RAND McNALLY

ANNIVERSARY EDITION

The New International Atlas
Der Neue Internationale Atlas
El Nuevo Atlas Internacional
Le Nouvel Atlas International
O Nôvo Atlas Internacional

RAND McNALLY CHICAGO / NEW YORK / SAN FRANCISCO

International Planning Conference
Internationale Planungskonferenz
Conferencia Internacional de Consultores
Conférence Internationale de Planning
Conferência Internacional de Consultores

International Atlas Staff
Redaktion des Internationalen Atlasses
Personal del Atlas Internacional
Personnel de l'Atlas International
Redação do Atlas Internacional

ADVISERS AND CONSULTANTS

The editors wish to express their special appreciation to these geographers, cartographers, and regional specialists who assisted in the refinement of the basic concepts of the atlas or who participated in the review of many of the regional maps.

ALLGEMEINE UND KARTOGRAPHISCHE BERATER

Die Herausgeber möchten ihren besonderen Dank den Geographen, Kartographen und Landeskundlern aussprechen, die mitgeholfen haben bei der Klärung des Atlaskonzepts oder beteiligt waren an der Durchsicht vieler Regionalkarten.

ASESORES Y CONSULTORES

Los redactores quieren expresar su más profundo agradecimiento a los geógrafos, cartógrafos y especialistas en mapas regionales, que han colaborado en la determinación exacta de los conceptos básicos del atlas o que han participado en la revisión de gran número de los mapas regionales.

CONSEILLERS ET CONSULTANTS

Les éditeurs veulent exprimer ici leur gratitude aux géographes, cartographes et spécialistes régionaux qui ont collaboré à la mise au point de la conception de base de l'Atlas ou qui ont participé à la révision de nombreuses cartes régionales.

CONSELHEIROS E CONSULTORES

Os editores desejam expressar seu profundo agradecimento aos geógrafos, cartógrafos e especialistas regionais que assistiram no refinamento dos conceitos básicos do atlas ou que tenham participado na revisão de um grande número de mapas regionais.

Dr. MANLIO CASTIGLIONI
Italy

Dr. ARCH C. GERLACH
United States

Dr. Ir. CORNELIS KOEMAN
Netherlands

Dr. ANDRÉ LIBAULT
Brazil

Brig. D. E. O. THACKWELL
United Kingdom

ROBERT J. VOSKUIL
United States

Dr. AKIRA WATANABE
Japan

Map Advisers
Kartographische Berater
Consejeros Cartográficos
Conseillers Cartographes
Conselheiros Cartográficos

Europe
Prof. Dr. EMIL MEYNEN
Germany

Dr. SANDOR RADO
Hungary

Asia
Dr. HISASHI SATO
Japan

Australia
R. O. BUCHANAN
United Kingdom

Anglo-America
Dr. ARCH C. GERLACH
United States

Latin America
Dr. ANDRÉ LIBAULT
Brazil

Dra. CONSUELO SOTO MORA
Mexico

Dr. JORGE A. VIVÓ ESCOTO
Mexico

Metropolitan Area Maps
Prof. HAROLD M. MAYER
United States

Rand McNally
Corporate Advisory Group
Thomas J. Hermes
Dennis O'Shea
Carl Mapes, Ph.D.
Bruce C. Ogilvie, Ph.D.
Paul T. Tiddens

The New International Atlas

RAND McNALLY

Publisher
Andrew McNally III
Andrew McNally IV

Editorial and Cartographic Direction
Russell L. Voisin
Michael W. Dobson, Ph.D.
Jon M. Leverenz

Art and Design Direction
Chris Arvetis
Gordon Hartshorne

Coordination
V. Patrick Healy
Arlen H. Winterfeld
John E. Zych

Geographic Research and Index
Susan Hudson
Keith Jennerjohn
Felix A. Lopez
Raymond T. Tobiaski
Richard L. Forstall (Consultant)

Cartographic Editorial
Robert K. Argersinger
Winifred V. Farbman

Cartographic Compilation
Ernest A. Dahl
Esther A. Grene
Lynn N. Jasmer
Han Sik Lee
Larry K. Tyler

Cartographic Production
Timothy J. Carter
Ronald Peters
Barbara Smith
Walter E. Erck
Joseph H. Funke
Ruthe Garner
Raymond J. Nitch

Composition and Typesetting
Sam Wilen
Rajani Veeramachaneni

Terrain Illustrators
Ivan Barcaba
Evelyn Mitchell
Mary Jo Schrader

MONDADORI McNALLY GmbH, Stuttgart

General Manager
Helmut Schaub
and Cartographic Staff

CARTOGRAPHIA, Budapest

Coordinator
Ervin Földi
and Cartographic Staff

ESSELTE MAP SERVICE, Stockholm

Editorial and Cartographic Direction
Paul R. Kraske,
Jürgen Jansch,
and Cartographic Staff

GEORGE PHILIP & SON, London

Editorial and Cartographic Direction
Harold Fullard,
A. G. Poynter,
and Cartographic Staff

TEIKOKU-SHOIN CO., LTD., Tokyo

Supervisor
Kimio Moriya
and Cartographic Staff

Foreword

THE HISTORY OF MAPS is as old as travel, discovery, and curiosity about the world. Since the earliest times, cartographers have served mariners with guidance for their explorations, monarchs with portraits of their territories, and scholars with a record of the earth's surface. Today, maps play an even more important role by providing men with the evidence of the ties which link the world's countries and peoples to one another.

The prime function of a map is to portray the earth's surface and the patterns of human occupance that have developed upon it. If a map were no more than an objective record, it would not need revision; however, a map is more than just a simple picture. Greatly reduced in scale from the reality it represents, it must abstract and generalize from that reality, selecting and interpreting the facts deemed to be of greatest significance. Thus, not only must cartography map new regions of the world, but it must also reflect a steady improvement in the techniques of portraying geographic information for the user.

The present century has offered a great challenge to map makers. Not only has it witnessed the increasing demand for specialized map information from governments, teachers, and scientists, it has also seen growing numbers of non-specialists eager to use maps in their business, for travel, or simply for enjoyment.

The Editors of *The International Atlas* feel, then, that a new work should be more than an updated version of older ones. The goal should be to produce an atlas of the greatest possible value and interest to a wide range of specialists and laymen. In this Foreword, we call the attention of users to several aspects which are new to the traditional framework of atlas publishing. The two most significant of these are the internationality of its planning and execution, and the designing of the maps as components of five distinctive series.

From the beginning, this Atlas has been international in concept, planning, editorial policy, and production. It was felt by Rand McNally & Company that there would be important gains in source material and expertise from the participation of organizations with previous cartographic experience in widely varying regions of the world. The advice and guidance of the senior personnel of these organizations has borne out this belief, although Rand McNally & Company as publisher has retained prime responsibility.

The editorial policies of the Atlas have been established with international use in mind, being designed for those whose native tongue is German, Spanish, French or Portuguese, as well as English. This international approach has been carried into the maps through the utilization of the metric system of measurement, and particularly by a strong emphasis on the use of local forms for geographic names. Essentially all names are in the local language, and English is used only for names of major features which extend across international borders. The names of countries appear on most of the maps both in English and in the locally official forms.

Generic terms for physical features (mountain, island, cape, etc.) also appear in their local forms, not in English. Short glossaries translating the most common of these terms appear in the margins of most maps. There is also a comprehensive glossary of all the generic terms. In the index to the Atlas, translation of generic terms is aided by the use of a system of symbols.

The coverage of the world's regions has also been planned with international utilization in mind. The space allotted to each region reflects its relative economic and cultural significance on the world scene, as well as its total population and area. There is an approximate balance between Anglo-America, Europe, and Asia, each with over one-fifth of the total map pages. Africa, Oceania, and Latin America together account for the remaining one-third. The index maps on pages xiii-xv show the map coverage according to scale.

The second of the Atlas' significant new aspects is the planning of the maps as components of five separate series. Each series has a distinctive style and content. In the first of these series, the continents are portrayed at 1:24,000,000 in natural colors, as they might appear from about 4,000 miles in space. The series also includes maps of the oceans at 1:48,000,000 and the world at 1:75,000,000.

In the next series, the major world regions are uniformly portrayed at 1:12,000,000 (190 miles to the inch). These maps are primarily political in style and content. The third series covers virtually the entire inhabited area of the earth at either 1:6,000,000 (95 miles to the inch), for the less dense regions, or 1:3,000,000 (47 miles to the inch), for Europe, most of North America, and the densest portions of South and East Asia. Physical and cultural detail are given approximately equal emphasis in this series.

In the fourth series, the scale of 1:1,000,000 (16 miles to the inch) has been used to portray key regions in each continent, selected for their exceptional importance, high population density, or complexity of development. The emphasis is on cultural detail, though shaded relief also appears. A final series maps the world's major urban areas at 1:300,000 (4.7 miles to the inch). This series emphasizes the complex patterns characteristic of large urban areas, omitting relief portrayal.

Each of the map series is comprehensive in a significant sense. The first three are territorially comprehensive, except for a few remote areas, and the last two are comprehensive for the most densely settled regions of the earth.

The sequence of maps in the Atlas begins with the series of world, continent, and ocean maps. Next are the three series of regional maps, arranged within major regions from smallest scale (1:12,000,000) to largest scale (1:1,000,000). The metropolitan map series (1:300,000) has been kept together in one section following the regional maps.

The individual map layouts have usually been planned to portray geographic and economic regions rather than individual countries. Thus there are maps of the Iberian Peninsula and of Southeastern Europe, but no separate maps of Portugal or Romania. In a few instances, this has necessitated the omission of some small portion of the region or country described in the map title. Inset maps have also been avoided, though exceptions have been made to portray some isolated islands or island groups.

The map symbols used for given features (Legend to Maps, pages x-xii) are generally alike on all of the map scales, though reduced in size on smaller scales. The symbols most often used have been arranged on page xi.

No aspect of map design has shown more dramatic advances in recent years than the cartographic rendering of relief. The Editors believe that the most effective method to depict this is the bird's-eye view or hill shading technique, which uses variation from light through dark tones to indicate slope and shape of relief features pictorially. This Atlas uses shaded relief on all but one of its five map series. On the 1:6,000,000 and 1:3,000,000 maps, it appears in combination with altitude tints, which show variations in elevation by means of light reflection, hue and intensity.

In the concluding portion of the Atlas are various tables and summaries for general reference. Next is the comprehensive glossary of geographic terms (pages 289-295). The World Information Table (pages 296-299) lists the area, population, and political status for each major political unit. The world's largest metropolitan areas are listed on page 300, followed by a comprehensive list of the world's major cities with population (pages 301-316). Finally, the Index provides map location references—map page, latitude and longitude—for more than 160,000 names.

Vorwort

DIE GESCHICHTE DER KARTE ist so alt wie das Reisen, die Entdeckungsfahrten und die Wissbegier über die Welt. Seit alten Zeiten haben Kartographen den Seefahrern mit Unterlagen für ihre Erkundungen gedient, den Herrschern Aufnahmen ihres Besitzes und den Gelehrten Darstellungen der Erdoberfläche geliefert. Heute spielen Karten eine noch bedeutendere Rolle, weil sie den Menschen vor Augen führen, wie eng die Länder und Völker der Welt miteinander verbunden sind.

Wichtigste Aufgabe einer Karte ist es, die Oberfläche der Erde und die vom Menschen geschaffenen Formen darzustellen. Wäre eine Karte nichts anderes als eine objektive Bestandsaufnahme, brauchte sie nicht bearbeitet zu werden; eine Karte ist jedoch mehr als nur ein Bild. Da sie eine vielfache Verkleinerung der Wirklichkeit wiedergibt, muss sie abstrahieren und durch Auswahl und Symbolisierung der wesentlichsten Tatsachen vereinfachen. So hat die Kartographie neue Regionen der Erde aufzunehmen und den neuesten Stand der Darstellung geographischer Informationen für den Benutzer aufzuzeigen.

Unser Jahrhundert bedeutet für die Kartographen eine grosse Herausforderung. Karten werden nicht nur in zunehmendem Masse von Regierungen, Wissenschaftlern und Pädagogen gefordert, sondern auch von interessierten Laien, die in ihrem Beruf, auf Reisen oder einfach zu ihrer Freude Karten benutzen.

Die Herausgeber des *Internationalen Atlas* meinen, dass ein neues Atlaswerk mehr sein sollte als nur die laufend gehaltene Ausgabe eines alten. Das Ziel sollte sein, einen Atlas von höchstem Gebrauchswert und Interesse sowohl für Fachleute als auch Laien zu schaffen.

In diesem Sinne möchten wir auf Besonderheiten hinweisen, die sich von dem traditionellen Aufbau eines Atlas wesentlich unterscheiden. Die beiden wichtigsten sind die Internationalität in Planung und Ausführung sowie die einheitliche Gestaltung der Karten zu fünf Gruppen.

Von Anfang an war dieser Atlas international in Planung, Redaktion und Herstellung. Rand McNally & Company war überzeugt, dass die Beteiligung von Partnern aus verschiedenen Teilen der Welt mit ihrer kartographischen Erfahrung einen grossen Gewinn an Quellen und Rat ergeben würde. Der Rat und die Mitarbeit dieser Fachleute haben diese Ansicht voll bestätigt, wobei Rand McNally als Verleger die letzte Entscheidung zufiel.

Die redaktionelle Bearbeitung des Atlas erfolgte mit Blick auf einen internationalen Interessentenkreis, vor allem aber für Benutzer, deren Muttersprache Deutsch, Spanisch, Französisch, Portugiesisch oder Englisch ist. Diese internationale Einstellung zeigt sich im Karteninhalt selbst, in der Benutzung des metrischen Masssystems und vor allem in der Bevorzugung der lokalen Schreibweise geographischer Namen. Grundsätzlich werden alle Namen in der Landessprache wiedergegeben; nur Namen grösserer Objekte, die sich über nationale Grenzen erstrecken, erscheinen in Englisch. Die Ländernamen stehen auf den meisten Karten sowohl in Englisch als auch in der offiziellen nationalen Form.

Namen für physische Objekte (Berg, Insel, Kap usw.) sind ebenfalls in ihrer lokalen Form wiedergegeben, nicht in Englisch. Die am häufigsten vorkommenden Begriffe stehen am Rande der meisten Karten erläutert. Der Atlas enthält ausserdem ein umfangreiches Verzeichnis aller Gattungsbegriffe. Im Register wird das Verständnis dieser Gattungsbegriffe durch ein System von Symbolen erleichtert.

Die Kartenausschnitte der verschiedenen Regionen der Erde wurden gleichfalls mit Blick auf einen internationalen Benutzerkreis gewählt. In diesem Atlas entspricht der einer Region zugemessene Kartenanteil ihrer relativen wirtschaftlichen und kulturellen Bedeutung in der Welt wie ihrer Gesamtbevölkerung und Fläche. Auf Anglo-Amerika, Europa und Asien entfällt mit je etwas mehr als einem Fünftel der Gesamtkartenzahl ungefähr der gleiche Anteil. Das verbleibende Drittel teilen sich Afrika, Australien, Ozeanien und Lateinamerika. Auf den Seiten XIII-XV sind die Karteauschnitte den Massstäben entsprechend auf Übersichtskarten ersichtlich.

Die zweite wesentliche Besonderheit des Atlas ist seine Gliederung der Karten in fünf charakteristische Gruppen. Jede Gruppe ist gekennzeichnet durch einen bestimmten Stil und Inhalt. In der ersten Gruppe werden die Kontinente (1:24 Mill.) abgebildet, wie sie sich aus einer ungefähren Entfernung von 6 500 km aus dem Weltraum darbieten. Diese Gruppe schliesst Karten der Ozeane (1:48 Mill.) und der Erde (1:75 Mill.) ein. In der folgenden Gruppe werden Grossregionen einheitlich (1:12 Mill.) dargestellt. Diese Karten sind in erster Linie politische Karten. Die dritte Serie deckt im wesentlichen das bewohnte Gebiet der Erde, entweder 1:6 Mill. für weniger dicht besiedelte Gebiete oder 1:3 Mill. für Europa, den Grossteil von Nordamerika und die dichtest besiedelten Teile Süd- und Ostasiens. Physische und kulturgeographische Einzelheiten werden in ungefähr gleichem Umfang wiedergegeben.

Für die vierte Gruppe wurde der Massstab 1:1 Mill. gewählt, um zentrale Räume jedes Kontinents abzubilden; sie sind entsprechend ihrer aussergewöhnlichen Bedeutung, hohen Bevölkerungsdichte oder komplexen Entwicklung gewählt. Betont werden kulturgeographische Einzelheiten, dazu enthalten die Karten eine Reliefschummerung. Die letzte Gruppe umfasst die bedeutendsten Stadtregionen der Erde (1:300 000). Diese Serie hebt das charakteristische, komplexe Gefüge grosser städtischer Ballungsgebiete hervor; auf Reliefdarstellung wurde verzichtet.

Jede der Kartenserien ist in sich abgeschlossen: Die ersten drei sind in bezug auf die Landflächen umfassend, ausgenommem einige entlegene Gebiete; die zwei letzten sind es hinsichtlich der Darstellung der dichtest besiedelten Räume der Erde.

Der Atlas beginnt mit der Gruppe der Welt-, Kontinent- und Ozeankarten. Es folgen drei Gruppen Regionalkarten, innerhalb jeder Grossregion geordnet vom kleinsten Massstab (1:12 Mill.) zum grössten (1:1 Mill.). Die Serie der Stadtregionen (1:300 000) wurde in einem einzigen Kapitel zusammengefasst, im Anschluss an die Regionalkarten.

Die Festlegung der einzelnen Kartenausschnitte zielte gewöhnlich mehr darauf ab, geographische und wirtschaftliche Regionen darzustellen als einzelne Staaten. Es gibt daher eine Karte der Iberischen Halbinsel oder von Südosteuropa, aber keine Einzelkarte von Portugal oder Rumänien. In einigen Fällen sind hierdurch kleinere Flächen des Landes oder der Region nicht erfasst, die im Kartentitel genannt sind. Die Verwendung von Einsatzkärtchen wurde möglichst vermieden, dennoch waren Ausnahmen erforderlich, um entlegene Inseln oder Inselgruppen darstellen zu können.

Die Kartensignaturen für bestimmte Objekte (Zeichenerklärung Seite X-XII) gleichen sich im

allgemeinen in allen Massstäben, auch wenn sie in Karten kleinerer Massstäbe verkleinert sind. Die am häufigsten vorkommenden Signaturen sind auf Seite XI dargestellt.

Auf kaum einem Gebiet der Kartengestaltung gab es in den vergangenen Jahren so eindrucksvolle Fortschritte wie auf dem der Geländedarstellung. Die Herausgeber glauben, dass die wirkungsvollste Darstellungsmethode die Reliefschummerung ist. Sie benutzt Tonabstufungen von Hell zu Dunkel, um Neigungen und Geländeformen plastisch hervorzuheben. Dieser Atlas bringt die Schummerung bei vier der fünf Kartenserien. In den Karten 1:6 und 1:3 Mill. wird sie kombiniert mit farbigen Höhenschichten, die unterschiedliche Höhenlagen durch ihren Farb- und Tonwert abgestuft wiedergeben.

Der letzte Teil des Atlas enthält zahlreiche Tabellen und Übersichten. Auf Seite 289-295 folgt eine Zusammenstellung geographischer Begriffe. In einer Länderübersicht (Seite 296-299) sind Daten über Fläche, Bevölkerung und politischen Status der wichtigsten politischen Einheiten zusammengefasst. Die grössten Stadtregionen der Erde werden auf Seite 300 dargestellt. Weiter folgt eine umfangreiche Liste der wichtigsten Weltstädte mit Einwohnerzahlen (Seite 301-316). Im Register werden für über 160 000 Namen die Kartenseite sowie die geographische Länge und Breite aufgeführt.

Prefacio

LA HISTORIA DE LOS MAPAS es tan antigua como la de los viajes, los descubrimientos y la curiosidad del hombre por el mundo. Desde hace mucho tiempo los cartógrafos han proporcionado guías a los navegantes en sus exploraciones, descripciones de sus territorios a los monarcas y registros de la superficie de la tierra a los eruditos. Más importante todavía es el papel que desempeñan los mapas en la actualidad, proporcionando al hombre en todas partes prueba de los lazos que vinculan entre sí a los diferentes países y pueblos del globo.

La función primordial de un mapa es la representación de la superficie de la tierra y de los patrones de ocupación humana que se han desarrollado sobre ella. Si un mapa no fuera sino un registro objetivo, no necesitaría ser revisado; sin embargo, un mapa es algo más que una simple representación gráfica. Representando una realidad enormemente reducida a escala, el mapa, forzosamente, debe abstraer y generalizar de esa realidad, seleccionando e interpretando los hechos que se juzguen de mayor significación. En consecuencia, la cartografía no debe limitarse al trazo de mapas de las nuevas regiones del mundo, sino que debe reflejar en ellos un continuo adelanto en las técnicas de representación de la información geográfica en provecho de quien los utiliza.

El siglo actual ha venido a presentar a los cartógrafos una desafiante tarea. Es época que no sólo ha presenciado una creciente demanda de información cartográfica especializada por parte de los gobiernos, maestros y científicos, sino que durante ella ha surgido un público cada vez mayor de gentes no especializadas, ávidas de aprovechar los mapas en sus negocios y viajes o que los adquieren simplemente por placer.

Los directores del *Atlas Internacional* consideran, por lo tanto, que una nueva obra debe ser algo más que una versión al día de trabajos anteriores. El objetivo debe ser producir un atlas del mayor valor e interés posibles para un vasto número de especialistas y de legos en la materia. En este prefacio, queremos llamar la atención de quienes consulten esta obra sobre varias innovaciones introducidas en el diseño tradicional de un atlas. De ellas, las más significativas son la internacionalidad de su preparación, y el diseño de los mapas como componentes de cinco series con características propias.

Desde un principio, este atlas ha tenido carácter internacional en cuanto a su concepto básico, su planeamiento, política editorial y producción. Rand McNally y Compañía consideró que con la participación de organizaciones con experiencia en cartografía en una gran variedad de regiones del mundo, se obtendría importante progreso en cuanto a fuentes de material y de conocimientos. Esta creencia originó el asesoramiento y guía recibidos del personal directivo de estas organizaciones, aunque Rand McNally y Compañía ha retenido la responsabilidad principal como casa editora.

Las normas o política editorial del atlas se ha establecido teniendo en cuenta su uso internacional, y éste ha sido diseñado para el público de habla alemana, española, francesa, portuguesa e inglesa. Este carácter internacional se introdujo en los mapas mediante la utilización del sistema métrico y en particular, dando marcada preferencia al uso de vocablos locales en la nomenclatura. Virtualmente todo nombre se da en el idioma de la localidad, usándose el inglés únicamente en la identificación de elementos geográficos de mayor importancia que se extienden a través de las fronteras internacionales. En la mayoría de los mapas, los nombres de los países aparecen en inglés y en la forma oficial localmente utilizada.

Los términos genéricos de geografía física (montañas, islas, cabos, etc.), también aparecen en el idioma local, no en inglés. Al margen de la mayoría de los mapas se incluyen breves glosarios con la traducción de los más comunes de dichos términos. Se incluye también un glosario completo de los términos genéricos y en el índice del atlas, mediante un sistema de símbolos, se facilita la traducción de los mismos.

Igualmente, la amplitud que el atlas da a las distintas regiones del mundo, fue preparada con un criterio de utilización internacional. El espacio asignado a cada región refleja su posición económica y cultural relativa dentro del escenario mundial, así como su población y superficie. El resultado de esto ha sido el equilibrio aproximado resultante entre Angloamérica, Europa y Asia, ocupando, cada cual, más de la quinta parte del total de páginas dedicadas a mapas. Africa, Oceanía y América Latina juntas, cubren el resto del volumen. Los mapas índices, en las páginas xiii a xv, muestran, a escala, la extensión de las regiones que los mapas comprenden.

El segundo de los nuevo aspectos significativos del atlas, es el planeamiento de los mapas como componentes de cinco series separadas. Cada serie tiene un estilo y contenido propios. En la primera de estas series, los continentes están representados a una escala de 1:24 000 000, en colores naturales, como aparecerían al observar la tierra desde el espacio a una distancia de cerca de 6 500 kilómetros. La serie incluye también mapas de los océanos a escala 1:48 000 000 y del mundo a escala 1:75 000 000.

En la serie siguiente, las principales regiones del mundo están uniformemente representadas a escala 1:12 000 000 (120 km por cm). Estos mapas son básicamente políticos en su estilo y contenido. La tercera serie cubre prácticamente el total de la superficie habitada de la tierra, a una de dos escalas: 1:6 000 000 (60 km por cm), para las regiones menos densas, o 1:3 000 000 (30 km por cm), para Europa, la mayor parte de Norteamérica y las regiones de mayor densidad de población del Sur y Sureste de Asia. En esta serie se hace aproximadamente igual énfasis a los detalles de orden físico y cultural.

En la cuarta serie se ha usado la escala 1:1 000 000 (10 km por cm), para representar las regiones más notables en cada continente, seleccionadas por su excepcional importancia, alta densidad de población o complejidad de desarrollo. Acá, el énfasis es en el detalle cultural aunque también aparece el relieve utilizando la técnica de sombreado. La serie final la componen los mapas de las principales áreas urbanas del mundo a una escala de 1:300 000 (3 km por cm). Esta serie recalca los complejos patrones culturales característicos de las grandes áreas urbanas, omitiendo la representación del relieve.

Cada una de las series es en sí una serie integral desde el punto de vista de significación. Las tres primeras, con excepción de unas cuantas áreas remotas, son territorialmente completas; las dos últimas, son completas en cuanto a las regiones más densamente pobladas de la tierra.

La sucesión de los mapas en el atlas principia con la serie del mundo, los continentes y los océanos. Luego vienen las tres series de mapas regionales distribuídos dentro de cada región principal, de la escala menor, (1:12 000 000), a la escala mayor, (1:1 000 000). La serie de mapas de áreas metropolitanas (1:300 000), se ofrece en una sección, inmediatamente después de los mapas regionales.

En general, el trazado de cada mapa se hizo con miras a representar regiones geográficas y económicas, y no necesariamente países individuales. Así, el atlas contiene mapas de la Península Ibérica y de Europa Sudoriental, pero no mapas separados de Portugal o de Rumania. En unos pocos casos, esto impuso la necesidad de omitir alguna pequeña porción de la región o país descrito en el título del mapa. También se evitó la inserción de mapas detallando determinada área, aunque se hicieron excepciones para representar algunas islas o grupos de islas.

Los símbolos utilizados para ciertos elementos (Leyenda para Mapas, páginas x a xii), son en general similares en todas las escalas, aunque reducidos en tamaño en los mapas de escala más pequeña. Los usados más frecuentemente se encuentran en la página xi.

En ningún aspecto del diseño cartográfico se han hecho progresos tan notables en años recientes como en la representación del relieve del terreno. Los editores opinan, sin embargo, que el método más efectivo en este sentido es la vista a vuelo de pájaro o técnica de sombreado: la variación de tonos claros a obscuros indica gráficamente la pendiente y la configuración del relieve. Este atlas utiliza el sombreado en cuatro de las cinco series de mapas. En los mapas a escala 1:6 000 000 y 1:3 000 000, el sombreado se combina con tintes que indican los cambios de altitud mediante reflexión de la luz, colorido e intensidad variables.

En la última parte del atlas se ofrecen varias tablas y resúmenes para consulta. En seguida se encuentra un glosario completo de términos geográficos (páginas 289-295). La Tabla de Información Mundial, (páginas 296 a 299), muestra el área, la población y la situación de cada una de las principales unidades políticas. La lista de las áreas metropolitanas más grandes del mundo aparece en la página 300, y está seguida por una lista completa de las principales ciudades del mundo con indicación del número de habitantes, (páginas 301-316). Finalmente, el índice ofrece referencias para localizar en los mapas más de 160 000 nombres: página del mapa, latitud y longitud.

Avant-propos

L'HISTOIRE DES CARTES géographiques remonte aussi loin que celle des voyages, des découvertes et du sentiment de curiosité touchant le globe terrestre. Depuis les temps les plus reculés, les cartographes ont servi les marins en les aidant à s'orienter dans leurs voyages d'explorations, les monarques en leur fournissant des représentations de leurs territoires, les savants en les documentant sur la surface terrestre. De nos jours, les cartes jouent un rôle plus important encore, en ce qu'elles procurent aux hommes l'évidence tangible des liens joignant les uns aux autres peuples et nations du monde.

La fonction primordiale d'une carte consiste à représenter la surface du globe et la répartition des concentrations humaines qui s'y sont développées. Une carte ne fût-elle qu'un document objectif, point ne serait besoin de la réviser; mais justement, elle constitue bien davantage qu'une simple image. Considérablement réduite relativement à la réalité qu'elle représente, elle doit abstraire et généraliser à partir de cette réalité, par la sélection et l'interprétation des données jugées les plus significatives. De sorte que la cartographie doit non seulement établir les cartes des nouvelles régions du globe, mais il lui faut en outre refléter les progrès constants des techniques d'exposé de la documentation géographique à l'intention du lecteur.

Le siècle actuel a porté un défi suprême aux cartographes. Non seulement en ce que l'on y est témoin d'une demande toujours croissante de cartes à l'usage des spécialistes, de la part des gouvernements, des professeurs et des savants, mais aussi bien en ce que l'on y constate une proportion de plus en plus élevée de non-initiés avides d'utiliser des cartes de vulgarisation pour leurs affaires, leurs voyages, ou simplement leur plaisir.

Les Editeurs de *L'Atlas International* estiment, dès lors, qu'un nouvel ouvrage se doit d'être plus qu'une ancienne version mise à jour. Le but qu'ils se proposent consiste à sortir un atlas qui soit du plus haut intérêt et de la plus profonde valeur pour un vaste public de spécialistes et de profanes. Les Editeurs attirent l'attention des lecteurs sur plusieurs innovations apportées ici au cadre traditionnel de publication des atlas. Deux des plus significatives de ces innovations résident dans l'internationalisation de la conception et de l'exécution d'une part, d'autre part dans la disposition des cartes réparties en cinq séries distinctives. Envisagé et entrepris sur un mode international dès le début, cet Atlas s'est développé selon une conception, une forme éditoriale et une réalisation du même ordre. Rand McNally & Company jugeait que de sérieux avantages—apports importants en matériaux de documentation et en connaissances spécialisées faisant autorité—résulteraient d'une collaboration avec des organisations possédant de longue date une expérience cartographique des régions les plus diversifiées du globe. Les avis et les opinions émanant du personnel de cadres de ces organisations ont corroboré iette conviction, encore que Rand McNally en tant que société d'édition en assume la responsabilité principale.

D'usage international, destiné à des lecteurs de langue allemande, espagnole , française ou portugaise, tout autant qu'anglaise, cet Atlas a dû être édité sous une forme qui tînt compte de sa raison d'être. Cette conception internationale de l'Atlas a été réalisée sur les cartes elles-mêmes avec d'une part l'utilisation du système métrique, avec

d'autre part l'emploi délibéré des noms géographiques sous leur forme nationale. Essentiellement, tous les noms apparaissent sous leur forme nationale, l'anglais n'étant utilisé que pour les noms d'importantes structures du relief qui s'étendent par-delà les frontières internationales. Sur la plupart des cartes, les noms des pays apparaissent à la fois en anglais et sous leur forme nationale officielle.

Les termes génériques désignant des structures de relief (montagne, île, cap, etc.) apparaissent également sous leur forme nationale, et non pas en anglais. En marge de la plupart des cartes, de courtes listes lexicales donnent la traduction des plus communs de ces termes. En outre, un glossaire donne tous les termes génériques dont la traduction se trouve par ailleurs facilitée grâce au système de symboles décrit dans l'Index de l'Atlas.

La répartition des régions du globe a été également déterminée en tenant compte de l'usage international qu'il sera fait de l'Atlas. L'espace attribué à chaque région reflète son importance économique et culturelle relative dans le monde, aussi bien que sa superficie et sa population. Il y a un équilibre approximatif entre l'Amérique du Nord, l'Europe et l'Asie, chacune avec plus d'un cinquième de la totalité des pages. L'Afrique, l'Océanie et l'Amérique du Sud occupent le tiers restant. Les cartes index des pages xiii-xv présentent la répartition des cartes en fonction de l'échelle à laquelle elles sont reproduites.

La seconde des innovations importantes de cet Atlas réside dans la conception des cartes en tant qu'éléments constitutifs de cinq séries séparées. Style et contenu distinctifs caractérisent nettement chacune de ces cinq séries. Dans la première, les continents sont représentés à l'échelle de 1:24 000 000, en couleurs naturelles, tels qu'ils apparaîtraient, vus de l'espace, à 6 500 km. Cette série comprend également les cartes de océans à l'échelle de 1:48 000 000 et du monde à l'échelle de 1:75 000 000.

Dans la série suivante, les régions majeures du globe sont représentées de facon uniforme à l'échelle de 1:12 000 000 (120 km au cm). Par leur style et leur contenu, celles-ci sont essentiellement des cartes politiques. Dans la troisième série, virtuellement toute las surface habitée de la terre est représentée, soit à l'échelle de 1:6 000 000 (60 km au cm) pour les régions de moindre densité de population, soit à l'échelle de 1:3 000 000 (30 km au cm) pour l'Europe, la plus grande partie de l'Amérique du Nord et les portions de plus forte densité du Sud et de l'Est de l'Asie. Dans cette série, une importance à peu près égale a été accordée aux détails physiques et aux détails culturels.

Dans la quatrième série, l'échelle de 1:1 000 000 (10 km au cm) a été employée pour représenter certaines régions-clefs de chaque continent, choisies pour leur importance exceptionnelle, leur densité de population, ou la complexité de leur développement. L'accent porte sur les détails culturels, bien que le relief ombré apparaisse également. Une série finale souligne la répartition culturelle complexe, caractéristique des vastes zones urbaines, omettant le relief.

Chacune de ces séries est complète dans un mode significatif. Les trois premières sont complètes du point de vue territorial, exception faite de quelques lointaines contrées, et les deux dernières sont complètes en ce qui concerne les régions du globe de plus forte densité de population.

La succession des cartes de l'Atlas s'ouvre avec la série qui comprend les cartes du monde, des continents, et des océans. A sa suite, viennent les trois séries de cartes régionales disposées pour chaque région principale depuis les plus petites échelles (1:12 000 000), aux plus grandes (1:1 000 000). La série des cartes métropolitaines est groupée en une section qui fait suite aux cartes régionales.

La répartition individuelle des cartes a généralement été conçue en fonction des régions géographiques et économiques, plutôt qu'en fonction des frontières politiques nationales. De sorte qu'il y a des cartes de la Péninsule Ibérique et de l'Europe du Sud-Est, mais pas de cartes séparées pour le Portugal ou la Roumanie. Dans quelques cas, ceci a nécessité l'omission de quelque petite portion de la région ou du pays décrit dans le titre de la carte. Les insertions d'extensions ont également été évitées, encore que plusieurs exceptions aient été faites pour représenter certaines îles isolées ou certains groupes d'îles.

Les symboles employés sur les cartes sont en général identiques pour toutes les échelles de cartes, quoique de taille réduite sur les cartes à petite échelle. Les symboles les plus fréquemment employés ont été réunis à la page xi.

Aucun de aspects de la réalisation des cartes n'a fait de progrès plus prodigieux durant ces dernières années que la représentation cartographique du relief. Les Editeurs estiment que la méthode la plus efficace est celle de la "vue à vol d'oiseau", ou technique du relief ombré; celle-ci utilise toute la gamme des tons, des plus clairs aux plus foncés, pour indiquer picturalement l'inclinaison des pentes et la forme des structures du relief. Le relief ombré apparaît sur quatre des cinq séries de cartes. Sur les cartes au 1:6 000 000e et au 1:3 000 000e, il apparaît en combinaison avec les teintes d'altitude qui indiquent les variations d'élévation au moyen de la réflexion de la lumière, de la nuance et de l'intensité.

Dans la dernière partie de l'Atlas, qui constitue sa conclusion, se trouvent divers tableaux de récapitulations et de références. A sa suite se trouve le lexique complet des termes géographiques (pages 289-295). Puis une table d'informations mondiales donne la liste de toutes les unités politiques principales, avec superficie, population et statut politique de chacune (pages 296-299). La liste des plus importants centres urbains du monde est à la page 300. A la suite de cette table se trouve une liste complète des principales villes du monde avec leur population (pages 301-316). Enfin, l'Index fournit des références de cartes—numéros de pages, longitude et latitude—pour permettre de situer plus de 160 000 noms géographiques.

Prefácio

A HISTÓRIA DOS MAPAS é tão antiga quanto as das viagens, descobertas, e curiosidades sobre o mundo. Desde os primórdios tempos, cartógrafos têm servido à marinheiros orientando-os em suas explorações, monarcas com reproduções dos seus territórios, e acadêmicos com o registro da superfície da terra. Hoje, os mapas têm um papel mais importante-ainda, fornecendo ao homem provas das ligações que unem os países e os povos do mundo.

A função fundamental do mapa é de retratar a superfície da terra e os padrões da ocupação humana que sobre ela se desenvolveu. Se o mapa não fosse nada mais que um registro objetivo, não necessitaria de revisão; contudo, um mapa é mais do que um simples retrato. Grandemente reduzido em escala, em relação à realidade que representa, ele deve absorver e ao mesmo tempo generalizar a realidade, selecionando e interpretando os fatos supostamente de maior significado. Portanto, não somente é preciso que o cartógrafo registre novas regiões do mundo, mas também tente refletir um melhoramento contínuo nas técnicas de retratamento de informação geográfica para o usuário.

O século atual tem oferecido um grande desafio para confeccionadores de mapas. Não há somente o testemunho da crescente demanda por mapas de informações especializadas, pelos governos, professores e cientistas, mas também tem-se notado um número crescente de leigos, ansiosos em usar mapas em seus negócios, viagens, ou simplesmente como-passatempo.

Os Editores do *Atlas Internacional* sentem, que um novo trabalho deveria ser mais do que uma versão renovada dos trabalhos anteriores. O objetivo deveria ser de produzir um atlas de máximo valor e interêsse possível, para uma grande gama de especialistas e leigos. Neste prefácio, chamamos a atenção dos usuários para os vários aspectos-que são novos para os esquemas tradicionais de publicação de atlas. Os dois mais significantes são: a internacionalidade do seu planejamento e execução, e o arranjo de mapas como componentes de cinco séries distintas.

Desde o início, o atlas tem sido internacional em conceito, planejamento, política editorial e produção. Rand McNally & Company sentiu que haveriam ganhos importantes na fonte de material e conhecimento, pela participação de organizações com experiências cartográficas anteriores, nas mais diversas regiões do mundo. O conselho e orientação do quadro pessoal dessas organizações têm comprovado esta crença, apesar da Rand McNally & Company, como editor, ter retido a responsabilidade principal.

As políticas editoriais do Atlas têm sido estabelecidas visando o uso internacional, sendo designado para aqueles cuja língua nativa é Alemão, Espanhol, Francês ou Português, bem como Inglês. Essa técnica internacional tem sido executada em mapas, através da utilização do sistema métrico de medidas, e particularmente, pela grande ênfase no uso dos estilos locais para nomes geográficos. Essencialmente, todos os nomes estão em linguagem local, e o Inglês é usado somente para nomes de acidentes geográficos importantes, que se extendam através de fronteiras internacionais. Os nomes dos países-aparecem na maioria dos mapas, em Inglês, e em linguagem oficial local.

Termos genéricos para características físicas (montanhas, ilhas, cabos, etc.) aparecem também nas suas formas locais, não em Inglês. Pequenos glossários traduzindo estes têrmos mais comuns aparecem nas margens da maioria dos mapas. Há também um glossário completo de todos os termos genéricos. No índice dos atlas, a tradução dos termos genéricos é auxiliada pelo uso de um sistema de símbolos.

A cobertura das regiões do mundo tem sido visando a utilização internacional. O espaço atribuído para cada região reflete seu relativo significado econômico e cultural no cenário mundial, bem como sua população e área. Há um balanço aproximado entre Anglo-América, Europa e Ásia, cada qual com mais de um quinto do total de páginas. África, Oceania e América Latina, juntos, contam com o restante um terço. O mapa índice nas páginas xiii-xv mostra a cobertura do mapa de acordo com a escala.

Um novo aspecto secundário do Atlas, é o planejamento de mapas como componentes de cinco séries separadas. Cada série tem um estilo e conteúdo distinto. Na primeira dessas séries, os continentes são ilustrados em 1:24 000 00 em cores naturais, tal como elas apareceriam a 6.500 km de espaço. A série também inclui mapas dos oceanos em 1:48 000 000 e do mundo em 1:75 000 000.

Na série seguinte, as regiões principais do mundo estão uniformemente ilustradas em 1:12 000 000 (120 km por cm). Estes mapas são principalmente políticos no estilo e conteúdo. A terceira série virtualmente, cobre toda a área habitada da terra em 1:6 000 000 (60 km por cm) para as regiões menos densas, ou 1:3 000 000 (47 km por cm) para Europa, maioria da América do Norte, e a mais densa porção do Sul e Leste da Ásia. É dado ênfase de igual valor aos detalhes físicos e culturais nesta série.

Na quarta série, a escala de 1:1 000 000 (10 km por cm) tem sido usada para ilustrar regiões chaves em cada continente, selecionado pela sua excepcional importância, alta densidade populacional ou complexidade de desenvolvimento. A ênfase está no detalhe cultural, apesar de relêvo sombreado também aparecer. A série final mapeia as principais áreas urbanas mundiais em 1:300 000 (3 km por cm). Esta série enfatiza padrões complexos característicos de grandes áreas urbanas, omitindo a ilustração do relêvo.

Cada série de mapas é completa em um determinado senso. As três primeiras são territorialmente completas, exceto as poucas áreas remotas, e as duas últimas são também completas para as regiões mais densamente habitadas da terra.

A sequência de mapas no Atlas começa com a série de mapas do mundo, continentes e oceanos. Em seguida, estão as três séries de mapas regionais, arranjados dentro de regiões principais de escala mínima (1:12 000 000) para escala máxima (1:1 000 000). As séries de mapas metropolitanos (1:300 000) têm sido mantidas juntas em uma secção seguindo os mapas regionais.

As apresentações individuais dos mapas têm sido normalmente planejadas para ilustrar regiões geográficas e econômicas em vez de países individuais. Portanto, existem mapas da Península Ibérica e do Sudeste Europeu, mas não existem mapas separados para Portugal ou Romênia. Em alguns casos, foi necessária a omissão de pequena porção de uma região ou país, descrito no título do mapa. Têm sido evitados os mapas embutidos, apesar de terem sido feitas exceções para ilustrar algumas ilhas ou grupos de ilhas isolados.

Os símbolos dos mapas usados para as características dadas (legendas para mapas, páginas x-xii) são geralmente semelhantes em todas as escalas dos mapas, apesar de serem reduzidos em tamanho nas escalas menores. Os símbolos mais usados foram dispostos na página xi.

Nenhum aspecto de apresentação de mapas, mostrou-se mais dramático recentemente, do que a reprodução cartográfica do relêvo. Os editores acreditam que o método mais efetivo para representá-lo é a reprodução vista do alto ou a técnica do sombreamento das colinas, que usa variações de tonalidades claras para escuras, para indicar o declive e a forma dos aspectos dos relêvos, por meio de ilustrações. Este Atlas usa relêvo sombreado em todas as cinco séries de mapas, com exceção de uma. Nos mapas de 1:6 000 000 e 1:3 000 000, aparece em combinação com variações de cores das altitudes, que mostram variações em elevação por meio de reflexão da luz, matiz e intensidade.

Na porção conclusiva do Atlas, estão várias tabelas e sumários para referências gerais. Em seguida, está um glossário completo de termos geográficos (páginas 289-295). A tabela de informação mundial (páginas 296-299). Registra a área, população e "status" político para cada unidade política principal. As maiores áreas metropolitanas do mundo, estão relacionadas na página 300. É seguido por uma lista completa das principais cidades do mundo, com as respectivas populações (páginas 301-316). Finalmente, o índice dá referências para a localização do mapa—página do mapa, latitude e longitude—com mais de 160 000 nomes.

List of Maps

*Scale in millions

Kartenverzeichnis

Lista de Mapas

Liste des Cartes

*Escalas em milhões

ix

Legend to Maps / Zeichenerklärung
Leyendas Para Mapas / Légende des Cartes / Legendas dos Mapas

The design and color of the map symbols are consistent throughout the Regional and Metropolitan Area maps, although the size of the symbol varies with scale. An asterisk marks those symbols which appear only on the 1:300,000 scale maps. Symbols for inhabited localities, boundaries, and capitals are given on page xi.

The symbol $\overrightarrow{80\text{-}81}$ in the margin of a map directs the reader to a map of the adjoining area.

A separate legend on page 1 identifies the land and submarine features which appear on the World, Ocean, and Continent maps.

Der Entwurf und die Farbe der Kartensymbole sind einheitlich für alle Regionalkarten und Karten von Stadtregionen, während die Grösse des Symbols sich mit dem Massstab ändert. Ein Stern kennzeichnet diejenigen Symbole, welche nur auf den Karten im Massstab 1:300 000 erscheinen. Symbole für bewohnte Orte, für Grenzen und Hauptstädte sind auf Seite xi angeführt.

Kennzeichen $\overrightarrow{80\text{-}81}$ am Rande einer Karte ist ein Hinweis für den Leser, die Karte eines angrenzenden Gebietes nachzuschlagen.

El diseño y el color de los símbolos cartográficos son uniformes para todas los mapas regionales y de las áreas metropolitanas, aunque el tamaño del símbolo varía según la escala. Un asterisco distingue los símbolos que aparecen sólo en los mapas a 1:300 000. Los símbolos de lugares poblados, de límites y de capitales se hallan en la página xi.

El símbolo $\overrightarrow{80\text{-}81}$ al margen de un mapa dirige al lector a un mapa del área adyacente.

Otra leyenda, en la página 1, identifica la topografía terrestre y submarina que se encuentra en los mapas del Mundo, Océanos y Continentes.

La couleur et la forme des symboles cartographiques des cartes régionales et des cartes des zones métro-politaines sont identiques, bien que la grandeur des signes varie selon l'échelle. Un astérisque accompagne les symboles qui n'apparaissent que sur les cartes au 1:300 000? La légende des signes conventionnels pour les lieux habités, les frontières et les capitales se trouve à la page xi.

Le symbole $\overrightarrow{80\text{-}81}$ en marge d'une carte renvoie le lecteur à une carte de la région voisine.

Pour les cartes du monde, des océans et des continents une légende séparée, à la page 1, donne le sens des symboles représentant les paysages continentaux et les formes de relief sous-marin.

A cor e a forma dos símbolos cartográficos dos mapas regionais e das áreas metropolitanas são idênticos, ainda que a dimensão do símbolo varie segundo a escala. Um asterisco distingue os símbolos que só aparecem nos mapas da escala de 1:300 000. As legendas dos símbolos convencionais dos lugares povoados, fronteiras e capitais encontram-se à pág. xi.

O símbolo $\overrightarrow{80\text{-}81}$ à margem de um mapa, remete o leitor a um mapa da região vizinha.

Nos mapas do mundo, dos oceanos e dos continentes uma legenda separada, na pág. 1, indica o sentido dos símbolos representativos das paisagens continentais e das formas do relevo submarino.

Hydrographic Features / Hydrographische Objekte / Elementos Hidrográficos
Données Hydrographiques / Acidentes Hidrográficos

Shoreline / Uferlinie
Línea costanera / Trait de côte
Linha costeira

Undefined or Fluctuating Shoreline
Unbestimmte oder Veränderliche Uferlinie
Línea costanera indefinida o fluctuante
Trait de côte indéfini ou fluctuant
Linha costeira indefinida ou flutuante

River, Stream / Fluss, Strom
Río, Corriente / Rivière, Cours d'eau
Rio, curso d'água

Intermittent Stream / Periodischer Fluss
Corriente intermitente / Cours d'eau périodique
Rio, curso d'água intermitente

Rapids, Falls / Stromschnellen, Wasserfälle
Rápidos, Cascadas / Rapides, Chutes d'eau
Corredeiras, quedas d'água

Depth of Water / Wassertiefe
Profundidad del agua / Profondeur bathymétrique
Profundidade da água

Greatest Depth (Atlantic, Indian, Pacific oceans)
Grösste Tiefe (Atlantischer, Indischer, Pazifischer Ozean)
Profundidad más grande (Océanos Atlántico, Índico, Pacífico)
Profondeur maximum (océans Atlantique, Indien, Pacifique)
Profundidade máxima (oceanos Atlântico, Índico, Pacífico)

Navigable Canal / Schiffbarer Kanal
Canal navegable / Canal navigable
Canal navegável

Irrigation or Drainage Canal
Be- oder Entwässerungskanal
Canal de irrigación o desagüe
Canal d'irrigation ou de drainage
Canal de irrigação ou drenagem

Aqueduct / Aquädukt
Acueducto / Aqueduc
Aqueduto

Pier, Breakwater / Landungsbrücke, Wellenbrecher
Embarcadero, Rompeolas / Jetée, Brise-lames
Cais, Quebra-mar

Reef / Riff
Arrecife / Récif
Recife

Uninhabited Oasis / Unbewohnte Oase
Oasis deshabitado / Oasis inhabitée
Oásis desabitado

Lake, Reservoir / See, Stausee
Lago, Embalse / Lac, Réservoir
Lago, reservatório (represa)

Intermittent Lake, Reservoir
Periodischer See, Stausee
Lago o Embalse intermitente
Lac ou Réservoir périodique
Lago, reservatório (represa) intermitente

Salt Lake / Salzsee
Lago salado / Lac salé
Lago salgado

Dry Lake Bed / Trockener Seeboden
Lecho de lago seco / Fond de lac asséché
Leito de lago seco

Swamp / Sumpf
Pantano / Marais
Pântano

Glacier / Gletscher
Glaciar / Glacier
Geleira

Lake Surface Elevation
Seehöhe
Elevación del lago
Cote du niveau du lac
Altitude do nível do lago

Topographic Features / Topographische Objekte / Elementos Topográficos
Données Topographiques / Acidentes Topográficos

Elevation Above Sea Level
Höhe über dem Meeresspiegel
Elevación sobre del nivel del mar
Cote au-dessus du niveau de la mer
Altitude acima do nível do mar

Elevation Below Sea Level
Höhe unter dem Meeresspiegel
Elevación bajo del nivel del mar
Cote au-dessous du niveau de la mer
Altitude abaixo do nível do mar

Highest Elevation in Country
Höchster Punkt des Landes
Elevación más alta en el país
Cote la plus élevée d'un pays
Altitude mais elevada de um país

Lowest Elevation in Country
Tiefster Punkt des Landes
Elevación más baja en el país
Cote la plus basse d'un pays
Altitude mais baixa de um país

Elevation of City
Höhenangabe einer Stadt
Elevación de ciudad
Altitude d'une ville
Altitude de uma cidade

Mountain Pass / Pass
Paso / Col de montagne
Passo (de montanha)

Rock / Fels
Roca / Rocher
Rocha

Lava / Lava
Lava / Lave
Lava

Sand Area / Sandgebiet
Area de arena / Région sableuse, Erg
Região arenosa, Erg

Salt Flat / Salzebene
Salar / Dépression salée
Depressão salgada

Elevations and depths are given in meters
Höhen und Tiefen sind in Metern angegeben
Elevaciones y profundidades se dan en metros
Cotes et profondeurs sont indiquées en mètres
Altitudes e profundidades são apresentadas em metros

Mountain Range, Plateau, Valley, etc.
Gebirge, Hochebene, Tal, usw.
Sierra, Meseta, Valle, etc.
Chaîne de montagnes, Plateau, Vallée, etc.
Cadeia de montanhas. Planalto, Vale etc.

Island
Insel
Isla
Île
Ilha

Peninsula, Cape, Point, etc.
Halbinsel, Kap, Landspitze, usw.
Península, Cabo, Punta, etc.
Péninsule, Cap, Pointe, etc.
Península, Cabo, Ponta etc.

Highest Elevation and Lowest Elevation of
  a continent are underlined
Höchster und tiefster Punkt innerhalb
  eines Erdteils sind unterstrichen
Elevación más alta y más baja de
  un continente se subrayan
La cote la plus haute et la cote la plus basse
  d'un continent sont soulignées
As altitudes mais e menos elevadas de um
  continente são sublinhadas

Inhabited Localities / Bewohnte Orte / Lugares Poblados / Lieux Habités / Lugares Habitados

The symbol represents the number of inhabitants within the locality/Die Signatur entspricht der Einwohnerzahl des Ortes
El símbolo representa el número de habitantes dentro del lugar/Le symbole représente le nombre d'habitants de la localité
O símbolo representa o número de habitantes do lugar

1:300,000	1:1,000,000			1:12,000,000			1:24,000,000		
1:3,000,000	1:6,000,000	.	0—10,000		.	0—50,000	1:48,000,000	.	0—100,000
		o	10,000—25,000		⊛	50,000—100,000		⊛	100,000—1,500,000
		⊛	25,000—100,000		⊡	100,000—250,000		■	>1,500,000
		⊡	100,000—250,000		▣	250,000—1,000,000			
		▣	250,000—1,000,000		■	>1,000,000			
		■	>1,000,000						

The size of type indicates the relative economic and political importance of the locality
Die Schriftgrösse entspricht der relativen wirtschaftlichen und politischen Bedeutung des Ortes
El tamaño del tipo de imprenta indica la relativa importancia económica y política del lugar
La dimension des caractères indique l'importance économique et politique relative d'une localité
A dimensão dos caracteres tipográficos indica a importância econômica e política relativa do lugar

Écommoy	Lisieux	**Rouen**
Trouville	**Orléans**	**PARIS**

Hollywood □ — **Section of a City, Neighborhood/Stadtteil, Nachbarschaft**
Westminster — **Sección de una ciudad, Barrio/Arrondissement, Quartier**
Seção de uma cidade, Bairro

Northland ■ — * **Major Shopping Center/Haupteinkaufszentrum/Mercado principal**
Center — **Centre commercial important/Centro comercial importante**

BYRD □ — **Scientific Station/Wissenschaftliche Station/Estación científica**
Station scientifique/Estação científica

Bi'r Safâjah ° — **Inhabited Oasis/Bewohnte Oase/Oasis habitado**
Oasis habitée/Oásis habitado

Kumdah ° — **Uninhabited Oasis/Unbewohnte Oase/Oasis deshabitado**
Oasis inhabitée/Oásis desabitado

Urban Area (area of continuous industrial, commercial, and residential development)
Stadtgebiet (ausgedehntes industrie-, Geschäfts- und Wohngebiet)
Zona urbanizada (área de desarrollo industrial, comercial y residencial)
Zone urbanisée (zone d'occupation continue par des industries, des commerces, des habitations)
Zona urbanizada (área de ocupação contínua por indústrias, estabelecimentos comerciais e habitações)

* **Major Industrial Area/Hauptindustriegebiet/Zona principal industrial**
Région industrielle importante/Zona industrial importante

* **Wooded Area/Wald/Área de bosque**
Région boisée/Área verde

* **Local Park or Recreational Area/Park oder Erholungsgebiet**
Parque municipal o área de recreo/Parc municipal ou zone de loisirs
Parque municipal ou área de lazer

Political Boundaries / Politische Grenzen / Límites Políticos / Frontières Politiques / Fronteiras e Limites

International (First-order political unit) /**Staatsgrenze** (Politische Einheit erster Ordnung)
Internacionales (Unidad política de primer orden) /**Internationales** (Entités politiques de premier ordre)
Internacionais (Unidade política de primeiro nível)

Capitals of Political Units
Hauptstädte politischer Einheiten
Capitales de Unidades Políticas
Capitales d'Entités Politiques
Capitais de Unidades Políticas

1:1,000,000	1:300,000 1:3,000,000 1:6,000,000	1:24,000,000 1:48,000,000	1:12,000,000	
	HUNGARY			**Demarcated, Undemarcated, and Administrative** / **Markiert, unmarkiert, verwaltungstechnisch** / **Demarcado, No demarcado, y Administrativo** / **Délimitées, Non-délimitées, Administratives** / **Delimitados, Não delimitados, Administrativos**

Disputed de facto/Umstritten de facto
Disputado de hecho/Contestées de facto
Contestados de fato

Disputed de jure/Umstritten de jure
Disputado de derecho/Contestées de jure
Contestados de direito

Indefinite or Undefined/Unklar oder Unbestimmt
Indefinido o No determinado/Imprécises ou Non définies
Imprecisos ou Não definidos

Demarcation Line/Demarkationslinie
Línea de demarcación/Ligne de démarcation
Linha de demarcação

BUDAPEST — **Independent Nation**
Unabhängiger Staat
Nación independiente
État indépendant
Estado independente

Cayenne — **Dependency** (Colony, protectorate, etc.)
Abhängiges Gebiet (Kolonie, Protektorat, usw.)
Dependencia (Colonia, protectorado, etc.)
Territoire dépendant (Colonie, protectorat, etc.)
Dependência (Colônia, protetorado, etc.)

GALAPAGOS (Ecuador) — **Administering Country**
Verwaltender Staat
País administrador
Pays administrateur
País administrador

Internal/Verwaltungsgrenze/Internos/Intérieures/Limites Internos

PERNAMBUCO — **State, Province, etc.** (Second-order political unit)
Land, Provinz, usw. (Politische Einheit zweiter Ordnung)
Estado, Provincia, etc. (Unidad política de segundo orden)
État, Province, etc. (Subdivision administrative de deuxième ordre)
Estado, Província, etc. (Unidade política de segundo nível)

Recife — **State, Province, etc./Land, Provinz, usw.**
Estado, Provincia, etc./État, Province, etc.
Estado, Província, etc.

SIENA WESTCHESTER — **County, Oblast, etc.** (Third-order political unit)/**Grafschaft, Oblast, usw.** (Politische Einheit dritter Ordnung)
Condado, Oblast, etc. (Unidad política de tercer orden)
Comté, Oblast, etc. (Subdivision administrative de troisième ordre)
Condado, Oblast, etc. (Unidade política de terceiro nível)

Ambala — **County, Oblast, etc./Grafschaft, Oblast, usw.**
Johnstown — **Condado, Oblast, etc./Comté, Oblast, etc.**
Condado, Oblast, etc.

ISERLOHN — **Okrug, Kreis, etc.** (Fourth-order political unit)/**Okrug, Kreis, usw.** (Politische Einheit vierter Ordnung)
Okrug, Kreis, etc. (Unidad política de cuarto orden)
Okrug, Kreis, etc. (Subdivision administrative de quatrième ordre)
Okrug, Kreis, etc. (Unidade política de quarto nível)

Iserlohn — **Okrug, Kreis, etc./Okrug, Kreis, usw.**
Okrug, Kreis, etc./Okrug, Kreis, etc.
Okrug, Kreis, etc.

City or Municipality (may appear in combination with another boundary symbol)
Stadt oder Gemeinde (kann zusammen mit einem anderen Begrenzungssymbol erscheinen)
Ciudad o Municipio (puede aparecer en combinación con otro símbolo de límite)
Ville ou Municipalité (peut paraître en combinaison avec un autre symbole de limites politiques)
Cidade ou Municipalidade (Pode aparecer em combinação com outro símbolo de limite político)

NORMANDIE — **Historical Region** (No boundaries indicated)
Historische Landschaft (Grenzen werden nicht gezeigt)
Región Histórica (Sin indicación de límites)
Région Historique (Sans indication de frontières)
Região Histórica (Sem indicação de fronteiras)

Legend to Maps/Zeichenerklärung
Leyendas Para Mapas/Légende des Cartes/Legendas dos Mapas

Transportation / Verkehr / Transporte / Transports / Transporte

	1:300,000	1:1,000,000	1:3,000,000 / 1:6,000,000	1:12,000,000

Road/Strasse/Camino/Route/Rodovia

Primary/Erster Ordnung/Principal/de premier ordre/Principal — PASSAIC EXPWY. (I-80) — PENNSYLVANIA TURNPIKE

Secondary/Zweiter Ordnung/Secundario/de second ordre/Secundária — BERLINER RING

Tertiary/Dritter Ordnung/Terciario/de troisième ordre/Terciária

Minor Road, Trail/Weg, Pfad
Rodera, Vereda/Route secondaire, Piste/Caminho, trilha

Railway/Eisenbahn/Ferrocarril/Voie ferrée/Ferrovia

Primary/Hauptbahn/Principal/Principale/Principal — CANADIAN NATIONAL — SANTA FE

Secondary/Sonstige Bahn/Secundario/Secondaire/Secundária

*Rapid Transit/Schnellverkehr/Tránsito rápido/Métro/Trânsito rápido (metrô)

Airport/Flughafen/Aeropuerto/Aéroport/Aeroporto — LONDON (HEATHROW) AIRPORT — DULLES INTERNATIONAL AIRPORT

*Rail or Air Terminal/Bahnhof oder Flughafengebäude
Terminal ferroviaria o aéro/Gare ou aérogare
Terminal ferroviário ou aéreo (estação) — SÜD-BAHNHOF

REICHS-BRÜCKE — Bridge/Brücke/Puente/Pont/Ponte

GREAT ST. BERNARD TUNNEL — Tunnel/Tunnel/Túnel/Tunnel/Túnel

Houston Ship Channel — Shipping Channel/Schiffahrtsrinne
Canal maritimo/Chenal maritime
Canal maritimo

Canal du Midi — Navigable Canal/Schiffbarer Kanal
Canal navegable/Canal navigable
Canal navegável

Intracoastal Waterway/Küstenschiffahrtsweg
Via fluvial Intracostera/Canal côtier
Via costeira interna

TO MALMÖ — Ferry/Fähre
Balsadera/Bac
Balsa

Miscellaneous Cultural Features / Sonstige Objekte / Elementos Culturales Misceláneos
Éléments Culturels Divers / Acidentes Culturais Diversos

PARQUE NACIONAL LANÍN — National or State Park or Monument
National- oder Naturpark oder Denkmal
Parque o Monumento nacional o provincial
Parc ou Monument national ou régional
Parque ou Monumento nacional ou regional

SORBONNE — Point of Interest (Battlefield, museum, temple, university, etc.)
Sehenswürdigkeit (Schlachtfeld, Museum, Tempel, Universität, usw.)
Punto de interés (Campo de batalla, museo, templo, universidad, etc.)
Curiosité (Champ de bataille, musée, temple, université, etc.)
Pontos de interesse (Campo de batalha, museu, templo, universidade, etc.)

ASWÃN DAM — Dam/Damm/Presa/Barrage
Represa (barragem)

EDISON NAT. HIST. SITE — National or State Historic(al) Site, Memorial
Historische Stätte, Gedenkstätte
Sitio histórico nacional o provincial, Monumento
Site historique national ou régional, Mémorial
Sitio histórico nacional ou regional, Monumento histórico

<> * Lock/Schleuse/Esclusa
Écluse/Eclusa

SEMINOLE IND. RES. — Indian Reservation/Indianerreservation
Reserva de indios/Réserve indienne
Reserva indígena

STEPHANSDOM — Church, Monastery/Kirche, Kloster
Iglesia, Monasterio/Église, Monastère
Igreja, Mosteiro

Crib — * Water Intake Crib/Wasseraufnahmestation
Toma de agua/Prise d'eau/Captação de água

UXMAL — Ruins/Ruinen/Ruinas/Ruines/Ruínas

Quarry or Surface Mine
Steinbruch oder Tagebau
Cantera o Mina de hoyo abierto
Carrière ou Mine à ciel ouvert
Pedreira ou mina a céu aberto

FORT DIX — Military Installation/Militäranlage
Instalación militar/Installation militaire
Instalação militar

WINDSOR CASTLE — Castle/Burg, Schloss/Castillo/Château/Castelo

Subsurface Mine/Bergwerk
Mina subterránea/Mine souterraine
Mina subterrânea

* Lighthouse/Leuchtturm
Faro/Phare/Farol

* Oil Well/Ölbohrturm
Pozo de petróleo/Puits de pétrole
Poço de petróleo

GREENWOOD CEMETERY — * Cemetery/Friedhof
Cementerio/Cimetière/Cemitério

Metric-English Equivalents / Umrechnung metrischer Masse in englische Masse / Métrico-Equivalentes Ingleses
Equivalences métriques des mesures anglaises / Equivalentes métricos das medidas inglesas

Areas represented by one square centimeter at various map scales
Flächen die einem cm² in den verschiedenen Kartenmassstäben entsprechen
Áreas representados por un centimetro cuadrado a varias escalas de mapas
Surface représentée par un cm² aux échelles indiquées
Áreas representadas por cm² nas escalas indicadas nos mapas

Meter=3.28 feet   Meter² (m²)=10.76 square feet

Kilometer=0.62 mile   Kilometer² (km²)=0.39 square mile

1:300,000
9 km²
3.48 square miles

1:6,000,000
3,600 km²
1,390 square miles

1:48,000,000
230,400 km²
88,934 square miles

1:1,000,000
100 km²
39 square miles

1:12,000,000
14,400 km²
5,558 square miles

1:3,000,000
900 km²
348 square miles

1:24,000,000
57,600 km²
22,234 square miles

Elevation tints shown only on 1:3,000,000 and 1:6,000,000 scale maps

Höhenschichten erscheinen nur auf Karten im Massstab 1:3 000 000 und 1:6 000 000

Se indica las tintas de elevación sólo en los mapas de escala 1:3 000 000 y 1:6 000 000

Teintes hypsométriques exprimées seulement sur cartes à 1:3 000 000 et 1:6 000 000

Indicaram-se as graduações de cor hipsométricas somente nos mapas de escalas 1:3 000 000 e 1:6 000 000

Meters	Feet
6000	19685
4000	13124
3000	9843
2000	6562
1000	3281
500	1640
200	656
Land 0	0
Below Sea Level 0	0
200	656
1000	3281
3000	9843
6000	19685
9000	29520

Alternate Names / Alternative Namensformen / Nombres Alternativos
Variantes Toponymiques / Variantes Toponímicas

MOSKVA
MOSCOW

English or second official language names are shown in reduced size lettering
Englische Namen oder Namen in einer zweiten offiziellen Sprache erscheinen in kleineren Schriftgrössen

Basel
Bâle

Los nombres en inglés o un segundo idioma oficial se muestran en tipo de imprenta mas pequeño
Les toponymes en anglais ou dans la seconde langue officielle sont indiqués en caractères plus petits
Os topônimos em inglês ou num segundo idioma oficial aparecem em tipologia menor

VOLGOGRAD
(STALINGRAD)

Historical or other alternates in the local language are shown in parentheses
Historische oder alternative Namensformen einheimischen Sprache erscheinen in Klammern

Ventura
(San Buenaventura)

Los nombres históricos y alternativos locales se muestran en paréntesis
Les noms historiques de lieux ou les variantes toponymiques locales sont mis entre parenthèses
Os topônimos históricos ou as variantes toponímicas locais aparecem entre parênteses

180
BRITISH
182
COLUMBIA
ALBERTA
SASKATCHEWAN
MANITOBA
184
C A N A D A
ONTARIO
QUEBEC
186
P. E. I.
N. B.
NOVA SCOTIA
NEWFOUNDLAND
224
WASH.
MONTANA
NORTH DAKOTA
MINN.
OREGON
202
IDAHO
190
WISCONSIN
MICHIGAN
206
Montreal
275
VT.
MAINE
N.H.
212
Toronto
275
Buffalo 284
NEW YORK
210
207
Boston
283
MASS.
CONN.
SOUTH DAKOTA
198
WYOMING
Detroit
281
Cleveland
279
Pittsburgh
279
214
216
Chicago
278
IOWA
NEBRASKA
N.J.
New York 276
PA.
Philadelphia
285
San Francisco
282
226
NEVADA
204
UTAH
U N I T E D
S T A T E S
COLORADO
ILL.
IND.
OHIO
Baltimore 284
Washington
284
188
W. VA.
219
218
CALIFORNIA
200
KANSAS
MISSOURI
KENTUCKY
VIRGINIA
208
Los Angeles
280
228
ARIZONA
NEW MEXICO
OKLAHOMA
194
TENNESSEE
NORTH CAROLINA
ARKANSAS
SOUTH CAROLINA
BAJA CAL. NORTE
ALABAMA
GEORGIA
MISS.
192
196
TEXAS
222
LOUISIANA
SONORA
232
CHIHUAHUA
FLA.
220
BAJA CAL. SUR
COAHUILA
M E X I C O
NUEVO LEON
SINALOA
DURANGO
TAMAULIPAS
238

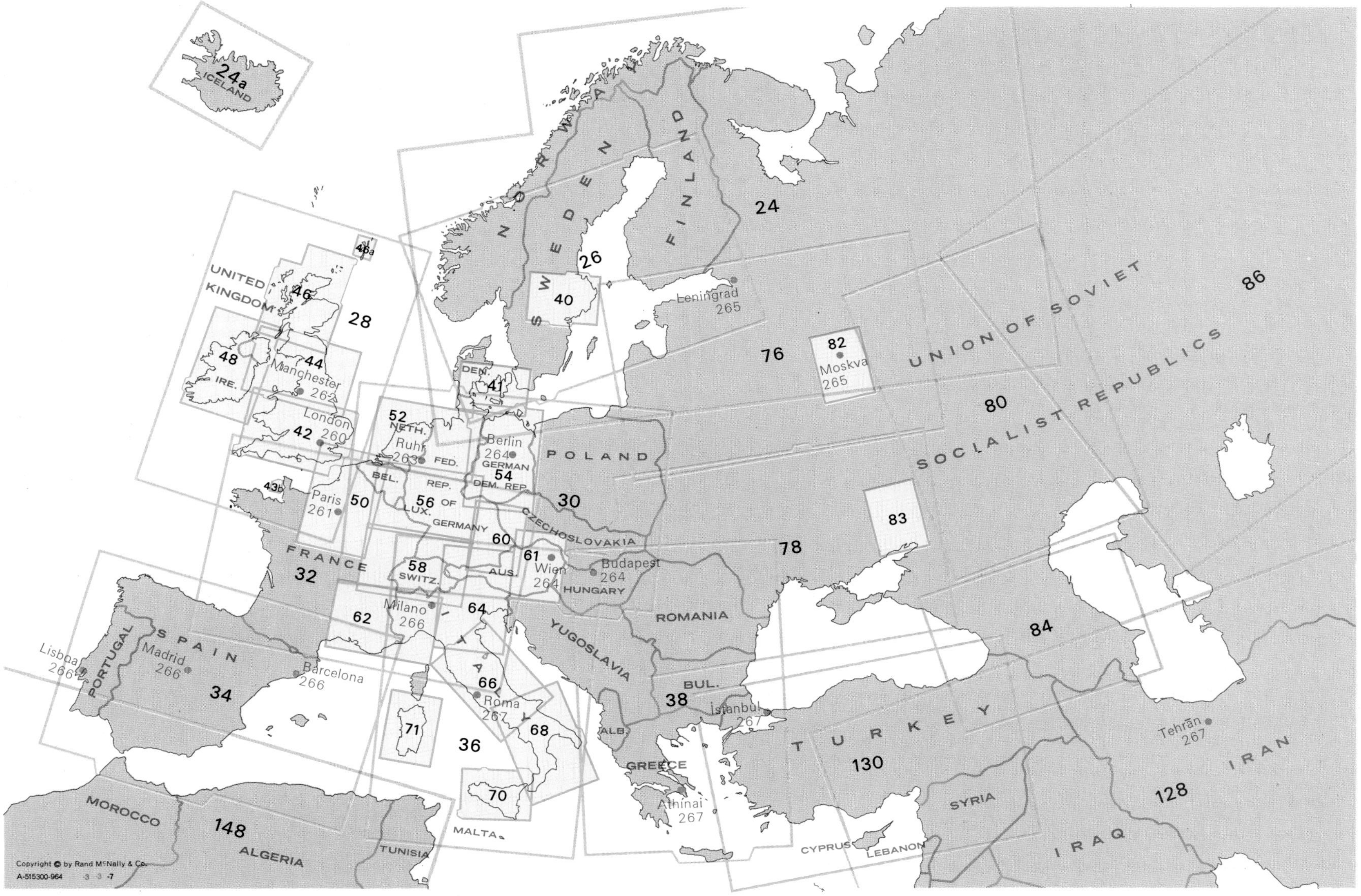
24a
ICELAND
N O R W A Y
S W E D E N
F I N L A N D
24
26
40
Leningrad
265
46a
UNITED KINGDOM
46
28
48
IRE.
44
Manchester
262
76
82
Moskva
265
U N I O N O F S O V I E T
S O C I A L I S T R E P U B L I C S
86
80
DEN.
41
52
NETH.
Ruhr
263
FED.
London
260
42
Berlin
264
GERMAN
DEM. REP.
54
P O L A N D
BEL.
REP.
OF
GERMANY
LUX.
43b
Paris
261
50
56
30
CZECHOSLOVAKIA
83
60
F R A N C E
32
61
Wien
264
Budapest
264
HUNGARY
AUS.
58
SWITZ.
78
62
Milano
266
64
ROMANIA
84
S P A I N
Madrid
266
34
PORTUGAL
Lisboa
266
Barcelona
266
I T A L Y
66
Roma
267
YUGOSLAVIA
BUL.
38
İstanbul
267
71
68
36
ALB.
T U R K E Y
130
Tehrān
267
I R A N
GREECE
70
Athinai
267
SYRIA
128
MOROCCO
148
ALGERIA
TUNISIA
MALTA
CYPRUS
LEBANON
I R A Q
Copyright © by Rand McNally & Co.
A-515300-964 -3 -3 -7

World Index Maps / Welt Indexkarten / Indice de Mapas del Mundo
Index des Cartes du Monde / Índice de Mapas do Mundo

MAP COVERAGE / KARTENAUSSCHNITTE
CONTENIDO DEL ATLAS / TABLEAU D'ASSEMBLAGE
ABRANGÊNCIA DO MAPA

Map Scale

Manila 269 • 1:300,000

▢ 1:1,000,000   ▢ 1:6,000,000

▢ 1:3,000,000   ▢ 1:12,000,000

148   Page Reference / Seitenangabe
      Página de Referencia / Page de Référence / Página de Referência

Enlarged maps of Anglo-America and Europe on page xiii.
Vergrösserte Karten von Anglo-Amerika und Europa auf Seite xiii.
Mapas aumentados de América Anglosajona y Europa, página xiii.
Cartes à grande échelle de l'Ámerique anglo-saxonne et de l'Europe à la page xiii.
Mapas ampliados da América Anglo-saxônica e da Europa, página xiii.

World, Ocean, and Continent maps on pages 2-19.
Weltkarten, Karten der Ozeane und Erdteile auf Seiten 2-19.
Mapas del Mundo, Océanos y Continentes, páginas 2-19.
Cartes du Monde, des Océans et des Continents aux pages 2-19.
Mapas do Mundo, dos Oceanos e dos Continentes, páginas 2-19.

Additional Pacific Ocean Island maps on pages 174-175.
Zusätzliche Karten der Inseln des Pazifischen Ozeans auf Seite 174-175.
Mapas adicionales de las Islas del Océano Pacífico, páginas174-175.
Cartes supplémentaires des Îles de l'Océan Pacifique aux pages 174-175.
Mapas suplementares das ilhas do Oceano Pacífico, páginas 174-175.

UNION OF SOVIET SOCIALIST REPUBLICS
Pacific Ocean
Indian Ocean
MONGOLIA
CHINA
JAPAN
KOREA
TURKEY
SYRIA
IRAQ
IRAN
AFGHANISTAN
PAKISTAN
INDIA
NEPAL
BURMA
THAILAND
LAOS
VIETNAM
CAMBODIA
MALAYSIA
INDONESIA
BORNEO
JAVA
SUMATRA
PHILIPPINES
TAIWAN
EGYPT
SAUDI ARABIA
OMAN
YEMEN
SUDAN
ETHIOPIA
SOMALIA
KENYA
TANZANIA
ZAMBIA
ZIMBABWE
MOZAMBIQUE
MADAGASCAR
SRI LANKA
PAPUA NEW GUINEA
NEW GUINEA
SOLOMON ISLANDS
AUSTRALIA
NEW ZEALAND
TASMANIA
Black Sea
Caspian Sea
Red Sea
Tehrān 267
Delhi 272
Calcutta 272
Bombay 272
Shanghai 269
Hong Kong
Singapore 271
Jakarta 268
Sydney 274
Melbourne
24 76 78 80 84 85 86 88 89 92 92a 93b 94 98 100 102 104 105 106 107 110 112 114 115a 115b 116 120 122 123 124 126 128 130 132 140 142 144 154 157a 157b 157c 162 164 166 168a 168b 169 170 171a 171b 172 174m 175b 175c 175d 175e 175f 175g

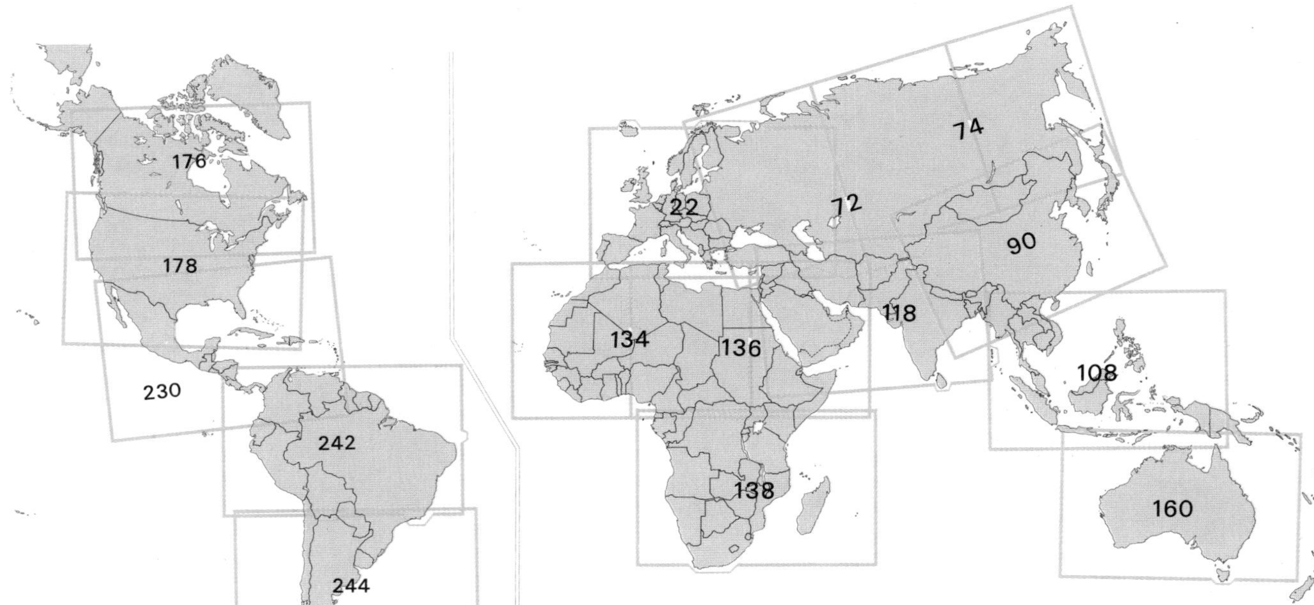
176 178 230 242 244 22 72 74 90 118 134 136 138 108 160

World Scene

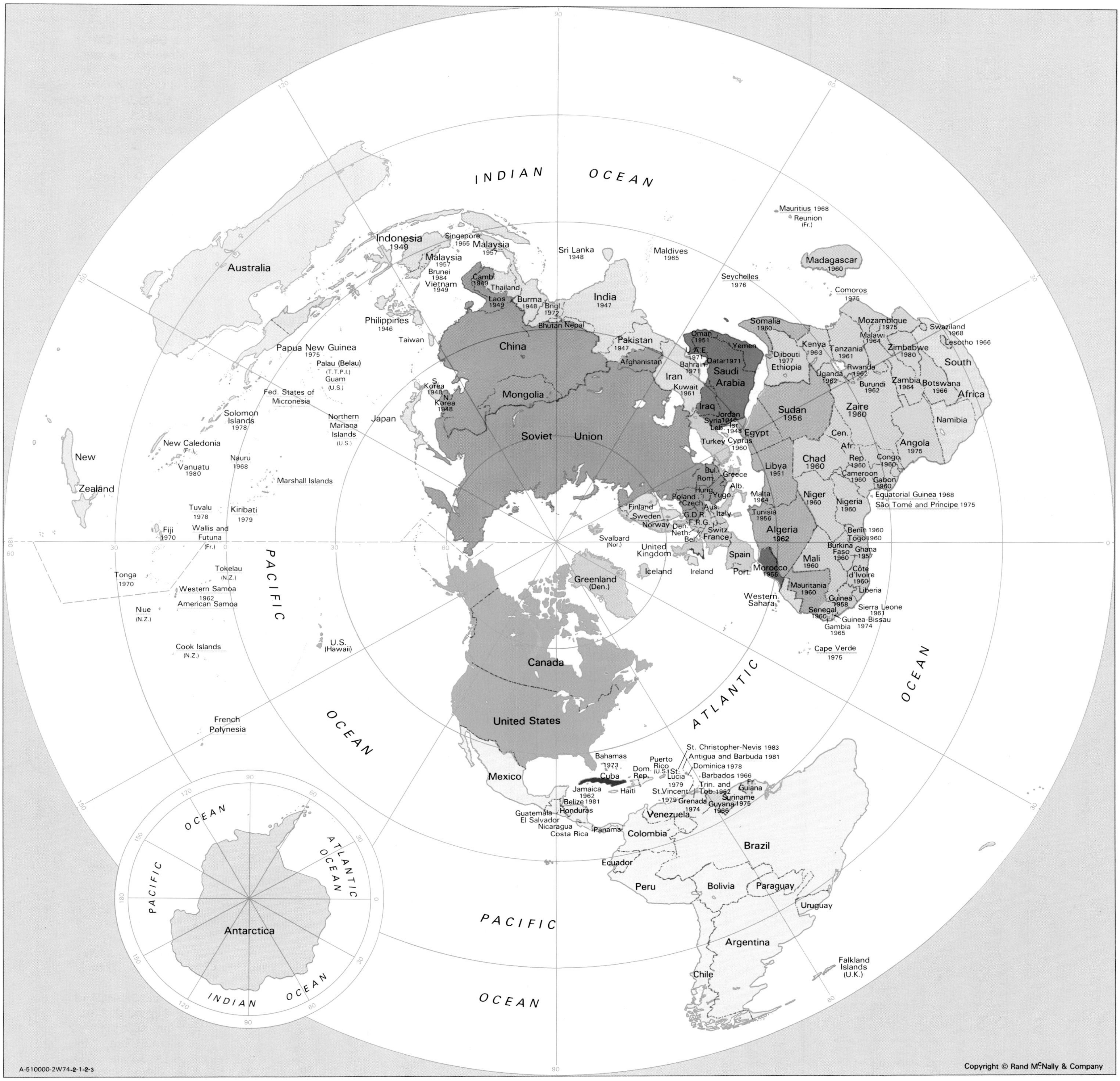

Copyright © Rand McNally & Company

Intergovernmental Organizations

The rise and evolution of the nation-state in the Twentieth century has many parallels with the history of smaller states in earlier times. The gradual admission of scores of new countries to the world community after World War II, indicated on the map above by the dates of their independence, also created certain opportunities for these new countries that had formerly been the prerogative of a much smaller community of independent states. Until the 19th century, the countries to which international law was applicable was confined to the principal states of Europe and such others, like those of the Americas, as had asserted their independence and right to be treated as equals, or those older kingdoms and states like Siam and Ethiopia that had preserved their independence in an era of colonialism and had, perforce, to be treated as equals in treaty relationships. But equality as a matter of international law does not constitute equality of opportunity, identity of national interest, or safety from aggression. Consequently, despite the aims and achievements of the United Nations, there remains the need for intergovernmental organizations as a means for small and large countries to promote economic advancement, military security, or to assert their cultural identity with a stronger voice than a single country might possess. The organizations shown represent some of the principal regional and mutual-interest organizations created to advance those interests.

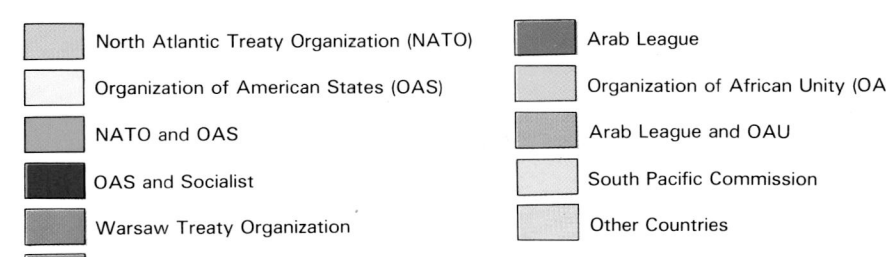

- North Atlantic Treaty Organization (NATO)
- Organization of American States (OAS)
- NATO and OAS
- OAS and Socialist
- Warsaw Treaty Organization
- Other Socialist
- Arab League
- Organization of African Unity (OAU)
- Arab League and OAU
- South Pacific Commission
- Other Countries

Seaward Claims

Common territorial sea claims

- 3 nautical miles
- 6 nautical miles
- 12 nautical miles

Less common claims

- 4 nautical miles
- 10 nautical miles
- Over 12 nautical miles
- Unusual claim

Other features

- Landlocked countries
- Continental shelf

Note: Territorial claims of outlying islands to their offshore waters are the same as those of the administering country.

The growth of international law on the legal status of the portions of the seas claimed by coastal states probably began in the early 17th century, when conflicting claims to parts of the high seas by colonial and exploring European sea powers induced the Dutch jurist Hugo Grotius to write *Mare liberum* (1609), on the concept of the "free, or open, sea." His work was answered in 1617-18 by John Selden's *Mare clausum*, proposing that the seas were as subject to property rights and claims as land areas. The first successful synthesis of the two positions was Cornelis van Bynkershoek's *De dominio maris* (1702) in which he suggested that the seaward limit of a national claim should be that of its effective land-based control (the distance of a cannon-shot, three nautical miles). Though never universally accepted, that standard persisted well into the twentieth century.

After World War II, however, both traditional sea-based economic activity—fishing, commercial navigation—and activities made newly possible or intensified by technological change—exploitation of the seabed, pollution, scientific investigation—led coastal states to make increasingly wider claims to both territorial seas, those wholly subject to national law, and to zones in which some, but not all, sovereign rights were claimed, usually to protect economic, but especially fishing, interests. The first Law of the Sea Conference in 1958 attempted under UN auspices to codify international law in these areas. More than 14 years later at the final meeting of the Third Conference, a text representing the efforts of some 150 countries was opened for signature on Dec. 10, 1982 as the *United Nations Convention on the Law of the Sea*. Accessions were deposited that day by 119 states to a document providing definitions, guidelines, procedures, and institutions to govern a wide range of maritime law and activities.

Among the subjects relating to sovereignty delimited by the Convention were sections defining the rights, jurisdiction, and duties of coastal states in matters relating to the territorial sea, the right of innocent passage, international straits, archipelagic (island) states, exclusive economic zones (EEZ's), the continental shelf, the high seas, as well as access to, and use of, areas of the sea beyond the jurisdiction of a single national power.

Territorial sea may be claimed up to a distance of 12 nautical miles (n.m.) from either the shoreline of a coastal state (measured from low water on navigational charts), or from a straight baseline defined by the state when its shoreline is very irregular, as is that of Norway. Waters directly connected to the sea behind this baseline are called internal waters, and include bays (which may be closed at the mouth by a single baseline if they are less than 24 n.m. wide, and river mouths and estuaries. A zone contiguous to the territorial sea not wider than 24 n.m. beyond the baselines defining the territorial sea is defined in which states may exercise *limited* control for customs, immigration, fiscal, or sanitary reasons. Another zone, defined in relation to the continental shelf (the seaward prolongation of the coastal landmass beneath the sea) permits extension of the national sovereignty over the seabed and subsoil of the zone to the edge of the continental margin (the lower termination of the continental slope and rise) for purposes of exploration, scientific study, or economic exploitation of either biological or mineral resources.

In areas of the seas where coastal states lie in close proximity, the seaward extension of a national boundary may necessitate the drawing or negotiation of an international boundary in the sea. Where claims permissible under the Convention overlap, as in the Persian Gulf, median lines must be drawn so as to accommodate each state's maximum claim without disadvantaging bordering states.

The table opposite provides a description of the nature of current national claims to territorial seas and of the economic, usually fishing, zones that have been declared *within* the permissible 200-n.m. limits of the potential EEZ permitted by the Convention.

Offshore zones

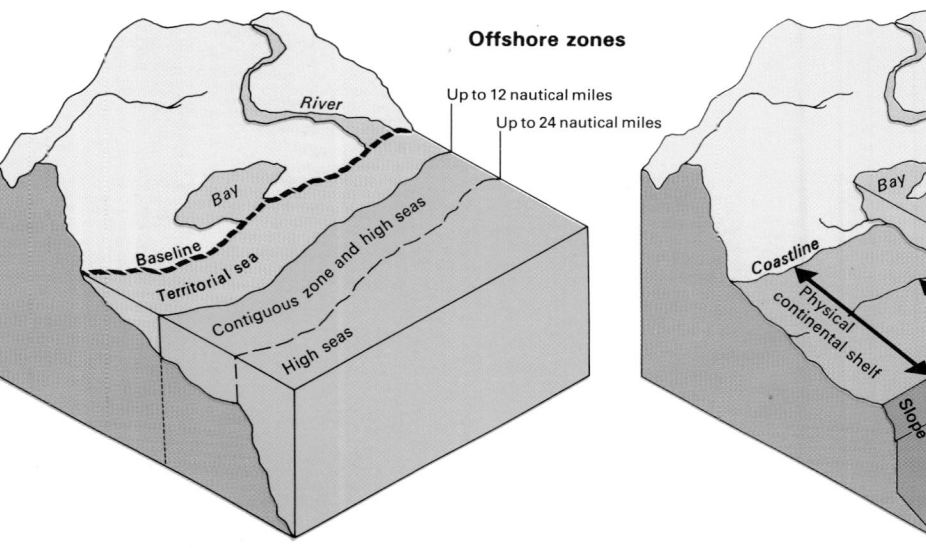

Up to 12 nautical miles
Up to 24 nautical miles

Irregular coastline of Norway

Norway measures its territorial sea from a straight baseline, which in general runs along the outer fringe of offshore islands and coastal promontories. The Law of the Sea Convention permits this type of claim in the case of highly irregular coastlines fringed with islands. In other cases the coastal features do not justify such claims to additional waters, and the claims may not be recognized.

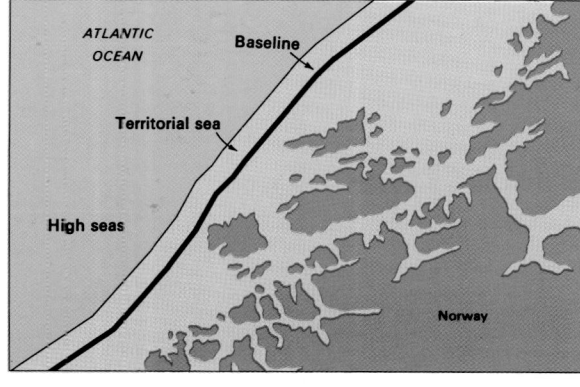

Overlapping claims in the Persian Gulf

The waters of the Persian Gulf are less than 200 meters in depth and the entire seabed is continental shelf. To determine the extent of jurisdiction that each state has over the resources of the seabed beyond its territorial sea, the Law of the Sea Convention provides for median lines, measured from the same baseline as the territorial sea. The median lines divide the continental shelf between opposite and adjacent states.

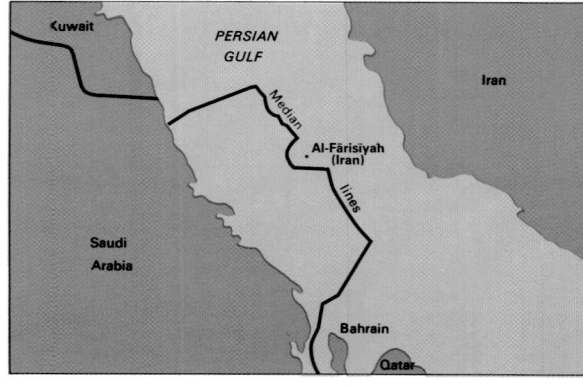

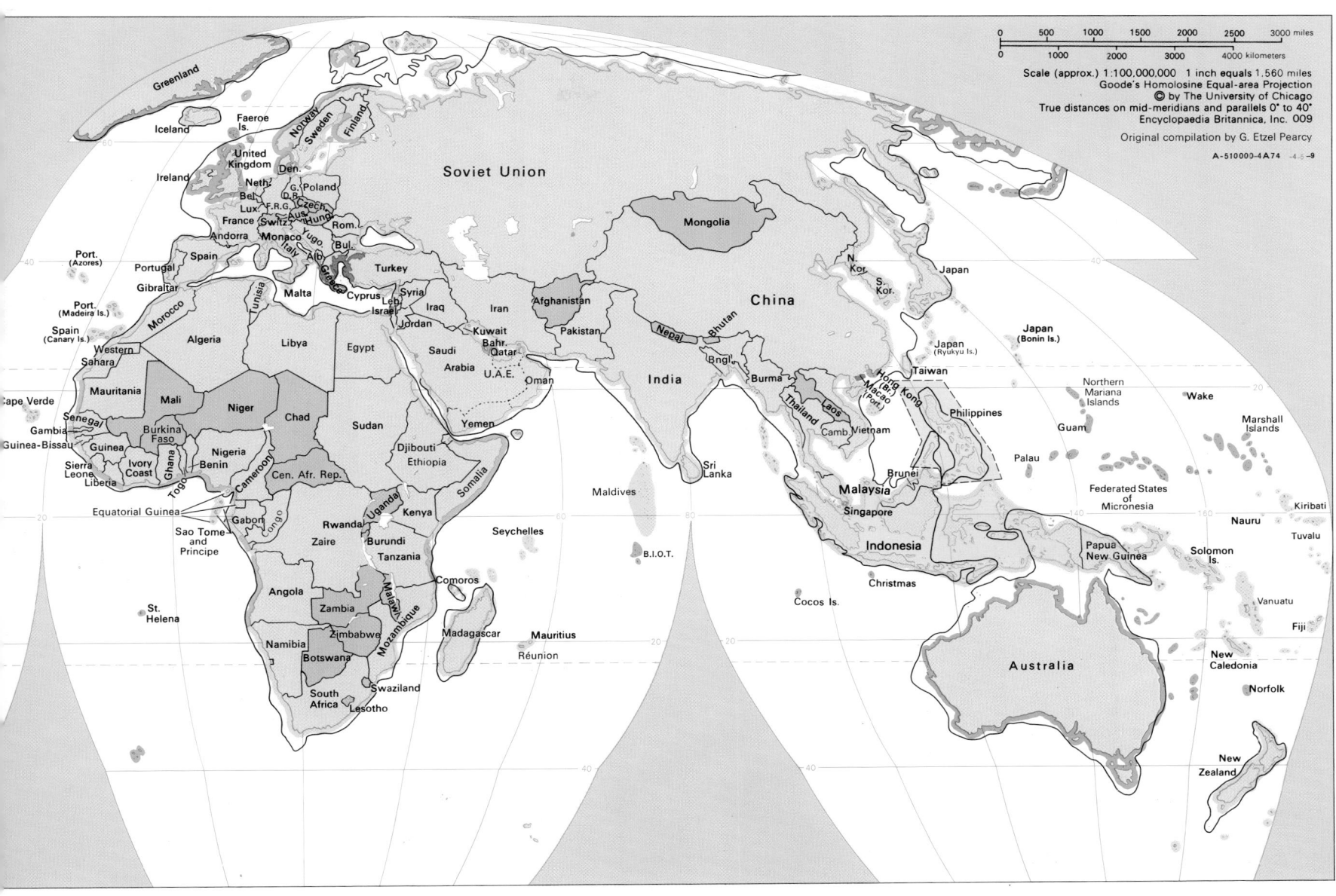

Scale (approx.) 1:100,000,000   1 inch equals 1,560 miles
Goode's Homolosine Equal-area Projection
© by The University of Chicago
True distances on mid-meridians and parallels 0° to 40°
Encyclopaedia Britannica, Inc. 009

Original compilation by G. Etzel Pearcy

A-510000-4A74

Political unit	Territorial sea claim*	Fishing claim*†	Political unit	Territorial sea claim*	Fishing claim*†	Political unit	Territorial sea claim*	Fishing claim*†
Albania	15 A		Gibraltar	3 B		Oman	12 A	200 D
Algeria	12 A		Greece	6		Pakistan	12	200 D
Angola	20 A	200	Greenland	3 B	200	Palau	3 B	200 D
Antigua and Barbuda	12	200 D	Grenada	12	200 D	Panama	200 A	
Argentina	200 A		Guatemala	12 A	200 D	Papua New Guinea	12 C	200 D
Aruba	12 B		Guinea	12 A	200 D	Peru	200	
Australia	3 A	200	Guinea-Bissau	12 A	200 D	Philippines		200 D
Bahamas	3	200	Guyana	12	200	Poland	12 A	200
Bahrain	3		Haiti	12 A	200 D	Portugal	12 A	200 D
Bangladesh	12 A	200 D	Honduras	12	200 D	Puerto Rico	3 B	200 D
Barbados	12	200 D	Hong Kong	3 B		Qatar	3	200 D
Belgium	3	200	Iceland	12 A	200 D	Romania	12	200 D
Belize	200		India	12	200 D	St. Christopher-Nevis	12	200 D
Benin	200		Indonesia	12 C	200 D	St. Lucia	12	200 D
Bermuda	3 B	200	Iran	12 A	50	St. Pierre and Miquelon	12 B	200 D
Brazil	200 A		Iraq	12		St. Vincent and the Grenadines	12	200 D
Brunei	12	200	Ireland	3 A	200	Sao Tome and Principe	12 C	200 D
Bulgaria	12 A		Israel	6		Saudi Arabia	12 A	
Burma	12 A	200 D	Italy	12		Senegal	12 A	200
Cambodia	12 A	200 D	Ivory Coast	12	200 D	Seychelles	12	200 D
Cameroon	50 A		Jamaica	12		Sierra Leone	200	
Canada	12 A	200 D	Japan	12	200	Singapore	3	12
Cape Verde	12 C	200 D	Jordan	3		Solomon Islands	12 C	200 D
Chile	12 A	200	Kenya	12 A	200 D	Somalia	200 A	
China	12 A		Kiribati	12	200	South Africa	12	200
Colombia	12 A	200 D	Korea, North	12	200 D	Soviet Union	12 A	200 D
Comoros	12 C	200 D	Korea, South	12 A		Spain	12 AC	200 D
Congo	200		Kuwait	12 A		Sri Lanka	12 A	200 D
Cook Islands	12 B	200 D	Lebanon	12		Sudan	12 A	
Costa Rica	12	200 D	Liberia	200		Suriname	12	200 D
Cuba	12 A	200 D	Libya	12 A		Sweden	12 A	200
Cyprus	12		Madagascar	12 A	200 D	Syria	35 A	
Denmark	3 A	200	Malaysia	12 A	200 D	Taiwan	12	200 D
Djibouti	12	200 D	Maldives	12	37-310 D	Tanzania	50 A	
Dominica	12	200 D	Malta	12 A	25	Thailand	12 A	200 D
Dominican Republic	6 A	200 D	Marshall Islands	3 B	200 D	Togo	30	200 D
Ecuador	200 A		Mauritania	70 A	200 D	Tonga	12 A	200 D
Egypt	12 A	200 D	Mauritius	12 A	200 D	Trinidad and Tobago	12	200 D
El Salvador	200		Mexico	12 A	200 D	Tunisia	12 A	
Equatorial Guinea	12	200 D	Micronesia, Fed. States of	3 B	200 D	Turkey	6-12 A	200
Ethiopia	12 A		Monaco	12		Tuvalu	12	200 D
Faeroe Islands	3 B	200	Morocco	12 A	200 D	United Arab Emirates	12	200 D
Falkland Islands	3	200	Mozambique	12 A	200 D	United Kingdom	3 A	200
Fiji	12 C	200 D	Namibia	12	200	United States	3	200 D
Finland	4 A	12	Nauru	12	200	Uruguay	200	
France	12 A	200 D	Netherlands	12 A	200	Vanuatu	12 C	200 D
French Guiana	12 B	200 D	Netherlands Antilles	12		Venezuela	12 A	200 D
French Polynesia	12 B	200 D	New Caledonia	12 B	200 D	Vietnam	12 A	200 D
Gabon	12	200 D	New Zealand	12	200 D	Western Samoa	12	200 D
Gambia	200		Nicaragua	200		Yemen	12	
German Dem. Republic	12 A	200	Nigeria	30	200 D	Yugoslavia	12 A	
Germany, Fed. Republic of	3-16 A	200	Northern Mariana Islands	3 B	200 D	Zaire	12	200
Ghana	200		Norway	4 A	200 D			

* Nautical miles
† When claim is beyond the territorial sea.

A. Measured from a straight baseline.
B. Same as that of administering country.
C. Extends beyond a perimeter drawn around archipelago.

D. Exclusive economic zone.

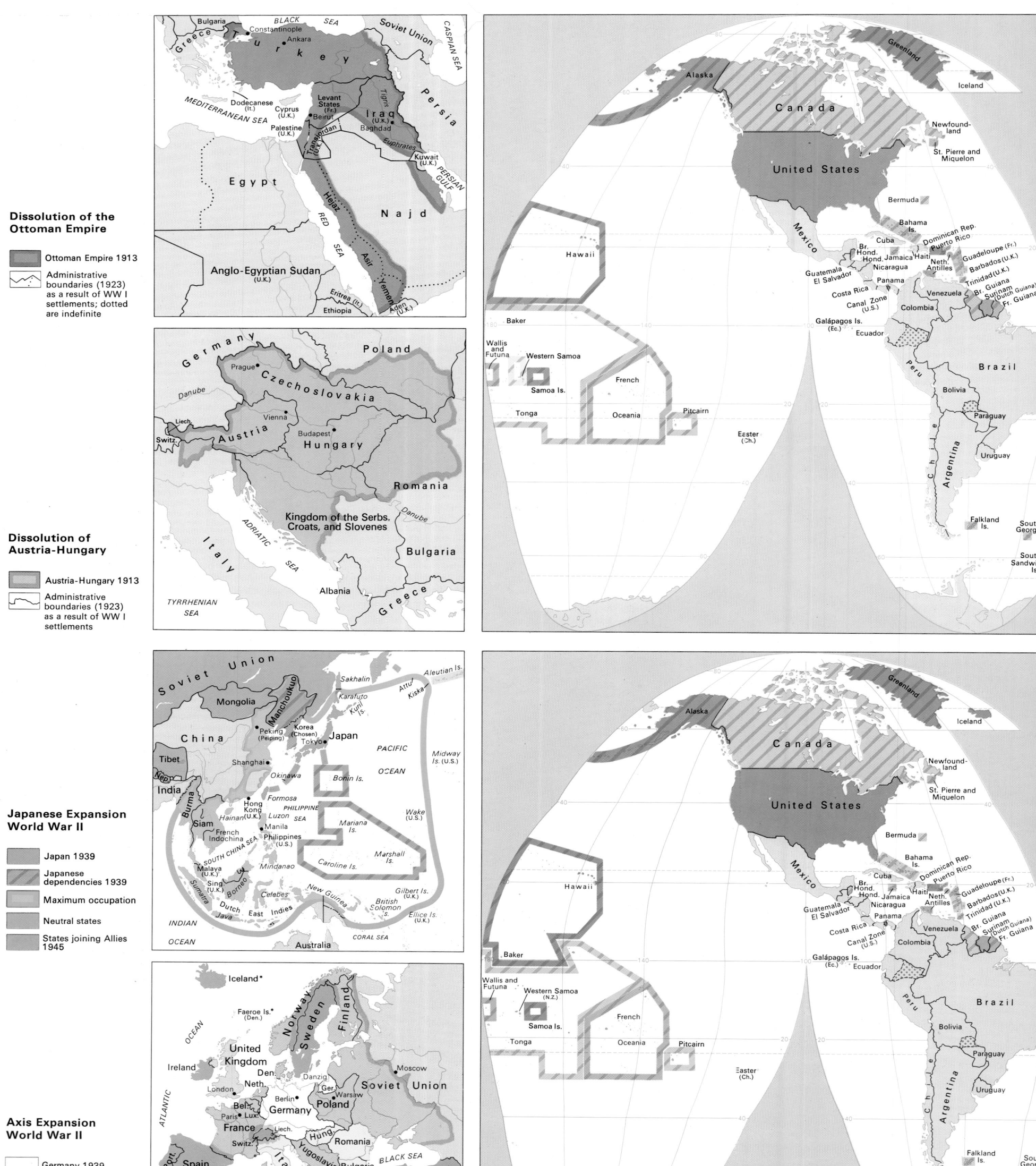

Dissolution of the Ottoman Empire

- Ottoman Empire 1913
- Administrative boundaries (1923) as a result of WW I settlements; dotted are indefinite

Dissolution of Austria-Hungary

- Austria-Hungary 1913
- Administrative boundaries (1923) as a result of WW I settlements

Japanese Expansion World War II

- Japan 1939
- Japanese dependencies 1939
- Maximum occupation
- Neutral states
- States joining Allies 1945

Axis Expansion World War II

- Germany 1939
- Other Axis Powers 1940-45
- Maximum occupation
- Neutral states
- States joining Allies 1943-45

*Occupied by Allies

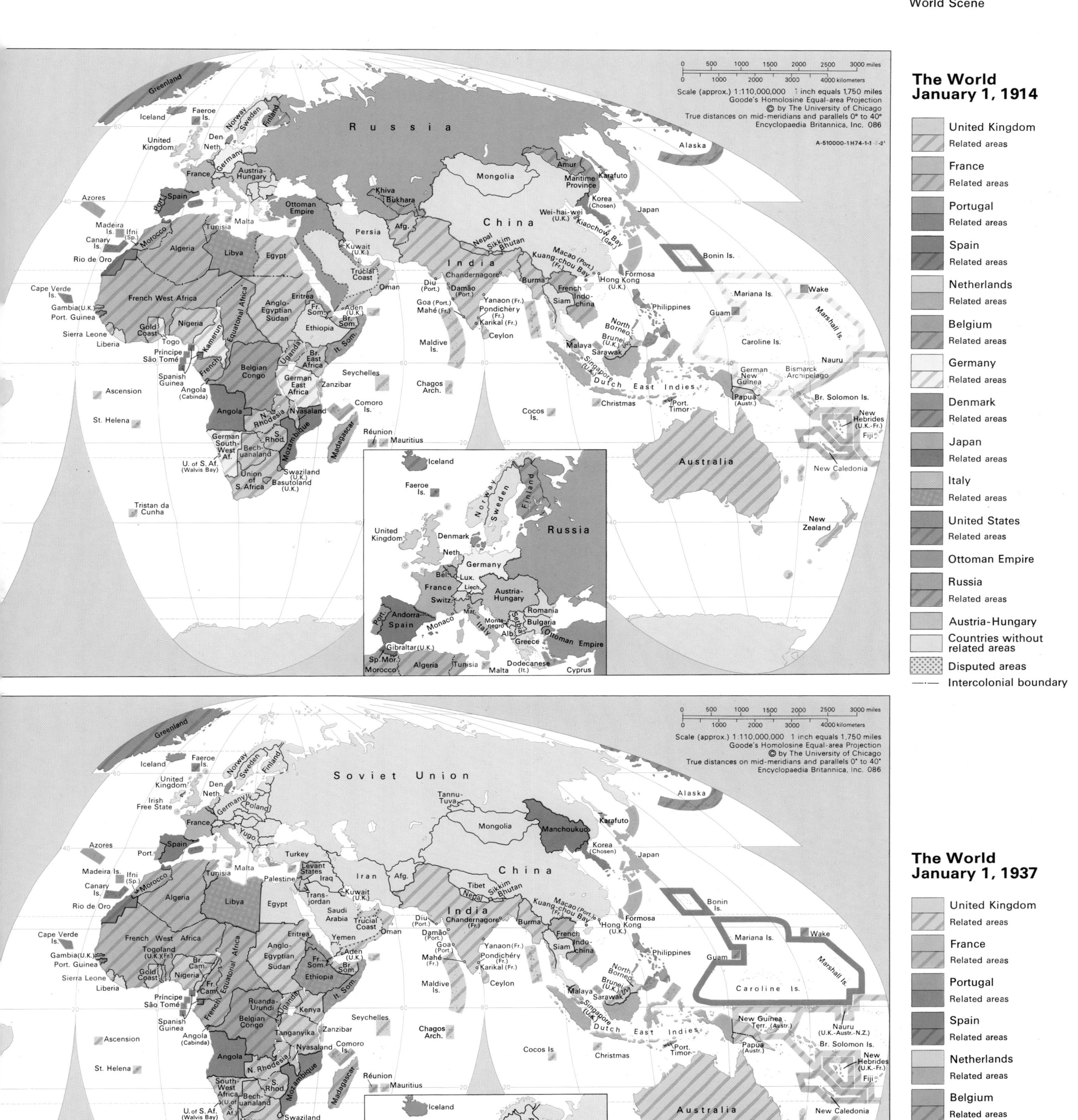

Scale (approx.) 1:110,000,000   1 inch equals 1,750 miles
Goode's Homolosine Equal-area Projection
© by The University of Chicago
True distances on mid-meridians and parallels 0° to 40°
Encyclopaedia Britannica, Inc. 086

A-510000-1 H74-1-1 -2'

The World January 1, 1914

United Kingdom
Related areas

France
Related areas

Portugal
Related areas

Spain
Related areas

Netherlands
Related areas

Belgium
Related areas

Germany
Related areas

Denmark
Related areas

Japan
Related areas

Italy
Related areas

United States
Related areas

Ottoman Empire

Russia
Related areas

Austria-Hungary

Countries without related areas

Disputed areas

Intercolonial boundary

Scale (approx.) 1:110,000,000   1 inch equals 1,750 miles
Goode's Homolosine Equal-area Projection
© by The University of Chicago
True distances on mid-meridians and parallels 0° to 40°
Encyclopaedia Britannica, Inc. 086

The World January 1, 1937

United Kingdom
Related areas

France
Related areas

Portugal
Related areas

Spain
Related areas

Netherlands
Related areas

Belgium
Related areas

Denmark
Related areas

Japan
Related areas

Italy
Related areas

United States
Related areas

Countries without related areas

Disputed areas

Intercolonial boundary

Population

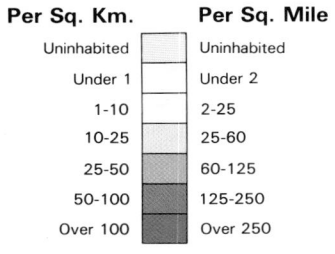

Per Sq. Km.	Per Sq. Mile
Uninhabited	Uninhabited
Under 1	Under 2
1-10	2-25
10-25	25-60
25-50	60-125
50-100	125-250
Over 100	Over 250

● Metropolitan areas over 2,000,000 population
○ Metropolitan areas 1,000,000 to 2,000,000 population

Some cities are identified by initial letter only.

The numbers and distribution of human beings on their planet and the forms that their occupance takes are controlled by a variety of factors. The main population map opposite focuses on identifying the location and density of the most populous regions and cities of the earth. The Urbanization inset highlights the propensity of man to congregate in cities and the group of "age pyramids" below illustrates some of the diversity that is concealed within apparently simple population totals.

Population

The patterns of distribution shown display certain characteristics worldwide: relative densities decline with altitude (and the capacity of the land to support higher densities); settlement patterns follow rivers, or focus on harbours opening on large bodies of water connecting populous, economically interrelated areas; populations tend to fill up contiguous areas of similar topographical and climatic opportunity, whether in coastal plains, intermontane basins, along railroad right-of-ways, or in biologically and climatically defined regions of similar soil, vegatative response, or access from more populous areas.

The main map also identifies the largest cities of the world, distinguishing between those of 1-2 million and more than 2 million population. The selection of cities is determined by the concept of "city proper," that is, usually the smallest contiguous civilly or adminstratively defined and named entity. The meaning of the concept in terms of local practice worldwide, however, is considerable. A city of 100,000 may in one country be a single social, economic, and administrative place, bound together fully by its transportation infrastructure and representing a single *urban* entity in its population's collective mind. A city of the same apparent size in another country, however, might represent something more nearly characterizable as 100 villages of 1,000 persons, pursuing separate economic activities in separate neighbourhoods, often poorly interconnected, sometimes still predominately rural in terms of economic activity, and perhaps not universally understood by its own people as the greater place seen by others.

Urbanization

The concept of "urban" exemplified on the inset map of urbanization is particularly elusive in international studies of population, as most countries have their own definition of the concept, appropriate to local conditions and discourse, but often unsuitable for international comparisons. It is that local concept which is mapped here. Size is a useful indicator as to whether a place is classifiable as "urban," but as indicated above, the "size" of a place, even in the presence of administrative requirements may be misleading. Japan defines a place as "urban" if it has 50,000 or more population and meets certain criteria for their location within the city. A smaller country with a less hospitable landscape, like Iceland or Norway, might, by the same token, define a place as small as 200 as "urban" if it had predominately non-rural employment patterns, administrative function, or its houses were closer together than some set distance. The concept of "metropolitan area," or urban areas contiguous with a central city that are economically dependent on it is also complex and interpreted differently throughout the world. The inset map of urbanization extends the city proper concept of the main map by showing metropolitan areas of more than 2 million. As can be seen from comparison of the two maps, sometimes high urbanization may correlate with relatively low numbers or densities of population. This occurs when the majority of a population lives in large settlements, rather than distributed across an entire landscape and may happen either because of localized economic and employment opportunities in the city, or because the countryside is unsuitable for agricultural or other exploitation. The strong correlation, however, is still between highly populous areas and large cities.

Age and sex composition

Among the characteristics of a population having the greatest significance both in terms of current needs and future trends, the age and sex composition of a population is perhaps the most important. Several examples are presented at the right of a graphic called an "age pyramid," which summarizes the relative proportion of males and females in each age cohort of a population. These examples, drawn by five-year age groups, often illuminate the effects on the whole population of the recent history of the relative growth or diminution of smaller parts of the whole: war losses, emigration of the young for work abroad, natural causes like disasters. The origins of the concern of many countries and organizations with uncontrolled population growth may be inferred from examples like Brazil, where the high proportion of young people means enormous numbers (both absolutely and relatively) in or near their childbearing years resulting in growth rates for the total population that can outrun the far more difficult-to-attain economic growth rates that determine the relative prosperity of a country. Japan, on the other hand, shows a pattern typical of a demographically mature population, that is, a population which is growing slowly or not at all, resulting in lower, more predictable, and more economically supportable demographic rates, but also foreshadowing the movement of large numbers of its people into the pensionable and financially dependent age groups without large numbers of younger workers to support them. The Japanese example also shows, in a somewhat smoothed form, the effects of some of the viscissitudes of Twentieth century history on the relative size of certain age groups.

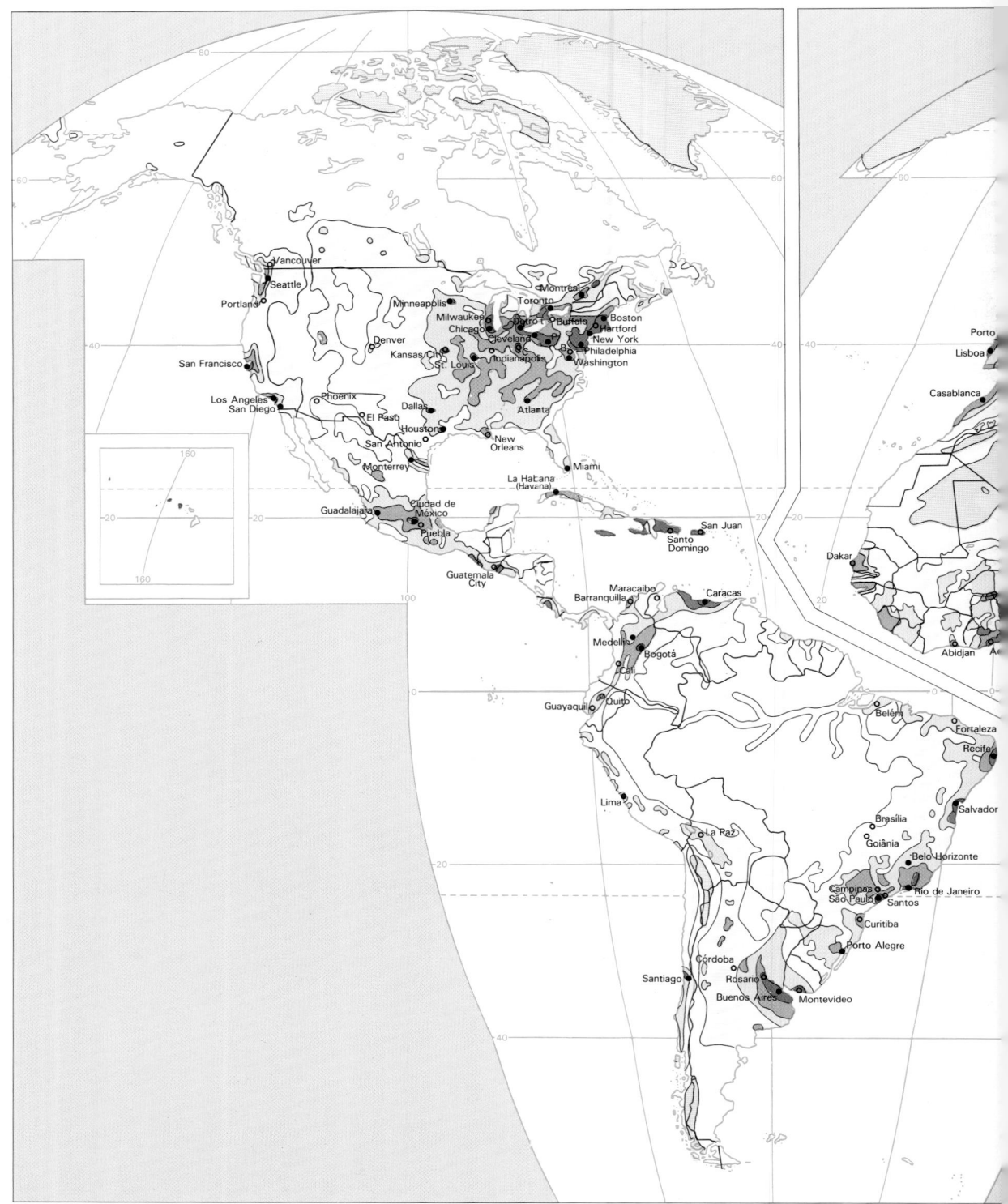

Age and sex composition

■ Male
■ Female

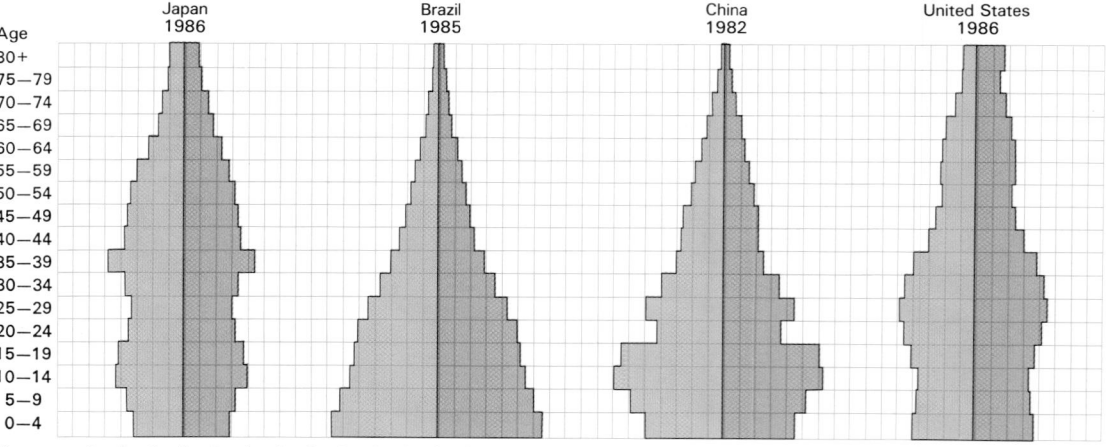

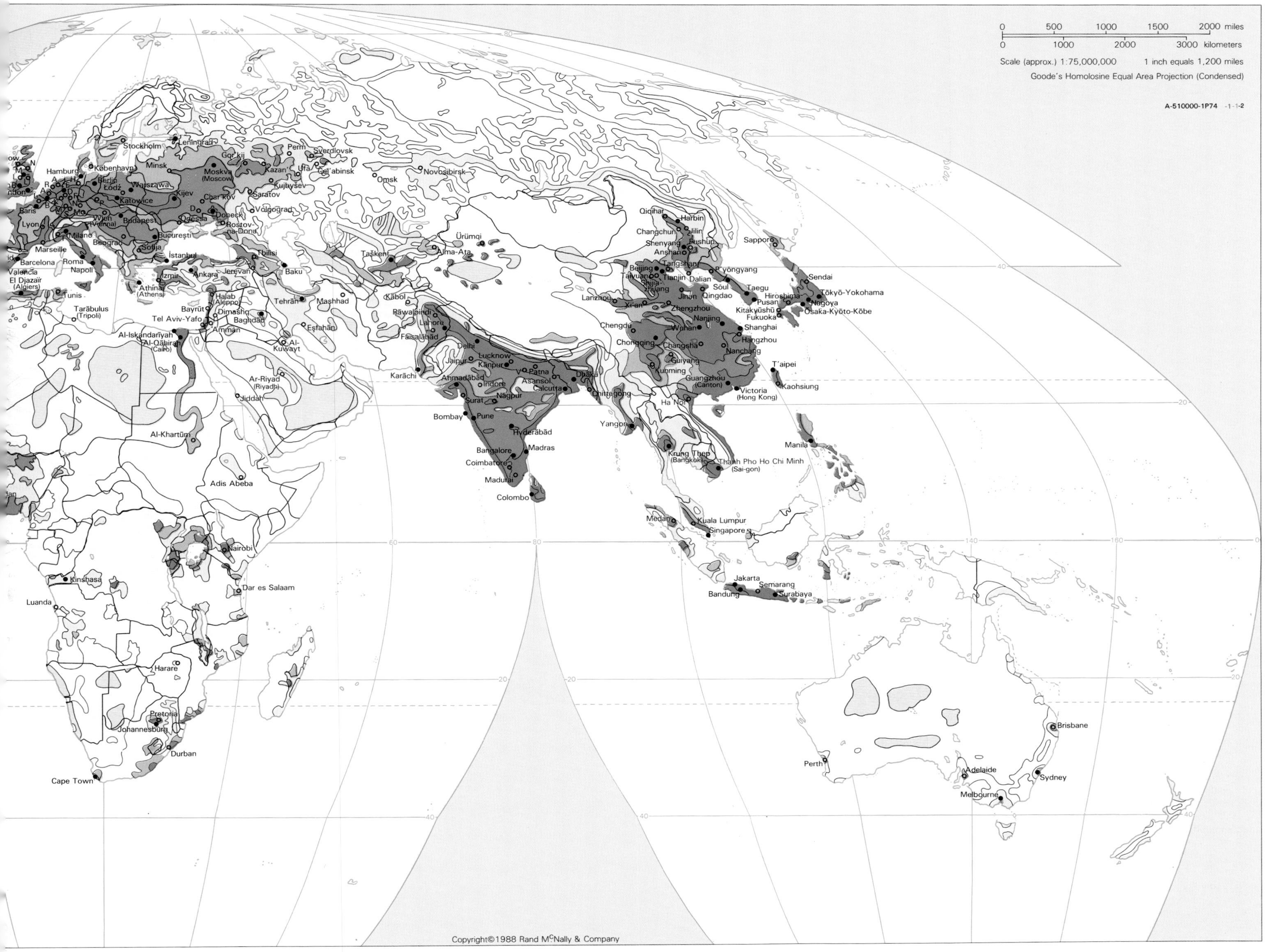

0   500   1000   1500   2000 miles
0   1000   2000   3000 kilometers
Scale (approx.) 1:75,000,000   1 inch equals 1,200 miles
Goode's Homolosine Equal Area Projection (Condensed)
A-510000-1P74   -1-1-2

Stockholm Leningrad Perm' Sverdlovsk
Hamburg København Minsk Gor'kij Čeljabinsk Omsk Novosibirsk
Berlin Łódź Kijev Kazan' Ufa Saratov
Wien Wrocław Moskva (Moscow) Kujbyšev
Katowice Don- Rostov-na-Donu Volgograd
Lyon Beograd Bucureşti
Marseille Roma Sofia Istanbul Tbilisi Taškent Alma-Ata Ürümqi
Barcelona Napoli İzmir Ankara Jerevan Baku
Valencia Athina (Athenai) Tel Aviv-Yafo Tehrān Mashhad Kābol
El Djazaïr (Algiers) Tarābulus (Tripoli) Halab (Aleppo) Dimashq Rawalpindi Islāmābād
Tunis Bayrūt Baghdād Esfahān Faisalābād
Al-Iskandariyah Amman Al-Kuwayt Karāchi Lahore Jaipur Lucknow Kanpur Patna
Al-Qāhirah (Cairo) Ar-Riyāḍ (Riyadh) Ahmadābād Indore Asansol Calcutta Dhaka
Jiddah Nagpur Chittagong
Surat Bombay Pune Hyderābād
Al-Khartūm Bangalore Madras
Coimbatore
Madurai
Colombo

Qiqihar Harbin
Changchun Jilin
Shenyang Fushun Sapporo
Anshan
Beijing Tangshan Pyŏngyang Sendai
Tianjin Dalian Sŏul Pusan Tōkyō-Yokohama
Lanzhou Jinan Qingdao Taegu Hiroshima Nagoya
Xi'an Zhengzhou Kitakyūshū Osaka-Kyōto-Kōbe
Chengdu Wuhan Nanjing Fukuoka
Chongqing Changsha Nanchang Shanghai
Guiyang Hangzhou
Kunming Guangzhou (Canton) Taipei
Ha Nôi Victoria (Hong Kong) Kaohsiung
Yangon
Krung Thep (Bangkok) Thanh Pho Ho Chi Minh (Sai-gon) Manila

Medan Kuala Lumpur Singapore

Jakarta Semarang
Bandung Surabaya

Adis Abeba

Nairobi

Kinshasa Dar es Salaam
Luanda

Harare

Pretoria
Johannesburg
Durban
Cape Town

Perth Adelaide Brisbane
Melbourne Sydney

Copyright©1988 Rand McNally & Company

Urbanization

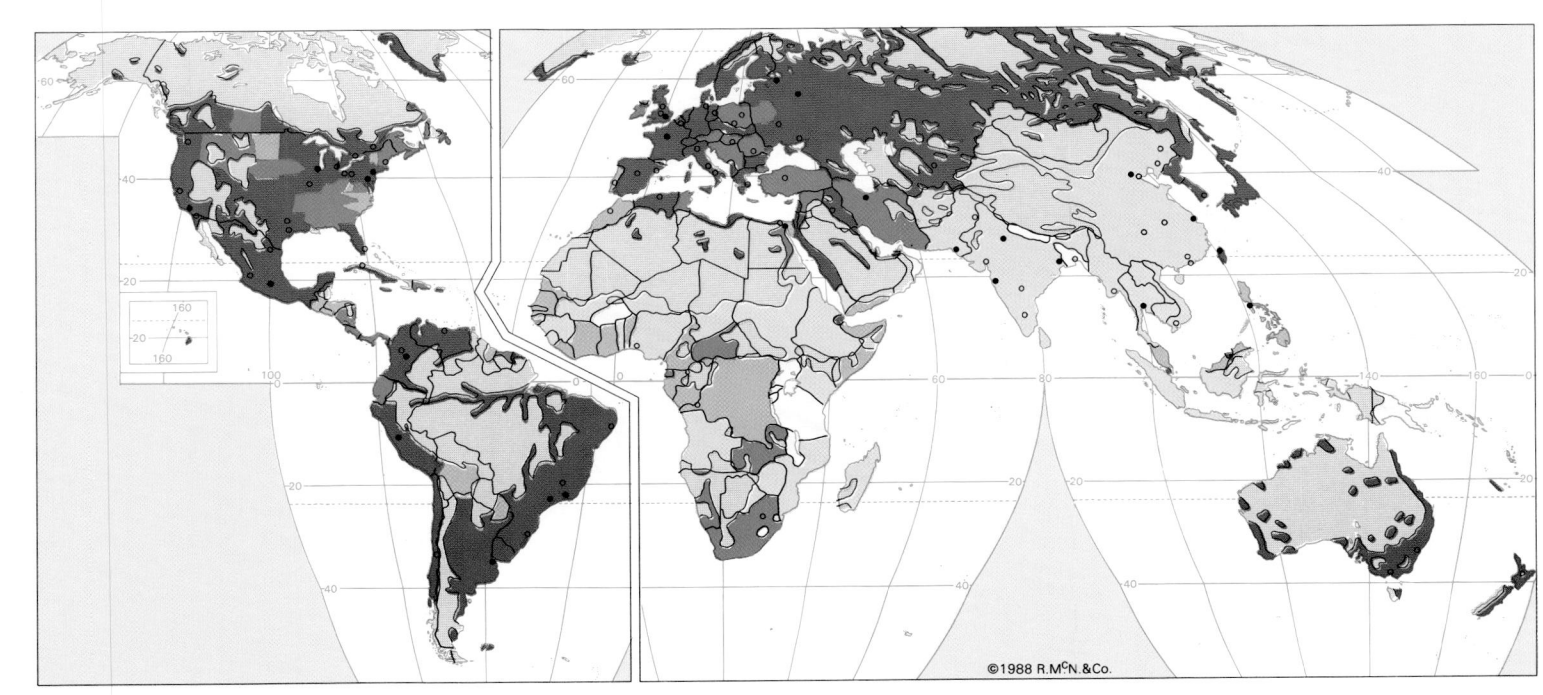

World Av. 42% →

- >60%
- 45-60
- 30-45
- 15-30
- <15
- Uninhabited or sparsely populated

- ● Metropolitan areas over 5,000,000 population
- ○ Metropolitan areas 2,000,000 to 5,000,000 population

©1988 R.McN.&Co.

Religions

The majority of the inhabitants in each of the areas colored on the map share the religious tradition indicated. Letter symbols show religious traditions shared by at least 25% of the inhabitants within areal units no smaller than one thousand square miles. Therefore minority religions of city-dwellers have generally not been represented.

	R	Roman Catholicism
	P	Protestantism
	E	Eastern Orthodox religions (including Armenian, Coptic, Ethiopian, Greek, and Russian Orthodox)
	M	Mormonism
	C	Christianity, undifferentiated by branch (chiefly mingled Protestantism and Roman Catholicism, neither predominant)
	I	Islam, predominantly Sunni
	Sh	Islam, predominantly Shia
		Theravada Buddhism
	L	Lamaism
	H	Hinduism
	J	Judaism
	Ch	Chinese religions *
	Ja	Japanese religions *
		Korean religions *
		Vietnamese religions *
	T	Simple ethnic (tribal) religions
	Sk	Sikhism
		Countries under Communist regimes; traditional religions often subject to restraint
		Uninhabited

*In certain Eastern Asian areas, most of the people have plural religious affiliations. Chinese, Korean, and Vietnamese religions include Mahayana Buddhism, Taoism, Confucianism, and folk cults. The Japanese religions include Shinto and Mahayana Buddhism.

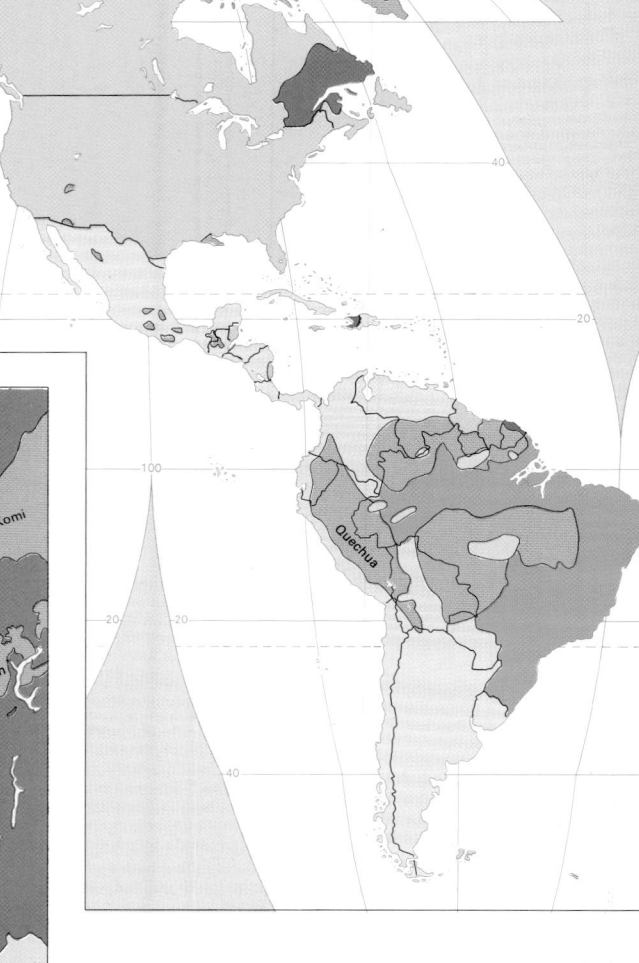

New World religions copyright by Encyclopaedia Britannica, Inc. Old World religions adapted by permission from *Geography of Religions*, D. E. Sopher, copyright, 1967, by Prentice-Hall, Inc.

Languages

Languages of Europe

The following languages are ranked in descending order by number of speakers. Languages spoken by more than 4.5 million people are indicated by color. Others listed, spoken by fewer than 4.5 million persons, are named on the map.

Russian	Norwegian	Basque	Karelian
German	Lithuanian	Irish-Gaelic	Icelandic
Italian	Chuvash	Mari	Adyge
English	Slovenian	Welsh	Scots-Gaelic
French	Macedonian	Friulian	Romansh
Ukrainian	Latvian	Komi	Lappish
Polish	Mordvinian	Frisian	Lusatian
Spanish	Estonian	Sardinian	Ladin
Romanian	Breton	Maltese	
Serbo-Croatian			
Dutch-Flemish			
Hungarian			
Portuguese			
Czech			
Belorussian			
Greek			
Bulgarian			
Swedish			
Catalan			
Danish			
Turkish			
Slovak			
Albanian			
Finnish			
All others			

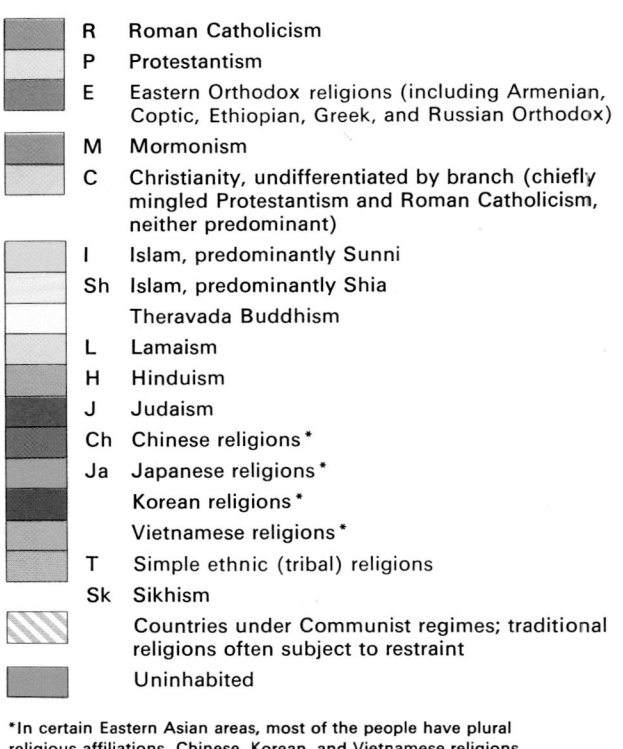

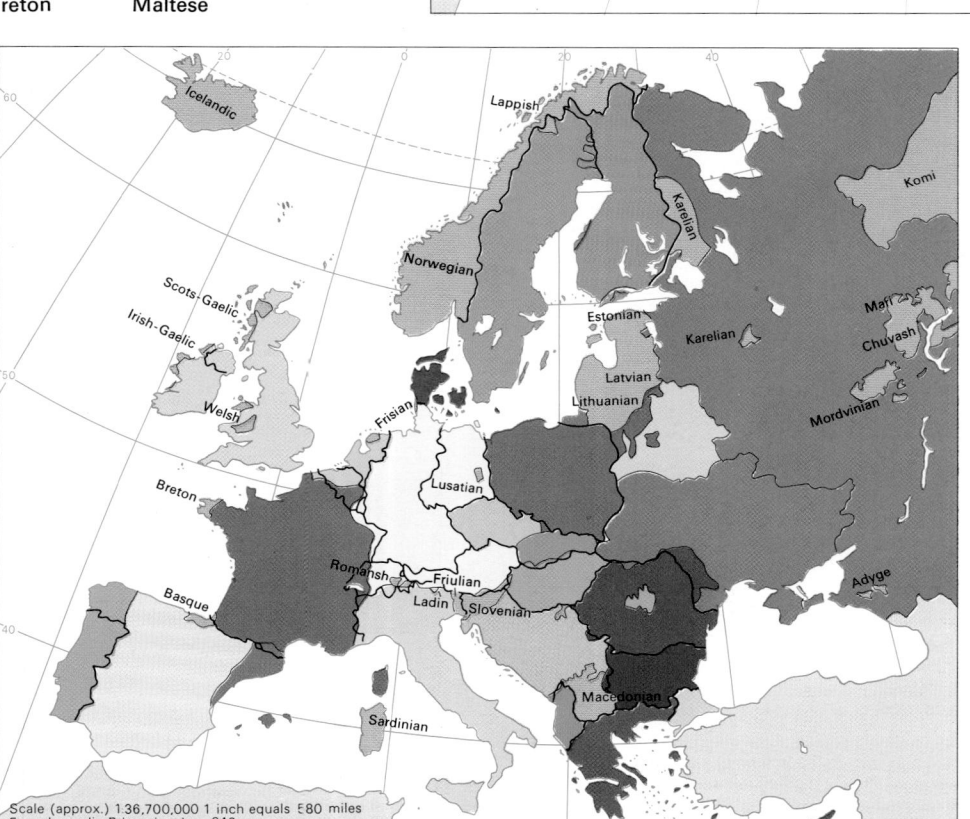

Scale (approx.) 1:36,700,000 1 inch equals 580 miles
Encyclopaedia Britannica, Inc. 048
Compiled by Philip L. Wagner.

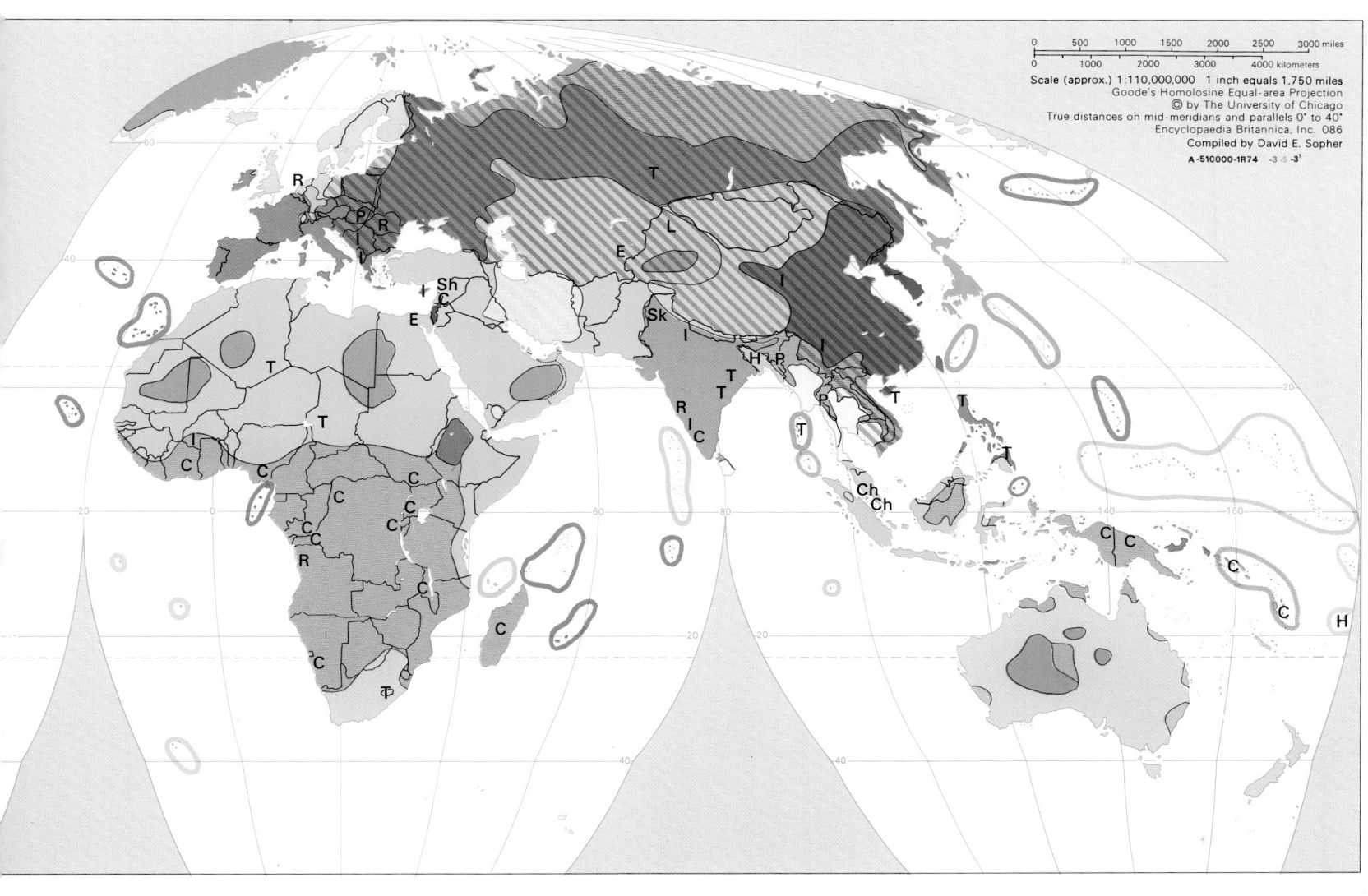

Scale (approx.) 1:110,000,000 1 inch equals 1,750 miles
Goode's Homolosine Equal-area Projection
© by The University of Chicago
True distances on mid-meridians and parallels 0° to 40°
Encyclopaedia Britannica, Inc. 086
Compiled by David E. Sopher
A-510000-1R74 -3 -5 -3ᵗ

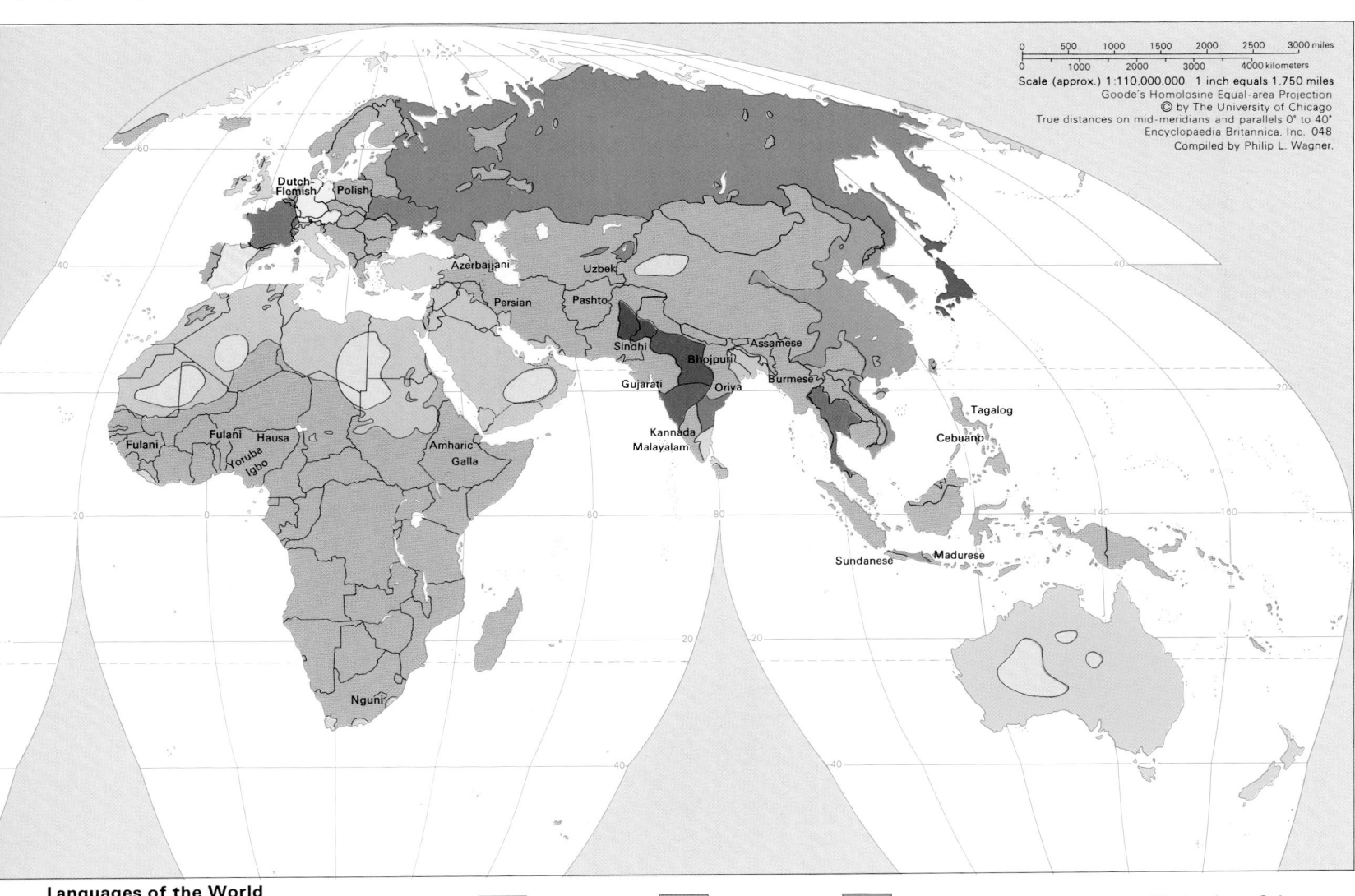

Scale (approx.) 1:110,000,000 1 inch equals 1,750 miles
Goode's Homolosine Equal-area Projection
© by The University of Chicago
True distances on mid-meridians and parallels 0° to 40°
Encyclopaedia Britannica, Inc. 048
Compiled by Philip L. Wagner.

Languages of the World

The following languages are ranked in descending order by number of speakers. Languages spoken by more than 40 million persons are indicated by color. Others listed, spoken by 10-40 million persons, are named on the map.

 Chinese   English

Spanish   Hindi

Bengali	Javanese	Vietnamese
Arabic	Korean	Urdu
Russian	Telugu	Turkish
Portuguese	Marathi	Ukrainian
Japanese	French	Thai
German	Italian	All others
Punjabi	Tamil	Uninhabited

Polish	Bhojpuri	Cebuano
Gujarati	Yoruba	Azerbaijani
Malayalam	Dutch-	Nguni
Kannada	Flemish	Tagalog
Oriya	Pashtu	Assamese
Burmese	Fulani	Sindhi
Persian	Igbo	Amharic
Hausa	Uzbek	Madurese
Sundanese	Galla	

Agricultural Regions

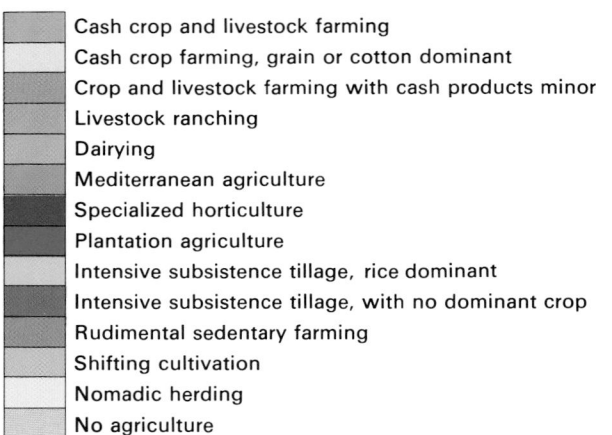

- Cash crop and livestock farming
- Cash crop farming, grain or cotton dominant
- Crop and livestock farming with cash products minor
- Livestock ranching
- Dairying
- Mediterranean agriculture
- Specialized horticulture
- Plantation agriculture
- Intensive subsistence tillage, rice dominant
- Intensive subsistence tillage, with no dominant crop
- Rudimental sedentary farming
- Shifting cultivation
- Nomadic herding
- No agriculture

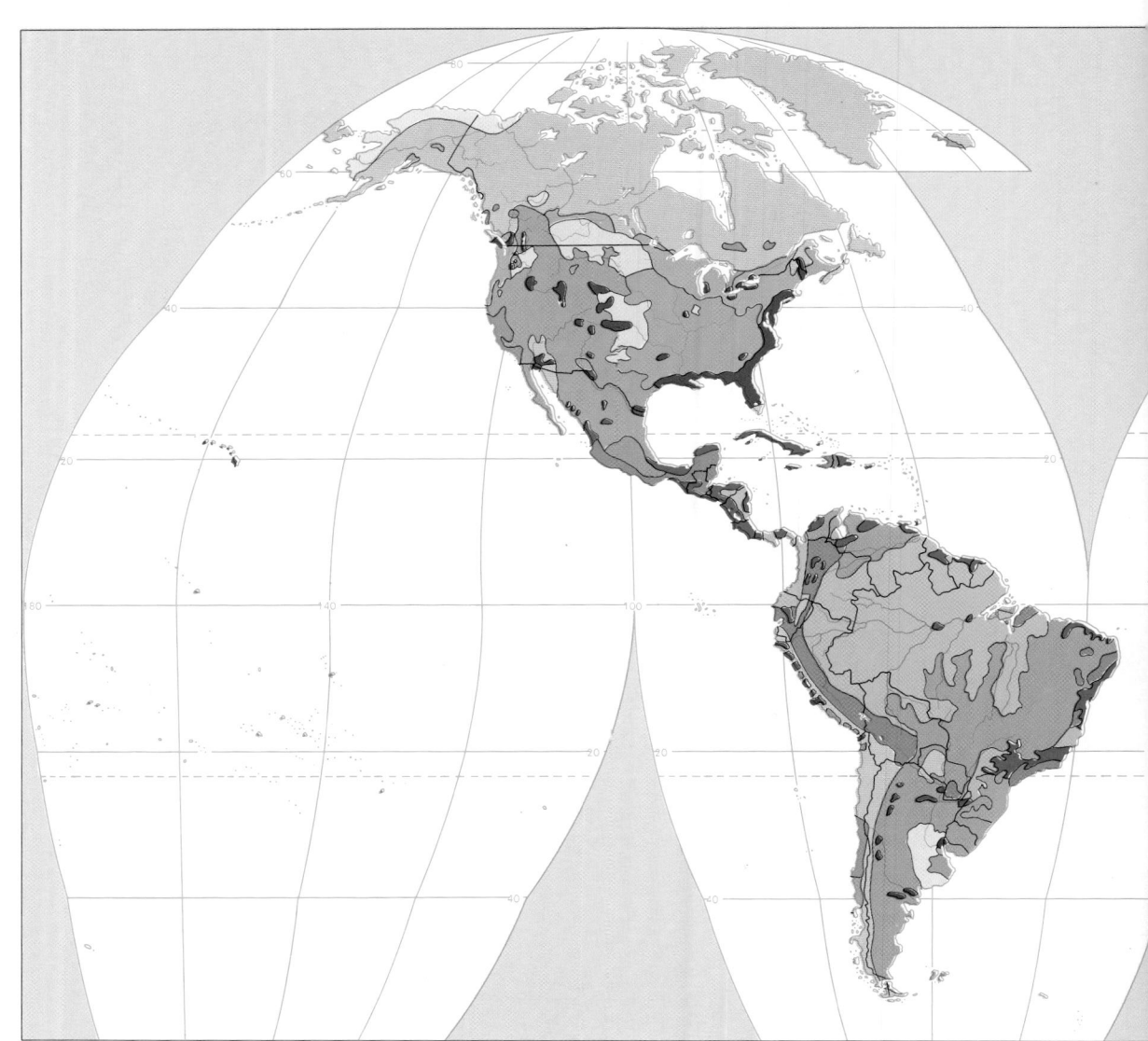

The agricultural systems classified and mapped here represent the primary *agricultural*, rather than economic, activity in the areas shown, since in many developed countries farm population may now constitute less than 5 percent of the total population. No particular level of technology is implied by the classification, as reindeer herding can be carried out with dogs or snowmobiles, crops be irrigated with bucket wheels or electric pumps, dairy cows milked by hand or by machine. Much of the activity shown is controlled, or more specifically, limited by topography and climate. Thus while it is easier to farm on flat land, terracing can create flat land where none exists; intermediate slopes can either be cropped by special techniques, as in Switzerland, or planted in a crop like tea or wine grapes for which slope, or attitude toward the sun and other climatic elements might determine the crop's success. Density of natural vegetation usually declines with altitude and rainfall and so livestock ranching can take place in the compass of a North American feedlot, an Australian cattle station, or a Papua New Guinean butterfly farm. Among the types of occupance listed, "Mediterranean" agriculture may be the least familiar to North Americans. It refers to a system developed in the Mediterranean basin's hot, dry summers that concentrates on hardy tree crops (olive, citrus) or vines (grape), interspersed with small plantings of vegetables or grain; few livestock are kept except in uplands, though small ruminants like goats may be kept lower down.

Forests and Fisheries

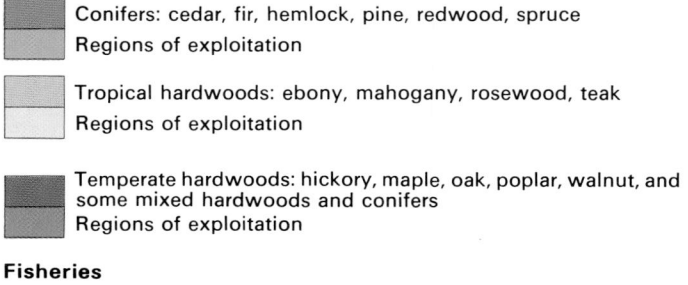

Forests

- Conifers: cedar, fir, hemlock, pine, redwood, spruce
  Regions of exploitation
- Tropical hardwoods: ebony, mahogany, rosewood, teak
  Regions of exploitation
- Temperate hardwoods: hickory, maple, oak, poplar, walnut, and some mixed hardwoods and conifers
  Regions of exploitation

Fisheries

- Pelagic fishing regions: anchoveta, anchovy, herring, menhaden, pilchard, sardine, sprat, tuna
- Ground fishing regions: cod, haddock, hake, horse mackerel, mackerel, pollack, redfish
- Mixed ground and pelagic fishing regions
- Shellfish: clam, crab, lobster, mussel, oyster, scallop, shrimp, squid

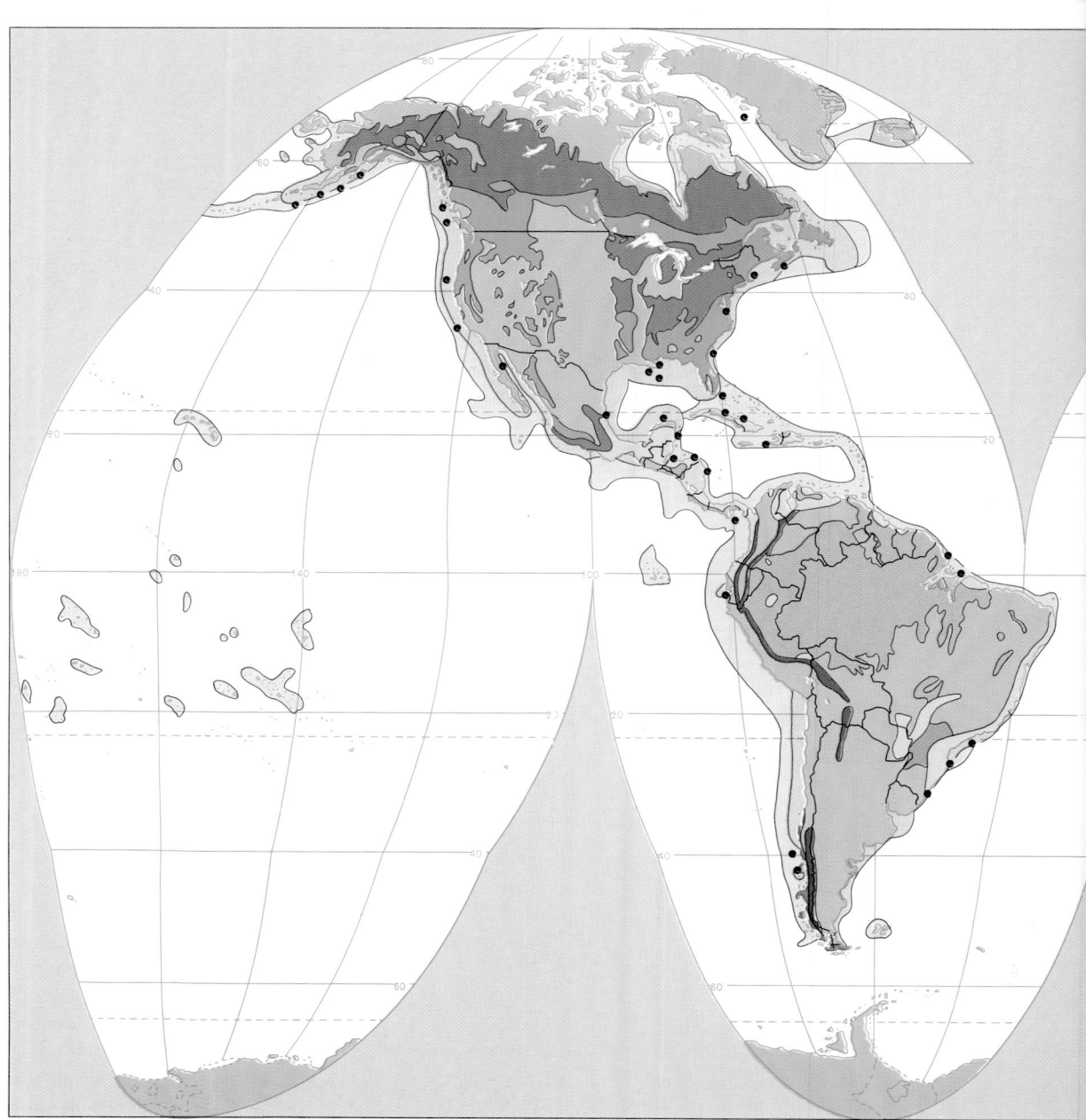

Two principal *commercial* activities are summarized on the map opposite: forestry, classified by type of forests exploited, and fisheries, classified by type of fishing grounds. Three forest types are shown, classified by the woods of chief economic interest within them, rather than by the predominant vegetation. For example, while the softwood conifers listed may actually predominate in many of the regions shown, there are very few areas where the temperate or tropical hardwoods listed will actually constitute the predominant or characteristic tree. Commercial exploitation concentrates on regions where the tree stock has reached economically significant size, is not diluted by other, uneconomical woods, and where transportation infrastructure permits economical removal.

Of the ocean fisheries shown, the term 'Pelagic' refers to near-surface fisheries, either near-shore or on the high seas. 'Ground' fisheries are those which exploit bottom-dwelling fish, or shellfish but should not be confused with the term 'fishing grounds,' which may be either pelagic or ground. The types of fish listed are the principal species exploited in terms of quantities landed. Ocean areas of greatest biological diversity may support both kinds of fish populations, such as those of the Grand Banks of Newfoundland. Commercial whaling is no longer significant although some traditional whaling from small boats still takes place.

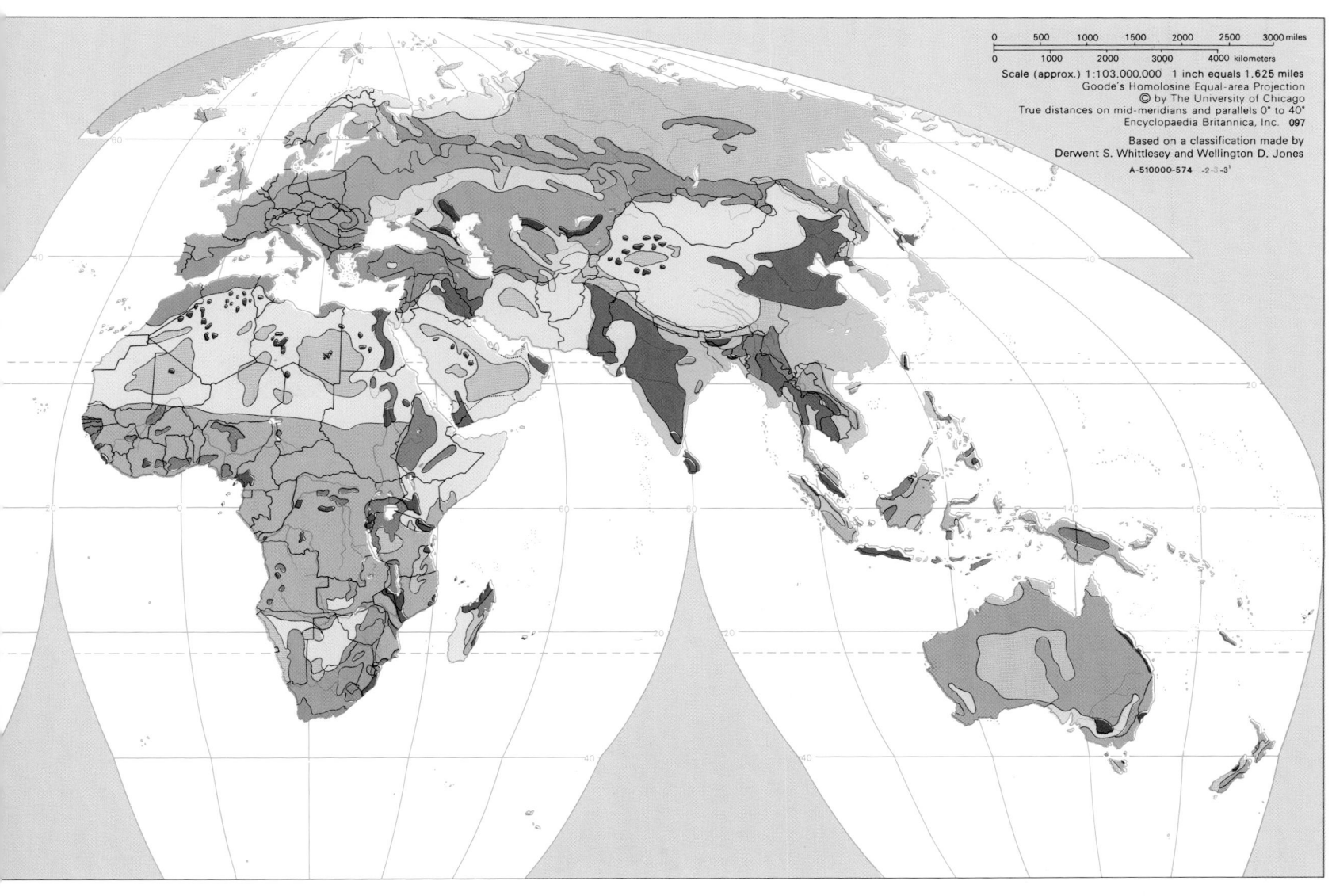

0   500   1000   1500   2000   2500   3000 miles

0   1000   2000   3000   4000 kilometers

Scale (approx.) 1:103,000,000   1 inch equals 1,625 miles
Goode's Homolosine Equal-area Projection
© by The University of Chicago
True distances on mid-meridians and parallels 0° to 40°
Encyclopaedia Britannica, Inc. 097

Based on a classification made by
Derwent S. Whittlesey and Wellington D. Jones

A-510000-574 -2-3-3¹

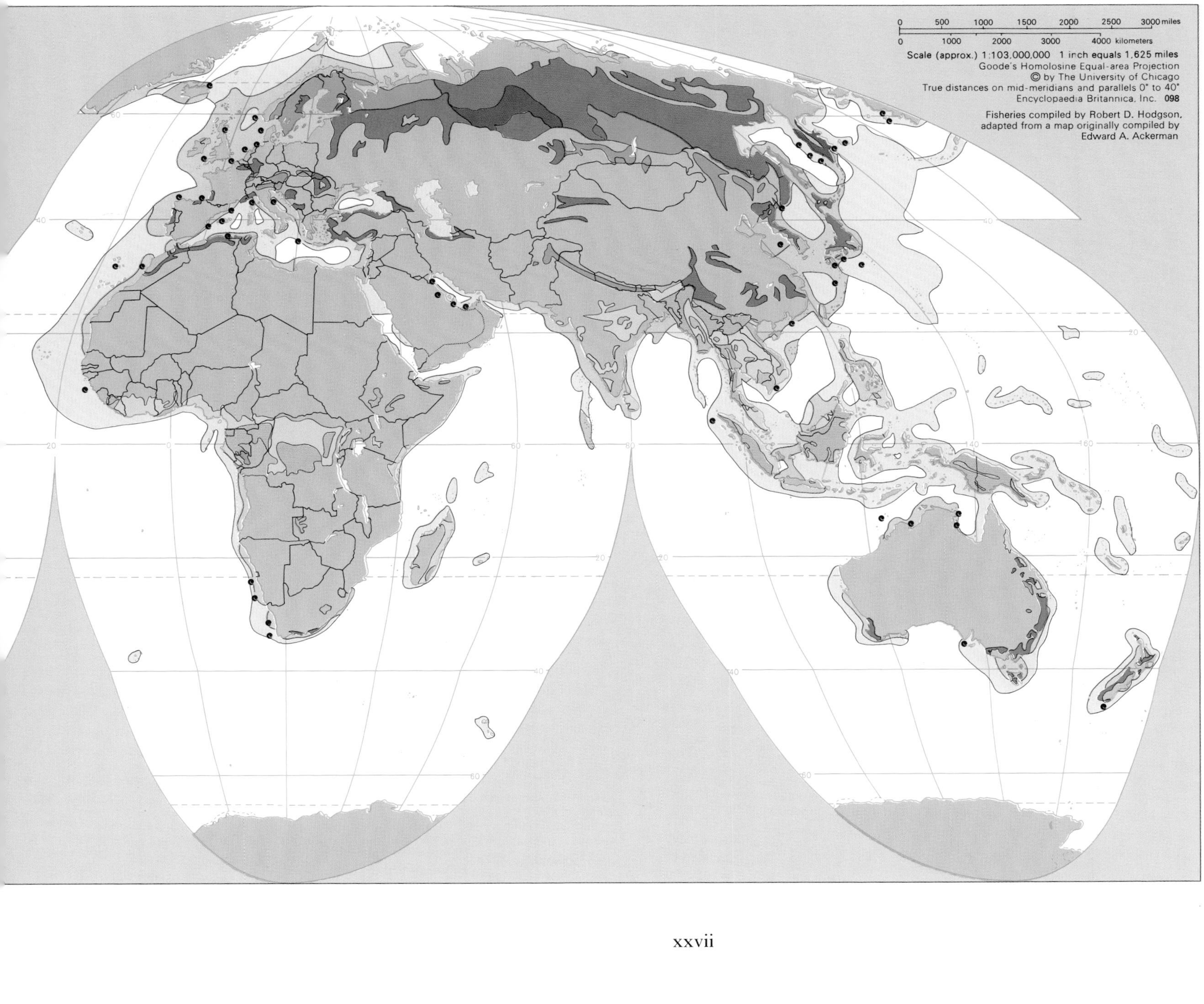

0   500   1000   1500   2000   2500   3000 miles

0   1000   2000   3000   4000 kilometers

Scale (approx.) 1:103,000,000   1 inch equals 1,625 miles
Goode's Homolosine Equal-area Projection
© by The University of Chicago
True distances on mid-meridians and parallels 0° to 40°
Encyclopaedia Britannica, Inc. 098

Fisheries compiled by Robert D. Hodgson,
adapted from a map originally compiled by
Edward A. Ackerman

Minerals

4-year world
average production
shown in graphs.
Producing areas
shown on maps

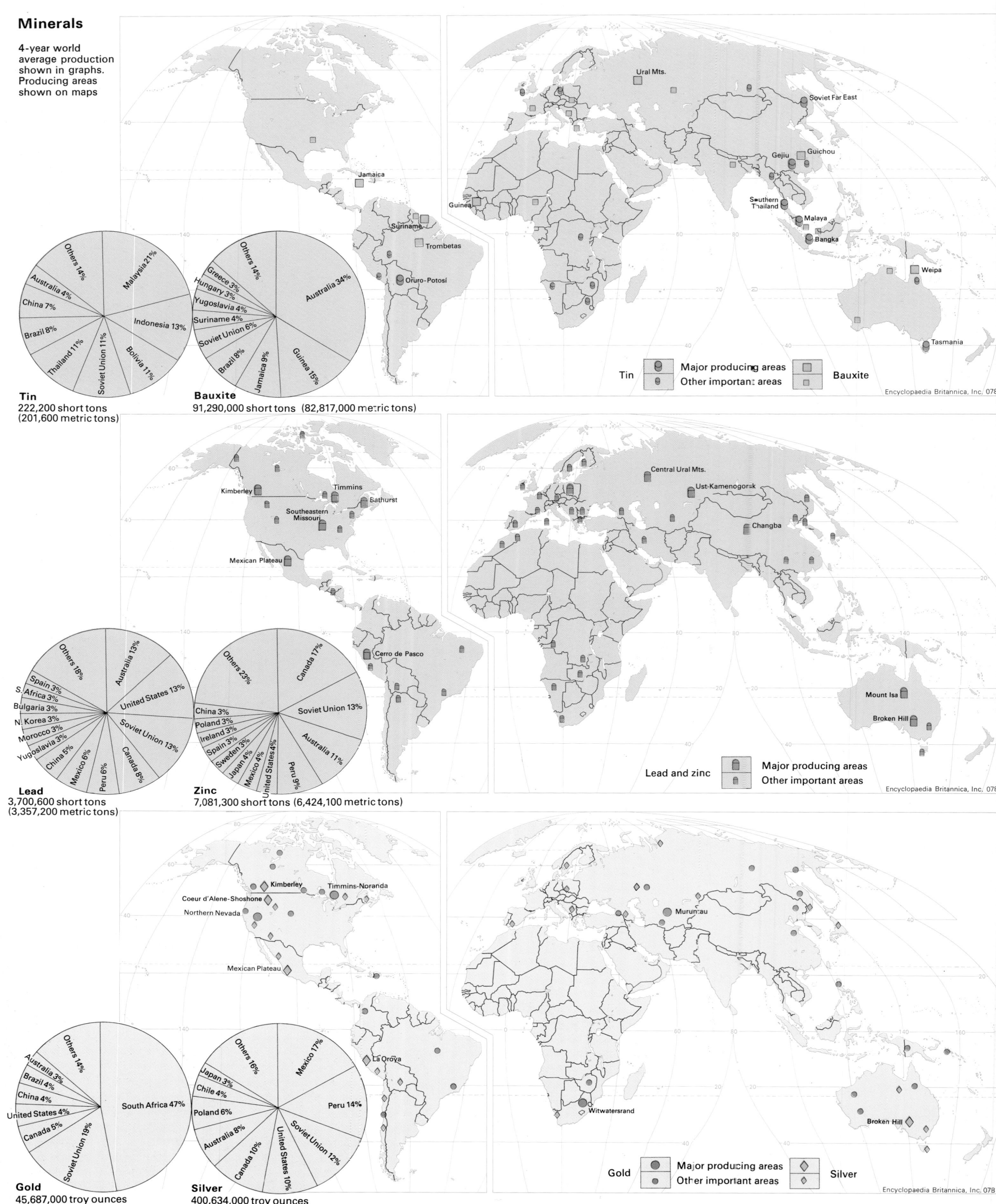

Tin
222,200 short tons
(201,600 metric tons)

Tin pie chart: Malaysia 21%, Indonesia 13%, Bolivia 11%, Soviet Union 11%, Thailand 11%, Brazil 8%, China 7%, Australia 4%, Others 14%

Bauxite
91,290,000 short tons (82,817,000 metric tons)

Bauxite pie chart: Australia 34%, Guinea 15%, Jamaica 9%, Brazil 8%, Soviet Union 6%, Suriname 4%, Yugoslavia 4%, Hungary 3%, Greece 3%, Others 14%

Map labels (Tin/Bauxite): Jamaica, Suriname, Trombetas, Oruro-Potosí, Guinea, Ural Mts., Soviet Far East, Gejiu, Guichou, Southern Thailand, Malaya, Bangka, Weipa, Tasmania

Tin — Major producing areas / Other important areas   Bauxite

Encyclopaedia Britannica, Inc. 078

Lead
3,700,600 short tons
(3,357,200 metric tons)

Lead pie chart: Australia 13%, United States 13%, Soviet Union 13%, Canada 8%, Peru 6%, Mexico 6%, China 5%, Yugoslavia 3%, Morocco 3%, N. Korea 3%, Bulgaria 3%, S. Africa 3%, Spain 3%, Others 16%

Zinc
7,081,300 short tons (6,424,100 metric tons)

Zinc pie chart: Canada 17%, Soviet Union 13%, Australia 11%, Peru 9%, United States 4%, Mexico 4%, Japan 4%, Sweden 3%, Spain 3%, Ireland 3%, Poland 3%, China 3%, Others 22%

Map labels (Lead and zinc): Kimberley, Timmins, Bathurst, Southeastern Missouri, Mexican Plateau, Cerro de Pasco, Central Ural Mts., Ust-Kamenogorsk, Changba, Mount Isa, Broken Hill

Lead and zinc — Major producing areas / Other important areas

Encyclopaedia Britannica, Inc. 078

Gold
45,687,000 troy ounces
(1,421,000 kilograms)

Gold pie chart: South Africa 47%, Soviet Union 19%, Canada 5%, United States 4%, China 4%, Brazil 4%, Australia 3%, Others 14%

Silver
400,634,000 troy ounces
(12,461,000 kilograms)

Silver pie chart: Mexico 17%, Peru 14%, Soviet Union 12%, United States 10%, Canada 10%, Australia 8%, Poland 6%, Chile 4%, Japan 3%, Others 16%

Map labels (Gold/Silver): Kimberley, Timmins-Noranda, Coeur d'Alene-Shoshone, Northern Nevada, Mexican Plateau, La Oroya, Muruntau, Witwatersrand, Broken Hill

Gold — Major producing areas / Other important areas   Silver

Encyclopaedia Britannica, Inc. 078

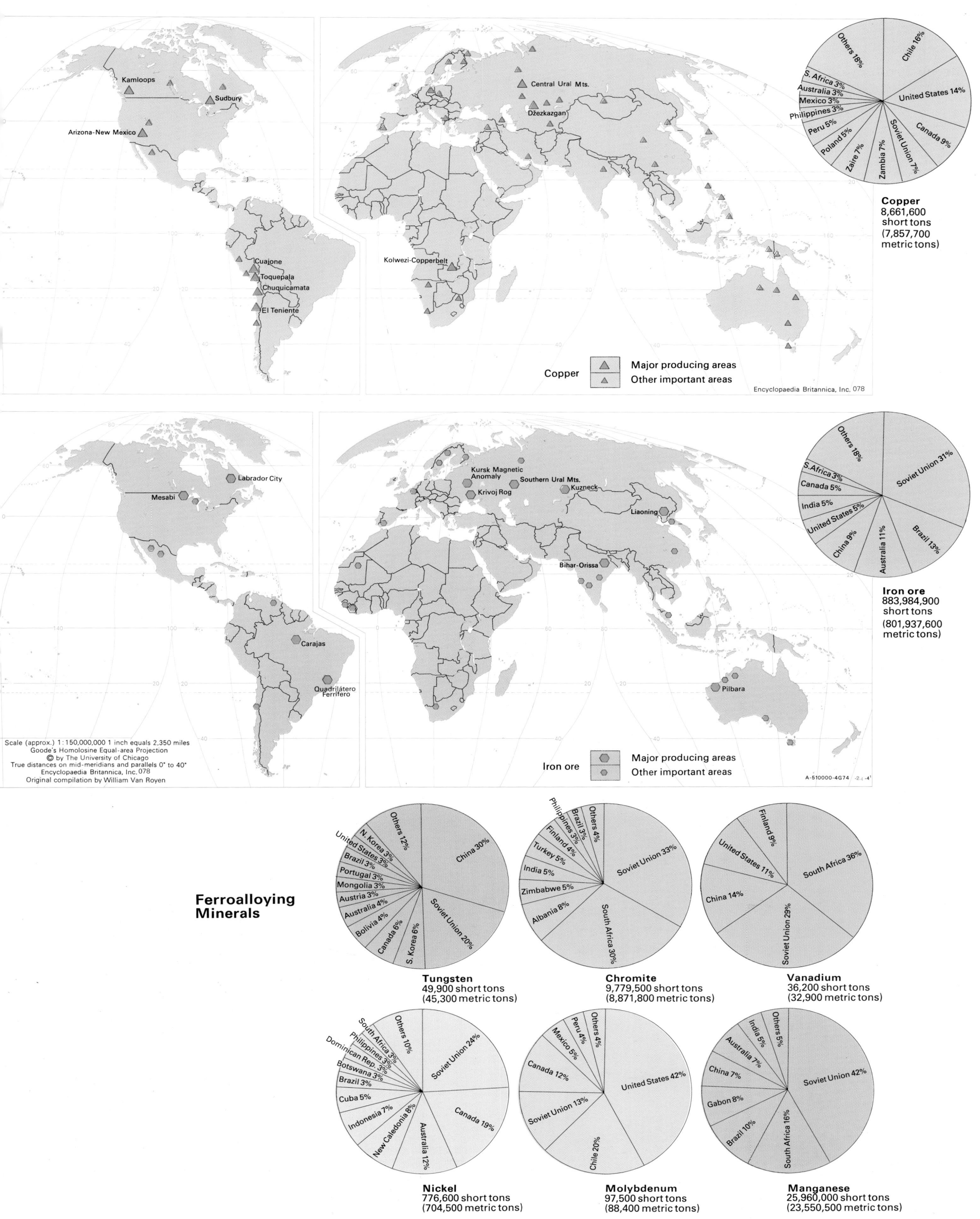

Copper
8,661,600
short tons
(7,857,700
metric tons)

Copper ▲ Major producing areas
▲ Other important areas

Encyclopaedia Britannica, Inc. 078

Iron ore
883,984,900
short tons
(801,937,600
metric tons)

Scale (approx.) 1 : 150,000,000 1 inch equals 2,350 miles
Goode's Homolosine Equal-area Projection
© by The University of Chicago
True distances on mid-meridians and parallels 0° to 40°
Encyclopaedia Britannica, Inc. 078
Original compilation by William Van Royen

Iron ore ⬡ Major producing areas
⬡ Other important areas

A-510000-4G74 -2-⌐-4'

Ferroalloying Minerals

Tungsten
49,900 short tons
(45,300 metric tons)

Chromite
9,779,500 short tons
(8,871,800 metric tons)

Vanadium
36,200 short tons
(32,900 metric tons)

Nickel
776,600 short tons
(704,500 metric tons)

Molybdenum
97,500 short tons
(88,400 metric tons)

Manganese
25,960,000 short tons
(23,550,500 metric tons)

Energy Production and Consumption
Unit of measure is metric tons coal equivalent (m.t.c.e.)

Production

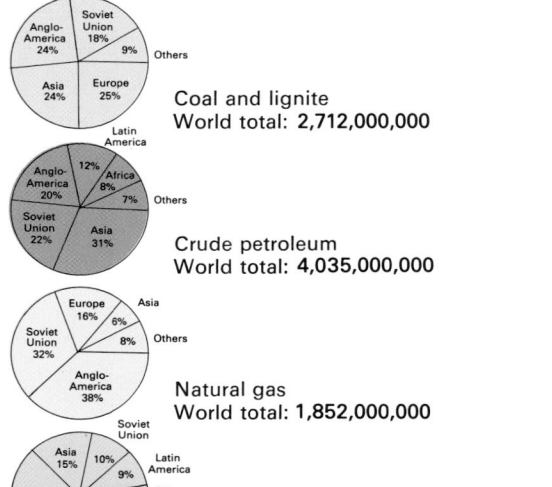

Coal and lignite
World total: 2,712,000,000

Anglo-America 24%, Soviet Union 18%, Europe 25%, Asia 24%, Others 9%

Crude petroleum
World total: 4,035,000,000

Anglo-America 20%, Latin America 12%, Africa 8%, Soviet Union 22%, Asia 31%, Others 7%

Natural gas
World total: 1,852,000,000

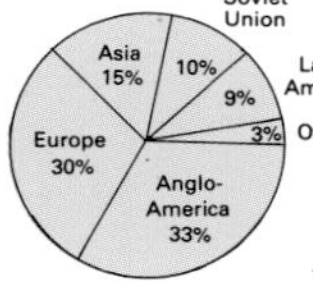

Europe 16%, Asia 8%, Soviet Union 32%, Anglo-America 38%, Others 6%

Primary electricity (hydro-, geothermal, and nuclear)
World total: 334,000,000

Europe 30%, Asia 15%, Soviet Union 10%, Latin America 9%, Anglo-America 33%, Others 3%

Table of equivalents

Coal, anthracite and bituminous	1 metric ton = 1.0 m.t.c.e.
Lignite	1 metric ton = 0.3 – 0.6 m.t.c.e.
Petroleum	1 metric ton = 1.5 m.t.c.e.
Natural gas	1,000 cubic meters = 1.33 m.t.c.e.
Hydro-, geothermal, and nuclear electricity	1.0 megawatt-hour = 0.125 m.t.c.e.

Potential energy of 1 metric ton of coal equals 28,000,000 B.T.U.

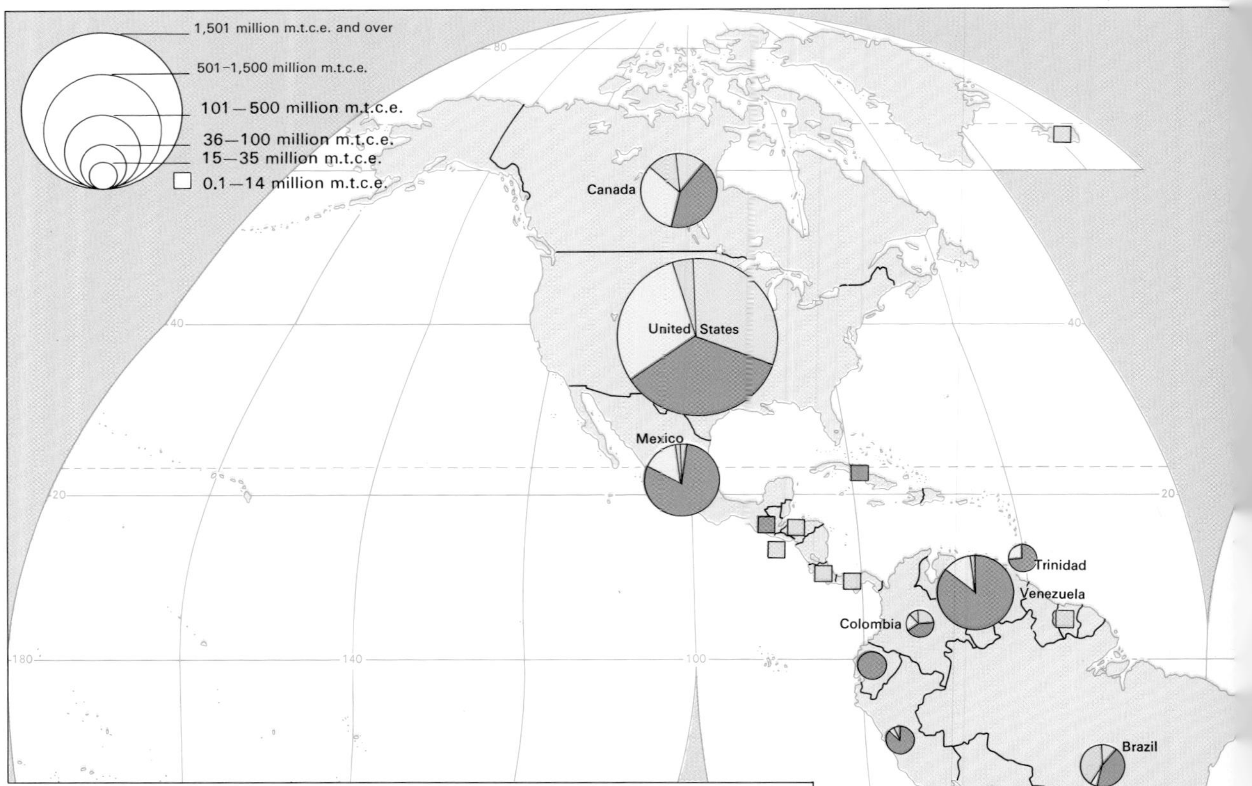

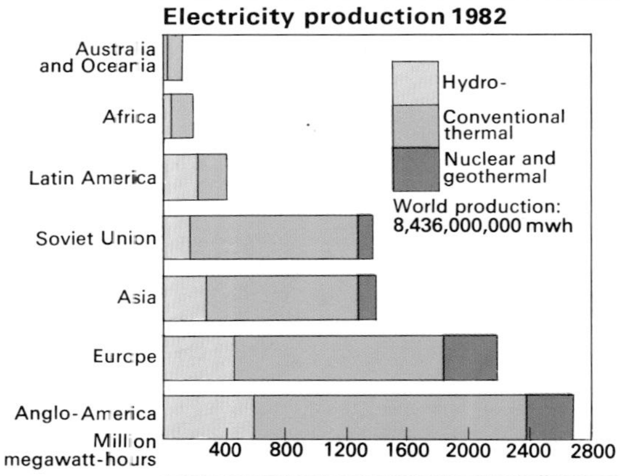

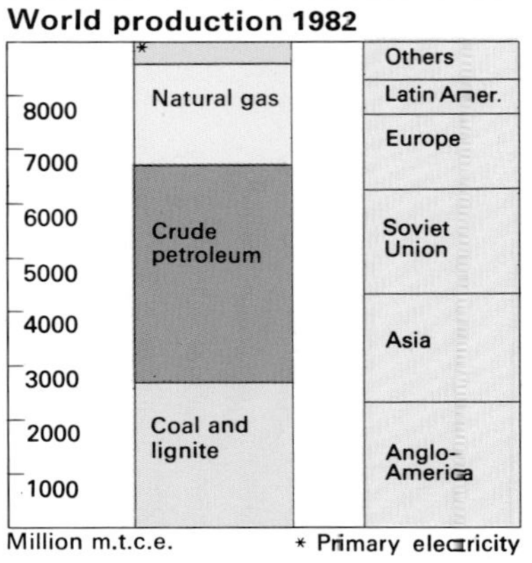

Consumption

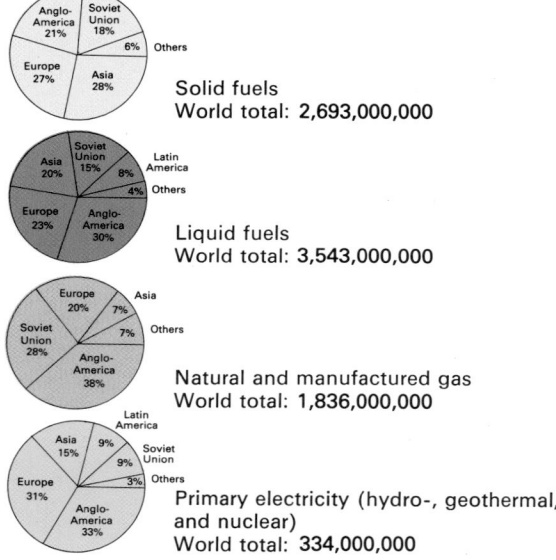

Solid fuels
World total: 2,693,000,000

Anglo-America 21%, Soviet Union 18%, Europe 27%, Asia 28%, Others 6%

Liquid fuels
World total: 3,543,000,000

Asia 20%, Soviet Union 15%, Latin America 8%, Europe 23%, Anglo-America 30%, Others 4%

Natural and manufactured gas
World total: 1,836,000,000

Europe 20%, Asia 7%, Soviet Union 28%, Anglo-America 38%, Others 7%

Primary electricity (hydro-, geothermal, and nuclear)
World total: 334,000,000

Europe 31%, Asia 15%, Latin America 9%, Soviet Union 9%, Anglo-America 33%, Others 3%

Consumption totals exclude noncommercial fuels, fuels consumed by vessels engaged in international trade, and nonfuel petroleum products.

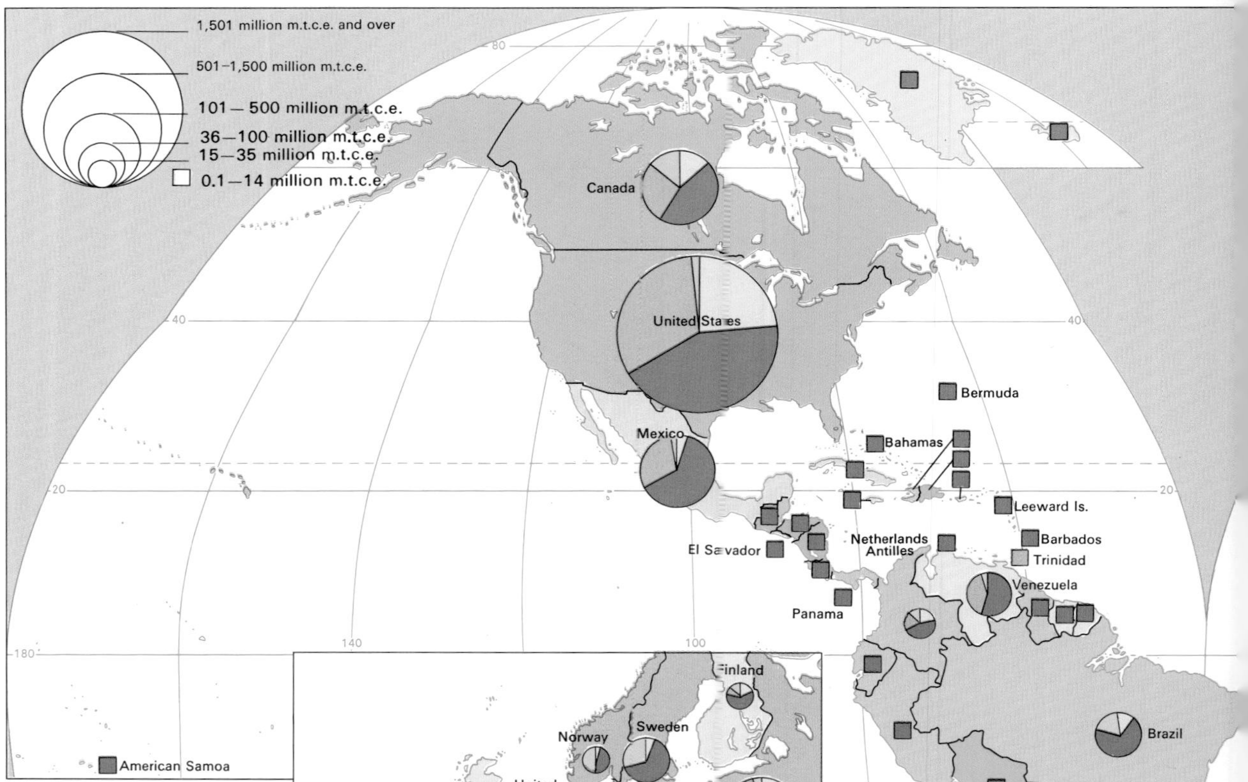

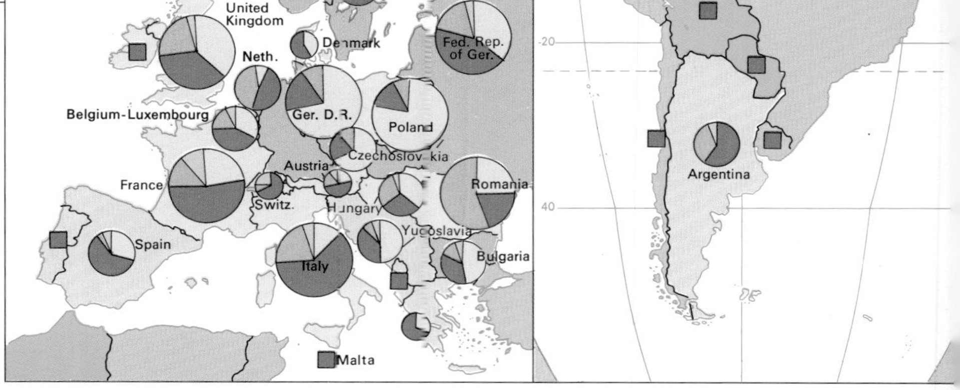

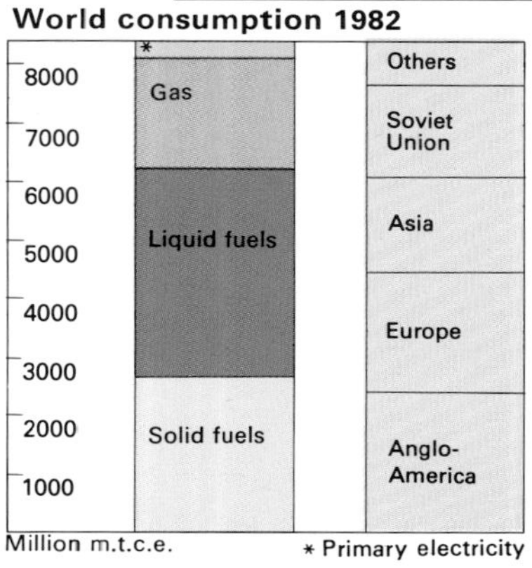

Per capita consumption

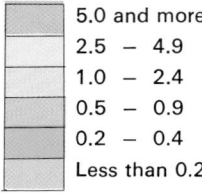

- 5.0 and more
- 2.5 – 4.9
- 1.0 – 2.4
- 0.5 – 0.9
- 0.2 – 0.4
- Less than 0.2

Map legend (Production):

- 1,501 million m.t.c.e. and over
- 501–1,500 million m.t.c.e.
- 101–500 million m.t.c.e.
- 36–100 million m.t.c.e.
- 15–35 million m.t.c.e.
- 0.1–14 million m.t.c.e.

Canada, United States, Mexico, Trinidad, Venezuela, Colombia, Brazil, Argentina

Electricity production 1982

Hydro-
Conventional thermal
Nuclear and geothermal

World production: 8,436,000,000 mwh

Australia and Oceania, Africa, Latin America, Soviet Union, Asia, Europe, Anglo-America

Million megawatt-hours: 400 800 1200 1600 2000 2400 2800

World production 1982

Natural gas, Crude petroleum, Coal and lignite

Others, Latin Amer., Europe, Soviet Union, Asia, Anglo-America

Million m.t.c.e. 1000–8000

* Primary electricity

Map legend (Consumption):

- 1,501 million m.t.c.e. and over
- 501–1,500 million m.t.c.e.
- 101–500 million m.t.c.e.
- 36–100 million m.t.c.e.
- 15–35 million m.t.c.e.
- 0.1–14 million m.t.c.e.

Canada, United States, Mexico, Bermuda, Bahamas, Leeward Is., Barbados, Trinidad, El Salvador, Netherlands Antilles, Panama, Venezuela, Brazil, Argentina, American Samoa

Finland, Norway, Sweden, United Kingdom, Neth., Denmark, Fed. Rep. of Ger., Belgium-Luxembourg, Ger. D.R., Poland, France, Austria, Czechoslovakia, Switz., Hungary, Romania, Spain, Italy, Yugoslavia, Bulgaria, Malta

World consumption 1982

Gas, Liquid fuels, Solid fuels

Others, Soviet Union, Asia, Europe, Anglo-America

Million m.t.c.e. 1000–8000

* Primary electricity

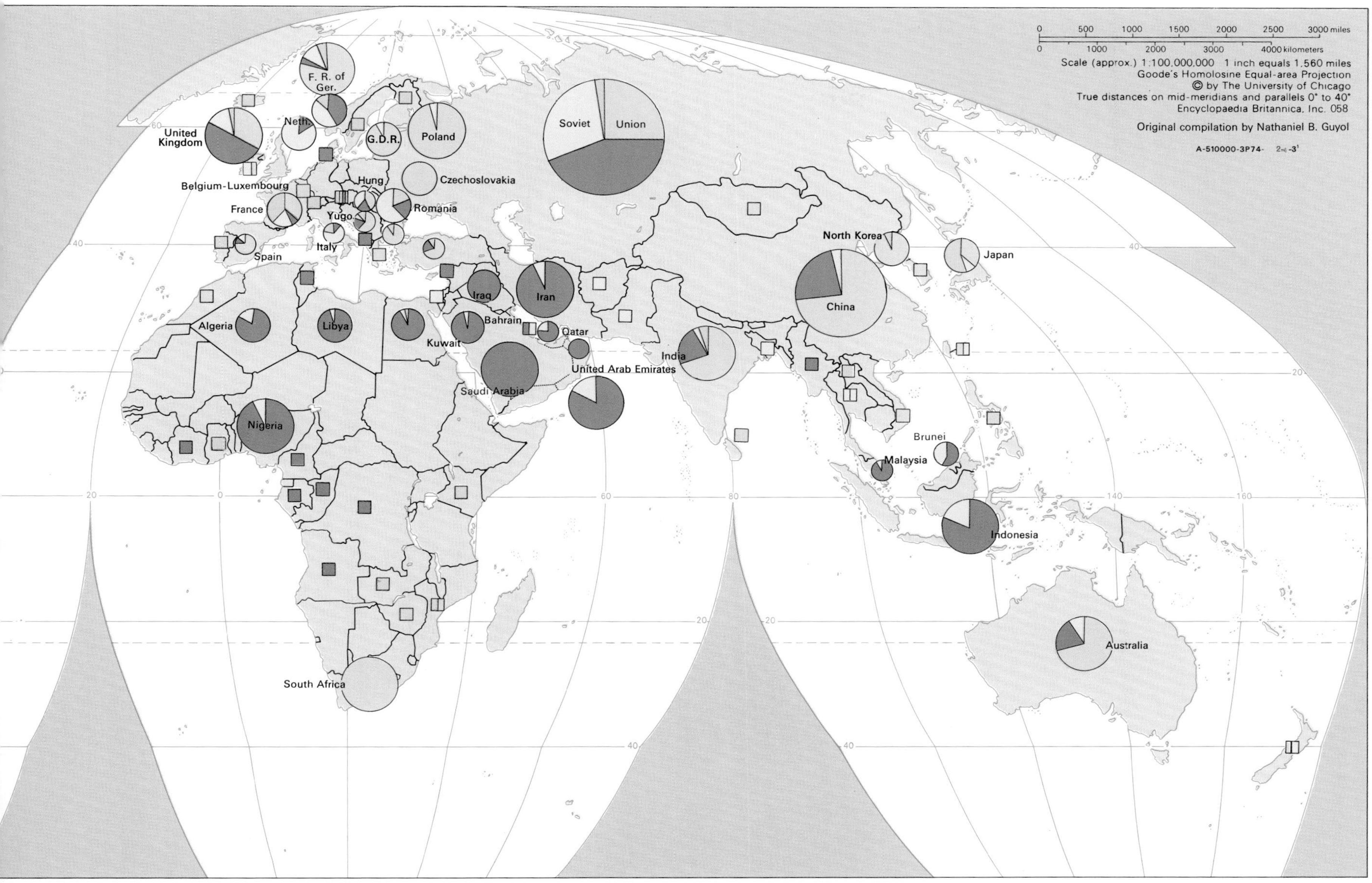

Top map

0 500 1000 1500 2000 2500 3000 miles
0 1000 2000 3000 4000 kilometers
Scale (approx.) 1:100,000,000 1 inch equals 1,560 miles
Goode's Homolosine Equal-area Projection
© by The University of Chicago
True distances on mid-meridians and parallels 0° to 40°
Encyclopaedia Britannica, Inc. 058
Original compilation by Nathaniel B. Guyol
A-510000-3P74- 2-c -3'

F. R. of Ger. · Neth. · United Kingdom · G.D.R. · Poland · Soviet Union · Belgium-Luxembourg · Hung. · Czechoslovakia · France · Yugo. · Romania · Spain · Italy · Algeria · Libya · Iraq · Iran · Kuwait · Bahrain · Qatar · North Korea · Japan · China · India · United Arab Emirates · Saudi Arabia · Nigeria · Brunei · Malaysia · Indonesia · South Africa · Australia

Bottom map

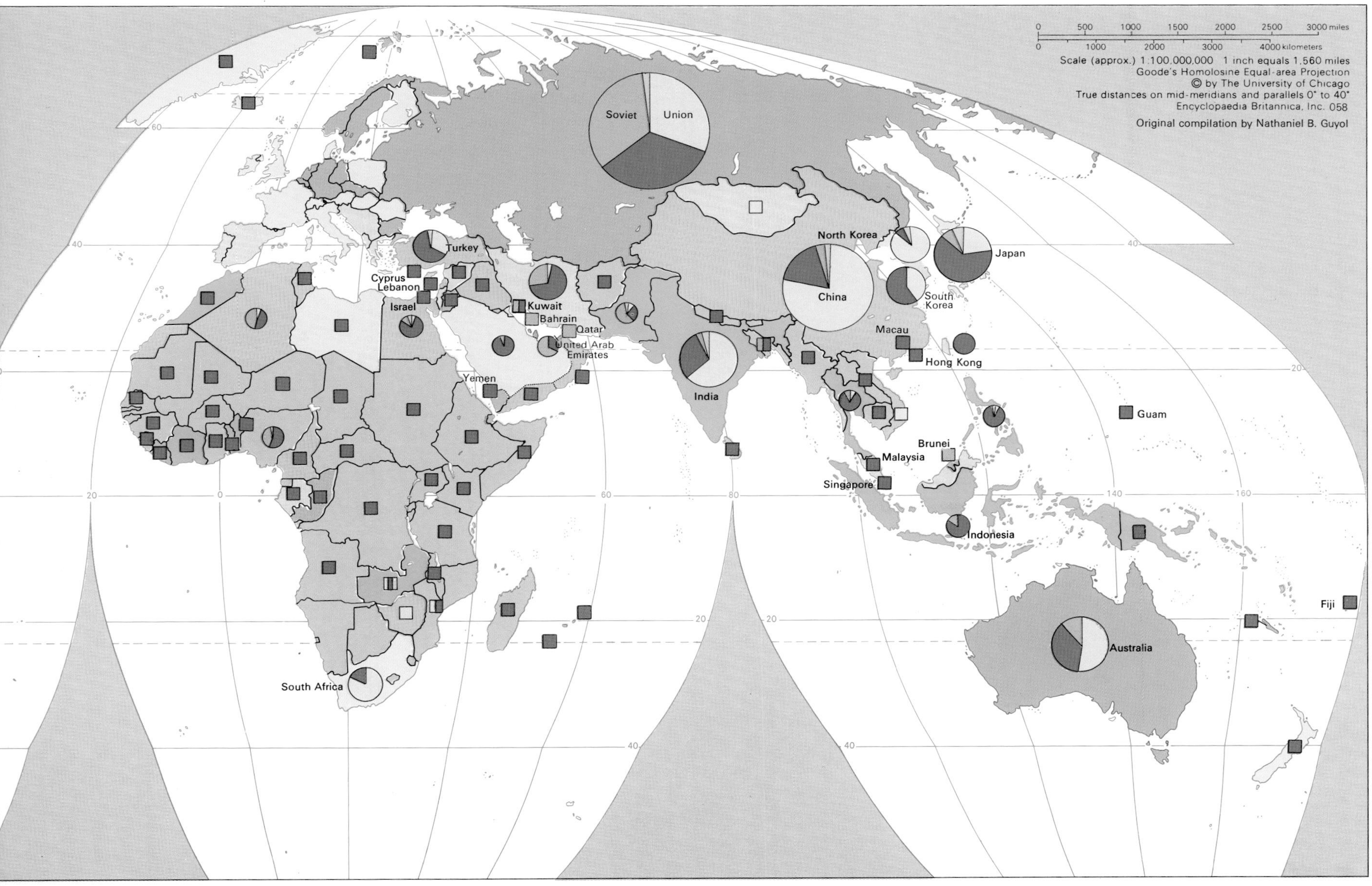

0 500 1000 1500 2000 2500 3000 miles
0 1000 2000 3000 4000 kilometers
Scale (approx.) 1:100,000,000 1 inch equals 1,560 miles
Goode's Homolosine Equal-area Projection
© by The University of Chicago
True distances on mid-meridians and parallels 0° to 40°
Encyclopaedia Britannica, Inc. 058
Original compilation by Nathaniel B. Guyol

Soviet Union · Turkey · Cyprus · Lebanon · Israel · Kuwait · Bahrain · Qatar · United Arab Emirates · Yemen · North Korea · Japan · China · South Korea · Macau · Hong Kong · India · Guam · Brunei · Malaysia · Singapore · Indonesia · Fiji · South Africa · Australia

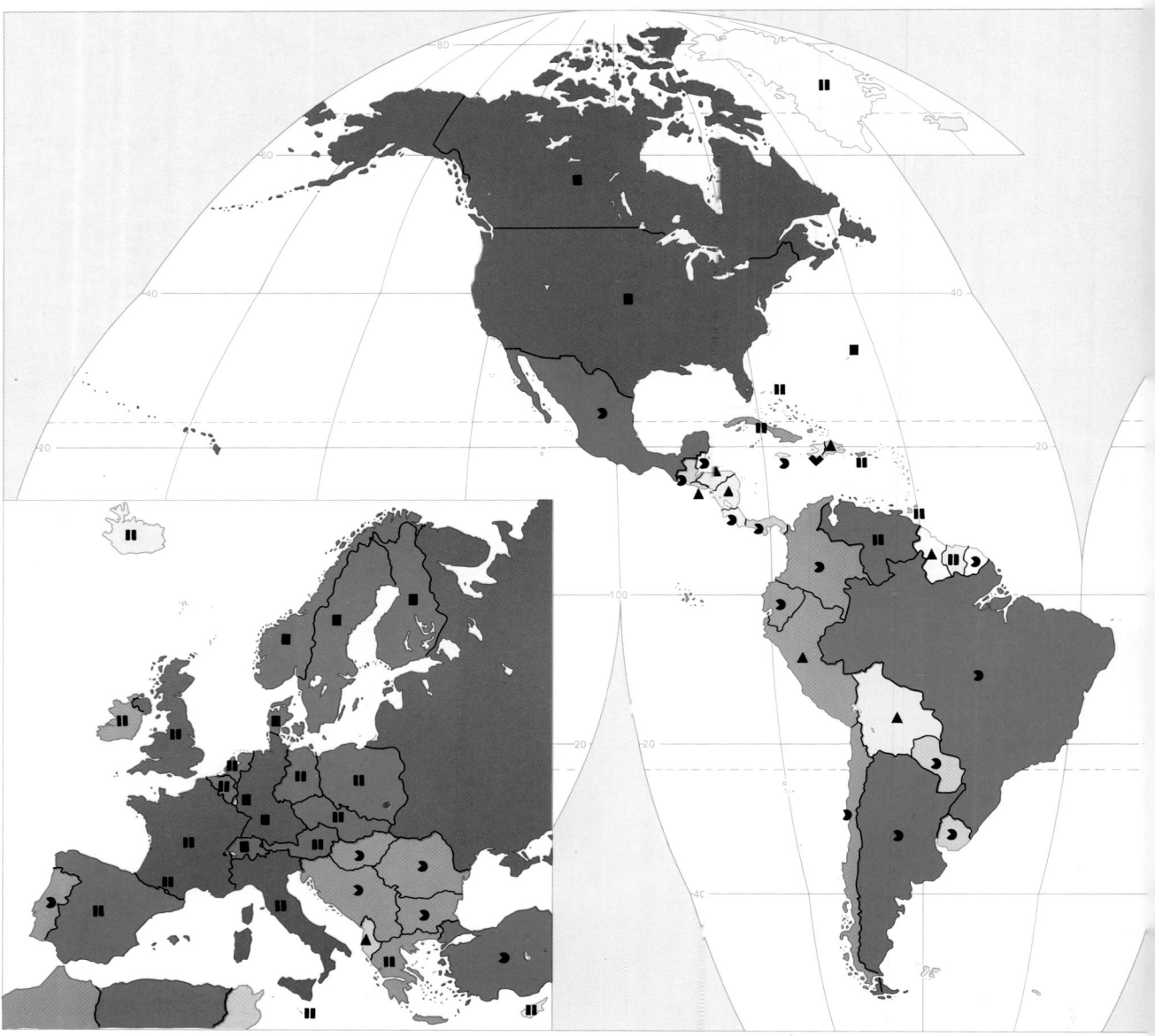

Gross National Product

Total per country
at market price
In billions of U.S. dollars

		Number of countries
	300–3,670	9
	50–300	27
	10–50	28
	3–10	34
	1–3	33
	Less than 1	21
	No data available	

Per capita
In U.S. dollars

■	10,000–22,300	18
❚❚	3,000–10,000	35
➋	1,000–3,000	32
▲	400–1,000	30
♥	200–400	27
●	Less than 200	15

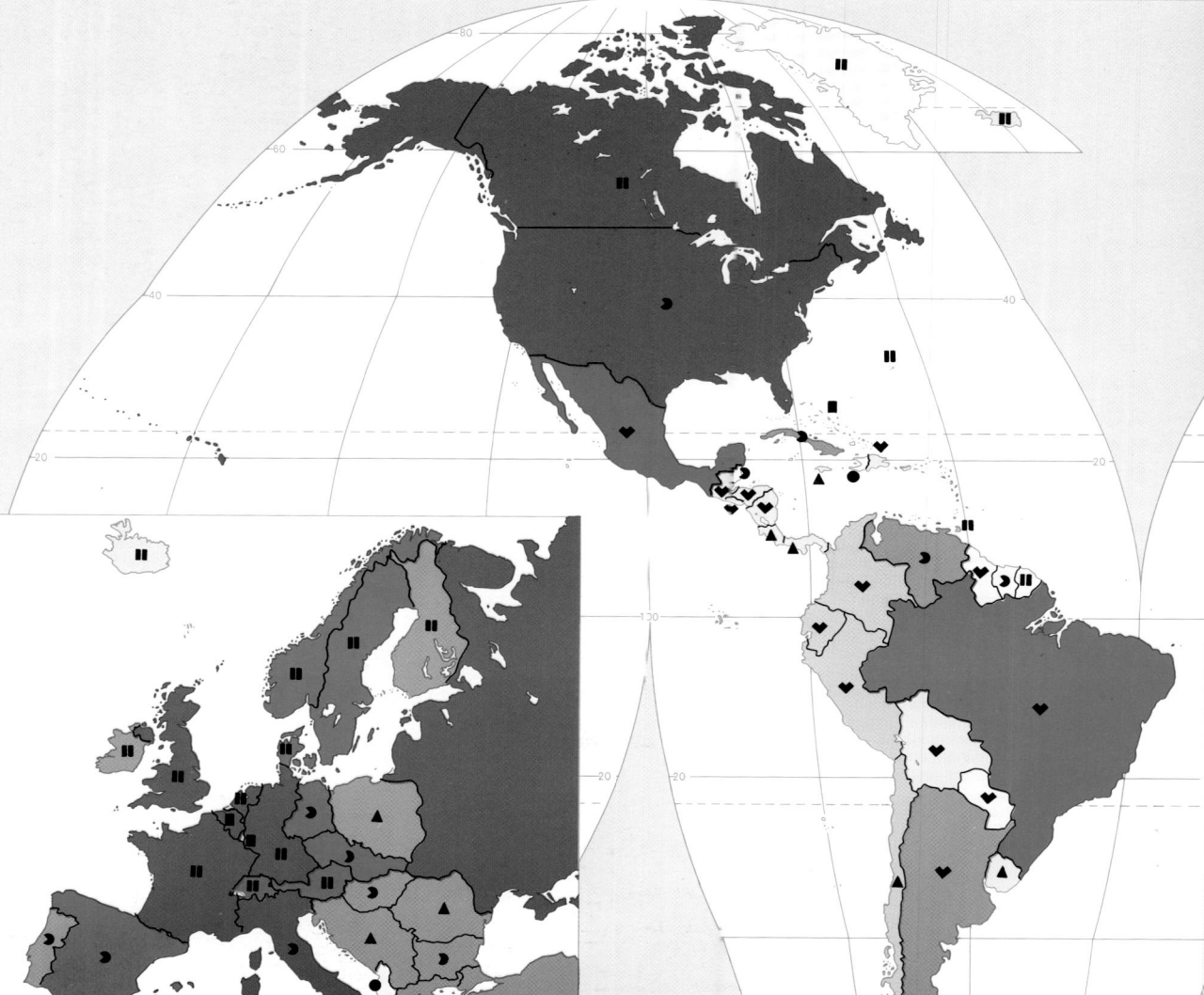

International Trade

Total per country
In billions of U.S. dollars

		Number of countries
	100–560	10
	30–100	19
	10–30	25
	3–10	19
	1–3	34
	Less than 1	46
	No data available	

Per capita
In U.S. dollars

■	10,000–45,000	11
❚❚	3,000–10,000	25
➋	1,000–3,000	28
▲	500–1,000	19
♥	200–500	36
●	Less than 200	39

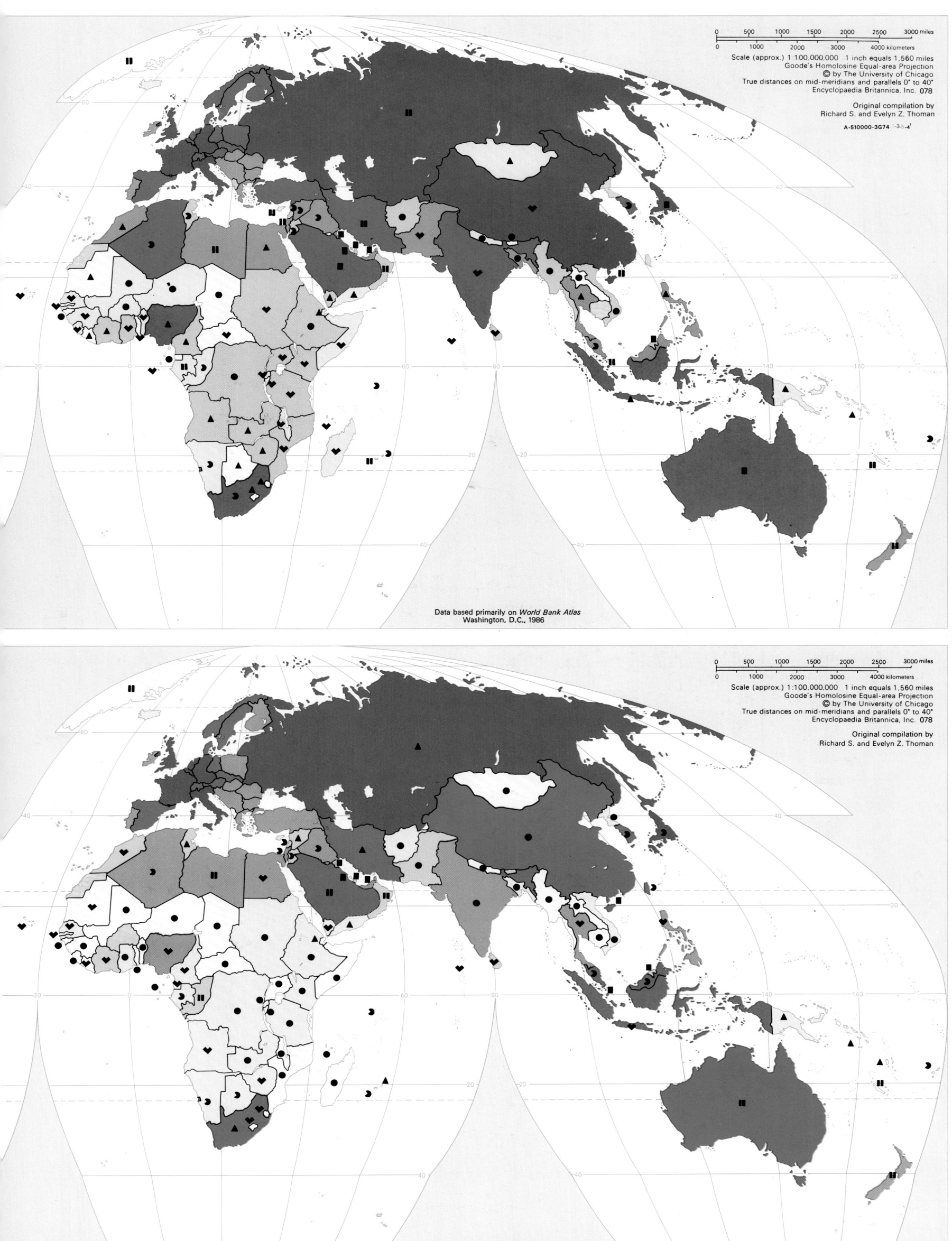

Scale (approx.) 1:100,000,000 1 inch equals 1,560 miles
Goode's Homolosine Equal-area Projection
© by The University of Chicago
True distances on mid-meridians and parallels 0° to 40°
Encyclopaedia Britannica, Inc. 078

Original compilation by
Richard S. and Evelyn Z. Thoman

A-510000-3G74

Data based primarily on *World Bank Atlas*
Washington, D.C., 1986

Scale (approx.) 1:100,000,000 1 inch equals 1,560 miles
Goode's Homolosine Equal-area Projection
© by The University of Chicago
True distances on mid-meridians and parallels 0° to 40°
Encyclopaedia Britannica, Inc. 078

Original compilation by
Richard S. and Evelyn Z. Thoman

Based primarily on United Nations data, 1986

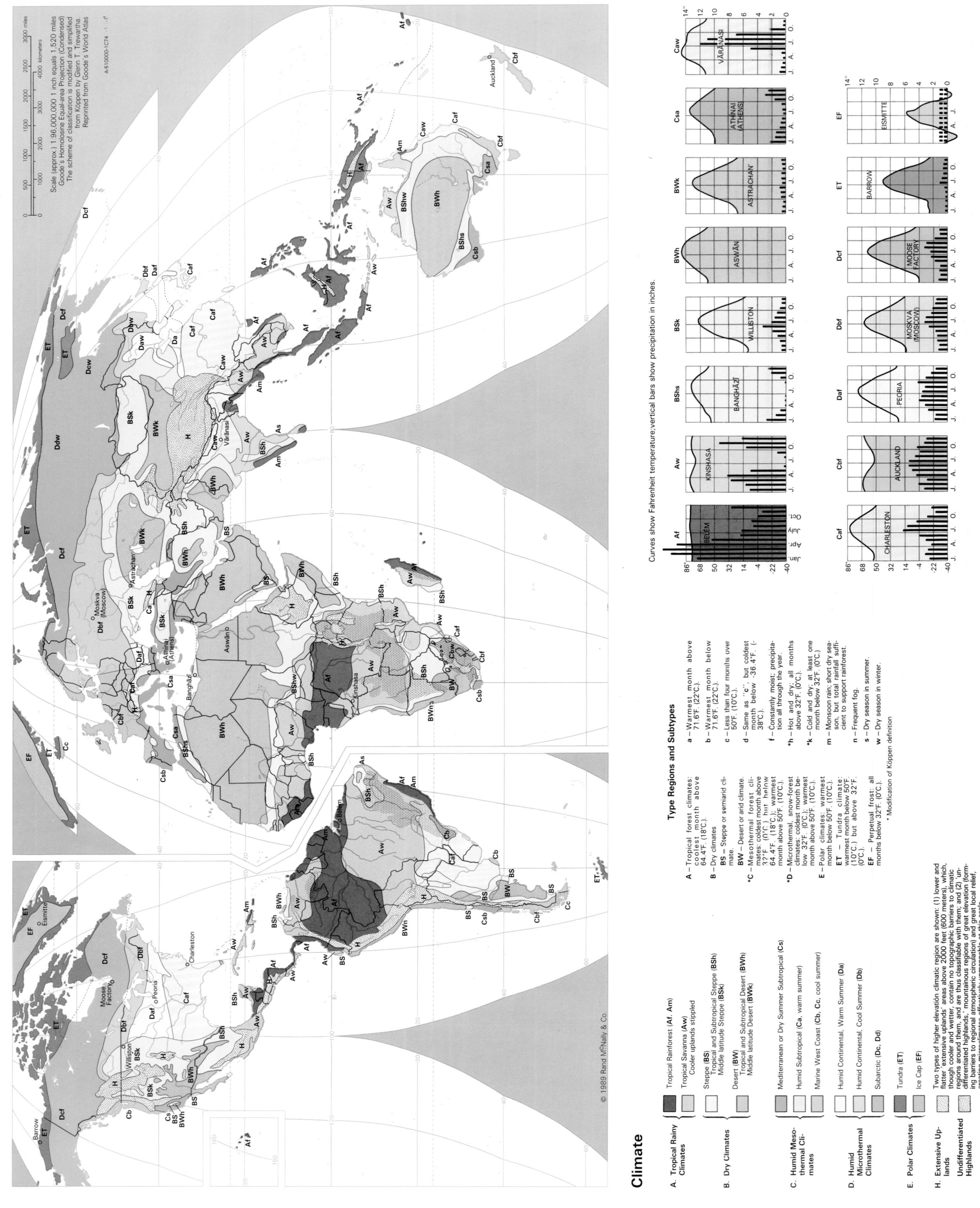

Climate

Curves show Fahrenheit temperature; vertical bars show precipitation in inches.

Type Regions and Subtypes

A – Tropical forest climates: coolest month above 64.4°F. (18°C.)

B – Dry climates
BS – Steppe or semiarid climate.
BW – Desert or arid climate.

*C – Mesothermal forest climates: coldest month above 32°F. (0°C.) but below 64.4°F. (18°C.); warmest month above 50°F. (10°C.).

*D – Microthermal, snow-forest climates: coldest month below 32°F. (0°C.); warmest month above 50°F. (10°C.).

E – Polar climates:
ET – Tundra climate: warmest month below 50°F. (10°C.) but above 32°F. (0°C.).
EF – Perpetual frost: all months below 32°F. (0°C.).

a – Warmest month above 71.6°F. (22°C.).
b – Warmest month below 71.6°F. (22°C.).
c – Less than four months over 50°F. (10°C.).
d – Same as "c" but coldest month below -36.4°F. (-38°C.).
f – Constantly moist; precipitation all through the year.

*h – Hot and dry; all months above 32°F. (0°C.).
*k – Cold and dry; at least one month below 32°F. (0°C.).
m – Monsoon rain; short dry season, but total rainfall sufficient to support rainforest.
n – Frequent fog.
s – Dry season in summer.
w – Dry season in winter.

* Modification of Köppen definition

A. Tropical Rainy Climates
- Tropical Rainforest (Af, Am)
- Tropical Savanna (Aw) Cooler uplands stippled

B. Dry Climates
- Steppe (BS) Tropical and Subtropical Steppe (BSh) Middle latitude Steppe (BSk)
- Desert (BW) Tropical and Subtropical Desert (BWh) Middle latitude Desert (BWk)

C. Humid Mesothermal Climates
- Mediterranean or Dry Summer Subtropical (Cs)
- Humid Subtropical (Ca, warm summer)
- Marine West Coast (Cb, Cc, cool summer)

D. Humid Microthermal Climates
- Humid Continental, Warm Summer (Da)
- Humid Continental, Cool Summer (Db)
- Subarctic (Dc, Dd)

E. Polar Climates
- Tundra (ET)
- Ice Cap (EF)

H. Extensive Uplands
- Undifferentiated Highlands

Two types of higher elevation climatic region are shown: (1) lower and flatter "extensive uplands" areas above 2000 feet (600 meters), which, though cooler and wetter, contain no topographic barriers to climatic regions around them, and are thus classifiable with them; and (2) undifferentiated highlands," mountainous regions of great elevation (forming barriers to regional atmospheric circulation) and great local relief, creating microclimates effectively unmappable at this scale.

Scale (approx.) 1:96,000,000 1 inch equals 1,520 miles
Goode's Homolosine Equal-area Projection (Condensed)
The scheme of classification is modified and simplified
from Köppen by Glenn T. Trewartha.
Reprinted from Goode's World Atlas

© 1989 Rand McNally & Co.

xxxiv

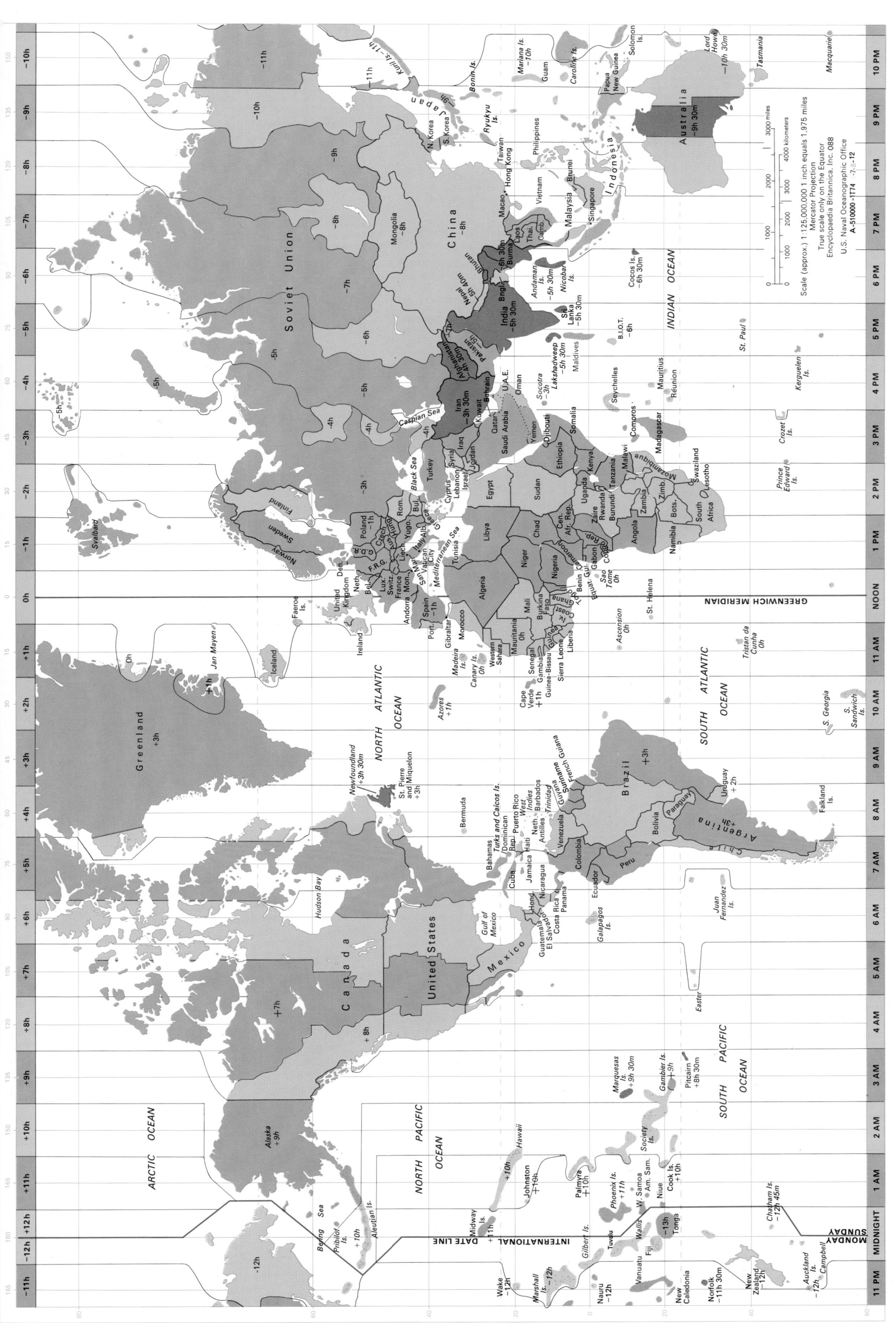

Time Zones

The standard time zone system, fixed by international agreement and by law in each country, is based on a theoretical division of the globe into 24 zones of 15° longitude each. The mid-meridian of each zone fixes the hour for the entire zone. The zero time zone extends 7½° east and 7½° west of the Greenwich meridian, 0° longitude. Since the earth rotates toward the east, time zones to the west of Greenwich are earlier, to the east, later.

Plus and minus hours at the top of the map are added to or subtracted from local time to find Greenwich time. Local standard time can be determined for any area in the world by adding one hour for each time zone counted in an easterly direction from one's own, or by subtracting one hour for each zone counted in a westerly direction. To separate one day from the next, the 180th meridian has been designated as the international date line. On both sides of the line the time of day is the same, but west of the line it is one day later than it is to the east. Countries that adhere to the international zone system adopt the zone applicable to their location. Some countries, however, establish time zones based on political boundaries, or adopt the time zone of a neighboring unit. For all or part of the year some countries also advance their time by one hour, thereby utilizing more daylight hours each day.

Standard time zone of even-numbered hours from Greenwich time

Standard time zone of odd-numbered hours from Greenwich time

Time varies from the standard time zone by half an hour

Time varies from the standard time zone by other than half an hour

h m   hours, minutes

XXXV

Surface Configuration

Smooth lands

Level plains: nearly all slopes gentle; local relief less than 100 ft. (30 m.)

Irregular plains: majority of slopes gentle; local relief 100-300 ft. (30-90 m.)

Broken lands

Tablelands and plateaus: majority of slopes gentle, with the gentler slopes on the uplands; local relief more than 300 ft. (90 m.)

Hill-studded plains: majority of slopes gentle, with the gentler slopes in the lowlands; local relief 300-1,000 ft. (90-300 m.)

Mountain-studded plains: majority of slopes gentle, with the gentler slopes in the lowlands; local relief more than 1,000 ft. (300 m.)

Rough lands

Hill lands: steeper slopes predominate; local relief less than 1,000 ft. (300 m.)

Mountains: steeper slopes predominate; local relief 1,000-5,000 ft. (300-1,500 m.)

Mountains of great relief: steeper slopes predominate; local relief more than 5,000 ft. (1,500 m.)

Other surfaces

Ice caps: permanent ice

Maximum extent of glaciation

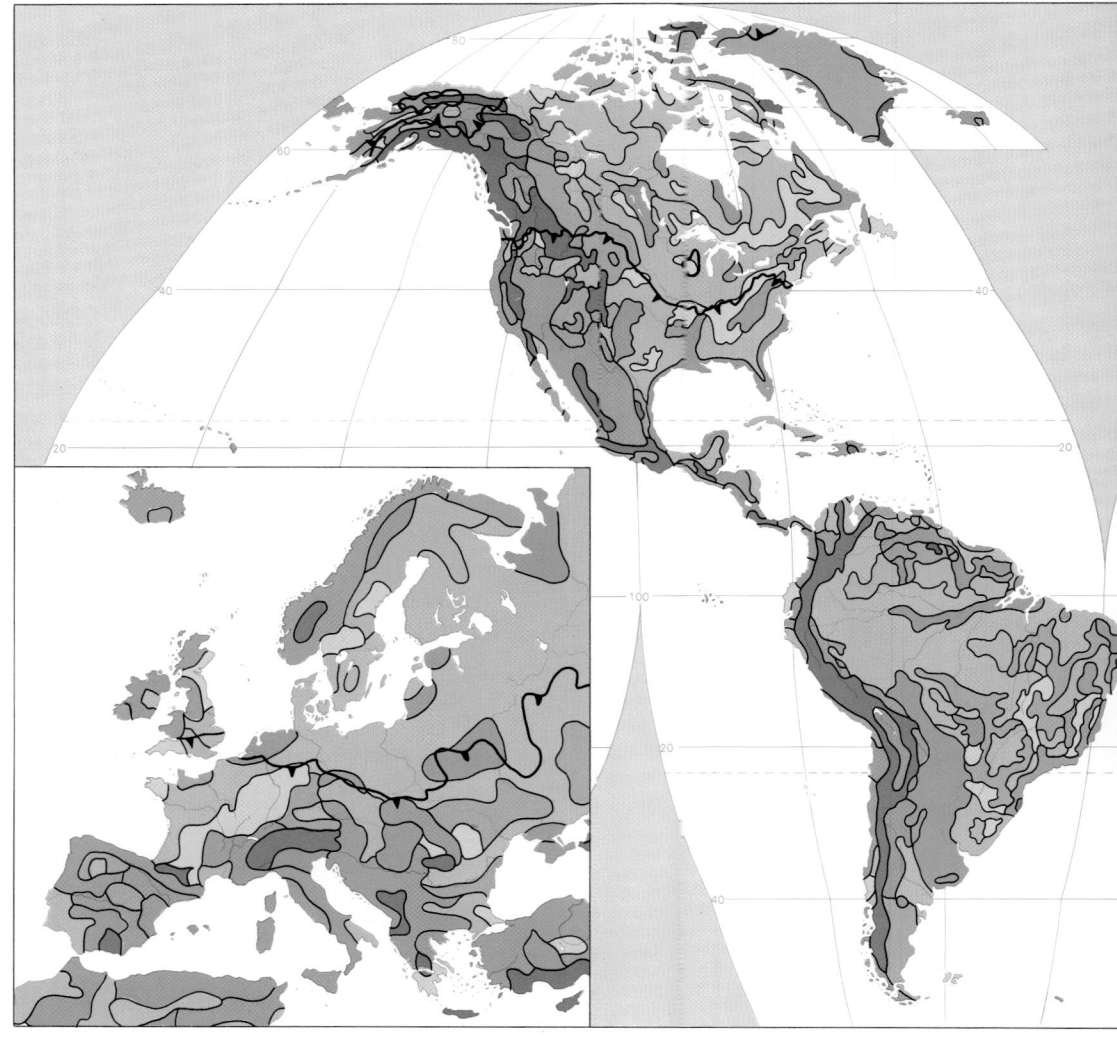

Earth Structure and Tectonics

Precambrian stable shield areas

Exposed Precambrian rock

Paleozoic and Mesozoic flat-lying sedimentary rocks

Principal Paleozoic and Mesozoic folded areas

Cenozoic sedimentary rocks

Principal Cenozoic folded areas

Lava plateaus

Major trends of folding

Geologic time chart

Precambrian—from formation of the earth (at least 4 billion years ago) to 600 million years ago

Paleozoic—from 600 million to 200 million years ago

Mesozoic—from 200 million to 70 million years ago

Cenozoic—from 70 million years ago to present time

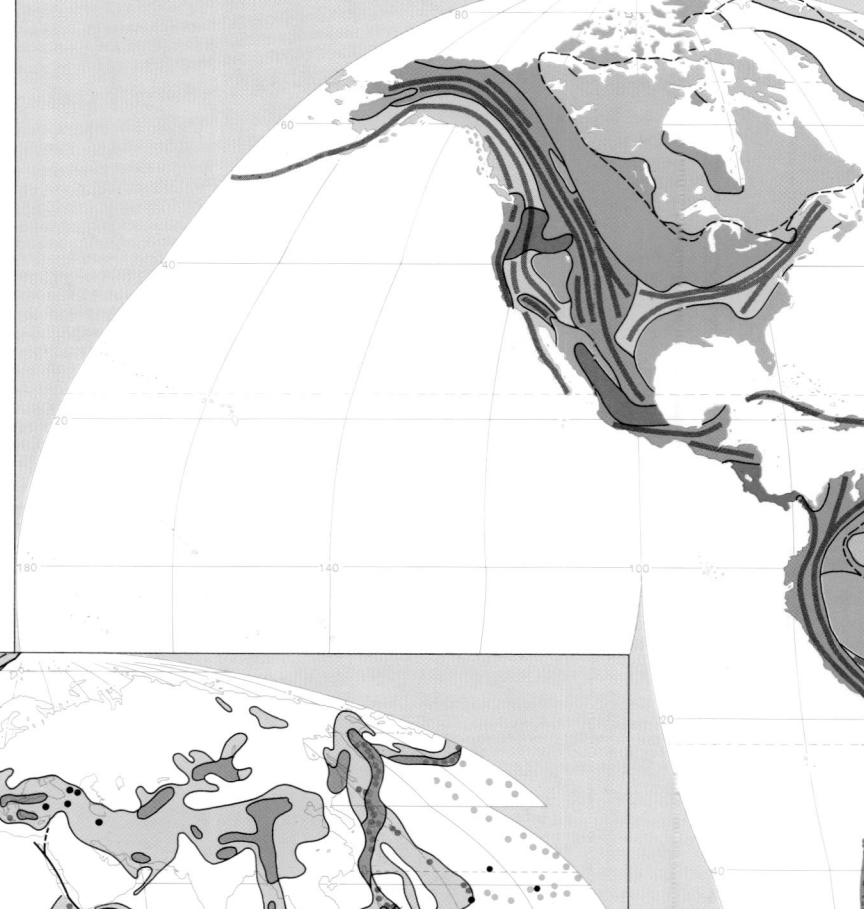

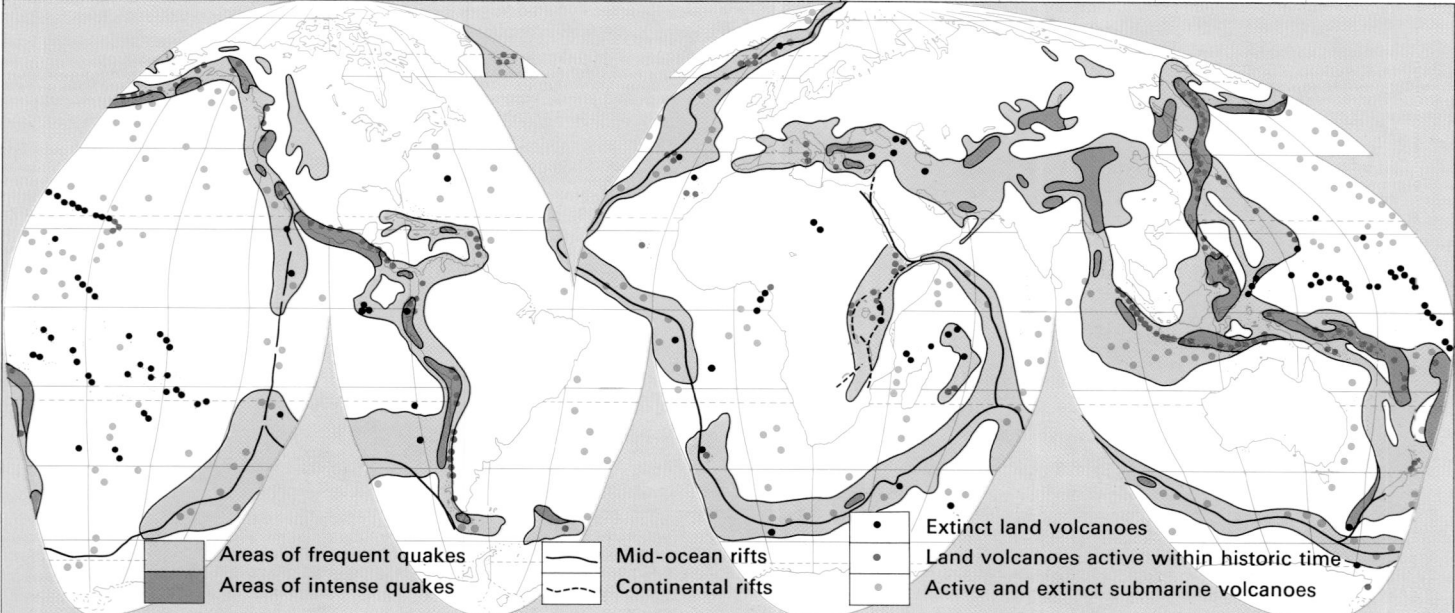

Areas of frequent quakes

Areas of intense quakes

Mid-ocean rifts

Continental rifts

Extinct land volcanoes

Land volcanoes active within historic time

Active and extinct submarine volcanoes

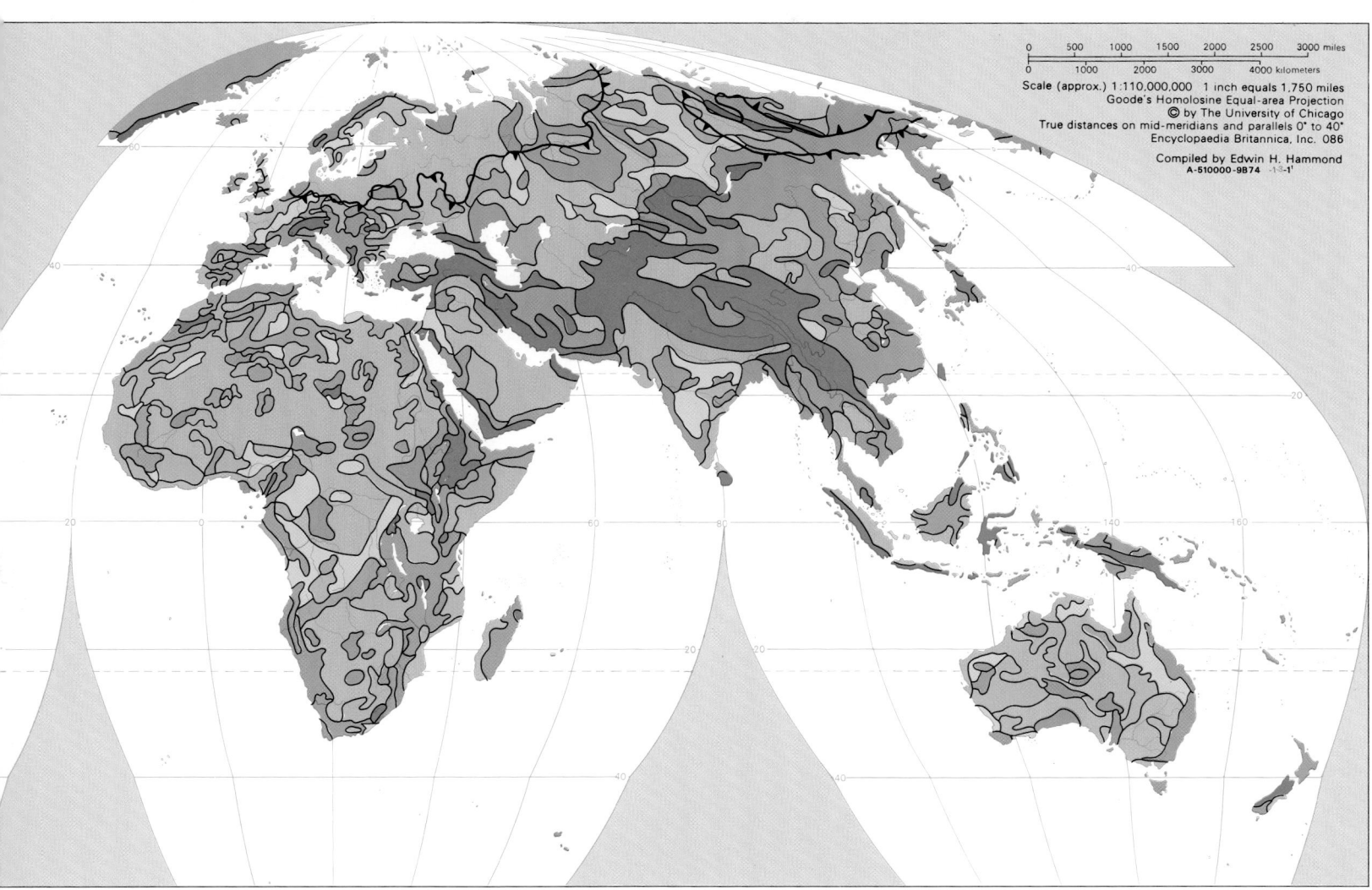

Scale (approx.) 1:110,000,000   1 inch equals 1,750 miles
Goode's Homolosine Equal-area Projection
© by The University of Chicago
True distances on mid-meridians and parallels 0° to 40°
Encyclopaedia Britannica, Inc. 086

Compiled by Edwin H. Hammond
A-510000-9B74

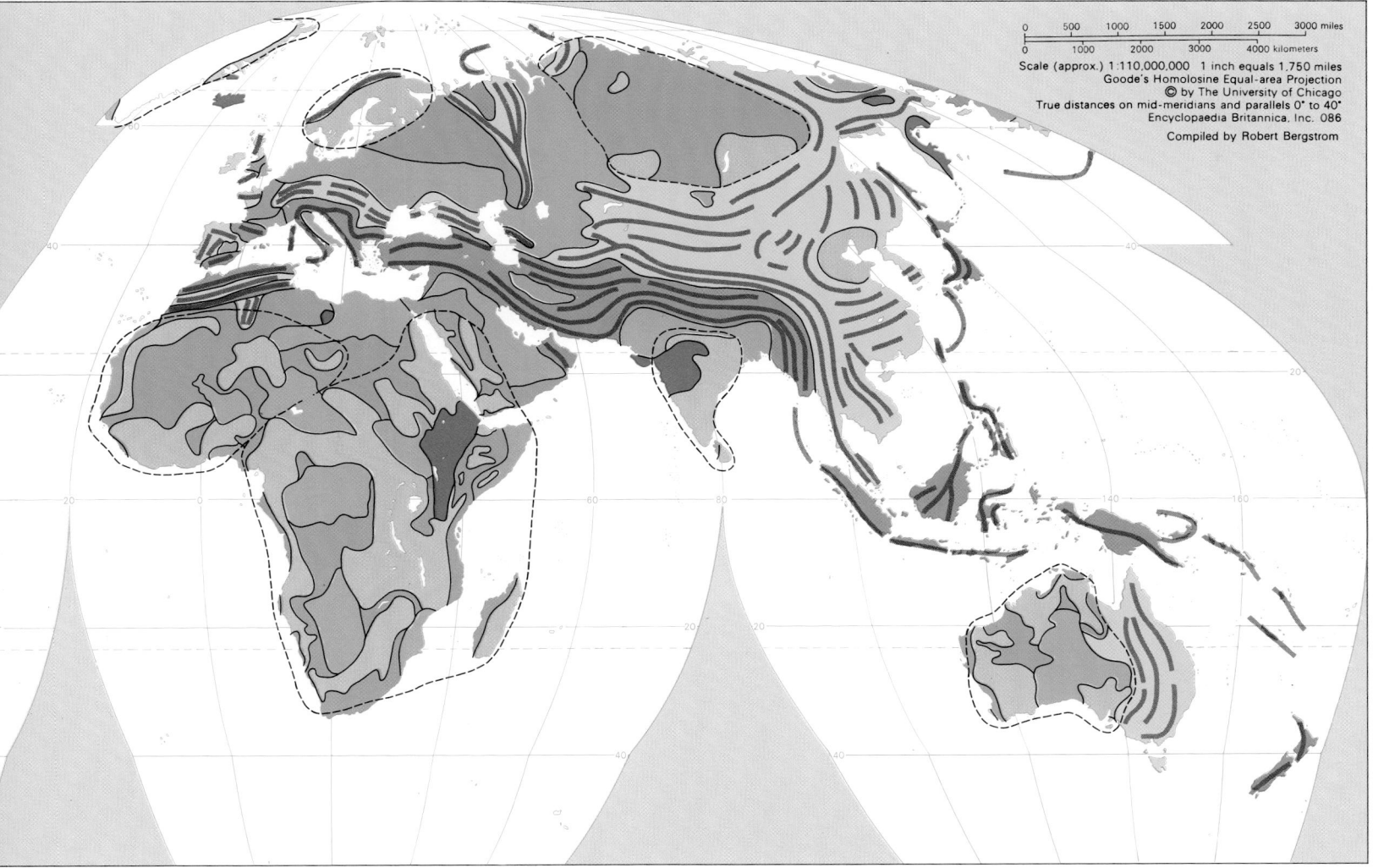

Scale (approx.) 1:110,000,000   1 inch equals 1,750 miles
Goode's Homolosine Equal-area Projection
© by The University of Chicago
True distances on mid-meridians and parallels 0° to 40°
Encyclopaedia Britannica, Inc. 086

Compiled by Robert Bergstrom

Development of the earth's structure

The earth is in process of constant transformation. Movements in the hot, dense interior of the earth result in folding and fracture of the crust and transfer of molten material to the surface. As a result, large structures such as mountain ranges, volcanoes, lava plateaus, and rift valleys are created. The forces that bring about these structural changes are called *tectonic forces.*

The present continents have developed from stable nuclei, or *shields,* of ancient (Precambrian) rock. Erosive forces such as water, wind, and ice have worn away particles of the rock, depositing them at the edges of the shields, where they have accumulated and ultimately become sedimentary rock. Subsequently, in places, these extensive areas of flat-lying rock have been elevated, folded, or warped, by the action of tectonic forces, to form mountains. The shape of these mountains has been altered by later erosion. Where the forces of erosion have been at work for a long time, the mountains tend to have a low relief and rounded contours, like the Appalachians. Mountains more recently formed are high and rugged, like the Himalayas.

The map above depicts some of the major geologic structures of the earth and identifies them according to the period of their formation. A geologic time chart is included in the legend. The inset map shows the most important areas of earthquakes, rifts, and volcanic activity. Comparison of all the maps will show the close correlation between present-day mountain systems, recent (Cenozoic) mountain-building, and the areas of frequent earthquakes and active volcanoes.

Natural Vegetation

Broad-leaved evergreen vegetation

Broad-leaved evergreen forest
Broad-leaved evergreen shrub formation
Scattered broad-leaved evergreen shrubs
Scattered broad-leaved evergreen dwarf shrubs

Broad-leaved deciduous vegetation

Broad-leaved deciduous forest
Broad-leaved deciduous shrub formation
Scattered broad-leaved deciduous shrubs
Scattered broad-leaved deciduous dwarf shrubs

Coniferous vegetation

Needle-leaved evergreen forest
Scattered needle-leaved evergreen trees
Needle-leaved deciduous forest

Mixed vegetation without grass

Forest of broad-leaved evergreen and deciduous trees
Forest of broad-leaved and needle-leaved evergreen trees
Broad-leaved deciduous forests with broad-leaved evergreen shrubs
Forest of broad-leaved deciduous and needle-leaved evergreen trees

Mixed vegetation with grass

Grassland with scattered broad-leaved evergreen trees
Grassland with broad-leaved evergreen shrubs
Grassland with scattered broad-leaved deciduous trees
Grassland with broad-leaved deciduous shrubs

Grassland, tundra, barren

Grassland
Patches of grass
Lichens and grasses
Lichens and mosses
Barren

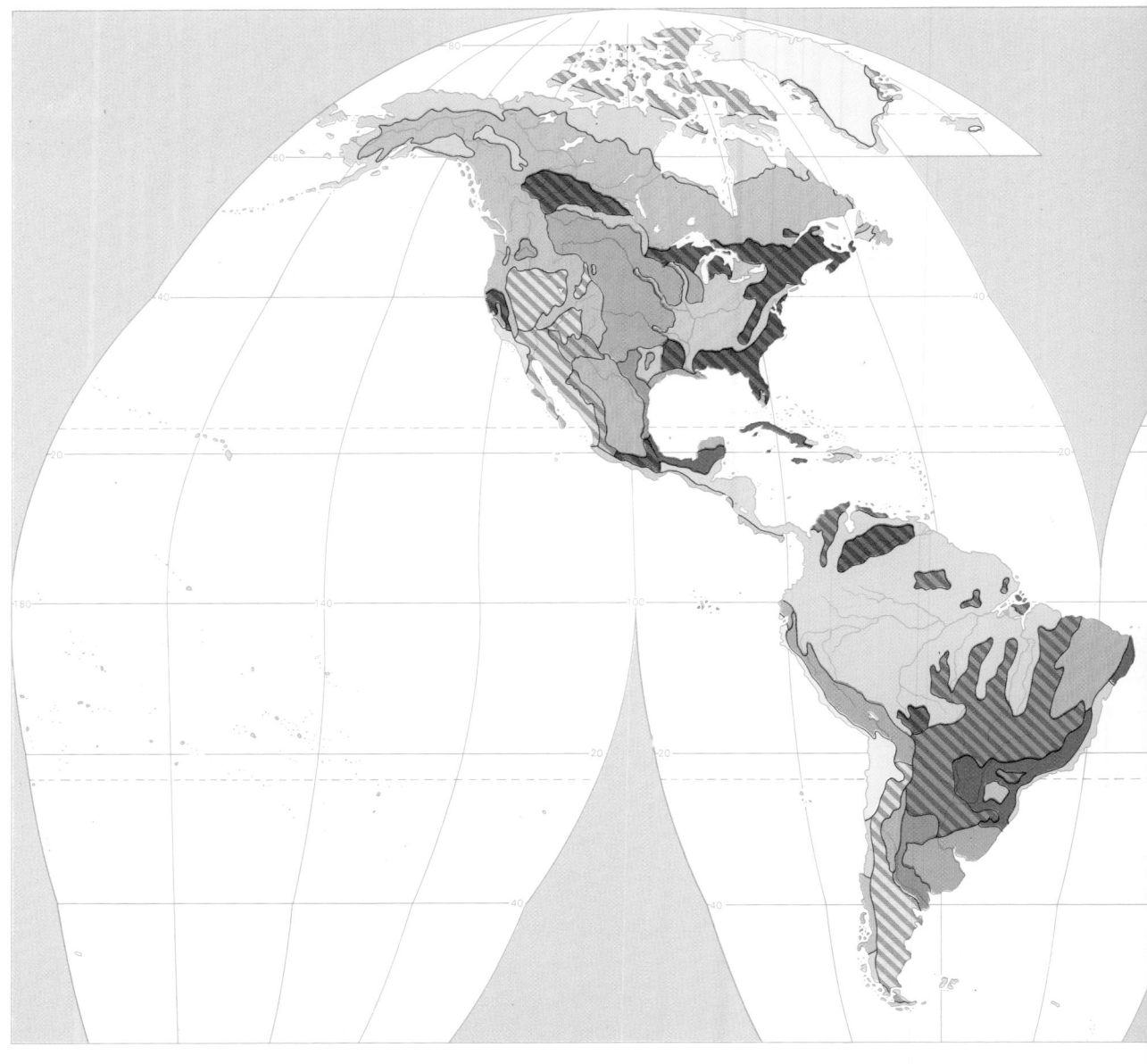

Soils

Tundra soils of frigid climates; commonly with permanently frozen subsoil; supports dwarf shrubs, mosses, and lichens; some used for reindeer pasture

Podzolic soils of humid, cool climates; covered with predominantly coniferous forest; some farming, mainly subsistence

Podzolic soils of humid, temperate climates; originally covered with predominantly deciduous forest, much of it removed to accommodate extensive general farming, industry, and cities

Podzolic soils of humid, warm climates; covered with coniferous or mixed forest; general farming

Chernozemic soils of subhumid and semiarid, cool to tropical climates; supports mainly grasslands; extensive grain and livestock farming

Latosolic soils of humid or wet-dry tropical and subtropical climates; supports forest or savanna; shifting cultivation with some plantation agriculture

Grumusolic soils of humid to semiarid and temperate to tropical climates, with distinct wet and dry seasons; mainly grass-covered; livestock and grain farming

Desertic soils of arid climates; includes many areas of shallow, stony soils; sparse cover of shrubs and grass, some suitable for grazing; fertile if irrigated; dry farming possible in some areas

Mountain soils of all climates; shallow, stony; barren, grass-covered, or forested, depending on climate; includes many areas of other soils

Alluvial soils of all climates; deposited by water in flood plains and deltas of rivers; intensive farming in most temperate and some tropical regions (many smaller areas not shown)

Ice cap of polar regions

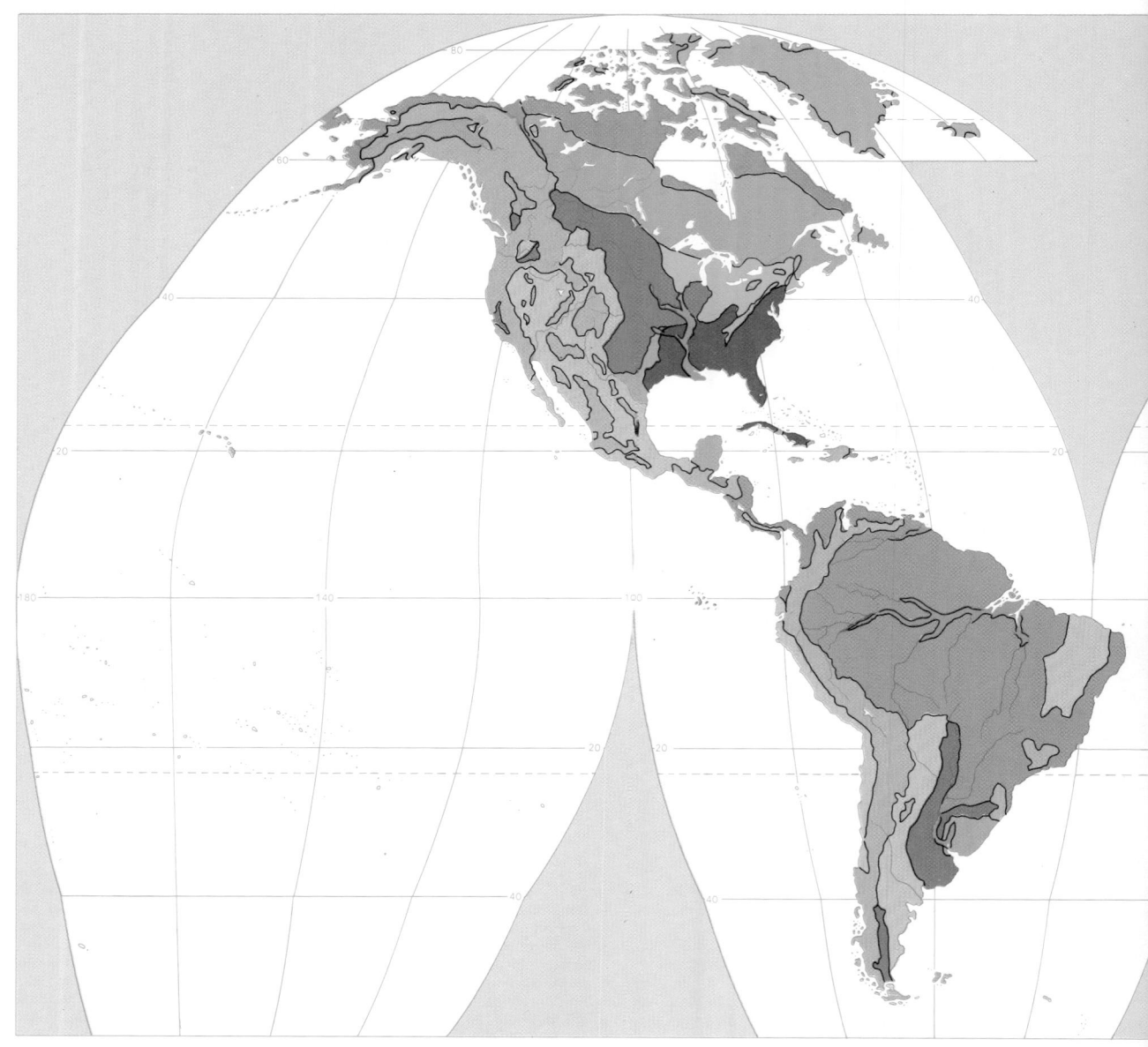

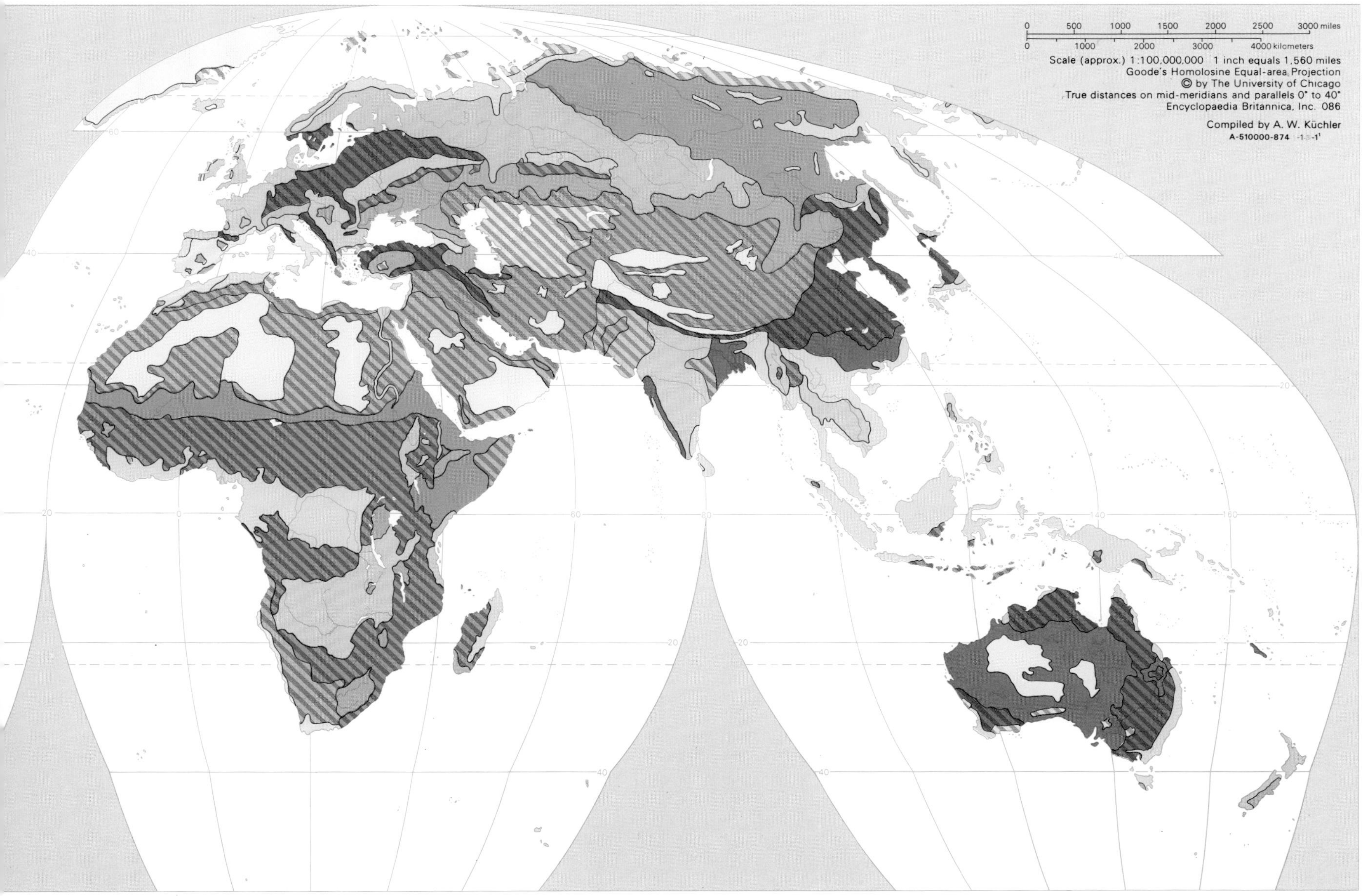

Scale (approx.) 1:100,000,000 1 inch equals 1,560 miles
Goode's Homolosine Equal-area Projection
© by The University of Chicago
True distances on mid-meridians and parallels 0° to 40°
Encyclopaedia Britannica, Inc. 086

Compiled by A. W. Küchler
A-510000-874 -1-2-1'

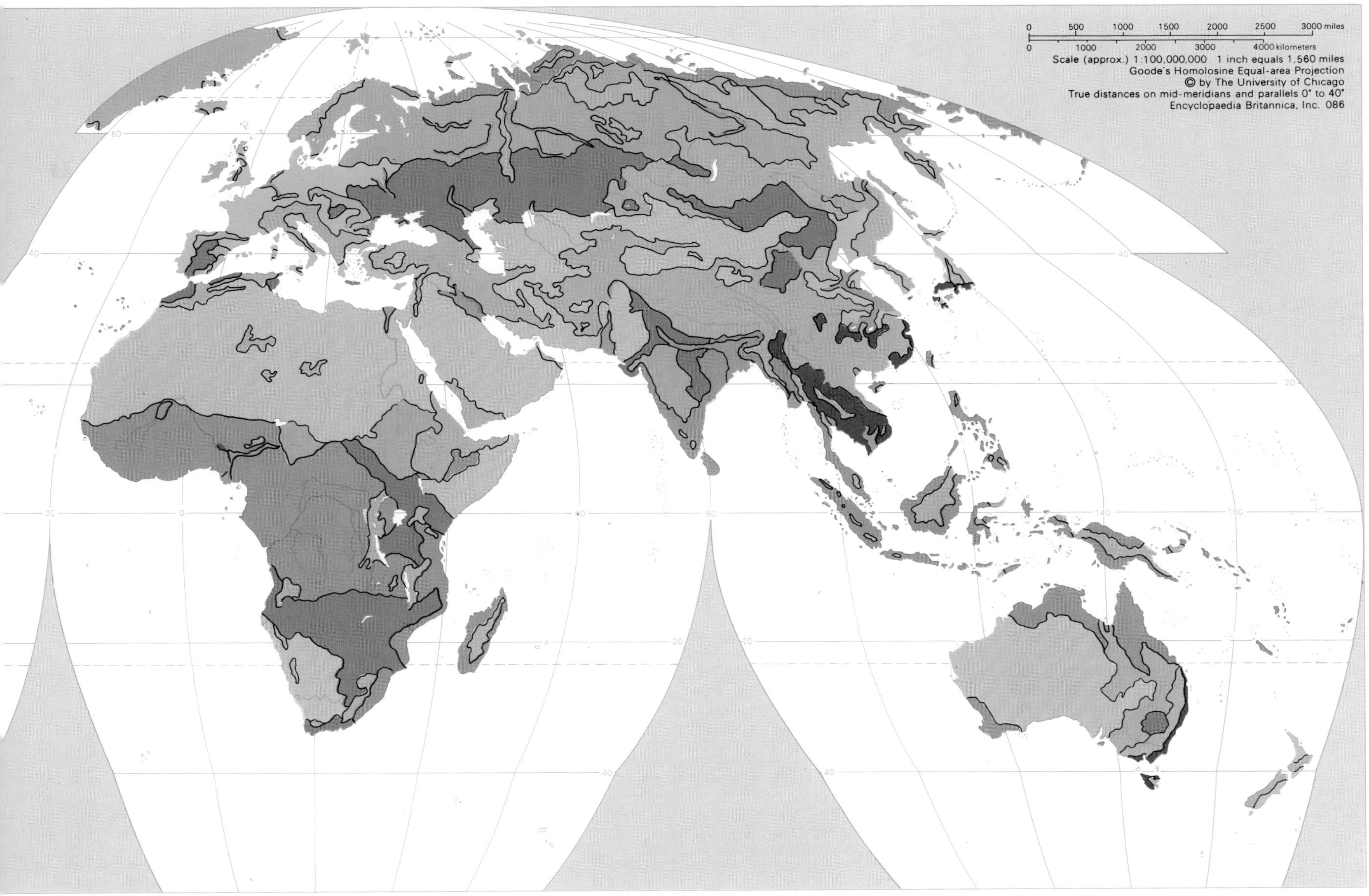

Scale (approx.) 1:100,000,000 1 inch equals 1,560 miles
Goode's Homolosine Equal-area Projection
© by The University of Chicago
True distances on mid-meridians and parallels 0° to 40°
Encyclopaedia Britannica, Inc. 086

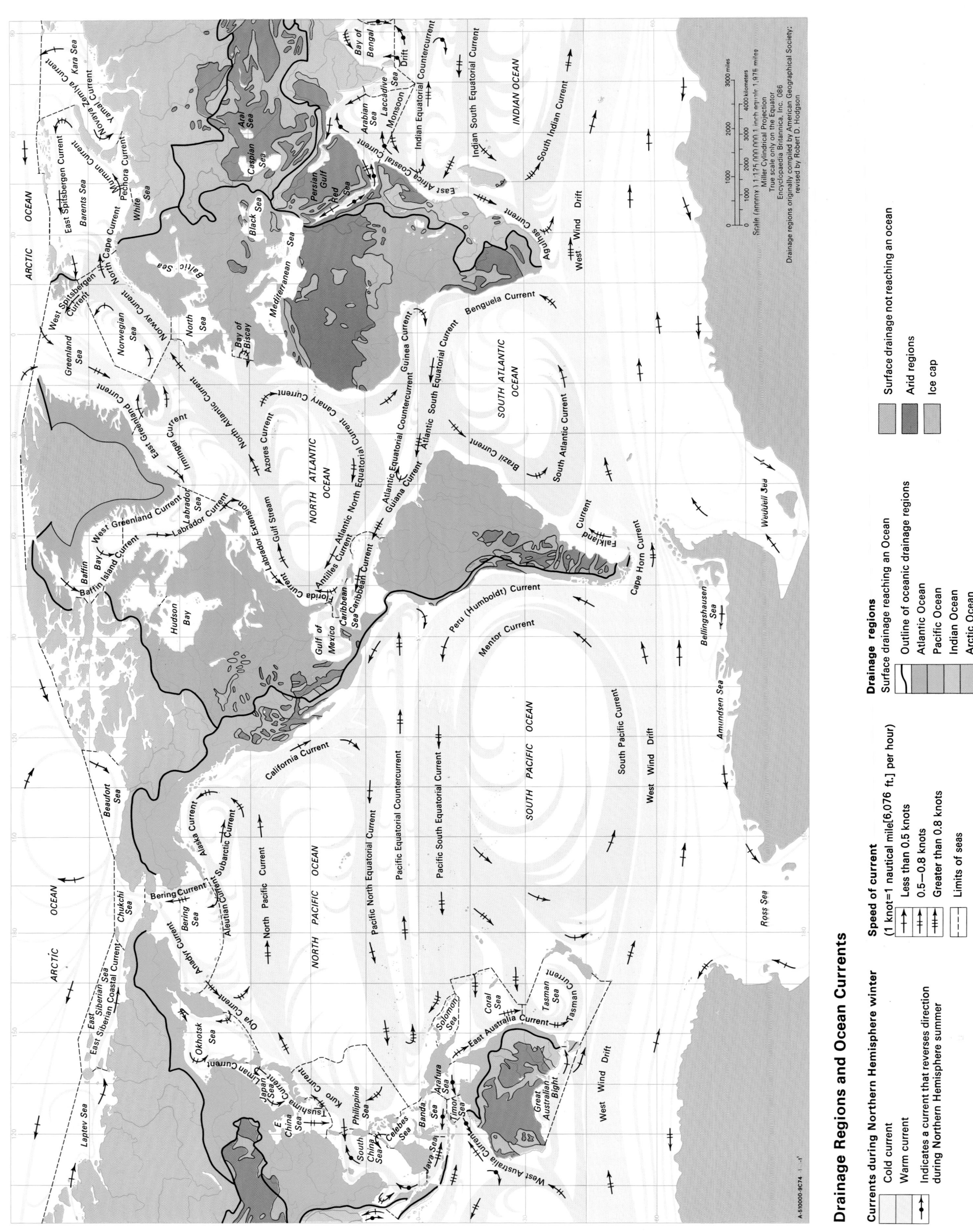

Drainage Regions and Ocean Currents

Currents during Northern Hemisphere winter

Cold current

Warm current

↑ Indicates a current that reverses direction
during Northern Hemisphere summer

Speed of current
(1 knot=1 nautical mile[6,076 ft.] per hour)

Less than 0.5 knots

0.5—0.8 knots

Greater than 0.8 knots

Limits of seas

Drainage regions

Surface drainage reaching an Ocean

Outline of oceanic drainage regions

Atlantic Ocean

Pacific Ocean

Indian Ocean

Arctic Ocean

Surface drainage not reaching an ocean

Arid regions

Ice cap

Scale (mmm) 1:1?5,000,000 1 inch equals 1,976 miles
Miller Cylindrical Projection
True scale only on the Equator
Encyclopaedia Britannica, Inc. 086
Drainage regions originally compiled by American Geographical Society;
revised by Robert D. Hodgson

A 510000-9C74 i - x'

World, Ocean, and Continent Maps / Weltkarten, Karten der Ozeane und Erdteile
Mapas del Mundo, Océanos y Continentes / Cartes du Monde, des Océans et des Continents
Mapas do Mundo, dos Oceanos e dos Continentes

1

THIS SECTION OPENS with World Political and World Physical maps at the scale of 1:75,000,000. There follow maps of the Pacific, Indian, and Atlantic oceans at the scale 1:48,000,000, the largest scale at which the total expanse of these bodies of water could be portrayed. Finally, a series of continent relief maps at the scale of 1:24,000,000 show a global view of the earth as it would appear from about 4,000 miles in space. The Azimuthal Equal-Area projection is used for the 1:24,000,000 maps, the scale being approximately that of a globe 20 inches in diameter.

The colors of the continent maps portray the land areas as if viewed from space during the growing season, without regard to the fact that the growing seasons are not concurrent in all areas. Underwater features and varying water depths are represented by shaded relief and different color tones. The result is a strong physical portrait of the earth's major land and submarine forms. The legend below shows how these different kinds of terrain and vegetation have been represented. The names of physical features—plateaus, basins, mountain ranges, seas, rivers, lakes, gulfs, trenches, bays, islands—predominate on these maps.

DIESER KARTENTEIL BEGINNT mit politischen und physischen Weltkarten im Massstab 1:75 Millionen. Dann folgen Karten des Pazifischen, Indischen und Atlantischen Ozeans in 1:48 Millionen, dem grössten Massstab, in dem diese Wasserflächen in ihrer ganzen Ausdehnung abgebildet werden konnten. Schliesslich folgt eine Reihe von Reliefkarten der Erdteile in 1:24 Millionen. Sie geben eine Übersicht der Erde, wie sie aus einer Entfernung von ungefähr 6 400 Kilometer aus dem Weltraum gewonnen würde. Den Karten im Massstab 1:24 Millionen liegt ein flächentreuer azimutaler Entwurf zugrunde, dieser Massstab entspricht ungefähr dem eines Globus von 50 cm Durchmesser.

Die Farben der Erdteilkarten bilden jedes Landgebiet so ab, wie es in der Vegetationsperiode aus der Vogelperspektive erschiene, ohne zu berücksichtigen, dass die Vegetationsperioden nicht in allen Gebieten gleichzeitig eintreten. Die Gliederung des Meeresbodens und die unterschiedlichen Meerestiefen werden durch Schummerung und verschiedene Farbstufen dargestellt. Das Ergebnis ist eine anschauliche physische Darstellung der wichtigsten terrestrischen und untermeerischen Formen der Erde. Die untenstehende Zeichenerklärung zeigt, wie diese verschiedenen Geländeformen und Vegetationsgebiete veranschaulicht werden. Namen physischer Objekte—Hochebenen, Becken, Gebirgszüge, Meere, Flüsse, Seen, Buchten, Gräben, Inseln—herrschen in diesen Karten vor.

ESTA SECCIÓN DA PRINCIPIO con los Mapas Políticos y Físicos del Mundo, a una escala de 1:75 000 000. A continuación están los mapas de los océanos Pacífico, Indico y Atlántico a una escala de 1:48 000 000, que es la mayor escala utilizable para la representación de esas masas de agua en toda su extensión. Por último, una serie de mapas del relieve de los continentes, a una escala de 1:24 000 000, proporcionan una vista global de la tierra tal como se apreciaría desde el espacio a una distancia aproximada de 6 400 kilómetros. La proyección azimutal equiárea se usa, para los mapas de 1:24 000 000, a una escala según la cual la tierra se reduciría a un globo de unos 50 cm de diámetro.

Los colores utilizados en los mapas de los continentes representan las diversas regiones de la tierra tal como se verían desde el espacio durante la estación en que la vegetación se desarrolla, sin tomar en cuenta que este fenómeno no se produce simultáneamente en todas las áreas. Las estructuras características del fondo marino y las variaciones de profundidad de los océanos se representan mediante relieve sombreado y distintos matices de color. El resultado es una imagen elocuente de las formas terrestres y submarinas más notables del planeta. La leyenda abajo explica cómo se representan estos diferentes tipos de terreno y vegetación. En estos mapas predomina la nomenclatura de elementos físicos: mesetas, cuencas, sierras, mares, ríos, lagos, golfos, bahías, trincheras, islas.

CETTE PARTIE comprend d'abord des cartes du monde politique et du monde physique à l'échelle de 1:75 000 000. Viennent ensuite les cartes des océans Pacifique, Indien et Atlantique à l'échelle de 1:48 000 000, la plus grande échelle qui a permis la reproduction complète de ces étendues d'eau. Pour terminer, une série de cartes en relief des continents à l'échelle de 1:24 000 000 donne une vue globale de la terre, telle qu'elle apparaîtrait vue de l'espace à une distance d'environ 6 400 kilomètres.

La projection azimutale équivalente a été utilisée pour les cartes au 1:24 000 000e, dont l'échelle équivaut à celle d'un globe de 50 cm de diamètre environ.

Les couleurs des cartes font apparaître les continents tels qu'on les verrait de l'espace, pendant la saison de croissance végétale, mais sans tenir compte du fait que cette saison n'apparaît pas partout simultanément. Le relief sous-marin est représenté par un estompage et la profondeur des océans par une variation de la couleur. Il en résulte une reproduction vigoureuse des principaux paysages continentaux et des principales formes sousmarines. La légende ci-dessous indique de quelle façon ils sont cartographiés. Les noms d'éléments topographiques tels que plateaux, bassins, chaînes de montagnes, mers, cours d'eau, lacs, golfes, baies, crêtes, îles et fosses océaniques, prédominent dans ces cartes.

ESTA SEÇÃO PRINCIPIA com os mapas políticos e físicos do Mundo, em escala de 1:75 000 000. Seguem-se os mapas dos oceanos Pacifico, Índico e Atlântico na escala de 1:48 000 000, a maior escala que se pode utilizar para a representação dessas massas de água em toda a sua extensão. Finalmente, uma série de mapas de relevo dos continentes, na escala de 1:24 000 000, proporciona uma visão global da Terra tal como apareceria do espaço a uma distância aproximada de cerca de 6 400 km. A projeção azimutal equiárea foi usada para os mapas da escala de 1:24 000 000, segundo a qual a Terra se apresentaria como um globo de cerca de 50 cm de diâmetro.

As cores utilizadas nos mapas dos continentes representam as massas terrestres tal como apareceriam vistas do espaço durante a estação do crescimento vegetal, sem levar em conta que este fenômeno não se produz simultaneamente em todas as regiões. As características do fundo do mar e as variações de profundidade das águas são representadas por um relevo sombreado e por diferentes matizes de cor. O resultado proporciona uma imagem física eloqüente das principais formas terrestres e submarinas da Terra. As legendas abaixo explicam como foram representados os diversos tipos de terreno e vegetação. Nestes mapas predomina a nomenclatura dos elementos físicos: planaltos, bacias, cadeias de montanhas, mares, rios, lagos, golfos, baías, fossas, ilhas.

Land Features / Land Phänomene / Elementos de la Tierra
Paysages Continentaux / Acidentes Continentais

Submarine Features / Untermeerische Phänomene
Elementos Submarinos / Formes de Relief Sous-marin / Acidentes do Revelo Submarino

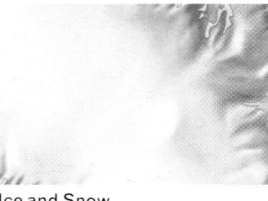

Ice and Snow
Eis und Schnee
Hielo y nieve
Glace et neige
Gelo e neve

High Barren Area
Hochgebirgswüste
Alta zona árida
Région haute et aride
Alta zona árida

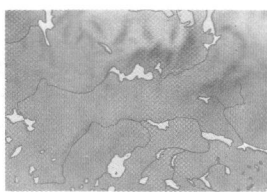

Tundra and Alpine
Tundra und Alpine Vegetation
Tundra y alpina
Toundra et végétation alpine
Tundra e vegetação alpina

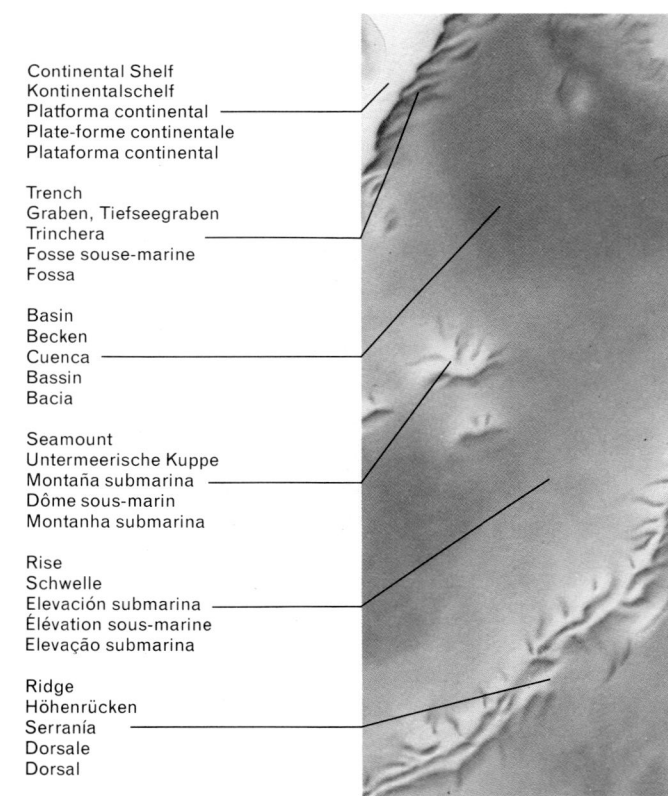

Continental Shelf
Kontinentalschelf
Platforma continental
Plate-forme continentale
Plataforma continental

Trench
Graben, Tiefseegraben
Trinchera
Fosse souse-marine
Fossa

Basin
Becken
Cuenca
Bassin
Bacia

Seamount
Untermeerische Kuppe
Montaña submarina
Dôme sous-marin
Montanha submarina

Rise
Schwelle
Elevación submarina
Élévation sous-marine
Elevação submarina

Ridge
Höhenrücken
Serranía
Dorsale
Dorsal

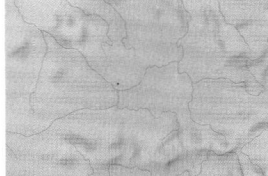

Needleleaf Trees
Nadelwälder
Coníferas
Forêt de conifères
Coníferas

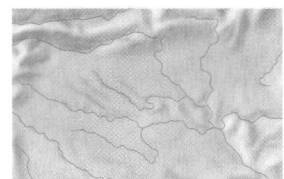

Broadleaf Trees
Laubwälder
Árboles de hojas anchas
Forêt à feuilles caduques
Árvores de folhas caducas

Tropical Rainforest
Tropischer Regenwald
Bosque tropical lluvioso
Forêt tropicale humide
Floresta tropical úmida

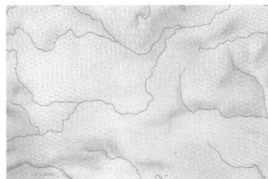

Grassland
Grasland
Pradera
Formations herbacées
Pradaria

Dry Scrub
Trockenes Buschland
Matorral
Brousse sèche
Caatinga

Desert
Wüste
Desierto
Désert
Deserto

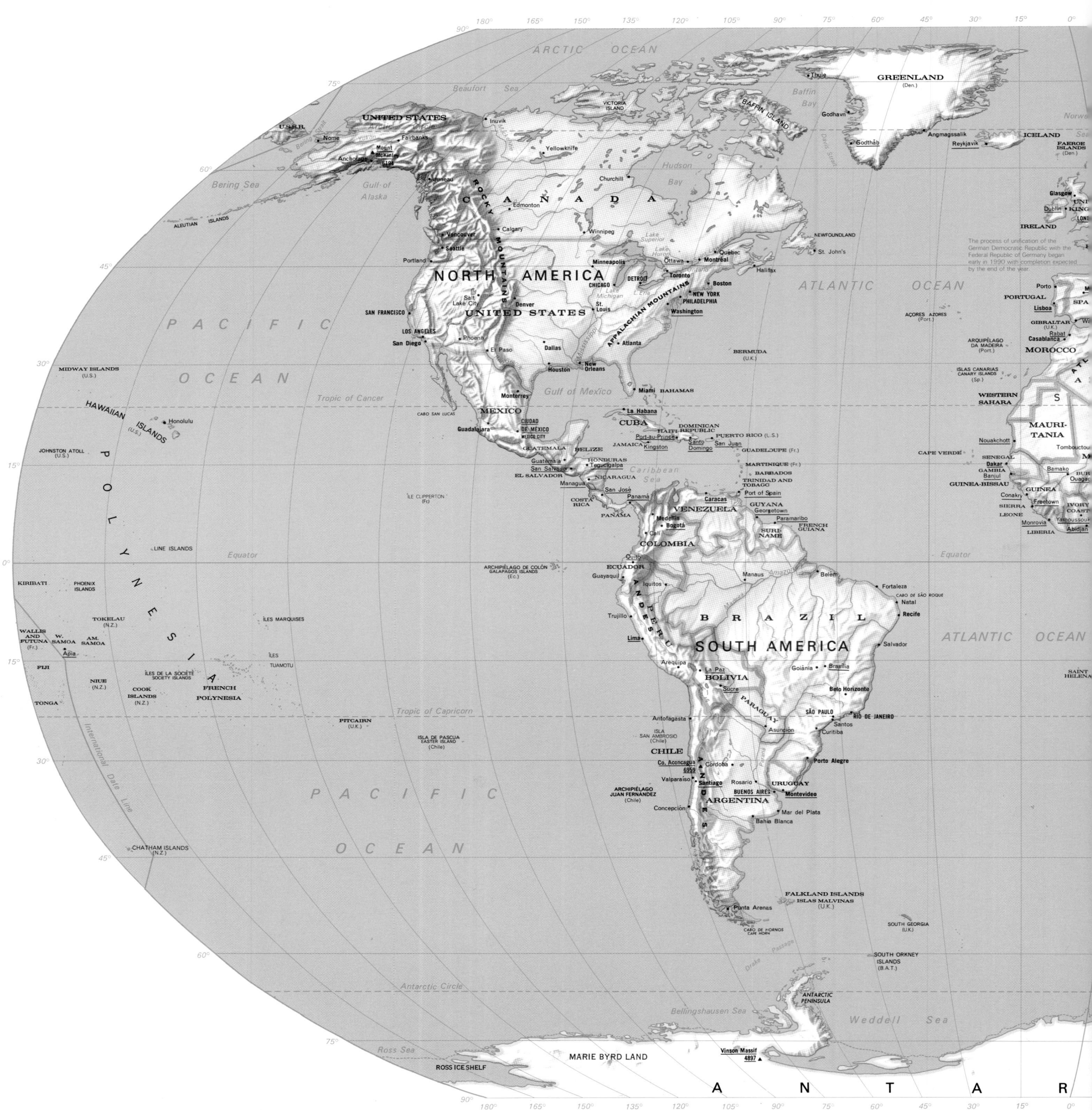

The process of unification of the
German Democratic Republic with the
Federal Republic of Germany began
early in 1990 with completion expected
by the end of the year.

Kilometers
Statute Miles

One centimeter represents 750 kilometers.
One inch represents approximately 1200 miles.
Robinson Projection
Scale 1:75,000,000

One centimeter represents 750 kilometers.
One inch represents approximately 1200 miles.
Robinson Projection
Scale 1:75,000,000

GREENLAND
Greenland Sea
Norwegian Sea
Arctic Circle
ICELAND
REYKJANES RIDGE
FAEROE IS.
UNITED KINGDOM
IRELAND
North Sea
Baltic Sea
FRANCE
SWEDEN
FINLAND
NORWAY
POLAND
HUNGARY
ROMANIA
BULGARIA
YUGO.
ITALY
GREECE
TURKEY
ASIA MINOR
Black Sea
Caspian Sea
Barents Sea
NOVAJA ZEMLJA
Karskoje more
UNION OF SOVIET SOCIALIST REPUBLICS
URAL'SKIJE GORY
URAL MOUNTAINS
ZAPADNO-SIBIRSKAJA RAVNINA
SIBERIA
SREDNESIBIRSKOJE PLOSKOGORJE
more Laptevych
Sea of Okhotsk
MONGOLIA
GOBI
CHINA
TIBET
KUNLUN SHAN
QING ZANG GAOYUAN
HIMALAYAS
Mount Everest
NEPAL
BHUTAN
INDIA
PAKISTAN
AFGHANISTAN
IRAN
IRAQ
SYRIA
SAUDI ARABIA
YEMEN
OMAN
EGYPT
LIBYA
SAHARA
Tropic of Cancer
MEDITERRANEAN SEA
TUNISIA
SUDAN
ETHIOPIA
SOMALIA
KENYA
UGANDA
TANZANIA
ZAMBIA
ZIMBABWE
MOZAMBIQUE
BOTSWANA
SOUTH AFRICA
MADAGASCAR
AFRICA
Equator
ARABIAN SEA
Bay of Bengal
SRI LANKA
MALDIVES
BURMA
THAILAND
VIET-NAM
INDOCHINA
MALAYSIA
South China Sea
PHILIPPINES
Philippine Sea
JAPAN
Sea of Japan
Yellow Sea
East China Sea
TAIWAN
BORNEO
SUMATERA
JAWA
GREATER SUNDA ISLANDS
INDONESIA
NEW GUINEA
PAPUA NEW GUINEA
Arafura Sea
Timor Sea
Gulf of Carpentaria
Coral Sea
AUSTRALIA
GREAT SANDY DESERT
GREAT VICTORIA DESERT
Great Australian Bight
GREAT DIVIDING RANGE
GREAT BARRIER REEF
TASMANIA
INDIAN OCEAN
Tropic of Capricorn
MID-INDIAN BASIN
NINETY EAST RIDGE
CHAGOS-LACCADIVE PLATEAU
MID-INDIAN RIDGE
SOUTHWEST INDIAN RIDGE
WHARTON BASIN
PERTH BASIN
BROKEN RIDGE
SOUTH AUSTRALIAN BASIN
SOUTHERN OCEAN
SOUTHEAST INDIAN RIDGE
SOUTH INDIAN BASIN
KERGUELEN PLATEAU
CROZET BASIN
AGULHAS BASIN
ATLANTIC-INDIAN RIDGE
ATLANTIC-INDIAN BASIN
Antarctic Circle
ENDERBY LAND
AMERICAN HIGHLAND
WILKES LAND
ANTARCTICA

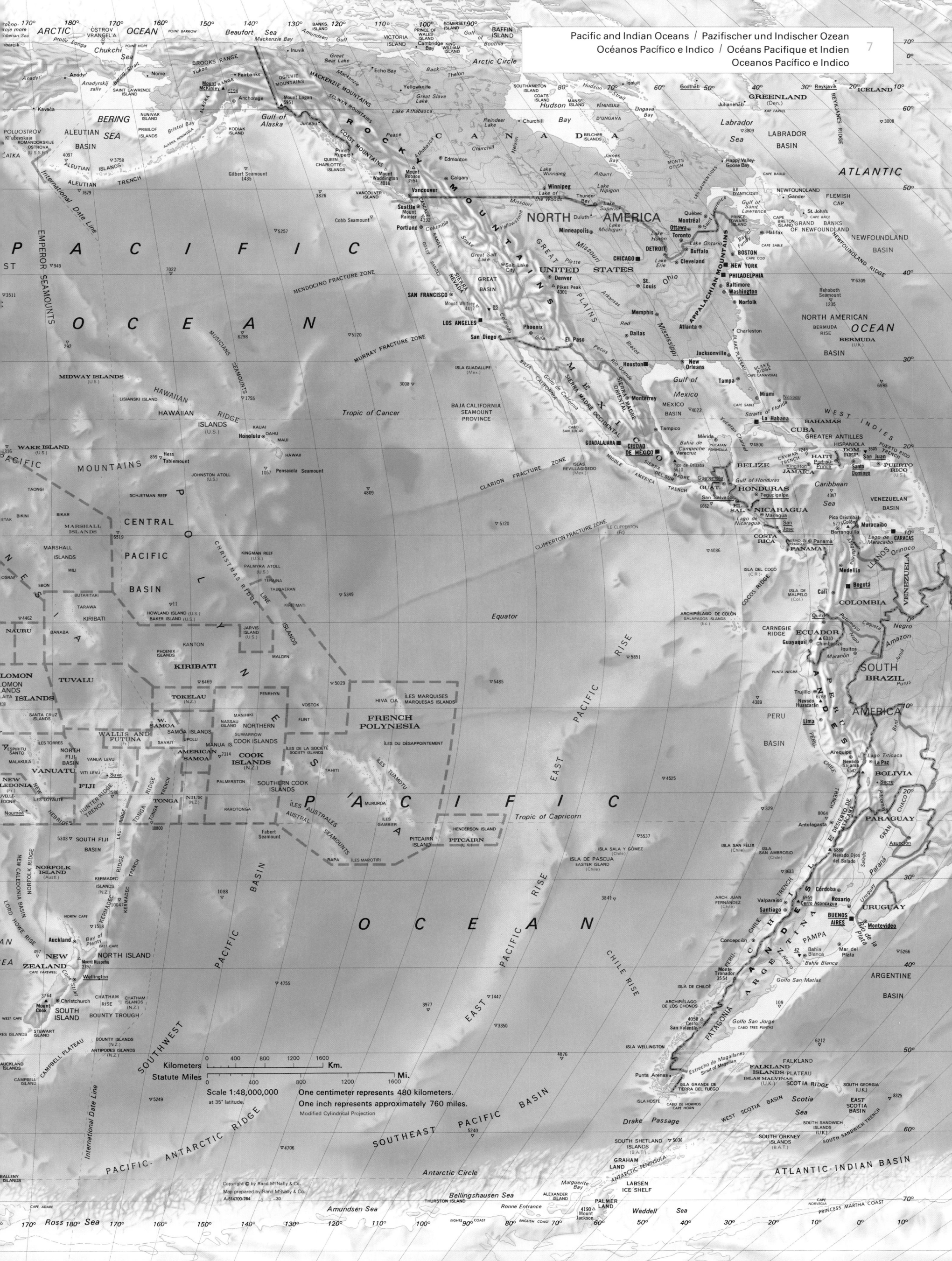

Pacific and Indian Oceans / Pazifischer und Indischer Ozean
Océanos Pacífico e Indico / Océans Pacifique et Indien
Oceanos Pacífico e Indico
7

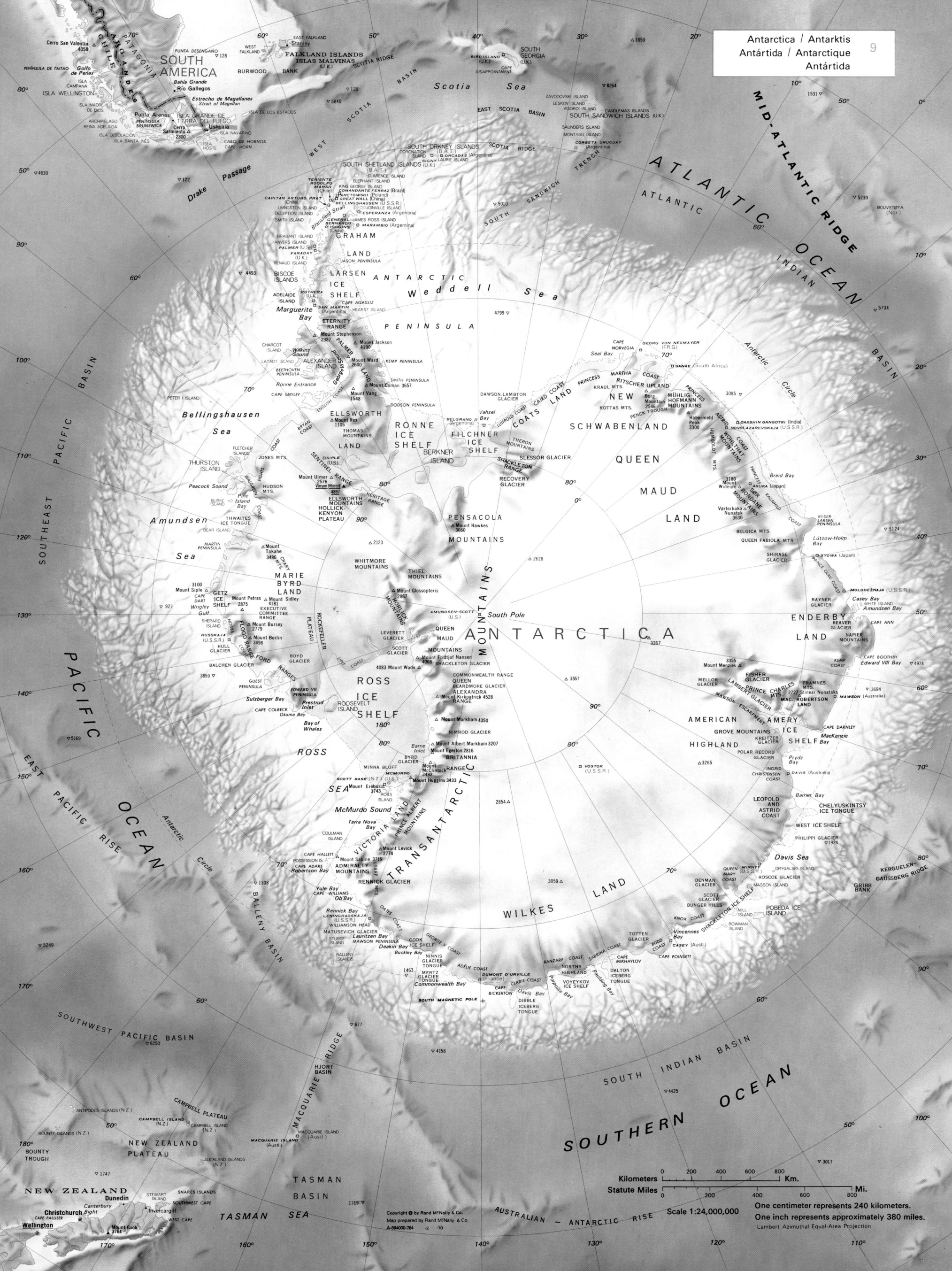

Copyright © by Rand McNally & Co.
Map prepared by Rand McNally & Co.
A-594000-764   -2 -10

Scale 1:24,000,000

One centimeter represents 240 kilometers.
One inch represents approximately 380 miles.
Lambert Azimuthal Equal-Area Projection

Kilometers
Km.
Statute Miles
Mi.
0   200   400   600   800
0   200   400   600   800

CANADA
GREENLAND (Den.)
Davis Strait
Labrador Sea
LABRADOR BASIN
Arctic Circle
Denmark Strait
ICELAND
Reykjavík
IRMINGER BASIN
REYKJANES RIDGE
ICELAND BASIN
ROCKALL RISE
JAN MAYEN RIDGE
NORWEGIAN BASIN
Norwegian Sea
LOFOTEN BASIN
GREENLAND BASIN
Greenland Sea
MOHNS RIDGE
SPITSBERGEN
SVALBARD (Nor.)
BJØRNØYA BEAR ISLAND (Nor.)
Barents Sea
MURMANSK RISE
Karskoje more
Kara Sea
FAEROE ISLANDS (Den.)
ATLANTIC OCEAN
MID-ATLANTIC RIDGE
WEST EUROPEAN BASIN
AZORES-GIBRALTAR RIDGE
AZORES
AÇORES (Port.)
Ponta Delgada
CANARY BASIN
ARQUIPÉLAGO DA MADEIRA (Port.)
Funchal
ISLAS CANARIAS CANARY ISLANDS (Sp.)
Santa Cruz
Las Palmas
CAPE VERDE
CAPE VERDE TERRACE
Tropic of Cancer
NORWAY
SWEDEN
FINLAND
Gulf of Bothnia
Oslo
Stockholm
Helsinki
Trondheim
Bergen
Göteborg
DENMARK
København
North Sea
Baltic Sea
UNITED KINGDOM
IRELAND
Dublin
LONDON
Edinburgh
Glasgow
Belfast
Manchester
Liverpool
Birmingham
Cardiff
Plymouth
Cork
English Channel
CELTIC SHELF
NETH.
Amsterdam
Rotterdam
BEL.
Bruxelles
Antwerpen
LUXE.
FRANCE
PARIS
Lille
Brest
Nantes
Bordeaux
Lyon
Marseille
Nice
Bay of Biscay
SPAIN
MADRID
BARCELONA
Bilbao
La Coruña
València
ANDORRA
PORTUGAL
Lisboa
Porto
Gibraltar (U.K.)
Strait of Gibraltar
FED. REP. OF GER.
GER. DEM. REP.
BERLIN
Hamburg
Frankfurt
München
Stuttgart
Köln
Bonn
Essen
Leipzig
SWITZ.
Zürich
Genève
Basel
AUSTRIA
WIEN VIENNA
Graz
ITALY
ROMA
MILANO
Torino
Venezia
Napoli
Palermo
Trieste
Cagliari
Tyrrhenian Sea
Adriatic Sea
Ionian Sea
MALTA
ALPS
APENNINO
POLAND
WARSZAWA
Gdańsk
Kraków
Katowice
CZECHOSLOVAKIA
Praha
HUNGARY
BUDAPEST
YUGOSLAVIA
Beograd
Zagreb
ALBANIA
Tiranë
GREECE
Athinai
Thessaloniki
BULGARIA
Sofija
BALKAN PENINSULA
ROMANIA
BUCUREŞTI
CARPATHIAN MOUNTAINS
Danube
Black Sea
Aegean Sea
Mediterranean Sea
LENINGRAD
MOSKVA MOSCOW
KIEV
CHAR'KOV
VOLGOGRAD
ODESSA
Minsk
Riga
Tallinn
Vilnius
Murmansk
Archangel'sk
Beloje more White Sea
Gor'kij
Kazan'
Kujbyšev
Saratov
Rostov-na-Donu
Doneck
Dnepropetrovsk
Sevastopol'
Volga
Dnepr
Don
Ural
UNION OF SOVIET SOCIALIST REPUBLICS
EUROPE
URAL'SKIJE GORY URAL MOUNTAINS
ZAPADNO-SIBIRSKAJA RAVNINA
ASIA
SVERDLOVSK
Čel'abinsk
Omsk
Perm'
Ufa
Orenburg
Vorkuta
Caspian Sea
Aral'skoje more Aral Sea
KYZYLKUM
KARAKUMY
BOL'ŠOJ KAVKAZ CAUCASUS
TBILISI
Jerevan
BAKU
TURKEY
ANKARA
İSTANBUL
İzmir
ASIA MINOR
CYPRUS
NORTH CYPRUS
Nicosia
SYRIA
DIMASHQ
LEBANON
Bayrūt
ISRAEL
Tel Aviv-Yafo
Yerushalayim Jerusalem
JORDAN
'Ammān
IRAQ
BAGHDĀD
IRAN
TEHRĀN
KUWAIT
Al-Kuwayt
NEUTRAL ZONE
SAUDI ARABIA
Ar-Riyāḍ
Makkah
Jiddah
Al-Madīnah
BAHRAIN
QATAR
UNITED ARAB EMIRATES
OMAN
Persian Gulf
Gulf of Oman
ARABIAN PENINSULA
AR-RUB' AL-KHĀLĪ
Red Sea
EGYPT
AL-QĀHIRAH CAIRO
AL-ISKANDARĪYAH ALEXANDRIA
Aswān
Nile
LIBYA
Ṭarābulus Tripoli
Banghāzī
TUNISIA
Tunis
ALGERIA
EL DJAZAÏR ALGIERS
MOROCCO
Rabat
CASABLANCA
Marrakech
ATLAS MOUNTAINS
SAHARA
WESTERN SAHARA
MAURITANIA
Nouakchott
MALI
NIGER
SUDAN
Būr Sūdān

Europe and Africa / Europa und Afrika
Europa y África / Europe et Afrique
Europa e África
11

ARCTIC OCEAN
ATLANTIC OCEAN
North Pole
GREENLAND (Den.)
ICELAND
Reykjavik
Greenland Sea
Norwegian Sea
Barents Sea
Kara Sea
Karskoje more
more Laptevych
Laptev Sea
Vostočno-Sibirskoje more
East Siberian Sea
Chukchi Sea
Bering Sea
Bering Strait
UNITED STATES
ALEUTIAN BASIN
Sea of Okhotsk
Ochotskoje more
OKHOTSK BASIN
SVALBARD
ZEML'A FRANCA-IOSIFA
FRANZ JOSEF LAND
SEVERNAJA ZEML'A
NOVAJA ZEML'A
NOVOSIBIRSKIJE OSTROVA
OSTROV VRANGEL'A
POLUOSTROV KAMČATKA
OSTROV SACHALIN
SACHALIN
KURIL'SKIJE OSTROVA
KURIL ISLANDS
UNION OF SOVIET SOCIALIST REPUBLICS
ZAPADNO-SIBIRSKAJA RAVNINA
SREDNESIBIRSKOJE PLOSKOGORJE
SIBERIA
URAL'SKIJE GORY
URAL MOUNTAINS
CHREBET ČERSKOGO
UNITED KINGDOM
IRELAND
NORWAY
SWEDEN
FINLAND
DENMARK
POLAND
CZECHOSLOVAKIA
HUNGARY
ROMANIA
BULGARIA
TURKEY
SYRIA
IRAQ
IRAN
AFGHANISTAN
MONGOLIA
GOBI
NORTH KOREA
SOUTH KOREA
JAPAN
ASIA
EUROPE
LONDON
Dublin
Oslo
Stockholm
Helsinki
København
Amsterdam
BERLIN
Warszawa
Praha
WIEN
BUDAPEST
Bucurešti
Sofija
ISTANBUL
ANKARA
LENINGRAD
MOSKVA
KIJEV
ODESSA
VOLGOGRAD
SVERDLOVSK
Novosibirsk
Krasnojarsk
Irkutsk
Jakutsk
Magadan
Vladivostok
Ulaanbaatar
BEIJING
SHANGHAI
TEHRĀN
BAGHDĀD
TAŠKENT
BAKU
TBILISI
Caspian Sea
Black Sea
Aral'skoje more
Aral Sea
Baltic Sea
North Sea
Sea of Japan
Yellow Sea
EAST CHINA SEA
ozero Bajkal
Lake Baikal
ozero Balchaš
Lake Balkhash
TIEN SHAN
ALTAI
PAMIR
HINDU KUSH
KUNLUN SHAN
TARIM PENDI
BOL'ŠOJ KAVKAZ
CAUCASUS
Arctic Circle

AUSTRALIA

Perth

PHILIPPINE
Sea

Philippine
Trench

SULU
Sea

Celebes
Sea

SUNDA

INDONESIA

SULAWESI
CELEBES

NUSA TENGGARA

JAVA

NORTH
AUSTRALIAN
BASIN

Darling Range

SOUTH
CHINA
SEA

GUANGZHOU
CANTON

HONG KONG

MANILA

Quezon City

VICTORIA

HAINAN DAO

MALAYSIA

BRUNEI

BORNEO

KALIMANTAN

Balikpapan

Banjarmasin

GREATER SUNDA ISLANDS

JAVA
TRENCH

CHRISTMAS
ISLAND

WHARTON
BASIN

VIETNAM

LAOS

THAILAND

CAMBODIA

Ha Noi

Hai Phong

Gulf of
Tonkin

THANH PHO
HO CHI MINH
SAIGON

PHNUM
PENH

KRUNG
THEP
BANGKOK

Gulf of
Thailand

SINGAPORE

Kuala
Lumpur

SUMATRA

Padang

Palembang

JAKARTA

Bandung

SURABAYA

Equator

MALAY
PENINSULA

George
Town

Medan

SUNDA
SHELF

COCOS
ISLANDS

BURMA

Mandalay

YANGON
RANGOON

Andaman
Sea

ANDAMAN
BASIN

COCO ISLANDS

ANDAMAN
ISLANDS
(India)

NICOBAR
ISLANDS
(India)

HIMALAYAS

Lhasa

NEPAL

BHUTAN

BANGLADESH

DHAKA

Chittagong

Ganges

CALCUTTA

Patna

Bay of
Bengal

MID-
INDIAN
BASIN

INDIAN
BASIN

INDIA

DELHI

New Delhi

Kānpur

Vārānasi

Nāgpur

SRI LANKA

Colombo

MADRAS

Hyderābād

BANGALORE

Pune

BOMBAY

COROMANDEL
COAST

Pak Strait

Gulf of
Mannar

CAPE
COMORIN

MALABAR
COAST

WESTERN
GHĀTS

EASTERN
GHĀTS

DECCAN

AHMADĀBĀD

Amritsar

PAKISTAN

KARĀCHI

Hyderābād

Sukkur

KIRTHAR
RANGE

INDIAN
DESERT

THAR
DESERT

Tropic of Cancer

ARABIAN
SEA

ARABIAN
BASIN

Laccadive
Sea

LAKSHADWEEP
(India)

LACCADIVE
PLATEAU

MALDIVES

Eight Degree Channel

CHAGOS
ARCHIPELAGO

CHAGOS-LACCADIVE PLATEAU

NINETYEAST RIDGE

BROKEN RIDGE

INDIAN

OCEAN

CARLSBERG RIDGE

MID- INDIAN RIDGE

MASCARENE
PLATEAU

MASCARENE
BASIN

SEYCHELLES

SAYA DE MALHA
BANK

NAZARETH
BANK

CARGADOS CARAJOS

MAURITIUS

RÉUNION
(France)

MADAGASCAR

OWEN
FRACTURE
ZONE

OMAN

UNITED ARAB
EMIRATES

QATAR

AR-RUB-AL-KHĀLĪ

ARABIAN
PENINSULA

YEMEN

Gulf of
Aden

Gulf of
Oman

Strait of Hormuz

Red
Sea

Bab el Mandeb

DJIBOUTI

SOMALIA

ETHIOPIA

Mogadisho

SOMALI
BASIN

MADAGASCAR
BASIN

Antananarivo

Tropic of Capricorn

Equator

SOUTHWEST
INDIAN
RIDGE

RODRIGUES
(Mau.)

Mi.
800

600

400

200

Km.
800

600

400

200

0

Kilometers

Statute Miles

One centimeter represents 240 kilometers.
One inch represents approximately 380 miles.
Lambert Azimuthal Equal-Area Projection

Scale 1:24,000,000

Copyright © by Rand McNally & Co.
Map prepared by Rand McNally & Co.
A-951200-764

ASIA
CHINA
INDIA
HIMALAYAS
BURMA
THAILAND
LAOS
VIETNAM
CAMBODIA
INDOCHINA
MALAYSIA
BRUNEI
SINGAPORE
INDONESIA
GREATER SUNDA ISLANDS
SUMATERA
SUMATRA
BORNEO
KALIMANTAN
SULAWESI
CELEBES
MALUKU
MOLUCCAS
NUSA TENGGARA
JAWA
JAVA
PHILIPPINES
TAIWAN
NEW GUINEA
PAPUA NEW GUINEA
BISMARCK ARCHIPELAGO
CAROLINE ISLANDS
FEDERATED STATES OF MICRONESIA
MARIANA ISLANDS
NORTHERN MARIANA ISLANDS
PALAU
AUSTRALIA
TASMANIA
CHONGQING
Changsha
Nanchang
Wenzhou
Fuzhou
Guiyang
Kunming
Liuzhou
Xiamen
Amoy
T'AIPEI
GUANGZHOU
CANTON
VICTORIA
HONG KONG
Macau
Nanning
Zhanjiang
Ha Noi
Hai Phong
Haikou
Mandalay
Chiang Mai
Viangchan
Udon Thani
Da Nang
Mawlamyine
KRUNG THEP
BANGKOK
Phnum Penh
THANH PHO HO CHI MINH
(SAIGON)
MANILA
Quezon City
Cebu
Davao
George Town
Kuala Lumpur
Medan
Padang
Palembang
JAKARTA
Bandung
SURABAYA
Kuching
Balikpapan
Banjarmasin
Ujungpandang
Manado
Dili
Jayapura
Port Moresby
Lae
Rabaul
Darwin
Broome
Birdum
Mount Isa
Alice Springs
Townsville
Cairns
Rockhampton
Brisbane
Newcastle
SYDNEY
Canberra
MELBOURNE
Adelaide
Broken Hill
Kalgoorlie
Perth
Launceston
Hobart
East China Sea
SOUTH CHINA SEA
PHILIPPINE SEA
PHILIPPINE BASIN
Sulu Sea
Celebes Sea
Java Sea
Laut Jawa
Banda Sea
Arafura Sea
Timor Sea
CORAL SEA
Bismarck Sea
Solomon Sea
Gulf of Carpentaria
Gulf of Thailand
Gulf of Tonkin
Great Australian Bight
INDIAN OCEAN
SOUTHERN OCEAN
JAVA TRENCH
WHARTON BASIN
NORTH AUSTRALIAN BASIN
PERTH BASIN
SOUTH AUSTRALIAN BASIN
BROKEN RIDGE
DIAMANTINA FRACTURE ZONE
GREAT BARRIER REEF
GREAT DIVIDING RANGE
GREAT SANDY DESERT
GIBSON DESERT
GREAT VICTORIA DESERT
NULLARBOR PLAIN
SIMPSON DESERT
KIMBERLEY PLATEAU
BARKLY TABLELAND
ARNHEM LAND
MACDONNELL RANGES
Tropic of Cancer
Tropic of Capricorn
Equator
CHRISTMAS ISLAND (Austl)
COCOS ISLANDS (Austl)
Challenger Deep 10915
Kilometers 0 200 400 600 800 Km.
Statute Miles 0 200 400 600 800 Mi.
Scale 1:24,000,000
One centimeter represents 240 kilometers.
One inch represents approximately 380 miles.
Lambert Azimuthal Equal-Area Projection
Copyright © by Rand McNally & Co.
Map prepared by Rand McNally & Co.

Australia and Oceania / Australien und Ozeanien
Australia y Oceanía / Australie et Océanie
Austrália e Oceania
15

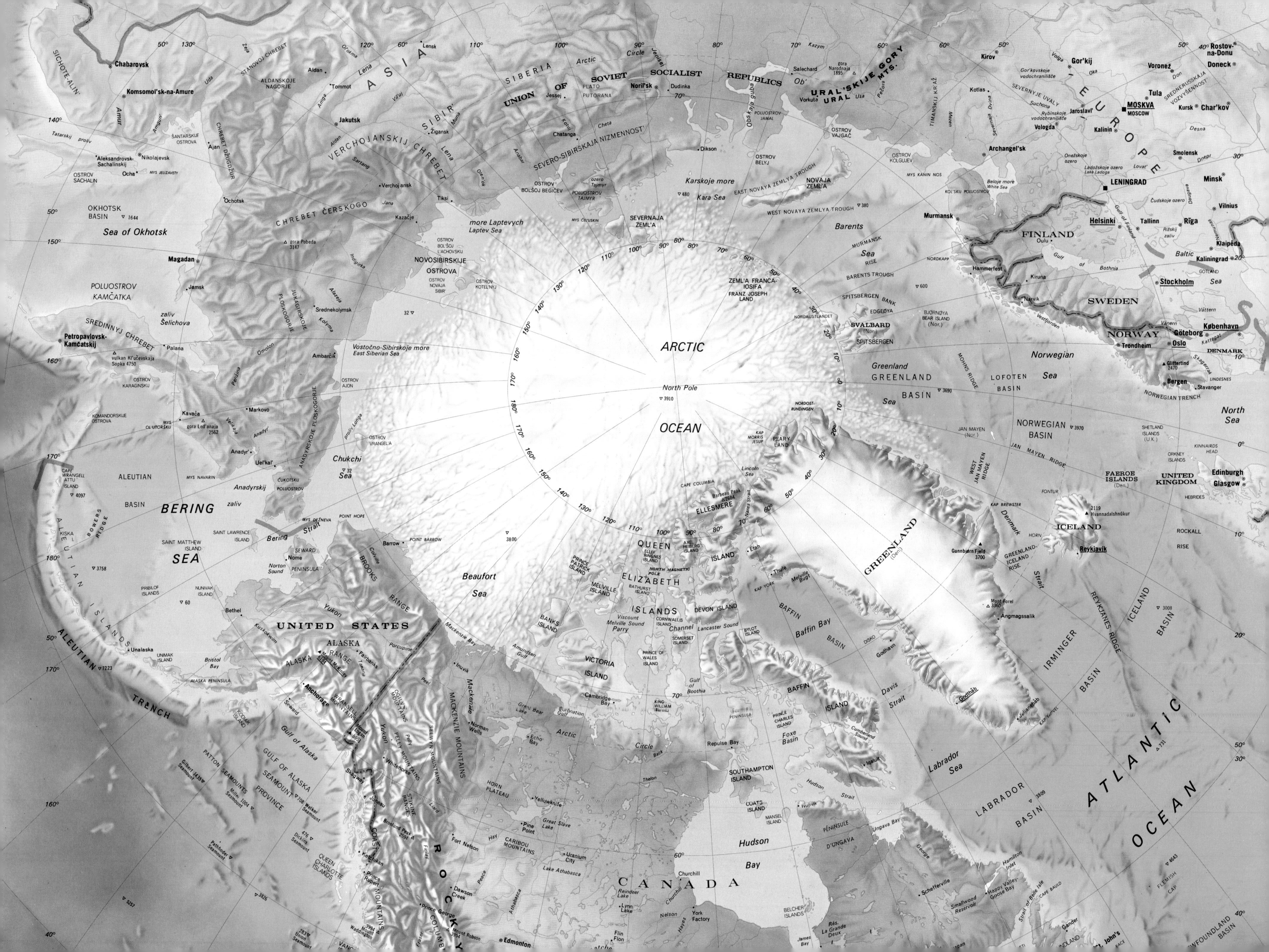

ARCTIC OCEAN
North Pole
ASIA
UNION OF SOVIET SOCIALIST REPUBLICS
SIBERIA
EUROPE
FINLAND
SWEDEN
NORWAY
DENMARK
UNITED KINGDOM
ICELAND
GREENLAND
CANADA
UNITED STATES
ALASKA
ATLANTIC OCEAN
BERING SEA
Sea of Okhotsk
Barents Sea
Kara Sea
Laptev Sea
East Siberian Sea
Chukchi Sea
Beaufort Sea
Norwegian Sea
Greenland Sea
Labrador Sea
Baffin Bay
Hudson Bay
Gulf of Alaska
North Sea
Davis Strait
Denmark Strait
Bering Strait
QUEEN ELIZABETH ISLANDS
ELLESMERE ISLAND
BAFFIN ISLAND
VICTORIA ISLAND
BANKS ISLAND
SVALBARD
ZEML'A FRANCA-IOSIFA
FRANZ JOSEPH LAND
NOVAJA ZEML'A
SEVERNAJA ZEML'A
NOVOSIBIRSKIJE OSTROVA
ALEUTIAN ISLANDS
ALEUTIAN TRENCH
BROOKS RANGE
MACKENZIE MOUNTAINS
ROCKY
URAL'SKIJE GORY
URAL MTS.
VERCHOJANSKIJ CHREBET
CHREBET ČERSKOGO
POLUOSTROV KAMČATKA
MOSKVA
LENINGRAD
Helsinki
Stockholm
Oslo
København
Reykjavík
Edmonton
Anchorage
Murmansk
Arctic Circle

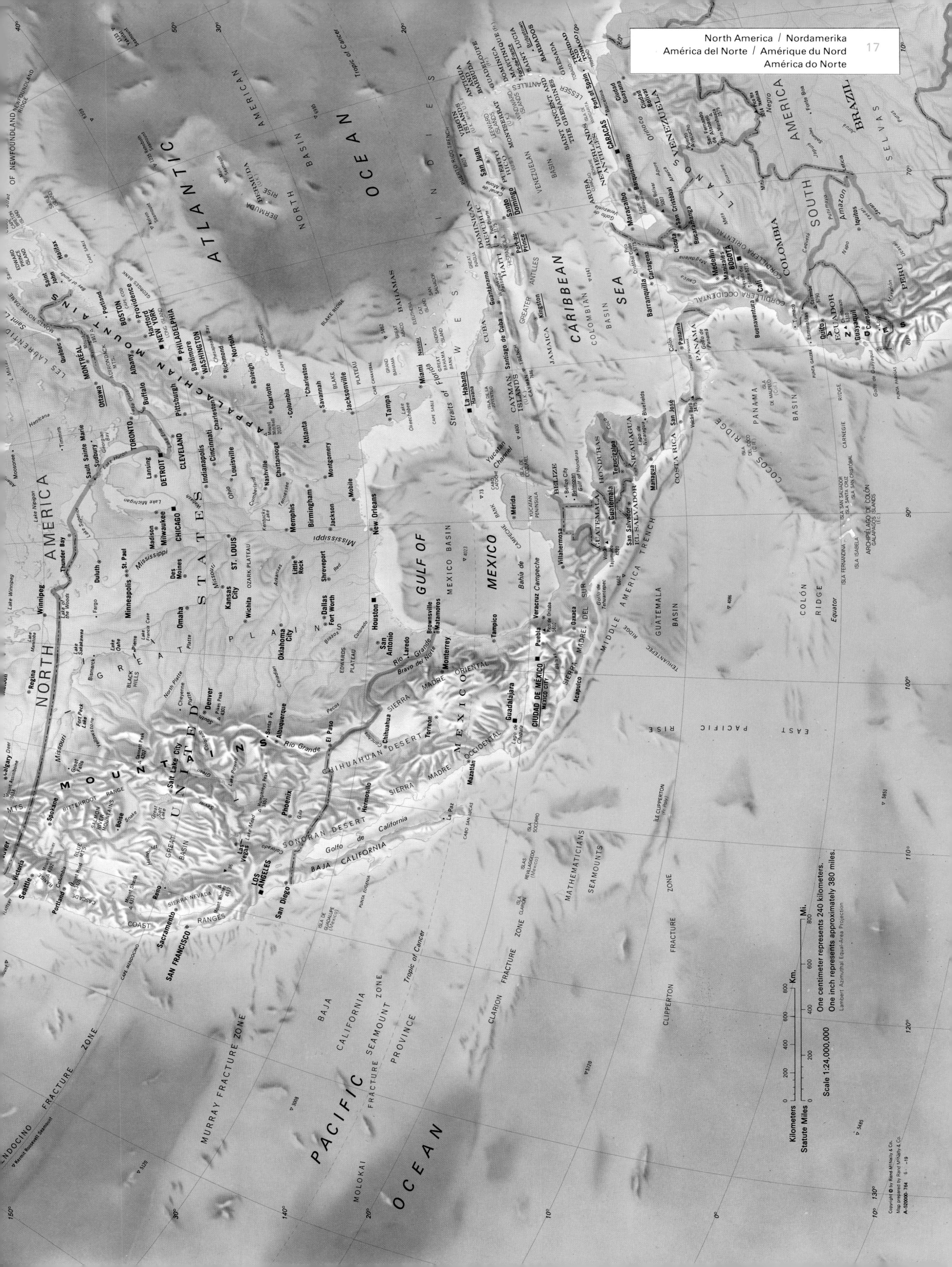

NORTH AMERICA

UNITED STATES

ATLANTIC OCEAN

PACIFIC OCEAN

GULF OF MEXICO

CARIBBEAN SEA

SOUTH AMERICA

BRAZIL

MEXICO

GREAT PLAINS

ROCKY MOUNTAINS

APPALACHIAN MOUNTAINS

WEST INDIES

SIERRA MADRE ORIENTAL

SIERRA MADRE OCCIDENTAL

SIERRA MADRE DEL SUR

CHIHUAHUAN DESERT

SONORAN DESERT

BAJA CALIFORNIA

GREAT BASIN

SIERRA NEVADA

CASCADE RANGE

COAST RANGES

VENEZUELA

COLOMBIA

ECUADOR

PERU

PANAMA

COSTA RICA

NICARAGUA

HONDURAS

GUATEMALA

EL SALVADOR

BELIZE

YUCATAN PENINSULA

CUBA

HAITI

DOMINICAN REPUBLIC

JAMAICA

BAHAMAS

BERMUDA

CAYMAN ISLANDS

GREATER ANTILLES

LESSER ANTILLES

PUERTO RICO

VIRGIN ISLANDS

ANTIGUA AND BARBUDA

GUADELOUPE

DOMINICA

MARTINIQUE

SAINT LUCIA

BARBADOS

GRENADA

TRINIDAD AND TOBAGO

NETHERLANDS ANTILLES

COCOS RIDGE

COLÓN RIDGE

EAST PACIFIC RISE

MIDDLE AMERICA TRENCH

MURRAY FRACTURE ZONE

MOLOKAI FRACTURE ZONE

CLARION FRACTURE ZONE

CLIPPERTON FRACTURE ZONE

MATHEMATICIANS SEAMOUNTS

New York
Boston
Philadelphia
Washington
Baltimore
Chicago
Detroit
Cleveland
Pittsburgh
Buffalo
Toronto
Montréal
Ottawa
Québec
Halifax
Saint John
Los Angeles
San Diego
San Francisco
Sacramento
Seattle
Portland
Spokane
Boise
Reno
Las Vegas
Salt Lake City
Denver
Phoenix
Albuquerque
Santa Fe
El Paso
San Antonio
Houston
Dallas
Fort Worth
Oklahoma City
Wichita
Kansas City
Omaha
Des Moines
Minneapolis
St. Paul
Madison
Milwaukee
Duluth
Fargo
Bismarck
Winnipeg
Regina
Calgary
Victoria
St. Louis
Memphis
Little Rock
Shreveport
New Orleans
Jackson
Birmingham
Montgomery
Mobile
Atlanta
Nashville
Chattanooga
Louisville
Cincinnati
Indianapolis
Columbus
Lansing
Charlotte
Columbia
Charleston
Savannah
Jacksonville
Tampa
Miami
Raleigh
Richmond
Norfolk
Albany
Hartford
Providence
Portland

La Habana
Santiago de Cuba
Guantánamo
Kingston
Port-au-Prince
Santo Domingo
San Juan
Fort-de-France
Port of Spain
Caracas
Maracaibo
Barquisimeto
Ciudad Guayana
Ciudad Bolívar
Bogotá
Medellín
Cali
Barranquilla
Cartagena
Cúcuta
Bucaramanga
Manizales
Buenaventura
Quito
Guayaquil
Cuenca
Iquitos
Leticia

Ciudad de México
Guadalajara
Monterrey
Puebla
Veracruz
Tampico
Mérida
Oaxaca
Acapulco
Mazatlán
Hermosillo
Chihuahua
Torreón
Matamoros
Brownsville
Laredo
Nuevo Laredo
Villahermosa
Ciudad Victoria
Guatemala
Guatemala City
Belize City
Tegucigalpa
Managua
San Salvador
San José
Panamá
Colón

Mississippi
Missouri
Río Grande
Bravo del Norte
Colorado
Ohio
Tennessee
Arkansas
Red
Platte
Columbia
Snake
Yellowstone
Amazon
Orinoco
Magdalena
Cauca
Negro

Lake Superior
Lake Michigan
Lake Huron
Lake Erie
Lake Ontario
Lake Winnipeg
Lake Manitoba
Great Salt Lake
Lake Mead
Lake Powell
Lake of the Woods
Lake Okeechobee
Lake Nicaragua

Scale 1:24,000,000
One centimeter represents 240 kilometers.
One inch represents approximately 380 miles.
Lambert Azimuthal Equal-Area Projection

Kilometers
Statute Miles

Copyright © by Rand McNally & Co.
Map prepared by Rand McNally & Co.
A-500000-704

Tropic of Cancer
Equator

NORTH AMERICA
UNITED STATES
ROCKY MTS.
APPALACHIAN MOUNTAINS
GREAT PLAINS
OZARK PLATEAU
EDWARDS PLATEAU
CHICAGO
CLEVELAND
NEW YORK
PHILADELPHIA
Baltimore
WASHINGTON
Pittsburgh
Indianapolis
Cincinnati
Charleston
Louisville
Nashville
Chattanooga
Knoxville
Richmond
Norfolk
Raleigh
Charlotte
Columbia
Atlanta
Birmingham
Montgomery
Savannah
Charleston
Jacksonville
Tampa
Miami
Memphis
Jackson
Mobile
New Orleans
Houston
Dallas
Fort Worth
Shreveport
Little Rock
Oklahoma City
Wichita
Kansas City
ST. LOUIS
Omaha
Des Moines
Denver
Cheyenne
Pikes Peak 4301
Santa Fe
Albuquerque
El Paso
San Antonio
Laredo
Brownsville
LONG ISLAND
GEORGES BANK
CAPE HATTERAS
CAPE LOOKOUT
CAPE FEAR
CAPE CANAVERAL
CAPE SABLE
Lake Okeechobee
BLAKE PLATEAU
BLAKE RIDGE
MEXICO
SIERRA MADRE ORIENTAL
SIERRA MADRE DEL SUR
Monterrey
Matamoros
Torreón
Tampico
Guadalajara
Lago de Chapala
CIUDAD DE MÉXICO
Puebla
Veracruz
Pico de Orizaba 5610
Oaxaca
Acapulco
Villahermosa
Mérida
YUCATAN PENINSULA
Bahía de Campeche
CAMPECHE BANK
GULF OF MEXICO
MEXICO BASIN
Yucatan Channel
Straits of Florida
BAHAMAS
GREAT BAHAMA BANK
Nassau
ELEUTHERA
CAT ISLAND
SAN SALVADOR
GREAT ABACO
ANDROS ISLAND
CUBA
La Habana
Havana
ISLA DE LA JUVENTUD
Santiago de Cuba
Guantánamo
CAYMAN ISLANDS
CAYMAN TRENCH
JAMAICA
Kingston
HAITI
Port-au-Prince
HISPANIOLA
Pico Duarte 3175
DOMINICAN REPUBLIC
Santo Domingo
PUERTO RICO
San Juan
PUERTO RICO TRENCH
VIRGIN ISLANDS (U.K. and U.S.)
WEST INDIES
ANTILLES
ANTIGUA AND BARBUDA
MONTSERRAT
GUADELOUPE (Fr.)
DOMINICA
MARTINIQUE (Fr.)
Fort-de-France
SAINT LUCIA
BARBADOS
Bridgetown
SAINT VINCENT AND THE GRENADINES
GRENADA
TRINIDAD AND TOBAGO
Port of Spain
NETHERLANDS ANTILLES
ARUBA
CURAÇAO
BONAIRE
CARIBBEAN SEA
VENEZUELAN BASIN
COLOMBIAN BASIN
BELIZE
Belmopan
Belize City
Gulf of Honduras
GUATEMALA
Guatemala
HONDURAS
Tegucigalpa
EL SALVADOR
San Salvador
NICARAGUA
Managua
Lago de Nicaragua
Bluefields
COSTA RICA
San José
PANAMA
Panamá
Golfo de Panamá
Colón
ISTMO DE PANAMÁ
Golfo de Tehuantepec
MIDDLE AMERICA TRENCH
TEHUANTEPEC RIDGE
GUATEMALA BASIN
PANAMA BASIN
COCOS RIDGE
CARNEGIE RIDGE
COLÓN RIDGE
ISLA DEL COCO (C.R.)
ISLA DE MALPELO (Col.)
ARCHIPIÉLAGO DE COLÓN
GALAPAGOS ISLANDS (Ec.)
ISLA ISABELA
ISLA FERNANDINA
ISLA SAN SALVADOR
ISLA SANTA CRUZ
ISLA SAN CRISTÓBAL
Equator
SOUTH AMERICA
VENEZUELA
CARACAS
Maracaibo
Lago de Maracaibo
Barquisimeto
Barcelona
Ciudad Bolívar
Ciudad Guayana
Orinoco
LLANOS
San Cristóbal
Puerto Ayacucho
San Fernando de Atabapo
Salto Ángel (Angel Falls)
Mt. Roraima 2772
PAKARAIMA MTS.
SA. PARIMA
Pico da Neblina 3014
GUYANA
Georgetown
SURINAME
Paramaribo
FRENCH GUIANA
Cayenne
COLOMBIA
BOGOTÁ
Barranquilla
Cartagena
Cúcuta
Bucaramanga
Medellín
Manizales
Cali
Buenaventura
Nevado del Tolima 5215
CORDILLERA OCCIDENTAL
CORDILLERA ORIENTAL
Mitú
ECUADOR
Quito
Guayaquil
Cuenca
Chimborazo 6310
Cayambe 5790
Golfo de Guayaquil
PERU
Iquitos
Chiclayo
Trujillo
Cajamarca
Huaraz
Nevado Huascarán 6768
Nevado Yerupaja 6634
Cerro de Pasco
Huancayo
LIMA
Cuzco
Puerto Maldonado
Lago Titicaca
Puno
ANDES
CORDILLERA
PERU-CHILE TRENCH
BRAZIL
SELVAS
Amazon
Negro
Manaus
Leticia
Fonte Boa
Santarém
Pôrto de Moz
Belém
ILHA DE MARAJÓ
Macapá
Amapá
São Luís
Teresina
Fortaleza
Natal
João Pessoa
Recife
Campina Grande
Caruaru
Maceió
Aracaju
Salvador
Pico das Almas 1850
Porto Velho
Rio Branco
Cobija
Riberalta
Guajará-Mirim
Mato Grosso
Cuiabá
CHAPADA DOS PARECIS
SA. DO TOMBADOR
SA. FORMOSA
SA. DO RONCADOR
SA. DO CACHIMBO
CHAPADA DAS MANGABEIRAS
ILHA DO BANANAL
PLANALTO
TUMUC-HUMAC MTS.
ACARAI MTS.
ATOL DAS ROCAS
ILHA FERNANDO DE NORONHA (Braz.)
CABO DE SÃO ROQUE
ATLANTIC OCEAN
NORTH AMERICAN BASIN
BERMUDA RISE (U.K.)
BERMUDA
MID-ATLANTIC RIDGE
GUIANA BASIN
CAPE VERDE BASIN
AZORES PLATEAU
AÇORES (AZORES) (Port.)
Tropic of Cancer
Kelvin Seamount
Rehoboth Seamount 1235
Muir Seamount
Yakutat Seamount 1133
Great Meteor Tablemount 269

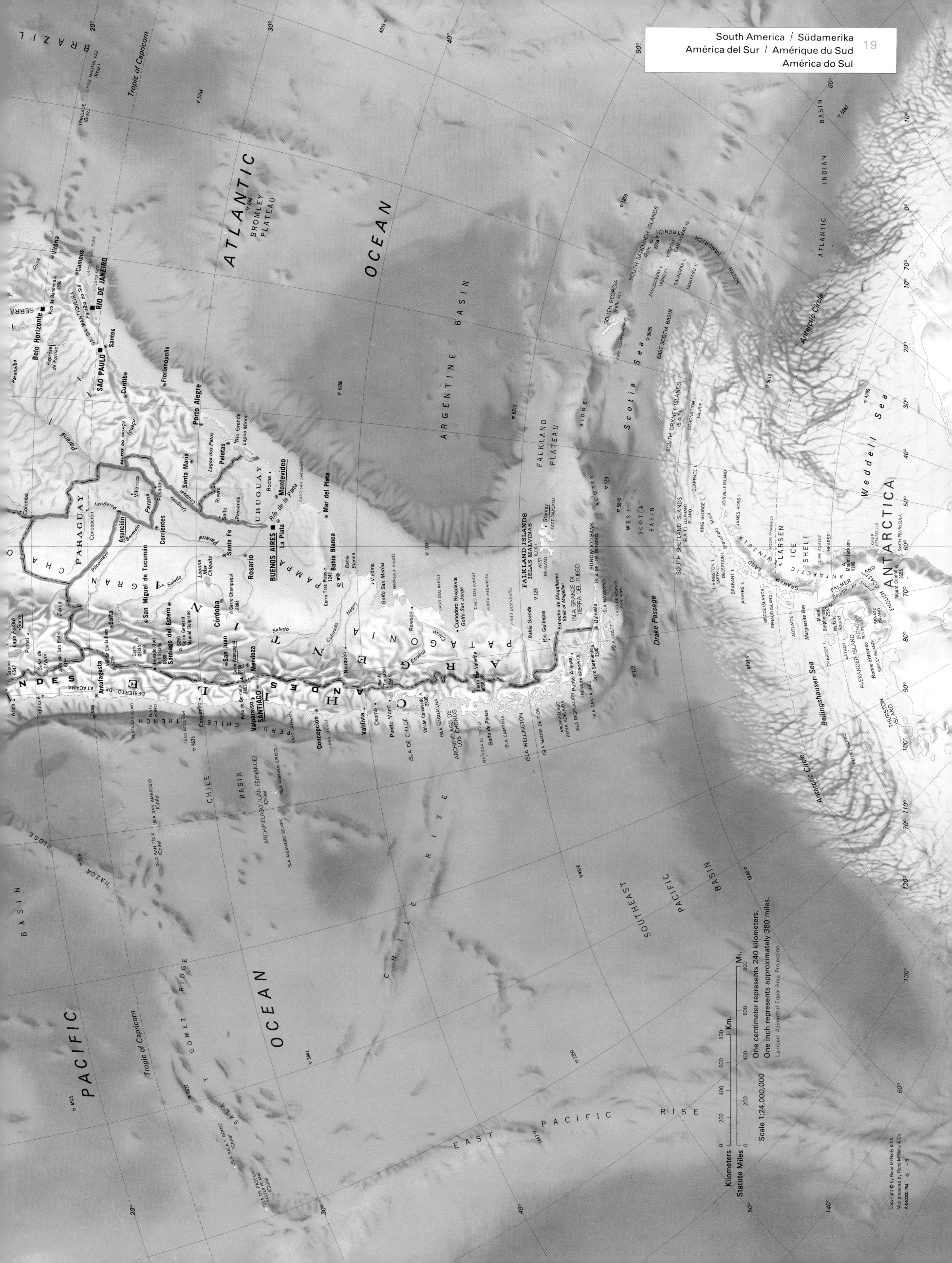
ATLANTIC
OCEAN
PACIFIC
OCEAN
ARGENTINE BASIN
BROMLEY PLATEAU
FALKLAND PLATEAU
Scotia Sea
Weddell Sea
Bellingshausen Sea
Drake Passage
ANTARCTICA
Antarctic Circle
Tropic of Capricorn
CHILE BASIN
CHILE RISE
SOUTHEAST PACIFIC BASIN
EAST PACIFIC RISE
NAZCA RIDGE
SALA Y GOMEZ RIDGE
SOUTH SANDWICH ISLANDS
SOUTH GEORGIA
SOUTH ORKNEY ISLANDS
SOUTH SHETLAND ISLANDS
FALKLAND ISLANDS
ISLAS MALVINAS
BURDWOOD BANK
ISLA GRANDE DE TIERRA DEL FUEGO
PATAGONIA
ANDES
GRAN CHACO
PAMPA
PARAGUAY
URUGUAY
BRAZIL
BUENOS AIRES
Montevideo
SANTIAGO
Asunción
SÃO PAULO
RIO DE JANEIRO
Belo Horizonte
Porto Alegre
Curitiba
Florianópolis
Córdoba
Rosario
Mendoza
Valparaíso
Concepción
Valdivia
Puerto Montt
Antofagasta
Salta
San Miguel de Tucumán
Santiago del Estero
Bahía Blanca
Mar del Plata
La Plata
Punta Arenas
Ushuaia
Stanley
LARSEN ICE SHELF
ALEXANDER ISLAND
THURSTON ISLAND
PALMER LAND
ENGLISH COAST
Kilometers
Statute Miles
Scale 1:24,000,000
One centimeter represents 240 kilometers.
One inch represents approximately 380 miles.
Lambert Azimuthal Equal-Area Projection
Copyright © by Rand McNally & Co.
Map prepared by Rand McNally & Co.

THE REGIONAL MAPS consist of three basic series, each distinctive in style, but using common symbols to ensure ease of understanding (see Legend to Maps, pages x-xii). Every major land region, continent or subcontinent, is introduced by one or more maps at the scale of 1:12,000,000. There follow maps at 1:6,000,000 and 1:3,000,000 which cover the region in sections, in greater detail. Except for scale, the 1:6,000,000 and 1:3,000,000 maps are alike. Finally, selected areas of special importance in the region are shown at 1:1,000,000. Each scale is identified by a color bar, and a locater map with the same color may be found in the margin of the map page. A sample area at each of the scales, including centimeter-kilometer and inch-mile equivalents, appears on page 21.

The three basic series differ in content and emphasis. The 1:12,000,000 maps, which are primarily political, present an overview of each region. They show national boundaries and, in some cases, subordinate administrative subdivisions as well. These introductory maps make it possible to compare location, areal extent, and shape among the nations of the world. The distribution of cities, towns and metropolitan areas is shown in the context of broad physical configurations. A selection of the most important railways and highways also appears.

The 1:6,000,000 and 1:3,000,000 maps together constitute about half of the map pages and provide the basic reference coverage of the Atlas. They show sections of regions in great detail—in some cases individual countries (Japan and New Zealand), in others, parts of countries (central Mexico), in still others, larger regions (the Middle East). The more densely settled areas appear at the larger 1:3,000,000 scale, the remaining areas at 1:6,000,000. Maps at these two scales present political and cultural information against the background of a detailed physical portrait of the terrain, which is depicted by both shaded relief and a spectrum of altitude tints. Bathymetric tints are used to show offshore water depths. The transportation pattern shown includes major railways, two classes of roads, and airports that offer either international or jet service. The names and boundaries of political subdivisions are given for selected countries.

In the 1:1,000,000 series, strategic areas that are of special interest because of economic importance, dense settlement, or both, appear in even greater detail. This series is designed to show the pattern of cities, towns, roads, railways, bridges, airports, dams, reservoirs, and other interrelated features reflecting man's dense occupancy in these areas. The most important parks, places of historical interest, and recreational facilities are indicated. Three classes of highways and two classes of railways are shown, and major roads are named. All features are portrayed against a topographic background of shaded relief.

Inhabited places on the regional maps are classified in two distinct ways. Cities and towns of different *population size* are distinguished by the *size and shape of the symbol* that locates the place. The symbol reflects the population within the municipal or corporate limits, exclusive of any suburbs. In countries where the limits of a municipality include rural areas, the symbol represents only the urban or agglomerated population. The *relative political and economic importance* of a place which may be independent of the number of its inhabitants, is indicated by the *size of type* in which its name appears.

A key to all symbols and type sizes is shown on page xi of the Legend to Maps.

DIE REGIONALKARTEN bestehen aus drei Serien, die im Stil verschieden sind, der besseren Lesbarkeit halber aber gemeinsame Kartensignaturen verwenden (siehe "Zeichenerklärung" S. x-xii). Jede Grossregion, jeder Kontinent oder Subkontinent werden durch eine oder mehrere Karten im Massstab 1:12 Millionen eingeleitet. Es folgen sodann Karten in den Massstäben 1:6 und 1:3 Millionen, welche die Region in Teilen und grösseren Einzelheiten darstellen. Die Karten in 1:6 Millionen und 1:3 Millionen unterscheiden sich nur im Massstab. Schliesslich werden ausgewählte Gebiete von besonderer Bedeutung innerhalb der Region in 1:1 Million dargestellt. Jede Massstabsangabe ist durch ein Farbfeld gekennzeichnet, und ein Lagekärtchen in derselben Farbe erscheint am Rand der Kartenseite. Kartenausschnitte als Beispiele für jeden dieser Massstäbe mit Angabe des Verhältnisses Zentimeter zu Kilometer und Zoll zu Meilen sind auf Seite 21 aufgeführt.

Die drei Kartenreihen unterscheiden sich in Inhalt und Betonung. Die Karten im Massstab 1:12 Millionen, die vor allem politische Karten sind, geben einen Überblick über jede Region. Sie zeigen die Staatsgrenzen und in manchen Fällen auch die Grenzen von nachgeordneten Verwaltungseinheiten. Diese einführenden Karten ermöglichen einen Vergleich der Lage, Ausdehnung und Gestalt der Staaten der Erde. Die Verteilung der städtischen Ballungsgebiete, Grossstädte und Städte wird in ihrem Zusammenhang mit dem grossräumigen Formenschatz des Reliefs dargestellt. Gezeigt wird auch eine Auswahl der wichtigsten Eisenbahnlinien und Fernverkehrsstrassen.

Die Karten 1:6 Millionen und 1:3 Millionen machen zusammen mehr als die Hälfte der Kartenseiten aus und bilden den grundlegenden Teil des Atlas. Sie zeigen sehr inhaltsreiche Ausschnitte von Regionen—in einigen Fällen einzeln Länder (Japan und Neuseeland), in anderen Landesteile (Zentralmexiko) und wieder anderen Grossräume (Mittlerer Osten).

Die dichter besiedelten Gebiete sind im Massstab 1:3 Millionen dargestellt, die übrigen Gebiete im Massstab 1:6 Millionen. Die Karten in diesen beiden Massstäben liefern politische und kulturgeographische Informationen vor dem Hintergrund einer detaillierten Geländedarstellung, gekennzeichnet durch Reliefschummerung und eine Skala von Höhenschichten. Tiefenstufen werden verwendet, um die Meerestiefen jenseits der Küsten zu gliedern. Das abgebildete Verkehrsnetz umfasst wichtige Eisenbahnlinien, zwei Klassen von Strassen und Flughäfen, die entweder im internationalen Verkehr oder von Düsenflugzeugen angeflogen werden. Die Verwaltungsgliederung wird für eine grosse Zahl von Staaten gezeigt.

In der Kartenserie 1:1 Million sind mit noch zahlreicheren Einzelheiten zentrale Räume dargestellt, denen infolge ihrer wirtschaftlichen Bedeutung, dichten Besiedlung oder durch beide Faktoren bedingt besonderes Interesse zukommt. Diese Kartenserie wurde entwikelt, um die Verteilung der Grossstädte, Städte, Strassen, Eisenbahnen, Brücken, Flughäfen, Dämme, Stauseen und anderer Objekte zu zeigen, die Ausdruck sind für die dichte Besiedlung. Verzeichnet sind auch die wichtigsten Parks, Örtlichkeiten von historischem Interesse und Erholungsstätten. Drei Strassenklassen und zwei Klassen von Eisenbahnlinien werden unterschieden. Die Darstellung ist mit einer Reliefschummerung unterlegt.

Die Siedlungen auf den Regionalkarten sind auf zwei bestimmte Arten klassifiziert. Grossstädte und Städte unterschiedlicher *Einwohnerzahl* sind durch *Grösse und Form der Signatur* unterschieden, den den Ort lokalisiert. Die Signatur entspricht der Zahl der Einwohner innerhalb der Stadtgrenzen, schliesst also nicht eingemeindete Vororte aus. In Staaten, in denen ländliche Gebiete in die Stadtgemeinden einbezogen sind, entsprechen die Signaturen nur der in den zentralen Siedlungen ansässigen Bevölkerung. Die *relative politische und wirtschaftliche Bedeutung* eines Ortes, die von der Zahl seiner Einwohner unabhängig sein kann, ist ausgedrückt durch die *Schriftgrösse*, in welcher der Ortsname erscheint.

Ein Schlüssel zu allen Signaturen und Schriftgrössen findet sich auf Seite xi der "Zeichenerklärung".

LOS MAPAS REGIONALES integran tres series básicas, cada una con su estilo propio; pero los símbolos usados son en todas los mismos para facilitar su comprensión (véanse las Leyendas para Mapas, páginas x-xii). Cada una de las grandes regiones, continentes o subcontinentes, se presenta a través de uno o varios mapas a la escala de 1:12 000 000. A continuación hay mapas a escalas de 1:6 000 000 y 1:3 000 000 que presentan la región correspondiente en secciones, con mayores detalles. Con excepción de su escala, los mapas de 1:6 000 000 y 1:3 000 000 tienen las mismas características. Por ultimo, aparecen a la escala de 1:1 000 000 áreas de cada región seleccionadas por su importancia. Cada escala se identifica por una barra de color, y un mapa-guía con el mismo color se presenta en el margen de la página de cada mapa. La página 21 ofrece como ejemplo un área-muestra a cada una de las escalas, incluyendo equivalentés en centímetros-kilómetros y pulgadas-millas.

Las tres series básicas son diferentes en contenido y en énfasis. Los mapas a escala de 1:12 000 000, fundamentalmente políticos, ofrecen una vista general de cada región. Indican las fronteras nacionales y, en algunos casos, las subdivisiones administrativas secundarias. Son mapas introductivos que permiten comparar la ubicación, extensión territorial y forma de las distintas naciones. La distribución de ciudades, poblados y áreas metropolitanas se aprecia en un contexto físico esbozado a grandes rasgos. Los detalles incluyen una selección de las vías férras y las carreteras más importantes.

Las series de mapas a 1:6 000 000 y a 1:3 000 000 ocupan entre ambas cerca de la mitad de los mapas del atlas y en ellas se concentra el material de consulta básico de la obra. Los mapas muestran secciones de regiones en gran detalle: en algunos casos países enteros, como Japón y Nueva Zelandia; en otros, partes de países, como el centro de México; y en otros, regiones mas extensas, como el Medio Oriente. Las áreas con mayor densidad de establecimientos humanos se presentan a una escala mayor, la de 1:3 000 000, y las demás a la escala de 1:6 000 000. En estas dos escalas los mapas contienen información política y cultural, sobre un fondo que ilustra en detalle la configuración física del terreno, utilizando sombreado para el relieve y toda una gama de tintes para indicar las altitudes. Un colorido batimétrico señala las variaciones de profundidad en el suelo marino. El esquema de las vías de comunicación incluye las principales vías férreas, dos clases de caminos, y los aeropuertos que ofrecen servicio nacional o internacional de jets. Las subdivisiones políticas secundarias se dan para una selección de varios países.

En la serie de mapas de 1:1 000 000, las áreas estratégicas de especial interés por su importancia económica, su densidad de población, o ambos factores combinados, aparecen aún con mayor detalle. Esta serie se diseñó para mostrar la distribución de ciudades, poblados, caminos, vías férreas, puentes, aeropuertos, presas, embalses y otros elementos similares, que reflejan la densidad de la ocupación humana. También se consignan los parques más importantes, los sitios de interés histórico, los campos de recreo, tres clases de carreteras, y dos de ferrocarriles, se da los nombres de los caminos más importantes. Todos estos elementos aparecen sobre un fondo topográfico de relieve sombreado.

En los mapas regionales se hacen dos clasificaciones distintas de los lugares habitados. Las ciudades y las poblaciones *de diferente densidad de habitantes* se distinguen por la *forma y tamaño del símbolo* que las localiza en el mapa. Este símbolo refleja el tamaño de la población dentro de sus límites municipales, sin tomar en cuenta los suburbios. En los países donde los límites de una municipalidad incluyen áreas rurales, el símbolo se limita a representar el conglomerado urbano de habitantes. La *importancia económica y política de un lugar*, la cual puede ser independiente del número de sus habitantes, se indica mediante el *tamaño del tipo de imprenta* en que aparece su nombre.

La clave de los símbolos y el valor de los tamaños de las letras se dan en la página xi de las Leyendas para Mapas.

LES CARTES RÉGIONALES sont de trois types principaux, chacun d'un style différent mais avec des symboles communs pour faciliter la compréhension (voir la légende des cartes pages x-xii). Chaque grande région, continent ou subcontinent, est représentée par une ou plusieurs cartes à l'échelle de 1:12 000 000ᵉ. Viennent ensuite des cartes au 1:6 000 000ᵉ et au 1:3 000 000ᵉ qui couvrent la région par sections plus détaillées; hormis la différence d'échelle, ces cartes sont semblables. Enfin, des secteurs particulièrement importants sont représentés au 1:1 000 000ᵉ. À chaque échelle correspond une bande colorée et une carte repère de même couleur, dans la marge de chaque page. Un échantillon de cartes aux diverses échelles est représenté à droite. Chaque carte est accompagnée d'une double échelle graphique donnant les rapports centimètre/kilomètre et inch/mille correspondants.

Les trois catégories de cartes diffèrent par le contenu et par ce qu'elles mettent en relief. Les cartes au 1:12 000 000ᵉ, qui sont essentiellement politiques, donnent un aperçu général de chaque région. Elles indiquent les frontières nationales et, dans certains cas, les subdivisions administratives intérieures. Ces cartes d'introduction permettent de comparer la localisation, la superficie et la forme des pays du monde. La répartition des villes et des zones métropolitaines y apparaît dans le cadre des grandes régions naturelles. Les routes et les voies ferrées les plus importantes y figurent également.

Les cartes au 1:6 000 000ᵉ et au 1:3 000 000ᵉ forment la moitié de l'Atlas et en constituent la série cartographique essentielle. Elles représentent de façon plus détaillée une partie de pays (centre du Mexique), ou encore des régions plus vestes (Moyen-Orient) ou, parfois, des pays entiers (Japon, Nouvelle-Zélande). Les régions les plus peuplées sont représentées à plus grande échelle (1:3 000 000ᵉ) que les autres (1:6 000 000ᵉ). Ces cartes offrent des informations d'ordre politique et culturel sur un fond topographique précis où le relief est indiqué à la fois par un estompage et par des variations de couleur. Différentes teintes de bleu sont utilisées pour symboliser les profondeurs marines. Les réseaux de transport représentés comprennent les principales voies ferrées, deux catégories de routes et les aéroports internationaux ou desservis par des avions à réaction. Les subdivisions politiques d'un certain nombre de pays sont aussi tracées.

Dans la série de cartes au 1:1 000 000ᵉ, des régions très importantes, soit du fait de leur densité de population, soit du fait de leur rôle économique, sont représentées d'une manière encore plus détaillée. L'objectif de cette série de cartes est de montrer la répartition des villes, routes, voies ferrées, ponts, aéroports, barrages, lacs de barrages et autres données associées qui traduisent la densité de l'occupation humaine dans ces régions. Les parcs les plus importants, les sites historiques essentiels et les centres de loisirs sont indiqués. Toutes les informations se détachent sur un fond topographique où le relief apparaît en estompage.

Les centres urbains des cartes régionales sont classés de deux manières différentes. *L'importance de la population* des villes est indiquée par *la dimension et la forme du symbole* qui les situe sur la carte. Seule la population comprise dans les limites municipales est prise en considération; dans les pays où des espaces ruraux sont inclus dans les limites d'une municipalité, seule la population urbaine entre en ligne de compte. *L'importance politique et économique relative* d'une ville, qui n'est pas nécessairement liée au nombre d'habitants, est indiquée par la dimension des caractères qui composent son nom.

La signification de tous les symboles utilisés dans les cartes régionales est donnée par la légende des cartes aux pages x-xii.

OS MAPAS REGIONAIS compreendem três séries básicas, cada uma em estilo diferente, mas que empregam os mesmos símbolos para facilitar sua compreensão (Ver as *Legendas dos mapas*, pág. x-xii). Os mapas de cada uma das principais regiões terrestres, continentes ou subcontinentes, são introduzidos por um ou mais mapas na escala 1:12 000 000. Em seguida, vêm mapas, nas escalas de 1:6 000 000 e 1:3 000 000, que apresentam, com maiores detalhes, seções da região considerada. Exceto quanto à escala, os mapas de 1:6 000 000 e 1:3 000 000 têm as mesmas características. Finalmente, aparecem, na escala de 1:1 000 000, os mapas das áreas mais importantes da região considerada. A cada escala corresponde uma barra colorida e um indicador da mesma cor, que se encontra à margem da página de cada mapa. À página 21, acha-se um exemplo de cada escala, bem como a equivalência das relações centímetro/ quilômetro e polegada/milha.

As três séries básicas de mapas são diferentes quanto ao conteúdo e à apresentação. Os mapas em escala de 1:12 000 000, que são essencialmente políticos, oferecem uma visão geral de cada região. Indicam as fronteiras nacionais e, em alguns casos, as subdivisões administrativas internas. Esses mapas servem de introdução e permitem avaliar e comparar a posição, superfície e forma dos países do Mundo. Neles está claramente indicada a distribuição das cidades e outros centros urbanos, bem como as principais características da configuração do solo. Encontra-se neles também uma seleção das ferrovias e rodovias mais importantes.

A série de mapas das escalas de 1:6 000 000 e de 1:3 000 000 constituem o principal material de referência do Atlas e representa cerca de metade do conjunto de mapas. Entre eles há mapas detalhados de parte de um país (centro do México), de um país inteiro (Japão e a Nova Zelândia) ou de uma região mais extensa (Oriente Médio). As áreas de maior densidade demográfica são apresentadas em escala maior, a de 1:3 000 000, e as demais, na de 1:6 000 000. Nessas duas escalas, os mapas fornecem informações de ordem política e cultural sobre um fundo que indica a configuração detalhada das particularidades físicas do solo, cujo relevo se destaca por contrastes de sombras e cores. Diversos matizes do azul traduzem o mapa batimétrico da profundidade ao largo das costas. Indicam também os aeroportos internacionais, as principais ferrovias, duas categorias de rodovias. As subdivisões políticas internas de numerosos países estão igualmente assinaladas.

Na série de mapas da escala de 1:1 000 000, certas áreas, de interesse estratégico conjugado à importância econômica, densidade demográfica, ou ambos os elementos combinados, aparecem em forma ainda mais detalhada. O objetivo dessa série é representar a distribuição dos grandes centros urbanos, cidades, rodovias, ferrovias, pontes, aeroportos, represas, reservatórios e outras características associadas às grandes densidades demográficas. Indicam-se, também, os parques mais importantes, os lugares de interesse histórico, as áreas de lazer, três categorias de rodovias, e duas de ferrovias; e a nomenclatura dos grandes itinerários rodoviários. Todos esses elementos destacam-se sobre um fundo topográfico do relevo, executado em matizes das diversas cores.

Nos mapas regionais, assinalam-se os centros urbanos de dois modos. A *grandeza da população* das grandes cidades e dos centros urbanos secundários é representada pela *dimensão e forma do símbolo* que as localiza no mapa. O símbolo só reflete a população situada dentro de limites administrativos, sem levar em conta os subúrbios. Nos países onde os limites de uma municipalidade incluem zonas rurais, o símbolo representa apenas a população. A *importância política e econômica* de uma cidade, que não se relaciona necessariamente com o número de seus habitantes, é indicada pela *dimensão* dos caracteres tipográficos com que se compõe o seu nome.

A chave dos símbolos e caracteres tipográficos empregados figura na pág. xi, nas *Legendas dos mapas*.

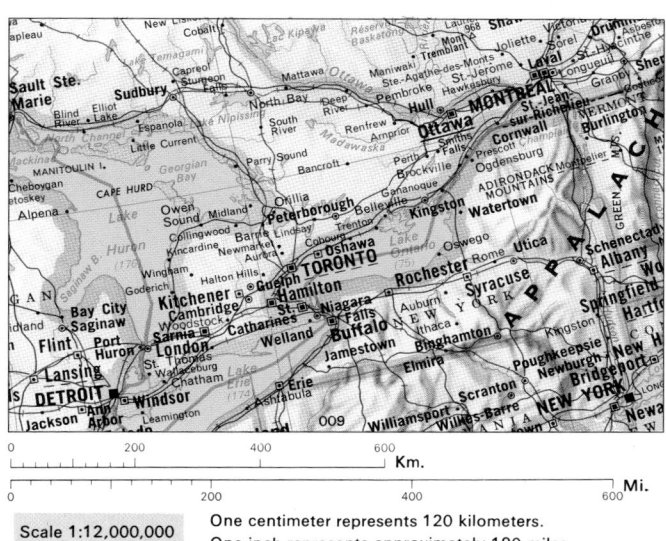

Scale 1:12,000,000   One centimeter represents 120 kilometers.
One inch represents approximately 190 miles.

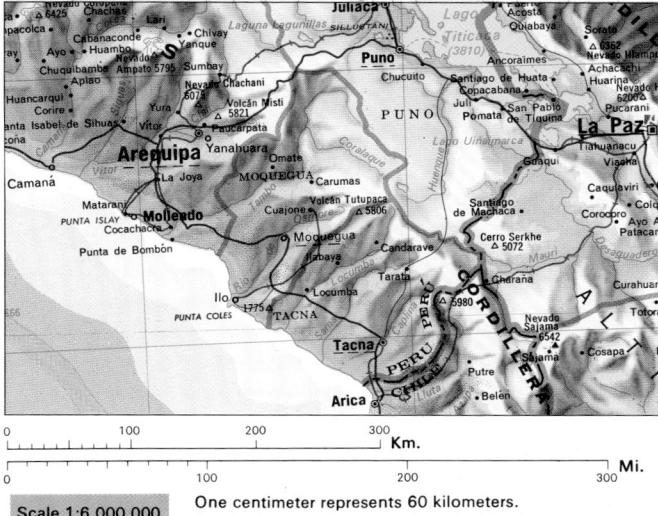

Scale 1:6,000,000   One centimeter represents 60 kilometers.
One inch represents approximately 95 miles.

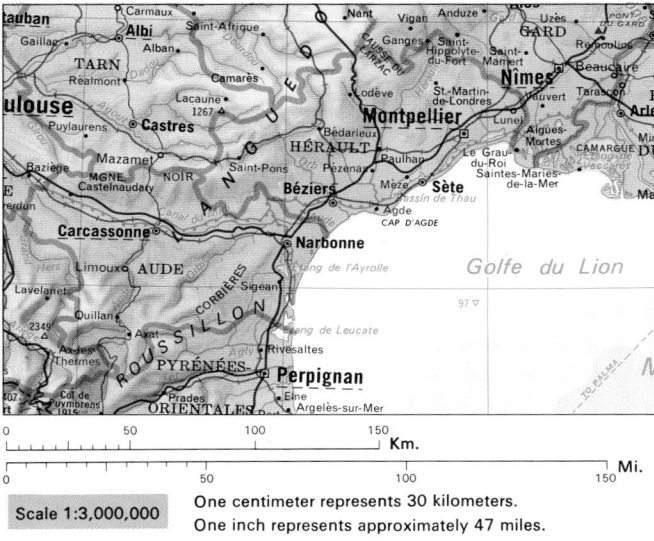

Scale 1:3,000,000   One centimeter represents 30 kilometers.
One inch represents approximately 47 miles.

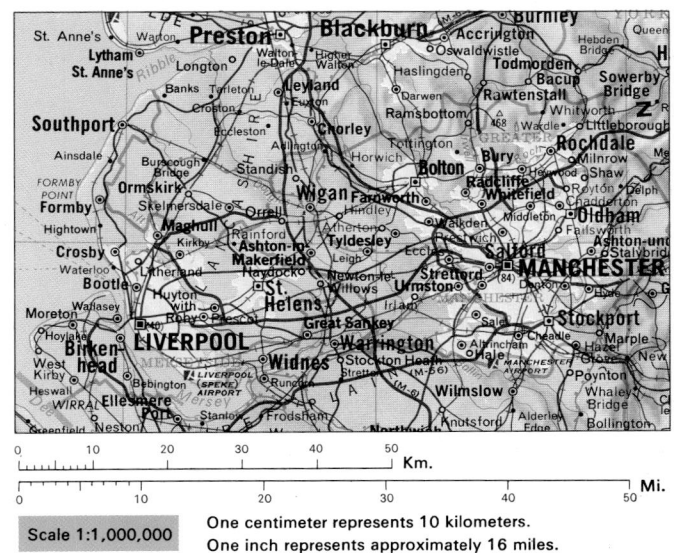

Scale 1:1,000,000   One centimeter represents 10 kilometers.
One inch represents approximately 16 miles.

ATLANTIC OCEAN

NORWEGIAN SEA

NORTH SEA

Arctic Circle

ICELAND

FAEROE ISLANDS (Den.)

SHETLAND ISLANDS

ORKNEY ISLANDS

NORWAY

SWEDEN

DENMARK

IRELAND

SCOTLAND

UNITED KINGDOM

GREAT BRITAIN

ENGLAND

WALES

NETHERLANDS

GERMAN DEMOCRATIC REPUBLIC

FEDERAL REPUBLIC OF GERMANY

POLAND

BELGIUM

LUXEMBOURG

CZECHOSLOVAKIA

FRANCE

SWITZERLAND

AUSTRIA

HUNGARY

PORTUGAL

SPAIN

ANDORRA

ILLES BALEARS BALEARES ISLANDS

ITALY

CORSE CORSICA (Fr.)

SARDEGNA SARDINIA (It.)

YUGOSLAVIA

ALBANIA

MEDITERRANEAN SEA

Tyrrhenian Sea

Ionian Sea

MOROCCO

ALGERIA

TUNISIA

ATLAS MOUNTAINS

ATLAS TELLIEN

ATLAS SAHARIEN

MALTA

SICILY SICILIA

CELTIC SEA

Bay of Biscay

English Channel

The process of unification of the German Democratic Republic with the Federal Republic of Germany began early in 1990 with completion expected by the end of the year.

The annexation of Lithuania, Latvia, and Estonia in 1940 by the Soviet Union has never been officially recognized by the United States government.

In March, 1990 the parliament of Lithuania voted for secession from the Soviet Union.

Copyright © by Rand McNally & Co.
Map prepared by Esselte Map Service AB, Stockholm.

A-550000-264   —81   —16

MAP FORM	-älven	gora	Ile	islands	-øya	ozero	sea	vodochranilišče
ENGLISH	river	mountain	island	islands	island	lake	sea	reservoir
DEUTSCH	Fluss	Berg	Insel	Inseln	Insel	See	Meer	Stausee
ESPAÑOL	rio	montaña	isla	islas	isla	lago	mar	embalse
FRANÇAIS	rivière	montagne	île	îles	île	lac	mer	réservoir
PORTUGUÊS	rio	montanha	ilha	ilhas	ilha	lago	mar	reservatório

Map continues
pages 134-135

BARENTS SEA

Map continues
pages 72-73 →

Map continues
pages 118-119 →

Kilometers 0 200 400 600 Km.

Statute Miles 0 200 400 600 Mi.

Scale 1:12,000,000

One centimeter represents 120 kilometers.
One inch represents approximately 190 miles.

Miller Oblated Stereographic Projection

MAP FORM	-älven	-fjorden	guba	-joki	-jökull	laani		-øya	ozero
ENGLISH	river	fjord, lake	bay	river	glacier	province		island	lake
DEUTSCH	Fluss	Fjord, See	Bucht	Fluss	Gletscher	Provinz		Insel	See
ESPAÑOL	río	fiordo, lago	bahía	río	glaciar	provincia		isla	lago
FRANÇAIS	rivière	fjord, lac	baie	rivière	glacier	province		île	lac
PORTUGUÊS	rio	fiorde, lago	baía	rio	geleira	provincia		ilha	lago

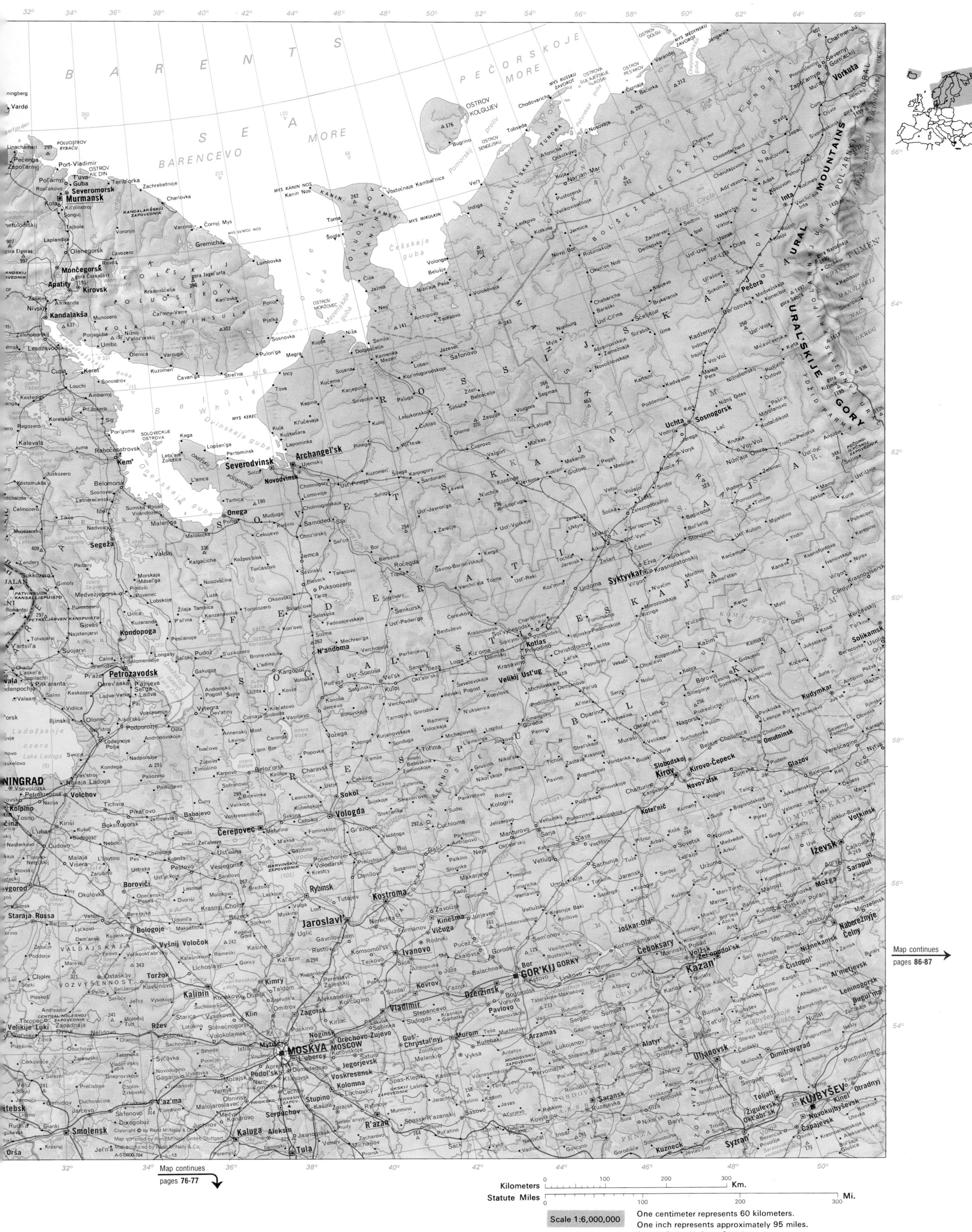

Map continues
pages 86-87

Map continues
pages 76-77

Kilometers

Statute Miles

One centimeter represents 60 kilometers.
One inch represents approximately 95 miles.

Scale 1:6,000,000

Lambert Conformal Conic Projection

Copyright © by Rand McNally & Co.

Map compiled by Rand McNally & Co.
Map produced by Rand McNally & Co.-Stuttgart
A-575000-764

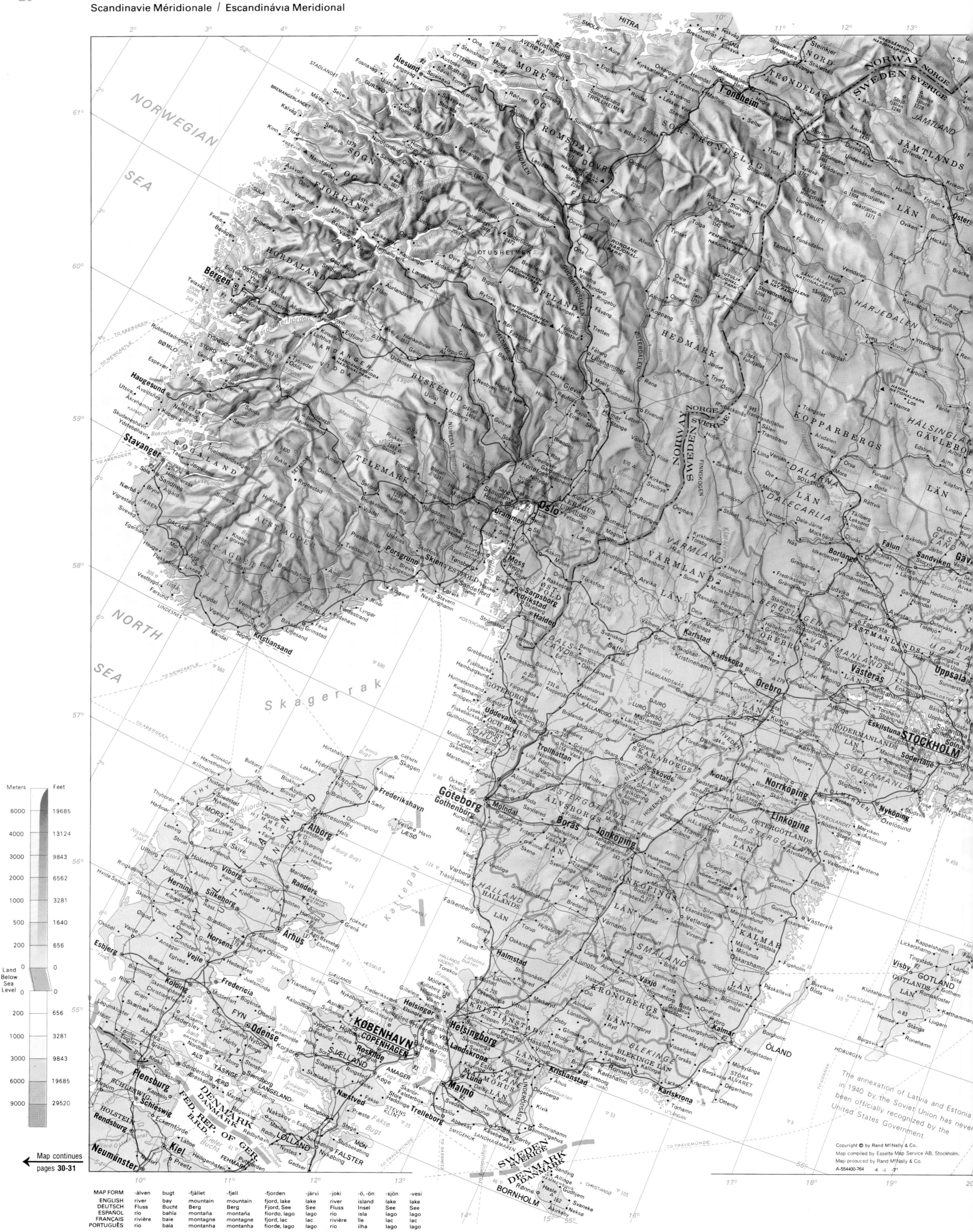

← Map continues
pages **30-31**

	Meters	Feet
	6000	19685
	4000	13124
	3000	9843
	2000	6562
	1000	3281
	500	1640
	200	656
	0	0
Land Below Sea Level	0	0
	200	656
	1000	3281
	3000	9843
	6000	19685
	9000	29520

The annexation of Latvia and Estonia
in 1940 by the Soviet Union has never
been officially recognized by the
United States Government.

MAP FORM	-älven	bugt	-fjället	-fjell	-fjorden	-järvi	-joki	-ö, -ön	-sjön	-vesi
ENGLISH	river	bay	mountain	mountain	fjord, lake	lake	river	island	lake	lake
DEUTSCH	Fluss	Bucht	Berg	Berg	Fjord, See	See	Fluss	Insel	See	See
ESPAÑOL	río	bahía	montaña	montaña	fiordo, lago	lago	río	isla	lago	lago
FRANÇAIS	rivière	baie	montagne	montagne	fjord, lac	lac	rivière	île	lac	lac
PORTUGUÊS	rio	baía	montanha	montanha	fiorde, lago	lago	rio	ilha	lago	lago

Map continues
pages **24-25**

Map continues
pages **76-77**

Map continues
pages 76-77

Kilometers

Km.

Statute Miles

Mi.

Scale 1:3,000,000

One centimeter represents 30 kilometers.
One inch represents approximately 47 miles.
Conic Projection, Two Standard Parallels

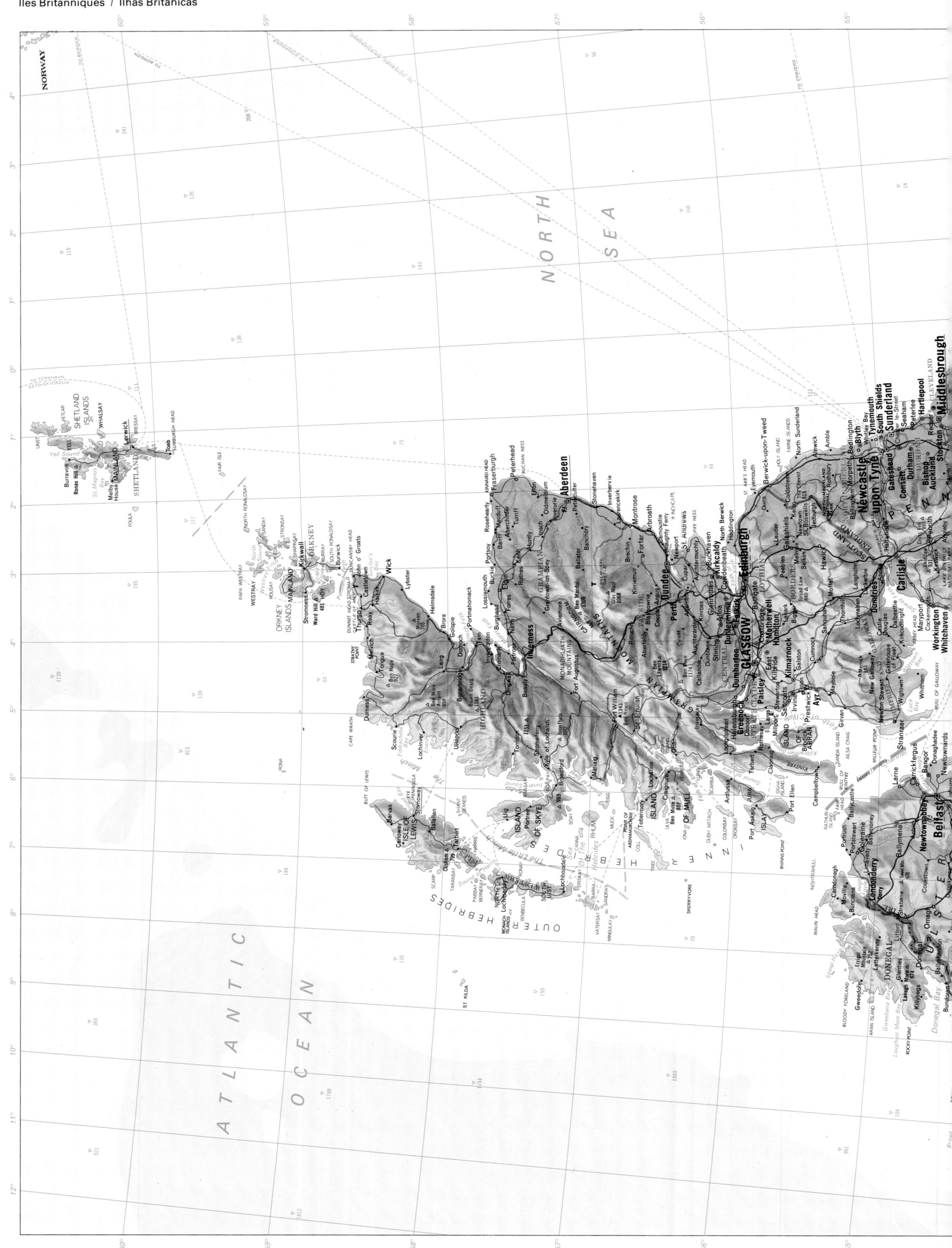

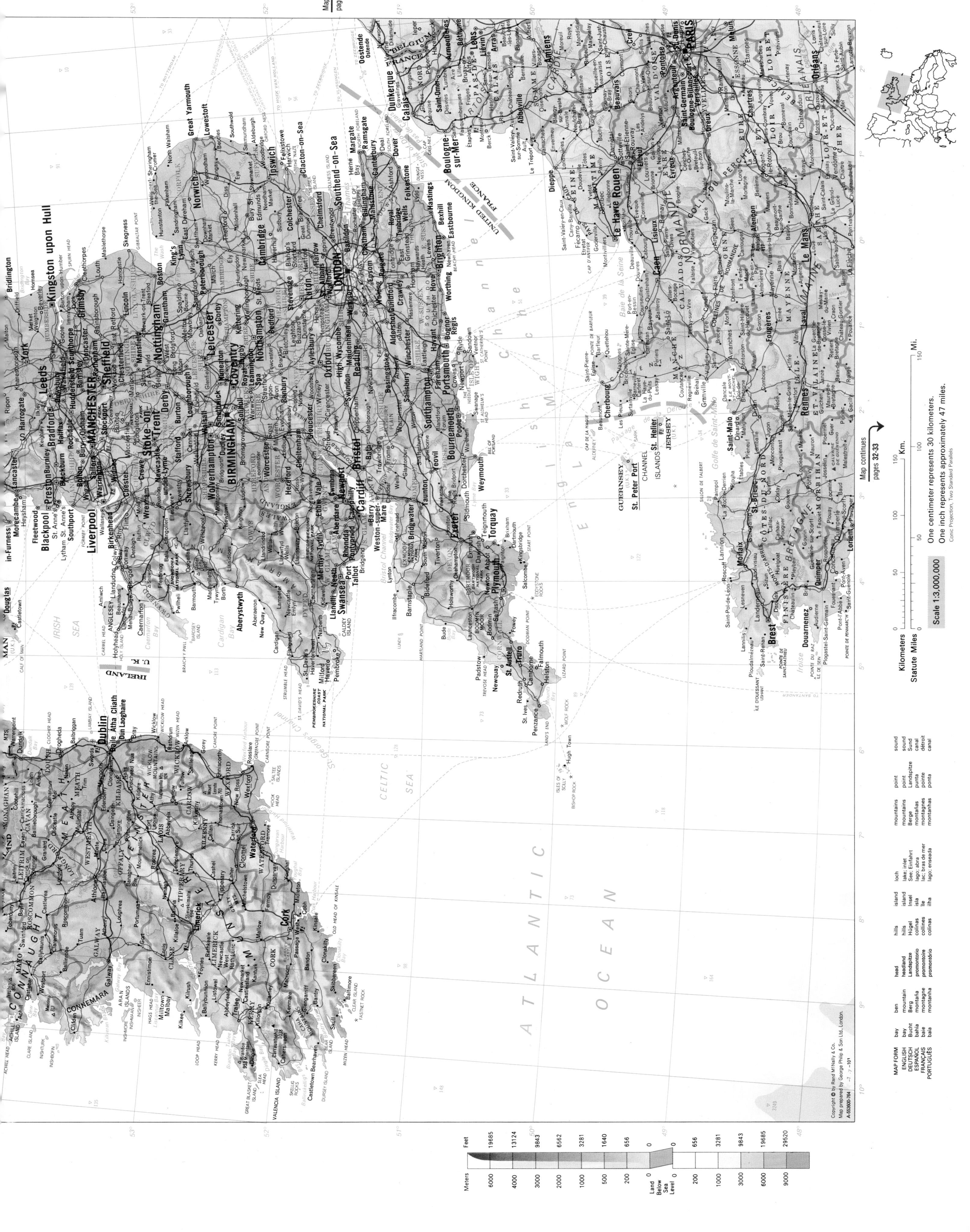

Map continues pages 30-31

Map continues pages 32-33

Scale 1:3,000,000

Conic Projection, Two Standard Parallels

One centimeter represents 30 kilometers.
One inch represents approximately 47 miles.

Kilometers: 0 50 100 150 Km.
Statute Miles: 0 50 100 150 Mi.

MAP FORM					
ENGLISH	bay	ben	head	hills	island
DEUTSCH	bay	mountain	headland	hills	island
ESPAÑOL	Bucht	Berg	Landspitze	Hügel	Insel
FRANÇAIS	bahía	montaña	promontorio	colinas	isla
PORTUGUÊS	baie	montagne	promontoire	collines	île
	baía	montanha	promontorio	colinas	ilha

loch	mountains	point	sound
lake; inlet	mountains	point	sound
See; Einfahrt	Berge	Landspitze	Sund
lago; abra	montañas	punta	canal
lac; bras de mer	montagnes	pointe	détroit
lago; enseada	montanhas	ponta	canal

Elevation scale:

Meters	Feet
6000	19685
4000	13124
3000	9843
2000	6562
1000	3281
500	1640
200	656
0	0
Land Below Sea Level	
0	0
200	656
1000	3281
3000	9843
6000	19685
9000	29520

Map continues
pages 26-27

Map continues
pages 28-29

The process of unification of the
German Democratic Republic with the
Federal Republic of Germany began
early in 1990 with completion
expected by the end of the year

NORTH SEA

FRISIAN ISLANDS

MAP FORM	Bucht	Gebirge	jezioro	Kanal	park narodowy	See	Wald
ENGLISH	bay	range	lake, lagoon	canal	national park	lake	forest, mountains
DEUTSCH	Bucht	Gebirge	See, Haff	Kanal	Nationalpark	See	Wald
ESPAÑOL	bahía	sierra	lago, laguna	canal	parque nacional	lago	bosque, montañas
FRANÇAIS	baie	chaîne	lac, lagune	canal	parc national	lac	forêt, montagnes
PORTUGUÊS	baía	serra	lago, laguna	canal	parque nacional	lago	floresta, montanhas

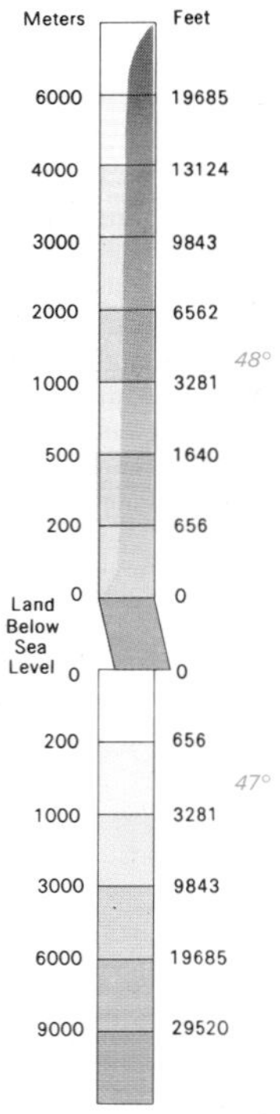

Meters	Feet
6000	19685
4000	13124
3000	9843
2000	6562
1000	3281
500	1640
200	656
Land Below Sea Level 0	0
200	656
1000	3281
3000	9843
6000	19685
9000	29520

Kilometers   0   50   100   150 Km.
Statute Miles   0   50   100   150 Mi.

Scale 1:3,000,000

One centimeter represents 30 kilometers.
One inch represents approximately 47 miles.
Conic Projection, Two Standard Parallels.

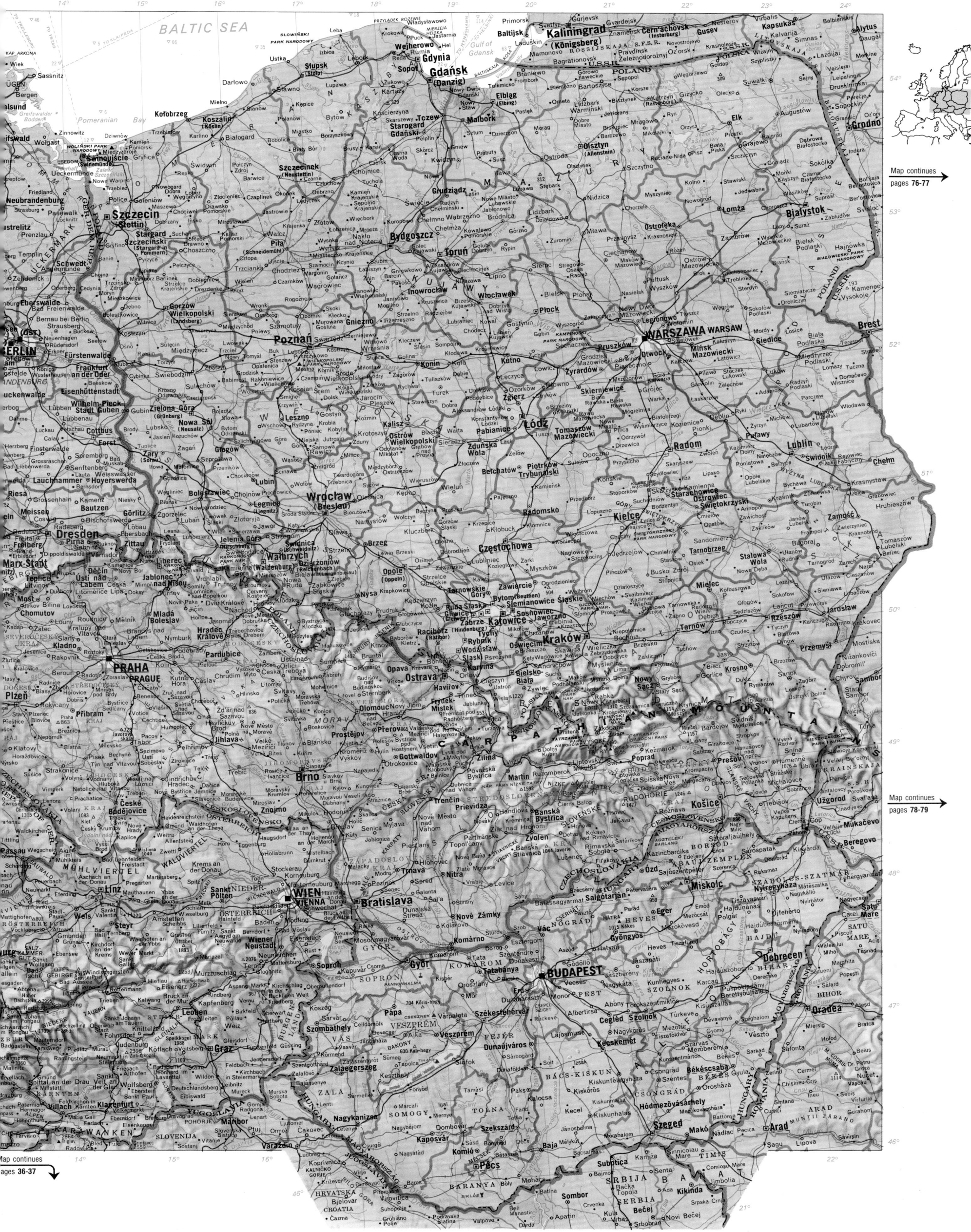

Map continues
pages 76-77

Map continues
pages 78-79

Map continues
pages 36-37

Map continues
pages 28-29

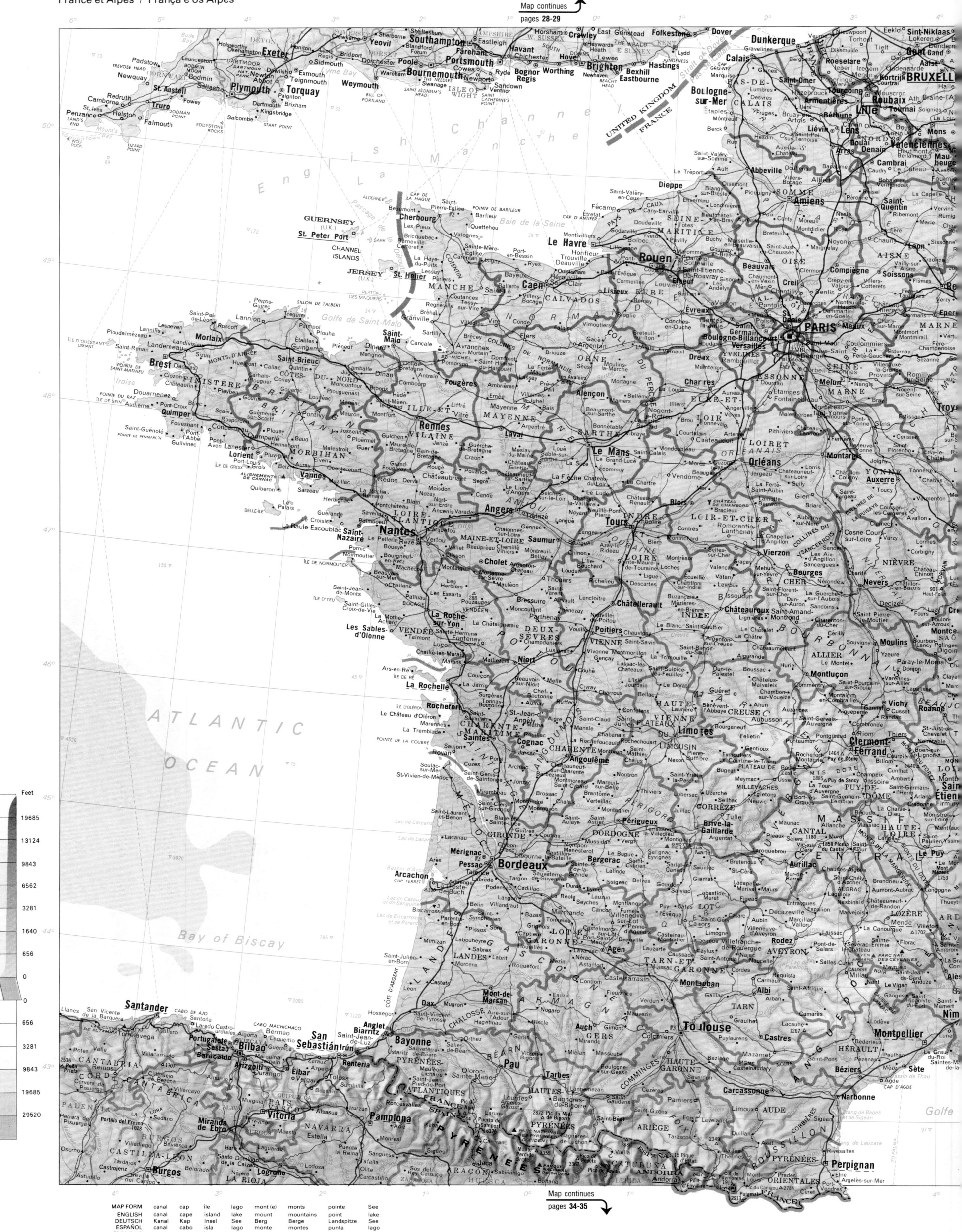

Map continues
pages 34-35

Meters	Feet
6000	19685
4000	13124
3000	9843
2000	6562
1000	3281
500	1640
200	656
Land Below Sea Level 0	0
200	656
1000	3281
3000	9843
6000	19685
9000	29520

MAP FORM	canal	cap	île	lago	mont (e)	monts	pointe	See
ENGLISH	canal	cape	island	lake	mount	mountains	point	lake
DEUTSCH	Kanal	Kap	Insel	See	Berg	Berge	Landspitze	See
ESPAÑOL	canal	cabo	isla	lago	monte	punta	lac
FRANÇAIS	canal	cap	île	lac	mont	monts	pointe	lac
PORTUGUÊS	canal	cabo	ilha	lago	monte	montes	ponta	lago

Map continues
pages 30-31

Map continues
pages 36-37

Kilometers   0   50   100   150   Km.
Statute Miles   0   50   100   150   Mi.

Scale 1:3,000,000

One centimeter represents 30 kilometers.
One inch represents approximately 47 miles.
Lambert Conformal Conic Projection

	ESPAÑOL	bahía	cabo	isla	embalse	puerto	punta	Valdoviño	sierra
	ENGLISH	bay	cape	island	reservoir	port	point	ria	mountains
	DEUTSCH	Bucht	Kap	Insel	Stausee	Hafen	Landspitze	Trichtermündung	Berge
	FRANÇAIS	baie	cap	île	réservoir	port	pointe	estuaire	montagnes
	PORTUGUÊS	baía	cabo	ilha	reservatório	porto	ponta	estuário	serra

Map continues
pages 32-33

Map continues
pages 148-149

Kilometers
Statute Miles

Km.
Mi.

Scale 1:3,000,000

One centimeter represents 30 kilometers.
One inch represents approximately 47 miles.
Conic Projection, Two Standard Parallels

Map continues
pages 38-39

Map continues
pages 30-31

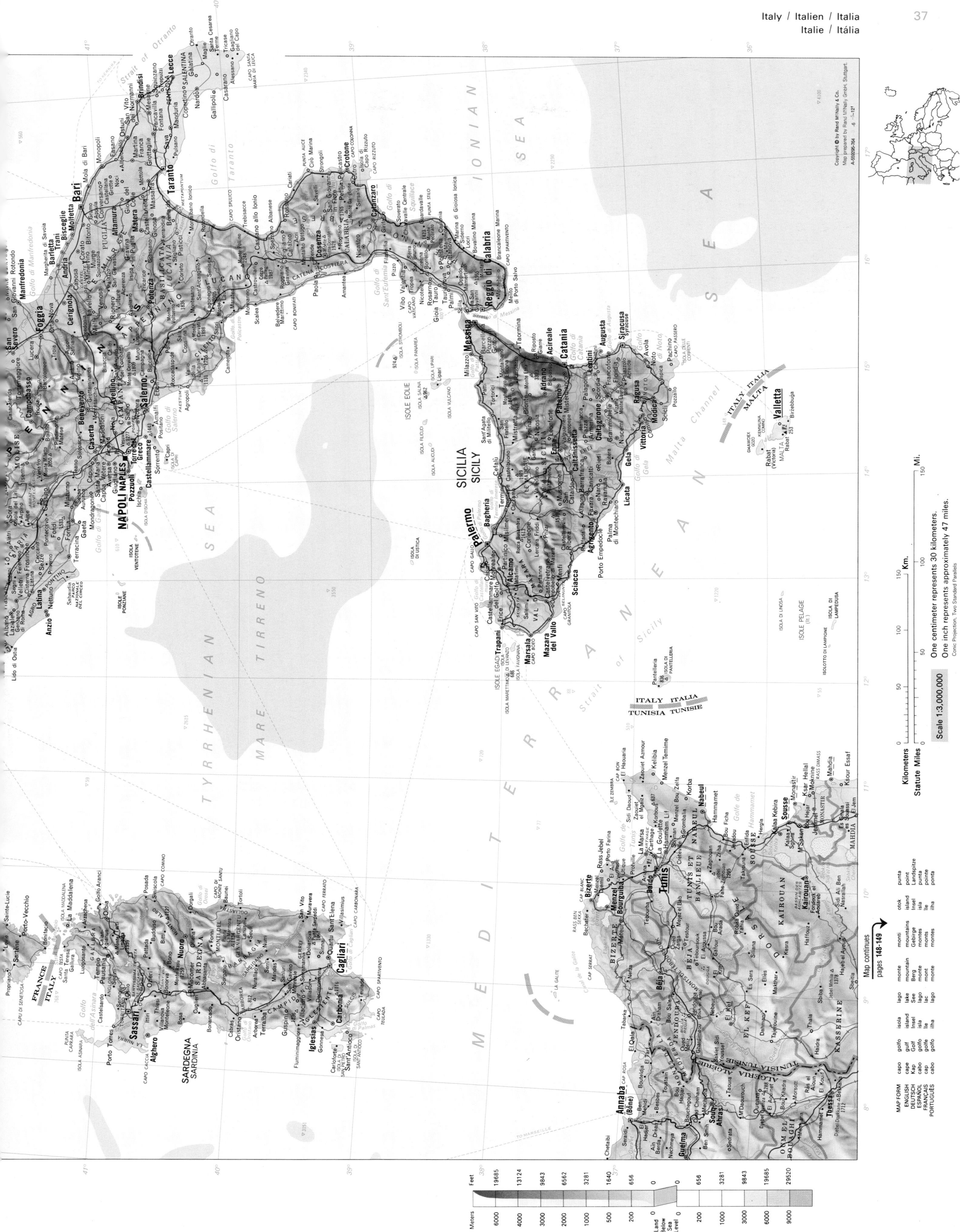
TYRRHENIAN SEA
MARE TIRRENO
IONIAN SEA
MEDITERRANEAN SEA
SICILIA
SICILY
SARDEGNA
SARDINIA
NAPOLI NAPLES
Palermo
Messina
Catania
Reggio di Calabria
Taranto
Bari
Brindisi
Lecce
Cagliari
Sassari
Tunis
Valletta
MALTA
Strait of Otranto
Strait of Sicily
Malta Channel
Scale 1:3,000,000
One centimeter represents 30 kilometers.
One inch represents approximately 47 miles.
Conic Projection, Two Standard Parallels
Kilometers
Statute Miles
Map continues pages 148-149
Copyright © by Rand McNally & Co.
Map prepared by Rand McNally GmbH, Stuttgart.
MAP FORM capo golfo isola lago monte monti otok punta
ENGLISH cape gulf island lake mountain mountains island point
DEUTSCH Kap Golf Insel See Berg Gebirge Insel Landspitze
ESPAÑOL cabo golfo isla lago monte montes isla punta
FRANÇAIS cap golfe île lac mont monts île pointe
PORTUGUÊS cabo golfo ilha lago monte montes ilha ponta
Meters
Feet
Land Below Sea Level

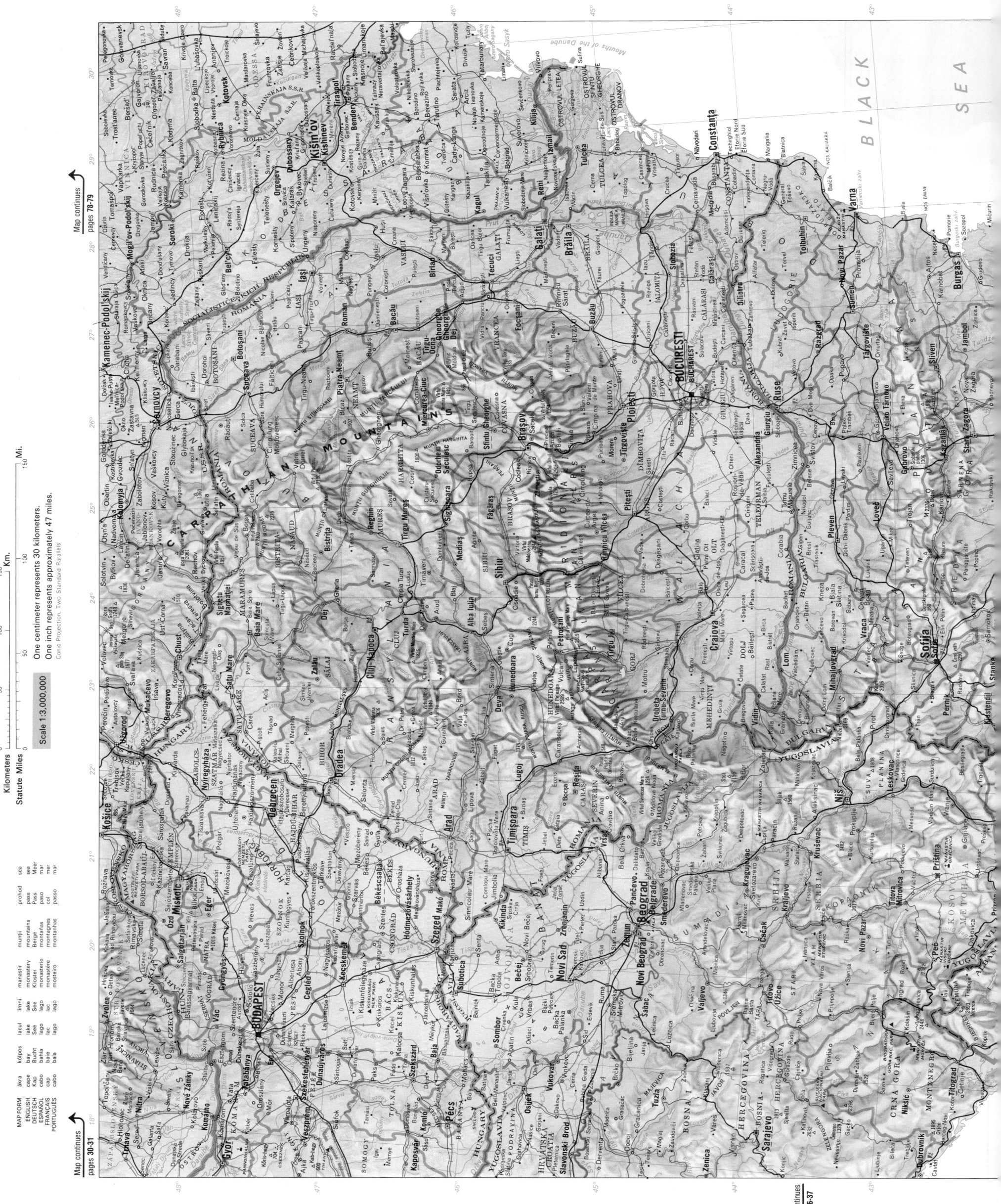

Map continues
pages 78-79

Map continues
pages 30-31

Map continues
pages 36-37

Mi.
150

Km.
100

150

Kilometers   Statute Miles

100

50

50

0

Scale 1:3,000,000

One centimeter represents 30 kilometers.
One inch represents approximately 47 miles.
Conic Projection, Two Standard Parallels

MAP FORM				
ENGLISH	ákra	lacul	limni	manastir
DEUTSCH	Kap	lake	lake	monastery
ESPAÑOL	Kap	See	See	Kloster
FRANÇAIS	cabo	lago	lago	monasterio
PORTUGUÊS	cabo	lac	lago	monastère
	cabo	lago	lago	mosteiro

	köpos	muntii	prohod	sea
	bay	mountains	pass	sea
	Bucht	Berge	Pass	Meer
	bahia	montañas	paso	mar
	baie	montagnes	col	mer
	baía	montanhas	passo	mar

BLACK SEA

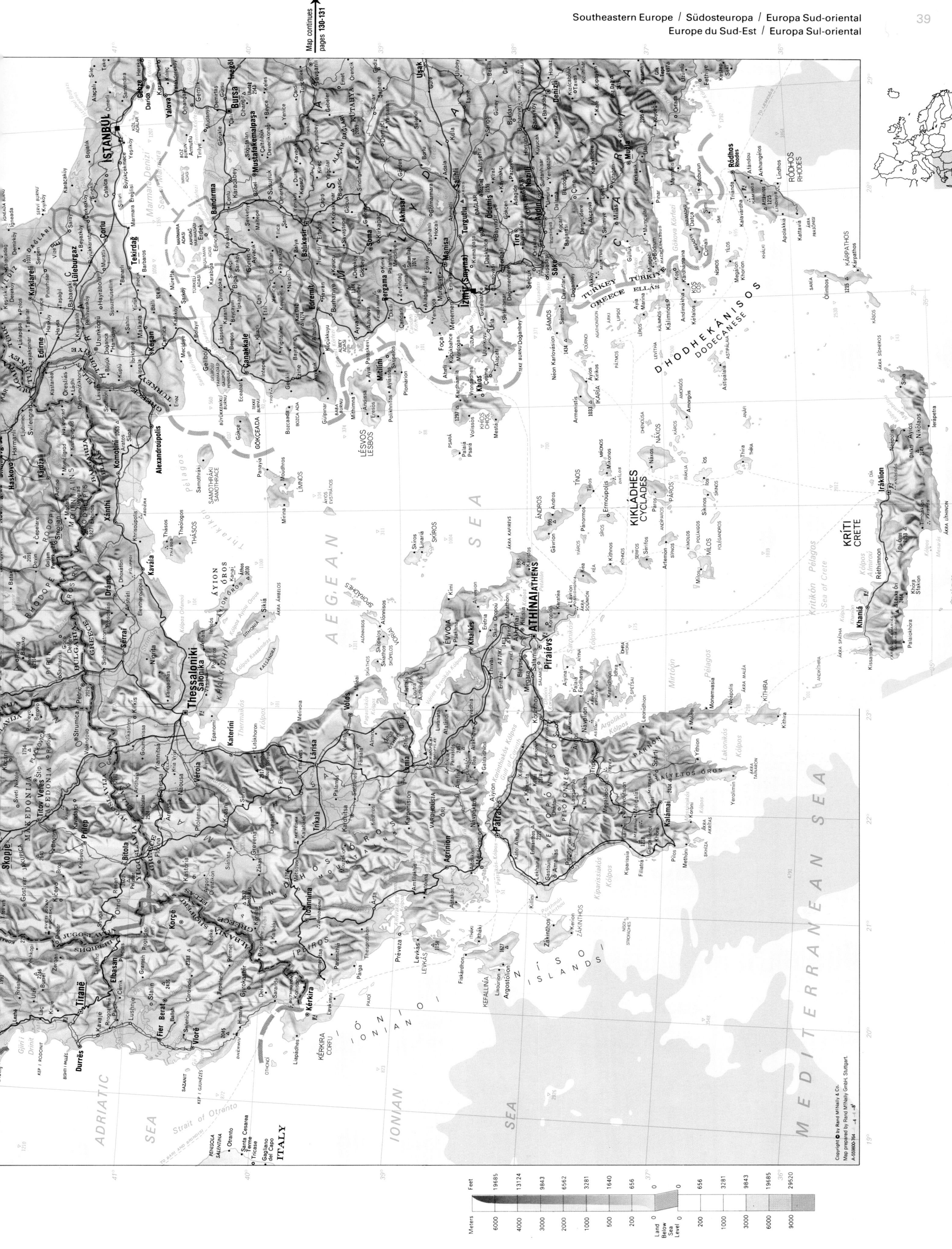

Map continues
pages 130-131

ISTANBUL

Bursa

Mustafakemalpaşa

Bandırma

Tekirdağ

Çanakkale

Edirne

Kırklareli
Lüleburgaz

Corlu

Yalova

Gebze

İnegöl

Balıkesir

Soma

Akhisar

Manisa

Turgutlu

İzmir Smyrna

Bergama

Edremit

Mitilíni

Aydın

Denizli

Uşak

Kütahya

Salihli

Ödemiş

Tire

Söke

Muğla

Ródhos
Rhodes

RÓDHOS
RHODES

Lindhos

TURKEY TÜRKIYE
GREECE ELLAS

DHODHEKÁNISOS
DODECANESE

KÁRPATHOS
Kárpathos

SÁMOS

IKARÍA
IKARIA

Khíos

LÉSVOS
LESBOS

SAMOTHRÁKI
SAMOTHRACE

LÍMNOS

THÁSOS

Alexandroúpolis

Komotiní

Xánthi

Kaválla

ÁYION ÓROS

KIKLÁDHES
CYCLADES

NÁXOS

PÁROS

ÁNDROS

SKÍROS

KRÍTI
CRETE

Iráklion

Khaniá

Réthimnon

A E G E A N   S E A

Haskovo

Kürdžali

RODOPI MOUNTAINS

Dráma

Sérrai

Thessaloníki
Salóniki

Kateríni

Vólos

Lárisa

KHALKIDHIKÍ

Véroia

Trikala

SPORÁDHES

ÉVVOIA

Khalkís

ATHÍNAI ATHENS

Piraiévs

SKÓPJE

Titov Veles Štip

Bitola

PELOPÓNNISOS

PÉTROS

Pátrai

Ioánnina

Agrínion

Pirgos

Kalámai

Spárti

Trípolis

Kérkira
CORFU

IÓNIOI NÍSOI
IONIAN ISLANDS

KEFALLINÍA

ZÁKINTHOS

LÉVKAS

PÉVKI

Vlorë

Fier

Berat

Durrës

Tiranë

Elbasan

Korçë

SHQIPËRIA
ALBANIA

MAKEDONIJA
MACEDONIA

JUGOSLAVIJA
YUGOSLAVIA

BULGARIA
GREECE GRÈCE

ADRIATIC SEA

Strait of Otranto

ITALY

Santa Cesarea
Terme

Otranto

Gagliano
del Capo

PENISOLA
SALENTINA

I O N I A N   S E A

M E D I T E R R A N E A N   S E A

Kíthira
KÍTHIRA

Monemvasía

Neápolis

Kalamata

Feet													
19685	13124	9843	6562	3281	1640	656	0	0	656	3281	9843	19685	29520

Meters							Land Below Sea Level						
6000	4000	3000	2000	1000	500	200	0	0	200	1000	3000	6000	9000

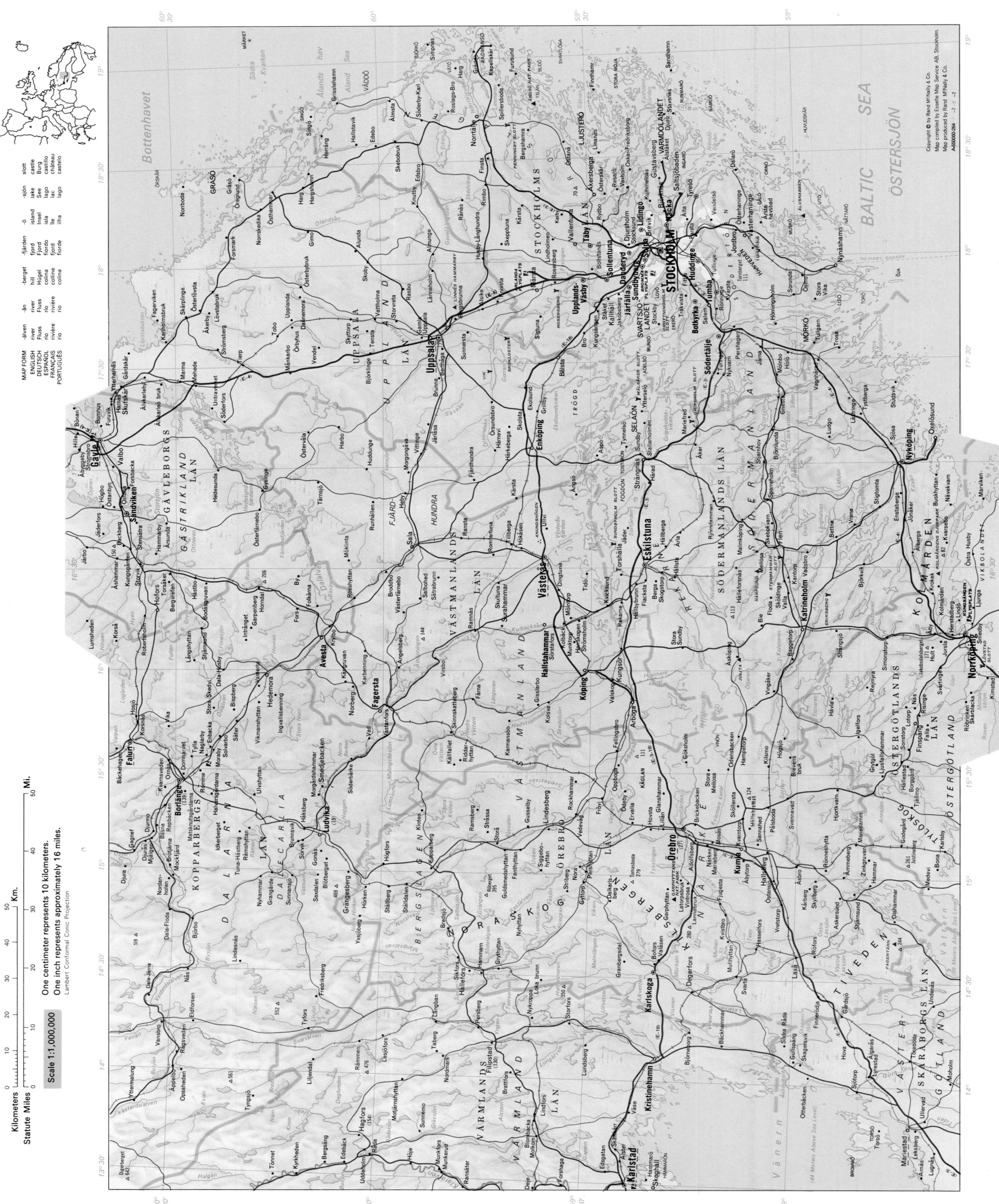
MAP FORM
ENGLISH
DEUTSCH
ESPAÑOL
FRANÇAIS
PORTUGUÊS
-älven river Fluss rio rivière rio
-ån river Fluss rio rivière rio
-berget hill Hügel colina colline colina
-fjärden fjord Fjord fiordo fjord fiorde
-ö island Insel isla île ilha
-sjön lake See lago lac lago
slott castle Burg castillo château castelo
Kilometers
Statute Miles
Scale 1:1,000,000
One centimeter represents 10 kilometers.
One inch represents approximately 16 miles.
Lambert Conformal Conic Projection
Copyright © by Rand McNally & Co.
Map compiled by Esselte Map Service AB, Stockholm.
Map produced by Rand McNally & Co.
STOCKHOLM
Uppsala
Västerås
Örebro
Karlstad
Bottenhavet
BALTIC SEA
ÖSTERSJÖN

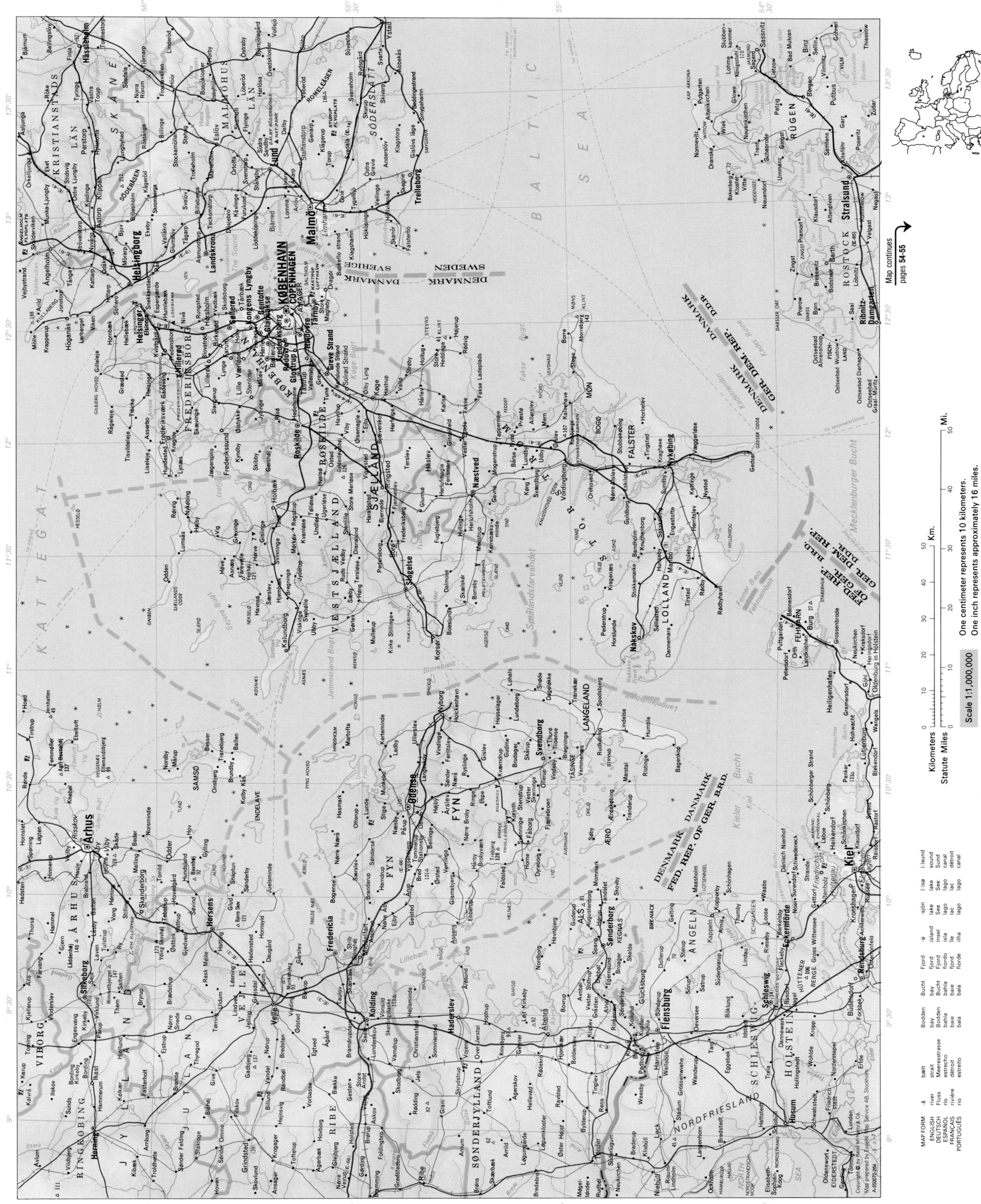

Map continues
pages 54-55

Scale 1:1,000,000

One centimeter represents 10 kilometers.
One inch represents approximately 16 miles.

Lambert Conformal Conic Projection

Kilometers

Km.

Statute Miles

Mi.

MAP FORM									
ENGLISH	river	bay	strait	bay	island	lake	sound	canal	
DEUTSCH	Fluss	Bodden	Meeresstrasse	Bucht	Insel	See	Sund	Kanal	
ESPAÑOL	río	bahía	estrecho	bahía	isla	lago	lago	canal	
FRANÇAIS	rivière	Bodden	détroit	fjord	île	lac	lac	canal	
PORTUGUÊS	rio	baía	estreito	baía	ilha	lago	lago	canal	
	-å	Bodden	-beit	Bucht	-ø	-sjön	i-isø	i-/sund	
				Fjord					

Copyright © by Rand McNally & Co.
Map prepared by Esselte Map Service AB, Stockholm.
A-650072-264

← Map continues pages 48-49

ENGLISH	bay	drain	forest	head	hill	isle	marsh	point	vale
DEUTSCH	Bucht	Abzugsgraben	Wald	Landspitze	Hügel	Insel	Marsch	Landspitze	Tal
ESPAÑOL	bahía	acequia	bosque	promontorio	colina	isla	pantano	punta	valle
FRANÇAIS	baie	drainage	forêt	promontoire	colline	île	marais	pointe	depression
PORTUGUÊS	baía	drenagem	floresta	promontório	colina	ilha	pântano	ponta	vale

Copyright © by Rand McNally & Co.
Map prepared by Rand McNally & Co.
A-556900-264

Map continues
pages 44-45

Map continues
pages 50-51

b

GUERNSEY
(U.K.)

St. Sampson
Vale
Castel
St. Peter Port
Torteval
SARK

CHANNEL

ISLANDS

JERSEY
(U.K.)

St. John
St. Helier
Aubin

Kilometers 0 10 20 30 40 50 Km.
Statute Miles 0 10 20 30 40 50 Mi.

Scale 1:1,000,000
One centimeter represents 10 kilometers.
One inch represents approximately 16 miles.
Lambert Conformal Conic Projection

Map continues
pages 46-47

Map continues
pages 48-49

Copyright © by Rand McNally & Co.
Map prepared by Rand McNally & Co.
A-556800-264   -10-) -13

MAP FORM	bay	dale	firth	forest	head	loch	moor	water
ENGLISH	bay	dale	estuary	forest	head	lake; inlet	moor	water (lake, river)
DEUTSCH	Bucht	Weites Tal	Trichtermündung	Wald	Landspitze	See; Einfahrt	Moor	See, Fluss
ESPAÑOL	bahía	valle	estuario	bosque	promontorio	lago; abra	páramo	lago, río
FRANÇAIS	baie	vallée	estuaire	forêt	promontoire	lac; bras de mer	lande	lac, rivière
PORTUGUÊS	baía	vale	estuário	floresta	promontório	lago; enseada	pântano	lago, rio

Map continues
pages 42-43

Kilometers 0 10 20 30 40 50 Km.
Statute Miles 0 10 20 30 40 50 Mi.

Scale 1:1,000,000

One centimeter represents 10 kilometers.
One inch represents approximately 16 miles.
Lambert Conformal Conic Projection

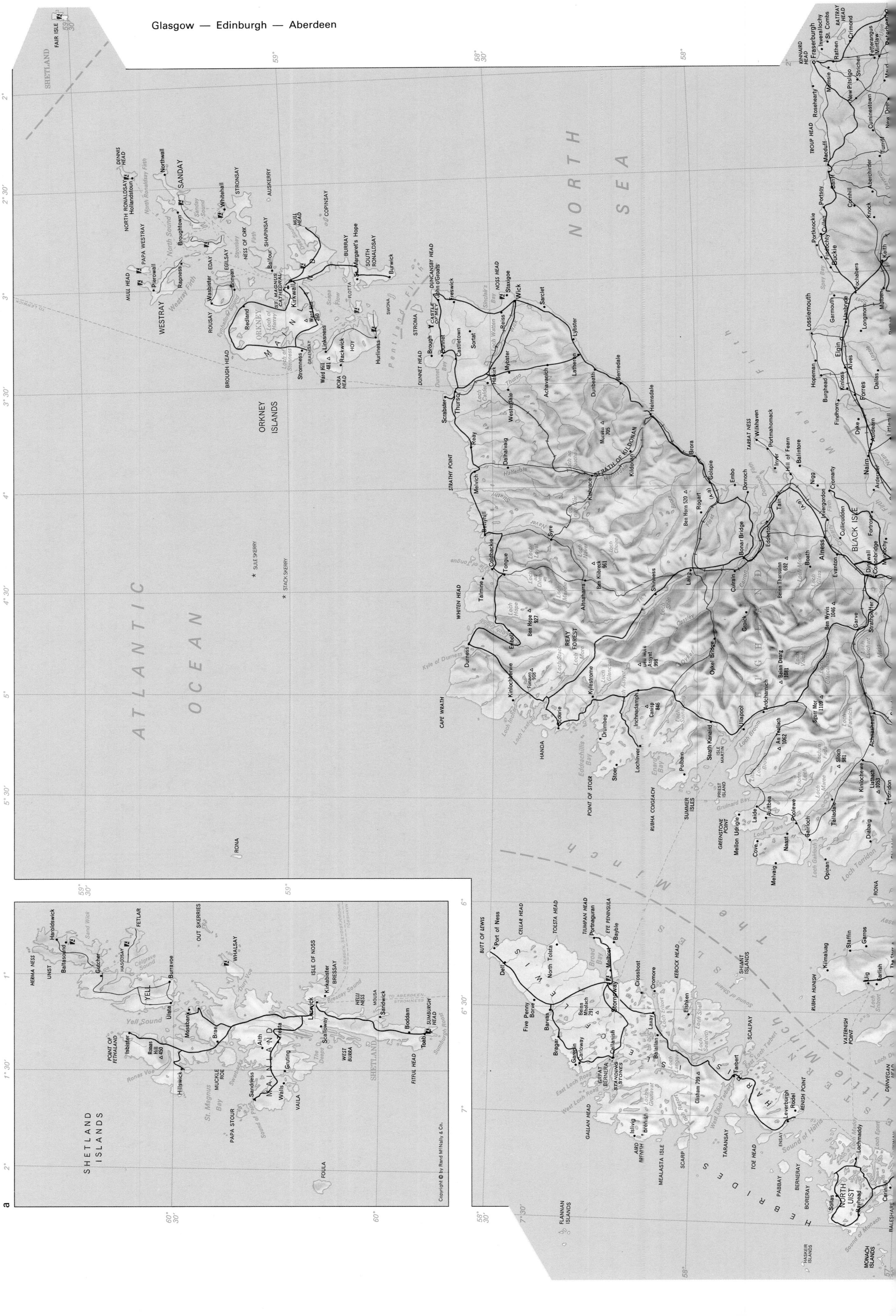
ATLANTIC OCEAN
NORTH SEA
ORKNEY ISLANDS
SHETLAND ISLANDS
WESTRAY
SANDAY
STRONSAY
EDAY
ROUSAY
SHAPINSAY
HOY
SOUTH RONALDSAY
BURRAY
FLOTTA
STROMA
SWONA
NORTH RONALDSAY
PAPA WESTRAY
AUSKERRY
COPINSAY
Kirkwall
Stromness
Pierowall
Hollandstoun
Balfour
St. Margaret's Hope
Burwick
Hurliness
Rackwick
Linksness
Redland
Wasbister
Rapness
Broughtown
Whitehall
Northwall
Pentland Firth
Scapa Flow
DUNNET HEAD
DUNCANSBY HEAD
NOSS HEAD
John O'Groats
Thurso
Scrabster
Castletown
Wick
Staxigoe
Reiss
Sarclet
Lybster
Latheron
Dunbeath
Berriedale
Helmsdale
Brora
Golspie
Dornoch
Embo
Tain
Invergordon
Alness
Cromarty
Nigg
Nairn
Forres
Elgin
Lossiemouth
Buckie
Cullen
Portsoy
Banff
Macduff
Fraserburgh
Moray Firth
Dornoch Firth
BLACK ISLE
Dingwall
Strathpeffer
Garve
Bonar Bridge
Lairg
Shinness
Altnaharra
Tongue
Bettyhill
Melvich
Reay
Durness
Kinlochbervie
Scourie
Kylestrome
Lochinver
Inchnadamph
Ullapool
Gairloch
Poolewe
Aultbea
Kinlochewe
Torridon
Achnasheen
CAPE WRATH
WHITEN HEAD
STRATHY POINT
HANDA
SULE SKERRY
STACK SKERRY
RONA
Ben Hope 927
Ben Klibreck 961
Ben Wyvis 1046
Beinn Dearg 1081
An Teallach 1062
Liathach 1053
SUMMER ISLES
The Minch
Little Minch
OUTER HEBRIDES
LEWIS
HARRIS
NORTH UIST
BUTT OF LEWIS
Port of Ness
Stornoway
Barvas
Callanish
Tarbert
Leverburgh
Rodel
Lochmaddy
FLANNAN ISLANDS
SHIANT ISLANDS
MONACH ISLANDS
SCALPAY
TARANSAY
PABBAY
BERNERAY
Sound of Harris
Staffin
Uig
UNST
YELL
FETLAR
WHALSAY
BRESSAY
MAINLAND
FOULA
PAPA STOUR
OUT SKERRIES
MOUSA
Lerwick
Scalloway
Sandwick
Baltasound
Haroldswick
Brae
Walls
Hillswick
SUMBURGH HEAD
FITFUL HEAD
FAIR ISLE
Copyright © by Rand McNally & Co.

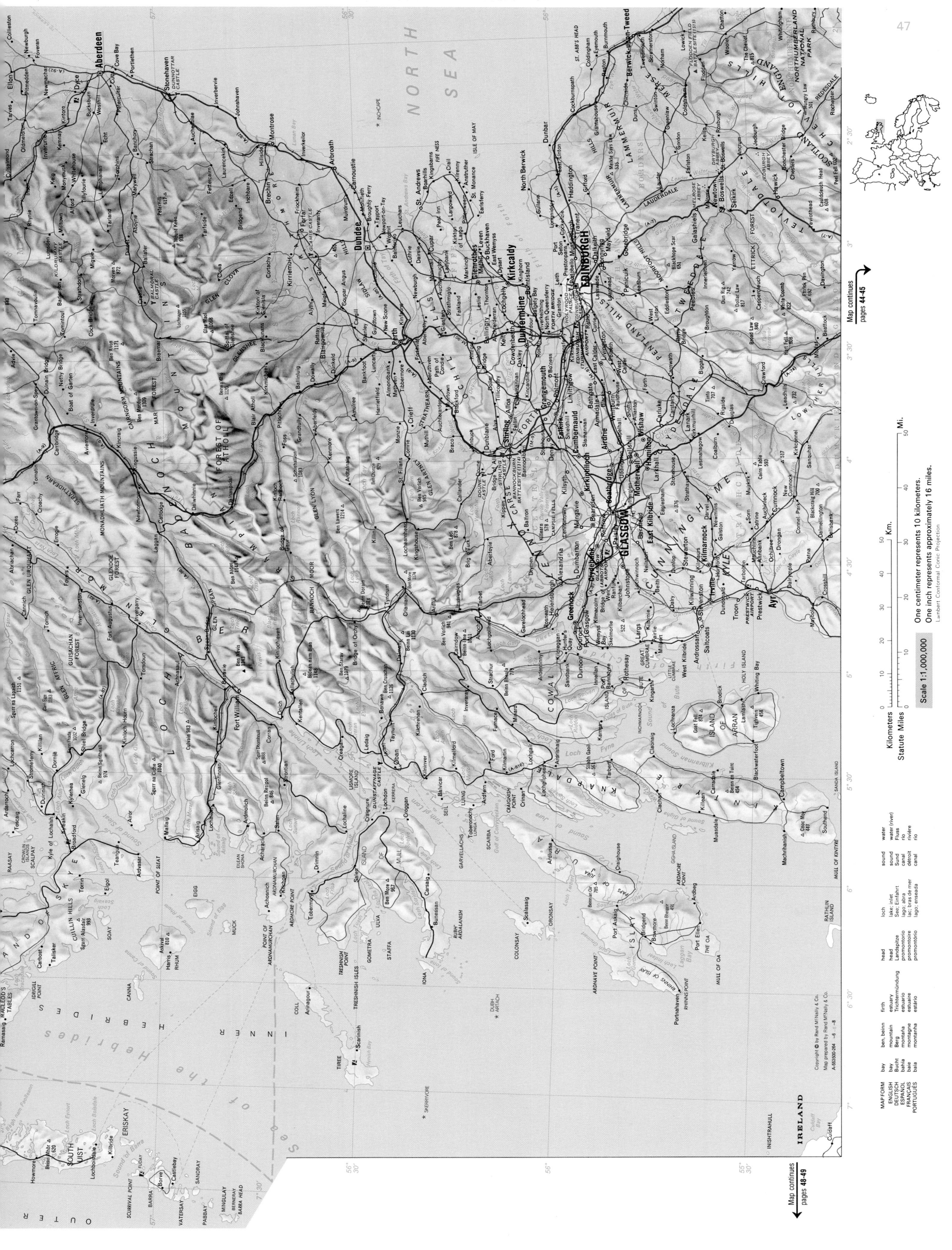

Map continues pages 44-45

Map continues pages 48-49

MAP FORM	bay	ben, beinn	firth	head	loch	sound	water
ENGLISH	bay	mountain	estuary	head	lake; inlet	sound	water (river)
DEUTSCH	Bucht	Berg	Trichtermündung	Landspitze	See; Einfahrt	Sund	Fluss
ESPAÑOL	bahía	montaña	estuario	promontorio	lago; abra	canal	río
FRANÇAIS	baie	montagne	estuaire	promontoire	lac; bras de mer	détroit	rivière
PORTUGUÊS	baía	montanha	estário	promontório	lago; enseada	canal	rio
Kilometers 0 10 20 30 40 50 Km.
Statute Miles 0 10 20 30 40 50 Mi.
Scale 1:1,000,000
One centimeter represents 10 kilometers.
One inch represents approximately 16 miles.
Lambert Conformal Conic Projection

Map continues
pages 46-47

Map continues
pages 44-45

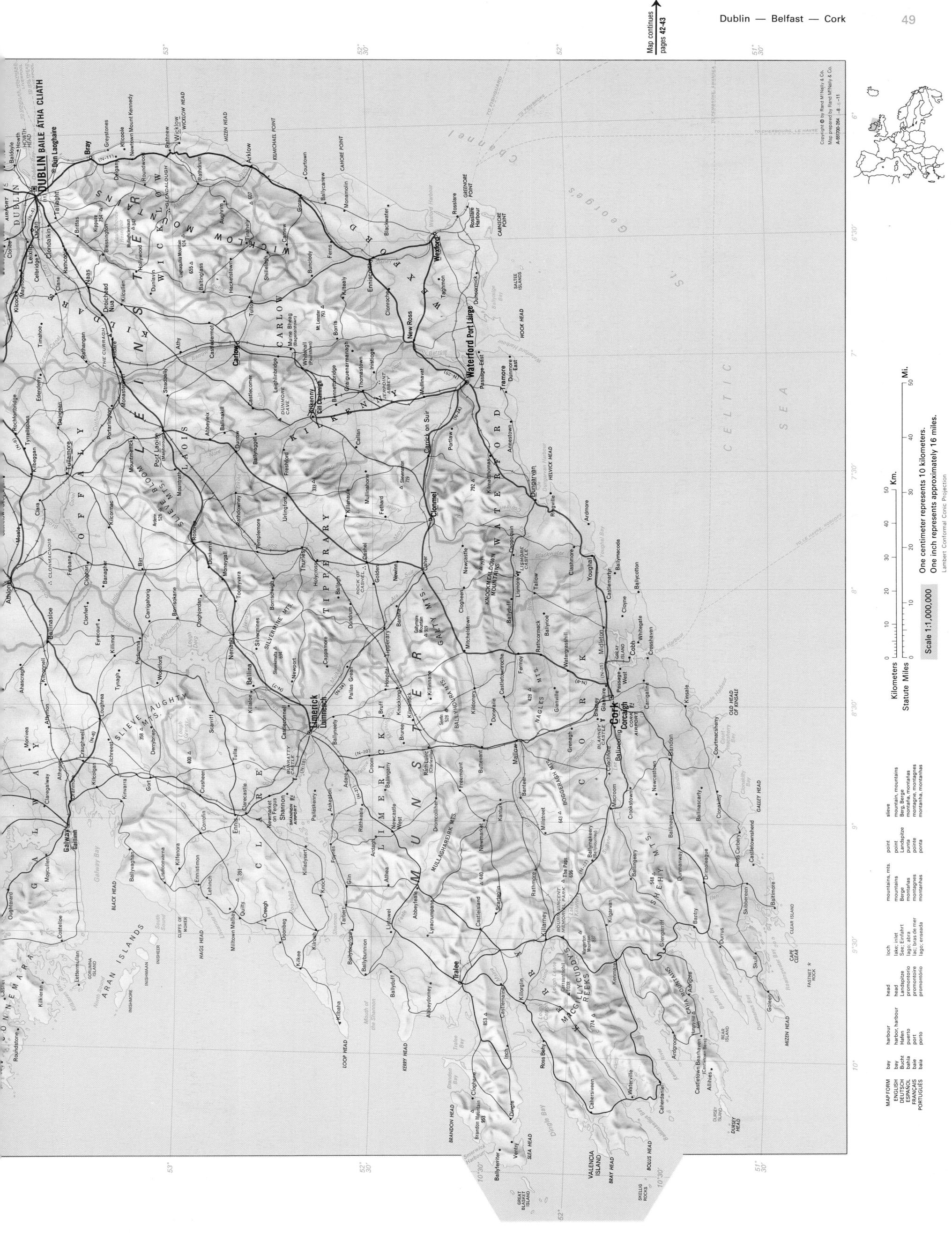

Map continues pages 42-43

DUBLIN BAILE ÁTHA CLIATH

Howth
HOWTH HEAD
Baldoyle
Dún Laoghaire
Bray
(N-11)
Greystones
Kilcoole
Newtown Mount Kennedy
Delgany
Rathnew
Wicklow
WICKLOW HEAD
Roundwood
Ashford
MIZEN HEAD

Clontarf
Tallaght
Rathcoole
Clondalkin
Lucan
Leixlip
Maynooth
Celbridge
Clane
Naas
Sallins
Kilcock
Brittas
Blessington
Hollywood
Kilbride
754
Lugnaquilla Mountain 924
655
Baltinglass
Hacketstown
Rathdrum
Avoca
Aughrim
Arklow
KILMICHAEL POINT
Courtown
Ballycanew
Monamolin
CAHORE POINT

Maynooth
Kilcullen
Dunlavin
Rathangan
Monasterevin
Athy
Castledermot
Tullow
Carnew
Ferns
Bunclody

DUBLIN
AIRPORT
DUBLIN

Kildare

Droichead Nua
The Curragh

THE CURRAGH

Rochfortbridge
Edenderry
Rathangan
Portarlington

PORT LAOISE
Portlaoise (Maryborough)

Mountmellick
Stradbally

Abbeyleix
Ballinakill
Durrow
Castlecomer
DUNMORE CAVE

Leighlinbridge
Bagenalstown
Muine Bheag
(Bagenalstown)

CARLOW
Carlow
Graiguenamanagh

Kilkenny
Cill Chainnigh

KILKENNY

Thomastown
Inistioge
New Ross

WEXFORD
Wexford
Rosslare
Rosslare Harbour
GREENORE POINT
CARNSORE POINT

Taghmon
Clonroche
Enniscorthy

JERPOINT ABBEY

Callan
Mullinavat

Passage-East
DUNMORE EAST
Tramore

WATERFORD Port Láirge
HOOK HEAD

Duncannon

Kilmacthomas

WATERFORD

Dungarvan
HELVICK HEAD
792

Lismore
LISMORE CASTLE
Tallow
Clashmore
Ardmore

Cahir
Clonmel
Carrick on Suir
Portlaw

CELTIC SEA

Athlone

OFFALY

Clara
Kilbeggan
Tullamore
Ferbane
Clonony
Cloghan
Banagher

CLONMACNOIS

Birr

Shinrone
Roscrea

Templemore

Thurles
Holycross
ROCK OF CASHEL
Cashel
Golden
Tipperary
Cahir

Moate

SLIEVE BLOOM MTS.

Shannonbridge

Ballinasloe

Clonfert
Eyrecourt
Portumna
Carrigahorig
Borrisokane
Nenagh
Silvermines
Newport
SILVERMINE MTS.
Toomyvara

Killimor

Laurencetown
Woodford
Scarriff

GALWAY
Gaillimh

Galway

Oranmore
Clarinbridge
Craughwell
Athenry
Loughrea
Kilcolgan
Kinvara
Gort

SLIEVE AUGHTY MTS.

KNOCKMEALDOWN MOUNTAINS

GALTEE MTS.
Galtymore Mountain 919

Mitchelstown

Fermoy
Castletownroche
Rathcormack

Watergrasshill
Glanmire
CORK Corcaigh
Cork
BLARNEY CASTLE
Blarney
Ballincollig
Carrigaline
Passage West
Cobh
GREAT ISLAND
Crosshaven
Midleton
Cloyne
Whitegate
Ballycotton
Youghal

Macroom
Coachford
Ballyvourney
Inchigeelagh
Dunmanway
Drimoleague
Bantry

BOGGERAGH MTS.
Mallow
Buttevant
Doneraile
Kanturk
Newmarket
Freemount

Castleisland
Farranfore
Killorglin
Killarney
Kenmare
MACGILLYCUDDY'S REEKS
Carrauntoohil

KILLARNEY
Killarney

Tralee
Castlegregory
Dingle
Ventry
SLEA HEAD

LIMERICK
Luimneach

Limerick

Bruff
Kilmallock
Charleville
Bruree

Ballingarry
Rathkeale
Adare
Croom
Askeaton
Foynes
Newcastle West
Abbeyfeale

Tarbert
Listowel
Ballybunion
Ballylongford

KERRY HEAD

LOOP HEAD

CLARE

Ennis
Ennistimon
Lisdoonvarna
Corofin
CLIFFS OF MOHER
HAGS HEAD
Kilrush
Kilkee
Kildysart
Doonbeg
Miltown Malbay
Quilty

BUNRATTY CASTLE
SHANNON
Shannon
Newmarket on Fergus
Clarecastle
Quin
Tulla

Scarriff
Killaloe

GALWAY
Gort

ARAN ISLANDS
INISHMORE
INISHMAAN
INISHEER

SHEEHY MTS.
CAHA MOUNTAINS

Kilgarvan
Glengarriff
Castletownbere
Adrigole
Allihies
BEAR ISLAND
DURSEY ISLAND
DURSEY HEAD
MIZEN HEAD

Skibbereen
Ballydehob
Schull
CLEAR ISLAND
CAPE CLEAR
FASTNET ROCK

Bandon
Clonakilty
Rosscarbery
Castletownshend
GALLEY HEAD
Kinsale
OLD HEAD OF KINSALE
Courtmacsherry
Timoleague

VALENCIA ISLAND
Cahersiveen
Waterville
SKELLIG ROCKS
BOLUS HEAD
BRAY HEAD

GREAT BLASKET ISLAND

BRANDON HEAD
Brandon Mountain 953
Cloghane

MAP FORM				
ENGLISH	bay	harbour	head	loch
DEUTSCH	Bucht	harbour, harbour	head	lake; inlet
ESPAÑOL	bahía	Hafen	Landspitze	See; Einfahrt
FRANÇAIS	baie	puerto	promontorio	lago; abra
PORTUGUÊS	baía	porto	promontorio	lac; bras de mer
		porto	promontorio	lago; enseada

mountains, mts.	point	slieve
mountains	point	mountain, mountains
Berge	Landspitze	Berg, Berge
montañas	punta	montaña, montañas
montagnes	pointe	montagne, montagnes
montanhas	ponta	montanha, montanhas

Scale 1:1,000,000

Kilometers
Statute Miles
Km.
Mi.

One centimeter represents 10 kilometers.
One inch represents approximately 16 miles.
Lambert Conformal Conic Projection

EUROPE

Map continues pages 56-57

Map continues pages 52-53

Map continues pages 42-43

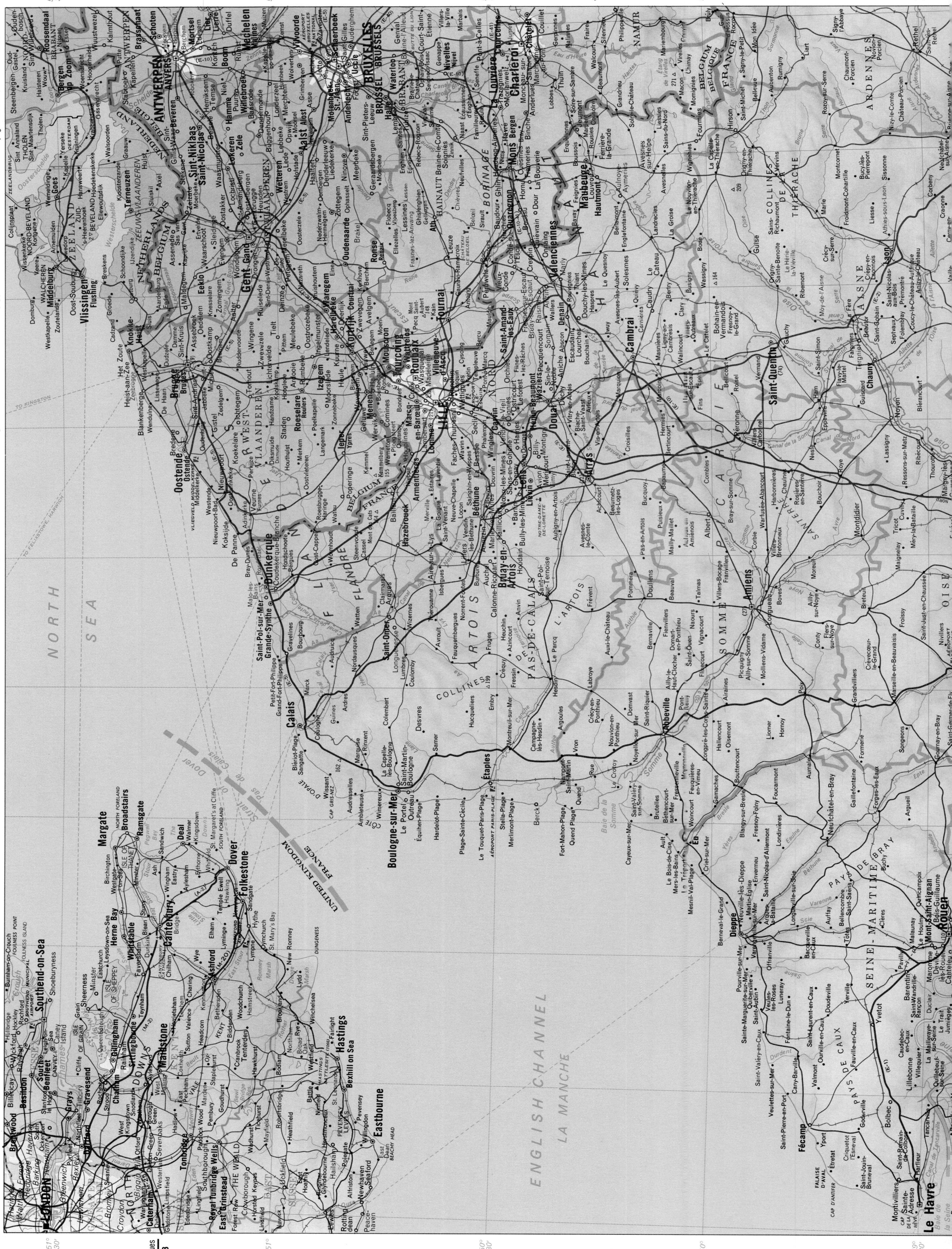

NORTH SEA

ENGLISH CHANNEL · LA MANCHE

Straits of Dover · Pas de Calais

UNITED KINGDOM · FRANCE

NEDERLAND

BELGIË · BELGIQUE · BELGIUM

BELGIË · BELGIQUE

NAMUR

BRABANT

HAINAUT

BORINAGE

FLANDRE

WEST-VLAANDEREN

OOST-VLAANDEREN

ZEELAND

NORD

PAS-DE-CALAIS

ARTOIS

PICARDIE

THIÉRACHE

AISNE

SOMME

OISE

SEINE-MARITIME

PAYS DE CAUX

PAYS DE BRAY

COLLINES DE L'ARTOIS

KENT

THE WEALD

NORTH DOWNS

SOUTH DOWNS

ROMNEY MARSH

ISLE OF SHEPPEY

ISLE OF THANET

Cities and towns:

ANTWERPEN · ANVERS · BRUSSEL · BRUSSELS · BRUXELLES · Gent · Gand · Charleroi · NAMUR · Mons · Bergen · Maubeuge · Valenciennes · Cambrai · Saint-Quentin · LILLE · Roubaix · Tournai · Kortrijk · Courtrai · Roeselare · Brugge · Bruges · Oostende · Ostende · Dunkerque · Calais · Boulogne-sur-Mer · Saint-Omer · Béthune · Lens · Arras · Douai · Amiens · Abbeville · Dieppe · Fécamp · Le Havre · Rouen · Hastings · Eastbourne · Folkestone · Dover · Canterbury · Margate · Ramsgate · Maidstone · Southend-on-Sea · LONDON · Aalst · Alost · Mechelen · Bergen op Zoom · Roosendaal · Vlissingen · Flushing · Middelburg · Goes · Terneuzen · Sint-Niklaas · Saint-Nicolas · Lokeren · Wetteren · Oudenaarde · Ronse · Ninove · Waterloo · Nivelles · La Louvière · Châtelet · Philippeville · Avesnes · Le Cateau · Bapaume · Albert · Doullens · Montreuil-sur-Mer · Étaples · Le Touquet-Paris-Plage · Berck · Eu · Neufchâtel-en-Bray

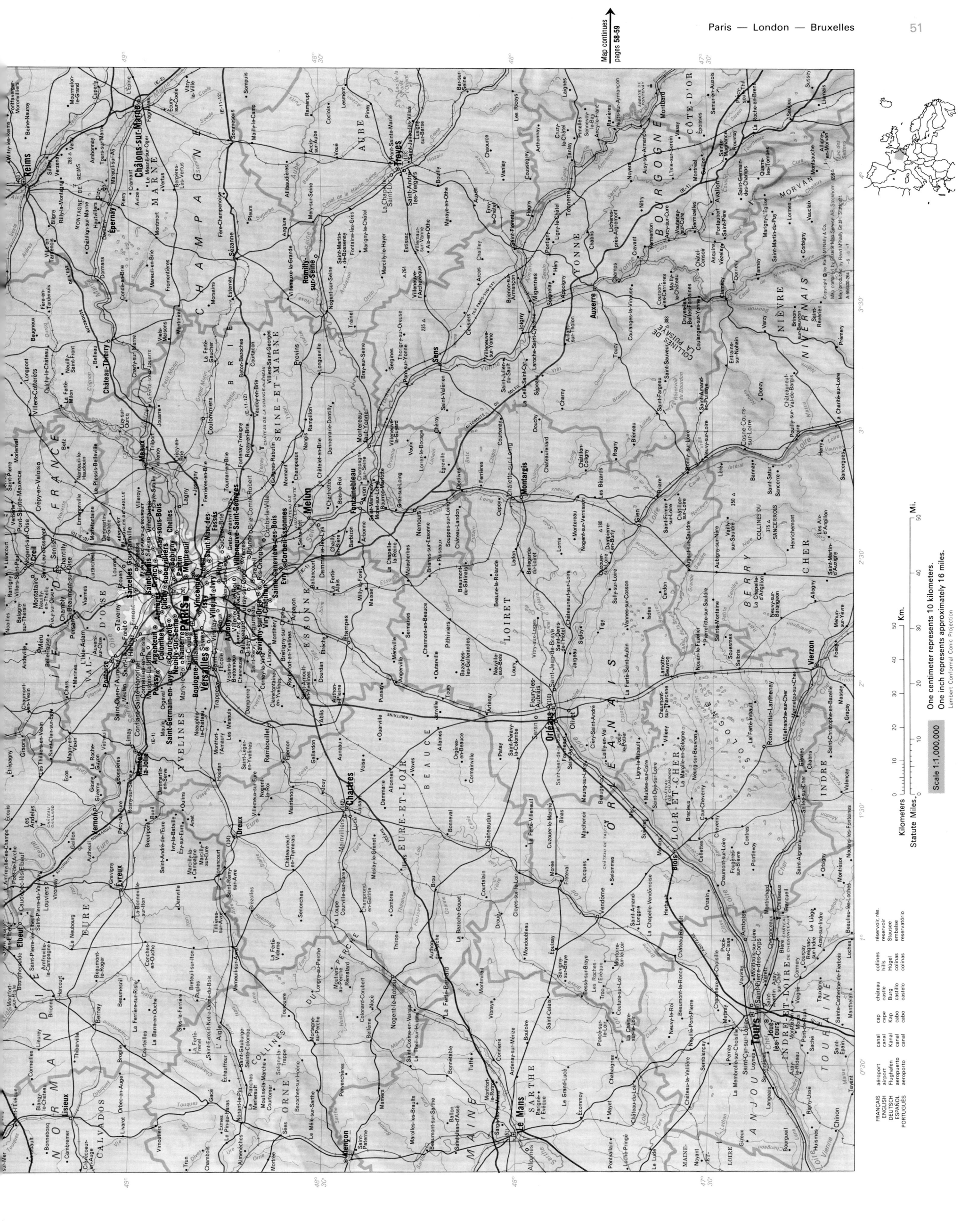

Map continues pages 58-59

One centimeter represents 10 kilometers.
One inch represents approximately 16 miles.
Lambert Conformal Conic Projection

Scale 1:1,000,000

Kilometers 0 10 20 30 40 50 Km.
Statute Miles 0 10 20 30 Mi.
FRANÇAIS	aéroport	canal	cap	château	collines	réservoir, rés.
ENGLISH	airport	canal	cape	castle	hills	reservoir
DEUTSCH	Flughafen	Kanal	Kap	Burg	Hügel	Stausee
ESPAÑOL	aeropuerto	canal	cabo	castillo	colinas	embalse
PORTUGUÊS	aeroporto	canal	cabo	castelo	colinas	reservatório

← Map continues pages 50-51

Map continues pages 56-57

DEUTSCH	Gebirge	Kanal	Moor	Naturpark	Stausee	Talsperre	Wald
ENGLISH	range	canal	moor	reserve	reservoir	dam	forest, mountains
ESPAÑOL	sierra	canal	páramo	reserva	reservoir	presa	bosque, montañas
FRANÇAIS	chaîne	canal	lande	réserve	réservoir	barrage	forêt, montagnes
PORTUGUÊS	serra	canal	pântano	reserva natural	reservatório	represa	floresta, montanhas

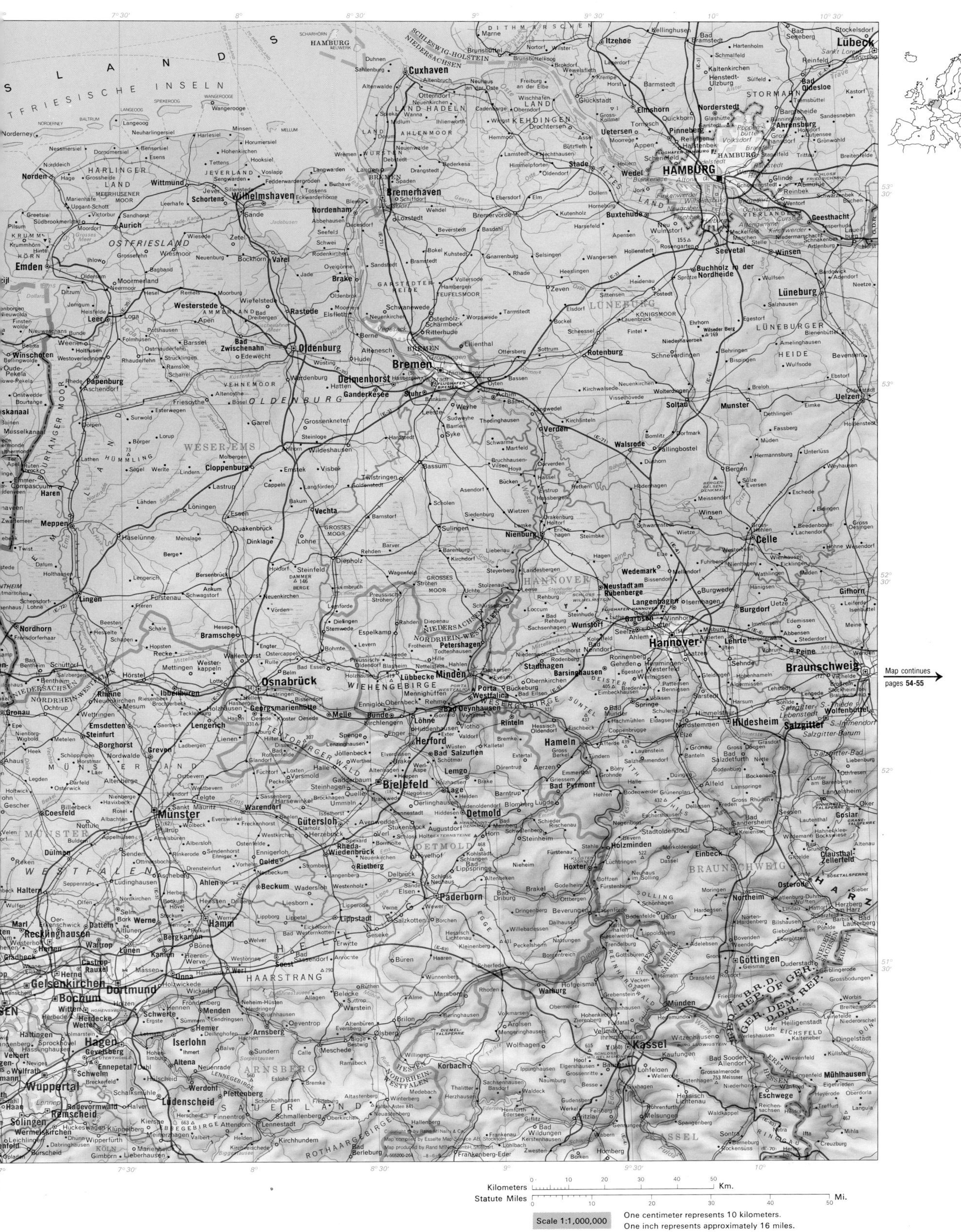

Map continues
pages 54-55 →

Kilometers 0 10 20 30 40 50 Km.
Statute Miles 0 10 20 30 40 50 Mi.

Scale 1:1,000,000

One centimeter represents 10 kilometers.
One inch represents approximately 16 miles.
Lambert Conformal Conic Projection

BALTIC SEA
Pomeranian Bay
Mecklenburger Bucht
Kieler Bucht
Rostock
Stralsund
Greifswald
Wismar
Schwerin
Güstrow
Neubrandenburg
Neustrelitz
Szczecin (Stettin)
Lübeck
Kiel
HAMBURG
Lüneburg
Uelzen
Salzwedel
Stendal
Wittenberge
Brandenburg
Potsdam
BERLIN (WEST)
Frankfurt
Fürstenwalde
Wolfsburg
MECKLENBURG
VORPOMMERN
UCKERMARK
PRIGNITZ
ALTMARK
HAVELLAND
BARNIM
WENDLAND
GER. DEM. REP.
FED. REP. OF GER.
POLAND

Map continues page 41

Map continues pages 52-53

Map continues
page 60

Map continues
pages 56-57

Scale 1:1,000,000

One centimeter represents 10 kilometers.
One inch represents approximately 16 miles.
Lambert Conformal Conic Projection

Kilometers
Statute Miles

DEUTSCH	Berg, Bg.	Boden	Bucht	Gebirge	Heide	Kanal	See
ENGLISH	mountain	mountain	bay	range	heath	canal	lake
ESPAÑOL	montaña	bajo	bahía	sierra	matorral	canal	lago
FRANÇAIS	montagne	baie	baie	chaîne	lande	canal	lac
PORTUGUÊS	montanha	baixo	baía	serra	charneca	canal	lago

Talsperre
dam
presa
barrage
represa

Map continues pages 52-53

Map continues pages 50-51

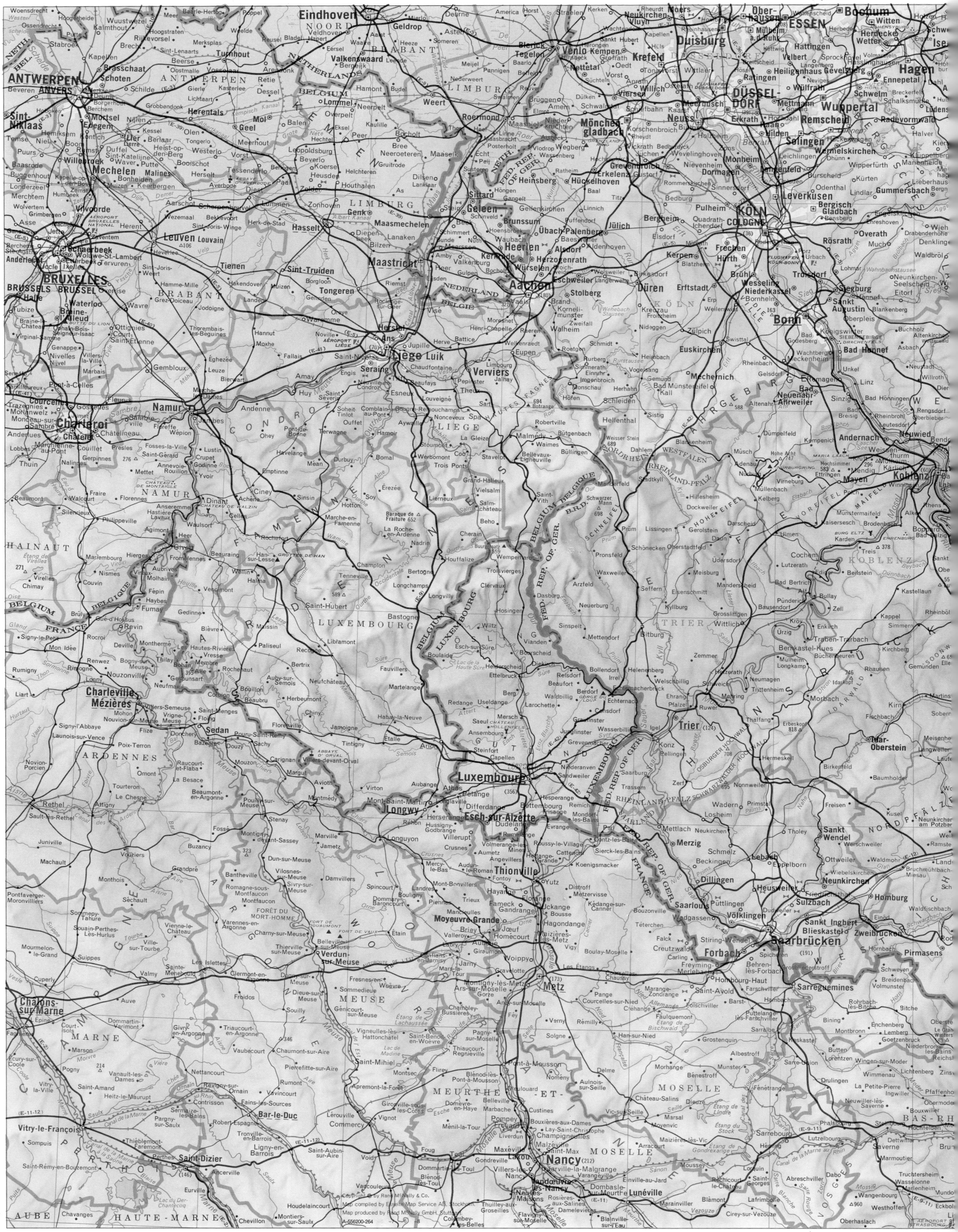

Map continues pages 58-59

MAP FORM	aéroport	Berg	canal	château	étang	Gebirge	Naturpark	Stausee
ENGLISH	airport	mountain	canal	castle	pond	range	reserve	reservoir
DEUTSCH	Flughafen	Berg	Kanal	Burg	Teich	Gebirge	Naturpark	Stausee
ESPAÑOL	aeropuerto	montaña	canal	castillo	charca	cordillera	reserva	embalse
FRANÇAIS	aéroport	montagne	canal	château	étang	chaine	réservoir	réservoir
PORTUGUÊS	aeroporto	montanha	canal	castelo	lagoa	cordilheira	reserva	reservatório

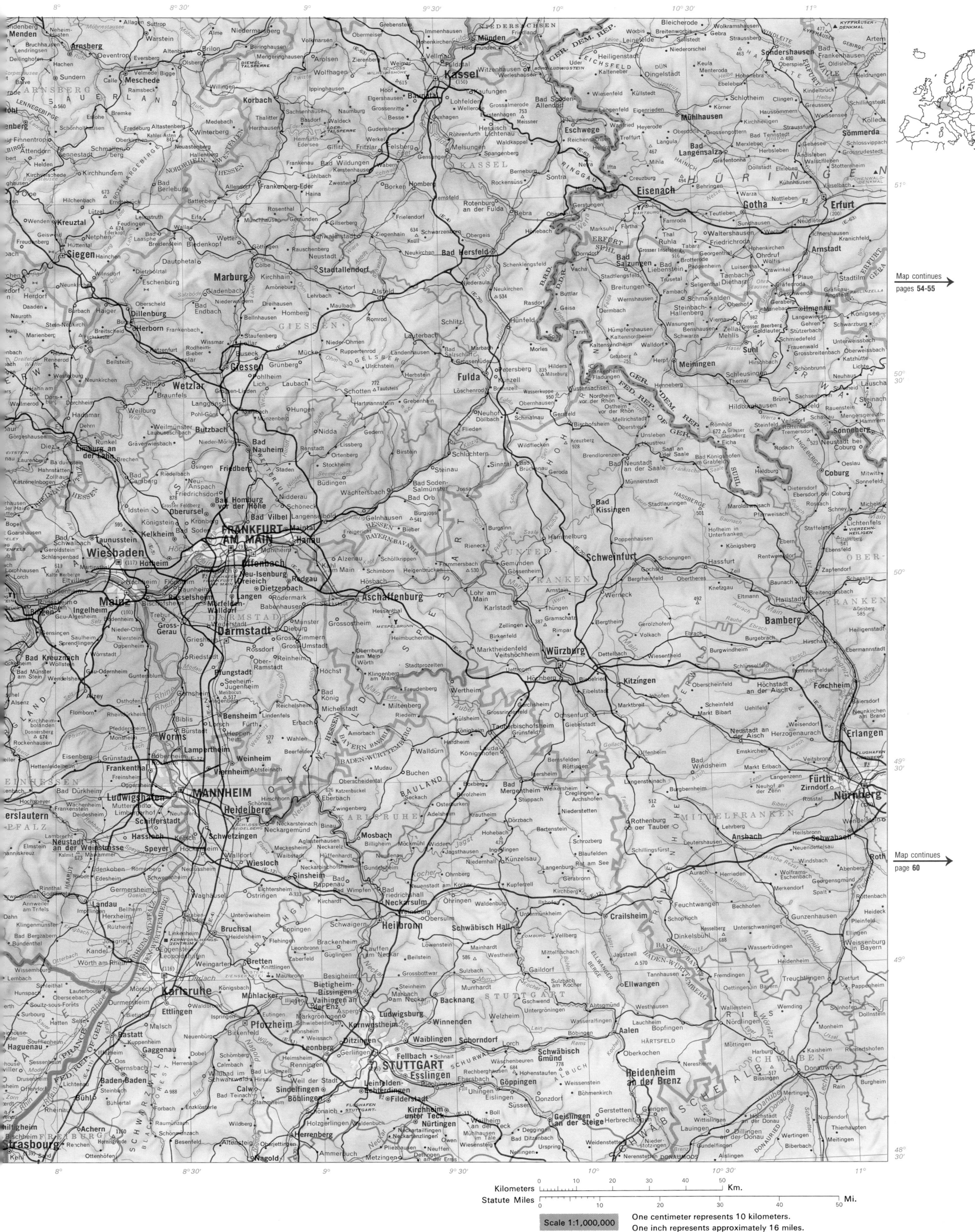

Map continues
pages 54-55 →

Map continues
page 60 →

Kilometers |||||||||| 0 10 20 30 40 50 — Km.

Statute Miles 0 10 20 30 40 50 Mi.

Scale 1:1,000,000

One centimeter represents 10 kilometers.
One inch represents approximately 16 miles.

Lambert Conformal Conic Projection

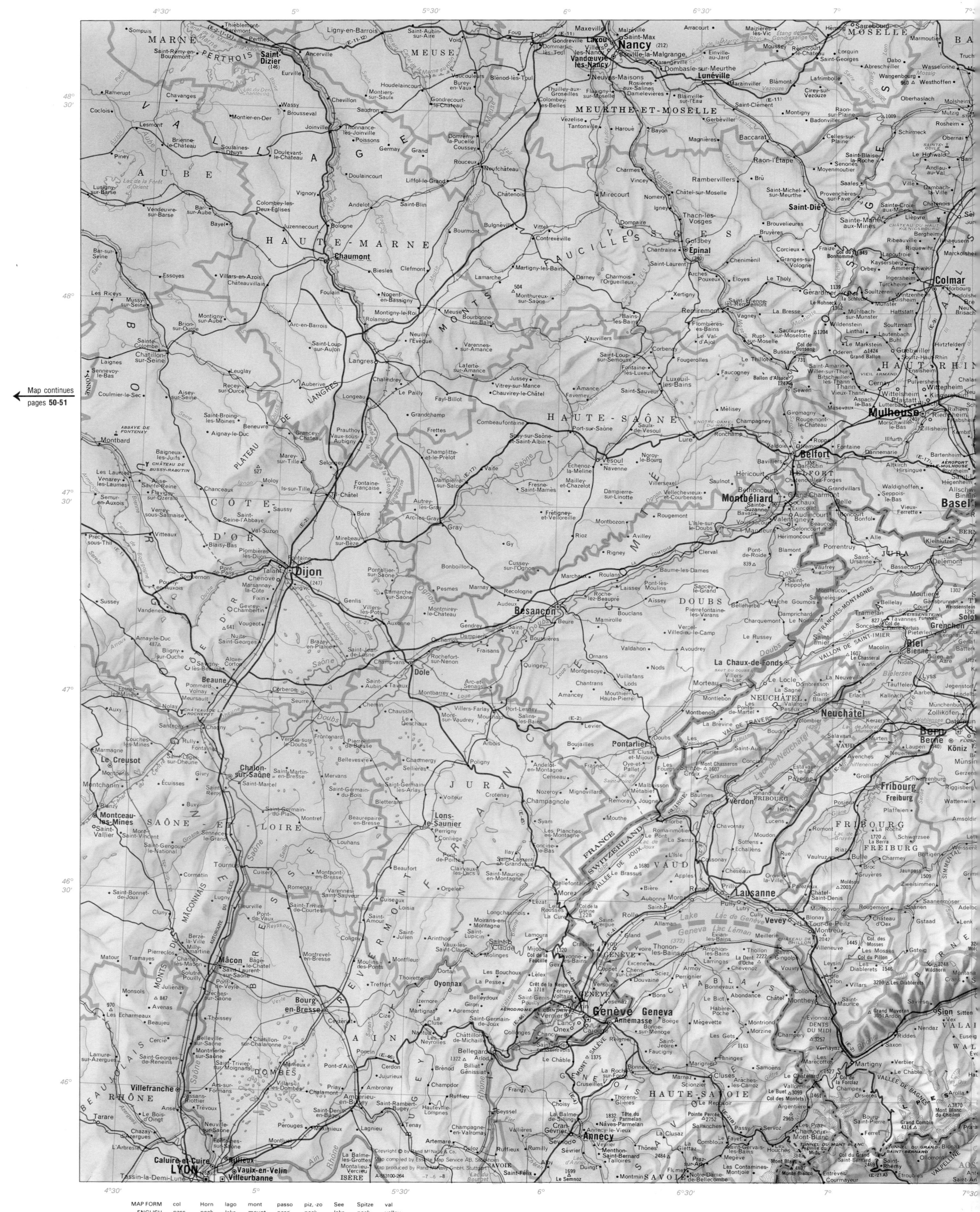

◄ Map continues
pages 50-51

MAP FORM	col	Horn	lago	mont	passo	piz, -zo	See	Spitze	val
ENGLISH	pass	peak	lake	mount	pass	peak	See	peak	valley
DEUTSCH	Pass	Horn	See	Berg	Pass	Gipfel	See	Spitze	Tal
ESPAÑOL	paso	pico	lago	monte	paso	pico	lago	pico	valle
FRANÇAIS	col	cime	lac	mont	col	cime	lac	cime	val
PORTUGUÊS	passo	pico	lago	monte	passo	pico	lago	pico	vale

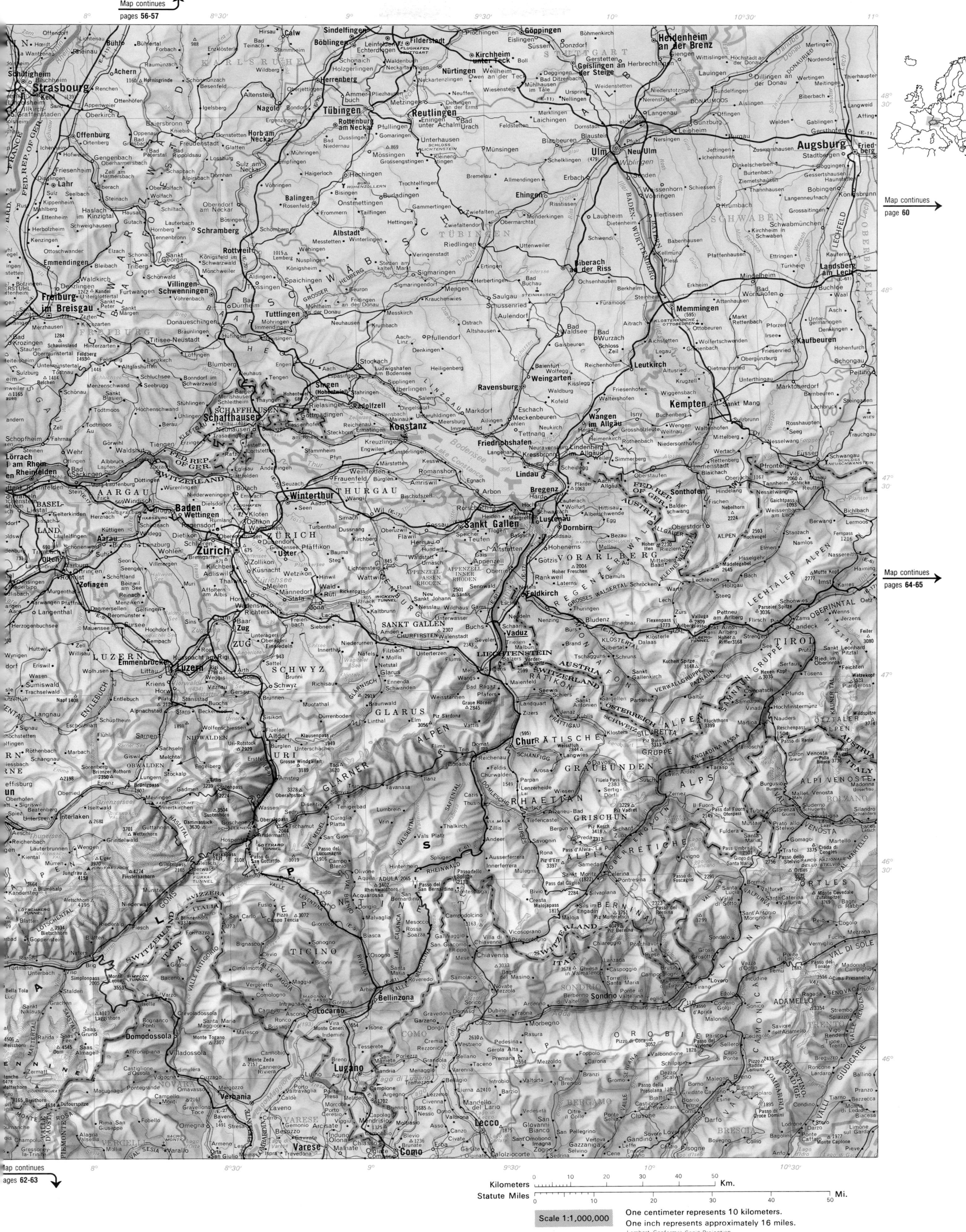

Map continues
pages 56-57

Map continues
page 60

Map continues
pages 64-65

Map continues
pages 62-63

Kilometers

Statute Miles

Scale 1:1,000,000

One centimeter represents 10 kilometers.
One inch represents approximately 16 miles.

Lambert Conformal Conic Projection

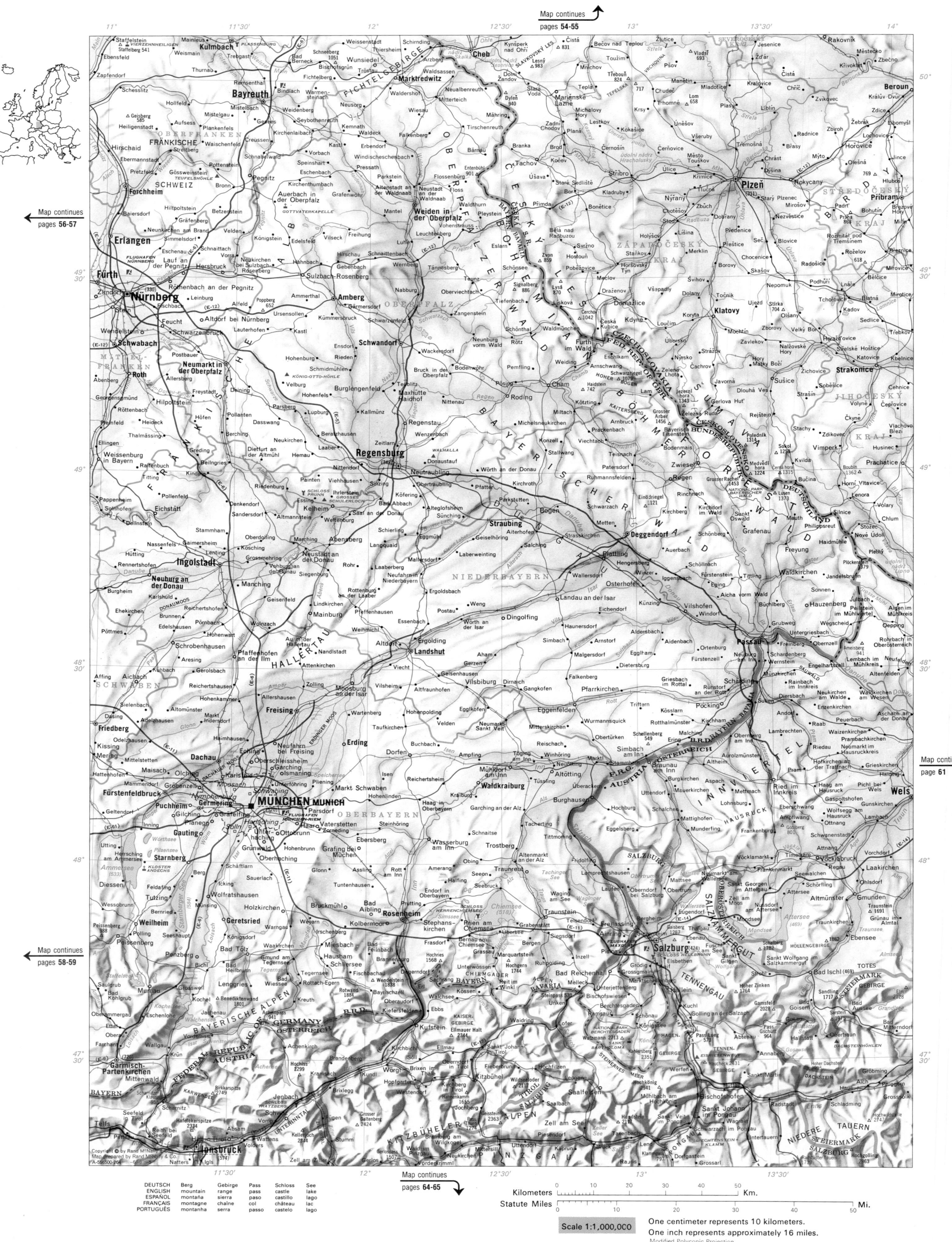

Map continues
pages 54-55

Map continues
pages 56-57

Map continues
page 61

Map continues
pages 58-59

Map continues
pages 64-65

DEUTSCH	Berg	Gebirge	Pass	Schloss	See
ENGLISH	mountain	range	pass	castle	lake
ESPAÑOL	montaña	sierra	paso	castillo	lago
FRANÇAIS	montagne	chaîne	col	château	lac
PORTUGUÊS	montanha	serra	passo	castelo	lago

Kilometers

Statute Miles

Scale 1:1,000,000

One centimeter represents 10 kilometers.
One inch represents approximately 16 miles.

Modified Polyconic Projection

DEUTSCH	Alpe, -n	Berg	Gebirge	Sattel	Schloss	Wald
ENGLISH	mountains	mountain	range	saddle	castle	forest; mountains
ESPAÑOL	montañas	montaña	sierra	paso	castillo	bosque; montañas
FRANÇAIS	montagnes	montagne	chaîne	col	château	forêt; montagnes
PORTUGUÊS	montanhas	montanha	serra	passo	castelo	Floresta; montanhas

Kilometers 0 10 20 30 40 50 Km.

Statute Miles 0 10 20 30 40 50 Mi.

Scale 1:1,000,000
One centimeter represents 10 kilometers.
One inch represents approximately 16 miles.
Lambert Conformal Conic Projection

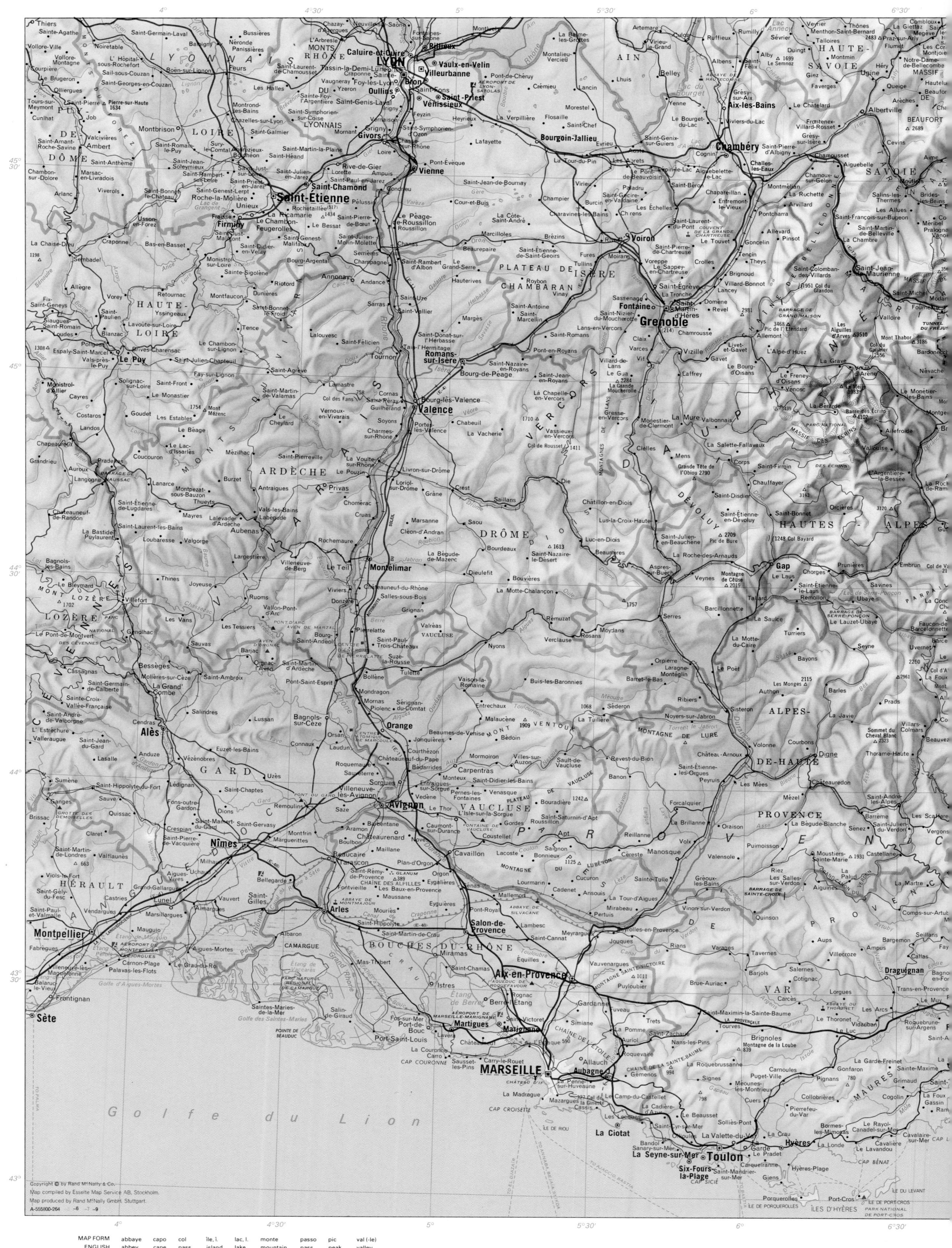

MAP FORM	abbaye	capo	col	île, l.	lac, l.	monte	passo	pic	val (-le)
ENGLISH	abbey	cape	pass	island	lake	mountain	pass	peak	valley
DEUTSCH	Abtei	Kap	Pass	Insel	See	Berg	Pass	Gipfel	Tal
ESPAÑOL	abadía	cabo	paso	isla	lago	montaña	paso	valle	
FRANÇAIS	abbaye	cap	col	île	lac	montagne	col	cime	val
PORTUGUÊS	abadia	cabo	passo	ilha	lago	montanha	passo	pico	vale

Map continues pages 58-59

Map continues pages 64-65

Golfo di Genova

L i g u r i a n   S e a

Mar Ligure

M E D I T E R R A N E A N   S E A

Kilometers
Statute Miles

Scale 1:1,000,000   One centimeter represents 10 kilometers.
One inch represents approximately 16 miles.
Lambert Conformal Conic Projection

Map continues
page 61

Map continues
page 60

Map continues
pages 58-59

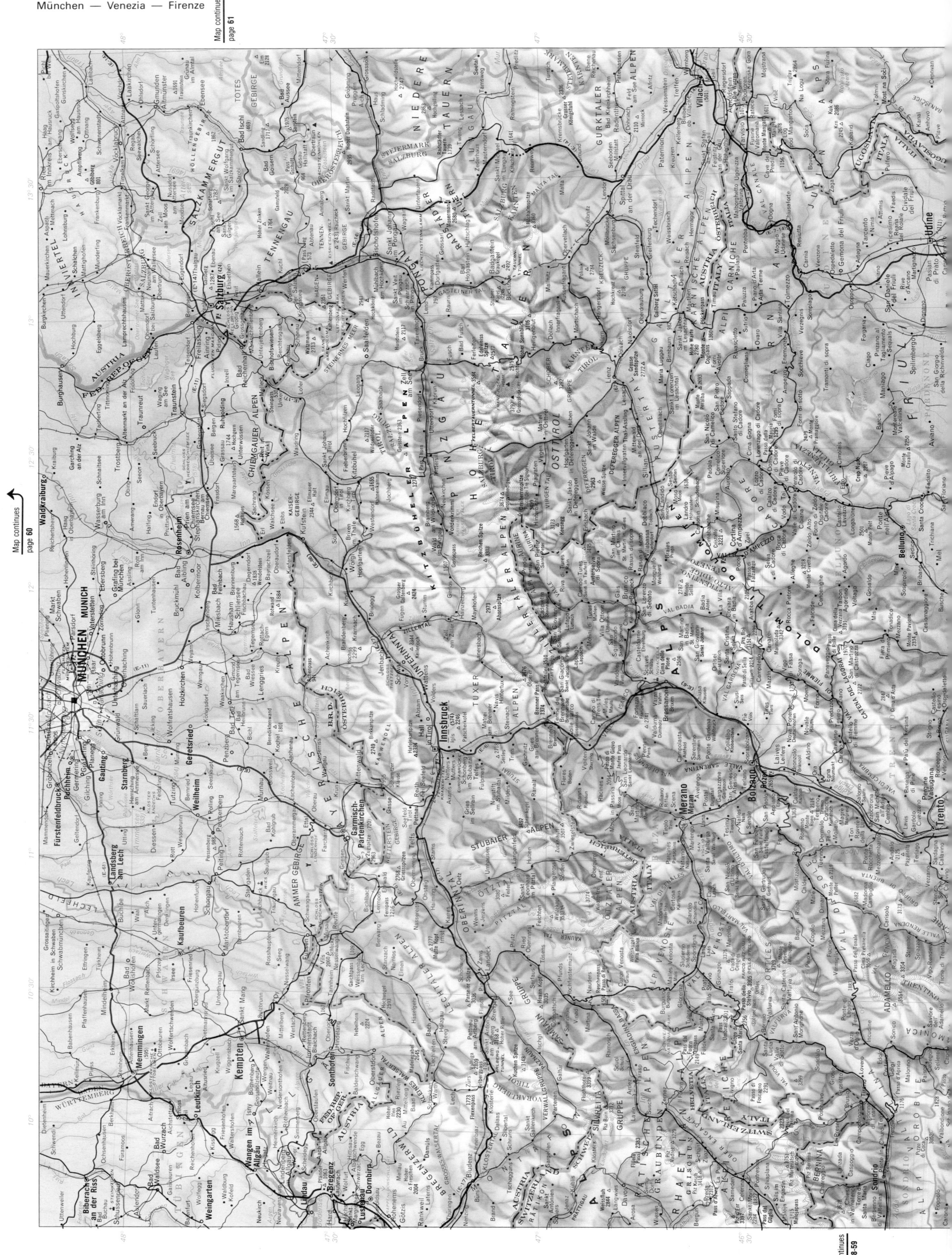

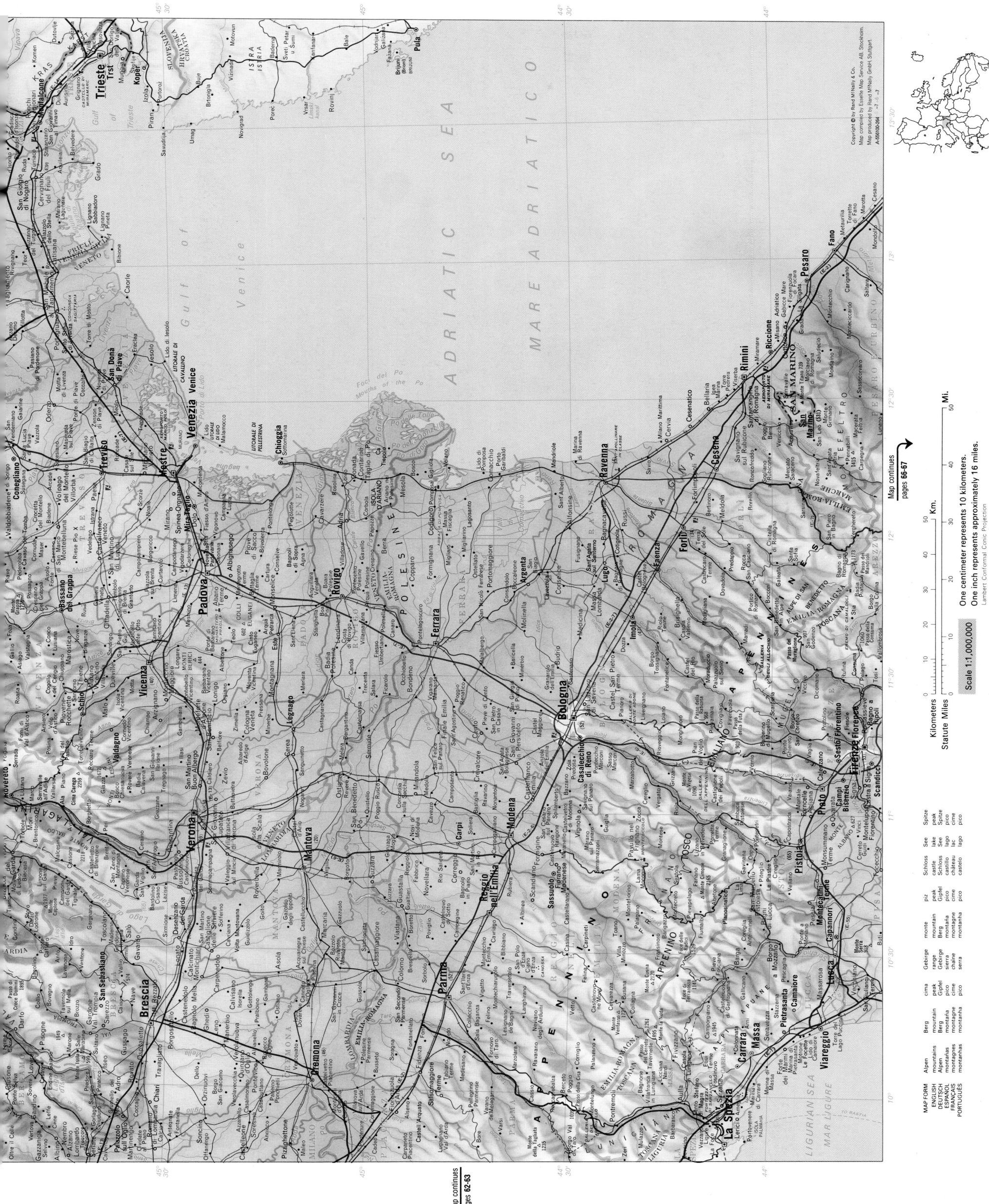

Map continues
pages 66-67

Map continues
pages 62-63

Scale 1:1,000,000

One centimeter represents 10 kilometers.
One inch represents approximately 16 miles.

Lambert Conformal Conic Projection

Kilometers

Statute Miles

MAP FORM							
ENGLISH	Alpen	Berg	cima	monte	Gebirge	piz	Schloss	See	Spitze
DEUTSCH	mountains	mountain	peak	mountain	range	peak	castle	lake	peak
ESPAÑOL	Alpen	Berg	Gipfel	mountain	Berg	Gipfel	Schloss	See	Spitze
FRANÇAIS	montañas	montaña	pico	montaña	sierra	pico	castillo	lago	pico
PORTUGUÊS	montanhas	montagne	cime	montagne	chaîne	cime	château	lac	cime
	montanhas	montanha	pico	montanha	serra	pico	castelo	lago	pico

Copyright © by Rand McNally & Co.
Map compiled by Esselte Map Service AB, Stockholm.
Map produced by Rand McNally GmbH, Stuttgart.
A-586100-264 -7 -7 -7

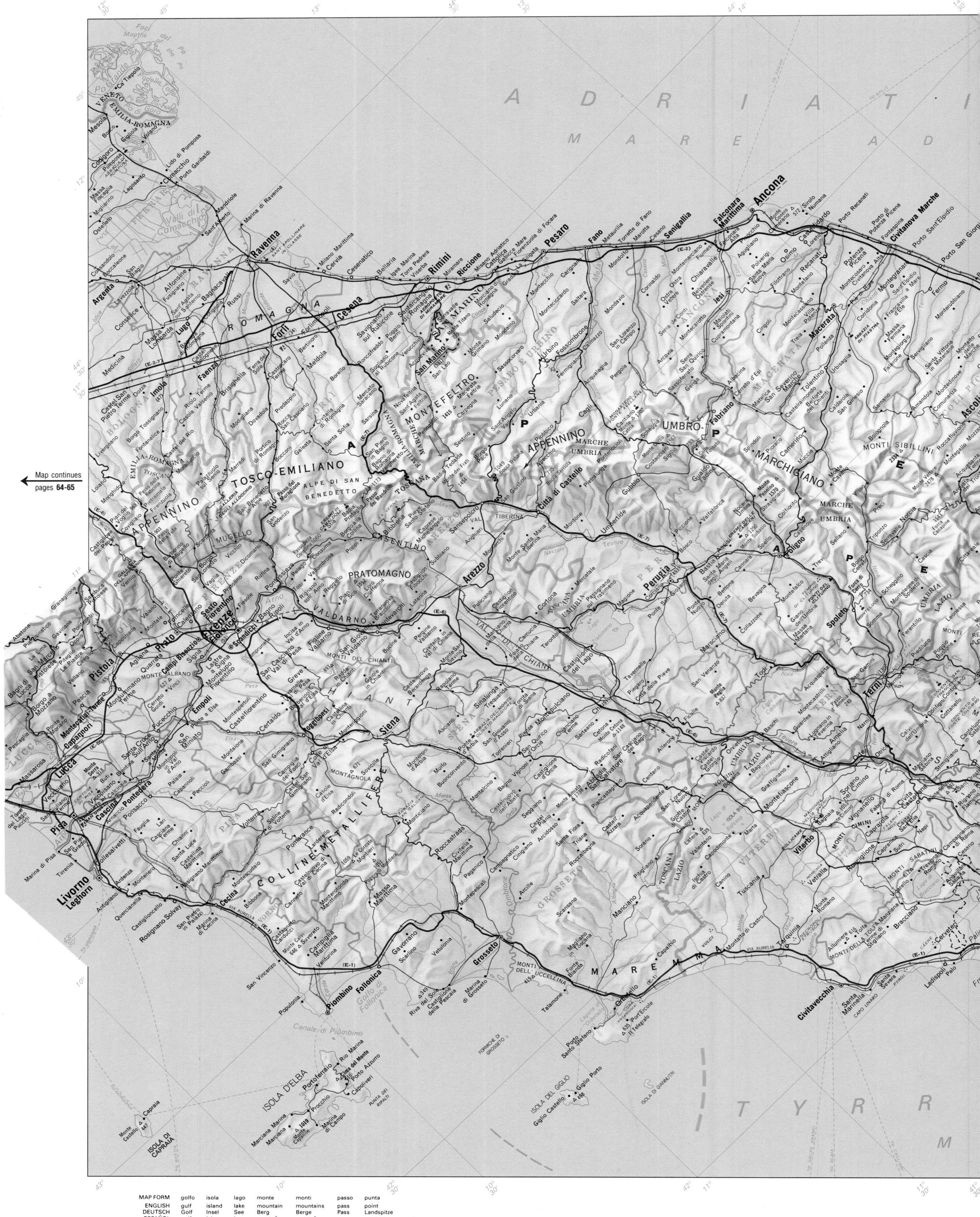

← Map continues
pages 64-65

MAP FORM	golfo	isola	lago	monte	monti	passo	punta
ENGLISH	gulf	island	lake	mountain	mountains	pass	point
DEUTSCH	Golf	Insel	See	Berg	Berge	Pass	Landspitze
ESPAÑOL	golfo	isla	lago	montaña	montañas	paso	punta
FRANÇAIS	golfe	île	lac	montagne	montagnes	col	pointe
PORTUGUÊS	golfo	ilha	lago	montanha	montanhas	passo	ponta

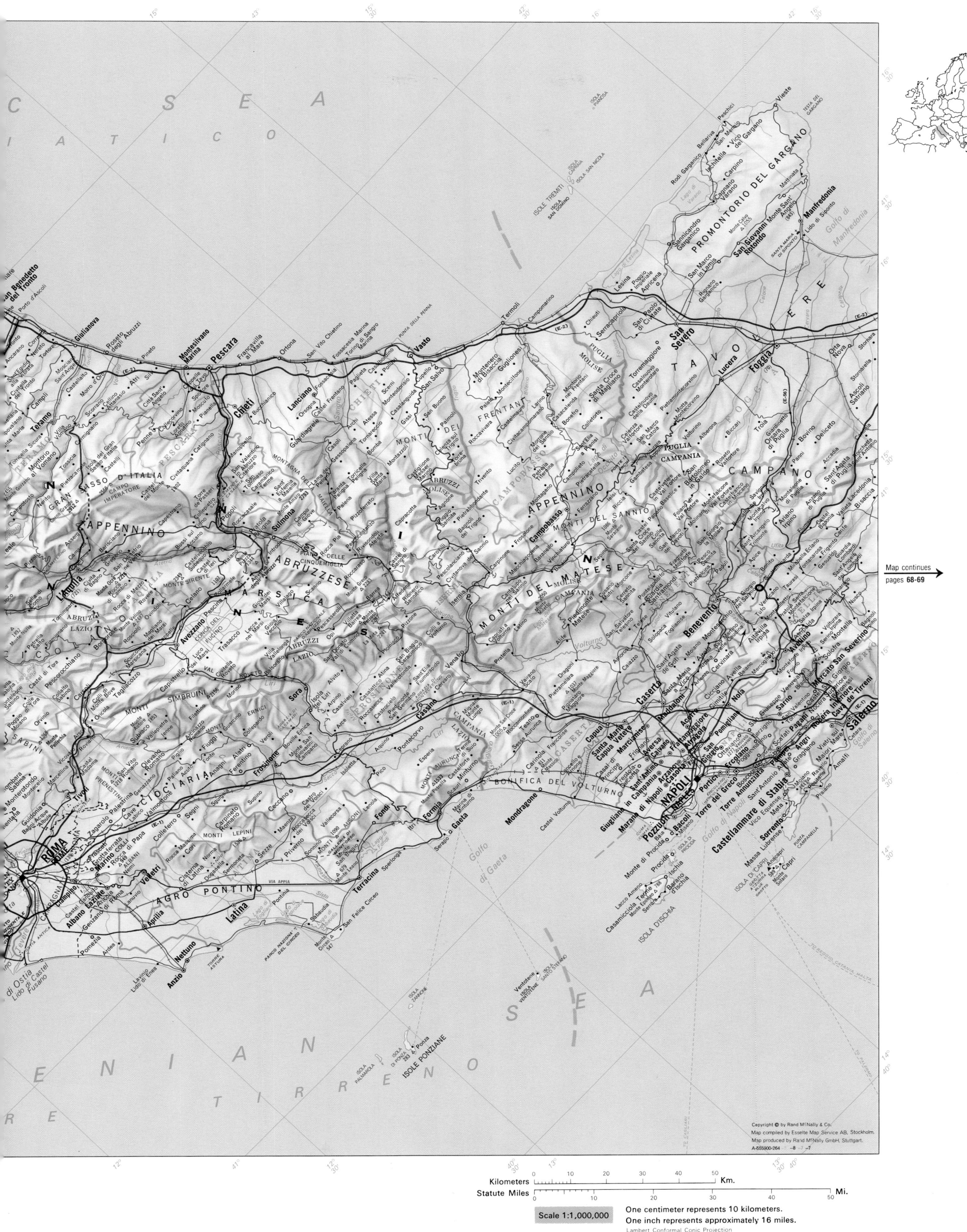

Map continues
pages 68-69 →

Kilometers
Statute Miles

Scale 1:1,000,000

One centimeter represents 10 kilometers.
One inch represents approximately 16 miles.
Lambert Conformal Conic Projection

Map continues pages 66-67

MAP FORM	capo	golfo	isola	lago	monte	monti	punta
ENGLISH	cape	gulf	island	lake	mountain	mountains	point
DEUTSCH	Kap	Golf	Insel	See	Berg	Berge	Landspitze
ESPAÑOL	cabo	golfo	isla	lago	montaña	montañas	punta
FRANÇAIS	cap	golfe	île	lac	montagne	montagnes	pointe
PORTUGUÉS	cabo	golfo	ilha	lago	montanha	montanhas	ponta

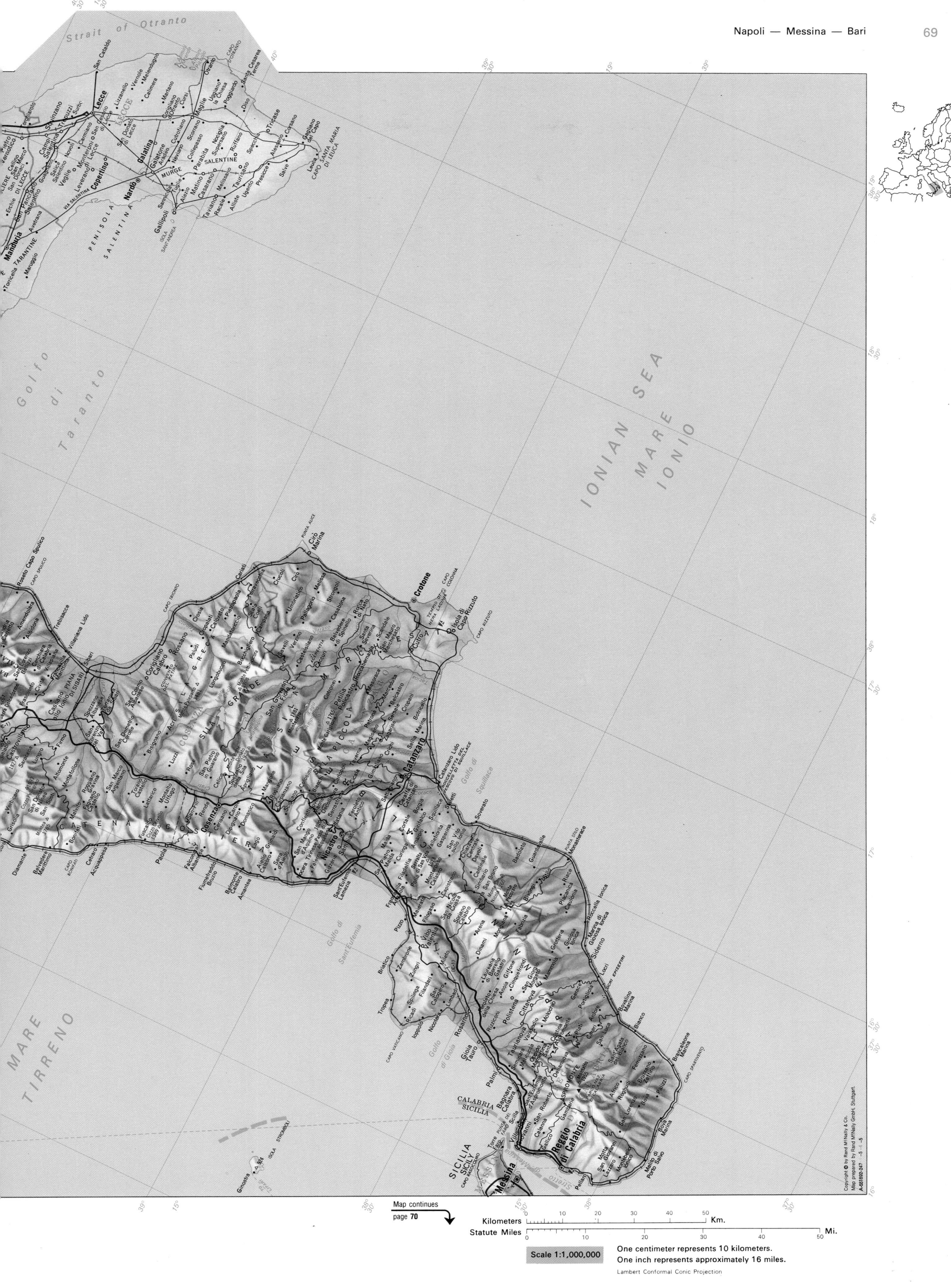

Map continues
page **70**

Kilometers
Statute Miles

Scale 1:1,000,000

One centimeter represents 10 kilometers.
One inch represents approximately 16 miles.

Lambert Conformal Conic Projection

Map continues pages 68-69

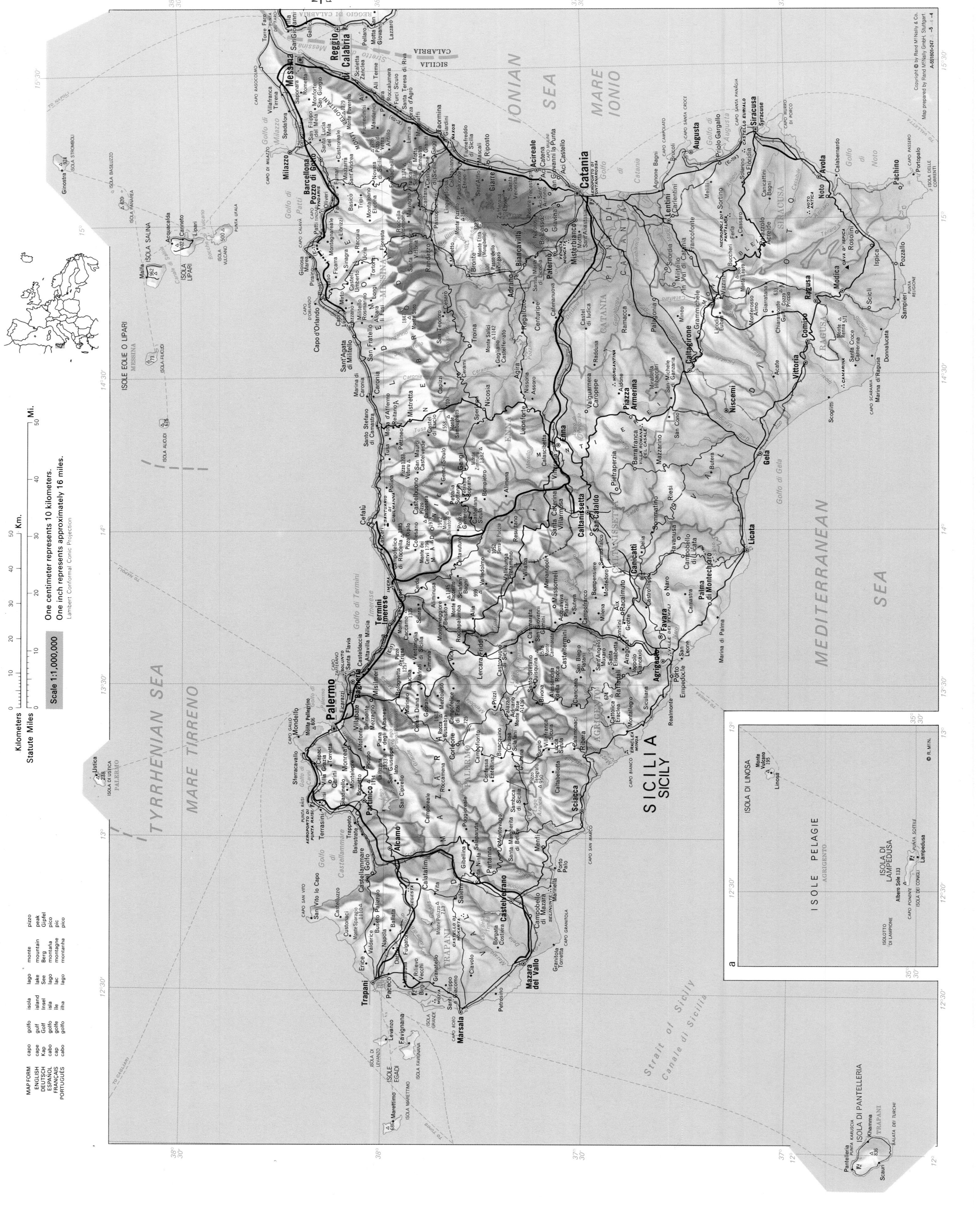

Kilometers

Mi.

Km.

Statute Miles

One centimeter represents 10 kilometers.
One inch represents approximately 16 miles.

Lambert Conformal Conic Projection

Scale 1:1,000,000

MAP FORM				
ENGLISH	cape	gulf	island	lake
DEUTSCH	Kap	Golf	Insel	See
ESPAÑOL	cabo	golfo	isla	lago
FRANÇAIS	cap	golfe	île	lac
PORTUGUÊS	cabo	golfo	ilha	lago

monte	pizzo
mountain	peak
Berg	Gipfel
montaña	pico
montagne	pic
montanha	pico

TYRRHENIAN SEA

MARE TIRRENO

IONIAN SEA

MARE IONIO

MEDITERRANEAN SEA

Strait of Sicily

Canale di Sicilia

ISOLE EOLIE O LIPARI

ISOLE PELAGIE

SICILIA SICILY

Palermo

Catania

Messina

Reggio di Calabria

Siracusa

Marsala

Mazara del Vallo

Trapani

Agrigento

ISOLA DI PANTELLERIA

ISOLA DI LINOSA

ISOLA DI LAMPEDUSA

Copyright © by Rand McNally & Co.

Map prepared by Rand McNally GmbH, Stuttgart

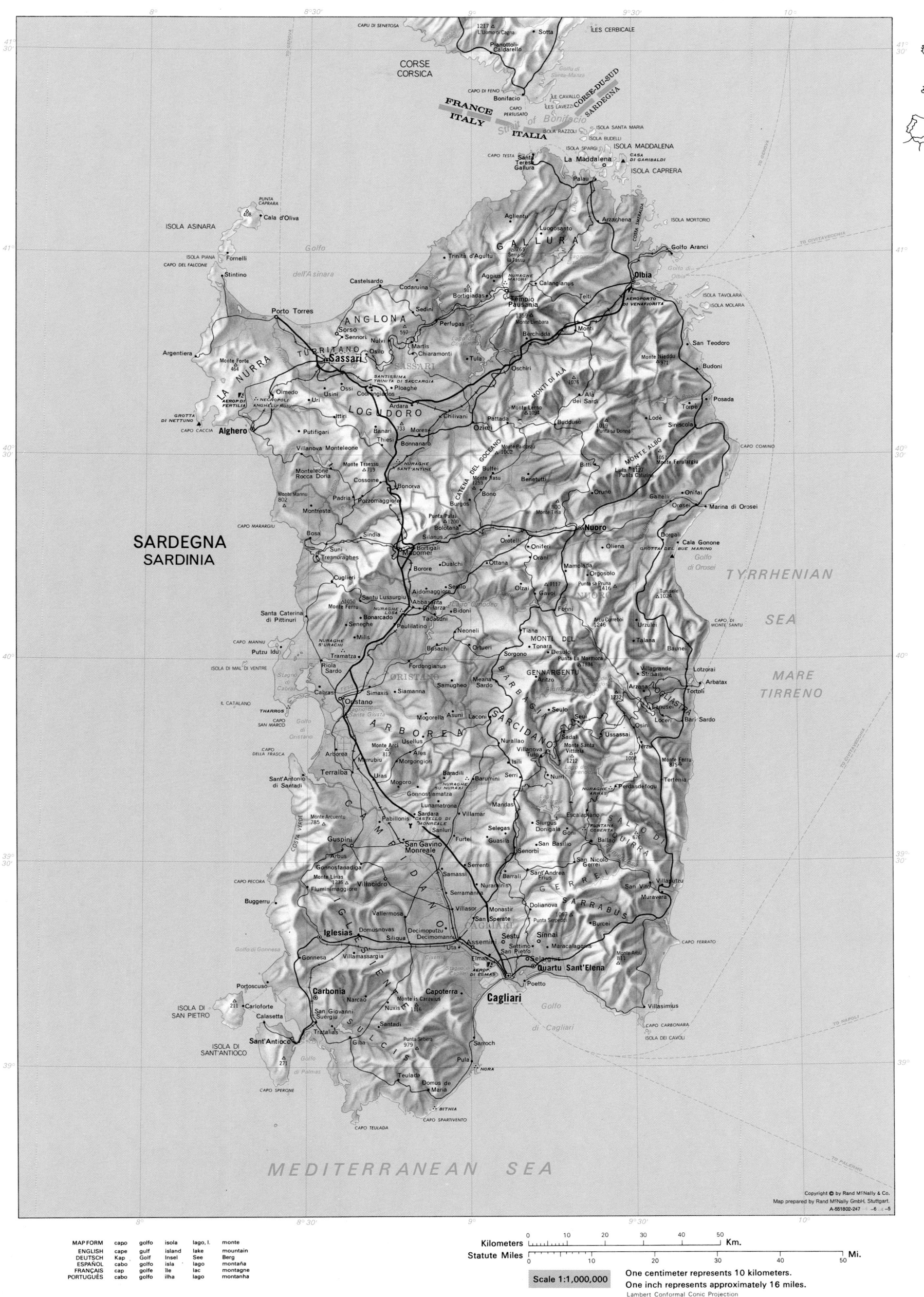

SARDEGNA
SARDINIA

MEDITERRANEAN SEA

TYRRHENIAN
SEA

MARE
TIRRENO

CORSE
CORSICA

FRANCE
ITALY
ITALIA

GALLURA

ANGLONA

LOGUDORO

ARBOREA

GENNARGENTU

BARBAGIA

MONTI DEL
GENNARGENTU

Cagliari

Sassari

Olbia

Alghero

Nuoro

Iglesias

Carbonia

Quartu Sant'Elena

MAP FORM	capo	golfo	isola	lago, l.	monte
ENGLISH	cape	gulf	island	lake	mountain
DEUTSCH	Kap	Golf	Insel	See	Berg
ESPAÑOL	cabo	golfo	isla	lago	montaña
FRANÇAIS	cap	golfe	île	lac	montagne
PORTUGUÉS	cabo	golfo	ilha	lago	montanha

Kilometers ... Km.
Statute Miles ... Mi.
0 10 20 30 40 50

Scale 1:1,000,000

One centimeter represents 10 kilometers.
One inch represents approximately 16 miles.
Lambert Conformal Conic Projection

The annexation of Lithuania, Latvia, and Estonia in 1940 by the Soviet Union has never been officially recognized by the United States government.

In March, 1990 the parliament of Lithuania voted for secession from the Soviet Union.

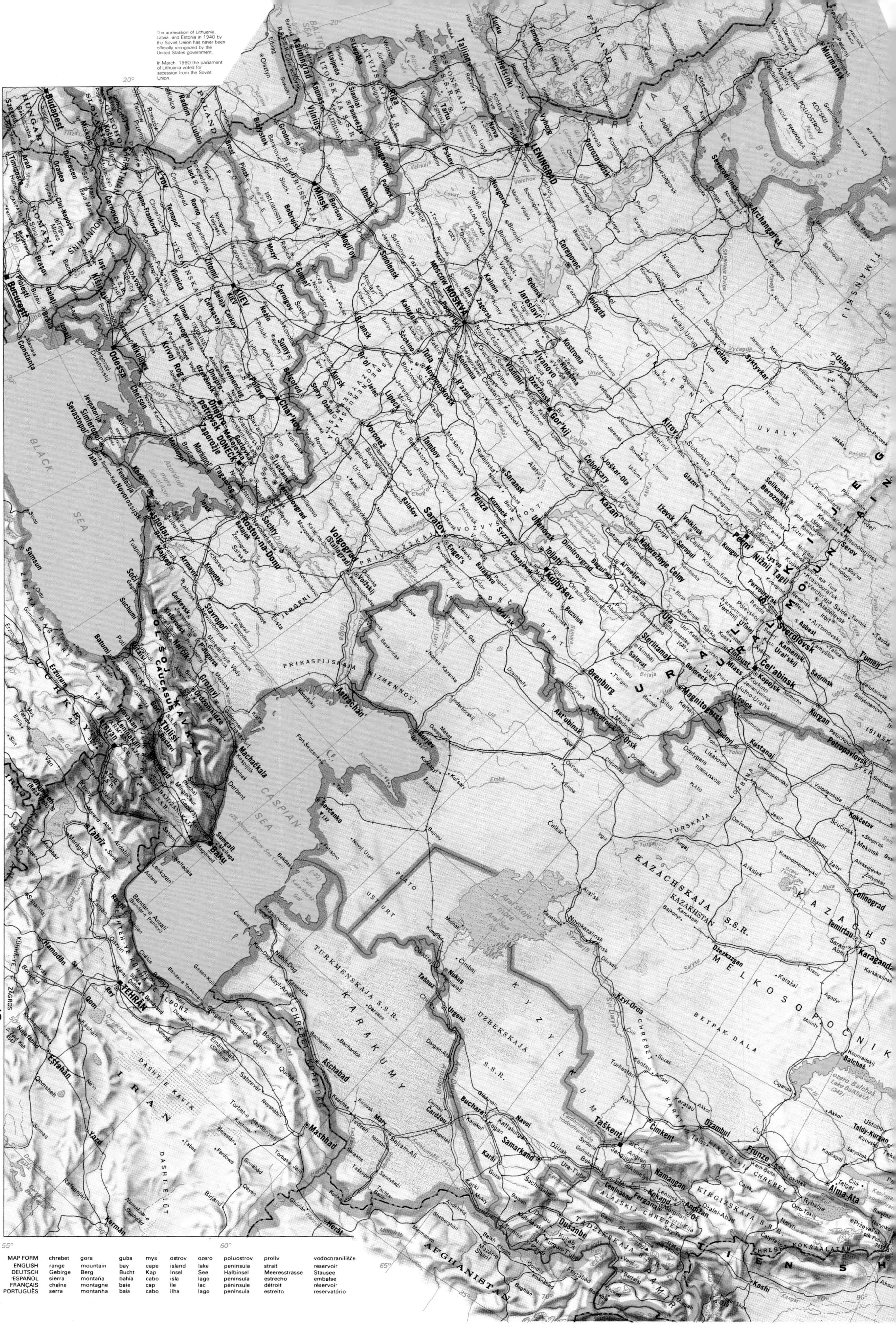

Map continues pages 22-23

Map continues pages 118-119

MAP FORM	chrebet	gora	guba	mys	ostrov	ozero	poluostrov	proliv	vodochranilišče
ENGLISH	range	mountain	bay	cape	island	lake	peninsula	strait	reservoir
DEUTSCH	Gebirge	Berg	Bucht	Kap	Insel	See	Halbinsel	Meeresstrasse	Stausee
ESPAÑOL	sierra	montaña	bahía	cabo	isla	lago	península	estrecho	embalse
FRANÇAIS	chaîne	montagne	baie	cap	île	lac	péninsule	détroit	reservoir
PORTUGUÊS	serra	montanha	baía	cabo	ilha	lago	península	estreito	reservatório

Western and Central Soviet Union / Westliche und zentrale Sowjetunion / Unión Soviética Occidental y Central
Union Soviétique Occidentale et Centrale / União Soviética Ocidental e Central

73

Map continues
pages 74-75

Map continues
pages 90-91

Kilometers 0 200 400 600 Km.
Statute Miles 0 200 400 600 Mi.

Scale 1:12,000,000   One centimeter represents 120 kilometers.
One inch represents approximately 190 miles.
Lambert Conformal Conic Projection

Copyright © by Rand McNally & Co.
Map prepared by Esselte Map Service AB, Stockholm.
A-579594-264   -6 9 -13

Eastern and Central Soviet Union / Östliche und zentrale Sowjetunion / Unión Soviética Oriental y Central
Union Soviétique Orientale et Centrale / União Soviética Oriental e Central

Map continues pages 72-73

Map continues pages 90-91

MAP FORM	chrebet	gora	guba	mys	ostrov	ozero	poluostrov	proliv	vodochranilišče
ENGLISH	range	mountain	bay	cape	island	lake	peninsula	strait	reservoir
DEUTSCH	Gebirge	Berg	Buchf	Kap	Insel	See	Halbinsel	Meeresstrasse	Stausee
ESPAÑOL	sierra	montaña	bahía	cabo	isla	lago	península	estrecho	embalse
FRANÇAIS	chaîne	montagne	baie	cap	île	lac	péninsule	détroit	réservoir
PORTUGUÊS	serra	montanha	baía	cabo	ilha	lago	península	estreito	reservatório

Kilometers

Statute Miles

Scale 1:12,000,000

One centimeter represents 120 kilometers.
One inch represents approximately 190 miles.
Lambert Conformal Conic Projection

Copyright © by Rand McNally & Co.
Map prepared by Esselte Map Service AB, Stockholm.
A-579395-264

ALASKA
UNITED STATES

Chukchi Sea

OSTROV VRANGELA

VOSTOČNO-SIBIRSKOJE MORE
EAST SIBERIAN SEA

Bering Sea

OSTROVA ANŽU
OSTROV ŽOCHOVA
OSTROVA DE-LONGA
OSTROV NOVAJA SIBIR

OSTROV KOTEL'NYJ

KOLYMSKAJA NIZMENNOST'

JUKAGIRSKOJE PLOSKOGORJE

KORJAKSKOJE NAGORJE

SREDINNYJ CHREBET

MOMSKIJ CHREBET

ČERSKOGO

SIBERIA
CHREBET

CHREBET SETTE-DABAN

SUNTAR CHAJATA

Jakutsk

POLUOSTROV KAMČATKA
KAMCHATKA

Magadan

Ochotsk

Petropavlovsk-
Kamčatskij

REPUBLICS

CHREBET DŽUGDŽUR

SEA OF OKHOTSK
OCHOTSKOJE MORE

ALDANSKOJE NAGORJE

STANOVOJ CHREBET

ŠANTARSKIJE OSTROVA

OSTROV SACHALIN
SACHALIN
SAKHALIN

KURIL'SKIJE OSTROVA
KURIL ISLANDS

Komsomol'sk-
na-Amure

BUREINSKIJ CHREBET

Svobodnyj

Belogorsk

Blagoveščensk

Chabarovsk

Užno-Sachalinsk

SICHOTE-ALIN'

DA HINGGAN LING

NEI MONGGOL ZIZHIQU
MONGOLIA

HEILONGJIANG

Beian

Qiqihar Tsitsihar

Yichun

Hegang

Jiamusi

Shuangyashan

MANCHURIA

Harbin

Mudanjiang

Ussurijsk

Art'om

Nachodka

Vladivostok

Asahikawa

Kushiro

Obihiro

HOKKAIDO

Otaru

Sapporo

Muroran

Hakodate

Wakkanai

SEA OF JAPAN

JAPAN

Aomori

Hachinohe

Hirosaki

Akita

Morioka

HONSHŪ

PACIFIC OCEAN

Habomai, Shkotan, Kunashiri, and
Etorofu, occupied by the U.S.S.R.
since 1945, are claimed by Japan
pending a final peace treaty.

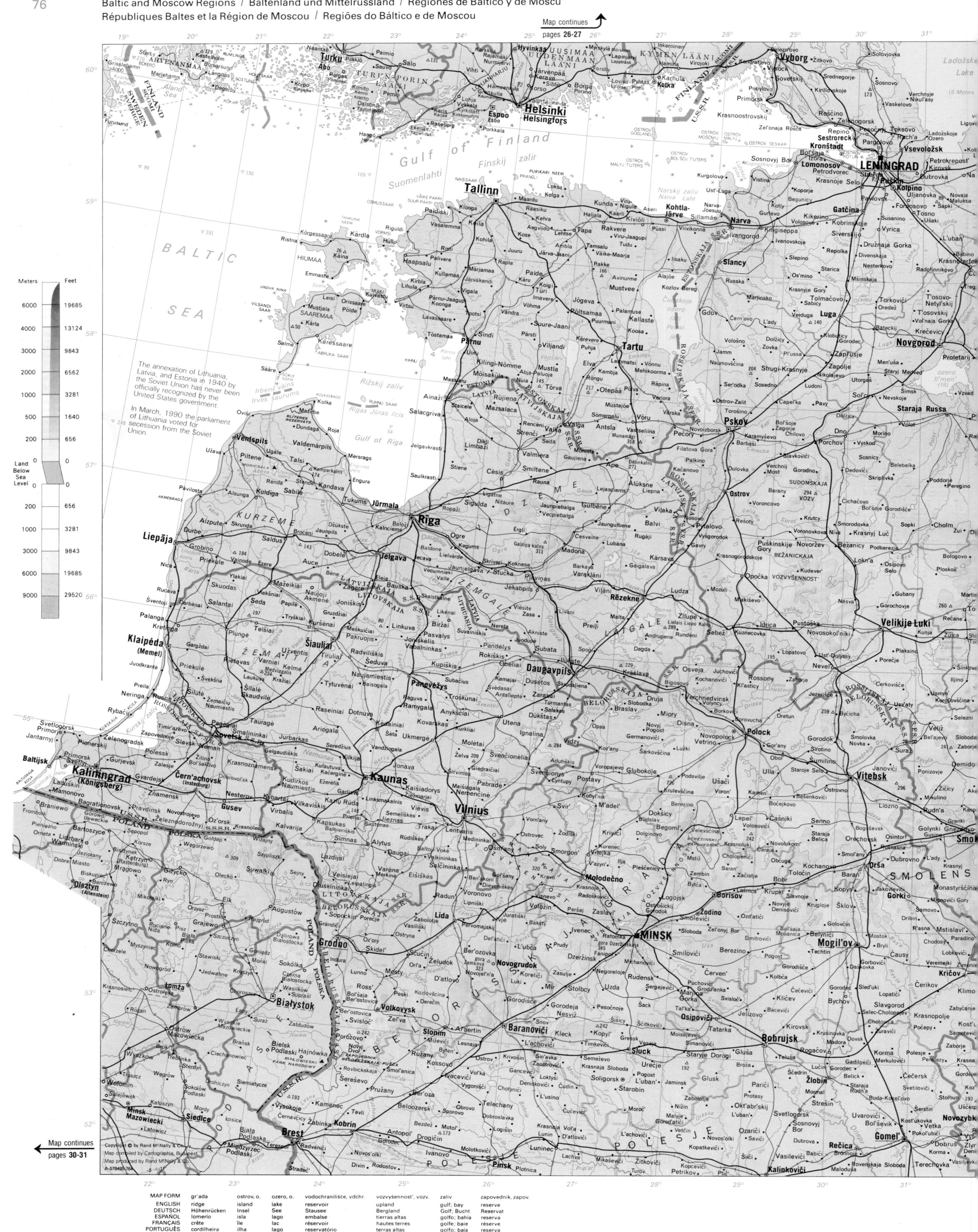

Baltic and Moscow Regions / Baltenland und Mittelrussland / Regiones de Báltico y de Moscú
Républiques Baltes et la Région de Moscou / Regiões do Báltico e de Moscou

Map continues pages 26-27

The annexation of Lithuania, Latvia, and Estonia in 1940 by the Soviet Union has never been officially recognized by the United States government.

In March, 1990 the parliament of Lithuania voted for secession from the Soviet Union.

Meters	Feet
6000	19685
4000	13124
3000	9843
2000	6562
1000	3281
500	1640
200	656
Land Below Sea Level	0
0	0
200	656
1000	3281
3000	9843
6000	19685
9000	29520

Map continues pages 30-31

MAP FORM	gr'ada	ostrov, o.	ozero, o.	vodochranilišče, vdchr.	vozvyšennost', vozv.	zaliv	zapovednik, zapov.
ENGLISH	ridge	island	lake	reservoir	upland	gulf; bay	reserve
DEUTSCH	Höhenrücken	Insel	See	Stausee	Bergland	Golf; Bucht	Reservat
ESPAÑOL	lomerío	isla	lago	embalse	tierras altas	golfo; bahía	reserva
FRANÇAIS	crête	île	lac	réservoir	hautes terres	golfe; baie	réserve
PORTUGUÊS	cordilheira	ilha	lago	reservatório	terras altas	golfo; baía	reserva

Baltic and Moscow Regions / Baltenland und Mittelrussland / Regiones de Báltico y de Moscú
Républiques Baltes et la Région de Moscou / Regiões do Báltico e de Moscou

77

Map continues
pages 24-25

Map continues
pages 80-81

Map continues
pages 78-79

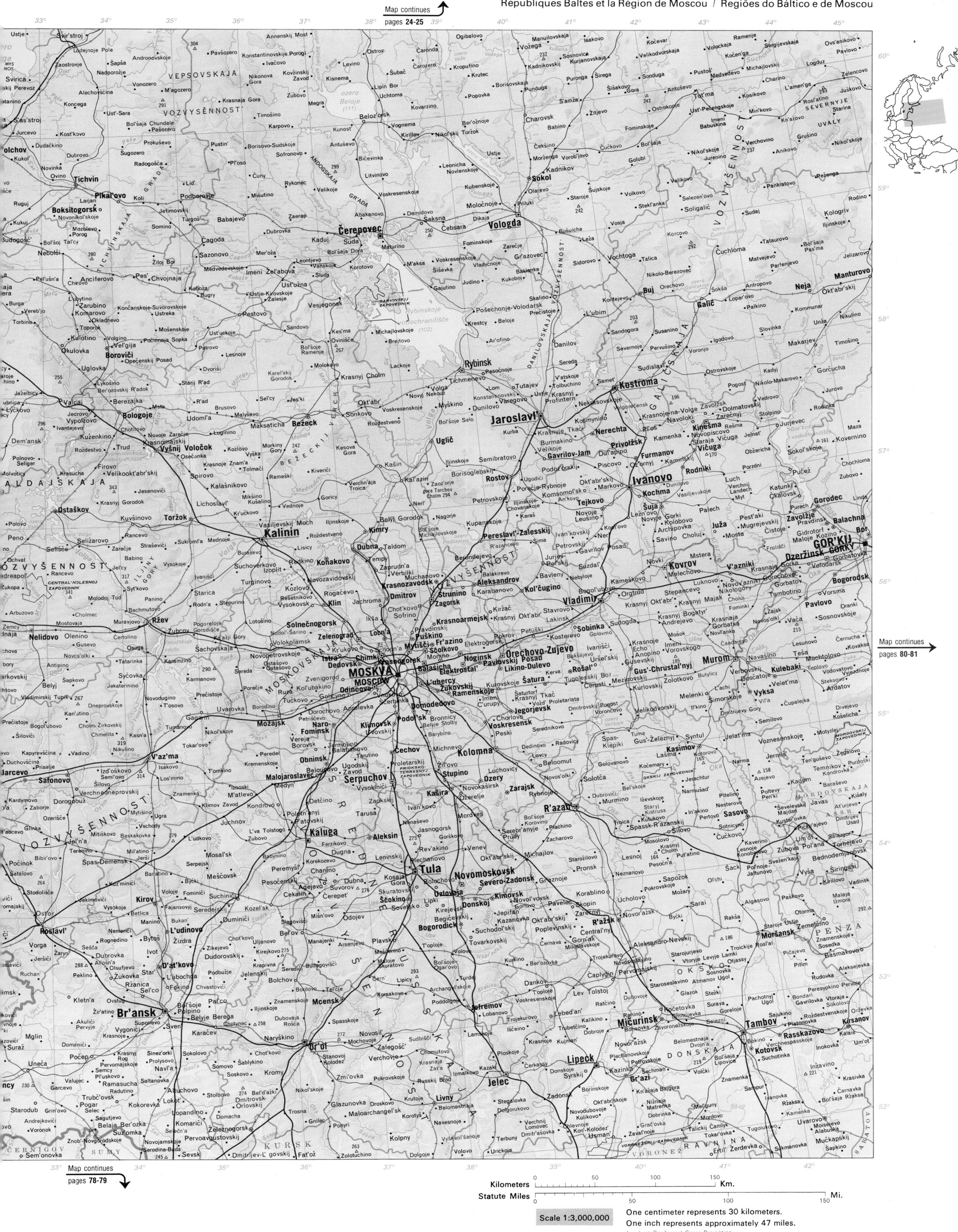

Kilometers
Statute Miles

Scale 1:3,000,000
One centimeter represents 30 kilometers.
One inch represents approximately 47 miles.
Lambert Conformal Conic Projection

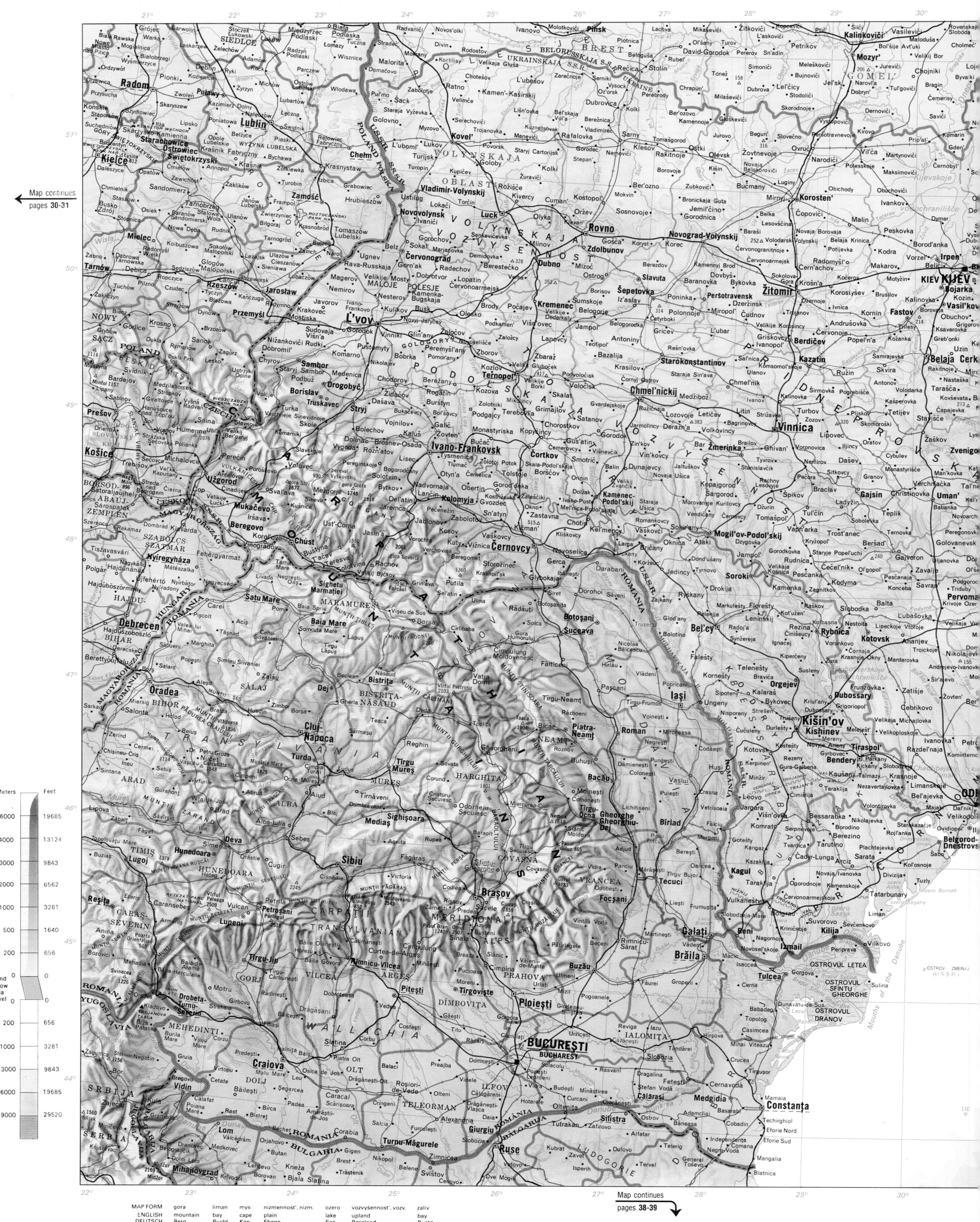

← Map continues
pages 30-31

Meters	Feet
6000	19685
4000	13124
3000	9843
2000	6562
1000	3281
500	1640
200	656
0	0
Land Below Sea Level	
0	0
200	656
1000	3281
3000	9843
6000	19685
9000	29520

MAP FORM	gora	liman	mys	nizmennost', nizm.	ozero	vozvyšennost', vozv.	zaliv
ENGLISH	mountain	bay	cape	plain	lake	upland	bay
DEUTSCH	Berg	Bucht	Kap	Ebene	See	Bergland	Bucht
ESPAÑOL	montaña	bahía	cabo	llano	lago	tierras altas	bahía
FRANÇAIS	montagne	baie	cap	plaine	lac	hautes terres	baie
PORTUGUÊS	montanha	baía	cabo	planície	lago	terras altas	baía

Map continues
pages 38-39 →

Map continues
pages 76-77

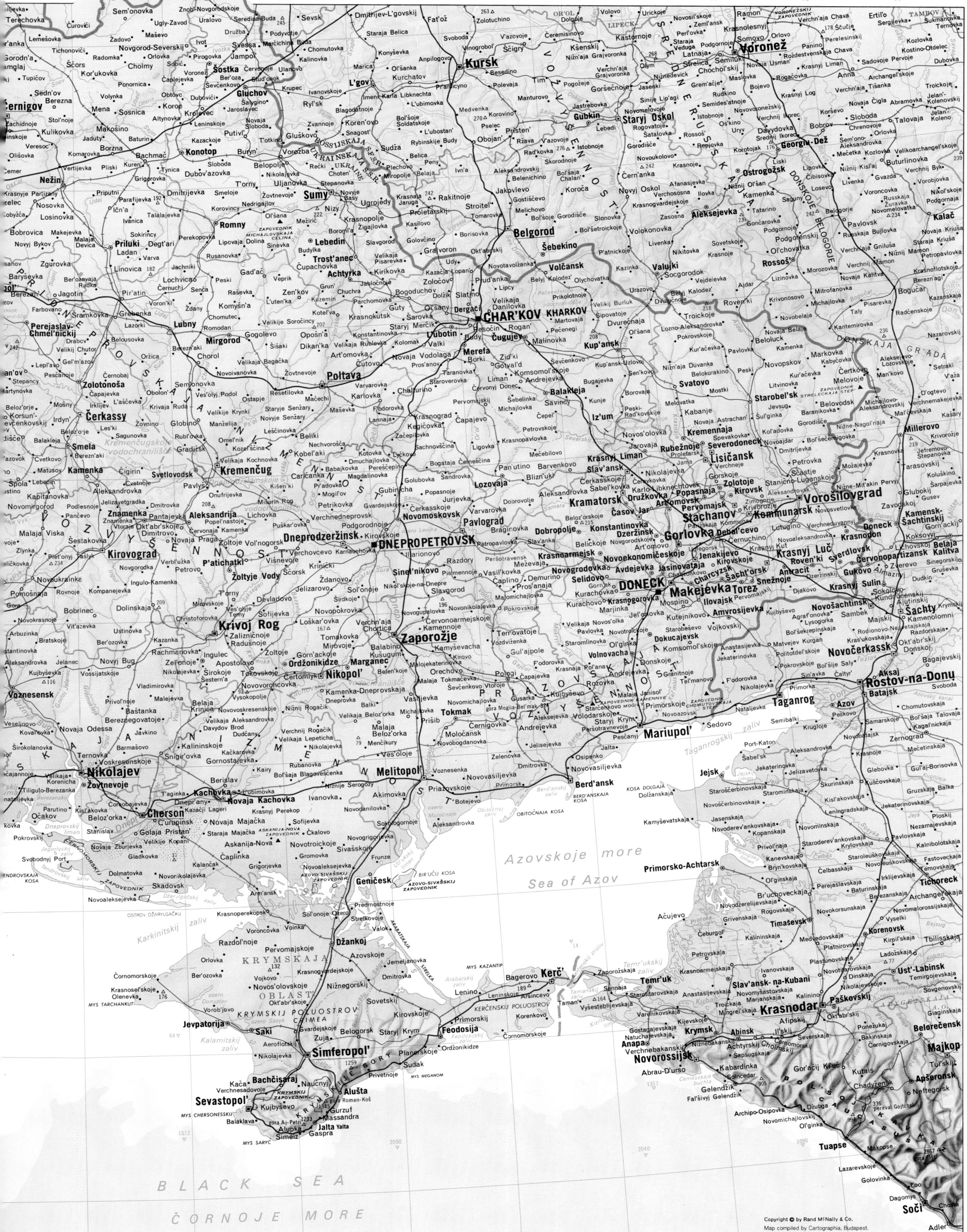

Map continues
pages 80-81

Map continues
page 84

BLACK SEA
ČORNOJE MORE

Azovskoje more
Sea of Azov

CHAR'KOV KHARKOV
DNEPROPETROVSK
DONECK
Kursk
Voronež
Belgorod
Poltava
Zaporožje
Krivoj Rog
Kirovograd
Čerkassy
Kremenčug
Kišinëv
Nikolajev
Cherson
Simferopol'
Sevastopol'
Jalta Yalta
Krasnodar
Novorossijsk
Rostov-na-Donu
Taganrog
Mariupol'
Melitopol'
Kerč'
Vorošilovgrad
Makejevka

Kilometers
Statute Miles

Scale 1:3,000,000

One centimeter represents 30 kilometers.
One inch represents approximately 47 miles.
Lambert Conformal Conic Projection

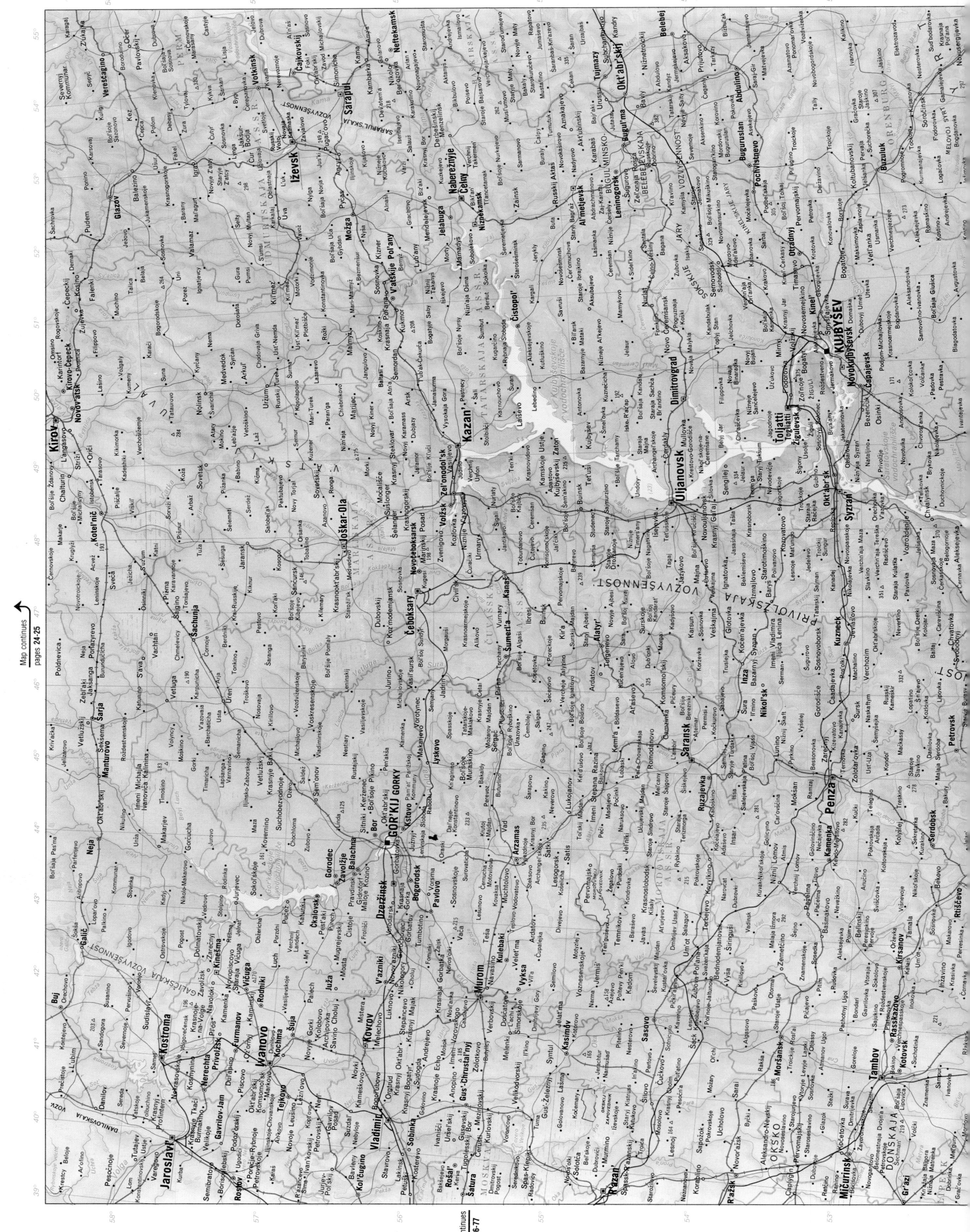

Map continues
pages 24-25

Map continues
pages 76-77

Map continues
pages 86-87

Map continues
pages 78-79

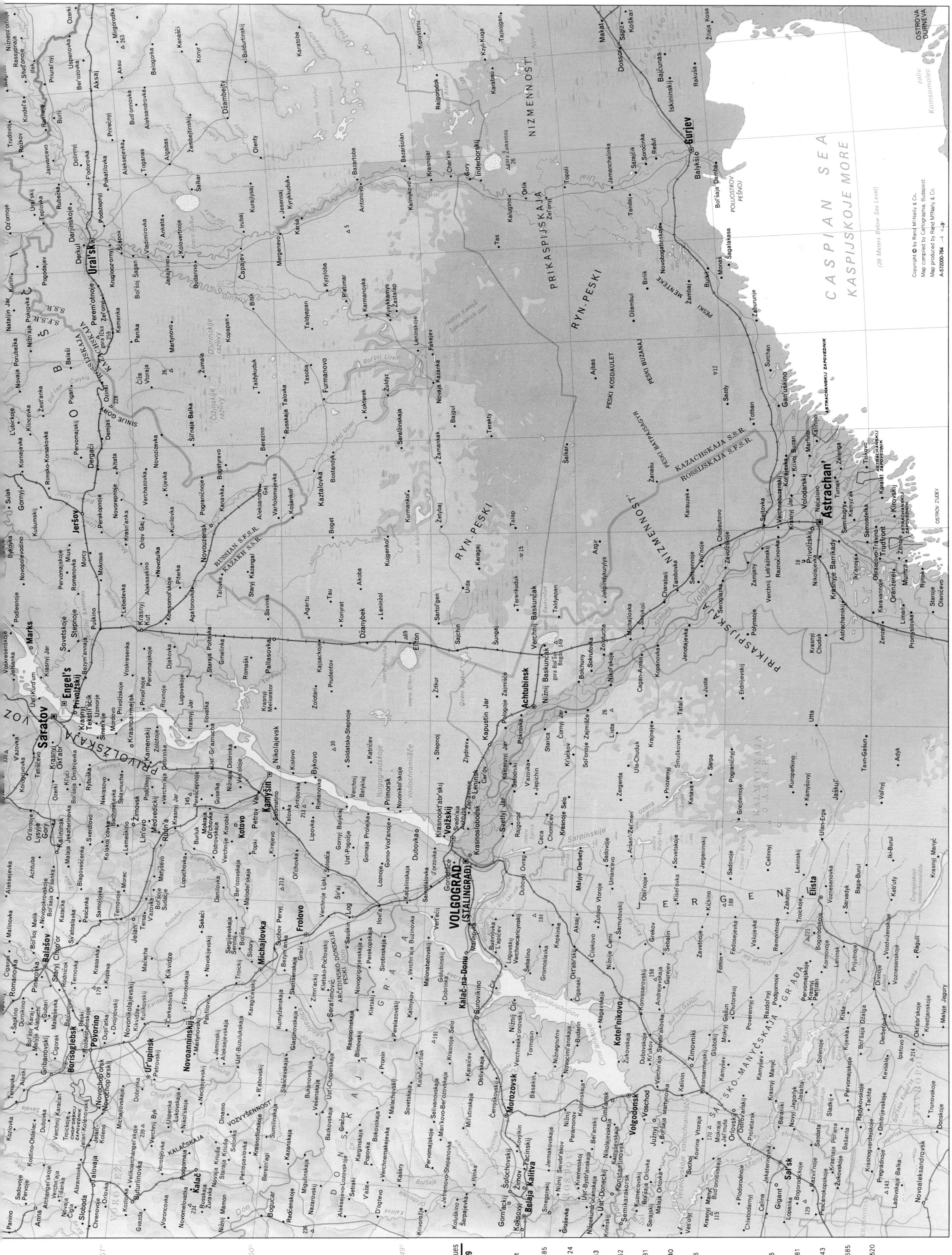

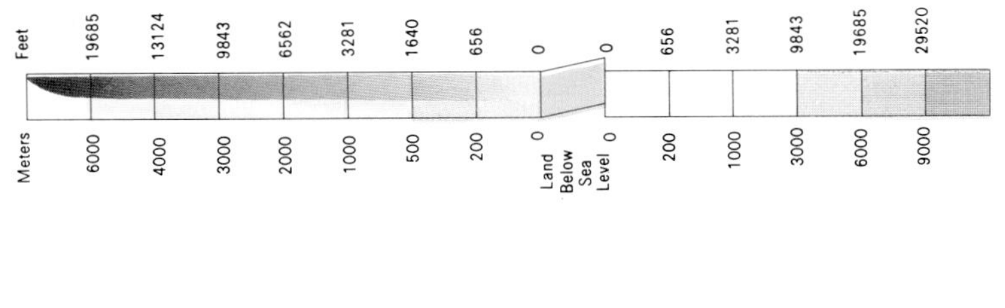

Map continues
page 84

CASPIAN SEA
KASPIJSKOJE MORE
(26 Meters Below Sea Level)

PRIKASPIJSKAJA NIZMENNOST'

RYN-PESKI

PESKI KOSDAULET

KAZACHSKAJA S.S.R.
ROSSIJSKAJA S.F.S.R.

S K O - M A N Y Č S K A J A

G R J A D A

E R G E N I

KALMYCKAJA A.S.S.R.

PRIVOLŽSKAJA VOZVYŠENNOSТЬ

Major cities: Guŕjev, Ural'sk, Saratov, Engel's, Marks, Privolžskij, Kamyšin, Volžskij, VOLGOGRAD (STALINGRAD), Astrachan', Elista, Sal'sk, Kalač-na-Donu, Volgodonsk, Kotel'nikovo, Michajlovka, Frolovo, Novoanninskij, Uŕupinsk, Balašov, Borisoglebsk, Povorino, Bogučar, Kalač, Belaja Kalitva, Morozovsk

Copyright notice:
Copyright © by Rand McNally & Co.
Map compiled by Cartographia, Budapest.
Map produced by Rand McNally & Co.
A-672000-764 —4 —4-gr

Scale 1:3,000,000

One centimeter represents 30 kilometers.
One inch represents approximately 47 miles.
Lambert Conformal Conic Projection

Km.
0   50   100   150

Mi.
0   50   100   150

Kilometers
Statute Miles

MAP FORM						
ENGLISH	gory mountains	ostrov island	ozero lake	peski desert	vodochranilišče reservoir	vozvyšennost' upland	zapovednik reserve
DEUTSCH	Berge	Insel	See	Wüste	Stausee	Bergland	Reservat
ESPAÑOL	montañas	isla	lago	desierto	embalse	tierras altas	reserva
FRANÇAIS	montagnes	île	lac	désert	réservoir	hautes terres	réserve
PORTUGUÊS	montanhas	ilha	lago	deserto	reservatório	terras altas	reserva

Elevation legend:

Feet	Meters
19685	6000
13124	4000
9843	3000
6562	2000
3281	1000
1640	500
656	200
0	Land Below Sea Level
656	200
3281	1000
9843	3000
19685	6000
29520	9000

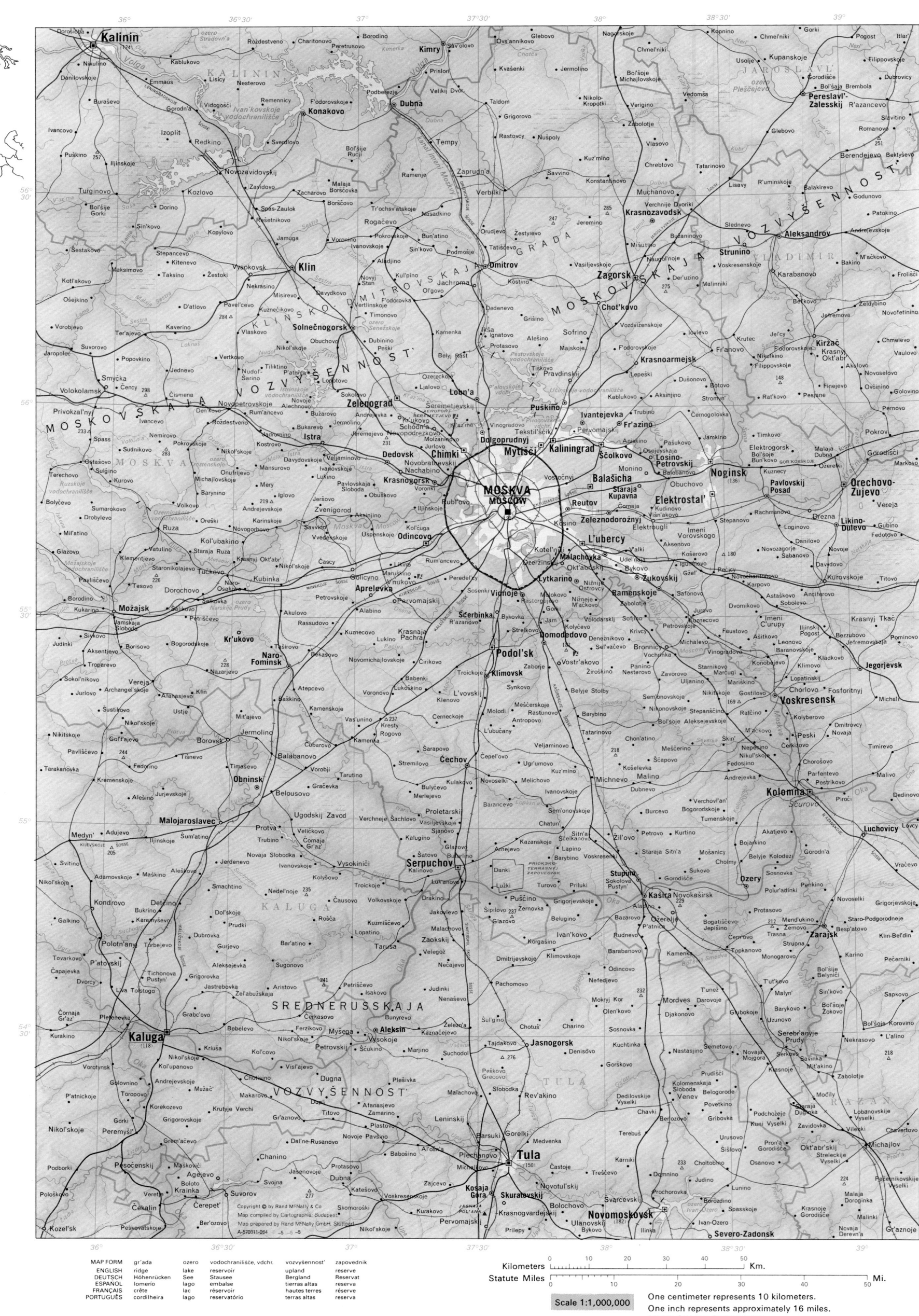

MAP FORM	gr'ada	ozero	vodochranilišče, vdchr.	vozvyšennost'	zapovednik
ENGLISH	ridge	lake	reservoir	upland	reserve
DEUTSCH	Höhenrücken	See	Stausee	Bergland	Reservat
ESPAÑOL	lomerío	lago	embalse	tierras altas	reserva
FRANÇAIS	crête	lac	réservoir	hautes terres	réserve
PORTUGUÊS	cordilheira	lago	reservatório	terras altas	reserva

Kilometers

Statute Miles

Scale 1:1,000,000

One centimeter represents 10 kilometers.
One inch represents approximately 16 miles.

Lambert Conformal Conic Projection

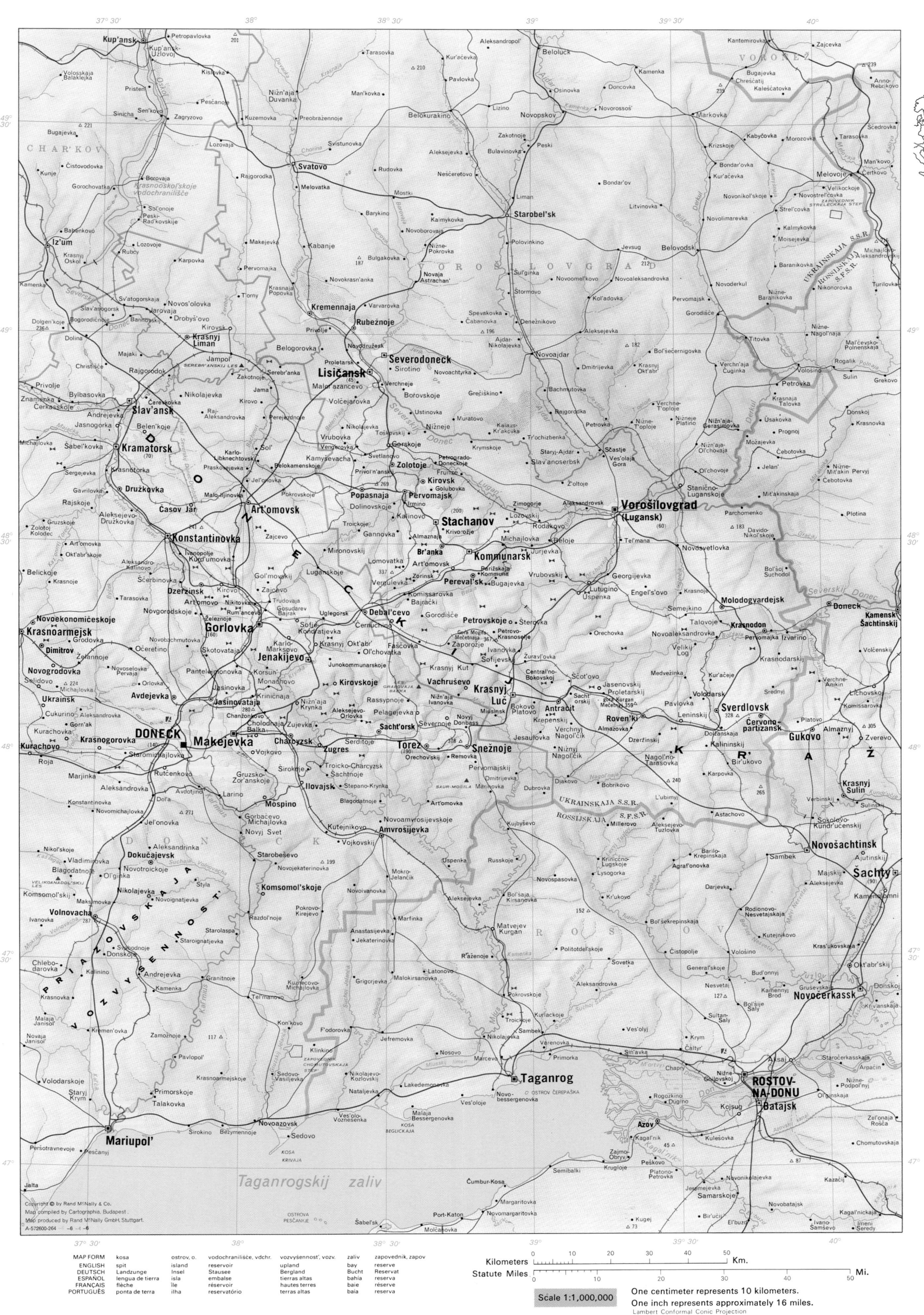

MAP FORM	kosa	ostrov, o.	vodochranilišče, vdchr.	vozvyšennost', vozv.	zaliv	zapovednik, zapov
ENGLISH	spit	island	reservoir	upland	bay	reserve
DEUTSCH	Landzunge	Insel	Stausee	Bergland	Bucht	Reservat
ESPAÑOL	lengua de tierra	isla	embalse	tierras altas	bahía	reserva
FRANÇAIS	flèche	île	réservoir	hautes terres	baie	réserve
PORTUGUÊS	ponta de terra	ilha	reservatório	terras altas	baía	reserva

Kilometers
Statute Miles

0   10   20   30   40   Km.
0   10   20   30   40   50 Mi.

Scale 1:1,000,000

One centimeter represents 10 kilometers.
One inch represents approximately 16 miles.
Lambert Conformal Conic Projection

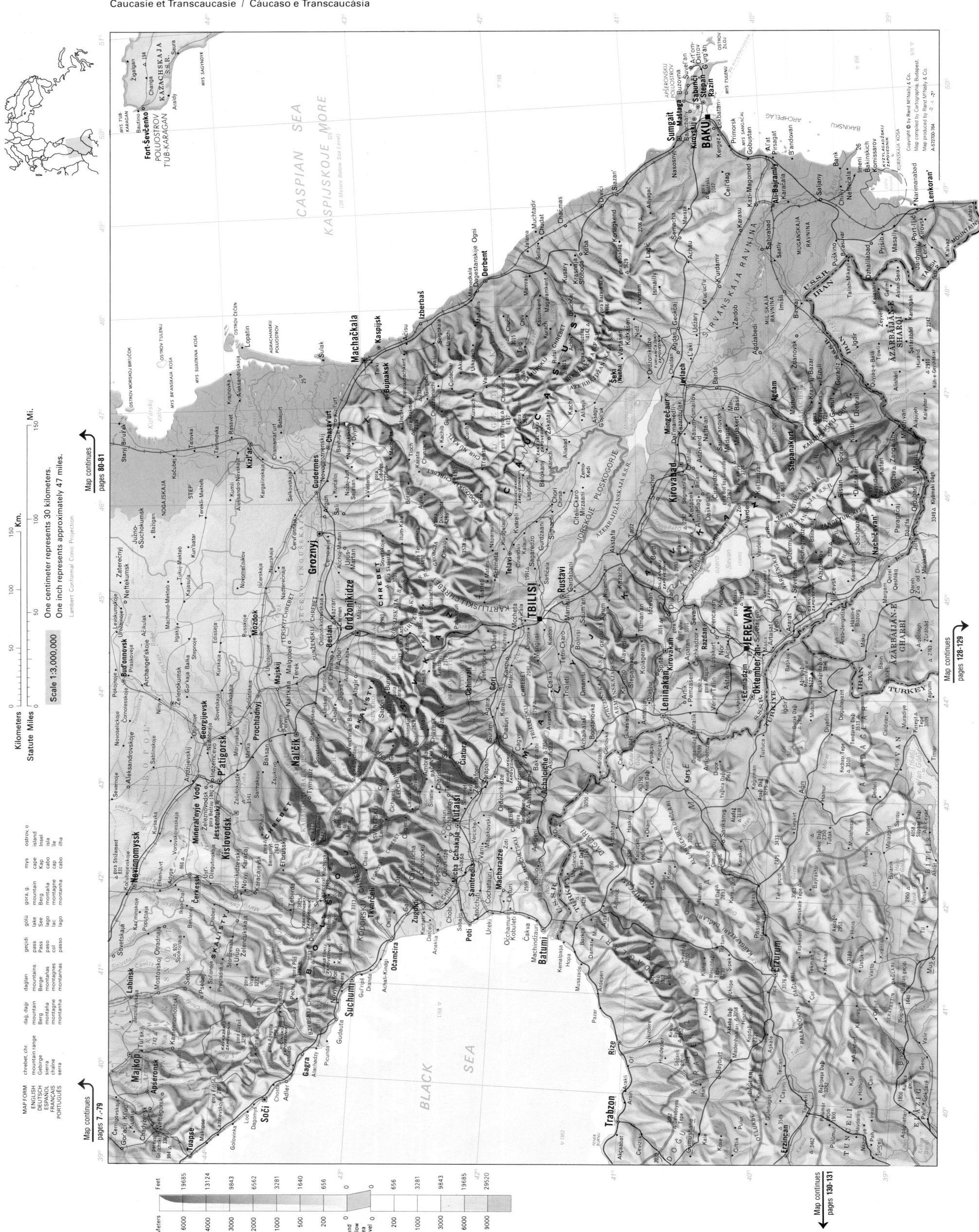

CASPIAN SEA
KASPIJSKOJE MORE
(28 Meters Below Sea Level)

BLACK SEA

Scale 1:3,000,000

One centimeter represents 30 kilometers.
One inch represents approximately 47 miles.

Lambert Conformal Conic Projection

Kilometers
Statute Miles

Map continues
pages 7.–79

Map continues
pages 80-81

Map continues
pages 128–129

Map continues
pages 130-131

BAKU
Sumgait
Tbilisi
JEREVAN
Groznyj
Machačkala
Derbent
Nal'čik
Ordžonikidze
Kutaisi
Batumi
Suchumi
Majkop
Nevinnomyssk
Kislovodsk
Pjatigorsk
Trabzon
Erzurum
Kirovabad
Stepanakert
Nachičevan'
Rize

Eastern Soviet Central Asia / Östliches Sowjet-Mittelasien / Asia Central Soviética: zona oriental
Asia Centrale Soviétique, partie Orientale / Ásia Central Soviética: zona oriental

85

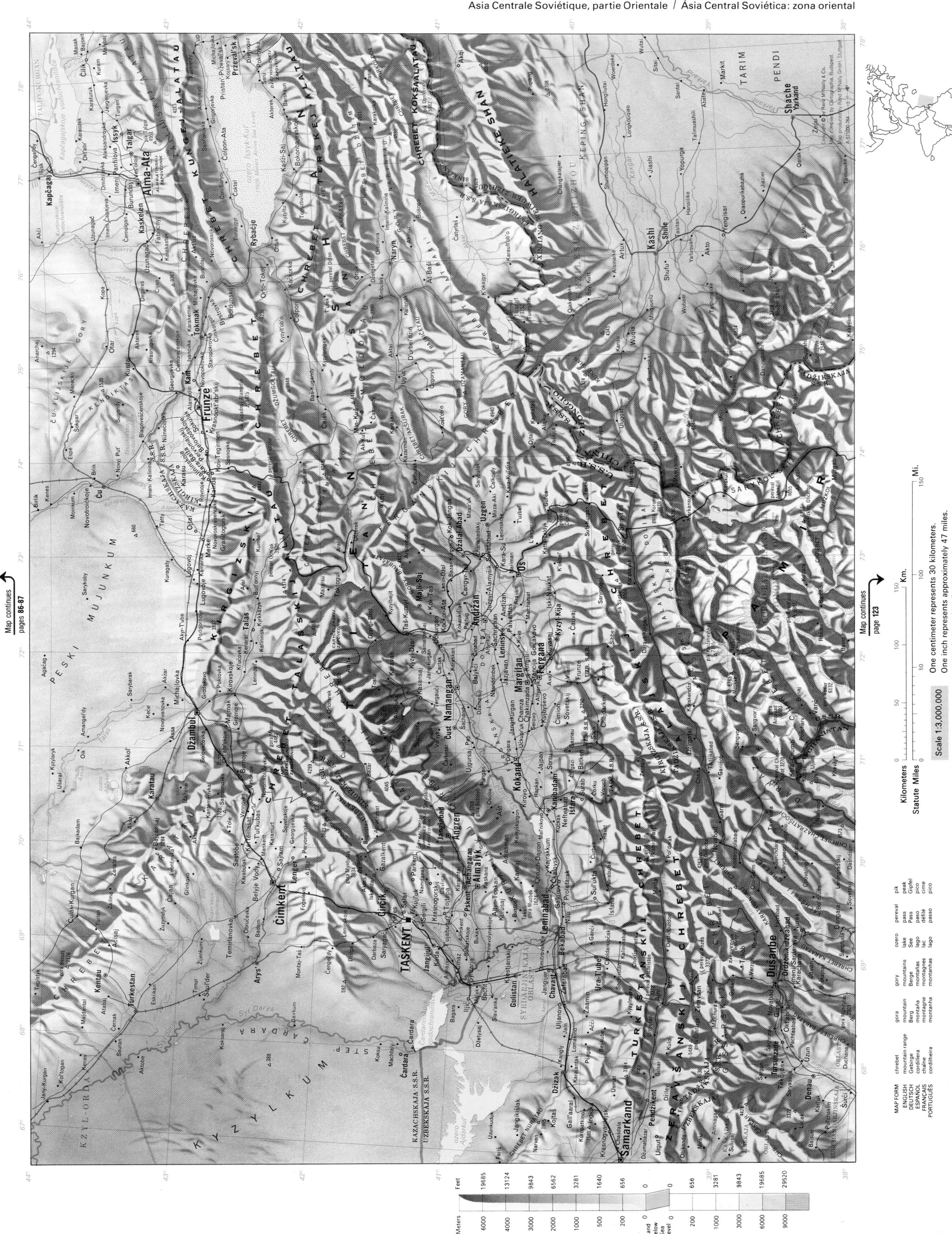

Map continues pages 86-87

Map continues page 123

Kilometers
Statute Miles

One centimeter represents 30 kilometers.
One inch represents approximately 47 miles.

Scale 1:3,000,000

Lambert Conformal Conic Projection

MAP FORM					
ENGLISH	mountain	mountains	mountain range	lake	pass	peak
DEUTSCH	Berg	Berge	Gebirge	See	Pass	Gipfel
ESPAÑOL	montaña	montañas	cordillera	lago	paso	pico
FRANÇAIS	montagne	montagnes	chaîne	lac	défilé	cime
PORTUGUÊS	montanha	montanhas	cordilheira	lago	passo	pico

gora / gory / chrebet / ozero / pereval / pik

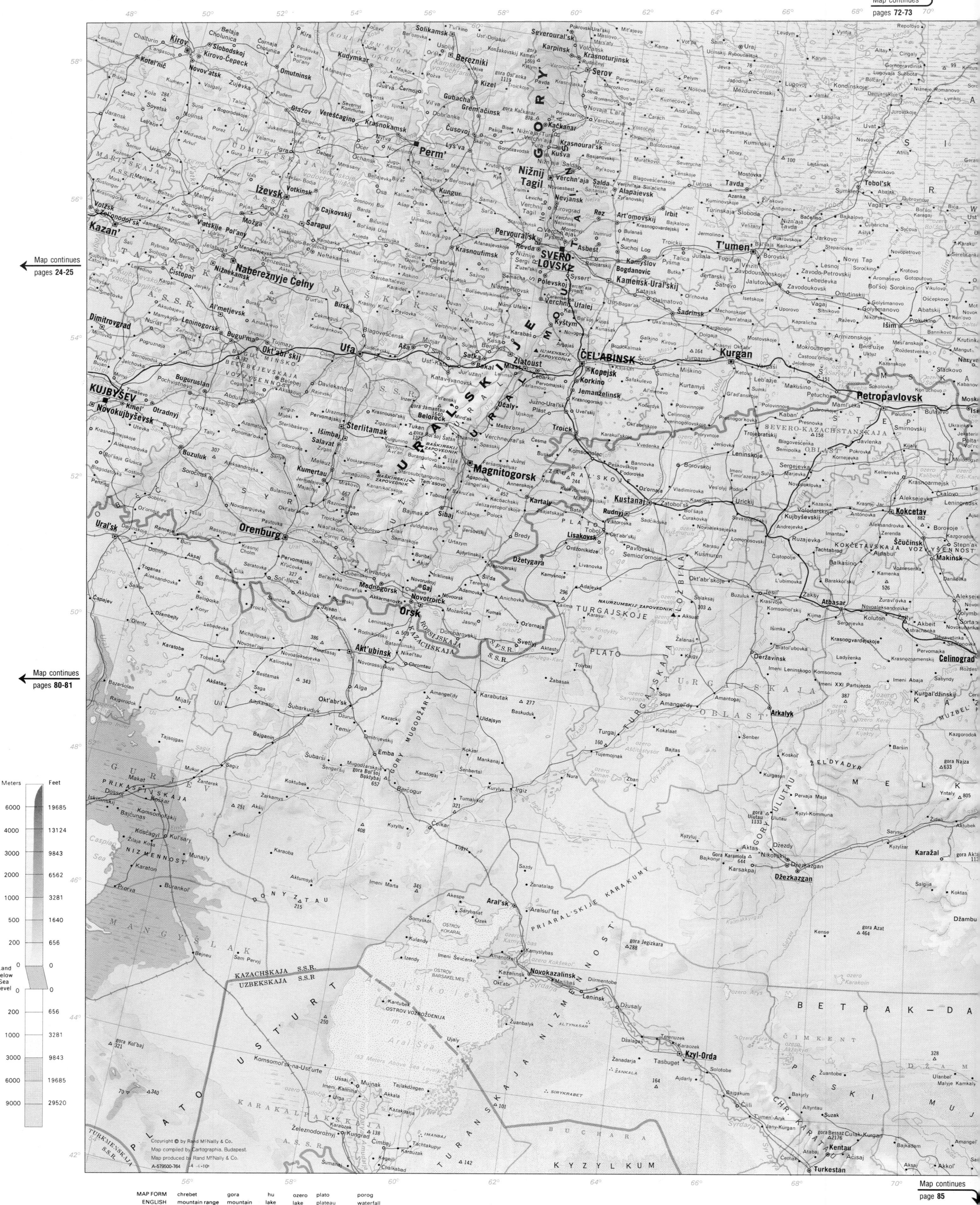

Map continues
pages 72-73

Map continues
pages 24-25

Map continues
pages 80-81

Map continues
page 85

Meters	Feet
6000	19685
4000	13124
3000	9843
2000	6562
1000	3281
500	1640
200	656
Land Below Sea Level	0
0	0
200	656
1000	3281
3000	9843
6000	19685
9000	29520

MAP FORM	chrebet	gora	hu	ozero	plato	porog
ENGLISH	mountain range	mountain	lake	lake	plateau	waterfall
DEUTSCH	Gebirge	Berg	See	See	Hochebene	Wasserfall
ESPAÑOL	cordillera	montaña	lago	lago	meseta	cascada
FRANÇAIS	chaîne	montagne	lac	lac	plateau	chute d'eau
PORTUGUÊS	cordilheira	montanha	lago	lago	planalto	queda d'água

Copyright © by Rand McNally & Co.
Map compiled by Cartographia, Budapest.
Map produced by Rand McNally & Co.
A-579500-764

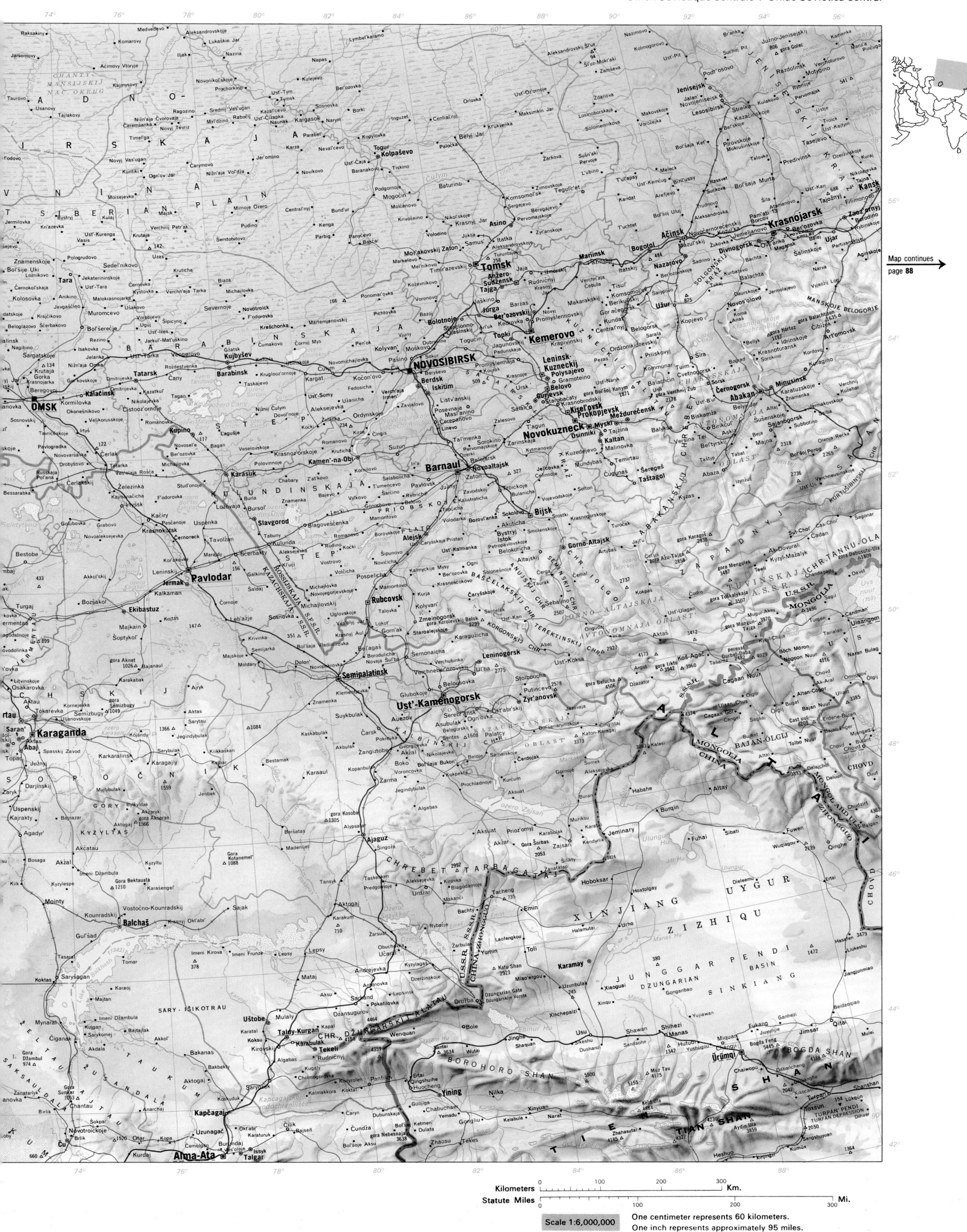

Map continues
page 88 ➜

Kilometers
Statute Miles

Scale 1:6,000,000

One centimeter represents 60 kilometers.
One inch represents approximately 95 miles.
Lambert Conformal Conic Projection

Lake Baikal Region / Baikalseegebiet / Región del Lago Baikal
Région du Lac Baïkal / Região do Lago Baikal

Map continues page 89

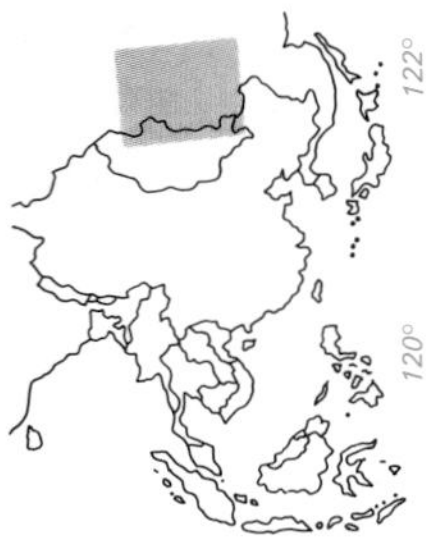

Map continues pages 74-75

Map continues pages 102-103

Map continues pages 86-87

Kilometers 0 100 200 300 Km.
Statute Miles 0 100 200 300 Mi.

Scale 1:6,000,000

One centimeter represents 60 kilometers.
One inch represents approximately 95 miles.
Lambert Conformal Conic Projection

MAP FORM	chrebet	gora	nuruu	nuur	ozero, o.	porog	uul
ENGLISH	mountain range	mountain	mountain range	lake	lake	waterfall	mountains
DEUTSCH	Gebirge	Berg	Gebirge	See	See	Wasserfall	Berge
ESPAÑOL	cordillera	montaña	cordillera	lago	lago	cascada	montañas
FRANÇAIS	chaîne	montagne	chaîne	lac	lac	chute d'eau	montagnes
PORTUGUÊS	cordilheira	montanha	cordilheira	lago	lago	queda d'água	montanhas

Meters	Feet
6000	19685
4000	13124
3000	9843
2000	6562
1000	3281
500	1640
200	656
0	0
Land Below Sea Level 0	0
200	656
1000	3281
3000	9843
6000	19685
9000	29520

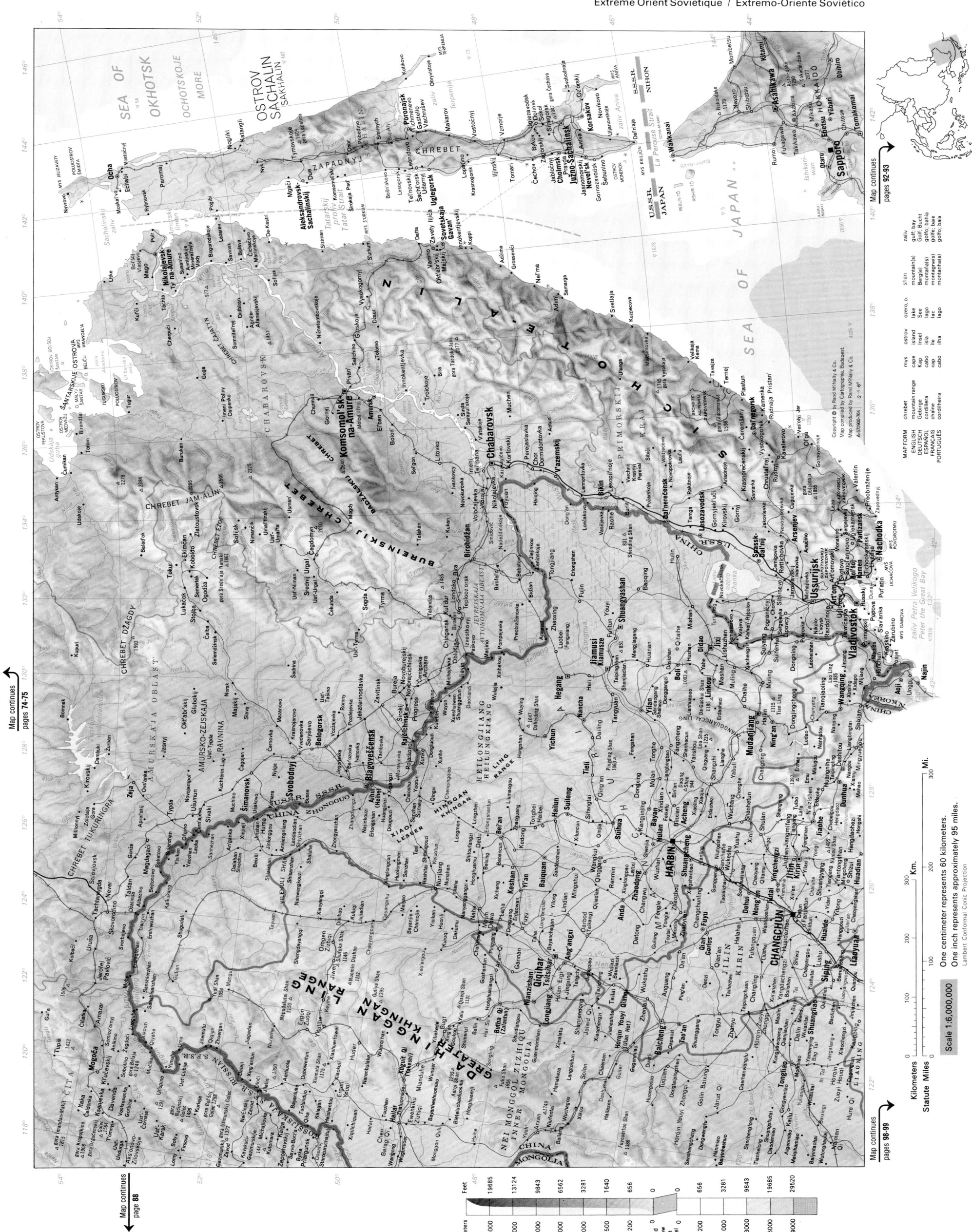

Map continues pages 92-93

Map continues pages 74-75

Map continues page 88

Map continues pages 98-99

Scale 1:6,000,000

One centimeter represents 60 kilometers.
One inch represents approximately 95 miles.

Lambert Conformal Conic Projection

Mi.
Km.

Kilometers
Statute Miles

MAP FORM		
ENGLISH	zaliv	gulf, bay
DEUTSCH		Golf, Bucht
ESPAÑOL		golfo, bahía
FRANCAIS		golfe, baie
PORTUGUÊS		golfo, baía

	ozero, o.	lake
		See
		lago
		lac
		lago

	ostrov	island
		Insel
		isla
		île
		ilha

	mys	cape
		Kap
		cabo
		cap
		cabo

	chrebet	mountain range
		Gebirge
		cordillera
		chaîne
		cordilheira

	shan	mountain(s)
		Berg(e)
		montaña(s)
		montagne(s)
		montanha(s)

Copyright © by Rand McNally & Co.
Map compiled by Cartographia, Budapest.
Map produced by Rand McNally & Co.
A-572000-764   - 2 - 4 - 61

Feet   19685 13124 9843 6562 3281 1640 656 0 0 656 3281 9843 19685 29520
Meters 6000 4000 3000 2000 1000 500 200 Land Below Sea Level 0 200 1000 3000 6000 9000

Map continues
pages 74-75

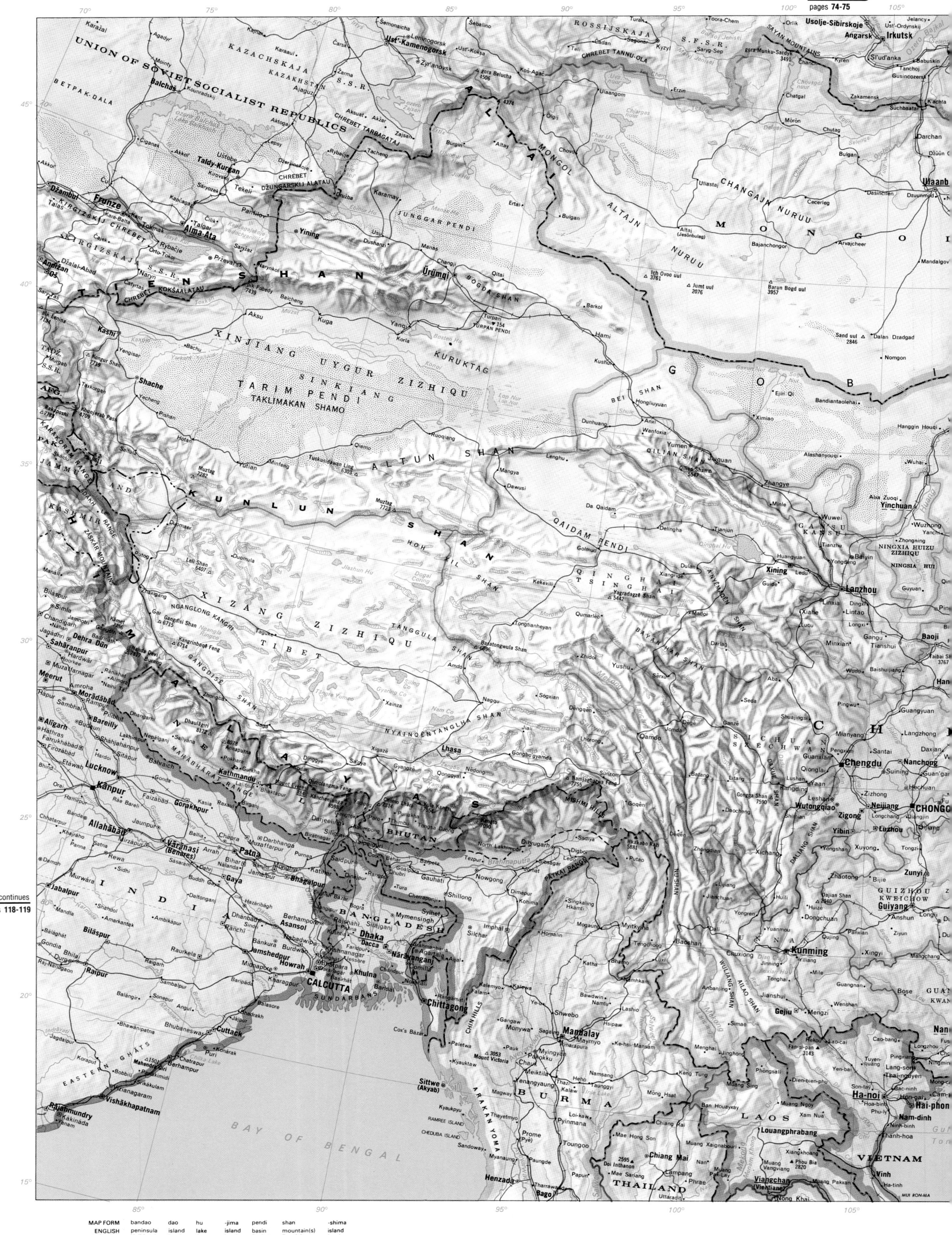

Map continues
pages 118-119

MAP FORM	bandao	dao	hu	-jima	pendi	shan	-shima
ENGLISH	peninsula	island	lake	island	basin	mountain(s)	island
DEUTSCH	Halbinsel	Insel	See	Insel	Becken	Berg(e)	Insel
ESPAÑOL	península	isla	lago	isla	cuenca	montaña(s)	isla
FRANÇAIS	péninsule	île	lac	île	bassin	montagne(s)	île
PORTUGUÊS	península	ilha	lago	ilha	bacia	montanha(s)	ilha

SEA OF OKHOTSK

U.S.S.R.

S.F.S.R.

ROSSIJSKAJA S.F.S.R.

OSTROV SACHALIN
SAKHALIN

Chabarovsk

HOKKAIDO

Sapporo

MANCHURIA

HEILONGJIANG
HEILUNGKIANG

Harbin

Vladivostok

DA HINGGAN LING

NEI MONGGOL ZIZHIQU
INNER MONGOLIA

JILIN
KIRIN

Changchun

NORTH KOREA

P'yŏngyang

SEA OF JAPAN

JAPAN

HONSHŪ

TŌKYŌ
Yokohama

SHENYANG
MUKDEN

LIAONING

Beijing
PEKING

TIANJIN
TIENTSIN

HEBEI
HOPEH

SHANXI
SHANSI

Taiyuan

Dalian

SOUTH KOREA

SŎUL
SEOUL

Taegu

Pusan

ŌSAKA
Kyōto
Nagoya

Kōbe

Yellow Sea

SHANDONG
SHANTUNG

Qingdao
Tsingtao

Jinan
Tsinan

JIANGSU
KIANGSU

Nanjing

SHANGHAI

HENAN
HONAN

Zhengzhou

WUHAN

HUBEI
HUPEH

ANHUI
ANHWEI

Hefei

Hangzhou

Ningbo

EAST CHINA SEA

ZHEJIANG
CHEKIANG

Wenzhou

KYŪSHŪ

Nagasaki

Kagoshima

HUNAN

Changsha

JIANGXI
KIANGSI

Nanchang

FUJIAN
FUKIEN

Fuzhou

SHIKOKU

RYUKYU ISLANDS

NANSEI-SHOTŌ

Naha

OKINAWA-JIMA

Tropic of Cancer

NAN LING

GUANGDONG
KWANGTUNG

GUANGXI ZHUANGZU ZIZHIQU

GUANGZHOU
CANTON

HONG KONG
(U.K.)

Macau
Aomen
(Port.)

HAINAN

Haikou

T'aipei
Chilung

TAIWAN
T'AIWAN

T'ainan

Kaohsiung

PACIFIC OCEAN

PHILIPPINE SEA

SOUTH CHINA SEA

PHILIPPINES

LUZON

Luzon Strait

Copyright © by Rand McNally & Co.
Map prepared by Esselte Map Service AB, Stockholm.
A-569700-264   -7 -7-13

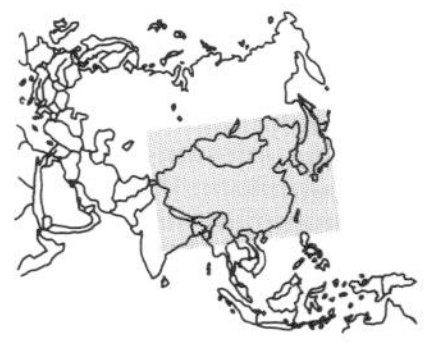

Map continues
pages 108-109

Kilometers   0   200   400   600   Km.

Statute Miles   0   200   400   600   Mi.

Scale 1:12,000,000   One centimeter represents 120 kilometers.
One inch represents approximately 190 miles.
Lambert Conformal Conic Projection

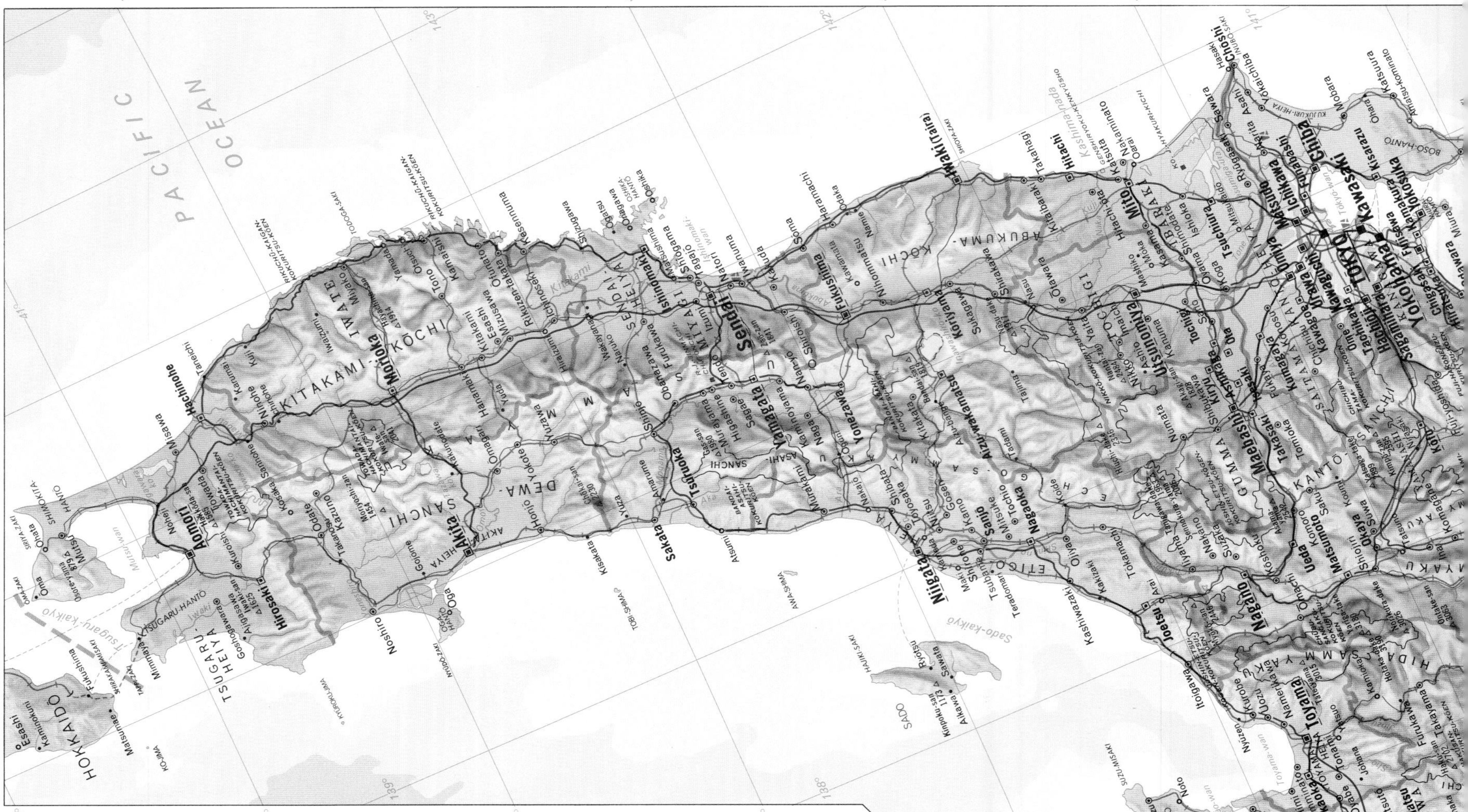

Japan / Japan / Japón
Japon / Japão

PACIFIC OCEAN

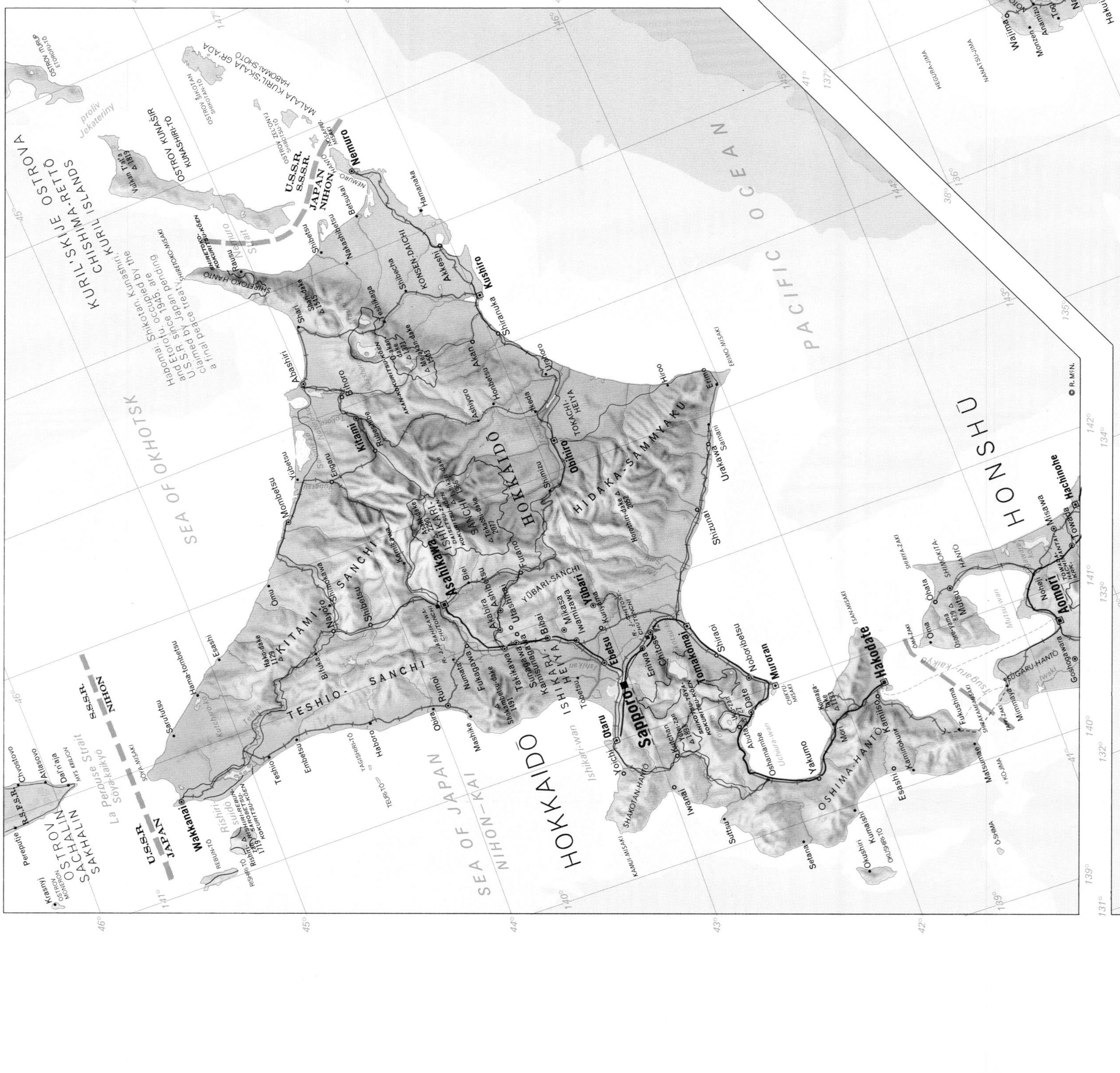

HOKKAIDŌ

HONSHŪ

SEA OF OKHOTSK

SEA OF JAPAN
NIHON-KAI

KURIL'SKIJE OSTROVA
CHISHIMA-RETTŌ
KURIL ISLANDS

OSTROV SACHALIN
SACHALIN
SAKHALIN

U.S.S.R.
S.S.S.R.
JAPAN
NIHON

Wakkanai

Asahikawa
Sapporo
Otaru
Ebetsu
Muroran
Hakodate

Aomori
Hachinohe

Sendai
Akita
Niigata
Nagano
Toyama
Kanazawa
Nagaoka
Joetsu
Sakata
Yamagata
Hirosaki
Morioka

Iwaki(Taira)
Hitachi

TŌKYŌ
Yokohama
Kawasaki
Chiba

HIDAKA-SAMMYAKU
ISHIKARI
KITAMI-SANCHI
TESHIO-SANCHI
TOKACHI-HEIYA

KITAKAMI
IWATE
DEWA
SANCHI
KANTŌ

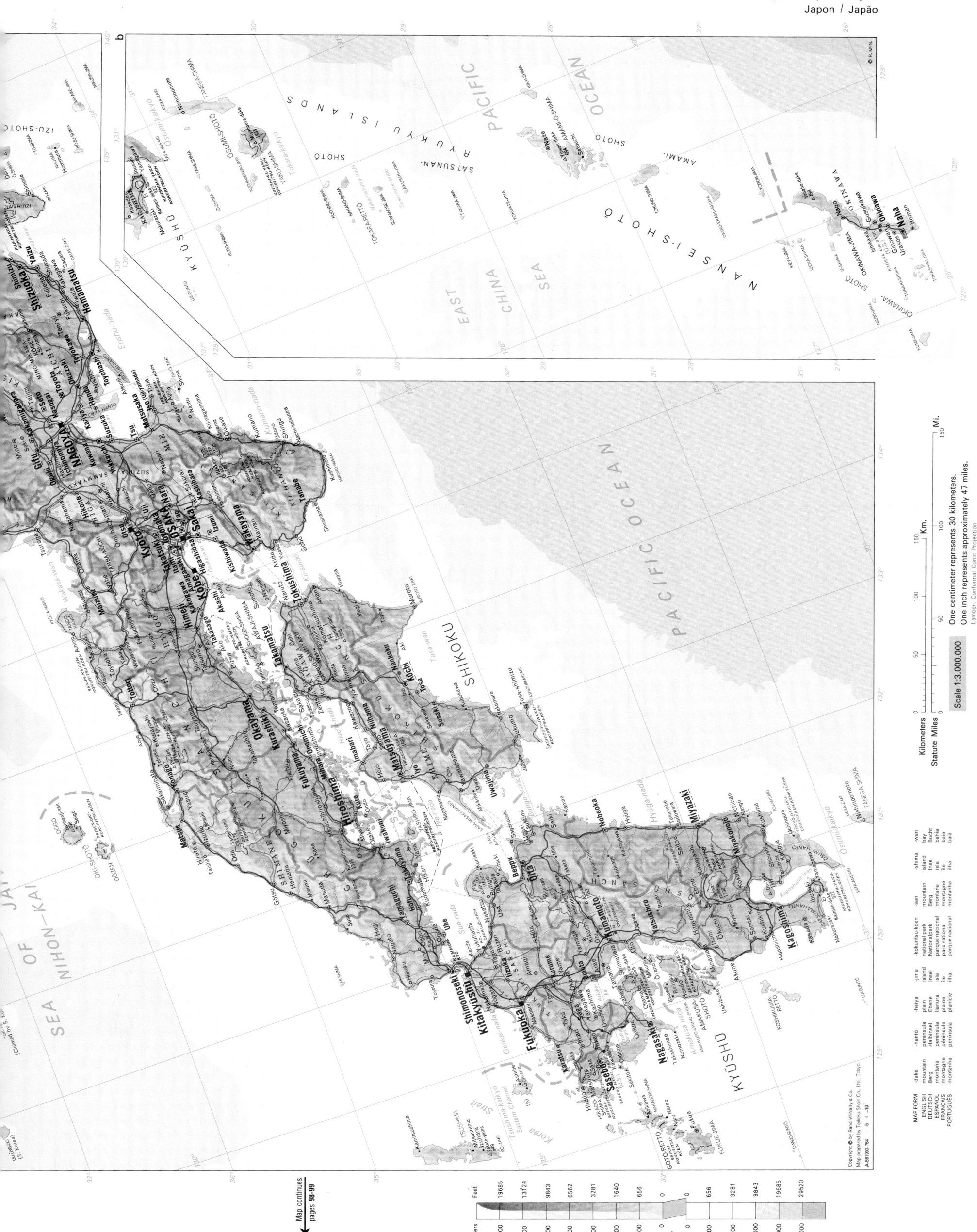

PACIFIC OCEAN

EAST CHINA SEA

RYUKYU ISLANDS

NANSEI-SHOTŌ

SEA OF JAPAN
NIHON-KAI

SHIKOKU

KYŪSHŪ

NAGOYA
Kyōto
ŌSAKA
Kōbe
Nara
Wakayama
Tokushima
Takamatsu
Kōchi
Okayama
Kurashiki
Fukuyama
Hiroshima
Matsue
Tottori
Ube
Shimonoseki
Kitakyūshū
Fukuoka
Nagasaki
Sasebo
Kumamoto
Beppu
Ōita
Miyazaki
Kagoshima
Matsuyama
Imabari
Noboka

Naha
OKINAWA
Okinawa
Gushikawa
Ginowan
Urasoe

Naze
AMAMI-ŌSHIMA

Map continues
pages 98-99

MAP FORM	-dake	-heiya	-jima	-kokuritsu kōen	-san	-shima	-wan	-hantō
ENGLISH	mountain	plain	island	national park	mountain	island	bay	peninsula
DEUTSCH	Berg	Ebene	Insel	Nationalpark	Berg	Insel	Bucht	Halbinsel
ESPAÑOL	montaña	llanura	isla	parque nacional	montaña	isla	bahía	peninsula
FRANÇAIS	montagne	plaine	île	parc national	montagne	île	baie	péninsule
PORTUGUÊS	montanha	planície	ilha	parque nacional	montanha	ilha	baia	peninsula

Kilometers
Statute Miles
Km.
Mi.

Scale 1:3,000,000

One centimeter represents 30 kilometers.
One inch represents approximately 47 miles.

Lambert Conformal Conic Projection

Copyright © by Rand McNally & Co.
Map prepared by Teikoku-Shoin Co., Ltd., Tokyo.
A-561000-784   -5 -4 -10

Feet
19685
13124
9843
6562
3281
1640
656
0
Meters
6000
4000
3000
2000
1000
500
200
0
Land Below Sea Level
0
200
1000
3000
6000
9000
0
656
3281
9843
19685
29520

Map continues
pages 96-97

MAP FORM	-dake	-hantō	-kokutei-kōen	-misaki	-san	-tōge	-wan	-yama	-zaki
ENGLISH	mountain	peninsula	national park	cape	mountain	pass	bay	mountain	point
DEUTSCH	Berg	Halbinsel	Nationalpark	Kap	Berg	Pass	Bucht	Berg	Landspitze
ESPAÑOL	montaña	peninsula	parque nacional	cabo	montaña	paso	bahia	montaña	punta
FRANÇAIS	montagne	peninsule	parc national	cap	montagne	col	baie	montagne	pointe
PORTUGUÊS	montanha	peninsula	parque nacional	cabo	montanha	passo	baia	montanha	ponta

Kilometers
Statute Miles

Scale 1:1,000,000   One centimeter represents 10 kilometers.
One inch represents approximately 16 miles.
Lambert Conformal Conic Projection

SEA OF JAPAN

NIHON-KAI

MAP FORM	-jima	-misaki	-san	-sen	-shima	-tōge	-yama	-zen
ENGLISH	island	cape	mountain	mountain	island	pass	mountain	mountain
DEUTSCH	Insel	Kap	Berg	Berg	Insel	Pass	Berg	Berg
ESPAÑOL	isla	cabo	montaña	montaña	isla	paso	montaña	montaña
FRANÇAIS	île	cap	montagne	montagne	île	col	montagne	montagne
PORTUGUÊS	ilha	cabo	montanha	montanha	ilha	passo	montanha	montanha

Map continues
pages 94-95

PACIFIC   OCEAN

Kilometers
Statute Miles

One centimeter represents 10 kilometers.
One inch represents approximately 16 miles.

Scale 1:1,000,000

Copyright © by Rand McNally & Co.
Map prepared by Teikoku-Shoin Co., Ltd., Tokyo.
A-566600-264   -4 -5 -6

Lambert Conformal Conic Projection

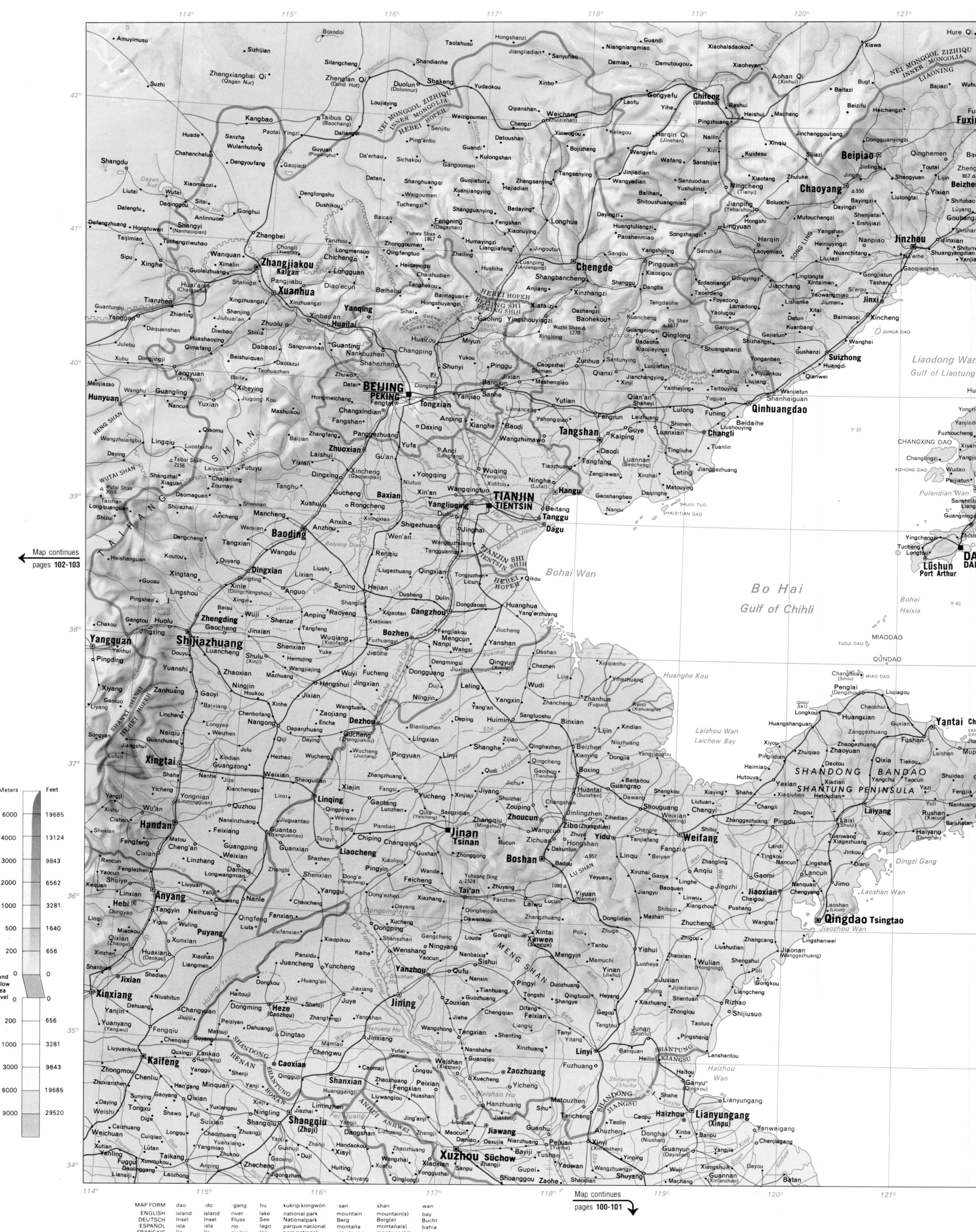

Map continues
pages 102-103

Map continues
pages 100-101

MAP FORM	dao	-do	-gang	hu	kukrip kongwôn	-san	shan	wan
ENGLISH	island	island	river	lake	national park	mountain	mountain(s)	bay
DEUTSCH	Insel	Insel	Fluss	See	Nationalpark	Berg	Berg(e)	Bucht
ESPAÑOL	isla	isla	río	lago	parque nacional	montaña	montaña(s)	bahía
FRANÇAIS	île	île	rivière	lac	parc national	montagne	montagne(s)	baie
PORTUGUÊS	ilha	ilha	rio	lago	parque nacional	montanha	montanha(s)	baía

Meters   Feet
6000   19685
4000   13124
3000   9843
2000   6562
1000   3281
500   1640
200   656
0   0
Land
Below
Sea
Level   0
0   0
200   656
1000   3281
3000   9843
6000   19685
9000   29520

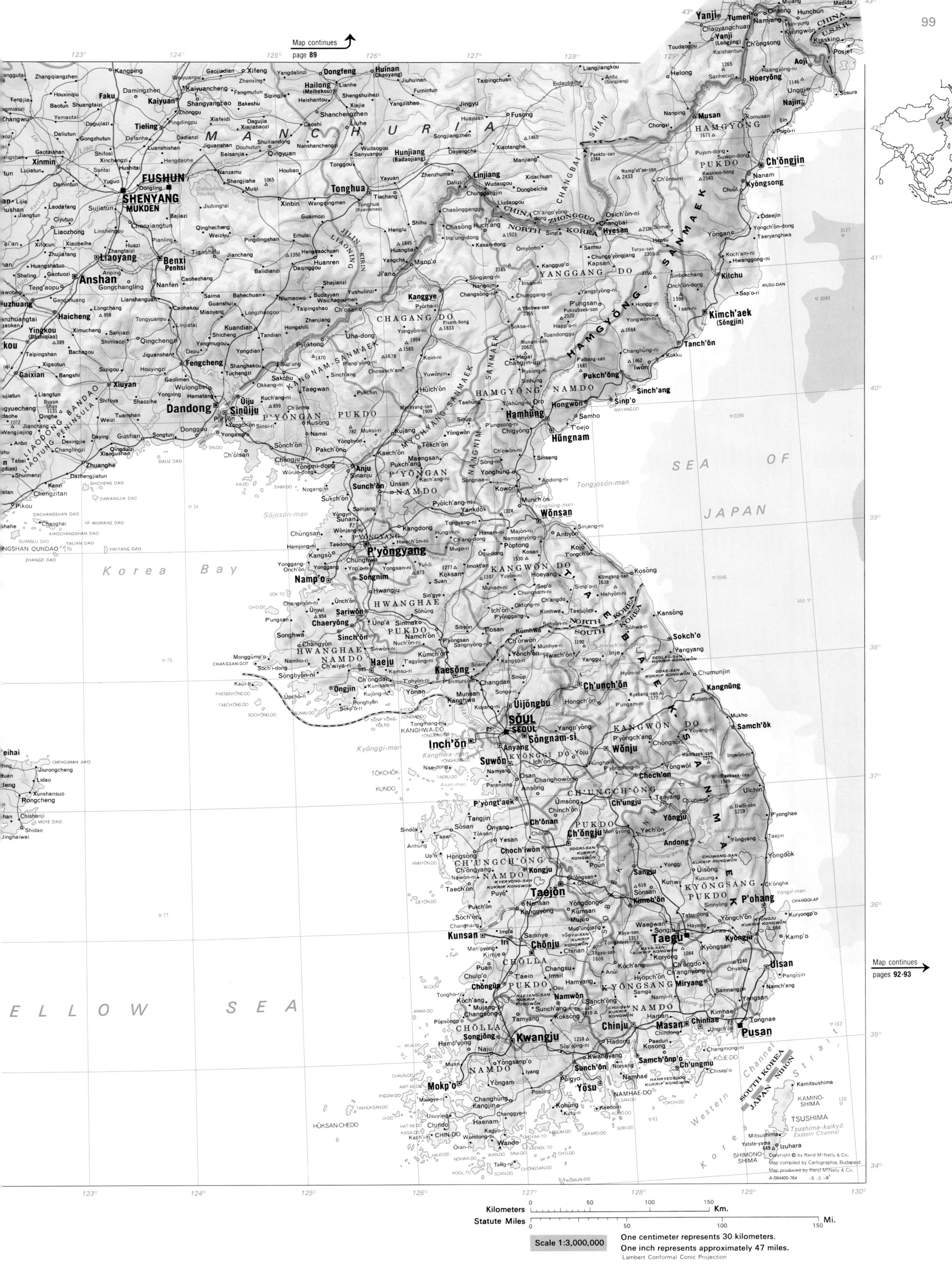

Map continues
page 89

Map continues
pages 92-93

43°

MANCHURIA

CHINA
USSR

Yanji
Tumen
Namyang
Onsong
Hunchun
CHINA
USSR
Kraskino
Posjet

Toudaogou
Helong
Sanhecun
Haeyong-ni
Aoji
Sosura
Najin

Kangping
Gaojiadian
Xifeng
Dongfeng
Huinan
(Chaoyang)
Liangjiangkou
Nanping
Musan
Komusan
Iljin

42°

Faku
Kaiyuan
Shangyangtao
Hailong
(Meihekou)
Lianhe
Shengshuihezi
Jiuhuinan
Fumintun
Fusong
Chongxi
Pugo-ri
HAMGYONG
Hoeryong
1146
Musan
Kyongsong

FUSHUN
Tieling
Kuanyuanpu
Zhenxing
Shanchengzhen
Jingyu
Huayuan
Chungmu
Chongsong
Ch'ongjin

SHENYANG
MUKDEN
Tonghua
Linjiang
Chasong
Huch'ang
Sinp'a
Hyesan
Soman
Nanam

Kilchu

CHAGANG DO
YANGGANG DO
HAMGYONG
NAMDO

Kanggye

P'YONGAN PUKDO

Dandong
Sinuiju

P'YONGAN NAMDO

P'YONGYANG
Wonsan

SEA OF JAPAN

Korea Bay

Namp'o
Songnim

HWANGHAE PUKDO
HWANGHAE NAMDO

Haeju
Kaesong

KANGWON DO

SOUL
SEOUL
Inch'on
Suwon
Wonju
Kangnung
Samch'ok

KYONGGI DO
KANGWON DO

CH'UNGCH'ONG
PUKDO

Taejon
CH'UNGCH'ONG
NAMDO
KYONGSANG
PUKDO
P'ohang

Kunsan
Chonju
Taegu
Ulsan

CHOLLA
PUKDO
KYONGSANG
NAMDO

Kwangju
Chinju
Masan
Chinhae
Pusan

CHOLLA
NAMDO

Mokp'o
Sunch'on
Yosu

YELLOW SEA

SOUTH KOREA
JAPAN NIHON

TSUSHIMA

Kilometers
Statute Miles

Scale 1:3,000,000

One centimeter represents 30 kilometers.
One inch represents approximately 47 miles.
Lambert Conformal Conic Projection

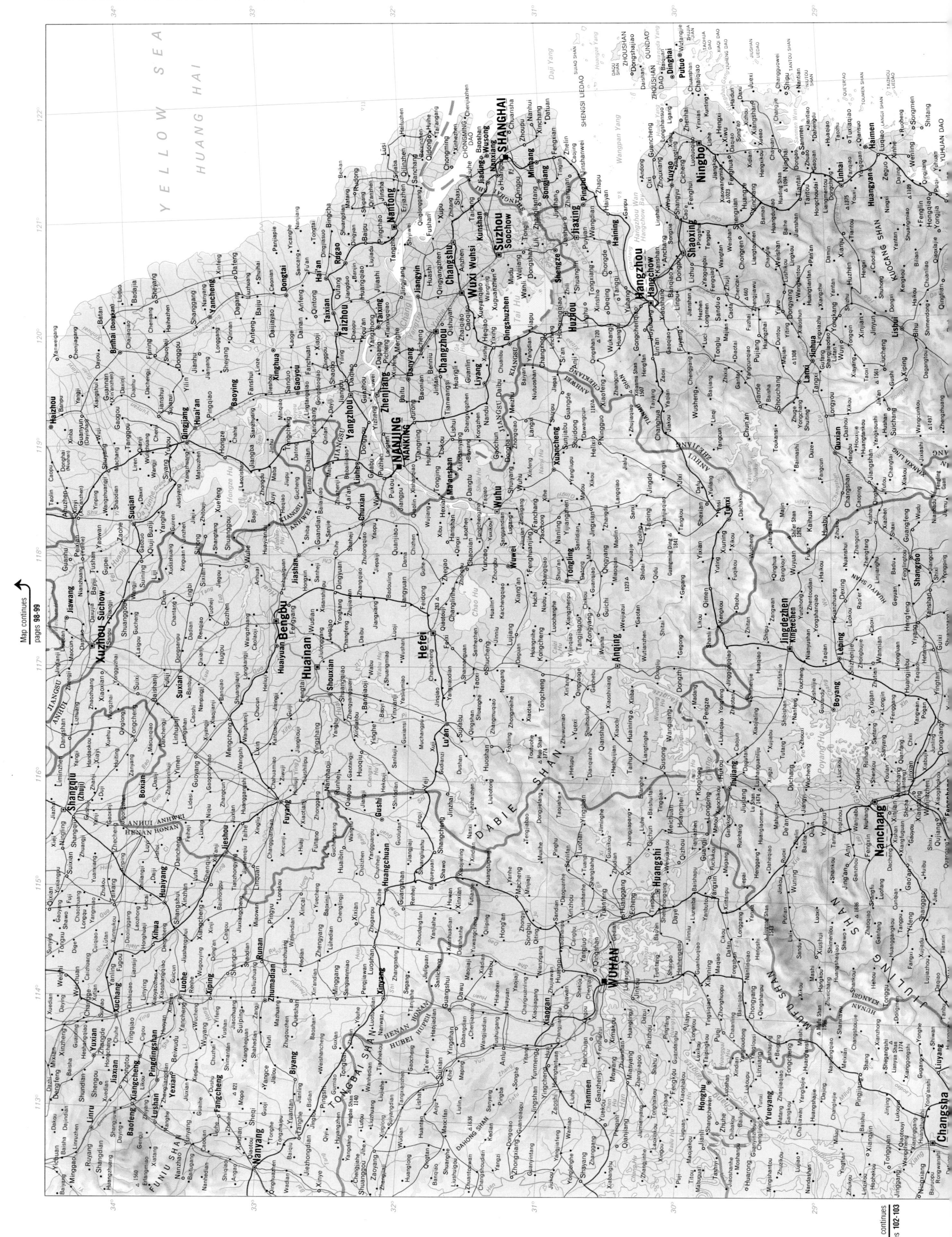

Map continues pages 98·99

Map continues pages 102·103

East and Southeast China / Ost- und Südostchina / Este y Sudeste de la China
Chine de l'Est et du Sud-Est / Leste e Sudeste da China

101

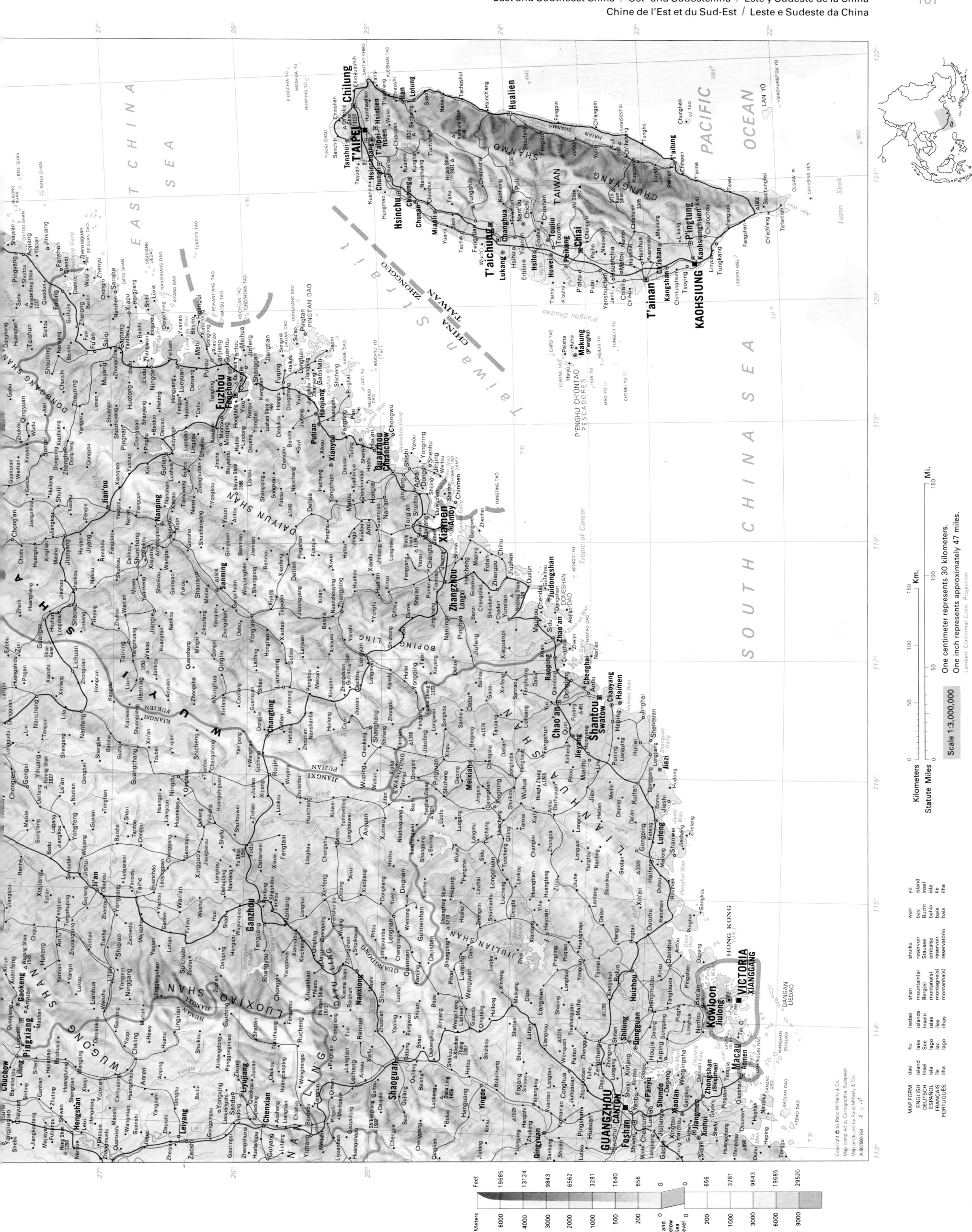

EAST CHINA SEA

PACIFIC OCEAN

SOUTH CHINA SEA

TAIWAN STRAIT / TAIWAN ZHONGGTO

Chilung
TAIPEI
T'aichung
T'ainan
KAOHSIUNG
Hualien

Fuzhou
Foochow

Xiamen
Amoy

Shantou
Swatow

GUANGZHOU
CANTON

VICTORIA
XIANGGANG

HONG KONG

Macau

Tropic of Cancer

Luzon Strait

MAP FORM							
ENGLISH	dao	hu	liedao	shan	shuiku	wan	yü
DEUTSCH	Insel	lake	islands	mountain(s)	reservoir	bay	island
ESPAÑOL	isla	See	Inseln	Berg(e)	Stausee	Bucht	Insel
FRANCAIS	île	lago	islas	montaña(s)	embalse	bahía	isla
PORTUGUÊS	ilha	lac	lies	montagne(s)	réservoir	baie	île
		lago	ilhas	montanha(s)	reservatório	baía	ilha

Kilometers
Statute Miles

Scale 1:3,000,000

One centimeter represents 30 kilometers.
One inch represents approximately 47 miles.

Lambert Conformal Conic Projection

Mi.
Km.

Feet
19685
13124
9843
6562
3281
1640
656
0

Land
Below
Sea
Level

656
3281
9843
19685
29520

Meters
6000
4000
3000
2000
1000
500
200
0

0
200
1000
3000
6000
9000

Map continues pages 98-99

Map continues page 88

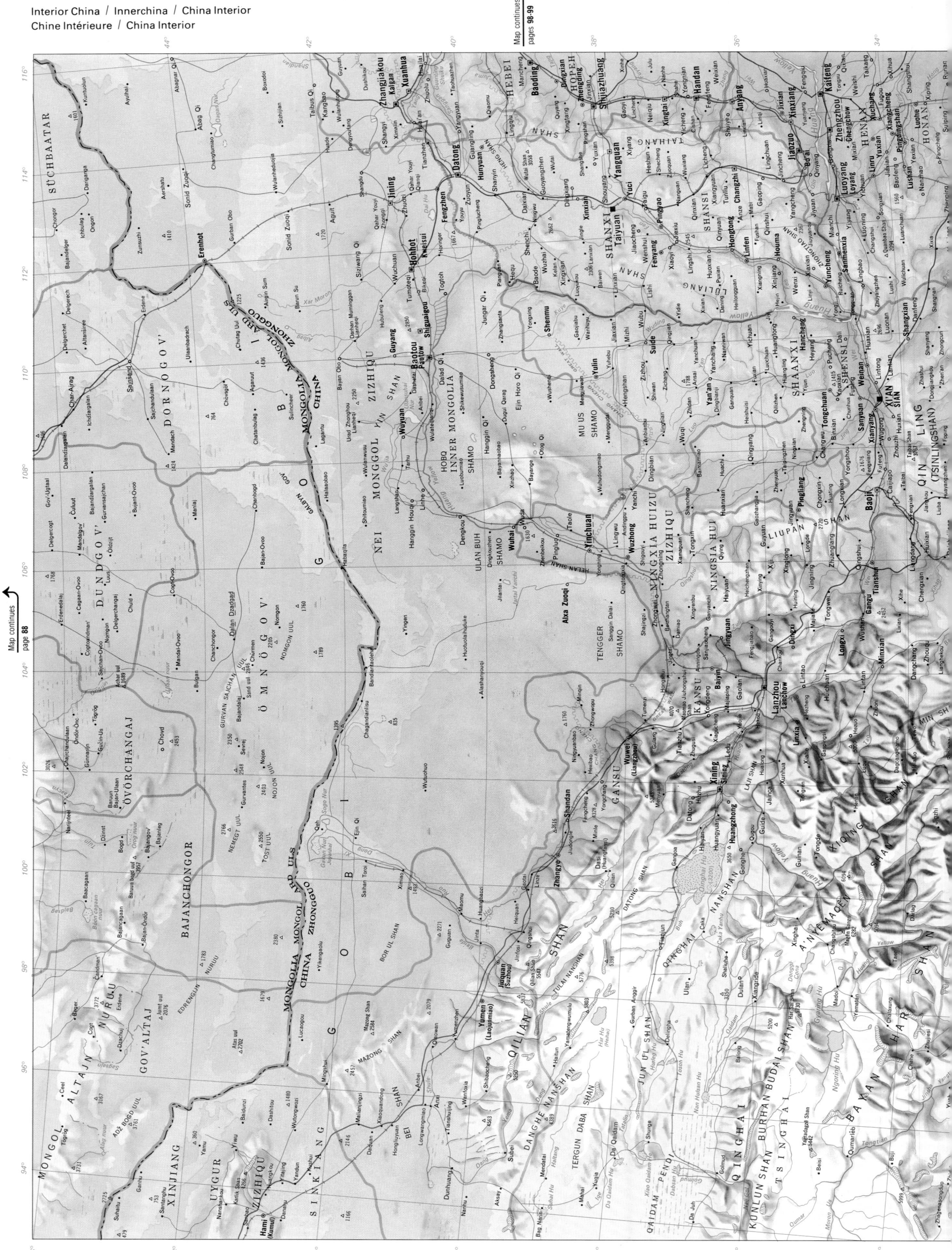
SÜCHBAATAR
DORNOGOV'
DUNDGOV'
ÖMNÖGOV'
ÖVÖRCHANGAJ
BAJANCHONGOR
GOV'ALTAJ
MONGOL ALTAJN NURUU
MONGOLIA MONGOL ARD ULS
CHINA ZHONGGUO
GOBI
NEI MONGGOL ZIZHIQU
INNER MONGOLIA
HOBQ SHAMO
MU US SHAMO
TENGGER SHAMO
ULAN BUH SHAMO
YIN SHAN
HEBEI
HOPEH
SHANXI
SHANSI
SHAANXI
SHENSI
HENAN
HONAN
NINGXIA HUIZU ZIZHIQU
NINGSIA HUI
GANSU
KANSU
QINGHAI
TSINGHAI
XINJIANG UYGUR ZIZHIQU
SINKIANG
QILIAN SHAN
QIN LING (TSINLINGSHAN)
LIUPAN SHAN
HELAN SHAN
TAIHANG SHAN
LÜLIANG SHAN
A'NYÊMAQÊN SHAN
BAYAN HAR SHAN
KUNLUN SHAN
BURHAN BUDAI SHAN
QAIDAM PENDI
Qinghai Hu
Lanzhou
Xining
Yinchuan
Baotou
Hohhot
Datong
Taiyuan
Xi'an
Zhengzhou
Luoyang
Kaifeng
Shijiazhuang
Baoding
Zhangjiakou
Erenhot
Hami (Kumul)
Dunhuang
Yumen (Laojunmiao)
Jiuquan (Suzhou)
Zhangye
Wuwei (Liangzhou)
Tianshui
Baoji

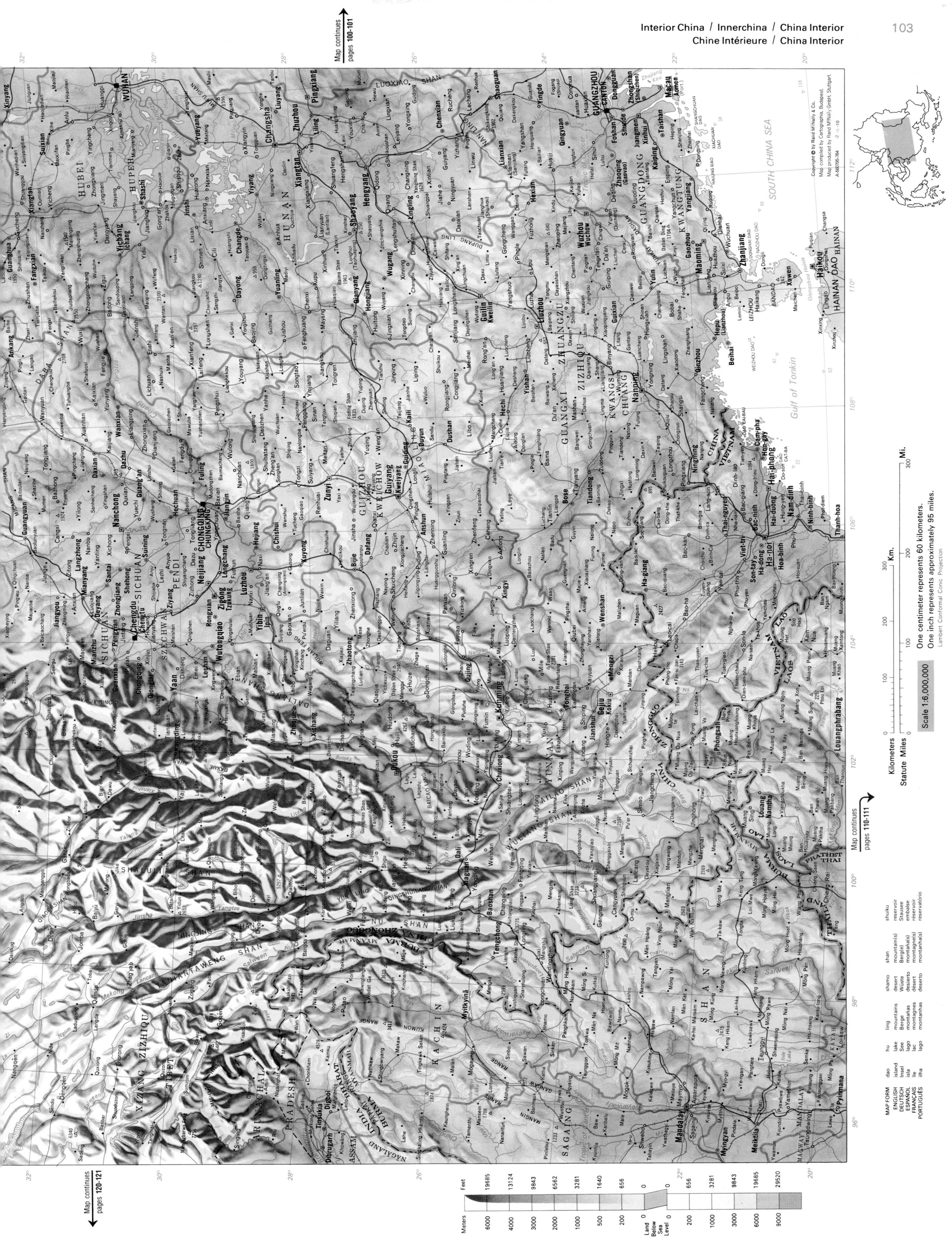

Map continues
pages 100-101

Map continues
pages 110-111

Map continues
120-121

SOUTH CHINA SEA

Gulf of Tonkin

Scale 1:6,000,000

One centimeter represents 60 kilometers.
One inch represents approximately 95 miles.

Lambert Conformal Conic Projection

Kilometers

Statute Miles

MAP FORM					
ENGLISH	dao	hu	ling	shamo	shan	shuiku
	island	lake	mountains	desert	mountain(s)	reservoir
DEUTSCH	Insel	See	Berge	Wüste	Berg(e)	Stausee
ESPAÑOL	isla	lago	montañas	desierto	montaña(s)	embalse
FRANÇAIS	île	lac	montagnes	désert	montagne(s)	réservoir
PORTUGUÊS	ilha	lago	montanhas	deserto	montanha(s)	reservatório

Feet
19685
13124
9843
6562
3281
1640
656
0
Land
Below
Sea
Level

656
3281
9843
19685
29520

Meters
6000
4000
3000
2000
1000
500
200
0
0
200
1000
3000
6000
9000

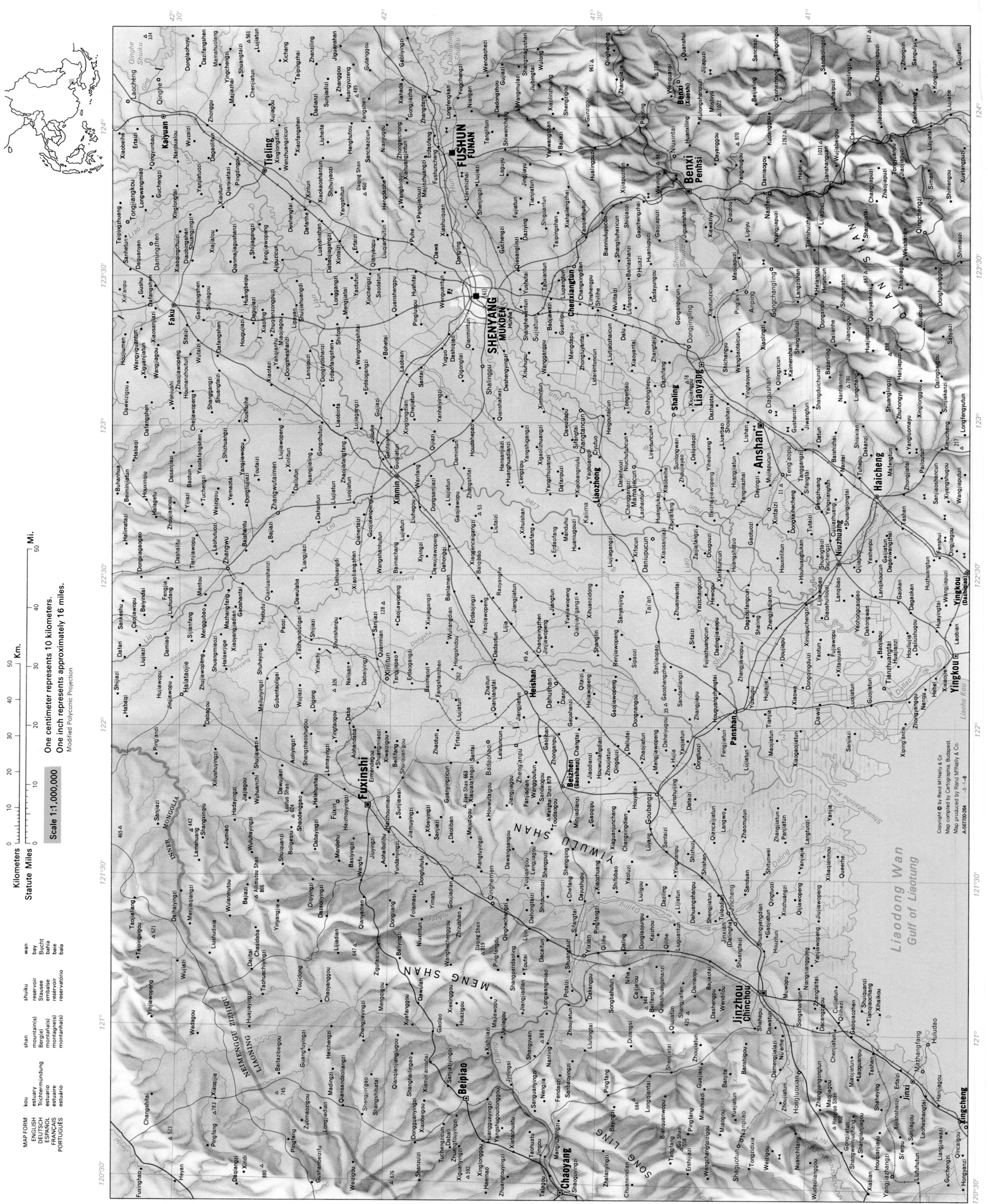

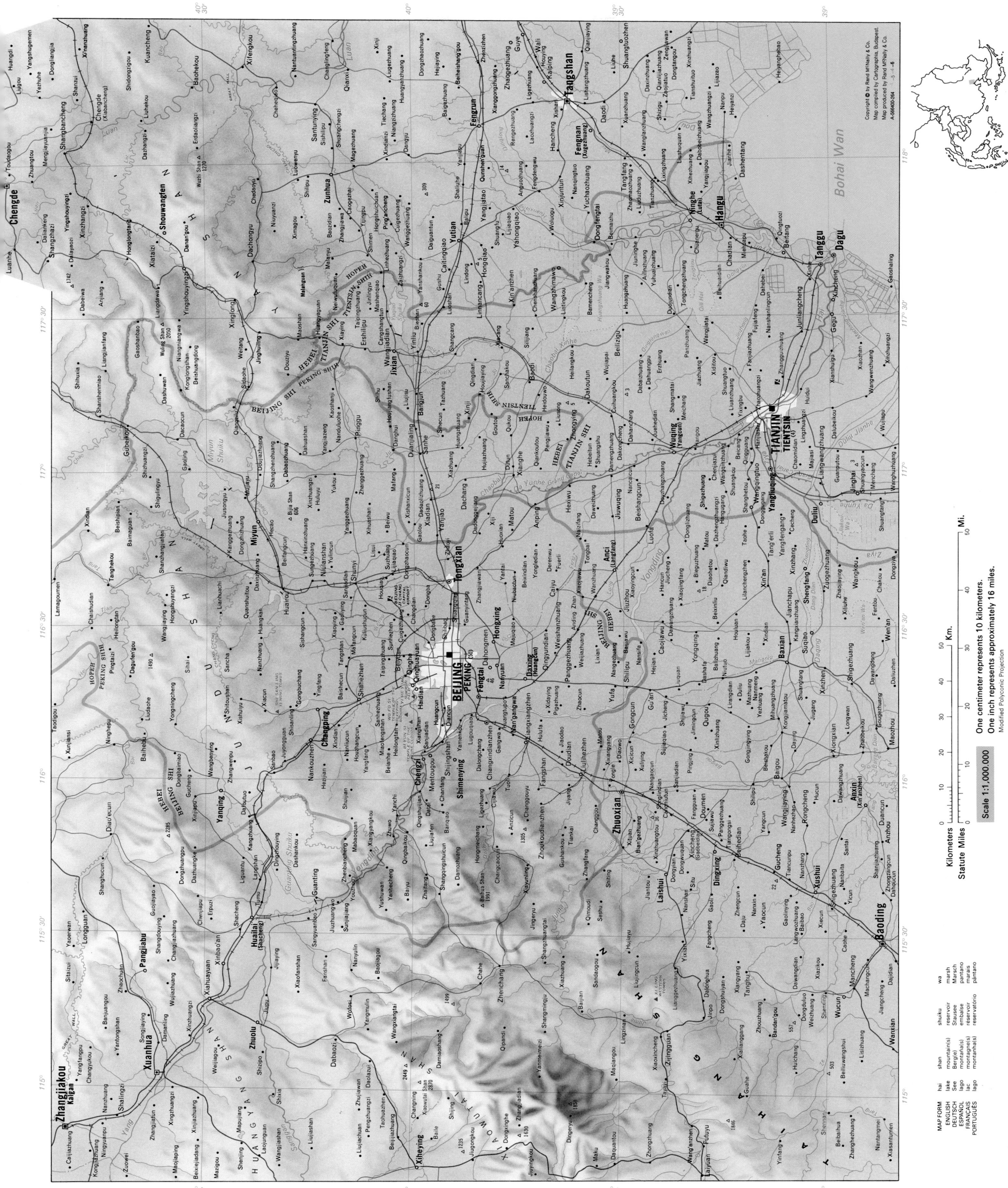

Bohai Wan

MAP FORM				
ENGLISH	hai	lake	shan	mountain(s)	shuiku	reservoir	wa	marsh
DEUTSCH		See		Berg(e)		Stausee		Marsch
ESPAÑOL		lago		montaña(s)		embalse		pantano
FRANÇAIS		lac		montagne(s)		réservoir		marais
PORTUGUÊS		lago		montanha(s)		reservatório		pântano

Kilometers
Statute Miles

Scale 1:1,000,000

One centimeter represents 10 kilometers.
One inch represents approximately 16 miles.
Modified Polyconic Projection

Km.
Mi.

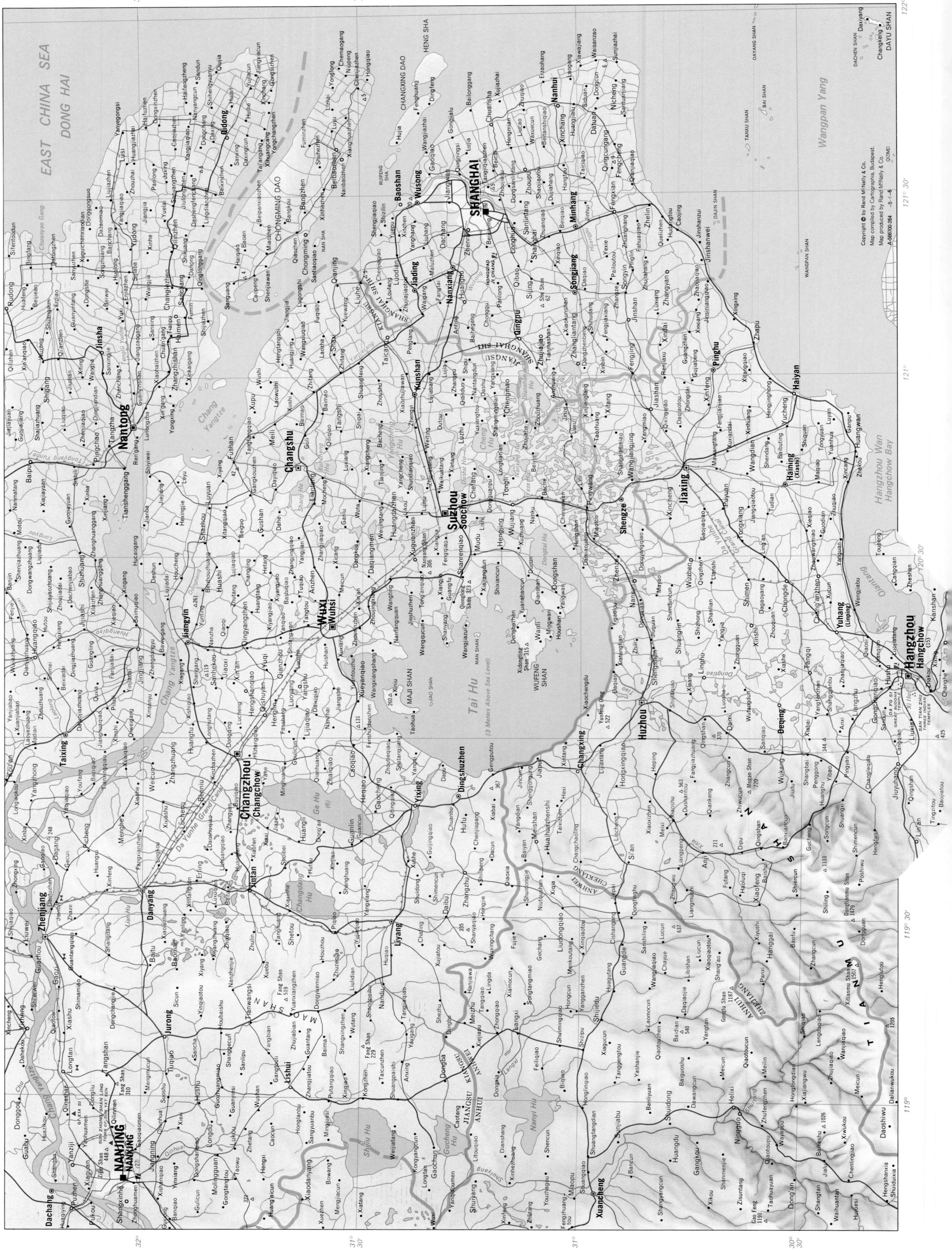
EAST CHINA SEA
DONG HAI
SHANGHAI
NANJING
NANKING
Suzhou
Soochow
Wuxi
Wuhsi
Changzhou
Changchow
Hangzhou
Hangchow
Nantong
Tai Hu
Hangzhou Wan
Hangchow Bay
Wangpan Yang
Kilometers 0 10 20 30 40 50 Km.
Statute Miles 0 10 20 30 40 50 Mi.
Scale 1:1,000,000
One centimeter represents 10 kilometers.
One inch represents approximately 16 miles.
Lambert Conformal Conic Projection
MAP FORM dao hu sha shan si wan
ENGLISH island lake island mountain(s); island temple bay
DEUTSCH Insel See Insel Berg(e); Insel Tempel Bucht
ESPAÑOL isla lago isla montaña(s); isla templo bahía
FRANÇAIS île lac île montagne(s); île temple baie
PORTUGUÊS ilha lago ilha montanha(s); ilha templo baía
Copyright © by Rand McNally & Co.
Map compiled by Cartographia, Budapest.
Map produced by Rand McNally & Co.

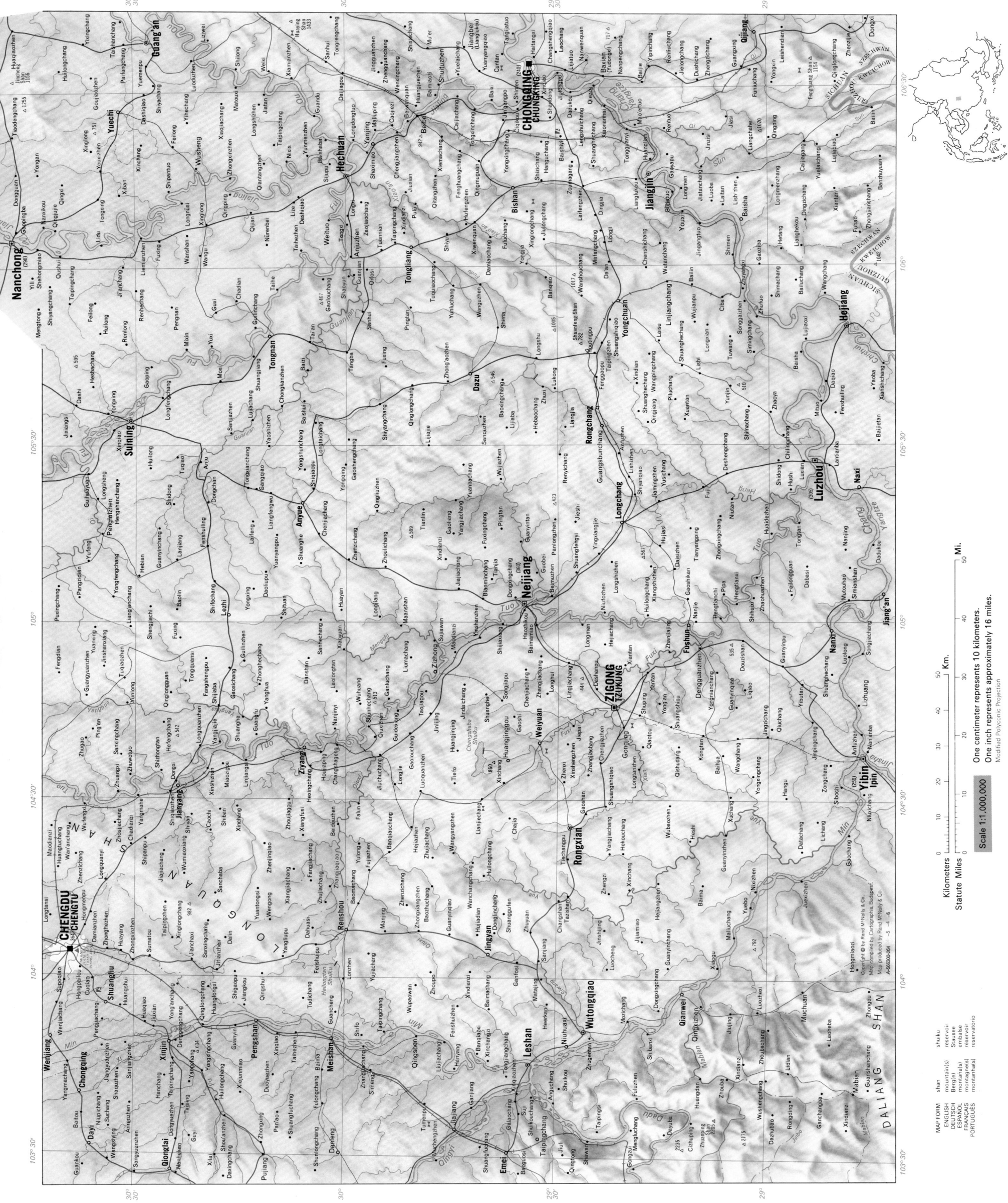

Map continues
pages 90-91

Map continues
pages 118-119

MAP FORM	gulf	gunung	island	kepulauan	pulau	sea	selat	strait
ENGLISH	gulf	mountain	island	islands	island	sea	strait	strait
DEUTSCH	Golf	Berg	Insel	Inseln	Insel	Meer	Meeresstrasse	Meeresstrasse
ESPAÑOL	golfo	montaña	isla	islas	isla	mar	estrecho	estrecho
FRANÇAIS	golfe	montagne	île	lies	île	mer	détroit	détroit
PORTUGUÊS	golfo	montanha	ilha	ilhas	ilha	mar	estreito	estreito

120° 125° 130° 135° 140° 145°

Tropic of Cancer

TAIWAN

Chiai
Yü Shan 3997
T'aitung
P'ingtung
SIUNG
OWAN PI

Bashi Channel

Luzon
AMIANAN ISLAND
ITBAYAT ISLAND
BATAN ISLANDS
Strait
Basco • BATAN ISLAND
Balintang Channel
DALUPIRI ISLAND
CALAYAN ISLAND
BABUYAN ISLANDS
BOJEADOR FUGA ISLAND
CAMIGUIN ISLAND
ESCARFADA POINT
Laoag BABUYAN ISLAND
Aparri
Tuguegarao
Vigan Ilagan
Bontoc
Lagawe
San Mount Pulog 2934
Fernando Bayombong
gayen Bambang
Dagupan LUZON
San Carlos
Tarlac Cabanatuan
Angeles San Fernando POLLO ISLANDS
zapo Dungalan Bay
MANILA Quezon City
Cavite
Tagaytay San Pablo
Lipa Daet CATANDUANES ISLAND
Batangas **PHILIPPINES**
Calapan Naga Virac
MARINDUQUE Legaspi Mayon Volcano 2462
MINDORO ISLAND Bulan Sorsogon
San Jose BURIAS Catarman
TABLAS ISLAND Masbate Laoang
SIBUYAN ISLAND
BUSUANGA ISLAND MASBATE Calbayog
CALAMIAN GROUP CUYO ISLAND **SAMAR**
CUYO Romblon Catbalogan
DUMARAN ISLAND Kalibo Basey
Roxas BILIRAN Tacloban
PANAY Ormoc **LEYTE**
Iloilo Bogo Guiuan
Bacolod San Leyte Gulf
CAGAYAN Carlos **Cebu** Libagon DINAGAT ISLAND
ISLANDS GUIMARAS ISLAND BOHOL Tagbilaran SIARGAO ISLAND
NEGROS Santander Surigao
Dumaguete SIQUIJOR ISLAND Butuan Tandag
Dipolog Iligan Bislig
Siocon Ozamiz Malaybalay
Liloy Pagadian **Cagayan de Oro**
Zamboanga **MINDANAO**
Isabela Cotabato **Davao**
PANGUTARAN Datu Piang 2956 Mount Apu
GROUP BASILAN ISLAND Lebak
Jolo Kiamba **General** CAPE SAN AGUSTIN
JOLO ISLAND Santos
Tinaca Point
SULU ARCHIPELAGO
TAWI-TAWI PULAU MANGAS
SARANGANI ISLANDS

PHILIPPINE

SEA

OKINO-TORI-SHIMA PARECE VELA (Japan)
FARALLON DE PAJAROS
MAUG ISLANDS
NORTHERN MARIANA ISLANDS (U.S.)
ASUNCION ISLAND
AGRIHAN
MARIANA PAGAN
ALAMAGAN
GUGUAN
ISLANDS SARIGAN
ANATAHAN
FARALLON DE MEDINILLA
SAIPAN
TINIAN
AGUIJAN
ROTA
Agana **GUAM** (U.S.)

PACIFIC OCEAN

ULITHI
YAP FAIS GAFERUT
FEDERATED STATES OF MICRONESIA
NGULU SOROL FARAULEP
KAYANGEL ISLANDS OLIMARAO
PALAU ISLANDS BABELTHUAP WOLEAI
NGERUKTABEL Koror IFALIK
PELELIU EAURIPIK
ANGAUR

CAROLINE ISLANDS

SONSOROL ISLANDS
PULO ANNA
MERIR
PALAU BELAU (T.T.P.I.)
TOBI
HELEN ISLAND

KEPULAUAN NANUSA
PULAU KARAKELONG
KEPULAUAN TALAUD
PULAU SALEBABU
Tahuna PULAU KABURUANG
PULAU SANGIHE
KEPULAUAN ASIA
KEPULAUAN MAPIA

CELEBES SEA

KEPULAUAN
SANGIHE
TANJUNG PULAU SAU
TORAWITAN PULAU TAHULANDANG
PULAU BIARO Wayabula MOROTAI
Galela
Manado Bitung Tobelo
MINAHASA 2022 Gunung Klabat
Tolitoli Tondano Jailolo
Bukit Matino Kotamobagu Ternate **HALMAHERA**
2440 Tidore Weda
Gorontalo
Moutong KEPULAUAN ASIA
Tomini KEPULAUAN AYU
Palu
LAUT MALUKU
Teluk Tomini **MOLUCCA SEA**
Poso Danau TOGIAN PULAU KASIRUTA PULAU WAIGEO
Poso Luwuk PULAU BACAN *Laut Halmahera* BIAK
Teluk Banggai PULAU MANDIOLI *"Halmahera" Sea*
Tolo KEPULAUAN PULAU OBILATU PULAU GEBE Manokwari
BANGGAI PULAU BISA Selat Dampier PULAU NUMFOOR
SULAWESI KEPULAUAN Sorong Bosnik
CELEBES KEPULAUAN OBI SALAWATI PULAU TANJUNG D'URVILLE
nale SULA KEPULAUAN BATANTA YAPEN Sarmi
Palopo SANANA PULAU MISOOL JAZIRAH DOBERAI Serui Demta
3455 Kolaka Inanwatan Teminabuan **Jayapura** (Sukarnapura) **PAPUA**
peng Watampone PULAU MANUI Fakfak *Teluk Berau* Babo *Teluk Cenderawasih* Waren Vanimo **NEW GUINEA**
jungpandang KEPULAUAN WOWONI Piru **SERAM CERAM** Bula SEMENANJUNG Nabire Aitape
PULAU KABAENA Namlea **CERAM SEA** Amahai BOMBERAI PEGUNUNGAN VAN REES Dagua
PULAU BUTON **BURU** Wahai Karufa Kaimana Demta Wewak
Sinjai Kendari PULAU AMBON **Ambon** Geser Modowi PEGUNUNGAN MAOKE Angoram MANAM ISLAND
Bantaeng PULAU AMBELAU KEPULAUAN Puncak Jaya 5030 **NEW** Amunti Sepik
PULAU WATUBELA KEPULAUAN 4750 Ambunti
Bulukumba TUKANGBESI BANDA Puncak Trikora 4760 **GUINEA** Wabag Mount
PULAU **LAUT BANDA** Kokenau Puncak Mandala Telefomin Wilhelm 4509
SELAYAR KEPULAUAN Lake Tari Mount
BANDA SEA WUCIPARA KEPULAUAN **KAI** Murray Mount Hagen
KEPULAUAN PENTU KAI KECIL Tual Kepi Mendi Giluwe 4368 Goroka
PULAU BINONGKO NUHU CUT Dobo PULAU WOKAM Mount Bosavi
DAYA PULAU KEPULAUAN 2397
PULAU SERUA MAIKOOR **ARU** Kikori
PULAU SELAYAR PULAU NILA KEPULAUAN Balimo Kikori
PULAU MOLU PULAU TRANGAN Gulf
BARAT PULAU TELUN Tanahmerah **PULAU** of Papua
KEPULAUAN PULAU DAMAR PULAU **YOS** Okaba
PULAU ROMANG WULIARU **SUDARSO** Balimo
PULAU MAMBERA PULAU LARAT Merauke
PULAU WETAR KISAR PULAU **PULAU**
Ilwaki PULAU MOA SELU **YAMDENA** BOIGU
FLORES Maumere Kalabahi ALOR Tepa Saumlaki **KEPULAUAN TANIMBAR** ISLAND SABAI ISLAND
Ende ADONARA PULAU SERMATA TANJUNG VALS WARRIOR REEFS
GGARA PANTAR KEPULAUAN **Dili** PRINCE OF WALES ISLAND
DA ISLANDS Ruteng LOMBLEN LETI BABAR Torres Strait CAPE YORK
Waingapu PULAU ATAURO KEPULAUAN SELARU MOA ISLAND
Baing **TIMOR**
SUMBA Soe **ARAFURA SEA** CAPE YORK
PULAU SEMAU Kupang PENINSULA
PULAU SAWU Savu Sea **TIMOR SEA**
PULAU ROTI CAPE CROKER **AUSTRALIA** Endeavour GREAT BARRIER
CAPE WESSEL

20°
15°
10°
5°
Equator 0°
5°
10°

Map continues
pages **160-161**

120° 125° 130° 135° 140° 145°

Kilometers 0 200 400 600 Km.
Statute Miles 0 200 400 600 Mi.

Scale 1:12,000,000

One centimeter represents 120 kilometers.
One inch represents approximately 190 miles.
Lambert Conformal Conic Projection

Burma, Thailand and Indochina / Burma, Thailand und Indochina / Birmania, Siam e Indochina
Birmanie, Thaïlande et Indochine / Birmânia, Tailândia e Indochina

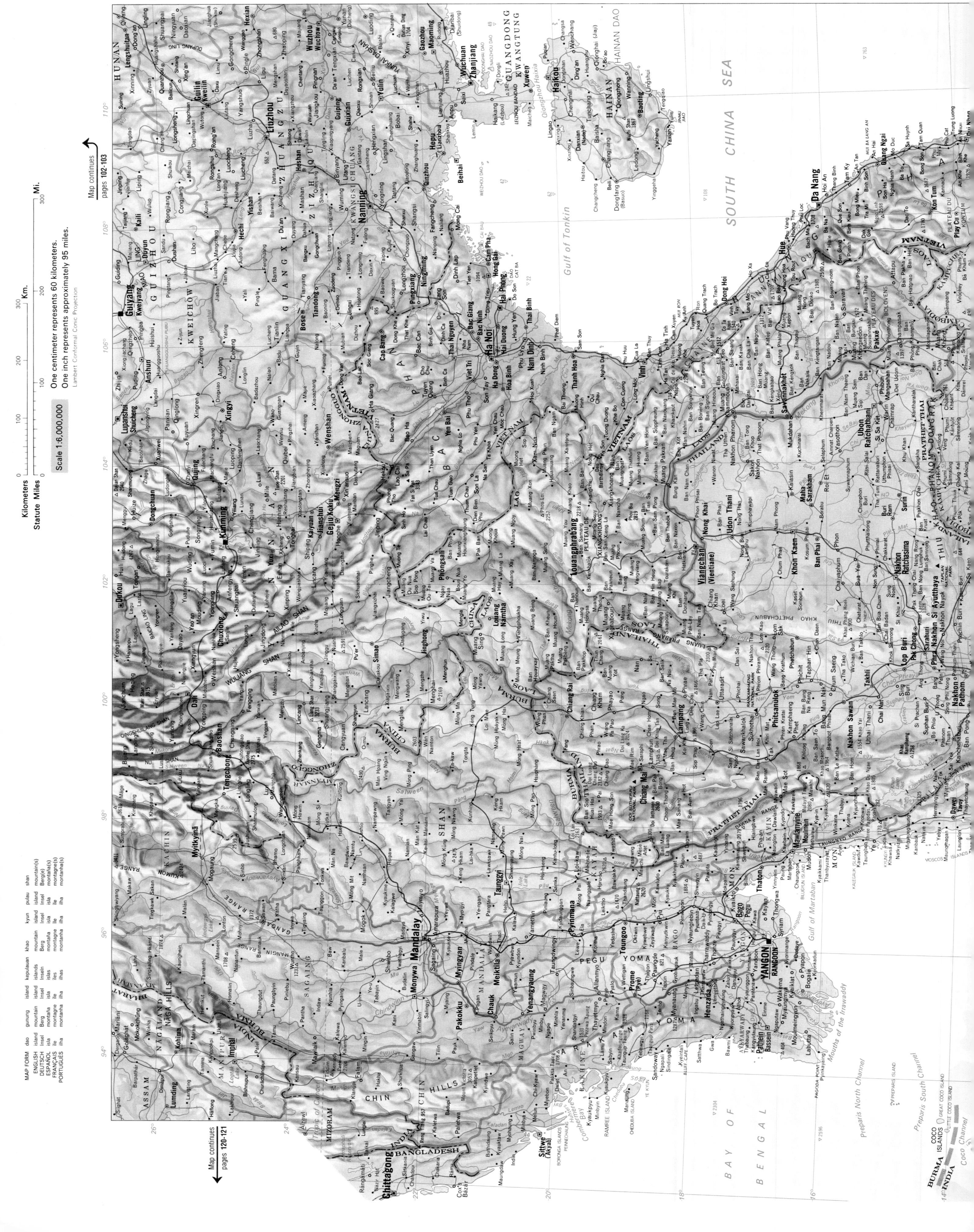

Scale 1:6,000,000

One centimeter represents 60 kilometers.
One inch represents approximately 95 miles.

Lambert Conformal Conic Projection

Kilometers
Statute Miles

Map continues
pages 102-103

Map continues
pages 120-121

MAP FORM						
ENGLISH	dao island	gurung mountain	kyun island	khao mountain	kepulauan islands	shan mountain(s)
DEUTSCH	Insel	Berg	Insel	Berg	Inseln	Berg(e)
ESPAÑOL	isla	montaña	isla	montaña	islas	montaña(s)
FRANÇAIS	île	montagne	île	montagne	îles	montagne(s)
PORTUGUÊS	ilha	montanha	ilha	montanha	ilhas	montanha(s)

pulau island Insel isla île ilha

SOUTH CHINA SEA

Gulf of Tonkin

BAY OF BENGAL

Gulf of Martaban

Mouths of the Irrawaddy

Burma, Thailand and Indochina / Burma, Thailand und Indochina / Birmania, Siam e Indochina
Birmanie, Thaïlande et Indochine / Birmânia, Tailândia e Indochina

111

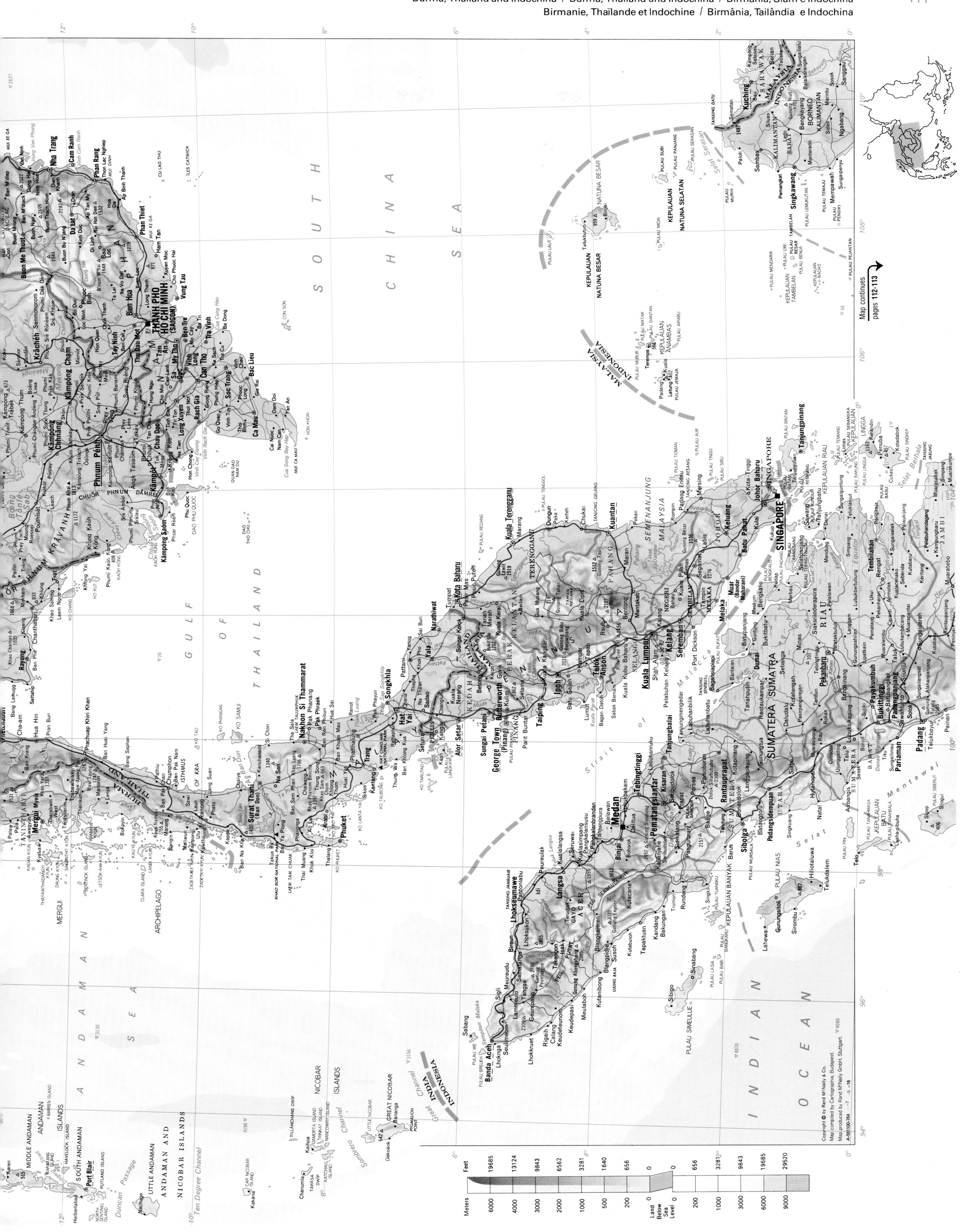

Malaysia and Western Indonesia / Malaysia und westliches Indonesien / Malasia e Indonesia Occidental
Malaisie et Indonésie Occidentale / Malásia e Indonésia Ocidental

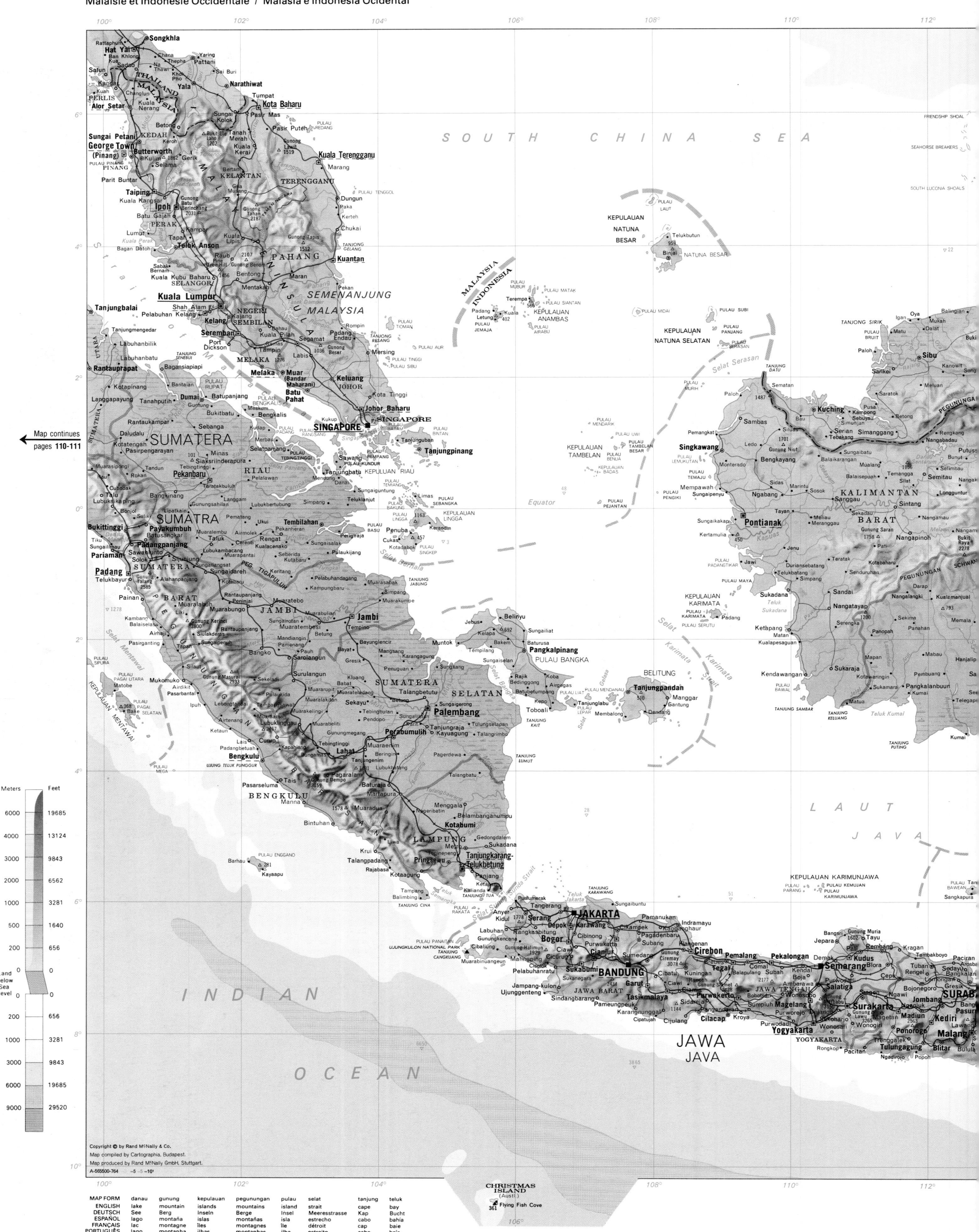

SOUTH CHINA SEA

SUMATERA

SINGAPORE

KALIMANTAN
BARAT

INDIAN
OCEAN

JAWA
JAVA

LAUT
JAWA

CHRISTMAS
ISLAND
(Austl.)
361 Flying Fish Cove

MAP FORM	danau	gunung	kepulauan	pegunungan	pulau	selat	tanjung	teluk
ENGLISH	lake	mountain	islands	mountains	island	strait	cape	bay
DEUTSCH	See	Berg	Inseln	Berge	Insel	Meeresstrasse	Kap	Bucht
ESPAÑOL	lago	montaña	islas	montañas	isla	estrecho	cabo	bahía
FRANÇAIS	lac	montagne	îles	montagnes	île	détroit	cap	baie
PORTUGUÊS	lago	montanha	ilhas	montanhas	ilha	estreito	cabo	baía

Meters	Feet
6000	19685
4000	13124
3000	9843
2000	6562
1000	3281
500	1640
200	656
0	0
Land Below Sea Level 0	0
200	656
1000	3281
3000	9843
6000	19685
9000	29520

Map continues pages 110-111

Malaysia and Western Indonesia / Malaysia und westliches Indonesien
Malasia e Indonesia Occidental / Malaisie et Indonésie Occidentale
Malásia e Indonésia Ocidental

113

Map continues
pages 116-117

Map continues
pages 164-165

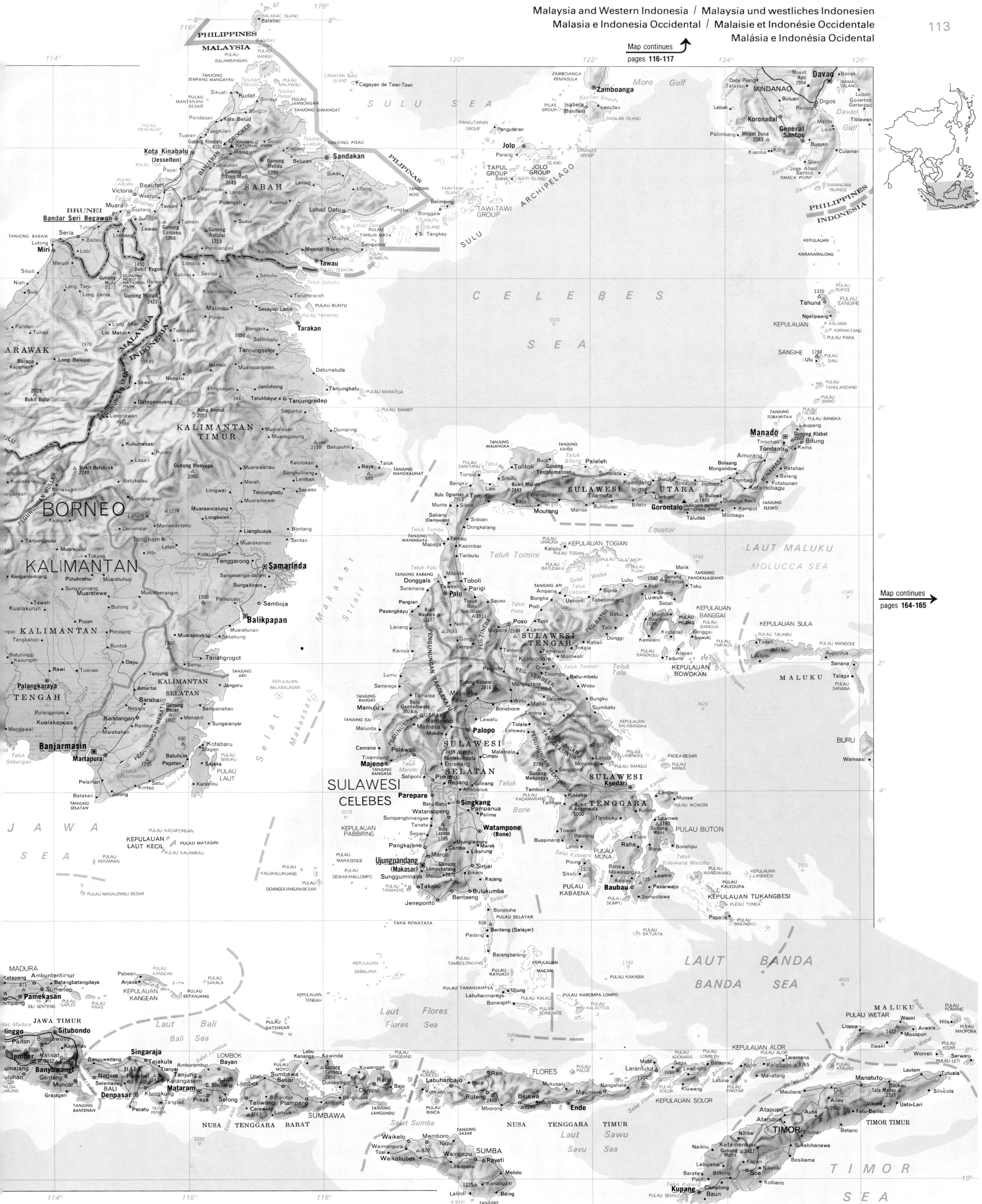

PHILIPPINES
MALAYSIA

SULU SEA

CELEBES SEA

MINDANAO
Davao
Zamboanga
General Santos
Koronadal
PHILIPPINES
INDONESIA

SABAH
Kota Kinabalu (Jesselton)
Sandakan
Tawau
Lahad Datu
BRUNEI
Bandar Seri Begawan
Miri
SARAWAK

BORNEO

KALIMANTAN TIMUR

KALIMANTAN

Samarinda
Balikpapan

KALIMANTAN TENGAH
Palangkaraya

KALIMANTAN SELATAN
Banjarmasin
Martapura

Tarakan

SULAWESI UTARA
Manado
Gorontalo
Tahuna

SULAWESI TENGAH
Palu
Donggala
Poso

SULAWESI
CELEBES

SULAWESI SELATAN
Palopo
Majene
Parepare
Singkang
Watampone (Bone)
Ujungpandang (Makasar)

SULAWESI TENGGARA
Kendari
Baubau

PULAU BUTON
PULAU MUNA
PULAU KABAENA

MALUKU
BURU
BANDA SEA
LAUT BANDA
LAUT MALUKU
MOLUCCA SEA

JAWA SEA
JAWA TIMUR
Pamekasan
MADURA

BALI
Denpasar
Singaraja
Mataram
LOMBOK
SUMBAWA

NUSA TENGGARA BARAT

FLORES
Ende
Labuhanbajo

NUSA TENGGARA TIMUR

SUMBA
Waingapu
Waikabubak

TIMOR
Kupang
Dili
TIMOR TIMUR

LAUT SAWU
Savu Sea

TIMOR SEA

Laut Flores
Flores Sea
Laut Bali
Bali Sea

Selat Makasar
Makasar Strait

Teluk Tomini
Teluk Tolo
Teluk Bone

Kilometers 0 100 200 300 Km.
Statute Miles 0 100 200 300 Mi.
Scale 1:6,000,000
One centimeter represents 60 kilometers.
One inch represents approximately 95 miles.
Mercator Projection

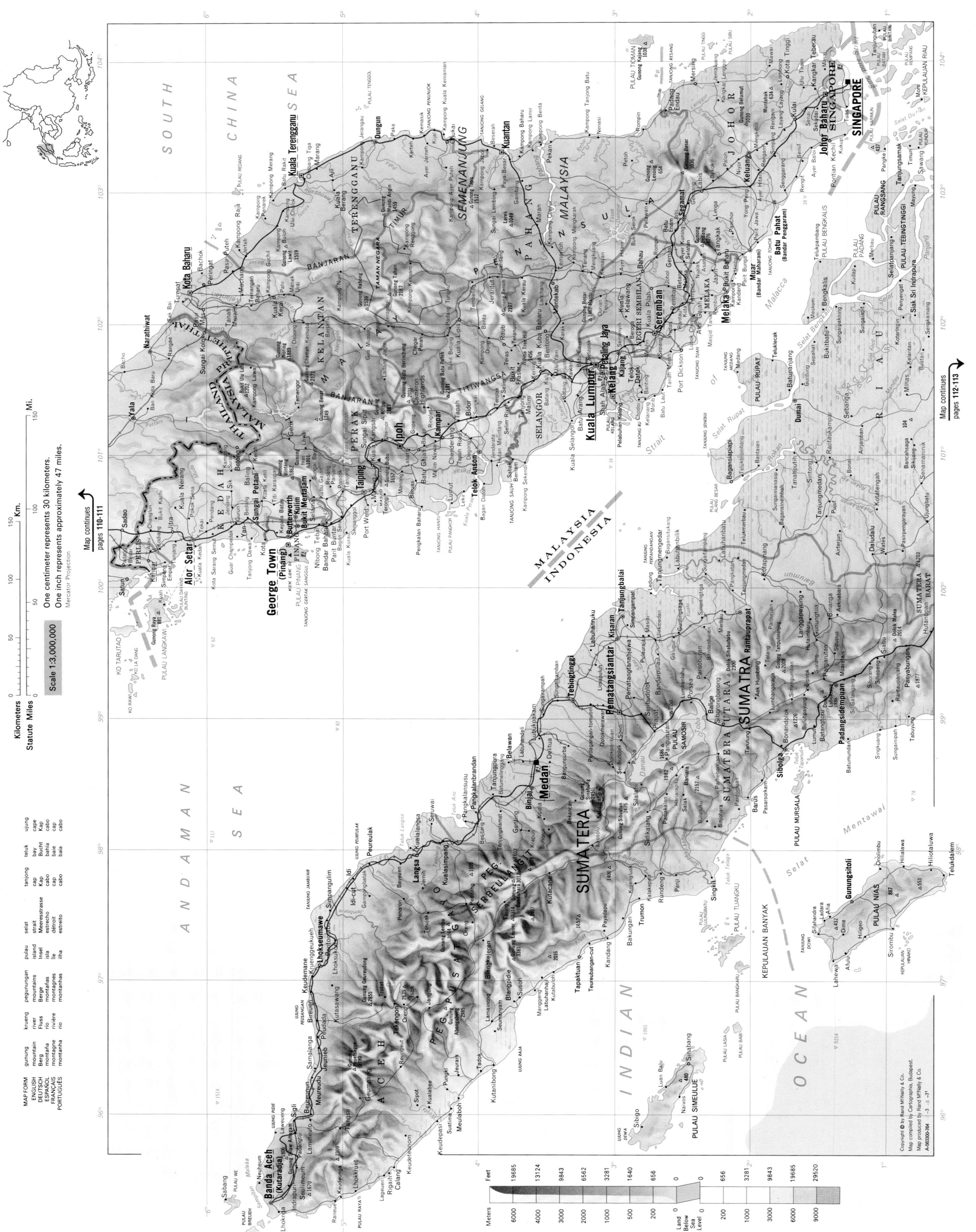

Kilometers
Statute Miles

Scale 1:3,000,000

One centimeter represents 30 kilometers.
One inch represents approximately 47 miles.
Mercator Projection

Map continues
pages 110-111

Map continues
pages 112-113

MAP FORM				
ENGLISH	gunung	krueng	peguningan	ujung
DEUTSCH	mountain	river	mountains	cape
ESPAÑOL	Berg	Fluss	Berge	Kap
FRANÇAIS	montaña	río	montañas	cabo
PORTUGUÊS	montanha	rio	montanhas	cabo

gunung	mountain	teluk	bay
Berg	montaña	Bucht	bahía
montagne	montanha	baie	baía

tanjong	cap	selat	strait
Kap	cabo	Meeresstrasse	estrecho
cap	cabo	détroit	estreito

pulau	island
Insel	isla
île	ilha

MALAYSIA
INDONESIA

SOUTH CHINA SEA

ANDAMAN SEA

INDIAN OCEAN

Banda Aceh (Kutaradja)

SUMATERA

Medan

SINGAPORE

Kuala Lumpur

George Town (Pinang)

Feet / Meters elevation scale
19685 / 6000
13124 / 4000
9843 / 3000
6562 / 2000
3281 / 1000
1640 / 500
656 / 200
0 / Land Below Sea Level
656 / 200
3281 / 1000
9843 / 3000
19685 / 6000
29520 / 9000

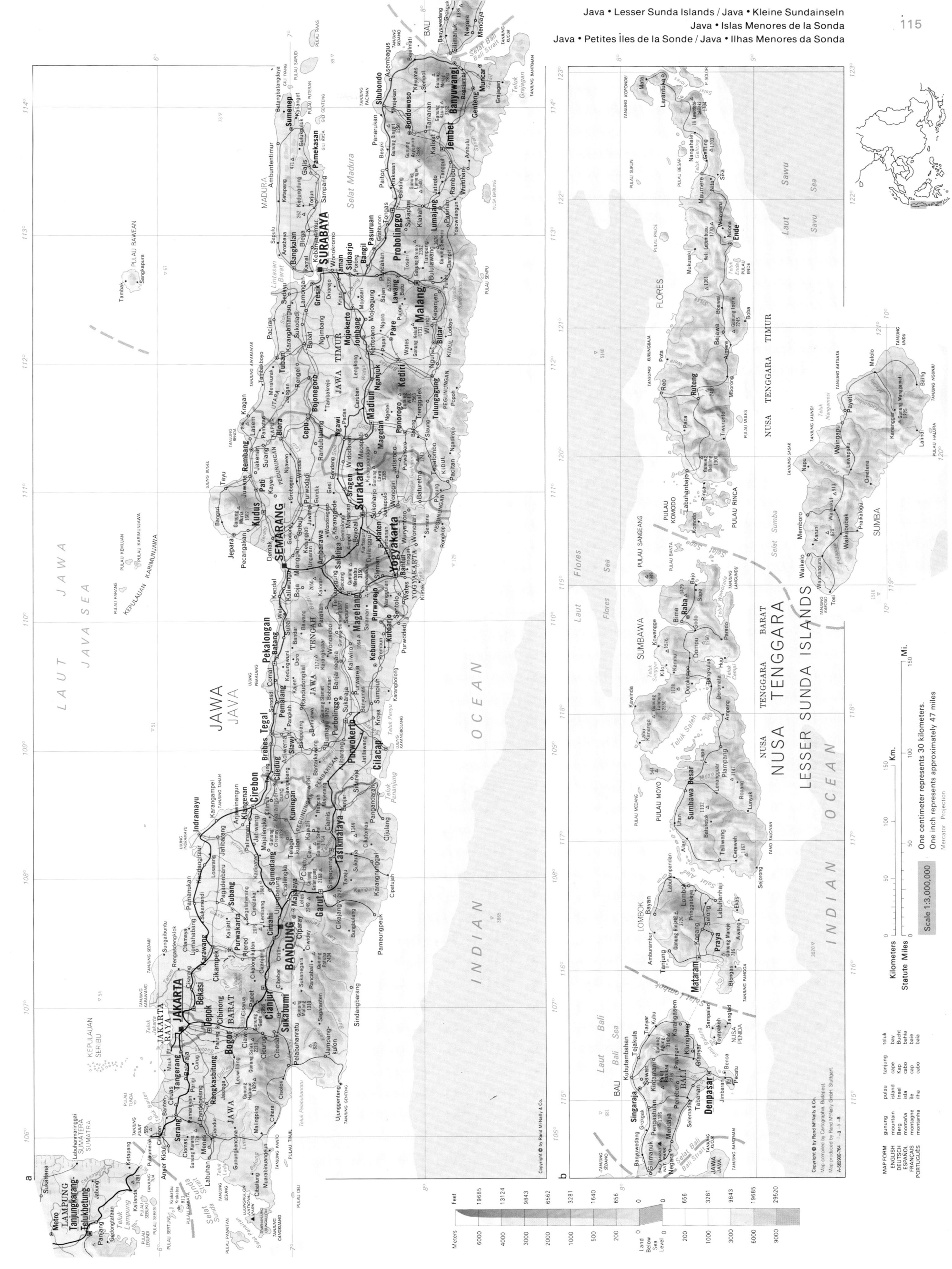

Java • Lesser Sunda Islands / Java • Kleine Sundainseln
Java • Islas Menores de la Sonda
Java • Petites Îles de la Sonde / Java • Ilhas Menores da Sonda

LESSER SUNDA ISLANDS

NUSA TENGGARA

NUSA TENGGARA BARAT

NUSA TENGGARA TIMUR

JAWA
JAVA

LAUT JAWA
JAVA SEA

INDIAN OCEAN

LAUT FLORES
FLORES SEA

LAUT SAWU
SAWU SEA

BALI

FLORES

SUMBA

SUMBAWA

LOMBOK

MADURA

Scale 1:3,000,000

One centimeter represents 30 kilometers.
One inch represents approximately 47 miles.
Mercator Projection

Kilometers
Statute Miles
Km.
Mi.

MAP FORM		
ENGLISH	gunung	mountain
DEUTSCH		Berg
ESPAÑOL		montaña
FRANÇAIS		montagne
PORTUGUÊS		montanha

	tanjung	cape
		Kap
		cabo
		cap
		cabo

	teluk	bay
		Bucht
		bahía
		baie
		baía

	pulau	island
		Insel
		isla
		île
		ilha

Feet
19685
13124
9843
6562
3281
1640
656
0

Meters
6000
4000
3000
2000
1000
500
200
0
Land Below Sea Level

Meters
200
1000
3000
6000
9000

Feet
656
3281
9843
19685
29520

Copyright © by Rand McNally & Co.

a

b

Scale 1:3,000,000

One centimeter represents 30 kilometers.
One inch represents approximately 47 miles.

Lambert Conformal Conic Projection

Mi.
150
100
50
0

Km.
150
100
50
0

Kilometers
Statute Miles

MAP FORM	bay	channel	island, i.	mount, mt.	passage	peak, pk.	point	strait
ENGLISH	bay	channel	island	mount	passage	peak	point	strait
DEUTSCH	Bucht	Kanal	Insel	Berg	Durchfahrt	Gipfel	Landspitze	Meeresstrasse
ESPAÑOL	bahia	canal	isla	montaña	pasaje	pico	punta	estrecho
FRANÇAIS	baie	détroit	île	mont	passage	cime	pointe	détroit
PORTUGUÊS	baja	canal	ilha	montanha	passagem	pico	ponta	estreito

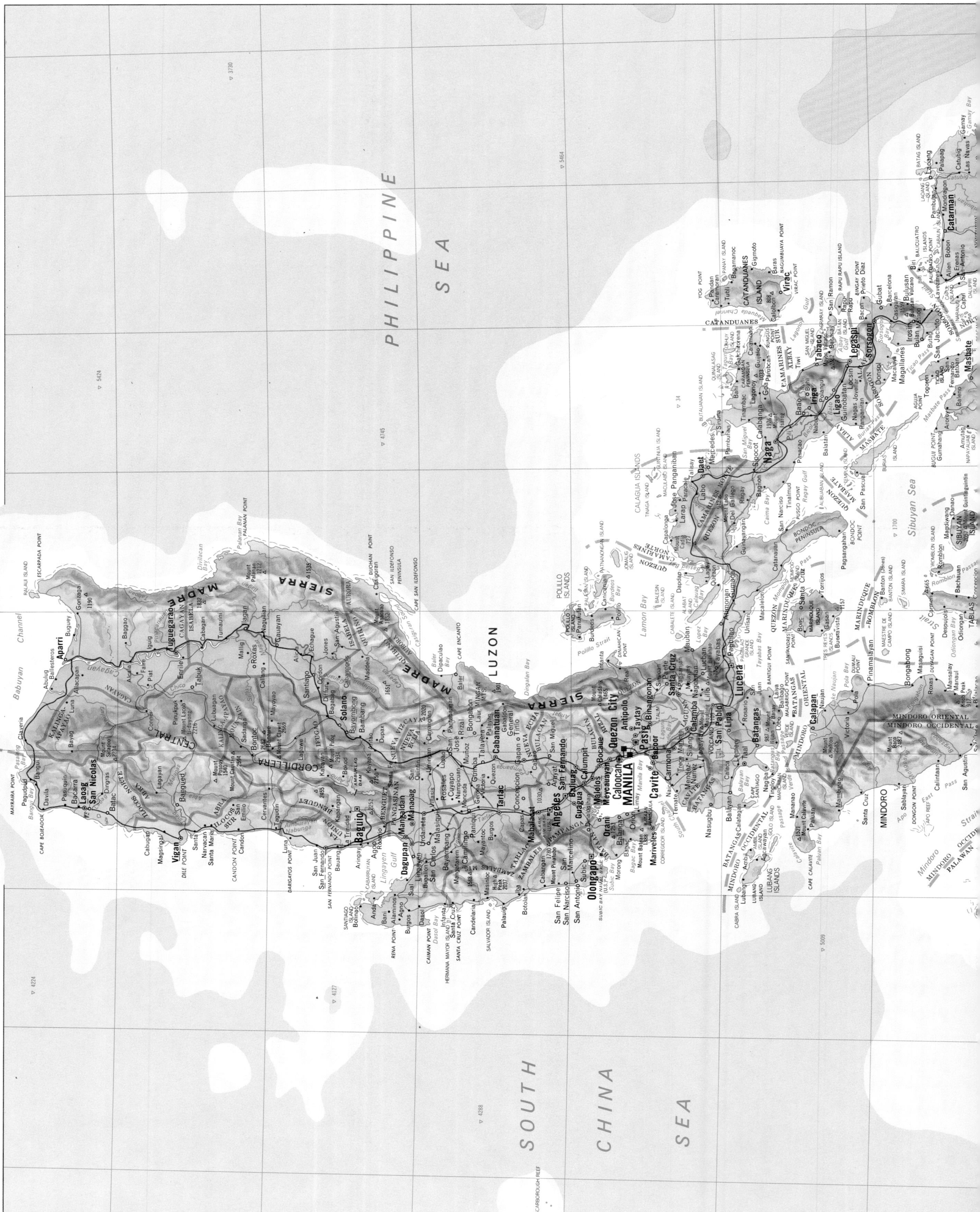

PHILIPPINE SEA

SOUTH CHINA SEA

LUZON

SIERRA MADRE

CORDILLERA CENTRAL

CAGAYAN

BABUYAN ISLANDS

Luzon Strait

Babuyan Channel

MANILA

Quezon City

Caloocan

Cavite

Baguio

Dagupan

Mangaldan

Tarlac

Angeles

San Fernando

Olongapo

Aparri

Laoag

Vigan

San Nicolas

Bacarra

Santa Cruz

Lucena

San Pablo

Batangas

Lipa

Calamba

Naga

Legaspi

Tabaco

Sorsogon

Daet

Virac

CATANDUANES ISLAND

MASBATE

MINDORO

MINDORO ORIENTAL

MINDORO OCCIDENTAL

PALAWAN

MARINDUQUE

ROMBLON

TABLAS ISLAND

SIBUYAN ISLAND

Sibuyan Sea

Catarman

QUEZON

BONDOC PENINSULA

CAMARINES NORTE

CAMARINES SUR

ALBAY

SCARBOROUGH REEF

	Feet
	19685
	13124
	9843
	6562
	3281
	1640
	656
	0

Meters	
6000	
4000	
3000	
2000	
1000	
500	
200	
0	Land
	Below
	Sea
	Level

0	656	3281	9843	19685	29520	Feet
0	200	1000	3000	6000	9000	Meters

SAMAR

Catbalogan

Tacloban

LEYTE

CEBU

Cebu · Lapu-Lapu (Opon)
Mandaue

Cadiz
Victorias
Silay · Talisay
San Carlos
La Carlota
Bacolod
Pulupandan
Binalbagan

NEGROS

Iloilo
Roxas (Capiz)

PANAY

GUIMARAS ISLAND

MASBATE

CAMOTES ISLANDS

Dumaguete

Tagbilaran

BOHOL

Bohol Sea

Visayan Sea

Sulu Sea

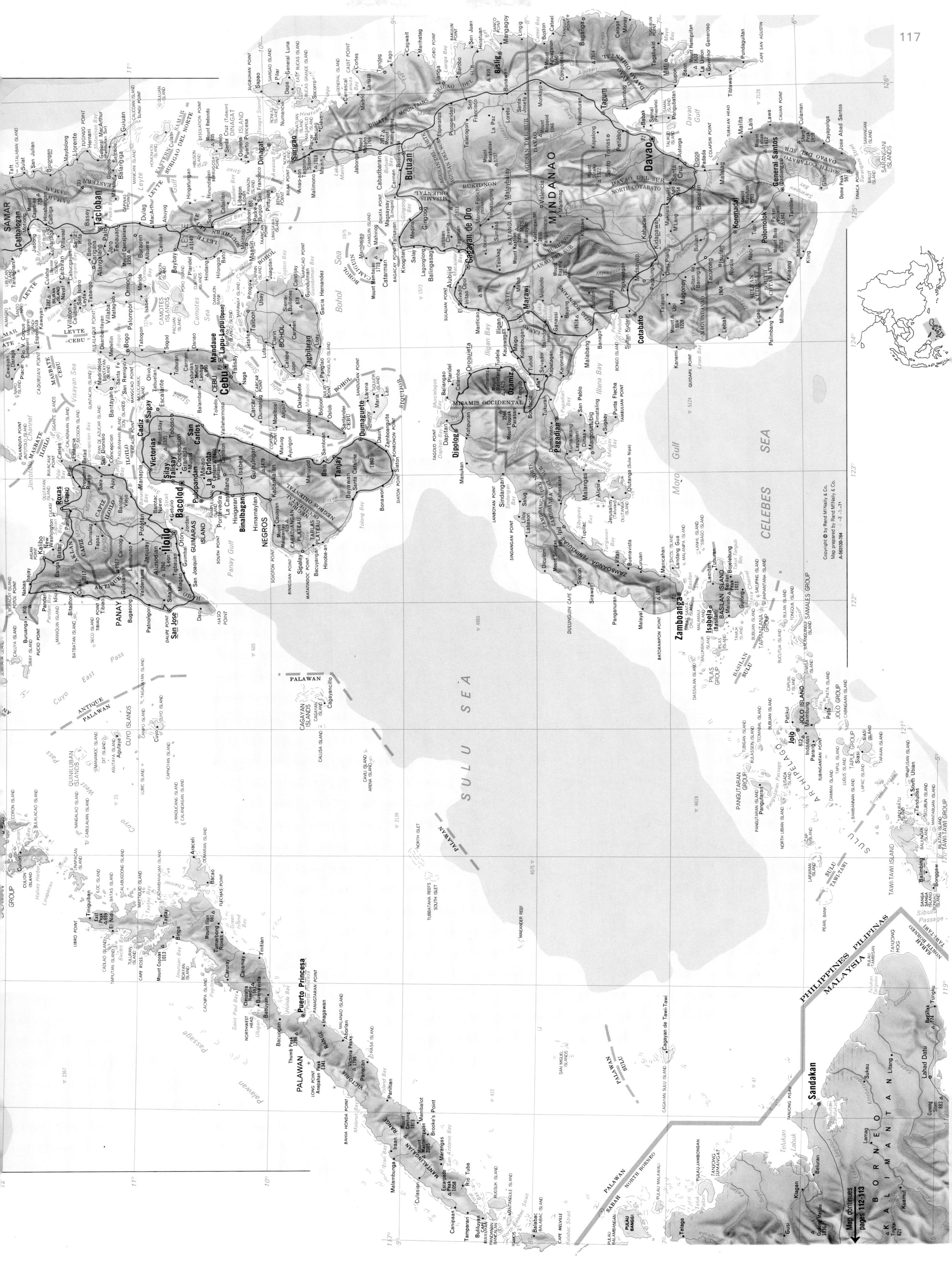

SULU SEA

CELEBES SEA

MINDANAO

Surigao
Butuan
Cagayan de Oro
Marawi
Iligan Bay
Ozamiz
Dipolog
Pagadian
Cotabato
Davao
General Santos
Koronadal
Polomoloc
Tagum
Bislig

Davao Gulf

Moro Gulf

Zamboanga
Isabela (Basilan)
BASILAN ISLAND

SULU ARCHIPELAGO

Jolo
JOLO ISLAND

TAWI-TAWI ISLAND
TAWI-TAWI GROUP

PALAWAN

Puerto Princesa

San Jose

CUYO ISLANDS

CAGAYAN ISLANDS

Cagayancillo

ANTIQUE
PALAWAN

PHILIPPINES · PILIPINAS
MALAYSIA

Sandakan

SABAH
NORTH BORNEO

BORNEO

KALIMANTAN

Copyright © by Rand McNally & Co.
Map prepared by Rand McNally & Co.
A-567100-764   -3-3-71

Map continues
pages 112-113

Map continues
pages 22-23

Map continues
pages 134-135

MAP FORM	gulf	jabal	jazirat	range	ra's	shan
ENGLISH	gulf	mountain	island	range	cape	shan
DEUTSCH	Golf	Berg	Insel	Gebirge	Kap	Berg(e)
ESPAÑOL	golfo	montaña	isla	sierra	cabo	montaña(s)
FRANÇAIS	golfe	montagne	ile	chaîne	cap	montagne(s)
PORTUGUÊS	golfo	montanha	ilha	serra	cabo	montanha(s)

Kilometers 0   200   400   600 Km.
Statute Miles 0   200   400   600 Mi.

Scale 1:12,000,000   One centimeter represents 120 kilometers.
One inch represents approximately 190 miles.
Lambert Conformal Conic Projection

India, Pakistan and Southwest Asia / Indien, Pakistan und Südwestasien / India, Pakistán y Asia Sud-occidental
Inde, Pakistan et Asie du Sud-Ouest / Índia, Paquistão e Ásia do Sudoeste

119

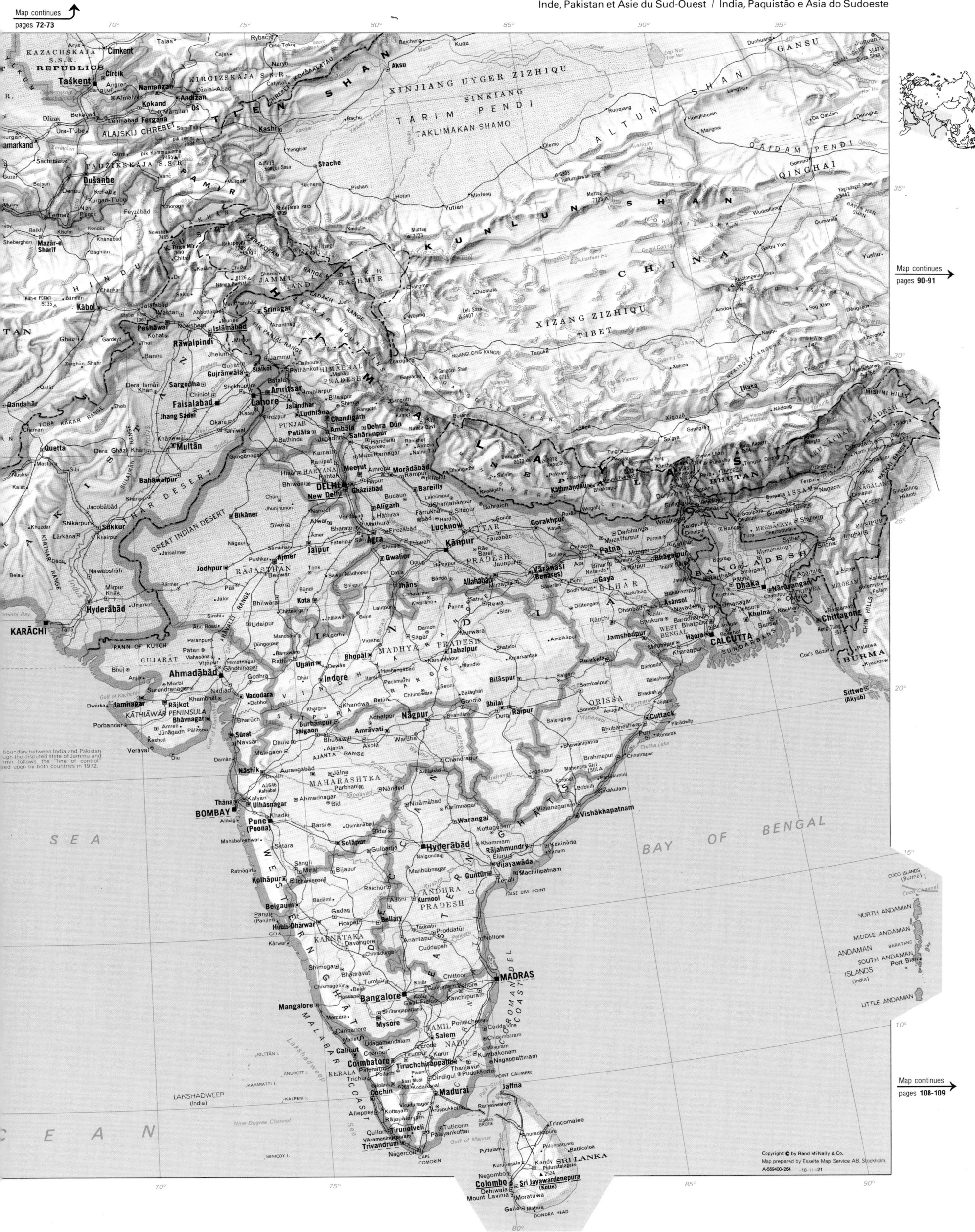

Map continues
pages 72-73

Map continues
pages 90-91

Map continues
pages 108-109

Copyright © by Rand McNally & Co.
Map prepared by Esselte Map Service AB, Stockholm.
A-569400-264   -10-11-21

120

Northern India and Pakistan / Nordindien und Pakistan / India Septentrional y Pakistán
Inde Septentrionale et Pakistan / Índia Setentrional e Paquistão

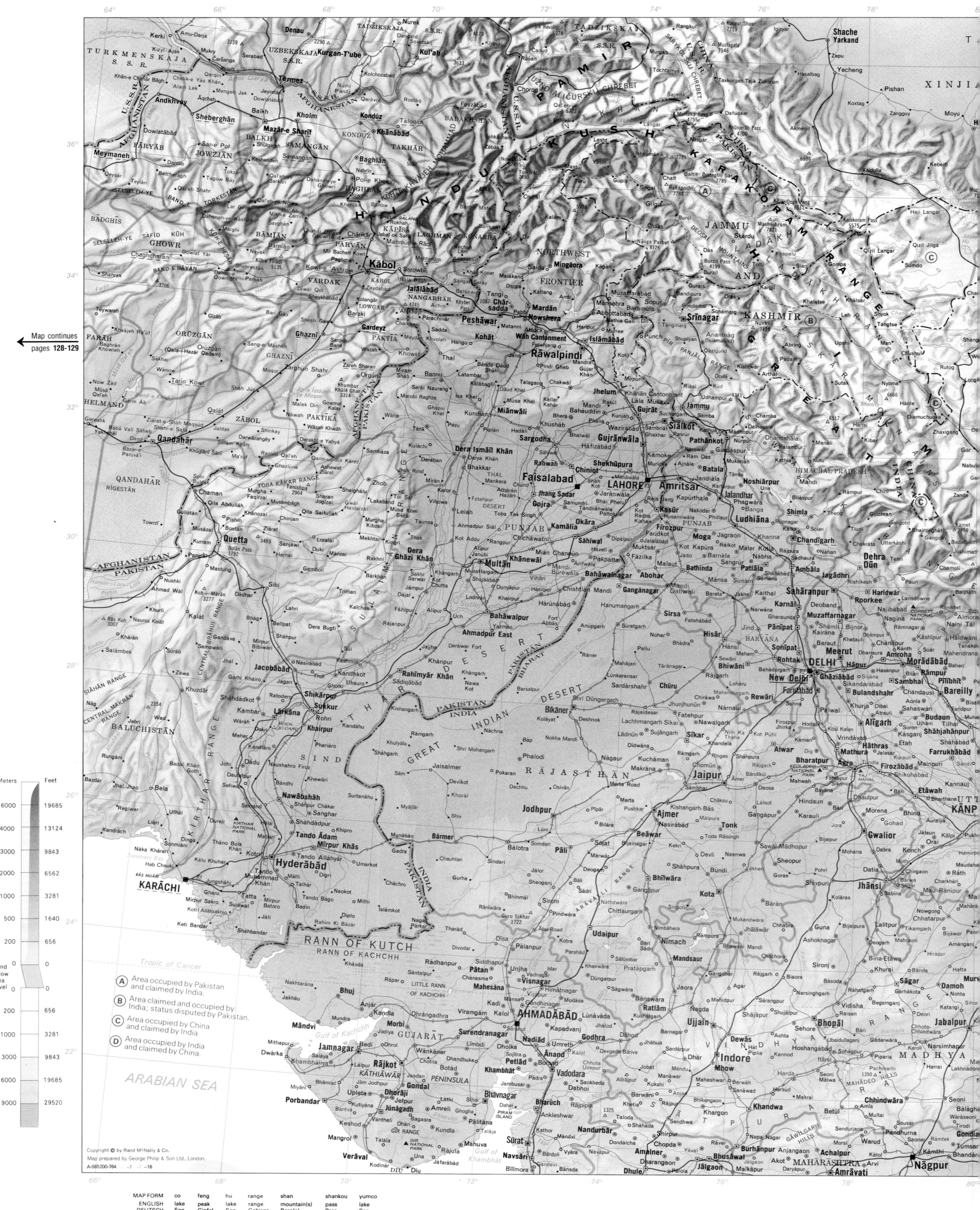

Map continues
pages 128-129

Meters   Feet

6000   19685

4000   13124

3000   9843

2000   6562

1000   3281

500   1640

200   656

Land   0
Below
Sea
Level   0

200   656

1000   3281

3000   9843

6000   19685

9000   29520

Tropic of Cancer

(A) Area occupied by Pakistan
     and claimed by India.

(B) Area claimed and occupied by
     India; status disputed by Pakistan.

(C) Area occupied by China
     and claimed by India.

(D) Area occupied by India
     and claimed by China.

ARABIAN SEA

MAP FORM	co	feng	hu	range	shan	shankou	yumco
ENGLISH	lake	peak	lake	range	mountain(s)	pass	lake
DEUTSCH	See	Gipfel	See	Gebirge	Berg(e)	Pass	See
ESPAÑOL	lago	pico	lago	sierra	montaña(s)	paso	lago
FRANÇAIS	lac	cime	lac	chaîne	montagne(s)	col	lac
PORTUGUÊS	lago	pico	lago	serra	montanha(s)	passo	lago

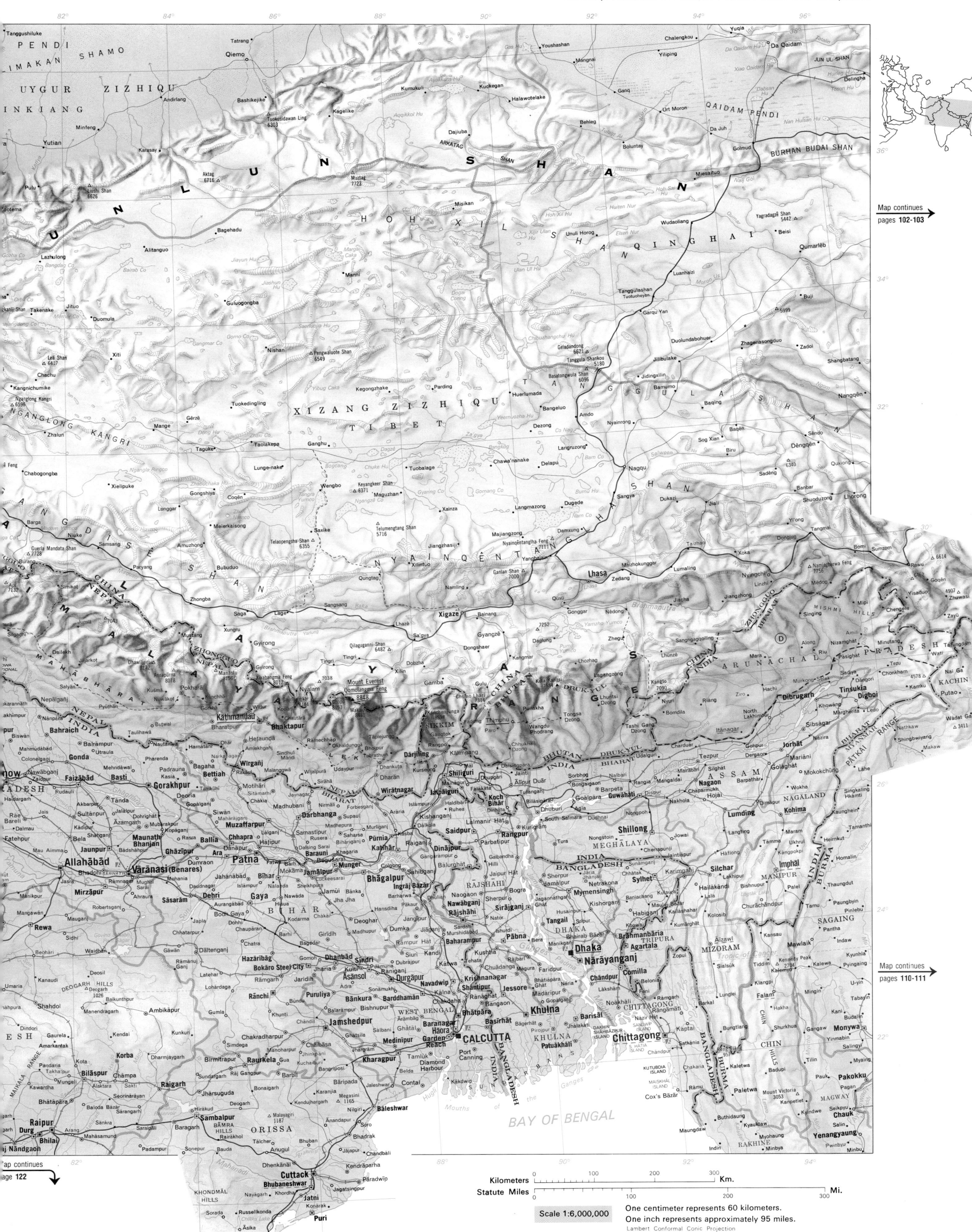

Kilometers
Statute Miles

Scale 1:6,000,000

One centimeter represents 60 kilometers.
One inch represents approximately 95 miles.
Lambert Conformal Conic Projection

Map continues
pages 102-103

Map continues
pages 110-111

Map continues
page 122

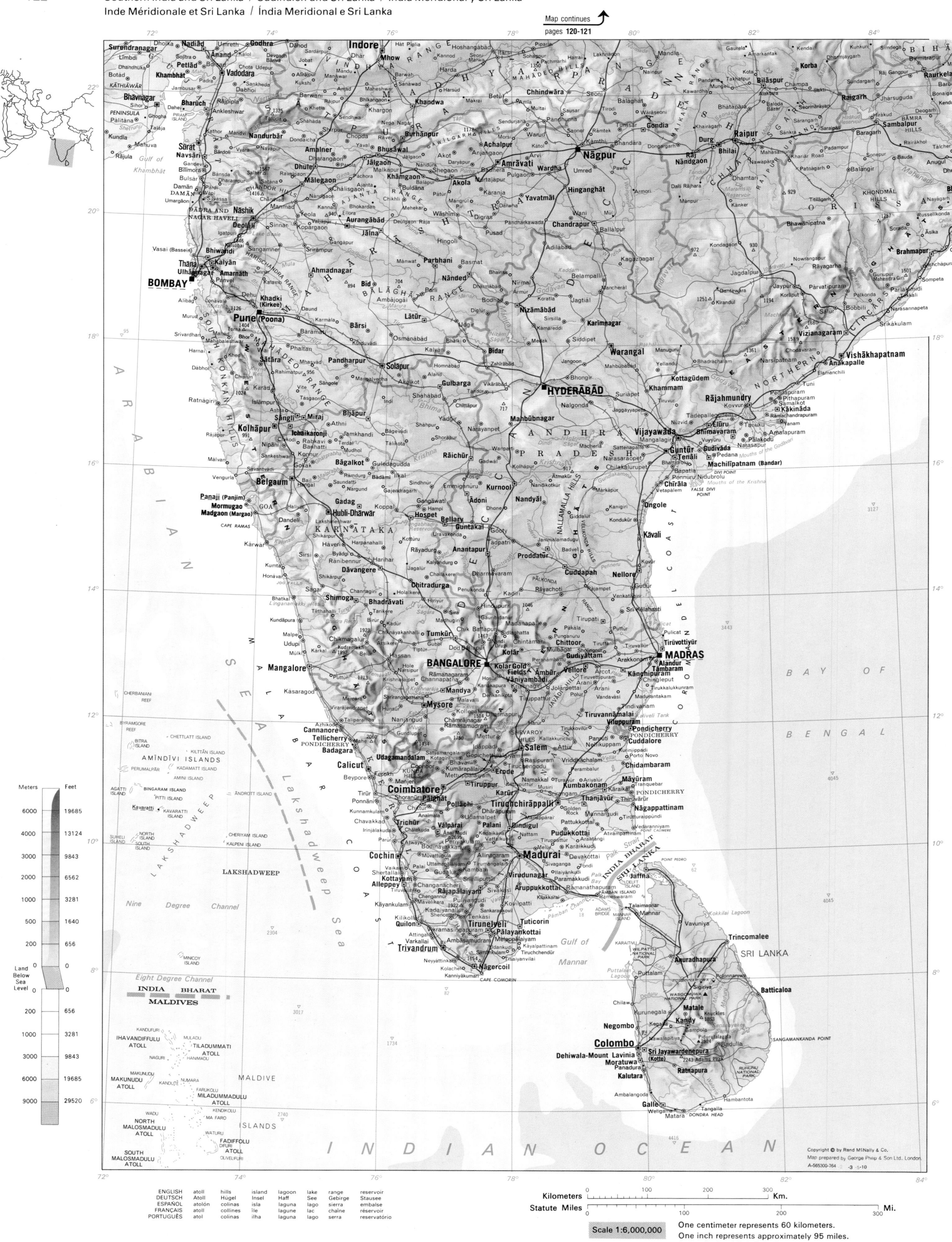

122

Southern India and Sri Lanka / Südindien und Sri Lanka / India Meridional y Sri Lanka
Inde Méridionale et Sri Lanka / Índia Meridional e Sri Lanka

Map continues
pages **120-121**

Meters | Feet

Meters	Feet
6000	19685
4000	13124
3000	9843
2000	6562
1000	3281
500	1640
200	656
Land Below Sea Level 0	0
200	656
1000	3281
3000	9843
6000	19685
9000	29520

ENGLISH	atoll	hills	island	lagoon	lake	range	reservoir
DEUTSCH	atoll	Hügel	Insel	Haff	See	Gebirge	Stausee
ESPAÑOL	atolón	colinas	isla	laguna	lago	sierra	embalse
FRANÇAIS	atoll	collines	île	lagune	lac	chaîne	réservoir
PORTUGUÊS	atol	colinas	ilha	laguna	lago	serra	reservatório

Kilometers
Statute Miles

Scale 1:6,000,000

One centimeter represents 60 kilometers.
One inch represents approximately 95 miles.
Lambert Conformal Conic Projection

Copyright © by Rand McNally & Co.
Map prepared by George Philip & Son Ltd., London.
A-565300-764   -3 -5-10

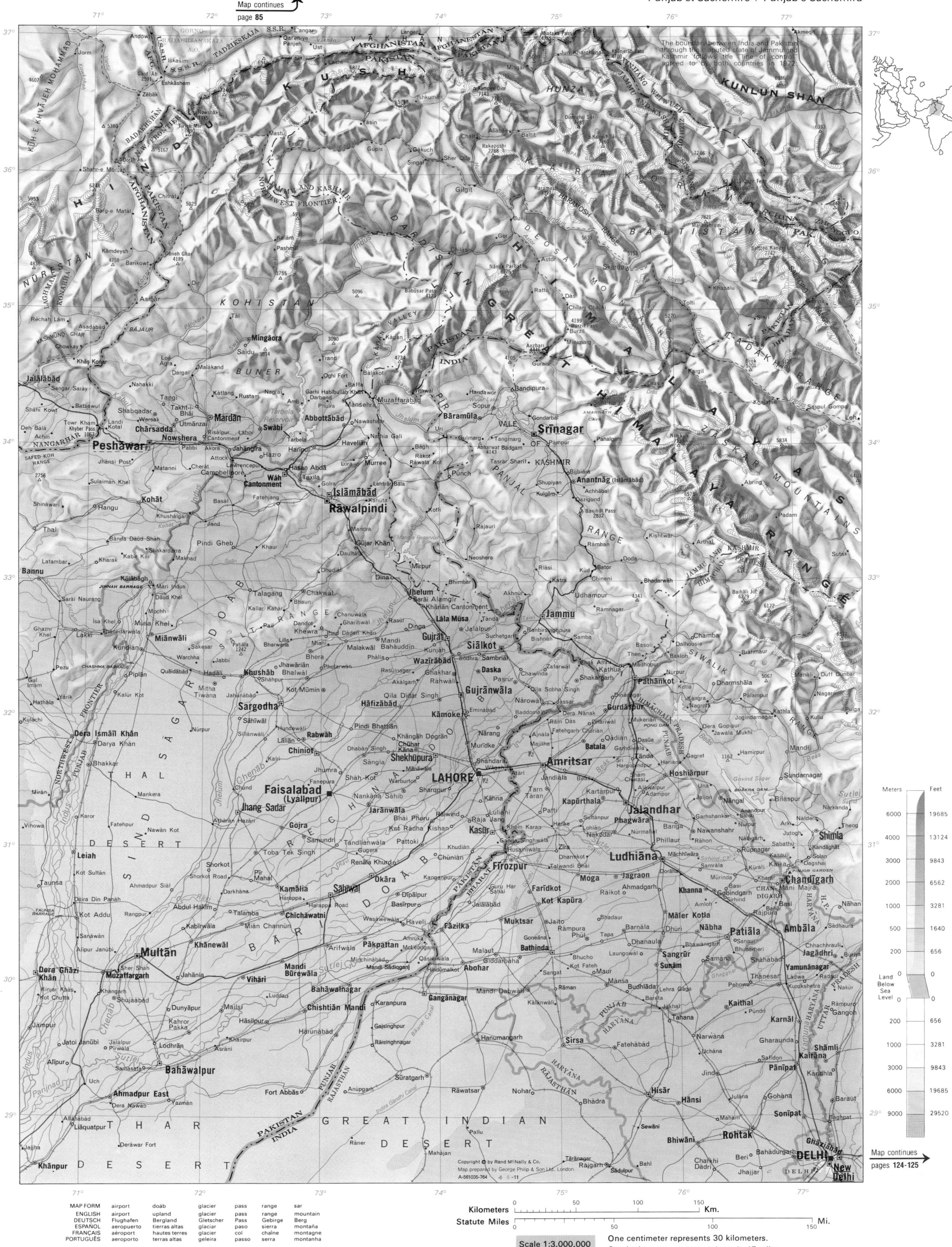

Scale 1:3,000,000
One centimeter represents 30 kilometers.
One inch represents approximately 47 miles.
Lambert Conformal Conic Projection

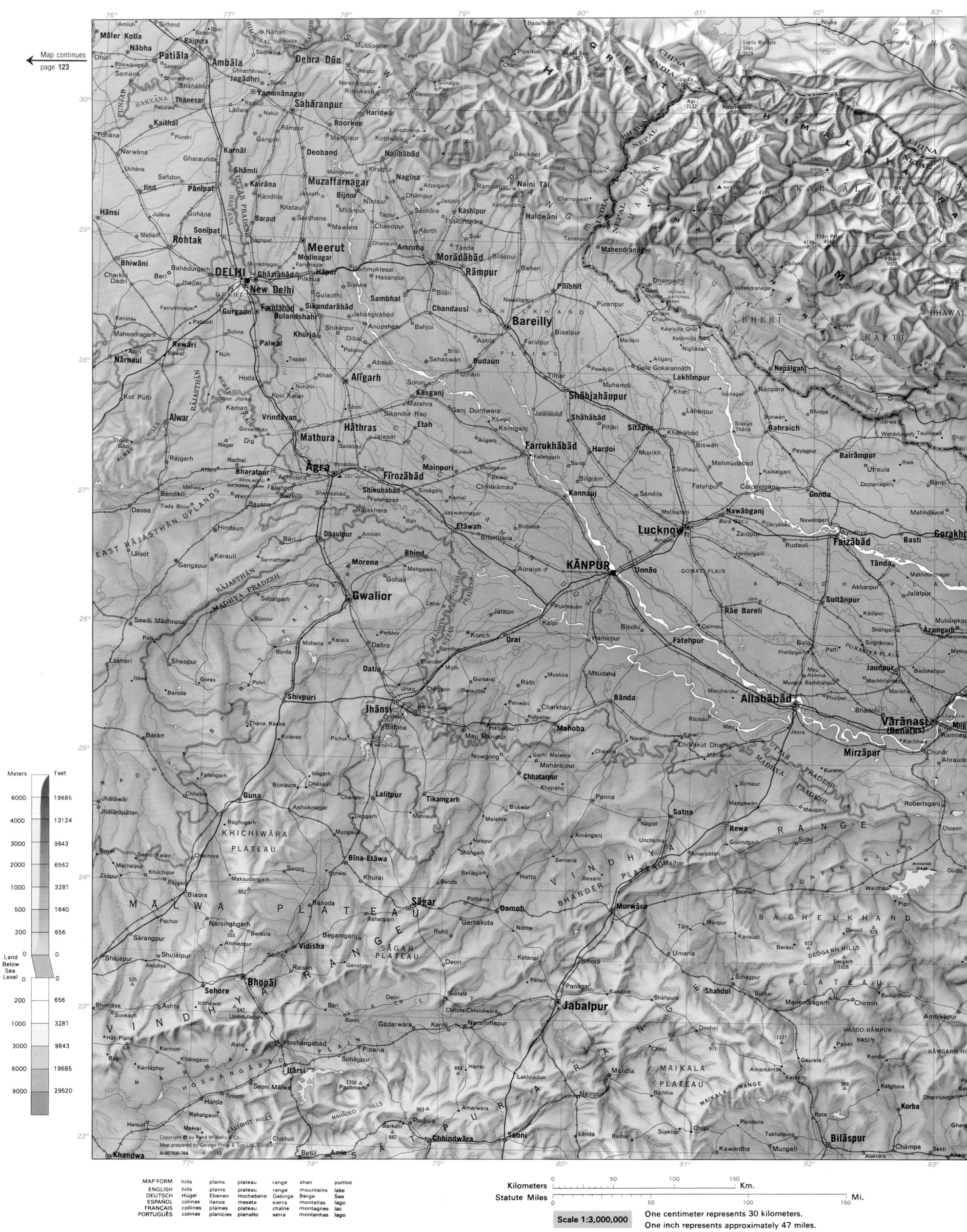

Map continues
page 123

Meters	Feet
6000	19685
4000	13124
3000	9843
2000	6562
1000	3281
500	1640
200	656
0	0
Land Below Sea Level	
0	0
200	656
1000	3281
3000	9843
6000	19685
9000	29520

MAP FORM	hills	plains	plateau	range	shan	yumco
ENGLISH	hills	plains	plateau	range	mountains	lake
DEUTSCH	Hügel	Ebenen	Hochebene	Gebirge	Berge	See
ESPAÑOL	colinas	llanos	meseta	sierra	montañas	lago
FRANÇAIS	collines	plaines	plateau	chaîne	montagnes	lac
PORTUGUÊS	colinas	planicies	planalto	serra	montanhas	lago

Kilometers   0   50   100   150   Km.
Statute Miles   0   50   100   150   Mi.

Scale 1:3,000,000

One centimeter represents 30 kilometers.
One inch represents approximately 47 miles.
Lambert Conformal Conic Projection

Ganges Lowland and Nepal / Gangestiefland und Nepal / Llanuras del Ganges y Nepal
Plaine du Gange et Népal / Planície do Ganges e Nepal

125

BAY OF BENGAL

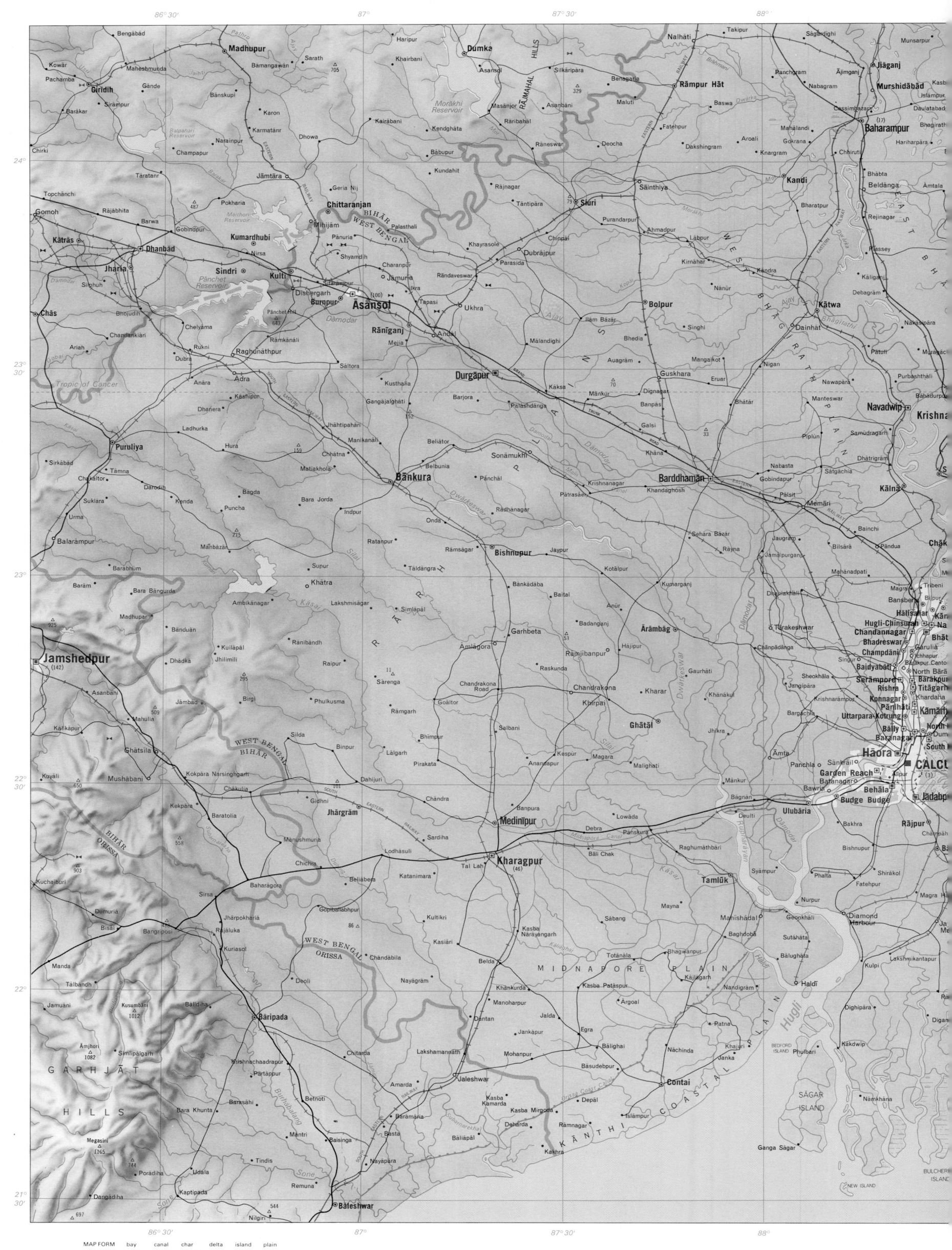

Kilometers 0 10 20 30 40 50 Km.

Statute Miles 0 10 20 30 40 50 Mi.

Scale 1:1,000,000   One centimeter represents 10 kilometers.
One inch represents approximately 16 miles.
Lambert Conformal Conic Projection

Map continues page 84

Map continues pages 130-131

Map continues pages 140-141

Map continues pages 144-145

The Turkish Republic of Northern Cyprus unilaterally declared its independence on November 15, 1983.

Area occupied by Israel since June 1967

Administrative Boundary

Area administered by Sudan

Meters	Feet
6000	19685
4000	13124
3000	9843
2000	6562
1000	3281
500	1640
200	656
0	0
Land Below Sea Level 0	0
200	656
1000	3281
3000	9843
6000	19685
9000	29520

MAP FORM	harrat	jabal	jazireh	küh	ra's	sabkhat	wādi
ENGLISH	lava flow	mountain	island	mountain	cape	salt marsh	wadi
DEUTSCH	Lavastrom	Berg	Insel	Berg	Kap	Salzmarsch	Wadi
ESPAÑOL	corriente de lava	montaña	isla	montaña	cabo	pantano salado	uadi
FRANÇAIS	coulée de lave	montagne	île	montagne	cap	marais salé	uadi
PORTUGUÊS	corrente de lava	montanha	ilha	montanha	cabo	pântano salgado	uádi

Kilometers
Statute Miles

Scale 1:6,000,000
One centimeter represents 60 kilometers.
One inch represents approximately 95 miles.
Lambert Conformal Conic Projection

Map continues
pages 120-121

Map continues pages 38-39

The Turkish Republic of Northern Cyprus unilaterally declared its independence on November 15, 1983.

Meters	Feet
6000	19685
4000	13124
3000	9843
2000	6562
1000	3281
500	1640
200	656
0	0
Land Below Sea Level	
0	0
200	656
1000	3281
3000	9843
6000	19685
9000	29520

Copyright © by Rand McNally & Co.
Map prepared by George Philip & Son Ltd., London.
A-563900-764   -6 -7 -10

MAP FORM	burnu	dağ, dağı	dağları	gölü	jabal	körfezi	sabkhat
ENGLISH	cape	mountain	mountains	lake	mountains	bay, gulf	salt marsh
DEUTSCH	Kap	Berg	Berge	See	Berge	Bucht, Golf	Salzmarsch
ESPAÑOL	cabo	montaña	montañas	lago	montañas	bahía, golfo	pantano salado
FRANÇAIS	cap	montagne	montagnes	lac	montagnes	baie, golfe	marais salé
PORTUGUÊS	cabo	montanha	montanhas	lago	montanhas	baía, golfo	pântano salgado

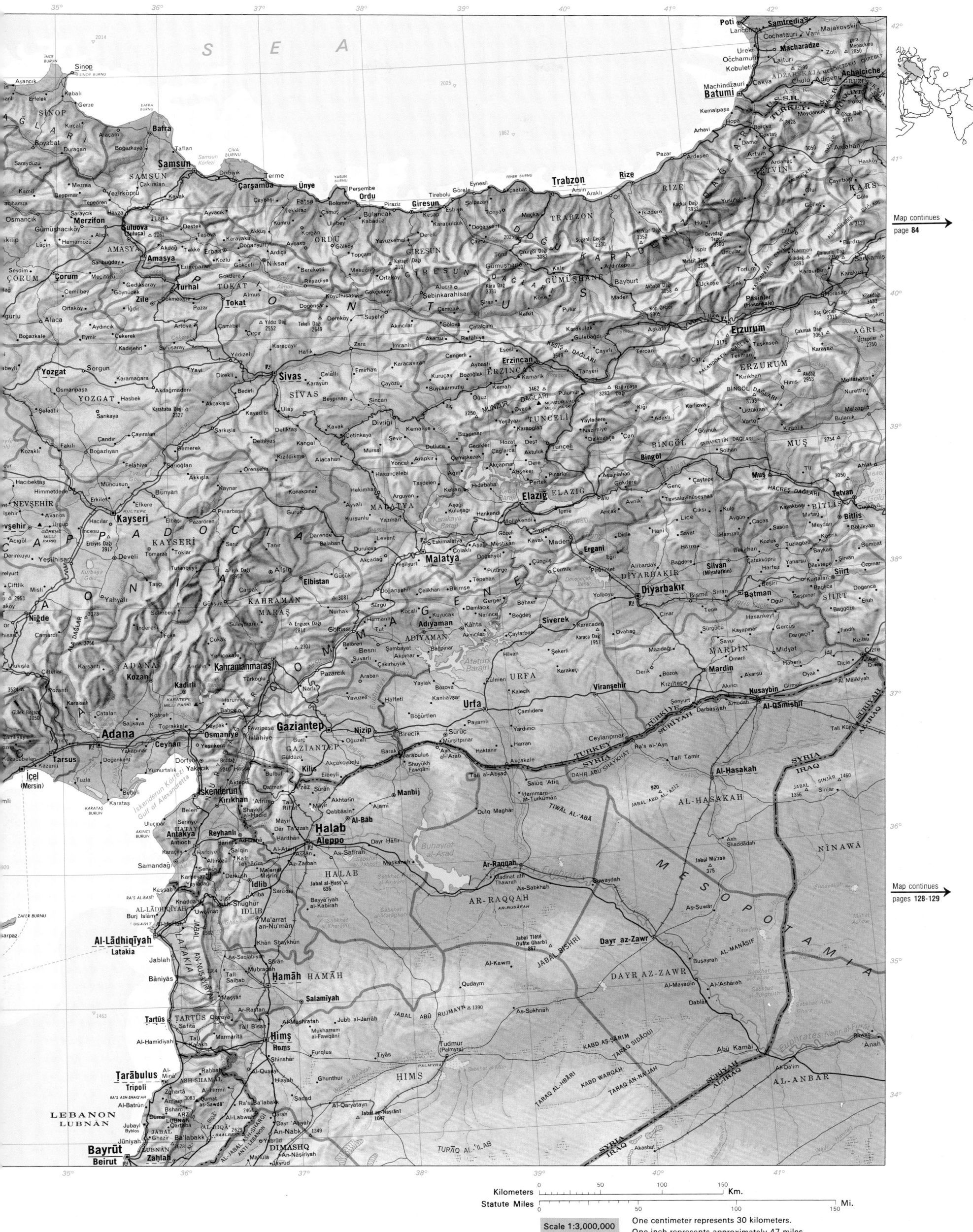

Map continues page 84

Map continues pages 128-129

Kilometers 0   50   100   150 Km.

Statute Miles 0   50   100   150 Mi.

Scale 1:3,000,000
One centimeter represents 30 kilometers.
One inch represents approximately 47 miles.
Conic Projection, Two Standard Parallels

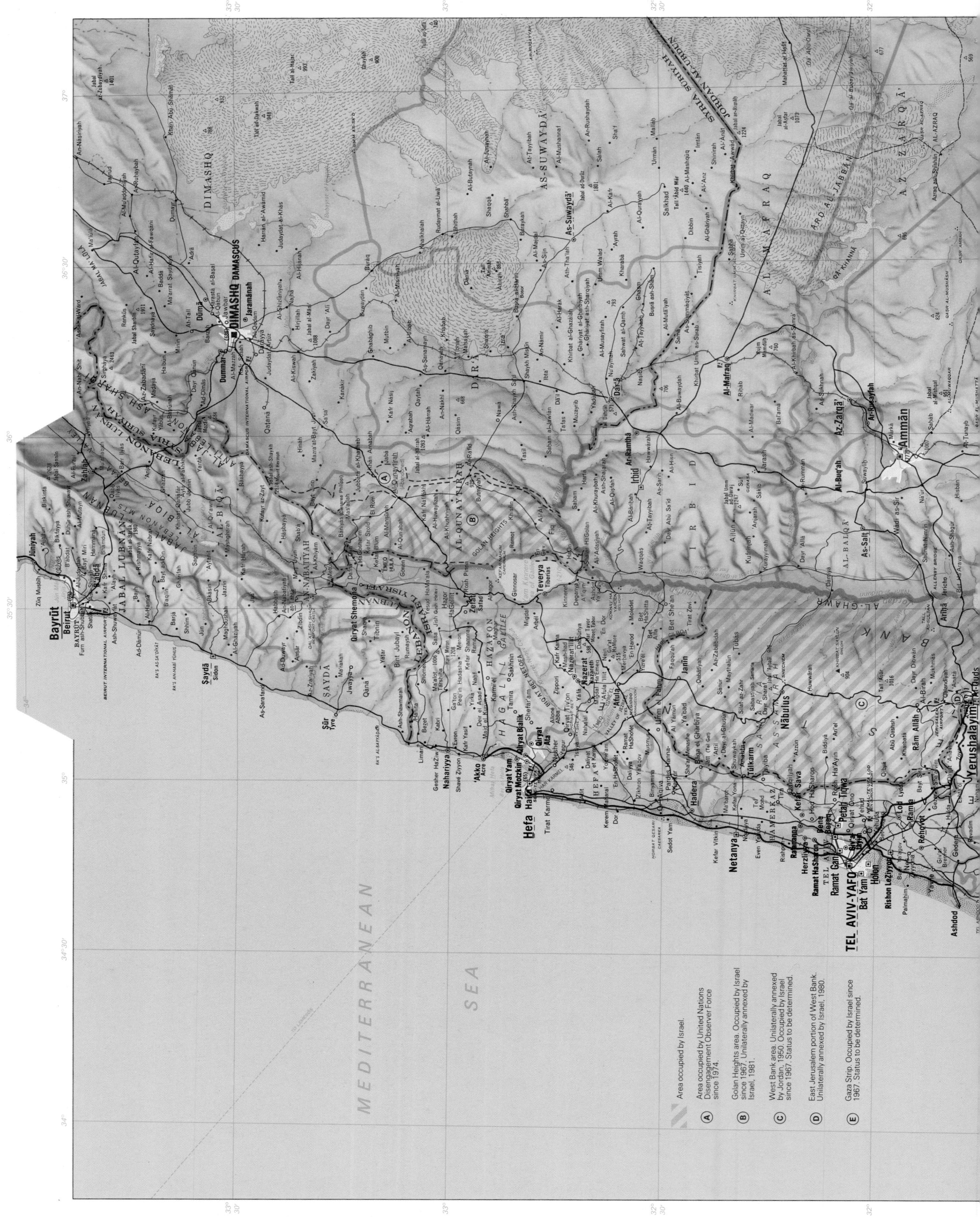

MEDITERRANEAN

SEA

Area occupied by Israel.

(A) Area occupied by United Nations Disengagement Observer Force since 1974.

(B) Golan Heights area. Occupied by Israel since 1967. Unilaterally annexed by Israel, 1981.

(C) West Bank area. Unilaterally annexed by Jordan, 1950. Occupied by Israel since 1967. Status to be determined.

(D) East Jerusalem portion of West Bank. Unilaterally annexed by Israel, 1980.

(E) Gaza Strip. Occupied by Israel since 1967. Status to be determined.

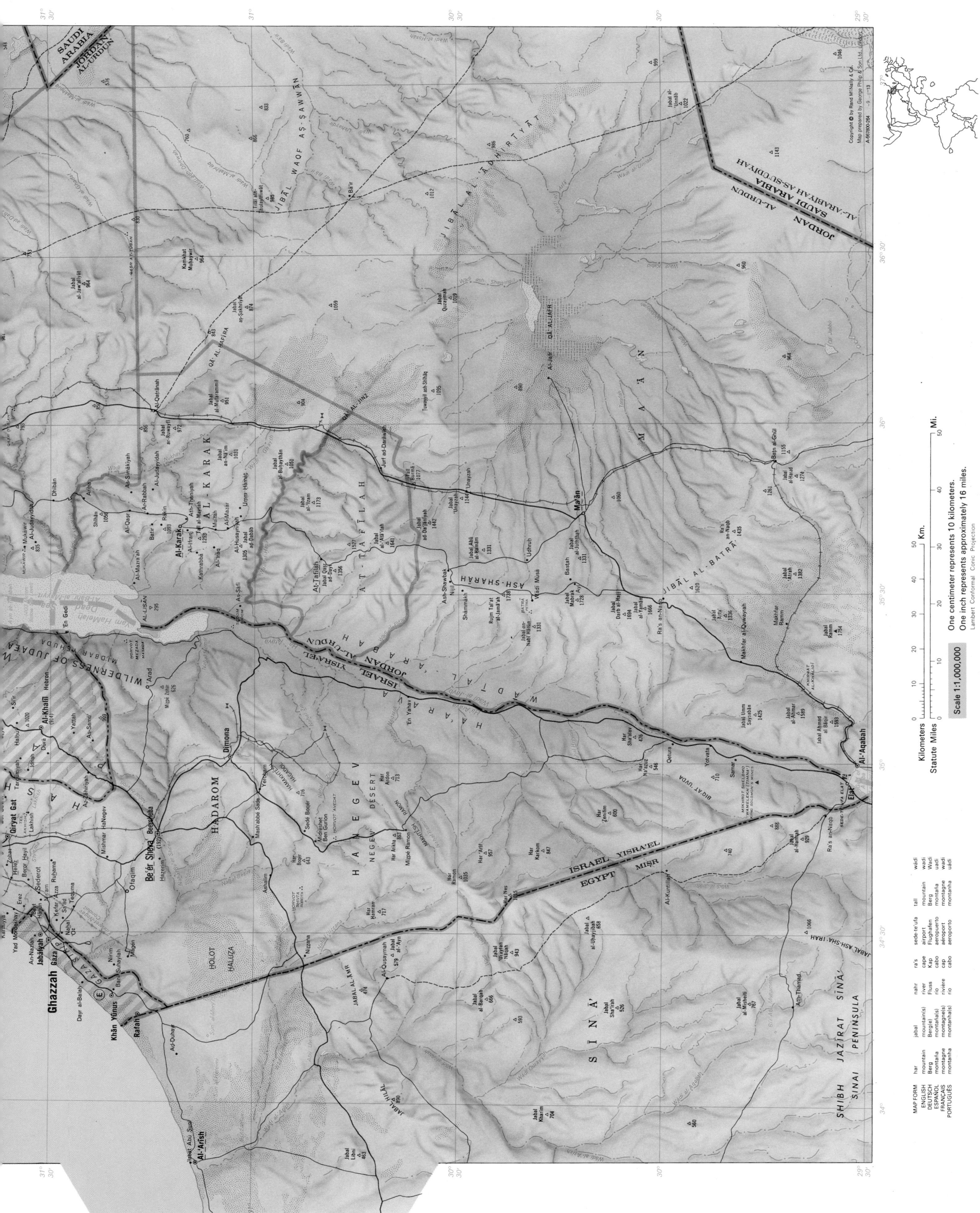

Scale 1:1,000,000

Kilometers

Statute Miles

Km.

Mi.

One centimeter represents 10 kilometers.
One inch represents approximately 16 miles.

Lambert Conformal Conic Projection

MAP FORM	har	jabal	nahr	ra's	sede-te'ula	tall	wadi
ENGLISH	mountain	mountain(s)	river	cape	airport	mountain	wadi
DEUTSCH	Berg	Berg(e)	Fluss	Kap	Flughafen	Berg	uadi
ESPAÑOL	montaña	montaña(s)	río	cabo	aeropuerto	montaña	uadi
FRANCAIS	montagne	montagne(s)	rivière	cap	aeroport	montagne	wadi
PORTUGUÊS	montanha	montanha(s)	rio	cabo	aeroporto	montanha	uádi

MAP FORM	bahr, baḥr	chott	jabal	lake	mountains	oued	wahât
ENGLISH	river, sea	salt marsh	mountain(s)	lake	mountains	wadi	oasis
DEUTSCH	Fluss, Meer	Salzmarsch	Berg(e)	See	Berge	Wadi	Oase
ESPAÑOL	rio, mar	pantano salado	montaña(s)	lago	montañas	uadi	oasis
FRANÇAIS	rivière, mer	marais salé	montagne(s)	lac	montagnes	wadi	oasis
PORTUGUÊS	rio, mar	pântano salgado	montanha(s)	lago	montanhas	uádi	oásis

Western North Africa / West Nordafrika / Región Occidental de Africa Septentrional
Afrique du Nord Occidentale / África do Norte Ocidental

135

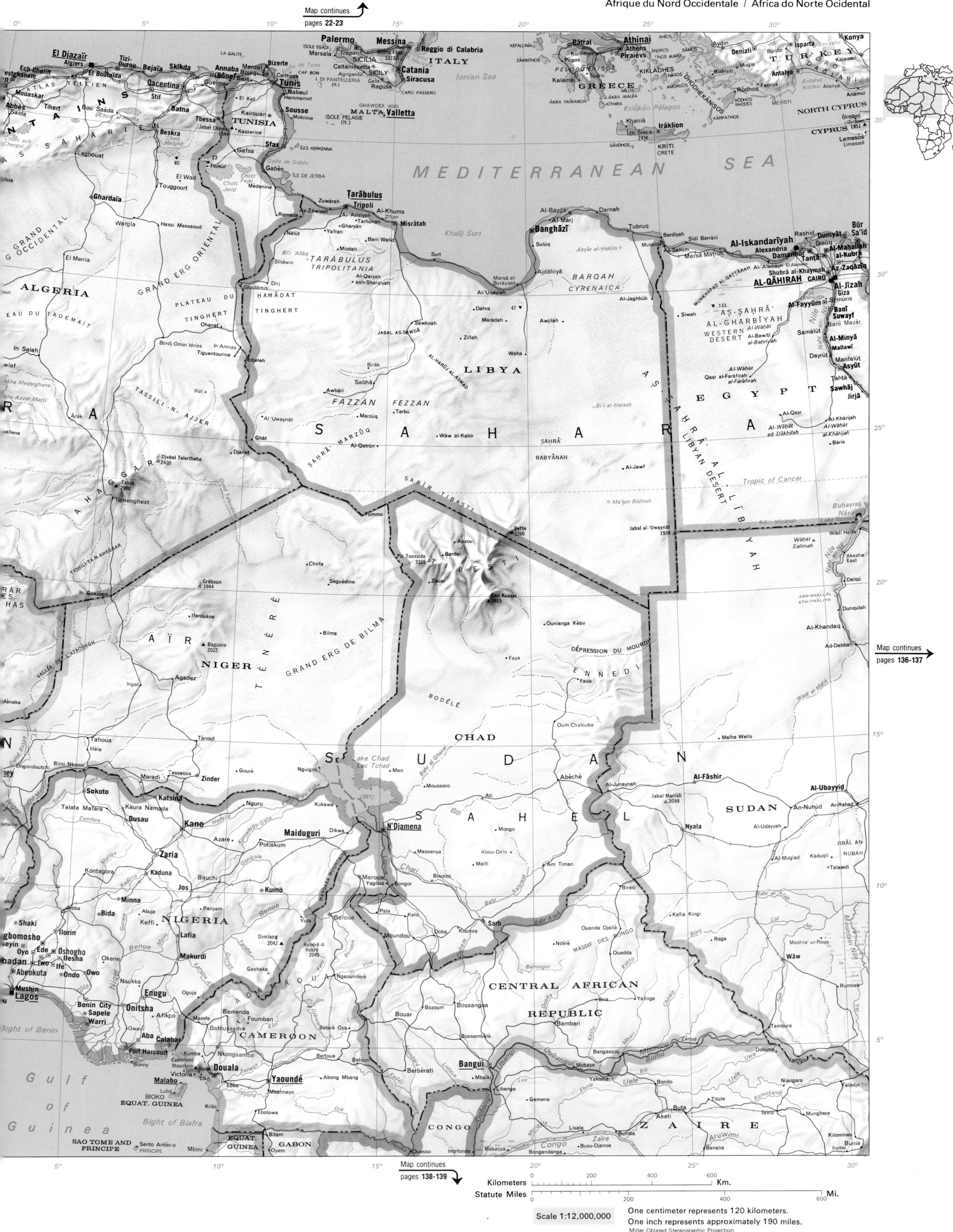

Map continues
pages 22-23

Map continues
pages 136-137

Map continues
pages 138-139

Kilometers
0   200   400   600   Km.

Statute Miles
0   200   400   600   Mi.

Scale 1:12,000,000

One centimeter represents 120 kilometers.
One inch represents approximately 190 miles.
Miller Oblated Stereographic Projection

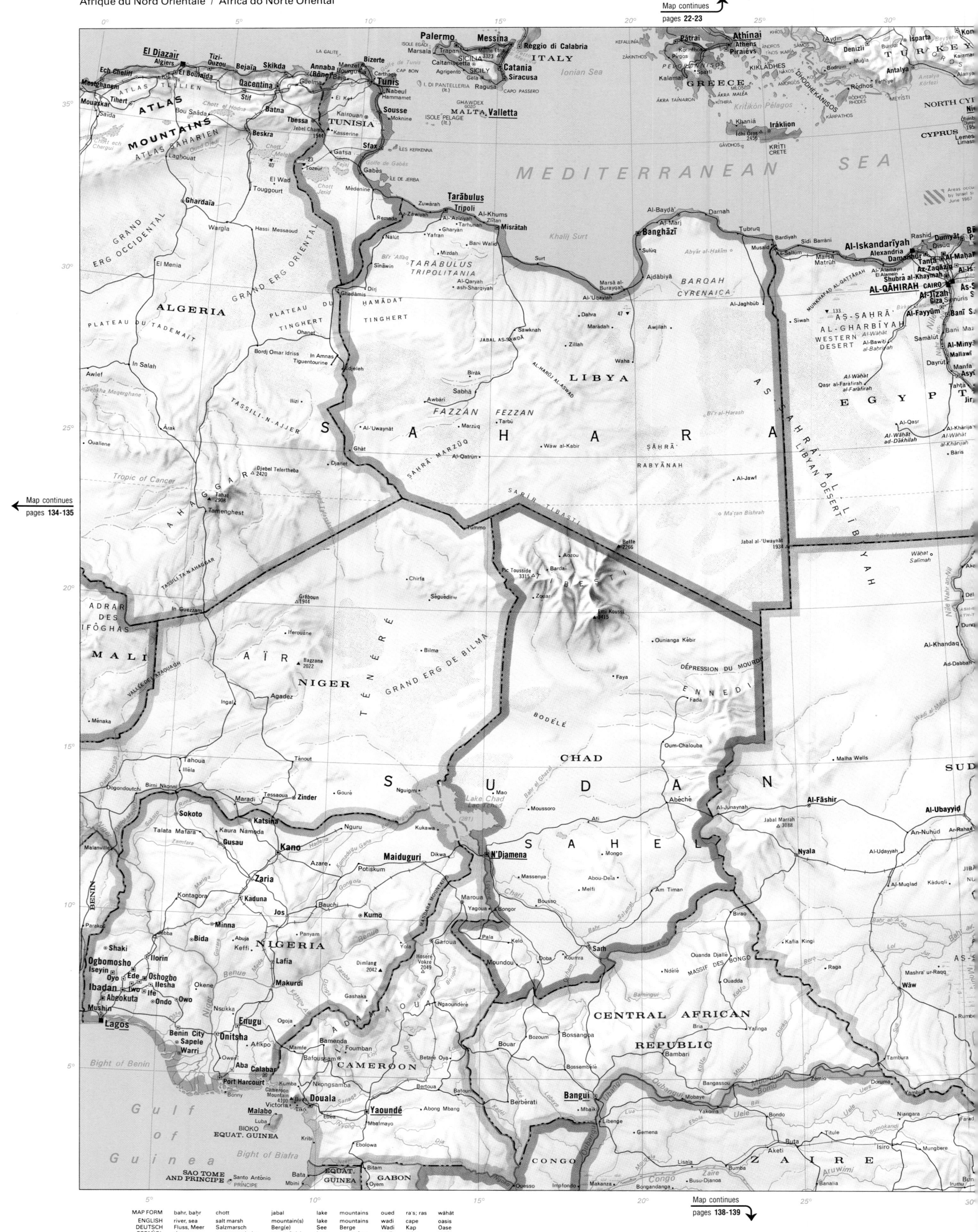

Map continues
pages 22-23

Map continues
pages 134-135

Map continues
pages 138-139

MAP FORM	bahr, bahr	chott	jabal	lake	mountains	oued	ra's; ras	wāhāt
ENGLISH	river, sea	salt marsh	mountain(s)	lake	mountains	wadi	cape	oasis
DEUTSCH	Fluss, Meer	Salzmarsch	Berg(e)	See	Berge	Wadi	Kap	Oase
ESPAÑOL	río, mar	pantano salado	montaña(s)	lago	montañas	uadi	cabo	oasis
FRANÇAIS	rivière, mer	marais salé	montagne(s)	lac	montagnes	wadi	cap	oasis
PORTUGUÊS	rio, mar	pântano salgado	montanha(s)	lago	montanhas	uádi	cabo	oásis

Eastern North Africa / Ost Nordafrika / Región Oriental de Africa Septentrional
Afrique du Nord Orientale / África do Norte Oriental

137

Map continues
pages 118-119

Kilometers 0   200   400   600 Km.
Statute Miles 0   200   400   600 Mi.

Scale 1:12,000,000   One centimeter represents 120 kilometers.
One inch represents approximately 190 miles.
Miller Oblated Stereographic Projection

Copyright © by Rand McNally & Co.
Map prepared by Esselte Map Service AB, Stockholm.
A-589391 -264 -8- -20

Map continues
pages 136-137

SAO TOME AND
PRINCIPE

PRINCIPE ● Santo António

SÃO TOMÉ ○ São Tomé

Q. ANNOBÓN
(Equat. Gui.)

EQUATORIAL
GUINEA

CAMEROON

GABON

Libreville

CAP LOPEZ
Port Gentil

ATLANTIC

OCEAN

ANGOLA

Luanda

Lobito
Benguela

Namibe

Tombua

CABINDA
(Angola)

KINSHASA
(LEOPOLDVILLE)

Brazzaville

Pointe-Noire

Boma
Matadi

ZAIRE

Mbandaka
(Coquilhatville)

Bandundu

Kikwit

Kananga
(Luluabourg)

Mbuji-Mayi
(Bakwanga)

Kisangani
(Stanleyville)

Bukavu

KATANGA

Kamina

Kolwezi
Likasi
(Jadotville)
Lubumbashi
(Elisabethville)

RWANDA
Kigali

BURUNDI
Bujumbura

Kalemie
(Albertville)

Lake
Tanganyika

Chililabombwe
(Bancroft)
Chingola
Kitwe
Luanshya

ZAMBIA

Mufulira
Sakania
Ndola

Kabwe
(Broken Hill)

Lusaka

Livingstone

ZIMBABWE

Bulawayo

Gweru

Harare
(Salisb...)

OVAMBOLAND

KAOKOVELD

CAPE FRIA

CAPRIVI ZIPFEL

Etosha Pan

Tsumeb
Grootfontein

OKAVANGO
DELTA

KAUKAU VELD

NAMIBIA

Windhoek

Swakopmund
Walvisbaai
Walvis Bay
(S. Afr.)

Tropic of Capricorn

HOLLANDSBIRD
ISLAND

DAMARALAND

BOTSWANA

KALAHARI

DESERT

Gaborone

GREAT
NAMAQUALAND

Lüderitz

Keetmanshoop

BUSHMAN

LAND

Oranjemund
Alexander Bay

Port Nolloth

Kimberley

Bloemfontein

BOPHUTHATSWANA

Pretoria

JOHANNESBURG
Springs
Germiston
Vereeniging

Klerksdorp

Kroonstad

Welkom
Virginia

SOUTH

AFRICA

LESOTHO

Durban

Pietermaritzburg

GREAT

KARROO

East London
Oos-London

Port Elizabeth

Cape Town
Kaapstad

CAPE OF
GOOD HOPE

MAP FORM	cape	île	island	lake	mountains	plateau
ENGLISH	cape	island	island	lake	mountains	plateau
DEUTSCH	Kap	Insel	Insel	See	Berge	Hochebene
ESPAÑOL	cabo	isla	isla	lago	montañas	meseta
FRANÇAIS	cap	isla	île	lac	montagnes	plateau
PORTUGUÊS	cabo	ilha	ilha	lago	montanhas	planalto

Kilometers

Statute Miles

Scale 1:12,000,000   One centimeter represents 120 kilometers.
One inch represents approximately 190 miles.
Miller Oblated Stereographic Projection

Map continues pages 128-129

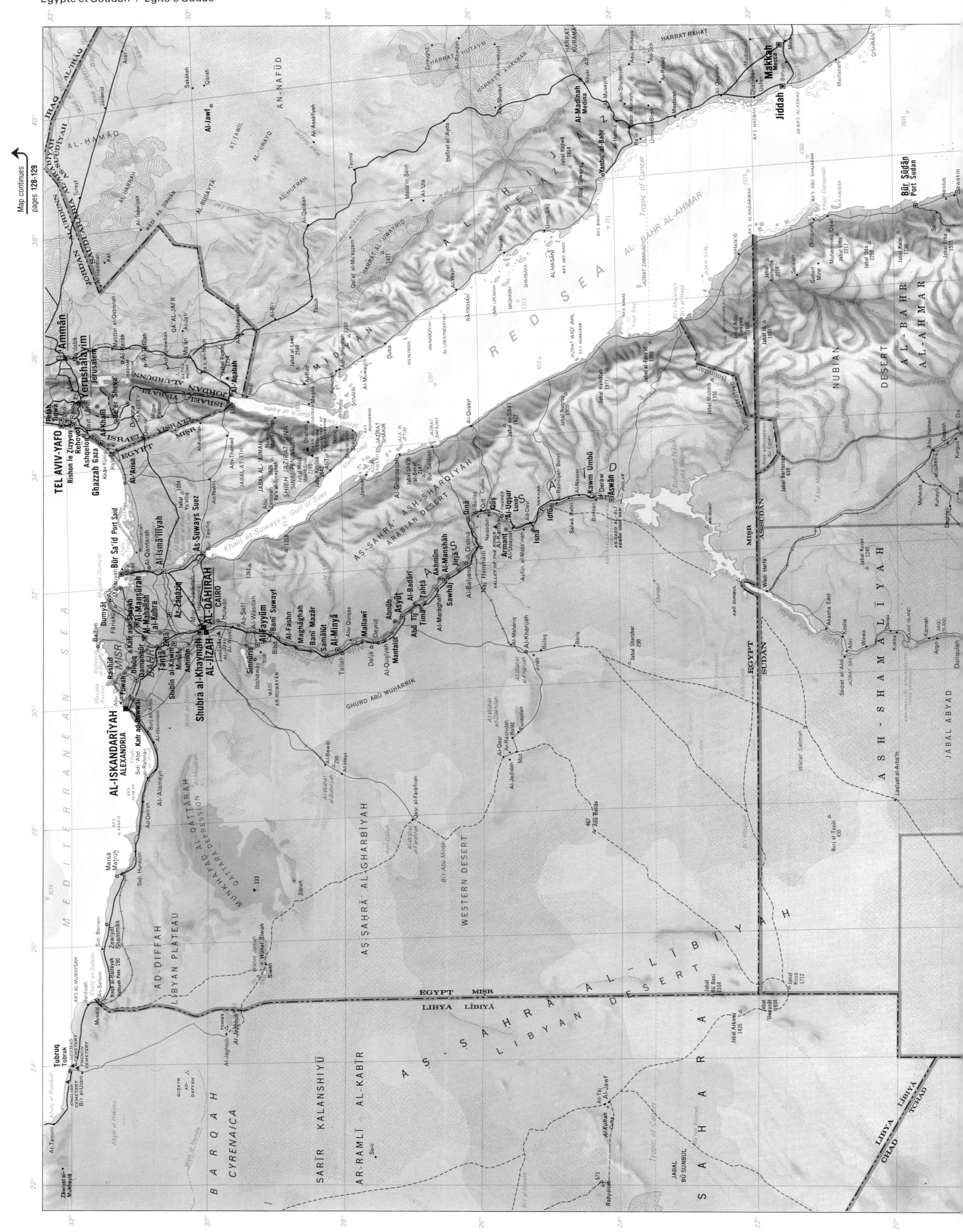
MEDITERRANEAN SEA
RED SEA
AL-BAHR AL-AHMAR
AL-QAHIRAH
CAIRO
AL-ISKANDARĪYAH
ALEXANDRIA
AL-JĪZAH
Shubrā al-Khaymah
TEL AVIV-YAFO
Yerushalayim
Jerusalem
'Ammān
Makkah
Mecca
Jiddah
Al-Madīnah
Medina
Būr Sūdān
Port Sudan
Būr Sa'īd Port Said
As-Suways Suez
Al-Ismā'īlīyah
Aswān
Luxor
Asyūt
Al-Minyā
Al-Fayyūm
Tanṭā
Dumyāṭ
Marsā Maṭrūḥ
Tubruq
Tobruk
Wādī Ḥalfā
EGYPT
MIṢR
SUDAN
AS-SŪDĀN
LIBYA
LĪBIYĀ
CHAD
TCHAD
ISRAEL
YISRA'EL
JORDAN
AL-URDUN
SAUDI ARABIA
IRAQ
AL-'IRĀQ
WESTERN DESERT
ARABIAN DESERT
AS-SAHRĀ' ASH-SHARQĪYAH
AṢ-ṢAḤRĀ' AL-GHARBĪYAH
LIBYAN DESERT
AṢ-ṢAḤRĀ' AL-LĪBĪYAH
NUBIAN DESERT
AS-SAHRĀ' AN-NŪBĪYAH
MUNKHAFAḌ AL-QAṬṬĀRAH
QATTARA DEPRESSION
SHIBH JAZĪRAT SĪNĀ'
SINAI PENINSULA
LIBYAN PLATEAU
AD-DIFFAH
BARQAH
CYRENAICA
AL-HIJAZ
AN-NAFŪD
AL-HAMAD
SARĪR KALANSHIYŪ
AR-RAMLĪ AL-KABĪR
JABAL ABYAD
Tropic of Cancer
Khalīj as-Suways
Gulf of Suez
Gulf of Aqaba
Buhayrat Nasir
Lake Nasser
Nile

Map continues pages 144-145

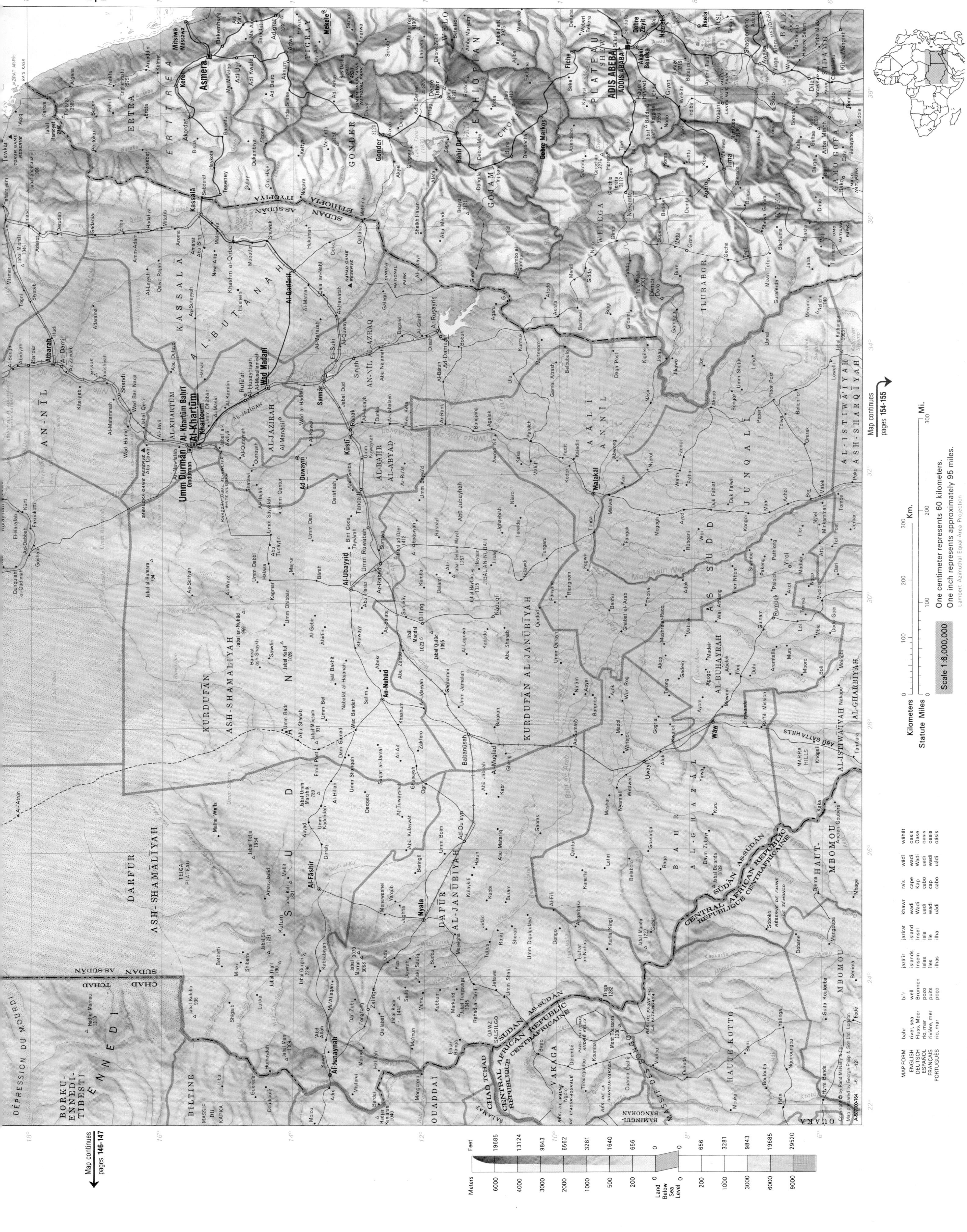

Map continues pages 146-147

Map continues pages 154-155

Scale 1:6,000,000

One centimeter represents 60 kilometers.
One inch represents approximately 95 miles.

Lambert Azimuthal Equal-Area Projection

MAP FORM						
ENGLISH	river, sea	well	islands	island	cape	oasis
DEUTSCH	Fluss, Meer	Brunnen	Inseln	Insel	Kap	Oase
ESPAÑOL	río, mar	pozo	islas	isla	cabo	oasis
FRANÇAIS	rivière, mer	puits	îles	île	cap	oasis
PORTUGUÊS	rio, mar	poço	ilhas	ilha	cabo	oásis
	bahr	bi'r	jazā'ir	jazīrat	ra's	wāhāt
					khawr	wadi
					wadi	wadi

Feet / Meters elevation legend:
19685 / 6000
13124 / 4000
9843 / 3000
6562 / 2000
3281 / 1000
1640 / 500
656 / 200
0 / 0 Land Below Sea Level
656 / 200
3281 / 1000
9843 / 3000
19685 / 6000
29520 / 9000

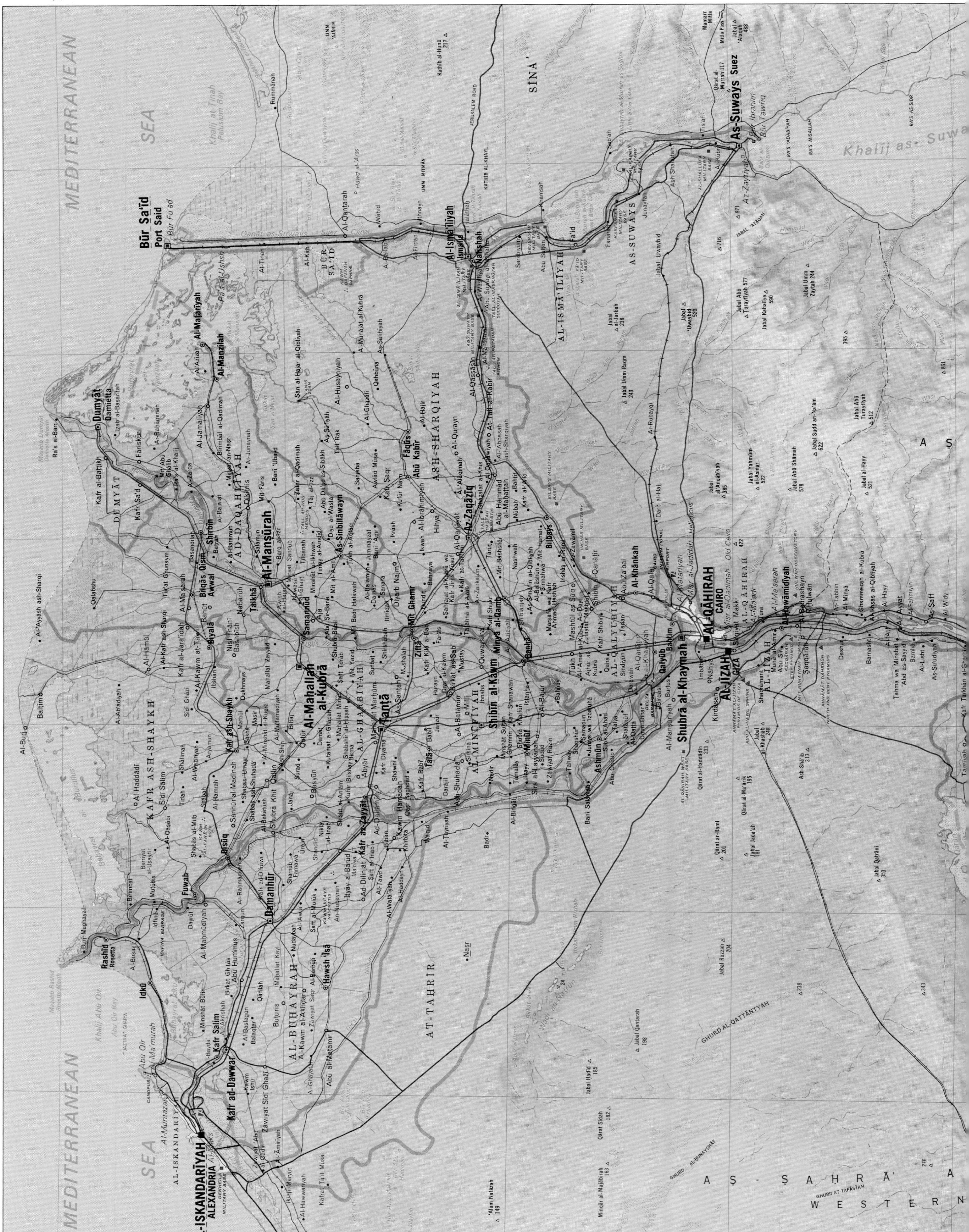
MEDITERRANEAN SEA
Būr Sa'īd
Port Said
Būr Fu'ād
Dumyāṭ
Damietta
Rashīd
Rosetta
AL-ISKANDARĪYAH
ALEXANDRIA
Al-Manṣūrah
Al-Maḥallah al-Kubrā
Ṭanṭā
Damanhūr
Az-Zaqāzīq
Al-Ismā'īlīyah
AL-QĀHIRAH
CAIRO
AL-JĪZAH
GIZA
Shubrā al-Khaymah
As-Suways
Suez
SĪNĀ'
Khalīj as-Suways
AS-SAḤRĀ' AL-GHARBĪYAH
WESTERN
AT-TAḤRĪR
Qanāt as-Suways

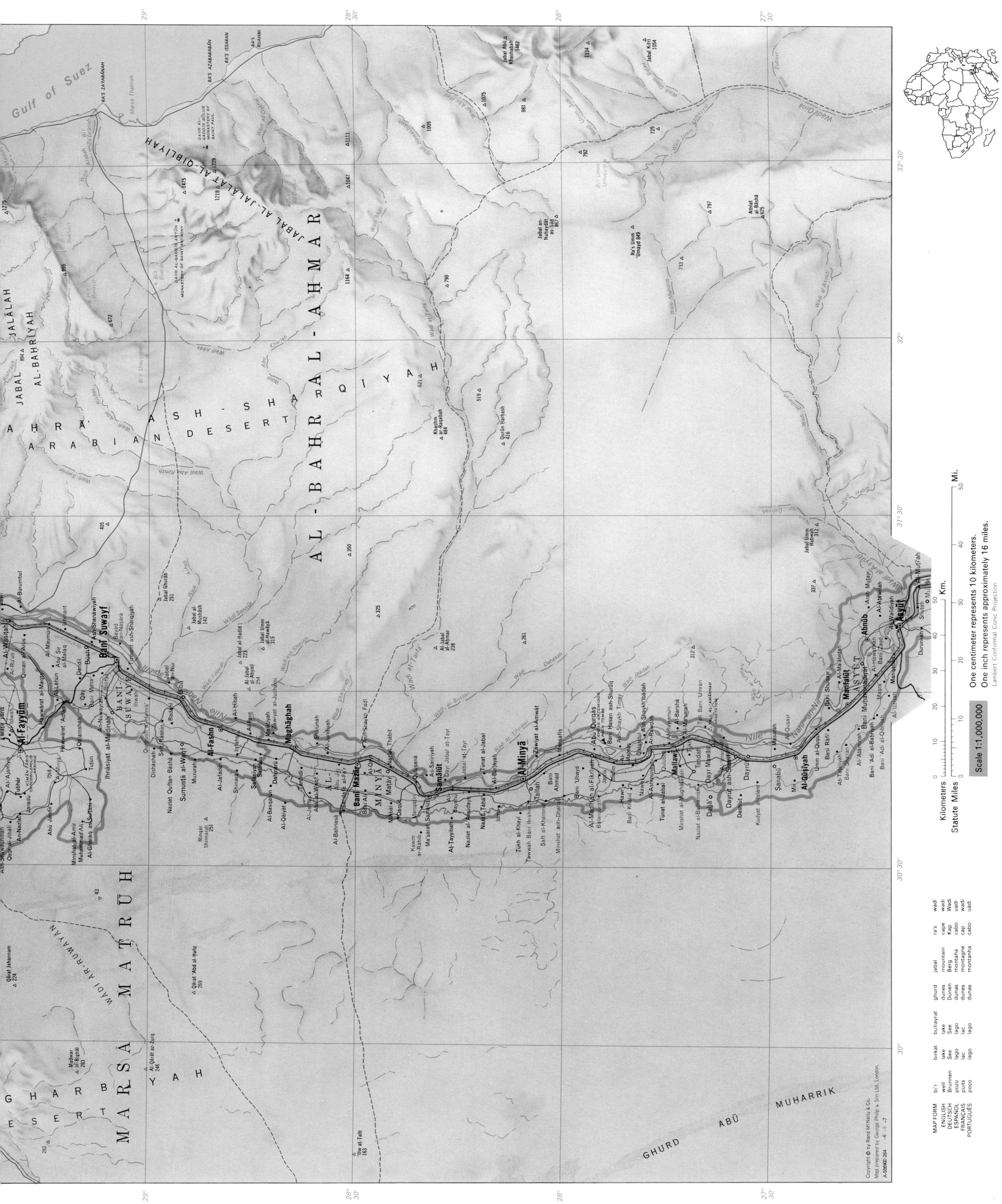

Gulf of Suez

JABAL AL-QIBLIYAH
JABAL AL-BAHRIYAH
JALĀLAH

AHRĀ' ASH-SHARQIYAH
ARABIAN DESERT

AL-BAHR AL-AHMAR

MARSĀ MAṬRŪḤ

WĀDĪ AR-RUWAYĀN

GHARBĪYAH
ESERT

GHURD ABŪ MUHARRIK

Al-Fayyūm

Banī Suwayf

Al-Fashn

Maghāghah

Banī Mazār
AL-MINYĀ

Samālūṭ

Al-Minyā

Mallawī

Abū Qurqāṣ

Manfalūṭ

ASYŪṬ
Asyūṭ

Abnūb

Al-Qūṣīyah

MAP FORM
ENGLISH   bi'r   birkat   buhayrat   ghurd   jabal   ra's   wadi
DEUTSCH   well   lake   lake   dunes   mountain   cape   wadi
ESPAÑOL   Brunnen   See   See   Dünen   Berg   Kap   Wadi
FRANÇAIS   pozo   lago   lago   dunas   montaña   cabo   uadi
PORTUGUÊS   puits   lac   lac   dunes   montagne   cap   uadi
            poço   lago   lago   dunas   montanha   cabo   uádi

Copyright © by Rand McNally & Co.
Map prepared by George Philip & Son Ltd., London.

Scale 1:1,000,000

Kilometers

Statute Miles

Km.

Mi.

One centimeter represents 10 kilometers.
One inch represents approximately 16 miles.
Lambert Conformal Conic Projection

144

Ethiopia, Somalia and Yemen / Äthiopien, Somalia und Jemen / Etiopía, Somalía y Yemen
Ethiopie, Somalie et Yemen / Etiópia, Somália e Iêmen

Map continues
pages 128-129

Map continues
pages 140-141

Ethiopia, Somalia and Yemen / Äthiopien, Somalia und Jemen / Etiopía, Somalía y Yemen
Ethiopie, Somalie et Yemen / Etiópia, Somália e Iêmen

145

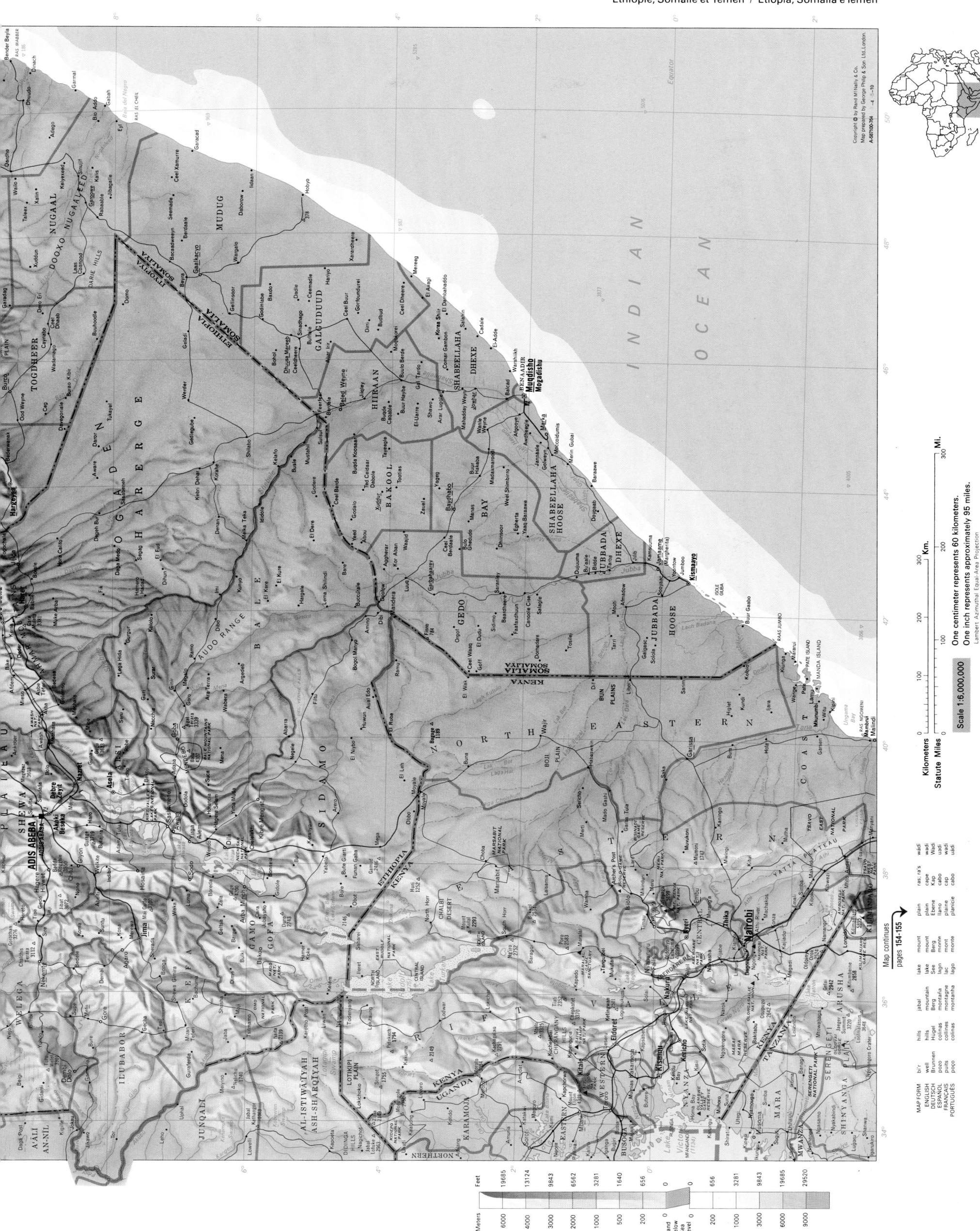

Scale 1:6,000,000

One centimeter represents 60 kilometers.
One inch represents approximately 95 miles.
Lambert Azimuthal Equal-Area Projection

Kilometers

Km.

Statute Miles

Mi.

MAP FORM					
ENGLISH	bir	hills	jabal	lake	plain	ras, ra's
DEUTSCH	well	hills	mountain	lake	plain	cape
ESPAÑOL	Brunnen	Hügel	Berg	See	Ebene	Kap
FRANCAIS	pozo	colinas	montaña	lago	llano	cabo
PORTUGUÊS	puits	collines	montagne	lac	plaine	cap
	poço	colinas	montanha	lago	planície	cabo

wadi
wadi
uadi
wadi
uádi

Map continues
pages 154-155

INDIAN OCEAN

Feet
19685
13124
9843
6562
3281
1640
656
0

Land
Below
Sea
Level 0

656
3281
9843
19685
29520

Meters
6000
4000
3000
2000
1000
500
200
0

0
200
1000
3000
6000
9000

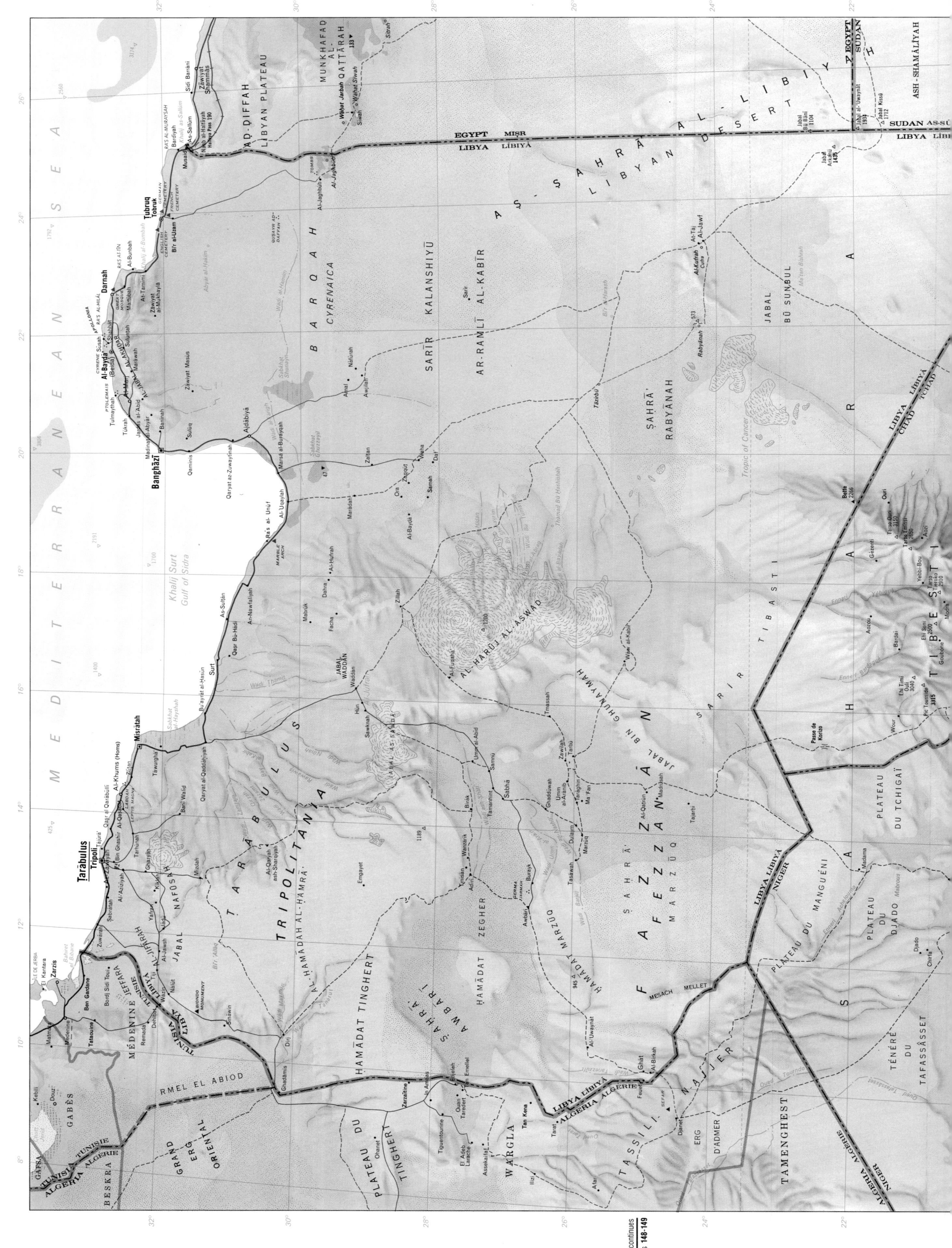
MEDITERRANEAN SEA
Khalij Surt
Gulf of Sidra
Tarābulus
Tripoli
Misratah
Banghāzī
Ṭubruq
Tobruk
Darnah
Al-Bayḍā'
TRIPOLITANIA
ṬARĀBULUS
CYRENAICA
BARQAH
FAZZĀN
AS-SAḤRĀ' AL-LĪBĪYAH
LIBYAN DESERT
AL-HARŪJ AL-ASWAD
SAHARA
TIBESTI
EGYPT
MIṢR
LIBYA
LĪBIYĀ
SUDAN
CHAD
TCHAD
NIGER
ALGERIA
ALGÉRIE
TUNISIA
TUNISIE
GRAND ERG ORIENTAL
ṢAḤRĀ' RABYĀNAH
SARĪR KALANSHIYŪ
AR-RAMLĪ AL-KABĪR
JABAL BŪ SUNBUL
ḤAMĀDAT TINGHERT
TASSILI-N-AJJER
PLATEAU DU DJADO
PLATEAU DU MANGUÉNI
PLATEAU DU TCHIGAÏ
TÉNÉRÉ DU TAFASSÂSSET
Tropic of Cancer

Map continues pages 148-149

Map continues
pages 140-141

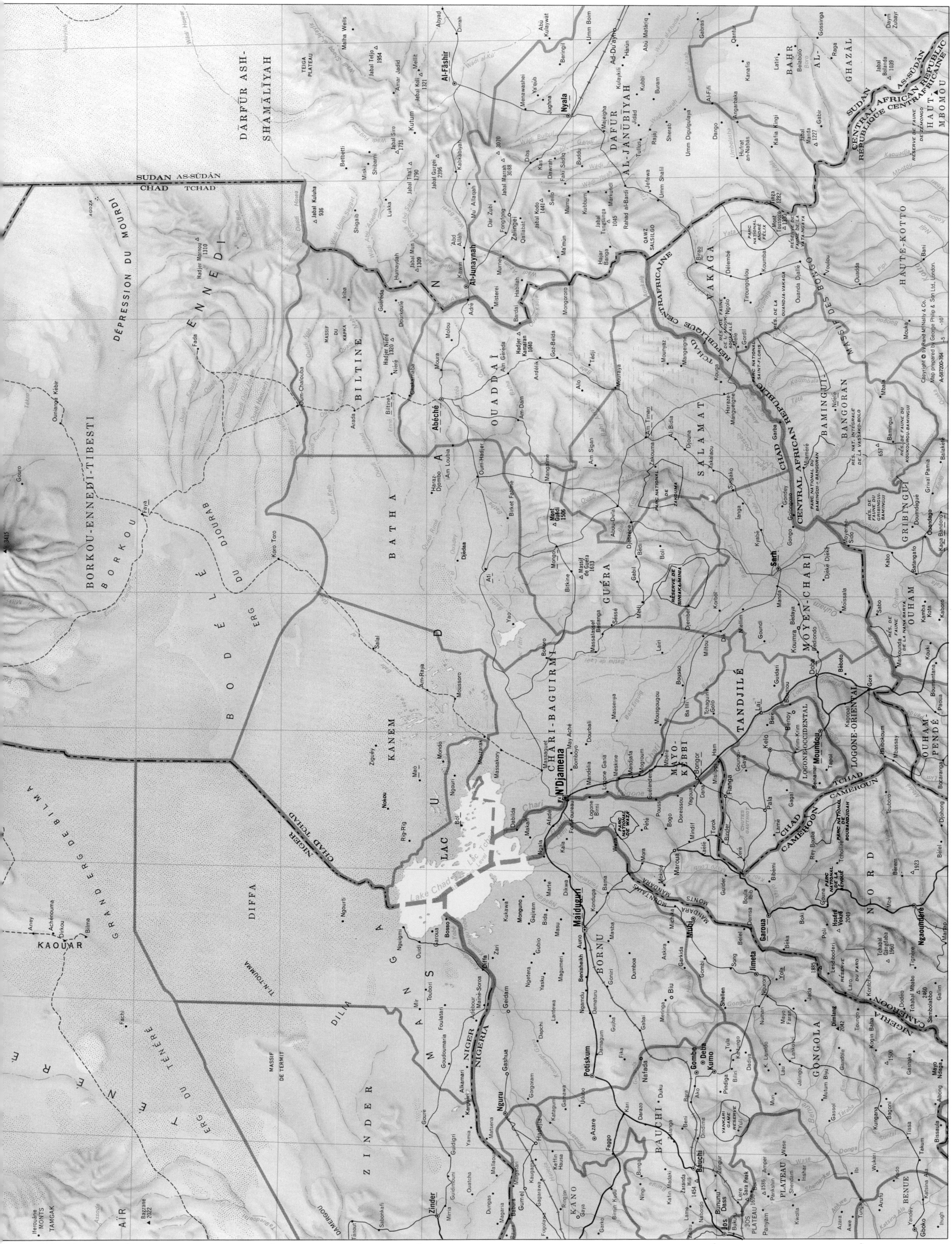

Map continues
pages 150-151

Map continues
pages 152-153

Scale 1:6,000,000

One centimeter represents 60 kilometers.
One inch represents approximately 95 miles.

Lambert Azimuthal Equal-Area Projection

Kilometers

Statute Miles

MAP FORM					
ENGLISH	bahr	hadjer	jabal	massif	plateau
DEUTSCH	river	mountain	mountain	Gebirgsmassiv	
ESPAÑOL	Fluss	Berg	Berg	macizo	
FRANÇAIS	rio	montaña	montaña	massif	
PORTUGUÊS	rivière	montagne	montagne	montanha	
	rio	montanha	montanha	maciço	

ouadi	ra's	sarir
wadi	cape	desert
Wadi	Kap	Wüste
uadi	cabo	desierto
wadi	cap	désert
uadi	cabo	deserto

wadi
wadi
Wadi
uadi
wadi
uadi

Feet: 19685 13124 9843 6562 3281 1640 656 0 / 0 656 3281 9843 19685 29520

Meters: 6000 4000 3000 2000 1000 500 200 0 / 0 200 1000 3000 6000 9000

Land Below Sea Level

Northwestern Africa / Nordwestafrika / África Nor-occidental
Afrique du Nord-Ouest / África Norte-ocidental

Map continues
pages 34-35

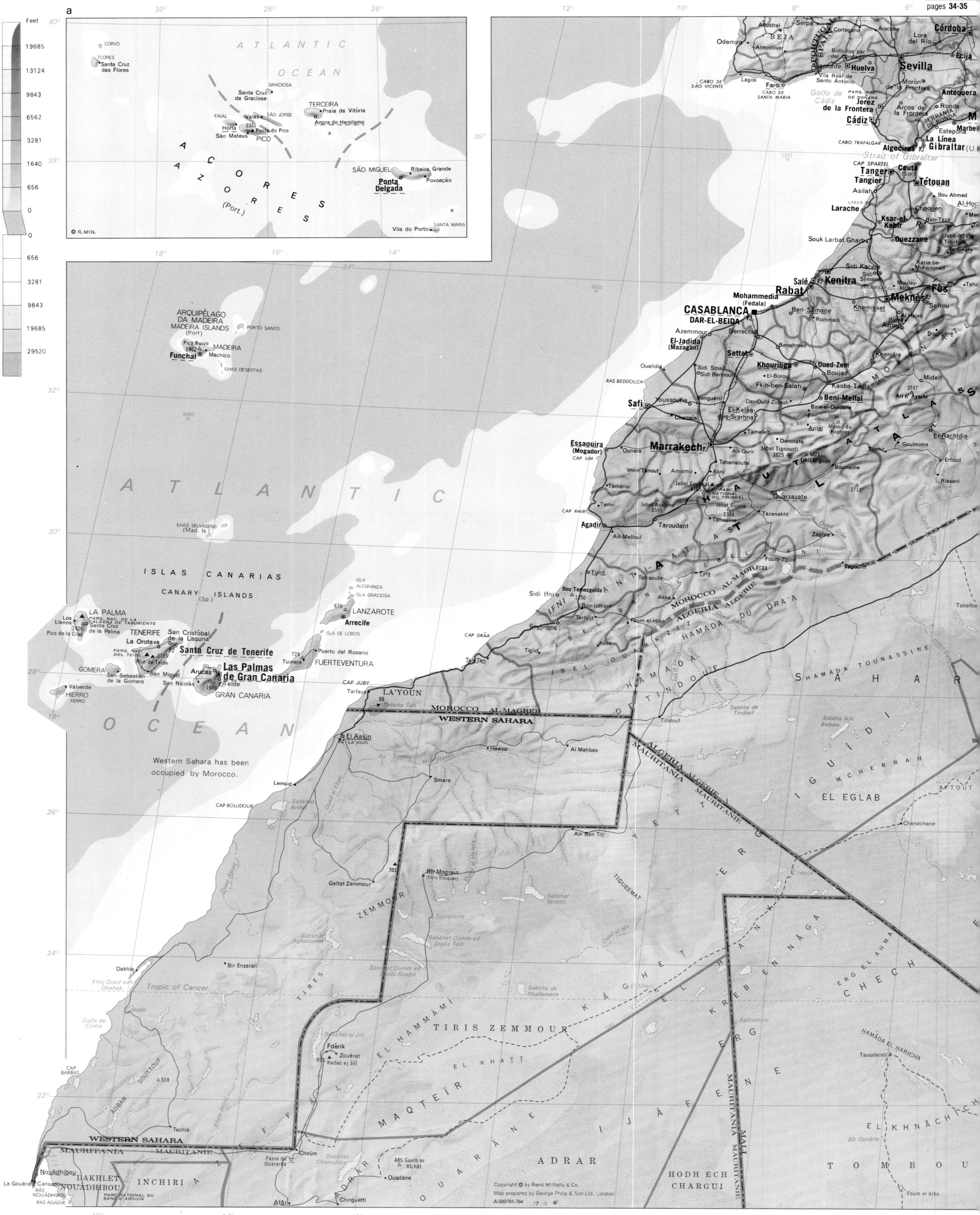

Scale (left margin):

Meters	Feet
6000	19685
4000	13124
3000	9843
2000	6562
1000	3281
500	1640
200	656
Land Below Sea Level 0	0
0	0
200	656
1000	3281
3000	9843
6000	19685
9000	29520

a (inset — Azores):

ATLANTIC OCEAN

CORVO
FLORES
Santa Cruz das Flores
GRACIOSA
Santa Cruz da Graciosa
TERCEIRA
Praia da Vitória
Angra do Heroísmo
SÃO JORGE
FAIAL — Velas
Horta
São Mateus — Ponta do Pico
PICO
A Ç O R E S
(Port.)
SÃO MIGUEL — Ribeira Grande
Ponta Delgada — Povoação
SANTA MARIA
Vila do Porto
© R. MtN.

ATLANTIC OCEAN

ARQUIPÉLAGO DA MADEIRA
MADEIRA ISLANDS (Port.)
PORTO SANTO
Pico Ruivo 1862 MADEIRA
Funchal — Machico
ILHAS DESERTAS

ILHAS SELVAGENS (Mad. Is.)

ISLAS CANARIAS
CANARY ISLANDS (Sp.)

LA PALMA
Los Llanos — PARQ. NAC. DE LA CALDERA DE TABURIENTE
Santa Cruz de la Palma
Pico de la Cruz
TENERIFE
La Orotava — San Cristóbal de la Laguna
PARQ. NAC. DEL TEIDE — Pico de Teide
GOMERA — San Sebastián de la Gomera
Valverde
HIERRO — FERRO
Santa Cruz de Tenerife
San Miguel — Güimar
San Nicolás — Arucas
Las Palmas de Gran Canaria
GRAN CANARIA

ISLA ALEGRANZA
ISLA GRACIOSA
LANZAROTE
Arrecife
ISLA DE LOBOS
Puerto del Rosario
FUERTEVENTURA

CAP JUBY
Tarfaya
LA'YOUN
Sebkha Tah
El Aaiún (La'youn)
MOROCCO AL-MAGREB
WESTERN SAHARA

Western Sahara has been occupied by Morocco.

CAP BOUJDOUR
Lemsid
Smara
Al Mahbas
Hawza

CAP BARBAS
Dakhla
Bir Enzaran
Tropic of Cancer
Golfe de Cintra
Khlij Oued edh Dheheb

Bîr Mogreïn (Fort-Trinquet)
Galtat Zemmour
ZEMMOUR
TIRIS ZEMMOUR
Fdérik — Zouérat
Kediet ej Jill 915

CAP AGÂDIR
RAS NOUADHIBOU
La Guera — Cansado
Nouâdhibou
DAKHLET NOUADHIBOU
INCHIRI
PARC NATIONAL DU BANC D'ARGUIN
Atâr
Techlé
Fasse de Ouarâne
Choûm — Chenchâmé
ADRAR
Ouadâne
Chinguetti
MAURITANIA — MAURITANIE

MOROCCO AL-MAGREB
ALGERIA ALGÉRIE
MAURITANIA MAURITANIE
ALGERIA ALGÉRIE MAURITANIE
MALI MAURITANIE

HAMADA DU DRÂA
JBEL OUARKZIZ
EL EGLAB
SHAMADA TOUNASSINE
SAHARA
ERG IGUIDI
EL MREÏTI
TIGUESMAT
EL HAMMÂMI
EL KHATT
MAQTEÎR
OUÂRÂNE
ERG CHECH
HAMÂDA EL HARICHA
Taoudenni
HODH ECH CHARGUI
ADRAR
EL KHNÂCHÎCH
TOMBOU

Morocco / east side:

BEJA
Odemira
CABO DE SÃO VICENTE
Lagos — Faro
Huelva
Sevilla
Écija
Córdoba
Antequera
Ronda
Jerez
Cádiz
Arcos de la Frontera
Algeciras — Gibraltar
La Línea
Strait of Gibraltar
Ceuta (Sp.)
Tanger — Tangier
Tétouan
Asilah
Larache
Ksar-el-Kebir
Souk Larbat Gharb
Ouezzane
Sidi Kacem
Salé — Kenitra
Rabat
Meknès
Fès
CASABLANCA
DAR-EL-BEIDA
Mohammedia (Fedala)
Ben-Slimane
Khemisset
Settat
El-Jadida (Mazagan)
Azemmour
Berrechid
Oualidia
Khouribga
Oued-Zem
Boujad
RAS BEDDOUZA
Safi
Youssoufia
Beni-Mellal
Kasba-Tadla
Bine-el-Ouidane
El-Kelaâ-es-Srarhna
Chemaïa
Midelt
Er-Rachidia
Essaouira (Mogador)
CAP SIM
Marrakech
Tahanaoute — Asni
Demnate
Jebel Tignousti 3825
Jebel Toubkal 4165
Tamanar
CAP RHIR
Tamri
Agadir
Aït-Melloul
Taroudant
Ouarzazate
Tazenakht
Taliouine
Zagora
Foum-Zguid
ANTI-ATLAS
HAUT ATLAS
MOYEN ATLAS
Goulimima
Erfoud
Rissani
CAP DRAA
Tiznit
Tarhjijt
Tafraoute
Tata
Akka
Sidi Ifni
Bou Izakarn
Goulimime
Tan-Tan
Tiglit
Assa
Foum-el-Hisn
Zag
JBEL BANI
HAMADA DU DRÂA
DESERT DU TINDOUF
Tindouf
Sebkha de Tindouf
Sebkha Ain Bêlbela
IGUIDI
MCHERRAH
Chenachane

Map continues
pages 150-151

Glossary (bottom):

MAP FORM	cap	chott	djebel	erg	hamada	jbel	oued	sebkha
ENGLISH	cape	intermittent lake	mountain	sand desert	desert	mountain	wadi	salt flat
DEUTSCH	Kap	periodischer See	Berg	Sandwüste	Wüste	Berg	Wadi	Salzebene
ESPAÑOL	cabo	lago intermitente	montaña	desierto arenoso	desierto	montaña	uadi	salar
FRANÇAIS	cap	lac périodique	montagne	désert de sable	désert	montagne	wadi	saline
PORTUGUÊS	cabo	lago intermitente	montanha	deserto arenoso	deserto	montanha	uádi	salina

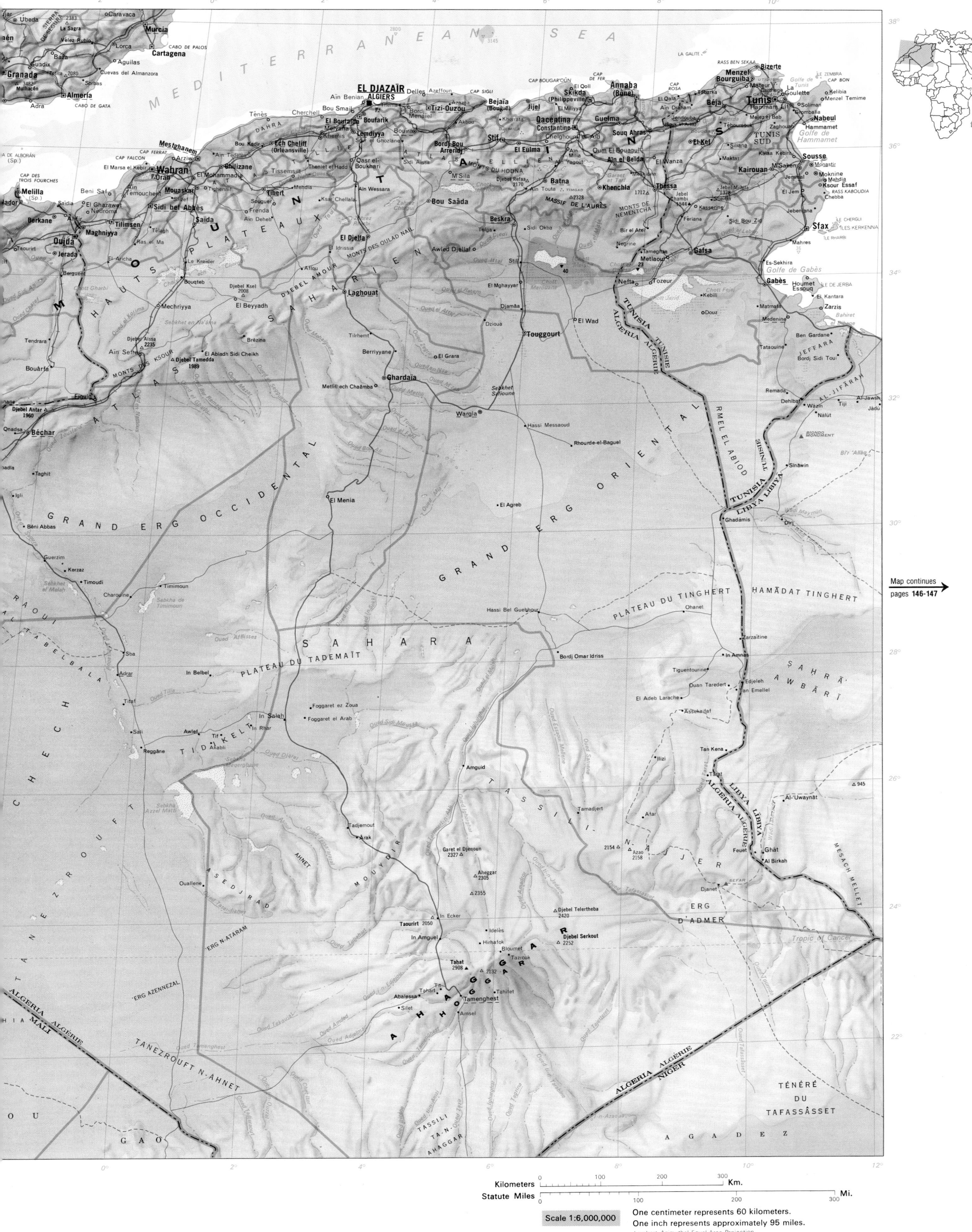

Map continues
pages 146-147

Kilometers
Statute Miles

Km.
Mi.

Scale 1:6,000,000

One centimeter represents 60 kilometers.
One inch represents approximately 95 miles.

Lambert Azimuthal Equal-Area Projection

West Africa / Westafrika / África Occidental
Afrique Occidentale / África Ocidental

Meters	Feet
6000	19685
4000	13124
3000	9843
2000	6562
1000	3281
500	1640
200	656
0	0
Land Below Sea Level 0	0
200	656
1000	3281
3000	9843
6000	19685
9000	29520

Copyright © by Rand M9Nally & Co.
Map prepared by George Philip & Son Ltd, London.
A-589792-764   -5 0 -14'

CAPE VERDE
CABO VERDE

MAP FORM							
ENGLISH	coast	escarpment	game reserve	island	lake	mountains	valley
DEUTSCH	Küste	Landstufe	Wildpark	Insel	See	Berge	Tal
ESPAÑOL	costa	escarpa	vedado de caza	isla	lago	montañas	valle
FRANÇAIS	côte	escarpement	réserve à gibier	île	lac	montagnes	vallée
PORTUGUÊS	costa	escarpa	reserva de caça	ilha	lago	montes	vale

MAP FORM — coast — dhar — escarpment — game reserve — ilha — lac — monts — mountains — vallée

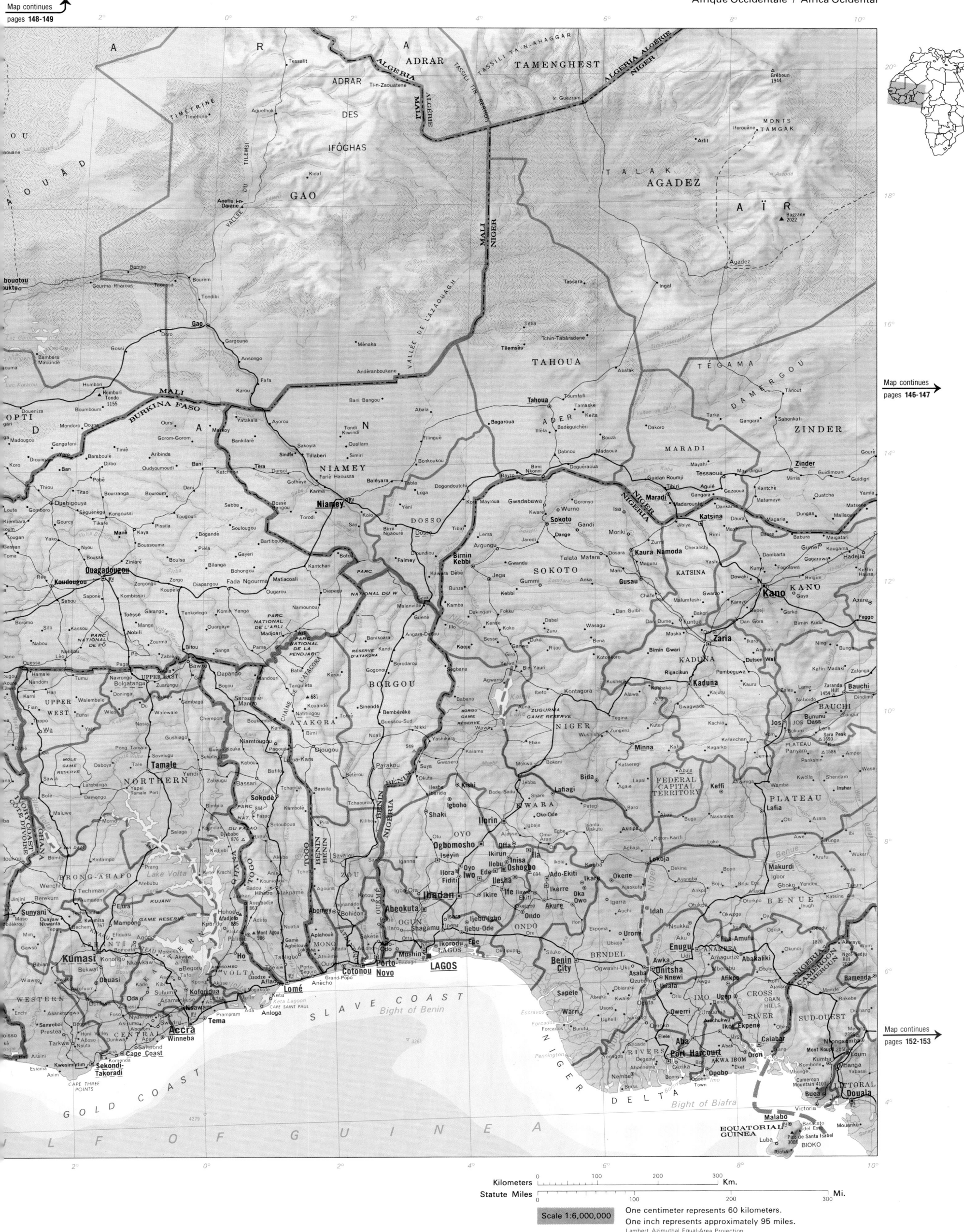

Map continues
pages 148-149

Map continues
pages 146-147

Map continues
pages 152-153

Kilometers 0 100 200 300 Km.
Statute Miles 0 100 200 300 Mi.

Scale 1:6,000,000
One centimeter represents 60 kilometers.
One inch represents approximately 95 miles.
Lambert Azimuthal Equal-Area Projection

152

Western Congo Basin / Westliches Kongobecken / Cuenca Occidental del Congo
Bassin du Congo, partie Occidentale / Bacia Ocidental do Congo

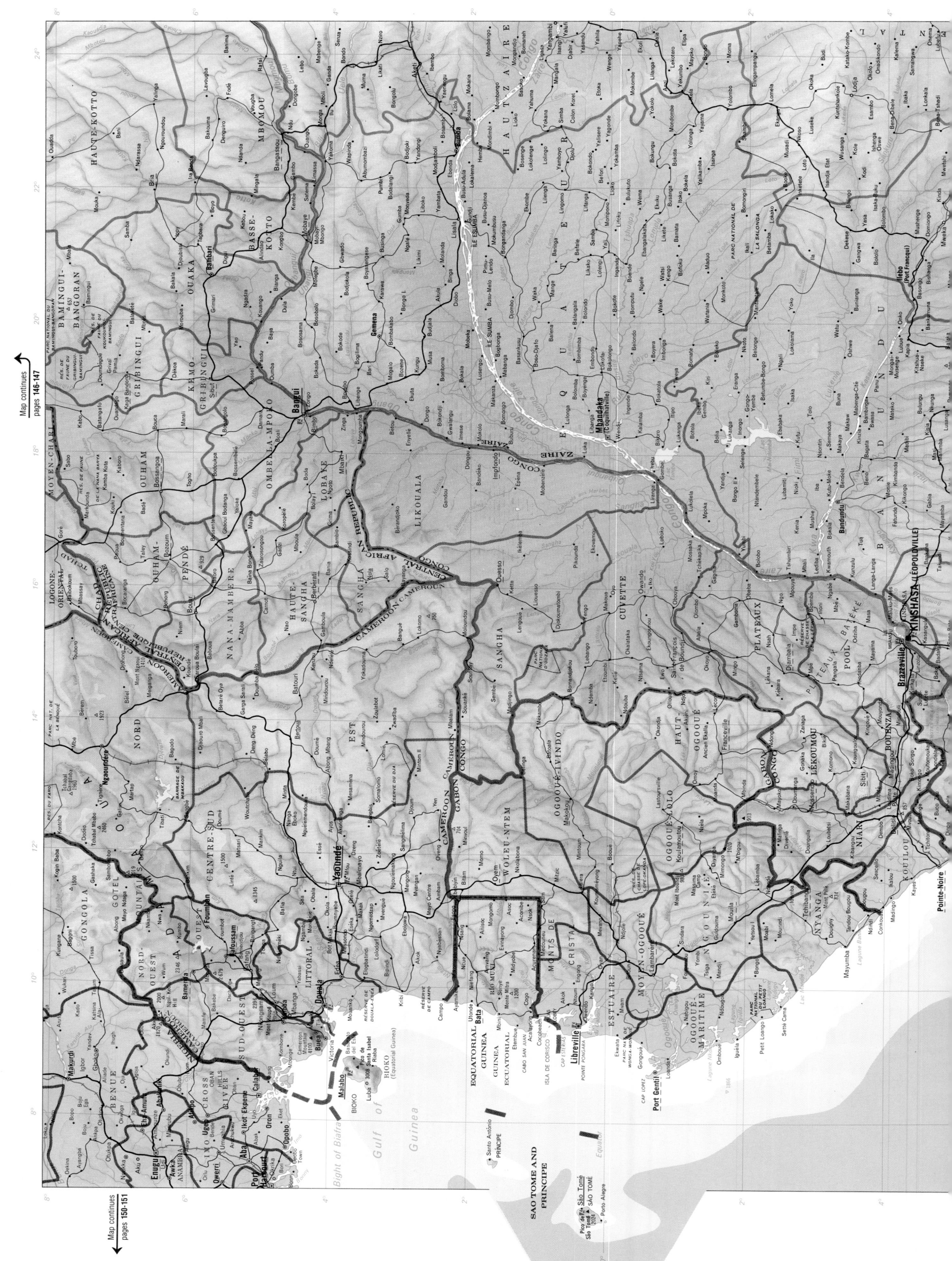

Map continues
pages 146-147

Map continues
pages 150-151

Map continues
pages 154-155

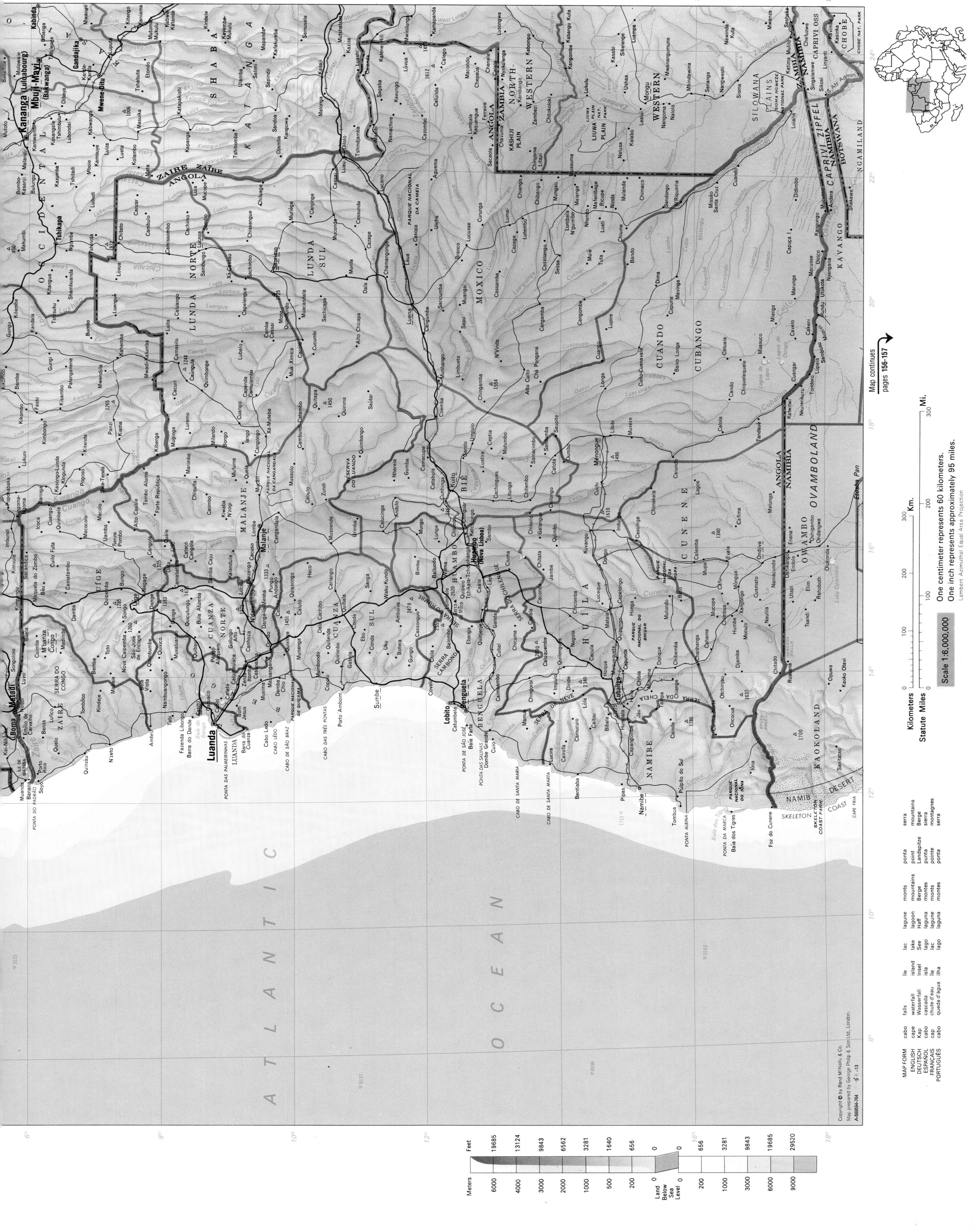

Map continues
pages 156-157

Scale 1:6,000,000

One centimeter represents 60 kilometers.
One inch represents approximately 95 miles.

Lambert Azimuthal Equal Area Projection

Kilometers

Statute Miles

MAP FORM								
ENGLISH	cape	waterfall	island	lake	lagoon	mountains	point	mountains
DEUTSCH	Kap	Wasserfall	Insel	See	Haff	Berge	Landspitze	Berge
ESPAÑOL	cabo	cascada	isla	lago	laguna	sierra	punta	sierra
FRANÇAIS	cap	chute d'eau	île	lac	lagune	montagnes	pointe	montes
PORTUGUÊS	cabo	queda d'água	ilha	lago	laguna	serra	ponta	montes

cabo — falls — ilie — lac — laguna — monts — ponta — serra

Copyright © by Rand McNally & Co.
Map prepared by George Philip & Son Ltd., London.

Meters	Feet
6000	19685
4000	13124
3000	9843
2000	6562
1000	3281
500	1640
200	656
0	0
Land	Below Sea Level
0	0
200	656
1000	3281
3000	9843
6000	19685
9000	29520

ATLANTIC OCEAN

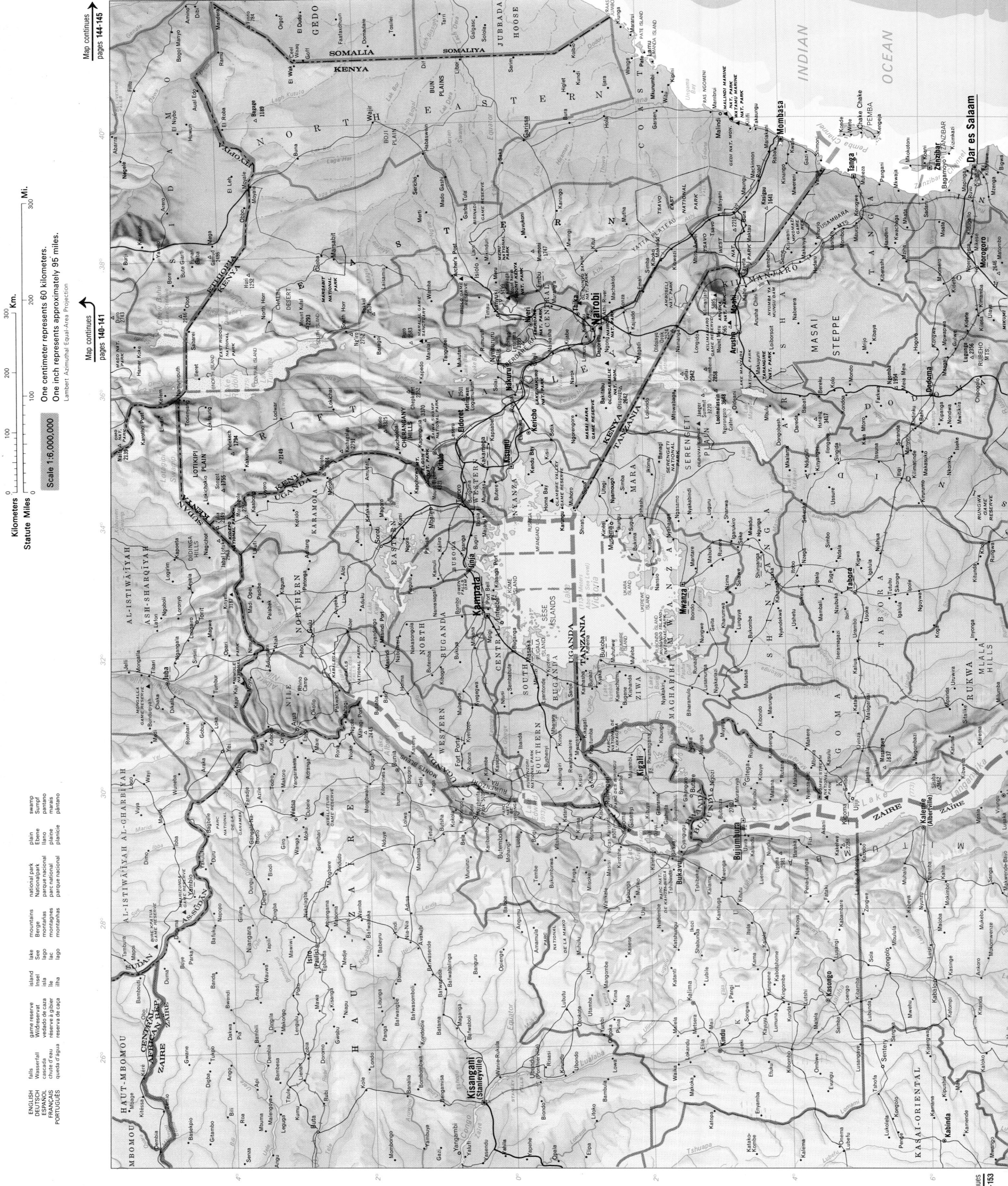

Scale 1:6,000,000

One centimeter represents 60 kilometers.
One inch represents approximately 95 miles.

Lambert Azimuthal Equal-Area Projection

East Africa and Eastern Congo Basin / Ostafrika und Östliches Kongobecken / África Oriental y Cuenca Oriental del Congo
Afrique Orientale et Bassin du Congo, partie Orientale / África Oriental e Bacia Oriental do Congo

155

Map continues
pages 156-157

	Feet
	19685
	13124
	9843
	6562
	3281
	1640
	656
	0
	656
	3281
	9843
	19685
	29520

Meters	
6000	
4000	
3000	
2000	
1000	
500	
200	
0	
Land Below Sea Level	0
200	
1000	
3000	
6000	
9000	

Southern Africa and Madagascar / Südafrika und Madagaskar / África Meridional y Madagascar
Afrique Méridionale et Madagascar / África Meridional e Madagascar

Map continues
pages 152-153

ATLANTIC OCEAN

NAMIB DESERT

KALAHARI DESERT

ANGOLA

BOTSWANA

ZIMBABWE

NAMIBIA / SÜDWESTAFRIKA

Windhoek

Walvis Bay

Lüderitz

Swakopmund

Keetmanshoop

CAPE TOWN
KAAPSTAD

Port Elizabeth

Bloemfontein

Kimberley

Gaborone

Livingstone

MAP FORM	bay	berg, berge	cape	game reserve	ilha	lake	national park
ENGLISH	bay	mountain, mountains	cape	game reserve	island	lake	national park
DEUTSCH	Bucht	Berg, Berge	Kap	Wildpark	Insel	See	Nationalpark
ESPAÑOL	bahía	montaña, montañas	cabo	vedado de caza	isla	lago	parque nacional
FRANÇAIS	baie	montagne, montagnes	cap	réserve à gibier	île	lac	parc national
PORTUGUÊS	baía	montanha, montanhas	cabo	reserva de caça	ilha	lago	parque nacional

Meters / Feet

Meters	Feet
6000	19685
4000	13124
3000	9843
2000	6562
1000	3281
500	1640
200	656
0	0

Land Below Sea Level

0	0
200	656
1000	3281
3000	9843
6000	19685
9000	29520

Kilometers 0 100 200 300 Km.
Statute Miles 0 100 200 300 Mi.

Scale 1:6,000,000
One centimeter represents 60 kilometers.
One inch represents approximately 95 miles.
Lambert Azimuthal Equal-Area Projection

Southern Africa and Madagascar / Südafrika und Madagaskar / África Meridional y Madagascar
Afrique Méridionale et Madagascar / África Meridional e Madagascar

157

Map continues
pages **154-155**

a

INDIAN OCEAN

Mitsamiouli
N'Tsaouéni NJAZIDJA
Hahaïa (GRANDE COMORE)
Moroni Koimbani
Kartala 2361 COMOROS
Salimani COMORES
Dembéni POINTE SUD

Sima Mutsamudu
Fomboni Moya Domoni
NZWANI M'Ramani
MWALI (ANJOUAN)
(MOHÉLI)

ARCHIPEL DES COMORES

Chingoni Mamoutzou
Boeni Bandeli
Dzaoudzi
MAYOTTE
(Fr.)

MOZAMBIQUE CHANNEL

© R. MEN.

b

c

INDIAN

MAURITIUS

Port Louis CAP MALHEUREUX
Triolet
Rivière du Rempart
Vacoas Rose-Hill
Curepipe
MAURITIUS Mahébourg
RÉUNION Piton de la Petite
Rivière Noire 828

Saint-Denis
Le Port Saint-André
Saint-Paul Saint-Benoît
Piton des Neiges 3069
Saint-Louis Piton de la Fournaise 2631
Saint-Pierre Saint-Joseph
RÉUNION

MASCARENE
OCEAN

© R. MEN.

INDIAN

OCEAN

Bophuthatswana, Ciskei, Transkei, and Venda
are not internationally recognized.

MADAGASCAR
MADAGASIKARA

INDIAN

OCEAN

Tropic of Capricorn

Map continues
pages 156-157

MAP FORM	bay	berge	cape	dam	game reserve	national park	pass	point
ENGLISH	bay	mountains	cape	dam	game reserve	national park	pass	point
DEUTSCH	Bucht	Berge	Kap	Damm	Wildpark	Nationalpark	Pass	Landspitze
ESPAÑOL	bahía	montañas	cabo	presa	vedado de caza	parque nacional	paso	punta
FRANÇAIS	baie	montagnes	cap	barrage	réserve à gibier	parc national	col	pointe
PORTUGUÊS	baía	montanhas	cabo	represa	reserva de caça	parque nacional	passo	ponta

South Africa / Republik Südafrika / Sudáfrica

Pretoria • Johannesburg • Soweto • Krugersdorp • Roodepoort-Maraisburg • Randfontein • Carletonville • Vereeniging • Vanderbijlpark • Potchefstroom • Klerksdorp • Stilfontein • Orkney • Kroonstad • Welkom • Virginia • Bloemfontein • Maseru • LESOTHO • Queenstown • King William's Town • East London / Oos-Londen • Grahamstown • Port Elizabeth

Rustenburg • Sonop • Lichtenburg • Coligny • Vredefort • Parys • Sasolburg • Heilbron • Frankfort • Reitz • Bethlehem • Harrismith • Ladybrand • Ladysmith • Dundee • Newcastle • Volksrust • Charlestown • Vryheid • Piet Retief • Ermelo • Bethal • Witbank • Middelburg • Pretoria • Carolina • SWAZILAND • Mbabane • Manzini • Piggs Peak • Maputo (Lourenço Marques) • MOZAMBIQUE / MOÇAMBIQUE

DRAKENSBERG • TRANSVAAL • NATAL • ZULULAND • TRANSKEI • GRIQUALAND EAST • PONDOLAND • KAFFRARIA • CISKEI • STORMBERGE • WITTEBERGE • WINTERBERGE • SOUTH AFRICA / SUID-AFRIKA

Pietermaritzburg • DURBAN • Richard's Bay • Umtata • Stanger

INDIAN OCEAN

Bophuthatswana, Ciskei, Transkei, and Venda
are not internationally recognized.

Copyright © by Rand McNally & Co.
Map prepared by George Philip & Son Ltd., London
A-584600-764

Kilometers | 0   50   100   150 | Km.
Statute Miles | 0   50   100   150 | Mi.

Scale 1:3,000,000
One centimeter represents 30 kilometers.
One inch represents approximately 47 miles.
Lambert Conformal Conic Projection

Australia / Australien / Australia
Australie / Austrália

Map continues ↑
pages **108-109**

110°   115°   120°   125°   130°

G. Slamet
1428
Tasik-
malaya Citacap Magelang Kedin Malang Jember Singaraja Mataram Sumbawa Basar NUSA FLORES TENGGARA ISLANDS
Yogyakarta Surakarta Madiun Bitar Banyuwangi Bali Denpasar Praya SUMBAWA LESSER SUNDA Ara
JAWA JAVA LOMBOK Waikabubak Waingapu SUMBA Baing Laut Sawu PULAU SEMAU Kupang TIMOR Soba
I N D O N E S I A Savu Sea PULAU ROTI MELVILLE
PULAU Timor ISLAND CAPE CROKER
SAWU BATHURST COBURG PENINSULA
HIBERNIA REEF ISLAND CAPE
10° ASHMORE ISLANDS CARTIER ISLANDS Sea Darwin Humpty Doo
(Austl.) POINT BLAZE Rum Jungle ARNHEM
CAPE Pine Creek
BROWSE LONDONDERRY Joseph Katherine
ISLAND BONAPARTE Bonaparte
SCOTT REEF ARCHIPELAGO York Sound Gulf
BEAGLE Wyndham Kununurra
ADÈLE ISLAND REEF Lake Victoria
BUCCANEER Collier KIMBERLEY PLATEAU Argyle River Downs Daly Wate
ARCHIPELAGO Bay KING LEOPOLD RANGES DURACK RANGES
CAPE LEVEQUE Derby Mount Ord Wave Hill
15° Mount Ord 937 Fitzroy Crossing Halls Creek NORTHE
ROWLEY SHOALS Broome TANAMI Barro
CAPE LATOUCHE TREVILLE TERRITO
La Grange Lake Gregory
I N D I A N EIGHTY MILE BEACH DESERT
Goldsworthy GREAT SANDY DESERT Lake Barro
MONTE BELLO DAMPIER Port Hedland Shay Gap Willis
ISLANDS ARCHIPELAGO Grey Lake Lake Mackay
O C E A N Dampier Roebourne Marble Bar Dora Lake Auld
BARROW ISLAND Karratha Nullagine
MUIRON ISLANDS Onslow Pannawonica HAMERSLEY RANGE Wittenoom Lake
20° NORTH WEST CAPE Mount Brockman Mount Bruce Disappointment Mount Leisler Mount Ze
Exmouth 1132 1235 897 1524 1511
Gulf Tom Price Savory MACDONN
POINT CLOATES Mount Mahanry Newman Lake RANGE
1251 Macdonald
Paraburdoo Lake Neale
CAPE CUVIER Mount Augustus 1105 W E S T E R N GIBSON DESERT Lake Amadeus
Tropic of Capricorn 1105 906 Mount Olga A U S T
Geographe Chan. Mount Essendon 1069 Ayers Rock
105° Carnarvon Peak Hill Mount Aloysius 867 Mount Cockburn Mount Woodroffe
BERNER ISLAND Gascoyne ROBINSON RANGE 1085 1138 1440
DORRE ISLAND Shark Lake Carnegie Lake Giles
Naturaliste Channel Bay Woodleigh Lake Wells
DIRK HARTOG Denham Meekatharra Wiluna
ISLAND Nannine A U S T R A L I A GREAT VICTORIA DESERT
25° STEEP POINT Cue Lake Austin Mara-inga
Kalbarri Sandstone Agnew Yeo Lake Oldea
Mount Magnet Mount Redcliffe Laverton SOU
Northampton Yalgoo 562 Malcolm Lake Carey
HOUTMAN Mullewa Pindar Leonora Lake Maurice
ABROLHOS Geraldton Mongers Lake Lake Raeside Lake
Dongara Lake Barlee Menzies Lake Mingwal
Tallering Lake Moore
Springs Lake
GREEN HEAD Dalwallinu Bonnie Rock Kalgoorlie NULLARBOR PLAIN
Moora Bencubbin Boulder Zanthus Rawlinna Haig Forrest Deakin
30° Wanneroo Bullfinch Coolgardie Lake Lefroy Eucla
Northam Southern Cross Lake Cowan CAPE ADIEU
Perth York Merredin SAINT PETER ISL
Fremantle Beverley Kellerberrin Norseman Stre
Pinjarra Brookton Lake Johnston Lake Dundas
Nerrogin Hyden POINT CULVER
Bunbury Wagin Newdegate Great Australian Bight
Collie Nyabing Ravensthorpe CAPE ARID
Busselton Bridgetown Katanning ARCHIPELAGO
CAPE NATURALISTE Gnowangerup Hopetoun OF THE
Augusta Manjimup Bluff Knoll HOOD POINT RECHERCHE
Geographe 1096 Great Australian Bight
CAPE LEEUWIN Pemberton Mount Barker S O U T H E R N O C E
POINT D'ENTRECASTEAUX Denmark Albany
CAPE VANCOUVER
WEST CAPE HOWE George Sound

35°

40°

105°   110°   115°   120°   125°   130°

ENGLISH	bay	cape	island	lake	mount	point	range	reef
DEUTSCH	Bucht	Kap	Insel	See	Berg	Landspitze	Gebirge	Riff
ESPAÑOL	bahía	cabo	isla	lago	montaña	punta	cordillera	arrecife
FRANÇAIS	baie	cap	île	lac	mont	pointe	chaîne	récif
PORTUGUÊS	baía	cabo	ilha	lago	monte	ponta	cordilheira	recife

Australia / Australien / Australia
Australie / Austrália

a S e a

CAPE WESSEL
WESSEL ISLANDS
THE ENGLISH COMPANYS ISLANDS
CAPE ARNHEM
CAPE GREY
GROOTE EYLANDT
CAPE BEATRICE
Limmen Bight
BLUE MUD ISLAND
SIR EDWARD PELLEW GROUP
VANDERLIN ISLAND
Borroloola

Gulf

of

Carpentaria

BARKLY TABLEABLE
Nicholson
Ranken Store

SIMPSON

DESERT

A L I A

AUSTRALIA

Oodnadatta

BOIGU ISLAND
SAIBAI ISLAND
Daru
Torres Strait
PRINCE OF WALES ISLAND
Thursday Island
MOA ISLAND
CAPE YORK
Bamaga
Endeavour Strait

CAPE
YORK
PENINSULA

DUIFKEN POINT
Albatross Bay
Weipa
Archer Bay
Aurukun
CAPE KEER-WEER
Coen
MORNINGTON ISLAND
WELLESLEY ISLANDS
BENTINCK ISLAND
Karumba
Normanton
Burketown
Croydon
Forsayth
Einasleigh
Greenvale
Mount Isa
Cloncurry
SELWYN RA.
Selwyn
Duchess
Dajarra
Richmond
Hughenden
Boulia
Hamilton
Winton
GREAT

Carnoowweal
Avon Downs

Birdsville
Bedourie
Cooper
Innamincka
STURT STONY DESERT
GREY
RANGE

Lake Eyre North
16
Lake Eyre South
Marree
Copley
Lake Torrens
Pinba
Woomera
Lake Gairdner
Kimba
GAWLER RANGES
EYRE PENINSULA
Port Lincoln
Whyalla
Iron Knob
Port Augusta
Quorn
Hawker
N. FLINDERS RANGE
Saint Mary Peak 1182
Peterborough
Jamestown
Burra

NEW GUINEA

NEW GUINEA

Kokoda
Mount Victoria 4035
OWEN STANLEY RANGE
Garara
Popondetta
Wanigela
Abau
Esa'ala
Samarai

Port Moresby
Rigo
Papua

PAPUA
NEW GUINEA

Losuia
KIRIWINA ISLANDS
D'ENTRECASTEAUX ISLANDS
Kulumadau
MUYUA ISLAND
LOUISIADE ARCHIPELAGO
MISIMA
TAGULA ISLAND
YELA ISLAND
LONG REEF

C o r a l   S e a

OSPREY REEF

BOUGAINVILLE REEF

HOLMES REEF

WILLIS GROUP (Austl.)

FLINDERS REEFS
MALAY REEF
ABINGTON REEFS
CHILCOTT ISLAND (Austl.)
DIAMOND ISLETS (Austl.)
LIHOU REEF AND CAYS
TREGOSSE ISLETS (Austl.)

MARION REEF

ÎLES CHESTERFIELD (N. Cal.)

VELLA LAVELLA
RANONGGA
Gizo
KOLOMBANGARA
NEW GEORGIA
VANGUNU
RENDOVA
RUSSELL ISLANDS
CHOISEUL
SANTA ISABEL
Tulaghi
GUADALCANAL
Mt. Makarakomburu 2447
Honiara

SOLOMON ISLANDS

S o l o m o n   S e a

RENNELL

INDISPENSABLE REEFS

MELLISH REEF

ÎLE DE SABLE (N. Cal.)

CAYE DE L'OBSERVATOIRE (N. Cal.)
RÉCIFS
BELLONA

KENN REEF
BIRD ISLET (Austl.)
WRECK REEF
SAUMAREZ REEF
CATO ISLAND

Tropic of Capricorn

P A C I F I C

O C E A N

GREAT DIVIDING RANGE

Chillagoe
Mareeba
Atherton
Ravenshoe
Cairns
Babinda
Bellenden Ker 1622
Innisfail
CAPE GRAFTON

HINCHINBROOK ISLAND
Ingham
Halifax Bay
Townsville
Charters Towers
CAPE CLEVELAND
Ayr
Home Hill
Bowen
Proserpine
CUMBERLAND ISLANDS
Collinsville
NORTHUMBERLAND ISLES
Mackay
Sarina
CAPE PALMERSTON
TOWNSHEND ISLAND

GREAT

BARRIER

REEF

SWAIN REEFS

Laura
Cooktown
Musgrave

Coleman
Staaten

Mitchell

GREGORY RANGE

QUEENSLAND

GREAT ARTESIAN

BASIN

RANGE

Longreach
Ilfracombe
Barcaldine
Blackall
Aramac
Jericho
Alpha
Tambo
Windorah
Adavale
Yaraka
Quilpie
Charleville
Eromanga
Thargomindah
Cunnamulla

DENHAM RANGE
CONNORS RA.
Clermont
Blair Athol
Emerald
Rockhampton
Yeppoon
CAPICORN GROUP
CURTIS ISLAND
Port Curtis
BUNKER GROUP
Gladstone
Biloela
Morgan
Springsure
Theodore
Taroom
Monto
Biggenden
Childers
Bundaberg
SANDY CAPE
FRASER ISLAND

NEW SOUTH WALES

Tibooburra
Wilcannia
Menindee
Ivanhoe
Broken Hill
BARRIER RANGE
Olary
Tilpa
Bourke
Darling
Wentworth
Balranald
Hay
Hillston
West Wyalong
Griffith
Leeton
Narrandera
Jerilderie
Deniliquin
Echuca

Walgett
Brewarrina
Nyngan
Cobar
Nymagee
Condobolin
Parkes
Forbes
Cowra
Young
Temora
Cootamundra
Junee
Wagga Wagga
Coonamble
Gilgandra
Dubbo
Wellington
Mudgee
Orange
Bathurst
Lithgow
Katoomba
RIVERINA

Narromine
Gunnedah
Tamworth
Quirindi
Scone
Muswellbrook
Singleton
Cessnock
Maitland
Newcastle
SUGARLOAF POINT
Gosford
Wyong

Narrabri
Coonabarabran
Coolah
Armidale
Round Mountain 1586
Kempsey
Port Macquarie
SMOKY CAPE
Tamworth

Goondiwindi
Moree
Narrabri
Inverell
Warialda
Glen Innes
Tenterfield
Casino
Lismore
Grafton
Maclean
CAPE BYRON
Ballina
Murwillumbah
Warwick
Stanthorpe

Dalby
Kingaroy
Nanango
Nambour
MORETON ISLAND
Brisbane
Ipswich
Southport
NORTH STRADBROKE ISLAND
Toowoomba
Beaudesert
Boonah
Gympie
Maryborough
Murgon
Wondai

GREAT DIVIDING RANGE

Wyndham
Narromine
Dubbo
Parramatta
SYDNEY
Campbelltown
Wollongong
Moss Vale
Goulburn
Yass
Nowra
Queanbeyan
Jervis Bay
Canberra
A.C.T.
Cooma
Tumut
Gundagai
SHOALHAVEN

VICTORIA

Adelaide
Elizabeth
GULF ST. VINCENT
KANGAROO ISLAND
Victor Harbor
Encounter Bay
Murray Bridge
Tailem Bend
Pinnaroo
Bordertown
Keith
Naracoorte
Penola
Millicent
Mount Gambier
Kingston Southeast
CAPE JAFFA
Robe
Portland
CAPE NELSON
Warrnambool
Port Fairy
Colac
CAPE OTWAY
SOUTH EAST POINT

Renmark
Loxton
Mildura
Swan Hill
Kerang
Horsham
Ararat
Stawell
Hamilton
Ballarat
Geelong
MELBOURNE
Moe
Sale
Bairnsdale
NINETY MILE BEACH
Morwell
Wonthaggi
Foster
WILSONS PROMONTORY
PHILLIP ISLAND

Albury
Wangaratta
Benalla
Shepparton
Seymour
Bendigo
Maryborough
Mount Bogong 1986
Mount Kosciuszko 2228
Bombala
Orbost
CAPE HOWE
POINT HICKS

KING ISLAND

Bass Strait

HUNTER ISLAND
CAPE GRIM
FLINDERS ISLAND
FURNEAUX GROUP
CAPE BARREN ISLAND

Smithton
Burnie
Wynyard
Devonport
Ulverstone
Beaconsfield
Scottsdale
Launceston
Saint Marys
Zeehan
Mount Ossa 1617
Queenstown
Strahan
CAPE SORELL

TASMANIA

TASMANIA
New Norfolk
Huonville
Hobart
Geeveston
Bothwell
LOW ROCKY POINT
SOUTH WEST CAPE
Port Arthur
SOUTH EAST CAPE
BRUNY ISLAND
Freycinet Peninsula
MARIA ISLAND

T a s m a n

S e a

Kilometers 0   200   400   600 Km.
Statute Miles 0   200   400   600 Mi.

Scale 1:12,000,000

One centimeter represents 120 kilometers.
One inch represents approximately 190 miles.
Lambert Conformal Conic Projection

162

Western and Central Australia / West-und Mittelaustralien / Australia Centro-occidental
Australie Occidentale et Centrale / Austrália Ocidental e Central

Meters		Feet
6000		19685
4000		13124
3000		9843
2000		6562
1000		3281
500		1640
200		656
0		0
Land Below Sea Level		
0		0
200		656
1000		3281
3000		9843
6000		19685
9000		29520

	bay	cape	creek, cr.	island, i.	lake, l.	mount	point	range
ENGLISH	bay	cape	creek, cr.	island, i.	lake, l.	mount	point	range
DEUTSCH	Bucht	Kap	Bach.	Insel	See	Berg	Landspitze	Gebirge
ESPAÑOL	bahía	cabo	riachuelo	isla	lago	montaña	punta	cordillera
FRANÇAIS	baie	cap	crique	île	lac	mont	pointe	chaîne
PORTUGUÊS	baía	cabo	riacho	ilha	lago	monte	ponta	cordilheira

Western and Central Australia / West- und Mittelaustralien / Australia Centro-occidental
Australie Occidentale et Centrale / Austrália Ocidental e Central

163

Map continues pages 164-165

Map continues pages 166-167

164

Northern Australia and New Guinea / Nordaustralien und Neuguinea / Australia Septentrional y Nueva Guinea
Australie Septentrionale et Nouvelle Guinée / Austrália Setentrional e Nova Guiné

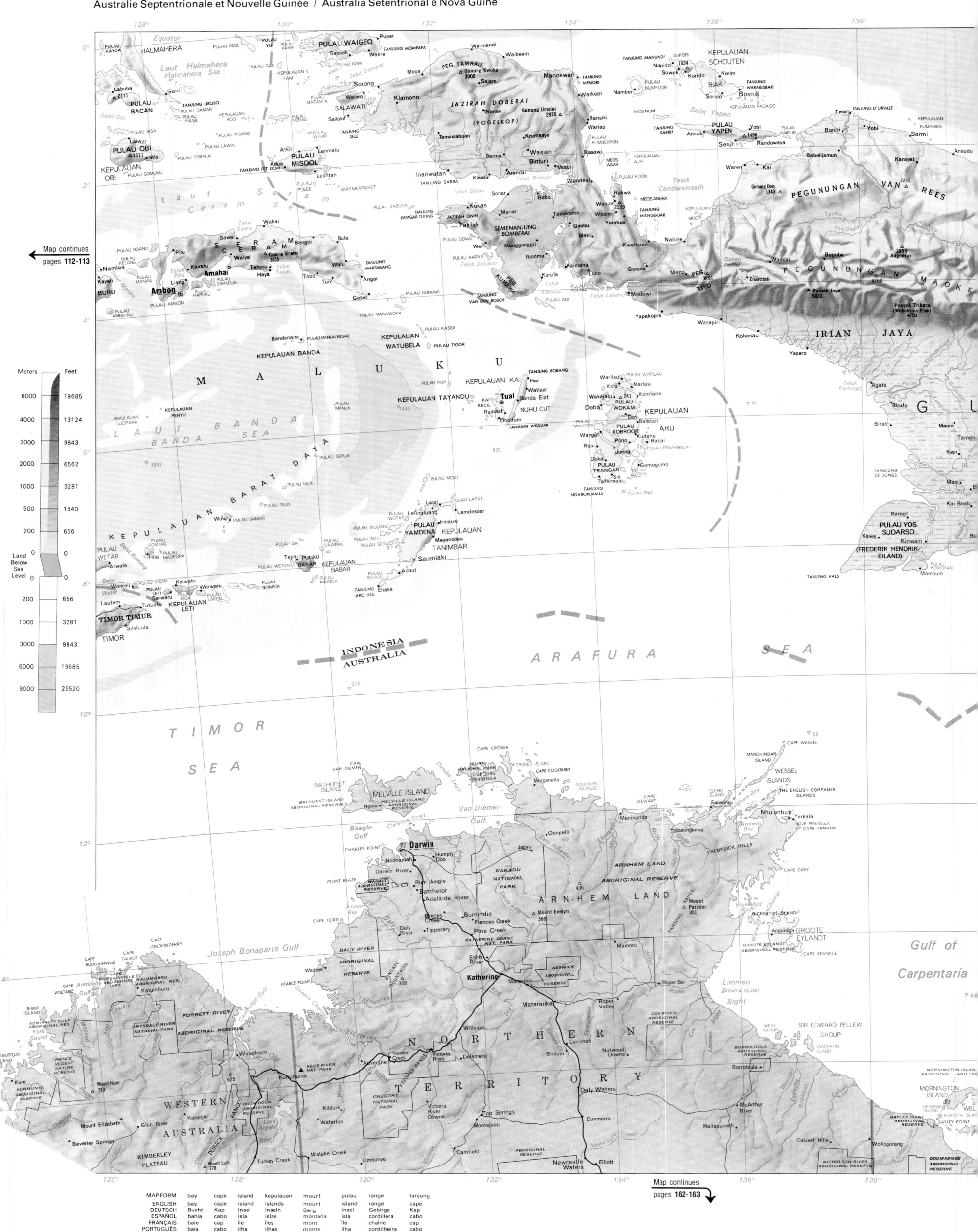

Map continues
pages 112-113

Map continues
pages 162-163

MAP FORM	bay	cape	island	kepulauan	mount	pulau	range	tanjung
ENGLISH	bay	cape	island	islands	mount	island	range	cape
DEUTSCH	Bucht	Kap	Insel	Inseln	Berg	Insel	Gebirge	Kap
ESPAÑOL	bahía	cabo	isla	islas	montaña	isla	cordillera	cabo
FRANÇAIS	baie	cap	île	îles	mont	île	chaîne	cap
PORTUGUÊS	baía	cabo	ilha	ilhas	monte	ilha	cordilheira	cabo

Northern Australia and New Guinea / Nordaustralien und Neuguinea / Australia Septentrional y Nueva Guinea
Australie Septentrionale et Nouvelle Guinée / Austrália Setentrional e Nova Guiné

165

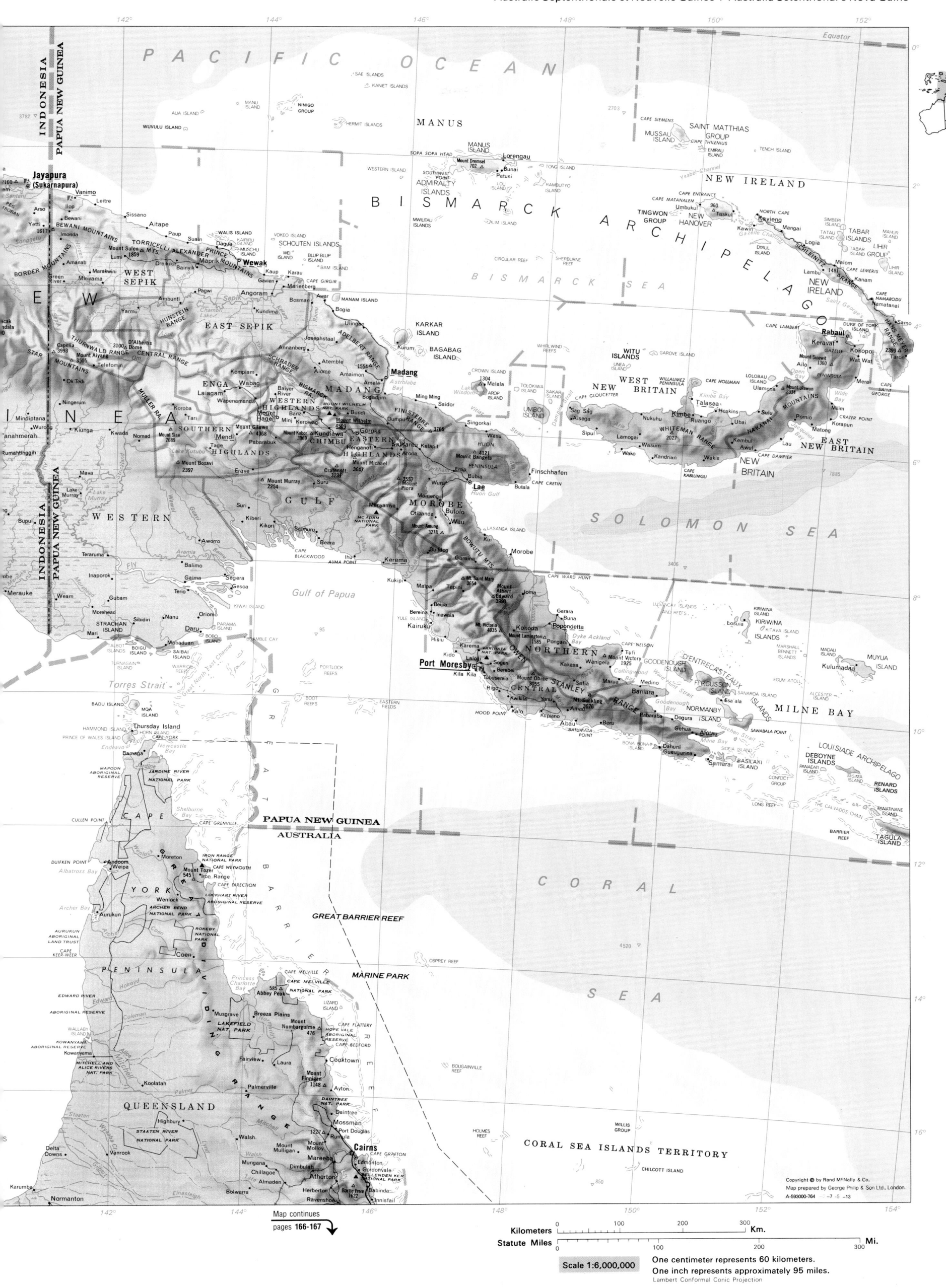

Map continues
pages 166-167

Kilometers

Statute Miles

Scale 1:6,000,000
One centimeter represents 60 kilometers.
One inch represents approximately 95 miles.
Lambert Conformal Conic Projection

Copyright © by Rand McNally & Co.
Map prepared by George Philip & Son Ltd., London.
A-593000-764   -7 -5 -13

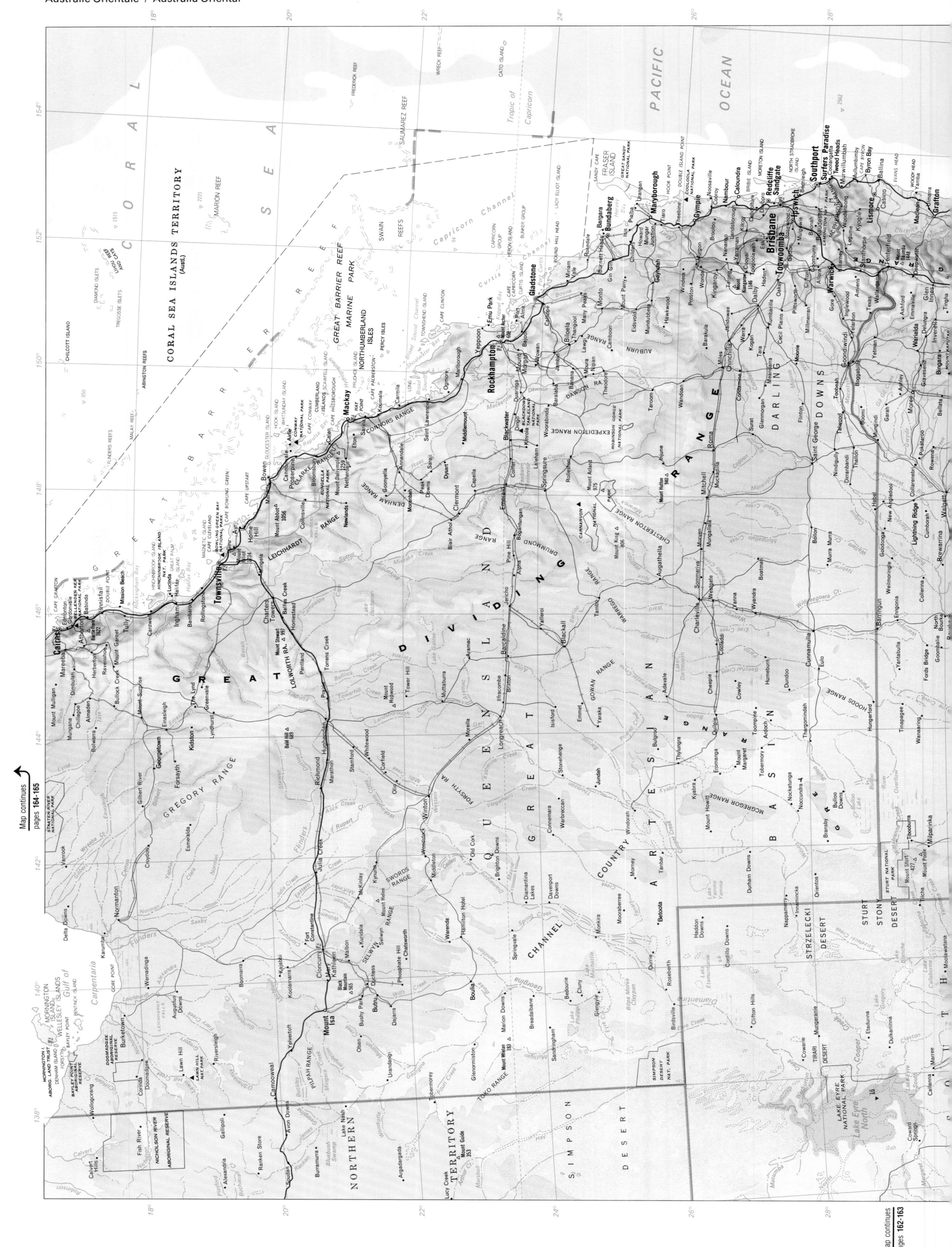

Map continues
pages 164-165

Map continues
pages 162-163

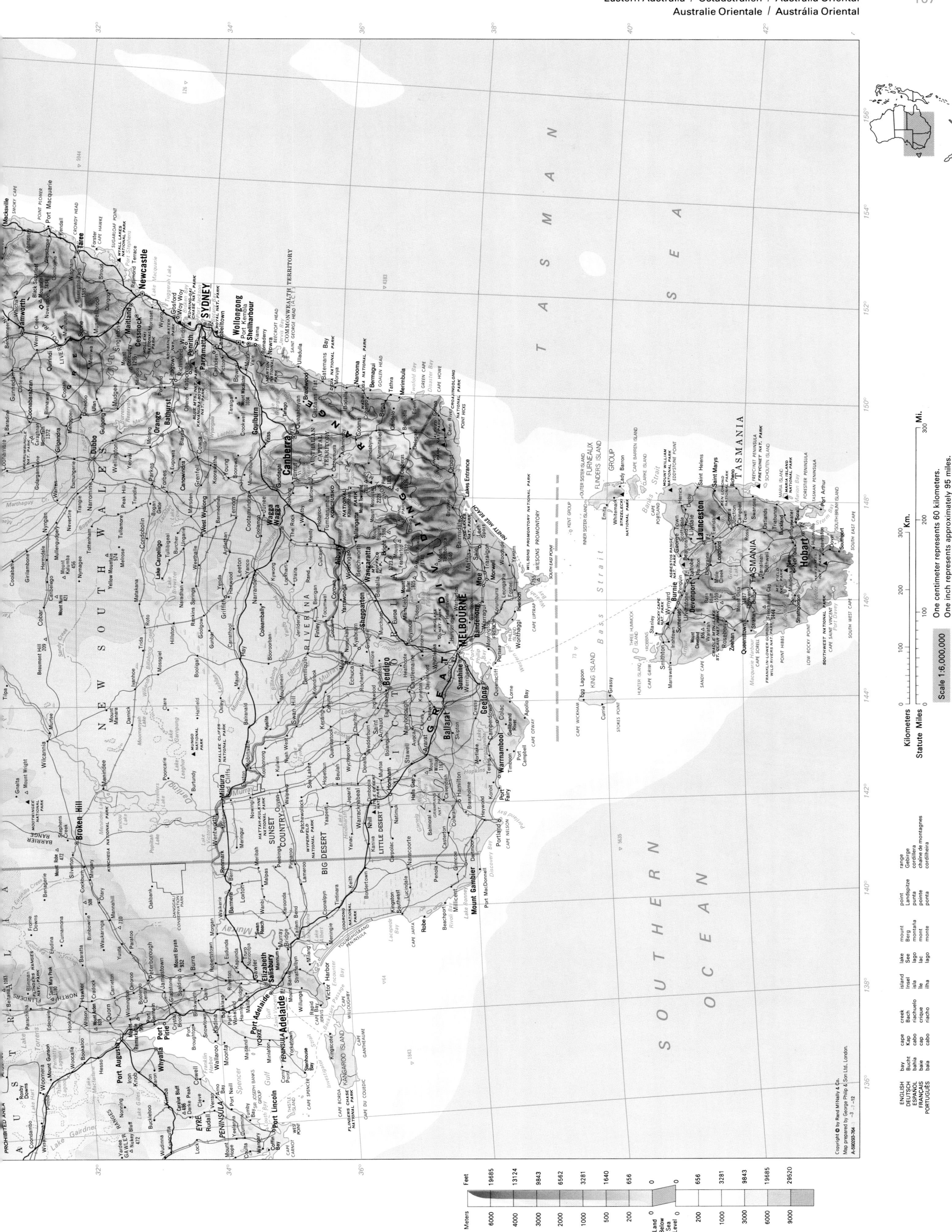

Scale 1:6,000,000

One centimeter represents 60 kilometers.
One inch represents approximately 95 miles.
Lambert Conformal Conic Projection

Kilometers
Statute Miles

Meters	Feet
6000	19685
4000	13124
3000	9843
2000	6562
1000	3281
500	1640
200	656
0	0
Land Below Sea Level	0
200	656
1000	3281
3000	9843
6000	19685
9000	29520

ENGLISH	bay	cape	creek	island	lake	mount	point	range
DEUTSCH	Bucht	Kap	Bach	Insel	See	Berg	Landspitze	Gebirge
ESPAÑOL	bahía	cabo	riachuelo	isla	lago	montaña	punta	cordillera
FRANÇAIS	baie	cap	crique	île	lac	mont	pointe	chaîne de montagnes
PORTUGUÊS	baía	cabo	riacho	ilha	lago	monte	ponta	cordilheira

Copyright © by Rand McNally & Co.
Map prepared by George Philip & Son, Ltd., London.

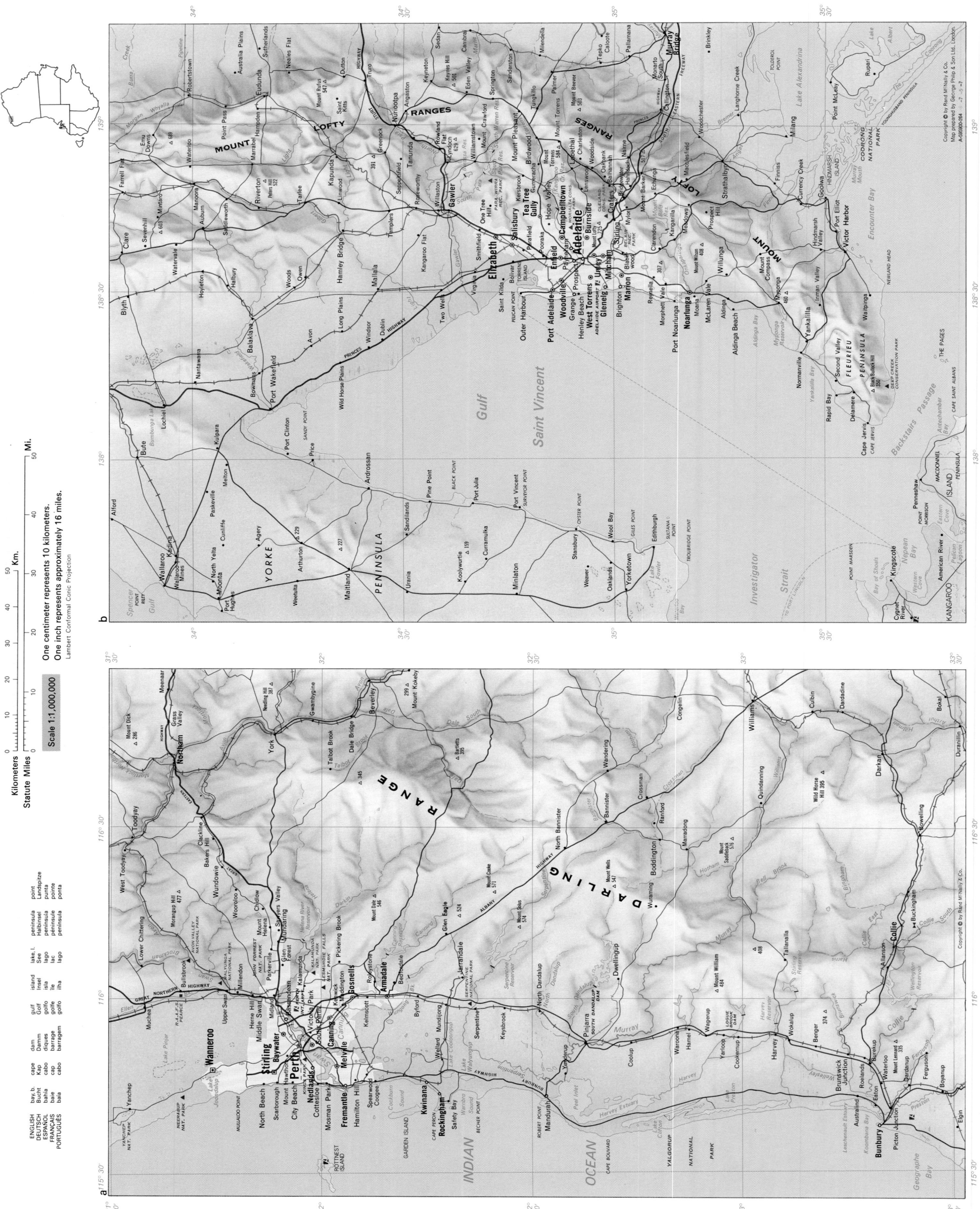

Scale 1:1,000,000

One centimeter represents 10 kilometers.
One inch represents approximately 16 miles.
Lambert Conformal Conic Projection

Kilometers

Statute Miles

ENGLISH	bay, b.	cape	dam	gulf	island	lake, l.	peninsula	point
DEUTSCH	Bucht	Kap	Damm	Golf	Insel	See	Halbinsel	Landspitze
ESPAÑOL	bahía	cabo	dique	golfo	isla	lago	península	punta
FRANÇAIS	baie	cap	barrage	golfe	île	lac	péninsule	pointe
PORTUGUÊS	baía	cabo	barragem	golfo	ilha	lago	península	ponta

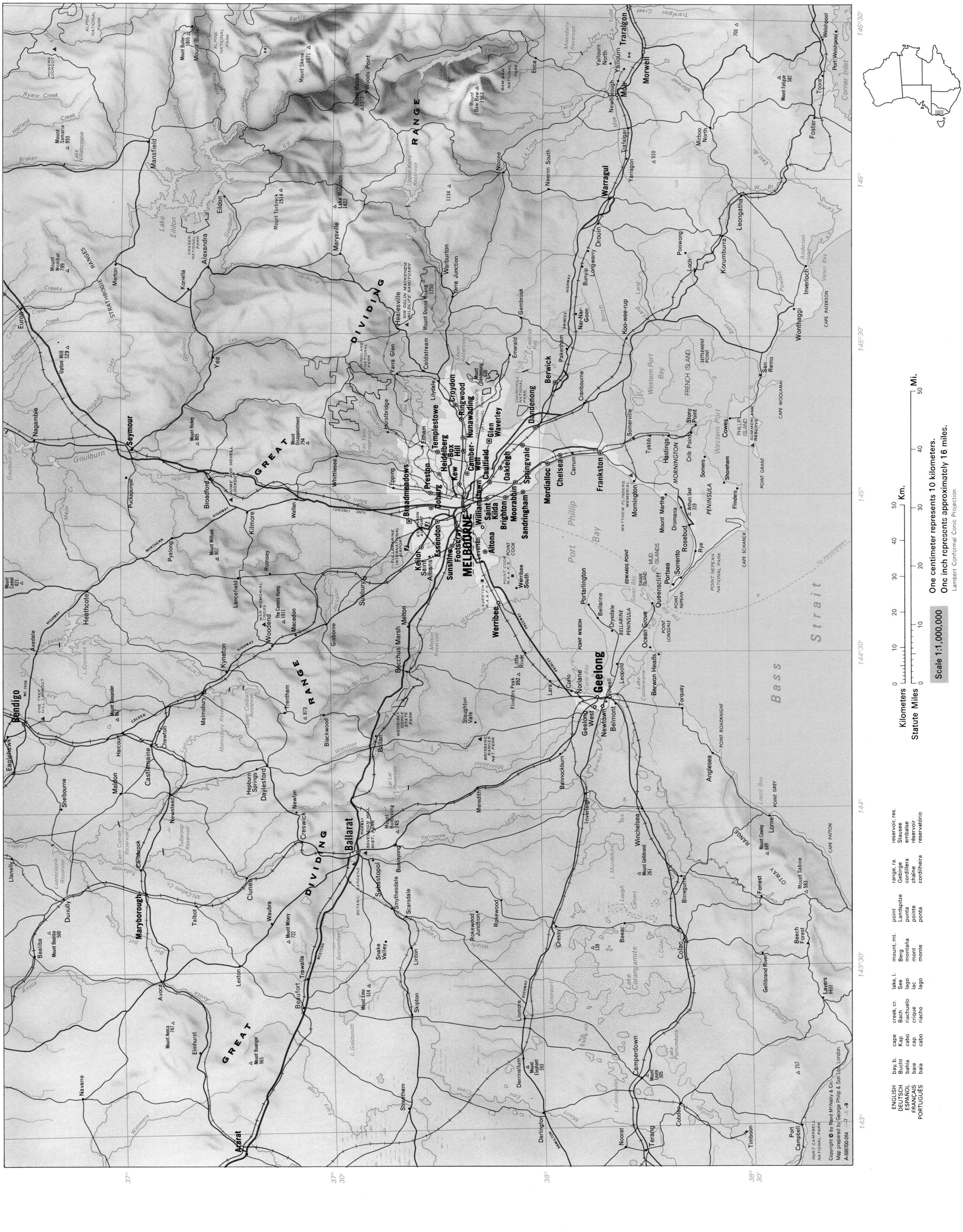
MELBOURNE
Geelong
Ballarat
Bendigo
Port Phillip Bay
Bass Strait
GREAT DIVIDING RANGE
Scale 1:1,000,000
Kilometers
Statute Miles
One centimeter represents 10 kilometers.
One inch represents approximately 16 miles.
Lambert Conformal Conic Projection
ENGLISH bay, b. cape creek, cr. lake, l. mount, mt. point range, ra. reservoir, res.
DEUTSCH Bucht Kap Bach See Berg Landspitze Gebirge Stausee
ESPAÑOL bahía cabo riachuelo lago montaña punta cordillera embalse
FRANÇAIS baie cap crique lac mont pointe chaîne réservoir
PORTUGUÊS baía cabo riacho lago monte ponta cordilheira reservatório
Copyright © by Rand McNally & Co.
Map prepared by George Philip & Son Ltd. London.

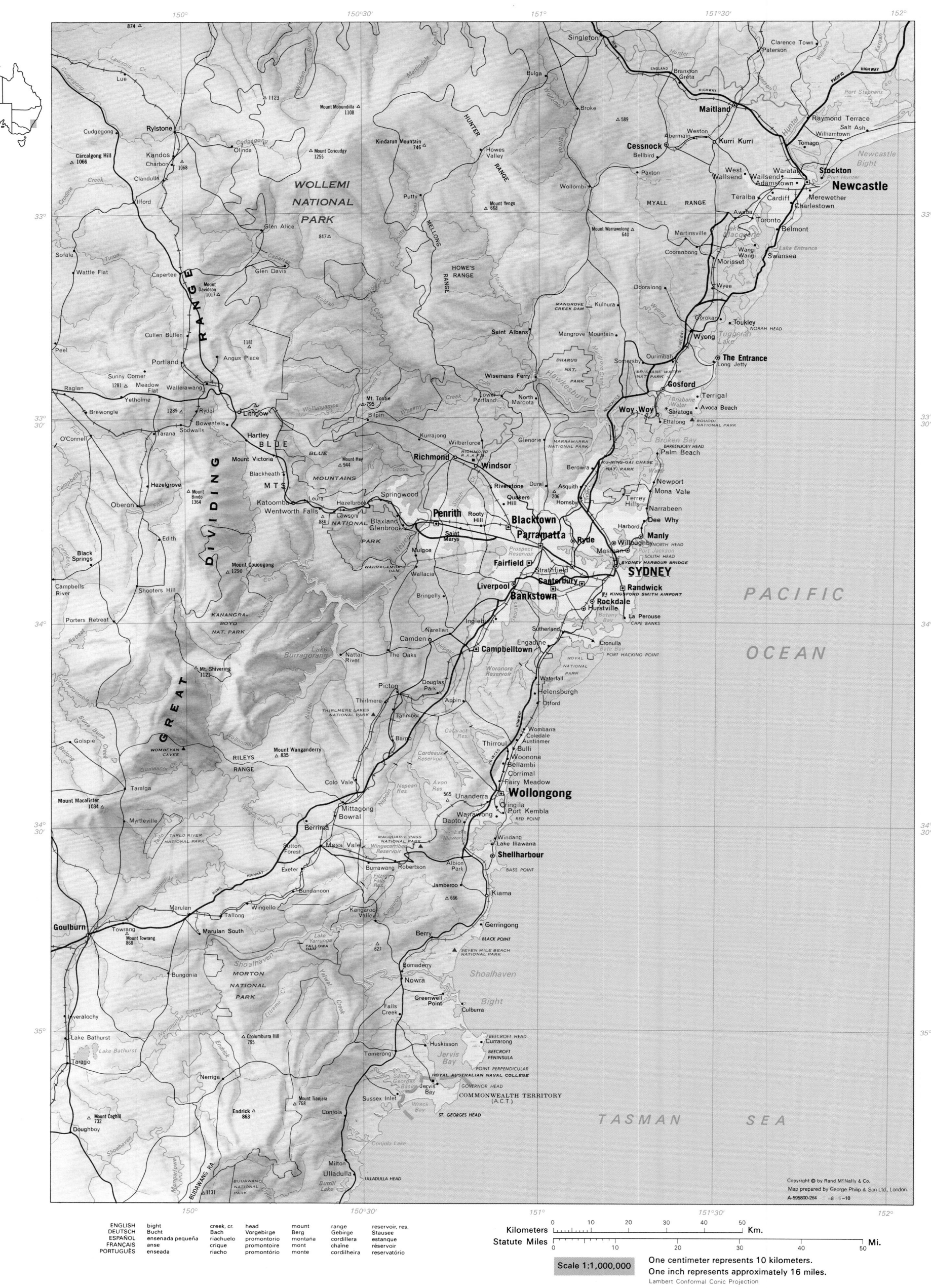

ENGLISH   bight   creek, cr.   head   mount   range   reservoir, res.
DEUTSCH   Bucht   Bach   Berg   Gebirge   Stausee
ESPAÑOL   ensenada pequeña riachuelo   montaña   monte   cordillera   estanque
FRANÇAIS   anse   crique   promontoire   mont   chaine   réservoir
PORTUGUÊS   enseada   riacho   promontório   monte   cordilheira   reservatório

Kilometers

Statute Miles

Scale 1:1,000,000
One centimeter represents 10 kilometers.
One inch represents approximately 16 miles.
Lambert Conformal Conic Projection

Copyright © by Rand McNally & Co.
Map prepared by George Philip & Son Ltd., London.
A-595800-264   -8--11--10

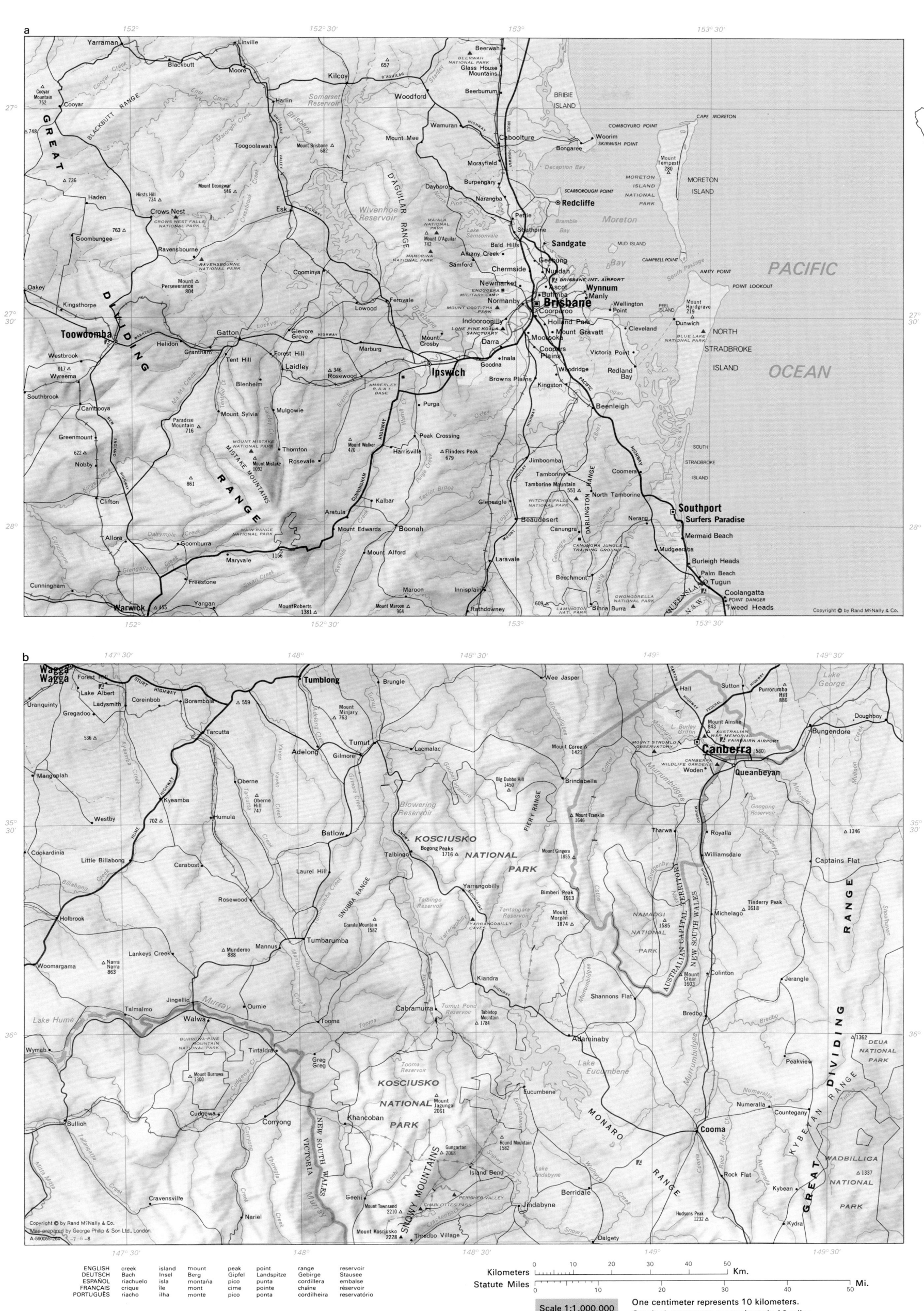

New Zealand / Neuseeland / Nueva Zelanda
Nouvelle Zélande / Nova Zelândia

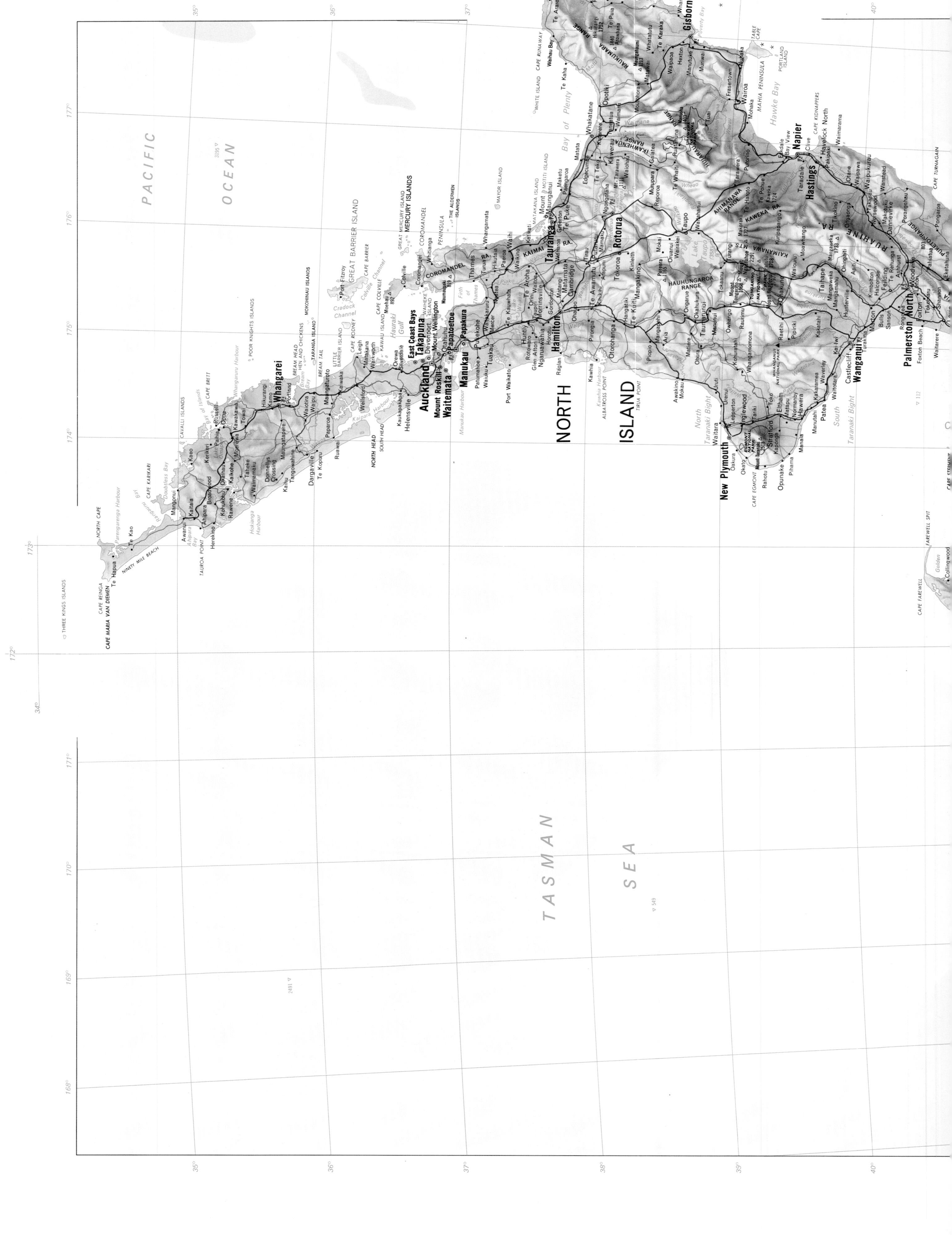

PACIFIC OCEAN

TASMAN SEA

NORTH ISLAND

Bay of Plenty

Hawke Bay

MAHIA PENINSULA

Auckland
Whangarei
Hamilton
Rotorua
Tauranga
Gisborne
Napier
Hastings
New Plymouth
Wanganui
Palmerston North

Mount Roskill
Mount Wellington
Manukau
Waitemata
Takapuna
Papatoetoe
Papakura
East Coast Bays

GREAT BARRIER ISLAND
LITTLE BARRIER ISLAND
MERCURY ISLANDS
GREAT MERCURY ISLAND
MOKOHINAU ISLANDS
POOR KNIGHTS ISLANDS
CAVALLI ISLANDS
THREE KINGS ISLANDS
MAYOR ISLAND
WHITE ISLAND
THE ALDERMEN ISLANDS
PORTLAND ISLAND
KAWAU ISLAND
TARANGA ISLAND

COROMANDEL PENINSULA

NORTH CAPE
CAPE REINGA
CAPE MARIA VAN DIEMEN
CAPE KARIKARI
CAPE BRETT
CAPE RODNEY
CAPE COLVILLE
CAPE RUNAWAY
EAST CAPE
CAPE KIDNAPPERS
CAPE TURNAGAIN
CAPE EGMONT
CAPE FAREWELL
FAREWELL SPIT

RUAHINE RA.
KAIMANAWA MTS.
KAWEKA RANGE
KAIMAI RA.
RAUKUMARA RANGE
HAUHUNGAROA RANGE
AHIMANAWA RANGE
TE WHAITI
MOUNT EGMONT / TARANAKI

NINETY MILE BEACH
Ninety Mile Beach

Kaipara Harbour
Manukau Harbour
Hauraki Gulf
Firth of Thames
Lake Taupo
North Taranaki Bight
South Taranaki Bight
Doubtless Bay
Hokianga Harbour
Whangaroa Harbour
Golden Bay

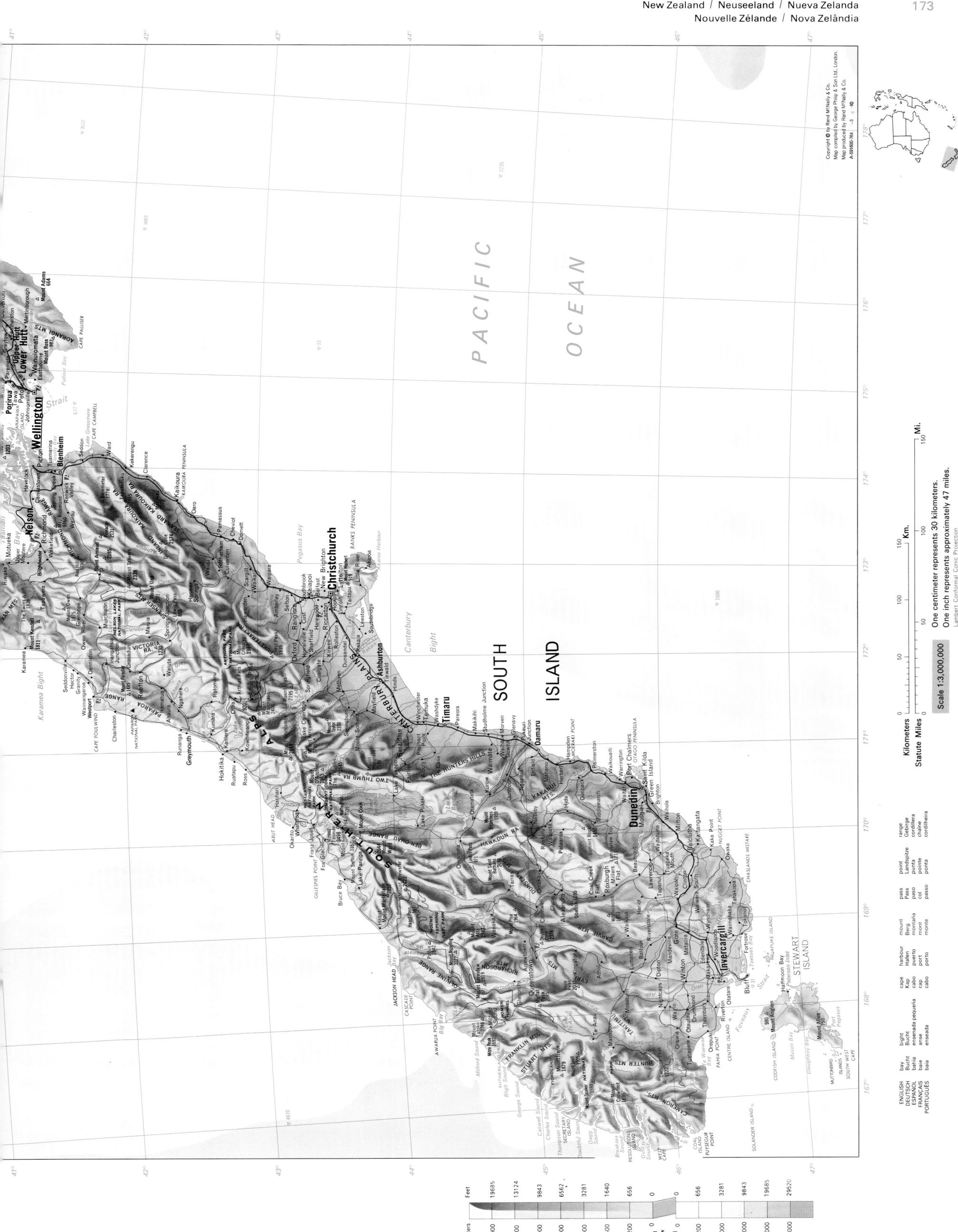

PACIFIC

OCEAN

SOUTH

ISLAND

STEWART
ISLAND

ENGLISH	DEUTSCH	ESPAÑOL	FRANÇAIS	PORTUGUÊS
bay	Bucht	bahía	baie	baía
bight	Bucht	ensenada pequeña	anse	enseada
cape	Kap	cabo	cap	cabo
harbour	Hafen	puerto	port	porto
mount	Berg	montaña	mont	monte
pass	Pass	paso	col	passo
point	Landspitze	punta	pointe	ponta
range	Gebirge	cordillera	chaîne	cordilheira

Kilometers
Statute Miles

Scale 1:3,000,000

One centimeter represents 30 kilometers.
One inch represents approximately 47 miles.
Lambert Conformal Conic Projection

Meters	Feet
6000	19685
4000	13124
3000	9843
2000	6562
1000	3281
500	1640
200	656
0	0
Land Below Sea Level	0
200	656
1000	3281
3000	9843
6000	19685
9000	29520

Islands of the Pacific / Pazifische Inseln / Islas del Pacífico
Îles du Pacifique / Ilhas do Pacífico

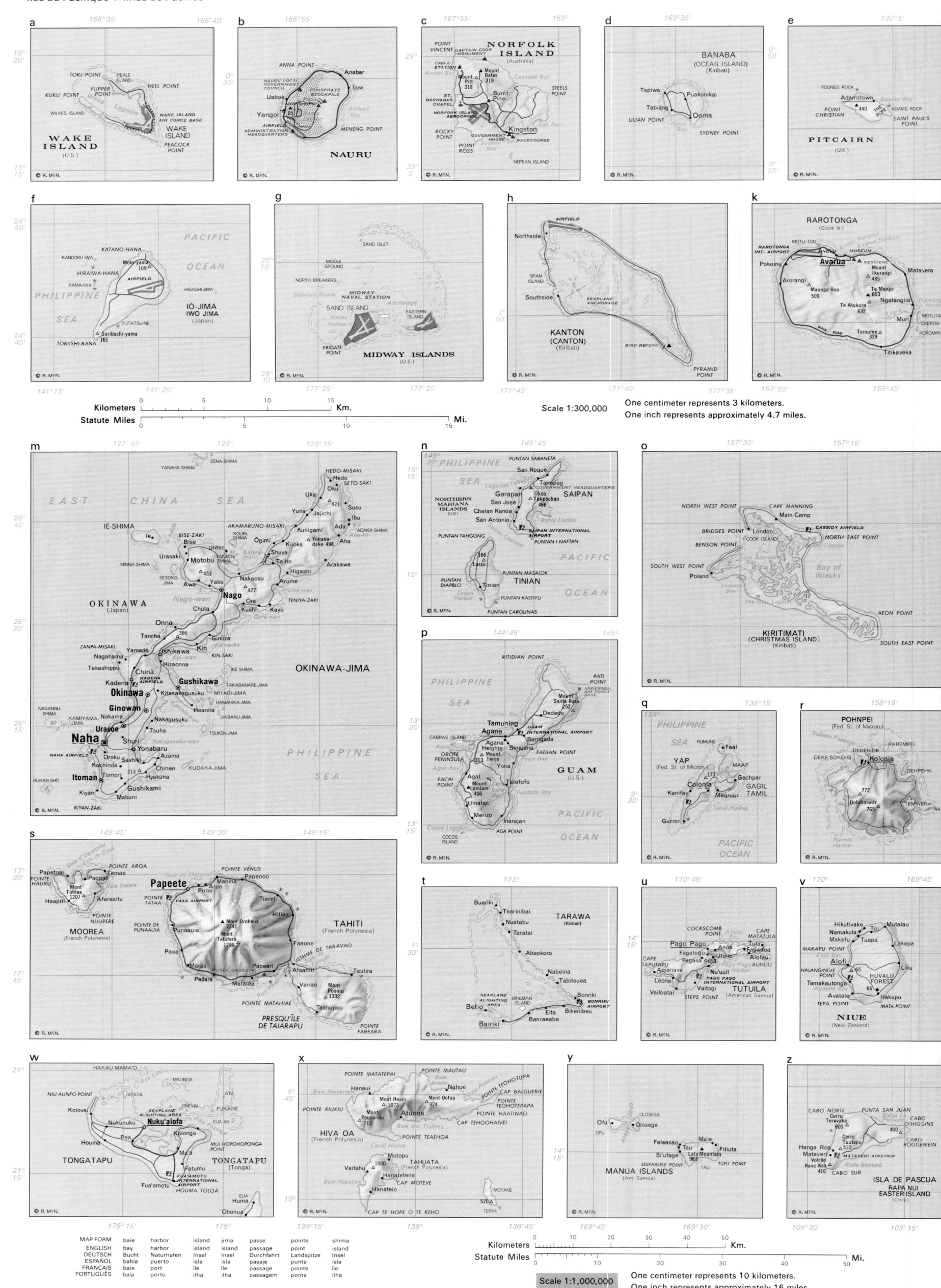

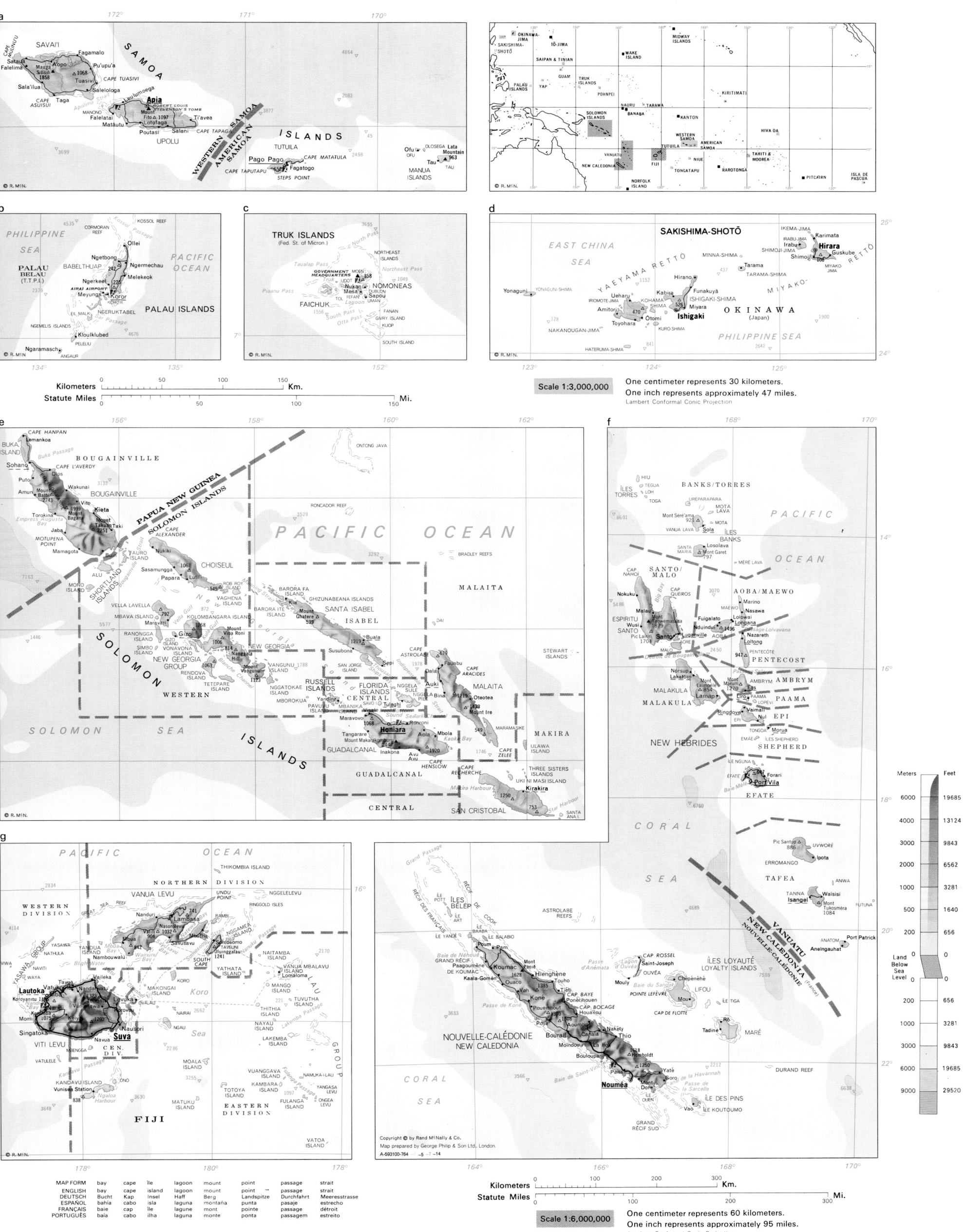

Map continues
pages **178-179** →

ENGLISH	bay	cape	island	lake, l.	mountains, mts.	point	range	strait
DEUTSCH	Bucht	Kap	Insel	See	Berge	Landspitze	Gebirge	Meeresstrasse
ESPAÑOL	bahía	cabo	isla	lago	montañas	punta	sierra	estrecho
FRANÇAIS	baie	cap	île	lac	montagnes	pointe	chaîne	détroit
PORTUGUÊS	baía	cabo	ilha	lago	montanhas	ponta	serra	estreito

Kilometers 0   200   400   600
     Km.
Statute Miles 0   200   400   600
     Mi.

Scale 1:12,000,000   One centimeter represents 120 kilometers.
One inch represents approximately 190 miles.
Lambert Conformal Conic Projection

United States (excluding Alaska and Hawaii) / Vereinigte Staaten
Estados Unidos / États-Unis / Estados Unidos

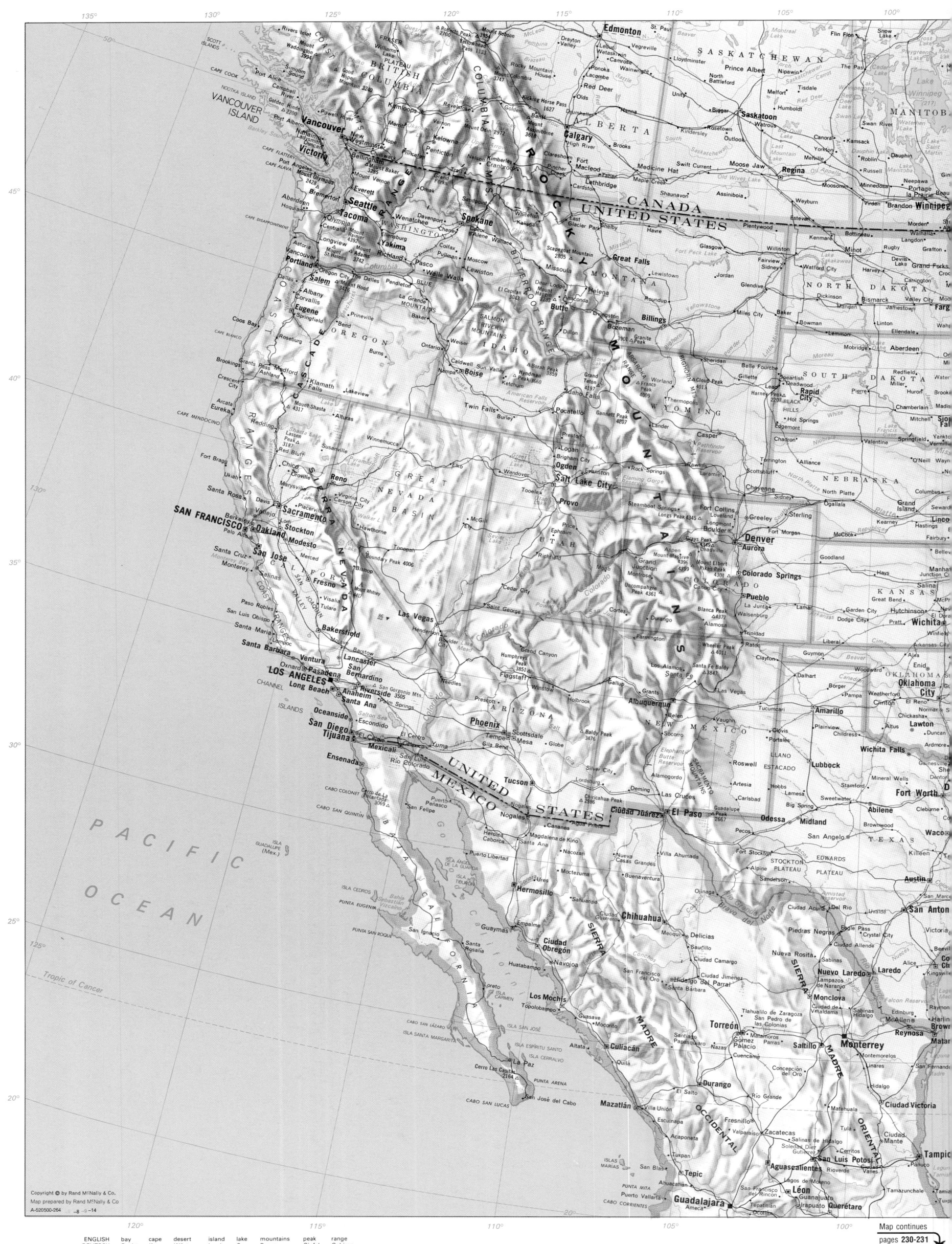

Map continues
pages 230-231

	bay	cape	desert	island	lake	mountains	peak	range
ENGLISH	bay	cape	desert	island	lake	mountains	peak	range
DEUTSCH	Bucht	Kap	Wüste	Insel	See	Berge	Gipfel	Gebirge
ESPAÑOL	bahía	cabo	desierto	isla	lago	montañas	pico	sierra
FRANÇAIS	baie	cap	désert	île	lac	montagnes	cime	chaîne
PORTUGUÊS	baía	cabo	deserto	ilha	lago	montanhas	pico	serra

Map continues
pages **176-177**

Kilometers
Statute Miles

Scale 1:12,000,000

One centimeter represents 120 kilometers.
One inch represents approximately 190 miles.

Albers Conical Equal-Area Projection

Map continues
pages 176-177

Map continues
pages 182-183

Kilometers 0   100   200   300 Km.
Statute Miles 0   100   200   300 Mi.

Scale 1:6,000,000

One centimeter represents 60 kilometers.
One inch represents approximately 95 miles.
Lambert Conformal Conic Projection

Copyright © by Rand McNally & Co.
Map prepared by Rand McNally & Co.
A-520502-764 -8—6 91

Southwestern Canada / Südwestkanada / Canadá Sud-occidental
Sud-Ouest du Canada / Canadá: Sudoeste

Map continues
pages 180-181

PRINCE OF WALES ISLAND

REVILLAGIGEDO ISLAND

BRITISH COLUMBIA

ALASKA

Prince Rupert

QUEEN CHARLOTTE ISLANDS

GRAHAM ISLAND

MORESBY ISLAND

Dixon Entrance

Hecate Strait

Queen Charlotte Sound

COAST MOUNTAINS

KITIMAT RANGES

Kitimat

Smithers

HAZELTON MOUNTAINS

BABINE RANGE

OMINECA MOUNTAINS

NECHAKO PLATEAU

Prince George

TWEEDSMUIR PROVINCIAL PARK

PACIFIC RANGES

Bella Coola

Monarch Mountain 3533

Mount Waddington 3994

FRASER PLATEAU

Williams Lake

Quesnel

VANCOUVER ISLAND

STRATHCONA PROVINCIAL PARK

Golden Hinde 2200

Campbell River

Courtenay

Port Alberni

Nanaimo

VANCOUVER

Burnaby

New Westminster

North Vancouver

West Vancouver

Powell River

GARIBALDI PROVINCIAL PARK

Mount Garibaldi 2678

Squamish

Victoria

Esquimalt

Oak Bay

SAN JUAN ISLANDS

Bellingham

Mount Vernon

OLYMPIC NATIONAL PARK

Port Angeles

Everett

CANADA

UNITED STATES

PACIFIC OCEAN

Strait of Juan de Fuca

Meters	Feet
6000	19685
4000	13124
3000	9843
2000	6562
1000	3281
500	1640
200	656
0	0
Land Below Sea Level	
0	0
200	656
1000	3281
3000	9843
6000	19685
9000	29520

Copyright © by Rand McNally & Co.
Map prepared by Rand McNally & Co.
A-520220-764

ENGLISH	creek	Indian reserve	inlet	island	lake, l.	mountain	peak	provincial park	sound
DEUTSCH	Bach	Indianerreservation	Einfahrt	Insel	See	Berg	Gipfel	Provinz-Park	Sund
ESPAÑOL	riachuelo	reserva de Indios	abra	isla	lago	montaña	pico	parque de provincia	sonda
FRANÇAIS	crique	réserve indienne	bras de mer	île	lac	montagne	cime	parc provincial	détroit
PORTUGUÊS	riacho	reserva indígena	enseada	ilha	lago	montanha	pico	parque provincial	estreito

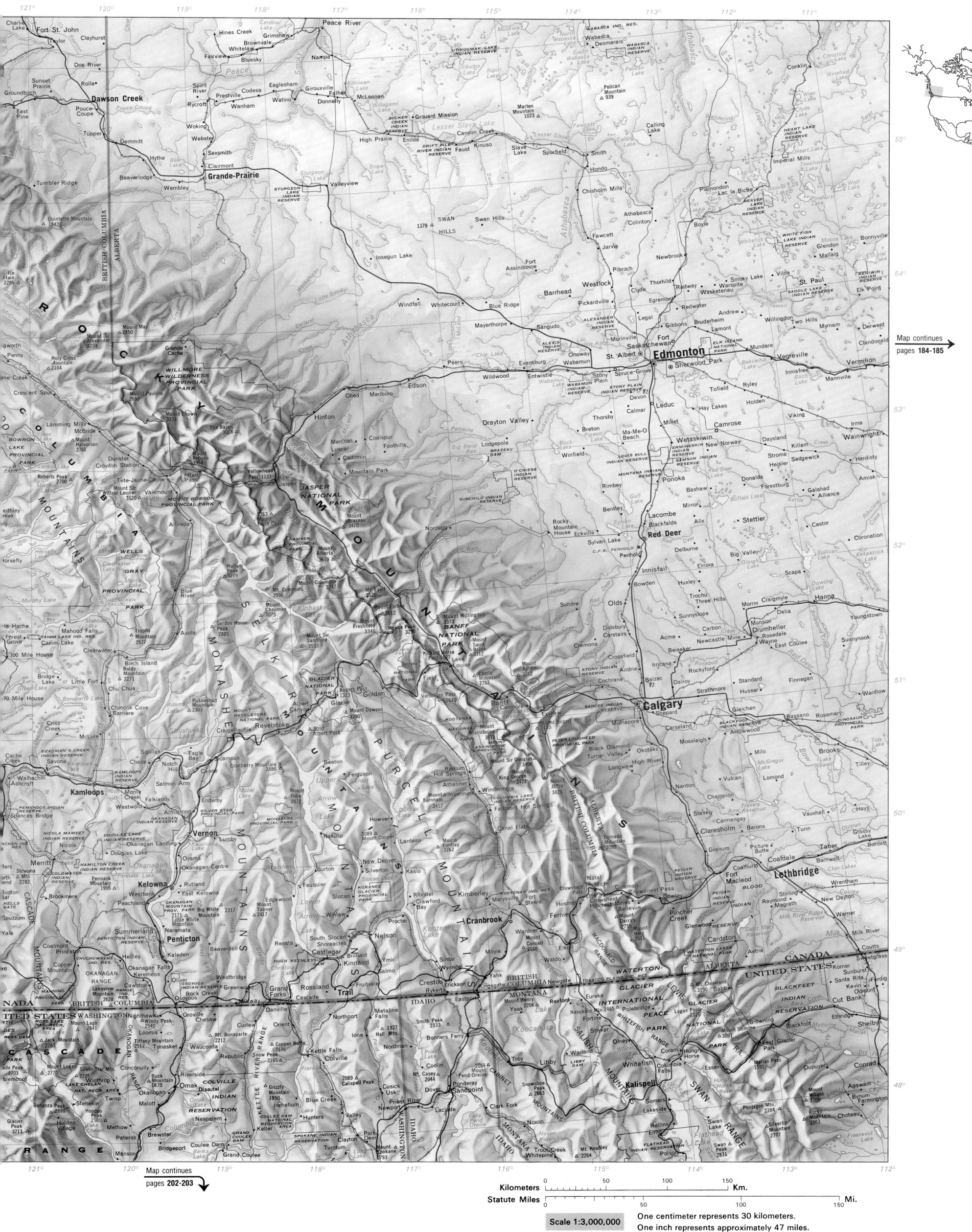

Map continues
pages 184-185

Map continues
pages 202-203

Kilometers 0   50   100   150   Km.

Statute Miles 0   50   100   150   Mi.

Scale 1:3,000,000

One centimeter represents 30 kilometers.
One inch represents approximately 47 miles.
Lambert Conformal Conic Projection

South-Central Canada / Südliches Mittelkanada / Centro Meridional del Canadá
Canada Central, partie Méridionale / Canadá Central, parte meridional

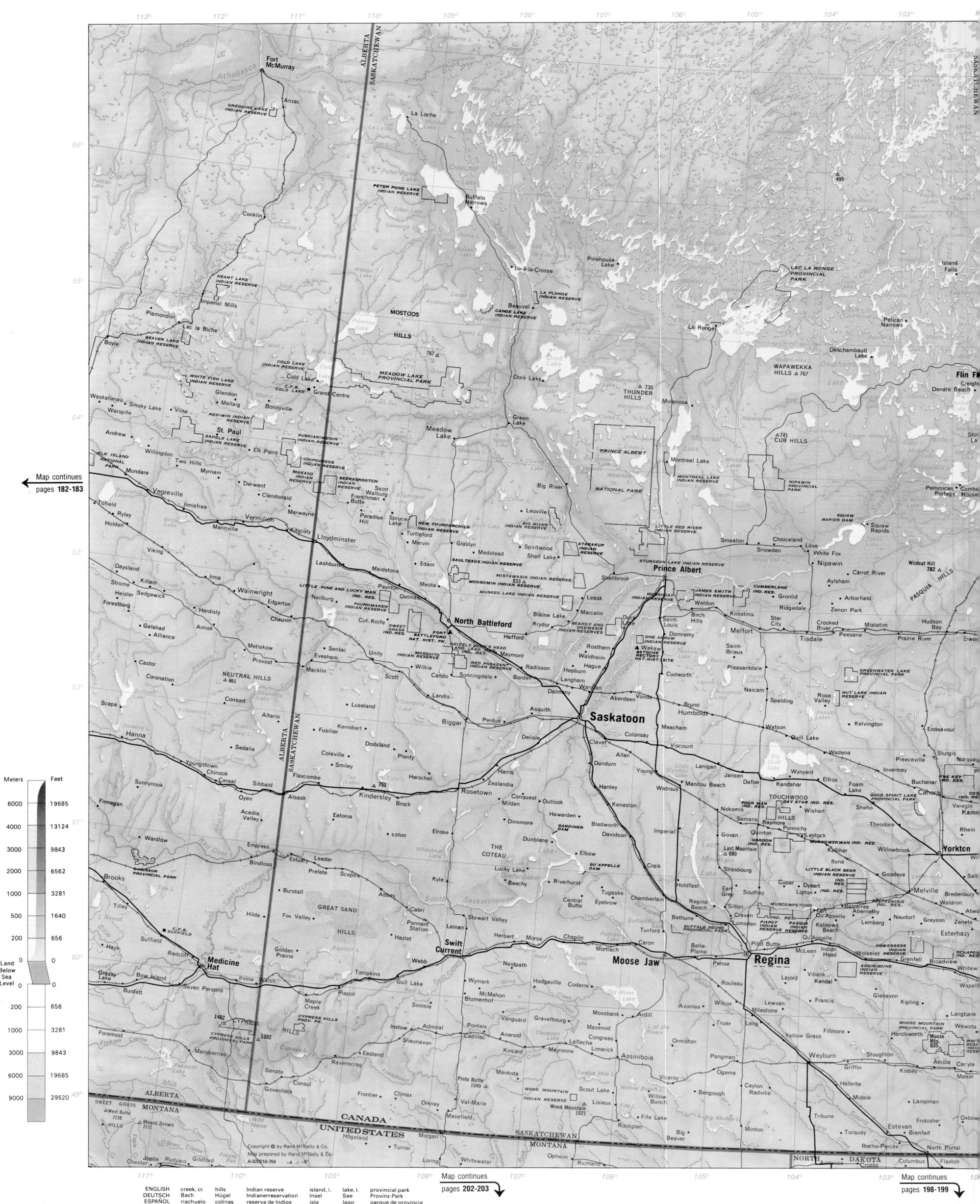

← Map continues pages 182-183

Map continues pages 202-203 ↓

Map continues pages 198-199 ↓

ENGLISH	creek, cr.	hills	Indian reserve	island, i.	lake, l.	provincial park
DEUTSCH	Bach	Hügel	Indianerreservation	Insel	See	Provinz-Park
ESPAÑOL	riachuelo	colinas	reserva de Indios	isla	lago	parque de provincia
FRANÇAIS	crique	collines	réserve indienne	île	lac	parc provincial
PORTUGUÊS	riacho	colinas	reserva indigena	ilha	lago	parque provincial

Meters / Feet

Meters	Feet
6000	19685
4000	13124
3000	9843
2000	6562
1000	3281
500	1640
200	656
0	0
Land Below Sea Level 0	0
200	656
1000	3281
3000	9843
6000	19685
9000	29520

South-Central Canada / Südliches Mittelkanada / Centro Meridional del Canadá
Canada Central, partie Méridionale / Canadá Central, parte meridional

185

Port Nelson
York Factory
Thibadeau
△250
Weir River
KETTLE RAPIDS DAM
Amery
Gillam
Shamattawa

MANITOBA
ONTARIO

South Indian Lake
Iliford

Kississing
Sherridon
HIGHROCK INDIAN RESERVE
Nelson House
○ Thompson
Pikwitonei
Sipiwesk
Thicket Portage

Snow Lake
GRASS RIVER PROVINCIAL PARK
Herb Lake
Wabowden
BEAR ISLAND
Oxford House
OXFORD HOUSE INDIAN RESERVE
Gods Lake

WETIKO HILLS

Optic Lake
Cranberry Portage
Cormorant
JENPEG DAM
Cross Lake
ROSS ISLAND

Island Lake

Pas
CLEARWATER LAKE PROVINCIAL PARK
Moose Lake
LIMESTONE POINT
BIG MOSSY POINT
Norway House

Opasquia

Grand Rapids
Lake

Cedar Lake
LONG POINT
Winnipeg (217)

Pelican Rapids
Mafeking
(253)
BIRCH I.
REINDEER ISLAND
Berens River
Poplar Hill

Bowsman
Duck Bay
PINE CREEK INDIAN RESERVE
BERENS ISLAND
Pikangikum

Minitonas
Camperville
Skownan
Sturgeon Bay
Casummit Lake
△480

Pine River
Winnipegosis
Gypsumville
Anama Bay
Jackhead Harbour
Matheson Island

DUCK MOUNTAIN PROVINCIAL PARK
DUCK MOUNTAIN
Ethelbert
CRANE RIVER IND. RES.
Steep Rock
MOOSE L.
Little Bullhead

Baldy Mountain 832
Sifton
Rorketon
Magnet
PEGUIS INDIAN RESERVE
FISHER RIVER INDIAN RESERVE
HECLA PROVINCIAL PARK
McKenzie Island
Balmertown
Red Lake
Uchi Lake

RIDING MOUNTAIN
Grandview
Gilbert Plains
Dauphin
Ochre River
Ste-Rose-du-Lac
Ashern
Hodgson
Fisher Branch
BLACK L.
Hecla
Manigotagan
Bissett
Madsen
Bruce Lake
499 △

RIDING MOUNTAIN NATIONAL PARK
751 △
McCreary
Ste-Amélie
Laurier
EBB AND FLOW INDIAN RESERVE
Eriksdale
Riverton
Arborg
HECLA I.
Lake Winnipeg
Ear Falls

Rossburn
LIZARD POINT INDIAN RESERVE
Oakburn
Elphinstone
Strathclair
ROLLING RIVER INDIAN RESERVE
Amaranth
Lundar
ELK ISLAND
FORT ALEXANDER INDIAN RESERVE
Perrault Falls
LAC SEUL
LAC SEUL INDIAN RESERVE
Sioux Lookout

Binscarth
Russell
St-Lazare
Birtle
Shoal Lake
Minnedosa
Plumas
Arden
Gladstone
Langruth
St-Laurent
Oak Point
Gimli
Winnipeg Beach
Grand Beach
Pine Falls
Great Falls
Red Lake Road
Vermilion Bay

McAuley
Hamiota
Rapid City
Neepawa
Westbourne
Poplar Point
LOWER FORT GARRY NATIONAL HISTORIC PARK
Stonewall
Selkirk
Beausejour
Dryden

Miniota
Rivers
Douglas
Austin
MacGregor
Oakville
Portage-la-Prairie
Winnipeg
Lockport
Whitemouth
Rennie
WHITESHELL PROVINCIAL PARK
Kenora
Hawk Lake
Keewatin
Dinorwic
Dyment

Elkhorn
Alexander
Griswold
Brandon
C.F.B. SHILO
SPRUCE WOODS PROV. PARK
Carberry
Starbuck
La Salle
Ste-Anne
Ste-Chemin
Niverville
Richer
East Braintree
Waugh
Gold Rock

Virden
Oak Lake
Souris
Treherne
Rathwell
Haywood
Elm Creek
Ste-Agathe
La Broquerie
Sioux Narrows

Reston
Hartney
Minto
Ninette
Glenboro
Belmont
Cypress River
Swan Lake
Holland
Notre-Dame-de-Lourdes
Carman
Roland
St-Pierre-Jolys
Grunthal
Woodridge
Crow Lake
AULNEAU PENINSULA

Napinka
Melita
Deloraine
Goodlands
Nunga
Killarney
Baldur
Pilot Mound
Manitou
Darlingford
Miami
Winkler
St-Jean-Baptiste
Dominion City
Vita
Sprague
Middlebro
Moskosit
Flanders

Gainsborough
Waskada
Cartwright
Mather
Crystal City
Clearwater
Morden
Altona
Ridgeville
Gardenton
MANITOBA
ONTARIO
Mine Centre

Westhope
TURTLE MTN. P. P.
INTERNATIONAL PEACE GARDEN
Hannah
Gretna
Emerson
Neche
Pembina
St-Vincent
Roseau
Warroad
Baudette
Roosevelt
Williams
Rainy River
Black Hawk
Emo
Fort Frances
International Falls

CANADA
UNITED STATES
MANITOBA
MINNESOTA

Kilometers
Statute Miles
0   50   100   150 Km.
0   50   100   150 Mi.

Scale 1:3,000,000
One centimeter represents 30 kilometers.
One inch represents approximately 47 miles.
Lambert Conformal Conic Projection

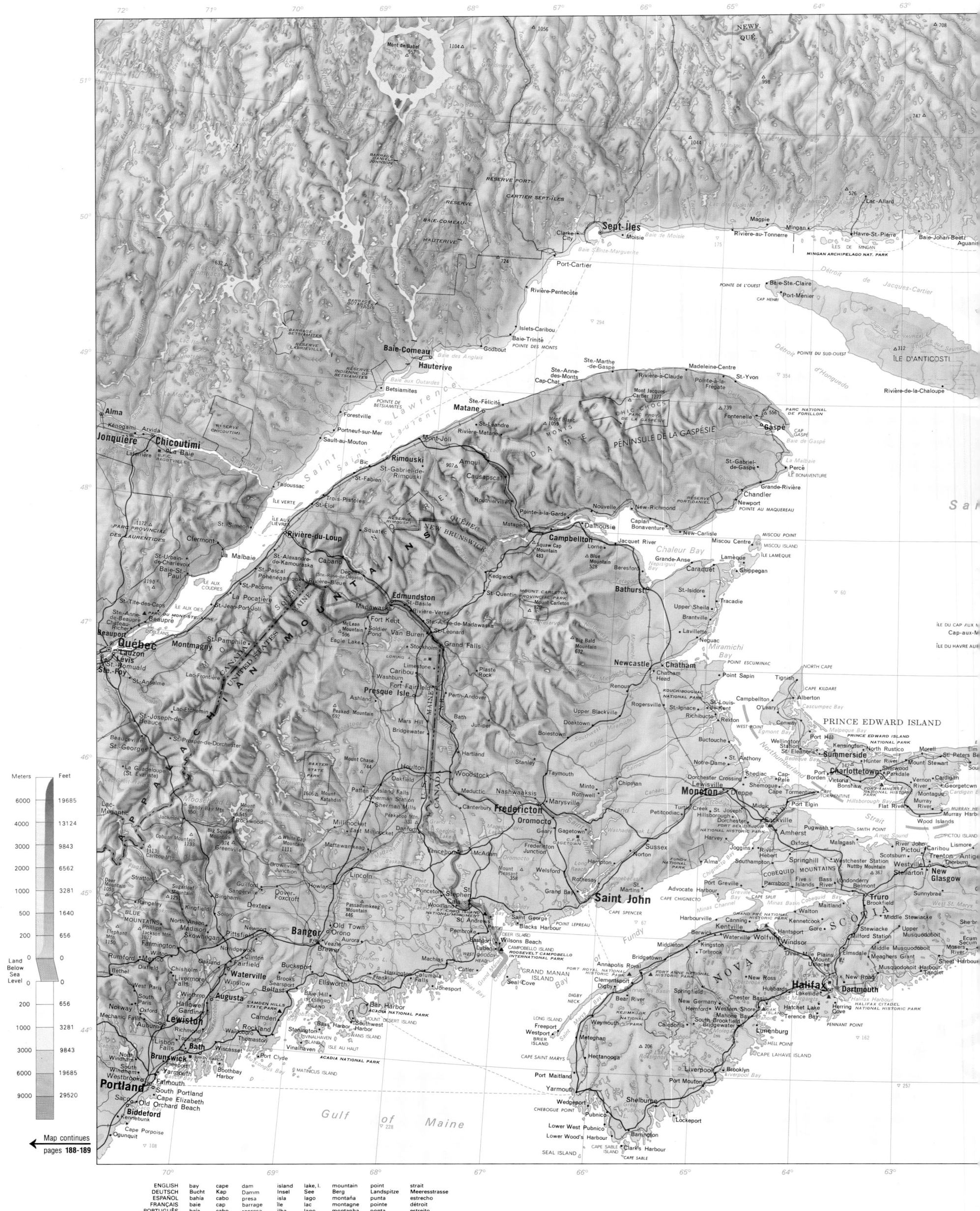

← Map continues
pages **188-189**

	Meters	Feet
	6000	19685
	4000	13124
	3000	9843
	2000	6562
	1000	3281
	500	1640
	200	656
	Land Below Sea Level 0	0
	200	656
	1000	3281
	3000	9843
	6000	19685
	9000	29520

	bay	cape	dam	island	lake, l.	mountain	point	strait
ENGLISH	bay	cape	dam	island	lake, l.	mountain	point	strait
DEUTSCH	Bucht	Kap	Damm	Insel	See	Berg	Landspitze	Meeresstrasse
ESPAÑOL	bahía	cabo	presa	isla	lago	montaña	punta	estrecho
FRANÇAIS	baie	cap	barrage	île	lac	montagne	pointe	détroit
PORTUGUÊS	baía	cabo	represa	ilha	lago	montanha	ponta	estreito

LABRADOR
SEA

NEWFOUNDLAND

LONG RANGE MOUNTAINS

Corner Brook

St. John's

SAINT PIERRE
AND MIQUELON
(France)

SAINT-PIERRE-
ET-MIQUELON

CANADA

CAPE BRETON
ISLAND

Sydney
Glace Bay
North Sydney
Sydney Mines

ATLANTIC

OCEAN

SABLE ISLAND
(N.S.)

Kilometers
Statute Miles

0   50   100   150   Km.

0   50   100   150   Mi.

Scale 1:3,000,000

One centimeter represents 30 kilometers.
One inch represents approximately 47 miles.

Lambert Conformal Conic Projection

188

Northeastern United States / Nordöstliche Vereinigte Staaten / Nor-este de los Estados Unidos
Nord-Est des États-Unis / Estados Unidos: Nordeste

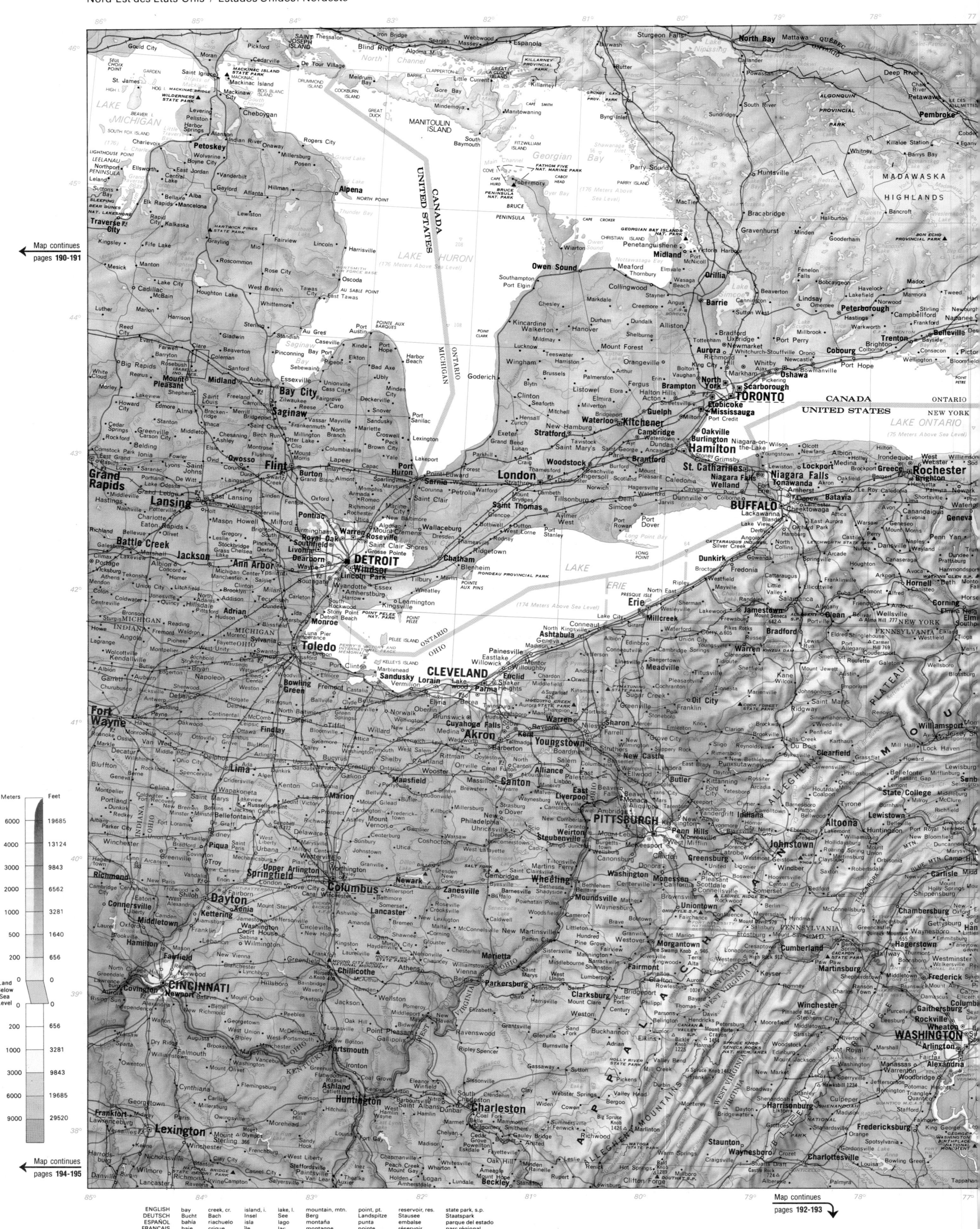

← Map continues
pages 190-191

← Map continues
pages 194-195

Map continues
pages 192-193 ↓

Meters	Feet
6000	19685
4000	13124
3000	9843
2000	6562
1000	3281
500	1640
200	656
0	0
Land Below Sea Level	
0	0
200	656
1000	3281
3000	9843
6000	19685
9000	29520

ENGLISH	bay	creek, cr.	island, i.	lake, l.	mountain, mtn.	point, pt.	reservoir, res.	state park, s.p.
DEUTSCH	Bucht	Bach	Insel	See	Berg	Landspitze	Stausee	Staatspark
ESPAÑOL	bahía	riachuelo	isla	lago	montaña	punta	embalse	parque del estado
FRANÇAIS	baie	crique	île	lac	montagne	pointe	réservoir	parc régional
PORTUGUÊS	baía	riacho	ilha	lago	montanha	ponta	reservatório	parque estadual

Northeastern United States / Nordöstliche Vereinigte Staaten / Nor-este de los Estados Unidos
Nord-Est des États-Unis / Estados Unidos: Nordeste

189

Map continues
pages 186-187

Kilometers

Statute Miles

Scale 1:3,000,000

One centimeter represents 30 kilometers.
One inch represents approximately 47 miles.

Albers Conical Equal-Area Projection

190
Great Lakes Region / Grosse Seen-Region / Región de los Grandes Lagos
Région des Grands Lacs / Região dos Grandes Lagos

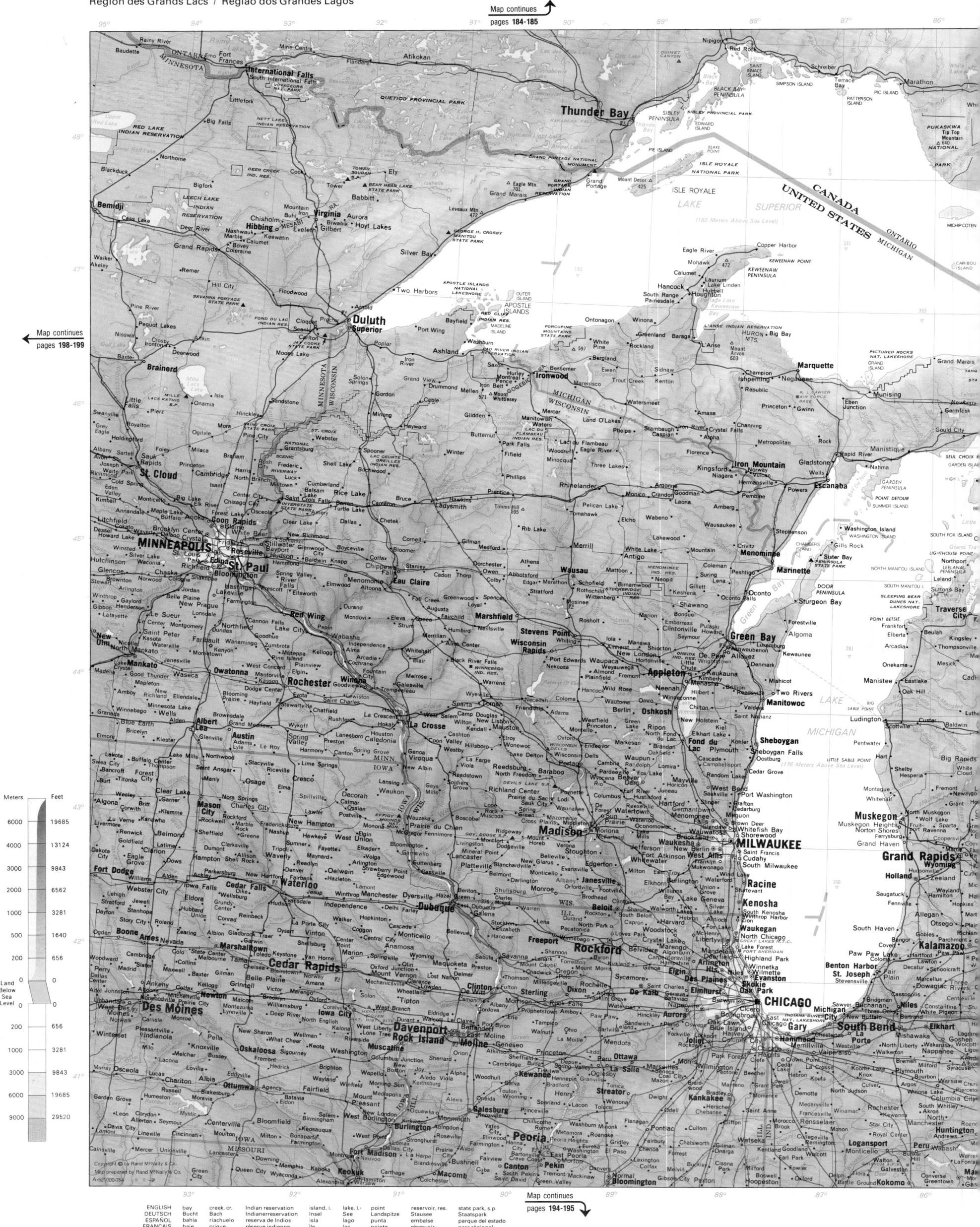

Map continues
pages 184-185

Map continues
pages 198-199

Map continues
pages 194-195

ENGLISH	bay	creek, cr.	Indian reservation	island, i.	lake, l-	point	reservoir, res.	state park, s.p.
DEUTSCH	Bucht	Bach	Indianerreservation	Insel	See	Landspitze	Stausee	Staatspark
ESPAÑOL	bahía	riachuelo	reserva de Indios	isla	lago	punta	embalse	parque del estado
FRANÇAIS	baie	crique	réserve indienne	île	lac	pointe	réservoir	parc régional
PORTUGUÊS	baía	riacho	reserva indígena	ilha	lago	ponta	reservatório	parque estadual

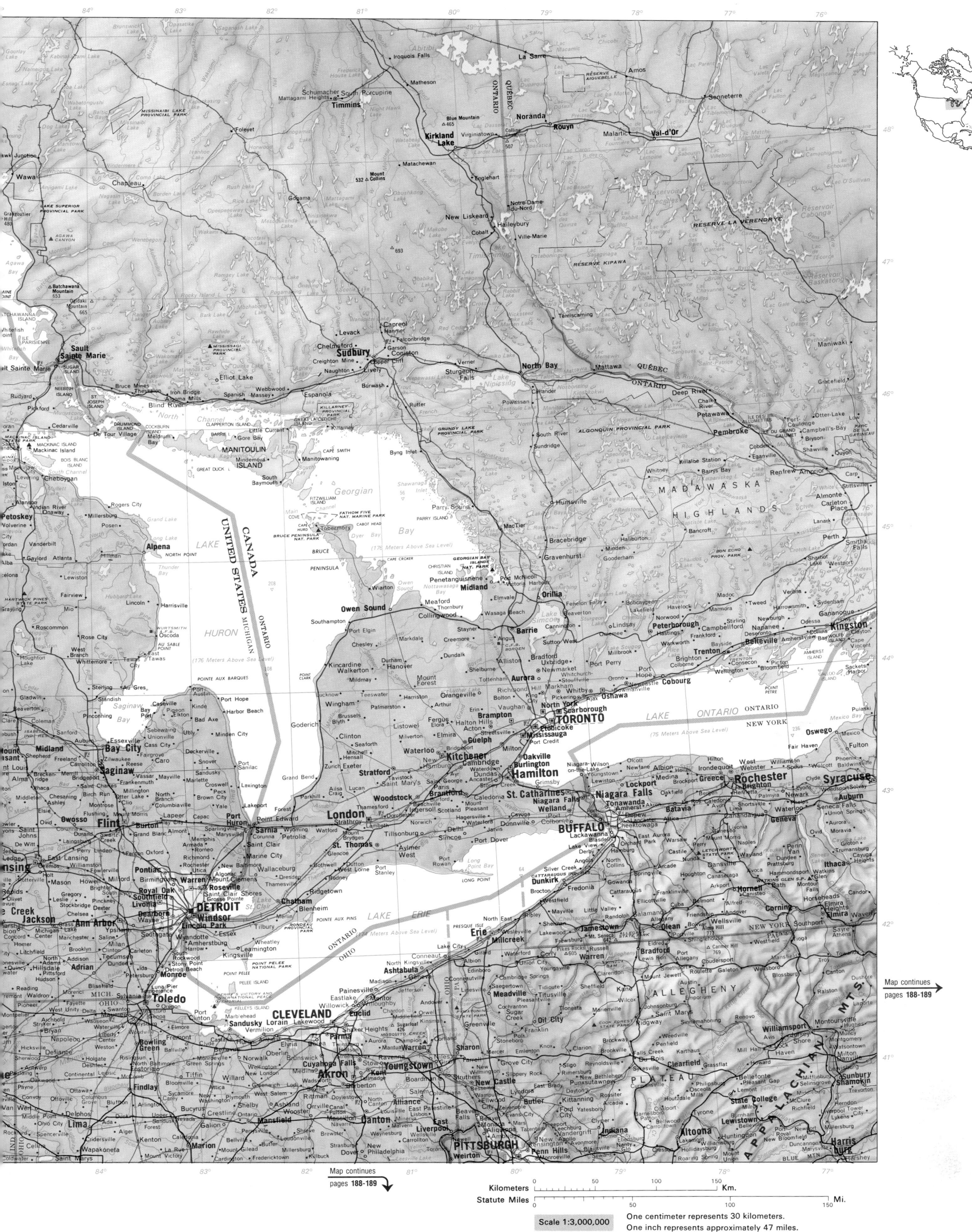

Kilometers 0   50   100   150 Km.

Statute Miles 0   50   100   150 Mi.

Scale 1:3,000,000

One centimeter represents 30 kilometers.
One inch represents approximately 47 miles.
Albers Conical Equal-Area Projection

Map continues
pages 188-189

Map continues
pages 188-189

Southeastern United States / Südöstliche Vereinigte Staaten / Sud-este de los Estados Unidos
Sud-Est des États-Unis / Estados Unidos: Sudeste

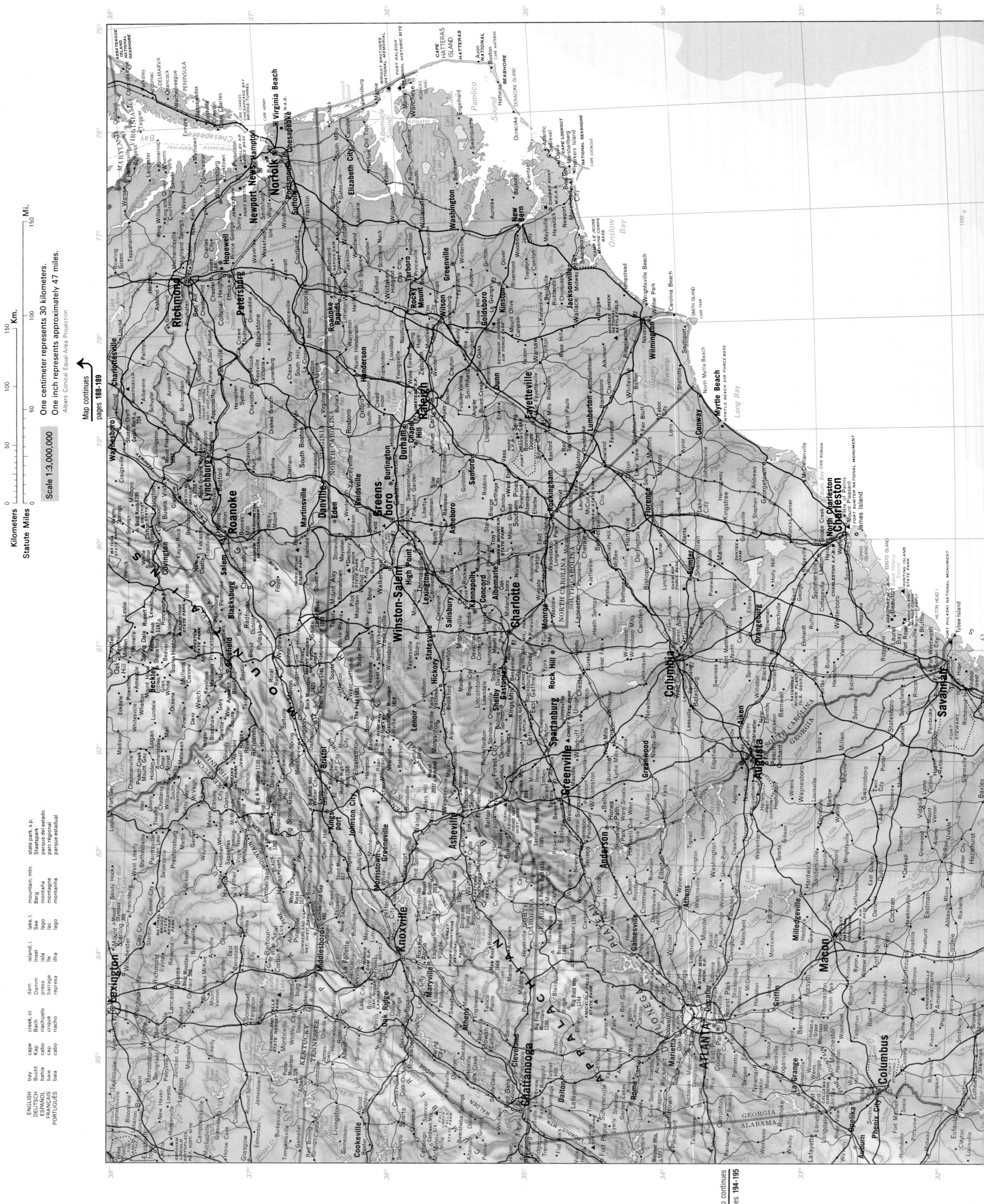

Mi.

Km.

Kilometers

Statute Miles

Scale 1:3,000,000

One centimeter represents 30 kilometers.
One inch represents approximately 47 miles.

Albers Conical Equal-Area Projection

Map continues
pages 188-189

Map continues
pages 194-195

ENGLISH	DEUTSCH	ESPAÑOL	FRANÇAIS	PORTUGUÊS
bay	Bucht	bahía	baie	baía
cape	Kap	cabo	cap	cabo
creek, cr.	Bach	riachuelo	ruisseau	riacho
dam	Damm	presa	barrage	represa
island, i.	Insel	isla	île	ilha
lake, l.	See	lago	lac	lago
mountain, mtn.	Berg	montaña	montagne	montanha
state park, s.p.	Staatspark	parque del estado	parc régional	parque estadual

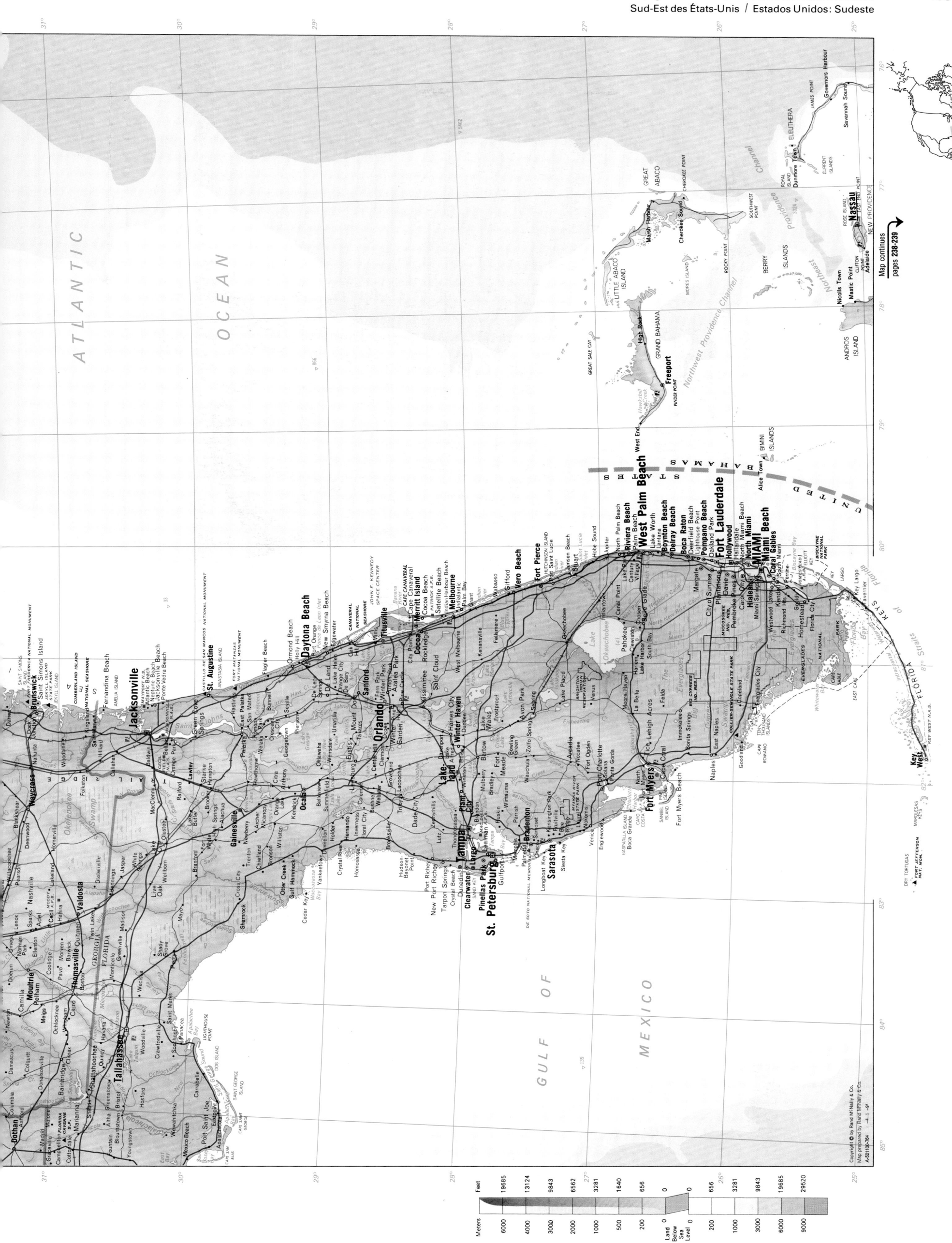

Map continues
pages 238-239

ATLANTIC   OCEAN

GULF   OF   MEXICO

Feet		Meters
19685		6000
13124		4000
9843		3000
6562		2000
3281		1000
1640		500
656		200
0	Land Below Sea Level	0
0		0
656		200
3281		1000
9843		3000
19685		6000
29520		9000

Copyright by Rand McNally & Co.
Map prepared by Rand McNally & Co.
A-321100-764

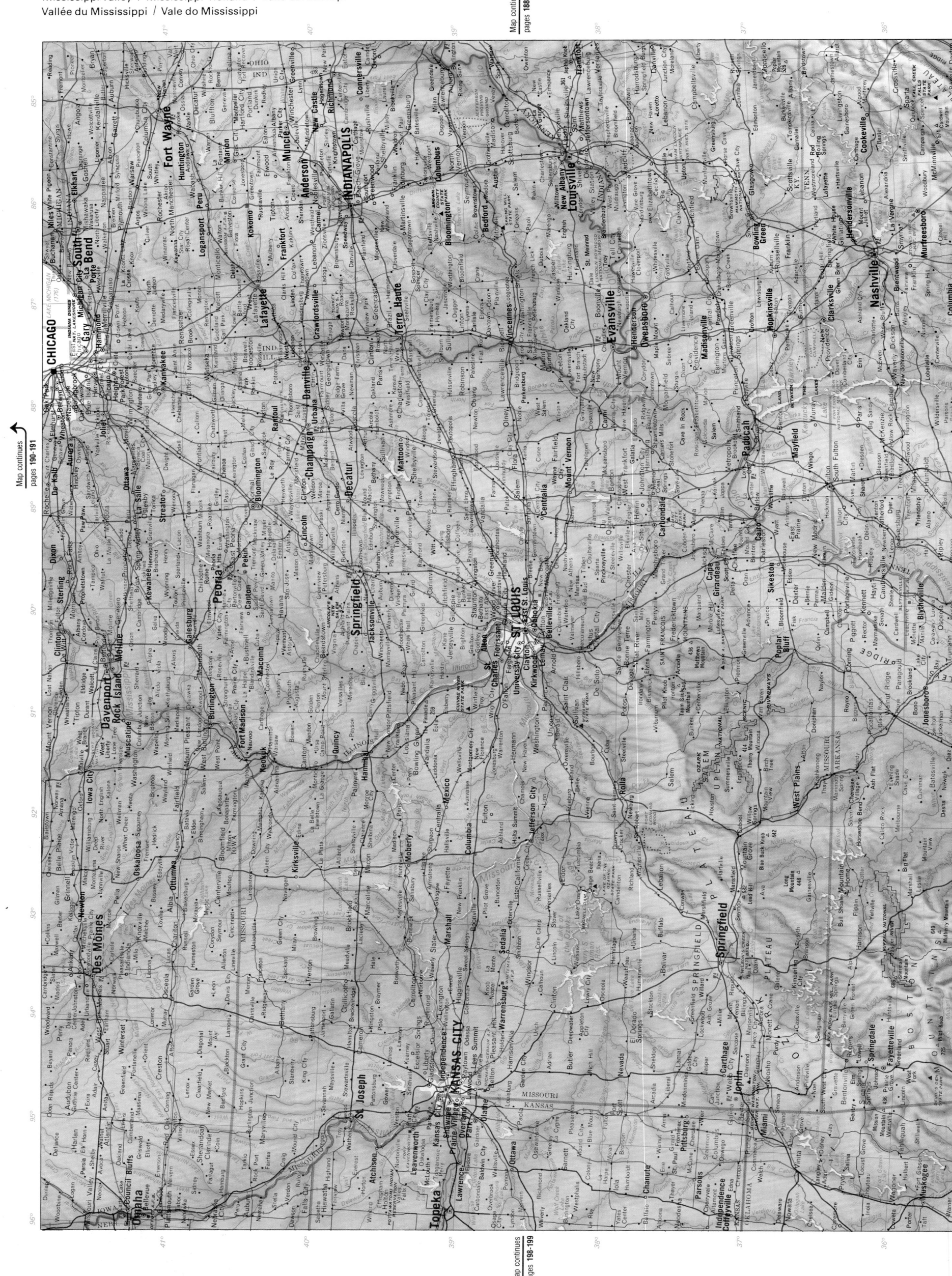

Map continues
pages 188-189

Map continues
pages 190-191

Map continues
pages 198-199

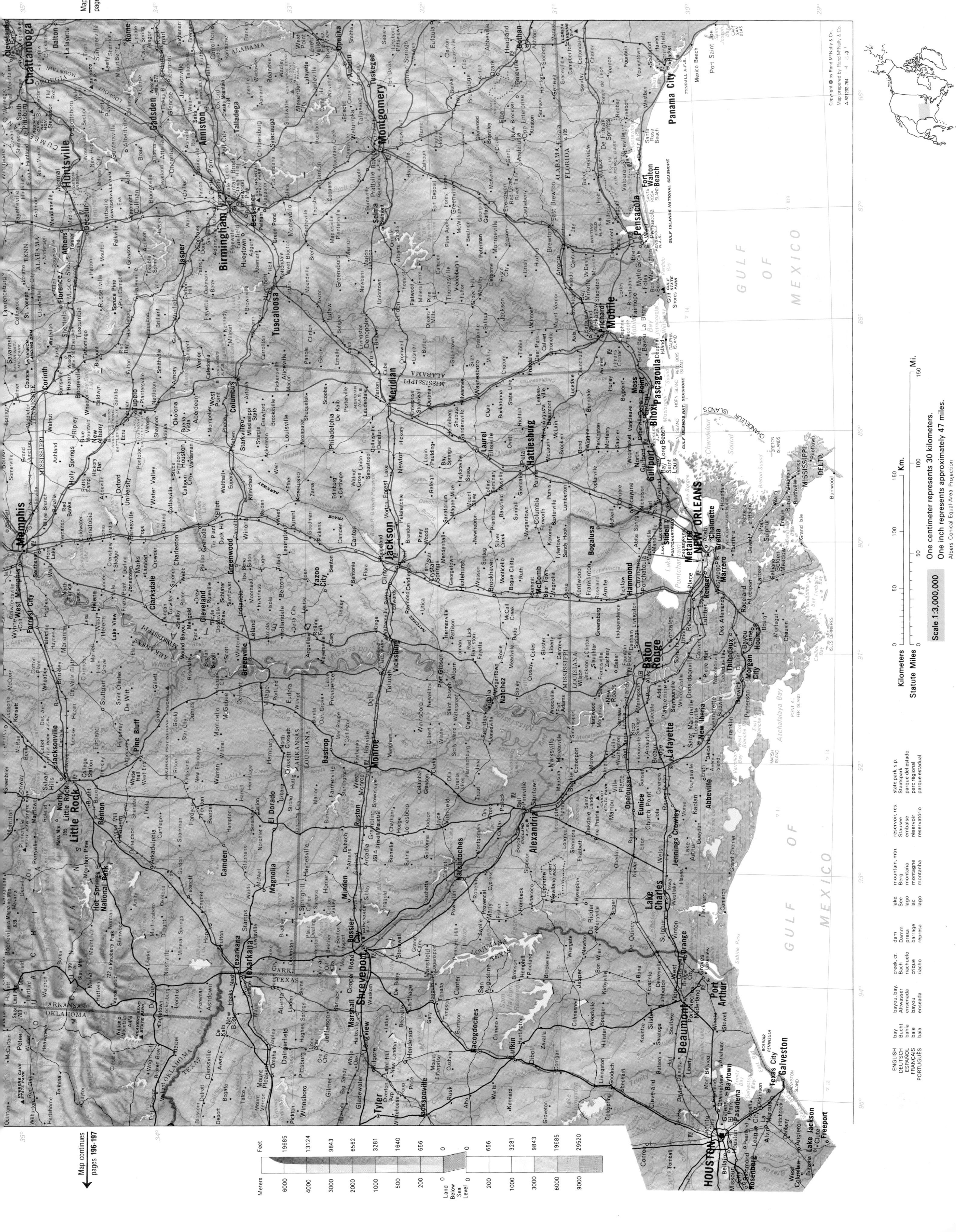

Map continues pages 192-193

Map continues pages 196-197

Copyright © by Rand McNally & Co.
Map prepared by Rand McNally & Co.
A-591290-764

Scale 1:3,000,000

One centimeter represents 30 kilometers.
One inch represents approximately 47 miles.
Albers Conical Equal-Area Projection

Kilometers
Km.
0   50   100   150

Statute Miles
Mi.
0   50   100   150

ENGLISH	DEUTSCH	ESPAÑOL	FRANÇAIS	PORTUGUÊS
bay	Bucht	bahía	baie	baía
bayou, bay.	Altwasser	ensenada	bayou	enseada
creek, cr.	Bach	riachuelo	crique	riacho
dam	Damm	presa	barrage	represa
lake	See	lago	lac	lago
mountain, mtn.	Berg	montaña	montagne	montanha
reservoir, res.	Stausee	embalse	réservoir	reservatório
state park, s.p.	Staatspark	parque del estado	parc régional	parque estadual

Feet	Meters
19685	6000
13124	4000
9843	3000
6562	2000
3281	1000
1640	500
656	200
0	0
	Land Below Sea Level
0	0
656	200
3281	1000
9843	3000
19685	6000
29520	9000

GULF OF MEXICO

NEW ORLEANS

Memphis

Birmingham

Montgomery

Jackson

Shreveport

Houston

Mobile

Baton Rouge

196
Southern Great Plains / Südliche Grosse Ebenen / Grandes Llanos: zona meridional
Grandes Plaines, partie Méridionale / Grandes Planícies: zona meridional

Map continues
pages 194-195

Map continues
pages 198-199

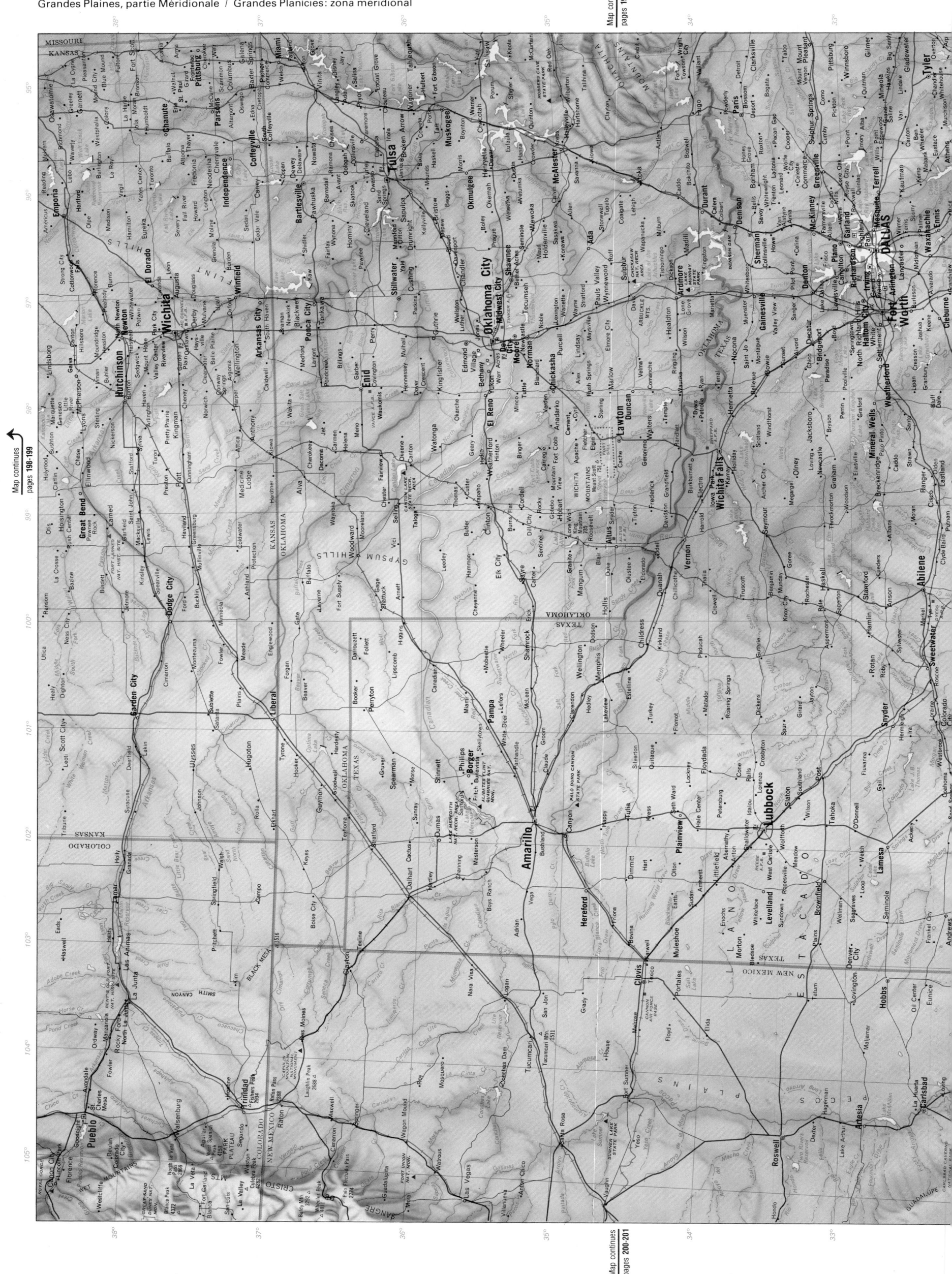

Map continues
pages 200-201

Southern Great Plains / Südliche Grosse Ebenen / Grandes Llanos: zona meridional
Grandes Plaines, partie Méridionale / Grandes Planícies: zona meridional

197

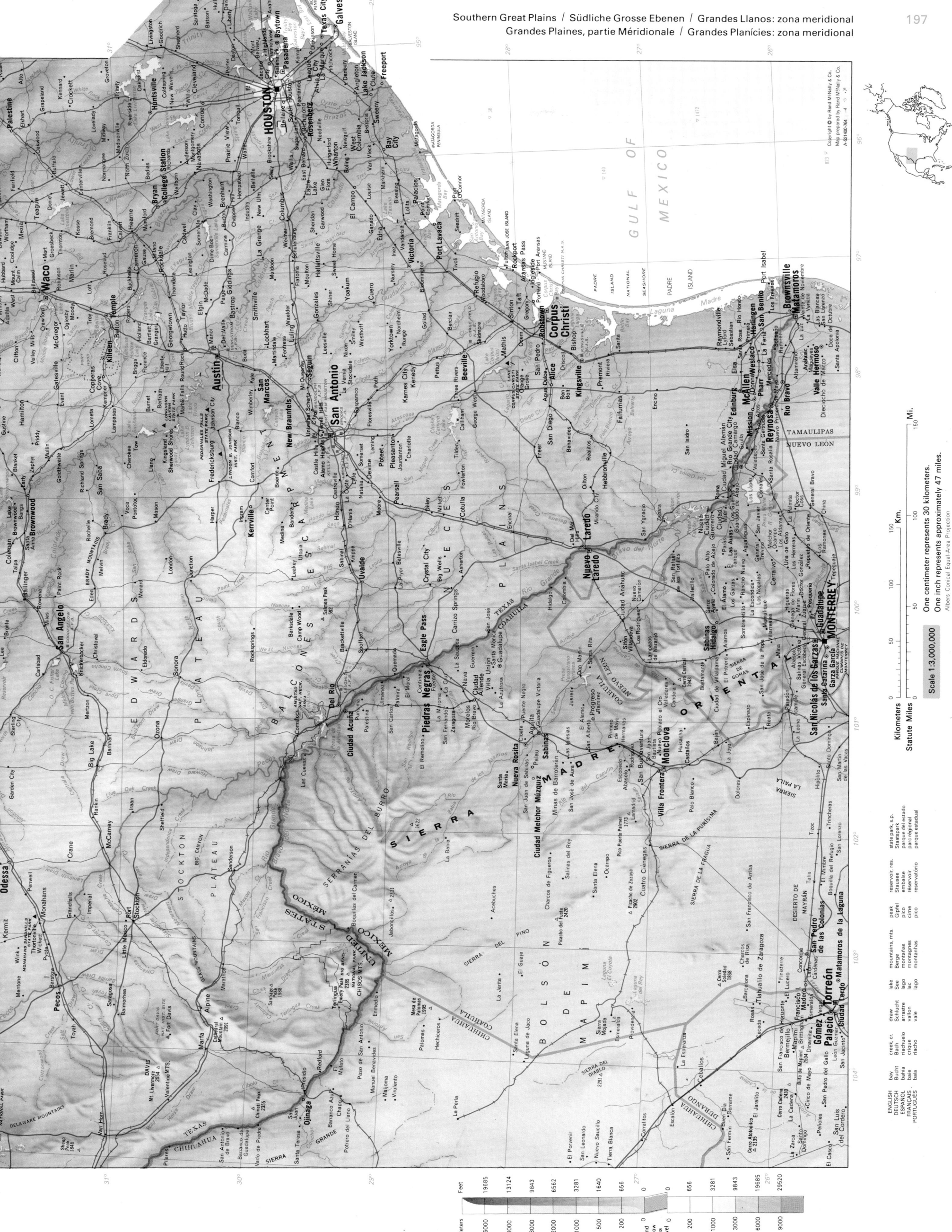

One centimeter represents 30 kilometers.
One inch represents approximately 47 miles.

Albers Conical Equal-Area Projection

Scale 1:3,000,000

ENGLISH	DEUTSCH	ESPAÑOL	FRANÇAIS	PORTUGUÊS
bay	Bucht	bahía	baie	baía
creek, cr.	Bach	riachuelo	crique	riacho
draw	Schlucht	arroyo	vallon	vale
lake	See	lago	lac	lago
mountains, mts.	Berge	montañas	montagnes	montanhas
peak	Gipfel	pico	cime	pico
reservoir, res.	Stausee	embalse	réservoir	reservatório
state park, s.p.	Staatspark	parque del estado	parc régional	parque estadual

Map continues
pages 190-191

Map continues
pages 184-185

Map continues
pages 202-203

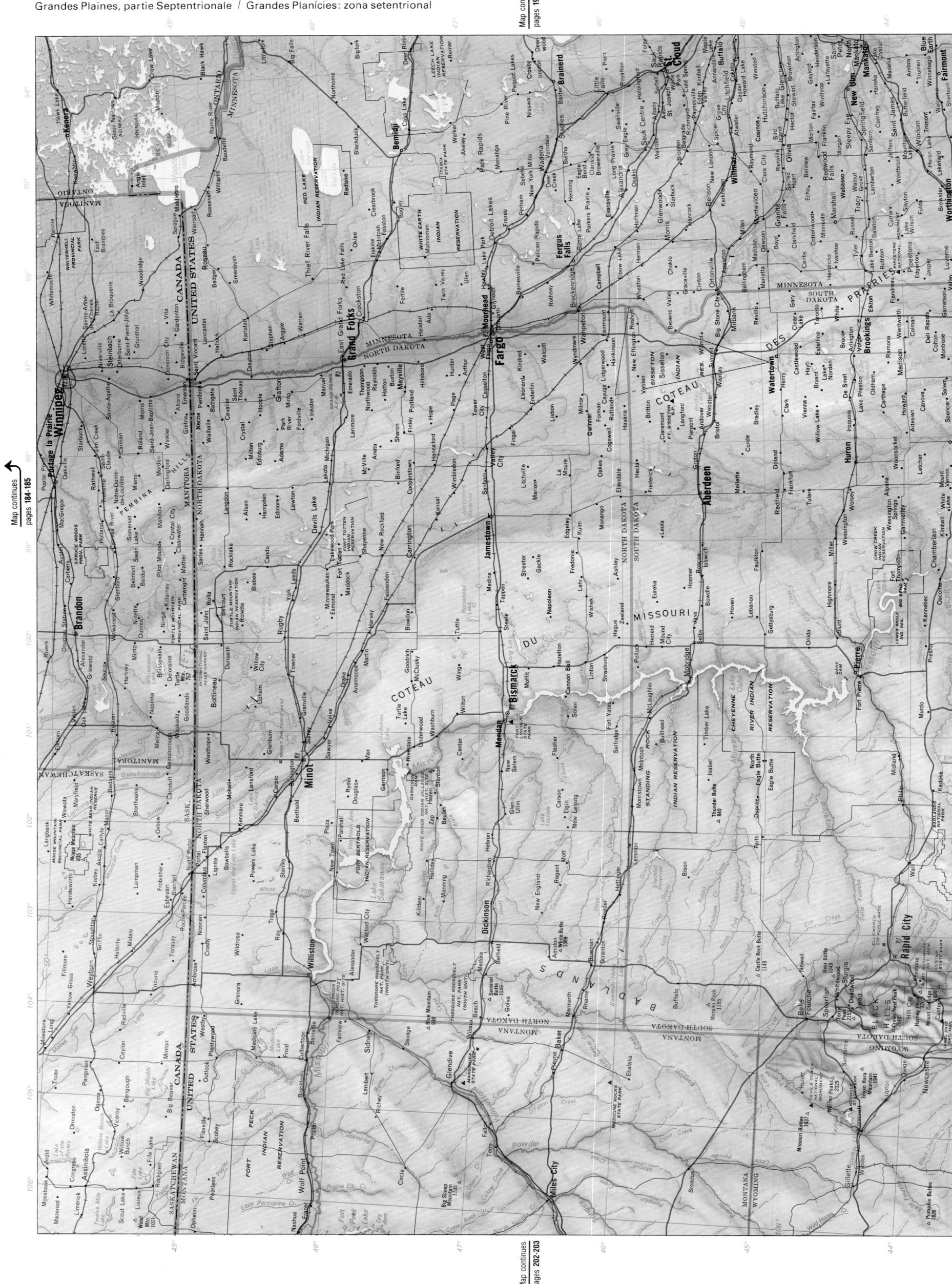

Northern Great Plains / Nördliche Grosse Ebenen / Grandes Llanos: zona septentrional
Grandes Plaines, partie Septentrionale / Grandes Planícies: zona setentrional

199

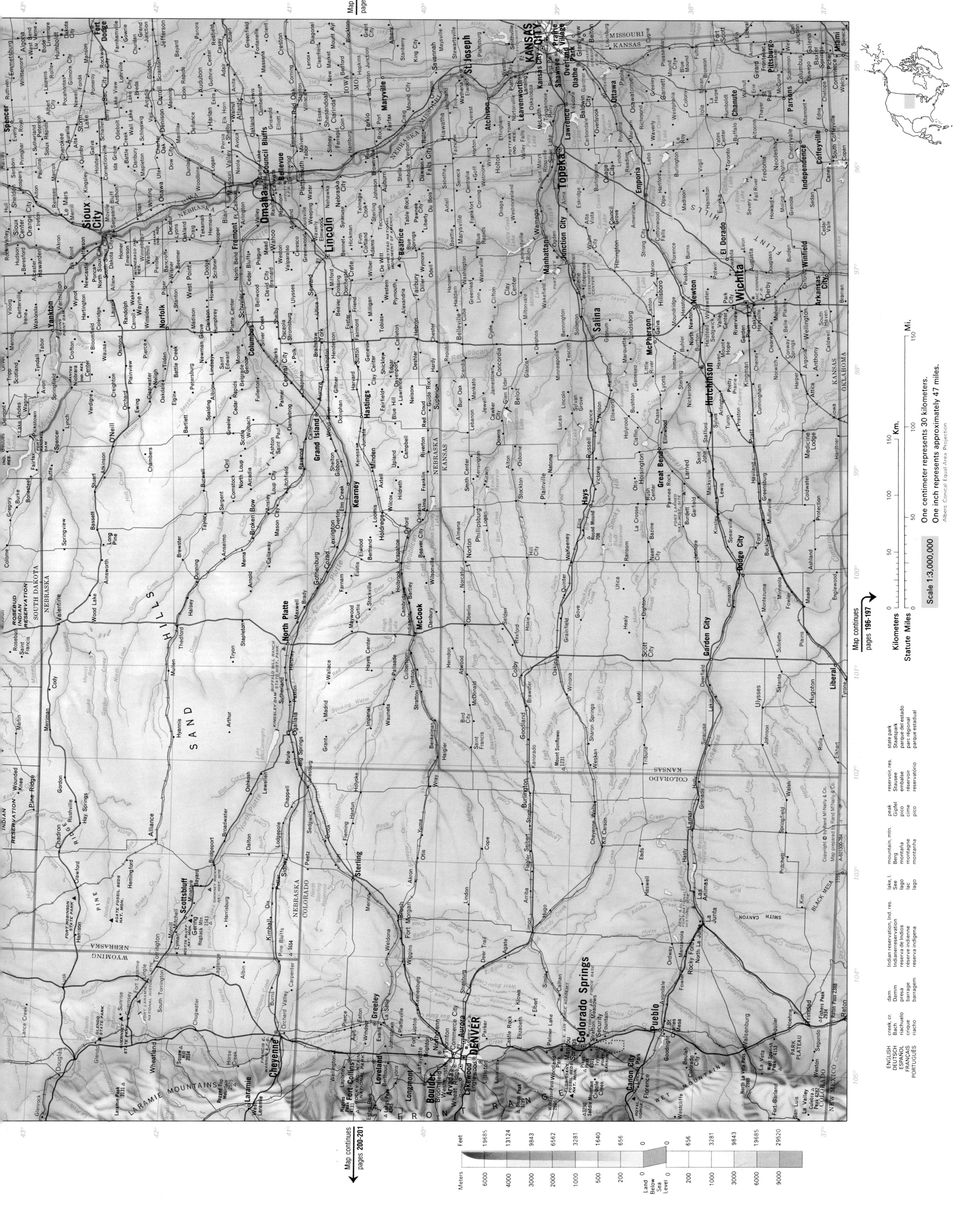

Map continues pages 194-195
Map continues pages 196-197
Map continues pages 200-201

Scale 1:3,000,000

One centimeter represents 30 kilometers.
One inch represents approximately 47 miles.

Albers Conical Equal Area Projection

Kilometers 0 50 100 150 Km.
Statute Miles 0 50 100 150 Mi.

ENGLISH	DEUTSCH	ESPAÑOL	FRANÇAIS	PORTUGUÊS
creek, cr.	Bach	riachuelo	crique	córrego
dam	Damm	presa	barrage	barragem
Indian reservation, Ind. res.	Indianerreservation	reserva de indios	réserve indienne	reserva indígena
lake, l.	See	lago	lac	lago
mountain, mtn.	Berg	montaña	montagne	montanha
peak	Gipfel	pico	cime	pico
reservoir, res.	Stausee	embalse	réservoir	reservatório
state park	Staatspark	parque del estado	parc regional	parque estadual

Copyright © by Rand McNally & Co.
Map prepared by Rand McNally & Co.

Feet / Meters
19685 / 6000
13124 / 4000
9843 / 3000
6562 / 2000
3281 / 1000
1640 / 500
656 / 200
0 / 0
Land Below Sea Level
0 / 0
656 / 200
3281 / 1000
9843 / 3000
19685 / 6000
29520 / 9000

200

Southern Rocky Mountains / Südliches Felsengebirge / Montañas Rocosas: zona meridional
Montagnes Rocheuses, partie Méridionale / Montanhas Rochosas: zona meridional

Map continues pages 198-199

Map continues pages 202-203

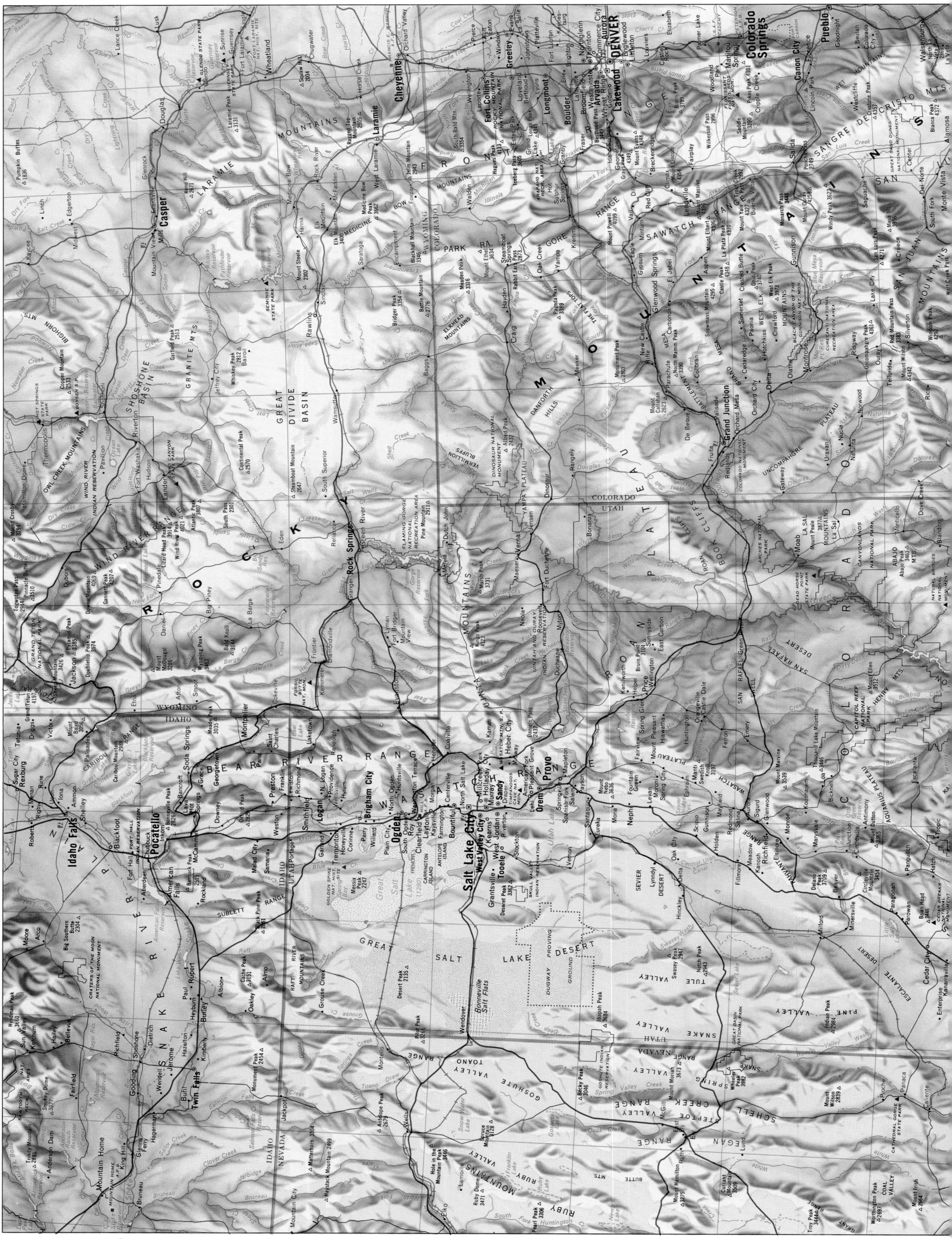

Map continues pages 204-205

Southern Rocky Mountains / Südliches Felsengebirge / Montañas Rocosas: zona meridional
Montagnes Rocheuses, partie Méridionale / Montanhas Rochosas: zona meridional

201

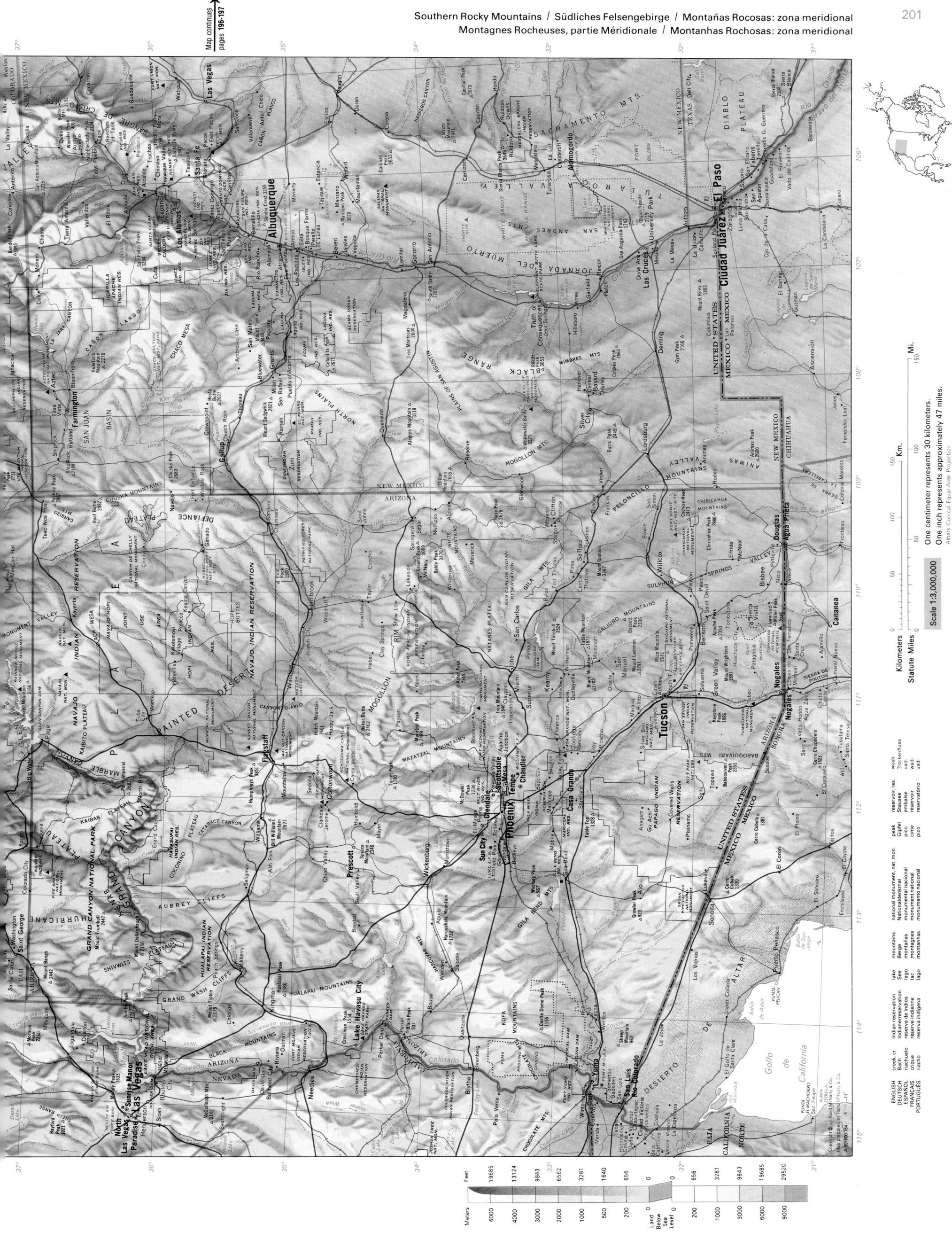

Map continues pages 196–197

Kilometers

Statute Miles

One centimeter represents 30 kilometers.
One inch represents approximately 47 miles.
Albers Conical Equal-Area Projection

Scale 1:3,000,000

ENGLISH	DEUTSCH	ESPAÑOL	FRANÇAIS	PORTUGUÊS
creek, cr.	Bach	riachuelo	crique	riacho
lake	See	lago	lac	lago
Indian reservation	Indianerreservation	reserva de Indios	réserve indienne	reserva indígena
mountains	Berge	montañas	montagnes	montanhas
national monument, nat. mon.	Nationaldenkmal	monumento nacional	monument national	monumento nacional
peak	Gipfel	pico	cime	pico
reservoir, res.	Stausee	embalse	réservoir	reservatório
wash	Trockenfluss	uadi	wadi	uadi

Feet
19685
13124
9843
6562
3281
1640
656
0
656
3281
9843
19685
29520

Meters
6000
4000
3000
2000
1000
500
200
0
Land Below Sea Level
200
1000
3000
6000
9000

Copyright by Rand McNally & Co.

Northwestern United States / Nordwestliche Vereinigte Staaten / Nor-oeste de los Estados Unidos
Nord-Ouest des États-Unis / Noroeste dos Estados Unidos

Map continues
pages 182-183

Map continues
pages 204-205

ENGLISH	creek, cr.	Indian reservation	lake, l.	mountain, mtn.	pass	peak	range	reservoir, res.
DEUTSCH	Bach	Indianerreservation	See	Berg	Pass	Gipfel	Gebirge	Stausee
ESPAÑOL	riachuelo	reserva de indios	lago	montaña	paso	pico	sierra	embalse
FRANÇAIS	crique	reserve indienne	lac	montagne	col	cime	chaîne	réservoir
PORTUGUÊS	riacho	reserva indigena	lago	montanha	passo	pico	serra	reservatório

Northwestern United States / Nordwestliche Vereinigte Staaten / Nor-oeste de los Estados Unidos
Nord-Ouest des États-Unis / Noroeste dos Estados Unidos

203

Map continues
pages 184-185

Map continues
pages 198-199

Map continues
pages 200-201

Kilometers

Statute Miles

Scale 1:3,000,000

One centimeter represents 30 kilometers.
One inch represents approximately 47 miles.
Albers Conical Equal-Area Projection

Map continues pages 200-201

Map continues pages 202-203

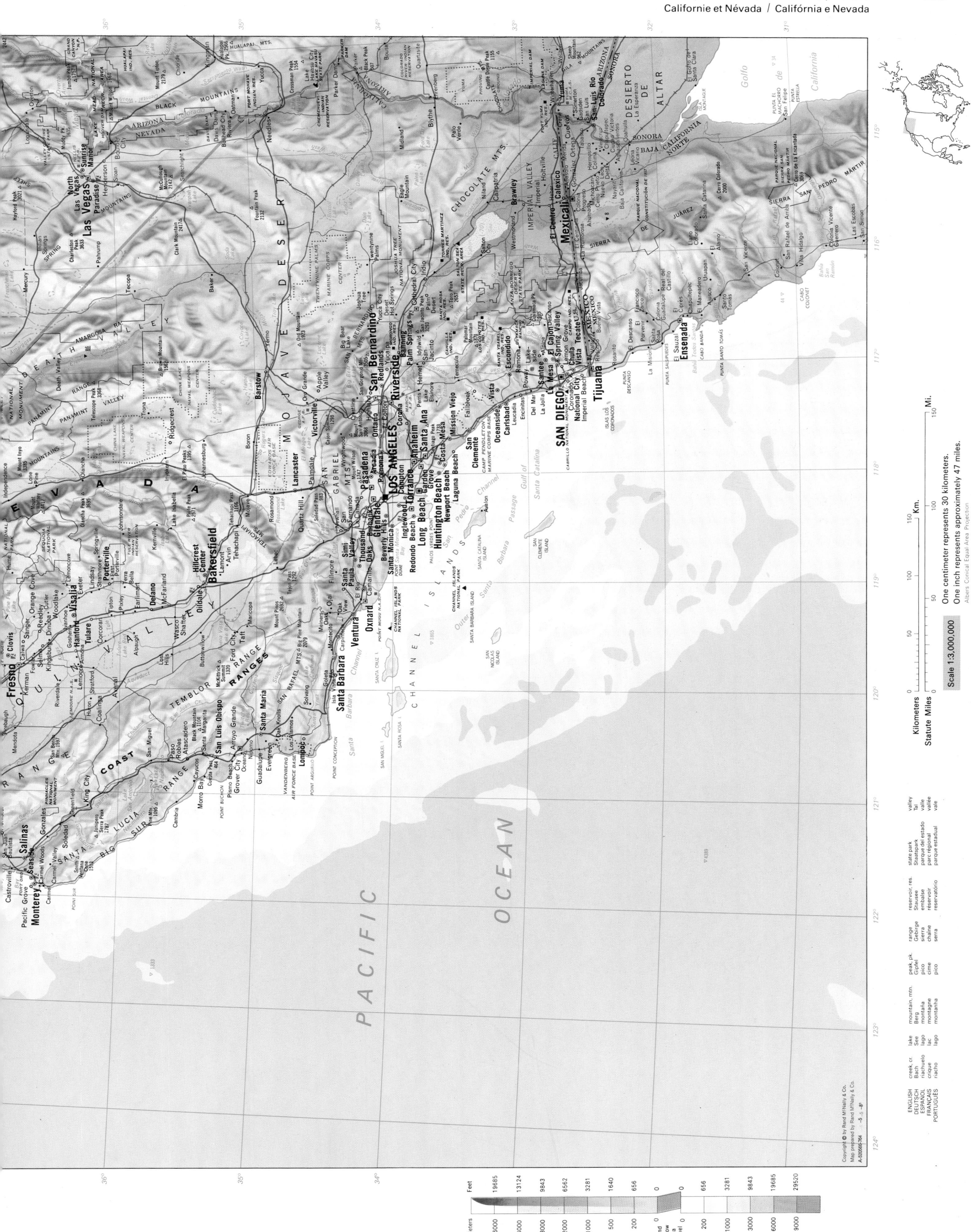

One centimeter represents 30 kilometers.
One inch represents approximately 47 miles.

Albers Conical Equal-Area Projection

Scale 1:3,000,000

ENGLISH	creek, cr.	lake	mountain, mtn.	peak, pk.	range	reservoir, res.	state park	valley
DEUTSCH	Bach	See	Berg	Gipfel	Gebirge	Stausee	Staatspark	Tal
ESPAÑOL	riachuelo	lago	montaña	pico	sierra	embalse	parque del estado	valle
FRANÇAIS	crique	lac	montagne	cime	chaîne	réservoir	parc régional	vallée
PORTUGUÊS	riacho	lago	montanha	pico	serra	reservatório	parque estadual	vale

Copyright © by Rand McNally & Co.
Map prepared by Rand McNally & Co.
A-800266/764

Feet	Meters
19685	6000
13124	4000
9843	3000
6562	2000
3281	1000
1640	500
656	200
0	0
Land Below Sea Level	
0	0
656	200
3281	1000
9843	3000
19685	6000
29520	9000

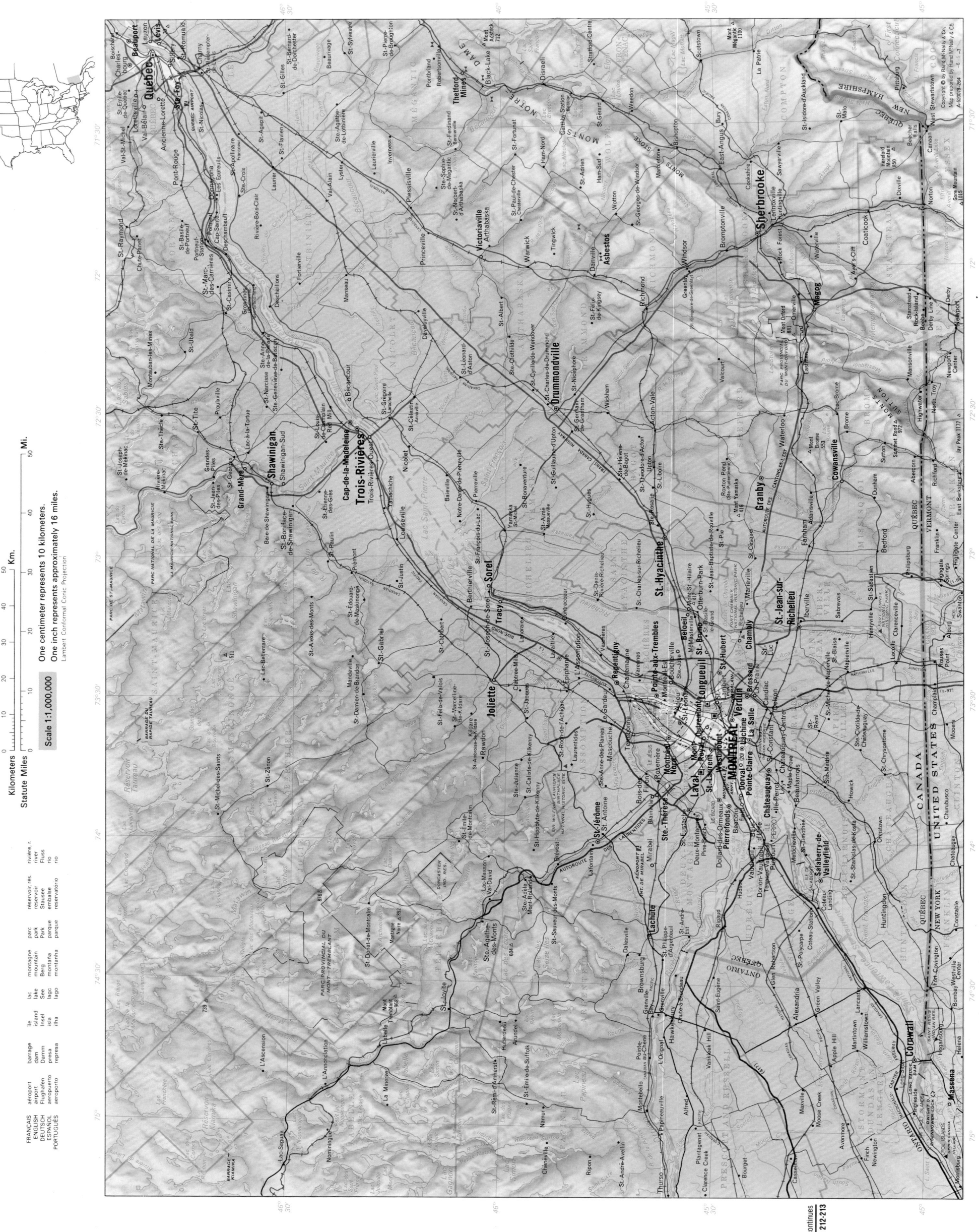

Scale 1:1,000,000
One centimeter represents 10 kilometers.
One inch represents approximately 16 miles.
Lambert Conformal Conic Projection

FRANCAIS	aeroport	barrage	île	lac	montagne	parc	réservoir, rés.	rivière, r.
ENGLISH	airport	dam	island	lake	mountain	park	reservoir	river
DEUTSCH	Flughafen	Damm	Insel	See	Berg	Park	Stausee	Fluss
ESPAÑOL	aeropuerto	presa	isla	lago	montaña	parque	embalse	río
PORTUGUÊS	aeroporto	represa	ilha	lago	montanha	parque	reservatório	rio

Map continues
pages 212-213

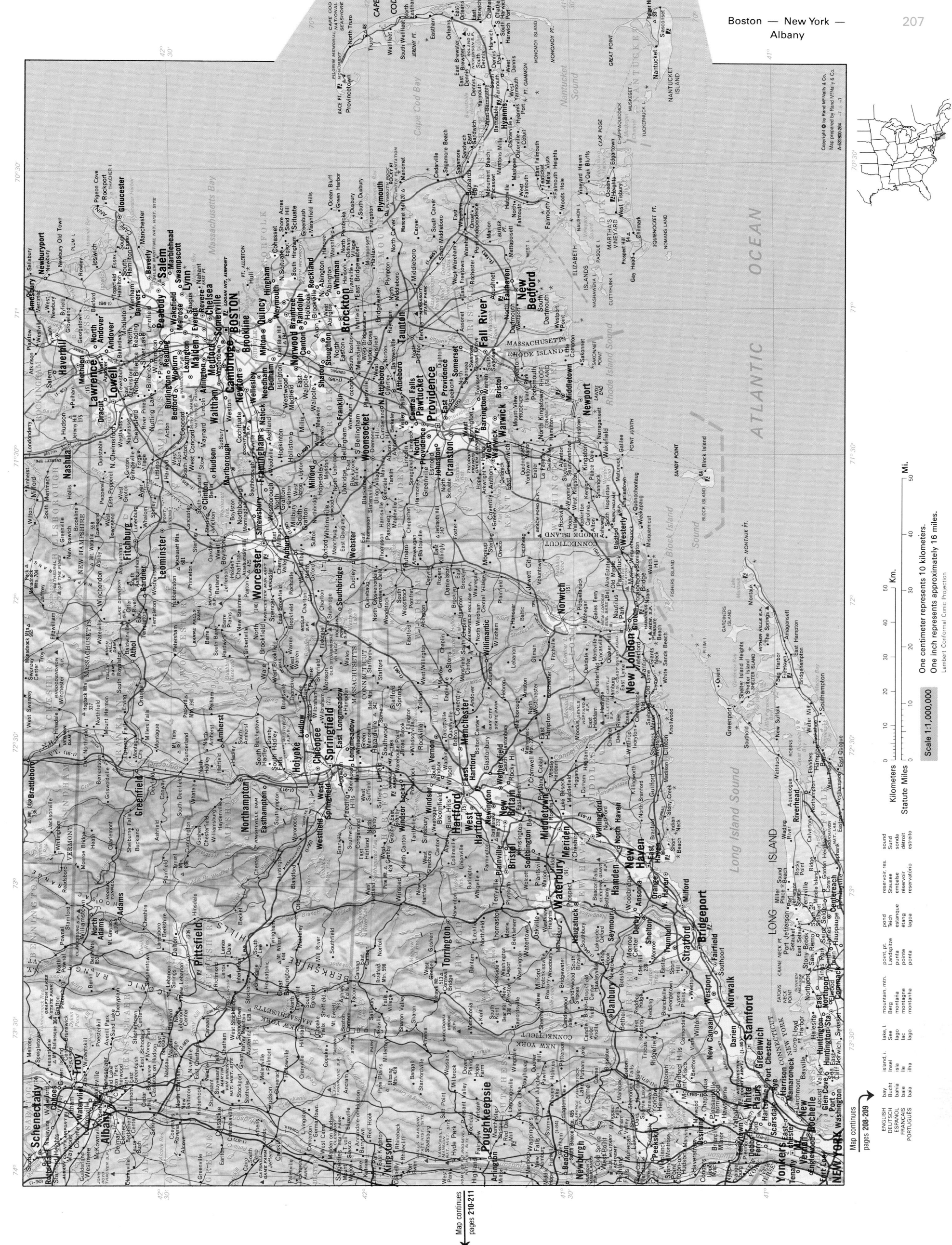

Copyright © by Rand McNally & Co.
Map prepared by Rand McNally & Co.
A-623800-264   -7-I,-7

Map continues
pages 208-209

Map continues
pages 210-211

One centimeter represents 10 kilometers.
One inch represents approximately 16 miles.
Lambert Conformal Conic Projection

Scale 1:1,000,000

Kilometers

Statute Miles

Km.

Mi.

ENGLISH	island, i.	lake, l.	mountain, mtn.	point, pt.	pond	reservoir, res.	sound
DEUTSCH	Insel	See	Berg	Landspitze	Teich	Stausee	Sund
ESPAÑOL	isla	lago	montaña	punta	estanque	embalse	sonda
FRANÇAIS	île	lac	montagne	pointe	étang	réservoir	détroit
PORTUGUÊS	ilha	lago	montanha	ponta	lagoa	reservatório	estreito

CAPE COD

ATLANTIC OCEAN

Massachusetts Bay

Cape Cod Bay

Nantucket Sound

Rhode Island Sound

Long Island Sound

NEW HAMPSHIRE

VERMONT

MASSACHUSETTS

CONNECTICUT

RHODE ISLAND

NEW YORK

LONG ISLAND

BOSTON

Worcester

Springfield

Hartford

New Haven

Providence

New Bedford

Fall River

Bridgeport

Stamford

Albany

Schenectady

Troy

Pittsfield

Poughkeepsie

NEW YORK

Yonkers

New Rochelle

White Plains

Map continues pages 210-211

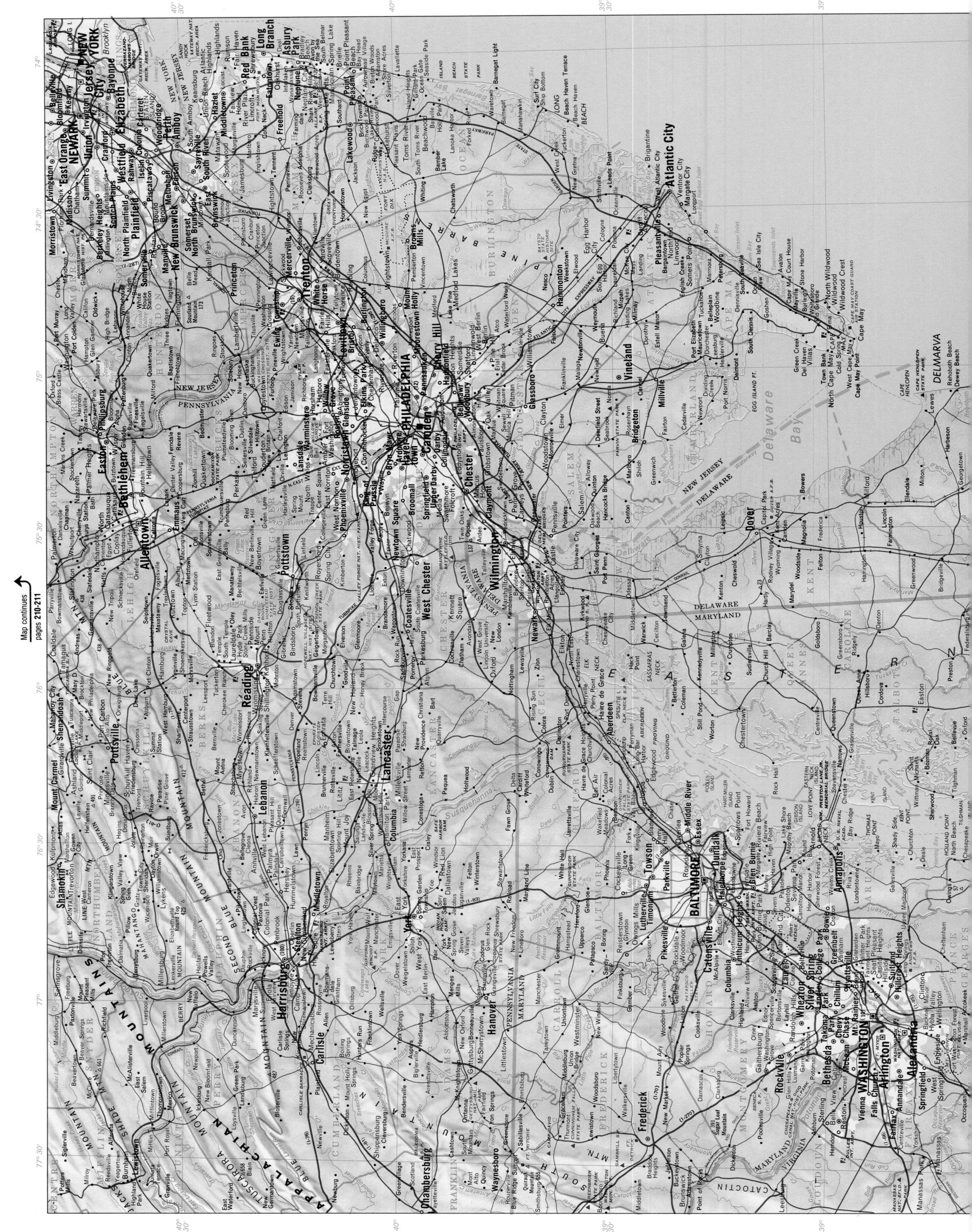
NEW YORK
NEWARK
Jersey City
Elizabeth
Trenton
PHILADELPHIA
Camden
Wilmington
Atlantic City
Vineland
Allentown
Bethlehem
Reading
Lancaster
Harrisburg
York
BALTIMORE
WASHINGTON
Alexandria
Arlington
Annapolis
Frederick
Dover
Delaware Bay
NEW JERSEY
PENNSYLVANIA
DELAWARE
MARYLAND
DELMARVA
APPALACHIAN
BLUE
MOUNTAIN
SOUTH
CATOCTIN

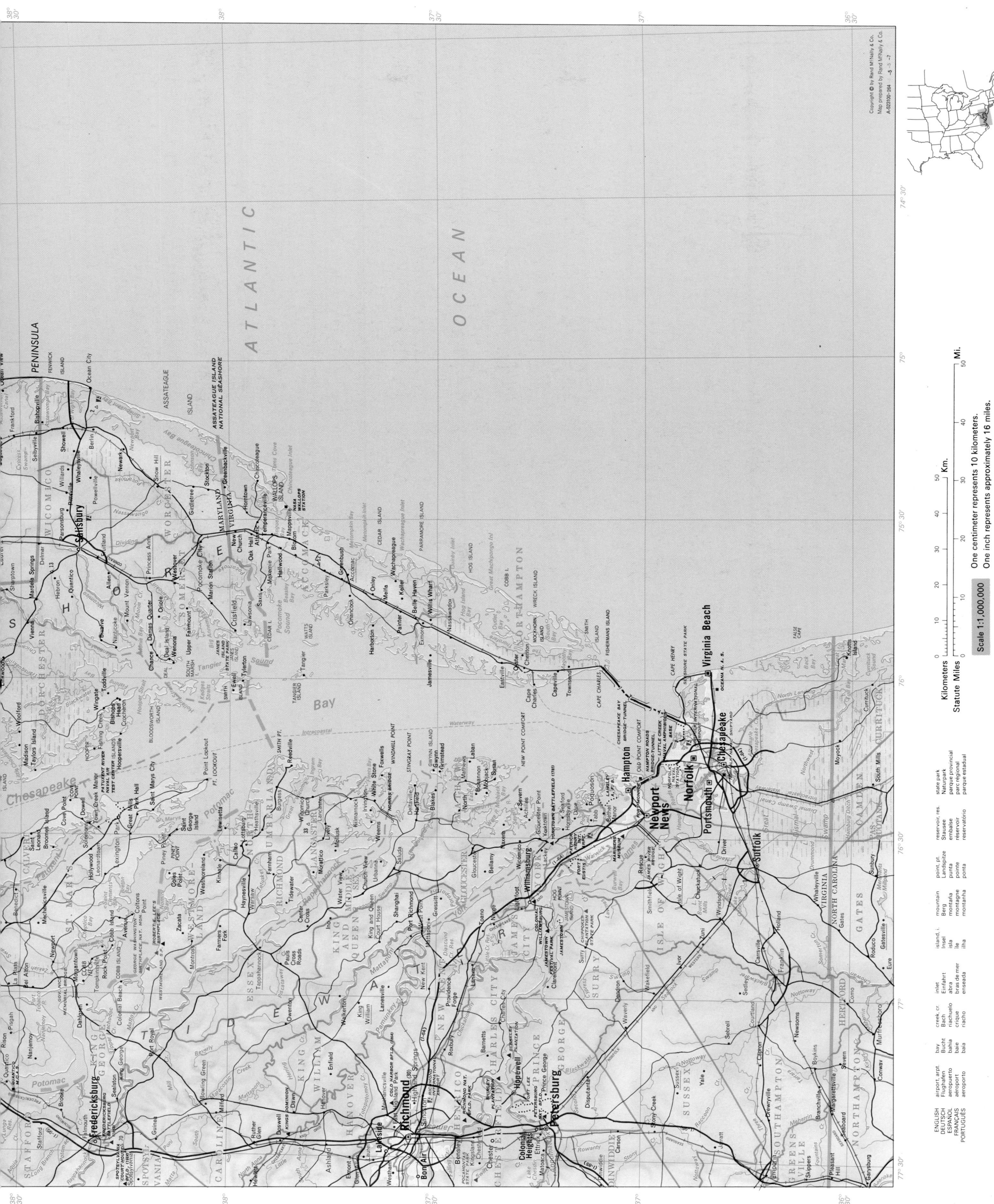

Scale 1:1,000,000

One centimeter represents 10 kilometers.
One inch represents approximately 16 miles.

Kilometers
Km.

Statute Miles
Mi.

Lambert Conformal Conic Projection

ENGLISH	airport, arpt.	bay	creek, cr.	inlet	island, i.	mountain	point, pt.	reservoir, res.	state park
DEUTSCH	Flughafen	Bucht	Bach	Einfahrt	Insel	Berg	Landspitze	Stausee	Naturpark
ESPAÑOL	aeropuerto	bahía	riachuelo	abra	isla	montaña	punta	embalse	parque provincial
FRANÇAIS	aéroport	baie	crique	bras de mer	île	montagne	pointe	réservoir	parc régional
PORTUGUÊS	aeroporto	baía	riacho	enseada	ilha	montanha	ponta	reservatório	parque estadual

Map continues
pages 212-213

Map continues
pages 214-215

LAKE ONTARIO (75)

MONROE   ORLEANS   GENESEE   WYOMING   LIVINGSTON   ONTARIO   YATES   SENECA   CAYUGA   ONONDAGA   WAYNE   SCHUYLER   TOMPKINS   TIOGA   STEUBEN   CHEMUNG   ALLEGANY   CATTARAUGUS   ERIE   WARREN

NEW YORK
PENNSYLVANIA

McKEAN   POTTER   TIOGA   BRADFORD   SULLIVAN   LYCOMING   CLINTON   CAMERON   ELK   FOREST   JEFFERSON   CLEARFIELD   CENTRE   UNION   SNYDER   NORTHUMBERLAND   MONTOUR   COLUMBIA   MIFFLIN   JUNIATA   HUNTINGDON   BLAIR   CAMBRIA   INDIANA   PERRY   DAUPHIN   SCHUYLKILL

Niagara Falls   BUFFALO   Lockport   Tonawanda   Batavia   Rochester   Brighton   Auburn   Geneva   Canandaigua   Hornell   Corning   Elmira   Ithaca   Cortland   Olean   Bradford   Williamsport   Lock Haven   Clearfield   State College   Altoona   Lewistown   Sunbury   Shamokin   Bloomsburg   Berwick   Pottsville   Sayre   Syracuse

Copyright © by Rand McNally & Co.
Map prepared by Rand McNally & Co.
A-523000-264   A-5—6

	airport, arpt.	bay	creek, cr.	hill	Island	lake	mountain	reservoir	state park, s.p.
ENGLISH	airport, arpt.	bay	creek, cr.	hill	Island	lake	mountain	reservoir	state park, s.p.
DEUTSCH	Flughafen	Bucht	Bach	Hügel	Insel	See	Berg	Stausee	Naturpark
ESPAÑOL	aeropuerto	bahía	riachuelo	colina	isla	lago	montaña	embalse	parque provincial
FRANÇAIS	aéroport	baie	crique	colline	île	lac	montagne	réservoir	parc régional
PORTUGUÊS	aeroporto	baía	riacho	colina	ilha	lago	montanha	reservatório	parque estadual

Map continues
page **207** →

Map continues
pages **208-209** ↓

Kilometers 0 10 20 30 40 50
Statute Miles 0 10 20 30 40 50

Scale 1:1,000,000   One centimeter represents 10 kilometers.
One inch represents approximately 16 miles.
Lambert Conformal Conic Projection

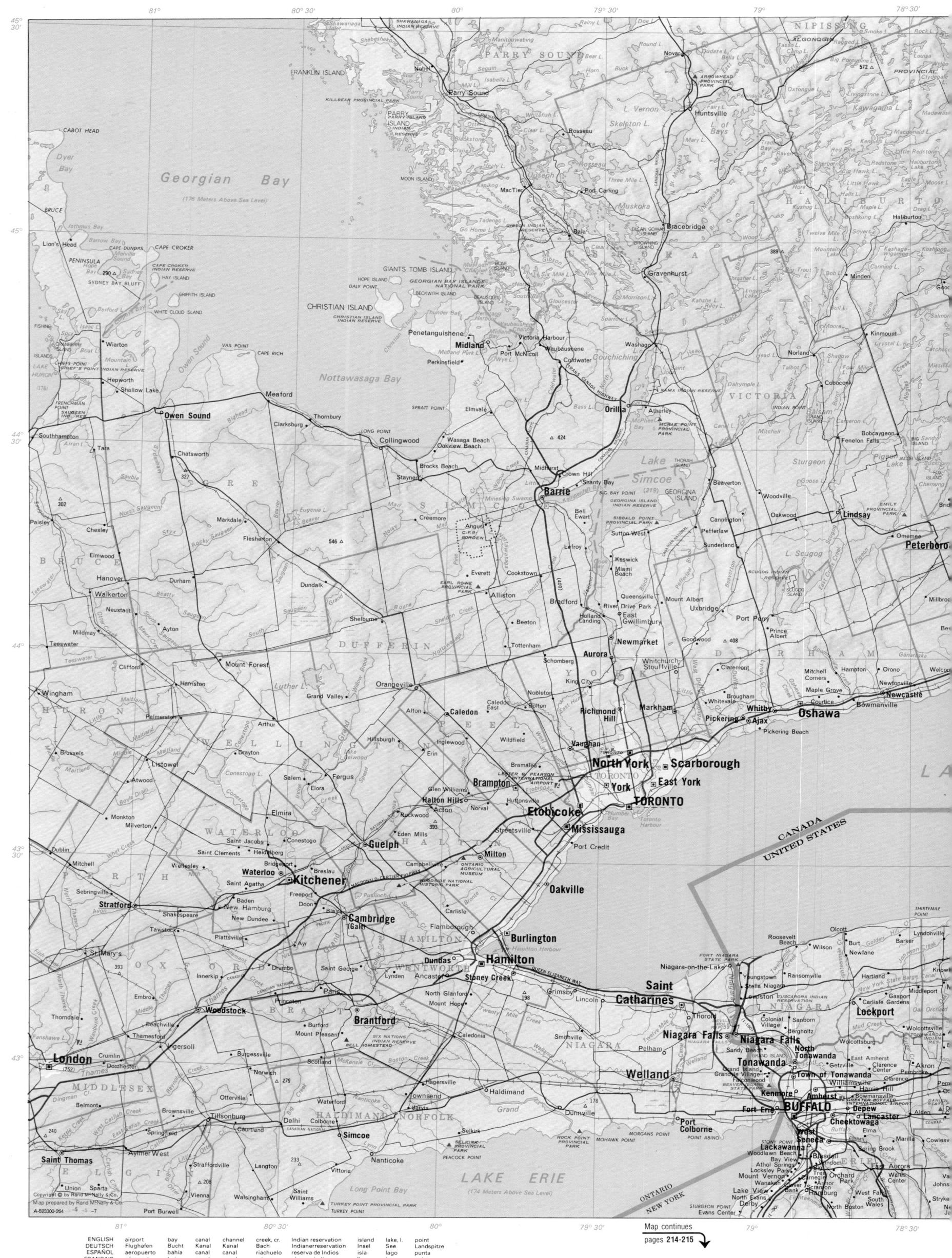

Map continues
pages 214-215

ENGLISH	airport	bay	canal	channel	creek, cr.	Indian reservation	island	lake, l.	point
DEUTSCH	Flughafen	Bucht	Kanal	Kanal	Bach	Indianerreservation	Insel	See	Landspitze
ESPAÑOL	aeropuerto	bahía	canal	canal	riachuelo	reserva de Indios	isla	lago	punta
FRANÇAIS	aéroport	baie	canal	canal	crique	réserve indienne	île	lac	pointe
PORTUGUÊS	aeroporto	baía	canal	canal	riacho	reserva indígena	ilha	lago	ponta

Map continues page 206

Map continues pages 210-211

Kilometers Km.
Statute Miles Mi.

Scale 1:1,000,000

One centimeter represents 10 kilometers.
One inch represents approximately 16 miles.
Lambert Conformal Conic Projection

← Map continues
pages 216-217

Map continues
page 218 ↓

	ENGLISH	airport	creek, cr.	hill	lake, l.	mountain, mtn.	point, pt.	reservoir, res.	state park
	DEUTSCH	Flughafen	Bach	Hügel	See	Berg	Landspitze	Stausee	Naturpark
	ESPAÑOL	aeropuerto	riachuelo	colina	lago	montaña	punta	embalse	parque provincial
	FRANÇAIS	aéroport	crique	colline	lac	montagne	pointe	réservoir	parc régional
	PORTUGUÊS	aeroporto	riacho	colina	lago	montanha	ponta	reservatório	parque estadual

Map continues
pages 212-213

Map continues
pages 210-211

Kilometers ⊢⊢⊢⊢⊢⊢⊢ 0   10   20   30   40   50 Km.
Statute Miles ⊢⊢⊢⊢⊢⊢⊢ 0   10   20   30   40   50 Mi.

Scale 1:1,000,000
One centimeter represents 10 kilometers.
One inch represents approximately 16 miles.
Lambert Conformal Conic Projection

Map continues
page 219 →

ENGLISH	airport	creek, cr.	ditch	lake, l.	reservoir	state park, s.p.
DEUTSCH	Flughafen	Bach	Graben	See	Stausee	Naturpark
ESPAÑOL	aeropuerto	riachuelo	acequia	lago	embalse	parque provincial
FRANÇAIS	aéroport	crique	fossé	lac	réservoir	parc régional
PORTUGUÊS	aeroporto	riacho	fosso	lago	reservatório	parque estadual

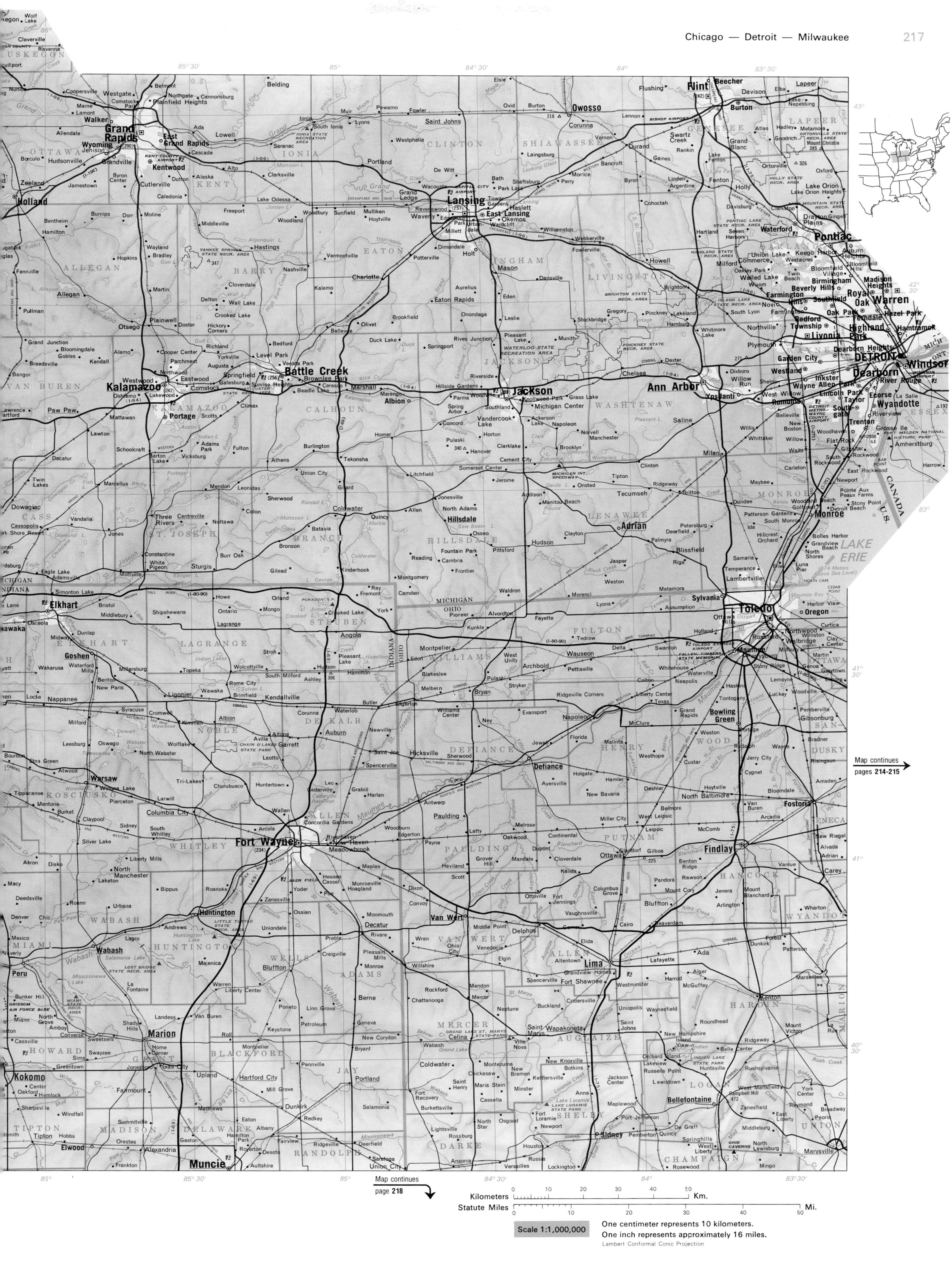

Grand Rapids
Wyoming
East Grand Rapids
Kentwood
Holland
Kalamazoo
Portage
Battle Creek
Lansing
East Lansing
Jackson
Ann Arbor
Ypsilanti
Flint
Burton
Owosso
Pontiac
Waterford
DETROIT
Dearborn
Windsor
Warren
Royal Oak
Southfield
Livonia
Westland
Monroe
Toledo
Maumee
Bowling Green
Findlay
Fostoria
Lima
Van Wert
Defiance
Fort Wayne
Huntington
Wabash
Marion
Kokomo
Muncie
Elkhart
Goshen
Warsaw
Columbia City
Auburn
Angola
Sturgis
Three Rivers
Coldwater
Hillsdale
Adrian
Sylvania

LAKE ERIE

CANADA
U.S.

Map continues pages 214-215 →

Map continues page 218 ↓

Kilometers
0 10 20 30 40 50 Km.
Statute Miles
0 10 20 30 40 50 Mi.

Scale 1:1,000,000
One centimeter represents 10 kilometers.
One inch represents approximately 16 miles.
Lambert Conformal Conic Projection

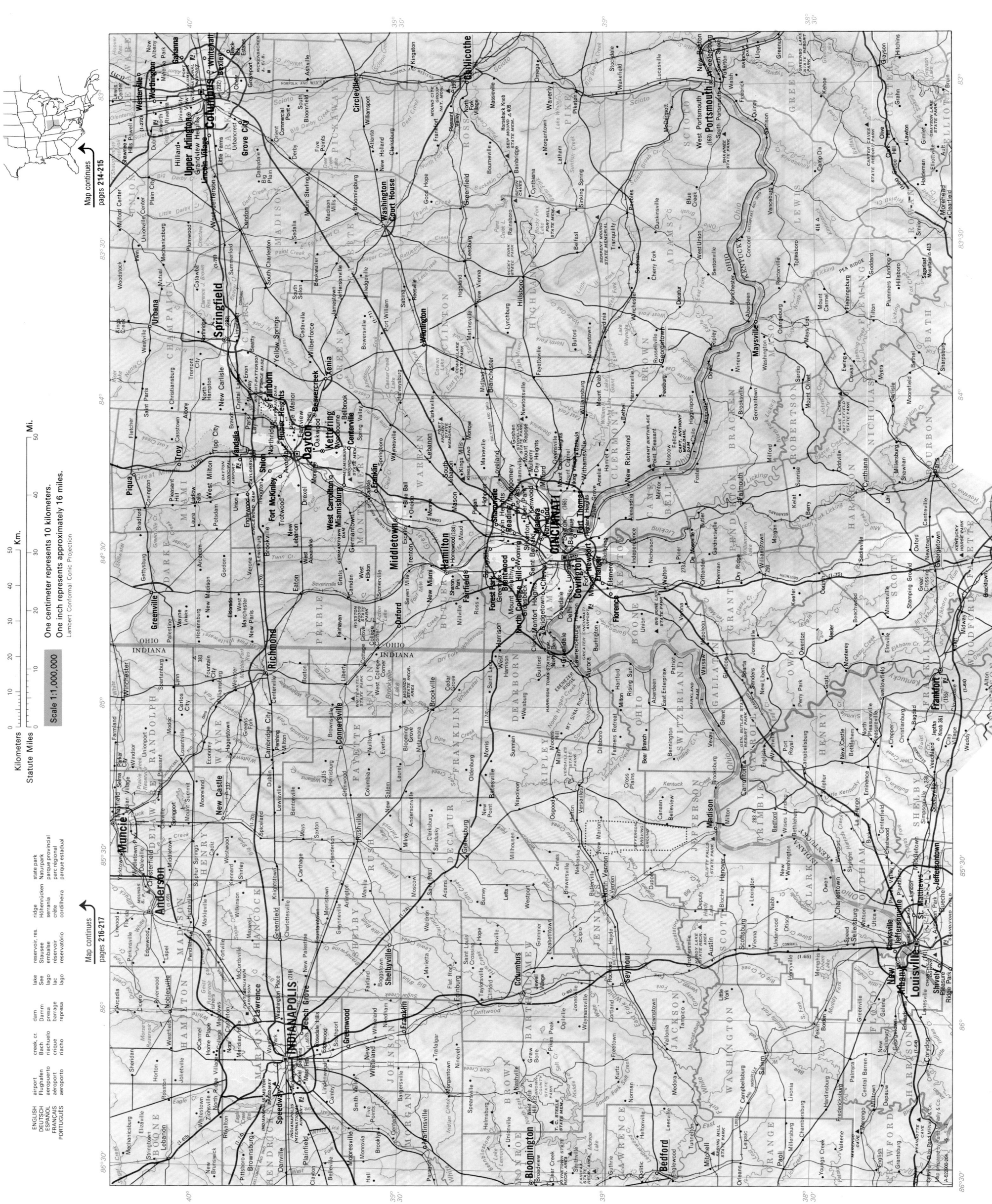

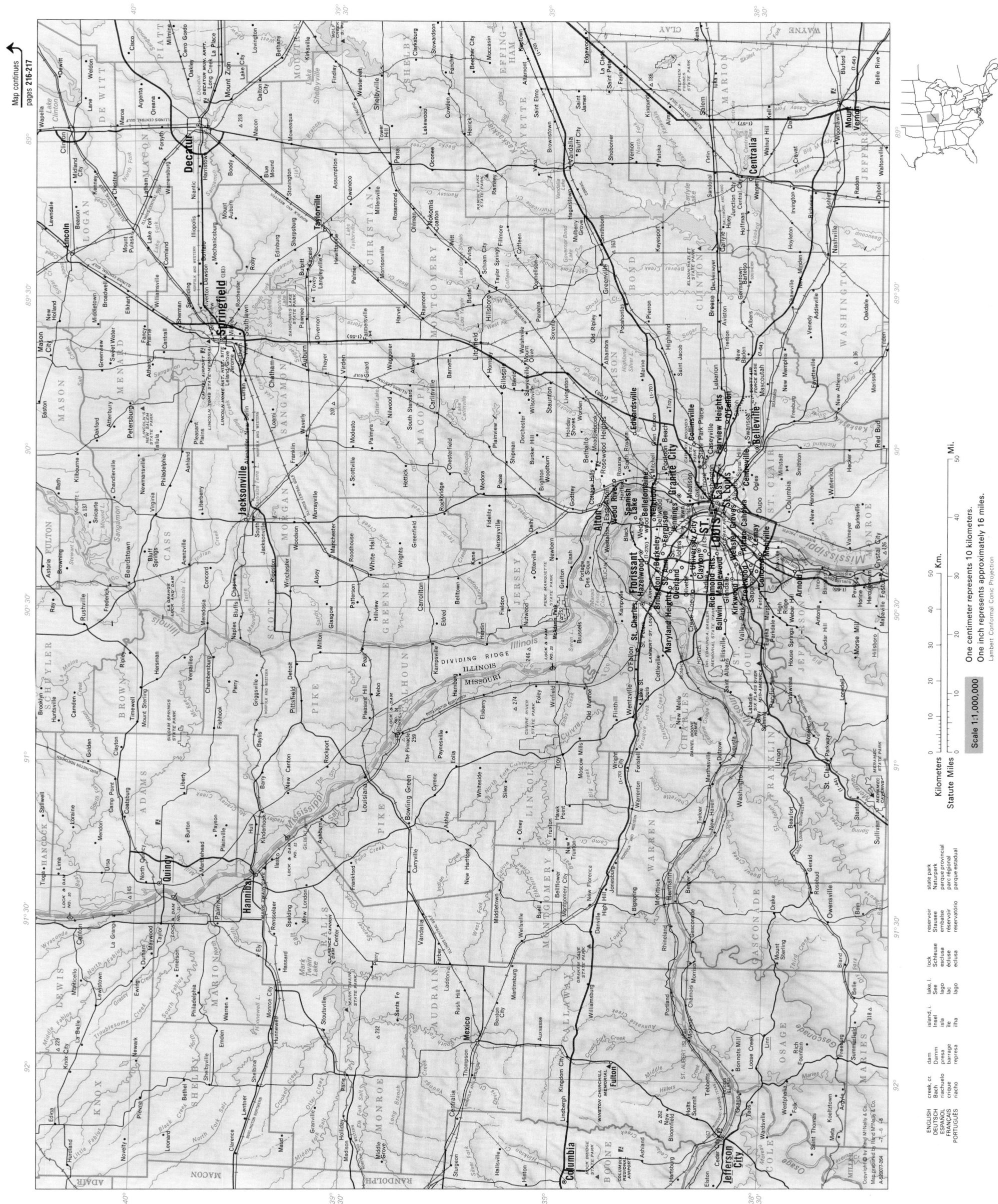

Map continues pages 216-217

Scale 1:1,000,000

Kilometers

Statute Miles

Mi.

Km.

One centimeter represents 10 kilometers.
One inch represents approximately 16 miles.

Lambert Conformal Conic Projection

ENGLISH	creek, cr.	dam	lake, l.	island, i.	lock	reservoir	state park
DEUTSCH	Bach	Damm	See	Insel	Schleuse	Stausee	Naturpark
ESPAÑOL	riachuelo	presa	lago	isla	esclusa	embalse	parque provincial
FRANÇAIS	critique	represa	lac	île	écluse	barrage	parque provincial
PORTUGUÊS	riacho	represa	lago	ilha	eclusa	reservatório	parque estadual

Copyright © by Rand McNally & Co.
Made in U.S.A.
A-300077-264

Kilometers
Statute Miles
Mi.
Km.

Scale 1:1,000,000

One centimeter represents 10 kilometers.
One inch represents approximately 16 miles.
Lambert Conformal Conic Projection

ENGLISH	bay	canal	cape cr.	creek, cr.	inlet	lake l.	key	island	cape	swamp
DEUTSCH	Bucht	Kanal	Kap	Bach	Einfahrt	See	Klippe	Insel	Kap	Sumpf
ESPAÑOL	bahía	canal	cabo	riachuelo	abra	lago	cayo	isla	cabo	pantano
FRANÇAIS	baie	canal	cap	cr.	bras de mer	lac	cayo	île	cap	marais
PORTUGUÊS	baía	canal	cabo	riacho	ensenada	lago	recife	ilha	cabo	pântano

ATLANTIC   OCEAN

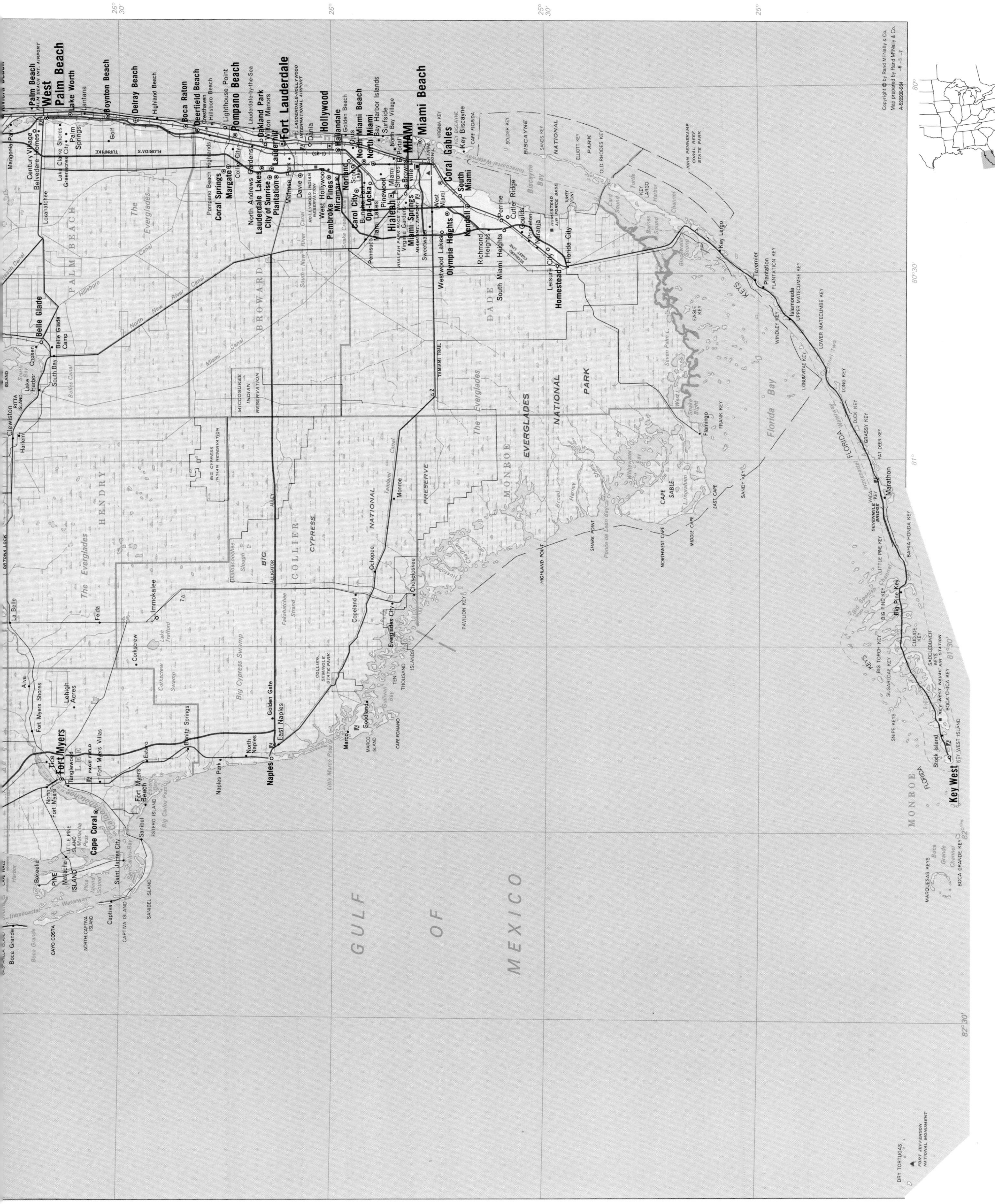
West Palm Beach
Palm Beach
Lake Worth
Lantana
Boynton Beach
Delray Beach
Highland Beach
Boca Raton
Deerfield Beach
Pompano Beach
Lighthouse Point
Fort Lauderdale
Oakland Park
Wilton Manors
Lauderdale Lakes
City of Sunrise
Plantation
Coral Springs
Margate
Hollywood
Hallandale
Dania
Davie
Miramar
Pembroke Pines
West Hollywood
North Miami Beach
North Miami
Miami Beach
MIAMI
Coral Gables
Hialeah
Opa-Locka
Carol City
Miami Springs
Kendall
South Miami
Key Biscayne
Perrine
Cutler Ridge
Goulds
Naranja
Homestead
Florida City
Leisure City
Olympia Heights
Westwood Lakes
Richmond Heights
South Miami Heights
Sweetwater
Key Largo
Tavernier
Plantation
Islamorada
Marathon
Big Pine Key
Stock Island
Key West
Flamingo
Belle Glade
Clewiston
Immokalee
Felda
La Belle
Corkscrew
Naples
North Naples
East Naples
Naples Park
Golden Gate
Bonita Springs
Estero
Fort Myers
Fort Myers Beach
Fort Myers Shores
North Fort Myers
Lehigh Acres
Cape Coral
Sanibel
Captiva
Bokeelia
Saint James City
Boca Grande
Everglades City
Chokoloskee
Copeland
Ochopee
Monroe
Marco
Goodland
PALM BEACH
BROWARD
DADE
HENDRY
COLLIER
MONROE
LEE
EVERGLADES NATIONAL PARK
BIG CYPRESS NATIONAL PRESERVE
BISCAYNE NATIONAL PARK
Florida Bay
GULF OF MEXICO
FLORIDA KEYS
TAMIAMI TRAIL
The Everglades
Big Cypress Swamp
DRY TORTUGAS
FORT JEFFERSON NATIONAL MONUMENT
MARQUESAS KEYS
Copyright © by Rand McNally & Co.

DALLAS
Fort Worth
Waco
Tyler
Longview
Nacogdoches
Lufkin
Palestine
Corsicana
Athens
Denton
McKinney
Greenville
Sulphur Springs
Mount Pleasant
Jacksonville
Kilgore
Henderson
Terrell
Ennis
Waxahachie
Cleburne
Weatherford
Hillsboro
Mexia
Garland
Irving
Arlington
Grand Prairie
Mesquite
Plano
Richardson
Killeen
Temple
Crockett
Fairfield
Kaufman
Canton
Mineola
Rusk
Marlin
Groesbeck
Gatesville
HARRISON
SMITH
RUSK
CHEROKEE
NACOGDOCHES
ANGELINA
HOUSTON
ANDERSON
HENDERSON
VAN ZANDT
KAUFMAN
DALLAS
TARRANT
PARKER
WISE
DENTON
COLLIN
HUNT
HOPKINS
FRANKLIN
TITUS
CAMP
UPSHUR
WOOD
RAINS
ROCKWALL
ELLIS
JOHNSON
HILL
NAVARRO
FREESTONE
LIMESTONE
LEON
MCLENNAN
BOSQUE
CORYELL
FALLS
TRINITY
MORRIS
CASS
MARION
GREGG
PANOLA
SOMERVELL
HOOD
FORT HOOD

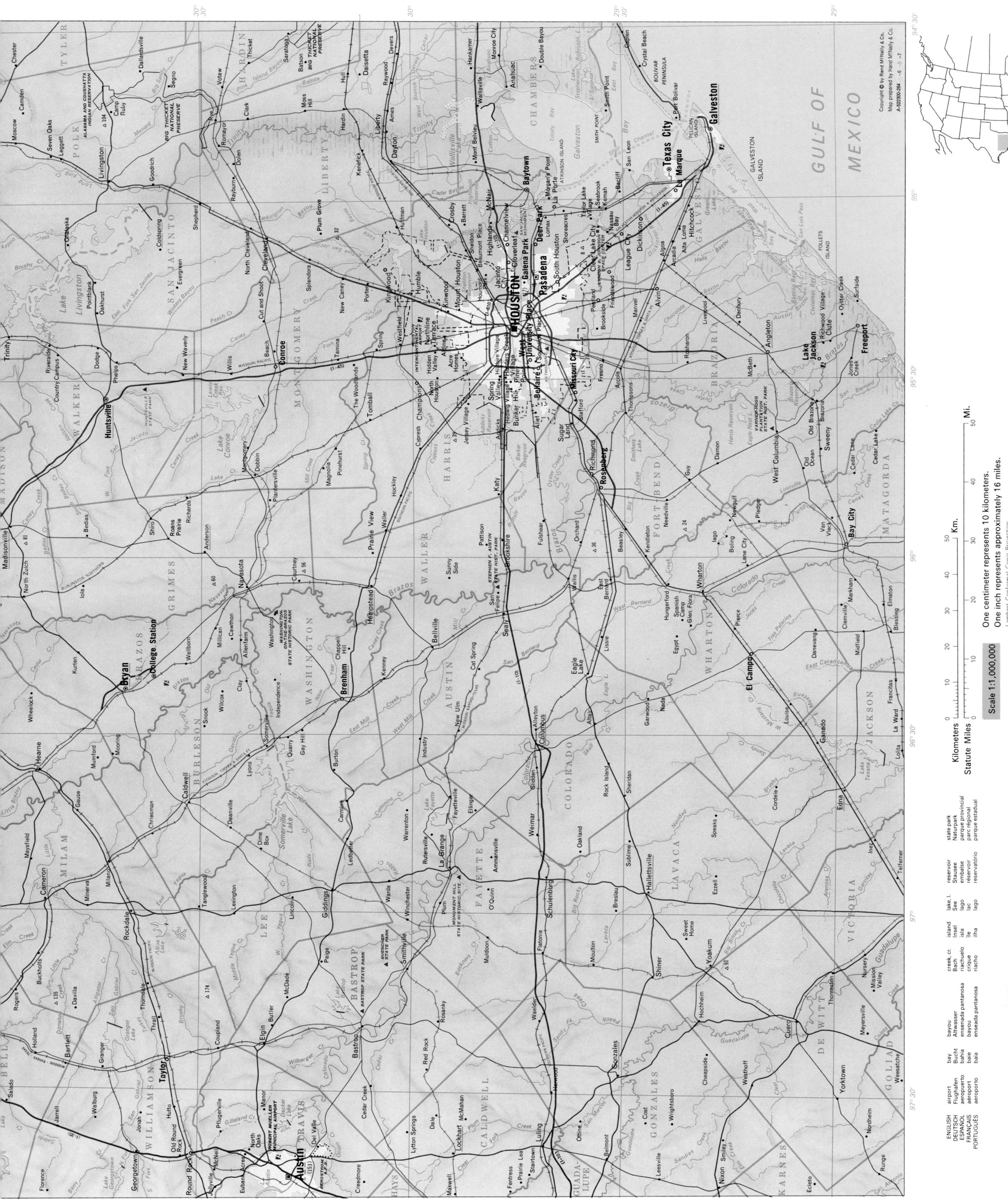

One centimeter represents 10 kilometers.
One inch represents approximately 16 miles.
Lambert Conformal Conic Projection

Scale 1:1,000,000

Kilometers

Statute Miles

ENGLISH	airport	bay	bayou	creek, cr.	island	lake, l.	reservoir	state park
DEUTSCH	Flughafen	Bucht	Altwasser	Bach	Insel	See	Stausee	Naturpark
ESPAÑOL	aeropuerto	bahía	ensenada pantanosa	riachuelo	isla	lago	embalse	parque provincial
FRANÇAIS	aéroport	baie	bayou	crique	île	lac	réservoir	parc provincial
PORTUGUÊS	aeroporto	baía	ensada pantanosa	riacho	ilha	lago	reservatório	parque estadual

VANCOUVER
New Westminster
Burnaby
North Vancouver
Richmond
Victoria
Nanaimo
Bellingham
Mount Vernon
Everett
SEATTLE
Bremerton
Tacoma
Port Angeles
Strait of Georgia
Strait of Juan de Fuca
CANADA
UNITED STATES
BRITISH COLUMBIA
WASHINGTON
CASCADE MOUNTAINS
OLYMPIC MOUNTAINS
VANCOUVER ISLAND RANGES
SEYMOUR RANGE

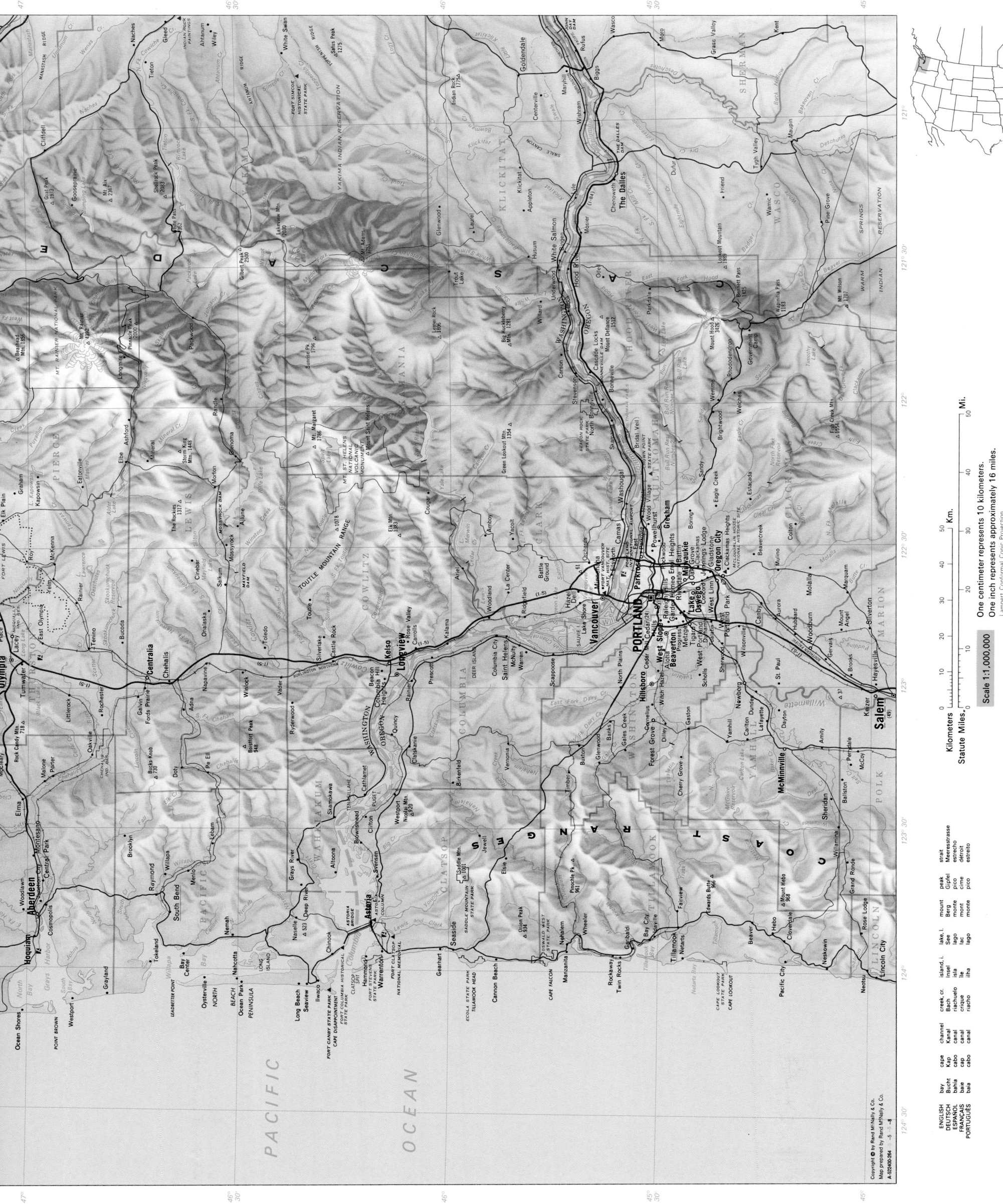

ENGLISH	bay	cape	channel	creek, cr.	island, i.	lake, l.	mount	peak	strait
DEUTSCH	Bucht	Kap	Kanal	Bach	inset	See	Berg	Gipfel	Meeresstrasse
ESPAÑOL	bahia	cabo	canal	riachuelo	isla	lago	monte	pico	estrecho
FRANÇAIS	baie	cap	canal	crique	île	lac	mont	cime	détroit
PORTUGUÊS	baia	cabo	canal	riacho	ilha	lago	monte	pico	estreito

Kilometers

One centimeter represents 10 kilometers.

Statute Miles

One inch represents approximately 16 miles.

Scale 1:1,000,000

Lambert Conformal Conic Projection

Reno · Sparks · Sun Valley · Carson City · South Lake Tahoe · Lake Tahoe · Virginia City · Dayton · Minden · Gardnerville · Markleeville · Yerington

NEVADA · CALIFORNIA

SIERRA · NEVADA · PLACER · EL DORADO · AMADOR · CALAVERAS · TUOLUMNE · MARIPOSA

Truckee · Nevada City · Grass Valley · Auburn · Colfax · Placerville · Georgetown · Coloma · Diamond Springs · El Dorado · Jackson · San Andreas · Angels Camp · Sonora · Jamestown · Groveland · Mariposa

Downieville · Sierra City · Alleghany · Washington · Camptonville · North San Juan · Forest Hill

Oroville · South Oroville · Marysville · Yuba City · Gridley · Biggs · Live Oak · Sutter · Colusa · Williams · Maxwell · Princeton · Willows

BUTTE · SUTTER · YUBA · COLUSA · GLENN · SACRAMENTO VALLEY

Roseville · Citrus Heights · Orangevale · Fair Oaks · Rancho Cordova · Carmichael · Arden · Arcade · North Highlands · Sacramento · West Sacramento · Woodland · Davis · Dixon · Lincoln · Rocklin · Loomis · Folsom · Galt · Elk Grove · Lodi · Stockton · Manteca · Modesto · Oakdale · Riverbank · Ceres · Turlock · North Turlock

YOLO · SACRAMENTO · SAN JOAQUIN · STANISLAUS

Winters · Vacaville · Fairfield · Suisun City · Rio Vista · Antioch · Pittsburg · Tracy · Livermore · Pleasanton

SOLANO · CONTRA COSTA · ALAMEDA

Napa · St. Helena · Calistoga · Santa Rosa · Sonoma · Petaluma · Novato · San Rafael · Vallejo · Benicia · Martinez · Concord · Walnut Creek · Pleasant Hill · Lafayette · Orinda · Berkeley · Oakland · Alameda · San Leandro · Hayward · Union City · Fremont · Newark

SONOMA · NAPA · MARIN · SAN FRANCISCO

San Francisco · Daly City · Pacifica · South San Francisco · San Bruno · Millbrae · Burlingame · San Mateo · Foster City · Redwood City · Palo Alto · East Palo Alto · Half Moon Bay

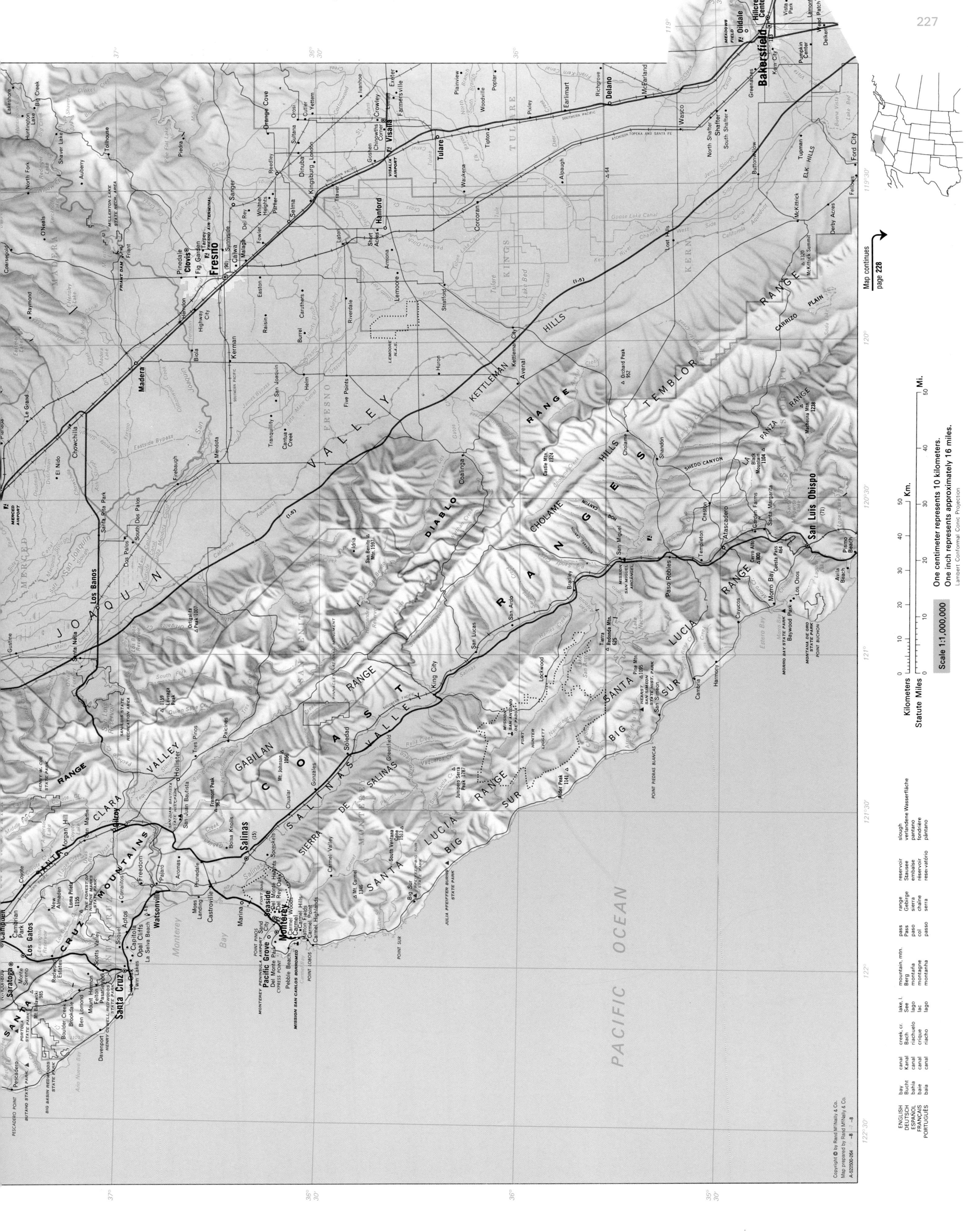

PACIFIC OCEAN

Fresno
Bakersfield
Visalia
Tulare
Hanford
Madera
Salinas
Santa Cruz
Monterey
San Luis Obispo
Los Gatos
Saratoga
Watsonville

COAST RANGE
DIABLO RANGE
GABILAN RANGE
SANTA LUCIA RANGE
BIG SUR
SALINAS VALLEY
SAN JOAQUIN VALLEY
FRESNO VALLEY
TEMBLOR RANGE
CHOLAME HILLS
KETTLEMAN HILLS
SANTA CRUZ MOUNTAINS
KINGS
KERN

Scale 1:1,000,000

One centimeter represents 10 kilometers.
One inch represents approximately 16 miles.

Lambert Conformal Conic Projection

Kilometers
Statute Miles

Map continues page 228

Copyright © by Rand McNally & Co.
Map prepared by Rand McNally & Co.

ENGLISH   DEUTSCH   ESPAÑOL   FRANÇAIS   PORTUGUÊS
bay   Bucht   bahía   baie   baía
canal   Kanal   canal   canal   canal
creek, cr.   Bach   riachuelo   crique   riacho
lake, l.   See   lago   lac   lago
mountain, mtn.   Berg   montaña   montagne   montanha
pass   Pass   paso   col   passo
range   Gebirge   sierra   chaîne   serra
reservoir   Stausee   embalse   réservoir   reservatório
slough   verlandene Wasserfläche   pantano   fondrière   pântano

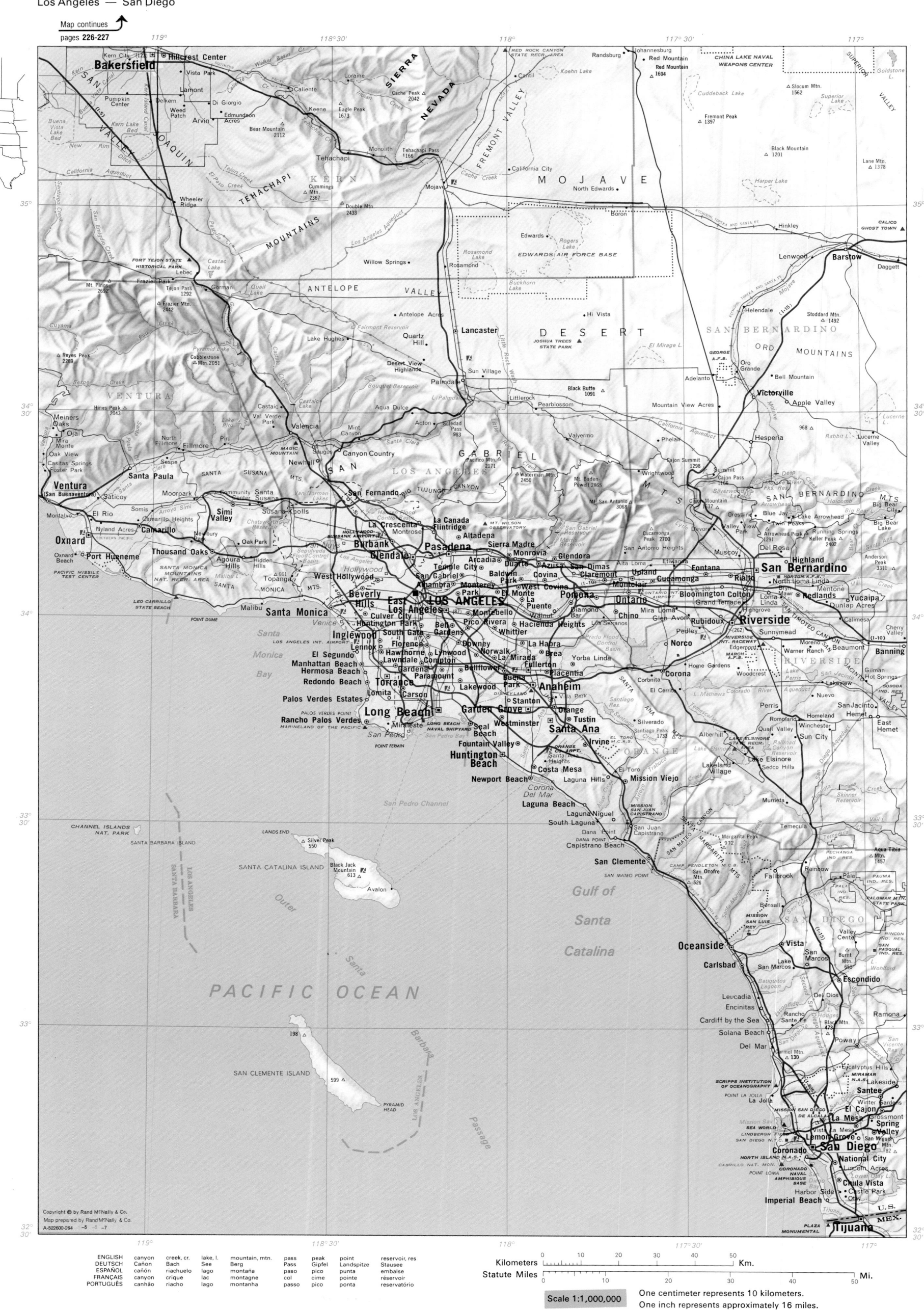

Map continues
pages 226-227

Copyright © by Rand McNally & Co.
Map prepared by Rand McNally & Co.
A-522600-264

ENGLISH	canyon	creek, cr.	lake, l.	mountain, mtn.	pass	peak	point	reservoir, res
DEUTSCH	Cañon	Bach	See	Berg	Pass	Gipfel	Landspitze	Stausee
ESPAÑOL	cañon	riachuelo	lago	montaña	paso	pico	punta	embalse
FRANÇAIS	canyon	crique	lac	montagne	col	cime	pointe	réservoir
PORTUGUÊS	canhão	riacho	lago	montanha	passo	pico	ponta	reservatório

Kilometers
Statute Miles

Scale 1:1,000,000

One centimeter represents 10 kilometers.
One inch represents approximately 16 miles.
Lambert Conformal Conic Projection

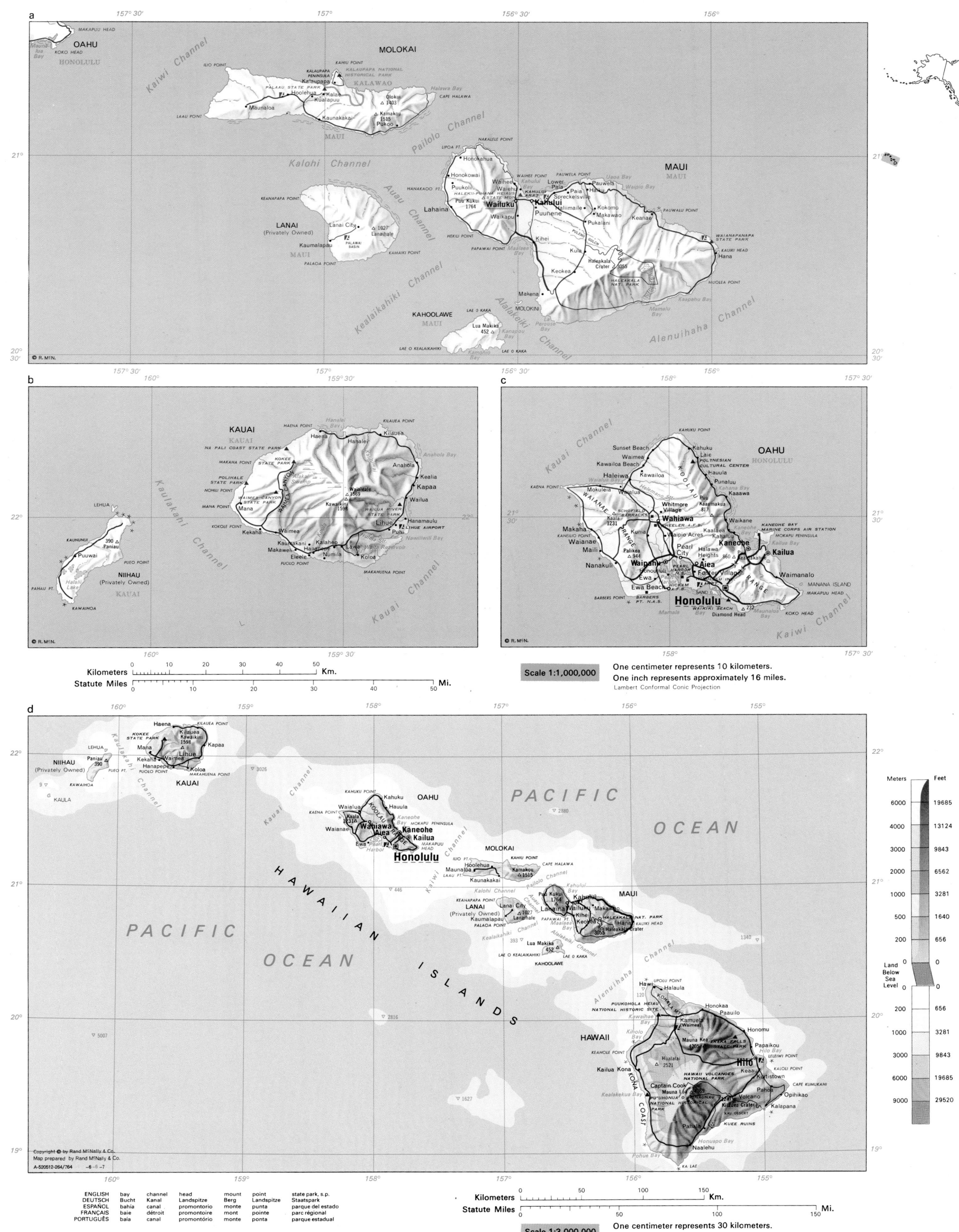

Scale 1:1,000,000
One centimeter represents 10 kilometers.
One inch represents approximately 16 miles.
Lambert Conformal Conic Projection

Scale 1:3,000,000
One centimeter represents 30 kilometers.
One inch represents approximately 47 miles.
Lambert Conformal Conic Projection

ENGLISH	bay	channel	head	mount	point	state park, s.p.
DEUTSCH	Bucht	Kanal	Landspitze	Berg	Landspitze	Staatspark
ESPAÑOL	bahía	canal	promontorio	monte	punta	parque del estado
FRANÇAIS	baie	détroit	promontoire	mont	pointe	parc régional
PORTUGUÊS	baía	canal	promontório	monte	ponta	parque estadual

Copyright © by Rand McNally & Co.
Map prepared by Rand McNally & Co.
A-520512-264/764 —6-6—7

230

Middle America / Mittelamerika / México, Centroamérica y Las Antillas
Mexique, Amérique Centrale et Région des Caraïbes / México, América Central e Antilhas

Map continues
pages **178-179**

ESPAÑOL	cabo	cordillera	golfo	isla, i.	lago, l.	punta	sierra	volcán, vol.
ENGLISH	cape	mountains	gulf	island	lake	point	mountains	volcano
DEUTSCH	Kap	Berge	Golf	Insel	See	Landspitze	Berge	Vulkan
FRANÇAIS	cap	montagnes	golfe	île	lac	pointe	montagnes	volcan
PORTUGUÊS	cabo	cordilheira	golfo	ilha	lago	ponta	serra	vulcão

Middle America / Mittelamerika / México, Centroamérica y Las Antillas
Mexique, Amérique Centrale et Région des Caraïbes / México, América Central e Antilhas

231

ATLANTIC OCEAN

BERMUDA
(U.K.)
Hamilton

Tropic of Cancer

WEST INDIES

BAHAMAS

Nassau

CUBA

La Habana Havana
Matanzas
Cárdenas
Pinar del Río
Santa Clara
Cienfuegos
Sancti Spíritus
Ciego de Avila
Camagüey
Holguín
Bayamo
Manzanillo
Santiago de Cuba
Guantánamo

ISLA DE LA
JUVENTUD

GREATER

CAYMAN IS.
(U.K.)

JAMAICA
Montego Bay
Kingston

HAITI
Port-au-Prince

HISPANIOLA

DOMINICAN
REPUBLIC
Santiago
Santo Domingo

San Juan

PUERTO
RICO (U.S.)

VIRGIN
ISLANDS

ANGUILLA (U.K.)
SAINT-MARTIN (Guad. and Neth. Ant.)

ANTIGUA
AND
BARBUDA
Saint Johns

SAINT
CHRISTOPHER-
NEVIS

MONTSERRAT (U.K.)

GUADELOUPE (Fr.)

DOMINICA
Roseau

ANTILLES

MARTINIQUE
(Fr.)
Fort-de-France
Castries
SAINT LUCIA

BARBADOS
Bridgetown

SAINT
VINCENT
AND THE
GRENADINES
Kingstown

GRENADA
Saint George's

CARIBBEAN SEA

LESSER

TRINIDAD
AND
TOBAGO
Port-of-Spain

ARUBA
(Neth.)
Oranjestad

NETHERLANDS
ANTILLES
Willemstad

NICARAGUA

COSTA
RICA
San José

PANAMA
Colón

COLOMBIA

Barranquilla
Cartagena
Santa Marta
Maracaibo
Cabimas

VENEZUELA
CARACAS
Valencia
Barquisimeto
Maracay
Barcelona
Cumaná
Ciudad Bolívar
Ciudad Guayana

Medellín
Manizales
Pereira
Cartago
Armenia
BOGOTÁ
Cali
Buenaventura

LA GRAN
SABANA

GUYANA

PAKARAIMA
MTS.

BRAZIL

Map continues
pages 242-243

Kilometers
0   200   400   600   Km.

Statute Miles
0   200   400   600   Mi.

Scale 1:12,000,000
One centimeter represents 120 kilometers.
One inch represents approximately 190 miles.
Oblique Conic Conformal Projection

Mexico / Mexiko / México
Mexique / México

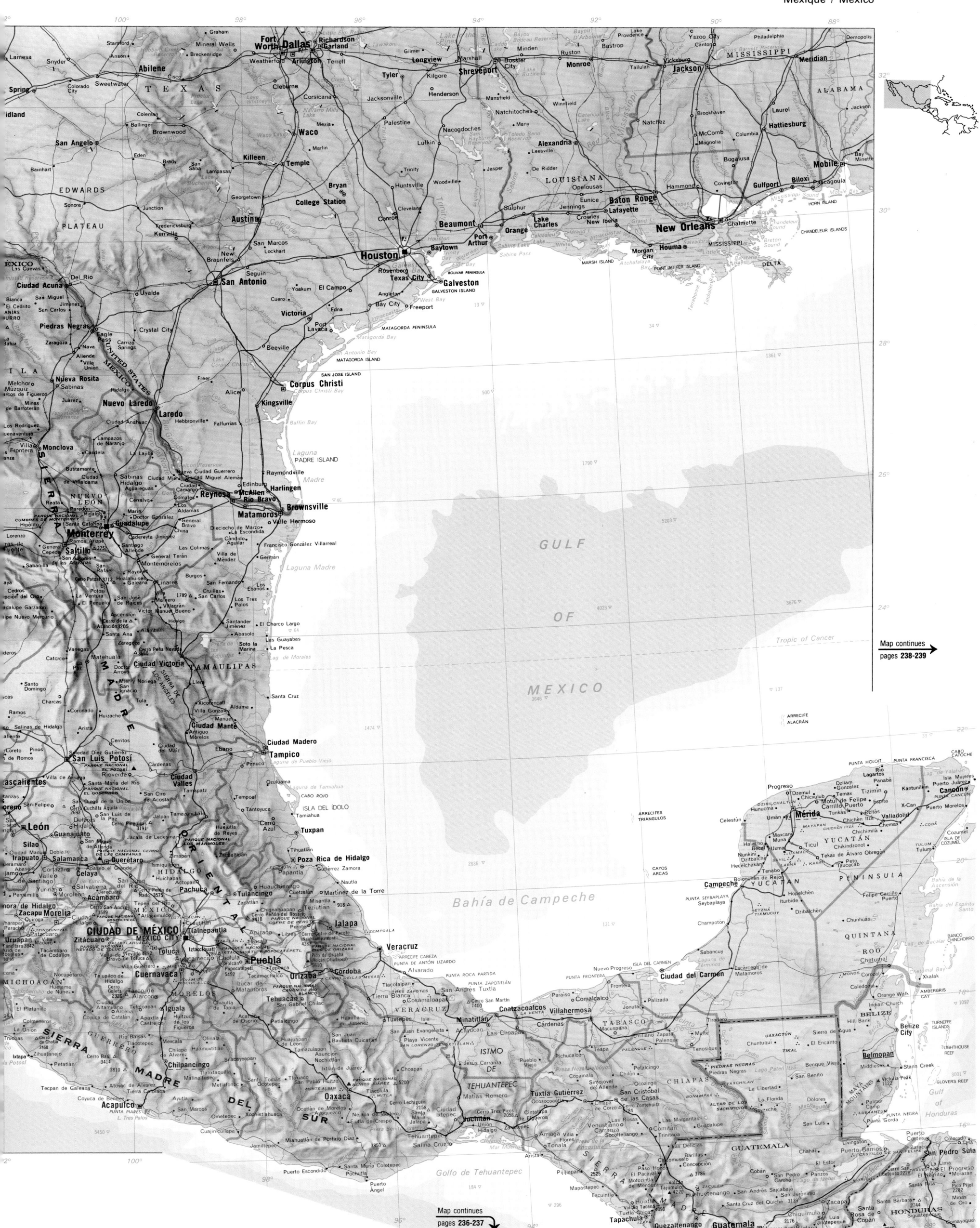

GULF

OF

MEXICO

Bahía de Campeche

Golfo de Tehuantepec

Map continues
pages 238-239 ➜

Map continues
pages 236-237 ⬇

Central Mexico / Mittelmexiko / México Central
Mexique Central / México Central

Map continues
pages 232-233

PACIFIC OCEAN

Major cities and features (selection):

Durango, Mazatlán, Villa Unión, Fresnillo, Zacatecas, Aguascalientes, San Luis Potosí, Matehuala, Tepic, Puerto Vallarta, GUADALAJARA, Tlaquepaque, Zapopan, León, Guanajuato, San Miguel de Allende, Irapuato, Salamanca, Querétaro, Celaya, Lagos de Moreno, Colima, Manzanillo, Tecomán, Ciudad Guzmán, Zamora de Hidalgo, Sahuayo, La Piedad, Morelia, Uruapan, Apatzingán, Zitácuaro, Ciudad Hidalgo, Pátzcuaro, Zacapu, Acámbaro, Moroleón, Taxco de Alarcón, Iguala, Chilpancingo, Zihuatanejo, Acapulco

Scale:

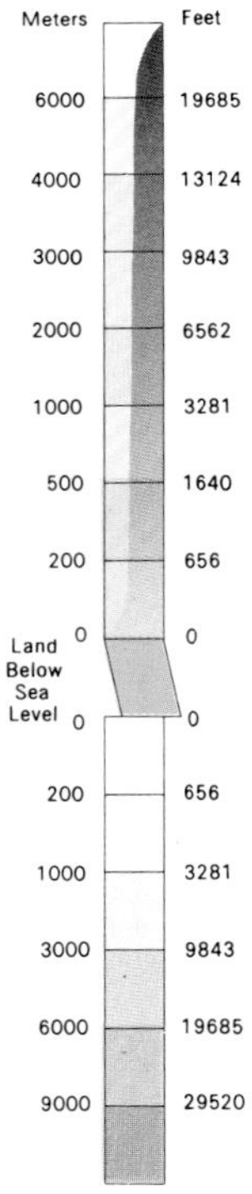

Meters	Feet
6000	19685
4000	13124
3000	9843
2000	6562
1000	3281
500	1640
200	656
Land Below Sea Level 0	0
200	656
1000	3281
3000	9843
6000	19685
9000	29520

Copyright © by Rand McNally & Co.
Map prepared by Rand McNally & Co.
A-531606-764

ESPAÑOL	ENGLISH	DEUTSCH	FRANÇAIS	PORTUGUÊS
arroyo	brook	Bach	ruisseau	riacho
boca	entrance	Einfahrt	entrée	entrada
cerro	butte	Restberg	butte	cerro
lago	lake	See	lac	lago
laguna	lagoon	Haff	lagune	laguna
punta	point	Landspitze	pointe	ponta
río	river	Fluss	rivière	rio
sierra	ranges	Bergketten	chaîne	serra
volcán	volcano	Vulkan	volcan	vulcão

GULF OF

MEXICO

Bahía de Campeche

Tropic of Cancer

Ciudad
Victoria

SIERRA

Ciudad Mante

Tampico

Ciudad Madero

Ciudad
Valles

Poza Rica
de Hidalgo

Papantla

Tuxpan

Pachuca

Tulancingo

Teziutlán

Jalapa

CIUDAD DE MÉXICO

MEXICO CITY

Puebla

Veracruz

Córdoba

Orizaba
Ciudad
Mendoza

Tehuacán

Tierra Blanca

San Andrés Tuxtla

Cosamaloapan

Coatzacoalcos

Minatitlán

Villahermosa

Izúcar de
Matamoros

Oaxaca

Tuxtla
Gutiérrez

San
Cristóbal de
las Casas

Juchitán

Salina
Cruz

ISTMO DE
VERACRUZ

OAXACA
TEHUANTEPEC

Golfo de
Tehuantepec

Map continues
pages 232-233

Map continues
pages 236-237

Kilometers   0   50   100   150   Km.

Statute Miles   0   50   100   150   Mi.

Scale 1:3,000,000

One centimeter represents 30 kilometers.
One inch represents approximately 47 miles.
Lambert Conformal Conic Projection

Map continues pages 232-233

Map continues pages 234-235

PETÉN

MÉXICO
GUATEMALA
MÉXICO

BELIZE

Gulf of Honduras

ISLA DE ROATÁN
ISLAS DE LA BAHÍA

CHIAPAS

SIERRA MADRE

ALTA VERAPAZ

QUICHÉ

HUEHUETENANGO

SIERRA DE LOS CUCHUMATANES

Puerto Cortés
Puerto Barrios

San Pedro Sula
El Progreso

HONDURAS

SANTA BÁRBARA

ATLÁNTIDA
La Ceiba

CORDILLERA NOMBRE DE DIOS

TOTONICAPÁN

BAJA VERAPAZ

SIERRA DE LAS MINAS

Tapachula

Quezaltenango
QUEZALTENANGO

SOLOLÁ

CHIMALTENANGO

Guatemala

Escuintla

ZACAPA
Zacapa

COPÁN
Santa Rosa de Copán

CHIQUIMULA

OCOTEPEQUE

COMAYAGUA
Comayagua

INTIBUCÁ

FRANCISCO MORAZÁN

Tegucigalpa
EL PARAÍSO

SUCHITEPÉQUEZ

RETALHULEU

ESCUINTLA

SANTA ROSA

JUTIAPA

JALAPA

Santa Ana
Chalchuapa

Ahuachapán

EL SALVADOR

LEMPIRA

LA PAZ

Sonsonate

Nueva San Salvador
San Salvador

San Vicente

San Miguel

VALLE

La Unión

CHOLUTECA
Choluteca

ESTELÍ
Estelí

MADRIZ

NUEVA SEGOVIA

Bahía de Jiquilisco

Golfo de Fonseca

CHINANDEGA

El Viejo
Chinandega

Corinto

León
LEÓN

Lago de Managua

Managua

Masaya

CARAZO

PACIFIC

OCEAN

Meters	Feet
6000	19685
4000	13124
3000	9843
2000	6562
1000	3281
500	1640
200	656
0	0
Land Below Sea Level 0	0
200	656
1000	3281
3000	9843
6000	19685
9000	29520

ESPAÑOL	bahía	cerro	cordillera	isla	lago	laguna	punta	sierra	volcán
ENGLISH	bay	mountain	mountains	island	lake	lagoon	point	mountains	volcano
DEUTSCH	Bucht	Berg	Berge	Insel	See	Haff	Landspitze	Berge	Vulkan
FRANÇAIS	baie	montagne	montagnes	île	lac	lagune	pointe	montagnes	volcan
PORTUGUÊS	baía	cerro	cordilheira	ilha	lago	laguna	ponta	serra	vulcão

Kilometers

Km.

Statute Miles

Mi.

Scale 1:3,000,000

One centimeter represents 30 kilometers.
One inch represents approximately 47 miles.
Lambert Conformal Conic Projection

Caribbean Region / Mittelamerikanische Inselwelt / Región del Caribe
Région des Caraïbes / Região do Caribe

Map continues
pages 232-233

Map continues
pages 236-237

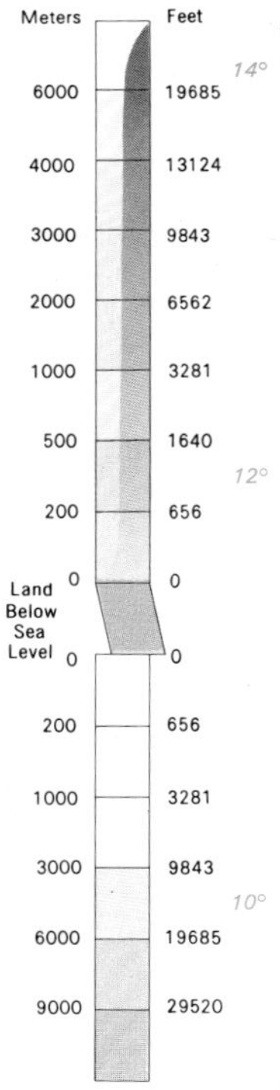

Meters	Feet
6000	19685
4000	13124
3000	9843
2000	6562
1000	3281
500	1640
200	656
Land Below Sea Level 0	0
0	0
200	656
1000	3281
3000	9843
6000	19685
9000	29520

Copyright © by Rand McNally & Co.
Map prepared by Rand McNally & Co.
A-530100-764   -7 -5 -17¹

MAP FORM	bahía	cabo	cerro	channel	golfo	isla	passage	pico	punta
ENGLISH	bay	cape	mountain	channel	gulf	isle	passage	peak	point
DEUTSCH	Bucht	Kap	Berg	Kanal	Golf	Insel	Durchfahrt	Gipfel	Landspitze
ESPAÑOL	bahía	cabo	cerro	canal	golfo	isla	pasaje	pico	punta
FRANÇAIS	baie	cap	montagne	détroit	golfe	île	passage	cime	pointe
PORTUGUÊS	baía	cabo	montanha	canal	golfo	ilha	passagem	pico	ponta

ATLANTIC

OCEAN

Tropic of Cancer

W E S T

I N D I E S

HAITI
HAÏTI

HISPANIOLA

DOMINICAN REPUBLIC
REPÚBLICA DOMINICANA

Santo
Domingo

Port-au-Prince

A N T I L L E S

C A R I B B E A N

S E A

PUERTO RICO

SAN
JUAN

VIRGIN ISLANDS

Charlotte
Amalie

Road Town

ANGUILLA

SAINT CHRISTOPHER-
NEVIS

Basseterre

MONTSERRAT
(U.K.)

ANTIGUA
AND
BARBUDA

Saint Johns

L E E W A R D   ISLANDS

GUADELOUPE
(Fr.)

Basse-Terre

Pointe-à-Pitre

GRANDE-TERRE

DOMINICA

Roseau

MARTINIQUE

Fort-de-France

SAINT LUCIA

Castries

SAINT VINCENT
AND THE
GRENADINES

Kings-
town

Bridgetown

BARBADOS

W I N D W A R D   ISLANDS

GRENADA

Saint George's

L E S S E R   A N T I L L E S

NETHERLANDS ANTILLES
NEDERLANDSE ANTILLEN

ARUBA
(Neth.)

Oranjestad

CURAÇAO

Willemstad

BONAIRE

Kralendijk

TRINIDAD

Port of Spain

AND

TOBAGO

TOBAGO

Scarborough

PENÍNSULA DE
LA GUAJIRA

LA GUAJIRA

COLOMBIA

VENEZUELA

Maracaibo

Lago de
Maracaibo

ZULIA

CARACAS

Barquisimeto

Valencia

Maracay

FALCÓN

LARA

SUCRE

MONAGAS

ORINOCO

AMACURO

DELTA

TURKS AND CAICOS ISLANDS
(U.K.)

Map continues
pages 246-247

Kilometers
Statute Miles
0 100 200 300 Km.
0 100 200 300 Mi.

Scale 1:6,000,000

One centimeter represents 60 kilometers.
One inch represents approximately 95 miles.
Lambert Conformal Conic Projection

Islands of the West Indies / Westindische Inseln / Islas de las Antillas
Îles des Antilles / Ilhas do Caribe (Índias Ocidentais)

a — BERMUDA (U.K.)

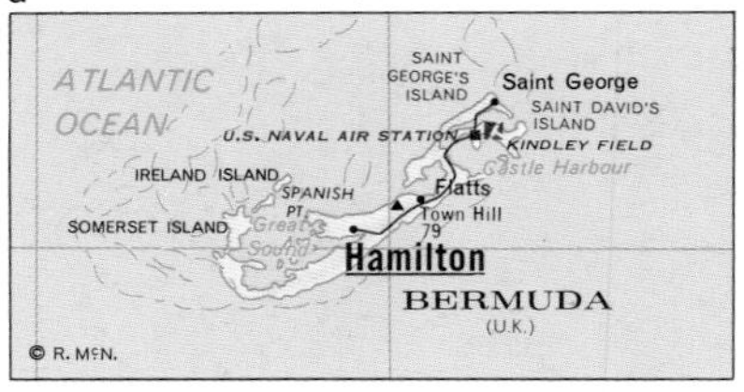

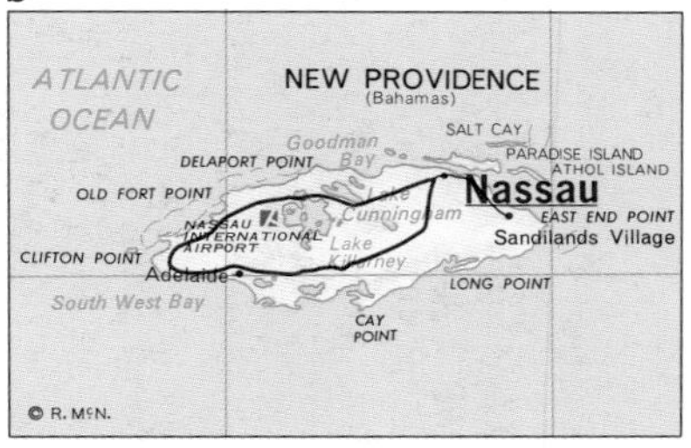

ATLANTIC OCEAN
SAINT GEORGE'S ISLAND
SAINT DAVID'S ISLAND
Saint George
U.S. NAVAL AIR STATION
KINDLEY FIELD
Castle Harbour
IRELAND ISLAND
SPANISH POINT
SOMERSET ISLAND
Platts
Hamilton
Town Hill

b — NEW PROVIDENCE (Bahamas)

ATLANTIC OCEAN
DELAPORT POINT
SALT CAY
PARADISE ISLAND
ATHOL ISLAND
Goodman Bay
OLD FORT POINT
NASSAU INTERNATIONAL AIRPORT
Nassau
EAST END POINT
Sandilands Village
CLIFTON POINT
Adelaide
LONG POINT
South West Bay
CAY POINT

c — ANTIGUA AND BARBUDA

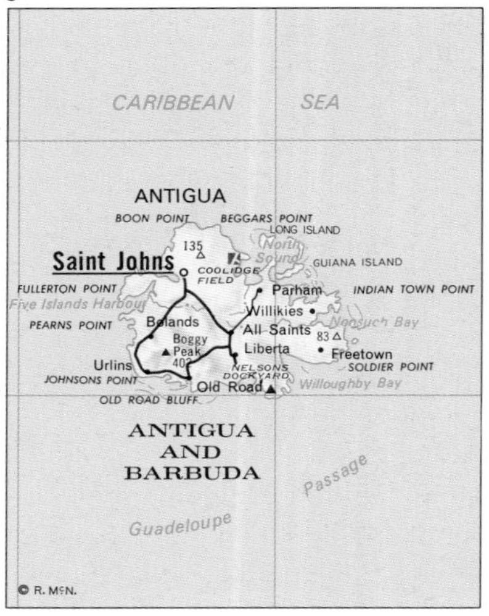

CARIBBEAN SEA
ANTIGUA
BOON POINT
BEGGARS POINT
LONG ISLAND
GUIANA ISLAND
Saint Johns
Parham
INDIAN TOWN POINT
FULLERTON POINT
COOLIDGE FIELD
Willikies
Five Islands Harbour
PEARNS POINT
Bolands
All Saints
Liberta
Boggy Peak
Freetown
SOLDIER POINT
Urlins
OLD ROAD BLUFF
Old Road
WILLOUGHBY BAY
JOHNSONS POINT
Passage
Guadeloupe

d — DOMINICA

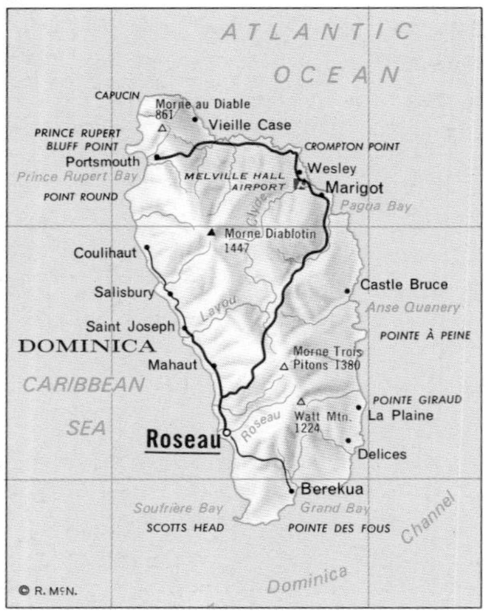

ATLANTIC OCEAN
CAPUCIN
Morne au Diable
Vieille Case
PRINCE RUPERT BLUFF POINT
Portsmouth
CROMPTON POINT
Prince Rupert Bay
MELVILLE HALL AIRPORT
Wesley
POINT ROUND
Marigot
Pagua Bay
Coulihaut
Salisbury
Castle Bruce
Saint Joseph
Anse Quanery
Morne Diablotin 1447
Mahaut
Pointe À Peine
Roseau
Morne Trois Pitons 1386
Pointe Giraud
La Plaine
Watt Mtn. 1224
Delices
Berekua
Soufrière Bay
SCOTTS HEAD
POINTE DES FOUS
CARIBBEAN SEA

e — MARTINIQUE (Fr.)

Dominica Channel
CAP SAINT-MARTIN
Grand' Rivière
POINTE DE MACOUBA
Le Prêcheur
Basse-Pointe
Le Lorrain
Montagne Pelée 1397
Sainte-Marie
POINTE TÉNOS
POINTE LA MARE
Morne-Rouge
Saint-Pierre
Morne Jacob 868
La Trinité
POINTE DU DIABLE
PRESQU'ÎLE DE LA CARAVELLE
POINTE DE LA BATTERIE
Le Carbet
Pitons du Carbet 1196
Gros-Morne
Le Robert
Bellefontaine
Saint-Joseph
Case-Pilote
Le Lamentin
Fort-de-France
POINTE DES NÈGRES
FORT-DE-FRANCE/LE LAMENTIN AÉROPORT
504
Le Vauclin
François
MARTINIQUE
Trois-Îlets
CAP SALOMON
Rivière-Salée
Saint-Esprit
Morne Bigot 460
Les Anses-d'Arlet
Le Diamant
Rivière-Pilote
Saint-Luce
Le Marin
POINTE DU DIAMANT
POINTE BORGNESSE
Sainte-Anne
Sainte-Luce
CARIBBEAN SEA
POINTE DES SALINES
POINTE D'ENFER
Saint Lucia Channel

m — PUERTO RICO

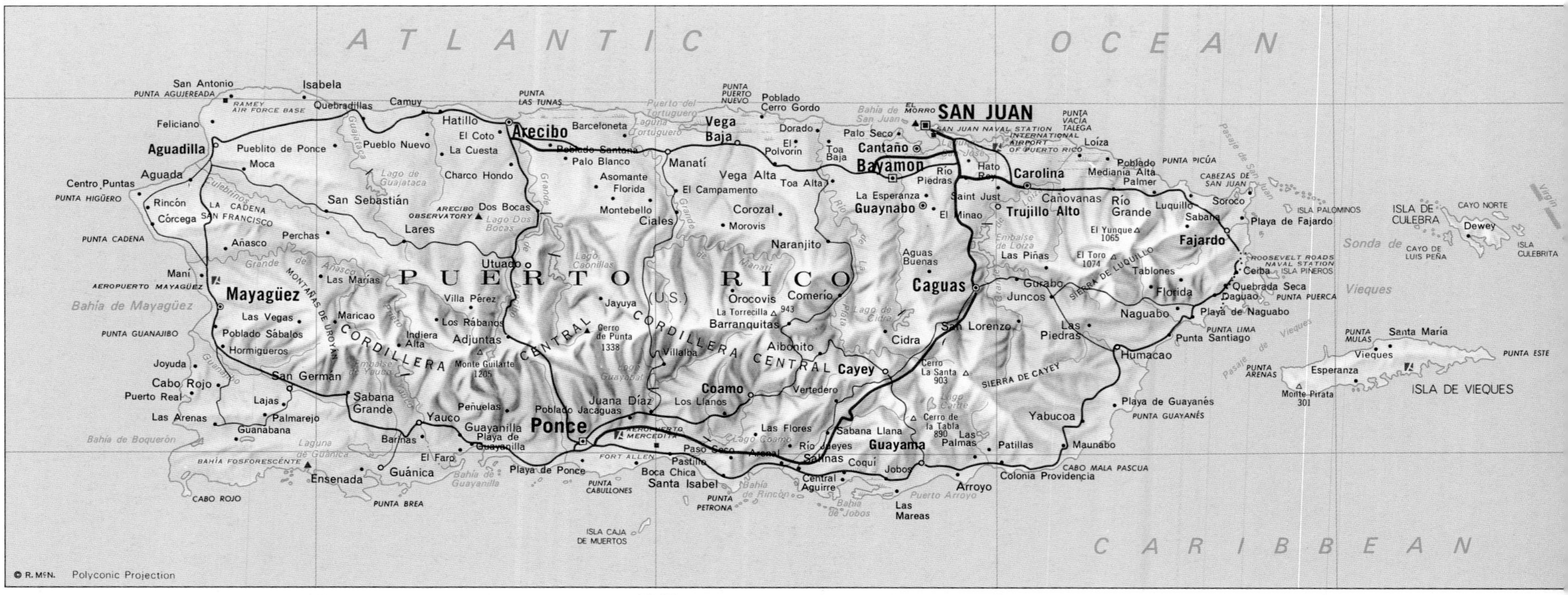

ATLANTIC OCEAN
San Antonio
Isabela
Quebradillas
Camuy
Punta Las Tunas
Poblado Cerro Gordo
PUNTA AGUJEREADA
RAMEY AIR FORCE BASE
Hatillo
Barceloneta
Vega Baja
Dorado
SAN JUAN
PUNTA VACIA TALEGA
Feliciano
Arecibo
Toa Baja
Cantaño
Loíza
Aguadilla
Pueblito de Ponce
El Coto
La Cuesta
Palo Seco
El Polvorín
Bayamon
Río Piedras
Hato Rey
Carolina
Poblado Mediania Alta
PUNTA PICÚA
Aguada
Pueblo Nuevo
Charco Hondo
Manatí
Vega Alta
Toa Alta
Guaynabo
Trujillo Alto
Río Grande
Luquillo
Sabana
CABEZAS DE SAN JUAN
Centro-Puntas
Rincón
Córcega
Moca
San Sebastián
Asomante
Florida
Montebello
Corozal
El Minao
Las Piñas
El Yunque 1065
Soroco
ISLA PALOMINOS
ISLA DE CULEBRA
PUNTA HIGÜERO
Añasco
Perchas
Lares
Dos Bocas
ARECIBO OBSERVATORY 320
Ciales
Morovis
Naranjito
Aguas Buenas
El Toro 1074
Fajardo
Sabana
Ceiba
PUNTA PUERCA
Dewey
PUNTA CADENA
LA CADENA DE SAN FRANCISCO
Utuado
El Campamento
Orocovis
Comerío
Caguas
Florida
Quebrada Seca
Daguao
ISLA CULEBRITA
Mani
Las Marias
PUERTO RICO
Jayuya
Cidra
San Lorenzo
Naguabo
Playa de Naguabo
Mayagüez
Las Vegas
Villa Pérez
La Torrecilla 941
Barranquitas
Aibonito
Las Piedras
Humacao
Punta Santiago
PUNTA ESTE
Santa María
Vieques
Marícao
Poblado Sábalos
Indiera Alta
Los Rábanos
Cerro de Punta 1338
CORDILLERA CENTRAL
Villalba
Cayey
CERRO DE CAYEY
Yabucoa
Playa de Guayanés
Esperanza
ISLA DE VIEQUES
Joyuda
Hormigueros
Monte Guilarte 1205
Coamo
Los Llanos
SIERRA DE CAYEY
Monte Pirata 301
PUNTA ARENAS
Cabo Rojo
San German
Juana Díaz
Vertedero
Sabana Llana
Guayama
Maunabo
Puerto Real
Lajas
Sabana Grande
Poblado Jacaguas
Cerro La Santa 903
Patillas
Las Arenas
Yauco
Barinas
Peñuelas
Ponce
Las Flores
Río Reyes
Coquí
Guayama
Arroyo
Colonia Providencia
CABO MALA PASCUA
Guanabana
El Faro
Guayanilla
Playa de Ponce
Santa Isabel
Salinas
Central Aguirre
Las Mareas
Ensenada
Guánica
Playa de Guayanilla
Boca Chica
Jobos
Bahía de Jobos
CABO ROJO
PUNTA BREA
Bahía Fosforescente
Laguna Guánica
PUNTA CABULLONES
PUNTA PETRONA
Puerto Arroyo
ISLA CAJA DE MUERTOS
Bahía de Rincón
CARIBBEAN
Bahía de Mayagüez
Bahía de Boquerón
Lago Guayabal
Sonda de Vieques
Polyconic Projection

p — CUBA

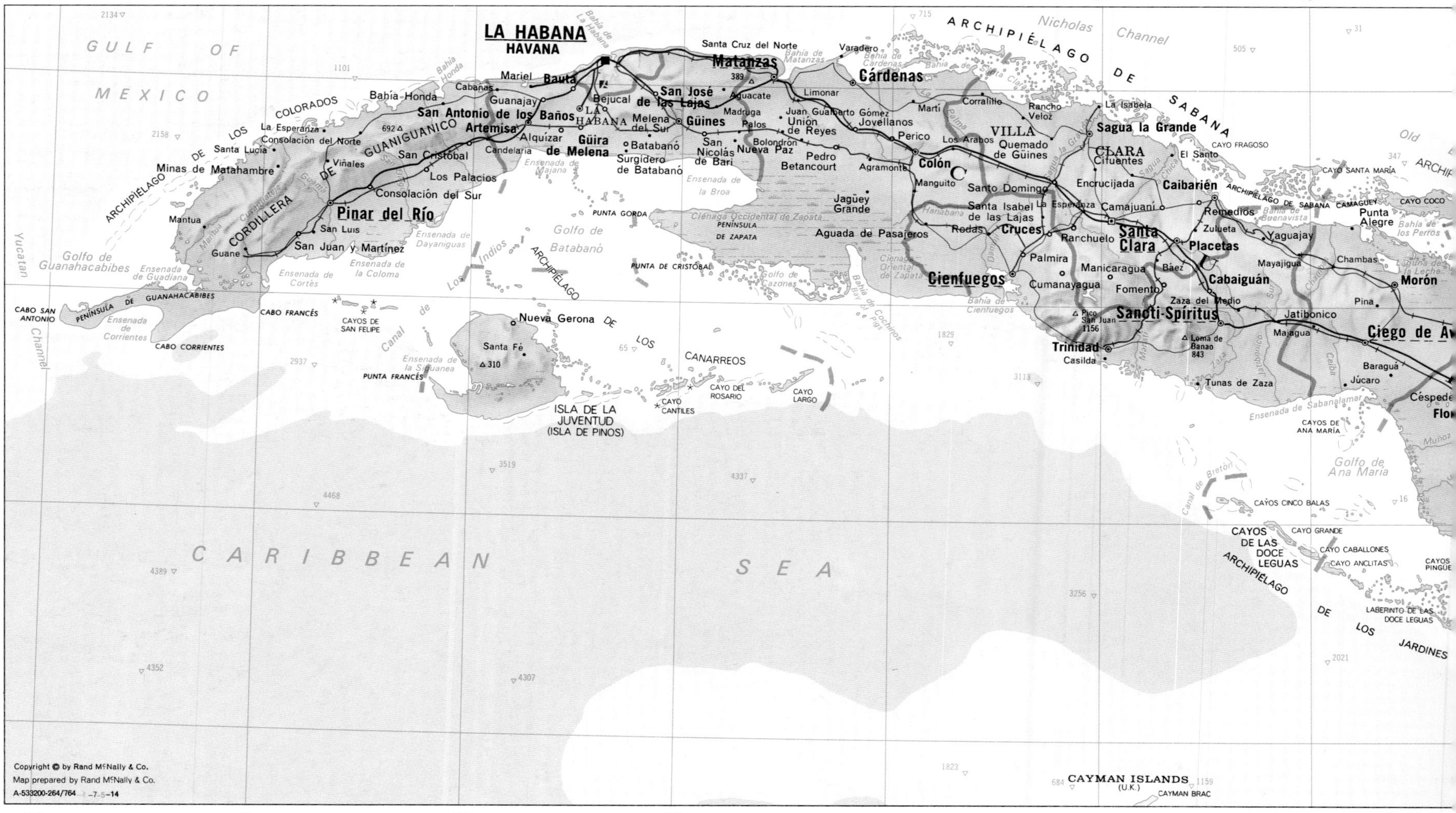

GULF OF MEXICO
LA HABANA / HAVANA
Mariel
Bauta
Santa Cruz del Norte
Varadero
Matanzas
Cárdenas
ARCHIPIÉLAGO DE SABANA
Nicholas Channel
Bahía Honda
Cabañas
Guanajay
Guanabo
San José de las Lajas
Aguacate
Limonar
Corralillo
Rancho Veloz
La Isabela
Sagua la Grande
COLORADOS
La Esperanza
Consolación del Norte
Bejucal
Artemisa
Madruga
Jovellanos
Quemado de Güines
El Santo
CAYO FRAGOSO
San Antonio de los Baños
Güira de Melena
Güines
Unión de Reyes
Perico
Los Arabos
Encrucijada
Caibarién
ARCHIPIÉLAGO DE SABANA
Minas de Matahambre
Santa Lucía
Viñales
San Cristóbal
Alquízar
Melena del Sur
San Nicolás de Bari
Pedro Betancourt
Manguito
Santo Domingo
Camajuaní
Remedios
Zulueta
Yaguajay
Punta Alegre
CAMAGUEY
ARCHIPIÉLAGO DE CAMAGÜEY
Mantua
CORDILLERA DE LOS
Pinar del Río
Candelaria
Surgidero de Batabanó
Jagüey Grande
Aguada de Pasajeros
Santa Isabel de las Lajas
La Esperanza
Rodas
Cruces
Ranchuelo
Palmira
Santa Clara
Placetas
VILLA CLARA
Cifuentes
Esperanza
Mayajigua
Chambas
Morón
Guane
San Luis
Los Palacios
Consolación del Sur
Batabanó
Bolondrón
Agramonte
Colón
Manicaragua
Báez
Cabaiguán
Pina
Guala
San Juan y Martínez
PUNTA GORDA
Nueva Paz
Jagüey
PUNTA DE CRISTÓBAL
Cienfuegos
Cumanayagua
Fomento
Zaza del Medio
Jatibonico
Ciego de Ávila
Nueva Gerona
Santa Fé 310
Trinidad
Casilda
Sancti Spíritus 1156
Loma de Banao 843
Casilda
Tunas de Zaza
Júcaro
Baraguá
Céspedes
Flo
ISLA DE LA JUVENTUD (ISLA DE PINOS)
CAYOS DE SAN FELIPE
CANARREOS
CAYO DEL ROSARIO
CAYO LARGO
CABO SAN ANTONIO
PENÍNSULA DE GUANAHACABIBES
CABO FRANCÉS
CABO CORRIENTES
PUNTA FRANCÉS
Golfo de Batabanó
Golfo de Ana María
Golfo de Guacanayabo
CAYOS DE ANA MARÍA
CAYOS CINCO BALAS
CAYO GRANDE
CAYO CABALLONES
CAYOS PINGÜE
CAYOS DE LAS DOCE LEGUAS
ARCHIPIÉLAGO DE LOS JARDINES
LABERINTO DE LAS DOCE LEGUAS
CARIBBEAN SEA
CAYMAN ISLANDS (U.K.)
GRAND CAYMAN BRAC
Yucatan Channel
Golfo de Guanahacabibes
PENÍNSULA DE GUANAHACABIBES
Ensenada de la Broa
CIÉNAGA OCCIDENTAL DE ZAPATA
PENÍNSULA DE ZAPATA

Copyright © by Rand McNally & Co.
Map prepared by Rand McNally & Co.
A-533200-264/764 — -7-5-14

Meters	Feet
6000	19685
4000	13124
3000	9843
2000	6562
1000	3281
500	1640
200	656
Land Below Sea Level 0	0
0	0
200	656
1000	3281
3000	9843
6000	19685
9000	29520

MAP FORM								
ENGLISH	bahia bay	cayo cay	channel channel	ensenada bayou	golfo gulf	island island	mount mount	passage passage	point point
DEUTSCH	Bucht	Klippe	Kanal	Altwasser	Golf	Insel	Berg	Durchfahrt	Landspitze
ESPAÑOL	bahía	cayo	canal	ensenada	golfo	isla	montaña	pasaje	punta
FRANÇAIS	baie	caye	détroit	bayou	golfe	île	mont	passage	pointe
PORTUGUÊS	baía	baixio	canal	enseada	golfo	ilha	montanha	passagem	ponta

Islands of the West Indies / Westindische Inseln / Islas de las Antillas
Îles des Antilles / Ilhas do Caribe (Índias Ocidentais)

241

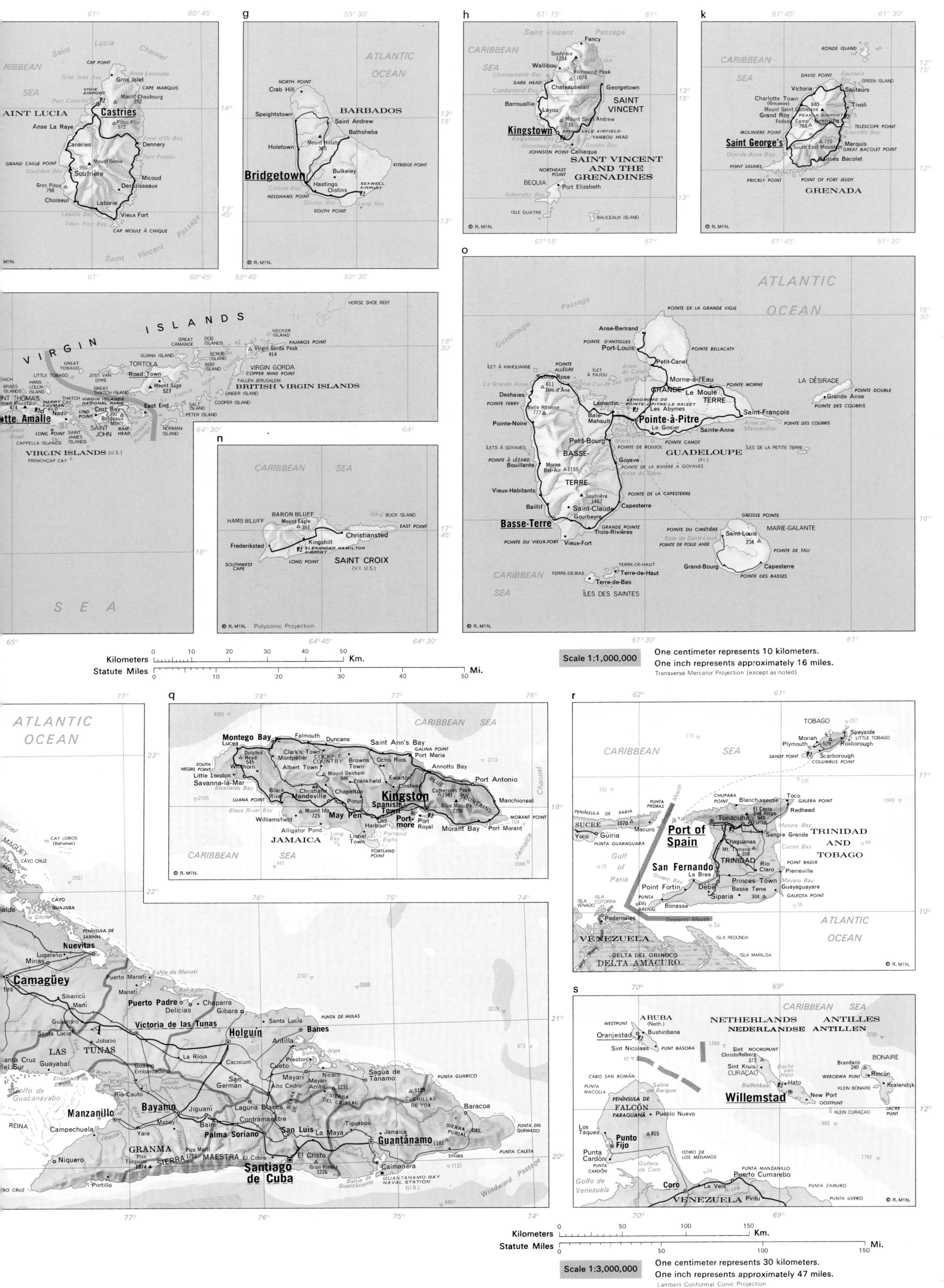

Northern South America / Südamerika, nördlicher Teil / América del Sur: zona septentrional
Amérique du Sud Septentrionale / América do Sul: zona setentrional

Map continues
pages 230-231

Kilometers
Km.
Statute Miles
Mi.

Scale 1:12,000,000

One centimeter represents 120 kilometers.
One inch represents approximately 190 miles.
Oblique Conic Conformal Projection

Copyright © by Rand McNally & Co.
Map prepared by Esselte Map Service AB, Stockholm.
A-549100-254   -7 -5 -12

Northern South America / Südamerika, nördlicher Teil / América del Sur: zona septentrional
Amérique du Sud Septentrionale / América do Sul: zona setentrional

243

A T L A N T I C   O C E A N

BARBADOS
Bridgetown

Georgetown

SURINAME

FRENCH GUIANA

Paramaribo

Cayenne

ACARAI MTS.

TUMUC-HUMAC MTS.

Equator 0°

10°

5°

Amazon

Amazonas

Santarém

Macapá

ILHA DE MARAJÓ

Belém

São Luís

Parnaíba

Fortaleza

Teresina

Natal

João Pessoa

Campina Grande

Olinda
Recife

Caruaru

Maceió

Aracaju

B R A Z I L

SERRA DO CACHIMBO

SERRA DOS CARAJÁS

ILHA DO BANANAL

PLANALTO DO MATO GROSSO

Cuiabá

Brasília

Goiânia

Salvador

Vitória da Conquista

Ilhéus
Itabuna

P L A N A L T O   C E N T R A L

Montes Claros

Campo Grande

Presidente Prudente

Uberaba

Uberlândia

Governador Valadares

Belo Horizonte

Vitória

Campos

Juiz de Fora

São Paulo

Santos

RIO DE JANEIRO

Niterói

Tropic of Capricorn

15°

20°

Map continues
pages 244-245

MAP FORM	cerro	cordillera	ilha	lago	nevado	peninsula	serra
ENGLISH	mountain	range	island	lake	mountain	peninsula	mountains
DEUTSCH	Berg	Gebirge	Insel	See	Berg	Halbinsel	Berge
ESPAÑOL	montaña	cordillera	isla	lago	montaña	península	montañas
FRANÇAIS	montagne	chaîne	île	lac	montagne	péninsule	montagnes
PORTUGUÊS	montanha	cordilheira	ilha	lago	montanha	península	montanhas

55° 50° 45° 40° 35°

Southern South America / Südamerika, südlicher Teil / América del Sur: zona meridional
Amérique du Sud Méridionale / América do Sul: zona meridional

Map continues
pages **242-243**

Tropic of Capricorn

BOLIVIA

PARA

CHILE

ARGENTINA

P A C I F I C

O C E A N

PATAGONIA

ANDES

ARCHIPIÉLAGO
JUAN FERNÁNDEZ
(Chile)

ISLA SAN FÉLIX · ISLA SAN AMBROSIO
(Chile)

FALKLAND
ISLAND
ISLAS MALV
(U.K.)

WEST
FALKLAND

EAS
FALKL

TIERRA
DEL FUEGO

MAP FORM	cerro, co.	golfo	ilha	isla	lago	lagoa	monte	salar
ENGLISH	butte	gulf	island	isle	lake	lake	mountain	saltflat
DEUTSCH	Restberg	Golf	Insel	Insel	See	See	Berg	Salzebene
ESPAÑOL	cerro	golfo	isla	isla	lago	lago	montaña	salobral
FRANÇAIS	butte	golfe	île	île	lac	lac	montagne	salina
PORTUGUÊS	colina	golfo	ilha	ilha	lago	lago	montanha	salina

20°
25°
Tropic of Capricorn
25°
30°
35°

A T L A N T I C

O C E A N

40°

45°

TRINIDADE
(Brazil)
ILHAS
MARTIN VAZ
(Brazil)

SHAG ROCKS
BLACK ROCK
BIRD ISLAND
ANNENKOV ISLAND
SOUTH GEORGIA
(Falkland Is.)
2934 Mount Paget
CAPE DISAPPOINTMENT
CLERKE ROCKS

Kilometers 0   200   400   600 Km.
Statute Miles 0   200   400   600 Mi.

Scale 1:12,000,000   One centimeter represents 120 kilometers.
One inch represents approximately 190 miles.
Oblique Conic Conformal Projection

BRAZIL
SÃO PAULO
RIO DE JANEIRO
Curitiba
Porto Alegre
Florianópolis

Colombia, Ecuador, Venezuela and Guyana / Kolumbien, Ecuador, Venezuela und Guayana / Colombia, Ecuador, Venezuela y Guyana
Colombie, Équateur, Venezuela et Guyane / Colômbia, Equador, Venezuela e Guiana

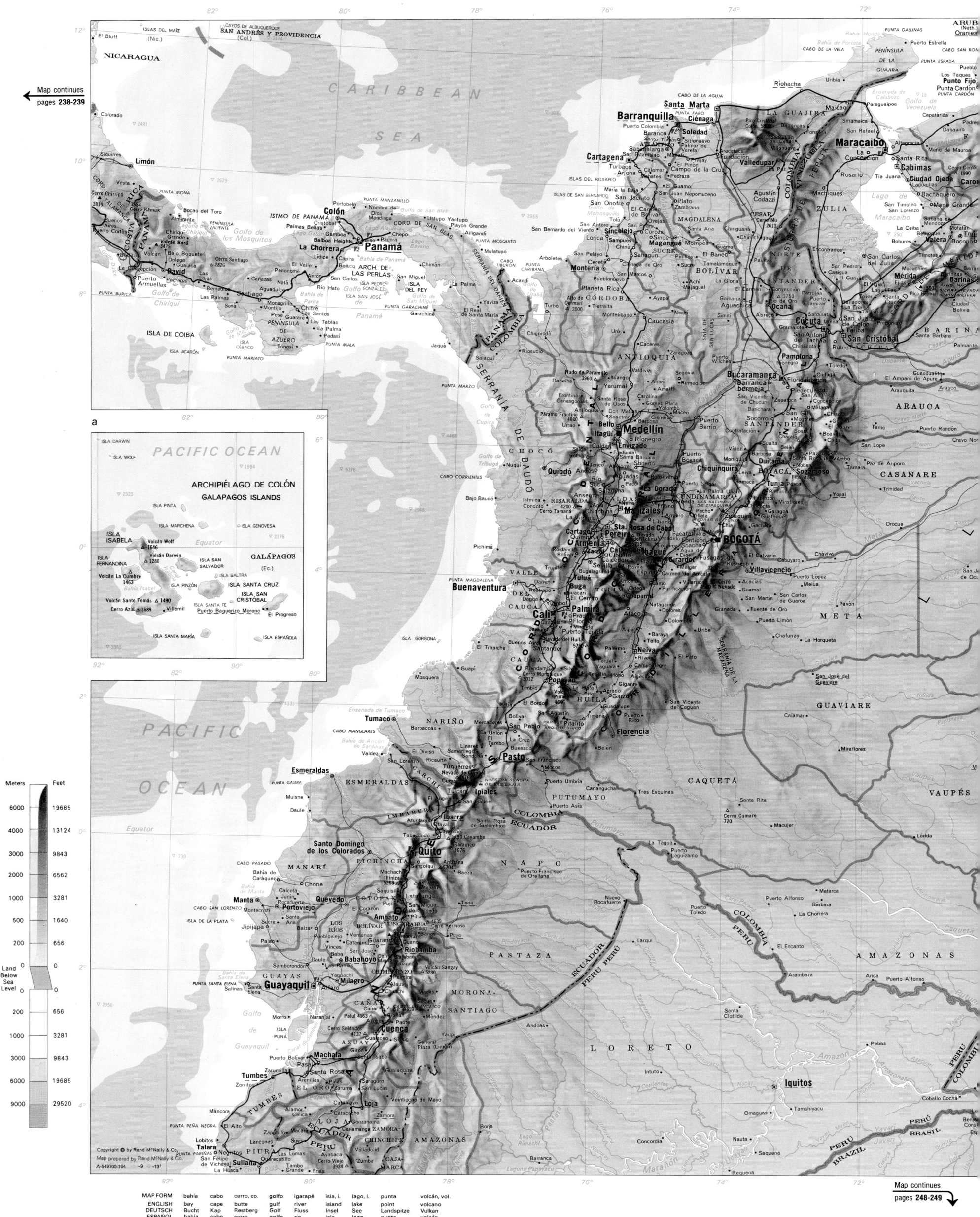

Map continues pages **238-239**

Map continues pages **248-249**

MAP FORM	bahía	cabo	cerro, co.	golfo	igarapé	isla, i.	lago, l.	punta	volcán, vol.
ENGLISH	bay	cape	butte	gulf	river	island	lake	point	volcano
DEUTSCH	Bucht	Kap	Restberg	Golf	Fluss	Insel	See	Landspitze	Vulkan
ESPAÑOL	bahía	cabo	cerro	golfo	río	isla	lago	punta	volcán
FRANÇAIS	baie	cap	butte	golfe	rivière	île	lac	pointe	volcan
PORTUGUÊS	baía	cabo	colina	golfo	rio	ilha	lago	ponta	vulcão

Colombia, Ecuador, Venezuela and Guyana / Kolumbien, Ecuador, Venezuela und Guayana / Colombia, Ecuador, Venezuela y Guyana
Colombie, Équateur, Venezuela et Guyane / Colômbia, Equador, Venezuela e Guiana

247

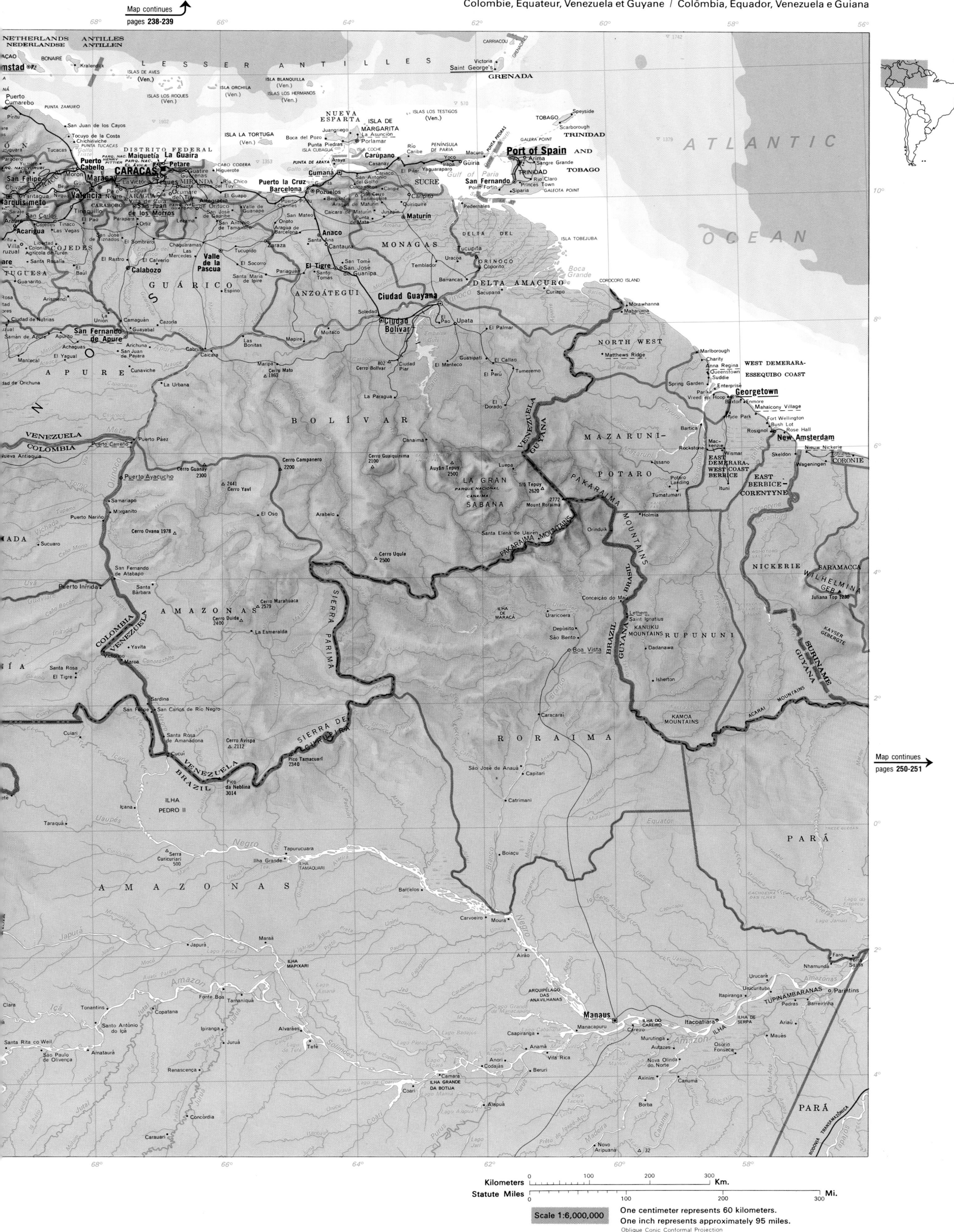

Map continues
pages 238-239

Map continues
pages 250-251

Kilometers
Statute Miles

Scale 1:6,000,000
One centimeter represents 60 kilometers.
One inch represents approximately 95 miles.
Oblique Conic Conformal Projection

Peru, Bolivia and Western Brazil / Peru, Bolivien und westliches Brasilien / Perú, Bolivia y Brasil Occidental
Pérou, Bolivie et Brésil Occidental / Peru, Bolívia e Brasil Ocidental

MAP FORM	cerro	cordillera	isla, i.	lago, l.	nevado	punta	rio	serra
ENGLISH	mountain	mountains	island	lake	mountain	point	river	mountains
DEUTSCH	Berg	Berge	Insel	See	Berg	Landspitze	Fluss	Berge
ESPAÑOL	montaña	montañas	isla	lago	nevado	punta	río	sierra
FRANÇAIS	montagne	montagnes	île	lac	montagne	pointe	rivière	montagnes
PORTUGUÊS	montanha	montanhas	ilha	lago	pico nevado	ponta	rio	serra

Peru, Bolivia and Western Brazil / Peru, Bolivien und westliches Brasilien / Perú, Bolivia y Brasil Occidental
Pérou, Bolivie et Brésil Occidental / Peru, Bolívia e Brasil Ocidental

249

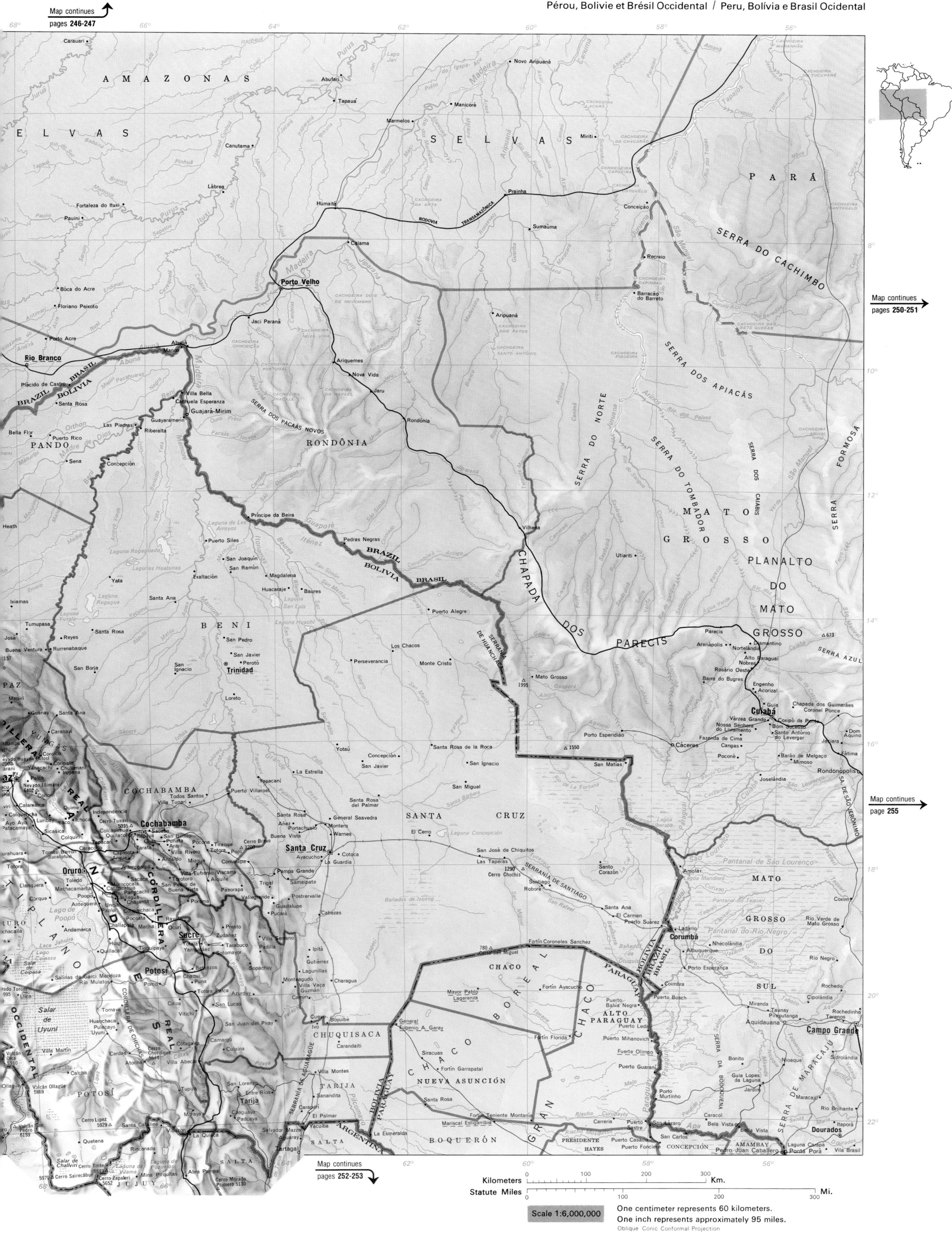

Map continues
pages 246-247

Map continues
pages 250-251

Map continues
page 255

Map continues
pages 252-253

Kilometers
Statute Miles

Scale 1:6,000,000

One centimeter represents 60 kilometers.
One inch represents approximately 95 miles.
Oblique Conic Conformal Projection

56° 54° 6° 52° 50° 48° 46°

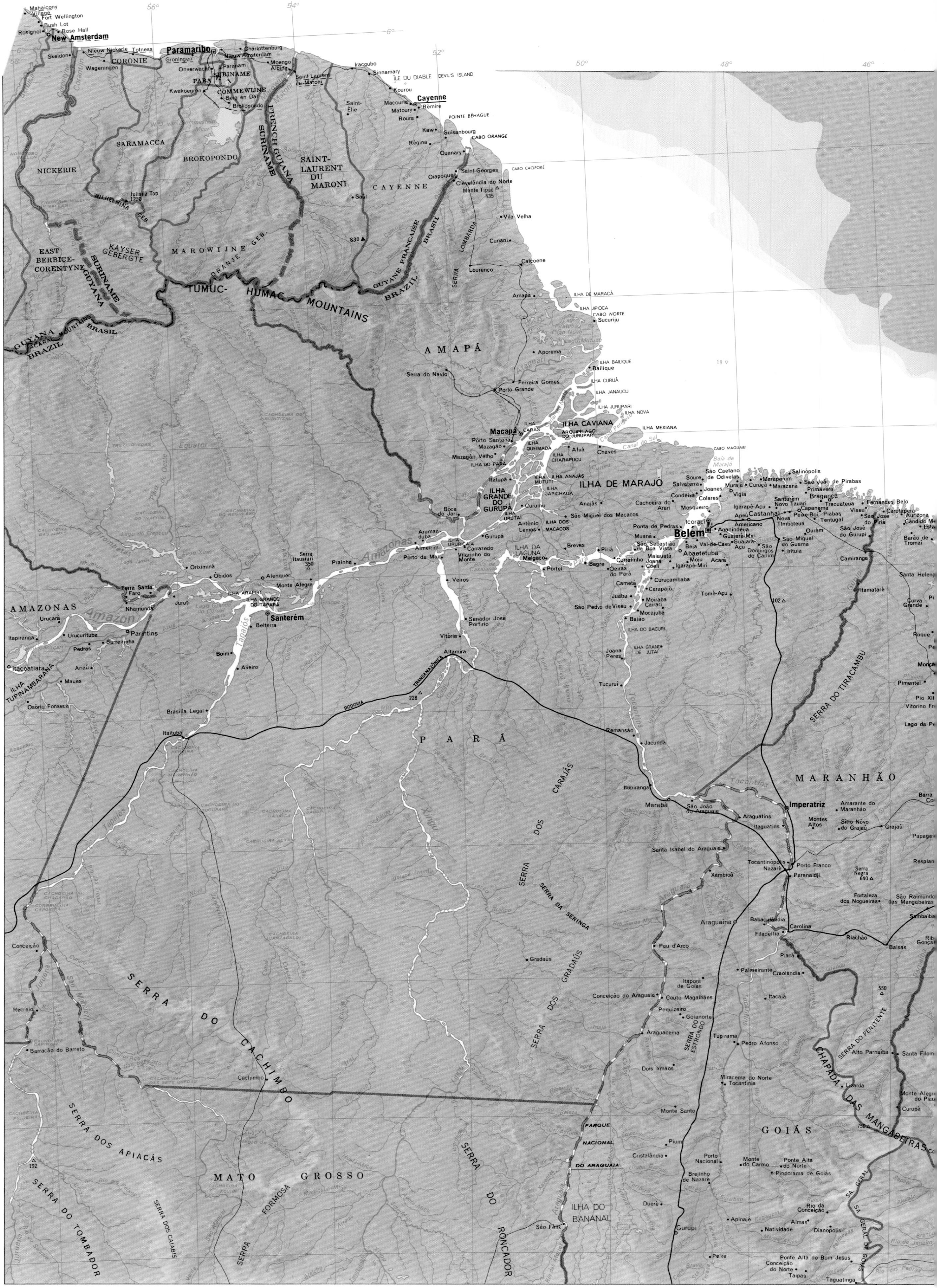

Mahaicony
Village
Fort Wellington
Bush Lot
Rosignol Rose Hall
New Amsterdam
Skeldon
Nieuw Nickerie Totness
Wagingen
Paramaribo
Groningen
Charlottenburg
Onverwacht Nieuw Amsterdam
Paranam
Kwakoegron Moengo
Moengo Tapoe
Belo en Dam
Brokopondo
CORONIE
PARA
SURINAME
COMMEWIJNE
Iracoubo
Sinnamary
ÎLE DU DIABLE DEVIL'S ISLAND
Kourou
Saint-Laurent du Maroni
Saint-Élie
Macouria Remire
Cayenne
Matoury
Roura
Kaw Guisanbourg
Régina
Ouanary
CABO ORANGE
Oiapoque
Saint-Georges
Clevelândia do Norte
Monte Tipac 435
CABO CACIPORÉ

NICKERIE
SARAMACCA
BROKOPONDO
Juliana Top 1230
WILHELMINA GEB.
EAST BERBICE-CORENTYNE
KAYSER GEBERGTE
SURINAME
GUYANA
BRAZIL
SAINT-LAURENT DU MARONI
CAYENNE
FRENCH GUIANA
SURINAMB
MAROWIJNE GEB.
ORANJE GEB.
GUYANE FRANÇAISE
BRAZIL
BRASIL
SERRA LOMBARDA
Vila Velha
Cunani
Saul
830 ▲
Caiçoene
Lourenço
Amapá

GUYANA BRAZIL
BRASIL
TUMUC-HUMAC MOUNTAINS

AMAPÁ

ILHA DE MARACÁ
ILHA JIPIOCA
CABO NORTE
Sucuriju
Aporema
ILHA BAILIQUE
Bailique
Serra do Navio ILHA CURUÁ
Ferreira Gomes
Porto Grande ILHA JANAUCU
ILHA JURUPARI
ILHA NOVA
Macapá
ILHA CAVIANA
ILHA MEXIANA
Pôrto Santana ARQUIPÉLAGO DO JURUPARI
Mazagão
ILHA QUEIMADA
Mazagão Velho Atuá Chaves
CABO MAGUARI
ILHA DO PARÁ
Itatupa
ILHA ANAJÁS
ILHA MUTUÍ
ILHA DE MARAJÓ
São Caetano de Odivelas
Salinópolis
São João de Pirabas
Soure
ILHA GRANDE DO GURUPÁ
ILHA JAPICHAUA
Salvaterra
Anajás
Cachoeira do Arari
Muraná Curuçá Maracanã
Primavera
Bragança
Condeixa Colares
Igarapé-Açu Maracanã
Novo Tauari
Tracuateua
Fernandes Belo
Bôca do Jari
ILHA URUTAÍ Curumu
São Miguel dos Macacos
Ponta de Pedras
Apeú Castanhal
Capanema
Viseu
Almeirim Antônio ILHA DOS MACACOS
Mosqueiro
Igarapé-Açu
Nova Timboteua Tentugal
São José do Piriá
Carrazedo Gurupá
Belém
Americano Ourém
Aurinona
Vilarinho do Monte
ILHA DA LAGUNA
Anapindeua
Guamá-Miri
São Miguel do Guamá
Candido Mendes
Pôrto de Moz
Breves
Melgaço
Val-de-Cães
Irituia
Barão de Tromai
Aruman-duba
São Sebastião da Boa Vista
São Domingos do Capim
Camiranga
Porto Santana
Portel
Currralinho
Maiauatá Moju Acará
Bagre
Pирá
Quéiras do Pará
Curuçá-Miri

Amazonas AMAZONAS
Óbidos
Oriximiná
Alenquer
Monte Alegre
Prainha
Santa Helena
Santarém
ILHA GRANDE DE AITAI
ILHA DO SACURI
Cametá
Carapajó
Curva Grande
Terra Santa
Faro
Nhamundá
Juruti
ILHA ARAPIRI
ILHA GRANDE DO TAPARÁ
Santarém
Belterra
Vitória
Senador José Porfírio
Juaba
Moirana Cairari Mocajuba
Tomé-Açu
São Pedro de Viseu
Baião
Roque
Monção
Serra Itauaiuri 350
Urucuritube
Barreirinha
Parintins
Boim
Aveiro
Altamira
Tucuruí
Pimentel
Pio XII
Vitório Freire
Itacoatiara
Ariaú
Mauás
Pedras
ILHA TUPINAMBARANA
Osório Fonseca
Brasília Legal
Tucuruí
Ramansão
Jacundá
SERRA DO TIRACAMBU
Lago da Pe
Resplan
Barra
Amarante do Maranhão

PARÁ
SERRA DOS CARAJÁS
Itaituba
RODOVIA 228
TRANSAMAZÔNICA
Itupiranga
Marabá São João do Araguaia
Imperatriz
MARANHÃO
Tocantins
Araguatins
Itaguatins
Sítio Nôvo do Grajaú
Montes Altos
Grajaú
Papagai
Santa Isabel do Araguaia
Tocantinópolis
Porto Franco
Nazaré
Paranaidji
Serra Negra 640 ▲
Fortaleza dos Noqueiras
São Raimundo das Mangabeiras
Sambaíba
Xambioá
Babaçulândia
Carolina
Riachão
Balsas

Conceição
SERRA DO CACHIMBO
SERRA DA SERINGA
Araguaína
Filadélfia
Piaca
Croalândia
SERRA DAS MANGABEIRAS
Gradaús
Pau d'Arco
Palmeirante
Recreio
Itapora de Goiás
Itacajá
Barracão do Barreto
Conceição do Araguaia
Pequizeiro
SERRA DO ESTRONDO
Couto Magalhães
Goianorte
Tupirama
Pedro Afonso
Alto Parnaíba
Santa Ana
Araguacema
CHAPADA DAS MANGABEIRAS
Dois Irmãos
Cachimbo
Miracema do Norte
Tocantinia
Monte Santo
SERRA DO RONCADOR
GOIÁS
SERRA DOS APIACÁS
PARQUE NACIONAL DO ARAGUAIA
Cristalândia
Porto Nacional
Monte do Carmo
Ponte Alta do Norte
SERRA FORMOSA
Pindorama de Goiás
MATO GROSSO
SERRA DOS CARAIS
Brejinho de Nazaré
Rio da Conceição
Monte Alegre de Goiás
ILHA DO BANANAL
Duerê
Apinajé
Natividade
Dianópolis
Chapada
SERRA DO TOMBADOR
São Félix
Gurupi
Peixe
Ponte Alta do Bom Jesus
Conceição do Norte
Taipas
Taguatinga
Lizarda

Equator 0° 2° 4° 6° 8° 10° 12°
4° 2° 58° 56° 54° 52° 50° 48° 46°

← Map continues pages 246-247

← Map continues pages 248-249

Map continues page 255 →

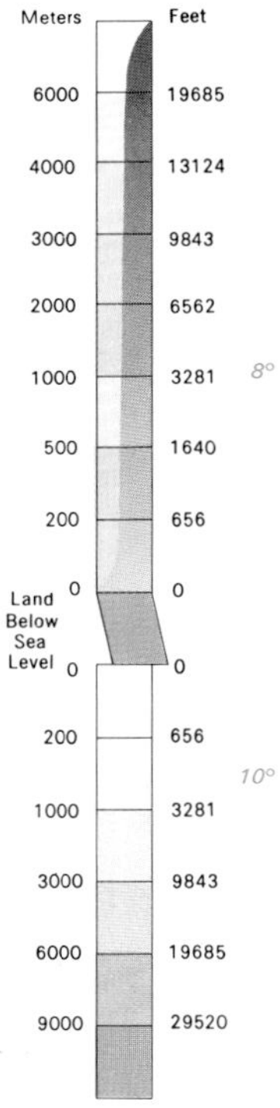

Meters	Feet
6000	19685
4000	13124
3000	9843
2000	6562
1000	3281
500	1640
200	656
Land Below Sea Level 0	0
0	0
200	656
1000	3281
3000	9843
6000	19685
9000	29520

MAP FORM	cabo	cachoeira, cach.	ilha, i.	lago, l.	riacho	ribeirão, râo.	rio, r.	serra, sa.
ENGLISH	cape	waterfall	island	lake	creek	creek	river	mountains
DEUTSCH	Kap	Wasserfall	Insel	See	Bach	Bach	Fluss	Berge
ESPAÑOL	cabo	cascada	isla	lago	riachuelo	riachuelo	río	montañas
FRANÇAIS	cap	chute d'eau	île	lac	crique	crique	rivière	montagnes
PORTUGUÊS	cabo	queda d'água	ilha	lago	riacho	riacho	rio	montanhas

ATLANTIC

OCEAN

Equator

FERNANDO DE
NORONHA

ATOL DAS ROCAS   ILHA FERNANDO
DE NORONHA

CEARÁ

RIO   GRANDE   DO   NORTE

CABO DE SÃO ROQUE

Natal

Fortaleza

Sobral

Parnaíba

São Luís
Anil

Caxias

Teresina

Crateús

PIAUÍ

Floriano

SERRA GRANDE

Juàzeiro
do Norte

Crato

CHAPADA DO ARARIPE

PERNAMBUCO

Arcoverde

Garanhuns

Petrolina
Juàzeiro

Paulo Afonso
PARQUE NACIONAL
DE PAULO AFONSO

SERGIPE

Aracaju

ALAGOAS

Maceió

Arapiraca

BAHIA

Mossoró

PARAÍBA

Campina
Grande

João Pessoa
Cabedelo

Caruaru

RECIFE
Olinda
Jaboatão
Muribeca dos Guararapes
Palmares

Alagoinhas

Kilometers   0   100   200   300   Km.
Statute Miles   0   100   200   300   Mi.

Scale 1:6,000,000
One centimeter represents 60 kilometers.
One inch represents approximately 95 miles.
Oblique Conic Conformal Projection

252

Central Argentina and Chile / Mittelargentinien und Mittelchile / Argentina y Chile: zonas centrales
Argentine et Chili, parties Centrales / Argentina e Chile: zonas centrais

Map continues
pages 248-249

Map continues
page 254

MAP FORM	cabo	cerro	cuchilla	ilha	laguna	punta	salar	sierra	volcán
ENGLISH	cape	mountain	hills	island	lagoon; lake	point	saltflat	mountains	volcano
DEUTSCH	Kap	Berg	Hügel	Insel	Haff; See	Landspitze	Salzebene	Berge	Vulkan
ESPAÑOL	cabo	cerro	cuchilla	isla	laguna; lac	punta	salobral	sierra	volcan
FRANÇAIS	cap	montagne	collines	île	lagune; lac	pointe	salobral	montagnes	volcan
PORTUGUÊS	cabo	montanha	colina	ilha	laguna	ponta	salina	serra	vulcão

Central Argentina and Chile / Mittelargentinien und Mittelchile / Argentina y Chile: zonas centrales
Argentine et Chili, parties Centrales / Argentina e Chile: zonas centrais

253

Map continues
page 255

Kilometers 0   100   200   300   Km.
Statute Miles 0   100   200   300   Mi.

Scale 1:6,000,000   One centimeter represents 60 kilometers.
One inch represents approximately 95 miles.
Oblique Conic Conformal Projection

Southern Argentina and Chile / Südliches Argentinien und südliches Chile / Argentina y Chile: zonas meridionales
Argentine et Chili, parties Méridionales / Argentina e Chile: zonas meridionais

Map continues
pages 252-253

PACIFIC OCEAN

ATLANTIC OCEAN

PACIFIC OCEAN

FALKLAND ISLANDS
ISLAS MALVINAS
(U.K.)

Meters	Feet
6000	19685
4000	13124
3000	9843
2000	6562
1000	3281
500	1640
200	656
Land Below Sea Level 0	0
0	0
200	656
1000	3281
3000	9843
6000	19685
9000	29520

MAP FORM	bahia	cabo	cerro	isla	lago	monte	punta
ENGLISH	bay	cape	mountain, hill	isle	lake	mountain	point
DEUTSCH	Bucht	Kap	Berg, Hügel	Insel	See	Berg	Landspitze
ESPAÑOL	bahía	cabo	cerro	isla	lago	monte	punta
FRANÇAIS	baie	cap	montagne, colline	île	lac	montagne	pointe
PORTUGUÊS	baía	cabo	montanha, colina	ilha	lago	monte	ponta

Kilometers 0 100 200 300 Km.
Statute Miles 0 100 200 300 Mi.

Scale 1:6,000,000
One centimeter represents 60 kilometers.
One inch represents approximately 95 miles.
Oblique Conic Conformal Projection

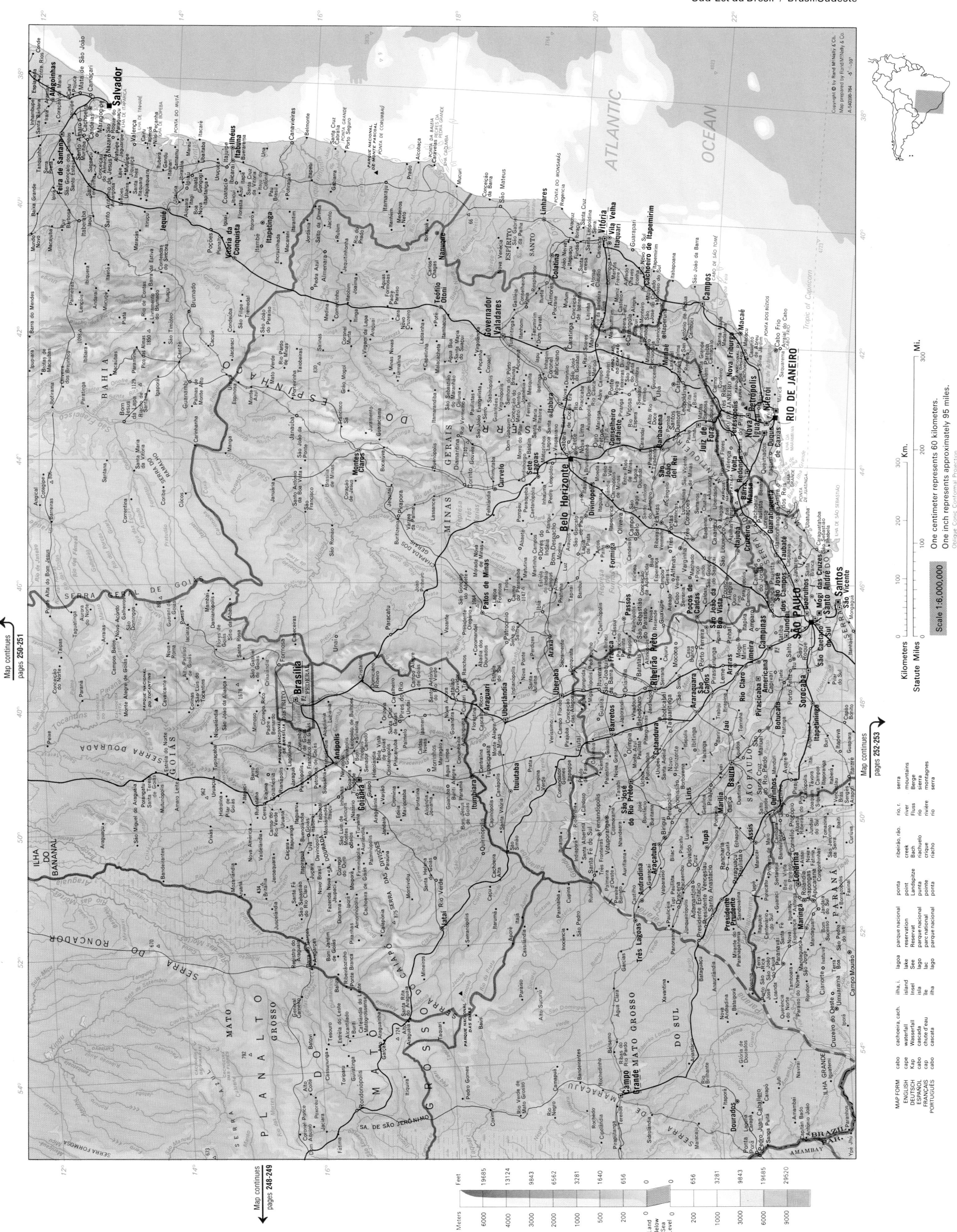

Map continues
pages 250-251

Map continues
pages 248-249

Map continues
pages 252-253

Scale 1:6,000,000

One centimeter represents 60 kilometers.
One inch represents approximately 95 miles.

Oblique Conic Conformal Projection

MAP FORM	cabo	cachoeira, cach.	ilha, i.	lagoa	ponta	ribeirão, rio.	rio. r.	serra
ENGLISH	cape	waterfall	island	lake	point	creek	river	mountains
DEUTSCH	Kap	Wasserfall	Insel	See	Landspitze	Bach	Fluss	Gebirge
ESPAÑOL	cabo	cascada	isla	lago	punta	riachuelo	río	sierra
FRANÇAIS	cap	chute d'eau	île	lac	pointe	crique	rivière	montagnes
PORTUGUÊS	cabo	cascata	ilha	lago	ponta	riacho	rio	serra

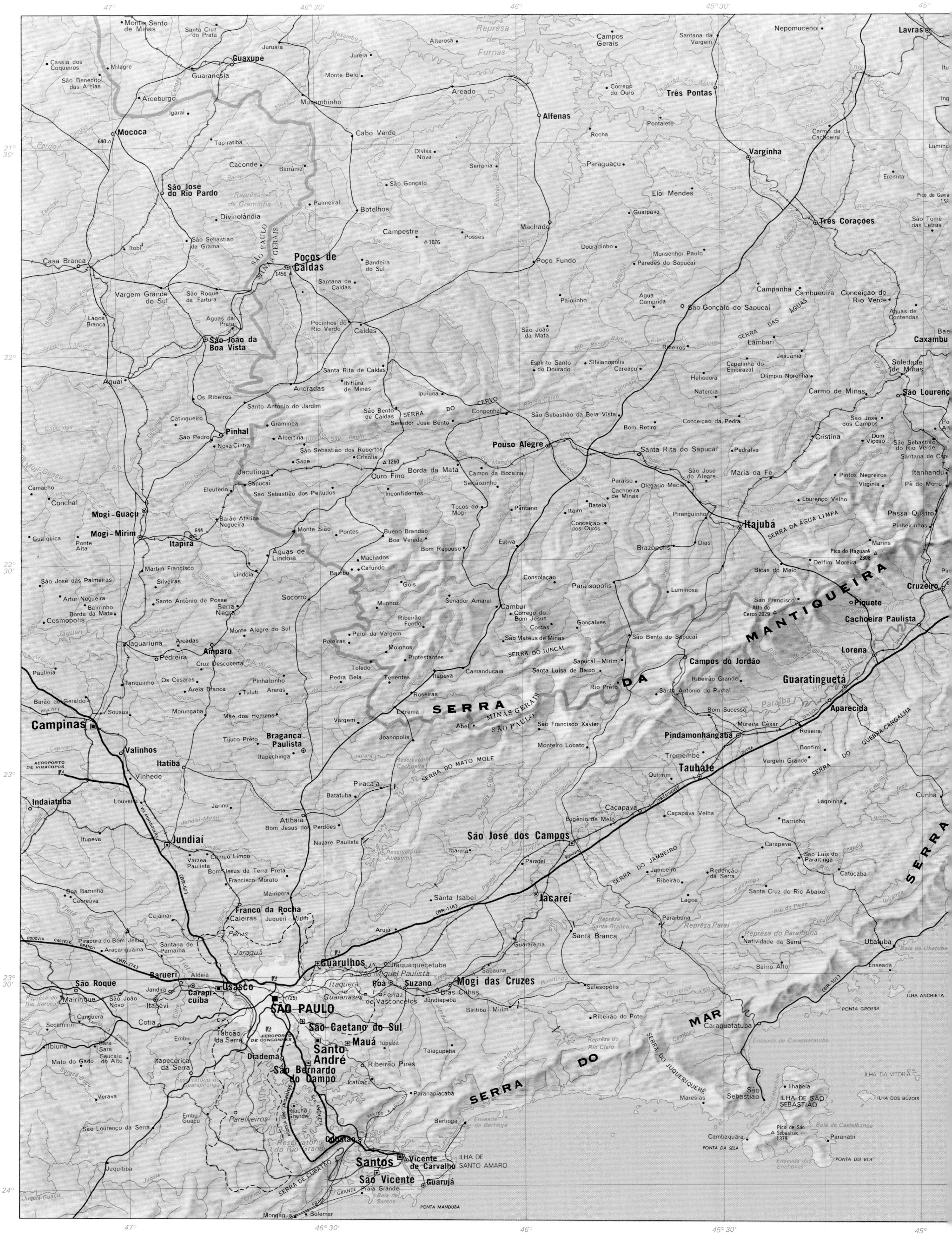

MAP FORM	baía	enseada	ilha	pico	ponta	represa	ribeirão	rio	serra
ENGLISH	bay	bay	island	peak	point	reservoir	stream	river	mountains
DEUTSCH	Bucht	Bucht	Insel	Gipfel	Landspitze	Stausee	Bach	Fluss	Berge
ESPAÑOL	bahía	bahía	isla	pico	punta	estanque	corriente de agua	río	sierra
FRANÇAIS	baie	baie	île	cime	pointe	réservoir	cours d'eau	rivière	montagnes
PORTUGUÊS	baía	enseada	ilha	pico	ponta	represa	ribeirão	rio	serra

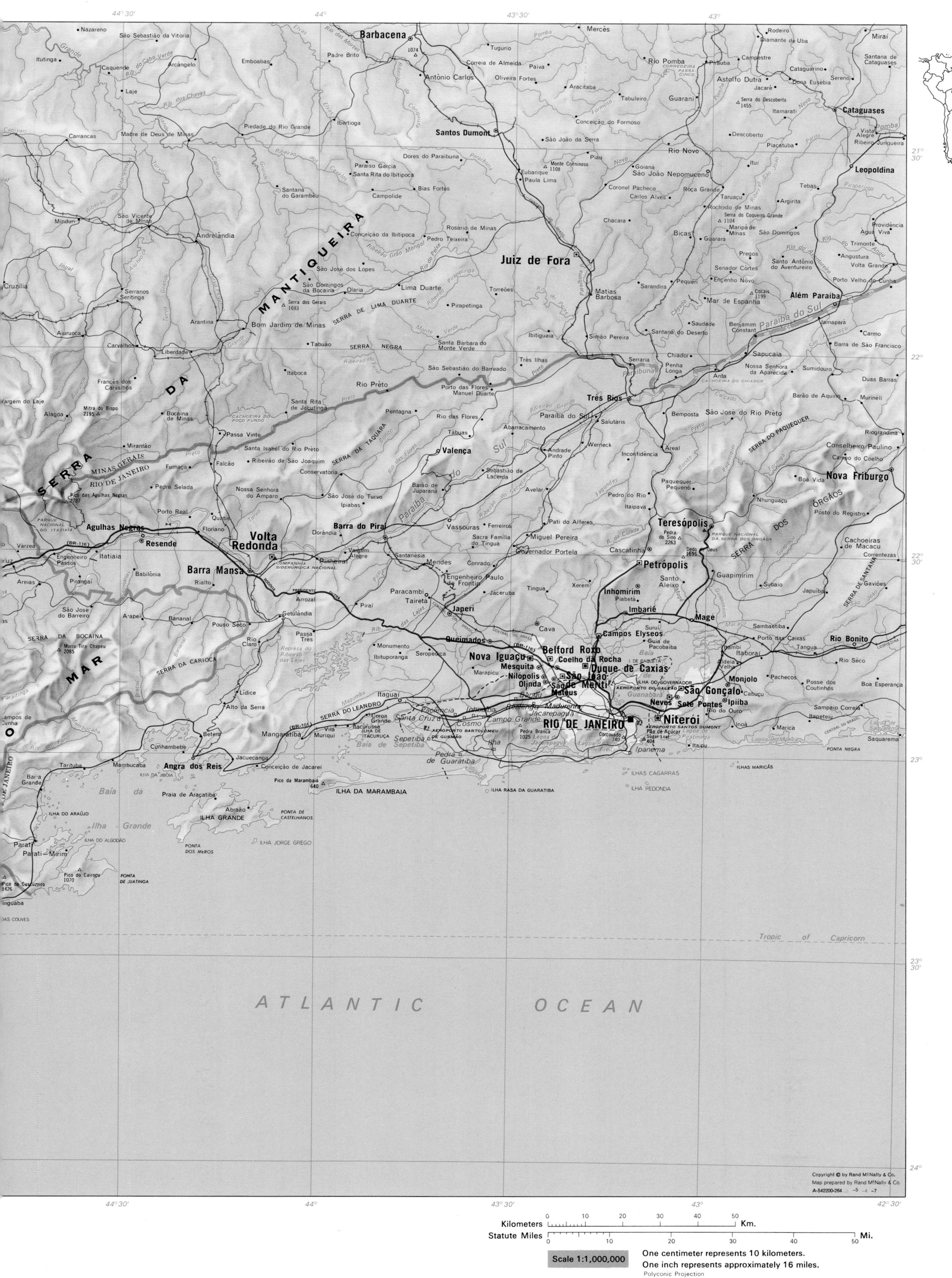

Kilometers |0 10 20 30 40 50| Km.

Statute Miles |0 10 20 30 40 50| Mi.

Scale 1:1,000,000

One centimeter represents 10 kilometers.
One inch represents approximately 16 miles.

Polyconic Projection

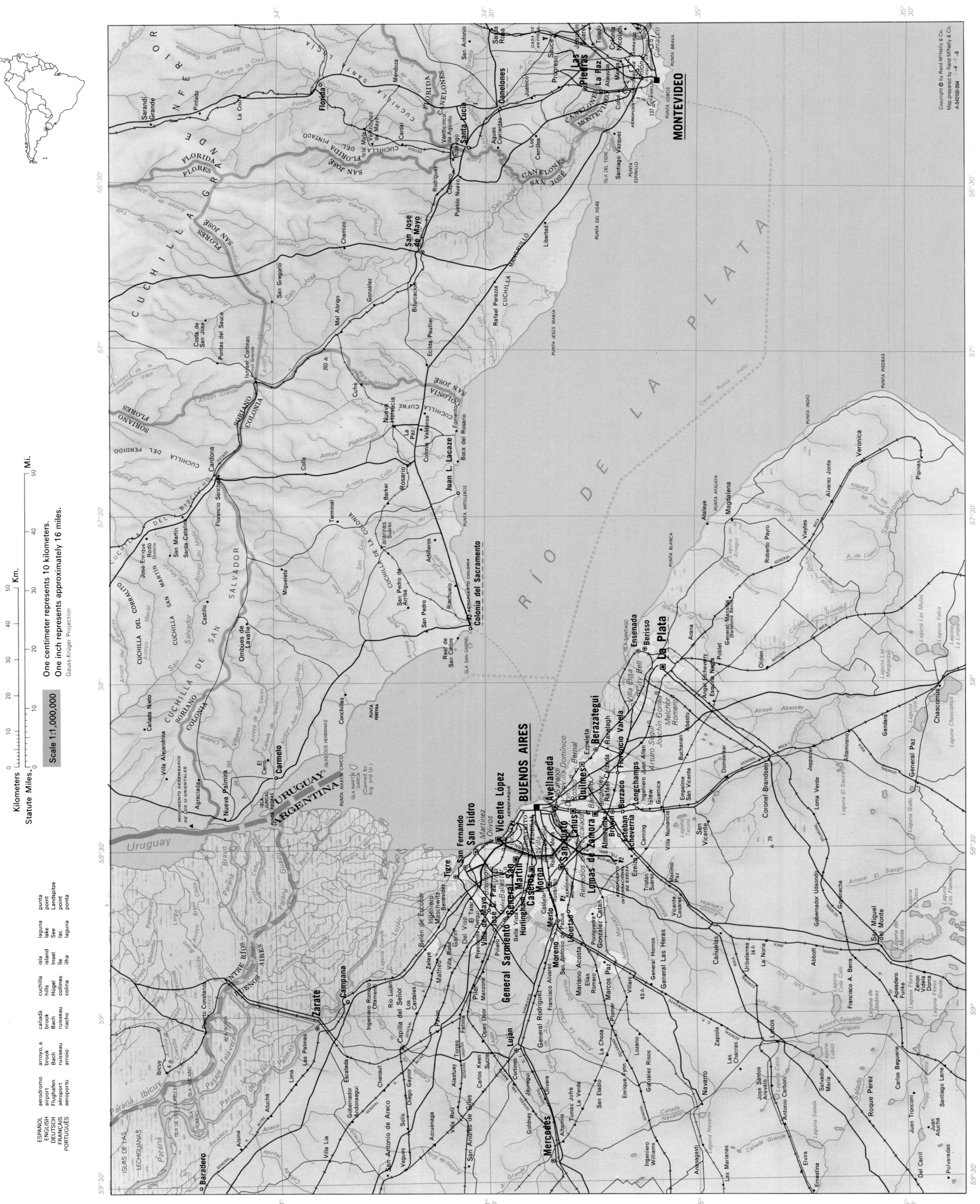

Kilometers
Mi.
50
40
Km.
50
40
30
20
Statute Miles
10
0
10
20
30
40

Scale 1:1,000,000

One centimeter represents 10 kilometers.
One inch represents approximately 16 miles.
Gauss-Krüger Projection

ESPAÑOL	ENGLISH	DEUTSCH	FRANÇAIS	PORTUGUÊS
aeródromo	airport	Flughafen	aéroport	aeroporto
arroyo, a.	brook	Bach	ruisseau	arroio
cañada	brook	Bach	ruisseau	riacho
cuchilla	hills	Hügel	collines	colina
isla	island	Insel	île	ilha
laguna	lake	See	lac	laguna
punta	point	Landspitze	point	ponta

THIS SECTION CONSISTS of 60 maps of the world's major metropolitan areas, at the scale of 1:300,000. The maps show the generalized land-use patterns in and around each city—the total urban extent, major industrial areas, parks and preserves, and wooded areas. Airports are shown, as are many details of the highway and rail transportation networks. Selected points of interest appear, such as Fisherman's Wharf and Chinatown in San Francisco, the Welcome monument in Jakarta, the Temple of the Jade Buddha in Shanghai, and the Cristo Redentor statue in Rio de Janeiro.

The maps name and locate a great number of towns, villages, and suburbs, and also sections or neighborhoods within limits of the larger cities. Prominent physical features, including elevations, named and unnamed, have been indicated to give a general impression of the local topography. Shaded relief has been omitted, however, to permit display of such details as streams, parks, airport runways, important public buildings and monuments, and the names of major streets. The corporate limits of major cities are also outlined. For the symbols used on these maps see the Legend to Maps, pages x-xii.

Maps of major world cities usually vary widely in scale, and heretofore have not been consistent in design and coverage. For this section, a special effort has been made to portray these varied metropolitan areas in as standard and comparable a fashion as possible. However, for a few cities (notably several in Asia) there has not been adequate source material to include certain information, such as major industrial areas and corporate limits.

The order of presentation is generally regional, with some exceptions where for ease of comparison major capitals or industrial centers or cities located in similar physical surroundings have been juxtaposed. Many American cities and some European cities, with their lower densities and more extensive areas, require larger maps than do Asiatic cities of comparable population. The total land area and population within the confines of each map are stated in the margin as a further aid to comparison.

DIESER KARTENTEIL UMFASST 60 Karten der bedeutendsten Stadtregionen der Erde im Massstab 1:300 000. Die Karten zeigen in generalisierter Form die Landnutzung in und um jede Stadt: die gesamte Ausdehnung des verstädterten Gebietes, wichtige Industriegebiete, Parks, Landflächen in Gemeinbesitz und Wald. Flughäfen werden ebenso dargestellt wie viele Einzelheiten des Strassen- und Eisenbahnnetzes. Bekannte Sehenswürdigkeiten sind eingetragen wie die "Fisherman's Wharf" und "Chinatown" in San Francisco, das Willkomm-Denkmal in Jakarta, der Tempel des Jade-Buddhas in Shanghai und die "Cristo Redentor"-Statue in Rio de Janeiro.

Die Karten verzeichnen Name and Lage einer grossen Zahl von Städten, Dörfern, Vororten ebenso wie eingemeindete Ortsteile bei grösseren Städten. Hervortretende physische Formen wie benannte und unbenannte Erhebungen sind aufgenommen, um eine allgemeine Vorstellung des lokalen Reliefs zu geben. Auf die Schummerung wurde jedoch verzichtet, um klar solche Einzelheiten wie Flüsse, Parks, Start- und Landebahnen der Flughäfen, bedeutende öffentliche Gebäude und Denkmäler sowie die Namen der wichtigsten Strassen herausstellen zu können. Eingetragen sind ferner die Gemeindegrenzen der wichtigsten Städte. Zu den auf diesen Karten verwendeten Signaturen siehe "Zeichenerklärung" Seite x-xii.

Karten der bedeutendsten Weltstädte differieren normalerweise sehr stark in ihren Massstäben und sind daher uneinheitlich in ihrer Gestaltung und Begrenzung. Deshalb wurde in diesem Kartenteil besonderer Wert darauf gelegt, die verschiedenen städtischen Ballungsgebiete in möglichst einheitlicher und vergleichbarer Form darzustellen. Für einige Städte, vor allem mehrere asiatische, war das Quellenmaterial jedoch nicht ausreichend genug, um gewisse Informationen wie Hauptindustriegebiete oder Stadtgrenzen einzutragen.

Im allgemeinen sind diese Karten nach regionalen Gesichtspunkten geordnet. Um Vergleiche zu erleichtern wurden einige Ausnahmen gemacht, indem wichtige Hauptstädte, Industriezentren oder Städte in vergleichbarer landschaftlicher Lage einander gegenübergestellt wurden. Viele americkanische und einige europäische Städte mit ihrer geringen Bevölkerungsdichte, aber ausgedehnteren Fläche erfordern eine grössere Kartenfläche als asiatische Städte von vergleichbarer Bevölkerungszahl. Die gesamte Landfläche und die Bevölkerung innerhalb des dargestellten Gebietes ist am Kartenrand verzeichnet als ein weiteres Hilfsmittel für Vergleiche.

INTEGRAN ESTA SECCION 60 mapas de las áreas metropolitanas más importantes del mundo, a la escala de 1:300 000. Los mapas muestran los patrones de uso del suelo dentro de cada ciudad y en sus alrededores—la extensión total del conglomerado urbano, las principales áreas industriales, parques y reservas, y zonas boscosas. Aparecen los aeropuertos, así como muchos otros detalles de las redes de carreteras y ferrocarriles. Se seleccionaron también puntos de interés, como el Muelle de los Pescadores y el Barrio Chino de San Francisco, el monumento de Bienvenida de Jakarta, el Templo del Buda de Jade de Shanghai y la estatua del Cristo Redentor de Rio de Janeiro.

Los mapas incluyen los nombres y la ubicación de gran número de ciudades, poblaciones menores, suburbios, e inclusive barrios y distritos de algunas de las ciudades más importantes. Las características físicas sobresalientes, e incluso algunas elevaciones con o sin nombre, están indicados para dar una impresión general de la topografía local. Se omitió sin embargo el relieve sombreado, lo cual permite mostrar detalles como ríos y arroyos, parques, pistas de aterrizaje, edificios y monumentos públicos notables y los nombres de las calles principales. También están marcados los límites territoriales de las ciudades más grandes. Para la interpretación de los símbolos usados en estos mapas, véanse Leyendas para Mapas en las páginas x-xii.

Los mapas de las ciudades más importantes del mundo varían generalmente en escala, y hasta ahora no han sido consistentes ni en diseño ni en contenido. En esta sección hemos hecho un esfuerzo de presentar las distintas áreas metropolitanas en la forma más uniforme posible, para facilitar sus comparaciones. Para algunas ciudades (la mayoría de ellas en Asia), no fué posible obtener de las propias fuentes material adecuado para la inclusión de ciertos datos, tales como las mayores áreas industriales y los límites municipales.

Los mapas de áreas metropolitanas se presentan por regiones, a excepción de unos cuantos que aparecen yuxtapuestos para facilitar la comparación entre grandes capitales, o centros comerciales, o ciudades ubicadas en contextos físicos similares. Muchas ciudades de América y algunas ciudades de Europa, por su baja densidad de población y su área extensa, requieren mapas más grandes que los ocupados por ciudades asiáticas con poblaciones comparables. Al margen de cada mapa se anotaron el área total y la población de territorio representado, lo cual facilita también las comparaciones.

CETTE PARTIE COMPREND 60 cartes des principales zones métropolitaines à l'échelle du 1:300 000ᵉ. Les cartes représentent les principaux types d'occupation du sol des villes et de leurs environs, c'est-à-dire de toute la zone urbanisée, les principales zones industrielles, les parcs et réserves naturelles, et les régions boisées. Les aéroports sont aussi représentés ainsi que de nombreux éléments des réseaux routier et ferroviaire. Certains lieux particulièrement intéressants sont indiqués, tels que le quai des pêcheurs et la ville chinoise à San Francisco, le monument de la Bienvenue à Jakarta, le temple du Bouddha de Jade à Shanghai et la statue du Christ Rédempteur à Rio de Janeiro.

Les cartes permettent de localiser un grand nombre de villes, villages et banlieues, ainsi que des quartiers de grandes villes. Les caractéristiques topographiques notables, comme les hauteurs sont indiquées même si elles ne portent pas de nom, pour donner une idée du site de l'aire métropolitaine. L'estompage du relief est omis cependant pour permettre de représenter cours d'eau, parcs, pistes d'envol des aéroports, monuments et bâtiments publics importants, noms des principales rues, ainsi que les limites municipales des grandes villes. (Pour la signification des symboles voir légende, pages x-xii.)

En général, les échelles des cartes des grandes villes du monde varient considérablement, et jusqu'ici la présentation et le contenu de ces cartes n'étaient pas comparables. Dans cette partie de l'Atlas, un effort spécial a été fait pour représenter les diverses zones métropolitaines de manière aussi homogène que possible. Cependant, dans certains cas (en Asie notamment), les documents de base n'étaient pas assez complets pour qu'il fût possible d'inclure avec précision des données comme les zones industrielles et les limites municipales.

L'ordre de présentation est régional, avec des exceptions quand, pour faciliter les comparaisons, de grandes capitales de grands centres industriels ou encore des villes possédant un même environnement naturel, sont juxtaposés. Beaucoup de villes américaines et quelques villes européennes ont une faible densité de population et une étendue considérable; elles requièrent, par conséquent, des cartes plus grandes que des villes asiatiques de population similaire. La superficie et la population de chaque carte sont indiquées dans la marge.

INTEGRAM ESTA SEÇÃO 60 mapas das áreas metropolitanas mais importantes do mundo, em escala de 1:300 000. Os mapas mostram os principais tipos de uso do solo em cada cidade e seus arredores, seja, a extensão total da zona urbanizada, as principais áreas industriais, os parques e reservas, e as áreas florestais. Mostram os aeroportos, e muitos detalhes das redes rodo e ferroviária. Indicam também pontos de interesse, selecionados, tais como o Cais dos Pescadores e o Bairro Chinês de San Francisco, o monumento de Boasvindas, em Jakarta, o templo do Buda de Jade, em Shanghai, e a Estátua do Cristo Redentor, no Rio de Janeiro.

Os mapas apresentam o nome e a localização de grande número de cidades, vilas e subúrbios, e incluem bairros das cidades mais importantes. Foram indicadas as características físicas principais, inclusive elevações, com ou sem nome, com o objetivo de proporcionar uma idéia geral da topografia local. No entanto, omitiu-se o sombreado do relevo, para permitir a indicação de detalhes tais como cursos d'água, parques, pistas de aeroportos, edifícios públicos e monumentos notáveis, e os nomes das principais ruas, bem como os limites municipais das grandes cidades. Para a interpretação dos símbolos usados nesses mapas, ver as *Legendas dos mapas*, nas pág. x-xii.

Os mapas das cidades mais importantes do mundo variam consideravelmente, de modo geral, quanto à escala, e até o presente não são comparáveis nem na forma de apresentação nem no conteúdo. Nesta seção, fez-se um esforço especial para representar as diversas áreas metropolitanas do modo mais uniforme e comparável possível. No entanto, para algumas cidades, a maioria das quais da Ásia, não foi possível obter fontes fidedignas de informações, tais como áreas industriais principais e limites municipais.

A ordem de apresentação dos mapas das áreas metropolitanas é geralmente regional, exceto em certos casos em que, para facilidade de comparação, capitais ou centros industriais e cidades importantes localizadas em meio físico semelhante foram justapostos. Muitas cidades da América e algumas da Europa, por sua baixa densidade demográfica e áreas mais extensas, exigem mapas maiores que as cidades asiáticas de população comparável. À margem de cada mapa indicam-se a área terrestre e a população total do território representado, também para maior facilidade de comparação.

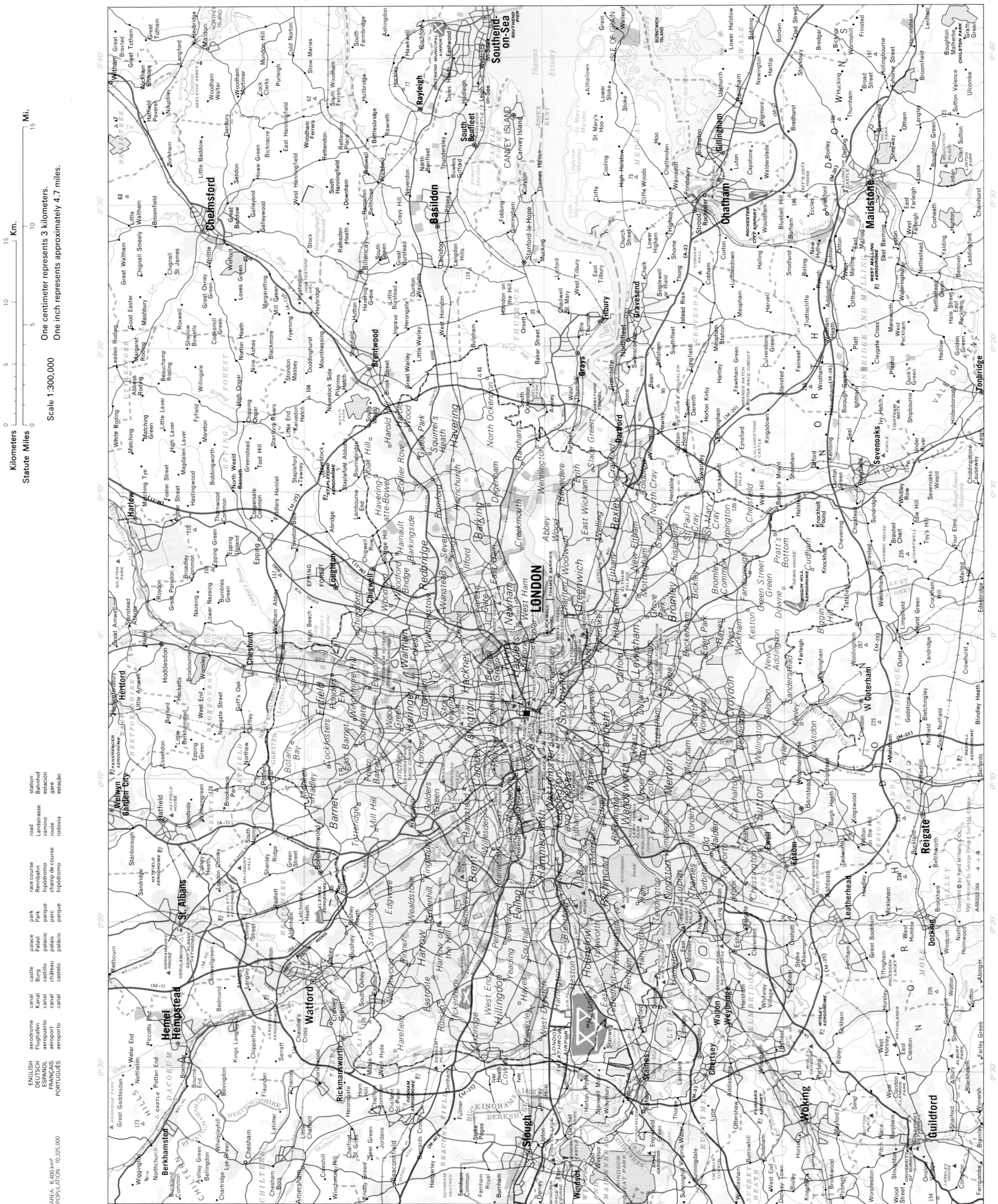

Mi.
Km.

Kilometers
Statute Miles

One centimeter represents 3 kilometers.
One inch represents approximately 4.7 miles.

Scale 1:300,000

ENGLISH	aerodrome	canal	castle	palace	park	race course	station
DEUTSCH	Flughafen	Kanal	Burg	Palast	Park	Rennbahn	Bahnhof
ESPAÑOL	aeropuerto	canal	castillo	palacio	parque	hipódromo	estación
FRANÇAIS	aéroport	canal	château	palais	parc	champ de course	gare
PORTUGUÊS	aeroporto	canal	castelo	palácio	parque	hipódromo	estação

road
Landstrasse
camino
route
rodovia

AREA 6,400 km²
POPULATION 10,325,000

Berkhamsted
Hemel Hempstead
Rickmansworth
Watford
St. Albans
Welwyn Garden City
Hertford
Cheshunt
Harlow
Chelmsford
Witham
Brentwood
Basildon
Rayleigh
Southend-on-Sea
South Benfleet
Canvey Island
Tilbury
Grays
Gravesend
Chatham
Gillingham
Maidstone
Sevenoaks
W. Coterham
Reigate
Dorking
Leatherhead
Guildford
Woking
Slough
Windsor
Weybridge
Walton

LONDON

EPPING FOREST
LITTLE THURROCK
THAMES
MEDWAY

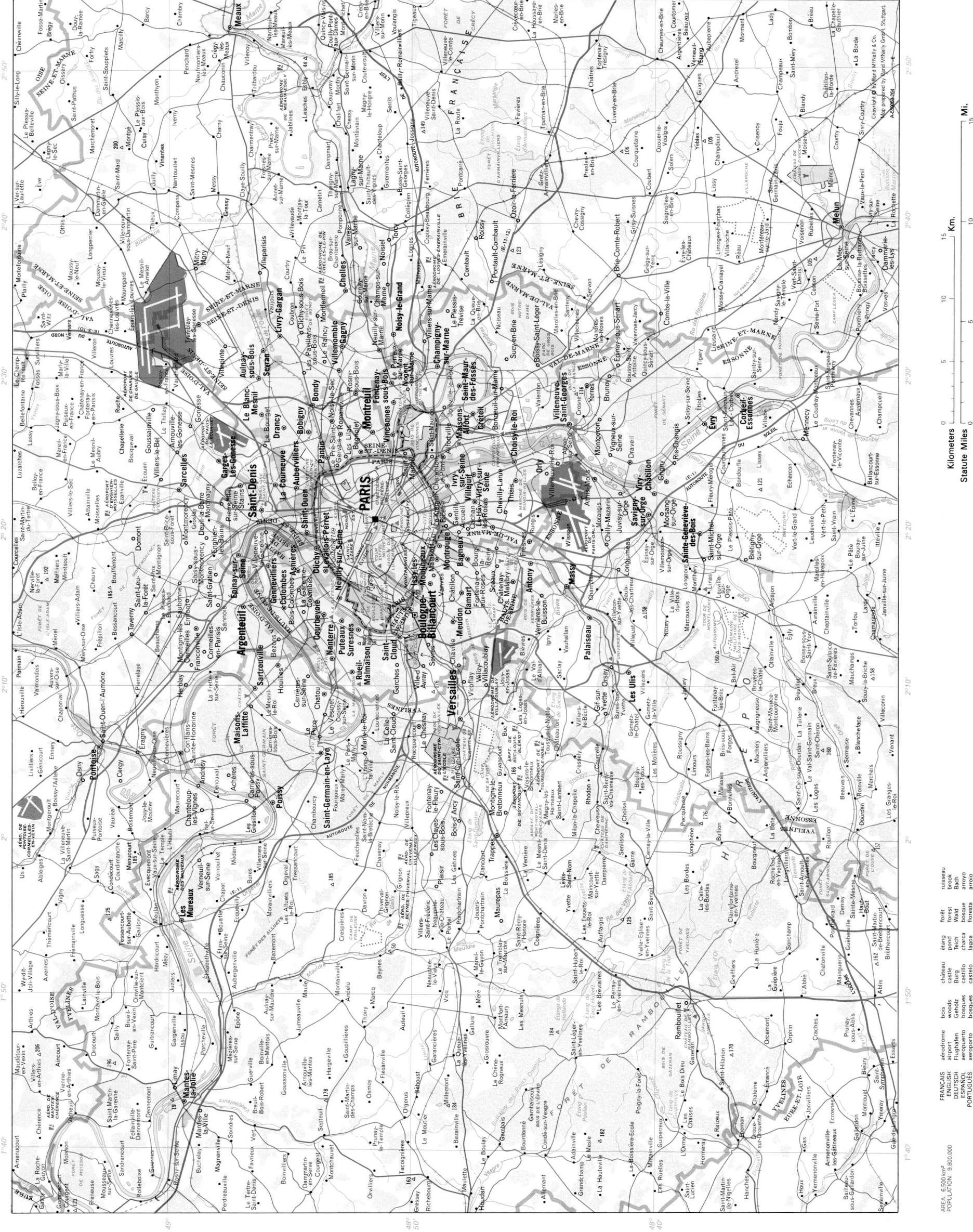

Scale 1:300,000

One centimeter represents 3 kilometers.
One inch represents approximately 4.7 miles.

FRANÇAIS	aérodrome	bois	château	forêt	ruisseau	étang
ENGLISH	airport	woods	castle	forest	brook	
DEUTSCH	Flughafen	Gehölz	Burg	Wald	Bach	Teich
ESPAÑOL	aeropuerto	bosques	castillo	bosque	arroyo	charca
PORTUGUÊS	aeroporto	bosques	castelo	floresta	arroio	lagoa

AREA 6,500 km²
POPULATION 9,600,000

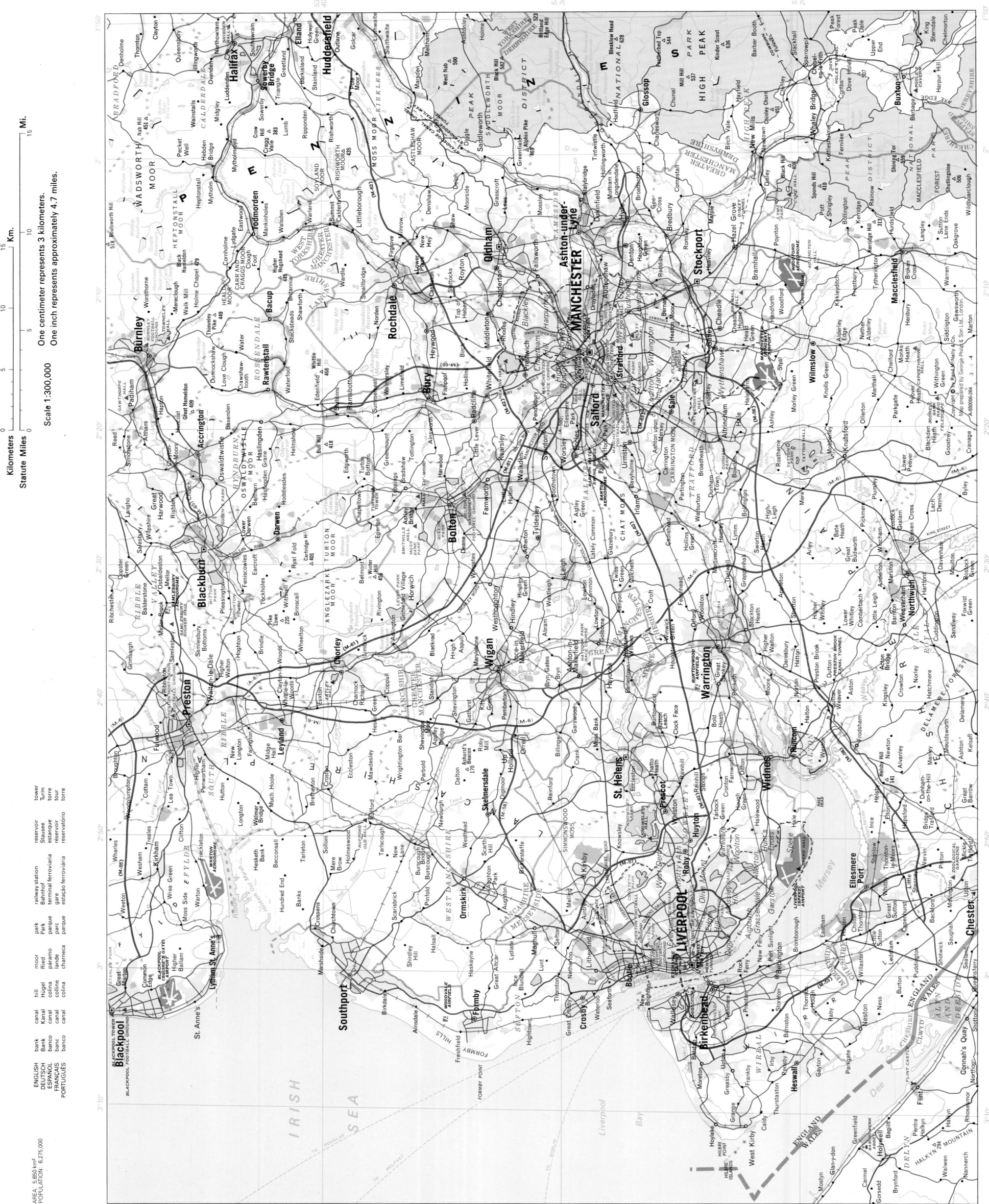

AREA: 5,650 km²
POPULATION: 6,275,000

ENGLISH	DEUTSCH	ESPAÑOL	FRANÇAIS	PORTUGUÊS
bank	Bank	banco	banc	banco
hill	Hügel	colina	colline	colina
moor	Ried	páramo	lande	charneca
park	Park	parque	parc	parque
railway station	Bahnhof	terminal ferroviaria	gare	estação ferroviária
reservoir	Stausee	estanque	réservoir	reservatório
tower	Turm	torre	tour	torre

Scale 1:300,000

One centimeter represents 3 kilometers.
One inch represents approximately 4.7 miles.

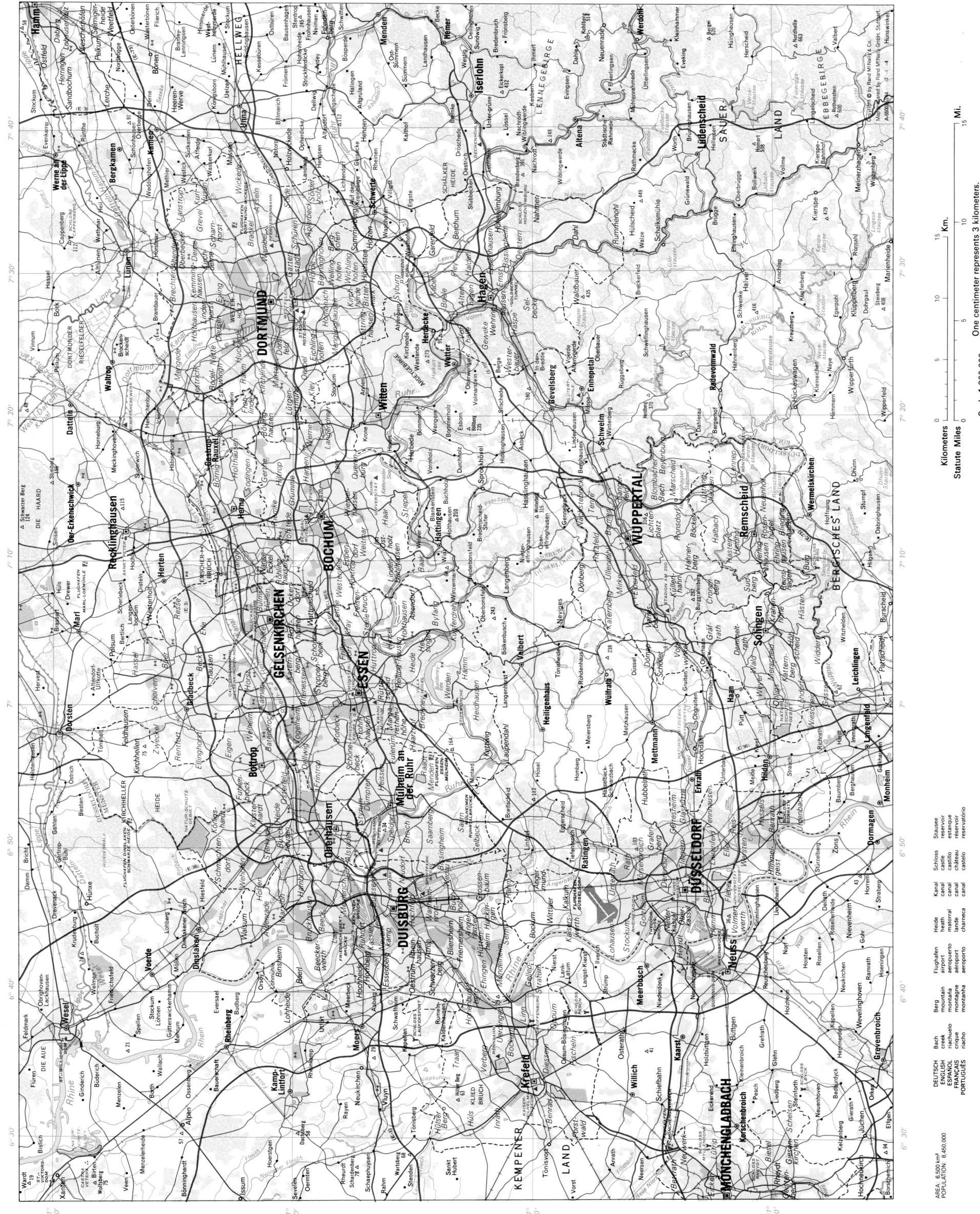

Kilometers

Statute Miles

One centimeter represents 3 kilometers.

One inch represents approximately 4.7 miles.

Scale 1:300,000

DEUTSCH	Bach	Berg	Flughafen	Heide	Kanal	Schloss	Stausee
ENGLISH	creek	mountain	airport	heath	canal	castle	reservoir
ESPAÑOL	riachuelo	montaña	aeropuerto	matorral	canal	castillo	estanque
FRANÇAIS	crique	montagne	aéroport	lande	canal	château	reservoir
PORTUGUES	riacho	montanha	aeroporto	charneca	canal	castelo	reservatório

AREA 6,500 km²
POPULATION 8,450,000

© by Rand M°Nally & Co.

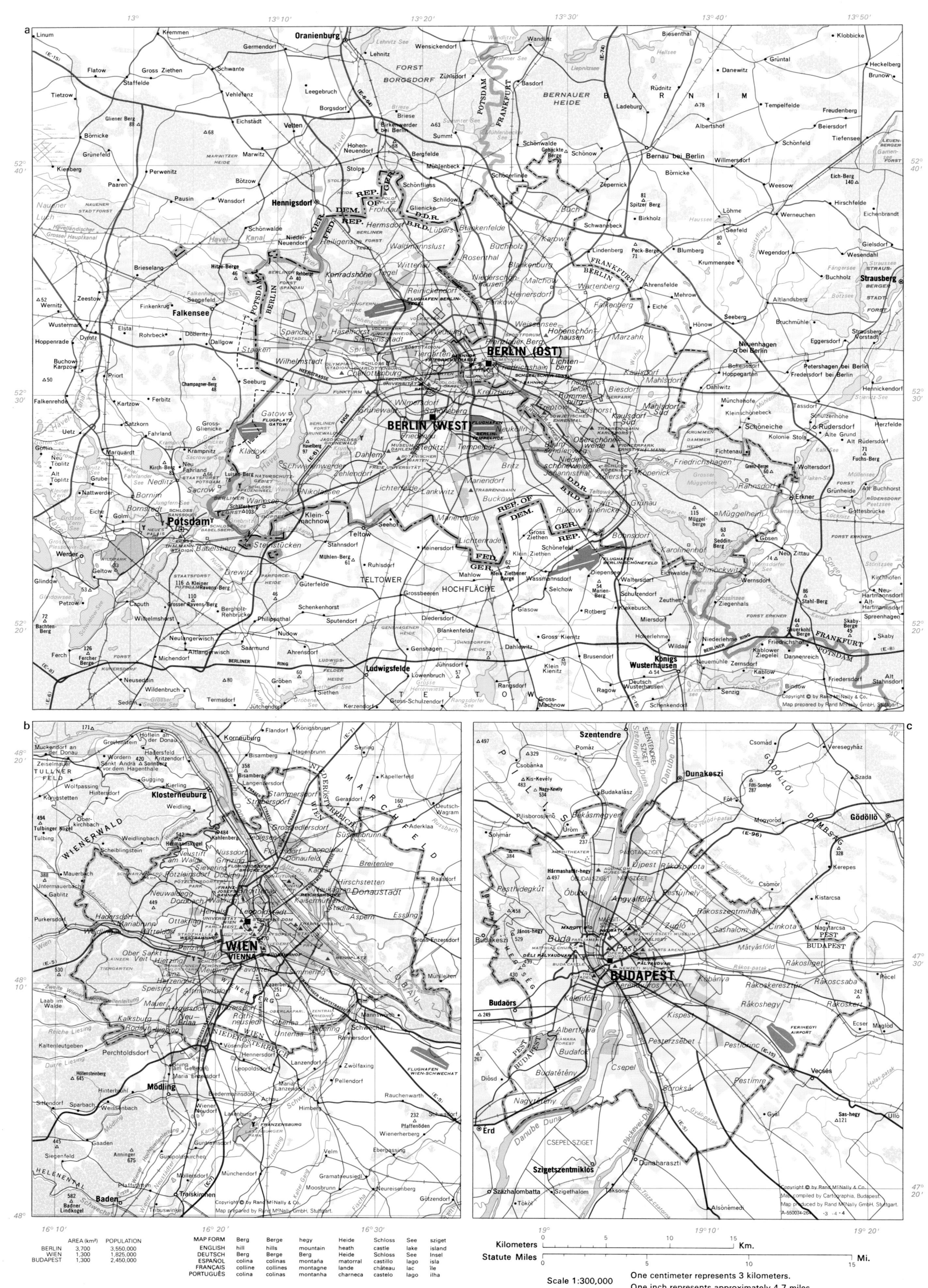

	AREA (km²)	POPULATION
BERLIN	3,700	3,550,000
WIEN	1,300	1,825,000
BUDAPEST	1,300	2,450,000

MAP FORM					
ENGLISH	hill	hills	mountain	heath	castle	lake	island
DEUTSCH	Berg	Berge	Berg	Heide	Schloss	See	Insel
ESPAÑOL	colina	colinas	montaña	matorral	castillo	lago	isla
FRANÇAIS	colline	collines	montagne	lande	château	lac	île
PORTUGUÊS	colina	colinas	montanha	charneca	castelo	lago	ilha

Scale 1:300,000

One centimeter represents 3 kilometers.
One inch represents approximately 4.7 miles.

a

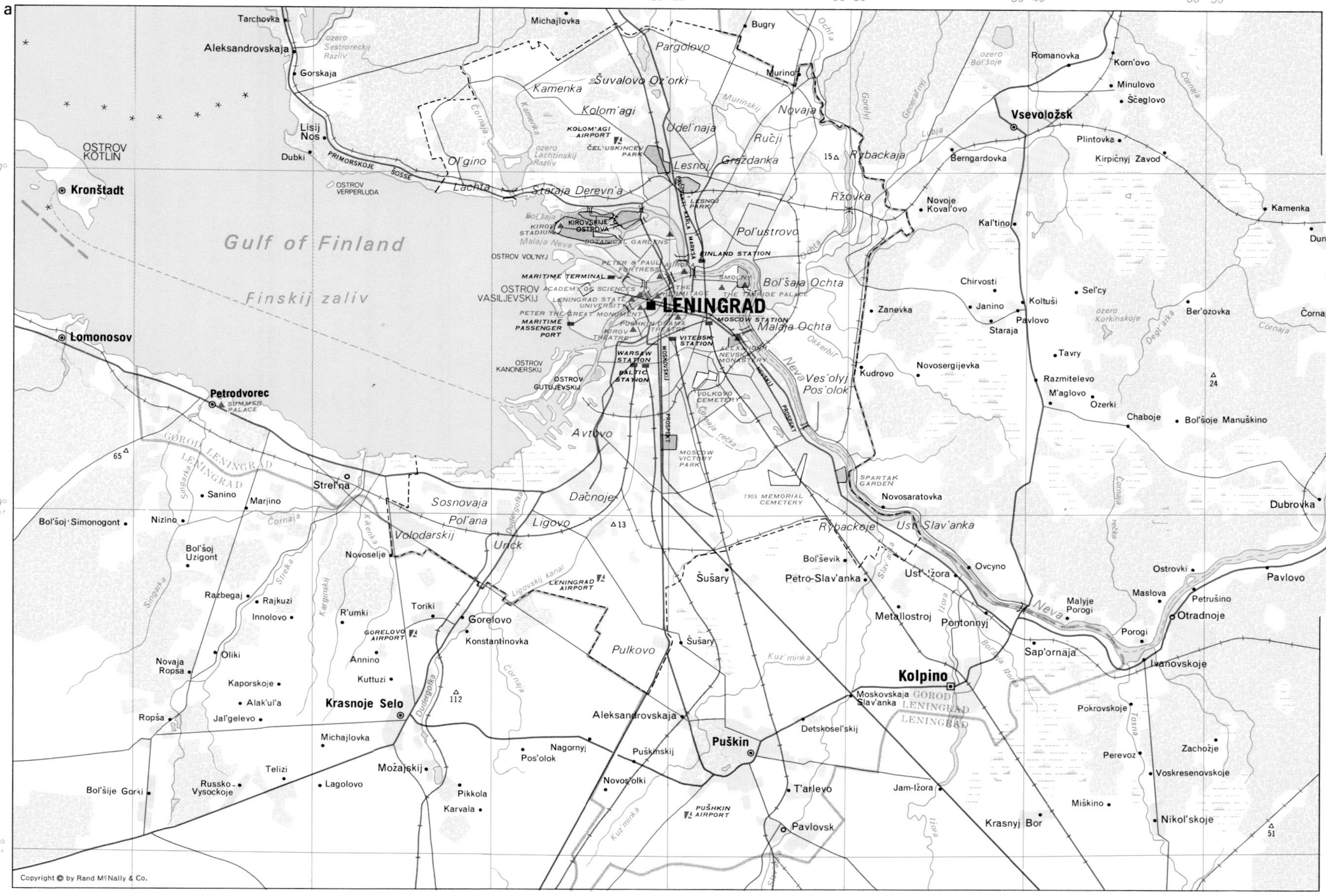

b

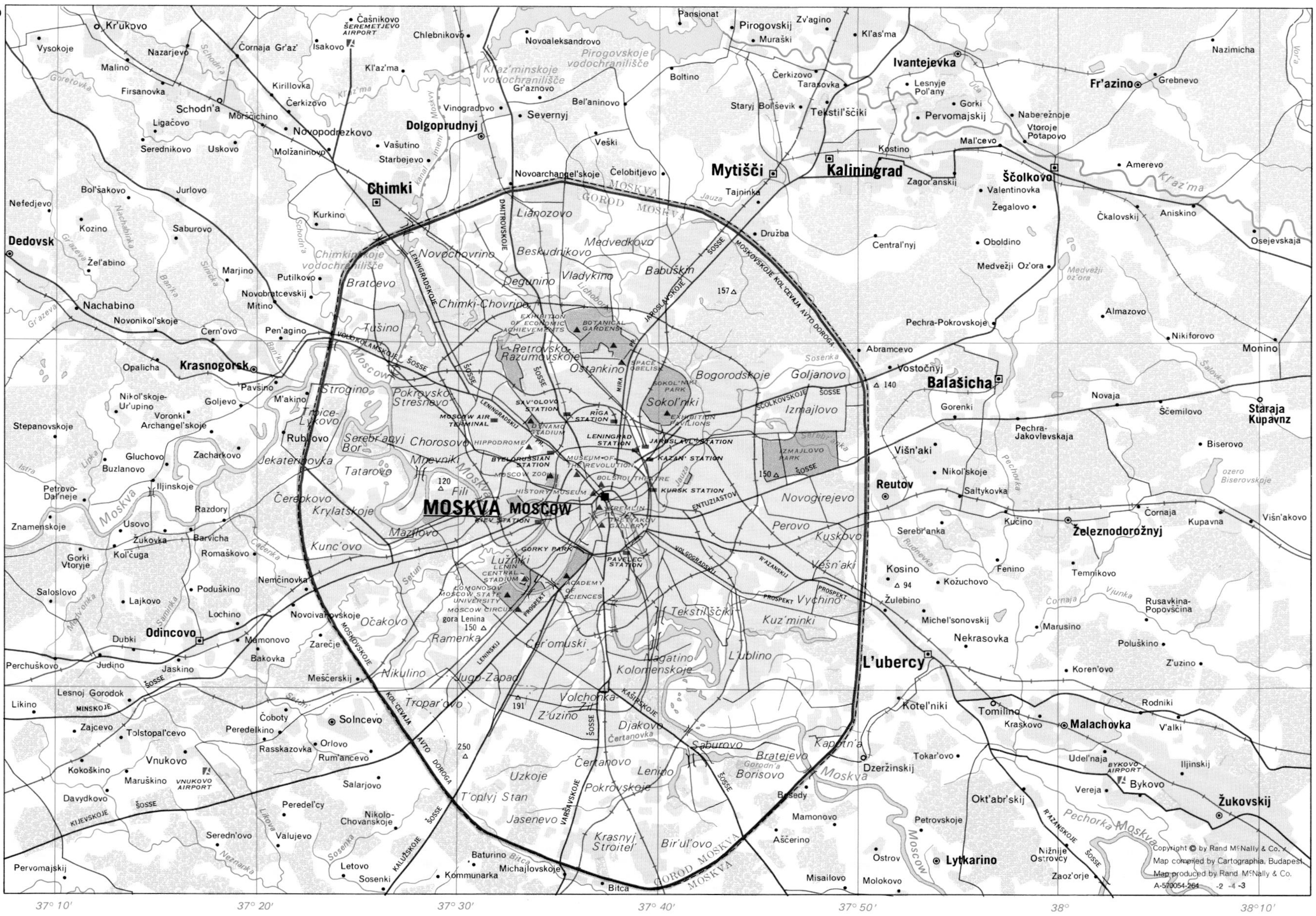

	AREA (km²)	POPULATION
LENINGRAD	2,800	4,850,000
MOSKVA	3,200	9,950,000

MAP FORM	ostrov	ozero	stadion	vodochranilišče	vokzal
ENGLISH	island	lake	stadium	reservoir	rail terminal
DEUTSCH	Insel	See	Stadion	Stausee	Bahnhof
ESPAÑOL	isla	lago	estadio	estanque	terminal ferroviaria
FRANÇAIS	île	lac	stade	réservoir	gare
PORTUGUÊS	ilha	lago	estádio	reservatório	estação ferroviária

Kilometers 0 5 10 15 Km.

Statute Miles 0 5 10 15 Mi.

Scale 1:300,000

One centimeter represents 3 kilometers.
One inch represents approximately 4.7 miles.

	AREA (km²)	POPULATION
MADRID	1,250	3,875,000
MILANO	1,900	3,975,000
LISBOA	1,150	2,150,000
BARCELONA	950	3,825,000

MAP FORM	aeroporto	arroyo	estación	ponta	ribeira	riera
ENGLISH	airport	brook	station	point	creek	creek
DEUTSCH	Flughafen	Bach	Bahnhof	Landspitze	Bach	Bach
ESPAÑOL	aeropuerto	arroyo	estación	punta	riachuelo	riera
FRANÇAIS	aéroport	ruisseau	gare	pointe	crique	crique
PORTUGUÊS	aeroporto	arroio	estação	ponta	riacho	riacho

Kilometers 0 5 10 15 Km.
Statute Miles 0 5 10 15 Mi.

Scale 1:300,000
One centimeter represents 3 kilometers.
One inch represents approximately 4.7 miles

a

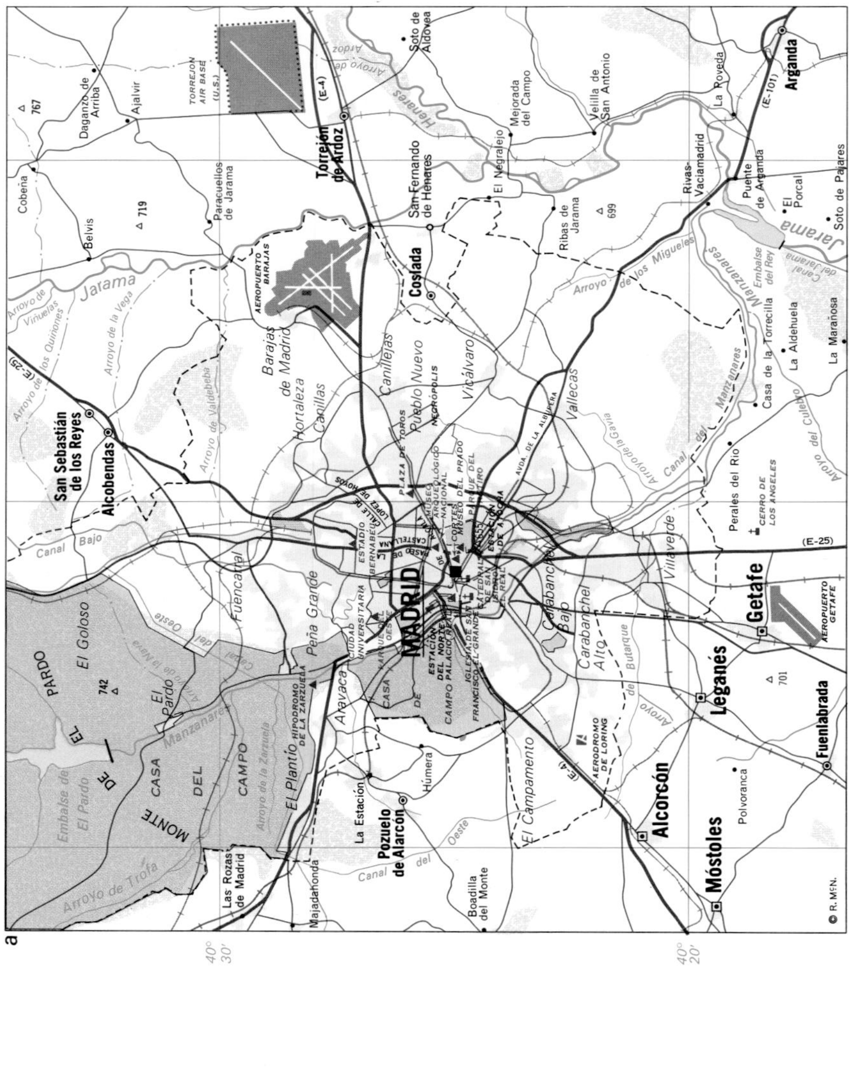

b

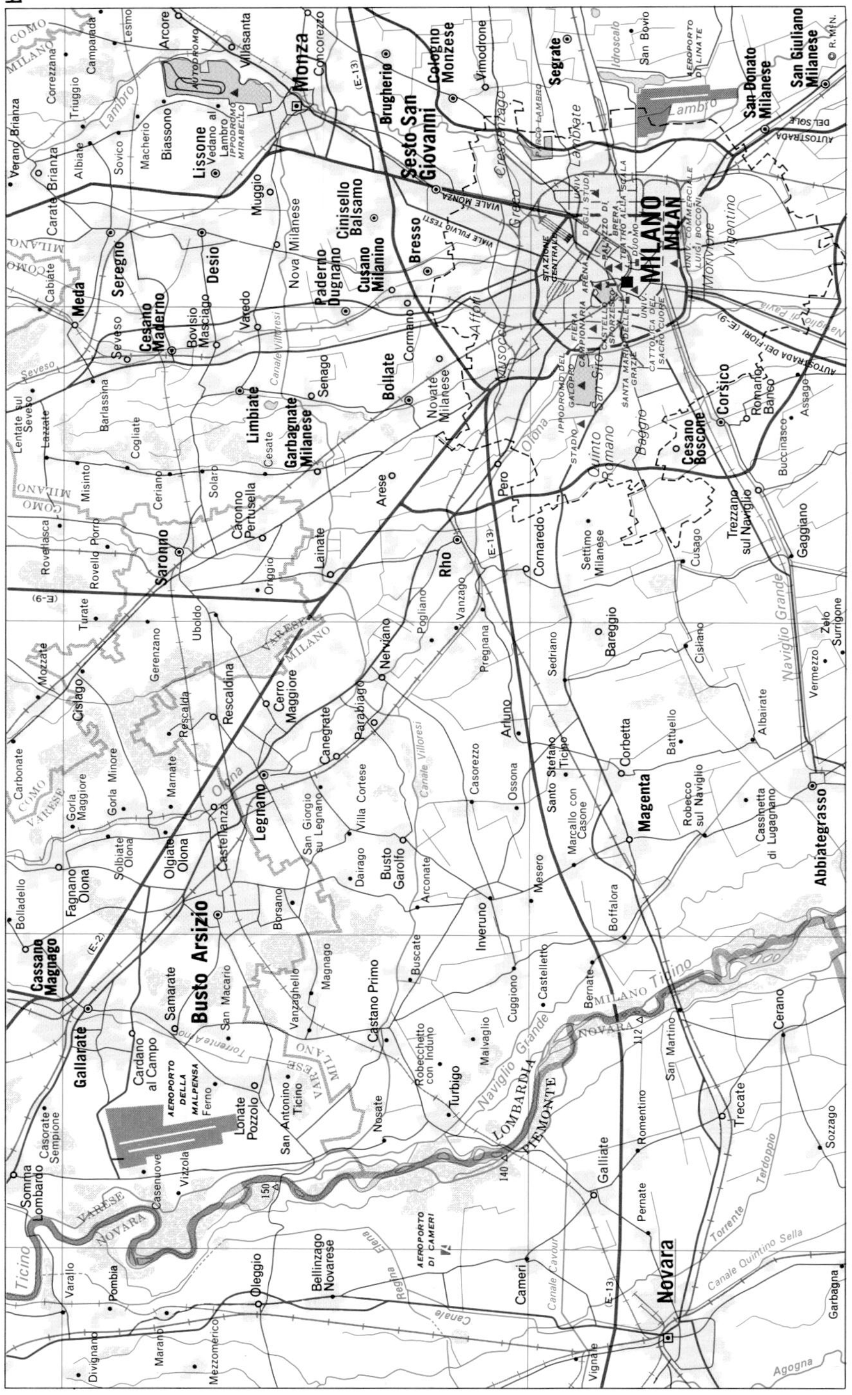

c

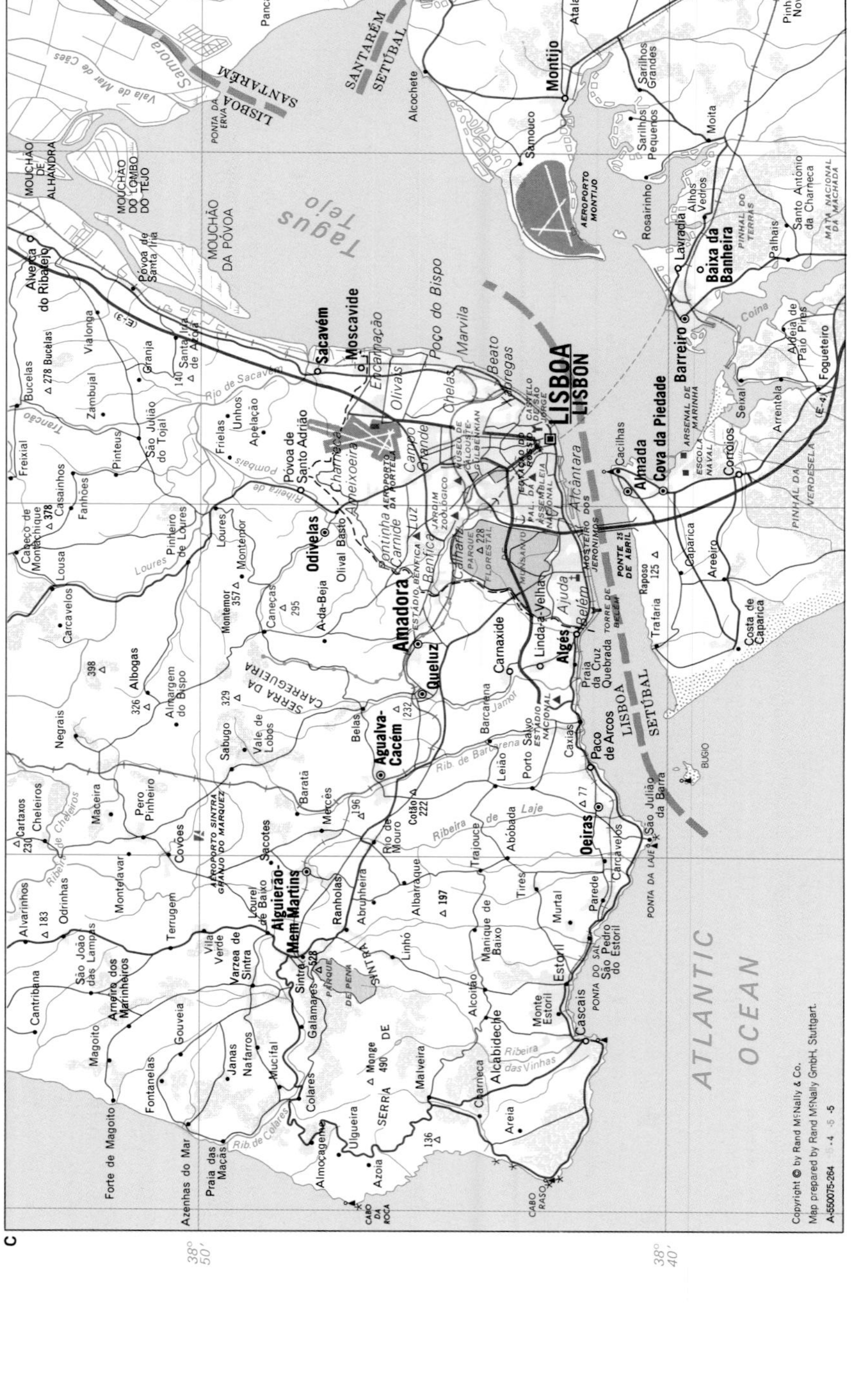

d

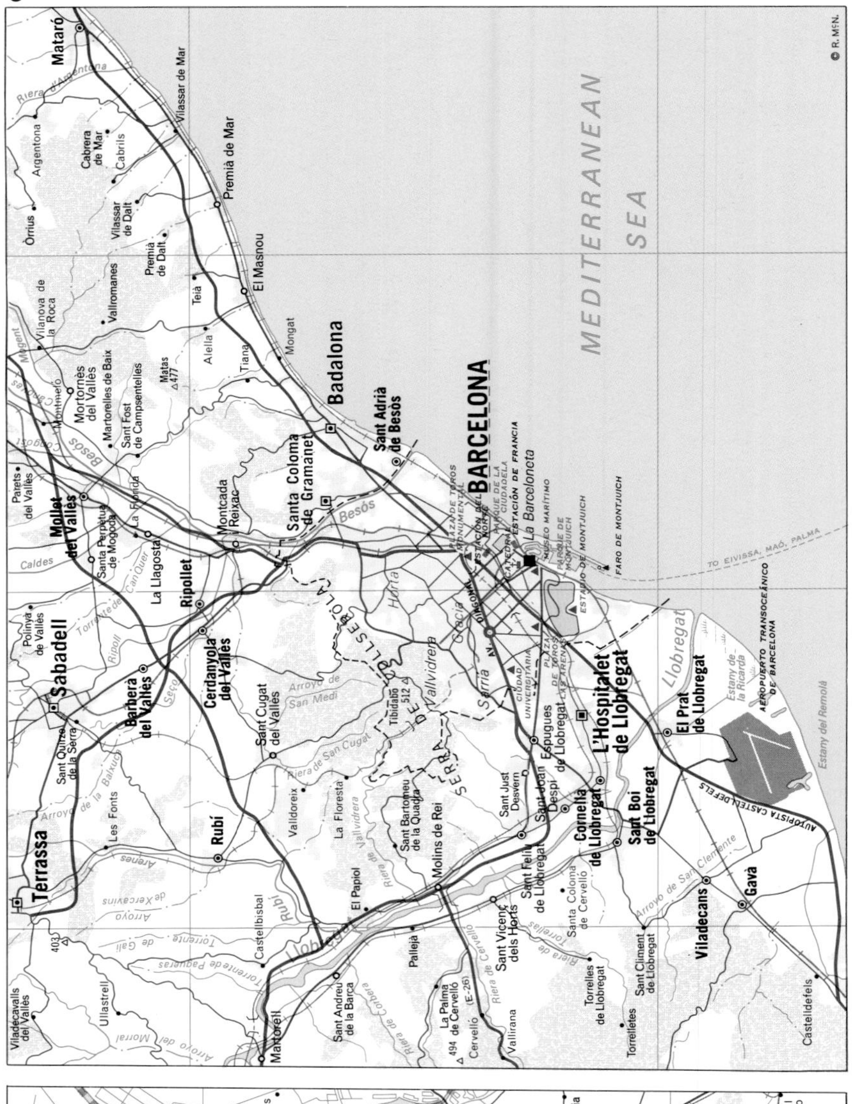

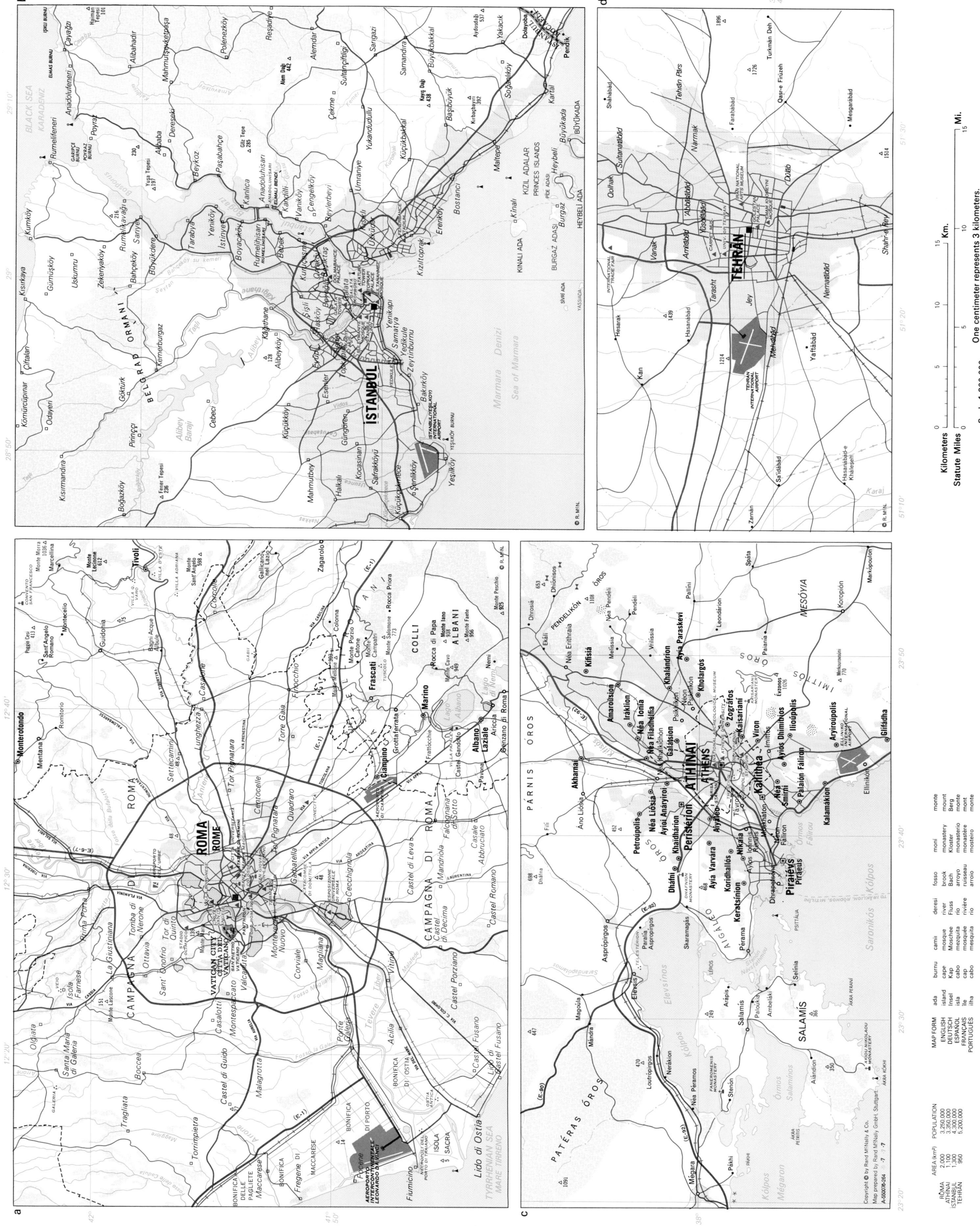

Copyright © by Rand McNally & Co.
Map prepared by Rand McNally GmbH, Stuttgart.
A-550078-264

Scale 1:300,000

One centimeter represents 3 kilometers.
One inch represents approximately 4.7 miles.

MAP FORM						
ENGLISH	island	cape	mosque	river	brook	monastery	mount
DEUTSCH	Insel	Kap	Moschee	Fluss	Bach	Kloster	Berg
ESPAÑOL	isla	cabo	mezquita	río	arroyo	monasterio	monte
FRANÇAIS	île	cap	mosquée	rivière	ruisseau	monastère	mont
PORTUGUÊS	ilha	cabo	mesquita	rio	arroio	mosteiro	monte
	ada	burnu	cami	deresi	fosso	moni	

	AREA (km²)	POPULATION
ROMA	2,000	3,250,000
ATHÍNAI	1,100	3,350,000
İSTANBUL	1,300	4,300,000
TEHRĀN	950	5,200,000

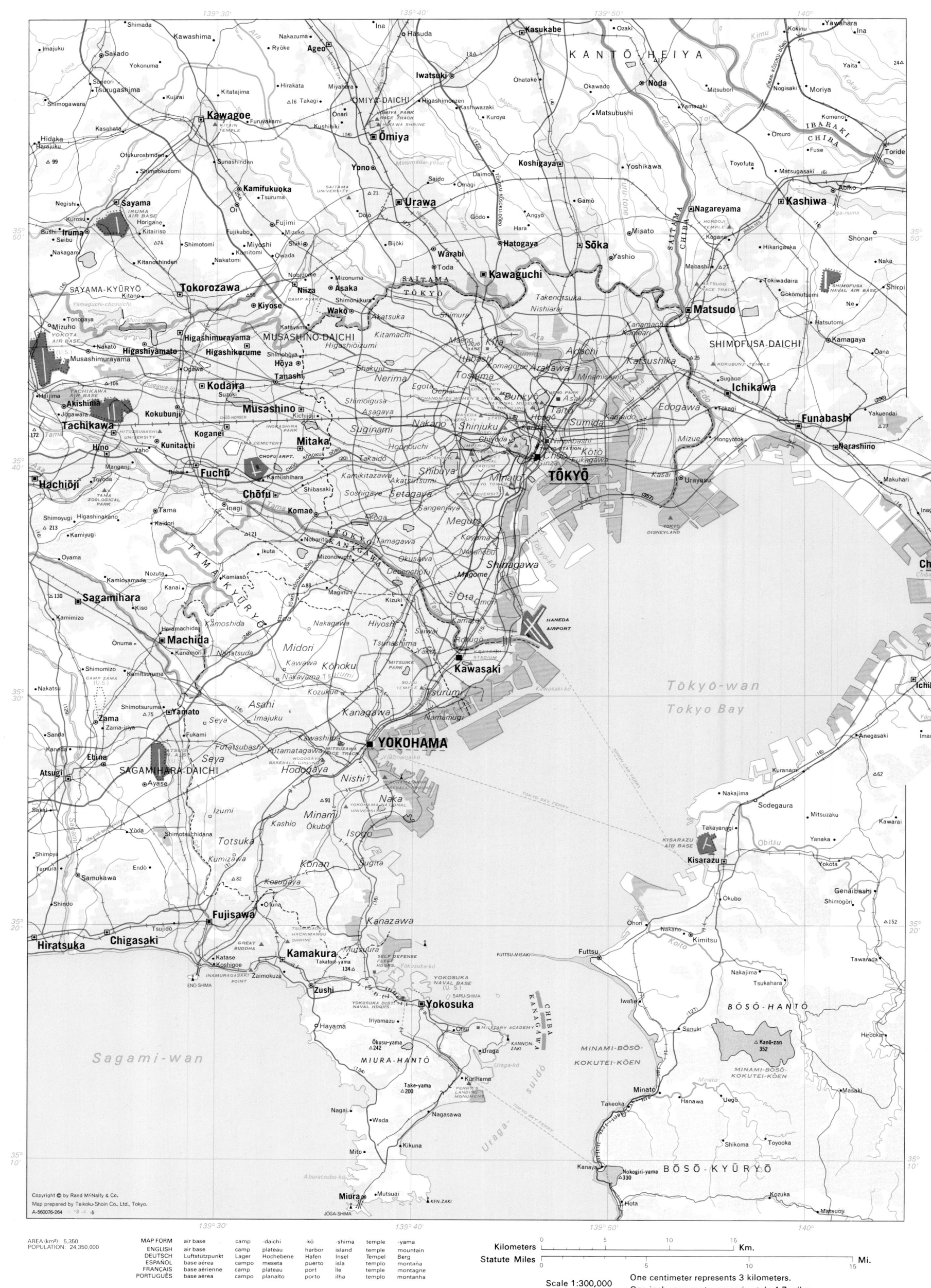

Copyright © by Rand McNally & Co.
Map prepared by Teikoku-Shoin Co., Ltd., Tokyo.
A-560076-264 -3 -4 -5

AREA (km²): 5,350
POPULATION: 24,350,000

MAP FORM						
ENGLISH	air base	camp	-daichi	-kō	-shima	temple	-yama
DEUTSCH	air base	camp	plateau	harbor	island	temple	mountain
ESPAÑOL	Luftstützpunkt	Lager	Hochebene	Hafen	Insel	Tempel	Berg
FRANÇAIS	base aérea	campo	meseta	puerto	isla	templo	montaña
PORTUGUÊS	base aérienne	campo	plateau	port	île	temple	montagne
	base aérea	campo	planalto	porto	ilha	templo	montanha

Kilometers 0   5   10   15 Km.
Statute Miles 0   5   10   15 Mi.

Scale 1:300,000

One centimeter represents 3 kilometers.
One inch represents approximately 4.7 miles.

a

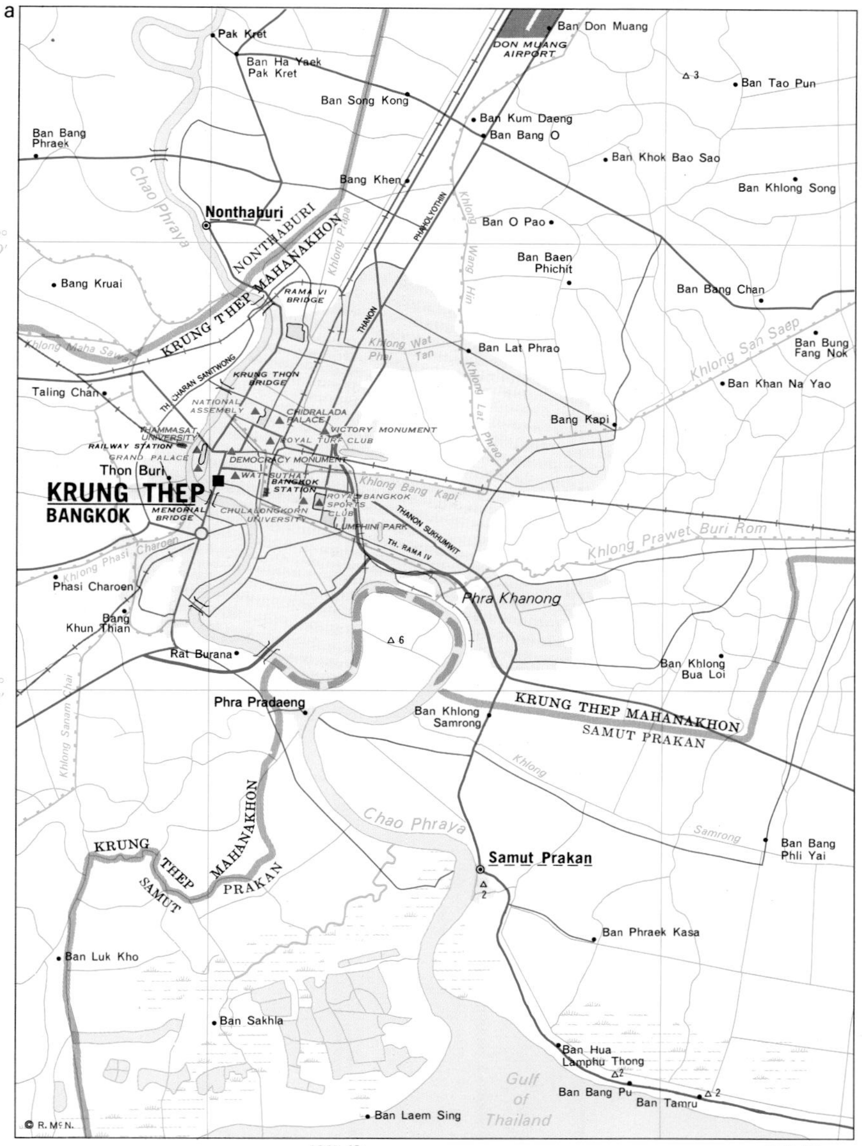

b

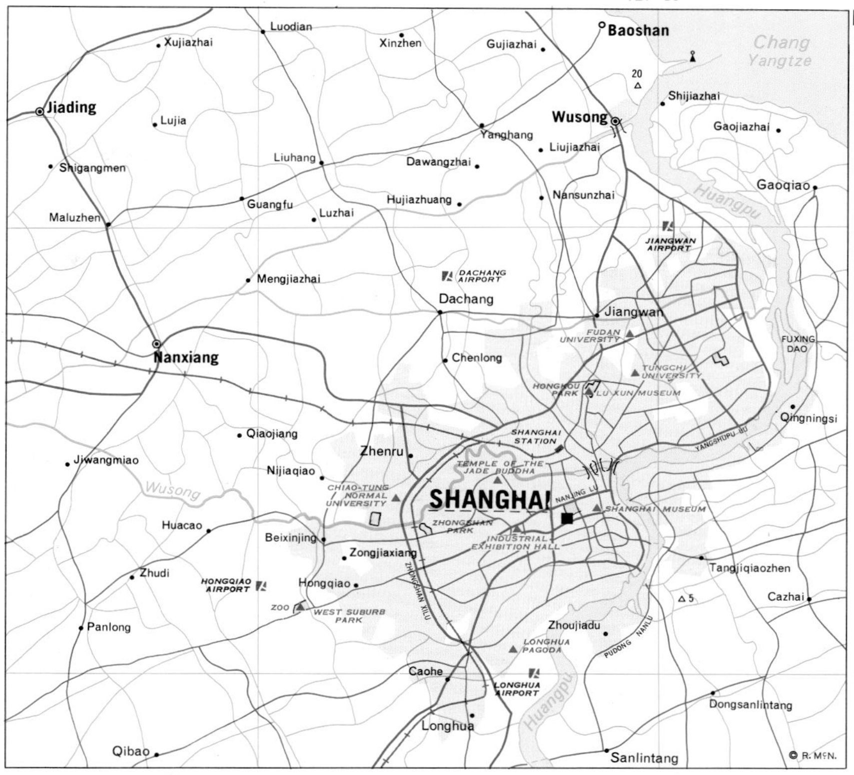

d

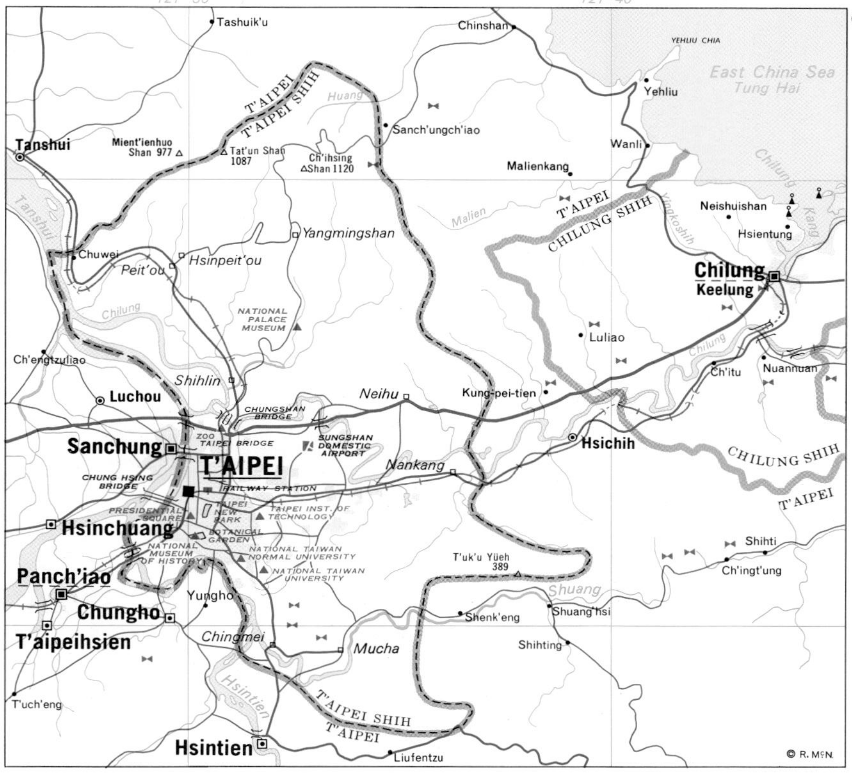

c

e

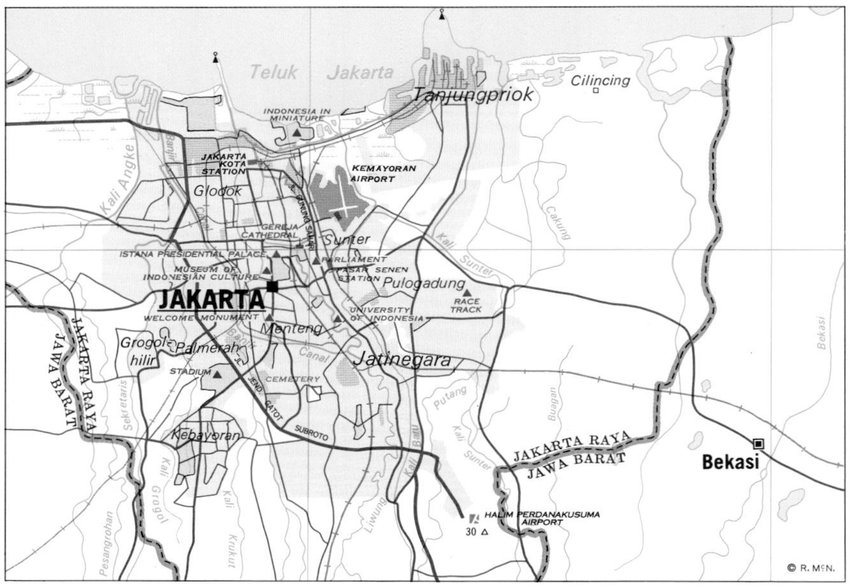

f

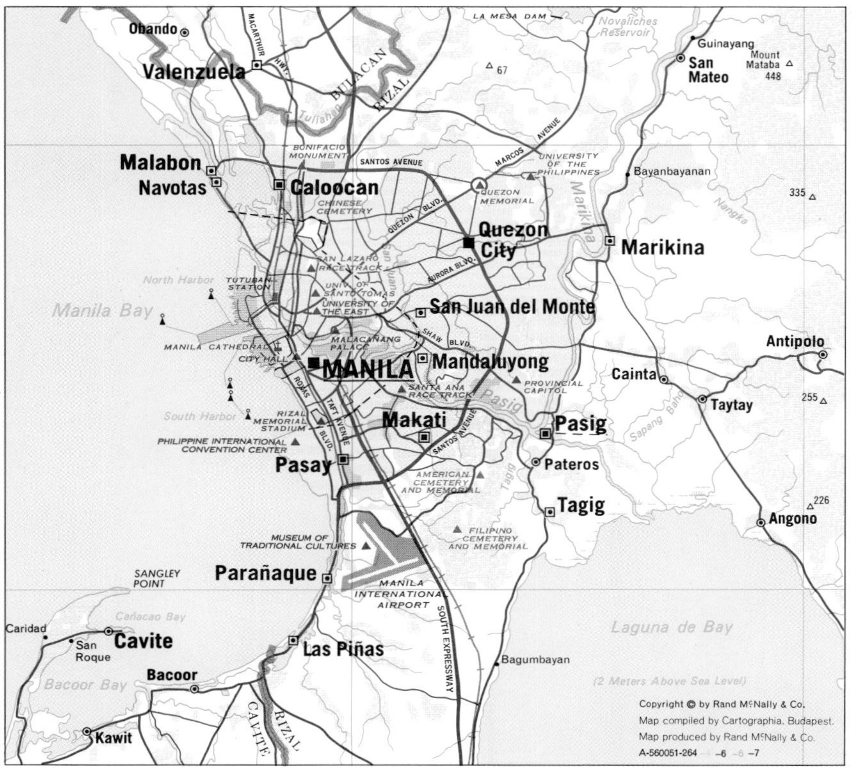

	AREA (km²)	POPULATION
KRUNG THEP (BANGKOK)	1,450	5,300,000
SAI-GON	750	2,400,000
JAKARTA	700	6,450,000
SHANGHAI	1,000	8,400,000
T'AIPEI	950	4,125,000
MANILA	650	5,900,000

MAP FORM	kali	khlong	monument	shan
ENGLISH	stream	stream	monument	mountain
DEUTSCH	Bach	Bach	Denkmal	Berg
ESPAÑOL	corriente de agua	corriente de agua	monumento	montaña
FRANÇAIS	cours d'eau	cours d'eau	monument	montagne
PORTUGUÊS	corrente de água	corrente de água	monumento	montanha

Kilometers 0 5 10 15 Km.
Statute Miles 0 5 10 15 Mi.

Scale 1:300,000

One centimeter represents 3 kilometers.
One inch represents approximately 4.7 miles.

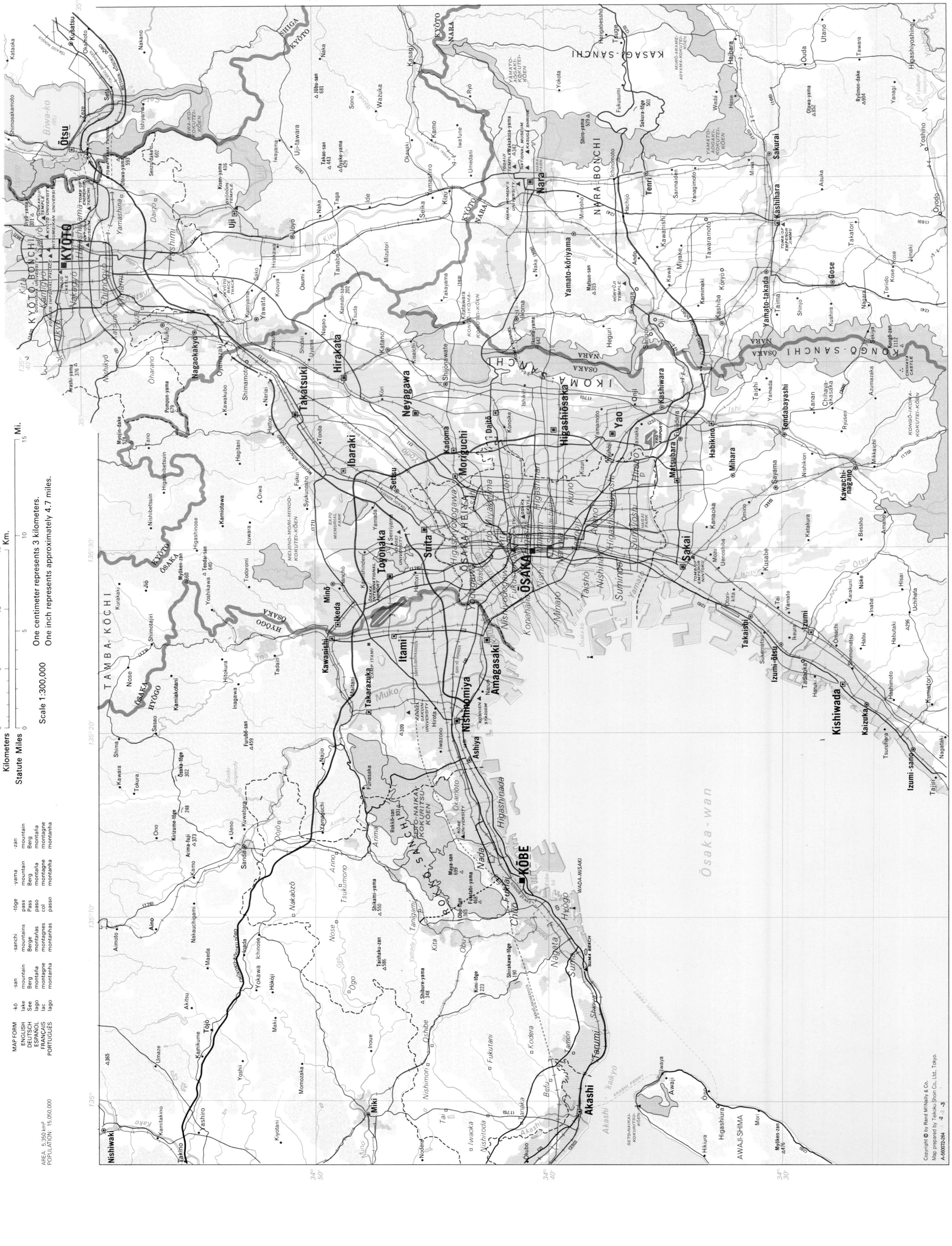

MAP FORM	-kō	-san	-sanchi	-tōge	-yama	-zan
ENGLISH	lake	mountain	mountains	pass	mountain	mountain
DEUTSCH	See	Berg	Berge	Pass	Berg	Berg
ESPAÑOL	lago	montaña	montañas	paso	montaña	montaña
FRANÇAIS	lac	montagne	montagnes	col	montagne	montagne
PORTUGUÊS	lago	montanha	montanhas	passo	montanha	montanha

AREA: 5,350 km²
POPULATION: 15,050,000

a
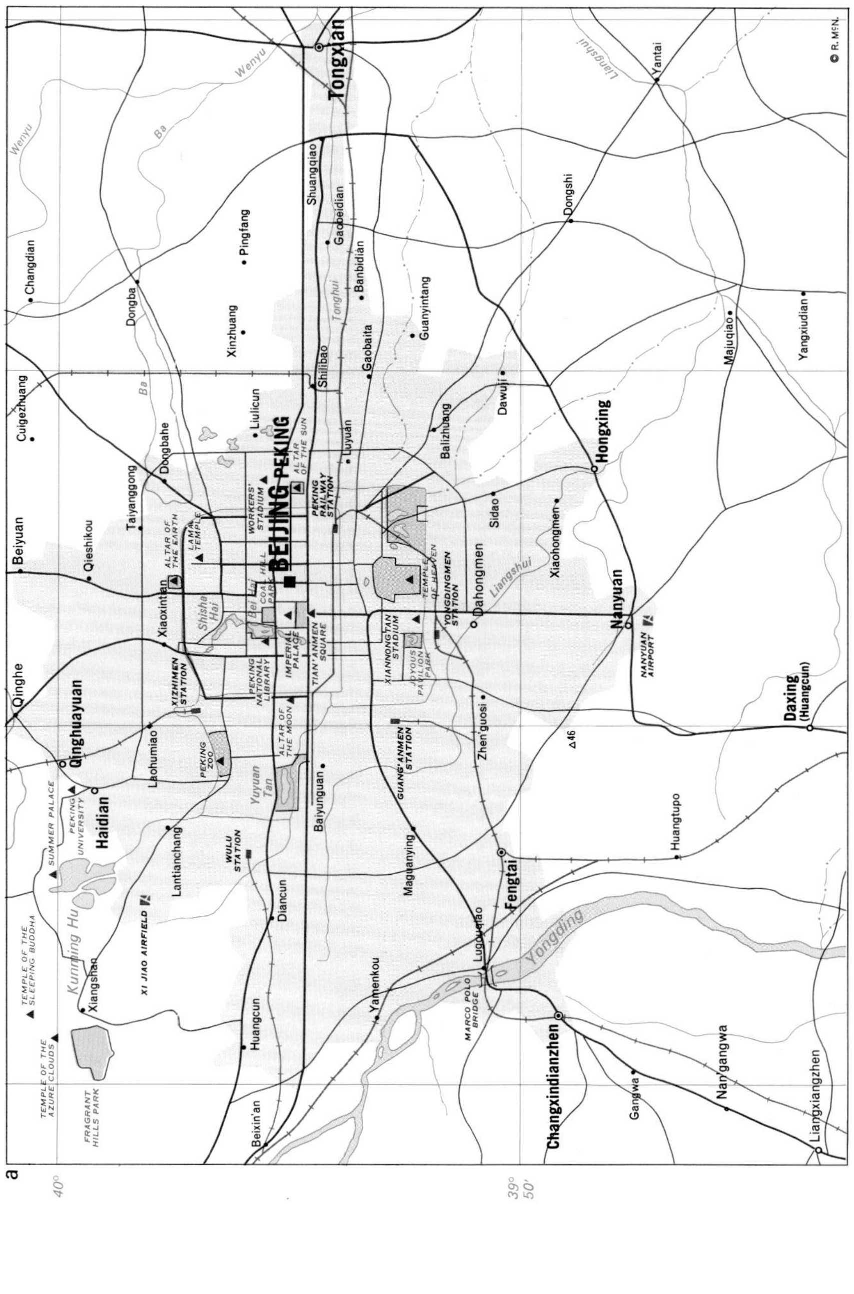

b
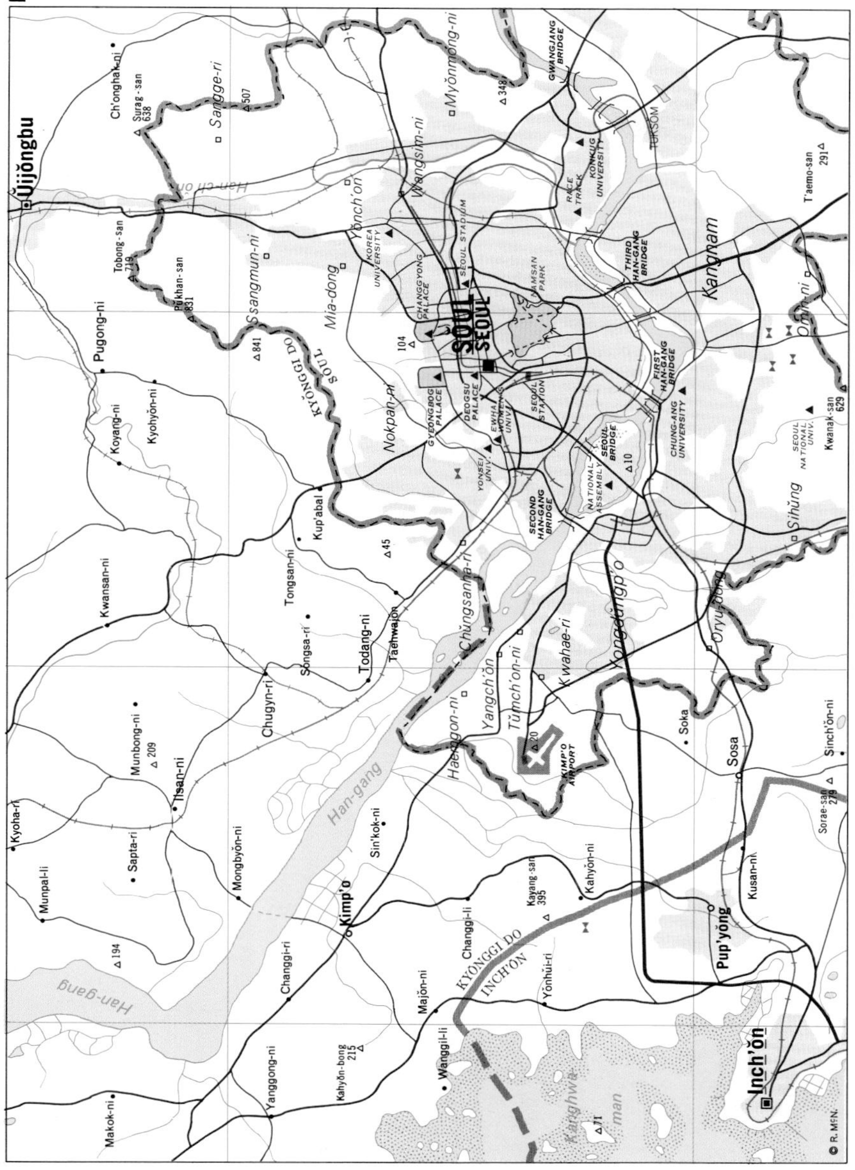

c
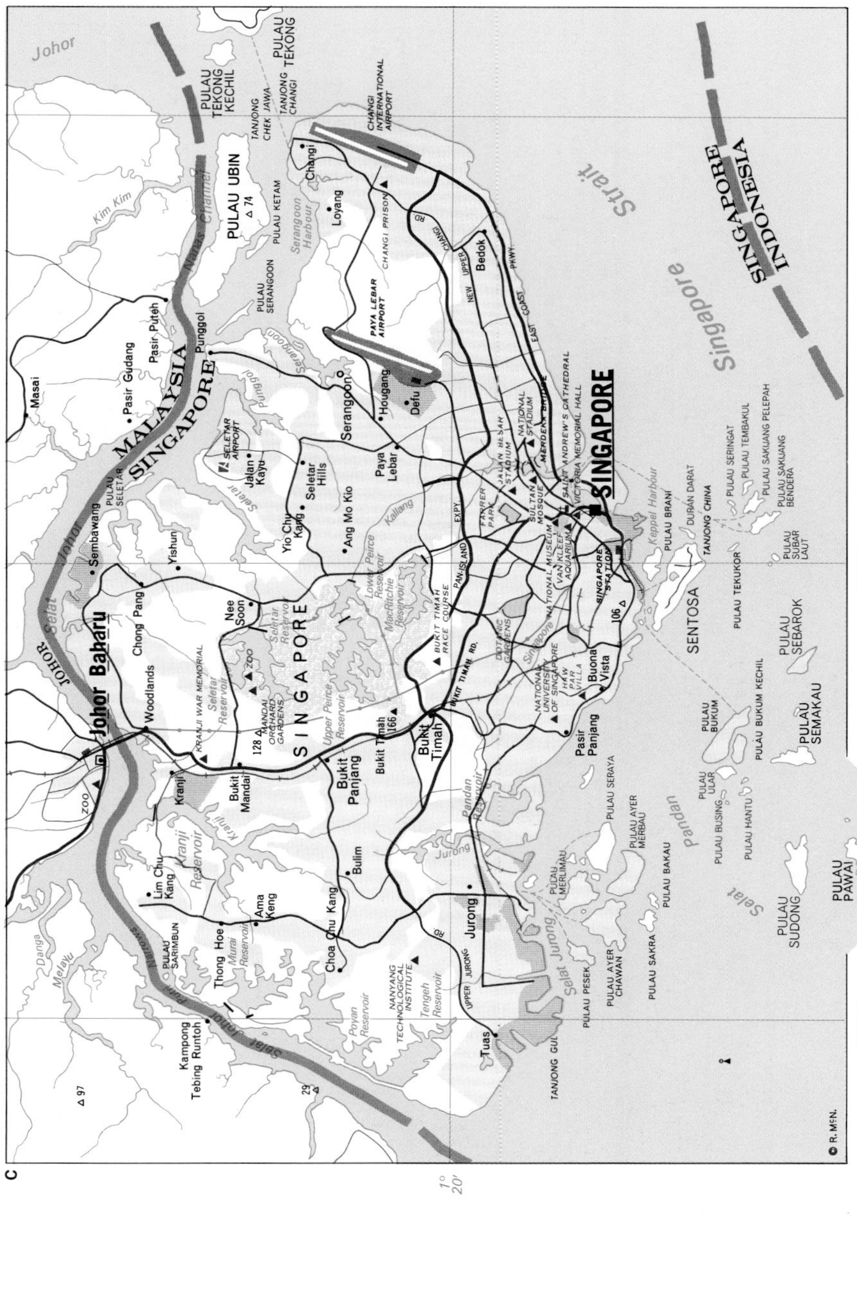

d

Scale 1:300,000

Kilometers 0 5 10 15 Km.

Statute Miles 0 5 10 15 Mi.

One centimeter represents 3 kilometers.
One inch represents approximately 4.7 miles.

	AREA (km²)	POPULATION
BEIJING (PEKING)	1,550	5,300,000
SŎUL	1,450	9,300,000
SINGAPORE	900	2,600,000
HONG KONG	650	4,450,000

MAP FORM	airport	chau	island	park	peak	reservoir	wan
ENGLISH	airport	island	island	park	peak	reservoir	bay
DEUTSCH	Flughafen	Insel	Insel	Park	Gipfel	Stausee	Bucht
ESPAÑOL	aeropuerto	isla	isla	parque	pico	estanque	bahía
FRANÇAIS	aéroport	île	île	parc	cime	réservoir	baie
PORTUGUÊS	aeroporto	ilha	ilha	parque	pico	reservatório	baía

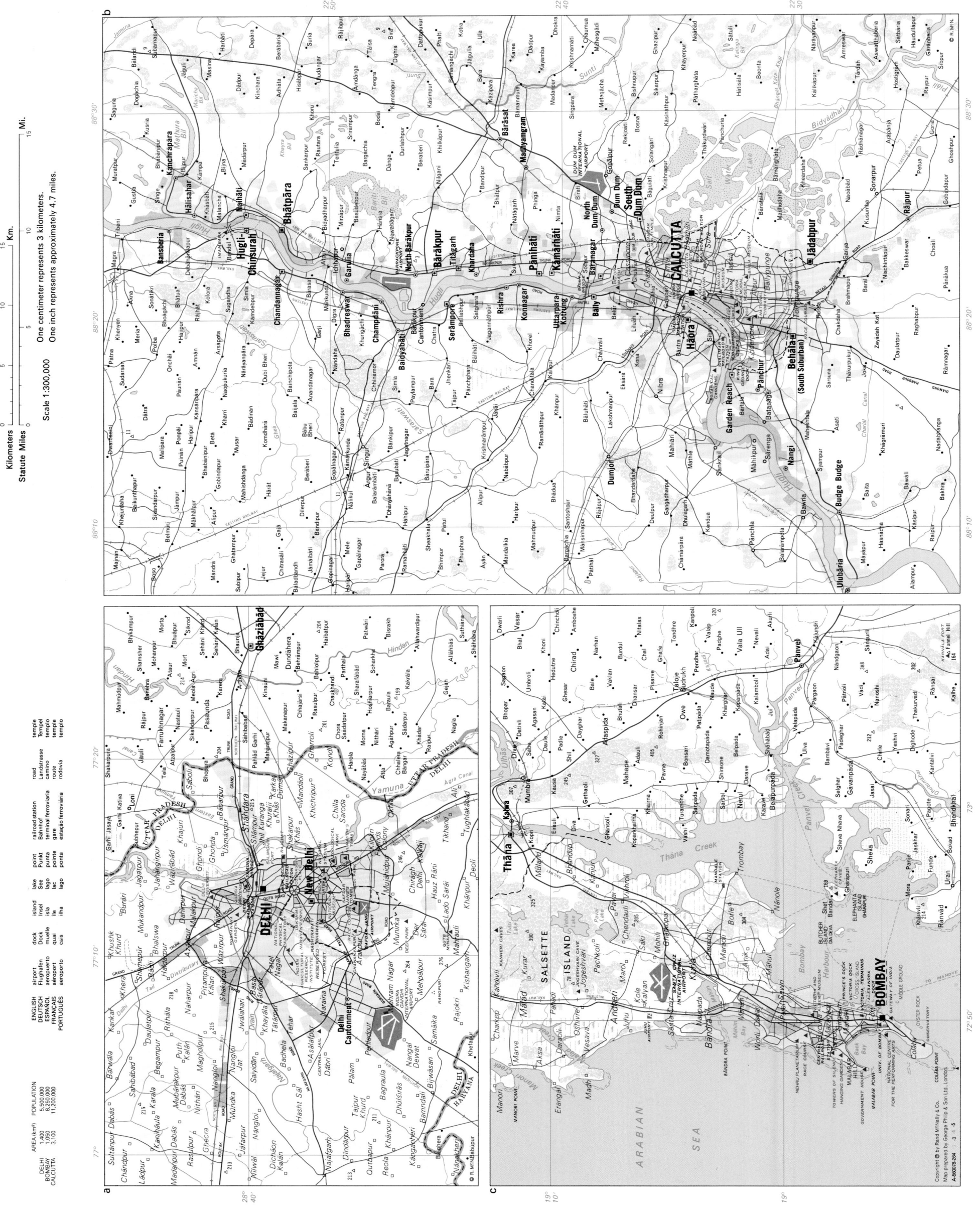

One centimeter represents 3 kilometers.
One inch represents approximately 4.7 miles.

Scale 1:300,000

Kilometers
Statute Miles

	AREA (km²)	POPULATION
DELHI	1,400	5,500,000
BOMBAY	1,050	8,250,000
CALCUTTA	3,100	11,200,000

ENGLISH	airport	dock	island	lake	point	railroad station	road	temple
DEUTSCH	Flughafen	Dock	Insel	Insel	Punkt	Bahnhof	Landstrasse	Tempel
FRANÇAIS	aéroport	quai	île	lac	pointe	gare	route	temple
ESPAÑOL	aeropuerto	muelle	isla	lago	punta	terminal ferroviaria	camino	templo
PORTUGUÊS	aeroporto	cais	ilha	lago	ponta	estação ferroviária	rodovia	templo

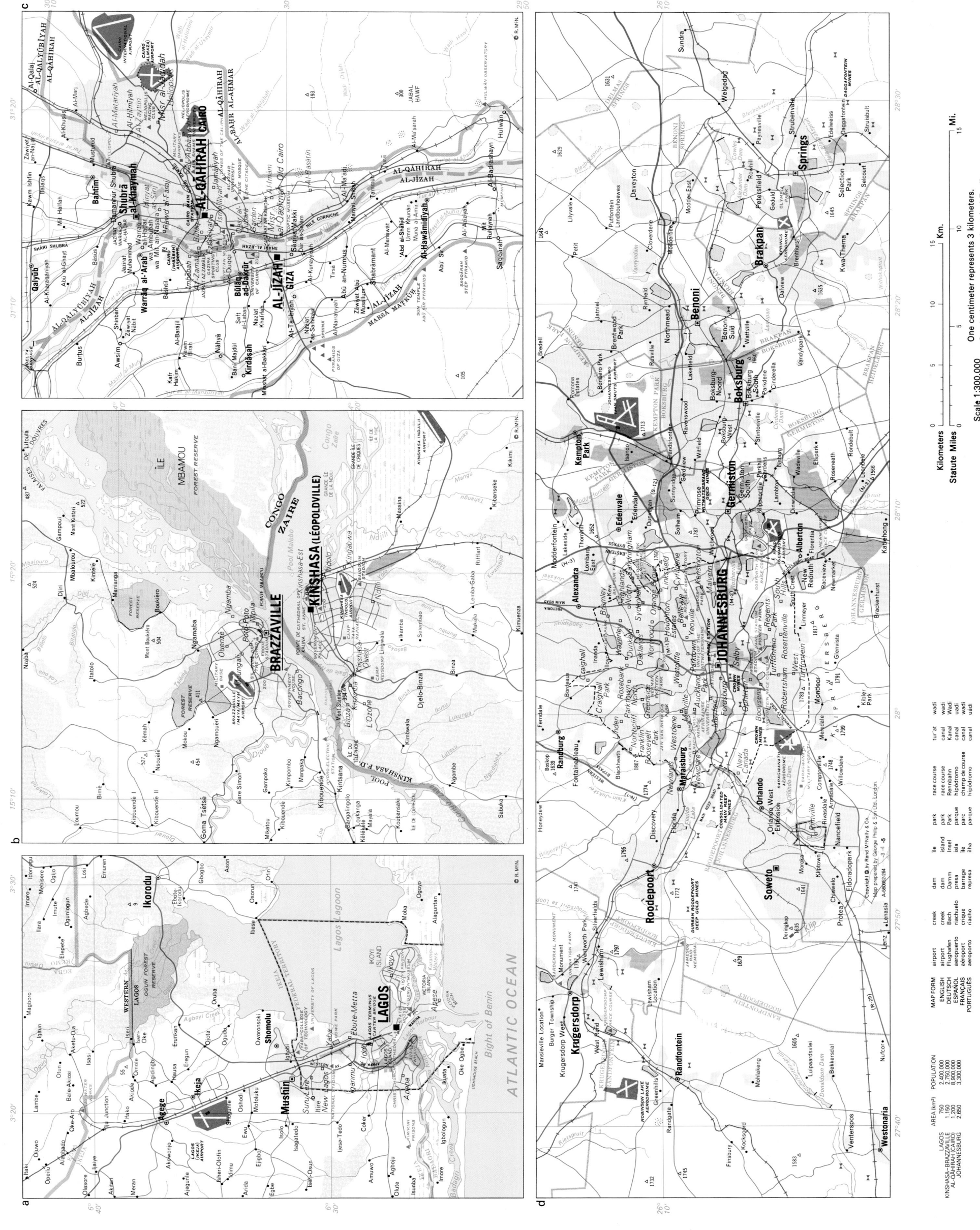

Scale 1:300,000

One centimeter represents 3 kilometers.
One inch represents approximately 4.7 miles.

MAP FORM							
ENGLISH	airport	creek	dam	Iie	island	park	race course	turf at
DEUTSCH	airport	creek	dam	island	inset	park	race course	wadi
ESPAÑOL	Flughafen	Bach	Damm	isla		Park	Rennbahn	Kanal
FRANÇAIS	aeropuerto	riachuelo	presa	isla		parque	hipódromo	canal
	aéroport	crique	barrage	île		parc	champ de course	canal
PORTUGUÊS	aeroporto	riacho	represa	ilha		parque	hipódromo	canal

Copyright by Rand McNally & Co.
Map prepared by George Philip & Son Ltd, London.
A-560062-264 -3 -4 -5

	AREA (km²)	POPULATION
LAGOS	750	1,150,000
KINSHASA-BRAZZAVILLE	1,200	2,750,000
AL-QĀHIRAH (CAIRO)	1,200	8,900,000
JOHANNESBURG	2,650	3,300,000

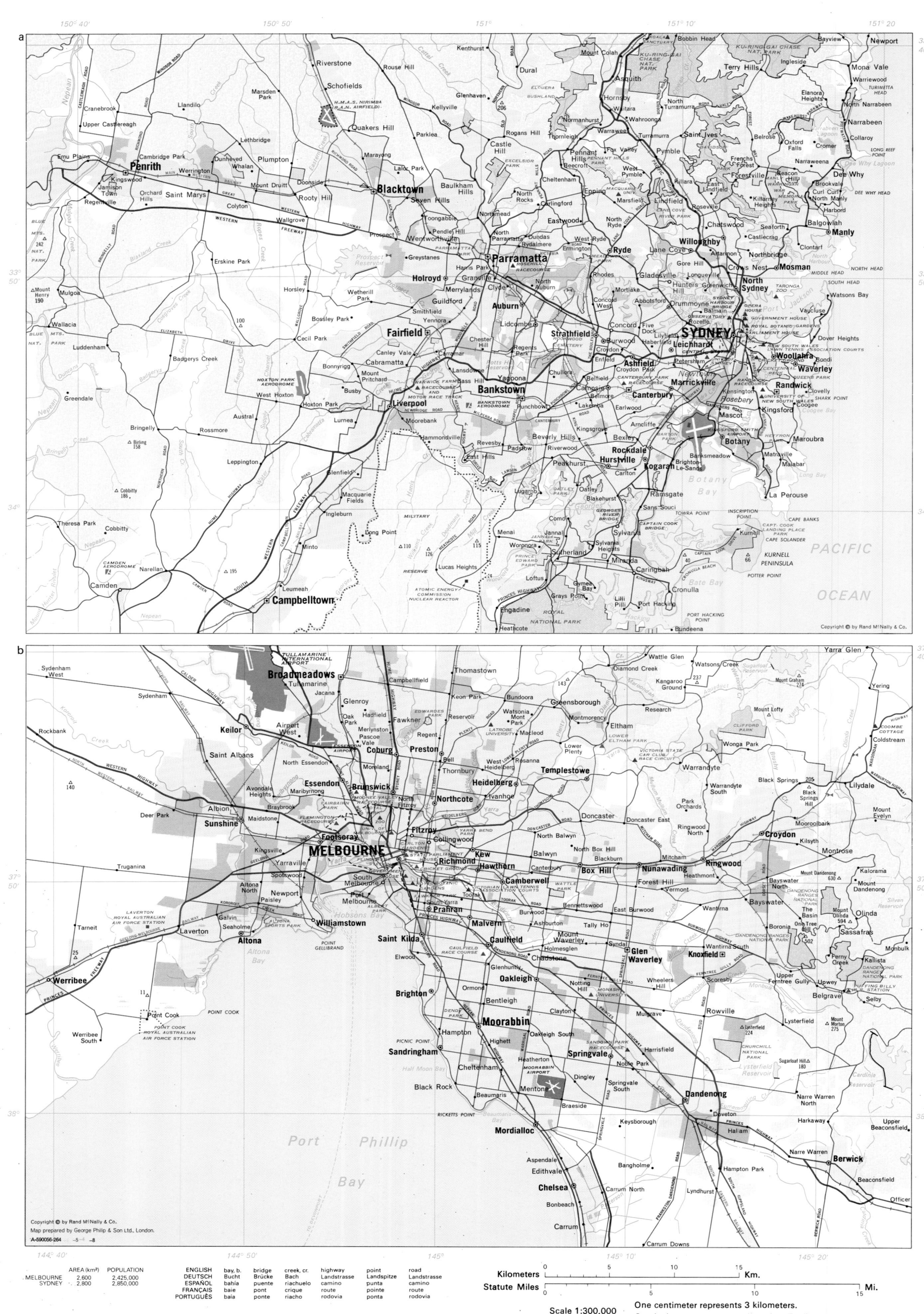

	AREA (km²)	POPULATION
MELBOURNE	2,600	2,425,000
SYDNEY	2,800	2,850,000

	bay, b.	bridge	creek, cr.	highway	point	road
ENGLISH	bay, b.	bridge	creek, cr.	highway	point	road
DEUTSCH	Bucht	Brücke	Bach	Landstrasse	Landspitze	Landstrasse
ESPAÑOL	bahía	puente	riachuelo	camino	punta	camino
FRANÇAIS	baie	pont	crique	route	pointe	route
PORTUGUÊS	baía	ponte	riacho	rodovia	ponta	rodovia

Kilometers   0   5   10   15   Km.

Statute Miles   0   5   10   15   Mi.

Scale 1:300,000   One centimeter represents 3 kilometers.
One inch represents approximately 4.7 miles.

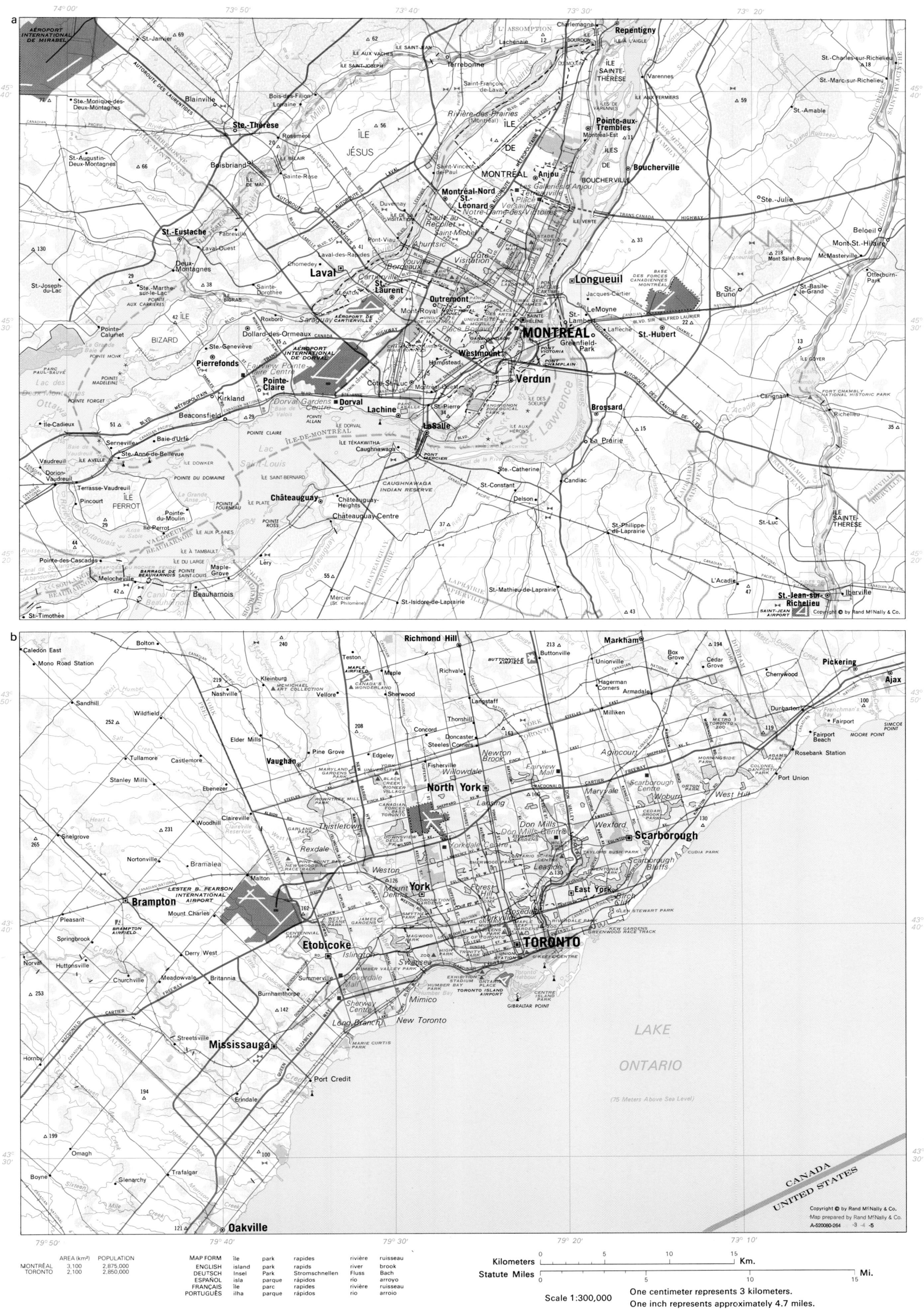

a

b

	AREA (km²)	POPULATION
MONTRÉAL	3,100	2,875,000
TORONTO	2,100	2,850,000

MAP FORM					
ENGLISH	île	park	rapides	rivière	ruisseau
	island	park	rapids	river	brook
DEUTSCH	Insel	Park	Stromschnellen	Fluss	Bach
ESPAÑOL	isla	parque	rápidos	rio	arroyo
FRANÇAIS	île	parc	rapides	rivière	ruisseau
PORTUGUÊS	ilha	parque	rápidos	rio	arroio

Kilometers   0   5   10   Km.

Statute Miles   0   5   10   15   Mi.

Scale 1:300,000

One centimeter represents 3 kilometers.
One inch represents approximately 4.7 miles.

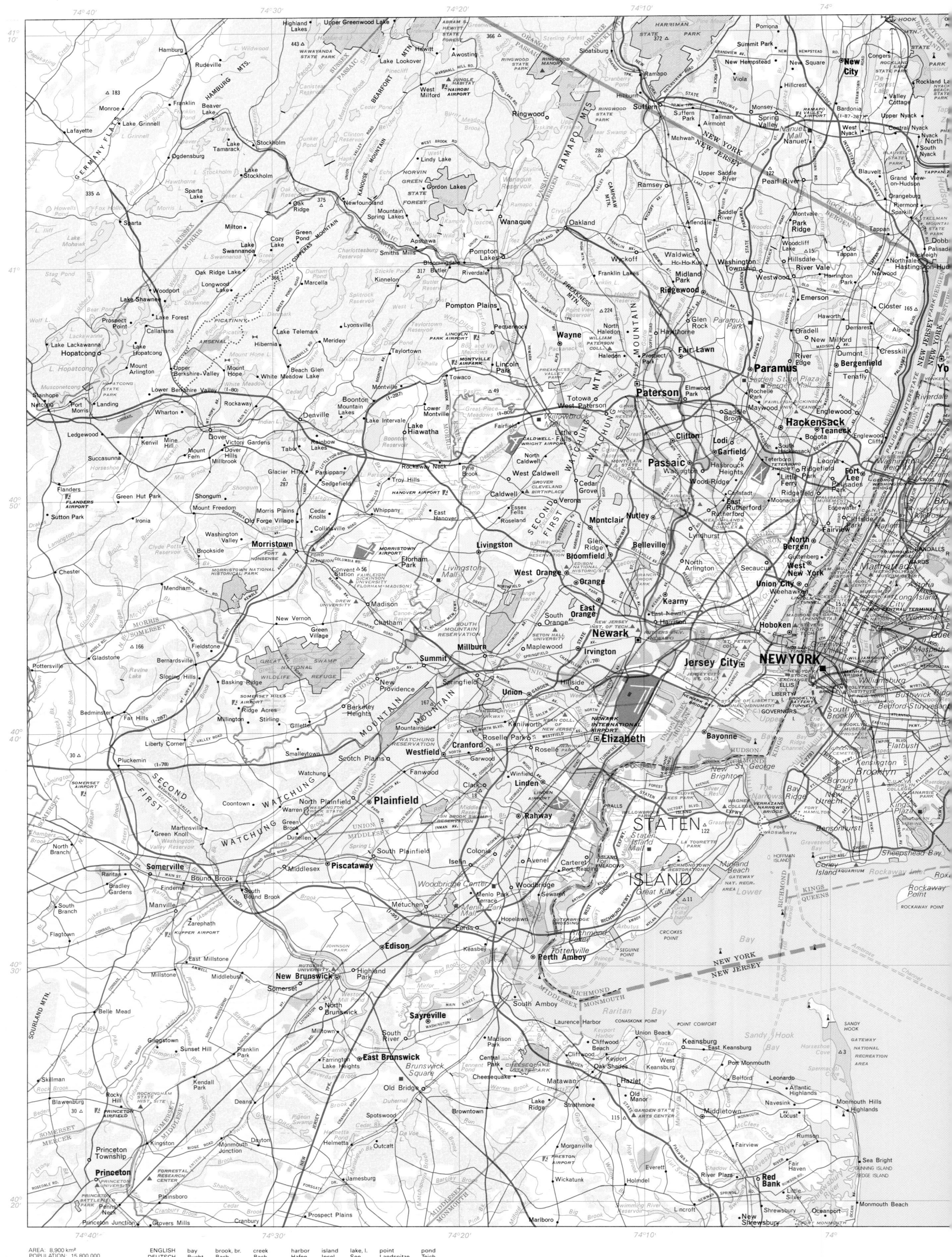

AREA: 8,900 km²
POPULATION: 15,800,000

ENGLISH	bay	brook, br.	creek	harbor	island	lake, l.	point	pond
DEUTSCH	Bucht	Bach	Bach	Hafen	Insel	See	Landspitze	Teich
ESPAÑOL	bahia	arroyo	riachuelo	puerto	isla	lago	punta	charca
FRANÇAIS	baie	ruisseau	crique	port	île	lac	pointe	étang
PORTUGUÊS	baia	arroio	riacho	porto	ilha	lago	ponta	lagoa

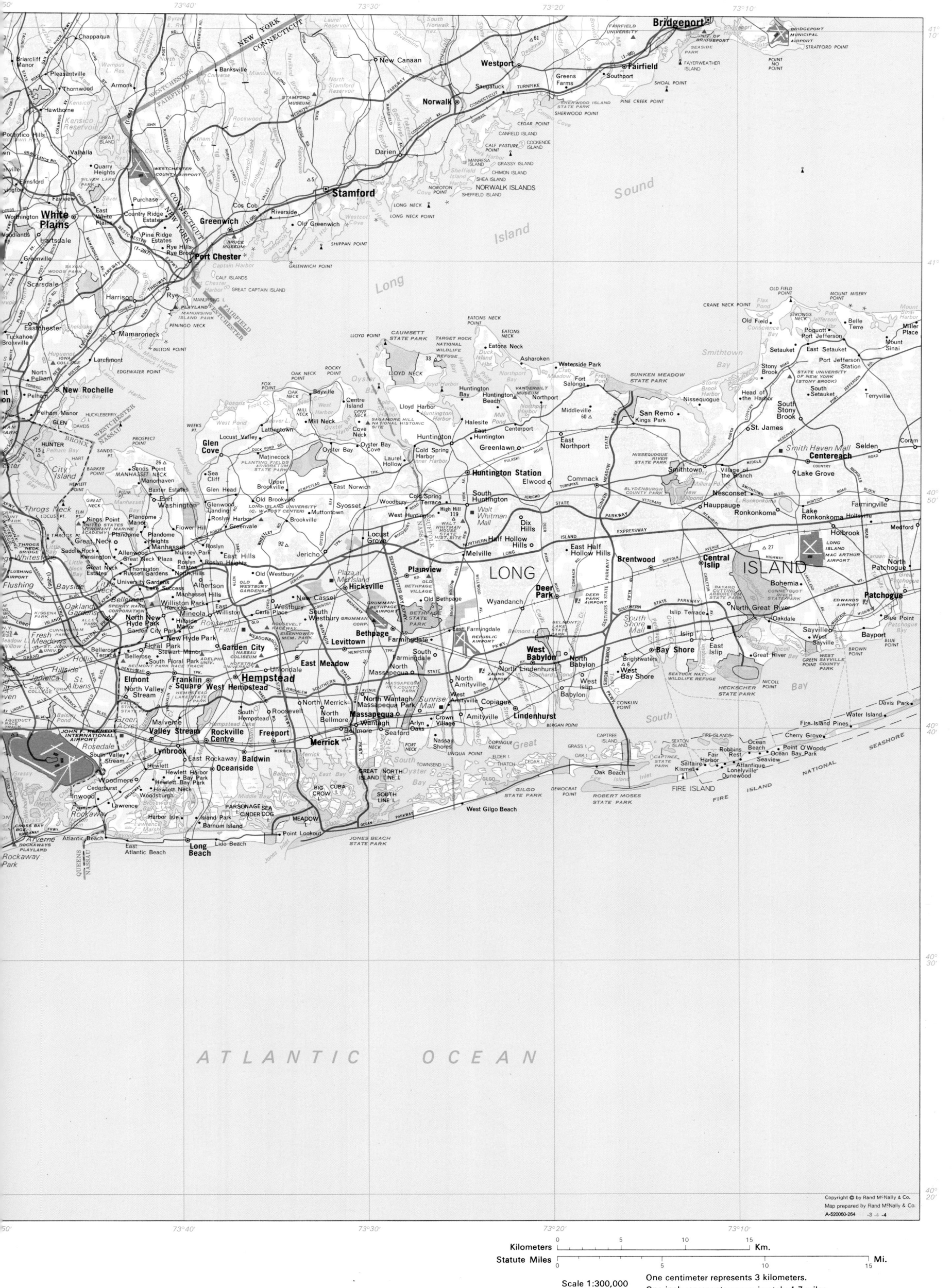

Scale 1:300,000

One centimeter represents 3 kilometers.
One inch represents approximately 4.7 miles.

AREA: 4,500 km²
POPULATION: 6,700,000

ENGLISH	airport	creek, cr.	harbor	lake, l.	park	woods
DEUTSCH	Flughafen	Bach	Hafen	See	Park	Gehölz
ESPAÑOL	aeropuerto	riachuelo	puerto	lago	parque	bosques
FRANÇAIS	aéroport	crique	port	lac	parc	bois
PORTUGUÊS	aeroporto	riacha	porto	lago	parque	bosques

Kilometers

Statute Miles

Scale 1:300,000   One centimeter represents 3 kilometers.
One inch represents approximately 4.7 miles.

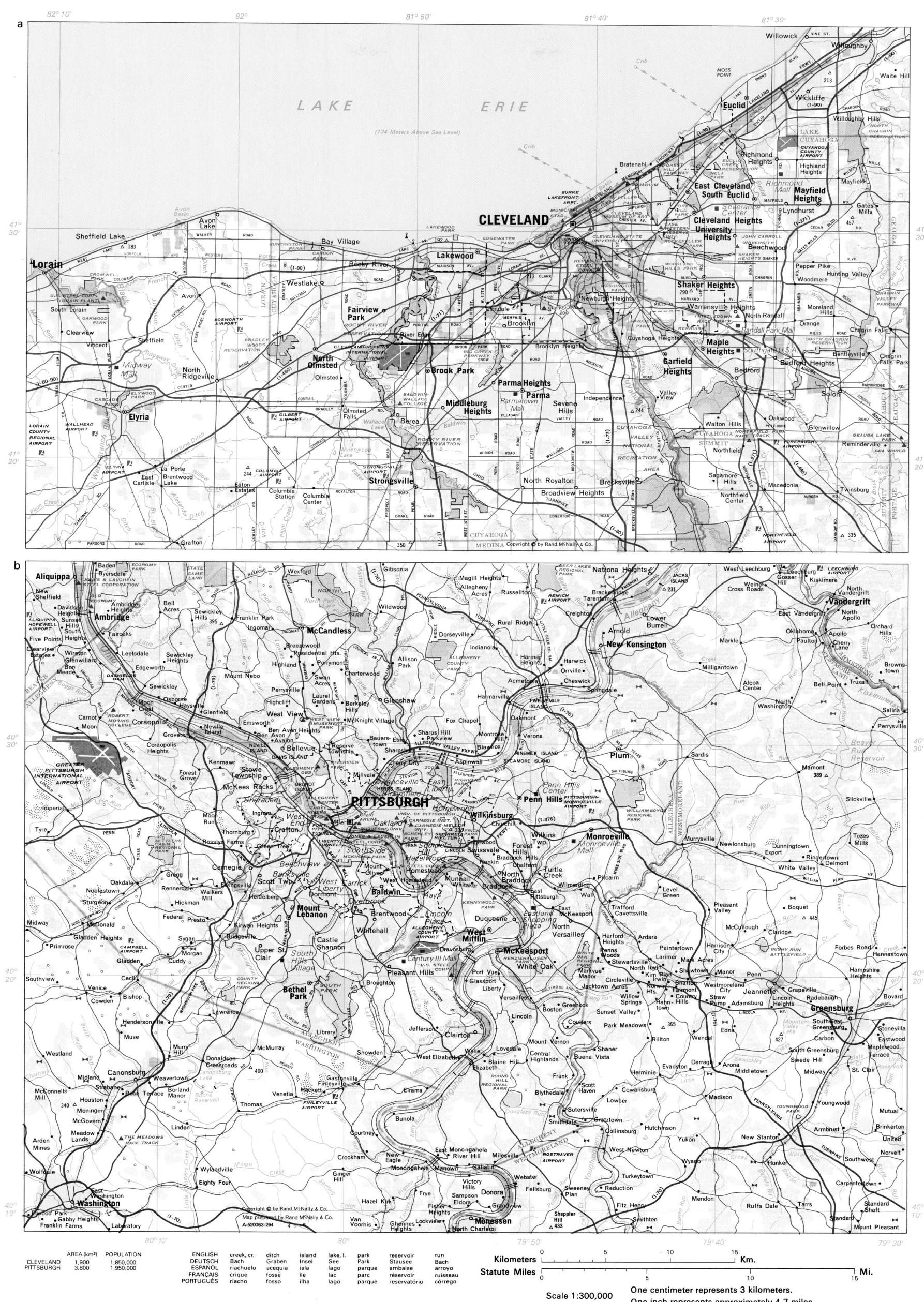

a

b

	AREA (km²)	POPULATION
CLEVELAND	1,900	1,850,000
PITTSBURGH	3,800	1,950,000

	creek, cr.	ditch	island	lake, l.	park	reservoir	run
ENGLISH	creek, cr.	ditch	island	lake, l.	park	reservoir	run
DEUTSCH	Bach	Graben	Insel	See	Park	Stausee	Bach
ESPAÑOL	riachuelo	acequia	isla	lago	parque	embalse	arroyo
FRANÇAIS	crique	fossé	île	lac	parc	réservoir	ruisseau
PORTUGUÊS	riacho	fosso	ilha	lago	parque	reservatório	córrego

Kilometers 0   5   10   15 Km.

Statute Miles 0   5   10   15 Mi.

Scale 1:300,000

One centimeter represents 3 kilometers.
One inch represents approximately 4.7 miles.

Copyright © by Rand McNally & Co.
Map prepared by Rand McNally & Co.
A-520063-264

AREA: 5,900 km²
POPULATION: 8,375,000

ENGLISH	DEUTSCH	ESPAÑOL	FRANÇAIS	PORTUGUÊS
canyon	Canon	cañón	canyon	canhão
college	College	escuela	collège	colégio
creek	Bach	riachuelo	crique	riacho
dam	Damm	dique	barrage	represa
hills	Hügel	colinas	collines	colinas
mount	Berg	montaña	mont	monte
park	Park	parque	parc	parque
peak	Gipfel	pico	pic	pico
reservoir	Stausee	estanque	réservoir	reservatório

Kilometers 0 5 10 15 Km.
Statute Miles 0 5 10 15 Mi.
Scale 1:300,000
One centimeter represents 3 kilometers.
One inch represents approximately 4.7 miles.
SAN GABRIEL MOUNTAINS
ANGELES NATIONAL FOREST
SANTA MONICA MOUNTAINS
SANTA ANA MOUNTAINS
PACIFIC OCEAN
Santa Monica Bay
San Pedro Bay
LOS ANGELES
Pasadena
Glendale
Burbank
Santa Monica
Long Beach
Anaheim
Santa Ana
Pomona
Torrance
Inglewood
Compton
Fullerton
Copyright © by Rand McNally & Co.
Map prepared by Rand McNally & Co.
A-520064-264

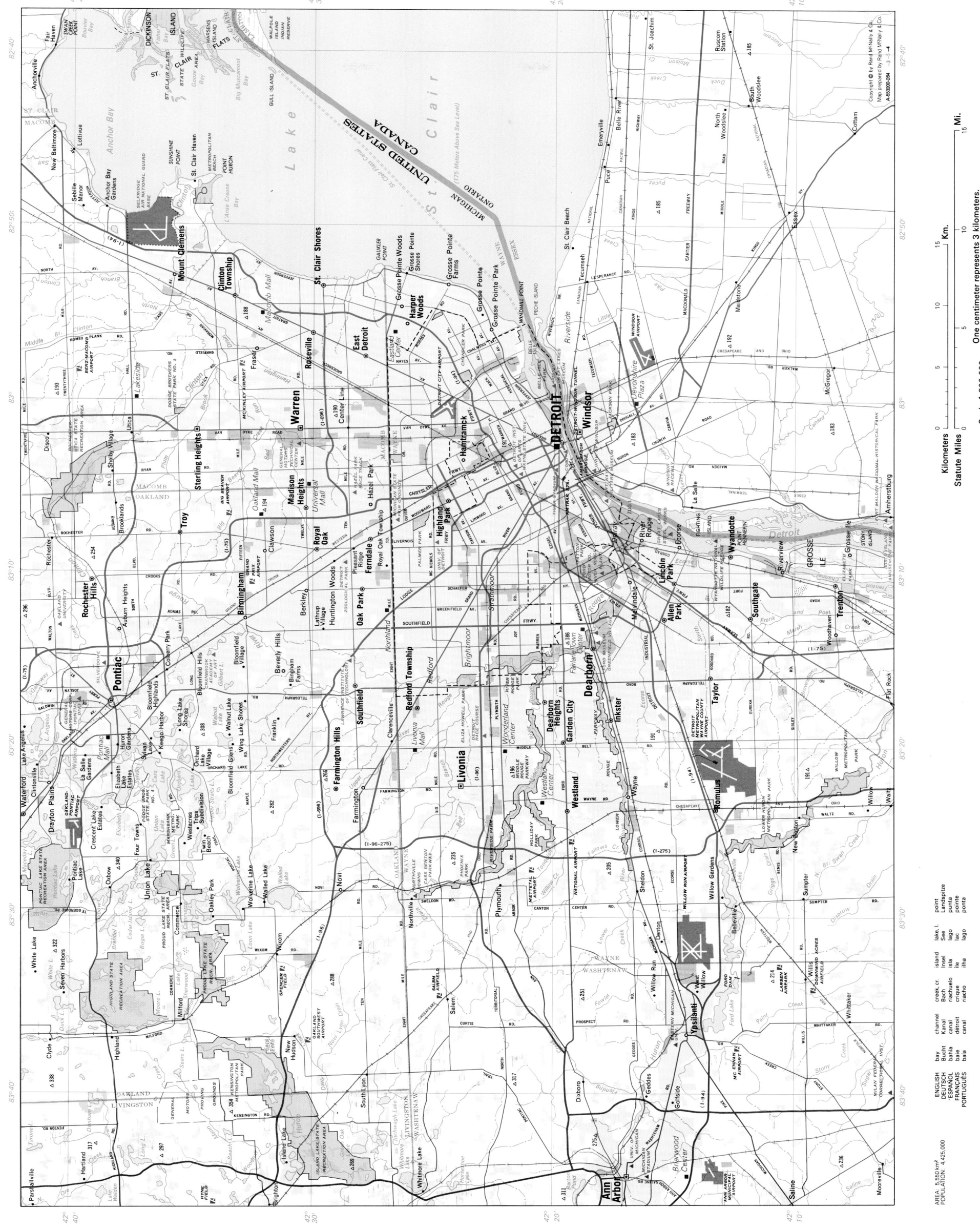

Scale 1:300,000

One centimeter represents 3 kilometers.
One inch represents approximately 4.7 miles.

Mi.

| Kilometers | 0 | 5 | 10 | 15 | Km. |

| Statute Miles | 0 | 5 | 10 | 15 |

ENGLISH	bay	channel	creek, cr.	island	lake, l.	point
DEUTSCH	Bucht	Kanal	Bach	Insel	See	Landspitze
ESPAÑOL	bahía	canal	riachuelo	isla	lago	punta
FRANÇAIS	baie	canal	crique	île	lac	pointe
PORTUGUÊS	baía	canal	riacho	ilha	lago	ponta

AREA 5,550 km²
POPULATION 4,425,000

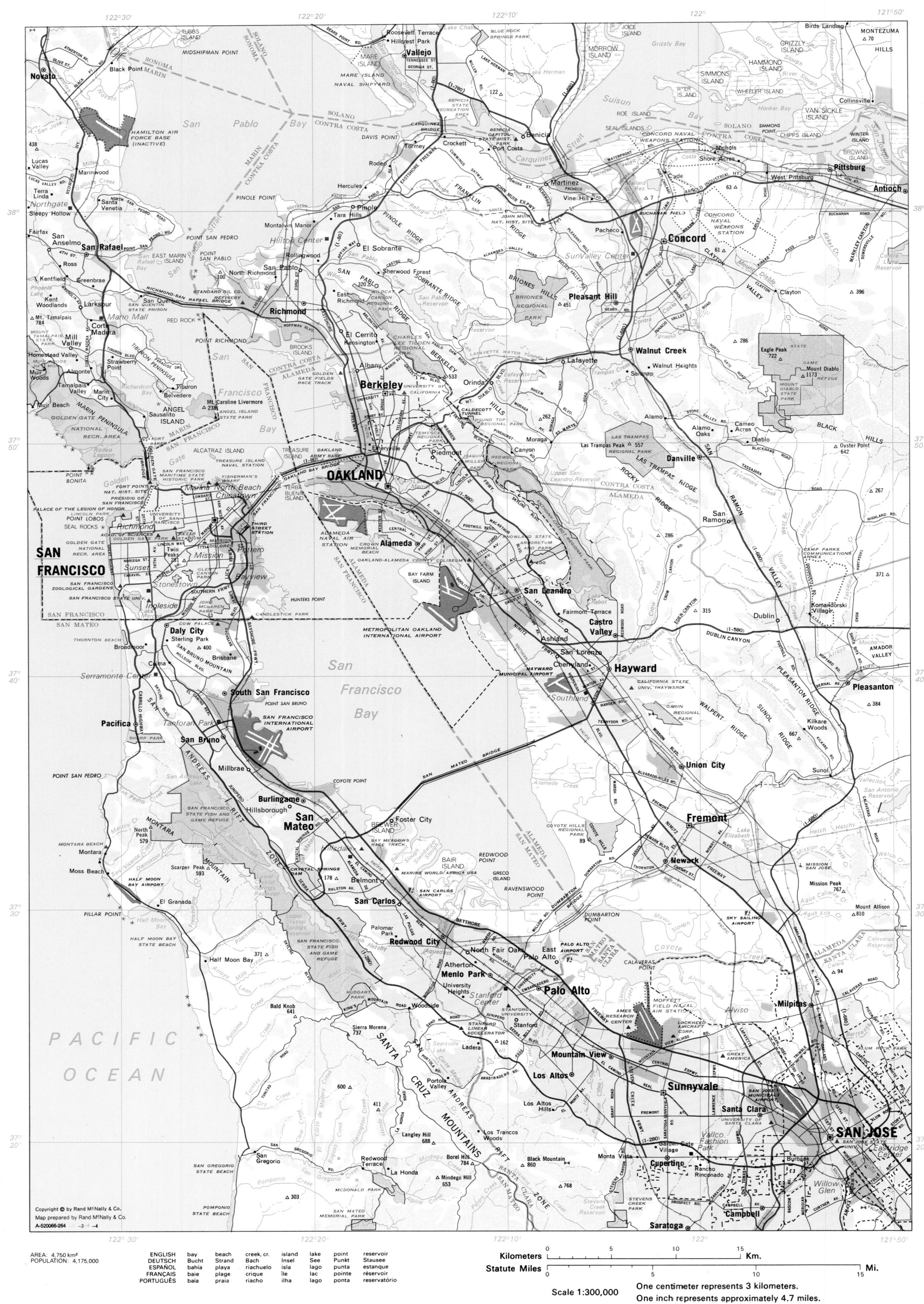

AREA: 4,750 km²
POPULATION: 4,175,000

ENGLISH	bay	beach	creek, cr.	island	lake	point	reservoir
DEUTSCH	Bucht	Strand	Bach	Insel	See	Punkt	Stausee
ESPAÑOL	bahia	playa	riachuelo	isla	lago	punta	estanque
FRANÇAIS	baie	plage	crique	île	lac	pointe	réservoir
PORTUGUÊS	baia	praia	riacho	ilha	lago	ponta	reservatório

Copyright © by Rand McNally & Co.
Map prepared by Rand McNally & Co.
A-520066-264 -3- -4

Kilometers 0   5   10   15 Km.
Statute Miles 0   5   10   15 Mi.

Scale 1:300,000
One centimeter represents 3 kilometers.
One inch represents approximately 4.7 miles.

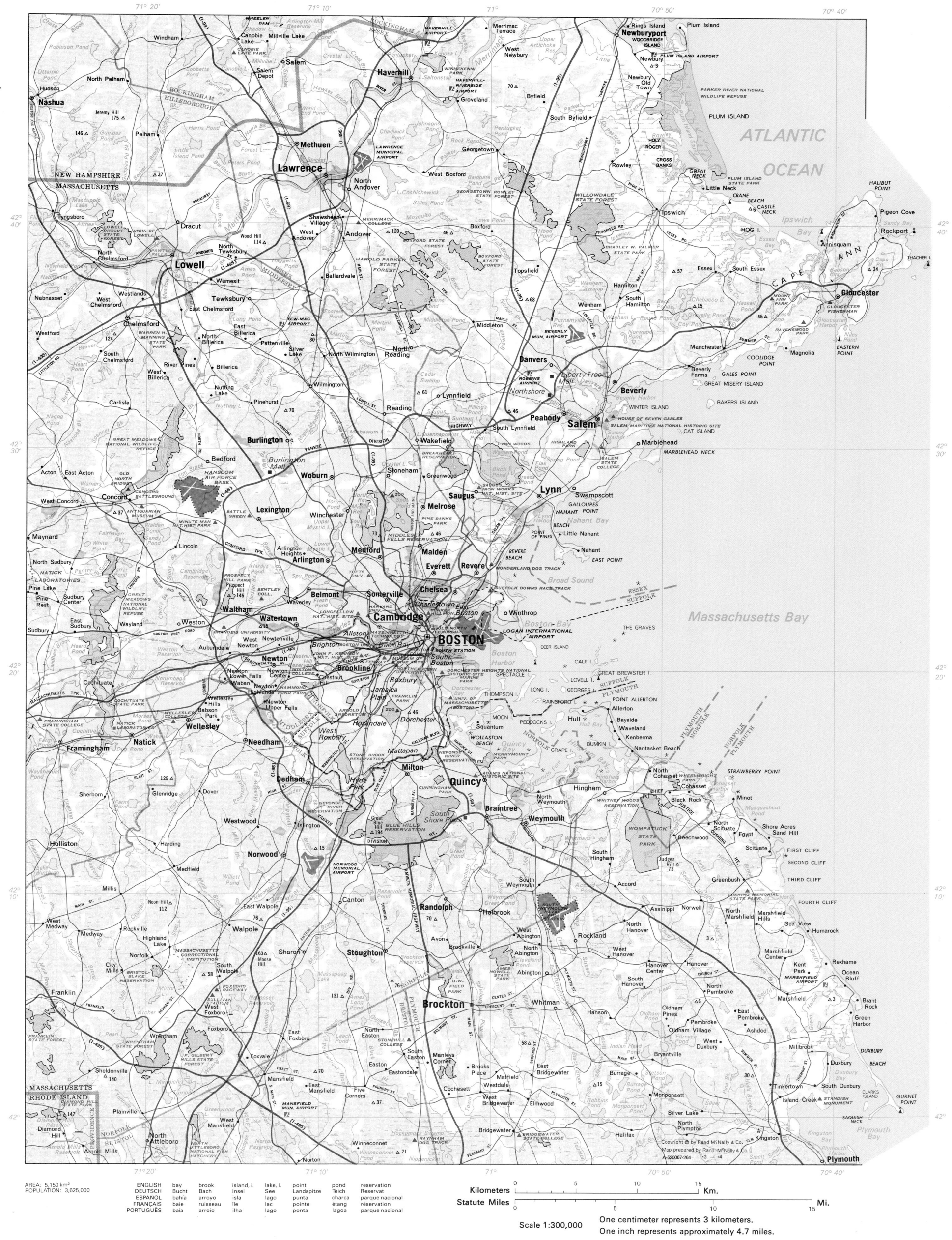

AREA: 5,150 km²
POPULATION: 3,625,000

	ENGLISH	DEUTSCH	ESPAÑOL	FRANÇAIS	PORTUGUÊS
	bay	Bucht	bahía	baie	baía
	brook	Bach	arroyo	ruisseau	arroio
	island, i.	Insel	isla	île	ilha
	lake, l.	See	lago	lac	lago
	point	Landspitze	punta	pointe	ponta
	pond	Teich	charca	étang	lagoa
	reservation	Reservat	parque nacional	réservation	parque nacional

Kilometers 0   5   10   15   Km.

Statute Miles 0   5   10   15   Mi.

Scale 1:300,000

One centimeter represents 3 kilometers.
One inch represents approximately 4.7 miles.

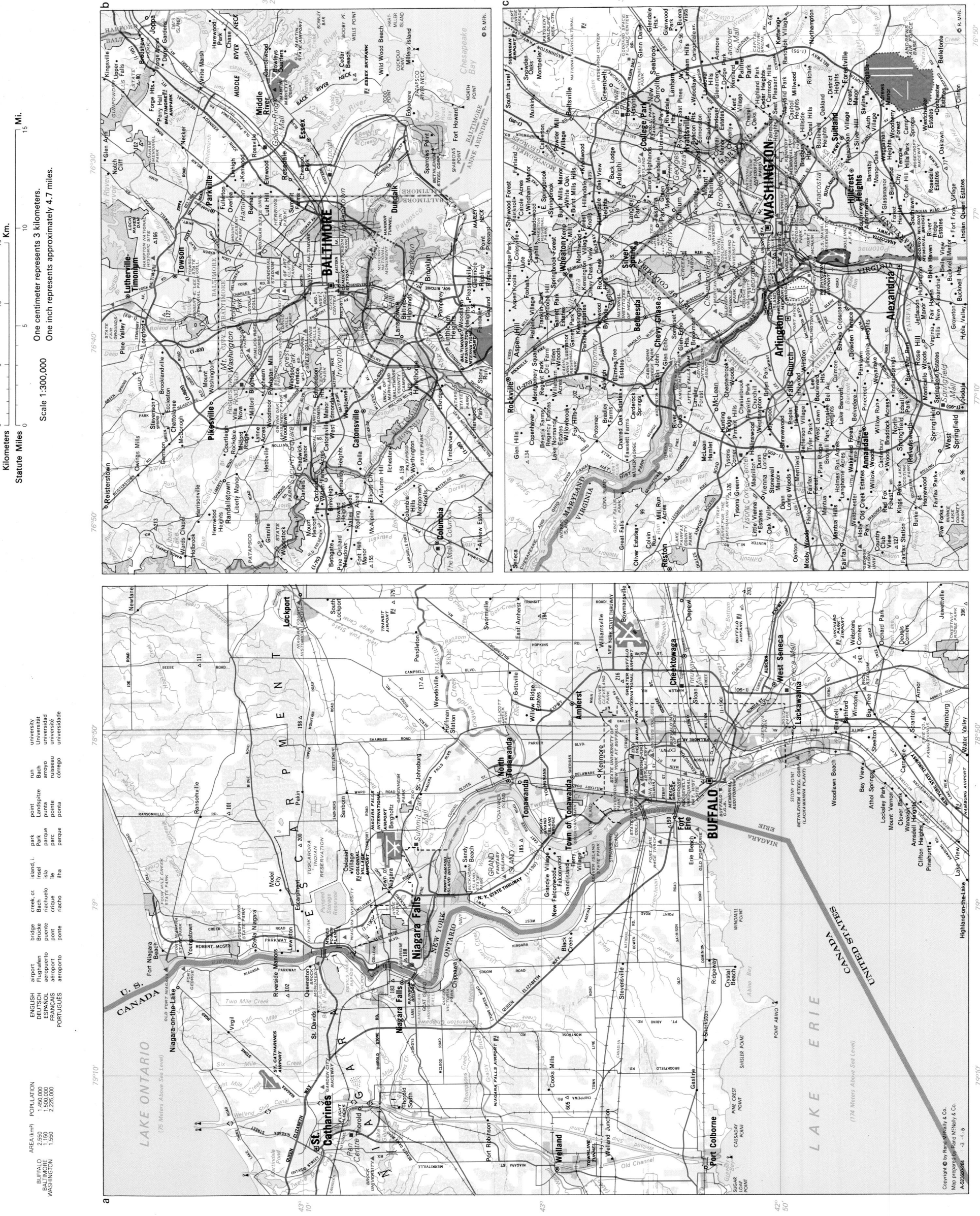

Kilometers   Mi.

Statute Miles

One centimeter represents 3 kilometers.

One inch represents approximately 4.7 miles.

Scale 1:300,000

	AREA (km²)	POPULATION
BUFFALO	2,550	1,450,000
BALTIMORE	1,150	1,500,000
WASHINGTON	1,550	2,225,000

ENGLISH	airport	bridge	creek, cr.	island, i.	park	point	run
DEUTSCH	Flughafen	Brücke	Bach	Insel	Park	Landspitze	Bach
ESPAÑOL	aeropuerto	puente	riachuelo	isla	parque	punta	arroyo
FRANÇAIS	aéroport	pont	ruisseau	île	parc	pointe	ruisseau
PORTUGUÉS	aeroporto	ponte	riacho	ilha	parque	ponta	córrego

					university
					Universität
					universidad
					université
					universidade

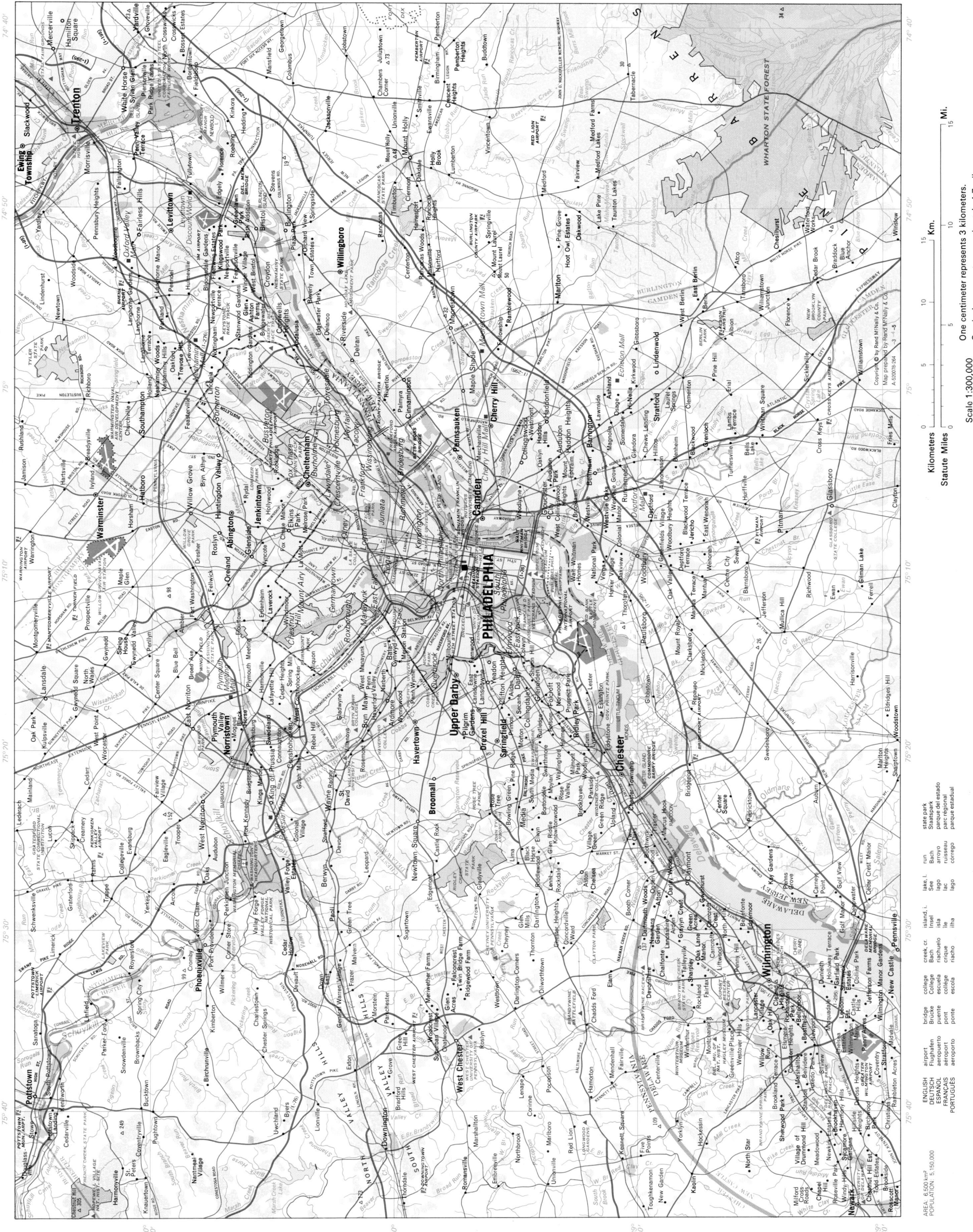

Scale 1:300,000

One centimeter represents 3 kilometers.
One inch represents approximately 4.7 miles.

Kilometers
Statute Miles

Km.
Mi.

Copyright © by Rand McNally & Co.
Map produced by Rand McNally & Co.
A-530079-394

state park
Staatspark
parc regional
parque del estado
parque estadual

ENGLISH	DEUTSCH	ESPAÑOL	FRANÇAIS	PORTUGUÊS
airport	Flughafen	aeropuerto	aéroport	aeroporto
bridge	Brücke	puente	pont	ponte
college	College	colegio	collège	escola
creek, cr.	Bach	arroyo	ruisseau	córrego
island, I.	Insel	isla	île	ilha
lake, I.	See	lago	lac	lago
run		arroyo	ruisseau	córrego

AREA 6,500 km²
POPULATION 5,150,000

a

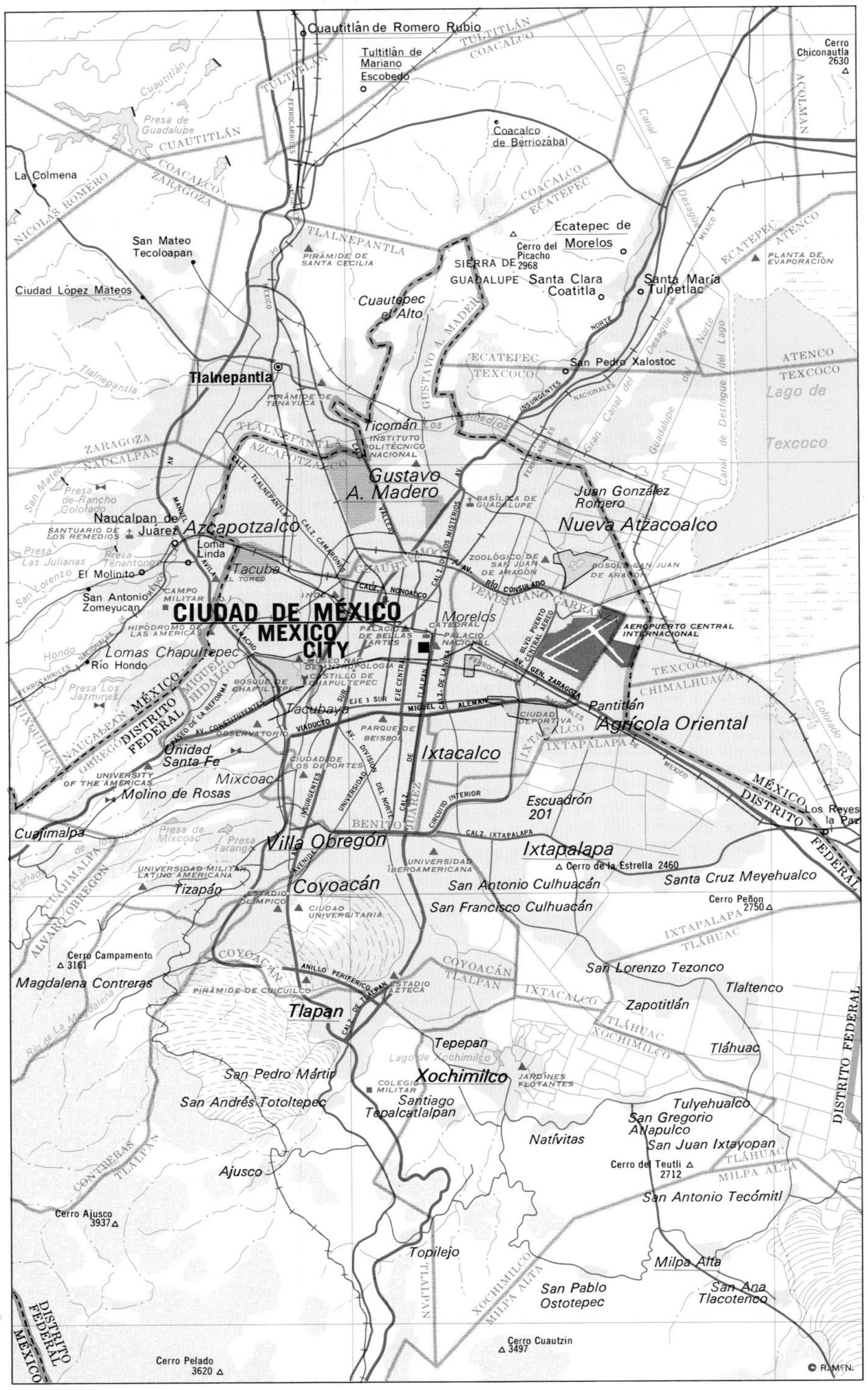

b

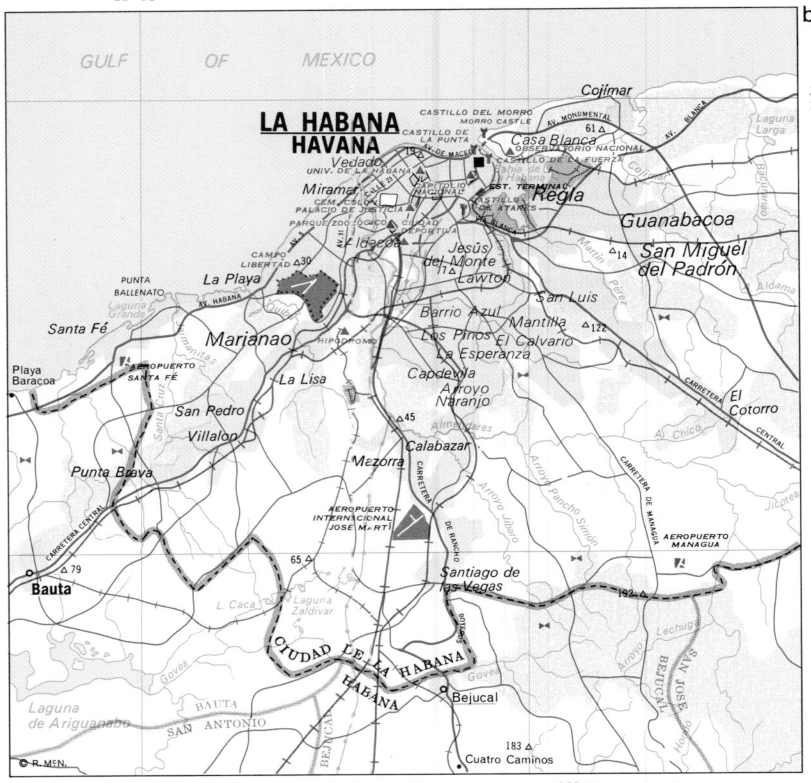

c

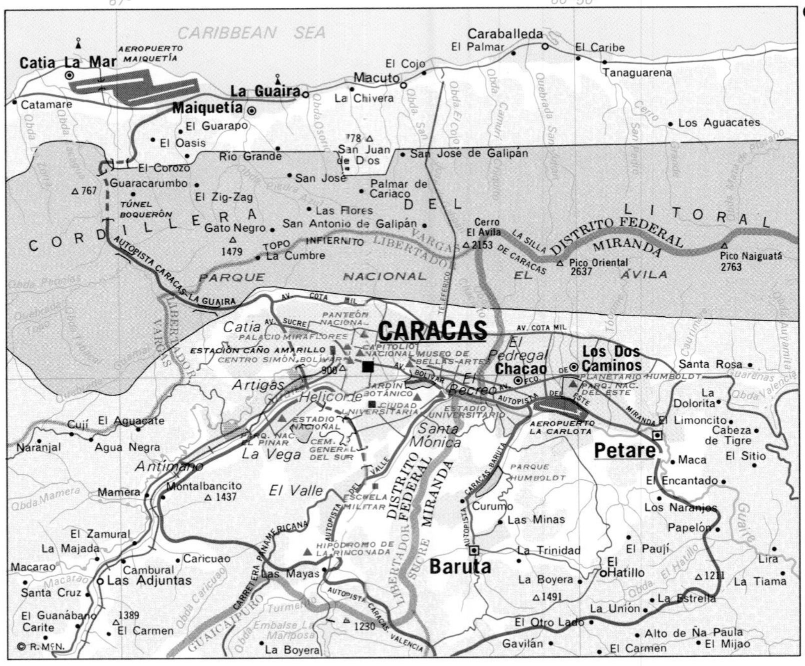

d

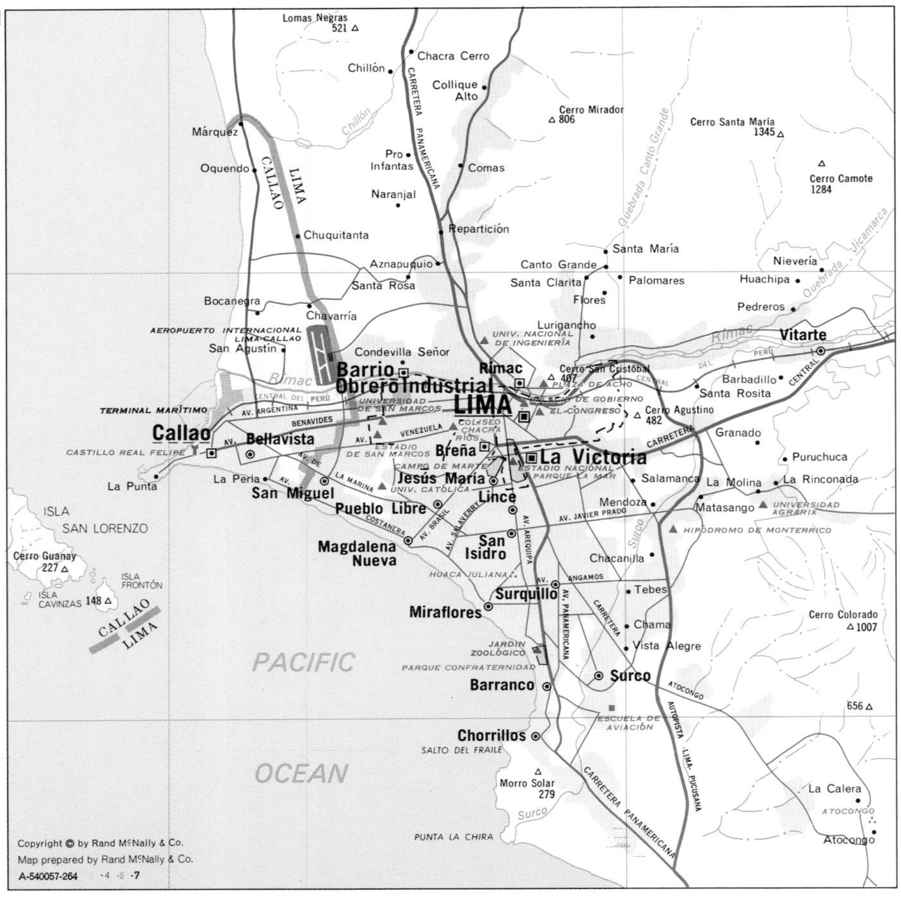

e

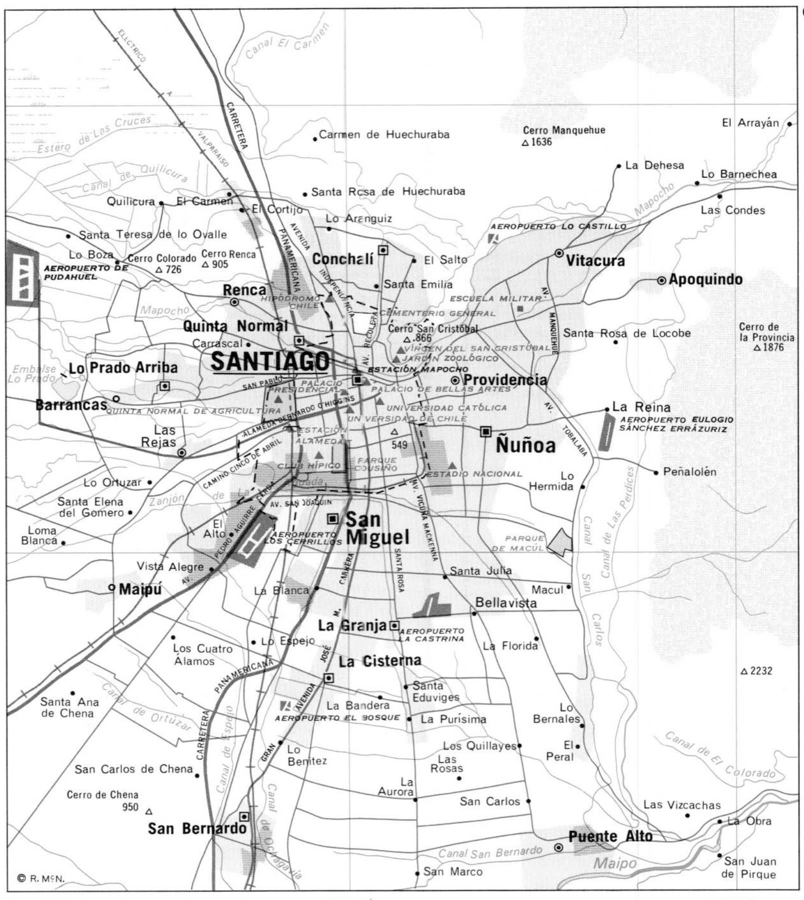

	AREA (km²)	POPULATION
CIUDAD DE MÉXICO	2,050	13,250,000
LA HABANA	750	2,050,000
CARACAS	750	2,950,000
LIMA	750	4,300,000
SANTIAGO	1,100	3,700,000

ESPAÑOL	arroyo	castillo	isla	laguna	presa	quebrada
ENGLISH	brook	castle	island	lagoon	reservoir	creek
DEUTSCH	Bach	Burg	Insel	Haff	Stausee	Bach
FRANÇAIS	ruisseau	château	île	lagune	réservoir	crique
PORTUGUÊS	arroio	castelo	ilha	laguna	reservatório	riacho

Kilometers 0 5 10 15 Km.
Statute Miles 0 5 10 15 Mi.

Scale 1:300,000
One centimeter represents 3 kilometers.
One inch represents approximately 4.7 miles.

a

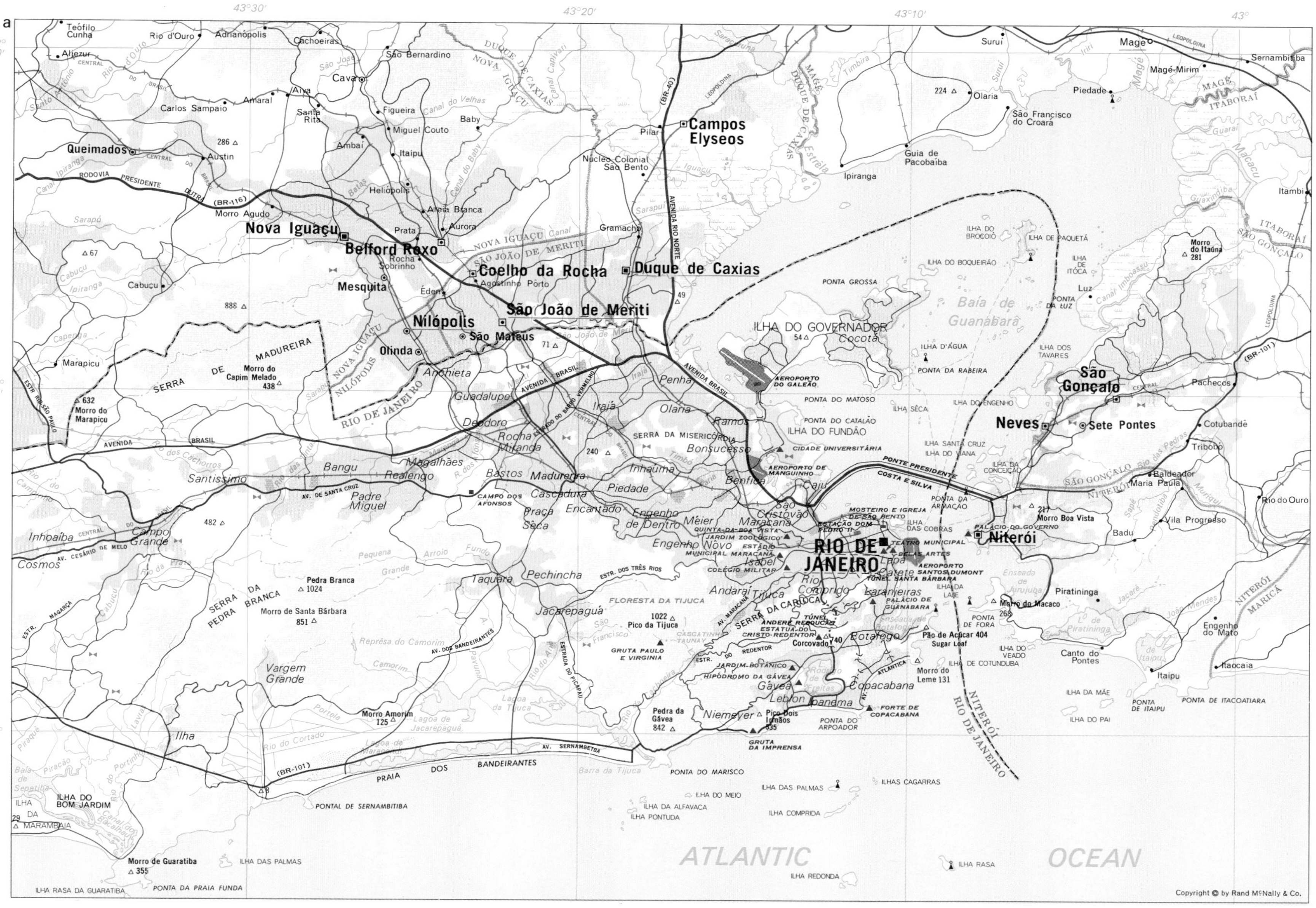

b

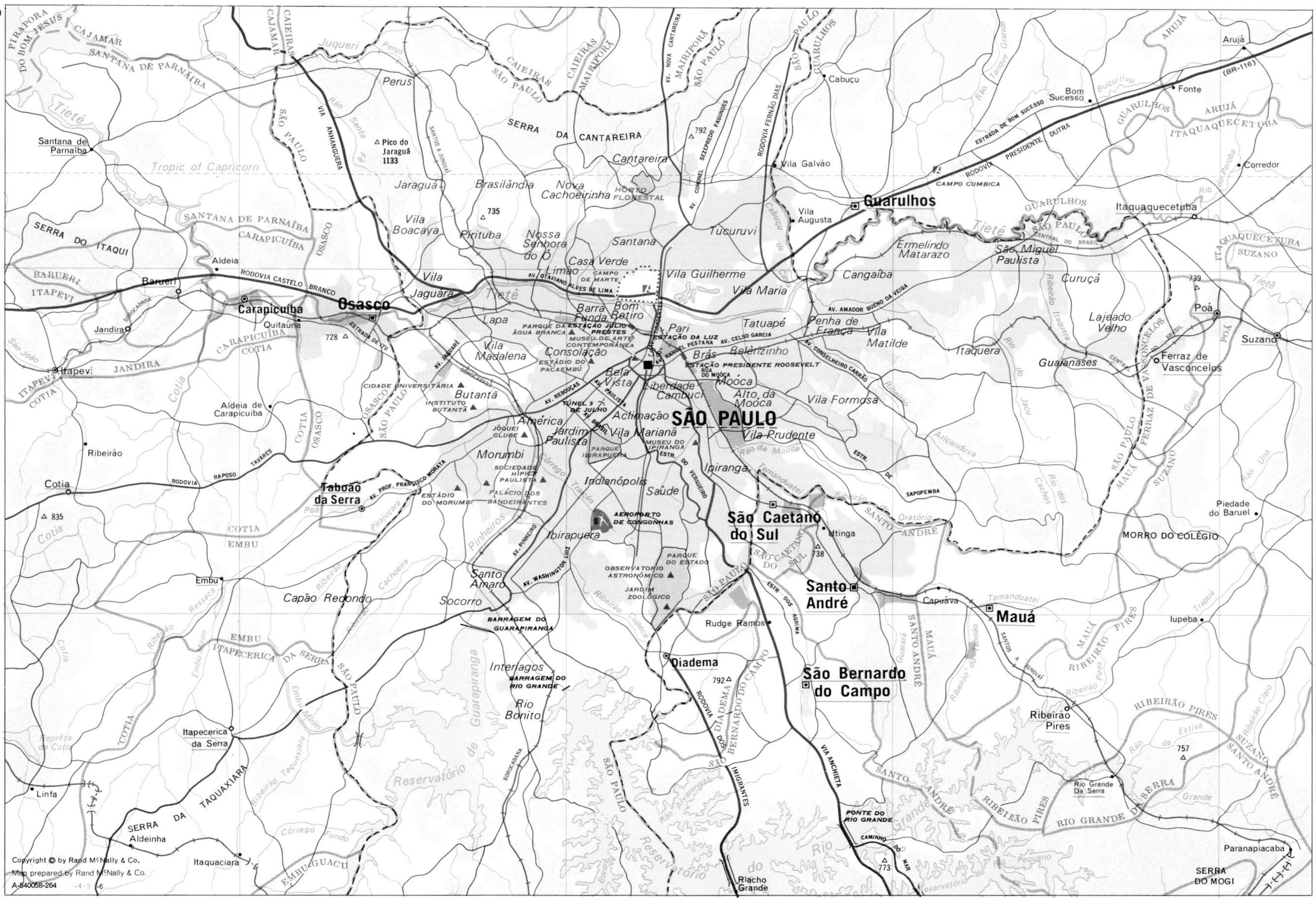

	AREA (km²)	POPULATION
RIO DE JANEIRO	2,200	8,200,000
SÃO PAULO	3,200	11,000,000

PORTUGUÊS	ilha	lagoa, l.	morro	ponta	reservatório	ribeirão, raõ.
ENGLISH	island	lagoon	hill	point	reservoir	creek
DEUTSCH	Insel	Haff	Hügel	Landspitze	Stausee	Bach
ESPAÑOL	isla	laguna	colina	punta	embalse	riachuelo
FRANÇAIS	île	lagune	colline	pointe	réservoir	crique

Kilometers 0 5 10 15 Km.

Statute Miles 0 5 10 15 Mi.

Scale 1:300,000

One centimeter represents 3 kilometers.
One inch represents approximately 4.7 miles.

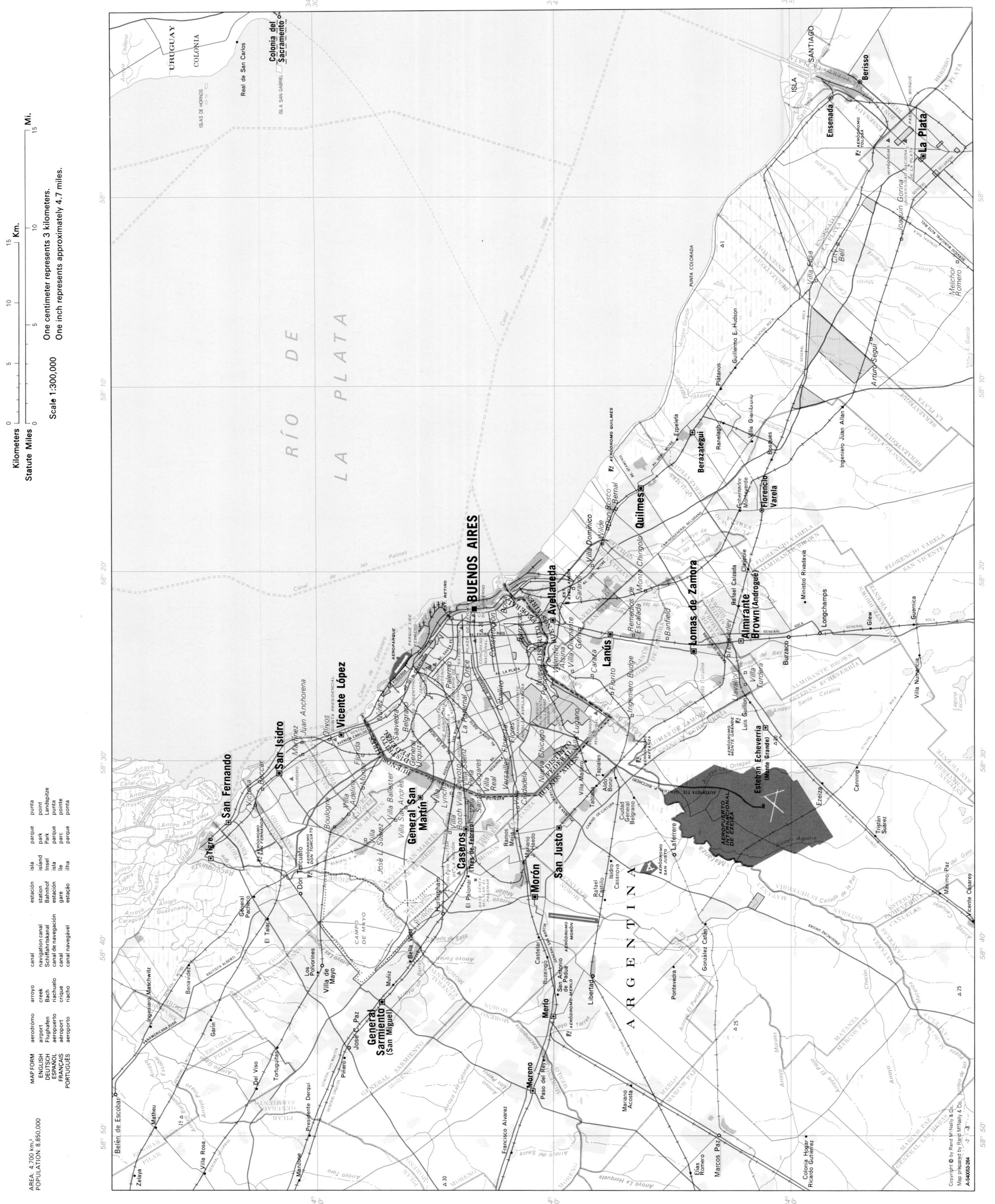

AREA 4,700 km²
POPULATION 8,850,000

MAP FORM					
ENGLISH	aerodrome	arroyo	canal	estación	isla	parque	punta
DEUTSCH	airport	creek	navigation canal	station	island	park	point
ESPAÑOL	Flughafen	Bach	Schiffahrtskanal	Bahnhof	Insel	Park	Landspitze
FRANÇAIS	aeropuerto	riachuelo	canal de navegación	estación	isla	parque	punta
PORTUGUÊS	aeroport	crique	canal	gare	île	parc	pointe
	aeroporto	riacho	canal navegável	estação	ilha	parque	ponta

Scale 1:300,000

One centimeter represents 3 kilometers.
One inch represents approximately 4.7 miles.

Kilometers
Statute Miles

Km.
Mi.

RÍO DE LA PLATA

BUENOS AIRES

ARGENTINA

URUGUAY

COLONIA

Colonia del Sacramento

THE MAP FORM column of the Glossary lists in alphabetical order the geographical terms, including any abbreviations, that appear on the maps. Terms preceded by a hyphen are those which commonly appear as endings in map names (for example, -san in Fuji-san, -älven in Dalälven). The languages of the terms are identified by abbreviations in *italics* (see Abbreviations of Language Names below). The Glossary provides the English, German, Spanish, French, and Portuguese equivalent for each term.

As a rule, the translations were made from the map form to English, then from English into the other four languages. Since the glossary terms and translations refer to specific map features, some may vary from the customary dictionary definitions of the terms.

IN DER SPALTE "Geographische Begriffe" werden alle Begriffe und Abkürzungen in alphabetischer Ordnung aufgeführt, die in den Karten erscheinen. Begriffe mit vorgesetztem Bindestrich erscheinen normalerweise als Wortendungen in Kartennamen (z.B. -san in Fuji-san, -älven in Dalälven). In *Kursivschrift* sind die jeweiligen Abkürzungen angegeben für die Sprachen, in denen der Begriff wiedergegeben ist (siehe unten: Abkürzungen der Sprachen). Das Verzeichnis gibt für jeden Begriff den entsprechenden Ausdruck in englisch, deutsch, spanisch, französisch, und portugiesisch.

In der Regel wurde der Begriff in der Karte ins Englische übersetzt und dann vom Englischen in die vier anderen Sprachen. Da die Begriffe und Übersetzungen sich auf bestimmte Objekte in der Karte beziehen, können einige von ihnen von den in den üblichen Wörterbüchern aufgeführten Begriffsbestimmungen abweichen.

LOS TÉRMINOS GEOGRÁFICOS que aparecen en los mapas, incluyendo abreviaciones, son presentados en la columna de Términos Geográficas del Glosario, en orden alfabético. Los términos que están precedidos por un guión aparecen frecuentemente como terminaciones de los nombres en los mapas (por ejemplo, -san en Fuji-san, -älven en Dalälven). Los idiomas que representan los términos están identificados por medio de abreviaciones en *cursiva* (véase abajo, Abreviaciones de los Idiomas Extranjeros). El Glosario provee el equivalente para cada término en inglés, alemán, español, francés y portugués.

Generalmente las traducciones están hechas de las formas originales de la terminología de los mapas que aparecen primero en inglés, y luego se traducen a las otras cuatro lenguas. Algunos términos y traducciones pueden aparecer distintas a las usadas en los diccionarios generales porque se refieren a los rasgos particulares de los mapas.

LE GLOSSAIRE cite par ordre alphabétique les termes géographiques et les abréviations utilisées. Les mots précédés d'un tiret sont des suffixes (par exemple -san dans Fuji-san, -älven dans Dalälven). La langue d'origine du nom cité est indiquée par une abréviation en *italique* (voir Abréviations des noms de langues, ci-dessous). Le Glossaire donne chaque nom en anglais, allemand, espagnol, français, et portugais.

En général, les termes géographiques des cartes ont d'abord été traduits en anglais, puis de l'anglais dans les quatre autres langues. Les définitions de certains termes sont adaptées aux particularités de l'Atlas. Il peut arriver qu'elles diffèrent des définitions habituelles données par les dictionnaires.

A COLUNA 'TERMINOLOGIA', do *Glossário*, contém todos os termos geográficos que figuram nos mapas, em ordem alfabética e com as respectivas abreviações. Os termos precedidos por um hífen são os que freqüentemente aparecem nos mapas como sufixos de nomes tais como *-san* (em Fuji-san), *-älven* (em Dalälven). As línguas em que os termos são expressos estão identificadas por abreviações em *grifo* (ver abaixo, 'Abreviações das línguas estrangeiras'). O Glossário fornece o equivalente de cada termo em inglês, alemão, espanhol, português e francês.

De modo geral, as traduções foram feitas das formas originais da terminologia usada nos mapas para o inglês, e, em seguida, do inglês para as outras quatro línguas. Uma vez que os termos geográficos e traduções do *Glossário* referem-se a acidentes específicos de cada mapa, é possível que algumas definições sejam diferentes das consignadas nos dicionários gerais das línguas.

Abbreviations of Language Names / Abkürzungen der Nationalsprachen / Abreviaciones de los Idiomas Extranjeros / Abréviations des Noms de Langues / Abreviações dos Idiomas Estrangeiros

	ENGLISH	DEUTSCH	ESPAÑOL	FRANÇAIS	PORTUGUÊS
Afk.	Afrikaans	Afrikaans	Africano	Afrikaans	Afrikaans
Alb.	Albanian	Albanisch	Albanesa	Albanais	Albanês
Ara.	Arabic	Arabisch	Árabe	Arabe	Árabe
Ber.	Berber	Berberisch	Bereber	Berbère	Berbere
Ben.	Bengali	Bengali	Bengali	Bengali	Bengali
Blg.	Bulgarian	Bulgarisch	Búlgaro	Bulgare	Búlgaro
Bur.	Burmese	Burmanisch	Birmano	Birman	Birmanês
Cat.	Catalan	Katalanisch	Catalán	Catalan	Catalão
Cbd.	Cambodian	Kambodschanisch	Camboyano	Cambodgien	Cambojano
Ch.	Chinese	Chinesisch	Chino	Chinois	Chinês
Czech	Czech	Tschechisch	Checo	Tchèque	Tcheco
Dan.	Danish	Dänisch	Danés	Danois	Dinamarquês
Du.	Dutch	Niederländisch	Holandés	Néerlandais	Holandês
Eng.	English	Englisch	Inglés	Anglais	Inglês
Est.	Estonian	Estnisch	Estonio	Esthonien	Estoniano
Finn.	Finnish	Finnisch	Finés	Finnois	Finlandês
Flm.	Flemish	Flämisch	Flamenco	Flamand	Flamengo
Fr.	French	Französisch	Francés	Français	Francês
Gae.	Gaelic	Gälisch	Gaélico	Gaélique	Gaélico
Ger.	German	Deutsch	Alemán	Allemand	Alemão
Gr.	Greek	Griechisch	Griego	Grec	Grego
Hau.	Hausa	Haussa	Hausa	Haoussa	Haussa
Heb.	Hebrew	Hebräisch	Hebreo	Hébreu	Hebraico
Hung.	Hungarian	Ungarisch	Húngaro	Hongrois	Húngaro
Ice.	Icelandic	Isländisch	Islandés	Islandais	Islandês
Indon.	Indonesian	Indonesisch	Indonesio	Indonésien	Indonésio
It.	Italian	Italienisch	Italiano	Italien	Italiano
Jap.	Japanese	Japanisch	Japonés	Japonais	Japonês
Kor.	Korean	Koreanisch	Coreano	Coréen	Coreano
Lao.	Laotian	Laotisch	Laosiano	Laotien	Laosiano
Lapp.	Lappish	Lappisch	Lapón	Lapon	Lapão
Latv.	Latvian	Lettisch	Letón	Letton	Letão
Lith.	Lithuanian	Litauisch	Lituano	Lithuanien	Lituano
Mal.	Malay	Malaiisch	Malayo	Malais	Malaio
Mong.	Mongolian	Mongolisch	Mogol	Mongol	Mongol
Nor.	Norwegian	Norwegisch	Norvego	Norvégien	Norueguês
Pas.	Pashto	Paschtu	Pushtu	Pachtou	Pachtu
Per.	Persian	Persisch	Persa	Persan	Persa
Pol.	Polish	Polnisch	Polaco	Polonais	Polonês
Poly.	Polynesian	Polynesisch	Polinesio	Polynésien	Polinésio
Port.	Portuguese	Portugiesisch	Portugués	Portugais	Português
Rom.	Romanian	Rumänisch	Rumano	Roumain	Romeno
Rus.	Russian	Russisch	Ruso	Russe	Russo
S./C.	Serbo-Croatian	Serbokroatisch	Servio-croata	Serbo-croate	Servo-croata
Sin.	Sinhalese	Singhalesisch	Cingalés	Cinghalais	Cingalês
Slo.	Slovak	Slowakisch	Eslovaco	Slovaque	Eslovaco
Sp.	Spanish	Spanisch	Español	Espagnol	Espanhol
Swe.	Swedish	Schwedisch	Sueco	Suédois	Sueco
Thai	Thai	Thai	Tai	Thaï	Tailandês
Tib.	Tibetan	Tibetisch	Tibetano	Tibétain	Tibetano
Tur.	Turkish	Türkisch	Turco	Turc	Turco
Viet.	Vietnamese	Vietnamesisch	Vietnamita	Vietnamien	Vietnamita
Welsh	Welsh	Walisisch	Galés	Gallois	Galês

A

ENGLISH	DEUTSCH	Map Form / Geographische Begriffe / Términos Geográficos / Termes Géographiques / Termos Geográficos	ESPAÑOL	FRANÇAIS	PORTUGUÊS
river	Fluss	**-å** *Dan., Nor., Swe.*	río	rivière	rio
brook	Bach	**a., arroyo** *Sp.*	arroyo	ruisseau	córrego
river	Fluss	**āb** *Per.*	río	rivière	rio
army base	Heeresstützpunkt	**a.b., army base** *Eng.*	base del ejército	base d'armée	base militar
well	Brunnen	**ābār** *Ara.*	pozo	puits	poço
abbey	Abtei	**abb., abbazia** *It.*	abadía	abbaye	abadia
abbey	Abtei	**abbaye** *Fr.*	abadía	abbaye	abadia
abbey	Abtei	**abbazia** *It.*	abadía	abbaye	abadia
abbey	Abtei	**abbey** *Eng.*	abadía	abbaye	abadia
aboriginal reserve	Eingeborenenschutzgebiet	**aboriginal reserve** *Eng.*	zona de aborígenes	réserve des indigènes	reserva indígena
abbey	Abtei	**Abtei** *Ger.*	abadía	abbaye	abadia
ditch	Graben	**acequia** *Sp.*	acequia	fossé	fosso
reservoir	Stausee	**açude** *Port.*	embalse	réservoir	açude
island(s)	Insel(n)	**ada(lar)** *Tur.*	isla(s)	île(s)	ilha(s)
island	Insel	**adası** *Tur.*	isla	île	ilha
mountains	Berge	**adrar** *Ber.*	montañas	montagnes	montanhas
Atomic Energy Commission	Atomenergiekommission	**A.E.C., Atomic Energy Commission** *Eng.*	Comisión de Energía Atomica	Commission de l'Énergie Atomique	Comissão de Energia Atômica
airport	Flughafen	**aérd., aérodrome** *Fr.*	aeródromo	aérodrome	aeródromo
airport	Flughafen	**aeródromo** *Port., Sp.*	aeródromo	aérodrome	aeródromo
airport	Flughafen	**aeroparque** *Sp.*	aeroparque	aéroport	aeroporto
airport	Flughafen	**aéroport** *Fr.*	aeropuerto	aéroport	aeroporto
airport	Flughafen	**aeroporto** *It., Port.*	aeropuerto	aéroport	aeroporto
airport	Flughafen	**aeropuerto** *Sp.*	aeropuerto	aéroport	aeroporto
air force base	Luftwaffenstützpunkt	**a.f.b., air force base** *Eng.*	base aeronáutica	base aérienne	base aérea
wadi	Wadi	**ahzar** *Ara.*	uadi	wadi	uádi
peak	Gipfel	**aiguille** *Fr.*	pico	aiguille	pico
air base	Luftstützpunkt	**air base** *Eng.*	base aérea	base aérienne	base aérea
airfield	Flugplatz	**airfield** *Eng.*	camp de aviación	aérodrome	campo de pouso
air force base	Luftwaffenstützpunkt	**air force base** *Eng.*	base aeronáutica	base aérienne	base aérea
airport	Flughafen	**airport** *Eng.*	aeropuerto	aéroport	aeroporto
cape	Kap	**ákra, akrotírion** *Gr.*	cabo	cap	cabo
hill	Hügel	**'alam, 'alāmat** *Ara.*	colina	colline	colina
avenue	Allee	**alameda** *Sp.*	alameda	avenue	avenida
alps	Alpen	**alpes** *Fr.*	alpes	alpes	alpes
alps	Alpen	**alpi** *It.*	alpes	alpes	alpes
mountains, hills	Berge, Hügel	**altos** *Sp.*	altos	montagnes, collines	montanhas, colinas
river	Fluss	**-älv, -älven** *Swe.*	río	rivière	rio
amusement park	Vergnügungspark	**amusement park** *Eng.*	parque de diversiones	parc récréatif	parque de diversões
river	Fluss	**-ån** *Swe.*	río	rivière	rio
anchorage	Ankerplatz	**anchorage** *Eng.*	ancladero	ancrage	ancoradouro
bay	Bucht	**angra** *Sp.*	angra	baie	baía
cove	kleine Bucht	**anse** *Fr.*	ensenada	anse	enseada
bay	Bucht	**ao** *Thai*	bahía	baie	baía
aqueduct	Aquädukt	**aqueduc** *Fr.*	acueducto	aqueduc	aqueduto
aqueduct	Aquädukt	**aqueduct** *Eng.*	acueducto	aqueduc	aqueduto
archipelago	Archipel	**archipel** *Fr.*	archipiélago	archipel	arquipélago
archipelago	Archipel	**archipelag** *Rus.*	archipiélago	archipel	arquipélago
archipelago	Archipel	**archipelago** *Eng.*	archipiélago	archipel	arquipélago
archipelago	Archipel	**archipiélago** *Sp.*	archipiélago	archipel	arquipélago
arm	Arm	**arm** *Eng.*	brazo	bras	braço de rio
army base	Heeresstützpunkt	**army base** *Eng.*	base del ejército	base d'armée	base militar
airport	Flughafen	**arpt., aéroport** *Fr.* **aeroporto** *It., Port.* **aeropuerto** *Sp.* **airport** *Eng.*	aeropuerto	aéroport	aeroporto
archipelago	Archipel	**arquipélago** *Port.*	archipiélago	archipel	arquipélago
reef	Riff	**arrecife** *Sp.*	arrecife	récif	recife
brook	Bach	**arroyo** *Sp.*	arroyo	ruisseau	córrego, arroio
hills	Hügel	**-ås,-åsen** *Swe.*	colinas	collines	colinas
ridge	Höhenrücken	**'assâbet** *Ara.*	sierra	crête	serra
atoll	Atoll	**atol** *Port.*	atolón	atoll	atol
atoll	Atoll	**atoll** *Eng., Fr.*	atolón	atoll	atol
auditorium	Auditorium	**aud., auditorium** *Eng.*	auditorio	auditorium	auditório
race course	Rennbahn	**autodrome** *Fr.*	autódromo	autodrome	autódromo
race course	Rennbahn	**autodromo** *It.*	autódromo	autodrome	autódromo
expressway	Autobahn	**autopista** *Sp.*	autopista	autoroute	via expressa
avenue	Allee	**av., avenida** *Port., Sp.* **avenue** *Eng., Fr.*	avenida	avenue	avenida
channel	Kanal	**ava** *Poly.*	canal, estrecho	canal, détroit	canal, estreito
avenue	Allee	**avenida** *Port., Sp.*	avenida	avenue	avenida
avenue	Allee	**avenue** *Eng., Fr.*	avenida	avenue	avenida
spring	Quelle	**'ayn** *Ara.*	manantial	source	manancial, fonte

290 Glossary and Abbreviations of Geographical Terms / Verzeichnis und Abkürzungen Geographischer Begriffe
Glosario y Abreviaciones de Términos Geográficos / Glossaire et Abréviations de Termes Géographiques
Glossário e Abreviações de Termos Geográficos

ENGLISH	DEUTSCH	Map Form / Geographische Begriffe / Términos Geográficos / Termes Géographiques / Termos Geográficos	ESPAÑOL	FRANÇAIS	PORTUGUÊS

B

ENGLISH	DEUTSCH	Map Form	ESPAÑOL	FRANÇAIS	PORTUGUÊS
bay	Bucht	**baai** *Du.*	bahía	baie	baía
strait	Meeresstrasse	**bab** *Ara.*	estrecho	détroit	estreito
brook, creek	Bach	**Bach** *Ger.*	arroyo, riachuelo	ruisseau, crique	córrego, arroio
hill	Hügel	**-backen** *Swe.*	colina	colline	colina
desert	Wüste	**bādiyat** *Ara.*	desierto	désert	deserto
strait	Meeresstrasse	**bælt** *Dan.*	estrecho	détroit	estreito
bay	Bucht	**bahía** *Sp.*	bahía	baie	baía
inlet	Einfahrt	**bahiret** *Ara.*	abra	bras de mer	enseada, estuário
railroad station	Bahnhof	**Bahnhof** *Ger.*	estación de ferrocarril	gare	estação ferroviária
river; sea	Fluss; Meer	**bahr, baḥr** *Ara.*	río; mar	rivière; mer	rio; mar
reservoir	Stausee	**baḥrat** *Ara.*	embalse	réservoir	reservatório
bay	Bucht	**baía** *Port.*	bahía	baie	baía
bay	Bucht	**baie** *Fr.*	bahía	baie	baía
reef, sand bar	Riff, Sandbarre	**bajo** *Sp.*	bajo	récif, banc de sable	recife, banco de areia
gorge	Schlucht	**balka** *Rus.*	garganta	gorge	garganta
dome	Kuppe	**ballon** *Fr.*	domo	ballon	domo
marsh	Marsch	**balta** *Rom.*	pantano	marais	pântano
cape	Kap	**-bana** *Jap.*	cabo	cap	cabo
marsh	Marsch	**bañados** *Sp.*	bañados	marais	pântano
island	Insel	**-banare** *Jap.*	isla	île	ilha
bank	Bank	**banco** *Sp.*	banco	banc	banco
peninsula	Halbinsel	**-bandao** *Ch.*	península	péninsule	península
bank	Bank	**bank** *Eng.*	banco	banc	banco
shoal	Untiefe	**-banken** *Swe.*	bajo	haut-fond	escolho
sand bar	Sandbarre	**barra** *Sp.*	barra	banc de sable	banco de areia
dam	Damm	**barrage** *Fr.*	presa	barrage	represa
ravine	Tobel	**barranca** *Sp.*	barranca	ravin	ravina
air base	Luftstützpunkt	**base aérea** *Sp.*	base aérea	base aérienne	base aérea
basilica	Basilika	**basílica** *Sp.*	basílica	basilique	basílica
basilica	Basilika	**basilique** *Fr.*	basílica	basilique	basílica
basin	Becken	**basin** *Eng.*	cuenca	bassin	bacia
basin	Becken	**bassin** *Fr.*	cuenca	bassin	bacia
marsh	Marsch	**batakliği** *Tur.*	pantano	marais	pântano
river	Fluss	**batang** *Indon.*	río	rivière	rio
river	Fluss	**batha** *Ara.*	río	rivière	rio
marsh	Marsch	**bāṭlāq** *Per.*	pantano	marais	pântano
battlefield	Schlachtfeld	**battlefield** *Eng.*	campo de batalla	champ de bataille	campo de batalha
mountain	Berg	**batu** *Mal.*	montaña	montagne	montanha
bay	Bucht	**bay** *Eng.*	bahía	baie	baía
bayou	Altwasser	**bayou** *Fr., Eng.*	ensenada pantanosa	bayou	enseada pantanosa
beach	Strand	**beach** *Eng.*	playa	plage	praia
mountain	Berg	**bein, beinn** *Gae.*	montaña	montagne	montanha
snowcapped mountains	Schneegipfel	**belogorje** *Rus.*	nevados	montagnes neigeuses	picos nevados
mountain	Berg	**ben** *Gae.*	montaña	montagne	montanha
mountain, hill	Berg	**Berg** *Ger.*	montaña, colina	montagne, colline	montanha, colina
mountains	Berge	**berg** *Afk.*	montañas	montagnes	montanhas
hill(s), mountain(s)	Hügel, Berg(e)	**-berg** *Swe.*	colina(s), montaña(s)	colline(s), montagne(s)	colina(s), montanha(s)
mountains	Berge	**Berge** *Ger.*	montañas	montagnes	montanhas
mountains	Berge	**berge** *Afk.*	montañas	montagnes	montanhas
hills, mountains	Hügel, Berge	**-bergen** *Swe.*	colinas, montañas	collines, montagnes	colinas, montanhas
hill, mountain	Hügel, Berg	**-berget** *Swe.*	colina, montaña	colline, montagne	colina, montanha
upland	Bergland	**Bergland** *Ger.*	tierras altas	hautes terres	terras altas
battlefield	Schlachtfeld	**bfld., battlefield** *Eng.*	campo de batalla	champ de bataille	campo de batalha
mountain, hill	Berg	**Bg., Berg** *Ger.*	montaña, colina	montagne, colline	montanha, colina
bridge	Brücke	**bge., bridge** *Eng.*	puente	pont	ponte
bight	Bucht	**bight** *Eng.*	bahía	baie	baía, enseada
bill (point)	Landspitze	**bill** *Eng.*	punta	pointe	ponta
valley	Tal	**biq'at** *Heb.*	valle	vallée	vale
well	Brunnen	**bi'r** *Ara.*	pozo	puits	poço
lake	See	**birkat** *Ara.*	lago	lac	lago
mountains	Berge	**bjeshkët** *Alb.*	montañas	montagnes	montanhas
brook	Bach	**bk., brook** *Eng.*	arroyo	ruisseau	córrego, arroio
upland	Bergland	**blaenau** *Welsh*	tierras altas	hautes terres	terras altas
bluff(s)	Steilufer	**bluff(s)** *Eng.*	acantilado(s)	falaise(s)	falésia(s)
boulevard	Boulevard	**blvd., boulevard** *Fr., Eng.*	bulevar	boulevard	bulevar
mountain	Berg	**b'nom** *Viet.*	montaña	montagne	montanha
lake	See	**-bo** *Ch.*	lago	lac	lago
river mouth	Flussmündung	**boca** *Sp.*	boca	embouchure	foz
river mouth; pass	Flussmündung; Pass	**bocca** *It.*	boca; paso	embouchure; col	foz; passo
bay	Bucht	**bocht** *Du.*	bahía	baie	baía
bay	Bodden	**Bodden** *Ger.*	bahía	baie	baía
bog	Moor	**bog** *Eng.*	pantano	fondrière	pântano
strait	Meeresstrasse	**boğazı** *Tur.*	estrecho	détroit	estreito
range	Gebirge	**bogd** *Mong.*	sierra	chaîne	cordilheira
woods	Gehölz	**bois** *Fr.*	bosque	bois	bosque
enclosed basin	Becken	**bolsón** *Sp.*	bolsón	bassin fermée	bacia fechada
forest	Wald	**bory** *Pol.*	bosque	forêt	floresta
forest	Wald	**bosque** *Sp.*	bosque	forêt	floresta
boulevard	Boulevard	**boulevard** *Fr., Eng.*	boulevar	boulevard	bulevar
branch	Arm	**br., branch** *Eng.*	brazo	bras	braço
stream distributary	Flussarm	**braţul** *Rom.*	brazo de río	bras	braço de rio
breakwater	Wellenbrecher	**breakwater** *Eng.*	rompeolas	brise-lames	quebra-mar
glacier	Gletscher	**-breen** *Nor.*	glaciar	glacier	geleira
bridge	Brücke	**bridge** *Eng.*	puente	pont	ponte
brook	Bach	**brook** *Eng.*	arroyo	ruisseau	córrego
marsh	Bruch	**Bruch** *Ger.*	pantano	marais	pântano
bridge	Brücke	**Brücke** *Ger.*	puente	pont	ponte
bridge	Brücke	**brug** *Du.*	puente	pont	ponte
bay	Bucht	**Bucht** *Ger.*	bahía	baie	baía
bay	Bucht	**buchta** *Rus.*	bahía	baie	baía
mountain	Berg	**bufa** *Sp.*	bufa	montagne	montanha
bay	Bucht	**bugt** *Dan.*	bahía	baie	baía
lake	See	**buḥayrah** *Ara.*	lago	lac	lago
lake, lagoon	See, Lagune, Haff	**buḥayrat** *Ara.*	lago, laguna	lac, lagune	lago, laguna
mountain, hill	Berg, Hügel	**bukit** *Indon., Mal.*	montaña, colina	montagne, colline	montanha, colina
bay	Bucht	**-bukten** *Swe.*	bahía	baie	baía
mountain	Berg	**bulu** *Indon.*	montaña	montagne	montanha
castle	Burg	**Burg** *Ger.*	castillo	château	castelo
hill	Hügel	**burj** *Ara.*	colina	colline	colina
creek	Bach	**burn** *Ger.*	riachuelo	crique	riacho
cape	Kap	**burnu, burun** *Tur.*	cabo	cap	cabo
bay	Busen	**Busen** *Ger.*	bahía	baie	baía
butte(s)	Restberg(e)	**butte(s)** *Eng., Fr.*	butte(s)	butte(s)	colina, outeiro

C

ENGLISH	DEUTSCH	Map Form	ESPAÑOL	FRANÇAIS	PORTUGUÊS
cape	Kap	**c., cabo** *Sp.* **cap** *Fr.* **cape** *Eng.*	cabo	cap	cabo
street	Strasse	**c., calle** *Sp.*	calle	rue	rua
peaks	Gipfel	**cabezas** *Sp.*	cabezas	cimes	picos
cape	Kap	**cabo** *Port., Sp.*	cabo	cap	cabo
waterfall	Wasserfall	**cachoeira** *Port.*	cascada	chute d'eau	cachoeira
street	Strasse	**calle** *Sp.*	calle	rue	rua
parkway	Ferienstrasse	**calzada** *Sp.*	calzada	allée de parc	alameda de parque
mosque	Moschee	**camii** *Tur.*	mezquita	mosquée	mesquita
road	Weg	**camino** *Sp.*	camino	route	rodovia
camp	Lager	**camp** *Eng., Fr.*	campo	camp	campo
plain	Ebene	**campo** *It.*	llanura	plaine	planície
brook; ravine	Bach; Tobel	**cañada** *Sp.*	cañada	ruisseau; ravin	ravina
canal	Kanal	**canal** *Eng.*	canal	canal	canal
canal, channel	Kanal	**canal** *Fr., Port., Sp.*	canal	canal	canal
canal, channel	Kanal	**canale** *It.*	canal	canal	canal
stream distributary	Flussarm	**caño** *Sp.*	caño	bras	braço de rio, igarapé
canyon	Cañon	**cañón** *Sp.*	cañón	canyon	canhão
canyon	Cañon	**canyon** *Eng.*	cañón	canyon	canhão
plateau	Hochebene	**cao nguyen** *Viet.*	meseta	plateau	planalto
cape	Kap	**cap** *Fr.*	cabo	cap	cabo
cape	Kap	**cape** *Eng.*	cabo	cap	cabo
capitol	Kapitol	**capitolio** *Sp.*	capitolio	capitole	capitólio
cape	Kap	**capo** *It.*	cabo	cap	cabo
captain	Kapitän	**capt., captain** *Eng.*	capitán	capitaine	capitão
highway	Strasse	**carretera** *Sp.*	carretera	route	rodovia
valley	Tal	**carse** *Gae.*	valle	vallée	vale
waterfall	Wasserfall	**cascada** *Sp.*	cascada	chute d'eau	queda d'água
waterfall	Wasserfall	**cascata** *It.*	cascada	chute d'eau	queda d'água
castle	Burg, Schloss	**castel, castello** *It.*	castillo	château	castelo
castle	Burg, Schloss	**castelo** *Port.*	castillo	château	castelo
castle	Burg, Schloss	**castillo** *Sp.*	castillo	château	castelo
castle	Burg, Schloss	**castle** *Eng.*	castillo	château	castelo
cataracts	Katarakten	**cataratas** *Port., Sp.*	cataratas	cataractes	cataratas
cathedral	Kathedrale	**catedral** *Sp.*	catedral	cathédrale	catedral
range	Gebirge	**catena** *Sp.*	catena	chaîne	cordilheira
cathedral	Kathedrale	**cathedral** *Eng.*	catedral	cathédrale	catedral
causeway	Dammweg	**causeway** *Eng.*	calzada	chaussée	calçada
upland	Bergland	**causse** *Fr.*	tierras altas	causse	terras altas
cave(s)	Höhle(n)	**cave(s)** *Eng.*	cueva(s)	caverne(s)	caverna(s)
cay	Klippe	**cay** *Eng.*	cayo	caye	baixio
cay(s)	Klippe(n)	**cayo(s)** *Sp.*	cayo(s)	cave(s)	baixio(s)
cemetery	Friedhof	**cementerio** *Sp.*	cementerio	cimetière	cemitério
cemetery	Friedhof	**cemetery** *Eng.*	cementerio	cimetière	cemitério
mountain(s), hill(s)	Berg(e), Hügel	**cerro(s)** *Sp.*	cerro(s)	montagne(s), colline(s)	montanha(s), colina(s)
range	Gebirge	**chaîne** *Fr.*	sierra	chaîne	cordilheira
channel	Kanal	**channel** *Eng.*	canal, estrecho	canal, détroit	canal, estreito
hills	Hügel	**chapada** *Port.*	colinas	collines	chapada
island	Insel	**char** *Ben.*	isla	île	ilha
castle	Burg, Schloss	**château** *Fr.*	castillo	château	castelo
island	Insel	**chau** *Ch.*	isla	île	ilha
road	Landstrasse	**chemin** *Fr.*	camino	chemin	rodovia
bay	Bucht	**chhâk** *Cbd.*	bahía	baie	baía
river	Fluss	**ch'i** *Ch.*	río	rivière	rio
lake	See	**-chi** *Ch.*	lago	lac	lago
cape	Kap	**chia** *Ch.*	cabo	cap	cabo
harbor	Hafen	**chiang** *Ch.*	puerto	port	porto
cape	Kap	**chiao** *Ch.*	cabo	cap	cabo
road	Landstrasse	**chin., chemin** *Fr.*	camino	chemin	rodovia
river	Fluss	**-ch'ŏn** *Kor.*	río	rivière	rio
reservoir	Stausee	**-chŏsuji** *Kor.*	embalse	réservoir	reservatório
intermittent lake, salt marsh	periodischer See, Salzmarsch	**chott** *Ara.*	lago intermitente, pantano salado	lac périodique, marais salé	lago intermitente, pântano salgado
range	Gebirge	**chr., chrebet** *Rus.*	sierra	chaîne	cordilheira
river	Fluss	**ch'uan** *Ch.*	río	rivière	rio
mountains	Berge	**chuŏr phnum** *Cbd.*	montañas	montagnes	montanhas
church	Kirche	**church** *Eng.*	iglesia	église	igreja
waterfalls	Wasserfälle	**chutes** *Fr.*	cascadas	chutes d'eau	quedas d'água
marsh	Marsch	**ciénaga** *Sp.*	ciénaga	marais	pântano
peak	Gipfel	**cima** *It., Sp.*	cima	cime	pico
peak	Gipfel	**cime** *Fr.*	cima	cime	pico
cemetery	Friedhof	**cimetière** *Fr.*	cementerio	cimetière	cemitério
city	Stadt	**città** *It.*	ciudad	ville	cidade
city	Stadt	**city** *Eng.*	ciudad	ville	cidade
city	Stadt	**ciudad** *Sp.*	ciudad	ville	cidade
claypan	Tonpfanne	**claypan** *Eng.*	capa de arcilla	couche argilleuse	camada de argila
cliff(s)	Kliff(e)	**cliff(s)** *Eng.*	risco(s)	falaise(s)	falésia(s)
mountain	Berg	**co** *Viet.*	montaña	montagne	montanha
mountain, hill	Berg, Hügel	**co., cerro** *Sp.*	cerro	montagne, colline	montanha, colina
coast	Küste	**coast** *Eng.*	costa	côte	costa
coast guard station	Küstenwacht-station	**coast guard station** *Eng.*	estación de los guardacostas	station des gardes de la côte	estação de guarda costeira
pass	Pass	**col** *Fr.*	paso	col	passo
college	Hochschule	**colegio** *Sp.*	colegio	collège	colégio
hill(s)	Hügel	**colina(s)** *Sp.*	colina(s)	colline(s)	colina(s)
college	Hochschule	**coll., college** *Eng.*	colegio	collège	colégio
hills	Hügel	**colli** *It.*	colinas	collines	colinas
hills	Hügel	**colline** *It.*	colinas	collines	colinas
hills	Hügel	**collines** *Fr.*	colinas	collines	colinas
common	Gemeindeland	**common** *Eng.*	campo común	commune	terra comum
islands	Inseln	**con** *Viet.*	islas	îles	ilhas
plain	Ebene	**conca** *It.*	llanura	plaine	planície
convent	Nonnenkloster	**convent** *Eng.*	convento	couvent	convento
convent	Nonnenkloster	**convento** *It., Port., Sp*	convento	couvent	convento
range	Gebirge	**cord., cordillera** *Sp.*	cordillera	chaîne	cordilheira
mountain	Berg	**corno** *It.*	montaña	montagne	montanha
brook	Bach	**córrego** *Port.*	arroyo	ruisseau	córrego
coast	Küste	**costa** *Sp.*	costa	côte	costa
coast, hills	Küste, Hügel	**côte** *Fr.*	costa, colinas	côte	costa, colinas
hills	Hügel	**coteau** *Fr.*	colinas	coteau	colinas
coulee	breite Schlucht	**coulee** *Eng.*	rambla	coulée	barranco
coulee	breite Schlucht	**coulée** *Fr.*	rambla	coulée	barranco
county park	Park	**county park** *Eng.*	parque del condado	parc de comté	parque de condado
convent	Nonnenkloster	**couvent** *Fr.*	convento	couvent	convento
cove	kleine Bucht	**cove** *Eng.*	ensenada	anse	enseada
creek	Bach	**cr., creek** *Eng.*	riachuelo	crique	riacho
crag	Felsspitze	**crag** *Eng.*	despeñadero	pointe de rocher	despenhadeiro
crater	Krater	**crater** *Eng.*	cráter	cratère	cratera
crater	Krater	**cratère** *Fr.*	cráter	cratère	cratera
creek	Bach	**creek** *Eng.*	riachuelo	crique	riacho
peak	Gipfel	**croda** *It.*	pico	cime	pico
canal	Kanal	**csatorna** *Hung.*	canal	canal	canal
bay	Bucht	**cua** *Viet.*	bahía	baie	baía
hills, ridge	Hügel, Höhenrücken	**cuchilla** *Sp.*	cuchilla	collines, crête	coxilha
caves	Höhen	**cuevas** *Sp.*	cuevas	cavernes	cavernas
cove	kleine Bucht	**cul-de-sac** *Fr.*	ensenada	cul-de-sac	enseada
mountains	Berge	**culmea** *Rom.*	montañas	montagnes	montanhas
summit	Gipfel	**cumbre** *Sp.*	cumbre	sommet	cume

D

ENGLISH	DEUTSCH	Map Form	ESPAÑOL	FRANÇAIS	PORTUGUÊS
mountain	Berg	**dağ, dağı** *Tur.*	montaña	montagne	montanha
mountains	Berge	**dāgh** *Per.*	montañas	montagnes	montanhas
mountains	Berge	**dağlar, dağları** *Tur.*	montañas	montagnes	montanhas
hill	Hügel	**ḍahr** *Ara.*	colina	colline	colina
plateau	Hochebene	**-dai, -daichi** *Jap.*	meseta	plateau	planalto

Glossary and Abbreviations of Geographical Terms / Verzeichnis und Abkürzungen Geographischer Begriffe
Glosario y Abreviaciones de Términos Geográficos / Glossaire et Abréviations de Termes Géographiques
Glossário e Abreviações de Termos Geográficos 291

ENGLISH	DEUTSCH	Map Form Geographische Begriffe Términos Geográficos Termes Géographiques Termos Geográficos	ESPAÑOL	FRANÇAIS	PORTUGUÊS
mountain	Berg	**-dake** *Jap.*	montaña	montagne	montanha
valley	Tal	**-dal, -dalen** *Nor., Swe.*	valle	vallée	vale
dale	weites Tal	**dale** *Eng.*	valle ancho	vallée large	vale aberto
dam	Damm	**dam** *Eng.*	presa	barrage	represa
lake	See	**danau** *Indon.*	lago	lac	lago
island	Insel	**-dao** *Ch., Viet.*	isla	île	ilha
marsh	Marsch	**daqq** *Per.*	pantano	marais	pântano
lake	See	**daryācheh** *Per.*	lago	lac	lago
desert	Wüste	**dasht** *Per.*	desierto	désert	deserto
monastery	Kloster	**dayr** *Ara.*	monasterio	monastère	mosteiro
deep	Tiefe	**deep** *Eng.*	fosa marina	fossé marin	fossa submarina
delta	Delta	**delta** *Eng., Fr., Sp.*	delta	delta	delta
sea	Meer	**deniz, denizi,** *Tur.*	mar	mer	mar
monument	Denkmal	**Denkmal** *Ger.*	monumento	monument	monumento
pass	Pass	**deo** *Viet.*	paso	col	passo
depression	Senke	**depression** *Eng.*	depresión	dépression	depressão
river	Fluss	**deresi** *Tur.*	río	rivière	rio
desert	Wüste	**desert** *Eng.*	desierto	désert	deserto
desert	Wüste	**desierto** *Sp.*	desierto	désert	deserto
strait	Meeresstrasse	**détroit** *Fr.*	estrecho	détroit	estreito
escarpment	Landstufe	**dhar** *Ara.*	escarpa	escarpement	escarpa
canal	Kanal	**dhiórix** *Gr.*	canal	canal	canal
lake	See	**-dian** *Ch.*	lago	lac	lago
channel	Kanal	**diep** *Du.*	canal, estrecho	canal, détroit	canal, estreito
dike	Deich	**dijk** *Du.*	dique	digue	dique
district	Distrikt	**district** *Eng.*	distrito	district	distrito
district	Distrikt	**distrito** *Sp.*	distrito	district	distrito
ditch	Graben	**ditch** *Eng.*	acequia	fossé	fosso
peninsula	Halbinsel	**djazirah** *Indon.*	península	péninsule	península
mountain(s)	Berg(e)	**djebel** *Ara.*	montaña(s)	montagne(s)	montanha(s)
fjord	Fjord	**-djúp** *Ice.*	fiordo	fjord	fiorde
channel, sound	Kanal, Sund	**-djupet** *Swe.*	canal, sonda	canal, détroit	canal, estreito
zoo	Zoo	**djurpark** *Swe.*	parque zoológico	zoo	jardim zoológico
island	Insel	**-do** *Kor.*	isla	île	ilha
interfluve	Erhebung	**doāb** *Per.*	interfluvio	interfluve	interflúvio
dock	Dock	**dock** *Eng.*	muelle	quai	doca
mountain	Berg	**doi** *Thai*	montaña	montagne	montanha
valley	Tal	**dolina** *Rus.*	valle	vallée	vale
mountain	Berg	**dolok** *Indo.*	montaña	montagne	montanha
hills	Hügel	**dombrovidék** *Hung.*	colinas	collines	colinas
hills	Hügel	**dombvidék** *Hung.*	colinas	collines	colinas
peak	Gipfel	**dos** *Fr.*	pico	dos	pico
downs (hills)	Hügelland	**downs** *Eng.*	colinas	collines	terras baixas (colinas)
drive	Fahrweg	**dr., drive** *Eng.*	calzada	avenue	avenida
drain	Abzugsgraben	**drain** *Eng.*	desaguadero	drainage	escoadouro
draw	kleines Tal	**draw** *Eng.*	valle pequeño	ravine	bacia, vale
drive	Fahrweg	**drive** *Eng.*	calzada	avenue	avenida
dry lake	Trockensee	**dry lake** *Eng.*	lago seco	lac asséché	lago seco
dunes	Dünen	**dunes** *Eng., Fr.*	dunas	dunes	dunas

E

ENGLISH	DEUTSCH	Map Form	ESPAÑOL	FRANÇAIS	PORTUGUÊS
east	Ost	**e., east** *Eng.*	este	est	leste
school	Schule	**école** *Fr.*	escuela	école	escola
mountain	Berg	**-egga** *Nor.*	montaña	montagne	montanha
memorial	Ehrenmal	**Ehrenmal** *Ger.*	monumento	memorial	monumento
river	Fluss	**-elv, -elva** *Nor.*	río	rivière	rio
reservoir	Stausee	**embalse** *Sp.*	embalse	réservoir	reservatório
pier	Landungsbrücke	**embarcadero** *Sp.*	embarcadero	jetée	cais
valley	Tal	**'emeq** *Heb.*	valle	vallée	vale
monument	Denkmal	**emlékmű** *Hung.*	monumento	monument	monumento
spring	Quelle	**'en** *Heb.*	manantial	source	fonte, manancial
cove	kleine Bucht	**enseada** *Port.*	ensenada	anse	enseada
cove	kleine Bucht	**ensenada** *Sp.*	ensenada	anse	enseada
entrance	Einfahrt	**entrance** *Eng.*	entrada	entrée	entrada
forest	Wald	**erdő** *Hung.*	bosque	forêt	floresta
sand desert	Sandwüste	**erg** *Ara.*	desierto arenoso	désert de sable	deserto arenoso
escarpment	Landstufe	**escarpment** *Eng.*	escarpa	escarpement	escarpa
school	Schule	**escuela** *Sp.*	escuela	école	escola
highland	Hochland	**espigão** *Port.*	región montañosa	pays montagneux	espigão
station	Bahnhof, Stützpunkt	**est., estação** *Port.* **estación** *Sp.*	estación	station	estação
stadium	Stadion	**estadio** *Sp.*	estadio	stade	estádio
reservoir	Stausee	**estanque** *Sp.*	estanque	réservoir	reservatório
estuary	Trichtermündung	**estero** *Sp.*	estero	estuaire	estuário
road	Landstrasse	**estr., estrada** *Port.*	camino	route	estrada
strait	Meeresstrasse	**estrecho** *Sp.*	estrecho	détroit	estreito
estuary	Trichtermündung	**estuary** *Eng.*	estuario	estuaire	estuário
pond	Teich	**étang** *Fr.*	charca	étang	lagoa, açude
expressway	Autobahn	**expy., expressway** *Eng.*	autopista	autoroute	via expressa
island	Insel	**-ey** *Ice.*	isla	île	ilha
lake	See	**ežeras** *Lith.*	lago	lac	lago
lake	See	**ezers** *Latv.*	lago	lac	lago

F

ENGLISH	DEUTSCH	Map Form	ESPAÑOL	FRANÇAIS	PORTUGUÊS
faculty (school)	Fakultät	**faculté** *Fr.*	facultad	faculté	faculdade
fairground	Ausstellungsgelände	**fairground** *Eng.*	campo para ferias	champ de foire	terreno para feiras
cliff	Kliff	**falaise** *Fr.*	risco	falaise	falésia
waterfall	Wasserfall	**fall(s)** *Eng.*	cascada	chute d'eau	queda d'água
waterfall	Wasserfall	**Fall** *Ger.*	cascada	chute d'eau	queda d'água
waterfall	Wasserfall	**-fallet** *Swe.*	cascada	chute d'eau	queda d'água
river	Fluss	**far'** *Ara.*	río	rivière	rio
lighthouse	Leuchtturm	**faro** *Sp.*	faro	phare	farol
upland	Bergland	**farsh** *Ara.*	tierras altas	hautes terres	terras altas
fell (mountain, hill)	ödes Hügelland	**fell** *Eng.*	colina rocosa	colline rocheuse	colina rochosa
mountain	Berg	**-fell** *Ice.*	montaña	montagne	montanha
mountain	Berg	**-feng** *Ch.*	montaña	montagne	montanha
upland	Bergland	**fennsík** *Hung.*	tierras altas	hautes terres	terras altas
ferry	Fähre	**ferry** *Eng.*	balsadera	bac	balsa
lake	See	**fertő** *Hung.*	lago	lac	lago
fortress	Feste	**Feste** *Ger.*	fortaleza	fort	fortaleza
estuary, strait	Trichtermündung, Meeresstrasse	**firth** *Gae.*	estuario, estrecho	estuaire, détroit	estuário, estreito
mountain(s)	Berg(e)	**fjäll(en)** *Swe.*	montaña(s)	montagne(s)	montanha(s)
mountain	Berg	**fjället** *Swe.*	montaña	montagne	montanha
fjord	Fjord	**fjärden** *Swe.*	fiordo	fjord	fiorde
mountain	Berg	**-fjell, -fjellet** *Nor.*	montaña	montagne	montanha
mountain	Berg	**fjöll** *Ice.*	montaña	montagne	montanha
fjord	Fjord	**-fjord** *Nor.*	fiordo	fjord	fiorde
fjord, lake	Fjord, See	**-fjorden** *Nor., Swe.*	fiordo, lago	fjord, lac	fiorde, lago
fjord, bay	Fjord, Bucht	**fjördur** *Ice.*	fiordo, bahía	fjord, baie	fiorde, baía
fork	Arm	**fk., fork** *Eng.*	brazo	bras	braço de rio
flat	Flachland	**flat** *Eng.*	llano	plat	planície
river	Fluss	**-fljót** *Ice.*	río	rivière	rio
bay	Bucht	**-flói** *Ice.*	bahía	baie	baía
flood control basin	Hochwasserrückhaltebecken	**flood control basin** *Eng.*	cuenca para controlar la inundación	bassin de contrôle d'inondation	bacia de controle de inundações
airport	Flughafen	**Flughafen** *Ger.*	aeropuerto	aéroport	aeroporto
airport	Flugplatz	**Flugplatz** *Ger.*	aeropuerto	aéroport	aeroporto
airport	Flugplatz	**flygplats** *Swe.*	aeropuerto	aéroport	aeroporto
river mouth; pass	Flussmündung; Pass	**foce** *It.*	desembocadura; paso	embouchure; col	desembocadura; foz; passo

ENGLISH	DEUTSCH	Map Form Geographische Begriffe Términos Geográficos Termes Géographiques Termos Geográficos	ESPAÑOL	FRANÇAIS	PORTUGUÊS
canal	Kanal	**föcsatorna** *Hung.*	canal	canal	canal
glacier	Gletscher	**-fonn** *Nor.*	glaciar	glacier	geleira
spring	Quelle	**fontaine** *Fr.*	manantial	fontaine	fonte, manancial
pass	Pass	**forca** *It.*	paso	col	passo
inlet	Förde	**Förde** *Ger.*	abra	bras de mer	enseada
foreland	Vorland	**foreland** *Eng.*	promontorio	promontoire	promontório
forest	Wald	**forest** *Eng.*	bosque	forêt	floresta
forest reserve	Waldreservat	**forest reserve** *Eng.*	reserva de bosque	réserve forestière	reserva florestal
forest	Wald	**forêt** *Fr.*	bosque	forêt	floresta
waterfall	Wasserfall	**-forsen** *Swe.*	cascada	chute d'eau	queda d'água
forest	Forst	**Forst** *Ger.*	bosque	forêt	floresta
fort	Fort	**fort** *Eng., Fr.*	fuerte	fort	forte
waterfall	Wasserfall	**-foss** *Ice.*	cascada	chute d'eau	queda d'água
waterfall	Wasserfall	**-fossen** *Nor.*	cascada	chute d'eau	queda d'água
brook	Bach	**fosso** *It.*	arroyo	ruisseau	córrego
pass	Pass	**foum** *Ara.*	paso	col	passo
fracture zone	Bruchzone	**fracture zone** *Eng.*	zona de fractura	zone de faille	zona de fratura
freeway	Autobahn	**frwy., freeway** *Eng.*	autopista	autoroute	via expressa
fort	Fort	**ft., fort** *Eng., Fr.*	fuerte	fort	forte
stream distributary	Flussarm	**furo** *Port.*	brazo de río	bras	furo

G

ENGLISH	DEUTSCH	Map Form	ESPAÑOL	FRANÇAIS	PORTUGUÊS
mountain, hill	Berg, Hügel	**g., gora** *Rus.*	montaña, colina	montagne, colline	montanha, colina
mountain	Berg	**g., gunong** *Mal.* **gunung** *Indon.*	montaña	montagne	montanha
mountain	Berg	**-gai'sa** *Lapp.*	montaña	montagne	montanha
tunnel	Tunnel	**galleria** *It.*	túnel	tunnel	túnel
gallery	Galerie	**gallery** *Eng.*	galería	galerie	galeria
game farm	Wildfarm	**game farm** *Eng.*	criadero de caza	ferme de gibier	fazenda de caça
game park	Wildpark	**game park** *Eng.*	vedado de caza	parc à gibier	parque de caça
game refuge	Wildgehege	**game refuge** *Eng.*	refugio de caza	refuge de gibier	refúgio de caça
game reserve	Wildreservat	**game reserve** *Eng.*	vedado de caza	réserve à gibier	reserva de caça
game sanctuary	Wildschutzgebiet	**game sanctuary** *Eng.*	vedado de caza	réserve à gibier	santuário de caça
bay	Bucht	**-gang** *Ch.*	bahía	baie	baía
river	Fluss	**-gang** *Kor.*	río	rivière	rio
gap	Pass	**gap** *Eng.*	paso	col	passo
intermittent lake	periodischer See	**garaet** *Ara.*	lago intermitente	lac périodique	lago intermitente
garden	Garten	**gard., garden** *Eng.*	jardín	jardin	jardim
gardens	Gärten	**gardens** *Eng.*	jardines	jardins	jardins
mountain	Berg	**garet** *Ara.*	montaña	montagne	montanha
station	Bahnhof, Stützpunkt	**garı** *Tur.*	estación	station	estação
lake	See	**-gata** *Jap.*	lago	lac	lago
gate	Tor	**gate** *Eng.*	puerta	porte	portão
mountain torrent	Wildbach	**gave** *Fr.*	torrente	gave	torrente
range	Gebirge	**gebergte** *Du.*	sierra	chaîne	cordilheira
range	Gebirge	**Gebirge** *Ger.*	sierra	chaîne	cordilheira
pass	Pass	**geçidi** *Tur.*	paso	col	passo
oasis, well	Oase, Brunnen	**ghadīr** *Ara.*	oasis, pozo	oasis, puits	oásis, poço
mountains	Berge	**ghar** *Pas.*	montañas	montagnes	montanhas
spring	Quelle	**ghayl** *Ara.*	manantial	source	manancial
bay	Bucht	**ghubbat** *Ara.*	bahía	baie	baía
dunes	Dünen	**ghurd** *Ara.*	dunas	dunes	dunas
island	Insel	**gili** *Indon.*	isla	île	ilha
peak	Gipfel	**Gipfel** *Ger.*	pico	cime	pico
hill	Hügel	**giva't** *Heb.*	colina	colline	colina
bay	Bucht	**gji** *Alb.*	bahía	baie	baía
glacier	Gletscher	**glacier** *Eng., Fr.*	glaciar	glacier	geleira
river	Fluss	**gol** *Mong.*	río	rivière	rio
lake	See	**göl** *Tur.*	lago	lac	lago
bald mountains	kahle Berge	**gol'cy** *Rus.*	montañas calvas	monts chauves	montanhas calvas
golf course	Golfplatz	**golf course** *Eng.*	campo de golf	champ de golf	campo de golfe
gulf	Golf	**golfe** *Fr.*	golfo	golfe	golfo
bay	Bucht	**golfete** *Sp.*	golfete	baie	baía
gulf	Golf	**golfo** *It., Sp.*	golfo	golfe	golfo
lake	See	**gölü** *Tur.*	lago	lac	lago
mountain, hill	Berg, Hügel	**gora** *Rus.*	montaña, colina	montagne, colline	montanha, colina
mountains	Berge	**gora** *S./C.*	montañas	montagnes	montanhas
mountain	Berg	**góra** *Pol.*	montaña	montagne	montanha
gorge	Schlucht	**gorge** *Eng., Fr.*	garganta	gorge	garganta
mountains, hills	Berge, Hügel	**gorje** *S./C.*	montañas, colinas	montagnes, collines	montanhas, colinas
ruins	Ruinen	**gorodišče** *Rus.*	ruinas	ruines	ruínas
mountains, hills	Berge, Hügel	**gory** *Rus.*	montañas, colinas	montagnes, collines	montanhas, colinas
mountains	Berge	**góry** *Pol.*	montañas	montagnes	montanhas
river	Fluss	**-gou** *Ch.*	río	rivière	rio
sinkhole	Schluckloch	**gouffre** *Fr.*	sumidero	gouffre	sumidouro
wadi	Wadi	**goulbin** *Hau.*	uadi	wadi	uádi
ditch	Graben	**Graben** *Ger.*	acequia	fossé	fosso
ridge	Höhenrücken	**gr'ada** *Rus.*	sierra	crête	cordilheira
mountain	Berg	**gradište** *Blg.*	montaña	montagne	montanha
ridges	Höhenrücken	**gr'ady** *Rus.*	sierras	crêtes	cordilheira
general	General	**gral., general** *Eng., Sp.*	general	général	geral
ridge	Grat	**Grat** *Ger.*	sierra	crête	cordilheira
grotto	Grotte	**grotta** *It.*	gruta	grotte	gruta
grotto	Grotte	**grotte** *Fr.*	gruta	grotte	gruta
group	Gruppe	**group** *Eng.*	grupo	groupe	grupo
island	Insel	**-grund** *Swe.*	isla	île	ilha
group	Gruppe	**grupo** *Sp.*	grupo	groupe	grupo
group	Gruppe	**gruppo** *It.*	grupo	groupe	grupo
pass	Pass	**-guan** *Ch.*	paso	col	passo
bay	Bucht	**guba** *Rus.*	bahía	baie	baía
mountain	Berg	**guelb** *Ara.*	montaña	montagne	montanha
gulch	Wildbachschlucht	**gulch** *Eng.*	quebrada	ravin	quebrada
gulf	Golf	**gulf** *Eng.*	golfo	golfe	golfo
mountain	Berg	**gunong** *Mal.*	montaña	montagne	montanha
mountain	Berg	**gunung** *Indon.*	montaña	montagne	montanha
islands	Inseln	**-guntō** *Jap.*	islas	îles	ilhas

H

ENGLISH	DEUTSCH	Map Form	ESPAÑOL	FRANÇAIS	PORTUGUÊS
upland	Bergland	**haḍabat** *Ara.*	tierras altas	hautes terres	terras altas
mountain	Berg	**hadjer** *Ara.*	montaña	montagne	montanha
lagoon	Haff	**Haff** *Ger.*	laguna	lagune	laguna
sea, lake	Meer, See	**-hai** *Ch.*	mar, lago	mer, lac	mar, lago
strait	Meeresstrasse	**-haixia** *Ch.*	estrecho	détroit	estreito
reef	Riff	**hakau** *Poly.*	arrecife	récif	recife
peninsula	Halbinsel	**Halbinsel** *Ger.*	península	péninsule	península
hall	Halle	**hall** *Eng., Fr.*	salón	hall	hall
peninsula	Halbinsel	**-halvøya** *Nor.*	península	péninsule	península
beach	Strand	**-hama** *Jap.*	playa	plage	praia
desert	Wüste	**hamada** *Ara.*	desierto	désert	deserto
plateau	Hochebene	**ḥammādat** *Ara.*	meseta	plateau	planalto
lake, marsh	See, Marsch	**hāmūn** *Per.*	lago, pantano	lac, marais	lago, pântano
point	Landspitze	**-hana** *Jap.*	punta	pointe	ponta
peninsula	Halbinsel	**-hantō** *Jap.*	península	péninsule	península
mountain, hill	Berg, Hügel	**har** *Heb.*	montaña, colina	montagne, colline	montanha, colina
harbor, harbour	Hafen	**harbor, harbour** *Eng.*	puerto	port	porto
mountains, hills	Berge, Hügel	**hare** *Heb.*	montañas, colinas	montagnes, collines	montanhas, colinas
ridge	Höhenrücken	**-harju** *Finn.*	sierra	crête	cordilheira
lava flow	Lavastrom	**ḥarrat** *Ara.*	corriente de lava	coulée de lave	corrente de lava
hills	Hügel	**hauteurs** *Fr.*	colinas	hauteurs	colinas

292 Glossary and Abbreviations of Geographical Terms / Verzeichnis und Abkürzungen Geographischer Begriffe
Glosario y Abreviaciones de Términos Geográficos / Glossaire et Abréviations de Termes Géographiques
Glossário e Abreviações de Termos Geográficos

ENGLISH	DEUTSCH	Map Form / Geographische Begriffe / Términos Geográficos / Termes Géographiques / Termos Geográficos	ESPAÑOL	FRANÇAIS	PORTUGUÊS
sea, bay	Meer, Bucht	**-hav** *Swe.*	mar, bahía	mer, baie	mar, baía
harbor	Hafen	**havre** *Fr.*	puerto	havre	porto
oasis	Oase	**ḥawḍ** *Ara.*	oasis	oasis	oásis
lake	See	**hawr** *Ara.*	lago	lac	lago
harbor, harbour	Hafen	**hbr., harbor, harbour** *Eng.*	puerto	port	porto
headquarters	Hauptquartier	**hdqrs., headquarters** *Eng.*	cuartel general	quartier général	quartel-general
river	Fluss	**-he** *Ch.*	río	rivière	rio
head (headland)	Landspitze	**head** *Eng.*	promontorio	promontoire	promontório
heath	Heide	**heath** *Eng.*	matorral	lande	charneca
mountain(s)	Berg(e)	**hegy(ség)** *Hung.*	montaña(s)	montagne(s)	montanha(s)
heath	Heide	**Heide** *Ger.*	matorral	lande	charneca
plain	Ebene	**-heiya** *Jap.*	llanura	plaine	planície
river mouth	Flussmündung	**-hekou** *Ch.*	desembocadura	embouchure	desembocadura
hills	Hügel	**heuwells** *Afk.*	colinas	collines	colinas
highland	Hochland	**highland** *Eng.*	región montañosa	pays montagneux	terras altas
highway	Strasse	**highway** *Eng.*	carretera	route	rodovia
hill(s)	Hügel	**hill(s)** *Eng.*	colina(s)	colline(s)	colina(s)
race course	Rennbahn	**hipódromo** *Sp.*	hipódromo	hippodrome	hipódromo
race course	Rennbahn	**hippodrome** *Fr.*	hipódromo	hippodrome	hipódromo
historical	historisch	**hist., historical** *Eng.*	histórico	historique	histórico
historical park	historischer Park	**historical park** *Eng.*	parque histórico	parc historique	parque histórico
historic(al) site	historische Stätte	**historic(al) site** *Eng.*	sitio histórico	site historique	sitio histórico
river	Fluss	**hka** *Bur.*	río	rivière	rio
Her Majesty's Air Station (U.K.)	Luftwaffenstützpunkt (U.K.)	**H.M.A.S., Her Majesty's Air Station** *Eng.*	Real Estación Aeronáutica (U.K.)	Station Aérienne Royale (U.K.)	Estação Aérea Real (R.U.)
river	Fluss	**ho** *Ch.*	río	rivière	rio
reservoir	Stausse	**-ho** *Kor.*	embalse	réservoir	reservatório
mountain	Berg	**-hø** *Nor.*	montaña	montagne	montanha
plateau	Hochebene	**Hochebene** *Ger.*	meseta	plateau	planalto
forest	Hochwald	**Hochwald** *Ger.*	bosque	forêt	floresta
mountain	Berg	**-högarna** *Swe.*	montaña	montagne	montanha
height	Höhe	**Höhe** *Ger.*	altura	hauteur	elevação
cave(s)	Höhle(n)	**Höhle(n)** *Ger.*	cueva(s)	caverne(s)	caverna(s)
bay	Bucht	**hoi** *Ch.*	bahía	baie	baía
island	Insel	**-holm** *Dan.*	isla	île	ilha
hook	Haken	**hook** *Eng.*	gancho	crochet	cabo, promontório
mountain	Berg	**hora** *Czech., Slo.*	montaña	montagne	montanha
point; peak	Horn	**Horn** *Ger.*	punta; pico	pointe; cime	ponta; pico
ruin	Ruine	**ḥorva** *Heb.*	ruina	ruine	ruína
mountains	Berge	**hory** *Czech., Slo.*	montañas	montagnes	montanhas
hospital	Krankenhaus	**hospital** *Eng., Sp.*	hospital	hôpital	hospital
point	Landspitze	**houma** *Poly.*	punta	pointe	ponta
house	Haus	**house** *Eng.*	casa	maison	casa
island	Insel	**hsü** *Ch.*	isla	île	ilha
lake	See	**-hu** *Ch.*	lago	lac	lago
hill	Hügel	**Hügel** *Ger.*	colina	colline	colina
cape	Huk	**Huk** *Ger.*	cabo	cap	cabo
cape	Huk	**-huk** *Swe.*	cabo	cap	cabo
highway	Strasse	**hy., highway** *Eng.*	carretera	route	rodovia

I

island	Insel	**i., isla** *Sp.* **island** *Eng.*	isla	île	ilha
icefield	Eisdecke	**icefield** *Eng.*	helero	champ de glace	geleira
ice shelf	Schelfeis	**ice shelf** *Eng.*	corniza glacial	barrière de glace	banco de gelo
ice tongue	Eiszunge	**ice tongue** *Eng.*	lengua de glaciar	langue glaciaire	língua de geleira
dunes	Dünen	**idehan** *Ber.*	dunas	dunes	dunas
river	Fluss	**ig., igarapé** *Port.*	río	rivière	igarapé
church	Kirche	**iglesia** *Sp.*	iglesia	église	igreja
lake	See	**-ike** *Jap.*	lago	lac	lago
island(s)	Insel(n)	**île(s)** *Fr.*	isla(s)	île(s)	ilha(s)
islet(s)	kleine Insel(n)	**îlet(s)** *Fr.*	isleta(s)	îlet(s)	ilhota(s)
island(s)	Insel(n)	**ilha(s)** *Port.*	isla(s)	île(s)	ilha(s)
islet(s)	kleine Insel(n)	**ilhéu(s)** *Port.*	isleta(s)	îlot(s)	ilhéu(s)
hill, upland	Hügel, Bergland	**'ilw** *Ara.*	colina, tierras altas	colline, hautes terres	colina, terras altas
hill	Hügel	**'ilwat** *Ara.*	colina	colline	colina
lake	See	**in** *Bur.*	lago	lac	lago
Indian reservation	Indianerreservation	**Ind. res., Indian reservation, Indian reserve** *Eng.*	reserva de Indios	réserve Indienne	reserva indígena
inlet	Einfahrt	**inlet** *Eng.*	abra	bras de mer	enseada
island(s)	Insel(n)	**Insel(n)** *Ger.*	isla(s)	île(s)	ilha(s)
institute	Institut	**inst., institute** *Eng.*	instituto	institut	instituto
international	international	**int., international** *Eng.*	internacional	international	internacional
race course	Rennbahn	**ippodromo** *It.*	hipódromo	hippodrome	hipódromo
wadi	Wadi	**irhazer** *Ber.*	uadi	wadi	uádi
dunes	Dünen	**'irq** *Ara.*	dunas	dunes	dunas
islands	Inseln	**is., islands** *Eng.* **islas** *Sp.*	islas	îles	ilhas
island	Insel	**isla** *Sp.*	isla	île	ilha
island(s)	Insel(n)	**island(s)** *Eng.*	isla(s)	île(s)	ilha(s)
islands	Inseln	**islas** *Sp.*	islas	îles	ilhas
isle(s)	Insel(n)	**isle(s)** *Eng.*	isla(s)	île(s)	ilha(s)
islet(s)	kleine Insel(n)	**islet(s)** *Eng.*	isleta(s)	îlot(s)	ilhota(s)
islet	kleine Insel	**islote** *Sp.*	islote	îlot	ilhota
island	Insel	**isola** *It.*	isla	île	ilha
islands	Inseln	**isole** *It.*	islas	îles	ilhas
islet	kleine Insel	**isolotto** *It.*	isleta	îlot	ilhota
isthmus	Landenge	**isthme** *Fr.*	istmo	isthme	istmo
isthmus	Landenge	**isthmus** *Eng.*	istmo	isthme	istmo
isthmus	Landenge	**istmo** *Sp.*	istmo	isthme	istmo
island	Insel	**-iwa** *Jap.*	isla	île	ilha

J

mountain(s)	Berg(e)	**jabal** *Ara.*	montaña(s)	montagne(s)	montanha(s)
garden	Garten	**jardin** *Fr.*	jardín	jardin	jardim
garden	Garten	**jardín** *Sp.*	jardín	jardin	jardim
gardens	Gärten	**jardines** *Sp.*	jardines	jardins	jardins
lake	See	**järv** *Est.*	lago	lac	lago
lake	See	**-järvi** *Finn.*	lago	lac	lago
mountains	Berge	**jary** *Rus.*	montañas	montagnes	montanhas
cave	Höhle	**jaskyně** *Slo.*	cueva	caverne	caverna
lake	See	**-jaur** *Lapp.*	lago	lac	lago
islands	Inseln	**jazā'ir** *Ara.*	islas	îles	ilhas
island	Insel	**jazīrat** *Ara.*	isla	île	ilha
island	Insel	**jazīreh** *Per.*	isla	île	ilha
reservoir	Stausee	**jazovir** *Blg.*	embalse	réservoir	reservatório
mountain(s)	Berg(e)	**jbel** *Ara.*	montaña(s)	montagne(s)	montanha(s)
lake	See	**jezero** *S./C.*	lago	lac	lago
lake, lagoon	See, Lagune, Haff	**jezioro** *Pol.*	lago, laguna	lac, lagune	lago, laguna
river	Fluss	**-jiang** *Ch.*	río	rivière	rio
cape	Kap	**-jiao** *Ch.*	cabo	cap	cabo
mountains	Berge	**jibāl** *Ara.*	montañas	montagnes	montanhas
island	Insel	**-jima** *Jap.*	isla	île	ilha
saddle	Joch	**Joch** *Ger.*	paso	col	passo
river	Fluss	**-joki** *Finn.*	río	rivière	rio
glacier	Gletscher	**-jøkulen** *Nor.*	glaciar	glacier	geleira
glacier	Gletscher	**-jökull** *Ice.*	glaciar	glacier	geleira
gulf	Golf	**jūras līcis** *Latv.*	golfo	golfe	golfo
islands	Inseln	**juzur** *Ara.*	islas	îles	ilhas

K

ENGLISH	DEUTSCH	Map Form / Geographische Begriffe / Términos Geográficos / Termes Géographiques / Termos Geográficos	ESPAÑOL	FRANÇAIS	PORTUGUÊS
mountains	Berge	**kabīr** *Per.*	montañas	montagnes	montanhas
dunes	Dünen	**kahal** *Ara.*	dunas	dunes	dunas
sea	Meer	**-kai** *Jap.*	mar	mer	mar
strait	Meeresstrasse	**-kaikyō** *Jap.*	estrecho	détroit	estreito
mountain	Berg	**-kaise** *Lapp.*	montaña	montagne	montanha
navy installation	Anlage der Marine	**ka.j., kaijō-jieitai** *Jap.*	estación de la marina	installation navale	instalação naval
creek	Bach	**kali** *Indon.*	riachuelo	crique	riacho
mountain	Berg	**kalns** *Latv.*	montaña	montagne	montanha
ridge	Kamm	**Kamm** *Ger.*	sierra	crête	serra
canal	Kanal	**kanaal** *Du.*	canal	canal	canal
canal, channel	Kanal	**Kanal** *Ger.*	canal	canal	canal
canal, channel	Kanal	**kanal** *Rus., S./C., Swe.*	canal	canal	canal
canal, channel	Kanal	**kanał** *Pol.*	canal	canal	canal
canal, channel	Kanal	**Kanalen** *Swe.*	canal	canal	canal
canal, channel	Kanal	**kanava** *Finn.*	canal	canal	canal
pass	Pass	**kandao** *Pas.*	paso	col	passo
river	Fluss	**-kang** *Kor.*	río	rivière	rio
moor	Moor	**-kangas** *Finn.*	páramo	lande	charneca
national park	Nationalpark	**kansallis-puisto** *Finn.*	parque nacional	parc national	parque nacional
island	Insel	**kaôh** *Cbd.*	isla	île	ilha
cape	Kap	**Kap** *Ger.*	cabo	cap	cabo
gorge	Schlucht	**kapija** *S./C.*	garganta	gorge	garganta
cape	Kap	**-kapp** *Nor.*	cabo	cap	cabo
dunes	Dünen	**kathīb** *Ara.*	dunas	dunes	dunas
desert	Wüste	**kavīr** *Per.*	desierto	désert	deserto
mountain	Berg	**kawlat** *Ara.*	montaña	montagne	montanha
hill	Hügel	**kawm** *Ara.*	colina	colline	colina
mountain	Berg	**kediet** *Ara.*	montaña	montagne	montanha
lake	See	**kenohan** *Indon.*	lago	lac	lago
cape	Kap	**kep** *Alb.*	cabo	cap	cabo
islands	Inseln	**kepulauan** *Indon.*	islas	îles	ilhas
key(s), cay(s)	Klippe(n)	**key(s)** *Eng.*	cayo(s)	caye(s)	baixio(s)
intermittent lake	periodischer See	**khabrat** *Ara.*	lago intermitente	lac périodique	lago intermitente
gulf	Golf	**khalīj** *Ara.*	golfo	golfe	golfo
mountain	Berg	**khao** *Bur., Thai*	montaña	montagne	montanha
mountain	Berg	**khashm** *Ara.*	montaña	montagne	montanha
wadi	Wadi	**khatt** *Ara.*	uadi	wadi	uádi
wadi, river	Wadi, Fluss	**khawr** *Ara.*	uadi, río	wadi, rivière	uádi, rio
dam	Damm	**khazzān** *Ara.*	presa	barrage	represa
river, canal	Fluss, Kanal	**khlong** *Thai*	río, canal	rivière, canal	rio, canal
dunes	Dünen	**khubb** *Ara.*	dunas	dunes	dunas
kill (river, channel)	Fluss, Kanal	**kill** *Eng.*	río, canal	rivière, canal	rio, canal
cemetery	Friedhof	**kladb., kladbišče** *Rus.*	cementerio	cimetière	cemitério
cloister	Kloster	**klasztory** *Pol.*	claustro	cloître	claustro, convento
cloister, monastery	Kloster	**Kloster** *Ger.*	claustro, monasterio	cloître, monastère	claustro, mosteiro
knob	Kuppe	**knob** *Eng.*	protuberancia	bosse	cerro, colina
island	Insel	**ko** *Thai*	isla	île	ilha
lake, lagoon	See, Lagune, Haff	**-ko** *Jap.*	lago, laguna	lac, lagune	lago, laguna
harbor	Hafen	**-kō** *Jap.*	puerto	port	porto
highland	Hochland	**-kōchi** *Jap.*	región montañosa	pays montagneux	terras altas
mountain	Kogel	**Kogel** *Ger.*	montaña	montagne	montanha
plateau	Hochebene	**-kogen** *Jap.*	meseta	plateau	planalto
mountains	Berge	**koh** *Per.*	montañas	montagnes	montanhas
air force installation	Anlage der Luftwaffe	**ko.j., kōkū-jieitai** *Jap.*	estación aeronáutica	installation aérienne	instalação da força aérea
national park	Nationalpark	**-kokuritsu-kōen** *Jap.*	parque nacional	parc national	parque nacional
national park	Nationalpark	**-kokutei-kōen** *Jap.*	parque nacional	parc national	parque nacional
bay	Bucht	**kólpos** *Gr.*	bahía	baie	baía
bay	Bucht	**kong** *Ch.*	bahía	baie	baía
mountain	Berg	**kong** *Indon.*	montaña	montagne	montanha
peak	Kopf	**Kopf** *Ger.*	pico	cime	pico
bridge	Brücke	**köprüsü** *Tur.*	puente	pont	ponte
gulf, bay	Golf, Bucht	**körfezi** *Tur.*	golfo, bahía	golfe, baie	golfo, baía
spit	Landzunge	**kosa** *Rus.*	lengua de tierra	flèche	ponta de terra
rapids	Stromschnellen	**-koski** *Finn.*	rápidos	rapides	rápidos
pass	Pass	**kotal** *Per.*	paso	col	passo
basin	Becken	**kotlina** *Pol.*	cuenca	bassin	bacia
bay; pass	Bucht; Pass	**-kou** *Ch.*	bahía; paso	baie; col	baía; passo
mountains	Berge	**kras** *Slo.*	montañas	montagnes	montanhas
ridge	Höhenrücken	**kr'až** *Rus.*	sierra	crête	serra
escarpment	Landstufe	**kreb** *Ara.*	escarpa	escarpement	escarpa
fort	Fort	**krepost'** *Rus.*	fuerte	fort	forte
national park	Nationalpark	**krk., kokuritsu-kōen** *Jap.*	parque nacional	parc national	parque nacional
river	Fluss	**krueng** *Indon.*	río	rivière	rio
national park	Nationalpark	**ktk., kokutei-kōen** *Jap.*	parque nacional	parc national	parque nacional
river mouth	Flussmündung	**-ku** *Ch.*	desembocadura	embouchure	desembocadura
bay	Bucht	**kuala** *Mal.*	bahía	baie	baía
mountain(s)	Berg(e)	**kūh(ha)** *Per.*	montaña(s)	montagne(s)	montanha(s)
hill	Hügel	**-kulle** *Swe.*	colina	colline	colina
dome	Kuppe	**Kuppe** *Ger.*	domo	dôme	domo
strait	Meeresstrasse	**-kurkku** *Finn.*	estrecho	détroit	estreito
channel	Kanal	**kyle** *Gae.*	canal, estrecho	canal, détroit	canal, estreito
island	Insel	**kyun** *Bur.*	isla	île	ilha
hills	Hügel	**-kyūryū** *Jap.*	colinas	collines	colinas

L

lake	See	**l., lac** *Fr.* **lago** *It., Sp.* **lagoa** *Port.* **lake** *Eng.*	lago	lac	lago, lagoa
pass	Pass	**la** *Tib.*	paso	col	passo
province	Provinz	**lääni** *Finn.*	provincia	province	província
lake(s)	See(n)	**lac(s)** *Fr.*	lago(s)	lac(s)	lago(s)
lake	See	**lacul** *Rom.*	lago	lac	lago
river	Fluss	**lae** *Indon.*	río	rivière	rio
cape	Kap	**laem** *Thai*	cabo	cap	cabo
lagoon, lake	Lagune, Haff, See	**lag., laguna** *Sp.*	laguna	lagune, lac	laguna
lake	See	**lago** *It., Port., Sp.*	lago	lac	lago
lake, lagoon	See, Lagune, Haff	**lagoa** *Port.*	lago, laguna,	lac, lagune	lagoa
lagoon	Lagune, Haff	**lagoon** *Eng.*	laguna	lagune	laguna
lakes	Seen	**lagos** *Port., Sp.*	lagos	lacs	lagos
lagoon, lake	Lagune, Haff, See	**laguna** *Sp.*	laguna	lagune, lac	laguna, lago
lagoon	Lagune, Haff	**lagune** *Fr.*	laguna	lagune	laguna
bay	Bucht	**laht** *Est.*	bahía	baie	baía
gulf	Golf	**-lahti** *Finn.*	golfo	golfe	golfo
lake(s)	See(n)	**lake(s)** *Eng.*	lago(s)	lac(s)	lago(s)
county	Grafschaft	**län** *Swe.*	condado	comté	condado
lake	Lanke (See)	**Lanke** *Ger.*	lago	lac	lago
sea	Meer	**laut** *Indon.*	mar	mer	mar
lava flow	Lavastrom	**lava flow** *Eng.*	corriente de lava	coulée de lave	corrente de lava
hill, mountain	Hügel, Berg	**law** *Gae.*	colina, montaña	colline, montagne	colina montanha
mountains; forest	Berge; Wald	**les** *Czech*	montañas; bosque	montagnes; forêt	montanhas; floresta
forest	Wald	**les** *Rus.*	bosque	forêt	floresta
level (plain)	Niveau (Ebene)	**level** *Eng.*	nivel (llano)	niveau (plaine)	planície
islands	Inseln	**liehtao** *Ch.*	islas	îles	ilhas
lighthouse	Leuchtturm	**lighthouse** *Eng.*	faro	phare	farol
estuary	Trichtermündung	**liman** *Rus.*	estuario	estuaire	estuário

Glossary and Abbreviations of Geographical Terms / Verzeichnis und Abkürzungen Geographischer Begriffe
Glosario y Abreviaciones de Términos Geográficos / Glossaire et Abréviations de Termes Géographiques
Glossário e Abreviações de Termos Geográficos
293

ENGLISH	DEUTSCH	Map Form / Geographische Begriffe / Términos Geográficos / Termes Géographiques / Termos Geográficos	ESPAÑOL	FRANÇAIS	PORTUGUÊS
bay	Bucht	**limanı** *Tur.*	bahía	baie	baía
lake	See	**límni** *Gr.*	lago	lac	lago
peak	Gipfel	**-ling** *Ch.*	pico	cime	pico
plain	Ebene	**llano** *Sp.*	llano	plaine	planície
plains	Ebenen	**llanos** *Sp.*	llanos	plaines	planícies
lake, inlet	See, Einfahrt	**loch** *Gae.*	lago, abra	lac, bras de mer	lago, angra
lock	Schleuse	**lock** *Eng.*	esclusa	écluse	eclusa
lock and dam	Damm mit Schleuse	**lock and dam** *Eng.*	presa y esclusa	écluse et barrage	represa e eclusa
gorge	Schlucht	**log** *Rus.*	garganta	gorge	garganta
mountain	Berg	**loi** *Bur.*	montaña	montagne	montanha
hills	Hügel	**lomas** *Sp.*	lomas	collines	colinas
lake	See	**lough** *Gae.*	lago	lac	lago
lowland	Tiefland	**lowland** *Eng.*	tierra baja	terrain bas	terras baixas
marsh	Luch (Bruch)	**Luch** *Ger.*	pantano	marais	pântano
airport	Flughafen	**luchthaven** *Du.*	aeropuerto	aéroport	aeroporto
island	Insel	**-luoto** *Finn.*	isla	île	ilha

M

ENGLISH	DEUTSCH	Map Form	ESPAÑOL	FRANÇAIS	PORTUGUÊS
mountains	Berge	**m., munţii** *Rom.*	montañas	montagnes	montanhas
island	Insel	**-maa** *Est.*	isla	île	ilha
river	Fluss	**mae** *Thai*	río	rivière	rio
strait	Meeresstrasse	**maḏiq** *Ara.*	estrecho	détroit	estreito
depression	Senke	**makhtesh** *Heb.*	depresión	dépression	depressão
bay	Bucht	**-man** *Kor.*	bahía	baie	baía
monastery	Kloster	**manastir** *S./C.*	monasterio	monastère	mosteiro
sea	Meer	**mar** *Sp.*	mar	mer	mar
marsh	Marsch	**marais** *Fr.*	pantano	marais	pântano
sea	Meer	**mare** *It.*	mar	mer	mar
Marine Corps Air Station	Flugstützpunkt des Marine-Corps	**Marine Corps Air Station** *Eng.*	estación aeronáutica de la infantería de marina	station aérienne des fusiliers marins	estação aérea de fuzileiros navais
Marine Corps Base	Marine-Corps-Stützpunkt	**Marine Corps Base** *Eng.*	base de la infantería de marina	base des fusiliers marins	base de fuzileiros navais
bay	Bucht	**marsā** *Ara.*	bahía	baie	baía
marsh	Marsch	**Marsch** *Ger.*	pantano	marais	pântano
marsh(es)	Marsch(en)	**marsh(es)** *Eng.*	pantano(s)	marais	pântano(s)
river mouth	Flussmündung	**maşabb** *Ara.*	desembocadura	embouchure	desembocadura
canal	Kanal	**maşrif** *Ara.*	canal	canal	canal
massif	Gebirgsmassiv	**massif** *Eng., Fr.*	macizo	massif	maciço
Marine Corps Air Station	Flugstützpunkt des Marine-Corps	**M.C.A.S., Marine Corps Air Station** *Eng.*	estación aeronáutica de la infantería de marina	station aérienne des fusiliers marins	estação aérea de fuzileiros navais
Marine Corps Base	Marine-Corps-Stützpunkt	**M.C.B., Marine Corps Base** *Eng.*	base de la infantería de marina	base des fusiliers marins	base de fuzileiros navais
meadow	Wiese	**meadow** *Eng.*	prado	prairie	pradaria
dunes	Dünen	**médanos** *Sp.*	médanos	dunes	dunas
sea, lake	Meer	**Meer** *Ger.*	mar, lago	mer, lac	mar, lago
sea, lake	Meer	**meer** *Afk., Du.*	mar, lago	mer, lac	mar, lago
hills	Hügel	**melkosopočnik** *Rus.*	colinas	collines	colinas
memorial	Gedenkstätte	**mem., memorial** *Eng., Fr.*	monumento	memorial	monumento
peninsula	Halbinsel	**menandjung** *Indon.*	península	péninsule	península
sea	Meer	**mer** *Fr.*	mar	mer	mar
mesa	Tafelberg	**mesa** *Sp.*	mesa	mesa	mesa
plateau	Hochebene	**meseta** *Sp.*	meseta	plateau	planalto
middle	Mittel-	**mid., middle** *Eng.*	medio	moyen	médio, central
spit	Landzunge	**mierzeja** *Pol.*	lengua de tierra	flèche	ponta de terra
bay	Bucht	**mifraz** *Heb.*	bahía	baie	baía
mines	Bergwerke	**mikhrot** *Heb.*	minas	mines	minas
military	militärisch	**mil., military** *Eng.*	militar	militaire	militar
harbor	Hafen	**-minato** *Jap.*	puerto	port	porto
mine	Bergwerk	**mine** *Eng., Fr.*	mina	mine	mina
mountain	Berg	**-mine** *Jap.*	montaña	montagne	montanha
cliff	Kliff	**minqār** *Ara.*	risco	falaise	falésia
cape	Kap	**-misaki** *Jap.*	cabo	cap	cabo
mission	Mission	**mission** *Eng., Fr.*	misión	mission	missão
monument	Denkmal	**mon., monument** *Eng. Fr.*	monumento	monument	monumento
monastery	Kloster	**monasterio** *Sp.*	monasterio	monastère	mosteiro
monastery	Kloster	**monastero** *It.*	monasterio	monastère	mosteiro
monastery	Kloster	**monastery** *Eng.*	monasterio	monastère	mosteiro
monastery	Kloster	**moní** *Gr.*	monasterio	monastère	mosteiro
mount	Berg	**mont** *Fr.*	monte	mont	monte
mountain	Berg	**montagna** *It.*	montaña	montagne	montanha
mountain(s)	Berg(e)	**montagne(s)** *Fr.*	montaña(s)	montagne(s)	montanha(s)
mountain(s)	Berg(e)	**montaña(s)** *Sp.*	montaña(s)	montagne(s)	montanha(s)
mount	Berg	**monte** *It., Port., Sp.*	monte	mont	monte
mountains	Berge	**montes** *Port., Sp.*	montes	monts	montes
mountains	Berge	**monti** *It.*	montes	monts	montes
mountains	Berge	**monts** *Fr.*	montes	monts	montes
monument	Denkmal	**monument** *Eng., Fr.*	monumento	monument	monumento
moor	Moor	**moor** *Eng.*	páramo	lande	pântano
moor	Moos	**Moos** *Ger.*	páramo	lande	pântano
sea	Meer	**more** *Rus.*	mar	mer	mar
mountain	Berg	**-mori** *Jap.*	montaña	montagne	montanha
mountain	Berg	**morne** *Fr.*	montaña	morne	montanha
hill, mountain	Hügel, Berg	**morro** *Port., Sp.*	morro	colline, montagne	morro
mosque	Moschee	**mosque** *Eng.*	mezquita	mosquée	mesquita
island, rock	Insel, Fels	**motu** *Poly.*	isla, roca	île, rocher	ilha, rochedo
island	Insel	**mouchão** *Port.*	isla	île	mouchão
mound	Erdhügel	**mound** *Eng.*	montículo	tertre	montículo
mount	Berg	**mount** *Eng.*	monte	mont	monte
mountain(s)	Berg(e)	**mountain(s)** *Eng.*	montaña(s)	montagne(s)	montanha(s)
mouth	Mündung	**mouth** *Eng.*	desembocadura	embouchure	desembocadura
mount	Berg	**mt., mount** *Eng.*	monte	mont	monte
mountain	Berg	**mtn., mountain** *Eng.*	montaña	montagne	montanha
mountains	Berge	**mts., mountains** *Eng.*	montañas	montagnes	montanhas
point	Landspitze	**mui** *Viet.*	punta	pointe	ponta
headland	Landspitze	**mull** *Gae.*	promontorio	promontoire	promontório
channel	Kanal	**mun** *Ch.*	canal,estrecho	canal, détroit	canal, estreito
depression	Senke	**munkhafaḍ** *Ara.*	depresión	dépression	depressão
mountain	Berg	**muntele** *Rom.*	montaña	montagne	montanha
mountains	Berge	**munţii** *Rom.*	montañas	montagnes	montanhas
museum	Museum	**museo** *It., Sp.*	museo	musée	museu
museum	Museum	**Museum** *Ger.*	museo	musée	museu
museum	Museum	**museum** *Eng.*	museo	musée	museu
museum	Museum	**múzeum** *Hung.*	museo	musée	museu
museum	Museum	**muzej** *Rus.*	museo	musée	museu
cape	Kap	**mys** *Rus.*	cabo	cap	cabo

N

ENGLISH	DEUTSCH	Map Form	ESPAÑOL	FRANÇAIS	PORTUGUÊS
north	Nord	**n., north** *Eng.*	norte	nord	norte
sea, gulf	Meer, Golf	**-nada** *Jap.*	mar, golfo	mer, golfe	mar, golfo
desert	Wüste	**nafūd** *Ara.*	desierto	désert	deserto
plateau, mountains	Hochebene, Berge	**nagorje** *Rus.*	meseta, montañas	plateau, montagnes	planalto, montanhas
river	Fluss	**nahr** *Ara.*	río	rivière	rio
sea	Meer	**-naikai** *Jap.*	mar	mer	mar
salt flat	Salzebene	**namakzār** *Per.*	salar	saline	salina
narrows	Meeresenge	**narrows** *Eng.*	angostura	goulet	estreito
peninsula	Halbinsel	**-näs** *Swe.*	península	péninsule	península
naval air station	Flugstützpunkt der Marine	**n.a.s., naval air station** *Eng.*	estación aeronáutica de la marina	station des forces aériennes navales	estação aérea da marinha
National Aeronautics and Space Administration	Nationale Aeronautik- und Weltraum-Behörde	**N.A.S.A., National Aeronautics and Space Administration** *Eng.*	Administración Nacional Aeronáutica y Espacial	Administration Nationale de l'Espace et Aéronautique	Administração Nacional do Espaço e Aeronáutica
national park	Nationalpark	**nasjonal park** *Nor.*	parque nacional	parc national	parque nacional
national	national	**nat., national** *Eng., Fr.*	nacional	national	nacional
national battlefield site	Schlachtfeld	**national battlefield site** *Eng.*	campo de batalla nacional	champ de bataille national	campo de batalha nacional
national cemetery	National-friedhof	**national cemetery** *Eng.*	cementerio nacional	cimetière national	cemitério nacional
national forest	Wald in Gemeinbesitz	**national forest** *Eng.*	bosque nacional	forêt nationale	floresta nacional
national historical park	Park an historischer Stätte	**national historical park** *Eng.*	parque histórico nacional	parc historique national	parque histórico nacional
national historical site	historische Stätte	**national historical site** *Eng.*	lugar histórico nacional	site historique national	sítio histórico nacional
national laboratory	staatliche Forschungsanstalt	**national laboratory** *Eng.*	laboratorio nacional	laboratoire national	laboratório nacional
national memorial	nationale Gedenkstätte	**national memorial** *Eng.*	monumento nacional	memorial national	monumento nacional
national military park	Park bei einem Schlachtfeld	**national military park** *Eng.*	parque militar nacional	parc militaire national	parque militar nacional
national monument	Nationaldenkmal	**national monument** *Eng.*	monumento nacional	monument national	monumento nacional
national park	Nationalpark	**national park** *Eng.*	parque nacional	parc national	parque nacional
natioanal recreation area	Ausflugsgebiet	**national recreation area** *Eng.*	campo nacional de recreo	région de récréation nationale	área de lazer nacional
national seashore	öffentlicher Badestrand	**national seashore** *Eng.*	playa nacional	plage nationale	praia nacional
reserve	Naturpark	**Naturpark** *Ger.*	reserva natural	réserve naturelle	reserva natural
nature reserve	Naturschutzgebiet	**Naturschutzgebiet** *Ger.*	reserva natural	réserve naturelle	reserva natural
naval air station	Flugstützpunkt der Marine	**naval air station** *Eng.*	estación aeronáutica de la marina	station des forces aériennes navales	estação aérea da marinha
naval base	Flottenstützpunkt	**naval base** *Eng.*	base naval	base navale	base naval
naval station	Marinestation	**naval station** *Eng.*	estación naval	station navale	estação naval
naval base	Flottenstützpunkt	**n.b., naval base** *Eng.*	base naval	base navale	base naval
rock	Fels	**-ne** *Jap.*	roca	rocher	rochedo
neck	Landenge	**neck** *Eng.*	istmo	isthme	istmo
necropolis	Friedhof	**necrópolis** *Sp.*	necrópolis	nécropole	necrópole
cape	Kap	**neem** *Est.*	cabo	cap	cabo
peninsula, point	Halbinsel, Landspitze	**-nes** *Ice., Nor.*	península, punta	péninsule, pointe	península, ponta
promontory	Vorgebirge	**ness** *Gae.*	promontorio	promontoire	promontório
snowcapped mountain(s)	Schneegipfel	**nev(s)., nevado(s)** *Sp.*	nevado(s)	montagne(s) neigeuse(s)	pico(s) nevado(s)
mountain	Berg	**ngoc** *Viet.*	montaña	montagne	montanha
cape	Kap	**nina** *Est.*	cabo	cap	cabo
islands	Inseln	**nísoi** *Gr.*	islas	îles	ilhas
island	Insel	**nísos** *Gr.*	isla	île	ilha
lowland	Tiefland	**nizina** *Rus.*	tierra baja	terrain bas	terras baixas
lowland	Tiefland	**nižina** *Slo.*	tierra baja	terrain bas	terras baixas
lowland	Tiefland	**nizmennost'** *Rus.*	tierra baja	terrain bas	terras baixas
cape	Kap	**nos** *Blg.*	cabo	cap	cabo
naval station	Marinestation	**n.s., naval station** *Eng.*	estación naval	station navale	estação naval
nature reserve	Naturschutzgebiet	**Nsg., Naturschutzgebiet** *Ger.*	reserva natural	réserve naturelle	reserva natural
mountain	Berg	**nui** *Viet.*	montaña	montagne	montanha
lake	See	**-numa** *Jap.*	lago	lac	lago
mountains	Berge	**nuruu** *Mong.*	montañas	montagnes	montanhas
island	Insel	**nusa** *Indon.*	isla	île	ilha
lake	See	**nuur** *Mong.*	lago	lac	lago

O

ENGLISH	DEUTSCH	Map Form	ESPAÑOL	FRANÇAIS	PORTUGUÊS
bay	Bucht	**o** *Ch.*	bahía	baie	baía
island	Insel	**-ø** *Dan., Nor.*	isla	île	ilha
island	Insel	**-ö** *Swe.*	isla	île	ilha
island	Insel	**o., ostrov** *Rus.*	isla	île	ilha
islands	Inseln	**-öarna** *Swe.*	islas	îles	ilhas
oasis	Oase	**oasis** *Eng., Fr., Sp.*	oasis	oasis	oásis
observatory	Observatorium	**observatorio** *Sp.*	observatorio	observatoire	observatório
observatory	Observatorium	**observatory** *Eng.*	observatorio	observatoire	observatório
ocean	Ozean	**ocean** *Eng.*	océano	océan	oceano
island	Insel	**-ön** *Swe.*	isla	île	ilha
mountains	Berge	**óri** *Gr.*	montañas	montagnes	montanhas
bay	Bucht	**órmos** *Gr.*	bahía	baie	baía
mountain(s)	Berg(e)	**óros** *Gr.*	montaña(s)	montagne(s)	montanha(s)
island(s)	Insel(n)	**ostrov(a)** *Rus.*	isla(s)	île(s)	ilha(s)
island	Insel	**ostrovul** *Rom.*	isla	île	ilha
islands	Inseln	**otoci** *S./C.*	islas	îles	ilhas
island	Insel	**otok** *S./C.*	isla	île	ilha
wadi	Wadi	**ouadi** *Ara.*	uadi	wadi	uádi
wadi	Wadi	**oued** *Ara.*	uadi	wadi	uádi
outlet	Abfluss	**outlet** *Eng.*	desagüe	débouché	escoadouro
island	Insel	**-øy, -øya** *Nor.*	isla	île	ilha
lake	See	**oz., ozero** *Rus.*	lago	lac	lago
lakes	Seen	**ozera** *Rus.*	lagos	lacs	lagos

P

ENGLISH	DEUTSCH	Map Form	ESPAÑOL	FRANÇAIS	PORTUGUÊS
hills	Hügel	**pahorkatina** *Czech.*	colinas	collines	colinas
palace	Palast	**pal., palace** *Eng.*	palacio	palais	palácio
palace	Palast	**palacio** *Sp.*	palacio	palais	palácio
palace	Palast	**palais** *Fr.*	palacio	palais	palácio
palace	Palast	**palazzo** *It.*	palacio	palais	palácio
palace	Palast	**paleis** *Du.*	palacio	palais	palácio
railroad station	Bahnhof	**pályaudvar** *Hung.*	estación ferrocarril	gare	estação ferroviária
monument	Denkmal	**pam'atnik** *Rus.*	monumento	monument	monumento
plain	Ebene	**pampa** *Sp.*	pampa	plaine	pampa
basin	Becken	**pánev** *Czech*	cuenca	bassin	bacia
swamp	Sumpf	**pantanal** *Port., Sp.*	pantanal	marais	pantanal
marsh, swamp; reservoir	Marsch, Sumpf; Stausee	**pantano** *Sp.*	pantano	marais; réservoir	pântano
moor	Moor	**páramo** *Sp.*	páramo	lande	pântano
park	Park	**parc** *Fr.*	parque	parc	parque
national park	National park	**parc national** *Fr.*	parque nacional	parc national	parque nacional
park	Park	**parco** *It.*	parque	parc	parque
national park	Nationalpark	**parco nazionale** *It.*	parque nacional	parc national	parque nacional
provincial park	Naturpark	**parc provincial** *Fr.*	parque de la provincia	parc provincial	parque provincial
park	Park	**Park** *Ger.*	parque	parc	parque
park	Park	**park** *Eng.*	parque	parc	parque
national park	Nationalpark	**park narodowy** *Pol.*	parque nacional	parc national	parque nacional
parkway	Ferienstrasse	**parkway** *Eng.*	calzada	allée de parc	alameda de parque
park	Park	**parque** *Port., Sp.*	parque	parc	parque
national park	Nationalpark	**parq. nac., parque nacional** *Port., Sp.*	parque nacional	parc national	parque nacional
beach	Strand	**part** *Hung.*	playa	plage	praia
strait	Meeresstrasse	**pas** *Fr.*	estrecho	détroit	estreito
passage	Durchfahrt	**pasaje** *Sp.*	pasaje	passage	passagem
pass	Pass	**paso** *Sp.*	paso	col	passo
pass	Pass	**Pass** *Ger.*	paso	col	passo
pass	Pass	**pass** *Eng.*	paso	col	passo
passage	Durchfahrt	**passage** *Eng., Fr.*	pasaje	passage	passagem
passage	Durchfahrt	**passe** *Fr.*	pasaje	passe	passagem

294 Glossary and Abbreviations of Geographical Terms / Verzeichnis und Abkürzungen Geographischer Begriffe
Glosario y Abreviaciones de Términos Geográficos / Glossaire et Abréviations de Termes Géographiques
Glossário e Abreviações de Termos Geográficos

ENGLISH	DEUTSCH	Map Form / Geographische Begriffe / Términos Geográficos / Termes Géographiques / Termos Geográficos	ESPAÑOL	FRANÇAIS	PORTUGUÊS
pass	Pass	**passo** *It.*	paso	col	passo
pass	Pass	**pasul** *Rom.*	paso	col	passo
creek	Bach	**patak** *Hung.*	riachuelo	crique	riacho
peak(s)	Gipfel	**peak(s)** *Eng.*	pico(s)	pic(s)	pico(s)
cave	Höhle	**pećina** *S./C.*	cueva	caverne	caverna
mountains	Berge	**peg., pegunungan** *Indon.*	montañas	montagnes	montanhas
sea	Meer	**pélagos** *Gr.*	mar	mer	mar
bay	Bucht	**pellg** *Alb.*	bahía	baie	baía
peninsula	Halbinsel	**pen., peninsula** *Eng.*	península	péninsule	península
peak; rock	Gipfel; Fels	**peña** *Sp.*	peña	pic; rocher	penha
peak; large rock	Gipfel; grosser Fels	**peñasco** *Sp.*	peñasco	pic; rocher	penhasco
basin	Becken	**-pendi** *Ch.*	cuenca	bassin	bacia
peninsula	Halbinsel	**peninsula** *Eng.*	península	péninsule	península
peninsula	Halbinsel	**península** *Sp.*	península	péninsule	península
peninsula	Halbinsel	**péninsule** *Fr.*	península	péninsule	península
rock	Fels	**peñón** *Sp.*	peñón	rocher	rochedo
pass	Pass	**pereval** *Rus.*	paso	col	passo
strait	Meeresstrasse	**pertuis** *Fr.*	estrecho	pertuis	estreito
sand desert	Sandwüste	**peski** *Rus.*	desierto arenoso	désert de sable	deserto arenoso
mountain	Berg	**phnum** *Cbd.*	montaña	montagne	montanha
mountain	Berg	**phou** *Lao.*	montaña	montagne	montanha
mountain	Berg	**phu** *Thai*	montaña	montagne	montanha
cape	Kap	**pi** *Ch.*	cabo	cap	cabo
plain	Ebene	**piano** *It.*	llanura	plaine	planície
peak	Gipfel	**pic** *Fr.*	pico	pic	pico
peak	Gipfel	**picacho** *Sp.*	picacho	pic	pico
peak	Gipfel	**picco** *It.*	pico	pic	pico
peak(s)	Gipfel	**pico(s)** *Port., Sp.*	pico(s)	pic(s)	pico(s)
pier	Landungsbrücke	**pier** *Eng.*	embarcadero	jetée	cais
mountain	Berg	**-piggen** *Nor.*	montaña	montagne	montanha
peak	Gipfel	**pik** *Rus.*	pico	pic	pico
forest	Wald	**pinhal** *Port.*	bosque	forêt	pinhal
peak	Gipfel	**pique** *Fr.*	pico	pique	pico
pyramid	Pyramide	**pirámide** *Sp.*	pirámide	pyramide	pirâmide
peak(s)	Gipfel	**piton(s)** *Fr.*	pico(s)	piton(s)	pico(s)
peak	Gipfel	**piz, pizzo** *It.*	pico	pic	pico
peak	Gipfel	**pk., peak** *Eng.*	pico	pic	pico
parkway	Ferienstrasse	**pkwy., parkway** *Eng.*	calzada	allée de parc	avenida
plain	Ebene	**plain** *Eng.*	llanura	plaine	planície
plain	Ebene	**plaine** *Fr.*	llanura	plaine	planície
plains	Ebenen	**plains** *Eng.*	llanura	plaines	planícies
plateau	Hochebene	**planalto** *Port.*	meseta	plateau	planalto
planetarium	Planetarium	**planetario** *Sp.*	planetario	planétarium	planetário
planetarium	Planetarium	**planetarium** *Eng.*	planetario	planétarium	planetário
mountain, range	Berg, Gebirge	**planina** *S./C.*	montaña, sierra	montagne, chaîne	montanha, cordilheira
plateau	Hochebene	**plateau** *Eng., Fr.*	meseta	plateau	planalto
plateau	Hochebene	**plato** *Afk., Blg., Rus.*	meseta	plateau	planalto
beach	Strand	**playa** *Sp.*	playa	plage	praia
square	Platz	**plaza** *Sp.*	plaza	place	praça
plateau	Hochebene	**plošina** *Czech*	meseta	plateau	planalto
plateau	Hochebene	**ploskogorje** *Rus.*	meseta	plateau	planalto
pass	Pass	**poarta** *Rom.*	paso	col	passo
hill	Hügel	**poggio** *It.*	colina	colline	colina
mountains	Berge	**pohorie** *Slo.*	montañas	montanges	montanhas
point	Landspitze	**point** *Eng.*	punta	pointe	ponta
point	Landspitze	**pointe** *Fr.*	punta	pointe	ponta
island	Insel	**pol** *Du.*	isla	île	ilha
plain, basin	Ebene, Becken	**polje** *S./C.*	llanura, cuenca	plaine, bassin	planície, bacia
peninsula	Halbinsel	**poluostrov** *Rus.*	península	péninsule	península
peninsula	Halbinsel	**poluotok** *S./C.*	península	péninsule	península
pond	Teich	**pond** *Eng.*	charca	étang	lago
peak	Gipfel	**-pong** *Kor.*	pico	cime	pico
bridge	Brücke	**pont** *Fr.*	puente	pont	ponte
point	Landspitze	**ponta, pontal** *Port.*	punta	pointe	ponta, pontal
bridge	Brücke	**ponte** *Port.*	puente	pont	ponte
pool	Tümpel	**pool** *Eng.*	charco	étang	charco
rapids	Stromschnellen	**porog** *Rus.*	rápidos	rapides	rápidos
port	Hafen	**port** *Eng., Fr.*	puerto	port	porto
port	Hafen	**porto** *It.*	puerto	port	porto
strait	Meeresstrasse	**porthmós** *Gr.*	estrecho	détroit	estreito
provincial park	Naturpark	**p.p., provincial park** *Eng.*	parque de la provincia	parc provincial	parque provincial
beach	Strand	**praia** *Port.*	playa	plage	praia
reservoir	Stausee	**přehr., přehradová nádrž** *Czech*	embalse	réservoir	reservatório
reservoir, dam	Stausee, Damm	**presa** *Sp.*	presa	réservoir, barrage	represa
peninsula	Halbinsel	**presqu'île** *Fr.*	península	presqu'île	península
pass	Pass	**priesmyk** *Slo.*	paso	col	passo
reservoir	Stausee	**priehradová nádrž** *Slo.*	embalse	réservoir	reservatório
prison	Gefängnis	**prison** *Eng.*	prisión	prison	prisão
pass	Pass	**prohod** *Blg.*	paso	col	passo
strait	Meeresstrasse	**proliv** *Rus.*	estrecho	détroit	estreito
promontory	Vorgebirge	**promontorio** *It., Sp.*	promontorio	promontoire	promontório
promontory	Vorgebirge	**promontory** *Eng.*	promontorio	promontoire	promontório
provincial park	Naturpark	**prov. park, provincial park** *Eng.*	parque de la provincia	parc provincial	parque provincial
reservoir	Stausee	**prudy** *Rus.*	embalse	réservoir	reservatório
pass	Pass	**průsmyk** *Czech*	paso	col	passo
pass	Pass	**przełęcz** *Pol.*	paso	col	passo
cape	Kap	**przylądek** *Pol.*	cabo	cap	cabo
point	Landspitze	**pt., point** *Eng.*	punta	pointe	ponta
railroad station	Bahnhof	**pu., pályaudvar** *Hung.*	estación de ferrocarril	gare	estação ferroviária
port	Hafen	**puerto** *Sp.*	puerto	port	porto
peak	Gipfel	**puig** *Cat.*	pico	cime	pico
island	Insel	**pulau** *Indon., Mal.*	isla	île	ilha
islands	Inseln	**pulau-pulau** *Indon.*	islas	îles	ilhas
upland	Bergland	**puna** *Sp.*	puna	hautes terres	terras altas
point	Landspitze	**punt** *Du.*	punta	pointe	ponta
point, peak	Landspitze, Gipfel	**punta** *It., Sp.*	punta	pointe, cime	ponta
point	Landspitze	**puntilla** *Sp.*	puntilla	pointe	ponta pequena
peak	Gipfel	**puntjak** *Indon.*	pico	cime	pico
forest	Wald	**puszcza** *Pol.*	bosque	forêt	floresta
pyramid	Pyramide	**pyramid** *Eng.*	pirámide	pyramide	pirâmide

Q

ENGLISH	DEUTSCH	Map Form	ESPAÑOL	FRANÇAIS	PORTUGUÊS
salt flat	Salzebene	**qâ'** *Ara.*	salar	saline	salina
pass	Pass	**qaf'** *Alb.*	paso	col	passo
canal	Kanal	**qanât** *Ara.*	canal	canal	canal
hill	Hügel	**qārat** *Ara.*	colina	colline	colina
hills	Hügel	**qārāt** *Ara.*	colinas	collines	colinas
dunes	Dünen	**qawz** *Ara.*	dunas	dunes	dunas
creek	Bach	**qbda, quebrada** *Sp.*	quebrada	crique	arroio
mountain	Berg	**qolleh** *Per.*	montaña	montagne	montanha
canal	Kanal	**-qu** *Ch.*	canal	canal	canal
quarry	Steinbruch	**quarry** *Eng.*	cantera	carrière	pedreira
creek	Bach	**quebrada** *Sp.*	quebrada	crique	arroio
rapids	Stromschnellen	**quedas** *Port.*	rápidos	rapides	quedas
islands	Inseln	**-qundao** *Ch.*	islas	îles	ilhas
hill	Hügel	**qūr** *Ara.*	colina	colline	colina
mountain	Berg	**qurnat** *Ara.*	montaña	montagne	montanha

R

ENGLISH	DEUTSCH	Map Form	ESPAÑOL	FRANÇAIS	PORTUGUÊS
river	Fluss	**r., rio** *Port.* **río** *Sp.* **river** *Eng.* **rivière** *Fr.*	río	rivière	rio
range	Gebirge	**ra., range** *Eng.*	sierra	chaîne	cordilheira
Royal Australian Air Force Station	Luftwaffenstützpunkt (Austl.)	**R.A.A.F.S., Royal Australian Air Station** *Eng.*	Real Estación Aeronáutica (Austl.)	Station Aérienne Royale (Austl.)	Real Estação da Força Aérea Australiana
race course	Rennbahn	**race course** *Eng.*	hipódromo	champ de course	hipódromo
race track	Rennbahn	**race track** *Eng.*	hipódromo	champ de course	hipódromo
raceway	Rennbahn	**raceway** *Eng.*	hipódromo	champ de course	hipódromo
river	Fluss	**rach** *Viet.*	río	rivière	rio
anchorage	Ankerplatz	**rada** *Sp.*	rada	ancrage	ancoradouro
cape	Kap	**rags** *Latv.*	cabo	cap	cabo
railroad	Eisenbahn	**railroad** *Eng.*	ferrocarril	chemin de fer	ferrovia
railway	Eisenbahn	**railway** *Eng.*	ferrocarril	chemin de fer	ferrovia
railway station	Bahnhof	**railway station** *Eng.*	estación de ferrocarril	gare	estação ferroviária
dunes	Dünen	**ramlat** *Ara.*	dunas	dunes	dunas
range(s)	Gebirge	**range(s)** *Eng.*	sierra(s)	chaîne(s)	cordilheira(s)
river	Fluss	**rão., ribeirão** *Port.*	río	rivière	rio, ribeirão
rapids	Stromschnellen	**rapides** *Fr.*	rápidos	rapides	rápidos
rapids	Stromschnellen	**rapids** *Eng.*	rápidos	rapides	rápidos
wadi	Wadi	**raqabat** *Ara.*	uadi	wadi	uádi
cape	Kap	**ras, ra's** *Ara.*	cabo	cap	cabo
cape	Kap	**râs** *Per.*	cabo	cap	cabo
ravine	Tobel	**ravine** *Eng.*	barranca	ravin	ravina
plain	Ebene	**ravnina** *Rus.*	llanura	plaine	planície
canal	Kanal	**rayyāh** *Ara.*	canal	canal	canal
flood plain	Überschwemmungsebene	**razlivy** *Rus.*	llanura de inundación	lit d'inondation	planície de inundação
road	Landstrasse	**rd., road** *Eng.*	camino	route	rodovia
reef	Riff	**récif** *Fr.*	arrecife	récif	recife
reefs	Riffe	**recifes** *Port.*	arrecifes	récifs	recifes
reefs	Riffe	**récifs** *Fr.*	arrecifes	récifs	recifes
reef(s)	Riff(e)	**reef(s)** *Eng.*	arrecife(s)	récif(s)	recife(s)
regional park	Regionalpark	**regional park** *Eng.*	parque regional	parc régional	parque regional
mountain	Berg	**-rei** *Jap.*	montaña	montagne	montanha
race course	Rennbahn	**Rennbahn** *Ger.*	hipódromo	champ de course	hipódromo
dam; reservoir	Damm; Stausee	**represa** *Port.*	presa; embalse	barrage; réservoir	represa
airport	Flughafen	**repülőtér** *Hung.*	aeropuerto	aéroport	aeroporto
reservoir	Stausee	**res., reservoir** *Eng.*	embalse	réservoir	reservatório
reservation	Reservat	**reservation** *Eng.*	reservación	réservation	reserva
reservoir	Stausee	**reservatório** *Port.*	embalse	rèservoir	reservatório
reserve	Reservat	**reserve** *Eng.*	reserva	réserve	reserva
reserve	Reservat	**rèserve** *Fr.*	reserva	réserve	reserva
game reserve	Wildreservat	**rèserve de chasse** *Fr.*	vedado de caza	réserve de chasse	reserva de caça
reservoir	Stausee	**reservoir** *Eng.*	embalse	réservoir	reservatório
reservoir	Stausee	**réservoir** *Fr.*	embalse	réservoir	reservatório
islands	Inseln	**-retto** *Jap.*	islas	îles	ilhas
ria	Ria	**ría** *Sp.*	ría	ria	ria
creek	Bach	**riacho** *Port., Sp.*	riacho	crique	riacho
creek	Bach	**riachuelo** *Sp.*	riachuelo	crique	riacho
creek	Bach	**rib., ribeira** *Port.*	riachuelo	crique	ribeira
river	Fluss	**ribeirão** *Port.*	río	rivière	ribeirão
ridge	Höhenrücken	**ridge** *Eng.*	sierra	crête	serra
moor	Ried	**Ried** *Ger.*	páramo	lande	pântano
creek	Bach	**riera** *Sp.*	riera	crique	riacho
national museum	Reichsmuseum	**rijksmuseum** *Du.*	museo nacional	musée national	museu nacional
army installation	Anlage des Heeres	**rikujō-jieitai** *Jap.*	estación del ejército	installation militaire	instalação militar
river	Fluss	**rio** *Port.*	río	rivière	rio
river	Fluss	**río** *Sp.*	río	rivière	rio
river	Fluss	**riozinho** *Port.*	río	rivière	riozinho
rise (submarine)	Schwelle (untermeerische)	**rise** *Eng.*	elevación (submarina)	élévation (sous-marine)	elevação (submarina)
river	Fluss	**river** *Eng.*	río	rivière	rio
brook	Bach	**rivera** *Sp.*	rivera	ruisseau	córrego
coast	Küste	**riviera** *It.*	costa	côte	costa
river	Fluss	**rivière** *Fr.*	río	rivière	rio
army installation	Anlage des Heeres	**r.j., rikujō-jieitai** *Jap.*	estación del ejército	installation militaire	instalação do exército
road	Landstrasse	**road** *Eng.*	camino	route	rodovia
roads (anchorage)	Ankerplatz	**roads** *Eng.*	ancladero	ancrage	ancoradouro
rock	Fels	**roca** *Sp.*	roca	rocher	rochedo
rock, mountain	Fels, Berg	**rocca** *It.*	roca, montaña	rocher, montagne	rochedo, montanha
rock(s)	Fels(en)	**rock(s)** *Eng.*	roca(s)	rocher(s)	rochedo(s)
cape	Kap	**rt** *S./C.*	cabo	cap	cabo
brook	Bach	**rû** *Fr.*	arroyo	rû	córrego
mountains	Berge	**rudohorie** *Slo.*	montañas	montagnes	montanhas
brook	Bach	**ruisseau** *Fr.*	arroyo	ruisseau	córrego
mountain	Berg	**rujm** *Ara.*	montaña	montagne	montanha
run	Bach	**run** *Eng.*	arroyo	ruisseau	córrego

S

ENGLISH	DEUTSCH	Map Form	ESPAÑOL	FRANÇAIS	PORTUGUÊS
south	süd	**s., south** *Eng.*	sur	sud	sul
range	Gebirge	**sa., serra** *Port.*	sierra	chaîne	cordilheira
island	Insel	**saar** *Est.*	isla	île	ilha
savanna	Savanne	**sabana** *Sp.*	sabana	savane	savana
salt marsh; lagoon	Salzmarsch; Lagune, Haff	**sabkhat** *Ara.*	pantano salado; laguna	marais salé; lagune	pântano salgado; laguna
dam	Damm	**sadd** *Ara.*	presa	barrage	represa
wadi	Wadi	**saguia** *Ara.*	uadi	wadi	uádi
desert	Wüste	**ṣaḥrā'** *Ara.*	desierto	désert	deserto
cape	Kap	**-saki** *Jap.*	cabo	cap	cabo
salt flat	Salzebene	**salar** *Sp.*	salar	saline	salina
salt marsh, salt flat	Salzmarsch, Salzebene	**salina(s)** *Sp.*	salina(s)	marais salé, saline	salina(s)
salt marsh, salt flat	Salzmarsch, Salzebene	**salines** *Fr.*	pantano salado, salinas, salar	salines	pântano salgado, salinas
salt flat	Salzebene	**salt flat** *Eng.*	salar	saline	salina
salt lake	Salzsee	**salt lake** *Eng.*	lago salado	lac salé	lago salgado
salt marsh	Salzmarsch	**salt marsh** *Eng.*	pantano salado	marais salé	pântano salgado
waterfall	Wasserfall	**salto(s)** *Port., Sp.*	salto(s)	chute d'eau	salto(s)
reservoir	Stausee	**samudra** *Sin.*	embalse	réservoir	reservatório
range	Gebirge	**-sammyaku** *Jap.*	sierra	chaîne	cordilheira
mountain	Berg	**-san** *Jap., Kor.*	montaña	montagne	montanha
mountains	Berge	**-sanchi** *Jap.*	montañas	montagnes	montanhas
mountains	Berge	**-sanmaek** *Kor.*	montañas	montagnes	montanhas
shrine	Schrein	**santuario** *It., Sp.*	santuario	châsse	santuário
mountain	berg	**sar** *Pas.*	montaña	montagne	montanha
island	Insel	**sari** *Est.*	isla	île	ilha
desert	Wüste	**sarīr** *Ara.*	desierto	désert	deserto
saddle	Sattel	**Sattel** *Ger.*	paso	col	passo
strait	Meeresstrasse	**šaurums** *Latv.*	estrecho	détroit	estreito
waterfall	Wasserfall	**saut** *Fr.*	cascada	saut	queda d'água
castle	Schloss	**Schloss** *Ger.*	castillo	château	castelo
gorge	Schlucht	**Schlucht** *Ger.*	garganta	gorge	garganta
school	Schule	**school** *Eng.*	escuela	école	escola
sea	Meer	**sea** *Eng.*	mar	mer	mar
seamount	untermeerische Kuppe	**seamount** *Eng.*	montaña submarina	montagne sous-marine	montanha submarina
sea scarp	Abbruch	**sea scarp** *Eng.*	cantil	escarpement sous-marine	escarpa submarina
dry lake	Trockensee	**sebjet** *Ara.*	lago seco	lac asséché	lago seco
salt flat	Salzebene	**sebkha** *Ara.*	salar	saline	salina
intermittent lake	periodischer See	**sebkra** *Ara.*	lago intermitente	lac périodique	lago intermitente
salt marsh	Salzmarsch	**sebkret** *Ara.*	pantano salado	marais salé	pântano salgado
airport	Flughafen	**sede-te'ufa** *Heb.*	aeropuerto	aéroport	aeroporto
saddle	Sattel	**sedlo** *Czech*	paso	col	passo
lake(s)	See(n)	**See(n)** *Ger.*	lago(s)	lac(s)	lago(s)

Glossary and Abbreviations of Geographical Terms / Verzeichnis und Abkürzungen Geographischer Begriffe
Glosario y Abreviaciones de Términos Geográficos / Glossaire et Abréviations de Termes Géographiques
Glossário e Abreviações de Termos Geográficos
295

ENGLISH	DEUTSCH	**Map Form Geographische Begriffe Términos Geográficos Termes Géographiques Termos Geográficos**	ESPAÑOL	FRANÇAIS	PORTUGUÊS
strait	Meeresstrasse	**selat** *Indon.*	estrecho	détroit	estreito
peninsula	Halbinsel	**semenandjung** *Indon.*	península	péninsule	península
seminary	Seminar	**seminary** *Eng.*	seminario	séminaire	seminário
mountain	Berg	**-sen** *Jap.*	montaña	montagne	montanha
sound	Sund	**seno** *Sp.*	seno	détroit	estreito
range, mountain	Gebirge, Berg	**serra** *Port.*	sierra	chaîne, montagne	serra
ridge(s)	Höhenrücken	**serranía(s)** *Sp.*	serranía(s)	crête(s)	serrania(s)
rapids	Stromschnellen	**shallāl** *Ara.*	rápidos	rapides	rápidos
mountain(s); island	Berg(e); Insel	**-shan** *Ch.*	montaña(s); isla	montagne(s); île	montanha(s) ilha
pass	Pass	**-shankou** *Ch.*	paso	col	passo
mountains	Berge	**-shanling, -shanmai, -shanmo** *Ch.*	montañas	montagnes	montanhas
bay	Bucht	**sharm** *Ara.*	bahía	baie	baía
peninsula	Halbinsel	**shibh jazīrat** *Ara.*	península	péninsule	península
island	Insel	**-shima** *Jap.*	isla	île	ilha
reef	Riff	**-shō** *Jap.*	arrecife	récif	recife
shoal(s)	Untiefe(n)	**shoal(s)** *Eng.*	bajo(s)	haut-fond(s)	baixio(s)
islands	Inseln	**-shotō** *Jap.*	islas	îles	ilhas
shrine	Schrein	**shrine** *Eng.*	santuario	châsse	santuário
river	Fluss	**-shui** *Ch.*	río	rivière	rio
reservoir	Stausee	**-shuiku** *Ch.*	embalse	réservoir	reservatório
strait	Meeresstrasse	**shuitao** *Ch.*	estrecho	détroit	estreito
temple	Tempel	**-si** *Ch.*	templo	temple	templo
range, ridge	Gebirge, Höhenrücken	**sierra** *Sp.*	sierra	chaîne, crête	serra
range	Gebirge	**silsilesi** *Tur.*	sierra	chaîne	cordilheira
rapids	Stromschnellen	**šivera** *Rus.*	rápidos	rapides	rápidos
lake	See	**-sjø** *Nor.*	lago	lac	lago
lakes	Seen	**-sjöarna** *Swe.*	lagos	lacs	lagos
lake	See	**-sjøen** *Nor.*	lago	lac	lago
lake, bay	See, Bucht	**-sjön** *Swe.*	lago, bahía	lac, baie	lago, baía
island	Insel	**-skär** *Swe.*	isla	île	ilha
forest	Wald	**-skog, -skogen** *Swe.*	basque	forêt	floresta
mountain	Berg	**slieve** *Gae.*	montaña	montagne	montanha
castle	Schloss	**slot** *Du.*	castillo	château	castelo
castle	Schloss	**slott** *Swe.*	castillo	château	castelo
slough	verlandende Wasserfläche	**slough** *Eng.*	pantano	fondrière	pântano, brejo
ridge	Höhenrücken	**snía., serranía** *Sp.*	serranía	crête	serrania
snowfield	Schneefeld	**snowfield** *Eng.*	ventisquero	champ de neige	campo de neve
lake	See	**-sø** *Dan.*	lago	lac	lago
sound	Sund	**sonda** *Sp.*	sonda	détroit	estreito
sound	Sund	**sound** *Eng.*	sonda	détroit	estreito
cave, tunnel	Höhle, Tunnel	**souterrain** *Fr.*	cueva, túnel	souterrain	caverna, túnel
state park	Naturpark	**s.p., state park** *Eng.*	parque provincial	parc régional	parque estadual
cave	Höhle	**špilja** *S./C.*	cueva	caverne	caverna
spit	Landzunge	**spit** *Eng.*	lengua de tierra	flèche	ponta de terra
peak	Spitze	**Spitze** *Ger.*	pico	cime	pico
spring	Quelle	**spr., spring** *Eng.*	manantial	source	fonte, manancial
square	Platz	**sq., square** *Eng.*	plaza	place	praça
range, ridge	Gebirge Höhenrücken	**srra., sierra** *Sp.*	sierra	chaîne, crête	serra
saint	Sankt	**st., saint** *Eng., Fr.*	san, santa, santo	saint	são, santa, santo
street	Strasse	**st., street** *Eng.*	calle	rue	rua
saint	Sankt	**sta., santa** *Port., Sp.*	santa	sainte	santa
station	Bahnhof, Stützpunkt	**sta., station** *Eng., Fr.*	estación	station	estação
stadium	Stadion	**stad., stadium** *Eng.*	estadio	stade	estádio
stadium	Stadion	**stadio** *It.*	estadio	stade	estádio
stadium	Stadion	**Stadion** *Ger.*	estadio	stade	estádio
stadium	Stadion	**stadion** *Rus.*	estadio	stade	estádio
stadium	Stadion	**stadium** *Eng.*	estadio	stade	estádio
state beach	öffentlicher Badestrand	**state beach** *Eng.*	playa provincial	plage régionale	praia estadual
state forest	Wald in Gemeinbesitz	**state forest** *Eng.*	bosque provincial	forêt régionale	floresta estadual
state historical park	Park an historischer Stätte	**state historical park** *Eng.*	parque histórico provincial	parc historique régional	parque histórico estadual
state park	Naturpark	**state park** *Eng.*	parque provincial	parc régional	parque estadual
state recreation area	Ausflugsgebiet	**state recreation area** *Eng.*	zona de recreo provincial	zone récréative regional	área de lazer estadual
station	Bahnhof, Stützpunkt	**station** *Eng., Fr.*	estación	station	estação
reservoir	Stausee	**Stausee** *Ger.*	embalse	réservoir	reservatório
station	Bahnhof, Stützpunkt	**stazione** *It.*	estación	station	estação
saint	Sankt	**ste., sainte** *Fr.*	santa	sainte	santa
mountains	Berge	**stěny** *Czech*	montañas	montagnes	montanhas
steppe	Steppe	**step'** *Rus.*	estepa	steppe	estepe
peak	Gipfel	**štít** *Slo.*	pico	cime	pico
saint	Sankt	**sto., santo** *Port., Sp.*	santo	saint	santo
strait(s)	Meeresstrasse	**strait(s)** *Eng.*	estrecho	détroit	estreito
stream	Strom	**stream eng.**	corriente de agua	cours d'eau	curso d'água
street	Strasse	**street** *Eng.*	calle	rue	rua
strait	Meeresstrasse	**stretto** *It.*	estrecho	détroit	estreito
stream	Strom	**Strom** *Ger.*	corriente de agua	cours d'eau	curso d'água
stream	Strom	**-ström, -strömmen** *Swe.*	corriente de agua	cours d'eau	curso d'água
river	Fluss	**-su** *Kor.*	río	rivière	rio
channel	Kanal	**-suidō** *Jap.*	canal, estrecho	canal, détroit	canal, estreito
sound	Sund	**Sund** *Ger.*	sonda	détroit	estreito
sound	Sund	**-sund** *Swe.*	sonda	détroit	estreito
river	Fluss	**suyu** *Tur.*	río	rivière	rio
swamp	Sumpf	**swamp** *Eng.*	pantano	marais	pântano
ridge	Höhenrücken	**syrt** *Tur.*	sierra	crête	serra
island	Insel	**sziget** *Hung.*	isla	île	ilha

T

ENGLISH	DEUTSCH	Map Form	ESPAÑOL	FRANÇAIS	PORTUGUÊS
tableland	Tafelland	**tableland** *Eng.*	mesa, altiplano	plateau	planalto
woods	Gehölz	**taillis** *Fr.*	bosque	taillis	bosque
reef	Riff	**taka** *Indon.*	arrecife	récif	recife
mountain	Berg	**-take** *Jap.*	montaña	montagne	montanha
waterfall	Wasserfall	**-taki** *Jap.*	cascada	chute d'eau	queda d'água
valley	Tal	**Tal** *Ger.*	valle	vallée	vale
mountain	Berg	**tall** *Ara.*	montaña	montagne	montanha
mountain, hill	Berg, Hügel	**tallat** *Ara.*	montaña, colina	montagne, colline	montanha, colina
hills	Hügel	**tallāt** *Ara.*	colinas	collines	colinas
dam	Talsperre	**Talsperre** *Ger.*	presa	barrage	represa
cape	Kap	**tandjung** *Indon.*	cabo	cap	cabo
point	Landspitze	**-tangar, -tangi** *Ice.*	punta	pointe	ponta
cape	Kap	**tanjong** *Mal.*	cabo	cap	cabo
island	Insel	**tao** *Ch.*	isla	île	ilha
hills	Hügel	**ţaraq** *Ara.*	colinas	collines	colinas
lake	See	**tasek** *Mal.*	lago	lac	lago
lake	See	**tasik** *Indon.*	lago	lac	lago
plateau	Hochebene	**tassili** *Ber.*	meseta	plateau	planalto
mountain	Berg	**taung** *Bur.*	montaña	montagne	montanha
range	Gebirge	**taungdan** *Bur.*	sierra	chaîne	cordilheira
theatre	Theater	**teatro** *It., Sp.*	teatro	théâtre	teatro
bay	Bucht	**teluk** *Indon.*	bahía	baie	baía
temple	Tempel	**temple** *Eng., Fr.*	templo	temple	templo
church	Kirche	**templom** *Hung.*	iglesia	église	igreja
desert	Wüste	**ténéré** *Ber.*	desierto	désert	deserto
peak, hill	Gipfel, Hügel	**tepe, tepesi** *Tur.*	pico, colina	cime, colline	pico, colina
territory	Territorium	**territory** *Eng.*	territorio	territoire	território
lagoon	Lagune, Haff	**thale** *Thai*	laguna	lagune	laguna
mountains	Berge	**thiu khao** *Thai*	montañas	montagnes	montanhas
mountain	Berg	**-tind, -tinderne** *Nor.*	montaña	montagne	montanha
ridge	Höhenrücken	**ţiwāl** *Ara.*	sierra	crête	serra
mountain	Berg	**-tjåkko, -tjöure** *Lapp.*	montaña	montagne	montanha
island	Insel	**-to** *Kor.*	isla	île	ilha
island	Insel	**-tō** *Jap.*	isla	île	ilha
lake	See	**tó** *Hung.*	lago	lac	lago
pass	Pass	**-tōge** *Jap.*	paso	col	passo
island	Insel	**tokong** *Mal.*	isla	île	ilha
lake	See	**tônlé** *Cbd.*	lago	lac	lago
mountain torrent	Wildbach	**torrente** *It., Sp.*	torrente	torrent	torrente
tower	Turm	**tower** *Eng.*	torre	tour	torre
turnpike	gebührenpflichtige Autobahn	**tpk., turnpike** *Eng.*	camino con peaje	grande route à péage	rodovia com pedágio
lake	See	**-träsk** *Swe.*	lago	lac	lago
trench	Tiefseegraben	**trench** *Eng.*	trinchera	tranchée	fossa submarina
trough	Tiefseegraben	**trough** *Eng.*	trinchera	tranchée	fossa submarina
volcano	Vulkan	**tulūl** *Ara.*	volcán	volcan	vulcão
tunnel	Tunnel	**túnel** *Sp.*	túnel	tunnel	túnel
tunnel	Tunnel	**tunnel** *Eng., Fr.*	túnel	tunnel	túnel
hill, mountain	Hügel, Berg	**-tunturi** *Finn.*	colina, montaña	colline, montagne	colina, montanha
island	Insel	**-tuo** *Ch.*	isla	île	ilha
canal	Kanal	**tur'at** *Ara.*	canal	canal	canal
turnpike	gebührenpflichtige Autobahn	**turnpike** *Eng.*	camino con peaje	grande route à péage	rodovia com pedágio

U-V

ENGLISH	DEUTSCH	Map Form	ESPAÑOL	FRANÇAIS	PORTUGUÊS
cape	Kap	**udjung** *Indon.*	cabo	cap	cabo
lagoon	Lagune, Haff	**-umi** *Jap.*	laguna	lagune	laguna
United Nations	Vereinte Nationen	**U.N., United Nations** *Eng.*	Naciones Unidas	Nations Unies	Nações Unidas
canal	Kanal	**-unga** *Jap.*	canal	canal	canal
university	Universität	**univ., universidad** *Sp.* **universidade** *Port.* **università** *It.* **university** *Eng.*	universidad	université	universidade
university	Universität	**Universität** *Ger.*	universidad	université	universidade
university	Universität	**université** *Fr.*	universidad	université	universidade
university	Universität	**universitet** *Rus.*	universidad	université	universidade
upland	Bergland	**upland** *Eng.*	tierras altas	hautes terres	terras altas
lake	See	**-ura** *Jap.*	lago	lac	lago
mountain(s)	Berg(e)	**uul** *Mong.*	montaña(s)	montagne(s)	montanha(s)
elevation(s)	Höhe(n)	**uval(y)** *Rus.*	altura(s)	élévation(s)	elevação(ões)
spring	Quelle	**'uyūn** *Ara.*	manantial	source	fonte, manancial
hill	Hügel	**-vaara** *Finn.*	colina	colline	colina
strait	Meeresstrasse	**väin** *Est.*	estrecho	détroit	estreito
valley	Tal	**val** *Fr., It.*	valle	val	vale
valley	Tal	**valle** *It., Sp.*	valle	vallée	vale
valley	Tal	**vallée** *Fr.*	valle	vallée	vale
waterfall	Wasserfall	**vallen** *Du.*	cascada	chute d'eau	queda d'água
valley	Tal	**valley** *Eng.*	valle	vallée	vale
valley	Tal	**vallon** *Fr.*	valle	vallon	vale
lake	See	**-vatn** *Ice., Nor.*	lago	lac	lago
lake	See	**-vatnet** *Nor.*	lago	lac	lago
lake	See	**-vattnett** *Swe.*	lago	lac	lago
reservoir	Stausee	**vdchr., vodochranilišče** *Rus.*	embalse	réservoir	reservatório
hills	Hügel	**-veden** *Swe.*	colinas	collines	colinas
upland	Bergland	**verch** *Rus.*	tierras altas	hautes terres	terras altas
lake	See	**-vesi** *Finn.*	lago	lac	lago
viaduct	Viadukt	**viaducto** *Sp.*	viaducto	viaduc	viaduto
plateau	Hochebene	**-vidda** *Nor.*	meseta	plateau	planalto
gulf	Golf	**-viken** *Swe.*	golfo	golfe	golfo
bay	Bucht	**vinh** *Viet.*	bahía	baie	baía
mountain	Berg	**vîrful** *Rom.*	montaña	montagne	montanha
airport	Flughafen	**vliegveld** *Du.*	aeropuerto	aéroport	aeroporto
channel	Kanal	**vliet** *Du.*	canal, estrecho	canal, détroit	canal, estreito
canal	Kanal	**vodnyj put'** *Rus.*	canal	canal	canal
reservoir	Stausee	**vodochranilišče** *Rus.*	embalse	réservoir	reservatório
railroad station	Bahnhof	**vokzal** *Rus.*	estación de ferrocarril	gare	estação ferroviária
volcano	Vulkan	**vol., volcán** *Sp.* **volcano** *Eng.*	volcán	volcan	vulcão
pass	Pass	**vorota** *Rus.*	paso	col	passo
upland	Bergland	**vozvyšennost'** *Rus.*	tierras altas	hautes terres	terras altas
mountain	Berg	**vrâh** *Blg.*	montaña	montagne	montanha
mountains	Berge	**vrchovina** *Czech, Slo.*	montañas	montagnes	montanhas
peak	Gipfel	**vrh** *S./C.*	pico	cime	pico
volcano	Vulkan	**vulkan** *Rus.*	volcán	volcan	vulcão
bay	Bucht	**vung** *Viet.*	bahía	baie	baía
mountain, hill	Berg, Hügel	**-vuori** *Finn.*	montaña, colina	montagne, colline	montanha, colina

W-Z

ENGLISH	DEUTSCH	Map Form	ESPAÑOL	FRANÇAIS	PORTUGUÊS
west	West	**w., west** *Eng.*	oeste	ouest	oeste
wadi	Wadi	**wādī** *Ara.*	uadi	wadi	uádi
oasis	Oase	**wāḥat, wāḥāt** *Ara.*	oasis	oasis	oásis
forest; mountains	Wald	**Wald** *Ger.*	bosque; montañas	forêt; montagnes	floresta; montanhas
bay	Bucht	**-wan** *Ch., Jap.*	bahía	baie	baía
wash	Wadi	**wash** *Eng.*	uadi	wadi	uádi
waterfalls	Wasserfälle	**Wasserfälle** *Ger.*	cascadas	chutes d'eau	quedas d'água
water (lake; river)	Wasser (See; Fluss)	**water** *Eng.*	agua (lago;rio)	eau (lac; rivière)	água (lago, rio)
waterway	Wasserstrasse	**waterway** *Eng.*	canal	canal	canal
pond	Weiher	**Weiher** *Ger.*	charca	étang	charco
well	Brunnen	**well** *Eng.*	pozo	puits	poço
bay	Wiek	**Wiek** *Ger.*	bahía	baie	baía
woods	Gehölz	**woods** *Eng.*	bosque	bois	bosque
water (lake; river)	Wasser (See; Fluss)	**wr., water** *Eng.*	agua (lago; rio)	eau (lac; rivière)	água (lago, rio)
river	Fluss	**-xi** *Ch.*	río	rivière	rio
strait	Meeresstrasse	**-xia** *Ch.*	estrecho	détroit	estreito
lake, sea	See, Meer	**yam** *Heb.*	lago, mar	lac, mer	lago, mar
mountain	Berg	**-yama** *Jap.*	montaña	montagne	montanha
sea, bay, lake	Meer, Bucht, See	**-yang** *Ch.*	mar, bahía, lago	mer, baie, lac	mar, baía, lago
peninsula	Halbinsel	**yarımadası** *Tur.*	península	péninsule	península
mountain	Berg	**yebel** *Ara.*	montaña	montagne	montanha
rock, island	Fels, Insel	**yen** *Ch.*	roca, isla	rocher,île	rochedo, ilha
mountains	Berge	**yoma** *Bur.*	montañas	montagnes	montanhas
island	Insel	**-yu** *Ch.*	isla	île	ilha
intermittent lake	periodischer See	**zahrez** *Ara.*	lago intermitente	lac périodique	lago intermitente
point	Landspitze	**-zaki** *Jap.*	punta	pointe	ponta
lagoon	Lagune, Haff	**zalew** *Pol.*	laguna	lagune	laguna
gulf, bay	Golf, Bucht	**zaliv** *Rus.*	golfo, bahía	golfe, baie	golfo, baía
reserve	Reservat	**zapov., zapovednik** *Rus.*	reserva	réserve	reserva
sea, lake	Meer, See	**zee** *Du.*	mar, lago	mer, lac	mar, lago
autonomous province	autonome Provinz	**zizhiqu** *Ch.*	provincia autónoma	province autonome	província autônoma
autonomous district	autonomer Distrikt	**zizhizhou** *Ch.*	distrito autónomo	district autonome	distrito autônomo
zoo	Zoo	**zoo** *Eng.*	parque zoológico	zoo	jardim zoológico

THIS TABLE gives the area, population, population density, capital, and political status for every country in the world. The political units listed are categorized by political status in the last column of the table, as follows: A—independent countries; B—internally independent political entities which are under the protection of another country in matters of defense and foreign affairs; C—colonies and other dependent political units; and D—the major administrative subdivisions of Australia, Canada, China, the Soviet Union, the United Kingdom, and the United States. For comparison, the table also includes the continents and the world. For units categorized B, the names of protecting countries are specified in the political-status column. For units categorized C, the names of administering countries are given in parentheses in the first column.

The populations are estimates for January 1, 1990, made by Rand McNally on the basis of official data, United Nations estimates, and other available information.

IN DIESER ÜBERSICHT sind Fläche, Bevölkerung, Bevölkerungsdichte, Hauptstadt und politischer Status für jedes Land der Erde aufgeführt. Die politischen Einheiten sind in der letzten Spalte der Tabelle nach ihrem politischen Status wie folgt gegliedert: A—souveräne Staaten; B—innenpolitisch unabhängige Länder unter der Protektion eines anderen Landes in Angelegenheiten der Aussenpolitik und Verteidigung; C—Kolonien oder anderweitig abhängige Gebiete; D—die wichtigsten Verwaltungseinheiten von Australien, Kanada, China, der Sowjetunion, dem Vereinigten Königreich und den Vereinigten Staaten. Für Vergleiche enthält die Übersicht auch Angaben über die Kontinente und die Welt. Für die unter B eingestuften Einheiten ist der Name des Schutzstaates in der Spalte Politischer Status aufgeführt. Für die unter C eingestuften Gebiete steht der Name des die Verwaltung ausübenden Landes in Klammern in der ersten Spalte.

Die Bevölkerungsangaben sind Schätzungen zum 1. Januar 1990, die Rand McNally auf der Grundlage amtlicher Zahlen, Schätzungen der Vereinten Nationen und anderer zugänglicher Informationen berechnet hat.

EL CUADRO ABAJO incluye la extensión, población y densidad de población, la capital y el estado político de todos los países del mundo. Las entidades políticas nombradas están clasificadas de acuerdo a su estado político en la última columna de la tabla, de esta manera: A—países independientes; B—entidades políticas internamente independientes las cuales se encuentran bajo la protección de otro país en cuanto a asuntos de defensa nacional y relaciones con el extranjero; C—colonias y otras entidades políticas dependientes; y D—las mayores subdivisiones administrativas de Australia, Canadá, China, la Unión Soviética, el Reino Unido, y los Estados Unidos. Para servir de medida comparativa, el cuadro también incluye los continentes y el mundo. Para las entidades de la clasificación B, los nombres de los países protectores están especificados en la columna de estado político. Para las unidades bajo la categoría C, los nombres de los países administradores se encuentran entre paréntesis en la primera columna.

Las poblaciones son los estimados de Rand McNally, tomados el 1o. de Enero de 1990, en base a datos oficiales, estimados de las Naciones Unidas y varias otras informaciones disponibles.

CETTE TABLE donne, pour chaque pays du monde, les renseignements suivants: superficie, population, densité de population, capitale, statut politique. Les entités politiques sont classées, selon leur statut, dans la dernière colonne du tableau: A—pays indépendants; B—entités politiques indépendants intérieurement, mais qui se trouvent sous la protection d'un autre pays pour leur défense et leurs relations extérieures; C—colonies et autres entités politiques dépendantes; D—principales subdivisions administratives de l'Australie, du Canada, de la Chine, de l'U.R.S.S., du Royaume-Uni, des États-Unis. Pour permettre les comparaisons, la table comprend aussi les continents et le monde. Pour les entités politiques de la catégorie B, les noms des pays protecteurs sont spécifiés dans la colonne "statut politique". Pour celles de la catégorie C, les noms des pays administrateurs sont mis entre parenthèses dans la première colonne.

Les chiffres concernant la population sont des estimations au 1er janvier 1990, établies par Rand McNally, d'après les sources officielles, les estimations des Nations Unies et autres informations disponibles.

A TABELA que se segue apresenta a área, a população, a densidade demográfica, a capital e o estatuto político de todos os países do mundo. As unidades políticas relacionadas na tabela estão classificadas de acordo com o respectivo estatuto político na última coluna, do seguinte modo: A—países independentes; B—unidades políticas internamente independentes mas que se encontram sob a proteção de outro país no tocante a assuntos de defesa nacional e negócios extrenos; C—colônias e outras unidades políticas dependentes; e D—subdivisões administrativas principais da Austrália, Canadá, China, União Soviética, Reino Unido e Estados Unidos. Para fins de comparabilidade, a tabela também inclui os continentes e o mundo. No tocante ás unidades classificadas em B, os nomes dos países protetores estão especificados na coluna relativa ao estatuto político. Para as unidades da categoria C, os nomes dos países administradores figuram entre parênteses na primeira coluna.

Os dados relativos à população são estimativas de Rand McNally para 1 de janeiro de 1990, com base em dados oficiais, estimativas das Nações Unidas e outras informações disponíveis.

NAME / NAME / NOMBRE / NOM / NOME English / Englisch Inglés / Anglais / Inglês	Local / Einheimisch Local / Local / Local	AREA / FLÄCHE AREA / SUPERFICIE / ÁREA sq. km.	sq. mi.	POPULATION BEVÖLKERUNG POBLACIÓN POPULATION POPULAÇÃO	DENSITY PER BEVÖLKERUNGSDICHTE PRO / DENSIDAD POR DENSITÉ / DENSIDADE POR sq. km.	sq. mi.	CAPITAL HAUPSTADT CAPITAL CAPITALE CAPITAL	POLITICAL STATUS POLITISCHER STATUS ESTADO POLITICO STATUS POLITIQUE ESTATUTO POLITICO
†Afghanistan	Afghānestān	652,225	251,826	15,210,000	23	60	Kābol	A
Africa	. . .	30,300,000	11,700,000	648,300,000	21	55	. . .	. . .
Alabama, U.S.	Alabama	133,913	51,704	4,203,000	31	81	Montgomery	D
Alaska, U.S.	Alaska	1,530,693	591,004	543,000	0.4	0.9	Juneau	D
†Albania	Shqipëri	28,748	11,100	3,233,000	112	291	Tiranë	A
Alberta, Can.	Alberta	661,190	255,287	2,475,000	3.7	9.7	Edmonton	D
†Algeria	Algérie (French) / Djazaïr (Arabic)	2,381,741	919,595	24,880,000	10	27	El Djazaïr (Algiers)	A
American Samoa (U.S.)	American Samoa (English) / Amerika Samoa (Samoan)	199	77	44,000	221	571	Pago Pago	C
Andorra	Andorra	453	175	51,000	113	291	Andorra	B(Sp., Fr.)
†Angola	Angola	1,246,700	481,354	8,668,000	7.0	18	Luanda	A
Anguilla (U.K.)	Anguilla	91	35	7,000	77	200	The Valley	B(U.K.)
Anhwei, China	Anhui	139,000	53,668	53,840,000	387	1,003	Hefei	D
Antarctica	. . .	14,000,000	5,400,000	(1)	. . .	. . .	. . .	. . .
†Antigua and Barbuda	Antigua and Barbuda	443	171	79,000	178	462	St. John's	A
†Argentina	Argentina	2,780,092	1,073,400	32,680,000	12	30	Buenos Aires	A
Arizona, U.S.	Arizona	295,264	114,002	3,577,000	12	31	Phoenix	D
Arkansas, U.S.	Arkansas	137,764	53,191	2,451,000	18	46	Little Rock	D
Armenian S.S.R., U.S.S.R.	Arm'anskaja S.S.R.	29,800	11,506	3,324,000	112	289	Jerevan	D
Aruba	Aruba	193	75	63,000	326	840	Oranjestad	B(Neth.)
Asia	. . .	44,900,000	17,300,000	3,156,100,000	70	182	. . .	. . .
†Australia	Australia	7,682,300	2,966,155	16,950,000	2.2	5.7	Canberra	A
Australian Capital Territory, Austl.	Australian Capital Territory	2,400	927	280,000	117	302	Canberra	D
†Austria	Österreich	83,855	32,377	7,644,000	91	236	Wien (Vienna)	A
Azerbaijan S.S.R., U.S.S.R.	Azerbajdžanskaja S.S.R.	86,600	33,436	7,081,000	82	212	Baku	D
†Bahamas	Bahamas	13,934	5,380	251,000	18	47	Nassau	A
†Bahrain	Al-Baḥrayn	691	267	478,000	692	1,790	Al-Manāmah	A
†Bangladesh	Bangladesh	143,998	55,598	107,510,000	747	1,934	Dhaka (Dacca)	A
†Barbados	Barbados	430	166	255,000	593	1,536	Bridgetown	A
†Belgium	Belgique (French) / België (Flemish)	30,518	11,783	9,877,000	324	838	Bruxelles (Brussels)	A
†Belize	Belize	22,963	8,866	189,000	8.2	21	Belmopan	A
†Belorussia, U.S.S.R.	Belorusskaja S.S.R.	207,600	80,155	10,290,000	50	128	Minsk	D
†Benin	Bénin	112,600	43,475	4,667,000	41	107	Porto-Novo and Cotonou	A
Bermuda (U.K.)	Bermuda	54	21	57,000	1,056	2,714	Hamilton	C
†Bhutan	Druk-Yul	46,500	17,954	1,550,000	33	86	Thimphu	B(India)
†Bolivia	Bolivia	1,098,581	424,165	7,298,000	6.6	17	La Paz and Sucre	A
Bophuthatswana(2)	Bophuthatswana	40,509	15,641	2,251,000	56	144	Mmabatho	B(S. Afr.)
†Botswana	Botswana	582,000	224,711	1,280,000	2.2	5.7	Gaborone	A
†Brazil	Brasil	8,511,965	3,286,488	148,980,000	18	45	Brasília	A
British Columbia, Can.	British Columbia (English) / Colombie-Britannique (French)	947,800	365,948	3,011,000	3.2	8.2	Victoria	D
British Indian Ocean Territory (U.K.)	British Indian Ocean Territory	60	23	(1)	. . .	. . .	. . .	C
†Brunei	Brunei	5,765	2,226	253,000	44	114	Bandar Seri Begawan	A
†Bulgaria	Bâlgarija	110,912	42,823	9,015,000	81	211	Sofija (Sofia)	A
†Burkina Faso	Burkina Faso	274,200	105,869	9,019,000	33	85	Ouagadougou	A
†Burma	Myanmar	676,577	261,228	40,865,000	60	156	Yangon (Rangoon)	A
†Burundi	Burundi	27,830	10,745	5,380,000	193	501	Bujumbura	A
California, U.S.	California	411,041	158,704	28,815,000	70	182	Sacramento	D
†Cambodia	Kâmpŭchéa	181,035	69,898	8,153,000	45	117	Phnum Pénh (Phnom Penh)	A
†Cameroon	Cameroun (French) / Cameroon (English)	475,442	183,569	11,580,000	24	63	Yaoundé	A
†Canada	Canada	9,970,610	3,849,674	26,415,000	2.6	6.9	Ottawa	A
†Cape Verde	Cabo Verde	4,033	1,557	370,000	92	238	Praia	A
Cayman Islands (U.K.)	Cayman Islands	259	100	25,000	97	250	Georgetown	C
†Central African Republic	République centrafricaine	622,984	240,535	2,843,000	4.6	12	Bangui	A
†Chad	Tchad	1,284,000	495,755	4,984,000	3.9	10	N'Djamena	A
Chekiang, China	Zhejiang	101,800	39,305	42,045,000	413	1,070	Hangzhou	D
†Chile	Chile	756,626	292,135	13,140,000	17	45	Santiago	A
†China (excl. Taiwan)	Zhongguo	9,556,100	3,689,631	1,092,100,000	114	296	Beijing (Peking)	A
Christmas Island (Austl.)	Christmas Island	135	52	2,000	15	38	. . .	C
Ciskei(2)	Ciskei	7,760	2,996	1,268,000	163	423	Bisho	B(S. Afr.)
Cocos (Keeling) Islands (Austl.)	Cocos (Keeling) Islands	14	5.4	600	43	111	. . .	C
†Colombia	Colombia	1,141,748	440,831	30,860,000	27	70	Bogotá	A
Colorado, U.S.	Colorado	269,602	104,094	3,402,000	13	33	Denver	D
†Comoros	Comores (French) / Al-Qumur (Arabic)	2,235	863	452,000	202	524	Moroni	A
†Congo	Congo	342,000	132,047	2,267,000	6.6	17	Brazzaville	A
Connecticut, U.S.	Connecticut	12,999	5,019	3,302,000	254	658	Hartford	D
Cook Islands	Cook Islands	236	91	18,000	76	198	Avarua	B(N.Z.)
†Costa Rica	Costa Rica	51,100	19,730	2,958,000	58	150	San José	A
†Cuba	Cuba	110,861	42,804	10,640,000	96	249	La Habana (Havana)	A
†Cyprus	Kípros (Greek) / Kıbrıs (Turkish)	5,896	2,276	524,000	89	230	Nicosia (Levkosía)	A
Cyprus, North	Kuzey Kıbrıs	3,355	1,295	173,000	52	134	Nicosia (Lefkoşa)	A
†Czechoslovakia	Československo	127,900	49,382	15,670,000	123	317	Praha (Prague)	A
Delaware, U.S.	Delaware	5,297	2,045	650,000	123	318	Dover	D
†Denmark	Danmark	43,092	16,638	5,135,000	119	309	København (Copenhagen)	A
District of Columbia, U.S.	District of Columbia	179	69	625,000	3,492	9,058	Washington	D
†Djibouti	Djibouti	23,200	8,958	333,000	14	37	Djibouti	A
†Dominica	Dominica	790	305	86,000	109	282	Roseau	A

World Information Table / Welt-Informationstabelle / Table de Información Mundial
Table d'Informations Mondiales / Tabela de Informação Mundial

297

NAME / NAME / NOMBRE / NOM / NOME English / Englisch Inglés / Anglais / Inglês	Local / Einheimisch Local / Local / Local	AREA / FLÄCHE AREA / SUPERFICIE / ÁREA sq. km.	sq. mi.	POPULATION BEVÖLKERUNG POBLACIÓN POPULATION POPULAÇÃO	DENSITY PER BEVÖLKERUNGSDICHTE PRO / DENSIDAD POR DENSITÉ / DENSIDADE POR sq. km.	sq. mi.	CAPITAL HAUPSTADT CAPITAL CAPITALE CAPITAL	POLITICAL STATUS POLITISCHER STATUS ESTADO POLITICO STATUS POLITIQUE ESTATUTO POLÍTICO
†Dominican Republic	República Dominicana	48,442	18,704	7,094,000	146	379	Santo Domingo	A
†Ecuador	Ecuador	283,561	109,484	10,650,000	38	97	Quito	A
†Egypt	Misr	1,001,449	386,662	52,830,000	53	137	Al-Qāhirah (Cairo)	A
†El Salvador	El Salvador	21,041	8,124	5,260,000	250	647	San Salvador	A
England, U.K.	England	130,439	50,363	47,730,000	366	948	London	D
†Equatorial Guinea	Guinea Ecuatorial	28,051	10,831	357,000	13	33	Malabo	A
Estonia, U.S.S.R.	Estonskaja S.S.R.	45,100	17,413	1,590,000	35	91	Tallinn	D
†Ethiopia	Ityopiya	1,251,282	483,123	49,628,000	40	103	Adis Abeba	A
Europe	. . .	9,900,000	3,800,000	688,000,000	69	181	. . .	
Faeroe Islands	Føroyar	1,399	540	47,000	34	87	Tórshavn	B(Den.)
Falkland Islands (U.K.)[3]	Falkland Islands (English) / Islas Malvinas (Spanish)	12,173	4,700	2,000	0.2	0.4	Stanley	C
†Fiji	Fiji	18,333	7,078	720,000	39	102	Suva	A
†Finland	Suomi (Finnish) / Finland (Swedish)	338,145	130,559	4,985,000	15	38	Helsinki (Helsingfors)	A
Florida, U.S.	Florida	151,949	58,668	12,610,000	83	215	Tallahassee	D
†France (excl. Overseas Departments)	France	547,026	211,208	56,210,000	103	266	Paris	A
French Guiana (Fr.)	Guyane française	91,000	35,135	96,000	1.1	2.7	Cayenne	C
French Polynesia (Fr.)	Polynésie française	4,000	1,544	194,000	49	126	Papeete	C
Fukien, China	Fujian	120,000	46,332	28,395,000	237	613	Fuzhou	D
†Gabon	Gabon	267,667	103,347	1,065,000	4.0	10	Libreville	A
†Gambia	Gambia	11,295	4,361	805,000	71	185	Banjul	A
Georgia, U.S.	Georgia	152,587	58,914	6,504,000	43	110	Atlanta	D
Georgia, U.S.S.R.	Gruzinskaja S.S.R.	69,700	26,911	5,491,000	79	204	Tbilisi	D
†German Democratic Republic[9]	Deutsche Demokratische Republik	108,333	41,828	16,740,000	155	400	Berlin, Ost- (East Berlin)	A
†Germany, Federal Republic of[9]	Bundesrepublik Deutschland	248,708	96,028	61,460,000	247	640	Bonn	A
†Ghana	Ghana	238,533	92,098	14,160,000	59	154	Accra	A
Gibraltar (U.K.)	Gibraltar	6.0	2.3	31,000	5,167	13,478	Gibraltar	C
†Greece	Ellás	131,990	50,962	10,010,000	76	196	Athínai (Athens)	A
Greenland	Kalaallit Nunaat (Eskimo) / Grønland (Danish)	2,175,600	840,004	57,000	. . .	0.1	Godthåb (Nuuk)	B(Den.)
†Grenada	Grenada	344	133	97,000	282	729	St. George's	A
Guadeloupe (incl. Dependencies) (Fr.)	Guadeloupe	1,780	687	346,000	194	504	Basse-Terre	C
Guam (U.S.)	Guam	541	209	154,000	285	737	Agana	C
†Guatemala	Guatemala	108,889	42,042	9,059,000	83	215	Guatemala	A
Guernsey (incl. Dependencies) (U.K.)	Guernsey	78	30	57,000	731	1,900	St. Peter Port	C
†Guinea	Guinée	245,857	94,926	7,178,000	29	76	Conakry	A
†Guinea-Bissau	Guiné-Bissau	36,125	13,948	986,000	27	71	Bissau	A
†Guyana	Guyana	214,969	83,000	765,000	3.6	9.2	Georgetown	A
Hainan	Hainan	34,000	13,127	6,553,000	193	499	Haikou	D
†Haiti	Haïti	27,750	10,714	6,456,000	233	603	Port-au-Prince	A
Hawaii, U.S.	Hawaii	16,765	6,473	1,126,000	67	174	Honolulu	D
Heilungkiang, China	Heilongjiang	469,000	181,082	34,400,000	73	190	Harbin	D
Honan, China	Henan	167,000	64,479	80,800,000	484	1,253	Zhengzhou	D
†Honduras	Honduras	112,088	43,277	5,039,000	45	116	Tegucigalpa	A
Hong Kong (U.K.)	Hong Kong	1,072	414	5,888,000	5,493	14,222	Hong Kong (Victoria)	C
Hopeh, China	Hebei	190,000	73,359	57,990,000	305	790	Shijiazhuang	D
Hunan, China	Hunan	210,000	81,081	58,860,000	280	726	Changsha	D
†Hungary	Magyarország	93,033	35,920	10,565,000	114	294	Budapest	A
Hupeh, China	Hubei	187,400	72,356	51,550,000	275	712	Wuhan	D
†Iceland	Ísland	103,000	39,769	254,000	2.5	6.4	Reykjavík	A
Idaho, U.S.	Idaho	216,435	83,566	1,026,000	4.7	12	Boise	D
Illinois, U.S.	Illinois	149,888	57,872	11,780,000	79	204	Springfield	D
†India (incl. part of Jammu and Kashmir)	India (English) / Bharat (Hindi)	3,203,975	1,237,062	841,750,000	263	680	New Delhi	A
Indiana, U.S.	Indiana	94,320	36,417	5,653,000	60	155	Indianapolis	D
†Indonesia	Indonesia	1,919,443	741,101	189,460,000	99	256	Jakarta	A
Inner Mongolia, China	Nei Monggol	1,183,000	456,759	20,970,000	18	46	Hohhot	D
Iowa, U.S.	Iowa	145,752	56,275	2,877,000	20	51	Des Moines	D
†Iran	Īrān	1,648,000	636,296	55,280,000	34	87	Tehrān	A
†Iraq	Al-ʿIrāq	438,317	169,235	17,745,000	40	105	Baghdād	A
†Ireland	Ireland (English) / Éire (Gaelic)	70,285	27,137	3,536,000	50	130	Dublin (Baile Átha Cliath)	A
Isle of Man	Isle of Man	572	221	67,000	117	303	Douglas	B(U.K.)
†Israel	Yisra'el (Hebrew) / Isrā'īl (Arabic)	20,770	8,019	4,460,000	215	556	Yerushalayim (Jerusalem)	A
Israeli Occupied Areas[4]	. . .	7,632	2,947	1,876,000	246	637	. . .	. . .
†Italy	Italia	301,277	116,324	57,625,000	191	495	Roma (Rome)	A
†Ivory Coast	Côte d'Ivoire	322,500	124,518	11,845,000	37	95	Abidjan and Yamoussoukro[5]	A
†Jamaica	Jamaica	10,991	4,244	2,386,000	217	562	Kingston	A
†Japan	Nihon	377,801	145,870	123,350,000	326	846	Tōkyō	A
Jersey (U.K.)	Jersey	116	45	81,000	698	1,800	St. Helier	C
†Jordan	Al-Urdun	91,000	35,135	3,011,000	33	86	ʿAmmān	A
Kansas, U.S.	Kansas	213,109	82,282	2,527,000	12	31	Topeka	D
Kansu, China	Gansu	450,000	173,746	21,405,000	48	123	Lanzhou	D
Kazakh, U.S.S.R.	Kazachskaja S.S.R.	2,717,300	1,049,156	16,675,000	6.1	16	Alma-Ata	D
Kentucky, U.S.	Kentucky	104,672	40,414	3,802,000	36	94	Frankfort	D
†Kenya	Kenya	582,646	224,961	25,350,000	44	113	Nairobi	A
Kiangsi, China	Jiangxi	166,600	64,325	36,260,000	218	564	Nanchang	D
Kiangsu, China	Jiangsu	102,600	39,614	64,760,000	631	1,635	Nanjing (Nanking)	D
Kirghiz S.S.R., U.S.S.R.	Kirgizskaja S.S.R.	198,500	76,641	4,335,000	22	57	Frunze	D
Kiribati	Kiribati	726	280	70,000	96	250	Bairiki	A
Kirin, China	Jilin	187,000	72,201	23,915,000	128	331	Changchun	D
Korea, North	Chosòn-minjujuŭi-inmīn-konghwaguk	120,538	46,540	22,790,000	189	490	P'yŏngyang	A
Korea, South	Taehan-min'guk	99,016	38,230	42,590,000	430	1,114	Sŏul (Seoul)	A
†Kuwait	Al-Kuwayt	17,818	6,880	1,971,000	111	286	Al-Kuwayt (Kuwait)	A
Kwangsi Chuang, China	Guangxi Zhuangzu	236,300	91,236	40,735,000	172	446	Nanning	D
Kwangtung, China	Guangdong	178,000	68,726	58,970,000	331	858	Guangzhou (Canton)	D
Kweichow, China	Guizhou	170,000	65,637	31,125,000	183	474	Guiyang	D
†Laos	Lao	236,800	91,429	3,980,000	17	44	Viangchan (Vientiane)	A
Latvia, U.S.S.R.	Latvijskaja S.S.R.	63,700	24,595	2,717,000	43	110	Rīga	D
†Lebanon	Lubnān	10,400	4,015	3,377,000	325	841	Bayrūt (Beirut)	A
†Lesotho	Lesotho	30,355	11,720	1,772,000	58	151	Maseru	A
Liaoning, China	Liaoning	145,700	56,255	38,440,000	264	683	Shenyang (Mukden)	D
†Liberia	Liberia	99,067	38,250	2,670,000	27	70	Monrovia	A
†Libya	Lībiyā	1,759,540	679,362	4,143,000	2.4	6.1	Tarābulus (Tripoli)	A
Liechtenstein	Liechtenstein	160	62	28,000	175	452	Vaduz	A
Lithuania, U.S.S.R.[6]	Litovskaja S.S.R.	65,200	25,174	3,728,000	57	148	Vilnius	D
Louisiana, U.S.	Louisiana	123,672	47,750	4,503,000	36	94	Baton Rouge	D
†Luxembourg	Luxembourg	2,586	998	381,000	147	382	Luxembourg	A
Macau (Port.)	Macau	17	6.6	454,000	26,706	68,788	Macau	C
†Madagascar	Madagasikara (Malagasy) / Madagascar (French)	587,041	226,658	11,615,000	20	51	Antananarivo	A
Maine, U.S.	Maine	86,156	33,265	1,226,000	14	37	Augusta	D
†Malawi	Malaŵi	118,484	45,747	8,335,000	70	182	Lilongwe	A
†Malaysia	Malaysia	334,758	129,251	17,480,000	52	135	Kuala Lumpur	A
†Maldives	Maldives	298	115	211,000	708	1,835	Male	A
†Mali	Mali	1,240,000	478,767	9,293,000	7.5	19	Bamako	A
†Malta	Malta	316	122	347,000	1,098	2,844	Valletta	A
Manitoba, Can.	Manitoba	649,950	250,947	1,115,000	1.7	4.4	Winnipeg	D
Marshall Islands	Marshall Islands	181	70	43,000	238	614	Majuro (island)	B(U.S.)
Martinique (Fr.)	Martinique	1,100	425	347,000	315	816	Fort-de-France	C
Maryland, U.S.	Maryland	27,094	10,461	4,703,000	174	450	Annapolis	D
Massachusetts, U.S.	Massachusetts	21,461	8,286	5,954,000	277	719	Boston	D
†Mauritania	Mauritanie (French) / Mūrītāniyā (Arabic)	1,025,520	395,956	2,008,000	2.0	5.1	Nouakchott	A
†Mauritius (incl. Dependencies)	Mauritius	2,040	788	1,105,000	542	1,402	Port Louis	A

NAME / NAME / NOMBRE / NOM / NOME English / Englisch Inglés / Anglais / Inglês	Local / Einheimisch Local / Local / Local	AREA / FLÄCHE AREA / SUPERFICIE / ÁREA sq. km.	sq. mi.	POPULATION BEVÖLKERUNG POBLACIÓN POPULATION POPULAÇÃO	DENSITY PER BEVÖLKERUNGSDICHTE PRO / DENSIDAD POR DENSITÉ / DENSIDADE POR sq. km.	sq. mi.	CAPITAL HAUPSTADT CAPITAL CAPITALE CAPITAL	POLITICAL STATUS POLITISCHER STATUS ESTADO POLÍTICO STATUS POLITIQUE ESTATUTO POLÍTICO
Mayotte (Fr.)[7]	Mayotte	374	144	82,000	219	569	Dzaoudzi and Mamoudzou[5]	C
†Mexico	México	1,958,201	756,066	85,090,000	43	113	Ciudad de México (Mexico City)	A
Michigan, U.S.	Michigan	251,506	97,107	9,431,000	37	97	Lansing	D
Micronesia, Federated States of	Federated States of Micronesia	702	271	90,000	128	332	Kolonia	B(U.S.)
Midway Islands (U.S.)	Midway Islands	5.2	2.0	500	96	250	. . .	C
Minnesota, U.S.	Minnesota	224,329	86,614	4,378,000	20	51	St. Paul	D
Mississippi, U.S.	Mississippi	123,519	47,691	2,702,000	22	57	Jackson	D
Missouri, U.S.	Missouri	180,514	69,697	5,253,000	29	75	Jefferson City	D
Moldavian S.S.R., U.S.S.R.	Moldavskaja S.S.R.	33,700	13,012	4,365,000	130	335	Kišin'ov (Kishinev)	D
Monaco	Monaco	1.9	0.7	29,000	15,263	41,429	Monaco	A
†Mongolia	Mongol Ard Uls	1,565,000	604,250	2,155,000	1.4	3.6	Ulaanbaatar (Ulan Bator)	A
Montana, U.S.	Montana	380,845	147,045	825,000	2.2	5.6	Helena	D
Montserrat (U.K.)	Montserrat	102	39	12,000	118	308	Plymouth	C
†Morocco (excl. Western Sahara)	Al-Magrib	446,550	172,414	25,930,000	58	150	Rabat	A
†Mozambique	Moçambique	799,379	308,642	15,535,000	19	50	Maputo	A
Namibia (excl. Walvis Bay)	Namibia	823,144	317,818	1,386,000	1.7	4.4	Windhoek	A
Nauru	Nauru (English) / Naoero (Nauruan)	21	8.1	9,000	429	1,111	Yaren District	A
Nebraska, U.S.	Nebraska	200,336	77,350	1,626,000	8.1	21	Lincoln	D
†Nepal	Nepāl	147,181	56,827	18,930,000	129	333	Kāthmāndau	A
†Netherlands	Nederland	41,785	16,133	14,825,000	355	919	Amsterdam and 's-Gravenhage (The Hague)	A
Netherlands Antilles	Nederlandse Antillen	800	309	207,000	259	670	Willemstad	B(Neth.)
Nevada, U.S.	Nevada	286,354	110,562	1,076,000	3.8	9.7	Carson City	D
New Brunswick, Can.	New Brunswick (English) / Nouveau-Brunswick (French)	73,440	28,355	740,000	10	26	Fredericton	D
New Caledonia (Fr.)	Nouvelle-Calédonie	19,058	7,358	153,000	8.0	21	Nouméa	C
Newfoundland, Can.	Newfoundland (English) / Terre-Neuve (French)	405,720	156,649	592,000	1.5	3.8	St. John's	D
New Hampshire, U.S.	New Hampshire	24,030	9,278	1,101,000	46	119	Concord	D
New Jersey, U.S.	New Jersey	20,168	7,787	7,830,000	388	1,006	Trenton	D
New Mexico, U.S.	New Mexico	314,927	121,594	1,551,000	4.9	13	Santa Fe	D
New South Wales, Austl.	New South Wales	801,600	309,500	5,823,000	7.3	19	Sydney	D
New York, U.S.	New York	136,588	52,737	18,185,000	133	345	Albany	D
†New Zealand	New Zealand	268,112	103,519	3,408,000	13	33	Wellington	A
†Nicaragua	Nicaragua	130,000	50,193	3,555,000	27	71	Managua	A
†Niger	Niger	1,267,000	489,191	7,609,000	6.0	16	Niamey	A
†Nigeria	Nigeria	923,768	356,669	111,010,000	120	311	Lagos and Abuja[5]	A
Ningsia Hui, China	Ningxia Huizu	66,400	25,637	4,368,000	66	170	Yinchuan	D
Niue	Niue	263	102	1,600	6.1	16	Alofi	B(N.Z.)
Norfolk Island (Austl.)	Norfolk Island	36	14	1,900	53	136	Kingston	C
North America	. . .	24,400,000	9,400,000	423,600,000	17	45	. . .	. . .
North Carolina, U.S.	North Carolina	136,412	52,669	6,604,000	48	125	Raleigh	D
North Dakota, U.S.	North Dakota	183,117	70,702	699,000	3.8	9.9	Bismarck	D
Northern Ireland, U.K.	Northern Ireland	14,121	5,452	1,588,000	112	291	Belfast	D
Northern Mariana Islands	Northern Mariana Islands	477	184	24,000	50	130	Saipan (island)	B(U.S.)
Northern Territory, Austl.	Northern Territory	1,346,200	519,771	158,000	0.1	0.3	Darwin	D
Northwest Territories, Can.	Northwest Territories (English) / Territoires du Nord-Ouest (French)	3,426,320	1,322,910	55,000	. . .	. . .	Yellowknife	D
†Norway (incl. Svalbard and Jan Mayen)	Norge	386,975	149,412	4,202,000	11	28	Oslo	A
Nova Scotia, Can.	Nova Scotia (English) / Nouvelle-Écosse (French)	55,490	21,425	909,000	16	42	Halifax	D
Oceania (incl. Australia)		8,500,000	3,300,000	26,300,000	3.1	8.0	. . .	. . .
Ohio, U.S.	Ohio	115,995	44,786	11,005,000	95	246	Columbus	D
Oklahoma, U.S.	Oklahoma	181,188	69,957	3,352,000	19	48	Oklahoma City	D
†Oman	'Umān	212,457	82,030	1,325,000	6.2	16	Masqaṭ (Muscat)	A
Ontario, Can.	Ontario	1,068,580	412,581	9,495,000	8.9	23	Toronto	D
Oregon, U.S.	Oregon	251,426	97,076	2,777,000	11	29	Salem	D
Pacific Islands, Trust Territory of the	Trust Territory of the Pacific Islands	508	196	15,000	30	77	. . .	B(U.S.)
†Pakistan (incl. part of Jammu and Kashmir)	Pākistān	879,902	339,732	112,360,000	128	331	Islāmābād	A
Palau (Trust Territory)	Palau (English) / Belau (Palauan)	508	196	15,000	30	77	Koror	B(U.S.)
†Panama	Panamá	77,082	29,762	2,396,000	31	81	Panamá	A
†Papua New Guinea	Papua New Guinea	462,840	178,704	3,653,000	7.9	20	Port Moresby	A
†Paraguay	Paraguay	406,752	157,048	4,221,000	10	27	Asunción	A
Peking, China	Beijing	16,800	6,487	10,045,000	598	1,548	Beijing (Peking)	D
Pennsylvania, U.S.	Pennsylvania	119,261	46,047	12,155,000	102	264	Harrisburg	D
†Peru	Perú	1,285,216	496,225	22,085,000	17	45	Lima	A
†Philippines	Philippines (English) / Pilipinas (Tagalog)	300,000	115,831	60,835,000	203	525	Manila	A
Pitcairn (incl. Dependencies) (U.K.)	Pitcairn	49	19	60	1.2	3.2	Adamstown	C
†Poland	Polska	312,683	120,728	37,840,000	121	313	Warszawa (Warsaw)	A
†Portugal	Portugal	91,985	35,516	10,495,000	114	296	Lisboa (Lisbon)	A
Prince Edward Island, Can.	Prince Edward Island (English) / Île-du Prince-Édouard (French)	5,660	2,185	132,000	23	60	Charlottetown	D
Puerto Rico	Puerto Rico	9,104	3,515	3,368,000	370	958	San Juan	B(U.S.)
†Qatar	Qatar	11,437	4,416	417,000	36	94	Ad-Dawḥah (Doha)	A
Quebec, Can.	Québec	1,540,680	594,860	6,815,000	4.4	11	Québec	D
Queensland, Austl.	Queensland	1,727,200	666,876	2,843,000	1.6	4.3	Brisbane	D
Reunion (Fr.)	Réunion	2,510	969	590,000	235	609	Saint-Denis	C
Rhode Island, U.S.	Rhode Island	3,139	1,212	1,001,000	319	826	Providence	D
†Romania	România	237,500	91,699	23,210,000	98	253	Bucureşti (Bucharest)	A
Russian Soviet Federative Socialist Republic, U.S.S.R.	Rossijskaja S.F.S.R.	17,075,400	6,592,849	148,550,000	8.7	23	Moskva (Moscow)	D
†Rwanda	Rwanda	26,338	10,169	7,463,000	283	734	Kigali	A
†St. Christopher-Nevis	St. Christopher-Nevis	269	104	46,000	171	442	Basseterre	A
St. Helena (incl. Dependencies) (U.K.)	St. Helena	419	162	7,600	18	47	Jamestown	C
†St. Lucia	St. Lucia	616	238	151,000	245	634	Castries	A
St. Pierre and Miquelon (Fr.)	Saint-Pierre-et-Miquelon	242	93	6,800	28	73	Saint-Pierre	C
†St. Vincent and the Grenadines	St. Vincent and the Grenadines	388	150	114,000	294	760	Kingstown	A
San Marino	San Marino	61	24	24,000	393	1,000	San Marino	A
†Sao Tome and Principe	São Tomé e Príncipe	964	372	123,000	128	331	São Tomé	A
Saskatchewan, Can.	Saskatchewan	652,330	251,866	1,051,000	1.6	4.2	Regina	D
†Saudi Arabia	Al-'Arabīyah as-Su'ūdīyah	2,149,690	830,000	14,645,000	6.8	18	Ar-Riyāḍ (Riyadh)	A
Scotland, U.K.	Scotland	78,772	30,414	5,150,000	65	169	Edinburgh	D
†Senegal	Sénégal	196,722	75,955	7,367,000	37	97	Dakar	A
†Seychelles	Seychelles	453	175	69,000	152	394	Victoria	A
Shanghai, China	Shanghai	6,200	2,394	12,780,000	2,061	5,338	Shanghai	D
Shansi, China	Shanxi	156,000	60,232	27,410,000	176	455	Taiyuan	D
Shantung, China	Shandong	153,000	59,074	80,380,000	525	1,361	Jinan	D
Shensi, China	Shaanxi	205,000	79,151	31,450,000	153	397	Xi'an (Sian)	D
†Sierra Leone	Sierra Leone	72,325	27,925	4,116,000	57	147	Freetown	A
†Singapore	Singapore	636	246	2,710,000	4,261	11,016	Singapore	A
Sinkiang Uighur, China	Xinjiang Uygur	1,600,000	617,764	14,305,000	8.9	23	Ürümqi	D
†Solomon Islands	Solomon Islands	28,370	10,954	312,000	11	28	Honiara	A
†Somalia	Somaliya	637,657	246,201	8,332,000	13	34	Muqdisho (Mogadishu)	A
†South Africa (incl. Walvis Bay)	South Africa (English) / Suid-Afrika (Afrikaans)	1,123,226	433,680	36,790,000	33	85	Pretoria, Cape Town, and Bloemfontein	A
South America	. . .	17,800,000	6,900,000	293,700,000	17	43	. . .	. . .
South Australia, Austl.	South Australia	984,000	379,925	1,437,000	1.5	3.8	Adelaide	D
South Carolina, U.S.	South Carolina	80,590	31,116	3,552,000	44	114	Columbia	D

World Information Table / Welt-Informationstabelle / Table de Información Mundial
Table d'Informations Mondiales / Tabela de Informação Mundial

299

NAME / NAME / NOMBRE / NOM / NOME English / Englisch Inglés / Anglais / Inglês	Local / Einheimisch Local / Local / Local	AREA / FLÄCHE AREA / SUPERFICIE / ÁREA sq. km.	sq. mi.	POPULATION BEVÖLKERUNG POBLACIÓN POPULATION POPULAÇÃO	DENSITY PER BEVÖLKERUNGSDICHTE PRO / DENSIDAD POR DENSITÉ / DENSIDADE POR sq. km.	sq. mi.	CAPITAL HAUPSTADT CAPITAL CAPITALE CAPITAL	POLITICAL STATUS POLITISCHER STATUS ESTADO POLITICO STATUS POLITIQUE ESTATUTO POLITICO
South Dakota, U.S.	South Dakota	199,740	77,120	725,000	3.6	9.4	Pierre	D
South Georgia and the South Sandwich Islands (U.K.)	. . .	3,755	1,450	(1)	. . .	. . .	. . .	C
†Spain	España	504,750	194,885	39,520,000	78	203	Madrid	A
Spanish North Africa (Sp.)[8]	Plazas de Soberanía en el Norte de África	32	12	100,000	3,125	8,333	. . .	C
†Sri Lanka	Sri Lanka	64,652	24,962	16,935,000	262	678	Colombo and Sri Jayawardenapura	A
†Sudan	As-Sūdān	2,505,813	967,500	24,775,000	9.9	26	Al-Khartūm (Khartoum)	A
†Suriname	Suriname	163,820	63,251	405,000	2.5	6.4	Paramaribo	A
†Swaziland	Swaziland	17,364	6,704	787,000	45	117	Mbabane and Lobamba[5]	A
†Sweden	Sverige	449,964	173,732	8,503,000	19	49	Stockholm	A
Switzerland	Schweiz (German) / Suisse (French) / Svizzera (Italian)	41,293	15,943	6,623,000	160	415	Bern (Berne)	A
†Syria	Sūrīyah	185,180	71,498	11,915,000	64	167	Dimashq (Damascus)	A
Szechwan, China	Sichuan	570,000	220,078	106,590,000	187	484	Chengdu	D
Taiwan	T'aiwan	36,002	13,900	20,345,000	565	1,464	T'aipei	A
Tajik S.S.R., U.S.S.R.	Tajikskaja S.S.R.	143,100	55,251	5,144,000	36	93	Dušanbe	D
†Tanzania	Tanzania	945,087	364,900	25,220,000	27	69	Dar es Salaam and Dodoma[5]	A
Tasmania, Austl.	Tasmania	67,800	26,178	456,000	6.7	17	Hobart	D
Tennessee, U.S.	Tennessee	109,150	42,143	5,003,000	46	119	Nashville	D
Texas, U.S.	Texas	691,022	266,805	17,060,000	25	64	Austin	D
†Thailand	Prathet Thai	513,115	198,115	55,925,000	109	282	Krung Thep (Bangkok)	A
Tibet, China	Xizang	1,220,000	471,045	2,075,000	1.7	4.4	Lhasa	D
Tientsin, China	Tianjin	11,300	4,363	8,409,000	744	1,927	Tianjin (Tientsin)	D
†Togo	Togo	56,785	21,925	3,508,000	62	160	Lomé	A
Tokelau (N.Z.)	Tokelau	12	4.6	1,700	142	370	. . .	C
Tonga	Tonga	750	290	97,000	129	334	Nuku'alofa	A
Transkei[2]	Transkei	43,553	16,816	3,636,000	83	216	Umtata	B(S. Afr.)
†Trinidad and Tobago	Trinidad and Tobago	5,128	1,980	1,248,000	243	630	Port of Spain	A
Tsinghai, China	Qinghai	720,000	277,994	4,259,000	5.9	15	Xining	D
†Tunisia	Tunisie (French) / Tunis (Arabic)	163,610	63,170	8,079,000	49	128	Tunis	A
†Turkey	Türkiye	779,452	300,948	54,075,000	69	180	Ankara	A
Turkmen S.S.R., U.S.S.R.	Turkmenskaja S.S.R.	488,100	188,456	3,555,000	7.3	19	Ašchabad	D
Turks and Caicos Islands (U.K.)	Turks and Caicos Islands	430	166	11,000	26	66	Grand Turk	C
Tuvalu	Tuvalu	26	10	8,800	338	880	Funafuti	A
†Uganda	Uganda	241,139	93,104	17,300,000	72	186	Kampala	A
†Ukraine, U.S.S.R.	Ukrainskaja S.S.R.	603,700	233,090	52,110,000	86	224	Kijev (Kiev)	D
†Union of Soviet Socialist Republics	Sojuz Sovetskich Socialističeskich Respublik	22,274,900	8,600,387	289,010,000	13	34	Moskva (Moscow)	A
†United Arab Emirates	Al-Imārāt al-'Arabīyah al-Muttahidah	83,600	32,278	2,183,000	26	68	Abū Ẓaby (Abu Dhabi)	A
†United Kingdom	United Kingdom	244,100	94,248	57,335,000	235	608	London	A
†United States	United States	9,529,202	3,679,245	250,150,000	26	68	Washington	A
†Uruguay	Uruguay	177,414	68,500	3,120,000	18	46	Montevideo	A
Utah, U.S.	Utah	219,895	84,902	1,726,000	7.8	20	Salt Lake City	D
Uzbek S.S.R., U.S.S.R.	Uzbekskaja S.S.R.	447,400	172,742	20,055,000	45	116	Taškent	D
†Vanuatu	Vanuatu	12,189	4,706	158,000	13	34	Port Vila	A
Vatican City	Città del Vaticano	0.4	0.2	800	2,000	4,000	Città del Vaticano (Vatican City)	A
Venda[2]	Venda	6,198	2,393	588,000	95	246	Thohoyandou	B(S. Afr.)
†Venezuela	Venezuela	912,050	352,145	19,485,000	21	55	Caracas	A
Vermont, U.S.	Vermont	24,900	9,614	563,000	23	59	Montpelier	D
Victoria, Austl.	Victoria	227,600	87,877	4,355,000	19	50	Melbourne	D
†Vietnam	Viet Nam	329,556	127,242	65,475,000	199	515	Ha Noi	A
Virginia, U.S.	Virginia	105,576	40,763	6,104,000	58	150	Richmond	D
Virgin Islands (U.S.)	Virgin Islands (U.S.)	344	133	114,000	331	857	Charlotte Amalie	C
Virgin Islands, British (U.K.)	British Virgin Islands	153	59	13,000	85	220	Road Town	C
Wake Island (U.S.)	Wake Island	7.8	3.0	300	38	100	. . .	C
Wales, U.K.	Wales	20,768	8,019	2,867,000	138	358	Cardiff	D
Wallis and Futuna (Fr.)	Wallis et Futuna	255	98	16,000	63	163	Mata-Utu	C
Washington, U.S.	Washington	176,479	68,139	4,678,000	27	69	Olympia	D
Western Australia, Austl.	Western Australia	2,525,500	975,101	1,598,000	0.6	1.6	Perth	D
Western Sahara	. . .	266,000	102,703	196,000	0.7	1.9	El Aaiún (Laayone)	. . .
†Western Samoa	Western Samoa (English) / Samoa i Sisifo (Samoan)	2,831	1,093	184,000	65	168	Apia	A
West Virginia, U.S.	West Virginia	62,771	24,236	1,926,000	31	79	Charleston	D
Wisconsin, U.S.	Wisconsin	171,491	66,213	4,903,000	29	74	Madison	D
Wyoming, U.S.	Wyoming	253,322	97,808	500,000	2.0	5.1	Cheyenne	D
†Yemen	Al-Yaman	531,869	205,356	13,019,000	24	63	San'ā'	A
†Yugoslavia	Jugoslavija	255,804	98,766	23,765,000	93	241	Beograd (Belgrade)	A
Yukon Territory, Can.	Yukon Territory	483,450	186,661	25,000	0.1	0.1	Whitehorse	D
Yunnan, China	Yunnan	394,000	152,124	35,710,000	91	235	Kunming	D
†Zaire	Zaïre	2,345,095	905,568	35,165,000	15	39	Kinshasa	A
†Zambia	Zambia	752,614	290,586	7,995,000	11	28	Lusaka	A
†Zimbabwe	Zimbabwe	390,759	150,873	9,252,000	24	61	Harare (Salisbury)	A
WORLD	. . .	149,800,000	57,800,000	5,236,000,000	35	91	. . .	. . .

† Member of the United Nations (1989).
. . . None, or not applicable.
(1) No permanent population.
(2) Bophuthatswana, Ciskei, Transkei, and Venda are not recognized by the United Nations.
(3) Claimed by Argentina.
(4) Includes West Bank, Golan Heights, and Gaza Strip.
(5) Future capital.
(6) On March 11, 1990 Lithuania unilaterally declared its independence from the Soviet Union.
(7) Claimed by Comoros.
(8) Comprises Ceuta, Melilla, and several small islands.
(9) The process of unification of the German Democratic Republic with the Federal Republic of Germany began early in 1990 with completion expected by the end of the year.

† Mitglied der Vereinten Nationen (1989).
. . . Kein(e), oder nicht anwendbar.
(1) Bevölkerungszahl schwankend.
(2) Bophuthatswana, Ciskei, Transkei und Venda von Vereinten Nationen nicht anerkannt.
(3) Von Argentinien beansprucht.
(4) Westufer, Golan-Höhen und Gazastreifen einbegriffen.
(5) Zukünftige Hauptstadt.
(6) Am 11. März 1990 erklärte Litauen einseitig seine Unabhängigkeit von der Sowjetunion.
(7) Von Komoren beansprucht.
(8) Umfasst Ceuta, Melilla und mehrere kleine Inseln.
(9) Der Wiedervereinigungsprozess der Deutschen Demokratischen Republik mit der Bundesrepublik Deutschland hat zu Beginn des Jahres 1990 begonnen. Vollendung des Prozess ist am Jahresende erwartet.

† Miembro de las Naciones Unidas (1989).
. . . Ninguno, o no se aplica.
(1) Sin población permanente.
(2) Bophuthatswana, Ciskei, Transkei y Venda no reconocido por las Naciones Unidas.
(3) Reclamado por la Argentina.
(4) Incluye la ribera oeste, las alturas de Golán y la franja de Gaza.

(5) Capital futura.
(6) En 11 de marzo de 1990, Lituania declaró unilateralmente su independencia de la Unión Soviética.
(7) Reclamado por las Comores.
(8) Comprende Ceuta, Melilla y various islas pequeñas.
(9) El proceso de unificación de la República Democrática Alemana con la República Federal de Alemania comenzó a principios del año 1990 con la conclusión esperada para fines del año.

† Membre des Nations Unies (1989).
. . . Pas d'information, ou pas applicable.
(1) Pas de population permanente.
(2) Bophuthatswana, Ciskei, Transkei et Venda non reconnaissent pas les Nations Unies.
(3) Revendiqué par l'Argentine.
(4) Y compris Cisjordanie, hauteurs de Golan et la bande de Gaza.
(5) Capitale future.
(6) Le 11 mars 1990, la Lituanie s'est proclamée unilatéralement indépendante de l'Union soviétique.
(7) Revendiqué par les Comores.
(8) Inclus Ceuta, Melilla et plusieurs petites îles.
(9) Le processus de l'unification de la République démocratique allemande avec la République fédérale d'Allemagne commença au début de 1990 en anticipant son accomplissement avant la fin de l'année.

† Membro das Nações Unidas (1989).
. . . Inexistente ou não aplicável.
(1) Sem população permanente.
(2) Bophuthatswana, Ciskei, Transkei e Venda não son reconhecido pelas Nações Unidas.
(3) Reivindicado pela Argentina.
(4) Incluindo a margem oeste, as colinas de Golan e a faixa de Gaza.
(5) Capital futuro.
(6) A 11 de março de 1990, a Lituânia declarou unilateralmente sua independência da União Soviética.
(7) Reivindicado pelas Comores.
(8) Compreende Ceuta, Melilla e várias ilhas pequenas.
(9) O processo de unificação da República Democrática Alemã com a República Federal da Alemanha começou no princípio de 1990 espera-se o termino para o final do ano.

THIS TABLE lists the major metropolitan areas of the world according to their estimated population on January 1, 1989. For convenience in reference, the areas are grouped by major region with the total for each region given. The number of areas by population classification is given in parentheses with each size group.

For ease of comparison, each metropolitan area has been defined by Rand McNally & Company according to consistent rules. A metropolitan area includes a central city, neighboring communities linked to it by continuous built-up areas, and more distant communities if the bulk of their population is supported by commuters to the central city. Some metropolitan areas have more than one central city; in such cases each central city is listed.

IN DIESER TABELLE sind die Hauptmetropolen der Welt verzeichnet, gemessen nach ihrer Bevölkerung, die nach dem Stand vom 1. Januar 1989 geschätzt wurde. Zur besseren Übersicht sind die Zonen nach grösseren Regionen gruppiert, wobei die Gesamtzahl für jede Region angegeben ist. Die Anzahl der Zonen ist nach Bevölkerung klassifiziert und in Klammern hinter denen nach Grössen sortierten Gruppen angegeben.

Zum einfacheren Vergleich ist jede Metropole von Rand McNally & Company nach übereinstimmenden Massstäben definiert worden. Eine Metropole schliesst eine zentrale Stadt mit benachbarten Gemeinden, die mit ihr durch ununterbrochen bebaute Gebiete verbunden sind ein, sowie weiter entfernte Gemeinden, wenn der grösste Teil ihrer Bevölkerung von den Pendlern unterhalten wird. Einige Metropolen haben mehr als eine zentrale Stadt; in solchen Fällen ist jede dieser zentralen Städte angeführt.

ESTA TABLA indica las principales áreas metropolitanas del mundo, de acuerdo con su población calculada al 1 de enero de 1989. Para facilitar las referencias, las áreas se han agrupado por regiones principales, indicándose el total para cada región. El número de áreas, clasificadas por población, se indica entre paréntesis en los grupos de cada tamaño.

Para facilitar las comparaciones, Rand McNally y Compañía ha definido cada área metropolitana de acuerdo con reglas consistentes. Un área metropolitana incluye una ciudad central, localidades vecinas vinculadas con ella mediante sectores construídos y contínuos, y localidades más distantes, si el grueso de su población lo constituye un núcleo que diariamente viaja a la ciudad central. Algunas áreas metropolitanas incluyen más de una ciudad central; en tales casos se indica cada una dichas ciudades.

CETTE TABLE contient la liste des aires métropolitaines les plus considérables dans le monde pour ce qui est du peuplement a la date du 1 er janvier 1989. Afin de faciliter la consultation, on a groupé les aires par grandes régions en indiquant la population totale pour chaque région, et, entre parenthéses, le nombre d'aires comprises dans celle-ci.

Afin de rendre plus faciles les comparaisons, Rand McNally & Co. a défini chaque aire métropolitaine selorègles cohérentes: une aire métropolitaine englobe une cité centrale ou métropole et l'environnement urbain continu qui s'y rattache; elle inclut également des agglomérations éloignées de la métropole lorsque la population de ces dernières est pour sa májorité constituée d'habitants se rendant quotidiennement dans la cité ou est situé le lieu de travail de ceux-ci. On trouvera quelques aires métropolitaines pourvues de plus d'une métropole. Dans ce cas, chaque métropole est mentionnée.

A TABELA que se segúe relaciona as principais áreas metropolitanas do mundo, de acordo com as respectivas populações, estimadas para 1 de janeiro de 1989. Para facilidade de referência, as áreas metropolitanas foram agrupadas dentro das regiões maiores, indicando-se, entre parênteses, os totais de cada região maior e o número de áreas metropolitanas, classificadas segundo a população, compreendidas em cada uma.

Para fins de comparabilidade, Rand McNally & Company definiu cada área metropolitana de acordo com regras uniformes. Uma área metropolitana inclui uma cidade central, as localidades vizinhas ligadas a ela por áreas construídas contínuas, e as localidades mais distantes, desde que a maior parte de suas respectivas populações dependa economicamente da cidade central e que para ela viaje diariamente. Algumas áreas metropolitanas incluem mais de uma cidade central; em tais casos, indicam-se ambas as cidades.

CLASSIFICATION KLASSIFIZIERT CLASIFICADAS CLASSIFICATION CLASSIFICAÇÃO	ANGLO-AMERICA ANGLO-AMERIKA AMÉRICA ANGLOSAJONA AMÉRIQUE ANGLO-SAXONNE AMÉRICA ANGLO-SAXÔNICA	LATIN AMERICA LATEIN-AMERIKA AMÉRICA LATINA AMÉRIQUE LATINE AMÉRICA LATINA	EUROPE EUROPA EUROPA EUROPE EUROPA	U.S.S.R. U.S.S.R. U.R.S.S. U.R.S.S. U.R.S.S.	WEST ASIA WESTASIEN ASIA OCCIDENTAL ASIE OCCIDENTALE ÁSIA OCIDENTAL	EAST ASIA OSTASIEN ASIA ORIENTAL ASIE ORIENTALE ÁSIA ORIENTAL	AFRICA-OCEANIA AFRIKA-OZEANIEN AFRICA-OCEANÍA AFRIQUE-OCÉANIE ÁFRICA-OCEANIA
Over 15,000,000 (6)	New York	Ciudad de México (Mexico City) São Paulo				Ōsaka-Kōbe-Kyōto Sōul (Seoul) Tōkyō-Yokohama	
10,000,000-15,000,000 (9)	Los Angeles	Buenos Aires Rio de Janeiro	London Paris	Moskva (Moscow)	Bombay Calcutta		Al-Qāhirah (Cairo)
5,000,000-10,000,000 (18)	Chicago Philadelphia-Trenton- Wilmington San Francisco-Oakland-San Jose	Lima		Leningrad	Delhi-New Delhi İstanbul Karāchi Madras Tehrān	Beijing (Peking) Jakarta Krung Thep (Bangkok) Manila Shanghai T'aipei Tianjin (Tientsin) Victoria (Hong Kong)	
3,000,000-5,000,000 (38)	Boston Dallas-Fort Worth Detroit-Windsor Houston Miami-Fort Lauderdale Toronto Washington	Belo Horizonte Bogotá Caracas Guadalajara Santiago	Athínai (Athens) Barcelona Berlin Essen-Dortmund-Duisburg (Ruhr Area) Madrid Milano (Milan) Roma (Rome)		Baghdād Bangalore Dhaka (Dacca) Hyderābād, India Lahore	Guangzhou (Canton) Nagoya Pusan Yangon (Rangoon) Shenyang (Mukden) Singapore Thanh Pho Ho Chi Minh (Saigon) Wuhan	Al-Iskandarīyah (Alexandria) Johannesburg Kinshasa Lagos Melbourne Sydney
2,000,000-3,000,000 (49)	Atlanta Baltimore Cleveland Minneapolis-St. Paul Montréal Phoenix Pittsburgh St. Louis San Diego-Tijuana Seattle-Tacoma	Fortaleza La Habana (Havana) Medellín Monterrey Porto Alegre Recife Salvador	Birmingham Bruxelles (Brussels) Bucuresti (Bucharest) Budapest Hamburg Katowice-Bytom-Gliwice Lisboa (Lisbon) Manchester Napoli (Naples) Warszawa (Warsaw)	Baku Doneck-Makejevka Gor'kij (Gorkiy) Kijev (Kiev) Taškent	Ahmadābād Ankara Colombo Kānpur Pune (Poona)	Bandung Chongqing (Chungking) Harbin Kuala Lumpur Nanjing (Nanking) Sapporo-Otaru Surabaya Taegu Xi'an (Sian)	Cape Town Casablanca El Djazaïr (Algiers)
1,500,000-2,000,000 (57)	Cincinnati Denver	Brasília Cali Curitiba Guayaquil Montevideo San Juan Santo Domingo	Amsterdam Beograd (Belgrade) Frankfurt am Main Glasgow København (Copenhagen) Köln (Cologne) Leeds-Bradford Liverpool München (Munich) Stuttgart Torino (Turin) Wien (Vienna)	Char'kov (Kharkov) Dnepropetrovsk Kujbyšev (Kuybyshev) Minsk Novosibirsk Sverdlovsk	Al-Kuwayt (Kuwait) 'Amman Ar-Riyad (Riyadh) Bayrūt (Beirut) Chittagong Dimashq (Damascus) İzmir Jiddah Mashhad Nāgpur Tel Aviv-Yafo	Changchun (Hsinking) Chengdu (Chengtu) Dalian (Dairen) Fukuoka Ha Noi Hiroshima-Kure Jinan (Tsinan) Kaohsiung Kitakyūshū-Shimonoseki Medan P'yongyang Semarang Taiyuan	Abidjan Adis Abeba Al-Khartūm-Umm Durmān (Khartoum-Omdurman) Dakar Dar es Salaam Durban
1,000,000-1,500,000 (105)	Buffalo-Niagara Falls- St. Catharines Columbus El Paso-Ciudad Juárez Hartford-New Britain Indianapolis Kansas City Milwaukee New Orleans Portland Riverside-San Bernardino Sacramento St. Petersburg-Clearwater San Antonio Vancouver	Barranquilla Belém Campinas Córdoba Goiânia Guatemala La Paz Maracaibo Puebla Quito Rosario Santos	Antwerpen (Anvers) Dublin (Baile Átha Cliath) Düsseldorf Hannover Lille-Roubaix Łódź Lyon Mannheim Marseille Newcastle-Sunderland Nürnberg Porto Praha (Prague) Rotterdam Sofija (Sofia) Stockholm Valencia	Alma-Ata Čel'abinsk (Chelyabinsk) Jerevan Kazan' Odessa Omsk Perm Riga Rostov-na-Donu Saratov Tbilisi Ufa Volgograd	Asansol Coimbatore Esfahān Faisalabad Halab (Aleppo) Indore Jaipur Kābol (Kabul) Lucknow Madurai Patna Rāwalpindi-Islāmābād Surat Tabrīz Vārānasi (Benares)	Anshan Baotou Changsha Fushun Guiyang (Kweiyang) Hangzhou (Hangchow) Jilin (Kirin) Kunming Kwangju Lanzhou (Lanchow) Nanchang Palembang Qingdao (Tsingtao) Qiqihar (Tsitsihar) Sendai Shijiazhuang Tangshan Ujungpandang (Makasar) Ürümqi Zhengzhou (Chengchow)	Accra Adelaide Brisbane Douala Harare Ibadan Luanda Maputo Nairobi Perth Pretoria Rabat-Salé Tarābulus (Tripoli) Tunis
Total/Gesamtzahl Total/Total/Total (282)	38	36	48	26	43	61	30

ALL URBAN CENTERS of 50,000 or more population and many other important or well-known cities and towns are listed in the following table. The populations are from recent censuses (designated C) or official estimates (designated E) for the dates specified. For a few cities, only unofficial estimates are available (designated U). For comparison, the total population of each country is also given. For each country, the date stated for the total population also applies to the cities, except those for which another date is specified.

Population estimates for 1990 for countries may be found in the World Information Table.

A population figure in parentheses and preceded by a star (★) is the population of a city's entire metropolitan area. To permit meaningful comparisons of metropolitan areas, these have been defined by Rand McNally according to consistent rules (see introduction to Metropolitan Areas Table), and in some cases may differ somewhat from the officially recognized metropolitan areas. Where a town is located within the metropolitan area of another city, that city's name is given in parentheses preceded by a star (★). The capital of a country is denoted by CAPITAL letters.

ALLE STÄDTISCHEN ZENTREN mit 50 000 oder mehr Einwohnern und zahlreiche andere bedeutende oder bekannte Städte sind in der folgenden Tabelle zusammengestellt. Die Bevölkerungszahlen stammen von neuesten Zählungen (mit C gekennzeichnet) oder amtlichen Schätzungen (E) zu den angegebenen Zeitpunkten. Für einige wenige Städte waren lediglich inoffizielle Schätzungen erhältlich (U). Zu Vergleichszwecken ist ferner die Gesamtbevölkerung jedes Landes angegeben. Das Bezugsjahr für die Einwohnerzahl eines Landes betrifft auch die Städte mit Ausnahme jener, bei denen ein anderes Datum angegeben ist.

Schätzungen der Bevölkerungszahlen der Länder für 1990 finden sich in der Welt-Informationstabelle.

Bevölkerungszahlen in Klammern mit vorangestelltem Stern (★) beziehen sich auf die gesamte Stadtregion einer Stadt. Um sinnvolle Vergleiche von Stadtregionen zu ermöglichen, wurden diese von Rand McNally nach einheitlichen Regeln festgelegt (siehe Einleitung: Tabelle der Stadtregionen), weshalb sie in einigen Fällen etwas von der offiziellen Abgrenzung von Stadtregionen abweichen können. Ist eine Stadt in die Stadtregion einer anderen Grossstadt einbezogen, so wird der Name der Stadtregion mit vorangestelltem Stern (★) in Klammern aufgeführt. Die Hauptstadt eines Landes wird durch GROSSBUCHSTABEN hervorgehoben.

TODAS LOS CENTROS URBANOS de 50 000 habitantes o más y muchos otros de importancia así como bien conocidas ciudades y pueblos están incluídos en la tabla que se presenta a continuación. El número de habitantes indicados está tomado del censo más reciente (cifras identificadas con la letra C) o estimados oficiales (E) para las fechas especificadas. Para algunas ciudades, sólo existen informes no oficiales (U). Para medida de comparación, la población total de cada país se encuentra incluída también.

Para permitir una comparación, se da la población total de cada país, referente al mismo año que se usa para las ciudades principles, excepto para aquellas en las que se especifica otra fecha. El número de habitantes para 1990 para los países, se encuentra en la Tabla de Información Mundial.

La segunda cifra para la población que aparece en paréntesis y está precedida por una estrella (★) constituye la población de un área metropolitana entera. Para permitir comparaciones validas de áreas metropolitanas, éstas fueron definidas por Rand McNally siguiendo las reglas establecidas para estos propósitos (véase la Introducción a la Tabla de las Areas Metropolitanas), y en algunas ocasiones pueden ser un poco distintas de las áreas metropolitanas oficialmente reconocidas. Cuando una población se encuentra dentro de los límites de un área metropolitana de otra ciudad, el nombre de ésta se da entre paréntesis precedido por una (★). La capital de un país se indica con letras MAYÚSCULAS.

TOUTES LES VILLES de plus de 50 000 habitants et des villes moins peuplées, mais célèbres ou importantes, sont mentionnées dans la table ci-dessous. Les chiffres donnant la population proviennent de recensements récents (référence C), ou d'estimations officielles (référence E), aux dates indiquées. Pour quelques villes, on dispose seulement d'estimations non officielles (référence U). La population totale de chaque pays est également donnée, ce qui permet des comparaisons. Dans chaque pays, la date des renseignements est identique pour les villes et le pays, sauf indication contraire.

On trouvera dans la table d'informations mondiales les estimations de la population en 1990 pour chaque pays.

Les chiffres entre parenthèses, précédés d'une étoile (★), indiquent la population de l'ensemble de la zone métropolitaine. Pour permettre d'établir des comparaisons significatives entre les zones métropolitaines, ces dernières ont été définies selon des critères uniformes par Rand McNally & Company (voir l'introduction à la table des zones métropolitaines). Parfois, les limites des zones métropolitaines ainsi définies diffèrent des limites officielles. Quand une ville fait partie de la zone métropolitaine d'une autre ville, le nom de celle-ci, précédé d'une étoile (★), est mis entre parenthèses. Le nom des capitales de pays est écrit en lettres MAJUSCULES.

TODOS OS CENTROS URBANOS de 50 000 habitantes e mais, bem como muitas outras cidades e vilas importantes ou muito conhecidas figuram na tabela que se apresenta em sequida. Os dados relativos à população referem-se a censos recentes (identificadas com a letra C), ou a estimativas oficiais (E) nas datas indicadas. Para algumas cidades só existem estimativas não oficiais (U). Para fins de comparabilidade, apresenta-se também a população total de cada país.

Para cada país, a data de referência da população total aplica-se também às cidades exceto quando especificado em contrário. As estimativas da população dos países para 1990 encontra-se na *Tabela de informaçoes mundiais.*

Um dado de população apresentado entre parênteses e precedido por uma estrela (★), refere-se à população de toda a área metropolitana. Para fins de comparabilidade, as áreas metropolitanas foram definidas por Rand McNally segundo regras coerentes (ver a 'Introdução' à *Tabela das áreas metropolitanas),* e em certos casos podem ser um pouco diferentes das áreas metropolitanas oficialmente reconhecidas. Quando um centro urbano esta localizado dentro dos limites da área metropolitana de outro, seu nome figura entre parênteses precedido por uma estrela (★). A capital de um país é indicada por letras MAIÚSCULAS.

AFGHANISTAN / Afghānestān

1984 E	17,672,000
Herāt	160,000
Jalālābād (1982E)	58,000
• KĀBOL	1,179,000
Kondūz (1982E)	57,000
Mazār-e Sharīf	118,000
Qandahār	203,000

ALBANIA / Shqipëri

1983 E	2,841,300
Durrës	72,400
Elbasan	69,900
Korçë	57,100
Shkodër	71,200
• TIRANË (1984E)	210,800
Vlorë	61,100

ALGERIA / Algérie / Djazaïr

1987 C	23,038,942
Aïn el Beïda	61,997
Aïn Oussera	44,270
Aïn Témouchent	47,479
Annaba (Bône)	305,526
Bab Ezzouar (★El Djazaïr)	55,211
Barika	56,488
Batna	181,601
Béchar	107,311
Bejaïa (Bougie)	114,534
Beskra	128,281
Bordj Bou Arreridj	84,264
Bordj el Kiffan (★El Djazaïr)	61,035
Boufarik	41,305
Bou Saâda	66,688
Ech Cheliff (Orléansville)	129,976
El Boulaïda	170,935
• EL DJAZAÏR (ALGIERS) (★2,547,983)	1,507,241
El Djelfa	84,207
El Eulma	67,933
El Wad	70,073
Ghardaïa	89,415
Ghilizane	80,091
Guelma	77,821
Jijel	62,793
Khemis	55,335
Khenchla	69,743
Laghouat	67,214
Lemdiyya	85,195
Maghniyya	52,275
Messaad	47,460
Mestghanem	114,037
Mouaskar	64,691
M'Sila	65,805
Qacentina	440,842
Saïda	80,825
Sidi bel Abbès	152,778
Skikda	128,747
Souq Ahras	83,015
Stif	170,182
Tbessa	107,559
Tihert	95,821
Tilimsen	126,882
Tizi-Ouzou	61,163
Touggourt	70,645
Wahran	628,558
Wargla	81,721

AMERICAN SAMOA / Amerika Samoa

1980 C	32,279
• PAGO PAGO	3,075

ANDORRA

1986 C	46,976
• ANDORRA	18,463

ANGOLA

1989 E	9,739,100
Benguela (1983E)	155,000
Huambo (Nova Lisboa) (1983E)	203,000
Lobito (1983E)	150,000
• LUANDA	1,459,900
Lubango (1984E)	95,915
Namibe (1981E)	100,000

ANGUILLA

1984 C	6,680
South Hill	961
• THE VALLEY	1,042

ANTIGUA AND BARBUDA

1977 E	72,000
• SAINT JOHNS	24,359

ARGENTINA

1980 C	27,947,446
Almirante Brown (★Buenos Aires)	331,919
Avellaneda (★Buenos Aires)	334,145
Bahía Blanca	223,818
Berazategui (★Buenos Aires)	201,862
Berisso (★Buenos Aires)	66,152
• BUENOS AIRES (★10,750,000)	2,922,829
Campana (★Buenos Aires)	54,832
Caseros (Tres de Febrero) (★Buenos Aires)	345,424
Catamarca (★90,000)	78,799
Comodoro Rivadavia	96,817
Concordia	94,222
Córdoba (★1,070,000)	993,055
Corrientes	180,612
Esteban Echeverría (★Buenos Aires)	188,923
Florencio Varela (★Buenos Aires)	173,452
Formosa	93,603
General San Martín (★Buenos Aires)	385,625
General Sarmiento (San Miguel) (★Buenos Aires)	502,926
Godoy Cruz (★Mendoza)	142,408
Gualeguaychú	51,400
Junín	62,458
Lanús (★Buenos Aires)	466,980
La Plata (★Buenos Aires)	477,175
La Rioja	67,043
Las Heras (★Mendoza)	101,579
Lomas de Zamora (★Buenos Aires)	510,130
Mar del Plata	414,696
Mendoza (★650,000)	119,088
Mercedes	50,992
Merlo (★Buenos Aires)	292,587
Moreno (★Buenos Aires)	194,440
Morón (★Buenos Aires)	598,420
Necochea	51,069
Neuquén	90,089
Olavarría	64,097
Paraná	161,638
Pergamino	68,612
Pilar (★Buenos Aires)	84,429
Posadas	143,889
Presidencia Roque Sáenz Peña	49,341
Punta Alta	56,620
Quilmes (★Buenos Aires)	446,587
Rafaela	53,273
Resistencia	220,104
Río Cuarto	110,254
Rosario (★1,045,000)	938,120
Salta	260,744
San Carlos de Bariloche	48,980
San Fernando (★Buenos Aires)	133,624
San Francisco (★58,536)	51,932
San Isidro (★Buenos Aires)	289,170
San Juan (★300,000)	118,046
San Justo (★Buenos Aires)	949,566
San Lorenzo (★Rosario)	96,891
San Luis	70,999
San Miguel de Tucumán (★525,000)	392,888
San Nicolás de los Arroyos	98,495
San Rafael	70,959
San Salvador de Jujuy	124,950
Santa Fe	292,165
Santiago del Estero (★200,000)	148,758
San Vincente (★Buenos Aires)	55,803
Tandil	79,429
Tigre (★Buenos Aires)	206,349
Trelew	52,372
Vicente López (★Buenos Aires)	291,072
Villa Krause (★San Juan)	66,693
Villa María	67,560
Villa Nueva (★Mendoza)	164,670
Zárate	67,143

ARUBA

1987 E	64,763
• ORANJESTAD	19,800

AUSTRALIA

1986 C	15,602,156
Adelaide (★977,721)	14,157
Albury (★62,697)	38,704
Auburn (★Sydney)	47,147
Ballarat (★75,210)	34,806
Bankstown (★Sydney)	151,570
Bendigo (★62,380)	30,704
Berwick (★Melbourne)	48,677
Blacktown (★Sydney)	192,442
Blue Mountains (★Sydney)	63,866
Box Hill (★Melbourne)	45,785
Brisbane (★1,149,401)	705,755
Broadmeadows (★Melbourne)	101,144
Brunswick (★Melbourne)	41,362
Camberwell (★Melbourne)	83,792
Campbelltown (★Sydney)	121,297
CANBERRA (★271,362)	247,194
Canning (★Perth)	60,736
Canterbury (★Sydney)	128,502
Caulfield (★Melbourne)	67,718
Coburg (★Melbourne)	52,885
Dandenong (★Melbourne)	56,461
Darwin (★72,937)	66,131
Doncaster (★Melbourne)	99,269
Enfield (★Adelaide)	63,528
Essendon (★Melbourne)	53,977
Fairfield (★Sydney)	153,522
Footscray (★Melbourne)	47,330
Frankston (★Melbourne)	83,819
Geelong (★139,792)	13,441
Gosford	109,278
Gosnells (★Perth)	60,610
Heidelberg (★Melbourne)	61,917
Hobart (★175,082)	47,356
Holroyd (★Sydney)	78,237
Hurstville (★Sydney)	63,219

▲ Population of an entire municipality, commune, or district, including rural area.
• Largest city in country.
★ Population or designation of the metropolitan area, including suburbs.
C Census. **E** Official estimate.
U Unofficial estimate.

▲ Bevölkerung eines ganzen städtischen Verwaltungsgebietes, eines Kommunalbezirkes oder eines Distrikts, einschliesslich ländlicher Gebiete.
• Grösste Stadt des Landes.
★ Bevölkerung oder Bezeichnung der Stadtregion einschliesslich Vororte.
C Volkszählung. **E** Offizielle Schätzung.
U Inoffizielle Schätzung.

▲ Población de un municipio, comuna o distrito entero, incluyendo sus áreas rurales.
• Ciudad más grande de un país.
★ Población o designación de un área metropolitana, incluyendo los suburbios.
C Censo. **E** Estimado oficial.
U Estimado no oficial.

▲ Population d'une municipalité, d'une commune ou d'un district, zone rurale incluse.
• Ville la plus peuplée du pays.
★ Population de l'agglomération (ou nom de la zone métropolitaine englobante).
C Recensement. **E** Estimation officielle.
U Estimation non officielle.

▲ População de um municipio, comuna ou distrito, inclusive as respectivas áreas rurais.
• Maior cidade de um país.
★ População ou indicação de uma área metropolitana.
C Censo. **E** Estimativa oficial.
U Estimativa não oficial.

Ipswich (★Brisbane)	71,861
Keilor (★Melbourne)	93,327
Knox (★Melbourne)	104,207
Kogarah (★Sydney)	45,949
Lake Macquarie (★Newcastle)	153,540
Launceston (★88,486)	61,492
Leichhardt (★Sydney)	56,303
Liverpool (★Sydney)	93,215
Logan (★Brisbane)	117,191
Malvern (★Melbourne)	41,777
Marion (★Adelaide)	69,695
Marrickville (★Sydney)	81,647
Melbourne (★2,832,893)	60,828
Melville (★Perth)	67,131
Mitcham (★Adelaide)	61,213
Moorabbin (★Melbourne)	95,291
Newcastle (★405,089)	129,490
Noarlunga (★Adelaide)	69,809
Northcote (★Melbourne)	48,552
North Sydney (★Sydney)	49,927
Nunawading (★Melbourne)	93,482
Oakleigh (★Melbourne)	55,764
Parramatta (★Sydney)	130,783
Penrith (★Sydney)	135,342
Perth (★994,472)	79,409
Prahran (★Melbourne)	43,051
Preston (★Melbourne)	80,551
Randwick (★Sydney)	115,620
Rockdale (★Sydney)	83,350
Rockhampton (★59,056)	56,742
Ryde (★Sydney)	89,252
Saint Kilda (★Melbourne)	45,889
Salisbury (★Adelaide)	96,618
Shoalhaven	55,980
Southport (★215,663)	130,304
Springvale (★Melbourne)	83,385
Stirling (★Perth)	164,687
Sunshine (★Melbourne)	94,413
• Sydney (★3,364,858)	86,311
Tea Tree Gully (★Adelaide)	73,838
Toowoomba	73,390
Townsville (★106,416)	82,809
Wagga Wagga	49,401
Wanneroo (★Perth)	126,053
Waverley (★Sydney)	59,847
Waverley (★Melbourne)	122,935
West Torrens (★Adelaide)	43,639
Willoughby (★Sydney)	51,893
Wollongong (★225,178)	167,863
Woodville (★Adelaide)	79,886
Woollahra (★Sydney)	51,057

AUSTRIA / Österreich

1981 C	7,555,338
Bruck an der Mur (★52,000)	15,068
Graz (★325,000)	243,166
Innsbruck (★185,000)	117,287
Klagenfurt (★115,000)	87,321
Leoben (★52,000)	31,989
Linz (★335,000)	199,910
Neunkirchen (★45,000)	10,764
Salzburg (★220,000)	139,426
Sankt Pölten (★67,000)	50,419
Steyr (★65,000)	38,942
Villach (★65,000)	52,692
Wels (★76,000)	51,060
• WIEN (VIENNA) (★1,875,000) (1988E)	1,480,688

BAHAMAS

1982 E	218,000
Freeport	25,000
• NASSAU	135,000

BAHRAIN / Al-Baḥrayn

1981 C	350,798
• AL-MANĀMAH (★224,643)	115,054
Al-Muḥarraq (★Al-Manāmah)	57,688

BANGLADESH

1981 C	87,119,965
Barisāl	172,905
Begamganj	69,623
Bhairab Bāzār	63,563
Bogra	68,749
Brāhmanbāria	87,570
Chāndpur	85,656
Chittagong (★1,391,877)	980,000
Chuādanga	76,000
Comilla	184,132
• DHAKA (DACCA) (★3,430,312)	2,365,695
Dinājpur	96,718
Farīdpur	66,579
Gopālpur	31,725
Gulshan (★Dhaka)	215,444
Jamālpur	91,815
Jessore	148,927
Jhenida	47,953
Khulna	648,359
Kishorganj	52,302
Kurīgrām	47,641
Kushtia	74,892
Mādārīpur	63,917
Mīrpur (★Dhaka)	349,031
Mymensingh	190,991
Naogaon	52,975
Nārāyanganj (★Dhaka)	405,562
Narsinghdi	76,841
Nawābganj	87,724
Noākhāli	59,065
Pābna	109,065
Patuākhāli	48,121
Rājshāhi	253,740
Rangpur	153,174
Saidpur	126,608
Sātkhira	52,156
Sherpur	48,214
Sirājganj	106,774
Sītākunda (★Chittagong)	237,520
Sylhet	168,371
Tangail	77,518
Tongi (★Dhaka)	94,580

BARBADOS

1980 C	244,228
• BRIDGETOWN (★115,000)	7,466

BELGIUM / België / Belgique

1987 E	9,864,751
Aalst (Alost) (★Bruxelles)	77,113
Anderlecht (★Bruxelles)	88,849
Antwerpen (★1,100,000)	479,748
Bastogne (▲11,699)	6,900
Brugge (Bruges) (★223,000)	117,755
• BRUXELLES (★2,385,000)	136,920
Charleroi (★480,000)	209,395
Etterbeek (★Bruxelles)	44,240
Forest (★Bruxelles)	48,266
Genk (★Hasselt)	61,391
Gent (Gand) (★465,000)	233,856
Hasselt (★290,000)	65,563
Ixelles (★Bruxelles)	76,241
Kortrijk (Courtrai) (★202,000)	76,216
La Louvière (★147,000)	76,340
Leuven (Louvain) (★173,000)	84,583
Liège (Luik) (★750,000)	200,891
Mechelen (Malines) (★121,000)	75,808
Molenbeek-St.-Jean (★Bruxelles)	69,764
Mons (Bergen) (★242,000)	89,697
Mouscron (★Lille, France)	53,713
Namur (★147,000)	102,670
Oostende (Ostende) (★122,000)	68,318
Roeselare (Roulers)	51,963
Saint-Gilles (★Bruxelles)	42,482
Schaerbeek (★Bruxelles)	104,919
Seraing (★Liège)	61,731
Sint-Niklaas (Saint-Nicolas)	68,082
Spa	9,645
Tournai (Doornik) (▲66,998)	44,900
Uccle (★Bruxelles)	75,876
Verviers (★101,000)	53,498
Waterloo (★Bruxelles)	25,232
Woluwe-Saint-Lambert (Sint-Lambrechts-Woluwe) (★Bruxelles)	47,887

BELIZE

1985 E	166,400
• Belize City	47,000
BELMOPAN	4,500

BENIN / Bénin

1984 E	3,825,000
Abomey	53,000
• Cotonou	478,000
Natitingou (1975E)	51,000
Ouidah (1979E)	53,000
Parakou	92,000
PORTO-NOVO	164,000

BERMUDA

1985 E	56,000
• HAMILTON (★15,000)	1,676

BHUTAN / Druk-Yul

1982 E	1,333,000
• THIMPHU	12,000

BOLIVIA

1985 E	6,429,226
Cochabamba	317,251
• LA PAZ	992,592
Oruro	178,393
Potosí	113,380
Santa Cruz	441,717
SUCRE	86,609
Tarija	60,621

BOPHUTHATSWANA

1982 E	1,347,000
• Ga-Rankuwa (1980C)	48,300
Mafikeng (★16,000) (1980C)	6,500
MMABATHO (★Mafikeng) (1977E)	9,062

BOTSWANA

1986 E	1,127,900
Francistown	43,837
• GABORONE	95,163
Selebi Phikwe	41,382

BRAZIL / Brasil

1985 E	135,564,395
Alagoinhas (▲116,959)	87,500
Alegrete (▲71,898)	56,700
Alvorada	105,730
Americana	156,030
Anápolis	225,840
Apucarana (▲92,812)	73,700
Aracaju	360,013
Araçatuba	129,304
Araguari (▲96,035)	84,300
Arapiraca (▲147,879)	91,400
Araraquara (▲145,042)	87,500
Araras (▲71,652)	59,900
Araxá	61,418
Assis (▲74,238)	63,100
Bagé (▲106,155)	70,800
Barbacena (▲99,337)	80,200
Barra do Piraí (▲71,931)	55,700
Barra Mansa (★Volta Redonda)	149,200
Barretos	80,202
Bauru	220,105
Bayeux (★João Pessoa)	67,182
Belém (★1,200,000)	1,116,578
Belford Roxo (★Rio de Janeiro)	340,700
Belo Horizonte (★2,950,000)	2,114,429
Betim (★Belo Horizonte)	96,810
Blumenau	192,074
Botucatu (▲71,139)	62,600
Bragança Paulista (▲105,099)	76,300
BRASÍLIA	1,567,709
Caçapava (▲64,213)	56,600
Cachoeira do Sul (▲91,492)	58,900
Cachoeirinha (★Porto Alegre)	73,117
Cachoeiro de Itapemirim (▲138,156)	95,000
Campina Grande	279,929
Campinas (★1,125,000)	841,016
Campo Grande	384,398
Campos (▲366,716)	187,900
Campos Elyseos (★Rio de Janeiro)	188,200
Canoas (★Porto Alegre)	261,222
Carapicuíba (★São Paulo)	265,856
Carazinho (▲62,108)	48,500
Cariacica (★Vitória)	74,300
Caruaru (▲190,794)	152,100
Cascavel (▲200,485)	123,100
Castanhal (▲89,703)	71,200
Catanduva (▲80,309)	71,400
Caucaia (★Fortaleza)	78,500
Cavaleiro (★Recife)	106,600
Caxias (▲148,230)	66,300
Caxias do Sul	266,809
Chapecó (▲100,997)	64,200
Coelho da Rocha (★Rio de Janeiro)	164,400
Colatina (▲106,260)	58,600
Colombo (★Curitiba)	65,900
Conselheiro Lafaiete	77,958
Contagem (★Belo Horizonte)	152,700
Corumbá (▲80,666)	65,800
Crato (▲86,371)	52,700
Criciúma (▲128,410)	85,900
Cruz Alta (▲71,817)	58,300
Cruzeiro	63,918
Cubatão (★Santos)	98,322
Cuiabá (▲279,651)	220,400
Curitiba (★1,700,000)	1,279,205
Diadema (★São Paulo)	320,187
Divinópolis	139,940
Dourados (▲123,757)	89,200
Duque de Caxias (★Rio de Janeiro)	353,200
Embu (★São Paulo)	119,791
Erechim (▲70,709)	54,300
Esteio (★Porto Alegre)	58,964
Feira de Santana (▲355,201)	278,600
Ferraz de Vasconcelos (★São Paulo)	68,831
Florianópolis (★365,000)	178,400
Fortaleza (★1,825,000)	1,582,414
Foz do Iguaçu (▲182,101)	124,900
Franca	182,820
Garanhuns	73,100
Goiânia (★990,000)	923,333
Governador Valadares (▲216,957)	192,300
Guaratinguetá (▲93,534)	80,400
Guarujá (★Santos)	83,500
Guarulhos (★São Paulo)	571,700
Ijuí (▲82,064)	64,400
Ilhéus (▲145,810)	79,400
Imperatriz (▲235,453)	119,500
Ipatinga (★270,000)	149,100
Ipiíba (★Rio de Janeiro)	116,200
Itabira (▲81,771)	66,300
Itabuna (▲167,543)	142,200
Itajaí	104,232
Itajubá (▲69,675)	61,500
Itapecerica da Serra (★São Paulo)	65,500
Itapetininga (▲105,512)	76,700
Itapevi (★São Paulo)	66,825
Itaquaquecetuba (★São Paulo)	91,366
Itaquari (★Vitória)	163,900
Itaúna	61,446
Itu (▲92,786)	77,900
Ituiutaba (▲85,365)	74,900
Itumbiara (▲78,844)	57,200
Jaboatão (★Recife)	82,900
Jacareí	149,061
Jaú (▲92,547)	74,500
Jequié (▲127,070)	92,100
João Pessoa (★550,000)	348,500
Joinvile	302,877
Juàzeiro (★Petrolina)	78,600
Juàzeiro do Norte	159,806
Juiz de Fora	349,720
Jundiaí (▲313,652)	268,900
Lajes (▲143,246)	103,600
Lavras	52,100
Limeira	186,986
Linhares (▲122,453)	53,400
Londrina (▲346,676)	296,400
Lorena	63,230
Luziânia (▲98,408)	71,400
Macapá (▲168,839)	109,400
Maceió	482,195
Manaus	809,914
Marabá (▲133,559)	92,700
Marília (▲136,187)	116,100
Maringá	196,871
Mauá (★São Paulo)	269,321
Mesquita (★Rio de Janeiro)	161,300
Mogi das Cruzes (★São Paulo)	144,800
Mogi-Guaçu (▲91,994)	81,800
Mogi-Mirim (▲63,313)	52,300
Monjolo (★Rio de Janeiro)	113,900
Montes Claros (▲214,472)	183,500
Mossoró (▲158,723)	128,300
Muriaé (▲80,466)	57,600
Muribeca dos Guararapes (★Recife)	171,200
Natal	510,106
Neves (★Rio de Janeiro)	163,600
Nilópolis (★Rio de Janeiro)	112,800
Niterói (★Rio de Janeiro)	441,684
Nova Friburgo (▲143,529)	103,500
Nova Iguaçu (★Rio de Janeiro)	592,800
Novo Hamburgo (★Porto Alegre)	167,744
Olinda (★Recife)	316,600
Osasco (★São Paulo)	591,568
Ourinhos (▲65,841)	58,100
Paranaguá (▲94,809)	82,300
Paranavaí (▲75,511)	60,900
Parnaíba (▲116,206)	90,200
Parque Industrial (★Belo Horizonte)	228,400
Passo Fundo (▲137,843)	117,500
Passos (▲79,393)	65,500
Patos	74,298
Patos de Minas (▲99,027)	69,000
Paulo Afonso (▲86,182)	75,300
Pelotas (▲277,730)	210,300
Petrolina (★225,000)	92,100
Petrópolis (★Rio de Janeiro)	170,300
Pindamonhangaba (▲86,990)	64,100
Pinheirinho (★Curitiba)	51,600
Piracicaba (▲252,079)	211,000
Poá (★São Paulo)	66,006
Poços de Caldas	100,004
Ponta Grossa	223,154
Porto Alegre (★2,600,000)	1,272,121
Porto Velho (▲202,011)	152,700
Pouso Alegre (▲65,958)	58,300
Praia Grande (★Santos)	67,800
Presidente Prudente	155,883
Queimados (★Rio de Janeiro)	113,700
Recife (★2,625,000)	1,287,623
Ribeirão Prêto	383,125
Rio Branco (▲145,486)	109,800
Rio Claro	129,859
Rio de Janeiro (★10,150,000)	5,603,388
Rio Grande	164,221
Rio Verde (▲92,954)	59,400
Rondonópolis (▲101,642)	65,500
Salvador (★2,050,000)	1,804,438
Santa Bárbara d'Oeste	95,818
Santa Cruz do Sul (▲115,288)	60,300
Santa Maria (▲196,827)	163,900
Santana do Livramento	60,100
Santarém (▲226,618)	120,800
Santa Rita (★João Pessoa)	60,100
Santo André (★São Paulo)	635,129
Santo Ângelo (▲107,559)	57,700
Santos (★1,065,000)	460,100
São Bernardo do Campo (★São Paulo)	562,485
São Caetano do Sul (★São Paulo)	171,005
São Carlos	140,383
São Gonçalo (★Rio de Janeiro)	262,400
São João da Boa Vista (▲61,653)	50,400
São João del Rei (▲74,385)	61,400
São João de Meriti (★Rio de Janeiro)	241,700
São José do Rio Prêto	229,221
São José dos Campos	372,578
São José dos Pinhais (★Curitiba)	64,100
São Leopoldo (★Porto Alegre)	114,065
São Lourenco da Mata (★Recife)	65,936
São Luís (★600,000)	227,900
• São Paulo (★15,175,000)	10,063,110
São Vicente (★Santos)	239,778
Sapucaia do Sul (★Porto Alegre)	91,820
Sete Lagoas	121,418
Sete Pontes (★Rio de Janeiro)	72,300
Sobral (▲112,275)	69,400
Sorocaba	327,468
Suzano (★São Paulo)	128,924
Taboão da Serra (★São Paulo)	122,112
Tatuí (▲69,358)	56,000
Taubaté	205,120
Teófilo Otoni (▲126,265)	82,700
Teresina (★525,000)	425,300
Teresópolis (▲115,859)	92,600
Timon (★Teresina)	68,300
Tubarão (▲82,082)	70,400
Uberaba	244,875
Uberlândia	312,024
Uruguaiana (▲105,862)	91,500
Varginha	74,630
Vicente de Carvalho (★Santos)	102,700
Vila Velha (★Vitória)	91,900
Vitória (★735,000)	201,500
Vitória da Conquista (▲198,150)	145,800
Vitória de Santo Antão (▲100,450)	67,800
Volta Redonda (★375,000)	219,267

BRUNEI

1981 C	192,832
• BANDAR SERI BEGAWAN (★64,000)	22,777
Seria	23,415

BULGARIA / Bâlgarija

1986 E	9,913,000
Blagoevgrad	67,766
Burgas	186,369
Dimitrovgrad	54,898
Gabrovo	81,688
Haskovo	89,273
Jambol	92,321
Kârdžali	56,906
Kazanlâk	61,780
Kjustendil	54,773
Loveč (1985E)	48,862
Mihajlovgrad	53,529
Pazardžik	79,198
Pernik	96,277
Pleven	132,206
Plovdiv	349,148
Razgrad	51,277
Ruse	186,428
Silistra	54,627
Sliven	104,345
• SOFIJA (★1,205,000)	1,119,152
Stara Zagora	153,538
Šumen	102,886
Tolbuhin	110,471
Varna	303,071
Veliko Târnovo	70,610
Vidin	63,813
Vraca	77,934

BURKINA FASO

1985 C	7,964,705
Bobo Dioulasso	228,668
Koudougou	51,926
• OUSGADOUGOU	441,514
Ouahigouya	38,902

BURMA / Myanmar

1983 C	35,306,189
Bago (Pegu)	150,447
Dawei (Tavoy) (1970E)	53,000
Henzada (1970E)	85,000
Mandalay	532,895
Mawlamyine (Moulmein)	219,991
Monywa	106,873
Myingyan (1970E)	65,000

▲ Population of an entire municipality, commune, or district, including rural area.
• Largest city in country.
★ Population or designation of the metropolitan area, including suburbs.
C Census. E Official estimate. U Unofficial estimate.

▲ Bevölkerung eines ganzen städtischen Verwaltungsgebietes, eines Kommunalbezirkes oder eines Distrikts, einschliesslich ländlicher Gebiete.
• Grösste Stadt des Landes.
★ Bevölkerung oder Bezeichnung der Stadtregion einschliesslich Vororte.
C Volkszählung. E Offizielle Schätzung. U Inoffizielle Schätzung.

Population of Cities and Towns / Einwohnerzahlen von Grossstädten / Habitantes en las Ciudades y Poblaciones
Population des Grands Centres et des Villes / População dos Centros Urbanos
303

Pathein (Bassein)	144,092
Prome (Pyè) (1970E)	65,000
Sittwe (Akyab)	107,607
Taunggyi	107,907
• YANGON (RANGOON) (★2,800,000)	2,458,712

BURUNDI

1986 E	4,782,000
• BUJUMBURA	273,000

CAMBODIA / Kâmpŭchéa

1986 E	7,492,000
Kâmpóng Saôm (1981E)	53,000
• PHNUM PÉNH	700,000

CAMEROON / Cameroun

1986 E	10,446,000
Bafoussam (1985E)	89,000
Bamenda (1985E)	72,000
• Douala	1,029,731
Foumban (1985E)	50,000
Garoua (1985E)	96,000
Kumba (1985E)	67,000
Maroua	103,653
Ngaoundéré (1985E)	61,000
Nkongsamba	123,149
YAOUNDÉ	653,670

CANADA

1986 C	25,354,064

CANADA: ALBERTA

1986 C	2,375,278
Calgary (★671,326)	636,104
Edmonton (★785,465)	573,982
Lethbridge	58,841
Medicine Hat (★50,734)	41,804
Red Deer	54,425

CANADA: BRITISH COLUMBIA

1986 C	2,889,207
Burnaby (★Vancouver)	145,161
Kamloops	61,773
Kelowna (★89,730)	61,213
Matsqui (★88,420)	51,449
Nanaimo (★60,420)	49,029
Prince George	67,621
Richmond (★Vancouver)	108,492
Vancouver (★1,380,729)	431,147
Victoria (★255,547)	66,303

CANADA: MANITOBA

1986 C	1,071,232
Winnipeg (★625,304)	594,551

CANADA: NEW BRUNSWICK

1986 C	710,422
Fredericton (★65,768)	44,352
Moncton (★102,084)	55,468
Saint John (★121,265)	76,381

CANADA: NEWFOUNDLAND

1986 C	568,349
Saint John's (★161,901)	96,216

CANADA: NORTHWEST TERRITORIES

1986 C	52,238
Yellowknife	11,753

CANADA: NOVA SCOTIA

1986 C	873,199
Dartmouth (★Halifax)	65,243
Halifax (★295,990)	113,577
Sydney (★119,470)	27,754

CANADA: ONTARIO

1986 C	9,113,515
Barrie (★67,703)	48,287
Brampton (★Toronto)	188,498
Brantford (★90,521)	76,146
Burlington (★Hamilton)	116,675
Cambridge (Galt) (★Kitchener)	79,920
Cornwall (★51,719)	46,425
East York (★Toronto)	101,085
Etobicoke (★Toronto)	302,973
Gloucester (★Ottawa)	89,810
Guelph (★85,962)	78,235
Hamilton (★557,029)	306,728
Kingston (★122,350)	55,050
Kitchener (★311,195)	150,604
London (★342,302)	269,140
Markham (★Toronto)	114,597
Mississauga (★Toronto)	374,005
Nepean (★Ottawa)	95,490
Niagara Falls (★Saint Catharines)	72,107
North Bay (★57,422)	50,623
North York (★Toronto)	556,297
Oakville (★Toronto)	87,107
Oshawa (★203,543)	123,651
OTTAWA (★819,263)	300,763
Peterborough (★87,083)	61,049
Saint Catharines (★343,258)	123,455
Sarnia (★85,700)	49,033
Sault Sainte Marie (★84,617)	80,905
Scarborough (★Toronto)	484,676
Sudbury (★148,877)	88,717
Thunder Bay (★122,217)	112,272
• Toronto (★3,427,168)	612,289
Waterloo (★Kitchener)	58,718
Windsor (★253,988)	193,111
York (★Toronto)	135,401

CANADA: PRINCE EDWARD ISLAND

1986 C	126,646
Charlottetown (★53,868)	15,776

CANADA: QUÉBEC

1986 C	6,540,276
Beauport (★Québec)	62,869
Brossard (★Montréal)	57,441
Charlesbourg (★Québec)	68,996
Chicoutimi (★158,468)	61,083
Drummondville (★56,283)	36,020
Gatineau (★Ottawa)	81,244
Hull (★Ottawa)	58,722
Jonquière (★Chicoutimi)	58,467
La Salle (★Montréal)	75,621
Laval (★Montréal)	284,164
Longueuil (★Montréal)	125,441
Montréal (★2,921,357)	1,015,420
Montréal-Nord (★Montréal)	90,303
Québec (★603,267)	164,580
Sainte-Foy (★Québec)	69,615
Saint-Hubert (★Montréal)	66,218
Saint-Jean-sur-Richelieu (★59,958)	34,745
Saint-Laurent (★Montréal)	67,002
Saint-Léonard (★Montréal)	75,947
Shawinigan (★61,965)	21,470
Sherbrooke (★129,960)	74,438
Trois-Rivières (★128,888)	50,122
Verdun (★Montréal)	60,246

CANADA: SASKATCHEWAN

1986 C	1,010,198
Regina (★186,521)	175,064
Saskatoon (★200,665)	177,641

CANADA: YUKON

1986 C	23,504
Whitehorse	15,199

CAPE VERDE / Cabo Verde

1980 C	296,093
Mindelo	36,265
• PRAIA	37,480

CAYMAN ISLANDS

1988 E	25,900
• GEORGETOWN	13,700

CENTRAL AFRICAN REPUBLIC / République centrafricaine

1984 E	2,517,000
• BANGUI	473,817
Bouar (1982E)	48,000

CHAD / Tchad

1979 E	4,405,000
Abéché	54,000
Moundou	66,000
• N'DJAMENA	303,000
Sarh	65,000

CHILE

1982 C	11,329,736
Antofagasta	185,486
Apoquindo (★Santiago)	175,735
Arica	139,320
Calama	81,684
Cerrillos (★Santiago)	67,013
Cerro Navia (★Santiago)	137,777
Chillán	118,163
Concepción (★675,000)	267,891
Conchalí (★Santiago)	157,884
Copiapó	69,045
Coquimbo	62,186
Coronel (★Concepción)	65,918
Curicó	60,550
El Bosque (★Santiago)	143,717
Huechuraba (★Santiago)	56,313
Independencia (★Santiago) (1985E)	83,000
Iquique	110,153
La Cisterna (★Santiago)	95,863
La Florida (★Santiago)	191,883
La Granja (★Santiago)	109,168
La Pintana (★Santiago)	73,932
La Reina (★Santiago)	80,452
La Serena	83,283
Linares	46,433
Lo Barnechea (★Santiago)	24,258
Lo Espejo (★Santiago)	124,462
Lo Prado Arriba (★Santiago)	103,575
Los Ángeles	70,529
Lota (★Concepción)	47,133
Macul (★Santiago)	113,100
Maipú (★Santiago)	114,117
Ñuñoa (★Santiago)	168,919
Osorno	95,286
Ovalle	43,023
Pedro Aguirre Cerda (★Santiago)	145,207
Peñalolén (★Santiago)	137,298
Providencia (★Santiago)	115,449
Pudahuel (★Santiago)	97,578
Puente Alto (★Santiago)	109,239
Puerto Montt	84,410
Punta Arenas	95,332
Quilpué (★Valparaíso)	84,136
Quinta Normal (★Santiago)	128,989
Rancagua	139,925
Recoleta (★Santiago)	164,292
Renca (★Santiago)	93,928
San Antonio	61,486
San Bernardo (★Santiago)	117,132
San Joaquín (★Santiago)	123,904
San Miguel (★Santiago)	88,764
San Ramón (★Santiago)	99,410
• SANTIAGO (★4,100,000)	232,667
Talca	128,544
Talcahuano (★Concepción)	202,368
Temuco	157,297
Valdivia	100,046
Vallenar	38,375
Valparaíso (★675,000)	265,355
Villa Alemana (★Valparaíso)	55,766
Viña del Mar (★Valparaíso)	244,899
Vitacura (★Santiago)	72,038

CHINA / Zhongguo

1987 E	1,057,210,000
Abagnar Qi (▲100,700) (1986E)	71,700
Acheng (1985E)	100,304
Aihui (▲135,000) (1986E)	76,700
Aksu (▲345,900) (1986E)	143,100
Altay (▲141,700) (1986E)	62,800
Anci (Langfang) (▲522,800) (1986E)	122,100
Anda (▲425,500) (1986E)	130,200
Ankang (1985E)	89,188
Anqing (▲433,900) (1986E)	213,200
Anshan	1,300,000
Anshun (▲214,700) (1986E)	128,800
Anyang (▲541,900) (1986E)	361,200
Baicheng (▲282,000) (1986E)	198,600
Baiquan (1985E)	50,996
Baiyin (▲301,900) (1986E)	157,100
Baoding (▲535,100) (1986E)	423,200
Baoji (▲359,500) (1986E)	286,200
Baoshan (▲688,400) (1986E)	52,300
Baotou (Paotow)	1,120,000
Baoying (1985E)	50,479
Bei'an (▲440,500) (1986E)	199,500
Beihai (▲175,900) (1986E)	119,000
BEIJING (PEKING) (★6,450,000)	5,970,000
Beipiao (▲603,700) (1986E)	180,900
Bengbu (▲612,600) (1986E)	403,900
Benxi (Penhsi)	840,000
Bijie (1985E)	54,871
Binxian (1982C)	127,326
Binxian (▲177,900) (1986E)	86,700
Boli (1985E)	61,990
Bose (▲271,400) (1986E)	82,000
Boshan (1975U)	100,000
Boxian (1985E)	63,222
Boxing (1982C)	57,554
Boyang (1985E)	60,688
Butha Qi (Zalantun) (▲389,500) (1986E)	111,300
Cangshan (Bianzhuang) (1982C)	79,334
Cangzhou (▲293,600) (1986E)	196,700
Changchun (▲1,910,000)	1,740,000
Changde (▲220,800) (1986E)	178,200
Changge (1982C)	67,002
Changji (▲233,400) (1986E)	110,500
Changqing (1982C)	65,094
Changsha	1,190,000
Changshou (1985E)	51,923
Changshu (▲998,000) (1986E)	281,300
Changtu (1985E)	49,937
Changyi (1982C)	64,513
Changzhi (▲463,400) (1986E)	273,000
Changzhou (Changchow) (1986E)	522,700
Chao'an (▲1,214,500) (1986E)	265,400
Chaoxian (▲739,500) (1986E)	116,800
Chaoyang, Guangdong prov. (1985E)	85,968
Chaoyang, Liaoning prov. (▲318,900) (1986E)	180,300
Chengde (▲330,400) (1986E)	226,600
Chengdu (Chengtu) (▲2,640,000)	1,810,000
Chenghai (1985E)	50,631
Chenxian (▲191,900) (1986E)	143,500
Chifeng (Ulanhad) (▲882,900) (1986E)	299,000
Chongqing (Chungking) (▲2,830,000)	2,450,000
Chuxian (▲365,000) (1986E)	113,300
Chuxiong (▲379,400) (1986E)	67,700
Da'an (1985E)	70,552
Dachangzhen (1975U)	50,000
Dalian (Dairen)	1,680,000
Dandong (1986E)	579,800
Daqing (▲850,000)	620,000
Dashiqiao (1985E)	68,898
Datong (1985E)	55,529
Datong (▲1,020,000)	790,000
Dawa (1985E)	142,581
Daxian (▲209,400) (1986E)	142,000
Dehui (1985E)	60,247
Dengfeng (1982C)	49,746
Deqing (1982C)	48,726
Deyang (▲753,400) (1986E)	184,800
Dezhou (▲276,200) (1986E)	161,300
Didao (1975U)	50,000
Dinghai (1985E)	50,161
Dongchuan (Xincun) (▲275,100) (1986E)	67,400
Dongguan (▲1,208,500) (1986E)	254,900
Dongsheng (▲121,300) (1986E)	57,500
Dongtai (1985E)	65,788
Dongying (▲514,400) (1986E)	178,100
Dukou (▲551,200) (1986E)	380,200
Dunhua (▲448,000) (1986E)	217,100
Duyun (▲386,600) (1986E)	123,800
Echeng (▲938,000) (1986E)	217,400
Enshi (▲679,000) (1986E)	84,300
Erenhot (1986E)	7,200
Ergun Zuoqi (1985E)	55,970
Feixian (1982C)	73,246
Fengcheng (1985E)	66,745
Foshan (▲312,700) (1986E)	243,500
Fujin (1985E)	60,948
Fuling (▲973,500) (1986E)	166,300
Fushun (Funan)	1,270,000
Fuxian (Wafangdian) (▲960,700) (1986E)	246,200
Fuxin	690,000
Fuyang (▲195,200) (1986E)	143,400
Fuyu, Heilongjiang prov. (1985E)	48,670
Fuyu, Jilin prov. (1985E)	98,373
Fuzhou, Fujian prov. (▲1,210,000)	890,000
Fuzhou, Jiangxi prov. (▲171,800) (1986E)	106,700
Gaixian (1985E)	67,587
Ganhe (1985E)	48,128
Ganzhou (▲346,000) (1986E)	191,600
Gaoqing (Tianzhen) (1982C)	70,411
Gaoyou (1985E)	57,844
Gejiu (Kokiu) (▲341,700) (1986E)	193,600
Golmud (1986E)	60,300
Gongchangling (1982C)	49,281
Guanghua (▲420,000) (1986E)	104,400
Guangyuan (▲805,500) (1986E)	162,200
Guangzhou (Canton) (▲3,360,000)	3,050,000
Guanxian, Shandong prov. (1982C)	49,782
Guanxian, Sichuan prov. (1985E)	65,039
Guilin (Kweilin) (▲457,500) (1986E)	324,200
Guixian (1985E)	61,970
Guiyang (Kweiyang) (▲1,400,000)	1,010,000
Haicheng (▲984,800) (1986E)	210,700
Haifeng (1985E)	50,401
Haikou (▲289,600) (1986E)	209,200
Hailar (1986E)	180,000
Hailin (1985E)	58,909
Hailong (Meihekou) (▲534,200) (1986E)	117,500
Hailun (1985E)	83,448
Haiyang (Dongcun) (1982C)	77,098
Hami (Kumul) (▲270,300) (1986E)	146,400
Hancheng (▲304,200) (1986E)	66,600
Handan (▲1,010,000)	850,000
Hangu (1975U)	100,000
Hangzhou (Hangchow)	1,270,000
Hanzhong (▲415,000) (1986E)	151,700
Harbin	2,670,000
Hebi (▲321,600) (1986E)	158,500
Hechi (▲266,800) (1986E)	74,400
Hechuan (1985E)	65,237
Hefei (▲900,000)	720,000
Hegang (1986E)	588,300
Helong (1985E)	62,665
Hengshui (▲286,500) (1986E)	83,100
Hengyang (▲601,300) (1986E)	419,200
Heshan (▲109,600) (1986E)	42,000
Heze (Caozhou) (▲1,001,500) (1986E)	115,400
Hohhot (▲810,000)	650,000
Hongjiang (▲67,000) (1986E)	54,300
Horqin Youyi Qianqi (Ulan Hot) (▲192,100) (1986E)	129,100
Hotan (▲122,800) (1986E)	71,700
Houma (▲158,500) (1986E)	67,000
Huadian (1985E)	75,183
Huai'an (1985E)	65,673
Huaibei (▲447,200) (1986E)	252,100
Huaide (▲899,400) (1986E)	187,600
Huaihua (▲427,100) (1986E)	102,000
Huainan (▲1,090,000)	690,000
Huaiyin (Wangying) (▲382,500) (1986E)	201,700
Huanan (1985E)	66,596
Huanggang (1982C)	65,961
Huangshi (1986E)	451,900
Huayun (Huarong) (▲313,500) (1986E)	81,000
Huinan (Chaoyang) (1985E)	52,429
Huizhou (▲182,100) (1986E)	117,000
Hulan (1985E)	74,989
Hunjiang (Badaojiang) (▲687,700) (1986E)	442,600
Huzhou (▲964,400) (1986E)	208,500
Jiading (1985E)	60,718
Jiamusi (Kiamusze) (▲557,700) (1986E)	429,800
Ji'an (▲184,300) (1986E)	132,200
Jiangling (1985E)	77,887
Jiangmen (▲231,700) (1986E)	168,800
Jiangyin (1985E)	66,476
Jiangyou (1985E)	72,663
Jian'ou (1985E)	55,180
Jiaohe (1985E)	51,504
Jiaojiang (▲385,200) (1986E)	82,300
Jiaoxian (1985E)	51,869
Jiaozuo (▲509,900) (1986E)	335,400
Jiawang (1975U)	50,000
Jiaxing (▲686,500) (1986E)	210,200
Jiayuguan (▲102,100) (1986E)	73,800
Jiexiu (1985E)	51,300
Jieyang (1985E)	98,531
Jilin (Kirin)	1,170,000
Jinan (Tsinan)	1,460,000
Jinchang (Baijiazui) (▲136,000) (1986E)	90,500
Jincheng (▲612,700) (1986E)	99,900
Jingdezhen (Kingtechen) (▲569,700) (1986E)	304,000
Jingmen (▲946,500) (1986E)	227,000
Jinhua (▲799,900) (1986E)	147,800
Jining, Nei Monggol prov. (1986E)	163,300
Jining, Shandong prov. (▲765,700) (1986E)	222,600
Jinshi (▲219,700) (1986E)	73,700
Jinxi (▲634,300) (1986E)	223,100
Jinxian (1985E)	95,761
Jinzhou (Chinchou) (▲790,000)	690,000
Jishou (▲194,500) (1986E)	59,500
Jishu (1985E)	75,587
Jiujiang (▲382,300) (1986E)	248,500
Jiuquan (Suzhou) (▲269,900) (1986E)	56,300
Jiutai (1985E)	63,021
Jixi (▲820,000)	700,000
Jixian (1985E)	59,725
Juancheng (1982C)	54,110
Junan (Shizilu) (1982C)	90,222
Junxian (▲423,400) (1986E)	97,000
Juxian (1982C)	51,666
Kaifeng (▲629,100) (1986E)	458,800
Kaili (▲342,100) (1986E)	96,600
Kaiping (1985E)	54,145
Kaiyuan (1985E)	85,762
Kaiyuan (▲342,100) (1986E)	96,600
Karamay (1986E)	185,300
Kashi (▲194,500) (1986E)	146,300
Keshan (1985E)	65,088
Korla (▲219,000) (1986E)	129,400
Kunming (▲1,520,000)	1,280,000
Kunshan (1985E)	44,645
Kuqa (1985E)	63,847
Kuytun (1986E)	60,200
Laiwu (▲1,041,800) (1986E)	143,500
Langxiang (1985E)	64,658
Lanxi (1985E)	53,236
Lanxi (▲606,800) (1986E)	70,500
Lanzhou (Lanchow) (▲1,390,000)	1,270,000
Lechang (1986E)	56,913
Lengshuijiang (▲277,600) (1986E)	101,700

▲ Población de un municipio, comuna o distrito entero, incluyendo sus áreas rurales.
• Ciudad más grande de un país.
★ Población o designación de un área metropolitana, incluyendo los suburbios.
C Censo. **E** Estimado oficial. **U** Estimado no oficial.

▲ Population d'une municipalité, d'une commune ou d'un district, zone rurale incluse.
• Ville la plus peuplée du pays.
★ Population de l'agglomération (ou nom de la zone métropolitaine englobante).
C Recensement. **E** Estimation officielle. **U** Estimation non officielle.

▲ População de um municipio, comuna ou distrito, inclusive as respectivas áreas rurais.
• Maior cidade de um país.
★ População ou indicação de uma área metropolitana.
C Censo. **E** Estimativa oficial. **U** Estimativa não oficial.

Lengshuitan (▲362,000) (1986E)	60,900
Leshan (▲972,300) (1986E)	307,300
Lhasa (▲107,700) (1986E)	84,400
Lianyungang (Xinpu) (▲459,400) (1986E)	288,000
Liaocheng (▲724,300) (1986E)	119,000
Liaoyang (▲576,900) (1986E)	442,600
Liaoyuan (1986E)	370,400
Liling (▲856,300) (1986E)	107,100
Linfen (▲530,100) (1986E)	157,600
Lingling (▲515,300) (1986E)	72,700
Lingyuan (1985E)	66,825
Linhai (1985E)	52,653
Linhe (▲365,900) (1986E)	99,800
Linkou (1985E)	52,936
Linqing (▲603,000) (1986E)	87,000
Linqu (1982C)	84,196
Linxia (▲150,200) (1986E)	72,900
Liuzhou	660,000
Longjiang (1985E)	51,156
Longyan (▲378,500) (1986E)	114,500
Loudi (▲254,300) (1986E)	84,200
Lu'an (▲163,400) (1986E)	122,600
Lufeng (1985E)	53,015
Luohe (▲159,100) (1986E)	102,300
Luoyang (Loyang) (▲1,060,000)	740,000
Luzhou (▲360,300) (1986E)	237,800
Ma'anshan (▲367,000) (1986E)	258,900
Manzhouli (1986E)	116,600
Maoming (▲434,900) (1986E)	118,600
Meixian (▲740,600) (1986E)	169,100
Mengyin (1982C)	70,602
Mianyang, Sichuan prov. (▲848,500) (1986E)	233,900
Minhang (1975U)	60,000
Mishan (1985E)	54,919
Mixian (1982C)	64,776
Mudanjiang	630,000
Nahe (1985E)	49,725
N'aizishen (1985E)	51,982
Nancha (1975U)	50,000
Nanchang (▲1,190,000)	1,030,000
Nanchong (▲238,100) (1986E)	158,000
Nanjing (Nanking)	2,290,000
Nanning (▲960,000)	690,000
Nanpiao (1982C)	67,274
Nanping (▲420,800) (1986E)	157,100
Nantong (▲411,000) (1986E)	308,800
Nanyang (▲294,800) (1986E)	199,400
Neihuang (1982C)	56,039
Neijiang (▲298,500) (1986E)	191,100
Ning'an (1985E)	49,334
Ningbo (▲1,030,000)	560,000
Ningyang (1982C)	55,424
Nong'an (1985E)	55,966
Nunjiang (1985E)	59,276
Orogen Zizhiqi (1985E)	48,042
Panshan (▲343,100) (1986E)	248,100
Panshi (1985E)	59,270
Pingdingshan (▲819,900) (1986E)	363,200
Pingliang (▲362,500) (1986E)	85,400
Pingxiang, Jiangxi prov. (▲1,286,700) (1986E)	368,700
Pingyi (1982C)	89,373
Pingyin (1982C)	62,827
Potou (▲456,100) (1986E)	59,000
Puqi (1985E)	65,239
Putian (▲265,400) (1986E)	64,600
Putuo (1985E)	50,962
Puyang (▲1,086,100) (1986E)	131,000
Qian Gorlos (1985E)	79,494
Qingdao (Tsingtao)	1,270,000
Qinggang (1985E)	43,075
Qingjiang, Jiangsu prov. (▲246,617) (1982C)	150,000
Qingjiang, Jiangxi prov. (1985E)	42,698
Qingyuan (1985E)	51,756
Qinhuangdao (Chinwangtao) (▲436,000) (1986E)	307,500
Qinzhou (▲923,400) (1986E)	97,100
Qiqihar (Tsitsihar) (▲1,300,000)	1,150,000
Qitaihe (▲309,900) (1986E)	166,400
Qixia (1982C)	54,158
Qixian (1982C)	53,041
Quanzhou (Chuanchou) (▲436,000) (1986E)	157,000
Qujing (▲758,000) (1986E)	135,000
Quxian (▲704,800) (1986E)	124,000
Raoping (1985E)	54,831
Rizhao (▲970,300) (1986E)	93,300
Rongcheng (1982C)	52,878
Rugao (1985E)	50,643
Rui'an (1985E)	57,993
Sanmenxia (Shanxian) (▲150,000) (1986E)	79,000
Sanming (▲214,300) (1986E)	144,900
• Shanghai (★9,300,000)	7,100,000
Shangqiu (Zhuji) (▲199,400) (1986E)	135,400
Shangrao (▲142,500) (1986E)	113,000
Shangshui (1982C)	50,191
Shantou (Swatow) (▲770,000)	550,000
Shanwei (1985E)	61,234
Shaoguan (1986E)	363,100
Shaowu (▲266,700) (1986E)	81,400
Shaoxing (▲250,900) (1986E)	167,100
Shaoyang (▲465,900) (1986E)	218,600
Shashi (1986E)	253,700
Shenxian (1982C)	50,208
Shenyang (Mukden) (▲4,290,000)	3,840,000
Shenzhen (▲231,900) (1986E)	189,600
Shiguaigou (1975U)	50,000
Shihezi (▲549,300)	304,700
Shijiazhuang	1,190,000
Shiyan (▲332,600) (1986E)	227,300
Shizuishan (▲317,400) (1986E)	225,500
Shouguang (1982C)	83,400
Shuangcheng (1985E)	91,163
Shuangliao (1985E)	67,326
Shuangyashan (1986E)	427,300
Shuicheng (▲2,216,500) (1986E)	363,500
Shulan (1986E)	50,582
Shunde (1985E)	50,262
Siping (▲357,800) (1986E)	280,100
Sishui (1982C)	82,990
Songjiang (1985E)	71,864
Songjianghe (1985E)	53,023
Suifenhe (▲21,700) (1986E)	13,900
Suihua (▲732,100) (1986E)	200,400
Suileng (1985E)	68,399
Suining (▲1,174,900) (1986E)	118,500
Suixian (▲1,281,600) (1986E)	187,700
Suqian (1985E)	50,742
Suxian (▲218,600) (1986E)	123,300
Suzhou (Soochow)	720,000
Tai'an (▲1,325,400) (1986E)	215,900
Taiyuan (▲1,930,000)	1,660,000
Taizhou (▲210,800)	143,200
Tancheng (1982C)	61,857
Tangshan (▲1,410,000)	1,060,000
Tao'an (1985E)	76,269
Tengxian (1985E)	53,254
Tianjin (Tientsin) (▲5,460,000)	4,880,000
Tianshui (▲953,200) (1986E)	209,500
Tiefa (▲146,367) (1982C)	60,000
Tieli (1985E)	102,527
Tieling (▲454,100) (1986E)	326,100
Tongchuan (▲393,200) (1986E)	268,900
Tonghua (▲367,400) (1986E)	290,200
Tongliao (▲253,100) (1986E)	190,100
Tongling (▲216,400) (1986E)	182,900
Tongren (1985E)	50,307
Tongxian (1985E)	97,168
Tumen (▲99,700) (1986E)	77,600
Tunxi (▲104,500) (1986E)	61,800
Turpan (▲196,800) (1986E)	52,300
Ürümqi	1,040,000
Wangkui (1985E)	52,021
Wangqing (1985E)	61,237
Wanxian (▲280,800) (1986E)	138,700
Weifang (▲1,042,200) (1986E)	312,500
Weihai (▲220,800) (1986E)	83,000
Weinan (▲699,400) (1986E)	111,300
Weishan (Xiazhen) (1982C)	57,932
Weixian (Hanting) (1982C)	50,180
Wenzhou (▲530,600) (1986E)	372,200
Wuchang (1985E)	64,403
Wuhai (1986E)	266,000
Wuhan	3,490,000
Wuhu (▲502,200) (1986E)	396,000
Wulian (Hongning) (1982C)	51,718
Wusong (1982C)	64,017
Wuwei (Liangzhou) (▲804,000) (1986E)	115,500
Wuxi (Wuhsi)	860,000
Wuzhong (▲402,400) (1986E)	48,600
Wuzhou (Wuchow) (▲261,500) (1986E)	194,800
Xiaguan (▲395,800) (1986E)	112,100
Xiamen (Amoy) (▲546,400) (1986E)	343,700
Xi'an (Sian) (▲2,390,000)	2,050,000
Xiangfan (▲421,200) (1986E)	314,900
Xiangtan (▲511,100) (1986E)	389,500
Xianning (▲402,200) (1986E)	122,200
Xianyang (▲641,800) (1986E)	285,900
Xiaogan (▲1,204,400) (1986E)	125,500
Xiaoshan (1985E)	63,074
Xichang (▲161,000) (1986E)	105,000
Xinghua (1985E)	75,573
Xinglongzhen (1982C)	52,961
Xingtai (▲350,800) (1986E)	265,600
Xinhui (1985E)	77,381
Xining (Sining)	610,000
Xinmin (1985E)	47,900
Xintai (▲1,157,300) (1986E)	171,400
Xinwen (Suncun) (1975U)	50,000
Xinxian (▲398,600) (1986E)	74,200
Xinxiang (▲540,500) (1986E)	411,000
Xinyang (▲234,200) (1986E)	169,100
Xinyu (▲610,600) (1986E)	140,200
Xuancheng (1985E)	52,387
Xuanhua (1975U)	140,000
Xuanwei (1982C)	70,081
Xuchang (▲247,200) (1986E)	167,800
Xuguit Qi (Yakeshi) (1986E)	390,000
Xuzhou (Süchow)	840,000
Yaan (▲277,600) (1986E)	89,200
Yan'an (▲259,800) (1986E)	86,700
Yancheng (▲1,251,400) (1986E)	258,400
Yangcheng (1982C)	57,255
Yangjiang (1986E)	91,433
Yangquan (▲478,900) (1986E)	295,100
Yangzhou (▲417,300) (1986E)	321,500
Yanji (▲216,900) (1986E)	175,000
Yanji (Longjing) (1985E)	55,035
Yanling (1982C)	52,679
Yantai (Chefoo) (▲717,300) (1986E)	327,000
Yanzhou (1985E)	48,972
Yaxian (Sanya) (▲321,700) (1986E)	70,500
Yi'an (1986E)	54,253
Yibin (Ipin) (▲636,500) (1986E)	218,800
Yichang (Ichang) (1986E)	410,500
Yichuan (1982C)	58,914
Yichun, Heilongjiang prov.	830,000
Yichun, Jiangxi prov. (▲770,200) (1986E)	132,600
Yidu (1985E)	54,838
Yilan (1985E)	50,436
Yima (▲84,800) (1986E)	53,700
Yinan (Jiehu) (1982C)	67,803
Yinchuan (▲396,900) (1986E)	268,200
Yingchengzi (1985E)	59,072
Yingkou (▲480,000) (1986E)	366,900
Yingtan (▲116,200) (1986E)	64,500
Yining (Kuldja) (▲232,000) (1986E)	153,200
Yiyang (▲365,000) (1986E)	155,300
Yiyuan (Nanma) (1982C)	53,800
Yong'an (▲269,000) (1986E)	105,100
Yongchuan (1985E)	70,444
Yuci (▲420,700) (1986E)	171,000
Yueyang (▲411,300) (1986E)	239,500
Yulin, Guangxi Zhuangzu prov. (▲1,228,800) (1986E)	115,600
Yulin, Shaanxi prov. (1985E)	51,610
Yumen (Laojunmiao) (▲160,100) (1986E)	84,300
Yuncheng, Shandong prov. (1982C)	54,262
Yuncheng, Shansi prov. (▲434,900) (1986E)	87,000
Yunyang (1982C)	54,903
Yushu (1985E)	57,222
Yuyao (▲772,700) (1986E)	169,700
Zaozhuang (▲1,592,000) (1986E)	292,200
Zhangjiakou (Kalgan) (▲626,500) (1986E)	492,800
Zhangye (▲394,200) (1986E)	73,000
Zhangzhou (Longxi) (▲310,400) (1986E)	159,400
Zhanjiang (▲920,900) (1986E)	335,500
Zhaodong (1985E)	99,836
Zhaoqing (Gaoyao) (▲187,600) (1986E)	145,700
Zhaotong (▲546,600) (1986E)	77,500
Zhaoyuan (1985E)	42,426
Zhaoyuan (1982C)	56,389
Zhengzhou (Chengchow) (▲1,610,000)	1,170,000
Zhenjiang (1986E)	412,400
Zhongshan (Shiqizhen) (▲1,059,700) (1986E)	238,700
Zhoucun (1975U)	50,000
Zhoukouzhen (▲220,400) (1986E)	110,500
Zhuhai (▲155,000) (1986E)	88,800
Zhumadian (▲149,500) (1986E)	99,400
Zhuoxian (1985E)	54,523
Zhuzhou (Chuchow) (▲499,600) (1986E)	344,800
Zibo (Zhangdian) (▲2,330,000)	830,000
Zigong (Tzukung) (▲909,300) (1986E)	361,700
Zixing (▲334,300) (1986E)	97,100
Ziyang (1985E)	57,349
Zouping (1982C)	49,274
Zouxian (1985E)	61,578
Zunyi (▲347,600) (1986E)	236,600

CISKEI

1986 E	882,200
BISHO	2,850
• Mdantsane (★East London, S. Afr.)	242,823

COLOMBIA

1985 C	27,867,326
Armenia	187,130
Barrancabermeja	137,406
Barranquilla (★1,140,000)	899,781
Bello (★Medellín)	212,861
• BOGOTÁ (★4,260,000)	3,982,941
Bucaramanga (★550,000)	352,326
Buenaventura	160,342
Buga	82,992
Cali (★1,400,000)	1,350,565
Cartagena	531,426
Cartago	97,791
Ciénaga	56,860
Cúcuta (★445,000)	379,478
Dos Quebradas (★Pereira)	101,480
Duitama	56,390
Envigado (★Medellín)	91,391
Florencia	66,430
Floridablanca (★Bucaramanga)	143,824
Girardot	70,078
Ibagué	292,965
Itagüí (★Medellín)	137,623
Magangué	49,160
Maicao	46,033
Malambo (★Barranquilla)	52,584
Manizales (★330,000)	299,352
Medellín (★2,095,000)	1,468,089
Montería	157,466
Neiva	194,556
Ocaña	51,443
Palmira	175,186
Pasto	197,407
Pereira (★390,000)	233,271
Popayán	141,964
Santa Marta	177,922
Sincelejo	120,537
Soacha (★Bogotá)	109,051
Sogamoso	64,437
Soledad (★Barranquilla)	165,791
Tuluá	99,721
Tunja	93,792
Valledupar	142,771
Villa Rosario (★Cúcuta)	63,615
Villavicencio	178,685
Zipaquirá	45,676

COMOROS / Al-Qumur / Comores

1990 E	452,742
• MORONI	23,432

CONGO

1984 C	1,912,429
• BRAZZAVILLE	585,812
Dolisie	49,134
Pointe-Noire	294,203

COOK ISLANDS

1986 C	18,155
• AVARUA	9,678

COSTA RICA

1984 C	2,416,809
Alajuela (▲34,556)	29,273
Desamparados (★San José)	43,352
Limón (▲52,602)	33,925
Puntarenas	29,224
• SAN JOSÉ (★670,000)	241,464

CUBA

1981 C	9,723,605
Bayamo (1985E)	105,302
Camagüey (1985E)	260,782
Cárdenas	59,352
Ciego de Avila (1985E)	80,500
Cienfuegos (1985E)	109,304
Guantánamo (1985E)	174,383
Holguín (1985E)	194,728
• LA HABANA (HAVANA) (★2,125,000) (1987E)	2,036,800
Manzanillo	87,830
Matanzas (1985E)	105,382
Palma Soriano	55,851
Pinar del Río (1985E)	100,906
Sancti-Spíritus (1985E)	75,600
Santa Clara (1985E)	178,278
Santiago de Cuba (1985E)	358,764
Victoria de las Tunas (1985E)	91,400

CYPRUS / Kıbrıs / Kípros

1982 C	512,097
Lárnax (Larnaca) (★48,330)	35,823
Lemesós (Limassol) (★107,161)	74,782
• NICOSIA (LEVKOSÍA) (★185,000)	48,221

CYPRUS, NORTH / Kuzey Kıbrıs

1985 E	160,287
Gazimağusa (Famagusta)	19,428
• NICOSIA (LEFKOŞA)	37,400

CZECHOSLOVAKIA / Československo

1989 E	15,624,021
Banská Bystrica	85,327
Bratislava	435,499
Brno (★450,000)	389,892
České Budějovice (★114,000)	97,340
Chomutov (★80,000)	56,715
Děčín (★72,000)	56,200
Frýdek-Místek (★Ostrava)	65,481
Gottwaldov (★124,000)	86,742
Havířov (★Ostrava)	92,279
Hradec Králové (★113,000)	100,454
Jihlava	53,987
Karlovy Vary (Carlsbad)	55,907
Karviná (★Ostrava)	71,742
Kladno (★88,500)	73,180
Košice	232,253
Liberec (★175,000)	103,752
Martin	65,218
Most (★135,000)	69,557
Nitra	89,306
Olomouc (★126,000)	106,662
Opava (★77,500)	63,084
Ostrava (★760,000)	330,614
Pardubice	95,668
Plzeň (★210,000)	174,635
Poprad	50,300
• PRAHA (★1,325,000)	1,211,106
Přerov	51,800
Prešov	87,396
Prievidza	51,200
Prostějov	51,900
Spišská Nová Ves	44,600
Teplice (★94,000)	55,756
Trenčín	56,843
Trnava	72,200
Ústí nad Labem (★115,000)	105,854
Žilina	96,418

DENMARK / Danmark

1988 E	5,129,254
Ålborg (▲154,739)	113,800
Århus (▲258,028)	199,700
Ballerup (★København)	45,791
Esbjerg (▲81,385)	71,800
Fredericia (▲45,970)	28,300
Frederiksberg (★København)	85,814
Gentofte (★København)	65,467
Gladsakse (★København)	61,424
Helsingør (Elsinore) (★København)	56,607
Horsens (▲54,776)	46,900
Hvidovre (★København)	49,332
• KØBENHAVN (★1,685,000)	468,704
Kolding (▲57,043)	42,000
Kongens Lyngby (★København)	49,601
Odense (▲174,016)	138,400
Randers	61,155
Rønne	15,397
Roskilde (★København)	39,700
Vejle (▲50,817)	44,800

DJIBOUTI

1976 E	226,000
• DJIBOUTI	120,000

DOMINICA

1984 E	77,000
• ROSEAU	9,348

DOMINICAN REPUBLIC / República Dominicana

1981 C	5,647,977
Barahona	49,334
La Romana	91,571
La Vega	52,432
San Cristóbal	58,520
San Francisco de Macorís	64,906
San Juan [de la Maguana]	49,764
San Pedro de Macorís	78,562
Santiago [de los Caballeros]	278,638
• SANTO DOMINGO	1,313,172

ECUADOR

1982 C	8,050,630
Alfaro (★Guayaquil)	51,023
Ambato	100,454
Cuenca	157,213
Esmeraldas	91,382
• Guayaquil (★1,255,000)	1,204,532
Ibarra	53,428
Loja	71,652
Machala	108,156
Manta	103,609
Milagro	77,010
Portoviejo	102,628
Quevedo	67,023
QUITO (★1,050,000)	890,355
Riobamba	75,455
Santo Domingo de los Colorados	69,235

EGYPT / Mişr

1986 C	48,205,049

▲ Population of an entire municipality, commune, or district, including rural area.
• Largest city in country.
★ Population or designation of the metropolitan area, including suburbs.
C Census. **E** Official estimate. **U** Unofficial estimate.

▲ Bevölkerung eines ganzen städtischen Verwaltungsgebietes, eines Kommunalbezirkes oder eines Distrikts, einschliesslich ländlicher Gebiete.
• Grösste Stadt des Landes.
★ Bevölkerung oder Bezeichnung der Stadtregion einschliesslich Vororte.
C Volkszählung. **E** Offizielle Schätzung. **U** Inoffizielle Schätzung.

Population of Cities and Towns / Einwohnerzahlen von Grossstädten / Habitantes en las Ciudades y Poblaciones
Population des Grands Centres et des Villes / População dos Centros Urbanos 305

Abnūb	48,519
Abū Kabīr	69,509
Abū Tīj	48,711
Akhmīm	70,602
Al-'Arīsh	67,638
Al-Fayyūm	212,523
Al-Ḥawāmidīyah (★Al-Qāhirah)	73,060
Al-Iskandarīyah (Alexandria) (★3,350,000)	2,917,327
Al-Ismā'īlīyah (★235,000)	212,567
Al-Jīzah (Giza) (★Al-Qāhirah)	1,870,508
Al-Maḥallah al-Kubrā	358,844
Al-Manṣūrah (★375,000)	316,870
Al-Manzilah	55,090
Al-Maṭarīyah	74,554
Al-Minyā	179,136
• AL-QĀHIRAH (CAIRO) (★9,300,000)	6,052,836
Al-Qanāṭir al-Khayrīyah	48,909
Al-Uqṣur (Luxor)	125,404
Armant	54,650
Ashmūn	54,450
As-Sinbillāwayn	60,285
As-Suways (Suez)	326,820
Aswān	191,461
Asyūṭ	273,191
Az-Zaqāzīq	245,496
Bahtīm (★Al-Qāhirah)	275,807
Banhā	115,571
Banī Mazār	47,964
Banī Suwayf	151,813
Bilbays	96,540
Bilqās Qism Awwal	73,162
Biyalā	47,781
Būlāq ad-Dakrūr (★Al-Qāhirah)	148,787
Būr Sa'īd (Port Said)	399,793
Būsh	54,482
Damanhūr	190,840
Disūq	78,119
Dumyāṭ (Damietta)	89,498
Fāqūs	48,625
Ḥawsh 'Īsā (1980C)	53,619
Idkū	70,729
Jirjā	70,899
Kafr ad-Dawwār (★Al-Iskandarīyah)	195,102
Kafr ash-Shaykh	102,910
Kafr az-Zayyāt	58,061
Kawm Umbū	52,131
Maghāghah	50,807
Mallawī	99,062
Manfalūṭ	52,644
Marsā Maṭrūḥ	43,192
Minūf	69,883
Mīt Ghamr (★100,000)	92,253
Qalyūb	86,684
Qinā	119,794
Rashīd (Rosetta)	52,014
Rummānah	50,014
Samālūṭ	62,404
Sāqiyat Makkī	51,062
Sawhāj	132,965
Shibīn al-Kawm	132,751
Shubrā al-Khaymah (★Al-Qāhirah)	710,794
Sinnūris	55,323
Ṭahṭā	58,516
Ṭalkhā (★Al-Manṣūrah)	55,757
Ṭanṭā	334,505
Ṭimā	47,223
Warrāq al-'Arab (★Al-Qāhirah)	127,108
Ziftā (★Mīt Ghamr)	69,050

EL SALVADOR

1985 E	5,337,896
Mejicanos (★San Salvador)	91,465
Nueva San Salvador (★San Salvador)	53,688
San Miguel	88,520
• SAN SALVADOR (★920,000)	462,652
Santa Ana	137,879
Soyapango (★San Salvador)	60,000
Villa Delgado (★San Salvador)	67,684

EQUATORIAL GUINEA / Guinea Ecuatorial

1983 C	300,000
• MALABO	30,710

ETHIOPIA / Ityopiya

1984 C	42,019,418
• ADIS ABEBA (★1,500,000)	1,412,575
Akaki Beseka (★Adis Abeba)	54,146
Asmera	275,385
Awasa	36,169
Bahir Dar	54,800
Debre Zeyit	51,143
Dese	68,848
Dire Dawa	98,104
Gonder	68,958
Harer	62,160
Jima	60,992
Mekele	61,583
Mitsiwa	15,441
Nazret	76,284

FAEROE ISLANDS / Føroyar

1988 E	47,653
• TÓRSHAVN	14,547

FALKLAND ISLANDS / Islas Malvinas

1986 C	1,916
• STANLEY	1,200

FIJI

1986 C	715,375
Lautoka (★39,057)	28,728
• SUVA (★141,273)	69,665

FINLAND / Suomi

1988 E	4,938,602
Espoo (Esbo) (★Helsinki)	164,569
• HELSINKI (HELSINGFORS) (★900,000)	490,034
Jyväskylä (★89,000)	65,719
Kouvola (★55,000)	31,933
Kuopio	78,916
Lahti (★109,000)	74,300
Lappeenranta (▲53,780)	47,400
Oulu (★112,000)	98,582
Pori	77,395
Tampere (★241,000)	170,533
Turku (Åbo) (★221,000)	160,456
Vaasa (Vasa)	53,737
Vantaa (Vanda) (★Helsinki)	149,063

FRANCE

1982 C	54,334,871
Aix-en-Provence (★126,552)	121,327
Ajaccio	54,089
Albi (★60,181)	45,947
Alès (★70,180)	43,268
Amiens (★154,498)	131,332
Angers (★195,859)	136,038
Angoulême (★103,552)	46,197
Annecy (★112,632)	49,965
Antibes (★Cannes)	62,859
Antony (★Paris)	54,610
Argenteuil (★Paris)	95,347
Arles (★52,547)	37,571
Armentières (★59,000)	24,834
Arras (★80,477)	41,736
Asnières [-sur-Seine] (★Paris)	71,077
Aubervilliers (★Paris)	67,719
Aulnay-sous-Bois (★Paris)	75,996
Avignon (★174,264)	89,132
Bastia (★50,596)	44,020
Bayonne (★127,477)	41,381
Beauvais (★55,817)	52,365
Belfort (★76,221)	51,206
Besançon (★120,772)	113,283
Béthune (★258,383)	25,508
Béziers (★81,347)	76,647
Blois (★61,049)	47,243
Bondy (★Paris)	44,301
Bordeaux (★640,012)	208,159
Boulogne-Billancourt (★Paris)	102,582
Boulogne-sur-Mer (★98,566)	47,653
Bourg-en-Bresse (★53,463)	41,098
Bourges (★92,202)	76,432
Brest (★201,145)	156,060
Brive-la-Gaillarde (★64,301)	51,511
Bruay-en-Artois (★Béthune)	22,893
Caen (★183,526)	114,068
Calais (★100,823)	76,527
Cambrai (★49,581)	35,272
Cannes (★295,525)	72,259
Carcassonne	41,153
Castres (★46,891)	45,578
Châlons-sur-Marne (★63,061)	51,137
Chalon-sur-Saône (★78,064)	56,194
Chambéry (★96,163)	53,427
Champigny-sur-Marne (★Paris)	76,176
Charleville-Mézières (★67,694)	58,667
Chartres (★77,795)	37,119
Châteauroux (★66,851)	51,942
Châtellerault	35,838
Cherbourg (★85,485)	28,442
Cholet	55,524
Clamart (★Paris)	48,353
Clermont-Ferrand (★256,189)	147,361
Clichy (★Paris)	46,895
Cognac (★31,189)	20,660
Colmar (★82,468)	62,483
Colombes (★Paris)	78,777
Compiègne (★62,778)	40,384
Courbevoie (★Paris)	59,830
Creil (★82,505)	34,709
Créteil (★Paris)	71,693
Denain (★Valenciennes)	21,825
Dieppe (★41,812)	35,957
Dijon (★215,865)	140,942
Douai (★202,366)	42,576
Drancy (★Paris)	60,183
Dunkerque (★195,705)	73,120
Elbeuf (★51,083)	17,224
Épinal (★51,495)	37,818
Épinay-sur-Seine (★Paris)	50,314
Évreux (★54,654)	46,045
Fontainebleau (★35,629)	15,679
Fontenay-sous-Bois (★Paris)	52,627
Forbach (★99,606)	27,187
Fréjus (★60,289)	31,662
Gennevilliers (★Paris)	45,396
Grenoble (★392,021)	156,637
Hagondange (★119,669)	9,091
Hayange (★Thionville)	17,848
Issy-les-Moulineaux (★Paris)	45,772
Ivry-sur-Seine (★Paris)	55,699
La Rochelle (★102,143)	75,840
La Seyne-sur-Mer (★Toulon)	57,659
Laval (★55,984)	50,360
Le Blanc-Mesnil (★Paris)	47,037
Le Havre (★254,595)	199,388
Le Mans (★191,080)	147,697
Lens (★327,383)	38,244
Le Puy (★42,382)	24,064
Levallois-Perret (★Paris)	53,500
Lille (★1,020,000)	168,424
Limoges (★171,689)	140,400
Longwy (★77,000)	17,338
Lorient (★104,025)	62,554
Lourdes	17,425
Lyon (★1,275,000)	413,095
Mâcon (★47,274)	38,404
Maisons-Alfort (★Paris)	51,065
Mantes-la-Jolie (★170,265)	43,564
Marseille (★1,225,000)	874,436
Maubeuge (★105,714)	36,061
Meaux (★55,797)	45,005
Melun (★82,479)	35,005
Menton (★Monaco, Monaco)	25,072
Mérignac (★Bordeaux)	51,306
Metz (★186,437)	114,232
Meudon (★Paris)	48,450
Montargis (★51,954)	16,110
Montbéliard (★128,194)	31,836
Montceau-les-Mines (★51,290)	26,925
Montluçon (★67,963)	49,912
Montpellier (★221,307)	197,231
Montreuil-sous-Bois (★Paris)	93,368
Moulins (★43,082)	25,159
Moyeuvre-Grande (★Hagondange)	10,287
Mulhouse (Mülhausen) (★220,613)	112,157
Nancy (★306,982)	96,317
Nanterre (★Paris)	88,578
Nantes (★464,857)	240,539
Neuilly-sur-Seine (★Paris)	64,170
Nevers (★59,274)	43,013
Nice (★449,496)	337,085
Nîmes (★132,343)	124,220
Niort (★61,959)	58,203
Noisy-le-Sec (★Paris)	36,880
Orléans (★220,478)	102,710
Orly (★Paris)	23,766
Pantin (★Paris)	43,553
• PARIS (★9,775,000) (1987E)	2,078,900
Pau (★131,265)	83,790
Périgueux (★59,716)	32,916
Perpignan (★137,915)	111,669
Pessac (★Bordeaux)	50,267
Poissy (★Paris)	36,389
Poitiers (★103,204)	79,350
Quimper	56,907
Reims (★199,388)	194,656
Rennes (★234,418)	117,234
Roanne (★81,786)	48,705
Rodez (★37,953)	24,368
Romans-sur-Isère (★47,083)	33,152
Roubaix (★Lille)	101,602
Rouen (★379,879)	101,945
Rueil-Malmaison (★Paris)	63,412
Saint-Brieuc (★83,900)	48,563
Saint-Chamond (★82,059)	40,267
Saint-Denis (★Paris)	90,829
Saint-Dizier	35,189
Saint-Étienne (★317,228)	204,955
Saint-Lô (★27,656)	23,212
Saint-Malo	46,347
Saint-Maur-des-Fossés (★Paris)	80,811
Saint-Nazaire (★130,271)	68,348
Saint-Ouen (★Paris)	43,606
Saint-Quentin (★71,887)	63,567
Sarcelles (★Paris)	53,630
Soissons (★47,305)	30,213
Strasbourg (★400,000)	248,712
Suresnes (★Paris)	35,187
Tarbes (★78,056)	51,422
Thionville (★138,034)	40,573
Toulon (★410,393)	179,423
Toulouse (★541,271)	347,995
Tourcoing (★Lille)	96,908
Tours (★262,786)	132,209
Troyes (★125,240)	63,581
Valence (★106,041)	66,356
Valenciennes (★349,505)	40,275
Vénissieux (★Lyon)	64,804
Verdun-sur-Meuse (★26,944)	21,516
Versailles (★Paris)	91,494
Vichy (★63,501)	30,527
Villefranche (★50,143)	28,881
Villejuif (★Paris)	52,448
Villeneuve-d'Ascq (★Lille)	59,527
Villeurbanne (★Lyon)	115,960
Vitry-sur-Seine (★Paris)	85,263
Wattrelos (★Lille)	44,626

FRENCH GUIANA / Guyane française

1982 C	73,022
• CAYENNE	38,091

FRENCH POLYNESIA / Polynésie française

1988 C	188,814
• PAPEETE (★80,000)	23,555

GABON

1985 E	1,312,000
Franceville	58,800
Lambaréné	49,500
• LIBREVILLE	235,700
Port Gentil	124,400

GAMBIA

1983 C	696,000
• BANJUL (★95,000)	44,536
Brikama	20,208

GERMAN DEMOCRATIC REPUBLIC (EAST GERMANY) / Deutsche Demokratische Republik

1987 E	16,639,877
Altenburg	53,602
Bautzen	52,354
• BERLIN (OST) (★Berlin)	1,236,248
Bitterfeld (★105,000)	20,869
Brandenburg	94,755
Cottbus	126,592
Dessau (★140,000)	103,538
Dresden (★670,000)	519,810
Eberswalde	54,566
Eisenach	49,534
Eisenhüttenstadt	51,729
Erfurt	217,134
Frankfurt an der Oder	86,441
Freiberg	50,415
Freital (★Dresden)	43,092
Gera	132,319
Görlitz	78,856
Gotha	57,423
Greifswald	67,298
Halberstadt	47,017
Halle (★475,000)	236,148
Halle-Neustadt (★Halle)	93,477
Hoyerswerda	69,113
Jena	107,610
Karl-Marx-Stadt (Chemnitz) (★450,000)	313,799
Leipzig (★700,000)	550,641
Magdeburg (★400,000)	288,975
Merseburg (★Halle)	46,188
Neubrandenburg	87,235
Nordhausen	47,681
Pirna	46,991
Plauen	77,514
Potsdam (★Berlin)	141,231
Riesa	49,108
Rostock	249,349
Schwedt	51,753
Schwerin	128,328
Stralsund	75,857
Suhl	55,295
Weimar	63,910
Wismar	58,066
Wittenberg	53,670
Zwickau (★165,000)	120,923

GERMANY, FEDERAL REPUBLIC OF (WEST GERMANY) / Bundesrepublik Deutschland

1987 E	61,140,461
Aachen (★535,000)	239,170
Aalen (★80,000)	63,337
Ahlen	51,895
Albstadt	45,973
Alsdorf (★Aachen)	45,925
Amberg	43,348
Arnsberg	74,641
Aschaffenburg (★145,000)	59,646
Augsburg (★405,000)	245,962
Baden-Baden	49,257
Bad Homburg (★Frankfurt am Main)	51,081
Bad Oeynhausen	43,237
Bad Salzuflen (★Herford)	51,187
Bamberg (★120,000)	69,591
Bayreuth (★90,000)	72,326
Berchtesgaden	8,051
Bergheim (★Köln)	54,413
Bergisch Gladbach (★Köln)	101,776
Bergkamen (★Essen)	47,912
Berlin (West) (★3,825,000)	1,879,225
Bielefeld (★515,000)	299,360
Bocholt	66,443
Bochum (★Essen)	381,216
BONN (★570,000)	291,439
Bottrop (★Essen)	112,256
Braunschweig (★330,000)	247,836
Bremen (★800,000)	521,976
Bremerhaven (★190,000)	132,194
Castrop-Rauxel (★Essen)	76,110
Celle	70,245
Cuxhaven	56,076
Dachau (★München)	32,871
Darmstadt (★305,000)	133,572
Delmenhorst (★Bremen)	70,512
Detmold	66,660
Dinslaken (★Essen)	61,330
Dormagen (★Köln)	57,513
Dorsten (★Essen)	74,115
Dortmund (★Essen)	568,164
Duisburg (★Essen)	514,628
Düren (★110,000)	84,100
Düsseldorf (★1,190,000)	560,572
Emden	49,557
Erlangen (★Nürnberg)	100,200
Eschweiler (★Aachen)	53,082
• Essen (★4,950,000)	615,421
Esslingen (★Stuttgart)	86,886
Euskirchen	45,676
Flensburg (★103,000)	85,714
Frankfurt am Main (★1,855,000)	592,411
Freiburg (★225,000)	186,156
Friedrichshafen	52,064
Fulda (★79,000)	54,131
Fürth (★Nürnberg)	98,203
Garbsen (★Hannover)	57,541
Garmisch-Partenkirchen	27,701
Gelsenkirchen (★Essen)	283,560
Giessen (★160,000)	71,095
Gladbeck (★Essen)	76,625
Göppingen (★155,000)	51,416
Goslar (★84,000)	49,034
Göttingen	133,796
Grevenbroich (★Düsseldorf)	57,463
Gummersbach	48,359
Gütersloh (★Bielefeld)	79,432
Hagen (★Essen)	206,070
Hamburg (★2,225,000)	1,571,267
Hameln (★72,000)	55,390
Hamm	165,957
Hanau (★Frankfurt am Main)	85,217
Hannover (★1,000,000)	505,718
Hattingen (★Essen)	54,964
Heidelberg (★Mannheim)	136,227
Heidenheim (★89,000)	47,611
Heilbronn (★230,000)	111,713
Herford (★120,000)	59,495
Herne (★Essen)	171,274
Herten (★Essen)	67,829
Hilden (★Düsseldorf)	53,820
Hildesheim (★140,000)	100,558
Hof	50,623
Hürth (★Köln)	51,286
Ingolstadt (★138,000)	92,593
Iserlohn	89,466
Kaiserslautern (★138,000)	96,766
Karlsruhe (★485,000)	268,309
Kassel (★360,000)	185,370
Kempten (Allgäu)	56,950
Kerpen (★Köln)	55,158
Kiel (★335,000)	243,626
Kleve	44,725
Koblenz (★180,000)	110,277
Köln (★1,760,000)	914,336
Konstanz	70,539
Krefeld (★Essen)	216,598
Landshut	57,067
Langenfeld (★Düsseldorf)	45,463
Leverkusen (★Köln)	154,703
Lippstadt	60,141
Lübeck (★260,000)	209,159
Lüdenscheid	73,442
Ludwigsburg (★Stuttgart)	76,898
Ludwigshafen (★Mannheim)	152,162
Lüneburg	59,497
Lünen (★Essen)	84,352
Mainz (★Wiesbaden)	189,005
Mannheim (★1,400,000)	294,648
Marburg	77,114
Marl (★Essen)	87,766
Meerbusch (★Düsseldorf)	49,158
Menden	52,175
Minden (★125,000)	75,384

▲ Población de un municipio, comuna o distrito entero, incluyendo sus áreas rurales.
• Ciudad más grande de un país.
★ Población o designación de un área metropolitana, incluyendo los suburbios.
C Censo. **E** Estimaco oficial. **U** Estimado no oficial.

▲ Population d'une municipalité, d'une commune ou d'un district, zone rurale incluse.
• Ville la plus peuplée du pays.
★ Population de l'agglomération (ou nom de la zone métropolitaine englobante).
C Recensement. **E** Estimation officielle. **U** Estimation non officielle.

▲ População de um município, comuna ou distrito, inclusive as respectivas áreas rurais.
• Maior cidade de um país.
★ População ou indicação de uma área metropolitana.
C Censo. **E** Estimativa oficial. **U** Estimativa não oficial.

Moers (★Essen) 95,407
Mönchengladbach (★410,000)... 255,087
Mülheim an der Ruhr (★Essen) 170,392
München (Munich) (★1,955,000) 1,274,716
Münster 267,628
Neumünster 77,877
Neunkirchen/Saar (★135,000) ... 49,536
Neuss (★Düsseldorf) 143,832
Neustadt an der Weinstrasse ... 48,391
Neu-Ulm (★Ulm) 46,409
Neuwied (★150,000) 58,263
Norderstedt (★Hamburg) 68,724
Nordhorn 48,015
Nürnberg (★1,030,000) 467,392
Oberammergau 4,664
Oberhausen (★Essen) 221,542
Offenbach (★Frankfurt am Main) 107,078
Offenburg 50,468
Oldenburg 139,256
Osnabrück (★270,000) 153,776
Paderborn 110,296
Passau 52,733
Peine 45,576
Pforzheim (★220,000) 104,452
Pirmasens 46,077
Ratingen (★Düsseldorf) 89,161
Ravensburg (★75,000) 43,245
Recklinghausen (★Essen) 117,585
Regensburg (★205,000) 123,821
Remscheid (★Wuppertal) 121,005
Reutlingen (★160,000) 97,920
Rheine 70,412
Rosenheim 53,168
Rüsselsheim (★Wiesbaden) 57,303
Saarbrücken (★385,000) 184,353
Saarlouis (★115,000) 37,411
Salzgitter 105,392
Sankt Augustin (★Bonn) 51,105
Schwäbisch Gmünd 56,137
Schweinfurt (★110,000) 50,568
Siegburg (★170,000) 34,085
Siegen (★200,000) 107,319
Sindelfingen (★Stuttgart) 55,715
Solingen (★Wuppertal) 158,401
Stolberg (★Aachen) 56,421
Stuttgart (★1,925,000) 565,486
Trier (★125,000) 93,076
Troisdorf (★Siegburg) • 61,832
Tübingen 76,122
Ulm (★210,000) 100,745
Unna (★Essen) 59,587
Velbert (★Essen) 88,573
Viersen (★Mönchengladbach) 78,124
Villingen-Schwenningen 76,155
Wesel 54,604
Wetzlar (★105,000) 50,284
Wiesbaden (★795,000) 266,542
Wilhelmshaven (★135,000) 94,896
Witten (★Essen) 102,232
Wolfenbüttel (★Braunschweig) 48,623
Wolfsburg 121,951
Worms (★Mannheim) 72,045
Wuppertal (★830,000) 374,217
Würzburg (★210,000) 127,050
Zweibrücken (★105,000) 32,722

GHANA
1984 C 12,205,574
• ACCRA (★1,250,000) 859,640
Ashiaman (★Accra) 49,427
Cape Coast 86,620
Koforidua 54,400
Kumasi (★600,000) 348,880
Obuasi 60,146
Sekondi (★175,352) 32,355
Tafo (★Kumasi) 50,432
Takoradi (★Sekondi) 61,527
Tamale (★168,091) 136,828
Tema (★Accra) 99,608
Teshie (★Accra) 62,954

GIBRALTAR
1987 E 30,000
• GIBRALTAR 30,000

GREECE / Ellás
1981 C 9,740,417
Aiyáleo (★Athínai) 81,906
Ampelókipoi (★Thessaloníki) 40,033
• ATHÍNAI (ATHENS)
(★3,027,331) 885,737
Áyios Dhimítrios (★Athínai) 51,421
Ermoúpolis (★16,595) 13,876
Galátsion (★Athínai) 50,096
Ilioúpolis (★Athínai) 69,560
Ioánnina 44,829
Iráklion (★110,958) 102,398
Kalámai (★43,235) 42,075
Kalamariá (★Thessaloníki) 51,676
Kallithéa (★Athínai) 117,319
Kardhítsa 27,291
Kateríni (★39,895) 38,404
Kavála 56,375
Keratsínion (★Athínai) 74,179
Khalándrion (★Athínai) 54,320
Khalkís 44,867
Khaniá (★61,976) 47,451
Khíos (★29,742) 24,070
Koridhallós (★Athínai) 61,313
Kórinthos (Corinth) 22,658
Lárisa 102,048
Návplion 10,609
Néa Ionía (★Athínai) 59,202
Néa Liósia (★Athínai) 72,427
Neápolis (★Thessaloníki) 31,464
Néa Smírni (★Athínai) 67,408
Níkaia (★Athínai) 90,368
Palaión Fáliron (★Athínai) 53,273
Pátrai (★154,596) 142,163
Peristérion (★Athínai) 140,858
Piraiévs (Piraeus) (★Athínai) 196,389
Ródhos (Rhodes) 40,392
Spárti (Sparta) (★14,388) 12,975
Thessaloníki (Salonika)
(★706,180) 406,413
Tríkala 40,857
Trípolis 21,311

Véroia 37,087
Víron (★Athínai) 57,880
Vólos (★107,407) 71,378
Zográfos (★Athínai) 84,548

GREENLAND / Grønland / Kalaallit Nunaat
1989 E 55,171
Egedesminde (Aasiaat) 3,601
• GODTHÅB (NUUK) 12,426
Holsteinsborg (Sisimiut) 5,024

GRENADA
1981 C 89,088
• SAINT GEORGE'S (★25,000) 4,788

GUADELOUPE
1982 C 328,400
BASSE-TERRE (★26,600) 13,656
Les Abymes (★Pointe-à-Pitre) ... 56,165
• Pointe-à-Pitre (★83,000) 25,310

GUAM
1980 C 105,979
• AGANA (★44,000) 896

GUATEMALA
1989 E 8,935,395
Escuintla 60,673
• GUSTEMALA (★1,400,000) 1,057,210
Quezaltenango 88,769

GUERNSEY
1986 C 55,482
• SAINT PETER PORT (★36,000) 16,085

GUINEA / Guinée
1986 E 6,225,000
• CONAKRY 800,000
Kankan 100,000
Kindia 80,000
Labé 110,000

GUINEA-BISSAU / Guiné-Bissau
1979 C 777,214
• BISSAU 109,486

GUYANA
1983 E 918,000
• GEORGETOWN (★188,000) 78,500

HAITI / Haïti
1987 E 5,531,802
Cap-Haïtien 72,161
Gonaïves 37,034
• PORT-AU-PRINCE (★880,000) 797,000

HONDURAS
1988 C 4,376,839
Choluteca 53,799
El Progreso 55,523
La Ceiba 68,289
San Pedro Sula 279,356
• TEGUCIGALPA 551,606

HONG KONG
1986 C 5,395,997
Kowloon (Jiulong) (★Victoria) 774,781
Kwai Chung (★Victoria) 131,362
New Kowloon (Xinjiulong)
(★Victoria) 1,526,910
Sha Tin (★Victoria) 355,810
Sheung Shui 87,206
Tai Po 119,679
Tsuen Wan (Quanwan)
(★Victoria) 514,241
Tuen Mun (★Victoria) 262,458
• VICTORIA (★4,770,000) 1,175,860
Yuen Long 75,740

HUNGARY / Magyarország
1989 E 10,589,000
Békéscsaba (▲70,978) 61,700
• BUDAPEST (★2,565,000) 2,113,645
Debrecen 219,251
Dunaújváros 62,386
Eger 67,252
Érd (★Budapest) 48,037
Györ 131,503
Hódmezövásárhely (▲53,311) ... 44,600
Kaposvár 76,834
Kecskemét (▲106,869) 85,400
Miskolc 207,826
Nagykanizsa 55,023
Nyíregyháza (▲119,333) 92,500
Ózd 44,617
Pécs 183,082
Salgótarján 48,785
Sopron 57,107
Szeged 189,484
Székesfehérvár 113,935
Szolnok 81,907
Szombathely 87,997
Tatabánya 76,455
Vác 36,070
Veszprém 66,280
Zalaegerszeg 63,785

ICELAND / Ísland
1987 E 247,357
Akureyri 13,856
• REYKJAVÍK (★137,941) 93,425

INDIA / Bharat
1981 C 685,184,692
Abohar 86,334
Achalpur 81,186
Ädiläbäd 53,482
Adîtyapur (★Jamshedpur) 53,421
Ädoni 108,939
Agartala 132,186
Ägra (★747,318) 694,191
Ahmadäbäd (★2,400,000) 2,059,725

Ahmadnagar (★181,210) 143,937
Äïzawl 74,493
Ajmer 375,593
Akola 225,412
Akot 51,936
Alandur (★Madras) 97,449
Alïgarh 320,861
Älïpur Duär (★71,573) 45,324
Allahäbäd (★650,070) 616,051
Alleppey 169,940
Alwar 145,795
Amalner 67,516
Amarnäth (★Bombay) 96,347
Ambäla (★233,110) 104,565
Ambäla Sadar (★Ambäla) 80,741
Ambäsamudram (★52,591) 29,761
Ambattur (★Madras) 115,901
Ämbür 66,042
Amrävati 261,404
Amreli (★58,241) 56,598
Amritsar 594,844
Amroha 112,682
Anakäpalle 73,179
Änand 83,936
Anantapur 119,531
Ara 125,111
Arakkonam 59,405
Arcot (★94,363) 38,836
Arni 49,365
Aruppukkottai 72,245
Asansol (★1,050,000) 183,375
Ashoknagar-Kalyangarh
(★Häbra) 55,176
Ättür 50,517
Aurangäbäd (★316,421) 284,607
Avadi (★Madras) 124,701
Äzamgarh 66,523
Badagara 64,174
Bägalkot 67,858
Baharampur (★102,311) 92,889
Bahraich 99,889
Baidyabäti (★Calcutta) 70,573
Bäläghät (★53,183) 49,564
Bälängïr 54,943
Bäleshwar 65,779
Ballarpur 61,398
Ballia 61,704
Bälly (★Calcutta) 147,735
Bälly (★Calcutta) 54,859
Balrämpur 46,058
Bälurghät (★112,621) 104,646
Bända 72,379
Bangalore (★2,950,000) 2,476,355
Bangaon 69,885
Bänkura 94,954
Bansberia (★Calcutta) 77,020
Bänswära (★48,070) 46,749
Bäpatla 55,347
Bäräkpur (★Calcutta) 115,253
Baranagar (★Calcutta) 170,343
Bäräsat (★Calcutta) 66,504
Barauni 56,366
Baraut 46,292
Barddhamän 167,364
Bareilly (★449,425) 386,734
Bäripada (★52,989) 40,314
Bärmer 55,554
Bärsi 72,537
Basïrhät 81,040
Basti 69,357
Batala (★101,966) 87,135
Bathinda (★127,363) 124,453
Beäwar 89,998
Begusarai (★68,305) 56,633
Behäla (South Suburban)
(★Calcutta) 378,765
Bela 49,932
Belgaum (★300,372) 274,430
Bellary 201,579
Bettiah 72,167
Betül 46,293
Bhadrak 60,600
Bhadrävati (★130,606) 53,551
Bhadrävati New Town
(★Bhadrävati) 77,055
Bhadreswar (★Calcutta) 58,858
Bhägalpur 225,062
Bhandära 56,025
Bharatpur 105,274
Bharüch (★120,524) 110,070
Bhätpära (★Calcutta) 260,761
Bhaväni (★80,472) 28,898
Bhävnagar (★308,642) 307,121
Bhilai (★490,214) 290,090
Bhïlwära 122,625
Bhïmavaram 101,894
Bhind 74,515
Bhiwandi (★Bombay) 115,298
Bhiwäni 101,277
Bhopäl 671,018
Bhubaneshwar 219,211
Bhuj (★70,211) 69,693
Bhusäwal (★132,142) 123,133
Bïd 80,287
Bïdar 78,856
Bihär 151,343
Bijäpur 147,313
Bijnor 56,713
Bïkäner (★287,712) 253,174
Bïläspur (★187,104) 147,218
Bïrlapur (★50,831) 20,470
Bïrnagar (★67,066) 14,581
Bishnupur 47,529
Bodhan 50,807
Bodinäyakkanür 59,168
Bokäro Steel City (★264,480) ... 224,099
Bombay (★9,950,000) 8,243,405
Botäd 50,274
Brahmapur 162,550
Brajrajnagar 54,033
Budaun 93,004
Budge Budge (★Calcutta) 66,424
Bulandshahr 103,436
Bulsär (★Bombay) 54,017
Bündi (★48,027) 47,736
Burhänpur 140,896
• Calcutta (★11,100,000) 3,305,006
Calicut (★546,058) 394,447

Cannanore (★157,797) 60,904
Chäkdaha 59,308
Chakradharpur (★44,532) 29,272
Chälisgaon 59,342
Champdäni (★Calcutta) 76,138
Chandannagar (★Calcutta) 101,925
Chandausi 66,970
Chandïgarh (★422,841) 373,789
Chandrapur 115,777
Changanächeri 51,955
Channapatna 50,725
Chäpra 111,564
Chhatarpur 51,959
Chhindwära 75,118
Chidambaram (★62,543) 55,920
Chikmagalür 60,582
Chilakalürupet 61,645
Chïräla 72,040
Chitradurga 74,580
Chittaranjan (★61,045) 50,748
Chittoor 86,230
Chüru (★62,070) 61,811
Cochin (★685,836) 513,249
Coimbatore (★965,000) 704,514
Coonoor (★92,242) 44,750
Cuddalore 127,625
Cuddapah 103,125
Cuttack (★327,412) 269,950
Dabgram 76,402
Dabhoi 44,357
Dähod (★82,256) 55,256
Dältenganj 51,952
Damoh (★76,758) 75,573
Dänäpur (★Patna) 58,684
Darbhanga 176,301
Darjiling 57,603
Datia 49,386
Dävangere 196,621
Dehra Dün (★293,010) 211,416
Dehri 90,409
Delhi (★7,200,000) 4,884,234
Delhi Cantonment (★Delhi) 85,166
Deoband 51,270
Deoghar (★59,120) 52,904
Deoläli (★Näsik) 77,666
Deoläli Cantonment (★Näsik) ... 57,745
Deoria 55,720
Dewäs 83,465
Dhamtari 55,797
Dhanbad (★825,000) 120,221
Dhär 48,870
Dharmapuri 51,223
Dharmavaram 50,969
Dhorâji (★77,716) 76,556
Dhrängadhra 51,280
Dhuburi (★45,580) (1971C) 36,503
Dhule 210,759
Dibrugarh (1971C) 80,348
Dindigul 164,103
Dombivli (★Bombay) 103,222
Dum Dum (★Calcutta) 33,604
Durg (★Bhilai) 114,637
Durgäpur 311,798
Elüru 168,154
Erode (★275,999) 142,252
Etah 53,784
Etäwah 112,174
Faizäbäd (★143,167) 101,873
Farïdäbäd New Township
(★Delhi) 330,864
Farrukhäbäd (★160,796) 145,793
Fatehpur 84,831
Fathpur, Räjasthän state 51,084
Fïrozäbäd 202,338
Fïrozpur (★105,840) 61,162
Gadag 117,368
Gandhidham (★61,489) 61,415
Gändhinagar 62,443
Ganganagar 123,692
Gangäwati 58,735
Garden Reach (★Calcutta) 191,107
Gärulia (★Calcutta) 57,061
Gaya 247,075
Ghäziäbäd (★287,170) 271,730
Ghäzïpur 60,725
Girïdïh 65,444
Godhra (★86,228) 85,784
Gonda 70,847
Gondal (★66,818) 66,096
Gondia 100,423
Gorakhpur (★307,501) 290,814
Gudiväda 80,198
Gudiyättam (★80,674) 75,044
Gulbarga 221,325
Guna (★64,659) 60,255
Guntakal 84,599
Guntür 367,699
Gurgaon (★100,877) 89,115
Guruvayur (★59,467) 17,858
Guwähäti (★200,377) (1971C) ... 123,783
Gwalior (★555,862) 539,015
Häbra (★129,610) 74,434
Häjïpur 62,520
Haldwäni 77,300
Hälisahar (★Calcutta) 95,579
Hänsi 50,365
Hanumängarh 60,071
Häora (★Calcutta) 744,429
Häpur 102,837
Hardoi 67,259
Haridwär (★145,946) 114,180
Harihar 52,334
Hassan 71,534
Häthras 92,962
Hazärïbäg 80,155
Hindupur 55,901
Hinganghät 59,075
Hisär (★137,369) 131,309
Hoshiärpur 85,648
Hospet (★115,351) 90,572
Hubli-Dhärwär 527,108
Hugli-Chinsurah (★Calcutta) 125,193
Hyderäbäd (★2,750,000) 2,187,262
Ichaikaronji 133,751
Imphäl 156,622
Indore (★850,000) 829,327
Ingräj Bäzär 79,010
Itärsi (★69,619) 62,499

▲ Population of an entire municipality, commune, or district, including rural area.
• Largest city in country.
★ Population or designation of the metropolitan area, including suburbs.
C Census. E Official estimate. U Unofficial estimate.

▲ Bevölkerung eines ganzen städtischen Verwaltungsgebietes, eines Kommunalbezirkes oder eines Distrikts, einschliesslich ländlichen Gebiete.
• Grösste Stadt des Landes.
★ Bevölkerung oder Bezeichnung der Stadtregion einschliesslich Vororte.
C Volkszählung. E Offizielle Schätzung. U Inoffizielle Schätzung.

Population of Cities and Towns / Einwohnerzahlen von Grossstädten / Habitantes en las Ciudades y Poblaciones 307
Population des Grands Centres et des Villes / População dos Centros Urbanos

Jabalpur (★757,303)	614,162
Jabalpur Cantonment (★Jabalpur)	61,026
Jādabpur (★Calcutta)	251,968
Jagādhri (★Yamunānagar)	43,102
Jagdalpur (★63,632)	51,286
Jagtiāl	53,213
Jaipur (★1,025,000)	977,165
Jalandhar (★441,552)	408,186
Jālgaon	145,335
Jālna	122,276
Jalpāiguri	61,743
Jamālpur	78,356
Jammu (★223,361)	206,135
Jamnagar (★317,362)	277,615
Jamshedpur (★669,580)	438,385
Jangoon	70,727
Jaora (★47,548)	47,129
Jaridih Bazar (★101,946)	46,477
Jaunpur	105,140
Jaypur	53,981
Jetpur (★63,074)	62,806
Jhānsi (★284,141)	246,172
Jharia (★Dhanbād)	57,496
Jhārsuguda	54,859
Jīnd	56,748
Jodhpur	506,345
Jorhāt (★70,674) (1971C)	30,247
Jūnāgadh (★120,416)	118,646
Kadaiyanallūr	60,306
Kadiri	52,774
Kaithal	58,385
Kākināda	226,409
Kālol (★Ahmadābād)	69,946
Kalyān (★Bombay)	136,052
Kāmārhāti (★Calcutta)	234,951
Kambam	50,340
Kāmthi (★Nāgpur)	67,364
Kānchipuram (★145,254)	130,926
Kānchrāpāra (★Calcutta)	88,798
Kānpur (★1,875,000)	1,481,789
Kānpur Cantonment (★Kānpur)	90,311
Kapūrthala	50,300
Karād	54,364
Kāraikkudi (★100,141)	66,993
Karīmnagar	86,125
Karnāl	132,107
Karūr (★93,810)	72,692
Kāsganj	61,402
Kāshīpur	51,773
Katihār (★122,005)	104,781
Kātwa (★44,430)	32,890
Kāvali	48,119
Kāyankulam	61,327
Kerkend (★Dhānbād)	75,186
Khadki Cantonment (★Pune)	80,835
Khambhāt	68,791
Khāmgaon	61,992
Khammam	98,757
Khandwa	114,725
Khanna	53,761
Kharagpur (★232,575)	150,475
Kharagpur Railway Settlement (★Kharagpur)	82,100
Khargone	52,749
Khurja	67,119
Kishanganj	51,790
Kishangarh Bās	62,032
Koch Bihār (★80,101)	62,127
Kolār	65,834
Kolār Gold Fields (★144,385)	77,679
Kolhāpur (★351,392)	340,625
Konnagar (★Calcutta)	51,211
Korba	83,387
Kota	358,241
Kot Kapūra	47,550
Kottagūdem	94,894
Kottayam	64,431
Kovilpatti	63,964
Krishnagiri	48,335
Krishnanagar	98,141
Kulti (★Asansol)	41,323
Kumbakonam (★141,794)	132,832
Kundla (★51,431)	49,740
Kurasia (★53,015)	12,963
Kurichi (★Coimbatore)	48,936
Kurnool	206,362
Lakhīmpur	61,003
Lalitpur	55,756
Lātūr	111,986
Lucknow (★1,060,000)	895,721
Lucknow Cantonment (★Lucknow)	59,614
Ludhiāna	607,052
Machilīpatnam (Bandar)	138,530
Madanapalle	54,938
Madgaon (Margao) (★64,858)	53,076
Madras (★4,475,000)	3,276,622
Madurai (★960,000)	820,891
Mahbūbnagar	87,503
Mahesāna (★73,024)	72,872
Mahuva (★56,072)	53,625
Mainpuri	58,928
Mālegaon	245,883
Māler Kotla	65,756
Malkajgiri (★Hyderābād)	65,776
Mandsaur	77,603
Mandya	100,285
Mangalore (★306,078)	172,252
Mango (★Jamshedpur)	67,284
Manjeri	53,959
Manmād	51,439
Mannārgudi	51,738
Mathura (★160,995)	147,493
Maunath Bhanjan	86,326
Māyūram	67,675
Medinīpur	86,118
Meerut (★536,615)	417,395
Meerut Cantonment (★Meerut)	94,210
Melappālaiyam (★Tirunelveli)	57,683
Mettuppālaiyam	59,537
Mhow (★76,037)	70,130
Miraj (★Sāngli)	105,455
Mirzāpur	127,787
Modinagar (★87,665)	78,243
Moga	80,272
Mokāma	51,047
Morādābād (★345,350)	330,051
Morbi	73,327
Morena	69,864
Mormugao	69,684
Motihāri (★63,212)	57,911
Muktsar	50,941
Munger	129,260
Murwāra (★123,017)	77,862
Muzaffarnagar	171,816
Muzaffarpur	190,416
Mysore (★479,081)	441,754
Nadiād	142,689
Nagaon (1971C)	56,537
Nāgappattinam (★90,650)	82,828
Nāgaur	48,005
Nagda	56,602
Nāgercoil	171,648
Nagīna	50,405
Nāgpur (★1,302,066)	1,219,461
Naihāti (★Calcutta)	114,607
Najībābād	55,109
Nalgonda	62,458
Nānded	191,269
Nandurbār	65,394
Nandyāl	88,185
Nangi (★Calcutta)	54,035
Narasapur	46,033
Narasaraopet	67,032
Nāshik (★429,034)	262,428
Navadwip (★129,800)	109,108
Navsāri (★129,266)	106,793
Nawābganj (★62,216)	51,518
Neemuch (★68,853)	65,860
Nellore	237,065
NEW DELHI (★Delhi)	273,036
Neyveli (★98,866)	88,000
Nizāmābād	183,061
North Bārākpur (★Calcutta)	81,758
North Dum Dum (★Calcutta)	96,418
Ongole	85,302
Orai	66,397
Outer Burnpur (★Asansol)	86,803
Pālakodu	46,146
Palani (★68,389)	64,444
Pālanpur	61,262
Pālayankottai (★Tirunelveli)	87,302
Pālghāt (★117,986)	111,245
Pāli	91,568
Pallavaram (★Madras)	83,901
Palwal	47,328
Panaji (Panjim) (★77,226)	43,165
Pānchur (★Calcutta)	51,223
Pandharpur	64,380
Pānihāti (★Calcutta)	205,718
Pānīpat	137,927
Panruti	43,042
Paramakkudi	61,149
Parbhani	109,364
Parli	48,946
Pātan	79,196
Pathānkot	110,039
Patiāla (★206,254)	205,141
Patna (★1,025,000)	776,371
Pattukkottai	49,484
Periyakulam	44,310
Petlād	47,020
Phagwāra (★75,961)	72,499
Pīlībhīt	88,548
Pimpri-Chinchwad (★Pune)	220,966
Pollāchi (★114,971)	82,354
Pondicherry (★251,420)	162,636
Ponmalai (★Tiruchchirāppalli)	55,995
Ponnāni	43,226
Ponnūru Nidubrolu	50,206
Porbandar (★133,307)	115,182
Port Blair	49,634
Proddatūr	107,070
Pudukkottai	87,952
Pune (Poona) (★1,775,000)	1,203,351
Pune Cantonment (★Pune)	85,986
Puri	100,942
Pūrnia (★109,875)	91,144
Puruliya	73,904
Quilon (★167,598)	137,943
Rabkavi Banhatti	51,693
Rāe Bareli	89,697
Rāichūr	124,762
Raiganj (★66,705)	60,343
Raigarh (★69,791)	68,060
Raipur	338,245
Rājahmundry (★268,370)	203,358
Rājapālaiyam	101,640
Rajhara-Jharandalli	55,307
Rājkot	445,076
Rāj Nāndgaon	86,367
Rājpur (★60,734)	43,985
Rājpura	58,645
Rāmanāthapuram	45,719
Rāmgarh (★65,268)	41,257
Rāmpur	204,610
Rānāghāt (★83,744)	58,356
Rānchi (★502,771)	489,626
Rānībennur	58,118
Rānīganj (★119,101)	48,702
Ratlām (★155,578)	142,319
Ratnāgiri	47,036
Raurkela (★322,610)	206,821
Raurkela Civil Township (★Raurkela)	96,000
Rewa	100,641
Rewāri	51,562
Rishra (★Calcutta)	81,001
Robertson Pet (★Kolār Gold Fields)	61,099
Rohtak	166,767
Roorkee (★79,076)	61,851
Sāgar (★207,479)	160,392
Sahāranpur	295,355
Saharsa	57,580
Sahijpur Bogha (★Ahmadābād)	65,327
Salem (★518,615)	361,394
Sambalpur (★162,214)	110,282
Sambhal	108,232
Sāngli (★268,988)	152,339
Sardarnagar (★Ahmadābād)	50,128
Sardārshahr (★56,388)	55,473
Sāsarām	73,457
Sātāra	83,336
Satna (★96,667)	90,476
Saunda (★99,990)	70,780
Sawāi Mādhopur (★59,083)	28,139
Secunderābād Cantonment (★Hyderābād)	135,994
Sehore	52,190
Seoni	54,017
Serampore (★Calcutta)	127,304
Shahdol (★49,631)	44,342
Shāhjahānpur (★205,095)	185,396
Shāmli	51,850
Shāntipur	82,980
Shikohābād	47,083
Shiliguri	154,378
Shillong (★174,703)	109,244
Shimoga	151,783
Shivpuri	75,738
Shrirampur	55,491
Siddhapur (★52,706)	51,953
Sīkar	102,970
Silchar (1971C)	52,596
Simla	70,604
Sindri (★Dhānbād)	70,645
Sirsa	89,068
Sītāpur	101,210
Sivakāsi (★83,072)	59,827
Siwān	51,284
Solāpur (★514,860)	511,103
Sonīpat	109,369
South Dum Dum (★Calcutta)	230,266
Srīkākulam	68,145
Srikalahasti	51,306
Srīnagar (★606,002)	594,775
Srīrangam (★Tiruchchirāppalli)	64,241
Srīvilliputtūr	61,458
Sujāngarh	55,546
Sultānpur	48,782
Sūrat (★913,806)	776,583
Surendranagar (★130,602)	89,619
Tādepallegūdem	62,574
Tādpatri	53,920
Tāmbaram (★Madras)	86,923
Tānda	54,474
Tanuku	53,618
Tellicherry (★98,704)	75,561
Tenāli	119,257
Tenkāsi	49,214
Thāna (★Bombay)	309,897
Thānesar	49,052
Thanjāvūr	184,015
Theni-Allinagaram	53,018
Tindivanam	56,520
Tinsukia (1971C)	54,911
Tiruchchirāppalli (★609,548)	362,045
Tiruchengodu	53,941
Tirunelveli (★323,344)	128,850
Tirupati	115,292
Tiruppattūr	52,422
Tiruppur (★215,859)	165,223
Tiruvannāmalai	89,462
Tirūvottiyūr (★Madras)	134,014
Titāgarh (★Calcutta)	104,534
Tonk	77,653
Trichūr (★170,122)	77,923
Trivandrum (★520,125)	483,086
Ttruchchendūr (★68,884)	24,233
Tumkūr	108,670
Tuticorin (★250,677)	192,949
Udagamandalam	78,277
Udaipur	232,588
Udamalpet	54,852
Udgīr	50,564
Ujjain (★282,203)	278,454
Ulhāsnagar (★Bombay)	273,668
Unnāo	75,983
Upleta	54,907
Uttarpara-Kotrung (★Calcutta)	79,598
Vadodara (★744,881)	734,473
Vālpārai	115,452
Vāniyambādi (★75,042)	59,107
Vārānasi (Benares) (★925,000)	708,647
Vasai (Bassein) (★52,398)	34,940
Vellore (★274,041)	174,247
Verāval (★105,307)	85,048
Vidisha	65,521
Vijayawāda (★543,008)	454,577
Vikramasingapuram	49,319
Viluppuram	77,091
Viramgām	48,275
Virudunagar	68,047
Vishākhapatnam (★603,630)	565,321
Visnagar	46,631
Vizianagaram	114,806
Warangal	335,150
Wardha	88,495
Yamunānagar (★160,424)	109,304
Yavatmāl	89,071
Yemmiganur	50,701

INDONESIA

1980 C	147,490,298
Ambon (▲207,702)	111,914
Balikpapan (▲279,852)	208,040
Banda Aceh (Kuturaja)	71,868
Bandung (★1,800,000)	1,461,407
Banjarmasin	380,884
Banyuwangi	90,378
Batang	49,328
Bekasi (★Jakarta)	144,290
Bengkulu (▲64,733)	32,478
Binjai	71,444
Blitar (★100,000)	78,503
Bogor (★560,000)	246,946
Bojonegoro	57,483
Bukittinggi (▲70,691)	55,577
Cianjur	105,655
Cibinong	87,580
Cilacap	127,017
Cimahi (★Bandung) (1971C)	72,367
Ciparay	66,854
Cirebon (★275,000)	223,504
Denpasar	159,233
Depok (★Jakarta)	126,693
Garut	145,624
Genteng	59,481
Gorontalo (▲97,610)	63,554
Gresik	86,418
• JAKARTA (★8,600,000) (1985E)	7,885,000
Jambi (▲230,046)	155,761
Jayapura (Sukarnapura)	60,641
Jember	171,284
Jombang	58,800
Karawang	72,195
Kediri (▲221,830)	176,261
Kisaran	58,129
Klangenang	64,013
Klaten	117,560
Kudus	154,478
Kupang	84,587
Langsa	16,426
Lumajang	58,495
Madiun (★180,000)	150,562
Magelang (★160,000)	123,358
Majalaya	87,474
Malang	511,780
Manado	217,091
Mataram	210,485
Medan	1,373,747
Mojokerto	68,849
Muncar	47,009
Padang (▲480,607)	296,675
Padangsidempuan	56,984
Palangkaraya (▲60,447)	51,686
Palembang	786,607
Pangkalpinang	90,078
Pare	47,262
Parepare (▲86,360)	62,865
Pasuruan (★125,000)	95,864
Pati	50,159
Pekalongan (★260,000)	132,413
Pekanbaru	186,199
Pemalang	72,663
Pematangsiantar (★175,000)	150,296
Ponorogo	55,523
Pontianak	304,490
Pringsewu	56,115
Probolinggo	100,296
Purwakarta	61,995
Purwokerto	143,787
Salatiga	85,740
Samarinda (▲264,012)	182,473
Semarang	1,024,940
Serang	78,209
Sibolga	59,466
Sidoarjo	56,090
Singaraja	53,368
Singkawang	58,693
Situbondo	58,299
Sorong	52,041
Subang	52,041
Sukabumi (★225,000)	109,898
Surabaya	2,027,913
Surakarta (★575,000)	469,532
Taman	64,358
Tangerang	97,091
Tanjungkarang-Telukbetung (★375,000)	284,167
Tarakan	46,657
Tasikmalaya	192,267
Tebingtinggi (▲92,068)	69,569
Tegal (★340,000)	131,440
Tembilahan	52,140
Tuban	48,558
Tulungagung	91,585
Ujungpandang (Makasar)	708,465
Yogyakarta (★510,000)	394,965

IRAN / Īrān

1986 C	49,445,010
Ābādān (1976C)	296,081
Āghā Jārī (1982E)	64,000
Ahar (1982E)	52,000
Ahvāz	579,826
Āmol	118,242
Andīmeshk (1982E)	53,000
Arāk	265,349
Ardabīl	281,973
Bābol	115,320
Bākhtarān (Kermānshāh)	560,514
Bandar-e ʿAbbās	201,642
Bandar-e Anzalī (Bandar-e Pahlavī) (1982E)	83,000
Bandar-e Būshehr	120,787
Bandar-e Māh Shahr (1982E)	88,000
Behbahān (1982E)	84,000
Bīrjand (1982E)	68,000
Bojnūrd (1982E)	82,000
Borāzjān (1982E)	53,000
Borūjerd	183,879
Dezfūl	151,420
Do Rūd (1982E)	52,000
Emāmshahr (Shāhrūd) (1982E)	68,000
Eṣfahān	986,753
Eslāmābād (1982E)	71,000
Eslāmshahr (★Tehrān)	215,129
Fasā (1982E)	67,000
Gonbad-e Qābūs (1982E)	75,000
Gorgān	139,430
Hamadān	272,499
Īlām (1982E)	75,000
Jahrom (1982E)	68,000
Karaj (★Tehrān)	275,100
Kāshān	138,599
Kāzerūn (1982E)	63,000
Kermān	257,284
Khomeynīshahr	104,647
Khorramābād	208,592
Khorramshahr (1976C)	146,709
Khvoy	115,343
Mahābād (1982E)	63,000
Malāyer	103,640
Marāgheh	100,679
Marand (1982E)	59,000
Marv Dasht (1982E)	72,000
Mashhad	1,463,508
Masjed-e Soleymān	104,787
Mīāndoāb (1982E)	52,000
Mīāneh (1982E)	57,000
Najafābād	129,058
Neyshābūr	109,258
Orūmīyeh (Reẕā'īyeh)	300,746
Qā'emshahr	109,288
Qazvīn	248,591

▲ Población de un municipio, comuna o distrito entero, incluyendo sus áreas rurales.
• Ciudad más grande de un país.
★ Población o designación de un área metropolitana, incluyendo los suburbios.
C Censo. **E** Estimado oficial. **U** Estimado no oficial.

▲ Population d'une municipalité, d'une commune ou d'un district, zone rurale incluse.
• Ville la plus peuplée du pays.
★ Population de l'agglomération (ou nom de la zone métropolitaine englobante).
C Recensement. **E** Estimation officielle. **U** Estimation non officielle.

▲ População de um municipio, comuna ou distrito, inclusive as respectivas áreas rurais.
• Maior cidade de um país.
★ População ou indicação de uma área metropolitana.
C Censo. **E** Estimativa oficial. **U** Estimativa não oficial.

Qom	543,139
Qomsheh (1982E)	67,000
Qūchān (1982E)	61,000
Rafsanjān (1982E)	61,000
Rāmhormoz (1982E)	53,000
Rasht	290,897
Sabzevār	129,103
Sanandaj	204,537
Saqqez (1982E)	76,000
Sārī	141,020
Semnān (1982E)	54,000
Shahr-e Kord (1982E)	63,000
Shīrāz	848,289
Sīrjān (1982E)	67,000
Tabrīz	971,482
• TEHRĀN (★6,400,000)	6,042,584
Torbat-e Heydarīyeh (1982E)	62,000
Varāmīn (1982E)	51,000
Yazd	230,483
Zābol (1982E)	58,000
Zāhedān	281,923
Zanjān	215,261
Zarrīn Shahr (1982E)	69,000

IRAQ / Al 'Irāq

1985 E	15,584,987
Ad-Dīwānīyah (1970E)	62,300
Al-'Amārah	131,758
Al-Başrah	616,700
Al-Hillah	215,249
Al-Mawşil	570,926
An-Najaf	242,603
An-Nāşirīyah	138,842
Ar-Ramādī	137,388
As-Sulaymānīyah	279,424
• BAGHDĀD (1987C)	3,841,268
Ba'qūbah	114,516
Irbīl	333,903
Karbalā'	184,574
Kirkūk (1970E)	207,900

IRELAND / Éire

1986 C	3,540,643
Cork (★173,694)	133,271
• DUBLIN (BAILE ÁTHA CLIATH) (★1,140,000)	502,749
Dún Laoghaire (★Dublin)	54,715
Galway	47,104
Limerick (★76,557)	56,279
Waterford (★41,054)	39,529

ISLE OF MAN

1986 C	64,282
• DOUGLAS (★28,500)	20,368

ISRAEL / Isrā'īl / Yisra'el

1989 E	4,386,000
Ashdod	74,700
Ashqelon	56,300
Bat Yam (★Tel Aviv-Yafo)	133,100
Be'ér Sheva (Beersheba)	113,200
Bene Beraq (★Tel Aviv-Yafo)	109,400
Elat	24,700
Giv'atayim (★Tel Aviv-Yafo)	45,600
Ḥefa (★435,000)	222,600
Herzliyya (★Tel Aviv-Yafo)	71,600
Ḥolon (★Tel Aviv-Yafo)	146,100
Kefar Sava (★Tel Aviv-Yafo)	54,800
Nazerat (Nazareth) (★74,000)	50,600
Netanya (★Tel Aviv-Yafo)	117,800
Petaḥ Tiqwa (★Tel Aviv-Yafo)	133,600
Ra'anana (★Tel Aviv-Yafo)	49,400
Ramat Gan (★Tel Aviv-Yafo)	115,700
Reḥovot (★Tel Aviv-Yafo)	72,500
Rishon LeẒiyyon (★Tel Aviv-Yafo)	123,800
• Tel Aviv-Yafo (★1,670,000)	317,800
YERUSHALAYIM (AL-QUDS) (JERUSALEM) (★490,000)	493,500

ISRAELI OCCUPIED TERRITORIES

1989 E	1,574,700
Al-Quds (Jerusalem) (★Yerushalayim) (1976E)	90,000
Arīḥā (Jericho) (1967C)	6,829
Bayt Laḥm (Bethlehem) (1971E)	25,000
• Ghazzah (1967C)	118,272
Khān Yūnis (1967C)	52,997
Nābulus (1971E)	64,000
Rafaḥ (1967C)	49,812

ITALY / Italia

1987 E	57,290,519
Afragola (★Napoli)	59,397
Alessandria (▲96,014)	76,100
Altamura	54,784
Ancona	104,409
Andria	88,348
Arezzo (▲91,681)	74,200
Asti (▲75,459)	63,600
Avellino	56,407
Aversa (★Napoli)	57,827
Bari (★475,000)	362,524
Barletta	86,954
Benevento (▲65,661)	54,400
Bergamo (★345,000)	118,959
Biella	51,788
Bitonto	51,962
Bologna (★525,000)	432,406
Bolzano	101,515
Brescia	199,286
Brindisi	92,280
Busto Arsizio (★Milano)	78,056
Cagliari (★305,000)	220,574
Caltanissetta	62,352
Campobasso (▲50,801)	44,000
Carpi (▲60,614)	49,500
Carrara (★Massa)	69,229
Caserta	65,974
Casoria (★Napoli)	54,100
Castellammare di Stabia (★Napoli)	68,491
Catania (★550,000)	372,486
Catanzaro	102,558
Cava de'Tirreni (★Salerno)	52,028
Cerignola	53,463
Cesena (▲90,012)	72,600
Chieti	55,827
Cinisello Balsamo (★Milano)	78,917
Civitavecchia	50,806
Collegno (★Torino)	49,334
Cologno Monzese (★Milano)	52,554
Como (★165,000)	91,738
Cosenza (★150,000)	106,026
Cremona	76,979
Crotone (▲61,005)	53,600
Cuneo (▲55,878)	47,900
Empoli (▲43,940)	33,200
Ercolano (★Napoli)	62,783
Ferrara (▲143,950)	113,300
Firenze (★640,000)	425,835
Foggia	155,051
Foligno (▲53,568)	42,500
Forlì (▲110,482)	91,200
Gela	79,378
Genova (Genoa) (★805,000)	727,427
Giugliano in Campania (★Napoli)	51,187
Grosseto (▲70,592)	56,400
Imola (▲61,587)	48,200
Imperia	41,481
L'Aquila (▲66,438)	42,200
La Spezia (★185,000)	108,937
Latina (▲98,479)	67,800
Lecce	100,981
Lecco	48,844
Legnano (★Milano)	48,711
Livorno	174,065
Lucca	88,024
Manfredonia	57,707
Mantova (▲56,817)	49,000
Marsala	80,468
Massa (★145,000)	66,872
Matera	52,819
Messina	268,896
Mestre (★Venezia)	189,700
• Milano (Milan) (★3,750,000)	1,495,260
Modena	176,880
Molfetta	64,519
Moncalieri (★Torino)	62,306
Monza (★Milano)	122,064
Napoli (Naples) (★2,875,000)	1,204,211
Nicastro (▲67,562)	52,100
Nocera Inferiore	48,151
Novara	102,742
Padova (★270,000)	225,769
Palermo	723,732
Parma	175,842
Paternò	45,513
Pavia	82,065
Perugia (▲146,713)	106,700
Pesaro (▲90,336)	78,700
Pescara	131,027
Piacenza	105,626
Pisa	104,384
Pistoia (▲90,689)	76,800
Pordenone	50,825
Portici (★Napoli)	76,302
Potenza (▲67,114)	57,600
Pozzuoli (★Napoli)	65,000
Prato (★215,000)	164,595
Quartu Sant'Elena	52,838
Ragusa	67,748
Ravenna (▲136,016)	86,500
Reggio di Calabria	178,821
Reggio nell'Emilia (▲130,086)	107,300
Rho (★Milano)	50,876
Rimini (▲130,698)	114,600
Rivoli (★Torino)	50,786
ROMA (★3,175,000)	2,815,457
Salerno (★250,000)	154,848
San Benedetto del Tronto	45,397
San Giorgio a Cremano (★Napoli)	63,656
San Remo	60,797
San Severo	55,239
Sassari	120,152
Savona (★112,000)	62,300
Scandicci (★Firenze)	54,367
Sesto Fiorentino (★Firenze)	46,355
Sesto San Giovanni (★Milano)	91,624
Siena	59,712
Siracusa	122,857
Taranto	244,997
Teramo (▲52,378)	36,000
Terni (▲111,157)	94,500
Torino (★1,550,000)	1,035,565
Torre Annunziata (★Napoli)	57,508
Torre del Greco (★Napoli)	105,066
Trapani (▲73,083)	63,000
Trento (▲100,202)	81,500
Treviso	85,083
Trieste (Triest)	239,031
Udine (★126,000)	100,211
Varese	88,353
Venezia (Venice) (★420,000)	88,700
Vercelli	51,008
Verona	259,151
Viareggio (▲59,146)	50,300
Vicenza	110,449
Vigevano	62,671
Viterbo (▲59,267)	47,900
Vittoria	54,795

IVORY COAST / Côte d'Ivoire

1983 E	9,300,000
• ABIDJAN	1,950,000
Bouaké	275,000
Daloa	70,000
Korhogo	125,000
Man	55,000
YAMOUSSOUKRO	80,000

JAMAICA

1982 C	2,190,357
• KINGSTON (★770,000)	586,930
Montego Bay	70,265
Portmore (★Kingston)	73,426
Spanish Town (★Kingston)	89,097

JAPAN / Nihon

1985 C	121,048,923
Abiko (★Tōkyō)	111,659
Ageo (★Tōkyō)	178,587
Aizu-wakamatsu	118,140
Akashi (★Ōsaka)	263,363
Akishima (★Tōkyō)	97,543
Akita	296,400
Akō	52,374
Amagasaki (★Ōsaka)	509,115
Anan (▲60,749)	48,100
Anjō	133,059
Aomori	294,045
Arao (★Ōmuta)	62,570
Asahikawa	363,631
Asaka (★Tōkyō)	94,431
Ashikaga	167,656
Ashiya (★Ōsaka)	87,127
Atami	49,374
Atsugi (★Tōkyō)	175,600
Ayase (★Tōkyō)	71,152
Beppu	134,775
Bisai (★Nagoya)	56,234
Chiba (★Tōkyō)	788,930
Chichibu	61,013
Chigasaki (★Tōkyō)	185,030
Chikushino (★Fukuoka)	63,242
Chiryū (★Nagoya)	50,506
Chita (★Nagoya)	70,013
Chitose	73,610
Chōfu (★Tōkyō)	191,071
Chōshi	87,883
Daitō (★Ōsaka)	122,441
Dazaifu (★Fukuoka)	57,737
Ebetsu (★Sapporo)	90,328
Ebina (★Tōkyō)	93,159
Eniwa	48,305
Fuchū	47,798
Fuchū (★Tōkyō)	201,972
Fuchū	48,833
Fuji (★370,000)	214,448
Fujieda (★Shizuoka)	111,985
Fujiidera (★Ōsaka)	65,252
Fujimi (★Tōkyō)	85,697
Fujinomiya (★Fuji)	112,642
Fujisawa (★Tōkyō)	328,387
Fuji-yoshida	54,796
Fukaya (▲89,121)	71,600
Fukuchiyama (▲65,995)	56,200
Fukui	250,261
Fukuoka (★1,750,000)	1,160,440
Fukushima	270,762
Fukuyama	360,261
Funabashi (★Tōkyō)	506,966
Fussa (★Tōkyō)	51,478
Gamagōri	85,580
Gifu	411,743
Ginowan	69,206
Gotemba	74,882
Gyōda	79,359
Habikino (★Ōsaka)	111,394
Hachinohe	241,430
Hachiōji (★Tōkyō)	426,654
Hadano (★Tōkyō)	141,803
Hagi	52,740
Hakodate	319,194
Hamada	51,071
Hamakita	77,228
Hamamatsu	514,118
Hanamaki (▲69,886)	54,500
Handa (★Nagoya)	92,883
Hannō (★Tōkyō)	66,550
Hashima	59,760
Hasuda (★Tōkyō)	53,991
Hatogaya (★Tōkyō)	55,424
Hatsukaichi (★Hiroshima)	52,020
Hekinan	63,778
Higashihiroshima (★Hiroshima)	84,717
Higashikurume (★Tōkyō)	110,079
Higashimatsuyama	70,426
Higashimurayama (★Tōkyō)	123,798
Higashiōsaka (★Ōsaka)	522,805
Higashiyamato (★Tōkyō)	69,881
Hikari (★Tokuyama)	49,246
Hikone	94,204
Himeji (★660,000)	452,917
Himi (▲62,112)	52,300
Hino (★Tōkyō)	156,031
Hirakata (★Ōsaka)	382,257
Hiratsuka (★Tōkyō)	229,990
Hirosaki (▲176,082)	134,800
Hiroshima (★1,575,000)	1,044,118
Hita (▲65,730)	57,900
Hitachi	206,074
Hōfu	118,067
Honjō	56,495
Hōya (★Tōkyō)	9,156
Hyūga	59,163
Ibaraki (★Ōsaka)	250,463
Ichihara (★Tōkyō)	237,617
Ichikawa (★Tōkyō)	397,822
Ichinomiya (★Nagoya)	257,388
Ichinoseki (▲60,941)	49,200
Iida (▲92,401)	65,000
Iizuka (★110,000)	81,868
Ikeda (★Ōsaka)	101,683
Ikoma (★Ōsaka)	86,293
Imabari	125,115
Imari (▲62,044)	50,700
Ina (▲59,010)	48,600
Inagi (★Tōkyō)	50,766
Inazawa (★Nagoya)	94,479
Inuyama (★Nagoya)	68,723
Iruma (★Tōkyō)	118,603
Isahaya	88,376
Ise (Uji-yamada)	105,455
Isehara (★Tōkyō)	7,776
Isesaki	112,459
Ishinomaki	122,674
Itami (★Ōsaka)	182,731
Itō	70,197
Iwaki (Taira)	350,569
Iwakuni	111,833
Iwamizawa	81,664
Iwata	80,810
Iwatsuki (★Tōkyō)	100,903
Izumi (★Sendai)	124,216
Izumi (★Ōsaka)	137,641
Izumi-ōtsu (★Ōsaka)	67,755
Izumi-sano (★Ōsaka)	91,563
Izumo (▲80,749)	68,000
Joetsu	130,659
Jōyō (★Ōsaka)	81,850
Kadoma (★Ōsaka)	140,590
Kaga	68,630
Kagoshima	530,502
Kainan (★Wakayama)	50,779
Kaizuka (★Ōsaka)	79,591
Kakamigahara	124,464
Kakegawa (▲68,724)	55,600
Kakogawa (★Ōsaka)	227,311
Kamagaya (★Tōkyō)	85,705
Kamaishi	60,007
Kamakura (★Tōkyō)	175,495
Kameoka	76,207
Kamifukuoka (★Tōkyō)	57,638
Kanazawa	430,481
Kani (★Nagoya)	69,630
Kanoya (▲76,029)	60,200
Kanuma (▲88,078)	73,200
Karatsu (▲78,744)	70,100
Kariya (★Nagoya)	112,403
Kasai	52,107
Kasaoka (▲60,598)	53,500
Kashihara (★Ōsaka)	112,888
Kashiwa (★Tōkyō)	273,128
Kashiwara (★Ōsaka)	73,252
Kashiwazaki (▲86,020)	73,350
Kasuga (★Fukuoka)	75,555
Kasugai (★Nagoya)	256,990
Kasukabe (★Tōkyō)	171,890
Katano (★	64,205
Katsuta	102,763
Kawachi-nagano (★Ōsaka)	91,313
Kawagoe (★Tōkyō)	285,437
Kawaguchi (★Tōkyō)	403,015
Kawanishi (★Ōsaka)	136,376
Kawasaki (★Tōkyō)	1,088,624
Kesennuma	68,137
Kimitsu (▲84,310)	71,900
Kiryū	131,267
Kisarazu	120,201
Kishiwada (★Ōsaka)	185,731
Kitaibaraki	51,035
Kitakyūshū (★1,525,000)	1,056,402
Kitami	107,281
Kitamoto (★Tōkyō)	58,114
Kiyose (★Tōkyō)	65,066
Kōbe (★Ōsaka)	1,410,834
Kōchi	312,241
Kodaira (★Tōkyō)	158,673
Kōfu	202,405
Koga (★Tōkyō)	57,541
Koganei (★Tōkyō)	104,642
Kokubunji (★Tōkyō)	95,467
Komae (★Tōkyō)	73,784
Komaki (★Nagoya)	113,284
Komatsu	106,041
Kōnan (★Nagoya)	92,049
Kōnosu (★Tōkyō)	60,565
Kōriyama	301,673
Koshigaya (★Tōkyō)	253,479
Kudamatsu (★Tokuyama)	54,445
Kuki (★Tōkyō)	58,636
Kumagaya	143,496
Kumamoto	555,719
Kunitachi (★Tōkyō)	64,881
Kurashiki	413,632
Kurayoshi (▲52,351)	43,000
Kure (★Hiroshima)	226,488
Kuroiso (▲49,742)	39,800
Kurume	222,847
Kusatsu (★Ōsaka)	87,542
Kushiro	214,541
Kuwana (★Nagoya)	94,731
Kyōto (★	1,479,218
Machida (★Tōkyō)	321,188
Maebashi	277,319
Maizuru	98,775
Marugame	74,272
Matsubara (★Ōsaka)	136,455
Matsudo (★Tōkyō)	427,473
Matsue	140,005
Matsumoto	197,340
Matsusaka	116,886
Matsuyama	426,658
Mihara	85,975
Miki (★Ōsaka)	74,527
Minō (★Ōsaka)	114,770
Misato (★Tōkyō)	107,964
Mishima (★Numazu)	99,600
Mitaka (★Tōkyō)	166,252
Mito	228,985
Miura (★Tōkyō)	50,471
Miyako	61,654
Miyakonojō (▲132,098)	107,600
Miyazaki	279,114
Mobara	76,929
Moriguchi (★Ōsaka)	159,400
Morioka	235,469
Moriyama	53,052
Mukō (★Ōsaka)	52,216
Munakata	60,971
Muroran (★195,000)	136,208
Musashimurayama (★Tōkyō)	60,930
Musashino (★Tōkyō)	138,783
Mutsu	49,292
Nabari	56,474
Nagahama	55,531
Nagano	336,973
Nagaoka	183,756
Nagaokakyō (★Ōsaka)	75,242
Nagareyama (★Tōkyō)	124,682
Nagasaki	449,382
Nagoya (★4,800,000)	2,116,381
Naha	303,674
Nakama (★Kitakyūshū)	50,294
Nakatsu	66,260
Nakatsugawa	53,277
Nanao	50,582
Nara (★Ōsaka)	327,702
Narashino (★Tōkyō)	136,365
Narita	77,181
Naruto	64,329
Naze	49,765
Neyagawa (★Ōsaka)	258,228
Niigata	475,630
Niihama	132,184
Niitsu (▲63,846)	55,600

▲ Population of an entire municipality, commune, or district, including rural area.
• Largest city in country.
★ Population or designation of the metropolitan area, including suburbs.
C Census. **E** Official estimate. **U** Unofficial estimate.

▲ Bevölkerung eines ganzen städtischen Verwaltungsgebietes, eines Kommunalbezirkes oder eines Distrikts, einschliesslich ländlicher Gebiete.
• Grösste Stadt des Landes.
★ Bevölkerung oder Bezeichnung der Stadtregion einschliesslich Vororte.
C Volkszählung. **E** Offizielle Schätzung. **U** Inoffizielle Schätzung.

Population of Cities and Towns / Einwohnerzahlen von Grossstädten / Habitantes en las Ciudades y Poblaciones
Population des Grands Centres et des Villes / População dos Centros Urbanos 309

Niiza (★Tōkyō)	129,287
Nishinomiya (★Ōsaka)	421,267
Nishio	91,930
Nobeoka	136,381
Noboribetsu (★Muroran)	58,370
Noda (★Tōkyō)	105,937
Nōgata	64,479
Noshiro (▲59,170)	50,400
Numazu (★495,000)	210,490
Obihiro	162,932
Ōbu (★Nagoya)	66,696
Ōdate (▲71,794)	60,900
Odawara	185,941
Ōgaki	145,910
Ōita	390,096
Ōkawa	47,837
Okaya	61,747
Okayama	572,479
Okazaki	284,996
Okegawa (★Tōkyō)	61,499
Okinawa	101,210
Ōme (★Tōkyō)	110,828
Ōmi-hachiman (★Ōsaka)	63,791
Ōmiya (★Tōkyō)	373,022
Ōmura	69,472
Ōmuta (★225,000)	159,424
Ōnojō (★Fukuoka)	69,435
Onomichi	100,640
Ōsaka (★16,450,000)	2,636,249
Ōta	133,670
Otaru (★Sapporo)	172,486
Ōtsu (★Ōsaka)	234,551
Owariashi (★Nagoya)	57,415
Oyama (▲134,242)	113,100
Sabae	61,452
Saga	168,252
Sagamihara (★Tōkyō)	482,778
Saijō	56,516
Saiki	54,708
Sakado (★Tōkyō)	87,586
Sakai (★Ōsaka)	818,271
Sakaide	66,087
Sakata	101,392
Saku (▲59,974)	48,400
Sakura (★Tōkyō)	121,213
Sakurai	58,894
Sanjō	86,325
Sano	80,753
Sapporo (★1,900,000)	1,542,979
Sasebo	250,633
Satte	51,462
Sayama (★Ōsaka)	50,246
Sayama (★Tōkyō)	144,366
Seki	64,149
Sendai, Kagoshima pref. (▲71,444)	57,800
Sendai, Miyagi pref. (★1,175,000)	700,254
Sennan (★Ōsaka)	60,059
Seto	124,623
Settsu (★Ōsaka)	86,332
Shibata (▲77,219)	62,800
Shibukawa	47,814
Shijōnawate (★Ōsaka)	50,352
Shiki (★Tōkyō)	58,935
Shimada (▲72,388)	63,200
Shimizu (★Shizuoka)	242,166
Shimodate (▲63,958)	52,400
Shimonoseki (★Kitakyūshū)	269,169
Shiogama (★Sendai)	61,825
Shizuoka (★975,000)	468,362
Sōka (★Tōkyō)	194,205
Suita (★Ōsaka)	348,948
Suwa	52,329
Suzuka	164,936
Tachikawa (★Tōkyō)	146,523
Tagajō (★Sendai)	54,436
Tagawa	59,727
Tajimi (★Nagoya)	84,829
Takaishi (★Ōsaka)	66,974
Takamatsu	326,999
Takaoka (★220,000)	175,780
Takarazuka (★Ōsaka)	194,273
Takasago (★Ōsaka)	91,434
Takasaki	231,766
Takatsuki (★Ōsaka)	348,784
Takayama	65,033
Takefu	69,148
Takikawa	52,004
Tama (★Tōkyō)	122,135
Tamano	76,954
Tanabe (▲70,835)	59,800
Tanashi (★Tōkyō)	71,331
Tatebayashi	75,141
Tenri	69,129
Tochigi	86,290
Toda (★Tōkyō)	76,960
Tōkai (★Nagoya)	95,278
Toki	65,308
Tokoname (★Nagoya)	53,077
Tokorozawa (★Tōkyō)	275,168
Tokushima	257,884
Tokuyama (★250,000)	112,638
• TŌKYŌ (★27,700,000)	8,354,615
Tomakomai	158,061
Tondabayashi (★Ōsaka)	102,619
Toride (★Tōkyō)	78,608
Tosu	55,791
Tottori	137,060
Toyama	314,111
Toyoake (★Nagoya)	57,969
Toyohashi	322,142
Toyokawa	107,430
Toyonaka (★Ōsaka)	413,213
Toyota	308,111
Tsu	150,690
Tsuchiura	120,175
Tsuruga	65,670
Tsuruoka	100,200
Tsushima (★Nagoya)	58,735
Tsuyama	86,837
Ube (★230,000)	174,855
Ueda	116,178
Ueno (▲60,812)	51,800
Uji (★Ōsaka)	165,411
Uozu	49,825
Urasoe	81,611
Urawa (★Tōkyō)	377,235
Urayasu (★Tōkyō)	93,756
Usa (▲52,217)	39,500
Ushiku	51,926
Utsunomiya	405,375
Uwajima	71,381
Wakayama (★495,000)	401,352
Wakkanai	51,854
Wakō (★Tōkyō)	55,212
Warabi (★Tōkyō)	70,408
Yachiyo (★Tōkyō)	142,184
Yaizu (★Shizuoka)	108,558
Yamagata	245,158
Yamaguchi	124,213
Yamato (★Tōkyō)	177,669
Yamato-kōriyama (★Ōsaka)	89,624
Yamato-takada (★Ōsaka)	65,223
Yame (▲40,286)	33,000
Yao (★Ōsaka)	276,394
Yashio (★Tōkyō)	67,635
Yatsushiro (▲108,790)	88,700
Yawata (★Ōsaka)	72,356
Yokkaichi	263,001
Yokohama (★Tōkyō)	2,992,926
Yokosuka (★Tōkyō)	427,116
Yonago	131,792
Yonezawa	93,721
Yono (★Tōkyō)	71,597
Yotsukaidō (★Tōkyō)	67,008
Yukuhashi	65,527
Zama (★Tōkyō)	100,000
Zushi (★Tōkyō)	57,656

JERSEY

1986 C	80,212
• SAINT HELIER (★46,500)	27,083

JORDAN / Al-Urdun

1986 E	2,796,100
Al-Baq'ah	57,860
• 'AMMĀN (★1,250,000)	833,500
Ar-Ruṣayfah (★'Ammān)	65,560
Az-Zarqā'	285,000
Irbid	150,000

KENYA

1989 E	24,506,000
Eldoret (1979C)	50,503
Kisumu (1984E)	167,100
Machakos (1983E)	92,300
Meru (1979C)	72,049
Mombasa (1985E)	442,369
• NAIROBI	1,286,200
Nakuru (1984E)	101,700

KIRIBATI

1988 E	68,207
BAIRIKI	2,230
• Bikenibeu	4,580

KOREA, NORTH / Chosŏn-minjujuŭi-inmīn-konghwaguk

1981 E	18,317,000
Ch'ŏngjin	490,000
Haeju (1983E)	213,000
Hamhŭng (1970E)	150,000
Hŭngnam (1976E)	260,000
Kaesŏng	259,000
Kanggye (1967E)	130,000
Kimch'aek (Sŏngjin) (1967E)	265,000
Namp'o	241,000
• P'YŎNGYANG (★1,600,000)	1,283,000
Sinŭiju	305,000
Songnim (1944C)	53,035
Wŏnsan	398,000

KOREA, SOUTH / Taehan-min'guk

1985 C	40,448,486
Andong	114,216
Anyang (★Sŏul)	361,577
Bucheon (★Sŏul)	456,292
Changwŏn (★Masan)	173,508
Chech'on	102,274
Cheju	202,911
Chinhae	121,341
Chinju	227,309
Ch'ŏnan	170,196
Ch'ŏngju	350,256
Chŏnju	79,323
Chŏnju, Chŏlla Pukdo prov.	426,473
Ch'unch'ŏn	162,988
Ch'ungju	113,331
Ch'ungmu	87,459
Inch'ŏn (★Sŏul) (1989E)	1,604,000
Iri	192,269
Kangnŭng	132,897
Kimch'ŏn	77,254
Kimhae	77,903
Kumi	142,094
Kŭmsŏng	58,897
Kunsan	185,649
Kwangju (1989E)	1,165,000
Kwangmyŏng (★Sŏul)	219,611
Kyŏngju	127,544
Masan (★625,000)	448,746
Mokp'o	236,085
Namwŏn	61,447
P'ohang	260,691
Pusan (★3,800,000) (1989E)	3,754,000
P'yŏngt'aek (▲180,513)	63,400
Samch'ŏnp'o	62,466
Sangju (▲180,575)	28,300
Sŏgwipo	82,311
Sŏkch'o	69,501
Songjŏng (▲136,612)	35,300
Sŏngnam (★Sŏul)	447,692
Songtan	66,357
• SŎUL (★15,850,000) (1989E)	10,513,000
Sunch'ŏn (▲116,323)	121,958
Suwŏn (★Sŏul)	430,752
T'aebaek	113,997
Taegu (1989C)	2,206,000
Taejŏn	866,148
Tongduchŏn	68,633
Tonghae	91,691
Ŭijŏngbu (★Sŏul)	162,700
Ulsan	551,014
Wŏnju	151,165
Yŏngch'ŏn	52,811
Yŏngju	84,742
Yŏsu	171,933

KUWAIT / Al-Kuwayt

1985 C	1,697,301
Abraq Khīṭān (★Al-Kuwayt)	45,120
Al-Aḥmadī (★285,000)	26,899
Al-Farwānīyah (★Al-Kuwayt)	68,701
Al-Fuḥayḥīl (★Al-Aḥmadī)	50,081
Al-Jahrah (★Al-Kuwayt)	111,222
• AL-KUWAYT (★1,375,000)	44,335
As-Sālimīyah (★Al-Kuwayt)	153,359
Aṣ-Ṣulaybīyah (★Al-Kuwayt)	51,314
Ḥawallī (★Al-Kuwayt)	145,126
Qalīb ash-Shuyūkh (★Al-Kuwayt)	114,771
South Khīṭān (★Al-Kuwayt)	69,256
Subahiya (★Al-Aḥmadī)	60,787

LAOS / Lao

1985 C	3,584,803
Savannakhét (1975E)	53,000
• VIANGCHAN (VIENTIANE)	377,409

LEBANON / Lubnān

1982 E	2,637,000
• BAYRŪT (★1,675,000)	509,000
Ṣaydā	105,000
Ṣūr (Tyre) (1970E)	12,500
Ṭarābulus (Tripoli)	198,000

LESOTHO

1986 C	1,577,536
• MASERU	109,382

LIBERIA

1986 E	2,221,000
• MONROVIA	465,000

LIBYA / Lībiyā

1984 C	3,637,488
Al-Bayḍā (Beida)	67,120
Banghāzī	435,886
Misrātah	131,031
• ṬARĀBULUS (TRIPOLI)	990,697
Ṭubruq (Tobruk)	75,282

LIECHTENSTEIN

1990 E	28,452
• VADUZ	4,874

LUXEMBOURG

1985 E	366,000
Esch-sur-Alzette (★83,000) (1981C)	25,142
• LUXEMBOURG (★133,000)	76,130

MACAU

1987 E	429,000
• MACAU	429,000

MADAGASCAR / Madagasikara

1984 E	9,731,000
• ANTANANARIVO (1985E)	663,000
Antsirabe (▲95,000)	50,100
Antsiranana	100,000
Fianarantsoa	130,000
Mahajanga	85,000
Toamasina	100,000
Toliara	55,000

MALAWI / Malaŵi

1987 C	7,982,607
• Blantyre	331,588
LILONGWE	233,973

MALAYSIA

1980 C	13,136,109
Alor Setar	69,435
Batu Pahat	64,727
Butterworth (★George Town)	77,982
George Town (Pinang) (★495,000)	248,241
Ipoh	293,849
Johor Baharu (★Singapore)	246,395
Kelang	192,080
Keluang	50,315
Kota Baharu	167,872
Kota Kinabalu (Jesselton)	55,997
• KUALA LUMPUR (★1,475,000)	919,610
Kuala Terengganu	180,296
Kuantan	131,547
Kuching	72,555
Melaka	87,494
Miri	52,125
Muar (Bandar Maharani)	65,151
Petaling Jaya (★Kuala Lumpur)	207,805
Sandakan	70,420
Seremban	132,911
Sibu	85,231
Taiping	146,000
Telok Anson	49,148

MALDIVES

1985 C	181,453
• MALE	46,334

MALI

1987 C	7,620,225
• BAMAKO	646,163
Gao	54,874
Kayes	48,216
Mopti	73,979
Ségou	88,877
Sikasso	73,050
Tombouctou (Timbuktu)	31,925

MALTA

1987 E	343,334
• VALLETTA (★215,000)	9,263

MARSHALL ISLANDS

1980 C	30,873
• Jarej-Uliga-Delap	8,583

MARTINIQUE

1982 C	328,566
• FORT-DE-FRANCE (★116,017)	99,844

MAURITANIA / Mauritanie / Mūrītānīyā

1987 E	2,007,000
• NOUAKCHOTT	285,000

MAURITIUS

1987 E	1,008,864
Beau Bassin-Rose Hill (★Port Louis)	93,125
Curepipe (★Port Louis)	64,243
• PORT LOUIS (★420,000)	139,730
Quatre Bornes (★Port Louis)	65,480
Vacoas-Phoenix (★Port Louis)	55,667

MAYOTTE

1985 E	67,205
• DZAOUDZI (★6,979)	5,865

MEXICO / México

1980 C	67,395,826
Acapulco [de Juárez]	301,902
Aguascalientes	293,152
Apatzingán	55,522
Atlixco	53,207
Campeche	128,434
Cancún	33,273
Celaya	141,675
Chetumal	56,709
Chihuahua	385,603
Chilpancingo	67,498
Ciudad del Carmen	72,489
• CIUDAD DE MÉXICO (★14,100,000)	8,831,079
Ciudad de Naucalpan de Juárez (★Ciudad de México)	723,723
Ciudad Guzmán	60,938
Ciudad Juárez (★El Paso, Tex., U.S.A.)	544,496
Ciudad Madero (★Tampico)	132,444
Ciudad Mante	70,647
Ciudad Obregón	165,572
Ciudad Valles	65,609
Ciudad Victoria	140,161
Coatzacoalcos	127,170
Colima	86,044
Córdoba	99,972
Cuernavaca	192,770
Culiacán	304,826
Delicias	65,504
Durango	257,915
Ecatepec de Morelos (★Ciudad de México)	741,821
Ensenada	120,483
Fresnillo	56,066
Garza García (★Monterrey)	81,974
Gómez Palacio (★Torreón)	116,967
Guadalajara (★2,325,000)	1,626,152
Guadalupe (★Monterrey)	370,524
Guanajuato	48,981
Guaymas	54,826
Hermosillo	297,175
Hidalgo del Parral	75,590
Iguala	66,005
Irapuato	170,138
Jalapa	204,594
La Paz	91,453
La Piedad [Cavadas]	47,441
Las Choapas	35,807
León	593,002
Los Mochis	122,531
Matamoros (★Brownsville, Tex., U.S.A.)	188,745
Mazatlán	199,830
Mérida	400,142
Mexicali (★365,000)	341,559
Minatitlán	106,765
Monclova	115,786
Monterrey (★2,015,000)	1,090,009
Morelia	297,544
Navojoa	62,901
Netzahualcóyotl (★Ciudad de México)	1,341,230
Nogales	65,603
Nuevo Laredo (★Laredo, Tex., U.S.A.)	201,731
Oaxaca [de Juárez]	154,223
Ocotlán	48,931
Orizaba (★215,000)	114,848
Pachuca	110,351
Piedras Negras	67,455
Poza Rica de Hidalgo	166,799
Puebla (★1,055,000)	835,759
Puerto Vallarta	38,645
Querétaro	215,976
Reynosa	194,693
Río Bravo	55,236
Salamanca	96,703
Saltillo	284,937
San Luis Potosí (★470,000)	362,371
San Luis Río Colorado	76,684
San Nicolás de los Garzas (★Monterrey)	280,696
Santa Catarina (★Monterrey)	87,673
Soledad Díez Gutiérrez (★San Luis Potosí)	49,173
Tampico (★435,000)	267,957
Tapachula	85,766
Tecomán	46,371
Tehuacán	79,547
Tepic	145,741
Tijuana (★San Diego, Calif., U.S.A.)	429,500

▲ Población de un municipio, comuna o distrito entero, incluyendo sus áreas rurales.
• Ciudad más grande de un país.
★ Población o designación de un área metropolitana, incluyendo los suburbios.
C Censo. **E** Estimado oficial. **U** Estimado no oficial.

▲ Population d'une municipalité, d'une commune ou d'un district, zone rurale incluse.
• Ville la plus peuplée du pays.
★ Population de l'agglomération (ou nom de la zone métropolitaine englobante).
C Recensement. **E** Estimation officielle. **U** Estimation non officielle.

▲ População de um município, comuna ou distrito, inclusive as respectivas áreas rurais.
• Maior cidade de um país.
★ População ou indicação de uma área metropolitana.
C Censo. **E** Estimativa oficial. **U** Estimativa não oficial.

Tlalnepantla (★Ciudad de México)	778,173
Tlaquepaque (★Guadalajara)	133,500
Toluca [de Lerdo]	199,778
Torreón (★575,000)	328,086
Tulancingo	53,400
Tuxpan	56,037
Tuxtla Gutiérrez	131,096
Uruapan [del Progreso]	122,828
Veracruz [Llave] (★385,000)	284,822
Villahermosa	158,216
Zacatecas	80,088
Zamora de Hidalgo	86,998
Zapopan (★Guadalajara)	345,390
Zitácuaro	47,520

MICRONESIA, FEDERATED STATES OF

1980 C	73,160
• KOLONIA	5,549

MONACO

1982 C	27,063
• MONACO (★87,000)	27,063

MONGOLIA / Mongol Ard Uls

1989 E	2,040,000
Darchan (1985E)	69,800
• ULAANBAATAR	548,400

MONTSERRAT

1980 C	11,606
• PLYMOUTH	1,568

MOROCCO / Al-Magreb

1982 C	20,419,555
Agadir	110,479
Beni-Mellal	95,003
Berkane	60,490
• Casablanca (Dar-el-Beida) (★2,475,000)	2,139,204
El-Jadida (Mazagan)	81,455
Fès (★535,000)	448,823
Kenitra	188,194
Khemisset	58,925
Khouribga	127,181
Ksar-el-Kebir	73,541
Larache	63,893
Marrakech (★535,000)	439,728
Meknès (★375,000)	319,783
Mohammedia (Fedala) (★Casablanca)	105,120
Nador	62,040
Oued-Zem	58,744
Oujda	260,082
RABAT (★980,000)	518,616
Safi	197,309
Salé (★Rabat)	289,391
Settat	65,203
Sidi Kacem	55,833
Sidi Slimane	50,457
Tanger (Tangier) (★370,000)	266,346
Tan-Tan	41,451
Taza	77,216
Temera (★Rabat)	48,644
Tétouan	199,615

MOZAMBIQUE / Moçambique

1989 E	15,326,476
Beira	291,604
Chimoio (1986E)	86,928
Inhambane (1986E)	64,274
• MAPUTO	1,069,727
Nacala	101,615
Nampula	197,379
Quelimane	78,520

NAMIBIA

1988 E	1,760,000
• WINDHOEK	114,500

NAURU / Naoero

1987 E	8,000

NEPAL / Nepāl

1981 C	15,022,839
Bhaktapur	48,472
• KĀTHMĀNDĀU (★320,000)	235,160
Wirātnagar	93,544

NETHERLANDS / Nederland

1986 E	14,529,430
Alkmaar (★121,000)	86,509
Almelo	62,421
Alphen aan den Rijn	55,812
Amersfoort (★130,158)	89,596
Amstelveen (★Amsterdam)	68,090
• AMSTERDAM (★1,860,000)	679,140
Apeldoorn	145,773
Arnhem (★294,085)	127,968
Assen	47,462
Bergen op Zoom	46,103
Breda (★154,565)	119,174
Delft (★'s-Gravenhage)	87,440
Den Helder	63,231
Deventer	64,806
Dordrecht (★200,396)	106,968
Ede (▲88,866)	46,700
Eindhoven (★376,185)	190,839
Emmen (▲91,775)	36,400
Enschede (★288,000)	144,048
Geleen (★177,243)	34,292
Gouda	60,927
Groningen (★207,060)	168,006
Haarlem (★Amsterdam)	149,776
Haarlemmermeer (★Amsterdam) (1984E)	11,400
Heerlen (★266,617)	93,871
Helmond	63,043
Hengelo (★Enschede)	76,694
Hilversum (★Amsterdam)	86,125
Hoorn	52,720
IJmuiden (★Amsterdam)	57,157
Kerkrade (★Heerlen)	52,885
Leeuwarden	84,966
Leiden (★178,731)	105,262
Maastricht (★158,915)	114,579
Nieuwegein (★Utrecht)	55,644
Nijmegen (★238,187)	147,182
Oss	50,343
Purmerend (★Amsterdam)	50,664
Ridderkerk (★Rotterdam)	46,419
Rijswijk (★'s-Gravenhage)	48,886
Roosendaal	57,385
Rotterdam (★1,110,000)	571,372
Schiedam (★Rotterdam)	69,078
'S-GRAVENHAGE (THE HAGUE) (★770,000)	443,961
's-Hertogenbosch (★189,067)	89,039
Soest (★Amersfoort)	40,562
Spijkenisse (★Rotterdam)	60,221
Tilburg (★223,043)	153,703
Utrecht (★511,195)	229,933
Venlo (★87,000)	63,475
Vlaardingen (★Rotterdam)	75,536
Vlissingen (Flushing) (▲45,339)	26,000
Zaanstad (★Amsterdam)	128,248
Zeist (★Utrecht)	59,743
Zoetermeer (★'s-Gravenhage)	82,334
Zwolle	88,438

NETHERLANDS ANTILLES / Nederlandse Antillen

1984 E	178,744
• WILLEMSTAD (★130,000) (1981C)	31,883

NEW CALEDONIA / Nouvelle-Calédonie

1989 C	164,173
• NOUMÉA (★88,000)	65,110

NEW ZEALAND

1986 C	3,307,084
• Auckland (★850,000)	149,046
Christchurch (★320,000)	168,200
Dunedin (★109,000)	76,964
Hamilton (★101,814)	94,511
Invercargill (★52,807)	48,197
Lower Hutt (★Wellington)	63,862
Manukau (★Auckland)	177,248
Napier (★107,060)	49,428
Palmerston North (★67,405)	60,503
Rotorua (★52,001)	40,597
Takapuna (★Auckland)	69,419
Tauranga (★59,435)	41,611
Waitemata (★Auckland)	96,365
WELLINGTON (★350,000)	137,495

NICARAGUA

1985 E	3,272,100
Chinandega	75,000
Granada (1981E)	64,642
León	101,000
• MANAGUA	682,000
Masaya	75,000
Matagalpa	68,000

NIGER

1988 C	7,250,383
Agadez	50,164
Maradi	112,965
• NIAMEY	398,265
Tahoua	51,607
Zinder	120,892

NIGERIA

1987 E	101,907,000
Aba	239,800
Abakaliki	56,800
Abeokuta	341,300
Ado-Ekiti	287,000
Afikpo	65,790
Agege	83,810
Akure	129,600
Amaigbo	53,690
Apomu	49,570
Aramoko	48,280
Asaba	47,410
Awka	88,800
Azare	50,020
Bauchi	68,840
Benin City	183,200
Bida	100,200
Calabar	139,800
Deba	110,600
Duku	52,880
Ede	245,200
Effon-Alaiye	122,300
Ejigbo	84,570
Emure-Ekiti	58,750
Enugu	252,500
Epe	80,560
Erin-Oshogbo	59,940
Eruwa	49,140
Fiditi	49,440
Gboko	49,390
Gbongan	53,990
Gombe	86,120
Gusau	126,200
Ibadan	1,144,000
Idah	50,550
Idanre	56,080
Ife	237,000
Ifon-Oshogbo	65,980
Igbasa-Odo	48,040
Igboho	85,230
Igbo-Ora	68,060
Igede-Ekiti	56,570
Ihiala	73,240
Ijebu-Igbo	78,680
Ijebu-Ode	124,900
Ijero-Ekiti	76,420
Ikare	112,500
Ikerre	195,400
Ikire	94,450
Ikirun	144,900
Ikole	71,860
Ikorodu	147,700
Ikot Ekpene	69,440
Ila	210,800
Ilawe-Ekiti	147,300
Ilesha	302,100
Ilobu	159,000
Ilorin	380,000
Inisa	95,630
Ipoti-Ekiti	53,220
Ise-Ekiti	82,580
Iseyin	173,500
Iwo	289,100
Jega (1985E)	47,000
Jimeta	66,130
Jos	164,700
Kaduna	273,200
Kano	538,300
Katsina	165,000
Kaura Namoda	52,910
Keffi	57,790
Kishi	77,210
Kumo	118,200
Lafia	97,810
Lafiagi	57,580
• LAGOS (★3,800,000)	1,213,000
Lalupon	56,130
Lere	49,670
Maiduguri	255,100
Makurdi	98,350
Minna	109,300
Mubi	51,190
Mushin (★Lagos)	266,100
Nguru	78,770
Nsukka	47,760
Ode-Ekiti	48,910
Offa	157,500
Ogbomosho	582,900
Oka	114,400
Oke-Mesi	55,040
Okwe	52,550
Olupona	65,720
Ondo	135,300
Onitsha	298,200
Opobo	64,620
Oron	62,260
Oshogbo	380,800
Owerri (1982E)	52,670
Owo	146,600
Oyan	50,930
Oyo	204,700
Pindiga	64,130
Port Harcourt	327,300
Potiskum	56,490
Sapele	111,200
Shagamu	93,610
Shaki	139,000
Shomolu (★Lagos)	120,700
Sokoto	163,700
Umuahia	52,550
Uyo	60,500
Warri	100,700
Zaria	302,800

NIUE

1986 C	2,531
• ALOFI	811

NORTHERN MARIANA ISLANDS

1980 C	16,780
• Chalan Kanoa	2,678
Garapan	2,063

NORWAY / Norge

1985 E	4,153,000
Bærum (★Oslo) (1982C)	86,724
Bergen (★239,000)	207,374
Drammen (★73,000)	50,700
Fredrikstad (★52,000) (1983E)	27,618
Hammerfest (1983E)	7,208
Kristiansand	62,200
Narvik (1983E)	19,080
• OSLO (★720,000)	447,304
Skien (★77,981)	46,700
Stavanger (★132,000)	94,200
Tromsø	47,800
Trondheim	134,019

OMAN / 'Umān

1981 E	919,000
• MASQAT (MUSCAT)	50,000
Maṭraḥ (1971E)	14,000
Sūr (1980E)	30,000

PAKISTAN / Pākistān

1981 C	84,253,644
Abbottābād (★65,996)	32,188
Ahmadpur East	56,979
Attock (★39,986)	26,233
Bahāwalnagar	74,533
Bahāwalpur (★180,263)	152,009
Bannu (★43,210)	35,170
Bhakkar	41,934
Chārsadda	62,530
Chīchāwatni	50,241
Chiniot	105,559
Chishtiān Mandi	61,959
Daska	55,555
Dera Ghāzi Khān	102,007
Dera Ismāīl Khān (★68,145)	64,358
Drigh Road Cantonment (★Karāchi)	56,742
Faisalabad (Lyallpur)	1,104,209
Gojra	68,000
Gujrānwāla (★658,753)	600,993
Gujrānwāla Cantonment (★Gujrānwāla)	57,760
Gujrāt	155,058
Hāfizābād	83,464
Hyderābād (★800,000)	702,539
Hyderābād Cantonment (★Hyderābād)	48,990
ISLĀMĀBĀD (★Rāwalpindi)	204,364
Jacobābād	79,365
Jarānwāla	69,459
Jhang Sadar	195,558
Jhelum (★106,462)	92,646
Kamālia	61,107
Kāmoke	71,097
• Karāchi (★5,300,000)	4,901,627
Karāchi Cantonment (★Karāchi)	181,981
Kasūr	155,523
Khairpur	61,447
Khānewāl	89,090
Khānpur	70,589
Khāriān Cantonment (★51,506)	16,042
Khushāb	56,274
Kohāt (★77,604)	55,832
Lahore (★3,025,000)	2,707,215
Lahore Cantonment (★Lahore)	245,474
Lārkāna	123,890
Leiah	51,482
Malir Cantonment (★Karāchi)	47,588
Mandi Būrewāla	86,311
Mardān (★147,977)	141,842
Miānwāli	59,159
Mingāora	88,078
Mīrpur Khās	124,371
Multān (★732,070)	696,316
Muzaffargarh	53,000
Nawābshāh	102,139
Nowshera (★74,913)	38,875
Okāra (★153,483)	127,455
Pākpattan	69,820
Peshāwar (★566,248)	506,896
Peshāwar Cantonment (★Peshāwar)	59,352
Quetta (★285,719)	244,842
Rahīmyār Khān (★132,635)	119,036
Rāwalpindi (★1,040,000)	457,091
Rāwalpindi Cantonment (★Rāwalpindi)	337,752
Sādiqābād	63,935
Sāhīwal	150,954
Sargodha (★291,362)	231,895
Sargodha Cantonment (★Sargodha)	59,467
Shekhūpura	141,168
Shikārpur	88,138
Shorkot (★50,568)	18,533
Siālkot (★302,009)	258,147
Sukkur	190,551
Tando Ādam	62,744
Turbat	52,337
Vihāri	53,799
Wāh Cantonment	122,335
Wazīrābād	62,725

PALAU / Belau

1980 C	12,116
• KOROR	6,222

PANAMA / Panamá

1980 C	1,795,012
Balboa (★Panamá)	1,904
Colón (★88,000) (1982E)	64,763
David	49,472
• PANAMÁ (★625,000) (1984E)	424,204
San Miguelito (★Panamá) (1984E)	200,584

PAPUA NEW GUINEA

1987 E	3,479,400
Lae	79,600
• PORT MORESBY	152,100
Rabaul (1980C)	14,954

PARAGUAY

1985 E	3,279,000
• ASUNCIÓN (★700,000)	477,100
Fernando de la Mora (★Asunción)	80,000
Lambaré (★Asunción)	84,000
Puerto Presidente Stroessner	64,000
San Lorenzo (★Asunción) (1982C)	74,632

PERU / Perú

1981 C	17,031,221
Arequipa (★446,942)	108,023
Ayacucho (★69,533)	57,432
Barranco (★Lima)	46,478
Barrio Obrero Industrial (★Lima)	404,856
Breña (★Lima)	112,398
Cajamarca	62,259
Callao (★Lima)	264,133
Cerro de Pasco (★66,373)	55,597
Chiclayo (★279,527)	213,095
Chimbote	223,341
Chorrillos (★Lima)	141,881
Chosica	65,139
Cuzco (★184,550)	89,563
Huacho	43,398
Huancayo (★164,954)	84,845
Huánuco	61,812
Ica	114,786
Iquitos	178,738
Jesús María (★Lima)	83,179
Juliaca	87,651
La Victoria (★Lima)	270,778
• LIMA (★4,608,010)	371,122
Lince (★Lima)	80,456
Magdalena Nueva (★Lima)	55,535
Miraflores (★Lima)	103,453
Pisco	55,604
Piura (★207,934)	144,609
Pucallpa	112,263
Pueblo Libre (★Lima)	83,985
Puno	67,397
Rímac (★Lima)	184,484
San Isidro (★Lima)	71,203
Sullana	89,037
Surco (★Lima)	146,636
Surquillo (★Lima)	134,158
Tacna	97,173
Talara	57,351
Trujillo (★354,301)	202,469
Tumbes	47,936
Vitarte (★Lima)	145,504

PHILIPPINES / Pilipinas

1980 C	48,098,460
Angeles (1984E)	213,305
Antipolo (▲68,912)	54,117
Bacolod (1984E)	287,830

▲ Population of an entire municipality, commune, or district, including rural area.
• Largest city in country.
★ Population or designation of the metropolitan area, including suburbs.
C Census. **E** Official estimate. **U** Unofficial estimate.

▲ Bevölkerung eines ganzen städtischen Verwaltungsgebietes, eines Kommunalbezirkes oder eines Distrikts, einschliesslich ländlicher Gebiete.
• Grösste Stadt des Landes.
★ Bevölkerung oder Bezeichnung der Stadtregion einschliesslich Vororte.
C Volkszählung. **E** Offizielle Schätzung. **U** Inoffizielle Schätzung.

Population of Cities and Towns / Einwohnerzahlen von Grossstädten / Habitantes en las Ciudades y Poblaciones
Population des Grands Centres et des Villes / População dos Centros Urbanos 311

Bacoor (★Manila)	90,364
Baguio (1984E)	133,726
Baliuag	70,555
Biñan (★Manila)	83,684
Binangonan	80,980
Bislig (▲81,615)	49,498
Bocaue	49,693
Butuan (▲172,489) (1984E)	74,900
Cabanatuan (▲153,899) (1984E)	67,300
Cagayan de Oro (▲275,938) (1984E)	207,000
Cainta (★Manila)	59,025
Calamba (▲121,175)	72,359
Caloocan (★Manila) (1984E)	524,624
Carmona (★Manila)	65,014
Cavite (★175,000)	87,666
Cebu (★600,000) (1984E)	552,155
Cotabato	83,871
Dagupan (1984E)	103,401
Davao (▲610,375)	408,775
Dumaguete	63,411
General Santos (Dadiangas) (▲183,255) (1984E)	115,600
Guagua	72,609
Iloilo (1984E)	263,422
Isabela (Basilan) (▲49,891)	11,491
Jolo	52,429
Lapu-Lapu (Opon)	98,723
Las Piñas (★Manila) (1984E)	190,364
Legaspi (▲108,864) (1984E)	56,600
Lucena (1984E)	124,355
Mabalacat (▲80,966)	54,988
Makati (★Manila) (1984E)	408,991
Malabon (★Manila) (1984E)	212,930
Malolos	95,699
Mandaluyong (★Manila) (1984E)	226,670
Mandaue (★Cebu) (1984E)	137,300
Mangaldan	50,434
• MANILA (★6,800,000) (1984E)	1,728,441
Marawi	53,812
Marikina (★Manila) (1984E)	248,183
Meycauayan (★Manila)	83,579
Muntinglupa (★Manila) (1984E)	172,421
Naga	90,712
Navotas (★Manila) (1984E)	146,899
Olongapo (1984E)	173,701
Parañaque (★Manila) (1984E)	252,791
Pasay (★Manila) (1984E)	320,889
Pasig (★Manila) (1984E)	318,853
Quezon City (★Manila) (1984E)	1,326,035
San Fernando	110,891
San Juan del Monte (★Manila) (1984E)	139,126
San Pablo (▲143,023) (1984E)	74,500
San Pedro	74,556
Santa Cruz	60,620
Santa Rosa (★Manila)	64,325
Tacloban (1984E)	117,243
Tagig (★Manila) (1984E)	130,719
Taytay (★Manila)	75,328
Valenzuela (★Manila) (1984E)	275,725
Zamboanga (▲379,194) (1984E)	91,300

PITCAIRN

1988 C	59
• ADAMSTOWN	59

POLAND / Polska

1988 E	37,663,800
Będzin (★Katowice)	77,300
Bełchatów	54,900
Biała Podlaska	49,700
Białystok	259,600
Bielsko-Biała	177,700
Bydgoszcz	372,600
Bytom (Beuthen) (★Katowice)	239,800
Chełm	62,700
Chorzów (★Katowice)	138,200
Częstochowa	252,900
Dąbrowa Górnicza (★Katowice)	140,000
Dzierżoniów (Reichenbach) (★89,000)	37,800
Elbląg (Elbing)	121,800
Gdańsk (Danzig) (★909,000)	469,100
Gdynia (★Gdańsk)	249,500
Gliwice (Gleiwitz) (★Katowice)	211,300
Głogów	70,100
Gniezno	70,000
Gorzów Wielkopolski (Landsberg an der Warthe)	119,500
Grudziądz	98,300
Inowrocław	74,600
Jastrzębie-Zdrój	102,200
Jaworzno (★Katowice)	97,500
Jelenia Góra (Hirschberg)	92,500
Kalisz	105,300
• Katowice (★2,778,000)	368,600
Kędzierzyn Kozle	72,900
Kielce	208,100
Konin	78,100
Koszalin (Köslin)	104,700
Kraków (★828,000)	744,900
Legnica (Liegnitz)	100,700
Leszno	56,300
Łódź (★1,061,000)	844,900
Łomża	54,800
Lubin	77,600
Lublin (★389,000)	333,000
Mielec	56,900
Mysłowice (★Katowice)	91,900
Nowy Sącz	73,200
Olsztyn (Allenstein)	154,900
Opole (Oppeln)	128,200
Ostrowiec Świętokrzyski	75,500
Ostrów Wielkopolski	70,400
Pabianice (★Łódź)	73,600
Piekary Śląskie (★Katowice)	69,400
Piła (Schneidemühl)	69,700
Piotrków Trybunalski	80,200
Płock	117,600
Poznań (★672,000)	585,900
Pruszków (★Warszawa)	53,700
Przemyśl	67,200
Puławy	51,200
Racibórz (Ratibor)	62,500
Radom	221,800
Radomsko	49,600
Ruda Śląska (★Katowice)	167,900
Rybnik	141,000
Rzeszów	147,300
Siedlce	68,400
Siemianowice Śląskie (★Katowice)	82,200
Skarżysko-Kamienna	49,500
Słupsk (Stolp)	96,200
Sopot (★Gdańsk)	49,700
Sosnowiec (★Katowice)	259,600
Stalowa Wola	68,800
Starachowice	56,000
Stargard Szczeciński (Stargard in Pommern)	68,500
Suwałki	55,900
Świdnica (Schweidnitz)	61,900
Świętochłowice (★Katowice)	60,900
Świnoujście (Swinemünde)	44,100
Szczecin (Stettin) (★449,000)	396,600
Tarnów	118,400
Tarnowskie Góry (★Katowice)	74,300
Tczew	59,000
Tomaszów Mazowiecki	67,400
Toruń	197,000
Tychy (★Katowice)	187,800
Wałbrzych (Waldenburg) (★207,000)	141,100
WARSZAWA (★2,323,000)	1,671,400
Włocławek	119,200
Wodzisław Śląski	111,500
Wrocław (Breslau)	640,200
Zabrze (Hindenburg) (★Katowice)	199,400
Zamość	58,400
Zawiercie	56,100
Zgierz (★Łódź)	56,200
Zielona Góra (Grünberg)	113,300
Żory	65,300

PORTUGAL

1981 C	9,833,014
Amadora (★Lisboa)	95,518
Barreiro (★Lisboa)	50,863
Braga	63,033
Coimbra	74,616
• LISBOA (★2,250,000)	807,167
Ponta Delgada	21,187
Porto (★1,225,000)	327,368
Setúbal	77,885
Vila Nova de Gaia (★Porto)	62,469

PUERTO RICO

1980 C	3,196,520
Arecibo (★160,336)	48,779
Bayamón (★San Juan)	185,087
Caguas (★San Juan)	87,214
Carolina (★San Juan)	147,835
Guaynabo (★San Juan)	65,075
Mayagüez (★200,464)	82,968
Ponce (★232,551)	161,739
• SAN JUAN (★1,775,260)	424,600

QATAR / Qatar

1986 C	369,079
• AD-DAWHAH (DOHA) (★310,000)	217,294
Ar-Rayyān (★Ad-Dawhah)	91,996

REUNION / Réunion

1982 C	515,814
• SAINT-DENIS (▲109,072)	84,400

ROMANIA / România

1986 E	22,823,479
Alba Iulia	66,100
Alexandria	52,802
Arad	187,744
Bacău	179,877
Baia Mare	139,704
Bîrlad	70,365
Bistriţa	77,267
Botoşani	108,775
Brăila	235,620
Braşov	351,493
• BUCUREŞTI (BUCHAREST) (★2,250,000)	1,989,823
Buzău	136,080
Călăraşi	69,350
Cluj-Napoca	310,017
Constanţa	327,676
Craiova	281,044
Deva	77,976
Drobeta-Turnu Severin	99,366
Focşani	86,411
Galaţi	295,372
Giurgiu	68,002
Hunedoara	88,514
Iaşi	313,060
Lugoj	53,665
Mediaş	72,816
Oradea	213,846
Petroşani (★74,000)	49,131
Piatra Neamţ	109,393
Piteşti	157,190
Ploieşti (★300,000)	234,886
Reşiţa	105,914
Rîmnicu Vîlcea	96,051
Roman	72,415
Satu Mare	130,082
Sfîntu-Gheorghe	67,587
Sibiu	177,511
Slatina	76,714
Suceava	96,317
Timişoara	325,272
Tîrgovişte	91,990
Tîrgu Jiu	87,693
Tîrgu-Mureş	158,998
Tulcea	86,336
Turda	61,594
Vaslui	65,070
Zalău	57,283

RWANDA

1983 E	5,762,000
• KIGALI	181,600

SAINT CHRISTOPHER-NEVIS

1980 C	44,404
• BASSETERRE	14,725
Charlestown	1,771

SAINT HELENA

1987 C	5,644
• JAMESTOWN	1,413

SAINT LUCIA

1987 E	142,342
• CASTRIES	53,933

SAINT PIERRE AND MIQUELON / Saint-Pierre-et-Miquelon

1982 C	6,041
• SAINT-PIERRE	5,371

SAINT VINCENT AND THE GRENADINES

1987 E	112,589
• KINGSTOWN (★28,936)	19,028

SAN MARINO

1988 E	22,304
• SAN MARINO	4,137

SAO TOME AND PRINCIPE / São Tomé e Príncipe

1970 C	73,631
• SÃO TOMÉ	17,380

SAUDI ARABIA / Al-ʿArabīyah as-Suʿūdīyah

1980 E	9,229,000
Abhā (1974C)	30,150
Ad-Dammām	200,000
Al-Hufūf (1974C)	101,271
Al-Khubar (1974C)	48,817
Al-Madīnah (Medina)	290,000
Al-Mubarraz (1974C)	54,325
AR-RIYĀD (RIYADH)	1,250,000
Aṭ-Ṭā'if	300,000
Buraydah (1974C)	69,940
Hā'il (1974C)	40,502
• Jiddah	1,300,000
Khamīs Mushayt (1974C)	49,581
Makkah (Mecca)	550,000
Najran (1974C)	47,501
Tabūk (1974C)	74,825

SENEGAL / Sénégal

1985 E	6,566,988
• DAKAR	1,428,084
Diourbel	76,409
Kaolack	132,386
Louga	49,436
Saint-Louis	91,485
Thiès	156,200
Ziguinchor	106,460

SEYCHELLES

1984 E	64,718
• VICTORIA	23,000

SIERRA LEONE

1985 C	3,515,812
Bo	59,768
• FREETOWN (★525,000)	469,776
Kenema	52,473
Koidu	82,474
Makeni	49,038

SINGAPORE

1989 E	2,673,000
• SINGAPORE (★3,025,000)	2,673,000

SOLOMON ISLANDS

1986 C	285,176
• HONIARA	30,413

SOMALIA / Somaliya

1984 E	5,423,000
Berbera	65,000
Hargeysa	70,000
Kismaayo	70,000
Marka	60,000
• MUQDISHO	600,000

SOUTH AFRICA / Suid-Afrika

1985 C	23,385,645
Alberton (★Johannesburg)	66,155
Alexandra (★Johannesburg)	67,276
Atteridgeville (★Pretoria)	73,439
Bellville (★Cape Town)	68,915
Benoni (★Johannesburg)	94,926
Bloemfontein (★235,000)	104,381
Boksburg (★Johannesburg)	110,832
Botshabelo (★Bloemfontein)	95,625
Brakpan (★Johannesburg)	46,416
CAPE TOWN (KAAPSTAD) (★1,790,000)	776,617
Carletonville (★120,499)	97,874
Daveyton (★Johannesburg)	99,056
Diepmeadow (★Johannesburg)	192,682
Durban (★1,550,000)	634,301
East London (Oos-Londen) (★320,000)	85,699
Edendale (★Pietermaritzburg)	47,001
Elsies River (★Cape Town)	70,067
Empumalanga (★Durban)	47,938
Evaton (★Vereeniging)	52,559
Galeshewe (★Kimberley)	63,238
Germiston (★Johannesburg)	116,718
Grassy Park (★Cape Town)	50,193
Guguleto (★Cape Town)	63,893
• Johannesburg (★3,650,000)	632,369
Kagiso (★Johannesburg)	50,647
Katlehong (★Johannesburg)	137,745
Kayamnandi (★Port Elizabeth)	220,548
Kempton Park (★Johannesburg)	87,721
Kimberley (★145,000)	74,061
Klerksdorp (★205,000)	48,947
Krugersdorp (★Johannesburg)	73,767
Kwa Makuta (★Durban)	71,378
Kwa Mashu (★Durban)	111,593
Kwanobuhle (★Port Elizabeth)	52,376
Kwa-Thema (★Johannesburg)	78,640
Ladysmith (★31,670)	25,102
Lekoa (Shapeville) (★Vereeniging)	218,392
Madadeni (★Newcastle)	65,832
Mamelodi (★Pretoria)	127,033
Mangaung (★Bloemfontein)	79,851
Ntuzuma (★Durban)	61,834
Nyanga (★Cape Town)	148,882
Ozisweni (★Newcastle)	51,934
Paarl (★Cape Town)	63,671
Parow (★Cape Town)	60,294
Pietermaritzburg (★230,000)	133,809
Pinetown (★Durban)	55,770
Port Elizabeth (★690,000)	272,844
PRETORIA (★960,000)	443,059
Randburg (★Johannesburg)	74,347
Randfontein (★Johannesburg)	43,763
Roodepoort-Maraisburg (★Johannesburg)	141,764
Sandton (★Johannesburg)	86,089
Soshanguve (★Pretoria)	68,598
Soweto (★Johannesburg)	521,948
Springs (★Johannesburg)	68,235
Tembisa (★Johannesburg)	149,282
Thabong (★Welkom)	43,470
Uitenhage (★Port Elizabeth)	54,987
Umlazi (★Durban)	194,933
Vanderbijlpark (★Vereeniging)	59,865
Vereeniging (★525,000)	60,584
Verwoerdburg (★Pretoria)	49,891
Vosloosrus (★Johannesburg)	52,061
Walvisbaai (Walvis Bay) (★16,607)	9,687
Welkom (★215,000)	54,488
Westonaria (★Johannesburg)	46,523

SPAIN / España

1987 E	38,606,576
Alacant (Alicante)	258,004
Albacete	125,764
Alcalá de Guadaira	50,567
Alcalá de Henares (★Madrid)	145,320
Alcobendas (★Madrid)	71,542
Alcoi (Alcoy)	66,312
Alcorcón (★Madrid)	138,448
Algeciras	97,601
Almería	154,911
Avilés (★131,000)	86,858
Badajoz (▲120,240)	104,500
Badalona (★Barcelona)	224,233
Baracaldo (★Bilbao)	114,090
Barcelona (★4,040,000)	1,703,744
Bilbao (★985,000)	382,413
Burgos	158,857
Cáceres	69,770
Cádiz (★240,000)	156,113
Cartagena (▲169,036)	68,500
Castelló de la Plana	128,664
Ciudad Real	55,072
Córdoba	298,372
Cornellà de Llobregat (★Barcelona)	86,971
Coslada (★Madrid)	65,598
Donostia (San Sebastián) (★285,000)	176,586
Dos Hermanas (▲67,330)	59,600
Elda	56,189
El Ferrol del Caudillo (★129,000)	86,329
El Prat de Llobregat (★Barcelona)	63,411
El Puerto de Santa María (▲61,032)	48,900
Elx (Elche) (▲177,629)	156,000
Fuenlabrada (★Madrid)	122,752
Gernika-Lumo (Guernica y Luno) (▲17,836) (1981C)	12,214
Getafe (★Madrid)	132,786
Gijón	258,759
Granada	256,800
Granollers (★Barcelona)	48,380
Guadalajara	59,492
Huelva	135,938
Irún	54,301
Jaén	103,698
Jerez de la Frontera (▲179,349)	153,100
La Coruña	242,437
La Línea	59,260
Las Palmas de Gran Canaria (▲358,272)	312,000
Leganés (★Madrid)	167,748
León (★159,000)	135,521
L'Hospitalet de Llobregat (★Barcelona)	277,688
Linares (▲57,401)	57,526
Lleida (Lérida) (▲108,207)	90,200
Logroño	116,273
Lugo (▲77,043)	67,200
• MADRID (★4,650,000)	3,100,507
Málaga	566,330
Manresa	65,285
Mataró	100,189
Mérida	52,225
Móstoles (★Madrid)	176,993
Murcia (▲305,278)	145,600
Orense	103,397
Oviedo (▲186,363)	165,600
Palencia	75,951
Palma (▲306,840)	242,900
Pamplona	178,666
Parla (★Madrid)	64,546
Portugalete (★Bilbao)	58,117
Puertollano	51,755
Reus	81,816
Sabadell (★Barcelona)	187,506
Salamanca	155,612
San Baudilio de Llobregat (★Barcelona)	76,008
San Cristóbal de la Laguna (▲107,593)	25,000
San Fernando (★Cádiz)	80,791

▲ Población de un municipio, comuna o distrito entero, incluyendo sus áreas rurales.
• Ciudad más grande de un país.
★ Población o designación de un área metropolitana, incluyendo los suburbios.
C Censo. **E** Estimado oficial. **U** Estimado no oficial.

▲ Population d'une municipalité, d'une commune ou d'un district, zone rurale incluse.
• Ville la plus peuplée du pays.
★ Population de l'agglomération (ou nom de la zone métropolitaine englobante).
C Recensement. **E** Estimation officielle. **U** Estimation non officielle.

▲ População de um município, comuna ou distrito, inclusive as respectivas áreas rurais.
• Maior cidade de um país.
★ População ou indicação de uma área metropolitana.
C Censo. **E** Estimativa oficial. **U** Estimativa não oficial.

San Sebastián de los Reyes (★Madrid)	50,531
Santa Coloma de Gramanet (★Barcelona)	135,310
Santa Cruz de Tenerife	211,209
Santander (▲187,222)	163,700
Santiago de Compostela (▲86,818)	67,800
Santurce-Antiguo (★Bilbao)	52,480
Segovia	53,849
Sevilla (★945,000)	655,435
Talavera de la Reina	67,680
Tarragona (▲107,356)	62,200
Tarrasa (★Barcelona)	160,245
Toledo	58,297
Torrejón de Ardoz (★Madrid)	81,658
Torrent (★València)	54,739
València (★1,270,000)	732,491
Valladolid	329,206
Vigo (▲262,560)	173,800
Vitoria (Gasteiz)	200,742
Zamora	60,708
Zaragoza	575,317

SPANISH NORTH AFRICA / Plazas de Soberanía en el Norte de África

1987 E	118,380
• Ceuta	65,141
Melilla	53,239

SRI LANKA

1985 E	15,837,000
Battaramulla (★Colombo) (1981C)	56,535
• COLOMBO (★2,050,000)	664,000
Dehiwala-Mount Lavinia (★Colombo)	188,000
Galle	102,000
Jaffna	138,000
Kandy	125,000
Matale	57,000
Moratuwa (★Colombo)	138,000
Negombo	76,000
Sri Jayawardenepura (Kotte) (★Colombo)	102,000

SUDAN / As-Sūdān

1983 C	20,564,364
Al-Fāshir (1973C)	51,932
• AL-KHARṬŪM (★1,450,000)	476,218
Al-Kharṭūm Baḥrī (★Al-Kharṭūm)	341,146
Al-Qaḍārif (1973C)	66,465
Al-Ubayyiḍ	140,000
'Aṭbarah	73,000
Būr Sūdān (Port Sudan)	206,727
Jūbā (1973C)	56,737
Kassalā	143,000
Kūstī (1973C)	65,257
Nyala (1973C)	59,852
Umm Durmān (Omdurman) (★Al-Kharṭūm)	526,287
Wad Madanī	141,000
Wāw (1973C)	52,752

SURINAME

1988 E	392,000
• PARAMARIBO	241,000

SWAZILAND

1986 C	712,131
LOBAMBA	...
Manzini (★30,000)	18,084
• MBABANE	38,290

SWEDEN / Sverige

1988 E	8,414,083
Borås	100,395
Eskilstuna	88,508
Gävle (▲87,474)	67,000
Göteborg (★710,894)	431,521
Halmstad (▲77,942)	50,000
Helsingborg	106,982
Huddinge (★Stockholm)	71,910
Järfälla (★Stockholm)	56,563
Jönköping	108,962
Karlstad	74,892
Linköping	118,602
Luleå	66,719
Lund (★Malmö)	84,342
Malmö (★445,000)	230,838
Mölndal (★Göteborg)	50,549
Nacka (★Stockholm)	61,084
Norrköping	119,001
Örebro	119,066
Södertälje (★Stockholm)	80,263
Sollentuna (★Stockholm)	49,757
Solna (★Stockholm)	50,450
• STOCKHOLM (★1,449,972)	666,810
Sundsvall (▲92,721)	50,200
Täby (★Stockholm)	55,661
Trollhättan	49,914
Tumba (★Stockholm)	67,536
Umeå (▲86,816)	56,600
Uppsala	159,962
Västerås	117,563
Växjö (▲67,350)	44,500

SWITZERLAND / Schweiz / Suisse / Svizzera

1987 E	6,523,413
Aarau (★57,900)	15,750
Arbon (★41,100)	12,292
Baden (★70,700)	14,058
Basel (Bâle) (★575,000)	173,160
BERN (BERNE) (★298,800)	137,134
Biel (Bienne) (★81,900)	51,341
Fribourg (Freiburg) (★56,800)	33,935
Genève (Geneva) (★460,000)	160,645
Lausanne (★259,900)	124,206
Locarno (★42,350)	14,473
Lugano (★94,800)	27,462
Luzern (★159,500)	59,904
Neuchâtel (★65,900)	32,650
Sankt Gallen (★125,000)	72,910
Schaffhausen (★53,000)	33,826
Thun (★77,200)	37,074
Vevey (★63,100)	15,021
Winterthur (★107,400)	84,548
Zug (★67,100)	21,569
• Zürich (★860,000)	349,549

SYRIA / Sūrīyah

1987 E	10,969,000
Al-Ḥasakah (1981C)	73,426
Al-Lādhiqīyah (Latakia)	241,000
Al-Qāmishlī (1988E)	126,236
Ar-Raqqah	126,700
Dar'ā (1981C)	49,534
Dārayyā (1988E)	53,204
Dayr az-Zawr (1986E)	106,500
• DIMASHQ (DAMASCUS) (★1,850,000) (1988E)	1,326,000
Dūmā (★Dimashq) (1988E)	66,130
Ḥalab (Aleppo)	1,216,000
Ḥamāh	214,000
Ḥimṣ	431,000
Idlib (1981C)	51,682
Jaramānah (★Dimashq) (1988E)	96,681
Kābir aṣ Ṣaghīr (1988E)	47,728
Madīnat ath Thawrah (1988E)	58,151
Ṭarṭūs (1981C)	52,589

TAIWAN / T'aiwan

1988 E	19,672,612
Changhua (▲206,603)	158,400
Chiai	254,875
Chilung	348,541
Chungho (★T'aipei)	343,389
Chungli	247,639
Chutung	104,797
Fangshan (★Kaohsiung)	276,259
Fengyüan (▲144,434)	115,300
Hsichih (★T'aipei) (1980C)	70,031
Hsinchu	309,899
Hsinchuang (★T'aipei)	259,001
Hsintien (★T'aipei)	205,094
Hualien	106,658
Ilan (▲81,751) (1980C)	70,900
Kangshan (1980C)	78,049
Kaohsiung (★1,845,000)	1,342,797
Lotung (1980C)	57,925
Lukang (1980C)	72,019
Miaoli (1980C)	81,500
Nant'ou (1980C)	84,038
P'ingchen (★T'aipei)	134,925
P'ingtung (▲204,990)	167,600
Sanchung (★T'aipei)	362,171
Shulin (★T'aipei) (1980C)	75,700
Tach'i (1980C)	67,209
T'aichung	715,107
T'ainan	656,927
• T'AIPEI (★6,130,000)	2,637,100
T'aipeihsien (★T'aipei)	506,220
T'aitung (▲109,358)	79,800
Taoyüan	220,255
T'oufen (1980C)	66,536
T'uch'eng (★T'aipei)	70,500
Yangmei (1980C)	84,353
Yüanlin (▲116,936)	51,300
Yungho (★T'aipei)	242,252
Yungkang (▲114,904)	59,600

TANZANIA

1984 E	21,062,000
Arusha	69,000
• DAR ES SALAAM	1,300,000
Dodoma	54,000
Iringa	67,000
Kigoma (1978C)	50,044
Mbeya	93,000
Morogoro	72,000
Moshi	62,000
Mtwara (1978C)	48,510
Mwanza (1978C)	110,611
Tabora	87,000
Tanga	121,000
Ujiji (1967C)	21,369
Zanzibar (1980E)	119,000

THAILAND / Prathet Thai

1986 E	52,969,204
Chiang Mai	157,843
Chon Buri	48,203
Hat Yai	131,302
Khon Kaen	130,773
• KRUNG THEP (BANGKOK) (★6,450,000)	5,468,915
Nakhon Ratchasima	206,758
Nakhon Sawan	101,498
Nakhon Si Thammarat	72,558
Pattaya	49,548
Phitsanulok	75,804
Phra Nakhon Si Ayutthaya	60,511
Sakon Nakhon	23,454
Samut Prakan (★Krung Thep)	69,218
Samut Sakhon	53,274
Saraburi	57,364
Songkhla	84,738
Ubon Ratchathani	100,145
Udon Thani	82,706
Yala	64,695

TOGO

1981 C	2,702,945
• LOMÉ (1984E)	400,000

TOKELAU

1986 C	1,690

TONGA

1986 C	94,535
• NUKU'ALOFA	21,265

TRANSKEI

1982 E	2,400,000
• UMTATA (1978E)	30,000

TRINIDAD AND TOBAGO

1987 E	1,217,100
• PORT OF SPAIN (★370,000)	58,300
San Fernando (★75,000)	33,100

TUNISIA / Tunis / Tunisie

1984 C	6,975,450
Ariana (★Tunis)	98,655
Bardo (★Tunis)	65,669
Ben Arous (★Tunis)	52,105
Bizerte	94,509
Gabès	92,258
Gafsa	60,970
Hammam Lif (★Tunis)	47,009
Houmt Essouk	92,269
Kairouan	72,254
Kasserine	47,606
La Goulette (★Tunis)	61,609
Menzel Bourguiba	51,399
Sfax (★310,000)	231,911
Sousse (★160,000)	83,509
• TUNIS (★1,225,000)	596,654
Zarzis	49,063

TURKEY / Türkiye

1985 C	50,664,458
Adana	777,554
Adapazarı	152,291
Adıyaman	71,644
Afyon	87,033
Ağrı	54,492
Akhisar	68,553
Aksaray	81,056
Amasya	53,431
ANKARA (★2,400,000)	2,235,035
Antakya (Antioch)	107,821
Antalya	261,114
Aydın	90,449
Bafra	53,482
Balıkesir	149,989
Bandırma	70,137
Batman	110,036
Bilecik	18,506
Bolu	50,288
Burdur	53,995
Bursa	612,510
Çanakkale	48,059
Ceyhan	72,624
Çorlu	59,107
Çorum	96,725
Denizli	169,130
Diyarbakır	305,940
Edirne	86,909
Elazığ	182,296
Elbistan	48,756
Ereğli, Konya prov.	68,749
Ereğli, Zonguldak prov.	54,837
Erzincan	82,616
Erzurum	246,053
Eskişehir	366,765
Gaziantep	478,635
Gebze (★İstanbul)	92,592
Gelibolu	16,715
Giresun	55,887
Gölcük	56,087
Gümüşhane	22,067
Hakkâri	20,754
İçel (Mersin)	314,350
İnegöl	54,659
İskenderun	152,096
Isparta	101,215
• İstanbul (★5,750,000)	5,475,982
İzmir (★1,550,000)	1,489,772
İzmit	233,338
Kadirli	47,609
Karabük	94,818
Karaman	64,735
Kars	69,293
Kastamonu	46,986
Kayseri	373,937
Kilis	59,876
Kırıkhan	52,780
Kırıkkale	208,018
Kırşehir	64,754
Konya	439,181
Kozan	50,324
Kütahya	118,773
Malatya	243,138
Manisa	127,012
Maraş	210,371
Muş	42,159
Nazilli	77,627
Nevşehir	50,204
Niğde	49,068
Nizip	50,067
Ödemiş	47,475
Ordu	80,828
Osmaniye	103,824
Polatlı	52,737
Rize	50,221
Salihli	63,759
Samsun	240,674
Siirt	53,884
Sincan (★Ankara)	50,869
Sinop	23,148
Sivas	198,553
Siverek	48,333
Tarsus	146,502
Tatvan	51,906
Tekirdağ	63,215
Tokat	73,008
Trabzon	142,008
Tunceli	18,471
Turgutlu	65,740
Turhal	60,097
Urfa	194,969
Uşak	88,267
Van	110,653
Yalova	53,857
Yarımca	48,420
Zonguldak (★210,000)	117,879

TURKS AND CAICOS ISLANDS

1980 C	7,436
• GRAND TURK	3,146

TUVALU

1979 C	7,349
• FUNAFUTI	2,191

UGANDA

1980 C	12,636,179
Jinja (1982E)	55,000
• KAMPALA (1982E)	460,000

UNION OF SOVIET SOCIALIST REPUBLICS / Sojuz Sovetskich Socialističeskich Respublik

1989 C	286,717,000
Abakan	154,000
Abovjan (1987E)	53,000
Achtubinsk (1987E)	53,000
Ačinsk	122,000
Akt'ubinsk	253,000
Alapajevsk (1987E)	51,000
Alatyr' (1974E)	46,000
Aleksandrija	103,000
Aleksandrov (1987E)	66,000
Aleksin (1987E)	72,000
Ali-Bajramly (1987E)	51,000
Alma-Ata (★1,190,000)	1,128,000
Almalyk	114,000
Al'metjevsk	129,000
Alytus (1987E)	71,000
Amursk (1987E)	54,000
Andižan	293,000
Angarsk	266,000
Angren	131,000
Antracit (★Krasnyj Luč) (1987E)	70,000
Anžero-Sudžensk	108,000
Apatity (1987E)	80,000
Archangel'sk	416,000
Arkalyk (1987E)	71,000
Armavir	161,000
Arsenjev (1987E)	67,000
Art'om (1987E)	73,000
Art'omovsk (1987E)	91,000
Arzamas	109,000
Asbest (1987E)	83,000
Aščhabad	398,000
Astrachan'	509,000
Azov (1987E)	81,000
Baku (★2,020,000)	1,150,000
Balakovo	198,000
Balašicha (★Moskva)	136,000
Balašov (1987E)	99,000
Balchaš (1987E)	84,000
Baranoviči	159,000
Barnaul (★665,000)	602,000
Batajsk (★Rostov-na-Donu) (1987E)	98,000
Batumi	136,000
Bekabad (1987E)	80,000
Belaja Cerkov'	197,000
Bel'cy	159,000
Belebej (1987E)	51,000
Belgorod	300,000
Belgorod-Dnestrovskij (1987E)	54,000
Belogorsk (1987E)	71,000
Beloreck (1987E)	75,000
Belovo (1987E)	118,000
Bendery	130,000
Berd'ansk	132,000
Berdičev (1987E)	89,000
Berdsk (★Novosibirsk) (1987E)	77,000
Berezniki	201,000
Ber'ozovskij (1987E)	51,000
Bijsk	233,000
Birobidžan (1987E)	82,000
Blagoveščensk	206,000
Bobrujsk	223,000
Bor (★Gor'kij) (1987E)	65,000
Borisoglebsk (1987E)	69,000
Borisov	144,000
Boroviči (1987E)	64,000
Br'anka (★Stachanov) (1987E)	65,000
Br'ansk	452,000
Bratsk	255,000
Brest	258,000
Brovary (★Kijev) (1987E)	73,000
Buchara	224,000
Bud'onnovsk (1987E)	54,000
Bugul'ma (1987E)	88,000
Buguruslan (1987E)	53,000
Bujnaksk (1987E)	53,000
Buzuluk (1987E)	82,000
Čajkovskij (1987E)	83,000
Čapajevsk (1987E)	87,000
Čardžou	161,000
Čeboksary	420,000
Čechov (1987E)	57,000
Čel'abinsk (★1,325,000)	1,143,000
Čelinograd	277,000
Čeremchovo (1987E)	73,000
Čerepovec	310,000
Čerkassy	290,000
Čerkessk	113,000
Černigov	296,000
Černogorsk (1987E)	80,000
Černovcy	257,000
Červonograd (1987E)	71,000
Chabarovsk	601,000
Charcyzsk (★Doneck) (1987E)	69,000
Char'kov (★1,940,000)	1,611,000
Chasavjurt (1987E)	74,000
Cherson	355,000
Chimki (★Moskva)	133,000
Chmel'nickij	237,000
Chodžejli (1987E)	55,000
Cholmsk (1987E)	50,000
Čimkent	393,000
Čirčik (★Taškent)	156,000
Čistopol' (1987E)	65,000
Čita	366,000
Čusovoj (1987E)	59,000
Daugavpils	127,000
Denau (1987E)	53,000
Derbent (1987E)	83,000
Dimitrov (★Krasnoarmejsk) (1987E)	62,000
Dimitrovgrad	124,000
Dmitrov (1987E)	64,000
Dneprodzeržinsk (★Dnepropetrovsk)	282,000
Dnepropetrovsk (★1,600,000)	1,179,000
Dolgoprudnyj (★Moskva) (1987E)	71,000
Domodedovo (★Moskva) (1987E)	51,000

▲ Population of an entire municipality, commune, or district, including rural area.
• Largest city in country.
★ Population or designation of the metropolitan area, including suburbs.
C Census. **E** Official estimate. **U** Unofficial estimate.

▲ Bevölkerung eines ganzen städtischen Verwaltungsgebietes, eines Kommunalbezirkes oder eines Distrikts, einschliesslich ländlicher Gebiete.
• Grösste Stadt des Landes.
★ Bevölkerung oder Bezeichnung der Stadtregion einschliesslich Vororte.
C Volkszählung. **E** Offizielle Schätzung. **U** Inoffizielle Schätzung.

Population of Cities and Towns / Einwohnerzahlen von Grossstädten / Habitantes en las Ciudades y Poblaciones
Population des Grands Centres et des Villes / População dos Centros Urbanos 313

Doneck (★2,200,000)	1,110,000
Drogobyč (1987E)	76,000
Družkovka (★Kramatorsk) (1987E)	70,000
Dubna (1987E)	64,000
Dušanbe	595,000
Džalal-Abad (1987E)	74,000
Džambul	307,000
Džankoj (1987E)	51,000
Dzeržinsk (★Gor'kij)	285,000
Džezkazgan	109,000
Džizak	102,000
Ečmiadzin (★Jerevan) (1987E)	53,000
Ekibastuz	135,000
Elektrostal'	153,000
Elista (1987E)	85,000
Engel's (★Saratov)	182,000
Fastov (1987E)	55,000
Feodosija (1987E)	83,000
Fergana	200,000
Fr'azino (★Moskva) (1987E)	52,000
Frunze	616,000
Gatčina (★Leningrad) (1987E)	81,000
Georgijevsk (1987E)	62,000
Georgiu-Dež (1987E)	54,000
Glazov	104,000
Gomel'	500,000
Gori (1987E)	62,000
Gor'kij (★2,025,000)	1,438,000
Gorlovka (★710,000)	337,000
Gorno-Altajsk (1974E)	39,000
Gr'azi (1974E)	42,000
Grodno	270,000
Groznyj	401,000
Gubkin (1987E)	75,000
Gukovo (1987E)	72,000
Gulistan (1987E)	51,000
Gurjev	149,000
Gus'-Chrustal'nyj (1987E)	75,000
Iljičovsk (★Odessa) (1987E)	52,000
Inta (1987E)	58,000
Irbit (1987E)	53,000
Irkutsk	626,000
Išim (1987E)	65,000
Išimbaj (1987E)	67,000
Iskitim (1987E)	69,000
Ivano-Frankovsk	214,000
Ivanovo	481,000
Ivantejevka (★Moskva) (1987E)	53,000
Iževsk	635,000
Izmail (1987E)	90,000
Iz'um (1987E)	63,000
Jakutsk	187,000
Jalta (1987E)	89,000
Jangijul' (1987E)	71,000
Jaroslavl'	633,000
Jefremov (1987E)	58,000
Jegorjevsk (1987E)	73,000
Jejsk (1987E)	77,000
Jelec	120,000
Jelgava (1987E)	72,000
Jenakijevo (★Gorlovka)	121,000
Jerevan (★1,315,000)	1,199,000
Jessentuki (1987E)	84,000
Jevpatorija	108,000
Joškar-Ola	242,000
Jurga (1987E)	92,000
Jūrmala (★Rīga) (1987E)	65,000
Južno-Sachalinsk	157,000
Kalinin	451,000
Kaliningrad (Königsberg)	401,000
Kaliningrad (★Moskva)	160,000
Kaluga	312,000
Kaluš (1987E)	67,000
Kamenec-Podol'skij	102,000
Kamensk-Šachtinskij (1987E)	75,000
Kamensk-Ural'skij	209,000
Kamyšin	122,000
Kanaš (1987E)	53,000
Kansk	110,000
Kara-Balta (1987E)	55,000
Karaganda	614,000
Karši	156,000
Kaspijsk (1987E)	61,000
Kattakurgan (1987E)	63,000
Kaunas	423,000
Kazan' (★1,140,000)	1,094,000
Kemerovo	520,000
Kentau (1987E)	60,000
Kerč'	174,000
Kijev (★2,900,000)	2,587,000
Kimry (1987E)	61,000
Kinel' (1974E)	40,000
Kinešma	105,000
Kiriši (1987E)	51,000
Kirov	441,000
Kirovabad	278,000
Kirovakan (1987E)	169,000
Kirovo-Čepeck (1987E)	89,000
Kirovograd	269,000
Kisel'ovsk (★Prokopjevsk)	128,000
Kišin'ov	665,000
Kislovodsk	114,000
Kizel (1974E)	42,000
Klaipėda (Memel)	204,000
Klimovsk (★Moskva) (1987E)	57,000
Klin (1987E)	95,000
Klincy (1987E)	72,000
Kohtla-Järve (1987E)	78,000
Kokand	182,000
Kokčetav	137,000
Kol'čugino (1974E)	43,000
Kolomna	162,000
Kolomyja (1987E)	63,000
Kolpino (★Leningrad)	142,000
Kommunarsk (★Stachanov)	126,000
Komsomol'sk-na-Amure	315,000
Konotop (1987E)	93,000
Konstantinovka	108,000
Kopejsk (★Čel'abinsk) (1987E)	99,000
Korkino (1981E)	63,000
Korosten' (1987E)	72,000
Korsakov (1974E)	40,000
Kostroma	278,000
Kotlas (1987E)	69,000
Kovel' (1987E)	66,000
Kovrov	160,000

Kramatorsk (★465,000)	198,000
Krasnoarmejsk (★175,000) (1987E)	70,000
Krasnodar	620,000
Krasnodon (1987E)	52,000
Krasnogorsk (★Moskva) (1987E)	89,000
Krasnojarsk	912,000
Krasnokamensk (1987E)	70,000
Krasnokamsk (1987E)	58,000
Krasnoturjinsk (1987E)	66,000
Krasnoufimsk (1974E)	40,000
Krasnoural'sk (1974E)	40,000
Krasnovodsk (1987E)	59,000
Krasnyj Luč (★250,000)	113,000
Krasnyj Sulin (1974E)	43,000
Kremenčug	236,000
Krivoj Rog	713,000
Kropotkin (1987E)	73,000
Krymsk (1983E)	50,000
Kstovo (★Gor'kij) (1987E)	64,000
Kujbyšev (1987E)	51,000
Kujbyšev (★1,505,000)	1,257,000
Kul'ab (1987E)	71,000
Kumertau (1987E)	62,000
Kungur (1987E)	83,000
Kurgan	356,000
Kurgan-T'ube (1987E)	55,000
Kursk	424,000
Kustanaj	224,000
Kutaisi	235,000
Kuzneck (1987E)	98,000
Kyzyl (1987E)	80,000
Kzyl-Orda	153,000
Labinsk (1987E)	58,000
Leninabad	160,000
Leninakan	120,000
Leningrad (★5,825,000)	4,456,000
Leninogorsk, Tatarskaja A. S. S. R. (1987E)	61,000
Leninogorsk, Vostočno-Kazachstanskaja oblast' (1987E)	69,000
Leninsk-Kuzneckij	165,000
Lida (1987E)	81,000
Liepāja	114,000
Lipeck	450,000
Lisičansk (★410,000)	127,000
Livny (1987E)	51,000
Lobn'a (★Moskva) (1987E)	59,000
Lozovaja (1987E)	68,000
L'ubercy (★Moskva)	165,000
Lubny (1987E)	58,000
Luck	198,000
L'vov	790,000
Lys'va (1987E)	77,000
Lytkarino (★Moskva) (1987E)	51,000
Machačkala	315,000
Magadan	152,000
Magnitogorsk	440,000
Majkop	149,000
Makejevka (★Doneck)	430,000
Marganec (1987E)	55,000
Margilan	125,000
Mariupol' (Ždanov)	517,000
Mary (1987E)	89,000
Melitopol'	174,000
Meždurečensk	107,000
Miass	168,000
Michajlovka (1987E)	58,000
Mičurinsk	109,000
Mineral'nyje Vody (1987E)	75,000
Mingečaur (1987E)	78,000
Minsk (★1,650,000)	1,589,000
Minusinsk (1987E)	72,000
Mogil'ov	356,000
Molodečno (1987E)	87,000
Mončegorsk (1987E)	65,000
Moršansk (1987E)	51,000
• MOSKVA (MOSCOW) (★13,100,000)	8,769,000
Mozyr'	101,000
Mukačevo (1987E)	88,000
Murmansk	468,000
Murom	124,000
Mytišči (★Moskva)	154,000
Naberežnyje Čelny	501,000
Nachičevan' (1987E)	51,000
Nachodka	165,000
Nal'čik	235,000
Namangan	308,000
Naro-Fominsk (1987E)	60,000
Narva (1987E)	81,000
Navoi	107,000
Nazarovo (1987E)	63,000
Nebit-Dag (1987E)	85,000
Neftejugansk (1987E)	86,000
Neftekamsk	107,000
Ner'ungri (1987E)	68,000
Nevinnomyssk	121,000
Nežin (1987E)	81,000
Nikolajev	503,000
Nikol'skij (1987E)	64,000
Nikopol'	158,000
Nižnekamsk	191,000
Nižnevartovsk	242,000
Nižnij Tagil	440,000
Noginsk	123,000
Nojabr'sk (1987E)	77,000
Noril'sk	174,000
Novaja Kachovka (1987E)	53,000
Novgorod	229,000
Novoaltajsk (★Barnaul) (1987E)	51,000
Novočeboksarsk	115,000
Novočerkassk	187,000
Novodvinsk (1987E)	50,000
Novograd-Volynskij (1987E)	52,000
Novokujbyševsk (★Kujbyšev)	113,000
Novokuzneck	600,000
Novomoskovsk, Dnepropetrovsk oblast' (1987E)	76,000
Novomoskovsk, Tula oblast' (★365,000)	146,000
Novopolock (1987E)	90,000
Novorossijsk	186,000
Novošachtinsk	106,000
Novosibirsk (★1,600,000)	1,436,000
Novotroick	106,000

Novovolynsk (1987E)	54,000
Novyj Urengoj (1987E)	79,000
Nukus	169,000
Obninsk	100,000
Odessa (★1,185,000)	1,115,000
Odincovo (★Moskva)	125,000
Okt'abr'skij	105,000
Omsk (★1,175,000)	1,148,000
Ordžonikidze	300,000
Orechovo-Zujevo (★205,000)	137,000
Orenburg	547,000
Or'ol	337,000
Orša	123,000
Orsk	271,000
Oš	213,000
Osinniki (1987E)	63,000
Panevėžys	126,000
Pärnu (1987E)	53,000
Partizansk (1974E)	49,000
P'atigorsk	129,000
Pavlodar	331,000
Pavlograd	131,000
Pavlovo (1987E)	72,000
Pavlovskij Posad (1987E)	71,000
Pečora (1987E)	64,000
Penza	543,000
Perm' (★1,160,000)	1,091,000
Pervomajsk (1987E)	79,000
Pervoural'sk	142,000
Petrodvorec (★Leningrad) (1987E)	77,000
Petropavlovsk	241,000
Petropavlovsk-Kamčatskij	269,000
Petrozavodsk	270,000
Pinsk	119,000
Podol'sk (★Moskva)	210,000
Polevskoj (1987E)	71,000
Polock (1987E)	80,000
Poltava	315,000
Poti (1977E)	54,000
Priluki (1987E)	73,000
Prochladnyj (1987E)	53,000
Prokopjevsk (★410,000)	274,000
Prževal'sk (1987E)	64,000
Pskov	204,000
Puškin (★Leningrad) (1987E)	97,000
Puškino (1987E)	74,000
Ramenskoje (1987E)	86,000
R'azan'	515,000
Razdan (1987E)	56,000
Rečica (1987E)	71,000
Reutov (★Moskva) (1987E)	68,000
Revda (1987E)	66,000
Rīga (★1,005,000)	915,000
Romny (1987E)	53,000
Roslavl' (1987E)	61,000
Rossoš' (1987E)	55,000
Rostov-na-Donu (★1,165,000)	1,020,000
Roven'ki (1987E)	68,000
Rovno	228,000
Rubcovsk	172,000
Rubežnoje (★Lisičansk) (1987E)	72,000
Rudnyj	124,000
Rustavi (★Tbilisi)	159,000
Ruzajevka (1987E)	53,000
Rybinsk	252,000
Rybnica (1987E)	58,000
Ržev (1987E)	70,000
Šachtinsk (1987E)	62,000
Šacht'orsk (★Torez) (1987E)	73,000
Šachty	224,000
Šadrinsk (1987E)	87,000
Safonovo (1987E)	56,000
Salavat	150,000
Sal'sk (1987E)	62,000
Samarkand	366,000
Saran' (1987E)	64,000
Saransk	312,000
Sarapul	111,000
Saratov (★1,155,000)	905,000
Ščelkovo (★Moskva)	109,000
Ščokino (1987E)	70,000
Ščučinsk (1987E)	53,000
Šeki (Nucha) (1987E)	54,000
Semipalatinsk	334,000
Serov	104,000
Serpuchov	144,000
Sevastopol'	356,000
Ševčenko	159,000
Severodoneck (★Lisičansk)	131,000
Severodvinsk	249,000
Severomorsk (1987E)	55,000
Šiauliai	145,000
Simferopol'	344,000
Slav'ansk (★Kramatorsk)	135,000
Slav'ansk-Na-Kubani (1987E)	57,000
Sluck (1987E)	55,000
Smela (1987E)	76,000
Smolensk	341,000
Snežnoje (★Torez) (1987E)	68,000
Soči	337,000
Sokol (1974E)	48,000
Soligorsk (1987E)	92,000
Solikamsk	110,000
Solncevo (★Moskva) (1984E)	62,000
Solnečnogorsk (★Moskva) (1987E)	53,000
Sosnovyj Bor (1987E)	56,000
Šostka (1987E)	87,000
Spassk-Dal'nij (1987E)	60,000
Stachanov (★610,000)	112,000
Staryj Oskol	174,000
Stavropol'	318,000
Sterlitamak	248,000
Stryj (1987E)	63,000
Stupino (1987E)	73,000
Suchumi	121,000
Šuja (1987E)	72,000
Sumgait (★Baku)	231,000
Sumy	291,000
Surgut	248,000
Sverdlovsk, Sverdlovsk oblast' (★1,620,000)	1,367,000
Sverdlovsk, Vorosilovgrad oblast' (1987E)	84,000
Svetlogorsk (1987E)	68,000
Svetlovodsk (1987E)	55,000

Svobodnyj (1987E)	78,000
Syktyvkar	233,000
Syzran'	174,000
Taganrog	291,000
Taldy-Kurgan	119,000
Tallinn	482,000
Talnach (1987E)	54,000
Tambov	305,000
Tartu	114,000
Tašauz	112,000
Taškent (★2,325,000)	2,073,000
Tbilisi (★1,460,000)	1,260,000
Temirtau	212,000
Termez (1987E)	72,000
Ternopol'	205,000
Tichoreck (1987E)	67,000
Tichvin (1987E)	70,000
Tiraspol'	182,000
Tobol'sk (1987E)	82,000
Tokmak (1987E)	71,000
Toljatti	630,000
Tomsk	502,000
Torez (★290,000) (1987E)	88,000
Toržok (1987E)	51,000
Troick (1987E)	91,000
Tuapse (1987E)	64,000
Tujmazy (1987E)	54,000
Tula (★640,000)	540,000
Tulun (1987E)	56,000
T'umen'	477,000
Turkestan (1987E)	77,000
Tyndinskij (1987E)	61,000
Uchta	111,000
Ufa (★1,100,000)	1,083,000
Uglič (1974E)	37,000
Ulan-Ude	353,000
Uljanovsk	625,000
Uman' (1987E)	89,000
Ural'sk	200,000
Urgenč	128,000
Usolje-Sibirskoje	107,000
Ussurijsk	162,000
Ust'-Ilimsk	109,000
Ust'-Kamenogorsk	324,000
Ust'-Kut (1987E)	58,000
Užgorod	117,000
UzlovajaNovomoskovsk) (1987E)	63,000
V'az'ma (1987E)	57,000
Velikije Luki	114,000
Ventspils (1987E)	52,000
Verchn'aja Salda (1987E)	56,000
Vičuga (1987E)	51,000
Vilnius	582,000
Vinnica	374,000
Vitebsk	350,000
Vladimir	350,000
Vladivostok	648,000
Volchov (1987E)	51,000
Volgodonsk	176,000
Volgograd (Stalingrad) (★1,360,000)	999,000
Vologda	283,000
Vol'sk (1987E)	66,000
Volžsk (1987E)	60,000
Volžskij (★Volgograd)	269,000
Vorkuta	116,000
Voronež	887,000
Vorošilovgrad	497,000
Voskresensk (1987E)	80,000
Votkinsk	103,000
Vyborg (1987E)	81,000
Vyksa (1987E)	60,000
Vyšnij Voločok (1987E)	70,000
Zagorsk	115,000
Žanatas (1987E)	53,000
Zaporožje	884,000
Zelenograd (★Moskva)	158,000
Železnodorožnyj (★Moskva) (1987E)	90,000
Železnogorsk (1987E)	81,000
Zel'onodol'sk (1987E)	93,000
Žigulevsk (1977E)	50,000
Zima (1987E)	51,000
Žitomir	292,000
Zlatoust	208,000
Žlobin (1987E)	52,000
Žodino (1987E)	51,000
Žoltyje Vody (1987E)	61,000
Žukovskij	101,000
Zyr'anovsk (1987E)	55,000

UNITED ARAB EMIRATES / Al-Imārāt al-'Arabīyah Al-Muttaḥidah

1980 C	980,000
ABŪ ZABY (ABU DHABI)	242,975
Al-'Ayn	101,663
Ash-Shāriqah	125,149
• Dubayy	265,702
Ra's al-Khaymah	42,000

UNITED KINGDOM

1981 C	55,678,079

UNITED KINGDOM: ENGLAND

1981 C	46,220,955
Aldershot (★London)	53,665
Ashton-under-Lyne (★Manchester)	43,605
Aylesbury	51,999
Barnsley	76,783
Barrow-in-Furness	50,174
Basildon (★London)	94,800
Basingstoke	73,027
Bath	84,283
Bebington (★Liverpool)	62,618
Bedford	75,632
Beeston and Stapleford (★Nottingham)	64,785
Benfleet (★London)	50,783
Birkenhead (★Liverpool)	99,075
Birmingham (★2,675,000)	1,013,995
Blackburn (★221,900)	109,564
Blackpool (★280,000)	146,297
Bognor Regis	50,323
Bolton (★Manchester)	143,960
Bootle	70,860

▲ Población de un municipio, comuna o distrito entero, incluyendo sus áreas rurales.
• Ciudad más grande de un país.
★ Población o designación de un área metropolitana, incluyendo los suburbios.
C Censo. **E** Estimado oficial. **U** Estimado no oficial.

▲ Population d'une municipalité, d'une commune ou d'un district, zone rurale incluse.
• Ville la plus peuplée du pays.
★ Population de l'agglomération (ou nom de la zone métropolitaine englobante).
C Recensement. **E** Estimation officielle. **U** Estimation non officielle.

▲ População de um municipio, comuna ou distrito, inclusive as respectivas áreas rurais.
• Maior cidade de um país.
★ População ou indicação de uma área metropolitana.
C Censo. **E** Estimativa oficial. **U** Estimativa não oficial.

Bournemouth (★315,000)	142,829
Bracknell (★London)	52,257
Bradford (★Leeds)	293,336
Brentwood (★London)	51,212
Brighton (★420,000)	134,581
Bristol (★630,000)	413,861
Burnley (★160,000)	76,365
Burton upon Trent	59,040
Bury (★Manchester)	61,785
Bury Saint Edmunds	30,563
Camberley see Frimley and Camberley	
Cambridge	87,111
Cannock (★Birmingham)	54,503
Canterbury	34,546
Carlisle	72,206
Carlton (★Nottingham)	46,053
Chatham (★London)	65,835
Cheadle and Gatley (★Manchester)	59,478
Chelmsford (★London)	91,109
Cheltenham	87,188
Cheshunt (★London)	49,616
Chester	80,154
Chesterfield (★127,000)	73,352
Clacton-on-Sea	39,618
Colchester	87,476
Corby	48,704
Coventry (★645,000)	318,718
Crawley (★London)	80,113
Crewe	59,097
Crosby (★Liverpool)	54,103
Darlington	85,519
Dartford (★London)	62,032
Derby (★275,000)	218,026
Dewsbury (★Leeds)	49,612
Doncaster	74,727
Dover	33,461
Dudley (★Birmingham)	186,513
Dunstable (★Luton)	48,436
Durham	38,105
Eastbourne	86,715
Eastleigh (★Southampton)	58,585
Ellesmere Port (★Liverpool)	65,829
Epsom and Ewell (★London)	65,830
Esher / Molesey (★London)	46,688
Exeter	88,235
Fareham / Portchester (★Portsmouth)	55,563
Farnborough (★London)	48,063
Folkestone	42,949
Frimley and Camberley (★London)	45,108
Gateshead (★Newcastle)	91,429
Gillingham (★London)	92,531
Gloucester (★115,000)	106,526
Gosport (★Portsmouth)	69,664
Gravesend (★London)	53,450
Grays (★London)	45,881
Greasby / Moreton (★Liverpool)	56,410
Great Yarmouth	54,777
Grimsby (★145,000)	91,532
Guildford (★London)	61,509
Halesowen (★Birmingham)	57,533
Halifax	76,675
Harlow (★London)	79,150
Harrogate	63,637
Hartlepool (★Middlesbrough)	91,749
Hastings	74,979
Havant (★Portsmouth)	50,098
Hemel Hempstead (★London)	80,110
Hereford	48,277
Hertford (★London)	21,350
High Wycombe (▲156,800)	69,575
Hove (★Brighton)	65,587
Huddersfield (▲377,400)	147,825
Huyton-with-Roby (★Liverpool)	62,011
Ipswich	129,661
Keighley (★Leeds)	49,188
Kidderminster	50,385
Kingston upon Hull (★350,000)	322,144
Kingswood (★Bristol)	54,736
Kirkby (★Liverpool)	52,825
Lancaster	43,902
Leeds (★1,540,000)	445,242
Leicester (★495,000)	324,394
Lincoln	79,980
Littlehampton	46,028
Liverpool (★1,525,000)	538,809
• LONDON (★11,100,000)	6,574,009
Loughborough	44,895
Lowestoft	59,430
Luton (★220,000)	163,209
Macclesfield	47,525
Maidenhead (★London)	59,809
Maidstone	86,067
Manchester (★2,775,000)	437,612
Mansfield (★198,000)	71,325
Margate	53,137
Middlesbrough (★580,000)	158,516
Middleton (★Manchester)	51,373
Milton Keynes	36,886
Newcastle-under-Lyme (★Stoke-on-Trent)	73,208
Newcastle upon Tyne (★1,300,000)	199,064
Northampton	154,172
Norwich (★230,000)	169,814
Nottingham (★655,000)	273,300
Nuneaton (★Coventry)	60,337
Oldbury / Smethwick (★Birmingham)	153,268
Oldham (★Manchester)	107,095
Oxford (★230,000)	113,847
Penzance	18,501
Peterborough	113,404
Plymouth (★290,000)	238,583
Poole (★Bournemouth)	122,815
Portsmouth (★485,000)	174,218
Preston (★250,000)	166,675
Ramsgate	36,678
Reading (★200,000)	194,727
Redditch (★Birmingham)	61,639
Reigate / Redhill (★London)	48,241
Rochdale (★Manchester)	97,292
Rotherham (★Sheffield)	122,374
Royal Leamington Spa (★Coventry)	56,552
Royal Tunbridge Wells	57,699
Rugby	59,039
Runcorn (★Liverpool)	63,995
Saint Albans (★London)	76,709
Saint Helens	114,397
Sale (★Manchester)	57,872
Salford (★Manchester)	96,525
Salisbury	36,890
Scarborough	36,665
Scunthorpe	79,043
Sheffield (★710,000)	470,685
Shrewsbury	57,731
Slough (★London)	106,341
Solihull (★Birmingham)	93,940
Southampton (★415,000)	211,321
Southend-on-Sea (★London)	155,720
Southport (★Liverpool)	88,596
South Shields (★Newcastle)	86,488
Stafford	60,915
Staines (★London)	51,949
Stapleford see Beeston and Stapleford	
Stevenage	74,757
Stockport (★Manchester)	135,489
Stockton-on-Tees (★Middlesbrough)	86,699
Stoke-on-Trent (★440,000)	272,446
Stourbridge (★Birmingham)	55,136
Stratford-upon-Avon	20,941
Stretford (★Manchester)	47,522
Sunderland (★Newcastle)	195,064
Sutton Coldfield (★Birmingham)	102,572
Swindon	127,348
Tamworth	63,260
Taunton	47,793
Torquay (★112,400)	54,430
Wakefield (★Leeds)	74,764
Wallasey (★Liverpool)	62,465
Walsall (★Birmingham)	177,923
Walton and Weybridge (★London)	50,031
Warrington	81,366
Washington (★Newcastle)	48,856
Waterlooville (★Portsmouth)	57,296
Watford (★London)	109,503
West Bromwich (★Birmingham)	153,725
Weston-super-Mare	60,821
Weybridge see Walton and Weybridge	
Widnes	55,973
Wigan (★Manchester)	88,725
Woking (★London)	92,667
Wolverhampton (★Birmingham)	263,501
Worcester	75,466
Worthing (★Brighton)	90,687
York (★145,000)	123,126

UNITED KINGDOM: NORTHERN IRELAND

1987 E	1,575,200
Bangor (★Belfast)	70,700
Belfast (★685,000)	303,800
Castlereagh (★Belfast)	57,900
Londonderry (★97,200)	97,500
Lurgan (★63,000) (1981C)	20,991
Newtownabbey (★Belfast)	72,300

UNITED KINGDOM: SCOTLAND

1981 C	5,035,315
Aberdeen	186,757
Ayr (★100,000)	48,493
Clydebank (★Glasgow)	51,832
Coatbridge	50,831
Cumbernauld (★Glasgow)	47,517
Dundee	172,294
Dunfermline (★125,817)	52,105
East Kilbride (★Glasgow)	70,454
Edinburgh (★630,000)	408,822
Falkirk (★148,171)	36,372
Glasgow (★1,800,000)	754,586
Greenock (★101,000)	58,436
Hamilton (★Glasgow)	51,666
Irvine (★94,000)	32,507
Kilmarnock (★84,000)	51,799
Kirkcaldy (★148,171)	46,356
Motherwell (★Glasgow)	30,616
Paisley (★Glasgow)	84,330
Perth	41,916
Stirling (★61,000)	36,640

UNITED KINGDOM: WALES

1981 C	2,790,462
Cardiff (★625,000)	262,313
Cwmbran (★Newport)	44,592
Llanelli	45,336
Merthyr Tydfil	38,893
Neath (★Swansea)	48,687
Newport (★310,000)	115,896
Pontypool (★Newport)	36,064
Port Talbot (★130,000)	40,078
Rhondda (★Cardiff)	70,980
Swansea (★275,000)	172,433
Wrexham	39,929

UNITED STATES

1980 C	226,549,248

UNITED STATES: ALABAMA

1980 C	3,894,046
Anniston (★102,900)	29,523
Auburn (★50,700)	28,471
Birmingham (★747,400)	286,799
Decatur (★76,700)	42,002
Dothan (★75,500)	48,750
Florence (★98,200)	37,029
Gadsden (★88,800)	47,565
Huntsville (★189,600)	142,513
Mobile (★361,900)	200,452
Montgomery (★225,000)	177,857
Tuscaloosa (★115,700)	75,211

UNITED STATES: ALASKA

1980 C	401,851
Anchorage (★184,300)	174,431
Fairbanks (★39,900)	22,645
Juneau	19,528

UNITED STATES: ARIZONA

1980 C	2,718,425
Glendale (★Phoenix)	97,172
Mesa (★Phoenix)	152,453
Nogales (★81,400)	15,683
Phoenix (★1,482,400)	790,044
Scottsdale (★Phoenix)	88,622
Tempe (★Phoenix)	106,920
Tucson (★495,600)	336,503
Yuma (★58,100)	43,950

UNITED STATES: ARKANSAS

1980 C	2,286,357
Fayetteville (★87,000)	36,608
Fort Smith (★129,500)	71,626
Hot Springs National Park (★57,600)	36,228
Jonesboro (★43,700)	31,530
Little Rock (★382,000)	167,744
North Little Rock (★Little Rock)	64,388
Pine Bluff (★72,250)	56,636

UNITED STATES: CALIFORNIA

1980 C	23,667,555
Alameda (★San Francisco)	63,852
Alhambra (★Los Angeles)	64,767
Anaheim (★Los Angeles)	219,494
Arden (★Sacramento)	52,000
Bakersfield (★245,100)	105,735
Baldwin Park (★Los Angeles)	50,554
Bellflower (★Los Angeles)	53,441
Berkeley (★San Francisco)	103,328
Buena Park (★Los Angeles)	64,165
Burbank (★Los Angeles)	84,625
Calexico (★365,000)	14,412
Carson (★Los Angeles)	81,221
Cerritos (★Los Angeles)	53,020
Chico (★57,300)	26,716
Chula Vista (★San Diego)	83,927
Citrus Heights (★Sacramento)	85,911
Compton (★Los Angeles)	81,230
Concord (★San Francisco)	103,763
Costa Mesa (★Los Angeles)	82,562
Cucamonga (★Los Angeles)	55,250
Daly City (★San Francisco)	78,427
Downey (★Los Angeles)	82,602
East Los Angeles (★Los Angeles)	110,017
El Cajon (★San Diego)	73,892
El Monte (★Los Angeles)	79,494
Escondido (★San Diego)	64,355
Eureka (★82,700)	24,153
Fairfield (★117,000)	58,099
Fountain Valley (★Los Angeles)	55,080
Fremont (★San Francisco)	131,945
Fresno (★389,500)	235,812
Fullerton (★Los Angeles)	102,246
Garden Grove (★Los Angeles)	123,307
Glendale (★Los Angeles)	139,060
Hawthorne (★Los Angeles)	56,437
Hayward (★San Francisco)	93,718
Hemet (★61,700)	24,438
Huntington Beach (★Los Angeles)	170,505
Inglewood (★Los Angeles)	94,162
Irvine (★Los Angeles)	62,134
Lakewood (★Los Angeles)	74,654
La Mesa (★San Diego)	50,308
Lancaster (★86,400)	48,027
Livermore (★San Francisco)	48,349
Lompoc (★43,400)	26,267
Long Beach (★Los Angeles)	361,355
Los Angeles (★9,763,600)	2,968,579
Lynwood (★Los Angeles)	48,409
Merced (★72,500)	36,499
Mission Viejo (★Los Angeles)	50,666
Modesto (★183,800)	106,963
Montebello (★Los Angeles)	52,929
Monterey (★127,900)	27,558
Monterey Park (★Los Angeles)	54,338
Mountain View (★San Francisco)	58,655
Napa (★71,500)	50,879
Newport Beach (★Los Angeles)	62,556
Norwalk (★Los Angeles)	84,901
Oakland (★San Francisco)	339,337
Oceanside (★129,100)	76,698
Ontario (★Los Angeles)	88,820
Orange (★Los Angeles)	91,450
Oxnard (★294,200)	108,195
Palm Springs (★80,900)	32,359
Palo Alto (★San Francisco)	55,225
Pasadena (★Los Angeles)	118,072
Pico Rivera (★Los Angeles)	53,387
Pomona (★Los Angeles)	92,742
Porterville (★46,300)	20,865
Redding (★96,300)	41,995
Redondo Beach (★Los Angeles)	57,102
Redwood City (★San Francisco)	54,951
Richmond (★San Francisco)	74,676
Riverside (★768,300)	170,591
Sacramento (★866,400)	275,741
Salinas (★109,400)	80,479
San Bernardino (★Riverside)	118,794
San Diego (★2,098,500)	875,538
San Francisco (★4,683,200)	678,974
San Jose (★San Francisco)	629,400
San Leandro (★San Francisco)	63,952
San Mateo (★San Francisco)	77,640
Santa Ana (★Los Angeles)	204,023
Santa Barbara (★170,300)	74,414
Santa Clara (★San Francisco)	87,700
Santa Cruz (★134,100)	41,483
Santa Maria (★67,500)	39,685
Santa Monica (★Los Angeles)	88,314
Santa Rosa (★153,300)	83,320
Simi Valley (★Los Angeles)	77,500
South Gate (★Los Angeles)	66,784
South San Francisco (★San Francisco)	49,393
Stockton (★213,000)	149,779
Sunnyvale (★San Francisco)	106,618
Thousand Oaks (★Los Angeles)	85,188
Torrance (★Los Angeles)	129,881
Vallejo (★San Francisco)	80,303
Ventura (San Buenaventura) (★Oxnard)	77,988
Visalia (★76,300)	49,729
Walnut Creek (★San Francisco)	56,125
Watsonville (★55,100)	23,662
West Covina (★Los Angeles)	80,292
Westminster (★Los Angeles)	71,133
Whittier (★Los Angeles)	68,558
Yuba City (★68,200)	18,736

UNITED STATES: COLORADO

1980 C	2,889,735
Arvada (★Denver)	84,576
Aurora (★Denver)	158,588
Boulder (★165,200)	76,685
Colorado Springs (★301,500)	214,821
Denver (★1,405,300)	492,365
Fort Collins (★87,600)	65,092
Grand Junction (★74,300)	27,956
Greeley (★69,900)	53,006
Lakewood (★Denver)	113,808
Loveland (★42,000)	30,215
Pueblo (★117,000)	101,686
Westminster (★Denver)	50,211

UNITED STATES: CONNECTICUT

1980 C	3,107,576
Bridgeport (★438,500)	142,546
Bristol (★Hartford)	57,370
Danbury (★New York)	60,470
East Hartford (★Hartford)	52,563
Fairfield (★Bridgeport)	54,849
Greenwich (★New York)	59,565
Hamden (★New Haven)	51,071
Hartford (★1,013,600)	136,392
Manchester (★Hartford)	49,761
Meriden (★New Haven)	57,118
Milford (★Bridgeport)	49,101
New Britain (★Hartford)	73,840
New Haven (★500,500)	126,101
New London (★250,800)	28,842
Norwalk (★New York)	77,767
Stamford (★New York)	102,466
Stratford (★Bridgeport)	50,541
Torrington (★54,300)	30,987
Waterbury (★205,000)	103,266
West Hartford (★Hartford)	61,301
West Haven (★New Haven)	53,184

UNITED STATES: DELAWARE

1980 C	594,317
Dover (★70,300)	23,507
Wilmington (★Philadelphia)	70,195

UNITED STATES: DISTRICT OF COLUMBIA

1980 C	638,432
WASHINGTON (★3,221,400)	638,432

UNITED STATES: FLORIDA

1980 C	9,747,117
Boca Raton (★Miami)	49,447
Clearwater (★Saint Petersburg)	85,528
Daytona Beach (★178,800)	54,176
De Land (★47,300)	15,354
Fort Lauderdale (★Miami)	153,279
Fort Myers (★163,200)	36,638
Fort Pierce (★83,300)	33,802
Fort Walton Beach (★88,900)	20,829
Gainesville (★123,100)	81,371
Hialeah (★Miami)	145,254
Hollywood (★Miami)	121,323
Jacksonville (★635,900)	540,920
Kendall (★Miami)	51,000
Lakeland (★138,900)	50,158
Largo (★Saint Petersburg)	58,977
Melbourne (★227,500)	46,536
Miami (★2,827,300)	346,865
Miami Beach (★Miami)	96,298
Naples (★66,600)	17,581
Ocala (★83,600)	37,170
Orlando (★619,300)	128,291
Panama City (★92,900)	33,346
Pensacola (★250,200)	57,619
Plantation (★Miami)	48,653
Pompano Beach (★Miami)	58,021
Saint Petersburg (★852,300)	238,647
Sarasota (★281,900)	48,868
Tallahassee (★136,900)	101,547
Tampa (★594,500)	271,598
Venice (★56,900)	12,153
West Palm Beach (★356,000)	63,305
Winter Haven (★85,300)	21,119

UNITED STATES: GEORGIA

1980 C	5,462,982
Albany (★105,200)	83,245
Athens (★102,500)	42,549
Atlanta (★1,962,500)	425,022
Augusta (★251,100)	47,532
Columbus (★233,400)	169,441
Macon (★227,400)	116,896
Rome (★74,200)	29,928
Savannah (★212,800)	141,651
Valdosta (★58,100)	37,596
Warner Robins (★Macon)	39,893

UNITED STATES: HAWAII

1980 C	964,691
Hilo (★43,200)	35,269
Honolulu (★762,600)	365,048

UNITED STATES: IDAHO

1980 C	944,127
Boise (★164,200)	102,160
Idaho Falls (★66,200)	39,734
Lewiston (★43,600)	27,986
Nampa (★64,600)	25,112
Pocatello (★56,200)	46,340

UNITED STATES: ILLINOIS

1980 C	11,427,414
Arlington Heights (★Chicago)	66,116
Aurora (★Chicago)	81,293
Bloomington (★85,300)	44,189
Champaign (★118,100)	58,267
Chicago (★7,717,100)	3,005,072
Cicero (★Chicago)	61,232

▲ Population of an entire municipality, commune, or district, including rural area.
• Largest city in country.
★ Population or designation of the metropolitan area, including suburbs.
C Census. **E** Official estimate. **U** Unofficial estimate.

▲ Bevölkerung eines ganzen städtischen Verwaltungsgebietes, eines Kommunalbezirkes oder eines Distrikts, einschliesslich ländlicher Gebiete.
• Grösste Stadt des Landes.
★ Bevölkerung oder Bezeichnung der Stadtregion einschliesslich Vororte.
C Volkszählung. **E** Offizielle Schätzung. **U** Inoffizielle Schätzung.

Population of Cities and Towns / Einwohnerzahlen von Grossstädten / Habitantes en las Ciudades y Poblaciones
Population des Grands Centres et des Villes / População dos Centros Urbanos 315

Danville (★72,900)	38,985
Decatur (★119,200)	93,896
De Kalb (★49,200)	33,157
Des Plaines (★Chicago)	55,374
East Saint Louis (★Saint Louis)	55,200
Elgin (★Chicago)	63,668
Evanston (★Chicago)	73,706
Galesburg (★43,500)	35,305
Joliet (★Chicago)	77,956
Kankakee (★83,300)	29,635
Mount Prospect (★Chicago)	52,634
Oak Lawn (★Chicago)	60,590
Oak Park (★Chicago)	54,887
Peoria (★319,700)	124,160
Quincy (★54,700)	42,554
Rockford (★280,700)	139,712
Schaumburg (★Chicago)	53,355
Skokie (★Chicago)	60,278
Springfield (★154,200)	100,054
Waukegan (★Chicago)	67,653

UNITED STATES: INDIANA

1980 C	5,490,212
Anderson (★143,200)	64,695
Bloomington (★91,400)	52,044
Columbus (★64,700)	30,614
Elkhart (★138,500)	41,305
Evansville (★223,900)	130,496
Fort Wayne (★284,300)	172,349
Gary (★Chicago)	151,953
Hammond (★Chicago)	93,714
Indianapolis (★1,072,500)	700,807
Kokomo (★85,300)	47,808
Lafayette (★113,000)	43,011
Marion (★83,900)	35,874
Michigan City (★60,600)	36,850
Muncie (★130,600)	77,216
Richmond (★66,800)	41,349
South Bend (★279,500)	109,727
Terre Haute (★119,100)	61,125

UNITED STATES: IOWA

1980 C	2,913,808
Ames (★63,300)	45,775
Cedar Rapids (★153,200)	110,243
Clinton (★44,200)	32,828
Council Bluffs (★Omaha)	56,449
Davenport (★320,400)	103,264
Des Moines (★308,000)	191,003
Dubuque (★78,100)	62,321
Iowa City (★68,000)	50,508
Mason City (★40,600)	30,144
Sioux City (★101,600)	82,003
Waterloo (★129,700)	75,985

UNITED STATES: KANSAS

1980 C	2,364,236
Hutchinson (★48,600)	40,284
Kansas City (★Kansas City, Mo.)	161,148
Lawrence (★54,200)	52,738
Manhattan (★42,000)	32,644
Overland Park (★Kansas City)	81,784
Salina (★42,200)	41,843
Topeka (★145,600)	118,690
Wichita (★372,200)	279,835

UNITED STATES: KENTUCKY

1980 C	3,660,330
Bowling Green (★52,700)	40,450
Covington (★Cincinnati)	49,567
Frankfort	25,973
Lexington (★255,600)	204,165
Louisville (★891,400)	298,694
Owensboro (★72,600)	54,450
Paducah (★69,700)	29,315

UNITED STATES: LOUISIANA

1980 C	4,206,098
Alexandria (★103,900)	51,565
Baton Rouge (★434,400)	238,876
Bossier City (★Shreveport)	50,817
Houma (★90,400)	32,602
Kenner (★New Orleans)	66,382
Lafayette (★164,800)	80,584
Lake Charles (★144,400)	75,226
Metairie (★New Orleans)	164,160
Monroe (★125,300)	57,597
New Iberia (★42,300)	32,766
New Orleans (★1,185,000)	557,927
Shreveport (★292,500)	205,820

UNITED STATES: MAINE

1980 C	1,125,043
Augusta (★55,300)	21,819
Bangor (★83,500)	31,643
Lewiston (★84,700)	40,481
Portland (★193,800)	61,572

UNITED STATES: MARYLAND

1980 C	4,216,941
Annapolis (★67,900)	31,740
Baltimore (★1,960,400)	786,741
Bethesda (★Washington)	63,022
Columbia (★Washington)	52,518
Cumberland (★83,100)	25,933
Dundalk (★Baltimore)	71,293
Hagerstown (★127,000)	34,132
Salisbury (★62,600)	16,429
Silver Spring (★Washington)	64,100
Towson (★Baltimore)	51,083
Wheaton (★Washington)	48,600

UNITED STATES: MASSACHUSETTS

1980 C	5,737,093
Amherst (★41,800)	17,773
Boston (★3,971,700)	562,994
Brockton (★Boston)	95,172
Brookline (★Boston)	55,062
Cambridge (★Boston)	95,322
Chicopee (★Springfield)	55,112
Fall River (★157,200)	92,574
Fitchburg (★94,000)	39,580
Framingham (★Boston)	65,113
Lawrence (★Boston)	63,175
Lowell (★Boston)	92,418
Lynn (★Boston)	78,471
Malden (★Boston)	53,386
Medford (★Boston)	58,076
New Bedford (★166,700)	98,478
Newton (★Boston)	83,622
Northampton (★34,600)	29,286
Pittsfield (★83,500)	51,974
Quincy (★Boston)	84,743
Somerville (★Boston)	77,372
Springfield (★485,900)	152,319
Taunton (★53,100)	45,001
Waltham (★Boston)	58,200
Weymouth (★Boston)	55,601
Worcester (★402,900)	161,799

UNITED STATES: MICHIGAN

1980 C	9,262,044
Ann Arbor (★Detroit)	107,969
Battle Creek (★102,600)	56,339
Benton Harbor (★102,200)	14,707
Clinton Township (★Detroit)	72,400
Dearborn (★Detroit)	90,660
Dearborn Heights (★Detroit)	67,706
Detroit (★4,691,900)	1,202,463
East Lansing (★Lansing)	51,392
Farmington Hills (★Detroit)	58,056
Flint (★521,200)	159,611
Grand Rapids (★503,800)	181,843
Holland (★75,800)	26,281
Jackson (★138,900)	39,739
Kalamazoo (★240,800)	79,722
Lansing (★352,600)	130,414
Livonia (★Detroit)	104,814
Monroe (★63,200)	23,531
Muskegon (★150,800)	40,823
Pontiac (★Detroit)	76,715
Port Huron (★164,700)	33,981
Redford Township (★Detroit)	58,441
Roseville (★Detroit)	54,311
Royal Oak (★Detroit)	70,893
Saginaw (★362,700)	77,508
Saint Clair Shores (★Detroit)	76,210
Sault Sainte Marie (★103,600)	14,448
Southfield (★Detroit)	75,568
Sterling Heights (★Detroit)	108,999
Taylor (★Detroit)	77,568
Troy (★Detroit)	67,102
Warren (★Detroit)	161,134
Westland (★Detroit)	84,603
Wyoming (★Grand Rapids)	59,616

UNITED STATES: MINNESOTA

1980 C	4,075,970
Bloomington (★Minneapolis)	81,831
Duluth (★145,800)	92,811
Mankato (★45,000)	28,646
Minneapolis (★2,012,400)	370,951
Rochester (★79,000)	57,890
Saint Cloud (★75,800)	42,566
Saint Paul (★Minneapolis)	270,230

UNITED STATES: MISSISSIPPI

1980 C	2,520,698
Biloxi (★196,900)	49,311
Columbus (★50,200)	27,503
Greenville (★51,700)	40,613
Gulfport (★Biloxi)	39,676
Hattiesburg (★66,400)	40,829
Jackson (★306,900)	202,895
Laurel (★47,200)	21,897
Meridian (★62,000)	46,577
Natchez (★47,600)	22,209
Pascagoula (★78,300)	29,318
Vicksburg (★47,000)	25,434

UNITED STATES: MISSOURI

1980 C	4,916,759
Cape Girardeau (★57,400)	34,361
Columbia (★81,800)	62,061
Florissant (★Saint Louis)	55,372
Independence (★Kansas City)	111,797
Jefferson City (★54,100)	33,619
Joplin (★76,100)	39,023
Kansas City (★1,272,400)	448,033
Saint Joseph (★87,300)	76,691
Saint Louis (★2,203,000)	452,801
Springfield (★192,600)	133,116

UNITED STATES: MONTANA

1980 C	786,690
Billings (★96,100)	66,842
Butte (★38,100)	37,205
Great Falls (★71,200)	56,725
Helena	23,938
Missoula (★64,900)	33,388

UNITED STATES: NEBRASKA

1980 C	1,569,825
Grand Island (★41,000)	33,180
Lincoln (★176,500)	171,932
Omaha (★538,600)	322,133

UNITED STATES: NEVADA

1980 C	800,508
Carson City	32,022
Las Vegas (★453,800)	164,674
Reno (★176,200)	100,756

UNITED STATES: NEW HAMPSHIRE

1980 C	920,610
Concord (★59,800)	30,400
Manchester (★129,300)	90,936
Nashua (★Boston)	67,865
Portsmouth (★170,200)	26,254

UNITED STATES: NEW JERSEY

1980 C	7,365,011
Atlantic City (★170,700)	40,199
Bayonne (★New York)	65,047
Bloomfield (★New York)	47,792
Brick Township (★New York)	53,629
Camden (★Philadelphia)	84,910
Cherry Hill (★Philadelphia)	68,785
Clifton (★New York)	74,388
East Orange (★New York)	77,878
Edison (★New York)	70,193
Elizabeth (★New York)	106,201
Irvington (★New York)	61,493
Jersey City	223,532
Middletown (★New York)	62,298
Newark (★New York)	329,248
Passaic (★New York)	52,463
Paterson (★New York)	137,970
Trenton (★Philadelphia)	92,124
Union (★New York)	50,184
Union City (★New York)	55,593
Vineland (★143,800)	53,753
Woodbridge (★New York)	90,074

UNITED STATES: NEW MEXICO

1980 C	1,303,542
Albuquerque (★453,200)	332,336
Farmington (★45,200)	31,222
Las Cruces (★65,200)	45,086
Roswell (★45,000)	39,676
Santa Fe (★54,400)	49,299

UNITED STATES: NEW YORK

1980 C	17,558,165
Albany (★729,100)	101,727
Amherst (★Buffalo)	66,100
Auburn (★52,900)	32,548
Binghamton (★230,600)	55,860
Buffalo (★1,483,000)	357,870
Cheektowaga (★Buffalo)	92,145
Elmira (★90,800)	35,327
Glens Falls (★64,500)	15,897
Greece (★Rochester)	63,700
Hicksville (★New York)	43,245
Irondequoit (★Rochester)	57,648
Ithaca (★76,700)	28,732
Jamestown (★68,400)	35,775
Kingston (★88,000)	24,481
Levittown (★New York)	57,045
Lockport (★54,800)	24,844
Middletown (★72,700)	21,454
Mount Vernon (★New York)	66,713
Newburgh (★91,900)	23,438
New Rochelle (★New York)	70,794
• New York (★16,800,900)	7,071,639
Niagara Falls (★Buffalo)	71,384
Poughkeepsie (★191,700)	29,757
Rochester (★816,200)	241,741
Schenectady (★Albany)	67,972
Syracuse (★518,600)	170,105
Town of Tonawanda (★Buffalo)	72,795
Troy (★Albany)	56,638
Utica (★224,000)	75,632
West Seneca (★Buffalo)	51,210
Yonkers (★New York)	195,351

UNITED STATES: NORTH CAROLINA

1980 C	5,880,965
Asheville (★159,900)	53,583
Burlington (★99,000)	37,266
Charlotte (★479,200)	315,473
Durham (★203,100)	100,538
Fayetteville (★236,200)	59,507
Gastonia (★125,400)	47,333
Goldsboro (★64,500)	34,705
Greensboro (★392,400)	155,642
Hickory (★81,600)	23,426
High Point (★Greensboro)	63,808
Jacksonville (★89,200)	22,586
Kannapolis (★103,100)	34,564
Raleigh (★282,800)	150,255
Rocky Mount (★67,400)	41,283
Salisbury (★61,500)	22,677
Wilmington (★109,700)	44,000
Winston-Salem (★278,400)	138,583

UNITED STATES: NORTH DAKOTA

1980 C	652,717
Bismarck (★65,000)	44,485
Fargo (★108,800)	61,383
Grand Forks (★53,500)	43,765
Minot (★38,300)	32,843

UNITED STATES: OHIO

1980 C	10,797,603
Akron (★614,100)	237,177
Alliance (★50,700)	24,315
Ashtabula (★44,700)	23,449
Brunswick (★51,700)	28,104
Canton (★311,200)	93,077
Cincinnati (★1,480,100)	385,457
Cleveland (★2,218,400)	573,822
Cleveland Heights (★Cleveland)	56,438
Columbus (★963,600)	565,032
Dayton (★768,200)	193,536
East Liverpool (★51,700)	16,687
Elyria (★Cleveland)	57,538
Euclid (★Cleveland)	59,999
Hamilton (★Cincinnati)	63,189
Kettering (★Dayton)	61,186
Lakewood (★Cleveland)	61,963
Lancaster (★52,500)	34,953
Lima (★108,000)	47,827
Lorain (★Cleveland)	75,416
Mansfield (★112,700)	53,927
Marion (★57,300)	37,040
Middletown (★105,500)	43,719
Newark (★83,400)	41,200
Parma (★Cleveland)	92,548
Portsmouth (★69,100)	25,943
Sandusky (★61,900)	31,360
Springfield (★128,000)	72,563
Steubenville (★135,000)	26,400
Toledo (★595,500)	354,635
Warren (★Youngstown)	56,629
Youngstown (★499,600)	115,436
Zanesville (★69,700)	28,655

UNITED STATES: OKLAHOMA

1980 C	3,025,487
Enid (★54,300)	50,363
Lawton (★96,800)	80,054
Midwest City (★Oklahoma City)	49,559
Muskogee (★49,600)	40,011
Norman (★Oklahoma City)	68,020
Oklahoma City (★742,000)	403,484
Tulsa (★567,100)	360,919

UNITED STATES: OREGON

1980 C	2,633,156
Corvallis (★95,100)	40,960
Eugene (★218,100)	105,664
Medford (★117,600)	39,603
Portland (★1,227,200)	368,139
Salem (★175,300)	89,233

UNITED STATES: PENNSYLVANIA

1980 C	11,864,751
Abington (★Philadelphia)	59,084
Allentown (★529,000)	103,758
Altoona (★128,900)	57,078
Bensalem (★Philadelphia)	52,368
Bethlehem (★Allentown)	70,419
Bristol (★Philadelphia)	58,773
Butler (★87,700)	17,026
Coatesville (★79,600)	10,698
Erie (★248,800)	119,123
Hanover (★56,000)	14,890
Harrisburg (★396,300)	53,264
Haverford (★Philadelphia)	52,371
Hazleton (★74,800)	27,318
Johnstown (★168,400)	35,496
Lancaster (★227,200)	54,725
Lebanon (★82,900)	25,711
Lower Merion Township (★Philadelphia)	59,629
New Castle (★76,400)	33,621
Oil City (★46,600)	13,881
Penn Hills (★Pittsburgh)	57,632
Philadelphia (★5,208,600)	1,688,210
Pittsburgh (★2,218,800)	423,959
Pottstown (★82,200)	22,729
Pottsville (★58,100)	18,195
Reading (★245,100)	78,686
Scranton (★492,700)	88,117
Sharon (★83,000)	19,057
State College (★82,100)	36,130
Uniontown (★60,100)	14,510
Upper Darby (★Philadelphia)	84,054
Washington (★69,100)	18,363
Wilkes-Barre (★Scranton)	51,551
Williamsport (★88,000)	33,401
York (★213,300)	44,619

UNITED STATES: RHODE ISLAND

1980 C	947,154
Cranston (★Providence)	71,992
East Providence (★Providence)	50,980
Newport (★60,700)	29,259
Pawtucket (★Providence)	71,204
Providence (★921,800)	156,804
Warwick (★Providence)	87,123

UNITED STATES: SOUTH CAROLINA

1980 C	3,122,717
Anderson (★74,500)	27,546
Charleston (★352,000)	69,855
Columbia (★375,900)	101,229
Florence (★60,800)	29,842
Greenville (★328,500)	58,242
North Charleston (★Charleston)	62,504
Rock Hill (★76,900)	35,327
Spartanburg (★172,100)	43,826
Sumter (★77,400)	24,921

UNITED STATES: SOUTH DAKOTA

1980 C	690,768
Pierre	11,973
Rapid City (★58,100)	46,492
Sioux Falls (★92,200)	81,343

UNITED STATES: TENNESSEE

1980 C	4,591,120
Bristol (★81,500)	23,986
Chattanooga (★359,200)	169,728
Clarksville (★91,200)	54,777
Jackson (★60,500)	49,258
Johnson City (★125,500)	43,617
Kingsport (★116,600)	32,027
Knoxville (★490,000)	175,045
Memphis (★852,900)	646,174
Murfreesboro (★45,700)	32,845
Nashville (★633,900)	455,651

UNITED STATES: TEXAS

1980 C	14,227,574
Abilene (★103,600)	98,315
Amarillo (★153,300)	149,230
Arlington (★Dallas)	160,113
Austin (★430,200)	345,890
Baytown (★Houston)	56,923
Beaumont (★346,300)	118,102
Brownsville (★299,800)	84,997
Bryan (★86,600)	45,917
Corpus Christi (★272,000)	231,134
Dallas (★2,727,300)	904,078
Denton	48,063
El Paso (★1,037,700)	425,259
Fort Worth (★Dallas)	385,164
Freeport (★82,700)	13,444
Galveston (★144,700)	61,902
Garland (★Dallas)	138,857
Grand Prairie (★Dallas)	71,462
Harlingen (★88,200)	43,543
Houston (★2,755,100)	1,595,138
Irving (★Dallas)	109,943
Killeen (★119,500)	46,296
Laredo (★298,900)	91,449
Longview (★89,300)	62,762
Lubbock (★198,100)	173,979
Lufkin (★52,500)	28,562
McAllen (★207,600)	66,281
Mesquite (★Dallas)	67,053
Midland (★78,000)	70,525
Odessa (★112,200)	90,027

▲ Población de un municipio, comuna o distrito entero, incluyendo sus áreas rurales.
• Ciudad más grande de un país.
★ Población o designación de un área metropolitana, incluyendo los suburbios.
C Censo. **E** Estimado oficial. **U** Estimado no oficial.

▲ Population d'une municipalité, d'une commune ou d'un district, zone rurale incluse.
• Ville la plus peuplée du pays.
★ Population de l'agglomération (ou nom de la zone métropolitaine englobante).
C Recensement. **E** Estimation officielle. **U** Estimation non officielle.

▲ População de um municipio, comuna ou distrito, inclusive as respectivas áreas rurais.
• Maior cidade de um país.
★ População ou indicação de uma área metropolitana.
C Censo. **E** Estimativa oficial. **U** Estimativa não oficial.

Pasadena (★Houston) ... 112,560
Plano (★Dallas) ... 72,331
Port Arthur (★Beaumont) ... 63,053
Richardson (★Dallas) ... 72,496
San Angelo (★77,300) ... 73,240
San Antonio (★968,200) ... 786,023
Sherman (★64,300) ... 30,413
Temple (★64,200) ... 42,354
Texarkana (★86,700) ... 31,271
Tyler (★97,500) ... 70,508
Victoria (★54,300) ... 50,695
Waco (★141,800) ... 101,261
Wichita Falls (★117,700) ... 94,201

UNITED STATES: UTAH
1980 C ... 1,461,037
Logan (★50,300) ... 26,844
Ogden (★217,300) ... 64,407
Orem (★Provo) ... 52,399
Provo (★215,200) ... 74,108
Salt Lake City (★682,400) ... 163,034
Sandy (★Salt Lake City) ... 52,210
West Valley City (★Salt Lake City) ... 72,509

UNITED STATES: VERMONT
1980 C ... 511,456
Burlington (★115,300) ... 37,712
Montpelier (★50,500) ... 8,241
Rutland (★49,800) ... 18,436

UNITED STATES: VIRGINIA
1980 C ... 5,346,797
Alexandria (★Washington) ... 103,217
Arlington (★Washington) ... 152,599
Charlottesville (★75,000) ... 39,916
Chesapeake (★Norfolk) ... 114,486
Danville (★77,800) ... 45,642
Hampton (★Newport News) ... 122,617
Lynchburg (★119,500) ... 66,743
Martinsville (★70,200) ... 18,149
Newport News (★314,600) ... 144,903
Norfolk (★795,600) ... 266,979
Portsmouth (★Norfolk) ... 104,577
Richmond (★690,600) ... 219,214
Roanoke (★216,000) ... 100,220
Suffolk (★Norfolk) ... 47,621
Virginia Beach (★Norfolk) ... 262,199

UNITED STATES: WASHINGTON
1980 C ... 4,132,353
Bellevue (★Seattle) ... 73,903
Bellingham (★75,300) ... 45,794
Bremerton (★115,900) ... 36,208
Everett (★Seattle) ... 54,413
Lakes District (★Seattle) ... 54,533
Longview (★65,500) ... 31,052
Olympia (★97,400) ... 27,447
Pasco (★126,300) ... 18,425
Seattle (★2,077,100) ... 493,846
Spokane (★303,200) ... 171,300
Tacoma (★Seattle) ... 158,501
Yakima (★103,600) ... 49,826

UNITED STATES: WEST VIRGINIA
1980 C ... 1,950,186
Beckley (★72,800) ... 20,492
Charleston (★236,300) ... 63,968
Clarksburg (★60,300) ... 22,371
Fairmont (★61,700) ... 23,863
Huntington (★273,900) ... 63,684
Morgantown (★71,500) ... 27,605
Parkersburg (★99,700) ... 39,946
Wheeling (★168,200) ... 43,070

UNITED STATES: WISCONSIN
1980 C ... 4,705,642
Appleton (★167,600) ... 58,913
Beloit (★62,000) ... 35,207
Eau Claire (★88,100) ... 51,509
Fond du Lac (★50,700) ... 35,863
Green Bay (★161,300) ... 87,899

Janesville (★73,500) ... 51,071
Kenosha (★96,700) ... 77,685
La Crosse (★87,500) ... 48,347
Madison (★294,300) ... 170,616
Manitowoc (★59,400) ... 32,547
Milwaukee (★1,374,700) ... 636,297
Oshkosh (★67,600) ... 50,016
Racine (★136,300) ... 85,725
Sheboygan (★77,100) ... 48,085
Waukesha (★Milwaukee) ... 50,365
Wausau (★74,800) ... 32,426
Wauwatosa (★Milwaukee) ... 51,308
West Allis (★Milwaukee) ... 63,982

UNITED STATES: WYOMING
1980 C ... 469,557
Casper (★67,000) ... 51,016
Cheyenne (★61,900) ... 47,716

URUGUAY
1985 C ... 2,940,200
Las Piedras (★Montevideo) ... 61,300
Melo ... 39,600
Mercedes ... 33,300
Minas ... 33,700
● MONTEVIDEO (★1,550,000) ... 1,246,500
Paysandú ... 75,200
Rivera ... 55,400
Salto ... 77,400

VANUATU
1986 C ... 140,154
● PORT VILA (★18,000) ... 14,184

VATICAN CITY / Città del Vaticano
1987 E ... 752

VENDA
1985 C ... 459,819
Makwarela ... 3,712
● Shayandima ... 4,853
THOHOYANDOU ... 3,641

VENEZUELA
1981 C ... 14,516,735
Acarigua ... 91,662
Barcelona ... 156,461
Barinas ... 110,462
Barquisimeto ... 497,635
Baruta (★Caracas) ... 200,063
Cabimas ... 140,435
Cagua ... 53,704
Calabozo ... 61,995
● CARACAS (★3,600,000) ... 1,816,901
Carora ... 58,694
Carúpano ... 64,579
Catia La Mar (★Caracas) ... 87,916
Chacao (★Caracas) ... 72,703
Ciudad Bolívar ... 182,941
Ciudad Guayana ... 314,497
Ciudad Ojeda (Lagunillas) ... 83,565
Coro ... 96,339
Cumaná ... 179,814
El Limón ... 65,122
El Tigre ... 73,595
Guacara ... 72,727
Guanare ... 64,025
Guarenas (★Caracas) ... 101,742
La Victoria ... 70,828
Los Dos Caminos (★Caracas) ... 63,346
Los Teques (★Caracas) ... 112,857
Maiquetía (★Caracas) ... 66,056
Maracaibo ... 890,643
Maracay ... 322,560
Mariara ... 47,242
Maturín ... 154,976
Mérida ... 143,209
Petare (★Caracas) ... 395,715
Porlamar ... 51,079
Pozuelos ... 80,342
Puerto Cabello ... 71,759
Puerto la Cruz ... 53,881

Punto Fijo ... 71,114
San Cristóbal ... 198,793
San Felipe ... 57,526
San Fernando de Apure ... 57,308
San Juan de los Morros ... 57,219
Turmero ... 111,186
Valencia ... 616,224
Valera ... 102,068
Valle de la Pascua ... 55,761

VIETNAM / Viet Nam
1979 C ... 52,741,766
Bac Giang ... 54,506
Bien Hoa ... 187,254
Buon Me Thuot ... 71,815
Ca Mau ... 67,484
Cam Pha ... 76,697
Cam Ranh (1973E) ... 118,111
Can Tho ... 182,856
Chau Doc ... 45,245
Da Lat ... 87,136
Da Nang ... 318,653
Dong Hoi ... 39,521
Hai Duong ... 54,579
Hai Phong (▲1,279,067) ... 385,210
HA NOI (★1,500,000) ... 897,500
Hoa Binh ... 51,187
Hon Gai ... 114,573
Hue ... 165,710
Long Xuyen ... 112,485
Minh Hai ... 72,517
My Tho ... 101,493
Nam Dinh ... 160,179
Nha Trang ... 172,663
Phan Thiet ... 75,241
Play Cu ... 58,088
Qui Nhon ... 127,211
Rach Gia ... 81,075
Sa Dec ... 73,104
Soc Trang ... 74,967
Tan An ... 43,364
Thai Binh ... 79,566
Thai Nguyen ... 138,023
Thanh Hoa ... 72,646
● Thanh Pho Ho Chi Minh (Saigon) (★3,100,000) ... 2,700,849
Tra Vinh ... 44,020
Tuy Hoa ... 46,617
Viet Tri ... 72,108
Vinh ... 159,753
Vinh Long ... 71,505
Vung Tau ... 81,694
Yen Bai ... 40,017

VIRGIN ISLANDS, BRITISH
1980 C ... 12,034
● ROAD TOWN ... 2,479

VIRGIN ISLANDS OF THE UNITED STATES
1980 C ... 96,569
● CHARLOTTE AMALIE (★32,000) ... 11,842

WALLIS AND FUTUNA / Wallis et Futuna
1983 E ... 12,408
● MATA-UTU ... 815
Ono (1976C) ... 624

WESTERN SAHARA
1982 E ... 142,000
● EL AAIÚN ... 93,875

WESTERN SAMOA / Samoa i Sisifo
1981 C ... 156,349
● APIA ... 33,170

YEMEN / Al-Yaman
1990 E ... 15,267,000
'Adan (★318,000) (1984E) ... 176,100
Al-Hudaydah (1986C) ... 155,110
Al-Mukallā (1984E) ... 58,000

● SAN'Ā' (1986C) ... 427,150
Ta'izz (1986C) ... 178,043

YUGOSLAVIA / Jugoslavija
1987 E ... 23,417,188
Banja Luka (▲193,890) ... 130,900
● BEOGRAD (★1,400,000) ... 1,130,000
Bitola (▲143,090) ... 76,200
Kragujevac (▲171,609) ... 94,800
Ljubljana (▲316,607) ... 233,200
Maribor (▲187,651) ... 107,400
Niš (▲240,219) ... 168,400
Novi Sad (▲266,772) ... 176,000
Osijek (▲162,490) ... 106,800
Pančevo (★Beograd) ... 62,700
Priština (▲244,830) ... 125,400
Rijeka (▲199,282) ... 166,400
Sarajevo (▲479,688) ... 341,200
Skopje (▲547,214) ... 444,900
Split ... 191,074
Subotica (▲153,306) ... 100,500
Titograd (▲145,163) ... 82,500
Tuzla (▲129,967) ... 67,300
Zagreb ... 697,925
Zenica (▲144,869) ... 67,500
Zrenjanin (▲140,009) ... 65,400

ZAIRE / Zaïre
1984 C ... 29,671,407
Bandundu ... 63,189
Beni ... 73,319
Boma ... 88,556
Bukavu ... 171,064
Bumba ... 46,823
Bunia ... 46,224
Butembo ... 78,633
Gandajika ... 60,263
Gemena ... 62,641
Goma ... 76,745
Ilebo (Port-Francqui) ... 48,831
Isiro ... 78,871
Kabinda ... 81,752
Kalemie (Albertville) ... 70,694
Kananga (Luluabourg) ... 290,898
Kikwit ... 146,784
Kindu ... 68,044
● KINSHASA (LÉOPOLDVILLE) (1986E) ... 3,000,000
Kisangani (Stanleyville) ... 282,650
Kolwezi ... 201,382
Likasi (Jadotville) ... 194,465
Lisala ... 40,471
Lubumbashi (Élisabethville) ... 543,268
Matadi ... 144,742
Mbandaka (Coquilhatville) ... 125,263
Mbuji-Mayi (Bakwanga) ... 423,363
Mwene-Ditu ... 72,567
Tshikapa ... 105,484
Yangambi ... 53,726

ZAMBIA
1980 C ... 5,661,801
Chililabombwe (Bancroft) (★56,582) ... 25,900
Chingola ... 130,872
Kabwe (Broken Hill) ... 127,420
Kalulushi ... 53,383
Kitwe (★283,962) ... 207,500
Livingstone ... 61,296
Luanshya (★113,422) ... 61,600
● LUSAKA ... 535,830
Mufulira (★138,824) ... 77,100
Ndola ... 250,490

ZIMBABWE
1982 C ... 7,539,000
Bulawayo ... 413,814
Chitungwiza (★Harare) ... 172,556
Gweru ... 78,918
● HARARE (★890,000) ... 656,011
Mutare ... 69,621

▲ Population of an entire municipality, commune, or district, including rural area.
● Largest city in country.
★ Population or designation of the metropolitan area, including suburbs.
C Census. E Official estimate.
U Unofficial estimate.

▲ Bevölkerung eines ganzen städtischen Verwaltungsgebietes, eines Kommunalbezirkes oder eines Distrikts, einschliesslich ländlicher Gebiete.
● Grösste Stadt des Landes.
★ Bevölkerung oder Bezeichnung der Stadtregion einschliess lich Vororte.
C Volkszählung. E Offizielle Schätzung.
U Inoffizielle Schätzung.

▲ Población de un municipio, comuna o distrito entero, incluyendo sus áreas rurales.
● Ciudad más grande de un país.
★ Población o designación de un área metropolitana, incluyendo los suburbios.
C Censo. E Estimado oficial.
U Estimado no oficial.

▲ Population d'une municipalité, d'une commune ou d'un district, zone rurale incluse.
● Ville la plus peuplée du pays.
★ Population de l'agglomération (ou nom de la zone métropolitaine englobante).
C Recensement. E Estimation officielle.
U Estimation non officielle.

▲ População de um município, comuna ou distrito, inclusive as respectivas áreas rurais.
● Maior cidade de um país.
★ População ou indicação de uma área metropolitana.
C Censo. E Estimativa oficial.
U Estimativa não oficial.

The Index includes in a single alphabetical list some 160,000 names appearing on the maps. Each name is followed by a page reference to one or more maps and by the location of the feature on the map, in coordinates of latitude and longitude. If a page contains several maps, a lowercase letter identifies the particular map. The page reference for two-page maps is always to the left-hand page.

Most map features are indexed to the largest-scale map on which they appear. However, a feature usually is not indexed to a Metropolitan Area map if it is also shown on another map where it can be seen in a broader setting. Countries, mountain ranges, and other extensive features are generally indexed to the largest-scale map that shows them in their entirety.

The order in which index information is presented is shown in the English, German, Spanish, French, and Portuguese headings at the center of each two-page spread.

For example:

ENGLISH

Name	Page	Lat.°′	Long.°′

The features indexed are of three types: *point, areal,* and *linear.* For *point* features (for example, cities, mountain peaks, dams), latitude and longitude coordinates give the location of the point on the map. For *areal* features (countries, mountain ranges, etc.), the coordinates generally indicate the approximate center of the feature. For *linear* features (rivers, canals, aqueducts), the coordinates locate a terminating point—for example, the mouth of a river, or the point at which a feature reaches the map margin.

Name Forms Names in the Index, as on the maps, are generally in the local language and insofar as possible are spelled according to official practice. Diacritical marks are included, except that those used to indicate tone, as in Vietnamese, are usually not shown. Most features that extend beyond the boundaries of one country have no single official name, and these are usually named in English. Many English, German, Spanish, French, and Portuguese names, which may not be shown on the maps, appear in the Index as cross references. All cross references are indicated by the symbol →. A name that appears in a shortened version on the map due to space limitations is given in full in the Index, with the portion that is omitted on the map enclosed in brackets, for example, Acapulco [de Juárez].

Transliteration For names in languages not written in the Roman alphabet, the locally official transliteration system has been used where one exists. Thus, names in the Soviet Union and Bulgaria have been transliterated according to the systems adopted by the academies of science of these countries. Similarly, the transliteration for mainland Chinese names follows the Pinyin system, which has been officially adopted in mainland China. For languages with no one locally accepted transliteration system, notably Arabic, transliteration in general follows closely a system adopted by the United States Board on Geographic Names.

Alphabetization Names are alphabetized in the order of the letters of the English alphabet. Spanish *ll* and *ch*, for example, are not treated as distinct letters. Furthermore, diacritical marks are disregarded in alphabetization—German or Scandinavian *ä* or *ö* are treated as *a* or *o*.

The names of physical features may appear inverted, since they are always alphabetized under the proper, not the generic, part of the name, thus: "Gibraltar, Strait of ⋓." Otherwise every entry, whether consisting of one word or more, is alphabetized as a single continuous entity. "Lakeland," for example, appears after "La Crosse" and before "La Salle." Names beginning with articles (Le Havre, Den Helder, Al-Qāhirah, As-Suways) are not inverted. Names beginning "Mc" are alphabetized as though spelled "Mac," and names beginning "St." and "Sainte" as though spelled "Saint."

In the case of identical names, towns are listed first, then political divisions, then physical features. Entries that are completely identical (including symbols, discussed below) are distinguished by abbreviations of their official country names and are sequenced alphabetically by country name. The many duplicate names in Canada, the United Kingdom, and the United States are further distinguished by abbreviations of the names of their primary subdivisions. (See list of abbreviations on pages 319-320).

Abbreviation and Capitalization Abbreviation and styling have been standardized for all languages. A period is used after every abbreviation even when this may not be the local practice. The abbreviation "St." is used only for "Saint." "Sankt" and other forms of the term are spelled out.

All names are written with an initial capital letter except for a few Dutch names, such as 's-Gravenhage. Capitalization of noninitial words in a name generally follows local practice.

Symbol The symbols that appear in the Index represent graphically the broad categories of the features named, for example, ▲ for mountain (Everest, Mount ▲). An abbreviated key to the symbols, in the five Atlas languages, appears at the foot of each pair of Index pages. Superior numbers following some symbols in the Index indicate finer distinctions, for example, $\blacktriangle^{1}$ for volcano (Fuji-san $\blacktriangle^{1}$). A complete list of the symbols and superior numbers is given on page I·1.

Das Register umfasst in alphabetischer Anordnung etwa 160 000 in den Karten erscheinende Namen. Nach jedem Namen folgt die Seitenangabe zu einer oder mehreren Karten und die Lageangabe des Objektes in der Karte mit geographischer Länge und Breite. Enthält eine Seite mehrere Karten, so wird die betreffende Karte durch einen Kleinbuchstaben gekennzeichnet. Die Seitenangabe für Doppelseiten bezieht sich immer auf die linke Seite.

Die Verweise für die meisten Objekte in den Karten beziehen sich auf die Karte mit dem grössten Massstab. Normalerweise werden jedoch Verweise auf Objekte in den Karten der Stadtregionen nicht gegeben, wenn sie auf einer anderen Karte in grösserem Zusammenhang dargestellt sind. Die Lageangaben für Länder, Gebirgszüge und andere ausgedehnte Objekte beziehen sich allgemein auf die Karte grössten Massstabes, die sie in ihrer ganzen Ausdehnung zeigt.

Die Anordnung, in welcher die Lageangabe erfolgt, geht aus den englischen, deutschen, spanischen, französischen und portugiesischen Überschriften in der Mitte jeder Doppelseite hervor.

Zum Beispiel:

DEUTSCH

Name	Seite	Breite°′	Länge°′ E = Ost

Die aufgeführten Objekte gliedern sich in drei Gruppen: *punkt-, flächen-* und *linienförmige* Objekte. Bei *punktförmigen* Objekten (z.B. Städte, Berge, Dämme) beziehen sich die Angaben nach Länge und Breite auf die Signatur in der Karte. Bei *flächenhaften* Objekten (Länder, Gebirgszüge usw.) verweisen die Koordinaten im allgemeinen auf das ungefähre Zentrum des Objektes. Bei *linienhaften* Objekten (Flüsse, Kanäle, Wasserleitungen) beziehen sich die Koordinaten auf einen bestimmten Punkt, z.B. die Mündung eines Flusses oder den Punkt, an dem das Objekt den Kartenrand schneidet.

Namengebung Wie in den Karten so sind auch im Register die Namen im allgemeinen in der örtlichen Namensform wiedergegeben und soweit als möglich in der amtlichen Schreibweise. Diakritische Zeichen wurden gesetzt; sie wurden nur dort weggelassen, wo sie, wie im Vietnamesischen, Tonhöhen kennzeichnen. Meist haben Objekte, die sich über die Grenzen eines Landes hinaus erstrecken, keinen einzelnen offiziellen Namen; normalerweise sind sie daher englisch beschriftet. Viele englische, deutsche, spanische, französische und portugiesische Namensformen, die nicht in den Karten enthalten sind, erscheinen im Register als Kreuzverweis. Alle Kreuzverweise werden durch das Symbol → gekennzeichnet. Namen, die aus Platzgründen in abgekürzter Form in der Karte erscheinen, werden im Register voll ausgeschrieben, wobei der auf der Karte weggelassene Teil in Klammern gesetzt ist, z.B. Acapulco [de Juárez].

Transkription Für die Transkription von Namen aus Sprachen, die nicht im lateinischen Alphabet geschrieben werden, wurde das offizielle Transkriptionssystem benutzt, sofern ein solches vorhanden ist. So wurden die Namen in der Sowjetunion und in Bulgarien nach dem von den wissenschaftlichen Akademien dieser Länder angewandten System transkribiert. Entsprechend wurden die Namen auf dem chinesischen Festland nach dem Pinyin-System übertragen, das offiziell in der Volksrepublik China eingeführt wurde. Bei Sprachen, für die ein allgemein anerkanntes Transkriptionssystem nicht vorliegt, vor allem für Arabisch, erfolgte die Transkription in enger Anlehnung an das vom United States Board on Geographic Names angewandte System.

Alphabetische Ordnung Die alphabetische Ordnung der Namen entspricht der Reihenfolge der Buchstaben im englischen Alphabet. So werden z.B. das spanische *ll* und *ch* nicht als besondere Buchstaben behandelt. Ferner wurden diakritische Zeichen beim Alphabetisieren nicht berücksichtigt, das deutsche oder skandinavische *ä* oder *ö* als *a* oder *o* behandelt.

Physische Objekte können umgestellt erscheinen, da sie immer nach dem Eigennamen und nicht nach dem Gattungsbegriff eingeordnet wurden, z.B. "Gibraltar, Strait of ⋓". Ansonsten wurde jeder Eintrag, ob er aus einem Wort oder aus mehreren besteht, als eine einzige Einheit behandelt. So ist z.B. "Lakeland" nach "La Crosse," aber vor "La Salle" aufgeführt. Namen, die mit einem Artikel beginnen, wurden nicht umgestellt (Le Havre, Den Helder, Al-Qāhirah, As-Suways), Namen, die mit "Mc" beginnen, sind der Schreibweise "Mac" nach eingeordnet und Namen, die mit "St." und "Sainte" beginnen, entsprechend der Schreibweise "Saint".

Wo Namensgleichheit besteht, werden zunächst die Städte aufgeführt, dann politische Einheiten und schliesslich physische Objekte. Eintragungen, die vollkommen identisch sind (einschliesslich der weiter unten erläuterten Symbole), werden durch Hinzufügung der Abkürzung des offiziellen Ländernamens unterschieden und sind den Ländernamen nach alphabetisch geordnet. Die zahlreichen identischen Namen in Kanada, dem Vereinigten Königreich und den Vereinigten Staaten sind darüber hinaus noch durch Abkürzungen der obersten Verwaltungseinheit unterschieden. (Siehe Verzeichnis der Abkürzungen, Seite 319-320).

Abkürzungen und Grossschreibung Abkürzung und Schreibweise wurden für alle Sprachen vereinheitlicht. Nach jeder Abkürzung steht ein Punkt, auch wenn dies nicht der jeweiligen Gepflogenheit entspricht. Die Abkürzung "St." wird ausschliesslich für "Saint" gebraucht. "Sankt" und andere Formen dieses Begriffes werden ausgeschrieben.

Der erste Buchstabe eines Namens wird gross geschrieben, ausgenommen einige holländische Namen wie 's-Gravenhage. Die Grossschreibung der weiteren Worte eines zusammengesetzten Namens folgt im allgemeinen der landesüblichen Schreibweise.

Symbole Die im Register verwendeten Symbole veranschaulichen graphisch die zahlreichen Kategorien der benannten Objekte, z.B. ▲ = Berg (Everest, Mount ▲). Eine kurzgefasste Erläuterung der Symbole erscheint in jeder der fünf Sprachen des Atlas am Fusse jeder Doppelseite des Registers. Hochgestellte Ziffern hinter Symbolen im Register bezeichnen feinere Unterscheidungen, z.B. $\blacktriangle^{1}$ = Vulkan (Fuji-san $\blacktriangle^{1}$). Eine vollständige Übersicht der Symbole und hochgestellten Ziffern findet sich auf Seite I·1.

El Índice contiene en una sola lista alfabética, alrededor de 160 000 nombres que aparecen en los mapas. Después de cada nombre está indicada la página o las páginas de referencia, en los cuales se encuentran los mismos, y las coordinadas de la latitud y la longitud del lugar del rasgo. Si una página contiene varios mapas, letras minúsculas identifican el mapa correspondiente. Para mapas que ocupan dos páginas, la página de referencia siempre es la de la izquierda.

La mayoría de los nombres que figuran en el Índice, se efiere a los mapas en la escala más grande. Sin embargo, un nombre no se refiere en un mapa metropolitano si ya aparece en otro mapa, donde se muestra en un marco de mayor proporción. Los países, sierras y otros rasgos extensivos se refieren generalmente en el Índice en los mapas de escalas mayores en que se muestran completos.

El orden en que la información del Índice se presenta, aparece en un encabezamiento al centro de cada par de páginas, en inglés, alemán, español, francés y portugués.

Por ejemplo:

ESPAÑOL

Nombre	Página	Lat.°′	Long.°′ W=Oeste

Los rasgos anotados en el Índice son de tres tipos: *el punto, el área y la extensión linear.* Para rasgos que indican *el punto* (como por ejemplo, las ciudades, picos de montañas, presas), las coordinadas de latitud y longitud indican la posición exacta del punto sobre el mapa. Respecto a *las áreas* (como países, sierras, etc.), las coordinadas indican usualmente el centro aproximado del rasgo particular. En cuanto a *los rasgos lineares* (ríos, canales, acueductos) las coordinadas indican los puntos terminales, por ejemplo, la boca de un río, o el punto en que un rasgo físico alcanza el margen del mapa.

Las Formas de los Nombres Los nombres que aparecen en el Índice, así como también en los mapas, se dan en general en el idioma local, y en tanto que es posible siguen la ortografía oficialmente aceptada. Incluímos también marcas diacríticas, excepto las que se usan para indicar tono, como en la lengua vietnamita. A causa de que la mayoría de los rasgos que se extienden más allá de las fronteras de un país no tienen un solo nombre oficial, éstos se denominan usualmente en inglés. Muchos nombres, en inglés, alemán, español, francés y portugués, que pueden no figurar en el mapa, se dan como referencia de una página a otra en el Índice. Todas las referencias que pasan a otras páginas se indican con el símbolo →. Un nombre que aparece en el mapa en forma abreviada, debido a la limitación de espacio, en el Índice figura en su forma completa, poniendo entre paréntesis angulares la parte omitida en el mapa, por ejemplo Acapulco [de Juárez].

"Trasliteración" Para los nombres escritos en los idiomas que no usan el alfabeto latino, el sistema oficial de trasliteración ha sido utilizado donde localmente existe. Así,

los nombres de la Unión Soviética y de Bulgaria se trasliteran conforme a los sistemas aceptados por las academias de las ciencias de sus respectivos países. De la misma manera, la trasliteración de los nombres en chino continental siguen el sistema Pinyin que ha sido oficialmente adoptado en este país. Para idiomas sin ningún sistema localmente aceptado de trasliteración, particularmente para el árabe, éstos se trasliteran usando por lo general un sistema adoptado por el United States Board on Geographic Names.

Alfabetización Los nombres se han ordenado de acuerdo con el alfabeto inglés. Las letras del alfabeto en español *ll* y *ch* por ejemplo, no se han considerado letras separadas. Además, los signos diacríticos no se toman en cuenta en la alfabetización—en alemán o escadinavo letras *ä* u *ö* se tratan como *a* u *o*.

Los nombres de los rasgos físicos algunas veces se invierten, ya que se ordenan alfabéticamente según la parte propia y no genérica del nombre. Así por ejemplo, en el caso del Estrecho de Gibraltar aparece: Gibraltar, Strait of ʉ. Por lo demás, cada renglón, sea una palabra o una frase, se alfabetiza como una unidad. Por ejemplo, "Lakeland" aparece después de "La Crosse" y antes de "La Salle". Los nombres que comienzan con artículos (Le Havre, Den Helder, Al-Qāhirah, As-Suways) no están invertidos. Nombres que empiezan con "Mc" se tratan como si fueran del grupo de "Mac", y los que comienzan con "St." y "Sainte" se incluyen con "Saint".

En los casos de nombres idénticos, las poblaciones aparecen primero, las divisiones políticas después y finalmente los rasgos físicos. En caso de ser completamente idénticos (incluyendo los símbolos, discutidos más abajo) se distinguen por medio de abreviaciones de los nombres oficiales de los países a que pertenecen y son puestos en orden alfabético, de acuerdo al nombre de cada país. Hay muchos nombres duplicados en Canadá, el Reino Unido y los Estados Unidos de América, y éstos se distinguen además, por sus subdivisiones primarias. (Vease abajo, la lista de abreviaciones en las páginas 319-320).

Abreviaciones y Mayúsculas Las abreviaciones y el uso de las mayúsculas se han hecho uniformes para todos los idiomas. Se usa un punto al final de la abreviación, aun cuando en algunos casos no sea ésta la práctica local. La abreviación "St." se usa sólo para "Saint". Las otras formas del mismo término, como "Sankt", se escriben completas.

La mayúscula se usa al comienzo de todos los nombres a excepción de algunos holandeses, como 's-Gravenhage. Las palabras que no son iniciales, se dan con mayúscula o minúscula, según la práctica local.

Símbolos Los símbolos que aparecen en el Índice representan gráficamente las grandes categorías de los rasgos que se han ido nombrando, por ejemplo, $\wedge$ para montaña (Everest, Mount $\wedge$). Una clave abreviada para los símbolos aparece en los cinco idiomas del Atlas al pie de cada par de páginas del Índice. Los números que siguen más arriba del símbolo indican alguna diferencia más precisa, por ejemplo, $\wedge^{1}$ para un volcán (Fuji-san $\wedge^{1}$). Una lista completa de símbolos y números superiores aparece en la página I•1.

L'index rassemble en une seule liste alphabétique, quelque 160 000 noms qui figurent sur les cartes. Chaque nom est suivi d'un renvoi à une ou plusieurs pages de cartes et de coordonnées géographiques qui permettent de localiser ce qu'il désigne. Si une page contient plusieurs cartes, une lettre minuscule permet d'identifier chaque carte. Pour les cartes en double page, la référence indiquée est toujours celle de la page de gauche.

En général, l'index renvoie aux cartes où l'information recherchée est reproduite à la plus grande échelle; cependant, les cartes de zones métropolitaines ne sont pas utilisées si le terme géographique figure sur une autre carte dans un contexte plus large. Pour les éléments de grande dimension comme les pays et les chaînes de montagnes, l'index renvoie généralement à la carte à grande échelle qui les représente en entier.

L'ordre des informations de l'index est rappelé en tête de chaque double page dans les cinq langues: anglais, allemand, espagnol, français et portugais.

Par exemple:

FRANÇAIS

Nom	Page	Lat.°'	Long.°' W=Ouest

Les termes de l'index désignent des réalités géographiques de type *ponctuel*, *spatial* ou *linéaire*. Leur position est déterminée par les coordonnées géographiques du lieu quand les données sont de type *ponctuel* (villes, sommets, barrages, etc.), quand elles sont de type *spatial* (pays, chaînes de montagnes, etc.) par les coordonnées du centre approximatif de la zone considérée, et, quand elles sont du type *linéaire* (aqueducs, canaux, etc.) par les coordonnées soit d'un point terminal comme l'embouchure d'un cours d'eau, soit du point où les limites de la carte les interrompent.

Forme des Toponymes Les noms de l'index comme ceux des cartes sont généralement reproduits dans la langue locale et, dans la mesure du possible, selon leur orthographe officielle. Les signes diacritiques sont conservés, à l'exclusion de ceux qui servent à indiquer le ton, comme en vietnamien. La plupart des données géographiques qui s'étendent au-delà des frontières d'un pays sont nommées souvent en anglais, car elles n'ont pas de nom officiel unique. Beaucoup de noms anglais, allemands, espagnols, français et portugais, qui ne se trouvent pas sur les cartes, sont cités dans l'index sous forme de renvois. Tous les renvois sont signalés par le symbole (→). Un nom écrit sur la carte sous forme abrégée, par manque de place, figure en entier dans l'index; la partie omise est entre crochets, par exemple: Acapulco [de Juárez].

Transcription des Noms Pour les noms qui viennent de langues n'utilisant pas l'alphabet romain, le système local et officiel de transcription a été utilisé là où il existait. Ainsi, les noms russes et bulgares ont été transcrits selon les systèmes adoptés par les académies des sciences de ces pays. De même, pour la transcription des noms de la Chine continentale, on a employé le système Pinyin, officiellement adopté en Chine continentale. Pour les langues qui n'ont pas de système officiel de transcription en alphabet romain, notamment l'arabe, la transcription suit généralement de près le système adopté par le United States Board on Geographic Names (Comité américain pour les noms géographiques).

Ordre Alphabétique Les noms sont classés dans l'ordre de l'alphabet anglais. Les *ll* et *ch* espagnols, par exemple, ne sont pas traités comme des lettres séparées. De plus, on ne tient pas compte des signes diacritiques: le *ä* et le *ö* allemand ou scandinave correspondent au *a* et *o* sans tréma.

Les noms des données physiques peuvent se trouver inversés car ils sont toujours classés suivant le nom propre. Exemple: "Gibraltar, Strait of ʉ". Par ailleurs, les noms composés d'un ou plusieurs mots sont considérés comme une seule entité. Exemple: "Lakeland" est inscrit après "La Crosse" et avant "La Salle". Les noms qui commencent par un article (Le Havre, Den Helder, Al-Qāhirah, As-Suways) ne sont pas inversés. Les noms qui commencent par "Mc" sont classés comme s'ils s'écrivaient "Mac" et les noms qui commencent par "St." ou "Sainte" sont classés comme s'ils s'écrivaient "Saint".

Dans le cas de noms identiques, les villes sont inscrites d'abord, puis les divisions politiques, et ensuite les données physiques. Les noms qui sont tout à fait identiques (y compris les symboles qui s'y rapportent) se distinguent par leur pays d'origine, noté en abrégé dans l'ordre alphabétique. Les noms que l'on rencontre plusieurs fois, au Canada, au Royaume-Uni et aux Etats-Unis se distinguent grâce à l'abréviation de la première subdivision administrative de ce pays (voir la liste des abréviations de la page 319-320).

Abréviations et Majuscules L'usage des abréviations a été standardisé pour toutes les langues. Un point suit chaque abréviation, même quand ce n'est pas l'usage dans certaines langues. L'abréviation "St." sert uniquement pour le mot "Saint". "Sankt" et les autres formes du mot "Saint" sont écrites en entier.

Tous les noms commencent par une majuscule, sauf quelques noms des Pays-Bas comme 's-Gravenhage. Certains noms prennent une majuscule, même s'ils ne se trouvent pas au début du terme; on a adopté, en général, l'orthographe locale.

Symboles Les symboles utilisés dans l'index donnent une représentation graphique des réalités géographiques mentionnées. Par exemple, $\wedge$ pour une montagne (Everest, Mount $\wedge$). Une explication abrégée des symboles dans les cinq langues de l'Atlas se trouve au bas de chaque double page de l'index. Les indices qui accompagnent certains symboles permettent une distinction plus précise. Par exemple, $\wedge^{1}$ pour volcan (Fujisan $\wedge^{1}$). Une liste complète des symboles et indices est donnée à la page I•1.

O Índice contém, numa só lista alfabética, cerca de 160 000 nomes que figuram nos mapas. Segue-se a cada nome a referência a um ou mais mapas e a localização do acidente geográfico no mapa pelas respectivas coordenadas de latitude e longitude. A referência a mapas que ocupam duas páginas fica sempre na página da esquerda. A maior parte dos acidentes geográficos estão indexados no mapa em que aparecem em escala maior. No entanto, um acidente geográfico não é geralmente indexado num mapa de Área Metropolitana se também figura em outro mapa em que aparece em contexto mais amplo. Os países, cordilheiras e outros acidentes geográficos de maior extensão estão geralmente indexados no mapa em escala maior que os apresente em seu todo.

A ordem em que as informações são apresentadas no Índice figura no cabeçalho, a cada duas páginas, em inglês, alemão, espanhol, francês e PORTUGUÊS.

Por exemplo:

PORTUGUÊS

Nome	Página	Lat.°'	Long.°' W=Oeste

Os acidentes indexados são de três tipos: *ponto*, *espacial* (área) e *linear* (extensão). Para acidentes que indicam *pontos* (como, por exemplo, cidades, picos de montanhas, represas), as coordenadas de latitude e longitude indicam a posição exata do ponto no mapa. No que se refere aos acidentes espaciais (como países, cordilheiras etc.), as coordenadas geralmente indicam o centro aproximado do acidente específico. Quanto aos *acidentes lineares* (rios, canais, aquedutos), as coordenadas localizam os pontos terminais, como, por exemplo, a foz de um rio, ou o ponto em que um acidente físico atinge a margem do mapa.

Formas dos nomes Os nomes que aparecem no Índice, assim como também nos mapas, são geralmente apresentados na língua local, e tanto quanto possível, seguem a ortografia oficial. Usam-se, também, os sinais diacríticos, exceto os que indicam tom, como na língua vietnamita. A maioria dos acidentes geográficos que se estendem além das fronteiras de um só país não possuem um nome oficial único; nesses casos, estão geralmente indicados em inglês. Muitos nomes em inglês, alemão, espanhol, português e francês podem não figurar nos mapas, mas aparecem no Índice como referências remissivas. Todas essas referências são indicadas pelo símbolo (→). Um nome que aparece no mapa em forma abreviada devido a limitações de espaço, figura no Índice em sua forma completa, com a parte omitida no mapa entre chaves (por exemplo, Acapulco [de Juárex]).

Transliteração Para os nomes escritos em línguas que não usam o alfabeto latino, foi utilizado o sistema oficial de transliteração, sempre que este existia. Assim, os nomes da União Soviética e da Bulgária foram transliterados de acordo com os sistemas adotados pelas academias de ciências desses países. Do mesmo modo, a transliteração dos nomes da China continental seguem o sistema Pinyin, que foi oficialmente adotado nesse país. Para as línguas que não possuem um sistema de transliteração adotado oficialmente, em especial o árabe, a transliteração geralmente segue de perto o sistema adotado pelo Conselho de Nomes Geográficos dos Estados Unidos (United States Board on Geographic Names).

Alfabetação Os nomes foram ordenados de acordo com o alfabeto inglês. Por exemplo, o espanhol *ll* e *ch* não foram considerados como letras separadas. Ademais, os sinais diacríticos não foram considerados na alfabetação. Por exemplo, em alemão ou escandinavo as letras *ä* ou *ö* foram tratradas como *a* ou *o*.

Os nomes dos acidentes físicos podem aparecer, às vezes, invertidos, já que foram sempre alfabetados pela parte específica e não genérica do nome, como, por exemplo, *Gibraltar, estreito de* ʉ. Por outro lado, cada entrada do Índice, quer constituída por uma só palavra ou mais de uma, foi alfabetada como uma unidade contínua. Por exemplo, "Lakeland" aparece depois de "La Grosse" e antes de "La Salle". Os nomes que começam por artigo (Le Havre, Den Helder, Al-Qāhirah, As-Suways) não são invertidos. Os nomes que começam por "Mc" são alfabetados como se fossem soletrados "Mac", e os que começam por "St." e "Sainte" como se fossem soletrados "Saint".

Nos casos de nomes idênticos, as cidades estão relacionadas em primeiro lugar; depois as divisões políticas e em seguida os acidentes físicos. As entradas completamente idênticas (inclusive símbolos, mencionados mais abaixo), distinguem-se pelas abreviaturas dos nomes oficiais dos países a que pertencem e são arrolados na ordem alfabética do nome do país. Os muitos nomes repetidos no Canadá, no Reino Unido e nos Estados Unidos, são ainda diferenciados pelas abreviaturas dos nomes das respectivas subdivisões primárias (Ver a lista de abreviaturas, das páginas 319-320).

Abreviações e uso de maiúsculas As abreviaturas e o estilo foram normalizados em todas as línguas. Usa-se um ponto depois de cada abreviatura, mesmo que não seja essa a prática local. A abreviatura "St." só é usada para "Saint". As outras formas do termo, tal como "Sankt", são escritas por extenso.

Todos os nomes são escritos com a inicial maiúscula exceto em alguns nomes holandeses, como 's-Gravenhage. O uso de maiúsculas em palavras não iniciais de um nome segue geralmente a prática local.

Símbolos Os símbolos que aparecem no Índice representam graficamente as grandes categorias dos acidentes indicados, por exemplo, $\wedge$ para montanha (Everest, Mount $\wedge$). Uma chave abreviada dos símbolos nas cinco línguas do Atlas figura no pé de cada par de páginas do Índice. Os números altos que acompanham certos símbolos do Índice indicam diferenças mais precisas, como, por exemplo, $\wedge^{1}$ para vulcão (Fuji-san $\wedge^{1}$). Uma lista completa de símbolos e números altos aparece à pág. I•1.

	LOCAL NAME	ENGLISH	DEUTSCH	ESPAÑOL	FRANÇAIS	PORTUGUÊS
Ab., Can.	Alberta	Alberta	Alberta	Alberta	Alberta	Alberta
Afg.	Afghānestān	Afghanistan	Afghanistan	Afganistán	Afghanistan	Afeganistão
Afr.	...	Africa	Afrika	Africa	Afrique	África
Ak., U.S.	Alaska	Alaska	Alaska	Alaska	Alaska	Alasca
Al., U.S.	Alabama	Alabama	Alabama	Alabama	Alabama	Alabama
Alg.	Algérie / Djazaïr	Algeria	Algerien	Argelia	Algérie	Argélia
Am. Sam.	American Samoa / Amerika Samoa	American Samoa	Amerikanisch-Samoa	Samoa Americana	Samoa américaines	Samoa Americana
And.	Andorra	Andorra	Andorra	Andorra	Andorre	Andorra
Ang.	Angola	Angola	Angola	Angola	Angola	Angola
Anguilla	Anguilla	Anguilla	Anguilla	Anguilla	Anguilla	Anguilla
Ant.	...	Antarctica	Antarktis	Antártida	Antarctique	Antártida
Antig.	Antigua and Barbuda	Antigua and Barbuda	Antigua und Barbuda	Antigua y Barbuda	Antigua-et-Barbuda	Antígua e Barbuda
Ar., U.S.	Arkansas	Arkansas	Arkansas	Arkansas	Arkansas	Arkansas
Arc. O.	...	Arctic Ocean	Nördliches Eismeer	Océano Artico	Océan Glacial arctique	Ártico, Oceano
Arg.	Argentina	Argentina	Argentinien	Argentina	Argentine	Argentina
Ar. Su.	Al-'Arabīyah as-Su'ūdīyah	Saudi Arabia	Saudi-Arabien	Arabia Saudita	Arabie saoudite	Arábia Saudita
Aruba	Aruba	Aruba	Aruba	Aruba	Aruba	Aruba
Asia	...	Asia	Asien	Asia	Asie	Ásia
Atl. O.	...	Atlantic Ocean	Atlantischer Ozean	Océano Atlántico	Océan Atlantique	Atlântico, Oceano
Austl.	Australia	Australia	Australien	Australia	Australie	Austrália
Az., U.S.	Arizona	Arizona	Arizona	Arizona	Arizona	Arizona
Ba.	Bahamas	Bahamas	Bahamas	Bahamas	Bahamas	Bahamas
Bahr.	Al-Bahrayn	Bahrain	Bahrain	Bahrein	Bahreïn	Bahrein
Barb.	Barbados	Barbados	Barbados	Barbados	Barbade	Barbados
B.A.T.	British Antarctic Territory	British Antarctic Territory	Britisches Antarktis-Territorium	Territorio Antártico Británico	Territoires britanniques de l'Antarctique	Território Antártico Británico
B.C., Can.	British Columbia / Colombie-Britannique	British Columbia	Britisch Kolumbien	Columbia Británica	Colombie britannique	Colúmbia Británica
Bdi.	Burundi	Burundi	Burundi	Burundi	Burundi	Burundi
Bel.	Belgique / België	Belgium	Belgien	Bélgica	Belgique	Bélgica
Belize	Belize	Belize	Belize	Belice	Belize	Belize
Bénin	Bénin	Benin	Benin	Benin	Bénin	Benin
Ber.	Bermuda	Bermuda	Bermuda	Bermudas	Bermudes	Bermudas
Ber. S.	...	Bering Sea	Beringmeer	Mar de Bering	Mer de Bering	Bering, Mar de
B.I.O.T.	British Indian Ocean Territory	British Indian Ocean Territory	Britisch-Indien Ozean-Territorium	Territorio Británico del Océano Indico	Territoire britannique de l'océan Indien	Território Británico do Oceano Indico
Blg.	Bâlgarija	Bulgaria	Bulgarien	Bulgaria	Bulgarie	Bulgária
Bngl.	Bangladesh	Bangladesh	Bangladesch	Bangladesh	Bangladesh	Bangladesh
Bol.	Bolivia	Bolivia	Bolivien	Bolivia	Bolivie	Bolívia
Boph.	Bophuthatswana	Bophuthatswana	Bophuthatswana	Bophuthatswana	Bophuthatswana	Bophuthatswana
Bots.	Botswana	Botswana	Botswana	Botswana	Botswana	Botsuana
Bra.	Brasil	Brazil	Brasilien	Brasil	Brésil	Brasil
B.R.D.	Bundesrepublik Deutschland	Federal Republic of Germany	Bundesrepublik Deutschland	República Federal de Alemania	République fédérale d'Allemagne	República Federal da Alemanha
Bru.	Brunei	Brunei	Brunei	Brunei	Brunéi	Brunei
Br. Vir. Is.	British Virgin Islands	British Virgin Islands	Britischen Jungferninseln	Islas Vírgenes Británicas	Îles Vierges britanniques	Virgens Británicas, Ilhas
Burkina	Burkina Faso	Burkina Faso	Burkina Faso	Burkina Faso	Burkina Faso	Burkina Faso
Ca., U.S.	California	California	Kalifornien	California	Californie	Califórnia
Cam.	Cameroun / Cameroon	Cameroon	Kamerun	Camerún	Cameroun	Camarão
Can.	Canada	Canada	Kanada	Canadá	Canada	Canadá
Carib. S.	...	Caribbean Sea	Karibisches Meer	Mar Caribe	Mer des Caraïbes	Caribe, Mar do
Cay. Is.	Cayman Islands	Cayman Islands	Caiman-Inseln	Islas Caimán	Îles Caïmanes	Cayman, Ilhas
Centraf.	République centrafricaine	Central African Republic	Zentralafrikanische Republik	República Centroafricana	République centrafricaine	Centro-Africana, República
Česko.	Československo	Czechoslovakia	Tschechoslowakei	Checoslovaquia	Tchécoslovaquie	Tchecoslováquia
Chile	Chile	Chile	Chile	Chile	Chili	Chile
Christ. I.	Christmas Island	Christmas Island	Weihnachtsinsel	Isla Christmas	Île Christmas	Christmas, Ilha
Ciskei	Ciskei	Ciskei	Ciskei	Ciskei	Ciskei	Ciskei
C. Iv.	Côte d'Ivoire	Ivory Coast	Elfenbeinküste	Costa de Marfil	Côte d'Ivoire	Costa do Marfim
C.M.I.K.	Chosón-minjujuùi-inmīn-konghwaguk	North Korea	Nordkorea	Corea del Norte	Corée du Nord	Coréia do Norte
Co., U.S.	Colorado	Colorado	Colorado	Colorado	Colorado	Colorado
Cocos Is.	Cocos (Keeling) Islands	Cocos (Keeling) Islands	Cokos-Inseln	Islas Cocos (Keeling)	Îles des Cocos (Keeling)	Cocos (Keeling), Ilhas
Col.	Colombia	Colombia	Kolumbien	Colombia	Colombie	Colômbia
Comores	Comores / Al-Qumur	Comoros	Komoren	Comoras	Comores	Comores
Congo	Congo	Congo	Kongo	Congo	Congo	Congo
Cook Is.	Cook Islands	Cook Islands	Cook-Inseln	Islas Cook	Îles Cook	Cook, Ilhas
C.R.	Costa Rica	Costa Rica	Costa Rica	Costa Rica	Costa Rica	Costa Rica
Ct., U.S.	Connecticut	Connecticut	Connecticut	Connecticut	Connecticut	Connecticut
Cuba	Cuba	Cuba	Kuba	Cuba	Cuba	Cuba
C.V.	Cabo Verde	Cape Verde	Kap Verde	Cabo Verde	Cap-Vert	Cabo Verde
Dan.	Danmark	Denmark	Dänemark	Dinamarca	Danemark	Dinamarca
D.C., U.S.	District of Columbia	District of Columbia	District of Columbia	District of Columbia	District of Columbia	Distrito de Columbia
D.D.R.	Deutsche Demokratische Republik	German Democratic Republic	Deutsche Demokratische Republik	República Democrática Alemana	République démocratique allemande	República Democrática Alemã
De., U.S.	Delaware	Delaware	Delaware	Delaware	Delaware	Delaware
Dji.	Djibouti	Djibouti	Djibouti	Djibouti	Djibouti	Djibouti
Dom.	Dominica	Dominica	Dominica	Dominica	Dominique	Dominica
D.Y.	Druk-Yul	Bhutan	Bhutan	Bhután	Bhoutan	Butã
Ec.	Ecuador	Ecuador	Ecuador	Ecuador	Équateur	Equador
Ellás	Ellás	Greece	Griechenland	Grecia	Grèce	Grécia
El Sal.	El Salvador	El Salvador	El Salvador	El Salvador	El Salvador	El Salvador
Eng., U.K.	England	England	England	Inglaterra	Angleterre	Inglaterra
Esp.	España	Spain	Spanien	España	Espagne	Espanha
Europe	...	Europe	Europa	Europa	Europe	Europa
Falk. Is.	Falkland Islands / Islas Malvinas	Falkland Islands	Falkland-Inseln	Islas Malvinas	Îles Falkland	Falkland, Ilhas
Fiji	Fiji	Fiji	Fidschi	Fiji	Fidji	Fiji (Fidji)
Fl., U.S.	Florida	Florida	Florida	Florida	Floride	Flórida
Før.	Føroyar	Faeroe Islands	Färöer	Islas Feroe	Îles Féroé	Faeroe, Ilhas
Fr.	France	France	Frankreich	Francia	France	França
Ga., U.S.	Georgia	Georgia	Georgia	Georgia	Georgie	Geórgia
Gabon	Gabon	Gabon	Gabun	Gabón	Gabon	Gabão
Gam.	Gambia	Gambia	Gambia	Gambia	Gambie	Gâmbia
Ghana	Ghana	Ghana	Ghana	Ghana	Ghana	Gana
Gib.	Gibraltar	Gibraltar	Gibraltar	Gibraltar	Gibraltar	Gibraltar
Gren.	Grenada	Grenada	Grenada	Granada	Grenade	Grenada
Guad.	Guadeloupe	Guadeloupe	Guadeloupe	Guadalupe	Guadeloupe	Guadalupe
Guam	Guam	Guam	Guam	Guam	Guam	Guam
Guat.	Guatemala	Guatemala	Guatemala	Guatemala	Guatemala	Guatemala
Guernsey	Guernsey	Guernsey	Guernsey	Guernsey	Guernesey	Guernsey
Gui.-B.	Guiné-Bissau	Guinea-Bissau	Guina-Bissau	Guinea-Bissau	Guinée-Bissau	Guiné-Bissau
Gui. Ecu.	Guinea Ecuatorial	Equatorial Guinea	Äquatorial-guinea	Guinea Ecuatorial	Guinée équatoriale	Guiné Equatorial
Guinée	Guinée	Guinea	Guinea	Guinea	Guinée	Guiné
Guy.	Guyana	Guyana	Guyana	Guyana	Guyane	Guiana
Guy. fr.	Guyane française	French Guiana	Französisch-Guayana	Guayana Francesa	Guyane française	Guiana Francesa
Haï.	Haïti	Haiti	Haiti	Haiti	Haïti	Haiti
Hi., U.S.	Hawaii	Hawaii	Hawaii	Hawaii	Hawaii	Havaí
H.K.	Hong Kong	Hong Kong	Hongkong	Hong Kong	Hong-Kong	Hong Kong
Hond.	Honduras	Honduras	Honduras	Honduras	Honduras	Honduras
Ia., U.S.	Iowa	Iowa	Iowa	Iowa	Iowa	Iowa
I.A.M.	Al-Imārāt al-'Arabīyah al-Muttahidah	United Arab Emirates	Vereinigte Arabische Emirate	Emiratos Arabes Unidos	Émirate arabes unis	Emirados Árabes Unidos
Id., U.S.	Idaho	Idaho	Idaho	Idaho	Idaho	Idaho
Il., U.S.	Illinois	Illinois	Illinois	Illinois	Illinois	Illinois
In., U.S.	Indiana	Indiana	Indiana	Indiana	Indiana	Indiana
India	India / Bharat	India	Indien	India	Inde	India
Ind. O.	...	Indian Ocean	Indischer Ozean	Océano Índico	Océan Indien	Índico, Oceano
Indon.	Indonesia	Indonesia	Indonesien	Indonesia	Indonésie	Indonésia
I. of Man	Isle of Man	Isle of Man	Insel Man	Isla de Man	Île de Man	Man, Ilha de
'Īrāq	Al-'Īrāq	Iraq	Irak	Irak	Iraq	Iraque
Ire.	Ireland / Éire	Ireland	Irland	Irlanda	Irlande	Irlanda
Ísland	Ísland	Iceland	Island	Islandia	Islande	Islândia
Isr. Occ.	...	Israeli Occupied Areas	Von Israel besetztes Gebiet	Áreas ocupadas por Israel	Territoires occupés par Israël	Áreas ocupadas por Israel
It.	Italia	Italy	Italien	Italia	Italie	Itália
Ityo.	Ityopiya	Ethiopia	Äthiopien	Etiopía	Éthiopie	Etiópia
Jam.	Jamaica	Jamaica	Jamaika	Jamaica	Jamaïque	Jamaica
Jersey	Jersey	Jersey	Jersey	Jersey	Jersey	Jersey
Jugo.	Jugoslavija	Yugoslavia	Jugoslawien	Yugoslavia	Yougoslavie	Iugoslávia
J.Y.D.S.	Al-Yaman	Yemen	Jemen	Yemen	Yémen	Iêmen
Kal. Nun.	Kalaallit Nunaat / Grønland	Greenland	Grönland	Groenlandia	Groenland	Groenlândia
Kam.	Kâmpúchéa	Cambodia	Kambodscha	Camboya	Cambodge	Camboja
Kenya	Kenya	Kenya	Kenia	Kenya	Kenya	Quênia
Kıbrıs	Kuzey Kıbrıs	North Cyprus (Turkish Republic of Northern Cyprus)	Türkischen Republik Nordzypern	República turca do Norte de Chipre	République turque du Nord de Chypre	República Turca de Chipre del Norte
Kípros	Kípros / Kıbrıs	Cyprus	Zypern	Chipre	Chypre	Chipre
Ks., U.S.	Kansas	Kansas	Kansas	Kansas	Kansas	Kansas
Ky., U.S.	Kentucky	Kentucky	Kentucky	Kentucky	Kentucky	Kentucky
La., U.S.	Louisiana	Louisiana	Louisiana	Luisiana	Louisiane	Louisiana
Lao	Lao	Laos	Laos	Laos	Laos	Lao
Leso.	Lesotho	Lesotho	Lesotho	Lesotho	Lesotho	Lesoto
Liber.	Liberia	Liberia	Liberia	Liberia	Libéria	Libéria
Lībiyā	Lībiyā	Libya	Libyen	Libia	Libye	Líbia
Liech.	Liechtenstein	Liechtenstein	Liechtenstein	Liechtenstein	Liechtenstein	Liechtenstein
Lubnān	Lubnān	Lebanon	Libanon	Líbano	Liban	Líbano
Lux.	Luxembourg	Luxembourg	Luxemburg	Luxemburgo	Luxembourg	Luxemburgo
Ma., U.S.	Massachusetts	Massachusetts	Massachusetts	Massachusetts	Massachusetts	Massachusetts
Macau	Macau	Macau	Macau	Macao	Macao	Macau
Madag.	Madagasikara / Madagascar	Madagascar	Madagaskar	Madagascar	Madagascar	Madagascar
Magreb	Al-Magreb	Morocco	Marokko	Marruecos	Maroc	Marrocos
Magy.	Magyarország	Hungary	Ungarn	Hungría	Hongrie	Hungria
Malaŵi	Malaŵi	Malawi	Malawi	Malawi	Malawi	Malaui
Malay.	Malaysia	Malaysia	Malaysia	Malasia	Malaisie	Malásia
Mald.	Maldives	Maldives	Malediven	Maldivas	Maldives	Maldivas
Mali	Mali	Mali	Mali	Malí	Mali	Mali
Malta	Malta	Malta	Malta	Malta	Malte	Malta
Marsh. Is.	Marshall Islands	Marshall Islands	Marshall Islands	Marshall Islands	Marshall Islands	Marshall Islands
Mart.	Martinique	Martinique	Martinique	Martinica	Martinique	Martinica
Maur.	Mauritanie / Mūrītāniyā	Mauritania	Mauretanien	Mauritania	Mauritanie	Mauritânia
Maus.	Mauritius	Mauritius	Mauritius	Mauricio	Maurice	Maurício
Mayotte	Mayotte	Mayotte	Mayotte	Mayotte	Mayotte	Mayotte
Mb., Can.	Manitoba	Manitoba	Manitoba	Manitoba	Manitoba	Manitoba
Md., U.S.	Maryland	Maryland	Maryland	Maryland	Maryland	Maryland
Me., U.S.	Maine	Maine	Maine	Maine	Maine	Maine
Medit. S.	...	Mediterranean Sea	Mittelmeer	Mar Mediterráneo	Méditerranée, Mer	Mediterrâneo, Mar
Méx.	México	Mexico	Mexiko	México	Mexique	México
Mi., U.S.	Michigan	Michigan	Michigan	Michigan	Michigan	Michigan
Micron.	Federated States of Micronesia	Federated States of Micronesia	Federated States of Micronesia	Estados Federated States of Micronesia	États Federated States of Micronesia	Estados Federated States of Micronesia
Mid. Is.	Midway Islands	Midway Islands	Midway-Inseln	Islas Midway	Îles Midway	Midway, Ilhas
Misr	Misr	Egypt	Ägypten	Egipto	Égypte	Egito
Mn., U.S.	Minnesota	Minnesota	Minnesota	Minnesota	Minnesota	Minnesota
Mo., U.S.	Missouri	Missouri	Missouri	Misuri	Missouri	Missouri
Moç.	Moçambique	Mozambique	Mosambik	Mozambique	Mozambique	Moçambique
Monaco	Monaco	Monaco	Monaco	Mónaco	Monaco	Mônaco
Mong.	Mongol Ard Uls	Mongolia	Mongolei	Mongolia	Mongolie	Mongólia
Monts.	Montserrat	Montserrat	Montserrat	Montserrat	Montserrat	Montserrat
Ms., U.S.	Mississippi	Mississippi	Mississippi	Misisipi	Mississippi	Mississippi
Mt., U.S.	Montana	Montana	Montana	Montana	Montana	Montana
Mya.	Myanmar	Burma	Birma	Birmania	Birmanie	Birmânia
N.A.	...	North America	Nordamerika	América del Norte	Amérique du Nord	América do Norte
Namibia	Namibia	Namibia	Namibia	Namibia	Namibie	Namíbia
Nauru	Nauru / Naoero	Nauru	Nauru	Nauru	Nauru	Nauru
N.B., Can.	New Brunswick / Nouveau-Brunswick	New Brunswick	Neubraunschweig	Nueva Brunswick	Nouveau-Brunswick	Nova Brunswick
N.C., U.S.	North Carolina	North Carolina	Nord Karolina	Carolina del Norte	Caroline du Nord	Carolina do Norte
N. Cal.	Nouvelle-Calédonie	New Caledonia	Neukaledonien	Nueva Caledonia	Nouvelle Calédonie	Nova Caledônia
N.D., U.S.	North Dakota	North Dakota	Nord Dakota	Dakota del Norte	Dakota du Nord	Dakota do Norte
Ne., U.S.	Nebraska	Nebraska	Nebraska	Nebraska	Nebraska	Nebraska
Ned.	Nederland	Netherlands	Niederlande	Países Bajos	Pays-Bas	Países Baixos
Ned. Ant.	Nederlandse Antillen	Netherlands Antilles	Niederländische Antillen	Antillas Neerlandeses	Antilles néerlandaises	Antilhas Holandesas
Nepāl	Nepāl	Nepal	Nepal	Nepal	Népal	Nepal
Nf., Can.	Newfoundland / Terre-Neuve	Newfoundland	Neufundland	Terranova	Terre-Neuve	Terra Nova
N.H., U.S.	New Hampshire	New Hampshire	New Hampshire	Nuevo Hampshire	New Hampshire	Nova Hampshire
Nic.	Nicaragua	Nicaragua	Nicaragua	Nicaragua	Nicaragua	Nicarágua
Nig.	Nigeria	Nigeria	Nigeria	Nigeria	Nigéria	Nigéria
Niger	Niger	Niger	Niger	Níger	Niger	Níger
Nihon	Nihon	Japan	Japan	Japón	Japon	Japão
N. Ire., U.K.	Northern Ireland	Northern Ireland	Nordirland	Irlanda del Norte	Irlande du Nord	Irlanda do Norte
Niue	Niue	Niue	Niue	Niue	Niue	Niue
N.J., U.S.	New Jersey	New Jersey	New Jersey	Nueva Jersey	New Jersey	Nova Jersey
N.M., U.S.	New Mexico	New Mexico	New Mexico	Nuevo Mexico	Nouveau-Mexique	Nova México
N. Mar. Is.	Northern Mariana Islands	Northern Mariana Islands	Northern Mariana Islands	Northern Mariana Islands	Northern Mariana Islands	Northern Mariana Islands
Nor.	Norge	Norway	Norwegen	Noruega	Norvège	Noruega
Norf. I.	Norfolk Island	Norfolk Island	Norfolk-Insel	Isla Norfolk	Île Norfolk	Norfolk, Ilha

	LOCAL NAME	ENGLISH	DEUTSCH	ESPAÑOL	FRANÇAIS	PORTUGUÊS
N.S., Can.	Nova Scotia / Nouvelle-Écosse	Nova Scotia	Neu Schottland	Nueva Escocia	Nouvelle-Écosse	Nova Scotia
N.T., Can.	Northwest Territories / Territoires du Nord-Ouest	Northwest Territories	Nord-West Territorien	Territorios del Noroeste	Territoires du Nord-Ouest	Territórios do Noroeste
Nv., U.S.	Nevada	Nevada	Nevada	Nevada	Nevada	Nevada
N.Y., U.S.	New York	New York	New York	Nueva York	New York	Nova York
N.Z.	New Zealand	New Zealand	Neuseeland	Nueva Zelandia	Nouvelle-Zélande	Nova Zelândia
Oc.	...	Oceania	Ozeanien	Oceanía	Océanie	Oceania
Oh., U.S.	Ohio	Ohio	Ohio	Ohio	Ohio	Ohio
Ok., U.S.	Oklahoma	Oklahoma	Oklahoma	Oklahoma	Oklahoma	Oklahoma
On., Can.	Ontario	Ontario	Ontario	Ontario	Ontario	Ontário
Or., U.S.	Oregon	Oregon	Oregon	Oregón	Oregon	Oregon
Öst.	Österreich	Austria	Österreich	Austria	Autriche	Austria
Pa., U.S.	Pennsylvania	Pennsylvania	Pennsylvanien	Pensilvania	Pennsylvanie	Pennsylvania
Pac. O.	...	Pacific Ocean	Pazifischer Ozean	Océano Pacífico	Océan Pacifique	Pacífico, Oceano
Pāk.	Pākistān	Pakistan	Pakistan	Pakistán	Pakistan	Paquistão
Palau	Palau	Palau	Palau	Palau	Palau	Palau
Pan.	Panamá	Panama	Panama	Panamá	Panama	Panamá
Pap. N. Gui.	Papua New Guinea	Papua New Guinea	Papua-Neuguinea	Papua Nueva Guinea	Papouasie-Nouvelle Guinée	Papua-Nova Guiné
Para.	Paraguay	Paraguay	Paraguay	Paraguay	Paraguay	Paraguai
P.E., Can.	Prince Edward Island / Île-du-Prince-Édouard	Prince Edward Island	Prinz Edward-Insel	Isla Príncipe Eduardo	Île-du-Prince Édouard	Príncipe Eduardo, Ilha do
Perú	Perú	Peru	Peru	Perú	Pérou	Peru
Pil.	Pilipinas / Philippines	Philippines	Philippinen	Filipinas	Philippines	Filipinas
Pit.	Pitcairn	Pitcairn	Pitcairn	Pitcairn	Pitcairn	Pitcairn
Pol.	Polska	Poland	Polen	Polonia	Pologne	Polônia
Poly. fr.	Polynésie française	French Polynesia	Französisch-Polynesien	Polinesia Francesa	Polynésie française	Polinésia Francesa
Port.	Portugal	Portugal	Portugal	Portugal	Portugal	Portugal
P.Q., Can.	Québec	Quebec	Quebec	Quebec	Québec	Québec
P.R.	Puerto Rico	Puerto Rico	Puerto Rico	Puerto Rico	Porto Rico	Porto Rico
P.S.N.Á.	Plazas de Soberanía en el Norte de África	Spanish North Africa	Spanisch-Nordafrika	Plazas de Soberanía en el Norte de África	Afrique du Nord espagnole	África do Norte Espanhola
Qatar	Qatar	Qatar	Katar	Qatar	Qatar	Qatar
Rep. Dom.	República Dominicana	Dominican Republic	Dominikanische Republik	República Dominicana	République dominicaine	Dominicana, República
Réu.	Réunion	Reunion	Réunion	Reunión	Réunion	Reunião
R.I., U.S.	Rhode Island	Rhode Island	Rhode Island	Rhode Island	Rhode Island	Rhode Island
Rom.	România	Romania	Rumänien	Rumania	Roumanie	Romênia
Rw.	Rwanda	Rwanda	Ruanda	Rwanda	Rwanda	Ruanda
S.A.	...	South America	Südamerika	América del Sur	Amérique du Sud	América do Sul
S. Afr.	South Africa / Suid-Afrika	South Africa	Südafrika	Sudáfrica	Afrique du Sud	África do Sul
S.C., U.S.	South Carolina	South Carolina	Süd Karolina	Carolina del Sur	Caroline du Sud	Carolina do Sul
S. Ch. S.	...	South China Sea	Südchinesisches Meer	Mar de China Meridional	Mer de Chine Méridionale	China do Sul, Mar da
Schw.	Schweiz / Suisse / Svizzera	Switzerland	Schweiz	Suiza	Suisse	Suiça
Scot., U.K.	Scotland	Scotland	Schottland	Escocia	Écosse	Escócia
S.D., U.S.	South Dakota	South Dakota	Süd Dakota	Dakota del Sur	Dakota du Sud	Dakota do Sul
Sén.	Sénégal	Senegal	Senegal	Senegal	Sénégal	Senegal
Sey.	Seychelles	Seychelles	Seschellen	Seychelles	Seychelles	Seychelles
Shq.	Shqipëri	Albania	Albanien	Albania	Albanie	Albânia
Sing.	Singapore	Singapore	Singapur	Singapur	Singapour	Cingapura
Sk., Can.	Saskatchewan	Saskatchewan	Saskatchewan	Saskatchewan	Saskatchewan	Saskatchewan
S.L.	Sierra Leone	Sierra Leone	Sierra Leone	Sierra Leone	Sierra Leone	Serra Leoa
S. Lan.	Sri Lanka	Sri Lanka	Sri Lanka	Sri Lanka	Sri Lanka	Sri Lanka
S. Mar.	San Marino	San Marino	San Marino	San Marino	Saint-Marin	San Marino
Sol. Is.	Solomon Islands	Solomon Islands	Salomonen	Islas Salomón	Îles Salomon	Salomão, Ilhas
Som.	Somaliya	Somalia	Somalia	Somalia	Somalie	Somália
S.S.S.R.	Sojuz Sovetskich Socialistiĉeskich Respublik	Union of Soviet Socialist Republics	Union der Sozialistischen Sowjetrepubliken	Unión de Repúblicas Socialistas Soviéticas	Union des Républiques socialistes soviétiques	União das Repúblicas Socialistas Soviéticas
St. C.-N.	St. Christopher-Nevis	St. Christopher-Nevis	Sankt Christopher-Nevis	San Cristóbal-Nevis	Saint-Christophe-Nièves	São Cristóvão-Neves
St. Hel.	St. Helena	St. Helena	Sankt Helena	Santa Elena	Sainte-Hélène	Santa Helena
St. Luc.	St. Lucia	St. Lucia	Sankt Lucia	Santa Lucía	Sainte-Lucie	Santa Lúcia

	LOCAL NAME	ENGLISH	DEUTSCH	ESPAÑOL	FRANÇAIS	PORTUGUÊS
S. Tom./P.	São Tomé e Príncipe	Sao Tome and Principe	São Tomé und Principe	São Tomé y Príncipe	Sao Tomé-et-Principe	São Tomé e Príncipe
St. P./M.	St.-Pierre-et-Miquelon	St. Pierre and Miquelon	Saint-Pierre und Miquelon	San Pedro y Miquelón	Saint-Pierre-et-Miquelon	São Pedro e Miquelon
St. Vin.	St. Vincent and the Grenadines	St. Vincent and the Grenadines	Sankt Vincent und die Grenadinen	San Vicente y las Granadinas	Saint-Vincent-et-Grenadines	São Vicente e Granadinas
Süd.	As-Südān	Sudan	Sudan	Sudán	Soudan	Sudão
Suomi	Suomi / Finland	Finland	Finnland	Finlandia	Finlande	Finlândia
Sur.	Suriname	Suriname	Suriname	Suriname	Suriname	Suriname
Sūrīy.	Sūrīyah	Syria	Syrien	Siria	Syrie	Síria
Sve.	Sverige	Sweden	Schweden	Suecia	Suède	Suécia
Swaz.	Swaziland	Swaziland	Swasiland	Swazilandia	Swaziland	Suazilândia
T.a.a.f.	Terres australes et antarctiques françaises	French Southern and Antarctic Territories	Französische Süd- und Antarktis-Gebiete	Tierras Australes y Antárticas Francesas	Terres australes et antarctiques françaises	Terras Austrais e Antárticas Francesas
Taehan	Taehan-min'guk	South Korea	Südkorea	Corea del Sur	Corée du Sud	Coréia do Sul
T'aiwan	T'aiwan	Taiwan	Taiwan	Taiwán	Taïwan	Taiwan (Formosa)
Tan.	Tanzania	Tanzania	Tansania	Tanzanía	Tanzanie	Tanzânia
Tchad	Tchad	Chad	Tschad	Chad	Tchad	Tchad
T./C. Is.	Turks and Caicos Islands	Turks and Caicos Islands	Turks- und Caicos-Irseln	Islas Turcas y Caicos	Îles Turques et Caïques	Turcas e Caicos, Ilhas
Thai	Prathet Thai	Thailand	Thailand	Tailandia	Thaïlande	Tailândia
Tn., U.S.	Tennessee	Tennessee	Tennessee	Tennessee	Tennessee	Tennessee
Togo	Togo	Togo	Togo	Togo	Togo	Togo
Tok.	Tokelau	Tokelau	Tokelau	Tokelau	Tokélaou	Tokelau
Tonga	Tonga	Tonga	Tonga	Tonga	Tonga	Tonga
Transkei	Transkei	Transkei	Transkei	Transkei	Transkei	Transkei
Trin.	Trinidad and Tobago	Trinidad and Tobago	Trinidad und Tobago	Trinidad y Tabago	Trinité-et-Tobago	Trinidad e Tobago
T.T.P.I.	Trust Territory of the Pacific Islands	Trust Territory of the Pacific Islands	Treuhandgebiet Pazifische Inseln	Territorio Fideicometido de las Islas Pacíficas	Territorie sous tutelle îles du Pacifique	Pacífico, Ilhas do (Território sob Tutela)
Tun.	Tunisie / Tunis	Tunisia	Tunesien	Túnez	Tunisie	Tunísia
Tür.	Türkiye	Turkey	Türkei	Turquía	Turquie	Turquia
Tuvalu	Tuvalu	Tuvalu	Tuvalu	Tuvalu	Tuvalu	Tuvalu
Tx., U.S.	Texas	Texas	Texas	Texas	Texas	Texas
Ug.	Uganda	Uganda	Uganda	Uganda	Ouganda	Uganda
U.K.	United Kingdom	United Kingdom	Vereinigtes Königreich	Reino Unido	Royaume-Uni	Reino Unido
'Umān	'Umān	Oman	Oman	Omán	Oman	Omã
Ur.	Uruguay	Uruguay	Uruguay	Uruguay	Uruguay	Uruguai
Urd.	Al-Urdun	Jordan	Jordanien	Jordania	Jordanie	Jordânia
U.S.	United States	United States	Vereinigte Staaten	Estados Unidos	États-Unis	Estados Unidos
Ut., U.S.	Utah	Utah	Utah	Utah	Utah	Utah
Va., U.S.	Virginia	Virginia	Virginia	Virginia	Virginie	Virgínia
Vanuatu	Vanuatu	Vanuatu	Vanuatu	Vanuatu	Vanuatu	Vanuatu
Vat.	Cittá del Vaticano	Vatican City	Vatikanstadt	Ciudad del Vaticano	Cité du Vatican	Vaticano
Ven.	Venezuela	Venezuela	Venezuela	Venezuela	Venezuela	Venezuela
Venda	Venda	Venda	Venda	Venda	Venda	Venda
Viet	Viet Nam	Vietnam	Vietnam	Viet-Nam	Viet Nam	Vietnam
Vir. Is., U.S.	Virgin Islands (U.S.)	Virgin Islands (U.S.)	Amerikanische Jungferninseln	Islas Vírgenes (americanas)	Îles Vierges (américaines)	Virgens Americanas, Ilhas
Vt., U.S.	Vermont	Vermont	Vermont	Vermont	Vermont	Vermont
Wa., U.S.	Wake Island	Wake Island	Wake	Isla Wake	Île de Wake	Wake
Wales, U.K.	Wales	Wales	Wales	Gales	Galles	Gales
Wal./F.	Wallis et Futuna	Wallis and Futuna	Wallis und Futuna	Wallis y Futuna	Wallis et Futuna	Wallis e Futuna
Wi., U.S.	Wisconsin	Wisconsin	Wisconsin	Wisconsin	Wisconsin	Wisconsin
W. Sah.	...	Western Sahara	Westliche Sahara	Sahara Occidental	Sahara occidental	Saara Ocidental
W. Sam.	Western Samoa / Samoa i Sisifo	Western Samoa	Westsamoa	Samoa Occidental	Samoa-Occidental	Samoa Ocidental
W.V., U.S.	West Virginia	West Virginia	West Virginia	Virginia Occidental	Virginie Occidentale	Virgínia Ocidental
Wy., U.S.	Wyoming	Wyoming	Wyoming	Wyoming	Wyoming	Wyoming
Yaman	Al-Yaman	Yemen	Jemen	Yemen	Yémen	Iêmen
Yis.	Yisra'el / Isrā'īl	Israel	Israel	Israel	Israël	Israel
Yk., Can.	Yukon Territory	Yukon	Yukon	Yukón	Yukon	Yukon
Zaïre	Zaïre	Zaire	Zaire	Zaire	Zaïre	Zaire
Zam.	Zambia	Zambia	Sambia	Zambia	Zambie	Zâmbia
Zhg.	Zhongguo	China	China	China	Chine	China
Zimb.	Zimbabwe	Zimbabwe	Simbabwe	Zimbabwe	Zimbabwe	Zimbabwe

Key to Index Symbols

The symbols below represent the categories into which the physical and cultural features are classified in the Index. Broad categories appear in **boldface** type. Symbols with superior numbers identify subcategories.

Schlüssel zu den Symbolen des Registers

Die folgenden Symbole veranschaulichen die Kategorien, nach denen physische und kulturgeographische Objekte im Register geordnet sind. Die Oberbegriffe sind in **Fettdruck** hervorgehoben. Symbole mit hochgestellten Nummern kennzeichnen Unterbegriffe.

Clave de los Símbolos del Índice

Los símbolos abajo representan las categorías dentro de las cuales están clasificados los rasgos físicos y culturales que están incluídos en el Índice. Las grandes categorías aparecen en **negrilla**. Los símbolos que tienen números en su parte superior identifican las subcategorías.

Signification des Symboles de l'Index

Les symboles ci-dessous représentent les catégories sous lesquelles les données physiques et culturelles sont classées dans l'index. Les symboles en caractèter **gras** correspondent aux catégories principales. Ceux suivis d'un indice désignent les subdivisions d'une même catégorie.

Chave dos Símbolos do Índice

Os símbolos abaixo representam as categorias em que estão classificados os acidentes físicos e culturais no Índice. As grandes categorias aparecem em **negrito**. Os símbolos acompanhados de números altos identificam as subcategorias.

ENGLISH	DEUTSCH	ESPANOL	FRANCAIS	PORTUGUES
Mountain	**Berg**	**Montaña**	**Montagne**	**Montanha**
Volcano	Vulkan	Volcán	Volcan	Vulcão
Hill	Hügel	Colina	Colline	Colina
Mountains	**Gebirge**	**Montañas**	**Montagnes**	**Montanhas**
Plateau	Hochebene	Meseta	Plateau	Planalto
Hills	Hügel	Colinas	Collines	Colinas
Pass	**Paß**	**Paso**	**Col**	**Passo**
Valley, Canyon	**Tal, Cañon**	**Valle, Cañón**	**Vallée, Canyon**	**Vale, Canhão**
Plain	**Ebene**	**Llano**	**Plaine**	**Planície**
Basin	Becken	Cuenca	Bassin	Bacia
Delta	Delta	Delta	Delta	Delta
Cape	**Kap**	**Cabo**	**Cap**	**Cabo**
Peninsula	Halbinsel	Península	Péninsule	Península
Spit, Sand Bar	Landzunge, Sandbarre	Lengua de Tierra, Bajo	Flèche, Banc de sable	Ponta de Terra, Banco de Areia
Island	**Insel**	**Isla**	**Île**	**Ilha**
Atoll	Atoll	Atolón	Atoll	Atol
Rock	Fels	Roca	Rocher	Rochedo
Islands	**Inseln**	**Islas**	**Îles**	**Ilhas**
Rocks	Felsen	Rocas	Rochers	Rochedos
Other Topographic Features	**Andere Topographische Objekte**	**Otros Elementos Topográficos**	**Autres données topographiques**	**Outros Acidentes Topográficos**
Continent	Erdteil	Continente	Continent	Continente
Coast, Beach	Küste, Strand	Costa, Playa	Côte, Plage	Costa, Praia
Isthmus	Landenge	Istmo	Isthme	Istmo
Cliff	Kliff	Risco	Falaise	Falésia
Cave, Caves	Höhle, Höhlen	Cueva, Cuevas	Caverne, Cavernes	Caverna, Cavernas
Crater	Krater	Cráter	Cratère	Cratera
Depression	Senke	Depresión	Depression	Depressão
Dunes	Dünen	Dunas	Dunes	Dunas
Lava Flow	Lavastrom	Corriente de Lava	Coulée de lave	Corrente de Lava
River	**Fluß**	**Río**	**Rivière, Fleuve**	**Rio**
River Channel	Flussarm	Brazo de Río	Bras de rivière	Canal de Rio
Canal	**Kanal**	**Canal**	**Canal**	**Canal**
Aqueduct	Aquädukt	Acueducto	Aqueduc	Aqueduto
Waterfall, Rapids	**Wasserfall, Stromschnellen**	**Cascada, Rápidos**	**Chute d'eau, Rapides**	**Quedas d'água, Rápidos**
Strait	**Meereßtrasse**	**Estrecho**	**Détroit**	**Estreito**
Bay, Gulf	**Bucht, Golf**	**Bahía, Golfo**	**Baie, Golfe**	**Baía, Golfo**
Estuary	Trichtermündung	Estuario	Estuaire	Estuário
Fjord	Fjord	Fiordo	Fiord	Fiorde
Bight	Bucht	Bahía	Baie	Enseada
Lake, Lakes	**See, Seen**	**Lago, Lagos**	**Lac, Lacs**	**Lago, Lagos**
Reservoir	Stausee	Embalse	Réservoir, Retenue	Reservatório
Swamp	**Sumpf**	**Pantano**	**Marais**	**Pântano**
Ice Features, Glacier	**Eis- und Gletscherformen**	**Accidentes Glaciales, Glaciar**	**Formes glaciaires, Glacier**	**Acidentes Glaciares, Geleira**
Other Hydrographic Features	**Andere Hydrographische Objekte**	**Otros Elementos Hidrográficos**	**Autres données hydrographiques**	**Outros Acidentes Hidrográficos**
Ocean	Ozean	Océano	Océan	Oceano
Sea	Meer	Mar	Mer	Mar
Anchorage	Ankerplatz	Ancladero	Ancrage	Ancoradouro
Oasis, Well, Spring	Oase, Brunnen, Quelle	Oasis, Pozo, Manantial	Oasis, Puits, Source	Oásis, Poço, Fonte, Manancial

ENGLISH	DEUTSCH	ESPANOL	FRANCAIS	PORTUGUES
Submarine Features	**Untermeerische Objekte**	**Accidentes Submarinos**	**Formes de relief sous-marin**	**Acidentes Submarinos**
Depression	Senke	Depresión	Dépression	Depressão
Reef, Shoal	Riff, Untiefe	Arrecife, Bajo	Récif, Haut-fond	Recife, Baixio
Mountain, Mountains	Berg, Gebirge	Montaña, Montañas	Montagne, Montagnes	Montanha, Montanhas
Slope, Shelf	Abhang, Schelf	Talud, Plataforma	Talus, Plateau continental	Talude, Plataforma
Political Unit	**Politische Einheit**	**Unidad Política**	**Entité politique**	**Unidade Política**
Independent Nation	Unabhängiger Staat	Nación Independiente	État indépendant	País Independente
Dependency	Abhángiges Gebiet	Dependencia	Dépendance	Dependência
State, Canton, Republic	Land, Kanton, Republik	Estado, Cantón, República	État, Canton, République	Estado, Cantão, República
Province, Region, Oblast	Provinz, Landschaft, Oblast	Provincia, Región, Oblast	Province, Région, Oblast	Província, Região, Oblast
Department, District, Prefecture	Département, Distrikt, Präfektur	Departamento, Distrito, Prefectura	Département, District, Préfecture	Departamento, Distrito, Prefeitura
County	Grafschaft	Condado	Comté	Condado
City, Municipality	Stadt, Stadtkreis	Ciudad, Municipalidad	Ville, Municipalité	Cidade, Municipalidade
Miscellaneous	Verschiedenes	Misceláneo	Divers	Diversos
Historical	Historisch	Histórico	Historique	Sítio Histórico
Cultural Institution	**Kulturelle Institution**	**Institución Cultural**	**Institution culturelle**	**Instituição Cultural**
Religious Institution	Religiöse Institution	Institución Religiosa	Institution religieuse	Instituição Religiosa
Educational Institution	Erziehungsinstitution	Institución Educacional	Établissement d'éducation	Estabelecimento de Ensino
Scientific, Industrial Facility	Wissenschaftliche, Industrielle Anlage	Institución Científica o Industrial	Établissement scientifique ou industriel	Estabelecimento Científico ou Industrial
Historical Site	**Historische Stätte**	**Sitio Históric**	**Site historique**	**Sítio Histórico**
Recreational Site	**Erholungs- und Ferienort**	**Sitio de Recreo**	**Centre de loisirs**	**Área de Lazer**
Airport	**Flughafen**	**Aeropuerto**	**Aéroport**	**Aeroporto**
Military Installation	**Militäranlage**	**Instalación Militar**	**Installation militaire**	**Instalação Militar**
Miscellaneous	**Verschiedenes**	**Misceláneo**	**Divers**	**Diversos**
Region	Region	Región	Région	Região
Desert	Wüste	Desierto	Désert	Deserto
Forest, Moor	Wald, Moor	Bosque, Páramo	Forêt, Lande	Floresta, Pântano
Reserve, Reservation	Reservat	Reserva, Reservación	Réserve	Reserva
Transportation	Verkehr	Transporte	Transport	Transporte
Dam	Damm	Presa	Barrage	Represa
Mine, Quarry	Bergwerk, Steinbruch	Mina, Cantera	Mine, Carrière	Mina, Pedreira
Neighborhood	Nachbarschaft	Barrio	Quartier	Arredores, Vizinhança
Shopping Center	Einkaufszentrum	Mercado	Centre commercial	Shopping Center

A

Ābādān	128	30.20 N	48.16 E	Abasolo, Méx.	232	25.18 N	104.40 W	Abbey Wood	260	51.29 N	0.08 E	Abel Tasman			
Ābādeh	128	31.10 N	52.37 E	Abasolo, Méx.	232	24.04 N	98.22 W	Abbiategrasso	82	45.24 N	8.54 E	National Park	172	40.55 S 173.00 E	
Abadia dos Dourados	255	18.28 S	47.24 W	Abasolo, Méx.	234	20.27 N	101.32 W	Abbot, Mount	166	20.03 S 147.45 E		Abelti	144	8.10 N 37.34 E	
Abadiânia	255	16.06 S	48.48 W	Abasolo del Valle	234	17.44 N	95.29 W	Abbots Bromley	42	52.48 N	1.52 W	Aberdour	46	56.03 N 3.19 W	
Abadla	148	31.01 N	2.44 W	Abasto	258	34.58 S	58.06 W	Abbotsbury	42	50.40 N	2.36 W	Aberdulais	42	51.41 N 3.48 W	
Abaeté	255	19.09 S	45.27 W	Abastumani	84	41.46 N	42.50 E	Abbotsford, Austl.	274a	33.51 S 151.08 E		Aberdyfi	42	52.33 N 4.02 W	
Abaeté ≃	255	18.02 S	45.12 W	Abate	85	39.03 N	77.36 E	Abbotsford, B.C.,				Aberfeldy	46	56.37 N 3.54 W	
Abaetetuba	250	1.42 S	48.54 W	Abate Alonia, Lago di				Can.	224	49.03 N 122.17 W		Aberfoyle	46	56.11 N 4.23 W	
Abagaitujī	88	49.35 N 117.49 E			85	41.01 N	15.45 E	Abbotsford, Wi., U.S.	190	44.56 N 90.18 W		Abergavenny	42	51.50 N 3.00 W	
Abagnar Qi	102	43.58 N 116.04 E		Abatiá	255	23.19 S	50.18 W	Abbots Langley	260	51.43 N 0.25 W		Abergele	44	53.17 N 3.34 W	
Abag Qi	102	43.53 N 114.33 E		Abatimbo el Gumas	144	10.36 N	35.13 E	Abbott, Arg.	258	35.17 S 58.48 W		Abergwynfi	42	51.40 N 3.35 W	
Abai	252	26.01 S	55.57 W	Abatskij	86	56.18 N	70.28 E	Abbott, Tx., U.S.	222	31.53 N 97.04 W		Abergwolwyn	42	42.40 N 3.58 W	
→ El Aaiún	148	27.09 N	13.12 W	Abau	164	10.11 S 148.42 E		Abbottābād	123	34.09 N 73.13 E		Aberjona ≃	283	42.27 N 71.08 W	
Aalen	56	48.50 N	10.05 E	Abava ≃	76	57.06 N	21.54 E	Abbott Butte	202	42.57 N 122.33 W		Abermain	170	32.49 S 151.25 E	
A' äll an-Nîl	140	9.30 N	31.00 E	Abay				Abbottstown	208	39.53 N 76.59 W		Abernathy	196	33.50 N 101.51 W	
Aalsmeer	52	52.16 N	4.45 E	→ Blue Nile ≃	140	15.38 N	32.31 E	Abchazskaja				Abernethy, Sk., Can.	184	50.45 N 103.25 W	
Aalst (Alost), Bel.	50	50.56 N	4.02 E	Abaya, Lake ⊜	144	6.20 N	37.55 E	Avtonomnaja				Abernethy, Scot.,			
Aalst, Ned.	52	51.23 N	5.29 E	Abayuba	258	34.51 S	56.14 W	Sovetskaja				U.K.	46	56.20 N 3.19 W	
Aalten	52	51.56 N	6.35 E	Abaza	86	52.39 N	90.06 E	Socialistíčeskaja				Aberporth	42	52.09 N 4.33 W	
Aalter	50	51.05 N	3.27 E	Abbabach ≃	263	51.28 N	7.41 E	Republika ☐³	84	43.10 N 41.00 E		Abersoch	42	52.50 N 4.29 W	
Aalwynsfontein	158	30.27 S	18.38 E	Abbadia San				Abcoude	52	52.16 N 4.58 E		Abersychan	42	51.44 N 3.04 W	
Äänekoski	28	62.36 N	25.44 E	Salvatore	82	42.53 N	11.41 E	Abercorn				Abert, Lake ⊜	202	42.38 N 120.13 W	
Aansluit	158	26.44 S	22.28 E	'Abbāsābād	130	36.25 N	40.20 E	→ Mbala, Zam.	154	8.50 S 31.22 E		Abertillery	42	51.45 N 3.09 W	
Aar ≃	56	50.23 N	8.00 E	Abbasanta	82	40.08 N	8.49 E	Abercrombie ≃	170	34.09 S 149.40 E		Aberuthven	46	56.19 N 3.39 W	
Aarau	58	47.23 N	8.03 E	'Abbāsābād	267d	35.44 N	51.25 E	'Abd al-'Azīz, Jabal				Aberystwyth	42	52.25 N 4.05 W	
Aarberg	58	47.03 N	7.16 E	Abbaye, Étang de l'	261	48.41 N 1.56 E		'Abd al-Hafiz, Qārat				Abessinien, Hochland			
Aarburg	58	47.19 N	7.54 E	Abbekås	41	55.24 N	13.36 E	^²	130	28.53 N 30.08 E		von			
Aardenburg	52	51.16 N	3.27 E	Abbekås	41	55.24 N	13.36 E	'Abd al-Kūrī I	118	12.12 N 52.13 E		→ Ethiopian			
Aare ≃	58	47.37 N	8.13 E	Abbensen	48	53.25 N	8.53 W	'Abd Allāh	124	30.00 N 48.20 E		Plateau ^¹	144	9.00 N 38.00 E	
Aareschlucht	58	46.44 N	8.12 E	Abbeville, Fr.	50	50.06 N	1.50 E	'Abd Allāh, Khawr ⨅	128	29.50 N 48.20 E		Abetone	66	44.08 N 10.40 E	
Aargau ☐³	58	47.30 N	8.10 E	Abbeville, Ga., U.S.	192	31.59 N	83.18 W	'Abd ash-Shāhīd	273c	29.55 N 31.19 E		Abez'	24	66.32 N 61.42 E	
Aarle-Rixtel	52	51.31 N	5.38 E	Abbeville, La., U.S.	194	29.58 N	92.08 W	Ābdānān	128	32.58 N 47.26 E		Abhā	144	18.13 N 42.30 E	
Aaronsburg	210	40.54 N	77.27 W	Abbeville, Ms., U.S.	194	34.30 N	89.30 W	Ābdera ☐⁴	38	40.59 N 24.58 E		Abharwat ^	123	34.02 N 74.25 E	
Aarschot	56	50.59 N	4.50 E	Abbeville, S.C., U.S.	192	34.10 N	82.22 W	Abdrachmanovo	80	54.46 N 52.30 E		Abhayāpur	124	26.20 N 90.40 E	
Aarwangen	58	47.15 N	7.46 E	Abbeyfeale	45	52.24 N	9.18 W	Abdul Hakīm	123	30.33 N 72.07 E		Abhaynagar	124	23.01 N 89.28 E	
Aazanäm	34	35.13 N	3.10 W	Abbey Head ⊁	44	54.46 N	3.58 W	Abdulino	80	54.16 N 53.27 E		Abico	94	35.52 N 140.03 E	
Aba, Nig.	150	5.06 N	7.21 E	Abbeyleix	48	52.55 N	7.20 W	Abe ≃	94	34.56 N 133.25 E		Abia ☐⁴	194	33.20 N 90.15 W	
Aba, Zaïre	154	3.52 N	30.14 E	Abbey Peak ^	164	14.18 S 144.29 E		Abe, Lake (Lac Abbé)				Ābidī, Oued el ≃	148	32.18 N 7.03 E	
Aba, Zhg.	102	33.06 N 101.59 E		Abbscay, Arroyo ≃	258	35.17 S	58.07 W	Abe, Lake (Lac Abbé)	144	11.06 N 41.50 E		Ābīdīn	140	13.33 N 29.38 E	
Abā al-Bawl, Qurayn				Abashiri	92a	44.01 N 144.17 E		Abejorral, Cerro ^	236	11.39 N 86.10 W		'Abidiyah	140	18.15 N 33.57 E	
^²	128	24.56 N	51.13 E	Abasolo, Méx.	196	27.12 N 101.24 W		Abejorral	240	5.47 N 75.26 W		Abīdjan	150	5.19 N 4.02 W	
Abā al-Waqf	142	28.35 N	30.46 E	Abasolo, Méx.	234	19.53 N 101.08 W		Abekr	140	12.43 N 28.55 E		Abīd Mār, Tall ^	132	32.26 N 36.42 E	
Abā as-Su'ūd	144	17.29 N	44.08 E	Abasolo, Méx.	234	25.57 N 100.24 W		Abel	256	22.54 S 46.08 W		Abiegama	154	2.35 N 27.34 E	
Abacexis ≃	242	3.54 S	58.47 W	Abasolo, Méx.	204	25.39 N 115.21 W		Abelek	140	7.23 N 28.46 E		Abiko	94	35.52 N 140.03 E	
Abadab, Jabal ^	140	18.53 N	35.59 E									Abilene, Ks., U.S.	198	38.55 N 97.12 W	
												Abilene, Tx., U.S.	196	32.26 N 99.43 W	

Aadorf	58	47.30 N	8.54 E	Abbott Butte				
Aaiun				Abau				
→ El Aaiún	148	27.09 N	13.12 W					

River	Fluß
Canal	Kanal
Waterfall, Rapids	Wasserfall, Stromschnellen
Strait	Meereßtraße
Bay, Gulf	Bucht, Golf
Lake, Lakes	See, Seen
Swamp	Sumpf
Ice Features, Glacier	Eis- und Gletscherformen
Other Hydrographic Features	Andere Hydrographische Objekte

Río	Rivière
Canal	Canal
Cascada, Rápidos	Chute d'eau, Rapides
Estrecho	Détroit
Bahía, Golfo	Baie, Golfe
Lago, Lagos	Lac, Lacs
Pantano	Marais
Accidentes Glaciales	Formes glaciaires
Otros Elementos Hidrográficos	Autres données hydrographiques

Rio	**Submarine Features** Untermeerische Objekte
Canal	**Political Unit** Politische Einheit
Cascata, Rápidos	**Cultural Institution** Kulturelle Institution
Estreito	**Historical Site** Historische Stätte
Baía, Golfo	**Recreational Site** Erholungs- und Ferienort
Lago, Lagos	**Airport** Flughafen
Pântano	**Military Installation** Militäranlage
Acidentes glaciares	**Miscellaneous** Verschiedenes
Outros acidentes hidrográficos	

Accidentes Submarinos	Formes de relief sous-marin	Acidentes submarinos
Unidad Política	Entité politique	Unidade política
Institución Cultural	Institution culturelle	Instituição cultural
Sitio Histórico	Site historique	Sítio histórico
Sitio de Recreo	Centre de loisirs	Área de Lazer
Aeropuerto	Aéroport	Aeroporto
Instalación Militar	Installation militaire	Instalação militar
Misceláneo	Divers	Diversos

Abingdon, Eng., U.K. 42 51.41 N 1.17 W
Abingdon, Il., U.S. 190 40.48 N 90.24 W
Abingdon, Il., U.S. 194 40.48 N 90.24 W
Abingdon, Va., U.S. 192 36.42 N 81.58 W
Abinger 260 51.12 N 0.24 W
Abington, Ct., U.S. 207 41.51 N 72.00 W
Abington, Ma., U.S. 207 42.06 N 70.56 W
Abington, Pa., U.S. 208 40.07 N 75.07 W
Abington Reefs ✢[2] 166 18.00 S 149.36 E
Abino, Point ≻ 212 42.50 N 79.05 W
Abino Bay ⊂ 284a 42.51 N 79.05 W
Abinsk 78 44.52 N 38.09 E
Abiod, Rmel el ≗[8] 148 31.30 N 9.30 E
Abiquiu 200 36.12 N 106.19 W
Abiquiu Reservoir ⊜[1] 200 36.18 N 106.32 W
Abisko 24 68.20 N 18.51 E
Abisko Nationalpark ♦ 24 68.20 N 18.30 E
Abita Springs 194 30.28 N 90.02 W
Abitau ≐ 176 59.53 N 109.03 W
Abitibi ≐ 176 51.03 N 80.55 W
Abitibi, Lake ⊜ 190 48.42 N 79.45 W
Abiy Adi 144 13.26 N 39.05 E
Abiyata, Lake ⊜ 144 7.37 N 38.36 E
Abja-Paluoja 76 58.08 N 25.21 E
Ableiges 261 49.05 N 1.59 E
Ablis 50 48.31 N 1.50 E
Ablon-sur-Seine 261 48.43 N 2.25 E
Abnūb 142 27.16 N 31.09 E
Åbo → Turku 26 60.27 N 22.17 E
Abóbada 266c 38.43 N 9.20 W
Abodom 150 5.32 N 0.49 W
Abohar 123 30.09 N 74.11 E
Aboisso 150 5.28 N 3.12 W
Abomey 150 7.11 N 1.59 E
Abondance 58 46.17 N 6.44 E
Abong 146 6.59 N 10.44 E
Abongabong, Gunung ▲ 114 4.15 N 96.48 E
Abong Mbang 152 3.59 N 13.10 E
Abonnema 150 4.43 N 6.47 E
Abony 30 47.11 N 20.01 E
Aborigen, pik ▲ 74 61.59 N 149.19 E
Aborlan 116 9.26 N 118.33 E
Aborrebjerg ▲[2] 41 54.59 N 12.32 E
Aboso 150 5.22 N 1.56 W
Abō-tōge ✕ 94 36.11 N 137.35 E
Abou 144 4.21 N 43.03 E
Abou-Deïa 146 11.27 N 19.17 E
Abounamy ≐ 250 4.24 N 54.26 W
Aboyne 46 57.05 N 2.50 W
Abra ⊏[4] 116 17.35 N 120.50 E
Abra ≐ 116 17.31 N 120.23 E
Abraão 256 23.08 S 44.10 W
Abraham Lake ⊜[1] 182 52.15 N 116.23 W
Abraham Lincoln Birthplace National Historic Site ⫫ 194 37.32 N 85.44 W
Abrahamsdam 158 29.08 S 22.39 E
Abraka 150 5.50 N 6.05 E
Abram 262 53.31 N 2.35 W
Abramcevo 265b 55.50 N 37.50 E
Abramovka 78 51.12 N 41.01 E
Abramovskaja 24 65.11 N 51.43 E
Abram S. Hewitt State Forest ♦ 276 41.11 N 74.22 W
Abrantes 34 39.28 N 8.12 W
Abra Pampa 252 22.43 S 65.42 W
Abraq, Wādī al- V 146 26.27 N 18.48 E
Abrau-D'urso 78 44.43 N 37.37 E
Abra Vieja, Arroyo ≐ 288 34.26 S 58.34 W
Abre Campo 255 20.18 S 42.29 W
Ábrego 246 8.05 N 73.13 W
Abreojos, Punta ≻ 232 26.42 N 113.35 W
Abreschviller 58 48.38 N 7.06 E
Abreu e Lima 250 7.54 S 34.53 W
'Abrī, Sūd. 140 11.40 N 30.28 E
'Abrī, Sūd. 140 20.48 N 30.20 E
Abriachan 46 57.22 N 4.24 W
Abridge 260 51.39 N 0.07 E
Abriès 62 44.47 N 6.56 E
Abring 123 33.42 N 76.35 E
Abriola 68 40.30 N 15.49 E
Abrud 38 46.17 N 23.04 E
Abruka saar I 76 58.10 N 22.30 E
Abrunheira 266c 38.46 N 9.21 W
Abruzzi ⊏[4] 66 42.20 N 13.45 E
Abruzzo, Parco Nazionale d' ♦ 66 41.45 N 13.45 E
Absam 64 47.18 N 11.30 E
Absaroka Range ⋀ 202 44.45 N 109.50 W
Absarokee 202 45.31 N 109.26 W
Abscon 50 50.20 N 3.18 E
Absdorf 61 48.24 N 15.59 E
Absecon 208 39.25 N 74.29 W
Absecon Bay ⊂ 208 39.24 N 74.28 W
Abşeker 130 38.55 N 39.11 E
Abtenau 64 47.33 N 13.21 E
Abtsgmünd 56 48.54 N 10.00 E
Abtsteinach 56 49.33 N 8.47 E
Abu 96 34.30 N 131.28 E
Abu ≐ 96 34.25 N 131.24 E
Abū Ahl ▾[4] 128 34.06 N 43.45 E
Abū 'Alāwī, Wādī V 142 30.07 N 31.51 E
Abū al-Ghayṭ 273c 30.09 N 31.11 E
Abū al-Ḥamām, Jabal ▲ 132 30.27 N 35.38 E
Abū al-Hawl (Sphinx) ⫫ 142 29.59 N 31.08 E
Abū 'Alī I 128 27.20 N 49.33 E
Abū al-Khaṣīb 128 30.27 N 47.59 E
Abū al-Maṭāmīr 142 30.55 N 30.11 E
Abū al-'Urūq, Bi'r ▾[4] 142 30.45 N 32.23 E
Abū an-Numrus 273c 29.57 N 31.12 E
Abū 'Aradeib, Wādī V 140 14.12 N 23.06 E
Abū 'Arīsh 144 16.57 N 42.50 E
Abū Ballās ▲[2] 140 24.26 N 27.39 E
Abū Daraj, Ra's ≻ 142 29.23 N 32.34 E
Abū Dā'ūd, Ra's ≻ 128 23.19 N 58.55 E
Abū Dā'ūd as-Sibākh 142 30.55 N 31.34 E
Abū Dawm 140 16.16 N 32.36 E
Abū Dawm, Wādī V 140 18.28 N 31.49 E
Abu Dhabi → Abū Ẓaby 128 24.28 N 54.22 E
Abū Dhi'ābah, Wādī V 142 29.37 N 32.06 E
Abū Dīs 140 19.08 N 33.34 E
Abū Dulayq 140 15.54 N 33.49 E
Abufari 248 5.25 S 62.59 W
Abū Gatta Hills ⋀[2] 140 6.06 N 27.44 E
Abū Gelba 140 13.11 N 31.52 E
Abū Ghālib 142 30.16 N 30.56 E
Abū Ḥabl, Khawr V 140 12.49 N 31.15 E
Abū Ḥād, Wādī V 142 28.20 N 32.49 E
Abū Ḥadīmah, Bi'r ▾[4] 142 30.44 N 29.51 E
Abū Ḥamad 140 19.32 N 33.19 E
Abū Ḥammād al-Mahaṭṭah 142 30.32 N 31.40 E
Abū Ḥarāz, Sūd. 140 12.58 N 29.52 E
Abū Ḥarāz, Sūd. 140 19.04 N 32.07 E
Abū Ḥasan, Jabal ▲ 144 17.42 N 42.54 E
Abū Ḥummuṣ 142 31.06 N 30.19 E
Abū Ḥushsh, Bi'r ▾[4] 142 30.49 N 29.57 E
Abuja 150 9.12 N 7.11 E
Abū Jābirah 140 11.04 N 26.51 E
Abū Jandīr 142 29.14 N 30.41 E
Abū Jirj 142 28.32 N 30.47 E
Abū Jubayhah 140 11.27 N 31.14 E
Abū Kabīr 142 30.44 N 31.40 E
Abū Kamāl 130 34.27 N 40.55 E
Abū Kharjah, Wādī V 142 28.38 N 31.44 E
Abū Khashabah, Jabal ▲ 142 28.08 N 32.52 E
Abūksāh 142 29.23 N 30.42 E
Abū Kulaywāt 140 12.20 N 26.00 E
Abukuma ≐ 92 38.02 N 140.56 E
Abukuma-kōchi ⋀ 92 37.30 N 140.45 E
Abū Latt I 144 19.58 N 40.08 E
Abulug 116 18.27 N 121.27 E
Abulug ≐ 116 18.29 N 121.25 E
Abū Madd, Ra's ≻ 128 24.50 N 37.07 E
Abū Makhlūf, Bi'r ▾[4] 142 30.45 N 29.42 E
Abū Maṭāriq 140 10.58 N 26.17 E
Abu Mendi 144 11.47 N 35.43 E
Abū Minqār, Bi'r ▾[4] 140 26.30 N 27.35 E
Abumombazi 152 3.42 N 22.10 E
Abū Muḥammad, Bi'r ▾[4] 132 29.43 N 34.13 E
Abū Muḥarrik, Ghurd ≗[8] 140 27.50 N 29.40 E
Abū Mūsā I 128 25.52 N 55.03 E
Abunã 248 9.42 S 65.23 W
Abuná (Abunã) ≐ 248 9.41 S 65.23 W
Abū Na'āmah 140 12.44 N 34.08 E
Abune Yosef ▲ 144 12.10 N 39.12 E
Abū Qardī, Qā' ≚ 132 32.08 N 37.11 E
Abū Qashsh 132 31.57 N 35.11 E
Abū Qīr ◆[8] 142 31.19 N 30.04 E
Abū Qīr, Khalīj (Abu Qir Bay) ⊂ 142 31.23 N 30.13 E
Abū Qurqāṣ 142 27.56 N 30.50 E
Aburatsubo-kō ⊂ 268 35.09 N 139.38 E
Abū Rimth, Wādī V, Miṣr 142 28.45 N 31.27 E
Abū Rimth, Wādī V, Miṣr 142 30.21 N 31.53 E
Abū Rīshat, Wādī V 142 28.54 N 31.37 E
Ābu Road 120 24.29 N 72.47 E
Abū Rubayq 128 23.44 N 39.42 E
Abū Rujmayn, Jabal ⋀ 130 34.52 N 38.20 E
Abū Sanṭ, Wādī V 140 14.11 N 23.06 E
Abū Shajarah, Ra's ≻ 140 21.04 N 37.14 E
Abū Shāmah, Jabal ▲ 142 29.52 N 31.38 E
Abū Shanab, Sūd. 140 10.47 N 29.32 E
Abū Shanab, Sūd. 140 13.57 N 27.47 E
Abū Shaykhāt, Ḍahr ▲[2] 130 36.36 N 39.40 E
Abu Simbel → Abū Sunbul ⫫ 140 22.22 N 31.38 E
Abū Ṣīr 273c 29.53 N 31.13 E
Abu Ṣīr al-Malaq 142 29.15 N 31.05 E
Abū Ṣīr-Banā 142 30.55 N 31.15 E
Abū Ṣīr Pyramids ⫫ 273c 29.54 N 31.12 E
Abū Sulṭān 142 30.25 N 32.19 E
Abū Sunbul ⫫ 140 22.22 N 31.38 E
Abū Ṣuwayr al-Mahaṭṭah 142 30.34 N 32.07 E
Abū Ṣuwayr Military Base ■ 142 30.34 N 32.06 E
Abuta 92a 42.33 N 140.46 E
Abū Ṭabarī ▾[4] 140 17.35 N 28.31 E
Abū Ṭarafah, Wādī V 132 30.12 N 36.13 E
Abut Head ≻ 172 43.07 S 170.15 E
Abū Tīj 140 27.02 N 31.19 E
Abū Ṭunayṭin 140 14.24 N 31.01 E
Abū Ṭurayfīyah, Jabal ▲, Miṣr 142 29.58 N 32.06 E
Abū Ṭurayfīyah, Jabal ▲, Miṣr 142 29.42 N 31.49 E
Abū 'Uwayjilah ▾[4] 132 30.50 N 34.07 E
Abuye Meda ▲ 144 10.28 N 39.44 E
Abuyog 116 10.45 N 125.01 E
Abū Zabad 140 12.21 N 29.15 E
Abū Za'bal 142 30.15 N 31.21 E
Abū Ẓaby (Abu Dhabi) 128 24.28 N 54.22 E
Abū Zanīmah 140 29.03 N 33.06 E
Abwong 140 9.07 N 32.12 E
Åby 40 58.40 N 16.11 E
Åby ◆[8] 41 56.09 N 10.10 E
Aby, Lagune ⊂ 150 5.15 N 3.14 W
Abyaḍ 140 13.46 N 26.28 E
Abyaḍ, Al-Baḥr al- → White Nile ≐ 140 15.38 N 32.31 E
Abyaḍ, Wādī al- V 142 29.38 N 32.13 E
Åbyälven ≐ 26 65.01 N 21.24 E
Abyār 142 30.50 N 30.52 E
Abyār 'Alī 128 24.25 N 39.32 E
Åbybro 26 57.09 N 9.45 E
Abydos 162 21.25 S 118.54 E
Abyei 140 9.36 N 28.26 E
Åbyggeby 40 60.44 N 17.07 E
Åbytorp 40 59.07 N 15.04 E
Abzanovo 86 53.50 N 58.36 E
Acacías 246 3.59 N 73.46 W
Acacio 232 24.50 N 102.44 W
Academia 214 40.25 N 82.28 W
Academy Corners 208 41.57 N 77.23 W
Academy of Sciences ⫫[3] 282 37.46 N 122.28 W
Acadia National Park ♦ 188 44.18 N 68.15 W
Acadia Valley 184 51.08 N 110.13 W
Acahay 252 25.55 S 57.09 W
Acajete 234 19.06 N 97.57 W
Acajutiba 250 11.40 S 38.01 W
Acajutla 236 13.36 N 89.50 W
Acala 234 16.34 N 92.48 W
Acalayong 152 1.05 N 9.40 E
Acámbaro 234 20.02 N 100.44 W
Acampo 226 38.10 N 121.13 W
Acandí 246 8.32 N 77.14 W
Acaponeta 234 22.30 N 105.22 W
Acaponeta, Río de ≐ 234 22.20 N 105.37 W
Acapulco [de Juárez] 234 16.51 N 99.55 W
Acará 250 1.57 S 48.11 W
Acará ≐ 250 1.40 S 48.25 W
Acará, Cachoeira ⌞ 248 5.47 S 59.12 W
Acará, Lago ⊜ 246 3.39 S 62.40 W
Acaraí ≐ 250 2.02 S 52.15 W
Acarai Mountains ⋀ 246 1.50 N 57.40 W
Acará-Mirim ≐ 250 1.58 S 48.12 W
Acaraú 250 2.53 S 40.07 W
Acaraú ≐ 250 2.51 S 40.08 W
Acaray ≐ 252 25.29 S 54.42 W
Acari, Bra. 250 6.31 S 36.38 W
Acarí, Perú 248 15.26 S 74.37 W
Acari ≐, Bra. 248 5.18 S 59.42 W
Acari ≐, Bra. 255 16.00 S 45.03 W
Acarí ≐, Perú 248 15.39 S 74.39 W
Acarigua 246 9.33 N 69.12 W
Acate 70 37.02 N 14.28 E
Acate ≐ 70 37.00 N 14.20 E
Acatic 234 20.47 N 102.53 W
Acatlán 234 20.09 N 98.27 W
Acatlán ≐ 234 18.04 N 98.19 W
Acatlán de Juárez 234 20.26 N 103.38 W
Acatlán de Osorio 234 18.12 N 98.03 W
Acatlán [de Pérez Figueroa] 234 18.32 N 96.37 W
Acatzingo [de Hidalgo] 234 18.59 N 97.47 W
Acay, Nevado de ▲ 252 24.21 S 66.12 W
Acayucan 234 17.57 N 94.55 W
Accadia 68 41.10 N 15.20 E
Acceglio 62 44.28 N 7.00 E
Aččen, mys ≻ 180 64.45 N 175.30 W
Accettura 68 40.29 N 16.09 E
Ačchoj-Martan 84 43.11 N 45.18 E
Ačči 85 39.57 N 68.14 E
Acciano 66 42.10 N 13.43 E
Accokeek 208 38.40 N 77.02 W
Accomac 208 37.43 N 75.39 W
Accomack ⊏[6] 208 37.45 N 75.40 W
Accord, Ma., U.S. 283 42.10 N 70.53 W
Accord, N.Y., U.S. 210 41.47 N 74.13 W
Accord Brook ≐ 283 42.10 N 70.53 W
Accord Pond ⊜ 283 42.10 N 70.53 W
Accotink Creek ≐ 284c 38.46 N 77.13 W
Accotink Creek, Bear Branch ≐ 284c 38.52 N 77.15 W
Accotink Creek, Long Branch ≐ 284c 38.48 N 77.13 W
Accoville 192 37.46 N 81.50 W
Accra 150 5.33 N 0.13 W
Accra ⊏[4] 150 5.40 N 0.10 W
Accrington 262 53.46 N 2.21 W
Accumoli 66 42.42 N 13.15 E
Acebal 252 33.14 S 60.50 W
Acebuches 232 28.15 N 102.43 W
Aceguá 252 31.52 S 54.09 W
Aceh ⊏[4] 114 4.00 N 97.00 E
Aceh ≐ 114 5.36 N 95.20 E
Acerentia ⫫ 68 39.16 N 16.49 E
Acerenza 68 40.48 N 15.57 E
Acerno 68 40.44 N 15.03 E
Acerra 68 40.57 N 14.22 E
Acevedo 252 33.45 S 60.27 W
Achacachi 248 16.03 S 68.43 W
Achaguas 246 7.46 N 68.14 W
Achalciche 84 41.38 N 42.59 E
Achali-Kindgi 84 42.48 N 41.16 E
Achalkalaki 84 41.25 N 43.29 E
Achalpur 120 21.16 N 77.31 E
Achangaran 85 40.54 N 69.37 E
Achao 254 42.28 S 73.30 W
Achar 252 32.25 S 56.10 W
Acharacle 46 56.44 N 5.47 W
Achar uul ▲ 102 45.10 N 103.45 E
Achau 264b 48.05 N 16.23 E
Achavanich 46 58.22 N 3.24 W
Achelouma, Enneri V 146 21.55 N 13.35 E
Achêne 56 50.16 N 5.03 E
Acheng 89 45.32 N 126.59 E
Achenkirch 64 47.31 N 11.42 E
Achénouma 146 19.08 N 12.55 E
Achen Pass ✕ 64 47.35 N 11.38 E
Achensee ⊜ 64 47.28 N 11.42 E
Achères 261 48.58 N 2.04 E
Achern 56 48.37 N 8.04 E
Acheron ≐, Austl. 169 37.14 S 145.42 E
Acheron ≐, N.Z. 172 42.24 S 172.58 E
Acheux-en-Amiénois 50 50.04 N 2.32 E
Achhābal 123 33.41 N 75.14 E
Achhnera 124 27.11 N 77.46 E
Achí, Col. 246 8.34 N 74.33 W
Achi, Nihon 94 35.27 N 137.45 E
Achiasi 150 5.52 N 1.00 W
Achicourt 50 50.16 N 2.46 E
Achigan, Lac de l' ⊜ 206 45.56 N 73.58 W
Achiguate ≐ 236 13.55 N 90.55 W
Achill 28 53.56 N 9.54 W
Achilles 208 37.17 N 76.27 W
Achill Head ≻ 48 53.59 N 10.13 W
Achill Island I 48 54.00 N 10.00 W
Achill Sound 48 53.55 N 9.58 W
Achim 52 53.00 N 9.02 E
Achīn 120 34.08 N 70.42 E
Achiras 252 33.10 S 65.00 W
Achir-Ula, gora ▲ 88 50.21 N 94.31 E
Achmeta 84 42.02 N 45.13 E
Achnasaul 46 56.58 N 4.59 W
Achnasheen 46 57.35 N 5.06 W
Acho, Plaza de ♦ 286d 12.02 S 77.02 W
Achol 140 6.34 N 31.31 E
Achosnich 46 56.45 N 6.06 W
Achsu 84 40.34 N 48.24 E
Achterwasser ⊂ 54 54.00 N 13.57 E
Achterwehr 41 54.19 N 9.57 E
Achthuizen 52 51.42 N 4.16 E
Achtuba 80 51.37 N 44.22 E
Achtuba ≐ 80 46.42 N 48.00 E
Achtubinsk 80 48.17 N 46.10 E
Achty 84 41.28 N 47.43 E
Achtyrka 78 50.19 N 34.55 E
Achtyrskij 78 44.52 N 38.20 E
Achur'an (Arpaçay) ≐ 84 40.06 N 43.39 E
Achwa ≐ 154 3.43 N 31.55 E
Ači 85 41.17 N 73.02 E
Aci Castello 70 37.33 N 15.08 E
Aci Catena 70 37.36 N 15.08 E
Acıgöl 130 38.35 N 34.31 E
Acı Göl ⊜ 130 37.50 N 29.54 E
Acikak 88 54.11 N 106.18 E
Ačikulak 84 44.34 N 44.50 E
Acilia ◆[8] 267a 41.47 N 12.22 E
Ačimovy Vtoryje 86 60.04 N 75.12 E
Ačinsk 86 56.17 N 90.30 E
Acıpayam 130 37.25 N 29.22 E
Acireale 70 37.37 N 15.10 E
Acîș 38 47.33 N 22.47 E
Ačisaj 85 43.35 N 68.53 E
Aci Sant'Antonio 70 37.36 N 15.07 E
Ačisu 84 42.38 N 47.40 E
Ačit 86 56.48 N 57.54 E
Ačit nuur ⊜ 86 49.30 N 90.30 E
Ackerly 196 32.32 N 101.43 W
Ackerman 194 33.18 N 89.10 W
Ackermanville 210 40.49 N 75.17 W
Ackerson Lake 216 42.11 N 84.20 W
Ackley 190 42.33 N 93.03 W
Acklins, The Bight of ⊂[3] 238 22.30 N 74.15 W
Acklins Island I 238 22.26 N 73.58 W
Acland, Mount ▲ 166 24.55 S 148.05 E
Acle 42 52.38 N 1.33 E
Aclimação ◆[8] 287b 23.34 S 46.37 W
Acme, Ab., Can. 182 51.30 N 113.30 W
Acme, Pa., U.S. 214 40.08 N 79.26 W
Acme, Wa., U.S. 224 48.43 N 122.12 W
Acmetonia 279b 40.32 N 79.49 W
Acobamba 248 12.48 S 74.34 W
Acolla 248 11.44 S 75.34 W
Acolman ⊏[7] 286a 19.37 N 98.58 W
Acoma Indian Reservation ◆[4] 200 34.52 N 107.40 W
Acomayo, Perú 248 13.55 S 71.41 W
Acomayo, Perú 248 9.46 S 76.05 W
Aconcagua, Cerro ▲ 252 32.39 S 70.01 W
Aconchi 232 29.50 N 110.12 W
Aconibe 152 1.18 N 10.56 E
Acopiara 250 6.06 S 39.27 W
Açores (Azores) II 148a 38.30 N 28.00 W
Acoria 248 12.37 S 74.53 W
Acorizal 248 15.12 S 56.22 W
Acornhoek 156 24.37 S 31.02 E
Acosta 214 40.07 N 79.04 W
Acoyapa 236 11.58 N 85.10 W
Acoyapa ≐ 236 11.48 N 85.16 W
Acquabona, Passo di ✕ 68 39.02 N 16.20 E
Acquacalda 70 38.31 N 14.57 E
Acqualagna 66 43.37 N 12.40 E
Acquanegra sul Chiese 64 45.10 N 10.26 E
Acquapendente 66 42.44 N 11.52 E
Acquappesa 68 39.29 N 15.57 E
Acquarossa 58 46.28 N 8.57 E
Acquasanta Terme 66 42.46 N 13.24 E
Acquasparta 66 42.41 N 12.33 E
Acquaviva 66 43.57 N 12.25 E
Acquaviva delle Fonti 68 40.54 N 16.50 E
Acquaviva Platani 70 37.34 N 13.42 E
Acqui Terme 62 44.41 N 8.28 E
Acra 210 42.19 N 74.03 W
Acraman, Lake ⊜ 162 32.02 S 135.26 E
Acre → 'Akko 132 32.55 N 35.05 E
Acre ⊏[3] 248 9.00 S 70.00 W
Acre ≐ 248 8.45 S 67.22 W
Acre Homes 222 29.53 N 95.27 W
Acri 68 39.29 N 16.23 E
Acropolis ⫫ 267c 37.58 N 23.43 E
Acrotambo, Cerro ▲ 248 8.50 S 76.50 W
Acton, On., Can. 212 43.37 N 80.02 W
Acton, Ca., U.S. 228 34.28 N 118.11 W
Acton, Ma., U.S. 207 42.29 N 71.26 W
Acton, Tx., U.S. 222 32.27 N 97.41 W
Acton ◆[8] 260 51.30 N 0.16 W
Acton Bridge 262 53.16 N 2.36 W
Acton Homes 158 28.36 S 29.26 E
Acton Lake ⊜ 218 39.34 N 84.45 W
Acton Turville 42 51.32 N 2.17 W
Acton-Vale 206 45.39 N 72.34 W
Actopan 234 20.16 N 98.56 W
Actopan ≐ 234 19.25 N 96.20 W
Açu 250 5.34 S 36.54 W
Açu, Igarapé ≐ 250 3.44 S 55.31 W
Açuã ≐ 248 7.12 S 64.11 W
Açucena 255 19.04 S 42.32 W
Acuitzio del Canje 234 19.29 N 101.20 W
Ačujevo 78 45.43 N 37.45 E
Acuña 252 29.55 S 57.58 W
Acuracay 248 5.35 S 74.10 W
Acurauá ≐ 248 7.37 S 70.48 W
Acurenam 152 1.02 N 10.40 E
Acushnet 207 41.41 N 70.55 W
Acuto 66 41.47 N 13.10 E
Acvež 80 58.21 N 47.46 E
Acworth 192 34.03 N 84.40 W
Ada, Ghana 150 5.47 N 0.24 E
Ada, Jugo. 38 45.48 N 20.08 E
Ada, Nihon 174m 26.44 N 128.19 E
Ada, Mi., U.S. 216 42.57 N 85.29 W
Ada, Mn., U.S. 198 47.18 N 96.31 W
Ada, Oh., U.S. 216 40.46 N 83.49 W
Ada, Ok., U.S. 196 34.46 N 96.40 W
Ada, Mount ▲ 180 56.41 N 134.41 W
Adaba 144 7.00 N 39.24 E
A-da-Beja 266c 38.47 N 9.14 W
'Adabīyah, Ra's ≻ 142 29.52 N 32.30 E
Adachi ◆[8] 268 35.45 N 139.48 E
Adachi-yama ▲ 96 33.51 N 130.55 E
Adado, Ras ≻ 144 11.20 N 48.40 E
Adâfer el Abiod ◆[1] 150 19.30 N 10.00 W
Adai 272c 19.01 N 73.08 E
Adailo 144 14.29 N 40.52 E
Adainville 261 48.43 N 1.39 E
Adair, Ia., U.S. 198 41.22 N 94.19 W
Adair, Ok., U.S. 196 36.26 N 95.16 W
Adair ⊏[6] 219 40.08 N 92.22 W
Adair, Bahía de ⊂ 232 31.30 N 113.48 W
Adair, Cape ≻ 176 71.24 N 71.13 W
Adairsville 192 34.22 N 84.56 W
Adairville 194 36.40 N 86.51 W
Adaja ≐ 34 41.32 N 4.52 W
Adajevka 86 51.47 N 62.06 E
Adak, S.S.S.R. 24 66.30 N 59.38 E
Adak, Ak., U.S. 180 51.54 N 176.35 W
Adaka-shima I 174m 26.45 N 128.20 E
Adak Island I 180 51.45 N 176.40 W
Adaklı 130 39.14 N 40.30 E
Ådalen V 26 63.10 N 17.16 E
Ādam 118 22.24 N 57.32 E
Adam, Mount ▲ 254 51.36 S 59.55 W
Adamantina 255 21.42 S 51.04 W
Adamaoua ⋀ 152 7.00 N 12.00 E
Adamawa → Adamaoua ⋀ 152 7.00 N 12.00 E
Adamclisi 38 44.05 N 27.57 E
Adamello ⋀ 64 46.10 N 10.35 E
Adaminaby 171b 36.03 S 148.43 E
Adami Tulu 144 7.52 N 38.42 E
Adamovka 86 51.32 N 59.56 E
Adamovskoje 82 54.52 N 35.57 E
Adamów 30 51.45 N 22.17 E
Ādampur 123 31.26 N 75.43 E
Adams, In., U.S. 218 39.22 N 85.33 W
Adams, Ma., U.S. 207 42.37 N 73.07 W
Adams, Mn., U.S. 190 43.33 N 92.43 W
Adams, Ne., U.S. 198 40.27 N 96.30 W
Adams, N.Y., U.S. 212 43.48 N 76.01 W
Adams, N.D., U.S. 198 48.25 N 98.04 W
Adams, Tn., U.S. 194 36.34 N 87.03 W
Adams, Wi., U.S. 190 43.57 N 89.49 W
Adams ⊏[6], Il., U.S. 219 39.56 N 91.23 W
Adams ⊏[6], In., U.S. 216 40.50 N 84.56 W
Adams ⊏[6], Oh., U.S. 218 38.48 N 83.32 W
Adams ⊏[6], Pa., U.S. 208 39.48 N 77.15 W
Adams ≐ 182 50.52 N 119.35 W
Adams, Mount ▲, N.Z. 172 41.19 S 175.46 E
Adams, Mount ▲, Wa., U.S. 224 46.12 N 121.28 W
Adams Bridge ✢[2] 122 9.04 N 79.37 E
Adamsburg 279b 40.19 N 79.40 W
Adams Center 212 43.51 N 76.00 W
Adams Creek ≐ 224 46.18 N 121.40 W
Adams Lake ⊜ 182 51.13 N 119.33 W
Adams Mills 214 40.09 N 81.57 W
Adams National Historic Site ⫫ 283 42.15 N 71.01 W
Adams Park 216 42.08 N 85.29 W
Adams Park ♦ 275b 43.48 N 79.09 W
Adams Peak ▲ 122 6.48 N 80.30 E
Adams Rock I[2] 174e 25.04 S 130.05 W
Adamston 208 40.02 N 74.05 W
Adamstown, Austl. 170 32.56 S 151.44 E
Adamstown, Pit. 174e 25.04 S 130.05 W
Adamstown, Md., U.S. 208 39.18 N 77.28 W
Adamstown, Pa., U.S. 208 40.14 N 76.03 W
Adamsville, P.Q., Can. 206 45.17 N 72.47 W
Adamsville, Mi., U.S. 216 41.47 N 86.00 W
Adamsville, Oh., U.S. 214 40.04 N 81.53 W
Adamsville, Pa., U.S. 214 41.31 N 80.22 W
Adamsville, Tn., U.S. 194 35.14 N 88.23 W
'Adan (Aden) 144 12.45 N 45.12 E
Adana 130 37.01 N 35.18 E
Adana ⊏[4] 130 37.20 N 35.45 E
Adanero 34 40.56 N 4.36 W
Adapazarı 130 40.46 N 30.24 E
Adarama 140 17.05 N 34.54 E
Adare 48 52.34 N 8.48 W
Adare, Cape ≻ 9 71.17 S 170.14 E
Adar Gwagwa, Jabal ▲ 140 22.15 N 35.20 E
Adarot 140 17.50 N 36.07 E
Adaševo 80 53.56 N 44.19 E
Adauli 272c 19.06 N 73.02 E
Adaut 164 8.08 S 131.07 E
Adavale 166 25.55 S 144.36 E
Adda ≐, It. 36 45.08 N 9.53 E
Adda ≐, Sūd. 140 9.51 N 24.50 E
Aḍ-Ḍab'ah 140 31.02 N 28.26 E
Ad-Dabbah 140 18.03 N 30.57 E
Ad-Dafīnah 128 23.18 N 41.58 E
Aḍ-Ḍafrah ◆[1] 128 23.25 N 53.25 E
Ad-Dahnā' ◆[2] 128 24.30 N 48.10 E
Ad-Daljamūn 142 30.48 N 30.50 E
Ad-Damazin 140 11.49 N 34.23 E
Ad-Dāmir 140 17.35 N 33.58 E
Ad-Dammām 128 26.26 N 50.07 E
Ad-Dāmūr 132 33.44 N 35.27 E
Ad-Dānā 130 36.13 N 36.46 E
Ad-Daqahlīyah ⊏[4] 142 31.10 N 31.30 E
Ad-Darb 144 17.43 N 42.15 E
Ad-Dawādimī 128 24.28 N 44.18 E
Ad-Dawḥah (Doha) 128 25.17 N 51.32 E
Ad-Dayr, Miṣr 140 25.20 N 32.35 E
Ad-Dayr, Miṣr 142 30.20 N 31.16 E
Adderbury 42 52.00 N 1.17 W
Ad-Dibdibah ◆[1] 128 28.00 N 46.30 E
Addicks 222 29.47 N 95.39 W
Addicks Reservoir ⊜[1] 222 29.49 N 95.40 W
Addieville 219 38.23 N 89.29 W
Aḍ-Ḍiffah (Libyan Plateau) ⋀[1] 140 30.30 N 25.30 E
Ad-Dilam 128 23.59 N 47.12 E
Ad-Dilinjāt 142 30.50 N 30.30 E
Ad-Dīmās 132 33.35 N 36.05 E
Addingham 44 53.57 N 1.53 W
Addington 260 51.18 N 0.23 E
Addis 194 30.21 N 91.15 W
Addis Ababa → Adis Abeba 144 9.02 N 38.42 E
Addison, Il., U.S. 216 41.55 N 87.59 W
Addison, Mi., U.S. 216 41.59 N 84.21 W
Addison, N.Y., U.S. 210 42.06 N 77.14 W
Addison, Tx., U.S. 222 32.57 N 96.49 W
Addison Creek ≐ 278 41.51 N 87.51 W
Ad-Dīwānīyah 128 31.59 N 44.56 E
Addlestone 260 51.22 N 0.30 W
Addo 158 33.32 S 25.45 E
Addo Elephant National Park ♦ 158 33.29 S 25.46 E
Ad-Du'ayn 140 11.26 N 26.09 E
Aḍ-Ḍuhayr 132 31.11 N 34.08 E
Ad-Duqqī 273c 30.04 N 31.15 E
Ad-Duwayd 128 30.15 N 42.17 E
Ad-Duwaym 140 14.00 N 32.19 E
Ad-Duwayr 132 33.23 N 35.25 E
Adébour 146 13.20 N 11.54 E
Adegem 50 51.12 N 3.29 E
Adego 144 8.58 N 49.35 E
Adel, Ga., U.S. 192 31.08 N 83.25 W

ENGLISH | Name | Page | Lat.°′ | Long.°′

Adel, Ia., U.S. 190 41.36 N 94.01 W
Adelaida → Adelaide 168b 34.55 S 138.35 E
Adelaide, Austl. 168b 34.55 S 138.35 E
Adelaide, Ba. 240b 25.00 N 77.31 W
Adelaide, S. Afr. 158 32.42 S 26.20 E
Adelaide Airport ⊠ 168b 34.58 S 138.32 E
Adelaide Island I 9 67.15 S 68.30 W
Adelaide Peninsula ≻[1] 176 68.09 N 97.45 W
Adelaide River 164 13.15 S 131.06 E
Adelanto 228 34.34 N 117.24 W
Adelbert Range ⋀ 164 4.35 S 145.10 E
Adelboden 58 46.30 N 7.33 E
Adelebsen 52 51.34 N 9.45 E
Adèle Island I 160 15.32 S 123.09 E
Adelfia 68 41.00 N 16.52 E
Adélie Coast ≗[2] 9 67.00 S 139.00 E
Adelong 171b 35.19 S 148.03 E
Adelong Creek ≐ 171b 35.06 S 148.02 E
Adelphi 284c 39.00 N 76.58 W
Adelphia 208 40.13 N 74.15 W
Adelphi University ⫫[2] 276 40.43 N 73.36 W
Adelsheim 56 49.24 N 9.23 E
Adelsö I 40 59.23 N 17.30 E
Adelzhausen 60 48.21 N 11.08 E
Aden → 'Adan 144 12.45 N 45.12 E
Aden, Gulf of ⊂ 136 12.30 N 48.00 E
Adena 214 40.13 N 80.52 W
Adenau 56 50.23 N 6.55 E
Adendorf 52 53.17 N 10.26 E
Adendorp 158 32.20 S 24.33 E
Ader ⋀[1] 150 14.50 N 5.15 E
Aderklaa 264b 48.17 N 16.32 E
Adéta 150 7.08 N 0.44 E
Adhāta 272b 22.52 N 88.32 E
'Ādhirīyāt, Jibāl al- ⋀[2] 132 30.25 N 36.48 E
Adi 154 3.24 N 30.48 E
Adi, Pulau I 164 4.18 S 133.26 E
Adiaké 150 5.16 N 3.17 W
Adi Arkay 144 13.27 N 37.57 E
Adi Dairo 144 14.23 N 38.12 E
Adieu, Cape ≻ 162 31.59 S 132.09 E
Adigala 144 10.25 N 42.14 E
Adige (Etsch) ≐ 64 45.10 N 12.20 E
Adigeni 84 41.42 N 42.42 E
Adigrat 144 14.17 N 39.28 E
Adıgüzel Barajı ⊜[1] 130 38.10 N 29.15 E
Adi Keyih 144 14.51 N 39.22 E
Adi Kwala 144 14.38 N 38.50 E
Ādilābād 122 19.40 N 78.32 E
Adilang 154 2.44 N 33.29 E
Adilcevaz 84 38.44 N 42.44 E
Adimi 89 47.20 N 138.56 E
Adin 204 41.11 N 120.56 W
Adinkerke 50 51.04 N 2.36 E
Adirondack Mountains ⋀ 188 44.00 N 74.00 W
Adirondack Park ♦ 188 44.00 N 74.20 W
Adis Abeba (Addis Ababa) 144 9.02 N 38.42 E
Adis Zemen 144 12.07 N 37.47 E
Adi Ugri 144 14.53 N 38.49 E
Adiwerna 115a 6.56 S 109.07 E
Adıyaman 130 37.46 N 38.17 E
Adıyaman ⊏[4] 130 37.45 N 38.30 E
Adjan 112 2.11 N 113.12 E
Adjelman, Oued V 148 22.09 N 3.47 E
Adjohon 150 6.42 N 2.28 E
Adjud 38 46.04 N 27.11 E
Adjumani 154 3.22 N 31.47 E
Adjuntas 240m 18.10 N 66.43 W
Adjuntas, Presa de las ⊜[1] 234 24.00 N 98.50 W
Adler 78 43.27 N 39.55 E
Adler Planetarium ⫫ 278 41.52 N 87.37 W
Adlershof ◆[8] 264a 52.26 N 13.33 E
Adlington 262 53.37 N 2.36 W
Adlington Hall ⫫ 262 53.19 N 2.09 W
Adliswil 58 47.19 N 8.32 E
Admer, Erg d' ◆[2] 148 24.00 N 9.15 E
Admiral 184 49.43 N 108.01 W
Admiralitäts-Inseln → Admiralty Islands II 164 2.10 S 147.00 E
Admiralty Bay ⊂, St. Vin. 241h 13.00 N 61.16 W
Admiralty Bay ⊂, Ak., U.S. 180 70.53 N 155.45 W
Admiralty Gulf ⊂ 160 14.20 S 125.50 E
Admiralty Gulf Aboriginal Reserve ◆[4] 164 14.40 S 125.30 E
Admiralty Inlet ⊂, N.T., Can. 176 73.00 N 86.00 W
Admiralty Inlet ⊂, Wa., U.S. 224 48.05 N 122.39 W
Admiralty Island I, N.T., Can. 176 69.30 N 101.00 W
Admiralty Island I, Ak., U.S. 180 57.50 N 134.30 W
Admiralty Islands II 164 2.10 S 147.00 E
Admiralty Mountains ⋀ 9 71.45 S 168.30 E
Admont 61 47.34 N 14.27 E
Adna 224 46.38 N 123.04 W
Ado ≐ 94 35.19 N 136.05 E
Adobe Creek ≐, Ca., U.S. 282 37.26 N 122.06 W
Adobe Creek ≐, Co., U.S. 198 38.05 N 103.18 W
Ado-Ekiti 150 7.38 N 5.12 E
Adogawa 94 35.20 N 136.02 E
Adok 140 8.11 N 30.19 E
Adolfo López Mateos, Presa ⊜[1] 232 25.13 N 107.25 W
Adolfo Ruíz Cortines 232 25.40 N 108.40 W
Adolfsberg 40 59.15 N 15.10 E
Adolphus Reach ⌞ 212 44.05 N 76.55 W
Adonara, Pulau I 112 8.20 S 123.10 E
Ādoni 122 15.38 N 77.17 E
Ado-Odo 150 6.36 N 2.56 E
Adorf 54 50.19 N 12.15 E
Adoua, Korén V 150 14.37 N 6.40 E
Adour ≐ 32 43.32 N 1.32 W
Adowa → Adwa 144 14.10 N 38.55 E
Adra, Esp. 34 36.44 N 3.01 W
Ādra, India 126 23.30 N 86.40 E
'Adrā, Sūrīy. 132 33.37 N 36.30 E
Adranga 154 2.54 N 30.26 E
Adrano 70 37.40 N 14.50 E
Adrar 148 27.54 N 0.17 W
Adrar ⊏[4] 150 20.05 N 11.00 W
Adrar ⊏[5] 148 26.00 N 1.00 W
Adrâr ◆[1] 134 20.30 N 13.30 W
Adraskan 128 33.39 N 62.16 E
Adrasman 85 40.38 N 69.58 E
Adré 146 13.28 N 22.12 E
Adrī 146 27.32 N 13.14 E
Adria 64 45.03 N 12.03 E
Adrian, Ga., U.S. 192 32.31 N 82.35 W
Adrian, Mi., U.S. 216 41.53 N 84.02 W
Adrian, Mn., U.S. 198 43.38 N 95.55 W
Adrian, Mo., U.S. 194 38.23 N 94.21 W
Adrian, Oh., U.S. 214 41.03 N 83.20 W
Adrian, Or., U.S. 202 43.44 N 117.04 W
Adrian, Pa., U.S. 214 40.53 N 79.32 W
Adrian, Tx., U.S. 196 35.16 N 102.40 W
Adrian, W.V., U.S. 188 38.54 N 80.16 W
Adrianople → Edirne 130 41.40 N 26.34 E
Adrianópolis 287a 22.39 S 43.30 W
Adrianovka 88 51.34 N 114.30 E
Adriatico, Mar → Adriatic Sea ▾[2] 22 42.30 N 16.00 E
Adriatic Sea ▾[2] 22 42.30 N 16.00 E
Adriatique, Mer → Adriatic Sea ▾[2] 22 42.30 N 16.00 E
Adriatisches Meer → Adriatic Sea ▾[2] 22 42.30 N 16.00 E

DEUTSCH | Name | Seite | Breite°′ | Länge°′ E = Ost

Adrigole 48 51.40 N 9.42 W
Adro 64 45.37 N 9.57 E
Adrogué → Almirante Brown 258 34.48 S 58.23 W
Adstock, Mont ▲ 206 46.02 N 71.12 W
Adua 164 1.55 S 129.50 E
Aduard 52 53.15 N 6.26 E
Adujevo 82 54.59 N 35.59 E
Aduku 154 2.01 N 32.43 E
A Dun ≐ 110 13.24 N 108.28 E
Adur ≐ 42 50.49 N 0.16 W
Adusa 154 1.23 N 28.01 E
Adutiškis 76 55.09 N 26.36 E
Advance 194 37.06 N 89.54 W
Adventure, Bahía ⌞ 254 44.50 S 74.45 W
Advie 46 57.23 N 3.27 W
Advocate Harbour 186 45.20 N 64.47 W
Adwa 144 14.10 N 38.55 E
Adwick le Street 44 53.34 N 1.11 W
Adyča ≐ 74 68.13 N 134.41 E
Adyge 84 44.19 N 41.57 E
Adygejskaja Avtonomnaja Oblast' ⊏[8] 78 45.00 N 40.00 E
Adyk 80 45.48 N 45.38 E
Adžarskaja Avtonomnaja Sovetskaja Socialističeskaja Respublika ⊏[3] 84 41.40 N 42.00 E
Adž Bogd uul ⋀ 102 44.52 N 95.10 E
Adžikend 84 40.31 N 46.21 E
Adžima 89 48.08 N 139.40 E
Adzopé 150 6.06 N 3.52 W
Adz'va ≐ 24 66.36 N 59.28 E
Adz'vavom 24 66.36 N 59.12 E
Ae, Water of ≐ 44 55.08 N 3.27 W
Æbelø I 41 55.38 N 10.12 E
Aegean Sea ▾[2] 38 38.30 N 25.00 E
Aegerisee ⊜ 58 47.07 N 8.38 E
Aegina → Aíyina I 38 37.46 N 23.26 E
Aegviidu 76 59.17 N 25.37 E
Aek Humbang 114 1.59 N 99.11 E
Aeknabara 114 1.17 N 99.45 E
Aeon Point ≻ 174o 1.46 N 157.11 W
Aerhuola 89 51.01 N 120.10 E
Aerku Hu ⊜ 120 30.43 N 82.55 E
Ærø I 41 54.53 N 10.20 E
Aeroflotskij 78 45.03 N 34.01 E
Aeron ≐ 42 52.14 N 4.16 W
Aeroparque ⊠ 288 34.35 S 58.24 W
Ærøskøbing 41 54.53 N 10.25 E
Aerqi Shan ▲ 89 48.35 N 121.07 E
Aershatu 102 44.11 N 113.36 E
Aerzen 52 52.03 N 9.16 E
Aesch 58 47.28 N 7.36 E
Aeschi 58 46.40 N 7.42 E
Aetna 182 49.08 N 113.15 W
Afaahiti 174s 17.43 S 149.19 W
Afadé 146 12.14 N 14.38 E
Afadjoto ▲[2] 150 7.05 N 0.35 E
'Afak 128 32.04 N 45.15 E
Afan ≐ 42 51.35 N 3.48 W
Afanasjevka 78 50.47 N 38.36 E
Afanasjevo, S.S.S.R. 24 58.52 N 53.12 E
Afanasjevo, S.S.S.R. 82 54.20 N 37.01 E
Afanasjevo, S.S.S.R. 82 55.18 N 36.12 E
Afanasjevskoje 86 56.49 N 58.17 E
Afándou 38 36.17 N 28.10 E
Afar 148 25.30 N 8.22 E
Afareaitu 174s 17.33 S 149.47 W
Afars and Issas → Djibouti ⊏[1] 144 11.30 N 43.00 E
Afaspida 272c 19.08 N 73.04 E
Afdem 144 9.28 N 41.00 E
Afferde, B.R.D. 52 52.06 N 9.25 E
Afferde, B.R.D. 263 51.34 N 7.39 E
Afféry 150 6.19 N 3.57 W
Affi 64 45.33 N 10.46 E
Affing 58 48.27 N 10.58 E
Afflisses, Oued V 148 28.29 N 1.09 E
Affoltern am Albis 58 47.17 N 8.27 E
Affori ◆[8] 266b 45.31 N 9.10 E
Affric ≐ 46 57.19 N 4.50 W
Affric, Glen V 46 57.17 N 4.56 W
Affton 219 38.33 N 90.19 W
Afghānestān → Afghanistan ⊏[1] 118 33.00 N 65.00 E
Afghanistan (Afghānestān) ⊏[1] 118 33.00 N 65.00 E
Afgooye 144 2.09 N 45.07 E
Afia 114 1.23 N 97.32 E
'Afīf 128 23.55 N 42.56 E
Afikpo 150 5.53 N 7.56 E
Afipskij 78 44.55 N 38.50 E
Afiqim 132 32.40 N 35.35 E
Åfjord 26 63.58 N 10.12 E
Aflao 150 6.05 N 1.08 E
Aflenz Kurort 61 47.32 N 15.14 E
Aflou 148 34.07 N 2.06 E
Afmadow 144 0.31 N 42.04 E
Afodo 144 10.14 N 34.39 E
Afogados da Ingàzeira 250 7.45 S 37.39 W
Afognak Island I 180 58.15 N 152.30 W
Afollé ⋀[2] 150 16.55 N 10.25 W
Afonicha 24 68.13 N 53.17 E
Afono Bay ⊂ 174u 14.15 S 170.39 W
Afonso Bezerra 250 5.30 S 36.30 W
Afonso Cláudio 255 20.05 S 41.08 W
Afonsos, Campo dos ■ 287a 22.53 S 43.23 W
Afonsos, Rio dos ≐ 287a 22.51 S 43.23 W
Afragola 68 40.55 N 14.18 E
Afram ≐ 150 7.00 N 0.52 W
Afrera YeChew Hayk ⊜ 144 13.17 N 40.54 E
Africa ≗[1] 4 10.00 N 22.00 E
Africa ≗[1] 10 10.00 N 22.00 E
Africa del Sur → South Africa ⊏[1] 156 30.00 S 26.00 E
Africo 68 38.04 N 15.59 E
Afrika → Africa ≗[1] 10 10.00 N 22.00 E
Afrikanda 24 67.25 N 32.43 E
'Afrīn 130 36.31 N 36.52 E
'Afrīn ≐ 130 36.22 N 36.28 E
Afrique → Africa ≗[1] 10 10.00 N 22.00 E
Afrique du Sud (République d') → South Africa ⊏[1] 156 30.00 S 26.00 E
Afritz 64 46.43 N 13.48 E
Afşin 130 38.15 N 36.55 E
Afsluitdijk ◆[5] 52 53.00 N 5.15 E
Afton, De., U.S. 285 39.49 N 75.29 W
Afton, Ia., U.S. 194 41.01 N 94.11 W
Afton, N.Y., U.S. 210 42.13 N 75.31 W
Afton, Ok., U.S. 196 36.41 N 94.57 W
Afton, Wi., U.S. 216 42.36 N 89.04 W
Afton, Wy., U.S. 200 42.43 N 110.55 W
Aftout ◆[1] 148 26.40 N 3.48 W
Afuá 250 0.10 S 50.23 W
'Afula 132 32.36 N 35.17 E
'Afula 'Illit 132 32.38 N 35.20 E
Afulu 114 1.17 N 97.15 E
Afyon 130 38.45 N 30.33 E
Afyon ⊏[4] 130 38.40 N 30.30 E
Afyonkarahisar → Afyon 130 38.45 N 30.33 E
Afzalgarh 124 29.24 N 78.41 E
Aga, Nor. 26 60.18 N 6.36 E
Aga, S.S.S.R. 88 51.12 N 115.10 E
Aga ≐ 88 51.30 N 115.50 E
Agačag 85 44.03 N 71.58 E
Ağaçören 130 38.52 N 33.56 E
Agadez 150 16.58 N 7.59 E
Agadez ⊏[5] 146 19.45 N 12.00 E
Agadez, Ighazer oua-n- V 150 17.28 N 6.26 E
Agadir 148 30.26 N 9.36 W

Symbols in the index entries represent the broad categories identified in the key at the right. Symbols with superior numbers (⋀[1]) identify subcategories (see complete key on page *I* · *1*).

Symbole im Register stellen die rechts im Schlüssel erklärten Kategorien dar. Symbole mit hochgestellten Ziffern (⋀[1]) bezeichnen Unterabteilungen einer Kategorie (vgl. vollständiger Schlüssel auf Seite *I* · *1*).

Los símbolos incluídos en el texto del índice representan las grandes categorías identificadas con la clave a la derecha. Los símbolos con numeros en su parte superior (⋀[1]) identifican las subcategorías (véase la clave completa en la página *I* · *1*).

Les symboles de l'index représentent les catégories indiquées dans la légende à droite. Les symboles suivis d'un indice (⋀[1]) représentent des sous-catégories (voir légende complète à la page *I* · *1*).

Os símbolos incluídos no texto do índice representam as grandes categorias identificadas com a chave à direita. Os símbolos com números em sua parte superior (⋀[1]) identificam as subcategorias (veja-se a chave completa à página *I* · *1*).

▲ Mountain	Berg	Montaña	Montagne	Montanha
⋀ Mountains	Gebirge	Montañas	Montagnes	Montanhas
✕ Pass	Paß	Paso	Col	Passo
V Valley, Canyon	Tal, Cañon	Valle, Cañón	Vallée, Canyon	Vale, Canhão
≚ Plain	Ebene	Llano	Plaine	Planície
≻ Cape	Kap	Cabo	Cap	Cabo
I Island	Insel	Isla	Île	Ilha
II Islands	Inseln	Islas	Îles	Ilhas
≗ Other Topographic Features	Andere Topographische Objekte	Otros Elementos Topográficos	Autres données topographiques	Outros acidentes topográficos

ESPAÑOL · FRANÇAIS · PORTUGUÊS

Nombre / Nom / Nome	Página / Page / Página	Lat.°′	Long.°′ W = Oeste / W = Ouest
Agadir □[4]	148	30.40 N	8.55 W
Agâdîr, Râs ›	148	20.34 N	16.32 W
Agadyr'	86	48.17 N	72.53 E
Agafonovka	80	50.36 N	47.26 E
Agāhpur	272a	28.34 N	77.22 E
Agaie	150	9.03 N	6.18 E
Ägäisches Meer → Aegean Sea ⊤[2]	38	38.30 N	25.00 E
Agalak	140	11.01 N	32.42 E
Agalega Islands II	138	10.24 S	56.37 E
Agal Terara ∧	144	6.57 N	40.08 E
Agan ≃	72	61.23 N	74.35 E
Agana	174p	13.28 N	144.45 E
Agana Heights	174p	13.28 N	144.45 E
Agano ≃	92	37.57 N	139.08 E
Agapa	74	71.27 N	89.15 E
Aga Point ›	174p	13.15 N	144.43 E
Agapovka	86	53.18 N	59.28 E
Agar	120	23.42 N	76.01 E
Agara	84	42.03 N	43.49 E
Agâraktem ⊤[4]	148	23.11 N	6.20 W
Ågård	41	55.35 N	9.26 E
Agaro	144	7.50 N	36.40 E
Agartala	120	23.49 N	91.16 E
Agartu	80	49.49 N	47.06 E
Agaru	140	10.59 N	34.44 E
Agaruut	102	43.10 N	109.26 E
Agasan	272c	19.11 N	73.04 E
Agassiz	224	49.14 N	121.46 W
Agassiz, Cape ›	9	68.29 S	62.56 W
Agassiz Pool ⊜	198	48.20 N	95.58 W
Agat	174p	13.24 N	144.39 E
Agat Bay ⊂	174p	13.24 N	144.39 E
Agate	198	39.27 N	103.56 W
Agate Beach	202	44.40 N	124.03 W
Agate Fossil Beds National Monument ♦	198	42.25 N	103.43 W
Agathonísion I	38	37.28 N	27.00 E
Agats	164	5.33 S	138.08 E
Agatsuma	94	36.34 N	138.50 E
Agatsuma ≃	94	36.30 N	139.01 E
Agatti Island I	122	10.50 N	72.12 E
Agattu Island I	181a	52.25 N	173.35 E
Agattu Strait ꓤ	181a	52.35 N	173.25 E
Agawa	96	33.34 N	133.10 E
Agawa ≃	190	47.21 N	84.38 W
Agawa Bay ⊂	190	47.20 N	84.42 W
Agawa Canyon V	190	47.27 N	84.29 W
Agawam, Ma., U.S.	207	42.04 N	72.36 W
Agawam, Mt., U.S.	182	48.00 N	112.10 W
Agay	62	43.26 N	6.51 E
Agazzano	62	44.57 N	9.31 E
Agbaja	150	7.58 N	6.38 E
Agbede	273a	6.40 N	3.29 E
Agbélouvé	150	6.40 N	1.10 E
Agboju	273a	6.28 N	3.17 E
Agboville	150	5.56 N	4.13 W
Agboyi Creek ≃	273a	6.34 N	3.25 E
Agcawayan	116	13.46 N	120.16 E
Agdam	84	39.59 N	46.57 E
Agdaš	84	40.38 N	47.28 E
Agde	32	43.19 N	3.28 E
Agde, Cap d' ›	32	43.16 N	3.30 E
Agdžabedi	84	40.03 N	47.28 E
Agege	273a	6.37 N	3.20 E
Agejevo	82	54.10 N	36.29 E
Agematsu	94	35.47 N	137.42 E
Agen	32	44.12 N	0.37 E
Agency	190	40.59 N	92.18 W
Agency Lake ⊜	202	42.32 N	121.58 W
Ageo	94	35.58 N	139.36 E
Agepsta, gora ∧	84	43.32 N	40.30 E
Ager ≃	60	48.05 N	13.51 E
Agerbæk	41	55.36 N	8.48 E
Agerskov	41	55.07 N	9.08 E
Agersø I	41	55.12 N	11.12 E
Agery	168b	34.10 S	137.44 E
Ágfalva	61	47.41 N	16.31 E
Aggeneis	158	29.03 S	18.51 E
Agger ≃	56	50.48 N	7.11 E
Aggherar	144	4.03 N	42.40 E
Aggius	71	40.46 N	9.04 E
Aggstein ⊥	61	48.18 N	15.25 E
Aggteleki Barlang •[5]	30	48.30 N	20.32 E
Āghā Jārī	128	30.42 N	49.50 E
Aghleam	48	54.08 N	10.07 W
Aghzoumal, Sabkhat ⊜	148	24.21 N	12.52 W
Agia	124	26.05 N	90.32 E
Agidingbi	273a	6.38 N	3.21 E
Agimont	56	50.10 N	4.48 E
Ağın	130	38.57 N	38.43 E
Agincourt ◆[8]	275b	43.48 N	79.17 W
Aginskij Bur'atskij Nacional'nyj Okrug □[3]	88	51.00 N	114.00 E
Aginskoje, S.S.S.R.	86	55.15 N	94.55 E
Aginskoje, S.S.S.R.	88	51.06 N	114.32 E
Agira	70	37.39 N	14.31 E
Aglasterhausen	56	49.21 N	8.59 E
Ağlasun	130	37.40 N	30.32 E
Agliana	66	43.54 N	11.00 E
Agliano	62	44.47 N	8.15 E
Aglientu	71	41.05 N	9.07 E
Agly ≃	32	42.47 N	3.02 E
Agna	64	45.10 N	11.58 E
Agnadello	62	45.26 N	9.33 E
Agnes, Mount ∧	162	26.51 S	128.59 E
Agnes Lake ⊜	190	48.13 N	91.21 W
Agnew	162	28.01 S	120.30 E
Agnew Lake ⊜[1]	190	46.22 N	81.45 W
Agnews Hill ∧[2]	48	54.51 N	5.56 W
Agnibilékrou	150	7.08 N	3.12 W
Agnije-Afanasjevskij	89	51.57 N	138.45 E
Agnita	38	45.59 N	24.38 E
Agno, Pil.	116	16.07 N	119.48 E
Agno, Schw.	58	46.00 N	8.54 E
Agno ≃, It.	64	45.15 N	11.28 E
Agno ≃, Pil.	116	16.02 N	120.08 E
Agnone	66	41.48 N	14.22 E
Agnone Bagni ◆[8]	70	37.18 N	15.06 E
Ago	92	34.20 N	136.51 E
Agogna ≃	62	45.04 N	8.54 E
Agogo, Ghana	150	6.47 N	1.04 W
Agogo, Sūd.	140	7.49 N	28.52 E
Agoo	116	16.20 N	120.22 E
Agordat → Akordat	144	15.33 N	37.53 E
Agordo	64	46.17 N	12.02 E
Agostinho Pôrto	287a	22.47 S	43.23 W
Agostitlán	234	19.33 N	100.41 W
Agou, Mont ∧	150	6.52 N	0.46 E
Agouna	150	7.34 N	1.42 E
Agoura Hills	228	34.08 N	118.44 W
Agout ≃	32	43.47 N	1.41 E
Agoza ⊥	146	18.30 N	23.45 E
Āgra	124	27.11 N	78.01 E
Āgra Canal ≅	272a	28.34 N	77.18 E
Agrachanskij poluostrov ›[1]	84	43.42 N	47.36 E
Agraciada	258	33.48 S	58.15 W
Agrado	246	2.15 N	75.46 W
Agraf'novka	83	47.45 N	39.29 E
Agram → Zagreb	36	45.48 N	15.58 E
Agramonte	240p	22.41 N	81.07 W
Agrate Brianza	62	45.34 N	9.21 E
Ágreda	34	41.51 N	1.56 W
Agrestina	250	8.27 S	35.57 W
Ağrı	84	39.44 N	43.03 E
Ağrı □[4]	84	39.30 N	43.15 E
Agri ≃	68	40.13 N	16.44 E
Agri Bavnehøj ∧[2]	41	56.14 N	10.33 E
Agrícola Oriental ◆[8]	286a	19.24 N	99.05 W
Ağrı Dağı (Mount Ararat) ∧	84	39.42 N	44.18 E
Agrigento	70	37.18 N	13.35 E
Agrigento □[4]	70	37.27 N	13.30 E
Agrihan I	108	18.46 N	145.40 E
Agrínion	38	38.37 N	21.24 E
Agrio ≃	252	38.21 S	69.43 W
Agronomia y Veterinaria, Facultad de ⊍[2]	288	36.36 S	58.29 W
Agropoli	68	40.21 N	15.00 E
Agro Pontino ◆[1]	66	41.25 N	12.55 E
Agryz	80	56.33 N	53.00 E
Agtuuganon, Mount ∧	116	7.48 N	126.12 E
Agua, Cayo I	236	9.09 N	82.02 W
Agua, Ilha d' I	287a	22.49 S	43.10 W
Agua, Volcán de ∧[1]	236	14.28 N	90.45 W
Água Boa	255	17.59 S	42.24 W
Água Branca, Bra.	250	9.17 S	37.55 W
Água Branca, Bra.	250	7.31 S	37.40 W
Água Branca, Bra.	250	5.53 S	42.38 W
Água Branca, Parque da ♦	287b	23.32 S	46.40 W
Agua Brava, Laguna de ⊂	234	22.10 N	105.32 W
Agua Caliente	234	23.20 N	105.20 W
Agua Caliente, Cerro ∧	232	26.27 N	106.12 W
Agua Caliente Creek ≃	282	37.29 N	121.56 W
Agua Caliente de Chínipas	232	27.27 N	108.32 W
Agua Caliente Grande de Gastelum	232	26.31 N	108.22 W
Aguacate	240p	22.59 N	81.49 W
Aguachica	246	8.19 N	73.38 W
Água Clara	255	20.27 S	52.52 W
Água Comprida, Bra.	255	20.04 S	48.08 W
Água Comprida, Bra.	256	21.54 S	45.40 W
Aguada	240m	18.23 N	67.11 W
Aguada Cecilio	254	40.51 S	65.51 W
Aguada de Guerra	254	41.04 S	68.25 W
Aguada de Pasajeros	240p	22.23 N	80.51 W
Aguadas	246	5.37 N	75.27 W
Agua de Afuera, Sierra del ⋏	234	23.53 N	99.45 W
Agua de Dios	246	4.23 N	74.40 W
Aguadilla	240m	18.26 N	67.09 W
Água Doce	252	27.00 S	51.33 W
Agua Dulce, Méx.	234	18.08 N	94.08 W
Aguadulce, Pan.	236	8.15 N	80.33 W
Agua Dulce, Ca., U.S.	228	34.30 N	118.23 W
Agua Dulce, Tx., U.S.	196	27.47 N	97.54 W
Agua Escondida	234	19.08 N	103.27 W
Agua Fria ≃	200	33.23 N	112.21 W
Agua Fria Creek ≃	282	37.28 N	121.56 W
Aguaí	256	22.04 S	46.58 W
Aguaje Copal, Cerro ∧	234	16.33 N	95.15 W
Agualeguas	232	26.18 N	99.34 W
Água Limpa	255	18.06 S	48.46 W
Água Limpa, Serra da ⋏	256	22.30 S	45.25 W
Agualva-Cacém	266c	38.46 N	9.18 W
Aguán ≃	236	15.57 N	85.44 W
Aguanaval ≃	232	25.28 N	102.53 W
Agua Negra	286c	10.28 N	67.01 W
Aguanish	186	50.13 N	62.05 W
Aguanus ≃	186	50.13 N	62.05 W
Aguapeí ≃	248	15.53 S	58.25 W
Aguapepito	232	24.33 N	107.39 W
Aguapey ≃	252	29.07 S	56.36 W
Água Preta, Igarapé ≃	246	1.41 S	63.48 W
Agua Prieta	232	31.18 N	109.34 W
Aguaragüe, Serranía de ⋏	248	21.30 S	63.40 W
Aguaray	252	22.16 S	63.44 W
Aguaray-Guazú ≃, Para.	252	24.05 S	56.40 W
Aguaray-Guazú ≃, Para.	252	24.47 S	57.19 W
Aguarico ≃	246	0.59 S	75.11 W
Aguaruto	232	24.47 N	107.29 W
Aguas ≃	34	37.09 N	1.49 W
Águas, Serra das ∧	256	21.55 S	45.25 W
Aguasabon ≃	190	48.46 N	87.07 W
Águas Belas	250	9.07 S	37.07 W
Aguas Buenas	240m	18.15 N	66.06 W
Aguascalientes, Méx.	200	32.18 N	115.10 W
Aguascalientes, Méx.	234	21.53 N	102.18 W
Aguascalientes □[3]	234	22.00 N	102.30 W
Aguascalientes, Río de ≃	234	21.23 N	102.28 W
Aguas Corrientes	258	34.31 S	56.24 W
Águas da Prata	256	21.56 S	46.43 W
Águas de Contendas	256	21.54 S	45.01 W
Águas de Lindóia	256	22.29 S	46.39 W
Águas Formosas	255	17.05 S	40.57 W
Aguasvivas ≃	34	41.20 N	0.25 W
Agua Tibia ∧	228	33.24 N	116.59 W
Água Verde ≃	248	13.42 S	56.43 W
Água Viva	256	21.41 S	42.33 W
Aguayo	252	31.40 S	65.54 W
Aguaytía ≃	248	8.08 S	74.37 W
Agua Zarca, Méx.	200	31.10 N	110.59 W
Agua Zarca, Méx.	234	23.10 N	104.28 W
Agu Bay ⊂	176	70.18 N	86.30 W
Agudo	252	29.38 S	53.15 W
Agudos	255	22.28 S	49.00 W
Águeda	34	40.34 N	8.27 W
Águeda ≃	34	41.02 N	6.56 W
Aguelhok	150	19.28 N	0.52 E
Aguema	152	12.03 S	21.49 E
Aguenier, Lac ⊜	186	50.43 N	68.13 W
Agugliano	66	43.32 N	13.23 E
Agui	94	34.55 N	136.55 E
Aguié	150	13.30 N	7.47 E
Aguijan I	108	14.51 N	145.34 E
Aguila	200	33.56 N	113.10 W
Águila, Cerro del ∧	232	26.58 N	112.28 W
Aguilar, Esp.	34	37.31 N	4.39 W
Aguilar, Co., U.S.	198	37.24 N	104.39 W
Aguilares, Arg.	252	27.26 S	65.37 W
Aguilares, El Sal.	236	13.58 N	89.12 W
Águilas	34	37.24 N	1.35 W
Aguililla	234	18.44 N	102.44 W
Aguirre ≃	246	8.28 N	61.02 W
Aguirre, Arroyo ≃	288	34.46 S	58.35 W
Aguirre, Bahía ⊂	254	54.57 S	65.50 W
Aguit	102	41.52 N	112.56 E
Aguja, Cerro ∧	254	42.11 S	71.51 W
Aguja, Punta ›	248	5.48 S	81.06 W
Aguja Point ›	116	12.42 N	123.23 E
Agujas, Cabo de las → Agulhas, Cape ›	158	34.52 S	20.00 E
Agujereada, Punta ›	240m	18.31 N	67.08 W
Agujita	196	27.53 N	101.09 W
Agul ≃	88	55.44 N	95.41 E
Agulai	144	13.41 N	39.35 E
Agulhas	158	34.50 S	20.00 E
Agulhas, Cape ›	158	34.52 S	20.00 E
Agulhas Basin ✦[1]	8	47.00 S	27.00 E
Agulhas Negras	256	22.28 S	44.27 W
Agulhas Negras, Pico das ∧	256	22.23 S	44.38 W
Agulhas Plateau ✦[3]	10	40.00 S	26.00 E
Agung, Gunung ∧	115b	8.21 S	115.30 E
Aguni-jima I	93b	26.35 N	127.14 E
Agusan ≃	116	9.00 N	125.31 E
Agusan del Norte □[4]	116	9.00 N	125.30 E
Agusan del Sur □[4]	116	8.30 N	125.40 E
Agustín Codazzi	246	10.02 N	73.14 W
Agustino, Cerro ∧	286d	12.04 S	77.00 W
Agutaya	116	11.09 N	120.56 E
Agutaya Island I	116	11.09 N	120.58 E
Ağva	130	41.09 N	29.50 E
Agvali	84	42.33 N	46.06 E
Agwarra	150	10.42 N	4.35 E
Ägypten → Egypt □[1]	140	27.00 N	30.00 E
Aha	174m	26.43 N	128.17 E
Ahaggar (Hoggar) ⋏	148	23.00 N	6.30 E
Ahaggar, Tassili ta-n- ⋏[1]	148	21.00 N	6.00 E
Aha Hills ⋏[2]	156	19.45 S	21.10 E
Aha-kō ⊂	174m	26.43 N	128.18 E
Aham	60	48.32 N	12.28 E
Ahar	128	38.28 N	47.04 E
Ahar ≃	128	38.32 N	47.31 E
Ahascragh	48	53.24 N	8.20 W
Ahaura	172	42.21 S	171.32 E
Ahaura ≃	172	42.21 S	171.31 E
Ahaus	52	52.04 N	7.00 E
Ahe ≃	263	51.13 N	7.43 E
Aheggar ∧	148	24.43 N	5.39 E
Ahfir	148	34.57 N	2.17 W
Ahimanawa Range ⋏	172	39.00 S	176.27 E
Ahipara	172	35.10 S	173.10 E
Ahipara Bay ⊂	172	35.10 S	173.07 E
'Āhirah	132	32.53 N	36.28 E
Ahırlı	130	37.14 N	32.08 E
Ahklun Mountains ⋏	180	59.15 N	161.00 W
Ahlat, Tür.	128	38.45 N	42.29 E
Ahlat, Tür.	130	38.45 N	42.29 E
Ahlbeck	54	53.40 N	14.11 E
Ahlem	52	52.23 N	9.40 E
Ahlen	52	51.46 N	7.53 E
Ahlenberg	263	51.25 N	7.28 E
Ahlenmoor ◆[3]	52	53.40 N	8.45 E
Ahlhorn	52	52.54 N	8.14 E
Ahlsdorf	54	51.32 N	11.28 E
Ahmadābād	120	23.02 N	72.37 E
Ahmadābād-e Sarjām	128	35.51 N	59.36 E
Aḥmad al-Bāqir, Jabal ∧	132	29.36 N	35.08 E
Ahmadgarh	123	30.41 N	75.50 E
Ahmadnagar	122	19.05 N	74.44 E
Ahmadpur, India	124	23.31 N	77.13 E
Ahmadpur, India	126	23.50 N	87.42 E
Ahmadpur East	123	29.09 N	71.16 E
Ahmadpur Siāl	123	30.41 N	71.46 E
Ahmad Wāl	120	29.25 N	65.56 E
Aḥmar, Al-Baḥr al- → Red Sea ⊤[2]	136	20.00 N	38.00 E
Aḥmar, 'Erg el ◆[2]	148	23.30 N	4.54 W
Aḥmar, Jabal al- ∧	132	29.40 N	35.09 E
Ahmar Mountains ⋏	144	9.15 N	41.00 E
Ahmedabad → Ahmadābād	120	23.02 N	72.37 E
Ahmetli	130	38.31 N	27.57 E
Ahmic Lake ⊜	190	45.37 N	79.42 W
Ahnet ⋏	148	24.58 N	2.57 E
Ahnet, Tanezrouft n- ◆[2]	148	22.15 N	1.30 E
Ahoada	150	5.05 N	6.38 E
Ahogados, Arroyo de los ≃	258	33.37 S	56.31 W
Ahoghill	48	54.51 N	6.22 W
Ahome	232	25.55 N	109.11 W
Ahon, Tarso ∧	146	20.23 N	18.18 E
Ahornspitz ∧	64	47.08 N	11.56 E
Ahoskie	192	36.17 N	76.59 W
Ahousat	182	49.17 N	126.04 W
Ahr ≃	56	50.33 N	7.17 E
Ahram	128	28.52 N	51.16 E
Ahrāmāt Dahshūr (North and Bent Pyramids) ⊥	142	29.48 N	31.13 E
Ahrāmāt Maydūm (Maydūm Pyramid) ⊥	142	29.23 N	31.10 E
Ahraura	124	25.01 N	83.01 E
Ahrensbök	54	54.00 N	10.34 E
Ahrensburg	52	53.40 N	10.14 E
Ahrensdorf, D.D.R.	54	52.10 N	14.05 E
Ahrensdorf, D.D.R.	264a	52.19 N	13.12 E
Ahrensfelde	264a	52.35 N	13.35 E
Ahrgebirge ⋏	56	50.30 N	6.50 E
Ahtanum	224	46.34 N	120.37 W
Ahtanum Creek ≃	202	46.32 N	120.31 W
Ahtanum Ridge ∧	224	46.30 N	120.50 W
Ähtäri	26	62.34 N	24.06 E
Ähtärinjärvi ⊜	26	62.40 N	24.03 E
Ähtävänjoki ≃	26	63.38 N	22.48 E
Ahtopol	38	42.06 N	27.57 E
Ahu	98	34.27 N	118.39 E
Ahuacatlán, Méx.	234	21.03 N	104.29 W
Ahuacatlán, Méx.	234	20.00 N	97.52 W
Ahuachapán	236	13.55 N	89.51 W
Ahuacuotzingo	234	17.42 N	98.56 W
Ahualulco de Mercado	234	20.42 N	103.59 W
Ahuijullo	234	19.05 N	103.05 W
Ahuijullo ≃	234	18.49 N	103.37 W
Ahumada	204	32.30 N	115.30 W
Ahun	32	46.05 N	2.05 E
Ahuntsic ◆[8]	275a	45.33 N	73.39 W
Ahunui I[1]	14	19.39 S	140.25 W
Ahuriri ≃	172	44.33 S	170.11 E
Åhus	26	55.55 N	14.17 E
Ahuzhen	98	34.27 N	118.39 E
Ahvāz	128	31.19 N	48.42 E
Ahvenanmaa □[4]	26	60.15 N	20.00 E
Ahwahnee	226	37.21 N	119.43 W
Aḥwar	144	13.31 N	46.42 E
Ahwa-ri	98	35.54 N	129.02 E
Ai ≃	98	40.13 N	124.30 E
Aialik Cape ›	180	59.42 N	149.31 W
Aiándion	267c	37.55 N	23.28 E
Aiapuá	246	4.29 S	62.04 W
Aiapuá, Lago ⊜	246	4.27 S	62.08 W
Aibag ≃	102	42.40 N	110.42 E
Aibonito	240m	18.08 N	66.16 W
Aich	64	47.25 N	13.49 E
Aichach	60	48.28 N	11.08 E
Aicha vorm Wald	60	48.41 N	13.18 E
Aichi □[5]	94	35.00 N	137.15 E
Aichi-kōgen-kokutei-kōen ♦	94	35.10 N	137.25 E
Aichi-yōsui ≅	94	34.42 N	136.57 E
Aichstetten	58	47.54 N	10.04 E
Aide ≃	42	52.10 N	1.27 E
Aidenbach	60	48.34 N	13.06 E
Aidomaggiore	71	40.10 N	8.51 E
Aidone	70	37.25 N	14.27 E
Aidong	102	24.46 N	107.21 E
Aiduma, Pulau I	164	3.58 S	134.06 E
Aiea	229c	21.22 N	157.56 W
Aiello Calabro	68	39.07 N	16.10 E
Aigáleo Óros ∧[2]	267c	38.00 N	23.37 E
Aigburth ◆[8]	262	53.22 N	2.55 W
Aigen im Mühlkreis	60	48.39 N	13.58 E
Aigenmiao	89	43.36 N	120.50 E
Aigle	58	46.19 N	6.58 E
Aigle, Île à l' I	275a	45.42 N	73.28 W
Aigle, Lac à l' ⊜	186	51.12 N	65.25 W
Aignay-le-Duc	58	47.40 N	4.44 E
Aigre	32	45.54 N	0.01 E
Aiguá	252	34.12 S	54.45 W
Aiguebelette, Lac d' ⊜	62	45.33 N	5.48 E
Aiguebelette-le-Lac	62	45.32 N	5.49 E
Aiguebelle	62	45.32 N	6.18 E
Aiguebelle, Réserve ♦	190	48.33 N	78.45 W
Aigueperse	32	46.01 N	3.12 E
Aigues ≃	62	44.07 N	4.43 E
Aigues-Mortes	62	43.34 N	4.11 E
Aigues-Mortes, Golfe d' ⊂	62	43.31 N	4.03 E
Aigüestortes, Parc National d' ♦	34	42.30 N	1.01 E
Aigues-Vives	62	43.44 N	4.10 E
Aiguilles	62	44.47 N	6.52 E
Aiguines	62	43.46 N	6.15 E
Aigurande	32	46.26 N	1.50 E
Aihui (Heihe)	89	50.16 N	127.28 E
Aija	248	9.46 S	77.38 W
Aikawa, Nihon	92	38.02 N	138.15 E
Aikawa, Nihon	94	35.32 N	139.17 E
Aiken	192	33.33 N	81.43 W
Aikens Lake ⊜	184	51.12 N	95.20 W
Ailao Shan ⋏	102	24.08 N	101.25 E
Ailefroide	62	44.53 N	6.27 E
Aileron	162	22.39 S	133.20 E
Ailette ≃	50	49.35 N	3.10 E
Aileu	112	8.43 S	125.34 E
Ailigandí	246	9.14 N	78.01 W
Ailimutou Shan ∧	104	42.19 N	121.25 E
Ailingen	58	47.41 N	9.29 E
Ailinglapalap I[1]	14	7.23 N	168.46 E
Ailinzhuang	105	39.27 N	117.36 E
Aillant-sur-Tholon	50	47.52 N	3.21 E
Aille ≃	62	43.26 N	6.30 E
Ailly-le-Haut-Clocher	50	50.05 N	2.00 E
Ailly-sur-Noye	50	49.45 N	2.22 E
Ailly-sur-Somme	50	49.55 N	2.12 E
Ailo	164	4.50 S	151.40 E
Ailsa Craig	190	43.08 N	81.33 W
Ailsa Craig I	44	55.16 N	5.07 W
Ailuk I[1]	14	10.20 N	169.56 E
Aim	74	58.50 N	134.12 E
Aimargues	62	43.41 N	4.12 E
Aime	62	45.33 N	6.39 E
Aimere	115b	8.50 S	120.52 E
Aimi	96	35.22 N	133.22 E
Aimogasta	252	28.33 S	66.49 W
Aimorés	255	19.30 S	41.04 W
Aimoto	270	34.59 N	135.10 E
Ain □[5]	32	46.10 N	5.20 E
Ain ≃	62	45.48 N	5.10 E
Aïn Arnat	34	36.11 N	5.19 E
Aïn Azel	34	35.49 N	5.31 E
Ainaži	76	57.52 N	24.21 E
'Aïn Belbela, Sebkha ≋	148	27.30 N	5.20 W
Aïn Benian	148	36.48 N	2.55 E
Aïn Ben Tili	148	26.00 N	9.32 W
Aïn Berda	36	36.39 N	7.35 E
Aïn Bessem	34	36.18 N	3.40 E
Aincourt	261	49.04 N	1.47 E
Aïn Defla	34	36.16 N	1.58 E
Aïn Deheb	148	34.51 N	1.33 E
Aïn Draham	148	36.47 N	8.42 E
Aine ≃	56	50.23 N	5.31 E
Aïn el Beïda	148	35.48 N	7.24 E
Aïn el Hadjel	34	35.40 N	3.53 E
Aïn el Kebira	34	36.22 N	5.30 E
Aïn Milia	148	36.02 N	6.34 E
Aino	270	34.57 N	135.10 E
Aino-shima I, Nihon	96	33.45 N	130.23 E
Aino-shima I, Nihon	96	33.59 N	130.50 E
Aïn Oulmène	34	35.55 N	5.18 E
Ainring	64	47.48 N	12.56 E
Ainsdale	262	53.36 N	3.02 W
Aïn Sefra	148	32.45 N	0.35 W
Ain Shams University ⊍[2]	273c	30.03 N	31.17 E
Ainslie, Mount ∧	171b	35.16 S	149.10 E
Ainslie Lake ⊜	186	46.08 N	61.12 W
Ainsworth, Eng., U.K.	262	53.35 N	2.22 W
Ainsworth, Ne., U.S.	198	42.33 N	99.51 W
Aïn Taghrout	34	36.08 N	5.05 E
Aïn Tedelès	148	36.00 N	0.18 E
Aïn Témouchent	148	35.18 N	1.08 W
Aïn Touta	148	35.23 N	5.54 E
Aintree	262	53.29 N	2.56 W
Aintree Race Course ♦	262	53.28 N	2.56 W
Aïn Wessara	148	35.27 N	2.54 E
Aïn Yagout	148	35.47 N	6.25 E
Aio	96	34.00 N	131.26 E
Aioi	96	34.48 N	134.28 E
Aiome	164	5.10 S	144.45 E
Aiora	34	39.04 N	1.03 W
Aipe	246	3.13 N	75.15 W
Aiquara	255	14.07 S	39.52 W
Aiquile	248	18.10 S	65.10 W
Aïr ⋏	150	18.00 N	8.30 E
Airabu, Pulau I	112	2.46 N	106.14 E
Airai Airport ⊠	175b	7.22 N	134.33 E
Airaines	50	49.58 N	1.57 E
Airão	246	1.56 S	61.22 W
Airasca	62	44.55 N	7.29 E
Airbangis	110	0.12 N	99.23 E
Airdikit	112	2.40 S	101.15 E
Airdrie, Ab., Can.	182	51.18 N	114.02 W
Airdrie, Scot., U.K.	46	55.52 N	3.59 W
Aire	32	43.42 N	0.16 W
Aire ≃, Fr.	56	49.19 N	4.49 E
Aire ≃, Eng., U.K.	44	53.44 N	0.54 W
Aire-sur-la-Lys	50	50.38 N	2.24 E
Air Force Island I	176	67.55 N	74.10 W
Airgegas	112	2.42 S	106.25 E
Airgin Sum	102	42.58 N	111.08 E
Airhaji	112	1.57 S	100.53 E
Airjamban	114	1.13 N	101.14 E
Airlie	166	20.16 S	148.43 E
Airmolek	112	0.22 S	102.17 E
Airmont	276	41.06 N	74.06 W
Airola	68	41.04 N	14.33 E
Airole	62	43.52 N	7.33 E
Airolo	58	46.32 N	8.37 E
Airor	46	57.04 N	5.46 W
Airport West	274b	37.44 S	144.53 E
Airtenang	112	3.08 S	101.43 E
Airterjun	114	1.20 N	100.27 E
Airuno	62	45.45 N	9.25 E
Airvault	32	46.50 N	0.08 W
Aisch ≃	60	49.46 N	11.01 E
Aisega	164	5.44 S	148.21 E
Aisén del General Carlos Ibáñez del Campo □[4]	254	46.30 S	73.30 W
Aisey-sur-Seine	58	47.45 N	4.35 E
Aishihik	180	61.35 N	137.30 W
Aishihik Lake ⊜	180	61.25 N	137.06 W
Ai-shima I	96	34.30 N	131.17 E
Aisinaike	85	39.47 N	75.47 E
Aislingen	56	48.30 N	10.27 E
Aisne □[5]	50	49.30 N	3.30 E
Aisne ≃	50	49.26 N	2.50 E
Aisne à la Marne, Canal de l' ≅	50	49.24 N	3.55 E
Aïssa, Djebel ∧	148	32.51 N	0.30 W
Aïssey	58	47.16 N	6.20 E
Aist ≃	61	48.14 N	14.35 E
Aisy-sur-Armançon	50	47.39 N	4.13 E
Aitana, Serra d' ∧	34	38.44 N	0.16 W
Aitape	164	3.08 S	142.21 E
Aiterach ≃	60	48.54 N	12.38 E
Aiterhofen	60	48.51 N	12.37 E
Aith	46a	60.16 N	1.23 W
Aitkin	190	46.31 N	93.42 W
Aït-Melloul	148	30.21 N	9.31 W
Aitolikón	38	38.27 N	21.22 E
Aït-Ourir	148	31.38 N	7.42 W
Aitrach	58	47.56 N	10.05 E
Aitutaki I[1]	14	18.52 S	159.45 W
Ait Youssef ou Ali	34	35.13 N	3.55 W
Aiuaba	250	6.38 S	40.07 W
Aiud	38	46.19 N	23.44 E
Aiún → El Aaiún	148	27.09 N	13.12 W
Aiuruoca	256	21.58 S	44.36 W
Aiuruoca ≃	256	21.42 S	44.22 W
Aiva	287a	22.42 S	43.28 W
Aiviekste ≃	76	56.37 N	25.45 E
Aix, Mount ∧	224	46.47 N	121.15 W
Aix-en-Othe	50	48.13 N	3.44 E
Aix-en-Provence	62	43.32 N	5.26 E
Aix-la-Chapelle → Aachen	56	50.47 N	6.05 E
Aix-les-Bains	62	45.42 N	5.55 E
Aiyáleo	267c	37.59 N	23.41 E
Aiyang, Mount ∧	164	5.05 S	141.19 E
Aiyansh	182	55.17 N	129.03 W
Aíyina	38	37.44 N	23.27 E
Aíyina I	38	37.46 N	23.26 E
Aiyínion	38	40.30 N	22.33 E
Aíyion	38	38.15 N	22.05 E
Āīzawl	120	23.44 N	92.43 E
Aizhaipuzi	104	40.57 N	124.01 E
Aizpute	76	56.43 N	21.38 E
Aizu-bange	92	37.34 N	139.49 E
Aizu-wakamatsu	92	37.30 N	139.56 E
Aj ≃	86	56.08 N	57.40 E
Ajā	142	30.57 N	31.17 E
Ajā', Jabal ⋏	128	27.20 N	41.45 E
'Ajab Shīr	128	37.28 N	45.54 E
Ajaccio	36	41.55 N	8.44 E
Ajaguz	86	47.56 N	80.23 E
Ajaguz ≃	86	46.42 N	79.15 E
Ajaijú ≃	246	0.59 N	72.20 W
Ajalpan	234	18.22 N	97.15 W
'Ajaltūn	132	33.58 N	35.41 E
Ajalvir	266a	40.32 N	3.29 W
'Ajamī	130	36.28 N	37.42 E
Ajan, S.S.S.R.	74	56.27 N	138.10 E
Ajan, S.S.S.R.	88	54.43 N	110.55 E
Ajan ≃	74	70.10 N	95.50 E
Ajana	162	27.57 S	114.38 E
Ajanta	122	20.32 N	75.45 E
Ajanta Range ⋏	122	20.30 N	76.00 E
Ajaokuta	150	7.28 N	6.39 E
Ajarani ≃	246	1.33 N	61.16 W
Ajasse	150	8.17 N	4.48 E
Ajasso	150	5.52 N	8.52 E
Ajat ≃	86	52.54 N	63.02 E
Ajax	212	43.51 N	79.02 W
Ajay ≃	126	23.39 N	88.08 E
Ajbas	80	47.51 N	49.37 E
Ajdābiyā	146	30.48 N	20.14 E
Ajdabul'	86	52.42 N	68.59 E
Ajdar	78	50.03 N	38.56 E
Ajdar ≃	83	48.42 N	39.13 E
Ajdarkul', ozero ⊜[1]	85	40.45 N	67.20 E
Ajdarly	86	44.32 N	65.50 E
Ajdar-Nikolajevka	83	48.58 N	38.58 E
Ajdovščina	64	45.53 N	13.53 E
Ajdyrlinskij	86	52.03 N	59.50 E
Ajegunle	273a	6.36 N	3.17 E
Ajgurka ≃	80	45.46 N	43.12 E
Ajgyrkol', ozero ⊜	80	48.15 N	52.50 E
Ajhūr al-Kubrā	142	30.18 N	31.09 E
Aji	96	34.23 N	134.08 E
Ajibar	144	10.52 N	38.40 E
Ajibarang	115a	7.25 S	109.04 E
Ajigasawa	92	40.47 N	140.12 E
'Ajīj, Wādī al- V	130	35.19 N	41.09 E
Ajijic	234	20.18 N	103.17 W
Ajil	114	5.05 N	103.05 E
Ājimganj	126	24.14 N	88.15 E
Ajimu	96	33.26 N	131.21 E
Ajipuzicun	104	42.16 N	123.33 E
Ajisu	96	34.00 N	131.22 E
Ajjer, Tassili-n- ⋏[1]	148	25.10 N	8.00 E
Ajka	30	47.07 N	17.34 E
Ajke, ozero ⊜	86	50.57 N	61.36 E
Ajkino	24	62.15 N	49.56 E
'Ajlūn	132	32.20 N	35.45 E
Ajlune	224	46.31 N	122.26 W
'Ajmah, Jabal al- ⋏	140	29.12 N	34.02 E
Ajmer	120	26.27 N	74.38 E
Ajnāla	123	31.51 N	74.48 E
Ajni	85	39.23 N	68.32 E
Ajo	200	32.22 N	112.51 W
Ajo, Cabo de ›	34	43.31 N	3.35 W
Ajok	140	9.15 N	28.27 E
Ajon, ostrov I	74	69.50 N	168.40 E
Ajoya	232	24.04 N	106.22 W
Aj-Petri, gora ∧	78	44.27 N	34.03 E
Ajrag nuur ⊜	88	48.54 N	93.28 E
'Ajramīyah, Bi'r al- ⊤[4]	142	29.39 N	31.50 E
Ajrum	84	41.13 N	44.53 E
Ajryk	86	50.30 N	76.48 E
Ajsary	86	53.18 N	71.52 E
Ajtos	38	42.42 N	27.15 E
Ajuchitlán del Progreso	234	18.09 N	100.29 W
Ajuda ◆[8]	266c	38.43 N	9.12 W
Ajusco	204	31.35 N	116.25 W
Ajusco ◆[8]	286a	19.14 N	99.12 W
Ajusco, Cerro ∧	286a	19.12 N	99.15 W
Ajuta ≃	83	47.34 N	40.07 E
Ajuterique	236	14.20 N	87.43 W
Ajutinskij	83	47.46 N	40.08 E
Ajuy	116	11.10 N	123.01 E
Ajuy Bay ⊂	116	11.10 N	123.02 E
Aka ≃	92	38.54 N	139.50 E
Akaba	150	7.57 N	1.03 E
Akabane	94	34.37 N	137.12 E
Akabira	92a	43.34 N	142.03 E
Akabli	148	26.42 N	1.22 E
Akabori	94	36.22 N	139.14 E
Akademii, zaliv ⊂	89	54.15 N	138.05 E
Akagera (Kagera) ≃	154	0.57 S	31.47 E
Akagera, Parc National de l' ♦	154	1.30 S	30.35 E
Akagi, Nihon	94	36.33 N	139.03 E
Akagi, Nihon	96	35.00 N	132.43 E
Akagi-san ∧	94	36.33 N	139.11 E
Akaishi-dake ∧	94	35.27 N	138.09 E
Akaishi-sammyaku ⋏	94	35.18 N	138.07 E
Akaka Falls State Park ♦	229d	19.52 N	155.09 W
Akaki Beseka	144	8.52 N	38.47 E
Akālgarh	123	32.16 N	73.49 E
Akalkot	122	17.32 N	76.13 E
Akamaruno-misaki ›	174m	26.44 N	128.09 E
Akámas, Akrotírion ›	130	35.06 N	32.17 E
Akan	92a	43.06 N	144.10 E
Akana-tōge)(	96	34.57 N	132.44 E
Akan-kokuritsu-kōen ♦	92a	43.30 N	144.15 E
Akaoka	96	33.32 N	133.43 E
Ak-Aral	86	49.10 N	90.57 E
Akaroa	172	43.48 S	172.58 E
Akaroa Harbour ⊂	172	43.50 S	172.56 E
Åkarp	41	55.39 N	13.07 E
Akarsu, Tür.	130	39.56 N	38.38 E
Akarsu, Tür.	130	37.14 N	41.04 E
Akasaki	96	35.31 N	133.38 E
'Akasha East	140	21.05 N	30.43 E
Akashat	130	33.45 N	39.58 E
Akashi	96	34.38 N	134.59 E
Akashi ≃	270	34.38 N	134.59 E
Akashi-kaikyō ꓤ	96	34.37 N	135.02 E
Akashina	94	36.21 N	137.56 E
Akatani-ko ⊜[1]	94	36.43 N	138.54 E
Akatjevo	82	54.59 N	38.45 E
Akatova	76	55.09 N	31.48 E
Akatsuka ◆[8]	268	35.46 N	139.39 E
Akatsutsumi ◆[8]	268	35.39 N	139.39 E
Akbaba ◆[8]	267b	41.09 N	29.06 E
Akbaba Dağı ∧	130	40.12 N	40.51 E
Akbajtal	85	38.32 N	73.49 E
Akbajtal, pereval)(	85	38.32 N	73.40 E
Akbarpur, India	124	24.39 N	83.58 E
Akbarpur, India	124	26.25 N	82.33 E
Akbeit	86	51.38 N	70.02 E
Akbou	148	36.28 N	4.32 E
Akbulak, S.S.S.R.	86	51.01 N	55.37 E
Akbulak, S.S.S.R.	86	49.26 N	80.28 E
Akbura ≃	85	40.39 N	72.36 E
Akçaabat	130	41.02 N	39.34 E
Akçadağ	130	38.21 N	37.59 E
Akçakale	130	36.41 N	38.56 E
Akcakışla	130	39.33 N	36.22 E
Akçakoca	130	41.05 N	31.09 E
Akçakoyunlu	130	36.46 N	37.38 E
Akçaova, Tür.	130	37.30 N	28.02 E
Akçaova, Tür.	130	41.03 N	29.57 E
Akçapınar	130	38.57 N	38.57 E
Akčatau	86	47.59 N	74.02 E
Akçay	130	36.36 N	29.45 E
Akçay ≃	130	37.50 N	28.15 E
Akchâr ◆[1]	150	20.00 N	14.30 W
Akči	85	44.00 N	76.20 E
Akdağ	130	40.43 N	36.00 E
Akdağ ∧	130	39.29 N	41.54 E
Akdağmadeni	130	39.40 N	35.54 E
Akdala	86	45.02 N	74.35 E
Akdoğan	130	35.06 N	33.41 E
Ak-Dovurak	86	51.16 N	90.31 E
Akechi	94	35.18 N	137.23 E
Akehama	96	33.19 N	132.26 E
Akeley	190	47.00 N	94.43 W
Aken	54	51.51 N	12.02 E
Akeno, Nihon	94	36.15 N	140.02 E
Akeno, Nihon	94	35.46 N	138.26 E
Åker	40	59.15 N	17.05 E
Akera ≃	84	39.09 N	46.51 E
Åkerby	40	60.25 N	17.46 E
Åkersberga	40	59.29 N	18.18 E
Akershus □[6]	26	60.00 N	11.10 E
Akersloot	52	52.34 N	4.44 E
Akespe	86	46.48 N	60.31 E
Aketi	152	2.44 N	23.46 E
Aketilepa	85	39.57 N	74.03 E
Aketu-Oja	273a	6.41 N	3.23 E
Åkforsån ≃	40	58.54 N	16.28 E
Akgöl ⊜	130	38.58 N	31.48 E
Akharnaí	38	38.05 N	23.44 E
Akhḍar, Al-Jabal al- ⋏, Lībiyā	146	32.30 N	21.30 E
Akhḍar, Al-Jabal al- ⋏, 'Umān	128	23.15 N	57.20 E
Akhelóös ≃	38	38.36 N	21.14 E
Akh Gol ⊜	84	39.33 N	44.47 E
Akhiok	180	56.57 N	154.10 W
Akhisar	130	38.55 N	27.51 E
Akhmīm	140	26.34 N	31.44 E
Akhnūr	123	32.54 N	74.44 E
Akhtarīn	130	36.31 N	37.20 E
Aki, Nihon	96	33.30 N	133.54 E
Aki, Nihon	96	33.28 N	131.43 E
Aki ≃, Nihon	94	35.41 N	139.21 E
Aki ≃, Nihon	96	33.30 N	133.55 E
Akiachak	180	60.55 N	161.27 W
Akiak	180	60.55 N	161.12 W
Akiéni	152	1.11 S	13.53 E
Akima	88	53.06 N	115.44 E
Akimiski Island I	176	53.00 N	81.20 W
Akimovka	78	46.42 N	35.09 E
Aki-nada ⊤[2]	96	34.05 N	132.48 E
Akıncı	130	37.10 N	40.52 E
Akıncı Burun ›	130	36.19 N	35.47 E
Akıncılar, Tür.	130	37.45 N	38.50 E
Akıncılar, Tür.	130	40.06 N	38.21 E
Akiode	273a	6.38 N	3.21 E
Åkirkeby	26	55.04 N	14.56 E
Akishima	94	35.41 N	139.22 E
Akišma ≃	89	52.08 N	132.40 E
Akita	92	39.43 N	140.07 E
Akita-heiya ≋	92	39.45 N	140.10 E
Akitan	273a	6.39 N	3.16 E
Akitipa	150	8.17 N	6.16 E
Akitkan, chrebet ⋏	88	57.05 N	109.05 E
Akitsu, Nihon	96	34.19 N	132.50 E
Akitsu, Nihon	270	34.56 N	135.06 E
Akiyama	94	35.34 N	139.05 E
Akiyoshi-dai ⋏[1]	96	34.15 N	131.15 E
Akiyoshi-dai-kokutei-kōen ♦	96	34.15 N	131.17 E
Akiyoshi-do •[5]	96	34.14 N	131.19 E
Akjar	86	51.50 N	58.14 E
Akjoujt	150	19.45 N	14.23 W
Akka	148	29.22 N	8.14 W
Akkala	86	43.43 N	59.31 E
Akkani	180	65.30 N	171.10 W
Akkerman → Belgorod-Dnestrovskij	78	46.12 N	30.20 E
Akkermanovka	86	51.11 N	58.12 E
Akkerwoude	52	53.17 N	5.58 E
Akkeshi	92a	43.02 N	144.51 E
Akkışla	130	39.00 N	36.11 E
'Akko (Acre)	132	32.55 N	35.05 E
Akkol', S.S.S.R.	85	43.25 N	70.47 E
Akkol', S.S.S.R.	86	45.02 N	75.40 E
Akkol', ozero ⊜	85	43.24 N	70.40 E
Akkol'skij	86	52.12 N	75.05 E
Akköy	130	37.29 N	27.15 E
Akkra → Accra	150	5.33 N	0.13 W
Akkrum	52	53.03 N	5.50 E
Ak-Kul'	85	41.41 N	74.16 E
Akkuş	130	40.49 N	37.01 E
Aklan □[4]	116	11.40 N	122.20 E
Aklan ≃	116	11.44 N	122.20 E
Aklan Point ›	116	11.44 N	122.22 E
Aklavik	180	68.12 N	135.00 W
'Aklé 'Aouâna ◆[1]	150	18.00 N	5.30 W
Akmenrags ›	76	56.51 N	21.03 E
Akmeqit	120	37.01 N	76.59 E
Akmeşe	130	40.51 N	30.12 E
Akmuz	85	41.16 N	76.09 E
Ākna	272b	22.59 N	88.21 E
Aknet, gora ∧	86	50.51 N	75.40 E
Aknīste	76	56.10 N	25.45 E
Aknoul	148	34.43 N	3.49 W
Ako, Nig.	146	10.17 N	10.58 E
Akō, Nihon	96	34.45 N	134.24 E
Akoba	80	49.28 N	47.25 E
Akobo	140	7.47 N	33.01 E
Akobo (Akūbū) ≃	140	7.47 N	33.03 E
Akodiya	124	23.23 N	76.36 E
Akok, Cam.	152	2.46 N	10.18 E
Akok, Gabon	152	0.31 N	9.45 E
Akola	122	20.44 N	77.00 E
Akonolinga	152	3.47 N	12.15 E
Akop	140	8.21 N	29.05 E
Akor	150	14.53 N	6.58 W
Akora	123	34.00 N	72.08 E
Akordat	144	15.33 N	37.53 E
Akören	130	37.27 N	32.23 E
Akosombo Dam ◆[6]	150	6.16 N	0.03 E
Akot, India	120	21.11 N	77.04 E
Akot, Sūd.	140	6.33 N	30.03 E
Akoupé	150	6.23 N	3.54 W
Akowonjo	273a	6.37 N	3.19 E
Akpatok Island I	176	60.25 N	68.00 W
Akpınar, Tür.	130	37.34 N	38.13 E
Akpınar, Tür.	130	39.17 N	33.40 E
Akqi	85	40.52 N	77.58 E
Åkrafjorden ⊂[2]	26	59.46 N	6.06 E
Akranes	24a	64.18 N	22.02 W
Åkrehamn	26	59.16 N	5.11 E
Akrítas, Ákra ›	38	36.43 N	21.54 E
Akrofuom	150	6.07 N	1.39 W
Akrokórinthos ⊥	38	37.54 N	22.56 E
Akron, Co., U.S.	198	40.09 N	103.12 W
Akron, In., U.S.	216	41.02 N	86.01 W
Akron, Ia., U.S.	198	42.49 N	96.33 W
Akron, N.Y., U.S.	210	43.01 N	78.29 W
Akron, Oh., U.S.	214	41.04 N	81.31 W
Akron, Pa., U.S.	208	40.09 N	76.12 W
Akron-Canton Regional Airport ⊠	214	40.55 N	81.27 W
Akron City Reservoir ⊜[1]	214	41.20 N	81.17 W
Akrotíri	130	34.36 N	32.57 E
Akša	88	50.16 N	113.17 E
Aksa ◆[8]	272c	19.10 N	72.48 E
Aksaj, S.S.S.R.	80	51.09 N	53.00 E
Aksaj, S.S.S.R.	80	47.58 N	43.59 E
Aksaj, S.S.S.R.	83	47.15 N	39.52 E
Aksaj, S.S.S.R.	85	43.22 N	70.12 E
Aksaj (Toxkan) ≃, Asia	85	40.55 N	78.16 E
Aksaj ≃, S.S.S.R.	83	47.15 N	39.53 E
Aksaj ≃, S.S.S.R.	84	43.32 N	46.51 E
Aksakovo	80	54.02 N	54.09 E
Aksaray	130	38.23 N	34.03 E
Aksarka	74	66.36 N	67.46 E
Akšatau	86	49.23 N	54.36 E
Aksaut ≃	84	43.55 N	41.42 E
Aksay	102	39.28 N	94.15 E
Aksayqin Hu ⊜	120	35.12 N	79.50 E
Akşehir	130	38.21 N	31.25 E
Akşehir Gölü ⊜	130	38.30 N	31.28 E
Akseki	130	37.02 N	31.48 E
Aksengir ≃	85	43.40 N	76.14 E
Aksenkino	80	53.59 N	53.06 E
Aksenovo	82	55.40 N	38.15 E
Aksentjevo	82	55.25 N	35.54 E
Akšij	86	47.37 N	55.56 E
Akšijrak, chrebet ⋏	85	41.20 N	74.15 E
Aksinjino, S.S.S.R.	82	55.44 N	36.59 E
Aksinjino, S.S.S.R.	82	56.02 N	38.12 E
Aks'onovo	88	58.51 N	101.43 E
Aks'onovo-Zilovskoje	88	53.04 N	117.32 E
Aksoran, gora ∧	86	48.27 N	75.32 E
Akstafa	84	41.08 N	45.28 E
Akstafa ≃	84	41.15 N	45.26 E
Aksu, S.S.S.R.	80	50.56 N	53.06 E
Aksu, S.S.S.R.	86	52.28 N	71.59 E

	English	Deutsch	Español	Français	Português
≃	River	Fluß	Río	Rivière	Rio
≅	Canal	Kanal	Canal	Canal	Canal
⌊	Waterfall, Rapids	Wasserfall, Stromschnellen	Cascada, Rápidos	Chute d'eau, Rapides	Cascata, Rápidos
ꓤ	Strait	Meeresstraße	Estrecho	Détroit	Estreito
⊂	Bay, Gulf	Bucht, Golf	Bahía, Golfo	Baie, Golfe	Baía, Golfo
⊜	Lake, Lakes	See, Seen	Lago, Lagos	Lac, Lacs	Lago, Lagos
≋	Swamp	Sumpf	Pantano	Marais	Pântano
⌂	Ice Features, Glacier	Eis- und Gletscherformen	Accidentes Glaciales	Formes glaciaires	Acidentes glaciares
⊤	Other Hydrographic Features	Andere Hydrographische Objekte	Otros Elementos Hidrográficos	Autres données hydrographiques	Outros acidentes hidrográficos
✦	Submarine Features	Untermeerische Objekte	Accidentes Submarinos	Formes de relief sous-marin	Acidentes submarinos
□	Political Unit	Politische Einheit	Unidad Politica	Entité politique	Unidade política
⊍	Cultural Institution	Kulturelle Institution	Institución Cultural	Institution culturelle	Instituição cultural
⊥	Historical Site	Historische Stätte	Sitio Histórico	Site historique	Sitio histórico
♦	Recreational Site	Erholungs- und Ferienort	Sitio de Recreo	Centre de loisirs	Area de Lazer
⊠	Airport	Flughafen	Aeropuerto	Aéroport	Aeroporto
■	Military Installation	Militäranlage	Instalación Militar	Installation militaire	Instalação militar
◆	Miscellaneous	Verschiedenes	Misceláneo	Divers	Diversos

Name	Page	Lat.°′	Long.°′	Name	Seite	Breite°′	Länge°′ E = Ost

Aksu, S.S.S.R.	86	45.37 N	79.30 E
Aksu, Tür.	130	38.58 N	30.50 E
Aksu, Zhg.	90	41.10 N	80.20 E
Aksu ≃, S.S.S.R.	85	43.22 N	73.54 E
Aksu ≃, S.S.S.R.	86	46.20 N	78.15 E
Aksu ≃, Tür.	130	36.51 N	30.54 E
Aksu ≃, Tür.	130	37.25 N	36.54 E
Aksuat, ozero @	86	51.24 N	64.28 E
Aksuat, S.S.S.R.	86	51.32 N	64.34 E
Aksuat, S.S.S.R.	86	47.45 N	82.40 E
Aksuat, S.S.S.R.	86	48.16 N	83.50 E
Aksubajevo	80	54.52 N	50.50 E
Aksu-Džabaglinskij zapovednik ✦	144	14.08 N	38.43 E
Aksum	120	36.45 N	84.40 E
Aktag ▲	85	41.25 N	75.03 E
Aktal	80	55.43 N	54.05 E
Aktanyš	85	42.57 N	70.04 E
Aktaš, S.S.S.R.	86	41.38 N	69.44 E
Aktaš, S.S.S.R.	86	50.18 N	87.44 E
Aktaš, S.S.S.R.	86	48.02 N	66.21 E
Aktaš, S.S.S.R.	86	49.47 N	72.59 E
Aktaš, S.S.S.R.	86	50.06 N	76.40 E
Aktaş Gölü @	84	41.15 N	43.12 E
Aktau	86	50.44 N	61.43 E
Aktau, gora ▲	86	50.16 N	73.02 E
Aktepe	130	36.44 N	36.27 E
Akterek, S.S.S.R.	85	43.22 N	75.18 E
Akterek, S.S.S.R.	85	42.14 N	77.45 E
Akto	85	39.08 N	75.57 E
Aktobe	85	49.58 N	67.46 E
Aktogaj, S.S.S.R.	86	44.27 N	76.42 E
Aktogaj, S.S.S.R.	86	48.18 N	74.58 E
Aktogaj, S.S.S.R.	86	46.57 N	79.40 E
Aktubek	86	48.37 N	71.06 E
Akt'ubinsk	86	50.17 N	57.10 E
Akt'ubinskij	80	54.49 N	52.47 E
Aktuluk	130	39.03 N	39.32 E
Aktumsyk	86	46.40 N	57.19 E
Akt'uz	85	42.54 N	76.07 E
Aku	150	6.42 N	7.20 E
Akūbū (Akobo) ≃	140	7.47 N	33.03 E
Akui	96	34.06 N	134.33 E
Akula	152	2.22 N	20.11 E
Akuliči Pervyje	76	53.11 N	33.13 E
Akulovo, S.S.S.R.	80	55.31 N	36.42 E
Akulovo, S.S.S.R.	82	56.05 N	38.59 E
Akumadan	150	7.24 N	1.57 W
Akune	92	32.01 N	130.11 E
Akun Island I	186	54.12 N	165.35 W
Akure	150	7.15 N	5.12 E
Akureyri	24a	65.44 N	18.08 W
Akurli	272c	19.01 N	73.08 E
Akuša	84	42.17 N	47.21 E
Akuse	150	6.06 N	0.08 E
Akuseki-jima I	93b	29.27 N	129.37 E
Akutan	180	54.08 N	165.46 W
Akutan Island I	180	54.10 N	165.55 W
Akutan Pass ⊔	180	54.00 N	166.10 W
Akuticha	86	52.27 N	84.29 E
Akwa Ibom ◻³	150	4.50 N	7.50 E
Akwanga	150	8.55 N	8.23 E
Akwatia	150	6.04 N	0.49 W
Akwaya ▲²	150	6.27 N	0.25 W
Akyab → Sittwe	152	6.30 N	9.42 E
Akyab → Sittwe	110	20.09 N	92.54 E
Akyazı	130	40.41 N	30.37 E
Akyel	144	12.33 N	37.04 E
Akyrt-T'ube	85	42.59 N	72.07 E
Akyurt	130	37.25 N	36.54 E
Akžajkyn, ozero @	86	44.55 N	67.46 E
Akžal, S.S.S.R.	86	47.47 N	74.02 E
Akžal, S.S.S.R.	86	49.13 N	81.25 E
Akžar, S.S.S.R.	86	47.33 N	83.42 E
Akžar, S.S.S.R.	86	48.34 N	75.30 E
Akžaryk	86	48.30 N	8.34 E
Al	26	60.38 N	8.34 E
Ala	64	45.45 N	11.00 E
Ala ⊃	64	44.42 N	89.12 E
Alà, Monti di ⋌	71	40.40 N	9.14 E
Al-Abʹādīyah	142	31.22 N	31.07 E
Alabama	210	43.06 N	78.23 W
Alabama ◻³, U.S.	178	32.50 N	87.00 W
Alabama ◻³, U.S.	194	32.30 N	87.00 W
Alabama ≃	194	31.08 N	87.57 W
Alabama and Coushatta Indian Reservation ✦⁴	222	30.13 N	94.42 W
Alabaster	194	33.14 N	86.48 W
Alabat Island I	116	14.07 N	122.03 E
Al-ʿAbbāsah ash-Sharqīyah	142	30.32 N	31.43 E
Al-ʿAbbāsīyah	140	12.10 N	31.18 E
Al-ʿAbbāsīyah ◻⁸	273c	30.04 N	31.17 E
Alabino	82	55.31 N	37.01 E
Alā ʿĀbis	144	18.04 N	43.10 E
Ala-Buga	85	41.26 N	74.41 E
Ala-Buka	85	41.23 N	71.30 E
Alaca	130	40.10 N	34.51 E
Alacahan	130	39.07 N	37.37 E
Alaçam	130	41.11 N	29.27 E
Alaçam	130	41.37 N	35.37 E
Alaçam Dağları ⋌	130	39.20 N	28.32 E
Alaçatı	34	38.21 N	0.29 W
Alaçatı	130	38.16 N	26.23 E
Alachadzy	84	43.14 N	40.18 E
Alachua	192	29.47 N	82.29 W
Alacrán, Arrecife ▲²	232	22.24 N	89.42 W
Aladağ	130	37.02 N	32.41 E
Aladağ ▲, Tür.	130	42.49 N	18.16 E
Aladağ ▲, Tür.	130	37.44 N	35.09 E
Aladağlar ▲, Tür.	130	39.20 N	43.35 E
Ala Dağlar ⋌, Tür.	130	37.55 N	35.13 E
Al-ʿAdasīyah	132	32.40 N	35.37 E
Ala dei Sardi	71	40.39 N	9.22 E
Aladino	88	58.24 N	95.29 E
Aladinskij, porog ⌊	86	56.21 N	37.04 E
Aladža manastir ⊽¹	84	43.18 N	28.01 E
Alafia ≃	220	27.52 N	82.23 W
Alafia, South Prong ≃	220	27.51 N	82.08 W
Alagir	72	43.03 N	44.14 E
Alagna Valsesia	62	45.51 N	7.56 E
Alago nuur @	90	44.28 E
Alagoa	258	22.05 N	44.38 W
Alagoa Grande	256	7.03 S	35.38 W
Alagoa Nova	256	7.05 S	36.00 W
Alagoinhas	255	12.07 S	38.26 W
Alagón	34	41.46 N	1.07 W
Alagón ≃	34	39.44 N	6.53 W
Alaguntan	273a	6.26 N	3.37 E
Alah ≃	116	6.53 N	124.33 E
Alahanpanjang	112	1.05 S	100.47 E
Alahärmä	26	63.14 N	22.51 E
Alajärvi	26	63.00 N	23.49 E
Al-ʿAjamīyīn	142	29.20 N	30.43 E
Alajõe	85	50.18 N	74.25 E
Alajskaja dolina V	85	39.45 N	72.00 E
Alajskij chrebet ⋌	85	39.30 N	72.00 E
Alajuela	236	10.30 N	84.12 W
Alajuela, Lago @	236	9.10 N	79.40 W
Alāʾijüjeh	138	38.57 N	46.41 E
Alakai Swamp ⯑	229b		
Alakamisy	157b	21.19 S	47.14 E
Alakanuk	186	62.41 N	164.37 W
Alakoʾada	124	30.18 N	48.15 E
Alakol', ozero @	86	46.10 N	81.45 E
Alaktara	124	22.01 N	82.26 E
Alak'ura	85	42.11 N	70.27 E
Alakurtti	24	66.57 N	30.18 E
Al-ʿĀl	132	32.48 N	35.44 E

Alalakeiki Channel ⊔	229a	20.35 N	156.30 W
Al-ʿAlamayn	140	30.49 N	28.57 E
Al-ʿAlāqimah	142	30.37 N	31.38 E
Alalaú ≃	246	0.30 S	61.09 W
Al-ʿAmādīyah	128	37.06 N	43.29 E
Alamagan I	100	17.36 N	145.50 E
Al-ʿAmārah	128	31.50 N	47.09 E
Al-ʿAmbar al-Kubrā	142	30.21 N	31.08 E
Alamata	144	12.25 N	39.33 E
Alamdānga	124	23.46 N	88.57 E
Alameda, Esp.	34	37.12 N	4.39 W
Alameda, Ca., U.S.	226	37.45 N	122.14 W
Alameda, N.M., U.S.	200	35.11 N	106.37 W
Alameda, Estación	226	37.35 N	121.55 W
Alamicho ≃⁵	286e	33.27 S	70.41 W
Alameda Creek ≃	226	37.35 N	122.09 W
Alameda Naval Air Station ▪	226	37.47 N	122.18 W
Alamein	85	44.51 N	84.58 W
→ Al-ʿAlamayn	140	30.49 N	28.57 E
Alamillo	200	31.02 N	110.35 W
Alaminos	116	16.10 N	119.59 E
Al-ʿĀmirīyah	142	31.01 N	29.48 E
Alam Lek	128	37.02 N	65.57 E
Alamo, Méx.	234	20.55 N	97.41 W
Alamo, Ca., U.S.	226	37.51 N	122.02 W
Alamo, Ga., U.S.	192	32.08 N	82.46 W
Alamo, Mi., U.S.	216	42.22 N	85.43 W
Alamo, Nv., U.S.	204	37.21 N	115.09 W
Alamo, Tn., U.S.	194	35.47 N	89.07 W
Alamo ≃	204	33.14 N	115.39 W
Alamo Creek ≃	282	37.42 N	121.55 W
Alamo Creek, West Branch ≃	282	37.45 N	121.55 W
Alamogordo	200	32.53 N	105.57 W
Alamogordo Creek ≃	196	34.40 N	104.23 W
Alamo Heights	196	29.29 N	98.27 W
Alamo Indian Reservation ✦⁴	200	34.30 N	107.30 W
Alamo Lake @¹	200	34.13 N	113.34 W
Alamo Oaks	282	37.51 N	121.59 W
Alamor	246	4.02 S	80.02 W
Alamos, Méx.	226	26.25 N	100.25 W
Álamos, Méx.	232	27.01 N	108.56 W
Álamos, Río de los ≃	232	27.53 N	101.12 W
Alamosa	200	37.28 N	105.52 W
Alamosa ≃	200	37.22 N	105.46 W
Alamosa Creek ≃, N.M., U.S.	196	34.26 N	103.58 W
Alamosa Creek ≃, N.M., U.S.	200	33.20 N	107.21 W
Álamos East	200	37.28 N	105.49 W
Álamos de San Felipe, Cerro ▲	232	30.41 N	112.35 W
Ālampur, Bngl.	126	23.49 N	89.06 E
Ālampur, India	272b	22.25 N	88.08 E
Alanäs	26	64.10 N	15.42 E
Al-ʿAnāt ≃	132	32.21 N	36.48 E
Al-Anbār ◻⁴	128	33.45 N	41.45 E
Åland	122	17.34 N	76.34 E
Åland (Ahvenanmaa) ◻	26	60.15 N	20.00 E
Åland ≃	54	53.02 N	11.34 E
Åland-Inseln → Åland ◻	26	60.15 N	20.00 E
Ålands hav ⫝̸² ≃	26	60.00 N	19.00 E
Alandur	122	13.02 N	80.15 E
Alangalang	116	11.12 N	124.51 E
Alang-besar, Pulau I	118	1.22 N	100.39 E
Alano di Piave	64	45.55 N	11.55 E
Alanson	190	45.26 N	84.47 W
Alanya	130	36.33 N	32.01 E
Al-ʿAnz	142	32.23 N	36.38 E
Alaotra, Lac @	157b	17.30 S	48.30 E
Alapaha	192	31.23 N	83.13 W
Alapaha ≃	192	30.26 N	83.06 W
Alapajevsk	86	57.52 N	61.42 E
Alapli	130	41.11 N	31.24 E
Al-ʿAqabah	132	29.31 N	35.00 E
Al-ʿAlaqah, Jabal ▲	142	29.59 N	32.53 E
Alaquines	234	22.08 N	99.36 W
Al-ʿArabīyah as-Suʿūdīyah → Saudi Arabia ◻¹	118	25.00 N	45.00 E
Alarcón, Embalse de @¹	34	39.33 N	2.05 W
Al-ʿArīsh	132	31.08 N	33.48 E
Al-ʿArmah ⫝̸¹	124	25.30 N	46.30 E
Alarobia Vohiposa	157b	20.59 S	47.09 E
Alas ≃, Indon.	114	3.05 N	97.55 E
Alaş ≃, S.S.S.R.	86	48.13 N	90.54 E
Alas, Selat ⊔	115b	8.40 S	116.40 E
Alasan	112	1.45 S	123.19 E
Alasdair, Sgurr ▲	46	57.12 N	6.14 W
Al-ʿAshārah	130	38.21 N	28.32 E
Al-ʿAshmūnayn	142	27.47 N	30.49 E
Alaska	230	42.50 N	85.29 W
Alaska ◻³	216	65.00 N	153.00 W
Alaska, Gulf of ⊂	180	58.00 N	146.00 W
Alaska Peninsula ▹¹	180	57.00 N	158.00 W
Alaska Range ⋌	180	62.30 N	150.00 W
Al-ʿAssāfīyah	124	28.21 N	39.09 E
Alassio	62	44.00 N	8.10 E
Alastaro	26	60.56 N	22.55 E
Alastuey	258	34.25 S	59.13 W
Al-Atābād	124	32.47 N	59.54 E
Al-ʿAṭāminah	142	29.26 N	30.50 E
Alatan'aola → Xin Barag Youqi	88	48.41 N	116.53 E
Alatri	68	41.43 N	13.21 E
Al-ʿAṭrūn	140	18.11 N	26.36 E
Alatyr'	80	54.51 N	46.36 E
Alatyr' ≃	80	54.52 N	46.36 E
Alausí	246	2.12 S	78.50 W
Alava, Cape ▹	224	48.10 N	124.43 W
Alaverdi	26	61.08 N	44.39 E
Alavieska	26	64.10 N	24.18 E
Alavus	26	62.35 N	23.37 E
Alaw, Llyn @¹	44	53.20 N	4.22 W
Alāwalpur	131	31.26 N	75.39 E
Al-ʿAwājā	126	26.49 N	41.41 E
Al-ʿAwshazīyah	128	26.49 N	41.41 E
ʿĀlayh	130	33.48 N	35.36 E
Al-ʿAyn	124	24.13 N	55.46 E
Al-ʿAyyāsh ash-Sharqī	142	31.33 N	31.13 E
Al-ʿAyyāt	142	29.37 N	31.15 E
Alazani ≃	84	41.05 N	46.40 E
Alazeja ≃	142	70.51 N	153.34 E
Al-Azhar University	273c	30.03 N	31.16 E
Alʾ-Azīzīyah, Lībyā	146	32.32 N	13.01 E
Alʾ-Azīzīyah, Lībyā	146	30.29 N	31.18 E
Alʾ-Azīzīyah, Miṣr	273c	29.52 N	31.15 E
Al-ʿAzraq ≃	132	32.32 N	36.50 E
Alb ⫝̸	58	47.35 N	8.08 E
Alba	62	44.42 N	8.02 E
Alba, Mi., U.S.	216	44.58 N	84.58 W
Alba, N.Y., U.S.	210	41.44 N	76.50 W
Alba, Tx., U.S.	196	32.48 N	95.38 W
Al-Bāb	130	36.22 N	37.31 E
Albacete	34	38.59 N	1.51 W
Albacita	66	37.55 N	13.01 E

Al-Badʾ	128	28.25 N	35.04 E
Al-Badārī	140	26.59 N	31.25 E
Alba de Tormes	34	40.49 N	5.31 W
Al-Badrashayn	142	29.51 N	31.16 E
Albæk	26	57.36 N	10.25 E
Al-Bahnasā	142	28.32 N	30.39 E
Al-Baḥr al-Abyaḍ ◻⁴	140	13.15 N	32.25 E
Al-Baḥr al-Aḥmar ◻⁴, Misr	142	28.45 N	32.00 E
Al-Baḥr al-Aḥmar ◻⁴, Süd.	140	20.00 N	35.15 E
Al-Baḥrayn → Bahrain ◻¹	128	26.00 N	50.30 E
Albaida	34	38.51 N	0.31 W
Albairate	266b	45.25 N	8.56 E
Alba Iulia	38	46.04 N	23.35 E
Al-Bajalāt	142	31.10 N	31.37 E
Al-Bājūr	142	30.26 N	31.02 E
Al-Bakātūsh	142	31.03 N	30.48 E
Al-Balāṣ ≃	142	30.26 N	31.26 E
Al-Balāshūn	142	30.26 N	31.26 E
Al-Ballah	142	30.46 N	32.19 E
Al-Ballāş	140	26.01 N	32.46 E
Al-Balqāʾ ◻⁸	132	32.00 N	35.40 E
Al-Balqāʾ ◻⁸	130	35.55 N	36.28 E
Al-Balyanā	140	26.14 N	32.00 E
Alban	32	43.54 N	2.28 E
Albanel, Lac @	176	50.55 N	73.12 W
Albanella	68	40.30 N	15.08 E
Albani, Colli ⋌²	68	41.45 N	12.45 E
Albania (Shqipëri) ◻¹, Europe	22	41.00 N	20.00 E
Albania (Shqipëri) ◻¹, Europe	38	41.00 N	20.00 E
Albanie → Albania ◻¹	38	41.00 N	20.00 E
Albanien → Albania ◻¹	38	41.00 N	20.00 E
Albano, Lago @	66	41.45 N	12.40 E
Albano, Monte ▲	66	43.50 N	10.58 E
Albano di Lucania	68	40.35 N	16.02 E
Albano Laziale	66	41.44 N	12.39 E
Al-Biqāʾ ≃¹	130	34.00 N	36.00 E
Al-Biqāʾ V	128	33.50 N	36.00 E
Al-Bīʾr	132	34.34 N	35.13 E
Al-Birīgāt	142	30.30 N	30.49 E
Al-Birk	144	18.13 N	41.33 E
Al-Birkah	142	24.54 N	10.11 E
Al-Birkah ≃⁴	144	22.12 N	40.43 E
Albisola Marina	62	44.19 N	8.30 E
Albisola Superiore	62	44.19 N	8.30 E
Albizzate	62	45.43 N	8.44 E
Albbasseraam	52	51.52 N	4.40 E
Albo, Monte ⋌	71	40.32 N	9.35 E
Albocàsser	34	40.21 N	0.02 E
Albogas	266c	38.51 N	9.15 W
Alboran, Isla de I	34	35.58 S	3.02 W
Alborán Sea ≃²	34	36.00 N	3.00 W
Ålborg	26	57.03 N	9.56 E
Ålborg Bugt ⊂	26	56.45 N	10.30 E
Al-Barājil	273c	30.04 N	31.09 E
Al-Barāmūn	142	31.07 N	31.26 E
Albardón ≃	258	31.26 S	68.32 W
Albarado d'Adige	64	45.19 N	11.16 E
Al-Barīhah	132	32.34 N	35.50 E
Al-Barnūjī	142	30.56 N	30.23 E
Albaron	62	43.37 N	4.28 E
Albarracín	34	40.25 N	1.26 W
Al-Barrah	128	24.55 N	45.52 E
Albarraque	266c	38.46 N	9.21 W
Al-Barun	140	11.44 N	33.30 E
Al-Basāṭīn ≃⁴	273c	29.59 N	31.16 E
Al-Başāqūn	142	31.06 N	30.08 E
Al-Başqalīn	142	28.42 N	30.44 E
Al-Başrah (Basra)	128	30.30 N	47.47 E
Al-Basrah ◻⁴	128	30.20 N	47.45 E
Al-Batānūn	142	30.37 N	30.59 E
Al-Bathāʾ	128	31.06 N	45.53 E
Al-Bāṭinah ≃¹	128	23.45 N	57.20 E
Albatross Bay ⊂	166	12.45 S	141.43 E
Albatross Point ▹	172	38.06 S	174.41 E
Al-Batrūn	130	34.15 N	35.39 E
Al-Batrūnah	132	33.39 N	36.02 E
Al-Bauga	140	18.16 N	33.55 E
Al-Bawīṭī	140	28.21 N	28.52 E
Albay	116	13.09 N	123.40 E
Albay, Gulf of ⊂	116	13.16 N	123.45 E
Albbruck	58	47.35 N	8.07 E
Albegna ≃	66	42.30 N	11.11 E
Albemarle	192	35.13 N	80.13 W
Albemarle and Chesapeake Canal ☰	208	36.43 N	76.15 W
Albemarle Sound ⊔	192	36.03 N	76.12 W
Albenga	62	44.03 N	8.13 E
Albens	62	45.47 N	5.57 E
Alberche ≃	34	39.58 N	4.46 W
Alberdi	252	26.10 S	58.09 W
Aberdeen	182	37.53 N	78.37 W
Alberga, Austl.	162	27.12 S	135.28 E
Alberga, Sve.	30	58.44 N	16.34 E
Alberga Creek ≃	162	27.06 S	135.33 E
Albergaria-a-Velha	34	40.42 N	8.29 W
Alberhill	228	33.44 N	117.23 W
Alberik	52	39.07 N	0.31 W
Alberni Inlet ⊂	182	49.07 N	124.50 W
Alberobello	68	40.47 N	17.15 E
Al-Berka	128	30.22 N	43.40 E
Albero Sole ▲	70a	35.31 N	12.32 E
Albers	219	38.32 N	89.37 W
Alberschwende	58	47.27 N	9.49 E
Albersloh	52	51.52 N	7.43 E
Albert ≃	30	50.00 N	2.39 E
Albert ≃	171a	27.42 S	153.15 E
Albert, Lake @, Afr.	154	1.40 N	31.00 E
Albert, Lake @, Austl.	162	35.38 S	139.17 E
Alberta	166	35.08 N	24.19 E
Alberta ◻⁴, Can.	176	54.00 N	113.00 W
Alberta ◻⁴, Can.	178	54.00 N	113.00 W
Alberta, Mount ▲	182	52.18 N	117.28 W
Alberta, Mount ▲	182	51.08 N	117.52 W
Albert Canyon	182	51.08 N	117.55 W
Albert City	198	42.46 N	94.56 W
Albert Edward, Mount ▲	164	8.23 S	147.24 E
Albert Edward Bay ⊂	176	69.32 N	103.00 W
Albert Falls	158	29.27 S	30.25 E
Albertfalva ≃⁸	264c	47.27 N	19.02 E
Alberti	252	35.02 S	60.16 W
Albertina	256	22.15 S	46.37 W
Albertina ≃	256	34.13 S	21.36 E
Albertirsa	60	47.15 N	19.38 E
Albert Lea	190	43.39 N	93.22 W
Albert Markham, Mount ▲	9	81.23 S	158.12 E
Albert Nile ≃	154	3.36 N	32.02 E
→ Albert, Lake @	154	1.40 N	31.00 E
Alberto Eduardo, Mount ▲	164	46.49 N	147.04 W
Alberton, P.E., Can.	176	46.49 N	64.04 W
Alberton, S. Afr.	273d	26.16 S	28.08 E
Albertson, Mt., U.S.	202	44.00 N	114.29 W
Albert Park ◻⁸	278	37.51 S	144.57 E
Albert Park ◻⁸	274b	32.51 S	151.22 E
Albert Peak ▲	182	51.02 N	117.51 W
Albert River ≃	264a	52.12 N	8.40 E
Albertson	276	40.46 N	73.38 W
Albertson Brook ≃	285	39.41 N	74.45 W

Albertson Brook, Blue Anchor Branch ≃	285	39.42 N	74.49 W
Albertson Brook, Pump Branch ≃	285	39.42 N	74.49 W
Albert Town	241q	18.17 N	77.33 W
Albertville, Fr.	62	45.41 N	6.23 E
Albertville, Al., U.S.	194	34.16 N	86.12 W
Albertville → Kalemie, Zaïre	154	5.56 S	29.12 E
Albestroff	56	48.56 N	6.51 E
Albettone	64	45.21 N	11.35 E
Albi	32	43.56 N	2.09 E
Albia, Ia., U.S.	190	41.01 N	92.48 W
Albia, N.Y., U.S.	210	42.43 N	73.39 W
Albiate	266b	45.39 N	9.15 E
Al Bidia	146	10.33 N	20.13 E
Albidona	68	39.55 N	16.28 E
Abignasego	64	45.21 N	11.52 E
Albin	198	41.25 N	104.05 W
Albina	64	5.30 N	54.03 W
Albina ≃	62	45.46 N	9.47 E
Albion, Austl.	274b	37.47 S	144.49 E
Albion, B.C., Can.	224	49.11 N	122.33 W
Albion, Ca., U.S.	204	39.13 N	123.46 W
Albion, Id., U.S.	202	42.24 N	113.34 W
Albion, Il., U.S.	194	38.22 N	88.03 W
Albion, In., U.S.	216	41.23 N	85.25 W
Albion, Ia., U.S.	190	42.06 N	92.59 W
Albion, Mi., U.S.	216	42.14 N	84.45 W
Albion, Ne., U.S.	198	41.41 N	98.00 W
Albion, N.J., U.S.	285	39.47 N	74.56 W
Albion, N.Y., U.S.	210	42.54 N	78.29 W
Albion, N.Y., U.S.	210	43.14 N	78.11 W
Albion, Pa., U.S.	214	41.53 N	80.22 W
Albion, Pa., U.S.	207	41.57 N	77.27 W
Albion, Wa., U.S.	202	46.47 N	117.14 W
Albion, Wi., U.S.	216	42.52 N	89.04 W
Albion Park	285	39.46 N	75.28 W
Aldbourne	42	51.31 N	1.37 W
Aldbrough	44	53.50 N	0.07 W
Aldbury	42	51.48 N	0.36 W
Alde ≃	42	52.03 N	1.28 E
Aldea Apeleg	254	44.49 N	71.03 E
Aldeburgh	42	52.09 N	1.35 E
Aldecoa ≃⁸	266b	23.07 N	82.22 W
Aldeia	256	23.30 S	46.51 W
Aldeia de Carapicuíba	287b	23.35 S	46.48 W
Aldeia de Paio Pires	266c	38.38 N	9.05 W
Aldeia Nova de Santo Bento	34	37.55 N	7.25 W
Aldeia Velha	256	22.47 S	42.55 W
Aldeinha	287b	23.45 S	46.53 W
Alden, Il., U.S.	216	42.27 N	88.31 W
Alden, Ia., U.S.	190	42.31 N	93.22 W
Alden, Mn., U.S.	190	43.40 N	93.34 W
Alden, N.Y., U.S.	210	42.54 N	78.29 W
Alden, N.Y., U.S.	210	41.16 N	76.00 W
Alden, Pa., U.S.	210	42.54 N	78.32 W
Aldenham	260	51.40 N	0.21 W
Aldenhoven	56	50.53 N	6.16 E
Aldenrade ≃⁸	263	51.31 N	6.44 E
Alder, Ben ▲	46	56.48 N	4.28 W
Alder Creek ≃	202	45.50 N	119.56 W
Aldergrove	224	49.04 N	122.28 W
Alder Lake @¹	224	46.44 N	122.15 W
Alderley Edge	262	53.18 N	2.14 W
Aldermaston	42	51.23 N	1.09 W
Alderney I	43b	49.43 N	2.12 W
Alder Peak ▲	226	35.53 N	121.22 W
Aldersbach	60	48.36 N	13.05 E
Aldershot	42	51.15 N	0.47 W
Alderson	192	37.44 N	80.38 W
Alderwood Manor	224	47.49 N	122.17 W
Aldine	222	29.54 N	95.24 W
Aldinga	168b	35.17 S	138.29 E
Aldinga Bay ⊂	168b	35.20 S	138.25 E
Aldinga Beach	168b	35.18 S	138.27 E
Aldino	64	46.23 N	11.20 E
Aldo Bonzi	288	34.42 S	58.31 W
Aldridge	42	52.36 N	1.55 W
Aldwell, Lake @¹	224	48.05 N	123.34 W
Aledo, Il., U.S.	190	41.11 N	90.45 W
Aledo, Tx., U.S.	222	32.42 N	97.36 W
Alefa	144	11.57 N	36.52 E
Aleg	150	17.03 N	13.55 W
Alegranza, Isla I	148	29.23 N	13.30 W
Alegre	256	20.46 S	41.32 W
Alegres Mountain ▲	200	34.09 N	108.11 W
Alegrete	252	29.46 S	55.46 W
Alej ≃	86	52.52 N	83.36 E
Alejandría	58	46.42 N	9.27 E
Alejandro, Isla I	254	36.47 N	3.12 W
Alejandro Roca	252	33.21 S	63.43 W
Alejo Ledesma	236	12.10 N	81.50 W
Alejsk	86	52.28 N	82.45 E
Aleknagik	180	59.17 N	158.38 W
Aleknagik, Lake @	180	59.20 N	158.45 W
Aleksandrija	78	48.40 N	33.07 E
Aleksandrijskaja	84	43.54 N	47.08 E
Aleksandro-Nevskaja	84	43.55 N	44.35 E
Aleksandro-Nevskij	80	53.28 N	40.13 E
Aleksandropol' → Leninakan	84	40.48 N	43.50 E
Aleksandrov	82	56.24 N	38.43 E
Aleksandrov Gaj	80	50.09 N	48.34 E
Aleksandrovac	38	43.28 N	21.05 E
Aleksandrovac	78	46.47 N	39.01 E
Aleksandrovka, Austl.	166	36.47 S	36.55 E
Aleksandrovka, N.Z.	172	38.53 N	32.14 E
Aleksandrovka, S. Afr.	158	48.57 N	32.14 E
Aleksandrovo	54	51.49 N	9.16 E
Aleksandrovo	78	47.42 N	31.16 E
Aleksandrovsk	80	59.09 N	57.36 E
Aleksandrovsk ▲	86	50.42 N	142.11 W
Aleksandrovskaja	78	45.40 N	33.07 E
Aleksandrovskaja	82	59.44 N	30.21 E
Aleksandrovsk-Sachalinskij	86	50.54 N	142.10 E
Aleksandrówów Łódzki	46	51.49 N	19.19 E
Aleksejevka, S.S.S.R.	86	50.57 N	73.23 E
Aleksejevka, S.S.S.R.	78	50.38 N	38.42 E
Aleksejevka, S.S.S.R.	82	52.40 N	58.04 E
Aleksejevka, S.S.S.R.	80	52.15 N	51.17 E
Aleksejevka, S.S.S.R.	80	52.08 N	49.08 E
Aleksejevskaja	78	50.12 N	41.43 E
Aleksejevskoje	80	55.18 N	50.06 E
Aleksin	82	54.31 N	37.05 E
Aleksinac	38	43.32 N	21.43 E
Alella	266d	41.30 N	2.18 E

Alcove Reservoir @¹	210	42.29 N	73.57 W
Alcoy ≃	192	33.26 N	83.50 W
Alcoy, Nevado ▲	248	11.17 S	76.30 W
Alcubierre	34	41.48 N	0.27 W
Alcudia	34	39.52 N	3.07 E
Alcúdia, Badia d' ⊂	34	39.48 N	3.13 E
Alcyon Lake @	285	39.44 N	75.08 W
Aldabra Island I	138	9.25 S	46.22 E
Aldama, Méx.	232	28.51 N	105.54 W
Aldama, Méx.	234	22.55 N	98.04 W
Aldan, Arroyo ≃	236b	23.05 N	82.15 W
Aldan, S.S.S.R.	74	58.37 N	125.24 E
Aldan, Pa., U.S.	235	39.55 N	75.17 W
Aldan ≃	74	63.28 N	129.35 E
Alemana, República Democrática → German Democratic Republic ◻¹	30	52.00 N	12.30 E
Alemania, Arg.	252	25.36 S	65.38 W
Alemania, Chile	252	25.10 S	69.55 W
Alemania, República Federal de → Germany, Federal Republic of ◻¹	30	51.00 N	9.00 E
Alem Dağı ▲	267b	41.04 N	29.12 E
Alemdar ≃⁸	267b	41.03 N	29.14 E
Além Paraíba	256	21.52 S	42.41 W
Alençon	32	48.26 N	0.05 E
Alengue	250	1.56 S	54.46 W
Alentejo ◻⁹	34	38.00 N	8.00 W
Alenuihaha Channel ⊔	229a	20.26 N	156.00 W
Alep → Ḥalab	130	36.12 N	37.10 E
Aleppo → Ḥalab	130	36.12 N	37.10 E
Alerces, Parque Nacional ✦	254	42.50 S	71.52 W
Aléria	36	42.05 N	9.30 E
Alert Bay	182	50.35 N	126.55 W
Alès, Fr.	62	44.04 N	4.05 E
Ales, It.	71	39.46 N	8.49 E
Alesd	38	47.04 N	22.24 E
Alešino, S.S.S.R.	82	56.09 N	37.45 E
Alešino, S.S.S.R.	82	55.04 N	36.05 E
Aleški	80	51.38 N	41.46 E
Aleškovo	54	54.53 N	36.23 E
Alessandria	62	44.54 N	8.37 E
Alessandria ◻⁴	62	44.49 N	8.42 E
Alessandria della Rocca	70	37.34 N	13.27 E
Alessano	68	39.53 N	18.20 E
Ålestrup	26	56.42 N	9.30 E
Alessio	68	62.28 N	6.09 E
Ålesund	26	46.28 N	8.00 E
Aleuten → Aleutian Islands II	180	52.00 N	176.00 E
Aleutian Basin ≃¹	16	57.00 N	177.00 E
Aleutian Islands II	180	52.00 N	176.00 E
Aleutian Range ⋌	180	58.00 N	155.00 W
Aleutian Trench ≃¹	74	51.00 N	170.00 E
Aleutka	74	45.57 N	150.10 E
Alevina, mys ▹	74	58.50 N	151.20 E
Ale Water ≃	46	55.31 N	2.35 W
Alex	196	34.54 N	97.46 W
Alexander, II., U.S.	219	39.43 N	90.02 W
Alexander, N.Y., U.S.	210	42.54 N	78.16 W
Alexander, N.D., U.S.	198	47.50 N	103.38 W
Alexander ≃	162	32.24 S	34.52 E
Alexander, Cape ▹	175e	6.35 S	156.30 E
Alexander, Mount ▲, Austl.	162	22.39 S	115.32 E
Alexander, Mount ▲, Austl.	166	36.59 S	144.18 E
Alexander Archipelago II	180	56.30 N	134.00 W
Alexander Bay	156	28.40 S	16.30 E
Alexander City	194	32.56 N	85.57 W
Alexander Dam ⊟¹	273d	33.28 S	28.25 E
Alexander Ditch ☰¹	279a	41.20 N	82.05 W
Alexander Hamilton Airport ◻	241n	17.42 N	64.48 W
Alexander Island I	9	71.00 S	70.00 W
Alexander Nevsky Monastery ⊽¹	265a	59.55 N	30.24 E
Alexandra, Austl.	166	37.12 S	145.43 E
Alexandra, N.Z.	173	45.15 S	169.24 E
Alexandra, S. Afr.	273d	26.06 S	28.05 E
Alexandra	166	18.14 S	139.54 E
Alexandra Canal ☰	274a	33.56 S	151.10 E
Alexandra Park ⌊	176	60.29 N	116.18 W
Alexandra Park Race Course ◍	260	51.36 N	0.08 W
Alexandria → İskenderun	130	36.37 N	36.07 E
Alexandretta, Gulf of → İskenderun Körfezi ⊂	130	36.30 N	35.40 E
Alexandria, Austl.	166	19.05 S	136.40 E
Alexandria, Bra.	256	6.25 S	38.01 W
Alexandria, B.C., Can.	182	52.38 N	122.27 W
Alexandria, On., Can.	206	45.19 N	74.38 W
Alexandria → Al-Iskandarīyah, Miṣr	142	31.12 N	29.54 E
Alexandria, Rom.	38	43.58 N	25.20 E
Alexandria, S. Afr.	158	33.40 S	26.24 E
Alexandria, In., U.S.	216	40.15 N	85.40 W
Alexandria, Ky., U.S.	218	38.58 N	84.23 W
Alexandria, La., U.S.	194	31.18 N	92.26 W
Alexandria, Mn., U.S.	190	45.53 N	95.22 W
Alexandria, Ne., U.S.	198	40.15 N	97.23 W
Alexandria, S.D., U.S.	198	43.39 N	97.47 W
Alexandria, S.D., U.S.	198	43.30 N	97.46 W
Alexandria, Va., U.S.	208	38.48 N	77.02 W
Alexandria Bay	206	44.20 N	75.55 W
Alexandrína, Lake @	168b	35.26 S	139.10 E
Alexandroúpolis	38	40.50 N	25.52 E
Alexis	190	41.03 N	90.33 W
Alexis Creek	182	52.06 N	123.17 W
Alexis Indian Reserve ✦⁴	182	53.46 N	114.30 W
Alf	56	50.03 N	7.07 E
Alfäldänga ≃⁸	267b	41.04 N	28.53 E
Alfambra	34	40.33 N	1.03 W
Alfambra ≃	34	40.31 N	1.07 W
Al-Fallūjah	128	33.21 N	43.46 E
Alfanta	266d	41.30 N	2.24 E
Al-Fardān	144	14.51 N	48.27 E
Alfaro, Esp.	34	42.11 N	1.45 W
Alfaro ≃	246	0.23 S	75.55 W
Al-Fāshir	140	13.38 N	25.21 E
Al-Fāshn	142	28.49 N	30.54 E
Al-Fayyūm	142	29.19 N	30.50 E

Symbols in the index entries represent the broad categories identified in the key at the right. Symbols with superior numbers (⋌¹) identify subcategories (see complete key on page *I · 1*).

Symbole im Register stellen die rechts im Schlüssel erklärten Kategorien dar. Symbole mit hochgestellten Ziffern (⋌¹) bezeichnen Unterteilungen einer Kategorie (vgl. vollständiger Schlüssel auf Seite *I · 1*).

Los símbolos incluídos en el texto del índice representan las grandes categorías identificadas con la clave a la derecha. Símbolos con numeros en su parte superior (⋌¹) identifican las subcategorías (véase la clave completa en la página *I · 1*).

Os símbolos incluídos no texto do índice representam as grandes categorias identificadas com a chave à direita. Os símbolos com números em sua parte superior (⋌¹) identificam as subcategorias (veja-se a clave completa à página *I · 1*).

Les symboles de l'index représentent les catégories indiquées dans la légende à droite. Les symboles suivis d'un indice (⋌¹) représentent les sous-catégories (voir légende complète à la page *I · 1*).

▲ Mountain	Berg	Montaña	Montagne	Montanha
⋌ Mountains	Gebirge	Montañas	Montagnes	Montanhas
⧟ Pass	Paß	Paso	Col	Passo
V Valley, Canyon	Tal, Cañon	Valle, Cañón	Vallée, Canyon	Vale, Canhão
≃ Plain	Ebene	Llano	Plaine	Planicie
▹ Cape	Kap	Cabo	Cap	Cabo
I Island	Insel	Isla	Île	Ilha
II Islands	Inseln	Islas	Îles	Ilhas
⯑ Other Topographic Features	Andere Topographische Objekte	Otros Elementos Topográficos	Autres données topographiques	Outros acidentes topográficos

Alfa-Alqa *I* · 5

ESPAÑOL

Nombre	Página	Lat.°′	Long.°′ W = Oeste
Al-Fayyūm □[4]	142	29.19 N	30.48 E
Al-Fāzah	144	14.08 N	43.05 E
Alfbach ≃	56	50.03 N	7.08 E
Alfedena	66	41.44 N	14.02 E
Alfeld, B.R.D.	52	51.59 N	9.50 E
Alfeld, B.R.D.	60	49.26 N	11.33 E
Alfenas	256	21.25 S	45.57 W
Alfianello	64	45.16 N	10.10 E
Al-Fifi	140	10.03 N	25.01 E
Alfiós ≃	38	37.40 N	21.33 E
Al-Firdān	142	30.41 N	32.20 E
Alföld ≚	30	47.00 N	20.00 E
Alfonsine	66	44.30 N	12.03 E
Alford, Austl.	168b	33.49 S	137.49 E
Alford, Eng., U.K.	44	53.16 N	0.10 E
Alford, Scot., U.K.	46	57.13 N	2.42 W
Alfortville	261	48.49 N	2.25 E
Ålfotbreen ⊓	26	61.45 N	5.40 E
Alfred, On., Can.	206	45.34 N	74.53 W
Alfred, Me., U.S.	188	43.28 N	70.43 W
Alfred, N.Y., U.S.	210	42.15 N	77.47 W
Alfred National Park ♠	166	37.35 S	149.20 E
Alfredo Chaves	255	20.38 S	40.45 W
Alfredo M. Terrazas	234	21.28 N	98.51 W
Alfreton	44	53.06 N	1.23 W
Alfriston	42	50.48 N	0.10 E
Alfta	26	61.21 N	16.05 E
Al-Fujayrah	128	25.06 N	56.21 E
Al-Fuqahā'	146	27.50 N	16.22 E
Al-Furzul	132	33.52 N	35.56 E
Alga	86	49.46 N	57.20 E
Algabas, S.S.S.R.	80	50.39 N	52.07 E
Algabas, S.S.S.R.	86	44.41 N	78.06 E
Algabas, S.S.S.R.	86	48.21 N	81.39 E
Algači	88	50.43 N	117.47 E
Älgarås	40	58.48 N	14.14 E
Ålgård	26	58.46 N	5.51 E
Al-Garef	140	12.03 N	34.19 E
Algarrobal	252	28.08 S	70.39 W
Algarrobo, Arg.	252	38.53 S	63.08 W
Algarrobo, Chile	252	33.22 S	71.40 W
Algarrobo del Águila	252	36.26 S	67.09 W
Algarrobo Verde	252	31.44 S	68.18 W
Algarve □[9]	34	37.10 N	8.15 W
Algás ≃	34	41.08 N	0.39 E
Algasovo	76	53.41 N	41.40 E
Al-Gebir	140	13.43 N	29.49 E
Algeciras, Col.	246	2.35 N	75.18 W
Algeciras, Esp.	34	36.08 N	5.30 W
Algemesí	34	39.11 N	0.26 W
Algena	144	17.19 N	38.31 E
Alger → El Djazaïr	148	36.47 N	3.03 E
Alger	216	40.42 N	83.50 W
Alger, Baie d' ⊂	34	36.50 N	3.15 E
Algeria (Algérie) □[1], Afr.	134	28.00 N	3.00 E
Algeria (Algérie) □[1], Afr.	148	28.00 N	3.00 E
Algérie → Algeria □[1]	148	28.00 N	3.00 E
Algerien → Algeria □[1]	148	28.00 N	3.00 E
Algermissen	52	52.15 N	9.58 E
Algés	266c	38.42 N	9.13 W
Al-Ghāb ◎	130	35.30 N	36.18 E
Al-Gharaq as-Sulṭānī	142	29.08 N	30.42 E
Al-Gharbīyah □[4]	142	30.45 N	31.00 E
Al-Ghāriyah	132	32.23 N	36.39 E
Al-Ghāṭ	128	26.00 N	45.03 E
Al-Ghawr ∨	132	31.50 N	35.30 E
Al-Ghayatah	142	30.57 N	30.06 E
Al-Ghayḍah	118	16.12 N	52.15 E
Al-Ghazālah	128	26.48 N	41.19 E
Al-Ghazālī	142	30.49 N	31.49 E
Al-Ghāzīyah	132	33.31 N	35.22 E
Alghero	71	40.34 N	8.19 E
Al-Ghurayfah	128	24.00 N	56.29 E
Al-Ghurdaqah	140	27.14 N	33.50 E
Algier → El Djazaïr	148	36.47 N	3.03 E
Algiers → El Djazaïr	148	36.47 N	3.03 E
Alginet	34	39.16 N	0.28 W
Algoa	222	29.24 N	95.11 W
Algoabaai ⊂	158	33.50 S	25.50 E
Algodão, Ilha do I	256	23.13 S	44.36 W
Algodón ≃	246	2.23 S	71.56 W
Algodones	200	35.22 N	106.28 W
Algodor ≃	34	39.55 N	3.53 W
Algoma	190	44.36 N	87.25 W
Algoma Mills	190	46.10 N	82.50 W
Algona, Ia., U.S.	190	43.04 N	94.13 W
Algona, Wa., U.S.	224	47.16 N	122.15 W
Algonac	214	42.37 N	82.31 W
Algonquin	216	42.09 N	88.17 W
Algonquin Lake ◎	216	42.40 N	85.20 W
Algonquin Provincial Park ♠	190	45.45 N	78.26 W
Algood	194	36.11 N	85.26 W
Algorta, Esp.	34	43.22 N	3.01 W
Algorta, Ur.	252	32.25 S	57.23 W
Alguierão-Mem Martins	266c	38.48 N	9.20 W
Al-Haddādī	142	31.20 N	30.47 E
Al-Haddayn	142	30.44 N	30.38 E
Al-Hadīthah	128	34.07 N	42.23 E
Al-Hadr	128	35.35 N	42.44 E
Al-Haffah	130	35.35 N	36.02 E
Al-Hafīr Al-Fawqānī	132	33.42 N	36.28 E
Al-Hajālīj	140	14.36 N	31.54 E
Al-Hajarah ◈[1]	128	30.00 N	44.00 E
Al-Hajar al-Gharbī ⩘	128	24.10 N	56.15 E
Al-Hajar ash-Sharqī ⩘	128	22.45 N	59.00 E
Al Hajeb	148	33.43 N	5.13 W
Al-Hājir	142	30.41 N	31.49 E
Al-Halfāyah	128	31.49 N	47.26 E
Al-Hamād ≚	128	32.00 N	39.30 E
Alhama de Granada	34	37.00 N	3.59 W
Alhama de Murcia	34	37.51 N	1.25 W
Al-Hamal ◈[1]	128	23.30 N	49.45 E
Alhambra, Ca., U.S.	228	34.05 N	118.07 W
Alhambra, Il., U.S.	219	38.53 N	89.44 W
Al-Hamīdīyah	130	34.43 N	35.56 E
Al-Hammām	140	30.50 N	29.23 E
Al-Hamrā', Ar. Su.	128	23.57 N	38.52 E
'Al-Hamrā', Lubnān	132	33.42 N	35.27 E
Al-Hamrah	142	31.10 N	30.52 E
Al-Hāmūl	142	31.19 N	31.10 E
Alhandra	250	7.26 S	34.54 W
Alhandra, Mouchão de I	266c	38.54 N	9.00 W
Al-Harāk	132	32.44 N	36.18 E
Al-Harīq	128	23.37 N	46.31 E
Al-Hārrah	132	33.03 N	36.00 E
Al-Harrah ♉[9]	128	31.00 N	38.30 E
Al-Harūj al-Aswad ⩘[2]	146	27.00 N	17.10 E
Al-Hasakah	130	36.29 N	40.45 E
Al-Hasakah □[8]	130	36.30 N	41.00 E
Al-Hasānī I	128	24.58 N	37.05 E
Alhaurín el Grande	34	36.38 N	4.41 W
Al-Hawāmidīyah	273c	29.54 N	31.15 E
Al-Hawātah	140	13.25 N	34.38 E
Al-Hawātikah	142	27.16 N	31.01 E
Al-Hawrah	144	13.49 N	47.37 E
Al-Hawṭah	144	15.50 N	48.27 E
Al-Hawwārīyah	142	30.58 N	29.41 E
Al-Hayy, 'Irāq	128	32.10 N	46.03 E
Al-Hayy, Miṣr	142	29.39 N	31.18 E
Al-Hayyānīyah	128	28.38 N	42.45 E
Al-Hayz	140	28.02 N	28.39 E
Al-Hībah	142	28.45 N	30.55 E
Al-Hijānah	132	33.21 N	36.33 E
Al-Hijāz ◈[1]	118	24.30 N	38.30 E
Al-Hillah, 'Irāq	128	32.29 N	44.25 E
Al-Hillah, Sūd.	140	13.27 N	27.08 E
Al-Hilmīyah ◈[8]	273c	30.07 N	31.19 E
Al-Hindīyah	128	32.33 N	44.13 E
Al-Hirmil	130	34.23 N	36.23 E
Al-Hiṣn	132	32.29 N	35.52 E
Al-Hoceïma	148	35.15 N	3.55 W
Al-Hoceïma □[4]	148	35.00 N	4.30 W

FRANÇAIS

Nom	Page	Lat.°′	Long.°′ W = Ouest
Al Hoceïma, Baie d' ⊂	34	35.20 N	3.50 W
Alhos Vedros	266c	38.39 N	9.02 W
Alhucemas, Peñón de I	34	35.13 N	3.53 W
Al-Huḍayb	140	13.00 N	32.50 E
Al-Ḥudaydah	144	14.48 N	42.57 E
Al-Ḥufrah	146	29.10 N	18.02 E
Al-Ḥufrah ◈[1]	128	28.40 N	38.30 E
Al-Hufūf	128	25.22 N	49.34 E
Al-Ḥulwah	128	23.27 N	46.47 E
Al-Humayshah	144	13.41 N	45.52 E
Al-Ḥumrah ◈[1]	128	23.20 N	54.30 E
Al-Ḥuṣayḥiṣah	140	14.44 N	33.18 E
Al-Ḥusaynīyah	142	30.52 N	31.55 E
Al-Ḥuṣaynīyah ∓[4]	144	17.48 N	44.27 E
Al-Ḥuwaylizah	132	33.02 N	35.51 E
Al-Ḥuwaymī	144	14.05 N	47.44 E
Al-Ḥuwayyiṭ	128	25.36 N	40.23 E
Alì	70	38.02 N	15.25 E
Ali ◈[8]	272a	28.31 N	77.18 E
'Ālī, As-Sadd al- (Aswān High Dam) ◈[6]	140	23.58 N	32.52 E
Alía, Esp.	34	39.27 N	5.13 W
Alia, It.	70	37.47 N	13.43 E
'Alīābād, Īrān	128	36.57 N	54.59 E
Alīābād, Pāk.	123	36.18 N	74.37 E
Aliabad, S.S.S.R.	84	41.29 N	46.37 E
Aliade	150	7.16 N	8.28 E
Aliaga, Esp.	34	40.40 N	0.42 W
Aliağa, Tür.	130	38.48 N	26.59 E
Aliákmon ≃	38	40.30 N	22.36 E
Aliákmonos, Tekhnití Límni ◎[1]	38	40.15 N	22.00 E
Aliaksin, Cape ≻	180	55.30 N	160.43 W
'Alī al-Gharbī	128	32.27 N	46.41 E
Aliança	250	7.35 S	35.13 W
Aliano	68	40.19 N	16.14 E
Alībāg	122	18.39 N	72.54 E
Alibahadır ◈[8]	267b	41.11 N	29.12 E
Ali-Bajramly	84	39.56 N	48.56 E
Alibardak	130	38.06 N	40.25 E
Alibates Flint Quarries National Monument ♠	196	35.35 N	101.39 W
Alibej, ozero ◎	78	45.48 N	30.02 E
Alibejli	84	41.23 N	46.49 E
Alibey ≃	267b	41.03 N	28.56 E
Alibey Adası I	130	39.20 N	26.38 E
Alibey Barajı ◎[1]	267b	41.07 N	28.55 E
Alibeyköy ◈[8]	267b	41.04 N	28.56 E
Alibijaban Island I	116	13.20 N	122.43 E
Alibori ≃	150	11.56 N	3.17 E
Al-Ibrāhīmīyah	142	30.57 N	31.35 E
Alibunar	38	45.05 N	20.58 E
Alicante → Alacant	34	38.21 N	0.29 W
Alice, Ciskei	158	32.47 S	26.50 E
Alice, Tx., U.S.	196	27.45 N	98.04 W
Alice ≃, Austl.	164	15.22 S	141.58 E
Alice ≃, Austl.	166	24.02 S	144.50 E
Alice, Punta ≻	68	39.24 N	17.10 E
Alice Arm	182	55.29 N	129.29 W
Alicedale	158	33.19 S	26.05 E
Alice Downs	162	17.45 S	127.56 E
Alice Springs	162	23.42 S	133.53 E
Alice Superiore	62	45.28 N	7.47 E
Alice Town	238	25.44 N	79.17 W
Aliceville	194	33.07 N	88.09 W
Alicia, Pil.	116	16.45 N	121.42 E
Alicia, Pil.	116	7.30 N	122.55 E
Alıcık	130	40.49 N	35.21 E
Alick Creek ≃	166	20.25 S	142.00 E
Alicudi, Isola I	70	38.32 N	14.21 E
Al-'Idwah	142	29.21 N	30.55 E
Alief	222	29.43 N	95.35 W
Alife	68	41.20 N	14.20 E
Al-Ifranj	132	31.11 N	35.41 E
Alīganj, India	124	28.07 N	80.36 E
Alīganj, India	124	27.30 N	79.11 E
Alīgarh	124	27.53 N	78.05 E
Alignements de Carnac ⊥	32	47.35 N	3.05 W
Alīgūdarz	128	33.24 N	49.41 E
Alijos, Escollos II[1]	232	24.57 N	115.44 W
'Alī Kheyl	120	33.57 N	69.43 E
Al-Ikhṣāṣ al-Qiblīyah	142	29.42 N	31.17 E
Al-Ikhwān II	118	12.08 N	53.10 E
Alikovo	80	55.45 N	46.45 E
Alima ≃	152	1.36 S	16.36 E
Al-Imām ◈[8]	273c	30.01 N	31.10 E
Al-Imārāt al-'Arabīyah al-Muttaḥidah → United Arab Emirates □[1]	128	24.00 N	54.00 E
Al-'Imārīyah	142	27.37 N	30.53 E
Alimena	70	37.42 N	14.07 E
Alimini Grande ◎	68	40.12 N	18.27 E
Alimini Piccolo ◎	68	40.10 N	18.27 E
Aliminusa	70	37.52 N	13.47 E
Alim Island I	164	2.55 S	147.05 E
Alimkent	85	40.58 N	69.11 E
Alimodian	116	10.49 N	122.26 E
Alindao	152	5.02 N	21.13 E
Alingsås	26	57.56 N	12.31 E
Ālipur, India	272b	22.43 N	88.12 E
Alipur, India	272b	22.55 N	88.11 E
Alīpur, Pāk.	123	29.23 N	70.55 E
Ālipur ◈[8]	126	22.31 N	88.20 E
Ālīpur Duār	124	26.29 N	89.44 E
Alīpur Janūbi	123	30.13 N	71.18 E
Aliquippa	214	40.38 N	80.14 W
Aliquippa-Hopewell Airport ⊠	279b	40.35 N	80.17 W
Alīrājpur	120	22.19 N	74.21 E
Al-'Irāq	132	31.05 N	35.39 E
Al-'Irāq → Iraq □[1]	128	33.00 N	44.00 E
Al-'Irqah	144	13.30 N	47.22 E
Ali-Sabieh	144	11.09 N	42.42 E
Al-'Īsāwīyah	128	30.38 N	37.53 E
Aliseda	34	39.26 N	6.41 W
Alise-Sainte-Reine	58	47.32 N	4.29 E
Alīshārī	84	39.02 N	47.15 E
Al-Iskandarīyah (Alexandria)	142	31.12 N	29.54 E
Al-Iskandarīyah □[4]	142	31.10 N	29.53 E
Al-Ismā'īlīyah (Ismailia)	142	30.35 N	32.16 E
Al-Ismā'īlīyah □[4]	142	30.30 N	32.15 E
Al-Ismā'īlīyah Military Base ■	142	30.35 N	32.14 E
Aliso Canyon ∨, Ca., U.S.	280	34.18 N	118.33 W
Aliso Canyon ∨, Ca., U.S.	280	33.53 N	117.40 W
Aliso Creek ≃	228	33.31 N	117.45 W
Al-Istiwā'īyah al-Gharbīyah □[4]	140	5.55 N	28.15 E
Al-Istiwā'īyah ash-Sharqīyah □[4]	154	4.30 N	33.00 E
Alistráti	38	41.04 N	23.57 E
Alitak, Cape ≻	180	56.51 N	154.21 W
Alitak Bay ⊂	180	57.00 N	154.05 W
Alitanguo	120	35.10 N	83.30 E
Alì Terme	70	38.01 N	15.26 E
Alivérion	38	38.24 N	24.02 E
Aliwal North	158	30.45 S	26.45 E
Alix	182	52.24 N	113.11 W
Al-'Izzīyah	142	27.13 N	30.59 E
Al-Jabal al-Abyaḍ ⋀[2]	142	28.46 N	31.00 E
Al-Jabal al-Aḥmar ⋀[2]	142	28.19 N	31.07 E
Al-Jabalayn	140	12.36 N	32.48 E
Al-Jadīdah	140	25.34 N	28.51 E
Al-Jafādūn	142	28.50 N	30.48 E
Al-Jafr	132	30.18 N	36.13 E
Al-Jāfūrah ◈[2]	128	24.14 N	50.00 E
Al-Jaghbūb	146	29.45 N	24.31 E
Al-Jaghbūb ∓[4]	146	29.40 N	24.43 E
Al-Jahrah	128	29.20 N	47.40 E
Al-Jamālīyah	142	31.11 N	31.51 E
Al-Jarnūs	142	28.36 N	30.43 E

PORTUGUÊS

Nome	Página	Lat.°′	Long.°′ W = Oeste
Al-Jawf, Ar. Su.	128	29.50 N	39.52 E
Al-Jawf, Lībiyā	146	24.11 N	23.19 E
Al-Jawsh	146	32.00 N	11.40 E
Al-Jaylī	140	16.01 N	32.36 E
Al-Jazā'ir → Algeria □[1]	148	28.00 N	3.00 E
Al-Jazīrah □[4]	140	14.30 N	33.20 E
Al-Jazīrah ◈[1]	140	14.25 N	33.00 E
Aljezur, Bra.	287a	22.40 S	43.36 W
Aljezur, Port.	34	37.19 N	8.48 W
Al-Jibāb	132	33.06 N	36.15 E
Al-Jifārah	128	23.59 N	45.11 E
Al-Jifārah (Jeffara) ≚	146	32.30 N	11.45 E
Al-Jīzah (Giza), Miṣr	142	30.01 N	31.13 E
Al-Jīzah, Urd.	132	31.43 N	35.58 E
Al-Jīzah □[4]	142	29.46 N	31.18 E
Al-Jubayl	128	27.01 N	49.40 E
Al-Jubayn	140	12.07 N	35.10 E
Aljucén ≃	34	38.56 N	6.25 W
Al-Judaydah	132	33.54 N	35.34 E
Al-Judayyidah, Urd.	132	31.15 N	35.49 E
Al-Judayyidah, Urd.	132	31.32 N	35.39 E
Al-Jufrah ∓[4]	146	29.10 N	16.00 E
Al-Julaydah ∓[4]	128	29.03 N	45.38 E
Al-Junaynah, Miṣr	142	31.06 N	31.41 E
Al-Junaynah, Sūd.	140	13.27 N	22.27 E
Al-Junaynah, Sūrīy.	132	32.54 N	36.44 E
Al-Jundīyah	142	28.34 N	30.50 E
Aljustrel	34	37.52 N	8.10 W
Al-Kāb	142	30.57 N	32.18 E
Al-Kabrit Military Base ■	142	30.15 N	32.29 E
Al-Kafr	132	32.38 N	36.38 E
Al-Kafr ash-Sharqī	142	37.17 N	31.10 E
Al-Kahfah	128	27.04 N	43.02 E
Alkali Creek ≃, Ab., Can.	184	50.52 N	110.30 W
Alkali Creek ≃, Wy., U.S.	202	43.16 N	107.40 W
Alkali Lake	182	51.47 N	122.14 W
Alkali Lake ◎, Nv., U.S.	204	41.42 N	119.50 W
Alkali Lake ◎, Or., U.S.	202	42.58 N	120.02 W
Alkamari	146	13.24 N	11.07 E
Al-Kāmilīn	140	15.05 N	33.11 E
Al-Karabah	140	18.33 N	33.42 E
Al-Karak	132	31.11 N	35.42 E
Al-Karak □[8]	132	31.10 N	35.45 E
Al-Karnak	140	25.43 N	32.39 E
Al-Kawah	140	13.44 N	32.30 E
Al-Kawd	144	13.05 N	45.22 E
Al-Kawm	130	35.11 N	38.52 E
Al-Kawm al-Akhḍar	142	30.58 N	30.17 E
Al-Kawm Aṭ-Ṭawīl	142	31.12 N	31.05 E
Alken	56	50.15 N	7.26 E
Al-Khabrā'	128	26.04 N	43.33 E
Al-Khābūrah	128	23.59 N	57.08 E
Al-Khafaqān ◎	128	23.24 N	40.24 E
Al-Khalīl (Hebron)	132	31.32 N	35.06 E
Al-Khālis	128	33.49 N	44.32 E
Al-Khandaq	140	18.36 N	30.34 E
Al-Khānkah	142	30.13 N	31.21 E
Al-Kharaqānīyah	273c	30.10 N	31.10 E
Al-Khārijah	140	25.26 N	30.33 E
Al-Kharṭūm (Khartoum)	140	15.36 N	32.32 E
Al-Kharṭūm □[4]	140	15.45 N	32.30 E
Al-Kharṭūm Baḥrī	140	15.38 N	32.33 E
Al-Khaṣab	128	26.12 N	56.15 E
Al-Khatam ◈[1]	128	24.00 N	55.10 E
Al-Khirbah as-Samrā'	132	32.11 N	36.10 E
Al-Khiyām	132	33.19 N	35.36 E
Al-Khubar	128	26.17 N	50.12 E
Al-Khums (Homs)	146	32.39 N	14.16 E
Al-Khuraybah, J.Y.D.S.	144	15.06 N	48.19 E
Al-Khuraybah, Urd.	132	32.40 N	35.52 E
Al-Khurmah	144	21.54 N	42.03 E
Al-Khushnīyah	132	33.00 N	35.48 E
Al-Khuṣūṣ	273c	30.09 N	31.19 E
Al-Kifl	128	32.14 N	44.22 E
Al-Kiswah	132	33.21 N	36.14 E
Alkmaar	52	52.37 N	4.44 E
Alkoven	61	48.17 N	14.06 E
Al-Kūbrī	142	30.02 N	32.33 E
Al-Kūfah	128	32.02 N	44.24 E
Al-Kufrah (Cufra) ∓[4]	146	24.20 N	23.15 E
Al-Kunayyisah	273c	29.59 N	31.11 E
Al-Kuntillah	140	30.00 N	34.41 E
Al-Kūt	128	32.25 N	45.49 E
Al-Kuwayt	128	29.20 N	47.59 E
Al-Kuwayt → Kuwait □[1]	128	29.30 N	47.45 E
Alkvettern ◎	40	59.25 N	14.21 E
Allaben	210	42.07 N	74.22 W
Al-Labwah	130	34.12 N	36.21 E
Allacapan	116	18.15 N	121.35 E
Allach-Jun'	74	61.08 N	138.03 E
Allada	150	6.39 N	2.09 E
Al-Lādhiqīyah (Latakia)	130	35.31 N	35.47 E
Al-Lādhiqīyah □[8]	130	35.30 N	36.00 E
Allagash ≃	186	47.05 N	69.02 W
Allagen	56	51.28 N	8.14 E
Al-Lagowa	140	11.24 N	29.08 E
Allahābād, India	124	25.27 N	81.51 E
Allāhābād, Pāk.	123	28.57 N	70.53 E
Allāhbās	272a	28.31 N	77.25 E
Allahüekber Dağları ⩘	130	40.35 N	42.32 E
Al-Lāhūn	142	29.13 N	30.59 E
Allāhwardipur	272a	28.33 N	77.26 E
Allaines	50	48.12 N	1.50 E
Allaire State Park ♠	208	40.08 N	74.08 W
Allakaket	180	66.34 N	152.41 W
Allaman	58	46.28 N	6.24 E
Allamuchy	210	40.55 N	74.48 W
Allan	184	51.53 N	106.04 W
Allan, Pointe ≻	275a	45.26 N	73.45 W
Allanche	32	45.14 N	2.56 E
Alland	61	48.03 N	16.05 E
Allan Island I	224	48.28 N	122.42 W
Allanmyo	110	19.22 N	95.13 E
Allanridge	158	27.55 S	26.44 E
Allanson	168a	33.20 S	116.06 E
Allanton	46	55.47 N	3.51 W
Allan Water ≃	46	56.08 N	3.56 W
Allapattah Flats ≚	220	27.29 N	82.34 W
'Allāq, Bi'r ∓[4]	146	31.05 N	11.42 E
'Allāqī, Wādī al- ∨	140	22.42 N	33.12 E
Allard, Lac ◎	186	50.32 N	63.31 W
Allardt	194	36.22 N	84.53 W
Allariz	34	42.11 N	7.48 W
Allatoona Lake ◎[1]	192	34.08 N	84.38 W
Allauch	62	43.20 N	5.29 E
Al-Layyah	140	16.16 N	35.25 E
Alldays	156	22.44 S	29.04 E
Alle, Bel.	56	49.51 N	4.58 E
Alle, Schw.	58	47.26 N	7.08 E
Ålleberg ⋀[2]	26	58.08 N	13.36 E
Allegan	216	42.31 N	85.51 W
Allegan □[6]	216	42.35 N	85.53 W
Allegan, Lake ◎	216	42.33 N	85.55 W
Allegany	210	42.05 N	78.29 W
Allegany □[6]	210	42.13 N	78.02 W
Allegany Indian Reservation ◈[4]	210	42.10 N	78.47 W
Allegany State Park ♠	210	42.04 N	78.44 W
Alleghany	226	39.28 N	120.51 W
Alleghe	64	46.24 N	12.01 E
Allegheny □[6]	214	40.26 N	79.59 W
Allegheny ≃	214	40.27 N	80.00 W
Allegheny Acres	279b	40.37 N	79.53 W
Allegheny Center ♉	279b	40.27 N	80.01 W
Allegheny County Airport ⊠	279b	40.21 N	79.56 W
Allegheny County Park ♠	279b	40.34 N	79.55 W
Allegheny Mountains ⩘	188	38.30 N	80.00 W
Allegheny Observatory ♉[3]	279b	40.29 N	80.01 W
Allegheny Plateau ⩘[1]	188	41.30 N	78.00 W
Allegheny Portage Railroad National Historic Site ⊥	214	40.28 N	78.32 W
Allegheny Reservoir ◎[1]	214	42.00 N	78.56 W
Allègre	62	45.12 N	3.42 E
Allègre, Pointe ≻	241o	16.22 N	61.45 W
Allemagne, République fédérale d' → Germany, Federal Republic of □[1]	30	51.00 N	9.00 E
Allemande, République démocratique → German Democratic Republic □[1]	30	52.00 N	12.30 E
Allemands, Lac Des ◎	194	29.55 N	90.35 W
Allemanskraaldam ◎[1]	158	28.16 S	27.07 E
Allemant	261	48.45 N	1.37 E
Allemont	62	45.08 N	6.02 E
Allen, Arg.	252	38.58 S	67.50 W
Allen, Pil.	116	12.30 N	124.17 E
Allen, Md., U.S.	208	38.17 N	75.41 W
Allen, Mi., U.S.	216	41.57 N	84.46 W
Allen, Ne., U.S.	198	42.24 N	96.50 W
Allen, Ok., U.S.	196	34.52 N	96.24 W
Allen, Pa., U.S.	208	40.10 N	77.05 W
Allen, S.D., U.S.	198	43.16 N	101.55 W
Allen, Tx., U.S.	222	33.06 N	96.40 W
Allen, Wa., U.S.	224	48.31 N	122.23 W
Allen □[6], In., U.S.	216	41.04 N	85.09 W
Allen □[6], Oh., U.S.	216	40.46 N	84.06 W
Allen ≃	44	54.58 N	2.19 W
Allen, Lough ◎	48	54.08 N	8.08 W
Allen, Mount ⋀, N.Z.	172	47.05 S	167.48 E
Allen, Mount ⋀, Ak., U.S.	180	62.14 N	142.13 W
Allenby Bridge ◈[5]	132	31.52 N	35.52 E
Allendale, Il., U.S.	194	38.32 N	87.43 W
Allendale, Mi., U.S.	216	42.58 N	85.57 W
Allendale, N.J., U.S.	276	41.02 N	74.07 W
Allendale, S.C., U.S.	192	33.00 N	81.18 W
Allendale Town	44	54.54 N	2.15 W
Allende, Méx.	232	25.17 N	100.01 W
Allende, Méx.	232	28.20 N	100.51 W
Allende, Méx.	234	18.09 N	94.16 W
Allendorf	56	51.02 N	8.38 E
Allenfarm	222	30.24 N	96.14 W
All England Lawn Tennis Club ♠	260	51.26 N	0.13 W
Allen Grove	216	42.35 N	88.41 W
Allen Park	216	42.15 N	83.12 W
Allenport, Pa., U.S.	214	40.20 N	77.53 W
Allenport, Pa., U.S.	214	40.06 N	79.51 W
Allensbach	58	47.43 N	9.03 E
Allenstein → Olsztyn	30	53.48 N	20.29 E
Allensville	214	40.32 N	77.49 W
Allenton, Mi., U.S.	214	42.55 N	82.57 W
Allenton, R.I., U.S.	207	41.32 N	71.28 W
Allentown, N.J., U.S.	208	40.10 N	74.35 W
Allentown, N.Y., U.S.	210	42.05 N	78.03 W
Allentown, Oh., U.S.	216	40.46 N	84.12 W
Allentown, Pa., U.S.	208	40.36 N	75.28 W
Allentsteig	61	48.42 N	15.20 E
Allenwood, N.J., U.S.	208	40.12 N	74.13 W
Allenwood, N.Y., U.S.	276	40.48 N	73.44 W
Allenwood, Pa., U.S.	210	41.07 N	76.54 W
Alleppey	122	9.29 N	76.19 E
Aller ≃	30	52.57 N	9.11 E
Allerona	66	42.49 N	11.58 E
Allersberg	60	49.15 N	11.15 E
Allershausen	60	48.26 N	11.36 E
Allerslev	41	55.05 N	12.03 E
Allerton, Ia., U.S.	190	40.42 N	93.21 W
Allerton, Ma., U.S.	283	42.18 N	70.53 W
Allerton ◈[8]	262	53.22 N	2.53 W
Allerton, Point ≻	207	42.18 N	70.53 W
Allestree	42	52.57 N	1.29 W
Allevard	62	45.24 N	6.04 E
Alley Park ♠	276	40.45 N	73.44 W
Alleyton	222	29.43 N	96.29 W
Allgäu ◈[1]	58	47.35 N	10.10 E
Allgäuer Alpen ⩘	58	47.20 N	10.25 E
Allhallows	260	51.28 N	0.39 E
Alli ≃	68	38.51 N	16.40 E
Alliance, Ab., Can.	182	52.26 N	111.47 W
Alliance, Ne., U.S.	198	42.12 N	102.58 W
Alliance, Oh., U.S.	214	40.54 N	81.06 W
Allibaudières	50	48.35 N	4.07 E
Al-Lidām	144	20.29 N	44.50 E
Allier □[5]	32	46.25 N	3.00 E
Allier ≃, Fr.	32	46.58 N	3.04 E
Allier ≃, Fr.	62	45.05 N	3.35 E
Alligator ≃	192	35.58 N	75.58 W
Alligator Creek ≃, Ga., U.S.	192	31.58 N	82.22 W
Alligator Creek ≃, Tx., U.S.	222	30.42 N	97.07 W
Alligator Lake ◎	220	28.13 N	81.13 W
Alligator Pond	241q	17.52 N	77.34 W
Alligny-en-Morvan	50	47.12 N	4.10 E
Allihies	48	51.38 N	10.03 W
Allinagaram	122	10.02 N	77.30 E
Allinge	26	55.16 N	14.49 E
Allington Castle ⊥	260	51.17 N	0.31 E
Al-Lisān ≻[1]	132	31.17 N	35.28 E
Al-Lisht	142	29.34 N	31.14 E
Allison	190	42.45 N	92.47 W
Allison, Mount ⋀	282	37.30 N	121.52 W
Allison Gulch ∨	280	34.16 N	117.44 W
Allison Park	214	40.34 N	79.57 W
Alliste	68	39.57 N	18.05 E
Alliston	212	44.09 N	79.52 W
Al-Līth	144	20.09 N	40.16 E
Allmendingen	58	48.20 N	9.43 E
Alloa	46	56.07 N	3.49 W
Allochio, Galleria degli ◈[5]	66	44.03 N	11.30 E
Allogny	50	47.13 N	2.19 E
Allonby	44	54.46 N	3.25 W
Alloné Abba	132	32.44 N	35.10 E
Allonnes, B.R.D.	50	47.58 N	0.09 E
Allonnes, Fr.	50	48.20 N	1.40 E
Allora	171a	28.02 S	151.59 E
Allos	62	44.14 N	6.38 E
Allott, Mount ⋀[2]	162	26.06 S	124.46 E
Allouez	190	44.28 N	88.00 W
Alloway	208	39.33 N	75.21 W
Alloway Creek ≃	208	39.27 N	75.30 W
Allport	214	40.58 N	78.12 W
Allred Peak ⋀	200	40.32 N	108.33 W
All Saints	240c	17.03 N	61.48 W
Allschwil	58	47.33 N	7.33 E
Allstedt	54	51.24 N	11.23 E
Allston ◈[8]	283	42.22 N	71.08 W
Alluets, Forêt des ♠	261	48.55 N	1.55 E
Al-Luḥayyah	144	15.42 N	42.42 E
Allumette Lake ◎	190	45.53 N	77.13 W
Allumettes, Île des I	190	45.50 N	77.05 W
Allumiere	66	42.09 N	11.54 E
Allview Estates	208	39.12 N	76.51 W
Allyn	224	47.23 N	122.49 W
Alm ≃	60	48.05 N	13.55 E
Alma, N.B., Can.	186	45.36 N	64.57 W
Alma, P.Q., Can.	186	48.33 N	71.39 W
Alma, Ar., U.S.	194	35.28 N	94.13 W
Alma, Ga., U.S.	192	31.32 N	82.27 W
Alma, Il., U.S.	219	38.43 N	88.55 W
Alma, Ks., U.S.	198	39.01 N	96.17 W
Alma, Mi., U.S.	190	43.22 N	84.39 W
Alma, Ne., U.S.	198	40.05 N	99.21 W
Alma, N.Y., U.S.	210	42.01 N	78.03 W
Alma, Wi., U.S.	190	44.19 N	91.54 W
Al-Ma'ābidah	142	27.20 N	31.01 E
Al-Ma'ādī ◈[8]	142	29.58 N	31.15 E
Alma-Ata	85	43.15 N	76.57 E
Alma-Ata □[4]	85	44.00 N	76.00 E
Alma-Atinskij zapovednik ♠	85	43.10 N	77.25 E
Alma Center	190	44.26 N	90.54 W
Almada	34	38.41 N	9.09 W
Almaden, Austl.	166	17.20 S	144.41 E
Almadén, Esp.	34	38.46 N	4.50 W
Almadén de la Plata	34	37.52 N	6.04 W
Al-Madīnah (Medina)	128	24.28 N	39.36 E
Al-Madīnah al-Fikrīyah	142	27.56 N	30.49 E
Al-Madwar	132	32.17 N	36.00 E
Al-Mafāzah	140	13.36 N	34.33 E
Al-Mafraq	132	32.21 N	36.12 E
Al-Mafraq □[8]	132	32.15 N	36.30 E
Almafuerte	252	32.12 S	64.15 W
Al-Maghārīm	144	15.01 N	47.51 E
Al-Maghrah ∓[4]	140	30.14 N	28.56 E
Almagor	132	32.55 N	35.36 E
Almagre, Laguna ⊂	234	23.48 N	97.48 W
Al-Magreb → Morocco □[1]	148	32.00 N	5.00 W
Almagro	34	38.53 N	3.43 W
Almagro Island I	116	11.56 N	124.18 E
Al-Maḥallah al-Kubrā	142	30.58 N	31.10 E
Al-Maḥārīq	140	25.37 N	30.39 E
Al Mahbas	148	27.13 N	9.44 W
Alma Hill ⋀[2]	210	42.03 N	78.01 W
Al-Maḥmūdīyah	142	31.11 N	30.32 E
Al-Maḥraṣ	142	27.49 N	30.48 E
Al-Maḥsamah	142	30.34 N	32.01 E
Al-Majdal	132	32.47 N	36.30 E
Al-Majma'ah	128	25.54 N	45.20 E
Almăjului, Munții ⩘	38	44.43 N	22.12 E
Al-Maks ◈[8]	142	31.09 N	29.51 E
Al-Mālikīyah	130	37.10 N	42.08 E
Almalyk	85	40.50 N	69.35 E
Al-Ma'mūrah ◈[3]	142	31.18 N	30.03 E
Al-Manāmah	128	26.13 N	50.35 E
Al-Manāqil	140	14.15 N	32.59 E
Al-Manāṣif ◈[1]	130	35.17 N	40.50 E
Al-Manāwāt	273c	29.55 N	31.14 E
Almanor, Lake ◎	204	40.15 N	121.08 W
Almansa	34	38.52 N	1.05 W
Al-Manshāh	140	26.28 N	31.48 E
Al-Manṣūrah, Isr. Occ	132	33.08 N	35.48 E
Al-Manṣūrah, Miṣr	142	31.03 N	31.23 E
Al-Manṣūrīyah	142	30.08 N	31.05 E
Almanza	34	42.39 N	5.02 W
Al-Manzilah	142	31.09 N	31.56 E
Almanzor ⋀	34	40.15 N	5.18 W
Almanzora ≃	34	37.14 N	1.46 W
Almar ≃	34	40.54 N	5.29 W
Al-Marāghah	140	26.42 N	31.36 E
Almargem do Bispo	266c	38.51 N	9.16 W
Al-Marj	146	32.30 N	20.54 E
Al-Marj ◈[8]	273c	30.09 N	31.20 E
Almas	250	11.33 S	47.09 W
Almaș ≃	38	47.14 N	23.19 E
Almas, Pico das ⋀	255	13.33 S	41.56 W
Almas, Rio das ≃	255	13.37 S	39.02 W
Al-Ma'ṣarah, Miṣr	142	27.42 N	30.52 E
Al-Ma'ṣarah, Miṣr	142	31.13 N	31.19 E
Al-Ma'ṣarah ◈[8]	142	29.54 N	31.17 E
Al-Mashqūq	132	32.24 N	36.43 E
Al-Mashrafah	130	34.50 N	36.52 E
Al-Masīd	140	15.15 N	32.57 E
Almassora	34	39.57 N	0.03 W
Al-Matammah	140	16.43 N	33.22 E
Al-Maṭarīyah	142	31.11 N	32.02 E
Al-Maṭarīyah ◈[8]	142	30.07 N	31.19 E
Al-Matnah	140	13.47 N	35.03 E
Al-Mawṣil (Mosul)	128	36.20 N	43.08 E
Al-Mayādīn	130	35.01 N	40.27 E
Al-Maymūn	142	29.14 N	31.12 E
Almazán	34	41.29 N	2.32 W
Almazar, S.S.S.R.	85	40.59 N	68.54 E
Al-Mazār, Urd.	132	31.04 N	35.42 E
Almaznaja ◈[8]	83	48.31 N	38.35 E
Almaznyj	83	48.02 N	40.03 E
Almazovka ◈[8]	83	48.04 N	39.18 E
Almazovo	265b	55.51 N	38.02 E
Al-Mazra'ah	132	31.16 N	35.31 E
Al-Mazzah	132	33.30 N	36.15 E
Alme	56	51.28 N	8.37 E
Almeer	52	52.20 N	5.14 E
Almeida	34	40.43 N	6.54 W
Almeirim, Bra.	250	1.32 S	52.34 W
Almeirim, Port.	34	39.12 N	8.38 W
Almejas, Bahía ⊂	232	24.29 N	111.44 W
Almelo	52	52.21 N	6.39 E
Almelo-Nordhorn. Kanaal ≡	52	52.20 N	6.40 E
Almena	198	39.53 N	99.42 W
Almenara	255	16.11 S	40.42 W
Almenar de Soria	34	41.41 N	2.12 W
Almendares ≃	286b	23.08 N	82.25 W
Almendra, Embalse de ◎[1]	34	41.15 N	6.10 W
Almendralejo	34	38.41 N	6.24 W
Almenêches	50	48.42 N	0.07 E
Al'menevo	86	54.57 N	63.34 E
Almenno San Salvatore	62	45.45 N	9.35 E
Almería	34	36.50 N	2.27 W
Almería, Golfo de ⊂	34	36.46 N	2.30 W
Al'metjevsk	80	54.53 N	52.20 E
Al'mež	24	60.03 N	48.03 E
Älmhult	26	56.33 N	14.08 E
Al-Midhnab	128	25.54 N	44.14 E
Al-Mīnā'	130	34.27 N	35.49 E
Almina, Punta ≻	34	35.53 N	5.15 W
Almino Afonso	250	6.09 S	37.46 W
Al-Minshāt al-Kubrā	142	31.03 N	30.54 E
Al-Minūfīyah □[4]	142	30.30 N	31.00 E
Al-Minyā, Miṣr	142	29.14 N	30.45 E
Al-Minyā, Miṣr	142	28.06 N	30.45 E
Al-Minyā, Miṣr	142	29.45 N	31.18 E
Al-Minyā □[4]	142	28.26 N	30.42 E
Al-Miqdādīyah	128	33.59 N	44.56 E
Almira	202	47.42 N	118.56 W
Almirantazgo, Islas → Admiralty Islands II	164	2.10 S	147.00 E
Almirantazgo, Montes → Admiralty Mountains ⩘	9	71.45 S	168.30 E
Almirante	236	9.18 N	82.24 W
Almirante, Bahía ⊂	236	9.20 N	82.18 W
Almirante Brown	258	34.48 S	58.23 W
Almirante Brown □[5]	288	34.50 S	58.20 W
Almirante Guillermo Brown, Parque ♠	288	34.40 S	58.28 W
Almirante Latorre	252	29.38 S	70.58 W
Almirante Montt, Golfo ʊ	254	51.55 S	72.45 W
Almirós	38	39.11 N	22.46 E
Almiroú, Kólpos ⊂	38	35.23 N	24.20 E
Al-Mismīyah	132	33.08 N	36.23 E
Almo	202	42.06 N	113.37 W
Almoçageme	266c	38.48 N	9.28 W
Almodôvar	34	37.31 N	8.04 W
Almodóvar del Campo	34	38.43 N	4.10 W
Almolonga	236	14.49 N	91.30 W
Almond, N.Y., U.S.	210	42.19 N	77.44 W
Almond, Wi., U.S.	190	44.15 N	89.24 W
Almond ≃, Scot., U.K.	46	55.58 N	3.18 W
Almond ≃, Scot., U.K.	46	56.25 N	3.27 W
Almondbank	46	56.24 N	3.33 W
Almondsbury	42	51.34 N	2.34 W
Almonesson	208	39.49 N	75.06 W
Almont	214	42.55 N	83.02 W
Almont ≃	261	48.32 N	2.40 E
Almonte, On., Can.	212	45.14 N	76.12 W
Almonte, Esp.	34	37.15 N	6.31 W
Almonte, Ca., U.S.	282	37.53 N	122.32 W
Almora	124	29.37 N	79.40 E
Almsee ◎	64	47.45 N	13.57 E
Älmsta	40	59.58 N	18.48 E
Al-Mu'addamīyah	132	33.45 N	36.39 E
Al-Mubarraz, Ar. Su.	128	25.55 N	49.36 E
Al-Mubarraz, Ar. Su.	144	22.17 N	46.44 E
Al-Mudawwarah	128	29.19 N	35.59 E
Almudébar	34	42.03 N	0.35 W
Al-Muglad	140	11.02 N	27.44 E
Al-Muḥarraq	128	26.16 N	50.37 E
Al-Mukallā	144	14.32 N	49.08 E
Al-Mukhā (Mocha)	144	13.19 N	43.15 E
Al-Munājāt al-Kubrā	142	30.50 N	32.01 E
Almuñécar	34	36.43 N	3.41 W
Almunge	40	59.53 N	18.03 E
Al-Muntazah ◈[8]	142	31.17 N	30.01 E
Almus	130	40.23 N	36.55 E
Al-Musallamīyah	140	14.34 N	33.21 E
Al-Musayfirah	132	32.37 N	36.20 E
Al-Musayjīd	128	24.05 N	39.06 E
Al-Musayyib	128	32.47 N	44.18 E
Almus Barajı ◎[1]	130	40.20 N	37.00 E
Al-Mushannaf	132	32.44 N	36.46 E
Al-Musharrak Qiblī	142	29.23 N	30.34 E
Al-Mutā'iyah	132	32.29 N	36.17 E
Al-Mu'tamadīyah	142	31.02 N	31.05 E
Al-Mutayn	132	33.54 N	35.44 E
Al-Muthannā □[4]	128	30.30 N	45.15 E
Al-Muṭī'ah	142	27.08 N	31.18 E
Al-Muwaqqar ⊥	132	31.49 N	36.06 E
Al-Muwassam	144	16.25 N	42.20 E
Al-Muwayh	144	22.45 N	41.36 E
Al-Muwayliḥ	128	27.41 N	35.27 E
Aln ≃	44	55.23 N	1.37 W
Alnarp	41	55.39 N	13.05 E
Al-Narrānīyah	273c	29.58 N	31.10 E
Al'n'aš	80	56.44 N	54.43 E
Alnaši	80	56.11 N	52.28 E
Al-Nasser	140	24.32 N	32.55 E
Alne ≃	42	52.13 N	1.52 W
Alness	46	57.41 N	4.15 W
Alnmouth	44	55.23 N	1.36 W
Alnön I	26	62.25 N	17.26 E
Alnor	41	54.55 N	9.36 E
Alnwick	44	55.25 N	1.42 W
Alnwick Indian Reserve ◈[4]	212	44.10 N	78.06 W
Alo	146	11.47 N	20.53 E
Aloândia	255	17.43 S	49.29 W
Alofau	174u	14.16 S	170.36 W
Alofi	174v	19.01 S	169.55 W
Alofi Bay ⊂	174v	19.01 S	169.56 W
Aloha	224	45.29 N	122.51 W
Aloha, Lake ◎	226	38.52 N	120.09 W
Aloi	154	2.17 N	33.10 E
Aloja	76	57.46 N	24.53 E
Alondra	280	33.55 N	118.15 W
Along	120	28.18 N	94.39 E
Alónnisos	38	39.08 N	23.50 E
Alónnisos I	38	39.13 N	23.55 E
Alor, Kepulauan II	112	8.15 S	124.30 E
Alor, Pulau I	112	8.15 S	124.45 E
Alor, Selat ʊ	112	8.20 S	123.48 E
Álora	34	36.48 N	4.42 W
Alor Gajah	114	2.23 N	102.13 E
Alor Setar	114	6.07 N	100.22 E
Alor Star → Alor Setar	114	6.07 N	100.22 E
Alorton	219	38.36 N	90.08 W
Al'oškino	88	58.35 N	100.32 E
Al'ošn'a, S.S.S.R.	76	53.38 N	33.29 E
Al'ošn'a, S.S.S.R.	82	54.14 N	37.16 E
Alosno	34	37.33 N	7.07 W
Alost → Aalst	50	50.56 N	4.02 E
Alotau	164	10.14 S	150.30 E
Alouette ≃	224	49.16 N	122.42 W
Alouette Lake ◎	224	49.19 N	122.28 W
Alovo	80	54.38 N	46.27 E
Aloxe-Corton	58	47.04 N	4.52 E
Aloysius, Mount ⋀	162	26.01 S	128.34 E
Alpachiri	252	37.22 S	63.46 W
Alpaugh	226	35.53 N	119.29 W
Alpen	52	51.35 N	6.30 E
Alpen → Alps ⩘	32	46.25 N	10.00 E
Alpena, Ar., U.S.	194	36.17 N	93.17 W
Alpena, Mi., U.S.	190	45.03 N	83.25 W
Alpena, S.D., U.S.	198	44.10 N	98.21 W
Alpercatas ≃	250	6.02 S	44.19 W
Alpes → Alps ⩘	32	46.25 N	10.00 E
Alpes-de-Haute-Provence □[5]	62	44.10 N	6.00 E
Alpes Dináricos → Dinara ⩘	36	43.50 N	16.35 E
Alpes Maritimes □[5]	62	44.00 N	7.10 E
Alpes Marítimos → Maritime Alps ⩘	62	44.15 N	7.10 E
Alpes Transilvanos → Carpații Meridionali ⩘	38	45.30 N	24.15 E
Alpha, Austl.	166	23.39 S	146.38 E
Alpha, Il., U.S.	190	41.12 N	90.23 W
Alpha, Mi., U.S.	190	46.02 N	88.22 W
Alpha, N.J., U.S.	210	40.40 N	75.09 W
Alpharetta	192	34.04 N	84.17 W
Alphen aan den Rijn	52	52.07 N	4.40 E
Alphington	42	50.42 N	3.31 W
Alphin Pike ⋀[2]	262	53.31 N	2.00 W
Alphonse Island I	138	7.00 S	52.45 E
Alpi → Alps ⩘	32	46.25 N	10.00 E
Alpi, Monte ⋀	68	40.07 N	15.59 E
Alpiarça	34	39.15 N	8.35 W
Alpi Dinariche → Dinara ⩘	36	43.50 N	16.35 E
Alpignano	62	45.06 N	7.31 E
Alpilles, Chaîne des ⩘[2]	62	43.45 N	4.50 E
Alpine, Az., U.S.	200	33.50 N	109.08 W
Alpine, Ca., U.S.	204	32.50 N	116.47 W
Alpine, N.J., U.S.	276	40.57 N	73.55 W
Alpine, N.Y., U.S.	210	42.19 N	76.44 W
Alpine, Tx., U.S.	196	30.21 N	103.39 W
Alpine □[6]	226	38.41 N	119.47 W
Alpine Creek ≃	282	37.19 N	122.17 W
Alpine National Park ♠	166	37.00 S	147.15 E
Alpinópolis	255	20.52 S	46.23 W
Alpi Retiche → Rhaetian Alps ⩘	58	46.30 N	10.00 E
Alpirsbach	58	48.21 N	8.23 E
Alplaus Kill ≃	210	42.51 N	73.54 W
Alpnachstad	58	46.57 N	8.17 E
Alps ⩘	22	46.25 N	10.00 E
Alpsee ◎	58	47.34 N	10.10 E
Alpu	130	39.47 N	30.58 E
Al-Qābil	128	23.57 N	55.48 E
Al-Qābūn	132	33.33 N	36.20 E
Al-Qadam	132	33.28 N	36.17 E
Al-Qaḍārif	140	14.02 N	35.24 E
Al-Qadīmah	144	22.21 N	39.09 E
Al-Qādisīyah □[4]	128	31.55 N	45.00 E
Al-Qāhirah (Cairo), Miṣr	142	30.03 N	31.15 E
Al-Qāhirah (Cairo), Miṣr	273c	30.03 N	31.15 E
Al-Qāhirah □[4]	142	30.02 N	31.17 E
Al-Qāhirah West Military Base ■	142	30.06 N	30.56 E
Al-Qahmah	144	18.00 N	41.41 E
Al-Qā'im	128	34.21 N	41.07 E
Al-Qā'īyah ∓[4]	128	26.27 N	45.35 E
Al-Qāiyāt	142	28.40 N	30.41 E
Al-Qalaj	142	30.11 N	31.21 E
Al-Qalībah	128	28.32 N	37.42 E
Al-Qalyūbīyah □[4]	142	30.18 N	31.18 E
Al-Qāmishlī	130	37.02 N	41.14 E
Al-Qanāṭir al-Khayrīyah	142	30.12 N	31.08 E
Al-Qanāyāt	142	30.37 N	31.28 E
Al-Qanṭarah	142	30.52 N	32.19 E
Al-Qaryah ash-Sharqīyah	146	30.24 N	13.36 E
Al-Qaryatayn	130	34.14 N	37.14 E
Al-Qaṣabāt	146	32.35 N	14.03 E
Al-Qaṣābī	142	31.16 N	30.41 E

Symbol	English	Deutsch	Español	Français	Português
≃	River	Fluß	Río	Rivière	Rio
≡	Canal	Kanal	Canal	Canal	Canal
∟	Waterfall, Rapids	Wasserfall, Stromschnellen	Cascada, Rápidos	Chute d'eau, Rapides	Cascata, Rápidos
ʊ	Strait	Meeresstraße	Estrecho	Détroit	Estreito
⊂	Bay, Gulf	Bucht, Golf	Bahía, Golfo	Baie, Golfe	Baía, Golfo
◎	Lake, Lakes	See, Seen	Lago, Lagos	Lac, Lacs	Lago, Lagos
≚	Swamp	Sumpf	Pantano	Marais	Pântano
⊓	Ice Features, Glacier	Eis- und Gletscherformen	Accidentes Glaciales	Formes glaciaires	Acidentes glaciares
∓	Other Hydrographic Features	Andere Hydrographische Objekte	Otros Elementos Hidrográficos	Autres données hydrographiques	Outros acidentes hidrográficos
✢	Submarine Features	Untermeerische Objekte	Accidentes Submarinos	Formes de relief sous-marin	Acidentes submarinos
□	Political Unit	Politische Einheit	Unidad Politica	Entité politique	Unidade política
♉	Cultural Institution	Kulturelle Institution	Institución Cultural	Institution culturelle	Instituição cultural
⊥	Historical Site	Historische Stätte	Sitio Histórico	Site historique	Sitio histórico
♠	Recreational Site	Erholungs- und Ferienort	Sitio de Recreo	Centre de loisirs	Area de Lazer
⊠	Airport	Flughafen	Aeropuerto	Aéroport	Aeroporto
■	Military Installation	Militäranlage	Instalación Militar	Installation militaire	Instalação militar
◈	Miscellaneous	Verschiedenes	Misceláneo	Divers	Diversos

ENGLISH: Name – Page – Lat.°′ – Long.°′
DEUTSCH: Name – Seite – Breite°′ – Länge°′ E = Ost

Al-Qaṣr, Miṣr 140 25.42 N 28.53 E
Al-Qaṣr, Urd. 132 31.19 N 35.45 E
Al-Qaṣṣāṣīn 142 30.34 N 31.56 E
Al-Qaṭīf 128 26.33 N 50.00 E
Al-Qaṭrānah 132 31.15 N 36.03 E
Al-Qaṭrūn 146 24.56 N 14.38 E
Al-Qaṭṭā 142 30.13 N 30.58 E
Al-Qaṭṭāwīyah 142 30.33 N 31.40 E
Al-Qays 142 28.29 N 30.47 E
Al-Qayṣūmah 128 28.16 N 46.03 E
Al-Qirʿawn 132 33.34 N 35.43 E
Al-Qiṣfah 132 32.38 N 35.52 E
Al-Quds
— Yerushalayim 132 31.46 N 35.14 E
Alquízar 240p 22.48 N 82.35 W
Al-Qunʿabah 132 33.08 N 35.40 E
Al-Qunayṭirah 132 33.07 N 35.49 E
Al-Qunayṭirah □8 132 33.00 N 35.50 E
Al-Qunfudhah 144 19.08 N 41.05 E
Al-Qurayn 142 30.37 N 31.44 E
Al-Qurayyah 132 32.32 N 36.36 E
Al-Qurnah 128 31.00 N 47.26 E
Al-Quṣaymah 132 30.40 N 34.22 E
Al-Quṣayr, Miṣr 128 26.06 N 34.17 E
Al-Quṣayr, Miṣr 142 27.27 N 30.52 E
Al-Quṣayr, Sūrīy. 130 34.31 N 36.35 E
Al-Qūṣīyah 142 27.26 N 30.49 E
Al-Quṭayfah 132 33.44 N 36.36 E
Al-Quṭaynah 140 14.52 N 32.21 E
Al-Quwayʿīyah 128 24.03 N 45.15 E
Al-Quwaysī 140 13.20 N 34.05 E
Alrø I 41 55.51 N 10.05 E
Alroy Downs 162 19.18 S 136.04 E
Als I 41 54.59 N 9.55 E
Alsace □9 58 48.30 N 7.30 E
Alsace, Ballon d' ʌ 58 47.50 N 6.51 E
Alsager 44 53.06 N 2.17 W
Alsask 184 51.23 N 109.59 W
Alsasua 34 42.54 N 2.10 W
Alsdorf 56 50.53 N 6.10 E
Alsea 202 44.22 N 123.35 W
Alsea ≃ 202 44.26 N 124.05 W
Alsek ≃ 180 59.10 N 138.10 W
Alsen 198 48.37 N 98.42 W
Alseno 64 44.54 N 9.59 E
Alsenz 56 49.43 N 7.49 E
Alsenz ≃ 56 49.49 N 7.51 E
Alsey 219 39.34 N 90.25 W
Alsfeld 56 50.45 N 9.16 E
Als Fjord c2 41 55.02 N 9.38 E
Alsh, Loch c 46 57.15 N 5.39 W
Al-Shallūfa Military
Base ■ 142 30.03 N 32.32 E
Alsike 40 59.45 N 17.45 E
Alsina 252 33.54 S 59.23 W
Alsip 216 41.40 N 87.44 W
Alsleben 54 51.42 N 11.41 E
Alsónémedi 264c 47.19 N 19.10 E
Alstaden ◆8 263 51.28 N 6.50 E
Ålstäket 40 59.20 N 18.28 E
Alstätte 52 52.08 N 6.55 E
Alstead ≃ 184 55.50 N 107.26 W
Alster 40 59.24 N 13.36 E
Alster ≃ 52 53.36 N 9.59 E
Alsterbro 26 56.57 N 15.55 E
Alstern ⊜ 40 59.40 N 13.55 E
Alston 44 54.49 N 2.26 W
Alsunga 76 56.59 N 21.34 E
Alswede 52 52.20 N 8.33 E
Alt ≃ 262 53.32 N 3.03 W
Alta, Nor. 24 69.55 N 23.12 E
Älta, Sve. 40 59.16 N 18.11 E
Alta, Ca., U.S. 226 39.12 N 120.49 W
Alta, Ia., U.S. 198 42.40 N 95.17 W
Alta, Cachoeira ∟ 250 5.46 S 54.28 W
Alta, Mount ʌ 172 44.30 S 168.58 E
Altadena 228 34.11 N 118.07 W
Alta Gracia, Arg. 252 31.40 S 64.26 W
Alta Gracia, Nic. 236 11.34 N 85.35 W
Altagracia, Ven. 246 10.43 N 71.32 W
Altagracia de Orituco 246 9.52 N 66.23 W
Alta Hill 226 39.14 N 121.04 W
Al Tahoe 226 38.57 N 119.59 W
Altai ⊀ 90 48.00 N 90.00 E
Altair 222 29.34 N 96.28 W
Altaj, Mong. 86 48.18 N 89.35 E
Altaj (Jesönbulag),
Mong. 90 46.20 N 96.18 E
Altaj, S.S.S.R. 86 53.27 N 91.48 E
Altajskij 86 51.58 N 85.22 E
Alta Loma, Ca., U.S. 228 34.07 N 117.36 W
Alta Loma, Tx., U.S. 222 29.22 N 95.04 W
Altamachi ≃ 248 16.08 S 66.50 W
Altamaha ≃ 192 31.19 N 81.17 W
Altamira, Arg. 258 34.40 S 59.22 W
Altamira, Bra. 250 3.12 S 52.12 W
Altamira, Chile 252 25.47 S 69.51 W
Altamira, C.R. 236 10.30 N 84.23 W
Altamira, Méx. 234 22.24 N 97.55 W
Altamira, Las Cuevas
de ±5 34 43.18 N 4.08 W
Altamirano, Arg. 258 35.21 S 58.09 W
Altamirano, Méx. 196 25.55 N 97.47 W
Altamont, Il., U.S. 219 39.03 N 88.44 W
Altamont, Ks., U.S. 198 37.11 N 95.17 W
Altamont, N.Y., U.S. 210 42.42 N 74.02 W
Altamont, Or., U.S. 202 42.12 N 121.44 W
Altamont, Tn., U.S. 194 35.25 N 85.43 W
Altamonte Springs 220 28.39 N 81.21 W
Altamura 68 40.50 N 16.33 E
Altamura, Isla I 232 25.00 N 108.10 W
Altan, S.S.S.R. 88 49.31 N 111.32 E
Altan, S.S.S.R. 88 49.53 N 109.04 E
Altanbulag, Mong. 88 50.19 N 106.30 E
Altanbulag, Mong. 88 47.41 N 106.22 E
Altan-Cögor 86 49.03 N 90.27 E
Altanširee 102 45.35 N 110.27 E
Altar 232 30.43 N 111.44 W
Altar ≃ 232 30.39 N 111.53 W
Altar, Desierto de ◆2 232 31.50 N 114.15 W
Altar de los
Sacrificios ⊥ 232 16.28 N 90.32 W
Altare 62 44.20 N 8.20 E
Altario 184 51.55 N 110.09 W
Altarnun 42 50.37 N 4.30 W
Altar of the Earth ⊕1 271a 39.57 N 116.24 E
Altar of the Moon ⊕1 271a 39.55 N 116.20 E
Altar of the Sun ⊕1 271a 39.54 N 116.27 E
Altar Wash V 200 32.05 N 111.19 W
Altaskij Kraj □8 86 52.30 N 83.00 E
Altastenberg 56 51.11 N 8.28 E
Altata, Méx. 232 24.38 N 107.55 W
Altata, S.S.S.R. 80 51.07 N 48.44 E
Alta Verapaz □5 236 15.40 N 90.00 W
Altavilla Irpina 68 41.00 N 14.47 E
Altavilla Milicia 70 38.02 N 13.32 E
Altavilla Silentina 68 40.32 N 15.08 E
Altaville 226 38.05 N 120.33 W
Alta Vista, Ks., U.S. 198 38.51 N 96.29 W
Altavista, Va., U.S. 192 37.06 N 79.17 W
Altay, S.S.S.R. 86 60.20 N 68.58 E
Altay, Zhg. 86 47.52 N 88.07 E
Alt Buchhorst 264a 52.26 N 13.51 E
Altdamm
— Dąbie ◆8 54 53.24 N 14.40 E
Altdöbern 54 51.39 N 14.02 E
Altdorf, B.R.D. 60 48.34 N 12.07 E
Altdorf, Schw. 58 46.53 N 8.39 E
Altdorf bei Nürnberg 60 49.23 N 11.21 E
Alte Donau ⊜ 264b 48.14 N 16.26 E
Alteelva ≃ 24 69.58 N 23.23 E
Altefähr 54 54.20 N 13.07 E
Alteglofsheim 60 48.55 N 12.12 E
Alte Grund 264a 52.28 N 13.47 E
Altena 56 51.17 N 7.40 E
Altenahr 56 50.31 N 6.59 E
Altenau 52 51.48 N 10.26 E
Altenbeken 52 51.46 N 8.56 E
Altenberg 54 50.46 N 13.45 E
Altenberge 52 52.03 N 7.27 E
Altenbruch 52 53.49 N 8.46 E
Altenbüren 56 51.23 N 8.30 E
Altenburg, D.D.R. 54 50.59 N 12.26 E
Altenburg, Öst. 61 48.38 N 15.35 E
Altenderne
Oberbecker ◆8 263 51.35 N 7.33 E
Altendorf 263 51.29 N 7.40 E
Altendorf ◆8 263 51.25 N 7.06 E
Altendorf-Ulfkotte 263 51.38 N 7.00 E
Altenesch 52 53.08 N 8.37 E
Altenessen ◆8 263 51.29 N 7.00 E
Altenfelden 60 48.29 N 13.58 E
Altengamme ◆8 52 53.25 N 10.16 E
Altenhagen, B.R.D. 52 52.03 N 8.38 E
Altenhagen, D.D.R. 54 53.45 N 13.06 E
Altenhagen ◆8 263 51.22 N 7.28 E
Altenhof 54 52.55 N 13.43 E
Altenholz 41 54.24 N 10.07 E
Altenkirchen
(Westerwald),
B.R.D. 56 50.41 N 7.38 E
Altenkirchen, D.D.R. 54 54.38 N 13.20 E
Altenkrempe 54 54.08 N 10.49 E
Altenkunstadt 54 50.07 N 11.14 E
Altenmarkt an der Alz 60 48.00 N 12.32 E
Altenoythe 52 53.02 N 7.52 E
Altenpleen 54 54.21 N 12.57 E
Altenstadt an der
Waldnaab 60 49.48 N 12.10 E
Altensteig 56 48.35 N 8.37 E
Altentreptow 54 53.42 N 13.14 E
Altenvoerde 263 51.18 N 7.22 E
Altenwalde 52 53.49 N 8.40 E
Altenweddingen 54 52.00 N 11.31 E
Alte Oder ≃ 54 52.52 N 14.09 E
Alter do Chão 34 39.12 N 7.40 W
Alterosa 256 21.15 S 46.08 W
Alter Rhein ≃ 263 51.35 N 6.36 E
Altes Land ◆1 52 53.33 N 9.38 E
Altevatnet ⊜ 24 68.32 N 19.30 E
Altfraunhofen 60 48.27 N 12.10 E
Altfriedland 54 52.38 N 14.12 E
Altglashütten 58 47.51 N 8.06 E
Alt-Glienicke ◆8 264a 52.25 N 13.32 E
Altgruland 263 51.27 N 7.41 E
Altha 192 30.34 N 85.07 W
Altham 262 53.47 N 2.21 W
Alt-Hartmannsdorf 264a 52.21 N 13.50 E
Althea Lake ⊜ 283 42.40 N 71.23 W
Altheim 60 48.15 N 13.13 E
Altheimer 194 34.19 N 91.50 W
Althofen 61 46.54 N 14.27 E
Altınekin 130 38.19 N 32.53 E
Altinho 250 8.29 S 36.04 W
Altınoluk 130 39.34 N 26.44 E
Altinópolis 255 21.02 S 47.23 W
Altınova 130 39.13 N 26.47 E
Altınözü 130 36.08 N 36.12 E
Altıntaş 130 39.04 N 30.07 E
Altınyaka 130 36.34 N 30.21 E
Altiplano ⊀1 248 18.00 S 68.00 W
Alt Käbelich 54 53.29 N 13.29 E
Altkirch 58 47.37 N 7.15 E
Altlandsberg 54 52.33 N 13.43 E
Altlangerwisch 264a 52.19 N 13.04 E
Altlewin 54 52.42 N 14.16 E
Altlüdersdorf 54 53.02 N 13.11 E
Altlünen 52 51.38 N 7.31 E
Altmannsdorf ◆8 264b 48.10 N 16.20 E
Altmannstein 60 48.54 N 11.39 E
Altmar 212 43.31 N 76.00 W
Altmark □9 54 52.40 N 11.20 E
Altmittweida 54 50.58 N 12.57 E
Altmühl ≃ 60 48.54 N 11.54 E
Altmünster 64 47.54 N 13.45 E
Altnaharra 46 58.16 N 4.27 W
Alto, Mi., U.S. 216 42.51 N 85.22 W
Alto, Tx., U.S. 222 31.39 N 95.04 W
Alto, Cerro ʌ, Méx. 234 20.50 N 100.22 W
Alto, Cerro ʌ, Ca.,
U.S. 226 35.25 N 120.43 W
Alto Anapu ≃ 250 2.15 S 51.27 W
Alto Araguaia 255 17.19 S 53.12 W
Alto Cauale 152 7.34 S 16.16 E
Alto Cedro 240p 20.31 N 75.58 W
Alto Chicapa 152 10.53 S 19.14 E
Alto Coité 255 15.47 S 54.20 W
Alto Cuito 152 13.27 S 18.49 E
Alto da Moóca ◆8 287b 23.34 S 46.35 W
Alto da Serra 256 22.53 S 44.14 W
Alto del Carmen 252 28.46 S 70.30 W
Alto de Ña Paula 286c 10.24 N 66.48 W
Altofonte 70 38.03 N 13.18 E
Alto Garças 255 16.56 S 53.32 W
Alto Ligonha 154 15.30 S 38.20 E
Alto Longá 250 5.15 S 42.12 W
Alto Lucero 234 19.37 N 96.43 W
Alto Madre de Dios
≃ 248 12.17 S 70.52 W
Alto Molócuè 154 15.38 S 37.42 E
Altomonte 68 39.42 N 16.08 E
Altomünster 60 48.23 N 11.15 E
Alton, On., Can. 212 43.52 N 80.04 W
Alton, Eng., U.K. 42 51.09 N 0.59 W
Alton, Il., U.S. 219 38.53 N 90.11 W
Alton, Ia., U.S. 198 42.59 N 96.00 W
Alton, Ks., U.S. 198 39.28 N 98.56 W
Alton, Ky., U.S. 218 38.04 N 84.55 W
Alton, Mo., U.S. 194 36.41 N 91.23 W
Alton, N.H., U.S. 188 43.27 N 71.13 W
Alton, N.Y., U.S. 210 43.13 N 76.59 W
Alton, R.I., U.S. 207 41.26 N 71.43 W
Altona, Austl. 162 27.34 S 120.00 E
Altona, Austl. 169 37.52 S 144.50 E
Altona, Mb., Can. 184 49.06 N 97.33 W
Altona, In., U.S. 216 41.21 N 85.09 W
Altona ◆8 52 53.32 N 9.56 E
Altona Bay c 274b 37.53 S 144.51 E
Altona North 274b 37.50 S 144.51 E
Altona Sports Park ♦ 274b 37.52 S 144.52 E
Altoona, Al., U.S. 194 34.01 N 86.19 W
Altoona, Fl., U.S. 220 28.57 N 81.38 W
Altoona, Ia., U.S. 190 41.39 N 93.28 W
Altoona, Ks., U.S. 198 37.31 N 95.39 W
Altoona, Pa., U.S. 214 40.31 N 78.23 W
Altoona, Wa., U.S. 224 46.16 N 123.39 W
Altoona, Wi., U.S. 190 44.48 N 91.26 W
Alto Pacajá ≃ 250 3.07 S 50.20 W
Alto Paraguai 248 14.30 S 56.31 W
Alto Paraguay □5 248 21.00 S 58.45 W
Alto Paraíso de Goiás 255 14.07 S 47.31 W
Alto Paraná □5 252 25.00 S 54.50 W
Alto Parnaíba 250 9.06 S 45.57 W
Alto Purús ≃ 248 9.34 S 70.36 W
Alto Rio Doce 255 21.02 S 43.25 W
Alto Río Senguerr 254 45.02 S 70.50 W
Altos 250 5.03 S 42.28 W
Alto Santo 250 5.31 S 38.15 W
Alto Sucuriú 255 19.19 S 52.47 W
Altotonga 234 19.46 N 97.14 W
Altötting 60 48.13 N 12.40 E
Alto Volta
— Burkina Faso □1 150 13.00 N 1.30 W
Alto Yurua ≃ 248 9.24 S 72.43 W
Altrincham 262 53.24 N 2.21 W
Alt Rüdersdorf 264a 52.28 N 13.49 E
Altruppin 54 52.56 N 12.50 E
Altshausen 58 47.56 N 9.32 E
Alt Stahnsdorf 264a 52.17 N 13.53 E
Altstätten, Öst. 36 47.28 N 9.30 E
Altstätten, Schw. 58 47.23 N 9.33 E
Alt Töplitz 264a 52.26 N 12.55 E
Altuchovo 76 52.40 N 34.20 E
Āltūn Kūprī 128 35.45 N 44.09 E
Altun Shan ⊀ 90 38.00 N 88.00 E
Alturas 204 41.29 N 120.32 W
Altus, Ar., U.S. 194 35.26 N 93.45 W
Altus, Ok., U.S. 196 34.38 N 99.20 W
Altus, Lake ⊜1 196 34.56 N 99.18 W
Altus Air Force Base
■ 196 34.40 N 99.16 W
Altusried 58 47.48 N 10.13 E
Altyagač 84 40.50 N 48.54 E
Altyaryk 85 40.23 N 71.30 E
Altykarasu 86 49.12 N 55.52 E
Altynaj 86 57.04 N 62.00 E
Altynasar ⊥ 86 45.10 N 63.07 E
Altynkul' 85 40.48 N 72.10 E
Altynovka 78 51.27 N 33.10 E
Altyntau 86 44.08 N 68.03 E
Altyn-Topkan 85 40.38 N 69.35 E
Alu I 175e 7.02 S 155.47 E
Al-Ubayyiḍ 140 13.11 N 30.13 E
Alubijid 116 8.35 N 124.29 E
Alucra 130 40.20 N 38.46 E
Al-ʿUdaysāt 140 25.35 N 32.29 E
Al-Uḍayyah 140 12.03 N 28.17 E
Aluk 140 8.26 N 27.27 E
Alūksne 76 57.25 N 27.03 E
Al-ʿUlā 128 26.37 N 37.52 E
Alum Bank 214 40.14 N 78.34 W
Alum Creek ≃ 218 39.53 N 82.54 W
Alum Creek Lake ⊜1 214 40.15 N 82.58 W
Aluminé 254 39.13 S 70.57 W
Aluminé ≃ 254 39.50 S 70.53 W
Aluminé, Lago ⊜ 252 38.55 S 71.09 W
Alum Rock 226 37.21 N 121.49 W
Alum Rock Park ♦ 282 37.24 N 121.49 W
Alunda 40 60.04 N 18.05 E
Alunitdag 84 40.32 N 46.03 E
Alupka 78 44.26 N 34.03 E
Al-ʿUqaylah 146 30.16 N 19.12 E
Al-ʿUqayr 128 25.39 N 50.12 E
Al-Uqṣur (Luxor) 140 25.41 N 32.39 E
Al-ʿUrayq ±8 128 29.10 N 39.15 E
Al-ʿUrayq ◆1 128 24.47 N 42.55 E
Al-Urdun
— Jordan □1 128 31.00 N 36.00 E
Al-Urdunn
— Jordan ≃ 132 31.46 N 35.33 E
Alušta 78 44.42 N 34.24 E
Al-ʿUṭayshān ⊤4 140 16.25 N 34.30 E
Al-ʿUwaynāt 146 25.46 N 10.34 E
Al-ʿUwaynidhīyah I 128 26.37 N 36.05 E
Al-ʿUyaynah 128 24.54 N 46.23 E
Alva, Scot., U.K. 46 56.09 N 3.48 W
Alva, Fl., U.S. 220 26.42 N 81.36 W
Alva, Ok., U.S. 196 36.48 N 98.39 W
Alva ≃ 34 40.18 N 8.15 W
Alvada 214 41.03 N 83.24 W
Alvaiázere 34 39.49 N 8.23 W
Alvaneu-Bad 58 46.40 N 9.39 E
Alvängen 26 57.58 N 12.07 E
Alvanley 262 53.16 N 2.45 W
Alvarado, Méx. 234 18.46 N 95.46 W
Alvarado, Tx., U.S. 222 32.24 N 97.12 W
Alvarado, Lake ⊜1 222 32.23 N 97.15 W
Alvarães 246 3.12 S 64.50 W
Alvarengas, Ribeirão
≃ 287b 23.45 S 46.37 W
Álvarez Jonte 258 35.19 S 57.28 W
Alvarinhos 266c 38.54 N 9.22 W
Álvaro Obregón 234 19.50 N 101.05 W
Alvaro Obregon □7 286a 19.22 N 99.16 W
Álvaro Obregón,
Presa ⊜1 232 27.55 N 109.52 W
Alvastra ⊥ 26 58.18 N 14.39 E
Alvdal 26 62.07 N 10.39 E
Älvdalen 26 61.14 N 14.02 E
Alvear 252 29.06 S 56.33 W
Alvechurch 42 52.21 N 1.57 W
Alverca 34 38.54 N 9.02 W
Alverda 214 40.38 N 78.52 W
Alvernia, Mount ʌ2 238 24.15 N 75.24 W
Alverton 214 40.08 N 79.35 W
Alves 46 57.38 N 3.27 W
Alvesta 26 56.54 N 14.33 E
Alveston 42 51.36 N 2.32 W
Alviano, Lago di ⊜1 66 42.36 N 12.15 E
Ålvik, Nor. 26 60.26 N 6.26 E
Alvik, Sve. 26 62.25 N 17.24 E
Alvin, Il., U.S. 216 40.19 N 87.37 W
Alvin, Tx., U.S. 222 29.25 N 95.14 W
Alvinópolis 255 20.06 S 43.03 W
Alvinston 214 42.49 N 81.52 W
Alviso ◆8 282 37.26 N 121.58 W
Alviso Slough ≃ 282 37.27 N 122.02 W
Alvito, It. 66 41.41 N 13.45 E
Alvito, Port. 34 38.15 N 7.59 W
Älvkarleby 40 60.34 N 17.27 E
Älvkarleö bruk 40 60.32 N 17.24 E
Alvord 196 33.22 N 97.42 W
Alvord Desert ◆2 202 42.30 N 118.25 W
Alvord Lake ⊜ 202 42.23 N 118.36 W
Alvordton 216 41.40 N 84.26 W
Alvra, Pass d')(58 46.35 N 9.50 E
Älvros 26 62.03 N 14.39 E
Älvsborgs Län □6 26 58.00 N 12.30 E
Älvsbyn 24 65.39 N 20.59 E
Älvsnabben ⊥ 40 58.59 N 18.10 E
Al-Wafāʾīyah 142 30.46 N 30.36 E
Al-Wajh 128 26.15 N 36.26 E
Al-Wakrah 128 25.10 N 51.36 E
Al-Walīdīyah 142 27.12 N 31.10 E
Alwar 124 27.34 N 76.36 E
Alwar Hills ⊀2 124 27.20 N 76.15 E
Al-Wāṣifīyah 142 30.35 N 32.10 E
Al-Wāsiṭah 142 29.20 N 31.12 E
Alwaye 122 10.07 N 76.21 E
Al-Wazīrīyah 142 31.11 N 30.57 E
Al-Wazz 140 15.01 N 30.10 E
Alwen ≃ 42 52.58 N 3.24 W
Al-Widy 142 29.31 N 31.16 E
Alxa Zuoqi 102 38.50 N 105.32 E
Al-Yamāmah
— As-
Sulaymānīyah 128 24.09 N 47.19 E
Al-Yaman
— Yemen □1 144 15.00 N 47.00 E
Al-Yaman ash-
Shaʿbīyah
— Yemen □1 144 15.00 N 47.00 E
Al Yāmūn 132 32.29 N 35.14 E
Alygdžer 88 53.38 N 98.16 E
Alyn and Deeside □8 262 53.16 N 3.02 W
Alypsatar 86 48.03 N 80.21 E
Alyth 46 56.37 N 3.13 W
Alytus 76 54.24 N 24.03 E
Alz ≃ 60 48.16 N 12.49 E
Alzamaj 88 55.33 N 98.39 E
Alzano Lombardo 62 45.44 N 9.43 E
Al-Zarqa 142 31.13 N 31.38 E
Alzenau 56 50.05 N 9.04 E
Alzette ≃ 56 49.22 N 6.09 E
Alzey 56 49.45 N 8.07 E
Alzira (Alcira) 34 39.09 N 0.26 W
Amab, Khawr V 140 17.08 N 34.51 E
Amacuro ≃ 246 8.32 N 60.28 W
Amacuzac ≃ 234 17.53 N 99.12 W
Amadeus, Lake ⊜ 162 24.50 S 130.45 E
Āmādi, Bngl. 126 22.28 N 89.19 E
Amadi, Zaïre 154 3.35 N 26.47 E
Amadjuak Lake ⊜ 176 65.00 N 71.00 W
Amador □6 226 38.21 N 120.46 W
Amadora 266c 38.45 N 9.14 W
Amador City 226 38.25 N 120.56 W
Amadores 234 22.51 N 99.43 W
Amador Valley V 282 37.41 N 121.51 W
Amagansett 207 40.58 N 72.08 W
Amagasaki 96 34.43 N 135.25 E
Amagase 96 33.15 N 131.02 E
Amager I 41 55.37 N 12.37 E
Amagi 96 33.25 N 130.39 E
Amagi-san ʌ 94 34.51 N 139.00 E
Amagi-yugashima 94 34.53 N 138.56 E
Amagoi-dake ʌ 94 35.01 N 136.23 E
Amagunze 150 6.20 N 7.40 E
Amahai 164 3.20 S 128.55 E
Amaichá del Valle 252 26.36 S 65.55 W
Amaimon 164 5.10 S 145.25 E
Amajac ≃ 234 21.15 N 98.46 W
Amaka ≃ 236 14.14 N 85.07 W
Ama Keng 271c 1.24 N 103.42 E
Amak Island I 180 55.25 N 163.07 W
Amakusa-nada ⊤2 92 32.35 N 130.05 E
Amakusa-shotō II 92 32.20 N 130.15 E
Amakuso-Shimo-
shima I 92 32.20 N 130.05 E
Amal, Lībiyā 146 29.25 N 21.10 E
Åmål, Sve. 26 59.03 N 12.42 E
Amalāpuram 122 16.35 N 82.01 E
Amalat ≃ 88 54.49 N 115.12 E
Amalfi, Col. 246 6.55 N 75.04 W
Amalfi, It. 68 40.38 N 14.36 E
Amalia 158 27.16 S 25.03 E
Amaliás 38 37.49 N 21.23 E
Amalner 120 21.03 N 75.04 E
Amamaki-zan ʌ 94 36.25 N 140.09 E
Amambaí 255 23.05 S 55.13 W
Amambaí ≃ 255 23.22 S 53.56 W
Amambay □5 252 23.00 S 56.00 W
Amambay, Cordillera
de ⊀ 252 23.10 S 55.30 W
Amami-Ō-shima I 93b 28.15 N 129.20 E
Amami-shotō II 93b 28.16 N 129.21 E
Amamula 154 0.18 S 27.50 E
Amana 190 41.48 N 91.52 W
Amanã ≃, Bra. 250 4.25 S 57.34 W
Amana ≃, Ven. 238 9.45 N 62.39 W
Amaná, Lago ⊜ 246 2.35 S 64.40 W
Amanab 164 3.35 S 141.13 E
Amanave 174u 14.19 S 170.49 W
Amance 58 47.48 N 6.04 E
Amancey 58 47.02 N 6.05 E
Amanda 188 39.38 N 82.44 W
Amanda Park 224 47.28 N 123.54 W
Amandola 66 42.59 N 13.21 E
Amānganj 124 24.26 N 80.02 E
Amangel'dy, S.S.S.R. 85 43.43 N 71.07 E
Amangel'dy, S.S.S.R. 86 50.10 N 65.13 E
Amangel'dy, S.S.S.R. 86 49.52 N 59.00 E
Åmänningen ⊜ 40 59.57 N 15.56 E
Amano 270 34.26 N 135.33 E
Amanotkel' 86 46.07 N 61.34 E
Amantea 68 39.08 N 16.05 E
Amantogaj 86 50.22 N 65.33 E
Amanu I1 14 17.48 S 140.46 W
Amanzimtofi 158 30.03 S 30.53 E
Amapá 250 2.03 N 50.48 W
Amapá □8 250 1.00 N 52.00 W
Amapala 236 13.17 N 87.40 W
Amapala, Punta > 236 13.10 N 87.54 W
Amapari ≃ 250 0.43 N 51.32 W
Amaraji 250 8.24 S 35.27 W
Amaral 287a 22.42 S 43.29 W
Amaramba, Lago ⊜ 154 14.30 S 35.55 E
Amarante 250 6.14 S 42.50 W
Amarante do
Maranhão 250 5.36 S 46.45 W
Amaranth 184 50.36 N 98.43 W
Amarapura 110 21.54 N 96.03 E
Amărăştii-de-Jos 38 43.59 N 24.10 E
ʿAmārat Abū Sinn 140 15.21 N 35.45 E
Amarāvati ≃ 122 10.51 N 78.11 E
Amarda 126 21.47 N 87.08 E
Amareleja 34 38.12 N 7.14 W
Amares 34 41.38 N 8.21 W
Amarete (Charazani) 248 15.14 S 68.58 W
Amargosa 255 13.02 S 39.36 W
Amargosa ≃ 204 36.13 N 116.48 W
Amargosa Range ⊀ 204 36.15 N 116.45 W
Amarillo 196 35.13 N 101.49 W
Amarillo, Mar
— Yellow Sea ⊤2 90 36.00 N 123.00 E
ʿAmar Jadīd 140 14.28 N 25.14 E
Amarkantak 124 22.40 N 81.45 E
Amarnāth 122 19.11 N 73.10 E
Amarnāth Cave ±5 123 34.13 N 75.31 E
Amaro, Monte ʌ 66 42.05 N 14.05 E
Amaro Leite 255 13.58 S 49.09 W
Amaroúsion 267c 38.03 N 23.49 E
Amarpātan 124 24.19 N 80.59 E
Amarube-saki > 96 35.40 N 134.32 E
Amarume 92 38.50 N 139.55 E
Amarwāra 124 22.18 N 79.10 E
Amasa 190 46.13 N 88.26 W
Amaseno ≃ 66 41.34 N 13.13 E
Amasija 84 40.58 N 43.46 E
Amasra 130 41.45 N 32.24 E
Amasya 130 40.39 N 35.51 E
Amasya □4 130 40.45 N 35.30 E
Amataurá 246 3.29 S 68.06 W
Amatenango de la
Frontera 236 15.26 N 92.07 W
Amatignak Island I 181a 51.15 N 179.08 W
Amatikulu 158 29.06 S 31.27 E
Amatique, Bahía de c 236 15.55 N 88.45 W
Amatitán 234 20.50 N 103.43 W
Amatitlán 236 14.29 N 90.37 W
Amatitlán, Lago de ⊜ 236 14.27 N 90.34 W
Amatlán de Cañas 234 20.52 N 104.27 W
Amatlán de los
Reyes 234 18.50 N 96.55 W
Amatrice 66 42.38 N 13.17 E
Amatsu-kominato 94 35.07 N 140.10 E
Amau 164 10.02 S 148.34 E
Amausi 124 26.46 N 80.51 E
Amawalk 210 41.17 N 73.46 W
Amay 56 50.33 N 5.19 E
Ama-zaki > 94 37.08 N 136.40 E
Amazar 89 53.54 N 120.53 E
Amazon (Solimões)
(Amazonas) ≃ 242 0.10 S 49.00 W
Amazonas □3 246 2.00 S 64.00 W
Amazonas □5, Col. 246 1.00 S 72.00 W
Amazonas □5, Perú 248 5.30 S 78.00 W
Amazonas □8 246 3.30 N 66.00 W
Amazonas
— Amazon ≃ 242 0.10 S 49.00 W
Amb 123 34.19 N 72.51 E
Ambāh 124 26.43 N 78.14 E
Ambahikily 157b 21.36 S 43.41 E
Ambahita 157b 24.01 S 45.16 E
Ambaí 287a 22.43 S 43.28 W
Ambājogāi 122 18.44 N 76.23 E
Ambakaka 157b 24.10 S 46.17 E
Ambāla 124 30.21 N 76.50 E
Ambāla Airport ⊠ 123 30.22 N 76.50 E
Ambalabe 157b 18.24 S 49.10 E
Ambalafany 157b 22.32 S 47.36 E
Ambalangoda 122 6.14 N 80.03 E
Ambalanjanakomby 157b 16.42 S 47.05 E
Ambalavao 157b 21.50 S 46.56 E
Ambalema 246 4.47 N 74.46 W
Ambam 152 2.23 N 11.17 E
Amba Maryam 144 11.26 N 39.17 E
Ambanja 157b 13.41 S 48.27 E
Ambar 248 10.44 S 77.16 W
Ambararata 157b 15.03 S 48.33 E
Ambarawa 115a 7.15 S 110.24 E
Ambarčik, S.S.S.R. 74 69.39 N 162.20 E
Ambarčik, S.S.S.R. 88 55.09 N 95.46 E
Ambargasta, Salinas
de ≚ 252 29.15 S 64.30 W
Ambarijeby 157b 14.56 S 47.41 E
Ambarnyj 24 65.56 N 33.43 E
Ambaro, Baie d' c 157b 13.23 S 48.38 E
Ambāsamudram 122 8.42 N 77.28 E
Ambassador Bridge
◆5 281 42.20 N 83.05 W
Ambato, Ec. 246 1.15 S 78.37 W
Ambato, Madag. 157b 13.24 S 48.29 E
Ambato Boeny 157b 16.28 S 46.43 E
Ambatofinandrahana 157b 20.33 S 46.48 E
Ambatolampy 157b 19.23 S 47.25 E
Ambatomainty 157b 17.41 S 45.40 E
Ambatomanoina 157b 18.18 S 47.37 E
Ambatondrazaka 157b 17.50 S 48.25 E
Ambatosoratra 157b 17.34 S 48.32 E
Ambeláki 267c 37.57 N 23.32 E
Ambelau, Pulau I 164 3.51 S 127.12 E
Ámbelos, Ákra > 38 39.56 N 23.55 E
Ambenja 157b 15.17 S 46.58 E
Amber ≃ 44 53.04 N 1.29 W
Amberes
— Antwerpen 50 51.13 N 4.25 E
Amberg, B.R.D. 60 49.27 N 11.52 E
Amberg, Wi., U.S. 190 45.30 N 87.59 W
Ambergris Cay I 232 18.03 N 87.56 W
Ambérieu-en-Bugey 58 45.57 N 5.21 E
Amberley 172 43.10 S 172.44 E
Amberley Royal
Australian Air
Force Base ■ 171a 27.37 S 152.41 E
Amberson 214 40.10 N 77.41 W
Ambert 62 45.33 N 3.45 E
Ambevongo 157b 15.27 S 47.27 E
Ambia 216 40.29 N 87.31 W
Ambidédi 150 14.35 N 11.47 W
Ambikānagar 126 22.57 N 86.46 E
Ambikāpur 124 23.07 N 83.12 E
Ambil 116 13.49 N 120.20 E
Ambil Island I 116 13.48 N 120.18 E
Ambilobe 157b 13.12 S 49.04 E
Ambinanindrano 157b 20.20 S 48.19 E
Ambinanitelo 157b 15.21 S 49.35 E
Ambinda 157b 16.25 S 45.52 E
Ambivy 157b 21.31 S 44.02 E
Ambjörby 26 60.30 N 13.10 E
Ambla 76 59.11 N 25.51 E
Amble 44 55.20 N 1.34 W
Amblecote 42 52.28 N 2.09 W
Ambler, Ak., U.S. 180 67.05 N 157.52 W
Ambler, Pa., U.S. 208 40.09 N 75.13 W
Ambleside 44 54.26 N 2.58 W
Ambleteuse 50 50.49 N 1.36 E
Amblève ≃ 56 50.28 N 5.36 E
Ambo 248 10.07 S 76.10 W
Amboahangy 157b 24.15 S 46.22 E
Amboasary, Madag. 157b 18.26 S 48.16 E
Amboasary, Madag. 157b 25.02 S 46.23 E
Ambodifototra 157b 16.59 S 49.52 E
Ambodilazana 157b 18.06 S 49.10 E
Ambodiriana 157b 17.55 S 49.18 E
Ambohibary 157b 19.20 S 46.17 E
Ambohidratrimo 157b 18.50 S 47.26 E
Ambohidray 157b 18.36 S 48.18 E
Ambohimahamasina 157b 21.56 S 47.11 E
Ambohimahasoa 157b 21.07 S 47.13 E
Ambohimanga du
Sud 157b 20.52 S 47.36 E
Ambohimitombo 157b 20.43 S 47.26 E
Amboina
— Ambon 164 3.43 S 128.12 E
Amboise 50 47.25 N 0.59 E
Amboíva 152 11.32 S 14.44 E
Ambon 164 3.43 S 128.12 E
Ambon, Pulau I 164 3.40 S 128.10 E
Ambondro 157b 25.13 S 45.44 E
Ambonnay 50 49.04 N 4.10 E
Amboseli, Lake ⊜ 154 2.37 S 37.08 E
Amboseli National
Park ♦ 154 2.30 S 37.15 E
Amboshe 272c 19.09 N 73.08 E
Ambositra 157b 20.31 S 47.15 E
Ambovombe 157b 25.11 S 46.05 E
Amboy, Il., U.S. 190 41.42 N 89.19 W
Amboy, In., U.S. 216 40.36 N 85.55 W
Amboy, Mn., U.S. 190 43.53 N 94.09 W
Amboy, Wa., U.S. 224 45.54 N 122.26 W
Ambre, Cap d' > 157b 11.57 S 49.17 E
Ambre, Montagne d'
ʌ 157b 12.30 S 49.10 E
Ambridge 214 40.35 N 80.13 W
Ambridge Heights 214 40.36 N 80.13 W
Ambridge Reservoir
⊜1 214 40.34 N 80.21 W
Ambrières 32 48.24 N 0.38 W
Ambriz 152 7.50 S 13.06 E
Ambrolauri 84 42.31 N 43.09 E
Ambronay 58 46.00 N 5.21 E
Ambrose 198 48.57 N 103.28 W
Ambrose Brook ≃ 276 40.33 N 74.32 W
Ambrose Channel ⊔ 276 40.32 N 74.02 W
Ambrosia Lake 200 35.25 N 107.49 W
Ambrym □8 175f 16.15 S 168.12 E
Ambrym I 175f 16.15 S 168.10 E
Ambuklao Dam ◆6 116 16.28 N 120.45 E
Ambulong Island I 116 12.12 N 121.01 E
Ambulu 115a 8.21 S 113.36 E
Ambuntentimur 115a 6.54 S 113.45 E
Ambunti 164 4.14 S 142.50 E
Āmbūr 122 12.47 N 78.42 E
Amburambur 115b 8.15 S 116.18 E
Amburayan Nabunga
≃ 116 16.55 N 120.27 E
Amby 56 50.53 N 5.44 E
Amchitka Island I 181a 51.30 N 179.00 E
Amchitka Pass ⊔ 181a 51.30 N 179.30 W
ʿAmd 144 15.18 N 48.00 E
Am-Dam 146 12.46 N 20.29 E
Āmdānga 272b 22.49 N 88.31 E
Amded, Oued V 148 22.09 N 3.15 E
Amden 58 47.09 N 9.11 E
Amderma 72 69.45 N 61.39 E
Amdo 120 32.18 N 91.04 E
Ameagle 188 37.56 N 81.25 W
Ameca 234 20.33 N 104.02 W
Ameca ≃ 234 20.41 N 105.18 W
Amecameca [de
Juárez] 234 19.07 N 98.46 W
Ameghino 252 34.50 S 62.27 W
Ameglia 64 44.04 N 9.57 E
Ameisberg ʌ 60 48.33 N 13.50 E
Ameixoeira ◆8 266c 38.47 N 9.10 W
Ameland I 52 53.25 N 5.45 E
Amele 164 5.16 S 145.42 E
Amelia, It. 66 42.33 N 12.25 E
Amelia, Oh., U.S. 218 39.01 N 84.13 W
Amelia, Passo d')(66 42.36 N 12.32 E
Amelia Court House 192 37.20 N 77.58 W
Amelia Earhart Peak
ʌ 226 37.47 N 119.17 W
Amelia Island I 192 30.37 N 81.27 W
Amelinghausen 52 53.08 N 10.13 E
Amelsbüren 52 51.53 N 7.37 E
Amendolara 68 39.57 N 16.35 E
Ameng 102 23.50 N 104.32 E
Amenia 210 41.50 N 73.33 W
Amenucourt 261 49.06 N 1.39 E
Āmer 120 26.59 N 75.52 E
Amerang 60 48.00 N 12.18 E
Amerevo 265b 55.55 N 38.03 E
America 52 51.26 N 5.59 E
América del Norte
— North America
±1 16 45.00 N 100.00 W
América del Sur
— South America
±1 18 15.00 S 60.00 W
American ≃, Ca.,
U.S. 226 38.36 N 121.30 W
American ≃, Wa.,
U.S. 224 46.58 N 121.08 W
American, Middle
Fork ≃ 226 38.55 N 121.02 W
American, North Fork
≃ 226 38.43 N 121.09 W
American, South
Fork ≃ 226 38.43 N 121.09 W
Americana 255 22.45 S 47.20 W
American Canyon 226 38.10 N 122.15 W
American Cemetery
and Memorial ◆ 269f 14.33 N 121.03 E
American Falls 202 42.47 N 112.51 W
American Falls ∟ 284a 43.05 N 79.04 W
American Falls
Reservoir ⊜1 202 42.45 N 112.45 W
American Fork 200 40.22 N 111.47 W
American Highland
⊀1 9 72.30 S 78.00 E
American Lake ⊜ 224 47.07 N 122.34 W
American Museum of
Natural History ⊕ 276 40.47 N 73.59 W
Americano 250 1.19 S 48.04 W
American River 168b 35.47 S 137.47 E
American Samoa □2,
Oc. 14 14.20 S 170.00 W
American Samoa □2,
Oc. 175a 14.20 S 170.00 W
American University
⊕2 284c 38.56 N 77.05 W
Américas, Hipódromo
de las ♦ 286a 19.26 N 99.13 W
Americas, University
of the ⊕2 286a 19.23 N 99.15 W
Americus, Ga., U.S. 192 32.04 N 84.13 W
Americus, Ks., U.S. 198 38.30 N 96.15 W
Amerikanisches
Hochland
— American
Highland ⊀1 9 72.30 S 78.00 E
Ameringkogel ʌ 61 47.04 N 14.48 E
Amérique du Nord
— North America
±1 16 45.00 N 100.00 W
Amern 56 51.14 N 6.15 E
Amerongen 52 52.00 N 5.27 E
Amersfoort, Ned. 52 52.09 N 5.24 E
Amersfoort, S. Afr. 158 27.01 S 29.51 E
Amersham 260 51.40 N 0.38 W
Amery, Austl. 162 31.09 S 117.05 E
Amery, Mb., Can. 184 56.34 N 94.03 W
Amery, Wi., U.S. 190 45.18 N 92.21 W
Amery Ice Shelf ⊓ 9 69.30 S 72.00 E
Ames, Ia., U.S. 190 42.02 N 93.37 W
Ames, N.Y., U.S. 210 42.50 N 74.36 W
Ames, Tx., U.S. 222 30.03 N 94.46 W
Amesbury, Eng., U.K. 42 51.10 N 1.45 W
Amesbury, Ma., U.S. 207 42.51 N 70.55 W
Ames Long Pond ⊜ 283 42.05 N 71.07 W
Ames Nowell State
Park ♦ 283 42.07 N 70.59 W
Ames Pond ⊜ 283 42.38 N 71.13 W
Ames Research
Center ⊕3 282 37.25 N 122.04 W
Amet Sound ⊔ 186 45.47 N 63.13 W
Amfíklia 38 38.38 N 22.35 E
Amfilokhía 38 38.51 N 21.10 E
Ámfissa 38 38.31 N 22.24 E
Amfreville-la-
Campagne 50 49.13 N 0.57 E
Amfreville-les-
Champs 50 49.19 N 1.19 E
Amga 74 60.53 N 132.00 E
Amga ≃ 74 62.38 N 134.32 E
Am Géréda 146 12.52 N 21.10 E
Amguema 180 66.58 N 179.16 W
Amguema ≃ 180 68.10 N 177.40 W
Amguid 148 26.26 N 5.22 E
Amgun' ≃ 89 52.56 N 139.40 E
Amherst, N.S., Can. 186 45.49 N 64.14 W
Amherst, Ma., U.S. 207 42.22 N 72.31 W
Amherst, N.H., U.S. 207 42.51 N 71.37 W
Amherst, N.Y., U.S. 210 42.58 N 78.48 W
Amherst, Oh., U.S. 214 41.23 N 82.13 W
Amherst, Tx., U.S. 196 34.01 N 102.25 W
Amherst, Va., U.S. 192 37.35 N 79.03 W
Amherst, Wi., U.S. 190 44.27 N 89.17 W
Amherst, Mount ʌ 162 18.11 S 126.59 E
Amherstburg 214 42.06 N 83.06 W
Amherstdale 188 37.47 N 81.48 W
Amherst Island I 212 44.08 N 76.45 W
Amherstview 212 44.13 N 76.38 W
Ami 94 36.02 N 140.14 E
Amianan Island I 108 21.07 N 121.57 E
Amiata, Monte ʌ 66 42.53 N 11.37 E
Amicalola Falls State
Park ♦ 192 34.33 N 84.15 W
Amidon 198 46.28 N 103.19 W
Amiens, Austl. 166 28.35 S 151.49 E
Amiens, Fr. 50 49.54 N 2.18 E
Amili, India 120 28.26 N 95.52 E
Amili, Zhg. 120 28.25 N 95.52 E
Amīn as-Samālūsī,
Biʾr ⊤4 142 29.52 N 30.02 E
Amīndīvi Islands II 122 11.23 N 72.23 E
Aminga 252 28.50 S 66.54 W
Amini Island I 122 11.07 N 72.44 E
Amino, Ityo. 144 4.31 N 41.49 E
Amino, Nihon 96 35.41 N 135.02 E
Aminuis 156 23.43 S 19.21 E
Amīrābād 128 36.04 N 54.10 E
Amīrābād ◆8 267d 35.43 N 51.23 E
Amirante Islands II 138 6.00 S 53.10 E
Amirauté, Îles de l'
— Admiralty
Islands II 164 2.10 S 147.00 E
Amisk 182 52.33 N 111.04 W
Amisk Lake ⊜ 184 54.35 N 102.13 W
Amistad, Presa de la
(Amistad Reservoir)
⊜1 196 29.34 N 101.15 W
Amistad National
Recreation Area ♦ 196 29.32 N 101.12 W
Amistad Reservoir
(Presa de la
Amistad) ⊜1 196 29.34 N 101.15 W
Amite 194 30.43 N 90.30 W
Amite ≃ 194 30.12 N 90.35 W
Amite, East Fork ≃ 194 30.58 N 90.51 W
Amiterno ⊥ 66 42.21 N 13.42 E
Amitori 175d 24.18 N 123.41 E
Amity, Ar., U.S. 194 34.15 N 93.27 W
Amity, Oh., U.S. 214 40.03 N 83.17 W
Amity, Or., U.S. 224 45.06 N 123.12 W
Amity Point > 171a 27.24 S 153.27 E
Amityville 276 40.40 N 73.25 W
Amixtlán 234 20.03 N 97.48 W
Amizmiz 148 31.14 N 8.14 W
Āmjhori ʌ 126 21.51 N 86.19 E
Āmjhupi 126 23.45 N 88.42 E
Āmla, Bngl. 126 23.54 N 88.56 E
Āmla, India 124 21.56 N 78.07 E
Āmlāgora 126 22.50 N 87.20 E
Āmlekhgañj 124 27.17 N 84.59 E
Åmli 26 58.47 N 8.30 E
Amlia Island I 180 52.06 N 173.30 W
Amloh 124 30.37 N 76.14 E
Am Loubia 146 13.39 N 20.08 E
Amlwch 44 53.25 N 4.20 W
ʿAmm-Adām 140 16.22 N 36.06 E
Ammagan 85 38.56 N 67.15 E
ʿAmmān 132 31.57 N 35.56 E
ʿAmmān □8 132 31.45 N 36.15 E
Ammanford 42 51.48 N 3.59 W
Ämmänsaari 26 64.53 N 28.55 E
Ammansville 222 29.47 N 96.51 W
ʿAmmār, Tall ʌ2 132 32.53 N 36.29 E
Ammarnäs 24 65.56 N 16.09 E
Ammaroo 162 21.45 S 135.15 E
Åmmeberg 40 58.52 N 15.00 E
Ammeloe 52 52.05 N 6.47 E
Ammendorf ◆8 54 51.25 N 11.59 E
Ammer ≃ 64 47.57 N 11.08 E
Ammerån ≃ 26 63.09 N 16.13 E
Ammerbuch 56 48.33 N 8.58 E
Ammer Gebirge ⊀ 64 47.35 N 10.55 E
Ammerland ◆1 52 53.15 N 8.00 E
Ammerman Mountain
ʌ 180 68.21 N 141.03 W
Ammerschwihr 58 48.07 N 7.17 E
Ammersee ⊜ 60 48.00 N 11.08 E
Ammerthal 60 49.26 N 11.45 E
Ammon 202 43.28 N 111.57 W
Ammonoosuc ≃ 188 44.10 N 72.02 W
Amnān 272b 22.56 N 88.18 E
Amnat Charoen 110 15.51 N 104.38 E
Amnay ≃ 116 12.58 N 120.46 E
Amne Machin Shan
— A'nyêmaqên
Shan ⊀ 102 34.30 N 100.00 E
Amnicon ≃ 190 46.41 N 91.52 W
Amnok-kang (Yalu) ≃ 98 39.55 N 124.22 E
Amo ≃, Asia 124 26.16 N 89.36 E
Amo ≃, Zhg. 102 22.58 N 101.44 E
Āmol 128 36.23 N 52.20 E
Amolar 248 18.01 S 57.30 W
Amöneburg 56 50.48 N 8.55 E
Amorbach 56 49.39 N 9.13 E
Amorgós 38 36.50 N 25.54 E
Amorgós I 38 36.50 N 25.59 E
Amorim, Morro ʌ2 287a 23.00 S 43.26 W
Amorinópolis 255 16.36 S 51.08 W
Amorosi 68 41.12 N 14.28 E

Symbols in the index entries represent the broad categories identified in the key at the right. Symbols with superior numbers (⊀1) identify subcategories (see complete key on page *I · 1*).

Symbole im Register stellen die rechts im Schlüssel erklärten Kategorien dar. Symbole mit hochgestellten Ziffern (⊀1) bezeichnen Unterabteilungen einer Kategorie (vgl. vollständiger Schlüssel auf Seite *I · 1*).

Los símbolos incluídos en el texto del índice representan las grandes categorías identificadas con la clave a la derecha. Los símbolos con numeros en su parte superior (⊀1) identifican las subcategorías (véase la clave completa en la página *I · 1*).

Les symboles de l'index représentent les catégories indiquées dans la légende à droite. Les symboles suivis d'un indice (⊀1) représentent des sous-catégories (voir légende complète à la page *I · 1*).

Os símbolos incluídos no texto do índice representam as grandes categorias identificadas com a chave à direita. Os símbolos com números em sua parte superior (⊀1) identificam as subcategorias (veja-se a chave completa à página *I · 1*).

	English	Deutsch	Español	Français	Português
ʌ	Mountain	Berg	Montaña	Montagne	Montanha
⊀	Mountains	Gebirge	Montañas	Montagnes	Montanhas
)(	Pass	Paß	Paso	Col	Passo
V	Valley, Canyon	Tal, Cañon	Valle, Cañón	Vallée, Canyon	Vale, Canhão
≚	Plain	Ebene	Llano	Plaine	Planície
>	Cape	Kap	Cabo	Cap	Cabo
I	Island	Insel	Isla	Île	Ilha
II	Islands	Inseln	Islas	Îles	Ilhas
±	Other Topographic Features	Andere Topographische Objekte	Otros Elementos Topográficos	Autres données topographiques	Outros acidentes topográficos

ESPAÑOL				FRANÇAIS				PORTUGUÊS			
Nombre	Página	Lat.°′	Long.°′ W=Oeste	Nom	Page	Lat.°′	Long.°′ W=Ouest	Nome	Página	Lat.°′	Long.°′ W=Oeste

Column 1 (ESPAÑOL)

- Amory 194 33.59 N 88.29 W
- Amos 190 48.35 N 78.07 W
- Åmose Å ≃ 41 55.35 N 11.18 E
- Åmot, Nor. 26 59.35 N 8.00 E
- Åmot, Nor. 26 59.54 N 9.54 E
- Amotfors 26 59.46 N 12.22 E
- Amour → Amur ≃ 74 52.56 N 141.10 E
- Amour, Djebel ⋌ 148 34.00 N 2.15 E
- Amoy → Xiamen 100 24.28 N 118.07 E
- Amozoc 234 19.02 N 98.03 W
- Ampana 112 0.51 S 121.32 E
- Ampanavoana 157b 15.41 S 50.22 E
- Ampang 115b 8.47 S 118.00 E
- Ampanihy 157b 24.42 S 44.45 E
- Ampaoid, Mount ⋀ 116 7.57 N 125.41 E
- Amparafaravola 157b 17.35 S 48.13 E
- Amparihy, Madag. 157b 16.40 S 44.43 E
- Amparihy, Madag. 157b 17.20 S 47.20 E
- Amparo 256 22.42 S 46.45 W
- Ampasibe 157b 22.56 S 46.58 E
- Ampasinambo 157b 20.31 S 48.00 E
- Ampasindava, Baie d' c 157b 13.16 S 48.43 E
- Ampasindava, Presqu'île d' ›1 157b 13.45 S 48.00 E
- Ampato, Nevado ⋀ 248 15.50 S 71.52 W
- Ampel 115a 7.27 S 110.32 E
- Amper 150 9.20 N 9.43 E
- Amper ≃ 60 48.30 N 11.58 E
- Ampezzo 64 46.25 N 12.48 E
- Ampezzo, Valle di ✔ 64 46.30 N 12.10 E
- Ampfing 60 48.16 N 12.25 E
- Ampflwang 60 48.05 N 13.34 E
- Amphion-les-Bains 58 46.23 N 6.32 E
- Ampisikina 157b 12.57 S 49.49 E
- Ampiyacu ≃ 246 3.19 S 71.51 W
- Ampleforth 44 54.12 N 1.06 W
- Ampollino, Lago ⊜ 68 39.12 N 16.37 E
- Ampombiantambo 157b 12.42 S 48.57 E
- Amposta 34 40.43 N 0.35 E
- Ampotaka 157b 25.03 S 44.41 E
- Ampoza 157b 22.20 S 44.44 E
- Ampthill 42 52.02 N 0.30 W
- Ampuis 62 45.29 N 4.49 E
- Ampus 62 43.36 N 6.23 E
- Amqui 186 48.28 N 67.26 W
- Amr, Jabal al- ⋌ 132 30.45 N 34.20 E
- Amraoti → Amrāvati 120 20.56 N 77.45 E
- Amrāvati 120 20.56 N 77.45 E
- Am-Raya 146 14.00 N 16.35 E
- Amreli 120 21.37 N 71.14 E
- Amreswar 272b 22.28 N 88.34 E
- Amriswil 58 47.33 N 9.18 E
- Amritsar 123 31.35 N 74.53 E
- Amroha 124 28.55 N 78.28 E
- Amrūka 123 30.19 N 73.53 E
- Amrum I 30 54.39 N 8.21 E
- Amsdell Heights 284a 42.45 N 78.54 W
- Amsden 214 41.13 N 83.20 W
- Amsel 148 22.37 N 5.26 E
- Amsele 26 64.32 N 19.20 E
- Am Sigan 146 11.41 N 19.51 E
- Amsoldingen 58 46.43 N 7.35 E
- Amsteg 58 46.46 N 8.41 E
- Amstel ≃ 52 52.22 N 4.54 E
- Amstelmeer ⊜ 52 52.52 N 4.45 E
- Amstelveen 52 52.18 N 4.51 E
- Amsterdam, Ned. 52 52.22 N 4.54 E
- Amsterdam, S. Afr. 158 26.35 S 30.45 E
- Amsterdam, N.Y., U.S. 210 42.56 N 74.11 W
- Amsterdam, Oh., U.S. 214 40.28 N 80.55 W
- Amsterdam, Île 6 37.52 S 77.32 E
- Amsterdam-Rijnkanaal ≊ 52 51.57 N 5.20 E
- Amstetten 61 48.07 N 14.53 E
- Amston 207 41.37 N 72.20 W
- Åmta 126 22.35 N 88.01 E
- Amt'ae-do I 98 34.50 N 126.02 E
- Amtala 126 23.55 N 88.27 E
- Amtāli 126 22.08 N 90.14 E
- Am Timan 148 11.02 N 20.17 E
- Amtrak Station ⟶5 281 42.19 N 83.04 W
- Amubri 236 9.31 N 82.56 W
- 'Āmūdah 130 37.06 N 40.54 E
- Amu-Darja 128 37.53 N 65.15 E
- Amu Darya (Amudarja) ≃ 72 43.40 N 59.01 E
- Amudat 154 1.57 N 34.57 E
- Amugulang → Xin Barag Zuoqi 88 48.14 N 118.18 E
- Amukta Island I 180 52.29 N 171.15 W
- Amukta Pass ⨆ 180 52.25 N 172.00 W
- Amulree 46 56.30 N 3.47 W
- Amun 175e 5.37 S 154.45 E
- Amundsen Bay c 6 66.55 S 50.00 E
- Amundsen Gulf c 176 71.00 N 124.00 W
- Amundsen-Scott ⬩3 9 90.00 S 0.00 E
- Amundsen Sea ⤳2 9 72.30 S 112.00 W
- Amung, Mount ⋀ 164 7.26 S 146.36 E
- Amungen ⊜ 26 61.09 N 15.39 E
- Amuntai 112 2.26 S 115.15 E
- Amur (Heilong) ≃ 74 52.56 N 141.10 E
- 'Amūr, Wādī ✔ 140 18.56 N 33.34 E
- Amurang 112 1.11 N 124.35 E
- Amuria 112 2.01 N 33.38 E
- Amursk 89 50.13 N 136.52 E
- Amurskaja Oblast' ⊡4 89 53.00 N 129.00 E
- Amurskij liman c 89 52.45 N 141.40 E
- Amursko-Zejskaja ravnina ⫢4 89 52.30 N 128.30 E
- Amurzet 89 47.42 N 131.05 E
- Amusgos 234 16.39 N 98.06 W
- Amutag 116 23.23 N 123.16 E
- Amvoso 273a 6.29 N 1.43 W
- Amuyunusu 98 42.25 N 113.21 E
- Amuzhong 120 30.33 N 84.28 E
- Amvamg 152 1.45 N 10.29 E
- Amvrakikós Kólpos c 38 39.00 N 21.00 E
- Amvrosijevka 83 47.47 N 38.54 E
- Amwom, Khawr ✔ 140 7.50 N 31.13 E
- Amyl ≃ 80 53.47 N 92.54 E
- Amyūn 130 34.18 N 35.49 E
- Amz'a 80 56.13 N 54.23 E
- Amzi, Oued ti-n- ✔ 148 20.30 N 4.35 E
- An 114 17.25 S 145.30 W
- Anaa I 14 17.25 S 145.30 W
- Anabanua 112 3.57 S 120.04 E
- Anabar 174b 0.30 S 166.57 E
- Anabar ≃ 74 73.03 N 113.36 E
- 'Anabtā 132 32.19 N 35.07 E
- Anabuki 96 34.02 N 134.11 E
- Anacapri 68 40.33 N 14.13 E
- Anaco 246 9.27 N 64.28 W
- Anacoco 246 31.15 N 93.20 W
- Anacoco, Bayou ≃ 194 30.52 N 93.34 W
- Anaconda 200 46.07 N 112.56 W
- Anaconda Range ⋌ 202 46.05 N 113.30 W
- Anacortes 184 48.30 N 122.36 W
- Anacostia ≃ 284c 38.52 N 76.59 W
- Anacostia ⬩8 284c 38.52 N 76.59 W
- Anacostia, Little Paint Branch ≃ 284c 39.01 N 76.56 W
- Anacostia, Northeast Branch ≃ 284c 38.57 N 76.57 W
- Anacostia Park ⬩ 284c 38.54 N 76.58 W
- Anacuao, Mount ⋀ 116 16.16 N 121.53 E
- Anadarko 196 35.04 N 98.14 W
- Anadia 34 40.26 N 8.26 W
- Anadolufeneri ⬩8 267b 41.12 N 29.09 E
- Anadoluhisarı ⬩8 267b 41.04 N 29.03 E
- Anadyr' 80 64.45 N 177.29 E
- Anadyr' ≃ 74 64.55 N 176.05 E
- Anadyrskaja nizmennost' ≃ 180 65.30 N 176.00 E
- Anadyrskij zaliv c 180 64.00 N 179.00 W

Column 2 (FRANÇAIS)

- Anadyrskoje ploskogorje ⋌1 180 67.00 N 174.00 E
- Anáfi I 38 36.21 N 25.50 E
- Anagni 66 41.44 N 13.09 E
- 'Ānah 128 34.28 N 41.56 E
- Anaheim 228 33.50 N 117.54 W
- Anaheim Shopping Center ⟶9 280 33.51 N 117.56 W
- Anaheim Stadium ⬩ 280 33.51 N 117.57 W
- Anaheim Union Canal ≊ 280 33.54 N 117.52 W
- Anahi, Baie c 174x 9.45 S 138.56 W
- Anáhola 182 52.28 N 125.18 W
- Anáhola Bay c 229b 22.08 N 159.18 W
- Anáhuac, Méx. 196 25.48 N 97.45 W
- Anáhuac, Méx. 232 28.25 N 106.40 W
- Anahuac, Tx., U.S. 222 29.46 N 94.41 W
- Anahuac, Lake ⊜ 222 29.48 N 94.41 W
- Anaimalai 255 10.35 N 76.56 E
- Anai Mudi ⋀ 122 10.10 N 77.04 E
- Anajás 250 0.59 S 49.57 W
- Anajás, Ilha I 250 0.20 S 50.30 W
- Anajatuba 250 3.16 S 44.37 W
- Anakápalle 122 17.41 N 83.01 E
- Anaklia 84 42.24 N 41.34 E
- Anaktuvuk ≃ 180 69.32 N 151.30 W
- Anaktuvuk Pass ⨆ 180 68.10 N 151.50 W
- Analalava 157b 14.38 S 47.45 E
- Analapatsy 157b 25.10 S 46.42 E
- Analavoka 157b 22.33 S 46.30 E
- Analomink 210 41.03 N 75.13 W
- Anamã 246 3.35 S 61.22 W
- Anamã, Lago ⊜ 246 3.32 S 61.35 W
- Anama Bay 184 51.56 N 98.05 W
- Ana María, Cayos de ⋯ 240p 21.29 N 78.46 W
- Ana María, Golfo de c 240p 21.25 N 78.40 W
- Anambas, Kepulauan II 112 3.00 N 106.00 E
- Anambra ⊡3 150 6.30 N 7.20 E
- Anambra ≃ 150 6.11 N 6.46 E
- Anamizu 94 37.14 N 136.54 E
- Anamoose 198 47.52 N 100.14 W
- Anamosa 190 42.06 N 91.17 W
- Anan 250 0.56 N 57.03 W
- Anamur 130 36.06 N 32.50 E
- Anamur Burnu › 130 36.03 N 32.48 E
- Anan, Nihon 94 35.19 N 137.49 E
- Anan, Nihon 96 33.55 N 134.39 E
- Ānand 120 22.34 N 72.56 E
- Ananda 150 7.17 N 4.16 W
- Anandanagar 272b 22.51 N 88.16 E
- Anandapur, India 272b 22.56 N 88.07 E
- Anandapur, India 126 22.34 N 87.25 E
- Anandpur Sahib 123 31.15 N 76.30 E
- Ananea 248 14.42 S 69.33 W
- Ananindeua 250 1.22 S 48.23 W
- Ananjev 78 47.40 N 29.55 E
- Ananjevo 85 42.45 N 77.40 E
- Anantapur 122 14.41 N 77.36 E
- Anantnāg (Islāmābād) 123 33.44 N 75.09 E
- Anao-aon 116 9.47 N 125.25 E
- Anapa 78 44.53 N 37.19 E
- Ana Pink, Bahía c 254 45.50 S 74.50 W
- Anápolis 255 16.20 S 48.58 W
- Anápu ≃ 250 1.53 S 50.53 W
- Anapu'us 250 3.40 S 43.06 W
- Anár, Īrān 128 30.53 N 55.18 E
- Anār, S.S.S.R. 86 50.38 N 72.27 E
- Anārak 126 33.20 N 53.42 E
- Anarchaj 85 44.02 N 75.15 E
- Anär Darreh 123 32.46 N 61.39 E
- Anaš 86 54.52 N 91.00 E
- Anasagasti 258 35.01 S 59.24 W
- Añasco 240m 18.17 N 67.08 W
- Anáset 26 64.28 N 21.03 E
- Anastasia Island I 192 29.48 N 81.16 W
- Anastasijevka 83 47.34 N 38.31 E
- Anastasijevskaja 78 45.13 N 37.53 E
- 'Anātā 132 31.49 N 35.16 E
- Anatahan I 108 16.22 N 145.40 E
- Anatuya 252 28.28 S 62.50 W
- Anauá ≃ 246 0.58 N 61.21 W
- Anaurilândia 255 22.03 S 52.45 W
- Anavilhanas, Arquipélago das II 246 2.42 S 60.45 W
- Anawalt 192 37.20 N 81.26 W
- Anbanjing 102 23.57 N 100.55 E
- Anbei, Zhg. 102 40.45 N 96.06 E
- Anbei, Zhg. 100 40.45 N 96.06 E
- Anbianbu 102 37.40 N 107.18 E
- Anbu 100 23.28 N 116.44 E
- Anbyon 100 39.01 N 127.32 E
- Ancash ⊡3 248 9.30 S 77.30 W
- Ancaster, On., Can. 212 43.13 N 80.00 W
- Ancaster, Eng., U.K. 44 52.59 N 0.32 W
- Ance ≃, Fr. 62 44.58 N 4.08 E
- Ance ≃, Fr. 62 45.17 N 3.40 E
- Ancenis 54 47.22 N 1.11 W
- Ancerville 56 48.38 N 5.00 E
- Ancha, Sierra de ⋌ 252 28.49 S 65.30 W
- Ancha, Sierra de ⋌ 204 34.20 N 111.10 W
- Anchang 102 30.09 N 120.30 E
- Anchieta ⬩8 256 20.48 S 40.39 W
- Anchieta, Ilha I 256 23.33 S 45.04 W
- Anch'ing → Anqing 100 30.31 N 117.02 E
- Ancho, Canal ⨆ 254 48.15 S 74.25 W
- Anchor 214 40.34 N 88.32 W
- Anchorage 180 61.13 N 149.54 W
- Anchor Bay c 214 42.49 N 82.45 W
- Anchor Bay Gardens 214 42.49 N 82.49 W
- Anchorena 258 35.41 S 65.27 W
- Anchor Point 180 59.46 N 151.52 W
- Anchor Point › 180 59.46 N 151.52 W
- Anchuras 34 39.29 N 4.50 W
- Anci (Langfang) 102 39.31 N 116.41 E
- Ancien Ekalla 152 1.27 S 14.00 E
- Ancienne-Lorette 208 46.47 N 71.21 W
- Anciferovo, S.S.S.R. 76 58.58 N 31.01 E
- Anciferovo, S.S.S.R. 76 59.25 N 31.01 E
- Ancipa, Lago di ⊜ 70 37.48 N 14.37 E
- Anclote ≃ 192 28.12 N 82.51 W
- Anclote Keys II 192 28.10 N 82.50 W
- Ancohuma ⋀ 248 15.51 S 68.36 W
- Ancón, Perú 248 11.47 S 77.11 W
- Ancon ⊜8 236 9.00 N 79.33 W
- Ancón de Sardinas, Bahía de c 246 1.30 N 79.00 W
- Ancoraimes 248 15.54 S 68.58 W
- Ancre ≃ 56 49.54 N 2.28 E
- Ancud 254 41.52 S 73.50 W
- Ancud, Golfo de c 254 41.52 S 73.00 W
- Ancy-sur-Moselle 56 49.03 N 6.04 E
- Anda, Fil. 116 16.18 N 120.12 E
- Anda, Zhg. 100 46.24 N 125.19 E
- Andacollo, Arg. 252 37.11 S 70.40 W
- Andacollo, Chile 252 30.14 S 71.06 W
- Andahuaylas 248 13.39 S 73.23 W
- Andal 124 23.36 N 87.12 E
- Andalgalá 252 27.36 S 66.19 W
- Andalo 64 46.10 N 11.00 E

Column 3 (PORTUGUÊS)

- Åndalsnes 26 62.34 N 7.42 E
- Andalucía ⊡4 34 37.30 N 4.30 W
- Andalucía ⊡9 34 37.36 N 4.30 W
- Andalusia, Al., U.S. 194 31.19 N 86.29 W
- Andalusia, Pa., U.S. 285 40.04 N 74.58 W
- Andaman and Nicobar Islands ⊡8 110 11.00 N 93.00 E
- Andaman Basin ⤳1 12 10.00 N 94.00 E
- Andaman Islands II 110 12.00 N 92.45 E
- Andaman Islands II 110 12.00 N 92.45 E
- Andaman Sea ⤳2 110 10.00 N 95.00 E
- Andamarca, Bol. 248 18.49 S 67.31 W
- Andamarca, Perú 248 11.46 S 74.44 W
- Andamooka 166 30.27 S 137.12 E
- Andance 62 45.14 N 4.47 E
- Andapa 157b 14.39 S 49.39 E
- Andara 152 18.03 S 21.27 E
- Andaraí 255 12.48 S 41.20 W
- Andaraí ⤳8 287a 22.56 S 43.15 W
- Andarax ≃ 34 36.48 N 2.26 W
- Andaray 248 15.49 S 72.50 W
- Andau 61 47.46 N 17.02 E
- Andechs, Kloster ⋎1 64 47.58 N 11.10 E
- Andée 58 46.36 N 9.26 E
- Andelfingen 58 47.36 N 8.41 E
- Andelle ≃ 50 49.19 N 1.44 E
- Andelot 58 48.15 N 5.18 E
- Andelot-en-Montagne 58 46.51 N 5.56 E
- Andelu 261 48.53 N 1.50 E
- Anden → Andes ⋌ 18 20.00 S 67.00 W
- Andenes 26 69.16 N 16.08 E
- Andenne 58 50.29 N 5.06 E
- Andéranboukane 150 15.26 N 3.02 E
- Anderdalen Nasjonalpark ⬩ 24 69.14 N 17.17 E
- Andermatt → Andros I 38 37.50 N 24.57 E
- Andes ⋌ 18 20.00 S 67.00 W
- Andoscoggin ≃ 188 43.55 N 69.55 W
- Andros Island I 238 24.26 N 77.57 W
- Andirlang ⬩ 80 52.41 N 49.35 E
- Andirlang 238 24.43 N 77.47 W
- Andırın 130 37.35 N 36.21 E
- Ândradina 255 20.54 S 51.23 W
- Andarko 246 10.43 S 48.42 W
- Andkhvoy 126 36.56 N 65.08 E
- Andalucía 34 37.30 N 4.30 W
- Andoas 246 2.54 S 76.24 W
- Andoga ≃ 76 59.10 N 37.27 E
- Andogskaja gr'ada ⋌ 76 59.10 N 37.30 E
- Andoharano 157b 15.59 S 45.23 E
- Andol 122 17.12 N 78.22 E
- Andong-chōsuji ⊜ 98 36.41 N 128.49 E
- Andong 100 36.35 N 128.44 E
- Andoom 168 12.27 S 141.52 E
- Andorf 60 48.22 N 13.34 E
- Andorinha 255 10.20 S 39.51 W
- Ándorra 22 42.30 N 1.31 E
- Andorra ⊡1, Europe 22 42.30 N 1.30 E
- Andorra → Andorra ⊡1 22 42.30 N 1.30 E
- Andover, Ct., U.S. 207 41.44 N 72.22 W
- Andover, Me., U.S. 188 44.38 N 70.45 W
- Andover, N.J., U.S. 210 41.00 N 74.44 W
- Andover, N.Y., U.S. 210 42.09 N 77.47 W
- Andover, Oh., U.S. 214 41.36 N 80.34 W
- Andover, S.D., U.S. 198 45.25 N 97.54 W
- Andowj ≃ 123 37.02 N 71.27 E
- Andøya I 26 69.08 N 15.54 E
- Andradas 256 22.04 S 46.34 W
- Andrade Araújo ⬩8 287a 22.45 S 43.23 W
- Andrade Pinto 256 22.35 S 44.05 W
- Andradina 255 20.54 S 51.23 W
- Andramasina 157b 19.11 S 47.35 E
- Andranopasy 157b 21.17 S 43.44 E
- Andrate 64 45.32 N 7.53 E
- Andreafsky ≃ 180 62.02 N 163.10 W
- Andreafsky, East Fork ≃ 180 62.03 N 163.07 W
- Andreanof Islands II 180 51.10 N 176.00 W
- Andreapol' 76 56.39 N 32.15 E
- Andrea, I. of Man 44 54.22 N 4.26 W
- Andreas, I. of Man 44 54.22 N 4.26 W
- Andreashütte → Zawadzkie 30 50.37 N 18.29 E
- André Félix, Parc National ⬩ 146 9.25 N 23.22 E
- Andrejevka, S.S.S.R. 78 47.06 N 36.35 E
- Andrejevka, S.S.S.R. 83 48.49 N 37.33 E

Column 4

- Andrejevka, S.S.S.R. 86 52.59 N 67.23 E
- Andrejevka, S.S.S.R. 86 45.50 N 80.35 E
- Andrejevo 80 55.56 N 41.08 E
- Andrejevo-Ivanovka 78 47.28 N 30.28 E
- Andrejevskaja 80 47.21 N 43.02 E
- Andrejevskoje, S.S.S.R. 82 54.23 N 36.12 E
- Andrejevskoje, S.S.S.R. 82 56.24 N 39.01 E
- Andrejevskoje, S.S.S.R. 82 55.46 N 36.35 E
- Andrejkovičí 76 52.25 N 33.00 E
- Andrelândia 256 21.44 S 44.18 W
- Andrésy 261 48.59 N 2.04 E
- Andretta 68 40.56 N 15.19 E
- Andrew 182 53.53 N 112.21 W
- Andrew, Mount ⋀ 162 32.52 S 122.56 E
- Andrews, In., U.S. 216 40.51 N 85.36 W
- Andrews, Mi., U.S. 216 41.57 N 86.22 W
- Andrews, N.C., U.S. 192 35.12 N 83.49 W
- Andrews, S.C., U.S. 192 33.18 N 79.17 W
- Andrews, Tx., U.S. 196 32.19 N 102.32 W
- Andrews Air Force Base ⬩ 208 38.48 N 76.52 W
- Andrews Manor 284c 38.49 N 76.54 W
- Andrezel 261 48.37 N 2.49 E
- Andrézieux Bouthéon 62 45.32 N 4.16 E
- Andria 68 41.13 N 16.18 E
- Andriamena 157b 17.26 S 47.30 E
- Andriandampy 157b 22.45 S 45.41 E
- Andrijevica 38 42.44 N 19.46 E
- Andrijevskaja 84 50.02 S 44.05 E
- Andronovskoje 76 60.39 N 34.46 E
- Andropov → Rybinsk 80 58.03 N 38.52 E
- Ándros 38 37.50 N 24.57 E
- Ándros I 38 37.45 N 24.42 E
- Androscoggin ≃ 188 43.55 N 69.55 W
- Andros Island I 238 24.26 N 77.57 W
- Andros Town 238 24.43 N 77.47 W
- Androtti Island I 122 10.50 N 73.41 E
- Andrupene 76 56.11 N 27.23 E
- Andr'ušino 86 59.12 N 62.59 E
- Andrušovka 78 50.01 N 29.01 E
- Andudu 154 2.29 N 29.19 E
- Andújar 34 38.03 N 4.04 W
- Andulo 152 11.30 S 16.45 E
- Anduze 62 44.03 N 3.59 E
- Andžievskij 84 44.14 N 43.05 E
- Ane, Dos d' ⋌ 241o 16.19 N 61.46 W
- Aneby 26 57.50 N 14.48 E
- Anecho 150 6.14 N 1.36 E
- Anecón Grande, Cerro ⋀ 254 41.25 S 70.16 W
- Anefis i-n-Darane 150 18.03 N 0.36 E
- Anegada I 240m 18.45 N 64.20 W
- Anegada, Bahía c 254 40.15 S 62.15 W
- Anegada Passage ⨆ 238 18.30 N 63.40 W
- Anegam 204 32.22 N 112.01 W
- Anegasaki 268 35.28 N 140.02 E
- Anelnqauhat 176f 20.14 N 169.44 E
- Anelo 254 38.21 S 68.47 W
- Anemata, Passe d' ⨆ 175f 20.31 S 166.12 E
- Anepahan Peak ⋀ 116 9.40 N 118.25 E
- Aneroid 184 49.43 N 107.20 W
- Anet 50 48.52 N 1.26 E
- Aneta 198 47.40 N 97.59 W
- Aneto, Pico de ⋀ 34 42.38 N 0.40 E
- Añez 248 19.19 S 61.13 W
- Añelo 254 38.21 S 68.47 W
- Anfeng, Zhg. 102 32.44 N 120.24 E
- Anfeng, Zhg. 100 33.06 N 120.08 E
- Anfengqiao 100 26.41 N 118.08 E
- Anfu 100 27.23 N 114.37 E
- Anfuzhen, Zhg. 107 28.47 N 104.41 E
- Anfuzhen, Zhg. 107 29.10 N 105.28 E
- Anga 74 52.58 N 106.12 E
- Angamacutiro [de la Unión] 234 20.10 N 101.41 W
- Angamos, Punta › 252 23.01 S 70.32 W
- Angangueo 234 19.37 N 100.18 W
- An'ganka 89 47.09 N 123.48 E
- Angara ≃ 74 58.06 N 93.00 E
- Angara-Débou 150 11.19 N 3.03 E
- Angarbaka 150 9.44 N 24.44 E
- Angarsk 74 52.34 N 103.54 E
- Angas ≃ 169b 35.23 S 138.59 E
- Angas Downs 166 25.02 S 132.14 E
- Angaston 169b 34.30 S 139.02 E
- Angaul 74 54.31 N 103.53 E
- Ange 26 62.31 N 15.39 E
- Angeja 34 40.38 N 8.20 W

Column 5

- Anghiari 66 43.32 N 12.03 E
- Angical 255 12.00 S 44.42 W
- Angical do Piauí 250 6.05 S 42.44 W
- Angicos 250 5.40 S 36.36 W
- Angier 192 35.30 N 78.44 W
- Angijak Island I 176 65.40 N 62.15 W
- Angikuni Lake ⊜ 176 62.13 N 99.50 W
- Angke, Kali ≃ 269e 6.06 S 106.46 E
- Angkor Wat ⊥ 110 13.26 N 103.52 E
- Ångk Tasaôm 110 11.01 N 104.41 E
- Anglais, Baie des c 186 49.15 N 68.07 W
- Anglais, Jardin ⬩ 261 48.38 N 1.49 E
- Anglais, Rivière des (English) ≃ 206 45.13 N 73.50 W
- Angle 42 51.41 N 5.06 W
- Angle Inlet 198 49.21 N 95.04 W
- Anglem, Mount ⋀ 172 46.44 S 167.56 E
- Anglesea 169 38.25 S 144.11 E
- Anglesey I 44 53.17 N 4.22 W
- Anglesey ⊡4 130 43.29 N 1.31 W
- Anglesey → England ⊡8 28 52.30 N 1.30 W
- Anglet 62 43.29 N 1.31 W
- Angليz 74 43.29 N 1.31 W
- Angleton 222 29.10 N 95.25 W
- Anglezarke Moor ⋌3 262 53.40 N 2.33 W
- Anglezarke Reservoir ⊜ 262 53.39 N 2.35 W
- Anglin ≃ 62 46.45 N 0.58 E
- Angling ≃ 184 56.45 N 93.36 W
- Angling Lake ⊜ 184 53.55 N 93.52 W
- Anglona ⋌1 71 40.50 N 8.45 E
- Anglo-Normandes, Îles → Channel Islands 157b 17.36 S 46.55 E
- Anglure 50 49.20 N 2.20 W
- Angmagssalik 176 65.36 N 37.41 W
- Angmering 42 50.48 N 0.28 W
- Ang Mo Kio 271c 1.22 N 103.51 E
- Angoche 154 16.15 S 39.54 E
- Angoche, Ilha I 154 16.20 S 39.50 E
- Angohrän 128 26.35 N 57.54 E
- Angol 252 37.48 S 72.43 W
- Angola, In., U.S. 216 41.38 N 84.59 W
- Angola, N.Y., U.S. 210 42.38 N 79.01 W
- Angola ⊡1, Afr. 138 12.30 S 18.30 E
- Angola Basin ⤳1 10 15.00 S 3.00 E
- Angola Lake Shore 214 42.37 N 79.05 W
- Angono 2691 14.31 N 121.09 E
- Angoon 180 57.30 N 134.35 W
- Angora → Ankara 130 39.56 N 32.52 E
- Angoram 164 4.04 S 144.04 E
- Angostura, Méx. 232 25.22 N 108.11 W
- Angostura → Ciudad Bolívar, Ven. 246 8.08 N 63.33 W
- Angostura, Presa de la ⊜1 234 16.10 N 92.40 W
- Angostura Reservoir ⊜ 198 43.18 N 103.27 W
- Angoulême 32 45.39 N 0.09 E
- Angoumois ⫟9 32 45.45 N 0.15 E
- Angra, Meos I 164 2.42 S 134.50 E
- Angra do Heroísmo 148a 38.39 N 27.13 W
- Angra dos Reis 256 23.00 S 44.18 W
- An-Nabatīyah ⊡4 132 33.20 N 35.30 E
- An-Nabatīyah at-Tahtā 132 33.23 N 35.29 E
- Annaberg, Öst. 61 47.52 N 15.22 E
- Annaberg, Öst. 61 47.31 N 13.26 E
- Annaberg-Buchholz 54 50.35 N 13.00 E
- An-Nabk, Sūrīy. 130 34.01 N 36.44 E
- An-Nabk 130 28.52 N 36.07 E
- An-Nabk ⋌ 132 28.52 N 36.01 E
- An-Nabqīyah I 128 26.44 N 36.01 E
- Annaburg 54 51.44 N 13.03 E

Column 6

- 'Anjarah 132 32.18 N 35.45 E
- Anjavimihavana 157b 12.32 S 49.16 E
- Anji 106 30.43 N 119.41 E
- Anjiabe 157b 12.07 S 49.20 E
- Anjiang 105 40.45 N 117.38 E
- Anjigami Lake ⊜ 190 47.51 N 84.34 W
- Anjō 94 34.57 N 137.05 E
- Anju 206 45.36 N 73.33 W
- Anju ⊡9 32 47.20 N 0.30 W
- Anjozorobe 157b 18.24 S 47.52 E
- Anju, C.M.I.K. 98 39.36 N 125.40 E
- Anju, Zhg. 100 31.45 N 113.11 E
- Anju, Zhg. 107 30.21 N 105.27 E
- Anjudin 107 32.33 N 58.12 E
- Anjuzhen 107 29.59 N 106.22 E
- Anka 150 12.07 N 5.55 E
- Ankang 122 32.42 N 109.05 E
- Ankara 130 39.56 N 32.52 E
- Ankara ⊡4 130 39.50 N 32.50 E
- Ankara ≃ 130 39.51 N 35.55 E
- Ankaramena 157b 21.57 S 46.39 E
- Ankaratra ⋌ 157b 19.25 S 47.12 E
- Ankarimbelo 157b 22.08 S 47.20 E
- Ankaroaka ≃ 157b 17.48 S 48.32 E
- Ankarsrum 26 57.42 N 16.19 E
- Ankasakasa 157b 16.21 S 44.52 E
- Ankata 80 50.44 N 51.34 E
- Ankavandra 157b 18.46 S 45.18 E
- Ankazoabo 157b 22.18 S 44.31 E
- Ankazobe 157b 18.21 S 47.07 E
- Ankazomiriotra 157b 19.38 S 46.32 E
- Ankeny 190 41.43 N 93.36 W
- An Khe 110 13.57 N 108.39 E
- Ankiliabo 157b 22.58 S 43.45 E
- Ankilizato 157b 20.25 S 45.01 E
- Anking → Anqing 100 30.31 N 117.02 E
- Ankisabe 157b 19.17 S 46.29 E
- Anklam 54 53.51 N 13.41 E
- Ankleshwar 120 21.36 N 73.00 E
- Ankober 144 9.35 N 39.44 E
- Ankoro 154 6.45 S 26.57 E
- Ankororoka 157b 25.30 S 45.11 E
- Ankou 100 25.03 N 118.11 E
- An'kovo 80 56.57 N 39.57 E
- Ankpa 150 7.23 N 7.37 E
- Ankum 52 52.32 N 7.52 E
- Ankwe ≃ 150 8.03 N 9.26 E
- Anliennuoer 98 41.11 N 114.31 E
- Anliu 100 23.42 N 115.42 E
- Anloga 150 5.47 N 0.50 E
- Anlong 102 25.02 N 105.31 E
- Ânlong Vêng 110 14.14 N 104.05 E
- Anlu 100 31.17 N 113.40 E
- Anmo-do I 98 36.30 N 126.22 E
- Anmyon-do I 98 36.30 N 126.22 E
- Ann, Cape ›, Ant. 9 66.10 S 51.22 E
- Ann, Cape ›, Ma., U.S. 283 42.39 N 70.38 W
- Anna, S.S.S.R. 78 51.29 N 40.25 E
- Anna, Il., U.S. 194 37.27 N 89.14 W
- Anna, Oh., U.S. 216 40.23 N 84.10 W
- Anna, Tx., U.S. 196 33.21 N 96.33 W
- Anna, Lake ⊜1 188 38.04 N 77.45 W
- Annaba (Bône) 148 36.54 N 7.46 E
- An-Nabatīyah ⊡4 132 33.20 N 35.30 E
- Annan 46 54.59 N 3.16 W
- Annan ≃ 46 54.58 N 3.16 W
- Annandale, Austl. 166 24.10 S 141.23 E
- Annandale, Mn., U.S. 198 45.16 N 94.07 W
- Annandale, Va., U.S. 208 38.50 N 77.11 W
- Annandale-on-Hudson 210 42.01 N 73.54 W
- Anna Plains 162 19.17 S 121.37 E
- Anna Point › 174b 0.30 S 166.56 E
- Annapolis 208 38.58 N 76.29 W
- Annapolis Basin c 186 44.43 N 65.37 W
- Annapolis Royal 186 44.45 N 65.31 W
- Annapūrna ⋌ 124 28.34 N 83.50 E
- Ann Arbor 216 42.16 N 83.43 W
- Ann Arbor Municipal Airport ⬩ 281 42.14 N 83.45 W
- Annfield Plain 42 54.52 N 1.45 W
- An Nhon 110 13.53 N 109.06 E
- Annidale 192 37.11 N 80.26 W
- Anniston 194 33.39 N 85.49 W
- An-Nādirīyah, 'Irāq 128 31.03 N 46.16 E
- An-Nāşirīyah, Sūrīy. 130 33.22 N 36.38 E
- Annobón I 136 1.25 S 5.36 E
- Annonay 62 45.14 N 4.40 E

Legend / symbols

≃ River	Fluß	Río	Rivière	Rio
≊ Canal	Kanal	Canal	Canal	Canal
⨆ Waterfall, Rapids	Wasserfall, Stromschnellen	Cascada, Rápidos	Cascade, Rapides	Cascata, Rápidos
c Strait	Meeresstraße	Estrecho	Détroit	Estreito
c Bay, Gulf	Bucht, Golf	Bahía, Golfo	Baie, Golfe	Baía, Golfo
⊜ Lake, Lakes	Seen	Lago, Lagos	Lac, Lacs	Lago, Lagos
≃ Swamp	Sumpf	Pantano	Marais	Pântano
⌀ Ice Features, Glacier	Eis- und Gletscherformen	Accidentes Glaciares	Formes glaciaires	Acidentes glaciares
⤳ Other Hydrographic Features	Andere Hydrographische Objekte	Otros Elementos Hidrográficos	Autres données hydrographiques	Outros acidentes hidrográficos
⤳ Submarine Features	Untermeerische Objekte	Accidentes Submarinos	Formes de relief sous-marin	Acidentes submarinos
⊡ Political Unit	Politische Einheit	Unidad Política	Entité politique	Unidade política
⊥ Cultural Institution	Kulturelle Institution	Institución Cultural	Institution culturelle	Instituição cultural
⊥ Historical Site	Historische Stätte	Sitio Histórico	Site historique	Sítio histórico
⬩ Recreational Site	Erholungs- und Ferienort	Sitio de Recreo	Centre de loisirs	Área de Lazer
⬩ Military Installation	Militäranlage	Instalación Militar	Installation militaire	Instalação militar
⬩ Miscellaneous	Verschiedenes	Misceláneo	Divers	Diversos

ENGLISH			DEUTSCH		Länge°′
Name	Page	Lat.°′ Long.°′	Name	Seite	Breite°′ E = Ost

Column 1

Name	Page	Lat.	Long.
Annopol	30	50.54 N	21.52 E
Anno-Rebrikovo	83	49.36 N	40.12 E
Annot	62	43.58 N	6.40 E
Annotto Bay	241q	18.16 N	76.46 W
Annsjön ⊜	40	58.48 N	15.26 E
An-Nubayrah	142	30.54 N	30.35 E
An-Nuhūd	140	12.42 N	28.26 E
An-Nu'mān I	128	27.08 N	35.46 E
An-Nu'māniyah	128	32.32 N	45.25 E
An-Nuwayrah	142	29.06 N	30.59 E
Annville, Ky., U.S.	192	37.19 N	83.58 W
Annville, Pa., U.S.	208	40.19 N	76.30 W
Annweiler am Trifels	56	49.12 N	7.58 E
Anõ	94	34.46 N	136.27 E
Anoia	68	38.27 N	16.05 E
Anoia ≃	34	41.28 N	1.56 E
Anoka	190	45.11 N	93.23 W
Año Liósia	267c	38.05 N	23.42 E
Año Nuevo Bay c	226	37.07 N	122.19 W
Anopino	80	55.42 N	40.40 E
Anori, Bra.	246	3.47 S	61.38 W
Anori, Col.	246	7.05 N	75.08 W
Anorotsangana	157b	13.56 S	47.55 E
Anosibe	157b	19.26 S	48.13 E
Anosyennes, Chaînes ⬩	157b	24.30 S	46.50 E
Anotaie ≃	250	3.29 N	52.04 W
Anpilogovo	78	51.47 N	36.01 E
Anping, Zhg.	98	38.16 N	115.30 E
Anping, Zhg.	100	26.33 N	113.22 E
Anping, Zhg.	104	41.11 N	123.26 E
Anping, Zhg.	105	39.43 N	116.53 E
Anping, Zhg.	100	12 27 N	110.00 E
Anpu	102	21.27 N	110.00 E
'Anqābīyah, Jabal al- ʌ [2]	142	30.01 N	31.37 E
Anqing	100	30.31 N	117.02 E
Anqiu	98	36.25 N	119.10 E
Anrath	56	51.17 N	6.28 E
Anren, Zhg.	100	28.04 N	119.20 E
Anren, Zhg.	100	26.42 N	113.16 E
Anrenzhen	107	30.31 N	103.38 E
Anröchte	52	51.33 N	8.19 E
Ans, Bel.	56	50.39 N	5.32 E
Ans, Dan.	41	56.19 N	9.36 E
Ansager	41	55.42 N	8.45 E
Ansal	132	36.54 N	109.10 E
'Ansār	132	33.23 N	35.21 E
Ansbach	56	49.17 N	10.34 E
Anschan → Anshan	104	41.08 N	122.59 E
Anschlag	263	51.10 N	7.29 E
Anse	58	45.56 N	4.43 E
Anse ≃	144	17.03 N	37.24 E
Anse-Bertrand	241q	16.29 N	61.31 W
Anse-d'Hainault	238	18.30 N	74.27 W
Anse La Raye	241f	13.57 N	61.03 W
Anselmo	198	41.37 N	99.51 W
Anseremme	56	50.15 N	4.54 E
Anserma	246	5.13 N	75.48 W
Ansfelden	61	48.13 N	14.17 E
Anshan	104	41.08 N	122.59 E
Anshun	102	26.15 N	105.56 E
Ansina	252	31.54 S	55.28 W
Ansley	198	41.17 N	99.22 W
Anson	196	32.45 N	99.53 W
Anson Bay c, Austl.	164	13.20 S	130.06 E
Anson Bay c, Norf. I.	174c	29.01 S	167.55 E
Anson Creek ≃	212	44.53 N	79.03 W
Ansòng	98	37.02 N	127.16 E
Ansongo	150	15.40 N	0.30 E
Ansonia, Ct., U.S.	207	41.20 N	73.04 W
Ansonia, Oh., U.S.	216	40.12 N	84.38 W
Ansonville, N.C., U.S.	192	35.06 N	80.06 W
Ansonville, Pa., U.S.	214	40.51 N	78.34 W
Ansouis	62	43.44 N	5.28 E
Anstey	188	38.05 N	81.05 W
Anstey	42	52.40 N	1.11 W
Anstruther	46	56.13 N	2.42 W
Anstruther Lake ⊜	212	44.45 N	78.12 W
Ansudu	164	2.08 S	139.20 E
Ansus	164	1.44 S	135.49 E
Anta, Perú	248	13.29 S	72.09 W
Anta, Cachoeira ⮾	255	13.06 S	48.09 W
Anta, Cachoeira da ⮾	248	7.29 S	61.51 W
Antabamba	248	14.19 S	72.55 W
Antakya (Antioch)	130	36.14 N	36.07 E
Antalaha	157b	14.53 S	50.16 E
Antalieptė	76	55.40 N	25.51 E
Antalovcy	78	48.38 N	22.31 E
Antalya	130	36.53 N	30.42 E
Antalya □⁴	130	37.00 N	31.00 E
Antalya, Gulf of → Antalya Körfezi c	130	36.30 N	31.00 E
Antalya Körfezi c	130	36.30 N	31.00 E
Antambohobe	157b	22.20 S	46.47 E
An Tan	110	15.26 N	108.39 E
Antanambao Manampotsy	157b	19.29 S	48.34 E
Antanambe	157b	16.26 S	49.52 E
Antananarivo	157b	18.55 S	47.31 E
Antananarivo □⁴	157b	19.00 S	47.00 E
Antanetibe	157b	18.27 S	46.42 E
Antanifotsy	157b	19.39 S	47.19 E
Antanimieva	157b	22.12 S	43.44 E
Antanimora	157b	24.49 S	45.40 E
Antar, Djebel ʌ	148	31.57 N	1.56 W
Antarctica ± ¹	9	87.00 S	60.00 E
Antarctic Peninsula ⊁¹	9	69.30 S	65.00 W
Antarctique, Péninsule → Antarctic Peninsula ⊁¹	9	69.30 S	65.00 W
Antarctiques territoires britanniques → British Antarctic Territory □²	9		
Antarktis → Antarctica ± ¹	9	87.00 S	60.00 E
Antártica, Península → Antarctic Peninsula ⊁¹	9	69.30 S	65.00 W
Antas	250	10.23 S	38.20 W
Antas, Ribeirão das ≃			
Antas, Rio das ≃	252	29.04 S	51.21 W
An Teallach ʌ	46	57.48 N	5.14 W
Antechamber Bay c	168b	35.48 S	138.05 E
Antegnate	62	45.29 N	9.47 E
Antela, Laguna de ⊜	34	42.07 N	7.41 W
Antelope Acres	228	34.44 N	118.19 W
Antelope Creek ≃, Nv., U.S.	204	40.00 N	117.24 W
Antelope Creek ≃, S.D., U.S.	198	45.19 N	102.27 W
Antelope Creek ≃, Wy., U.S.	198	43.29 N	105.23 W
Antelope Island I	202	40.57 N	112.12 W
Antelope Mine	154	21.02 S	28.27 E
Antelope Peak ʌ	204	41.19 N	114.58 W
Antelope Reservoir ⊜¹	202	42.54 N	117.13 W
Antelope Valley V	228	34.45 N	118.20 W
Antelope Wash ≃	204	39.33 N	116.17 W
Antenor Navarro	250	6.44 S	38.27 W
Antequera, Esp.	34	37.01 N	4.33 W
Antequera, Para.	252	24.08 S	57.07 W
Antero Reservoir ⊜¹	200	39.00 N	105.55 W
Anterselva, Lago di ⊜	63	46.52 S	12.10 E
Anterselva di Sopra	63	46.53 N	12.08 E
Antes Fort	210	41.12 N	77.12 W
Antetikireja	157b	14.42 S	47.29 E
Antevamena	157b	21.02 S	44.08 E
Antey-Saint-André	62	45.48 N	7.36 E
Anthon	200	42.23 N	96.01 W
Anthony	198	42.23 N	95.51 W
Anthony, Ks., U.S.	192	29.17 N	82.06 W
Anthony, Fl., U.S.	198	37.09 N	98.01 W

Column 2

Name	Page	Lat.	Long.
Anthony, N.M., U.S.	200	32.00 N	106.36 W
Anthony, R.I., U.S.	207	41.41 N	71.32 W
Anthony, Tx., U.S.	200	31.59 N	106.36 W
Anthony Chabot Regional Park ♦	282	37.45 N	122.06 W
Anthony Creek ≃	188	37.54 N	80.20 W
Anthony Lagoon	162	17.59 S	135.32 E
Anthony Peak ʌ	204	39.51 N	122.58 W
Anti-Atlas ⬩	148	30.00 N	8.30 W
Antibes	62	43.35 N	7.07 E
Antibes, Cap d' ⊁	62	43.32 N	7.07 E
Anticosti, Île d' I	186	49.30 N	63.00 W
Antiesen ≃	60	48.22 N	13.24 E
Antietam Creek, West Branch ≃	188	39.41 N	77.37 W
Antietam National Battlefield ♦	188	39.24 N	77.47 W
Antifer, Cap d' ⊁	50	49.41 N	0.10 E
Antignano	66	43.30 N	10.19 E
Antigo	190	45.08 N	89.09 W
Antigonish	186	45.35 N	61.55 W
Antigoris, Valle V	58	46.18 N	8.20 E
Antigua I	240c	17.03 N	61.48 W
Antigua and Barbuda □¹, N.A.	230	17.03 N	61.48 W
Antigua and Barbuda □¹, N.A.	240c	17.03 N	61.48 W
Antigua Guatemala	236	14.34 N	90.44 W
Antigues, Pointe d' ⊁	241q	16.26 N	61.33 W
Antiguo Morelos	234	22.33 N	99.05 W
Anti-Lebanon → Sharqī, Al-Jabal ash- ⬩	132	33.35 N	36.00 E
Antilla, Arg.	252	26.07 S	64.36 W
Antilla, Cuba	240p	20.50 N	75.45 W
Antillas, Archipiélago de las → West Indies II	230	19.00 N	70.00 W
Antillas Holandesas → Netherlands Antilles □²	241s	12.15 N	69.00 W
Antilles hollandaise → Netherlands Antilles □²	241s	12.15 N	69.00 W
Antilles néerlandaises → Netherlands Antilles □²	241s	12.15 N	69.00 W
Antillo	70	37.58 N	15.15 E
Antilýås	132	33.55 N	35.35 E
Antímano ⬩⁸	286c	10.28 N	66.59 W
Antimari ≃	248	9.04 S	67.23 W
Antimony	200	38.07 N	111.59 W
Anting	106	31.18 N	121.09 E
Antioch → Antakya, Tür.	130	36.14 N	36.07 E
Antioch, Ca., U.S.	226	38.00 N	121.48 W
Antioch, Il., U.S.	216	42.28 N	88.05 W
Antioquia	246	6.33 N	75.50 W
Antioquia □⁵	246	7.00 N	75.50 W
Antipino, S.S.S.R.	86	55.55 N	33.16 E
Antipino, S.S.S.R.	86	59.51 N	55.10 E
Antipino, S.S.S.R.	86	57.49 N	66.34 E
Antipodes Islands II	9	49.40 S	178.47 E
Antipolo	116	14.35 N	121.10 E
Antipovka	80	49.50 N	45.20 E
Antiquarian Museum ♦	283	42.27 N	71.20 W
Antique □⁴	116	11.00 N	121.45 E
Antisana ʌ¹	246	0.30 S	78.08 W
Antler ≃	198	49.08 N	101.00 W
Antlers	196	34.13 N	95.37 W
Antofagasta	252	23.39 S	70.24 W
Antofagasta □⁴	252	23.30 S	69.00 W
Antofagasta de la Sierra	252	26.04 S	67.25 W
Antofalla, Salar de ≃	252	25.44 S	67.45 W
Antofalla, Volcán ʌ¹	252	25.34 S	67.55 W
Antoing	50	50.34 N	3.27 E
Antón, Pan.	236	8.24 N	80.16 W
Anton, Tx., U.S.	196	33.49 N	102.10 W
Anton Chico	200	35.12 N	105.08 W
Antongila, Helodrano c	157b	15.45 S	49.50 E
Antonia	219	38.21 N	90.27 W
Antonine	157b	15.07 N	47.24 E
Antonina do Norte	250	6.43 S	39.58 W
Antoniny	78	49.49 N	26.52 E
Antonio Amaro	232	24.16 N	104.01 W
Antonio Carlos	258	35.12 S	59.20 W
Antônio Carlos	255	21.19 S	43.45 W
Antonio de Biedma	254	47.29 S	66.30 W
Antônio Diogo	250	4.18 S	38.45 W
Antonio Escobedo	234	20.46 N	103.57 W
Antônio João	255	23.15 S	55.31 W
Antônio Lemos	250	1.22 S	50.50 W
Antônio Prado	252	28.51 S	51.17 W
Antonito	200	37.05 N	106.00 W
Antón Lizardo, Punta de ⊁	234	19.03 N	95.58 W
Antonov	78	49.37 N	29.47 E
Antonovka, S.S.S.R.	80	54.55 N	49.30 E
Antonovka, S.S.S.R.	86	53.19 N	68.26 E
Antonovka, S.S.S.R.	86	45.38 N	80.15 E
Antonovka, S.S.S.R.	80	49.23 N	51.47 E
Antony	58	48.45 N	2.18 E
Antopol'	76	52.12 N	24.47 E
Antou	286	26.07 N	118.11 E
Antracit	83	48.06 N	39.06 E
Antraigues	62	44.43 N	4.21 E
Antratsit	32	48.27 N	1.29 W
Antrim ⬩⁸	44	58.06 N	39.06 E
Antrim, N. Ire., U.K.	56	50.54 N	9.15 E
Antrim, Oh., U.S.	214	40.06 N	81.20 W
Antrim, Pa., U.S.	210	41.37 N	77.18 W
Antrodoco	66	42.25 N	13.05 E
Antronapiana	58	46.03 N	8.07 E
Antropovo, S.S.S.R.	80	58.26 N	43.00 E
Antsakabary	157b	15.03 N	48.56 E
Antsalova	157b	18.40 S	44.37 E
Antsenavolo	157b	21.24 S	47.58 E
Antsiafabositra	157b	17.18 S	46.57 E
Antsirabe, Madag.	157b	19.51 S	47.02 E
Antsirabe, Madag.	157b	19.51 S	47.02 E
Antsirañana □⁴	157b	14.00 S	49.17 E
Antslohihy	157b	14.52 S	47.59 E
Anttu (Songjiang)	98	43.32 N	128.18 E
Antufash, Jazīrat I	144	15.42 N	42.25 E
Antulai, Gunong ʌ	112	4.40 N	116.21 E
Antung → Dandong	98	40.08 N	124.20 E
Antuševo, S.S.S.R.	80	59.54 N	37.40 E
Antwerp → Antwerpen, Bel.	50	51.13 N	4.25 E
Antwerp, N.Y., U.S.	212	44.11 N	75.36 W
Antwerp, Oh., U.S.	216	41.10 N	84.44 W
Antwerpen (Anvers)	50	51.13 N	4.25 E
Antwerpen □⁴	50	51.10 N	4.50 E
Anua	174u	14.16 S	170.40 W
Anučino, S.S.S.R.	89	43.58 N	133.02 E
An'uj ≃	89	49.18 N	136.27 E
An'ujskij chrebet ⬩	74	68.18 N	161.38 E

Column 3

Name	Page	Lat.	Long.
Anüpshahr	124	28.22 N	78.16 E
Anūr	126	22.55 N	87.39 E
Anuradhapura	122	8.21 N	80.23 E
Anvers → Antwerpen	50	51.13 N	4.25 E
Anversa degli Abruzzi	66	41.59 N	13.48 E
Anvers Island I	9	64.33 S	63.35 W
Anvik	180	62.40 N	160.12 W
Anvik ≃	180	62.39 N	160.14 W
Anvil Peak ʌ	181a	52.00 N	179.35 E
Anvil Range ⬩	180	62.30 N	133.50 W
Anvin	50	50.27 N	2.15 E
Anxi, Zhg.	100	25.06 N	118.12 E
Anxi, Zhg.	102	40.32 N	95.51 E
Anxi, Zhg.	106	30.25 N	120.01 E
Anxian	102	31.40 N	104.32 E
Anxiang	100	29.23 N	112.09 E
Anxin (Xin'anzhen)	105	38.55 N	115.55 E
Anxing	106	31.24 N	119.06 E
Anxious Bay c	162	33.25 S	134.35 E
Anyama	150	5.30 N	4.03 W
Anyang, Taehan	98	37.23 N	126.55 E
Anyang, Zhg.	98	36.06 N	114.21 E
Anyang ≃	98	36.01 N	114.46 E
Anyeke	154	2.24 N	32.31 E
A'nyêmaqên Shan ⬩	102	34.30 N	100.00 E
Anyer Kidul	115a	6.04 S	105.53 E
Anykščiai	76	55.32 N	25.06 E
Anyox	182	55.25 N	129.49 W
Anysberg	158	33.31 S	20.46 E
Anyuan, Zhg.	100	26.36 N	116.38 E
Anyuan, Zhg.	100	27.37 N	113.54 E
Anyuan, Zhg.	100	25.08 N	115.28 E
Anyuanyi → Tianzhu	102	37.14 N	102.59 E
Anyue	107	30.06 N	105.21 E
Anza ≃	58	46.00 N	8.17 E
Anza-Borrego Desert State Park ♦	204	33.16 N	116.26 W
Anzac	184	56.21 N	111.02 W
Anzaldo	248	17.50 S	65.55 W
Anzano di Puglia	68	41.07 N	15.17 E
Anzbari ʌ	123	34.40 N	74.50 E
Anze	102	36.11 N	112.16 E
Anzero-Sudžensk	86	56.08 N	86.08 E
Anzhen	106	31.36 N	120.28 E
Anzhou	105	38.52 N	115.49 E
Anzhuang	106	31.04 N	121.01 E
Anzi, It.	68	40.31 N	15.55 E
Anzi, Zaïre	152	0.52 S	23.24 E
Anzicun	105	39.46 N	116.53 E
Anzob	120	39.10 N	68.48 E
Anzoátegui □³	246	9.00 N	64.30 W
Anzob, pereval ⮾	120	39.10 N	68.52 E
Anzola dell'Emilia	64	44.33 N	11.11 E
Anzon ≃	62	45.45 N	3.57 E
Anzu, ostrova II	74	75.30 N	143.00 E
Aoba I	175f	15.25 S	167.50 E
Aoba / Maewo ⬩⁸	175f	15.05 S	168.00 E
Aogaki	95	35.14 N	135.00 E
Aoga-shima I	90	32.28 N	139.46 E
Aohanbolihu	104	42.01 N	121.32 E
Aohandaba	104	42.05 N	121.59 E
Aohan Qi (Xinhui)	104	42.19 N	119.59 E
Aoiz	34	42.47 N	1.22 W
Aoji	98	42.31 N	130.23 E
Aojiang	100	27.37 N	120.33 E
Aojiang ≃	100	27.39 N	117.26 E
Aola	175e	9.32 S	160.29 E
Aoliyingzi	104	42.14 N	121.58 E
Ao Luk	110	8.23 N	98.43 E
Aomar	34	36.30 N	3.47 E
Aomori → Macau	100	22.14 N	113.35 E
Aomori	92	40.49 N	140.45 E
Aonla	124	28.17 N	79.09 E
Aono-yama ʌ	96	34.27 N	131.48 E
Aöös (Vijosë) ≃	38	40.37 N	19.20 E
A'opo	175a	13.29 S	172.30 W
Aöral, Phnum ʌ	110	12.02 N	104.10 E
Aorangi Mountains ⬩	172	41.26 S	175.20 E
Aore I	175f	15.35 S	167.10 E
Aorere ≃	172	40.41 S	172.40 E
Aoshang	100	25.42 N	113.00 E
Ao-shima I, Nihon	96	31.26 N	131.24 E
Ao-shima I, Nihon	96	33.55 N	134.44 E
Aosta	62	45.44 N	7.20 E
Aosta □⁴	62	45.45 N	7.25 E
Aosta, Valle d' V	62	45.46 N	7.25 E
Aoste	62	45.35 S	5.36 E
Aoudaghost ⊥	150	17.25 N	10.40 W
Aouderas	150	17.37 N	8.26 E
Aoudour, Oued ≃	148	35.02 N	5.02 W
Aouk, Bahr ≃	146	8.51 N	18.53 E
Aoukâle ≃	146	9.17 N	22.42 E
Aoukâr-Aoukalé, Réserve de Faune de l' ♦⁴	146	10.00 N	21.15 E
Aoukâr ʌ¹	150	18.00 N	9.30 W
Aoulime, Jebel ʌ	148	30.48 N	8.50 W
Aoumou	175f	21.24 S	165.50 E
Aoya	96	35.32 N	133.59 E
Aoyama	94	34.37 N	136.11 E
Aoyama-tōge ⮾	94	34.40 N	136.16 E
Aozi	146	20.04 N	18.41 E
Aozou	146	21.49 N	17.25 E
Apa ≃	252	22.06 S	58.00 W
Apache	196	34.53 N	98.21 W
Apache Junction	200	33.25 N	111.32 W
Apache Lake ⊜¹	200	33.36 N	111.16 W
Apache Peak ʌ	200	31.49 N	110.25 W
Apalachee ≃	192	33.43 N	83.17 W
Apalachee Bay c	192	30.00 N	84.13 W
Apalaches → Appalachian Mountains ⬩	178	41.00 N	77.00 W
Apalachicola	192	29.44 N	84.59 W
Apalachicola ≃	192	29.44 N	84.58 W
Apalachicola Bay c	192	29.40 N	85.00 W
Apalachin	210	42.06 N	76.09 W
Apam, Ghana	150	5.17 N	0.44 W
Apam, Méx.	234	19.43 N	98.25 W
Apanás, Lago de ⊜¹	236	13.16 N	85.59 W
Apaporis ≃	246	1.23 S	69.25 W

Column 4

Name	Page	Lat.	Long.
Apen	52	53.13 N	7.48 E
Apenes	224	49.16 N	124.41 W
Apeninos → Appennino ⬩	36	43.00 N	13.00 E
Apennine → Appennino ⬩	36	43.00 N	13.00 E
Apennines → Appennino ⬩	36	43.00 N	13.00 E
Apennins → Appennino ⬩	36	43.00 N	13.00 E
Apensen	52	53.26 N	9.37 E
Apese ⬩⁸	273a	6.25 N	3.25 E
Apetlon	61	47.45 N	16.50 E
Apeú	250	1.18 S	47.59 W
Apex	192	35.43 N	78.51 W
Apex Mountain ʌ	180	62.28 N	138.04 W
Api ≃	154	3.40 N	25.26 E
Api ʌ	124	30.00 N	80.57 E
Apia, Col.	246	5.05 N	75.58 W
Apia, W. Sam.	175a	13.50 S	171.44 W
Apiacá ⬩	255	21.08 S	41.34 W
Apiacá ≃	250	9.16 S	57.03 W
Apiacás, Serra dos ⬩¹	248	10.15 S	57.15 W
Apiaí	252	24.31 S	48.50 W
Apiaú ≃	246	2.39 N	61.12 W
Apica	68	41.07 N	14.56 E
Apinajé	250	11.31 S	48.18 W
Apipilulco	234	18.11 N	99.41 W
Apisancho	248	7.18 S	76.50 W
Apishapa ≃	198	38.08 N	103.57 W
Apiti	172	39.58 S	175.53 E
Apizaco	234	19.25 N	98.09 W
Apoizlaya	232	24.50 N	102.15 W
Aplahoué	150	6.56 N	1.41 E
Aplao	248	16.05 S	72.31 W
Ap Lei Chau I	271d	22.15 N	114.09 E
Aplerbeck ⬩⁸	263	51.29 N	7.33 E
Aplinskij, porog ⮾	88	58.28 N	100.32 E
Apo, Mount ʌ	116	6.59 N	125.16 E
Apodi	250	5.39 S	37.48 W
Apodi ≃	250	4.56 S	37.10 W
Apo East Pass ⮾	116	12.40 N	120.40 E
Apolakkiá	38	36.06 N	27.50 E
Apolda	54	51.01 N	11.31 E
Apolima Strait ⮾	175a	13.50 S	172.10 W
Apolinario Saravia	252	24.25 S	64.02 W
Apollo	214	40.34 N	79.34 W
Apollo Bay	166	38.45 S	143.40 E
Apollo Beach	220	27.45 N	82.25 W
Apollonia ⊥	144	32.54 N	21.58 E
Apolo	248	14.43 S	68.31 W
Apón ≃	246	10.06 N	72.23 W
Aponguao ≃	246	4.48 N	61.36 W
Apopa	236	13.48 N	89.11 W
Apopka	220	28.37 N	81.38 W
Apopka, Lake ⊜	220	28.37 N	81.38 W
Aporá	250	11.39 S	38.05 W
Aporé ≃	255	18.58 S	52.01 W
Aporé ≃	255	19.27 S	50.57 W
Apo Reef ⊁²	116	12.40 N	120.29 E
Aporema	250	1.14 N	50.49 W
Aporo	234	19.41 N	100.25 W
Apostle Islands II	190	47.00 N	90.30 W
Apostle Islands National Lakeshore ♦	190	46.55 N	91.00 W
Apóstoles	252	27.55 S	55.46 W
Apostolovo	78	47.39 N	33.44 E
Apozol	234	21.22 N	104.00 W
Appalachen → Appalachian Mountains ⬩	178	41.00 N	77.00 W
Appalachee, Monts → Appalachian Mountains ⬩	178	41.00 N	77.00 W
Appalachia	192	36.54 N	82.46 W
Appalachian Mountains ⬩	178	41.00 N	77.00 W
Appelbo	40	60.30 N	14.00 E
Appelhülsen	52	51.54 N	7.25 E
Appen	52	53.40 N	9.44 E
Appengedam	52	53.19 N	6.52 E
Appennino ⬩	36	43.00 N	13.00 E
Appennino, Galleria dell' ⬩⁵	64	44.10 N	11.10 E
Appennino Abruzzese ⬩	66	42.00 N	14.00 E
Appennino Calabrese ⬩	68	39.00 N	16.30 E
Appennino Campano ⬩	68	41.30 N	15.00 E
Appennino Ligure ⬩	66	44.30 N	9.00 E
Appennino Lucano ⬩	68	40.30 N	16.00 E
Appennino Tosco-Emiliano ⬩	66	44.00 N	11.30 E
Appennino Umbro-Marchigiano ⬩	66	43.00 N	13.00 E
Appenzell	58	47.20 N	9.25 E
Appenzell-Ausser Rhoden □³	58	47.22 N	9.28 E
Appenzell-Inner Rhoden □³	58	47.18 N	9.25 E
Appiano (Eppan)	64	46.28 N	11.15 E
Appiano Gentile	62	45.44 N	8.59 E
Appin	170	34.12 S	150.47 E
Appingedam	52	53.19 N	6.52 E
Apple ≃, U.S.	190	45.09 N	92.45 W
Appleby, S. Afr.	158	27.39 S	30.06 E
Appleby, Eng., U.K.	44	54.36 N	2.29 W
Appleby, Tx., U.S.	222	31.43 N	94.36 W
Apple Creek ≃	214	40.45 N	81.50 W
Apple Creek ≃, Il., U.S.	219	39.22 N	90.37 W
Apple Creek ≃, Mo., U.S.	219		
Apple Creek ≃, N.D., U.S.	198	46.40 N	100.46 W
Applecross	46	57.25 N	5.49 W
Appledore ≃	42	51.03 N	4.12 W
Applegate ≃	202	42.26 N	123.27 W
Apple Hill	212	45.13 N	74.46 W
Apple Orchard Mountain ʌ	192	37.31 N	79.31 W
Apples	58	46.34 N	6.25 E
Apple Springs	222	31.13 N	94.58 W
Appleton, Mn., U.S.	198	45.11 N	96.01 W
Appleton, Wi., U.S.	190	44.15 N	88.24 W
Appleton City	218	38.11 N	94.01 W
Appley Bridge	44	53.33 N	2.43 W
Appling	192	33.33 N	82.18 W
Appomattox	192	37.21 N	78.49 W
Appomattox ≃	192	37.21 N	77.17 W
Appomattox Court House National Historical Park ♦	192	37.23 N	78.48 W
Apprieu	62	45.27 N	5.27 E
Approuague ≃	250	4.30 N	51.58 W
Apra Harbor c	174p	13.27 N	144.38 E
Aprelevka	82	55.32 N	37.04 E
Aprel'sk	88	58.10 N	114.34 E
Apremont	58	46.13 N	5.40 E
Apremont-la-Forêt	58	48.58 N	5.37 E
Aprica, Passo di ⮾	62	46.14 N	10.09 E
Apricena	68	41.47 N	15.27 E
April ≃	164	4.18 S	142.26 E
Aprília	66	41.36 N	12.39 E
Apscheron → Apšeronskij poluostrov ⊁¹	84	40.30 N	50.00 E
Apsley	212	44.45 N	78.06 W

Column 5

Name	Page	Lat.	Long.
Apšeronskij poluostrov ⊁¹	84	40.30 N	50.00 E
Apshawa	276	41.01 N	74.22 W
Apsley	212	44.45 N	78.06 W
Apt	62	43.53 N	5.24 E
Aptakisic	278	42.12 N	87.56 W
Ap Tan Hoa	269c	10.45 N	106.35 E
Ap Tan My	110	11.43 N	108.49 E
Aptos	226	36.58 N	121.53 W
Apuane, Alpi ⬩	64	44.09 N	10.15 E
Apuaú ≃	246	2.32 S	60.48 W
Apucarana	255	23.33 S	51.29 W
Apuiarés	250	3.56 S	39.24 W
Apulia Station	250	7.10 N	68.50 W
Apure □³	246	7.10 N	68.50 W
Apure ≃	246	7.37 N	66.25 W
Apurímac □⁵	248	14.00 S	73.00 W
Apurímac ≃	248	11.48 S	74.03 W
Apurito	246	7.56 N	68.27 W
Aqaba, Gulf of c	128	29.00 N	34.40 E
'Aqabah, Wādī al- V	132	30.14 N	33.55 E
Āqcheh	120	36.56 N	66.11 E
'Aqdā	128	32.26 N	53.38 E
'Aqiq	140	18.14 N	38.12 E
'Aqiq, Khalij c	140	18.20 N	38.10 E
'Aqiq, Wādī al- V	128	37.01 N	54.30 E
Aq'qel'nh	120	37.05 N	88.05 E
Aqqikkol Hu ⊜	123	37.05 N	88.05 E
'Aqrabah	132	33.06 N	36.00 E
'Aqrah	128	36.45 N	43.54 E
Aquarius Plateau ʌ¹	200	38.05 N	111.40 W
Aquasco	208	38.35 N	76.43 W
Aquashicola	210	40.49 N	75.35 W
Aquashicola Creek ≃	210	40.47 N	75.37 W
Aquatic Park ♦	282		
Aquatorial-Guinea → Equatorial Guinea □¹	152	2.00 N	9.00 E
Aquia Creek ≃	276	40.40 N	73.50 W
Aquiaulne ≃	50	47.37 N	2.30 E
Aquibí, Cachoeira ⮾	250	11.08 S	55.22 W
Aquidabã	250	10.17 S	37.02 W
Aquidabã ≃	246	6.47 N	73.43 W
Aquidabán ≃	252	23.11 S	57.32 W
Aquidauana	248	20.28 S	55.48 W
Aquidauana ≃	248	19.44 S	56.50 W
Aquila, Méx.	234	18.36 N	103.30 W
Aquila, Schw.	58	46.31 N	8.57 E
Aquidneck Island I	207	41.30 N	71.13 W
Aquila □⁴	62	45.46 N	13.22 E
Aquiles Serdán	232	28.35 N	105.53 W
Aquileia	64	45.46 N	13.22 E
Aquiles Serdán	232	28.35 N	105.53 W
Aquila Creek ≃	222	31.40 N	97.10 W
Aquilonia (S.M.)	68	41.00 N	15.29 E
Aquin	238	18.17 N	73.24 W
Aquincumi Museum ♦	264c	47.34 N	19.03 E
Aquio ≃	246	2.42 N	67.34 W
Ara ≃, Esp.	34	42.25 N	0.09 E
Ara ≃, Ire.	48	52.24 N	7.56 W
Ara ≃, Nihon	92	35.39 N	139.51 E
Ara ≃, Nihon	94	35.59 N	139.49 E
'Arab, Bahr al- ≃	140	9.02 N	29.28 E
'Arab, Khalīj al- c	144	30.55 N	29.02 E
Arab, Oued el V	148	34.41 N	6.31 E
'Arab, Shatt al- ≃	128	29.57 N	48.34 E
'Arab, Wādī al- V	132	32.35 N	35.35 E
'Arabah V	128	33.02 N	57.41 E
'Arabah, Wādī V	142	29.07 N	32.39 E
'Arabah, Wādī al- (Ha' Arava) V	132	30.10 N	35.10 E
Arabako □⁴	34	42.50 N	2.45 W
Arabatskaja strelka ⊁²	78	45.40 N	35.00 E
Arabba	64	46.30 N	11.52 E
Arabi	194	29.57 N	90.00 W
Arabian Basin ≃¹	12	11.30 N	65.00 E
Arabian Desert → Sharqīyah, Aṣ-Ṣahrā' ash- ⬩	140	28.00 N	32.00 E
Arabian Sea ⊁¹	118	25.00 N	65.00 E
Arabia Saudita → Saudi Arabia □¹	118	15.00 N	65.00 E
Arabie, Mer d' → Arabian Sea ⊀²	118	15.00 N	65.00 E
Arabie Saoudite → Saudi Arabia □¹	118	25.00 N	45.00 E
Arabique, Péninsule → Arabian Peninsula ⊁¹	118	25.00 N	45.00 E
Arabisches Meer → Arabian Sea ⊁²	118	15.00 N	65.00 E
Arab-Jengidža	84	39.29 N	44.58 E
Ara-Bure, porog ⮾	130	39.13 N	31.14 E
Araç	130	41.14 N	33.20 E
Aracaju	250	10.55 S	37.04 W
Aracati	250	4.34 S	37.46 W
Aracatuba	255	21.12 S	50.25 W
Arāch	124	26.08 N	87.24 E
Arăches-les-Carroz	58	46.03 N	6.39 E
Aracides, Cape ⊁	175e	8.25 S	161.01 E
Araçoiaba	250	7.46 S	35.28 W
Aracruz	255	19.49 S	40.16 W
Araçuaí	255	16.52 S	42.04 W
Araçuaí ≃	255	16.51 S	42.04 W
'Aradah	128	23.15 N	53.55 E
Arad □⁶	36	46.10 N	21.20 E
Arad, Rom.	36	46.11 N	21.20 E
Arad, Yis.	132	31.15 N	35.13 E
Arada, Hond.	236	15.06 N	87.14 W
Arada, Tchad	146	15.01 N	20.40 E
Aradhippou	132	34.55 N	33.37 E
Aradu Nou	36	46.09 N	21.23 E
Arafali	140	15.06 N	39.57 E
Arafura Sea ⊁²	158	9.00 S	133.00 E
Arafura Shelf ≃⁴	160	10.00 S	137.00 E
Aragarças	255	15.55 S	52.15 W
Aragats, gora ʌ	84	40.32 N	44.11 E
Aragón □⁹	34	41.25 N	1.00 W
Aragón ≃	34	42.13 N	1.44 W
Aragona	70	37.24 N	13.37 E
Aragonesa, Plataforma ≃	34	40.30 N	0.55 W
Aragua □³	246	10.00 N	67.10 W
Aragua de Barcelona	246	9.28 N	64.49 W
Aragua de Maturín	246	9.58 N	63.29 W
Araguacema	250	8.50 S	49.33 W
Araguaçu	255	12.56 S	49.49 W
Araguaia ≃	246	5.21 S	48.41 W
Araguaia, Braço Menor do ≃	250	12.10 S	50.30 W
Araguaia, Parque Nacional do ♦	250	10.50 S	50.20 W
Araguaiana	255	15.43 S	51.49 W
Araguaína	250	7.12 S	48.12 W
Araguao, Caño ≃¹	246	9.12 N	61.04 W
Araguari	255	18.38 S	48.11 W
Araguari ≃, Bra.	250	1.15 N	49.55 W
Araguari ≃, Bra.	255	18.21 S	48.04 W

Column 6

Name	Page	Lat.	Long.
Arai, Nihon	94	34.41 N	137.34 E
Arāihāzar	126	23.47 N	90.40 E
Araioses	250	2.53 S	41.55 W
Ārak, Alg.	148	25.18 N	3.45 E
Arāk, Īrān	128	34.05 N	49.41 E
Araka	154	4.20 N	30.23 E
Arakamčečen, ostrov I	180	64.45 N	172.30 W
Arakan, porog ⮾	88	57.35 N	96.36 E
Arakan Yoma ⬩	110	19.00 N	94.40 E
Arakawa, Nihon	94	35.57 N	139.02 E
Arakawa, Nihon	174m	26.39 N	128.15 E
Arakawa ⬩⁸	268	35.47 N	139.47 E
Arakawa ≃	94	35.30 N	138.10 E
Arākhova ≃	38	38.29 N	22.35 E
Arákhthos ≃	38	39.01 N	21.03 E
Arakkonam	122	13.06 N	79.40 E
Arakli	130	40.57 N	40.03 E
Arakmeer, gora ʌ	84	42.38 N	46.49 E
Araks (Aras) ≃	272a	28.58 N	48.28 E
Araks (Aras) ≃	84	39.56 N	48.28 E
Aral, S.S.S.R.	85	42.32 N	72.40 E
Aral, S.S.S.R.	85	51.30 N	73.03 E
Araldy	84	44.18 N	50.24 E
Aral Sea → Aral skoje more ≃²			
Aral'sk	86	46.48 N	61.40 E
Aral'skoje more (Aral Sea) ≃²	86	45.00 N	60.00 E
Aralsor, ozero ⊜, S.S.S.R.	80	48.42 N	52.24 E
Aralsor, ozero ⊜, S.S.S.R.	80	49.05 N	48.12 E
Aralsul'fat	86	46.50 N	61.58 E
Aramá ≃	250	1.06 S	50.40 W
Aramac	166	22.59 S	145.14 E
Aramari	250	11.27 S	38.47 W
Arambaré	252	30.54 S	51.30 W
Aramberri	232	24.06 N	99.49 W
Arambaza	246	2.04 S	73.06 W
Aramia ≃	164	7.55 S	143.22 E
Aramon	62	43.53 N	4.41 E
Arampampa	248	17.55 S	66.04 W
Arān	128	34.04 N	51.29 E
Arana	258	35.00 S	57.54 W
Arancio, Lago di ⊜	70	37.38 N	13.05 E
Aranda de Duero	34	41.41 N	3.41 W
Arandaí	164	2.10 S	133.01 E
Arandelovac	38	44.18 N	20.35 E
Arandas	234	20.42 N	102.21 W
Aran Fawddwy ʌ	42	52.47 N	3.41 W
Arang	120	21.12 N	81.58 E
Aranhegyi-patak ≃	264c	47.34 N	19.04 E
Ārāni, Bngl.	126	24.71 N	88.52 E
Ārāni, Bol.	248	17.34 S	65.46 W
Aran Island I	48	54.59 N	8.33 W
Aran Islands II	48	53.07 N	9.43 W
Aranjuez	34	40.02 N	3.36 W
Aranos	158	24.09 S	19.09 E
Aransas Pass	196	27.54 S	97.08 W
Arantāngi	122	10.10 N	78.59 E
Aranyaprathet	110	13.41 N	102.30 E
Arao	96	32.57 N	130.26 E
Araouane	150	18.54 N	3.33 W
Arapaho	196	35.35 N	98.58 W
Arapahoe, Co., U.S.	200	39.24 N	104.51 W
Arapahoe, Ne., U.S.	198	40.18 N	99.54 W
Arapahoe National Recreation Area ♦	200	40.07 N	105.48 W
Arapawa Island I	172	41.13 S	174.19 E
Arapei	256	22.41 S	44.27 W
Arapey	252	30.55 S	57.32 W
Arapey Chco ≃	252	30.57 S	57.30 W
Arapey Grande ≃	252	30.55 S	57.49 W
Arapiraca	250	9.45 S	36.39 W
Arapir, Ilha I	250	2.04 S	54.50 W
Arapis	267c	37.59 N	23.32 E
Arapiuns ≃	250	2.18 S	54.50 W
Arapongas	255	23.23 S	51.27 W
Araponga	255	20.39 S	42.31 W
Araputanga	248	15.28 S	58.21 W
Araquari	252	26.23 S	48.43 W
Araquém ≃	34	42.48 N	1.45 W
'Ar'ar	128	30.59 N	41.02 E
'Ar'ar, Wādī V	128	31.23 N	42.26 E
Araranguá	255	25.47 S	48.13 W
Araraquara	255	21.47 S	48.10 W
Araras, Bra.	255	22.22 S	47.23 W
Araras, Bra.	250	22.49 S	46.25 W
Araras, Açude ⊜¹	250	4.30 S	40.50 W
Araras, Ribeirão das ≃, Bra.	255	22.52 S	46.37 W
Araras, Serra das ⬩, Bra.	256	21.18 S	45.45 W
Araras, Serra das ⬩, Bra.	169	23.20 S	45.12 W
Ararat, Austl.	166	37.17 S	142.56 E
Ararat → Büyük Ağri Daği ʌ	84	39.42 N	44.18 E
Ararendá	250	4.44 S	40.47 W
Arari	250	3.28 S	44.47 W
Arari, Lago ⊜	250	0.35 S	49.10 W
Araria	124	26.08 N	87.24 E
Araripe	250	7.13 S	40.26 W
Araripe, Chapada do ⬩¹	250	7.20 S	40.00 W
Araripina	250	7.33 S	40.30 W
Araruama	256	22.53 S	42.20 W
Araruama, Lagoa de ⊜	256	22.50 S	42.15 W
Araruna	250	6.52 S	35.44 W
Aras → Araks ≃	84	39.56 N	48.28 E
'Aras, Hawd al- ≃⁴	84	40.05 N	46.50 E
Arāshi-vayal ʌ²	270	35.01 N	135.40 E
Aras Dağlari ⬩	84	40.05 N	44.10 E
Arašiyama	270	35.01 N	135.40 E
Arās-Terra	256	4.28 S	45.56 W
Araticu	250	1.55 S	49.51 W
Aratuípe	250	13.05 S	39.00 W
Aratos	38	41.06 N	25.33 E
Arauá ≃	248	5.38 S	40.05 W
Arauá, Bra.	250	11.16 S	37.37 W
Arauca, Col.	246	7.05 N	70.45 W
Arauca ≃	246	7.24 N	66.35 W
Arauca □³	246	6.40 N	71.00 W
Arauco	254	37.15 S	73.19 W
Arauco, Golfo de c	254	37.10 S	73.25 W
Araucária	255	25.35 S	49.24 W
Araure	246	9.34 N	69.13 W
Arauquita	246	6.59 N	71.25 W
Aravaca ⬩⁸	266a	40.28 N	3.46 W
Aravaipa Creek ≃	200	33.06 N	110.22 W
Aravalli Range ⬩	124	25.00 N	73.30 E
Arāwā	175f	6.15 S	155.34 E
Arawata ≃	172	44.02 S	168.37 E
Arba ≃	34	41.52 N	1.06 W
Arba Minch	154	6.02 N	37.40 E
Arbatax	71	39.56 N	9.42 E
Arbeca	34	41.32 N	0.55 E
Arbedo	58	46.11 N	9.03 E
Arbeláez	246	4.17 N	74.25 W
Arbel	132	32.49 N	35.25 E

	ENGLISH		DEUTSCH	ESPAÑOL	FRANÇAIS	PORTUGUÊS
ʌ	Mountain		Berg	Montaña	Montagne	Montanha
⬩	Mountains		Gebirge	Montañas	Montagnes	Montanhas
⮾	Pass		Paß	Paso	Col	Passo
V	Valley, Canyon		Tal, Cañon	Valle, Cañón	Vallée, Canyon	Vale, Canhão
⬩	Plain		Ebene	Llano	Plaine	Planície
⊁	Cape		Kap	Cabo	Cap	Cabo
I	Island		Insel	Isla	Île	Ilha
II	Islands		Inseln	Islas	Îles	Ilhas
±	Other Topographic Features		Andere Topographische Objekte	Otros Elementos Topográficos	Autres données topographiques	Outros acidentes topográficos

ESPAÑOL

Nombre	Página	Lat.°′	Long.°′ W = Oeste
Arbesbach	61	48.29 N	14.57 E
Arbia ≃	66	43.08 N	11.28 E
Arboga	40	59.24 N	15.50 E
Arbogaån ≃	40	59.26 N	16.04 E
Arbois	58	46.54 N	5.46 E
Arboledas	252	36.53 S	61.29 W
Arboletes	246	8.51 N	76.26 W
Arbon	58	47.31 N	9.26 E
Arbonne	50	48.25 N	2.34 E
Arborea	71	39.46 N	8.35 E
Arborea ◆[1]	71	39.50 N	8.50 E
Arborfield	184	53.06 N	103.39 W
Arborg	184	50.55 N	97.15 W
Arbrå	26	61.29 N	16.23 E
Arbroath	46	56.34 N	2.35 W
Arbu, Monte ∧	71	39.15 N	9.27 E
Arbuckle	226	39.01 N	122.03 W
Arbuckle, Lake ⊜	220	27.41 N	81.24 W
Arbuckle Creek ≃	220	27.26 N	81.17 W
Arbuckle Mountains ⋀	196	34.25 N	97.20 W
Arbuckles, Lake of the ⊜[1]	196	34.25 N	97.00 W
Arbury Hills	216	41.33 N	87.51 W
Arbus	71	39.32 N	8.36 E
Arbutus Lake ⊜	276	40.31 N	74.10 W
Arbuzinka	78	47.53 N	31.19 E
Arbuzovo	76	56.21 N	32.27 E
Arc ≃, Fr.	62	43.31 N	5.07 E
Arc ≃, Fr.	62	45.34 N	6.12 E
Arc, Bayou des ≃	194	35.00 N	91.30 W
Arcachon	32	44.37 N	1.12 W
Arcachon, Bassin d' ⊂	32	44.40 N	1.10 W
Arcadas	256	22.42 S	46.52 W
Arcade, It.	64	45.47 N	12.13 E
Arcade, Ca., U.S.	226	34.02 N	118.15 W
Arcade, N.Y., U.S.	210	42.32 N	78.25 W
Arcadia, Ca., U.S.	228	34.08 N	118.02 W
Arcadia, Fl., U.S.	220	27.12 N	81.51 W
Arcadia, In., U.S.	218	40.10 N	86.01 W
Arcadia, Ia., U.S.	198	42.01 N	95.02 W
Arcadia, Ks., U.S.	198	37.38 N	94.37 W
Arcadia, La., U.S.	194	32.32 N	92.55 W
Arcadia, Mi., U.S.	190	44.29 N	86.13 W
Arcadia, Mo., U.S.	194	37.35 N	90.37 W
Arcadia, Ne., U.S.	198	41.25 N	99.07 W
Arcadia, Oh., U.S.	216	41.06 N	83.31 W
Arcadia, Pa., U.S.	214	40.47 N	78.51 W
Arcadia, S.C., U.S.	192	34.57 N	81.59 W
Arcadia, Tx., U.S.	222	29.23 N	95.07 W
Arcadia, Wi., U.S.	190	44.15 N	91.30 W
Arcângelo	256	21.18 S	44.19 W
Arcanum	218	39.59 N	84.33 W
Arcas, Cayos II	232	20.12 N	91.58 W
Arcata	204	40.52 N	124.04 W
Arcatao	236	14.05 N	88.45 W
Arc de Triomphe ⊥	261	48.53 N	2.17 E
Arc Dome ∧	204	38.50 N	117.21 W
Arce	66	41.35 N	13.34 E
Arceburgo	256	21.22 S	46.56 W
Arčeda ≃	80	49.52 N	43.10 E
Arčedinsko-Donskije peski ◆[2]	80	49.33 N	43.15 E
Arcelia	234	18.17 N	100.16 W
Arcen	52	51.29 N	6.11 E
Arc-en-Barrois	58	47.57 N	5.00 E
Arces	50	43.05 N	3.36 E
Arc-et-Senans	58	47.02 N	5.46 E
Arcevia	66	43.30 N	12.56 E
Archambault, Lac ⊜	206	46.18 N	74.15 W
Archangaj □[8]	88	43.00 N	101.30 E
Archangel → Archangel'sk	24	64.34 N	40.32 E
Archangel'sk	24	64.34 N	40.32 E
Archangel'skaja	78	45.41 N	40.15 E
Archangel'skoje, S.S.S.R.	76	53.16 N	37.42 E
Archangel'skoje, S.S.S.R.	78	51.27 N	40.55 E
Archangel'skoje, S.S.S.R.	80	55.13 N	44.05 E
Archangel'skoje, S.S.S.R.	80	54.26 N	48.40 E
Archangel'skoje, S.S.S.R.	82	55.19 N	35.58 E
Archangel'skoje, S.S.S.R.	84	44.37 N	44.05 E
Archangel'skoje, S.S.S.R.	265b	55.47 N	37.18 E
Archara	89	49.27 N	130.07 E
Archara ≃	89	49.13 N	129.53 E
Archbald	210	41.29 N	75.32 W
Archbold	216	41.31 N	84.18 W
Archdale	192	35.54 N	79.58 W
Archer	192	29.31 N	82.31 W
Archer ≃	164	13.28 S	141.41 E
Archer, Lake ⊜	283	42.04 N	71.20 W
Archer, Mount ∧	166	23.20 S	150.34 E
Archer Bay ⊂	164	13.25 S	141.43 E
Archer Bend National Park ♠	164	13.30 S	142.20 E
Archer City	196	33.35 N	98.37 W
Archer's Post	154	0.39 N	37.41 E
Arches	58	48.07 N	6.32 E
Arches National Park ♠	200	38.42 N	109.45 W
Archi	66	42.05 N	14.23 E
Archiac	32	45.31 N	0.18 W
Archidona	34	37.05 N	4.23 W
Archipo-Osipovka	78	44.22 N	38.33 E
Archipovka	80	56.38 N	41.14 E
Archipovo	24	66.26 N	45.52 E
Archonskaja	84	43.07 N	44.30 E
Archshofen	56	49.27 N	10.04 E
Archville	276	41.07 N	73.52 W
Arci, Monte ∧	71	39.47 N	8.44 E
Arcidosso	66	42.52 N	11.33 E
Arcille	66	42.48 N	11.15 E
Arcinazzo Romano	66	41.48 N	13.12 E
Arcisate	62	45.54 N	8.52 E
Arcis-sur-Aube	50	48.32 N	4.08 E
Arciz	78	46.00 N	29.26 E
Arckaringa	162	27.56 S	134.45 E
Arckaringa Creek ≃	162	28.10 S	135.22 E
Arc-les-Gray	58	47.27 N	5.35 E
Arco, It.	64	45.55 N	10.53 E
Arco, Id., U.S.	202	43.38 N	113.17 W
Arco de Baúlhe	34	41.29 N	7.58 W
Arcola, Sk., Can.	184	49.37 N	102.30 W
Arcola, It.	64	44.07 N	9.54 E
Arcola, Il., U.S.	194	39.41 N	88.18 W
Arcola, In., U.S.	216	41.06 N	85.17 W
Arcola, Ms., U.S.	194	33.16 N	90.52 W
Arcola, Pa., U.S.	285	40.09 N	75.27 W
Arcola, Tx., U.S.	222	29.31 N	95.27 W
Arconate	266b	45.32 N	8.51 E
Arcore	266b	45.38 N	9.19 E
Arcos	255	20.17 S	45.32 W
Arcos de la Frontera	34	36.45 N	5.48 W
Arcot	122	12.54 N	79.20 E
Arcoverde	250	8.25 S	37.04 W
Arctic Bay	176	73.02 N	85.11 W
Arctic Ocean ⊤[1]	16	85.00 N	170.00 E
Arctic Red ≃	180	67.27 N	133.46 W
Arctic Red River	180	67.27 N	133.46 W
Arctic Village	180	68.08 N	145.19 W
Arctique, Océan Glacial → Arctic Ocean ⊤[1]	16	85.00 N	170.00 E
Arctowski ʊ[3]	9	62.09 S	58.28 W
Arcturus	154	17.47 S	31.20 E
Arcueil	261	48.48 N	2.20 E
Arcuentu, Monte ∧	71	39.35 N	8.33 E
Arcy-sur-Cure	50	47.36 N	3.45 E
Ard, Loch ⊜	46	56.11 N	4.28 W
Arḍ, Ra's al- ›	128	29.21 N	48.05 E
Arda ≃, Europe	38	41.39 N	26.29 E
Arda ≃, It.	64	45.02 N	10.02 E
Ardabīl	128	38.15 N	48.18 E
Ardagger	61	48.11 N	14.50 E
Ardagh	48	52.28 N	9.04 W

FRANÇAIS

Nom	Page	Lat.°′	Long.°′ W = Ouest
Ardahan	130	41.07 N	42.41 E
Ardakān, Īrān	128	30.16 N	52.01 E
Ardakān, Īrān	128	32.19 N	53.59 E
Ardal	128	31.59 N	50.39 E
Ardalanish, Rubh' ›	46	56.17 N	6.18 W
Årdalsfjorden ⊂[2]	26	61.12 N	7.30 E
Årdalstangen	26	61.14 N	7.43 E
Ardanuç	130	41.08 N	42.04 E
Ardara, Ire.	48	54.46 N	8.25 W
Árdara, It.	71	40.37 N	8.48 E
Ardara, Pa., U.S.	279b	40.22 N	79.44 W
Ardarroch	46	57.25 N	5.38 W
Ardatov, S.S.S.R.	80	55.15 N	43.06 E
Ardatov, S.S.S.R.	80	54.51 N	46.13 E
Ardbeg	46	55.39 N	6.05 W
Ardcharnich	46	57.51 N	5.05 W
Ardea	66	41.36 N	12.33 E
Ardèche □[5]	62	44.40 N	4.20 E
Ardèche ≃	62	44.16 N	4.39 E
Ardee	48	53.52 N	6.33 W
Ardélik	146	12.26 N	21.25 E
Arden, Mb., Can.	184	50.17 N	99.14 W
Arden, Ca., U.S.	226	38.36 N	121.23 W
Arden, De., U.S.	208	39.48 N	75.29 W
Arden, Forest of ◆[3]	42	52.23 N	1.42 W
Arden, Mount ∧	166	32.09 S	137.59 E
Ardenay-sur-Mérize	50	48.00 N	0.25 E
Arden Mines	279b	40.12 N	80.17 W
Ardennes □[5]	50	49.40 N	4.40 E
Ardennes ◆[1]	56	50.10 N	5.45 E
Ardennes, Canal des ≅	50	49.26 N	4.02 E
Ardenno	58	46.10 N	9.39 E
Ardentinny	46	56.03 N	4.55 W
Ardenza	66	43.31 N	10.19 E
Arderin ∧[2]	48	53.02 N	7.40 W
Ardersier	46	57.34 N	4.02 W
Ardeşen	130	41.12 N	41.00 E
Ardestān	128	33.22 N	52.23 E
Ardey	263	51.28 N	7.43 E
Ardeygebirge ⋀[2]	263	51.25 N	7.20 E
Ardez	58	46.46 N	10.11 E
Ardfern	46	56.10 N	5.32 W
Ardglass	48	54.16 N	5.37 W
Ardgroom	48	51.42 N	9.52 W
Ardıçlı	130	40.40 N	37.00 E
Ardila ≃	34	38.12 N	7.28 W
Ardill	184	49.53 N	105.49 W
Ardino	38	41.35 N	25.08 E
Ardlethan	166	34.21 S	146.54 E
Ardlui	46	56.18 N	4.43 W
Ardlussa	46	56.02 N	5.47 W
Ardmolich	46	56.49 N	5.41 W
Ardmore, Ire.	48	51.57 N	7.43 W
Ardmore, Al., U.S.	194	34.59 N	86.50 W
Ardmore, In., U.S.	216	41.41 N	86.19 W
Ardmore, Md., U.S.	284c	38.56 N	76.51 W
Ardmore, Ok., U.S.	196	34.10 N	97.08 W
Ardmore, Pa., U.S.	208	40.01 N	75.18 W
Ardmore Point ›, Scot., U.K.	46	56.39 N	6.07 W
Ardmore Point ›, Scot., U.K.	46	55.42 N	6.01 W
Ardnamurchan ›[1]	46	56.43 N	6.00 W
Ardnamurchan, Point of ›	46	56.44 N	6.13 W
Ardnaree	48	54.06 N	9.08 W
Ardnave Point ›	46	55.54 N	6.20 W
Ardoch	166	27.26 S	144.08 E
Ardon, Schw.	58	46.13 N	7.15 E
Ardon, S.S.S.R.	84	43.12 N	44.18 E
Ardon ≃	84	43.17 N	44.18 E
Ardon, Har ∧	132	30.38 N	34.57 E
Ardooie	50	50.59 N	3.12 E
Ardore	68	38.11 N	16.10 E
Ardoux ≃	50	47.42 N	1.35 E
Ardoz, Arroyo de ≃	266a	40.26 N	3.27 W
Ardres	50	50.51 N	1.59 E
Ardres ≃	50	49.18 N	3.40 E
Ardrishaig	46	56.01 N	5.27 W
Ardrossan, Austl.	168b	34.25 S	137.55 E
Ardrossan, Scot., U.K.	46	55.39 N	4.49 W
Ardsley, Eng., U.K.	44	53.32 N	1.28 W
Ardsley, N.Y., U.S.	276	41.00 N	73.50 W
Ardtalnaig	46	56.31 N	4.06 W
Arduan Island I	140	19.55 N	30.22 E
Ardusson ≃	50	48.30 N	3.32 E
Ardvasar	46	57.04 N	5.54 W
Åre	26	63.24 N	13.04 E
Areado	256	21.21 S	46.09 W
Areal	256	22.14 S	43.07 W
Arèches	62	45.41 N	6.34 E
Arecibo	240m	18.28 N	66.43 W
Arecibo Observatory ʊ[3]	240m	18.20 N	66.46 W
Areco ≃	258	33.56 S	59.16 W
Areeiro	266c	38.39 N	9.12 W
Arefjevo	86	57.01 N	90.40 E
Areguá	252	25.18 S	57.25 W
Areia, Bra.	250	6.58 S	35.42 W
Areia, Port.	266c	38.43 N	9.08 W
Areia, Ribeirão da ≃	255	16.07 S	45.52 W
Areia Branca, Bra.	250	4.56 S	37.07 W
Areia Branca, Bra.	256	22.48 S	46.51 W
Areia Branca, Bra.	287a	22.44 S	43.25 W
Areias	256	22.35 S	44.42 W
Arena	68	38.34 N	16.13 E
Arena, Point ›	204	38.57 N	123.44 W
Arena, Punta ›	232	23.33 N	109.28 W
Arena de la Ventana, Punta ›	232	24.04 N	109.52 W
Arena Island I	116	9.14 N	120.46 E
Arenal, C.R.	236	10.29 N	84.53 W
Arenal, P.R.	240m	17.59 N	66.19 W
Arenal, Laguna de ⊜	236	10.32 N	84.56 W
Arenal, Punta del ›	241r	10.03 N	61.56 W
Arenal, Volcán ∧[1]	236	10.28 N	84.44 W
Arenápolis	248	14.26 S	56.49 W
Arenas, Punta ›, Chile	248	21.39 S	70.10 W
Arenas, Punta ›, P.R.	240m	18.07 N	65.35 W
Arenas, Punta de ›	254	53.09 S	68.13 W
Arenas de San Pedro	34	40.12 N	5.05 W
Arendal	26	58.27 N	8.48 E
Arendonk	56	51.19 N	5.05 E
Arendsee	54	52.53 N	11.30 E
Arendsee ⊜	54	52.53 N	11.30 E
Arendtsville	208	39.55 N	77.18 W
Arenes ≃	266d	41.29 N	2.02 E
Arenig Fawr ∧	42	52.55 N	3.45 W
Arenillas	246	3.33 S	80.04 W
Arenosa Creek ≃	196	28.52 N	96.44 W
Arenys de Mar	34	41.35 N	2.33 E
Arenzano	62	44.24 N	8.41 E
Arenzville	219	39.53 N	90.22 W
Arequipa	248	16.24 S	71.33 W
Arequipa □[5]	248	16.00 S	72.15 W
Arequito	252	33.09 S	61.28 W
Arero	144	4.45 N	38.49 E
Arês, Bra.	250	6.11 S	35.09 W
Arès, Fr.	32	44.46 N	1.08 W
Arese	266b	45.33 N	9.05 E
Aresing	60	48.32 N	11.18 E
Åreskutan ∧	26	63.26 N	13.06 E
Areuse ≃	58	46.56 N	6.53 E
Arévalo	34	41.04 N	4.43 W
Arezzo	66	43.25 N	11.53 E
Arezzo □[4]	66	43.32 N	11.50 E
Arfa', Jabal ∧	132	29.51 N	35.27 E
'Arfā', Wādī al- V	132	30.16 N	36.34 E
Arga ≃	34	42.18 N	1.47 W
Argada	88	54.14 N	110.41 E
Argadargada	166	21.40 S	136.40 E
Argajaš	86	55.29 N	60.52 E
Argamasilla de Alba	34	39.07 N	3.06 W
Arganda	34	40.18 N	3.26 W
Argao	116	9.52 N	123.36 E
Arga-Sala ≃	74	68.30 N	112.12 E
Argedeb	144	6.10 N	41.10 E
Argegno	58	45.56 N	9.08 E
Argel → El Djazaïr	148	36.47 N	3.03 E

PORTUGUÊS

Nome	Página	Lat.°′	Long.°′ W = Oeste
Argelès-Gazost	32	43.01 N	0.06 E
Argelès-sur-Mer	32	42.33 N	3.01 E
Argelia → Algeria □[1]	148	28.00 N	3.00 E
Argen ≃	58	47.35 N	9.33 E
Argens ≃	62	43.24 N	6.44 E
Argent	158	26.04 S	28.50 E
Argent, Côte d' ⍊[2]	32	43.30 N	1.30 W
Argenta, It.	66	44.37 N	11.50 E
Argenta, Il., U.S.	219	39.58 N	88.49 W
Argentan	32	48.45 N	0.01 W
Argentario, Monte ∧	66	42.24 N	11.09 E
Argentat	32	45.06 N	1.56 E
Argentera	62	44.24 N	6.57 E
Argentera ∧	62	44.10 N	7.18 E
Argenteuil	50	48.57 N	2.15 E
Argenteuil □[6]	206	45.45 N	74.30 W
Argentia	186	47.18 N	53.59 W
Argentiera	71	40.44 N	8.09 E
Argentière	58	45.59 N	6.56 E
Argentières	261	48.39 N	2.52 E
Argentina □[1]	244	34.00 S	64.00 W
Argentina ≃	62	43.50 N	7.51 E
Argentine	216	42.47 N	83.51 W
Argentine → Argentina □[1]	244	34.00 S	64.00 W
Argentine Basin ✢[1]	18	45.00 S	45.00 W
Argentinien → Argentina □[1]	244	34.00 S	64.00 W
Argentino, Hipódromo ♠	288	34.34 S	58.26 W
Argentino, Lago ⊜	254	50.13 S	72.25 W
Argentona	266d	41.33 N	2.24 E
Argentona, Riera d' ≃	266d	41.31 N	2.26 E
Argenton-Château	32	46.59 N	0.27 W
Argenton-sur-Creuse	32	46.35 N	1.31 E
Argent-sur-Sauldre	50	47.33 N	2.27 E
Argeș □[6]	38	45.00 N	24.45 E
Argeș ≃	38	44.04 N	26.37 E
Arghandāb ≃	128	31.27 N	64.23 E
Arghastān ≃	120	31.23 N	65.45 E
Argirita	256	21.37 S	42.50 W
Argıthanı	130	38.17 N	31.43 E
Argo	140	19.31 N	30.25 E
Ārgoal	126	21.58 N	87.38 E
Argo Island I	140	19.25 N	30.27 E
Argolikós Kólpos ⊂	38	37.33 N	22.45 E
Argonia	198	37.15 N	97.45 W
Argonne	190	45.39 N	88.52 W
Argonne ◆[1]	56	49.30 N	5.00 E
Argonne National Laboratory ʊ[3]	216	41.43 N	87.58 W
Argopuro, Gunung ∧	115a	7.57 S	113.33 E
Árgos, Ellás	38	37.39 N	22.44 E
Argos, In., U.S.	216	41.14 N	86.15 W
Árgos Orestikón	38	40.28 N	21.16 E
Argostólion	38	38.10 N	20.30 E
Argoules	50	50.21 N	1.50 E
Argueil	50	49.32 N	1.31 E
Arguello, Point ›	204	34.35 N	120.39 W
Argun	84	43.16 N	45.52 E
Argun' (Ergun) ≃, Asia	74	53.20 N	121.28 E
Argun ≃, S.S.S.R.	84	43.22 N	45.55 E
Argungu	150	12.45 N	4.31 E
Arguni, Teluk ⊂	164	3.06 S	133.42 E
Ārgur	272b	22.48 N	88.13 E
Argut	86	49.51 N	87.03 E
Argut ≃	86	50.16 N	86.43 E
Arguvan	130	38.47 N	38.17 E
Argyle, Austl.	162	33.32 S	115.46 E
Argyle, Mn., U.S.	198	48.19 N	96.49 W
Argyle, Mo., U.S.	219	38.18 N	92.02 W
Argyle, N.Y., U.S.	210	43.14 N	73.30 W
Argyle, Tx., U.S.	222	33.07 N	97.11 W
Argyle, Lake ⊜[1]	164	16.15 S	128.45 E
'Arhāb, Wādī V	142	28.55 N	31.09 E
Arhavi	130	41.22 N	41.16 E
Arhéa Epídavros ⊥	38	37.37 N	23.02 E
Århus	41	56.09 N	10.13 E
Århus □[6]	41	56.15 N	10.05 E
Århus Bugt ⊂	41	56.09 N	10.18 E
Aria	172	38.33 S	174.59 E
Aria ≃	164	5.45 S	149.15 E
Ariadnoje	89	45.08 N	134.25 E
Ariah	126	23.33 N	86.20 E
Ariake-kai ⊂	92	33.00 N	130.20 E
Ariāl Khān ≃	126	23.56 N	90.46 E
Ariamácina, Lago di ⊜[1]	68	39.20 N	16.32 E
Ariamsvlei	156	28.07 S	19.49 E
Ariana	36	36.52 N	10.12 E
Ariano, Isola d' I	64	45.10 N	12.10 E
Ariano Irpino	68	41.09 N	15.05 E
Ariano nel Polesine	64	44.56 N	12.07 E
Ariari ≃	246	2.35 N	72.47 W
Arias	252	33.38 S	62.25 W
Arias, Arroyo de ≃	258	34.17 S	56.06 W
Arias, Cañada de ≃	258	34.39 S	58.59 W
Ariaú	250	3.11 S	57.14 W
Aribinda	150	14.14 N	0.52 W
Arica, Chile	248	18.29 S	70.20 W
Arica, Col.	246	2.08 S	71.47 W
Arıcak	130	38.33 N	39.48 E
Aricanduva, Ribeirão ≃	287b	23.32 S	46.33 W
Ariccia	66	41.43 N	12.40 E
Arichat	186	45.31 N	61.01 W
Arichuna	246	7.42 N	67.08 W
Arid, Cape ›	162	34.00 S	123.09 E
Arida, Nig.	273a	6.34 N	3.16 E
Arida, Nihon	96	34.05 N	135.07 E
Arida ≃	96	34.05 N	135.06 E
Aridal, Sabkhat ⊜	148	26.12 N	14.05 W
Aridhaía	38	40.59 N	22.03 E
Ariège □[5]	32	43.00 N	1.30 E
Ariège ≃	32	43.31 N	1.25 E
Ari'el, Isr. Occ	132	32.06 N	35.06 E
Ariel, Wa., U.S.	224	45.57 N	122.34 W
Arienzo	68	41.01 N	14.30 E
Arieș ≃	38	46.26 N	23.59 E
'Arif, Har ∧	132	30.26 N	34.44 E
Ārifwāla	123	30.17 N	73.04 E
Ariguanabo, Laguna de ⊜	286b	22.56 N	82.33 W
Ariguaní ≃	246	9.35 N	73.46 W
Arīḥā (Jericho), Isr. Occ	132	31.52 N	35.27 E
Arīḥā, Sūrīy.	130	35.48 N	36.36 E
Arīḥā, Urd.	132	31.25 N	35.47 E
Arikaree ≃	198	40.01 N	101.56 W
Arikaree, North Fork ≃	198	39.39 N	102.57 W
Arikawa	92	32.59 N	129.07 E
Arikha, Har ∧[2]	132	30.39 N	34.47 E
Arild	41	56.16 N	12.34 E
Arima	241r	10.38 N	61.17 W
Arima ◆[8]	270	34.48 N	135.15 E
Arima ≃	270	34.52 N	135.15 E
Arima-fuji ∧[2]	270	34.55 N	135.14 E
Arimine-dam ◆[6]	94	36.29 N	137.27 E
Arinagour	46	56.37 N	6.31 W
Aringay	116	16.26 N	120.21 E
Arino ◆[8]	270	34.50 N	135.14 E
Arinos ≃	248	10.25 S	58.20 W
Arinthod	58	46.23 N	5.34 E
Ario de Rosales	234	19.12 N	101.43 W
Ariogala	76	55.16 N	23.30 E
Aripeka	220	28.25 N	82.39 W
Ariporo ≃	246	6.03 N	69.54 W
Aripuanã	248	9.10 S	60.38 W
Aripuanã ≃	248	5.07 S	60.24 W
Ariquemes	248	9.56 S	63.04 W
Arisa ≃	246	7.32 N	64.00 W
Arisaig	46	56.51 N	5.51 W
Arisaig, Sound of ⊂	46	56.51 N	5.51 W
'Arīsh, Wādī al- V	140	31.09 N	33.49 E
Arismendi	246	8.29 N	68.22 W
Arista, Méx.	234	15.56 N	93.48 W
Arista, Méx.	234	22.39 N	100.50 W
Aristazabal Island I	182	52.30 N	129.05 W
Aristes	210	40.49 N	76.20 W

Aristizábal, Cabo ›	254	45.13 S	66.31 W
Aristovo	82	54.37 N	36.40 E
Arıt	130	41.41 N	32.39 E
Aritao	116	16.18 N	121.02 E
Ariton	194	31.36 N	85.43 W
Aritzo	71	39.57 N	9.12 E
Arivonimamo	157b	19.01 S	47.15 E
Ariyalūr	122	11.08 N	79.05 E
Arizaro, Salar de ⩦	252	24.42 S	67.45 W
Arizgoiti	34	43.13 N	2.54 W
Arizona	252	35.43 S	65.18 W
Arizona □[3], U.S.	178	34.00 N	112.00 W
Arizona □[3], U.S.	200	34.00 N	112.00 W
Arizpe	232	30.20 N	110.10 W
Arja	80	57.30 N	46.00 E
Årjäng	26	59.23 N	12.08 E
Arjasa	112	6.51 S	115.16 E
Arjawinangun	115a	6.39 S	108.24 E
Arjay	192	36.48 N	83.38 W
Arjeplog	24	66.00 N	17.58 E
Arjona, Col.	246	10.15 N	75.21 W
Arjona, Esp.	34	37.56 N	4.03 W
Arka	74	60.03 N	142.12 E
Arkabutla Lake ⊜[1]	194	34.45 N	90.06 W
Arkadak	80	51.58 N	43.28 E
Arkadelphia	194	34.07 N	93.03 W
Arkaig, Loch ⊜	46	56.58 N	5.08 W
Arkalyk	86	50.13 N	66.50 E
Arkansas □[3], U.S.	178	34.50 N	92.30 W
Arkansas □[3], U.S.	194	34.50 N	92.30 W
Arkansas ≃	178	33.48 N	91.04 W
Arkansas, Salt Fork ≃	196	36.36 N	97.03 W
Arkansas City, Ar., U.S.	194	33.36 N	91.12 W
Arkansas City, Ks., U.S.	198	37.03 N	97.02 W
Arkansas Post National Memorial ⊥	194	33.55 N	91.26 W
Arkanū, Jabal ∧	146	22.13 N	24.41 E
Arkatag Shan ⋀	120	36.48 N	89.10 E
Arken-Ahon ∧	146	20.05 N	18.25 E
Arkhangélos	38	36.12 N	28.08 E
Arkhangel'sk → Archangel'sk	24	64.34 N	40.32 E
Arki	123	31.09 N	76.58 E
Árki I	38	37.22 N	26.45 E
Arkit	85	41.47 N	71.58 E
Arklow	48	52.48 N	6.09 W
Arkoma	194	35.21 N	94.26 W
Arkona, Kap ›	54	54.41 N	13.26 E
Arkösund	26	58.30 N	16.56 E
Arkport	210	42.23 N	77.41 W
Arktičeskij, mys ›	74	81.15 N	95.45 E
Arktičeskogo Instituta, ostrova II	74	75.20 N	81.55 E
Arkul'	80	57.17 N	50.03 E
Arkville	210	42.08 N	74.37 W
Arkwright	207	41.43 N	71.33 W
Ärla	40	59.17 N	16.40 E
Arlan	80	55.58 N	54.15 E
Arlan, gora ∧	128	39.40 N	54.33 E
Arlanc	62	45.25 N	3.44 E
Arlanda flygplats ⊠	40	59.37 N	17.55 E
Arlanza ≃	34	42.06 N	4.09 W
Arlanzón ≃	34	42.03 N	4.17 W
Arlbergpass)(	64	47.08 N	10.12 E
Arlberg-Tunnel ◆[5]	58	47.08 N	10.12 E
Arlee	202	47.09 N	114.05 W
Arles	62	43.40 N	4.38 E
Arles à Port de Bouc, Canal d' ≅	62	43.40 N	4.37 E
Arlesey	42	52.01 N	0.14 W
Arlesheim	58	47.30 N	7.37 E
Arleta ◆[8]	280	34.15 N	118.26 W
Arleux	50	50.17 N	3.06 E
Arley	262	53.19 N	2.30 W
Arli	150	11.35 N	1.28 E
Arli, Parc National de l' ♠	150	11.35 N	1.30 E
Arlington, S. Afr.	158	28.06 S	27.54 E
Arlington, Ga., U.S.	192	31.26 N	84.43 W
Arlington, In., U.S.	218	39.38 N	85.34 W
Arlington, Ia., U.S.	190	42.44 N	91.40 W
Arlington, Ks., U.S.	198	37.53 N	98.10 W
Arlington, Ky., U.S.	194	36.47 N	89.00 W
Arlington, Ma., U.S.	207	42.24 N	71.09 W
Arlington, Mn., U.S.	190	44.36 N	94.04 W
Arlington, Ne., U.S.	198	41.27 N	96.21 W
Arlington, N.Y., U.S.	210	41.41 N	73.53 W
Arlington, Oh., U.S.	216	40.53 N	83.39 W
Arlington, Or., U.S.	202	45.43 N	120.11 W
Arlington, S.D., U.S.	198	44.21 N	97.07 W
Arlington, Tn., U.S.	194	35.18 N	89.40 W
Arlington, Tx., U.S.	222	32.44 N	97.06 W
Arlington, Vt., U.S.	210	43.04 N	73.09 W
Arlington, Va., U.S.	208	38.52 N	77.06 W
Arlington, Wa., U.S.	224	48.11 N	122.07 W
Arlington □[6]	284c	38.50 N	77.10 W
Arlington, Lake ⊜[1]	222	32.42 N	97.13 W
Arlington Heights, Il., U.S.	216	42.05 N	87.58 W
Arlington Heights, Ma., U.S.	283	42.25 N	71.11 W
Arlington Memorial Bridge ◆[5]	284c	38.53 N	77.03 W
Arlington Mill Reservoir ⊜[1]	283	42.48 N	71.13 W
Arlington National Cemetery ◆	284c	38.53 N	77.04 W
Arlit	150	19.00 N	7.38 E
Arlod	58	46.06 N	5.49 E
Arlon	56	49.41 N	5.49 E
Arlöv	41	55.39 N	13.05 E
Arltunga	162	23.26 S	134.41 E
Arl'uk	86	55.26 N	84.50 E
Arluno	62	45.30 N	8.56 E
Arly ≃	62	45.40 N	6.23 E
Arlyn Oaks	276	40.40 N	73.27 W
Arm ≃	184	50.46 N	105.00 W
Arma	198	37.32 N	94.42 W
Armação, Ponta da ›	287a	22.53 S	43.08 W
Armada	214	42.50 N	82.53 W
Armadale, Austl.	168a	32.09 S	116.00 E
Armadale, On., Can.	275b	43.50 N	79.15 W
Armadale, S. Afr.	273d	26.17 S	27.57 E
Armadale, Scot., U.K.	46	55.54 N	3.42 W
Arma di Taggia	62	43.50 N	7.51 E
Armageddon → Tel Megiddo ⊥	132	32.35 N	35.11 E
Armagh, N. Ire., U.K.	48	54.21 N	6.39 W
Armagh, Pa., U.S.	214	40.27 N	79.02 W
Armagnac □[9]	32	43.45 N	0.10 E
Armah, Wādī V	144	18.12 N	51.02 E
Armainvilliers, Étang d' ⊜	261	48.45 N	2.44 E
Armainvilliers, Forêt d' ♠	261	48.45 N	2.45 E
Armance ≃	50	47.26 N	3.33 E
Armançon ≃, Fr.	50	47.57 N	3.30 E
Armançon ≃, Fr.	58	47.33 N	4.17 E
Arm'ansk	78	46.07 N	33.41 E
Arm'anskaja Sovetskaja Socialističeskaja Respublika □[3]	84	40.00 N	45.00 E
Armant	140	25.37 N	32.32 E
Armavir	72	45.00 N	41.08 E
Armazém	252	28.16 S	49.01 W
Armbrust	214	40.13 N	79.33 W
Armells Creek ≃	202	47.37 N	108.40 W
Armenia	246	4.31 N	75.41 W
Armenia → Arm'anskaja Sovetskaja Socialističeskaja Respublika □[3]	84	40.00 N	45.00 E
Armenia □[9]	84	40.30 N	43.30 E
Armeniș	38	45.12 N	22.19 E
Armenistís	38	37.36 N	26.08 E
Armeno	62	45.49 N	8.26 E

Armenonville-les-Gâtineaux	261	48.33 N	1.39 E
Armentières	50	50.41 N	2.53 E
Armento	68	40.18 N	16.04 E
Armería	234	18.56 N	103.58 W
Armería ≃	234	18.52 N	103.59 W
Armero	246	4.58 N	74.54 W
Armidale	166	30.31 S	151.39 E
Armijo	200	35.03 N	106.40 W
Armitage	42	52.44 N	1.53 W
Armit Lake ⊜	176	64.10 N	91.32 W
Armizonskoje	86	55.57 N	67.42 E
Armona	226	36.19 N	119.42 W
Armonk	276	41.07 N	73.42 W
Armor	210	42.44 N	78.48 W
Armori	122	20.28 N	79.59 E
Armour	198	43.19 N	98.20 W
Armoy	58	46.21 N	6.31 E
Armstrong, Arg.	252	32.47 S	61.36 W
Armstrong, B.C., Can.	182	50.27 N	119.12 W
Armstrong, Il., U.S.	216	40.18 N	87.53 W
Armstrong, Ia., U.S.	198	43.23 N	94.28 W
Armstrong, Mo., U.S.	194	39.16 N	92.42 W
Armstrong □[6]	214	40.49 N	79.32 W
Armstrong ≃	164	16.46 S	131.12 E
Armstrong, Mount ∧	180	63.12 N	133.16 W
Armstrong Station	176	50.18 N	89.02 W
Armthorpe	44	53.32 N	1.03 W
Ārmūr	122	18.48 N	78.17 E
Armutlu	130	40.31 N	28.50 E
Arnå ≃	41	54.57 N	8.53 E
Arnaccio	66	43.40 N	10.17 E
Arnaía	38	40.29 N	23.35 E
Arnarfjörður ⊂[2]	24a	65.45 N	23.40 W
Arnäs	40	58.41 N	13.35 E
Arnaud ≃	176	59.59 N	69.46 W
Arnaudville	194	30.24 N	91.56 W
Arnavad, gora ∧	85	38.33 N	71.31 E
Arnavutköy ≃	267b	41.13 N	29.12 E
Arnay-le-Duc	58	47.08 N	4.29 E
Arnaz	62	45.38 N	7.43 E
Arnborg	41	56.01 N	8.59 E
Arnbruck	60	49.08 N	13.00 E
Arncliffe	274a	33.56 S	151.09 E
Arneburg	54	52.40 N	12.00 E
Arnedo	34	42.13 N	2.06 W
Arneiro dos Marinheiros	266c	38.51 N	9.25 W
Arneiroz	250	6.20 S	40.08 W
Arnejevo	82	54.58 N	37.35 E
Arnemuiden	52	51.30 N	3.41 E
Årnes	26	60.09 N	11.28 E
Arnett	196	36.08 N	99.46 W
Arney ≃	48	54.16 N	7.37 W
Arnhem	52	51.59 N	5.55 E
Arnhem, Cape ›	164	12.21 S	136.21 E
Arnhem Bay ⊂	164	12.20 S	136.12 E
Arnhem Land ◆[1]	164	13.10 S	134.30 E
Arnhem Land Aboriginal Reserve ◆[4]	164	13.10 S	134.30 E
Arni	64	44.04 N	10.15 E
Arnis	41	54.38 N	9.56 E
Árnissa	38	40.48 N	21.50 E
Arno I[1]	14	7.05 N	171.41 E
Arno ≃	66	43.41 N	10.17 E
Arno, Torrente ≃	266b	45.42 N	8.48 E
Arno Bay	166	33.54 S	136.34 E
Arnold, B.C., Can.	224	49.08 N	122.03 W
Arnold, Eng., U.K.	44	53.00 N	1.08 W
Arnold, Ca., U.S.	204	38.15 N	120.21 W
Arnold, Md., U.S.	208	39.01 N	76.30 W
Arnold, Mn., U.S.	190	46.52 N	92.05 W
Arnold, Mo., U.S.	219	38.25 N	90.22 W
Arnold, Ne., U.S.	198	41.25 N	100.11 W
Arnold, Pa., U.S.	214	40.34 N	79.46 W
Arnold ≃	164	15.19 S	134.06 E
Arnold Arboretum ♠	283	42.18 N	71.08 W
Arnold Mills	283	41.58 N	71.23 W
Arnold Mills Reservoir ⊜[1]	283	41.59 N	71.25 W
Arnolds Park	198	43.22 N	95.08 W
Arnoldstein	64	46.33 N	13.43 E
Arnon ≃	50	48.16 N	0.38 E
Arnos Vale Airfield ⊠	241h	13.09 N	61.13 W
Arnot	210	41.39 N	77.07 W
Arnouville-lès-Gonesse	261	49.00 N	2.25 E
Arnouville-lès-Mantes	261	48.55 N	1.44 E
Arnoya ≃	34	42.15 N	8.09 W
Arnprior	212	45.26 N	76.21 W
Arnsberg	56	51.24 N	8.03 E
Arnsberg □[5]	52	51.20 N	8.00 E
Arnschwang	60	49.16 N	12.49 E
Arnsdorf	54	51.05 N	13.59 E
Arnside	44	54.12 N	2.50 W
Arnstadt	54	50.50 N	10.57 E
Arnstein	56	49.58 N	9.58 E
Arnstorf	60	48.34 N	12.49 E
Arnum	41	55.15 N	8.59 E
Ærø I	41	55.15 N	9.45 E
Aro ≃	246	8.01 N	64.11 W
Aroa	246	10.26 N	68.54 W
Aroa ≃	246	10.40 N	68.19 W
Aroa, Pointe ›	174s	17.28 S	149.46 W
Aroab	156	26.47 S	19.40 E
Aroali	126	24.03 N	87.56 E
Arochukwu	150	5.23 N	7.55 E
Aroeiras	250	7.31 S	35.41 W
Ar'ofino	80	58.16 N	39.15 E
Arolla	58	46.02 N	7.29 E
Arolsen	56	51.23 N	9.01 E
Aroma	140	15.49 N	36.08 E
Aroma Park	216	41.04 N	87.48 W
Aromas	226	36.53 N	121.39 W
Aromaševo	86	56.52 N	68.39 E
Aron ≃	50	47.15 N	2.02 E
Arona, It.	62	45.46 N	8.34 E
Arona, Pap. N. Gui.	164	6.20 S	146.00 E
Arona, Pa., U.S.	279b	40.16 N	79.39 W
Aroostook ≃	186	46.48 N	67.45 W
Arop Island I	164	5.20 S	147.05 E
Aropuk Lake ⊜	180	61.12 N	163.50 W
Arorae I	14	2.38 S	176.49 E
Arorangi	174k	21.13 S	159.49 W
Aroroy	116	12.31 N	123.24 E
Arosa	58	46.47 N	9.41 E
Arosa, Ría de ⊂[1]	34	42.28 N	8.57 W
Arosbaya	115a	6.56 S	112.51 E
Ærøsund	41	55.16 N	9.45 E
Aro Usu, Tanjung ›	164	8.20 S	130.45 E
Arowhana ∧	172	38.07 S	177.52 E
Arp	222	32.13 N	95.03 W
Arpa ≃	84	39.28 N	44.57 E
Arpaçay	84	40.52 N	43.20 E
Arpaçay (Achur'an) ≃	84	40.06 N	43.39 E
Arpačin	83	47.14 N	40.11 E
Arpaia	68	41.02 N	14.33 E
Arpajon	50	48.35 N	2.15 E
Ārpāra	126	23.23 N	89.23 E
Arpino	66	41.39 N	13.36 E
Arpoador, Ponta do ›, Bra.	252	24.25 S	47.00 W
Arpoador, Ponta do ›, Bra.	287a	22.59 S	43.12 W
Arquà Petrarca	64	45.16 N	11.43 E
Arquà Polesine	64	45.01 N	11.45 E
Arquata del Tronto	66	42.46 N	13.18 E
Arquata Scrivia	62	44.41 N	8.53 E
Arque	248	17.48 S	66.23 W
Arques	50	50.44 N	2.17 E
Arques-la-Bataille	50	49.53 N	1.08 E
Ar-Rabaḍ	128	23.11 N	39.32 E
Ar-Rabbah	132	31.16 N	35.44 E
Arracourt	58	48.44 N	6.32 E
Ar-Radīsīyah Baḥrī	140	24.57 N	32.53 E
Ar-Rafīd	132	32.57 N	35.53 E
Arraga	252	28.04 S	64.14 W
Arrah	150	6.40 N	3.58 W
Ar-Rahad	140	12.43 N	30.39 E
Ar-Raḥāminah	142	31.18 N	31.45 E
Ar-Raḥmānīyah	142	31.06 N	30.38 E

Arraial do Cabo	255	22.58 S	42.01 W
Arraias	255	12.56 S	46.57 W
Arraias ≃, Bra.	250	11.10 S	53.35 W
Arraias ≃, Bra.	255	12.28 S	47.18 W
'Arrām, Wādī V	132	32.55 N	36.10 E
Ar-Ramādī	128	33.25 N	43.17 E
Ar-Ramthā	132	32.34 N	36.00 E
Arran, Island of I	46	55.35 N	5.15 W
Ar-Rank	140	11.45 N	32.48 E
Arran Lake ⊜	212	44.29 N	81.16 W
Ar-Raqqah	130	35.56 N	39.01 E
Ar-Raqqah □[8]	130	36.00 N	39.00 E
Arras	50	50.17 N	2.47 E
Arras, Nuraghe ⊥	71	39.40 N	9.25 E
Ar-Rāshidah	140	25.35 N	28.56 E
Ar-Rass	128	25.52 N	43.28 E
Ar-Rastan	130	34.55 N	36.44 E
Arrats ≃	32	44.06 N	0.52 E
Ar-Rawḍah, Ar. Su.	128	26.05 N	40.37 E
Ar-Rawḍah, J.Y.D.S.	144	14.28 N	47.17 E
Ar-Rawḍah, Miṣr	142	27.48 N	30.52 E
Ar-Rawḍah, Miṣr	142	29.27 N	31.00 E
Ar-Rāwuk	144	15.45 N	48.54 E
Ar-Rayramūn	142	27.45 N	30.52 E
Ar-Rayyāḥ ar-Minūfīya ≅	142	30.20 N	31.00 E
Ar-Rayyāḥ at-Tawfīqī ≅	142	30.11 N	31.07 E
Ar-Rayyān	128	25.18 N	51.27 E
Arrecife	148	28.57 N	13.32 W
Arrecifes	252	34.03 S	60.07 W
Arrée, Montagnes d' ⋀	32	48.26 N	3.55 W
Arregui, Laguna ⊜	258	35.05 S	57.33 W
Arrentela	266c	38.38 N	9.06 W
Arresø ⊜	41	55.58 N	12.08 E
Arrey	200	32.50 N	107.19 W
Arriaga	234	16.14 N	93.54 W
Arriba	198	39.17 N	103.16 W
Arrild	41	55.09 N	8.58 E
Ar-Riyāḍ (Riyadh)	128	24.38 N	46.43 E
Arrochar	46	56.12 N	4.44 W
Arroio Grande	252	32.14 S	53.05 W
Arrojado ≃	255	13.24 S	44.20 W
Arronches	34	39.07 N	7.17 W
Arrone ≃, It.	66	42.18 N	11.38 E
Arrone ≃, It.	66	41.52 N	12.11 E
Arros ≃	32	43.40 N	0.02 W
Arroscia ≃	62	44.03 N	8.11 E
Arroux ≃	32	46.29 N	3.58 E
Arrow ≃, Eng., U.K.	42	52.12 N	2.43 W
Arrow ≃, Eng., U.K.	42	52.09 N	1.53 W
Arrow, Lough ⊜	48	54.04 N	8.21 W
Arrow Creek ≃	202	47.43 N	109.50 W
Arrowhead, Lake ⊜[1], Ca., U.S.	228	34.15 N	117.11 W
Arrowhead, Lake ⊜[1], Tx., U.S.	196	33.40 N	98.20 W
Arrowhead Peak ∧	228	34.13 N	117.16 W
Arrowhead Provincial Park ♠	212	45.24 N	79.13 W
Arrowhead Village	208	40.04 N	74.07 W
Arrow Lake ⊜	190	48.08 N	90.18 W
Arrowrock Reservoir ⊜[1]	202	43.36 N	115.51 W
Arrowsmith	216	40.27 N	88.38 W
Arrowsmith, Mount ∧, Austl.	166	30.09 S	141.50 E
Arrowsmith, Mount ∧, B.C., Can.	224	49.13 N	124.36 W
Arrowsmith, Mount ∧, N.Z.	172	43.21 S	170.59 E
Arrowtown	172	44.56 S	168.50 E
Arrowwood	182	50.44 N	113.09 W
Arroyan, Arroyo ≃[1]	288	34.24 S	58.32 W
Arroyito	252	31.25 S	63.03 W
Arroyo	240m	17.58 N	66.04 W
Arroyo, Puerto ⊂	240m	17.58 N	66.05 W
Arroyo de la Luz	34	39.29 N	6.35 W
Arroyo Frío	234	17.26 N	100.35 W
Arroyo Grande, Ca., U.S.	204	35.07 N	120.35 W
Arroyo Grande → Ismael Cortinas, Ur.	258	33.58 S	57.06 W
Arroyo Hondo	200	36.32 N	105.40 W
Arroyo Naranjo ◆[8]	286b	23.02 N	82.23 W
Arroyo Seco Park ♠	280	34.06 N	118.12 W
Arroyos y Esteros	252	25.04 S	57.06 W
Arrozal	256	22.37 S	44.03 W
Ar-Ru'at	140	12.21 N	32.17 E
Ar-Rub' al-Khālī ◆[2]	118	20.00 N	51.00 E
Ar-Rubayqī	142	30.10 N	31.46 E
Ar-Ruḥaybah	132	33.45 N	36.42 E
Ar-Rukhaymīyah ⊤[4]	128	29.14 N	45.35 E
Ar-Rumaythah	128	31.32 N	45.12 E
Ar-Rummān	132	32.10 N	35.50 E
Ar-Ruqayyah ⊥	132	32.47 N	37.05 E
Ar-Ruṣāfah ⊥	130	35.37 N	38.45 E
Ar-Ruṣayfah	132	32.01 N	36.03 E
Ar-Ruṣayriṣ	140	11.51 N	34.23 E
Ar-Rushaydah	132	32.40 N	36.50 E
Ar-Ruṭbah	128	33.02 N	40.17 E
Ar-Ru'ūs	142	29.21 N	31.04 E
Ar-Ruways	128	26.08 N	51.13 E
Års	26	56.48 N	9.32 E
Aršan, S.S.S.R.	88	51.54 N	102.27 E
Aršan, S.S.S.R.	88	53.54 N	99.54 E
Arsanjān	128	29.56 N	53.18 E
Aršan'-Zel'men'	80	47.36 N	44.36 E
Ārsāpota	272b	22.55 N	88.18 E
Arsbeck	56	51.08 N	6.12 E
Arsenal de Marinha ■	266c	38.39 N	9.09 W
Arsenal Football Club ♠	260	51.33 N	0.06 W
Arsenault Lake ⊜	184	55.06 N	108.30 W
Arsenjev	89	44.10 N	133.15 E
Arsenjevka ≃	89	44.54 N	133.35 E
Arsenjevo	76	53.44 N	36.40 E
Ars-en-Ré	32	46.12 N	1.31 W
Arsi □[4]	144	8.00 N	39.40 E
Arsiè	64	45.59 N	11.45 E
Arsiero	64	45.48 N	11.21 E
Arsikere	122	13.20 N	76.15 E
Arsin	130	40.58 N	39.56 E
Aršincevo	78	45.17 N	36.25 E
Arsk	80	56.06 N	49.54 E
Arslanbob	85	41.21 N	72.56 E
Årslev	41	55.18 N	10.29 E
Arso	164	2.56 S	140.47 E
Arsoli	66	42.02 N	13.01 E
Ársos	130	34.50 N	32.46 E
Ars-sur-Formans	58	45.59 N	4.49 E
Ars-sur-Moselle	56	49.05 N	6.04 E
Årsta havsbad	40	59.05 N	18.10 E
Arsufhsa ≃	84	39.08 N	46.50 E
Arsunda	40	60.32 N	16.44 E
Art, Île I	175f	19.43 S	163.38 E
Árta, Ellás	38	39.09 N	20.59 E
Artà, Esp.	34	39.42 N	3.21 E
Artarmon	274a	33.49 S	151.11 E
Artašat	84	39.59 N	44.33 E
Arta Terme	64	46.28 N	13.01 E
Arteaga	234	18.28 N	102.25 W
Arteche	116	12.17 N	125.22 E
Artegna	64	46.14 N	13.09 E
Artemare	62	45.52 N	5.42 E
Artemisa	240p	22.49 N	82.46 W
Artemón	38	36.59 N	24.43 E
Artémou	150	15.31 N	12.16 W
Artemovsk → Art'omovsk	83	48.35 N	38.00 E
Artèn	64	46.00 N	11.50 E
Artenay	50	48.05 N	1.53 E
Artern	54	51.22 N	11.17 E
Artesia → Mosomane, Bots.	156	24.04 S	26.15 E
Artesia, Ca., U.S.	280	33.51 N	118.04 W
Artesia, Ms., U.S.	194	33.24 N	88.38 W
Artesia, N.M., U.S.	196	32.50 N	104.24 W
Artesia Lake ⊜	226	38.57 N	119.22 W
Artesian	198	44.00 N	97.55 W

≃	River	Fluß	Río	Rivière	Rio
≅	Canal	Kanal	Canal	Canal	Canal
⌊	Waterfall, Rapids	Wasserfall, Stromschnellen	Cascada, Rápidos	Chute d'eau, Rapides	Cascata, Rápidos
⨃	Strait	Meeresstraße	Estrecho	Détroit	Estreito
⊂	Bay, Gulf	Bucht, Golf	Bahía, Golfo	Baie, Golfe	Baía, Golfo
⊜	Lake, Lakes	See, Seen	Lago, Lagos	Lac, Lacs	Lago, Lagos
≋	Swamp	Sumpf	Pantano	Marais	Pântano
⍓	Ice Features, Glacier	Eis- und Gletscherformen	Accidentes Glaciales	Formes glaciaires	Acidentes glaciares
⊤	Other Hydrographic Features	Andere Hydrographische Objekte	Otros Elementos Hidrográficos	Autres données hydrographiques	Outros acidentes hidrográficos
✢	Submarine Features	Untermeerische Objekte	Accidentes Submarinos	Formes de relief sous-marin	Acidentes submarinos
□	Political Unit	Politische Einheit	Unidad Politica	Entité politique	Unidade política
ʊ	Cultural Institution	Kulturelle Institution	Institución Cultural	Institution culturelle	Instituição cultural
⊥	Historical Site	Historische Stätte	Sitio Histórico	Site historique	Sitio histórico
♠	Recreational Site	Erholungs- und Ferienort	Sitio de Recreo	Centre de loisirs	Area de Lazer
⊠	Airport	Flughafen	Aeropuerto	Aéroport	Aeroporto
■	Military Installation	Militäranlage	Instalación Militar	Installation militaire	Instalação militar
◆	Miscellaneous	Verschiedenes	Misceláneo	Divers	Diversos

I · 10 Arth-Athi
ENGLISH Name Page Lat.°′ Long.°′ — DEUTSCH Name Seite Breite°′ Länge°′ E = Ost

Arth 58 47.04 N 8.31 E
Arthabaska 206 46.02 N 71.55 W
Arthabaska □6 206 46.05 N 72.00 W
Arthal 123 33.16 N 76.11 E
Arthala 272a 28.40 N 77.24 E
Arthies 261 49.06 N 1.48 E
Arthonnay 50 47.56 N 4.13 E
Arthur, On., Can. 212 43.50 N 80.32 W
Arthur, Il., U.S. 194 39.43 N 88.28 W
Arthur, Ne., U.S. 198 41.34 N 101.41 W
Arthur, N.D., U.S. 198 47.06 N 97.13 W
Arthur, Tn., U.S. 192 36.32 N 83.40 W
Arthur ≃, Austl. 166 41.03 S 144.40 E
Arthur ≃, Austl. 168a 33.31 S 116.50 E
Arthur, Lake ⊜1 214 40.57 N 80.05 W
Arthur Creek ≃ 162 22.55 S 136.45 E
Arthur Kill ꓤ 276 40.30 N 74.15 W
Arthurs Pass 172 42.57 S 171.34 E
Arthurs Pass)(172 42.54 S 171.34 E
Arthur's Pass National Park ♦ 172 42.50 S 171.40 E
Arthurs Seat ʌ2 169 38.21 S 144.57 E
Arthurs Town 238 24.38 N 75.42 W
Arthurton 168b 34.16 S 137.45 E
Arti 86 56.26 N 58.32 E
Artibonite ≃ 238 19.15 N 72.47 W
Artico, Océano → Arctic Ocean ⚓1 16 85.00 N 170.00 E
Artigas 252 30.24 S 56.28 W
Artigas ◆8 286c 10.30 N 66.56 W
Artigas, Casa de ⊥ 258 34.39 S 56.03 W
Artik 84 40.37 N 43.59 E
Artilleros 258 34.22 S 57.34 W
Artilleros, Punta ≻ 258 34.28 S 57.32 W
Artillery Lake ⊜ 176 63.09 N 107.52 W
Artlenburg 52 53.22 N 10.29 E
Artney, Glen V 46 56.20 N 4.04 W
Artois □9 50 50.30 N 2.30 E
Artois, Collines de l' ⨯2 50 50.25 N 2.10 E
Art'om 89 43.22 N 132.13 E
Art'om-Ostrov 84 40.28 N 50.20 E
Art'omovka, S.S.S.R. 78 49.46 N 35.04 E
Art'omovka, S.S.S.R. 83 48.29 N 37.23 E
Art'omovka, S.S.S.R. 83 47.53 N 38.38 E
Art'omovo 83 48.22 N 37.53 E
Art'omovsk, S.S.S.R. 83 48.27 N 38.42 E
Art'omovsk, S.S.S.R. 83 48.35 N 38.00 E
Art'omovsk, S.S.S.R. 86 54.21 N 93.26 E
Art'omovskij, S.S.S.R. 86 57.21 N 61.54 E
Art'omovskij, S.S.S.R. 88 58.12 N 114.45 E
Art'omovskij, S.S.S.R. 89 43.27 N 132.22 E
Artova 130 40.03 N 36.19 E
Artpark ♦ 284a 43.10 N 79.03 W
Artrutx, Cap d' ≻ 34 39.56 N 3.48 E
Artuby ≃ 62 43.45 N 6.29 E
Artur Nogueira 256 22.35 S 47.09 W
Arturo Segui ◆8 258 34.51 S 58.09 W
Artvin 130 41.11 N 41.49 E
Artvin □4 130 41.05 N 42.00 E
Artybaš 86 51.48 N 87.16 E
Artyk 74 64.12 N 145.06 E
Aru, Kepulauan II 164 6.00 S 134.30 E
Aru, Tanjung ≻ 112 2.10 S 116.34 E
Aru, Teluk ᑕ 114 4.09 N 98.12 E
Arua 154 3.01 N 30.55 E
Aruã ≃ 250 2.39 S 55.38 W
Aruaddin 144 16.15 N 38.43 E
Aruanã 255 14.54 S 51.05 W
Aruângua (Luangwa) ≃ 154 15.36 S 30.25 E
Aruba □2 241s 12.30 N 69.58 W
Aru Basin ⚓1 14 5.00 S 134.00 E
Arucas 148 28.07 N 15.31 W
Arue 174s 17.32 S 149.32 W
Arufu 150 7.50 N 9.14 E
Arujá 256 23.24 S 46.20 W
Arujá □7 287b 23.24 S 46.20 W
Arumanduba 250 1.29 S 52.29 W
Arume 174m 26.36 N 128.07 E
Arume-wan ᑕ 174m 26.35 N 128.08 E
Arun (Pong) ≃, Asia 126 26.49 N 87.09 E
Arun ≃, Eng., U.K. 42 50.48 N 0.33 W
Arunāchal Pradesh □3 120 28.30 N 95.00 E
Arundel, P.Q., Can. 206 45.58 N 74.37 W
Arundel, Eng., U.K. 42 50.51 N 0.34 W
Arun Qi 89 48.07 N 123.28 E
Ārup 41 55.23 N 10.04 E
Aruppukkottai 122 9.31 N 78.06 E
Arurandéua ≃ 250 3.43 S 48.50 W
Arusha 154 3.22 S 36.41 E
Arusha □4 154 4.00 S 36.15 E
Arusha Chini 154 3.35 S 37.20 E
Arusha National Park ♦ 154 3.17 S 36.56 E
Arut ≃ 112 2.42 S 111.34 E
Aruvi ≃ 122 8.49 N 79.55 E
Aruwimi ≃ 138 1.13 N 23.36 E
Arvada 200 39.48 N 105.05 W
Arvagh 48 53.55 N 7.34 W
Arvajcheer 90 46.15 N 102.48 E
Arve ≃ 58 46.12 N 6.08 E
Arverne ◆8 276 40.35 N 73.48 W
Arves, Les Aiguilles d' ʌ 62 45.08 N 6.21 E
Arvi 120 20.59 N 78.14 E
Arvida 186 48.25 N 71.11 W
Arvidsjaur 24 65.35 N 19.07 E
Arvier 62 45.42 N 7.11 E
Arvieux 62 44.46 N 6.44 E
Arvika 26 59.39 N 12.36 E
Arvillard 62 45.27 N 6.07 E
Arvin 228 35.12 N 118.49 W
Arvo, Lago ⊜ 68 39.14 N 16.29 E
Arvon, Mount ʌ 190 46.45 N 88.09 W
Arvonia 192 37.40 N 78.20 W
Arvorezinha 252 28.53 S 52.10 W
Arwal 124 25.15 N 84.41 E
Arwala 112 7.41 S 126.49 E
Arxan 89 47.11 N 119.57 E
Aryamūn 142 31.11 N 30.54 E
Aryiroúpolis 267c 37.54 N 23.45 E
Arys → Orzysz, Pol. 30 53.49 N 21.56 E
Arys', S.S.S.R. 85 42.26 N 68.48 E
Arys' ≃ 85 42.45 N 68.15 E
Arys, ozero ⊜ 86 45.50 N 66.20 E
Arzachena 71 41.05 N 9.23 E
Arzamas 80 55.23 N 43.50 E
Arzana 71 39.55 N 9.31 E
Arzano 68 40.55 N 14.16 E
Arzberg 60 50.04 N 12.12 E
Arzew, Golfe d' ᑕ 34 35.50 N 0.10 W
Arzew, Salines d' ⊜ 34 35.40 N 0.15 W
Arzfeld 56 50.05 N 6.16 E
Arzignano 64 45.31 N 11.20 E
Arziw 148 35.51 N 0.19 W
Arz Lubnān ◆3 130 34.14 N 36.03 E
Arzni 84 40.19 N 44.36 E
Arzon ≃ 62 45.11 N 3.54 E
Arzúa 34 42.56 N 8.09 W
As, Bel. 56 51.01 N 5.35 E
Aš, Česko. 54 50.10 N 12.10 E
Ås, Nor. 26 59.40 N 10.48 E
Asa, Nihon 96 34.33 N 132.26 E
Aša, S.S.S.R. 86 55.00 N 57.16 E
Asa ≃, Nihon 94 35.39 N 139.26 E
Asa ≃, Nihon 96 34.01 N 131.09 E
Asa ≃, Ven. 246 6.50 N 63.18 W
Asab 156 25.29 S 17.59 E
Asaba, Nig. 150 6.12 N 6.44 E
Asaba, Nihon 94 34.42 N 137.56 E
Asad, Buhayrat al- ⊜1 130 36.00 N 38.10 E
Asadābād, Afg. 120 34.52 N 71.09 E
Asadābād, Īrān 128 34.47 N 48.07 E
Asafo 150 6.11 N 0.28 W
Asaga Strait ꓤ 174y 14.11 S 169.40 W
Asagaya ◆8 268 35.42 N 139.38 E
Aşağıbostancı 130 35.10 N 33.00 E
Aşağıçiğil 130 38.03 N 31.52 E
Aşağı Dağ ʌ 84 40.01 N 43.11 E
Aşağı Kuluşağı 130 38.39 N 38.39 E
Aşağılahan 130 38.50 N 39.59 E
Aşağı Mestikân 130 38.25 N 38.46 E
Ašagy-G'ojn'uk 84 41.18 N 47.00 E
Asahan 114 2.23 N 102.33 E
Asahan ≃ 114 3.02 N 99.52 E
Asahi, Nihon 94 36.07 N 137.52 E
Asahi, Nihon 94 35.14 N 137.22 E
Asahi, Nihon 94 36.57 N 137.34 E
Asahi, Nihon 94 35.43 N 140.39 E
Asahi, Nihon 94 35.59 N 136.07 E
Asahi, Nihon 94 36.05 N 137.21 E
Asahi, Nihon 94 35.02 N 136.40 E
Asahi, Nihon 96 34.59 N 133.50 E
Asahi, Nihon 96 34.51 N 132.16 E
Asahi, Nihon 96 34.17 N 131.28 E
Asahi ◆8, Nihon 268 35.29 N 139.33 E
Asahi ◆8, Nihon 270 34.44 N 135.34 E
Asahi ≃ 96 34.36 N 133.58 E
Asahi-dake ʌ, Nihon 92a 43.40 N 142.51 E
Asahi-dake ʌ, Nihon 94 37.14 N 139.21 E
Asahigawa → Asahikawa 92a 43.46 N 142.22 E
Asahi-gawa-daiichi-dam ◆6 94 34.53 N 133.22 E
Asahikawa 92a 43.46 N 142.22 E
Asahikawa-chūtonchi, Rikujō-Jieitai- ■ 92a 43.49 N 142.25 E
Asahi-ko ⊜1 96 34.56 N 133.51 E
Asahi-sanchi ⨯ 92 38.25 N 139.50 E
Ašt 85 40.41 N 70.20 E
Asaka 94 35.48 N 139.36 E
Asaka, Camp ■ 268 35.47 N 139.36 E
Asakanskij Golec, gora ʌ 88 50.18 N 109.55 E
Asakawa 94 37.05 N 140.25 E
Asake ≃ 94 35.00 N 136.41 E
Asako 96 35.14 N 134.48 E
Asakuchi 96 33.23 N 130.44 E
Asakusa ◆8 268 35.43 N 139.49 E
Asālatpur ◆8 272a 28.38 N 77.05 E
Asale 144 14.22 N 40.32 E
Asale, Lake ⊜ 144 14.19 N 40.18 E
Asamankese 150 5.52 N 0.42 W
Asama-yama ʌ 94 36.24 N 138.31 E
Asanbani, India 126 22.43 N 86.20 E
Asanbāni, India 126 24.07 N 87.27 E
Asani 154 4.25 S 29.05 E
Asankrangwa 150 5.48 N 2.26 W
Asan-man ᑕ 98 36.56 N 126.51 E
Āsānsol, India 126 24.14 N 87.17 E
Āsānsol, India 126 23.41 N 86.59 E
Asap 88 57.07 N 56.30 E
Asar 88 47.56 N 117.38 E
Åsarna 26 62.39 N 14.21 E
Åsarum 26 56.12 N 14.50 E
Asashina 94 36.16 N 138.25 E
Āšāsuni 126 22.32 N 89.10 E
Asati 272b 22.29 N 88.14 E
Asa-yama ʌ 96 34.47 N 132.23 E
Asayita 144 11.33 N 41.30 E
Asbach 56 50.40 N 7.25 E
Asbeck 263 51.28 N 7.11 E
Asberg 263 51.26 N 6.40 E
Asbesberg ʌ 158 28.55 S 23.15 E
Asbest 86 57.00 N 61.30 E
Asbestos 206 45.46 N 71.57 W
Asbestos Range National Park ♦ 166 41.08 S 146.39 E
Asbe Teferi 144 9.02 N 40.58 E
Åsbro 40 59.00 N 15.03 E
Asbury 210 40.41 N 75.00 W
Asbury Park 208 40.13 N 74.01 W
Ascea 68 40.08 N 15.11 E
Ascensión, Méx. 232 31.06 N 107.59 W
Ascensión, Méx. 232 24.20 N 99.55 W
Ascension I 10 7.57 S 14.22 W
Ascensión, Bahía de la ᑕ 232 19.40 N 87.30 W
Ascent 158 27.12 S 29.03 E
Aščerino 265b 55.36 N 37.46 E
Asch 58 47.57 N 10.49 E
Aschabad 128 37.57 N 58.23 E
Aschabad □4 128 38.30 N 58.25 E
Aschach an der Donau 61 48.22 N 14.02 E
Aschaffenburg 56 49.59 N 9.09 E
Aschbach Markt 61 48.04 N 14.45 E
Ascheberg, B.R.D. 52 51.47 N 7.37 E
Ascheberg, B.R.D. 54 54.08 N 10.20 E
Aschendorf 52 53.04 N 7.22 E
Aschersleben 54 51.45 N 11.27 E
Asciano 66 43.14 N 11.33 E
Aščikol', ozero ⊜ 86 45.05 N 67.15 E
Aščiozek ≃ 80 49.12 N 48.06 E
Aščitastysor, ozero ⊜ 86 49.19 N 63.59 E
Ascoli Piceno 66 42.51 N 13.34 E
Ascoli Piceno □4 66 43.01 N 13.34 E
Ascoli Satriano 68 41.12 N 15.34 E
Ascona 58 46.09 N 8.46 E
Ascope 248 7.43 S 79.07 W
Ascot, Austl. 171a 27.26 S 153.04 E
Ascot, Eng., U.K. 42 51.25 N 0.41 W
Ascot ≃ 206 45.21 N 71.51 W
Ascotán 252 21.44 S 68.18 W
Ascros 62 43.55 N 7.01 E
Aščykol', ozero ⊜ 85 43.32 N 70.35 E
Aščysu ≃ 86 49.54 N 78.58 E
Aseb 144 13.00 N 42.45 E
Åseda 26 57.10 N 15.20 E
Asedjrad ⨯1 148 24.28 N 1.52 E
Asekejevo 80 53.36 N 52.49 E
Asela 144 7.59 N 39.08 E
Åsele 26 64.10 N 17.20 E
Asem ≃ 115a 6.12 S 107.42 E
Asembagus 115a 7.45 S 114.14 E
Asembourg 56 49.43 N 6.02 E
Åsen 26 63.36 N 11.03 E
Asendabo 144 9.50 N 37.33 E
Asendorf 52 52.46 N 9.00 E
Asenovgrad 38 42.01 N 24.52 E
Åsensbruk 26 58.48 N 12.25 E
Aseri 76 59.27 N 26.52 E
Asfar, Jabal al- ʌ 132 32.12 N 36.54 E
Asfordby 42 52.46 N 0.57 W
Asfūn al-Maṭā'inah 140 25.23 N 32.32 E
Åsgårdstrand 26 59.21 N 10.28 E
Ash, Eng., U.K. 42 51.17 N 1.16 E
Ash, Eng., U.K. 42 51.15 N 0.44 W
Ashalim 132 30.58 N 34.40 E
Åshammar 40 60.39 N 16.32 E
Ashanti □4 150 6.45 N 1.30 W
'Ashārah, Wādī al- V 142 30.21 N 32.15 E
Asharoken 276 40.56 N 73.22 W
Ashaway 207 41.25 N 71.47 W
Ashbourne, Ire. 48 53.31 N 6.24 W
Ashbourne, Eng., U.K. 44 53.02 N 1.44 W
Ash Brook Swamp Reservation ♦ 276 40.37 N 74.21 W
Ashburn, Ga., U.S. 192 31.42 N 83.39 W
Ashburn, Mo., U.S. 219 39.33 N 91.10 W
Ashburn, Va., U.S. 208 39.02 N 77.29 W
Ashburnham 207 42.38 N 71.54 W
Ashburton, Austl. 274b 37.52 S 145.05 E
Ashburton, N.Z. 172 43.55 S 171.45 E
Ashburton, Eng., U.K. 42 50.31 N 3.45 W
Ashburton ≃, Austl. 162 21.40 S 114.56 E
Ashburton ≃, N.Z. 172 44.04 S 171.48 E
Ashburton, North Branch ≃ 172 43.54 S 171.44 E
Ashburton, South Branch ≃ 172 43.44 S 171.22 E
Ashburton Downs 162 23.24 S 117.04 E
Ashby 207 42.40 N 71.49 W
Ashby, Lake ⊜ 220 28.56 N 81.07 W
Ashby-de-la-Zouch 42 52.46 N 1.28 W
Ashchurch 42 52.00 N 2.07 W
Ash Creek ≃, Ca., U.S. 204 41.05 N 121.08 W
Ash Creek ≃, Ct., U.S. 276 41.08 N 73.14 W
Ashcroft 182 50.43 N 121.17 W
Ashdod, Ma., U.S. 283 42.04 N 70.45 W
Ashdod, Yis. 132 31.49 N 34.40 E
Ashdod, Tel ⊥ 132 31.45 N 34.40 E
Ashdot Ya'aqov 132 32.40 N 35.35 E
Ashdown 194 33.40 N 94.07 W
Asheboro 192 35.42 N 79.48 W
Ashern 184 51.11 N 98.21 W
Asherton 196 28.26 N 99.45 W
Asheville 192 35.36 N 82.33 W
Ashewat Ziārat 120 31.22 N 68.32 E
Asheweig ≃ 176 54.17 N 87.12 W
Ashfield, Austl. 274a 33.53 S 151.08 E
Ashfield, Ma., U.S. 207 42.31 N 72.47 W
Ash Flat 194 36.13 N 91.36 W
Ashford, Austl. 166 29.20 S 151.06 E
Ashford, Eng., U.K. 42 51.08 N 0.53 E
Ashford, Eng., U.K. 260 51.26 N 0.27 W
Ashford, Al., U.S. 194 31.10 N 85.14 W
Ashford, Wa., U.S. 224 46.46 N 122.02 W
Ashford Airport ⊠ 42 51.04 N 1.01 E
Ash Fork 200 35.13 N 112.28 W
Ash Grove 194 37.18 N 93.35 W
Ashhurst 172 40.18 S 175.45 E
Ashibe 92 33.48 N 129.46 E
Ashibetsu 92a 43.31 N 142.11 E
Ashida ≃ 96 34.26 N 133.25 E
Ashikaga 94 36.20 N 139.27 E
Ashikaga-gakkō ⊥ 94 36.22 N 139.30 E
Ashingdon 260 51.36 N 0.42 E
Ashington 44 55.12 N 1.35 W
Ashino-ko ⊜ 94 35.13 N 139.00 E
Ashio 94 36.38 N 139.27 E
Ashio-sanchi ⨯ 94 36.35 N 139.30 E
Ashippun 216 43.14 N 88.31 W
Ashippun ≃ 216 43.10 N 88.33 W
Ashitaka-yama ʌ 94 35.12 N 138.49 E
Ashiya, Nihon 96 33.53 N 130.40 E
Ashiya, Nihon 96 34.43 N 135.17 E
Ashiya ≃ 270 34.43 N 135.18 E
Ashiyasu 94 35.38 N 138.23 E
Ashiyoro 92a 43.15 N 143.30 E
Ashizuri-misaki ≻ 92 32.44 N 133.01 E
Ashizuri-Uwakai-kokuritsu-kōen ♦, Nihon 92 32.45 N 132.45 E
Ashizuri-Uwakai-kokuritsu-kōen ♦, Nihon 96 33.07 N 132.27 E
Ashkhabad → Aschabad 128 37.57 N 58.23 E
Ashkum 216 40.53 N 87.57 W
Ashland, Al., U.S. 194 33.16 N 85.50 W
Ashland, Ca., U.S. 226 37.41 N 122.06 W
Ashland, Il., U.S. 219 39.53 N 90.00 W
Ashland, Ks., U.S. 198 37.11 N 99.45 W
Ashland, Ky., U.S. 188 38.28 N 82.38 W
Ashland, Me., U.S. 186 46.37 N 68.24 W
Ashland, Ma., U.S. 207 42.15 N 71.27 W
Ashland, Ms., U.S. 194 34.49 N 89.10 W
Ashland, Mo., U.S. 219 38.46 N 92.15 W
Ashland, Mt., U.S. 202 45.35 N 106.16 W
Ashland, Ne., U.S. 198 41.02 N 96.22 W
Ashland, N.H., U.S. 188 43.41 N 71.37 W
Ashland, N.J., U.S. 285 39.51 N 75.00 W
Ashland, N.Y., U.S. 210 42.18 N 74.20 W
Ashland, Oh., U.S. 214 40.52 N 82.19 W
Ashland, Or., U.S. 202 42.11 N 122.42 W
Ashland, Pa., U.S. 210 40.46 N 76.20 W
Ashland, Va., U.S. 208 37.45 N 77.28 W
Ashland, Wi., U.S. 190 46.35 N 90.53 W
Ashland □6 214 40.52 N 82.19 W
Ashland, Mount ʌ 202 42.05 N 122.43 W
Ashland City 194 36.16 N 87.03 W
Ashley, Austl. 166 29.19 S 149.49 E
Ashley, Eng., U.K. 262 53.21 N 2.20 W
Ashley, Il., U.S. 219 38.20 N 89.11 W
Ashley, In., U.S. 216 41.32 N 85.04 W
Ashley, Mi., U.S. 190 43.11 N 84.28 W
Ashley, Mo., U.S. 219 39.15 N 91.14 W
Ashley, N.D., U.S. 198 46.01 N 99.22 W
Ashley, Oh., U.S. 214 40.24 N 82.57 W
Ashley, Pa., U.S. 210 41.12 N 75.53 W
Ashley ≃ 172 43.16 S 172.43 E
Ashley Creek ≃ 200 40.21 N 109.22 W
Ashley Falls 207 42.03 N 73.20 W
Ashley Green 260 51.44 N 0.35 W
Ashmore 194 39.32 N 88.01 W
Ashmore Islands II 160 12.14 S 123.05 E
Ashmūn 142 30.18 N 30.58 E
Ashokan Reservoir ⊜1 210 41.58 N 74.10 W
Ashoknagar 120 24.34 N 77.43 E
Ashqelon 132 31.40 N 34.35 E
Ashridge Park ♦ 260 51.48 N 0.34 W
Ash-Shabakah 128 30.49 N 43.39 E
Ash-Shabb ◆4 140 22.19 N 29.46 E
Ash-Shaddādah 130 36.03 N 40.45 E
Ash-Shāghūr 132 31.50 N 35.39 E
Ash-Shā'ib ⨯2 142 29.50 N 30.56 E
Ash-Shajarah 132 32.39 N 35.56 E
Ash-Shallūfah 142 30.07 N 32.34 E
Ash-Shamāl □4 140 34.30 N 36.00 E
Ash-Shamālīyah □4 140 19.15 N 29.00 E
Ash-Shāmīyah 128 31.57 N 44.36 E
Ash-Shanāwīyah 142 29.08 N 31.08 E
Ash-Sharāh ◆1 132 30.20 N 35.30 E
Ash-Shāriqah 128 25.22 N 55.23 E
Ash-Sharmah 128 28.01 N 35.18 E
Ash-Sharqāt 128 35.27 N 43.16 E
Ash-Sharqīyah □4 142 30.48 N 31.48 E
Ash-Sharqīyah ◆1 128 27.00 N 49.00 E
Ash-Shatrah 128 31.25 N 46.10 E
Ash-Shawāshinah 142 29.22 N 30.36 E
Ash-Shawbak 132 30.32 N 35.34 E
Ash-Shawmarah 132 33.07 N 35.08 E
Ash-Shaykh Fadl 142 28.29 N 30.50 E
Ash-Shaykh 'Ibādah 142 27.48 N 30.52 E
Ash-Shaykh Sa'd 132 32.50 N 36.02 E
Ash-Shaykh Timay 142 27.53 N 30.51 E
Ash-Shiḥr 144 14.44 N 49.35 E
Ash-Shīn 142 31.01 N 30.53 E
Ash-Shināfīyah 128 31.35 N 44.39 E
Ash-Shīyāḥ 132 33.51 N 35.30 E
Ash-Shufayyah 128 23.50 N 39.08 E
Ash-Shuhadā' 142 30.36 N 30.54 E
Ash-Shumlul 128 26.31 N 47.19 E
Ash-Shuqayq 144 17.43 N 42.01 E
Ash-Shurayf 128 25.43 N 39.14 E
Ash-Shurayk 140 18.48 N 33.34 E
Ash-Shuwayfāt 132 33.49 N 35.31 E
Ash Slough ≃ 226 37.02 N 120.32 W
Ashta, India 122 16.57 N 74.24 E
Ashta, India 124 23.01 N 76.43 E
Ashtabula 214 41.51 N 80.47 W
Ashtabula □6 214 41.44 N 80.46 W
Ashtabula ≃ 214 41.55 N 80.47 W
Ashtabula, East Branch ≃ 214 41.48 N 80.37 W
Ashtabula, Lake ⊜1 198 47.11 N 97.58 W
Ashtabula, West Branch ≃ 214 41.48 N 80.37 W
Ashtead 260 51.19 N 0.18 W
Ashton, S. Afr. 158 33.50 S 20.05 E
Ashton, Eng., U.K. 262 53.13 N 2.45 W
Ashton, Id., U.S. 202 44.04 N 111.26 W
Ashton, Il., U.S. 190 41.51 N 89.13 W
Ashton, Ia., U.S. 198 43.18 N 95.47 W
Ashton, Md., U.S. 208 39.08 N 77.00 W
Ashton, Ne., U.S. 198 41.14 N 98.47 W
Ashton, R.I., U.S. 207 41.46 N 71.25 W
Ashton-in-Makerfield 262 53.29 N 2.39 W
Ashton-under-Lyne 262 53.29 N 2.06 W
Ashton upon Mersey 262 53.26 N 2.19 W
Ashuanipi Lake ⊜ 176 52.35 N 66.10 W
Ashuelot ≃ 207 42.46 N 72.29 W
Ashurst's Beacon ⨯2 262 53.34 N 2.45 W
Ashville, Al., U.S. 194 33.52 N 86.17 W
Ashville, N.Y., U.S. 214 42.06 N 79.23 W
Ashville, Oh., U.S. 218 39.42 N 82.57 W
Ashville, Pa., U.S. 214 40.34 N 78.33 W
Ashwater 42 50.44 N 4.16 W
Ashwaubenon 190 44.30 N 88.06 W
Ashworth Moor Reservoir ⊜1 262 53.38 N 2.16 W
Asi (Nahr al-'Āṣī) ≃ 130 36.02 N 35.58 E
Asia ⊥1 4 50.00 N 100.00 E
Asia ⊥1 12 50.00 N 100.00 E
Asia, Kepulauan II 108 1.03 N 131.18 E
Asiago 64 45.52 N 11.30 E
Asia Menor → Asia Minor □9 22 39.00 N 32.00 E
Asia Minor □9 22 39.00 N 32.00 E
Asid Gulf ᑕ 116 12.07 N 123.30 E
Asie → Asia ⊥1 12 50.00 N 100.00 E
Asie Mineure → Asia Minor □9 22 39.00 N 32.00 E
Asien → Asia ⊥1 12 50.00 N 100.00 E
āsika 120 19.36 N 84.39 E
Asikuma 150 5.35 N 1.00 W
Asilah 148 35.32 N 6.00 W
Asinara, Golfo dell' ᑕ 71 41.00 N 8.32 E
Asinara, Isola I 71 41.04 N 8.16 E
Asinaro ≃ 70 36.53 N 15.08 E
Asino 86 57.00 N 86.09 E
Asipoquobah Lake ⊜ 184 53.40 N 91.15 W
'Asīr ◆1 144 19.00 N 42.00 E
Ašitkovo 82 55.26 N 38.36 E
Aşkale 130 39.55 N 40.42 E
Askam in Furness 44 54.11 N 3.13 W
Askanija-Nova 78 46.27 N 33.52 E
Askanija-nova zapovednik ♦ 78 46.37 N 33.54 E
Askarovo 86 53.21 N 58.30 E
Askeaton 48 52.36 N 8.58 W
Asker 26 59.50 N 10.26 E
Askern 44 53.37 N 1.09 W
Askersund 40 58.53 N 14.54 E
Askham 158 26.59 S 20.47 E
Askim 26 59.35 N 11.10 E
Askino 86 56.05 N 56.34 E
Askira 146 10.39 N 12.55 E
Askival ʌ 46 56.59 N 6.17 W
Askiz 86 53.08 N 90.32 E
Askja ʌ1 24a 65.00 N 16.46 W
Askø I 41 54.54 N 11.30 E
Asköping 40 59.09 N 16.04 E
Askov 41 55.28 N 9.06 E
Askraal 158 34.09 S 20.52 E
Askrigg 44 54.19 N 2.04 W
Askvoll 26 61.21 N 5.04 E
Aslanapa 130 39.13 N 29.52 E
Aslan-Sara 84 39.02 N 48.16 E
Aslantaş Barajı ⊜1 130 37.20 N 36.15 E
Asleigh 284c 39.01 N 77.10 W
Åsljunga 41 56.19 N 13.22 E
Ašlyk 86 57.53 N 68.40 E
Ašlyk ≃ 86 57.50 N 69.12 E
Asmār 120 35.02 N 71.22 E
Asmara → Asmera 144 15.20 N 38.53 E
Asmera 144 15.20 N 38.53 E
Asmundtorp 41 55.53 N 12.56 E
Asnæs 41 55.49 N 11.31 E
Asnæs ≻1 41 55.40 N 11.00 E
Asnebumskit Hill ʌ2 207 42.18 N 71.54 W
Åsnen ⊜ 26 56.38 N 14.42 E
Asni 148 31.14 N 7.55 W
Asnières [-sur-Seine] 50 48.55 N 2.17 E
Asō, Nihon 94 35.59 N 140.29 E
Aso, Nihon 96 32.58 N 131.02 E
Aso ≃ 66 43.06 N 13.51 E
Asoc 152 1.26 N 11.18 E
Aso-kokuritsu-kōen ♦ 92 33.00 N 131.07 E
Asola 64 45.13 N 10.24 E
Asola ≃ 64 45.48 N 11.54 E
Asomante 240m 18.23 N 66.35 W
Ason 273a 6.34 N 3.31 E
Asosa 144 10.03 N 34.32 E
Aso-san ʌ 92 32.53 N 131.05 E
Asoteriba, Jabal ʌ 140 21.51 N 36.33 E
Asotin 202 46.20 N 117.02 W
Asouf, Oued V 148 25.51 N 1.33 E
Asowsches Meer → Azovskoje more ⚓2 78 46.00 N 36.00 E
Asp 34 38.21 N 0.48 W
Aspach 60 48.11 N 13.18 E
Aspach-le-Bas 58 47.46 N 7.09 E
Aspang Markt 61 47.33 N 16.06 E
Aspara ≃ 85 43.17 N 73.28 E
Aspatria 44 54.46 N 3.20 W
Aspe, Gave d' ≃ 32 43.12 N 0.36 W
Aspen 200 39.11 N 106.49 W
Aspen Butte ʌ 202 42.19 N 122.05 W
Aspendale 274b 38.02 S 145.07 E
Aspendos ⊥ 130 37.00 N 31.10 E
Aspen Hill 284c 39.04 N 77.04 W
Aspen Knolls 284c 39.05 N 77.05 W
Aspen Lake ⊜ 202 42.18 N 122.00 W
Asperg 56 48.54 N 9.07 E
Aspermont 196 33.08 N 100.13 W
Aspern ◆8 264b 48.13 N 16.29 E
Aspers 208 39.59 N 77.13 W
Asperup 41 55.30 N 9.52 E
Aspid, Mount ʌ 180 53.30 N 167.33 W
Aspindza 84 41.36 N 43.15 E
Aspinwall → Colón, Pan. 236 9.22 N 79.54 W
Aspinwall, Pa., U.S. 279b 40.29 N 79.54 W
Aspiring, Mount ʌ 172 44.23 S 168.44 E
Aspö 40 59.29 N 17.02 E
Aspres-sur-Buëch 62 44.31 N 5.45 E
Aspromonte ⨯ 68 38.10 N 15.55 E
Asprópirgos 267c 38.04 N 23.35 E
Aspull 262 53.34 N 2.35 W
Aspy Bay ᑕ 186 46.55 N 60.25 W
Asquins 50 47.29 N 3.45 E
Asquith, Austl. 274a 33.41 S 151.06 E
Asquith, Sk., Can. 184 52.08 N 107.13 W
Asralt chajrchan ʌ 88 48.29 N 107.24 E
Asrāni 123 29.31 N 72.07 E
Assa, Magreb 148 28.34 N 9.27 W
Assa, S.S.S.R. 85 43.02 N 71.10 E
Assa ≃, S.S.S.R. 84 43.13 N 45.25 E
Assa ≃, S.S.S.R. 85 43.55 N 70.25 E
As-Sa'ata 140 13.37 N 29.59 E
Assab → Aseb 144 13.00 N 42.45 E
Assabet ≃ 283 42.28 N 71.21 W
As-Sabkhah 130 35.48 N 39.15 E
Aṣ-Ṣadārah 144 14.30 N 48.04 E
As-Sa'dīyah 128 34.11 N 45.07 E
Aṣ-Ṣaff 140 29.34 N 31.17 E
As-Saffānīyah 128 27.58 N 48.47 E
Aṣ-Ṣāfī 132 31.02 N 35.28 E
As-Safīrah 130 36.04 N 37.22 E
Aṣ-Ṣāfiyah 140 15.31 N 30.07 E
Assago 266b 45.24 N 9.08 E
Assaí 255 23.22 S 50.49 W
Aṣ-Ṣa'īd □9 140 26.00 N 32.00 E
Assaikwatamo ≃ 184 56.52 N 95.50 W
Assal, Lac ⊜ 144 11.41 N 42.25 E
'Assāl al-Ward 132 33.52 N 36.24 E
Aṣ-Ṣāliḥīyah 142 30.47 N 31.59 E
As-Salīmah 144 14.02 N 45.46 E
As-Sallūm 140 31.34 N 25.09 E
As-Salmān 128 30.30 N 44.32 E
As-Salṭ 132 32.03 N 35.44 E
Assam □3 120 26.00 N 93.00 E
As-Samāwah 128 31.18 N 45.17 E
As-Samū' 132 31.24 N 35.04 E
Assam Valley V 124 26.30 N 90.30 E
'Assān 130 36.05 N 37.14 E
Aṣ-Ṣanāfīn Al-Qiblīyah 142 30.27 N 31.18 E
Aṣ-Ṣanamayn 132 33.05 N 36.10 E
As-Santah 142 30.45 N 31.08 E
Assaq, Oued V 148 25.41 N 14.40 W
As-Saqlabiyah 130 35.22 N 36.23 E
Aṣ-Ṣarafand 132 33.27 N 35.18 E
Assaré 250 6.52 S 39.52 W
As-Sarīḥ 132 32.30 N 35.54 E
As-Sarīrīyah 142 28.20 N 30.45 E
Assateague Island I 208 38.05 N 75.10 W
Assateague Island National Seashore ♦ 208 38.00 N 75.15 W
Assawoman Bay ᑕ 208 38.25 N 75.05 W
Assawoman Canal ≛ 208 38.31 N 75.04 W
Assawompset Pond ⊜ 207 41.50 N 70.55 W
Asse 50 50.55 N 4.12 E
Asse ≃ 62 43.53 N 5.53 E
Assean Lake ⊜ 184 56.13 N 96.30 W
Assebroek 50 51.12 N 3.16 E
Assekaifaf 148 27.08 N 8.50 E
Assel 52 53.41 N 9.25 E
Asseln ◆8 263 51.32 N 7.35 E
Assembleia Nacional, Palacio da ⊎ 266c 38.43 N 9.09 W
Assemini 71 39.17 N 9.00 E
Assen 52 52.59 N 6.34 E
Assendelft 52 52.27 N 4.45 E
Assenede 50 51.14 N 3.45 E
Assens 41 55.16 N 9.55 E
Asserbo 41 56.01 N 12.01 E
Assergi 66 42.25 N 13.30 E
Asseria ⊥ 36 44.02 N 15.39 E
As-Sīb 128 23.41 N 58.11 E
As-Sidr 128 23.27 N 39.45 E
As-Sijn 132 32.47 N 36.28 E
As-Simākīyah 132 31.18 N 35.48 E
As-Sinbillāwayn 142 30.53 N 31.27 E
Assini ⊥ 38 37.36 N 22.48 E
Assiniboia 184 49.38 N 105.59 W
Assiniboine ≃ 184 49.53 N 97.08 W
Assiniboine, Mount ʌ 182 50.52 N 115.39 W
Assiniboine Indian Reserve ◆4 184 50.21 N 103.28 W
Assinika ≃ 184 52.37 N 96.10 W
Assinippi 283 42.09 N 70.51 W
Assis 255 22.40 S 50.25 W
Assiscunk Creek ≃ 208 40.05 N 74.51 W
Assisi 66 43.04 N 12.37 E
Asslar 56 50.35 N 8.28 E
Assling 60 48.00 N 12.00 E
Asso 62 45.52 N 9.16 E
Assodé ◆4 150 18.26 N 8.28 E
Assomada 150a 15.06 N 23.41 W
Assonet 207 41.47 N 71.04 W
Assoro 70 37.37 N 14.25 E
As-Subū' ⊥ 140 22.45 N 32.34 E
As-Sūdān → Sudan □1 140 15.00 N 30.00 E
As-Sudd ◆1 140 8.00 N 31.00 E
As-Sufāl 144 14.06 N 48.42 E
As-Sufayyah 140 15.30 N 34.42 E
As-Sūfīyah 142 30.55 N 31.46 E
As-Sukhnah, Sūriy. 130 34.52 N 38.52 E
As-Sukhnah, Urd. 132 32.08 N 36.04 E
As-Sulaymānīyah, Ar. Su. 128 24.09 N 47.19 E
As-Sulaymānīyah, 'Irāq 128 35.33 N 45.26 E
As-Sulaymānīyah □4 128 35.30 N 45.25 E
As-Sulaymī 128 26.17 N 41.21 E
As-Sulayyil 144 20.27 N 45.34 E
As-Sulṭān 146 31.07 N 17.10 E
As-Sumayh 140 9.49 N 27.39 E
As-Summān ◆1 128 25.00 N 47.00 E
As-Sumūmalīyāt 132 32.26 N 36.24 E
Assumption, Il., U.S. 219 39.31 N 89.02 W
Assumption, Oh., U.S. 216 41.40 N 83.54 W
Assumption Island I 138 9.45 S 46.30 E
Assunpink Creek ≃ 285 40.13 N 74.46 W
As-Su'ūdīyah 142 29.53 N 31.14 E
As-Suwār 130 35.30 N 40.39 E
As-Suwaydā' 132 32.42 N 36.34 E
As-Suwaydā' □8 132 32.45 N 36.45 E
As-Suways (Suez) 142 29.58 N 32.33 E
As-Suways □4 142 30.12 N 32.30 E
Assynt, Loch ⊜ 46 58.11 N 5.04 W
Asta, Cima d' ʌ 64 46.10 N 11.36 E
Astachovo 82 47.52 N 39.37 E
Astaffort 32 44.04 N 0.40 E
Astakós 38 38.32 N 21.05 E
Āstāneh, Īrān 128 37.17 N 49.59 E
Āstāneh, Īrān 128 33.53 N 49.22 E
Āstārā, Īrān 128 38.26 N 48.52 E
Astara, S.S.S.R. 84 38.28 N 48.52 E
Aštarak 84 40.18 N 44.22 E
Astaškovo 82 55.32 N 38.38 E
Astatula 220 28.43 N 81.44 W
Asten, Ned. 52 51.24 N 5.45 E
Asten, Öst. 61 48.13 N 14.25 E
Asti 62 44.54 N 8.12 E
Asti □4 62 44.55 N 8.10 E
Astica 252 30.56 S 67.23 W
Astico ≃ 64 45.37 N 11.37 E
Astillero 34 43.24 N 3.49 W
Astipalaia 38 36.30 N 26.20 E
Astipálaia I 38 36.35 N 26.25 E
Astley Bridge 262 53.36 N 2.26 W
Astley Green 262 53.29 N 2.27 W
Astley Hall ♦ 262 53.39 N 2.39 W
Astola Island I 120 25.07 N 63.51 E
Astolfo Dutra 256 21.19 S 42.52 W
Aston, Eng., U.K. 262 53.18 N 2.40 W
Aston, Pa., U.S. 285 39.52 N 75.26 W
Aston Clinton 260 51.48 N 0.44 W
Aston-on-Trent 42 52.52 N 1.23 W
Astor 123 35.22 N 74.51 E
Astor ≃ 123 35.34 N 74.41 E
Astorga, Bra. 255 23.13 S 51.40 W
Astorga, Esp. 34 42.27 N 6.03 W
Astorga, Pil. 116 6.54 N 125.27 E
Astoria, Il., U.S. 219 40.13 N 90.21 W
Astoria, Or., U.S. 224 46.11 N 123.49 W
Astoria ◆8 276 40.46 N 73.55 W
Astoria Bridge ◆5 224 46.13 N 123.52 W
Astoria Column ⊥ 224 46.11 N 123.50 W
Åstorp 41 56.08 N 12.57 E
Astove Island I 138 10.06 S 47.45 E
Astra 254 45.44 S 67.30 W
Astrachan' 80 46.21 N 48.03 E
Astrachanka 86 51.33 N 69.47 E
Astrachanskij zapovednik ◆4 80 46.00 N 48.32 E
Astrakhan → Astrachan' 80 46.21 N 48.03 E
Astrodome ♦ 222 29.41 N 95.25 W
Astrolabe, Cape ≻ 175e 8.20 S 160.34 E
Astrolabe Bay ᑕ 164 5.20 S 145.50 E
Astrolabe Reefs ◆2 175f 19.48 S 165.37 E
Astudillo 34 42.12 N 4.18 W
Astura, Torre ⊥ 66 41.24 N 12.46 E
Asturias 116 10.34 N 123.43 E
Asturias □4 34 43.20 N 6.00 W
Asturias □9 34 43.20 N 6.00 W
Astwood Bank 42 52.15 N 1.56 W
Asubulak 86 49.31 N 83.03 E
Asuisui, Cape ≻ 175a 13.47 S 172.29 W
Asuka 96 34.28 N 135.50 E
Asuka ⊎3 9 71.32 S 24.08 E
Asuke 94 35.08 N 137.19 E
Asunción 252 25.16 S 57.40 W
Asunción, Bahía ᑕ 232 27.06 N 114.11 W
Asunción, Cerro de la ʌ 232 24.15 N 99.56 W
Asuncion Island I 108 19.40 N 145.24 E
Asunción Mita 236 14.20 N 89.43 W
Asunción Nochixtlán 234 17.28 N 97.14 W
Åsunden ⊜, Sve. 26 57.58 N 15.50 E
Åsunden ⊜, Sve. 26 57.44 N 13.22 E
Asunga, Wādī V 146 13.21 N 22.17 E
Asuni 71 39.52 N 8.56 E
'Āṣūr, Tall ʌ 132 31.59 N 35.17 E
Asuwa 94 36.01 N 136.16 E
Asuwa ≃ 94 36.04 N 136.11 E
Aswad, Ar-Ra's al- ≻ 144 21.22 N 39.08 E
Aswān 140 24.05 N 32.53 E
Aswān High Dam → 'Ālī, As-Sadd al- ◆6 140 23.58 N 32.52 E
Aswatthaberia 272b 22.26 N 88.32 E
Asy ≃ 85 43.31 N 78.20 E
Asyūṭ 142 27.11 N 31.11 E
Asyūṭ □4 142 27.20 N 30.50 E
Asyūṭī, Wādī al- V 142 27.11 N 31.16 E
Aszód 30 47.39 N 19.31 E
'Ata I, Tonga 14 22.20 S 176.12 W
Ata I, Tonga 174w 21.03 S 175.00 W
Atabaj 85 43.30 N 68.20 E
Atabapo ≃ 246 4.03 N 67.42 W
Atabasca → Athabasca ≃ 176 58.40 N 110.50 W
Atabasca, Lago → Athabasca, Lake ⊜ 176 59.07 N 110.00 W
Atabey 130 37.57 N 30.39 E
Atacama □4 252 27.30 S 70.00 W
Atacama, Desierto de ◆2 18 24.30 S 69.15 W
Atacama, Puna de ⨯1 252 25.00 S 68.00 W
Atacama, Salar de ≚ 252 23.30 S 68.15 W
Ataco 246 3.35 N 75.23 W
Atacora, Chaîne de l' ⨯ 150 10.45 N 1.30 E
Atacuari ≃ 246 3.47 S 70.44 W
Atafu I[1] 14 8.33 S 172.30 W
Atagaj 88 55.06 N 99.23 E
Atago-yama ʌ, Nihon 94 35.07 N 139.59 E
Atago-yama ʌ, Nihon 96 35.03 N 135.37 E
Ātāi ≃1 126 22.51 N 89.33 E
'Aṭā'itah, Jabal al- ʌ 132 30.40 N 35.39 E
Atakakup Indian Reserve ◆4 184 53.24 N 106.55 W
Atakano-seki ⊥ 94 36.24 N 136.25 E
Ataki 78 48.25 N 27.47 E
Atakora □5 150 10.00 N 1.35 E
Atakora, Réserve d' ◆4 150 11.30 N 2.10 E
Atakpamé 150 7.32 N 1.08 E
Atalaia, Bra. 250 9.31 S 36.02 W
Atalaia, Port. 266c 38.42 N 8.55 W
Atalándi 38 38.39 N 23.00 E
Atalanka 88 54.50 N 103.05 E
Atalaya, Arg. 258 35.02 S 57.32 W
Atalaya, Pan. 236 8.03 N 80.56 W
Atalaya, Perú 248 10.44 S 73.45 W
Atalaya, Cerro ʌ, Chile 254 52.45 S 72.42 W
Atalaya, Cerro ʌ, Perú 248 12.38 S 71.56 W
Atalaya, Punta ≻ 258 35.01 S 57.31 W
Atamanovka 88 51.56 N 113.37 E
Atamanovo 86 56.24 N 93.36 E
Atambua 112 9.07 S 124.54 E
Atami 94 35.05 N 139.04 E
Atapupu 112 9.00 S 124.51 E
'Atāq 144 14.33 N 46.48 E
'Atāqah, Jabal ʌ 142 29.58 N 32.20 E
Atār 150 20.31 N 13.03 W
Ataram, 'Erg n- ◆2 148 23.46 N 1.44 E
Atarés, Castillo de ⊥ 286b 23.08 N 82.21 W
Atari 123 31.36 N 74.35 E
Atary 80 49.22 N 46.16 E
Atascadero 226 35.29 N 120.40 W
Atascosa ≃ 196 28.26 N 98.12 W
At'aševo 80 54.36 N 46.06 E
Atasu 86 48.42 N 71.38 E
Atas uul ʌ 102 43.18 N 96.36 E
Atata I 174w 21.03 S 175.15 W
Atatürk Tower ⊥ 267b 41.00 N 28.59 E
Ataur 272a 28.43 N 77.24 E
Atauro, Pulau I 112 8.13 S 125.35 E
Atbara ('Atbarah) ≃ 140 17.40 N 33.56 E
'Atbarah 140 17.42 N 33.59 E
'Atbarah (Atbara) ≃ 140 17.40 N 33.56 E
Atbasar 86 51.48 N 68.20 E
At-Baši 85 41.10 N 75.48 E
Atbaši ≃ 85 41.24 N 75.38 E
Atbaši, chrebet ⨯ 85 40.55 N 75.40 E
Atchafalaya ≃ 194 29.53 N 91.28 W
Atchafalaya Bay ᑕ 194 29.25 N 91.20 W
Atchison 198 39.33 N 95.07 W
Atco 208 39.46 N 74.53 W
Atebubu 150 7.45 N 0.59 W
Ateca 34 41.20 N 1.47 W
Atechu ≃ 255 12.05 S 53.46 W
Ateleta 66 41.51 N 14.12 E
Ateli 124 28.06 N 76.17 E
Atella 68 40.52 N 15.39 E
Atemajac de Brizuela 234 20.11 N 103.42 W
Atemajac del Valle 234 20.45 N 103.22 W
Atemar 80 54.11 N 45.24 E
Atemble 164 5.05 S 144.45 E
Atena Lucana 68 40.27 N 15.33 E
Atenango del Río 234 18.05 N 99.06 W
Atenas, C.R. 236 9.58 N 84.23 W
Atenas → Athínai, Ellás 38 37.58 N 23.43 E
Atencingo 234 18.30 N 98.36 W
Atenco □7 286a 19.34 N 99.00 W
Atengo ≃ 234 21.50 N 104.43 W
Atenguillo 234 20.25 N 104.31 W
Atenguillo ≃ 234 20.55 N 104.38 W
Atenquique 234 19.31 N 103.30 W
Atepcevo 82 55.20 N 36.46 E
Aterno ≃ 66 42.11 N 13.51 E
Aterrado, Ribeirão do ≃ 256 22.09 S 45.03 W
Atessa 66 42.04 N 14.27 E
Atfīh 142 29.24 N 31.15 E
Atfīḥ, Wādī al- V 142 29.23 N 31.16 E
Atgharia 126 24.06 N 89.14 E
Atglen 208 39.57 N 75.58 W
Ath 50 50.38 N 3.47 E
Athabasca 182 54.43 N 113.17 W
Athabasca ≃ 176 58.40 N 110.50 W
Athabasca, Lake ⊜ 176 59.07 N 110.00 W
Athalmer 182 50.32 N 116.02 W
Athapapuskow Lake ⊜ 184 54.33 N 101.40 W
Athārabānki ≃1 126 22.49 N 89.39 E
Athārban Hazāri 123 31.11 N 72.06 E
Athboy 48 53.37 N 6.55 W
Athea 48 52.28 N 9.17 W
Athen → Athínai 38 37.58 N 23.43 E
Athena 202 45.48 N 118.29 W
Athènes → Athínai 38 37.58 N 23.43 E
Athenry 48 53.18 N 8.45 W
Athens, On., Can. 212 44.38 N 75.57 W
Athens → Athínai, Ellás 38 37.58 N 23.43 E
Athens, Al., U.S. 194 34.48 N 86.58 W
Athens, Ga., U.S. 192 33.57 N 83.22 W
Athens, Il., U.S. 219 39.57 N 89.43 W
Athens, La., U.S. 194 32.39 N 93.01 W
Athens, Mi., U.S. 216 42.05 N 85.14 W
Athens, N.Y., U.S. 210 42.15 N 73.48 W
Athens, Oh., U.S. 188 39.19 N 82.06 W
Athens, Pa., U.S. 210 41.57 N 76.31 W
Athens, Tn., U.S. 192 35.26 N 84.35 W
Athens, Tx., U.S. 222 32.12 N 95.51 W
Athens, W.V., U.S. 192 37.25 N 81.00 W
Athens, Wi., U.S. 190 45.01 N 90.04 W
Athenstedt 54 51.56 N 10.55 E
Athens University ⊎2 267c 37.59 N 23.44 E
Atherley 212 44.36 N 79.22 W
Atherstone 42 52.35 N 1.31 W
Atherton, Austl. 166 17.16 S 145.29 E
Atherton, Eng., U.K. 262 53.31 N 2.31 W
Atherton, Ca., U.S. 226 37.27 N 122.11 W
Athi ≃ 154 2.59 S 38.31 E
Athiémé 150 6.35 N 1.40 E
Athies-sous-Laon 50 49.34 N 3.41 E
Athínai (Athens) 38 37.58 N 23.43 E
Athínai (Athens), Ellás 267c 37.58 N 23.43 E

Symbols in the index entries represent the broad categories identified in the key at the right. Symbols with superior numbers (⨯1) identify subcategories (see complete key on page *I · 1*).

Symbole im Register stellen die rechts im Schlüssel erklärten Kategorien dar. Symbole mit hochgestellten Ziffern (⨯1) bezeichnen Unterabteilungen einer Kategorie (vgl. vollständiger Schlüssel auf Seite *I · 1*).

Los símbolos incluidos en el texto del índice representan las grandes categorías identificadas con la clave a la derecha. Los símbolos con numeros en su parte superior (⨯1) identifican las subcategorías (véase la clave completa en la página *I · 1*).

Les symboles de l'index représentent les catégories indiquées dans la légende à droite. Les symboles suivis d'un indice (⨯1) représentent des sous-catégories (voir légende complète à la page *I · 1*).

Os símbolos incluídos no texto do índice representam as grandes categorias identificadas com a chave à direita. Os símbolos com números em sua parte superior (⨯1) identificam as subcategorias (veja-se a chave completa à página *I · 1*).

ʌ Mountain	Berg	Montaña	Montagne	Montanha
⨯ Mountains	Gebirge	Montañas	Montagnes	Montanhas
)(Pass	Paß	Paso	Col	Passo
V Valley, Canyon	Tal, Cañon	Valle, Cañón	Vallée, Canyon	Vale, Canhão
≚ Plain	Ebene	Llano	Plaine	Planície
≻ Cape	Kap	Cabo	Cap	Cabo
I Island	Insel	Isla	Île	Ilha
II Islands	Inseln	Islas	Îles	Ilhas
⊥ Other Topographic Features	Andere Topographische Objekte	Otros Elementos Topográficos	Autres données topographiques	Outros acidentes topográficos

ESPAÑOL · FRANÇAIS · PORTUGUÊS

Nombre / Nom / Nome	Página / Page	Lat.°′	Long.°′ W = Oeste / Ouest
Äthiopien → Ethiopia □1	144	9.00 N	39.00 E
Athi River	154	1.27 S	36.59 E
Athis-Mons	261	48.43 N	2.24 E
Athlat al-Bāshā ∧2	142	27.31 N	32.20 E
Athleague	48	53.34 N	8.15 W
Athlone	48	53.25 N	7.56 W
Athni	122	16.44 N	75.04 E
Athok	110	17.12 N	95.05 E
Athol, N.Z.	172	45.31 S	168.35 E
Athol, Ma., U.S.	207	42.35 N	72.13 W
Athol Bay ⊂	212	43.53 N	77.15 W
Athol Island I	240b	25.05 N	77.16 W
Atholl, Forest of ◆3	46	56.50 N	4.00 W
Athol Springs	210	42.46 N	78.52 W
Áthos ∧	38	40.09 N	24.19 E
Ath-Tha'lah	132	32.42 N	36.26 E
Ath-Thamad	140	29.41 N	34.18 E
Ath-Thanīyah	132	31.10 N	35.43 E
Athus	56	49.34 N	5.50 E
Athy	48	53.00 N	7.00 W
Ati	146	13.13 N	18.20 E
Atiak	154	3.15 N	32.07 E
Atibaia	256	23.07 S	46.33 W
Atibaia ≃	256	22.42 S	47.17 W
Atibainha, Reservatório ⊜1	256	23.10 S	46.20 W
Atico	248	16.14 S	73.39 W
Aticonipi, Lac ⊜	186	51.52 N	59.22 W
Atienza	34	41.12 N	2.52 W
Atigun Pass)(	180	68.08 N	149.29 W
Atik Lake ⊜	184	55.16 N	96.00 W
Atikokan	190	48.45 N	91.37 W
Atikonak Lake ⊜	176	52.40 N	64.30 W
Atil	200	30.50 N	111.35 W
Atimonan	116	14.00 N	121.55 E
Atina	66	41.37 N	13.48 E
Atiquizaya	236	13.58 N	89.46 W
Atirāmpattinam	122	10.21 N	79.24 E
Atitlán, Lago de ⊜	236	14.42 N	91.12 W
Atitlán, Volcán ∧1	236	14.35 N	91.11 W
Atiu I	14	20.02 S	158.07 W
Atka, S.S.S.R.	74	60.50 N	151.48 E
Atka, Ak., U.S.	180	52.12 N	174.12 W
Atka Island I	180	52.15 N	174.30 W
Atkaracalar	130	40.50 N	33.04 E
Atkarsk	80	51.52 N	45.00 E
Atkins	194	35.14 N	92.56 W
Atkinson, Il., U.S.	190	41.25 N	90.00 W
Atkinson, Ne., U.S.	198	42.31 N	98.58 W
Atkinson, N.H., U.S.	207	42.50 N	71.08 W
Atkinson, N.C., U.S.	192	34.31 N	78.10 W
Atkinson Island I	222	29.40 N	94.58 W
Atkinson Lake ⊜	184	55.59 N	94.48 W
Atkri	164	1.44 S	130.04 E
Atlacomulco de Fabela	234	19.48 N	99.53 W
Atlanta, Ga., U.S.	192	33.44 N	84.23 W
Atlanta, Il., U.S.	194	40.15 N	89.14 W
Atlanta, Mi., U.S.	190	45.00 N	84.08 W
Atlanta, Mo., U.S.	194	39.53 N	92.28 W
Atlanta, N.Y., U.S.	210	42.33 N	77.28 W
Atlanta, Oh., U.S.	218	39.34 N	83.11 W
Atlanta, Tx., U.S.	194	33.06 N	94.09 W
Atlantic, Ia., U.S.	198	41.24 N	95.00 W
Atlantic, N.C., U.S.	192	34.53 N	76.20 W
Atlantic, Pa., U.S.	214	41.30 N	80.21 W
Atlantic, Va., U.S.	208	37.54 N	75.30 W
Atlantic □6	208	39.27 N	74.44 W
Atlantic Beach, Fl., U.S.	192	30.20 N	81.23 W
Atlantic Beach, N.Y., U.S.	276	40.35 N	73.44 W
Atlantic City	208	39.21 N	74.25 W
Atlantic Highlands	208	40.24 N	74.02 W
Atlantic-Indian Basin ✦1	6	60.00 S	15.00 E
Atlantic-Indian Ridge ✦3	4	53.00 S	15.00 E
Atlántico □5	246	10.45 N	75.00 W
Atlántico, Océano → Atlantic Ocean ⚲1	8	5.00 S	25.00 W
Atlantic Ocean ⚲1	4	5.00 S	25.00 W
Atlantic Ocean ⚲1	8	5.00 S	25.00 W
Atlantic Peak ∧	200	42.37 N	109.00 W
Atlántida	252	34.46 S	55.45 W
Atlántida □5	236	15.40 N	87.00 W
Atlantique	276	40.39 N	73.10 W
Atlantique □5	150	6.35 N	2.15 E
Atlantique, Océan → Atlantic Ocean ⚲1	8	5.00 S	25.00 W
Atlantischer Ozean → Atlantic Ocean ⚲1	8	5.00 S	25.00 W
Atlas, Mi., U.S.	216	42.56 N	83.32 W
Atlas, Pa., U.S.	208	40.48 N	76.26 W
Atlasburg	214	40.20 N	80.23 W
Atlas Mountains ⋀	148	33.00 N	2.00 W
Atlasova, ostrov I	74	50.53 N	155.27 E
Atlasovo	92a	46.01 N	142.09 E
Atlas Saharien ⋀	148	33.25 N	1.20 E
Atlas Tellien ⋀	148	36.00 N	3.00 E
Atlin	180	59.35 N	133.42 W
Atlin Lake ⊜	180	59.20 N	133.45 W
'Atlit	132	32.41 N	34.56 E
Atlixco	234	18.54 N	98.26 W
Ātmakūr	122	15.53 N	78.35 E
Atmanov Ugol	80	53.07 N	41.23 E
Atmis	80	53.28 N	43.57 E
Atmore	194	31.01 N	87.29 W
Ätna → Etna, Monte ∧1	70	37.46 N	15.00 E
Atna ≃	26	61.44 N	10.49 E
Atna Peak ∧	182	53.57 N	128.03 W
Atnarko ≃	182	52.22 N	126.04 W
Atnis	86	58.48 N	69.38 E
Atnosen	26	61.44 N	10.49 E
Atō	96	34.24 N	131.43 E
Atocha	248	20.56 S	66.14 W
Atocha, Estación de ◆5	266a	40.24 N	3.41 W
Atocongo	286d	12.08 S	76.56 W
Atocongo ⊥	286d	12.12 S	76.55 W
Atoka	196	34.23 N	96.07 W
Atotonilco	234	23.35 N	104.20 W
Atotonilco, Cerro ∧	196	26.08 N	104.43 W
Atotonilco, Lago de ⊜	234	20.22 N	103.39 W
Atotonilco de los Martínez	232	24.15 N	102.45 W
Atotonilco de Tula	234	20.00 N	99.13 W
Atotonilco el Alto	234	20.33 N	102.31 W
Atoui, Khaṭṭ ∨	150	20.04 N	15.59 W
Atoyac	234	20.01 N	103.32 W
Atoyac ≃, Méx.	234	17.05 N	100.29 W
Atoyac ≃, Méx.	234	18.10 N	98.31 W
Atoyac ≃, Méx.	234	16.30 N	97.31 W
Atoyac de Alvarez	234	17.12 N	100.26 W
Atpur	272b	22.50 N	88.23 E
Atrå	26	59.59 N	8.45 E
'Aṭrah, Jabal ∧	132	29.40 N	35.34 E
Atrai ≃	124	24.29 N	89.03 E
Atrak (Atrek) ≃	128	37.28 N	53.57 E
Ätran ≃	26	56.53 N	12.30 E
Atrato ≃	246	8.17 N	76.58 W
Atrauli	124	28.02 N	78.17 E
Atrek (Atrak) ≃	128	37.28 N	53.57 E
Atri	66	42.35 N	13.58 E
Atripalda	68	40.55 N	14.50 E
Atrisco	200	34.59 N	106.41 W
Atrop ◆8	263	51.24 N	6.43 E
Atsion Lake ⊜	285	39.44 N	74.44 W
Atsugi	94	35.27 N	139.22 E
Atsugi-hikōjō ■	94	35.28 N	139.27 E
Atsumi, Nihon	92	38.37 N	139.35 E
Atsumi, Nihon	94	34.37 N	137.07 E
Atsumi-hantō ≻1	94	34.39 N	137.15 E
Atta	272a	28.34 N	77.20 E
At-Tabbīn	142	29.47 N	31.18 E
Aṭ-Ṭafīlah	132	30.50 N	35.36 E
Aṭ-Ṭafīlah □8	132	30.45 N	35.45 E
At-Tahrīr □4	142	30.40 N	30.15 E
Aṭ-Ṭā'if	144	21.16 N	40.24 E
Attainville	261	49.03 N	2.21 E
At-Tāj	146	24.13 N	23.18 E
Aṭ-Ṭalibīyah	273c	30.00 N	31.11 E
At-Tall	132	33.36 N	36.18 E
Attalla	194	34.01 N	86.05 W
At-Tall al-Kabīr	142	30.34 N	31.47 E
At-Ta'mīm □4	128	35.25 N	44.20 E
At-Tamīmī	146	32.20 N	23.04 E
Attapu	110	14.48 N	106.50 E
Attar, Oued el ∨	148	33.27 N	5.26 E
At-Taṭālīyah	142	27.20 N	30.50 E
Attáviros ∧	38	36.12 N	27.52 E
Attawapiskat	176	52.55 N	82.26 W
Attawapiskat ≃	176	52.57 N	82.18 W
Attawapiskat Lake ⊜	176	52.18 N	87.54 W
Attawaugan	207	41.52 N	71.52 W
Aṭ-Ṭawd	142	30.47 N	30.37 E
Aṭ-Ṭawīl ⋀	128	29.20 N	39.35 E
At-Tayrīyah	142	30.39 N	30.46 E
At-Taysīyah ≚	128	28.00 N	44.00 E
Aṭ-Ṭayyibah, Miṣr	142	28.16 N	30.39 E
Aṭ-Ṭayyibah, Sūrīy.	132	32.33 N	36.14 E
Aṭ-Ṭayyibah, Sūrīy.	132	32.48 N	36.46 E
Aṭ-Ṭayyibah, Urd.	132	32.33 N	35.43 E
Attel ≃	64	48.01 N	12.11 E
Attendorn	56	51.07 N	7.54 E
Attenhausen	58	47.59 N	10.20 E
Attenkirchen	60	48.30 N	11.46 E
Atterbury	219	40.04 N	89.55 W
Attersee	64	47.55 N	13.33 E
Attersee ⊜	64	47.52 N	13.33 E
Attert ≃	56	49.52 N	6.05 E
Attica, In., U.S.	216	40.17 N	87.14 W
Attica, Ks., U.S.	198	37.14 N	98.13 W
Attica, N.Y., U.S.	210	42.51 N	78.16 W
Attica, Oh., U.S.	214	41.03 N	82.53 W
Attichy	50	49.25 N	3.03 E
Attigliano	66	42.31 N	12.17 E
Attigny	56	49.29 N	4.35 E
Attikí □5	267c	38.00 N	23.40 E
Attikí □9	38	38.00 N	23.30 E
'Attīl	132	32.22 N	35.04 E
Attimis	64	46.11 N	13.16 E
At-Tīnah	142	31.03 N	32.18 E
Attingal	122	8.41 N	76.50 E
Attir	140	6.04 N	30.50 E
Attleboro	207	41.56 N	71.17 W
Attleborough	42	52.31 N	1.01 E
Attnang	60	48.01 N	13.43 E
Attock	123	33.54 N	72.15 E
Attoyac ≃	194	31.29 N	94.18 W
Attu	181a	52.56 N	173.14 E
At-Tubah	144	12.40 N	43.30 E
Attu Island I	181a	52.55 N	173.00 E
Aṭ-Ṭunayb	132	31.48 N	35.57 E
Āttūr, India	122	11.36 N	78.37 E
Aṭ-Ṭūr, Miṣr	140	28.14 N	33.37 E
Aṭ-Ṭuwayshah	140	12.21 N	26.32 E
Aṭ-Ṭuwayyah	128	27.36 N	41.13 E
Attymon	48	53.19 N	8.35 W
Atucatiquini ≃	248	7.44 S	67.57 W
Atucha	258	33.58 S	59.18 W
Atuel ≃	252	36.17 S	66.50 W
Atuel, Bañados del ≍	252	36.30 S	66.55 W
Atuntaqui	246	0.20 N	78.13 W
Atuona	174x	9.48 S	139.02 W
At'urjevo	80	54.21 N	43.19 E
Atushi	85	39.43 N	76.08 E
Åtvidaberg	26	58.12 N	16.00 E
Atwater, Sk., Can.	184	50.47 N	102.10 W
Atwater, Ca., U.S.	226	37.20 N	120.36 W
Atwater, Il., U.S.	219	39.20 N	89.44 W
Atwater, Mn., U.S.	198	45.08 N	94.46 W
Atwater, Oh., U.S.	214	41.01 N	81.10 W
Atwood, On., Can.	212	43.40 N	81.01 W
Atwood, Ca., U.S.	280	33.52 N	117.50 W
Atwood, Il., U.S.	194	39.48 N	88.28 W
Atwood, In., U.S.	216	41.15 N	85.58 W
Atwood, Ks., U.S.	198	39.48 N	101.02 W
Atwood, Tn., U.S.	194	35.58 N	88.40 W
Atwood Lake ⊜1	214	40.33 N	81.13 W
Atzacán	234	18.54 N	97.05 W
Atzalpur	272a	28.43 N	77.21 E
Atzendorf	54	51.55 N	11.35 E
Atzgersdorf ◆8	264b	48.09 N	16.18 E
Au	58	47.19 N	9.59 E
Auagrām	126	23.31 N	87.41 E
Auaiá-Miçu ≃	250	10.51 S	53.08 W
Aua Island I	164	1.27 S	143.04 E
Aual Edo	144	4.14 N	40.37 E
Auari ≃	246	3.33 N	63.48 W
Auati Paraná ≃1	246	1.51 S	65.37 W
Auau Channel ⊔	229a	20.51 N	156.45 W
Aub	56	49.33 N	10.04 E
Aubá	112	9.02 S	125.22 E
Aubagne	62	43.17 N	5.34 E
Aubange	56	49.35 N	5.48 E
Aube □5	50	48.15 N	4.05 E
Aube ≃	50	48.34 N	3.43 E
Aubenas	62	44.37 N	4.23 E
Aubenton	50	49.50 N	4.12 E
Aubepierre	261	48.38 N	2.53 E
Aubergenville	261	48.58 N	1.51 E
Auberive	58	47.47 N	5.03 E
Auberry	226	37.04 N	119.29 W
Aubervilliers	50	48.55 N	2.23 E
Aubetin ≃	50	48.49 N	3.01 E
Aubette ≃	261	49.00 N	1.54 E
Aubigny-en-Artois	50	50.21 N	2.35 E
Aubigny-sur-Nère	50	47.29 N	2.26 E
Aubin	32	44.32 N	2.14 E
Aubinadong ≃	190	46.51 N	83.22 W
Aubonne	58	46.28 N	6.24 E
Auboué	56	49.13 N	5.59 E
Aubrac ⋀	32	44.40 N	3.00 E
Aubrey Cliffs ≗4	200	35.45 N	113.00 W
Aubrey Lake ⊜1	190	46.54 N	83.11 W
Aubrives	56	50.06 N	4.46 E
Aubry Lake ⊜	180	67.23 N	126.30 W
Auburn, Austl.	168b	34.01 S	138.41 E
Auburn, Austl.	274a	33.51 S	151.02 E
Auburn, Al., U.S.	194	32.36 N	85.28 W
Auburn, Ca., U.S.	226	38.53 N	121.04 W
Auburn, Il., U.S.	219	39.35 N	89.44 W
Auburn, In., U.S.	216	41.22 N	85.03 W
Auburn, Ky., U.S.	194	37.02 N	86.54 W
Auburn, Me., U.S.	188	44.05 N	70.13 W
Auburn, Ma., U.S.	207	42.11 N	71.50 W
Auburn, Mi., U.S.	190	43.36 N	84.04 W
Auburn, Ne., U.S.	198	40.23 N	95.50 W
Auburn, N.J., U.S.	285	39.42 N	75.22 W
Auburn, N.Y., U.S.	210	42.55 N	76.33 W
Auburn, Pa., U.S.	208	40.35 N	76.05 W
Auburn, Wa., U.S.	224	47.18 N	122.13 W
Auburn ≃	166	25.38 S	151.12 E
Auburndale, Fl., U.S.	220	28.03 N	81.47 W
Auburndale, Ma., U.S.	283	42.21 N	71.22 W
Auburn Heights	216	42.38 N	83.13 W
Auburn Range ⋀	166	25.10 S	150.30 E
Auburn Ravine ∨	226	38.51 N	121.31 W
Auburn Southeast	210	42.54 N	76.32 W
Aubusson	32	45.57 N	2.11 E
Auby-sur-Semois	56	49.49 N	5.10 E
Auca Mahuida	252	37.53 S	68.31 W
Auca Mahuida, Cerro ∧	252	37.45 S	68.56 W
Aucará	248	14.15 S	74.05 W
Auce	76	56.28 N	22.53 E
Auch	32	43.39 N	0.35 E
Auchel	50	50.30 N	2.28 E
Auchenblae	46	56.54 N	2.26 W
Auchencairn	44	54.51 N	3.53 W
Auchi	150	7.02 N	6.14 E
Auchinleck	44	55.28 N	4.17 W
Auchterarder	46	56.18 N	3.43 W
Auchterderran	46	56.09 N	3.16 W
Auchtermuchty	46	56.17 N	3.15 W
Aucilla ≃	192	30.05 N	83.59 W
Auckland	172	36.52 S	174.46 E
Auckland Islands II	9	50.40 S	166.30 E
Auckland Park ◆8	273d	26.11 S	28.00 E
Auckland Park Race Course ♠	273d	26.11 S	28.00 E
Aude □5	32	43.05 N	2.30 E
Aude ≃	32	43.13 N	3.14 E
Audenge	32	44.41 N	1.00 W
Audenshaw	262	53.28 N	2.08 W
Audenshaw Reservoirs ⊜1	262	53.28 N	2.08 W
Auderghem	50	50.49 N	4.26 E
Audeux	58	47.16 N	5.53 E
Audierne	32	48.01 N	4.32 W
Audincourt	58	47.29 N	6.50 E
Audley	44	53.03 N	2.18 W
Audobon Park	285	39.54 N	75.05 W
Audo Range ⋀	144	6.30 N	41.30 E
Audrain □6	219	39.12 N	91.50 W
Audresselles	50	50.49 N	1.36 E
Audruicq	50	50.53 N	2.05 E
Audubon, Ia., U.S.	198	41.43 N	94.55 W
Audubon, N.J., U.S.	208	39.53 N	75.04 W
Audubon, Pa., U.S.	285	40.07 N	75.27 W
Audubon Lake ⊜1	198	47.35 N	101.10 W
Audubon Park	218	38.12 N	85.43 W
Audun-le-Roman	56	49.22 N	5.53 E
Aue	54	50.35 N	12.42 E
Aue ≃	52	53.05 N	8.04 E
Auer → Ora	64	46.21 N	11.18 E
Auerbach, B.R.D.	60	48.48 N	13.06 E
Auerbach, D.D.R.	54	50.30 N	12.23 E
Auerbach, D.D.R.	54	50.41 N	12.54 E
Auerbach in der Oberpfalz	60	49.42 N	11.38 E
Auersberg ∧	54	50.27 N	12.39 E
Auerswalde	54	50.54 N	12.55 E
Auezov	86	49.46 N	81.38 E
Auf dem Kreinberge	263	51.27 N	7.36 E
Auffargis	261	48.42 N	1.53 E
Auffay	50	49.43 N	1.06 E
Aufsess	60	49.54 N	11.13 E
Augarten ♠	264b	48.14 N	16.23 E
Augathella	166	25.48 S	146.35 E
Augher	48	54.26 N	7.09 W
Aughnacloy	48	54.25 N	6.58 W
Aughrim	48	52.51 N	6.17 W
Aughton, Eng., U.K.	44	53.22 N	1.18 W
Aughton, Eng., U.K.	262	53.32 N	2.56 W
Aughton Park	262	53.33 N	2.53 W
Aughwick Creek ≃	214	40.22 N	77.50 W
Auglaize □6	216	40.34 N	84.12 W
Auglaize ≃	216	41.17 N	84.21 W
Augrabies	158	28.37 S	20.20 E
Augrabies Falls National Park ♠	158	28.35 S	20.19 E
Augrabiesvalle ∟	158	28.35 S	20.19 E
Au Gres	190	44.02 N	83.41 W
Au Gres ≃	190	44.02 N	83.40 W
Au Gres, East Branch ≃	190	44.05 N	83.41 W
Augsburg	58	48.23 N	10.53 E
Augusta, Austl.	162	34.19 S	115.10 E
Augusta, It.	70	37.13 N	15.13 E
Augusta, Ar., U.S.	194	35.16 N	91.21 W
Augusta, Ga., U.S.	192	33.28 N	82.01 W
Augusta, Il., U.S.	194	40.13 N	90.57 W
Augusta, Ks., U.S.	198	37.41 N	97.58 W
Augusta, Ky., U.S.	218	38.46 N	84.00 W
Augusta, Me., U.S.	188	44.18 N	69.46 W
Augusta, Mi., U.S.	216	42.20 N	85.21 W
Augusta, Mo., U.S.	219	38.34 N	90.53 W
Augusta, Mt., U.S.	202	47.29 N	112.23 W
Augusta, N.J., U.S.	210	41.07 N	74.43 W
Augusta, Oh., U.S.	214	40.41 N	81.01 W
Augusta, Wi., U.S.	190	44.40 N	91.07 W
Augusta, Golfo di ⊂	70	37.12 N	15.13 E
Augustdorf	52	51.53 N	8.43 E
Augustenborg	41	54.57 N	9.53 E
Augustine Island I	180	59.22 N	153.28 W
Augusto Severo	250	5.52 S	37.19 W
Augustów	30	53.51 N	22.59 E
Augustowski, Kanał ≚	76	53.54 N	23.26 E
Augustus, Mount ∧	162	24.20 S	116.50 E
Augustusburg	54	50.49 N	13.06 E
Augustus Downs	166	18.33 S	139.52 E
Augustus Island I	164	15.20 S	124.30 E
Auiia, Ribeirão ≃	255	12.09 S	53.20 W
Au in der Hallertau	60	48.33 N	11.45 E
Aujon ≃	58	48.09 N	4.48 E
Auki	175e	8.46 S	160.42 E
Aulander	192	36.13 N	77.06 W
Aulanko	26	61.02 N	24.27 E
Auld, Lake ⊜	162	22.32 S	123.44 E
Auldearn	46	57.34 N	3.49 W
Aulendorf	58	47.57 N	9.38 E
Aulestad	26	61.13 N	10.17 E
Auletta	68	40.34 N	15.25 E
Aulla	64	44.12 N	9.58 E
Aulnay	32	46.01 N	0.21 W
Aulnay-sous-Bois	50	48.57 N	2.31 E
Aulnay-sur-Mauldre	261	48.56 N	1.51 E
Aulne ≃	32	48.17 N	4.16 W
Aulneau Peninsula ≻1	184	49.23 N	94.29 W
Aulnois-sur-Seille	56	48.52 N	6.19 E
Aulnoye-Aymeries	50	50.12 N	3.50 E
Ault, Fr.	50	50.06 N	1.27 E
Ault, Co., U.S.	200	40.34 N	104.43 W
Ault, Ky., U.S.	218	38.12 N	83.14 W
Aultbea	46	57.50 N	5.35 W
Aultman	214	40.34 N	79.16 W
Aultshire	216	40.13 N	85.19 W
Auma	54	50.42 N	11.54 E
Aumale	50	49.46 N	1.45 E
Auma Point ≻	164	7.55 S	145.25 E
Aumetz	56	49.25 N	5.56 E
Aumont-Aubrac	32	44.43 N	3.17 E
Aumühle	52	53.31 N	10.19 E
Auna	150	10.12 N	4.45 E
Auneau	50	48.27 N	1.46 E
Auneuil	50	49.22 N	2.00 E
Auning	26	56.26 N	10.23 E
Auno	146	11.50 N	12.53 E
Aunuu I	174u	14.17 S	170.33 W
Auob ≃	156	26.25 S	20.35 E
Auponhia	112	1.56 S	125.29 E
Aups	62	43.37 N	6.14 E
Aur, Pulau I	112	2.27 N	104.31 E
Aura	26	60.36 N	22.34 E
Aurach	56	49.15 N	10.25 E
Aurach ≃	56	49.34 N	10.59 E
Aurachmat	85	41.34 N	70.07 E
Auraiya	124	26.28 N	79.31 E
Aurangābād, India	122	19.53 N	75.20 E
Aurangābād, India	124	24.45 N	84.22 E
Auray	32	47.40 N	2.59 W
Aurdal	26	60.56 N	9.24 E
Aure	26	63.16 N	8.32 E
Aurelia	198	42.42 N	95.26 W
Aurelius	216	42.31 N	84.31 W
Aurès, Massif de l' ⋀	148	35.08 N	6.30 E
Auri, Kepulauan II	164	1.59 S	134.42 E
Aurich	52	53.28 N	7.29 E
Auriesville Shrine ʊ1	210	42.54 N	74.19 W
Auriflama	255	20.41 S	50.34 W
Aurigny → Alderney I	43b	49.43 N	2.12 W
Aurilândia	255	16.44 S	50.28 W
Aurillac	32	44.56 N	2.26 E
Aurina, Valle ∨	64	47.00 N	12.00 E
Aurine, Alpi (Zillertaler Alpen) ⋀	64	47.00 N	11.55 E
Aurino ≃	64	46.48 N	11.55 E
Auriol	62	43.23 N	5.38 E
Aurisina	64	45.45 N	13.41 E
Aurizona	250	1.17 S	45.46 W
Aurlandsfjorden ⊂2	26	61.05 N	7.02 E
Aurlandsvangen	26	60.54 N	7.11 E
Aurolzmünster	60	48.15 N	13.27 E
Auron	62	44.14 N	6.56 E
Auronzo di Cadore	64	46.33 N	12.26 E
Aurora, Bra.	250	6.57 S	38.58 W
Aurora, Bra.	287a	22.46 S	43.24 W
Aurora, On., Can.	212	44.00 N	79.28 W
Aurora, S. Afr.	158	32.42 S	18.29 E
Aurora, Co., U.S.	200	39.43 N	104.49 W
Aurora, Il., U.S.	216	41.45 N	88.19 W
Aurora, In., U.S.	218	39.03 N	84.54 W
Aurora, Me., U.S.	188	44.51 N	68.19 W
Aurora, Mn., U.S.	190	47.31 N	92.14 W
Aurora, Mo., U.S.	194	36.58 N	93.43 W
Aurora, Ne., U.S.	198	40.52 N	98.00 W
Aurora, N.Y., U.S.	210	42.45 N	76.42 W
Aurora, N.C., U.S.	192	35.18 N	76.47 W
Aurora, Oh., U.S.	214	41.19 N	81.20 W
Aurora, Or., U.S.	224	45.13 N	122.45 W
Aurora, Ut., U.S.	200	38.55 N	111.56 W
Aurora, W.V., U.S.	188	39.19 N	79.33 W
Aurora □4	116	16.00 N	121.40 E
Aurora ʊ	265a	59.57 N	30.21 E
Aurora do Norte	255	12.43 S	46.24 W
Aurora Pond ⊜	279a	41.20 N	81.23 W
Auroux	62	44.45 N	3.44 E
Aursunden ⊜	26	62.40 N	11.40 E
Aurukun	164	13.19 S	141.45 E
Aurukun Aboriginal Land Trust ◆4	164	13.45 S	141.45 E
Aurunci, Monti ⋀	66	41.22 N	13.40 E
Aus	156	26.40 S	16.15 E
Ausable ≃, On., Can.	190	43.19 N	81.46 W
Au Sable ≃, Mi., U.S.	190	44.25 N	83.20 W
Au Sable, North Branch ≃	190	44.40 N	84.23 W
Au Sable, South Branch ≃	190	44.40 N	84.23 W
Au Sable Forks	188	44.26 N	73.40 W
Au Sable Point ≻	190	44.20 N	83.20 W
Auschwitz → Oświęcim	30	50.03 N	19.12 E
Ausevik ⊥	26	61.32 N	5.16 E
Auskerry I	46	59.02 N	2.34 W
Ausoni, Monti ⋀	66	41.25 N	13.20 E
Ausserferrera	58	46.33 N	9.26 E
Ausserfragant	64	46.56 N	13.06 E
Aussig → Ústí nad Labem	54	50.40 N	14.02 E
Aussois	62	45.14 N	6.45 E
Aust-Agder □6	26	58.50 N	8.00 E
Austerlitz → Slavkov u Brna	61	49.09 N	16.52 E
Austerlitz, Ned.	52	52.05 N	5.19 E
Austerlitz, N.Y., U.S.	210	42.19 N	73.28 W
Austerlitz, Gare ◆5	261	48.50 N	2.22 E
Austin, Bra.	287a	22.43 S	43.32 W
Austin, Mb., Can.	184	49.57 N	98.56 W
Austin, In., U.S.	218	38.45 N	85.48 W
Austin, Mn., U.S.	190	43.40 N	92.58 W
Austin, Nv., U.S.	204	39.29 N	117.04 W
Austin, Pa., U.S.	214	41.37 N	78.05 W
Austin, Tx., U.S.	222	30.16 N	97.44 W
Austin □6	222	29.53 N	96.15 W
Austin ◆8	278	41.54 N	87.45 W
Austin, Lake ⊜	162	27.40 S	118.00 E
Austin, Lake ⊜1	222	30.19 N	97.46 W
Austin Bayou ≃	222	29.07 N	95.18 W
Austinburg	214	41.46 N	80.51 W
Austin Channel ⊔	176	75.35 N	103.25 W
Austin Lake ⊜	216	42.11 N	85.33 W
Austinmer	170	34.18 S	150.56 E
Austin's Post	158	29.32 S	25.49 E
Austintown	214	41.06 N	80.45 W
Austinville	192	36.51 N	80.54 W
Austnes	26	62.38 N	6.16 E
Austonio	222	31.11 N	95.38 W
Austonley	262	53.34 N	1.50 W
Austral	274a	33.56 S	150.48 E
Australes, Îles II	14	23.00 S	150.00 W
Australia □1	160	25.00 S	135.00 E
Australia Mountain ∧	180	63.36 N	138.08 W
Australian-Antarctic Rise ✦3	9	50.00 S	130.00 E
Australian Capital Territory □8	171b	35.30 S	149.00 E
Australian War Memorial ⊥	171b	35.17 S	149.09 E
Australia Plains	168b	34.06 S	139.09 E
Australie → Australia □1	160	25.00 S	135.00 E
Australien → Australia □1	160	25.00 S	135.00 E
Australind	168a	33.16 S	115.44 E
Austral Seamounts ✦3	14	22.40 S	152.45 W
Austråt	26	63.43 N	9.45 E
Austria (Österreich) □1, Europe	22	47.20 N	13.20 E
Austria (Österreich) □1, Europe	30	47.20 N	13.20 E
Austvågøya I	24	68.20 N	14.36 E
Autazes	246	3.35 S	59.08 W
Auteuil, Fr.	50	49.21 N	2.05 E
Auteuil, Fr.	261	48.50 N	1.49 E
Autheuil	50	49.06 N	1.17 E
Authie ≃	50	50.21 N	1.38 E
Authon	62	44.14 N	6.08 E
Authon-du-Perche	50	48.12 N	0.55 E
Authon-la-Plaine	50	48.27 N	1.57 E
Auth Village	284c	38.49 N	76.55 W
Autlán de Navarro	234	19.46 N	104.22 W
Autore, Monte ∧	66	41.58 N	13.12 E
Autrey-lès-Gray	58	47.29 N	5.30 E
Autriche → Austria □1	30	47.20 N	13.20 E
Autumn Hill	284b	39.16 N	76.48 W
Autun	32	46.57 N	4.18 E
Auve	56	49.02 N	4.42 E
Auvergne	164	15.41 S	130.01 E
Auvergne □9	32	45.25 N	2.30 E
Auvernaux	261	48.32 N	2.30 E
Auvers-sur-Oise	50	49.04 N	2.10 E
Auvézère ≃	32	45.12 N	0.51 E
Aux Cayes → Les Cayes	238	18.12 N	73.45 W
Auxerre	50	47.48 N	3.34 E
Auxier	192	37.44 N	82.45 W
Auxi-le-Château	50	50.14 N	2.07 E
Auxon	50	48.06 N	3.55 E
Auxonne	58	47.12 N	5.23 E
Aux Sable Creek ≃	216	41.23 N	88.20 W
Auxvasse	219	39.01 N	91.53 W
Auxvasse Creek ≃	219	38.41 N	91.49 W
Auxy	58	46.57 N	4.24 E
Auyamita, Quebrada ≃	286c	10.30 N	66.46 W
Auyán Tepuy ∧	246	5.55 N	62.32 W
Auzances	32	46.02 N	2.30 E
Auzangate, Nevado ∧	248	13.48 S	71.14 W
Auzon ≃, Fr.	58	48.00 N	4.20 E
Auzon ≃, Fr.	62	44.02 N	4.54 E
Ava, Il., U.S.	194	37.53 N	89.29 W
Ava, Mo., U.S.	194	36.57 N	92.39 W
Avadchara	84	43.31 N	40.39 E
Avadh Plains ≚	124	26.20 N	82.00 E
Avaí	255	22.08 S	49.22 W
Āvaj	128	35.34 N	49.13 E
Avakubi	154	1.20 N	27.34 E
Aval'	85	40.19 N	71.50 E
Aval, Falaise d' ≗4	50	49.45 N	0.10 E
Avala ⊥	38	44.45 N	20.35 E
Avaldsnes	26	59.21 N	5.16 E
Avallon	50	47.29 N	3.54 E
Avaloirs, Les ∧2	32	48.28 N	0.07 W
Avalon, Ca., U.S.	228	33.20 N	118.19 W
Avalon, N.J., U.S.	208	39.06 N	74.43 W
Avalon, Pa., U.S.	214	40.30 N	80.04 W
Avalon, Tx., U.S.	222	32.12 N	96.48 W
Avalon, Wi., U.S.	216	42.38 N	88.52 W
Avalon Peninsula ≻1	186	47.30 N	53.30 W
Avana ≃	174k	21.14 S	159.43 W
Avanley	262	53.16 N	2.45 W
Avanos	130	38.43 N	34.51 E
Avant	196	36.29 N	96.03 W
Avaré	255	23.05 S	48.55 W
Avarskoje Kojsu ≃	84	42.47 N	46.48 E
Avarua	174k	21.12 S	159.46 W
Avarua Harbour ⊂	174k	21.11 S	159.46 W
Avatanak Island I	180	54.03 N	165.19 W
Avatele	174v	19.06 S	169.55 W
Avatele Bay ⊂	174v	19.05 S	169.56 W
Avatiu	174k	21.12 S	159.47 W
Avatiu Harbour ⊂	174k	21.11 S	159.47 W
Avčala	84	41.48 N	44.48 E
Avdejevka	83	48.08 N	37.46 E
Avdotjino	83	47.55 N	37.51 E
Ave ≃	34	41.20 N	8.45 W
Avebury	42	51.27 N	1.51 W
Avebury Stone Circle ⊥	42	51.28 N	1.51 W
'Avedat, Ḥorvot ⊥	132	30.48 N	34.46 E
Avegbadje ∧	150	7.14 N	0.38 E
Aveiro, Bra.	250	3.15 S	55.10 W
Aveiro, Port.	34	40.38 N	8.39 W
Aveiro, Ria de ≃1	34	40.38 N	8.44 W
Avelar	256	22.20 S	43.25 W
Avelengo	64	46.38 N	11.13 E
Aveley	260	51.30 N	0.16 E
Avelgem	50	50.46 N	3.26 E
Avella, It.	68	40.58 N	14.36 E
Avella, Pa., U.S.	214	40.16 N	80.27 W
Avellaneda, Arg.	252	29.07 S	59.40 W
Avellaneda, Arg.	258	34.39 S	58.23 W
Avellaneda □5	288	34.40 S	58.20 W
Avellaneda, Estacion ◆5	288	34.41 S	58.22 W
Avelle, Île I	275a	45.24 N	74.00 W
Avellino	68	40.54 N	14.47 E
Avellino □4, It.	68	40.57 N	15.00 E
Avellino □4, It.	68	41.00 N	15.10 E
Avenal	226	36.00 N	120.07 W
Avenal Creek ≃	226	35.47 N	120.04 W
Aven Armand ≗5	32	44.15 N	3.22 E
Avenas	58	46.12 N	4.37 E
Avenches	58	46.53 N	7.02 E
Avenel	276	40.34 N	74.17 W
Aventureiro, Rio do ≃	256	21.52 S	42.39 W
Avenue	208	38.15 N	76.46 W
Avenwedde	52	51.55 N	8.27 E
Averbode	56	51.02 N	4.59 E
Averbode, Abbaye d' ʊ1	56	51.02 N	4.59 E
Averill Lake ⊜	206	44.59 N	71.44 W
Averill Park	210	42.38 N	73.33 W
Avern ⊜	40	58.54 N	15.32 E
Avernakø I	41	55.01 N	10.17 E
Avernes	261	49.05 N	1.52 E
Avernes, Ru des ≃	261	49.04 N	2.51 E
Averøya I	26	63.01 N	7.34 E
Aversa	68	40.58 N	14.12 E
Avery, Ca., U.S.	226	38.13 N	120.22 W
Avery, Id., U.S.	202	47.15 N	115.48 W
Avery, Tx., U.S.	194	33.33 N	94.47 W
Avery Island	194	29.54 N	91.54 W
Aves, Isla de I	238	15.42 N	63.38 W
Aves, Islas de II	246	12.00 N	67.30 W
Avesnelles	50	50.07 N	3.57 E
Avesnes	32	50.07 N	3.56 E
Avesnes-le-Comte	50	50.17 N	2.32 E
Avesnes-lès-Aubert	50	50.12 N	3.23 E
Avesnes-sur-Helpe	50	50.07 N	3.56 E
Avesta	40	60.09 N	16.12 E
Aveto ≃	62	44.42 N	9.23 E
Avetrana	68	40.21 N	17.43 E
Aveyron □5	32	44.15 N	2.40 E
Aveyron ≃	32	44.05 N	1.16 E
Avezzano	66	42.02 N	13.25 E
Avgustovka	80	52.16 N	50.44 E
Aviano	64	46.04 N	12.36 E
Avich, Loch ⊜	46	56.16 N	5.20 W
Aviemore	46	57.12 N	3.50 W
Avigliana	62	45.05 N	7.23 E
Avigliano	68	40.44 N	15.44 E
Avignon	62	43.57 N	4.49 E
Ávila	34	40.39 N	4.42 W
Ávila, Sierra de ⋀	34	40.35 N	5.08 W
Avila Beach	226	35.10 N	120.43 W
Avilés	34	43.33 N	5.55 W
Avilla	216	41.22 N	85.14 W
Avilley	58	47.26 N	6.16 E
Avinger	222	32.54 N	94.33 W
Avinurme	76	58.59 N	26.51 E
Avio	64	45.44 N	10.56 E
Avion	50	50.24 N	2.50 E
Avioth	56	49.34 N	5.24 E
Avis	210	41.11 N	77.18 W
Avisio ≃	64	46.07 N	11.05 E
Avispa, Cerro ∧	246	1.16 N	65.51 W
Aviston	219	38.36 N	89.36 W
Aviz	34	39.03 N	7.53 W
Avize	50	48.58 N	4.01 E
Avlan Gölü ⊜	130	36.34 N	29.57 E
Avlum	41	56.16 N	8.48 E
Avnbøl	41	54.58 N	9.39 E
Avnik	130	38.39 N	40.20 E
Avoca, Austl.	169	37.05 S	143.28 E
Avoca, Ia., U.S.	198	41.28 N	95.20 W
Avoca, N.Y., U.S.	210	42.24 N	77.25 W
Avoca, Pa., U.S.	210	41.20 N	75.44 W
Avoca ≃, Austl.	166	35.42 S	143.44 E
Avoca ≃, Ire.	48	52.48 N	6.09 W
Avoca, Mount ∧	169	37.07 S	143.21 E
Avoca Beach	170	33.29 S	151.29 E
Avocado Heights	280	34.08 N	117.54 W
Avola, B.C., Can.	182	51.47 N	119.19 W
Avola, It.	70	36.54 N	15.08 E
Avon, Austl.	168b	34.17 S	138.20 E
Avon, Fr.	50	48.24 N	2.43 E
Avon, Ct., U.S.	207	41.48 N	72.49 W
Avon, Il., U.S.	190	40.39 N	90.26 W
Avon, Ma., U.S.	207	42.07 N	71.02 W
Avon, Mn., U.S.	190	45.36 N	94.27 W
Avon, Mt., U.S.	202	46.35 N	112.36 W
Avon, N.Y., U.S.	210	42.54 N	77.44 W
Avon, N.C., U.S.	192	35.21 N	75.30 W
Avon, Oh., U.S.	214	41.27 N	82.02 W
Avon, Pa., U.S.	208	40.22 N	76.23 W
Avon, S.D., U.S.	198	43.00 N	98.03 W
Avon □6	42	51.30 N	2.40 W
Avon ≃, Austl.	168a	31.40 S	116.07 E
Avon ≃, N.S., Can.	186	45.10 N	64.15 W
Avon ≃, On., Can.	212	43.18 N	81.11 W
Avon ≃, Eng., U.K.	42	50.17 N	3.52 W
Avon ≃, Eng., U.K.	42	51.30 N	2.43 W
Avon ≃, Eng., U.K.	42	50.43 N	1.46 W
Avon ≃, Eng., U.K.	42	52.25 N	1.31 W
Avon ≃, Eng., U.K.	42	51.59 N	2.10 W
Avon ≃, Scot., U.K.	46	57.25 N	3.23 W
Avon ≃, Scot., U.K.	46	56.01 N	3.40 W
Avon, Ben ∧	46	57.05 N	3.27 W
Avon, Ru d' ≃	261	48.39 N	2.46 E
Avon Basin ⊂	279a	41.30 N	82.03 W
Avon by the Sea	208	40.11 N	74.00 W
Avondale, Az., U.S.	200	33.26 N	112.20 W
Avondale, Co., U.S.	198	38.14 N	104.21 W
Avondale, Md., U.S.	284c	38.56 N	76.59 W
Avondale, Oh., U.S.	214	39.47 N	84.08 W
Avondale Heights	274b	37.46 S	144.51 E
Avon Downs	166	20.05 S	137.30 E
Avondrust	158	34.21 S	21.51 E
Avon Lake	214	41.30 N	82.01 W
Avonlea	184	50.00 N	105.04 W
Avonmore, On., Can.	206	45.10 N	74.58 W
Avonmore, Pa., U.S.	214	40.31 N	79.27 W
Avonmore ≃	48	52.50 N	6.13 W
Avonmouth	42	51.31 N	2.42 W
Avon Park	220	27.35 N	81.30 W
Avon Reservoir ⊜1	170	34.24 S	150.40 E
Avontuur	158	33.44 S	23.11 E
Avon Valley National Park ♠	168a	31.41 S	116.06 E
Avon Water ≃	46	55.47 N	4.01 W
Avoudrey	58	47.08 N	6.26 E
Avrainville	261	48.34 N	2.15 E
Avranches	32	48.41 N	1.22 W
Avranlo	84	41.39 N	43.52 E
Avre ≃, Fr.	50	49.53 N	2.20 E
Avre ≃, Fr.	50	48.47 N	1.22 E
Avrieux	62	45.13 N	6.43 E
Avroult	50	50.38 N	2.09 E
Avtatkuul' ≃	180	64.06 N	178.10 E
Avtovo ◆8	265a	59.52 N	30.15 E
Avu Avu	175e	9.50 S	160.23 E
Awa, Nihon	96	34.04 N	134.12 E
Awa, Nihon	174m	26.36 N	127.56 E
Awaba	170	33.01 S	151.33 E
A'waj, Nahr al- ≃	132	33.20 N	36.34 E
Awaji	96	34.35 N	135.01 E
Awaji-shima I	96	34.21 N	134.51 E
Awakino	172	38.39 S	174.38 E
'Awālī	128	26.05 N	50.33 E
Awang	115b	8.54 S	116.24 E
Awano	94	36.31 N	139.41 E
Awanui	172	35.03 S	173.15 E
Awar	164	4.09 S	144.51 E
Awara	94	36.13 N	136.12 E
Awarawar, Tanjung ≻	115a	6.45 S	111.56 E
Aware	144	8.15 N	44.10 E
Awarua Point ≻	172	44.15 S	168.03 E
Awasa	144	6.45 N	38.15 E
Awasa, Lake ⊜	144	7.05 N	38.25 E
Awasan Bay ⊂	116	9.56 N	125.36 E
Awash	144	8.59 N	40.10 E
Awash ≃	144	11.45 N	41.05 E
Awa-shima I, Nihon	92	38.27 N	139.14 E
Awa-shima I, Nihon	96	34.16 N	133.38 E
Awash National Park ♠	144	9.05 N	40.00 E
Awaso	150	6.14 N	2.16 W
Awatere ≃	172	41.37 S	174.10 E
Awbārī	146	26.35 N	12.46 E
Awbārī, Ṣaḥrā' ≗8	146	28.00 N	11.30 E
Awdheegle	144	1.59 N	44.50 E
Awe	150	8.09 N	9.07 E
Awe, Loch ⊜	46	56.15 N	5.17 W
Awegyun	110	12.44 N	98.44 E
Awgu	150	6.04 N	7.29 E
Awīsh al-Ḥajar	142	31.01 N	31.19 E
'Awjā', Wādī al- ∨	132	31.56 N	35.31 E
Awjilah	146	29.09 N	21.15 E
Awka	150	6.12 N	7.05 E
Awlād Mūsā	142	30.48 N	31.44 E
Awled Djellal	148	34.28 N	5.02 E
Awlef	148	26.58 N	1.05 E
Aworo Kit	140	10.59 N	32.38 E
Aworro	164	7.45 S	143.10 E
Awosting	276	41.09 N	74.20 W
Awsīm	273c	30.07 N	31.08 E
Awul	164	6.00 S	151.00 E
Awuna ≃	180	69.04 N	155.30 W
Awwal, Ash-Shallāl al- (First Cataract) ∟	140	24.01 N	32.52 E
Awwalī, Nahr al- ≃	132	33.35 N	35.23 E
Axams	64	47.14 N	11.18 E
Axat	32	42.48 N	2.14 E
Axbridge	42	51.18 N	2.49 W
Axe ≃, Eng., U.K.	42	51.19 N	2.59 W
Axe ≃, Eng., U.K.	42	50.42 N	3.03 W
Axe Creek ≃	169	36.46 S	144.30 E
Axedale	169	36.47 S	144.30 E
Axe Edge ⋀2	262	53.14 N	1.57 W
Axel	52	51.16 N	3.55 E
Axel Heiberg Island I	16	79.45 N	91.00 W
Axim	150	4.52 N	2.14 W
Axinim	246	4.02 S	59.22 W
Axiós (Vardar) ≃	38	40.35 N	22.50 E
Axis	194	30.55 N	88.01 W
Axixá	250	2.51 S	44.04 W
Ax-les-Thermes	32	42.43 N	1.50 E
Axminster	42	50.47 N	3.00 W
Axmouth	42	50.42 N	3.02 W
Axochiapan	234	18.30 N	98.46 W
Axtell, Ks., U.S.	198	39.52 N	96.15 W
Axtell, Ne., U.S.	198	40.28 N	99.07 W
Axtell, Tx., U.S.	222	31.39 N	96.58 W
Aÿ	50	49.03 N	4.00 E
Ayabaca	246	4.38 S	79.43 W
Ayabe	96	35.18 N	135.15 E
Ayachi, Ari n' ∧	148	32.29 N	4.57 W
Ayacucho, Arg.	252	37.09 S	58.29 W
Ayacucho, Bol.	248	17.51 S	63.20 W
Ayacucho, Perú	248	13.07 S	74.13 W
Ayacucho □5	248	14.00 S	74.00 W
Ayakkum Hu ⊜	120	37.30 N	89.20 E
Ayamé	150	5.37 N	3.11 W
Ayamiken	152	2.07 N	10.01 E
Ayamonte	34	37.13 N	7.24 W
Āyān	272b	22.43 N	88.09 E
Ayancık	130	41.57 N	34.36 E
Ayangba	150	7.30 N	7.08 E
Ayapel	246	8.19 N	75.09 W
Ayarza, Laguna de ⊜	236	14.25 N	90.08 W
Ayas, It.	62	45.50 N	7.41 E
Ayaş, Tür.	130	40.01 N	32.21 E
Ayase	94	35.26 N	139.26 E
Ayase ≃	268	35.45 N	139.49 E
Ayauta	96	34.13 N	133.53 E
Ayaviri	248	14.52 S	70.35 W
Ayaviri ≃	248	15.01 S	70.22 W
'Aybāl, Jabal ∧	132	32.14 N	35.16 E
Aybastı, Tür.	130	39.42 N	39.02 E
Aybastı, Tür.	130	40.41 N	37.24 E
Ayden	192	35.28 N	77.24 W
Aydere	128	38.24 N	56.45 E
Aydın	130	37.51 N	27.51 E
Aydın □4	130	37.45 N	28.00 E
Aydıncık, Tür.	130	36.08 N	33.19 E
Aydıncık, Tür.	130	40.08 N	35.18 E
Aydın Dağları ⋀	130	38.00 N	28.00 E
Aydınkent	130	37.06 N	31.36 E
Aydıntepe	130	40.24 N	40.09 E
Aydin Ula ∧	86	42.55 N	87.35 E
Aydosdağı ∧	267b	40.56 N	29.15 E
Ayelu ∧	144	10.04 N	40.46 E
Ayer, Schw.	58	46.11 N	7.36 E
Ayer, Ma., U.S.	207	42.33 N	71.35 W
Ayer Baloi	114	1.35 N	103.20 E
Ayer Chawan, Pulau I	271c	1.17 N	103.42 E
Ayer Hitam, Malay.	114	2.56 N	102.24 E
Ayer Hitam, Malay.	114	1.55 N	103.11 E
Ayer Jerneh	114	4.24 N	103.24 E
Ayer Kuning Selatan	114	2.30 N	102.28 E
Ayer Merbau, Pulau I	271c	1.16 N	103.43 E
Ayers Cliff	206	45.10 N	72.03 W
Ayers Rock ∧	162	25.23 S	131.05 E
Ayersville	216	41.14 N	84.17 W
Ayeyarwady □8	110	17.00 N	95.00 E
Ayeyarwady (Irrawaddy) ≃	110	15.50 N	95.06 E
Aygün	130	38.26 N	41.17 E
Ayía Marína	38	37.09 N	26.52 E
Ayía Paraskeví, Ellás	38	39.15 N	26.16 E
Ayía Paraskeví, Ellás	267c	38.01 N	23.50 E
Ayiássos	38	39.05 N	26.23 E
Ayía Varvára	267c	37.59 N	23.39 E
Ayina ≃	152	1.48 N	13.10 E
Áyioi Anáryiroi	267c	38.02 N	23.43 E
Áyion Óros ≻1	38	40.15 N	24.15 E
Áyios Dhimítrios	267c	37.56 N	23.44 E
Áyios Evstrátios I	38	39.31 N	25.00 E
Áyios Ioánnis Réndis	267c	37.58 N	23.40 E
Áyios Kírikos	38	37.37 N	26.14 E
Áyios Nikólaos	38	35.11 N	25.42 E
Ayiou Nikolaou Monastery ʊ1	267c	37.53 N	23.27 E
Ayíou Órous, Kólpos ⊂	38	40.12 N	24.03 E
Ayl	132	30.13 N	35.32 E
Aylesbury	42	51.50 N	0.50 W
Aylesford	260	51.18 N	0.29 E
Aylesham	42	51.13 N	1.13 E
Aylmer	188	45.26 N	75.50 W
Aylmer, Lake ⊜	206	45.50 N	71.22 W
Aylmer, Mount ∧	182	51.19 N	115.26 W
Aylmer-East	212	45.26 N	75.50 W
Aylmer Lake ⊜	176	64.05 N	108.30 W
Aylmer West	212	42.46 N	80.59 W
Aylsham, Sk., Can.	184	53.11 N	103.49 W
Aylsham, Eng., U.K.	42	52.49 N	1.15 E
'Ayn al-'Arab	130	36.54 N	38.21 E
'Ayn Dār	128	25.59 N	49.23 E
'Ayn Dīwār	130	37.17 N	42.11 E
'Aynīn ⚲4	144	20.48 N	41.39 E

≃ River	Fluß	Río	Rivière	Rio
≚ Canal	Kanal	Canal	Canal	Canal
∟ Waterfall, Rapids	Wasserfall, Stromschnellen	Cascada, Rápidos	Chute d'eau, Rapides	Cascata, Rápidos
⊔ Strait	Meeresstraße	Estrecho	Détroit	Estreito
⊂ Bay, Gulf	Bucht, Golf	Bahía, Golfo	Baie, Golfe	Baía, Golfo
⊜ Lake, Lakes	See, Seen	Lago, Lagos	Lac, Lacs	Lago, Lagos
≍ Swamp	Sumpf	Pantano	Marais	Pântano
⊟ Ice Features, Glacier	Eis- und Gletscherformen	Accidentes Glaciales	Formes glaciaires	Acidentes glaciares
⚲ Other Hydrographic Features	Andere Hydrographische Objekte	Otros Elementos Hidrográficos	Autres données hydrographiques	Outros acidentes hidrográficos

✦ Submarine Features	Untermeerische Objekte	Accidentes Submarinos	Formes de relief sous-marin	Acidentes submarinos
□ Political Unit	Politische Einheit	Unidad Politica	Entité politique	Unidade política
ʊ Cultural Institution	Kulturelle Institution	Institución Cultural	Institution culturelle	Instituição cultural
⊥ Historical Site	Historische Stätte	Sitio Histórico	Site historique	Sitio histórico
♠ Recreational Site	Erholungs- und Ferienort	Sitio de Recreo	Centre de loisirs	Area de Lazer
⊠ Airport	Flughafen	Aeropuerto	Aéroport	Aeroporto
■ Military Installation	Militäranlage	Instalación Militar	Installation militaire	Instalação militar
◆ Miscellaneous	Verschiedenes	Misceláneo	Divers	Diversos

Aynor 192 33.59 N 79.11 W
'Aynūnah 128 28.05 N 35.08 E
Ayo 248 15.41 S 72.16 W
Ayo Ayo 248 17.05 S 68.00 W
Ayod 140 8.07 N 31.26 E
Ayodhya 124 26.48 N 82.12 E
Ayo el Chico 234 20.32 N 102.21 W
Ayom 140 7.52 N 28.23 E
Ayoquezco 234 16.41 N 96.50 W
Ayorou 150 14.44 N 0.55 E
Ayos 152 3.54 N 12.31 E
'Ayoûn el 'Atroûs 150 16.40 N 9.37 W
Ayr, Austl. 166 19.35 S 147.24 E
Ayr, On., Can. 212 43.17 N 80.27 W
Ayr, Scot., U.K. 44 55.28 N 4.38 W
Ayr ≃ 44 55.29 N 4.28 W
'Ayrah 132 32.37 N 36.32 E
Ayrancı 130 37.22 N 33.42 E
Ayre, Point of ➤ 44 54.26 N 4.22 W
Aysgarth 44 54.17 N 2.00 W
Aysha 144 10.46 N 42.37 E
'Aytā al-Fakhkhār 132 33.38 N 35.54 E
'Aytanīt 132 33.34 N 35.40 E
Ayton, Austl. 164 15.56 S 145.22 E
Ayton, On., Can. 212 44.03 N 80.56 W
Ayton, Eng., U.K. 44 54.14 N 0.29 W
Ayu, Kepulauan II 108 0.28 N 131.03 E
Ayubnagar 126 23.46 N 90.23 E
Ayulhai 102 44.36 N 115.36 E
Ayuñgon 116 9.51 N 123.08 E
Ayuquila ≃ 234 19.23 N 103.51 W
Ayutla 234 20.07 N 104.22 W
Ayutla [de los Libres] 234 16.54 N 99.13 W
Ayvacık, Tür. 130 39.36 N 26.24 E
Ayvacık, Tür. 130 41.00 N 36.39 E
Ayvalı 130 38.44 N 37.38 E
Ayvalık 130 39.18 N 26.41 E
Aywaille 56 50.28 N 5.40 E
Azabarabān, Ra's ➤ 142 28.51 N 32.43 E
Azacualpa, Hond. 236 15.19 N 88.33 W
Azacualpa, Hond. 236 14.27 N 86.09 W
Azādpur ✦8 272a 28.43 N 77.11 E
Azai 94 35.26 N 136.18 E
Azaila 34 41.17 N 0.29 W
Azalea Park 220 28.32 N 81.18 W
Azama 174m 26.11 N 127.49 E
Azamatovo 80 53.18 N 53.28 E
Azambuja 34 39.04 N 8.52 W
Āzamgarh 124 26.04 N 83.11 E
Azamiga-dake ∧ 96 34.20 N 131.47 E
Azángaro 248 14.55 S 70.13 W
Azángaro ≃ 248 15.17 S 70.10 W
Azanka 86 58.02 N 64.48 E
Azao ∧ 148 25.12 N 8.08 E
Azaouâd ✦1 150 19.00 N 3.00 W
Azaouagh, Vallée de l' V 150 15.30 N 3.18 E
Azapa, Quebrada de ≃ 248 18.30 S 70.17 W
Azar V 150 16.02 N 4.04 E
Azara 150 8.21 N 9.12 E
Āzārbāyjān-e Gharbī ▫4 128 37.40 N 45.00 E
Āzārbāyjān-e Sharqī ▫4 128 38.00 N 47.00 E
Azare 150 11.40 N 10.11 E
Āzar Shahr 128 37.45 N 45.59 E
Azas ≃ 88 52.26 N 96.15 E
Azat, gora ∧2 86 46.55 N 69.00 E
Azay-le-Rideau 50 47.16 N 0.28 E
Azay-sur-Cher 50 47.21 N 0.51 E
Azay-sur-Indre 50 47.12 N 0.57 E
A'zāz 130 36.35 N 37.03 E
Azazga 148 36.44 N 4.22 E
Azcapotzalco ▫7 286a 19.28 N 99.12 W
Azcapotzalco ✦8 286a 19.28 N 99.12 W
Azcuénaga 258 34.23 S 59.21 W
Aždaak, gora ∧ 84 40.13 N 44.56 E
Azdavay 130 41.39 N 33.18 E
Azeffâl ✦8 148 21.00 N 14.45 W
Azeffoun 148 36.53 N 4.25 E
Azejevo 80 54.41 N 42.02 E
Azemmour 148 33.20 N 8.25 W
Azenhas do Mar 266c 38.50 N 9.28 W
Azennezal, 'Erg V 148 22.50 N 0.25 E
Azerbaijan → Azerbajdžanskaja Sovetskaja Socialističeskaja Respublika ▫3 84 40.30 N 47.30 E
Azerbajdžanskaja Sovetskaja Socialističeskaja Respublika ▫3 84 40.30 N 47.30 E
Azergues ≃ 58 45.56 N 4.44 E
Azezo 144 12.35 N 37.28 E
Azgir 80 47.50 N 47.54 E
Azhikode 122 11.59 N 75.21 E
Azilal 148 31.58 N 6.34 W
Azilal ▫4 148 31.55 N 6.30 W
Azile 154 3.32 N 29.52 E
Azincourt 50 50.28 N 2.08 E
Azizbekov 84 39.40 N 45.30 E
Azle 222 32.53 N 97.32 W
Aznakajevo 80 54.53 N 53.04 E
Aznapuquio 286d 11.59 S 77.04 W
Azogues 246 2.44 S 78.50 W
Azoia 266c 38.46 N 9.29 W
Azor 132 32.01 N 34.48 E
Azores → Açores II 148a 38.30 N 28.00 W
Azores-Gibraltar Ridge ✦3 10 37.00 N 16.00 W
Azores Plateau ✦3 10 39.00 N 30.00 W
Azoum, Bahr (Wādī 'Azūm) V 146 10.53 N 20.15 E
Azov 83 47.07 N 39.25 E
Azov, Sea of → Azovskoje more ∓2 78 46.00 N 36.00 E
Azovo-Sivašskij zapovednik ✦4 78 46.08 N 35.08 E
Azovskij kanal ≍ 83 47.07 N 39.27 E
Azovskoje 78 45.34 N 34.34 E
Azovskoje more (Sea of Azov) ∓2 78 46.00 N 36.00 E
Azoyú 234 16.43 N 98.44 W
Azpeitia 34 43.11 N 2.16 W
Azraq, Al-Bahr al- → Blue Nile ≃ 140 15.38 N 32.31 E
Azraq, Bahr ≃ 146 10.52 N 20.35 E
Azraq, Wādī al- V 140 10.33 N 28.40 E
Azraq ash-Shīshān 132 31.50 N 36.48 E
Azrou 148 33.27 N 5.14 W
Aztalan State Park ♦ 216 43.04 N 88.51 W
Aztec 200 36.49 N 107.59 W
Azteca, Estadio ♦ 286a 19.18 N 99.09 W
Aztec Peak ∧ 200 33.48 N 110.55 W
Aztec Ruins National Monument ♦ 200 36.51 N 108.10 W
Azua 238 18.27 N 70.44 W
Azuaga 34 38.16 N 5.41 W
Azuay ▫4 246 3.00 S 79.00 W
Azucena 252 37.29 S 59.18 W
Azuchi 94 35.09 N 136.08 E
Azuchi-jō ⊥ 94 35.10 N 136.08 E
Azuer ≃ 34 39.08 N 3.36 W
Azuero, Península de ➤1 246 7.40 N 80.35 W
Azuga 38 45.27 N 25.33 E
Azul 252 36.47 S 59.51 W
Azul, Cerro ∧, C.R. 236 9.54 N 85.14 W
Azul, Cerro ∧, Ec. 246a 0.54 S 91.21 W
Azul, Cerro ∧, Hond. 236 14.32 N 88.23 W
Azul, Serra ⋀1 248 14.50 S 54.50 W
Azul, Sierra ⋀ 234 23.15 N 98.20 W
'Azūm, Wādī (Bahr Azoum) V 146 10.53 N 20.15 E
Azuma, Nihon 94 36.31 N 139.19 E
Azuma, Nihon 94 36.33 N 138.54 E
Azuma, Nihon 94 35.56 N 140.28 E
Azuma, Nihon 94 36.36 N 138.20 E
Azumaya-san ∧ 94 36.32 N 138.25 E
Azumazaka 270 34.26 N 135.39 E
Azumi 94 36.11 N 137.47 E
Azur, Côte D' ✦2 62 43.30 N 7.00 E
Azurduy 248 19.59 S 64.29 W
Azure Clouds, Temple of the ʊ1 271a 40.00 N 116.11 E
Azure Lake ⊜ 182 52.23 N 120.00 W
Azusa 228 34.08 N 117.54 W
Azusa ≃ 94 36.17 N 137.56 E
Ažu-Tajga, gora ∧ 86 51.35 N 88.45 E
Az-Zabābidah 132 32.23 N 35.20 E
Az-Zabadānī 132 33.43 N 36.05 E
Az-Zāb al-Kabīr → Great Zab ≃ 128 36.00 N 43.21 E
Az-Zāb aṣ-Ṣaghīr → Little Zab ≃ 128 35.12 N 43.25 E
Aẓ-Ẓāhirīyah 132 31.25 N 34.58 E
Aẓ-Ẓahrān (Dhahran) 128 26.18 N 50.08 E
Az-Zamālik ✦8 273c 30.04 N 31.13 E
Azzanello 64 45.18 N 9.55 E
Az-Zankalūn 142 30.33 N 31.27 E
Azzano Decimo 64 45.53 N 12.43 E
Az-Zaqāzīq 142 30.35 N 31.31 E
Az-Zarbah 130 36.04 N 36.59 E
Az-Zarqā' 132 32.05 N 36.06 E
Az-Zarqā' ▫8 132 32.00 N 36.45 E
Az-Zawāmil 142 30.21 N 31.26 E
Az-Zāwiyah 146 32.45 N 12.44 E
Az-Zaydāb 140 17.26 N 33.53 E
Az-Zaydīyah 144 15.18 N 43.04 E
Az-Zaytīyah ✦8 142 29.58 N 32.31 E
Az-Zaytūn ✦8 273c 30.06 N 31.19 E
Azzel Matti, Sebkha ≚ 148 25.55 N 0.56 E
Az-Zilfī 128 26.18 N 44.48 E
Az-Zrārīyah 132 33.21 N 35.20 E
Az-Zubayr 128 30.23 N 47.43 E
'Azzūn 132 32.11 N 35.03 E
Azzurra, Grotta (Blue Grotto) ✦5 68 40.35 N 14.14 E

B

Ba ≃, Viet. 110 13.02 N 109.03 E
Ba ≃, Zhg. 100 30.25 N 115.02 E
Ba ≃, Zhg. 102 31.03 N 107.08 E
Ba ≃, Zhg. 271a 39.57 N 116.38 E
Ba, Loch ⊜ 46 56.36 N 4.44 W
Baa 112 10.43 S 123.03 E
Baaba, Île I 175f 20.03 S 163.59 E
Baacagaan 102 45.35 N 99.27 E
Baad 58 47.19 N 10.07 E
Baah 112 10.28 S 121.59 E
Baak 263 51.25 N 7.10 E
Baal 56 51.02 N 6.17 E
Baao 116 13.27 N 123.22 E
Baar 58 47.12 N 8.32 E
Baar ✦1 58 48.00 N 8.30 E
Baarbach ≃ 263 51.27 N 7.39 E
Baardheere 144 2.20 N 42.17 E
Baardskeerdersbos 158 34.34 S 19.35 E
Baargaal 144 11.17 N 51.04 E
Baarle-Hertog 56 51.27 N 4.56 E
Baarle-Nassau 52 51.27 N 4.53 E
Baarlo 52 51.20 N 6.05 E
Baarn 52 52.13 N 5.16 E
Baasrode 50 51.02 N 4.10 E
Baba 246 1.47 S 79.40 W
Baba ≃ 152 6.25 N 17.07 E
Baba Burnu ➤, Tür. 130 41.17 N 31.24 E
Baba Burnu ➤, Tür. 130 39.29 N 26.04 E
Babaçulândia 250 7.13 S 47.46 W
Babadag, Rom. 38 44.54 N 28.43 E
Babadağ, Tür. 130 37.48 N 28.52 E
Babadag, gora ∧ 84 41.02 N 48.19 E
Babaeski 130 41.26 N 27.06 E
Babahoyo 246 1.49 S 79.31 W
Babaī (Sarju) ≃ 124 27.42 N 81.16 E
Babailiqiao 100 32.26 N 118.57 E
Babajevo 76 59.23 N 35.56 E
Babajkovka 78 49.01 N 34.32 E
Babajurt 84 43.36 N 46.47 E
Babak 112 7.08 N 125.41 E
Babakin 162 32.07 S 118.01 E
Babana 150 10.26 N 3.50 E
Babanango 158 28.30 S 31.00 E
Babanka 78 48.43 N 30.26 E
Babanūsah 140 11.20 N 27.48 E
Babar, Kepulauan II 164 7.50 S 129.45 E
Babar, Pulau I 164 7.55 S 129.45 E
Bābarpur ✦8 272a 28.41 N 77.17 E
Babat, Indon. 112 2.45 S 103.38 E
Babat, Indon. 115a 7.06 S 112.10 E
Babatag, chrebet ⋀ 85 38.15 N 68.20 E
Babati 154 4.13 S 35.45 E
Bābā Valī Ṣāheb 120 31.40 N 65.40 E
Babb 182 48.51 N 113.26 W
Babbacombe Bay ⊂ 42 50.30 N 3.25 W
Babb Creek ≃ 210 41.33 N 77.23 W
Babbitt, Mn., U.S. 190 47.43 N 91.57 W
Babbitt, Nv., U.S. 204 38.32 N 118.38 W
B'abdā 132 33.50 N 35.32 E
B'abdāt 132 33.53 N 35.40 E
Babel, Mont de ∧ 186 51.27 N 68.42 W
Babelijamun 164 2.04 S 137.43 E
Babelsberg ✦8 264a 52.24 N 13.05 E
Babelsberg, Schloss ⊥ 264a 52.24 N 13.05 E
Babelthuap I 175b 7.30 N 134.36 E
Babenhausen, B.R.D. 56 49.57 N 8.56 E
Babenhausen, B.R.D. 58 48.09 N 10.15 E
Babenki 82 55.21 N 37.11 E
Babenkovo 83 49.15 N 37.21 E
Babeyru 154 1.52 N 27.27 E
Babi, Pulau I 114 2.05 N 96.39 E
Babia, Arroyo de la ≃ 196 28.25 N 101.45 W
Babian ≃ 102 22.58 N 101.44 E
Babiči 76 52.17 N 30.00 E
Bābil 142 30.41 N 31.00 E
Bābil ▫4 128 32.40 N 44.35 E
Bābil, Aṭlāl (Babylon) ⊥ 128 32.33 N 44.24 E
Babile 144 9.15 N 42.19 E
Babilônia 256 22.33 S 44.28 W
Babilônia ≃ 255 17.10 S 53.05 W
Babimost 30 52.10 N 15.51 E
Babīna 124 25.15 N 78.28 E
Babina Greda 38 45.07 N 18.33 E
Babinda 166 17.20 S 145.55 E
Babine 182 55.19 N 126.37 W
Babine ≃ 182 55.42 N 127.40 W
Babine Lake ⊜ 182 54.45 N 126.00 W
Babine Range ⋀ 182 55.00 N 126.25 W
Babino, S.S.S.R. 76 56.44 N 34.17 E
Babino, S.S.S.R. 76 59.14 N 31.26 E
Babino, S.S.S.R. 76 59.50 N 40.49 E
Babino, S.S.S.R. 80 57.22 N 48.45 E
Babiogórski Park Narodowy ♦ 30 49.35 N 19.30 E
Babo 164 2.33 S 133.25 E
Bābol 128 36.34 N 52.42 E
Bābol Sar 128 36.43 N 52.39 E
Babonā ≃ 248 6.35 S 66.27 W
Baboon Point ➤ 158 32.19 S 18.20 E
Baboquivari Mountains ⋀ 200 31.45 N 111.35 W
Baboquivari Peak ∧ 200 31.46 N 111.35 W
Babor, Djebel ∧ 34 36.30 N 5.28 E
Baborów 30 50.09 N 17.59 E
Babošino 82 54.13 N 37.08 E
Baboua 152 5.48 N 14.49 E
Babrongan Tower ∧2 162 18.36 S 123.33 E
Babson Park, Fl., U.S. 220 27.49 N 81.31 W
Babson Park, Ma., U.S. 283 42.18 N 71.23 W
Babson Reservoir ⊜1 283 42.38 N 70.40 W
Babstovo 89 48.07 N 132.27 E
Bab-Taza 148 35.03 N 5.14 W
Bābu Bheri 272b 22.51 N 88.14 E
Bābupur, India 126 24.01 N 87.10 E
Bābūpur, India 272a 28.30 N 76.59 E
Babura 150 12.46 N 9.01 E
Bābūsar Pass)(123 35.09 N 74.03 E
Babuškin 88 51.41 N 105.54 E
Babuškin ✦8 265b 55.52 N 37.42 E
Babuyan 116 10.00 N 118.54 E
Babuyan Channel ʮ 116 18.44 N 121.40 E
Babuyan Island I 108 19.32 N 121.57 E
Babuyan Islands II 108 19.15 N 121.40 E
Baby 287a 22.42 S 43.23 W
Baby, Canal do ≍ 287a 22.42 S 43.21 W
Babylon 210 40.41 N 73.19 W
Babylon → Bābil, Aṭlāl ⊥ 128 32.33 N 44.24 E
Babynino 76 54.23 N 35.43 E
Bača ≃ 64 46.09 N 13.48 E
Bacaadweeyn 144 7.12 N 47.32 E
Bacaba, Igarapé ≃ 246 3.35 S 68.45 W
Bacabal 250 4.14 S 44.47 W
Bacacay 116 13.18 N 123.47 E
Bacajá ≃ 250 3.25 S 51.50 W
Bacajaí ≃ 250 3.27 S 51.53 W
Bacalar, Laguna de ⊜ 232 18.43 N 88.22 W
Bacalhau, Canal do ≍ 287a 23.03 S 43.35 W
Bacaligo 84 42.33 N 44.57 E
Bačalino 86 57.46 N 67.17 E
Bacan, Pulau I 164 0.35 S 127.30 E
Bacao 116 10.27 N 119.48 E
Bacarra 116 18.15 N 120.35 E
Bacatuba 250 5.40 S 43.42 W
Bacău 38 46.34 N 26.55 E
Bacău ▫6 38 46.30 N 26.45 E
Baccalieu Island I 186 48.08 N 52.48 W
Bac Can 110 22.08 N 105.50 E
Baccarat 58 48.27 N 6.45 E
Bacchiglione ≃ 64 45.11 N 12.14 E
Bacchus Marsh 169 37.41 S 144.27 E
Baceno 58 46.16 N 8.19 E
Bacerac 232 30.18 N 108.50 W
Baceviči 76 53.24 N 29.14 E
Bac Giang 110 21.16 N 106.12 E
Bach 58 47.16 N 10.24 E
Bachagou 98 40.36 N 122.54 E
Bachaquero 246 9.56 N 71.08 W
Bacharach 56 50.04 N 7.46 E
Bacharden 128 38.26 N 57.25 E
Bachardok 128 38.46 N 58.30 E
Bachauan 116 12.28 N 122.06 E
Bachčisaraj 78 44.45 N 33.51 E
Bache 106 31.05 N 120.40 E
Bacheng 106 31.27 N 120.52 E
Bachi 100 24.48 N 115.49 E
Bachíniva 232 28.45 N 107.15 W
Bach Ma 110 16.12 N 107.52 E
Bachmač 78 51.13 N 32.46 E
Bachmetjevka 80 51.06 N 44.46 E
Bachmut ≃ 83 48.56 N 38.03 E
Bachmutovka 83 48.52 N 39.03 E
Bachmutovo 76 56.22 N 34.03 E
Bacho 114 6.37 N 101.39 E
Bachok 114 6.04 N 102.24 E
Bacht 85 40.43 N 68.42 E
Bachta, S.S.S.R. 74 62.28 N 89.00 E
Bachta, S.S.S.R. 86 55.45 N 92.26 E
Bachtemir ≃ 80 45.43 N 47.38 E
Bachten-Berg ∧2 264a 52.20 N 12.54 E
Bachty, S.S.S.R. 86 46.39 N 82.42 E
Bachty, S.S.S.R. 86 55.45 N 92.26 E
Bachu 90 39.50 N 78.20 E
Bachuma 144 6.48 N 35.53 E
Back ≃, N.T., Can. 176 67.15 N 95.15 W
Back ≃, Va., U.S. 208 37.06 N 76.17 W
Bačka ✦1 38 45.50 N 19.30 E
Bačka Palanka 38 45.15 N 19.24 E
Bačka Topola 38 45.49 N 19.38 E
Back Bay ✦8 283 42.21 N 71.05 W
Back Bay ⊂, India 272c 18.56 N 72.49 E
Back Bay ⊂, Va., U.S. 208 36.35 N 75.57 W
Backberg 40 60.37 N 16.37 E
Backbone Ranges ⋀ 180 63.30 N 129.00 W
Back Branch ≃ 284c 38.50 N 76.48 W
Back Brook ≃ 276 40.26 N 74.39 W
Back Channel ≃1 279b 40.30 N 80.05 W
Back Creek ≃ 188 38.02 N 79.54 W
Backe 26 63.49 N 16.24 E
Bäckefors 26 58.48 N 12.10 E
Bäckehagen 40 60.39 N 15.34 E
Backford 262 53.15 N 2.54 W
Bäckhammar 40 59.10 N 14.11 E
Bački Petrovac 38 45.22 N 19.35 E
Backnang 56 48.56 N 9.25 E
Back River ⊂ 208 39.16 N 76.27 W
Back River Neck ➤1 284b 39.18 N 76.26 W
Backstairs Passage ʮ 168b 35.42 S 138.05 E
Bac Lieu 110 9.17 N 105.44 E
Bacliff 222 29.31 N 94.59 W
Bac Ninh 110 21.11 N 106.03 E
Baco, Mount ∧ 116 12.49 N 121.10 E
Bacoachi 232 30.38 N 109.56 W
Bacoli 68 40.48 N 14.05 E
Bacolod 116 10.40 N 122.57 E
Bacon 116 13.03 N 124.03 E
Baconga ✦8 273b 4.18 S 15.16 E
Bacon Peak ∧ 224 48.39 N 121.31 W
Bacons Run ≃ 285 40.06 N 74.41 W
Baconton 192 31.22 N 84.09 W
Bacoor 116 14.28 N 120.56 E
Bacoor Bay ⊂ 269f 14.28 N 120.54 E
Bac Phan ▫9 110 22.00 N 105.00 E
Bac Quang 110 22.29 N 104.52 E
Bacqueville-en-Caux 50 49.47 N 1.00 E
Bácsalmás 38 46.08 N 19.20 E
Bács-Kiskun ▫6 30 46.30 N 19.25 E
Bacton 42 52.52 N 1.28 E
Bacuag 116 9.37 N 125.38 E
Bacuit Bay ⊂ 116 11.07 N 119.23 E
Bácum 232 27.33 N 110.05 W
Bacungan 116 9.56 N 118.42 E
Bacup 262 53.43 N 2.12 W
Bacuranao ≃ 286b 23.10 N 82.14 W
Bacuri, Cachoeira ∟ 250 5.29 S 54.18 W
Bacuri, Ilha do I 250 2.55 S 49.43 W
Bacurituba 250 2.43 S 44.43 W
Bačurka 24 68.32 N 56.57 E
Bacuyangan 116 9.39 N 122.27 E
Bād 128 33.41 N 52.01 E
Bad ≃, Mi., U.S. 190 43.18 N 84.06 W
Bad ≃, S.D., U.S. 198 44.22 N 100.22 W
Bad ≃, Wi., U.S. 190 46.38 N 90.40 W
Bad', Wādī V 142 29.41 N 32.20 E
Bada 88 51.23 N 109.54 E
Bad Abbach 60 48.56 N 12.03 E
Badagara 122 11.36 N 75.35 E
Badagri 150 6.27 N 2.55 E
Badagri ▫8 273a 6.27 N 3.18 E
Badagri Creek ⊂ 273a 6.25 N 3.18 E
Badahl 142 28.56 N 30.54 E
Bad Aibling 64 47.52 N 12.00 E
Bada Jāmda 124 22.09 N 85.23 E
Badajia 100 33.57 N 120.17 E
Badajós ≃ 246 3.15 S 63.02 W
Badajós, Lago ⊜ 246 3.15 S 62.47 W
Badajoz 34 38.53 N 6.58 W
Badakani 152 4.46 S 14.52 E
Badakhshān ▫4 120 36.45 N 72.00 E
Badal Khān Goth 120 26.31 N 67.06 E
Badalona 34 41.27 N 2.15 E
Badalucco 62 43.55 N 7.51 E
Badam 85 42.23 N 69.15 E
Bādāmi 122 15.55 N 75.41 E
Bādāmpahār 124 22.06 N 86.06 E
Badana, Lach V 144 0.50 S 42.04 E
Badanah 128 30.59 N 41.02 E
Badanga 146 11.36 N 17.26 E
Badanganj 126 22.54 N 87.33 E
Badaohao 104 41.47 N 121.57 E
Badaohe, Zhg. 98 40.24 N 118.42 E
Badaohe, Zhg. 98 40.02 N 122.17 E
Badarīnāth 124 30.44 N 79.29 E
Badarma 88 57.46 N 102.36 E
Badas 112 4.36 N 114.27 E
Badas, Kepulauan II 112 0.35 N 107.06 E
Badata, gora ∧ 88 51.55 N 111.35 E
Bad Aussee 64 47.36 N 13.47 E
Bad Axe 190 43.48 N 83.00 W
Badaying 98 41.22 N 117.28 E
Badazhou 102 24.36 N 105.04 E
Bad Bentheim 52 52.19 N 7.10 E
Bad Bergzabern 56 49.07 N 8.00 E
Bad Berka 54 50.54 N 11.17 E
Bad Berleburg 52 51.03 N 8.23 E
Bad Berneck 60 50.03 N 11.40 E
Bad Bertrich 56 50.04 N 7.02 E
Bad Bibra 54 51.12 N 11.35 E
Bad Blankenburg 54 50.41 N 11.16 E
Bad Bramstedt 52 53.55 N 9.53 E
Bad Breisig 56 50.31 N 7.18 E
Bad Brückenau 56 50.18 N 9.47 E
Bad Buchau 58 48.03 N 9.36 E
Bad Camberg 56 50.18 N 8.16 E
Bad Creek ≃ 216 41.25 N 83.57 W
Baddā 132 33.41 N 36.26 E
Badda Rogghie ∧ 144 8.43 N 37.41 E
Baddeck 186 46.07 N 60.45 W
Bad Ditzenbach 56 48.35 N 9.41 E
Baddo ≃ 128 27.59 N 64.21 E
Bad Doberan 54 54.06 N 11.53 E
Baddomalhi 123 31.59 N 74.40 E
Bad Dreibergen 52 53.12 N 8.01 E
Bad Driburg 52 51.44 N 9.01 E
Bad Düben 54 51.36 N 12.34 E
Bad Dürkheim 56 49.28 N 8.10 E
Bad Dürrenberg 54 51.18 N 12.04 E
Bad Dürrheim 58 48.01 N 8.32 E
Badé, Centraf. 152 6.41 N 17.07 E
Bade, Indon. 164 7.10 S 139.35 E
Badeggi 150 9.05 N 6.08 E
Badéguichéri 150 14.31 N 5.22 E
Bad Eilsen 52 52.14 N 9.06 E
Badel 54 52.44 N 11.19 E
Bad Elster 54 50.17 N 12.14 E
Bad Ems 56 50.20 N 7.43 E
Baden, B.R.D. 52 53.00 N 9.04 E
Baden, On., Can. 212 43.24 N 80.39 W
Baden, Ityo. 144 17.00 N 38.00 E
Baden, Öst. 264b 48.00 N 16.14 E
Baden, Schw. 58 47.29 N 8.18 E
Baden, Pa., U.S. 214 40.38 N 80.13 W
Baden-Baden 56 48.46 N 8.14 E
Bad Endbach 56 50.45 N 8.32 E
Badenoch ▫9 46 56.57 N 4.19 W
Baden-Powell, Mount ∧ 228 34.21 N 117.46 W
Badenweiler 58 47.48 N 7.40 E
Baden-Württemberg ▫3 30 48.30 N 9.00 E
Badenyon 46 57.15 N 3.05 W
Baderna 64 45.12 N 13.46 E
Badersleben 54 51.59 N 10.53 E
Bad Essen 52 52.19 N 8.20 E
Bad Feilnbach 64 47.46 N 12.00 E
Badfish Creek ≃ 216 42.50 N 89.10 W
Bad Frankenhausen 54 51.21 N 11.06 E
Bad Freienwalde 54 52.47 N 14.01 E
Bad Friedrichshall 56 49.14 N 9.11 E
Bad Fusch 64 47.12 N 12.51 E
Badgam 123 34.01 N 74.43 E
Bad Gandersheim 52 51.52 N 10.01 E
Badgastein 64 47.07 N 13.08 E
Badger, Nf., Can. 186 48.59 N 56.02 W
Badger, Mn., U.S. 198 48.46 N 96.00 W
Badger Creek ≃, Co., U.S. 198 40.17 N 103.42 W
Badger Creek ≃, Co., U.S. 200 38.28 N 105.52 W
Badger Creek ≃, Or., U.S. 224 45.16 N 121.11 W
Badger Pass)(226 37.40 N 119.39 W
Badger's Mount 260 51.20 N 0.09 E
Badgery's Creek 274a 33.53 S 150.44 E
Badgerys Creek ≃ 274a 33.51 S 150.46 E
Bādghīs ▫4 128 35.00 N 63.45 E
Bad Gleichenberg 61 46.52 N 15.54 E
Bad Godesberg 56 50.41 N 7.10 E
Bad Goisern 64 47.38 N 13.37 E
Bad Gottleuba 54 50.51 N 13.56 E
Bad Griesbach 58 48.27 N 8.14 E
Bad Grund 52 51.48 N 10.14 E
Bad Hall 61 48.02 N 14.13 E
Bad Harzburg 54 51.53 N 10.33 E
Bad Heilbrunn 64 47.45 N 11.28 E
Badhela ✦8 272a 28.38 N 77.04 E
Bad Helmstedt 54 52.14 N 11.03 E
Bad Hersfeld 56 50.52 N 9.42 E
Badhoevedorp 52 52.21 N 4.46 E
Bad Hofgastein 64 47.10 N 13.06 E
Bad Homburg vor der Höhe 56 50.13 N 8.37 E
Bad Honnef 56 50.39 N 7.13 E
Bad Hönningen 56 50.31 N 7.19 E
Bāḍī ≃ 124 27.55 N 83.27 E
Badia (Abtei) 64 46.37 N 11.54 E
Badia, Val V 64 46.40 N 11.53 E
Badia Calavena 64 45.34 N 11.09 E
Badia Polesine 64 45.05 N 11.29 E
Badia Prataglia 66 43.47 N 11.52 E
Badia Tedalda 66 43.42 N 12.11 E
Badile Camuno, Pizzo ∧ 58 46.01 N 10.25 E
Badīn 120 24.39 N 68.50 E
Bādinan 272b 22.54 N 88.14 E
Badinko ≃ 150 13.42 N 9.35 W
Badin Lake ⊜1 192 35.27 N 80.06 W
Badiraguato 232 25.22 N 107.31 W
Bad Ischl 64 47.43 N 13.37 E
Bad Kissingen 56 50.12 N 10.04 E
Bad Kleinen 54 53.46 N 11.28 E
Bad Kleinkirchheim 64 46.49 N 13.49 E
Bad Klosterlausnitz 54 50.55 N 11.52 E
Bad Kohlgrub 64 47.40 N 11.03 E
Bad König 56 49.45 N 9.01 E
Bad Königshofen im Grabfeld 56 50.18 N 10.29 E
Bad Kösen 54 51.08 N 11.43 E
Bad Köstritz 54 50.56 N 12.01 E
Bad Kreuznach 56 49.52 N 7.51 E
Bad Krozingen 58 47.55 N 7.43 E
Bādkulla 126 23.17 N 88.32 E
Bad Laasphe 56 50.56 N 8.24 E
Badlands ⋀2, U.S. 198 46.45 N 103.30 W
Badlands ⋀2, S.D., U.S. 198 43.30 N 102.20 W
Badlands National Park ♦ 198 43.47 N 102.15 W
Bad Langensalza 56 51.06 N 10.38 E
Bad Lauchstädt 54 51.23 N 11.52 E
Bad Lausick 54 51.08 N 12.38 E
Bad Lauterberg [im Harz] 52 51.38 N 10.28 E
Bad Leonfelden 61 48.33 N 14.19 E
Bādli ✦8 272a 28.45 N 77.09 E
Bad Liebenstein 54 50.49 N 10.21 E
Bad Liebenwerda 54 51.31 N 13.23 E
Bad Liebenzell 56 48.46 N 8.44 E
Bad Lippspringe 52 51.46 N 8.49 E
Bad Meinberg 52 51.53 N 8.58 E
Bad Mergentheim 56 49.30 N 9.46 E
Bad Mukran 54 54.26 N 13.35 E
Bad Münder 52 52.12 N 9.27 E
Bad Münster am Stein 56 49.49 N 7.51 E
Bad Münstereifel 56 50.33 N 6.46 E
Bad Muskau 54 51.32 N 14.43 E
Bad Nauheim 56 50.22 N 8.44 E
Bad Nenndorf 52 52.20 N 9.22 E
Badnera 122 20.52 N 77.44 E
Badner Lindkogel ∧ 264b 48.01 N 16.11 E
Bad Neuenahr-Ahrweiler 56 50.33 N 7.08 E
Bad Neustadt an der Saale 56 50.19 N 10.13 E
Bad Niedernau 58 48.27 N 8.53 E

ENGLISH Name	Page	Lat.°′	Long.°′	DEUTSCH Name	Seite	Breite°′	Länge°′ E = Ost

Bad Oeynhausen 52 52.12 N 8.48 E
Badogo 150 11.02 N 8.13 W
Badolato 68 38.34 N 16.31 E
Bad Oldesloe 52 53.48 N 10.22 E
Ba Dong, Viet. 110 9.40 N 106.34 E
Badong, Zhg. 102 31.02 N 110.20 E
Badonviller 58 48.30 N 6.54 E
Bad Orb 56 50.14 N 9.20 E
Badou, Togo 150 7.35 N 0.36 E
Badou, Zhg. 98 36.27 N 117.55 E
Badouling 100 32.10 N 117.36 E
Badoumbé 150 13.38 N 10.13 W
Bad Peterstal 58 48.26 N 8.12 E
Badplaas 158 25.57 S 30.35 E
Bad Polzin → Połczyn Zdrój 30 53.46 N 16.06 E
Bad Pyrmont 52 51.59 N 9.15 E
Badr 142 30.33 N 30.43 E
Bad Radkersburg 61 46.41 N 15.59 E
Bad Ragaz 58 47.00 N 9.30 E
Bad Rappenau 56 49.14 N 9.06 E
Bad Rehburg 52 52.26 N 9.13 E
Bad Reichenhall 64 47.43 N 12.52 E
Badr Hunayn 128 23.44 N 38.46 E
Bad Rippoldsau 58 48.26 N 8.19 E
Bad River Indian Reservation ✦4 190 46.33 N 90.40 W
Bad Rothenfelde 52 52.06 N 8.09 E
Bad Saarow-Pieskow 54 52.17 N 14.03 E
Bad Sachsa 54 51.36 N 10.32 E
Bad Säckingen 58 47.33 N 7.56 E
Bad Salzdetfurth 52 52.03 N 10.01 E
Bad Salzig 56 50.12 N 7.38 E
Bad Salzschlirf 56 50.37 N 9.29 E
Bad Salzuflen 52 52.05 N 8.44 E
Bad Salzungen 56 50.48 N 10.13 E
Bad Sankt Leonhard im Lavanttal 61 46.58 N 14.48 E
Bad Sassendorf 52 51.35 N 8.10 E
Bad Schandau 54 50.55 N 14.10 E
Bad Schmiedeberg 54 51.41 N 12.44 E
Bad Schwalbach 56 50.08 N 8.04 E
Bad Schwartau 54 53.55 N 10.40 E
Bad Segeberg 52 53.56 N 10.17 E
Bādshāhpur 124 25.47 N 82.49 E
Bad Soden 56 50.08 N 8.30 E
Bad Soden-Salmünster 56 50.17 N 9.22 E
Bad Sooden-Allendorf 56 51.16 N 9.58 E
Bad Steben 54 50.22 N 11.38 E
Bad Stuer 54 53.22 N 12.19 E
Bad Suderode 54 51.44 N 11.07 E
Bad Sulza 54 51.05 N 11.37 E
Bad Sülze 54 54.06 N 12.38 E
Bad Tatzmannsdorf 61 47.20 N 16.13 E
Bad Teinach 56 48.41 N 8.41 E
Bad Tennstedt 54 51.09 N 10.50 E
Bad Tölz 64 47.46 N 11.34 E
Badu, Bra. 287a 22.54 S 43.04 W
Badu, Zhg. 100 26.51 N 119.35 E
Badu, Zhg. 100 28.32 N 117.57 E
Badu, Zhg. 102 24.15 N 105.41 E
Badu Island I 164 10.07 S 142.08 E
Badulla 122 6.59 N 81.03 E
Badung, Selat ʮ 115b 8.40 S 115.22 E
Badupi 120 21.36 N 93.25 E
Bādura 126 22.16 N 90.21 E
Bad Urach 58 48.29 N 9.23 E
Bāduria 126 22.44 N 88.47 E
Badvel 122 14.45 N 79.03 E
Bad Vellach 61 46.26 N 14.33 E
Bad Vilbel 56 50.12 N 8.42 E
Bad Vöslau 61 47.57 N 16.16 E
Bad Waldsee 58 47.55 N 9.45 E
Bad Warmbrunn → Cieplice Śląskie-Zdrój 30 50.52 N 15.41 E
Badwater Creek ≃ 202 43.17 N 108.08 W
Bad Westernkotten 52 51.38 N 8.21 E
Bad Wiessee 64 47.43 N 11.43 E
Bad Wildungen 56 51.07 N 9.07 E
Bad Wilsnack 54 52.57 N 11.57 E
Bad Wimpfen 56 49.14 N 9.09 E
Bad Windsheim 56 49.31 N 10.25 E
Bad Wörishofen 58 48.00 N 10.36 E
Bad Wurzach 58 47.54 N 9.54 E
Badžalskij chrebet ⋀ 89 50.40 N 134.50 E
Bad Zwischenahn 52 53.11 N 8.00 E
Baediam 150 15.03 N 11.51 W
Bække 41 55.34 N 9.09 E
Baena 34 37.37 N 4.19 W
Baependi 256 21.57 S 44.53 W
Baependi ≃ 256 21.52 S 45.04 W
Baer Field ⊠ 216 40.59 N 85.11 W
Baerl ✦8 263 51.29 N 6.41 E
Baesweiler 56 50.54 N 6.11 E
Báez 240p 22.13 N 79.45 W
Baeza, Ec. 246 0.27 S 77.53 W
Baeza, Esp. 34 37.59 N 3.28 W
Baezaeko ≃ 182 53.09 N 123.48 W
Bafang 152 5.09 N 10.11 E
Bafatá 150 12.10 N 14.40 W
Bafelé 150 10.09 N 10.08 W
Baffa 123 34.26 N 73.13 E
Baffin Basin ✦1 16 73.15 N 67.00 W
Baffin Bay ⊂, N.A. 16 73.00 N 66.00 W
Baffin Bay ⊂, Tx., U.S. 196 27.15 N 97.33 W
Baffin Island I 176 68.00 N 70.00 W
Bafia 152 4.44 N 11.16 E
Bafilo 150 9.21 N 1.16 E
Bafing ≃, Afr. 150 13.49 N 10.50 W
Bafing ≃, Mali 150 12.27 N 7.07 W
Bafing Makana 150 12.33 N 10.15 W
Bafoulabé 150 13.48 N 10.50 W
Bafoussam 152 5.29 N 10.24 E
Bāfq 128 31.35 N 55.24 E
Bafra 130 41.34 N 35.56 E
Bafra Burnu ➤ 130 41.44 N 35.58 E
Bāft 128 29.14 N 56.38 E
Bafuku 154 4.15 N 27.54 E
Bafwabaka 154 2.07 N 27.40 E
Bafwabalinga 154 0.51 N 27.04 E
Bafwaboli 154 0.39 N 26.10 E
Bafwangbe 154 1.39 N 26.51 E
Bafwapada 154 0.56 N 26.57 E
Bafwasende 154 1.05 N 27.16 E
Bafwasomboli 154 1.27 N 27.01 E
Baga 126 22.26 N 90.28 E
Bagabag 116 16.37 N 121.15 E
Bagabag Island I 164 4.50 S 146.15 E
Baga-Burul 80 46.00 N 44.36 E
Bagac 116 14.36 N 120.23 E
Bagacay Point ➤ 116 8.58 N 124.48 E
Bagac Bay ⊂ 116 14.36 N 120.22 E
Bagaces 236 10.31 N 85.15 W
Baga Chentej nuruu ⋀ 88 48.30 N 107.30 E
Bagage ∧ 154 3.23 N 40.12 E
Bagagem ≃, Bra. 250 11.37 S 48.12 W
Bagagem ≃, Bra. 255 13.58 S 48.21 W
Bagaha 124 27.06 N 84.05 E
Bagahak ∧ 116 5.03 N 118.44 E
Bagajevskij 78 47.19 N 40.23 E
Bāgalkot 122 16.11 N 75.42 E
Bagamanoc 116 13.57 N 124.17 E
Bagamoyo 154 6.26 S 38.54 E
Bagan 86 54.06 N 77.40 E
Bagana 80 54.22 N 51.25 E
Bagana, Mount ∧ 175e 6.09 S 155.12 E
Bagan Datoh 114 3.59 N 100.47 E
Bagañga 116 7.35 N 126.34 E
Bagan Serai 114 5.01 N 100.32 E
Bagansiapiapi 114 2.09 N 100.49 E
Bagansinembah 114 1.46 N 100.29 E
Bagansitukang 114 2.38 N 100.15 E
Baganza ≃ 64 44.47 N 10.19 E
Bagara 85 40.55 N 68.26 E
Bağarası 130 37.42 N 27.33 E
Bagaroua 150 14.38 N 4.21 E
Bagasra 120 21.29 N 70.57 E
Bagata 152 3.44 S 17.57 E
Bāgātipāra 126 24.18 N 88.57 E
Bagawi 140 12.19 N 34.21 E
Bagband 52 53.21 N 7.36 E
Bagbe ≃ 150 8.42 N 11.15 W
Bagbele 154 4.21 N 29.17 E
Bāgda 126 23.13 N 86.41 E
Bagdad → Baghdād, 'Īrāq 128 33.21 N 44.25 E
Bagdad, Az., U.S. 200 34.34 N 113.12 W
Bagdad, Fl., U.S. 194 30.35 N 87.01 W
Bagdad, Ky., U.S. 218 38.15 N 85.03 W
Bagdaha 126 23.13 N 88.53 E
Bagdanga 126 24.02 N 88.32 E
Bagdarin 88 54.26 N 113.36 E
Bağdere 130 38.07 N 40.44 E
Bagé 252 31.20 S 54.06 W
Bagehadu 120 35.25 N 84.50 E
Bâgé-le-Châtel 58 46.18 N 4.56 E
Bagenkop 41 54.45 N 10.41 E
Bāgerhāt 124 22.40 N 89.48 E
Bagerovo 78 45.23 N 36.17 E
Bages et de Sigean, Étang de ⊂ 32 43.05 N 3.03 E
Bāgevādi 122 16.35 N 75.58 E
Baggao 116 17.56 N 121.46 E
Baggeryd 24 57.30 N 14.07 E
Baggetorp 40 59.01 N 16.04 E
Baggio ✦8 266b 45.27 N 9.06 E
Bağgöze 130 37.43 N 41.55 E
Baggs 200 41.02 N 107.39 W
Baggy Point ➤ 42 51.09 N 4.16 W
Bāgh 123 33.59 N 73.47 E
Baghdād 128 33.21 N 44.25 E
Baghdād ▫4 128 33.30 N 44.30 E
Baghdobā 126 22.08 N 87.54 E
Baghelkhand Plateau ⋀1 124 23.45 N 82.20 E
Bāgh-e Malek 128 31.32 N 49.55 E
Bagheria 70 38.05 N 13.30 E
Bāgherpāra 126 23.14 N 89.21 E
Bāghia 126 23.27 N 90.29 E
Baghia Bīl ≋ 126 23.07 N 90.03 E
Bāghīn 128 30.12 N 56.48 E
Baghlān 120 36.13 N 68.46 E
Baghlān ▫4 120 35.45 N 69.00 E
Bāghmundi 124 23.12 N 86.03 E
Bāghpat 124 28.57 N 77.13 E
Baghrān Khowleh 120 33.01 N 64.58 E
Bagillt 262 53.16 N 3.10 W
Bagilt Bank ✦4 262 53.17 N 3.09 W
Bağırpaşa Dağı ∧ 130 39.30 N 40.06 E
Bağkonak 130 38.12 N 31.17 E
Bagley 198 47.31 N 95.23 W
Bāgli 124 22.39 N 76.21 E
Bağlıca 130 37.53 N 41.46 E
Bağlum 130 40.03 N 32.51 E
Bagmanl'ar 84 40.38 N 46.18 E
Bāgmāri ✦8 272b 22.34 N 88.25 E
Bāgmatī ▫6 124 27.45 N 85.30 E
Bāgmatī ≃ 124 25.31 N 86.44 E
Bagn 26 60.49 N 9.34 E
Bagnacavallo 66 44.25 N 12.00 E
Bagnaia 66 42.25 N 12.09 E
Bāgnān 126 22.28 N 87.59 E
Bagnara Calabra 68 38.18 N 15.49 E
Bagnara di Romagna 66 44.23 N 11.49 E
Bag Narin 102 38.57 N 94.08 E
Bagnasco 62 44.18 N 8.02 E
Bagnell Dam ✦6 194 38.11 N 92.39 W
Bagnères-de-Bigorre 32 43.04 N 0.09 E
Bagnères-de-Luchon 32 42.47 N 0.36 E
Bagnes, Vallée de V 58 46.03 N 7.18 E
Bagneux 261 48.48 N 2.18 E
Bagni Acque Albule, It. 66 41.57 N 12.43 E
Bagni Acque Albule, It. 267a 41.57 N 12.43 E
Bagni del Masino 58 46.15 N 9.36 E
Bagni di Lucca 66 44.01 N 10.35 E
Bagni di Rabbi 64 46.24 N 10.48 E
Bagno a Ripoli 66 43.45 N 11.19 E
Bagno di Romagna 66 43.50 N 11.57 E
Bagnolet 261 48.52 N 2.25 E
Bagnoli del Trigno 66 41.42 N 14.27 E
Bagnoli di Sopra 64 45.11 N 11.53 E
Bagnoli Irpino 68 40.50 N 15.04 E
Bagnolo in Piano 64 44.46 N 10.40 E
Bagnolo Mella 64 45.26 N 10.10 E
Bagnols-en-Forêt 62 43.32 N 6.42 E
Bagnols-sur-Cèze 62 44.10 N 4.37 E
Bagñon 116 13.44 N 122.50 E
Bagnone 64 44.19 N 10.00 E
Bagnoregio 66 42.37 N 12.05 E
Bagno Vignoni 66 43.02 N 11.39 E
Bago (Pegu) 110 17.20 N 96.29 E
Bago ▫8 110 18.00 N 96.00 E
Bågø I 41 55.18 N 9.49 E
Bago ≃ 116 10.33 N 122.50 E
Bagod 61 46.53 N 16.45 E
Bagodar 124 24.05 N 85.52 E
Bagodo 152 6.25 N 13.23 E
Bagoé ≃ 150 12.36 N 6.34 W
Bagolino 64 45.49 N 10.28 E
Bagoni 146 7.53 N 10.43 E
Bagot ▫6 206 45.40 N 72.45 W
Bagotville, Base des Forces canadiennes ■ 186 48.20 N 70.58 W
Bağpınar 130 37.35 N 38.19 E
Bagrationovsk 76 54.23 N 20.39 E
Bagraula ✦8 272a 28.34 N 77.04 E
Bagre 250 1.54 S 50.12 W
Bagrinovcy 78 49.17 N 27.56 E
Bagshot 42 51.22 N 0.42 W
Bag Tal 89 43.20 N 122.16 E
Bagua 248 5.40 S 78.31 W
Bāguiati 272b 22.36 N 88.26 E
Baguio 116 16.25 N 120.36 E
Bagula 126 23.19 N 88.39 E
Bagumbayan 269f 14.28 N 121.03 E
Bagyrlaj ≃ 80 48.08 N 51.14 E
Bagzane ∧ 150 17.43 N 8.45 E
Bāh 124 26.53 N 78.36 E
Bāhādurābād Ghāt 124 25.09 N 89.42 E
Bāhādurgarh 124 28.41 N 76.56 E
Bāhādurpur 126 23.25 N 88.28 E
Bahaia, Monte ∧ 144 11.20 N 49.45 E
Baha'i Temple ʊ1 278 42.05 N 87.41 W
Bahamas ▫1, N.A. 230 24.15 N 76.00 W
Bahamas ▫1, N.A. 238 24.15 N 76.00 W
Bahār 128 34.54 N 48.26 E
Baharāgora 126 22.17 N 86.43 E
Baharampur 126 24.06 N 88.15 E
Baharpur 126 23.41 N 89.34 E
Bahau 114 2.49 N 102.25 E
Bahau ≃ 112 2.34 N 116.20 E
Bahāwalnagar 123 29.59 N 73.16 E
Bahāwalpur 123 29.24 N 71.41 E
Bahçe 130 37.14 N 36.34 E
Bahçeköy ✦8 267b 41.11 N 28.59 E
Bahçeköy su kemeri ≍1 267b 41.03 N 28.59 E
Bahechuan 98 40.59 N 124.49 E
Baheri 124 28.47 N 79.30 E
Bahi, Pil. 116 13.53 N 123.38 E
Bahi, Tan. 154 5.59 S 35.19 E
Bahia → Salvador 255 12.59 S 38.31 W
Bahia ▫3 250 11.00 S 42.00 W
Bahía Blanca 252 38.43 S 62.17 W
Bahía Bustamante 254 45.08 S 66.32 W
Bahía de Caráquez 246 0.36 S 80.25 W
Bahía Honda 240p 22.54 N 83.10 W
Bahia Honda Key I 220 24.40 N 81.16 W
Bahia Honda Point ➤ 116 9.24 N 118.07 E
Bahía Kino 232 28.50 N 111.55 W
Bahía Laura 254 48.24 S 66.29 W
Bahīj 142 30.56 N 29.35 E
Bahir Dar 144 11.35 N 37.28 E
Bahi Swamp ≋ 154 6.05 S 35.10 E
Bahjoi 124 28.24 N 78.37 E
Bahl 123 28.38 N 75.38 E
Bahlolpur 272a 28.37 N 77.24 E

Symbols in the index entries represent the broad categories identified in the key at the right. Symbols with superior numbers (⋀1) identify subcategories (see complete key on page *I · 1).*

Symbole im Register stellen die rechts im Schlüssel erklärten Kategorien dar. Symbole mit hochgestellten Ziffern (⋀1) bezeichnen Unterabteilungen einer Kategorie (vgl. vollständiger Schlüssel auf Seite *I · 1).*

Los símbolos incluídos en el texto del índice representan las grandes categorias identificadas con la clave a la derecha. Los símbolos con numeros en su parte superior (⋀1) identifican las subcategorías (véase la clave completa en la página *I · 1).*

Les symboles de l'index représentent les catégories indiquées dans la légende à droite. Les symboles suivis d'un indice (⋀1) représentent des sous-catégories (voir légende complète à la page *I · 1).*

Os símbolos incluídos no texto do índice representam as grandes categorias identificadas com a chave à direita. Os símbolos com números em sua parte superior (⋀1) identificam as subcategorias (veja-se a chave completa à página *I · 1).*

∧ Mountain	Berg	Montaña	Montagne	Montanha
⋀ Mountains	Gebirge	Montañas	Montagnes	Montanhas
)(Pass	Paß	Paso	Col	Passo
V Valley, Canyon	Tal, Cañon	Valle, Cañón	Vallée, Canyon	Vale, Canhão
≚ Plain	Ebene	Llano	Plaine	Planície
➤ Cape	Kap	Cabo	Cap	Cabo
I Island	Insel	Isla	Île	Ilha
II Islands	Inseln	Islas	Îles	Ilhas
✦ Other Topographic Features	Andere Topographische Objekte	Otros Elementos Topográficos	Autres données topographiques	Outros acidentes topográficos

ESPAÑOL Nombre	Página	Lat.°′	Long.°′ W = Oeste
Bahn	150	7.05 N	8.45 W
Bahnāy	142	30.23 N	31.04 E
Bahnayā	142	30.41 N	31.23 E
Baḥrah	144	21.24 N	39.29 E
Bahraich	124	27.35 N	81.36 E
Bahrain (Al-Baḥrayn) □[1], Asia	118	26.00 N	50.30 E
Bahrain (Al-Baḥrayn) □[1], Asia	128	26.00 N	50.30 E
Baḥr al-Ghazāl □[4]	140	8.30 N	26.00 E
Bahrām Chāh	128	29.26 N	64.03 E
Baḥrānī, Ḥālat al- I	128	24.23 N	54.14 E
Baḥrayn, Khalīj al ⊂	128	25.45 N	50.40 E
Bahrdorf	54	52.23 N	11.00 E
Bahrein → Bahrain □[1]	128	26.00 N	50.30 E
Baḥrīyah, Al-Wāḥāt al- ⫧[4]	140	28.15 N	28.57 E
Bahser	130	37.57 N	39.18 E
Bahtīm	142	30.08 N	31.17 E
Baḥṭīṭ	142	30.29 N	31.38 E
Bāhū Kalāt	128	25.43 N	61.25 E
Bāhū Kalāt ≃	128	25.11 N	61.31 E
Bahulu, Pulau I	112	3.33 S	122.18 E
Bahu-mbelu	112	2.13 S	121.41 E
Bahūt	142	31.10 N	31.19 E
Baï	150	13.38 N	3.22 W
Bai ≃, Zhg.	102	32.10 N	112.20 E
Bai ≃, Zhg.	105	40.43 N	116.33 E
Baia	68	40.49 N	14.04 E
Baia-de-Aramă	38	45.00 N	22.49 E
Baía dos Tigres	152	16.36 S	11.43 E
Baía Farta	152	12.40 S	13.11 E
Baía Formosa	250	6.22 S	35.00 W
Baia Mare	38	47.40 N	23.35 E
Baiano	68	40.57 N	14.37 E
Baião	250	2.41 S	49.41 W
Baiardo	62	43.54 N	7.43 E
Baia Sprie	38	47.40 N	23.42 E
Baibao	105	39.04 N	115.31 E
Baibei	100	27.47 N	115.53 E
Baïbokoum	146	7.46 N	15.43 E
Baibuting	106	30.33 N	120.46 E
Baicang	124	30.14 N	90.44 E
Baicao	98	41.13 N	116.07 E
Baicaochang	102	32.08 N	103.59 E
Baicao Ling ∧∧	102	26.10 N	101.20 E
Baicha	100	29.11 N	115.37 E
Baicheng, Zhg.	89	45.38 N	122.46 E
Baicheng, Zhg.	90	41.46 N	81.52 E
Baidian	106	30.47 N	119.14 E
Baidiao	102	28.07 N	101.28 E
Baidunzi	102	43.11 N	95.19 E
Baidyabāti	126	22.47 N	88.20 E
Baidyanāth	124	24.29 N	86.42 E
Baidyer Bāzār	126	23.39 N	90.37 E
Baie-Comeau	186	49.13 N	68.10 W
Baie-Comeau-Hauterive, Réserve ♠	186	50.05 N	68.00 W
Baie-des-Ha90 Ha90	186	50.56 N	58.56 W
Baie-de-Shawinigan	206	46.34 N	72.45 W
Baie-des-Moutons	186	50.47 N	59.02 W
Baie-du-Renard	186	49.17 N	61.50 W
Baie-d'Urfé	206	45.25 N	73.55 W
Baie-Johan-Beetz	186	50.17 N	62.48 W
Baie-Mahault	241o	16.16 N	61.35 W
Baienfurt	64	47.49 N	9.38 E
Baiersbronn	58	48.30 N	8.22 E
Baiersdorf	60	49.39 N	11.01 E
Baies, Lac des ◎	190	47.18 N	77.40 W
Baie-Sainte-Claire	186	49.54 N	64.30 W
Baie-Saint-Paul	186	47.27 N	70.30 W
Baie-Trinité	186	49.25 N	67.18 W
Baie Verte	186	49.56 N	56.11 W
Baieville	206	46.08 N	72.43 W
Baigezhuang	105	39.54 N	118.09 E
Baigneux-les-Juifs	58	47.36 N	4.38 E
Baigong	100	24.18 N	116.14 E
Baigou	105	39.07 N	116.01 E
Baigou ≃	105	39.06 N	116.00 E
Baiguoshu	106	30.45 N	119.07 E
Baigusi	102	33.10 N	103.52 E
Baihāli Jot ∧	123	32.51 N	76.32 E
Baihar	124	22.06 N	80.33 E
Baihe, Zhg.	100	29.12 N	120.55 E
Baihe, Zhg.	102	32.17 N	110.02 E
Baihebu	105	40.39 N	116.10 E
Baihegang	106	31.16 N	121.08 E
Baihekou	102	31.46 N	110.13 E
Baihou	100	24.18 N	116.48 E
Baihua	107	29.07 N	104.37 E
Baihua Shan ∧	105	39.50 N	115.35 E
Baijala	272b	22.51 N	88.16 E
Baijian	105	39.36 N	115.16 E
Baijiang	100	29.51 N	119.20 E
Baijiawu	105	39.30 N	116.28 E
Baijie	107	29.17 N	106.31 E
Baijietan	107	28.44 N	105.30 E
Baijnāth	124	29.55 N	79.37 E
Baiju	100	33.04 N	120.20 E
Baikal, Lago → Bajkal, ozero ◎	88	53.00 N	107.40 E
Baikal, Lake → Bajkal, ozero ◎	88	53.00 N	107.40 E
Baikal-See → Bajkal, ozero ◎	88	53.00 N	107.40 E
Baikeshu	106	30.26 N	118.55 E
Baikonur → Bajkonyr	86	47 50 N	66.03 E
Baikunthapur	272b	22 59 N	88.13 E
Baikunthpur	124	23 15 N	82.33 E
Bailadores	246	8 15 N	71.50 W
Bailaiqiao	100	32 40 N	118.23 E
Bailang	89	46.57 N	120.05 E
Baildon	44	53.52 N	1.46 W
Baile	105	39.55 N	114.51 E
Baile Átha Cliath → Dublin	28	53.20 N	6.15 W
Baile Átha Luain → Athlone	48	53.25 N	7.56 W
Băile Govora	38	45.05 N	24.11 E
Băile Herculane	38	44.54 N	22.25 E
Bailén	34	38.06 N	3.46 W
Băile Olănești	38	45.11 N	24.16 E
Băilești	38	44.02 N	23.21 E
Bailey	192	35.46 N	78.07 W
Bailey Lakes	214	40.57 N	82.21 W
Bailey Run ≃	279b	40.35 N	79.47 W
Baileys Crossroads	284c	38.51 N	77.08 W
Bail Hongal	122	15.49 N	74.52 E
Bailian	102	24.09 N	112.22 E
Bailicun	102	25.45 N	110.33 E
Bailieborough	48	53.54 N	6.59 W
Bailin, Zhg.	100	27.12 N	120.10 E
Bailin, Zhg.	100	26.20 N	113.18 E
Bailin, Zhg.	107	29.11 N	105.57 E
Bailin, Zhg.	107	28.45 N	106.26 E
Bailingmiao → Darhan Muminggan Lianheqi	102	41.50 N	110.27 E
Bailique	250	0.58 N	50.04 W
Bailique, Ilha I	250	1.02 N	49.58 W
Bailleau-sous-Gallardon	261	48.32 N	1.39 E
Bailleul	50	50.44 N	2.44 E
Ba Illi	146	10.30 N	16.34 E
Baillie ≃	176	65.10 N	104.24 W
Baillie Islands II	176	70.33 N	128.10 W
Baillies Bacolet	241k	12.02 N	61.41 W
Baillif	241o	16.01 N	61.45 W
Bailly-Romainvilliers	261	48.50 N	2.49 E
Bailong ≃	102	32.18 N	105.42 E
Bailonggang	106	31.15 N	121.44 E
Bailu ≃	100	32.25 N	115.34 E
Bailuchang	107	28.56 N	105.57 E
Bailu Hu ◎	100	30.03 N	113.06 E
Bailundo	152	12.12 S	15.52 E
Bailuoji	100	29.37 N	113.15 E
Baima, Zhg.	106	31.35 N	119.10 E
Baima, Zhg.	107	30.03 N	103.44 E
Baima, Zhg.	107	29.09 N	104.16 E

FRANÇAIS Nom	Page	Lat.°′	Long.°′ W = Ouest
Baimachang, Zhg.	102	29.18 N	107.30 E
Baimachang, Zhg.	104	41.59 N	122.30 E
Baimachang, Zhg.	107	29.40 N	103.54 E
Baimaguan	105	40.41 N	116.52 E
Baimakou	102	25.55 N	102.06 E
Baimamiao, Zhg.	102	36.58 N	108.08 E
Baimamiao, Zhg.	107	29.33 N	104.59 E
Baimao, Zhg.	106	31.39 N	120.52 E
Baimao, Zhg.	106	31.35 N	120.54 E
Baima Shan ∧	102	27.12 N	110.32 E
Baimashi	100	29.15 N	118.42 E
Baimazhai	100	28.06 N	115.50 E
Baimiaozi, Zhg.	89	46.18 N	123.35 E
Baimiaozi, Zhg.	98	40.34 N	120.36 E
Baimiaozi, Zhg.	104	41.55 N	122.12 E
Baimiaozi, Zhg.	107	29.47 N	106.29 E
Baimuqiao	106	32.01 N	120.19 E
Baimuru	164	7.30 S	144.49 E
Bain ≃	44	53.05 N	0.12 W
Baïna Bondio	152	5.10 N	16.33 E
Bainang	120	29.11 N	89.12 E
Bainbridge, Ga., U.S.	192	30.54 N	84.34 W
Bainbridge, N.Y., U.S.	210	42.17 N	75.28 W
Bainbridge, Oh., U.S.	218	39.13 N	83.16 W
Bainbridge, Pa., U.S.	208	40.05 N	76.40 W
Bainbridge Island I	224	47.37 N	122.33 W
Bainchi	126	23.07 N	88.14 E
Bainchipota	272b	22.52 N	88.16 E
Bain-de-Bretagne	32	47.50 N	1.41 W
Baing	115b	10.14 S	120.34 E
Bainiqiao	100	29.35 N	114.09 E
Bains-les-Bains, Fr.	58	48.00 N	6.16 E
Bains-les-Bains, Fr.	58	48.20 N	6.20 E
Bainville	198	48.08 N	104.13 W
Bainyik	164	3.40 S	143.00 E
Baipeng	102	24.09 N	109.25 E
Baipu	106	32.15 N	120.46 E
Baiqibao	104	41.48 N	122.30 E
Baiqiu	100	32.44 N	112.38 E
Baiquan, Zhg.	89	47.36 N	126.07 E
Baiquan, Zhg.	100	30.06 N	122.08 E
Baiqueyuan	100	31.48 N	115.05 E
Bair, Pa., U.S.	208	39.54 N	76.50 W
Bā'ir, Urd.	132	30.46 N	36.41 E
Bā'ir, Wādī V	132	30.58 N	37.09 E
Bairab Co ◎	120	35.00 N	83.03 E
Baird	196	32.23 N	99.23 W
Baird, Mount ∧	202	43.22 N	111.06 W
Bairdford	214	40.37 N	79.52 W
Baird Inlet ⊂	180	60.45 N	164.00 W
Baird Mountains ∧∧	180	67.35 N	161.30 W
Baire	240p	20.19 N	76.20 W
Bairiki	174t	1.20 N	173.01 E
Bairin Zuoqi	90	44.00 N	119.00 E
Bair Island I	282	37.32 N	122.13 W
Bairkum	85	42.05 N	68.11 E
Bairnsdale	166	37.50 S	147.38 E
Bairoil	200	42.14 N	107.33 W
Bairrinho	256	22.36 S	47.06 W
Bairro Alto	256	23.29 S	45.21 W
Baïrsak (Sājūr) ≃	130	36.40 N	38.05 E
Bairuopu	100	28.12 N	112.46 E
Bais, Fr.	32	48.15 N	0.22 W
Bais, Pil.	116	9.35 N	123.07 E
Baïse ≃	32	44.17 N	0.18 E
Baisha, Zhg.	100	29.26 N	119.16 E
Baisha, Zhg.	100	26.58 N	115.22 E
Baisha, Zhg.	100	25.40 N	118.59 E
Baisha, Zhg.	100	24.39 N	113.31 E
Baisha, Zhg.	100	25.24 N	117.16 E
Baisha, Zhg.	100	34.20 N	113.14 E
Baisha, Zhg.	100	34.22 N	112.32 E
Baisha, Zhg.	107	28.55 N	105.45 E
Baisha, Zhg.	107	29.04 N	106.07 E
Baisha, Zhg.	110	19.17 N	109.27 E
Baishaba	107	30.03 N	106.21 E
Bai Shan I	106	30.35 N	121.43 E
Baishanji	100	33.48 N	116.40 E
Baishantu	104	42.21 N	122.35 E
Baishapu	100	29.58 N	115.04 E
Baishatan	98	36.52 N	121.38 E
Baishe	100	27.02 N	116.20 E
Baishecun	105	40.10 N	116.18 E
Baishi, Zhg.	100	27.18 N	119.45 E
Baishi, Zhg.	100	26.48 N	119.46 E
Baishi, Zhg.	102	22.36 N	110.55 E
Baishidu	100	25.26 N	113.01 E
Baishiyi	107	29.29 N	106.22 E
Baishizhai	104	40.57 N	122.58 E
Baishui, Zhg.	100	28.42 N	113.04 E
Baishui, Zhg.	106	30.34 N	119.39 E
Baishui, Zhg.	107	30.06 N	105.38 E
Baishuifan	100	30.17 N	115.43 E
Baishuijiang	102	33.29 N	106.01 E
Baishun	100	25.12 N	114.01 E
Baishuxia	100	27.22 N	113.41 E
Baisinga	126	21.39 N	86.54 E
Baisley Pond ◎	276	40.41 N	73.47 W
Baisogala	76	55.38 N	23.43 E
Bāisrasi	126	23.27 N	90.02 E
Baita, India	272b	22.27 N	88.11 E
Baita, Zhg.	106	31.48 N	119.35 E
Baitaḍī	124	29.32 N	80.26 E
Baital	126	22.57 N	87.28 E
Baitazi	98	42.19 N	120.19 E
Baitazibeigou	104	42.17 N	120.48 E
Bai Thuong	110	19.54 N	105.23 E
Baitings Reservoir ◎[1]	262	53.40 N	1.59 W
Baitou	107	30.37 N	103.36 E
Baitoutan	102	32.30 N	106.56 E
Baitu	106	31.59 N	119.21 E
Baitugang	100	33.28 N	112.22 E
Baiwang	102	24.14 N	108.32 E
Baiwen	102	38.15 N	111.06 E
Baixa da Banheira	266c	38.39 N	9.03 W
Baixa Grande	255	11.57 S	40.11 W
Baixi	107	29.39 N	106.28 E
Baixiang	98	37.32 N	114.34 E
Baixingt	89	43.08 N	121.03 E
Baixio	250	6.44 S	38.43 W
Baixo Longa	152	15.42 S	18.50 E
Baiyan, Zhg.	100	28.04 N	120.02 E
Baiyan, Zhg.	106	31.08 N	119.38 E
Baiyang	100	34.25 N	112.12 E
Baiyang Dian ◎	98	38.53 N	116.00 E
Baiyanghe	86	43.13 N	88.28 E
Baiyan Shan ∧	100	26.05 N	118.25 E
Baiyer River	164	5.35 S	144.10 E
Baiyin	102	36.47 N	104.07 E
Baiyinheshuo	89	44.31 N	119.51 E
Baiyintaohai	89	43.12 N	120.23 E
Baiyü, Zhg.	102	31.18 N	98.49 E
Baiyu, Zhg.	105	40.01 N	115.37 E
Baiyundu	100	26.10 N	118.47 E
Baiyunguan	271a	39.54 N	116.19 E
Baizhongpu	100	33.22 N	114.50 E
Baizi	107	30.06 N	105.43 E
Baja	30	46.11 N	18.57 E
Baja, Punta ≻, Méx.	232	29.58 N	115.49 W
Baja, Punta ≻, Méx.	232	28.28 N	111.45 W
Baja California	200	32.18 N	115.12 W
Baja California ≻[1]	232	28.00 N	113.30 W
Baja California Norte □[3]	232	30.00 N	115.00 W
Baja California Seamount Province ✣	16	26.00 N	124.00 W
Baja California Sur □[3]	232	26.00 N	112.00 W
Bajada del Agrio	252	38.23 S	70.02 W
Baján, Méx.	196	26.32 N	101.15 W
Bajan, S.S.S.R.	84	40.34 N	46.09 E
Bajan Adraga	88	48.32 N	111.03 E
Bajan Agt	88	49.02 N	102.05 E
Bajanaul	86	50.47 N	75.42 E
Bajancagaan	102	45.00 N	98.59 E
Bajan Chajrchan	88	49.18 N	96.20 E
Bajanchongor	90	46.08 N	100.43 E
Bajanchongor □[4]	102	45.00 N	99.30 E
Bajancogt	88	45.54 N	106.10 E
Bajandaj	88	53.04 N	105.30 E
Bajandalaj	102	43.28 N	103.28 E

PORTUGUÊS Nome	Página	Lat.°′	Long.°′ W = Oeste
Bajandelger, Mong.	88	47.44 N	108.07 E
Bajandelger, Mong.	102	45.40 N	112.20 E
Bajan Dün	88	49.13 N	113.23 E
Bajandžargalan	102	45.40 N	107.59 E
Bajan Dzürch	88	50.12 N	98.58 E
Bajan-Enger	86	48.25 N	90.50 E
Bajango	88	48.55 N	106.06 E
Bajan-Gol, S.S.S.R.	88	52.49 N	99.54 E
Bajangol, S.S.S.R.	88	50.44 N	103.27 E
Bajangov'	102	44.44 N	100.24 E
Bajanleg	102	44.33 N	100.50 E
Bajan Nuur	86	48.54 N	91.14 E
Bajanölgij □[4]	86	48.20 N	89.50 E
Bajan-Öndör	102	44.47 N	98.39 E
Bajan-Ovoo, Mong.	88	47.47 N	112.05 E
Bajan-Ovoo, Mong.	102	42.57 N	106.07 E
Bajánsenye	61	46.48 N	16.23 E
Bajan Tümen	88	48.04 N	114.24 E
Bajan Uul, Mong.	88	47.40 N	101.30 E
Bajan Uul, Mong.	88	49.10 N	112.50 E
Bajan Uul, Mong.	88	49.41 N	96.20 E
Bājaur □[9]	123	34.50 N	71.30 E
Baja Verapaz □[5]	236	15.05 N	90.20 W
Bajawa	115b	8.47 S	120.59 E
Bajbičetau ∧∧	85	41.12 N	75.15 E
Baj-Chak	88	51.13 N	94.34 E
Bajčunas	80	47.14 N	52.55 E
Bajčurovo	80	51.20 N	42.41 E
Bajdarackaja guba ⊂	72	69.00 N	67.30 E
Bajdonovo	88	54.17 N	104.38 E
Bajdrag ≃	102	45.38 N	99.15 E
Bājegūn, Kūh-e ∧	128	31.28 N	55.51 E
Bājengdoba	124	25.54 N	90.31 E
Bāje Phukura	126	23.09 N	89.45 E
Bajer	88	55.44 N	99.30 E
Bajestān	128	34.31 N	58.10 E
Bajevo	86	53.17 N	80.46 E
Bajgakum	86	44.18 N	66.28 E
Bajganin	86	48.43 N	55.53 E
Bajghera	272a	28.32 N	77.01 E
Bājgīrān	128	37.36 N	58.24 E
Bajgul	80	48.49 N	49.08 E
Bajiaotai	104	41.14 N	121.14 E
Bajiazi, Zhg.	104	42.21 N	121.27 E
Bajiazi, Zhg.	104	42.17 N	122.37 E
Bajiazi, Zhg.	104	41.36 N	123.53 E
Bājil	144	15.04 N	43.16 E
Bajimba, Mount ∧	166	29.18 S	152.07 E
Bajina Bašta	38	43.58 N	19.34 E
Bajkadam	85	43.44 N	69.55 E
Bajkal	88	51.53 N	104.47 E
Bajkal, ozero (Lake Baikal) ◎	88	53.00 N	107.40 E
Bajkalovo, S.S.S.R.	86	57.24 N	63.46 E
Bajkalovo, S.S.S.R.	86	57.45 N	67.40 E
Bajkal'sk	88	51.33 N	104.05 E
Bajkal'skij chrebet ∧∧	88	55.00 N	108.40 E
Bajkal'skij zapovednik ♠	88	51.25 N	105.10 E
Bajkal'skoje	88	55.21 N	109.12 E
Bajkit	74	61.41 N	96.25 E
Bajkonyr	86	47.50 N	66.03 E
Bajkovo	80	54.47 N	44.51 E
Bajmak	86	52.36 N	58.19 E
Bajmok	38	45.58 N	19.25 E
Bajnazar	86	48.32 N	73.42 E
Bajo, Indon.	112	0.27 N	120.48 E
Bajo, Indon.	115b	8.35 S	119.01 E
Bajo, Canal ≅	266a	40.27 N	3.43 W
Bajo Baudó	246	4.58 N	77.22 W
Bajo Boquete	236	8.47 N	82.26 W
Bajool	166	23.39 S	150.39 E
Bajos de Haina	238	18.25 N	70.02 W
Bajos del Balsamar	234	17.34 N	100.48 W
Bajrački	83	48.22 N	38.32 E
Bajr'aki	80	54.43 N	53.24 E
Bajram-Ali	128	37.37 N	62.10 E
Bajsa	88	53.58 N	113.33 E
Bajseit	85	43.35 N	78.20 E
Baj-Sot	88	51.42 N	95.22 E
Bajsun	85	38.14 N	67.12 E
Bajtajlak	86	45.15 N	75.00 E
Bajulmati	115a	7.56 S	114.23 E
Bajžansaj	85	43.13 N	69.56 E
Bak	61	46.43 N	16.51 E
Bakacak	130	40.12 N	27.06 E
Bakal	86	54.56 N	58.48 E
Bakala	152	6.11 N	20.22 E
Bakaldy	80	55.39 N	44.44 E
Bakali ≃	152	4.34 S	17.06 E
Bakaly	80	55.10 N	53.48 E
Bakambe	152	5.39 S	23.37 E
Bakanas	86	44.50 N	76.15 E
Bakanas ≃	86	47.05 N	79.18 E
Bakap	114	4.26 N	101.04 E
Bakar	116	7.09 N	125.42 E
Bākarganj	124	22.33 N	90.21 E
Bakaruma	124	22.32 N	83.25 E
Bakau, Pulau I	271c	1.16 N	103.43 E
Bakbakty	86	44.35 N	76.40 E
Bakčar	86	57.01 N	82.05 E
Bakčar ≃	86	57.37 N	82.18 E
Bake	112	3.03 S	100.16 E
Bakebe	152	5.35 N	9.33 E
Bakel	150	14.54 N	12.27 W
Bakem	112	1.58 S	105.54 E
Bakenberg ∧[2]	54	54.35 N	13.07 E
Bakenkop	158	28.01 S	23.02 E
Bakeoven Creek ≃	224	45.12 N	121.05 W
Baker, Ca., U.S.	204	35.15 N	116.04 W
Baker, Fl., U.S.	194	30.47 N	86.40 W
Baker, La., U.S.	194	30.35 N	91.10 W
Baker, Mt., U.S.	198	46.22 N	104.17 W
Baker, Or., U.S.	202	44.46 N	117.49 W
Baker ≃, Chile	254	47.49 S	73.37 W
Baker ≃, Wa., U.S.	224	48.38 N	121.41 W
Baker, Canal ʊ	254	48.00 S	74.00 W
Baker, Mount ∧	224	48.47 N	121.49 W
Baker Butte ∧	200	34.27 N	111.22 W
Baker Canyon V	280	33.47 N	117.38 W
Baker Creek ≃, B.C., Can.	182	52.59 N	122.30 W
Baker Creek ≃, Oh., U.S.	279a	41.21 N	81.54 W
Baker Creek ≃, Or., U.S.	224	45.15 N	123.14 W
Baker Island I, Oc.	14	0.15 N	176.27 W
Baker Island I, Ak., U.S.	182	55.20 N	133.36 W
Baker Lake	176	64.15 N	96.00 W
Baker Lake ◎, Austl.	162	26.54 S	126.05 E
Baker Lake ◎, N.T., Can.	176	64.10 N	95.30 W
Baker Lake ◎, Il., U.S.	278	42.08 N	88.07 W
Baker Lake ◎[1]	224	48.43 N	121.37 W
Bakersfield	226	35.22 N	119.01 W
Bakersfield South	228	35.20 N	119.03 W
Bakers Hill	168a	31.45 S	116.27 E
Bakers Island I	283	42.32 N	70.47 W
Bakerstown	214	40.39 N	79.56 W
Baker Street	260	51.30 N	0.21 E
Bakersville, N.C., U.S.	192	36.00 N	82.09 W
Bakersville, Oh., U.S.	214	40.21 N	81.39 W
Bakerville	158	26.00 S	26.06 E
Bakeshu	98	42.26 N	124.37 E
Bâ Kêv	110	13.42 N	107.12 E
Bakewell	44	53.13 N	1.40 W
Bakhra	126	22.24 N	88.11 E
Bākhrābād	126	23.43 N	90.53 E
Bakhri	124	25.35 N	86.16 E
Bākhtarān (Kermānshāh)	128	34.19 N	47.04 E
Bākhtarān □[4]	128	34.30 N	47.00 E
Bakhtegān, Daryācheh-ye ◎	128	29.20 N	54.05 E
Bakhtiyārpur	124	25.28 N	85.31 E
Bakile	154	13.58 S	35.15 E
Bakino	82	56.20 N	38.59 E
Bakinskaja	78	44.46 N	39.18 E
Bakinskij archipelag II	84	39.30 N	49.45 E
Bakır ≃	130	38.55 N	27.00 E

Bakitabu	154	1.29 S	35.34 E
Bakkafjörður	24a	66.04 N	14.45 W
Bakkaflói ⊂	24a	66.10 N	14.45 W
Bakkagerði	24a	65.32 N	13.48 W
Bakkeswar	272b	22.25 N	88.22 E
Bakkeveen	52	53.05 N	6.15 E
Baklan	130	37.58 N	29.36 E
Baklanka	76	58.43 N	40.06 E
Bakloh	123	32.28 N	75.55 E
Bakluši	80	52.07 N	43.22 E
Bako, C. Iv.	150	9.09 N	7.37 W
Bako, Ityo.	144	5.50 N	36.40 E
Bakony ∧∧	30	47.15 N	17.50 E
Bakool □[4]	144	4.00 N	44.00 E
Bakoondfontein	158	32.43 S	22.30 E
Bakori	150	11.34 N	7.27 E
Bakou → Baku	84	40.23 N	49.51 E
Bakouma	152	5.42 N	22.47 E
Bakovka	265b	55.41 N	37.20 E
Bakoy ≃	150	13.49 N	10.50 W
Bakruz'ak	86	52.59 N	58.42 E
Baksan	84	43.40 N	43.32 E
Baksan ≃	84	43.42 N	43.32 E
Bakšejevo, S.S.S.R.	80	55.44 N	39.53 E
Bakšejevo, S.S.S.R.	86	57.26 N	73.00 E
Baksir Chāndpur	126	23.30 N	89.44 E
Bakšty	76	53.56 N	26.11 E
Baksuk ≃	86	51.50 N	69.30 E
Baku	84	40.23 N	49.51 E
Bakulin Point ≻	116	8.33 N	126.22 E
Bakum	52	52.45 N	8.11 E
Bakumpai	112	1.26 S	113.05 E
Bakun	120	32.32 N	80.26 E
Bakung, Pulau I	112	0.04 N	104.27 E
Bakungan	114	2.56 N	97.30 E
Bakuriani	84	41.46 N	43.32 E
Bakury	80	52.22 N	44.42 E
Bakwa-Kenge	152	4.51 S	22.04 E
Bakwanga → Mbuji-Mayi	152	6.09 S	23.38 E
Bakyrly	86	44.21 N	67.48 E
Bal ≃	126	21.58 N	89.21 E
Bala, On., Can.	212	45.01 N	79.37 W
Bala, Sén.	150	14.02 N	13.10 W
Balâ, Tür.	130	39.34 N	33.08 E
Bala, Wales, U.K.	42	52.54 N	3.35 W
Balabac	116	7.59 N	117.04 E
Balabac Island I	116	7.57 N	117.01 E
Balabac Strait ʊ	112	7.35 N	117.00 E
Bālā Bāgh	120	34.24 N	70.14 E
Ba'labakk	130	34.00 N	36.12 E
Balabalagan, Kepulauan II	112	2.20 S	117.25 E
Balaban	130	38.28 N	37.36 E
Balabanovo	82	55.11 N	36.40 E
Balabino	78	47.44 N	35.13 E
Balabio, Île I	175f	20.07 S	164.11 E
Balachany	84	40.29 N	49.54 E
Balachčin	86	54.09 N	89.23 E
Balachna	80	56.30 N	43.36 E
Balachta	86	55.24 N	91.37 E
Balachtison, gora ∧	86	54.36 N	93.50 E
Balaci	38	44.21 N	24.55 E
Bala-Cynwyd	285	40.00 N	75.14 W
Balad	128	34.01 N	44.09 E
Baladbandh	272b	22.52 N	88.07 E
Balad'ok	89	53.41 N	133.07 E
Balagansk	88	53.57 N	103.02 E
Bālāghāt	120	21.48 N	80.11 E
Bālāghāt Range ∧∧	122	18.45 N	76.30 E
Balagny-sur-Thérain	50	49.18 N	2.20 E
Balaguer	34	41.47 N	0.49 E
Balaikarangan	112	0.50 N	110.26 E
Balaiselasa	112	1.48 S	100.50 E
Balaisepuah	112	0.27 N	111.13 E
Balaj	86	55.52 N	93.59 E
Balaka	152	4.51 S	19.57 E
Balakété	152	6.56 N	19.54 E
Balakirevo	82	56.30 N	38.51 E
Balaklava, Austl.	168b	34.09 S	138.25 E
Balaklava, S.S.S.R.	78	44.30 N	33.36 E
Balakleja, S.S.S.R.	78	49.14 N	31.44 E
Balakleja, S.S.S.R.	78	49.27 N	36.52 E
Bālākot	123	34.33 N	73.21 E
Balakovo	80	52.02 N	47.47 E
Balal, Laga ≃	154	3.25 N	37.15 E
Balallan	46	58.05 N	6.35 W
Balama, Moç.	154	13.20 S	38.30 E
Bal'amā, Urd.	132	32.14 N	36.05 E
Balamban	116	10.30 N	123.42 E
Balambangan, Pulau I	112	7.15 N	116.55 E
Bālā Morghāb	128	35.35 N	63.20 E
Bālandi	272b	22.58 N	88.32 E
Balanga	116	14.41 N	120.32 E
Balangala	152	0.24 N	19.45 E
Ba Lang An, Mui ≻	110	15.14 N	108.56 E
Balangero	62	45.16 N	7.31 E
Balangiga	116	11.07 N	125.23 E
Balāngīr	122	20.43 N	83.29 E
Balanguingui Island I	116	6.01 N	121.41 E
Bālān Ṣafar 'Alī	128	38.59 N	47.27 E
Balanṣūrah	142	27.55 N	30.41 E
Balantak, Gunung ∧	112	0.45 S	123.20 E
Balao ≃	246	2.54 S	79.50 W
Balapulang	115a	7.03 S	109.05 E
Bālāpur	122	20.40 N	76.46 E
Balaqs	273c	30.10 N	31.17 E
Balaqṭar	142	31.05 N	30.13 E
Balaraja	115a	6.12 S	106.27 E
Balarāmbāti	272b	22.48 N	88.13 E
Balarāmpota	272b	22.31 N	88.08 E
Balarāmpur	126	23.07 N	86.13 E
Balaruc-le-Vieux	62	43.27 N	3.41 E
Balaši	80	51.24 N	49.55 E
Balašicha	82	55.49 N	37.58 E
Balašov	80	51.32 N	43.08 E
Balassagyarmat	30	48.05 N	19.18 E
Balāṭ	140	25.33 N	29.16 E
Balatan, Indon.	164	6.05 S	134.45 E
Balatan, Pil.	116	13.20 N	123.10 E
Balaton	198	44.14 N	95.52 W
Balaton ◎	30	46.50 N	17.45 E
Balaurin	112	8.15 S	123.43 E
Balavé	150	12.23 N	4.09 W
Balayan	116	13.57 N	120.44 E
Balayan Bay ⊂	116	13.51 N	120.47 E
Balazote	34	38.53 N	2.08 W
Balbi, Mount ∧[1]	175e	5.55 S	154.59 E
Balbieriškis	76	54.32 N	23.52 E
Balbigny	62	45.49 N	4.11 E
Balboa	236	8.57 N	79.34 W
Balboa Heights	236	8.57 N	79.33 W
Balbriggan	48	53.37 N	6.11 W
Balcad	144	2.23 N	45.23 E
Balcanoona	166	30.31 S	139.18 E
Balcarce	252	37.50 S	58.15 W
Balcarres	184	50.48 N	103.33 W
Bălcești	38	44.37 N	23.56 E
Balchaš	86	46.49 N	74.59 E
Balchaš, ozero (Lake Balkhash) ◎	86	46.00 N	74.00 E
Balchen Glacier ⍓	9	76.46 S	145.30 W
Balch Springs	222	32.43 N	96.37 W
Balcı	130	38.43 N	34.06 E
Balčik	38	43.25 N	28.10 E
Balclutha	172	46.14 S	169.44 E
Balcombe	42	51.04 N	0.08 W
Balcones Escarpment ⏶[4]	196	29.30 N	99.15 W
Balcosna	252	27.53 S	65.43 W
Balde	252	33.20 S	66.38 W
Baldeador	287a	22.53 S	43.02 W
Bald Eagle	214	40.42 N	78.12 W
Bald Eagle Creek ≃	210	41.08 N	77.24 W
Bald Eagle Mountain ∧	214	41.00 N	77.45 W
Bald Eagle State Park ♠	214	41.00 N	77.40 W
Baldegger See ◎	58	47.12 N	8.16 E
Baldenburg → Biały Bór	30	53.54 N	16.51 E
Baldeneysee ◎	263	51.24 N	7.03 E

Balderschwang	58	47.28 N	10.06 E
Balderstone	262	53.47 N	2.34 W
Balderton	44	53.03 N	0.47 W
Bald Head ≻	162	35.07 S	118.01 E
Bald Hill ∧[2]	166	20.18 S	144.06 E
Bald Hill Branch ≃	284c	18.55 N	76.49 W
Baldhill Creek ≃	198	47.09 N	98.03 W
Bald Hills	171a	27.19 S	153.01 E
Baldichieri d'asti	62	44.54 N	8.07 E
Baldim	255	19.17 S	43.57 W
Bald Island I	162	34.55 S	118.27 E
Bald Knob	194	35.18 N	91.34 W
Bald Knob ∧, Ca., U.S.	282	37.25 N	122.21 W
Bald Knob ∧, Va., U.S.	192	37.56 N	79.51 W
Bald Knoll ∧	200	42.24 N	110.29 W
Bald Mountain ∧, Ct., U.S.	207	41.59 N	72.25 W
Bald Mountain ∧, Nv., U.S.	226	38.33 N	119.07 W
Bald Mountain ∧, Or., U.S.	202	44.48 N	123.33 W
Bald Mountain ∧, Or., U.S.	202	43.16 N	121.21 W
Bald Mountain ∧, Or., U.S.	202	44.36 N	117.53 W
Bald Mountain ∧, Vt., U.S.	210	42.55 N	73.09 W
Bald Mountain State Recreation Area ♠	216	42.46 N	83.14 W
Baldo, Monte ∧	64	45.47 N	10.48 E
Baldock	42	51.59 N	0.12 W
Baldock Lake ◎	184	56.33 N	97.57 W
Baldone	76	56.45 N	24.24 E
Baldovino, Arroyo ≃	288	34.46 S	58.07 W
Baldoyle	48	53.24 N	6.08 W
Baldpate Pond ◎	283	42.42 N	71.00 W
Balduinstein	56	50.20 N	7.58 E
Baldur	184	49.23 N	99.15 W
Baldwin, Fl., U.S.	192	30.18 N	81.58 W
Baldwin, La., U.S.	194	29.50 N	91.32 W
Baldwin, Mi., U.S.	190	43.54 N	85.51 W
Baldwin, N.Y., U.S.	210	40.39 N	73.36 W
Baldwin, Pa., U.S.	214	40.23 N	79.57 W
Baldwin, Wi., U.S.	190	44.58 N	92.22 W
Baldwin Bay ⊂	276	40.38 N	73.35 W
Baldwin City	198	38.46 N	95.11 W
Baldwin Creek ≃	279a	41.22 N	81.51 W
Baldwin Hills ∧∧[2]	280	34.00 N	118.22 W
Baldwin Lake ◎	279a	41.21 N	81.51 W
Baldwin Park	228	34.05 N	117.57 W
Baldwin Peninsula ≻[1]	180	66.44 N	162.15 W
Baldwinsville	210	43.09 N	76.19 W
Baldwinville	207	42.36 N	72.04 W
Baldwin-Wallace College ⊌[2]	279a	41.23 N	81.51 W
Baldwyn	194	34.31 N	88.38 W
Baldy Mountain ∧, B.C., Can.	182	51.28 N	120.02 W
Baldy Mountain ∧, Mb., Can.	184	51.28 N	100.44 W
Baldy Mountain ∧, Mt., U.S.	202	48.09 N	109.39 W
Baldy Mountain ∧, N.M., U.S.	200	36.38 N	105.13 W
Baldy Peak ∧	200	33.55 N	109.35 W
Bale, India	272c	19.08 N	73.06 E
Bale, Jugo.	64	45.02 N	13.48 E
Bâle → Basel, Schw.	58	47.33 N	7.35 E
Bale □[4]	144	6.20 N	41.30 E
Bale-Akiosi	273a	6.41 N	3.21 E
Balearen → Balears, Illes II	34	39.30 N	3.00 E
Baléares, Îles → Balears, Illes II	34	39.30 N	3.00 E
Balearic Islands → Balears, Illes II	34	39.30 N	3.00 E
Balears □[4]	34	39.30 N	3.00 E
Balears, Illes (Balearic Islands) II	34	39.30 N	3.00 E
Balease, Gunung ∧	112	2.24 S	120.33 E
Balegane	158	26.04 S	31.34 E
Baleh ≃	112	2.01 N	113.01 E
Baleia, Ponta da ≻	255	17.40 S	39.07 W
Baleine, Grande rivière de la ≃	176	55.16 N	77.47 W
Baleine, Petite rivière de la ≃	176	56.00 N	76.45 W
Baleine, Rivière à la ≃	176	58.15 N	67.40 W
Balej	88	51.36 N	116.38 E
Balelasberg ∧∧	158	27.30 S	30.07 E
Bale Mountains National Park ♠	144	7.00 N	39.40 E
Bâle-Mulhouse, Aéroport ⊠	58	47.35 N	7.32 E
Balen	56	51.10 N	5.09 E
Balena	152	0.55 N	20.00 E
Baleno	116	12.28 N	123.30 E
Baler	116	15.46 N	121.34 E
Baler Bay ⊂	116	15.50 N	121.35 E
Baleshare I	46	57.31 N	7.22 W
Bāleshwar	126	21.30 N	86.56 E
Balesin Island I	116	14.26 N	122.02 E
Balestrand	26	61.12 N	6.32 E
Balestrate	70	38.03 N	13.00 E
Baléya	150	9.15 N	10.29 W
Baléyara	150	13.47 N	2.57 E
Balezino	80	57.58 N	53.00 E
Balfate	236	15.48 N	86.25 W
Balfes Creek	166	20.13 S	145.55 E
Balfour, N.Z.	172	45.50 S	168.35 E
Balfour, S. Afr.	158	26.44 S	28.31 E
Balfour, Scot., U.K.	46	59.01 N	2.55 W
Balfour, N.C., U.S.	192	35.20 N	82.28 W
Balfour Downs	162	22.50 S	120.50 E
Balfour Park ♠	273d	26.08 S	28.06 E
Balfron	46	56.04 N	4.20 W
Balgach	58	47.25 N	9.35 E
Bâlgarija → Bulgaria □[1]	38	43.00 N	25.00 E
Balgazyn	88	51.08 N	95.00 E
Balgo	162	20.09 S	127.48 E
Balgowlah	274a	33.48 S	151.16 E
Balguerie, Cap ≻	174x	9.45 S	138.47 W
Balhannah	168b	35.00 S	138.50 E
Bāli	120	25.50 N	74.05 E
Bali □[4]	115b	8.30 S	115.00 E
Bali I	115b	8.20 S	115.00 E
Bali, Laut (Bali Sea) ⫧[2]	112	7.45 S	115.30 E
Bali, Selat ʊ	112	8.18 S	114.25 E
Bāliākāndi	126	23.38 N	89.33 E
Baliangao	116	8.40 N	123.36 E
Bāliāpāl	126	21.40 N	87.17 E
Bāliāti	126	23.59 N	90.03 E
Balibago	116	13.37 N	121.18 E
Bali Barat National Park ♠	115b	8.15 S	144.40 E
Baliceaux Island I	241h	12.57 N	61.08 W
Bāli Chak	126	22.22 N	87.33 E
Balicuatro Islands II	116	12.39 N	124.24 E
Balicuatro Point ≻	116	12.35 N	124.16 E
Balidianzi	98	41.13 N	124.49 E
Bālidiha	126	21.58 N	86.38 E
Balige	114	2.20 N	99.04 E
Bālighai	126	21.52 N	87.35 E
Balihan	98	41.29 N	118.41 E
Bālihāti	272b	22.44 N	88.19 E
Balıkesir	130	39.39 N	27.53 E
Balıkesir □[4]	130	39.45 N	27.50 E
Balık Gölü ◎	84	39.47 N	43.34 E
Balīkh ≃	130	35.52 N	39.12 E
Balıklıtohma ≃	130	38.50 N	37.41 E
Balikpapan	112	1.17 S	116.50 E
Balikumbat	152	5.54 N	10.23 E
Balimbing, Indon.	112	5.55 S	104.34 E
Balimbing, Pil.	116	5.05 N	119.58 E
Balimo	164	8.03 S	142.56 E
Balin, S.S.S.R.	78	48.52 N	26.40 E
Balin, Zhg.	89	48.19 N	122.19 E

Balincollig	48	51.53 N	8.35 W
Balindong (Watu)	116	7.55 N	124.12 E
Baling	114	5.40 N	100.55 E
Balingasag	116	8.45 N	124.47 E
Balingen	58	48.16 N	8.51 E
Balingian	112	2.55 N	112.32 E
Balingup	162	33.48 S	115.58 E
Balintang Channel ʊ	108	19.49 N	121.40 E
Balintore	46	57.45 N	3.54 W
Balipu	105	39.53 N	117.48 E
Balışeyh	130	39.56 N	33.43 E
Baliuag	116	14.57 N	120.54 E
Baliung ≃	115a	6.50 S	105.52 E
Baliungan Island I	116	5.09 N	120.12 E
Baliyingzi	104	41.59 N	121.14 E
Baliza	255	16.15 S	52.25 W
Balizhuang, Zhg.	105	39.16 N	116.28 E
Balizhuang, Zhg.	271a	39.52 N	116.28 E
Balk	52	52.54 N	5.34 E
Balkach, Lago → Balchaš, ozero ◎	86	46.00 N	74.00 E
Balkan Mountains → Stara Planina ∧∧	38	42.45 N	25.00 E
Balkan Peninsula ≻[1]	10	44.00 N	23.00 E
Balkašino	86	52.31 N	68.46 E
Balkbrug	52	52.36 N	6.24 E
Balkh	120	36.46 N	66.54 E
Balkh □[4]	120	36.30 N	67.00 E
Balkh ≃	120	36.39 N	66.56 E
Balkhash → Balchaš	86	46.49 N	74.59 E
Balkhash, Lake → Balchaš, ozero ◎	86	46.00 N	74.00 E
Balki	78	47.23 N	34.57 E
Ball	194	31.24 N	92.24 W
Balla	48	53.48 N	9.09 W
Balla Balla	154	20.26 S	29.02 E
Ballabhpur	272b	22.44 N	88.21 E
Ballachulish	46	56.40 N	5.10 W
Balladonia	162	32.27 S	123.51 E
Ballagh	48	52.35 N	7.59 W
Ballaghaderreen	48	53.55 N	8.36 W
Ballālpur	122	19.50 N	79.22 E
Ballan	169	37.36 S	144.14 E
Ballancourt	50	48.31 N	2.23 E
Ballangen	24	68.20 N	16.50 E
Ballantine	202	45.56 N	108.08 W
Ballantrae	44	55.06 N	5.00 W
Ballao	71	39.33 N	9.22 E
Ballarat	169	37.34 S	143.52 E
Ballard, Lake ◎	162	29.27 S	120.55 E
Ballardvale	207	42.37 N	71.09 W
Ballata	70	37.58 N	12.41 E
Ballater	46	57.03 N	3.03 W
Ballaugh	44	54.20 N	4.32 W
Ball Bay ⊂	174c	29.03 S	167.59 E
Ballé	150	15.20 N	8.35 W
Ballen	41	55.49 N	10.39 E
Ballenas, Bahía de ⊂	232	26.45 N	113.26 W
Ballenas, Canal de ʊ	232	29.10 N	113.29 W
Ballenato, Punta ≻	286b	23.06 N	82.30 W
Ballengeich	158	27.52 S	29.59 E
Ballenita, Punta ≻	252	25.46 S	70.44 W
Ballenstedt	54	51.43 N	11.14 E
Balleny Basin ✣[1]	9	67.00 S	170.00 E
Balleny Islands II	9	66.35 S	162.50 E
Balleroy	32	49.11 N	0.50 W
Ballerup	41	55.44 N	12.22 E
Ballesteros, Arg.	252	32.33 S	62.59 W
Ballesteros, Pil.	116	18.25 N	121.31 E
Ball Ground	192	34.20 N	84.22 W
Ballı	130	40.50 N	27.03 E
Ballia	124	25.45 N	84.10 E
Ballico	226	37.27 N	120.42 W
Ballidu	162	30.36 S	116.46 E
Ballina, Austl.	166	28.52 S	153.33 E
Ballina, Ire.	48	54.07 N	9.09 W
Ballina, Ire.	48	52.49 N	8.26 W
Ballinakill	48	52.53 N	7.18 W
Ballinalack	48	53.37 N	7.28 W
Ballinascarty	48	51.40 N	8.51 W
Ballinasloe	48	53.20 N	8.13 W
Ballinderry ≃	48	54.40 N	6.31 W
Ballindine	48	53.39 N	8.59 W
Ballineen	48	51.44 N	8.56 W
Ballingarry	48	52.29 N	8.52 W
Ballingeary	48	51.49 N	9.13 W
Ballinger	196	31.44 N	99.56 W
Ballingslöv	41	56.13 N	13.51 E
Ballinluig	46	56.38 N	3.39 W
Ballino	64	45.58 N	10.48 E
Ballinrobe	48	53.37 N	9.13 W
Ballinskelligs Bay ⊂	48	51.50 N	10.15 W
Ballintoy	48	55.14 N	6.22 W
Ballintra	48	54.35 N	8.08 W
Balloch	46	57.29 N	4.07 W
Ballon	50	48.10 N	0.14 E
Ballona Creek ≃	280	33.58 N	118.27 W
Ballos, Col d')(	62	44.18 N	6.36 E
Ballouville	207	41.52 N	71.51 W
Ballsh	38	40.36 N	19.44 E
Balls Pyramid I	160	31.45 S	159.15 E
Ballston	224	45.04 N	123.19 W
Ballston Lake	210	42.54 N	73.52 W
Ballston Spa	210	43.00 N	73.50 W
Ballville	214	41.20 N	83.09 W
Ballwin	219	38.35 N	90.32 W
Bālly, India	272b	22.38 N	88.21 E
Bally, Pa., U.S.	208	40.24 N	75.35 W
Bālly ◆[8]	272b	22.39 N	88.21 E
Ballybay	48	54.08 N	6.54 W
Ballybofey	48	54.48 N	7.47 W
Ballybogy	48	55.07 N	6.34 W
Bālly Bridge ◆[5]	272b	22.39 N	88.21 E
Ballybunnion	48	52.31 N	9.40 W
Ballycanew	48	52.36 N	6.19 W
Ballycastle, Ire.	48	54.16 N	9.23 W
Ballycastle, N. Ire., U.K.	48	55.12 N	6.15 W
Ballycastle Bay ⊂	44	55.13 N	6.15 W
Ballyclare	48	54.45 N	6.00 W
Ballyconneely	48	53.26 N	10.02 W
Ballyconnell	48	54.07 N	7.35 W
Ballycotton	48	51.50 N	8.01 W
Ballycroy	48	54.01 N	9.51 W
Ballyduff, Ire.	48	52.27 N	9.40 W
Ballyduff, Ire.	48	52.09 N	8.03 W
Ballyferriter	48	52.09 N	10.26 W
Ballyfinboy ≃	48	53.02 N	8.15 W
Ballygar	48	53.32 N	8.20 W
Ballygawley	48	54.28 N	7.02 W
Ballygorman	48	55.22 N	7.21 W
Ballygowan	48	54.30 N	5.48 W
Ballygunge ◆[8]	272b	22.31 N	88.21 E
Ballyhaise	48	54.03 N	7.19 W
Ballyhalbert	48	54.30 N	5.28 W
Ballyhaunis	48	53.46 N	8.46 W
Ballyhoura Mountains ∧∧	48	52.20 N	8.35 W
Ballyjamesduff	48	53.52 N	7.12 W
Ballylongford	48	52.33 N	9.28 W
Ballymacoda	48	51.57 N	7.54 W
Ballymahon	48	53.34 N	7.45 W
Ballymakeery (Ballyvourney)	48	51.55 N	9.09 W
Ballymena	48	54.52 N	6.17 W
Ballymoe	48	53.42 N	8.29 W
Ballymoney	48	55.04 N	6.31 W
Ballymote	48	54.06 N	8.31 W
Ballymurray	48	53.35 N	8.08 W
Ballynahinch	48	54.24 N	5.54 W
Ballyneety	48	52.35 N	8.33 W
Ballynoe	48	52.03 N	8.05 W
Ballyquintin Point ≻	48	54.20 N	5.30 W
Ballyragget	48	52.47 N	7.20 W
Ballysadare	48	54.13 N	8.31 W
Ballyshannon	48	54.30 N	8.11 W
Ballyteige Bay ⊂	48	52.11 N	6.39 W
Ballyvaghan	48	53.07 N	9.07 W
Ballyvoy	48	55.12 N	6.12 W
Ballywalter	48	54.33 N	5.30 W

≃ River	Fluß	Río	Rivière	Rio	
≅ Canal	Kanal	Canal	Canal	Canal	
↳ Waterfall, Rapids	Wasserfall, Stromschnellen	Cascada, Rápidos	Chute d'eau, Rapides	Cascata, Rápidos	
ʊ Strait	Meeresstraße	Estrecho	Détroit	Estreito	
⊂ Bay, Gulf	Bucht, Golf	Bahía, Golfo	Baie, Golfe	Baía, Golfo	
◎ Lake, Lakes	See, Seen	Lago, Lagos	Lac, Lacs	Lago, Lagos	
⋮ Swamp	Sumpf	Pantano	Marais	Pântano	
⍓ Ice Features, Glacier	Eis- und Gletscherformen	Accidentes Glaciales	Formes glaciaires	Acidentes glaciares	
⫧ Other Hydrographic Features	Andere Hydrographische Objekte	Otros Elementos Hidrográficos	Autres données hydrographiques	Outros acidentes hidrográficos	

✣ Submarine Features	Untermeerische Objekte	Accidentes Submarinos	Formes de relief sous-marin	Acidentes submarinos
□ Political Unit	Politische Einheit	Unidad Politica	Entité politique	Unidade política
⊌ Cultural Institution	Kulturelle Institution	Institución Cultural	Institution culturelle	Institução cultural
⊥ Historical Site	Historische Stätte	Sitio Histórico	Site historique	Sitio histórico
♠ Recreational Site	Erholungs- und Ferienort	Sitio de Recreo	Centre de loisirs	Area de Lazer
⊠ Airport	Flughafen	Aeropuerto	Aéroport	Aeroporto
■ Military Installation	Militäranlage	Instalación Militar	Installation militaire	Instalação militar
◆ Miscellaneous	Verschiedenes	Misceláneo	Divers	Diversos

Name	Page	Lat °'	Long °'
Balm	220	27.45 N	82.15 W
Balmaceda	254	45.55 S	71.41 W
Balmaceda, Cerro ▲	254	51.25 S	73.11 W
Balmain	274a	33.51 S	151.11 E
Balme	62	45.18 N	7.13 E
Balmerino	46	56.24 N	3.02 W
Balmertown	184	51.04 N	93.44 W
Balmhorn ▲	58	46.25 N	7.43 E
Balmoral, Austl.	168	37.15 S	141.51 E
Balmoral, S. Afr.	158	25.52 S	28.59 E
Balmoral Castle ⊥	46	57.02 N	3.14 W
Balmorhea	196	30.59 N	103.45 W
Balmville	210	41.32 N	74.00 W
Balnacra	46	57.28 N	5.23 W
Balnearia	252	31.00 S	62.40 W
Balobanovo	82	55.51 N	38.14 E
Balobe	154	0.05 N	28.00 E
Baloda Bāzār	120	21.40 N	82.10 E
Balombo	152	12.21 S	14.46 E
Balong, Indon.	115a	7.57 S	111.26 E
Balong, Zhg.	102	36.17 N	97.20 E
Balonne ≈	166	28.47 S	147.56 E
Bālotra	120	25.50 N	72.14 E
Baloži	76	56.53 N	24.06 E
Balpahari Reservoir @¹	126	24.04 N	86.28 E
Balrāmpur	124	27.26 N	82.11 E
Balranald	168	34.38 S	143.33 E
Bals	38	44.21 N	24.06 E
Balsam Lake	190	45.21 N	92.27 W
Balsam Lake @	212	44.35 N	78.50 W
Bálsamo	255	20.27 S	53.57 W
Balsas	250	7.31 S	46.02 W
Balsas ≈, Méx.	250	17.55 N	102.10 W
Balsas ≈, Pan.	246	8.15 N	77.59 W
Balsas, Rio das ≈, Bra.	250	9.58 S	47.52 W
Balsas, Rio das ≈, Bra.	250	7.14 S	44.33 W
Balseiros ≈	250	5.51 S	43.44 W
Balsham	42	52.08 N	0.20 E
Balsorano	66	41.49 N	13.34 E
Bålsta	40	59.35 N	17.30 E
Balsthal	58	47.19 N	7.42 E
Balta	78	47.55 N	29.37 E
Baltaj	80	54.55 N	46.38 E
Baltanás	34	41.56 N	4.15 W
Baltasar Brum	252	30.44 S	57.19 W
Baltasi	80	56.21 N	50.12 E
Baltazar, Arroyo ≈	258	33.45 S	58.58 W
Bălți → Bel'cy	78	47.46 N	27.56 E
Baltic, Ct., U.S.	207	41.37 N	72.05 W
Baltic, Oh., U.S.	214	40.26 N	81.41 W
Baltic Bay c	190	48.22 N	83.43 W
Baltico, Mar → Baltic Sea ⊤²	24	57.00 N	19.00 E
Baltic Sea ⊤²	24	57.00 N	19.00 E
Baltic Station ⊷⁵	265a	59.55 N	30.18 E
Baltijsk	76	54.39 N	19.55 E
Baltijskaja kosa ⊢²	30	54.25 N	19.35 E
Baltîm	142	31.33 N	31.05 E
Baltimore, Ire.	44	51.29 N	9.22 W
Baltimore, S. Afr.	156	23.15 S	28.20 E
Baltimore, Md., U.S.	208	39.17 N	76.36 W
Baltimore, Md., U.S.	284b	39.17 N	76.36 W
Baltimore, Oh., U.S.	188	39.50 N	82.36 W
Baltimore ◆	208	39.24 N	76.36 W
Baltimore, University of ◆²	284b	39.18 N	76.37 W
Baltimore Airpark ⊠	284b	39.16 N	76.25 W
Baltimore Highlands	284b	39.13 N	76.38 W
Baltimore-Washington International Airport ⊠	208	39.11 N	76.40 W
Baltinglass	48	52.55 N	6.41 W
Baltique, Mer → Baltic Sea ⊤²	24	57.00 N	19.00 E
Baltistān ◆¹	123	35.18 N	75.37 E
Baltit	123	36.20 N	74.40 E
Baltoji-Vokė	54	54.28 N	25.06 E
Baltoro Glacier ⋏	123	35.42 N	76.10 E
Baltra, Isla I	246a	0.26 S	90.16 W
Baltrum I	52	53.44 N	7.23 E
Bālu ≈, Bngl.	126	23.44 N	90.30 E
Ba Lu ≈, Viet.	110	14.18 N	107.52 E
Baluarte, Arroyo ≈	196	27.09 N	98.07 W
Baluarte, Boca del ≈¹	234	22.48 N	106.02 W
Baluarte, Río del ≈	234	22.48 N	106.02 W
Balucas, Barranca ≈	234	16.36 N	100.40 W
Baluchistān ◻⁹	120	29.00 N	67.00 E
Balud	116	12.02 N	123.12 E
Bālughāta	126	22.05 N	88.01 E
Bāluhāti	272b	22.39 N	88.16 E
Balui ≈	112	2.42 N	113.47 E
Balukbaluk Island I	116	6.40 N	121.43 E
Balurghāt	124	25.13 N	88.46 E
Bālut Island I	116	5.24 N	125.23 E
Balvano	68	40.39 N	15.31 E
Balve	56	51.20 N	7.51 E
Balvi	76	57.08 N	27.17 E
Balvicar	46	56.14 N	5.38 W
Balwina Aboriginal Reserve ◆⁴	162	20.30 S	128.00 E
Balwyn	274b	37.49 S	145.05 E
Balxuca, Arroyo de la ≈	266d	41.31 N	2.06 E
Balya	266d	49.37 N	27.35 E
Balygyčan	74	63.56 N	154.12 E
Balykši	85	53.25 N	89.05 E
Balykši	80	47.05 N	51.54 E
Balyktyg-Chem ≈	84	50.46 N	96.54 E
Balzac	182	51.10 N	114.01 W
Balzar	246	1.22 S	79.54 W
Balzers	58	47.04 N	9.30 E
Bal'zino	88	51.03 N	113.35 E
Bam	123	45.18 N	8.24 E
Bam, Īrān	128	36.58 N	57.59 E
Bam, Īrān	128	26.06 N	58.21 E
Bama, Nig.	146	11.30 N	13.41 E
Bama, Zhg.	102	24.21 N	107.08 E
Bamaga	166	10.52 S	142.24 E
Bamaji Lake @	184	51.09 N	91.34 W
Bamako	150	12.39 N	8.00 W
Bamangachi	272b	22.46 N	88.31 E
Bāmanghāti	126	22.11 N	86.49 E
Bāmanmura	272b	22.21 N	88.31 E
Bamba	100	29.26 N	120.59 E
Bamba, Indon.	115a	5.34 N	95.20 E
Bamba, Mali	150	17.02 N	01.24 W
Bamba, Zaïre	152	5.45 S	18.23 E
Bambamarca	246	6.41 S	78.31 W
Bambana ≈	236	13.27 N	83.50 W
Bambari	152	5.45 N	20.40 E
Bambaroo	166	18.52 S	146.12 E
Bambāri	272c	18.58 N	73.03 E
Bamberg, B.R.D.	30	49.53 N	10.53 E
Bamberg, S.C., U.S.	192	33.17 N	81.02 W
Bamber Lake	208	39.54 N	74.19 W
Bamberton	224	48.35 N	123.31 W
Bambesa	154	3.25 N	25.43 E
Bambesi	140	9.45 N	34.38 E
Bambez	154	20.00 S	28.56 E
Bambili	154	3.39 N	26.07 E
Bambinga	152	3.42 S	18.54 E
Bamboesberg ⋏	158	31.30 S	26.10 E
Bamboo Creek	162	20.56 S	120.13 E
Bamboo Springs	162	22.04 S	119.38 E
Bambouti	154	5.24 N	27.12 E
Bambu	256	22.31 S	46.26 W
Bambuí	255	20.01 S	46.00 W
Bambujka	88	55.47 N	115.48 E

Name	Page	Lat °'	Long °'
Bambula	154	1.17 S	25.38 E
Bamburgh	44	55.36 N	1.42 W
Bamburra ≃	248	20.10 S	58.07 W
Bambuto ⋏	200	30.51 N	110.52 W
Bam Co @	120	31.30 N	91.05 E
Bamencheng	105	39.35 N	117.37 E
Bamenda	152	5.56 N	10.10 E
Bamendjou	152	5.24 N	10.19 E
Bamfield	182	48.50 N	125.08 W
Bamhā	142	29.35 N	31.14 E
Bami	128	38.44 N	56.48 E
Bāmīān	120	34.50 N	67.50 E
Bāmīān ◻⁴	120	34.45 N	67.15 E
Bamiancheng	89	43.13 N	124.02 E
Bamingui	152	7.34 N	20.11 E
Bamingui ≈	146	8.33 N	19.05 E
Bamingui-Bangoran ◻⁵	146	8.15 N	20.15 E
Bamingui-Bangoran, Parc National du ◆	146	8.00 N	19.40 E
Bam Island I	164	3.35 S	144.50 E
Bāmna	126	22.19 N	90.06 E
Bamndali ◆⁸	272a	28.33 N	77.03 E
Bamol	164	7.38 S	138.37 E
Bampton, Eng., U.K.	42	51.44 N	1.33 W
Bampton, Eng., U.K.	42	51.00 N	3.29 W
Bāmpur	128	27.12 N	60.27 E
Bāmpūr ≈	128	27.18 N	59.06 E
Bāmra Hills ⋏²	120	21.30 N	84.30 E
Bamu ≈	164	8.01 S	143.33 E
Bamumo	120	32.30 N	93.15 E
Ban	150	14.05 N	2.27 W
Bana, Malawi	154	12.25 S	34.08 E
Ba Na, Viet.	110	15.59 N	107.59 E
Banā, Wādī V	144	13.03 N	45.24 E
Banaba (Ocean Island) I	174d	0.52 S	169.35 E
Banabuiú	250	5.07 S	38.06 W
Banabuiú, Açude @¹	250	5.20 S	39.05 W
Ban Aen	110	18.02 N	98.37 E
Banagher	48	53.11 N	7.59 W
Banagi	154	2.16 S	34.51 E
Banago	116	7.30 N	124.07 E
Banagrām	126	22.35 N	89.55 E
Banahao, Mount ▲	116	14.04 N	121.29 E
Banalia	154	1.33 N	25.20 E
Banamba	150	13.33 N	7.27 W
Banana, Austl.	166	24.28 S	150.07 E
Banana, Zaïre	152	6.01 S	12.24 E
Banana Creek ≈	220	28.36 N	80.38 W
Banana Islands II	150	8.07 N	13.13 W
Bananal	256	22.41 S	44.19 W
Bananal ≈, Bra.	250	8.33 S	49.26 W
Bananal ≈, Bra.	255	22.32 S	44.11 W
Bāndra Point ⊁	272c	19.03 N	72.49 E
Bananal, Ilha do I	250	11.30 S	50.15 W
Banana River c	220	28.25 N	80.38 W
Bananeiras	250	6.45 S	35.37 W
Bananga	110	6.56 N	93.54 E
Banao, Loma de ▲	240p	21.51 N	79.36 W
Bānār ≈	124	24.04 N	90.38 E
Banaras → Vārānasi	124	25.20 N	83.00 E
Banari	71	40.34 N	8.42 E
Bānaripāra	126	22.47 N	90.10 E
Banas ≈, India	120	25.54 N	76.45 E
Bānās, Ra's ⊁	140	23.54 N	35.48 E
Banat ◆¹	38	43.00 N	21.00 E
Banate Bay c	116	10.58 N	122.48 E
Banaue	116	16.55 N	121.04 E
Banavie	46	56.47 N	5.07 W
Banay, Mount ▲	116	14.32 N	121.10 E
Banaz	130	38.46 N	29.46 E
Ban Baen Phichit	269a	13.50 N	100.40 E
Ban Ban	110	19.38 N	103.34 E
Ban Bang Chan	269a	13.49 N	100.42 E
Ban Bang O	269a	13.53 N	100.36 E
Ban Bang Phli Yai	269a	13.36 N	100.42 E
Ban Bang Phraek	269a	13.53 N	100.29 E
Ban Bang Pu	269a	13.31 N	100.36 E
Banbar	120	30.49 N	94.59 E
Ban Bat	110	13.53 N	108.39 E
Banbidian	271a	39.54 N	116.32 E
Ban Blech	110	13.04 N	107.20 E
Ban Boneng	110	17.58 N	104.35 E
Ban Bouang-nom	110	15.47 N	106.47 E
Banbridge	48	54.21 N	6.16 W
Ban Bua Chum	110	15.15 N	101.12 E
Banbuji	100	33.34 N	116.44 E
Ban Bung Fang Nok	269a	13.48 N	100.43 E
Ban Bung Na Rang	110	16.11 N	100.09 E
Ban Bungxai	110	15.42 N	106.14 E
Banbury	42	52.04 N	1.20 W
Banchaiga	110	0.49 N	101.07 E
Bancalan Island I	116	8.14 N	117.06 E
Banc d'Arguin, Parc National du ◆	150	20.00 N	16.10 W
Ban Chak	110	14.17 N	105.25 E
Ban Cha La	110	17.11 N	106.05 E
Bānchhārāmpur	126	23.46 N	90.48 E
Banchory	46	57.03 N	2.31 W
Banco, Punta ⊁	236	8.23 N	83.09 W
Bancos, Isla → Banks Island I	182	73.15 N	121.30 W
Bancroft, On., Can.	212	45.03 N	77.51 W
Bancroft, Id., U.S.	202	42.43 N	111.53 W
Bancroft, Mi., U.S.	214	43.17 N	94.13 W
Bancroft, Ne., U.S.	198	42.00 N	96.34 W
Bancroft → Chillabombwe, Zam.	154	12.18 S	27.43 E
Bancun	108	30.53 N	118.48 E
Banda	124	25.29 N	80.20 E
Banda, Indon.	154	4.11 N	27.04 E
Banda, Zaïre	154	4.11 N	27.04 E
Banda, Kepulauan II	164	4.35 S	129.55 E
Banda, Laut (Banda Sea) ⊤²	108	4.35 S	128.00 E
Banda Aceh (Kutaraja)	110	5.34 N	95.20 E
Bānda Dāūd Shāh	124	33.16 N	71.11 E
Banda Elat	164	5.39 S	132.59 E
Bandahara, Gunung ▲	114	3.45 N	97.47 E

Name	Page	Lat °'	Long °'
Bandar Penggaram → Batu Pahat	114	1.51 N	102.56 E
Bandarpulau	114	2.41 N	99.31 E
Bandar Seri Begawan	112	4.56 N	114.55 E
Bande	34	42.02 N	7.58 W
Banded Peak ▲	200	37.06 N	106.38 W
Bandeira, Pico da ▲	255	20.26 S	41.47 W
Bandeira do Sul	256	21.47 S	46.23 W
Bandeirantes, Bra.	255	19.53 S	54.23 W
Bandeirantes, Bra.	255	23.06 S	50.21 W
Bandeirantes, Bra.	255	13.41 S	50.48 W
Bandeirantes, Palácio dos ⊥	287b	23.36 S	46.43 W
Bandeirantes, Praia dos ⊥²	287a	23.01 S	43.25 W
Bandéko	152	1.56 N	17.28 E
Bāndel	272b	22.56 N	88.22 E
Bandelier National Monument ◆	200	35.45 N	106.20 W
Bandera, Arg.	252	28.54 S	62.16 W
Bandera, Tx., U.S.	196	29.44 N	99.04 W
Bandera, Alto ▲	238	18.49 N	70.37 W
Bandera Bajada ⋏	234	22.40 N	105.25 W
Banderas	200	31.01 N	105.35 W
Banderas, Bahía de c	234	20.40 N	105.25 W
Banderilla	234	19.36 N	96.56 W
Bandholm	41	54.50 N	11.29 E
Bandiagara	150	14.21 N	3.37 W
Bandiantaolehai	102	41.41 N	104.06 E
Bāndīkūi	124	27.03 N	76.34 E
Bandipur, India	272b	22.44 N	88.26 E
Bandipur, India	272b	22.51 N	88.10 E
Bandirma	130	40.20 N	27.58 E
Bandırma Körfezi c	130	40.25 N	28.00 E
Bando	152	15.00 S	20.30 E
Bandol	62	43.08 N	5.45 E
Ban Don ≈	48	51.45 N	8.45 W
Ban Don → Surat Thani, Thai.	110	9.08 N	99.19 E
Bandon, Or., U.S.	202	43.07 N	124.24 W
Ban Don, Viet.	110	12.53 N	107.48 E
Bandon ≈	48	51.42 N	8.30 W
Ban Don, Ao c	110	9.20 N	99.25 E
Ban Donhiang	110	18.05 N	101.48 E
Ban Dônko	110	16.12 N	106.17 E
Ban Don Muang	269a	13.55 N	100.36 E
B'andovan ⊁	84	39.46 N	49.23 E
Bāndra ◆⁹	272c	19.03 N	72.49 E
Bāndra Point ⊁	272c	19.03 N	72.49 E
Bandula	156	19.02 S	33.07 E
Ban Dulad V	144	8.26 N	45.54 E
Banduk	152	3.18 S	17.20 E
Bandundu ◻⁴	152	4.30 S	18.30 E
Bandundu	152	3.18 S	17.20 E
Bandung	114	6.54 S	107.36 E
Bandura ≈	152	6.40 S	18.30 E
Bandya	162	27.40 S	122.05 E
Bäneasa	38	44.04 N	27.42 E
Banehra	272a	28.44 N	77.23 E
Banff, Ab., Can.	182	51.10 N	115.34 W
Banff, Scot., U.K.	46	57.40 N	2.33 W
Banff National Park ◆	182	51.38 N	116.22 W
Banfield ◆⁸	258	34.44 S	58.23 W
Banfora	150	10.38 N	4.46 W
Banga, India	124	31.11 N	75.59 E
Banga, Pil.	116	11.38 N	122.02 E
Banga, Zaïre	152	5.27 S	20.28 E
Banga ≃	116	6.44 N	124.34 E
Bangaduni Island I	126	21.34 N	88.52 E
Bangala Dam ≈⁶	154	20.40 S	31.15 E
Bangall	210	41.53 N	73.42 W
Bangalore	122	12.58 N	77.36 E
Bangalore → Bangalore	122	12.58 N	77.36 E
Bangangté	152	5.09 N	10.31 E
Bangassou	152	4.50 N	23.07 E
Bangdag Co @	102	27.59 N	98.40 E
Bangeluo	110	32.27 N	90.35 E
Bangeswari	164	2.29 S	89.44 E
Banggai, Mount ▲	164	6.15 S	147.04 E
Banggai, Kepulauan II	164	1.34 S	123.30 E
Banggai, Pulau I	164	1.30 S	123.15 E
Banggi, Pulau I	116	7.17 N	117.12 E
Banggong Co @	102	33.45 N	79.30 E
Banghazi	142	32.07 N	20.04 E
Banghiang ≈	110	16.03 N	105.15 E
Bangholme	274b	38.02 S	145.11 E

Name	Page	Lat °'	Long °'
Bangi	114	2.55 S	112.10 E
Bangil	115a	7.36 S	112.47 E
Bangjang	140	11.23 N	32.42 E
Bangka	105	39.59 N	117.16 E
Bangka, Pulau I, Indon.	114	2.15 S	106.00 E
Bangka, Pulau I, Indon.	112	1.48 N	125.09 E
Bangka, Selat ⋃	115a	2.15 S	105.45 E
Bangkalan	115a	7.02 S	112.44 E
Bangkiang	269a	13.56 N	100.36 E
Bangkinang	114	0.21 N	100.58 E
Bangko	114	2.05 S	102.17 E
Bangkok → Krung Thep	110	13.45 N	100.31 E
Bangkok Station ⊷⁵	269a	13.44 N	100.31 E
Bang Krathum	110	16.34 N	100.18 E
Bangkudu	164	3.10 S	116.16 E
Bangladesh ◻¹	120	24.00 N	90.00 E
Bang Lamung	110	13.05 N	100.55 E
Banglang	114	6.16 N	101.13 E
Ban Gnommarat Kéo	110	17.36 N	105.10 E
Bangolo	150	7.01 N	7.29 W
Bangong Co @	102	33.45 N	79.30 E
Bangor, Indon.	115a	7.02 S	109.47 E
Bangor, Ire.	48	54.04 N	9.45 W
Bangor, N. Ire., U.K.	48	54.40 N	5.40 W
Bangor, Wales, U.K.	42	53.13 N	4.08 W
Bangor, Ca., U.S.	204	39.23 N	121.24 W
Bangor, Me., U.S.	206	44.48 N	68.46 W
Bangor, Mi., U.S.	214	42.18 N	86.06 W
Bangor, Pa., U.S.	208	40.51 N	75.12 W
Bangor, Wi., U.S.	190	43.54 N	90.59 W
Bang Pa In	110	14.14 N	100.35 E
Bāngra ≈	126	21.44 N	89.43 E
Bangriposi	126	22.08 N	86.31 E
Bangs	196	31.43 N	99.08 W
Bangs, Mount ▲	200	36.48 N	113.51 W
Bangsalsari	115a	8.12 S	113.33 E
Bāngu	124	26.07 N	75.13 E
Bangued	116	17.36 N	120.37 E
Bangui, Centraf.	152	4.22 N	18.35 E
Bangui, Pil.	116	18.32 N	120.46 E
Bangui Bay c	116	18.34 N	120.44 E
Bangunpurba	114	3.01 N	99.09 E
Bangweulu, Lake @	154	11.05 S	29.45 E
Bangweulu Swamps ≈	154	11.30 S	30.15 E

Name	Page	Lat °'	Long °'
Bangzhen	106	31.39 N	121.29 E
Banhã	142	30.28 N	31.11 E
Ban Hatgnao	110	14.40 N	106.35 E
Ban Hatkiang	110	18.11 N	102.40 E
Ban Hat Yai → Hat Yai	110	7.01 N	100.28 E
Ban Ha Yaek Pak Kret	269a	13.54 N	100.31 E
Ban Hèt	110	14.44 N	107.29 E
Banhine, Parque Nacional de ◆	156	22.45 S	32.50 E
Ban Hin Heup	110	18.38 N	102.20 E
Ban Hom	110	15.33 N	98.46 E
Ban Hong	110	18.18 N	98.50 E
Ban Hong Muang	110	17.04 N	105.12 E
Ban Houayxay	110	20.18 N	100.26 E
Ban Huai Yang	110	11.36 N	99.40 E
Ban Hua Lamphu Thong	269a	13.32 N	100.38 E
Bani	150	14.02 N	0.02 W
Bani, Burkina	152	14.02 N	0.02 W
Bani, Centraf.	152	7.07 N	22.49 E
Bani, Pil.	116	16.11 N	119.52 E
Bani, Rep. Dom.	238	18.17 N	70.20 W
Bani ≈	152	14.30 N	4.12 W
Bani, Jbel ⋏	148	29.30 N	8.00 W
Baniachang	200	24.31 N	91.22 E
Banī ʿAḏī al-Baḥrīyah	142	27.15 N	30.55 E
Banī ʿAḏī al-Qiblīyah	142	27.15 N	30.56 E
Banī Aḥmad	142	28.03 N	30.46 E
Banī ʿAlī	142	28.29 N	30.43 E
Baniara, Indon.	164	9.46 S	149.53 E
Baniara, Pap. N. Gui.	164	9.46 S	149.53 E
Bānibāha	126	23.42 N	89.37 E
Banī Bangou	150	15.03 N	2.42 E
Banie	30	53.08 N	14.38 E
Banifing ≈	150	12.43 N	6.25 W
Banihāl Pass)(	123	33.31 N	75.13 E
Banī Hasan ash-Shurūq	142	27.54 N	30.51 E
Banī Khālid	142	27.50 N	30.44 E
Banikoara	150	11.18 N	2.26 E
Banima	273c	5.26 N	23.54 E
Banī Majdūl	142	28.30 N	30.48 E
Banī Mazār	142	28.30 N	30.48 E
Banī Muḥammadīyāt	142	27.17 N	31.05 E
Banī Mūsá	142	29.08 N	31.03 E
Banīnah	142	32.05 N	20.16 E
Banio, Lagune c	152	3.35 S	11.00 E
Baniou	34	35.25 N	4.21 E
Banī Rāfiʿ	142	27.22 N	30.53 E
Banī Salāmah	142	30.19 N	30.51 E
Banī Shaʿrān	142	27.19 N	30.51 E
Banī Shuqayr	142	27.23 N	30.56 E
Banister ≈	192	36.42 N	78.44 W
Banī Suhaylah	126	22.53 N	86.31 E
Banī Suwayf	142	29.05 N	31.05 E
Banī Suwayf ◻⁴	142	28.40 N	31.00 E
Banī ʿUbayd, Miṣr	142	31.01 N	31.36 E
Banī ʿUbayd, Miṣr	142	27.57 N	30.46 E
Banī Walīd	146	31.45 N	14.01 E
Ban Phya	110	17.35 N	102.55 E
Ban Pong	110	13.49 N	99.53 E

Name	Page	Lat °'	Long °'
Bao ≃, Zhg.	100	33.40 N	116.33 E
Bao ≃, Zhg.	105	40.31 N	118.17 E
Bao ≃, Zhg.	105	39.02 N	115.39 E
Bao, Ouadi V	146	16.36 N	23.55 E
Baoʼan, Zhg.	100	30.11 N	114.43 E
Baoʼan, Zhg.	100	22.34 N	114.07 E
Baoan → Zhuolu	105	40.22 N	115.12 E
Baoancun	89	48.13 N	125.52 E
Baochang → Taibus Qi	98	41.56 N	115.22 E
Baochang	106	32.04 N	121.25 E
Baochang	102	33.08 N	107.09 E
Baode	100	39.11 N	111.11 E
Baodi	105	39.44 N	117.17 E
Baoding	105	38.52 N	115.29 E
Baofeng	100	33.55 N	113.02 E
Baofu	100	30.31 N	119.29 E
Baoguosi	105	30.35 N	103.25 E
Bao Ha	110	22.11 N	104.21 E
Baohekou	105	40.32 N	118.15 E
Baoji, Zhg.	100	33.08 N	118.19 E
Baoji, Zhg.	102	34.23 N	107.09 E
Baojiagou	105	40.05 N	115.22 E
Baojiatou	106	30.11 N	119.48 E
Baojiawazi	104	41.38 N	123.24 E
Baojing	102	28.43 N	109.25 E
Baokang → Horqin Zuoyi Zhongqi	89	44.07 N	123.18 E
Bao Lac, Viet.	110	11.32 N	107.48 E
Bao Lac, Viet.	110	22.57 N	105.40 E
Baolin	107	30.24 N	105.02 E
Baolizhen	89	42.56 N	123.46 E
Baolunyuan	102	32.22 N	105.40 E
Baomachang	107	29.58 N	104.12 E
Baoqian	98	36.16 N	119.04 E
Baoqing	89	46.21 N	132.14 E
Baoquan	98	36.16 N	119.04 E
Baoshan, Zhg.	102	32.39 N	113.54 E
Baoshan, Zhg.	102	26.19 N	99.04 E
Baoshan, Zhg.	106	25.09 N	99.09 E
Baoshan, Zhg.	106	31.25 N	121.29 E
Baoting	110	18.42 N	109.45 E
Baotou (Paotow)	102	40.40 N	109.59 E
Baoué ≈, Afr.	150	11.06 N	6.34 W
Baoué ≈, Mali	150	13.33 N	5.54 W
Baowei	102	22.39 N	106.50 E
Baoxikou	100	23.16 N	115.14 E
Baoxingchang	107	29.38 N	105.41 E
Baoxinji	100	32.35 N	115.00 E
Baoyi	100	32.13 N	116.42 E
Baoying	100	33.16 N	119.20 E
Baozhichang	107	29.48 N	104.15 E
Baozidian	105	40.11 N	117.48 E
Bap	120	27.23 N	72.21 E
Bapaning	100	27.27 N	117.28 E
Bāpatla	122	15.54 N	80.28 E
Bapaume	50	50.06 N	2.51 E
Bapchule	200	33.08 N	111.52 W
Bapsfontein	158	26.08 S	28.25 E
Baptiste Lake @	212	45.07 N	78.02 W
Baptistown	208	40.31 N	75.00 W
Bāqa al Gharbīya, al-...	132	32.25 N	35.03 E
Baqar, Masrif Baḥr ≈	142	31.05 N	32.08 E
Baqar, Wādī al- V	146	27.49 N	18.37 E
Baqên	123	31.56 N	94.00 E
Baqing	100	32.15 N	93.30 E
B'aqlin	128	33.41 N	35.34 E

Name	Page	Lat °'	Long °'
Ban Ron Phibun	110	8.09 N	99.51 E
Ban Sa-ang	110	17.26 N	105.44 E
Ban Saen To	269a	13.54 N	100.36 E
Ban Sakhila	269a	13.58 N	100.55 E
Bansalan	116	6.47 N	125.14 E
Ban Salik	110	18.30 N	100.45 E
Ban Samang	110	19.43 N	102.36 E
Ban Sam Phan	110	8.33 N	99.09 E
Ban Samrong	110	14.23 N	102.54 E
Ban San Xieng La	110	19.27 N	102.28 E
Bansberia	272b	22.57 N	88.24 E
Bānsda	120	20.45 N	73.22 E
Banská Bystrica	30	48.44 N	19.09 E
Banská Štiavnica	30	48.27 N	18.55 E
Banshi	100	31.09 N	115.36 E
Banshigou	104	41.09 N	126.58 E
Bansi	124	27.11 N	82.56 E
Ban Signo	110	17.51 N	105.00 E
Banská →	62	48.28 N	3.21 W
Banstala	272b	22.34 N	88.21 E
Bansur	124	27.42 N	76.20 E
Ban Takhli	110	15.17 N	100.21 E
Bantam → Banten	115a	6.02 S	106.09 E
Bantam ≈	207	41.40 N	73.13 W
Bantam Lake @	207	41.42 N	73.13 W
Ban Tan	110	19.32 N	99.53 E
Ban Tao Pun	269a	13.51 N	100.32 E
Ban Tawai	110	18.34 N	98.52 E
Bantayan Island I	116	11.10 N	123.44 E
Banten	115a	6.02 S	106.09 E
Bantenan, Teluk c	115a	8.49 S	114.32 E
Ban Teung	110	18.24 N	101.50 E
Ban Thabok	110	18.22 N	103.53 E
Ban Thapuay	110	16.37 N	100.21 E
Bantiao	104	40.28 N	121.09 E
Banting	114	2.53 N	101.30 E
Banton (Jones)	116	12.55 N	122.05 E
Ban Tong Khop	110	15.49 N	102.41 E
Ban Tôp	110	16.12 N	106.27 E
Bantry	44	51.41 N	9.27 W
Bantry Bay c	44	51.38 N	9.48 W
Bantva	120	21.29 N	70.04 E
Bantval	122	12.54 N	75.02 E
Ban Van Viang	110	18.58 N	102.33 E
Banwel	122	19.02 N	73.02 E
Ban Xénklalôk	110	17.52 N	104.48 E
Banxi	100	28.13 N	118.19 E
Ban Xot	110	18.03 N	104.04 E
Banyak, Kepulauan II	114	2.10 N	97.15 E
Banyalbufar	34	39.42 N	2.31 E
Banyo	152	6.45 N	11.49 E
Banyoles	34	42.07 N	2.46 E
Banyuls	62	42.29 N	3.08 E
Banyumas	115a	7.31 S	109.17 E
Banyuwangi	115b	8.12 S	114.21 E
Banz	164	5.48 S	144.38 E

Symbols in the index entries represent the broad categories identified in the key at the right. Symbols with superior numbers (◆¹) identify subcategories (see complete key on page *I · 1*).

Symbole im Register stellen die rechts im Schlüssel erklärten Kategorien dar. Symbole mit hochgestellten Ziffern (◆¹) bezeichnen Unterteilungen einer Kategorie (vgl. vollständiger Schlüssel auf Seite *I · 1*).

Los símbolos incluidos en el texto del índice representan las grandes categorías identificadas con la clave a la derecha. Los símbolos con numeros en su parte superior (◆¹) identifican las subcategorías (véase la clave completa en la página *I · 1*).

Les symboles de l'index représentent les catégories indiquées dans la légende à droite. Les symboles suivis d'un indice (◆¹) représentent des sous-catégories (voir légende complète à la page *I · 1*).

Os símbolos incluídos no texto do índice representam as grandes categorias identificadas com a chave à direita. Os símbolos com números em sua parte superior (◆¹) identificam as subcategorias (veja-se a chave completa na página *I · 1*).

Symbol	English	Deutsch	(Español)	Français	Português
▲	Mountain	Berg	Montaña	Montagne	Montanha
⋏	Mountains	Gebirge	Montañas	Montagnes	Montanhas
)(	Pass	Paß	Paso	Col	Passo
V	Valley, Canyon	Tal, Cañon	Valle, Cañón	Vallée, Canyon	Vale, Canhão
≃	Plain	Ebene	Llano	Plaine	Planicie
⊃	Cape	Kap	Cabo	Cap	Cabo
I	Island	Insel	Isla	Île	Ilha
II	Islands	Inseln	Islas	Îles	Ilhas
⊥	Other Topographic Features	Andere Topographische Objekte	Otros Elementos Topográficos	Autres données topographiques	Outros acidentes topográficos

ESPAÑOL — Nombre | Página | Lat.°′ | Long.°′ W = Oeste
FRANÇAIS — Nom | Page | Lat.°′ | Long.°′ W = Ouest
PORTUGUÊS — Nome | Página | Lat.°′ | Long.°′ W = Oeste

Baranakovo 86 58.08 N 82.58 E
Barancevo 82 55.04 N 37.38 E
Baranello 66 41.32 N 14.34 E
Barangbarang 112 6.24 S 120.28 E
Barangeon ≃ 50 47.12 N 2.10 E
Barani 150 13.10 N 3.53 W
Baraniki 80 46.31 N 41.50 E
Baranikovka 83 49.10 N 39.50 E
Baranoa 246 10.48 N 74.55 W
Barano d'Ischia 61 40.42 N 13.55 E
Baranof 180 57.05 N 134.50 W
Baranof Island I 180 57.00 N 135.00 W
Baranoviči 76 53.08 N 26.02 E
Baranovka 78 50.18 N 27.40 E
Baranovskoje 82 55.25 N 38.45 E
Barany, S.S.S.R. 76 57.20 N 29.09 E
Barany, S.S.S.R. 80 57.38 N 52.16 E
Baranya □ [6] 30 46.05 N 18.15 E
Barão Ataliba Nogueira 256 22.24 S 46.45 W
Barão de Aquino 256 22.07 S 42.39 W
Barão de Cocais 255 19.56 S 43.28 W
Barão de Geraldo 256 22.49 S 47.06 W
Barão de Grajaú 250 6.45 S 43.01 W
Barão de Juparanã 256 22.21 S 43.41 W
Barão de Melgaço 248 16.13 S 55.58 W
Barão de Tromai 250 1.29 S 45.36 W
Baraolt 38 46.05 N 25.36 E
Baraque de Fraiture ∧ 56 50.15 N 5.44 E
Baras 116 13.40 N 124.22 E
Barasāhi 126 21.43 N 86.44 E
Bārāsat, India 126 22.43 N 88.29 E
Bārāsat, India 272b 22.51 N 88.22 E
Baraševo 80 54.32 N 42.53 E
Baraši 78 50.43 N 28.01 E
Baraški 24 65.40 N 52.10 E
Barat, Lintasan ʊ 115a 7.08 S 112.40 E
Baratã 266c 38.48 N 9.19 W
Baratang Island I 110 12.13 N 92.45 E
Barataria 194 29.43 N 90.07 W
Barataria Bay ⊂ 194 29.22 N 89.57 W
Barat Daya, Kepulauan II 108 7.25 S 128.00 E
Barate 112 9.54 S 123.38 E
Bar'atino, S.S.S.R. 76 54.19 N 34.31 E
Bar'atino, S.S.S.R. 82 54.43 N 36.49 E
Baratolia 126 22.25 N 86.37 E
Baratta 166 31.59 S 139.06 E
Baraula 272a 28.34 N 77.22 E
Baraúna ≃ 246 1.14 N 60.41 W
Barauni 124 25.29 N 85.59 E
Baraut 124 29.06 N 77.16 E
Baraya 246 3.10 N 75.04 W
Barbacena 256 21.14 S 43.46 W
Barbacoas 246 1.41 N 78.09 W
Barbades → Barbados □ [1] 241g 13.10 N 59.32 W
Barbadillo 286d 12.02 S 76.56 W
Barbadillo del Mercado 34 42.02 N 3.21 W
Barbadoes Island I 285 40.07 N 75.22 W
Barbados □ [1], N.A. 230 13.10 N 59.32 W
Barbados □ [1], N.A. 241g 13.10 N 59.32 W
Barbagia ◆ [1], It. 36 40.00 N 9.10 E
Barbagia ◆ [1], It. 71 39.55 N 9.12 E
Barbalha 250 7.19 S 39.17 W
Barbar 140 18.01 N 33.59 E
Bárbara 246 0.53 S 72.30 W
Barbarano Vicentino 64 45.24 N 11.32 E
Barbarasco 64 44.14 N 9.56 E
Barbareta, Isla I 236 16.26 N 86.09 W
Barbaria, Cap de › 34 38.38 N 1.23 E
Barbaros 130 40.54 N 27.27 E
Barbas, Cap › 148 22.18 N 16.41 W
Barbaši 76 57.42 N 28.24 E
Barbastro 34 42.02 N 0.08 E
Barbate ≃ 34 36.11 N 5.55 W
Barbate de Franco 34 36.12 N 5.55 W
Barbeau Peak ∧ 16 81.54 N 75.01 W
Barbentane 62 43.54 N 4.45 E
Barberà del Vallès 266d 41.31 N 2.08 E
Barber Booth 262 53.22 N 1.50 W
Barberena 236 14.18 N 90.22 W
Barberena, Río de ≃ 234 22.34 N 97.52 W
Barberino di Mugello 66 44.00 N 11.15 E
Barberino Val d'Elsa 66 43.32 N 11.10 E
Barbers Point › 229c 21.18 N 158.07 W
Barbers Point Naval Air Station ■ 229c 21.19 N 158.04 W
Barberton, S. Afr. 156 25.48 S 31.03 E
Barberton, Oh., U.S. 214 41.00 N 81.36 W
Barbezieux 32 45.28 N 0.09 W
Bar Bigha 124 25.13 N 85.44 E
Barbil 124 22.06 N 85.20 E
Barbis 54 51.37 N 10.25 E
Barbizon 50 48.27 N 2.36 E
Barbosa, Col. 246 6.26 N 75.20 W
Barbosa, Col. 246 5.57 N 73.37 W
Barboursville 188 38.24 N 82.17 W
Barbourville 192 36.51 N 83.53 W
Barbuda I 238 17.38 N 61.48 W
Barbuise ≃ 50 48.33 N 3.35 E
Barby 54 51.58 N 11.53 E
Barčadiv 85 38.19 N 72.29 E
Barca Grande ≃ 258 34.09 S 58.23 W
Barcaldine 166 23.33 S 145.17 E
Barcarena 266c 38.44 N 9.17 W
Barcarena, Ribeira de ≃ 266c 38.42 N 9.27 W
Barcarrota 34 38.31 N 6.51 W
Barcău (Berettyó) ≃ 38 46.59 N 21.07 E
Barce → Al-Marj 146 32.30 N 20.54 E
Barcellona Pozzo di Gotto 70 38.09 N 15.13 E
Barcelona, Esp. 34 41.23 N 2.11 E
Barcelona, Esp. 266d 41.23 N 2.11 E
Barcelona, Méx. 232 26.12 N 103.25 W
Barcelona, Pil. 116 12.52 N 124.09 E
Barcelona, Ven. 246 10.08 N 64.42 W
Barcelona ◆ [8] 266a 40.22 N 3.34 E
Barcelona, Aeropuerto Transoceánico de ⊠ 266d 41.18 N 2.05 E
Barcelone → Barcelona 34 41.23 N 2.11 E
Barceloneta 240m 18.27 N 66.32 W
Barcelonnette 62 44.23 N 6.39 E
Barcelos, Bra. 246 0.58 S 62.57 W
Barcelos, Port. 34 41.32 N 8.37 W
Barchaticha 80 57.34 N 45.13 E
Barchyn ≃ 88 48.43 N 110.17 E
Barcillonnette 62 44.26 N 5.55 E
Barcin 30 52.52 N 17.57 E
Barcis 64 46.11 N 12.33 E
Barclay 208 39.08 N 75.51 W
Barclay Brook ≃ 276 40.19 N 74.22 W
Barcoo ≃ 166 25.30 S 142.50 E
Barcroft, Lake ⊜ [1] 284c 38.51 N 77.09 W
Barcs 30 45.58 N 17.28 E
Barcy 261 49.01 N 2.53 E
Barczewo 30 53.50 N 20.42 E
Bard 62 45.36 N 7.45 E
Barda, S.S.S.R. 84 40.23 N 47.08 E
Barda, S.S.S.R. 86 56.54 N 55.38 E
Barda del Medio 252 38.43 S 68.10 W
Bardagué, Enneri ∨ 146 22.06 N 16.28 E
Bardai, Süd. 140 12.43 N 21.53 E
Bardaï, Tchad 146 21.22 N 16.59 E
Bardawīl, Sabkhat al- ≡ 140 31.10 N 33.10 E
Barddhamān 126 23.15 N 87.51 E
Bardejov 30 49.18 N 21.16 E
Bardenas Reales ⋏ [1] 34 42.10 N 1.25 W
Bardeskan 128 35.12 N 57.58 E
Bardi 62 44.38 N 9.44 E
Bardīyah 146 31.46 N 25.06 E
Bardız 130 40.26 N 42.20 E
Bardney 44 53.12 N 0.21 W
Bardo 36 36.50 N 10.06 E
Bardoc 162 30.20 S 121.17 E
Bārdoli 120 21.07 N 73.07 E
Bardolino 64 45.33 N 10.43 E
Bardonecchia 62 45.05 N 6.42 E
Bardonia 276 41.07 N 74.00 W
Bardoux, Lac ⊜ 186 51.09 N 67.50 W
Bardowick 52 53.18 N 10.23 E
Bardsey Island I 42 52.45 N 4.45 W
Bardsey Sound ʊ 42 52.47 N 4.45 W
Bardstown 194 37.48 N 85.28 W
Bardu 24 68.52 N 18.21 E
Bardufoss 24 69.04 N 18.30 E
Bardwell, Ky., U.S. 194 36.52 N 89.00 W
Bardwell, Tx., U.S. 222 32.16 N 96.42 W
Bardwell Lake ⊜ [1] 222 32.16 N 96.39 W
Bare 144 4.42 N 42.47 E
Bareggio 266b 45.29 N 9.00 E
Barei, Wādī ∨ 140 13.27 N 23.57 E
Bareilly 124 28.21 N 79.25 E
Bareli 124 23.00 N 78.14 E
Barenburg 52 52.37 N 8.47 E
Barendrecht 52 51.51 N 4.32 E
Bärenklau 54 51.56 N 14.34 E
Bärenstein, D.D.R. 54 50.48 N 13.47 E
Bärenstein, D.D.R. 54 50.30 N 13.02 E
Barentin 50 49.33 N 0.57 E
Barents Sea ⊤ [2] 12 74.00 N 36.00 E
Barents Trough ✦ [1] 12 75.00 N 29.00 E
Barentu 144 15.04 N 37.37 E
Bareo 112 3.45 N 115.27 E
Baresville 208 39.48 N 76.57 W
Bareta 123 29.52 N 75.42 E
Barfleur 32 49.40 N 1.15 W
Barfleur, Pointe de › 32 49.42 N 1.16 W
Barga 64 44.04 N 10.29 E
Bargāchia, India 126 22.39 N 88.07 E
Bargāchia, India 272b 22.48 N 88.27 E
Bargagli 62 44.27 N 9.05 E
Bargaintown 208 39.22 N 70.35 W
Bargara 166 24.49 S 152.27 E
Bargas 34 39.56 N 4.03 W
Barge, It. 62 44.43 N 7.20 E
Barge, Ityo. 144 6.14 N 36.58 E
Barg-e Matāl 120 35.40 N 71.21 E
Bargemon 62 43.37 N 6.32 E
Bargen 58 47.48 N 8.37 E
Bargersville 218 39.31 N 86.10 W
Barghanak 128 33.56 N 62.26 E
Bargnop 140 9.30 N 28.28 E
Bargo 170 34.18 S 150.35 E
Bargoed 42 51.43 N 3.15 W
Bargteheide 52 53.44 N 10.16 E
Bārguna 126 22.09 N 90.07 E
Barguzin 88 53.37 N 109.37 E
Barguzin ≃ 88 53.27 N 109.00 E
Barguzinskij chrebet ⋏ 88 54.30 N 110.20 E
Barguzinskij zapovednik ♠ 88 54.25 N 109.40 E
Bārh 124 25.29 N 85.43 E
Barhaj 124 26.17 N 83.44 E
Bar Harbor 188 44.23 N 68.12 W
Barharwa 124 24.52 N 87.47 E
Barhau 112 5.19 S 102.10 E
Barhi 124 24.18 N 85.25 E
Bar Hill 42 52.15 N 0.01 E
Barhiya 124 25.17 N 86.02 E
Bāri, India 124 23.03 N 78.05 E
Bāri, India 124 26.39 N 77.36 E
Bari, It. 68 41.07 N 16.52 E
Bari, Zaïre 152 3.19 N 19.23 E
Bari □ [4], It. 68 40.56 N 16.40 E
Bari □ [4], Som. 144 10.00 N 50.00 E
Baria ≃ 246 1.56 N 66.35 W
Baricella 64 44.39 N 11.32 E
Barichara 246 6.38 N 73.14 W
Barīdī, Ra's › 128 24.17 N 37.31 E
Bāri Doāb ⋏ [1] 123 30.25 N 73.00 E
Barī Gāv 120 33.52 N 67.49 E
Barigazzo 64 44.16 N 10.39 E
Barigua, Salina de ≃ 241s 12.08 N 69.59 W
Barika 34 35.23 N 5.22 E
Barika, Oued ≃ 34 35.22 N 5.18 E
Barikiwa 154 9.28 S 37.54 E
Barīkowt 120 35.18 N 71.32 E
Barile 68 40.57 N 15.40 E
Barillas 236 15.48 N 91.18 W
Bariloche → San Carlos de Bariloche 254 41.09 S 71.18 W
Barilo-Krepinskaja 83 47.45 N 39.32 E
Barīm (Perim) I 144 12.39 N 43.25 E
Barima ≃ 246 8.33 N 60.25 W
Barin 84 39.13 N 44.28 E
Barinas, P.R. 240m 18.01 N 66.51 W
Barinas, Ven. 246 8.38 N 70.12 W
Barinas □ [3] 246 8.10 N 69.50 W
Baring 224 47.46 N 121.29 W
Baring, Cape › 176 70.05 N 117.20 W
Baringa, Zaïre 152 6.17 S 16.55 E
Baringa, Zaïre 152 0.45 N 20.52 E
Baringo, Lake ⊜ 154 0.38 N 36.05 E
Båring Vig ⊂ 41 55.32 N 9.56 E
Barinitas 246 8.45 N 70.25 W
Bāripada 126 21.56 N 86.43 E
Bariri 255 22.04 S 48.44 W
Bārīs 140 24.40 N 30.36 E
Barisacho 84 42.28 N 44.54 E
Bari Sādri 120 24.25 N 74.28 E
Barisāl 124 22.42 N 90.22 E
Barisan, Pegunungan ⋏ 112 3.00 S 102.15 E
Bari Sardo 71 39.50 N 9.38 E
Barisciano 66 42.19 N 13.35 E
Bariti Bil ⊜ 272b 22.48 N 88.26 E
Barito ≃ 112 3.32 S 114.29 E
Barjā 132 33.39 N 35.26 E
Barjac 62 44.18 N 4.21 E
Barjols 62 43.33 N 6.00 E
Barjora 126 23.26 N 87.17 E
Barjūj, Wādī ∨ 146 25.57 N 13.12 E
Bark ≃ 216 42.55 N 88.50 W
Barka Kāna 124 23.37 N 85.29 E
Barkal 120 22.44 N 92.23 E
Barkam 102 31.50 N 102.40 E
Barkava 76 56.43 N 26.36 E
Barkelsby 41 54.30 N 9.50 E
Barker, N.Y., U.S. 210 43.19 N 78.33 W
Barker, Ur. 258 34.16 S 57.27 W
Barker Point › 276 40.51 N 73.44 W
Barker Reservoir ⊜ [1] 222 29.44 N 95.44 W
Barkers Brook ≃ 285 40.03 N 74.45 W
Barkerville 182 53.04 N 121.31 W
Barkerville Historic Park ⊥ 182 53.04 N 121.30 W
Barkeyville 214 41.12 N 79.58 W
Barkhamsted Reservoir ⊜ [1] 207 41.57 N 72.57 W
Bārkhān 120 29.54 N 69.31 E
Barkhanpur 126 23.50 N 89.33 E
Barking ◆ [8] 260 51.33 N 0.06 E
Barkingside ◆ [8] 260 51.36 N 0.05 E
Barki Saraiya 124 24.10 N 85.53 E
Barkisland 262 53.41 N 1.55 W
Bark Lake ⊜, On., Can. 190 46.54 N 82.28 W
Bark Lake ⊜, On., Can. 212 45.27 N 77.51 W
Barkley, Lake ⊜ [1] 194 36.40 N 87.55 W
Barkley Sound ʊ 182 48.53 N 125.20 W
Barkly ≃ 169 37.32 S 146.32 E
Barkly, Mount ∧ [2] 162 21.34 S 132.28 E
Barkly East 158 30.58 S 27.33 E
Barkly Tableland ⋏ [1] 162 18.00 S 136.00 E
Barkly West 158 28.05 S 24.31 E
Barkol 90 43.50 N 93.30 E
Barksdale 196 29.44 N 100.02 W
Barkuhi 124 22.13 N 78.42 E
Barla 130 38.01 N 30.47 E
Bârlad → Bîrlad 38 46.14 N 27.40 E
Barlassina 266b 45.39 N 9.08 E
Barlaston 42 52.57 N 2.10 W
Barlby 44 53.48 N 1.03 W
Barleben 54 52.12 N 11.37 E
Bar-le-Duc 56 48.47 N 5.10 E
Barlee, Lake ⊜ 162 29.10 S 119.30 E
Barlee, Mount ∧ [2] 162 24.37 S 128.06 E
Barlee Range ⋏ 162 23.35 S 116.00 E
Barles 62 44.16 N 6.16 E
Barletta 68 41.19 N 16.17 E
Barlin 50 50.27 N 2.37 E
Barlinek 30 53.00 N 15.12 E
Barling 194 35.19 N 94.18 W
Barlow 194 37.03 N 89.02 W
Barluk 88 54.32 N 101.43 E
Barma 164 1.54 S 133.00 E
Barmancak, ozero ⊜ 80 48.02 N 44.40 E
Barmašovo 78 47.07 N 32.26 E
Barmedman 166 34.09 S 147.23 E
Barmen ◆ [8] 263 51.17 N 7.13 E
Bārmer 120 25.45 N 71.23 E
Barmera 166 34.15 S 140.28 E
Barmouth 42 52.43 N 4.03 W
Barmouth Bay ⊂ 42 52.42 N 4.08 W
Barmstedt 52 53.47 N 9.46 E
Barnaby Manor Oaks 284c 38.50 N 76.58 W
Barnagar 120 23.03 N 75.22 E
Barnāla 123 30.23 N 75.33 E
Barnard Castle 44 54.33 N 1.55 W
Barnasht 142 29.41 N 31.15 E
Bärnau 60 49.49 N 12.26 E
Barnaul 86 53.22 N 83.45 E
Bärnbach 61 47.05 N 15.06 E
Barn Bluff ∧ 166 41.43 S 145.56 E
Barneberg 54 52.08 N 11.03 E
Barnegat 208 39.45 N 74.13 W
Barnegat Bay ⊂ 208 39.52 N 74.07 W
Barnegat Light 208 39.45 N 74.06 W
Barne Inlet ⊂ 9 80.15 S 160.15 E
Barnes 214 41.40 N 79.01 W
Barnes ◆ [8] 260 51.28 N 0.15 W
Barnesboro 214 40.39 N 78.46 W
Barnes Corners 212 43.49 N 75.49 W
Barnes Ice Cap ⊓ 176 70.00 N 73.15 W
Barnes Lake ⊜ 184 56.23 N 98.06 W
Barnes Sound ʊ 220 25.14 N 80.23 W
Barnesville, Ga., U.S. 192 33.03 N 84.09 W
Barnesville, Mn., U.S. 198 46.39 N 96.25 W
Barnesville, Oh., U.S. 188 39.59 N 81.10 W
Barnet ◆ [8] 260 51.40 N 0.13 W
Barnetby le Wold 44 53.35 N 0.25 W
Barnett 219 39.16 N 89.42 W
Barnetts 208 37.22 N 77.09 W
Barneveld, Ned. 52 52.08 N 5.35 E
Barneveld, N.Y., U.S. 210 43.16 N 75.12 W
Barneville-Carteret 32 49.23 N 1.47 W
Barnhart, Mo., U.S. 219 38.20 N 90.23 W
Barnhart, Tx., U.S. 196 31.08 N 101.10 W
Barnhill 214 40.27 N 81.21 W
Barnim ◆ [1] 54 52.40 N 13.45 E
Barnoldswick 44 53.55 N 2.11 W
Barnówko 54 52.48 N 14.45 E
Barnsboro 285 39.46 N 75.09 W
Barnsdall 196 36.33 N 96.09 W
Barnsley 44 53.34 N 1.28 W
Barnstable 207 41.42 N 70.18 W
Barnstable □ [6] 207 41.42 N 70.18 W
Barnstable Harbor ⊂ 207 41.43 N 70.18 W
Barnstaple 42 51.05 N 4.04 W
Barnstaple Bay ⊂ 42 51.05 N 4.20 W
Barnston 262 53.21 N 3.05 W
Barnstorf 52 52.42 N 8.30 E
Barnt Green 42 52.22 N 1.59 W
Barnton 262 53.16 N 2.33 W
Barntrup 52 51.59 N 9.06 E
Barnum Island 276 40.36 N 73.39 W
Barnwell, Ab., Can. 182 49.46 N 112.15 W
Barnwell, S.C., U.S. 192 33.14 N 81.21 W
Baro 150 8.37 N 6.25 E
Baro ≃ 144 8.26 N 33.13 E
Barobo 116 8.33 N 126.07 E
Baroda → Vadodara 122 22.18 N 73.12 E
Baroda, India 124 25.30 N 76.39 E
Baroda, Mi., U.S. 216 41.57 N 86.29 W
Baroe 158 33.13 S 24.33 E
Barometer ∧ 172 41.50 S 173.39 E
Baron Bluff ⊥ [4] 241n 17.47 N 64.47 W
Baronissi 68 40.44 N 14.45 E
Barons 182 50.00 N 113.05 W
Barora Fa Island I 175e 7.30 S 158.20 E
Barora Ite Island I 175e 7.35 S 158.24 E
Barossa Reservoir ⊜ [1] 168b 34.39 S 138.51 E
Barotac Nuevo 116 10.54 N 122.42 E
Barotac Viejo 116 11.03 N 122.51 E
Barouéli 150 13.04 N 6.50 W
Barpathār 120 26.17 N 93.53 E
Barpeta 120 26.19 N 91.00 E
Bar Point › 214 42.03 N 83.06 W
Barqa 120 30.57 N 81.20 E
Barqah (Cyrenaica) □ [9] 146 31.00 N 22.30 E
Barqah, Jabal al- ∧ 132 30.25 N 34.18 E
Barq al-ʿIzz 142 31.01 N 31.26 E
Barque Canada Reef ✦ [2] 108 8.12 N 113.19 E
Barques, Pointe aux › 190 44.04 N 82.58 W
Barquisimeto 246 10.04 N 69.19 W
Barr 58 48.24 N 7.27 E
Barra, Bra. 250 11.05 S 43.10 W
Barra, Gam. 150 13.20 N 16.36 W
Barra I 46 56.58 N 7.29 W
Barra, Ponta da › 156 23.47 S 35.32 E
Barra, Sound of ʊ 46 57.05 N 7.25 W
Barraba 166 30.22 S 150.36 E
Barracão 252 26.15 S 53.38 W
Barracão do Barreto 248 8.48 S 58.24 W
Barracas ◆ [8] 288 34.38 S 58.22 W
Barrackpore → Bārākpur 126 22.46 N 88.21 E
Barrackpore Airport ⊠ 272b 22.47 N 88.22 E
Barrackville 188 39.30 N 80.10 W
Barracouta, Cape › 158 34.26 S 21.22 E
Barra da Estiva 255 13.38 S 41.19 W
Barra de Río Grande 236 12.54 N 83.32 W
Barra de Santa Rosa 250 6.43 S 36.04 W
Barra de Santo Antônio 250 9.24 S 35.30 W
Barra de São Francisco 256 21.58 S 42.42 W
Barra do Bugres 248 15.05 S 57.11 W
Barra do Corda 250 5.30 S 45.15 W
Barra do Cuanza 152 9.09 S 13.00 E
Barra do Dande 152 8.28 S 13.22 E
Barra do Garças 255 15.53 S 52.15 W
Barra do Mendes 255 11.43 S 42.04 W
Barra do Piraí 256 22.28 S 43.49 W
Barra do Ribeiro 252 30.18 S 51.18 W
Barra dos Coqueiros 250 10.54 S 37.03 W
Barra Falsa, Ponta da › 156 22.55 S 35.37 E
Barrafranca 70 37.22 N 14.12 E
Barra Funda ◆ [8] 287b 23.31 S 46.39 W
Barra Grande 256 23.06 S 44.42 W
Barra Head › 46 56.46 N 7.38 W
Barrali 71 39.28 N 9.06 E
Barra Mansa 256 22.32 S 44.11 W
Barranca, Perú 248 10.45 S 77.46 W
Barranca, Perú 248 4.50 S 76.42 W
Barrancabermeja 246 7.03 N 73.52 W
Barranca del Cobre, Parque Nacional ♠ 232 27.15 N 107.41 W
Barrancas, Chile 252 33.27 S 70.46 W
Barrancas, Col. 246 10.57 N 72.50 W
Barrancas, Ven. 246 8.46 N 70.06 W
Barrancas, Ven. 246 8.42 N 62.11 W
Barrancas ≃ 252 36.52 S 69.45 W
Barranco 286d 12.09 S 77.02 W
Barranco Azul 196 29.21 N 104.17 W
Barranco de Guadalupe 196 30.02 N 104.44 W
Barranco do Velho 34 37.14 N 7.56 W
Barrancos 34 38.08 N 6.59 W
Barrânia 256 21.33 S 46.32 W
Barranqueras 252 27.29 S 58.56 W
Barranquilla 246 10.59 N 74.48 W
Barranquitas 240m 18.11 N 66.18 W
Barra Punta Gorda 236 11.31 N 83.47 W
Barras 250 4.15 S 42.18 W
Barrax 34 39.03 N 2.12 W
Barre, Ma., U.S. 207 42.25 N 72.06 W
Barre, Vt., U.S. 188 44.11 N 72.30 W
Barrea 66 41.45 N 13.59 E
Barreal 252 31.38 S 69.28 W
Barree 214 40.35 N 78.06 W
Barre Falls Dam ◆ [6] 207 42.26 N 72.02 W
Barreiras 255 12.08 S 45.00 W
Barreirinha 250 2.47 S 57.03 W
Barreirinhas 250 2.45 S 42.50 W
Barreiro 34 38.40 N 9.05 W
Barreiro ≃ 255 15.43 S 52.45 W
Barreiros 250 8.49 S 35.12 W
Barrême 62 43.57 N 6.22 E
Barren ≃ 194 37.11 N 86.37 W
Barren, Nosy II 157b 18.25 S 43.40 E
Barren Island I 110 12.16 N 93.51 E
Barren Islands II 180 58.55 N 152.15 W
Barrenjoey Head › 170 33.34 S 151.20 E
Barren River Lake ⊜ [1] 194 36.45 N 86.02 W
Barren Run ≃ 279b 40.09 N 79.42 W
Barre Plains 207 42.22 N 72.06 W
Barret-le-Bas 62 44.16 N 5.44 E
Barretos 255 20.33 S 48.33 W
Barrett 222 29.53 N 95.04 W
Barrett, Mount ∧ 162 18.10 S 127.33 E
Barrhead, Ab., Can. 182 54.08 N 114.24 W
Barrhead, Scot., U.K. 46 55.48 N 4.24 W
Barrhill 44 55.07 N 4.46 W
Barrie 212 44.24 N 79.40 W
Barriefield 212 44.14 N 76.28 W
Barrie Island I 190 45.55 N 82.40 W
Barrien 52 52.56 N 8.49 E
Barrier, Cape › 172 36.21 S 175.31 E
Barrier Bay ⊂ 9 67.45 S 81.10 E
Barrière 182 51.11 N 120.07 W
Barrier Range ⋏ 166 31.25 S 141.25 E
Barrier Reef ✦ [2] 164 11.36 S 153.00 E
Barrigada 174p 13.28 N 144.48 E
Barrilla Draw ∨ 196 31.21 N 103.23 W
Barr Ilyās 132 33.46 N 35.54 E
Barrington, N.S., Can. 186 43.34 N 65.34 W
Barrington, Il., U.S. 216 42.09 N 88.08 W
Barrington, N.J., U.S. 285 39.51 N 75.03 W
Barrington, R.I., U.S. 207 41.44 N 71.18 W
Barrington Hills 216 42.07 N 88.09 W
Barrington Lake ⊜ 184 56.55 N 100.15 W
Barrington Tops ∧ 166 32.00 S 151.28 E
Barrington Woods 278 42.09 N 88.04 W
Barringun 166 29.01 S 145.43 E
Barrinho 256 23.07 S 45.22 W
Barrio Azul ◆ [8] 286b 23.04 N 82.23 W
Barrio Obrero Industrial 286d 12.04 S 77.04 W
Barrita Vieja 236 13.55 N 90.54 W
Barrīyat al-Uṣayfir 142 31.18 N 30.40 E
Barro, Bra. 250 7.11 S 38.47 W
Barro, Gui.-B. 150 12.24 N 15.30 W
Barro Alto 255 15.04 S 48.58 W
Barro Duro 250 2.52 S 42.17 W
Barrois □ [9] 56 48.40 N 5.15 E
Barron 190 45.24 N 91.50 W
Barron Creek ≃ 282 37.27 N 122.05 W
Barron Lake 216 41.51 N 86.11 W
Barrouallie 241h 13.14 N 61.17 W
Barrow, Arg. 252 38.18 S 60.14 W
Barrow, Ak., U.S. 180 71.17 N 156.34 W
Barrow ≃ 48 52.15 N 7.00 W
Barrow, Point › 180 71.23 N 156.30 W
Barrow Bay ⊂ 212 44.58 N 81.13 W
Barrow Creek 162 21.33 S 133.53 E
Barrowford 44 53.52 N 2.13 W
Barrow-in-Furness 44 54.07 N 3.14 W
Barrow Island I 162 20.48 S 115.23 E
Barrow Range ⋏ 162 26.04 S 127.28 E
Barrows 184 52.49 N 101.27 W
Barrow Strait ʊ 176 74.21 N 94.10 W
Barrowsville 207 41.56 N 71.12 W
Barrow upon Humber 44 53.41 N 0.23 W
Barry, Wales, U.K. 42 51.24 N 3.18 W
Barry, Il., U.S. 219 39.41 N 91.02 W
Barry, Tx., U.S. 222 32.06 N 96.38 W
Barry □ [6] 216 42.35 N 85.18 W
Barrydale 158 33.55 S 20.43 E
Barrys Bay 212 45.29 N 77.41 W
Barrys Bay ⊂ 212 45.28 N 77.42 W
Barryton 190 43.45 N 85.08 W
Barrytown 210 42.00 N 73.56 W
Barryville 210 41.28 N 74.54 W
Barsakel'mes, ostrov I 86 45.40 N 59.58 E
Barsalpur 120 28.10 N 72.15 E
Baršatas 86 48.13 N 78.21 E
Bårse 41 55.07 N 11.58 E
Bārsi 122 18.14 N 75.42 E
Baršin 86 49.45 N 69.36 E
Barsinghausen 52 52.18 N 9.27 E
Barskaun 85 42.10 N 77.37 E
Barsø I 41 55.07 N 9.34 E
Barssel 52 53.10 N 7.44 E
Barst 56 49.04 N 6.50 E
Barstow, Ca., U.S. 228 34.53 N 117.01 W
Barstow, Tx., U.S. 196 31.28 N 103.24 W
Barsuki 82 54.15 N 37.30 E
Bar-sur-Aube 58 48.14 N 4.43 E
Bar-sur-Seine 50 48.07 N 4.22 E
Bart 208 39.56 N 76.05 W
Bārta ≃ 76 56.24 N 21.03 E
Bartala 272b 22.33 N 88.16 E
Bartang ≃ 120 37.56 N 71.34 E
Bartazuga, Jabal ∧ 140 21.44 N 33.33 E
Bartelso 219 38.32 N 89.28 W
Bartenheim 58 47.38 N 7.28 E
Bartenstein 56 49.21 N 9.53 E
Barter Island I 180 70.08 N 143.35 W
Barth 54 54.22 N 12.43 E
Barthe ≃ 54 54.22 N 12.41 E
Barthélemy, Deo)(110 19.26 N 104.06 E
Bartholomew □ [6] 218 39.13 N 85.55 W
Bartholomew, Bayou ≃ 194 32.43 N 92.04 W
Bartibougou 150 12.52 N 0.48 E
Bartica 246 6.24 N 58.37 W
Bartın 130 41.38 N 32.21 E
Bartle Frere ∧ 166 17.23 S 145.49 E
Bartlesville 196 36.44 N 95.58 W
Bartlett, Il., U.S. 216 41.59 N 88.11 W
Bartlett, Ne., U.S. 198 41.53 N 98.33 W
Bartlett, N.H., U.S. 188 44.04 N 71.17 W
Bartlett, Tn., U.S. 194 35.12 N 89.52 W
Bartlett, Tx., U.S. 222 30.48 N 97.26 W
Bartlett Brook ≃ 283 42.42 N 71.13 W
Bartlett Cove 180 58.27 N 135.55 W
Bartlett Reservoir ⊜ [1] 200 33.52 N 111.37 W
Bartletts ∧ [2] 168a 32.19 S 116.43 E
Bartletts Harbour 186 50.57 N 57.00 W
Bartley 198 40.14 N 100.18 W
Bartolomé Bavio → General Mansilla 258 35.05 S 57.45 W
Bartolomé de las Casas 252 25.24 S 59.34 W
Bartolomeu de Gusmão, Aeroporto ⊠ 256 22.56 S 43.43 W
Bartolomeu Dias 156 21.10 S 35.09 E
Barton, Austl. 162 30.31 S 132.39 E
Barton, N.Y., U.S. 210 42.03 N 76.27 W
Barton, Oh., U.S. 214 40.06 N 80.50 W
Barton, Vt., U.S. 188 44.44 N 72.10 W
Barton Aerodrome ⊠ 262 53.28 N 2.23 W
Barton Lake 216 42.06 N 85.35 W
Barton Lake ⊜ 184 52.00 N 94.06 W
Barton-le-Clay 42 51.57 N 0.25 W
Barton Mills 42 52.20 N 0.31 E
Barton Park ♠ 274a 33.57 S 151.09 E
Barton Run ≃ 285 39.53 N 74.51 W
Barton-under-Needwood 42 52.45 N 1.43 W
Barton-upon-Humber 44 53.41 N 0.27 W
Bartonville 190 40.39 N 89.39 W
Barton Water Swing Bridge ◆ [5] 262 53.28 N 2.21 W
Bartoszyce 30 54.16 N 20.49 E
Bartow, Fl., U.S. 220 27.53 N 81.50 W
Bartow, Ga., U.S. 192 32.52 N 82.28 W
Baru, Kali ≊ 269e 6.10 S 106.51 E
Barú, Volcán ∧ [1] 236 8.48 N 82.33 W
Barueri 256 23.31 S 46.53 W
Barugo 116 11.20 N 124.44 E
Bāruipāra 272b 22.46 N 88.14 E
Bāruipur 126 22.21 N 88.27 E
Bārūk, Jabal al- ∧ 132 33.43 N 35.45 E
Barumini 71 39.42 N 9.00 E
Barumun ≃ 114 2.30 N 100.09 E
Barun Bogd uul ∧ 90 44.57 N 100.15 E
Barung, Nusa I 115a 8.28 S 113.20 E
Barun Su 102 42.27 N 111.01 E
Barun-Torej, ozero ⊜ 88 50.10 N 115.30 E
Baruntse ∧ 124 27.51 N 86.59 E
Barus 114 2.00 N 98.24 E
Baruta 286c 10.26 N 66.53 W
Baruth 54 52.03 N 13.30 E
Baruun Bajan-Ulaan 102 45.10 N 101.24 E
Baruun bogd uul ∧ 102 44.57 N 100.15 E
Baruun-Urt 90 46.42 N 113.15 E
Barva, Volcán ∧ [1] 236 10.08 N 84.06 W
Barvas 46 58.22 N 6.32 W
Barvenkovo 78 48.54 N 37.02 E
Barver 52 52.37 N 8.35 E
Barvicha 265b 55.44 N 37.16 E
Barview 202 43.21 N 124.18 W
Barwa 126 23.51 N 86.26 E
Barwāh 120 22.16 N 76.03 E
Barwāla ◆ [8] 272a 28.46 N 77.04 E
Bärwalde → Mieszkowice 30 52.46 N 14.30 E
Barwāni 120 22.02 N 74.54 E
Barwa Sāgar 124 25.23 N 78.44 E
Barwell 42 52.32 N 1.21 W
Barwice 30 53.45 N 16.22 E
Barwick 192 30.54 N 83.44 W
Barwidgee 162 27.02 S 120.54 E
Barwon ≃, Austl. 166 30.00 S 148.05 E
Barwon ≃, Austl. 169 38.13 S 144.25 E
Barwon Heads (South Barwon) 169 38.17 S 144.30 E
Barybino, S.S.S.R. 82 55.16 N 37.54 E
Barybino, S.S.S.R. 82 54.56 N 37.47 E
Barycz ≃ 30 51.42 N 16.15 E
Barykino 83 49.17 N 38.24 E
Barykova, mys › 180 63.02 N 179.29 E
Barykovo 82 54.38 N 38.48 E
Barynino 82 55.47 N 36.21 E
Baryš 80 53.39 N 47.08 E
Baryš ≃ 80 54.35 N 46.48 E
Baryševka 78 50.22 N 31.19 E
Baryševo 86 54.58 N 83.11 E
Baryšniki 80 56.57 N 46.33 E
Barzah 132 33.34 N 36.19 E
Barzas 86 55.43 N 86.19 E
Barzio 58 45.57 N 9.27 E
Bas'a ≃ 76 53.46 N 31.01 E
Basacato del Este 152 3.37 N 8.54 E
Basai Dārāpur ◆ [8] 272a 28.40 N 77.08 E
Bāsaʿīdū 128 26.39 N 55.17 E
Basail, Arg. 252 27.52 S 59.18 W
Bāsāil, Bngl. 126 24.14 N 90.04 E
Basakin 80 48.11 N 42.18 E
Basāl 123 33.33 N 72.15 E
Basalt ≃ 166 19.38 S 145.52 E
Basalt Island I 271d 22.19 N 114.22 E
Basaluzzo 62 44.46 N 8.42 E
Basandīlah 142 31.12 N 31.26 E
Basankusu 152 1.14 N 19.48 E
Bašanta 80 46.05 N 41.56 E
Basanti 126 22.12 N 88.42 E
Basarabi 38 44.10 N 28.24 E
Basatongwula Shan ∧ 120 33.05 N 91.30 E
Basavakalyān 122 17.52 N 76.57 E
Basavilbaso 252 32.22 S 58.53 W
Baščelakskij chrebet ⋏ 86 51.15 N 84.30 E
Baschi 66 42.40 N 12.13 E
Basco 108 20.27 N 121.58 E
Bascom 214 41.07 N 83.17 W
Bascuñán, Cabo › 252 28.51 S 71.30 W
Basdahl 52 53.26 N 8.59 E
Basdorf, B.R.D. 56 51.12 N 8.58 E
Basdorf, D.D.R. 54 52.44 N 13.26 E
Basekpio 154 4.44 N 24.40 E
Basel (Bâle) 58 47.33 N 7.35 E
Baselga di Pinè 64 46.08 N 11.14 E
Baselice 68 41.24 N 14.58 E
Basel-Land □ [3] 58 47.30 N 7.50 E
Basel-Stadt □ [3] 58 47.38 N 7.40 E
Basen ≃ 96 34.48 N 132.51 E
Bas-en-Basset 62 45.18 N 4.06 E
Basentello ≃ 68 40.40 N 16.23 E
Basento ≃ 68 40.21 N 16.50 E
Başeu ≃ 38 47.44 N 27.15 E
Basey 116 11.17 N 125.04 E
Bashaw 182 52.35 N 112.58 W
Basher Kill ≃ 210 41.27 N 74.35 W
Bashi Channel ʊ 108 22.00 N 121.00 E
Bashikejike 120 37.30 N 85.50 E
Bashiqiao 106 31.40 N 120.22 E
Bashtīl 273c 30.05 N 31.11 E
Basi, India 123 30.36 N 76.50 E
Basi, India 123 30.41 N 76.24 E
Basiad Bay ⊂ 116 14.16 N 122.19 E
Basiano 112 1.16 S 122.50 E
Basibasy 157b 22.10 S 43.40 E
Başıbüyük ◆ [8] 267b 40.57 N 29.08 E
Basicò 70 38.04 N 15.04 E
Basid 85 38.07 N 72.09 E
Basilaki Island I 164 10.35 S 151.00 E
Basilan □ [4] 116 6.35 N 121.55 E
Basilan Island I 116 6.34 N 122.03 E
Basilan Peak ∧ 116 6.33 N 122.04 E
Basilan Strait ʊ 116 6.49 N 122.05 E
Basildon 260 51.35 N 0.25 E
Basildon □ [8] 260 51.35 N 0.29 E
Basile 194 30.29 N 92.35 W
Basiliano 64 46.01 N 13.06 E
Basilicata □ [4] 68 40.30 N 16.10 E
Basílio 252 31.53 S 53.01 W
Basiluzzo, Isola I 70 38.39 N 15.07 E
Basin, Mt., U.S. 202 46.16 N 112.15 W
Basin, Wy., U.S. 202 44.22 N 108.02 W
Bäsingen ⊜ 40 60.09 N 16.20 E
Basinger 220 27.24 N 81.01 W
Basingstoke 42 51.15 N 1.05 W
Basingstoke Canal ≊ 260 51.21 N 0.29 W
Basingwerk Abbey ⊌ [1] 262 53.17 N 3.12 W
Basin Lake ⊜ 184 52.38 N 105.18 W
Basīrhāt 126 22.40 N 88.53 E
Basīrpur 123 30.35 N 73.50 E
Basīṭ, Ra's al- › 130 35.51 N 35.48 E
Basiyingzi 104 42.05 N 121.37 E
Basjanovskij 86 58.19 N 60.44 E
Baška 36 44.58 N 14.46 E
Baskahegan Lake ⊜ 188 45.30 N 67.48 W
Baskakovka 76 54.36 N 34.19 E
Başkale 128 38.02 N 44.00 E
Baskatong, Réservoir ⊜ [1] 190 46.48 N 75.50 W
Baškaus ≃ 86 51.09 N 87.43 E
Baškend 84 40.38 N 45.32 E
Basket Lake ⊜ 184 49.43 N 92.00 W
Basking Ridge 276 40.42 N 74.32 W
Baškino 82 55.18 N 36.41 E
Baškirskaja Avtonomnaja Sovetskaja Socialističeskaja Respublika □ [3] 86 54.00 N 56.00 E
Baškirskij zapovednik ♠ 86 53.30 N 57.58 E
Baskomutan Milli Parkı ♠ 130 38.50 N 30.05 E
Başköy 84 39.53 N 44.32 E
Baskuduk 86 49.43 N 61.32 E
Baš-Kugandy 85 42.00 N 74.39 E
Baskunčak, ozero ⊜ 80 48.12 N 46.54 E
Baslow 44 53.15 N 1.38 W
Başmakçı 130 37.54 N 30.01 E
Bašmakovo 80 53.12 N 43.02 E
Basmat 122 19.19 N 77.10 E
Bäsna 40 60.32 N 15.12 E
Bāsoda 124 23.51 N 77.56 E
Basoko 152 1.14 N 23.36 E
Basoko ≃ 273b 4.19 S 15.16 E
Basoli 123 32.30 N 75.49 E
Basom 210 43.04 N 78.24 W
Basongo 152 4.20 S 20.24 E
Basora, Punt › 241s 12.25 N 69.52 W
Basovizza 64 45.38 N 13.52 E
Başpınar 130 39.12 N 38.42 E
Basque Lands → Euskal Herriko □ [4] 34 43.00 N 2.30 W
Basra → Al-Baṣrah 128 30.30 N 47.47 E
Bas-Rhin □ [5] 32 48.35 N 7.40 E
Bass ≃ 169 38.30 S 145.26 E
Bassano 182 50.47 N 112.28 W
Bassano del Grappa 64 45.46 N 11.44 E
Bassari 150 9.15 N 0.47 E
Bassas da India ✦ [2] 138 21.25 S 39.42 E
Bass Creek ≃ 216 42.37 N 89.04 W
Basse-Californie → Baja California › [1] 232 28.00 N 113.30 W
Bassecourt 58 47.20 N 7.15 E
Bassein → Pathein 110 16.47 N 94.44 E
Bassein ≃ [1] 110 15.56 N 94.18 E
Basse-Kotto □ [5] 152 5.00 N 21.30 E
Bassella 34 42.01 N 1.18 E
Bassen 52 53.04 N 9.04 E
Bassendean 168a 31.55 S 115.56 E
Bassenthwaite 44 54.41 N 3.12 W
Bassenthwaite Lake ⊜ 44 54.38 N 3.13 W
Basse-Pointe 240e 14.52 N 61.07 W
Basses, Pointe des › 241o 15.52 N 61.17 W
Basses-Alpes □ [5] 62 44.10 N 6.00 E
Basse Santa Su 150 13.19 N 14.13 W
Basse-Terre, Guad. 241o 16.00 N 61.44 W
Basseterre, St. C.-N. 238 17.18 N 62.43 W
Basse Terre, Trin. 241r 10.08 N 61.18 W
Basse-Terre I 241o 16.10 N 61.40 W
Bassett, Ne., U.S. 198 42.35 N 99.32 W
Bassett, Va., U.S. 192 36.45 N 79.59 W
Bassett Creek ≃ 194 31.25 N 87.56 W
Bassett Peak ∧ 200 32.30 N 110.17 W
Bassfield 194 31.30 N 89.44 W
Bass Harbor 188 44.14 N 68.20 W
Bass Hill 274a 33.54 S 151.00 E
Bassignana 62 45.00 N 8.44 E
Bassikounou 150 15.52 N 5.57 W
Bassila 150 9.01 N 1.40 E
Bassin des Aghlabites ⊥ 36 35.43 N 10.10 E
Bassingbourn 42 52.04 N 0.03 W
Bass Lake, Ca., U.S. 226 37.19 N 119.33 W
Bass Lake, In., U.S. 216 41.12 N 86.36 W
Bass Lake ⊜, On., Can. 212 44.49 N 76.08 W
Bass Lake ⊜, In., U.S. 216 41.13 N 86.36 W
Bass Lake ⊜ [1] 226 37.19 N 119.34 W
Bass Point › 170 34.36 S 150.54 E
Bass River 186 45.25 N 63.47 W
Bass Strait ʊ 166 39.20 S 145.30 E
Bassum 52 52.51 N 8.43 E
Basswood Lake ⊜, On., Can. 190 46.20 N 83.23 W
Basswood Lake ⊜, N.A. 190 48.06 N 91.40 W
Basta 126 21.41 N 87.03 E
Bästad 26 56.26 N 12.51 E
Baṣṭah 132 30.14 N 35.32 E
Bastak 128 27.14 N 54.22 E
Basṭām 128 36.29 N 55.04 E
Baštanka 78 47.24 N 32.25 E
Bastei ♠ 54 50.58 N 14.04 E
Bastelica 36 42.00 N 9.02 E
Basti 124 26.48 N 82.43 E
Bastia, Fr. 32 42.42 N 9.27 E
Bastia, It. 66 43.04 N 12.33 E
Bastian 192 37.09 N 81.09 W
Bastiglia 64 44.43 N 11.00 E
Bastimentos 236 9.21 N 82.12 W
Bastimentos, Isla I 236 9.18 N 82.08 W
Bastogne 56 50.00 N 5.43 E
Bastrop, La., U.S. 194 32.46 N 91.54 W
Bastrop, Tx., U.S. 222 30.06 N 97.18 W
Bastrop □ [6] 222 33.00 N 97.18 W
Bastrop, Lake ⊜ [1] 222 30.09 N 97.18 W
Bastrop Bay ⊂ 222 29.06 N 95.11 W
Bastrop State Park ♠ 222 30.07 N 97.17 W
Bastuträsk 26 64.47 N 20.02 E
Basu, Pulau I 112 0.18 S 103.36 E
Basubāti 272b 22.47 N 88.12 E
Bāsudebpur, India 126 21.49 N 87.38 E
Bāsudebpur, India 272b 22.49 N 88.25 E
Basuo → Dongfang 110 19.05 N 108.39 E
Bāsūs 273c 30.08 N 31.13 E
Baswa 126 24.08 N 87.52 E
Basyūn 142 30.57 N 30.49 E
Bas-Zaïre □ [4] 152 5.30 S 14.30 E
Bata 152 1.51 N 9.45 E
Bataan □ [4] 116 14.40 N 120.25 E
Bataan, Mount ∧ 116 14.31 N 120.28 E
Bataan Peninsula › [1] 116 14.40 N 120.25 E
Batabanó 240p 22.43 N 82.17 W
Batabanó, Golfo de ⊂ 240p 22.15 N 82.30 W
Batac 116 18.05 N 120.35 E
Batad 116 11.25 N 123.06 E
Batagaj 74 67.38 N 134.38 E
Batagaj-Alyta 74 67.48 N 130.25 E
Batag Island I 116 12.38 N 125.04 E
Batagol 88 52.22 N 100.45 E
Bataguaçu 255 21.42 S 52.22 W
Bataiporã 255 22.20 S 53.17 W
Batajsk 83 47.10 N 39.44 E
Batak 38 41.57 N 24.13 E
Batak, jazovir ⊜ [1] 38 41.59 N 24.11 E
Batakan 112 4.05 S 114.38 E
Batala 123 31.48 N 75.12 E
Batalha, Bra. 250 9.41 S 37.08 W
Batalha, Bra. 250 4.01 S 42.05 W
Batalha, Port. 34 39.39 N 8.50 W
Bataly 86 52.52 N 62.00 E
Batam, Pulau I 112 1.05 N 104.03 E
Batama, S.S.S.R. 88 53.53 N 101.36 E
Batama, Zaïre 154 0.56 N 26.39 E
Batamaj 74 63.31 N 129.27 E
Batamšinskij 86 50.36 N 58.16 E
Batan, Pil. 116 11.35 N 122.30 E
Batan, Zhg. 98 34.10 N 120.04 E
Batanagar 126 22.31 N 88.15 E
Batang, Indon. 115a 6.55 S 109.45 E
Batang, Zhg. 102 30.02 N 99.02 E
Batangafo 152 7.18 N 18.18 E
Batangas 116 13.45 N 121.03 E
Batangas □ [4] 116 13.50 N 121.00 E
Batangas Bay ⊂ 116 13.43 N 121.00 E
Batangbatangdaya 115a 6.56 S 113.59 E
Batang Berjuntai 114 3.23 N 101.25 E
Batang Kali 114 3.28 N 101.38 E
Batangtoru 114 1.29 N 99.03 E
Batan Island I, Pil. 108 20.26 N 121.58 E
Batan Island I, Pil. 116 13.15 N 124.00 E
Batan Islands II 108 20.30 N 121.50 E
Batanta, Pulau I 164 0.50 S 130.40 E
Batas ≃ 287a 22.44 S 43.24 W
Batas Island I 116 11.10 N 119.36 E
Bátaszék 30 46.12 N 18.44 E

Symbol	English	Deutsch	Español	Français	Português
≃	River	Fluß	Río	Rivière	Rio
≊	Canal	Kanal	Canal	Canal	Canal
⌊	Waterfall, Rapids	Wasserfall, Stromschnellen	Cascada, Rápidos	Chute d'eau, Rapides	Cascata, Rápidos
ʊ	Strait	Meeresstraße	Estrecho	Détroit	Estreito
⊂	Bay, Gulf	Bucht, Golf	Bahía, Golfo	Baie, Golfe	Baía, Golfo
⊜	Lake, Lakes	See, Seen	Lago, Lagos	Lac, Lacs	Lago, Lagos
≡	Swamp	Sumpf	Pantano	Marais	Pântano
⊓	Ice Features, Glacier	Eis- und Gletscherformen	Accidentes Glaciales	Formes glaciaires	Acidentes glaciares
⊤	Other Hydrographic Features	Andere Hydrographische Objekte	Otros Elementos Hidrográficos	Autres données hydrographiques	Outros acidentes hidrográficos
✦	Submarine Features	Untermeerische Objekte	Accidentes Submarinos	Formes de relief sous-marin	Acidentes submarinos
□	Political Unit	Politische Einheit	Unidad Politica	Entité politique	Unidade política
⊌	Cultural Institution	Kulturelle Institution	Institución Cultural	Institution culturelle	Instituição cultural
⊥	Historical Site	Historische Stätte	Sitio Histórico	Site historique	Sitio histórico
♠	Recreational Site	Erholungs- und Ferienort	Sitio de Recreo	Centre de loisirs	Area de Lazer
⊠	Airport	Flughafen	Aeropuerto	Aéroport	Aeroporto
■	Military Installation	Militäranlage	Instalación Militar	Installation militaire	Instalação militar
◆	Miscellaneous	Verschiedenes	Misceláneo	Divers	Diversos

Batatais 255 20.53 S 47.37 W
Batatuba 256 23.04 S 46.25 W
Batavia, Arg. 252 34.47 S 65.41 W
Batavia, Il., U.S. 216 41.51 N 88.18 W
Batavia, Ia., U.S. 190 40.59 N 92.10 W
Batavia, Mi., U.S. 216 41.55 N 85.06 W
Batavia, N.Y., U.S. 210 42.59 N 78.11 W
Batavia, Oh., U.S. 218 39.04 N 84.10 W
Batawa 212 44.10 N 77.36 W
Batbatan Island I 116 11.28 N 121.55 E
Batcengel 88 47.47 N 101.58 E
Batchawana ≃ 190 46.55 N 84.32 W
Batchawana Mountain ∧ 190 47.04 N 84.24 W
Batchawanna Island I 190 46.53 N 84.30 W
Batchelor 164 13.04 S 131.01 E
Bătdâmbâng 110 13.06 N 103.12 E
Bate Bay ⊂ 170 34.04 S 151.12 E
Bateckij 76 58.39 N 30.19 E
Bate Heath 262 53.19 N 2.28 W
Bateia 256 22.20 S 45.49 W
Batéké, Plateaux ⩘[1] 152 3.30 S 15.45 E
Batemans Bay 166 35.43 S 150.11 E
Batenbrock ◆[8] 263 51.31 N 6.57 E
Batepito ≃ 200 30.48 N 109.11 W
Bates, Mount ∧ 174c 29.01 S 167.56 E
Batesburg 192 33.54 N 81.32 W
Bates Creek ≃ 200 42.41 N 106.37 W
Bates Range ⩘ 162 27.25 S 121.13 E
Batesville, Ar., U.S. 194 35.46 N 91.38 W
Batesville, In., U.S. 218 39.18 N 85.13 W
Batesville, Ms., U.S. 194 34.18 N 89.56 W
Batesville, Tx., U.S. 196 28.57 N 99.37 W
Bath, N.B., Can. 186 46.31 N 67.36 W
Bath, On., Can. 212 44.11 N 76.47 W
Bath, Eng., U.K. 42 51.23 N 2.22 W
Bath, Il., U.S. 219 40.11 N 90.08 W
Bath, Me., U.S. 188 43.54 N 69.49 W
Bath, Mi., U.S. 216 42.49 N 84.26 W
Bath, N.Y., U.S. 210 42.20 N 77.19 W
Bath, Oh., U.S. 214 41.11 N 81.38 W
Bath, Pa., U.S. 208 40.43 N 75.23 W
Bath □[6] 218 38.14 N 83.48 W
Batha □[5] 146 14.00 N 19.00 E
Batha ≃ 146 12.47 N 17.34 E
Bath Addition 285 40.06 N 74.52 W
Bathgate, Scot., U.K. 46 55.55 N 3.39 W
Bathgate, N.D., U.S. 198 48.52 N 97.28 W
Bathinda 123 30.12 N 74.57 E
Bathsheba 241g 13.13 N 59.31 W
Bathurst, Austl. 166 33.25 S 149.35 E
Bathurst, N.B., Can. 186 47.36 N 65.39 W
Bathurst → Banjul, Gam. 150 13.28 N 16.39 W
Bathurst, S. Afr. 158 33.30 S 26.50 E
Bathurst, Cape › 176 70.35 N 128.00 W
Bathurst, Lake ⊜ 170 35.04 S 149.44 E
Bathurst Inlet 176 66.50 N 108.01 W
Bathurst Inlet ⊂ 176 68.10 N 108.50 W
Bathurst Island I, Austl. 164 11.37 S 130.23 E
Bathurst Island I, N.T., Can. 16 76.00 N 100.30 W
Bathurst Island Aboriginal Reserve ◆[4] 164 11.37 S 130.23 E
Bati 144 11.10 N 40.02 E
Batia 150 10.54 N 1.29 E
Batiāgarh 124 24.07 N 79.21 E
Batié 150 9.53 N 2.55 W
Bāṭin, Wādī al- V 128 29.35 N 47.00 E
Batina 38 45.51 N 18.51 E
Batiquitos Lagoon ⊂ 228 33.05 N 117.18 W
Batīr 132 31.16 N 35.42 E
Batiscan ≃ 206 46.31 N 72.15 W
Batiste Creek ≃ 222 30.04 N 94.28 W
Batkanu 150 9.05 N 12.25 W
Batken 85 40.03 N 70.50 E
Batley 44 53.44 N 1.37 W
Batlow 171b 35.31 S 148.09 E
Batman 130 37.52 N 41.07 E
Batna 148 35.34 N 6.11 E
Batna □[5] 148 35.30 N 6.10 E
Baṭn al-Ghūl 132 29.44 N 35.52 E
Batnorov 88 47.55 N 111.30 E
Batō, Nihon 94 36.44 N 140.10 E
Bato, Pil. 116 10.20 N 124.47 E
Ba To, Viet. 110 14.46 N 108.44 E
Bato, Lake ⊜ 116 13.19 N 123.21 E
Batoala 152 0.48 N 13.27 E
Batoche Rectory National Historic Site ⊥ 184 52.41 N 106.02 W
Batoka 154 16.47 S 27.15 E
Baton Rouge 194 30.27 N 91.09 W
Bator 123 33.06 N 75.19 E
Batorampon Point › 116 7.07 N 121.54 E
Batouri 152 4.26 N 14.22 E
Batovi 255 15.53 S 53.24 W
Batpajsagyr, peski ◆[2] 80 47.20 N 48.40 E
Baṭrā (Petra) ⊥ 132 30.20 N 35.26 E
Baṭrā', Jibāl al- ⩘ 132 29.53 N 35.38 E
Baṭrah 142 31.10 N 31.27 E
Ba Tri 110 10.02 N 106.36 E
Batsawul 120 34.15 N 70.52 E
Batson 222 30.15 N 94.37 W
Batsto ≃ 285 39.39 N 74.39 W
Batsto, Skit Branch ≃ 285 39.46 N 74.41 W
Batsto State Historic Site ⊥ 208 39.39 N 74.39 W
Bat Sûmber 88 48.29 N 106.42 E
Battaglia Terme 64 45.17 N 11.47 E
Battambang → Bătdâmbâng 110 13.06 N 103.12 E
Battenberg 56 51.01 N 8.38 E
Batten Kill ≃ 188 43.06 N 73.35 W
Batterie, Pointe de la › 240e 14.44 N 60.54 W
Bätterkinden 58 47.08 N 7.32 E
Battersea ◆[8] 260 51.28 N 0.10 W
Battersea Park ♠ 260 51.29 N 0.09 W
Batticaloa 122 7.43 N 81.42 E
Battice 56 50.39 N 5.49 E
Battin 224 45.29 N 122.34 W
Battipaglia 68 40.37 N 14.58 E
Battle 42 50.55 N 0.29 E
Battle ≃ 176 52.43 N 108.15 W
Battle Creek, Ia., U.S. 198 42.18 N 95.35 W
Battle Creek, Mi., U.S. 216 42.19 N 85.10 W
Battle Creek, Ne., U.S. 198 41.59 N 97.35 W
Battle Creek ≃, N.A. 202 48.36 N 109.11 W
Battle Creek ≃, Ca., U.S. 204 40.21 N 122.11 W
Battle Creek ≃, Id., U.S. 202 42.14 N 116.32 W
Battle Creek ≃, Mi., U.S. 216 42.19 N 85.12 W
Battle Creek ≃, Tx., U.S. 196 32.50 N 98.58 W
Battle Creek, North Fork ≃ 204 40.26 N 122.00 W
Battle Creek, South Fork ≃ 204 40.26 N 122.00 W
Battlefields 154 18.31 S 29.52 E
Battle Green ⊥ 283 42.27 N 71.14 W
Battle Ground, In., U.S. 216 40.30 N 86.50 W
Battle Ground, Wa., U.S. 224 45.46 N 122.31 W
Battle Harbour 176 52.16 N 55.35 W
Battle Lake 198 46.16 N 95.42 W
Battlement Mesa ∧ 200 39.20 N 108.00 W
Battlemount 158 26.57 S 23.46 E
Battle Mountain 204 40.38 N 116.56 W
Battle Mountain ∧ 200 41.02 N 107.16 W
Battlesbridge 260 51.37 N 0.34 E
Battonya 30 46.17 N 21.01 E
Battuello 266b 45.27 N 8.56 E
Batu 115a 7.52 S 112.31 E
Batu ∧ 144 6.55 N 39.46 E
Batu, Bukit ∧ 112 2.16 N 113.43 E
Batu, Kepulauan II 110 0.18 S 98.28 E
Batuan 116 12.25 N 123.47 E
Batu Arang 114 3.19 N 101.28 E
Batuata, Pulau I 112 6.12 S 122.42 E
Batuata, Tanjung › 115b 9.37 S 120.29 E
Batu-Batu 112 4.09 S 119.52 E
Batu Berinchang, Gunong ∧ 114 4.30 N 101.24 E
Batubetumpang 112 2.53 S 106.09 E
Batubrok, Bukit ∧ 112 1.10 N 114.36 E
Batuc 232 29.15 N 109.44 W
Batu Caves 114 3.14 N 101.40 E
Batudaka, Pulau I 112 0.28 S 121.48 E
Batu Enam 114 2.35 N 102.43 E
Batu Gajah 114 4.28 N 101.03 E
Batui 112 1.17 S 122.33 E
Batui, Pegunungan ⩘ 112 1.15 S 122.10 E
Batuidu 112 10.38 S 123.25 E
Batukau, Bukit ∧ 115b 8.20 S 115.05 E
Batukelau 112 0.48 N 115.01 E
Batu Laut 114 2.41 N 101.31 E
Batulicin 112 3.27 S 116.00 E
Batumata Point › 164 10.17 S 148.57 E
Batumi 84 41.38 N 41.38 E
Batumundan 114 1.17 N 98.50 E
Batu Pahat (Bandar Penggaram) 114 1.51 N 102.56 E
Batupanjang 114 1.43 N 101.31 E
Batu Puteh, Gunong ∧ 114 4.13 N 101.27 E
Batuputih 112 1.24 N 118.29 E
Baturaja 112 4.08 S 104.10 E
Batu Rakit 114 5.27 N 103.03 E
Baturetno 115a 7.59 S 110.56 E
Baturin 78 51.21 N 32.51 E
Baturino, S.S.S.R. 86 57.48 N 85.12 E
Baturino, S.S.S.R. 265b 55.35 N 37.31 E
Baturinskaja 78 45.47 N 39.22 E
Baturité 250 4.20 S 38.53 W
Baturotok 115b 8.42 S 117.10 E
Baturusa 112 2.02 S 106.07 E
Batusangkar 112 0.27 S 100.35 E
Batutinggi 112 1.55 S 113.19 E
Bat Yam 132 32.01 N 34.45 E
Batyrevo 80 55.04 N 47.38 E
Batyr-Mala, ozero ⊜ 80 47.35 N 44.45 E
Bau 112 1.25 N 110.08 E
Baú, Igarapé do ≃ 250 7.26 S 54.47 W
Bauang 116 16.31 N 120.20 E
Baubašata, gory ⩘ 85 41.20 N 72.45 E
Baubau 112 5.28 S 122.38 E
Bauchi 150 10.19 N 9.50 E
Bauchi □[3] 146 10.30 N 10.15 E
Baucina 70 37.55 N 13.32 E
Baud 32 47.52 N 3.01 W
Bauda 120 20.50 N 84.19 E
Baudette 190 48.42 N 94.35 W
Baudó ≃ 246 4.57 N 77.22 W
Baudó, Serranía de ⩘ 246 6.00 N 77.05 W
Baudouin Stadium ♠ 273b 4.20 S 15.20 E
Baudour 50 50.29 N 3.49 E
Bauernschaft 263 51.34 N 6.33 E
Bauerstown 279b 40.30 N 79.59 W
Baugo Creek ≃ 216 41.40 N 86.04 W
Baukau 112 8.27 S 126.27 E
Baúl, Cerro ∧ 234 17.38 N 100.19 W
Bauld, Cape › 186 51.38 N 55.25 W
Baulkham Hills 274a 33.46 S 151.00 E
Baulmes 58 46.48 N 6.32 E
Bauma 58 47.23 N 8.53 E
Baumberg 263 51.07 N 6.54 E
Baume ≃ 62 44.26 N 4.20 E
Baume-les-Dames 58 47.21 N 6.22 E
Baumholder 56 49.37 N 7.20 E
Baumschulenweg ◆[8] 264a 52.28 N 13.29 E
Baun 112 10.18 S 123.43 E
Baunach 56 49.59 N 10.50 E
Baunach ≃ 56 49.59 N 10.51 E
Baunatal 56 51.16 N 9.25 E
Baunei 71 40.02 N 9.40 E
Baunt 88 55.16 N 113.08 E
Baunt, ozero ⊜ 88 55.12 N 113.00 E
Bāuphal 126 22.25 N 90.33 E
Baure 150 12.50 N 8.45 E
Baures 248 13.35 S 63.35 W
Baures ≃ 248 12.30 S 64.18 W
Bauru 255 22.19 S 49.04 W
Baús 255 18.19 S 53.10 W
Bausendorf 56 50.01 N 6.59 E
Bausenhagen 263 51.31 N 7.48 E
Bauska 76 56.24 N 24.14 E
Bauta 240p 22.59 N 82.33 W
Bauta □[7] 286b 22.59 N 82.33 W
Bautino 84 44.33 N 50.15 E
Bautzen 54 51.11 N 14.26 E
Bauxite 194 34.33 N 92.31 W
Bauya 150 8.11 N 12.34 W
Bavans 58 47.29 N 6.44 E
Bavari 62 44.26 N 9.01 E
Bavaria → Bayern □[3] 30 49.00 N 11.30 E
Bavarian Alps → Bayerische Alpen ⩘ 64 47.30 N 11.00 E
Bavay 50 50.18 N 3.47 E
Båven ⊜ 40 59.01 N 16.56 E
Baveno 58 45.55 N 8.30 E
Bavilliers 58 47.37 N 6.50 E
Bavispe 232 30.24 N 108.50 W
Bavispe, Río de ≃ 232 29.15 N 109.11 W
Bavleny 80 56.24 N 39.34 E
Bavly 80 54.25 N 53.17 E
Bavnhöj ∧[2] 41 55.55 N 10.07 E
Bavtugaj 84 43.11 N 46.49 E
Baw 110 23.19 N 95.50 E
Bāwal 124 28.05 N 76.35 E
Bawal, Pulau I 112 2.44 S 110.06 E
Bāwāli 272b 22.25 N 88.12 E
Bawang 115a 7.06 S 109.55 E
Baw Baw, Mount ∧ 169 37.50 S 146.17 E
Baw Baw National Park ♠ 169 37.55 S 146.22 E
Baw Beese Lake ⊜ 216 41.54 N 84.36 W
Bawdeswell 42 52.45 N 1.01 E
Bawdwin 110 23.06 N 97.18 E
Bawean, Pulau I 115a 5.46 S 112.40 E
Baweigang 106 31.57 N 120.14 E
Bawku 150 11.05 N 0.14 W
Bawlake 110 19.11 N 97.21 E
Bawmi 110 17.19 N 94.35 E
Bawria 126 22.29 N 88.10 E
Bawtry 44 53.26 N 1.01 W
Baxdo 144 5.46 N 47.15 E
Baxenden 262 53.44 N 2.20 W
Baxian, Zhg. 105 39.06 N 116.23 E
Baxian (Yudongxi), Zhg. 107 29.23 N 106.32 E
Baxley 192 31.46 N 82.20 W
Baxter, Ia., U.S. 190 41.49 N 93.09 W
Baxter, Mn., U.S. 190 46.20 N 94.17 W
Baxter, Tn., U.S. 194 36.09 N 85.38 W
Baxter Estates 276 40.50 N 73.42 W
Baxter Springs 198 37.02 N 94.44 W
Baxter State Park ♠ 188 46.00 N 68.58 W
Baxterville 194 31.05 N 89.35 W
Bay 194 35.44 N 90.33 W
Bay □[4] 144 2.30 N 43.30 E
Bay, Laguna de ⊜ 116 14.23 N 121.15 E
Baya, Zaïre 152 4.57 N 19.43 E
Baya, Zaïre 154 11.52 S 27.27 E
Bayāḍah, Wādī al- V 146 26.08 N 18.35 E
Bayāḍ an-Naṣārā 142 29.04 N 31.08 E
Bayag 116 18.16 N 121.02 E
Bayala 158 27.47 S 32.08 E
Bay al-Kabīr, Wādī V 146 31.15 N 15.57 E
Bayambang 116 15.49 N 120.27 E
Bayamo 240p 20.23 N 76.39 W
Bayamo ≃ 240p 20.34 N 76.44 W
Bayamón 240m 18.24 N 66.09 W
Bayan, Indon. 115b 8.16 S 116.26 E
Bayan, Zhg. 89 46.05 N 127.24 E
Bāyan, Band-e ⩘ 120 34.20 N 65.30 E
Bayāna 124 26.54 N 77.17 E
Bayanbayanan 269f 14.39 N 121.06 E
Bayanchagan 89 47.19 N 124.03 E
Bayang 116 7.48 N 124.12 E
Bayanga 152 2.53 N 16.19 E
Bayange 102 39.19 N 107.31 E
Bayan Har Shan ⩘ 102 33.48 N 98.10 E
Bayanheshuomiao 89 48.51 N 119.46 E
Bayanjie 89 49.36 N 124.37 E
Bayanluke 89 50.52 N 119.33 E
Bayannaobao 102 39.44 N 107.40 E
Bayano, Lago ⊜[1] 246 9.10 N 78.40 W
Bayan Obo 102 41.58 N 110.02 E
Bayan Tal 89 43.44 N 123.16 E
Bayard, Ia., U.S. 198 41.51 N 94.33 W
Bayard, Ne., U.S. 198 41.45 N 103.19 W
Bayard, N.M., U.S. 200 32.45 N 108.07 W
Bayard, Oh., U.S. 214 40.46 N 81.04 W
Bayard, W.V., U.S. 188 39.16 N 79.21 W
Bayard, Col)(62 44.37 N 6.05 E
Bayard Cutting Arboretum State Park ♠ 276 40.45 N 73.10 W
Bayat, Indon. 112 2.06 S 103.38 E
Bayat, Tür. 130 38.59 N 30.56 E
Bayat, Tür. 130 40.39 N 34.15 E
Bayawan 116 9.22 N 122.48 E
Bayawan ≃ 116 9.22 N 122.48 E
Baybay 116 10.41 N 124.48 E
Bayberry 210 43.08 N 76.13 W
Bayble 46 58.12 N 6.13 W
Bayboro 192 35.08 N 76.46 W
Bay Bulls 186 47.19 N 52.49 W
Bayburt 130 40.16 N 40.15 E
Bay Center 224 46.37 N 123.57 W
Bay City, Mi., U.S. 190 43.35 N 83.53 W
Bay City, Or., U.S. 224 45.31 N 123.53 W
Bay City, Tx., U.S. 222 28.58 N 95.58 W
Bay Creek ≃, Il., U.S. 194 37.16 N 88.31 W
Bay Creek ≃, Il., U.S. 219 39.20 N 90.46 W
Bayḍā', Bi'r ⍑[4] 142 29.45 N 32.13 E
Bay de Verde 186 48.05 N 52.54 W
Baydhabo 144 3.07 N 43.39 E
Bay du Nord ≃ 186 47.44 N 55.25 W
Baye, Cap › 175f 20.57 S 165.25 E
Bayel 58 48.12 N 4.47 E
Bayerische Alpen ⩘ 64 47.30 N 11.00 E
Bayerisch Eisenstein 60 49.07 N 13.12 E
Bayerischer Wald ⩘ 60 49.00 N 12.40 E
Bayerischer Wald, Nationalpark ♠ 60 48.56 N 13.28 E
Bayern □[3] 30 49.00 N 11.30 E
Bayeuen 114 4.36 N 97.53 E
Bayeux, Bra. 250 7.08 S 34.56 W
Bayeux, Fr. 32 49.16 N 0.42 W
Bay Farm Island I 282 37.43 N 122.14 W
Bayfield, Co., U.S. 200 37.13 N 107.35 W
Bayfield, Wi., U.S. 190 46.48 N 90.49 W
Bayfield, Île I 186 51.13 N 58.23 W
Bayford 260 51.46 N 0.06 W
'Bayh 132 33.44 N 35.31 E
Bayḥān al-Qaṣāḍ 144 14.48 N 45.43 E
Bay Harbor Islands 220 25.53 N 80.08 W
Bayhead, Scot., U.K. 46 57.33 N 7.24 W
Bay Head, N.J., U.S. 208 40.04 N 74.03 W
Bayiji 98 34.18 N 117.41 E
Bayındır 130 38.13 N 27.40 E
Bayingzi 104 41.28 N 120.46 E
Baykan 130 38.09 N 41.47 E
Baykonur → Bajkonyr 86 47.50 N 66.03 E
Bay Kurt 85 39.58 N 75.33 E
Bay L'Argent 186 47.33 N 54.54 W
Bayley Point › 164 16.56 S 139.02 E
Bayley Point Aboriginal Reserve ◆[4] 166 16.57 S 138.55 E
Baylis 219 39.44 N 90.54 W
Bay Meadows Race Track ♠ 282 37.32 N 122.18 W
Bay Minette 194 30.52 N 87.46 W
Baynūnah ◆[1] 128 23.50 N 52.50 E
Bayo 34 43.09 N 8.58 W
Bayombong 116 16.29 N 121.09 E
Bayon 58 48.29 N 6.19 E
Bayona 34 42.07 N 8.51 W
Bayonne, Fr. 32 43.29 N 1.29 W
Bayonne, N.J., U.S. 210 40.40 N 74.06 W
Bayonne ≃ 206 46.05 N 73.10 W
Bayonne Bridge ◆[5] 276 40.38 N 74.09 W
Bayons 62 44.20 N 6.10 E
Bayou Bodcau Reservoir ⊜[1] 194 32.45 N 93.30 W
Bayou Cane 194 29.37 N 90.45 W
Bayou D'Arbonne Lake ⊜[1] 194 32.45 N 92.25 W
Bayou La Batre 194 30.24 N 88.14 W
Bayóvar 248 5.50 S 81.03 W
Bay Park 276 40.38 N 73.40 W
Bayport, Fl., U.S. 220 28.33 N 82.39 W
Bay Port, Mi., U.S. 190 43.50 N 83.22 W
Bayport, Mn., U.S. 190 45.01 N 92.46 W
Bayport, N.Y., U.S. 210 40.44 N 73.03 W
Bayramiç 130 39.48 N 26.37 E
Bayramören 130 40.57 N 33.12 E
Bayreuth 60 49.57 N 11.35 E
Bay Ridge 208 38.56 N 76.27 W
Bay Ridge ◆[8] 276 40.37 N 74.02 W
Bay Ridge Channel ⊔ 276 40.39 N 74.02 W
Bayrischzell 64 47.40 N 12.00 E
Bay Roberts 186 47.36 N 53.16 W
Bayrūt (Beirut) 130 33.53 N 35.30 E
Bayrūt □[4] 132 33.56 N 35.30 E
Bays, Lake of ⊜ 212 45.15 N 79.04 W
Bay Saint Louis 194 30.18 N 89.19 W
Bay Shore 210 40.43 N 73.14 W
Bayshore Gardens 220 27.25 N 82.35 W
Bayside, On., Can. 212 44.07 N 77.30 W
Bayside, Ma., U.S. 283 42.18 N 70.53 W
Bayside, Wi., U.S. 216 43.10 N 87.54 W
Bayside ◆[8] 276 40.46 N 73.46 W
Bay Springs 194 31.58 N 89.17 W
Bay Springs Lake ⊜[1] 194 34.35 N 88.20 W
Bayston Hill 42 52.40 N 2.45 W
Bayswater 274b 37.51 S 145.16 E
Bayswater North 274b 37.49 S 145.17 E
Bayt ad-Dīn 132 33.42 N 35.35 E
Bayt al-Faqīh 144 14.32 N 43.20 E
Bayt Ḥānūn 132 31.32 N 34.33 E
Bayt Jālā 132 31.43 N 35.11 E
Bayt Jinn 132 33.19 N 35.53 E
Bayt Laḥm (Bethlehem) 132 31.43 N 35.12 E
Bayt Mirī 132 33.52 N 35.36 E
Baytown 222 29.44 N 94.58 W
Bayt Sāḥūr 132 31.42 N 35.13 E
Bayt Sīrā 132 31.53 N 35.03 E
Bayunglencir 112 2.03 S 103.41 E
Bayview, Austl. 274a 33.40 S 151.18 E
Bay View, N.Z. 172 39.25 S 176.53 E
Bay View, N.Y., U.S. 210 42.47 N 78.51 W
Bay View, Oh., U.S. 214 41.28 N 82.50 W
Bayview ◆[8] 282 37.44 N 122.23 W
Bay Village 214 41.29 N 81.55 W
Bayville, N.J., U.S. 208 39.54 N 74.09 W
Bayville, N.Y., U.S. 210 40.54 N 73.33 W
Baywater 168a 31.55 S 115.56 E
Baywood Park 226 35.20 N 120.50 W
Bayyāḍah, Ra's al- › 132 33.10 N 35.10 E
Bayyā'īyah al-Kabīrah 130 35.42 N 37.09 E
Bayyūḍah ⍑[4] 140 17.32 N 32.07 E
Bayzo 150 13.52 N 4.45 E
Baza 34 37.29 N 2.46 W
Baza, Sierra de ⩘ 34 37.15 N 2.45 W
Bazai 100 24.32 N 114.10 E
Bazainville 261 48.48 N 1.40 E
Bazalija 78 49.43 N 26.27 E
Bazar 88 53.58 N 116.05 E
Bazarčaj 84 39.40 N 45.48 E
Bazard'uz'u, gora ∧ 84 41.13 N 47.51 E
Bāzār-e Panjvā'ī 120 31.32 N 65.28 E
Bazargic → Tolbuhin 38 43.34 N 27.50 E
Bazar-Kurgan 85 41.02 N 72.45 E
Bazarnyje Mataki 80 54.56 N 49.56 E
Bazarnyj Karabulak 80 52.16 N 46.25 E
Bazarnyj Syzgan 80 53.45 N 46.46 E
Bazarovo 82 54.47 N 38.10 E
Bazaršolan 80 49.04 N 51.56 E
Bazartobe 80 49.23 N 51.50 E
Bazaruto, Ilha do I 156 21.40 S 35.28 E
Bazas 32 44.26 N 0.13 W
Bazavluk ≃ 78 47.34 N 34.04 E
Bazdār 120 26.21 N 65.03 E
Bazeilles 56 49.40 N 4.59 E
Bazemont 261 48.56 N 1.52 E
Bazetta 214 41.20 N 80.47 W
Bazhong 102 31.51 N 106.39 E
Bazi 100 24.46 N 113.10 E
Baziège 32 43.27 N 1.37 E
Bažigan 84 44.33 N 45.41 E
Bazine 198 38.26 N 99.41 W
Baziqiao 106 32.07 N 119.52 E
Bazkovskaja 80 49.36 N 41.43 E
Bazmān 128 27.49 N 60.12 E
Bazmān, Kūh-e ∧ 128 28.04 N 60.00 E
Bazoches-les-Gallerandes 50 48.10 N 2.03 E
Bazoches-sur-Hoëne 50 48.33 N 0.28 E
Bazoj 86 55.45 N 83.22 E
Bazzano 64 44.30 N 11.05 E
Be ≃ 110 11.06 N 106.58 E
Be, Nosy I 157b 13.20 S 48.15 E
Beach, Il., U.S. 216 42.26 N 87.50 W
Beach, N.D., U.S. 198 46.55 N 104.00 W
Beach, Tx., U.S. 222 30.20 N 95.29 W
Beach Channel ⊔ 276 40.35 N 73.50 W
Beach City 214 40.39 N 81.34 W
Beach City Lake ⊜[1] 214 40.41 N 81.36 W
Beach Glen 276 40.56 N 74.29 W
Beach Haven, N.J., U.S. 208 39.33 N 74.14 W
Beach Haven, Pa., U.S. 210 41.04 N 76.11 W
Beach Haven Terrace 208 39.35 N 74.13 W
Beach Lake 210 41.36 N 75.09 W
Beach Lake ⊜ 281 42.33 N 83.43 W
Beach Pond State Park ♠ 207 41.35 N 71.45 W
Beachport 166 37.30 S 140.01 E
Beachville 212 43.05 N 80.49 W
Beachwood, N.J., U.S. 208 39.56 N 74.11 W
Beachwood, Oh., U.S. 214 41.27 N 81.30 W
Beachy Head › 42 50.44 N 0.16 E
Beacon, Austl. 162 30.26 S 117.51 E
Beacon, N.Y., U.S. 210 41.30 N 73.58 W
Beacon Falls 207 41.26 N 73.03 W
Beacon Heights 284c 38.57 N 76.54 W
Beacon Hill, Austl. 274a 33.45 S 151.15 E
Beacon Hill, Wa., U.S. 224 46.08 N 122.57 W
Beacon Hill ∧[2], H.K. 271d 22.21 N 114.09 E
Beacon Hill ∧[2], Wales, U.K. 42 52.23 N 3.12 W
Beacon Rock State Park ♠ 224 45.38 N 122.03 W
Beaconsfield, Austl. 166 41.12 S 146.43 E
Beaconsfield, Austl. 274b 38.03 S 145.22 E
Beaconsfield, P.Q., Can. 206 45.26 N 73.50 W
Beaconsfield, Eng., U.K. 260 51.37 N 0.39 W
Beaconsfield □[8] 260 51.34 N 0.35 W
Beadle Lake 216 42.18 N 85.12 W
Beagh, Slieve ∧[2] 48 54.21 N 7.12 W
Beagle, Canal ⊔ 254 54.53 S 68.10 W
Beagle Bay 162 16.58 S 122.40 E
Beagle Gulf ⊂ 164 12.00 S 130.20 E
Beagle Reef ✢[2] 160 15.20 S 123.29 E
Bealanana 157b 14.33 S 48.44 E
Beale, Cape › 182 48.44 N 125.20 W
Beale, Lake ⊜ 122 19.45 N 73.44 E
Beale Air Force Base ■ 226 39.08 N 121.20 W
Bealiba 169 36.48 S 143.33 E
Bealiba, Mount ∧[2] 169 36.49 S 143.38 E
Beallsville 214 40.04 N 80.01 W
Beals Creek ≃ 196 32.10 N 100.51 W
Beam ≃ 260 51.31 N 0.10 E
Beaminster 42 50.49 N 2.45 W
Bean 260 51.25 N 0.17 E
Beanblossom Creek ≃ 194 39.20 N 86.39 W
Bean Creek ≃ 216 41.35 N 84.19 W
Bear ≃, Sk., Can. 184 54.33 N 103.58 W
Bear ≃, U.S. 200 41.30 N 112.08 W
Bear ≃, Ca., U.S. 226 38.57 N 121.35 W
Bear, Mount ∧ 180 61.17 N 141.09 W
Beara 164 7.30 S 144.50 E
Bear Bay ⊂ 176 75.47 N 87.00 W
Bear Branch 218 38.55 N 85.05 W
Bear Brook ≃, On., Can. 212 45.25 N 75.10 W
Bear Brook ≃, N.J., U.S. 276 41.02 N 74.03 W
Bear Brook State Park ♠ 188 43.05 N 71.26 W
Bear Butte ∧ 198 44.28 N 103.26 W
Bear Canyon V 280 34.14 N 118.07 W
Bear Cove 182 50.44 N 127.27 W
Bear Creek 210 41.11 N 75.45 W
Bear Creek ≃, On., Can. 214 42.44 N 82.23 W
Bear Creek ≃, U.S. 194 34.46 N 88.05 W
Bear Creek ≃, U.S. 196 37.45 N 101.23 W
Bear Creek ≃, U.S. 216 41.17 N 83.57 W
Bear Creek ≃, Al., U.S. 194 33.11 N 88.05 W
Bear Creek ≃, Ca., U.S. 226 37.17 N 120.50 W
Bear Creek ≃, Ca., U.S. 226 38.56 N 122.20 W
Bear Creek ≃, Ca., U.S. 226 38.02 N 121.18 W
Bear Creek ≃, Ca., U.S. 228 34.10 N 117.01 W
Bear Creek ≃, Ca., U.S. 280 34.14 N 117.53 W
Bear Creek ≃, Co., U.S. 200 39.40 N 105.00 W
Bear Creek ≃, Il., U.S. 219 39.33 N 89.23 W
Bear Creek ≃, Il., U.S. 219 40.07 N 91.29 W
Bear Creek ≃, Md., U.S. 284b 39.13 N 76.30 W
Bear Creek ≃, Mo., U.S. 219 39.03 N 91.14 W
Bear Creek ≃, N.D., U.S. 198 46.10 N 98.06 W
Bear Creek ≃, Oh., U.S. 218 39.39 N 84.17 W
Bear Creek ≃, Or., U.S. 202 42.26 N 122.58 W
Bear Creek ≃, Or., U.S. 202 44.06 N 120.46 W
Bear Creek ≃, Pa., U.S. 214 41.23 N 78.50 W
Bear Creek ≃, Wy., U.S. 198 41.41 N 104.13 W
Bear Creek, South Fork ≃ 219 40.09 N 91.18 W
Bear Creek, West Fork ≃ 280 34.16 N 117.53 W
Bearden 194 33.43 N 92.36 W
Beardmore 176 49.36 N 87.57 W
Beardmore Glacier ⊓ 9 83.45 S 171.00 E
Beardsley Lake ⊜[1] 226 38.13 N 120.03 W
Beardstown, Il., U.S. 219 40.01 N 90.25 W
Beardstown, In., U.S. 216 41.08 N 86.36 W
Beardy and Okemasis Indian Reserves ◆[4] 184 52.48 N 106.20 W
Bearfort Mountain ∧ 276 41.09 N 74.23 W
Bear Head Creek ≃ 194 30.18 N 93.35 W
Bear Head Lake ⊜ 184 55.33 N 96.10 W
Bear Head Lake State Park ♠ 190 47.49 N 92.04 W
Bearhead Mountain ∧ 224 47.02 N 121.53 W
Bear Hill ∧[2], Ct., U.S. 207 41.39 N 73.24 W
Bear Hill ∧[2], N.Y., U.S. 210 41.18 N 74.00 W
Bear-in-the-Lodge Creek ≃ 198 43.41 N 101.50 W
Bear Island I, Ant. 9 74.30 S 110.45 W
Bear Island I, Mb., Can. 184 54.53 N 98.04 W
Bear Island I, Ire. 48 51.40 N 9.48 W
Bear Island → Bjørnøya I 12 74.25 N 19.00 E
Bear Island I 284c 38.59 N 77.14 W
Bear Lake, B.C., Can. 182 56.11 N 126.51 W
Bear Lake, Pa., U.S. 214 42.00 N 79.30 W
Bear Lake ⊜, Ab., Can. 182 55.16 N 119.00 W
Bear Lake ⊜, B.C., Can. 182 56.06 N 126.45 W
Bear Lake ⊜, Mb., Can. 184 55.08 N 96.00 W
Bear Lake ⊜, On., Can. 212 45.26 N 79.35 W
Bear Lake ⊜, U.S. 200 42.00 N 111.20 W
Bear Mountain ∧, Ca., U.S. 228 35.12 N 118.38 W
Bear Mountain ∧, Ky., U.S. 192 37.32 N 84.16 W
Bear Mountain ∧, Or., U.S. 202 43.51 N 122.53 W
Bear Mountain ∧[2] 210 41.18 N 74.01 W
Bear Mountain State Park ♠ 210 41.17 N 74.00 W
Béarn □[9] 32 43.20 N 0.45 W
Bear Pond ⊜ 276 40.58 N 74.40 W
Bear River 186 44.34 N 65.39 W
Bear River Range ⩘ 200 41.50 N 111.30 W
Bear Run ≃ 279b 40.33 N 80.04 W
Bearsden 46 55.56 N 4.20 W
Bears Paw Mountains ⩘ 202 48.15 N 109.30 W
Bearstead 260 51.16 N 0.35 E
Bearsville 210 42.02 N 74.09 W
Bear Swamp ≃ 285 39.54 N 74.47 W
Bear Swamp ≡ 285 39.53 N 74.45 W
Bear Swamp Brook ≃ 276 41.04 N 74.13 W
Bear Swamp Lake ⊜ 276 41.06 N 74.13 W
Beartooth Mountains ⩘ 202 45.00 N 109.30 W
Beartooth Pass)(202 44.58 N 109.28 W
Bear Town 194 31.13 N 90.27 W
Beās 123 31.31 N 75.17 E
Beās ≃ 123 31.10 N 74.59 E
Beasain 34 43.03 N 2.11 W
Beas de Segura 34 38.15 N 2.53 W
Beasley 222 29.30 N 95.55 W
Beasley Bay ⊂ 208 37.51 N 75.44 W
Beason 219 40.09 N 89.12 W
Beata, Cabo › 238 17.36 N 71.25 W
Beata, Isla I 238 17.35 N 71.31 W
Beatenberg 58 46.42 N 7.48 E
Beato ◆[8] 266c 38.44 N 9.06 W
Beaton 182 50.44 N 117.44 W
Beatrice, Al., U.S. 194 31.44 N 87.12 W
Beatrice, Ne., U.S. 198 40.16 N 96.44 W
Beatrice, Zimb. 154 18.15 S 30.55 E
Beatrice, Cape › 164 14.15 S 136.59 E
Beattie 198 39.51 N 96.25 W
Beattock 44 55.18 N 3.28 W
Beatton ≃ 176 56.10 N 120.25 W
Beatty, Nv., U.S. 204 36.54 N 116.45 W
Beatty, Oh., U.S. 218 39.53 N 83.50 W
Beatty Saugeen ≃ 212 44.08 N 81.02 W
Beattyville 192 37.34 N 83.42 W
Beaubru 56 49.46 N 5.05 E
Beaucaire 62 43.48 N 4.38 E
Beauce ◆[1] 50 48.22 N 1.50 E
Beauceville 188 46.12 N 70.46 W
Beauchamp 261 49.01 N 2.12 E
Beauchamp Roding 260 51.46 N 0.18 E
Beauchêne, Lac ⊜ 190 46.39 N 78.55 W
Beauchêne Island I 254 52.55 S 59.12 W
Beaucoup Creek ≃, Il., U.S. 194 37.47 N 89.17 W
Beaucoup Creek ≃, Il., U.S. 219 38.13 N 89.20 W
Beaucourt 58 47.29 N 6.55 E
Beaudesert 171a 27.59 S 153.00 E
Beaudette ≃ 206 45.12 N 74.19 W
Beaudry, Lac ⊜ 190 47.44 N 78.55 W
Beauduc, Pointe de › 62 43.22 N 4.34 E
Beaufays 56 50.34 N 5.38 E
Beaufort, Austl. 169 37.26 S 143.23 E
Beaufort, Fr. 58 46.34 N 5.26 E
Beaufort, Fr. 62 45.43 N 6.35 E
Beaufort, Lux. 56 49.51 N 6.18 E
Beaufort, Malay. 112 5.20 N 115.45 E
Beaufort, Mo., U.S. 219 38.26 N 91.12 W
Beaufort, N.C., U.S. 192 34.43 N 76.39 W
Beaufort, S.C., U.S. 192 32.25 N 80.40 W
Beaufort, Cape › 162 34.26 S 115.32 E
Beaufort, Massif de ⩘[1] 62 45.44 N 6.35 E
Beaufort Castle → Qal'At ash-Shaqīf ⊥ 132 33.19 N 35.32 E
Beaufort Island I 271d 22.11 N 114.15 E
Beaufort Marine Corps Air Station ■ 192 32.30 N 80.44 W
Beaufort Sea ⍑[2] 16 73.00 N 140.00 W
Beaufort West 158 32.18 S 22.36 E
Beaugency 50 47.47 N 1.38 E
Beauharnois 206 45.19 N 73.52 W
Beauharnois □[6] 206 45.15 N 74.00 W
Beauharnois, Barrage de ◆[6] 275a 45.19 N 73.55 W
Beauharnois, Canal de ≅ 206 45.19 N 73.54 W
Beaujeu 58 46.09 N 4.36 E
Beaujolais □[9] 32 46.05 N 4.10 E
Beaulieu 42 50.49 N 1.27 W
Beaulieu-lès-Loches 50 47.07 N 1.01 E
Beaulieu-sur-Mer 62 43.42 N 7.20 E
Beauly 46 57.29 N 4.29 W
Beauly ≃ 46 57.28 N 4.28 W
Beauly Firth ⊂[1] 46 57.30 N 4.23 W
Beaumaris, Austl. 274b 37.59 S 145.02 E
Beaumaris, Wales, U.K. 44 53.16 N 4.05 W
Beaumaris Bay ⊂ 274b 38.00 S 145.03 E
Beaumes-de-Venise 62 44.07 N 5.02 E
Beaumesnil 50 49.01 N 0.43 E
Beaumetz-lès-Loges 50 50.14 N 2.39 E
Beaumont, Bel. 50 50.14 N 4.14 E
Beaumont, Nf., Can. 186 49.37 N 55.41 W
Beaumont, Fr. 32 49.40 N 1.51 W
Beaumont, N.Z. 172 45.49 S 169.32 E
Beaumont, Ca., U.S. 228 33.55 N 116.58 W
Beaumont, Ms., U.S. 194 31.10 N 88.55 W
Beaumont, Tx., U.S. 194 30.05 N 94.06 W
Beaumont-du-Gâtinais 50 48.08 N 2.29 E
Beaumont-en-Argonne 56 49.32 N 5.03 E
Beaumont Hill ∧[2] 166 31.33 S 145.13 E
Beaumont-la-Ronce 50 47.34 N 0.40 E
Beaumont-le-Roger 50 49.05 N 0.47 E
Beaumont Place 222 29.50 N 95.14 W
Beaumont-sur-Oise 50 49.08 N 2.17 E
Beaumont-sur-Sarthe 50 48.13 N 0.08 E
Beaune 58 47.02 N 4.50 E
Beaune-la-Rolande 50 48.04 N 2.26 E
Beauport 206 46.52 N 71.11 W
Beaupré 186 47.03 N 70.54 W
Beaupréau 32 47.12 N 1.00 W
Beaupre Island I 212 44.26 N 76.19 W
Beaupré Lake ⊜ 184 54.30 N 107.10 W
Beauraing 56 50.07 N 4.58 E
Beaurepaire 62 45.20 N 5.03 E
Beaurepaire-en-Bresse 58 46.40 N 5.23 E
Beaurières 62 44.35 N 5.33 E
Beaurivage 206 46.25 N 71.14 W
Beaurivage ≃ 206 46.42 N 71.16 W
Beauséjour 184 50.04 N 96.33 W
Beausoleil 62 43.45 N 7.26 E
Beausoleil Island I 212 44.51 N 79.52 W
Beautor 50 49.39 N 3.20 E
Beauvais, Fr. 50 49.26 N 2.05 E
Beauvais, Fr. 261 48.32 N 2.03 E
Beauvais Creek ≃ 202 45.29 N 107.45 W
Beauvais-Tillé, Aéroport ⊠ 50 49.28 N 2.07 E
Beauval, Sk., Can. 184 55.09 N 107.37 W
Beauval, Fr. 50 50.06 N 2.20 E
Beauvezer 62 44.09 N 6.36 E
Beauville 32 44.17 N 0.52 E
Beauvoir 261 48.39 N 2.52 E
Beauvoir-sur-Mer 32 46.55 N 2.02 W
Beauvoir-sur-Niort 32 46.11 N 0.28 W
Beaux Arts 224 47.35 N 122.11 W
Beaver, Ak., U.S. 180 66.22 N 147.24 W
Beaver, Ok., U.S. 196 36.48 N 100.31 W
Beaver, Or., U.S. 224 45.16 N 123.49 W
Beaver, Pa., U.S. 214 40.41 N 80.18 W
Beaver, Ut,. U.S. 200 38.16 N 112.38 W
Beaver, Wa., U.S. 224 48.03 N 124.19 W
Beaver, W.V., U.S. 192 37.44 N 81.08 W
Beaver □[6] 214 40.40 N 80.25 W
Beaver ≃, Can. 176 59.43 N 124.16 W
Beaver ≃, Can. 184 55.25 N 107.45 W
Beaver ≃, On., Can. 212 44.34 N 80.27 W
Beaver ≃, U.S. 196 36.35 N 99.30 W
Beaver ≃, N.Y., U.S. 188 43.54 N 75.30 W
Beaver ≃, Pa., U.S. 214 40.40 N 80.18 W
Beaver ≃, Ut,. U.S. 200 39.10 N 112.57 W
Beaver Brook 210 40.55 N 75.59 W
Beaver Brook ≃, U.S. 207 42.40 N 71.19 W
Beaver Brook ≃, Ma., U.S. 283 42.03 N 70.58 W
Beaver Brook ≃, Ma., U.S. 283 42.23 N 71.14 W
Beaver Brook ≃, Ma., U.S. 283 42.36 N 71.21 W
Beaver Brook ≃, N.J., U.S. 276 40.58 N 74.35 W
Beaver Brook ≃, N.J., U.S. 276 40.54 N 74.30 W
Beaver City 198 40.08 N 99.49 W
Beaver Creek, Yk., Can. 180 62.22 N 140.52 W
Beavercreek, Oh., U.S. 218 39.43 N 84.03 W
Beavercreek, Or., U.S. 224 45.17 N 122.32 W
Beaver Creek ≃, On., Can. 212 44.30 N 77.42 W
Beaver Creek ≃, On., Can. 212 44.44 N 76.58 W
Beaver Creek ≃, On., Can. 275b 43.51 N 79.20 W
Beaver Creek ≃, On., Can. 284a 42.58 N 79.01 W
Beaver Creek ≃, U.S. 198 47.20 N 103.39 W
Beaver Creek ≃, U.S. 198 40.04 N 99.20 W
Beaver Creek ≃, U.S. 198 43.25 N 103.59 W
Beaver Creek ≃, U.S. 216 40.58 N 87.49 W
Beaver Creek ≃, Ak., U.S. 180 66.15 N 147.32 W
Beaver Creek ≃, Ca., U.S. 226 38.12 N 120.19 W
Beaver Creek ≃, Co., U.S. 198 40.20 N 103.33 W
Beaver Creek ≃, Co., U.S. 198 38.22 N 104.58 W
Beaver Creek ≃, Il., U.S. 216 42.16 N 88.56 W
Beaver Creek ≃, Il., U.S. 219 38.33 N 89.30 W
Beaver Creek ≃, Ky., U.S. 218 38.31 N 84.11 W
Beaver Creek ≃, Md., U.S. 208 39.32 N 77.42 W
Beaver Creek ≃, Mo., U.S. 194 36.38 N 93.02 W
Beaver Creek ≃, Mt., U.S. 202 48.29 N 107.24 W
Beaver Creek ≃, Ne., U.S. 198 40.42 N 97.20 W
Beaver Creek ≃, Ne., U.S. 198 41.26 N 97.42 W
Beaver Creek ≃, N.J., U.S. 285 39.45 N 75.23 W
Beaver Creek ≃, N.Y., U.S. 212 44.36 N 75.22 W
Beaver Creek ≃, N.D., U.S. 198 46.15 N 100.29 W
Beaver Creek ≃, Oh., U.S. 216 41.25 N 83.51 W
Beaver Creek ≃, Oh., U.S. 216 40.34 N 84.45 W
Beaver Creek ≃, Oh., U.S. 218 39.57 N 83.46 W
Beaver Creek ≃, Ok., U.S. 196 34.00 N 97.57 W
Beaver Creek ≃, Or., U.S. 224 44.56 N 121.22 W
Beaver Creek ≃, Pa., U.S. 285 40.00 N 75.42 W
Beaver Creek ≃, Tx., U.S. 196 33.53 N 98.49 W
Beaver Creek ≃, Wy., U.S. 202 42.58 N 108.26 W
Beaver Creek State Park ♠ 214 40.44 N 80.35 W
Beaver Crossing 198 40.46 N 97.16 W
Beaverdale 214 40.19 N 78.41 W
Beaver Dam, Ky., U.S. 194 37.24 N 86.52 W
Beaverdam, Oh., U.S. 216 40.50 N 83.59 W
Beaver Dam, Wi., U.S. 190 43.27 N 88.50 W
Beaverdam Brook ≃ 276 40.26 N 74.28 W
Beaverdam Creek ≃, U.S. 284c 38.55 N 76.57 W
Beaverdam Creek ≃, Md., U.S. 284c 39.01 N 76.54 W
Beaverdam Creek ≃, N.J., U.S. 285 39.56 N 74.45 W
Beaver Dams 210 42.17 N 76.58 W
Beaver Dams Creek ≃ 284a 43.06 N 79.11 W
Beaver Dam Wash V 200 36.54 N 114.55 W
Beaverdell 182 49.26 N 119.05 W
Beaver Falls, N.Y., U.S. 212 43.53 N 75.25 W
Beaver Falls, Pa., U.S. 214 40.45 N 80.19 W
Beaverhead ≃ 202 45.31 N 112.21 W
Beaverhead Mountains ⩘ 202 45.00 N 113.20 W
Beaverhill Lake ⊜, Ab., Can. 182 53.27 N 112.32 W
Beaver Hill Lake ⊜, Mb., Can. 184 54.16 N 94.53 W
Beaverhouse Lake ⊜ 190 48.32 N 92.05 W
Beaver Island I 190 45.40 N 85.31 W
Beaver Island State Park ♠ 210 42.58 N 78.57 W

Symbols in the index entries represent the broad categories identified in the key at the right. Symbols with superior numbers (⩘[1]) identify subcategories (see complete key on page *I · 1).*

Symbole im Register stellen die rechts im Schlüssel erklärten Kategorien dar. Symbole mit hochgestellten Ziffern (⩘[1]) bezeichnen Unterabteilungen einer Kategorie (vgl. vollständiger Schlüssel auf Seite *I · 1).*

Los símbolos incluídos en el texto del índice representan las grandes categorias identificadas con la clave a la derecha. Los símbolos con numeros en su parte superior (⩘[1]) identifican las subcategorías (véase la clave completa en la página *I · 1).*

Les symboles de l'index représentent les catégories indiquées dans la légende à droite. Les symboles suivis d'un indice (⩘[1]) représentent des sous-catégories (voir légende complète à la page *I · 1).*

Os símbolos incluídos no texto do índice representam as grandes categorias identificadas com a chave à direita. Os símbolos com números em sua parte superior (⩘[1]) identificam as subcategorias (veja-se a chave completa à página *I · 1).*

∧	Mountain	Berg	Montaña	Montagne	Montanha
⩘	Mountains	Gebirge	Montañas	Montagnes	Montanhas
)(	Pass	Paß	Paso	Col	Passo
V	Valley, Canyon	Tal, Cañon	Valle, Cañón	Vallée, Canyon	Vale, Canhão
≚	Plain	Ebene	Llano	Plaine	Planície
›	Cape	Kap	Cabo	Cap	Cabo
I	Island	Insel	Isla	Île	Ilha
II	Islands	Inseln	Islas	Îles	Ilhas
⊥	Other Topographic Features	Andere Topographische Objekte	Otros Elementos Topográficos	Autres données topographiques	Outros acidentes topográficos

ESPAÑOL Nombre	Página	Lat.°′	Long.°′ W = Oeste

FRANÇAIS Nom	Page	Lat.°′	Long.°′ W = Ouest

PORTUGUÊS Nome	Página	Lat.°′	Long.°′ W = Oeste

This is a multilingual geographic gazetteer index spanning names from "Beaver Kill" to "Belmopan," arranged in multiple columns with page numbers and latitude/longitude coordinates. The full entry list is too dense to reproduce reliably in its entirety.

Legend (bottom of page):

Symbol	Español	Français	(Other)
≃	River	Fluß / Rio / Rivière / Rio	
∟	Canal	Kanal / Canal / Canal / Canal	
∟	Waterfall, Rapids	Wasserfall, Stromschnellen / Cascada, Rápidos / Chute d'eau, Rapides / Cascata, Rápidos	
⊔	Strait	Meeresstraße / Estrecho / Détroit / Estreito	
c	Bay, Gulf	Buchт, Golf / Bahía, Golfo / Baie, Golfe / Baía, Golfo	
⊘	Lake, Lakes	See, Seen / Lago, Lagos / Lac, Lacs / Lago, Lagos	
≃	Swamp	Sumpf / Pantano / Marais / Pântano	
⛰	Ice Features, Glacier	Eis- und Gletscherformen / Otros Elementos / Autres données / Acidentes glaciares	
⊤	Other Hydrographic Features	Andere Hydrographische Objekte / Otros Elementos Hidrográficos / Autres données hydrographiques / Outros acidentes hidrográficos	
✦	Submarine Features	Untermeerische Objekte / Accidentes Submarinos / Formes de relief sous-marin / Acidentes submarinos	
○	Political Unit	Politische Einheit / Unidad Política / Entité politique / Unidade política	
⊥	Cultural Institution	Kulturelle Institution / Institución Cultural / Institution culturelle / Instituição cultural	
⊥	Historical Site	Historische Stätte / Sitio Histórico / Site historique / Sítio histórico	
⊞	Airport	Flughafen / Aeropuerto / Aéroport / Aeroporto	
■	Military Installation	Militäranlage / Instalación Militar / Installation militaire / Instalação militar	
⋄	Miscellaneous	Verschiedenes / Misceláneo / Divers / Diversos	
◆	Recreational Site	Erholungs- und Ferienort / Sitio de Recreo / Centre de loisirs / Área de Lazer	

ENGLISH — Name Page Lat.°′ Long.°′
DEUTSCH — Name Seite Breite°′ Länge°′ E = Ost

Belmore, Austl. 274a 33.55 S 151.05 E
Belmore, Oh., U.S. 216 41.09 N 83.56 W
Belmullet 48 54.14 N 10.00 W
Belmuri 272b 22.57 N 88.09 E
Belo 157b 19.42 S 44.33 E
Belœil, Bel. 50 50.33 N 3.43 E
Beloeil, P.Q., Can. 206 45.34 N 73.12 W
Belœil, Château de ʋ 50 50.35 N 3.44 E
Beloeil, Ruisseau ≃ 275a 45.39 N 73.12 W
Beloglazovo 86 56.05 N 72.40 E
Belogorje, S.S.S.R. 78 50.30 N 40.01 E
Belogorje, S.S.S.R. 78 50.01 N 26.25 E
Belogorka 80 50.42 N 53.27 E
Belogornoje 80 52.25 N 47.35 E
Belogorode 82 54.23 N 38.31 E
Belogorodka 78 50.00 N 26.39 E
Belogorovka 83 48.55 N 38.15 E
Belogorsk, S.S.S.R. 78 45.03 N 34.36 E
Belogorsk, S.S.S.R. 86 55.05 N 88.28 E
Belogorsk, S.S.S.R. 89 50.57 N 128.25 E
Belogorskij 86 49.27 N 83.10 E
Belogorskoje 80 53.35 N 48.12 E
Belogradčik 38 43.38 N 22.41 E
Beloguša 78 51.57 N 26.56 E
Beloha 157b 25.10 S 45.03 E
Belo Horizonte 255 19.55 S 43.56 W
Beloit, Ks., U.S. 198 39.27 N 98.06 W
Beloit, Oh., U.S. 214 40.55 N 80.59 W
Beloit, Wi., U.S. 216 42.30 N 89.01 W
Belo Jardim 250 8.20 S 36.26 W
Belojarsk 86 53.28 N 83.54 E
Belojarskij 86 56.45 N 61.24 E
Beloje, S.S.S.R. 80 58.23 N 39.24 E
Beloje, S.S.S.R. 83 48.31 N 39.04 E
Beloje, S.S.S.R. 86 48.55 N 82.58 E
Beloje, ozero ⊜ 76 60.11 N 37.37 E
Beloje more (White Sea) ⫧[2] 24 65.30 N 38.00 E
Belokamenskoje ◆[8] 83 48.41 N 38.06 E
Belokany 84 41.43 N 46.26 E
Belokurakino 83 49.33 N 38.44 E
Belokuricha 86 51.59 N 84.59 E
Beloluck 83 49.41 N 39.02 E
Belomestnaja 76 52.24 N 37.37 E
Belomestnaja Dvojn'a 80 52.42 N 41.03 E
Belomorsk 24 64.32 N 34.48 E
Belomorsko-Baltijskij kanal ≋ 24 62.48 N 34.48 E
Belondo 152 0.16 S 19.31 E
Belonge 152 2.06 S 19.32 E
Belonia 124 23.15 N 91.27 E
Beloomut 76 54.57 N 39.20 E
Beloozersk 76 52.28 N 25.11 E
Belopolje 78 51.09 N 34.18 E
Belorado 34 42.25 N 3.11 W
Belorečensk 78 44.46 N 39.52 E
Beloreck 86 53.58 N 58.24 E
Belören, Tür. 130 40.51 N 33.30 E
Belören, Tür. 130 37.12 N 32.33 E
Belören, Tür. 130 37.39 N 37.34 E
Belorussia → Belorusskaja Sovetskaja Socialističeskaja Respublika □[3] 76 53.35 N 28.00 E
Belorusskaja gr'ada ∧ 76 53.40 N 27.00 E
Belorusskaja Sovetskaja Socialističeskaja Respublika □[3] 76 53.50 N 28.00 E
Beloščelje 24 64.52 N 46.56 E
Belo-sur-mer 157b 20.44 S 44.00 E
Belot, Lac ⊜ 180 66.55 N 126.18 W
Belousovka, S.S.S.R. 78 49.57 N 32.20 E
Belousovka, S.S.S.R. 86 50.08 N 82.33 E
Belousovo 82 55.05 N 36.40 E
Bel'ov 76 53.48 N 36.08 E
Belo Vale 255 20.25 S 44.01 W
Beloveżskaja Pušča, zapovednik ♦ 76 52.40 N 23.50 E
Belovo, S.S.S.R. 86 52.57 N 82.16 E
Belovo, S.S.S.R. 86 54.25 N 86.18 E
Belovodsk 83 49.12 N 39.35 E
Belovodskoje 85 42.50 N 74.06 E
Beloz'orje, S.S.S.R. 78 49.29 N 31.35 E
Beloz'orje, S.S.S.R. 78 49.18 N 31.54 E
Beloz'orka 78 46.37 N 32.27 E
Beloz'orsk 76 60.02 N 37.48 E
Beloz'orskoje 78 48.33 N 37.04 E
Belp 58 46.53 N 7.30 E
Belpāda 272c 19.02 N 73.03 E
Belpasso 70 37.35 N 14.58 E
Belper 44 53.01 N 1.29 W
Belpre 188 39.16 N 81.34 W
Belrose 274a 33.44 S 151.13 E
Belsano 214 40.31 N 78.52 W
Belsele 50 51.09 N 4.05 E
Bel'skaja Vol'a 78 51.27 N 25.49 E
Bel'skoje, S.S.S.R. 80 54.44 N 40.22 E
Bel'skoje, S.S.S.R. 86 57.49 N 92.09 E
Belson Run ≃ 279b 40.12 N 79.37 W
Belspring 192 37.11 N 80.36 W
Belt 202 47.23 N 110.55 W
Beltana 166 30.48 S 138.25 E
Belt Creek ≃ 202 47.36 N 111.02 W
Belted Range ⋏ 204 37.25 N 116.10 W
Belterra 250 2.38 S 54.57 W
Belthorn 262 53.43 N 2.26 W
Beltinci 61 46.36 N 16.15 E
Belton, Eng., U.K. 42 52.34 N 1.41 E
Belton, Eng., U.K. 44 53.33 N 0.49 W
Belton, Mo., U.S. 194 38.48 N 94.31 W
Belton, S.C., U.S. 192 34.31 N 82.29 W
Belton, Tx., U.S. 222 31.03 N 97.27 W
Belton Lake ⊜[1] 222 31.08 N 97.32 W
Beltra 48 54.13 N 8.37 W
Beltrán 252 27.50 S 64.04 W
Beltsville, Md., U.S. 208 39.02 N 76.54 W
Beltsville, Md., U.S. 284c 39.02 N 76.54 W
Bel'tsy → Bel'cy 78 47.46 N 27.56 E
Belturbet 48 54.06 N 7.28 W
Beltway Plaza ◆[9] 284c 39.00 N 76.54 W
Bel'tyrskij 86 53.02 N 90.16 E
Beltzville Lake ⊜[1] 210 40.52 N 75.37 W
Beltzville State Park ♦ 210 40.52 N 75.36 W
Belucha, gora ∧ 86 49.48 N 86.40 E
Belucha, ozero ⊜ 80 49.20 N 46.05 E
Belugino 82 54.47 N 37.54 E
Belumut, Gunong ∧ 114 2.02 N 103.34 E
Belūr, India 122 13.10 N 75.52 E
Belur, India 272b 22.38 N 88.18 E
Beluran 112 5.54 N 117.33 E
Belur Math ʋ[1] 272b 22.38 N 88.22 E
Belušje 24 66.54 N 47.31 E
Belvedere, It. 64 45.44 N 13.23 E
Belvedere, Ca., U.S. 226 37.52 N 122.28 W
Belvedere, Va., U.S. 284c 38.50 N 77.10 W
Belvedere ◆[8] 260 51.29 N 0.09 E
Belvedere ʋ 264b 48.11 N 16.23 E
Belvedere di Spinello 68 39.12 N 16.53 E
Belvedere Homes 220 26.43 N 80.06 W
Belvedere Marittimo 68 39.37 N 15.52 E
Belvedere Ostrense 66 43.34 N 13.09 E
Belvès 32 44.47 N 1.00 E
Belvidere, De., U.S. 208 39.43 N 75.37 W
Belvidere, Il., U.S. 216 42.15 N 88.50 W
Belvidere, N.J., U.S. 210 40.49 N 75.04 W
Belview 198 44.36 N 95.19 W
Belvis 266a 40.33 N 3.33 W
Belvís de la Jara 34 39.45 N 4.57 W
Belvoir → Kokhav HaYarden ⊥ 132 32.36 N 35.31 E
Belvoir, Vale of V 42 52.57 N 0.53 W
Belyando ≃ 166 21.38 S 146.50 E
Belyj 76 55.50 N 32.56 E
Belyj, ostrov I 74 73.10 N 70.45 E
Belyje Berega 76 53.12 N 34.40 E
Belyje Kolodezi 82 54.55 N 38.42 E
Belyje Stolby 82 55.20 N 37.52 E
Belyje Vody 85 42.25 N 69.50 E
Belyj Gorodok 76 56.58 N 37.30 E
Belyj Jar, S.S.S.R. 80 53.57 N 48.58 E
Belyj Jar, S.S.S.R. 86 53.36 N 91.24 E
Belyj Jar, S.S.S.R. 86 58.26 N 85.01 E
Belyj Kalodez' 78 50.02 N 38.40 E
Belyj Kolodez' 78 50.12 N 37.08 E
Belyj Luch ≃ 80 57.43 N 43.42 E
Belyj Rast 82 56.08 N 37.26 E
Belyniči 76 53.59 N 29.42 E
Belynkoviči 76 53.15 N 32.08 E
Belz, Fr. 32 47.41 N 3.10 W
Belz, S.S.S.R. 78 50.23 N 24.01 E
Bełżec 30 50.24 N 23.26 E
Belzig 54 52.08 N 12.35 E
Belzoni 194 33.11 N 90.29 W
Bełżyce 30 51.11 N 22.18 E
Bem 219 38.15 N 91.28 W
Bemaraha, Plateau du ⋏[1] 157b 19.15 S 45.00 E
Bemarivo, Madag. 157b 16.56 S 44.21 E
Bemarivo, Madag. 157b 21.45 S 44.45 E
Bemarivo ≃, Madag. 157b 15.27 S 47.40 E
Bemarivo ≃, Madag. 157b 14.09 S 50.09 E
Bemavo 157b 21.37 S 45.24 E
Bembe 152 7.02 S 14.18 E
Bembéréké 150 10.13 N 2.40 E
Bembézar ≃ 34 37.45 N 5.13 W
Bembezi ≃ 154 18.57 S 27.47 E
Bembou Sambayabé 150 10.55 N 13.44 W
Bembridge 42 50.41 N 1.05 W
Bement 194 39.55 N 88.34 W
Bemidji 190 47.28 N 94.52 W
Bemis 194 35.34 N 88.49 W
Bemmel 52 51.54 N 5.54 E
Bemolanga 157b 17.44 S 45.06 E
Bemposta 256 22.09 S 43.07 W
Bemus Point 214 42.09 N 79.23 W
Bemyž 80 56.08 N 51.44 E
Ben, Kinh ≋ 269c 10.43 N 106.37 E
Bena 150 11.18 N 5.55 E
Benaadir □[4] 144 2.07 N 45.24 E
Benāb 128 37.20 N 46.04 E
Benabarre 34 42.07 N 0.29 E
Bena-Dibele 152 4.07 S 22.50 E
Benagaria 126 24.11 N 87.37 E
Benagerie 166 31.25 S 140.24 E
Benahmed 148 33.07 N 7.17 W
Benain ≃ 112 9.39 S 124.59 E
Ben'akoni 76 54.15 N 25.22 E
Bena-Leka 152 5.08 S 22.10 E
Benalla 166 36.33 S 145.59 E
Benamejí 34 37.16 N 4.32 W
Benares → Vārānasi 124 25.20 N 83.00 E
Bénat, Cap › 62 43.05 N 6.22 E
Benátky nad Jizerou 54 50.17 N 14.51 E
Bena-Tshadi 152 4.40 S 22.49 E
Benavente, Esp. 34 42.00 N 5.41 W
Benavente, Port. 34 38.59 N 8.48 W
Benavides 196 27.35 N 98.24 W
Benavidez 258 34.25 S 58.42 W
Ben Avon 279b 40.31 N 80.05 W
Ben Avon Heights 279b 40.31 N 80.04 W
Ben Badis 34 34.57 N 0.55 W
Benbane Head › 48 55.15 N 6.28 W
Benbecula I 46 57.26 N 7.21 W
Ben Bolt 196 27.39 N 98.05 W
Benbonyathe Hill ∧ 166 30.24 S 139.11 E
Benbrook 222 32.40 N 97.27 W
Benbrook Lake ⊜[1] 222 32.38 N 97.27 W
Ben Cat 110 11.09 N 106.36 E
Ben Cat, Rach ≃ 269c 10.50 N 106.42 E
Bencha, Khao Phanom ∧ 110 8.17 N 98.56 E
Ben-Chicao, Col de)(34 36.12 N 2.45 E
Bencubbin 162 30.48 S 117.52 E
Bend 202 44.03 N 121.18 W
Benda, Tanjung › 115a 6.37 S 111.29 E
Bendaja 150 7.10 N 11.15 W
Bende 150 5.36 N 7.39 E
Bendel □[3] 150 6.00 N 6.00 E
Bendela 152 3.18 S 17.36 E
Bendeleben, Mount ∧ 180 65.10 N 164.03 W
Bendemeer 166 30.53 S 151.10 E
Bender Beyla 144 9.29 N 50.49 E
Benderge ∧ 158 31.06 S 27.58 E
Bendersville 208 39.59 N 77.15 W
Bendery 78 46.48 N 29.29 E
Bendigo 169 36.46 S 144.17 E
Bendimahi ≃ 84 38.56 N 43.38 E
Bendorf 56 50.25 N 7.34 E
Bendugu 150 9.32 N 10.57 W
Bēne 76 56.29 N 23.04 E
Bene Beraq 132 32.05 N 34.50 E
Benedict 208 38.30 N 76.40 W
Benediktenwand ⊥[4] 64 47.39 N 11.28 E
Beneditinos 250 5.27 S 42.22 W
Benedito Leite 250 7.13 S 44.34 W
Benemérita de San Cristóbal 238 18.25 N 70.06 W
Bénéna 150 13.07 N 4.22 W
Benenitra 157b 23.27 S 45.05 E
Benepú, Rada ⫧[3] 174z 27.10 S 109.25 W
Beneraird ∧[2] 44 55.04 N 4.57 W
Benešov 30 49.47 N 14.43 E
Benešov nad Ploučnicí 54 50.45 N 14.22 E
Bénestroff 56 48.55 N 6.45 E
Benetutti 71 40.27 N 9.10 E
Beneuvre 58 47.42 N 4.57 E
Bene Vagienna 62 44.33 N 7.50 E
Bénévent-l'Abbaye 32 46.07 N 1.38 E
Benevento 68 41.08 N 14.45 E
Benevento □[4] 68 41.15 N 14.17 E
Benezett 214 41.19 N 78.23 W
Benfeld 58 48.22 N 7.36 E
Benfica ◆[8], Bra. 287a 22.53 S 43.15 W
Benfica ◆[8], Port. 266c 38.45 N 9.12 W
Benfica, Estádio ♦ 266c 38.45 N 9.11 W
Bèng ≃, Lao 110 19.53 N 101.08 E
Beng ≃, Zhg. 98 35.05 N 118.24 E
Benga 154 13.19 S 34.16 E
Bengābād 126 24.18 N 86.21 E
Bengal, Bay of c 12 15.00 N 90.00 E
Bengala, Golfo del → Bengal, Bay of c 12 15.00 N 90.00 E
Bengalen, Golf von → Bengal, Bay of c 12 15.00 N 90.00 E
Bengamisa 154 0.57 N 25.10 E
Bengara 112 3.11 N 117.12 E
Ben Gardane 148 33.08 N 11.13 E
Bengasi → Banghāzī 146 32.07 N 20.04 E
Bengbis 152 3.27 N 12.27 E
Bengbu 100 32.58 N 117.24 E
Benger 168a 33.11 S 115.52 E
Benghazi → Banghāzī 146 32.07 N 20.04 E
Ben Giang 110 15.41 N 107.47 E
Bengkalis 114 1.28 N 102.07 E
Bengkalis, Pulau I 114 1.30 N 102.15 E
Bengkalis, Selat ʮ 114 1.30 N 102.00 E
Bengkayang 112 0.50 N 109.29 E
Bengkoka ≃ 116 6.50 N 117.03 E
Bengkulu 112 3.48 S 102.16 E
Bengkulu □[4] 112 4.00 S 102.30 E
Bengo □[5] 152 8.30 S 13.20 E
Bengo ≃ 152 8.45 S 13.24 E
Bengo, Baía do c 152 8.43 S 13.21 E
Bengoi 164 3.01 S 130.12 E
Bengough 184 49.24 N 105.08 W
Bengtsfors 26 59.02 N 12.13 E
Benguela 152 12.35 S 13.25 E
Benguela □[5] 152 12.45 S 14.30 E
Benguerir 148 32.14 N 7.57 W
Benguet □[4] 116 16.30 N 120.40 E
Bengut, Cap › 34 36.55 N 3.54 E
Benha → Banhā 142 30.28 N 31.11 E
Benham 192 36.57 N 82.56 W
Ben Hur 222 31.30 N 96.44 W
Beni, Nig. 146 10.27 N 10.24 E
Beni, Zaïre 154 0.30 N 29.28 E
Beni □[5] 248 14.00 S 65.30 W
Beni ≃ 248 10.23 S 65.24 W
Béni Abbas 148 30.08 N 2.10 W
Benicarló 34 40.25 N 0.26 E
Benicia 226 38.02 N 122.09 W
Benicia Capitol State Historic Park ♦ 282 38.03 N 122.09 W
Benicia State Recreation Area ♦ 282 38.05 N 122.13 W
Benicito ≃ 248 11.32 S 65.47 W
Benidorm 34 38.32 N 0.08 W
Beni-Mellal 148 32.22 N 6.29 W
Beni-Mellal □[4] 148 32.22 N 6.27 W
Benin (Bénin) □[1], Afr. 134 9.30 N 2.15 E
Benin (Bénin) □[1], Afr. 150 9.30 N 2.15 E
Benin ≃ 150 5.45 N 5.04 E
Benin, Bight of c[3] 150 5.30 N 3.00 E
Benin City 150 6.19 N 5.41 E
Beni Saf 148 35.19 N 1.23 W
Benisheikh 146 11.49 N 12.29 E
Benissa 34 38.34 N 0.03 E
Beni Suef → Banī Suwayf 142 29.05 N 31.05 E
Benito 184 51.55 N 101.31 W
Benito Juárez, Méx. 234 19.14 N 100.28 W
Benito Juárez, Méx. 234 17.50 N 92.32 W
Benito Juárez □[7] 286a 19.22 N 99.10 W
Benito Juárez, Parque Nacional ♦ 234 17.07 N 96.43 W
Benito Juárez, Presa ⊜[1] 234 16.27 N 95.30 W
Benit Point › 116 9.54 N 125.17 E
Benjamim Constant 256 21.57 S 42.53 W
Benjamin 196 33.35 N 99.48 W
Benjamín, Isla I 254 44.40 S 74.08 W
Benjamín Aceval 252 24.58 S 57.34 W
Benjamin Constant 246 4.22 S 70.02 W
Benjamin Franklin Bridge ◆[5] 285 39.57 N 75.08 W
Benjamín Hill 232 30.10 N 111.10 W
Benjamín Zorrilla 252 39.06 S 65.29 W
Benkelman 198 40.02 N 101.31 W
Benken 54 52.10 N 12.28 E
Benkovac 36 44.02 N 15.37 E
Benld 219 39.05 N 89.48 W
Benllech 44 53.19 N 4.13 W
Ben Lomond 226 37.05 N 122.05 W
Ben Lomond National Park ♦ 166 41.34 S 147.11 E
Ben Mehidi 36 36.46 N 7.54 E
Benmore, Lake ⊜[1] 172 44.25 S 170.15 E
Benndale 194 30.52 N 88.48 W
Benndorf 54 51.34 N 11.29 E
Benneckenstein 54 51.40 N 10.45 E
Bennekom 52 52.00 N 5.40 E
Bennet 198 40.40 N 96.30 W
Bennett, Lake ⊜ 162 22.55 S 130.57 E
Bennetta, ostrov I 74 76.21 N 148.56 E
Bennett Lake ⊜, Can. 180 60.05 N 134.50 W
Bennett Lake ⊜, Mb., Can. 184 53.28 N 96.05 W
Bennett Lake ⊜, On., Can. 212 44.55 N 76.27 W
Bennett Pass)(224 45.18 N 121.39 W
Bennettsbridge 48 52.36 N 7.12 W
Bennetts Creek ≃ 210 42.16 N 77.35 W
Bennettsville 192 34.37 N 79.41 W
Bennettswood 274b 37.51 S 145.07 E
Bennigsen 52 52.14 N 9.40 E
Benninghofen ◆[8] 263 51.29 N 7.31 E
Bennington, In., U.S. 218 38.52 N 85.08 W
Bennington, Ks., U.S. 198 39.01 N 97.35 W
Bennington, Vt., U.S. 210 42.52 N 73.11 W
Bennington □[6] 207 42.50 N 73.08 W
Bennington Battle Monument ⊥ 210 42.53 N 73.13 W
Benniu 106 31.52 N 119.48 E
Bennstedt 54 51.29 N 11.49 E
Beno 152 3.37 S 17.48 E
Benoa 115b 8.46 S 115.13 E
Ben Ohau Range ⋏ 172 44.00 S 170.00 E
Benoit 194 33.39 N 91.00 W
Benom, Gunong ∧ 114 3.49 N 102.04 E
Benoni 158 26.11 S 28.19 E
Benoni □[5] 273d 26.08 S 28.22 E
Benoni-Suid 273d 26.13 S 28.18 E
Bénoué (Benue) ≃ 134 7.48 N 6.46 E
Bénoué, Parc National de la ♦ 146 8.20 N 13.50 E
Benover 260 51.13 N 0.26 E
Bénoy 146 8.59 N 16.19 E
Benque Viejo 232 17.05 N 89.08 W
Benrad ◆[8] 263 51.20 N 6.30 E
Benrath ◆[8] 56 51.10 N 6.51 E
Benrath, Schloss ⊥ 263 51.10 N 6.52 E
Bensbach ≃ 164 9.08 S 141.00 E
Bensberg 56 50.58 N 7.09 E
Bensdorf 54 52.24 N 12.20 E
Ben Sekka, Rass › 36 37.21 N 9.45 E
Bensenville 278 41.57 N 87.56 W
Bensersiel 52 53.40 N 7.34 E
Benshausen 54 50.38 N 10.35 E
Bensheim 56 49.41 N 8.37 E
Bensley 208 37.26 N 77.26 W
Ben-Slimane 148 33.41 N 7.10 W
Ben-Slimane □[4] 148 33.40 N 7.10 W
Ben Smih 36 36.23 N 7.31 E
Benson, Eng., U.K. 42 51.38 N 1.05 W
Benson, Az., U.S. 200 31.58 N 110.17 W
Benson, Md., U.S. 208 39.30 N 76.23 W
Benson, Mn., U.S. 198 45.18 N 95.35 W
Benson, N.C., U.S. 192 35.22 N 78.32 W
Bensonhurst ◆[8] 276 40.35 N 73.59 W
Benson Point › 174o 1.56 N 157.29 W
Bens Run ≃ 284b 39.19 N 76.48 W
Bent 128 26.17 N 59.31 E
Benta 114 4.01 N 101.58 E
Benteng (Salayar) 112 6.08 S 120.27 E
Bentheim, B.R.D. 52 52.17 N 7.10 E
Bentheim, Mi., U.S. 216 42.42 N 85.55 W
Ben Thuy 110 18.39 N 105.42 E
Bentiaba 152 14.15 S 12.21 E
Bentiaba ≃ 152 14.29 S 12.50 E
Bentinck Island I, Austl. 164 17.04 S 139.30 E
Bentinck Island I, Mya. 110 11.45 N 98.03 E
Bentiu 140 9.14 N 29.50 E
Bentleigh 274b 37.55 S 145.02 E
Bentley, Ab., Can. 182 52.28 N 114.04 W
Bentley, Eng., U.K. 44 53.33 N 1.09 W
Bentley College ʋ[2] 283 42.23 N 71.13 W
Bentleyville, Oh., U.S. 279a 41.25 N 81.26 W
Bentleyville, Pa., U.S. 214 40.07 N 80.00 W
Bento Gomes ≃ 248 16.40 S 57.12 W
Bento Gonçalves 252 29.10 S 51.31 W
Bentol 150 6.26 N 10.36 W
Benton, Ar., U.S. 194 34.33 N 92.35 W
Benton, Il., U.S. 194 37.59 N 88.55 W
Benton, In., U.S. 216 41.30 N 85.45 W
Benton, Ky., U.S. 194 36.51 N 88.21 W
Benton, La., U.S. 194 32.41 N 93.44 W
Benton, Ms., U.S. 194 32.49 N 90.15 W
Benton, Mo., U.S. 194 37.05 N 89.33 W
Benton, Oh., U.S. 214 40.36 N 81.51 W
Benton, Pa., U.S. 210 41.11 N 76.23 W
Benton, Tn., U.S. 192 35.10 N 84.39 W
Benton, Wi., U.S. 190 42.34 N 90.22 W
Benton □[6] 216 40.37 N 87.19 W
Benton City, Mo., U.S. 219 39.08 N 91.45 W
Benton City, Wa., U.S. 202 46.15 N 119.29 W
Bentong 114 3.32 N 101.55 E
Benton Harbor 216 42.07 N 86.26 W
Benton Heights 216 42.07 N 86.24 W
Bentonia 194 32.38 N 90.21 W
Benton Lake ⊜ 202 47.40 N 111.20 W
Benton Ridge 216 41.00 N 83.47 W
Bentonville, Ar., U.S. 194 36.22 N 94.12 W
Bentonville, In., U.S. 218 39.45 N 85.15 W
Bentonville, Oh., U.S. 218 38.45 N 83.37 W
Ben Tre 110 10.14 N 106.23 E
Bent's Old Fort National Historic Site ⊥ 198 38.05 N 103.28 W
Benua, Pulau I 112 0.56 N 107.27 E
Benue □[3] 150 7.15 N 8.00 E
Benue (Bénoué) ≃ 134 7.48 N 6.46 E
Benut 114 1.38 N 103.16 E
Benwee ∧ 48 53.35 N 9.31 W
Benwee Head › 48 54.20 N 9.50 W
Ben Wheeler 222 32.27 N 95.42 W
Benxi (Penhsi), Zhg. 104 41.18 N 123.45 E
Benxi (Xiaoshi), Zhg. 104 41.17 N 124.07 E
Benza 152 6.16 S 12.57 E
Beograd (Belgrade) 38 44.50 N 20.30 E
Beohāri 124 24.03 N 81.23 E
Beonta 272b 22.31 N 88.31 E
Béoumi 150 7.40 N 5.34 W
Beowawe 204 40.35 N 116.28 W
Beppu 96 33.17 N 131.30 E
Beppu-wan c 96 33.18 N 131.35 E
Bequia I 241h 13.01 N 61.13 W
Bequimão 250 2.26 S 44.47 W
Bera 126 24.05 N 89.37 E
Berābāria 272b 22.52 N 88.34 E
Beraberi, India 272b 22.46 N 88.27 E
Berāberi, India 272b 22.51 N 88.12 E
Beraketa, Madag. 157b 24.11 S 45.42 E
Beraketa, Madag. 157b 23.07 S 44.25 E
Beramanja 157b 13.13 S 48.56 E
Bérandjoko 152 3.06 N 17.17 E
Berāsi 124 23.36 N 81.51 E
Berasia 124 23.38 N 77.26 E
Berat 38 40.42 N 19.57 E
Beratzhausen 60 49.06 N 11.48 E
Berau 58 47.42 N 8.15 E
Berau ≃ 112 2.10 N 117.42 E
Berau, Teluk c 164 2.30 S 132.30 E
Beravina 157b 18.10 S 45.14 E
Berazategui 258 34.46 S 58.13 W
Berazategui □[5] 288 34.50 S 58.10 W
Berbenno di Valtellina 64 46.10 N 9.44 E
Berbera 144 10.25 N 45.02 E
Berbérati 152 4.16 N 15.47 E
Berbice ≃ 246 6.17 N 57.32 W
Berceto 64 44.31 N 9.59 E
Berchem, Bel. 50 51.12 N 4.26 E
Berchem, Bel. 50 50.47 N 3.30 E
Berchidda 71 40.47 N 9.10 E
Berching 60 49.07 N 11.27 E
Berchtesgaden 64 47.38 N 13.01 E
Berchtesgaden, Nationalpark ♦ 64 47.30 N 13.00 E
Berchum ◆[8] 263 51.23 N 7.32 E
Berck 50 50.24 N 1.34 E
Berclair 196 28.32 N 97.36 W
Berčogur 86 48.25 N 58.44 E
Bercu 50 50.31 N 3.17 E
Berd 84 40.53 N 45.23 E
Berda ≃ 78 46.48 N 36.52 E
Berdaale 144 7.04 N 47.51 E
Berdale 144 4.56 N 45.02 E
Berd'ansk 78 46.45 N 36.49 E
Berd'anskaja kosa ›[2] 78 46.42 N 36.48 E
Berd'anskij zaliv c 78 46.42 N 36.35 E
Berd'auš 86 55.09 N 59.09 E
Berdičev 78 49.54 N 28.36 E
Berdigest'ach 74 62.06 N 126.40 E
Berdniki 80 57.25 N 46.33 E
Berdorf 56 49.50 N 6.21 E
Berdsk 86 54.47 N 83.02 E
Berd'užje 86 55.48 N 68.19 E
Berdyansk → Berd'ansk 78 46.45 N 36.49 E
Bere, S.S.S.R. 128 39.47 N 58.06 E
Béré, Tchad 146 9.20 N 16.09 E
Berea, Ky., U.S. 192 37.34 N 84.17 W
Berea, Oh., U.S. 214 41.21 N 81.51 W
Berea, S.C., U.S. 192 34.53 N 82.27 W
Bere Alston 42 50.29 N 4.11 W
Berebei 164 9.31 S 147.27 E
Beregajevo 86 57.10 N 87.32 E
Beregomet 78 48.12 N 25.21 E
Beregovo 78 48.13 N 22.39 E
Beregovoj 86 55.12 N 73.12 E
Bereguardo 62 45.15 N 9.01 E
Bereina 164 8.40 S 146.30 E
Bereka ≃ 78 49.12 N 36.59 E
Bereketli 130 40.31 N 37.18 E
Bereku 154 4.27 S 35.44 E
Berekua 240d 15.14 N 61.19 W
Berekum 150 7.27 N 2.37 W
Bérem 152 7.33 N 13.55 E
Beren, liman ⊜ 80 46.52 N 44.55 E
Berenda Slough ≃ 226 37.00 N 120.29 W
Berendejevo 82 56.36 N 39.01 E
Berens ≃ 184 52.21 N 97.02 W
Berens Island I 184 52.18 N 97.17 W
Berens River 184 52.22 N 97.02 W
Bere Regis 42 50.46 N 2.14 W
Beresford, N.B., Can. 186 47.42 N 65.42 W
Beresford, S.D., U.S. 198 43.04 N 96.46 W
Beresina → Berezina ≃ 76 52.33 N 30.14 E
Berestečko 78 50.23 N 25.07 E
Berești 38 46.06 N 27.53 E
Berettyó (Barcău) ≃ 38 46.59 N 21.07 E
Berettyóújfalu 30 47.14 N 21.32 E
Berevo, Madag. 157b 17.14 S 44.17 E
Berevo, Madag. 157b 19.44 S 44.58 E
Berezajka 76 57.59 N 33.54 E
Berezan' 78 50.19 N 31.30 E
Berezanskaja 78 45.43 N 39.34 E
Berezanskij liman c[1] 78 46.43 N 31.30 E
Berežany 78 49.27 N 24.56 E
Berezdov 78 50.27 N 27.05 E
Berezina ≃, S.S.S.R. 76 53.48 N 25.59 E
Berezina ≃, S.S.S.R. 76 52.33 N 30.14 E
Berezino, S.S.S.R. 76 53.49 N 28.59 E
Berezino, S.S.S.R. 76 54.54 N 28.12 E
Berezino, S.S.S.R. 78 46.14 N 29.12 E
Berezino, S.S.S.R. 80 50.06 N 48.52 E
Berezinskij zapovednik ♦ 76 54.40 N 28.15 E
Berezna 78 51.34 N 31.47 E
Berezn'agi 78 49.59 N 41.06 E
Berezn'aki, S.S.S.R. 78 49.09 N 31.57 E
Berezn'aki, S.S.S.R. 78 49.51 N 33.01 E
Bereznegovatoje 78 47.20 N 32.49 E
Berežnica 78 51.27 N 26.27 E
Bereznik 24 62.51 N 42.40 E
Berezniki 86 59.24 N 56.46 E
Berford Lake ⊜ 212 44.48 N 81.11 W
Berg, B.R.D. 64 47.58 N 11.21 E
Berg, Lux. 56 49.49 N 6.05 E
Berg, Nor. 24 69.26 N 17.15 E
Berg, Öst. 64 46.45 N 13.09 E
Berga, D.D.R. 54 51.27 N 11.00 E
Berga, D.D.R. 54 50.45 N 12.10 E
Berga, Esp. 34 42.06 N 1.51 E
Berga, Sve. 40 59.21 N 16.26 E
Bergama 130 39.07 N 27.11 E
Bergambacht 52 51.56 N 4.46 E
Bergamo 62 45.41 N 9.43 E
Bergamo □[4] 64 45.50 N 9.48 E
Bergan Point › 276 40.40 N 73.20 W
Bergantín 246 10.01 N 64.22 W
Bergantino 64 45.05 N 11.15 E
Bergara 34 43.07 N 2.25 W
Bergby 26 60.56 N 17.02 E
Berge, B.R.D. 52 52.37 N 7.44 E
Berge, B.R.D. 263 51.21 N 7.22 E
Berge, D.D.R. 54 53.15 N 11.50 E
Bergedorf ◆[8] 52 53.29 N 10.13 E
Bergei ∧[2] 263 51.13 N 7.46 E
Bergeijk 52 51.19 N 5.22 E
Bergen → Mons, Bel. 50 50.27 N 3.56 E
Bergen, B.R.D. 52 52.48 N 9.58 E
Bergen, B.R.D. 54 52.53 N 10.58 E
Bergen, B.R.D. 64 47.48 N 12.35 E
Bergen, Ned. 52 52.40 N 4.41 E
Bergen, Nor. 26 60.23 N 5.20 E
Bergen, N.Y., U.S. 210 43.05 N 77.56 W
Bergen □[6] 210 40.53 N 74.03 W
Bergen aan Zee 52 52.38 N 4.37 E
Bergen [auf Rügen] 54 54.25 N 13.26 E
Bergen Basin c 276 40.39 N 73.49 W
Bergen-Belsen-Denkmal ⊥ 52 52.46 N 9.55 E
Berg en Dal 250 5.09 N 55.04 W
Bergenfield 210 40.55 N 73.59 W
Bergen Mall ◆[9] 276 40.55 N 74.04 W
Bergen op Zoom 52 51.30 N 4.17 E
Berger 219 38.40 N 91.20 W
Bergerac 32 44.51 N 0.29 E
Bergères-lès-Vertus 50 48.53 N 4.00 E
Bergerhof 263 51.12 N 7.21 E
Bergfelde 54 52.40 N 13.19 E
Berggiesshübel 54 50.52 N 13.57 E
Berghausen, B.R.D. 263 51.18 N 7.17 E
Berghausen, B.R.D. 263 51.07 N 6.55 E
Bergheim, B.R.D. 56 50.55 N 6.38 E
Bergheim, Fr. 58 48.12 N 7.22 E
Bergheim, Öst. 64 47.50 N 13.02 E
Berghem 52 51.46 N 5.34 E
Berghofen ◆[8] 263 51.29 N 7.32 E
Bergholtz 210 43.06 N 78.53 W
Bergholtz Creek ≃ 284a 43.05 N 78.57 W
Bergholz 214 40.31 N 80.53 W
Bergholz-Rehbrücke 54 52.20 N 13.05 E
Bergisches Land ◆[1] 56 51.00 N 7.10 E
Bergisch Gladbach 56 50.59 N 7.07 E
Bergkamen 52 51.38 N 7.38 E
Bergkvara 26 56.23 N 16.05 E
Bergland 190 46.35 N 89.34 W
Bergneustadt 56 51.01 N 7.39 E
Bergnicourt 50 49.25 N 4.15 E
Bergö I 26 62.58 N 21.11 E
Bergoo 188 38.29 N 80.18 W
Bergplaas 158 33.54 S 22.40 E
Bergrheinfeld 56 50.00 N 10.10 E
Bergsäng 40 60.06 N 13.33 E
Bergsbrunna 40 59.49 N 17.43 E
Bergsche Maas ≃ 52 51.45 N 5.08 E
Bergshamra 40 59.38 N 18.37 E
Bergsjö 26 61.59 N 17.04 E
Bergslagen ◆[1] 40 59.55 N 15.00 E
Bergstrom Air Force Base ■ 222 30.12 N 97.40 W
Bergtheim 56 49.54 N 10.04 E
Berguent 148 34.03 N 2.02 W
Bergues 50 50.58 N 2.26 E
Bergum 52 53.11 N 5.59 E
Bergün 58 46.38 N 9.45 E
Bergville 158 28.52 S 29.18 E
Bergvreten 40 60.31 N 16.26 E
Bergwitz 54 51.48 N 12.35 E
Berhala, Selat ʮ 112 0.48 S 104.25 E
Beri 124 28.42 N 76.35 E
Berici, Monti ⋏ 64 45.26 N 11.31 E
Berikul'skij 86 55.32 N 88.08 E
Beringa, ostrov I 74 55.00 N 165.15 E
Beringen 56 51.03 N 5.13 E
Bering Glacier ⍓ 180 60.15 N 143.30 W
Beringhausen 56 51.24 N 8.46 E
Beringil 140 12.10 N 25.41 E
Beringin 112 3.41 S 104.18 E
Beringovskij 180 63.03 N 179.19 E
Bering Sea ⫧[2] 16 60.00 N 175.00 W
Bering Strait ʮ 180 65.30 N 169.00 W
Berinsfield 42 51.40 N 1.11 W
Berislav 78 46.51 N 33.26 E
Berisso 258 34.52 S 57.53 W
Berisso □[5] 288 34.55 S 57.53 W
Berja 34 36.51 N 2.57 W
Berkåk 26 62.50 N 10.00 E
Berkakit 74 56.34 N 124.48 E
Berkane 148 34.59 N 2.20 W
Berkel ≃ 52 52.09 N 6.12 E
Berkeley, Eng., U.K. 42 51.42 N 2.27 W
Berkeley, Ca., U.S. 226 37.52 N 122.16 W
Berkeley, Il., U.S. 278 41.53 N 87.54 W
Berkeley, Mo., U.S. 219 38.45 N 90.19 W
Berkeley, R.I., U.S. 207 41.55 N 71.25 W
Berkeley, Vale of V 42 51.43 N 2.25 W
Berkeley Heights 210 40.41 N 74.26 W
Berkeley Hills 279b 40.32 N 80.00 W
Berkeley Hills ⋏[2] 282 37.54 N 122.16 W
Berkeley Plantation ⊥ 208 37.19 N 77.10 W
Berkeley Springs 188 39.37 N 78.13 W
Berkhamsted 260 51.46 N 0.35 W
Berkheim 58 48.02 N 10.04 E
Berkley, Ma., U.S. 207 41.50 N 71.05 W
Berkley, Mi., U.S. 281 42.30 N 83.11 W
Berkner Island I 9 79.30 S 49.30 W
Berks □[6] 208 40.20 N 75.50 W
Berkshire, Ma., U.S. 207 42.30 N 73.11 W
Berkshire, N.Y., U.S. 210 42.18 N 76.11 W
Berkshire □[6], Eng., U.K. 42 51.30 N 1.20 W
Berkshire □[6], Ma., U.S. 207 42.27 N 73.15 W
Berkshire Downs ⋏[1] 42 51.33 N 1.24 W
Berkshire Hills ⋏[2] 207 42.20 N 73.10 W
Berlaar 56 51.07 N 4.39 E
Berlaimont 50 50.12 N 3.49 E
Berland ≃ 182 54.01 N 116.50 W
Berlanga de Duero 34 41.28 N 2.51 W
Berlenga I 34 39.25 N 9.30 W
Berlengas ≃ 250 5.39 S 42.19 W
Berlevåg 24 70.51 N 29.06 E
Berlicum 52 51.42 N 5.23 E
Berlikum 52 53.15 N 5.39 E
Berlin (West), B.R.D. 54 52.31 N 13.24 E
Berlin (West), B.R.D. 264a 52.31 N 13.24 E
Berlin (Ost), D.D.R. 54 52.30 N 13.25 E
Berlin (Ost), D.D.R. 264a 52.30 N 13.25 E
Berlin, S. Afr. 158 32.54 S 27.35 E
Berlin, Ct., U.S. 207 41.37 N 72.44 W
Berlin, Md., U.S. 208 38.19 N 75.13 W
Berlin, Ma., U.S. 207 42.22 N 71.38 W
Berlin, N.H., U.S. 188 44.28 N 71.11 W
Berlin, N.J., U.S. 208 39.47 N 74.55 W
Berlin, N.Y., U.S. 210 42.42 N 73.23 W
Berlin, Oh., U.S. 214 40.34 N 81.48 W
Berlin, Pa., U.S. 188 39.55 N 78.57 W
Berlin, Wi., U.S. 190 43.58 N 88.56 W
Berlin □[5] 264a 52.33 N 13.30 E
Berlin, Mount ∧ 9 76.03 S 135.52 W
Berlin Center 214 41.01 N 80.57 W
Berlinchen 54 53.13 N 12.34 E
Berliner Brücke ◆[5] 263 51.27 N 6.47 E
Berliner Mauer (Berlin Wall) ⊥ 264a 52.35 N 13.22 E
Berlinguet Inlet c 176 71.10 N 85.35 W
Berlin Heights 214 41.20 N 82.30 W
Berlin-Ichthyosaur State Park ♦ 204 38.51 N 117.35 W
Berlin Lake ⊜[1] 214 41.00 N 81.00 W
Berlin Mountain ∧ 210 42.42 N 73.17 W
Berlin Park ♦ 285 39.47 N 74.57 W
Berlin-Schönefeld, Flughafen ⊠ 54 52.23 N 13.31 E
Berlinsville 210 40.47 N 75.35 W
Berlin-Tegel, Flughafen ⊠ 54 52.34 N 13.18 E
Berlin-Tempelhof, Flughafen ⊠ 54 52.29 N 13.25 E
Bermagui 166 36.25 S 150.04 E
Bermamyt, gora ∧ 84 43.41 N 42.27 E
Bermejillo 232 25.53 N 103.37 W
Bermejo 252 31.37 S 67.39 W
Bermejo ≃, Arg. 252 31.52 S 67.22 W
Bermejo ≃, S.A. 252 26.51 S 58.23 W
Bermejo, Paso de)(252 32.50 S 70.05 W
Bermen, Lac ⊜ 176 53.35 N 68.55 W
Bermeo 34 43.26 N 2.43 W
Bermillo de Sayago 34 41.22 N 6.06 W
Bermo 124 23.47 N 85.57 E
Bermondsey ◆[8] 260 51.30 N 0.04 W
Bermuda □[2], N.A. 230 32.20 N 64.45 W
Bermuda □[2], N.A. 240a 32.20 N 64.45 W
Bermuda Rise ✦[3] 16 32.30 N 65.00 W
Bermudes → Bermuda □[2] 240a 32.20 N 64.45 W
Bermudian Creek ≃ 208 40.01 N 76.55 W
Bern (Berne) 58 46.57 N 7.26 E
Bern (Berne) □[3] 58 46.55 N 7.35 E
Bern, Flughafen ⊠ 58 46.55 N 7.30 E
Berna → Bern 58 46.57 N 7.26 E
Bernabéu, Estadio ♦ 266a 40.27 N 3.41 W
Bernal ◆[8] 258 34.42 S 58.17 W
Bernalda 68 40.24 N 16.41 E
Bernalillo 200 35.18 N 106.33 W
Bernam ≃ 114 3.48 N 100.57 E
Bernardston 207 42.40 N 72.33 W
Bernardsville 210 40.43 N 74.34 W
Bernasconi 252 37.54 S 63.43 W
Bernate 266b 45.29 N 8.49 E
Bernau am Chiemsee 64 47.48 N 12.22 E
Bernau bei Berlin 54 52.40 N 13.35 E
Bernauer Heide ◆[3] 264a 52.43 N 13.30 E
Bernaville 50 50.08 N 2.10 E
Bernay 50 49.06 N 0.36 E
Bernbeuren 58 47.44 N 10.46 E
Bernburg 54 51.48 N 11.44 E
Berndorf 61 47.57 N 16.08 E
Berne, B.R.D. 52 53.11 N 8.29 E
Berne → Bern, Schw. 58 46.57 N 7.26 E
Berne, In., U.S. 216 40.39 N 84.57 W
Berne, N.Y., U.S. 210 42.38 N 74.08 W
Berneburg 56 51.04 N 9.53 E
Berner Alpen ⋏ 58 46.30 N 7.30 E
Berneray I 46 57.43 N 7.12 W
Berneval-le-Grand 50 49.57 N 1.12 E
Berngardovka 265a 60.01 N 30.36 E
Bernhardina 158 27.53 S 28.40 E
Bernhards Bay 210 43.15 N 75.56 W
Bernhardsthal 61 48.41 N 16.52 E
Bernice 194 32.49 N 92.39 W
Bernie 194 36.40 N 89.58 W
Bernier Bay c 176 71.00 N 87.30 W
Bernier Island I 162 24.52 S 113.08 E
Bernina ⋏ 58 46.22 N 9.50 E
Bernina, Passo del)(58 46.24 N 10.03 E
Bernina, Piz ∧ 58 46.21 N 9.51 E
Bernisdale 46 57.27 N 6.24 W
Bernkastel-Kues 56 49.55 N 7.04 E
Bernried 64 47.52 N 11.17 E
Bernsbach 54 50.34 N 12.46 E
Bernsdorf 54 51.22 N 14.04 E
Bernsfelden 56 49.34 N 9.53 E
Bernstadt, D.D.R. 54 51.03 N 14.50 E
Bernstadt → Bierutów, Pol. 30 51.08 N 17.32 E
Bernstein → Pełczyce 30 53.03 N 15.18 E
Bernville 208 40.26 N 76.07 W
Bero ≃ 152 15.10 S 12.09 E
Beroga 114 2.56 N 101.55 E
Beroldingen ⊥ 58 46.55 N 8.36 E
Berolzheim 56 49.28 N 9.32 E
Beromünster 58 47.12 N 8.11 E
Berón de Astrada 252 27.33 S 57.32 W
Beror Ḥayil 132 31.33 N 34.38 E
Beroroha 157b 21.41 S 45.10 E
Ber'ostovica 76 53.07 N 23.58 E
Beroun 30 49.58 N 14.04 E
Berounka ≃ 30 50.00 N 14.24 E
Berovo 38 41.42 N 22.51 E
Berowra 170 33.37 S 151.09 E
Ber'oza, S.S.S.R. 76 52.32 N 24.59 E
Ber'oza, S.S.S.R. 78 51.44 N 33.52 E
Ber'ozno 78 51.00 N 26.45 E
Ber'ožnoje 76 59.55 N 39.17 E
Ber'ozovaja ≃ 80 48.31 N 41.03 E
Ber'ozovaja Rudka 78 50.19 N 32.14 E
Ber'ozovka, S.S.S.R. 24 65.00 N 56.26 E
Ber'ozovka, S.S.S.R. 76 53.26 N 38.53 E
Ber'ozovka, S.S.S.R. 76 53.43 N 25.30 E
Ber'ozovka, S.S.S.R. 78 47.49 N 32.28 E
Ber'ozovka, S.S.S.R. 78 45.35 N 33.20 E
Ber'ozovka, S.S.S.R. 78 47.12 N 30.55 E
Ber'ozovka, S.S.S.R. 80 52.06 N 45.07 E
Ber'ozovka, S.S.S.R. 80 51.11 N 53.16 E
Ber'ozovka, S.S.S.R. 86 59.35 N 56.02 E
Ber'ozovka, S.S.S.R. 86 51.51 N 82.58 E
Ber'ozovka, S.S.S.R. 86 57.37 N 57.18 E
Ber'ozovka, S.S.S.R. 86 56.03 N 93.07 E
Ber'ozovka, S.S.S.R. 86 54.02 N 76.35 E
Ber'ozovka, S.S.S.R. 86 59.24 N 82.38 E
Ber'ozovka, S.S.S.R. 88 57.46 N 116.09 E
Ber'ozovka, S.S.S.R. 89 50.35 N 127.52 E
Ber'ozovka, S.S.S.R. 265a 59.56 N 30.49 E
Ber'ozovo, S.S.S.R. 74 63.56 N 65.02 E
Ber'ozovo, S.S.S.R. 78 51.35 N 27.20 E
Ber'ozovo, S.S.S.R. 80 51.56 N 48.28 E
Ber'ozovo, S.S.S.R. 82 54.03 N 36.24 E
Ber'ozovo, S.S.S.R. 82 54.19 N 38.17 E
Ber'ozovskaja 80 50.16 N 43.59 E
Ber'ozovskij 86 55.39 N 86.16 E
Ber'ozovskij R'adok 76 58.06 N 34.29 E
Ber'ozovskoje 86 55.50 N 89.36 E
Berra 64 44.59 N 11.58 E
Berras, Arroyo los ≃ 288 34.34 S 58.40 W
Berre ≃ 62 44.24 N 4.40 E
Berre, Étang de c 62 43.27 N 5.08 E
Berrechid 148 33.17 N 7.35 W
Berre-des-Alpes 62 43.50 N 7.19 E
Berre-L'Étang 62 43.28 N 5.11 E
Ber Remad, Oued V 148 31.45 N 1.10 E
Berri 166 34.17 S 140.36 E
Berridale 171b 36.22 S 148.50 E
Berriedale 46 58.11 N 3.29 W
Berrien □[6] 216 41.59 N 86.30 W
Berrien Springs 216 41.56 N 86.20 W
Berrigan 166 35.40 S 145.49 E
Berrima 170 34.30 S 150.20 E
Berriozábal 234 16.48 N 93.16 W
Berriyyane 148 32.50 N 3.46 E
Berrouaghia 34 36.08 N 2.55 E
Berrugosa Point › 116 10.23 N 125.33 E
Berry, Austl. 170 34.47 S 150.42 E
Berry, Al., U.S. 194 33.39 N 87.36 W
Berry, Ky., U.S. 218 38.31 N 84.23 W
Berry □[9] 50 47.20 N 2.10 E
Berry, Canal du ≋ 50 47.17 N 1.25 E
Berry-au-Bac 50 49.24 N 3.54 E
Berry Creek ≃, Ab., Can. 182 50.50 N 111.36 W
Berry Creek ≃, Tx., U.S. 222 30.40 N 97.36 W
Berryessa, Lake ⊜[1] 226 38.35 N 122.14 W
Berryessa Creek ≃ 282 37.24 N 121.53 W
Berryessa Peak ∧ 226 38.40 N 122.11 W
Berry Head › 42 50.24 N 3.29 W
Berry Islands II 238 25.34 N 77.45 W
Berry Mountain ∧ 208 40.31 N 77.02 W
Berrysburg 208 40.36 N 76.49 W
Berrys Creek ≃ 276 40.47 N 74.05 W
Berryville 194 36.21 N 93.34 W
Beršad' 78 48.23 N 29.30 E
Berseba 156 26.00 S 17.46 E
Bersenbrück 52 52.33 N 7.56 E
Bersut 80 55.32 N 50.54 E
Berta ≃ 130 41.09 N 41.53 E
Bertam 114 5.09 N 102.03 E
Berté, Lac ⊜ 186 50.48 N 68.30 W
Bertha 198 46.16 N 95.03 W
Berthåga 40 59.52 N 17.35 E
Berthelsdorf 54 51.05 N 14.13 E
Berthier □[6] 206 46.30 N 73.45 W
Berthierville 206 46.05 N 73.10 W
Berthold 198 48.18 N 101.44 W
Berthoud 200 40.18 N 105.04 W
Berthoud Pass)(200 39.45 N 105.45 W
Bertincourt 50 50.05 N 2.59 E
Bertinoro 66 44.09 N 12.08 E
Bertioga 256 23.51 S 46.09 W
Bertioga, Enseada da c 256 23.50 S 46.08 W
Bertkow 54 52.43 N 11.54 E
Bertlich 263 51.37 N 7.04 E
Bertogne 56 50.05 N 5.40 E

Symbols in the index entries represent the broad categories identified in the key at the right. Symbols with superior numbers (⋏[1]) identify subcategories (see complete key on page *I · 1).*

Symbole im Register stellen die rechts im Schlüssel erklärten Kategorien dar. Symbole mit hochgestellten Ziffern (⋏[1]) bezeichnen Unterabteilungen einer Kategorie (vgl. vollständiger Schlüssel auf Seite *I · 1).*

Los símbolos incluídos en el texto del índice representan las grandes categorias identificadas con la clave a la derecha. Los símbolos con numeros en su parte superior (⋏[1]) identifican las subcategorías (véase la clave completa en la página *I · 1).*

Les symboles de l'index représentent les catégories indiquées dans la légende à droite. Les symboles suivis d'un indice (⋏[1]) représentent des sous-catégories (voir légende complète à la page *I · 1).*

Os símbolos incluídos no texto do índice representam as grandes categorias identificadas com a chave à direita. Os símbolos com números em sua parte superior (⋏[1]) identificam as subcategorias (veja-se a chave completa à página *I · 1).*

	English	Deutsch	Español	Français	Português
∧	Mountain	Berg	Montaña	Montagne	Montanha
⋏	Mountains	Gebirge	Montañas	Montagnes	Montanhas
)(	Pass	Paß	Paso	Col	Passo
V	Valley, Canyon	Tal, Cañon	Valle, Cañón	Vallée, Canyon	Vale, Canhão
≚	Plain	Ebene	Llano	Plaine	Planície
›	Cape	Kap	Cabo	Cap	Cabo
I	Island	Insel	Isla	Île	Ilha
II	Islands	Inseln	Islas	Îles	Ilhas
⊥	Other Topographic Features	Andere Topographische Objekte	Otros Elementos Topográficos	Autres données topographiques	Outros acidentes topográficos

ESPAÑOL

Nombre	Página	Lat.°′	Long.°′ W = Oeste
Bertolínia	250	7.38 S	43.57 W
Bertoua	152	4.35 N	13.41 E
Bertram	196	30.45 N	98.03 W
Bertrand, Mi., U.S.	216	41.46 N	86.15 W
Bertrand, Ne., U.S.	198	40.31 N	99.38 W
Bertrix	56	49.51 N	5.15 E
Bertry	50	50.05 N	3.27 E
Beru I	14	1.20 S	176.00 E
Beruas	114	4.30 N	100.47 E
Beruri	246	3.54 S	61.22 W
Berville	214	42.55 N	82.53 W
Berville-sur-Mer	50	49.26 N	0.22 E
Berwang	58	47.24 N	10.45 E
Berwick, Austl.	169	38.02 S	145.21 E
Berwick, N.S., Can.	186	45.03 N	64.44 W
Berwick, La., U.S.	194	29.41 N	91.13 W
Berwick, Me., U.S.	188	43.15 N	70.51 W
Berwick, Pa., U.S.	210	41.03 N	76.14 W
Berwick-upon-Tweed	44	55.46 N	2.00 W
Berwyn, Il., U.S.	216	41.51 N	87.47 W
Berwyn, Pa., U.S.	208	40.02 N	75.26 W
Berwyn ⋏	42	52.53 N	3.24 W
Berwyn Heights	284c	38.59 N	76.54 W
Bērze ≃	76	56.41 N	23.37 E
Berzé-la-Ville	58	46.22 N	4.42 E
Berz-Macomb Airport ⊠	281	42.40 N	82.58 W
Bès ≃	62	44.08 N	6.14 E
Besalampy	157b	16.45 S	44.30 E
Besana in Brianza	62	45.42 N	9.17 E
Besançon	58	47.15 N	6.02 E
Besani	124	24.08 N	80.17 E
Besar, Gunong ∧, Malay.	114	2.30 N	103.10 E
Besar, Gunong ∧, Malay.	114	5.10 N	101.18 E
Besar, Gunung ∧	112	2.43 S	115.37 E
Besar, Pulau I	115b	8.28 S	122.22 E
Besar Hantu, Gunong ∧	114	3.12 N	102.02 E
Besaya ≃	34	43.21 N	4.04 W
Besbes	36	36.42 N	7.51 E
Besed' ≃	76	52.38 N	31.09 E
Besedino	78	51.42 N	36.28 E
Besedy	265b	55.37 N	37.47 E
Besenfeld	56	48.35 N	8.25 E
Bešenkoviči	76	55.03 N	29.27 E
Beserah	114	3.52 N	103.22 E
Besigheim	56	49.00 N	9.08 E
Besikama	112	9.36 S	124.57 E
Beşiktaş ◆[8]	267b	41.03 N	29.01 E
Beşiri	130	37.55 N	41.18 E
Besitang	114	4.02 N	98.12 E
Beškent	128	38.49 N	65.39 E
Beskid Mountains ⋏	30	49.40 N	20.00 E
Beşkonak	130	37.08 N	31.12 E
Beskra	148	34.51 N	5.44 E
Beskra □[5]	148	34.00 N	6.00 E
Beškube	85	39.50 N	68.18 E
Beskudnikovo ◆[8]	265b	55.52 N	37.34 E
Beslan	84	43.12 N	44.33 E
Beslenej	84	44.14 N	41.44 E
Besnard Lake ⊜	184	55.24 N	106.05 W
Besni	130	37.41 N	37.52 E
Besor, Naḥal V	132	31.28 N	34.22 E
Besós ≃	266d	41.25 N	2.04 E
Besozzo	62	45.51 N	8.39 E
Besp'atovo	82	54.45 N	38.54 E
Beşpınar, Tür.	130	37.51 N	41.36 E
Beşpınar, Tür.	130	41.09 N	35.14 E
Besputa ≃	82	54.50 N	37.58 E
Bessacarr	44	53.30 N	1.04 W
Bessancourt	261	49.02 N	2.13 E
Bessans	62	45.19 N	7.00 E
Bessarabia □[9]	78	47.00 N	28.30 E
Bessarabka, S.S.S.R.	78	46.20 N	28.58 E
Bessarabka, S.S.S.R.	86	53.37 N	73.17 E
Bessaz, gora ∧	85	43.49 N	68.40 E
Bessbrook	48	54.12 N	6.25 W
Besse, B.R.D.	56	51.13 N	9.23 E
Besse, Nig.	150	11.15 N	4.30 E
Bessèges	62	44.17 N	4.06 E
Bessemer, Al., U.S.	194	33.24 N	86.57 W
Bessemer, Mi., U.S.	190	46.28 N	90.03 W
Bessemer, Pa., U.S.	214	40.58 N	80.29 W
Bessemer City	192	35.17 N	81.17 W
Besser	41	55.52 N	10.39 E
Bessé-sur-Braye	50	47.50 N	0.45 E
Bessheim	26	61.31 N	8.51 E
Besshiyama	96	33.50 N	133.23 E
Bessho	270	34.27 N	135.31 E
Bessonovka	80	53.18 N	45.03 E
Best	52	51.31 N	5.24 E
Best'ach	74	61.52 N	129.55 E
Bestamak, S.S.S.R.	86	49.43 N	55.07 E
Bestamak, S.S.S.R.	86	49.13 N	78.21 E
Beštau, gora ∧	84	44.06 N	43.01 E
Besten	263	51.39 N	6.54 E
Bestensee	54	52.15 N	13.37 E
Bestfield	285	39.43 N	75.36 W
Bestobe	86	52.30 N	73.05 E
Beštor, gora ∧	85	42.03 N	70.50 E
Bestuževo	24	61.37 N	43.58 E
Bestwig	52	51.22 N	8.24 E
Besuki	115a	7.45 S	113.41 E
Besut ≃	114	5.48 N	102.35 E
Beswick Aboriginal Reserve ◆[4]	164	14.30 S	133.10 E
Betā	272b	22.55 N	88.14 E
Betafo	157b	19.50 S	46.51 E
Betāgi	126	22.25 N	90.11 E
Bet Alfa	132	32.31 N	35.26 E
Beta Main Canal ≊	226	36.34 N	120.11 W
Betamba	152	2.13 S	21.23 E
Betang Melaka	114	2.28 N	102.25 E
Betano	112	9.10 S	125.43 E
Betanzos, Bol.	248	19.34 S	65.27 W
Betanzos, Esp.	34	43.17 N	8.12 W
Betanzos, Ría de ⊂[1]	34	43.23 N	8.15 W
Betaré Oya	152	5.36 N	14.05 E
Betarsjön ⊜	26	63.44 N	16.52 E
Bet Bet Creek ≃	169	36.52 S	143.52 E
Betbetti	140	15.06 N	24.12 E
Betchworth	260	51.14 N	0.16 W
Bet Dagan	132	32.00 N	34.50 E
Bete Hor	144	11.37 N	39.02 E
Betém	256	22.52 S	44.17 W
Bétera	34	39.35 N	0.27 W
Bétérou	150	9.12 N	2.16 E
Bet Guvrin	132	31.36 N	34.54 E
Bet Ha'arava	132	31.48 N	35.32 E
Bethal	158	26.27 S	29.28 E
Bethalto	219	38.54 N	90.02 W
Bethanien	156	26.32 S	17.11 E
Bethanien □[5]	156	26.30 S	17.00 E
Bethany, Ct., U.S.	207	41.25 N	72.59 W
Bethany, Il., U.S.	219	39.38 N	88.44 W
Bethany, Mo., U.S.	194	40.16 N	94.01 W
Bethany, N.Y., U.S.	210	42.55 N	78.08 W
Bethany, Ok., U.S.	196	35.31 N	97.37 W
Bethany, Pa., U.S.	210	41.37 N	75.21 W
Bethany, W.V., U.S.	214	40.12 N	80.33 W
Bethany Reservoir ⊜[1]	226	37.47 N	121.37 W
Bet HaShitta	132	32.33 N	35.26 E
Bethel, Ak., U.S.	180	60.48 N	161.46 W
Bethel, Ct., U.S.	207	41.22 N	73.24 W
Bethel, De., U.S.	208	38.27 N	75.21 W
Bethel, Ky., U.S.	218	38.14 N	83.52 W
Bethel, Me., U.S.	188	44.24 N	70.47 W
Bethel, Mo., U.S.	219	39.52 N	92.01 W
Bethel, N.Y., U.S.	210	41.41 N	74.52 W
Bethel, N.C., U.S.	192	35.48 N	77.22 W
Bethel, Oh., U.S.	218	38.57 N	84.04 W
Bethel, Pa., U.S.	208	40.28 N	76.18 W
Bethel, Wa., U.S.	224	47.32 N	122.38 W
Bethel Acres	196	35.19 N	97.00 W
Bethel Island	226	38.01 N	121.39 W
Bethel Manor	208	37.06 N	76.25 W
Bethel Park	214	40.18 N	80.02 W
Bethelsdorp	158	33.52 S	25.34 E
Bethel Springs	194	35.14 N	88.36 W
Béthencourt-sur-Mer	50	50.05 N	1.30 E

FRANÇAIS

Nom	Page	Lat.°′	Long.°′ W = Ouest
Bethersden	42	51.08 N	0.48 E
Bethesda, Wales, U.K.	44	53.11 N	4.03 W
Bethesda, Md., U.S.	208	38.58 N	77.06 W
Bethesda, Oh., U.S.	188	40.00 N	81.04 W
Bethesdaweg	158	31.55 S	24.45 E
Bethford	284a	42.48 N	78.48 W
Bethgate	284b	39.18 N	76.51 W
Béthisy-Saint-Pierre	50	49.18 N	2.49 E
Bethlehem → Bayt Laḥm, Isr. Occ	132	31.43 N	35.12 E
Bethlehem, S. Afr.	158	27.10 S	24.00 E
Bethlehem, S. Afr.	158	28.15 S	28.15 E
Bethlehem, Ct., U.S.	207	41.38 N	73.12 W
Bethlehem, In., U.S.	218	38.32 N	85.25 W
Bethlehem, Ky., U.S.	218	38.24 N	85.04 W
Bethlehem, Pa., U.S.	210	40.37 N	75.22 W
Bethlehem, W.V., U.S.	188	40.02 N	80.41 W
Bethlehem Center	210	42.40 N	73.42 W
Bethlehem Steel Corporation ᵾ[3], Md., U.S.	284b	39.13 N	76.29 W
Bethlehem Steel Corporation (Lackawanna Plant) ᵾ[3], N.Y., U.S.	284a	42.49 N	78.52 W
Bethnal Green ◆[8]	260	51.32 N	0.03 W
Bethoncourt	58	47.32 N	6.48 E
Bethpage	210	40.44 N	73.28 W
Bethpage State Park ♠	210	40.45 N	73.27 W
Bethulie	158	30.32 S	25.59 E
Bethune, Sk., Can.	184	50.43 N	105.08 W
Béthune, Fr.	50	50.32 N	2.38 E
Bethune, S.C., U.S.	192	34.24 N	80.20 W
Béthune ≃	50	49.53 N	1.09 E
Beticos, Sistemas ⋏	34	37.00 N	4.00 W
Betijoque	246	9.23 N	70.44 W
Betil	126	24.14 N	89.43 E
Betio	174t	1.21 N	172.56 E
Betioky	157b	23.42 S	44.22 E
Betis ≃	114	4.53 N	101.48 E
Betlica	76	54.01 N	33.57 E
Betna ≃	126	22.34 N	89.12 E
Bet Netofa, Biq'at ≌	132	32.49 N	35.19 E
Betnoti	126	21.44 N	86.51 E
Beton-Bazoches	50	48.42 N	3.15 E
Betong, Malay.	112	1.24 N	111.31 E
Betong, Thai	110	5.45 N	101.05 E
Betoota	166	25.42 S	140.44 E
Bétou	152	3.03 N	18.31 E
Betpak-Dala ◆[2]	86	46.00 N	70.00 E
Betroka	157b	23.16 S	46.06 E
Betsham	260	51.25 N	0.19 E
Bet Sh'ean	132	32.30 N	35.30 E
Bet She'arim, Horbat ⊥	132	32.42 N	35.08 E
Bet Shemesh	132	31.45 N	35.00 E
Betsiamites	186	48.56 N	68.38 W
Betsiamites ≃	186	48.56 N	68.38 W
Betsiamites, Barrage ◆[6]	186	49.22 N	69.47 W
Betsiamites, Pointe de ›	186	48.55 N	68.37 W
Betsiamites, Réserve indienne de ◆[4]	186	49.05 N	68.37 W
Betsiboka ≃	157b	16.03 S	46.36 E
Betsie, Point ›	190	44.42 N	86.16 W
Betsioky	157b	21.31 S	44.28 E
Betsukai	92a	43.23 N	145.17 E
Betsy Layne	192	37.33 N	82.38 W
Betsy Ross Bridge ◆[5]	285	39.59 N	75.04 W
Bette ∧	146	22.00 N	19.12 E
Bettembourg	56	49.32 N	6.02 E
Bettendorf	190	41.31 N	90.30 W
Betterton	208	39.21 N	76.03 W
Bettiah	124	26.48 N	84.30 E
Bettie	222	32.48 N	94.58 W
Bettles Field	180	66.55 N	151.30 W
Bettola	62	44.47 N	9.36 E
Bettona	66	43.01 N	12.29 E
Bettrath ◆[8]	263	51.13 N	6.26 E
Bettsville	214	41.14 N	83.14 W
Bettyhill	46	58.32 N	4.14 W
Betty's Bay	158	34.22 S	18.52 E
Betūl	124	21.55 N	77.54 E
Betumbe-Bongo	152	2.11 S	18.46 E
Betung, Indon.	112	1.52 S	103.16 E
Betung, Indon.	112	2.50 S	104.14 E
Betuwe ◆[1]	52	51.55 N	5.30 E
Betwa ≃	124	25.55 N	80.12 E
Betws-y-Coed	44	53.05 N	3.48 W
Betz	50	49.09 N	2.57 E
Betz ≃	50	48.09 N	2.45 E
Betzdorf	56	50.47 N	7.53 E
Betzenstein	60	49.41 N	11.25 E
Béu	152	6.14 S	15.28 E
Beucha	54	51.19 N	12.34 E
Beugneux	50	49.14 N	3.25 E
Beuil	62	44.06 N	6.59 E
Beulah, Austl.	166	35.56 S	142.26 E
Beulah, Co., U.S.	200	38.04 N	104.59 W
Beulah, Mi., U.S.	190	44.37 N	86.05 W
Beulah, Ms., U.S.	194	33.47 N	90.58 W
Beulah, N.D., U.S.	198	47.15 N	101.46 W
Beulah, Lake ⊜	216	42.49 N	88.23 W
Beulah Beach	214	41.25 N	82.22 W
Beulah Reservoir ⊜[1]	202	43.56 N	118.09 W
Beulaville	192	34.55 N	77.46 W
Beult ≃	260	51.14 N	0.25 E
Beure	58	47.12 N	6.00 E
Beureunun	114	5.18 N	95.59 E
Beuron	58	48.03 N	8.58 E
Beuthen → Bytom	30	50.22 N	18.54 E
Beuvron ≃, Fr.	50	47.29 N	1.15 E
Beuvron ≃, Fr.	50	47.28 N	3.31 E
Beuvronne ≃	261	48.56 N	2.44 E
Beuvry	50	50.31 N	2.41 E
Beuzeville	50	49.20 N	0.21 E
Bevagna	66	42.56 N	12.36 E
Bevensen	52	53.05 N	10.34 E
Bever ≃	52	52.01 N	7.46 E
Bevera ≃	62	43.49 N	7.34 E
Beveren	50	51.13 N	4.15 E
B. Everett Jordan Lake ⊜[1]	192	35.45 N	79.00 W
Beverino	62	44.14 N	9.47 E
Beverley, Austl.	168a	32.06 S	116.56 E
Beverley, Eng., U.K.	44	53.52 N	0.26 W
Beverley Minster ᵾ[1]	44	53.50 N	0.27 W
Beverley Springs	162	16.43 S	125.28 E
Beverlo	56	51.05 N	5.12 E
Beverly, Ma., U.S.	207	42.33 N	70.52 W
Beverly, N.J., U.S.	208	40.03 N	74.55 W
Beverly, Tx., U.S.	222	31.30 N	97.10 W
Beverly ◆[8]	278	41.43 N	87.41 W
Beverly Farms, Md., U.S.	284c	39.04 N	77.11 W
Beverly Farms, Ma., U.S.	283	42.34 N	70.49 W
Beverly Harbor ⊂	283	42.32 N	70.53 W
Beverly Hills, Austl.	274a	33.57 S	151.05 E
Beverly Hills, Ca., U.S.	228	34.04 N	118.23 W
Beverly Hills, Fl., U.S.	220	28.56 N	82.28 W
Beverly Hills, Mi., U.S.	216	42.31 N	83.13 W
Beverly Lake ⊜	176	64.36 N	100.30 W
Beverly Municipal Airport ⊠	283	42.35 N	70.55 W
Beverly Run ≃	208	37.55 N	77.11 W
Beverly Shores	216	41.41 N	86.58 W
Bevern	52	51.51 N	9.29 E
Beverstausee ⊜[1]	263	51.09 N	7.23 E
Beverstedt	52	53.26 N	8.49 E
Beverungen	52	51.39 N	9.22 E
Beverwijk	52	52.28 N	4.40 E
Bevier	194	39.45 N	92.34 W
Bevin, Lac ⊜	206	45.57 N	74.35 W

PORTUGUÊS

Nome	Página	Lat.°′	Long.°′ W = Oeste
Bevoalavo	157b	25.13 S	45.26 E
Bewani	164	3.02 S	141.10 E
Bewani Mountains ⋏	164	3.10 S	141.25 E
Bewār	124	27.13 N	79.18 E
Bewdley, On., Can.	212	44.05 N	78.19 W
Bewdley, Eng., U.K.	42	52.22 N	2.19 W
Bewl Bridge Reservoir ⊜[1]	42	51.04 N	0.24 E
Bex	58	46.15 N	7.01 E
Bexhill	42	50.50 N	0.29 E
Bexley, Austl.	274a	33.57 S	151.08 E
Bexley, Oh., U.S.	218	39.58 N	82.56 W
Bexley ◆[8]	260	51.26 N	0.10 E
Beyazköy	130	41.21 N	27.42 E
Beybach ≃	56	50.13 N	7.23 E
Beyçayırı	130	40.15 N	26.55 E
Beycuma	130	41.19 N	31.59 E
Bey Dağları ⋏	130	36.40 N	30.15 E
Beydagları Olimpos Milli Parkı ♠	130	36.40 N	30.25 E
Beydili	130	40.10 N	31.01 E
Beyenburg ◆[8]	263	51.15 N	7.18 E
Beykoz ◆[8]	267b	41.08 N	29.05 E
Beyla	150	8.41 N	8.37 W
Beylerbeyi ◆[8]	267b	41.03 N	29.03 E
Beylikahır	130	39.42 N	31.13 E
Beylul	144	13.10 N	42.26 E
Beynes	261	48.51 N	1.53 E
Beynes-Thiverval, Aérodrome de ⊠	261	48.51 N	1.54 E
Beyoğlu ◆[8]	267b	41.02 N	28.59 E
Beypazarı	130	40.10 N	31.56 E
Beypınarı	130	39.31 N	37.44 E
Beypore	122	11.11 N	75.49 E
Beyra	144	6.57 N	47.19 E
Beyrouth → Bayrūt	130	33.53 N	35.30 E
Beyşehir	130	37.41 N	31.43 E
Beyşehir Gölü ⊜	130	37.40 N	31.30 E
Beytüşşebap	128	37.34 N	43.10 E
Bezaha	157b	23.30 S	44.31 E
Bežanickaja vozvyšennost' ⋏[1]	76	56.54 N	29.20 E
Bežanicy	76	56.58 N	29.53 E
Bezau	58	47.23 N	9.54 E
Bezavona ∧	157b	15.02 S	49.52 E
Bezdež	76	52.19 N	25.18 E
Bezděz ∧	54	50.32 N	14.43 E
Bezděz ⊥	54	50.32 N	14.46 E
Bèze	58	47.28 N	5.16 E
Bežeck	76	57.47 N	36.39 E
Bežeckij Verch ⋏[1]	76	57.36 N	36.54 E
Bezenčuk	80	52.59 N	49.26 E
Bezerra ≃	255	13.16 S	47.31 W
Bezerros	250	8.14 S	35.45 W
Beẓet	132	33.05 N	35.08 E
Béziers	32	43.21 N	3.15 E
Bezmein	128	38.05 N	58.12 E
Bezmenšur	80	56.29 N	51.17 E
Bezons	261	48.56 N	2.13 E
Bežta	84	42.08 N	46.08 E
Bezwada → Vijayawāda	122	16.31 N	80.37 E
Bezym'anka	80	49.56 N	43.15 E
Bezym'annaja	80	51.20 N	46.26 E
Bezymennoje	83	47.06 N	37.56 E
Bezzecca	64	45.55 N	10.43 E
Bezzubovo	82	55.27 N	38.55 E
Bhabānipur, India	272b	22.57 N	88.27 E
Bhabānipur, India	272b	22.56 N	88.13 E
Bhabhua	124	25.03 N	83.37 E
Bhābta	126	23.59 N	88.15 E
Bhadarwāh	123	32.59 N	75.43 E
Bhadaur	123	30.29 N	75.19 E
Bhādgāon → Bhaktapur	124	27.42 N	85.27 E
Bhadohi	124	25.25 N	82.34 E
Bhādra	123	29.07 N	75.10 E
Bhadra ≃[1]	126	22.19 N	89.31 E
Bhadrāchalam	122	17.40 N	80.53 E
Bhadrak	120	21.03 N	86.30 E
Bhadrapur	124	26.32 N	88.06 E
Bhadra Reservoir ⊜[1]	122	13.40 N	75.35 E
Bhadrāvati	122	13.52 N	75.43 E
Bhadreswar	126	22.50 N	88.21 E
Bhādua	272b	22.41 N	88.12 E
Bhāg	120	29.02 N	67.49 E
Bhagaiya	124	25.12 N	87.29 E
Bhāgalpur	124	25.15 N	87.00 E
Bhāgīrathi ≃, India	124	30.08 N	78.35 E
Bhāgīrathi ≃, India	126	23.25 N	88.23 E
Bhagirathpur	126	24.05 N	88.29 E
Bhagwānpur	126	22.07 N	87.45 E
Bhainsa	122	19.06 N	77.58 E
Bhāi Pheru	123	31.12 N	73.57 E
Bhairab ≃[1]	126	22.51 N	89.34 E
Bhairab Bāzār	120	24.04 N	90.58 E
Bhairhawā	124	27.31 N	83.24 E
Bhaironghāti	120	31.01 N	78.53 E
Bhakkar	123	31.38 N	71.04 E
Bhākra Dam ◆[6]	123	31.24 N	76.30 E
Bhaktapur	124	27.42 N	85.27 E
Bhal	272c	19.11 N	73.08 E
Bhālki	122	18.02 N	77.13 E
Bhalswa ◆[8]	272a	28.44 N	77.10 E
Bhalwāl	123	32.16 N	72.54 E
Bhamdūn	132	33.48 N	35.39 E
Bhamo	110	24.16 N	97.14 E
Bhandāra	120	21.10 N	79.39 E
Bhandārdaha	272b	22.37 N	88.13 E
Bhandāria	126	22.29 N	90.04 E
Bhānder	124	25.44 N	78.45 E
Bhānder Plateau ⋏[1]	124	24.10 N	80.20 E
Bhāndup ◆[8]	272c	19.09 N	72.57 E
Bhānga	126	23.22 N	89.59 E
Bhāngar	126	22.31 N	88.37 E
Bhāngar Kāta Khāl ≃	272b	22.31 N	88.33 E
Bhanvad	120	21.56 N	69.47 E
Bhārat → India □[1]	118	20.00 N	77.00 E
Bharatpur, India	124	27.13 N	77.29 E
Bharatpur, India	126	23.53 N	88.05 E
Bharatpur, Nepāl	124	27.14 N	84.21 E
Bharthana	124	26.45 N	79.14 E
Bharūch	120	21.42 N	72.58 E
Bhātai	126	23.36 N	89.11 E
Bhātāpāra	120	21.44 N	81.56 E
Bhātār	126	23.25 N	87.54 E
Bhatgaon → Bhaktapur	124	27.42 N	85.27 E
Bhātghar Lake ⊜[1]	122	18.12 N	73.49 E
Bhātiāpāra Ghāt	124	23.13 N	89.42 E
Bhatkal	122	13.58 N	74.34 E
Bhātpāra	126	22.52 N	88.24 E
Bhātpur	272b	22.43 N	88.25 E
Bhātsāla	126	22.33 N	90.30 E
Bhattapratāp	126	22.45 N	89.48 E
Bhattiprolu	122	16.06 N	80.47 E
Bhātua	272b	22.57 N	88.22 E
Bhaun	123	32.52 N	72.45 E
Bhaunja	272a	28.40 N	77.25 E
Bhavāni	122	11.27 N	77.41 E
Bhāvnagar	122	21.46 N	72.09 E
Bhawānīgarh	124	30.16 N	76.02 E
Bhawani Mandi	120	24.25 N	75.50 E
Bhawānipatna	122	19.54 N	83.10 E
Bhedia	126	23.36 N	87.42 E
Bheigeir, Beinn ∧[2]	46	55.44 N	6.05 W
Bhendkhal	272c	18.53 N	72.59 E
Bhera	123	32.29 N	72.55 E
Bheramara	126	24.02 N	88.58 E
Bherī □[8]	124	28.30 N	81.45 E
Bherī ≃	124	28.44 N	81.16 E
Bheula, Beinn ∧	46	56.08 N	4.58 W
Bhīkampur	272a	28.45 N	77.27 E
Bhīkangaon	120	21.52 N	75.57 E
Bhilai	120	21.13 N	81.26 E
Bhilainagar → Bhilai	120	21.13 N	81.26 E
Bhīlwāra	120	25.21 N	74.38 E
Bhīma ≃	122	16.24 N	77.18 E
Bhīmavaram	122	16.32 N	81.32 E
Bhimbar	123	32.59 N	74.04 E

Bhīmphedī	124	27.32 N	85.07 E
Bhīmpur, India	126	22.37 N	87.08 E
Bhimpur, India	272b	22.46 N	88.08 E
Bhind	124	26.34 N	78.48 E
Bhinga	124	27.43 N	81.56 E
Bhīnmāl	120	25.00 N	72.15 E
Bhiwandi	122	19.18 N	73.04 E
Bhiwāni	124	28.47 N	76.08 E
Bhoāgāchi	272b	22.57 N	88.20 E
Bhojpur	124	27.10 N	87.03 E
Bhojudih	126	23.38 N	86.27 E
Bhokardan	122	20.16 N	75.46 E
Bhola	124	22.41 N	90.39 E
Bhola ≃[1]	126	22.04 N	89.49 E
Bhongaon	124	27.15 N	79.11 E
Bhongīr	122	17.31 N	78.53 E
Bhonrāsa	124	22.59 N	76.12 E
Bhopāl	124	23.16 N	77.24 E
Bhopar	272c	19.12 N	73.05 E
Bhopura	272a	28.42 N	77.20 E
Bhoutan → Bhutan □[1]	120	27.30 N	90.30 E
Bhowali	124	29.23 N	79.31 E
Bhuāpur	272a	28.43 N	77.26 E
Bhuban	120	20.53 N	85.50 E
Bhubaneshwar	120	20.14 N	85.50 E
Bhucho	123	30.13 N	75.06 E
Bhuj	120	23.16 N	69.40 E
Bhunarheri	124	30.13 N	76.27 E
Bhunya	158	26.32 S	31.01 E
Bhusāwal	120	21.03 N	75.46 E
Bhūshana	126	23.24 N	89.40 E
Bhutali	272c	19.07 N	73.04 E
Bhutan (Druk-Yul) □[1], Asia	118	27.30 N	90.30 E
Bhutan (Druk-Yul) □[1], Asia	120	27.30 N	90.30 E
Bia ≃, Afr.	150	5.21 N	3.11 W
Biá ≃, Bra.	246	3.28 S	67.23 W
Bia, Phou ∧	110	18.59 N	103.09 E
Bīābānak	128	32.11 N	64.11 E
Biabo ≃	248	6.58 S	76.23 W
Biacesa	64	45.56 N	10.47 E
Biache-Saint-Vaast	50	50.18 N	2.57 E
Biadene	64	45.47 N	12.04 E
Biafra, Bight of ⊂[3]	134	4.00 N	8.00 E
Biak I	164	1.00 S	136.00 E
Biała	30	50.23 N	17.40 E
Biała ≃	30	50.03 N	20.55 E
Biała Piska	30	53.37 N	22.04 E
Biała Podlaska	30	52.02 N	23.06 E
Biała Podlaska □[4]	30	52.00 N	23.00 E
Biała Rawska	30	51.49 N	20.29 E
Białobrzegi	30	51.40 N	20.57 E
Białogard	30	54.01 N	16.00 E
Białowieski Park Narodowy ♠	30	52.40 N	23.50 E
Biały Bór	30	53.54 N	16.51 E
Białystok	30	53.09 N	23.09 E
Białystok □[4]	30	53.00 N	23.00 E
Bian ≃	164	8.07 S	139.56 E
Bian, Bidean nam ∧	46	56.38 N	5.02 W
Biancavilla	70	37.38 N	14.52 E
Bianchi	68	39.06 N	16.24 E
Bianco	68	38.05 N	16.09 E
Bianco, Canale ≊	64	45.02 N	11.30 E
Bianco, Capo ›	70	37.23 N	13.16 E
Bianco, Monte (Mont Blanc) ∧	62	45.50 N	6.52 E
Bian'er	102	31.14 N	101.28 E
Bianga	152	4.51 N	20.25 E
Bian'gezhuang	105	39.28 N	115.53 E
Biankouma	150	7.44 N	7.37 W
Bianlinzhen	98	37.26 N	116.32 E
Bianminchang	107	29.41 N	105.04 E
Bianniulupucun	104	41.30 N	123.42 E
Bianquanwopu	104	41.21 N	120.48 E
Bianzè	62	45.18 N	8.07 E
Biaora	124	23.55 N	76.54 E
Biaro, Pulau I	112	2.05 N	125.20 E
Biarritz	32	43.29 N	1.34 W
Biasca	58	46.22 N	8.58 E
Bias Fortes	256	21.36 S	43.46 W
Biassono	62	45.37 N	9.16 E
Biaza	86	56.38 N	78.18 E
Bibā	142	28.55 N	30.59 E
Bibai	92a	43.19 N	141.52 E
Bibala	152	14.46 S	13.21 E
Bībān	142	30.47 N	30.40 E
Bibane, Bahiret el ⊂	148	33.16 N	11.19 E
Bibanga	152	6.15 S	23.56 E
Bibban, Khawr V	140	11.00 N	32.41 E
Bibb City	192	32.30 N	84.59 W
Bibbiano	64	44.40 N	10.28 E
Bibbiena	66	43.42 N	11.49 E
Bibbona	66	43.16 N	10.35 E
Bibémi	146	9.19 N	13.53 E
Biberach	58	48.20 N	8.02 E
Biberach an der Riss	58	48.06 N	9.47 E
Biberbach	56	48.31 N	10.48 E
Biberonne ≃	261	48.59 N	2.41 E
Bibert ≃	56	49.27 N	10.59 E
Bibey ≃	34	42.24 N	7.13 W
Bibiani	150	6.28 N	2.20 W
Bībi Chīni	126	22.28 N	90.12 E
Bibione	64	45.38 N	13.00 E
Bibir'ovo	76	54.28 N	33.08 E
Biblián	246	2.42 S	78.52 W
Biblis	56	49.41 N	8.27 E
Bibo	102	29.02 N	99.20 E
Bic	186	48.22 N	68.42 W
Biča	86	57.53 N	70.37 E
Bicas	256	21.43 S	43.04 W
Bicas do Meio	256	22.31 S	45.21 W
Bicaz	38	46.54 N	26.05 E
Biccari	68	41.24 N	15.11 E
Bicester	42	51.54 N	1.09 W
Bičevinka	76	59.44 N	37.40 E
Biche, Lac la ⊜	182	54.50 N	112.03 W
Bichena	144	10.27 N	38.12 E
Bicheno	166	41.53 S	148.18 E
Bichhia	124	22.27 N	80.42 E
Bichl	64	47.43 N	11.24 E
Bichlbach	58	47.25 N	10.47 E
Bichota Canyon V	280	34.16 N	117.48 W
Biči ≃	89	52.10 N	139.50 E
Bičigt	88	47.06 N	95.05 E
Bickerstaffe	262	53.32 N	2.50 W
Bickerton, Cape ›	9	66.20 S	136.56 E
Bickerton Island I	164	13.45 S	136.12 E
Bickle Knob ∧	188	38.56 N	79.44 W
Bickley ◆[8]	260	51.24 N	0.03 E
Bicknacre, Eng., U.K.	42	51.41 N	0.35 E
Bicknacre, Eng., U.K.	260	51.42 N	0.35 E
Bicknell, In., U.S.	194	38.46 N	87.18 W
Bicknell, Ut,. U.S.	200	38.20 N	111.32 W
Bicknor	260	51.18 N	0.40 E
Bicol ≃	116	13.44 N	123.07 E
Bicske	30	47.29 N	18.37 E
Bicudo ≃	255	18.04 S	44.33 W
Bičura	88	50.36 N	107.35 E
Bičurina	86	56.51 N	55.25 E
Bīd	122	18.59 N	75.46 E
Bida, Nig.	146	12.20 N	13.25 E
Bida, Nig.	150	9.05 N	6.01 E
Bīdar	122	17.54 N	77.33 E
Bidde	144	0.58 N	42.37 E
Biddeford	188	43.29 N	70.27 W
Biddenden	42	51.07 N	0.39 E
Biddiyā	132	32.07 N	35.05 E
Biddulph	44	53.08 N	2.10 W
Bideford	42	51.01 N	4.13 W
Bidente ≃	66	44.24 N	12.12 E
Bidford-on-Avon	42	52.10 N	1.51 W
Bidhūna	124	26.49 N	79.31 E
Bidian	100	32.38 N	113.03 E
Bīdokht	128	34.21 N	58.46 E
Bidoni	71	40.07 N	8.56 E
Bidor	114	4.07 N	101.17 E
Bidston	262	53.24 N	3.05 W
Bidwell	188	38.55 N	82.17 W
Bidwell, Mount ∧	204	41.58 N	120.10 W
Bidya ≃[1]	126	21.56 N	88.42 E

Bidyādhari ≃	272b	22.23 N	88.35 E
Bidyādharpur	272b	22.50 N	88.24 E
Bidžan	89	47.58 N	131.58 E
Bidžan ≃	89	47.44 N	132.19 E
Bie	40	59.05 N	16.12 E
Bié □[5]	152	12.30 S	17.15 E
Biebelried	56	49.46 N	10.04 E
Bieber, B.R.D.	56	50.09 N	9.19 E
Bieber, Ca., U.S.	204	41.07 N	121.08 W
Biebrza ≃	30	53.13 N	22.25 E
Biecz	30	49.44 N	21.14 E
Biedenkopf	56	50.55 N	8.32 E
Biederitz	54	52.09 N	11.43 E
Biedermannsdorf	264b	48.05 N	16.21 E
Bieguzhuang	105	39.19 N	116.39 E
Biei	92a	43.35 N	142.28 E
Biel (Bienne)	58	47.10 N	7.12 E
Bielawa	30	50.41 N	16.38 E
Bielawski, Mount ∧	226	37.13 N	122.06 W
Bielefeld	52	52.01 N	8.31 E
Bieler Lake ⊜	176	70.20 N	73.00 W
Bielersee ⊜	58	47.05 N	7.10 E
Bielin	54	52.47 N	14.28 E
Biella	62	45.34 N	8.03 E
Bielsk	30	52.40 N	19.49 E
Bielsko-Biała	30	49.49 N	19.02 E
Bielsko-Biała □[4]	30	49.40 N	19.10 E
Bielsk Podlaski	30	52.47 N	23.12 E
Biemenhorst	52	51.49 N	6.36 E
Bienenbüttel	52	53.08 N	10.29 E
Bienfait	184	49.08 N	102.47 W
Bien Hoa	110	10.57 N	106.49 E
Bienne → Biel	58	47.10 N	7.12 E
Bienne ≃, Fr.	50	48.15 N	0.04 E
Bienne ≃, Fr.	58	46.20 N	5.38 E
Bienno	64	45.56 N	10.18 E
Bientina	66	43.42 N	10.37 E
Bienville	194	32.21 N	92.58 W
Bienville, Lac ⊜	176	55.05 N	72.40 W
Biere, D.D.R.	54	51.58 N	11.39 E
Bière, Schw.	58	46.33 N	6.20 E
Bierné	28	47.49 N	0.32 W
Bieruń Stary	30	50.06 N	19.06 E
Bierutów	30	51.08 N	17.32 E
Bierwart	56	50.34 N	5.01 E
Biesbos ◆[1]	52	51.45 N	4.50 E
Biesdorf ◆[8]	264a	52.31 N	13.33 E
Biese ≃	54	52.45 N	11.37 E
Biesel ◆[8]	263	51.10 N	6.29 E
Biesenthal	54	52.46 N	13.37 E
Bieshan	105	39.58 N	117.29 E
Biesiesvlei	158	26.22 S	25.55 E
Biesles	58	48.05 N	5.18 E
Bieszczadzki Park Narodowy ♠	30	49.05 N	22.45 E
Bieteluobaoluosika	89	48.35 N	119.56 E
Bietigheim	56	48.54 N	8.14 E
Bietigheim-Bissingen	56	48.58 N	9.07 E
Bietschhorn ∧	58	46.24 N	7.51 E
Bièvre	56	49.56 N	5.01 E
Bièvre ≃	261	48.47 N	2.20 E
Bièvres	261	48.45 N	2.13 E
Biferno ≃	66	41.59 N	15.02 E
Bifoun	152	0.22 S	10.23 E
Bifuka	92a	44.29 N	142.21 E
Bifurcación	258	34.19 S	56.48 W
Big ≃, Austl.	169	37.18 S	146.02 E
Big ≃, N.T., Can.	176	72.30 N	125.14 W
Big ≃, Sk., Can.	184	53.50 N	107.02 W
Big ≃, Ak., U.S.	180	63.00 N	154.56 W
Big ≃, Mo., U.S.	219	38.28 N	90.37 W
Biga	130	40.13 N	27.14 E
Bigadiç	130	39.23 N	28.08 E
Big A Mountain ∧	192	37.03 N	82.02 W
Big Annemessex River ⊂	208	38.03 N	75.50 W
Big Antelope Creek ≃	202	42.28 N	117.13 W
Big Bald Mountain ∧, N.B., Can.	186	47.12 N	66.25 W
Big Bald Mountain ∧, Ga., U.S.	192	34.45 N	84.19 W
Big Baldy ∧	202	44.47 N	115.13 W
Big Baldy Mountain ∧	202	46.58 N	110.37 W
Big Bar Creek	182	51.12 N	122.06 W
Big Basin Redwoods State Park ♠	226	37.09 N	122.17 W
Big Bay	190	46.49 N	87.44 W
Big Bay ⊂, N.Z.	172	44.18 S	168.05 E
Big Bay ⊂, Vanuatu	175f	15.06 S	166.54 E
Big Bay De Noc ⊂	190	45.46 N	86.43 W
Big Bay Point ›	212	44.24 N	79.31 W
Big Bear City	228	34.15 N	116.50 W
Big Bear Lake	228	34.15 N	116.53 W
Big Bear Lake ⊜	228	34.15 N	116.55 W
Big Beaver, Sk., Can.	184	49.08 N	105.10 W
Big Beaver, Pa., U.S.	214	40.50 N	80.20 W
Big Beaver Airport ⊠	281	42.33 N	83.06 W
Big Beaver Creek ≃, Mi., U.S.	281	42.32 N	83.01 W
Big Beaver Creek ≃, Oh., U.S.	218	39.01 N	83.03 W
Big Beaver Creek ≃, Wa., U.S.	224	48.40 N	121.08 W
Big Bell	162	27.21 S	117.40 E
Big Belt Mountains ⋏	202	46.40 N	111.25 W
Big Bend, Swaz.	158	26.50 S	31.57 E
Big Bend, Wi., U.S.	216	42.52 N	88.12 W
Big Bend National Park ♠	196	29.12 N	103.12 W
Big Bend Reservoir ⊜[1]	182	52.57 N	115.37 W
Big Black ≃	194	32.00 N	91.05 W
Big Blue ≃, U.S.	198	39.11 N	96.32 W
Big Blue ≃, In., U.S.	218	39.20 N	85.59 W
Big Blue, West Fork ≃	198	40.42 N	96.59 W
Big Bone Lick State Park ♠	218	38.53 N	84.45 W
Big Bonito Creek ≃	200	33.34 N	109.56 W
Big Brook ≃	276	40.19 N	74.10 W
Big Brushy Creek ≃, Tx., U.S.	222	32.32 N	96.20 W
Big Brushy Creek ≃, Tx., U.S.	222	29.12 N	96.55 W
Big Bureau Creek ≃	194	41.17 N	89.21 W
Bigbury Bay ⊂	42	50.16 N	3.48 W
Big Cabin Creek ≃	194	36.26 N	95.08 W
Big Canyon V	196	30.05 N	101.55 W
Big Carlos Pass ⊂	220	26.24 N	81.52 W
Big Cedar Lake ⊜	212	44.37 N	78.10 W
Big Chino Wash V	200	34.52 N	112.28 W
Big Clear Lake ⊜	212	44.43 N	76.55 W
Big Clifty	194	37.32 N	86.09 W
Big Coulee Creek ≃	202	46.17 N	108.56 W
Big Cow Creek ≃	194	30.34 N	93.44 W
Big Creek, B.C., Can.	182	51.44 N	123.03 W
Big Creek, Ca., U.S.	226	37.12 N	119.14 W
Big Creek ≃, B.C., Can.	182	51.40 N	122.50 W
Big Creek ≃, On., Can.	214	42.36 N	80.27 W
Big Creek ≃, On., Can.	214	42.19 N	82.27 W
Big Creek ≃, Ar., U.S.	194	34.21 N	91.03 W
Big Creek ≃, Ca., U.S.	226	37.12 N	119.19 W
Big Creek ≃, Ca., U.S.	226	36.53 N	119.15 W
Big Creek ≃, Id., U.S.	202	45.06 N	114.44 W
Big Creek ≃, Il., U.S.	219	39.07 N	88.52 W
Big Creek ≃, In., U.S.	216	40.38 N	86.46 W
Big Creek ≃, In., U.S.	218	38.48 N	85.39 W
Big Creek ≃, Ks., U.S.	198	38.47 N	98.55 W
Big Creek ≃, La., U.S.	194	32.10 N	91.53 W

Big Creek ≃, Mo., U.S.	194	40.02 N	94.07 W
Big Creek ≃, Mo., U.S.	219	38.52 N	90.50 W
Big Creek ≃, Oh., U.S.	279a	41.27 N	81.41 W
Big Creek ≃, Or., U.S.	224	46.11 N	123.35 W
Big Creek ≃, Tx., U.S.	222	31.09 N	96.52 W
Big Creek ≃, Tx., U.S.	222	29.22 N	95.34 W
Big Creek ≃, Wa., U.S.	224	47.15 N	121.10 W
Big Creek, East Fork ≃	194	40.16 N	94.03 W
Big Creek, West Fork ≃	194	40.16 N	94.03 W
Big Creek Parkway ♠	279a	41.24 N	81.45 W
Big Creek Peak ∧	202	44.28 N	113.32 W
Big Crow Island I	276	40.37 N	73.33 W
Big Cypress Creek ≃	222	33.00 N	94.51 W
Big Cypress Indian Reservation ◆[4]	220	26.14 N	80.49 W
Big Cypress National Preserve ♠	220	25.55 N	81.10 W
Big Cypress Swamp ⩩	220	26.10 N	81.38 W
Big Dalton Canyon V	280	34.10 N	117.48 W
Big Dalton Wash V	280	34.04 N	117.58 W
Big Darby Creek ≃	218	39.37 N	82.58 W
Big Delta	180	64.09 N	145.50 W
Big Desert ◆[2]	166	35.40 S	141.00 E
Big Diomede Island → Ratmanova, ostrov I	180	65.46 N	169.02 W
Big Ditch ≊	216	40.13 N	88.22 W
Big Dry Creek ≃	202	47.30 N	106.19 W
Big Dubbo Hill ∧	171b	35.25 S	148.36 E
Big Eau Pleine ≃	190	44.48 N	90.00 W
Big Elk Creek ≃	208	39.35 N	75.52 W
Big Elkhart Creek ≃	222	31.22 N	95.41 W
Big Elm Creek ≃	222	30.53 N	96.56 W
Bigelow Bight ⊂[3]	188	43.15 N	70.30 W
Big Escambia Creek ≃	194	30.58 N	87.14 W
Big Falls	190	48.11 N	93.48 W
Big Flat	194	36.00 N	92.24 W
Big Flat Creek ≃	194	31.33 N	87.31 W
Big Flats	210	42.08 N	76.56 W
Bigfork, Mn., U.S.	190	47.44 N	93.39 W
Bigfork, Mt., U.S.	202	48.04 N	114.04 W
Big Fork ≃	190	48.31 N	93.43 W
Big Four Ditch ≊	216	40.27 N	88.10 W
Big Frog Mountain ∧	192	35.00 N	84.32 W
Biggar, Sk., Can.	184	52.04 N	108.00 W
Biggar, Scot., U.K.	46	55.38 N	3.32 W
Biggarsberg ⋏	158	28.12 S	29.48 E
Bigge	56	51.21 N	8.28 E
Bigge Island I	164	14.35 S	125.10 E
Biggers	194	36.19 N	90.48 W
Biggestausee ⊜[1]	56	51.05 N	7.55 E
Biggin Hill ◆[8]	42	51.18 N	0.04 E
Biggin Hill Aerodrome ⊠	260	51.19 N	0.03 E
Biggleswade	42	52.05 N	0.17 W
Biggs, Ca., U.S.	226	39.24 N	121.42 W
Biggs, Or., U.S.	224	45.40 N	120.50 W
Big Gull Lake ⊜	212	44.50 N	76.58 W
Big Gully Creek ≃	184	53.13 N	109.03 W
Bighāi ≃[1]	126	22.10 N	90.13 E
Big Hawk Lake ⊜	212	45.10 N	78.44 W
Bighead ≃	212	44.36 N	80.35 W
Big Hole ≃	202	45.34 N	112.20 W
Big Hole National Battlefield ⊥	202	45.35 N	113.35 W
Bighorn ≃	202	46.09 N	107.28 W
Bighorn Basin ≌[1]	202	44.15 N	108.10 W
Bighorn Canyon National Recreation Area ♠	202	45.00 N	108.15 W
Big Horn Lake ⊜[1]	202	45.06 N	108.08 W
Bighorn Mountains ⋏	202	44.00 N	107.30 W
Bight, Head of ›	162	31.30 S	131.10 E
Big Huckleberry Mountain ∧	224	45.51 N	121.47 W
Big Island	192	37.32 N	79.21 W
Big Island I, N.T., Can.	176	62.43 N	70.43 W
Big Island I, On., Can.	184	49.10 N	94.40 W
Big Island I, On., Can.	212	44.33 N	78.30 W
Big Knob ∧	192	36.40 N	82.31 W
Big Koniuji Island I	180	55.06 N	159.33 W
Big Lake, Ak., U.S.	180	61.33 N	149.52 W
Big Lake, Mn., U.S.	190	45.19 N	93.44 W
Big Lake, Tx., U.S.	196	31.11 N	101.27 W
Big Lake, Wa., U.S.	224	48.24 N	122.14 W
Big Lake ⊜, Me., U.S.	188	45.10 N	67.40 W
Big Lake ⊜, Wa., U.S.	224	48.23 N	122.12 W
Bigler	214	40.59 N	78.19 W
Biglerville	208	39.55 N	77.14 W
Big Lick Creek ≃	216	40.22 N	85.27 W
Big Lookout Mountain ∧	202	44.37 N	117.17 W
Big Lost ≃	202	43.50 N	112.44 W
Big Monon Ditch ≊	216	40.52 N	86.46 W
Big Mossy Point ›	184	53.41 N	97.57 W
Big Mountain ∧, B.C., Can.	180	56.53 N	131.31 W
Big Mountain ∧, Nv., U.S.	204	41.17 N	119.04 W
Big Mountain Creek ≃	182	55.04 N	118.39 W
Big Muddy ≃	194	37.35 N	89.31 W
Big Muddy, Casey Fork ≃	194	38.06 N	88.57 W
Big Muddy Creek ≃, Mt., U.S.	198	48.08 N	104.36 W
Big Muddy Creek ≃, N.D., U.S.	198	46.37 N	101.24 W
Big Muddy Lake ⊜	184	49.08 N	104.54 W
Big Muscamoot Bay ⊂	281	42.33 N	82.40 W
Bignasco	58	46.20 N	8.36 E
Big Nasty Creek ≃	198	45.41 N	102.51 W
Big Nemaha, North Fork ≃	198	40.04 N	95.43 W
Bignona	150	12.49 N	16.14 W
Big Oak Flat	226	37.49 N	120.16 W
Bigosovo	76	55.49 N	27.43 E
Bigot, Morne ∧[2]	240e	14.31 N	61.04 W
Big Otter ≃	192	37.07 N	79.23 W
Big Otter Creek ≃	212	42.38 N	80.48 W
Big Ox Creek ≃	218	38.44 N	85.52 W
Big Pine	204	37.09 N	118.17 W
Big Pine Creek ≃	216	40.18 N	87.15 W
Big Pine Key	220	24.40 N	81.21 W
Big Pine Key I	220	24.42 N	81.23 W
Big Pine Mountain ∧	204	34.42 N	119.39 W
Big Piney	200	42.32 N	110.06 W
Big Piney ≃	194	37.53 N	92.04 W
Big Piney Creek ≃	194	35.20 N	93.20 W
Big Pipe Creek ≃	208	39.36 N	77.17 W
Big Plain	218	39.50 N	83.17 W
Big Pocono State Park ♠	210	41.03 N	75.19 W
Bigpoint	194	30.35 N	88.28 W
Big Pond	210	41.53 N	76.43 W
Big Porcupine Creek ≃	202	46.16 N	106.43 W
Big Porcupine Lake ⊜	212	45.27 N	78.36 W
Big Prairie	214	40.40 N	82.06 W
Big Prairie Creek ≃	194	32.35 N	87.45 W
Big Quilcene ≃	224	47.49 N	122.52 W
Big Quill Lake ⊜	184	51.55 N	104.22 W
Big Raccoon Creek ≃	194	39.46 N	87.22 W
Big Rapids	190	43.41 N	85.29 W
Bigras, Île I	275a	45.31 N	73.51 W

≃ River	Fluß	Río	Rivière	Rio
≊ Canal	Kanal	Canal	Canal	Canal
⌞ Waterfall, Rapids	Wasserfall, Stromschnellen	Cascada, Rápidos	Chute d'eau, Rapides	Cascata, Rápidos
≌ Strait	Meeresstraße	Estrecho	Détroit	Estreito
⊂ Bay, Gulf	Bucht, Golf	Bahía, Golfo	Baie, Golfe	Baía, Golfo
⊜ Lake, Lakes	See, Seen	Lago, Lagos	Lac, Lacs	Lago, Lagos
⩩ Swamp	Sumpf	Pantano	Marais	Pântano
⊓ Ice Features, Glacier	Eis- und Gletscherformen	Accidentes Glaciales	Formes glaciaires	Acidentes glaciares
⊤ Other Hydrographic Features	Andere Hydrographische Objekte	Otros Elementos Hidrográficos	Autres données hydrographiques	Outros acidentes hidrográficos

✢ Submarine Features	Untermeerische Objekte	Accidentes Submarinos	Formes de relief sous-marin	Acidentes submarinos
□ Political Unit	Politische Einheit	Unidad Politica	Entité politique	Unidade política
ᵾ Cultural Institution	Kulturelle Institution	Institución Cultural	Institution culturelle	Institução cultural
⊥ Historical Site	Historische Stätte	Sitio Histórico	Site historique	Sitio histórico
♠ Recreational Site	Erholungs- und Ferienort	Sitio de Recreo	Centre de loisirs	Area de Lazer
⊠ Airport	Flughafen	Aeropuerto	Aéroport	Aeroporto
■ Military Installation	Militäranlage	Instalación Militar	Installation militaire	Instalação militar
◆ Miscellaneous	Verschiedenes	Misceláneo	Divers	Diversos

Column 1

Name	Page	Lat.	Long.
Big Rib ≃	190	44.56 N	89.41 W
Big Rideau Lake ⊘	212	44.45 N	76.14 W
Big River	184	53.50 N	107.01 W
Big River Indian Reserve ⬩⁴	184	53.33 N	107.10 W
Big Rock	216	41.46 N	88.33 W
Big Rock Creek ≃	216	41.38 N	88.32 W
Big Rocky Creek ≃	222	29.34 N	96.50 W
Big Run	214	40.58 N	78.52 W
Big Sable ≻	190	44.02 N	86.31 W
Big Sable Point ≻	190	44.03 N	86.31 W
Big Salmon ≃	180	61.52 N	134.56 W
Big Salmon Range ⰾ	180	61.10 N	133.45 W
Big Sand Lake ⊘	176	57.45 N	99.42 W
Big Sandy, Mt., U.S.	202	48.10 N	110.06 W
Big Sandy, Tn., U.S.	194	34.14 N	88.05 W
Big Sandy, Tx., U.S.	222	32.35 N	95.07 W
Big Sandy ≃, Az., U.S.	188	38.25 N	82.36 W
Big Sandy ≃, Az., U.S.	200	34.19 N	113.31 W
Big Sandy ≃, Tn., U.S.	194	36.15 N	88.06 W
Big Sandy ≃, Wy., U.S.	202	41.51 N	109.47 W
Big Sandy Creek ≃, Ca., U.S.	226	35.47 N	120.43 W
Big Sandy Creek ≃, Co., U.S.	198	38.06 N	102.29 W
Big Sandy Creek ≃, Ga., U.S.	192	32.42 N	82.57 W
Big Sandy Creek ≃, Mt., U.S.	202	48.34 N	109.48 W
Big Sandy Creek ≃, Ne., U.S.	198	40.13 N	97.18 W
Big Sandy Creek ≃, Tx., U.S.	196	33.11 N	97.40 W
Big Sandy Creek ≃, Tx., U.S.	222	32.33 N	95.05 W
Big Sandy Creek ≃, Tx., U.S.	222	30.31 N	94.28 W
Big Sandy Lake ⊘, Sk., Can.	184	54.26 N	104.04 W
Big Sandy Lake ⊘, Mn., U.S.	190	46.45 N	93.17 W
Big Sandy Reservoir ⊘¹	200	42.16 N	109.26 W
Big Satilla Creek ≃	192	31.27 N	82.03 W
Bigsby Island I	184	49.04 N	94.35 W
Big Sewickley Creek ≃	279b	40.35 N	80.13 W
Big Shawnee Creek ≃	216	40.15 N	87.18 W
Big Sheep Mountain ⌃	202	47.03 N	105.43 W
Big Signal Peak ⌃	204	39.31 N	123.06 W
Big Sinking Creek ≃	194	37.55 N	86.31 W
Big Sioux ≃	198	43.30 N	96.25 W
Big Sixmile Creek ≃	284a	43.02 N	79.01 W
Big Sky	202	45.17 N	111.17 W
Big Slough ≃	192	30.56 N	84.33 W
Big Smoky Valley V	204	38.30 N	117.15 W
Big Snowy Mountains ⰾ	202	46.50 N	109.30 W
Big Southern Butte ⌃	202	43.23 N	113.01 W
Big Spanish Channel ⋃	220	24.44 N	81.20 W
Bigspring, Mo., U.S.	219	38.38 N	91.28 W
Big Spring, Tx., U.S.	196	32.15 N	101.28 W
Big Springs	198	41.03 N	102.04 W
Big Spruce Knob ⌃	188	38.10 N	80.12 W
Big Squaw Mountain ⌃	188	45.30 N	69.45 W
Bigstick Lake ⊘	184	50.16 N	109.20 W
Bigstone ≃	184	55.55 N	94.36 W
Big Stone City	184	45.17 N	96.27 W
Big Stone Gap	192	36.52 N	82.44 W
Bigstone Lake ⊘, Mb., Can.	184	53.42 N	95.44 W
Big Stone Lake ⊘, U.S.	198	45.18 N	96.40 W
Big Sunflower ≃	194	32.40 N	90.40 W
Big Sur	226	36.16 N	121.48 W
Big Sur ≃	226	36.17 N	121.51 W
Big Sur ⬩¹	226	35.45 N	121.20 W
Big Swamp Creek ≃	194	32.19 N	86.49 W
Big Swan Creek ≃	194	35.46 N	87.24 W
Big Thicket National Preserve ♦	222	32.35 N	94.40 W
Big Thompson ≃	200	40.21 N	104.45 W
Big Timber	202	45.50 N	109.57 W
Big Timber Creek ≃	285	39.53 N	75.08 W
Big Timber Creek, North Branch ≃	285	39.50 N	75.05 W
Big Timber Creek, South Branch ≃	285	39.50 N	75.05 W
Big Torch Key I	220	24.43 N	81.26 W
Big Tree	210	42.46 N	78.49 W
Big Trout Lake ⊘, On., Can.	176	53.45 N	90.00 W
Big Trout Lake ⊘, On., Can.	212	44.56 N	78.56 W
Big Tujunga Canyon V	228	34.16 N	118.18 W
Big Tujunga Dam ⬩⁶	228	34.18 N	118.12 W
Biguaçu	252	27.30 S	48.40 W
Big Valley	182	52.02 N	112.46 W
Bigwa	154	7.13 S	39.09 E
Big Walnut Creek ≃, In., U.S.	194	39.30 N	86.47 W
Big Walnut Creek ≃, Oh., U.S.	218	39.48 N	83.01 W
Big Warrambool ≃	166	30.05 S	147.33 E
Big Water	200	37.05 N	111.41 W
Big Wells	196	28.34 N	99.34 W
Big White Mountain ⌃	182	49.42 N	118.58 W
Big Wills Creek ≃	192	33.59 N	86.00 W
Big Wood ≃	202	42.52 N	114.54 W
Bihać	36	44.49 N	15.52 E
Bihar □³	124	25.11 N	85.31 E
Bihār	124	25.11 N	85.31 E
Biharamulo	152	2.38 S	31.20 E
Bihārīganj	124	25.44 N	86.59 E
Bihor □³	38	47.00 N	22.10 E
Bihor, Vîrful ⌃	38	46.27 N	22.42 E
Bihoro	92a	43.49 N	144.07 E
Bihu	100	28.21 N	119.48 E
Bija ≃	82	52.25 N	85.25 E
Bijagós, Arquipélago dos II	150	11.25 N	16.20 W
Bijainagar	120	25.56 N	74.38 E
Bijaipur	124	26.03 N	77.22 E
Bijaipura	124	27.14 N	77.48 E
Bijāpur	120	16.50 N	75.42 E
Bijār	128	35.52 N	47.36 E
Bijāwar	124	24.38 N	79.30 E
Bijbān Chāh	128	26.54 N	64.42 E
Bijbiāra	123	33.48 N	75.06 E
Bijelina	38	44.45 N	19.13 E
Bijeljina	38	43.02 N	19.44 E
Bijelo Polje	38	43.02 N	19.44 E
Bijiang	120	26.54 N	98.55 E
Bijia Shan ⌃	105	40.17 N	116.50 E
Bijie	102	27.18 N	105.20 E
Bijilkol', ozero ⊘	85	43.03 N	70.41 E
Bijni	124	26.29 N	90.40 E
Bijnor	124	29.22 N	78.08 E
Bijōki	128	26.37 N	89.27 E
Bijou Creek ≃	198	40.17 N	103.52 W
Bijpur	120	16.30 N	75.40 E
Bijsk	86	52.34 N	85.15 E
Bijuk-Karasu ≃	44	45.15 N	34.47 E
Biwāšan ⬩⁸	272a	38.32 N	77.03 E
Bikāner	120	28.01 N	73.18 E
Bikaner Canal ⩲	120	28.11 N	73.16 E
Bikar I	156	12.15 N	170.06 E
Bikbulovo	80	55.39 N	53.26 E
Bike	80	55.39 N	53.26 E
Bikeman Island I	174t	1.21 N	173.00 E
Bikeqi	104	40.45 N	111.17 E
Bikfayyā	132	33.55 N	35.41 E

Column 2

Name	Page	Lat.	Long.
Bikié	152	3.06 S	13.52 E
Bikin	89	46.48 N	134.16 E
Bikin ≃	89	46.51 N	134.02 E
Bikini I¹	14	11.35 N	165.23 E
Bikita	154	20.06 S	31.41 E
Bikl'an'	80	55.37 N	52.10 E
Bikoro	152	0.45 S	18.07 E
Bikuar, Parque Nacional do ♦	152	15.12 S	14.42 E
Bila	114	2.30 N	100.08 E
Bilaa Point ≻	116	9.49 N	125.26 E
Bilac	255	21.24 S	50.28 W
Billād Zahrān ⬩¹	144	20.16 N	41.14 E
Bila hora ⌃	54	50.10 N	14.10 E
Bilang, Teluk c	112	1.15 N	121.25 E
Bilanga	150	12.32 N	0.02 E
Bilāra	120	26.10 N	73.42 E
Bilāri	124	28.38 N	78.48 E
Bilāsipāra	124	26.14 N	90.14 E
Bilāspur, India	123	31.20 N	76.45 E
Bilāspur, India	124	28.53 N	79.16 E
Bilāspur, India	124	22.05 N	82.09 E
Bil'asuvar	84	39.24 N	48.24 E
Bilatan Island I	116	4.59 N	120.00 E
Bilati	112	0.32 N	122.38 E
Bilauktaung Range ⰾ	110	13.00 N	99.00 E
Bilbao	34	43.15 N	2.58 W
Bilbays	142	30.25 N	31.34 E
Bilbays Military Base ⬩	142	30.24 N	31.36 E
Bilbilis ⌿	34	41.25 N	1.39 W
Bil'čir	88	51.02 N	110.34 E
Bileća	38	42.53 N	18.26 E
Bilecik	130	40.09 N	29.59 E
Bilecik □⁴	130	40.10 N	30.10 E
Biles Island I	285	40.10 N	74.45 W
Biłgoraj	30	50.34 N	22.43 E
Bilgrām	124	27.11 N	80.02 E
Bili	154	4.09 N	25.10 E
Bili	136	4.09 N	22.29 E
Bilian	100	28.21 N	120.33 E
Bilifyā	142	29.07 N	31.03 E
Bilimora	120	20.45 N	72.57 E
Bilin	110	17.14 N	97.15 E
Bilin ≃	110	17.05 N	97.08 E
Bilina	54	50.35 N	13.45 E
Bilina ≃	54	50.40 N	14.02 E
Biloso ≃	68	40.39 N	16.24 E
Biliran Island I	116	11.35 N	124.28 E
Biliran Strait ⋃	116	11.30 N	124.28 E
Biliri	150	9.52 N	11.13 E
Biliu ≃	98	39.30 N	122.36 E
Bilk ⬩⁸	263	51.12 N	6.47 E
Billabong Creek ≃	166	35.06 S	144.02 E
Billeberga	41	55.53 N	13.00 E
Billerbeck	52	51.59 N	7.17 E
Billericay	260	51.38 N	0.25 E
Billesholm	41	56.03 N	13.00 E
Billiat	58	46.21 N	9.15 E
Billigheim	54	49.21 N	9.15 E
Billiluna	162	19.37 S	127.41 E
Billinge, Sve.	41	55.58 N	13.21 E
Billinge, Eng., U.K.	262	53.30 N	2.42 W
Billingham	26	54.36 N	1.17 W
Billings, Mo., U.S.	194	37.04 N	93.33 W
Billings, Mt., U.S.	202	45.46 N	108.30 W
Billings, Ok., U.S.	196	36.31 N	97.26 W
Billingsfors	26	58.59 N	12.15 E
Billings Heights	202	45.50 N	108.32 W
Billingshurst	42	51.01 N	0.28 W
Billmerich	263	51.30 N	7.47 E
Bilolo	273b	4.07 S	15.19 E
Bilom	32	45.44 N	3.21 E
Billund	41	55.44 N	9.07 E
Bill Williams ≃	200	34.17 N	114.03 W
Bill Williams Mountain ⌃	200	35.12 N	112.12 W
Billy Chinook, Lake ⊘¹	202	44.33 N	121.20 W
Billy-Montigny	50	50.26 N	2.52 E
Bilma	146	18.41 N	12.56 E
Biloela	166	24.24 S	150.30 E
Bilo Gora ⰾ	36	46.06 N	16.46 E
Biloxi	194	30.23 N	88.53 W
Biloxi Creek ≃	222	31.05 N	94.37 W
Bilpa Morea Claypan ⊟	166	25.00 S	140.00 E
Bilqās Qism Awwal	142	31.13 N	31.21 E
Bilsabrā	144	23.05 N	88.10 E
Bilshausen	52	51.37 N	10.10 E
Bilsi	124	28.08 N	78.55 E
Bilston	42	52.34 N	2.04 W
Bilthoven	52	52.07 N	5.17 E
Biltine	146	14.32 N	20.55 E
Biltine □⁵	146	15.00 N	21.00 E
Biltmore Forest	192	35.28 N	82.31 W
Bilugyun Island I	110	16.24 N	97.32 E
Bilwaskarma	188	14.45 N	83.53 W
Bilzen	56	50.45 N	5.31 E
Bimbān	142	24.05 N	32.53 E
Bimbe	152	11.49 S	15.49 E
Bimberi Peak ⌃	171b	35.40 S	148.47 E
Bimbila	150	8.55 N	0.04 E
Bimbo	152	4.18 N	18.23 E
Bimbowrie	166	32.03 S	140.09 E
Bimé	273b	4.05 S	15.11 E
Bimini Islands II	192	25.42 N	79.15 W
Bîna-Etāwa	124	24.11 N	78.11 E
Binaija, Gunung ⌃	114	3.11 S	129.26 E
Binalbagan	116	10.12 N	122.50 E
Binalbagan ≃	116	10.12 N	122.51 E
Binalong	171b	34.40 S	148.38 E
Binatang	114	2.10 N	111.38 E
Binatangon	116	14.28 N	121.11 E
Binas	50	47.59 N	1.28 E
Binasco	60	45.20 N	9.06 E
Binau	52	49.24 N	9.04 E
Binchuan	102	25.46 N	100.33 E
Bindal	24	65.06 N	12.30 E
Binder, Mong.	104	48.35 N	110.36 E
Binder, Tchad	146	9.58 N	14.28 E
Bindlach	54	49.59 N	11.37 E
Bindloss	182	50.52 N	110.16 W
Bindo, Mount ⌃	264a	52.17 N	13.45 E
Bindura	154	17.19 S	31.20 E
Bine-el-Ouidane	148	32.07 N	6.28 W
Binéfar	34	41.51 N	0.18 E
Binford	198	47.33 N	98.20 W
Binga, Pil.	116	10.45 N	119.19 E
Binga, Zaïre	152	2.23 N	20.30 E
Binga, Monte ⌃	156	19.45 S	33.04 E
Bingara	166	29.52 S	150.34 E
Bingay Point I	122	10.56 N	72.17 E
Bingcha	100	32.30 N	120.52 E
Bingen, B.R.D.	54	49.57 N	7.54 E
Bingen, Wa., U.S.	196	45.42 N	121.27 W
Bingerbrück	263	49.58 N	7.53 E
Bingerville	150	5.21 N	3.54 W
Bingfang	106	32.15 N	121.20 E
Bingham, Eng., U.K.	42	52.57 N	0.57 W
Bingham, Me., U.S.	188	45.03 N	69.52 W
Bingham Farms	281	42.31 N	83.16 W
Bin Ghashīr	146	32.41 N	13.11 E
Bini Ghunaymah, Jabal ⰾ	146	25.00 N	15.30 E

Column 3

Name	Page	Lat.	Long.
Bingi	154	0.24 S	29.05 E
Bingley	44	53.51 N	1.50 W
Bingöl	130	38.53 N	40.29 E
Bingöl □⁴	130	39.00 N	40.40 E
Bingöl Dağları ⰾ	130	39.20 N	41.20 E
Binhai (Dongkan)	100	34.03 N	119.51 E
Binh Ca	269c	10.40 N	106.34 E
Binh Chanh	269c	10.40 N	106.34 E
Binh Gia	110	21.59 N	106.21 E
Binh Hung Hoa	269c	10.49 N	106.37 E
Binh Khe	110	13.57 N	108.51 E
Binh Kieu	150	15.35 N	108.04 E
Binh-Houyé	150	6.47 N	8.19 W
Binh Son	110	15.18 N	108.46 E
Binh Trung	269c	10.47 N	106.46 E
Bingsian Point ≻	116	9.50 N	122.23 E
Bining	56	49.02 N	7.15 E
Binjai, Indon.	112	3.48 N	108.14 E
Binjai, Indon.	114	3.36 N	98.30 E
Binjohara	114	2.12 N	98.12 E
Binludi, Kūh-e ⌃	128	36.28 N	58.49 E
Binna Burra	171a	28.13 S	153.14 E
Binnah, Ras ≻	144	11.08 N	51.10 E
Binnaway	166	31.33 S	149.23 E
Binnian, Slieve ⌃	48	54.08 N	5.58 W
Binningen	58	47.32 N	7.34 E
Binodepur	126	23.26 N	89.30 E
Binongko, Pulau I	112	5.57 S	124.02 E
Binpur	126	22.36 N	86.55 E
Binscarth	184	50.37 N	101.16 W
Binsheim ⬩⁸	263	51.31 N	6.42 E
Bintan, Pulau I	112	1.05 N	104.30 E
Bintang	150	13.10 N	16.08 W
Bintang, Gunong ⌃	114	5.25 N	100.52 E
Bintang ≃	112	0.53 N	123.33 E
Bint Goda	140	13.17 N	31.33 E
Bintimani ⌃	150	9.13 N	11.07 W
Bint Jubayl	132	33.07 N	35.26 E
Bintuhan	112	4.48 S	103.22 E
Bintulu	112	3.10 N	113.02 E
Bintuni	164	2.07 S	133.32 E
Bintuni, Teluk c	164	2.20 S	133.30 E
Binxian, Zhg.	89	45.44 N	127.29 E
Binxian, Zhg.	98	37.28 N	117.56 E
Binxian, Zhg.	102	35.00 N	108.08 E
Binyamina	132	32.31 N	34.57 E
Bin Yauri	150	10.47 N	4.50 E
Binz	54	54.24 N	13.36 E
Binza	273b	4.21 S	15.14 E
Binza ⬩⁸	273b	4.20 S	15.14 E
Binza ≃	273b	4.21 S	15.14 E
Bio Addo	144	8.18 N	49.48 E
Biobío □⁴	252	37.00 S	72.30 W
Biobío ≃	252	36.49 S	73.10 W
Biodi	154	3.19 N	28.35 E
Biograd	36	43.56 N	15.27 E
Bioko I	152	3.30 N	8.40 E
Biola	226	36.48 N	120.00 W
Bionaz	62	45.52 N	7.28 E
Biondo	154	3.25 N	23.13 E
Biondo Monument ⌘	146	31.25 N	10.15 E
Biot	62	43.38 N	7.06 E
Bipindi	152	3.05 N	10.25 E
Bippus	216	40.56 N	85.37 W
Bir	120	18.59 N	75.46 E
Bir, Ras ≻	144	11.59 N	43.22 E
Bira, India	272b	22.47 N	88.24 E
Bira, S.S.S.R.	89	49.15 N	137.16 E
Bira, S.S.S.R.	89	49.02 N	132.30 E
Bira ≃	89	48.07 N	133.21 E
Birab	126	21.53 N	83.16 E
Biratnagar	124	26.29 N	87.17 E
Birāk	146	27.32 N	14.16 E
Biram	146	31.54 N	18.28 E
Bi'r 'Alī	144	14.01 N	48.19 E
Bir al-Uzam	146	31.54 N	23.58 E
Birama, Ensenada de c	240p	20.38 N	77.15 W
Birandža	89	54.35 N	136.18 E
Birao	146	10.17 N	22.47 E
Birati	272b	22.39 N	88.27 E
Birava	154	2.21 S	28.54 E
Bircao	138	1.40 S	41.35 E
→ Buur Gaabo	144	1.12 S	41.51 E
Biru'či kosa ≻²	88	46.08 N	35.05 E
Bir'učij	83	47.30 N	33.33 E
Birufu	164	5.52 S	138.24 E
Bir'ukovo	83	47.57 N	39.44 E
Bir'ul'ka	88	52.35 N	107.00 E
Birunga, Parc des ♦	152	1.25 S	29.30 E
Birur	122	13.37 N	75.58 E
Birūsa ≃	88	57.43 N	95.24 E
Birūsa (Ona) ≃	88	57.04 N	96.30 E
Bîrzava ≃	38	45.16 N	20.49 E
Bîrzebbuga	36	35.49 N	14.32 E
Bisa, Pulau I	164	1.15 S	127.28 E
Bisaccia	64	41.00 N	15.22 E
Bisalpur	124	28.18 N	79.48 E
Bisamberg	264b	48.19 N	16.22 E
Bisau	120	28.16 N	75.04 E
Bisbee, Az., U.S.	200	31.26 N	109.55 W
Bisbee, N.D., U.S.	198	48.37 N	99.22 W
Biscarrosse et de Parentis, Lac de c	32	44.20 N	1.10 W
Biscay, Bay of c	32	44.00 N	4.00 W
Biscayne, Key I	220	25.42 N	80.10 W
Biscayne Bay c	220	25.33 N	80.13 W
Biscayne National Park ♦	220	25.25 N	80.16 W
Biscéglie	68	41.14 N	16.31 E
Bischheim	263	48.36 N	7.45 E
Bischofsheim, B.R.D.	263	50.01 N	8.26 E
Bischofsheim an der Rhön	54	50.24 N	10.00 E
Bischofsgrün	54	50.04 N	11.47 E
Bischofshofen	61	47.25 N	13.13 E
Bischofstal → Ujazd	30	50.24 N	18.22 E
Bischofswerda	54	51.07 N	14.11 E
Bischofswiesen	54	47.38 N	12.58 E
Bischofszell	58	47.30 N	9.15 E
Bischwald, Étang de ⊘	263	49.04 N	6.42 E
Bischwiller	263	48.46 N	7.52 E
Biscoe, Ar., U.S.	194	34.49 N	91.24 W
Biscoe, N.C., U.S.	192	35.21 N	79.46 W
Biscoe Islands II	13	66.00 S	66.30 W
Biscotasi Lake ⊘	190	47.19 N	82.07 W
Biscucuy	246	9.22 N	69.59 W
Bisenti	64	42.36 N	13.48 E
Bisentina, Isola I	64	42.35 N	11.56 E
Biser	80	58.25 N	58.31 E
Biserovskoje, ozero ⊘	265b	55.46 N	38.07 E
Bi Yun Si (Temple of the Azure Clouds) ⵜ¹	105	40.00 N	116.11 E
Bizana	156	30.52 S	29.51 E
Bizard, Île I	275a	45.29 N	73.54 W

Column 4 (ENGLISH)

Name	Page	Lat.	Long.
Birgi Vecchio	70	37.53 N	12.29 E
Biri	116	12.41 N	124.22 E
Birigui	255	21.18 S	50.19 W
Biri Island I	116	12.40 N	124.22 E
Birkčul'	86	53.20 N	89.56 E
Biril'ussy	88	57.07 N	90.32 E
Birimbāl	142	31.21 N	30.30 E
Birimbāl al-Qadīmah	142	31.10 N	31.44 E
Birimşe	130	38.03 N	38.32 E
Biritiba-Mirim	256	23.35 S	46.02 W
Birjand	128	32.53 N	59.13 E
Birkat as-Sab'	142	30.38 N	31.05 E
Birkdale	262	53.37 N	3.02 W
Birkeland	26	58.20 N	8.14 E
Birken	182	54.41 N	122.36 W
Birkenfeld, B.R.D.	56	49.51 N	9.42 E
Birkenfeld, B.R.D.	56	49.39 N	7.10 E
Birkenfeld, Or., U.S.	224	45.59 N	123.20 W
Birkenhead	262	53.24 N	3.02 W
Birkenhead Park ♦	262	53.24 N	3.02 W
Birkenwerder bei Berlin	54	52.41 N	13.16 E
Birkerød	41	55.50 N	12.26 E
Birkesdorf	56	50.49 N	6.28 E
Birket Fatimé	146	12.54 N	19.05 E
Birkfeld	61	47.21 N	15.42 E
Birkholz	264a	52.38 N	13.34 E
Birkkarspitze ⌃	61	47.28 N	11.25 E
Birk-Nack ≻	41	54.48 N	9.55 E
Birksgate Range ⰾ	162	27.10 S	129.45 E
Bîrlad	38	46.14 N	27.40 E
Bîrlad ≃	38	45.36 N	27.31 E
Birla Museum ⰽ	272b	22.32 N	88.22 E
Birlik, S.S.S.R.	80	47.28 N	50.32 E
Birlik, S.S.S.R.	150	9.13 N	11.07 W
Birling	260	51.19 N	0.25 E
Birling	274a	33.57 S	150.43 E
Birmā	142	30.51 N	30.54 E
Birmaj	84	39.46 N	47.56 E
Birmania → Burma □¹	110	22.00 N	98.00 E
Birmenie → Burma →¹	110	22.00 N	98.00 E
Birmingham, Eng., U.K.	42	52.30 N	1.55 W
Birmingham, Al., U.S.	194	33.31 N	86.48 W
Birmingham, Ia., U.S.	190	40.52 N	91.56 W
Birmingham, Mi., U.S.	216	42.32 N	83.12 W
Birmingham, N.J., U.S.	285	39.58 N	74.42 W
Birmingham, Oh., U.S.	214	41.20 N	82.21 W
Birmingham Airport ⌖	42	52.27 N	1.45 W
Birmitrapur	124	22.24 N	84.46 E
Birnamwood	190	44.56 N	89.12 W
Birni	150	13.05 N	2.54 E
Birni Ngaouré	150	13.05 N	2.54 E
Birni N'Gwari	150	11.01 N	6.48 E
Birnin Kebbi	150	12.32 N	4.12 E
Birni Nkonni	150	13.48 N	5.15 E
Birnin Kudu	150	11.27 N	9.30 E
Birobidžan	89	48.48 N	132.57 E
Birofel'd	89	48.26 N	132.47 E
Birome	222	31.49 N	96.58 W
Bîrqāsh	142	30.10 N	31.02 E
Birr	26	53.05 N	7.54 W
Biregurra	168	38.20 S	143.48 E
Birrie ≃	166	29.43 S	146.37 E
Birrindudu	162	18.22 S	129.27 E
Birs ≃	58	47.22 N	7.22 E
Birsk	86	55.25 N	55.32 E
Birstall	42	52.41 N	1.07 W
Birstein	52	50.21 N	9.19 E
Birštonas	76	54.37 N	24.02 E
Birten	263	51.38 N	6.29 E
Birtle	184	50.25 N	101.03 W
Birtley	44	54.54 N	1.34 W
Biru	120	31.30 N	93.46 E
Bir'uči kosa ≻²	88	46.08 N	35.05 E
Bir'učij	83	47.30 N	33.33 E
Birufu	164	5.52 S	138.24 E
Biscucuy	246	9.22 N	69.59 W
→ Bitola	38	41.01 N	21.20 E
Bitam, Oued ≃	34	30.43 N	5.11 E
Bitatolo	273b	4.09 S	15.19 E
Bitca	265b	55.34 N	37.37 E
Bitche	56	49.03 N	7.26 E
Bitčú	88	57.50 N	96.30 E
Bitéa, Ouadi V	146	13.11 N	19.08 E
Bithlo	220	28.34 N	81.06 W
Bithynia □⁹	130	40.30 N	29.54 E
Bitia, Wâdî V	140	32.15 N	32.15 E
Bitik	80	50.09 N	50.30 E
Bitlis	130	38.23 N	42.06 E
Bitola	38	41.01 N	21.20 E
→ Bitola	38	41.01 N	21.20 E
Bitou	150	11.16 N	0.18 W
Bitra Island I	122	11.36 N	72.09 E
Bitritto	68	41.02 N	16.42 E
Bitscherland ⬩⁹	56	49.03 N	7.26 E
Bituima	244	4.52 N	74.32 W
Bituruna	252	26.10 S	51.34 W

Column 5 (DEUTSCH)

Name	Seite	Breite	Länge
Bizen	96	34.44 N	134.09 E
Bizerte	148	37.17 N	9.52 E
Bizerte □⁸	148	37.10 N	9.50 E
Bizerte, Lac de ⊘	36	37.12 N	9.52 E
Bizhanābād	128	27.55 N	58.03 E
Bizkaiko ⬩⁴	34	43.20 N	2.45 W
Bjæverskov	41	55.27 N	12.02 E
Bjala	38	43.27 N	25.44 E
Bjala Slatina	38	43.28 N	23.56 E
Bjargtangar ≻	24a	65.31 N	24.32 W
Bjärnum	41	56.17 N	13.42 E
Bjärred	41	55.43 N	13.01 E
Bārsjöägård	41	55.44 N	13.41 E
Bjästa	26	63.12 N	18.30 E
Bjelaja → Belaja ≃	72	55.54 N	53.33 E
Bjelovar	36	45.54 N	16.51 E
Bjerede	41	55.27 N	11.38 E
Bjerre Skov ⰾ²	41	55.47 N	9.53 E
Bjerringbro	26	56.23 N	9.40 E
Björbo	40	60.28 N	14.42 E
Björkelangen	26	59.53 N	11.34 E
Björklinge	40	60.02 N	17.33 E
Björknäs	40	59.19 N	18.14 E
Björkö I	40	59.53 N	19.00 E
Björkö	26	63.21 N	21.19 E
Björköfjärden c	40	59.53 N	18.56 E
Björkvik	48	58.50 N	16.31 E
Björna	26	63.34 N	18.33 E
Bjørnafjorden c²	24	60.06 N	5.22 E
Björndammen	40	59.12 N	16.49 E
Björneborg → Pori, Suomi	26	61.29 N	21.47 E
Björnesjön ≃	40	59.15 N	14.15 E
Bjørnesfjorden ⊘	26	60.10 N	7.41 E
Björnlunda	40	59.04 N	17.09 E
Bjørnøya (Bear Island) I	12	74.25 N	19.00 E
Bjurholm	26	63.56 N	19.13 E
Bjuv	41	56.05 N	12.54 E
Bkāssīn	132	33.34 N	35.35 E
Bla	150	12.57 N	5.46 W
Blaby	42	52.34 N	1.09 W
Blace	38	43.17 N	21.18 E
Black (Lixian) (Da) ≃, Asia	110	21.15 N	105.20 E
Black ≃, Mb., Can.	184	50.49 N	96.20 W
Black ≃, On., Can.	190	48.36 N	86.16 W
Black ≃, On., Can.	190	44.22 N	79.20 W
Black ≃, On., Can.	212	44.32 N	77.22 W
Black ≃, U.S.	194	35.38 N	91.19 W
Black ≃, Az., U.S.	200	66.39 N	144.50 W
Black ≃, Az., U.S.	200	33.44 N	110.13 W
Black ≃, La., U.S.	194	31.16 N	91.50 W
Black ≃, Mi., U.S.	190	46.40 N	90.03 W
Black ≃, Mi., U.S.	190	45.30 N	84.29 W
Black ≃, Mi., U.S.	214	43.00 N	82.25 W
Black ≃, N.Y., U.S.	188	43.59 N	76.04 W
Black ≃, N.Y., U.S.	214	41.28 N	82.11 W
Black ≃, S.C., U.S.	192	33.34 N	79.15 W
Black ≃, Vt., U.S.	188	43.36 N	72.19 W
Black ≃, Vt., U.S.	188	44.55 N	72.13 W
Black ≃, Wi., U.S.	224	46.49 N	123.13 W
Black ≃, Wi., U.S.	190	43.57 N	91.22 W
Black, East Branch ≃	214	44.26 N	90.42 W
Black, Middle Branch ≃	216	42.25 N	86.14 W
Black, South Branch ≃	216	42.25 N	86.15 W
Black, West Branch ≃	214	41.22 N	82.07 W
Blackadder Water ≃	44	55.46 N	2.15 W
Blackall	166	24.25 S	145.28 E
Black Bay c	190	48.40 N	88.30 W
Black Bay Peninsula ≻	190	48.38 N	88.21 W
Black Bear Island Lake ⊘	184	55.38 N	105.40 W
Blackberry Creek ≃	216	41.48 N	88.27 W
Black Birch Heights	216	41.45 N	88.23 W
Black Birch Lake ⊘	184	56.54 N	107.45 W
Black Brook ≃, Ma., U.S.	283	41.59 N	71.03 W
Black Brook ≃, N.J., U.S.	285	40.42 N	74.31 W
Black Bullock Hill ⌃	276	40.42 N	74.31 W
Blackburn, Austl.	274b	37.49 S	145.08 E
Blackburn, Eng., U.K.	44	53.45 N	2.29 W
Blackburn, Scot., U.K.	46	55.52 N	3.38 W
Blackburn, Mount ⌃	180	61.44 N	143.26 W
Blackburne ⌖	171a	26.53 S	152.06 E
Black Butte ⌃, Ca., U.S.	228	34.33 N	117.43 W
Black Butte ⌃, Mt., U.S.	202	46.47 N	110.56 W
Black Butte ⌃, Or., U.S.	224	44.24 N	121.38 W
Black Butte Lake ⊘¹	204	39.49 N	122.20 W
Blackburn Range ⰾ	171a	27.00 S	152.00 E
Black Canyon of the Gunnison National Monument ♦	200	38.35 N	107.42 W
Blackcraig Hill ⌃	44	55.18 N	4.08 W
Black Creek ≃, B.C., Can.	182	49.50 N	125.07 W
Black Creek ≃, On., Can.	284b	43.50 N	79.01 W
Black Creek ≃, N.Y., U.S.	210	43.05 N	78.00 W
Black Creek Park ♦	275b	43.47 N	79.32 W
Black Creek Pioneer Village ⵜ¹	275b	43.47 N	79.32 W
Black Cypress Creek ≃	222	32.53 N	94.26 W
Blackden Heath	262	53.14 N	2.28 W
Black Devon ≃	46	56.06 N	3.47 W
Black Diamond, Ab., Can.	182	50.42 N	114.14 W
Black Diamond, Wa., U.S.	224	47.18 N	122.00 W
Black Donald Lake ⊘	212	45.13 N	76.55 W

	English	Deutsch	Español	Français	Português
⌃	Mountain	Berg	Montaña	Montagne	Montanha
ⰾ	Mountains	Gebirge	Montañas	Montagnes	Montanhas
ⵜ	Pass	Paß	Paso	Col	Passo
V	Valley, Canyon	Tal, Cañon	Valle, Cañón	Vallée, Canyon	Vale, Canhão
≻	Cape	Kap	Cabo	Cap	Cabo
I	Island	Insel	Isla	Île	Ilha
II	Islands	Inseln	Islas	Îles	Ilhas
≃	Other Topographic Features	Andere Topographische Objekte	Otros Elementos Topográficos	Autres données topographiques	Outros acidentes topográficos

ESPAÑOL

Nombre	Página	Lat.°′	Long.°′ W = Oeste
Black Down Hills ⛰[2]	42	50.57 N	3.09 W
Blackdown Tableland National Park ♠	166	23.43 S	149.05 E
Blackduck	190	47.43 N	94.32 W
Black Duck ≃	176	56.51 N	89.02 W
Black Eagle	202	47.31 N	111.16 W
Black Esk ≃	44	55.12 N	3.10 W
Blackfalds	182	52.23 N	113.47 W
Blackfeet Indian Reservation ➧[4]	202	48.40 N	113.00 W
Blackfoot, Id., U.S.	202	43.11 N	112.20 W
Blackfoot, Mt., U.S.	182	48.34 N	112.52 W
Blackfoot ≃, Id., U.S.	202	43.08 N	112.30 W
Blackfoot ≃, Mt., U.S.	202	46.52 N	113.53 W
Blackfoot, North Fork ≃	202	46.59 N	113.07 W
Blackfoot Indian Reserve ➧[4]	182	50.45 N	113.00 W
Blackfoot Reservoir ⊜[1]	202	42.55 N	111.35 W
Blackford	46	56.15 N	3.46 W
Blackford □[6]	216	40.27 N	85.22 W
Black Forest → Schwarzwald ⛰	58	48.00 N	8.15 E
Blackhall Colliery	44	54.44 N	1.14 W
Blackhall Mountain ʌ	200	41.02 N	106.41 W
Black Hameldon ʌ[2]	262	53.44 N	2.08 W
Black Hawk	184	48.48 N	93.59 W
Black Hawk Creek ≃	190	42.30 N	92.21 W
Black Head ›, Ire.	48	53.08 N	9.17 W
Black Head ›, Eng., U.K.	42	50.01 N	5.06 W
Blackhead Bay ⊂	186	48.34 N	53.15 W
Blackheath, Austl.	170	33.38 S	150.17 E
Blackheath, S. Afr.	273d	26.08 S	27.58 E
Blackheath, Eng., U.K.	260	51.12 N	0.31 W
Black Hill ʌ[2], Eng., U.K.	262	53.20 N	2.01 W
Black Hill ʌ[2], Eng., U.K.	262	53.33 N	1.53 W
Black Hills ⛰	198	44.00 N	104.00 W
Black Hills ⛰[2]	282	37.50 N	121.52 W
Blackhope Scar ʌ	46	55.44 N	3.05 W
Black Horse, Oh., U.S.	214	41.09 N	81.18 W
Black Horse, Pa., U.S.	285	40.06 N	75.19 W
Black Horse, Pa., U.S.	285	39.55 N	75.25 W
Black Horse Creek ≃	285	40.05 N	75.43 W
Black Island ı	184	51.10 N	96.30 W
Black Isle ›[1]	46	57.35 N	4.15 W
Black Jack	219	38.47 N	90.16 W
Black Jack Mountain ʌ	228	33.23 N	118.24 W
Black-Lake	206	46.03 N	71.21 W
Black Lake ⊜, On., Can.	212	44.46 N	76.18 W
Black Lake ⊜, Sk., Can.	176	59.10 N	105.20 W
Black Lake ⊜, Mi., U.S.	190	45.28 N	84.15 W
Black Lake ⊜, N.Y., U.S.	212	44.31 N	75.35 W
Black Lake ⊜, Wa., U.S.	224	47.00 N	122.58 W
Black Lake Bayou ≃	194	32.01 N	93.09 W
Blacklegs Creek ≃	214	40.30 N	79.27 W
Blackley ➧[8]	262	53.31 N	2.13 W
Black Lick	214	40.28 N	79.11 W
Blacklick Creek ≃	214	40.28 N	79.13 W
Blacklick Creek, North Branch ≃	214	40.29 N	78.55 W
Blacklick Estates	218	39.54 N	83.22 W
Blacklog Mountain ʌ	214	40.20 N	77.45 W
Blacklunans	46	56.44 N	3.22 W
Black Mesa ʌ, U.S.	196	37.05 N	103.10 W
Black Mesa ʌ, Az., U.S.	200	36.35 N	110.20 W
Blackmoor ⛰[1]	42	50.24 N	4.46 W
Blackmoorfoot Reservoir ⊜[1]	262	53.37 N	1.51 W
Blackmoor Vale ∨	42	50.56 N	2.25 W
Blackmore	260	51.41 N	0.19 E
Blackmore, Mount ʌ	202	45.27 N	111.01 W
Black Moshannon State Park ♠	214	40.54 N	78.03 W
Black Mountain	192	35.37 N	82.19 W
Black Mountain ʌ, D.Y.	124	27.17 N	90.23 E
Black Mountain ʌ, Wales, U.K.	42	51.52 N	3.46 W
Black Mountain ʌ, U.S.	192	36.54 N	82.54 W
Black Mountain ʌ, Az., U.S.	200	32.46 N	110.57 W
Black Mountain ʌ, Ca., U.S.	226	35.24 N	120.21 W
Black Mountain ʌ, Ca., U.S.	228	35.08 N	117.14 W
Black Mountain ʌ, Ca., U.S.	282	37.19 N	122.09 W
Black Mountain ʌ, Id., U.S.	202	46.53 N	115.33 W
Black Mountain ʌ, Mt., U.S.	202	46.44 N	112.31 W
Black Mountain ʌ, Or., U.S.	202	45.13 N	119.17 W
Black Mountain ʌ, Wy., U.S.	202	44.45 N	107.22 W
Black Mountain ʌ[2], Austl.	166	21.08 S	139.41 E
Black Mountain ʌ[2], Ca., U.S.	228	32.59 N	117.07 W
Black Mountain ʌ[2], Tx., U.S.	222	31.09 N	97.44 W
Black Mountains ⛰, Wales, U.K.	42	51.57 N	3.08 W
Black Mountains ⛰, Az., U.S.	200	35.30 N	114.30 W
Black Nossob ≃	156	23.05 S	18.45 E
Black Oak	216	41.33 N	87.23 W
Black Peak ʌ	200	34.08 N	114.13 W
Black Pine Peak ʌ	202	42.08 N	113.08 W
Black Pipe Creek ≃	198	43.47 N	101.14 W
Black Point	226	38.07 N	122.31 W
Black Point ›, Austl.	168b	34.37 S	137.54 E
Black Point ›, Austl.	170	34.47 S	150.50 E
Black Point ›, Ak., U.S.	180	57.00 N	153.18 W
Blackpool	44	53.50 N	3.03 W
Blackpool □[8]	262	53.47 N	3.02 W
Blackpool (Squire's Gate) Airport ⊠	262	53.47 N	3.02 W
Blackpool Football Ground ♠	262	53.49 N	3.03 W
Blackpool Tower ʊ	262	53.49 N	3.03 W
Black Range ⛰	200	33.20 N	107.50 W
Black River, Jam.	241q	18.01 N	77.51 W
Black River, N.Y., U.S.	212	44.00 N	75.47 W
Black River Bay ⊂, Jam.	241q	18.00 N	77.51 W
Black River Bay ⊂, N.Y., U.S.	212	43.58 N	76.07 W
Black River Falls	190	44.17 N	90.51 W
Black Rock, Austl.	274b	37.59 S	145.01 E
Black Rock, Ar., U.S.	194	36.06 N	91.05 W
Black Rock, Ma., U.S.	283	42.14 N	70.49 W
Black Rock ı[2]	48	54.05 N	10.22 W
Black Rock ıı[1]	244	53.39 S	41.48 W
Black Rock Desert ➧[2]	204	41.10 N	119.00 W
Blackrod	262	53.35 N	2.35 W
Blacksburg, S.C., U.S.	192	35.07 N	81.30 W
Blacksburg, Va., U.S.	192	37.13 N	80.24 W
Blacks Creek ≃	285	40.08 N	74.43 W
Black Sea ⊤[2]	22	43.00 N	35.00 E
Blacks Fork ≃	200	41.24 N	109.38 W

FRANÇAIS

Nom	Page	Lat.°′	Long.°′ W = Ouest
Blacks Harbour	186	45.03 N	66.47 W
Blackshear	192	31.18 N	82.14 W
Blackshear, Lake ⊜[1]	192	31.56 N	83.56 W
Blacksod Bay ⊂	48	54.08 N	10.00 W
Black Springs, Austl.	170	33.52 S	149.42 E
Black Springs, Austl.	274b	37.46 S	145.19 E
Black Springs Hill ʌ[2]	274b	37.46 S	145.19 E
Black Star Canyon ∨	280	33.47 N	117.39 W
Blackstone, Ma., U.S.	207	42.01 N	71.32 W
Blackstone, Va., U.S.	192	37.04 N	77.59 W
Blackstone ≃, Ab., Can.	182	52.50 N	116.07 W
Blackstone ≃, Yk., Can.	180	65.51 N	137.12 W
Blackstone Lake ⊜	212	45.14 N	79.53 W
Black Sugarloaf Mountain ʌ	166	31.20 S	151.33 E
Black Thunder Creek ≃	198	43.33 N	104.41 W
Blacktown	170	33.46 S	150.55 E
Blackville	192	33.21 N	81.16 W
Black Volta (Volta Noire) ≃	150	8.41 N	1.33 W
Blackwall Tunnel ➧[5]	260	51.30 N	0.01 E
Blackwalnut Point ›	208	38.40 N	76.20 W
Black Warrior ≃	194	32.32 N	87.51 W
Blackwatch Hills	210	43.05 N	77.27 W
Blackwater, Austl.	166	23.35 S	148.53 E
Blackwater, Ire.	48	52.26 N	6.21 W
Blackwater ≃, Europe	44	54.31 N	6.34 W
Blackwater ≃, Ire.	48	53.39 N	6.43 W
Blackwater ≃, Ire.	48	51.51 N	7.50 W
Blackwater ≃, Eng., U.K.	260	51.45 N	1.00 E
Blackwater ≃, U.S.	194	30.36 N	87.02 W
Blackwater ≃, Md., U.S.	208	38.21 N	76.01 W
Blackwater ≃, Mo., U.S.	194	38.56 N	92.51 W
Blackwater ≃, Va., U.S.	208	36.33 N	76.55 W
Blackwater Creek ≃, Austl.	166	25.56 S	144.20 E
Black Water Creek ≃, Fl., U.S.	220	28.51 N	81.24 W
Blackwater Draw ∨	196	33.35 N	101.50 W
Blackwaterfoot	46	55.30 N	5.19 W
Blackwater Lake ⊜	180	64.00 N	123.05 W
Blackwater Reservoir ⊜[1]	46	56.41 N	4.46 W
Blackwater Sound ɰ	220	25.10 N	80.25 W
Blackwell, Ok., U.S.	196	36.48 N	97.16 W
Blackwell, Tx., U.S.	196	32.05 N	100.19 W
Blackwood, Austl.	168b	35.02 S	138.37 E
Blackwood, Austl.	169	37.29 S	144.19 E
Blackwood, N.J., U.S.	285	39.48 N	75.03 W
Blackwood ≃	162	34.19 S	115.11 E
Blackwood, Cape ›	164	7.50 S	144.30 E
Blackwood Terrace	285	39.48 N	75.05 W
Bladel	52	51.23 N	5.13 E
Bladenboro	192	34.32 N	78.47 W
Bladensburg, Md., U.S.	284c	38.56 N	76.56 W
Bladensburg, Oh., U.S.	214	40.17 N	82.17 W
Blades	208	38.38 N	75.36 W
Bladgrond	158	28.52 S	19.57 E
Bladnoch ≃	44	54.51 N	4.25 W
Bladworth	184	51.18 N	106.09 W
Blaenau Ffestiniog	42	52.59 N	3.56 W
Blaenavon	42	51.48 N	3.05 W
Bláfell ʌ	24a	64.32 N	19.53 W
Blagaj	36	43.15 N	17.50 E
Blagdon	42	51.20 N	2.43 W
Blagodarnoje	86	47.03 N	82.10 E
Blagodarnyj	72	45.06 N	43.27 E
Blagodatnoje, S.S.S.R.	78	51.32 N	34.54 E
Blagodatnoje, S.S.S.R.	83	47.53 N	38.29 E
Blagodatnoje, S.S.S.R.	83	47.42 N	37.25 E
Blagodatnoje, S.S.S.R.	86	51.18 N	72.49 E
Blagodatovka	80	52.14 N	50.27 E
Blagoevgrad	38	42.01 N	23.06 E
Blagoveščenka, S.S.S.R.	80	51.19 N	44.03 E
Blagoveščenka, S.S.S.R.	86	52.50 N	79.52 E
Blagoveščenka, S.S.S.R.	86	54.22 N	66.58 E
Blagoveščensk, S.S.S.R.	86	55.01 N	55.59 E
Blagoveščensk, S.S.S.R.	89	50.17 N	127.32 E
Blagoveščenskoje, S.S.S.R.	85	43.18 N	74.12 E
Blagoveščenskoje, S.S.S.R.	86	58.08 N	62.58 E
Blåhø ʌ	26	62.45 N	9.19 E
Blåhøj	41	55.51 N	9.01 E
Blaichach	58	47.34 N	10.15 E
Blaikfjället ʌ	26	64.33 N	16.12 E
Blain, Fr.	32	47.29 N	1.46 W
Blain, Pa., U.S.	208	40.20 N	77.31 W
Blaina	42	51.46 N	3.10 W
Blain City	214	40.45 N	78.34 W
Blaine, Mn., U.S.	190	45.09 N	93.14 W
Blaine, Wa., U.S.	224	48.59 N	122.44 W
Blaine Creek ≃	188	38.11 N	82.37 W
Blaine Hill	279b	40.16 N	79.53 W
Blaine Lake	184	52.50 N	106.54 W
Blaineys	224	48.53 N	123.47 W
Blainville	206	45.40 N	73.52 W
Blainville-sur-l'Eau	58	48.33 N	6.24 E
Blair, On., Can.	212	43.23 N	80.23 W
Blair, Ne., U.S.	198	41.32 N	96.07 W
Blair, Ok., U.S.	196	34.46 N	99.20 W
Blair, Wi., U.S.	190	44.18 N	91.14 W
Blair □[6]	214	40.30 N	78.25 W
Blair Athol	166	22.42 S	147.33 E
Blair Atholl	46	56.46 N	3.51 W
Blairgowrie	46	56.36 N	3.21 W
Blairs Mills	214	40.17 N	77.43 W
Blairstown, Ia., U.S.	190	41.54 N	92.05 W
Blairstown, N.J., U.S.	210	40.59 N	74.57 W
Blairsville, Ga., U.S.	192	34.52 N	83.57 W
Blairsville, Pa., U.S.	214	40.25 N	79.15 W
Blaise ≃, Fr.	50	48.46 N	1.25 E
Blaise ≃, Fr.	58	48.38 N	4.43 E
Blaisy-Bas	58	47.22 N	4.44 E
Blaj	38	46.11 N	23.55 E
Blakehurst	274a	33.59 S	151.07 E
Blakeley Canal ≊	226	36.09 N	119.48 W
Blakely, Ga., U.S.	192	31.22 N	84.56 W
Blakely, Pa., U.S.	210	41.28 N	75.35 W
Blakely Island ı	224	48.33 N	122.50 W
Blakeney, Eng., U.K.	42	52.58 N	1.00 E
Blakeney, Eng., U.K.	42	51.46 N	2.29 W
Blake Plateau ✣[4]	16	31.00 N	79.00 W
Blake Point ›	190	48.12 N	88.25 W
Blake Ridge ✣[3]	16	29.00 N	73.30 W
Blakes	208	37.30 N	76.22 W
Blakesburg	190	40.57 N	92.38 W
Blakeslee, Oh., U.S.	216	41.31 N	84.44 W
Blakeslee, Pa., U.S.	210	41.06 N	75.36 W
Blalock Island ı	202	45.53 N	119.41 W
Blâmont, Fr.	58	48.35 N	6.51 E
Blamont, Fr.	58	47.23 N	6.51 E
Blanc, Cap → Nouâdhibou, Râs ›	148	20.46 N	17.03 W
Blanc, Cap ›	36	37.20 N	9.51 E
Blanc, Mont ʌ, P.Q., Can.	186	48.47 N	66.52 W
Blanc, Mont (Monte Bianco) ʌ, Europe	62	45.50 N	6.52 E
Blanca	200	37.27 N	105.31 W
Blanca, Bahía ⊂	252	38.55 S	62.10 W
Blanca, Isla ı	248	9.06 S	78.38 W

PORTUGUÊS

Nome	Página	Lat.°′	Long.°′ W = Oeste
Blanca, Laguna ⊜	254	52.25 S	71.10 W
Blanca, Punta ›	258	34.57 S	57.40 W
Blanca, Sierra ʌ	200	31.15 N	105.26 W
Blanca Grande, Laguna ⊜	252	38.26 S	63.55 W
Blanca Lake ⊜	224	47.53 N	121.21 W
Blanca Peak ʌ	200	37.35 N	105.29 W
Blanc du Cheilon, Mont ʌ	58	45.59 N	7.25 E
Blanchard, Ok., U.S.	196	35.08 N	97.39 W
Blanchard, Pa., U.S.	210	41.04 N	77.36 W
Blanchard, Wa., U.S.	224	48.35 N	122.24 W
Blanchard ≃	216	41.02 N	84.18 W
Blanchardville	190	42.48 N	89.51 W
Blanche ≃, On., Can.	190	47.34 N	79.32 W
Blanche ≃, P.Q., Can.	206	46.40 N	72.08 W
Blanche, Cape ›	162	33.01 S	134.09 E
Blanche, Dent ʌ	58	46.03 N	7.36 E
Blanche, Lake ⊜, Austl.	162	22.25 S	123.17 E
Blanche, Lake ⊜, Austl.	166	29.15 S	139.39 E
Blanche, Mer → Beloje more ⊤[2]	24	65.30 N	38.00 E
Blanche Channel ɰ	175e	8.30 S	157.30 E
Blancheface	261	48.32 N	2.06 E
Blanchester	218	39.17 N	83.59 W
Blanchisseuse	241r	10.47 N	61.18 W
Blanco, S. Afr.	158	33.57 S	22.24 E
Blanco, Tx., U.S.	196	30.06 N	98.25 W
Blanco ≃, Arg.	252	30.12 S	69.05 W
Blanco ≃, Arg.	254	47.22 S	71.12 W
Blanco ≃, Bol.	248	13.09 S	63.46 W
Blanco ≃, Ec.	246	0.28 N	79.25 W
Blanco ≃, Perú	248	5.27 S	73.47 W
Blanco ≃, Tx., U.S.	196	29.51 N	97.55 W
Blanco, Cabo → Nouâdhibou, Râs ›	148	20.46 N	17.03 W
Blanco, Cabo ›	236	9.34 N	85.07 W
Blanco, Cañon ∨	200	35.20 N	105.05 W
Blanco, Cape ›	202	42.50 N	124.34 W
Blanco, Lago ⊜	254	54.03 S	69.00 W
Blanco, Mar → Beloje more ⊤[2]	24	65.30 N	38.00 E
Blanco, Monte → Blanc, Mont ʌ	62	45.50 N	6.52 E
Blanco, Rio ≃	200	37.07 N	107.03 W
Blanco Creek ≃	196	28.19 N	97.19 W
Blanc-Sablon	186	51.25 N	57.07 W
Bland, Mo., U.S.	219	38.18 N	91.37 W
Bland, Va., U.S.	192	37.06 N	81.06 W
Blanda ≃	24a	65.39 N	20.18 W
Blandburg	214	40.41 N	78.24 W
Blandford	207	42.10 N	72.55 W
Blandford Forum	42	50.52 N	2.11 W
Blanding	200	37.37 N	109.28 W
Blandinsville	190	40.33 N	90.51 W
Blandon	208	40.26 N	75.53 W
Blandy	261	48.34 N	2.47 E
Blanes	34	41.41 N	2.48 E
Blangkejeren	114	3.59 N	97.20 E
Blangpidie	114	3.45 N	96.51 E
Blangy-le-Château	50	49.14 N	0.17 E
Blangy-sur-Bresle	50	49.56 N	1.38 E
Blanice ≃	61	49.05 N	14.03 E
Blankenberg	56	50.45 N	7.22 E
Blankenberge	50	51.19 N	3.08 E
Blankenburg	54	51.48 N	10.58 E
Blankenburg ➧[8]	264a	52.35 N	13.28 E
Blankenese ➧[8]	52	53.33 N	9.48 E
Blankenfelde	54	52.20 N	13.23 E
Blankenfelde ➧[8]	264a	52.37 N	13.23 E
Blankenhain	54	50.51 N	11.21 E
Blankenheim, B.R.D.	56	50.26 N	6.39 E
Blankenheim, D.D.R.	54	51.31 N	11.25 E
Blankensee	54	52.14 N	13.08 E
Blankenstein	263	51.24 N	7.14 E
Blanket	196	31.49 N	98.47 W
Blanquilla, Isla ı	246	11.51 N	64.37 W
Blansko	30	49.22 N	16.39 E
Blanský Les ➧[3]	61	48.52 N	14.16 E
Blantyre	154	15.47 S	35.00 E
Blanzac	62	45.07 N	3.51 E
Blanzy	58	46.42 N	4.23 E
Blaricum	52	52.16 N	5.15 E
Blarney	48	51.56 N	8.34 W
Blarney Castle ⊥	48	51.56 N	8.34 W
Blasdell	210	42.47 N	78.49 W
Blasheim	52	52.18 N	8.34 E
Błaszki	30	51.39 N	18.27 E
Blatná	60	49.26 N	13.53 E
Blatnica	38	43.42 N	28.31 E
Blatten	58	46.25 N	7.50 E
Blatzheim	56	50.51 N	6.38 E
Blau ≃	58	48.23 N	9.49 E
Blaubeuren	58	48.24 N	9.47 E
Blauen ʌ	58	47.47 N	7.42 E
Blauer Nil → Blue Nile ≃	140	15.38 N	32.31 E
Blaufelden	56	49.18 N	9.58 E
Blaustein	58	48.25 N	9.53 E
Blauvelt	276	41.03 N	73.57 W
Blauvelt State Park ♠	276	41.04 N	73.56 W
Blåvands Huk ›	26	55.33 N	8.05 E
Blawenburg	276	40.24 N	74.42 W
Blawnox	279b	40.29 N	79.51 W
Blaxland	170	33.45 S	150.36 E
Blaxland Creek ≃	274a	33.48 S	150.46 E
Blaydon	44	54.58 N	1.42 W
Blaye-et-Sainte-Luce	32	45.08 N	0.39 W
Blayney	166	33.32 S	149.15 E
Blaze, Point ›	164	12.56 S	130.12 E
Błażowa	30	49.54 N	22.05 E
Bleaker Island ı	254	52.13 S	58.53 W
Bleaklow Head ʌ	262	53.28 N	1.50 W
Blean	42	51.19 N	1.02 E
Bleckede	54	53.17 N	10.44 E
Bled	36	46.22 N	14.06 E
Bledsoe	196	33.38 N	103.01 W
Bleecker	210	43.07 N	74.22 W
Blefjell ʌ	26	59.48 N	9.10 E
Blega	115a	7.08 S	113.03 E
Bleibach	58	48.07 N	8.01 E
Bleiberg ob Villach	64	46.37 N	13.41 E
Bleiburg	61	46.35 N	14.48 E
Bleicherode	54	51.26 N	10.34 E
Blekendorf	54	54.16 N	10.38 E
Blekinge □[9]	26	56.20 N	15.05 E
Blekinge Län □[6]	26	56.20 N	15.20 E
Blendecques	50	50.43 N	2.16 E
Bléneau	50	47.42 N	2.57 E
Blenheim, Austl.	171a	27.39 S	152.20 E
Blenheim, On., Can.	214	42.20 N	82.00 W
Blenheim, N.Z.	172	41.31 S	173.57 E
Blenheim, N.J., U.S.	285	39.48 N	75.05 W
Blenheim Palace ʊ	42	51.47 N	1.21 W
Blenio, Val ∨	58	46.27 N	8.58 E
Blénod-lès-Pont-à-Mousson	56	48.53 N	6.03 E
Blénod-lès-Toul	58	48.36 N	5.50 E
Bléone ≃	62	44.03 N	6.00 E
Blérancourt	50	49.31 N	3.09 E
Bléré	50	47.20 N	1.00 E
Blerick	52	51.23 N	6.10 E
Blériot-Plage	50	50.57 N	1.50 E
Blesbokspruit ≃	273d	26.14 S	28.29 E
Blessing	222	28.52 N	96.13 W
Blessington	48	53.10 N	6.32 W
Bletchingley	260	51.14 N	0.06 W
Bletchley	42	52.00 N	0.46 W
Bletterans	58	46.45 N	5.27 E
Bleu → Chang ≃	90	31.48 N	121.10 E
Bleue, Mer ≡	212	45.24 N	75.30 W
Bleury	261	48.31 N	1.45 E
Bleus, Monts ⛰	154	1.30 N	30.30 E
Blevio	62	45.50 N	9.05 E
Blewett Falls Lake ⊜[1]	192	35.03 N	79.54 W
Blexen	52	53.32 N	8.32 E
Blidö ı	40	59.37 N	18.54 E
Blidworth	44	53.06 N	1.07 W
Bliedinghausen ➧[8]	263	51.09 N	7.12 E
Bliersheim ➧[8]	263	51.23 N	6.43 E
Blies ≃	56	49.07 N	7.04 E
Blieskastel	56	49.14 N	7.16 E
Bligh Sound ɰ	172	44.50 S	167.32 E
Bligh Water ɰ	175g	17.00 S	178.00 E
Bligny	50	49.11 N	3.52 E
Bligny-sur-Ouche	58	47.06 N	4.40 E
Blik, Mount ʌ	116	6.58 N	124.15 E
Blina	162	17.46 S	124.32 E
Blind ≃	276	40.57 N	73.42 W
Blind Creek ≃	274b	37.54 S	145.12 E
Blindley Heath	260	51.12 N	0.04 W
Blind River	190	46.10 N	82.58 W
Blinman	166	31.06 S	138.41 E
Blinnenhorn ʌ	58	46.26 N	8.19 E
Blinovskij	80	49.23 N	42.19 E
Bliss	210	42.34 N	78.15 W
Blissfield, Mi., U.S.	216	41.49 N	83.51 W
Blissfield, Oh., U.S.	214	40.24 N	81.58 W
Blitar	115a	8.06 S	112.09 E
Blithe ≃	42	52.45 N	1.50 W
Blithfield Reservoir ⊜[1]	42	52.48 N	1.53 W
Blitta	150	8.19 N	0.59 E
Blizn'uki	78	48.52 N	36.33 E
Blocher	218	38.43 N	85.39 W
Block Dam ➧[6]	212	45.12 N	76.54 W
Block Island	207	41.10 N	71.33 W
Block Island ı	207	41.11 N	71.35 W
Block Island Sound ɰ	207	41.10 N	71.45 W
Blockley	42	52.01 N	1.45 W
Blockton	198	40.36 N	94.28 W
Blodgett Mills	210	42.34 N	76.08 W
Bloed ≃	158	28.15 S	30.30 E
Bloedel	182	50.07 N	125.23 W
Bloedrivier, S. Afr.	158	28.06 S	30.33 E
Bloedrivier, S. Afr.	158	27.53 S	30.30 E
Bloekomspruit	158	26.45 S	28.21 E
Bloemendaal	52	52.24 N	4.37 E
Bloemfontein	158	29.12 S	26.07 E
Bloemhof	158	27.38 S	25.32 E
Bloemhofdam ⊜[1]	158	27.40 S	25.40 E
Blois	50	47.35 N	1.20 E
Blokhus	26	57.15 N	9.35 E
Blokzijl	52	52.44 N	5.57 E
Blombacher Bach ➧[8]	263	51.15 N	7.14 E
Blombacka	40	59.37 N	13.47 E
Blomberg	52	51.56 N	9.05 E
Blomstermåla	26	56.59 N	16.20 E
Blonay	58	46.28 N	6.54 E
Blönduós	24a	65.39 N	20.15 W
Blongas	115b	8.53 S	116.02 E
Blonville-sur-Mer	50	49.19 N	0.02 E
Blood Indian Creek ≃	184	50.55 N	111.03 W
Blood Indian Reserve ➧[4]	182	49.30 N	113.10 W
Blood Mountain ʌ	192	34.44 N	83.56 W
Blood River ⊥	158	28.20 S	30.35 E
Bloodsworth Island ı	208	38.10 N	76.03 W
Bloodvein ≃	184	51.45 N	96.44 W
Bloody Foreland ›	48	55.09 N	8.17 W
Bloomdale	216	41.10 N	83.33 W
Bloomer	190	45.06 N	91.29 W
Bloomfield, On., Can.	212	43.59 N	77.14 W
Bloomfield, Ct., U.S.	207	41.49 N	72.43 W
Bloomfield, In., U.S.	194	39.01 N	86.56 W
Bloomfield, Ia., U.S.	190	40.45 N	92.24 W
Bloomfield, Ky., U.S.	194	37.54 N	85.19 W
Bloomfield, Mo., U.S.	194	36.53 N	89.55 W
Bloomfield, Ne., U.S.	198	42.35 N	97.38 W
Bloomfield, N.J., U.S.	210	40.48 N	74.11 W
Bloomfield, N.M., U.S.	200	36.42 N	107.59 W
Bloomfield, Oh., U.S.	214	40.03 N	81.44 W
Bloomfield ➧[8]	279b	40.27 N	79.56 W
Bloomfield Glens	281	42.33 N	83.20 W
Bloomfield Highlands	281	42.36 N	83.16 W
Bloomfield Hills	216	42.35 N	83.14 W
Bloomfield Village	216	42.33 N	83.15 W
Bloomingburg, N.Y., U.S.	210	41.33 N	74.26 W
Bloomingburg, Oh., U.S.	218	39.36 N	83.23 W
Bloomingdale, Il., U.S.	216	41.57 N	88.04 W
Bloomingdale, Mi., U.S.	216	42.22 N	85.57 W
Bloomingdale, N.J., U.S.	210	41.00 N	74.19 W
Bloomingdale, Oh., U.S.	214	40.21 N	80.49 W
Blooming Glen	208	40.22 N	75.15 W
Blooming Grove, In., U.S.	218	39.30 N	85.04 W
Blooming Grove, N.Y., U.S.	210	41.25 N	74.11 W
Blooming Grove, Pa., U.S.	210	41.21 N	75.09 W
Blooming Grove, Tx., U.S.	222	32.06 N	96.43 W
Blooming Prairie	190	43.52 N	93.03 W
Bloomington, Ca., U.S.	228	34.04 N	117.23 W
Bloomington, Il., U.S.	216	40.29 N	88.59 W
Bloomington, In., U.S.	218	39.09 N	86.31 W
Bloomington, Mn., U.S.	190	44.50 N	93.17 W
Bloomington, N.Y., U.S.	210	41.53 N	74.03 W
Bloomington, Tx., U.S.	196	28.38 N	96.53 W
Bloomington, Wi., U.S.	190	42.53 N	90.55 W
Bloomington, Lake ⊜[1]	216	40.37 N	88.55 W
Blooming Valley	214	41.40 N	80.03 W
Bloomsburg	210	41.00 N	76.27 W
Bloomsbury, Austl.	166	20.43 S	148.35 E
Bloomsbury, N.J., U.S.	210	40.39 N	75.05 W
Bloomsdale Gardens	285	40.07 N	74.52 W
Bloomville, N.Y., U.S.	210	42.20 N	74.48 W
Bloomville, Oh., U.S.	214	41.03 N	83.00 W
Blora	115a	6.57 S	111.25 E
Bloserville	208	40.12 N	77.24 W
Blossburg	210	41.40 N	77.03 W
Blossom	196	33.39 N	95.23 W
Blossom Hill	208	40.05 N	76.19 W
Blötberget	40	60.07 N	15.04 E
Blotzheim	58	47.36 N	7.29 E
Blouberg	156	23.08 S	28.56 E
Blouberg ʌ	156	23.01 S	28.59 E
Bloubergstrand	158	33.47 S	18.28 E
Blouin, Lac ⊜	190	48.10 N	77.44 W
Bloumet	148	23.27 N	6.06 E
Blountstown	192	30.26 N	85.02 W
Blountsville	194	34.04 N	86.35 W
Blountville	192	36.31 N	82.19 W
Blovice	60	49.35 N	13.33 E
Blovstrød	41	55.52 N	12.24 E
Blowering Reservoir ⊜[1]	171b	35.30 S	148.15 E
Blowing Rock	192	36.08 N	81.40 W
Bloxham	42	52.02 N	1.22 W
Bloxom	208	37.49 N	75.37 W
Blšanka ≃	54	50.10 N	13.34 E
Blšany	54	50.10 N	13.29 E
Bludenz	58	47.09 N	9.49 E
Bludnaja ≃	88	51.24 N	110.39 E
Blue ≃, Az., U.S.	200	33.13 N	109.11 W
Blue ≃, Co., U.S.	200	40.03 N	106.24 W
Blue ≃, In., U.S.	216	41.07 N	85.30 W
Blue ≃, In., U.S.	218	38.11 N	86.19 W
Blue ≃, Ok., U.S.	196	33.53 N	95.56 W
Blue, Middle Fork ≃	218	38.33 N	86.07 W
Blue, South Fork ≃	218	38.26 N	86.11 W
Blue, West Fork ≃	218	38.33 N	86.07 W
Blue Anchor	285	39.41 N	74.52 W
Blue Anchor Brook ≃	285	39.42 N	74.49 W
Blue Ash	218	39.13 N	84.22 W
Blue Ball	218	39.29 N	84.21 W
Blue Bell	208	40.09 N	75.16 W
Bluebell Hill	260	51.20 N	0.30 E
Blue Bonnets, Champ de Course ♠	275a	45.29 N	73.39 W
Blue Brook ≃	276	40.40 N	74.25 W
Blue Buck Knob ʌ[2]	194	36.57 N	92.07 W
Bluebush Swamp ≡	162	20.30 S	137.25 E
Blue Creek, Oh., U.S.	218	38.47 N	83.20 W
Blue Creek, Wa., U.S.	182	48.19 N	117.49 W
Blue Creek, Wa., U.S.	202	48.19 N	117.49 W
Blue Creek ≃, Ca., U.S.	226	38.28 N	120.22 W
Blue Creek ≃, Id., U.S.	202	42.02 N	116.08 W
Blue Creek ≃, Ne., U.S.	198	41.19 N	102.10 W
Blue Creek ≃, Oh., U.S.	216	41.07 N	84.26 W
Blue Creek ≃, Ut., U.S.	200	41.31 N	112.24 W
Blue Cypress Lake ⊜	220	27.44 N	80.45 W
Blue Earth	190	43.38 N	94.06 W
Blue Earth ≃	190	44.09 N	94.02 W
Bluefield, Va., U.S.	192	37.15 N	81.16 W
Bluefield, W.V., U.S.	192	37.16 N	81.13 W
Bluefields	236	12.00 N	83.45 W
Bluefields, Bahía de ⊂	236	12.02 N	83.44 W
Bluefields Bay ⊂	241q	18.10 N	78.03 W
Blue Grass Airport ⊠	218	38.02 N	84.36 W
Blue Grotto → Azzurra, Grotta ⊥[5]	68	40.35 N	14.14 E
Blue Hill, Me., U.S.	188	44.24 N	68.35 W
Blue Hill, Ne., U.S.	198	40.19 N	98.26 W
Blue Hill Bay ⊂	188	44.15 N	68.30 W
Blue Hills	207	41.40 N	72.56 W
Blue Hills of Couteau ⛰[2]	186	47.59 N	57.43 W
Blue Hills Reservation ♠	283	42.13 N	71.05 W
Blue Island	216	41.39 N	87.40 W
Blue Jay	228	34.15 N	117.13 W
Bluejoint Lake ⊜	202	42.35 N	119.40 W
Blue Knob ʌ	214	40.17 N	78.34 W
Blue Knob State Park ♠	214	40.16 N	78.35 W
Blue Lagoon National Park ♠	154	15.30 S	27.25 E
Blue Lake National Park ♠	171a	27.31 S	153.29 E
Blue Licks Battlefield State Park ♠	218	38.26 N	84.00 W
Blue Marsh Lake ⊜[1]	208	40.25 N	76.05 W
Blue Mesa Reservoir ⊜[1]	200	38.27 N	107.10 W
Blue Mosque ʊ[1]	273c	30.02 N	31.15 E
Blue Mound, Il., U.S.	219	39.42 N	89.07 W
Blue Mound, Ks., U.S.	198	38.05 N	95.00 W
Blue Mound, Tx., U.S.	222	32.51 N	97.19 W
Blue Mountain, Ms., U.S.	194	34.40 N	89.01 W
Blue Mountain, N.Y., U.S.	210	42.07 N	74.01 W
Blue Mountain ʌ, N.B., Can.	186	47.49 N	66.19 W
Blue Mountain ʌ, Nf., Can.	186	50.24 N	57.10 W
Blue Mountain ʌ, Ar., U.S.	194	34.41 N	94.03 W
Blue Mountain ʌ, Mt., U.S.	198	47.16 N	104.10 W
Blue Mountain ʌ, N.H., U.S.	188	44.47 N	71.28 W
Blue Mountain ʌ, Pa., U.S.	188	40.15 N	77.30 W
Blue Mountain ʌ[2], On., Can.	190	48.15 N	80.07 W
Blue Mountain ʌ[2], On., Can.	212	44.40 N	77.58 W
Blue Mountain Peak ʌ	241q	18.03 N	76.35 W
Blue Mountains ⛰, Austl.	170	33.37 S	150.17 E
Blue Mountains ⛰, Jam.	241q	18.06 N	76.40 W
Blue Mountains ⛰, U.S.	202	45.30 N	118.15 W
Blue Mountains ⛰, Me., U.S.	188	44.50 N	70.35 W
Blue Mountains National Park ♠	170	33.40 S	150.25 E
Blue Mud Bay ⊂	164	13.26 S	135.56 E
Blue Nile (Al-Bahr al-Azraq) (Abay) ≃	140	15.38 N	32.31 E
Bluenose Lake ⊜	180	68.25 N	119.45 W
Blue Point	276	40.45 N	73.02 W
Blue Point ›	276	40.44 N	73.02 W
Blue Rapids	198	39.40 N	96.39 W
Blue Ridge, Ab., Can.	182	54.08 N	115.22 W
Blue Ridge, Ga., U.S.	192	34.51 N	84.19 W
Blue Ridge, Il., U.S.	216	40.17 N	88.29 W
Blue Ridge ⛰	178	37.00 N	82.00 W
Blue Ridge Summit	208	39.43 N	77.28 W
Blue River	182	52.05 N	119.17 W
Blue Rock Springs Park ♠	282	38.08 N	122.12 W
Bluesky	182	56.04 N	118.14 W
Blue Springs	198	40.08 N	96.39 W
Blue Stack Mountains ⛰	48	54.45 N	8.05 W
Bluestone ≃	192	37.34 N	80.59 W
Bluestone Dam ➧[6]	192	37.36 N	80.53 W
Bluestone Lake ⊜[1]	192	37.30 N	80.50 W
Bluestone State Park ♠	192	37.37 N	80.56 W
Bluewater	200	35.15 N	107.59 W
Blue Water Bridge ➧[5]	214	43.00 N	82.25 W
Bluff, N.Z.	172	46.36 S	168.20 E
Bluff, Ut., U.S.	200	37.17 N	109.33 W
Bluff Cape ›	110	18.00 N	94.26 E
Bluff City, Il., U.S.	219	38.57 N	89.02 W
Bluff City, Tn., U.S.	192	36.28 N	82.15 W
Bluff Cove ⊂	280	33.48 N	118.24 W
Bluff Creek ≃, U.S.	196	36.58 N	97.26 W
Bluff Creek ≃, Ks., U.S.	198	37.02 N	99.29 W
Bluff Dale	196	32.21 N	98.01 W
Bluff Head ›	271d	22.11 N	114.12 E
Bluff Island ı	271d	22.19 N	114.21 E
Bluff Knoll ʌ	162	34.23 S	118.20 E
Bluff Park	194	33.24 N	86.51 W
Bluff Point ›	162	27.50 S	114.06 E
Bluffs	219	39.45 N	90.32 W
Bluff Springs	219	39.59 N	90.21 W
Bluffton, In., U.S.	216	40.44 N	85.10 W
Bluffton, Oh., U.S.	216	40.53 N	83.53 W
Bluffton, S.C., U.S.	192	32.14 N	80.51 W
Bluffy Lake ⊜	184	50.47 N	92.55 W
Bluford	219	38.20 N	88.45 W
Blum	222	32.09 N	97.24 W
Blumberg, B.R.D.	58	47.50 N	8.31 E
Blumberg, D.D.R.	54	52.36 N	13.37 E
Blumenau	252	26.56 S	49.03 W
Blumenhof	184	50.01 N	107.41 W
Blümlisalp ʌ	58	46.30 N	7.47 E
Blunt	198	44.30 N	99.59 W
Blup Blup Island ı	164	3.30 S	144.37 E
Bly	202	42.23 N	121.02 W
Blying Sound ɰ	180	59.50 N	149.15 W
Blyth, Austl.	168b	33.51 S	138.29 E
Blyth, On., Can.	190	43.44 N	81.26 W
Blyth, Eng., U.K.	44	55.07 N	1.30 W
Blyth ≃, Austl.	164	12.04 S	134.35 E
Blyth ≃, Eng., U.K.	42	52.18 N	1.40 E
Blyth ≃, Eng., U.K.	44	55.08 N	1.31 W
Blyth Bridge	46	55.42 N	3.24 W
Blythe	204	33.36 N	114.35 W
Blythedale	214	40.15 N	79.48 W
Blytheswood	214	42.07 N	82.36 W
Blytheville	194	35.55 N	89.55 W
Blytheville Air Force Base ■	194	35.57 N	89.57 W
Blyth Range ⛰	162	26.50 S	129.00 E
Bnei Braq → Bene Beraq	132	32.05 N	34.50 E
Bø, Nor.	24	68.37 N	14.33 E
Bø, Nor.	26	59.25 N	9.04 E
Bo, S.L.	150	7.56 N	11.21 W
Boa	154	10.32 S	28.06 E
Boa Barrinha	256	23.18 S	47.10 W
Boac	116	13.27 N	121.50 E
Boaco	236	12.28 N	85.40 W
Boaco □[5]	236	12.30 N	85.30 W
Boadilla del Monte	266a	40.24 N	3.53 W
Boa Esperança, Bra.	255	21.05 S	45.34 W
Boa Esperança, Bra.	256	22.48 S	42.34 W
Boa Esperança, Represa ⊜[1]	250	6.50 S	44.00 W
Bo'ai	102	35.10 N	113.04 E
Boali	152	4.48 N	18.07 E
Boalia	126	23.35 N	88.57 E
Boalsburg	214	40.46 N	77.48 W
Boane	156	26.06 S	32.19 E
Boano, Pulau ı	164	2.56 S	127.56 E
Boa Nova	255	14.22 S	40.10 W
Bo'ao	110	19.14 N	110.34 E
Boara Pisani	64	45.08 N	11.47 E
Boara Polesine	64	45.07 N	11.48 E
Board Camp Mountain ʌ	204	40.42 N	123.43 W
Boardman	214	41.01 N	80.39 W
Boardman ≃	190	44.46 N	85.38 W
Boarhills	46	56.19 N	2.42 W
Boario Terme	64	45.54 N	10.10 E
Boat Basin	182	49.29 N	126.25 W
Boat Channel ɰ	212	44.10 N	76.31 W
Boath	46	57.44 N	4.23 W
Boat Lake ⊜	212	44.44 N	81.13 W
Boatman	166	27.16 S	146.55 E
Boat of Garten	46	57.20 N	3.44 W
Boa Vereda	256	22.27 S	46.14 W
Boa Viagem	250	5.07 S	39.44 W
Boa Vida	256	22.18 S	42.47 W
Boa Vista, Bra.	246	2.49 N	60.40 W
Boa Vista, Bra.	252	26.17 S	48.50 W
Boa Vista ı	150a	16.05 N	22.50 W
Boa Vista, Morro ʌ[2]	287a	22.53 S	43.06 W
Boavita	246	6.20 N	72.35 W
Boawai	115b	8.46 S	121.10 E
Boayan Island ı	116	10.34 N	119.09 E
Boaz	194	34.12 N	86.09 W
Boba	115b	8.57 S	121.04 E
Bobai	102	22.12 N	109.52 E
Bobbau	54	51.41 N	12.16 E
Bobbili	122	18.34 N	83.22 E
Bobbing	260	51.21 N	0.43 E
Bobbingworth	260	51.44 N	0.13 E
Bobbin Head	274a	33.39 S	151.08 E
Bobbio	62	44.46 N	9.23 E
Bobbio Pellice	62	44.48 N	7.07 E
Bobbys Run ≃	285	39.58 N	74.48 W
Bobcaygeon	212	44.33 N	78.33 W
Bobenheim-Roxheim	56	49.35 N	8.21 E
Bobigny	50	48.54 N	2.27 E
Böbingen, B.R.D.	56	48.49 N	9.54 E
Bobingen, B.R.D.	58	48.16 N	10.50 E
Bobitz	54	53.47 N	11.20 E
Bob Lake ⊜	212	44.55 N	78.47 W
Böblingen	56	48.41 N	9.01 E
Boblo Island Amusement Park ♠	281	42.06 N	83.07 W
Bobo Dioulasso	150	11.12 N	4.18 W
Boboiob, gora ʌ	85	40.52 N	70.21 E
Bobo Island ı	164	9.08 S	143.14 E
Bobolice	30	53.57 N	16.36 E
Bobonaza ≃	246	2.36 S	76.38 W
Bobonong	156	21.58 S	28.17 E
Bobotsari	115a	7.18 S	109.22 E
Bobr	76	54.20 N	29.16 E
Bóbr ≃, Pol.	30	52.04 N	15.04 E
Bobr ≃, S.S.S.R.	76	54.03 N	28.51 E
Bobrik ≃	76	52.08 N	26.46 E
Bobrikovo	83	47.56 N	39.13 E
Bobrinec	78	48.03 N	32.09 E
Bobrka	78	49.38 N	24.18 E
Bobrov	78	51.06 N	40.02 E
Bobrovica	78	50.44 N	31.22 E
Bobrujsk	76	53.09 N	29.14 E
Bobs Creek ≃	219	38.57 N	90.42 W
Bobs Lake ⊜	212	44.40 N	76.35 W
Bobtown	188	39.45 N	79.58 W
Bobuk	140	11.30 N	34.05 E
Bobures	246	9.15 N	71.11 W
Boby, Pic ʌ	157b	22.12 S	46.55 E
Boca ➧[8]	288	34.38 S	58.21 W
Bôca, Cachoeira da ᒪ	250	5.27 S	54.24 W
Boca Brava, Isla ı	236	8.13 N	82.16 W
Boca Chica	240m	17.59 N	66.32 W
Boca Chica Key ı	220	24.34 N	81.42 W
Bôca da Mata	250	9.41 S	36.11 W
Boca del Monte	236	8.21 N	82.07 W
Boca del Pozo	246	11.00 N	64.23 W
Boca del Río	234	19.06 N	96.06 W
Boca del Rosario	258	34.26 S	57.17 W
Boca de Quadra ɰ	182	55.08 N	130.50 W
Bôca do Acre	248	8.45 S	67.23 W
Bôca do Jari	250	1.07 S	51.58 W
Bocage, Cap ›	175f	21.12 S	165.35 E
Boca Grande	220	26.44 N	82.15 W
Boca Grande Channel ɰ	220	24.34 N	82.03 W
Boca Grande Key ı	220	24.32 N	82.00 W
Bocaina ≃	256	22.40 S	45.00 W
Bocaina, Serra da ⛰	256	22.43 S	44.40 W
Bocaina de Minas	256	22.10 S	44.24 W
Bocaiúva	255	17.07 S	43.49 W
Bocanda	150	7.04 N	4.30 W
Bocanegra	286d	12.01 S	77.07 W
Bocaranga	152	6.59 N	15.39 E
Boca Raton	220	26.21 N	80.05 W
Boca Reservoir ⊜[1]	226	39.24 N	120.06 W
Bocas del Toro	236	9.20 N	82.15 W
Bocas del Toro □[4]	236	8.50 N	82.10 W
Bocas del Toro, Archipiélago de ıı	236	9.20 N	82.10 W
Bocaue	116	14.48 N	120.55 E
Bocay	236	14.19 N	85.10 W
Bocay ≃	236	14.20 N	85.10 W
Boccaleone	66	44.39 N	11.48 E
Boccea ➧[8]	267a	41.58 N	12.19 E
Bocchigliero	68	39.25 N	16.45 E
Boccon	64	45.19 N	11.39 E
Bocconi	64	44.01 N	11.46 E
Bočejkovo	76	55.01 N	29.09 E
Bochan	88	53.09 N	103.48 E
Bochil	234	16.59 N	92.55 W
Böch Möron	86	49.40 N	90.20 E
Bochnia	30	49.58 N	20.26 E
Bocholt, Bel.	56	51.10 N	5.35 E
Bocholt, B.R.D.	52	51.50 N	6.36 E
Bocholtz	56	50.49 N	6.00 E
Bochov	54	50.06 N	13.02 E
Bochum, B.R.D.	56	51.28 N	7.13 E
Bochum, B.R.D.	263	51.28 N	7.13 E
Bochum, S. Afr.	156	23.17 S	29.07 E
Bockel	52	53.12 N	9.17 E
Böckel ➧[8]	263	51.13 N	7.12 E
Bockenem	52	52.00 N	10.07 E
Bockhorn	52	53.23 N	8.01 E
Böckstein	64	47.05 N	13.07 E
Bockum ➧[8], B.R.D.	263	51.20 N	6.44 E
Bockum ➧[8], B.R.D.	263	51.21 N	6.38 E
Bockum-Hövel	52	51.42 N	7.46 E
Bocognano	36	42.05 N	9.03 E
Bocón, Caño ≃	246	3.42 N	67.53 W
Boconó	246	9.15 N	70.16 W
Bocq ≃	56	50.20 N	4.53 E

≃ River	Fluß	Río	Rivière	Rio
≊ Canal	Kanal	Canal	Canal	Canal
ᒪ Waterfall, Rapids	Wasserfall, Stromschnellen	Cascada, Rápidos	Chute d'eau, Rapides	Cascata, Rápidos
ɰ Strait	Meeresstraße	Estrecho	Détroit	Estreito
⊂ Bay, Gulf	Bucht, Golf	Bahía, Golfo	Baie, Golfe	Baía, Golfo
⊜ Lake, Lakes	See, Seen	Lago, Lagos	Lac, Lacs	Lago, Lagos
≡ Swamp	Sumpf	Pantano	Marais	Pântano
⍓ Ice Features, Glacier	Eis- und Gletscherformen	Accidentes Glaciales	Formes glaciaires	Acidentes glaciares
⊤ Other Hydrographic Features	Andere Hydrographische Objekte	Otros Elementos Hidrográficos	Autres données hydrographiques	Outros acidentes hidrográficos

✣ Submarine Features	Untermeerische Objekte	Accidentes Submarinos	Formes de relief sous-marin	Acidentes submarinos
□ Political Unit	Politische Einheit	Unidad Politica	Entité politique	Unidade política
ʊ Cultural Institution	Kulturelle Institution	Institución Cultural	Institution culturelle	Instituição cultural
⊥ Historical Site	Historische Stätte	Sitio Histórico	Site historique	Sitio histórico
♠ Recreational Site	Erholungs- und Ferienort	Sitio de Recreo	Centre de loisirs	Area de Lazer
⊠ Airport	Flughafen	Aeropuerto	Aéroport	Aeroporto
■ Military Installation	Militäranlage	Instalación Militar	Installation militaire	Instalação militar
➧ Miscellaneous	Verschiedenes	Misceláneo	Divers	Diversos

Bocşa	38	45.23 N	21.47 E
Bocsów	54	52.19 N	14.58 E
Boda, Centraf.	152	4.19 N	17.28 E
Boda, Sve.	26	61.01 N	15.13 E
Böda, Sve.	26	57.15 N	17.03 E
Bodafors	26	57.30 N	14.42 E
Boda Glasbruk	26	56.44 N	15.40 E
Bodäi	272b	22.48 N	88.29 E
Bodajbo	88	57.51 N	114.10 E
Bodalangi	152	3.14 N	22.14 E
Bodalla	166	36.05 S	150.03 E
Bodallin	162	31.22 S	118.52 E
Bodåsgruvan	40	60.25 N	16.26 E
Bodcau Creek ≃	194	33.01 N	93.31 W
Boddam, Scot., U.K.	46	57.28 N	1.47 W
Boddam, Scot., U.K.	46a	59.55 N	1.17 W
Boddington	168a	32.48 S	116.28 E
Bode	198	42.52 N	94.17 W
Bode ≃	54	52.01 N	11.12 E
Bodega Bay c	204	38.15 N	123.00 W
Bodegraven	52	52.05 N	4.45 E
Bodélé +¹	146	16.30 N	16.30 E
Bodelschwingh +⁸	263	51.33 N	7.22 E
Boden — Fleres, It.	64	46.58 N	11.21 E
Boden, Sve.	26	65.50 N	21.42 E
Bodenburg	52	52.01 N	10.01 E
Bodenfelde	52	51.38 N	9.33 E
Bodenheim	56	49.56 N	8.18 E
Bodenmais	60	49.04 N	13.06 E
Bodensee (Lake Constance) @	58	47.35 N	9.25 E
Bodenteich	52	52.50 N	10.41 E
Bodenwerder	52	51.59 N	9.31 E
Bodenwies ∧	61	47.45 N	14.34 E
Bodenwöhr	60	49.16 N	12.19 E
Boderg, Lough @	48	53.52 N	7.58 W
Bode Sadu	150	9.00 N	4.47 E
Bodhan	122	18.40 N	77.54 E
Bodh Gaya	124	24.42 N	84.59 E
Bodiam¹	42	51.00 N	0.33 E
Bodinäyakkanür	122	10.01 N	77.21 E
Bodine, Mount ∧	182	55.37 N	125.49 W
Bodjoki	152	2.59 N	22.18 E
Bodjokola	152	3.54 N	20.17 E
Bodmin	42	50.29 N	4.43 W
Bodmin Moor ∧³	42	50.33 N	4.33 W
Boda	24	67.17 N	14.23 E
Bodocó	250	7.47 S	39.55 W
Bodoquena, Serra da ∧¹	248	21.00 S	56.50 W
Bodoukpa	152	5.43 N	17.36 E
Bodri ≃	115a	6.52 S	110.10 E
Bodroǵ ≃	38	48.07 N	21.25 E
Bodrum	130	37.02 N	27.26 E
Bodstedt	54	54.22 N	12.37 E
Bo Duc	110	11.58 N	106.48 E
Bodzentyn	30	50.56 N	20.57 E
Boĕ, Piz ∧	64	46.31 N	11.48 E
Boëge	58	46.13 N	6.25 E
Boekelo	52	53.13 N	6.47 E
Boele +⁸	263	51.24 N	7.28 E
Boémbé	152	2.54 S	15.39 E
Boende	152	0.13 S	20.52 E
Boeng Lvea	110	12.36 N	105.34 E
Boeni	157a	12.55 S	45.06 E
Boen-sur-Lignon	62	45.44 N	3.59 E
Boeo, Capo ⊁	70	37.48 N	12.25 E
Boerboonfontein	158	33.43 S	20.32 E
Boerne	196	29.47 N	98.43 W
Boeslunde	41	55.18 N	11.17 E
Boesmanland ≃⁵	156	19.30 S	20.00 E
Boesmans ≃, S. Afr.	158	28.46 S	30.09 E
Boesmans ≃, S. Afr.	158	33.42 S	26.39 E
Boetsap	158	27.59 S	24.30 E
Boeuf ≃	194	31.52 N	91.47 W
Boeuf Creek ≃	219	38.36 N	91.09 W
Boffa	150	10.10 N	14.02 W
Boffalora	266b	45.28 N	8.50 E
Boffzen	52	51.45 N	9.23 E
Bofoku	152	0.57 S	20.53 E
Bofors	40	59.20 N	14.32 E
Bofosso	150	8.40 N	9.42 W
Böfu — Höfu	96	34.03 N	131.34 E
Boga	154	1.03 N	29.56 E
Bogachiel ≃	222	47.55 N	124.28 W
Bogadjim	164	5.25 S	145.45 E
Bogal, Lagh ≃	154	0.45 N	40.52 E
Bogale	110	16.17 N	95.24 E
Bogalusa	194	30.47 N	89.50 W
Bogan ≃	166	29.57 S	146.21 E
Bogandé	150	12.59 N	0.08 W
Bog and Vly Meadows +⁴	210	40.56 N	74.19 W
Bogan Gate	166	33.07 S	147.48 E
Bogangolo	152	5.34 N	18.15 E
Bogantungan	166	23.39 S	147.18 E
Bogart, Mount ∧	182	50.55 N	115.14 W
Bogastow Brook ≃	283	42.12 N	71.22 W
Bogata	196	33.28 N	95.13 W
Bogataja Černečšina	78	48.59 N	35.35 E
Bogatišvo-Jepišino	82	54.47 N	38.25 E
Bogatyje Saby	80	56.01 N	50.27 E
Bogatynia	54	50.54 N	51.24 E
Bogatyr'	80	53.25 N	50.02 E
Bogatyrevo	82	54.32 N	48.46 E
Boğazkale	130	40.02 N	34.37 E
Boğazkaya	130	41.27 N	35.54 E
Boğazköy +⁸	267b	41.11 N	28.46 E
Boğazliyan	130	39.12 N	35.15 E
Bogbonga	152	1.35 N	19.25 E
Bogcang ≃	120	31.56 N	87.24 E
Bogd	92	45.11 N	100.43 E
Bogdanovič, S.S.S.R.	86	56.47 N	62.01 E
Bogdanovka, S.S.S.R.	80	52.42 N	50.46 E
Bogdanovka, S.S.S.R.	80	52.10 N	52.37 E
Bogda Shan ∧	84	43.18 N	43.35 E
Bogdo Ula ∧	90	43.30 N	89.45 E
Bogel	56	50.11 N	7.48 E
Bogembaj	86	52.29 N	72.20 E
Bogen	60	52.22 N	12.43 E
Bogense	41	55.34 N	10.06 E
Boger City	192	35.29 N	81.12 W
Boges	41	55.10 N	7.48 E
Bogess Creek ≃	282	37.18 N	122.19 W
Boget	89	49.40 N	47.59 E
Boggabilla	166	28.37 S	150.21 E
Boggeragh Mountains ∧	48	52.03 N	8.55 W
Boggola, Mount ∧	162	23.48 S	117.40 E
Boggs Run ≃	279b	40.02 N	80.44 W
Boggstown	218	39.34 N	85.55 W
Boggy Creek ≃	222	31.07 N	95.46 W
Boggy Peak ∧	240c	17.03 N	61.51 W
Bogia	164	4.15 S	144.55 E
Bogie Lake @	281	42.37 N	83.31 W
Bogilima	152	3.34 N	19.16 E
Bogliasco	266a	44.23 N	9.04 E
Bognanco Fonti	58	46.07 N	8.12 E
Bognes	24	68.10 N	16.00 E
Bognor Regis	42	50.47 N	0.41 W
Bogny-sur-Meuse	54	49.51 N	4.46 E
Bogo, Cam.	146	10.44 N	14.36 E
Bogo, Pil.	116	11.03 N	124.00 E
Bogo ≃	54	54.56 N	12.04 E
Bogo Bay c	116	11.05 N	124.00 E
Boguchuvin	78	50.10 N	35.30 E
Bogol Manyo	144	4.31 N	41.32 E

Bogong Peaks ∧	171b	35.34 S	148.28 E
Bogor	115a	6.35 S	106.47 E
Bogoria, Lake @	154	0.15 N	36.06 E
Bogoro	154	1.24 N	30.17 E
Bogorodčany	78	48.48 N	24.32 E
Bogorodick	76	53.46 N	38.08 E
Bogorodickoje	80	46.20 N	41.10 E
Bogorodnoje	83	49.01 N	37.30 E
Bogorodsk, S.S.S.R.	24	62.16 N	52.28 E
Bogorodsk, S.S.S.R.	80	56.06 N	43.31 E
Bogorodskoje, S.S.S.R.	80	57.51 N	50.45 E
Bogorodskoje, S.S.S.R.	80	46.20 N	43.53 E
Bogorodskoje, S.S.S.R.	82	55.02 N	38.29 E
Bogorodskoje, S.S.S.R.	82	55.26 N	36.14 E
Bogorodskoje +⁸	89	52.22 N	140.30 E
Bogorodskoje ≃	265b	55.49 N	37.44 E
Bogoso	150	5.34 N	2.01 W
Bogosskij Chrebet ≃	84	42.15 N	46.05 E
Bogotá, Col.	246	4.36 N	74.05 W
Bogota, N.J., U.S.	276	40.52 N	74.01 W
Bogotol	86	56.12 N	89.33 E
Bogou	150	10.39 N	0.11 E
Bogovarovo	24	58.59 N	47.01 E
Bogra	124	24.51 N	89.22 E
Bograd	86	54.13 N	90.51 E
Bogrie Hill ∧²	44	55.08 N	3.55 W
Bogučany	88	58.23 N	97.29 E
Bogučar	78	49.57 N	40.33 E
Bogué	150	16.35 N	14.16 W
Bogue Chitto	194	31.26 N	90.27 W
Bogue Chitto ≃	194	30.35 N	89.49 W
Bogue Chitto Creek ≃	194	32.10 N	87.14 W
Bogue Phalia ≃	194	33.15 N	90.44 W
Bogus Bay c	208	32.52 N	75.29 W
Bögürtlen	130	37.10 N	38.04 E
Boguševsk	76	54.51 N	30.13 E
Boguslav	78	49.33 N	30.53 E
Bogustan	85	41.41 N	70.05 E
Bo Hai (Gulf of Chihli) c	98	38.30 N	120.00 E
Bohai Haixia ᴜ	98	38.15 N	121.00 E
Bohain-en-Vermandois	50	49.59 N	3.27 E
Bohai Wan c	98	38.40 N	118.20 E
Bohan	56	49.52 N	4.53 E
Bohannon	208	37.24 N	76.22 W
Böheimkirchen	61	48.12 N	15.46 E
Bohemia	210	40.46 N	73.06 W
Bohemia — Čechy □⁹	30	49.50 N	14.00 E
Bohemia ≃	208	39.29 N	75.55 W
Bohemia Downs	162	18.53 S	126.14 E
Bohemian Forest ∧	30	49.15 N	12.45 E
Bohetal	104	42.01 N	123.13 E
Bohicon	150	7.12 N	2.04 E
Bohin	144	11.44 N	51.15 E
Bohinjska Bistrica	36	46.17 N	13.57 E
Böhlen	54	51.12 N	12.23 E
Böhlitz-Ehrenberg ≃⁸	54	51.21 N	12.17 E
Böhme ≃	52	52.46 N	9.28 E
Böhmen — Čechy □⁹	30	49.50 N	14.00 E
Böhmenkirch	56	48.41 N	9.55 E
Böhmerwald — Bohemian Forest ∧	30	49.15 N	12.45 E
Böhmte	52	52.22 N	8.19 E
Bohners Lake	216	42.37 N	88.17 W
Böhnsdorf +⁸	264a	52.24 N	13.33 E
Bohodou	150	9.46 N	9.04 W
Bohol I	116	9.50 N	124.10 E
Bohol Sea ᵀ²	116	9.20 N	124.25 E
Bohon	116	18.30 N	120.35 E
Bohon	152	12.30 N	0.42 E
Bohong	152	6.23 N	15.37 E
Bohorok	114	3.30 N	98.12 E
Bohsdorf	54	51.38 N	14.32 E
Bohuslän □⁹	26	58.15 N	11.50 E
Bohušovice nad Ohří	60	50.24 N	14.07 E
Bohutín	60	49.40 N	13.55 E
Boi ≃	150	9.34 N	9.27 E
Boi, Ponta do ⊁	256	23.58 S	45.15 W
Boiaçu	246	0.27 S	61.46 W
Boiceville	210	41.59 N	74.15 W
Boinao	166	33.46 N	147.19 W
Boigu Island I	166	9.16 S	142.12 E
Boila	154	16.10 S	39.56 E
Boiling Springs, N.C., U.S.	192	35.30 N	81.37 W
Boiling Springs, Pa., U.S.	208	40.08 N	77.07 W
Boim	250	2.49 S	55.10 W
Boinville-en-Mantois	261	48.56 N	1.46 E
Boinvilliers	261	48.56 N	1.40 E
Boipeba, Ilha de I	255	13.39 S	38.55 W
Bois ≃	34	42.39 N	8.54 W
Bois, Lac des @, N.T., Can.	180	66.40 N	125.15 W
Bois, Lac des ≃ — Woods, Lake of the @, N.A.	184	49.15 N	94.45 W
Bois-Colombes	261	48.55 N	2.16 E
Boisdale, Loch c	46	57.08 N	7.19 W
Bois d'Arc Creek ≃	196	33.50 N	95.50 W
Bois-d'Arcy	261	48.48 N	2.01 E
Bois-des-Filion	261	45.40 N	73.45 W
Bois de Sioux ≃	198	46.16 N	96.36 W
Boise ≃	202	43.49 N	117.01 W
Boise, Middle Fork ≃	202	43.42 N	115.38 W
Boise, North Fork ≃	202	43.42 N	115.38 W
Boise, South Fork ≃	202	43.40 N	115.30 W
Boise City	196	36.43 N	102.30 W
Boissevain	184	49.14 N	100.03 W
Boissise-la-Bertrand	261	48.32 N	2.35 E
Boissy-l'Aillerie	261	49.05 N	2.05 E
Boissy-Saint-Léger	261	48.45 N	2.31 E
Boissy-sous-Saint-Yon	261	48.34 N	2.13 E
Boistfort Peak ∧	222	46.29 N	123.12 W
Boitzenburg	54	53.16 N	13.37 E
Boizenburg	52	53.22 N	10.43 E
Bojador, Cape ⊁	146	26.08 N	14.30 W
Bojano	68	41.29 N	14.28 E
Bojanowo	54	51.41 N	16.48 E
Bojeador, Cape ⊁	116	18.30 N	120.34 E
Bojelupang	78	51.24 N	39.19 E
Bojevo	80	56.55 N	37.30 E
Boji Plain ≃	154	1.30 N	38.50 E
Bojnegro	115a	7.09 S	111.52 E
Bojnurd	126	37.29 N	57.21 E
Boju	150	7.23 N	7.52 E
B'ojuk-Kirs, gora ∧	84	39.41 N	46.44 E
Bojuru	252	31.38 S	51.26 W
Bokad	272d	18.53 N	73.03 E
Bokada	152	4.18 N	19.23 E
Bokal	168a	33.23 S	115.54 E
Bokala, Zaïre	152	3.07 S	17.02 E

Bokala, Zaïre	152	2.03 N	18.59 E
Bokani	150	9.26 N	5.13 E
Bokāro Steel City	124	23.45 N	86.07 E
Bokatola	152	0.38 S	18.46 E
Bokchito	196	34.01 N	96.08 W
Boké	150	10.56 N	14.18 W
Bokeelia	220	26.42 N	82.09 W
Bokel	52	53.23 N	8.46 E
Bokela	152	1.08 S	21.56 E
Bokes Creek ≃	188	40.19 N	83.10 W
Bokfontein	158	32.48 S	19.16 E
Bokhara	158	27.57 S	20.30 E
Bokhara ≃	166	29.55 S	146.42 E
Boki	146	8.48 N	13.32 E
Bokino	80	52.38 N	41.26 E
Bokkol ∧	154	1.50 N	37.02 E
Bok Koŭ	110	10.37 N	104.03 E
Böklund	41	54.36 N	9.34 E
Boknafjorden c²	26	59.10 N	5.35 E
Boko, Congo	152	4.47 S	14.38 E
Boko, S.S.S.R.	86	49.55 N	81.38 E
Bokode	116	16.30 N	120.50 E
Bokode	152	3.58 N	19.29 E
Bokolako	150	13.36 N	12.33 W
Bokonbajevskoje	85	42.07 N	77.00 E
Bokondji	152	2.22 N	18.42 E
Bokondo	152	0.15 N	22.32 E
Bokoro	146	12.23 N	17.03 E
Boko Songo	152	4.26 S	13.37 E
Bokote	152	0.05 S	20.08 E
Bokovo-Antratsit			
— Antracit	83	48.06 N	39.06 E
Bokovo Platovo	83	48.07 N	39.01 E
Bokovskaja	80	49.15 N	41.49 E
Bokpyin	110	11.16 N	98.46 E
Boksburg	194	33.15 N	90.44 W
Boksburg □⁵	273d	26.12 S	28.14 E
Boksburg-Noord	273d	26.12 S	28.15 E
Boksburg-South	273d	26.14 S	28.15 E
Boksburg-West	273d	26.13 S	28.14 E
Boksitogorsk	76	59.28 N	33.51 E
Bokungu	152	0.41 S	22.19 E
Bol, Jugo.	36	43.16 N	16.40 E
Bol, Tchad	146	13.28 N	14.43 E
Bolaang Mongondow	112	0.56 N	124.10 E
Bolama, Gui.-B.	150	11.35 N	15.28 W
Bolama, Zaïre	152	1.57 N	22.58 E
Bolaman	130	41.03 N	37.37 E
Bolán ≃	120	28.38 N	67.42 E
Bolanda, Jabal ∧	144	7.44 N	25.28 E
Bol'andikik ≃	85	39.11 N	72.17 E
Bolands	240c	17.02 N	61.53 W
Bolaños	234	21.41 N	104.08 W
Bolaños ≃	234	21.14 N	104.08 W
Bolaños de Calatrava	34	38.54 N	3.40 W
Bolán Pass ᴜ	120	29.45 N	67.35 E
Bolayir	130	40.31 N	26.45 E
Bolbec	50	49.34 N	0.29 E
Bolchov	76	53.27 N	36.01 E
Bolchuny	80	47.59 N	46.25 E
Bolda ≃	80	46.10 N	48.14 E
Boldasevo	80	54.43 N	45.33 E
Boldekow	54	53.43 N	13.35 E
Bolderslev	41	54.59 N	9.18 E
Bold Heath	262	53.24 S	2.42 W
Boldon	44	54.57 N	1.27 W
Boldu	38	45.35 N	27.12 E
Bol'džuan	85	38.19 N	69.40 E
Bole, Ghana	150	9.02 N	2.29 W
Bole, Zhg.	86	44.53 N	82.05 E
Bolekov	78	49.04 N	23.52 E
Bolero	116	10.59 S	33.45 E
Bolesh	194	34.46 N	94.02 W
Bolesławiec	30	51.16 N	15.34 E
Bolesławkowice	52	52.44 N	14.36 E
Boletice nad Labem	54	50.45 N	14.13 E
Boley	196	35.29 N	96.29 W
Bolgarčaj ≃	84	39.28 N	48.36 E
Bolgart	162	31.16 S	116.30 E
Bolgatanga	150	10.46 N	0.52 W
Bolgrad	78	45.41 N	28.36 E
Boli, Süd.	144	6.01 N	28.43 E
Boli, Tchad	146	10.50 N	18.43 E
Boli, Zhg.	89	45.46 N	130.31 E
Bolia	152	1.36 S	18.23 E
Boliden	26	64.52 N	20.23 E
Boligee	194	32.45 N	88.01 W
Bolikov	85	49.02 N	15.22 E
Bolinao	116	16.23 N	119.54 E
Boline	116	9.16 S	142.12 E
Boling	222	29.15 N	95.56 W
Bolingbrook	216	41.41 N	88.04 W
Bolinger Creek ≃	283	37.47 N	122.00 W
Bolintin-Vale	38	44.27 N	25.46 E
Bolishan	98	40.08 N	122.20 E
Bolívar, Austl.	168b	34.45 S	138.36 E
Bolívar, Col.	246	5.50 N	76.01 W
Bolívar, Col.	246	1.50 N	76.58 W
Bolívar, Perú	246	7.18 S	77.48 W
Bolívar, Mo., U.S.	194	37.36 N	93.24 W
Bolívar, N.Y., U.S.	208	42.04 N	78.09 W
Bolívar, Oh., U.S.	214	40.40 N	81.27 W
Bolívar, Pa., U.S.	214	40.23 N	79.09 W
Bolívar, Tn., U.S.	194	35.15 N	88.59 W
Bolívar □⁴	246	8.00 N	74.00 W
Bolívar ≃	246	1.35 N	74.15 W
Bolívar, Cerro ∧	244	7.28 N	63.25 W
Bolívar, Pico ∧	246	8.30 N	71.02 W
Bolívar Peninsula ⊁¹	196	29.27 N	94.39 W
Bolívar Run ≃	214	41.59 N	78.39 W
Bolivia, Col.	246	17.00 S	65.00 W
Bolivia, N.C., U.S.	208	34.04 N	78.09 W
Bolivia □¹	248	17.00 S	65.00 W
Bolivien — Bolivia □¹	248	17.00 S	65.00 W
Boljarovo	38	42.09 N	26.49 E
Boljoon	116	9.38 N	123.29 E
Bolkar Dağları ∧	130	37.15 N	34.20 E
Bölkenbusch	263	51.22 N	7.34 E
Bollado	266b	45.41 N	8.50 E
Bollate	266b	45.33 N	9.07 E
Bollberg ∧²	263	51.23 N	7.19 E
Bollène	62	44.17 N	4.45 E
Bollensdorf	264a	52.31 N	13.43 E
Bolles Canal ≃	220	26.34 N	80.34 W
Bolles Harbor	216	41.51 N	83.24 W
Bolling Air Force Base ■	284c	38.51 N	77.02 W
Bollington, Eng., U.K.	262	53.22 N	10.43 E
Bollington, Eng., U.K.	262	53.18 N	2.06 W
Bollnäs	26	61.21 N	16.25 E
Bollon	166	28.02 S	147.29 E
Bollstabruk	26	63.00 N	17.73 E
Bollstanäs	40	59.30 N	17.56 E
Bollullos par del Condado	34	37.20 N	6.32 W
Bolmen @	26	56.55 N	13.40 E
Bolmsö I	26	56.55 N	13.40 E
Bolo	144	4.18 N	43.22 E
Bolobo	152	2.10 S	16.14 E
Bolochovo	82	54.05 N	37.50 E
Bolod Islands II	116	6.15 N	120.33 E
Bologna, Fr.	58	44.12 N	5.28 E
Bologna — Bologna, It.	64	44.29 N	11.20 E
Bologna, It.	64	44.29 N	11.20 E
Bolognola	66	42.59 N	13.14 E

Bologoje	76	57.54 N	34.02 E
Bologovo	76	56.54 N	31.42 E
Bololo	152	3.50 S	21.08 E
Bolomba	152	0.29 N	19.12 E
Bolombo	152	3.59 S	21.22 E
Bolombo ≃	152	1.32 N	21.14 E
Bolon'	89	49.55 N	136.07 E
Bolon', ozero @	89	49.51 N	136.22 E
Bolonchén de Rejón	232	20.00 N	89.49 W
Bolondo	152	0.27 N	20.01 E
Bolondrón	240p	22.46 N	81.27 W
Bolong ≃	170	34.15 S	149.36 E
Bolonia			
— Bologna	64	44.29 N	11.20 E
Bolótana	71	40.20 N	8.57 E
Bolotino	78	47.42 N	27.21 E
Bolotnoje	86	55.41 N	84.23 E
Bolotoje	82	54.10 N	36.20 E
Bolotovskoje	86	58.33 N	62.28 E
Bolovens, Plateau des ∧¹	110	15.20 N	106.20 E
Bolpur	126	23.40 N	87.43 E
Bol'šaja, S.S.S.R.	76	59.36 N	41.48 E
Bol'šaja, S.S.S.R.	88	45.59 N	42.42 E
Bol'šaja Atn'a	80	48.36 N	41.00 E
Bol'šaja Balachn'a ≃	74	73.37 N	107.05 E
Bol'šaja Ber'ostovica	76	53.11 N	24.01 E
Bol'šaja Blagoveščenka	78	46.51 N	34.03 E
Bol'šaja Brembola	80	56.45 N	38.55 E
Bol'šaja Bukon'	86	48.53 N	82.43 E
Bol'šaja Čalykla ≃	80	51.51 N	49.34 E
Bol'šaja Černigovka	80	52.07 N	50.52 E
Bol'šaja Chalan'	78	50.56 N	37.26 E
Bol'šaja Cheta ≃	74	69.33 N	84.15 E
Bol'šaja Chobda ≃	86	50.56 N	54.34 E
Bol'šaja Chundala ≃	74	44.35 N	34.18 E
Bol'šaja Čuja ≃	88	58.56 N	112.13 E
Bol'šaja Čurakovka	86	53.03 N	64.20 E
Bol'šaja Damba	80	46.57 N	51.47 E
Bol'šaja Dmitrijevka	80	51.21 N	45.15 E
Bol'šaja Dora	76	59.05 N	37.38 E
Bol'šaja Džalga	80	45.59 N	42.41 E
Bol'šaja Glušica	80	52.24 N	50.28 E
Bol'šaja Ižorka	265a	59.56 N	29.34 E
Bol'šaja Kakša ≃	80	57.53 N	45.28 E
Bol'šaja Kamenka ≃	80	53.39 N	50.31 E
Bol'šaja Kamenka ≃	88	48.22 N	40.04 E
Bol'šaja Kandala	80	54.32 N	49.22 E
Bol'šaja Kaskara	86	57.11 N	65.58 E
Bol'šaja Ket'	86	57.39 N	91.45 E
Bol'šaja Kinel' ≃	80	53.14 N	50.30 E
Bol'šaja Kirsanovka	83	47.40 N	38.54 E
Bol'šaja Konkudera	88	56.08 N	47.47 E
Bol'šaja Kugul'ta ≃	88	57.34 N	112.30 E
Bol'šaja Kuonamka	88	45.45 N	41.57 E
Bol'šaja Laba ≃	84	44.16 N	40.53 E
Bol'šaja Lipovica	82	52.33 N	41.20 E
Bol'šaja Martynovka	80	47.17 N	41.40 E
Bol'šaja Mošanica	76	53.58 N	29.37 E
Bol'šaja Murta	86	56.55 N	93.07 E
Bol'šaja Neva ≃	265a	59.58 N	30.13 E
Bol'šaja Norja ≃	80	56.41 N	52.43 E
Bol'šaja Ochta +⁸	265a	59.57 N	30.25 E
Bol'šaja Orlovka	80	47.28 N	41.16 E
Bol'šaja Osinovaja ≃	88	64.30 N	174.00 E
Bol'šaja Pas'ma	80	58.38 N	43.53 E
Bol'šaja Rečka	88	51.57 N	104.44 E
Bol'šaja Ržaksa ≃	82	52.08 N	42.13 E
Bol'šaja Sestra ≃	82	56.16 N	35.56 E
Bol'šaja Sojana ≃	24	65.07 N	44.20 E
Bol'šaja Sosnova	80	57.40 N	54.36 E
Bol'šaja Talovaja ≃	80	51.00 N	43.00 E
Bol'šaja Tarel'	88	53.45 N	106.40 E
Bol'šaja Tavoložka	80	52.07 N	49.04 E
Bol'šaja Uča	80	56.51 N	52.15 E
Bol'šaja Ussurka ≃	89	45.57 N	133.42 E
Bol'šaja Višera	76	58.38 N	32.08 E
Bol'šaja Vladimirovka	80	50.53 N	79.31 E
Bol'šaja Vys' ≃	78	48.45 N	30.54 E
Bol'šakovo, S.S.S.R.	226	36.44 N	121.38 W
Bol'šakovo, S.S.S.R.	82	54.55 N	21.40 E
Bol'šakovo, S.S.S.R.	265b	55.54 N	37.17 E
Bol'šakovo, ostrov I	74	78.40 N	102.30 E
Bol'šaja Theatre ⁊	265b	55.46 N	37.37 E
Bol'šije Algaši	80	55.20 N	46.30 E
Bol'šije Belyniči	80	58.40 N	53.31 E
Bol'šije Berezniki	80	54.14 N	45.20 E
Bol'šije Gorki	80	57.25 S	45.29 E
Bol'šije Gorki, S.S.S.R.	80	56.28 N	35.35 E
Bol'šije Kizi, ozero @	89	51.38 N	140.22 E
Bol'šije Ključi	80	53.17 N	50.45 E
Bol'šije Ligauči	80	54.01 N	45.40 E
Bol'šije Malачicyny	80	57.25 N	45.10 E
Bol'šije Ozerki	80	52.01 N	46.50 E
Bol'šije Puči	80	57.17 N	45.34 E
Bol'šije Soli	80	57.41 N	40.39 E
Bol'šije Uki	86	56.53 N	72.25 E
Bol'šije Ždanovy	80	58.23 N	47.23 E
Bol'šije Zmejinogorsk ≃	80	51.38 N	140.00 E
Bol'šoj An'uj ≃	88	68.30 N	160.49 E
Bol'šoj Azbulat, ozero @	80	53.17 N	77.25 E
Bol'šoj Begičev, ostrov I	74	74.20 N	112.30 E
Bol'šoj Bogdo, gora ∧	80	48.08 N	46.52 E
Bol'šoj Boktybaj, gora ∧	86	48.27 N	54.30 E
Bol'šoj Čeremšan ≃	80	54.11 N	49.39 E
Bol'šoj Civil' ≃	80	55.54 N	47.28 E
Bol'šoj Irgiz ≃	80	52.06 N	47.33 E
Bol'šoj Jugan ≃	86	61.05 N	74.44 E
Bol'šoj Kemčug ≃	86	56.26 N	91.16 E
Bol'šoj Konej, ozero @	86	61.00 N	68.00 E
Bol'šoj Luluj ≃	86	61.04 N	68.20 E
Bol'šoj Murtinskoje @	80	56.17 N	43.25 E
Bol'šoj Načar ≃	86	57.20 N	90.42 E
Bol'šoj Nimnyr	88	57.51 N	125.30 E
Bol'šoj Pit ≃	86	58.32 N	93.25 E

Bol'šoje Mikuškino	80	53.56 N	51.42 E
Bol'šoje Muraškino	80	55.47 N	44.46 E
Bol'šoje Nagatkino	80	54.31 N	47.58 E
Bol'šoje Nurkejevo	80	55.22 N	52.40 E
Bol'šoje Nyrsy	80	55.44 N	50.19 E
Bol'šoje Ogar'ovo	76	53.33 N	37.43 E
Bol'šoje Pikino	80	56.25 N	44.22 E
Bol'šoje Polpino	76	53.14 N	34.30 E
Bol'šoje Ramenje	80	58.21 N	36.40 E
Bol'šoje Rybuškino	80	55.25 N	45.48 E
Bol'šoje Sazonovo	80	58.06 N	53.21 E
Bol'šoje Šelo	76	57.43 N	38.56 E
Bol'šoje Šem'akino	80	55.03 N	48.38 E
Bol'šoje Soldatskoje	76	51.21 N	35.31 E
Bol'šoje Sudačje	80	50.49 N	44.05 E
Bol'šoje Topol'noje, ozero @	86	53.20 N	78.00 E
Bol'šoje Uro	88	53.32 N	109.48 E
Bol'šoje Zokovo	82	54.35 N	38.57 E
Bol'šoj Gašun ≃	80	47.22 N	42.43 E
Bol'šoj Ginaldag, gora ∧	84	42.20 N	45.57 E
Bol'šoj Golec, gora ∧	88	51.52 N	119.24 E
Bol'šoj Irgiz ≃	80	52.01 N	47.24 E
Bol'šoj Jenisej (Bij-Chem) ≃	88	51.43 N	94.26 E
Bol'šoj Kamen'	89	43.06 N	132.21 E
Bol'šoj Kandarat ≃	80	54.25 N	47.00 E
Bol'šoj Kanym, gora ∧	86	54.13 N	88.20 E
Bol'šoj Karagaj	86	57.57 N	70.15 E
Bol'šoj Karaman ≃	80	51.41 N	46.38 E
Bol'šoj Kavkaz (Caucasus) ∧	84	42.30 N	45.00 E
Bol'šoj Ketmen'	85	43.21 N	80.24 E
Bol'šoj Kujal'nik ≃	78	46.46 N	30.36 E
Bol'šoj Kujaš	86	55.50 N	61.06 E
Bol'šoj Kundyš ≃	80	56.32 N	47.23 E
Bol'šoj Kuvaj	80	54.37 N	47.05 E
Bol'šoj Kymynej, gora ∧	180	66.34 N	172.32 W
Bol'šoj L'achovskij, ostrov I	74	73.35 N	142.00 E
Bol'šoj Lug	88	52.07 N	104.10 E
Bol'šoj Matačynaj, gora ∧	180	66.28 N	179.25 W
Bol'šoj Melik	80	51.38 N	43.18 E
Bol'šoj Nesvetaj ≃	83	47.27 N	39.54 E
Bol'šoj Onguren	88	53.38 N	107.36 E
Bol'šoj Patom ≃	88	59.15 N	113.56 E
Bol'šoj Porog	86	59.11 N	91.44 E
Bol'šoj Porog	202	45.30 N	84.52 E
Bol'šoj Šagan	80	50.57 N	51.08 E
Bol'šoj Sajan ∧	86	52.00 N	99.30 E
Bol'šoj Šalym, ostrov I	86	60.55 N	70.25 E
Bol'šoj Šantar, ostrov I	89	55.00 N	137.42 E
Bol'šoj Šatan, gora ∧	85	53.41 N	57.36 E
Bol'šoj Simonogort	265a	59.50 N	29.49 E
Bol'šoj Sorokino	86	56.38 N	69.53 E
Bol'šoj Suchodol	80	48.25 N	39.53 E
Bol'šoj Sundyr'	80	56.07 N	46.46 E
Bol'šoj Tal'cy	90	59.13 N	30.00 E
Bol'šoj Tokjag	88	53.30 N	51.57 E
Bol'šoj T'uters, ostrov I	80	59.51 N	27.13 E
Bol'šoj Uluj	86	56.39 N	90.36 E
Bol'šoj Uran ≃	80	52.24 N	53.15 E
Bol'šoj Uvat, ozero @	86	57.35 N	70.30 E
Bol'šoj Uzen' ≃	80	48.30 N	174.00 E
Bol'šoj Uzignort	265a	59.48 N	29.53 E
Bol'šoj Vjass	80	53.48 N	45.30 E
Bol'šoj Vlasjevo	89	53.24 N	140.55 E
Bol'šoj Zelenčuk ≃	84	44.36 N	41.56 E
Bol'šovcy	78	49.12 N	24.44 E
Bolsover	44	53.14 N	1.18 W
Bolsward	52	53.03 N	5.31 E
Boltaña	34	42.27 N	0.04 E
Boltigen	58	46.38 N	7.24 E
Boltino	265b	55.58 N	37.41 E
Bolton, On., Can.	212	43.53 N	79.44 W
Bolton, Eng., U.K.	262	53.35 N	2.26 W
Bolton, Ct., U.S.	207	41.45 N	72.26 W
Bolton, Ms., U.S.	194	32.22 N	90.27 W
Bolton, N.C., U.S.	192	34.19 N	78.24 W
Bolton □⁶	262	53.35 N	2.28 W
Bolton Abbey	262	53.59 N	1.53 W
Bolton Abbey ⁊¹	262	53.59 N	1.54 W
Bolton Bridge	262	53.58 N	1.52 W
Bolton Center	207	41.45 N	72.26 W
Bolton Creek ≃	212	43.58 N	79.41 W
Bolton Lake @	207	41.54 N	72.20 W
Bolton-le-Sands	44	54.06 N	2.47 W
Bolton upon Dearne	262	53.31 N	1.19 W
Bolton Wanderers Football Ground ♦	262	53.34 N	2.25 W
Bolu	130	40.44 N	31.37 E
Bölükyazı	130	40.40 N	31.30 E
Boluntay	90	36.18 N	92.38 E
Boluo, Zhg.	100	23.11 N	114.17 E
Bolukokeng	98	34.05 N	113.22 E
Bolus Head ⊁	48	51.46 N	10.21 W
Bolva ≃	76	53.26 N	34.13 E
Bolvadin	130	38.43 N	31.03 E
Bolwarra	171a	32.44 S	151.36 E
Bolwerk	73	52.25 N	4.35 E
Bolyarovo	38	42.09 N	26.49 E
Bolzano (Bozen)	64	46.31 N	11.22 E
Bolzano ≃	64	46.45 N	11.40 E
Boma	152	5.51 S	13.03 E
Bomaderry	170	34.51 S	150.37 E
Bomandjoku	152	0.20 S	23.32 E
Bomarsund	208	60.13 N	20.14 E
Bomate	152	0.11 S	20.53 E
Bombala	166	36.54 S	149.14 E
Bombarral	34	39.16 N	9.09 W
Bombedougou	150	11.05 N	4.55 W
Bomberai, Jazirah ⊁¹	164	3.00 S	133.00 E
Bombetoka, Baie de c	157b	15.50 S	46.17 E
Bombay, India	122	18.58 N	72.50 E
Bombay, N.Y., U.S.	210	44.56 N	74.34 W
Bombay, University of ⁊	272c	18.57 N	72.50 E
Bombay Harbour c	272c	18.55 N	72.55 E
Bombi ≃	154	1.03 N	30.31 E
Bombón Alto, Cerro ∧	246	8.30 N	71.11 W

Bom Jesus da Terra Preta	256	23.15 S	46.36 W
Bom Jesus de Goiás	255	18.12 S	49.44 W
Bom Jesus dos Perdões	256	23.08 S	46.28 W
Bømlafjorden c²	26	59.39 N	5.20 E
Bömnitz	52	52.54 N	9.37 E
Bömki I	26	59.46 N	5.12 E
Bommerholz	263	51.23 N	7.18 E
Bommern	263	51.25 N	7.20 E
Bomnak	89	54.46 N	128.51 E
Bomokandi ≃	154	3.39 N	26.08 E
Bomongiri	152	1.57 S	21.13 E
Bomongo	152	1.22 N	18.21 E
Bompata	150	6.38 N	1.04 W
Bompensiere	70	37.28 N	13.47 E
Bompietro	70	37.44 N	14.06 E
Bomputu	152	0.20 S	20.06 E
Bom Repouso	256	22.28 S	46.09 W
Bom Retiro, Bra.	252	27.48 S	49.31 W
Bom Retiro, Bra.	256	22.10 S	45.40 W
Bom Retiro ⁊⁸	287b	23.32 S	46.38 W
Bom Retiro do Sul	252	29.37 S	51.56 W
Bom Sucesso, Bra.	255	15.43 S	56.07 W
Bom Sucesso, Bra.	255	23.42 S	51.45 W
Bom Sucesso, Bra.	256	22.52 S	45.33 W
Bomu (Mbomou) ≃	287b	23.25 S	46.24 W
Bon, Cap ⊁	136	4.08 N	22.26 E
Bona	36	37.05 N	11.03 E
Bona ∧	40	58.34 N	15.03 E
Boná, Isla I	236	8.34 N	79.36 W
Bona Bona Island I	164	10.30 S	149.50 E
Bon Accord	158	25.38 S	28.11 E
Bonaduz	58	46.49 N	9.25 E
Bonaero Park	273d	26.07 S	28.16 E
Bonai	114	1.16 N	100.52 E
Bonaigarh	120	21.50 N	84.57 E
Bonair, In., U.S.	278	41.31 N	87.22 W
Bon Air, Va., U.S.	208	37.31 N	77.33 W
Bon Aire	214	40.54 N	79.55 W
Bonaire I	241a	12.10 N	68.15 W
Bonampak ⊥	232	16.44 N	91.05 W
Bönan	40	60.44 N	17.18 E
Bonandolok	114	1.47 N	98.48 E
Bonanza, Nic.	236	14.01 N	84.35 W
Bonanza, Or., U.S.	202	42.11 N	121.24 W
Bonanza, Ut., U.S.	200	40.01 N	109.10 W
Bonanza Peak ∧	224	48.14 N	120.52 W
Bonao	238	18.56 N	70.25 W
Bonaparte	190	40.41 N	91.48 W
Bonaparte ≃	182	50.46 N	121.17 W
Bonaparte, Lake @	212	44.09 N	75.23 W
Bonaparte, Mount ∧	202	48.47 N	119.09 W
Bonaparte Archipelago II	160	14.17 S	125.18 E
Bonaparte Lake @	182	51.16 N	120.35 W
Bonar Bridge	46	57.53 N	4.21 W
Bonarcado	71	40.04 N	8.38 E
Bonasila Dome ∧	180	62.19 N	160.30 W
Bonasse	241r	10.05 N	61.52 W
Bonassola	66	44.11 N	9.35 E
Bonaventure	186	48.03 N	65.29 W
Bonaventure, Île I	186	48.30 N	64.10 W
Bonavista	186	48.39 N	53.07 W
Bonavista, Cape ⊁	186	48.42 N	53.05 W
Bonavista Bay c	186	48.45 N	53.20 W
Bonawon	116	9.08 N	122.55 E
Bonbeach	274b	38.04 S	145.08 E
Bonbillon	58	46.22 N	5.42 E
Bon Bon	162	30.26 S	135.28 E
Bonbonort Point ⊁	116	9.03 N	123.08 E
Bonchester Bridge	44	55.24 N	2.39 W
Boncourt	58	47.30 N	6.56 E
Boncuk Dağı ∧¹	130	36.53 N	29.17 E
Bond	194	30.54 N	89.10 W
Bond □⁶	219	38.53 N	89.25 W
Bondar'ov	83	50.18 N	35.00 E
Bondar'ovka	83	49.22 N	39.10 E
Bondeno	64	44.53 N	11.25 E
Bondo, Indon.	115a	6.28 S	110.45 E
Bondo, Zaïre	152	3.49 N	23.40 E
Bondoc Peninsula ⊁¹	116	13.10 N	122.36 E
Bondoc Point ⊁	116	13.10 N	122.36 E
Bondorf	56	48.31 N	8.49 E
Bondoufle	261	48.37 N	2.22 E
Bondoukou	150	8.02 N	2.48 W
Bondowoso	115a	7.55 S	113.49 E
Bondsville	207	42.12 N	72.20 W
Bond Street ≃	150	10.48 N	5.30 W
Bonduci	152	0.44 N	22.48 E
Bondy	261	48.54 N	2.29 E
Bondy, Forêt de ✦⁴	261	48.55 N	2.35 E
Bône — Annaba, Alg.	148	36.54 N	7.46 E
Bone, Indon.	112	5.09 S	122.37 E
Bone, Indon.	112	4.46 S	122.52 E
Bone, Teluk c	112	4.00 S	120.40 E
Bone Echo Provincial Park ⁊	212	44.52 N	77.15 W
Bonelipu	112	4.09 N	123.03 E
Bonelohe	116	5.48 S	120.27 E
Bonen	263	51.36 N	7.44 E
Bönen	263	51.36 N	7.46 E
Bonerate, Pulau I	112	7.25 S	121.05 E
Bon Espérance, Cap de — Good Hope, Cape of ⊁	158	34.24 S	18.30 E
Bo'ness	44	56.01 N	3.37 W
Bonesteel	198	43.04 N	98.56 W
Bonete, Cerro ∧	252	27.50 S	68.47 W
Bonete Chico, Cerro ∧	252	28.01 S	68.45 W
Bonétice	54	49.41 N	12.49 E
Bonfim	246	3.08 N	59.52 W
Bonfinópolis	255	16.38 S	48.58 W
Bonfol	58	47.28 N	7.09 E
Bongabon	116	15.37 N	121.08 E
Bongaigaon	124	26.28 N	90.34 E
Bongandanga	152	1.30 N	21.03 E
Bongor	146	10.17 N	15.22 E
Bongouanou	150	6.39 N	4.12 W
Bong Range ∧	150	6.47 N	10.30 W
Bonham	196	33.34 N	96.10 W
Bonheiden	53	51.01 N	4.32 E
Bonhomme, Col du ᴜ	58	48.10 N	7.06 E
Bonhomme, Morne ∧	238	19.05 N	72.36 W
Bonhomme Island I	219	38.43 N	90.38 W
Boni	146	15.23 N	0.56 W
Bonifacio	66	41.23 N	9.10 E
Bonifacio, Strait of ᴜ			

Symbols in the index entries represent the broad categories identified in the key at the right. Symbols with superior numbers (∧¹) identify subcategories (see complete key on page I · 1).

Symbole im Register stellen die rechts im Schlüssel erklärten Kategorien dar. Symbole mit hochgestellten Ziffern (∧¹) bezeichnen Unterteilungen einer Kategorie (vgl. vollständiger Schlüssel auf Seite I · 1).

Los símbolos incluidos en el texto del índice representan las grandes categorías identificadas con la clave a la derecha. Los símbolos con numeros en su parte superior (∧¹) identifican las subcategorías (véase la clave completa en la página I · 1).

Les symboles de l'index représentent les catégories indiquées dans la légende à droite. Les symboles suivis d'un indice (∧¹) représentent des sous-catégories (voir légende complète à la page I · 1).

Os símbolos incluídos no texto do índice representam as grandes categorias identificadas com a chave à direita. Os símbolos com números em sua parte superior (∧¹) identificam as subcategorias (veja-se a chave completa à página I · 1).

Symbol	ENGLISH	DEUTSCH	Montaña	Montagne	Montanha
∧	Mountain	Berg	Montaña	Montagne	Montanha
∧¹	Mountains	Gebirge	Montañas	Montagnes	Montanhas
)(	Pass	Paß	Paso	Col	Passo
V	Valley, Canyon	Tal, Cañon	Valle, Cañón	Vallée, Canyon	Vale, Canhão
≃	Plain	Ebene	Llano	Plaine	Planície
⊁	Cape	Kap	Cabo	Cap	Cabo
I	Island	Insel	Isla	Île	Ilha
II	Islands	Inseln	Islas	Îles	Ilhas
≃	Other Topographic Features	Andere Topographische Objekte	Otros Elementos Topográficos	Autres données topographiques	Outros acidentes topográficos

Boni-Bovr I · 23

ESPAÑOL Nombre / FRANÇAIS Nom / PORTUGUÊS Nome	Página / Page	Lat.°′	Long.°′ W = Oeste / W = Ouest
Bonifacio Monument ⊥	269f	14.39 N	120.59 E
Bonifati	68	39.35 N	15.54 E
Bonifati, Capo ⊳	68	39.35 N	15.52 E
Bonifay	194	30.47 N	85.40 W
Bonifica del Volturno ≍	68	41.01 N	14.00 E
Bonilla Island ı	182	53.29 N	130.36 W
Bonin Islands → Ogasawara-guntō ıı	14	27.00 N	142.10 E
Bonita	194	32.55 N	91.40 W
Bonita, Point ⊳	282	37.49 N	122.32 W
Bonita Springs	220	26.20 N	81.46 W
Bonito, Bra.	248	21.08 S	56.28 W
Bonito, Bra.	250	8.29 S	35.44 W
Bonito, It.	68	41.06 N	15.00 E
Bonito ≃, Bra.	255	16.31 S	51.23 W
Bonito ≃, Bra.	256	22.12 S	43.02 W
Bonito ≃, Bra.	256	22.09 S	43.40 W
Bonito, Pico ʌ	236	15.38 N	86.55 W
Bonito, Rio ≃	200	33.23 N	105.16 W
Bonito de Santa Fé	250	7.19 S	38.31 W
Bonjol	112	0.01 S	100.13 E
Bonkoukou	150	14.01 N	3.13 E
Bon Meade	279b	40.33 N	80.14 W
Bonn	56	50.44 N	7.05 E
Bonnanaro	71	40.32 N	8.45 E
Bonndorf im Schwarzwald	58	47.49 N	8.20 E
Bonneauville	208	39.46 N	77.10 W
Bonne Bay (Woody Point)	186	49.30 N	57.56 W
Bonne Bay ⊂	186	49.33 N	57.55 W
Bonnebosq	50	49.12 N	0.05 E
Bonnechere ≃	190	45.31 N	76.33 W
Bonneia	144	5.41 N	37.45 E
Bonnelles	261	48.37 N	2.02 E
Bonner	202	46.52 N	113.51 W
Bonners Ferry	202	48.41 N	116.18 W
Bonne-sur-Ménoge	58	46.10 N	6.20 E
Bonnet, Lac du ⊜	184	50.22 N	95.55 W
Bonnétable	50	48.11 N	0.26 E
Bonne Terre	194	37.55 N	90.33 W
Bonnet Plume ≃	180	65.55 N	134.58 W
Bonneuil-sur-Marne	261	48.46 N	2.29 E
Bonneval	50	48.11 N	1.24 E
Bonneval-sur-Arc	62	45.22 N	7.03 E
Bonnevaux	58	46.18 N	6.40 E
Bonneville, Fr.	58	46.05 N	6.25 E
Bonneville, Or., U.S.	224	45.38 N	121.57 W
Bonneville Dam ◆⁶	224	45.39 N	121.56 W
Bonneville Peak ʌ	202	42.46 N	112.08 W
Bonneville Salt Flats ≍	200	40.45 N	113.52 W
Bonney, Lake ⊜	166	37.48 S	140.22 E
Bonney Lake	224	47.10 N	122.11 W
Bonnie Doone	192	35.05 N	78.57 W
Bonnières	50	49.02 N	1.35 E
Bonnie Rock	162	30.32 S	118.21 E
Bonnieux	62	43.49 N	5.18 E
Bonnievale	158	33.57 S	20.06 E
Bönninghardt	263	51.35 N	6.28 E
Bönninghardt ⋀²	263	51.34 N	6.27 E
Bonnots Mill	219	38.34 N	91.58 W
Bonny	150	4.27 N	7.10 E
Bonny ≃¹	150	4.20 N	7.10 E
Bonnyrigg, Austl.	274a	33.54 S	150.54 E
Bonnyrigg, Scot., U.K.	46	55.52 N	3.08 W
Bonny-sur-Loire	50	47.34 N	2.50 E
Bonnyville	182	54.16 N	110.44 W
Bono, It.	71	40.25 N	9.02 E
Bono, Ar., U.S.	194	35.54 N	90.48 W
Bono, Oh., U.S.	214	41.38 N	83.16 W
Bonoi	164	1.51 S	137.48 E
Bonorva	71	40.25 N	8.46 E
Bonoua	150	5.16 N	3.36 W
Bonpas Creek ≃	194	38.16 N	87.59 W
Bonriki	174t	1.23 N	173.09 E
Bonriki Airport ✈	174t	1.22 N	173.10 E
Bons	58	46.16 N	6.23 E
Bonsall	228	33.17 N	117.13 W
Bonsari	272c	19.04 N	73.02 E
Bon Secour	194	30.18 N	87.43 W
Bon-Secours, Bel.	50	50.30 N	3.36 E
Bonsecours, Fr.	50	49.26 N	1.08 E
Bonshaw	186	46.12 N	63.21 W
Bonsucesso ◆⁸	287a	22.52 S	43.15 W
Bontang	112	0.08 N	117.30 E
Bontberg ʌ	158	32.21 S	21.04 E
Bontebok National Park ♦	158	34.07 S	20.23 E
Bonthe	150	7.32 N	12.30 W
Bontoc	116	17.05 N	120.58 E
Bon Wier	194	30.44 N	93.39 W
Bonyhád	30	46.19 N	18.32 E
Boo, Kepulauan ıı	164	1.12 S	129.24 E
Booby Point ⊳	284b	39.17 N	76.23 W
Boock	54	53.29 N	14.15 E
Boody	219	39.46 N	89.03 W
Boogardie	162	28.02 S	117.47 E
Booischot	56	51.03 N	4.46 E
Bookabie	162	31.50 S	132.41 E
Bookaloo	166	31.55 S	137.22 E
Book Cliffs ⊥⁴	200	39.20 N	109.00 W
Booke	152	2.33 S	22.00 E
Booker	196	36.27 N	100.32 W
Booker T. Washington National Monument ♦	192	37.01 N	79.45 W
Bookwalter	218	39.42 N	83.32 W
Boola	150	8.22 N	8.43 W
Boolaloo	162	22.35 S	115.51 E
Booleroo Centre	166	32.53 S	138.21 E
Booligal	166	33.52 S	144.53 E
Boologooro	162	24.21 S	114.02 E
Boom	50	51.05 N	4.22 E
Boomarra	166	19.33 S	140.20 E
Boomer	188	38.09 N	81.17 W
Boomi	166	28.44 S	149.35 E
Boomrivier	158	29.33 S	20.27 E
Boonah	171a	28.00 S	152.41 E
Böön cagaan nuur ⊜	102	45.35 N	99.09 E
Boone, Ia., U.S.	190	42.03 N	93.52 W
Boone, N.C., U.S.	192	36.13 N	81.40 W
Boone ◻⁶, Il., U.S.	216	42.15 N	88.50 W
Boone ◻⁶, In., U.S.	218	40.03 N	86.28 W
Boone ◻⁶, Ky., U.S.	218	38.57 N	84.45 W
Boone ◻⁶, Mo., U.S.	219	38.55 N	92.15 W
Boone ≃	190	42.19 N	93.56 W
Boone Draw V	196	33.51 N	103.42 W
Boone Grove	216	41.21 N	87.08 W
Boone Lake ⊜¹	192	36.25 N	82.25 W
Boone Reservoir ⊜¹	279b	40.15 N	80.08 W
Boones Mill	192	37.06 N	79.57 W
Booneville, Ar., U.S.	194	35.08 N	93.55 W
Booneville, Ky., U.S.	192	37.28 N	83.40 W
Booneville, Ms., U.S.	194	34.39 N	88.34 W
Boon Point ⊳	240c	17.10 N	61.50 W
Boons	158	25.59 S	27.13 E
Boonsboro	208	39.30 N	77.39 W
Boonsville	222	33.04 N	97.52 W
Boonton	210	40.54 N	74.24 W
Boonton Reservoir ⊜¹	276	40.53 N	74.25 W
Boonville, Ca., U.S.	204	39.00 N	123.21 W
Boonville, In., U.S.	194	38.02 N	87.16 W
Boonville, Mo., U.S.	194	38.58 N	92.44 W
Boonville, N.Y., U.S.	212	43.29 N	75.20 W
Boopi ≃	248	15.41 S	67.15 W
Boorabbin National Park ♦	162	31.13 S	120.10 E
Boorama	144	9.56 N	43.11 E
Boorindal	166	30.21 S	146.08 E
Booroorban	166	34.56 S	144.46 E
Boorowa	166	34.26 S	148.43 E
Boos	50	49.23 N	1.12 E
Boosaaso	144	11.17 N	49.11 E
Boossen	54	52.22 N	14.29 E
Boot	44	54.24 N	3.17 W
Bootahnie Indian Reserve ◆⁴	182	50.24 N	121.31 W
Booth	194	32.30 N	86.34 W
Booth, Lac ⊜	190	46.45 N	78.34 W
Boothbay Harbor	188	43.51 N	69.37 W
Boothby, Cape ⊳	9	66.34 S	57.16 E
Booth Corner	285	39.51 N	75.29 W
Boothia, Gulf of ⊂	176	71.00 N	91.00 W
Boothia Peninsula ⊳¹	176	70.30 N	95.00 W
Boothstown	262	53.30 N	2.25 W
Boothville	194	29.20 N	89.25 W
Booth Wood Reservoir ⊜¹	262	53.38 N	1.58 W
Boothwyn	285	39.49 N	75.26 W
Bootle	262	53.28 N	3.00 W
Boot Reefs ✢²	164	10.00 S	144.40 E
Booué	152	0.06 S	11.56 E
Booysens ◆⁸	273d	26.14 S	28.01 E
Booze Creek ≃	284c	38.59 N	77.07 W
Bopfingen	56	48.51 N	10.21 E
Bo Phloi	110	14.19 N	99.31 E
Bophuthatswana ◻¹, Afr.	138	26.00 S	25.35 E
Bophuthatswana ◻¹, Afr.	156	26.00 S	25.35 E
Boping	98	36.36 N	116.07 E
Boping Ling ⋀	100	25.00 N	117.00 E
Bopo	150	7.37 N	7.52 E
Bopolu	150	7.03 N	10.32 W
Boppard	56	50.14 N	7.35 E
Boqér, Har ʌ	132	30.52 N	34.43 E
Boqueirão, Ilha do ı	287a	22.46 S	43.09 W
Boqueirão, Serra do ⋀²	250	11.30 S	43.45 W
Boquerón	236	8.30 N	82.34 W
Boquerón ◻⁵	252	21.30 S	60.00 W
Boquerón, Bahía de ⊂	240m	18.01 N	67.12 W
Boquerón, Túnel ◆⁵	286c	10.34 N	67.00 W
Boquet	279b	40.23 N	79.36 W
Boquilla, Presa de la ⊜¹	232	27.30 N	105.30 W
Boquilla del Refugio	196	25.33 N	102.28 W
Boquillas del Carmen	232	29.17 N	102.53 W
Bor, Česko.	60	49.43 N	12.47 E
Bor, Jugo.	38	44.05 N	22.07 E
Bor, S.S.S.R.	24	63.00 N	42.38 E
Bor, S.S.S.R.	80	56.22 N	44.05 E
Bor, Sūd.	140	6.12 N	31.33 E
Bor, Tür.	130	37.54 N	34.34 E
Bor, Lak ≃	154	1.18 N	40.40 E
Bora-Bora ı	14	16.30 S	151.45 W
Borabu	110	16.02 N	103.07 E
Boracay Island ı	116	11.59 N	121.55 E
Boraha, Nosy ı	157b	16.50 S	49.55 E
Borah Peak ʌ	202	44.08 N	113.48 W
Boraldaj ≃	85	42.33 N	69.07 E
Borale	144	9.10 N	42.35 E
Borambola	171b	35.12 S	147.41 E
Borang, Tanjung ⊳	164	5.16 S	133.07 E
Boraré ≃	287b	23.46 S	46.39 W
Borås	26	57.43 N	12.55 E
Borāzjān	128	29.16 N	51.12 E
Borba, Bra.	246	4.24 S	59.35 W
Borba, Port.	34	38.48 N	7.27 W
Borbeck ◆⁸	263	51.29 N	6.57 E
Borbera ≃	62	44.42 N	8.52 E
Borborema	255	21.37 S	49.04 W
Borca di Cadore	64	46.26 N	12.13 E
Borcea, Braţul ≃	38	44.40 N	27.53 E
Borchen	52	51.39 N	8.44 E
Borçka	130	41.22 N	41.40 E
Borculo, Ned.	52	52.07 N	6.31 E
Borculo, Mi., U.S.	216	42.53 N	86.01 W
Borda, Cape ⊳	166	35.45 S	136.34 E
Borda da Mata, Bra.	256	22.16 S	46.10 W
Borda da Mata, Bra.	256	22.37 S	47.01 W
Bordeaux, Fr.	32	44.50 N	0.34 W
Bordeaux, S. Afr.	273d	26.06 S	28.01 E
Bordeaux ◆⁸	275a	45.33 N	73.41 W
Bordeaux Mountain ʌ²	240m	18.20 N	64.44 W
Borden, Austl.	162	34.05 S	118.16 E
Borden, Sk., Can.	184	52.25 N	107.13 W
Borden, Eng., U.K.	260	51.20 N	0.42 E
Borden, In., U.S.	218	38.28 N	85.57 W
Borden, Canadian Forces Base ■	212	44.17 N	79.55 W
Borden Lake ⊜	190	47.50 N	83.18 W
Borden Peninsula ⊳¹	176	73.00 N	83.00 W
Bordentown	208	40.08 N	74.42 W
Border Mountains ⋀	164	3.40 S	141.05 E
Borders ◻⁴	46	55.37 N	3.15 W
Bordertown	166	36.19 S	140.47 E
Bordesholm	30	54.11 N	10.01 E
Borðeyri	24a	65.15 N	21.10 W
Bordighera	62	43.46 N	7.39 E
Bording	41	56.12 N	9.17 E
Bording Kirkeby	41	56.10 N	9.15 E
Bordino, Fiume di ≃	70	37.53 N	12.37 E
Bordj Bou Arreridj	148	36.04 N	4.46 E
Bordj Bounaama	34	35.51 N	1.36 E
Bordj Menaïel	148	36.44 N	3.43 E
Bordj Omar Idriss	148	28.09 N	6.43 E
Bordj Sidi Toui	148	32.44 N	11.22 E
Bordunskij	85	42.40 N	75.37 E
Bore, It.	62	44.43 N	9.47 E
Bore, Ityo.	144	4.40 N	37.40 E
Boré, Mali	150	15.08 N	3.29 W
Boreda	144	6.32 N	37.48 E
Boreham	260	51.46 N	0.33 E
Borehamwood	260	51.40 N	0.16 W
Borel Hill ʌ	282	37.19 N	122.12 W
Borello, It.	64	41.55 N	14.18 E
Borello, It.	66	44.03 N	12.11 E
Borensberg	26	58.34 N	15.17 E
Boreray ı	46	57.42 N	7.18 W
Boretto	64	44.54 N	10.33 E
Borgå → Porvoo	26	60.24 N	25.40 E
Borgallo, Galleria del ◆⁵	62	44.25 N	9.53 E
Borgarnes	24a	64.35 N	21.53 W
Borgata Costiera	70	37.43 N	12.39 E
Børgefjell Nasjonalpark ♦	24	65.10 N	14.00 E
Borgentreich	52	51.34 N	9.14 E
Börger, B.R.D.	52	52.54 N	7.32 E
Borger, Ned.	52	52.55 N	6.46 E
Borger, Tx., U.S.	196	35.40 N	101.23 W
Borgerhout	50	51.13 N	4.26 E
Borgetto	70	38.03 N	13.08 E
Borggård	40	58.44 N	15.32 E
Borghetto	64	45.41 N	10.56 E
Borghetto di Vara	62	44.13 N	9.43 E
Borghetto Lodigiano	62	45.13 N	9.30 E
Borghetto Santo Spirito	62	44.06 N	8.14 E
Borgholm	26	56.53 N	16.39 E
Borghorst	52	52.07 N	7.23 E
Borgia	68	38.49 N	16.30 E
Borgio-Verezzi	62	44.10 N	8.18 E
Borgloon	56	50.48 N	5.20 E
Borg Mountain ʌ	9	72.42 S	3.30 W
Borgne, Lake ⊂	194	30.05 N	89.40 W
Borgnesse, Pointe ⊳	240e	14.27 N	60.54 W
Borgo	64	46.03 N	11.27 E
Borgo alla Collina	66	43.45 N	11.43 E
Borgo a Mozzano	66	43.59 N	10.33 E
Borgo Cerreto	66	42.49 N	12.54 E
Borgo d'Ale	62	45.21 N	8.03 E
Borgoforte	64	45.03 N	10.45 E
Borgofranco d'Ivrea	62	45.30 N	7.51 E
Borgolavezzaro	62	45.19 N	8.42 E
Borgomanero	62	45.42 N	8.28 E
Borgomaro	62	43.58 N	7.56 E
Borgonovo Val Tidone	62	45.01 N	9.26 E
Borgo Pace	66	43.39 N	12.17 E
Borgoricco	64	45.32 N	11.58 E
Borgorose	66	42.11 N	13.13 E
Borgo San Dalmazzo	62	44.20 N	7.30 E
Borgo San Giacomo	64	45.21 N	9.58 E
Borgo San Lorenzo	66	43.57 N	11.23 E
Borgosatollo	64	45.28 N	10.14 E
Borgosesia	62	45.43 N	8.16 E
Borgo Ticino	266b	45.41 N	8.36 E
Borgo Tossignano	66	44.16 N	11.35 E
Borgou ◻⁵	150	10.30 N	2.50 E
Borgo Val di Taro	62	44.29 N	9.46 E
Borgo Vercelli	62	45.21 N	8.28 E
Borgsdorf	54	52.42 N	13.14 E
Borgsdorf, Forst ◆³	264a	52.42 N	13.19 E
Borgu Game Reserve ◆⁴	150	10.15 N	4.10 E
Borgund ʋ¹	26	61.03 N	7.49 E
Bori	150	4.42 N	7.21 E
Borig Delijn els ◆²	88	50.00 N	94.00 E
Borikhan	110	18.33 N	103.43 E
Borilovo	76	53.22 N	35.58 E
Borinage ◻⁹	50	50.30 N	4.00 E
Boring, Md., U.S.	208	39.31 N	76.49 W
Boring, Or., U.S.	224	45.25 N	122.22 W
Borinskoje	76	52.27 N	39.22 E
Borislav	78	49.16 N	23.27 E
Borisoglebsk	80	51.23 N	42.06 E
Borisoglebskij	80	57.16 N	39.09 E
Borisov, S.S.S.R.	76	54.15 N	28.30 E
Borisov, S.S.S.R.	78	50.11 N	26.31 E
Borisovka, S.S.S.R.	76	52.50 N	39.58 E
Borisovka, S.S.S.R.	78	50.36 N	36.01 E
Borisovo	82	55.25 N	36.03 E
Borisovo ◆⁸	265b	55.38 N	37.45 E
Borisovo-Sudskoje	76	59.54 N	36.01 E
Borisovskaja	76	60.12 N	39.48 E
Borispol'	78	50.21 N	30.57 E
Borja, Esp.	34	41.50 N	1.32 W
Borja, Perú	246	4.26 S	77.33 W
Bork	52	51.40 N	7.30 E
Borken, B.R.D.	52	51.51 N	6.51 E
Borken, B.R.D.	56	51.03 N	9.16 E
Borkenwirthe	52	51.53 N	6.50 E
Borki, S.S.S.R.	78	49.42 N	36.02 E
Borki, S.S.S.R.	86	59.08 N	82.15 E
Borkoldoj, chrebet ⋀	85	41.25 N	77.50 E
Børkop	41	55.39 N	9.39 E
Borkou ◆¹	146	18.15 N	18.50 E
Borkou-Ennedi-Tibesti ◻⁵	146	18.15 N	18.50 E
Borkoviči	76	55.40 N	28.20 E
Borkum	52	53.35 N	6.40 E
Borkum ı	52	53.35 N	6.41 E
Borland Manor	279b	40.15 N	80.09 W
Borlänge	40	60.29 N	15.25 E
Borle ◆⁸	272c	19.02 N	72.55 E
Borlu	130	38.44 N	28.27 E
Bormes-les-Mimosas	62	43.09 N	6.20 E
Bormida ≃	62	44.23 N	8.13 E
Bormida di Millesimo ≃	62	44.40 N	8.20 E
Bormida di Spigno ≃	62	44.40 N	8.20 E
Bormio	64	46.28 N	10.22 E
Born, D.D.R.	41	54.23 N	12.31 E
Born, D.D.R.	54	52.22 N	11.28 E
Born, D.D.R.	54	45.22 N	12.31 E
Borna, D.D.R.	54	51.07 N	12.30 E
Borna, D.D.R.	54	51.19 N	13.11 E
Borndiep ⊂	52	53.25 N	5.35 E
Borne	52	52.18 N	6.45 E
Borne ≃	62	45.03 N	3.54 E
Borneo (Kalimantan) ı	112	0.30 N	114.00 E
Bornheim	56	50.46 N	6.59 E
Bornholm ı	26	55.10 N	15.00 E
Bornholte	52	51.52 N	8.29 E
Bornhöved	54	54.04 N	10.16 E
Börnicke, D.D.R.	54	52.41 N	12.56 E
Börnicke, D.D.R.	264a	52.40 N	13.38 E
Börnig ◆⁸	263	51.33 N	7.16 E
Bornim ◆⁸	264a	52.26 N	13.00 E
Borno	64	45.56 N	10.12 E
Bornos, Embalse de ⊜¹	34	36.50 N	5.30 W
Bornsdorf	54	51.46 N	13.41 E
Bornstedt ◆⁸	264a	52.25 N	13.02 E
Bornu ◻³	146	12.00 N	12.45 E
Boro ≃	140	8.52 N	26.11 E
Borobudur ⊥	115a	7.36 S	110.12 E
Borod'anka	78	50.39 N	29.56 E
Borodarou	150	10.59 N	2.53 E
Borodino, S.S.S.R.	78	46.18 N	29.13 E
Borodino, S.S.S.R.	82	55.32 N	35.50 E
Borodino, S.S.S.R.	82	56.53 N	37.00 E
Borodino, S.S.S.R.	88	55.55 N	94.55 E
Borodulicha	86	50.43 N	80.55 E
Borodulino	80	57.59 N	54.20 E
Borogoncy	74	62.42 N	131.08 E
Borohoro Shan ⋀	86	44.06 N	83.10 E
Boroko	112	0.55 N	123.16 E
Boroml'a	78	50.37 N	34.59 E
Boromo	150	11.45 N	2.56 W
Boron, Mali	150	14.01 N	7.30 W
Boron, Ca., U.S.	228	34.59 N	117.38 W
Boronga Islands ıı	110	19.58 N	93.06 E
Borongan	116	11.37 N	125.26 E
Boronia	274b	37.52 S	145.17 E
Boron'ki	76	53.09 N	32.08 E
Borore	71	40.13 N	8.48 E
Borotou	150	8.44 N	7.30 W
Boroughbridge	44	54.06 N	1.23 W
Borough Green	260	51.17 N	0.19 E
Borough Park ◆⁸	276	40.38 N	74.00 W
Borovaja, S.S.S.R.	78	50.12 N	30.07 E
Borovaja, S.S.S.R.	83	49.24 N	37.40 E
Borovaja ≃	83	48.58 N	38.24 E
Borovan	38	43.26 N	23.45 E
Borovany	61	48.54 N	14.39 E
Borovič̌i	76	58.24 N	33.55 E
Borovik ≃	83	49.11 N	38.33 E
Borovka ≃	80	52.54 N	52.00 E
Borovl'anka	86	52.38 N	84.29 E
Borovoj	24	59.55 N	51.38 E
Borovoje, S.S.S.R.	78	51.06 N	27.13 E
Borovoje, S.S.S.R.	86	53.04 N	70.19 E
Borovsk	82	55.12 N	36.30 E
Borovskaja	24	60.46 N	41.06 E
Borovskij	86	57.03 N	65.44 E
Borovskoj	86	53.48 N	64.12 E
Borovskoje, S.S.S.R.	83	48.51 N	38.34 E
Borovskoje, S.S.S.R.	86	52.39 N	82.08 E
Borovucha	76	55.36 N	28.37 E
Borovy	60	49.33 N	13.18 E
Borozdino	82	54.07 N	38.22 E
Borraan	144	10.14 N	48.44 E
Borrachudo ≃	255	18.12 S	45.16 W
Borrazópolis	255	23.56 S	51.36 W
Borrby	26	55.27 N	14.10 E
Borre	41	55.00 N	12.28 E
Borre ⊥	26	59.23 N	10.28 E
Borreby	41	55.14 N	11.19 E
Borriana, Esp.	34	39.53 N	0.05 W
Borriana, It.	62	45.30 N	8.02 E
Borris	48	52.35 N	6.06 W
Borrisokane	48	52.59 N	8.07 W
Borrisoleigh	48	52.45 N	7.57 W
Borroloola	164	16.04 S	136.17 E
Borroloola Aboriginal Reserve ◆⁴	164	16.00 S	136.15 E
Borrowdale	44	54.31 N	3.10 W
Börry	52	52.01 N	9.27 E
Borş	38	47.07 N	21.49 E
Borşa, Rom.	38	47.39 N	24.40 E
Borşa, Rom.	38	46.56 N	23.40 E
Borsad	120	22.25 N	72.54 E
Borsano	266b	45.35 N	8.51 E
Borschemich	263	51.04 N	6.25 E
Borščov	78	48.48 N	26.03 E
Borščovo	82	56.30 N	36.51 E
Borščovočnyj chrebet ⋀	88	52.00 N	117.00 E
Borsdorf	54	51.21 N	12.32 E
Borskoje	80	53.02 N	51.43 E
Borsod-Abaúj-Zemplén ◻⁶	30	48.15 N	21.00 E
Börssum	54	52.04 N	10.35 E
Borstendorf	54	50.46 N	13.10 E
Bortala ≃	86	44.50 N	82.45 E
Borth, B.R.D.	52	51.36 N	6.33 E
Borth, Wales, U.K.	42	52.29 N	4.03 W
Borthwick Water ≃	44	55.24 N	2.50 W
Bortigali	71	40.17 N	8.50 E
Bortigiadas	71	40.53 N	9.02 E
Bort-les-Orgues, Fr.	32	43.49 N	2.53 E
Bort-les-Orgues, Fr.	32	45.24 N	2.30 E
Bortniči	78	50.22 N	30.41 E
Borto	88	53.35 N	111.53 E
Bortondale	285	39.54 N	79.24 W
Boru	164	10.14 S	148.50 E
Boruca	236	9.00 N	83.20 W
Borūjen	128	31.59 N	51.18 E
Borūjerd	128	33.54 N	48.46 E
Bor Ul Shan ⋀	102	41.20 N	98.55 E
Borve	46	56.58 N	7.32 W
Borz'a	88	50.24 N	116.31 E
Borz'a ≃	88	50.38 N	115.38 E
Borzna	78	51.15 N	32.25 E
Boržomi	84	41.50 N	43.21 E
Boržomskij zapovednik ♦	84	41.50 N	43.10 E
Borzonasca	62	44.25 N	9.23 E
Borzyszkowy	30	54.03 N	17.22 E
Bosa	71	40.18 N	8.30 E
Bosaga	86	47.55 N	72.58 E
Bosambi	152	2.24 N	22.39 E
Bosanska Dubica	36	45.11 N	16.49 E
Bosanska Gradiška	36	45.09 N	17.15 E
Bosanska Krupa	36	44.53 N	16.10 E
Bosanski Novi	36	45.03 N	16.23 E
Bosanski Petrovac	36	44.33 N	16.22 E
Bosanski Šamac	38	45.03 N	18.28 E
Bosansko Grahovo	36	44.11 N	16.22 E
Bősárkány	61	47.41 N	17.14 E
Bosau	54	54.06 N	10.25 E
Bosavi, Mount ʌ	164	6.35 S	142.50 E
Boscastle	42	50.41 N	4.42 W
Bosco, It.	66	43.08 N	12.28 E
Bosco, It.	66	44.53 N	12.14 E
Boscobel	190	43.08 N	90.42 W
Bosco Chiesanuova	64	45.37 N	11.02 E
Bosco Marengo	62	44.49 N	8.41 E
Boscoreale	68	40.46 N	14.28 E
Bose	102	23.54 N	106.37 E
Bösel	52	53.00 N	7.58 E
Bosencheve, Parque Nacional ♦	234	19.36 N	100.15 W
Bosenge	152	1.18 N	22.19 E
Bósforo, Estrecho del → İstanbul Boğazı ʯ	130	41.06 N	29.04 E
Bosham	42	50.49 N	0.52 W
Boshan	98	36.29 N	117.50 E
Boshkung Lake ⊜	212	45.04 N	78.44 W
Boshoek	156	25.30 S	27.09 E
Boshof	158	28.34 S	25.04 E
Boshrūyeh	128	33.53 N	57.26 E
Bosilegrad	38	42.29 N	22.28 E
Bösingen	58	48.14 N	8.34 E
Bosjökloster	41	55.54 N	13.31 E
Boškajnar	85	38.13 N	68.51 E
Boskoop	52	52.04 N	4.35 E
Boskop	158	26.34 S	27.08 E
Boskop ʌ	273d	26.05 S	27.57 E
Boskovice	30	49.29 N	16.40 E
Boskuil	158	27.23 S	25.51 E
Bosman	164	4.10 S	144.40 E
Bosna	272b	22.37 N	88.30 E
Bosna ≃	38	45.04 N	18.29 E
Bosna i Hercegovina ◻³	36	44.15 N	17.30 E
Bošn'akovo	89	49.38 N	142.10 E
Bosnik	164	1.10 S	136.14 E
Boso	272b	22.58 N	88.08 E
Bosobolo	152	4.11 N	19.54 E
Boso-Djafo	152	1.06 N	19.14 E
Bosogo	85	41.09 N	76.25 E
Bōsō-hantō ⊳¹	94	35.18 N	140.10 E
Bōsō-kyūryō ⋀²	268	35.08 N	139.56 E
Bososama	152	4.18 N	20.00 E
Bösperde	263	51.28 N	7.46 E
Bosphore, Détroit du → İstanbul Boğazı ʯ	130	41.06 N	29.04 E
Bosporus → İstanbul Boğazı ʯ	130	41.06 N	29.04 E
Bosque ◻⁶	222	31.55 N	97.35 W
Bosque, Paseo del ♦	288	34.55 S	57.56 W
Bosque Farms	200	34.53 N	106.40 W
Bosques	288	34.49 S	58.14 W
Bosques Petrificados, Monumento Natural ♦	254	47.39 S	68.07 W
Bosqueville	222	31.38 N	97.13 W
Bossangoa	152	6.29 N	17.27 E
Bossdorf	54	51.59 N	12.40 E
Bossé Bangou	150	13.21 N	1.18 E
Bossembélé	152	5.16 N	17.39 E
Bossentele	152	5.41 N	16.38 E
Bossert Estates	285	40.09 N	74.44 W
Bossier City	194	32.30 N	93.43 W
Bossley Park	274a	33.52 S	150.54 E
Bosso	146	13.42 N	13.19 E
Bosso, Dallol V	150	12.25 N	2.50 E
Bossolasco	62	44.32 N	8.02 E
Bossut, Cape ⊳	162	18.43 S	121.38 E
Bostān, Īrān	128	31.43 N	48.00 E
Bostān, Pāk.	120	30.26 N	67.02 E
Bostancı ◆⁸	267b	40.57 N	29.05 E
Bostandyk	80	49.38 N	48.54 E
Bosten Hu ⊜	90	42.00 N	87.00 E
Bostock Green	262	53.13 N	2.30 W
Boston, Pil.	116	7.52 N	126.22 E
Boston, Eng., U.K.	44	52.59 N	0.01 W
Boston, Ga., U.S.	192	30.47 N	83.47 W
Boston, In., U.S.	218	39.44 N	84.51 W
Boston, Ma., U.S.	207	42.21 N	71.03 W
Boston, Ma., U.S.	283	42.21 N	71.03 W
Boston, N.Y., U.S.	210	42.38 N	78.44 W
Boston, Pa., U.S.	279b	40.18 N	79.49 W
Boston Bar	182	49.52 N	121.26 W
Boston Bay ⊂	283	42.22 N	70.54 W
Boston Brook ≃	283	42.37 N	71.00 W
Boston College ʋ²	283	42.20 N	71.10 W
Boston Common ♦	283	42.21 N	71.05 W
Boston Corners	210	42.03 N	73.31 W
Boston Creek ≃	212	43.02 N	79.56 W
Boston Harbor	224	47.08 N	122.54 W
Boston Harbor ⊂	283	42.20 N	70.58 W
Boston Heights	214	41.15 N	81.30 W
Boston Mill	214	41.16 N	81.34 W
Boston Mountains ⋀	194	35.50 N	93.20 W
Boston Spa	44	53.54 N	1.21 W
Boston University ʋ²	283	42.21 N	71.07 W
Bosumtwi, Lake ⊜	150	6.30 N	1.25 W
Bosut ≃	38	44.57 N	19.22 E
Boswell, In., U.S.	216	40.31 N	87.22 W
Boswell, Ok., U.S.	196	34.01 N	95.52 W
Boswell, Pa., U.S.	214	40.09 N	79.01 W
Boswell Bay	180	60.24 N	146.08 W
Bosworth	194	39.28 N	93.20 W
Bosworth Airport ✈	279a	41.26 N	82.00 W
Bosworth Field ⊥	42	52.36 N	1.25 W
Botād	120	22.10 N	71.40 E
Botafogo ◆⁸	287a	22.57 S	43.11 W
Botafogo, Enseada de ⊂	287a	22.57 S	43.10 W
Botany	274a	33.57 S	151.12 E
Botany Bay ◆⁸	260	51.41 N	0.07 W
Botany Bay ⊂	170	33.59 S	151.12 E
Botejevo	78	46.41 N	35.52 E
Botelhos	256	21.39 S	46.24 W
Botera	152	11.37 S	14.17 E
Botersleegte	158	30.35 S	21.22 E
Botesdale	42	52.20 N	1.01 E
Boteti ≃	156	20.08 S	23.23 E
Botev ʌ	38	42.43 N	24.55 E
Botevgrad	38	42.54 N	23.47 E
Botha's Hill	158	29.45 S	30.45 E
Bothaville	158	27.27 S	26.36 E
Bothell	224	47.45 N	122.12 W
Bothe-Napa Valley State Park ♦	226	38.32 N	122.32 W
Bothnia, Gulf of ⊂	26	63.00 N	20.00 E
Bothwell, Austl.	166	42.23 S	147.00 E
Bothwell, On., Can.	214	42.38 N	81.52 W
Boticas	34	41.41 N	7.40 W
Botija, Isla ı	258	33.52 S	59.02 W
Botkins	216	40.28 N	84.10 W
Botkul', ozero ⊜	80	48.46 N	46.40 E
Botkyrka	40	59.14 N	17.49 E
Botlich	84	42.39 N	46.14 E
Bot Makak	152	4.00 N	10.55 E
Botna ≃	78	46.45 N	29.34 E
Botnia, Golfo de → Bothnia, Gulf of ⊂	26	63.00 N	20.00 E
Botola	152	1.17 S	18.13 E
Botolan	116	15.17 N	120.01 E
Botoşani	38	47.45 N	26.40 E
Botoşani ◻⁶	38	48.00 N	26.45 E
Botoşaniţa	38	47.53 N	26.07 E
Botou	150	12.40 N	2.03 E
Botovo	82	56.03 N	38.26 E
Bo Trach	110	17.35 N	106.32 E
Botrange ʌ	56	50.30 N	6.08 E
Botricello	68	38.56 N	16.51 E
Botro	150	7.51 N	5.19 W
Botsford	210	41.21 N	73.15 W
Botswana ◻¹, Afr.	138	22.00 S	24.00 E
Botswana ◻¹, Afr.	156	22.00 S	24.00 E
Botte Donato, Monte ʌ	68	39.17 N	16.26 E
Bottenhavet (Selkämeri) ⊂	26	62.00 N	20.00 E
Bottenviken (Perämeri) ⊂	26	65.00 N	23.00 E
Bottesford	42	52.56 N	0.48 W
Bottineau	198	48.49 N	100.26 W
Bottisham	42	52.13 N	0.16 E
Bottnischer Meerbusen → Bothnia, Gulf of ⊂	26	63.00 N	20.00 E
Bottoms Reservoir ⊜¹	262	53.28 N	1.58 W
Bottrop	52	51.31 N	6.55 E
Botucatu	255	22.52 S	48.26 W
Botwood	186	49.09 N	55.21 W
Boty	88	52.24 N	118.32 E
Bötzingen	58	48.04 N	7.44 E
Bötzow	54	52.39 N	13.08 E
Bötzsee ⊜	264a	52.34 N	13.50 E
Bouaflé, C. Iv.	150	6.59 N	5.45 W
Bouafle, Fr.	261	48.58 N	1.54 E
Bou Ahmed	148	35.25 N	5.00 W
Bouaké	150	7.41 N	5.02 W
Bou Ali, Oued V	148	31.14 N	4.16 E
Bouânane	148	32.03 N	3.03 W
Bouandougou	150	8.13 N	5.40 W
Bouar	152	5.57 N	15.36 E
Bou Arada	36	36.20 N	9.38 E
Bou Areg, Sebkha ⊂	34	35.10 N	2.45 W
Bouârfa	148	32.30 N	1.59 W
Bouaye	32	47.09 N	1.42 W
Boubandjidah, Parc National de ♦	146	8.45 N	14.45 E
Bou Bernous	148	27.18 N	2.59 W
Boubín ʌ	60	48.59 N	13.51 E
Bouca	152	6.30 N	18.17 E
Bouchain	50	50.17 N	3.19 E
Bouchegouf	36	36.28 N	7.44 E
Boucher ≃	186	49.10 N	69.06 W
Boucher, Lac ⊜	186	51.07 N	59.35 W
Boucherville	206	45.36 N	73.27 W
Boucherville, Îles de ıı	275a	45.37 N	73.28 W
Bouches-du-Rhône ◻⁵	62	43.30 N	5.00 E
Bouchoir	50	49.45 N	2.41 E
Bouclans	58	47.14 N	6.15 E
Boucle du Baoulé, Parc National de la ♦	150	13.50 N	9.00 W
Bouddi National Park ♦	170	33.31 S	131.24 E
Boudjellil	34	36.20 N	4.21 E
Boudnib	148	31.57 N	4.38 W
Boudouaou	34	36.43 N	3.25 E
Boudry	58	46.57 N	6.50 E
Boué	50	50.01 N	3.42 E
Bouenza ◻⁵	152	4.00 S	13.45 E
Boufarik	148	36.34 N	2.55 E
Bouffémont	261	49.03 N	2.18 E
Bou Ficha	36	36.18 N	10.29 E
Bougaa	34	36.20 N	5.05 E
Bougainville ◻⁵	175e	6.00 S	155.00 E
Bougainville ı	175e	6.00 S	155.00 E
Bougainville, Cape ⊳	164	13.54 S	126.06 E
Bougainville, Détroit de ʯ	175f	15.50 S	167.10 E
Bougainville Reef ✢²	164	15.30 S	147.06 E
Bougainville Strait ʯ	175e	6.40 S	156.10 E
Bougar'oûn, Cap ⊳	34	37.06 N	6.28 E
Bough Beech Reservoir ⊜¹	260	51.13 N	0.08 E
Boughton	44	53.12 N	1.00 W
Boughton Green	260	51.14 N	0.32 E
Boughton Malherbe	260	51.13 N	0.42 E
Boughton Place ʋ	260	51.13 N	0.32 E
Bougie → Bejaïa	148	36.45 N	5.05 E
Bougou	152	3.45 S	11.12 E
Bougouni	150	11.25 N	7.29 W
Bougouriba ≃	150	10.42 N	2.56 W
Bougzoul	34	35.42 N	2.51 E
Bou Hadjar	36	36.30 N	8.06 E
Bou Hajar	36	35.42 N	10.48 E
Bouillante	241o	16.06 N	61.45 W
Bouillon	56	49.48 N	5.04 E
Bouilly	50	48.12 N	4.00 E
Bouïra	148	36.23 N	3.54 E
Bouïra ◻⁵	148	36.00 N	4.00 E
Bouisy, Ru de ≃	261	48.34 N	2.45 E
Bou Izakarn	148	29.09 N	9.44 W
Boujad	148	32.48 N	6.26 W
Boujailles	58	46.53 N	6.05 E
Boujdour, Cap ⊳	148	26.08 N	14.30 W
Bouka ≃	150	11.00 N	10.50 W
Bou Kadir	148	36.04 N	1.07 E
Bou Khadra	36	35.45 N	8.02 E
Boukiéro	273b	4.12 S	15.18 E
Boukiéro, Mont ʌ²	273b	4.11 S	15.17 E
Boukombé	150	10.11 N	1.06 E
Boula Ibib	146	9.34 N	13.46 E
Boulaide	56	49.54 N	5.49 E
Boularderie Island ı	186	46.15 N	60.30 W
Boulay-Moselle	56	49.11 N	6.30 E
Boulbon	62	43.52 N	4.41 E
Boulder, Austl.	162	30.47 S	121.29 E
Boulder, Co., U.S.	200	40.00 N	105.16 W
Boulder, Mt., U.S.	202	46.14 N	112.07 W
Boulder ≃	202	45.52 N	111.57 W
Boulder City	204	35.58 N	114.49 W
Boulder Creek	226	37.07 N	122.07 W
Boulder Creek ≃	200	37.47 N	111.22 W
Boulder Hill	216	41.41 N	88.25 W
Bouleaux, Lac des ⊜	275a	45.33 N	73.19 W
Bouli ≃	150	13.15 N	0.03 E
Boulia	166	22.54 S	139.54 E
Bouligny	56	49.17 N	5.45 E
Boullay-les-Troux	261	48.41 N	2.03 E
Boulmane	148	33.22 N	4.45 W
Boulmane ◻⁴	148	33.00 N	4.00 W
Boulogne ◆⁸	258	34.31 S	58.34 W
Boulogne, Bois de ♦	261	48.50 N	2.15 E
Boulogne-Billancourt	50	48.50 N	2.15 E
Boulogne-sur-Gesse	32	43.18 N	0.39 E
Boulogne-sur-Mer	50	50.43 N	1.37 E
Bouloire	50	47.58 N	0.33 E
Boulouli	150	15.34 N	9.21 W
Bouloupari	175f	21.52 S	166.04 E
Boulouris-sur-Mer	62	43.25 N	6.48 E
Boulsa	150	12.39 N	0.34 W
Boulsworth Hill ʌ	262	53.48 N	2.06 W
Bouly	150	15.19 N	11.48 W
Bou Maad, Djebel ʌ	34	36.26 N	2.08 E
Boumalne	148	31.32 N	5.27 W
Boumba ≃	152	2.02 N	15.12 E
Boumbé I ≃	152	4.04 N	15.23 E
Boumbé II ≃	152	4.08 N	15.08 E
Boumboum	150	15.01 N	1.42 W
Boûmdeïd	150	17.26 N	9.50 W
Bou Medfaa	34	36.22 N	2.28 E
Boumentana	152	6.59 N	16.56 E
Boumnyebe	152	3.52 N	10.49 E
Boumou	146	9.02 N	16.26 E
Bouna	150	9.16 N	3.00 W
Boundary	180	64.04 N	141.06 W
Boundary Bay ⊂	224	49.00 N	122.58 W
Boundary Peak ʌ	204	37.51 N	118.21 W
Boundary Ranges ⋀	180	59.00 N	134.00 W
Bound Brook	210	40.34 N	74.32 W
Bound Brook ≃, Ma., U.S.	283	42.13 N	70.47 W
Bound Brook ≃, N.J., U.S.	276	40.35 N	74.30 W
Boundiali	150	9.31 N	6.29 W
Boun Nua	110	21.38 N	101.54 E
Bountiful	200	40.53 N	111.52 W
Bounty Bay ⊂	174e	25.04 S	130.05 W
Bounty Islands ıı	14	47.42 S	179.04 E
Bounty Trough ✢¹	14	46.00 S	178.00 E
Bouqteb	148	34.02 N	0.05 E
Bouquet Reservoir ⊜¹	228	34.35 N	118.24 W
Bouqueval	261	49.01 N	2.26 E
Boura	150	12.25 N	4.33 W
Bouradière	62	43.58 N	5.19 E
Bourail	175f	21.34 S	165.30 E
Bouray-sur-Juine	261	48.31 N	2.18 E
Bourbeuse ≃	194	38.24 N	90.53 W
Bourbeuse, Dry Fork ≃	194	38.16 N	91.26 W
Bourbon, In., U.S.	216	41.17 N	86.06 W
Bourbon, Mo., U.S.	194	38.09 N	91.14 W
Bourbon ◻⁶	218	38.14 N	84.14 W
Bourbon ≃	206	46.17 N	71.55 W
Bourbon-Lancy	32	46.38 N	3.46 E
Bourbonnais	216	41.08 N	87.52 W
Bourbonnais ◻⁹	32	46.20 N	3.00 E
Bourbonne-les-Bains	58	47.57 N	5.45 E
Bourbourg	50	50.57 N	2.12 E
Bourbre ≃	62	45.47 N	5.11 E
Bourdeaux	62	44.35 N	5.08 E
Bourdon, Île ı	275a	45.43 N	73.29 W
Bourdon, Réservoir du ⊜¹	50	47.36 N	3.07 E
Bourdonné	261	48.45 N	1.40 E
Bou Regreg, Oued ≃	148	34.03 N	6.50 W
Bourem	150	16.57 N	0.21 W
Bourg	194	29.33 N	90.36 W
Bourg-Achard	50	49.21 N	0.49 E
Bourganeuf	32	45.57 N	1.46 E
Bourg-Argental	62	45.18 N	4.33 E
Bourg-de-Péage	62	45.02 N	5.03 E
Bourg-en-Bresse	58	46.12 N	5.13 E
Bourges	32	47.05 N	2.24 E
Bourget	206	45.26 N	75.09 W
Bourget, Lac du ⊜	62	45.44 N	5.52 E
Bourg-la-Reine	261	48.47 N	2.19 E
Bourg-Lastic	32	45.39 N	2.33 E
Bourg-lés-Valence	62	44.57 N	4.53 E
Bourgneuf	261	48.36 N	2.00 E
Bourgneuf-en-Retz	32	47.02 N	1.57 W
Bourgogne	50	49.21 N	4.04 E
Bourgogne (Burgundy) ◻⁹	32	47.00 N	4.30 E
Bourgogne, Canal de ≡	50	47.58 N	3.30 E
Bourgoin-Jallieu	62	45.35 N	5.17 E
Bourg-Saint-Andéol	62	44.22 N	4.39 E
Bourg-Saint-Maurice	62	45.37 N	6.46 E
Bourg-Saint-Pierre	58	45.57 N	7.12 E
Bourgtheroulde	50	49.18 N	0.53 E
Bourgueil	50	47.17 N	0.10 E
Bou Rjeïmât ⫪⁴	150	19.04 N	15.08 W
Bourke	166	30.05 S	145.56 E
Bourmont	58	48.12 N	5.35 E
Bourne	42	52.46 N	0.23 W
Bourne ≃, Fr.	62	45.04 N	5.15 E
Bourne ≃, Eng., U.K.	42	51.02 N	1.47 W
Bournebridge	260	51.38 N	0.11 E
Bourne End	260	51.45 N	0.32 W
Bournemouth	42	50.43 N	1.54 W
Bourneville, Fr.	50	49.23 N	0.37 E
Bourneville, Oh., U.S.	218	39.17 N	83.09 W
Bourn Vincent Memorial Park ♦	48	52.01 N	9.30 W
Bouroum	150	13.37 N	0.39 W
Bourron-Marlotte	50	48.20 N	2.42 E
Bourscheid	56	49.55 N	6.04 E
Bourtange	52	53.00 N	7.11 E
Bourtanger Moor ◆³	52	53.00 N	7.15 E
Bourton-on-the-Water	42	51.53 N	1.45 W
Bourzanga	150	13.41 N	1.33 W
Bou Saâda	148	35.12 N	4.11 E
Bou Salem	36	36.36 N	8.59 E
Bousbecque	50	50.46 N	3.05 E
Bouse	200	33.55 N	114.00 W
Bou Sellam, Oued ≃	34	36.26 N	4.34 E
Bouse Wash V	200	34.02 N	114.20 W
Bou Smail	148	36.38 N	2.41 E
Boussac	32	46.21 N	2.13 E
Boussé, Burkina	150	12.39 N	1.53 W
Bousse, Fr.	56	49.17 N	6.12 E
Boussières	58	47.09 N	5.54 E
Bousso	146	10.29 N	16.43 E
Boussois	50	50.17 N	4.03 E
Boussouma	150	12.55 N	1.05 W
Boussu	50	50.26 N	3.48 E
Boussy-Saint-Antoine	261	48.41 N	2.32 E
Bout, Pointe du ⊳	240e	14.34 N	61.03 W
Bouteille, Lac de la ⊜	206	46.42 N	73.41 W
Bouteldja	36	36.47 N	8.12 E
Bou Temezguida ʌ	148	29.21 N	9.55 W
Boutilimit	150	17.33 N	14.42 W
Bouttencourt	50	49.56 N	1.38 E
Bouvard, Cape ⊳	168a	32.41 S	115.37 E
Bouvetøya ı	9	54.26 S	3.24 E
Bouvier Bay ⊂	281	42.39 N	82.38 W
Bouvières	62	44.30 N	5.13 E
Bouxières-aux-Dames	56	48.45 N	6.10 E
Bouxwiller	56	48.49 N	7.29 E
Bouyon	62	43.50 N	7.07 E
Bouza	150	14.25 N	6.02 E
Bou Zadjar	34	35.35 N	1.09 W
Bouzonville	56	49.18 N	6.32 E
Bov	41	54.50 N	9.23 E
Bova	68	38.00 N	15.56 E
Bøvågen	26	60.40 N	4.58 E
Bovalino Marina	68	38.10 N	16.11 E
Bova Marina	68	37.56 N	15.55 E
Bovard	279b	40.19 N	79.30 W
Bovec	36	46.20 N	13.33 E
Bovegno	64	45.48 N	10.16 E
Bovenden	52	51.35 N	9.55 E
Bovenkarspel	52	52.42 N	5.15 E
Bøverdal	26	61.43 N	8.21 E
Boves, Fr.	50	49.51 N	2.23 E
Boves, It.	62	44.19 N	7.33 E
Bovey	190	47.17 N	93.25 W
Bovey ≃	42	50.34 N	3.37 W
Bovey Tracey	42	50.36 N	3.40 W
Bovill	202	46.51 N	116.23 W
Boville Ernica	66	41.38 N	13.28 E
Bovina	196	34.31 N	102.53 W
Bovina Center	210	42.16 N	74.47 W
Bovingdon	260	51.44 N	0.32 W
Bövinghausen ◆⁸	263	51.31 N	7.19 E
Bovington Camp	42	50.42 N	2.14 W
Bovino	68	41.15 N	15.20 E
Bovisio Masciago	266b	45.37 N	9.09 E
Bovolenta	64	45.16 N	11.56 E
Bovolone	64	45.15 N	11.07 E
Bovril	252	31.21 S	59.26 W
Bovrup	41	54.59 N	9.36 E

Symbol	English	Deutsch	Español	Français	Português
≃	River	Fluß	Río	Rivière	Rio
≡	Canal	Kanal	Canal	Canal	Canal
⌞	Waterfall, Rapids	Wasserfall, Stromschnellen	Cascada, Rápidos	Chute d'eau, Rapides	Cascata, Rápidos
ʯ	Strait	Meeresstraße	Estrecho	Détroit	Estreito
⊂	Bay, Gulf	Bucht, Golf	Bahía, Golfo	Baie, Golfe	Baía, Golfo
⊜	Lake, Lakes	See, Seen	Lago, Lagos	Lac, Lacs	Lago, Lagos
≍	Swamp	Sumpf	Pantano	Marais	Pântano
⍓	Ice Features, Glacier	Eis- und Gletscherformen	Accidentes Glaciales	Formes glaciaires	Acidentes glaciares
⫪	Other Hydrographic Features	Andere Hydrographische Objekte	Otros Elementos Hidrográficos	Autres données hydrographiques	Outros acidentes hidrográficos
✢	Submarine Features	Untermeerische Objekte	Accidentes Submarinos	Formes de relief sous-marin	Acidentes submarinos
◻	Political Unit	Politische Einheit	Unidad Politica	Entité politique	Unidade política
ʋ	Cultural Institution	Kulturelle Institution	Institución Cultural	Institution culturelle	Institução cultural
⊥	Historical Site	Historische Stätte	Sitio Histórico	Site historique	Sitio histórico
♦	Recreational Site	Erholungs- und Ferienort	Sitio de Recreo	Centre de loisirs	Area de Lazer
✈	Airport	Flughafen	Aeropuerto	Aéroport	Aeroporto
■	Military Installation	Militäranlage	Instalación Militar	Installation militaire	Instalação militar
◆	Miscellaneous	Verschiedenes	Misceláneo	Divers	Diversos

I · 24 **Bow-Bria**

Name	Page	Lat.°′	Long.°′
Bow	224	48.33 N	122.23 W
Bow ≃, Austl.	162	16.32 S	128.39 E
Bow ≃, Ab., Can.	182	49.56 N	111.42 W
Bow ≃, Sk., Can.	184	54.56 N	105.13 W
Bo-Wadrif	158	32.26 S	20.07 E
Bowang	106	31.34 N	118.50 E
Bowbells	198	48.48 N	102.14 W
Bow Brook ≃	42	52.04 N	2.07 W
Bowburn	44	54.43 N	1.31 W
Bow Creek ≃	198	39.35 N	99.14 W
Bowden	182	51.55 N	114.02 W
Bowdle	198	45.27 N	99.39 W
Bowdoin, Lake ⊜	202	48.24 N	107.41 W
Bowdon, Eng., U.K.	262	53.23 N	2.22 W
Bowdon, Ga., U.S.	192	33.32 N	85.15 W
Bowdon, N.D., U.S.	198	47.28 N	99.42 W
Bowelling	168a	33.25 S	116.29 E
Bowen, Arg.	252	35.00 S	67.31 W
Bowen, Austl.	166	20.01 S	148.15 E
Bowen, Il., U.S.	194	40.14 N	91.04 W
Bowen ≃	166	20.24 S	147.21 E
Bowenfels	170	33.31 S	150.07 E
Bowens Creek ≃	170	33.21 S	150.35 E
Bowers	208	39.15 N	75.36 W
Bowers Gifford	260	51.34 N	0.32 E
Bowers Mansion ⊥	226	39.17 N	119.50 W
Bowers Marshes ≡	260	51.33 N	0.32 E
Bowers Ridge ✣ 3	16	54.00 N	179.00 E
Bowerston	214	40.25 N	81.11 W
Bowersville	218	39.34 N	83.43 W
Bowgreave	44	53.52 N	2.45 W
Bowie, Az., U.S.	200	32.19 N	109.29 W
Bowie, Md., U.S.	208	39.00 N	76.46 W
Bowie, Tx., U.S.	196	33.33 N	97.50 W
Bowie Creek ≃	194	31.26 N	89.24 W
Bow Island	184	49.52 N	111.22 W
Bowland, Forest of ◆ 3	44	53.58 N	2.32 W
Bowles Creek ≃	222	32.02 N	94.59 W
Bowley Bar ≻ 2	284b	39.18 N	76.23 W
Bowleys Quarters	284b	39.19 N	76.24 W
Bowling Green, Fl., U.S.	220	27.38 N	81.49 W
Bowling Green, Ky., U.S.	194	36.59 N	86.26 W
Bowling Green, Mo., U.S.	219	39.20 N	91.11 W
Bowling Green, Oh., U.S.	216	41.22 N	83.39 W
Bowling Green, Pa., U.S.	285	39.55 N	75.23 W
Bowling Green, Va., U.S.	208	38.02 N	77.20 W
Bowling Green, Cape ≻	166	19.19 S	147.25 E
Bowling Green Bay National Park ♠	166	19.28 S	147.14 E
Bowman, Ca., U.S.	226	38.57 N	121.03 W
Bowman, Ga., U.S.	192	34.12 N	83.01 W
Bowman, N.D., U.S.	198	46.10 N	103.23 W
Bowman, S.C., U.S.	192	33.20 N	80.40 W
Bowman, Mount ∧	182	51.10 N	121.55 W
Bowman Creek ≃, Pa., U.S.	210	41.31 N	75.58 W
Bowman Creek ≃, Wa., U.S.	224	45.50 N	121.03 W
Bowman-Haley Lake ⊜ 1	198	46.00 N	103.20 W
Bowman Island I	9	65.17 S	103.08 E
Bowman Lake ⊜ 1	226	39.27 N	120.38 W
Bowmans	168b	34.09 S	138.16 E
Bowmansdale	208	40.10 N	76.59 W
Bowmanstown	208	40.48 N	75.40 W
Bowmansville, N.Y., U.S.	212	42.56 N	78.41 W
Bowmansville, Pa., U.S.	208	40.10 N	76.04 W
Bowmanville	212	43.55 N	78.41 W
Bowmanville Creek ≃	212	43.53 N	78.40 W
Bowmont Water ≃	44	55.34 N	2.09 W
Bowmore	46	55.45 N	6.17 W
Bowness-on-Windermere	44	54.22 N	2.55 W
Bowokan, Kepulauan II	112	2.05 S	123.35 E
Bowral	170	34.28 S	150.25 E
Bowraville	166	30.39 S	152.51 E
Bowron ≃	182	54.04 N	121.48 W
Bowron Lake Provincial Park ♠	182	53.10 N	121.06 W
Bowsman	184	52.14 N	101.14 W
Bowwood	154	17.07 S	26.17 E
Box	42	51.26 N	2.15 W
Boxberg	56	49.29 N	9.38 E
Box Butte Creek ≃	198	42.28 N	102.37 W
Box Creek ≃, Tx., U.S.	222	31.35 N	95.10 W
Box Creek ≃, Tx., U.S.	222	31.33 N	95.43 W
Box Elder	202	48.19 N	110.00 W
Boxelder Creek ≃, U.S.	198	45.59 N	103.57 W
Boxelder Creek ≃, Co., U.S.	198	40.33 N	105.00 W
Box Elder Creek ≃, Co., U.S.	198	40.23 N	104.28 W
Box Elder Creek ≃, Mt., U.S.	202	46.57 N	108.04 W
Boxelder Creek ≃, S.D., U.S.	198	44.01 N	102.27 W
Boxey	186	47.25 N	55.34 W
Boxey Point ≻	186	47.24 N	55.35 W
Boxford	207	42.39 N	70.59 W
Boxford State Forest ♠	283	42.39 N	71.02 W
Box Grove	275b	43.51 N	79.14 W
Box Hill	169	37.49 S	145.08 E
Boxholm	26	58.12 N	15.03 E
Boxian	100	33.53 N	115.45 E
Boxing	98	37.08 N	118.07 E
Boxley	260	51.18 N	0.33 E
Boxmeer	52	51.39 N	5.57 E
Boxmoor	260	51.45 N	0.29 W
Boxodoi	98	42.34 N	115.18 E
Boxtel	52	51.35 N	5.20 E
Boyabat	130	41.28 N	34.47 E
Boyabo	152	3.43 N	18.46 E
Boyacá □ 5	246	5.30 N	73.30 W
Boyacıköy ◆ 8	267b	41.06 N	29.02 E
Boyadel → Bojadła	30	51.57 N	15.50 E
Boyalı	130	41.02 N	33.19 E
Boyalık	130	41.15 N	28.37 E
Boyang	100	28.59 N	116.40 E
Boyanup	168a	33.29 S	115.44 E
Boyasengese	152	3.29 N	20.33 E
Boyce	194	31.23 N	92.40 W
Boyceville	190	45.02 N	92.02 W
Boyd, Mn., U.S.	198	44.50 N	95.54 W
Boyd, Tx., U.S.	222	33.05 N	97.34 W
Boyd ≃	166	29.51 S	152.35 E
Boyd Glacier ⊓	9	77.14 S	145.25 W
Boyd's Cove	186	49.27 N	54.39 W
Boydton	192	36.40 N	78.23 W
Boyenge	152	0.25 N	18.51 E
Boyer ≃	198	41.28 N	95.55 W
Boyera	152	0.38 S	19.25 E
Boyer Aḥmadī va Kohkīlūyeh □ 4	128	30.40 N	50.40 E
Boyer Run ≃	279b	40.13 N	79.32 W
Boyers	214	41.06 N	79.54 W
Boyer's Creek ≃	284a	43.00 N	79.02 W
Boyertown	208	40.20 N	75.38 W
Boyes Hot Springs	226	38.19 N	122.29 W
Boykins	208	36.34 N	77.12 W
Boyle, Ab., Can.	182	54.35 N	112.49 W
Boyle, Ire.	48	53.58 N	8.18 W
Boyle, Ms., U.S.	194	33.42 N	90.50 W
Boyle Drain ≃	212	43.42 N	81.06 W
Boyle Heights ◆ 8	280	34.02 N	118.13 W
Boylston, Al., U.S.	194	32.26 N	86.17 W
Boylston, Ma., U.S.	207	42.23 N	71.42 W
Boyne	275b	43.29 N	79.50 W
Boyne ≃, Austl.	166	23.56 S	151.21 E
Boyne ≃, Mb., Can.	184	49.34 N	97.52 W
Boyne ≃, On., Can.	212	44.10 N	79.49 W
Boyne ≃, Ire.	48	53.43 N	6.15 W
Boyne Battlesite ⊥	48	53.42 N	6.23 W
Boyne City	190	45.12 N	85.00 W
Boynton	196	35.38 N	95.39 W
Boynton Beach	220	26.31 N	80.04 W
Boyo	152	5.43 N	21.33 E
Boyolali	115a	7.32 S	110.35 E
Boysen Reservoir ⊜ 1	202	43.19 N	108.11 W
Boysen State Park ♠	202	43.23 N	108.07 W
Boys Ranch	196	35.32 N	102.15 W
Boyuibe	248	20.25 S	63.17 W
Boyup Brook	162	33.50 S	116.24 E
Bozburun	130	36.41 N	28.04 E
Boz Burun ≻	130	40.32 N	28.46 E
Bozburun Yarımadası ≻ 1	130	36.40 N	28.10 E
Bozcaada	130	39.50 N	26.04 E
Boz Dağ ∧, Tür.	130	37.18 N	29.12 E
Bozdağ ∧, Tür.	130	36.50 N	36.22 E
Boz Dağ ∧, Tür.	130	38.19 N	28.08 E
Boz Dağlar ⋀	130	38.20 N	27.45 E
Bozdoğan	130	37.40 N	28.19 E
Bozel	62	45.27 N	6.39 E
Bozeman	202	45.40 N	111.02 W
Bozen → Bolzano	64	46.31 N	11.22 E
Bozene	152	2.56 N	19.12 E
Bozhen	98	38.07 N	116.32 E
Boží Dar	54	50.24 N	12.55 E
Bozkır	130	37.11 N	32.15 E
Bozkurt, Tür.	130	41.57 N	34.01 E
Bozkurt, Tür.	130	37.49 N	29.37 E
Bozman	208	38.46 N	76.16 W
Bozoğlak	130	39.38 N	38.49 E
Bozok	130	37.18 N	40.22 E
Bozoum	152	6.19 N	16.23 E
Bozova, Tür.	130	37.22 N	38.31 E
Bozova, Tür.	130	37.13 N	30.18 E
Bozovici	38	44.55 N	21.59 E
Bozšakol'	86	51.50 N	74.20 E
Bozum	52	53.05 N	5.42 E
Bozüyük	130	39.54 N	30.03 E
Bozzolo	64	45.06 N	10.29 E
Bra	62	44.42 N	7.51 E
Braan ≃	46	56.33 N	3.35 W
Braås	26	57.04 N	15.03 E
Brabant □ 4	56	50.45 N	4.30 E
Brabante, Isla de → Brabant Island I	9	64.15 S	62.20 W
Brabant Island I	9	64.15 S	62.20 W
Brabant Lake ⊜	184	56.00 N	103.43 W
Brabrand	41	56.09 N	10.07 E
Brač, Otok I	36	43.20 N	16.40 E
Bracadale, Loch ⊂	46	57.19 N	6.30 W
Bracciano	66	42.06 N	12.10 E
Bracciano, Lago di ⊜	66	42.07 N	12.14 E
Bracco, Passo del)(	62	44.15 N	9.34 E
Bracebridge	212	45.02 N	79.19 W
Bracebridge Heath	44	53.13 N	0.33 W
Braceville, Il., U.S.	216	41.14 N	88.16 W
Braceville, Oh., U.S.	214	41.14 N	80.58 W
Brachfield	222	32.03 N	94.39 W
Bracieux	50	47.33 N	1.33 E
Bracigliano	68	40.49 N	14.42 E
Bracigovo	38	42.01 N	24.22 E
Bräcke	26	62.43 N	15.27 E
Brackel ◆ 8	263	51.32 N	7.33 E
Bracken □ 6	218	38.40 N	84.06 W
Brackendale	182	49.46 N	123.09 W
Brackenheim	56	49.05 N	9.03 E
Brackenhurst	273d	26.19 S	28.06 E
Bracken Lake ⊜	184	53.37 N	99.50 W
Brackenridge	214	40.36 N	79.44 W
Brackett Field ⊠	280	34.05 N	117.47 W
Brackettville	196	29.18 N	100.25 W
Brački Kanal ⊍	36	43.24 N	16.40 E
Brackley	42	52.02 N	1.09 W
Bracknell	42	51.26 N	0.45 W
Bracktown	218	38.04 N	84.31 W
Brackwede	52	51.59 N	8.31 E
Braclav	78	48.50 N	28.55 E
Braco	46	56.15 N	3.53 W
Braço do Norte	252	28.17 S	49.11 W
Braço Grande, Igarapé ≃	250	3.43 S	48.49 W
Bracuí ≃	256	22.57 S	44.24 W
Brad	38	46.08 N	22.47 E
Bradano ≃	68	40.23 N	16.51 E
Bradbury	280	34.08 N	117.59 W
Bradbury Heights	284c	38.52 N	76.56 W
Braddock, N.J., U.S.	285	39.42 N	74.53 W
Braddock, Pa., U.S.	214	40.24 N	79.52 W
Braddock Acres	284c	38.49 N	77.10 W
Braddock Heights, Md., U.S.	208	39.25 N	77.30 W
Braddock Heights, N.Y., U.S.	210	43.19 N	77.42 W
Braddock Hills	279b	40.25 N	79.51 W
Braddock Point ≻	210	43.19 N	77.43 W
Braddocks Millpond ⊜	285	39.49 N	74.51 W
Braden ≃	220	27.30 N	82.32 W
Bradenton	220	27.29 N	82.34 W
Bradenton Beach	220	27.28 N	82.42 W
Bradenville	214	40.19 N	79.20 W
Braderup	41	54.50 N	8.53 E
Bradford, On., Can.	212	44.07 N	79.34 W
Bradford, Eng., U.K.	44	53.48 N	1.45 W
Bradford, Ar., U.S.	194	35.25 N	91.27 W
Bradford, Il., U.S.	190	41.10 N	89.39 W
Bradford, N.Y., U.S.	210	42.22 N	77.07 W
Bradford, Oh., U.S.	218	40.08 N	84.26 W
Bradford, Pa., U.S.	214	41.57 N	78.38 W
Bradford, R.I., U.S.	207	41.23 N	71.44 W
Bradford, Tn., U.S.	194	36.04 N	88.48 W
Bradford, Vt., U.S.	188	43.59 N	72.09 W
Bradford □ 6	210	41.56 N	78.40 W
Bradford □ 8	262	53.47 N	1.52 W
Bradford Hills	285	40.01 N	75.39 W
Bradford Mountain ∧	207	41.59 N	73.18 W
Bradford-on-Avon	42	51.20 N	2.15 W
Bradford Regional Airport ⊠	214	41.48 N	78.38 W
Bradfordwoods	214	40.38 N	80.05 W
Brading	42	50.41 N	1.09 W
Bradley, Ar., U.S.	194	33.05 N	93.39 W
Bradley, Ca., U.S.	226	35.51 N	120.47 W
Bradley, Fl., U.S.	220	27.48 N	81.59 W
Bradley, Il., U.S.	216	41.08 N	87.51 W
Bradley, Mi., U.S.	216	42.38 N	85.39 W
Bradley, S.D., U.S.	198	45.05 N	97.38 W
Bradley Beach	208	40.12 N	74.01 W
Bradley Farms	284c	39.00 N	77.11 W
Bradley Gardens	276	40.34 N	74.39 W
Bradley Institute	154	17.02 S	31.27 E
Bradley International Airport ⊠	207	41.55 N	72.40 W
Bradley Reefs ✣ 2	175e	6.52 S	160.48 E
Bradley Woods Reservation ♠	279a	41.25 N	81.58 W
Bradley W. Palmer State Park ♠	283	42.39 N	70.54 W
Bradner, B.C., Can.	224	49.06 N	122.25 W
Bradner, Oh., U.S.	214	41.19 N	83.26 W
Bradninch	42	50.50 N	3.25 W
Bradore-Bay	186	51.28 N	57.14 W
Bradshaw, Eng., U.K.	262	53.36 N	2.24 W
Bradshaw, Md., U.S.	208	39.25 N	76.22 W
Bradshaw, Ne., U.S.	198	40.53 N	97.44 W
Bradshaw, W.V., U.S.	192	37.21 N	81.47 W
Bradwell-on-Sea	42	51.44 N	0.54 E
Bradworthy	42	50.54 N	4.22 W
Brady, Mt., U.S.	202	48.02 N	111.50 W
Brady, Ne., U.S.	198	41.01 N	100.22 W
Brady, Tx., U.S.	196	31.08 N	99.20 W
Brady Creek ≃	196	31.07 N	98.59 W
Brady Lake	214	41.09 N	81.19 W
Brady Mountains ⋀ 2	196	31.20 N	99.40 W
Brae	46a	60.23 N	1.21 W
Brædstrup	41	55.58 N	9.37 E
Braemar	46	57.01 N	3.23 W
Braeside, Austl.	162	21.12 S	121.01 E
Braeside, Austl.	274b	37.59 S	145.07 E
Braeside, On., Can.	212	45.28 N	76.24 W
Braga	34	41.33 N	8.26 W
Bragado	252	35.08 S	60.30 W
Bragança, Bra.	250	1.03 S	46.46 W
Bragança, Port.	34	41.49 N	6.45 W
Bragança Paulista	256	22.57 S	46.34 W
Bragar	46	58.24 N	6.40 W
Bragin	78	51.47 N	30.14 E
Braginka ≃	78	51.22 N	30.24 E
Braginovka	78	48.29 N	36.21 E
Braham	190	45.43 N	93.10 W
Brahetrolleborg ⊥	41	55.09 N	10.22 E
Brahma Island I	220	27.52 N	81.15 W
Brāhmanbāria	120	23.59 N	91.07 E
Brāhmani ≃, India	120	20.39 N	86.46 E
Brāhmani ≃, India	126	24.09 N	88.01 E
Brahmapur, India	122	19.19 N	84.47 E
Brahmapur, India	272b	22.28 N	88.22 E
Brahmaputra (Yarlung) ≃	120	24.02 N	90.59 E
Brāhmaur	123	32.27 N	76.32 E
Braich y Pwll ≻	42	52.48 N	4.36 W
Braidwood, Austl.	166	35.27 S	149.48 E
Braidwood, Il., U.S.	216	41.15 N	88.12 W
Braies (Prags)	64	46.42 N	12.08 E
Brăila	38	45.16 N	27.58 E
Brăila □ 6	38	45.00 N	27.40 E
Brailov	78	49.06 N	28.09 E
Brain ≃	42	51.48 N	0.39 E
Brainard, Ne., U.S.	198	41.11 N	97.00 W
Brainard, N.Y., U.S.	210	42.30 N	73.31 W
Braine	50	49.20 N	3.32 E
Braine-l'Alleud	50	50.41 N	4.22 E
Braine-le-Château	50	50.41 N	4.16 E
Braine-le-Comte	50	50.36 N	4.08 E
Brainerd	190	46.21 N	94.12 W
Braint ≃	44	53.08 N	4.19 W
Braintree, Eng., U.K.	42	51.53 N	0.32 E
Braintree, Ma., U.S.	207	42.13 N	71.00 W
Braintree □ 8	260	51.47 N	0.36 E
Brak ≃, S. Afr.	158	31.32 S	21.33 E
Brak ≃, S. Afr.	158	29.35 S	22.55 E
Brake, B.R.D.	52	53.19 N	8.28 E
Brake, B.R.D.	52	52.04 N	8.35 E
Brake, B.R.D.	52	52.01 N	8.55 E
Brakel, Bel.	50	50.48 N	3.46 E
Brakel, B.R.D.	52	51.43 N	9.10 E
Brakna □ 4	150	17.30 N	13.30 W
Brakpan	158	26.14 S	28.22 E
Brakpan □ 5	273d	26.16 S	28.21 E
Brakpoort	158	31.20 S	23.22 E
Brakputs	158	29.29 S	18.24 E
Brakwater	156	22.24 S	17.06 E
Brålanda	26	58.34 N	12.22 E
Bralorne	182	50.47 N	122.49 W
Bramalea	212	43.44 N	79.43 W
Bramall Hall ⊥	262	53.23 N	2.09 W
Braman	196	36.55 N	97.20 W
Brambauer	263	51.35 N	7.27 E
Bramberg am Wildkogel	64	47.16 N	12.21 E
Bramble Bay ⊂	171a	27.17 S	153.05 E
Bramble Cay I	164	9.08 S	143.52 E
Bramdrupdam	41	55.31 N	9.28 E
Bramey-Lenningsen	263	51.34 N	7.46 E
Bramfeld ◆ 8	52	53.37 N	10.04 E
Bramford	42	52.04 N	1.06 E
Bramhall	262	53.22 N	2.10 W
Bramhope	44	53.53 N	1.37 W
Bramley	260	51.12 N	0.34 W
Bramley ◆ 8	273d	26.08 S	28.05 E
Bramley Mountain ∧	210	42.18 N	74.49 W
Bramming	41	55.28 N	8.42 E
Brampton, On., Can.	212	43.41 N	79.46 W
Brampton, Eng., U.K.	42	52.19 N	0.14 W
Brampton, Eng., U.K.	44	54.57 N	2.43 W
Brampton Airfield ⊠	275b	43.40 N	79.47 W
Bramsche	52	52.24 N	7.58 E
Bramsöfjärden ⊜	40	60.20 N	17.10 E
Bramstedt	52	53.22 N	8.41 E
Brancaleone Marina	68	37.58 N	16.06 E
Brancaster	42	52.58 N	0.39 E
Brancaster Roads ⚓ 3	42	53.00 N	0.41 E
Branch	186	46.53 N	53.57 W
Branch □ 6	216	41.55 N	85.03 W
Branch Brook Park ♠	276	40.46 N	74.10 W
Branch Dale	208	40.41 N	76.20 W
Branchport	210	42.36 N	77.09 W
Branchville, Ct., U.S.	207	41.16 N	73.26 W
Branchville, N.J., U.S.	210	41.08 N	74.45 W
Branchville, S.C., U.S.	192	33.15 N	80.48 W
Branchville, Va., U.S.	208	36.34 N	77.14 W
Branco	152	12.30 S	20.32 E
Branco ≃, Bra.	246	1.24 S	61.51 W
Branco ≃, Bra.	248	10.03 S	67.51 W
Branco ≃, Bra.	248	7.44 S	61.46 W
Branco ≃, Bra.	248	6.41 S	66.41 W
Branco ≃, Bra.	248	9.12 S	64.22 W
Branco ≃, Bra.	248	9.37 S	60.33 W
Branco ≃, Bra.	248	13.41 S	60.44 W
Branco ≃, Bra.	248	21.00 S	57.48 W
Branco ≃, Bra.	250	12.00 S	44.56 W
Branco ≃, Bra.	250	7.01 S	51.42 W
Branco ≃, Bra.	256	24.09 S	46.48 W
Branco, Ilhéu I	150a	16.39 N	24.41 W
Brand, B.R.D.	56	50.43 N	6.09 E
Brand, Öst.	58	47.06 N	9.44 E
Brandamore	208	40.03 N	75.50 W
Brandaris ∧ 2	241s	12.17 N	68.24 W
Brandberg ∧	156	21.10 S	14.33 E
Brandbu	26	60.28 N	10.30 E
Brande	41	55.57 N	9.07 E
Brandebourg → Brandenburg	54	52.24 N	12.32 E
Brandeis University ❦ 2	283	42.22 N	71.16 W
Brandenberg	64	47.29 N	11.53 E
Brandenberg ∧ 2	263	51.20 N	7.37 E
Brandenburg, D.D.R.	54	52.24 N	12.32 E
Brandenburg, Ky., U.S.	194	38.00 N	86.10 W
Brandenburg □ 9	54	52.00 N	13.30 E
Brandenburger Tor ⊥	264a	52.31 N	13.23 E
Brand-Erbisdorf	54	50.52 N	13.19 E
Brandfort	158	28.47 S	26.30 E
Br'andino	80	54.23 N	49.23 E
Brandis, D.D.R.	54	51.20 N	12.36 E
Brandis, D.D.R.	54	51.48 N	13.10 E
Brandizzo	62	45.11 N	7.51 E
Brandkop	158	31.13 S	19.13 E
Brandon, Mb., Can.	184	49.50 N	99.57 W
Brandon, Eng., U.K.	42	52.27 N	0.37 E
Brandon, Eng., U.K.	44	54.46 N	1.39 W
Brandon, Fl., U.S.	220	27.56 N	82.17 W
Brandon, Ms., U.S.	194	32.16 N	89.59 W
Brandon, S.D., U.S.	198	43.35 N	96.34 W
Brandon, Tx., U.S.	222	32.03 N	96.58 W
Brandon, Vt., U.S.	188	43.47 N	73.05 W
Brandon, Wi., U.S.	190	43.44 N	88.46 W
Brandon Bay ⊂	48	52.15 N	10.05 W
Brandon Head ≻	48	52.16 N	10.14 W
Brandon Mountain ∧	48	52.14 N	10.15 W
Brandon Road Lock and Dam ◆ 5	278	41.30 N	88.06 W
Brandonville	210	40.52 N	76.10 W
Brand Park ♠	280	34.11 N	118.16 W
Brands Hatch Motor Race Circuit ♠	260	51.22 N	0.16 E
Brandsø I	41	55.21 N	9.43 E
Brandt	218	39.54 N	84.05 W
Brandvlei	158	30.25 S	20.30 E
Brandy Camp	214	41.19 N	78.41 W
Brandy Peak ∧	202	42.36 N	123.53 W
Brandýsek	54	50.10 N	14.10 E
Brandýs nad Labem	54	50.10 N	14.41 E
Brandywine Battlefield ⊥	208	39.53 N	75.35 W
Brandywine Creek ≃, U.S.	285	39.44 N	75.32 W
Brandywine Creek ≃, In., U.S.	218	39.31 N	85.52 W
Brandywine Creek ≃, Oh., U.S.	279a	41.17 N	81.34 W
Brandywine Creek, East Branch ≃	208	39.55 N	75.39 W
Brandywine Creek, West Branch ≃	208	39.55 N	75.39 W
Brandywine Creek State Park ♠	285	39.48 N	75.35 W
Brandywine Park ♠	285	39.45 N	75.33 W
Brandywine Raceway ♠	285	39.50 N	75.32 W
Brandywine Springs Park ♠	285	39.45 N	75.38 W
Branford, Ct., U.S.	207	41.16 N	72.48 W
Branford, Fl., U.S.	192	29.57 N	82.55 W
Brani, Pulau I	271c	1.15 N	103.50 E
Braniewo	30	54.24 N	19.50 E
Branka, Česko.	60	49.50 N	12.33 E
Br'anka, S.S.S.R.	83	48.29 N	38.39 E
Br'anka, S.S.S.R.	86	59.08 N	93.27 E
Branlin ≃	50	47.51 N	3.06 E
Brannenburg	64	47.44 N	12.05 E
Branquinho ≃	248	5.45 S	71.27 W
Bransby	166	28.14 S	142.04 E
Bransfield Strait ⊍	9	63.00 S	59.00 W
Bransgore	42	50.47 N	1.44 W
Brańsk, Pol.	30	52.45 N	22.51 E
Br'ansk, S.S.S.R.	76	53.15 N	34.22 E
Br'ansk □ 4, S.S.S.R.	76	53.00 N	34.00 E
Br'ansk □ 4, S.S.S.R.	78	52.30 N	33.00 E
Br'anskaja Kosa, mys ≻	84	44.22 N	47.00 E
Branson	194	36.38 N	93.13 W
Brant	210	42.35 N	79.01 W
Brant □ 6	212	43.10 N	80.20 W
Brant ≃	44	53.09 N	0.35 W
Br'anta ≃	89	54.27 N	127.42 E
Brantas ≃	115a	7.28 S	112.25 E
Brantford	212	43.08 N	80.16 W
Brantingham Lake ⊜	212	43.42 N	75.17 W
Brant Lake	188	43.40 N	73.45 W
Brantley	194	31.34 N	86.15 W
Brantôme	32	45.22 N	0.39 E
Brant Rock	283	42.05 N	70.38 W
Brantville	186	47.22 N	64.58 W
Branxholme	166	37.51 S	141.47 E
Branxton	170	32.39 S	151.22 E
Branzi	64	46.00 N	9.46 E
Brás ◆ 8	287b	23.32 S	46.36 W
Brás Cubas	256	23.32 S	46.13 W
Bras d'Or Lake ⊜	186	45.52 N	60.50 W
Brashear	222	33.07 N	95.44 W
Brasil → Brazil □ 1	242	10.00 S	55.00 W
Brasilândia ◆ 8	287b	23.28 S	46.41 W
Brasiléia	248	11.00 S	68.44 W
Brasília	255	15.47 S	47.55 W
Brasília, Lago de ⊜	255	15.48 S	47.50 W
Brasília, Parque Nacional de ♠	255	15.36 S	48.08 W
Brasília de Minas	255	16.12 S	44.26 W
Brasília Legal	250	3.49 S	55.36 W
Brasilien → Brazil □ 1	242	10.00 S	55.00 W
Braslav	76	55.38 N	27.02 E
Brașov	38	45.39 N	25.37 E
Brașov □ 6	38	45.45 N	25.15 E
Brass	150	4.19 N	6.14 E
Brass Castle	210	40.47 N	74.58 W
Brasschaat	50	51.17 N	4.27 E
Brassert	263	51.40 N	7.05 E
Brassey, Banjaran ⋀	112	4.54 N	117.30 E
Brassey, Mount ∧	162	23.05 S	134.38 E
Brass Islands II	240m	18.24 N	64.58 W
Brassó → Brașov	38	45.39 N	25.37 E
Brasstown Bald ∧	192	34.52 N	83.48 W
Brastad	26	58.23 N	11.29 E
Brasted	260	51.16 N	0.17 E
Brasted Chart	260	51.16 N	0.06 E
Břasy	60	49.50 N	13.35 E
Bratca	38	46.56 N	22.37 E
Bratcevo ◆ 8	265b	55.51 N	37.24 E
Bratejevo ◆ 8	265b	55.38 N	37.45 E
Bratenahl	279a	41.32 N	81.37 W
Brateș, Lacul ⊜	38	45.30 N	28.05 E
Bratislava	30	48.09 N	17.07 E
Bratol'ubovka	86	51.13 N	66.46 E
Bratsk	88	56.05 N	101.48 E
Bratskaja Kada	88	55.02 N	102.06 E
Bratskoje	78	47.52 N	31.34 E
Bratskoje vodochranilišče ⊜ 1	88	56.10 N	102.10 E
Brattfors	40	59.40 N	14.01 E
Brattleboro	207	42.51 N	72.33 W
Bratto	64	45.55 N	10.04 E
Brattvåg	26	62.36 N	6.27 E
Braubach	56	50.16 N	7.40 E
Braúnas	255	19.04 S	42.43 W
Braunau am Inn	60	48.15 N	13.02 E
Braunfels	56	50.31 N	8.23 E
Braunlage	54	51.44 N	10.37 E
Bräunlingen	58	47.55 N	8.26 E
Braunsbedra	54	51.15 N	11.49 E
Braunsberg → Braniewo	30	54.24 N	19.50 E
Braunschweig, B.R.D.	52	52.16 N	10.31 E
Braunschweig, S. Afr.	158	32.48 S	27.22 E
Braunschweig □ 6	54	52.10 N	10.30 E
Braunston	42	52.17 N	1.12 W
Braunton	42	51.07 N	4.10 W
Braunwald	58	46.56 N	9.00 E
Brava I	150a	14.52 N	24.43 W
Brava, Costa ⊥ 2	34	41.45 N	3.04 E
Brava, Laguna ⊜	252	28.22 S	68.50 W
Brava, Punta ≻	258	34.56 S	56.10 W
Brave	188	39.44 N	80.16 W
Bravića	78	47.22 N	28.26 E
Bråviken ⊂	40	58.38 N	16.32 E
Bravo, Cerro ∧, Bol.	248	17.40 S	64.35 W
Bravo, Cerro ∧, Perú	248	5.32 S	79.15 W
Bravo del Norte (Rio Grande) ≃	178	25.55 N	97.09 W
Brawley	204	32.58 N	115.31 W
Brawley Peaks ⋀	204	38.15 N	118.55 W
Brawley Wash V	200	32.34 N	111.26 W
Bray, Bel.	50	50.26 N	4.06 E
Bray, Ire.	48	53.12 N	6.06 W
Bray ≃	42	50.59 N	3.53 W
Bray, Pays de ◆ 1	50	49.46 N	1.26 E
Braybrook	274b	37.47 S	144.51 E
Bray-Dunes	50	51.05 N	2.31 E
Braye ≃	50	47.45 N	0.42 E
Bray Head ≻	48	51.53 N	10.26 W
Bray Island I	176	69.20 N	76.45 W
Braymer	194	39.35 N	93.47 W
Braysur-Seine	50	48.25 N	3.14 E
Bray-sur-Somme	50	49.56 N	2.43 E
Brayton	44	53.46 N	1.05 W
Brazeau ≃	182	52.55 N	115.15 W
Brazeau, Mount ∧	182	52.33 N	117.21 W
Brazeau Dam ◆ 6	182	52.45 N	115.30 W
Brazen Head ≻	158	31.43 S	29.25 E
Brazey-en-Plaine	58	47.08 N	5.13 E
Brazil	194	39.31 N	87.07 W
Brazil (Brasil) □ 1	242	10.00 S	55.00 W
Brazil Basin ✣ 1	8	15.00 S	25.00 W
Brazo Chico, Arroyo ≃	258	33.45 S	58.32 W
Brazo Largo, Arroyo ≃	258	33.47 S	58.36 W
Brazópolis	256	22.28 S	45.37 W
Brazoria	222	29.02 N	95.34 W
Brazoria □ 6	222	29.12 N	95.25 W
Brazoria Reservoir ⊜ 1	222	29.05 N	95.01 W
Brazos □ 6	222	30.40 N	96.18 W
Brazos ≃	196	28.53 N	95.23 W
Brazos, Clear Fork ≃	196	33.01 N	98.40 W
Brazos, Double Mountain Fork ≃	196	33.15 N	100.00 W
Brazos, Salt Fork ≃	196	33.15 N	100.00 W
Brazo Sur [del Rio Coig] ≃	254	51.32 S	70.04 W
Brazzaville, Congo	152	4.16 S	15.17 E
Brazzaville, Congo	273b	4.16 S	15.17 E
Brazzaville (Maya Maya) Airport ⊠	273b	4.15 S	15.15 E
Brčko	38	44.53 N	18.48 E
Brda ≃	30	53.07 N	18.08 E
Brdy ⋀	60	49.40 N	13.50 E
Bré → Bray	48	53.12 N	6.06 W
Brea	228	33.55 N	117.53 W
Brea, Punta ≻	240m	17.56 N	66.55 W
Brea Canyon V	280	33.55 N	117.55 W
Brea Creek ≃	280	33.53 N	117.59 W
Breadalbane	166	23.49 S	139.35 E
Brea Dam ◆ 6	280	33.54 N	117.56 W
Breaden Bluff ∧ 2	162	26.56 S	124.32 E
Breadysville	285	40.13 N	75.04 W
Breakenridge, Mount ∧	182	49.43 N	121.56 W
Breakheart Reservation ♠	283	42.29 N	71.02 W
Breaksea Sound ⊍	172	45.35 S	166.40 E
Breaks Interstate Park ♠	192	37.17 N	82.18 W
Bream	42	51.45 N	2.34 W
Bream Bay ⊂	172	35.55 S	174.30 E
Bream Head ≻	172	35.51 S	174.35 E
Breamish ≃	44	55.31 N	1.56 W
Bream Tail ≻	172	36.03 S	174.35 E
Brea Pozo	252	28.15 S	63.57 W
Breaston	44	52.54 N	1.19 W
Bréau	261	48.34 N	2.53 E
Breaux Bridge	194	30.16 N	91.53 W
Breaza	38	45.11 N	25.40 E
Brebes	115a	6.53 S	109.03 E
Brécey	32	48.44 N	1.10 W
Brechen	56	50.20 N	8.14 E
Brechfa	42	51.54 N	4.36 W
Brechin	46	56.44 N	2.40 W
Brecht	56	51.21 N	4.38 E
Brechten ◆ 8	263	51.35 N	7.28 E
Breckenridge, Co., U.S.	200	39.28 N	106.02 W
Breckenridge, Mi., U.S.	190	43.24 N	84.28 W
Breckenridge, Mn., U.S.	198	46.15 N	96.35 W
Breckenridge, Mo., U.S.	194	39.45 N	93.48 W
Breckenridge, Tx., U.S.	196	32.45 N	98.54 W
Breckerfeld	56	51.16 N	7.28 E
Breckland ◆ 1	42	52.28 N	0.37 E
Brecknock → Brecon	42	51.57 N	3.24 W
Brecknock, Península ≻ 1	254	54.35 S	71.50 W
Brecksville	214	41.19 N	81.37 W
Břeclav	30	48.46 N	16.53 E
Brecon	42	51.57 N	3.24 W
Brecon Beacons ∧	42	51.53 N	3.31 W
Brecon Beacons National Park ♠	42	51.52 N	3.25 W
Bred	41	55.22 N	10.07 E
Breda, Ned.	52	51.35 N	4.46 E
Breda, Ia., U.S.	198	42.10 N	94.58 W
Bredaryd	26	57.10 N	13.44 E
Bredasdorp	158	34.32 S	20.02 E
Bredbo	171b	35.57 S	149.10 E
Bredbo ≃	171b	35.58 S	149.08 E
Bredbury	262	53.25 N	2.06 W
Bredbyn	26	63.27 N	18.06 E
Breddin	54	52.52 N	12.13 E
Brede Å ≃	41	55.09 N	8.42 E
Bredebro	41	55.03 N	8.49 E
Bredell	273d	26.05 S	28.17 E
Bredenbeck	52	52.15 N	9.37 E
Bredenbruch	263	51.21 N	7.45 E
Bredenbury	184	50.57 N	102.03 W
Bredene	50	51.14 N	2.58 E
Bredeney ◆ 8	263	51.24 N	6.59 E
Bredenscheid-Stüter	263	51.22 N	7.11 E
Bredereiche	54	53.08 N	13.14 E
Bredgar	260	51.18 N	0.42 E
Bredhurst	260	51.20 N	0.35 E
Bredon Hill ∧ 2	42	52.06 N	2.03 W
Bredsjö	40	59.50 N	14.44 E
Bredsjön ⊜	40	60.13 N	13.55 E
Bredstedt	41	54.37 N	8.59 E
Bredsten	41	55.42 N	9.24 E
Bredy	86	52.26 N	60.21 E
Bree	56	51.08 N	5.36 E
Breë ≃	158	34.24 S	20.50 E
Breeches, Lac ⊜	206	45.54 N	71.28 W
Breedoge ≃	48	53.55 N	8.27 W
Breeds Pond ⊜	283	42.28 N	70.59 W
Breedsville	216	42.21 N	86.08 W
Breese	219	38.36 N	89.31 W
Breesport	210	42.10 N	76.44 W
Breeza Plains	164	14.50 S	144.07 E
Breezewood	279b	40.34 N	80.03 W
Breg ≃	58	47.57 N	8.31 E
Bregalnica ≃	38	41.43 N	22.09 E
Breganze	64	45.42 N	11.34 E
Bregenz	58	47.30 N	9.46 E
Bregenzer Wald ⋀	58	47.20 N	10.00 E
Bregninge, Dan.	41	55.41 N	11.19 E
Bregninge, Dan.	41	55.01 N	10.37 E
Bregovo	38	44.09 N	22.39 E
Breguzzo	64	46.00 N	10.42 E
Brégy	261	49.05 N	2.52 E
Bréhal	32	48.54 N	1.31 W
Brehna	54	51.33 N	12.12 E
Breiðafjörður ⊂	24a	65.15 N	23.15 W
Breidbach	158	32.54 S	27.27 E
Breid Bay ⊂	9	70.15 S	24.15 E
Breidenbach	56	49.08 N	7.25 E
Breidenstein	56	50.55 N	8.28 E
Breil-sur-Roya	62	43.56 N	7.30 E
Breinizer	214	40.24 N	79.16 W
Breisach	58	48.01 N	7.40 E
Breisgau □ 9	58	47.45 N	7.45 E
Breitenbrunn	54	50.29 N	12.46 E
Breitenfelde	52	53.36 N	10.38 E
Breitenfurt bei Wien	61	48.08 N	16.08 E
Breitengüssbach	56	49.58 N	10.53 E
Breitenlee ◆ 8	264b	48.15 N	16.30 E
Breitenstein	54	51.37 N	10.56 E
Breitenworbis	54	51.24 N	10.25 E
Breithorn ∧	58	45.56 N	7.45 E
Breitlingsee ⊜	54	52.23 N	12.28 E
Breitscheid, B.R.D.	56	50.41 N	8.11 E
Breitscheid, B.R.D.	56	51.22 N	6.52 E
Breitsetten	61	48.12 N	16.42 E
Breitungen	54	50.45 N	10.20 E
Brejinho de Nazaré	250	11.01 S	48.34 W
Brejo	250	3.41 S	42.47 W
Brejo, Riacho do ≃	250	8.08 S	42.49 W
Brejo de São Felix	250	5.24 S	43.24 W
Brejões	255	13.06 S	39.48 W
Brejo Grande	250	10.26 S	36.28 W
Brejo Santo	250	7.29 S	39.00 W
Brejtovo	76	58.18 N	37.52 E
Brekken	26	62.39 N	11.53 E
Brekstad	26	63.41 N	9.41 E
Breloh	52	53.01 N	10.04 E
Bremangerlandet I	26	61.51 N	5.02 E
Brembio	62	45.13 N	9.34 E
Brembo ≃	62	45.35 N	9.32 E
Brême → Bremen	52	53.04 N	8.49 E
Bremelau	58	48.20 N	9.32 E
Bremen, B.R.D.	52	53.04 N	8.49 E
Bremen, Ga., U.S.	192	33.43 N	85.08 W
Bremen, In., U.S.	216	41.26 N	86.08 W
Bremen, Oh., U.S.	188	39.42 N	82.25 W
Bremen □ 3	52	53.05 N	8.50 E
Bremen, Flughafen ⊠	52	53.03 N	8.46 E
Bremer ≃, Austl.	168b	35.23 S	139.02 E
Bremer ≃, Austl.	171a	27.39 S	152.45 E
Bremer Bay	162	34.24 S	119.22 E
Bremer Bay ⊂	162	34.23 S	119.25 E
Bremerhaven	52	53.33 N	8.34 E
Bremerton	224	47.34 N	122.37 W
Bremerton East	224	47.35 N	122.38 W
Bremervörde	52	53.29 N	9.08 E
Bremgarten	58	47.21 N	8.21 E
Bremke, B.R.D.	52	52.07 N	9.06 E
Bremke, B.R.D.	56	51.15 N	8.12 E
Bremke, B.R.D.	263	51.23 N	7.41 E
Bremner ≃	190	48.41 N	85.31 W
Bremond	222	31.09 N	96.40 W
Brem River	182	50.26 N	124.39 W
Breña	286d	12.04 S	77.04 W
Brendel Lake ⊜	281	42.38 N	83.30 W
Brenderup	41	55.29 N	9.59 E
Brendlorenzen	56	50.20 N	10.13 E
Brendon Hills ⋀ 2	42	51.07 N	3.25 W
Brenham	222	30.10 N	96.23 W
Brenig, Llyn ⊜ 1	44	53.05 N	3.32 W
Brenish	46	58.08 N	7.08 W
Brenish, Aird ≻	46	58.08 N	7.08 W
Bren Mar Park	284c	38.48 N	77.09 W
Brenne ≃	50	47.38 N	4.16 E
Brennero (Brenner)	64	47.00 N	11.30 E
Brennero, Passo del → Brenner Pass)(	64	47.00 N	11.30 E
Brenner Pass)(	64	47.00 N	11.30 E
Breno, It.	64	45.57 N	10.18 E
Breno, Schw.	58	46.02 N	8.53 E
Brénod	58	46.04 N	5.36 E
Brent, Al., U.S.	194	32.56 N	87.09 W
Brent, Fl., U.S.	194	30.28 N	87.14 W
Brent ◆ 8	260	51.34 N	0.17 W
Brent ≃	260	51.28 N	0.18 W
Brenta ≃	64	45.11 N	12.18 E
Brenta, Gruppo di ⋀	64	46.11 N	10.54 E
Brentford ◆ 8	260	51.29 N	0.18 W
Brenthurst	273d	26.16 S	28.23 E
Brentino	64	45.40 N	10.55 E
Brentonico	64	45.49 N	10.57 E
Brent Reservoir ⊜ 1	260	51.35 N	0.15 W
Brentwood, Eng., U.K.	260	51.38 N	0.18 E
Brentwood, Ca., U.S.	226	37.55 N	121.41 W
Brentwood, Md., U.S.	208	38.56 N	76.57 W
Brentwood, N.Y., U.S.	210	40.46 N	73.14 W
Brentwood, Oh., U.S.	218	39.13 N	84.31 W
Brentwood, Pa., U.S.	214	40.22 N	79.58 W
Brentwood, Tn., U.S.	194	36.01 N	86.46 W
Brentwood □ 8	260	51.37 N	0.20 E
Brentwood Bay	224	48.35 N	123.28 W
Brentwood Estates	214	40.25 N	80.45 W
Brentwood Heights ◆ 8	280	34.04 N	118.30 W
Brentwood Lake	214	41.19 N	82.05 W
Brentwood Park	273d	26.08 S	28.18 E
Brenz ≃	56	48.34 N	10.24 E
Breo	62	44.23 N	7.49 E
Bréon, Ruisseu du ≃	261	48.40 N	2.49 E
Brera, Palazzo di ❦	266b	45.28 N	9.11 E
Brereton Park	158	26.55 S	30.30 E
Brescello	64	44.54 N	10.31 E
Brescia	64	45.33 N	13.15 E
Brescia □ 4	64	45.38 N	10.18 E
Bresewitz	54	54.24 N	12.40 E
Brésil → Brazil □ 1	242	10.00 S	55.00 W
Breskens	52	51.24 N	3.34 E
Breslau, On., Can.	212	43.28 N	80.25 W
Breslau → Wrocław, Pol.	30	51.06 N	17.00 E
Breslau, Tx., U.S.	222	29.31 N	97.00 W
Bresle ≃	50	50.04 N	1.22 E
Bresles	50	49.25 N	2.15 E
Bresnahan, Mount ∧	162	23.50 S	117.55 E
Bressanone (Brixen)	64	46.43 N	11.39 E
Bressay I	46a	60.08 N	1.05 W
Bressay Sound ⊍	46a	60.07 N	1.09 W
Bresse ◆ 1	58	46.30 N	5.15 E
Bresso	266b	45.32 N	9.11 E
Bressuire	32	46.51 N	0.30 W
Brest, Blg.	38	43.38 N	24.35 E
Brest, Fr.	32	48.24 N	4.29 W
Brest, S.S.S.R.	76	52.06 N	23.42 E
Brestanica	36	45.59 N	15.29 E
Bretagne (Brittany) □ 9	32	48.00 N	3.00 W
Bretenoux	32	44.55 N	1.50 E
Breteuil	50	49.38 N	2.18 E
Breteuil-sur-Iton	50	48.50 N	0.55 E
Bréthencourt	261	48.30 N	1.55 E
Bretherton	262	53.41 N	2.48 W
Brétigny ■	261	48.35 N	2.20 E
Brétigny-sur-Orge	50	48.37 N	2.19 E
Bretnig	54	51.08 N	14.04 E
Breton	182	53.07 N	114.28 W
Bretón, Canal de ⊍	240p	21.10 N	79.30 W
Breton, Pertuis ⊍	32	46.25 N	1.20 W
Breton Bay ⊂	208	38.16 N	76.39 W
Breton Islands II	194	29.28 N	89.11 W
Breton Sound ⊍	194	29.30 N	89.30 W
Breton Woods	208	40.02 N	74.06 W
Brett ≃	42	51.58 N	0.58 E
Brett, Cape ≻	172	35.10 S	174.20 E
Bretten	56	49.02 N	8.42 E
Breu, Rio do ≃	246	3.29 S	66.20 W
Breueh, Pulau I	110	5.41 N	95.05 E
Breuil-Bois-Robert	261	48.57 N	1.43 E
Breuil-Cervinia	58	45.56 N	7.38 E
Breuillet	261	48.34 N	2.10 E
Breuilpont	50	48.58 N	1.26 E
Breukelen	52	52.10 N	5.00 E
Breux	261	48.34 N	2.11 E
Brevard	192	35.14 N	82.44 W
Brevard □ 6	220	28.18 N	80.42 W
Brévenne ≃	62	45.51 N	4.40 E
Brevens bruk	40	59.01 N	15.35 E
Breves	250	1.40 S	50.29 W
Brevig Mission	180	65.20 N	166.29 W
Brevik, Nor.	26	59.04 N	9.42 E
Brevik, Sve.	40	59.21 N	18.12 E
Brevoort Island I	176	63.30 N	64.20 W
Brewarrina	166	29.57 S	146.52 E
Brewer	188	44.47 N	68.45 W
Brewer Island I	282	37.33 N	122.16 W
Brewersville	218	39.05 N	85.37 W
Brewerton	210	43.14 N	76.08 W
Brewerville	150	6.26 N	10.47 W
Brewongle	170	33.29 S	149.43 E
Brewood	42	52.41 N	2.10 W
Brewster, Ks., U.S.	198	39.22 N	101.22 W
Brewster, Ma., U.S.	207	41.45 N	70.05 W
Brewster, Mn., U.S.	198	43.41 N	95.28 W
Brewster, Ne., U.S.	198	41.56 N	99.51 W
Brewster, N.Y., U.S.	210	41.23 N	73.37 W
Brewster, Oh., U.S.	214	40.42 N	81.35 W
Brewster, Wa., U.S.	202	48.05 N	119.46 W
Brewster, Kap ≻	16	70.19 N	22.05 W
Brewster, Lake ⊜	166	33.28 S	146.00 E
Brewster, Mount ∧	172	44.04 S	169.27 E
Brewton	194	31.06 N	87.04 W
Breyten	158	26.16 S	30.00 E
Břežany	61	48.52 N	16.20 E
Brežice	36	45.54 N	15.36 E
Brézina	148	33.04 N	1.14 E
Brézins	62	45.21 N	5.19 E
Březnice	60	49.33 N	13.57 E
Breznik	38	42.44 N	22.54 E
Brezno, Česko.	30	48.50 N	19.39 E
Březno, Česko.	54	50.24 N	13.26 E
Brézolles	50	48.41 N	1.04 E
Březová	54	50.06 N	12.39 E
Březové Hory	60	49.41 N	13.58 E
Bria	152	6.32 N	21.59 E
Brian Boru Peak ∧	182	55.05 N	127.35 W
Briançon	62	44.54 N	6.39 E
Brian Head ∧	200	37.41 N	112.50 W

Symbols in the index entries represent the broad categories identified in the key at the right. Symbols with superior numbers (⋀ 1) identify subcategories (see complete key on page *I* · *1*).

Symbole im Register stellen die rechts im Schlüssel erklärten Kategorien dar. Symbole mit hochgestellten Ziffern (⋀ 1) bezeichnen Unterabteilungen einer Kategorie (vgl. vollständiger Schlüssel auf Seite *I* · *1*).

Los símbolos incluídos en el texto del índice representan las grandes categorias identificadas con la clave a la derecha. Los símbolos con numeros en su parte superior (⋀ 1) identifican las subcategorías (véase la clave completa en la página *I* · *1*).

Les symboles de l'index représentent les catégories indiquées dans la légende à droite. Les symboles suivis d'un indice (⋀ 1) représentent des sous-catégories (voir légende complète à la page *I* · *1*).

Os símbolos incluídos no texto do índice representam as grandes categorias identificadas com a chave à direita. Os símbolos com números em sua parte superior (⋀ 1) identificam as subcategorias (veja-se a chave completa à página *I* · *1*).

	English	Deutsch	Español	Français	Português
∧	Mountain	Berg	Montaña	Montagne	Montanha
⋀	Mountains	Gebirge	Montañas	Montagnes	Montanhas
)(	Pass	Paß	Paso	Col	Passo
V	Valley, Canyon	Tal, Cañon	Valle, Cañón	Vallée, Canyon	Vale, Canhão
≃	Plain	Ebene	Llano	Plaine	Planície
≻	Cape	Kap	Cabo	Cap	Cabo
I	Island	Insel	Isla	Île	Ilha
II	Islands	Inseln	Islas	Îles	Ilhas
⊥	Other Topographic Features	Andere Topographische Objekte	Otros Elementos Topográficos	Autres données topographiques	Outros acidentes topográficos

ESPAÑOL — FRANÇAIS — PORTUGUÊS

Nombre / Nom / Nome	Página / Page / Página	Lat.°′	Long.°′ W = Oeste / W = Ouest / W = Oeste
Brianza □[9]	62	45.40 N	9.10 E
Briar	222	33.00 N	97.34 W
Briarcliff Manor	210	41.08 N	73.49 W
Briar Creek	210	40.10 N	76.46 W
Briar Creek ≃	222	32.06 N	96.22 W
Briare	50	47.38 N	2.44 E
Briare, Canal de ≋	50	48.02 N	2.43 E
Briarres-sur-Essonne	50	48.14 N	2.25 E
Briarwood Beach	214	41.06 N	81.54 W
Briarwood Center ⬥[9]	281	42.14 N	83.45 W
Briatico	68	38.43 N	16.02 E
Bribano	64	46.06 N	12.05 E
Bribie Island I	171a	27.00 S	153.07 E
Bričany	78	48.22 N	27.04 E
Bricelyn	190	43.33 N	93.48 W
Brice Run ≃	284b	39.19 N	76.50 W
Brices Cross Roads National Battlefield Site ⊥	194	34.31 N	88.41 W
Briceville	192	36.10 N	84.11 W
Bricherasio	62	44.49 N	7.18 E
Bricht	263	51.41 N	6.51 E
Brickebacken	40	59.15 N	15.15 E
Brick Lake ⊜	220	28.10 N	81.12 W
Brick Township	208	40.04 N	74.08 W
Briçonnet, Lac ⊜	186	51.27 N	60.11 W
Bricquebec	32	49.28 N	1.38 W
Bridal Veil	224	45.33 N	122.10 W
Bridalveil Fall ⌊	226	37.43 N	119.39 W
Bride	44	54.22 N	4.22 W
Bride ≃	48	52.04 N	7.52 W
Bridesburg ⬥[8]	285	40.00 N	75.04 W
Bridge	42	51.14 N	1.07 E
Bridge ≃	182	50.45 N	121.55 W
Bridge City	194	30.01 N	93.50 W
Bridge Creek ≃	224	48.26 N	120.52 W
Bridgehampton	207	40.56 N	72.18 W
Bridge Lake	182	51.29 N	120.43 W
Bridgend, Scot., U.K.	46	55.48 N	6.16 W
Bridgend, Scot., U.K.	46	56.48 N	2.45 W
Bridgend, Wales, U.K.	42	51.31 N	3.35 W
Bridgenorth	212	44.23 N	78.23 W
Bridge of Allan	46	56.09 N	3.57 W
Bridge of Gaur	46	56.41 N	4.27 W
Bridge of Orchy	46	56.30 N	4.46 W
Bridge of Weir	46	55.52 N	4.35 W
Bridgeport, On., Can.	212	43.29 N	80.29 W
Bridgeport, Al., U.S.	194	34.56 N	85.42 W
Bridgeport, Ca., U.S.	226	38.10 N	119.13 W
Bridgeport, Ct., U.S.	207	41.10 N	73.12 W
Bridgeport, Il., U.S.	194	38.42 N	87.45 W
Bridgeport, Mi., U.S.	190	43.21 N	83.52 W
Bridgeport, Ne., U.S.	198	41.39 N	103.05 W
Bridgeport, N.J., U.S.	285	39.48 N	75.20 W
Bridgeport, N.Y., U.S.	210	43.09 N	75.58 W
Bridgeport, Oh., U.S.	214	40.04 N	80.44 W
Bridgeport, Pa., U.S.	285	40.06 N	75.21 W
Bridgeport, Tx., U.S.	222	33.12 N	97.45 W
Bridgeport, Wa., U.S.	202	48.00 N	119.40 W
Bridgeport, W.V., U.S.	188	39.17 N	80.15 W
Bridgeport ⬥[8]	278	41.51 N	87.39 W
Bridgeport, Lake ⊜[1]	222	33.13 N	97.48 W
Bridgeport, University of ʊ[2]	276	41.10 N	73.12 W
Bridgeport Airport ⊠	285	39.47 N	75.20 W
Bridgeport Harbor c	276	41.10 N	73.11 W
Bridgeport Municipal Airport ⊠	276	41.10 N	73.08 W
Bridgeport Reservoir ⊜[1]	226	38.22 N	119.14 W
Bridger	202	45.17 N	108.54 W
Bridge River Indian Reserve ⬥[4]	182	50.45 N	122.00 W
Bridger Peak ∧	200	41.12 N	107.02 W
Bridges Point ›	174o	1.58 N	157.28 W
Bridgeton, Mo., U.S.	219	38.44 N	90.24 W
Bridgeton, N.J., U.S.	208	39.25 N	75.14 W
Bridgetown, Austl.	162	33.57 S	116.08 E
Bridgetown, Barb.	241g	13.06 N	59.37 W
Bridgetown, N.S., Can.	186	44.51 N	65.18 W
Bridgetown, Oh., U.S.	218	39.09 N	84.38 W
Bridge Trafford	262	53.14 N	2.49 W
Bridgeview	278	41.45 N	87.48 W
Bridgeville, De., U.S.	208	38.44 N	75.36 W
Bridgeville, Pa., U.S.	214	40.21 N	80.06 W
Bridgewater, Austl.	166	42.44 S	147.14 E
Bridgewater, Austl.	168b	35.02 S	138.47 E
Bridgewater, N.S., Can.	186	44.23 N	64.31 W
Bridgewater, Ct., U.S.	210	41.32 N	73.22 W
Bridgewater, Me., U.S.	186	46.25 N	67.50 W
Bridgewater, Ma., U.S.	207	41.59 N	70.58 W
Bridgewater, N.Y., U.S.	210	42.58 N	75.15 W
Bridgewater, Pa., U.S.	285	40.05 N	74.55 W
Bridgewater, S.D., U.S.	198	43.33 N	97.30 W
Bridgewater, Va., U.S.	188	38.22 N	78.58 W
Bridgewater Canal ≋	262	53.20 N	2.45 W
Bridgewater State College ʊ[2]	283	41.59 N	70.58 W
Bridgman	216	41.57 N	86.33 W
Bridgnorth	42	52.33 N	2.25 W
Bridgton	188	44.03 N	70.42 W
Bridgwater	42	51.08 N	3.00 W
Bridgwater Bay c	42	51.16 N	3.12 W
Bridlington	44	54.05 N	0.12 W
Bridlington Bay c	44	54.04 N	0.08 W
Bridport	42	50.44 N	2.46 W
Brie ⬥[1]	50	48.40 N	3.20 E
Briec	32	48.06 N	4.00 W
Brie-Comte-Robert	50	48.41 N	2.37 E
Brie Française ⬥[1]	261	48.40 N	2.50 E
Brieg → Brzeg	30	50.52 N	17.27 E
Brielle, Ned.	52	51.54 N	4.10 E
Brielle, N.J., U.S.	208	40.06 N	74.03 W
Brienne-le-Château	58	48.24 N	4.32 E
Brienne-sur-Aisne	50	49.26 N	4.03 E
Brienno	58	45.55 N	9.07 E
Brienon-sur-Armançon	50	48.00 N	3.37 E
Brien Run ≃	284b	39.20 N	76.28 W
Brienz	58	46.46 N	8.03 E
Brienza	68	40.29 N	15.37 E
Brienzer Rothorn ∧	58	46.48 N	8.04 E
Brienzersee ⊜	58	46.43 N	7.57 E
Brier Creek ≃	192	32.47 N	81.26 W
Brierfield	44	53.50 N	2.14 W
Brier Hill	212	44.32 N	75.40 W
Brier Island I	186	44.16 N	66.22 W
Brierley Hill	42	52.29 N	2.07 W
Brier Mountain ∧	210	41.37 N	77.02 W
Briese	264a	52.42 N	13.18 E
Briese ≃	264a	52.41 N	13.15 E
Brieselang	54	52.35 N	13.00 E
Briesen	54	52.20 N	14.16 E
Brieske	54	51.29 N	13.57 E
Brieskow-Finkenheerd	54	52.16 N	14.35 E
Briest	54	52.31 N	12.08 E
Briey	56	49.15 N	5.56 E
Brig	58	46.19 N	8.00 E
Brigach ≃	58	47.58 N	8.30 E
Brigantine	208	39.24 N	74.21 W
Brig Bay	186	51.04 N	56.55 W
Brigden	214	42.49 N	82.17 W
Brigg	44	53.34 N	0.30 W
Briggs	196	30.53 N	97.56 W
Brigham City	200	41.30 N	112.00 W
Brighouse	44	53.42 N	1.47 W
Brighstone	42	50.38 N	1.24 W
Bright	166	36.44 S	146.58 E
Brightlingsea	42	51.49 N	1.02 E
Brightmoor ⬥[8]	281	42.24 N	83.14 W
Brighton, Austl.	168b	35.01 S	138.31 E
Brighton, Austl.	169	37.55 S	145.00 E
Brighton, On., Can.	212	44.02 N	77.44 W
Brighton, N.Z.	172	45.57 S	170.20 E
Brighton, Eng., U.K.	42	50.50 N	0.08 W
Brighton, Co., U.S.	200	39.59 N	104.49 W
Brighton, Fl., U.S.	220	27.14 N	81.06 W
Brighton, Il., U.S.	219	39.02 N	90.08 W
Brighton, Ia., U.S.	190	41.10 N	91.49 W
Brighton, Md., U.S.	284b	39.21 N	76.43 W
Brighton, Mi., U.S.	216	42.31 N	83.46 W
Brighton, N.Y., U.S.	210	43.08 N	77.33 W
Brighton ⬥[8]	283	42.21 N	71.08 W
Brighton Downs	166	23.22 S	141.34 E
Brighton Indian Reservation ⬥[4]	220	27.04 N	81.05 W
Brighton-Le-Sands	274a	33.58 S	151.09 E
Brighton Park ⬥[8]	278	41.49 N	87.42 W
Brighton State Recreation Area ♦	216	42.30 N	83.48 W
Brightsand Lake ⊜	184	53.36 N	108.52 W
Brightwater	172	41.23 S	173.07 E
Brightwaters	276	40.43 N	73.16 W
Brightwood	224	45.23 N	122.01 W
Brightwood ⬥[8]	284c	38.58 N	77.02 W
Brigittenau ⬥[8]	264b	48.14 N	16.22 E
Brignoles	62	43.24 N	6.04 E
Brignoud	62	45.15 N	5.54 E
Brig o' Turk	46	56.13 N	4.22 W
Brigstock	42	52.27 N	0.36 W
Brigus	186	47.32 N	53.13 W
Brihuega	34	40.45 N	2.52 W
Briis-sous-Forges	261	48.38 N	2.07 E
Brijuni I	64	44.55 N	13.46 E
Brikama	150	13.15 N	16.39 W
Brilhante ≃	255	21.58 S	54.18 W
Brill	42	51.49 N	1.03 W
Brilliant, B.C., Can.	182	49.19 N	117.38 W
Brilliant, Al., U.S.	194	34.01 N	87.45 W
Brilliant, Oh., U.S.	214	40.15 N	80.37 W
Brillion	190	44.10 N	88.03 W
Brilon	56	51.24 N	8.34 E
Brilyn Park	284c	38.54 N	77.10 W
Brimfield, Eng., U.K.	42	52.18 N	2.42 W
Brimfield, In., U.S.	216	41.27 N	85.24 W
Brimfield, Ma., U.S.	207	42.07 N	72.12 W
Brimfield, Oh., U.S.	214	41.06 N	81.21 W
Brimington	44	53.16 N	1.23 W
Brindabella	171b	35.23 S	148.45 E
Brindisi	68	40.38 N	17.56 E
Brindisi □[4]	68	40.35 N	17.40 E
Brindisi Montagna	68	40.37 N	15.57 E
Brindle	262	53.43 N	2.36 W
Brindley Heath	260	51.12 N	0.03 W
Bringelly	170	33.56 S	150.44 E
Bringelly Creek ≃	274a	33.58 S	150.38 E
Brinje	36	45.00 N	15.08 E
Brinkerton	279b	40.13 N	79.32 W
Brinkhaven	214	40.28 N	82.12 W
Brinkleigh	284b	39.18 N	76.50 W
Brinkley, Austl.	168b	35.14 S	139.13 E
Brinkley, Ar., U.S.	194	34.53 N	91.11 W
Brinkum	52	53.00 N	8.47 E
Brinkworth	166	33.42 S	138.24 E
Brinnon	224	47.40 N	122.53 W
Brinon-sur-Beuvron	50	47.17 N	3.30 E
Brins, Ābār al- ⊤[4]	142	30.29 N	30.05 E
Brinscall	262	53.41 N	2.34 W
Brinyan	46	59.07 N	2.59 W
Brion, Île I	186	47.48 N	61.28 W
Brione	58	46.18 N	8.47 E
Briones Hills ⋏[2]	282	37.56 N	122.08 W
Briones Regional Park ♦	282	37.56 N	122.08 W
Briones Reservoir ⊜[1]	282	37.55 N	122.12 W
Brioni	64	44.55 N	13.46 E
Brionne	50	49.12 N	0.43 E
Brion-sur-Ource	58	47.55 N	4.39 E
Brioso ≃	255	20.21 S	52.05 W
Brioude	32	45.18 N	3.23 E
Briouze	32	48.42 N	0.22 W
Brisbane, Austl.	171a	27.28 S	153.02 E
Brisbane, Ca., U.S.	226	37.41 N	122.24 W
Brisbane ≃	171a	27.24 S	153.09 E
Brisbane, Mount ∧	171a	27.05 S	152.32 E
Brisbane International Airport ⊠	171a	27.27 S	153.11 E
Brisbane Ranges National Park ♦	169	37.52 S	144.14 E
Brisbane Water c	170	33.28 S	151.20 E
Brisbane Water National Park ♦	170	33.30 S	151.15 E
Brisben	210	42.22 N	75.41 W
Brisbin	214	40.50 N	78.21 W
Briseñas de Matamoros	234	20.16 N	102.33 W
Brisighella	66	44.13 N	11.46 E
Brissac	62	43.52 N	3.42 E
Brissago	58	46.07 N	8.43 E
Bristol, Eng., U.K.	42	51.27 N	2.35 W
Bristol, Ct., U.S.	207	41.41 N	72.57 W
Bristol, Fl., U.S.	192	30.25 N	84.58 W
Bristol, Il., U.S.	216	41.39 N	88.27 W
Bristol, In., U.S.	216	41.43 N	85.49 W
Bristol, N.H., U.S.	188	43.35 N	71.44 W
Bristol, Pa., U.S.	208	40.06 N	74.51 W
Bristol, R.I., U.S.	207	41.40 N	71.16 W
Bristol, S.D., U.S.	198	45.20 N	97.44 W
Bristol, Tn., U.S.	192	36.35 N	82.11 W
Bristol, Vt., U.S.	188	44.08 N	73.04 W
Bristol, Va., U.S.	192	36.35 N	82.11 W
Bristol, Wi., U.S.	216	42.33 N	88.02 W
Bristol □[6], Ma., U.S.	207	41.54 N	71.06 W
Bristol □[6], R.I., U.S.	207	41.42 N	71.18 W
Bristol (Lulsgate) Airport ⊠	42	51.23 N	2.43 W
Bristol Bay c	180	58.00 N	159.00 W
Bristol-Blake Reservation ♦	283	42.06 N	71.19 W
Bristol Center	210	42.49 N	77.23 W
Bristol Channel ⊔	42	51.20 N	4.00 W
Bristol Lake ⊜	204	34.28 N	115.41 W
Bristolville	214	41.23 N	80.52 W
Bristow	196	35.49 N	96.23 W
Britânia	255	15.14 S	51.09 W
Británicas, Islas → British Isles II	4	54.00 N	4.00 W
Britannia	275b	43.37 N	79.41 W
Britannia Beach	182	49.38 N	123.12 W
Britannia Range ⋏	9	80.00 S	158.00 E
Britische Jungfern-Inseln → British Virgin Islands □[2]	240m	18.30 N	64.30 W
Britisches Antarktis-Territorium → British Antarctic Territory □[2]	9	60.00 S	45.00 W
British Antarctic Territory □[2]	9	60.00 S	45.00 W
British Columbia □[4], Can.	176	54.00 N	125.00 W
British Columbia □[4], Can.	182	54.00 N	125.00 W
British Honduras → Belize □[1]	232	17.15 N	88.45 W
British Indian Ocean Territory □[2]	12	7.00 S	72.00 E
British Isles II	4	54.00 N	4.00 W
British Mountains ⋏	180	69.00 N	140.20 W
British Museum ʊ	260	51.31 N	0.08 W
British Solomon Islands → Solomon Islands □[1]	175e	8.00 S	159.00 E
British Virgin Islands □[2], N.A.	230	18.30 N	64.30 W
British Virgin Islands □[2], N.A.	240m	18.30 N	64.30 W
Britland Edge Hill ∧[2]	262	53.31 N	1.50 W
Briton Ferry	42	51.38 N	3.49 W
Brits	158	25.42 S	27.45 E
Britstown	158	30.37 S	23.30 E
Britt	190	43.05 N	93.48 W
Brittany → Bretagne □[9]	32	48.00 N	3.00 W
Brittas	48	53.14 N	6.27 W
Britten	158	27.42 S	25.17 E
Brittingham	196	25.45 N	103.24 W
Britton, Mi., U.S.	216	41.59 N	83.49 W
Britton, S.D., U.S.	198	45.47 N	97.45 W
Britton, Tx., U.S.	222	32.33 N	97.04 W
Britton, Mount ∧[2]	162	26.31 S	134.43 E
Britz	54	52.53 N	13.49 E
Britz ⬥[8]	264a	52.27 N	13.26 E
Brive-la-Gaillarde	32	45.10 N	1.32 E
Brives-Charensac	62	45.03 N	3.56 E
Briviesca	34	42.33 N	3.19 W
Brivio	62	45.44 N	9.27 E
Brixen im Thale	64	47.27 N	12.15 E
Brixham	42	50.24 N	3.30 W
Brixlegg	64	47.25 N	11.53 E
Brixton	166	23.32 S	144.57 E
Brixworth	42	52.20 N	0.54 W
Brlik	85	43.40 N	73.49 E
Brloh	61	48.56 N	14.13 E
Brno	30	49.12 N	16.37 E
Bro	40	59.31 N	17.38 E
Broa, Ensenada de la c	240p	22.35 N	82.00 W
Broad ≃, U.S.	192	34.00 N	81.04 W
Broad ≃, Fl., U.S.	220	25.28 N	81.09 W
Broad ≃, Ga., U.S.	192	33.59 N	82.39 W
Broadalbin	210	43.03 N	74.11 W
Broad Arrow	162	30.20 S	121.27 E
Broad Axe	285	40.10 N	75.15 W
Broadback ≃	176	51.21 N	78.52 W
Broad Bay c	46	58.15 N	6.15 W
Broadbottom	262	53.26 N	2.01 W
Broad Brook	207	41.54 N	72.32 W
Broad Chalke	42	51.02 N	1.57 W
Broadclyst	42	50.46 N	3.26 W
Broad Creek c	208	38.45 N	76.15 W
Broad Creek ≃	208	39.42 N	76.14 W
Broadford, Austl.	169	37.13 S	145.03 E
Broadford, Scot., U.K.	46	57.14 N	5.54 W
Broad Haven c	48	54.18 N	9.55 W
Broadheath	262	53.24 N	2.21 W
Broadhurst Range ⋏	162	22.23 S	122.09 E
Broadkill ≃	208	38.47 N	75.10 W
Broad Law ∧	46	55.30 N	3.22 W
Broadley Common	260	51.45 N	0.04 E
Broadmeadows	169	37.40 S	144.54 E
Broadmoor	226	37.41 N	122.29 W
Broad Neck ›[1]	208	39.03 N	76.27 W
Broad Oak	42	50.57 N	0.36 E
Broad Pass)(	180	63.18 N	149.09 W
Broad Run ≃, Pa., U.S.	285	39.56 N	75.41 W
Broad Run ≃, Pa., U.S.	285	39.59 N	75.40 W
Broad Run ≃, Va., U.S.	208	38.41 N	77.29 W
Broad Sound ⊔, Austl.	166	22.10 S	149.45 E
Broad Sound ⊔, Ma., U.S.	283	42.25 N	70.58 W
Broad Sound Channel ⊔	166	22.05 S	150.20 E
Broadstairs	42	51.22 N	1.27 E
Broad Street	260	51.17 N	0.38 E
Broad Top	214	40.12 N	78.08 W
Broadus	198	45.26 N	105.24 W
Broadview, Sk., Can.	184	50.20 N	102.30 W
Broadview, Il., U.S.	216	41.51 N	87.51 W
Broadview, In., U.S.	218	39.10 N	87.33 W
Broadview Heights	214	41.18 N	81.41 W
Broadwater	198	41.35 N	102.51 W
Broadway, Eng., U.K.	42	52.02 N	1.51 W
Broadway, Oh., U.S.	214	40.20 N	83.24 W
Broadway, Va., U.S.	188	38.38 N	78.46 W
Broadwell	219	40.04 N	89.27 W
Broadwindsor	42	50.49 N	2.48 W
Broadwood	172	35.16 S	173.23 E
Broager	41	54.53 N	9.41 E
Brobo	150	7.43 N	4.42 W
Broby	26	56.15 N	14.05 E
Brobyværk	41	55.14 N	10.15 E
Broc	58	46.36 N	7.06 E
Brocēni	76	56.42 N	22.35 E
Brochel	46	57.26 N	6.01 W
Brochet	176	57.53 N	101.40 W
Brochet, Lac au ⊜	186	49.40 N	69.37 W
Brochterbeck	52	52.13 N	7.44 E
Brock	184	51.27 N	108.42 W
Brock ≃	44	53.52 N	2.47 W
Brock Creek ≃	285	40.15 N	74.50 W
Brocken ∧	54	51.48 N	10.36 E
Brockenhurst	42	50.49 N	1.34 W
Brockenscheidt	263	51.38 N	7.25 E
Brockhagen	52	51.59 N	8.20 E
Brockham	260	51.14 N	0.17 W
Brockman ≃	168a	31.41 S	116.07 E
Brockman, Mount ∧	162	22.28 S	117.18 E
Brock Monument ⊥	284a	43.09 N	79.04 W
Brockport, N.Y., U.S.	210	43.12 N	77.56 W
Brockport, Pa., U.S.	214	41.16 N	78.44 W
Brocks Beach	212	44.27 N	80.06 W
Brocks Creek	164	13.28 S	131.25 E
Brockton, Ma., U.S.	207	42.05 N	71.01 W
Brockton, Mt., U.S.	198	48.09 N	104.54 W
Brockton, Pa., U.S.	208	40.45 N	76.04 W
Brockton Reservoir ⊜[1]	283	42.07 N	71.03 W
Brock University ʊ[2]	284a	43.07 N	79.15 W
Brockville	212	44.35 N	75.41 W
Brockway	214	41.15 N	78.47 W
Brockworth	42	51.51 N	2.09 W
Brocoió, Ilha do I	287a	22.45 S	43.07 W
Brocton	214	42.23 N	79.26 W
Brod, Česko.	60	49.51 N	12.45 E
Brod, Jugo.	38	41.31 N	21.12 E
Broddbo	40	59.59 N	16.28 E
Brodenbach	56	50.14 N	7.26 E
Broderick	226	38.35 N	121.30 W
Brodeur Peninsula ›[1]	176	73.00 N	88.00 W
Brodhead, Ky., U.S.	192	37.24 N	84.24 W
Brodhead, Wi., U.S.	190	42.37 N	89.22 W
Brodhead Creek ≃	210	40.59 N	75.08 W
Brodheadsville	210	40.55 N	75.24 W
Brodick	46	55.35 N	5.09 W
Brodnax	192	36.42 N	78.01 W
Brodnica	30	53.16 N	19.23 E
Brodokalmak	86	55.35 N	62.06 E
Brody, Pol.	30	51.45 N	14.45 E
Brody, S.S.S.R.	78	50.06 N	25.10 E
Broedersput	158	26.49 S	25.08 E
Broek [op Langendijk]	52	52.40 N	4.48 E
Brogan	202	44.14 N	117.30 W
Broglie	50	49.01 N	0.32 E
Brohlbach ≃	56	50.29 N	7.20 E
Broich ⬥[8]	263	51.25 N	6.51 E
Broichweiden	56	50.49 N	6.09 E
Broitzem	52	52.14 N	10.29 E
Brok	30	52.43 N	21.52 E
Brok ∧	123	34.32 N	76.35 E
Brokdorf	52	53.52 N	9.19 E
Broke	170	32.45 S	151.06 E
Broke Inlet c	162	34.55 S	116.25 E
Broken ≃	169	36.41 S	146.00 E
Broken Arrow	196	36.03 N	95.47 W
Broken Bay c	170	33.34 S	151.18 E
Broken Bow, Ne., U.S.	198	41.24 N	99.38 W
Broken Bow, Ok., U.S.	194	34.01 N	94.44 W
Broken Bow Lake ⊜[1]	194	34.10 N	94.40 W
Broken Cross, Eng., U.K.	262	53.15 N	2.29 W
Broken Cross, Eng., U.K.	262	53.15 N	2.10 W
Brokenhead ≃	184	50.25 N	96.40 W
Broken Hill, Austl.	166	31.57 S	141.27 E
Broken Hill → Kabwe, Zam.	154	14.27 S	28.27 E
Broken Ridge ✣[3]	12	31.30 S	95.00 E
Brokenstraw Creek ≃	214	41.51 N	79.09 W
Broken Sword Creek ≃	214	40.46 N	83.11 W
Brokopondo	250	5.04 N	54.58 W
Brokopondo □[5]	250	4.20 N	55.20 W
Brölbach ≃	56	50.47 N	7.18 E
Brolo	70	38.09 N	14.50 E
Bromberg → Bydgoszcz	30	53.08 N	18.00 E
Bromborough	262	53.19 N	2.59 W
Brome, B.R.D.	54	52.36 N	10.56 E
Brome, P.Q., Can.	206	45.12 N	72.34 W
Brome □[6]	206	45.10 N	72.30 W
Brome, Lac ⊜	206	45.15 N	72.30 W
Brome, Mont ∧	206	45.17 N	72.38 W
Bromham	42	52.09 N	0.31 W
Bromley ⬥[8]	260	51.24 N	0.02 E
Bromley Common ⬥[8]	260	51.22 N	0.03 E
Bromley Plateau ✣[3]	18	32.00 S	35.00 W
Bromma ⬥[8]	40	59.21 N	17.55 E
Bromma flygplats ⊠	40	59.21 N	17.55 E
Brommö I	40	58.50 N	13.41 E
Bromo, Gunung ∧	115a	7.57 S	112.57 E
Bromölla	26	56.04 N	14.28 E
Brompton, Eng., U.K.	44	54.22 N	1.25 W
Brompton, Eng., U.K.	260	51.23 N	0.33 E
Brompton, Lac ⊜	206	45.27 N	72.09 W
Bromptonville	206	45.28 N	71.57 W
Bromsgrove	42	52.20 N	2.03 W
Bromyard	42	52.11 N	2.30 W
Bron	62	45.44 N	4.55 E
Bron, Aéroport de ⊠	62	45.43 N	4.56 E
Brønderslev	26	57.16 N	9.58 E
Bronevskaja	24	61.43 N	39.10 E
Brong-Ahafo □[4]	150	7.45 N	1.30 W
Broni	62	45.04 N	9.16 E
Bronickaja Guta	78	50.56 N	27.19 E
Bronkhorstspruit	158	25.48 S	28.44 E
Bronkhorstspruitdam ⊜[1]	158	25.55 S	28.42 E
Bronkow	54	51.40 N	13.55 E
Bronllys	42	52.01 N	3.16 W
Bronlund Peak ∧	176	57.26 N	126.38 W
Bronn	60	49.44 N	11.28 E
Bronnicy	82	55.25 N	38.16 E
Bronnikovo	86	58.32 N	68.25 E
Bronnoje	76	52.19 N	30.29 E
Brønnøysund	24	65.30 N	12.10 E
Bronnzell	56	50.31 N	9.41 E
Brøns	41	55.11 N	8.44 E
Bronson, Fl., U.S.	192	29.26 N	82.38 W
Bronson, Ks., U.S.	198	37.54 N	95.04 W
Bronson, Mi., U.S.	216	41.52 N	85.11 W
Bronson, Tx., U.S.	194	31.21 N	94.01 W
Bronson Lake ⊜	184	53.52 N	109.43 W
Bronte, It.	70	37.47 N	14.50 E
Bronte, Tx., U.S.	196	31.53 N	100.18 W
Bronte Creek ≃	212	43.23 N	79.43 W
Bronwood	192	31.49 N	84.21 W
Bronx □[6]	210	40.49 N	73.56 W
Bronx ⬥[8]	276	40.49 N	73.56 W
Bronx ≃	276	40.49 N	73.52 W
Bronx Park ♦	276	40.52 N	73.53 W
Bronxville	276	40.56 N	73.49 W
Bronx-Whitestone Bridge ⬥[5]	276	40.48 N	73.50 W
Bronx Zoo ♦	276	40.51 N	73.53 W
Bronzolo (Branzoll)	64	46.24 N	11.19 E
Brooch, Lac ⊜	186	50.44 N	67.58 W
Broodsnyersplaas	158	26.03 S	29.29 E
Brook	216	40.51 N	87.21 W
Brookdale	226	37.06 N	122.06 W
Brooke	208	38.23 N	77.22 W
Brooke □[6]	214	40.18 N	80.33 W
Brookeborough	48	54.19 N	7.24 W
Brookeland	194	31.09 N	94.00 W
Brooker	192	29.53 N	82.19 W
Brooke's Point	116	8.47 N	117.50 E
Brookfield, N.S., Can.	186	45.15 N	63.17 W
Brookfield, Ct., U.S.	207	41.28 N	73.24 W
Brookfield, Il., U.S.	216	41.49 N	87.51 W
Brookfield, Ma., U.S.	207	42.12 N	72.06 W
Brookfield, Mi., U.S.	216	42.27 N	84.47 W
Brookfield, Mo., U.S.	194	39.47 N	93.04 W
Brookfield, N.Y., U.S.	210	42.48 N	75.19 W
Brookfield, Oh., U.S.	214	41.14 N	80.34 W
Brookfield, Wi., U.S.	216	43.03 N	88.06 W
Brookfield Center	207	41.27 N	73.23 W
Brookfield Zoo ♦	278	41.50 N	87.50 W
Brookford	192	35.42 N	81.20 W
Brookhaven, De., U.S.	285	39.42 N	75.41 W
Brookhaven, Ms., U.S.	194	31.34 N	90.26 W
Brookhaven, Pa., U.S.	285	39.52 N	75.22 W
Brookhaven Manor	278	41.44 N	87.58 W
Brookhaven National Laboratory ʊ[3]	207	40.54 N	72.52 W
Brookings, Or., U.S.	202	42.03 N	124.16 W
Brookings, S.D., U.S.	198	44.18 N	96.47 W
Brookland, Eng., U.K.	42	50.59 N	0.50 E
Brookland, Ar., U.S.	194	35.54 N	90.34 W
Brookland ⬥[8]	284c	38.56 N	76.59 W
Brooklands	214	42.38 N	83.06 W
Brookland Terrace	285	39.44 N	75.37 W
Brooklandville	284b	39.25 N	76.40 W
Brooklawn	285	39.52 N	75.07 W
Brooklet	192	32.22 N	81.39 W
Brooklin	212	43.57 N	78.57 W
Brookline, Ma., U.S.	207	42.21 N	71.07 W
Brookline, N.H., U.S.	207	42.44 N	71.39 W
Brooklyn, N.S., Can.	186	44.03 N	64.42 W
Brooklyn, Ct., U.S.	207	41.47 N	71.57 W
Brooklyn, Il., U.S.	219	40.14 N	90.46 W
Brooklyn, In., U.S.	218	39.32 N	86.22 W
Brooklyn, Ia., U.S.	190	41.44 N	92.26 W
Brooklyn, Md., U.S.	284b	39.14 N	76.37 W
Brooklyn, Mi., U.S.	216	42.06 N	84.14 W
Brooklyn, Ms., U.S.	194	31.03 N	89.11 W
Brooklyn, Oh., U.S.	214	41.26 N	81.44 W
Brooklyn, Pa., U.S.	210	41.45 N	75.48 W
Brooklyn, Wa., U.S.	224	46.47 N	123.31 W
Brooklyn, Wi., U.S.	216	42.51 N	89.22 W
Brooklyn ⬥[8], Md., U.S.	284b	39.14 N	76.36 W
Brooklyn ⬥[8], N.Y., U.S.	210	40.42 N	74.00 W
Brooklyn Battery Tunnel ⬥[5]	276	40.42 N	74.01 W
Brooklyn Bridge ⬥[5]	276	40.42 N	74.00 W
Brooklyn Center	190	45.04 N	93.19 W
Brooklyn Heights	279a	41.24 N	81.40 W
Brooklyn Marine Park ♦	276	40.35 N	73.55 W
Brooklyn Museum ʊ	276	40.40 N	73.58 W
Brookmans Park	260	51.43 N	0.12 W
Brookmere	182	49.49 N	120.53 W
Brookmont	284c	38.57 N	77.07 W
Brookneal	192	37.03 N	78.56 W
Brook Park	214	41.23 N	81.48 W
Brookport	194	37.07 N	88.37 W
Brooks, Ab., Can.	182	50.35 N	111.53 W
Brooks, Ca., U.S.	226	38.45 N	122.09 W
Brooks, Me., U.S.	188	44.33 N	69.07 W
Brooks, Or., U.S.	224	45.02 N	122.57 W
Brooks, Mount ∧	180	63.11 N	150.40 W
Brooks Air Force Base ■	196	29.21 N	98.25 W
Brooks Bay c	182	50.13 N	127.55 W
Brooksburg	218	38.44 N	85.15 W
Brookshire	222	29.47 N	95.57 W
Brookside, De., U.S.	285	39.40 N	75.43 W
Brookside, N.J., U.S.	276	40.48 N	74.34 W
Brookside, Pa., U.S.	214	42.08 N	80.00 W
Brookside, Tx., U.S.	222	29.35 N	95.18 W
Brookside Park ♦	279a	41.27 N	81.43 W
Brooks Island I	282	37.54 N	122.21 W
Brooks Mountain ∧	180	65.33 N	167.09 W
Brooks Place	283	42.02 N	71.01 W
Brooks Range ⋏	180	68.00 N	154.00 W
Brookston	216	40.36 N	86.52 W
Brook Street	260	51.37 N	0.17 E
Brooksville, Fl., U.S.	220	28.33 N	82.23 W
Brooksville, Ky., U.S.	218	38.40 N	84.03 W
Brooksville, Ms., U.S.	194	33.14 N	88.34 W
Brookton	162	32.22 S	117.01 E
Brooktondale	210	42.23 N	76.24 W
Brookvale	274a	33.46 S	151.17 E
Brookview	210	42.32 N	73.43 W
Brookville, In., U.S.	218	39.25 N	85.00 W
Brookville, Ma., U.S.	207	42.07 N	71.00 W
Brookville, N.Y., U.S.	276	40.48 N	73.34 W
Brookville, Oh., U.S.	218	39.50 N	84.24 W
Brookville, Pa., U.S.	214	41.09 N	79.05 W
Brookville Lake ⊜[1]	218	39.30 N	85.00 W
Brookwood, Eng., U.K.	260	51.18 N	0.38 W
Brookwood, In., U.S.	278	40.30 N	87.22 W
Brooloo	166	26.29 S	152.42 E
Broom, Little Loch c	46	57.54 N	5.22 W
Broom, Loch c	46	57.52 N	5.08 W
Broomall	285	39.58 N	75.21 W
Broome	162	17.58 S	122.14 E
Broome □[6]	210	42.08 N	75.54 W
Broome County Airport ⊠	210	42.13 N	75.59 W
Broomes Island	208	38.25 N	76.32 W
Broomfield, Eng., U.K.	260	51.46 N	0.28 E
Broomfield, Eng., U.K.	260	51.14 N	0.38 E
Broomfield, Co., U.S.	200	39.55 N	105.05 W
Broons	32	48.19 N	2.16 W
Brooten	198	45.30 N	95.07 W
Brophy, Mount ∧[2]	162	19.11 S	128.51 E
Brora	46	58.01 N	3.51 W
Brora ≃	46	58.01 N	3.52 W
Brørup	41	55.29 N	9.01 E
Broseley	42	52.37 N	2.29 W
Brosewere Bay c	276	40.37 N	73.42 W
Brosna ≃	48	53.13 N	7.58 W
Brošnev-Osada	78	49.00 N	24.13 E
Brossac	32	45.20 N	0.03 W
Brossard	206	45.26 N	73.29 W
Brossasco	62	44.34 N	7.21 E
Brosso	62	45.30 N	7.48 E
Brotas de Macaúbas	255	12.00 S	42.38 W
Brothers Brook ≃	276	41.02 N	73.36 W
Brötjärna	40	60.30 N	15.01 E
Broto	34	42.36 N	0.06 W
Brotterode	54	50.49 N	10.26 E
Brotton	44	54.34 N	0.56 W
Brou	50	48.13 N	1.11 E
Brough, Eng., U.K.	44	54.32 N	2.19 W
Brough, Eng., U.K.	44	53.44 N	0.35 W
Brough, Scot., U.K.	46	58.39 N	3.20 W
Brougham	212	43.55 N	79.06 W
Brough Head ›	46	59.08 N	3.17 W
Broughshane	48	54.54 N	6.12 W
Broughton, Eng., U.K.	42	52.23 N	0.46 W
Broughton, Eng., U.K.	44	53.49 N	2.44 W
Broughton, Eng., U.K.	44	53.34 N	0.33 W
Broughton, Eng., U.K.	262	53.49 N	2.43 W
Broughton, Scot., U.K.	46	55.37 N	3.25 W
Broughton, Wales, U.K.	44	53.10 N	2.59 W
Broughton, Pa., U.S.	214	40.21 N	79.59 W
Broughton in Furness	44	54.17 N	3.12 W
Broughton Island I	176	67.35 N	63.50 W
Broughtown	46	59.15 N	2.36 W
Broughty Ferry	46	56.28 N	2.53 W
Broumov	30	50.35 N	16.20 E
Brousseval	58	48.29 N	4.58 E
Brou-sur-Chantereine	261	48.53 N	2.38 E
Brouvelieures	58	48.14 N	6.44 E
Brouwersdam ⬥[6]	52	51.46 N	3.51 E
Brouwershaven	52	51.44 N	3.54 E
Brovary	78	50.31 N	30.46 E
Brovst	26	57.06 N	9.32 E
Broward □[6]	220	26.09 N	80.29 W
Browerville	198	46.05 N	94.51 W
Brown □[6], Il., U.S.	219	39.59 N	90.45 W
Brown □[6], In., U.S.	218	39.12 N	86.15 W
Brown □[6], Oh., U.S.	218	38.52 N	83.54 W
Brown, Mount ∧	202	48.52 N	111.09 W
Brown, Point ›	224	46.56 N	124.10 W
Brownbacks	285	40.11 N	75.37 W
Brown City	190	43.12 N	82.59 W
Brown Clee Hill ∧[2]	42	52.28 N	2.35 W
Brown County State Park ♦	218	39.09 N	86.14 W
Brown Creek ≃	276	40.43 N	73.04 W
Browndale	210	41.40 N	75.27 W
Brown Deer	216	43.09 N	87.57 W
Browne Bay c	176	73.08 N	97.30 W
Brownfield	196	33.10 N	102.16 W
Brown Gelly ∧[2]	42	50.32 N	4.32 W
Brownhills	42	52.39 N	1.55 W
Browning, Il., U.S.	219	40.08 N	90.22 W
Browning, Mo., U.S.	194	40.02 N	93.09 W
Browning, Mt., U.S.	202	48.33 N	113.00 W
Browning Entrance c	182	53.41 N	130.30 W
Browning Island I	212	45.00 N	79.25 W
Brown Lake ⊜	176	65.55 N	91.15 W
Brownlee Park	216	42.18 N	85.05 W
Brownlee Reservoir ⊜[1]	202	44.40 N	117.05 W
Brown Mountain ∧, Ca., U.S.	204	35.41 N	117.01 W
Brown Mountain ∧, Ca., U.S.	280	34.14 N	118.08 W
Brown Mountain ∧[2]	222	31.51 N	97.39 W
Brown Point ›	276	40.43 N	73.04 W
Brownsboro	222	32.18 N	95.37 W
Browns Brook ≃	276	41.09 N	73.17 W
Brownsburg, P.Q., Can.	206	45.41 N	74.25 W
Brownsburg, In., U.S.	218	39.50 N	86.23 W
Browns Canyon V	280	34.18 N	118.35 W
Brownsdale	190	43.44 N	92.52 W
Browns Island I	282	38.02 N	121.52 W
Browns Lake	216	42.42 N	88.14 W
Brownsmead	224	46.13 N	123.32 W
Browns Mills	208	39.58 N	74.35 W
Browns Plains	171a	36.03 S	146.38 E
Browns Point	224	47.18 N	122.21 W
Browns Town, Jam.	241q	18.24 N	77.22 W
Brownstown, Il., U.S.	219	38.59 N	88.57 W
Brownstown, In., U.S.	218	38.52 N	86.02 W
Brownstown, Pa., U.S.	208	40.08 N	76.13 W
Brownstown Creek ≃	281	42.06 N	83.13 W
Browns Valley, Ca., U.S.	226	39.15 N	121.23 W
Browns Valley, Mn., U.S.	198	45.35 N	96.49 W
Brownsville, On., Can.	212	42.52 N	80.50 W
Brownsville, Ca., U.S.	226	39.28 N	121.16 W
Brownsville, Fl., U.S.	220	25.50 N	80.17 W
Brownsville, In., U.S.	218	39.39 N	85.00 W
Brownsville, Ky., U.S.	194	37.11 N	86.16 W
Brownsville, La., U.S.	194	32.30 N	92.10 W
Brownsville, Or., U.S.	202	44.23 N	122.59 W
Brownsville, Pa., U.S.	188	40.01 N	79.53 W
Brownsville, Tn., U.S.	194	35.35 N	89.15 W
Brownsville, Tx., U.S.	196	25.54 N	97.29 W
Brownton	190	44.43 N	94.21 W
Browntown	276	40.24 N	74.19 W
Brownvale	182	56.08 N	117.53 W
Brownville, Al., U.S.	194	33.23 N	87.45 W
Brownville, Me., U.S.	188	45.18 N	69.02 W
Brownville, Ne., U.S.	198	40.23 N	95.39 W
Brownville, N.Y., U.S.	212	44.00 N	75.59 W
Brownville Junction	188	45.21 N	69.03 W
Brown Willy ∧[2]	42	50.35 N	4.36 W
Brownwood	196	31.42 N	98.59 W
Brownwood, Lake ⊜[1]	196	31.51 N	99.02 W
Browse Island I	160	14.07 S	123.33 E
Broxbourne	260	51.45 N	0.01 W
Broxbourne □[8]	260	51.44 N	0.04 W
Broxton	192	31.37 N	82.53 W
Broye ≃	58	46.55 N	7.02 E
Broyhill Park	284c	38.51 N	77.11 W
Broža	76	52.57 N	29.07 E
Brozas	34	39.37 N	6.46 W
Brozzo	64	45.43 N	10.14 E
Brtonigla	64	45.23 N	13.38 E
Brû	58	48.21 N	6.41 E
Bruay-en-Artois	50	50.29 N	2.33 E
Bruay-sur-l'Escaut	50	50.23 N	3.32 E
Bruce, Ms., U.S.	194	33.59 N	89.20 W
Bruce, S.D., U.S.	198	44.26 N	96.53 W
Bruce, Wi., U.S.	190	45.27 N	91.16 W
Bruce □[6]	212	44.30 N	81.15 W
Bruce, Mount ∧	162	22.36 S	118.08 E
Bruce Bay	172	43.35 S	169.41 E
Bruce Creek ≃	275b	43.52 N	79.18 W
Bruce Lake	184	50.48 N	93.24 W
Bruce Lake ⊜	184	50.49 N	93.20 W
Bruce Mines	190	46.18 N	83.48 W
Bruce Museum ʊ	276	41.01 N	73.37 W
Bruce Peninsula ›[1]	190	44.50 N	81.20 W
Bruce Peninsula National Park ♦	190	45.12 N	81.40 W
Bruce Rock	162	31.53 S	118.09 E
Bruceville	222	31.19 N	97.14 W
Bruchberg ∧	54	51.47 N	10.29 E
Bruchhausen	56	51.26 N	8.01 E
Bruchhausen-Vilsen	52	52.50 N	9.00 E
Bruchmühlbach-Miesau	56	49.24 N	7.26 E
Bruchmühle	264a	52.33 N	13.47 E
Br'uchoveckaja	78	45.48 N	38.59 E
Bruchsal	56	49.07 N	8.35 E
Brück, D.D.R.	54	52.12 N	12.46 E
Bruck, Öst.	64	47.17 N	12.49 E
Bruck an der Leitha	61	47.57 N	16.44 E
Bruck an der Mur	61	47.25 N	15.16 E
Bruckhausen ⬥[8]	263	51.29 N	6.44 E
Bruck in der Oberpfalz	60	49.15 N	12.18 E
Brückl	61	46.45 N	14.32 E
Bruckmühl	64	47.53 N	11.54 E
Brucoli ⬥[8]	70	37.17 N	15.11 E
Brudager	41	55.07 N	10.41 E
Bruderheim	182	53.47 N	112.56 W
Brue ≃	42	51.13 N	3.00 W
Brue-Auriac	62	43.32 N	5.57 E
Brueil-en-Vexin	261	49.02 N	1.49 E
Brüel	54	53.44 N	11.43 E
Bruff	48	52.29 N	8.33 W
Bruges → Brugge	50	51.13 N	3.14 E
Brugg	58	47.29 N	8.12 E
Brugge (Bruges), Bel.	50	51.13 N	3.14 E
Brügge, B.R.D.	263	51.13 N	7.34 E
Brüggen	56	51.14 N	6.11 E
Brugherio	62	45.33 N	9.18 E
Brugnato	62	44.14 N	9.43 E
Brühl	56	50.48 N	6.54 E
Bruin, Ky., U.S.	218	38.11 N	83.01 W
Bruin, Pa., U.S.	214	41.04 N	79.44 W
Bruinisse	52	51.40 N	4.06 E
Bruin Point ∧	200	39.39 N	110.22 W
Bruit, Pulau I	112	2.35 N	111.20 E
Bruja, Cerro ∧	236	9.29 N	79.34 W
Brule	198	41.05 N	101.53 W
Brule ≃	190	45.57 N	88.12 W
Brûlé, Lac ⊜, Can.	176	52.17 N	63.52 W
Brûlé, Lac ⊜, P.Q., Can.	190	46.57 N	77.12 W
Brule Lake ⊜	212	45.03 N	77.04 W
Brûly	50	49.58 N	4.31 E
Brumadinho	255	20.08 S	44.13 W
Brumado	255	14.13 S	41.40 W
Brumath	56	48.44 N	7.43 E
Brumby Creek ≃	162	24.09 S	118.39 E
Brummen	52	52.05 N	6.09 E
Brumunddal	26	60.53 N	10.56 E
Bruna ≃	66	42.45 N	10.53 E
Brunate	62	45.49 N	9.06 E
Brunau	54	52.45 N	11.28 E
Brundall	42	52.37 N	1.26 E
Brundby	41	55.49 N	10.37 E
Brundidge	194	31.43 N	85.48 W
Brune ≃	50	49.45 N	3.47 E
Bruneau	202	42.52 N	115.47 W
Bruneau ≃	202	42.57 N	115.58 W
Brunei → Bandar Seri Begawan	112	4.56 N	114.55 E
Brunei □[1], Asia	108	4.30 N	114.40 E
Brunei □[1], Asia	112	4.30 N	114.40 E
Brunei, Teluk c	112	5.05 N	115.18 E
Brünen	52	51.43 N	6.39 E
Brunette Creek ≃	162	18.47 S	135.41 E
Brunette Downs	162	18.38 S	135.57 E
Brunette Island I	186	47.16 N	55.54 W
Brunflo	26	63.05 N	14.49 E
Brungle	171b	35.10 S	148.14 E
Brunico (Bruneck)	64	46.48 N	11.56 E
Brünigpass)(	58	46.46 N	8.09 E
Brüninghausen	263	51.13 N	7.41 E
Brunkeberg	26	59.26 N	8.29 E
Brünn → Brno, Česko.	30	49.12 N	16.37 E
Brunn, D.D.R.	54	53.40 N	13.22 E
Brünn, D.D.R.	54	50.27 N	10.51 E
Brunna	40	59.51 N	17.26 E
Brunn am Gebirge	61	48.07 N	16.17 E
Brunnen, B.R.D.	60	48.38 N	11.18 E
Brunnen, Schw.	58	47.00 N	8.36 E
Brunner, Lake ⊜	172	42.37 S	171.27 E
Brunnerville	208	40.11 N	76.17 W
Brunni	58	47.03 N	8.42 E
Brunnsvik	40	60.12 N	15.08 E
Bruno	184	52.15 N	105.30 W
Brunot Island I	279b	40.28 N	80.03 W
Brunow	264a	52.44 N	13.52 E
Brunoy	50	48.42 N	2.30 E
Brunsbüttel	52	53.54 N	9.07 E
Brunsbüttelkoog	52	53.54 N	9.08 E
Brunson	192	32.55 N	81.11 W
Brunssum	56	50.56 N	5.59 E
Brunswick, Austl.	274b	37.46 S	144.58 E
Brunswick → Braunschweig, B.R.D.	52	52.16 N	10.31 E
Brunswick, Ga., U.S.	192	31.08 N	81.29 W
Brunswick, Me., U.S.	188	43.54 N	69.57 W
Brunswick, Md., U.S.	208	39.18 N	77.37 W
Brunswick, Mo., U.S.	194	39.25 N	93.07 W
Brunswick, Oh., U.S.	214	41.14 N	81.50 W
Brunswick ≃	168a	33.15 S	115.45 E
Brunswick, Península ›[1]	254	53.30 S	71.25 W
Brunswick Junction	168a	33.15 S	115.51 E
Brunswick Lake ⊜	190	49.00 N	83.23 W
Brunswick Naval Air Station ■	188	43.54 N	69.56 W
Brunswick Square ⬥[9]	276	40.25 N	74.23 W
Bruntál	30	49.59 N	17.28 E
Bruree	48	52.26 N	8.36 W
Brus, Laguna de c	236	15.50 N	84.35 W
Brus'any	80	53.13 N	49.24 E
Brusasco	62	45.09 N	8.04 E
Bruselas → Bruxelles	50	50.50 N	4.20 E
Brusendorf	264a	52.19 N	13.31 E
Brush	198	40.15 N	103.37 W
Brush Creek ≃, Oh., U.S.	216	41.26 N	84.24 W

Symbol	English	Deutsch	Español	Français	Português
≃	River	Fluß	Río	Rivière	Rio
≋	Canal	Kanal	Canal	Canal	Canal
⌊	Waterfall, Rapids	Wasserfall, Stromschnellen	Cascada, Rápidos	Chute d'eau, Rapides	Cascata, Rápidos
⊔	Strait	Meeresstraße	Estrecho	Détroit	Estreito
c	Bay, Gulf	Bucht, Golf	Bahía, Golfo	Baie, Golfe	Baía, Golfo
⊜	Lake, Lakes	See, Seen	Lago, Lagos	Lac, Lacs	Lago, Lagos
⁞	Swamp	Sumpf	Pantano	Marais	Pântano
⌂	Ice Features, Glacier	Eis- und Gletscherformen	Accidentes Glaciales	Formes glaciaires	Acidentes glaciares
⊤	Other Hydrographic Features	Andere Hydrographische Objekte	Otros Elementos Hidrográficos	Autres données hydrographiques	Outros acidentes hidrográficos
✣	Submarine Features	Untermeerische Objekte	Accidentes Submarinos	Formes de relief sous-marin	Acidentes submarinos
□	Political Unit	Politische Einheit	Unidad Política	Entité politique	Unidade política
ʊ	Cultural Institution	Kulturelle Institution	Institución Cultural	Institution culturelle	Instituição cultural
⊥	Historical Site	Historische Stätte	Sitio Histórico	Site historique	Sitio histórico
♦	Recreational Site	Erholungs- und Ferienort	Sitio de Recreo	Centre de loisirs	Area de Lazer
⊠	Airport	Flughafen	Aeropuerto	Aéroport	Aeroporto
■	Military Installation	Militäranlage	Instalación Militar	Installation militaire	Instalação militar
⬥	Miscellaneous	Verschiedenes	Misceláneo	Divers	Diversos

Brush Creek ≃, Pa., U.S. 279b 40.23 N 79.46 W
Brush Run ≃, Pa., U.S. 279b 40.16 N 80.10 W
Brush Run ≃, Pa., U.S. 279b 40.18 N 80.07 W
Brush Valley 214 40.32 N 79.04 W
Brushy Creek ≃, Austl. 274b 37.43 S 145.17 E
Brushy Creek ≃, Ok., U.S. 196 34.55 N 95.34 W
Brushy Creek ≃, Tx., U.S. 222 29.04 N 96.34 W
Brushy Creek ≃, Tx., U.S. 222 32.59 N 96.12 W
Brushy Creek ≃, Tx., U.S. 222 30.48 N 95.09 W
Brushy Creek ≃, Tx., U.S. 222 31.55 N 95.26 W
Brushy Creek ≃, Tx., U.S. 222 30.43 N 97.03 W
Brusilov 78 50.17 N 29.32 E
Brusio 58 46.14 N 10.07 E
Brus Laguna 236 15.47 N 84.35 W
Brusovo 76 57.51 N 35.24 E
Brusque 252 27.06 S 48.56 W
Brussel → Bruxelles 50 50.50 N 4.20 E
Brussels → Bruxelles, Bel. 50 50.50 N 4.20 E
Brussels, On., Can. 212 43.44 N 81.15 W
Brussels, Il., U.S. 219 38.57 N 90.36 W
Brusson 62 45.45 N 7.44 E
Brüssow 54 53.24 N 14.07 E
Brusy 30 53.53 N 17.45 E
Brutelles 50 50.08 N 1.31 E
Bruthen 166 37.43 S 147.48 E
Bruton 42 51.07 N 2.27 W
Brüx → Most 54 50.32 N 13.39 E
Bruxelles (Brussels) (Brussel) 56 50.50 N 4.20 E
Bruxelles National, Aéroport ⊠ 50 50.54 N 4.30 E
Bruyères 58 48.12 N 6.43 E
Bruyères-le-Châtel 261 48.36 N 2.11 E
Bruzual 246 8.03 N 69.19 W
Bruzzano Zeffirio 68 38.02 N 16.05 E
Brwinów 30 52.09 N 20.43 E
Bryan, Oh., U.S. 216 41.28 N 84.33 W
Bryan, Tx., U.S. 222 30.40 N 96.22 W
Bryan, Mount ∧ 166 33.26 S 138.59 E
Bryan Coast ⊥[2] 9 73.45 S 82.00 W
Bryansk → Br'ansk 76 53.15 N 34.22 E
Bryans Road 208 38.37 N 77.04 W
Bryant, Ar., U.S. 194 34.35 N 92.29 W
Bryant, In., U.S. 216 40.32 N 84.58 W
Bryant, S.D., U.S. 198 44.35 N 97.28 W
Bryant Creek ≃ 194 36.36 N 92.17 W
Bryant Mountain ∧ 207 42.28 N 72.58 W
Bryantville 207 42.02 N 70.50 W
Bryas, Lac ⊜ 206 46.44 N 73.05 W
Bryce Canyon National Park ♦ 200 37.29 N 112.12 W
Bryher I 42a 49.57 N 6.20 W
Brykalansk 24 65.30 N 54.12 E
Brykovka 80 52.32 N 48.35 E
Bryli 76 53.54 N 30.33 E
Brymbo 44 53.06 N 3.04 W
Bryn 262 53.30 N 2.39 W
Brynamman 42 51.49 N 3.52 W
Bryn Athyn 285 40.08 N 75.04 W
Bryn Brawd ∧[2] 42 52.09 N 3.54 W
Bryncethin 42 51.33 N 3.34 W
Bryne 26 58.44 N 5.39 E
Brynford 262 53.16 N 3.14 W
Bryn Gates 262 53.30 N 2.37 W
Bryn'kovskaja 78 46.02 N 38.35 E
Brynmawr, Wales, U.K. 42 51.49 N 3.11 W
Bryn Mawr, Ca., U.S. 228 34.03 N 117.14 W
Bryn Mawr, Pa., U.S. 208 40.01 N 75.18 W
Bryn Mawr College ✦[2] 285 40.02 N 75.19 W
Bryrup 41 56.01 N 9.31 E
Bryson, P.Q., Can. 188 45.41 N 76.37 W
Bryson, Tx., U.S. 196 33.10 N 98.23 W
Bryson City 192 35.25 N 83.26 W
Bryte 226 38.36 N 121.33 W
Brza Palanka 38 44.28 N 22.27 E
Brzeg 30 50.52 N 17.27 E
Brześć Kujawski 30 52.37 N 18.55 E
Brześć nad Bugiem 76 52.06 N 23.42 E
Brzesko 30 49.59 N 20.36 E
Brzeszcze 30 49.59 N 19.08 E
Brzeziny 30 51.48 N 19.46 E
Brzozów 30 49.42 N 22.02 E
Bsharrī 130 34.15 N 36.01 E
Bua ≃ 154 12.42 S 34.13 E
Bu'aale 144 1.05 N 42.35 E
Buada Lagoon ⊂ 174b 0.31 S 166.55 E
Buad Island I 116 11.40 N 124.51 E
Buagan ≃ 269e 6.17 S 106.55 E
Buala 175e 8.08 S 159.35 E
Bū al-Ḥīḍān, Wādī V 146 27.25 N 19.22 E
Buangor, Mount ∧ 169 37.18 S 143.13 E
Buapinang 112 4.46 S 121.34 E
Buariki 174t 1.36 N 172.58 E
Buatan 114 0.44 N 101.51 E
Bua Yai 110 15.35 N 102.25 E
Buayan ≃ 116 6.06 N 125.14 E
Bu'ayrāt al-Ḥasūn 146 31.24 N 15.44 E
Buba 150 11.36 N 14.55 W
Bubai 268 35.40 N 139.29 E
Bū Bānī, Jabal ∧ 140 22.38 N 25.00 E
Bubanza 154 3.06 S 29.23 E
Bubaque 150 11.17 N 15.50 W
Bubendorf 58 47.27 N 7.44 E
Bubia 164 6.40 S 146.55 E
Būbiyān I 128 29.45 N 48.15 E
Bublitz → Bobolice 30 53.57 N 16.36 E
Bubu ≃ 154 6.03 S 35.19 E
Bubu, Gunong ∧ 114 4.42 N 100.47 E
Bubuan Island I, Pil. 116 6.21 N 121.58 E
Bubuan Island I, Pil. 116 6.11 N 120.58 E
Bubuduo 120 30.06 N 84.38 E
Buburu 152 1.26 N 18.03 E
Bubye ≃ 154 22.20 S 31.07 E
Buc 261 48.46 N 2.08 E
Bučač 78 49.04 N 25.23 E
Bucak 130 37.28 N 30.36 E
Bucakkışla 130 36.57 N 33.02 E
Bucaramanga 246 7.08 N 73.09 W
Bucarest → București 38 44.26 N 26.06 E
Bucas Grande Island I 116 9.40 N 125.57 E
Buccaneer Archipelago II 160 16.17 S 123.20 E
Buccheri 70 37.08 N 14.51 E
Bucchianico 66 42.18 N 14.11 E
Buccinasco 266b 45.24 N 9.07 E
Buccino 68 40.37 N 15.23 E
Buccurale 144 4.31 N 42.01 E
Bucelas 266c 38.54 N 9.07 W
Bucelas ∧[2] 266c 38.53 N 9.07 W
Buch ◆[8] 264a 52.38 N 13.30 E
Buchanan, Arg. 258 34.58 S 58.13 W
Buchanan, Sk., Can. 184 51.43 N 102.45 W
Buchanan, Liber. 150 5.57 N 10.02 W
Buchanan, Ga., U.S. 192 33.48 N 85.11 W
Buchanan, Mi., U.S. 216 41.49 N 86.21 W
Buchanan, N.Y., U.S. 210 41.16 N 73.56 W
Buchanan, Va., U.S. 192 37.31 N 79.40 W
Buchanan, Lake ⊜ 166 21.28 S 145.52 E
Buchanan, Lake ⊜[1] 196 30.48 N 98.25 W
Buchanan Creek ≃ 162 19.11 S 136.16 E
Buchanan Field ⊠ 282 37.59 N 122.03 W
Buchanan Hills ⋏[2] 162 18.53 S 131.02 E
Buchan Ness ⟩ 46 57.28 N 1.45 W
Buchans 186 48.49 N 56.52 W
Buchara 128 39.48 N 64.25 E
Buchara □[4] 128 40.00 N 64.00 E
Buchardo 252 34.43 S 63.31 W
Bucharest → București 38 44.26 N 26.06 E
Buchbach 60 48.19 N 12.17 E
Buchelay 261 48.59 N 1.40 E
Büchen, B.R.D. 52 53.29 N 10.36 E
Buchen, B.R.D. 56 49.32 N 9.17 E
Buchenberg 58 47.42 N 10.14 E
Büchenbeuren 56 49.55 N 7.16 E
Buchenwald-Denkmal ⊥ 54 51.01 N 11.15 E
Buchholz, B.R.D. 56 50.41 N 7.23 E
Buchholz, B.R.D. 263 51.23 N 7.15 E
Buchholz, D.D.R. 54 52.10 N 12.55 E
Buchholz, D.D.R. 264a 52.35 N 13.47 E
Buchholz ◆[8], B.R.D. 263 51.23 N 6.46 E
Buchholz ◆[8], D.D.R. 264a 52.36 N 13.26 E
Buchholz in der Nordheide 52 53.20 N 9.52 E
Büchlberg 60 48.40 N 13.30 E
Buchloe 58 48.02 N 10.44 E
Bucholt 263 51.39 N 6.43 E
Buchon, Point ⟩ 226 35.15 N 120.54 W
Buchow-Karpzow 264a 52.31 N 12.57 E
Buchs, Schw. 58 47.23 N 8.04 E
Buchs, Schw. 58 47.10 N 9.28 E
Buchufontein 158 30.18 S 19.36 E
Buchy 50 49.35 N 1.22 E
Bučina 60 48.58 N 13.36 E
Bucine 66 43.29 N 11.37 E
Buck, Lake ⊜ 162 19.38 S 130.21 E
Buckatunna 194 31.32 N 88.31 W
Buckatunna Creek ≃ 194 31.30 N 88.32 W
Buck Branch ≃ 284b 39.01 N 77.10 W
Buck Creek 216 40.29 N 86.46 W
Buck Creek ≃, U.S. 196 34.35 N 99.58 W
Buck Creek ≃, In., U.S. 218 39.37 N 85.56 W
Buck Creek ≃, In., U.S. 218 40.11 N 85.30 W
Buck Creek ≃, Ky., U.S. 192 36.59 N 84.29 W
Buck Creek ≃, Oh., U.S. 218 39.56 N 83.51 W
Buck Creek ≃, Pa., U.S. 285 40.15 N 74.50 W
Buckden, Eng., U.K. 42 52.17 N 0.16 W
Buckden, Eng., U.K. 44 54.12 N 2.05 W
Bückeburg 52 52.16 N 9.02 E
Bücken 52 52.46 N 9.07 E
Buckeye 200 33.22 N 112.34 W
Buckeye Creek ≃ 226 38.54 N 121.55 W
Buckeye Lake 188 39.56 N 82.28 W
Buckeystown 208 39.20 N 77.25 W
Buckfastleigh 42 50.29 N 3.46 W
Buckhannon 188 38.59 N 80.13 W
Buckhaven 46 56.11 N 3.03 W
Buck Hill Falls 210 41.11 N 75.15 W
Buck Hollow ≃ 224 45.10 N 120.50 W
Buckholts 222 30.52 N 97.08 W
Buckhorn ≃ 180 66.13 N 161.10 W
Buckhorn Draw V 196 30.39 N 100.52 W
Buckhorn Island State Park ♦ 284a 43.03 N 78.59 W
Buckhorn Lake ⊜, On., Can. 212 44.28 N 78.23 W
Buckhorn Lake ⊜, Ca., U.S. 228 34.50 N 117.59 W
Buckie 46 57.40 N 2.58 W
Buckingham, Austl. 168a 33.24 S 116.19 E
Buckingham, P.Q., Can. 188 45.35 N 75.25 W
Buckingham, Eng., U.K. 42 52.00 N 1.00 W
Buckingham, Pa., U.S. 208 40.18 N 75.01 W
Buckingham, Va., U.S. 192 37.32 N 78.37 W
Buckingham Bay ⊂ 164 12.10 S 135.46 E
Buckingham Palace ✦ 260 51.30 N 0.08 W
Buckinghamshire □[6] 42 51.45 N 0.48 W
Buck Island I 241n 17.48 N 64.37 W
Buck Lake ⊜, Ab., Can. 182 53.00 N 114.45 W
Buck Lake ⊜, On., Can. 212 45.25 N 79.24 W
Buckland, Austl. 166 42.37 S 147.43 E
Buckland, Eng., U.K. 260 51.15 N 0.15 W
Buckland, Ak., U.S. 180 65.59 N 161.07 W
Buckland, Ma., U.S. 207 42.35 N 72.47 W
Buckland, Oh., U.S. 216 40.37 N 84.16 W
Buckland Brewer 42 50.57 N 4.14 W
Buckland Common 260 51.45 N 0.39 W
Bucklands 158 29.03 S 23.44 E
Buckleboo 166 32.55 S 136.12 E
Buckley, Wales, U.K. 44 53.09 N 3.04 W
Buckley, Il., U.S. 216 40.36 N 88.02 W
Buckley, Wa., U.S. 224 47.09 N 122.01 W
Buckley ≃ 166 20.22 S 137.57 E
Buckley Bay ⊂ 9 68.16 S 148.12 E
Bucklin, Ks., U.S. 198 37.32 N 99.38 W
Bucklin, Mo., U.S. 194 39.46 N 92.53 W
Buck Lodge 284c 39.01 N 76.58 W
Buck Mountain ∧, Va., U.S. 192 36.40 N 81.15 W
Buck Mountain ∧, Wa., U.S. 202 48.26 N 119.50 W
Bucknell Heights 284c 38.46 N 77.04 W
Bucknell Manor 208 38.46 N 77.04 W
Buckner 218 38.23 N 85.26 W
Buckner Creek ≃ 198 38.11 N 99.34 W
Buckners Creek ≃ 222 29.53 N 96.53 W
Buckow 54 52.34 N 14.04 E
Buckow ◆[8] 264a 52.25 N 13.26 E
Bucks □[6] 208 40.19 N 75.08 W
Bucksburn 46 57.12 N 2.18 W
Buckshot Lake ⊜ 212 45.00 N 77.04 W
Buckskin Creek ≃ 218 39.14 N 83.17 W
Buckskin Gulch V 200 37.01 N 111.52 W
Bucks Knob ∧ 224 46.41 N 123.20 W
Bucksport 188 44.34 N 68.47 W
Bucktown 285 40.10 N 75.43 W
Bückwitz 54 52.52 N 12.29 E
Buc-Louis-Blériot, Aérodrome de ⊠ 261 48.45 N 2.05 E
Bučmany 78 51.04 N 28.04 E
Bucoda 224 46.47 N 122.52 W
Buco Zau 152 4.46 S 12.33 E
Bucquoy 50 50.08 N 2.42 E
Buctouche 186 46.28 N 64.43 W
Bucun 98 36.37 N 117.27 E
București (Bucharest) 38 44.26 N 26.06 E
Bucutua Island I 116 6.09 N 121.49 E
Bucy-lès-Pierrepont 50 49.39 N 3.54 E
Bucyrus 214 40.48 N 82.58 W
Bud 26 62.55 N 6.55 E
Buda, Il., U.S. 190 41.19 N 89.40 W
Buda, Tx., U.S. 196 30.05 N 97.51 W
Buda ◆[8] 264c 47.30 N 19.02 E
Buda Castle ⊥ 264c 47.30 N 19.02 E
Budafok ◆[8] 264c 47.26 N 19.02 E
Budagovo 88 54.38 N 100.08 E
Budai-hegység ⋏ 264c 47.31 N 18.58 E
Budakalász 264c 47.37 N 19.03 E
Budakeszi 264c 47.31 N 18.56 E
Buda-Kosel'ovo 76 52.43 N 30.34 E
Budalin 110 22.22 N 95.08 E
Budaörs 264c 47.27 N 18.58 E
Budapest, Magy. 30 47.30 N 19.05 E
Budapest, Magy. 264c 47.30 N 19.05 E
Budapest □[7] 264c 47.30 N 19.05 E
Búðardalur 24a 65.10 N 21.42 W
Budarin 80 47.54 N 42.36 E
Budarino 80 50.31 N 51.04 E
Budatétény ◆[8] 264c 47.25 N 19.01 E
Budaun 124 28.03 N 79.07 E
Budawang National Park ♦ 170 35.26 S 150.02 E
Budawang Range ⋏ 170 35.20 S 150.03 E
Budayuan 98 40.56 N 125.19 E
Budberg 263 51.32 N 6.38 E
Budbud 144 4.11 N 46.28 E
Budd Coast ⊥[2] 9 66.30 S 113.00 E
Buddh Gaya → Bodh Gaya 124 24.42 N 84.59 E
Budd Inlet ⊂ 224 47.06 N 122.54 W
Budd Lake 210 40.52 N 74.44 W
Buddtown 285 39.56 N 74.42 W
Buddu 140 11.54 N 24.08 E
Buddusò 71 40.35 N 9.15 E
Bude, Eng., U.K. 42 50.50 N 4.33 W
Bude, Ms., U.S. 194 31.27 N 90.51 W
Bude Bay ⊂ 42 50.50 N 4.37 W
Budel 52 51.17 N 5.35 E
Budelli, Isola I 71 41.17 N 9.21 E
Büdelsdorf 41 54.18 N 9.40 E
Büderich 52 51.37 N 6.34 E
Buderus 263 51.33 N 7.38 E
Budești 38 44.14 N 26.28 E
Budge Budge 126 22.27 N 88.10 E
Budhāthum 124 28.04 N 84.50 E
Budhhāta 126 22.36 N 89.10 E
Budhī Gaṇḍakī ≃ 124 27.48 N 84.45 E
Budhlāda 123 29.56 N 75.34 E
Budi 152 3.04 S 23.56 E
Büdingen 56 50.17 N 9.07 E
Búðir 24a 64.56 N 13.58 W
Budišov nad Budišovkou 30 49.47 N 17.38 E
Budjala 152 2.39 N 19.42 E
Budkov 61 49.03 N 15.39 E
Budleigh Salterton 42 50.38 N 3.20 W
Budogošč' 76 59.17 N 32.27 E
Budogovišči 76 53.36 N 36.18 E
Budoni 71 40.43 N 9.42 E
Bud'onnovka 80 50.52 N 52.48 E
Bud'onnovsk 84 44.46 N 44.09 E
Bud'onnovskaja 80 46.56 N 41.33 E
Bud'onnyj, S.S.S.R. 83 47.27 N 39.46 E
Bud'onnyj, S.S.S.R. 85 42.30 N 72.35 E
Budrio 64 44.32 N 11.32 E
Budslav 76 54.47 N 27.27 E
Budweis → České Budějovice 30 48.59 N 14.28 E
Budworth Mere ⊜ 262 53.17 N 2.31 W
Budy 78 49.53 N 36.02 E
Budylka 78 50.30 N 34.26 E
Budyně nad Ohří 54 50.22 N 14.09 E
Budžak ⋏[1] 78 46.10 N 29.00 E
Buea 152 4.09 N 9.14 E
Buëch ≃ 62 44.12 N 5.57 E
Buechel 218 38.11 N 85.39 W
Buehl Airport ⊠ 285 40.11 N 74.54 W
Bueil 50 48.56 N 1.27 E
Buela 152 5.55 S 14.33 E
Buell 219 39.02 N 91.27 W
Bue Marino, Grotta del ⊥[5] 71 40.15 N 9.38 E
Buena 208 39.30 N 74.55 W
Buena Esperanza 252 34.45 S 65.15 W
Buena Esperanza, Cabo de → Good Hope, Cape of ⟩ 158 34.24 S 18.30 E
Buena Park, Ca., U.S. 228 33.52 N 117.59 W
Buena Park, Wi., U.S. 216 42.48 N 88.14 W
Buenaventura, Col. 246 3.53 N 77.04 W
Buenaventura, Méx. 232 29.51 N 107.29 W
Buena Vista, Bol. 248 17.27 S 63.40 W
Buena Vista, Guat. 236 13.49 N 90.19 W
Buena Vista, Méx. 204 32.32 N 116.44 W
Buenavista, Méx. 234 22.36 N 100.09 W
Buenavista, Méx. 234 22.30 N 103.10 W
Buena Vista, Para. 252 26.08 S 56.03 W
Buenavista, Pil. 116 8.59 N 125.24 E
Buenavista, Pil. 116 13.15 N 121.57 E
Buenavista, Pil. 116 10.04 N 118.49 E
Buenavista, Pil. 116 7.15 N 122.16 E
Buena Vista, Co., U.S. 200 38.50 N 106.07 W
Buena Vista, Fl., U.S. 220 28.11 N 82.44 W
Buena Vista, Ga., U.S. 192 32.19 N 84.31 W
Buena Vista, Md., U.S. 284c 38.57 N 76.50 W
Buena Vista, Ms., U.S. 194 33.53 N 88.50 W
Buena Vista, Pa., U.S. 279b 40.17 N 79.48 W
Buena Vista, Va., U.S. 192 37.44 N 79.21 W
Buenavista, Bahía de ⊂ 240p 22.30 N 79.08 W
Buena Vista Canal ≍ 228 35.21 N 119.06 W
Buenavista de Cuéllar 234 18.27 N 99.25 W
Buena Vista Lake Bed ⊜ 204 35.11 N 119.17 W
Buenavista Revolución Mexicana 234 16.03 N 93.04 W
Buenavista Tomatlán 234 19.12 N 102.36 W
Buen Día 196 26.21 N 104.32 W
Buendia, Embalse de ⊜[1] 34 40.25 N 2.43 W
Buenga ≃ 152 6.07 S 15.58 E
Bueno ≃ 254 40.13 S 73.43 W
Bueno Brandão 256 22.27 S 46.21 W
Buenolândia 255 15.48 S 50.17 W
Buenópolis 255 17.54 S 44.11 W
Buenos Aires, Arg. 258 34.36 S 58.27 W
Buenos Aires, Arg. 288 34.36 S 58.27 W
Buenos Aires, Col. 246 3.02 N 76.38 W
Buenos Aires, C.R. 236 9.10 N 83.20 W
Buenos Aires □[4] 252 36.00 S 60.00 W
Buenos Aires, Lago (Lago General Carrera) ⊜ 254 46.35 S 72.00 W
Buen Pasto 254 45.05 S 69.28 W
Buer ◆[8] 263 51.36 N 7.03 E
Buerarema 255 14.57 S 39.19 W
Buerāt, Bi'r ⊤[4] 142 28.59 N 32.10 E
Buertuokai 85 39.35 N 74.58 E
Buesaco 246 1.23 N 77.09 W
Buescher State Park ♦ 222 30.02 N 97.09 W
Buet, Le ∧ 58 46.02 N 6.52 E
Buey ≃ 240p 20.28 N 77.05 W
Bufalotta, Fosso della ≃ 267a 41.59 N 12.30 E
Buffalo, Il., U.S. 219 39.51 N 89.25 W
Buffalo, In., U.S. 216 40.53 N 86.45 W
Buffalo, Ks., U.S. 198 37.42 N 95.41 W
Buffalo, Mn., U.S. 190 45.10 N 93.52 W
Buffalo, Mo., U.S. 194 37.38 N 93.05 W
Buffalo, N.Y., U.S. 210 42.53 N 78.52 W
Buffalo, N.Y., U.S. 284a 42.53 N 78.52 W
Buffalo, Oh., U.S. 188 39.54 N 81.31 W
Buffalo, Ok., U.S. 196 36.50 N 99.37 W
Buffalo, S.C., U.S. 192 34.43 N 81.41 W
Buffalo, S.D., U.S. 198 45.35 N 103.32 W
Buffalo, Tx., U.S. 222 31.28 N 96.04 W
Buffalo, Wy., U.S. 202 44.20 N 106.41 W
Buffalo ≃, Can. 176 60.55 N 115.00 W
Buffalo ≃, S. Afr. 158 28.43 S 30.37 E
Buffalo ≃, Ar., U.S. 194 36.10 N 92.26 W
Buffalo ≃, Mn., U.S. 198 47.06 N 96.49 W
Buffalo ≃, Ms., U.S. 194 31.04 N 91.34 W
Buffalo ≃, N.Y., U.S. 284a 42.53 N 78.53 W
Buffalo ≃, Tn., U.S. 194 36.00 N 87.50 W
Buffalo ≃, Wi., U.S. 190 44.22 N 91.55 W
Buffalo, State University College at ✦[2] 284a 42.56 N 78.53 W
Buffalo Airpark ⊠ 284a 42.52 N 78.43 W
Buffalo Bayou ≃ 222 29.46 N 95.05 W
Buffalo Bill Ranch State Historical Park ♦ 198 41.10 N 100.48 W
Buffalo Bill Reservoir ⊜[1] 202 44.29 N 109.13 W
Buffalo Bill State Park ♦ 202 44.30 N 109.14 W
Buffalo Center 190 43.23 N 93.56 W
Buffalo Coast Guard Base ■ 284a 42.52 N 78.54 W
Buffalo Creek ≃, U.S. 198 45.57 N 102.56 W
Buffalo Creek ≃, U.S. 214 40.16 N 80.37 W
Buffalo Creek ≃, Il., U.S. 278 42.08 N 87.55 W
Buffalo Creek ≃, Ia., U.S. 190 42.06 N 91.18 W
Buffalo Creek ≃, Ks., U.S. 198 39.35 N 97.43 W
Buffalo Creek ≃, Ky., U.S. 218 38.28 N 83.03 W
Buffalo Creek ≃, Mn., U.S. 198 44.51 N 94.00 W
Buffalo Creek ≃, N.Y., U.S. 210 42.52 N 78.47 W
Buffalo Creek ≃, Ok., U.S. 196 36.47 N 99.15 W
Buffalo Creek ≃, Pa., U.S. 208 40.29 N 77.08 W
Buffalo Creek ≃, Pa., U.S. 210 40.58 N 76.53 W
Buffalo Creek ≃, Pa., U.S. 214 40.40 N 79.41 W
Buffalo Grove 216 42.09 N 87.57 W
Buffalo Harbor ⊂ 284a 42.51 N 78.52 W
Buffalo Lake 198 44.44 N 94.37 W
Buffalo Lake ⊜, Ab., Can. 182 52.27 N 112.54 W
Buffalo Lake ⊜, N.T., Can. 176 60.10 N 115.30 W
Buffalo Lake ⊜[1] 196 34.54 N 102.07 W
Buffalo Museum of Science ✦ 284a 42.54 N 78.51 W
Buffalo Narrows 184 55.51 N 108.30 W
Buffalo National River ♦ 194 35.58 N 92.53 W
Buffalo Pound Lake ⊜ 184 50.39 N 105.30 W
Buffalo Pound Provincial Park ♦ 184 50.36 N 105.30 W
Buffalo Run ≃ 279b 40.12 N 79.37 W
Buffalo Zoo ♦ 284a 42.56 N 78.51 W
Buffels ≃, S. Afr. 156 29.41 S 17.03 E
Buffels ≃, S. Afr. 158 33.45 S 21.11 E
Buffington Harbor ⊂ 278 41.38 N 87.25 W
Buffum, Lake ⊜ 220 27.48 N 81.40 W
Buford, Ga., U.S. 192 34.07 N 84.00 W
Buford, Oh., U.S. 218 39.04 N 83.50 W
Buford Dam ◆[6] 192 34.11 N 84.03 W
Buftea 38 44.34 N 25.57 E
Bug ≃ 22 52.31 N 21.05 E
Buga, Col. 246 3.54 N 76.17 W
Buga, Nig. 150 8.30 N 7.21 E
Bugajevka, S.S.S.R. 83 48.25 N 38.53 E
Bugajevka, S.S.S.R. 83 49.39 N 39.42 E
Bugajevka, S.S.S.R. 83 49.28 N 37.23 E
Bugalagrande 246 4.11 N 76.09 W
Bugala Island I 154 0.40 S 32.20 E
Bugallon 116 15.57 N 120.13 E
Buganga 154 0.03 S 31.59 E
Bugasong 116 11.03 N 122.04 E
Bugat, Mong. 86 48.59 N 90.10 E
Bugat, Mong. 88 47.55 N 101.16 E
Bugbrooke 42 52.12 N 1.01 W
Bug Catooti 144 10.44 N 50.35 E
Buğdaylı 130 40.13 N 27.46 E
Bugeat 32 45.35 N 1.59 E
Bugel, Ujung ⟩ 115a 6.26 S 111.03 E
Bugene 154 1.35 S 31.08 E
Bugey ◆[1] 58 45.55 N 5.30 E
Buggenhout 50 51.01 N 4.12 E
Buggerru 71 39.24 N 8.24 E
Bugio I 266c 38.39 N 9.18 W
Bugiri 154 0.34 N 33.45 E
Bugle 42 50.24 N 4.47 W
Bug Méridional → Južnyj Bug ≃ 78 46.59 N 31.58 E
Bugojno 36 44.03 N 17.27 E
Bugøynes 24 69.58 N 29.39 E
Bugrino 24 68.48 N 49.09 E
Bugry, S.S.S.R. 76 58.46 N 35.15 E
Bugry, S.S.S.R. 265a 60.04 N 30.24 E
Bugsanga ≃ 116 12.26 N 120.59 E
Bugsuk Island I 116 8.15 N 117.18 E
Bugt, Zhg. 89 48.46 N 121.57 E
Bugt, Zhg. 98 42.20 N 120.43 E
Buguba 164 3.41 S 137.30 E
Buguey 116 18.17 N 121.50 E
Bugui Point ⟩ 116 12.36 N 123.14 E
Bugul'dejka 88 52.33 N 106.05 E
Bugul'ma 80 54.33 N 52.48 E
Bugul'minsko-Belebejevskaja vozvyšennost' ⋏[1] 80 54.54 N 52.42 E
Bugun' ≃ 85 42.58 N 68.35 E
Bugun'skoje vodochranilišče ⊜[1] 85 42.45 N 69.05 E
Buguruslan 80 53.39 N 52.26 E
Buh ≃ 102 36.58 N 99.48 E
Buhanhua 104 42.39 N 122.46 E
Bū Ḥashīshah, Thamad ⊤[4] 146 26.23 N 18.47 E
Buḩayrah, Rayyāḩ al- ≍ 142 30.43 N 30.45 E
Buḩaythān, Jabal al- ∧ 132 30.55 N 35.53 E
Buhera 154 19.18 S 31.29 E
Buhi 116 13.26 N 123.31 E
Buhi, Lake ⊜ 116 13.26 N 123.31 E
Bühl, B.R.D. 56 48.42 N 8.08 E
Buhl, Fr. 58 47.56 N 7.11 E
Buhl, Id., U.S. 202 42.35 N 114.45 W
Buhl, Mn., U.S. 190 47.29 N 92.46 W
Buhler 198 38.08 N 97.46 W
Bühler ≃ 56 49.10 N 9.47 E
Bühlertal 56 48.41 N 8.10 E
Buhuai 120 33.22 N 80.36 E
Buhuși 38 46.43 N 26.41 E
Bui Dam ◆[6] 150 8.22 N 2.10 W
Buie, Loch ⊂ 46 56.20 N 5.52 W
Buile Hill Park ♦ 262 53.29 N 2.18 W
Builth Wells 42 52.09 N 3.24 W
Buin, Chile 252 33.44 S 70.45 W
Buin, Pap. N. Gui. 175e 6.50 S 155.44 E
Buin, Piz ∧ 58 46.50 N 10.08 E
Buinen 52 52.55 N 6.50 E
Buinsk, S.S.S.R. 80 55.12 N 47.03 E
Buinsk, S.S.S.R. 80 54.57 N 48.17 E
Buíque 250 8.37 S 37.09 W
Buis-les-Baronnies 62 44.16 N 5.16 E
Buitenpost 52 53.15 N 6.09 E
Buj 80 58.30 N 41.30 E
Buj ≃ 80 56.13 N 54.12 E
Bujaki 24 59.03 N 48.40 E
Bujalance 34 37.54 N 4.22 W
Bujant, Mong. 86 48.33 N 89.34 E
Bujant, Mong. 86 48.10 N 91.55 E
Bujant ≃ 88 47.08 N 97.38 E
Bujant-Ovoo 102 44.58 N 107.05 E
Bujaraloz 34 41.30 N 0.09 W
Buje 36 45.24 N 13.40 E
Buji 102 33.58 N 95.22 E
Bujnaksk 84 42.49 N 47.07 E
Bujnoviči 78 51.52 N 28.33 E
Bujr nuur ⊜ 88 47.48 N 117.42 E
Bujukly 89 49.30 N 142.47 E
Bujumbura 154 3.23 S 29.22 E
Bük, Magy. 61 47.23 N 16.45 E
Buk, Pol. 30 52.22 N 16.31 E
Buka 85 40.48 N 69.11 E
Bukačača 88 52.59 N 116.55 E
Bukačevcy 78 49.15 N 24.29 E
Buka Island I 175e 5.15 S 154.35 E
Bukama 154 9.12 S 25.51 E
Būkān, Īrān 128 36.31 N 46.12 E
Bukan', S.S.S.R. 76 53.55 N 34.42 E
Bukanovskaja 80 49.42 N 42.18 E

ENGLISH
Name Page Lat.°' Long.°'

Buka Passage)(175e 5.25 S 154.41 E
Bukarest → București 38 44.26 N 26.06 E
Bukarevo 82 55.57 N 36.44 E
Bukavu 154 2.30 S 28.52 E
Bukene 154 4.14 S 32.53 E
Bukhara → Buchara 128 39.48 N 64.25 E
Bukhayt, Bi'r ⊤[4] 142 29.13 N 32.17 E
Bukide, Pulau I 112 3.47 N 125.36 E
Bukidnon □[4] 116 8.00 N 125.00 E
Bukima 154 1.48 S 33.25 E
Bukit Baharu 114 2.13 N 102.16 E
Bukitbatu 114 1.27 N 102.00 E
Bukit Betong 114 4.15 N 101.56 E
Bukit Fraser 114 3.43 N 101.45 E
Bukit Kachi 114 6.24 N 100.32 E
Bukit Mandai 271c 1.25 N 103.45 E
Bukit Mertajam 114 5.22 N 100.28 E
Bukit Panjang 271c 1.23 N 103.46 E
Bukit Serok 114 2.55 N 102.50 E
Bukit Timah 271c 1.20 N 103.47 E
Bukit Timah Race Course ♦ 271c 1.20 N 103.48 E
Bukittinggi 112 0.19 S 100.22 E
Bükk ⋏ 30 48.05 N 20.30 E
Bukoba 154 1.20 S 31.49 E
Bukombe 154 3.31 S 32.03 E
Bukovica ◆[1] 36 44.10 N 15.40 E
Bukovina □[9] 78 48.00 N 25.30 E
Bukrino 82 54.48 N 36.14 E
Bukuka 88 51.11 N 116.39 E
Bukukun 88 49.27 N 111.08 E
Bukum, Pulau I 271c 1.14 N 103.47 E
Bukumbirwa 154 0.46 S 28.44 E
Bukum Kechil, Pulau I 271c 1.14 N 103.46 E
Bukunga 154 7.41 S 25.56 E
Bukuru 150 9.48 N 8.51 E
Bukuya 154 0.41 N 31.50 E
Bula 164 3.06 S 130.30 E
Bula ≃ 80 55.12 N 48.23 E
Bula Atumba 152 8.40 S 14.48 E
Bulacan □[4] 116 15.00 N 121.05 E
Bulacaue Point ⟩ 116 11.36 N 123.09 E
Bülach 58 47.31 N 8.32 E
Bulajevo 86 54.54 N 70.26 E
Bulak 88 51.02 N 115.21 E
Bulaka ≃ 164 8.06 S 139.12 E
Bulak Gölü ⊜ 130 38.32 N 32.55 E
Bulalacao 116 12.20 N 121.20 E
Bulalacao Island I 116 11.45 N 120.10 E
Bulalacui Point ⟩ 116 11.17 N 124.03 E
Bulan, Pil. 116 12.40 N 123.52 E
Bulan, Pil. 116 6.44 N 124.47 E
Bulan, Ky., U.S. 192 37.18 N 83.09 W
Bulanaš 86 57.16 N 62.00 E
Bulancak 130 40.57 N 38.14 E
Bulandshahr 124 28.24 N 77.51 E
Bulanicha 86 52.48 N 84.57 E
Bulanık 130 39.05 N 42.15 E
Bulan Island I 116 6.08 N 121.50 E
Bulanovo 86 52.27 N 55.10 E
Būlāq 140 25.12 N 30.32 E
Būlāq ◆[8] 273c 30.04 N 31.14 E
Būlāq ad-Dakrūr 273c 30.02 N 31.11 E
Bulava 89 51.55 N 140.25 E
Bulavinovka 83 49.25 N 38.58 E
Bulawa, Gunung ∧ 112 0.30 N 123.34 E
Bulawayo 154 20.09 S 28.36 E
Bulbjerg ∧[2] 26 57.09 N 9.02 E
Bulbul 130 36.46 N 36.49 E
Bulbul, Wādī V 140 10.59 N 24.33 E
Bulcherry Island I 126 21.33 N 88.31 E
Buldan 130 38.03 N 28.51 E
Buldāna 122 20.32 N 76.11 E
Buldern 52 51.52 N 7.22 E
Buldibuyo 248 8.07 S 77.22 W
Buldir Island I 181a 52.21 N 175.54 E
Buldon 116 7.33 N 124.25 E
Buldurtinskij 80 50.05 N 53.11 E
Buldyrty ≃ 80 49.48 N 52.34 E
Bulembu 158 25.56 S 31.06 E
Bulga 170 32.39 S 151.01 E
Bulgakovka 83 49.11 N 38.33 E
Bulgakovo 76 55.14 N 32.08 E
Bulgan, Mong. 86 46.53 N 91.05 E
Bulgan, Mong. 88 48.45 N 103.34 E
Bulgan, Mong. 102 44.05 N 103.32 E
Bulgan □[4] 88 49.00 N 103.30 E
Bulgaria (Bâlgarija) □[1], Europe 22 43.00 N 25.00 E
Bulgaria (Bâlgarija) □[1], Europe 38 43.00 N 25.00 E
Bulgarie → Bulgaria □[1] 38 43.00 N 25.00 E
Bulgarien → Bulgaria □[1] 38 43.00 N 25.00 E
Bulger 214 40.23 N 80.20 W
Bulgnéville 58 48.13 N 5.50 E
Bulgroo 166 25.48 S 143.59 E
Bulhale 144 5.20 N 46.29 E
Buliluyan 116 8.20 N 117.12 E
Buliluyan, Cape ⟩ 116 8.20 N 117.11 E
Bulim 271c 1.22 N 103.43 E
Bulimba 171a 27.25 S 153.04 E
Bulkeley 241g 13.07 N 59.32 W
Bulki 144 6.10 N 36.40 E
Bulkington 42 52.29 N 1.25 W
Bulkley ≃ 182 55.13 N 127.40 W
Bulkley Ranges ⋏ 182 54.30 N 127.30 W
Bull ≃ 182 49.28 N 115.26 W
Bullabulling 162 31.01 S 120.32 E
Bullaque ≃ 34 38.59 N 4.17 W
Bullara 162 22.40 S 114.03 E
Bullard 222 32.08 N 95.19 W
Bulla Regia ⊥ 36 36.34 N 8.46 E
Bullas 34 38.03 N 1.40 W
Bullaxaar 144 10.23 N 44.25 E
Bullay 56 50.03 N 7.08 E
Bull Creek ≃, Nv., U.S. 204 38.43 N 115.34 W
Bull Creek ≃, N.Y., U.S. 284a 43.03 N 78.50 W
Bull Creek ≃, Oh., U.S. 214 40.42 N 80.32 W
Bull Creek ≃, S.D., U.S. 198 43.41 N 99.28 W
Bull Creek ≃, S.D., U.S. 198 45.40 N 103.18 W
Bull Creek ≃, Tx., U.S. 196 32.36 N 101.10 W
Bulldog 164 7.45 S 146.25 E
Bulle 58 46.37 N 7.04 E
Bullenbaai ⊂ 241s 12.11 N 69.04 W
Buller ≃ 172 41.44 S 171.35 E
Buller, Mount ∧ 169 37.09 S 146.26 E
Bullfinch 162 30.59 S 119.06 E
Bullfrog Creek ≃ 200 37.19 N 110.44 W
Bull Harbour 182 50.54 N 127.55 W
Bullhead 198 45.45 N 101.04 W
Bullhead City 204 35.08 N 114.34 W
Bull Hide Creek ≃ 222 31.23 N 97.01 W
Bull Hill ∧[2] 262 53.40 N 2.21 W
Bulli 170 34.20 S 150.55 E
Bullicame ♦ 66 42.22 N 12.04 E
Büllingen 56 50.25 N 6.16 E
Bullich 171b 36.12 S 147.20 E
Bullion 261 48.37 N 2.00 E
Bull Lake ⊜[1] 202 43.11 N 109.07 W
Bull Lake Creek ≃ 202 43.14 N 109.02 W
Bull Mountain ∧ 202 46.05 N 112.04 W
Bullock 192 36.30 N 78.33 W
Bullock Creek 166 17.43 S 144.31 E
Bullock Creek ≃ 166 21.40 S 145.09 E
Bulloo ≃ 166 28.43 S 142.30 E
Bulloo Downs 166 28.31 S 142.57 E
Bulloo Lake ⊜ 166 28.43 S 142.25 E
Bulloo River Overflow ≚ 166 28.50 S 142.40 E
Bullpound Creek ≃ 182 51.05 N 111.58 W
Bull Run ≃, Or., U.S. 224 45.26 N 122.15 W
Bull Run ≃, Va., U.S. 208 38.43 N 77.23 W

DEUTSCH
Name Seite Breite°' Länge°' E = Ost

Bull Run Lake ⊜ 224 45.27 N 121.50 W
Bull Run Reservoir Number 1 ⊜[1], Or., U.S. 224 45.30 N 122.04 W
Bull Run Reservoir Number 2 ⊜[1], Or., U.S. 224 45.28 N 122.10 W
Bullrun Rock ∧ 202 44.21 N 118.17 W
Bulls 172 40.10 S 175.23 E
Bulls Bay ⊂ 192 32.59 N 79.33 W
Bullsbrook 168a 31.40 S 116.01 E
Bulls Gap 192 36.15 N 83.05 W
Bull Shoals 194 36.23 N 92.34 W
Bull Shoals Lake ⊜[1] 194 36.30 N 92.50 W
Bullskin Creek ≃ 218 38.10 N 85.19 W
Bullville 210 41.33 N 74.22 W
Bully Creek ≃ 202 43.58 N 117.15 W
Bully Hill 214 41.22 N 79.50 W
Bully-les-Mines 50 50.26 N 2.43 E
Bulmke-Hüllen ◆[8] 263 51.31 N 7.06 E
Bulnaj nuruu ⋏ 88 49.05 N 98.30 E
Bulnes 252 36.44 S 72.18 W
Bulo Ghedudo 144 2.52 N 43.01 E
Bulolo 164 7.10 S 146.40 E
Bulpham 260 51.33 N 0.22 E
Bulpitt 219 39.35 N 89.26 W
Bulsār 122 20.38 N 72.56 E
Bulstrode ≃ 206 46.02 N 72.15 W
Bultei 71 40.27 N 9.03 E
Bultfontein 158 28.20 S 26.05 E
Buluan 116 6.44 N 124.47 E
Buluan ≃ 116 6.47 N 124.47 E
Buluan, Lake ⊜ 115 6.40 N 124.49 E
Buluduku 114 2.20 N 98.14 E
Bulugansk 88 52.24 N 110.23 E
Bulukumba 112 5.33 S 120.11 E
Bulukuto 152 0.12 S 21.42 E
Bululawang 115a 8.05 S 112.38 E
Bulungu, Zaïre 152 4.33 S 18.36 E
Bulungu, Zaïre 152 6.04 S 21.54 E
Bulupayung 114 1.38 N 99.11 E
Bulusan 116 12.45 N 124.08 E
Bulusan Volcano ∧ 116 12.46 N 124.03 E
Bulwater 158 32.29 S 21.48 E
Bulwer 158 29.46 S 29.47 E
Bulyčevo 82 55.06 N 37.15 E
Bulyee 162 32.22 S 117.31 E
Bumba 152 2.11 N 22.28 E
Bumbah, Khalīj al- ⊂ 146 32.20 N 23.10 E
Bumbire Island I 154 1.40 S 31.53 E
Bumbles Green 260 51.44 N 0.02 E
Bumbo 152 6.55 S 19.16 E
Bumbu ≃ 273b 4.23 S 15.18 E
Bumbulan 112 0.29 N 122.04 E
Bumbun, Pulau I 112 4.27 N 118.40 E
Bumbuna 150 9.03 N 11.44 W
Bumbunga Lake ⊜ 168b 33.54 S 138.11 E
Bumiayu 115a 7.15 S 109.00 E
Bumijawa 115a 7.10 S 109.07 E
Bumkin Island I 283 42.17 N 70.54 W
Bumping ≃ 224 46.59 N 121.06 W
Bumping Lake ⊜ 224 46.52 N 121.19 W
Bumpus, Mount ∧[2] 176 69.33 N 112.40 W
Bumtang ≃ 124 26.56 N 90.51 E
Bumu Hu ⊜ 120 31.15 N 91.10 E
Buna, Kenya 154 2.47 N 39.31 E
Buna, Pap. N. Gui. 164 8.40 S 148.25 E
Buna, Tx., U.S. 194 30.26 N 93.58 W
Buna, Zaïre 152 3.15 S 18.59 E
Bunagāti 126 23.19 N 89.25 E
Bunai 164 2.11 S 147.14 E
Bunaj 85 38.26 N 71.32 E
Bun'atino 82 56.24 N 37.15 E
Bunavista 196 35.39 N 101.28 W
Bunawan 116 8.12 N 125.57 E
Bunazi 154 1.13 S 31.24 E
Bunbeg 48 55.03 N 8.18 W
Bunbury 168a 33.19 S 115.38 E
Bunceton 194 38.47 N 92.47 W
Bunclody 48 52.38 N 6.40 W
Buncrana 48 55.08 N 7.27 W
Bundaberg 166 24.52 S 152.21 E
Bundanoon 170 34.39 S 150.18 E
Bundarra 166 30.10 S 151.05 E
Bunde, B.R.D. 52 53.11 N 7.16 E
Bünde, B.R.D. 52 52.12 N 8.35 E
Bunde, Ned. 56 50.54 N 5.45 E
Bundeena 274a 34.05 S 151.09 E
Bundenthal 56 49.06 N 7.48 E
Bundesrepublik Deutschland → Germany, Federal Republic of □[1] 30 51.00 N 9.00 E
Bundey ≃ 162 21.46 S 135.37 E
Bündheim 54 51.53 N 10.32 E
Būndi, India 120 25.27 N 75.39 E
Bundi, Pap. N. Gui. 164 5.40 S 145.15 E
Bundick Creek ≃ 194 30.36 N 92.57 W
Bundoora 274b 37.42 S 145.04 E
Bundoran 48 54.28 N 8.17 W
Būndu, India 124 23.11 N 85.35 E
Bundu, S. Afr. 158 29.45 S 22.02 E
Bunduqiyah 154 5.06 N 30.53 E
Bund'ur 86 57.32 N 82.01 E
Buner □[9] 123 34.35 N 72.35 E
Bunessan 46 56.19 N 6.14 W
Bunga 150 11.04 N 9.38 E
Bunga ≃ 150 11.23 N 9.56 E
Bungamas 112 3.42 S 102.23 E
Bungay 42 52.28 N 1.26 E
Bungbulang 115a 7.27 S 107.35 E
Bunge 26 57.51 N 19.01 E
Bungegep 164 7.48 S 139.52 E
Bungendore 171b 35.15 S 149.27 E
Bunger Hills ⋏[2] 9 66.17 S 100.47 E
Bung Kan 110 18.23 N 103.37 E
Bungku 112 2.33 S 121.58 E
Bungo 152 7.26 S 15.23 E
Bungoma 154 0.34 N 34.34 E
Bungonia 170 34.51 S 149.57 E
Bungo-suidō)(92 33.00 N 132.13 E
Bungo-takada 96 33.33 N 131.27 E
Bungsberg ∧[2] 54 54.12 N 10.43 E
Bungtlang 120 22.20 N 92.46 E
Bungu 154 7.38 S 39.03 E
Buni ≃ 115a 7.26 S 106.47 E
Bunia 154 1.34 N 30.15 E
Bunianga 152 3.34 S 20.06 E
Būnīken, Kūh-e ∧ 128 26.46 N 58.12 E
Buninyong 169 37.39 S 143.53 E
Buninyong, Mount ∧ 169 37.39 S 143.56 E
Bunji 123 35.40 N 74.36 E
Bunkeflo strand 41 55.33 N 12.57 E
Bunker 194 37.27 N 91.12 W
Bunker Group II 166 23.48 S 152.20 E
Bunker Hill, Il., U.S. 219 39.02 N 89.57 W
Bunker Hill, In., U.S. 216 40.40 N 86.06 W
Bunker Hill, Or., U.S. 202 43.21 N 124.12 W
Bunker Hill, Tx., U.S. 222 29.46 N 95.32 W
Bunker Hill ∧ 204 39.15 N 117.08 W
Bunker Hill Monument ⊥ 283 42.22 N 71.04 W
Bunkeya 154 10.07 S 27.17 E
Bunkie 194 30.57 N 92.10 W
Bunkyō ◆[8] 268 35.43 N 139.45 E
Bunnahowen 48 54.11 N 9.54 W
Bunnell 192 29.27 N 81.15 W
Bunnik 52 52.04 N 5.12 E
Bünningstedt 52 53.41 N 10.13 E
Bunola 214 40.14 N 79.56 W
Bun Plains ≚ 154 0.44 N 40.42 E
Bunratty Castle ⊥ 48 52.42 N 8.48 W
Bunschoten 52 52.14 N 5.22 E
Bunsuru ≃ 150 13.21 N 6.23 E
Bunta 112 0.48 S 122.10 E
Buntine 162 29.59 S 116.34 E
Buntingford 42 51.57 N 0.01 W
Buntok 112 1.42 S 114.48 E
Bununu Dass 150 10.00 N 9.31 E
Bunut 112 0.46 N 112.30 E
Bunyambili 154 2.21 S 29.25 E
Bünyan 130 38.51 N 35.52 E

Symbols in the index entries represent the broad categories identified in the key at the right. Symbols with superior numbers (⋏[1]) identify subcategories (see complete key on page I · 1).

Symbole im Register stellen die rechts im Schlüssel erklärten Kategorien dar. Symbole mit hochgestellten Ziffern (⋏[1]) bezeichnen Unterabteilungen einer Kategorie (vgl. vollständiger Schlüssel auf Seite I · 1).

Los símbolos incluídos en el texto del índice representan las grandes categorias identificadas con la clave a la derecha. Los símbolos con numeros en su parte superior (⋏[1]) identifican las subcategorias (véase la clave completa en la página I · 1).

Les symboles de l'index représentent les catégories indiquées dans la légende à droite. Les symboles suivis d'un indice (⋏[1]) représentent des sous-catégories (voir légende complète à la page I · 1).

Os símbolos incluídos no texto do índice representam as grandes categorias identificadas com a chave à direita. Os símbolos com números em sua parte superior (⋏[1]) identificam as subcategorias (veja-se a chave completa à página I · 1).

∧ Mountain	Berg	Montaña	Montagne	Montanha
⋏ Mountains	Gebirge	Montañas	Montagnes	Montanhas
)(Pass	Paß	Paso	Col	Passo
V Valley, Canyon	Tal, Cañon	Valle, Cañón	Vallée, Canyon	Vale, Canhão
≚ Plain	Ebene	Llano	Plaine	Planície
⟩ Cape	Kap	Cabo	Cap	Cabo
I Island	Insel	Isla	Île	Ilha
II Islands	Inseln	Islas	Îles	Ilhas
♦ Other Topographic Features	Andere Topographische Objekte	Otros Elementos Topográficos	Autres données topographiques	Outros acidentes topográficos

ESPAÑOL

Nombre	Página	Lat.°′	Long.°′ W = Oeste
Bunyip	169	38.06 S	145.43 E
Bunyip ≃	169	38.13 S	145.27 E
Bunyolo	34	39.25 N	0.47 W
Bunyrevo	82	54.34 N	37.09 E
Bunyu, Pulau I	112	3.30 N	117.50 E
Bunza	150	12.08 N	4.00 E
Buochs	58	46.58 N	8.22 E
Buol	112	1.10 N	121.26 E
Buolkalach	74	72.56 N	119.50 E
Buonalbergo	68	41.13 N	14.59 E
Buona Vista	271c	1.16 N	103.47 E
Buon Bu N'jang	110	12.06 N	107.40 E
Buonconvento	66	43.08 N	11.29 E
Buon Me Thuot	110	12.40 N	108.03 E
Buon Mrong	110	12.48 N	108.28 E
Buon Ngo	110	12.30 N	108.28 E
Buon Thach Hom	110	12.17 N	108.48 E
Buon Ya Soup	110	13.05 N	107.52 E
Buor-Chaja, guba c	74	71.30 N	131.00 E
Buor-Chaja, mys ›	74	71.56 N	132.40 E
Bupul	164	7.31 S	140.52 E
Buqay'āwīyah, Qā' al- ≃	132	32.03 N	37.07 E
Buqayq	128	25.56 N	49.40 E
Buqda Koosaar	144	4.31 N	44.49 E
Buqde Caqable	144	4.04 N	45.15 E
Buquim	250	11.09 S	37.37 W
Buquira ≃	256	23.10 S	45.54 W
Buquirivu ≃	287b	23.28 S	46.28 W
Buqūm, Ḥarrat al- ▴9	144	20.54 N	42.00 E
Bur	88	58.47 N	107.01 E
Bura, Kenya	154	3.30 S	38.18 E
Bura, Kenya	154	1.06 S	39.57 E
Bura Gaurānga ≃1	126	22.00 N	90.33 E
Burakin	162	30.31 S	117.10 E
Buraly	80	55.04 N	52.52 E
Buram	140	10.49 N	25.10 E
Buran	86	48.04 N	85.15 E
Burang	120	30.16 N	81.14 E
Burangulovo	86	53.26 N	58.23 E
Buranhém ≃	255	16.27 S	39.04 W
Burankol'	86	46.14 N	54.12 E
Burannoje	86	50.59 N	54.28 E
Burano ≃	66	43.37 N	12.40 E
Burao Kibir	144	8.42 N	45.29 E
Burāq	132	33.10 N	36.29 E
Burāri ⬌8	272a	28.46 N	77.12 E
Buras	194	29.21 N	89.31 W
Buraševo	82	56.44 N	35.52 E
Bur'atskaja Avtonomnaja Sovetskaja Socialističeskaja Respublika □3	88	53.00 N	109.00 E
Burauen	116	10.58 N	124.53 E
Burayd, Bi'r ⊤4	142	29.08 N	32.07 E
Buraydah	128	26.20 N	43.59 E
Burayk	146	26.33 N	13.08 E
Buraykah	132	32.50 N	36.34 E
Burbach	56	50.45 N	8.05 E
Burbage, Eng., U.K.	42	51.20 N	1.40 W
Burbage, Eng., U.K.	262	53.15 N	1.56 W
Burbank, Ca., U.S.	226	37.19 N	121.55 W
Burbank, Ca., U.S.	228	34.10 N	118.18 W
Burbank, Il., U.S.	216	41.45 N	87.45 W
Burbank, Oh., U.S.	214	40.59 N	81.59 W
Burbank, Wa., U.S.	202	46.12 N	119.00 W
Burbank Studios ʊ3	280	34.09 N	118.21 W
Burbure	50	50.32 N	2.28 E
Burç	130	37.02 N	37.10 E
Burcei	71	39.21 N	9.21 E
Burcevo	82	55.02 N	38.09 E
Burcher	166	33.32 S	147.18 E
Burcin	62	45.26 N	5.26 E
Burco	144	9.31 N	45.34 E
Burda	124	25.50 N	77.35 E
Burdalyk	128	38.25 N	64.20 E
Burdekin ≃	166	19.39 S	147.30 E
Burdekin Falls ∟	166	20.39 S	147.09 E
Burden	198	37.18 N	96.45 W
Burdeos → Bordeaux, Fr.	32	44.50 N	0.34 W
Burdeos, Pil.	116	14.51 N	121.58 E
Burdeos Bay c	116	14.44 N	122.06 E
Burdett, Ab., Can.	182	49.50 N	111.32 W
Burdett, Ks., U.S.	198	38.11 N	99.31 W
Burdett, N.Y., U.S.	210	42.25 N	76.50 W
Burdul	272c	19.07 N	73.07 E
Burdur	130	37.43 N	30.17 E
Burdur □4	130	37.30 N	30.00 E
Burdur Gölü ◎	130	37.44 N	30.12 E
Burdwood Bank ✧3	18	54.15 S	59.00 W
Bure, Ityo.	144	8.15 N	35.09 E
Bure, Ityo.	144	10.47 N	37.06 E
Bure ≃	42	52.37 N	1.43 E
Bure, Pic de ∧	62	44.38 N	5.56 E
Bureå	26	64.37 N	21.12 E
Bureälven ≃	26	64.37 N	21.13 E
Bureg Changaj	88	48.14 N	103.57 E
Bureinskij chrebet ⋀	89	50.35 N	133.35 E
Bureja	89	49.52 N	129.48 E
Bureja ≃	89	49.25 N	129.35 E
Burekup	168a	33.19 S	115.49 E
Büren, B.R.D.	52	51.33 N	8.33 E
Büren, Mong.	88	47.13 N	95.54 E
Büren an der Aare	58	47.08 N	7.23 E
Büren Chaan	88	49.29 N	99.14 E
Bürengijn nuruu ⋀	88	49.15 N	104.30 E
Bures	261	48.57 N	1.58 E
Bures-sur-Yvette	261	48.42 N	2.10 E
Burey-en-Vaux	58	48.34 N	5.40 E
Burfjord	24	69.56 N	22.00 E
Burford, On., Can.	212	43.06 N	80.26 W
Burford, Eng., U.K.	42	51.49 N	1.38 W
Būr Fu'ād ⬌8	142	31.15 N	32.19 E
Burg, B.R.D.	56	50.42 N	8.19 E
Burg, D.D.R.	54	51.49 N	14.08 E
Burg, D.D.R.	54	52.16 N	11.51 E
Burg ⬌8	263	51.08 N	7.09 E
Burg, Schloss ⊥	263	51.08 N	7.10 E
Burga	76	58.45 N	32.29 E
Burgas	38	42.30 N	27.28 E
Burgas □4	130	42.10 N	27.00 E
Burgaski zaliv c	38	42.30 N	27.33 E
Burgau	58	48.26 N	10.25 E
Burg [auf Fehmarn]	54	54.26 N	11.12 E
Burgaw	192	34.33 N	77.55 W
Burgaz ⬌8	267b	40.53 N	29.03 E
Burgaz Adası I	267b	40.53 N	29.04 E
Burgbernheim	56	49.27 N	10.19 E
Burgdorf, B.R.D.	52	52.27 N	10.00 E
Burgdorf, Schw.	58	47.04 N	7.37 E
Burgebrach	56	49.50 N	10.44 E
Bürgel	54	50.56 N	11.45 E
Burgenland □3	61	47.30 N	16.20 E
Burgeo	186	47.37 N	57.37 W
Burgersdorp	158	31.00 S	26.20 E
Burger Township	273d	26.05 S	27.46 E
Burges, Mount ∧2	162	30.50 S	121.06 E
Burgess	208	37.53 N	76.21 W
Burgess Hill	42	50.57 N	0.07 W
Burgessville	212	43.01 N	80.39 W
Burgettstown	214	40.22 N	80.23 W
Burggrafenberg ∧2	263	51.13 N	7.07 E
Burghausen	60	48.09 N	12.49 E
Burghead	46	57.42 N	3.30 W
Burgheim	60	48.42 N	11.01 E
Burgh Heath	260	51.18 N	0.13 W
Burghill	214	41.22 N	80.34 W
Burgh le Marsh	44	53.09 N	0.15 E
Burghūth, Sabkhat al- ◎	130	34.58 N	41.06 E
Burgin	194	37.45 N	84.46 W
Burgio	70	37.36 N	13.17 E
Burgjoss	56	50.12 N	9.29 E
Burgkirchen	60	48.12 N	13.06 E
Burgkunstadt	54	50.08 N	11.14 E
Bürglen, Schw.	58	46.53 N	8.40 E
Bürglen, Schw.	58	47.33 N	9.09 E
Burglengenfeld	60	49.13 N	12.03 E
Burgoon	214	41.16 N	83.15 W
Burgos, Esp.	34	42.21 N	3.42 W
Burgos, It.	71	40.23 N	8.59 E

FRANÇAIS

Nom	Page	Lat.°′	Long.°′ W = Ouest
Burgos, Méx.	232	24.57 N	98.47 W
Burgos, Pil.	116	15.30 N	120.24 E
Burgos, Pil.	116	16.04 N	119.52 E
Burgos □4	34	42.20 N	3.40 W
Burgsinn	56	50.09 N	9.38 E
Burgstädt	54	50.55 N	12.49 E
Burgstall, D.D.R.	54	52.24 N	11.41 E
Burgstall → Postal, It.	64	46.36 N	11.11 E
Burg Stargard	54	53.29 N	13.18 E
Burgsvik	26	57.03 N	18.16 E
Burgueño, Arroyo ≃	288	34.24 S	58.47 W
Burgund → Bourgogne □9	32	47.00 N	4.30 E
Burgundy → Bourgogne □9	32	47.00 N	4.30 E
Burgusio (Burgeis)	64	46.42 N	10.31 E
Burgwedel, B.R.D.	52	52.30 N	9.52 E
Burgwedel, B.R.D.	52	52.29 N	9.51 E
Burgwindheim	56	49.49 N	10.35 E
Burhābalang ≃	126	21.28 N	87.04 E
Burham	260	51.20 N	0.29 E
Burhan Budai Shan ⋀	102	36.00 N	96.00 E
Burhaniye, Tür.	130	37.57 N	28.45 E
Burhaniye, Tür.	130	39.30 N	26.58 E
Burhānpur	120	21.18 N	76.14 E
Burhar	124	23.13 N	81.32 E
Burhave	52	53.34 N	8.21 E
Burholme ⬌8	285	40.03 N	75.05 W
Buri	255	23.48 S	48.35 W
Burias Island I	116	12.57 N	123.08 E
Burias Pass ʯ	116	13.00 N	123.15 E
Buribaj	86	51.57 N	58.11 E
Būr Ibrāhīm ⬌8	142	29.57 N	32.34 E
Burica, Punta ›	236	8.03 N	82.53 W
Burien	224	47.28 N	122.20 W
Burigi, Lake ◎	154	2.05 S	31.15 E
Burila Mare	38	44.27 N	22.34 E
Burin	186	47.02 N	55.10 W
Burin Peninsula ›1	186	47.00 N	55.40 W
Buri Ram	110	15.00 N	103.07 E
Buriswar ≃1	126	21.58 N	90.02 E
Buritama	255	21.03 S	50.08 W
Buriti, Bra.	250	3.55 S	42.57 W
Buriti, Bra.	255	16.27 S	53.27 W
Buriti ≃	248	12.50 S	58.28 W
Buriti Alegre	255	18.09 S	49.03 W
Buriti Bravo	250	5.50 S	43.50 W
Buriti Cortado	250	5.11 S	43.06 W
Buriticupu ≃	250	4.13 S	46.33 W
Buriti dos Lopes	250	3.10 S	41.52 W
Buritizal, Cachoeira do ∟	250	0.17 N	54.40 W
Buritizeiro	255	17.21 S	44.58 W
Būrīya	124	30.09 N	77.21 E
Burj al-'Arab	140	30.55 N	29.32 E
Burjassot	34	39.31 N	0.25 W
Burji	144	5.20 N	37.57 E
Burj Islām	130	35.41 N	35.48 E
Burj Mughayzil	142	31.27 N	30.23 E
Burkan ≃	85	41.43 N	76.46 E
Burkau	54	51.10 N	14.10 E
Burkburnett	196	34.05 N	98.34 W
Burke, S.D., U.S.	198	43.10 N	99.17 W
Burke, Tx., U.S.	222	31.14 N	94.46 W
Burke, Va., U.S.	284c	38.47 N	77.16 W
Burke ≃	166	23.12 S	139.33 E
Burke Channel ʯ	182	52.07 N	127.38 W
Burke Island I	9	73.15 S	104.35 W
Burke Lake County Park ♠	284c	38.45 N	77.18 W
Burke Lakefront Airport ⊠	279a	41.31 N	81.41 W
Burkesville	194	36.47 N	85.22 W
Burket	216	41.09 N	85.58 W
Burketown	166	17.43 S	139.34 E
Burkett Gardens	226	37.57 N	121.15 W
Burkettsville	216	40.21 N	84.39 W
Burkhardtsdorf	54	50.44 N	12.55 E
Burkina Faso □1, Afr.	134	13.00 N	1.30 W
Burkina Faso □1, Afr.	150	13.00 N	1.30 W
Burkit	80	47.03 N	50.42 E
Burksville	219	38.16 N	90.09 W
Burla	86	53.19 N	78.21 E
Burla ≃	86	53.20 N	78.02 E
Burladingen	58	48.17 N	9.07 E
Burleigh	208	39.02 N	74.51 W
Burleigh Falls	212	44.34 N	78.13 W
Burleigh Heads	171a	28.06 S	153.27 E
Burleson	222	32.32 N	97.19 W
Burleson □6	222	30.30 N	96.43 W
Burley, Id., U.S.	202	42.32 N	113.47 W
Burley, Wa., U.S.	224	47.25 N	122.37 W
Burley Griffin, Lake ◎	171b	35.13 S	149.05 E
Burli, S.S.S.R.	80	51.25 N	52.44 E
Burli, S.S.S.R.	86	53.36 N	61.55 E
Burlingame, Ca., U.S.	226	37.35 N	122.21 W
Burlingame, Ks., U.S.	198	38.45 N	95.00 W
Burlingame State Park ♠	207	41.22 N	71.43 W
Burlington, Nf., Can.	186	49.45 N	56.02 W
Burlington, On., Can.	212	43.19 N	79.47 W
Burlington, Co., U.S.	198	39.18 N	102.16 W
Burlington, Ct., U.S.	207	41.46 N	72.57 W
Burlington, Il., U.S.	216	42.03 N	88.33 W
Burlington, In., U.S.	216	40.29 N	86.24 W
Burlington, Ia., U.S.	190	40.48 N	91.06 W
Burlington, Ks., U.S.	198	38.11 N	95.44 W
Burlington, Ky., U.S.	218	39.01 N	84.43 W
Burlington, Ma., U.S.	207	42.30 N	71.11 W
Burlington, Mi., U.S.	216	42.06 N	85.05 W
Burlington, N.J., U.S.	208	40.04 N	74.51 W
Burlington, N.C., U.S.	192	36.05 N	79.26 W
Burlington, N.D., U.S.	198	48.16 N	101.25 W
Burlington, Pa., U.S.	210	41.47 N	76.37 W
Burlington, Tx., U.S.	222	31.01 N	96.60 W
Burlington, Vt., U.S.	188	44.28 N	73.12 W
Burlington, Wa., U.S.	224	48.28 N	122.19 W
Burlington, Wi., U.S.	216	42.40 N	88.16 W
Burlington, Wy., U.S.	202	44.26 N	108.25 W
Burlington □6	208	39.50 N	74.47 W
Burlington Beach	216	41.30 N	87.03 W
Burlington County Airpark ⊠	285	39.56 N	74.50 W
Burlington Island I	285	40.05 N	74.51 W
Burlington Junction	194	40.26 N	95.03 W
Burlington Mall ⬌9	283	42.29 N	71.13 W
Burlit	89	46.33 N	134.14 E
Burluk	80	50.34 N	44.33 E
Burma (Myanmar) □1	110	22.00 N	98.00 E
Burmā, Tall ∧	132	30.38 N	35.50 E
Burmakino	80	57.27 N	40.20 E
Burn ≃	44	54.12 N	1.38 W
Burnaby	224	49.15 N	122.57 W
Burnaby Island I	182	52.24 N	131.20 W
Burnage	262	53.26 N	2.12 W
Burnas, ozero ◎	78	45.52 N	30.08 E
Burnet	196	30.45 N	98.13 W
Burnett ≃	166	24.46 S	152.25 E
Burnett Bay c	176	73.53 N	124.00 W
Burnett Brook ≃	276	40.46 N	74.38 W
Burnett Heads	166	24.46 S	152.25 E
Burnettsville	216	40.46 N	86.36 W
Burney, Ca., U.S.	204	40.52 N	121.39 W
Burney, In., U.S.	218	39.19 N	85.38 W
Burnham, Eng., U.K.	260	51.33 N	0.39 W
Burnham, Il., U.S.	278	41.39 N	87.34 W
Burnham, Pa., U.S.	208	40.38 N	77.34 W
Burnham Beeches ⬌3	260	51.34 N	0.38 W
Burnham Market	42	52.57 N	0.44 E
Burnham-on-Crouch	42	51.38 N	0.49 E
Burnham-on-Sea	42	51.15 N	3.00 W
Burnhamthorpe	275b	43.37 N	79.36 W
Burnhaven	46	57.29 N	1.47 W
Burnie	166	41.04 S	145.54 E
Burning Tree Estates	284c	39.01 N	77.12 W
Burnips	216	42.44 N	85.50 W
Burniston	44	54.19 N	0.26 W
Burnley	44	53.48 N	2.14 W
Burnley □8	262	53.46 N	2.15 W
Burnley Creek ≃	212	44.13 N	77.51 W

PORTUGUÊS

Nome	Página	Lat.°′	Long.°′ W = Oeste
Burnley Football Ground ♠	262	53.48 N	2.14 W
Burnmouth	46	55.50 N	2.04 W
Burnoje	85	42.37 N	70.46 E
Burno-Okt'abr'skoje	85	42.42 N	70.49 E
Burnpur	126	23.40 N	86.57 E
Burns, Ks., U.S.	198	38.05 N	96.53 W
Burns, Or., U.S.	202	43.35 N	119.03 W
Burns, Tn., U.S.	194	36.03 N	87.18 W
Burns, Wy., U.S.	198	41.11 N	104.21 W
Burns Creek ≃	198	47.22 N	104.25 W
Burns Flat	196	35.20 N	99.10 W
Burns Harbor	216	41.37 N	87.10 W
Burnside, Austl.	168b	34.57 S	138.40 E
Burnside, Ky., U.S.	192	36.59 N	84.36 W
Burnside, Pa., U.S.	214	40.49 N	78.47 W
Burnside ≃	176	66.51 N	108.04 W
Burnside, Lake ◎	162	25.33 S	123.02 E
Burns Lake	182	54.14 N	125.46 W
Burnsville, Al., U.S.	194	32.28 N	86.53 W
Burnsville, Ms., U.S.	194	34.50 N	88.18 W
Burnsville, N.C., U.S.	192	35.55 N	82.18 W
Burnsville, W.V., U.S.	188	38.51 N	80.39 W
Burnt ≃, On., Can.	212	44.35 N	78.46 W
Burnt ≃, Or., U.S.	202	44.22 N	117.14 W
Burnt Cabins	214	40.05 N	77.54 W
Burnt Corn Creek ≃	194	31.06 N	87.04 W
Burnt Hills	210	42.54 N	73.53 W
Burnt Island, Nf., Can.	186	47.36 N	58.53 W
Burntisland, Scot., U.K.	46	56.03 N	3.15 W
Burnt Meadow Brook ≃	276	41.05 N	74.18 W
Burnt Mills, Lake ◎	208	36.50 N	76.38 W
Burnt Mills Hills	284c	39.02 N	77.00 W
Burnt Mills Manor	284c	39.02 N	77.00 W
Burnt Mountain ∧	228	33.12 N	117.04 W
Burntop	158	26.49 S	30.54 E
Burnt Pine	174c	29.02 S	167.56 E
Burnt Pond ◎	186	48.11 N	57.24 W
Burntwick Island I	260	51.25 N	0.41 E
Burntwood	42	52.41 N	1.56 W
Burntwood ≃	184	56.08 N	96.30 W
Burntwood Lake ◎	184	55.29 N	100.07 W
Burnyj, porog ∟	86	57.43 N	95.18 E
Buro	144	11.28 N	49.41 E
Buron	84	42.48 N	44.03 E
Buronzo	62	45.29 N	8.16 E
Burow	54	53.46 N	13.16 E
Burpengary	171a	27.10 S	152.57 E
Burpham	260	51.15 N	0.33 W
Burqin	86	47.43 N	86.53 E
Burqin ≃	86	47.40 N	86.55 E
Burra	166	33.40 S	138.56 E
Burra Burra Creek ≃	170	34.10 S	149.38 E
Burracoppin	162	31.23 S	118.29 E
Burra Creek ≃	168b	33.51 S	139.18 E
Burrage	283	42.02 N	70.51 W
Burrage Pond ◎	283	42.01 N	70.52 W
Burragorang, Lake ◎1	170	33.57 S	150.26 E
Burramurra	166	20.30 S	137.20 E
Burravoe	46a	60.32 N	1.28 W
Burrawang	170	34.36 S	150.31 E
Burray I	46	58.51 N	2.54 W
Burrel, Shq.	38	41.37 N	20.00 E
Burrel, Ca., U.S.	226	36.30 N	119.59 W
Burrendong Reservoir ◎1	166	32.39 S	149.15 E
Burren Junction	166	30.06 S	148.58 E
Burrill Lake c	170	35.23 S	150.27 E
Burrinjuck Reservoir ◎1	166	35.00 S	148.45 E
Burro, Serranías del ⋀	196	29.10 N	102.05 W
Burr Oak, In., U.S.	216	41.15 N	86.25 W
Burr Oak, Ks., U.S.	198	39.51 N	98.18 W
Burr Oak, Mi., U.S.	216	41.50 N	85.19 W
Burroburro ≃	246	4.48 N	58.51 W
Burro Creek ≃	200	34.32 N	113.35 W
Burro Peak ∧	200	32.35 N	108.26 W
Burrowa, Mount ∧	171b	36.05 S	147.42 E
Burrowa-Pine Mountain National Park ♠	171b	36.06 S	147.44 E
Burrow Head ›	44	54.41 N	4.24 W
Burrowhill	260	51.21 N	0.36 W
Burrows	216	40.40 N	86.30 W
Burrows Island I	224	48.29 N	122.42 W
Burr Ridge	278	41.46 N	87.55 W
Burrs Mill Brook ≃	285	39.53 N	74.42 W
Burrton	198	38.01 N	97.40 W
Burrumbeet, Lake ◎	169	37.30 S	143.39 E
Burrundie	164	13.32 S	131.42 E
Burruyacú	252	26.30 S	64.45 W
Burrwood	194	28.58 N	89.22 W
Burry Holms I	42	51.37 N	4.18 W
Burry Port	42	51.42 N	4.15 W
Bürs	58	47.09 N	9.48 E
Bursa	130	40.11 N	29.04 E
Bursa □4	130	40.10 N	29.00 E
Būr Safājah	140	26.44 N	33.56 E
Būr Sa'īd (Port Said)	142	31.16 N	32.18 E
Būr Sa'īd □4	142	30.36 N	32.15 E
Burscheid	56	51.05 N	7.06 E
Burscough	262	53.35 N	2.51 W
Burscough Bridge, Eng., U.K.	44	53.36 N	2.52 W
Burscough Bridge, Eng., U.K.	262	53.36 N	2.51 W
Bursey, Mount ∧	9	76.00 S	132.40 W
Bursol'	86	53.11 N	78.27 E
Bürstadt	56	49.38 N	8.27 E
Burstall	184	50.40 N	109.54 W
Burštyn	78	49.17 N	24.37 E
Būr Sūdān (Port Sudan)	140	19.37 N	37.14 E
Burt, Ia., U.S.	190	43.11 N	94.13 W
Burt, N.Y., U.S.	210	43.19 N	78.43 W
Būr Tawfīq ⬌8	128	29.57 N	32.34 E
Burtenbach	58	48.20 N	10.26 E
Burt Lake ◎	190	45.27 N	84.40 W
Burtnieku ezers ◎	76	57.45 N	25.16 E
Burton, B.C., Can.	182	49.59 N	117.54 W
Burton, Eng., U.K.	42	50.44 N	1.45 W
Burton, Eng., U.K.	262	53.16 N	3.01 W
Burton, Il., U.S.	219	39.55 N	91.15 W
Burton, Mi., U.S.	216	43.01 N	84.16 W
Burton, Mi., U.S.	216	43.02 N	83.36 W
Burton, Oh., U.S.	214	41.28 N	81.08 W
Burton, Tx., U.S.	222	30.11 N	96.36 W
Burton, Wa., U.S.	224	47.23 N	122.27 W
Burton, Lake ◎1	192	34.50 N	83.33 W
Burton Fleming	44	54.08 N	0.20 W
Burton Latimer	42	52.23 N	0.41 W
Burtons Bridge	216	42.17 N	88.14 W
Burton Seamount ✧3	14	32.00 S	171.45 W
Burtonsville	208	39.07 N	76.56 W
Burton upon Stather	44	53.39 N	0.41 W
Burton upon Trent	42	52.49 N	1.36 W
Burtonwood	262	53.26 N	2.39 W
Burtonwood Airfield ⊠	262	53.24 N	2.39 W
Burträsk	26	64.31 N	20.39 E
Burtundy	166	33.44 S	142.16 E
Burṭus	142	30.09 N	31.08 E
Buru I	108	3.24 S	126.40 E
Buruanga	116	11.51 N	121.53 E
Burukan	89	53.02 N	136.03 E
Buruldaj	85	42.48 N	75.52 E
Burullus, Buḥayrat al- ◎	142	31.30 N	30.50 E
Burūm	144	14.22 N	48.57 E
Burundaj	85	43.23 N	76.51 E
Burundi □1, Afr.	138	3.15 S	30.00 E
Burundi □1, Afr.	154	3.15 S	30.00 E
Burundučicha	80	58.21 N	46.07 E
Burun-Šibertuj, gora ∧	88	49.42 N	109.59 E
Bururi	154	3.57 S	29.37 E
Burutu	150	5.21 N	5.31 E
Buruz Bāgān	126	23.03 N	89.00 E
Burwash	190	46.19 N	80.48 W
Burwash Landing	180	61.21 N	139.00 W
Burwell, Eng., U.K.	42	52.16 N	0.19 E
Burwell, Ne., U.S.	198	41.46 N	99.07 W
Burwell Bay c	208	37.04 N	76.38 W
Burwick	46	58.44 N	2.57 W
Burwood, Austl.	274a	33.53 S	151.06 E
Burwood, Austl.	274b	37.51 S	145.06 E
Bury, P.Q., Can.	206	45.28 N	71.30 W
Bury, Eng., U.K.	42	50.54 N	0.34 W
Bury, Eng., U.K.	262	53.36 N	2.17 W
Bury □8	262	53.35 N	2.19 W
Buryn'	78	51.13 N	33.49 E
Bury Saint Edmunds	42	52.15 N	0.43 E
Burzaco	258	34.49 S	58.24 W
Burzet	62	44.44 N	4.15 E
Burzil	123	34.52 N	75.07 E
Burzil Pass)(	123	34.54 N	75.06 E
Būṣ, Ghubbat al- c	142	29.36 N	32.22 E
Busa, Mount ∧	116	6.08 N	124.39 E
Busachi	71	40.02 N	8.54 E
Busalla	62	44.34 N	8.57 E
Busambra, Rocca ∧	70	37.51 N	13.24 E
Busan → Pusan	98	35.06 N	129.03 E
Busana	64	44.22 N	10.19 E
Busanga	152	0.51 S	22.04 E
Busanga Swamp ≋	154	14.10 S	25.50 E
Busangu	154	8.32 S	25.31 E
Buṣayrah	130	35.09 N	40.26 E
Busby, Austl.	274a	33.54 S	150.53 E
Busby, Mt., U.S.	202	45.32 N	106.57 W
Busca	62	44.31 N	7.29 E
Buscate	266b	45.32 N	8.49 E
Buscbusc ≃	144	1.08 S	41.49 E
Buschberg ∧2	61	48.34 N	16.23 E
Busche	64	46.02 N	11.59 E
Busch Gardens ♠	280	34.13 N	118.28 W
Buschhausen ⬌8	263	51.30 N	6.51 E
Busdorf	41	54.29 N	9.32 E
Buseck	56	50.36 N	8.47 E
Buseto Palizzolo	70	38.01 N	12.43 E
Būsh	142	29.09 N	31.08 E
Bush ≃, N. Ire., U.K.	44	55.13 N	6.32 W
Bush ≃, S.C., U.S.	192	34.08 N	81.36 W
Būshehr □4	128	28.50 N	51.20 E
Bushenyi	154	0.32 S	30.11 E
Bushey	260	51.39 N	0.22 W
Bushey Heath	260	51.38 N	0.20 W
Bushi	268	35.50 N	139.22 E
Bushimaie ≃	152	6.02 S	23.45 E
Bushiribana	241s	12.33 N	69.58 W
Bushkill	210	41.06 N	75.00 W
Bush Kill ≃	210	41.05 N	74.59 W
Bushkill Falls ∟	210	41.09 N	75.01 W
Bushland	196	35.11 N	102.04 W
Bush Lot	246	6.12 N	57.16 W
Bushman Land □9	158	29.15 S	20.00 E
Bushmills	48	55.12 N	6.32 W
Bushnell, Fl., U.S.	220	28.39 N	82.06 W
Bushnell, Il., U.S.	190	40.33 N	90.30 W
Bush River ≃	208	39.21 N	76.14 W
Bushton	198	38.30 N	98.23 W
Bū Shubayrim, Wādī ∨	146	27.07 N	19.30 E
Bushwick ⬌8	276	40.42 N	73.55 W
Bushy Park	166	21.16 S	139.43 E
Bushy Park ♠	260	51.25 N	0.20 W
Bushy Run ≃	279b	40.20 N	79.40 W
Bushy Run Battlefield ⊥	279b	40.21 N	79.38 W
Busia	154	0.28 N	34.05 E
Busigny	50	50.02 N	3.28 E
Busing, Pulau I	271c	1.14 N	103.45 E
Businga	152	3.20 N	20.53 E
Büsingen	58	47.42 N	8.41 E
Busira ≃	152	0.15 S	18.59 E
Busjön ◎, Sve.	40	60.06 N	13.28 E
Busjön ◎, Sve.	40	60.31 N	13.58 E
Busk	78	49.58 N	24.37 E
Buskerud □6	26	60.25 N	9.12 E
Buskhyttan	40	58.40 N	16.56 E
Busko Zdrój	30	50.28 N	20.44 E
Buskul'	86	53.45 N	61.12 E
Busle	144	5.28 N	44.25 E
Busoga □5	154	0.40 N	33.30 E
Busovača	36	44.06 N	17.53 E
Buṣrā al-Ḥarīrī (Bosor)	132	32.50 N	36.20 E
Buṣrá ash-Shām	132	32.31 N	36.29 E
Bussana	62	43.49 N	7.51 E
Bussang	58	47.53 N	6.51 E
Bussang, Col de)(	58	47.54 N	6.54 E
Busse	89	51.16 N	126.58 E
Busselton	162	33.39 S	115.20 E
Busseri ≃	140	7.41 N	28.03 E
Busseto	64	44.59 N	10.02 E
Bussey	190	41.12 N	92.52 W
Bussières	62	45.50 N	4.16 E
Bussi sul Tirino	66	42.12 N	13.49 E
Busskoje	84	43.50 N	44.37 E
Bussolengo	64	45.28 N	10.51 E
Bussoleno	62	45.08 N	7.09 E
Bussum	52	52.16 N	5.10 E
Bussy-Rabutin, Château de ⊥	58	47.35 N	4.31 E
Bussy-Saint-Georges	261	48.51 N	2.42 E
Bustamante, Méx.	232	26.33 N	100.30 W
Bustamante, Méx.	234	23.26 N	99.47 W
Bustān, Wādī al- ∨	142	28.24 N	30.49 E
Buštěhrad	54	50.09 N	14.10 E
Buşteni	38	45.25 N	25.32 E
Busti	214	42.02 N	79.17 W
Bustleton ⬌8	285	40.05 N	75.02 W
Busto Arsizio	62	45.37 N	8.51 E
Busto Garolfo	62	45.33 N	8.53 E
Buston, S.S.S.R.	85	40.31 N	69.19 E
Buston, S.S.S.R.	128	40.04 N	64.49 E
Buštyna	78	48.04 N	23.27 E
Busu-Adula	152	2.05 N	21.40 E
Busuanga	116	12.10 N	119.55 E
Busuanga Island I	116	12.05 N	120.05 E
Busu-Djanoa	152	1.43 N	21.23 E
Bušuicha	76	59.02 N	40.26 E
Bušulej	88	52.45 N	117.13 E
Büsum	30	54.08 N	8.51 E
Busu-Melo	152	1.48 N	20.15 E
Bū Sunbul, Jabal ⋀2	146	23.10 N	22.21 E
Buta, S.S.S.R.	80	55.02 N	51.57 E
Buta, Zaïre	154	2.48 N	24.44 E
Butag	116	12.38 N	123.56 E
Butajira	144	8.07 N	38.22 E
Butala	164	6.42 S	147.37 E
Butan	38	43.39 N	23.45 E
Bután → Bhutan □1	120	27.30 N	90.30 E
Butand State Park ♠	226	37.13 N	122.20 W
Butantã ⬌8	287b	23.34 S	46.43 W
Butantã, Instituto ʊ3	287b	23.34 S	46.43 W
Buta Ranquil	252	37.03 S	69.50 W
Butare	154	2.36 S	29.44 E
Butaritari I1	14	3.07 N	172.48 E
Butarque, Arroyo de ≃	266a	40.19 N	3.39 W
Butauanan Island I	116	14.07 N	123.17 E
Butchart Gardens ♠	224	48.33 N	123.28 W
Butcher Island (Dia Deva) I	272c	18.58 N	72.54 E
Bute	168b	33.52 S	138.01 E
Bute, Island of I	46	55.50 N	5.06 W
Bute, Kyles of ʯ	46	55.53 N	5.13 W
Bute, Sound of ʯ	46	55.44 N	5.12 W
Büteelijn nuruu ⋀	88	50.00 N	104.50 E
Bute Giarti	144	4.33 N	37.45 E
Bute Inlet c	182	50.37 N	124.53 W
Butemba	154	1.09 N	31.36 E
Butembo	154	0.09 N	29.17 E
Butendorf ⬌8	263	51.33 N	6.59 E
Butera	70	37.11 N	14.11 E
Butere	154	0.13 N	34.30 E
Bütgenbach	56	50.26 N	6.12 E
Butha Buthe	158	28.45 S	28.15 E
Butha Qi (Zalantun)	89	48.02 N	122.43 E
Buthidaung	110	20.52 N	92.32 E
Buthier ≃	62	45.44 N	7.22 E
Buthroton ⊥	38	39.46 N	20.00 E
Buti	66	43.44 N	10.35 E
Butiá	252	30.07 S	51.58 W
Butiaba	154	1.49 N	31.19 E
Butig Mountains ⋀	116	7.39 N	124.20 E
Butka	86	56.47 N	63.47 E
Butler, Al., U.S.	194	32.05 N	88.13 W
Butler, Ga., U.S.	192	32.33 N	84.14 W
Butler, Il., U.S.	219	39.12 N	89.32 W
Butler, In., U.S.	216	41.25 N	84.52 W
Butler, Ky., U.S.	218	38.47 N	84.22 W
Butler, Mo., U.S.	194	38.15 N	94.19 W
Butler, N.J., U.S.	210	41.00 N	74.20 W
Butler, Oh., U.S.	214	40.35 N	82.25 W
Butler, Ok., U.S.	196	35.38 N	99.11 W
Butler, Pa., U.S.	214	40.51 N	79.53 W
Butler, Tx., U.S.	222	30.19 N	97.18 W
Butler, Wi., U.S.	216	43.06 N	88.04 W
Butler □6, Oh., U.S.	218	39.26 N	84.30 W
Butler □6, Pa., U.S.	214	40.52 N	79.54 W
Butler, Lake ◎	220	28.28 N	81.33 W
Butler Lake ◎	278	42.17 N	87.58 W
Butler Point ›	207	41.40 N	70.43 W
Butler Reservoir ◎1	276	40.59 N	74.23 W
Butlers Bridge	48	54.02 N	7.22 W
Butlerville	218	39.02 N	85.30 W
Butmīyah	132	32.56 N	35.53 E
Butnau Lake ◎	184	56.13 N	95.20 W
Butner	192	36.07 N	78.45 W
Buto	152	15.46 S	15.09 E
Buton, Pulau I	112	5.00 S	122.55 E
Butong	112	1.06 S	114.50 E
Bütow → Bytów	30	54.11 N	17.30 E
Butru	166	21.30 S	139.43 E
Butsha	154	0.57 N	29.13 E
Buttapietra	64	45.20 N	11.00 E
Butte, Mt., U.S.	202	46.00 N	112.32 W
Butte, Ne., U.S.	198	42.54 N	98.50 W
Butte □6	226	39.27 N	121.30 W
Butte City	226	39.28 N	121.59 W
Butte Creek ≃, Ca., U.S.	204	39.12 N	121.56 W
Butte Creek ≃, Or., U.S.	224	45.09 N	122.46 W
Butte du Lion ♠	50	50.40 N	4.24 E
Butte Falls	202	42.32 N	122.33 W
Buttelstedt	54	51.05 N	11.20 E
Butte Mountains ⋀	204	39.50 N	115.05 W
Butten	56	48.58 N	7.13 E
Butter Brook ≃	283	42.31 N	71.24 W
Butter Creek ≃	202	45.52 N	119.19 W
Butterfield, Il., U.S.	278	41.50 N	88.02 W
Butterfield, Mn., U.S.	198	43.57 N	94.47 W
Butterfield Creek ≃	278	41.33 N	87.37 W
Butterfield Lake ◎	212	44.19 N	75.46 W
Butterley Reservoir ◎1	262	53.35 N	1.56 W
Buttermere	44	54.33 N	3.17 W
Butternut	190	46.00 N	90.29 W
Butternut Creek ≃, N.Y., U.S.	210	42.25 N	75.22 W
Butternut Creek ≃, N.Y., U.S.	210	43.06 N	76.00 W
Butterwick	44	52.59 N	0.05 E
Butterworth, Malay.	114	5.25 N	100.24 E
Butterworth, Transkei	158	32.23 S	28.04 E
Buttevant	48	52.14 N	8.40 W
Büttgen	56	51.12 N	6.36 E
Buttlar	56	50.45 N	9.57 E
Buttle Lake ◎	182	49.46 N	125.36 W
Button Islands II	176	60.35 N	64.45 W
Buttonville	275b	43.52 N	79.22 W
Buttonville Airfield ⊠	275b	43.52 N	79.23 W
Buttonwillow	226	35.24 N	119.28 W
Buttrio	64	46.01 N	13.20 E
Buttstädt	54	51.07 N	11.25 E
Butty Head ›	162	33.54 S	121.38 E
Buttzville	210	40.49 N	75.00 W
Butuan	116	8.57 N	125.33 E
Butuan Bay c	116	9.06 N	125.20 E
Butuj	88	53.27 N	112.22 E
Bū Tumayyim, Wādī ∨	146	26.56 N	19.13 E
Butūris	142	31.00 N	30.15 E
Buturlino, S.S.S.R.	80	55.34 N	44.55 E
Buturlino, S.S.S.R.	82	54.55 N	37.29 E
Buturlinovka	78	50.50 N	40.36 E
Butwal	124	27.42 N	83.27 E
Butylicy	80	55.32 N	41.31 E
Butzbach	56	50.26 N	8.40 E
Bützfleth	52	53.39 N	9.28 E
Bützow	54	53.50 N	11.59 E
Bützsee ◎	54	52.49 N	12.53 E
Butztown	208	40.39 N	75.22 W
Buuhoodle	144	8.15 N	46.20 E
Buulo Berde	144	3.51 N	45.34 E
Buur Gaabo	144	1.12 S	41.51 E
Buurgplaatz ∧	56	50.10 N	6.01 E
Buur Hakaba	144	2.47 N	44.05 E
Buur Haybe	144	3.57 N	45.07 E
Buwarah, Sabkhat al- ≋	130	35.09 N	41.12 E
Buwaydān	132	33.12 N	36.26 E
Buxar	124	25.35 N	83.59 E
Buxtehude	52	53.28 N	9.41 E
Buxton, Boph.	158	27.38 S	24.42 E
Buxton, Guy.	246	6.47 N	58.02 W
Buxton, Eng., U.K.	262	53.15 N	1.55 W
Buxton, N.C., U.S.	192	35.16 N	75.32 W
Buxton, N.D., U.S.	198	47.36 N	97.05 W
Buxton, Or., U.S.	224	45.41 N	123.11 W
Buxton, Mount ∧	182	51.35 N	127.55 W
Buxy	58	46.43 N	4.41 E
Buye	154	4.38 N	27.30 E
Buyiqiao	106	31.47 N	119.48 E
Buyo	150	6.16 N	7.03 W
Buyo, Barrage de ⬌6	150	6.15 N	7.05 W
Buyuan ≃	102	21.51 N	101.13 E
Büyükada	130	40.52 N	29.07 E
Büyükada I	267b	40.52 N	29.07 E
Büyükarmutlu	130	39.35 N	38.26 E
Büyükbakkal ⬌8	267b	40.59 N	29.11 E
Büyükçeçeli	130	39.43 N	33.52 E
Büyükçekmece	130	41.01 N	28.34 E
Büyükdere ⬌8	267b	41.09 N	29.02 E
Büyükeceli	130	36.11 N	33.40 E
Büyükkale	130	38.01 N	27.34 E
Büyükkarıştıran	130	41.18 N	27.32 E
Büyükkemikli Burnu ›	130	40.18 N	26.14 E
Büyükmenderes ≃	130	37.28 N	27.11 E
Büyükzap → Great Zab ≃	128	36.00 N	43.21 E
Buyun Shan ∧	98	40.06 N	122.42 E
Buyun Uzun	128	39.13 N	63.19 E
Buzan ≃	80	46.18 N	49.06 E
Buzanaj, peski ⬌2	80	47.30 N	49.50 E
Buzançais	32	46.53 N	1.25 E
Buzancy	56	49.25 N	4.57 E
Bužaninovo	82	56.23 N	38.18 E
Bužarovo	82	55.59 N	36.47 E
Buzău	38	45.09 N	26.49 E
Buzău □6	38	45.15 N	26.45 E
Buzău ≃	38	45.26 N	27.44 E
Buzen	96	33.37 N	131.08 E
Búzi ≃	156	19.50 S	34.43 E
Buziaş	38	45.39 N	21.36 E
Buziji	100	33.49 N	118.14 E
Buzinovka	80	48.32 N	43.53 E
Búzios, Ilha dos I	256	23.48 S	45.08 W
Búzios, Ponta dos ›	255	22.44 S	41.53 W
Buzlanovo	265b	55.46 N	37.13 E
Buzovna	84	40.31 N	50.04 E
Buzuluk, S.S.S.R.	80	52.47 N	52.15 E
Buzuluk, S.S.S.R.	86	51.55 N	66.16 E
Buzuluk ≃, S.S.S.R.	80	50.13 N	42.12 E
Buzuluk ≃, S.S.S.R.	80	52.47 N	52.16 E
Buzzards Bay	207	41.44 N	70.37 W
Buzzards Bay c	207	41.33 N	70.47 W
Bwana Mkubwa	154	13.01 S	28.42 E
Bwasa	152	3.53 S	18.25 E
Bwendi	154	4.01 N	26.41 E
Bwlch	42	51.54 N	3.15 W
By	40	60.12 N	16.28 E
Byādgi	122	14.41 N	75.29 E
Byam Channel ʯ	176	75.20 N	105.20 W
Byam Martin Channel ʯ	176	75.45 N	104.00 W
Byam Martin Island I	176	75.15 N	104.00 W
Byberry Creek ≃	285	40.04 N	74.59 W
Byblos → Jubayl	130	34.07 N	35.39 E
Byček ≃	83	48.26 N	37.47 E
Bychawa	30	51.01 N	22.32 E
Bychov	76	53.32 N	30.12 E
Byčicha	76	55.41 N	29.58 E
Byčki, S.S.S.R.	76	54.15 N	34.39 E
Byčki, S.S.S.R.	80	53.38 N	40.54 E
Byculla ⬌8	272c	18.58 N	72.49 E
Byczyna	30	51.07 N	18.11 E
Bydalen	26	63.06 N	13.47 E
Bydgoszcz	30	53.08 N	18.00 E
Bydgoszcz □4	30	53.15 N	18.00 E
Byelorussian Station ⬌5	265b	55.47 N	37.35 E
Byers, Pa., U.S.	285	40.05 N	75.41 W
Byers, Tx., U.S.	196	34.04 N	98.11 W
Byersdale	279b	40.37 N	80.13 W
Byers Run ≃	279b	40.24 N	79.42 W
Byesville	188	39.58 N	81.32 W
Byfang ⬌8	263	51.24 N	7.06 E
Byfield, Eng., U.K.	42	52.11 N	1.14 W
Byfield, Ma., U.S.	207	42.45 N	70.56 W
Byfleet	260	51.20 N	0.29 W
Byford	168a	32.13 S	116.00 E
Byforde	284c	39.01 N	77.05 W
Bygdeå	26	64.04 N	20.51 E
Bygdeträsket ◎	26	64.26 N	20.32 E
Bygdin	26	61.20 N	8.48 E
Bygdin ◎	26	61.21 N	8.36 E
Bygi	80	57.13 N	53.44 E
Byglandsfjord	26	58.41 N	7.48 E
Byglandsfjorden ◎	26	58.48 N	7.50 E
Byhalia	194	34.52 N	89.41 W
Byk ≃	78	46.55 N	29.28 E
Bykle	26	59.21 N	7.20 E
Bykov	89	47.21 N	142.32 E
Bykovec	78	47.13 N	28.27 E
Bykovka, S.S.S.R.	78	50.17 N	27.58 E
Bykovka, S.S.S.R.	82	55.29 N	37.40 E
Bykovo, S.S.S.R.	80	49.47 N	45.22 E
Bykovo, S.S.S.R.	82	54.01 N	37.54 E
Bykovo, S.S.S.R.	82	55.37 N	38.04 E
Bykovo Airport ⊠	265b	55.36 N	38.05 E
Bylas	200	33.08 N	110.07 W
Bylbasovka	83	48.51 N	37.30 E
Bylderup	41	54.57 N	9.07 E
Byley	262	53.13 N	2.25 W
Bylkyldak	86	48.38 N	75.16 E
Bylnice	30	49.04 N	18.01 E
Bylot Island I	176	73.13 N	78.34 W
Byng Inlet	190	45.46 N	80.33 W
Bynum, Mt., U.S.	182	47.58 N	112.18 W
Bynum, N.C., U.S.	192	35.46 N	79.08 W
Bynum, Tx., U.S.	222	31.58 N	97.00 W
Byōdōin Temple ʊ1	270	34.53 N	135.48 E
Byram ≃	276	40.59 N	73.39 W
Byramgore Reef ✧2	122	11.54 N	71.49 E
Byram Lake Reservoir ◎1	276	41.10 N	73.41 W
Byrd, Lac ◎	190	47.01 N	76.56 W
Byrd Glacier ⊓	9	80.15 S	160.20 E
Byrdstown	194	36.34 N	85.07 W
Byrka	88	50.39 N	118.31 E
Byrnedale	214	41.17 N	78.30 W
Byro	162	26.05 S	116.09 E
Byrock	166	30.40 S	146.24 E
Byron, Ca., U.S.	226	37.52 N	121.38 W
Byron, Ga., U.S.	192	32.39 N	83.45 W
Byron, Il., U.S.	190	42.07 N	89.15 W
Byron, Mi., U.S.	216	42.49 N	83.57 W
Byron, N.Y., U.S.	210	43.04 N	78.03 W
Byron, Wy., U.S.	202	44.47 N	108.30 W
Byron, Cape ›	166	28.39 S	153.38 E
Byron, Isla I	254	47.47 S	75.12 W
Byron Bay	166	28.39 S	153.37 E
Byron Center	216	42.49 N	85.42 W
Byrranga, gory ⋀	74	75.00 N	104.00 E
Byšice-Liblice	54	50.19 N	14.38 E
Bysjön ◎	40	60.23 N	14.30 E
Byske	26	64.57 N	21.12 E
Byskeälven ≃	26	64.57 N	21.13 E
Bystraja ≃	80	47.58 N	41.00 E
Bystřany	54	50.38 N	13.51 E
Bystrica ≃	80	58.38 N	49.05 E
Bystřice	30	49.45 N	14.41 E
Bystřice pod Hostýnem	30	49.24 N	17.40 E
Bystrij Tanyp ≃	86	55.46 N	54.35 E
Bystrovka	85	42.47 N	75.43 E
Bystryj	86	57.50 N	73.58 E
Bystryj Istok	86	52.23 N	84.24 E
Bystrzyca Kłodzka	30	50.18 N	16.38 E
Bytantaj ≃	74	68.46 N	134.20 E
Bytča, Česko.	30	49.14 N	18.36 E
Bytča, S.S.S.R.	76	54.18 N	28.24 E
Byten'	76	52.54 N	25.29 E
Bytkov	78	48.38 N	24.26 E
Bytom (Beuthen)	30	50.22 N	18.54 E
Bytoš'	76	53.50 N	34.06 E
Bytów	30	54.11 N	17.30 E
Byumba	154	1.35 S	30.04 E
Byvalki	78	51.51 N	30.37 E
Byxelkrok	26	57.20 N	17.00 E
Bzyb' ≃	84	43.12 N	40.18 E
Bzybskij chrebet ⋀	84	41.18 N	40.41 E

C

Ça ≃	110	18.46 N	105.47 E
Čaa-Chol'	86	51.32 N	92.23 E
Caacupé	252	25.23 S	57.09 W
Čaadajevka	80	53.09 N	45.56 E
Čaadajevo	80	55.40 N	42.02 E
Caaguazú	252	25.26 S	56.02 W
Caaguazú □5	252	25.00 S	55.45 W
Caála	152	12.51 S	15.33 E
Caamaño Sound ʯ	182	52.49 N	129.28 W
Caapiranga	246	3.18 S	61.13 W
Caapucú	252	26.13 S	57.12 W
Caazapá	252	26.09 S	56.24 W
Caazapá □5	252	26.10 S	56.00 W
Cabaçal ≃	248	16.00 S	57.42 W
Cabaceiras	250	7.30 S	36.17 W
Cabadbaran	116	9.10 N	125.38 E
Cabadiangan Plateau ⋀1	116	9.50 N	122.36 E
Cabagan	116	17.26 N	121.46 E
Cabaiguán	240p	22.05 N	79.30 W
Cabalete Island I	116	14.17 N	121.50 E
Cabalian	116	10.16 N	125.10 E
Cabaliana, Lago ◎	246	3.20 S	60.50 W
Cabalian Bay c	116	10.13 N	125.10 E
Cabalian Point ›	116	12.06 N	122.01 E
Caballero Creek ≃	280	34.11 N	118.32 W
Caballito ⬌8	288	34.37 S	58.27 W
Caballones, Cayo I	240p	20.52 N	79.00 W
Caballo Reservoir ◎1	200	32.58 N	107.18 W
Caballos, Cerro de los ∧	234	23.04 N	102.55 W
Cabana	248	8.24 S	78.02 W
Cabanaconde	248	15.37 S	71.59 W
Cabañas	240p	22.58 N	82.55 W
Cabanatuan	116	15.29 N	120.58 E
Cabangan	116	15.10 N	120.03 E
Cabano	186	47.41 N	68.53 W
Čabanovka	83	49.02 N	38.46 E
Cabarroguis	116	16.33 N	121.32 E
Cabarruyan Island I	116	16.18 N	119.59 E
Cabaun Island I	116	12.34 N	124.30 E
Cabeceiras	255	15.48 S	46.59 W

≃ River	Fluß	Río	Rivière	Rio	⬌ Submarine Features	Untermeerische Objekte	Accidentes Submarinos	Formes de relief sous-marin	Acidentes submarinos
≊ Canal	Kanal	Canal	Canal	Canal	□ Political Unit	Politische Einheit	Unidad Política	Entité politique	Unidade política
∟ Waterfall, Rapids	Wasserfall, Stromschnellen	Cascada, Rápidos	Chute d'eau, Rapides	Cascata, Rápidos	ʊ Cultural Institution	Kulturelle Institution	Institución Cultural	Institution culturelle	Instituição cultural
ʯ Strait	Meeresstraße	Estrecho	Détroit	Estreito	⊥ Historical Site	Historische Stätte	Sitio Histórico	Site historique	Sitio histórico
c Bay, Gulf	Bucht, Golf	Bahía, Golfo	Baie, Golfe	Baía, Golfo	♠ Recreational Site	Erholungs- und Ferienort	Sitio de Recreo	Centre de loisirs	Area de Lazer
◎ Lake, Lakes	See, Seen	Lago, Lagos	Lac, Lacs	Lago, Lagos	⊠ Airport	Flughafen	Aeropuerto	Aéroport	Aeroporto
≋ Swamp	Sumpf	Pantano	Marais	Pântano	⊞ Military Installation	Militäranlage	Instalación Militar	Installation militaire	Instalação militar
⊓ Ice Features, Glacier	Eis- und Gletscherformen	Accidentes Glaciales	Formes glaciaires	Acidentes glaciares	⬌ Miscellaneous	Verschiedenes	Misceláneo	Divers	Diversos
⊤ Other Hydrographic Features	Andere Hydrographische Objekte	Otros Elementos Hidrográficos	Autres données hydrographiques	Outros acidentes hidrográficos					

Cabecera de Dupí 236 8.22 N 81.54 W
Cabeço de Montachique 266c 38.54 N 9.11 W
Cabedelo 250 6.58 S 34.50 W
Cabellera, Sierra de la ⋏ 200 30.55 N 109.07 W
Cabery 216 41.00 N 88.12 W
Cabeza, Arrecife ✢² 234 19.04 N 95.51 W
Cabeza del Buey 34 38.43 N 5.13 W
Cabeza de Tigre 286c 10.28 N 66.46 W
Cabezas 248 18.46 S 63.24 W
Cabiao 116 15.15 N 120.51 E
Cabiate 266b 45.40 N 9.10 E
Cabildo, Arg. 252 38.29 S 61.54 W
Cabildo, Chile 252 32.26 S 71.05 W
Cabimas 246 10.23 N 71.28 W
Cabin Branch ≃, Md., U.S. 284b 39.13 N 76.35 W
Cabin Branch ≃, Md., U.S. 284c 38.51 N 76.48 W
Cabin Creek ≃ 198 46.55 N 104.52 W
Cabinda 152 5.33 S 12.12 E
Cabinda □⁵ 152 5.00 S 12.30 E
Cabinet Mountains ⋏ 202 48.20 N 116.00 W
Cabingaan Island I 116 5.41 N 121.03 E
Cabin John 208 38.58 N 77.09 W
Cabin John Creek ≃ 284b 38.58 N 77.09 W
Cabin John Creek Park ♠ 284c 38.59 N 77.09 W
Cabin John Regional Park ♠ 284c 39.02 N 77.09 W
Cabiri 152 8.52 S 13.39 E
Cable 190 46.12 N 91.17 W
Cable Airport ⊠ 280 34.08 N 117.41 W
Cables 162 27.59 S 123.23 E
Cabo 250 8.17 S 35.02 W
Cabo Blanco 254 47.12 S 65.45 W
Cabo Delgado □⁵ 154 12.35 S 39.00 E
Cabo Frio 255 22.53 S 42.01 W
Cabo Gracias a Dios 236 14.59 N 83.10 W
Cabo Ledo 152 9.39 S 13.17 E
Cabonga, Réservoir ⊜¹ 190 47.20 N 76.35 W
Cabool 194 37.07 N 92.06 W
Caboolture 166 27.05 S 152.57 E
Cabora Bassa 154 15.35 S 32.48 E
Cabora Bassa Dam ◆⁶ 154 15.35 S 32.42 E
Cabo Raso 254 44.21 S 65.14 W
Cabo Rojo 240m 18.05 N 67.09 W
Cabot, Ar., U.S. 194 34.58 N 92.00 W
Cabot, Pa., U.S. 214 40.46 N 79.46 W
Cabot, Mount ∧ 188 44.31 N 71.24 W
Cabot Head ≻ 212 45.14 N 81.17 W
Cabot Strait ⊔ 186 47.20 N 59.30 W
Cabo Verde 256 21.28 S 46.24 W
Cabo Verde → Cape Verde □¹ 150a 16.00 N 24.00 W
Cabo Verde ≃ 256 21.28 S 46.17 W
Cabo Verde, Ribeirão do ≃ 256 21.20 S 44.32 W
Cabra 34 37.28 N 4.27 W
Cabra Island I 116 13.53 N 120.02 E
Cabral 238 18.15 N 71.13 W
Cabramatta 274a 33.54 S 150.56 E
Cabramatta Creek ≃ 274a 33.54 S 150.57 E
Cabramurra 171b 35.58 S 148.23 E
Cabras 71 39.56 N 8.32 E
Cabras, Ribeirão das ≃ 256 23.08 S 46.05 W
Cabras, Stagno di ⊜ 71 39.57 N 8.29 E
Cabras Island I 174p 13.27 N 144.40 E
Cabrel 234 20.06 N 105.14 W
Cabrera ≃, Col. 246 3.26 N 75.07 W
Cabrera ≃, Esp. 34 42.25 N 6.49 W
Cabrera, Illa de I 34 39.09 N 2.56 E
Cabrera, Sierra de la ⋏ 34 42.12 N 6.40 W
Cabrera de Mar 266d 41.32 N 2.24 E
Cabreúva 256 23.18 S 47.08 W
Cabri 184 50.37 N 108.28 W
Cabriel ≃ 34 39.14 N 1.03 W
Cabrillo National Monument ♠ 228 32.41 N 117.15 W
Cabrils 266d 41.32 N 2.22 E
Cabrobó 250 8.31 S 39.19 W
Cabruta 246 7.38 N 66.15 W
Cabucgayan 116 11.29 N 124.34 E
Cabuçu, Bra. 256 22.50 S 42.55 W
Cabuçu, Bra. 287a 22.47 S 43.32 W
Cabuçu, Bra. 287b 23.25 S 46.32 W
Cabuçu ≃, Bra. 287a 22.59 S 43.37 W
Cabuçu ≃, Bra. 287a 22.48 S 43.37 W
Cabuçu de Cima ≃ 287b 23.31 S 46.33 W
Cabugao 116 17.48 N 120.27 E
Cabulauan Island I 116 11.23 N 120.06 E
Cabullones, Punta ≻ 240m 17.58 N 66.35 W
Cabulo 152 10.15 S 16.40 E
Cabure 246 11.08 N 69.38 W
Cabuta 152 9.50 S 14.48 E
Cabuya 236 9.36 N 85.06 W
Cabuyal 236 10.40 N 85.40 W
Cabuyaro 246 4.18 N 72.49 W
Caca 80 48.11 N 44.40 E
Caca, Laguna ⊜ 286b 22.57 N 82.27 W
Caçador 252 26.47 S 51.00 W
Cacahoatán 236 14.59 N 92.10 W
Čačak 38 43.53 N 20.21 E
Cacaluta 234 20.03 N 104.52 W
Cacaoui, Lac ⊜ 186 50.53 N 66.58 W
Caçapava 256 23.06 S 45.42 W
Caçapava do Sul 252 30.30 S 53.30 W
Caçapava Velha 256 23.07 S 45.39 W
Cacapon ≃ 188 39.37 N 78.16 W
Cacapon State Park ♠ 188 39.32 N 78.23 W
Cacas 130 38.23 N 41.17 E
Caccamo 70 37.56 N 13.40 E
Caccia, Capo ≻ 71 40.34 N 8.09 E
Caccuri 68 39.14 N 16.47 E
Čačenka ≃ 265b 55.46 N 37.18 E
Cacequi 252 29.53 S 54.49 W
Cáceres, Bra. 248 16.04 S 57.41 W
Cáceres, Col. 246 7.35 N 75.20 W
Cáceres, Esp. 34 39.29 N 6.22 W
Cachan 261 48.48 N 2.20 E
Cachán ≃ 234 18.11 N 103.08 W
Cacharí 252 36.24 S 59.32 W
Cache 196 34.37 N 98.37 W
Cache ≃, Ar., U.S. 194 34.42 N 91.20 W
Cache ≃, Il., U.S. 194 37.04 N 89.10 W
Caché, Lac ⊜ 206 46.21 N 74.39 W
Cache Creek 182 50.48 N 121.19 W
Cache Creek ≃, Ca., U.S. 226 38.42 N 121.42 W
Cache Creek ≃, Ca., U.S. 228 35.06 N 117.58 W
Cache Creek, North Fork ≃ 226 38.59 N 122.30 W
Cache la Poudre ≃ 200 40.25 N 104.36 W
Cache la Poudre, North Fork ≃ 198 40.54 N 105.22 W
Cache Mountain ∧ 180 65.31 N 147.20 W
Cache Peak ∧, Ca., U.S. 228 35.13 N 118.15 W
Cache Peak ∧, Id., U.S. 202 42.11 N 113.40 W
Cache Slough ≃ 226 38.11 N 121.40 W
Cacheu 150 12.16 N 16.10 W
Cacheu ⊂¹ 150 12.10 N 16.21 W
Cachí 252 25.06 S 66.11 W
Cachimbo 250 9.24 S 54.56 W
Cachimbo, Serra do ⋏ 250 8.30 S 55.50 W
Cachimo 152 8.21 S 21.20 E
Cachingues 152 13.05 S 16.43 E
Cachir 88 48.06 N 98.52 E
Cáchira ≃ 246 7.52 N 73.40 W
Cachkadzor 84 40.33 N 44.43 E
Cachoeira 255 12.36 S 38.58 W
Cachoeira, Reservatório ⊜¹ 256 23.03 S 46.15 W
Cachoeira, Ribeirão ≃ 287b 23.38 S 46.43 W
Cachoeira, Rio da ≃ 287a 23.00 S 43.18 W
Cachoeira Alta 255 18.48 S 50.58 W
Cachoeira de Goiás 255 16.44 S 50.38 W
Cachoeira de Minas 256 22.21 S 45.47 W
Cachoeira do Arari 250 1.01 S 48.58 W
Cachoeira do Sul 252 30.02 S 52.54 W
Cachoeira Paulista 256 22.40 S 45.01 W
Cachoeiras 287a 22.39 S 43.28 W
Cachoeiras de Macacu 256 22.28 S 42.39 W
Cachoeirinha 250 8.29 S 36.14 W
Cachoeiro de Itapemirim 255 20.51 S 41.06 W
Cachorros, Rio dos ≃ 287a 22.52 S 43.34 W
Cachos, Punta ≻ 252 27.39 S 71.02 W
Cachos, Rio dos ≃ 287b 23.36 S 46.26 W
Čachrov 60 49.16 N 13.18 E
Cachuela Esperanza 248 10.32 S 65.38 W
Cachuma, Lake ⊜¹ 204 34.35 N 119.55 W
Cacilhas 266c 38.41 N 9.09 W
Cacimbinhas 250 9.24 S 36.59 W
Cacine 150 11.08 N 14.57 W
Caciporé ≃ 250 3.51 N 51.08 W
Caciporé, Cabo ≻ 250 3.55 N 51.07 W
Căciulați 38 44.38 N 26.10 E
Cacnipa Island I 116 10.30 N 119.04 E
Cacocum 240p 20.44 N 76.23 W
Cacólo 152 10.07 S 19.17 E
Caconda 152 13.43 S 15.06 E
Caconde 256 21.33 S 46.38 W
Cacra 248 12.48 S 75.48 W
Cactus 196 36.04 N 102.00 W
Cactus Flat ≚ 204 37.45 N 116.45 W
Cactus Peak ∧ 204 37.47 N 116.53 W
Caçu 255 18.37 S 51.04 W
Cacuaco 152 8.47 S 13.22 E
Cacula 152 14.29 S 14.10 E
Caculé 255 14.30 S 42.13 W
Caculuvar ≃ 152 16.46 S 14.36 E
Caçumba, Ilha I 255 17.46 S 39.17 W
Cacuri 152 8.14 S 18.20 E
Cacuso 152 9.26 S 15.43 E
Čadale 144 2.45 N 46.19 E
Čadan 86 51.17 N 91.35 E
Cadaqués 34 42.17 N 3.17 E
Čadariri ≃ 248 6.20 S 57.46 W
Čadca 30 49.26 N 18.48 E
Caddington 42 51.51 N 0.27 W
Caddo, Ok., U.S. 196 34.07 N 96.15 W
Caddo, Tx., U.S. 196 32.38 N 98.40 W
Caddo ≃ 194 34.10 N 93.03 W
Caddo Creek ≃ 196 34.14 N 96.59 W
Caddo Lake ⊜¹ 194 32.42 N 94.01 W
Caddo Mills 222 33.04 N 96.14 W
Caddo Peak ∧ 222 32.29 N 97.24 W
Caddy Vista 216 42.50 N 87.54 W
Cadell ≃ 166 22.51 S 141.55 E
Cadena, Arroyo de la ≃ 196 26.17 N 104.00 W
Cadena, Cerro ∧ 196 25.50 N 104.04 W
Cadena, Punta ≻ 240m 18.18 N 67.14 W
Cadenberge 52 53.46 N 9.04 E
Cadenet 62 43.44 N 5.22 E
Cadeo 62 44.58 N 9.48 E
Cader Bronwyn ∧ 42 52.54 N 3.22 W
Cadereyta Jiménez 232 25.36 N 100.00 W
Cader Idris ∧ 42 52.42 N 3.54 W
Cadibarrawirracanna, Lake ⊜ 162 28.52 S 135.27 E
Cadig, Mount ∧ 116 14.09 N 122.27 E
Cadillac, Sk., Can. 184 49.44 N 107.43 W
Cadillac, Fr. 32 44.38 N 0.19 W
Cadillac, Mi., U.S. 190 44.15 N 85.24 W
Cadipietra (Steinhaus) 64 46.59 N 11.59 E
Cadishead 262 53.25 N 2.26 W
Cadix → Cádiz 34 36.32 N 6.18 W
Cádiz, Esp. 34 36.32 N 6.18 W
Cadiz, Pil. 116 10.57 N 123.18 E
Cadiz, In., U.S. 218 39.57 N 85.30 W
Cadiz, Ky., U.S. 194 36.51 N 87.50 W
Cadiz, Oh., U.S. 214 40.16 N 80.59 W
Cádiz, Bahía de ⊂ 34 36.32 N 6.16 W
Cádiz, Golfo de ⊂ 34 36.50 N 7.10 W
Cadiz Lake ⊜ 204 34.18 N 115.24 W
Cadlao Island I 116 11.13 N 119.21 E
Çadnam 42 50.55 N 1.35 W
Čadobec 88 58.40 N 98.51 E
Čadobec ≃ 88 58.40 N 98.50 E
Cadogan 214 40.45 N 79.34 W
Cadomin 182 53.02 N 117.20 W
Cadoneghe 64 45.26 N 11.55 E
Cadore ◆¹ 64 46.30 N 12.20 E
Cadosia 210 41.58 N 75.16 W
Cadott 190 44.56 N 91.09 W
Cadoux 162 30.47 S 117.08 E
Caduruan Point ≻ 116 11.45 N 124.05 E
Caduta, Fosso delle ≃ 267a 41.56 N 12.12 E
Cadwell 192 32.20 N 83.02 W
Cady Marsh Ditch ≅ 278 41.33 N 87.29 W
Cady Mountain ∧² 224 48.33 N 123.07 W
Čadyr-Lunga 78 46.03 N 28.47 E
Cadzand 52 51.22 N 3.25 E
Caen 32 49.11 N 0.21 W
Caengo (Kwenge) ≃ 152 4.50 S 18.42 E
Caerano di San Marco 64 45.47 N 12.00 E
Caere ⊥ 66 42.02 N 12.07 E
Caergwrle 44 53.07 N 3.03 W
Caerleon 42 51.37 N 2.57 W
Caernarfon 44 53.08 N 4.16 W
Caernarfon Bay ⊂ 44 53.05 N 4.30 W
Caernarfon Castle ⊥ 44 53.08 N 4.16 W
Caerphilly 42 51.35 N 3.14 W
Caerphilly Castle ⊥ 42 51.34 N 3.14 W
Caersws 42 52.31 N 3.25 W
Caesar Creek ≃ 218 39.29 N 84.06 W
Caesar Creek, Anderson Fork ≃ 218 39.33 N 83.58 W
Caesar Creek Lake ⊜¹ 218 39.30 N 84.00 W
Cæsarea → Qesari, Ḫorbat ⊥ 132 32.30 N 34.53 E
Caetanópolis 255 19.18 S 44.24 W
Caeté 255 19.54 S 43.40 W
Caeté ≃ 248 9.03 S 68.39 W
Caetité 255 14.04 S 42.29 W
Cafayate 252 26.05 S 65.58 W
Cafelândia do Leste Matogrossense 255 16.40 S 53.25 W
Cafima 152 16.39 S 16.27 E
Cafu 152 16.27 S 15.14 E
Cafuini ≃ 246 1.17 N 57.11 W
Cafundó 256 22.31 S 46.25 W
Cagaan Chajrchan 88 49.25 N 94.15 E
Cagaan Gol 86 48.57 N 89.07 E
Cagaan Nuur, Mong. 86 49.32 N 89.42 E
Cagaannuur, Mong. 88 50.20 N 105.03 E
Cagaan-Ovoo 102 45.51 N 105.17 E
Cagaan Uul 88 49.28 N 98.30 E
Cagaan-Üür 88 50.32 N 101.30 E
Çágado ≃ 256 22.02 S 43.09 W
Čagan ≃ 80 51.12 N 51.20 E
Cagan-Aman 80 47.34 N 46.43 E
Cagan-Churtej, chrebet ⋏ 88 51.32 N 110.00 E
Cagarras, Ilhas II 287a 23.02 S 43.12 W
Cagayan □⁴ 116 18.00 N 121.50 E
Cagayan ≃ 116 18.22 N 121.37 E
Cagayancillo 116 9.34 N 121.12 E
Cagayan de Oro 116 8.29 N 124.39 E
Cagayan de Tawi-Tawi 116 7.01 N 118.30 E
Cagayan Island I 116 9.36 N 121.14 E
Cagayan Islands II 116 9.40 N 121.16 E
Çagayan Sulu Island I 116 7.01 N 118.30 E
Čagda 74 58.45 N 130.37 E
Cageri 84 42.39 N 42.45 E
Caggiano 68 40.34 N 15.29 E
Çağış 130 39.30 N 28.01 E
Çağlarca 130 39.05 N 39.10 E
Cagli 66 43.33 N 12.39 E
Cagliari 71 39.13 N 9.07 E
Cagliari □⁴ 71 39.30 N 8.45 E
Cagliari, Golfo di ⊂ 71 39.08 N 9.11 E
Çagliari, Stagno di ⊜ 71 39.13 N 9.02 E
Čaglinka ≃ 86 53.59 N 69.47 E
Cagnano Varano 68 41.49 N 15.47 E
Çagnes-sur-Mer 62 43.40 N 7.09 E
Čagoda 76 59.10 N 35.17 E
Čagoda ≃ 76 59.05 N 35.18 E
Čagodošča ≃ 76 58.57 N 36.35 E
Čagojan 89 52.08 N 128.15 E
Čagra ≃ 80 52.37 N 48.15 E
Cagraray Island I 116 13.18 N 123.52 E
Cagua 246 10.11 N 67.27 W
Caguán ≃ 246 0.08 S 74.18 W
Caguas 240m 18.14 N 66.02 W
Cagveri 84 41.48 N 43.29 E
Cagwait 116 8.55 N 126.18 E
Cahaba ≃ 194 32.20 N 87.05 W
Cahabón 236 15.34 N 89.49 W
Cahabón ≃ 236 15.25 N 89.36 W
Cahama 152 16.17 S 14.19 E
Caha Mountains ⋏ 48 51.45 N 9.45 W
Caher 48 52.21 N 7.56 W
Caherdaniel 48 51.45 N 10.05 W
Cahersiveen 48 51.57 N 10.13 W
Cahokia 219 38.34 N 90.11 W
Cahokia Creek ≃ 219 38.47 N 90.01 W
Cahokia Mounds State Park ♠ 219 38.39 N 90.03 W
Cahoon Creek ≃ 279a 41.29 N 81.55 W
Cahoon Park ♠ 279a 41.29 N 81.56 W
Cahoonzie 210 41.26 N 74.43 W
Cahore Point ≻ 48 52.34 N 6.11 W
Cahors 32 44.27 N 1.26 E
Cahto Peak ∧ 204 39.41 N 123.35 W
Cahuilla Indian Reservation ◆⁴ 204 33.30 N 116.43 W
Cahuinari ≃ 246 1.21 S 70.44 W
Cahuita, Punta ≻ 236 9.45 N 82.49 W
Caí ≃ 252 29.56 S 51.16 W
Caia ≃ 34 38.50 N 7.05 W
Caiabis, Serra dos ⋏¹ 248 11.30 S 56.30 W
Caianda 152 11.02 S 23.31 E
Caiapó ≃, Bra. 250 8.52 S 49.36 W
Caiapó ≃, Bra. 255 15.49 S 51.53 W
Caiapó, Serra do ⋏ 255 17.00 S 52.00 W
Caiapônia 255 16.57 S 51.49 W
Caiazzo 68 41.11 N 14.22 E
Caibarién 240p 22.31 N 79.28 W
Cai Bau, Dao I 110 21.10 N 107.27 E
Caibiran 116 11.34 N 124.35 E
Caiçara, Bra. 250 6.36 S 35.29 W
Caiçara, Bra. 250 5.04 S 36.03 W
Caiçara, Bra. 255 15.34 S 50.12 W
Caicara, Ven. 246 7.37 N 66.10 W
Caiçara ≃ 246 3.11 S 64.49 W
Caicara, Caño ≃ 246 7.44 N 69.04 W
Caicara de Maturín 246 9.49 N 63.36 W
Caicedonia 246 4.20 N 75.50 W
Caicó 250 6.27 S 37.06 W
Caicos Islands II 238 21.56 N 71.58 W
Caicos Passage ⊔ 238 22.00 N 72.30 W
Caieiras 256 23.22 S 46.44 W
Caieiras □⁷ 287b 23.23 S 46.41 W
Caigou 100 33.16 N 114.32 E
Caiguna 162 32.17 S 125.25 E
Caihuaping 100 26.54 N 113.23 E
Caijiachang 107 29.44 N 106.29 E
Caijiagang 107 28.55 N 106.21 E
Caijialou 104 41.24 N 121.06 E
Caijiapo 102 34.17 N 107.39 E
Caijiazhuang 105 40.48 N 114.44 E
Caille 62 43.46 N 6.44 E
Cailloma 248 15.12 S 71.46 W
Caillou Bay ⊂ 194 29.06 N 90.56 W
Caima Bay ⊂ 116 13.42 N 122.48 E
Caimán, Islas → Cayman Islands □² 238 19.30 N 80.40 W
Caimanera 240p 19.59 N 75.09 W
Caïmanes → Cayman Islands □² 238 19.30 N 80.40 W
Caiman Point ≻ 116 15.55 N 119.46 E
Caimbambo 152 12.58 S 14.01 E
Cain ≃ 42 52.46 N 3.08 W
Cain Creek ≃ 198 44.17 N 98.10 W
Cainde 152 15.42 S 13.12 E
Caine ≃ 248 18.23 S 65.21 W
Caino 64 45.38 N 10.18 E
Cains ≃ 186 46.40 N 65.47 W
Cainsdorf 54 50.41 N 12.29 E
Cainsville 194 40.28 N 93.59 W
Cainta 269f 14.35 N 121.07 E
Cai Nuoc 110 8.56 N 105.01 E
Cairano 68 40.54 N 15.22 E
Cairari 250 2.33 S 49.07 W
Caird Coast ⊥² 9 76.00 S 24.30 W
Caire, Le → Al-Qāhirah 142 30.03 N 31.15 E
Cairnbrook 214 40.07 N 78.49 W
Cairn Curran Reservoir ⊜¹ 169 37.04 S 143.59 E
Cairndow 46 56.15 N 4.56 W
Cairngorm Mountains ⋏ 46 57.04 N 3.50 W
Cairn Mountain ∧ 180 61.10 N 155.20 W
Cairnryan 44 54.58 N 5.02 W
Cairns 166 16.55 S 145.46 E
Cairns Lake ⊜ 184 51.42 N 94.30 W
Cairnsmore of Carsphairn ∧ 44 55.15 N 4.12 W
Cairnsmore of Fleet ∧ 44 54.59 N 4.20 W
Cairn Table ∧ 44 55.29 N 4.02 W
Cairn Water ≃ 44 55.07 N 3.45 W
Cairo → Al-Qāhirah, Miṣr 142 30.03 N 31.15 E
Cairo, Ga., U.S. 192 30.52 N 84.12 W
Cairo, Il., U.S. 194 37.00 N 89.10 W
Cairo, Ne., U.S. 198 41.00 N 98.36 W
Cairo, N.Y., U.S. 210 42.17 N 73.59 W
Cairo, Oh., U.S. 216 40.49 N 84.05 W
Cairo, W.V., U.S. 188 39.12 N 81.09 W
Cairo (Almaza) Airport ⊠, Miṣr 273c 30.06 N 31.22 E
Cairo (Imbābah) Airport ⊠, Miṣr 273c 30.04 N 31.12 E
Cairo, University of ♁² 273c 30.02 N 31.12 E
Cairoçu, Pico do ∧ 256 23.18 S 44.36 W
Cairofa 152 14.05 S 12.54 E
Cairo International Airport ⊠ 142 30.08 N 31.24 E
Cairo Main Station ◆⁵ 273c 30.04 N 31.15 E
Cairo Montenotte 62 44.24 N 8.16 E
Cairu 255 13.30 S 39.03 W
Caister-on-Sea 42 52.39 N 1.44 E
Caistor 44 53.30 N 0.20 W
Caitingqiao 105 39.54 N 117.39 E
Caitou 152 14.28 S 13.06 E
Caiundo 152 15.46 S 17.28 E
Caivano 68 40.57 N 14.18 E
Caiwan 102 25.50 N 110.50 E
Caixi 100 25.15 N 116.28 E
Caiyu 105 39.39 N 116.37 E
Caiza 248 20.02 S 65.40 W
Caizhuang 98 34.17 N 114.08 E
Çaizi Hu ⊜ 100 30.48 N 117.05 E
Čaja ≃, S.S.S.R. 86 58.08 N 82.57 E
Čaja ≃, S.S.S.R. 88 58.15 N 109.35 E
Cajabamba, Ec. 246 1.42 S 78.45 W
Cajabamba, Perú 248 7.37 S 78.03 W
Cajacay 248 10.10 S 77.26 W
Caja de Muertos, Isla I 240m 17.54 N 66.32 W
Cajamar 256 23.21 S 46.53 W
Cajamarca 248 7.10 S 78.31 W
Çajamarca □⁵ 248 6.15 S 78.50 W
Čajan 85 43.02 N 69.23 E
Čajan ≃ 85 42.52 N 68.56 E
Cajapió 250 2.58 S 44.48 W
Cajarc 32 44.29 N 1.50 E
Cajari 250 3.20 S 45.01 W
Cajari ≃ 250 0.48 S 51.43 W
Çajatambo 248 10.29 S 77.02 W
Čajatyn, chrebet ⋏ 89 52.25 N 138.25 E
Çajàzeiras 250 6.54 S 38.34 W
Čajek 85 41.56 N 74.30 E
Čajkovskij 80 56.47 N 54.09 E
Čajniče 38 43.33 N 19.04 E
Cajones ≃ 234 17.45 N 95.55 W
Cajones, Cayos II 236 16.05 N 83.12 W
Cajon Mountain ∧ 228 34.16 N 117.25 W
Cajon Pass)(228 34.19 N 117.26 W
Cajon Summit)(228 34.21 N 117.27 W
Caju ◆⁸ 287a 22.53 S 43.13 W
Cajueiro 250 9.25 S 36.08 W
Cajuru 255 21.17 S 47.18 W
Caka 102 36.48 N 99.19 E
Çaka Yanhu ⊜ 102 36.40 N 99.20 E
Čakčar, chrebet ⋏ 85 38.35 N 67.28 E
Cakeni 152 17.48 S 19.27 E
Cakir 88 50.27 N 103.35 E
Çakıralan 130 41.10 N 35.47 E
Çakırgöl Dağı ∧ 130 40.34 N 39.42 E
Çakırhüyük 130 37.34 N 37.50 E
Çakmak 130 37.37 N 34.19 E
Çakmak Dağı ∧ 130 39.46 N 42.12 E
Čakovec 61 46.23 N 16.26 E
Čakovice ◆⁸ 54 50.08 N 14.31 E
Cakung ≃ 269e 6.06 S 106.56 E
Çal 130 38.05 N 29.24 E
Cala, Transkei 158 31.30 S 27.37 E
Cala, Tür. 84 41.05 N 43.21 E
Cala, Embalse de ⊜¹ 34 37.50 N 6.00 W
Calabacillas 234 23.13 N 99.45 W
Calabanga 116 13.42 N 123.12 E
Calabar 150 4.57 N 8.19 E
Calabasas, Arroyo ≃ 280 34.12 N 118.36 W
Calabazar ◆⁸ 286b 23.01 N 82.22 W
Calabazas Creek ≃ 282 37.25 N 121.58 W
Calabernardo 70 36.52 N 15.08 E
Calabogie 212 45.18 N 76.43 W
Calabogie Lake ⊜ 212 45.16 N 76.45 W
Calabozo 246 8.56 N 67.26 W
Calabozo, Ensenada de ⊂ 246 11.30 N 71.45 W
Calabria □⁴ 68 39.00 N 16.30 E
Calabria, Parco Nazionale di ♠ 68 38.09 N 15.54 E
Calabritto 68 40.47 N 15.13 E
Calabro ≃ 70 37.53 N 14.11 E
Calabugdong Island I 116 11.06 N 119.41 E
Calaca 116 13.56 N 120.49 E
Calacuccia 36 42.20 N 9.03 E
Caladang, Mount ∧ 116 14.49 N 121.21 E
Caladesi Island I 220 28.02 N 82.49 W
Caladesi Island State Park ♠ 220 28.02 N 82.48 W
Cala d'Oliva 71 41.05 N 8.20 E
Calafat 38 43.59 N 22.56 E
Calafate 254 50.20 S 72.18 W
Calafquen, Lago ⊜ 254 39.31 S 72.10 W
Calagnaan Island I 116 11.29 N 123.13 E
Cala Gonone 71 40.18 N 9.38 E
Calagua Islands II 116 14.27 N 122.55 E
Calahorra 34 42.18 N 1.58 W
Calais, Fr. 50 50.57 N 1.50 E
Calais, Me., U.S. 188 45.11 N 67.16 W
Calais, Canal de ≅ 50 50.57 N 1.51 E
Calais, Pas de (Strait of Dover) ⊔ 50 51.00 N 1.30 E
Calala 152 12.59 S 23.30 E
Calalaste, Sierra de ⋏ 252 25.30 S 67.30 W
Calalzo di Cadore 64 46.27 N 12.23 E
Calama, Bra. 248 8.03 S 62.53 W
Calama, Chile 252 22.28 S 68.56 W
Calamar, Col. 246 10.15 N 74.55 W
Calamar, Col. 246 1.58 N 72.41 W
Calamarca 248 16.55 S 68.09 W
Calamba, Pil. 116 14.13 N 121.10 E
Calamba, Pil. 116 8.35 N 123.39 E
Calamian Group II 116 12.00 N 120.00 E
Calamity Creek ≃ 196 29.41 N 103.42 W
Calamocha 34 40.55 N 1.18 W
Calamonaci 70 37.31 N 13.17 E
Calamus ≃ 198 41.48 N 99.09 W
Calañas 34 37.39 N 6.53 W
Calanca, Val ∨ 58 46.22 N 9.07 E
Calanda 34 40.56 N 0.14 W
Calandagan Island I 116 10.39 N 120.15 E
Calang 114 4.38 N 95.34 E
Calangianus 71 40.56 N 9.11 E
Calanna 68 38.11 N 15.43 E
Calapan 116 13.25 N 121.10 E
Calape 116 9.54 N 123.52 E
Calapooia ≃ 202 44.38 N 123.08 W
Calapooya Mountains ⋏ 202 43.30 N 122.50 W
Călărași 38 44.11 N 27.20 E
Călărași □⁶ 38 44.20 N 27.10 E
Calarcá 246 4.31 N 75.38 W
Calascibetta 70 37.35 N 14.16 E
Calasetta 71 39.07 N 8.22 E
Calatabiano 70 37.49 N 15.14 E
Calatafimi 70 37.55 N 12.52 E
Calatagan 116 13.50 N 120.38 E
Calatayud 34 41.21 N 1.38 W
Calau 54 51.45 N 13.56 E
Calauag Bay ≃ 116 14.02 N 122.13 E
Calavá, Capo ≻ 70 38.11 N 14.55 E
Calaveras □⁶ 226 38.12 N 120.4[illegible] W
Calaveras ≃ 226 37.58 N 121.22 W
Calaveras, North Fork ≃ 226 38.12 N 120.43 W
Calaveras Big Trees State Park ♠ 226 38.16 N 120.19 W
Calaveras Point ≻ 282 37.28 N 122.03 W
Calaveras Reservoir ⊜¹ 226 37.28 N 121.49 W
Calaveritas Creek ≃ 226 38.10 N 120.40 W
Calavino 64 46.03 N 10.59 E
Calavite, Cape ≻ 116 13.27 N 120.18 E
Calavite, Mount ∧ 116 13.29 N 120.24 E
Calavite Passage ⊔ 116 13.36 N 120.25 E
Calavon ≃ 62 43.51 N 5.00 E
Calawah ≃ 224 47.56 N 124.27 W
Calawah, North Fork ≃ 224 47.58 N 124.20 W
Calawah, South Fork ≃ 224 47.58 N 124.20 W
Calayan 116 19.16 N 121.28 E
Çalayan Island I 116 19.20 N 121.27 E
Čalba 89 52.43 N 131.27 E
Calbayog 116 12.04 N 124.36 E
Calbe 54 51.54 N 11.46 E
Calbiga 116 11.38 N 125.01 E
Calbuco 254 41.46 S 73.08 W
Calca 248 13.20 S 71.57 W
Calçado ≃ 256 22.05 S 43.04 W
Calcasieu ≃ 194 30.05 N 93.20 W
Calcasieu Lake ⊜ 194 29.50 N 93.17 W
Calceta 246 0.51 S 80.10 W
Calcha 248 21.06 S 67.31 W
Calchaquí 252 29.54 S 60.18 W
Calchaquí ≃ 252 26.03 S 65.50 W
Calciano 68 40.35 N 16.11 E
Calcinaia 66 43.41 N 10.37 E
Calcinato 64 45.27 N 10.24 E
Calcio 62 45.30 N 9.50 E
Calcium 212 44.01 N 75.51 W
Calçoene 250 2.30 N 50.57 W
Calçoene ≃ 250 2.30 N 50.50 W
Calcutta, India 126 22.32 N 88.22 E
Calcutta, India 272b 22.32 N 88.22 E
Calcutta, Oh., U.S. 214 40.40 N 80.34 W
Calcutta University ♁² 272b 22.35 N 88.22 E
Caldaro (Kaltern) 64 46.25 N 11.14 E
Caldarola 66 43.08 N 13.13 E
Caldas, Bra. 256 21.56 S 46.23 W
Caldas, Col. 246 6.05 N 75.38 W
Caldas □⁵ 246 5.15 N 75.30 W
Caldas da Rainha 34 39.24 N 9.08 W
Caldas de Reyes 34 42.36 N 8.38 W
Caldas Novas 255 17.45 S 48.38 W
Caldè 58 45.57 N 8.38 E
Caldecott Tunnel ◆⁵ 282 37.52 N 122.12 W
Calder ≃, Eng., U.K. 44 53.44 N 1.21 W
Calder ≃, Eng., U.K. 262 53.49 N 2.24 W
Calder, Loch ⊜ 46 58.31 N 3.36 W
Caldera 252 27.04 S 70.50 W
Caldera de Taburiente, Parque Nacional de la ♠ 148 28.48 N 17.52 W
Calder and Hebble Navigation Canal ≅ 262 53.43 N 1.54 W
Calder Bridge 44 54.27 N 3.29 W
Calderbrook 262 53.39 N 2.05 W
Calderdale □⁸ 262 53.44 N 2.00 W
Calderstones Park ♠ 262 53.23 N 2.54 W
Caldes 64 46.22 N 10.56 E
Caldes ≃ 266d 41.31 N 2.13 E
Caldew ≃ 44 54.54 N 2.56 W
Caldey Island I 42 51.38 N 4.41 W
Caldicot 42 51.36 N 2.45 W
Caldiero 64 45.22 N 11.11 E
Çaldıran 84 39.09 N 43.55 E
Čaldonazzo 64 45.59 N 11.16 E
Caldonazzo, Lago di ⊜ 64 46.01 N 11.15 E
Čaldonka 88 53.47 N 119.12 E
Caldwell, Id., U.S. 202 43.39 N 116.41 W
Caldwell, Ks., U.S. 198 37.01 N 97.36 W
Caldwell, N.J., U.S. 276 40.51 N 74.17 W
Caldwell, Oh., U.S. 188 39.44 N 81.31 W
Caldwell, Tx., U.S. 222 30.31 N 96.41 W
Caldwell □⁶ 222 29.50 N 97.40 W
Caldwell Creek ≃ 214 41.37 N 79.37 W
Caldwell-Wright Airport ⊠ 276 40.53 N 74.17 W
Caldy 262 53.21 N 3.10 W
Cale ≃ 42 50.59 N 2.20 W
Caledon, On., Can. 212 43.52 N 80.00 W
Caledon, S. Afr. 158 34.12 S 19.23 E
Caledon (Mohokare) ≃ 158 30.31 S 26.05 E
Caledon East 212 43.52 N 79.52 W
Caledonia, Belize 232 18.14 N 88.29 W
Caledonia, N.S., Can. 186 44.22 N 65.02 W
Caledonia, On., Can. 212 43.04 N 79.56 W
Caledonia, Il., U.S. 216 42.22 N 88.53 W
Caledonia, Mi., U.S. 216 42.47 N 85.31 W
Caledonia, Mn., U.S. 190 43.38 N 91.29 W
Caledonia, Ms., U.S. 194 33.40 N 88.19 W
Caledonia, N.Y., U.S. 210 42.58 N 77.51 W
Caledonia, Oh., U.S. 214 40.38 N 82.58 W
Caledonia, Pa., U.S. 214 41.17 N 78.27 W
Caledonian Canal ≅ 46 56.50 N 5.06 W
Caledonia State Park ♠ 208 39.56 N 77.29 W
Calego 152 12.10 S 23.36 E
Calella 34 41.37 N 2.40 E
Calemba 152 16.04 S 15.44 E
Calen 166 20.54 S 148.46 E
Calendžicha 84 42.37 N 42.04 E
Calenzano 66 43.51 N 11.09 E
Calera, Al., U.S. 194 33.06 N 86.45 W
Calera, Ok., U.S. 196 33.56 N 96.25 W
Calera Creek ≃ 282 37.27 N 121.54 W
Calera Víctor Rosales 234 22.57 N 102.42 W
Caleta, Punta ≻ 240p 20.04 N 74.18 W
Caleta Olivia 254 46.26 S 67.32 W
Caleufú 252 35.35 S 64.33 W
Calexico 204 32.40 N 115.29 W
Calf Island I 283 42.20 N 70.54 W
Calf Islands II 276 40.59 N 73.38 W
Calfkiller ≃ 194 35.49 N 85.29 W
Calf of Man I 44 54.03 N 4.48 W
Calfpasture ≃ 188 37.58 N 79.28 W
Calf Pasture Point ≻ 276 41.05 N 73.24 W
Calgary 182 51.03 N 114.05 W
Calhan 198 39.02 N 104.17 W
Calhariz ◆⁸ 266c 38.44 N 9.12 W
Calhoun, Al., U.S. 194 32.03 N 86.32 W
Calhoun, Ga., U.S. 192 34.30 N 84.57 W
Calhoun, Ky., U.S. 194 37.32 N 87.15 W
Calhoun, Mo., U.S. 194 38.28 N 93.37 W
Calhoun, Tn., U.S. 192 35.17 N 84.44 W
Calhoun □⁶, Il., U.S. 219 39.09 N 90.37 W
Calhoun □⁶, Mi., U.S. 216 42.14 N 85.00 W
Calhoun City 194 33.51 N 89.18 W
Calhoun Falls 192 34.05 N 82.35 W
Cali, Col. 246 3.27 N 76.31 W
Çalı, Tür. 130 40.10 N 28.54 E
Čalian Point ≻ 116 6.07 N 125.42 E
Calicoan Island I 116 10.59 N 125.48 E
Calico Ghost Town ⊥ 228 34.57 N 116.52 W
Calico Rock 194 36.07 N 92.08 W
Calicut 122 11.15 N 75.46 E
Caliente, Ca., U.S. 228 35.17 N 118.37 W
Caliente, Nv., U.S. 204 37.36 N 114.30 W
Caliente Creek ≃ 228 35.17 N 118.48 W
Califon 210 40.43 N 74.50 W
California, Mo., U.S. 194 38.37 N 92.33 W
California, Pa., U.S. 214 40.03 N 79.53 W
California □³, U.S. 178 37.30 N 119.30 W
California □³, U.S. 204 37.30 N 119.30 W
California, Golfo de ⊂ 232 28.00 N 112.00 W
California, University of ♁² 282 37.52 N 122.15 W
California Aqueduct ≅¹ 204 33.52 N 117.12 W
California City 228 35.08 N 117.58 W
California Creek ≃ 196 33.05 N 99.33 W
California Institute of Technology ♁² 280 34.08 N 118.08 W
California Institution for Men ♁ 280 33.59 N 117.40 W
California Institution for Women ♁ 280 33.57 N 117.38 W
California-Los Angeles, University of (U.C.L.A.) ♁² 280 34.04 N 118.26 W
California State Polytechnic University ♁² 280 34.04 N 117.49 W
California State University (Los Angeles) ♁², Ca., U.S. 280 34.04 N 118.10 W
California State University (Dominguez Hills) ♁², Ca., U.S. 280 33.52 N 118.17 W
California State University (Fullerton) ♁², Ca., U.S. 280 33.53 N 117.53 W
California State University (Long Beach) ♁², Ca., U.S. 280 33.47 N 118.06 W
California State University (Northridge) ♁², Ca., U.S. 280 34.14 N 118.32 W
California State University (Hayward) ♁², Ca., U.S. 282 37.39 N 122.04 W
Calihualá 234 17.35 N 98.10 W
Calilegua 252 23.47 S 64.47 W
Călimănești 38 45.14 N 24.20 E
Călimani, Munții ⋏ 38 47.07 N 25.03 E
Calimera 68 40.15 N 18.17 E
Calimere, Point ≻ 122 10.18 N 79.52 E
Calimesa 228 34.00 N 117.03 W
Calindó ≃ 255 14.26 S 43.51 W
Calingasta 252 31.19 S 69.25 W
Calingiri 162 31.06 S 116.27 E
Calinog 116 11.07 N 122.32 E
Calintaan 116 12.35 N 120.56 E
Calion 194 33.19 N 92.32 W
Calipatria 204 33.07 N 115.30 W
Calispell Peak ∧ 202 48.26 N 117.30 W
Calistoga 226 38.34 N 122.34 W
Calitri 68 40.54 N 15.27 E
Calitzdorp 158 33.33 S 21.42 E
Calixtlahuaca ⊥ 234 19.20 N 99.42 W
Calizzano 62 44.14 N 8.07 E
Calka 84 41.37 N 44.05 E
Calkinskoje vodochranilišče ⊜¹ 84 41.38 N 44.03 E
Čalkojdy 85 40.44 N 73.39 E
Calla 226 37.46 N 121.11 W
Callabonna, Lake ⊜ 166 29.45 S 140.04 E
Callabonna Creek ≃ 166 29.38 S 140.08 E
Callac 32 48.24 N 3.26 W
Callaghan, Mount ∧ 204 39.42 N 116.57 W
Callahan 192 30.33 N 81.49 W
Callahan, Mount ∧ 200 39.26 N 108.07 W
Callahans 276 40.58 N 74.37 W
Callan 48 52.33 N 7.23 W
Callander, On., Can. 190 46.13 N 79.23 W
Callander, Scot., U.K. 46 56.15 N 4.14 W
Callang 116 17.02 N 121.38 E
Callanish 46 58.12 N 6.43 W
Callanmarca 248 12.52 S 74.38 W
Callanna 166 29.38 S 137.55 E
Callantsoog 52 52.49 N 4.41 E
Callao, Perú 248 12.04 S 77.09 W
Callao, Va., U.S. 208 37.58 N 76.33 W
Callao □⁴ 286d 12.04 S 77.09 W
Callas 62 43.35 N 6.32 E
Callaway 198 41.17 N 99.55 W
Callaway □⁶ 219 38.50 N 91.52 W
Callaway Gardens ♠ 192 32.51 N 84.52 W
Calle 56 51.20 N 8.13 E
Callensburg 214 41.08 N 79.33 W
Callery 214 40.45 N 80.02 W
Call Hill ∧² 210 42.13 N 77.40 W
Calliano, It. 62 45.00 N 8.15 E
Calliano, It. 64 45.56 N 11.05 E
Calliaqua 241h 13.08 N 61.12 W
Callicoon 210 41.46 N 75.03 W
Callicoon Center 210 41.50 N 74.57 W
Calliham 196 28.29 N 98.21 W
Calling Lake 182 55.15 N 113.12 W
Calling Lake ⊜ 182 55.13 N 113.15 W
Callington, Austl. 168b 35.07 S 139.02 E
Callington, Eng., U.K. 42 50.30 N 4.18 W
Calliope 166 24.00 S 151.12 E
Callosa d'En Sarrià 34 38.39 N 0.07 W
Callosa de Segura 34 38.08 N 0.52 W
Calloway Canal ≅ 226 35.24 N 119.01 W
Calmar, Ab., Can. 182 53.16 N 113.49 W
Calmar → Kalmar, Sve. 26 56.40 N 16.22 E
Calmar, Ia., U.S. 190 43.11 N 91.51 W
Călmățui ≃ 38 44.50 N 27.50 E
Calmazzo 66 43.40 N 12.46 E
Calmbach 56 48.46 N 8.35 E
Çalm Lake ⊜ 190 48.46 N 92.04 W
Čal'mny-Varre 24 67.10 N 37.33 E
Čalna 24 61.55 N 34.01 E
Calnalí 234 20.55 N 98.35 W
Calne 42 51.27 N 2.00 W
Calobre 236 8.19 N 80.51 W
Calola 152 16.30 S 17.51 E
Calolbon 116 13.36 N 124.06 E
Calólo 152 10.00 S 14.53 E
Calolziocorte 62 45.48 N 9.26 E
Calonne-Ricouart 50 50.29 N 2.29 E
Caloocan 116 14.39 N 120.58 E
Caloosahatchee ≃ 220 26.31 N 82.01 W
Caloosahatchee Canal ≅ 220 26.46 N 81.27 W
Caloote 168b 34.58 S 139.16 E
Calore ≃, It. 68 41.11 N 14.28 E
Calore ≃, It. 68 40.31 N 15.01 E
Calotlán ≃ 234 22.06 N 103.42 W
Caloundra 166 26.48 S 153.09 E
Calouste-Gulbenkian, Museu de ♁ 266c 38.44 N 9.08 W
Caloveto 68 39.30 N 16.45 E
Calp 34 38.39 N 0.03 E
Calpan 234 19.06 N 98.27 W
Çalpulalpan 234 19.35 N 98.35 W
Čalpy 80 55.05 N 53.06 E
Calshot 42 50.49 N 1.19 W
Calstock 42 50.30 N 4.12 W
Caltabellotta 70 37.34 N 13.13 E
Caltagirone 70 37.14 N 14.31 E
Caltagirone ≃ 70 37.21 N 14.42 E
Caltanissetta 70 37.29 N 14.04 E
Caltanissetta □⁴ 70 37.29 N 14.04 E
Caltavuturo 70 37.49 N 13.53 E
Çaltılıbük 130 39.57 N 28.36 E
Çaltra 48 53.26 N 8.25 W
Čaltyr' 83 47.17 N 39.30 E
Caluango 152 8.21 S 19.40 E
Calubian 116 11.27 N 124.26 E
Calucinga 152 11.18 S 16.12 E
Călugăreni 38 44.07 N 26.01 E
Caluire-et-Cuire 62 45.48 N 4.51 E
Calumbolaca 152 9.09 S 13.48 E
Calumet, Mi., U.S. 190 47.14 N 88.27 W
Calumet, Mn., U.S. 190 47.19 N 93.16 W
Calumet, Pa., U.S. 214 40.13 N 79.28 W
Calumet ≃ 278 41.44 N 87.32 W
Calumet, Lake ⊜ 216 41.41 N 87.35 W
Calumet City 216 41.36 N 87.31 W
Calumet Harbor ⊂ 278 41.44 N 87.32 W
Calumet Park 278 41.39 N 87.39 W
Calumet Park ♠ 278 41.43 N 87.32 W
Calumet Sag Channel ≅ 278 41.42 N 87.57 W
Calumpit 116 14.55 N 120.46 E
Calunda 152 12.06 S 23.23 E
Caluquembe 152 13.47 S 14.44 E
Calusa Island I 116 9.37 N 121.01 E
Caluso 62 45.18 N 7.53 E
Caluula 144 11.58 N 50.45 E
Caluula, Raasiga ≻ 144 11.59 N 50.47 E
Caluya Island I 116 11.55 N 121.34 E
Calvados □⁵ 32 49.10 N 0.30 W
Calvello 68 40.28 N 15.51 E
Calver 44 53.16 N 1.38 W
Calvera 68 40.09 N 16.09 E
Calvert, Al., U.S. 194 31.09 N 88.01 W
Calvert, Tx., U.S. 222 30.58 N 96.40 W
Calvert □⁶ 208 38.33 N 76.35 W
Calvert ≃ 164 16.17 S 137.44 E
Calvert, Lough ⊜ 169 38.11 S 143.42 E
Calvert City 194 37.02 N 88.21 W
Calvert Hills 166 17.15 S 137.20 E
Calvert Island I 182 51.35 N 128.00 W
Calverton, Eng., U.K. 44 53.02 N 1.05 W
Calverton, Md., U.S. 284c 39.03 N 76.56 W
Calverton, N.Y., U.S. 207 40.55 N 72.45 W
Calvi 32 42.34 N 8.45 E
Calvi, Monte ∧ 66 43.05 N 10.37 E
Calvia 34 39.34 N 2.31 E
Calvi dell'Umbria 66 42.24 N 12.34 E
Calvillo 234 21.51 N 102.43 W
Calvin, Ok., U.S. 196 34.58 N 96.14 W
Calvin, Pa., U.S. 214 40.20 N 78.02 W
Calvinia 158 31.25 S 19.45 E
Calvisano 64 45.20 N 10.20 E
Calvo, Monte ∧ 68 41.44 N 15.46 E
Calvörde 54 52.23 N 11.17 E
Calw 56 48.43 N 8.44 E
Calwa 226 36.42 N 119.45 W
Calypso 192 35.09 N 78.06 W
Calzada 248 6.02 S 77.02 W
Cam ≃ 42 52.21 N 0.15 E
Camabatela 152 8.11 S 15.22 E
Camaçari 255 12.41 S 38.18 W
Camachigama, Lac ⊜ 190 47.50 N 76.19 W
Camacho, Bra. 256 22.20 S 47.13 W
Camacho, Méx. 232 24.25 N 102.18 W
Camacosni 236 14.57 N 85.08 W
Camacupa 152 12.03 S 17.30 E
Camaguán 246 8.06 N 67.36 W

Symbols in the index entries represent the broad categories identified in the key at the right. Symbols with superior numbers (⋏¹) identify subcategories (see complete key on page *I · 1).*

Symbole im Register stellen die rechts im Schlüssel erklärten Kategorien dar. Symbole mit hochgestellten Ziffern (⋏¹) bezeichnen Unterabteilungen einer Kategorie (vgl. vollständiger Schlüssel auf Seite *I · 1).*

Los símbolos incluídos en el texto del índice representan las grandes categorias identificadas con la clave a la derecha. Los símbolos con numeros en su parte superior (⋏¹) identifican las subcategorías (véase la clave completa en la página *I · 1).*

Les symboles de l'index représentent les catégories indiquées dans la légende à droite. Les symboles suivis d'un indice (⋏¹) représentent des sous-catégories (voir légende complète à la page *I · 1).*

Os símbolos incluídos no texto do índice representam as grandes categorias identificadas com a chave à direita. Os símbolos com números em sua parte superior (⋏¹) identificam as subcategorias (veja-se a chave completa à página *I · 1).*

∧ Mountain	Berg	Montaña	Montagne	Montanha
⋏ Mountains	Gebirge	Montañas	Montagnes	Montanhas
)(Pass	Paß	Paso	Col	Passo
∨ Valley, Canyon	Tal, Cañon	Valle, Cañón	Vallée, Canyon	Vale, Canhão
≚ Plain	Ebene	Llano	Plaine	Planície
≻ Cape	Kap	Cabo	Cap	Cabo
I Island	Insel	Isla	Île	Ilha
II Islands	Inseln	Islas	Îles	Ilhas
⊥ Other Topographic Features	Andere Topographische Objekte	Otros Elementos Topográficos	Autres données topographiques	Outros acidentes topográficos

ESPAÑOL

Nombre	Página	Lat.°′	Long.°′ W = Oeste
Camagüey	240p	21.23 N	77.55 W
Camagüey □[4]	240p	21.30 N	78.00 W
Camagüey, Archipiélago de II	240p	22.18 N	78.00 W
Camaiore	64	43.56 N	10.18 E
Camaiú ≃	248	5.30 S	59.42 W
Camajuaní	240p	22.28 N	79.44 W
Camaldoli, Eremo di ʋ[1]	66	43.46 N	11.47 E
Camamu	255	13.57 S	39.07 W
Camaná	248	16.37 S	72.42 W
Camaná ≃	248	16.39 S	72.46 W
Camananaú ≃	246	1.51 S	61.14 W
Camanche	190	41.47 N	90.15 W
Camanche Reservoir ⊜[1]	226	38.13 N	120.58 W
Camandag Island I	116	11.59 N	124.25 E
Camanducaia	256	22.46 S	46.09 W
Camanducaia ≃, Bra.	256	22.39 S	46.58 W
Camanducaia ≃, Bra.	256	22.55 S	46.25 W
Camano Island I	224	48.10 N	122.30 W
Camaoi ≃	250	3.12 S	48.04 W
Camapuã	255	19.30 S	54.05 W
Camaquã	252	30.51 S	51.49 W
Camaquã ≃	252	31.17 S	51.47 W
Camará	246	3.55 S	62.44 W
Camarajibe	250	8.01 S	34.58 W
Camararé ≃	248	12.15 S	58.55 W
Camarat, Cap >	62	43.12 N	6.41 E
Camarda	66	42.23 N	13.29 E
Çamardı	130	37.50 N	35.00 E
Camarès	32	43.49 N	2.53 E
Camargo	248	20.39 S	65.13 W
Camargue ◆[1]	62	43.34 N	4.34 E
Camargue, Parc Naturel Regional de ♦	62	43.30 N	4.28 E
Camarillo	228	34.12 N	119.02 W
Camarillo Heights	228	34.14 N	119.02 W
Camarina ⊥	70	36.52 N	14.27 E
Camariñas	34	43.07 N	9.10 W
Camarines Norte □[4]	116	14.10 N	122.40 E
Camarines Sur □[4]	116	13.35 N	123.20 E
Camarón, Arroyo ≃	196	27.08 N	100.00 W
Camarón, Cabo >	236	16.00 N	85.05 W
Camaronero, Laguna c	234	23.00 N	106.07 W
Camarones	254	44.48 S	65.42 W
Camarones, Bahía c	254	44.45 S	65.34 W
Camas, Esp.	34	37.24 N	6.02 W
Çamaş, Tür.	130	40.55 N	37.32 E
Camas, Wa., U.S.	224	45.35 N	122.23 W
Camas Creek ≃, Id., U.S.	202	44.53 N	114.44 W
Camas Creek ≃, Id., U.S.	202	43.20 N	114.24 W
Camas Creek ≃, Id., U.S.	202	43.53 N	112.21 W
Camas Creek ≃, Or., U.S.	202	45.01 N	118.59 W
Camastra	70	37.15 N	13.47 E
Camatambo	152	6.30 S	15.18 E
Ca Mau	110	9.11 N	105.08 E
Ca Mau, Mui >	110	8.38 N	104.44 E
Camaxilo	152	8.21 S	18.56 E
Camba	112	4.54 S	119.50 E
Camba Cassai	152	9.40 S	19.18 E
Cambados	34	42.30 N	8.48 W
Cambaquara	256	23.54 S	45.27 W
Cambará	255	23.03 S	50.05 W
Camberley	42	51.21 N	0.45 W
Camberwell	169	37.50 S	145.04 E
Camberwell ◆[8]	260	51.28 N	0.05 W
Cambiano	62	44.58 N	7.47 E
Cambo	44	55.10 N	1.57 W
Cambo ≃	152	7.40 S	17.17 E
Cambodia □[1], Asia	108	13.00 N	105.00 E
Cambodia (Kâmpŭchéa) □[1], Asia	110	13.00 N	105.00 E
Cambois	44	55.10 N	1.31 W
Cambonda, Serra ⩘	152	12.06 S	14.00 E
Camboon	166	25.03 S	150.26 E
Cambooya	171a	27.42 S	151.52 E
Camboriú	252	27.01 S	48.38 W
Camboriú, Ponta >	252	25.10 S	47.55 W
Camborne	42	50.12 N	5.19 W
Cambra	210	41.11 N	76.18 W
Cambrai, Austl.	168b	34.39 S	139.17 E
Cambrai, Fr.	50	50.10 N	3.14 E
Cambremer	50	49.09 N	0.03 E
Cambria, Ca., U.S.	226	35.33 N	121.04 W
Cambria, In., U.S.	216	40.22 N	86.33 W
Cambria, Mi., U.S.	216	41.49 N	84.39 W
Cambria, Wi., U.S.	190	43.32 N	89.06 W
Cambria □[6]	214	40.29 N	79.16 W
Cambria Ice Field ⊓	182	55.55 N	129.30 W
Cambrian Mountains ⩘	42	52.35 N	3.35 W
Cambrian Park	226	37.15 N	121.55 W
Cambridge (Galt), On., Can.	212	43.22 N	80.19 W
Cambridge, N.Z.	172	37.53 S	175.28 E
Cambridge, Eng., U.K.	42	52.13 N	0.08 E
Cambridge, Id., U.S.	202	44.34 N	116.41 W
Cambridge, Il., U.S.	190	41.18 N	90.11 W
Cambridge, Ia., U.S.	190	41.53 N	93.31 W
Cambridge, Md., U.S.	208	38.33 N	76.04 W
Cambridge, Ma., U.S.	207	42.22 N	71.06 W
Cambridge, Mn., U.S.	190	45.34 N	93.13 W
Cambridge, Ne., U.S.	198	40.16 N	100.09 W
Cambridge, N.Y., U.S.	210	43.01 N	73.22 W
Cambridge, Oh., U.S.	188	40.02 N	81.35 W
Cambridge, Wi., U.S.	216	43.00 N	89.01 W
Cambridge Bay	176	69.03 N	105.05 W
Cambridge City	218	39.48 N	85.10 W
Cambridge Fiord c[2]	176	71.20 N	74.44 W
Cambridge Gulf c	164	14.55 S	128.15 E
Cambridge Park	274a	33.45 S	150.43 E
Cambridge Reservoir ⊜[1]	283	42.24 N	71.16 W
Cambridgeshire □[6]	42	52.20 N	0.05 E
Cambridge Springs	214	41.48 N	80.03 W
Cambrils	34	41.04 N	1.03 E
Cambuci	255	21.34 S	41.55 W
Cambuci ◆[8]	287b	23.34 S	46.37 W
Cambuí	256	22.37 S	46.04 W
Cambulo	152	7.48 S	21.14 E
Cambundi-Catembo	152	10.09 S	17.31 E
Cambuquira	256	21.51 S	45.18 W
Cambural	286c	10.26 N	66.59 W
Camburg	54	51.03 N	11.42 E
Camburu ≃	256	23.41 S	45.28 W
Camby	218	39.40 N	86.19 W
Čamčakly	128	37.56 N	63.06 E
Camden, Austl.	170	34.03 S	150.42 E
Camden, S. Afr.	158	26.38 S	30.07 E
Camden, Al., U.S.	194	31.59 N	87.17 W
Camden, Ar., U.S.	194	33.35 N	92.50 W
Camden, De., U.S.	208	39.06 N	75.32 W
Camden, Il., U.S.	219	40.09 N	90.46 W
Camden, In., U.S.	216	40.36 N	86.32 W
Camden, Me., U.S.	188	44.12 N	69.03 W
Camden, Mi., U.S.	216	41.45 N	84.45 W
Camden, Ms., U.S.	194	32.46 N	89.50 W
Camden, N.J., U.S.	208	39.55 N	75.07 W
Camden, N.Y., U.S.	210	43.20 N	75.44 W
Camden, N.C., U.S.	192	36.19 N	76.10 W
Camden, Oh., U.S.	218	39.37 N	84.38 W
Camden, S.C., U.S.	192	34.14 N	80.36 W
Camden, Tn., U.S.	194	36.03 N	88.05 W
Camden, Tx., U.S.	222	30.55 N	94.44 W
Camden □[6], N.J., U.S.	208	39.57 N	75.07 W
Camden □[6], N.C., U.S.	208	36.28 N	76.21 W
Camden ◆[8]	260	51.33 N	0.10 W
Camden, Grupo II	254	54.40 S	71.58 W
Camden Aerodrome ⊠	274a	34.03 S	150.41 E
Camden Bay c	180	70.00 N	145.00 W

FRANÇAIS

Nom	Page	Lat.°′	Long.°′ W = Ouest
Camden Hills State Park ♦	188	44.17 N	69.05 W
Camden Lake ⊜	212	44.25 N	76.52 W
Camden Station ◆[5]	284b	39.17 N	76.37 W
Camdenton	194	38.00 N	92.44 W
Camedo	58	46.09 N	8.37 E
Cameia, Parque Nacional da ♦	152	11.45 S	21.20 E
Camel ≃	42	50.33 N	4.55 W
Camel, Mount ∧[2]	169	36.45 S	144.43 E
Camelback Mountain ∧, Ak., U.S.	180	62.33 N	157.20 W
Camelback Mountain ∧, Pa., U.S.	210	41.03 N	75.21 W
Camelford	42	50.37 N	4.41 W
Çameli	130	37.05 N	29.20 E
Camels Hump ∧	188	44.19 N	72.53 W
Cameo Acres	282	37.51 N	121.58 W
Camerano	66	43.32 N	13.33 E
Cameri	62	45.30 N	8.39 E
Cameri, Aeroporto di ⊠	266b	45.32 N	8.40 E
Camerino	66	43.08 N	13.04 E
Cameron, Ca., U.S.	226	38.39 N	120.56 W
Cameron, La., U.S.	194	29.47 N	93.19 W
Cameron, Mo., U.S.	194	39.44 N	94.14 W
Cameron, N.Y., U.S.	210	42.12 N	77.24 W
Cameron, Pa., U.S.	214	41.27 N	78.10 W
Cameron, S.C., U.S.	192	33.33 N	80.42 W
Cameron, Tx., U.S.	222	30.51 N	96.58 W
Cameron, W.V., U.S.	188	39.49 N	80.34 W
Cameron, Wi., U.S.	190	45.24 N	91.44 W
Cameron □[6]	214	41.31 N	78.14 W
Cameron ≃	224	49.17 N	124.38 W
Cameron, Lac ⊜	206	46.06 N	74.50 W
Cameron Highlands	114	4.29 N	101.27 E
Cameron Hills ⩘[2]	176	59.48 N	118.00 W
Cameron Lake ⊜, B.C., Can.	224	49.17 N	124.37 W
Cameron Lake ⊜, On., Can.	212	44.34 N	78.45 W
Cameron Mills	210	42.11 N	77.22 W
Cameron Mountains ⩘	172	46.00 S	167.00 E
Cameron Run ≃	284c	38.48 N	77.04 W
Cameroon (Cameroun) □[1]	134	6.00 N	12.00 E
Cameroon Mountain ∧	152	4.12 N	9.11 E
Camerota	68	40.02 N	15.23 E
Camerun → Cameroon □[1]	134	6.00 N	12.00 E
Camerún → Cameroon □[1]	134	6.00 N	12.00 E
Cametá	250	2.15 S	49.30 W
Camfield	164	17.09 S	131.21 E
Çamiçi Gölü ⊜	130	37.30 N	27.25 E
Camiguin □[4]	116	9.15 N	124.40 E
Camiguin Island I, Pil.	116	9.11 N	124.42 E
Camiguin Island I, Pil.	116	18.56 N	121.55 E
Camiling	116	15.42 N	120.24 E
Camilla	192	31.13 N	84.12 W
Camillus	210	43.02 N	76.19 W
Camin	54	53.27 N	10.58 E
Camiña	248	19.18 S	69.26 W
Caminha	34	41.52 N	8.50 W
Camino	226	38.44 N	120.40 W
Camiranga	250	1.48 S	46.17 W
Camiri	248	20.03 S	63.31 W
Camisano Vicentino	64	45.31 N	11.43 E
Camissombo	152	8.10 S	20.39 E
Camlad ≃	42	52.36 N	3.10 W
Çamlıbel	130	40.05 N	36.29 E
Çamlıdere, Tür.	130	40.30 N	32.29 E
Çamlıdere, Tür.	130	37.08 N	39.03 E
Çamlıyayla	130	37.09 N	34.36 E
Cam Lo	110	16.49 N	106.59 E
Čamlyk ≃	84	44.45 N	40.45 E
Cammal	210	41.24 N	77.28 W
Cammarata	70	37.38 N	13.38 E
Cammarta, Monte ∧	70	37.37 N	13.36 E
Cammin → Kamień Pomorski	30	53.58 N	14.46 E
Camoapa	236	12.23 N	85.31 W
Camocim	250	2.54 S	40.50 W
Camogli	62	44.21 N	9.09 E
Çamoluk	130	40.08 N	38.45 E
Camonica, Val V	64	46.00 N	10.20 E
Camooweal	166	19.55 S	138.07 E
Camopi ≃	250	3.11 N	52.20 W
Camorim ≃	287a	22.59 S	43.25 W
Camorim, Represa do ⊜[1]	287a	22.58 S	43.27 W
Camorta Island I	110	8.08 N	93.30 E
Camote, Cerro ∧	286d	11.57 S	77.06 W
Camotes Islands II	116	10.40 N	124.24 E
Camotes Sea ⊤[2]	116	10.30 N	124.15 E
Camotlán ≃	234	22.01 N	104.15 W
Camowen ≃	48	54.36 N	7.18 W
Camp □[6]	222	33.00 N	94.58 W
Campagna	68	40.40 N	15.08 E
Campagna di Roma ◆[1]	66	41.50 N	12.35 E
Campagna Lupia	64	45.21 N	12.06 E
Campagnano di Roma	66	42.08 N	12.23 E
Campagnatico	66	42.53 N	11.16 E
Campagne-lès-Hesdin	50	50.24 N	1.52 E
Campaign	194	35.46 N	85.37 W
Campamento	236	14.33 N	86.42 W
Campamento, Cerro ∧	286a	19.18 N	99.17 W
Campana, Arg.	258	34.10 S	58.57 W
Campana, It.	68	39.24 N	16.50 E
Campana, Isla I	254	48.20 S	75.15 W
Campanario	34	38.52 N	5.37 W
Campanario, Cerro de ∧	248	5.57 S	77.31 W
Campanella, Punta >	68	40.34 N	14.19 E
Campanero, Cerro ∧	246	5.54 N	65.12 W
Campanha	256	21.50 S	45.24 W
Campania □[4]	68	40.55 N	14.50 E
Campania Island I	182	53.05 N	129.30 W
Camparada	266b	45.39 N	9.19 E
Campaspe ≃, Austl.	166	21.00 S	146.24 E
Campaspe ≃, Austl.	169	36.41 S	144.31 E
Campbell, S. Afr.	158	28.48 S	23.44 E
Campbell, Ca., U.S.	226	37.17 N	121.56 W
Campbell, Mn., U.S.	198	46.05 N	96.24 W
Campbell, Mo., U.S.	194	36.29 N	90.04 W
Campbell, Ne., U.S.	198	40.18 N	98.44 W
Campbell, N.Y., U.S.	210	42.13 N	77.11 W
Campbell, Oh., U.S.	214	41.04 N	80.35 W
Campbell, Tx., U.S.	222	33.09 N	95.57 W
Campbell □[6]	218	38.55 N	84.20 W
Campbell, Cape >	172	41.44 S	174.17 E
Campbell Airport ⊠	279b	40.21 N	80.11 W
Campbellfield	274b	37.41 S	144.57 E
Campbellford	212	44.18 N	77.48 W
Campbell Hall	210	41.27 N	74.16 W
Campbell Hill ∧[2]	216	40.22 N	83.43 W
Campbell Island	182	52.10 N	128.09 W
Campbell Island I	9	52.30 S	169.05 E
Campbell Lake ⊜	182	50.01 N	125.27 W
Campbell Plateau ✣[3]	9	51.00 S	170.00 E
Campbell Point >	171a	27.22 S	153.55 E
Campbellpore	123	33.46 N	72.22 E
Campbell Range ⩘	180	61.08 N	129.45 W
Campbell River	182	50.01 N	125.15 W
Campbells ≃	170	33.42 S	149.37 E
Campbell's Airport ⊠	278	42.20 N	88.04 W
Campbell's-Bay	188	45.44 N	76.36 W
Campbellsburg, In., U.S.	218	38.39 N	86.15 W
Campbellsburg, Ky., U.S.	218	38.31 N	85.12 W
Campbell Slough ≃	226	39.22 N	121.51 W
Campbellsport	190	43.35 N	88.16 W
Campbells River	170	33.54 S	149.37 E
Campbells Run ≃	279b	40.24 N	80.05 W
Campbellsville	194	37.20 N	85.20 W

PORTUGUÊS

Nome	Página	Lat.°′	Long.°′ W = Oeste
Campbellton, N.B., Can.	186	48.00 N	66.40 W
Campbellton, Nf., Can.	186	49.17 N	54.56 W
Campbellton, P.E., Can.	186	46.47 N	64.18 W
Campbellton, Fl., U.S.	192	30.56 N	85.24 W
Campbell Town, Austl.	166	41.56 S	147.29 E
Campbelltown, Austl.	168b	34.53 S	138.40 E
Campbelltown, Austl.	170	34.04 S	150.49 E
Campbelltown, Pa., U.S.	208	40.17 N	76.35 W
Campbellville	212	43.29 N	79.59 W
Campbeltown	44	55.26 N	5.36 W
Camp Creek ≃, Ca., U.S.	226	38.38 N	120.40 W
Camp Creek ≃, Mo., U.S.	219	39.02 N	91.12 W
Camp Creek Lake ⊜[1]	222	31.03 N	96.19 W
Camp David ʋ	208	39.38 N	77.28 W
Camp de Frileuse ■	261	48.52 N	1.55 E
Camp de Satory ■	261	48.47 N	2.06 E
Camp Dix	218	38.29 N	83.17 W
Camp Douglas	190	43.55 N	90.16 W
Campeche	232	19.51 N	90.32 W
Campeche, Bahía de c	232	20.00 N	94.00 W
Campeche Bank ✣[4]	16	22.00 N	90.00 W
Campechuela	240p	20.14 N	77.17 W
Campegine	64	44.45 N	10.32 E
Campello Monti	58	45.56 N	8.15 E
Camperdown, Austl.	169	38.14 S	143.09 E
Camperdown, S. Afr.	158	29.42 S	30.33 E
Camperville	184	51.59 N	100.09 W
Campestre, Bra.	256	21.16 S	42.56 W
Campestre, Bra.	256	21.43 S	46.15 W
Cam Pha	110	21.01 N	107.19 E
Camp Hill, Al., U.S.	194	32.48 N	85.39 W
Camp Hill, Pa., U.S.	208	40.14 N	76.55 W
Campi Bisenzio	66	43.49 N	11.08 E
Campidano ◆[1]	71	39.30 N	8.47 E
Campiglia dei Fosci	66	43.27 N	11.03 E
Campiglia Marittima	66	43.03 N	10.37 E
Campillo de Llerena	34	38.30 N	5.50 W
Campillos	34	37.03 N	4.51 W
Campina ◆[1]	34	37.45 N	4.45 W
Campina Grande	250	7.13 S	35.53 W
Campinas	256	22.54 S	47.05 W
Campina Verde	255	19.31 S	49.28 W
Campinho, Rio do ≃	287a	22.52 S	43.37 W
Campione del Garda	64	45.45 N	10.45 E
Campi Salentina	68	40.24 N	18.01 E
Campitello	64	46.28 N	11.44 E
Camp King	150	4.55 N	7.58 W
Camp Lake	216	42.32 N	88.09 W
Camp Lake ⊜	212	45.27 N	78.54 W
Camp Leger ■	261	48.34 N	2.34 E
Camp Lejeune Marine Corps Base ■	192	34.40 N	77.21 W
Campli	66	42.43 N	13.41 E
Camplong	112	10.02 S	123.55 E
Campo, Cam.	152	2.22 N	9.49 E
Campo, Moç.	156	17.44 S	36.21 E
Campo, Co., U.S.	198	37.06 N	102.34 W
Campo, Réserve de ◆[4]	152	2.35 N	9.57 E
Campoalegre	246	2.41 N	75.20 W
Campo Alegre ≃	250	9.19 S	50.06 W
Campo Alegre de Goiás	255	17.39 S	47.45 W
Campobasso	66	41.34 N	14.39 E
Campobasso □[4]	66	41.38 N	14.35 E
Campobello di Licata	70	37.15 N	13.55 E
Campobello di Mazara	70	37.38 N	12.45 E
Campobello Island I	186	44.53 N	66.55 W
Campo Belo	255	20.53 S	45.16 W
Campo Blenio	58	46.34 N	8.56 E
Campo Catino	66	41.48 N	13.20 E
Campocologno	58	46.13 N	10.08 E
Campo Cumbica ■	287b	23.27 S	46.28 W
Campo da Bocaina	256	22.17 S	46.06 W
Campodarsego	64	45.30 N	11.54 E
Campo de Criptana	34	39.24 N	3.07 W
Campo de la Cruz	246	10.23 N	74.53 W
Campo de Marte ♦	286d	12.04 S	77.03 W
Campo de Marte ■	287b	23.30 S	46.37 W
Campo de Mayo ■	288	34.32 S	58.38 W
Campo di Giove	66	42.01 N	14.03 E
Campo di Trens (Trens)	64	46.52 N	11.29 E
Campo do Coelho	256	22.15 S	42.39 W
Campodolcino	58	46.24 N	9.21 E
Campo Erê	252	26.23 S	53.03 W
Campofelice di Fitalia	70	37.50 N	13.29 E
Campofelice di Roccella	70	37.59 N	13.53 E
Campofiorito	70	37.45 N	13.16 E
Campo Florido	255	19.47 S	48.35 W
Campoformido	64	46.01 N	13.09 E
Campo Formoso	250	10.31 S	40.20 W
Campofranco	70	37.30 N	13.43 E
Campogalliano	64	44.41 N	10.50 E
Campo Gallo	252	26.35 S	62.51 W
Campo Grande, Arg.	252	27.13 S	54.58 W
Campo Grande, Bra.	255	20.27 S	54.37 W
Campo Grande ◆[8], Bra.	256	22.54 S	43.34 W
Campo Grande ◆[8], Port.	266c	38.45 N	9.09 W
Campo Indian Reservation ◆[4]	204	32.40 N	116.20 W
Campo Largo, Arg.	252	26.48 S	60.50 W
Campo Largo, Bra.	252	25.26 S	49.32 W
Campolaro	64	45.55 N	10.20 E
Campolasta (Astfeld)	64	46.40 N	11.22 E
Campolato, Capo >	70	37.17 N	15.12 E
Campo Libertad ■	286b	23.05 N	82.26 W
Campolide	256	21.36 S	43.53 W
Campolieto	66	41.38 N	14.46 E
Campo Ligure	62	44.32 N	8.42 E
Campo Limpo	256	23.12 S	46.48 W
Campo Maior, Bra.	250	4.49 S	42.10 W
Campo Maior, Port.	34	39.01 N	7.04 W
Campomarino	66	41.57 N	15.02 E
Campo Militar Número Uno ■	286a	19.27 N	99.14 W
Campo Morado	234	17.35 N	100.05 W
Campomorone	62	44.30 N	8.53 E
Campo Mourão	255	24.03 S	52.22 W
Campo Nôvo	252	27.42 S	53.48 W
Campo Pequeno ♦	266c	38.44 N	9.08 W
Campo Quijano	252	24.55 S	65.39 W
Campora	68	40.19 N	15.17 E
Camporeale	70	37.54 N	13.06 E
Camporgiano	64	44.09 N	10.20 E
Camporredondo	248	6.07 S	78.21 W
Campos	255	21.45 S	41.18 W
Campos Altos	255	19.41 S	46.10 W
Camposampiero	64	45.34 N	11.56 E
Campo Santo, Arg.	252	24.40 S	65.06 W
Camposanto, It.	64	44.47 N	11.08 E
Campos Belos	255	13.03 S	46.53 W
Campos de Cunha	256	22.55 S	44.49 W
Campos do Jordão	256	22.44 S	45.35 W
Campos Elyseos	256	22.42 S	43.17 W
Campos Gerais	256	21.14 S	45.46 W
Campos Novos	252	27.24 S	51.12 W
Campos Sales	250	7.04 S	40.23 W
Campo Tencia, Pizzo ∧	58	46.26 N	8.43 E
Campotosto	66	42.33 N	13.22 E
Campotosto, Lago di ⊜	66	42.32 N	13.22 E
Campo Tures (Sand in Taufers)	64	46.55 N	11.57 E
Campovalano	66	42.44 N	13.40 E
Camp Parks Communications Annex ■	282	37.44 N	121.54 W
Camp Pendleton Marine Corps Base ■	228	33.19 N	117.18 W
Camp Point	219	40.02 N	91.04 W
Camp Ruby	222	30.42 N	94.45 W
Campsie	274a	33.55 S	151.06 E
Campsie Fells ⩘[2]	46	56.02 N	4.12 W
Camp Springs	208	38.48 N	76.54 W
Campti	194	31.53 N	93.07 W
Campton	192	37.44 N	83.32 W
Camptonville	226	39.27 N	121.03 W
Camptown	210	41.43 N	76.14 W
Campus	216	41.01 N	88.18 W
Campuya ≃	246	1.43 S	73.30 W
Camp Verde	200	34.33 N	111.51 W
Campville	210	42.06 N	76.09 W
Camp Wood	196	29.40 N	100.01 W
Cam Ranh	110	11.54 N	109.09 E
Cam Ranh, Vinh c	110	11.53 N	109.10 E
Camrose, Ab., Can.	182	53.01 N	112.50 W
Camrose, Wales, U.K.	42	51.51 N	5.01 W
Camsell ≃	176	65.40 N	118.07 W
Camu ≃	250	1.15 N	57.09 W
Camucia	66	43.16 N	11.58 E
Camucuio	152	14.12 S	13.20 E
Camurí Chiquito, Quebrada ≃	286c	10.37 N	66.52 W
Çamurlu Dağ ∧	130	40.21 N	42.26 E
Camuy	240m	18.29 N	66.51 W
Çam Xuyen	110	18.15 N	106.00 E
Čamyndy	85	41.37 N	74.20 E
Čamzinka	80	54.24 N	45.47 E
Çan, Tür.	130	40.02 N	27.03 E
Çan, Tür.	130	39.09 N	40.13 E
Çan ≃	260	51.48 N	0.25 E
Čaňa	30	48.37 N	21.18 E
Canaan, Ct., U.S.	207	42.01 N	73.19 W
Canaan, Fl., U.S.	220	28.48 N	81.14 W
Canaan, In., U.S.	218	38.52 N	85.25 W
Canaan, N.Y., U.S.	210	42.25 N	73.27 W
Canaan, Vt., U.S.	206	44.59 N	71.32 W
Canaan ≃	186	45.55 N	65.47 W
Canaan Lake ⊜	276	40.47 N	73.01 W
Canaan Valley State Park ♦	188	39.02 N	79.32 W
Cana Brava ≃, Bra.	255	13.11 S	48.11 W
Cana Brava ≃, Bra.	255	12.12 S	48.40 W
Cañacao Bay c	269f	14.29 N	120.55 E
Canaçarí, Lago ⊜	250	2.57 S	58.15 W
Canachal	232	24.04 N	107.05 W
Canada □[1]	176	60.00 N	95.00 W
Canada Bay c	186	50.43 N	56.10 W
Cañada de Caracheo	234	20.22 N	100.57 W
Cañada de Gómez	252	32.49 S	61.24 W
Cañada Honda	252	31.59 S	68.33 W
Canada Lake ⊜	210	43.10 N	74.32 W
Cañada Nieto	258	33.43 S	58.05 W
Canadarago Lake ⊜	210	42.48 N	75.01 W
Canada's Wonderland ♦	275b	43.51 N	79.33 W
Cañada Verde → Villa Huidobro	252	34.50 S	64.35 W
Canadaway Creek ≃	214	42.28 N	79.22 W
Canadensis	210	41.11 N	75.15 W
Canadian	196	35.54 N	100.22 W
Canadian ≃, U.S.	196	35.27 N	95.03 W
Canadian ≃, Co., U.S.	200	40.53 N	106.20 W
Canadian, Deep Fork ≃	196	35.28 N	95.50 W
Canadian Forces Base Trenton ■	212	44.07 N	77.33 W
Canadice Lake ⊜	210	42.43 N	77.34 W
Cañadón Seco	254	46.33 S	67.35 W
Canaguá ≃	246	7.57 N	69.36 W
Canaima	246	6.14 N	62.52 W
Canaima, Parque Nacional ♦	246	4.27 N	62.00 W
Canajoharie	210	42.54 N	74.34 W
Çanakkale	130	40.09 N	26.24 E
Çanakkale □[4]	130	40.10 N	26.45 E
Çanakkale Boğazı (Dardanelles) ʊ	130	40.15 N	26.25 E
Canal, Anse du c	241o	16.23 N	61.30 W
Canal, Islas del → Channel Islands II	28	49.20 N	2.20 W
Canala	175f	21.32 S	165.57 E
Canale	62	44.48 N	8.00 E
Canale, Val V	64	46.29 N	13.30 E
Canale del Ferro ≃	64	46.21 N	13.07 E
Canalejas	234	19.57 N	99.39 W
Canal Flats	182	50.09 N	115.48 W
Canal Fulton	214	40.53 N	81.35 W
Canal Lake ⊜	212	44.34 N	79.03 W
Canal Lewisville	214	40.18 N	81.50 W
Canal Point	220	26.51 N	80.38 W
Canals	252	33.33 S	62.53 W
Canal Winchester	188	39.51 N	82.48 W
Canandaigua	210	42.52 N	77.20 W
Canandaigua Lake ⊜	210	42.49 N	77.16 W
Canandaigua Outlet ≃	210	43.04 N	77.00 W
Cananea	232	30.57 N	110.18 W
Cananéia	252	25.01 S	47.57 W
Cananguchal	246	0.51 N	75.47 W
Canan Station	214	40.28 N	78.26 W
Canapine, Forca)(	66	42.45 N	13.12 E
Canápolis	255	18.44 S	49.13 W
Canapville	50	49.19 N	0.08 E
Cañar	246	2.33 S	78.56 W
Cañar □[4]	246	2.30 S	79.00 W
Canard ≃	214	42.09 N	83.06 W
Canard, Lac au ⊜	206	45.48 N	71.31 W
Canarias, Islas (Canary Islands) II	148	28.00 N	15.30 W
Canaries	241f	13.55 N	61.04 W
Canaro	64	44.56 N	11.40 E
Canarreos, Archipiélago de los II	240p	21.50 N	82.30 W
Canarsie ◆[8]	276	40.38 N	73.53 W
Canarsie Park ♦	276	40.38 N	73.53 W
Canarsie Pol I	276	40.37 N	73.52 W
Canary Basin ✣[1]	10	30.00 N	25.00 W
Canary Islands → Canarias, Islas II	148	28.00 N	15.30 W
Cañas	236	10.25 N	85.07 W
Cañas, Río de las ≃	234	22.29 N	105.36 W
Canaseraga	210	42.27 N	77.46 W
Canaseraga Creek ≃	210	42.45 N	77.50 W
Cañasgordas	246	6.45 N	76.01 W
Canastota	210	43.04 N	75.45 W
Canastra ≃	250	11.23 S	49.41 W
Canatlán	232	24.31 N	104.47 W
Canaveral, Cape >	220	28.27 N	80.32 W
Canaveral Bight c[3]	220	28.26 N	80.33 W
Canaveral National Seashore ♦	220	28.45 N	80.45 W
Canaveral Peninsula >[1]	220	28.28 N	80.34 W
Cañaveras	34	40.22 N	2.24 W
Canavese □[9]	62	45.20 N	7.40 E
Canavieiras	255	15.39 S	38.57 W
Cañazas	236	8.19 N	81.13 W
Canazei	64	46.28 N	11.46 E
Canbelego	166	31.33 S	146.19 E
Canberra	171b	35.17 S	149.08 E
Canberra Wildlife Gardens ♦	171b	35.20 S	149.09 E
Canby, Ca., U.S.	204	41.26 N	120.52 W
Canby, Mn., U.S.	198	44.42 N	96.16 W
Canby, Or., U.S.	224	45.15 N	122.41 W
Cancajanang, Mount ∧	116	11.04 N	124.47 E
Cancale	32	48.41 N	1.51 W
Cancano, Lago di ⊜	64	46.31 N	10.18 E
Cance ≃	62	45.12 N	4.48 E
Cancellara	68	40.44 N	15.56 E
Cancello e Arnone	68	41.04 N	14.03 E
Canchaque	248	5.24 S	79.36 W
Canche ≃	50	50.31 N	1.39 E
Cancon	32	44.32 N	0.38 E
Cancún	232	21.05 N	86.46 W
Çancún, Punta >	232	21.08 N	86.45 W
Čančur	88	53.49 N	106.59 E
Canda	64	45.03 N	11.30 E
Candala → Qandala	144	11.28 N	49.52 E
Candarave	248	17.16 S	70.15 W
Çandarlı	130	38.56 N	26.56 E
Çandarlı Körfezi c	130	38.52 N	26.55 E
Čandás	34	43.35 N	5.46 W
Candé	32	47.34 N	1.02 W
Candeias, Bra.	255	12.40 S	38.33 W
Candeias, Bra.	255	20.47 S	45.16 W
Candeias ≃	248	8.39 S	63.31 W
Candela, It.	68	41.08 N	15.31 E
Candela, Méx.	232	26.50 N	100.40 W
Candela, Río de ≃	232	27.16 N	100.18 W
Candelaria, Arg.	252	27.28 S	55.44 W
Candelaria, Arg.	252	32.04 S	65.49 W
Candelária, Bra.	252	29.40 S	52.48 W
Candelaria, Col.	246	3.25 N	76.20 W
Candelaria, Cuba	240p	22.44 N	82.58 W
Candelaria, Pil.	116	15.38 N	119.56 E
Candelaria ≃	232	18.37 N	91.14 W
Candelaria, Cerro ∧	234	23.25 N	103.43 W
Candelaria Loxicha	234	15.54 N	96.31 W
Candelaro ≃	68	41.34 N	15.53 E
Candeleda	34	40.09 N	5.14 W
Candelo, Austl.	166	36.46 S	149.42 E
Candelo, It.	62	45.33 N	8.07 E
Candia → Iráklion	38	35.20 N	25.09 E
Candiac	206	45.23 N	73.31 W
Candia Canavese	62	45.20 N	7.53 E
Candia Lomellina	62	45.11 N	8.36 E
Cándido Aguilar	232	25.30 N	98.02 W
Cândido de Abreu	252	24.35 S	51.20 W
Cândido Mendes	250	1.27 S	45.43 W
Candies Creek ≃	192	35.18 N	84.51 W
Candijay	116	9.49 N	124.30 E
Çandır, Tür.	130	40.16 N	33.29 E
Çandır, Tür.	130	39.15 N	35.32 E
Candle	180	65.55 N	161.56 W
Candle Lake ⊜	184	53.50 N	105.18 W
Candlemas Islands II	18	57.03 S	26.40 W
Candlestick	194	32.15 N	90.20 W
Candlestick Park ♦	282	37.43 N	122.23 W
Candlewood, Lake ⊜	207	41.32 N	73.27 W
Candlewood Isle	207	41.28 N	73.27 W
Candlewood Knolls	207	41.28 N	73.27 W
Candlewood Shores	207	41.28 N	73.26 W
Çandman', Mong.	86	50.02 N	92.03 E
Čandman', Mong.	102	45.20 N	97.59 E
Cando, Ang.	152	16.30 S	18.19 E
Cando, Sk., Can.	184	52.23 N	108.14 W
Cando, N.D., U.S.	198	48.29 N	99.12 W
Candombé ≃	152	16.54 S	21.52 E
Candon	116	17.12 N	120.27 E
Candon Point >	116	17.13 N	120.24 E
Candor, N.Y., U.S.	210	42.13 N	76.20 W
Candor, N.C., U.S.	192	35.17 N	79.44 W
Candover	158	27.28 S	31.57 E
Cane ≃, Austl.	162	21.33 S	115.23 E
Cane ≃, La., U.S.	194	31.31 N	92.43 W
Cane ≃, N.C., U.S.	192	36.00 N	82.16 W
Canea → Khaniá	38	35.31 N	24.02 E
Caneadea	210	42.23 N	78.09 W
Caneças	266c	38.49 N	9.14 W
Cane Creek ≃	194	36.29 N	90.28 W
Canegrate	266b	45.34 N	8.56 E
Canela	252	29.22 S	50.50 W
Canelles, Embalse de ⊜[1]	34	42.10 N	0.30 E
Canelli	62	44.43 N	8.17 E
Canelón Chico, Arroyo ≃	258	34.29 S	56.20 W
Canelones	258	34.32 S	56.17 W
Canelones □[5]	258	34.35 S	56.15 W
Canelón Grande, Arroyo ≃	258	34.30 S	56.24 W
Canendiyu □[5]	252	24.05 S	55.45 W
Cane Run ≃	218	38.13 N	84.37 W
Cañete, Chile	252	37.48 S	73.24 W
Cañete, Esp.	34	40.03 N	1.35 W
Caneva	64	45.58 N	12.26 E
Caney	198	37.00 N	95.56 W
Caney ≃	196	36.20 N	95.42 W
Caney Brook ≃	276	41.07 N	73.50 W
Caney Creek ≃, Ar., U.S.	194	33.46 N	93.07 W
Caney Creek ≃, Tx., U.S.	196	28.46 N	95.39 W
Caney Creek ≃, Tx., U.S.	222	32.48 N	95.33 W
Caney Creek ≃, Tx., U.S.	222	30.07 N	95.10 W
Caney Creek ≃, Tx., U.S.	222	30.28 N	95.38 W
Caney Creek ≃, Tx., U.S.	222	30.04 N	96.08 W
Caney Creek ≃, Tx., U.S.	222	31.52 N	96.13 W
Caney Creek ≃, Tx., U.S.	222	31.03 N	94.33 W
Caney Creek ≃, Tx., U.S.	222	30.53 N	95.48 W
Canfield	214	41.01 N	80.45 W
Canfield Island I	276	41.06 N	73.23 W
Canfranc	34	42.43 N	0.31 W
Cangaíba ◆[8]	287b	23.30 S	46.31 W
Cangallo	248	13.33 S	74.12 W
Cangamba	152	13.40 S	19.54 E
Cangandala	152	9.45 S	16.33 E
Cangandala, Parque Nacional da ♦	152	9.45 S	16.50 E
Cangas, Bra.	248	16.05 S	56.33 W
Cangas, Esp.	34	42.16 N	8.47 W
Cangas de Narcea	34	43.11 N	6.33 W
Cangas de Onís	34	43.21 N	5.07 W
Cangbu	100	30.49 N	114.35 E
Can Gioc ≃	269c	10.42 N	106.37 E
Cangkuang, Tanjung >	115a	6.51 S	105.15 E
Cangniutun	105	39.23 N	115.54 E
Cango Caves ⊥[5]	158	33.23 S	22.14 E
Cangola	152	7.58 S	15.52 E
Cangombe	152	14.24 S	19.59 E
Cangongo	152	9.24 S	17.30 E
Cangqian, Zhg.	106	30.17 N	120.25 E
Cangqian, Zhg.	106	30.18 N	120.00 E
Cangshangtun	105	40.03 N	117.32 E
Canguaretama	250	6.24 S	35.08 W
Canguçu	252	31.24 S	52.41 W
Canguera	256	23.36 S	47.09 W
Cangumbe	152	12.00 S	19.17 E
Cangwu	102	23.22 N	111.13 E
Çangxi	102	31.48 N	105.57 E
Čangyrtas	85	40.53 N	72.50 E
Cangyuan	102	23.12 N	99.16 E
Cangzhou	98	38.19 N	116.51 E
Canhoca	152	9.15 S	14.41 E
Canhotinho	250	8.53 S	36.12 W
Caniapiscau ≃	176	57.40 N	69.30 W
Caniapiscau, Lac ⊜	176	54.10 N	69.55 W
Canicanian	116	14.46 N	122.01 E
Canicattì	70	37.21 N	13.51 E
Canicattini Bagni	70	37.02 N	15.04 E
Canigao Channel ʊ	116	10.15 N	124.42 E
Canigou, Pic du ∧	32	42.31 N	2.27 E
Canillas ◆[8]	266a	40.28 N	3.38 W
Canillejas ◆[8]	266a	40.27 N	3.37 W
Canimã ≃	248	8.45 S	59.15 W
Canim Lake	182	51.46 N	120.54 W
Canim Lake ⊜	182	51.52 N	120.45 W
Canim Lake Indian Reserve ◆[4]	182	51.47 N	121.00 W
Canindé	250	4.22 S	39.19 W
Canindé ≃	250	6.15 S	42.52 W
Canindé de São Francisco	250	9.39 S	37.48 W
Canino	66	42.28 N	11.45 E
Canipaan	116	8.35 N	117.16 E
Canipo Island I	116	10.59 N	120.57 E
Canisius College ʋ[2]	284a	42.55 N	78.52 W
Canisp ∧	46	58.07 N	5.03 W
Canistear Reservoir ⊜[1]	276	41.08 N	74.29 W
Canisteo	210	42.16 N	77.36 W
Canisteo ≃	210	42.07 N	77.08 W
Canistota	198	43.35 N	97.17 W
Cañitas de Felipe Pescador	234	23.36 N	102.43 W
Canjáyar	34	37.00 N	2.44 W
Canjinge	152	10.12 S	21.17 E
Cankhor	144	10.46 N	46.13 E
Çankırı	130	40.36 N	33.37 E
Çankırı □[4]	130	40.45 N	33.25 E
Čanlaon	116	10.22 N	123.12 E
Canlaon Volcano ∧[1]	116	10.25 N	123.08 E
Canley Vale	274a	33.53 S	150.57 E
Canmore	182	51.05 N	115.21 W
Canna	68	40.05 N	16.30 E
Canna I	46	57.04 N	6.34 W
Canna, Sound of ʊ	46	57.03 N	6.25 W
Cannanore	122	11.51 N	75.22 E
Cannara	66	43.00 N	12.35 E
Canne ⊥	68	41.18 N	16.09 E
Cannel City	192	37.47 N	83.16 W
Cannelton	194	37.54 N	86.44 W
Canner ≃	56	49.24 N	6.16 E
Cannero-Riviera	58	46.01 N	8.41 E
Cannes	62	43.33 N	7.01 E
Cannes, Bayou des ≃	194	30.12 N	92.35 W
Canneto, It.	66	43.12 N	10.44 E
Canneto, It.	70	38.29 N	14.58 E
Canneto sull'Oglio	64	45.09 N	10.25 E
Cannich	46	57.21 N	4.46 W
Cannich ≃	46	57.21 N	4.44 W
Cannifton	212	44.12 N	77.23 W
Canning, Arg.	288	34.53 S	58.30 W
Canning, Austl.	168a	32.02 S	115.56 E
Canning, N.S., Can.	186	45.09 N	64.25 W
Canning ≃, Austl.	168a	32.01 S	115.51 E
Canning ≃, Ak., U.S.	180	70.05 N	145.30 W
Canning Hill ∧[2]	162	28.50 S	117.49 E
Canning Lake ⊜	212	44.56 N	78.38 W
Canning Reservoir ⊜[1]	168a	32.10 S	116.09 E
Cannington, On., Can.	212	44.21 N	79.02 W
Cannington, Eng., U.K.	42	51.09 N	3.04 W
Cannobio	58	46.04 N	8.42 E
Cannock	42	52.42 N	2.09 W
Cannock Chase ◆[4]	42	52.43 N	2.00 W
Cannon ≃	190	44.35 N	92.33 W
Cannon Air Force Base ■	196	34.23 N	103.18 W
Cannon Ball	198	46.23 N	100.35 W
Cannonball ≃	198	46.26 N	100.38 W
Cannon Beach	224	45.53 N	123.57 W
Cannondale	207	41.12 N	73.25 W
Cannon Falls	190	44.30 N	92.54 W
Cannonsburg	216	43.03 N	85.28 W
Cannonsville Reservoir ⊜[1]	210	42.08 N	75.19 W
Cannonvale	166	20.17 S	148.42 E
Cann River	166	37.34 S	149.10 E
Caño, Isla del I	236	8.44 N	83.53 W
Caño Amarillo, Estación ◆[5]	286c	10.31 N	66.55 W
Canoas	252	29.56 S	51.11 W
Canoas ≃, Bra.	252	27.36 S	51.25 W
Canoas ≃, Bra.	256	21.30 S	47.09 W
Canobie Lake	283	42.48 N	71.14 W
Canobie Lake ⊜	283	42.49 N	71.15 W
Canobie Lake Park ♦	283	42.48 N	71.15 W
Canoe	182	50.45 N	119.13 W
Canoe ≃, B.C., Can.	182	52.09 N	118.27 W
Canoe ≃, Ma., U.S.	283	41.58 N	71.08 W
Canoe Brook ≃	276	40.45 N	74.22 W
Canoe Brook Reservoirs ⊜[1]	276	40.45 N	74.21 W
Canoe Creek Indian Reserve ◆[4]	182	51.32 N	122.15 W
Canoe Lake ⊜	184	55.11 N	108.15 W
Canoe Lake Indian Reserve ◆[4]	184	55.08 N	108.12 W
Canoga Park ◆[8]	280	34.12 N	118.35 W
Canoinhas	252	26.10 S	50.24 W
Canol	180	65.14 N	126.56 W
Canon	192	34.21 N	83.07 W
Canon ≃	224	46.36 N	123.53 W
Canonbie	44	55.05 N	2.57 W
Canon City	200	38.24 N	105.13 W
Cañón de Río Blanco, Parque Nacional ♦	234	18.38 N	97.06 W
Caño Negro	236	10.54 N	84.44 W
Canonsburg	214	40.15 N	80.11 W
Canonsburg Lake ⊜	279b	40.16 N	80.07 W
Canoochee ≃	192	31.59 N	81.18 W
Canoole Cise	144	2.02 N	42.19 E
Canopus ⊥	142	31.18 N	30.03 E
Canora	184	51.37 N	102.26 W
Canosa di Puglia	68	41.13 N	16.04 E
Canossa ⊥	64	44.35 N	10.27 E
Canot, Pointe >	241o	16.12 N	61.28 W
Canouan I	238	12.43 N	61.20 W
Canova	198	43.52 N	97.30 W
Canova Beach	220	28.08 N	80.34 W
Cañovanas	240m	18.23 N	65.54 W
Cánoves ≃	266d	41.37 N	2.22 E
Canow	54	53.12 N	12.54 E
Canowindra	166	33.34 S	148.38 E
Can Quer, Torrente de ≃	266d	41.31 N	2.11 E
Cansado	148	20.51 N	17.02 W
Cansanção	250	10.41 S	39.31 W
Canso	186	45.20 N	61.00 W
Canso, Strait of ʊ	186	45.37 N	61.25 W
Canta	248	11.25 S	76.38 W
Cantabria	234	19.50 N	101.44 W
Cantabria □[4]	34	43.15 N	4.00 W
Cantábrica, Cordillera ⩘	34	43.00 N	5.00 W
Cantabriques → Cantábrica, Cordillera ⩘	34	43.00 N	5.00 W
Cantagalo	255	21.58 S	42.22 W
Cantagalo, Cachoeira ⌊	250	7.18 S	54.52 W
Cantal □[5]	32	45.05 N	2.45 E
Cantalejo	34	41.15 N	3.55 W
Cantalupo in Sabina	66	42.18 N	12.39 E
Çantalupo nel Sannio	66	41.31 N	14.24 E
Čantal'vejergyn ≃	180	67.38 N	179.22 W
Cantanhede, Bra.	250	3.39 S	44.24 W
Cantanhede, Port.	34	40.21 N	8.36 W
Cantareira ◆[8]	287b	23.27 S	46.37 W
Cantareira, Serra da ∧	287b	23.25 S	46.39 W
Cantário ≃	248	12.13 S	64.34 W
Cantaura	246	9.19 N	64.21 W
Cant Clough Reservoir ⊜[1]	262	53.46 N	2.09 W
Canteleu	50	49.27 N	1.02 E
Canterbury, Austl.	274a	33.55 S	151.07 E
Canterbury, Austl.	274b	37.49 S	145.05 E
Canterbury, N.B., Can.	186	45.53 N	67.29 W
Canterbury, Eng., U.K.	42	51.17 N	1.05 E
Canterbury Bight c[3]	172	44.15 S	171.38 E
Canterbury Cathedral ʋ[1]	42	51.17 N	1.05 E
Canterbury Park Racecourse ♦	274a	33.54 S	151.07 E
Canterbury Plains ≚	172	44.00 S	171.45 E
Canterbury Woods	284c	38.49 N	77.15 W
Can Tho	110	10.02 N	105.47 E
Cantiano	66	43.28 N	12.38 E
Cantil	228	35.18 N	117.58 W

≃ River	Fluß	Río	Rivière	Rio
≅ Canal	Kanal	Canal	Canal	Canal
⌊ Waterfall, Rapids	Wasserfall, Stromschnellen	Cascada, Rápidos	Chute d'eau, Rapides	Cascata, Rápidos
ʊ Strait	Meeresstraße	Estrecho	Détroit	Estreito
c Bay, Gulf	Bucht, Golf	Bahía, Golfo	Baie, Golfe	Baía, Golfo
⊜ Lake, Lakes	See, Seen	Lago, Lagos	Lac, Lacs	Lago, Lagos
≣ Swamp	Sumpf	Pantano	Marais	Pântano
⊓ Ice Features, Glacier	Eis- und Gletscherformen	Accidentes Glaciales	Formes glaciaires	Acidentes glaciares
⊤ Other Hydrographic Features	Andere Hydrographische Objekte	Otros Elementos Hidrográficos	Autres données hydrographiques	Outros acidentes hidrográficos

✣ Submarine Features	Untermeerische Objekte	Accidentes Submarinos	Formes de relief sous-marin	Acidentes submarinos
□ Political Unit	Politische Einheit	Unidad Politica	Entité politique	Unidade política
ʋ Cultural Institution	Kulturelle Institution	Institución Cultural	Institution culturelle	Instituição cultural
⊥ Historical Site	Historische Stätte	Sitio Histórico	Site historique	Sitio histórico
♦ Recreational Site	Erholungs- und Ferienort	Sitio de Recreo	Centre de loisirs	Area de Lazer
⊠ Airport	Flughafen	Aeropuerto	Aéroport	Aeroporto
■ Military Installation	Militäranlage	Instalación Militar	Installation militaire	Instalação militar
◆ Miscellaneous	Verschiedenes	Misceláneo	Divers	Diversos

Cantiles, Cayo ı 240p 21.36 N 82.02 W
Cantin Lake ☐ 184 33.27 N 95.10 W
Canto do Buriti 250 8.07 S 42.58 W
Canto do Pontes 287a 22.58 S 43.04 W
Canto Grande 286d 11.59 S 77.01 W
Canto Grande, Quebrada V 286d 11.59 S 77.01 W
Cantoira 62 45.21 N 7.23 E
Canton, Ct., U.S. 207 41.49 N 72.53 W
Canton, Ga., U.S. 192 34.14 N 84.29 W
Canton, Il., U.S. 190 40.33 N 90.02 W
Canton, Ks., U.S. 198 38.23 N 97.25 W
Canton, Ma., U.S. 207 42.09 N 71.08 W
Canton, Mn., U.S. 194 43.31 N 91.55 W
Canton, Ms., U.S. 194 32.36 N 90.02 W
Canton, Mo., U.S. 194 40.07 N 91.37 W
Canton, N.J., U.S. 208 39.28 N 75.24 W
Canton, N.Y., U.S. 188 44.35 N 75.10 W
Canton, N.C., U.S. 192 35.31 N 82.50 W
Canton, Oh., U.S. 214 40.47 N 81.22 W
Canton, Ok., U.S. 196 36.03 N 98.35 W
Canton, Pa., U.S. 210 41.39 N 76.51 W
Canton, S.D., U.S. 198 43.18 N 96.35 W
Canton, Tx., U.S. 222 32.33 N 95.51 W
Canton → Guangzhou, Zhg. 100 23.06 N 113.16 E
Canton → Kanton ı 174h 2.50 S 171.40 W
Canton Airport 174h 2.04 S 171.43 W
Canton Lake ☺¹ 196 36.08 N 98.36 W
Canton Lake State Recreational Area 196 36.08 N 98.39 W
Cantonment 194 30.36 N 87.20 W
Cantorbéry → Canterbury 42 51.17 N 1.05 E
Cantrall 62 39.56 N 89.41 W
Cantribana 266c 38.53 N 9.25 W
Cantù 62 45.44 N 9.08 E
Cantu ☐ 252 24.46 S 52.54 W
Cantua Creek 226 36.30 N 120.19 W
Cantua Creek ≃ 226 36.28 N 120.17 W
Cantwell 180 63.23 N 148.57 W
Cañuelas ☐⁵ 288 35.03 S 58.44 W
Cañuelas ☐⁵ 288 34.56 S 58.41 W
Cañuelas, Arroyo ≃ 258 34.55 S 58.38 W
Canumã 246 4.02 S 59.04 W
Canumã ≃ 246 3.55 S 59.10 W
Canungra 171a 28.01 S 153.10 E
Canungra Creek ≃ 171a 27.55 S 153.06 E
Canungra Jungle Training Ground ■ 171a 28.02 S 153.10 E
Canutama 248 6.32 S 64.20 W
Canutillo 200 31.54 N 106.35 W
Canvastown 172 41.18 S 173.40 E
Canvey Island ı 52 51.32 N 0.36 E
Canvey Island ı 260 51.33 N 0.34 E
Čany 86 55.19 N 76.46 E
Cany, ozero ☺ 86 54.50 N 77.30 E
Cany-Barville 50 49.47 N 0.38 E
Canyon, Yk., Can. 180 60.52 N 137.02 W
Canyon, Ca., U.S. 282 37.49 N 122.09 W
Canyon, Tx., U.S. 196 34.58 N 101.55 W
Canyon City 202 44.23 N 118.56 W
Canyon Country 234 34.25 N 118.28 W
Canyon Creek 182 55.22 N 115.05 W
Canyon Creek ≃, Az., U.S. 200 33.49 N 110.40 W
Canyon Creek ≃, Ca., U.S. 226 39.22 N 120.45 W
Canyon Creek ≃, Id., U.S. 202 42.59 N 115.59 W
Canyon Creek ≃, Wa., U.S. 224 45.57 N 122.22 W
Canyon Creek ≃, Wa., U.S. 224 48.43 N 120.55 W
Canyon de Chelly National Monument ♦ 200 36.01 N 109.26 W
Canyon Ferry Lake ☺¹ 202 46.33 N 111.37 W
Canyon Lake ☺¹ 196 29.52 N 98.16 W
Canyonlands National Park ♦ 200 38.10 N 110.00 W
Canyonville 202 42.55 N 123.16 W
Canzar 152 7.38 S 21.32 E
Canzo 62 45.51 N 9.16 E
Cao ≃, Zhg. 98 40.29 N 124.08 E
Caobanal 234 17.37 N 93.22 W
Cao Bang 102 22.40 N 106.15 E
Caochi 107 30.19 N 104.24 E
Caocun 106 31.42 N 118.56 E
Caodian, Zhg. 100 33.21 N 112.39 E
Caodian, Zhg. 100 28.39 N 120.23 E
Caodian, Zhg. 100 32.32 N 111.11 E
Cao'e 100 30.01 N 120.52 E
Cao'e ≃ 100 30.06 N 120.46 E
Caofang 100 26.04 N 116.35 E
Caogezhai 105 40.09 N 117.50 E
Caohe, Zhg. 100 38.57 N 115.32 E
Caohe, Zhg. 269b 31.09 N 121.25 E
Caohecheng 100 40.46 N 124.02 E
Caohekou 104 41.04 N 123.53 E
Caohezhang 104 41.04 N 124.03 E
Caojian 102 25.38 N 99.07 E
Caojiaowopeng 104 42.00 N 122.20 E
Caojiawu 105 42.37 N 122.19 E
Caojiazhen 105 39.24 N 116.31 E
Caojiezi 100 31.55 N 121.38 E
Caojing 105 30.47 N 121.24 E
Caojing 100 29.41 N 116.17 E
Cao Lanh 110 10.27 N 105.38 E
Caolaoji 100 33.06 N 117.22 E
Caolisport, Loch c 46 55.54 N 5.37 W
Coomaji 98 52.34 N 116.17 E
Coombo 100 8.43 S 16.51 E
Caonao ☐⁵ 240p 22.05 N 78.05 W
Caonian 102 32.56 N 120.20 E
Caonillas, Lago ☺ 240m 18.16 N 66.39 W
Caopeng 62 31.44 N 121.17 E
Caoping 100 28.48 N 118.22 E
Caopu 98 34.34 N 118.32 E
Caoqiao 100 31.32 N 119.59 E
Caorle 64 45.36 N 12.53 E
Caorso 62 45.03 N 9.52 E
Caoshi, Zhg. 104 42.17 N 125.16 E
Caoshi, Zhg. 100 33.32 N 116.29 E
Caota 100 29.42 N 120.08 E
Caotang 106 31.16 N 118.59 E
Caoxi 100 28.42 N 117.18 E
Caoxian 100 34.33 N 115.33 E
Caoyangxi 100 26.34 N 118.47 E
Cap, Le → Cape Town 158 33.55 S 18.22 E
Capac 190 43.00 N 82.55 W
Capaccio 66 40.25 N 15.05 E
Capaci 66 38.04 N 13.14 E
Capage 152 13.21 S 21.05 E
Čapajevka, S.S.S.R. 80 52.52 N 51.10 E
Čapajevka ≃, S.S.S.R. 78 49.33 N 32.06 E
Čapajevo, S.S.S.R. 78 49.23 N 30.26 E
Čapajevo, S.S.S.R. 78 47.29 N 36.20 E
Čapajevsk 80 53.00 N 49.42 E
Čapajevsk 82 49.21 N 35.54 E
Čapajevsk 78 49.43 N 49.41 E
Capala 152 13.37 S 14.45 E
Capalbio 66 42.27 N 11.25 E
Capalonga 116 14.20 N 122.30 E
Capanaparo ≃ 246 7.01 N 67.07 W
Capanema, Bra. 250 1.12 S 47.11 W
Capanema, Bra. 252 25.40 S 53.48 W
Capangombe 152 15.05 S 13.08 E
Capanne, Monte ∧ 64 42.46 N 10.10 E
Capannoli 64 43.35 N 10.41 E
Capannori 64 43.50 N 10.34 E
Capão Bonito 252 24.00 S 48.21 W

Capão Doce, Morro do ∧ 252 26.43 S 51.25 W
Capão Redondo ☐⁸ 287b 23.40 S 46.46 W
Capaotigamau, Lac ☺ 186 50.18 N 68.14 W
Caparaó, Parque Nacional do ♦ 255 20.33 S 41.45 W
Caparica 266c 38.40 N 9.12 W
Caparo ≃ 246 7.46 N 70.23 W
Capas 116 15.20 N 120.35 E
Capatárida 246 11.11 N 70.37 W
Cap-aux-Meules (Grindstone Island) 186 47.23 N 61.52 W
Cap aux Meules, Île du ı 186 47.23 N 61.54 W
Capay 226 38.32 N 122.03 W
Cap-Chat 186 49.06 N 66.42 W
Cap-de-la-Madeleine 206 46.22 N 72.31 W
Capdevila ☐⁸ 286b 23.03 N 82.24 W
Cape (Kaap) ☐⁴ 156 31.00 S 23.00 E
Cape ≃ 166 20.49 S 146.51 E
Cape Arid National Park ♦ 162 33.40 S 123.25 E
Cape Barren Island ı 166 40.25 S 148.12 E
Cape Basin ✦¹ 8 37.00 S 7.00 E
Cape Bougainville Aboriginal Reserve ♦⁴ 164 14.10 S 126.30 E
Cape Breton Highlands National Park ♦ 186 46.45 N 60.45 W
Cape Breton Island ı 186 46.00 N 60.30 W
Cape Broyle 186 47.06 N 52.57 W
Cape Canaveral 220 28.24 N 80.36 W
Cape Canaveral Air Force Station ■ 220 28.29 N 80.35 W
Cape Charles 208 37.16 N 76.01 W
Cape Coast 150 5.05 N 1.15 W
Cape Cod Bay c 207 41.52 N 70.22 W
Cape Cod Canal ☰ 207 41.47 N 70.30 W
Cape Cod National Seashore ♦ 207 41.56 N 70.00 W
Cape Comorin → Kanniyākumari 122 8.05 N 77.34 E
Cape Coral 220 26.33 N 81.56 W
Cape Croker Indian Reserve ♦ 212 44.55 N 81.01 W
Cape Dorset 176 64.14 N 76.32 W
Cape Elizabeth 188 43.33 N 70.12 W
Cape Fear ≃ 192 33.53 N 78.00 W
Cape Girardeau 194 37.18 N 89.31 W
Cape Hatteras National Seashore ♦ 192 35.30 N 76.35 W
Cape Henlopen State Park ♦ 208 38.45 N 75.06 W
Cape Jervis 168b 35.36 S 138.06 E
Cape Johnson Tablemount ✦³ 14 17.08 N 177.15 W
Cape Krusenstern National Monument ♦ 180 67.30 N 163.40 W
Capela, Bra. 250 9.25 S 36.04 W
Capela, Bra. 250 10.30 S 37.04 W
Cape LaHave Island ı 186 44.12 N 64.22 W
Cape la Hune 186 47.33 N 56.52 W
Capel Curig 44 53.06 N 3.54 W
Capelinha 152 9.12 S 19.43 E
Capelinha 255 17.42 S 42.31 W
Capelinha do Embirazal 256 22.02 S 45.26 W
Cape Lisburne 180 68.52 N 166.05 W
Capel'ka 66 58.03 N 28.59 E
Capel·la 166 23.05 S 148.02 E
Capella 164 52.05 S 141.05 E
Capelle [aan de IJssel] 52 51.55 N 4.35 E
Capellen 56 49.38 N 5.59 E
Capelongo 152 14.54 S 15.08 E
Cape Lookout National Seashore ♦ 192 34.40 N 76.23 W
Cape Lookout State Park ♦ 224 45.21 N 123.59 W
Capel Saint Mary 42 52.00 N 1.04 E
Cape May ı 208 38.56 N 74.54 W
Cape May ☐⁶ 208 38.56 N 74.55 W
Cape May Coast Guard Air Station ■ 208 38.57 N 74.53 W
Cape May Court House 208 39.04 N 74.49 W
Cape May Point 208 39.04 N 74.46 W
Capembé ≃ 152 16.10 S 21.00 E
Cape Melville National Park ♦ 164 14.23 S 144.30 E
Capenda Camulemba 152 9.24 S 18.27 E
Capenga ☐ 287a 22.49 S 43.37 W
Capenhurst 262 53.15 N 2.57 W
Cape of Good Hope Nature Reserve ♦⁴ 158 34.18 S 18.26 E
Cape Pole 180 56.58 N 133.48 W
Cape Pond ☺ 283 42.38 N 70.38 W
Cape Porpoise 188 43.22 N 70.26 W
Cape Range National Park ♦ 162 22.10 S 113.55 E
Cape Rise ✦³ 8 42.00 S 15.00 E
Capernaum → Kefar Naḥum ı 132 32.53 N 35.34 E
Cape Romanzof 180 61.49 N 165.56 W
Capertee 170 33.09 S 149.59 E
Capertee ≃ 170 33.12 S 150.28 E
Cape Sable Island ı 186 43.25 N 65.37 W
Cape Scott Provincial Park ♦ 182 50.45 N 128.20 W
Capesterre, Guad. 241o 16.03 N 61.34 W
Capesterre, Guad. 241o 15.54 N 61.13 W
Capesterre, Pointe de la ⟩ 241o 16.03 N 61.33 W
Capesthorne Hall ⟂ 262 53.15 N 2.14 W
Capestrano 66 42.16 N 13.46 E
Capetinga ≃ 256 22.04 S 47.14 W
Cape Tormentine 186 46.08 N 63.47 W
Cape Town (Kaapstad) 158 33.55 S 18.22 E
Cape Verde (Cabo Verde) ☐¹, Afr. 134 16.00 N 24.00 W
Cape Verde (Cabo Verde) ☐¹, Afr. 150a 16.00 N 24.00 W
Cape Verde Basin ✦¹ 8 15.00 N 30.00 W
Cape Verde Islands → Cape Verde ☐¹ 150a 16.00 N 24.00 W
Cape Verde Terrace ✦³ 10 18.00 N 20.00 W
Capeville 208 37.12 N 75.57 W
Cape Vincent 212 44.07 N 76.19 W
Cape Yakataga 180 60.04 N 142.26 W
Cape York Peninsula ⟩¹ 164 14.00 S 142.30 E
Cap-Haïtien 238 19.45 N 72.12 W
Capilla de Farruco 252 33.05 S 55.25 W
Capilla del Monte 252 30.51 S 64.31 W
Capilla del Señor 258 34.18 S 59.06 W
Capim ≃ 250 1.40 S 47.47 W
Capim Melado, Morro do ∧ 287a 32.55 S 43.29 W
Capinas Point ⟩ 116 11.05 N 125.14 E
Capinópolis 255 18.41 S 49.35 W
Capinota 248 17.43 S 66.14 W
Capinzal 252 27.20 S 51.36 W
Capira 238 8.42 N 79.53 W
Capitan Island ı 116 5.57 N 120.06 E
Capistrano, Bra. 250 4.30 S 38.55 W
Capistrano, It. 66 38.41 N 16.19 E
Capistrano Beach 228 33.27 N 117.40 W
Capitachouane ≃ 186 47.36 N 76.54 W
Capitachouane, Lac ☺ 190 48.05 N 75.55 W
Capital Airport ⊡ 219 39.51 N 89.41 W

Capital Centre Arena 284c 38.54 N 76.51 W
Capital City Airport ⊡ 216 42.47 N 84.35 W
Capitan 200 33.32 N 105.34 W
Capitán Aracena, Isla ı 254 54.10 S 71.20 W
Capitán Arturo Prat [Base] 9 62.30 S 59.41 W
Capitán Bado 252 23.16 S 55.32 W
Capitán Bermúdez 252 32.49 S 60.43 W
Capitán Meza 252 26.55 S 55.15 W
Capitão de Campos 250 4.28 S 41.57 W
Capitán Sarmiento 252 34.10 S 59.48 W
Capitola 226 36.58 N 121.57 W
Capitol Heights 208 38.53 N 76.54 W
Capitol Park ☐ 208 39.08 N 75.30 W
Capitol Peak ∧ 204 41.50 N 117.18 W
Capitol Reef National Park ♦ 200 38.11 N 111.20 W
Capitol View 192 33.57 N 80.56 W
Capivari 255 23.00 S 47.31 W
Capivari ≃, Bra. 255 23.00 S 43.10 W
Capivari ≃, Bra. 116 7.20 N 126.34 E
Capivari ≃, Bra. 116 7.20 N 126.34 E
Capivari ≃, Bra. 256 22.26 S 45.47 W
Capivari ≃, Bra. 256 22.14 S 44.57 W
Capivari ≃, Bra. 256 22.56 S 47.16 W
Capivari ≃, Bra. 256 21.53 S 46.15 W
Capivari ≃, Bra. 256 21.30 S 44.20 W
Capivari ≃, Bra. 256 21.12 S 44.52 W
Capivari, Canal ☰ 287a 22.42 S 43.21 W
Capiz → Roxas 116 11.35 N 122.45 E
Capiz ☐⁴ 116 11.30 N 122.30 E
Capizzi 70 37.51 N 14.29 E
Caplan 186 48.06 N 65.41 W
Caplejevka 78 51.43 N 33.12 E
Caples Lake ☺¹ 226 38.42 N 120.03 W
Caplina ≃ 248 18.14 S 70.33 W
Caplinka 78 46.23 N 33.32 E
Caplino, S.S.S.R. 78 48.09 N 36.14 E
Caplino, S.S.S.R. 180 64.25 N 172.15 W
Čapljina 36 43.07 N 17.42 E
Caplone, Monte ∧ 64 45.48 N 10.38 E
Caplygin 62 53.14 N 39.58 E
Capnor'ja Island ı 180 64.44 N 123.23 W
Capoche ≃ 154 15.23 S 32.53 E
Capodichino, Aeroporto di ⊡ 68 40.50 N 14.17 E
Capodimonte 66 42.33 N 11.55 E
Capo di Ponte 64 46.02 N 10.21 E
Capo d'Orlando 70 38.10 N 14.53 E
Capolago 250 6.48 S 58.21 W
Capoliveri 66 42.45 N 10.22 E
Capoosie 68 40.49 N 15.13 E
Caposele 66 43.57 N 10.54 E
Capostrada 66 43.57 N 10.54 E
Capot ≃ 241l 14.51 N 61.05 W
Capoterra 71 39.11 N 8.58 E
Capoti-an, Mount ∧ 116 11.45 N 125.15 E
Capotoan, Mount ∧ 116 12.09 N 124.57 E
Cappadócia ☐³ 130 38.30 N 36.00 E
Cappamore 48 52.37 N 8.20 W
Cap-Pelé 186 46.13 N 64.18 W
Cappella Islands ıı 240m 18.17 N 64.54 W
Cappelle 66 42.13 N 13.22 E
Cappelle sul Tavo 66 42.28 N 14.06 E
Cappel 52 52.48 N 8.07 E
Cappenberg 263 51.39 N 7.32 E
Cappenberg, Schloss ⟂ 263 51.39 N 7.32 E
Cappercleuch 44 55.29 N 3.12 W
Cap Point ⟩ 241l 14.07 N 60.57 W
Cappracotta 66 41.50 N 14.16 E
Capraia 66 43.03 N 9.50 E
Capraia, Isola ı 66 42.08 N 15.31 E
Capraia, Isola di ı 66 43.02 N 9.49 E
Capranica 66 42.16 N 12.11 E
Caprara, Punta ⟩ 71 41.07 N 8.19 E
Caprarola 66 42.19 N 12.14 E
Capreol 190 46.43 N 80.56 W
Caprera, Isola ı 71 41.12 N 9.28 E
Caprese Michelangelo 64 43.39 N 11.59 E
Capri 68 40.33 N 14.14 E
Capri, Isola di ı 68 40.33 N 14.14 E
Capriati a Volturno 68 41.28 N 14.08 E
Capricorn, Cape ⟩ 166 23.30 S 151.13 E
Capricorn Channel ⊔ 166 22.30 S 152.20 E
Capricorn Group ıı 166 23.30 S 152.00 E
Capri Leone 70 38.05 N 14.44 E
Caprino Veronese 64 45.36 N 10.47 E
Caprivi Oos ☐⁵ 156 17.45 S 24.00 E
Caprivi Zipfel (Caprivi Strip) ☐⁹ 156 17.59 S 23.00 E
Caprolace, Lago di ☺ 66 41.21 N 12.58 E
Capron, Il., U.S. 216 42.24 N 88.44 W
Capron, Va., U.S. 208 36.42 N 77.12 W
Cap Saint Jacques → Vung Tau 110 10.21 N 107.04 E
Cap-Santé 206 46.40 N 71.47 W
Capstone 260 51.21 N 0.34 E
Captain Anthony Meldahl Dam ✦⁶ 218 38.48 N 84.11 W
Captain Cook 229d 19.29 N 155.55 W
Captain Cook Bridge ☰ 274a 34.00 S 151.14 E
Captain Cook Landing Place Park ♦ 274a 34.00 S 151.14 E
Captain Cook Monument ♦ 174c 29.00 S 167.56 E
Captain Daniel Wright [Woods] 278 42.13 N 87.56 W
Captain Harbor c 284 41.00 N 73.36 W
Captain Pond ☺ 283 42.48 N 71.10 W
Captains Flat 171b 35.35 S 149.27 E
Captieux 32 44.18 N 0.16 W
Captina Creek ≃ 188 39.52 N 80.48 W
Captiva 220 26.31 N 82.11 W
Captiva Island ı 220 26.31 N 82.11 W
Captree State Park ♦ 276 40.39 N 73.16 W
Capua 68 41.06 N 14.12 E
Capual Island ı 116 6.02 N 121.24 E
Capuáva 287b 23.39 S 46.30 W
Capuava 246 17.22 S 65.18 W
Capucin ⟩ 246 1.45 S 58.35 W
Capul, Río del ≃ 116 12.26 N 124.10 E
Capulin Mountain National Monument ♦ 196 27.31 N 101.33 W

Capulin, Río del ≃ 232 19.16 N 100.33 W
Capunda 152 10.02 S 17.31 E
Capupa 152 14.57 S 14.03 E
Caquená 248 18.05 S 69.15 W
Caquetá (Japurá) ≃ 246 1.00 N 74.00 W
Caquiaviri 248 17.03 S 68.38 W
Car ≃ 86 57.03 N 63.38 E
Çara, Ityo. 150 5.52 N 37.12 E
Čara, S.S.S.R. 88 56.54 N 118.12 E
Čara ≃ 88 60.23 N 120.50 E
Carabanchel Alto ☐⁸ 266a 40.22 N 3.45 W
Carabanchel Bajo ☐⁸ 266a 40.23 N 3.47 W
Carabao Island ı 116 12.04 N 121.56 E
Carabaya, Cordillera ∧ 248 13.50 S 70.10 W
Carabelas 258 33.47 S 59.45 W
Carabinani ≃ 246 1.58 S 61.31 W
Carabobo ☐³ 246 10.10 N 68.05 W
Carabost 171b 35.36 S 147.44 E
Caracal 38 44.07 N 24.21 E
Caracalla, Terme di ⁂ 267a 41.53 N 12.29 E
Caracarai 246 1.50 N 61.08 W
Caracas, Ven. 246 10.30 N 66.56 W
Caracas, Ven. 286c 10.30 N 66.56 W
Čarach 86 59.03 N 62.15 E
Carache 246 9.38 N 70.14 W
Caracol, Bra. 250 9.17 S 43.20 W
Caracol, Bra. 252 22.01 S 57.02 W
Caracollo 248 17.39 S 67.10 W
Caracorum → Karakoram Range ∧ 120 35.30 N 77.00 E
Carácuaro de Morelos 234 18.46 N 101.02 W
Caradoc Indian Reserve ♦ 214 42.48 N 81.29 W
Caraffa di Catanzaro 68 38.53 N 16.29 E
Caraga 116 7.20 N 126.34 E
Caraga ≃ 116 7.20 N 126.34 E
Caragh, Lough ☺ 48 52.03 N 9.52 W
Caraghnan Mountain ∧ 166 31.20 S 149.03 E
Caraglio 62 44.25 N 7.26 E
Caraguata, Arroyo ≃ 288 34.24 S 58.38 W
Caraguatatuba 256 23.37 S 45.25 W
Caraguatatuba, Enseada de c 256 23.40 S 45.20 W
Caraguatay 252 25.14 S 56.52 W
Caraí 255 17.12 S 41.42 W
Caraíbamba 248 14.24 S 73.09 W
Caraibes, Îles des → West Indies ıı 230 19.00 N 70.00 W
Caraïbes, Mer des → Caribbean Sea ⁷² 230 15.00 N 73.00 W
Caraigres, Cerro ∧ 236 9.43 N 84.05 W
Caraíva ≃ 255 16.48 S 39.08 W
Carajari ≃ 250 4.45 S 54.20 W
Carajás, Serra dos ∧ 250 6.00 S 51.20 W
Caralue Bluff ∧² 168 33.26 S 136.16 E
Caramagna-Piemonte 62 44.46 N 7.44 E
Caramanico Terme 66 42.09 N 14.00 E
Caramanta 246 5.33 N 75.38 W
Caramay 116 10.11 N 119.14 E
Caramoan 116 13.46 N 123.52 E
Caramoan Peninsula ⟩¹ 116 13.48 N 123.40 E
Caramy ≃ 32 43.26 N 6.12 E
Caransebeş 38 45.25 N 22.13 E
Carandaí 255 20.57 S 43.48 W
Carangola 255 20.44 S 42.02 W
Carano 64 46.16 N 11.27 E
Caranavi 248 4.18 S 75.15 W
Carapá ≃ 252 24.30 S 54.20 W
Carapachay ☐¹ 288 34.25 S 58.35 W
Carapajó 250 2.16 S 49.22 W
Cará-Paraná ≃ 246 1.45 S 73.13 W
Carapari 248 21.49 S 63.46 W
Carapeguá 252 25.48 S 57.14 W
Carapicuiba 255 23.31 S 46.50 W
Carapicuíba ☐⁷ 287b 23.31 S 46.53 W
Carapó 252 22.38 S 54.48 W
Carapo ≃ 246 4.48 N 64.57 W
Caraquet 186 47.48 N 64.57 W
Caras 248 9.03 S 77.45 W
Carás, Ilha ı 250 0.01 S 50.50 W
Caraş-Severin ☐⁶ 38 45.00 N 22.00 E
Caratasca, Laguna de c 236 15.23 N 83.55 W
Caratinga 255 19.47 S 42.08 W

Caravelas Grande ≃ 258 34.15 S 58.43 W
Carabas 246 1.58 S 61.31 W
Caraúbas ≃ 250 4.52 S 66.54 W
Caraúbas, Bra. 250 5.47 S 37.34 W
Caraúbas, Bra. 250 5.25 S 36.31 W
Caraúna ≃ 255 16.50 S 40.17 W
Carauari 248 4.52 S 66.54 W
Caravaca 34 38.06 N 1.51 W
Caravaggio 62 45.30 N 9.38 E
Caravelas 255 17.45 S 39.15 W
Caravelí 248 15.46 S 73.22 W
Caravelle, Presqu'île de la ⟩¹ 240e 14.45 N 60.55 W
Caravius, Monte ∧ 71 39.09 N 8.49 E
Caraway 194 35.45 N 90.19 W
Carayaó 252 25.10 S 56.26 W
Carazes ☐⁸ 246 25.10 S 56.26 W
Carazinho 252 28.18 S 52.48 W
Carazo ☐⁵ 236 11.45 N 86.15 W
Carballedo 34 42.26 N 7.48 W
Carballo 34 43.13 N 8.41 W
Carberry 184 49.52 N 99.20 W
Carbet, Pitons du ∧ 240e 14.42 N 61.07 W
Carbo 232 29.42 N 110.58 W
Carbó, Pil. 116 14.29 N 120.53 E
Carbon ≃ 70 32.16 N 12.59 E
Carbon, Ab., Can. 182 51.29 N 113.09 W
Carbon, Pa., U.S. 279b 40.17 N 79.34 W
Carbon, Tx., U.S. 222 32.16 N 98.50 W
Carbón ≃ 234 20.50 N 97.01 W
Carbon, Cap ⟩ 34 36.47 N 5.06 E
Carbonado 224 47.05 N 122.03 W
Carbonara, Capo ⟩ 71 39.06 N 9.31 E
Carbonara, Pizzo ∧ 70 37.54 N 14.02 E
Carbonate 64 45.41 N 11.13 E
Carbon-Blanc 32 44.53 N 0.31 W
Carbondale, Il., U.S. 194 37.43 N 89.13 W
Carbondale, Ks., U.S. 198 38.49 N 95.41 W
Carbondale, Pa., U.S. 210 41.34 N 75.30 W
Carbone 68 40.09 N 16.05 E
Carbonear 186 47.44 N 53.13 W
Carboneras de Guadazaón 34 39.53 N 1.48 W
Carbon Hill 194 33.53 N 87.31 W
Carbonia 71 39.10 N 8.31 E
Carbost 46 57.19 N 6.21 W
Carbost 46 57.17 N 6.22 W
Carcaixent 34 39.07 N 0.27 W
Carcajou 182 57.47 N 117.06 W
Carcar 116 10.07 N 123.38 E
Carcar Point ⟩ 116 10.05 N 123.41 W
Carcassonne 32 43.13 N 2.21 E
Carcastillo 34 42.23 N 1.27 W
Carcavelos, Port. 266c 38.41 N 9.20 W
Carcavelos, Port. 266c 38.53 N 9.14 W
Carcès 32 43.28 N 6.11 E
Carchi ☐³ 246 0.45 N 78.00 W
Carcross 180 60.10 N 134.42 W
Cardabia 162 23.05 S 113.46 E
Cardak, S.S.S.R. 82 41.37 N 69.56 E
Cardak, Tür. 130 37.49 N 29.39 E
Cardal 252 34.16 S 56.23 W
Cárdano al Campo 62 45.39 N 8.46 E
Cardedeu 34 41.38 N 2.21 E
Cardenete 34 39.46 N 1.41 W
Carden Place ⟂ 46 57.16 N 2.45 W
Cardeña 34 38.16 N 4.20 W

Cárdenas, Méx. 234 17.59 N 93.22 W
Cárdenas, Nic. 236 11.12 N 85.31 W
Cárdenas, Bahía de c 240p 23.05 N 81.10 W
Cardener ≃ 34 41.41 N 1.51 E
Carderock Springs 284c 38.59 N 77.10 W
Cardiel, Lago ☺ 254 48.55 S 71.15 W
Cardiff, Austl. 170 32.57 S 151.41 E
Cardiff, Wales, U.K. 42 51.29 N 3.13 W
Cardiff, Md., U.S. 208 39.43 N 76.20 W
Cardiff, N.J., U.S. 208 39.24 N 74.35 W
Cardiff by the Sea 228 33.01 N 117.16 W
Cardigan, P.E., Can. 186 46.14 N 62.37 W
Cardigan, Wales, U.K. 42 52.06 N 4.40 W
Cardigan Bay c, P.E., Can. 186 46.10 N 62.30 W
Cardigan Bay c, Wales, U.K. 42 52.30 N 4.20 W
Cardigan Island ı 42 52.08 N 4.41 W
Cardigan State Park ♦ 188 43.38 N 71.54 W
Cardinal 212 44.47 N 75.23 W
Cardinale 68 38.38 N 16.23 E
Cardinal Heights 242 52.03 N 75.37 W
Cardinal Lake ☺ 182 56.14 N 117.47 W
Cardington, Boph. 158 27.11 S 23.30 E
Cardington, Oh., U.S. 214 40.30 N 82.53 W
Cardinia Reservoir ☺¹ 169 37.58 S 145.25 E
Cardón, Punta ⟩ 246 11.37 N 70.14 W
Cardona 34 41.55 N 1.41 E
Cardona 255 20.04 S 49.54 W
Cardozo 252 33.53 S 57.23 W
Card Sound ⊔ 220 25.20 N 80.18 W
Cardston 182 49.12 N 113.18 W
Cardwell, Austl. 166 18.16 S 146.02 E
Cardwell, Mo., U.S. 194 36.02 N 90.17 W
Cardwell Mountain ∧ 194 35.41 N 85.44 W
Cärdžou 128 39.06 N 63.34 E
Cärdžou ☐⁴ 128 38.51 N 63.34 E
Careaçu 256 22.02 S 45.42 W
Careen Lake ☺ 184 57.00 N 108.10 W
Carega, Cima ∧ 64 45.44 N 11.08 E
Carei 38 47.42 N 22.28 E
Careiro, Ilha do ı 246 3.12 S 59.45 W
Çaren 252 3.10 S 59.44 W
Çarençavan 84 40.51 N 44.38 E
Carencro 194 30.19 N 92.02 W
Carentan 32 49.18 N 1.14 W
Carey 68 38.30 N 16.07 E
Carey, Lake ☺ 162 29.05 S 122.15 E
Carey Downs 162 25.38 S 115.27 E
Carey Island ı 150 6.30 N 10.32 W
Carey, Wales, U.K. 42 53.17 N 3.15 W
Cargados Carajos Shoals ıı 12 16.38 S 59.38 E
Cargill 46 56.30 N 3.22 W
Carhaix-Plouguer 32 48.17 N 3.35 W
Carhuamayo 248 10.55 S 76.02 W
Carhuanca 248 13.45 S 73.48 W
Carhué 252 37.11 S 62.44 W
Caria ☐⁹ 130 37.30 N 28.00 E
Cariaciaca 255 20.16 S 40.25 W
Cariaco, Golfo de c 246 10.30 N 64.00 W
Cariamanga 246 4.20 S 79.35 W
Cariango 152 10.55 S 15.20 E
Cariati 68 39.30 N 16.56 E
Caribana, Punta ⟩ 246 8.37 N 76.52 W
Cariboo Mountains ∧ 182 53.00 N 121.00 W
Caribou, N.S., Can. 186 45.44 N 62.42 W
Caribou, Me., U.S. 186 46.51 N 68.00 W
Caribou ≃ 176 59.20 N 94.44 W
Caribou, Lac du ☺ 206 46.56 N 72.50 W
Caribou Island ı 190 47.22 N 85.49 W
Caribou Mountain ∧, Id., U.S. 202 43.06 N 111.18 W
Caribou Mountains ∧ 176 59.12 N 115.40 W
Caribou Range ∧ 202 43.05 N 111.15 W
Cariçanha 78 48.57 N 34.29 E
Carichic 232 27.56 N 107.03 W
Caricuao, Quebrada ≃ 286c 10.26 N 66.59 W
Caribe, Mar → Caribbean Sea ⁷² 230 15.00 N 73.00 W
Cariboo 182 53.00 N 121.00 W
Caridad, Pil. 116 14.29 N 120.53 E
Caridad, Pil. 269f 14.29 N 120.53 E
Carife 68 41.01 N 15.12 E
Carigara 116 11.18 N 124.41 E
Carigara Bay c 116 11.24 N 124.40 E
Carignan 50 49.38 N 5.10 E
Carignano 62 44.55 N 7.40 E
Carilinga 255 21.56 S 42.37 W
Carmo ≃ 254 41.07 S 69.30 W
Carmo 255 21.56 S 42.37 W
Carmo, Monte ∧ 64 44.11 N 8.11 E
Carmo, Ribeirão do ≃ 256 21.20 S 45.10 W
Carmo do Paranaíba 255 18.59 S 46.21 W
Carmo do Rio Verde 255 15.21 S 49.42 W
Carmody Hills 284c 38.54 N 76.54 W
Carmona, Esp. 34 37.28 N 5.38 W
Carmona, S. Afr. 252 53.23 S 14.02 E
Carnaíba 250 10.12 S 40.29 W
Carnamah 162 29.42 S 115.53 E
Carnarvon, Austl. 162 24.53 S 113.40 E
Carnarvon, S. Afr. 158 30.59 S 22.08 E
Carnarvon → Caernarfon 44 53.08 N 4.16 W
Carnarvon National Park ♦ 166 25.00 S 148.00 E
Carnatic ⁹ 118 12.00 N 78.00 E
Carnaxide 266c 38.43 N 9.15 W
Carndonagh 48 55.15 N 7.15 W
Carnduff 184 49.10 N 101.47 W
Carnedd Llewelyn ∧ 44 53.10 N 3.58 W
Carnegie, Austl. 162 25.43 S 122.59 E
Carnegie, Pa., U.S. 279b 40.24 N 80.05 W
Carnegie, Lake ☺ 162 26.10 S 122.30 E
Carnegie Institute ⁂² 279b 40.27 N 79.57 W
Carnegie-Mellon University ⁂² 279b 40.27 N 79.57 W
Cärnes 261 48.51 N 2.42 E
Carney 208 39.24 N 76.32 W
Carneys Point 208 39.42 N 75.28 W
Carnia 64 46.40 N 13.00 E
Carnic Alps (Karnische Alpen) ∧ 64 46.40 N 13.00 E
Carnic Nicobar Island ı 118 9.11 N 92.45 E
Carnide 266c 38.46 N 9.11 W
Carnières 50 50.10 N 3.18 E

Carini, Golfo di c 70 38.08 N 13.11 E
Carinhanha 255 14.18 S 43.47 W
Carinhanha ≃ 255 14.20 S 43.47 W
Carini 70 38.08 N 13.11 E
Carmen, Méx. 232 18.38 N 91.50 W
Carmen, Pil. 116 12.37 N 122.07 E
Carmen, Pil. 116 8.59 N 125.17 E
Carmen, Pil. 116 11.53 N 124.01 E
Carmen, Pil. 116 9.50 N 124.12 E
Carmen, Ok., U.S. 196 36.34 N 98.27 W
Carmen, Ur. 252 33.15 S 56.01 W
Carmen, Isla ı 232 25.57 N 111.12 W
Carmen, Isla del ı 232 18.42 N 91.40 W
Carmen, Laguna del c 234 18.17 N 93.48 W
Carmen, Río del ≃, Chile 252 28.45 S 70.30 W
Carmen, Río del ≃, Méx. 232 30.42 N 106.29 W
Carmen Alto 252 23.11 S 69.40 W
Carmen de Apicalá 246 4.09 N 74.44 W
Carmen de Areco 252 34.22 S 70.43 W
Carmen de Huechuraba 286e 33.21 S 70.40 W
Carmen de Patagones 254 40.48 S 62.59 W
Carmen Hill ∧ 214 41.54 N 77.58 W

Carlisle Bay c 241g 13.05 N 59.37 W
Carlisle Gardens 210 43.11 N 78.39 W
Carlisle Island ı 180 52.52 N 170.02 W
Carlisle Springs 208 40.16 N 77.10 W
Carl Junction 194 37.10 N 94.33 W
Carls ⊙ 276 40.41 N 73.20 W
Carloforte 71 39.08 N 8.18 E
Carlópoli 68 39.05 N 16.27 E
Cariápolis 255 23.05 S 49.41 W
Carlos, Isla ı 254 54.03 S 73.20 W
Carlos Alves 256 21.37 S 43.07 W
Carlos Barbosa 252 29.19 S 51.30 W
Carlos Beguerie 252 35.29 S 59.06 W
Carlos Casares 252 35.38 S 61.21 W
Carlos Chagas 255 17.43 S 40.45 W
Carlos City 218 40.02 N 85.02 W
Carlos Keen 258 34.29 S 59.14 W
Carlos Pellegrini 252 32.03 S 61.48 W
Carlos Reyles 252 33.03 S 56.29 W
Carlos Sampaio 287a 22.42 S 43.43 W
Carlos Tejedor 252 35.23 S 62.25 W
Carlow ☐⁶ 48 52.50 N 6.55 W
Carlow 48 52.50 N 6.55 W
Carlow ☐⁶ 46 58.17 N 6.48 W
Carl Sandburg Home National Historic Site ♦ 192 35.16 N 82.27 W
Carlsbad → Karlovy Vary, Česko. 54 50.11 N 12.52 E
Carlsbad, Ca., U.S. 228 33.09 N 117.20 W
Carlsbad, N.M., U.S. 196 32.25 N 104.14 W
Carlsbad, Tx., U.S. 196 31.36 N 100.38 W
Carlsbad Caverns National Park ♦ 196 32.08 N 104.35 W
Carlsberg Ridge ✦³ 12 6.00 N 61.00 E
Carlsborg 224 48.05 N 123.10 W
Carlsfeld 54 50.26 N 12.35 E
Carlstadt 276 40.50 N 74.05 W
Carlton, Austl. 274a 33.58 S 151.08 E
Carlton, Eng., U.K. 42 52.58 N 1.05 W
Carlton, Eng., U.K. 44 53.42 N 1.01 W
Carlton, Mn., U.S. 190 46.39 N 92.25 W
Carlton, Or., U.S. 224 45.18 N 123.11 W
Carlton, Tx., U.S. 196 31.55 N 98.10 W
Carlton Gardens ♦ 274b 37.48 S 144.59 E
Carlton Lake ☺ 224 45.18 N 123.11 W
Carluke 46 55.45 N 3.51 W
Carlyle, Sk., Can. 184 49.38 N 102.16 W
Carlyle, Il., U.S. 219 38.36 N 89.22 W
Carlyle Lake ☺¹ 219 38.40 N 89.18 W
Carmacks 180 62.05 N 136.18 W
Carmagnola 62 44.51 N 7.43 E
Carman 184 49.32 N 98.00 W
Carmanah Creek ≃ 224 48.37 N 124.44 W
Carmangay 182 50.08 N 113.07 W
Carmanville 186 49.23 N 54.17 W
Carmarthen 42 51.52 N 4.19 W
Carmarthen Bay c 42 51.40 N 4.30 W
Carmaux 32 44.03 N 2.09 E
Carmel, Wales, U.K. 262 53.17 N 3.15 W
Carmel, In., U.S. 216 39.58 N 86.07 W
Carmel, N.J., U.S. 210 39.58 N 75.07 W
Carmel, N.Y., U.S. 210 41.26 N 73.41 W
Carmel ≃ 226 36.32 N 121.56 W
Carmel, Mount ∧ 226 36.32 N 121.47 W
Carmel → Karmel, Har ∧ 132 32.44 N 35.02 E
Carmel Bay c 226 36.33 N 121.57 W
Carmel Head ⟩ 44 53.24 N 4.34 W
Carmel Highlands 226 36.28 N 121.56 W
Carmel Hills 226 36.32 N 121.53 W
Carmel Mountain ∧² 228 32.55 N 117.13 W
Carmel Point ⟩ 226 36.31 N 121.56 W
Carmel Valley 226 36.31 N 121.54 W
Carmel Woods 226 36.34 N 121.54 W
Carmen → Ciudad del Carmen, Méx. 232 18.38 N 91.50 W

	ENGLISH	DEUTSCH		
∧	Mountain	Berg	Montaña	Montagne · Montanha
∧	Mountains	Gebirge	Montañas	Montagnes · Montanhas
⟩	Pass	Paß	Paso	Col · Passo
V	Valley, Canyon	Tal, Cañon	Valle, Cañón	Vallée, Canyon · Vale, Canhão
⟩	Plain	Ebene	Llano	Plaine · Planicie
⟩	Cape	Kap	Cabo	Cap · Cabo
ı	Island	Insel	Isla	Île · Ilha
ıı	Islands	Inseln	Islas	Îles · Ilhas
⟂	Other Topographic Features	Andere Topographische Objekte	Otros Elementos Topográficos	Autres données topographiques · Outros acidentes topográficos

ESPAÑOL Nombre / FRANÇAIS Nom / PORTUGUÊS Nome	Página / Page / Página	Lat.°′	Long.°′ W = Oeste / W = Ouest
Carniques → Karnische Alpen ⋏	64	46.40 N	13.00 E
Carnlough	48	54.59 N	6.00 W
Carno	42	52.33 N	3.31 W
Carnon-Plage	62	43.32 N	3.59 E
Carnot, Centraf.	152	4.56 N	15.52 E
Carnot, Pa., U.S.	214	40.31 N	80.13 W
Carnot, Cape ⊁	166	34.57 S	135.38 E
Carnoules	62	43.18 N	6.11 E
Carnoustie	46	56.30 N	2.44 W
Carnsore Point ⊁	48	52.10 N	6.22 W
Carnwath	46	55.43 N	3.38 W
Carnwath ≃	180	68.26 N	128.50 W
Caro	190	43.29 N	83.23 W
Caroga Creek ≃	210	42.58 N	74.38 W
Caroga Lake	210	43.08 N	74.29 W
Carol Beach Estates	216	42.31 N	87.49 W
Carol City	220	25.56 N	80.14 W
Carole Acres	284c	39.04 N	77.00 W
Caroleen	192	35.16 N	81.47 W
Carole Highlands	284c	38.58 N	76.59 W
Carolei	68	39.15 N	16.13 E
Carolina, Bra.	250	7.20 S	47.28 W
Carolina, Col.	246	6.43 N	75.17 W
Carolina, El Sal.	236	13.51 N	88.19 W
Carolina, P.R.	240m	18.23 N	65.57 W
Carolina, S. Afr.	158	26.05 S	30.06 E
Carolina, R.I., U.S.	207	41.27 N	71.39 W
Carolina Beach	192	34.02 N	77.53 W
Carolinas, Puntan ⊁	174n	14.55 N	145.38 E
Caroline □[6], Md., U.S.	208	38.53 N	75.50 W
Caroline □[6], Va., U.S.	208	38.00 N	77.20 W
Caroline I[1]	14	9.58 S	150.13 W
Caroline du Nord → North Carolina □[3]	192	35.30 N	80.00 W
Caroline du Sud → South Carolina □[3]	192	34.00 N	81.00 W
Caroline Islands II	14	8.00 N	147.00 E
Caroline Livermore, Mount ⋏[2]	282	37.52 N	122.26 W
Caroline Peak ⋏	172	45.56 S	167.13 E
Carol Stream	278	41.54 N	88.08 W
Caron	184	50.28 N	105.52 W
Caron, Lac ◎	190	48.00 N	78.53 W
Carona	64	46.01 N	9.47 E
Caronda	76	60.34 N	38.59 E
Caroní ≃	246	8.21 N	62.43 W
Caronia	70	38.01 N	14.26 E
Caronia ≃	70	38.03 N	14.26 E
Caronno Pertusella	266b	45.36 N	9.03 E
Carora	246	10.11 N	70.05 W
Carosino	68	40.27 N	17.23 E
Carouge	58	46.11 N	6.09 E
Car'ov	80	48.40 N	45.22 E
Carovigno	68	40.42 N	17.39 E
Carovilli	66	41.43 N	14.17 E
Car'ovščina	80	53.37 N	44.45 E
Carozero	76	60.28 N	38.39 E
Carp	212	45.21 N	76.02 W
Carp ≃, On., Can.	212	45.29 N	76.14 W
Carp ≃, Mi., U.S.	190	46.02 N	84.42 W
Carpaneto Piacentino	62	44.55 N	9.47 E
Carpanzano	68	39.09 N	16.18 E
Carpates → Carpathian Mountains ⋏	22	48.00 N	24.00 E
Carpathian Mountains ⋏	22	48.00 N	24.00 E
Carpaţii Meridionali ⋏	38	45.30 N	24.15 E
Cárpatos → Carpathian Mountains ⋏	22	48.00 N	24.00 E
Carpegna	66	43.47 N	12.20 E
Carpenedolo	64	45.22 N	10.26 E
Carpentaria, Gulf of ⊂	164	14.00 S	139.00 E
Carpenter	198	41.02 N	104.21 W
Carpenter Creek ≃	216	40.54 N	87.12 W
Carpenter Lake ◎	182	50.50 N	122.30 W
Carpentersville	216	42.07 N	88.15 W
Carpentertown	279b	40.11 N	79.31 W
Carpentras	62	44.03 N	5.03 E
Carpet Museum ⊍	267d	35.43 N	51.24 E
Carpi	64	44.47 N	10.53 E
Carpignano Sesia	62	45.32 N	8.25 E
Carpina	250	7.51 S	35.15 W
Carpineti	64	44.28 N	10.31 E
Carpineto Romano	66	41.36 N	13.05 E
Carpino	68	41.51 N	15.51 E
Carpinone	66	41.35 N	14.19 E
Carpinteria	204	34.23 N	119.31 W
Carpio	198	48.26 N	101.42 W
Carp Lake ◎	182	54.45 N	123.20 W
Carpolac	166	36.44 S	141.19 E
Carquefou	32	47.18 N	1.30 W
Carqueiranne	62	43.05 N	6.05 E
Carquinez Bridge ◆[5]	282	38.04 N	122.14 W
Carquinez Strait ʮ	282	38.02 N	122.12 W
Carra, Lough ◎	48	53.42 N	9.16 W
Carrabelle	192	29.51 N	84.39 W
Carradale	46	55.35 N	5.28 W
Carramar	274a	33.53 S	150.58 E
Carrancas	256	21.30 S	44.39 W
Carr and Craggs Moor ◆[3]	262	53.43 N	2.09 W
Carrangalan	116	15.58 N	121.04 E
Carranza, Cabo ⊁	252	35.36 S	72.38 W
Carrao ≃	246	6.17 N	62.51 W
Carrara	64	44.05 N	10.06 E
Carrascal, Chile	286e	33.25 S	70.43 W
Carrascal, Fil.	116	9.22 N	125.56 E
Carrasco ◆[8]	258	34.54 S	56.05 W
Carrasco, Aeropuerto Nacional de ⊠	258	34.52 S	56.02 W
Carrathool	166	34.24 S	145.26 E
Carrauntoohil ⋏	48	51.59 N	9.45 W
Carrazedo	256	21.57 S	48.47 W
Carrboro	192	35.54 N	79.04 W
Carr Bridge	46	57.17 N	3.49 W
Carrcroft	285	39.47 N	75.30 W
Carrcroft Crest	285	39.47 N	75.30 W
Carrefour Pompadour ◆[8]	261	43.46 N	2.26 E
Carregueira, Serra da ⋏[2]	266c	33.48 N	9.15 W
Carreria	252	21.59 S	58.35 W
Carreta, Punta ⊁	248	14.13 S	76.18 W
Carreta Quemada, Arroyo ≃	258	34.21 S	56.41 W
Carriacou I	238	12.30 N	61.27 W
Carrick ◆[8]	279b	40.23 N	79.59 W
Carrick ◆[1]	44	55.12 N	4.38 W
Carrickart	48	55.10 N	7.47 W
Carrickfergus	48	54.43 N	5.49 W
Carrickmacross	48	53.58 N	6.43 W
Carrick-on-Shannon	48	53.57 N	8.05 W
Carrick on Suir	48	52.21 N	7.25 W
Carrie, Mount ⋏	224	47.53 N	123.39 W
Carriere	194	30.37 N	89.39 W
Carrière, Lac ◎	190	47.14 N	77.12 W
Carrières, Pointe aux ⊁	275a	45.31 N	73.54 W
Carrières-sous-Bois	261	48.57 N	2.07 E
Carrières-sous-Poissy	261	48.57 N	2.03 E
Carrières-sur-Seine	261	48.55 N	2.11 E
Carriers Mills	194	37.41 N	88.38 W
Carrieton	166	32.26 S	138.32 E
Carrigahorig	48	53.04 N	8.09 W
Carrigaline	48	51.48 N	8.24 W
Carrigallen	48	53.59 N	7.39 W
Carrillo, C.R.	236	9.52 N	85.30 W
Carrillo, Méx.	232	26.54 N	103.55 W
Carrillo Puerto, Méx.	234	19.08 N	102.42 W
Carrillo Puerto, Méx.	234	21.09 N	104.52 W
Carrington, Eng., U.K.	262	53.26 N	2.24 W
Carrington, N.D., U.S.	198	47.26 N	99.07 W
Carrington Island I	202	41.00 N	112.37 W
Carrington Moss ◆[3]	262	53.25 N	2.23 W
Carr Inlet ⊂	224	47.17 N	122.42 W
Carrión ≃	34	41.53 N	4.32 W
Carrión de los Condes	34	42.20 N	4.36 W
Carrizal ≃	234	18.01 N	102.32 W
Carrizal, Cerro ⋏	196	26.43 N	100.36 W
Carrizal, Río del ≃	234	23.03 N	97.46 W
Carrizal Bajo	252	28.05 S	71.10 W
Carrizo	34	42.35 N	5.50 W
Carrizo Creek ≃, U.S.	196	36.05 N	102.36 W
Carrizo Creek ≃, N.M., U.S.	196	35.40 N	103.43 W
Carrizo Mountain ⋏	200	33.41 N	105.42 W
Carrizo Mountains ⋏	200	36.45 N	109.10 W
Carrizo Plain ≃	226	35.25 N	120.00 W
Carrizo Springs	196	28.31 N	99.51 W
Carrizo Wash V, U.S.	200	34.36 N	109.26 W
Carrizo Wash V, Ca., U.S.	204	33.05 N	115.56 W
Carrizozo	200	33.38 N	105.52 W
Carro	62	43.20 N	5.02 E
Carrodano	62	44.14 N	9.39 E
Carroll, Ia., U.S.	198	42.03 N	94.52 W
Carroll, Ne., U.S.	198	42.16 N	97.11 W
Carroll □[6], In., U.S.	216	40.36 N	86.41 W
Carroll □[6], Ky., U.S.	218	38.39 N	85.06 W
Carroll □[6], Md., U.S.	208	39.35 N	77.00 W
Carroll □[6], Oh., U.S.	214	40.34 N	81.05 W
Carroll Lake ◎	184	51.07 N	95.05 W
Carroll Park ♦	284b	39.17 N	76.39 W
Carrolls	224	46.05 N	122.52 W
Carrollton, Al., U.S.	194	33.10 N	88.06 W
Carrollton, Ga., U.S.	192	33.35 N	85.05 W
Carrollton, Il., U.S.	219	39.18 N	90.24 W
Carrollton, Ky., U.S.	218	38.40 N	85.10 W
Carrollton, Mi., U.S.	190	43.27 N	83.55 W
Carrollton, Ms., U.S.	194	33.30 N	89.55 W
Carrollton, Mo., U.S.	194	39.21 N	93.29 W
Carrollton, Oh., U.S.	214	40.34 N	81.05 W
Carrollton, Tx., U.S.	222	32.57 N	96.53 W
Carrollton Manor	208	39.05 N	76.35 W
Carrolltown	214	40.36 N	78.43 W
Carrollwood	284b	39.20 N	76.23 W
Carron ≃, Austl.	166	17.42 S	141.06 E
Carron ≃, Scot., U.K.	46	56.02 N	3.44 W
Carron ≃, Scot., U.K.	46	57.53 N	4.21 W
Carron ≃, Scot., U.K.	46	57.25 N	5.27 W
Carron, Loch ⊂	46	57.22 N	5.31 W
Carronbridge	44	55.16 N	3.48 W
Carron Valley Reservoir ◎[1]	46	56.02 N	4.05 W
Carros	62	43.48 N	7.11 E
Carrot ≃	184	53.50 N	101.17 W
Carrot River	184	53.17 N	103.35 W
Carrouges	28	48.34 N	0.09 W
Carrowmore Lake ◎	48	54.12 N	9.47 W
Carrsville	208	36.43 N	76.50 W
Carrù	62	44.29 N	7.52 E
Carrum	169	38.05 S	145.08 E
Carrum Downs	274b	38.06 S	145.11 E
Carrum North	274b	38.03 S	145.09 E
Carrville	192	32.16 N	85.52 W
Carryduff	48	54.31 N	5.53 W
Carry Falls Reservoir ◎[1]	188	44.25 N	74.45 W
Carry-le-Rouet	62	43.20 N	5.09 E
Carsaig	46	56.17 N	6.00 W
Çarşamba	130	41.12 N	36.44 E
Čaršanga	128	37.30 N	66.01 E
Carseland	182	50.51 N	113.28 W
Carshalton ◆[8]	260	51.22 N	0.10 W
Čarsk	86	49.35 N	81.05 E
Carsoli	66	42.06 N	13.05 E
Carson, Ca., U.S.	228	33.49 N	118.16 W
Carson, N.D., U.S.	198	46.25 N	101.33 W
Carson, Va., U.S.	208	37.02 N	77.23 W
Carson, Wa., U.S.	224	45.43 N	121.49 W
Carson ≃	204	39.45 N	118.40 W
Carson, East Fork ≃	226	38.59 N	119.49 W
Carson, West Fork ≃	226	38.59 N	119.49 W
Carson City, Mi., U.S.	190	43.10 N	84.50 W
Carson City, Nv., U.S.	226	39.10 N	119.46 W
Carsondale	284c	38.57 N	76.50 W
Carson Lake ◎, On., Can.	212	45.31 N	77.46 W
Carson Lake ◎, Nv., U.S.	204	39.19 N	118.43 W
Carson Range ⋏	226	39.15 N	120.20 W
Carson Sink ◎	204	39.45 N	118.30 W
Carson Valley V	226	39.00 N	119.48 W
Carstairs, Ab., Can.	182	51.34 N	114.06 W
Carstairs, Scot., U.K.	46	55.42 N	3.42 W
Carstensz-Toppen → Jaya, Puncak ⋏	164	4.05 S	137.11 E
Carswell Air Force Base ■	222	32.47 N	97.26 W
Cartagena, Chile	252	33.33 S	71.37 W
Cartagena, Col.	246	10.25 N	75.32 W
Cartagena, Esp.	34	37.36 N	0.59 W
Cartago, Col.	246	4.45 N	75.55 W
Cartago, C.R.	236	9.52 N	83.55 W
Cartago □[4]	236	9.50 N	83.45 W
Čartak	85	41.05 N	71.50 E
Cartaxo	34	39.09 N	8.47 W
Cartaxos ⋏[2]	266c	38.54 N	9.20 W
Cartaya	34	37.17 N	7.09 W
Carter	196	35.13 N	99.30 W
Carter □[6]	218	38.20 N	83.05 W
Carter Bridge ◆[5]	273a	6.28 N	3.23 E
Carter Caves State Resort Park ♦	218	38.22 N	83.10 W
Carteret	210	40.34 N	74.13 W
Carter Lake	198	41.17 N	95.55 W
Carter Mountain ⋏	202	44.12 N	109.25 W
Carters Lake ◎[1]	192	34.35 N	84.35 W
Cartersville	192	34.09 N	84.48 W
Carterton, N.Z.	172	41.02 S	175.31 E
Carterton, Eng., U.K.	42	51.45 N	1.35 W
Carterville	194	37.45 N	89.04 W
Carthage, Tun.	148	36.51 N	10.21 E
Carthage, Ar., U.S.	194	34.04 N	92.33 W
Carthage, Il., U.S.	190	40.24 N	91.08 W
Carthage, In., U.S.	218	39.44 N	85.34 W
Carthage, Ms., U.S.	194	32.43 N	89.32 W
Carthage, Mo., U.S.	194	37.10 N	94.18 W
Carthage, N.Y., U.S.	212	43.58 N	75.36 W
Carthage, N.C., U.S.	192	35.20 N	79.25 W
Carthage, S.D., U.S.	198	44.10 N	97.42 W
Carthage, Tn., U.S.	194	36.15 N	85.57 W
Carthage, Tx., U.S.	194	32.09 N	94.20 W
Carthage ⊥	36	36.52 N	10.20 E
Cartier Islands II	160	12.32 S	123.32 E
Cartierville ◆[8]	275a	45.32 N	73.42 W
Cartierville, Aéroport de ⊠	275a	45.31 N	73.43 W
Cartridge Hill ⋏[2]	262	53.41 N	2.30 W
Cartura	64	45.16 N	11.50 E
Cartwright, Mb., Can.	184	49.06 N	99.20 W
Cartwright, Nf., Can.	176	53.42 N	57.01 W
Caruaru	250	8.17 S	35.58 W
Caruban	115a	7.33 S	111.39 E
Carumas	248	16.49 S	70.43 W
Čarungol	88	49.14 N	106.29 E
Carunjamba ≃	152	13.57 S	12.25 E
Carúpano	246	10.40 N	63.14 W
Caruray	116	10.20 N	119.00 E
Carutapera	250	1.13 S	46.01 W
Caruthers	226	36.32 N	119.50 W
Caruthersville	194	36.11 N	89.39 W
Carvalhos	256	22.00 S	44.28 W
Carver	207	41.53 N	70.45 W
Carversville	208	40.23 N	75.04 W
Carvin	50	50.29 N	2.58 E
Carvoeiro	246	1.24 S	61.59 W
Carvoeiro, Cabo ⊁	34	39.21 N	9.24 W
Cary, Il., U.S.	216	42.12 N	88.14 W
Cary, Ms., U.S.	194	32.48 N	90.55 W
Cary, N.C., U.S.	192	35.47 N	78.46 W
Cary ≃	42	51.09 N	2.59 W
Caryčelekskij zapovednik ♦	85	41.50 N	71.55 E
Čaryk, ozero ◎	80	46.13 N	42.43 E
Čarymovo	86	58.31 N	77.42 E
Čaryn	86	43.46 N	79.24 E
Čaryš ≃	86	52.22 N	83.45 E
Čaryšskoje	86	51.24 N	83.35 E
Caryville, Fl., U.S.	194	30.46 N	85.48 W
Caryville, Tn., U.S.	192	36.17 N	84.13 W
Casablanca (Dar-el-Beida)	148	33.39 N	7.35 W
Casablanca □[4]	148	33.35 N	7.30 W
Casa Blanca ◆[8]	286b	23.09 N	82.20 W
Casabona	68	39.15 N	16.57 E
Casa Branca	256	21.46 S	47.04 W
Casacalenda	66	41.44 N	14.51 E
Casa de la Torrecilla	266a	40.19 N	3.37 W
Casa del Campo ♦	266a	40.32 N	3.47 W
Casa Grande	200	32.52 N	111.45 W
Casa Grande National Monument ♦	200	32.59 N	111.32 W
Casainhos	266c	38.53 N	9.10 W
Casalanguida	66	42.03 N	14.30 E
Casalattico	66	41.37 N	13.43 E
Casalbordino	66	42.09 N	14.35 E
Casalbuono	68	40.13 N	15.41 E
Casalbuttano	64	45.15 N	9.58 E
Casal di Principe	68	41.00 N	14.08 E
Casale Abbruciato ◆[8]	267a	41.44 N	12.33 E
Casalecchio di Reno	64	44.28 N	11.16 E
Casale Monferrato	62	45.08 N	8.27 E
Casale sul Sile	64	45.36 N	12.19 E
Casaletto Spartano	68	40.09 N	15.37 E
Casalmaggiore	64	44.59 N	10.26 E
Casalmorano	62	45.17 N	9.54 E
Casalnuovo Monterotaro	68	41.37 N	15.06 E
Casa Loma ⊍	275b	43.41 N	79.25 W
Casalone ◆[8]	267a	41.56 N	12.41 E
Casalotti ◆[8]	267a	41.55 N	12.22 E
Casalpusterlengo	62	45.11 N	9.39 E
Casal Velino	68	40.11 N	15.06 E
Casalvieri	66	41.38 N	13.43 E
Casamance ≃	150	12.33 N	16.46 W
Casamari, Abbazia di ⊍[1]	66	41.41 N	13.29 E
Casamassima	68	40.57 N	16.55 E
Casamicciola Terme	68	40.45 N	13.54 E
Casanare □[3]	246	5.45 N	72.00 W
Casanare ≃	246	6.02 N	69.51 W
Casanay	246	10.30 N	63.25 W
Casa Nova	250	9.25 S	41.08 W
Casarano	68	40.00 N	18.10 E
Casar de Cáceres	34	39.34 N	6.25 W
Casarsa della Delizia	64	45.57 N	12.50 E
Casas	234	23.44 N	98.45 W
Casas Adobes	200	32.19 N	110.59 W
Casas Grandes ≃	232	31.22 N	107.31 W
Casas Ibáñez	34	39.17 N	1.28 W
Casasimarro	34	39.22 N	2.02 W
Casauman ≃	116	7.16 N	126.31 E
Casa Verde ◆[8]	287b	23.30 S	46.39 W
Casavieja	34	40.17 N	4.46 W
Casbas	252	36.45 S	62.30 W
Casca	252	28.34 S	51.59 W
Casca, Rio da ≃	248	14.52 S	55.52 W
Cascade, B.C., Can.	182	49.01 N	118.13 W
Cascade, Id., U.S.	202	44.30 N	116.02 W
Cascade, Ia., U.S.	190	42.17 N	91.00 W
Cascade, Mi., U.S.	216	42.55 N	85.30 W
Cascade, Mt., U.S.	202	47.16 N	111.41 W
Cascade, Wi., U.S.	190	43.39 N	88.00 W
Cascade ≃, N.Z.	172	44.02 S	168.22 E
Cascade ≃, Wa., U.S.	224	48.32 N	121.26 W
Cascade Bay ⊂	174c	29.01 S	167.58 E
Cascade Locks	224	45.40 N	121.53 W
Cascade Mountains (Cascade Range) ⋏	202	45.00 N	121.30 W
Cascade Park ♦	279a	41.23 N	82.06 W
Cascade Point ⊁	172	44.00 S	168.22 E
Cascade Range ⋏	178	45.00 N	121.30 W
Cascade Reservoir ◎[1]	202	44.35 N	116.06 W
Cascade Tunnel ◆[5]	224	47.40 N	121.03 W
Cascadura ◆[8]	287a	22.53 S	43.20 W
Cascais	34	38.42 N	9.25 W
Cascalho Rico	255	18.34 S	47.52 W
Cascapédia ≃	186	48.11 N	65.54 W
Cascatinha	256	22.29 S	43.09 W
Cascavel, Bra.	250	4.07 S	38.14 W
Cascavel, Bra.	252	24.57 S	53.28 W
Cascia	66	42.43 N	13.01 E
Casciana Terme	66	43.31 N	10.32 E
Cascina	64	43.41 N	10.33 E
Casco Bay ⊂	188	43.40 N	70.00 W
Cascumpec Bay ⊂	186	46.45 N	64.03 W
Čascy	82	55.37 N	36.52 E
Casei Gerola	62	45.00 N	8.55 E
Case Inlet ⊂	224	47.19 N	122.53 W
Casekow	54	53.12 N	14.12 E
Casella	62	44.32 N	9.00 E
Caselle, Aeroporto di ⊠	62	45.13 N	7.40 E
Caselle in Pittari	68	40.10 N	15.33 E
Caselle Torinese	62	45.10 N	7.39 E
Cà Selva, Lago di ◎[1]	64	46.16 N	12.40 E
Casemero Palma	236	16.20 N	88.47 W
Casenove	66	42.58 N	12.50 E
Casentino V	66	43.40 N	11.50 E
Casenuove	266b	45.38 N	8.42 E
Case-Pilote	240e	14.38 N	61.08 W
Caseros	258	34.36 S	58.33 W
Caserta	68	41.04 N	14.20 E
Caserta □[4]	68	41.14 N	14.10 E
Caseville	190	43.56 N	83.16 W
Case Western Reserve University ⊍[2]	279a	41.30 N	81.36 W
Casey, Il., U.S.	194	39.17 N	87.59 W
Casey, Ia., U.S.	198	41.30 N	94.31 W
Casey ⊍[3]	9	66.17 S	110.32 E
Casey, Mount ⋏	202	48.26 N	116.42 W
Casey Bay ⊂	9	67.20 S	48.00 E
Casey Key I	220	27.10 N	82.30 W
Caseyr ⊁	144	11.49 N	51.15 E
Caseyville	219	38.38 N	90.02 W
Cash	222	32.59 N	96.07 W
Cashel, Ire.	48	53.25 N	9.48 W
Cashel, Ire.	48	52.31 N	7.53 W
Cashie ≃	192	35.53 N	76.49 W
Cashiers	192	35.06 N	83.05 W
Cashmere	202	47.31 N	120.28 W
Cashmere Downs	162	28.58 S	119.35 E
Cashton	190	43.44 N	90.46 W
Cashtown	208	39.53 N	77.22 W
Casiguran, Fil.	116	12.52 N	124.00 E
Casiguran, Pil.	116	16.17 N	122.07 E
Casiguran Sound ʮ	116	16.06 N	121.58 E
Casilda, Arg.	252	33.03 S	61.10 W
Casilda, Cuba	240p	21.45 N	79.59 W
Casimcea	38	44.43 N	28.23 E
Casimiro Castillo	234	19.38 N	104.28 W
Casimiro de Abreu	255	22.29 S	42.12 W
Casina	64	44.30 N	10.30 E
Casino	166	28.52 S	153.03 E
Casiquiare ≃	246	2.01 N	67.07 W
Casita	200	31.00 N	110.53 W
Casitas Springs	228	34.22 N	119.18 W
Čáslav	30	49.54 N	15.23 E
Casma	248	9.28 S	78.19 W
Časniki	76	54.52 N	29.08 E
Časnikovo	265b	55.59 N	37.25 E
Časnočor, gora ⋏	24	67.45 N	33.25 E
Casola in Lunigiana	64	44.14 N	10.10 E
Casola Valsenio	66	44.13 N	11.37 E
Casole d'Elsa	66	43.20 N	11.02 E
Casoli	66	42.07 N	14.18 E
Cason	222	33.02 N	94.49 W
Casorate Primo	62	45.19 N	9.01 E
Casorate Sempione	62	45.40 N	8.44 E
Casorezzo	266b	45.31 N	8.54 E
Casoria	68	40.54 N	14.17 E
Časov Jar	83	48.35 N	37.50 E
Časovo	24	62.01 N	50.36 E
Caspe	34	41.14 N	0.02 W
Casper	200	42.50 N	106.18 W
Casper Creek, Middle Fork ≃	200	43.01 N	106.29 W
Caspian	190	46.03 N	88.37 W
Caspian Sea ∓[2]	72	42.00 N	50.30 E
Caspienne, Mer → Caspian Sea ∓[2]	72	42.00 N	50.30 E
Caspio, Depresión del → Prikaspijskaja nizmennost' ≃	80	48.00 N	52.00 E
Caspio, Mar → Caspian Sea ∓[2]	72	42.00 N	50.30 E
Caspoggio	64	46.16 N	9.52 E
Cass □[6], Il., U.S.	219	39.57 N	90.13 W
Cass □[6], In., U.S.	216	40.45 N	86.21 W
Cass □[6], Mi., U.S.	216	41.55 N	86.01 W
Cass □[6], Tx., U.S.	222	33.05 N	94.32 W
Cass ≃	190	43.23 N	83.59 W
Cassadaga	214	42.20 N	79.18 W
Cassadaga Creek ≃	214	42.05 N	79.08 W
Cassadaga Lakes ◎	214	42.21 N	79.19 W
Cassaday Point ⊁	284a	42.52 N	79.13 W
Cassagnas	62	44.16 N	3.45 E
Cassai	152	10.33 S	21.59 E
Cassai (Kasai) ≃	152	3.02 S	16.57 E
Cassamba	152	13.06 S	20.18 E
Cassandra	214	40.24 N	78.38 W
Cassange ≃	248	17.06 S	57.23 W
Cassano allo Ionio	68	39.47 N	16.20 E
Cassano d'Adda	62	45.32 N	9.31 E
Cassano delle Murge	68	40.53 N	16.46 E
Cassano Magnago	62	45.41 N	8.50 E
Cassaro	70	37.07 N	14.56 E
Cass Benton Parkway ♦	281	42.25 N	83.28 W
Cass City	190	43.36 N	83.10 W
Cassel	50	50.48 N	2.29 E
Casselberry	220	28.40 N	81.19 W
Cassella	216	40.25 N	84.34 W
Casselman	206	45.19 N	75.05 W
Casselton	198	46.54 N	97.12 W
Cássia, Bra.	255	20.36 S	46.56 W
Cassia, Fl., U.S.	220	28.53 N	81.28 W
Cássia dos Coqueiros	256	21.17 S	47.10 W
Cassiar	180	59.16 N	129.40 W
Cassiar Mountains ⋏	176	59.00 N	129.00 W
Cassibile ≃	70	36.57 N	15.11 E
Cassidy	224	49.04 N	123.53 W
Cassidy Airfield ⊠	174o	1.57 N	157.18 W
Cassilândia	255	19.09 S	51.45 W
Cassimbazar	126	24.07 N	88.16 E
Cassine	62	44.45 N	8.31 E
Cassinetta di Lugagnano	266b	45.25 N	8.54 E
Cassinga	152	15.08 S	16.05 E
Cassino, Bra.	252	32.11 S	52.10 W
Cassino, It.	66	41.30 N	13.49 E
Cassio	64	44.35 N	10.02 E
Cassipore ◆[8]	272b	22.37 N	88.22 E
Cassis	62	43.13 N	5.32 E
Cass Lake	190	47.22 N	94.36 W
Cass Lake ◎, Mi., U.S.	281	42.36 N	83.22 W
Cass Lake ◎, Mn., U.S.	190	47.25 N	94.32 W
Cassley ≃	46	57.58 N	4.35 W
Cassoalala	152	9.30 S	14.22 E
Cassoango	152	13.42 S	20.56 E
Cassolnovo	62	45.22 N	8.48 E
Cassone	64	45.44 N	10.46 E
Cassongue	152	11.51 S	15.03 E
Cassopolis	216	41.54 N	86.00 W
Casstown	218	40.03 N	84.07 W
Cassunda	152	10.57 S	21.03 E
Cassununga	255	16.03 S	53.38 W
Cassville, In., U.S.	216	40.33 N	86.08 W
Cassville, Mo., U.S.	194	36.40 N	93.52 W
Cassville, N.Y., U.S.	210	42.57 N	75.15 W
Cassville, Pa., U.S.	214	40.18 N	78.02 W
Cassville, Wi., U.S.	190	42.42 N	90.59 W
Castac Lake ◎	228	34.50 N	118.51 W
Castagnaro	64	45.07 N	11.24 E
Castagneto Carducci	66	43.10 N	10.36 E
Castaic	228	34.30 N	118.37 W
Castaic Creek ≃	228	34.25 N	118.37 W
Castaic Lake ◎[1]	228	34.32 N	118.37 W
Castalia	214	41.24 N	82.48 W
Castanea	210	41.07 N	77.25 W
Castanhal	250	1.18 S	47.55 W
Castanheira de Pêra	34	40.00 N	8.13 W
Castaños	196	26.47 N	101.25 W
Castañones, Punta ⊁	236	12.28 N	87.11 W
Castano Primo	62	45.33 N	8.47 E
Casteggio	62	45.00 N	9.07 E
Castel	43b	49.28 N	2.34 W
Castelar	258	34.40 S	58.40 W
Castel Baronia	68	41.03 N	15.11 E
Castel Bolognese	66	44.19 N	11.48 E
Castelbuono	70	37.56 N	14.05 E
Castelcivita	68	40.30 N	15.15 E
Castelcucco	64	45.50 N	11.53 E
Castel d'Ario	64	45.11 N	10.58 E
Casteldarne (Ehrenburg)	64	46.48 N	11.50 E
Casteldelfino	62	44.35 N	7.04 E
Castel del Monte	66	42.22 N	13.43 E
Castel del Piano	66	42.53 N	11.32 E
Castel del Rio	64	44.12 N	11.30 E
Castel di Decima ◆[8]	267a	41.45 N	12.26 E
Castel di Guido ◆[8]	267a	41.54 N	12.17 E
Castel di Ieri	66	42.06 N	13.44 E
Castel di Iudica	70	37.30 N	14.38 E
Castel di Leva ◆[8]	267a	41.47 N	12.32 E
Castel di Lucio	70	37.53 N	14.19 E
Castel di Sangro	66	41.47 N	14.06 E
Castel di Tora	66	42.13 N	12.58 E
Castelfidardo	66	43.28 N	13.33 E
Castelfiorentino	66	43.36 N	10.58 E
Castelfondo	64	46.27 N	11.07 E
Castelforte	66	41.18 N	13.49 E
Castelfranco Emilia	64	44.37 N	11.03 E
Castelfranco in Miscano	68	41.18 N	15.05 E
Castelfranco Veneto	64	45.40 N	11.55 E
Castel Frentano	66	42.12 N	14.22 E
Castel Fusano ◆[8]	267a	41.44 N	12.19 E
Castel Gandolfo	66	41.45 N	12.39 E
Castel Giorgio	66	42.42 N	11.59 E
Castelgrande	68	40.47 N	15.26 E
Castelhanos, Baía de ⊂	256	23.51 S	45.15 W
Castelhanos, Ponta dos ⊁	256	23.10 S	44.06 W
Casteljaloux	32	44.19 N	0.05 E
Castellabate	68	40.17 N	14.57 E
Castell'Alfero	62	44.59 N	8.13 E
Castellammare, Golfo di ⊂	70	38.08 N	12.54 E
Castellammare del Golfo	70	38.01 N	12.53 E
Castellammare di Stabia	68	40.42 N	14.29 E
Castellamonte	62	45.23 N	7.42 E
Castellana, Grotte di ⊥[5]	68	40.53 N	17.07 E
Castellana Grotte	68	40.53 N	17.11 E
Castellana Sicula	70	37.47 N	14.02 E
Castellane	62	43.51 N	6.31 E
Castellaneta	68	40.37 N	16.57 E
Castellarano	64	44.30 N	10.44 E
Castell'Arquato	62	44.51 N	9.52 E
Castell'Azzara	66	42.46 N	11.42 E
Castellazzo Bormida	62	44.51 N	8.34 E
Castellbisbal	266d	41.29 N	1.59 E
Castelldefels	266d	41.17 N	1.59 E
Castelleone	62	45.18 N	9.46 E
Castelletto	266b	45.30 N	8.48 E
Castelletto di Brenzone	64	45.41 N	10.45 E
Castelli, Arg.	252	36.06 S	57.47 W
Castelli, It.	66	42.29 N	13.43 E
Castellina in Chianti	66	43.28 N	11.17 E
Castellina Marittima	66	43.25 N	10.35 E
Castelli Romani ◆[1]	267a	41.46 N	12.42 E
Castelló □[4]	34	40.10 N	0.10 W
Castello, Monte ⋏	66	43.03 N	9.49 E
Castello d'Annone	62	44.53 N	8.19 E
Castelló de la Plana	34	39.59 N	0.02 W
Castello di Fiemme	64	46.17 N	11.26 E
Castello Lavazzo	64	46.17 N	12.18 E
Castellote	34	40.48 N	0.19 W
Castello Tesino	64	46.04 N	11.38 E
Castellucchio	64	45.09 N	10.39 E
Castelluccio	68	40.00 N	15.58 E
Castell'Umberto	70	38.05 N	14.48 E
Castelluzzo	70	38.06 N	12.44 E
Castel Madama	66	41.58 N	12.52 E
Castel Maggiore	64	44.34 N	11.22 E
Castelmagno	62	44.24 N	7.13 E
Castelmassa	64	45.01 N	11.18 E
Castelmauro	66	41.50 N	14.43 E
Castelmezzano	68	40.32 N	16.03 E
Castelmoron-sur-Lot	32	44.24 N	0.30 E
Castelnaudary	32	43.19 N	1.57 E
Castelnau-Montratier	32	44.16 N	1.21 E
Castelnovo di Sotto	64	44.49 N	10.34 E
Castelnovo ne'Monti	64	44.26 N	10.24 E
Castelnuovo	64	45.26 N	10.47 E
Castelnuovo Berardenga	66	43.21 N	11.30 E
Castelnuovo dell'Abate	66	43.00 N	11.31 E
Castelnuovo della Daunia	68	41.35 N	15.07 E
Castelnuovo di Garfagnana	64	44.06 N	10.24 E
Castelnuovo di Porto	66	42.07 N	12.30 E
Castelnuovo di Val di Cecina	66	43.12 N	10.59 E
Castelnuovo Don Bosco	62	45.03 N	7.58 E
Castelnuovo Nigra	62	45.26 N	7.41 E
Castelnuovo Rangone	64	44.33 N	10.56 E
Castelnuovo Scrivia	62	44.59 N	8.53 E
Castelo	255	20.36 S	41.12 W
Castelo Branco	34	39.49 N	7.30 W
Castelo do Piauí	250	5.20 S	41.33 W
Castel Pagano	68	41.24 N	14.48 E
Castel Porziano ◆[8]	267a	41.44 N	12.24 E
Castelraimondo	66	43.12 N	13.04 E
Castel Romano ◆[8]	267a	41.44 N	12.27 E
Castel San Gimignano	66	43.24 N	11.00 E
Castel San Giorgio	68	40.47 N	14.42 E
Castel San Giovanni	62	45.04 N	9.26 E
Castel San Lorenzo	68	40.25 N	15.14 E
Castel San Pietro Terme	66	44.24 N	11.35 E
Castel Sant'Elia	66	42.15 N	12.22 E
Castelsaraceno	68	40.10 N	16.00 E
Castelsardo	71	40.55 N	8.43 E
Castelsarrasin	32	44.02 N	1.06 E
Castelsilano	68	39.16 N	16.46 E
Casteltermini	70	37.32 N	13.39 E
Castelvecchio Subequo	66	42.08 N	13.44 E
Castelvetere in Val Fortore	68	41.27 N	14.56 E
Castelvetrano	70	37.41 N	12.47 E
Castelvetro di Modena	64	44.30 N	10.57 E
Castelvetro Piacentino	64	45.05 N	9.59 E
Castel Viscardo	66	42.45 N	12.00 E
Castel Volturno, It.	66	44.13 N	11.37 E
Castel Volturno, It.	68	41.02 N	13.56 E
Castenaso	64	44.30 N	11.28 E
Castenedolo	64	45.28 N	10.18 E
Casterton	166	37.35 S	141.24 E
Castets	32	43.53 N	1.09 W
Castiglioncello	66	43.24 N	10.24 E
Castiglione Chiavarese	62	44.16 N	9.31 E
Castiglione d'Adda	62	45.13 N	9.41 E
Castiglione dei Pepoli	64	44.08 N	11.09 E
Castiglione del Lago	66	43.07 N	12.03 E
Castiglione della Pescaia	66	42.46 N	10.53 E
Castiglione delle Stiviere	64	45.23 N	10.29 E
Castiglione del Pepoli	66	44.08 N	11.09 E
Castiglione di Sicilia	70	37.53 N	15.07 E
Castiglione d'Orcia	66	43.00 N	11.37 E
Castiglione d'Ossola	58	46.03 N	8.13 E
Castiglione Messer Marino	66	41.52 N	14.27 E
Castiglione Olona	62	45.46 N	8.52 E
Castiglion Fibocchi	66	43.32 N	11.46 E
Castiglion Fiorentino	66	43.20 N	11.55 E
Castile	210	42.37 N	78.03 W
Castilho	255	20.52 S	51.29 W
Castilla	248	5.12 S	80.38 W
Castilla, Playa de ⊥[2]	34	37.00 N	6.33 W
Castilla-La Mancha □[4]	34	39.30 N	3.00 W
Castilla la Nueva □[9]	34	40.00 N	3.45 W
Castilla la Vieja □[9]	34	41.30 N	4.00 W
Castilla-León □[4]	34	41.30 N	5.00 W
Castillo	258	33.53 S	57.40 W
Castillo, Cerro ⋏	254	43.03 S	71.57 W
Castillo, Pampa del ≃	254	45.58 S	68.24 W
Castillo de San Marcos National Monument ♦	192	29.44 N	81.20 W
Castillo Incaico de Ingapirca ⊥	246	2.34 S	78.50 W
Castillon-la-Bataille	32	44.51 N	0.03 W
Castillos	252	34.12 S	53.50 W
Castillos, Laguna de ◎	252	34.20 S	53.54 W
Castillo Velasco	234	16.45 N	96.35 W
Castine	188	44.23 N	68.48 W
Castione della Presolana	64	45.54 N	10.04 E
Castions di Strada	64	45.54 N	13.11 E
Castle Acre	42	52.42 N	0.41 E
Castle Air Force Base ■	226	37.22 N	120.34 W
Castlebar	48	53.52 N	9.17 W
Castlebay	46	56.57 N	7.28 W
Castlebellingham	48	53.54 N	6.23 W
Castleberry	194	31.17 N	87.01 W
Castleblayney	48	54.07 N	6.44 W
Castle Bruce	240d	15.26 N	61.16 W
Castle Cape ⊁	180	56.15 N	158.06 W
Castle Cary	42	51.06 N	2.31 W
Castlecliff	172	39.57 S	174.59 E
Castlecomer	48	52.48 N	7.12 W
Castleconnell	48	52.43 N	8.30 W
Castlecrag	274a	33.48 S	151.13 E
Castle Crags State Park ♦	204	41.10 N	122.20 W
Castle Creek	210	42.14 N	75.55 W
Castle Creek ≃, Austl.	169	36.41 S	145.29 E
Castle Creek ≃, Id., U.S.	202	43.03 N	116.16 W
Castle Dale	200	39.13 N	111.01 W
Castledawson	48	54.47 N	6.33 W
Castlederg	48	54.42 N	7.36 W
Castledermot	48	52.55 N	6.50 W
Castle Dome Peak ⋏	200	33.05 N	114.08 W
Castle Donington	42	52.51 N	1.19 W
Castle Douglas	44	54.57 N	3.56 W
Castlefinn	48	54.47 N	7.35 W
Castleford	44	53.44 N	1.21 W
Castlegar	182	49.19 N	117.40 W
Castle Harbour ⊂	240a	32.21 N	64.40 W
Castle Hill	274a	33.44 S	151.00 E
Castle Hills, De., U.S.	208	39.41 N	75.33 W
Castle Hills, Tx., U.S.	196	29.32 N	98.31 W
Castleisland	48	52.14 N	9.27 W
Castlemaine, Austl.	169	37.04 S	144.13 E
Castlemaine, Ire.	48	52.09 N	9.43 W
Castlemartyr	48	51.55 N	8.03 W
Castlemore	275b	43.47 N	79.41 W
Castle Mountain ⋏, Ab., Can.	182	51.18 N	115.55 W
Castle Mountain ⋏, Yk., Can.	180	64.32 N	135.25 W
Castle Mountain ⋏, Ca., U.S.	226	35.56 N	120.20 W
Castle Neck ⊁[1]	283	42.41 N	70.45 W
Castle Neck ≃	283	42.40 N	70.44 W
Castle Park	228	32.36 N	117.04 W
Castle Peak ⋏, Co., U.S.	200	39.01 N	106.52 W
Castle Peak ⋏, Id., U.S.	202	44.02 N	114.35 W
Castle Peak ⋏, Wa., U.S.	224	48.58 N	120.51 W
Castlepoint	172	40.54 S	176.13 E
Castle Point ◆[8]	260	51.33 N	0.35 E
Castlepollard	48	53.40 N	7.17 W
Castlerea	48	53.46 N	8.29 W
Castlereagh ≃	166	30.12 S	147.32 E
Castle Rock, Co., U.S.	200	39.22 N	104.51 W
Castle Rock, Pa., U.S.	285	39.58 N	75.26 W
Castle Rock, Wa., U.S.	224	46.16 N	122.54 W
Castle Rock ⋏, Or., U.S.	202	44.02 N	118.11 W
Castle Rock ⋏, Va., U.S.	192	37.57 N	78.44 W
Castle Rock Butte ⋏	198	45.00 N	103.27 W
Castle Rock Lake ◎[1]	190	43.56 N	89.58 W
Castle Shannon	279b	40.21 N	80.01 W
Castleshaw Moor ◆[3]	262	53.36 N	2.00 W
Castleside	44	54.50 N	1.52 W
Castleton, Eng., U.K.	44	54.28 N	0.56 W
Castleton, Eng., U.K.	44	53.21 N	1.46 W
Castleton, Eng., U.K.	262	53.35 N	2.11 W
Castleton, In., U.S.	218	39.54 N	86.03 W
Castleton, Vt., U.S.	188	43.36 N	73.10 W
Castleton on Hudson	210	42.32 N	73.45 W
Castletown, I. of Man	44	54.04 N	4.40 W
Castletown, Scot., U.K.	46	58.35 N	3.23 W
Castletown Bearhaven (Castletown Bere)	48	51.39 N	9.55 W
Castletown Bere → Castletown Bearhaven	48	51.39 N	9.55 W
Castletown Geoghegan	48	53.26 N	7.38 W
Castletownroche	48	52.10 N	8.28 W
Castletownshend	48	51.32 N	9.11 W
Castlewellan	48	54.16 N	5.57 W
Castlewood, Ky., U.S.	218	38.04 N	84.27 W
Castlewood, S.D., U.S.	198	44.43 N	97.01 W
Castlewood, Va., U.S.	192	36.53 N	82.16 W
Častoje	82	54.11 N	37.47 E
Častooz'ornoje	86	55.34 N	67.53 E
Castor	182	52.13 N	111.53 W
Castor ≃, On., Can.	212	45.18 N	75.10 W
Castor ≃, Mo., U.S.	194	36.51 N	89.44 W
Castorano	66	42.54 N	13.43 E
Castor Creek ≃	194	31.47 N	92.20 W
Castorland	212	43.53 N	75.30 W
Castra Vetera ⊥	263	51.39 N	6.28 E
Castres	32	43.36 N	2.15 E
Castricum	52	52.33 N	4.39 E
Castries, Fr.	62	43.40 N	3.59 E
Castries, St. Luc.	241f	14.01 N	61.00 W
Castries, Port ⊂	241f	14.01 N	61.00 W
Castro, Bra.	252	24.47 S	50.00 W
Castro, Chile	254	42.29 S	73.46 W
Castro, It.	64	45.48 N	10.04 E
Castro, Arroyo de ≃	258	33.37 S	56.10 W
Castro, Punta ⊁	254	43.22 S	65.03 W
Castro Barros	252	30.35 S	65.44 W
Castrocaro Terme	66	44.10 N	11.57 E
Castrocielo	66	41.32 N	13.42 E
Castro Daire	34	40.54 N	7.56 W
Castro dei Volsci	66	41.30 N	13.24 E
Castro del Río	34	37.41 N	4.28 W
Castrofilippo	70	37.21 N	13.46 E
Castrojeriz	34	42.17 N	4.08 W
Castro Marim	34	37.13 N	7.26 W
Castronuño	34	41.23 N	5.16 W
Castronuovo di Sant'Andrea	68	40.11 N	16.11 E
Castronuovo di Sicilia	70	37.41 N	13.36 E
Castropignano	66	41.37 N	14.33 E
Castropol	34	43.32 N	7.02 W
Castrop-Rauxel	52	51.34 N	7.18 E
Castroreale	70	38.06 N	15.12 E
Castro-Urdiales	34	43.23 N	3.13 W
Castro Valley	226	37.41 N	122.05 W
Castro Verde	34	37.42 N	8.05 W
Castrovillari	68	39.49 N	16.13 E
Castroville, Ca., U.S.	226	36.45 N	121.45 W
Castroville, Tx., U.S.	196	29.21 N	98.52 W
Castrovirreyna	248	13.16 S	75.19 W
Castuera	34	38.43 N	5.33 W
Cast uul ⋏	86	48.40 N	90.45 E
Častyje	80	57.19 N	54.59 E
Casummit Lake	184	51.28 N	92.24 W
Casupá	252	34.07 S	55.38 W
Caswell Sound ʮ	172	45.00 S	167.10 E
Çat	130	39.40 N	41.00 E
Cat ≃	184	51.07 N	91.25 W
Catabola	152	12.09 S	17.16 E
Cataby	162	30.43 S	115.31 E
Catacamas	236	14.54 N	85.56 W
Catacaos	248	5.16 S	80.41 W
Catacocha	246	4.04 S	79.38 W
Cataguarino	256	21.18 S	42.43 W
Cataguases	256	21.24 S	42.41 W
Catahoula Lake ◎	194	31.30 N	92.06 W
Çatak	128	38.01 N	43.07 E
Çatakköprü	130	38.09 N	41.12 E
Catalaban Island I	116	11.51 N	125.28 E
Çatalan	130	37.14 N	35.16 E
Catalão	255	18.10 S	47.57 W
Catalão, Ponta do ⊁	287a	22.51 S	43.13 W
Çatalca	130	41.09 N	28.27 E
Çatalçam	130	40.00 N	38.51 E
Catalfaro ≃	70	37.22 N	14.43 E
Catalina, Nf., Can.	186	48.31 N	53.05 W
Catalina, Chile	252	25.13 S	69.43 W
Catalina → Santa Catalina Island I	228	33.23 N	118.24 W
Catalina, Punta ⊁	254	52.32 S	68.47 W
Catalonia → Catalunya □[4]	34	42.00 N	2.00 E
Catalunya □[4]	34	41.40 N	1.30 E
Catalzeytin	130	41.57 N	34.13 E
Catamarca □[4]	252	27.00 S	67.00 W
Catamare	286c	10.36 N	67.02 W
Catamayo	246	3.59 S	79.21 W
Catamayo ≃	246	4.18 S	80.09 W
Catanauan	116	13.36 N	122.19 E
Catanduanes □[4]	116	13.47 N	124.16 E
Catanduanes Island I	116	13.45 N	124.15 E
Catanduva	255	21.08 S	48.58 W
Catane → Catania	70	37.30 N	15.06 E
Catania	70	37.30 N	15.06 E
Catania □[4]	70	37.23 N	14.40 E

Symbol	English	Deutsch	Español	Français	Italiano	Português
≃	River	Fluß	Río	Rivière	Fiume	Rio
⊏	Canal	Kanal	Canal	Canal	Canale	Canal
⌊	Waterfall, Rapids	Wasserfall, Stromschnellen	Cascada, Rápidos	Chute d'eau, Rapides	Cascata, Rapide	Cascata, Rápidos
ʮ	Strait	Meeresstraße	Estrecho	Détroit	Stretto	Estreito
⊂	Bay, Gulf	Bucht, Golf	Bahía, Golfo	Baie, Golfe	Baia, Golfo	Baía, Golfo
◎	Lake, Lakes	See, Seen	Lago, Lagos	Lac, Lacs	Lago, Laghi	Lago, Lagos
⊞	Swamp	Sumpf	Pantano	Marais	Palude	Pântano
⊓	Ice Features, Glacier	Eis- und Gletscherformen	Accidentes Glaciales	Formes glaciaires	Forme glaciali	Acidentes glaciares
∓	Other Hydrographic Features	Andere Hydrographische Objekte	Otros Elementos Hidrográficos	Autres données hydrographiques	Altri elementi idrografici	Outros acidentes hidrográficos

Symbol	English	Deutsch	Español	Français	Italiano	Português
✣	Submarine Features	Untermeerische Objekte	Accidentes Submarinos	Formes de relief sous-marin	Forme del fondo marino	Acidentes submarinos
□	Political Unit	Politische Einheit	Unidad Política	Entité politique	Unità politica	Unidade política
⊍	Cultural Institution	Kulturelle Institution	Institución Cultural	Institution culturelle	Istituzione culturale	Instituição cultural
⊥	Historical Site	Historische Stätte	Sitio Histórico	Site historique	Sito storico	Sítio histórico
♦	Recreational Site	Erholungs- und Ferienort	Sitio de Recreo	Centre de loisirs	Area ricreativa	Área de Lazer
⊠	Airport	Flughafen	Aeropuerto	Aéroport	Aeroporto	Aeroporto
■	Military Installation	Militäranlage	Instalación Militar	Installation militaire	Installazione militare	Instalação militar
◆	Miscellaneous	Verschiedenes	Misceláneo	Divers	Varie	Diversos

I · *32* **Cata-Cent**

ENGLISH Name Page Lat.°′ Long.°′ — **DEUTSCH** Name Seite Breite°′ Länge°′ E = Ost

Catania, Golfo di ⊂ 70 37.24 N 15.09 E
Catania, Piana di ≚ 70 37.25 N 14.51 E
Cataño 240m 18.27 N 66.07 W
Catanzaro 68 38.54 N 16.36 E
Catanzaro □4 68 38.54 N 16.36 E
Catanzaro Lido 68 38.49 N 16.36 E
Cataonia □9 130 38.00 N 35.00 E
Catára ≃ 152 13.34 S 12.35 E
Cataract Canyon V 200 36.03 N 112.35 W
Cataract Reservoir ◎1 170 34.16 S 150.48 E
Catarama 246 1.35 S 79.28 W
Cataraqui 212 44.16 N 76.32 W
Cataraqui ≃ 212 44.13 N 76.28 W
Cataricahua 248 18.14 S 66.49 W
Catarina 250 6.12 S 39.54 W
Catarman, Pil. 116 12.30 N 124.38 E
Catarman, Pil. 116 9.08 N 124.40 E
Catarroja 34 39.24 N 0.24 W
Catasauqua 208 40.39 N 75.29 W
Catatumbo ≃ 246 9.22 N 71.45 W
Catawba 218 40.00 N 83.37 W
Catawba ≃ 192 34.36 N 80.54 W
Catawba Island 214 41.35 N 82.50 W
Catawissa, Mo., U.S. 219 38.25 N 90.47 W
Catawissa, Pa., U.S. 210 40.57 N 76.27 W
Catawissa Creek ≃ 210 40.57 N 76.28 W
Cataxa 154 15.58 S 33.12 E
Cat Ba, Dao I 110 20.50 N 107.00 E
Catbalogan 116 11.46 N 124.53 E
Catchabutan, Punta > 236 15.50 N 86.32 W
Catchacoma Lake ◎ 212 44.45 N 78.20 W
Cateco Cangola 152 8.27 S 15.48 E
Cateel 116 7.48 N 126.27 E
Cateel ≃ 116 7.47 N 126.27 E
Cateel Bay ⊂ 116 7.54 N 126.25 E
Catemaco 234 18.25 N 95.07 W
Catemaco, Lago ◎ 234 18.25 N 95.05 W
Catembe 156 26.00 S 32.33 E
Catenanuova 70 37.34 N 14.41 E
Caterham 260 51.17 N 0.04 W
Catete 152 9.06 S 13.43 E
Catete ✦8 287a 22.55 S 43.10 W
Catete ≃ 250 6.04 S 54.09 W
Catfish Creek ≃, On., Can. 212 42.39 N 81.01 W
Catfish Creek ≃, N.Y., U.S. 212 43.31 N 76.19 W
Catfish Creek ≃, Tx., U.S. 222 31.47 N 95.56 W
Catford ✦8 260 51.27 N 0.01 W
Catharine Creek ≃ 210 42.21 N 76.51 W
Cathcart 158 32.18 S 27.09 E
Cathead Mountain ∧ 210 43.17 N 74.17 W
Cathedral City 204 33.46 N 116.27 W
Cathedral Gorge State Park ♦ 204 37.50 N 114.30 W
Cathedral Mountain ∧ 196 30.10 N 103.40 W
Cathedral of the Pines ⌂1 207 42.47 N 71.58 W
Cathedral Provincial Park ♦ 202 49.05 N 120.10 W
Cathedral Range ⋏ 226 37.47 N 119.21 W
Catherines Peak ∧ 241q 18.04 N 76.42 W
Catheys Valley 226 37.25 N 120.06 W
Cathlamet 224 46.12 N 123.22 W
Catholic University ⌂2 284c 38.56 N 77.00 W
Catia ✦8 286c 10.31 N 66.57 W
Catia La Mar 286c 10.36 N 67.02 W
Ca' Tiepolo 66 44.56 N 12.22 E
Catignano 66 42.21 N 13.57 E
Catingueira 250 7.08 S 37.37 W
Catingueiro 256 22.10 S 46.52 W
Catió 150 11.13 N 15.10 W
Catirina, Punta > 71 40.29 N 9.32 E
Cat Island I, Ba. 238 24.27 N 75.30 W
Cat Island I, Ma., U.S. 283 42.31 N 70.49 W
Cat Island I, Ms., U.S. 194 30.13 N 89.06 W
Čatkal ≃ 85 41.38 N 70.01 E
Čatkal'skij chrebet ⋏ 85 41.40 N 71.05 E
Cat Lake ◎ 184 51.40 N 91.50 W
Catlettsburg 188 38.24 N 82.36 W
Catlin 194 40.03 N 87.42 W
Catlins ≃ 172 46.29 S 169.43 E
Catlodge 46 57.00 N 4.15 W
Catnip Mountain ∧ 204 41.52 N 119.23 W
Cato 210 43.10 N 76.34 W
Catoche, Cabo > 232 21.35 N 87.05 W
Catoctin Creek ≃ 208 39.18 N 77.33 W
Catoctin Mountain ∧ 208 39.26 N 77.31 W
Cato Island I 166 23.15 S 155.32 E
Catolé do Rocha 250 6.21 S 37.45 W
Católica, Universidad ⌂2, Chile 286e 33.27 S 70.39 W
Católica, Universidad ⌂2, Perú 286d 12.04 S 77.05 W
Caton 44 54.04 N 2.43 W
Catonsville 208 39.16 N 76.43 W
Catonsville Manor 284b 39.18 N 76.44 W
Catoosa 196 36.11 N 95.44 W
Catorce 234 23.42 N 100.54 W
Catorce, Sierra de ⋏ 234 23.36 N 100.52 W
Catota 152 13.52 S 17.15 E
Catria, Monte ∧ 66 43.28 N 12.42 E
Catriló 252 36.26 S 63.24 W
Catrimani 246 0.27 N 61.41 W
Catrimani ≃ 246 0.28 N 61.44 W
Catrine 46 55.30 N 4.20 W
Cats, Mont des ∧2 50 50.47 N 2.40 E
Catshill 42 52.22 N 2.03 W
Catskill 210 42.13 N 73.51 W
Catskill Aqueduct ≃ 276 41.11 N 73.48 W
Catskill Creek ≃ 210 42.12 N 73.51 W
Catskill Game Farm ♦ 210 42.15 N 74.01 W
Catskill Mountains ⋏ 210 42.10 N 74.30 W
Catskill Park ♦ 210 42.00 N 74.30 W
Cat Spring 222 29.51 N 96.20 W
Catt, Mount ∧ 182 54.21 N 128.47 W
Cattai Creek ≃ 274a 33.40 S 150.56 E
Cattaraugus 210 42.19 N 78.52 W
Cattaraugus □6 214 42.15 N 78.45 W
Cattaraugus Creek ≃ 214 42.35 N 79.10 W
Cattaraugus Creek, South Branch ≃ 214 42.26 N 78.53 W
Cattaraugus Indian Reservation ✦4 210 42.33 N 78.56 W
Cattenom 56 49.25 N 6.15 E
Catterick 44 54.22 N 1.38 W
Catterick Garrison 44 54.22 N 1.43 W
Cattle Canyon V 280 34.14 N 117.46 W
Cattolica 66 43.58 N 12.44 E
Cattolica del Sacro Cuore, Università ⌂2 266b 45.27 N 9.11 E
Cattolica Eraclea 70 37.26 N 13.24 E
Catton 44 54.55 N 2.15 W
Catu 255 12.21 S 38.23 W
Catuala 152 16.29 S 19.03 E
Catuane 156 26.48 S 32.18 E
Catubig 116 12.24 N 125.03 E
Catubig ≃ 116 12.34 N 125.01 E
Catuçaba 256 23.15 S 45.12 W
Catumbela 152 12.25 S 13.34 E
Catumbela ≃ 152 12.27 S 13.29 E
Catur 154 13.45 S 35.30 E
Catus 32 44.34 N 1.20 E
Catwick, Îles II 110 10.00 N 109.00 E
Čatyrk'ol', ozero ◎ 85 40.38 N 75.17 E
Čatyrtaš 85 40.55 N 76.26 E
Cau ≃ 110 21.07 N 106.18 E
Cau, Rach ≃ 269c 10.51 N 106.49 E
Cauaburi ≃ 246 0.17 S 65.56 W
Cauaxi ≃ 250 3.50 S 48.10 W
Cauayan, Pil. 116 9.58 N 122.37 E
Cauayan, Pil. 116 16.56 N 121.46 E
Caubvick, Mount (Mont d'Iberville) ∧ 176 58.53 N 63.43 W
Cauca □5 246 2.30 N 76.50 W
Cauca ≃ 246 8.54 N 74.28 W
Caucaia 250 3.42 S 38.39 W
Caucaia do Alto 256 23.41 S 47.02 W
Caucase, Monts du → Bol'šoj Kavkaz ⋏ 84 42.30 N 45.00 E
Caucasia 246 8.00 N 75.12 W
Caucaso → Bol'šoj Kavkaz ⋏ 84 42.30 N 45.00 E
Caucasus → Bol'šoj Kavkaz ⋏ 84 42.30 N 45.00 E
Caucete 252 31.39 S 68.17 W
Cauchari, Salar de ≚ 252 23.50 S 66.50 W
Cauchon Lake ◎ 184 55.25 N 96.30 W
Caudebec-en-Caux 50 49.32 N 0.44 E
Caudebec-lés-Elbeuf 50 49.17 N 1.02 E
Caudry 50 50.08 N 3.25 E
Caughdenoy 210 43.16 N 76.12 W
Caughnawaga 275a 45.25 N 73.41 W
Caughnawaga Indian Reserve ✦4 206 45.23 N 73.41 W
Cauitan, Mount ∧ 116 17.16 N 121.00 E
Cauit Point >, Pil. 116 12.16 N 122.38 E
Cauit Point >, Pil. 116 9.18 N 126.12 E
Cauldcleuch Head ∧ 44 55.18 N 2.51 W
Caulfield 169 37.53 S 145.03 E
Caulfield Racecourse ♦ 274b 37.53 S 145.02 E
Caulkerbush 44 54.54 N 3.40 W
Caulonia 68 38.23 N 16.25 E
Caumont-sur-Durance 62 43.54 N 4.57 E
Caumsett State Park ♦ 276 40.55 N 73.28 W
Caúngula 152 8.25 S 18.40 E
Čaunskaja guba ⊂ 74 69.20 N 170.00 E
Cauquenes 252 35.58 S 72.21 W
Caura ≃ 246 7.38 N 64.53 W
Caurés ≃ 246 1.21 S 62.20 W
Caurimare ≃ 286c 10.28 N 66.48 W
Causapscal 186 48.22 N 67.14 W
Čausovo 82 54.49 N 36.55 E
Caussade 32 44.10 N 1.32 E
Čausy 76 53.48 N 30.58 E
Caution, Cape > 182 51.10 N 127.47 W
Cauto ≃ 240p 20.33 N 77.14 W
Čauvaj 85 40.08 N 72.13 E
Caux, Pays de ✦1 50 49.40 N 0.40 E
Cava 256 22.41 S 43.26 W
Cava de' Tirreni 68 40.42 N 14.42 E
Cávado ≃ 34 41.32 N 8.48 W
Cavaglià 62 45.24 N 8.05 E
Cavaillon 62 43.50 N 5.02 E
Cavalaire-sur-Mer 62 43.10 N 6.32 E
Cavalcante 255 13.48 S 47.30 W
Cavalese 64 46.17 N 11.27 E
Cavalheiro 255 17.15 S 48.02 W
Cavalier 198 48.47 N 97.37 W
Cavalière 62 43.09 N 6.26 E
Cavalla (Cavally) ≃ 150 4.22 N 7.32 W
Cavalleria, Cap de > 34 40.05 N 4.05 E
Cavallermaggiore 62 44.43 N 7.41 E
Cavalli Islands II 172 35.02 S 173.58 E
Cavallino, Litorale di ≗2 64 45.27 N 12.30 E
Cavallo, Île I 71 41.21 N 9.16 E
Cavallo, Monte ∧ 64 46.08 N 12.30 E
Cavally (Cavalla) ≃ 150 4.22 N 7.32 W
Cavalos, Ribeirão dos ≃ 256 21.29 S 44.13 W
Cava Manara 62 45.08 N 9.07 E
Cavan 48 54.00 N 7.21 W
Cavan □6 48 53.55 N 7.15 W
Cavanaugh, Lake ◎ 224 48.23 N 122.00 W
Čavan'ga 24 66.06 N 37.47 E
Cavarzere 64 45.08 N 12.05 E
Cavaso del Tomba 64 45.51 N 11.52 E
Çavdır 130 37.09 N 29.42 E
Cave, It. 66 41.49 N 12.56 E
Cave, N.Z. 172 44.19 S 170.57 E
Cave City, Ar., U.S. 194 35.56 N 91.32 W
Cave City, Ky., U.S. 194 37.08 N 85.57 W
Cave Creek ≃ 200 33.34 N 112.07 W
Cave del Predil 64 46.26 N 13.34 E
Cavedine 64 45.59 N 10.59 E
Cave In Rock 194 37.29 N 88.10 W
Caveiras ≃ 252 27.35 S 50.56 W
Cavelo 152 17.33 S 19.21 E
Cavendish 166 37.31 S 142.02 E
Cavernago 62 45.38 N 9.46 E
Cavertitz 54 51.23 N 13.08 E
Cave Run Lake ◎1 188 38.03 N 83.30 W
Cave Spring 192 34.14 N 85.20 W
Cavettsville 279b 40.22 N 79.46 W
Cavezzo 64 44.50 N 11.02 E
Cavi 62 44.17 N 9.22 E
Caviana, Ilha I 250 0.10 N 50.10 W
Cavili Island I 116 9.17 N 120.50 E
Cavinzas, Isla I 286d 12.07 S 77.13 W
Cavite 116 14.29 N 120.55 E
Cavite □4 116 14.15 N 120.50 E
Čavka 84 41.44 N 41.45 E
Čavlisaj 85 41.08 N 69.44 E
Cavo, Monte ∧ 267a 41.45 N 12.42 E
Cavoli, Isola dei I 71 39.05 N 9.33 E
Cavonne ≃ 68 40.17 N 16.47 E
Cavour 62 44.47 N 7.22 E
Cavour, Canale ≋ 62 45.11 N 7.54 E
Cavriago 64 44.42 N 10.31 E
Cavriana 64 45.21 N 10.36 E
Cavtat 38 42.35 N 18.13 E
Çavuş 130 37.36 N 31.56 E
Çavuşbaşı ≃ 267b 40.58 N 28.51 E
Çavuşçu Gölü ◎ 130 38.25 N 31.53 E
Cawatose, Lac ◎ 190 47.20 N 77.07 W
Cawayan 116 11.56 N 123.46 E
Cawdor 46 57.31 N 3.56 W
Cawker City 198 39.30 N 98.26 W
Cawnpore → Kānpur 124 26.28 N 80.21 E
Cawood, Eng., U.K. 44 53.50 N 1.07 W
Cawood, Ky., U.S. 192 36.47 N 83.13 W
Cawston, B.C., Can. 182 49.11 N 119.45 W
Cawston, Eng., U.K. 42 52.46 N 1.10 E
Cawthon 222 30.25 N 96.14 W
Caxambu 256 21.59 S 44.56 W
Caxias, Bra. 250 4.50 S 43.21 W
Caxias, Port. 266c 38.42 N 9.16 W
Caxias do Sul 252 29.10 S 51.11 W
Caxinas, Punta > 236 16.01 N 86.02 W
Caxito 152 8.33 S 13.36 E
Caxiuana, Baía de ⊂ 250 1.45 S 51.20 W
Caxopa 152 11.52 S 20.52 E
Çay 130 38.35 N 31.02 E
Çayağzı ✦8 267b 41.13 N 29.12 E
Çayağzı ≃ 267b 41.14 N 29.12 E
Cayambe 246 0.03 N 78.08 W
Cayambe ∧1 246 0.02 N 77.59 W
Cayapoñga 116 5.48 N 125.33 E
Çaybaşı 130 41.02 N 37.06 E
Cayce 192 33.57 N 81.04 W
Çaycuma 130 41.25 N 32.05 E
Caycuse 224 48.53 N 124.22 W
Caycuse ≃ 224 48.48 N 124.41 W
Cay Duong, Vinh ⊂ 110 10.10 N 104.45 E
Cayenne 250 4.56 N 52.20 W
Cayenne □8 250 4.00 N 52.30 W
Cayes → Les Cayes 238 18.12 N 73.45 W
Cayeux-sur-Mer 50 50.11 N 1.29 E
Cayey 240m 18.07 N 66.10 W
Cayey, Sierra de ⋏ 240m 18.07 N 66.02 W
Çayıralan 130 39.18 N 35.40 E
Çayırbaşı 130 40.53 N 42.36 E
Çayırhan 130 40.06 N 31.37 E
Çayırlı 130 39.48 N 40.01 E
Çaylarbası 130 37.41 N 39.00 E
Caylus 32 44.14 N 1.46 E
Cayman Brac I 238 19.43 N 79.49 W
Cayman Islands □2, N.A. 230 19.30 N 80.40 W
Cayman Islands □2, N.A. 238 19.30 N 80.40 W
Cayman Trench ✧1 16 19.00 N 80.00 W
Cayna 248 10.11 S 76.20 W
Caynabo 144 8.57 N 46.26 E
Çayözü 130 39.36 N 38.11 E
Cay Point > 240b 24.59 N 77.25 W
Çayra 130 40.41 N 39.06 E
Cayres 62 44.55 N 3.48 E
Cay Sal Bank ✧2 238 23.45 N 80.00 W
Çaytepe 130 38.48 N 40.41 E
Cayucos 226 35.27 N 120.54 W
Cayuga, In., U.S. 194 39.56 N 87.27 W
Cayuga, N.Y., U.S. 210 42.55 N 76.44 W
Cayuga, N.D., U.S. 198 46.04 N 97.23 W
Cayuga, Tx., U.S. 222 31.57 N 95.57 W
Cayuga □6 210 42.56 N 76.34 W
Cayuga and Seneca Canal ≋ 210 42.56 N 76.44 W
Cayuga Creek ≃, N.Y., U.S. 210 42.52 N 78.47 W
Cayuga Creek ≃, N.Y., U.S. 284a 43.04 N 78.57 W
Cayuga Heights 210 42.27 N 76.29 W
Cayuga Lake ◎ 210 42.45 N 76.45 W
Cayuta 210 42.17 N 76.42 W
Cayuta Creek ≃ 210 41.59 N 76.30 W
Cazage 152 11.02 S 20.45 E
Cazalla de la Sierra 34 37.56 N 5.45 W
Căzănești 38 44.37 N 27.01 E
Cazaux et de Sanguinet, Lac de ⊂ 32 44.30 N 1.10 W
Cazenovia 210 42.55 N 75.51 W
Cazenovia Creek ≃ 210 42.52 N 78.50 W
Cazenovia Creek, East Branch ≃ 210 42.46 N 78.38 W
Cazenovia Creek, West Branch ≃ 210 42.46 N 78.39 W
Cazenovia Lake ◎ 210 42.57 N 75.53 W
Cazenovia Park ♦ 284a 42.51 N 78.48 W
Cazères 32 43.13 N 1.05 E
Cazhai 269b 31.12 N 121.34 E
Cazin 36 44.58 N 15.57 E
Cazis 58 46.43 N 9.25 E
Čazma 36 45.45 N 16.37 E
Cazombo 152 11.54 S 22.52 E
Cazones ≃ 234 20.44 N 97.12 W
Cazones, Golfo de ⊂ 240p 21.55 N 81.20 W
Cazorla, Esp. 34 37.55 N 3.00 W
Cazorla, Ven. 246 8.01 N 67.00 W
Cazula 154 15.25 S 33.40 E
Ccapi 248 13.52 S 72.05 W
Cchaltubo 84 42.20 N 42.35 E
Cchenisckali ≃ 84 42.07 N 42.18 E
Cchinvali 84 42.13 N 43.56 E
Čchorocku 84 42.32 N 42.07 E
Cchunkuri 84 42.23 N 42.34 E
Cea ≃ 34 42.00 N 5.36 W
Ceanannus Mór 48 53.44 N 6.53 W
Ceará → Fortaleza 250 3.43 S 38.30 W
Ceará □3 250 5.00 S 40.00 W
Ceará-Mirim 250 5.38 S 35.26 W
Ceará-Mirim ≃ 250 5.40 S 35.13 W
Ceatharlach → Carlow 48 52.50 N 6.55 W
Cébaco, Isla I 246 7.32 N 81.09 W
Ceballos, Méx. 232 26.32 N 104.09 W
Ceballos, Méx. 234 23.23 N 104.50 W
Čebarkul' 86 54.58 N 60.25 E
Çebeci ✦8 267b 41.07 N 28.52 E
Čeboksary 80 56.09 N 47.15 E
Cebolla Creek ≃ 200 38.29 N 107.13 W
Cebollar 252 29.06 S 66.33 W
Cebollatí 252 33.16 S 53.47 W
Cebollatí ≃ 252 33.09 S 53.38 W
Cebollita Peak ∧ 200 34.43 N 107.51 W
Céboruco, Volcán ∧1 234 21.09 N 104.30 W
Čebosarskoje vodochranilišče ◎1 24 56.10 N 46.00 E
Čebotovka, S.S.S.R. 83 48.42 N 39.51 E
Čebotovka, S.S.S.R. 83 48.41 N 40.00 E
Cebreros 34 40.27 N 4.28 W
Čebrikovo 78 47.09 N 30.06 E
Čebsara 76 59.12 N 38.50 E
Cebu 116 10.18 N 123.54 E
Cebu □4 116 10.20 N 123.45 E
Cebu I 116 10.20 N 123.45 E
Čeburgol' 78 45.34 N 38.07 E
Cebu Strait ⊔ 116 9.45 N 123.40 E
Ceccano 66 41.34 N 13.20 E
Cecchignola ✦8 267a 41.49 N 12.29 E
Ceceda 196 26.04 N 103.25 W
Čečel'nik 78 48.14 N 29.21 E
Čečen', ostrov I 84 43.58 N 47.45 E
Čečeno-Ingušskaja Avtonomnaja Sovetskaja Socialističeskaja Respublika □3 84 43.15 N 45.40 E
Cecer Chaan → Öndörchaan 88 47.19 N 110.39 E
Cecerleg, Mong. 88 47.30 N 101.27 E
Cecerleg, Mong. 88 49.30 N 97.36 E
Cecerleg, Mong. 88 48.52 N 101.14 E
Čečersk 76 52.55 N 30.55 E
Čečeviči 76 53.31 N 29.51 E
Cecheng 105 39.06 N 116.48 E
Čechov, S.S.S.R. 82 55.09 N 37.27 E
Čechov, S.S.S.R. 89 47.28 N 141.59 E
Čechova, gora ∧ 89 47.03 N 142.50 E
Čechtice 30 49.37 N 15.03 E
Čechy □9 30 49.50 N 14.00 E
Cecil, Ga., U.S. 192 31.02 N 83.23 W
Cecil, Oh., U.S. 216 41.13 N 84.35 W
Cecil, Pa., U.S. 214 40.19 N 80.10 W
Cecil □6 208 39.36 N 75.50 W
Cecil Field Naval Air Station ■ 192 30.12 N 81.52 W
Cecilia 194 37.39 N 85.57 W
Cecilia, Mount ∧2 162 20.45 S 120.55 E
Cecil Park 274a 33.52 S 150.51 E
Cecil Plains 166 27.32 S 151.12 E
Cecil Rhodes, Mount ∧ 162 25.26 S 121.26 E
Cecilton 208 39.24 N 75.52 W
Cecina 66 43.19 N 10.31 E
Cecina ≃ 66 43.18 N 10.29 E
Cecita, Lago di ◎ 68 39.24 N 16.30 E
Čečuj ≃ 88 58.12 N 109.18 E
Čečujsk 88 58.05 N 108.42 E
Cedar ≃, U.S. 190 41.17 N 91.21 W
Cedar ≃, Mi., U.S. 190 43.53 N 84.29 W
Cedar ≃, Mi., U.S. 190 45.25 N 87.21 W
Cedar ≃, Ne., U.S. 198 41.22 N 97.57 W
Cedar ≃, N.Y., U.S. 188 43.51 N 74.11 W
Cedar ≃, Wa., U.S. 224 47.30 N 122.12 W
Cedar, Middle Branch ≃ 216 42.38 N 84.05 W
Cedar, West Branch ≃ 216 42.41 N 84.09 W
Cedar, West Fork ≃ 190 42.37 N 92.29 W
Cedar Bayou ≃ 222 29.41 N 94.56 W
Cedar Beach 284b 39.17 N 76.25 W
Cedar Bluff Reservoir ◎1 198 38.47 N 99.47 W
Cedar Bluffs 198 41.23 N 96.36 W
Cedar Breaks National Monument ♦ 200 37.29 N 112.53 W
Cedar Brook 208 39.42 N 74.54 W
Cedar Brook ≃, N.J., U.S. 276 40.19 N 74.33 W
Cedar Brook ≃, N.J., U.S. 276 40.23 N 74.23 W
Cedar Brook ≃, N.J., U.S. 285 39.40 N 74.43 W
Cedar Brook Park ♦ 275b 43.45 N 79.14 W
Cedarburg 190 43.17 N 87.59 W
Cedar City, Mo., U.S. 219 38.35 N 92.10 W
Cedar City, Ut,. U.S. 200 37.40 N 113.03 W
Cedar Creek 222 30.05 N 97.30 W
Cedar Creek ≃, Al., U.S. 194 32.13 N 87.06 W
Cedar Creek ≃, Az., U.S. 200 33.48 N 110.18 W
Cedar Creek ≃, Ct., U.S. 276 41.09 N 73.13 W
Cedar Creek ≃, De., U.S. 208 38.55 N 75.20 W
Cedar Creek ≃, Ga., U.S. 194 34.08 N 85.19 W
Cedar Creek ≃, Id., U.S. 202 42.24 N 114.49 W
Cedar Creek ≃, In., U.S. 216 41.12 N 85.02 W
Cedar Creek ≃, Ia., U.S. 190 40.58 N 91.40 W
Cedar Creek ≃, Ia., U.S. 198 42.24 N 94.59 W
Cedar Creek ≃, Ky., U.S. 218 38.25 N 84.53 W
Cedar Creek ≃, Mo., U.S. 219 38.38 N 92.13 W
Cedar Creek ≃, N.D., U.S. 198 46.07 N 101.18 W
Cedar Creek ≃, Oh., U.S. 214 41.38 N 83.17 W
Cedar Creek ≃, Pa., U.S. 279b 40.10 N 79.47 W
Cedar Creek ≃, Tx., U.S. 196 32.53 N 98.37 W
Cedar Creek ≃, Tx., U.S. 222 30.51 N 96.12 W
Cedar Creek ≃, Tx., U.S. 222 32.04 N 96.05 W
Cedar Creek ≃, Tx., U.S. 222 30.02 N 97.17 W
Cedar Creek ≃, Wa., U.S. 224 45.56 N 122.37 W
Cedar Creek Reservoir ◎1 222 32.20 N 96.10 W
Cedar Crest Manor 285 39.41 N 75.28 W
Cedaredge 200 38.54 N 107.55 W
Cedar Falls 190 42.31 N 92.26 W
Cedar Grove, On., Can. 275b 43.52 N 79.12 W
Cedar Grove, In., U.S. 218 39.21 N 84.56 W
Cedar Grove, N.J., U.S. 276 40.51 N 74.13 W
Cedar Grove, W.V., U.S. 188 38.13 N 81.25 W
Cedar Grove, Wi., U.S. 190 43.34 N 87.49 W
Cedar Grove Reservoir ◎1 276 40.52 N 74.13 W
Cedar Heights, Md., U.S. 284c 38.54 N 76.54 W
Cedar Heights, Pa., U.S. 285 40.05 N 75.17 W
Cedar Hill, Mo., U.S. 219 38.21 N 90.39 W
Cedar Hill, N.Y., U.S. 210 42.33 N 73.47 W
Cedar Hill, Tn., U.S. 194 36.33 N 86.59 W
Cedar Hill, Tx., U.S. 222 32.35 N 96.57 W
Cedar Hills 224 45.30 N 122.47 W
Cedar Hollow 285 40.04 N 75.31 W
Cedarhurst, Md., U.S. 208 39.07 N 76.41 W
Cedarhurst, N.Y., U.S. 276 40.37 N 73.43 W
Cedar Island I, Md., U.S. 208 37.56 N 75.52 W
Cedar Island I, N.Y., U.S. 276 40.38 N 73.21 W
Cedar Island I, Va., U.S. 208 37.39 N 75.36 W
Cedar Island Lake ◎ 281 42.38 N 83.28 W
Cedar Key 192 29.08 N 83.02 W
Cedar Knolls 276 40.49 N 74.26 W
Cedar Lake, In., U.S. 216 41.21 N 87.26 W
Cedar Lake, Tx., U.S. 222 28.54 N 95.35 W
Cedar Lake ◎, On., Can. 190 46.02 N 78.30 W
Cedar Lake ◎, In., U.S. 216 41.22 N 87.26 W
Cedar Lake ◎, N.J., U.S. 276 40.55 N 74.28 W
Cedar Lake ◎, Tx., U.S. 196 32.49 N 102.17 W
Cedar Lake ◎1 184 53.15 N 100.10 W
Cedar Lake Creek ≃ 222 28.50 N 95.35 W
Cedar Lane 222 28.54 N 95.38 W
Cedar Mill 224 45.32 N 122.51 W
Cedarmont 158 26.50 S 29.01 E
Cedar Mountain ∧ 204 41.36 N 120.16 W
Cedar Point 216 41.16 N 89.08 W
Cedar Point >, Ct., U.S. 276 41.06 N 73.22 W
Cedar Point >, Oh., U.S. 214 41.42 N 83.20 W
Cedar Point >, Oh., U.S. 214 41.30 N 82.41 W
Cedar Pond ◎ 276 41.07 N 74.06 W
Cedar Rapids, Ia., U.S. 190 41.59 N 91.40 W
Cedar Rapids, Ne., U.S. 198 41.34 N 98.09 W
Cedar Ridge 226 39.12 N 121.01 W
Cedar Run ≃ 208 38.41 N 77.29 W
Cedars 285 40.13 N 75.22 W
Cedars of Lebanon → Arz Lubnān ✦3 130 34.14 N 36.03 E
Cedar Springs, On., Can. 214 42.17 N 82.02 W
Cedar Springs, Mi., U.S. 190 43.13 N 85.33 W
Cedar Swamp ≡, Ma., U.S. 283 42.33 N 71.05 W
Cedar Swamp ≡, N.J., U.S. 285 39.48 N 75.20 W
Cedartown 192 34.03 N 85.15 W
Cedarvale, B.C., Can. 182 55.01 N 128.20 W
Cedar Vale, Ks., U.S. 198 37.06 N 96.30 W
Cedarville, S. Afr. 158 30.23 S 29.03 E
Cedarville, Ca., U.S. 204 41.31 N 120.10 W
Cedarville, In., U.S. 216 41.12 N 85.01 W
Cedarville, Ma., U.S. 207 41.48 N 70.33 W
Cedarville, Mi., U.S. 190 46.00 N 84.22 W
Cedarville, N.J., U.S. 208 39.19 N 75.12 W
Cedarville, N.Y., U.S. 210 42.56 N 75.07 W
Cedarville, Oh., U.S. 218 39.44 N 83.48 W
Cedarville, Pa., U.S. 285 40.14 N 75.40 W
Cedarville Reservoir ◎1 216 41.12 N 85.01 W
Cedar Wash V 200 35.53 N 111.25 W
Cedarwood Park 208 40.03 N 74.08 W
Cedegolo 64 46.05 N 10.21 E
Cedeira 34 43.39 N 8.03 W
Čeder 88 51.25 N 94.45 E
Cedillo, Embalse de ◎1 34 39.40 N 7.25 W
Cedral 234 23.48 N 100.44 W
Cedrino ≃ 71 40.23 N 9.44 E
Cedro 250 6.36 S 39.03 W
Cedros, Hond. 236 14.35 N 87.08 W
Cedros, Méx. 232 24.41 N 101.47 W
Cedros, Isla I 232 28.12 N 115.15 W
Ceduna 162 32.07 S 133.40 E
Cedynia 30 52.50 N 14.14 E
Ceel 102 45.36 N 95.51 E
Ceelaayo 144 11.15 N 48.54 E
Ceel Afweyne 144 9.55 N 47.15 E
Ceel Berdaale 144 3.14 N 43.11 E
Ceel Berde 144 4.50 N 43.39 E
Ceel Buur 144 4.40 N 46.37 E
Ceel Dhaab 144 8.56 N 46.30 E
Ceel Dheere, Som. 144 3.51 N 47.12 E
Ceeldheere, Som. 144 5.22 N 46.11 E
Ceel Doofaar 144 10.38 N 49.02 E
Ceel Waaq 144 2.44 N 41.01 E
Ceel Xamurre 144 7.13 N 48.54 E
Ceemadle 144 5.14 N 46.56 E
Ceepeecee 182 49.52 N 126.43 W
Ceerigaabo 144 10.37 N 47.22 E
Cefalà Diana 70 37.54 N 13.28 E
Cefalonia → Kefallinía I 38 38.15 N 20.35 E
Cefalú 70 38.02 N 14.01 E
Cefni ≃ 44 53.12 N 4.23 W
Cefn-mawr 42 52.58 N 3.04 W
Ceg 144 8.58 N 45.20 E
Cega ≃ 34 41.33 N 4.46 W
Čeganly 80 53.54 N 53.34 E
Čegdomyn 89 51.07 N 133.05 E
Čegem ≃ 84 43.38 N 43.48 E
Čegem Pervyj 84 43.34 N 43.35 E
Čegitun' 180 66.34 N 171.06 W
Cegléd 30 47.10 N 19.48 E
Ceglie Messapico 68 40.39 N 17.31 E
Cehegín 34 38.06 N 1.48 W
Ceheng 102 25.10 N 105.48 E
Cehnice 60 49.12 N 14.02 E
Cehu-Silvaniei 38 47.25 N 23.11 E
Ceiba 240m 18.16 N 65.39 W
Ceiba ≃ 240p 21.38 N 78.52 W
Ceibo, Arroyo ≃ 258 33.57 S 58.27 W
Ceilán → Sri Lanka □1 122 7.00 N 81.00 E
Čeil'dag 84 40.17 N 49.18 E
Ceiriog ≃ 42 52.57 N 3.02 W
Ceirw ≃ 42 52.59 N 3.27 W
Čejč 61 48.57 N 16.57 E
Čekalin 82 54.06 N 36.15 E
Čekan 80 54.51 N 53.34 E
Čekanovskij 88 56.13 N 101.25 E
Çekerek 130 40.04 N 35.31 E
Çekerek ≃ 130 40.34 N 35.46 E
Čekmaguš 86 55.08 N 54.40 E
Çekme ✦8 267b 41.03 N 29.10 E
Čekšino 76 59.39 N 40.33 E
Čekujevo 24 63.34 N 38.56 E
Čekunda 89 50.48 N 132.10 E
Čel'abinsk 86 55.10 N 61.24 E
Čelákovice 54 50.10 N 14.46 E
Celâlli 130 39.42 N 37.26 E
Celano 66 42.05 N 13.33 E
Celanova 34 42.09 N 7.58 W
Celaya 234 20.31 N 100.49 W
Čelbas ≃ 78 46.06 N 38.59 E
Čelbasskaja 78 45.59 N 39.22 E
Celbridge 48 53.20 N 6.33 W
Celebes → Sulawesi I 112 2.00 S 121.00 E
Celebes Basin ✧1 14 4.00 N 122.00 E
Celebes Sea ⊤2 112 3.00 N 122.00 E
Čeleken 128 39.26 N 53.07 E
Celendín 248 6.52 S 78.09 W
Celenza sul Trigno 66 41.52 N 14.35 E
Celenza Valfortore 68 41.34 N 14.58 E
Celerina 58 46.31 N 9.51 E
Celeryville 214 41.02 N 82.45 W
Celeste 196 33.18 N 96.12 W
Celestún 232 20.52 N 90.24 W
Celica 246 4.07 S 79.59 W
Celico 68 39.19 N 16.20 E
Çelikhan 130 38.02 N 38.15 E
Čelina, S.S.S.R. 80 46.32 N 41.02 E
Celina, Oh., U.S. 216 40.32 N 84.34 W
Celina, Tn., U.S. 194 36.33 N 85.30 W
Celina, Tx., U.S. 196 33.19 N 96.47 W
Celinnoje, S.S.S.R. 86 53.04 N 85.40 E
Celinnoje, S.S.S.R. 86 54.31 N 63.39 E
Celinnyj 80 46.40 N 44.32 E
Celinograd 86 51.10 N 71.30 E
Celinogradskaja □4 86 51.00 N 71.00 E
Celje 36 46.14 N 15.16 E
Čelkar 86 47.50 N 59.36 E
Cellar Head > 46 58.26 N 6.10 W
Celldömölk 30 47.16 N 17.09 E
Celle 52 52.37 N 10.05 E
Celle, Ruisseau la ≃ 261 48.35 N 2.01 E
Celle Ligure 62 44.20 N 8.33 E
Celles 56 50.14 N 5.01 E
Celles-sur-Plaine 58 48.28 N 6.57 E
Cellettes 50 47.32 N 1.23 E
Cellina ≃ 64 46.02 N 12.47 E
Cellino Attanasio 66 42.36 N 13.52 E
Cellino San Marco 68 40.28 N 17.58 E
Čelmozero 24 64.18 N 31.48 E
Čelno-Veršiny 80 54.26 N 51.06 E
Čelobitjevo 265b 55.55 N 37.40 E
Celone ≃ 68 41.36 N 15.41 E
Celorico da Beira 34 40.38 N 7.23 W
Celoron 214 42.06 N 79.17 W
Celtic Sea ⊤2 28 51.00 N 6.30 W
Celtic Shelf ✧4 10 49.15 N 7.00 W
Çeltikçi, Tür. 130 40.20 N 32.28 E
Çeltikçi, Tür. 130 37.32 N 30.29 E
Čel'uš 86 51.32 N 87.46 E
Čel'uskin, mys > 74 77.45 N 104.20 E
Čel'uskincev park ♦ 265a 60.01 N 30.19 E
Cemaes Head > 42 52.07 N 4.44 W
Čemal 86 51.25 N 86.01 E
Čembilej 80 55.19 N 45.43 E
Cembra 64 46.10 N 11.13 E
Cembra, Val di V 64 46.10 N 11.13 E
Cement 196 34.55 N 98.08 W
Cement City 216 42.04 N 84.19 W
Cementon, N.Y., U.S. 210 42.09 N 73.55 W
Cementon, Pa., U.S. 208 40.41 N 75.30 W
Čemer 78 51.07 N 31.13 E
Čemerisy 78 51.42 N 30.24 E
Čemerno 36 43.11 N 18.37 E
Čemerno ✕ 38 43.14 N 18.37 E
Čemerovcy 78 49.01 N 26.21 E
Cemesskaja buchta ⊂ 78 44.40 N 37.50 E
Cemilbey 130 40.21 N 35.04 E
Çemişkezek 130 39.04 N 38.55 E
Cemmaes 42 52.37 N 3.42 W
Čemolgan 85 43.23 N 76.37 E
Cempi, Teluk ⊂ 115b 8.44 S 118.25 E
Čenča 88 55.57 N 110.59 E
Cencenighe 64 46.21 N 11.58 E
Čenchermandal 88 47.37 N 109.05 E
Čency 82 56.03 N 36.01 E
Cenderawasih, Teluk ⊂ 164 2.30 S 135.20 E
Cendras 62 44.09 N 4.04 E
Cene 62 45.47 N 9.49 E
Cenepa ≃ 246 4.35 S 78.12 W
Ceneri, Monte ✕ 58 46.08 N 8.55 E
Čengel 86 48.56 N 89.10 E
Čengel'dy, S.S.S.R. 85 43.59 N 77.26 E
Čengel'dy, S.S.S.R. 85 41.51 N 68.59 E
Çengelköy ✦8 267b 41.03 N 29.03 E
Çengerli 130 39.48 N 38.52 E
Cengles, Croda di ∧ 64 46.34 N 10.38 E
Ceno ≃ 36 44.41 N 10.05 E
Cenovo 38 43.32 N 25.39 E
Cenrana 112 3.18 S 118.50 E
Censeau 58 46.49 N 6.04 E
Centallo 62 44.30 N 7.35 E
Centenario 252 38.48 S 68.08 W
Centenário do Sul 255 22.48 S 51.37 W
Centennial Lake ◎ 285 39.50 N 74.51 W
Centennial Lake ◎1 212 45.10 N 72.05 W
Centennial Mountains ⋏ 202 44.35 N 111.55 W
Centennial Park ♦, Austl. 274a 33.54 S 151.14 E
Centennial Park ♦, On., Can. 275b 43.39 N 79.35 W
Centennial Wash V 200 33.14 N 112.46 W
Centeno 66 42.48 N 11.49 E
Center, Co., U.S. 200 37.45 N 106.06 W
Center, In., U.S. 216 40.26 N 86.04 W
Center, Mo., U.S. 219 39.30 N 91.31 W
Center, Ne., U.S. 198 42.36 N 97.52 W
Center, N.D., U.S. 198 47.06 N 101.17 W
Center, Tx., U.S. 194 31.47 N 94.10 W
Centerbrook 207 41.21 N 72.24 W
Center Brunswick 210 42.45 N 73.37 W
Centerburg 214 40.18 N 82.41 W
Center City 190 45.23 N 92.48 W
Center Cross 208 37.48 N 76.46 W
Centereach 210 40.51 N 73.06 W
Centerfield 218 38.21 N 83.24 W
Center Hill 220 28.38 N 81.59 W
Center Hill Lake ◎1 194 36.00 N 85.45 W
Center Line 214 42.29 N 83.01 W
Center Moriches 188 40.48 N 72.47 W
Center Mountain ∧ 202 45.06 N 115.13 W
Center Point, Al., U.S. 194 33.37 N 86.41 W
Center Point, Ia., U.S. 190 42.11 N 91.47 W
Center Point, Tx., U.S. 196 29.57 N 99.02 W
Centerport, N.Y., U.S. 210 40.54 N 73.22 W
Centerport, Pa., U.S. 208 40.29 N 76.01 W
Center Square, N.J., U.S. 285 39.46 N 75.23 W
Center Square, Pa., U.S. 208 40.10 N 75.18 W
Centerton, In., U.S. 218 39.30 N 86.23 W
Centerton, N.J., U.S. 285 39.31 N 75.10 W
Center Valley 208 40.32 N 75.24 W
Centerville, De., U.S. 285 39.49 N 75.37 W
Centerville, In., U.S. 218 39.49 N 84.59 W
Centerville, Ia., U.S. 190 40.43 N 92.52 W
Centerville, Ma., U.S. 207 41.38 N 70.20 W
Centerville, Mo., U.S. 194 37.26 N 90.57 W
Centerville, N.Y., U.S. 210 42.29 N 78.15 W
Centerville, Oh., U.S. 218 39.37 N 84.09 W
Centerville, Pa., U.S. 188 40.02 N 79.58 W
Centerville, S.D., U.S. 198 43.07 N 96.57 W
Centerville, Tn., U.S. 194 35.46 N 87.28 W
Centerville, Tx., U.S. 222 31.15 N 95.58 W
Centerville, Ut,. U.S. 200 40.55 N 111.52 W
Centerville, Wa., U.S. 224 45.45 N 120.54 W
Centinela 196 28.47 N 100.34 W
Cento 64 44.43 N 11.17 E
Centocelle ✦8 267a 41.53 N 12.34 E
Cento Croci, Passo di ✕ 62 44.25 N 9.37 E
Centola 68 40.04 N 15.19 E
Central, Bra. 250 11.08 S 42.08 W
Central, Ak., U.S. 180 65.34 N 144.48 W
Central, Az., U.S. 200 32.52 N 109.47 W
Central, N.M., U.S. 200 32.46 N 108.08 W
Central, S.C., U.S. 192 34.43 N 82.46 W
Central, Tx., U.S. 222 31.26 N 94.49 W
Central □4, Ghana 150 5.30 N 1.00 W
Central □4, Kenya 154 0.45 S 37.00 E
Central □4, Malawi 154 13.00 S 34.00 E
Central □4, Sol.Is. 175e 9.10 S 159.50 E
Central □4, Scot., U.K. 46 56.05 N 4.20 W
Central □4, Zam. 154 14.30 S 29.00 E
Central □5, Bots. 156 21.30 S 26.00 E
Central □5, Pap. N. Gui. 164 9.00 S 147.00 E
Central □5, Para. 252 25.30 S 57.30 W
Central □5, Ug. 154 0.10 N 32.00 E
Central, Cordillera ⋏, Col. 246 5.00 N 75.00 W
Central, Cordillera ⋏, C.R. 236 10.10 N 84.05 W
Central, Cordillera ⋏, Perú 248 8.00 S 77.00 W
Central, Cordillera ⋏, Pil. 116 17.20 N 120.57 E
Central, Cordillera ⋏, P.R. 240m 18.10 N 66.35 W
Central, Macizo → Central, Massif ⋏ 32 45.00 N 3.10 E
Central, Massif ⋏ 32 45.00 N 3.10 E
Central, Planalto ⋏1 242 18.00 S 47.00 W
Central, Sistema ⋏ 34 40.30 N 5.00 W
Central African Republic □1 136 7.00 N 21.00 E
Central Aguirre 240m 17.57 N 66.13 W
Central Barren 218 38.22 N 86.06 W
Central Brāhui Range ⋏ 120 29.20 N 66.55 E
Central Bridge 210 42.42 N 74.20 W
Central Butte 184 50.47 N 106.30 W
Central City, Il., U.S. 219 38.32 N 89.07 W
Central City, Ia., U.S. 190 42.12 N 91.31 W
Central City, Ky., U.S. 194 37.17 N 87.07 W
Central City, Ne., U.S. 198 41.06 N 98.00 W
Central City, Pa., U.S. 214 40.06 N 78.48 W
Central Division □5 175g 18.05 S 178.30 E
Central Falls 207 41.53 N 71.23 W
Central Heights 200 33.24 N 110.48 W
Central Highlands 279b 40.16 N 79.50 W
Centralia, Il., U.S. 219 38.31 N 89.08 W
Centralia, Ks., U.S. 198 39.43 N 96.07 W
Centralia, Mo., U.S. 219 39.12 N 92.08 W
Centralia, Tx., U.S. 222 31.16 N 95.02 W
Centralia, Wa., U.S. 224 46.42 N 122.57 W
Centralia, Lake ◎ 219 38.32 N 88.59 W
Centralia Draw V 196 31.27 N 101.16 W
Centralia Reservoir ◎1 219 38.32 N 89.08 W
Centralina 255 18.34 S 49.13 W
Central Intelligence Agency ⌂ 284c 38.57 N 77.09 W
Central Internacional, Aeropuerto ⊠ 286a 19.26 N 99.04 W
Central Island I 154 3.30 N 36.03 E
Central Islip 210 40.47 N 73.12 W
Central Kalahari Game Reserve ✦4 156 22.15 S 23.45 E
Central Lake 190 45.04 N 85.15 W
Central Makrān Range ⋏ 128 26.40 N 64.30 E
Central'no-Bokovskoj ✦8 83 48.11 N 39.03 E
Central'nolesnoj Zapovednik ✦4 76 56.32 N 32.50 E
Central Nyack 276 41.06 N 73.57 W
Central'nyj, S.S.S.R. 76 53.41 N 39.38 E
Central'nyj, S.S.S.R. 86 55.12 N 87.40 E
Central'nyj, S.S.S.R. 86 58.45 N 84.28 E
Central'nyj, S.S.S.R. 86 57.41 N 80.57 E
Central'nyj, S.S.S.R. 265b 55.53 N 37.52 E
Central'nyje Karakumy ✦2 128 39.00 N 60.00 E
Centralnyj park imeni Gor'kogo ♦ 265b 55.44 N 37.36 E
Central Pacific Basin ✧1 14 5.00 N 175.00 W
Central Park, N.J., U.S. 276 40.26 N 74.18 W
Central Park, Wa., U.S. 224 46.58 N 123.41 W
Central Park ♦ 276 40.47 N 73.58 W
Central Point 202 42.22 N 122.54 W
Central Railroad Station ✦5 272c 18.58 N 72.50 E
Central Range ⋏, Leso. 158 29.35 S 28.35 E
Central Range ⋏, Pap. N. Gui. 164 5.00 S 142.30 E
Central Square 210 43.17 N 76.08 W
Central Utah Canal ≋ 200 39.35 N 112.12 W
Central Valley, Ca., U.S. 204 40.40 N 122.22 W
Central Valley, N.Y., U.S. 210 41.19 N 74.07 W
Central Village 207 41.43 N 71.54 W
Centre 194 34.09 N 85.40 W
Centre □6 210 40.55 N 77.47 W
Centre, Canal du ≋ 32 46.27 N 4.07 E
Centre Atomique de Marcoule ⌂3 62 44.08 N 4.42 E
Centre City 285 39.46 N 75.10 W
Centre d'Énergie de Pierrelatte ⌂3 62 44.21 N 4.44 E
Centre Hall 214 40.50 N 77.41 W
Centre Island 276 40.54 N 73.32 W
Centre Island I 172 46.28 S 167.51 E
Centre Island Park ♦ 275b 43.37 N 79.23 W
Centre Lake ◎ 212 44.36 N 75.51 W
Centre Peak ∧ 182 55.41 N 126.26 W

Symbols in the index entries represent the broad categories identified in the key at the right. Symbols with superior numbers (⋏1) identify subcategories (see complete key on page *I · 1)*.

Symbole im Register stellen die rechts im Schlüssel erklärten Kategorien dar. Symbole mit hochgestellten Ziffern (⋏1) bezeichnen Unterabteilungen einer Kategorie (vgl. vollständiger Schlüssel auf Seite *I · 1)*.

Los símbolos incluídos en el texto del índice representan las grandes categorias identificadas con la clave a la derecha. Los símbolos con numeros en su parte superior (⋏1) identifican las subcategorías (véase la clave completa en la página *I · 1)*.

Les symboles de l'index représentent les catégories indiquées dans la légende à droite. Les symboles suivis d'un indice (⋏1) représentent des sous-catégories (voir légende complète à la page *I · 1)*.

Os símbolos incluídos no texto do índice representam as grandes categorias identificadas com a chave à direita. Os símbolos com números em sua parte superior (⋏1) identificam as subcategorias (veja-se a chave completa à página *I · 1)*.

∧ Mountain	Berg	Montaña	Montagne	Montanha
⋏ Mountains	Gebirge	Montañas	Montagnes	Montanhas
✕ Pass	Paß	Paso	Col	Passo
V Valley, Canyon	Tal, Cañon	Valle, Cañón	Vallée, Canyon	Vale, Canhão
≚ Plain	Ebene	Llano	Plaine	Planície
> Cape	Kap	Cabo	Cap	Cabo
I Island	Insel	Isla	Île	Ilha
II Islands	Inseln	Islas	Îles	Ilhas
≗ Other Topographic Features	Andere Topographische Objekte	Otros Elementos Topográficos	Autres données topographiques	Outros acidentes topográficos

ESPAÑOL / **FRANÇAIS** / **PORTUGUÊS**

Nombre / Nom / Nome	Página / Page	Lat.°′	Long.°′ W = Oeste / W = Ouest
Centre-Sud □[4]	152	4.10 N	12.00 E
Centreville, Al., U.S.	194	32.56 N	87.08 W
Centreville, Il., U.S.	219	38.35 N	90.07 W
Centreville, Ky., U.S.	218	38.13 N	84.24 W
Centreville, Md., U.S.	208	39.02 N	76.04 W
Centreville, Mi., U.S.	216	41.55 N	85.31 W
Centreville, Ms., U.S.	194	31.05 N	91.04 W
Centreville, Va., U.S.	208	38.50 N	77.25 W
Centro Puntas	240m	18.22 N	67.16 W
Centro Río Mayo	254	45.35 S	71.06 W
Centro Simón Bolívar ◆[9]	286c	10.30 N	66.55 W
Centuripe	70	37.37 N	14.44 E
Century, Fl., U.S.	194	30.58 N	87.15 W
Century, W.V., U.S.	188	39.05 N	80.11 W
Century City ◆[8]	280	34.03 N	118.26 W
Century III Mall ◆[9]	279b	40.21 N	79.57 W
Century Village	220	26.42 N	80.05 W
Cenxi	102	22.59 N	111.00 E
Čepca	80	57.54 N	53.25 E
Čepca ≐	80	58.36 N	50.04 E
Čepeckij	80	58.29 N	51.12 E
Čepel'	78	49.19 N	36.55 E
Čepelare	38	41.44 N	24.41 E
Čepel'ovo	82	55.11 N	37.30 E
Čepovan	64	46.03 N	13.47 E
Cepoy	50	48.03 N	2.44 E
Ceprano	66	41.33 N	13.31 E
Čepřovice	60	49.10 N	13.59 E
Ceptia	152	12.56 S	17.35 E
Cepu	115a	7.09 S	111.35 E
Ceraino	64	45.35 N	10.50 E
Ceram → Seram I	164	3.00 S	129.00 E
Cerami	70	37.49 N	14.30 E
Cerami ≐	70	37.42 N	14.29 E
Ceram Sea → Seram, Laut ⫫[2]	108	2.30 S	128.00 E
Cerano, It.	62	45.25 N	8.47 E
Cerano, Méx.	234	20.07 N	101.23 W
Ceraso	68	40.11 N	15.15 E
Cerbicale, Îles II	71	41.34 N	9.24 E
Čerčany	30	49.51 N	14.43 E
Cerchiara di Calabria	68	39.51 N	16.23 E
Čerchov ∧	60	49.23 N	12.47 E
Cercié	58	46.07 N	4.40 E
Cerco, Alto do ∧	256	22.38 S	45.22 W
Cercola	66	40.51 N	14.21 E
Cerda	70	37.54 N	13.49 E
Čerdakly	80	54.23 N	48.51 E
Cerdanyola del Vallès	266d	41.30 N	2.09 E
Cerdas	248	20.48 S	66.29 W
Cerdeña, Isla de → Sardegna I	71	40.00 N	9.00 E
Čerdojak	86	48.48 N	84.00 E
Cerdon, Fr.	50	47.38 N	2.22 E
Cerdon, Fr.	58	46.05 N	5.28 E
Čerdyn'	24	60.23 N	56.24 E
Cère ≐	32	44.55 N	1.53 E
Cerea	64	45.12 N	11.13 E
Cereal	184	51.25 N	110.48 W
Cereales	252	36.49 S	63.51 W
Čerecha ≐	76	57.46 N	28.21 E
Cereglio	64	44.18 N	11.04 E
Čereja	76	54.37 N	29.17 E
Čerek ≐	84	43.42 N	44.03 E
Čeremchovo	88	53.09 N	103.05 E
Čeremisinovo	78	51.54 N	37.15 E
Čeremoš ≐	78	48.23 N	25.37 E
Čeremšan, S.S.S.R.	80	55.15 N	48.07 E
Čeremšan, S.S.S.R.	80	54.40 N	51.30 E
Čeremšanka, S.S.S.R.	86	56.07 N	60.19 E
Čeremšanka, S.S.S.R.	86	59.10 N	76.51 E
Čeremšany	89	44.42 N	135.43 E
Cerenti	112	0.30 S	101.52 E
Čerepanovka	80	57.07 N	54.10 E
Čerepanovo	86	54.13 N	83.22 E
Čerepaška, ostrov I	83	47.11 N	38.59 E
Čerepet'	82	54.07 N	36.23 E
Čerepkovo ◆[8]	265b	55.46 N	37.23 E
Čerepovec	76	59.08 N	37.54 E
Ceres, Arg.	252	29.53 S	61.57 W
Ceres, Bra.	255	15.17 S	49.35 W
Ceres, It.	62	45.19 N	7.23 E
Ceres, S. Afr.	158	33.21 S	19.18 E
Ceres, Ca., U.S.	226	37.35 N	120.57 W
Ceres, N.Y., U.S.	210	42.00 N	78.16 W
Ceresco, Mi., U.S.	216	42.16 N	85.04 W
Ceresco, Ne., U.S.	198	41.03 N	96.38 W
Ceresole Reale	62	45.26 N	7.15 E
Céreste	62	43.51 N	5.35 E
Céret	32	42.29 N	2.45 E
Cereté	246	8.53 N	75.48 W
Čerevkovka	78	48.50 N	37.40 E
Čerevkovka ◆[8]	83	48.50 N	37.40 E
Čerevkovo	24	61.46 N	45.12 E
Cereweh	115b	8.52 S	116.51 E
Cerf Island I	138	9.32 S	50.59 E
Čerga	86	51.35 N	85.38 E
Cergy	261	49.02 N	2.04 E
Ceri ≐	42	52.03 N	4.29 W
Ceriale	62	44.06 N	8.14 E
Ceriana	62	43.53 N	7.46 E
Ceriano	266b	45.38 N	9.05 E
Cerignola	68	41.16 N	15.54 E
Čerikov	76	53.34 N	31.23 E
Cérilly	32	46.37 N	2.49 E
Cerisano	68	39.16 N	16.11 E
Cerisiers	50	48.08 N	3.29 E
Čerkašina	88	58.37 N	108.30 E
Čerkasovo	82	54.33 N	36.48 E
Čerkasskoje, S.S.S.R.	78	48.44 N	35.22 E
Čerkasskoje, S.S.S.R.	80	52.26 N	47.13 E
Čerkasskoje, S.S.S.R.	83	48.50 N	37.23 E
Čerkassy, S.S.S.R.	76	52.41 N	38.43 E
Čerkassy, S.S.S.R.	78	49.26 N	32.04 E
Çerkeş	130	40.50 N	32.54 E
Čerkesovskij	80	50.41 N	42.34 E
Čerkessk	84	44.14 N	42.04 E
Çerkezköy	130	41.17 N	28.00 E
Čerkizovo, S.S.S.R.	82	55.12 N	38.45 E
Čerkizovo, S.S.S.R.	265b	55.58 N	37.48 E
Čerkizovo, S.S.S.R.	265b	55.57 N	37.22 E
Cerknica	36	45.48 N	14.22 E
Čerkovišče	76	55.54 N	30.51 E
Čerlak	86	54.09 N	74.48 E
Čerlakskij	86	53.47 N	74.31 E
Cermei	38	46.33 N	21.51 E
Čermen	84	43.11 N	44.42 E
Cermignano	66	42.35 N	13.47 E
Çermik	130	38.09 N	39.27 E
Čermoz	86	58.53 N	56.08 E
Čern'	76	53.27 N	36.55 E
Cerna, Jugo.	38	45.11 N	18.42 E
Cerna, Rom.	38	45.04 N	28.18 E
Čern'achov	78	50.27 N	28.39 E
Čern'achovsk (Insterburg)	76	54.38 N	21.49 E
Černá hora ∧	60	48.58 N	13.48 E
Čern'ajevo	89	52.45 N	126.00 E
Černak	85	43.24 N	68.02 E
Čern'anka	78	50.55 N	37.49 E
Cernăuți → Černovcy	78	48.18 N	25.56 E
Černava	76	53.37 N	39.09 E
Černavčicy	76	52.13 N	23.44 E
Černavka, S.S.S.R.	80	52.18 N	47.14 E
Černavka, S.S.S.R.	80	52.11 N	42.25 E
Cernavodă	38	44.21 N	28.01 E
Černá v Pošumaví	61	48.44 N	14.07 E
Cernay	58	47.49 N	7.10 E
Cernay-la-Ville	50	48.40 N	1.58 E
Cerne Abbas	42	50.49 N	2.29 W
Černeckoje	82	55.15 N	37.20 E
Cernei, Munții ⋏	38	45.02 N	22.31 E
Černelica	78	48.48 N	25.26 E
Černevcy	78	48.33 N	28.09 E
Černigov	78	51.30 N	31.18 E
Černigov □[4]	76	52.13 N	32.45 E
Černigovka, S.S.S.R.	78	47.13 N	36.14 E
Černigovka, S.S.S.R.	86	50.28 N	71.27 E
Černigovka, S.S.S.R.	89	49.37 N	129.57 E
Černigovka, S.S.S.R.	89	44.21 N	132.33 E
Černigovskaja	78	44.41 N	39.40 E
Černi vrăh ∧	38	42.34 N	23.17 E
Černobaj	78	49.41 N	32.19 E
Cernobbio	62	45.50 N	9.04 E
Černobyl'	78	51.16 N	30.14 E
Černogolovka	82	56.00 N	38.22 E
Černogorsk	86	53.49 N	91.18 E
Černokol'skaja	86	56.42 N	72.49 E
Černomorskij zapovednik ◆[4]	78	46.10 N	32.00 E
Černorečenskoje	85	43.00 N	74.55 E
Černorečje	84	43.15 N	45.41 E
Černošín	60	49.49 N	12.53 E
Černovcy	78	48.18 N	25.56 E
Černovice	60	49.49 N	13.06 E
Černovka, S.S.S.R.	86	56.47 N	76.28 E
Černovka, S.S.S.R.	89	51.43 N	128.12 E
Čern'ovo, S.S.S.R.	76	58.39 N	28.14 E
Čern'ovo, S.S.S.R.	82	54.43 N	38.36 E
Čern'ovo, S.S.S.R.	265b	55.50 N	37.18 E
Černovskije Kopi	88	52.00 N	113.15 E
Černovskoje, S.S.S.R.	80	58.42 N	47.23 E
Černovskoje, S.S.S.R.	80	57.29 N	54.36 E
Černucha	80	55.36 N	43.46 E
Černuchi	78	50.16 N	32.57 E
Černuchino	83	48.19 N	38.30 E
Cernusco sul Naviglio	62	45.31 N	9.19 E
Černuška, S.S.S.R.	86	56.29 N	56.03 E
Černuška, S.S.S.R.	88	52.58 N	101.55 E
Cerny-en-Laonnois	50	49.27 N	3.40 E
Černyševsk	88	52.35 N	117.00 E
Černyševskij	74	63.00 N	112.15 E
Černyškovskij	80	48.27 N	42.14 E
Černyšova, gr'ada ⋏	24	66.30 N	59.00 E
Čer'omuchova	80	54.57 N	51.09 E
Čer'omuski ◆[8]	265b	55.41 N	37.35 E
Cerralvo	232	26.06 N	99.37 W
Cerralvo, Isla I	232	24.15 N	109.55 W
Cerreto, Passo del)(	64	44.18 N	10.13 E
Cerreto d'Esi	66	43.19 N	12.59 E
Cerreto Guidi	66	43.45 N	10.53 E
Cerreto Sannita	68	41.17 N	14.33 E
Cerrigydrudion	44	53.02 N	3.33 W
Cërrik	38	41.02 N	19.57 E
Cerrillos, Arg.	252	24.54 S	65.29 W
Cerrillos, N.M., U.S.	200	35.26 N	106.07 W
Cerrina	62	45.07 N	8.13 E
Cerritos, Méx.	234	22.26 N	100.17 W
Cerritos, Ca., U.S.	280	33.52 N	118.05 W
Cerro	58	45.54 N	8.36 E
Cerro, Forca di)(	66	42.45 N	12.47 E
Cerro Azul, Arg.	252	27.38 S	55.29 W
Cêrro Azul, Bra.	252	24.50 S	49.15 W
Cerro Azul, Méx.	234	21.12 N	97.44 W
Cerro Azul, Perú	248	13.02 S	76.30 W
Cerro Chato	252	33.06 S	55.08 W
Cerro Colorado	252	33.52 S	55.33 W
Cêrro Corá	250	6.03 S	36.21 W
Cerro de Garnica, Parque Nacional ♠	234	19.35 N	100.47 W
Cerro de las Campanas, Parque Nacional ♠	234	20.40 N	100.30 W
Cerro de las Mesas ⊥	234	18.47 N	96.05 W
Cerro de los Angeles ⚲[1]	266a	40.19 N	3.41 W
Cerro de Pasco	248	10.41 S	76.16 W
Cerro Gordo	219	39.53 N	88.43 W
Cerro Grande ≐	286c	10.37 N	66.49 W
Cêrro Largo	252	28.09 S	54.45 W
Cerro Maggiore	266b	45.36 N	8.58 E
Cerro Moreno	252	23.28 S	70.25 W
Cerrón, Cerro ∧	246	10.19 N	70.39 W
Cerrón Grande, Embalse ⊜[1]	236	14.00 N	89.00 W
Cerro Prieto	204	32.27 N	115.17 W
Cerros Colorados, Embalse ⊜[1]	252	38.35 S	68.40 W
Cerro Vera	252	33.11 S	57.28 W
Čerskij	74	68.45 N	161.45 E
Čerskogo, chrebet ⋏, S.S.S.R.	74	65.00 N	144.00 E
Čerskogo, chrebet ⋏, S.S.S.R.	88	52.00 N	114.00 E
Čerskogo, gora ∧	88	55.05 N	108.40 E
Cersosimo	68	40.03 N	16.21 E
Certaldo	66	43.33 N	11.02 E
Čertanovka ≐	265b	55.38 N	37.47 E
Čertanovo ◆[8]	265b	55.38 N	37.37 E
Čertkovo	83	49.23 N	40.10 E
Čertolino	76	56.12 N	33.54 E
Čertomlyk	78	47.37 N	34.09 E
Certosa (Karthaus)	64	46.42 N	10.54 E
Certosa di Pavia	62	45.15 N	9.09 E
Čerusti	76	55.33 N	40.01 E
Červ'anka	88	57.41 N	99.33 E
Cervantes, Austl.	162	30.30 S	115.04 E
Cervantes, Pil.	116	16.59 N	120.44 E
Cervarezza	64	44.23 N	10.20 E
Cervaro	66	41.29 N	13.54 E
Cervaro ≐	68	41.30 N	15.52 E
Cervati, Monte ∧	68	40.17 N	15.29 E
Cervelló	266d	41.24 N	1.57 E
Cervello, Cozzo ∧	68	39.24 N	16.05 E
Cervelló, Riera de ≐	266d	41.24 N	2.01 E
Červen'	76	53.42 N	28.26 E
Červen Brjag	38	43.16 N	24.06 E
Červený Kostelec	30	50.29 N	16.06 E
Cervera	34	41.40 N	1.17 E
Cervera del Río Alhama	34	42.01 N	1.57 W
Cervera de Pisuerga	34	42.52 N	4.30 W
Cerveteri	66	42.00 N	12.06 E
Cervi, Monte dei ∧	70	37.53 N	13.58 E
Cervia	66	44.15 N	12.22 E
Cervialto, Monte ∧	68	40.47 N	15.08 E
Cervignano del Friuli	64	45.49 N	13.20 E
Cervin, Mont → Matterhorn ∧	58	45.59 N	7.43 E
Cervinara	68	41.01 N	14.37 E
Cervino (Matterhorn) ∧	58	45.59 N	7.43 E
Cervione	36	42.20 N	9.31 E
Červl'onnaja	84	43.30 N	45.54 E
Cervo, Esp.	34	43.40 N	7.25 W
Cervo, It.	62	43.55 N	8.07 E
Cervo ≐	62	45.22 N	8.24 E
Cervo, Capo ›	62	43.55 N	8.08 E
Cervo, Rio do ≐, Bra.	256	22.07 S	45.49 W
Cervo, Rio do ≐, Bra.	256	21.12 S	45.10 W
Cervo, Serra do ∧	256	22.06 S	46.07 W
Červonaja Kamenka	78	48.38 N	33.26 E
Červonoarmejsk, S.S.S.R.	78	50.08 N	25.16 E
Červonoarmejsk, S.S.S.R.	78	50.28 N	28.14 E
Červonoarmejskoje, S.S.S.R.	78	45.47 N	28.44 E
Červonoarmejskoje, S.S.S.R.	78	47.57 N	35.27 E
Červonograd	78	50.24 N	24.14 E
Červonogranitnoje	78	50.34 N	28.33 E
Červonoje, S.S.S.R.	78	51.46 N	34.04 E
Červonoje, S.S.S.R.	78	49.57 N	28.53 E
Červonoje, ozero ⊜	76	52.24 N	27.57 E
Červonopartizansk	83	48.04 N	39.50 E
Červonyj Donec	78	49.29 N	36.34 E
Cesana Torinese	62	44.57 N	6.47 E
Cesano, It.	66	42.07 N	12.21 E
Cesano, It.	66	43.45 N	13.10 E
Cesano ≐	66	43.45 N	13.10 E
Cesano Boscone	266b	45.27 N	9.06 E
Cesano Maderno	62	45.38 N	9.08 E
Cesar □[5]	246	9.20 N	73.30 W
César ≐	246	9.00 N	73.58 W
Cesaró	70	37.50 N	14.43 E
Cesate	266b	45.36 N	9.05 E
Cesena	66	44.08 N	12.15 E
Cesenatico	66	44.12 N	12.24 E
Cesi, Poggio ∧[2]	267a	42.02 N	12.44 E
Cesiomaggiore	64	46.05 N	11.59 E
Cēsis	76	57.18 N	25.15 E
Česká Kamenice	54	50.47 N	14.26 E
Česká Kublice	60	49.22 N	12.52 E
Česká Lípa	54	50.42 N	14.32 E
Česká Socialistická Republika □[3]	30	49.40 N	15.10 E
Česká Třebová	30	49.54 N	16.27 E
České Budějovice	61	48.59 N	14.28 E
České středohoří ⋏	54	50.35 N	14.09 E
Českomoravská vrchovina ⋏[1]	30	49.20 N	15.30 E
Československo → Czechoslovakia □[1]	30	49.30 N	17.00 E
Český Brod	54	50.02 N	14.58 E
Český Krumlov	61	48.49 N	14.19 E
Česma	86	53.50 N	60.40 E
Çeşme	130	38.18 N	26.19 E
Céspedes	240p	21.35 N	78.17 W
Cessalto	64	45.42 N	12.36 E
Češskaja guba c	24	67.30 N	46.30 E
Cessnock	170	32.50 S	151.21 E
Cesson	261	48.34 N	2.36 E
Cestos ≐	150	5.40 N	9.10 W
Cesvaine	76	56.58 N	26.19 E
Čet' ≐	86	56.51 N	86.48 E
Cetara	68	40.39 N	14.42 E
Cetate	38	44.06 N	23.03 E
Cetatea Albă → Belgorod-Dnestrovskij	78	46.12 N	30.20 E
Četbulak	85	41.17 N	73.58 E
Cetian	100	25.44 N	116.22 E
Cetina ≐	36	43.26 N	16.42 E
Cetinje	38	42.23 N	18.55 E
Çetinkaya	130	39.15 N	37.38 E
Cetona	66	42.58 N	11.54 E
Cetona, Monte ∧	66	42.56 N	11.52 E
Cetraro	68	39.31 N	15.56 E
Cetronia	208	40.35 N	75.31 W
Četyrboki	78	50.02 N	27.01 E
Céüse, Montagne de ∧	62	44.31 N	5.57 E
Ceuta	34	35.53 N	5.19 W
Ceva	62	44.23 N	8.02 E
Cevedale, Monte (Zufallspitze) ∧	64	46.27 N	10.37 E
Cevennen → Cévennes ◆[1]	32	44.00 N	3.30 E
Cévennes ◆[1]	32	44.00 N	3.30 E
Cévennes, Parc National des ♠	32	44.15 N	3.40 E
Cevins	62	45.35 N	6.28 E
Cevio	58	46.19 N	8.36 E
Çevizli	130	37.12 N	31.45 E
Ceyhan	130	37.04 N	35.47 E
Ceyhan ≐	130	36.45 N	35.41 E
Ceylanpınar	130	36.51 N	40.02 E
Ceylon, Sk., Can.	184	49.28 N	104.36 W
Ceylon, Mn., U.S.	198	43.32 N	94.37 W
Ceylon → Sri Lanka □[1]	122	7.00 N	81.00 E
Ceyzériat	58	46.10 N	5.19 E
Cèze ≐	62	44.06 N	4.42 E
Chaam, Ned.	52	51.31 N	4.52 E
Cha-am, Thai	110	12.48 N	99.58 E
Chaanling	100	29.39 N	113.49 E
Chaatl Island I	182	53.00 N	132.25 W
Chabanais	32	45.52 N	0.43 E
Chabang Tiga	114	5.19 N	103.08 E
Chabaricha	24	65.50 N	52.16 E
Chabařovice	54	50.40 N	13.56 E
Chabarovo	72	69.39 N	60.24 E
Chabarovsk	89	48.27 N	135.06 E
Chabarovsk □[4]	89	54.00 N	136.00 E
Chabarowsk → Chabarovsk	89	48.27 N	135.06 E
Chabary	86	53.37 N	79.33 E
Chabás	252	33.15 S	61.22 W
Chabeuil	62	44.54 N	5.01 E
Chabez	84	44.02 N	41.47 E
Chābi	124	22.49 N	80.41 E
Chabjuwardoo Bay c	162	22.57 S	113.48 E
Chablais ◆[1]	58	46.18 N	6.39 E
Chablis	50	47.49 N	3.48 E
Chabogongba	120	31.47 N	81.14 E
Chaboje	265a	59.53 N	30.46 E
Chabot, Lake ⊜, Ca., U.S.	282	38.08 N	122.14 W
Chabot, Lake ⊜, Ca., U.S.	282	37.43 N	122.07 W
Chabris	50	47.15 N	1.39 E
Chabuchaer	86	43.42 N	81.04 E
Chabu-Rabot, pereval)(	85	38.40 N	70.43 E
Chacabuco	252	34.38 S	60.29 W
Chacaito, Quebrada ≐	286c	10.29 N	66.52 W
Chacaltianguis	234	18.20 N	95.50 W
Chacanilla	248	6.13 S	77.51 W
Chacao	286c	10.30 N	66.51 W
Chácara	256	21.41 S	43.13 W
Chacarão, Cachoeira do ᒪ	250	6.32 S	58.12 W
Chacarilla	286d	12.02 S	77.01 W
Chacarita, Cementerio de la ◆	288	34.33 S	58.28 W
Chacayán	248	10.24 S	76.25 W
Chachani, Nevado ∧	248	16.12 S	71.33 W
Chachapoyas, Perú	242	6.13 S	77.51 W
Chachapoyas, Perú	248	6.13 S	77.51 W
Chachas	248	15.30 S	72.16 W
Chachoengsao	110	13.42 N	101.05 E
Chāchora	124	24.10 N	76.59 E
Chāchro	120	25.07 N	70.15 E
Chachu	120	33.16 N	81.41 E
Chačinčaj ≐	84	40.13 N	47.18 E
Chačmas	84	41.28 N	48.48 E
Chaco □[4]	252	26.25 S	60.30 W
Chaco □[5]	248	20.00 S	60.30 W
Chaco ≐	200	36.46 N	108.39 W
Chaco Austral ◆[1]	252	26.30 S	61.30 W
Chaco Boreal ◆[1]	252	23.00 S	60.00 W
Chaco Central ◆[1]	252	25.00 S	59.45 W
Chaco Culture National Historical Park ♠	200	36.06 N	108.00 W
Chaco Mesa ∧	200	35.47 N	107.35 W
Chacón, Arroyo ≐	288	34.53 S	58.39 W
Chacon, Cape ›	182	54.42 N	132.00 W
Chacra Cerro	286d	11.55 S	77.04 W
Chacra Ríos, Coliseo ♠	286d	12.03 S	77.04 W
Chacuaco Creek ≐	196	37.34 N	103.38 W
Chad (Tchad) □[1], Afr.	136	15.00 N	19.00 E
Chad (Tchad) □[1], Afr.	146	15.00 N	19.00 E
Chad, Lake (Lac Tchad) ⊜	146	13.20 N	14.00 E
Chada-Bulak	88	50.38 N	116.18 E
Chadbourn	192	34.19 N	78.49 W
Chadderton	262	53.33 N	2.08 W
Chadds Ford	285	39.52 N	75.35 W
Chādegān	128	32.46 N	50.39 E
Chadian, Zhg.	102	26.48 N	105.48 E
Chadian, Zhg.	105	39.14 N	117.45 E
Chadian, Zhg.	107	30.14 N	105.56 E
Chadianzi	107	30.31 N	104.22 E
Chadiza	154	14.05 S	32.28 E
Chadron	198	42.49 N	103.00 W
Chadstone	274b	37.53 S	145.05 E
Chadwell Saint Mary	260	51.29 N	0.22 E
Chadwick	190	42.01 N	89.53 W
Chadwick Manor	284b	39.19 N	76.46 W
Chadwick Pond ⊜	283	42.44 N	71.05 W
Chadwicks	210	43.01 N	75.16 W
Chadyžensk	78	44.25 N	39.33 E
Chadžalmachi	84	42.26 N	47.13 E
Chadžibejskij liman ⊜	78	46.39 N	30.33 E
Chae Hom	110	18.43 N	99.35 E
Chaem ≐	110	18.11 N	98.38 E
Chaersen	89	46.19 N	121.54 E
Chaeryŏng	98	38.24 N	125.36 E
Chafarinas, Islas II	34	35.11 N	2.26 W
Chafe	150	11.56 N	6.55 E
Chaffee	194	37.10 N	89.39 W
Chaffins	207	42.21 N	71.51 W
Chafurray	246	3.10 N	73.14 W
Chāgai	128	29.18 N	64.42 E
Chāgai Hills ⋏[2]	128	29.30 N	64.15 E
Chagandianlisu	102	41.47 N	103.29 E
Chagang Do □[4]	98	40.50 N	126.30 E
'Chaghcharān	120	34.32 N	65.15 E
Chagny	58	46.55 N	4.45 E
Chagos Archipelago II	12	6.00 S	72.00 E
Chagos-Laccadive Plateau ✣[3]	12	3.00 N	73.00 E
Chagrin ≐	214	41.40 N	81.27 W
Chagrin, Aurora Branch ≐	279a	41.25 N	81.25 W
Chagrin Falls	214	41.26 N	81.24 W
Chagrin Falls Park	214	41.21 N	81.32 W
Chagrin Valley Parkway ♠	279a	41.26 N	81.25 W
Chaguanas	241r	10.31 N	61.25 W
Chaguaramas	246	9.20 N	66.16 W
Chaguaya	248	21.49 S	64.50 W
Chahaignes	50	47.44 N	0.31 E
Chāhak	128	33.17 N	58.54 E
Chahal	236	15.45 N	89.34 W
Chahancheluo	98	41.39 N	114.22 E
Chahanwusu → Dulan	102	36.16 N	98.28 E
Chahār Borjak	128	30.17 N	62.03 E
Chahār Deh-ye Ghowrband	120	34.59 N	68.44 E
Chahār Maḥāl va Bakhtīārī □[4]	128	32.00 N	51.00 E
Chahayang	89	48.24 N	124.15 E
Chahe, Zhg.	100	33.16 N	119.02 E
Chahe, Zhg.	102	33.48 N	97.22 E
Chahe, Zhg.	105	39.50 N	115.21 E
Chāh Gheybī, Hāmūn-e ⋮	128	28.06 N	60.50 E
Chahuamiao	100	33.00 N	115.56 E
Chahuites	234	16.17 N	94.11 W
Chai ≐	104	42.20 N	123.52 E
Chai Badan	110	15.04 N	101.05 E
Chāībāsa	124	22.34 N	85.49 E
Chaigou	98	36.15 N	119.36 E
Chaihe	89	44.47 N	129.42 E
Chaijiawan	100	29.10 N	113.06 E
Chaillé-les-Marais	32	46.24 N	1.01 W
Chailley	50	48.05 N	3.42 E
Chailly-en-Bière	50	48.28 N	2.35 E
Chai Nat	110	15.11 N	100.08 E
Chainhurst	260	51.12 N	0.29 E
Chain O'Lakes State Park ♠, Il., U.S.	216	42.27 N	88.11 W
Chain O'Lakes State Park ♠, In., U.S.	216	41.20 N	85.26 W
Chainpur	124	23.08 N	84.15 E
Chaipudyrskaja guba c	24	68.30 N	59.30 E
Chaiqiao	100	29.51 N	121.56 E
Chairel, Laguna de c	234	22.17 N	97.57 W
Chaishudian	105	40.46 N	116.30 E
Chaiši	84	42.57 N	42.12 E
Chait	85	39.11 N	70.53 E
Chaital	126	22.31 N	88.47 E
Chaitén	254	42.55 S	72.43 W
Chaiwopu	86	43.33 N	87.59 E
Chaiya	110	9.23 N	99.14 E
Chaiyaphum	110	15.48 N	102.02 E
Chajarí	252	30.46 S	57.59 W
Chajdarken	85	39.57 N	71.21 E
Chajia	107	29.37 N	104.27 E
Chajian	100	32.40 N	118.46 E
Chajianling	98	39.14 N	114.36 E
Chajiaqiao	100	34.00 N	120.07 E
Chajrchan	88	48.35 N	101.56 E
Chajrchandulaan	102	45.57 N	102.03 E
Chajul	236	15.30 N	91.02 W
Chaka	154	4.49 N	31.14 E
Chakachamna Lake ⊜	180	61.13 N	152.35 W
Chakāltor	126	23.14 N	86.22 E
Chak Amru	123	32.22 N	75.11 E
Chakari	154	18.05 S	29.51 E
Chakaria	120	21.45 N	92.05 E
Chakarnaba	146	14.13 N	20.51 E
Chakasskaja Avtonomnaja Oblast' □[8]	86	53.00 N	90.00 E
Chākdaha, India	126	23.05 N	88.31 E
Chakdaha, India	272b	22.20 N	88.20 E
Chake Chake	154	5.15 S	39.46 E
Chakhānsūr	128	31.10 N	62.04 E
Chākia	124	26.25 N	85.03 E
Chakkarat	110	15.00 N	102.16 E
Chakou, Zhg.	98	38.03 N	113.36 E
Chakou, Zhg.	105	38.53 N	116.41 E
Chakradharpur	124	22.42 N	85.38 E
Chakrāta	120	30.42 N	77.51 E
Chāksu	120	26.36 N	75.57 E
Chākulia	126	22.29 N	86.43 E
Chakwadām	102	27.29 N	98.31 E
Chakwāl	123	32.56 N	72.52 E
Chal	272c	19.06 N	73.08 E
Chala	248	15.52 S	74.16 W
Chalabesa	154	11.22 S	31.01 E
Chalais	32	45.16 N	0.02 E
Chālakuda	122	10.18 N	76.20 E
Chalamont	58	46.00 N	5.10 E
Chalampé	58	47.49 N	7.33 E
Chalan Kanoa	174n	15.08 N	145.43 E
Chalatenango	236	14.03 N	88.56 W
Chalaua	154	16.06 S	39.11 E
Chalaux ≐	50	47.23 N	3.54 E
Chalaxung	102	34.10 N	97.44 E
Chalbi Desert ◆[2]	154	3.00 N	37.20 E
Chalcatongo de Hidalgo	234	17.02 N	97.35 W
Chalchgol	88	48.11 N	114.54 E
Chalchihuites	234	23.29 N	103.53 W
Chalchis Terara ∧	144	9.08 N	36.44 E
Chalchuapa	236	13.59 N	89.41 W
Chalchyn ≐	88	47.55 N	117.47 E
Chalcis → Khalkís	38	38.28 N	23.36 E
Chalco [de Díaz Covarrubias]	234	19.16 N	98.54 W
Chaldan	84	40.43 N	47.15 E
Chaldon	260	51.17 N	0.07 W
Chaleine	261	48.36 N	1.43 E
Chalengkou	120	38.02 N	93.54 E
Châlette-sur-Loing	50	48.01 N	2.44 E
Chaleur Bay c	186	48.00 N	65.45 W
Chalfant	279b	40.25 N	79.52 W
Chalfant Run ≐	279b	40.25 N	79.48 W
Chalfont	208	40.17 N	75.13 W
Chalfont Common	260	51.38 N	0.33 W
Chalfonte	285	39.49 N	75.32 W
Chalfont Saint Giles	260	51.38 N	0.34 W
Chalfont Saint Peter	260	51.37 N	0.33 W
Chalford	42	51.45 N	2.09 W
Chalhuanca	248	14.17 S	73.15 W
Chalifert	261	48.53 N	2.46 E
Chalihuey	234	22.43 N	104.04 W
Chalilovo	86	51.24 N	58.04 E
Chalindrey	58	47.48 N	5.26 E
Chaling	100	26.47 N	113.33 E
Chālisgaon	122	20.28 N	75.01 E
Chalisi	102	32.55 N	102.04 E
Chaliun	88	48.50 N	103.59 E
Chalk	260	51.26 N	0.25 E
Chalkabad	86	42.42 N	59.43 E
Chalk Draw V	196	29.36 N	103.15 W
Chalk River	190	46.01 N	77.27 W
Chalkyitsik	180	66.39 N	143.43 W
Challakere	122	14.19 N	76.39 E
Challans	32	46.51 N	1.53 W
Challapata	248	18.54 S	66.47 W
Challenge	226	39.29 N	121.13 W
Challenger, Mount ∧	224	48.50 N	121.20 W
Challenger Deep ✣[1]	14	11.21 N	142.12 E
Challes-les-Eaux	62	45.33 N	5.59 E
Challis	202	44.30 N	114.13 W
Challviri, Salar de ⋮	248	22.32 S	67.34 W
Chal'mer-Ju	24	67.58 N	64.50 E
Chalmers	216	40.39 N	86.52 W
Chalmette	194	29.56 N	89.57 W
Chalone Creek ≐	226	36.21 N	121.14 W
Chalonnes-sur-Loire	32	47.21 N	0.46 W
Châlons-sur-Marne	50	48.57 N	4.22 E
Chalon-sur-Saône	58	46.47 N	4.51 E
Chalosse ◆[1]	32	43.45 N	0.30 W
Chalt	123	36.15 N	74.20 E
Chaltel, Cerro (Monte Fitzroy) ∧	254	49.17 S	73.05 W
Chalturin	80	58.33 N	48.50 E
Chalturino	78	49.31 N	35.17 E
Châlus, Fr.	32	45.39 N	0.59 E
Chālūs, Īrān	128	36.38 N	51.26 E
Cham, B.R.D.	60	49.13 N	12.41 E
Cham, Schw.	58	47.11 N	8.28 E
Chama, Perú	286d	12.08 S	77.00 W
Chama, N.M., U.S.	200	36.54 N	106.34 W
Chama ≐	246	9.03 N	71.40 W
Chama, Rio ≐	200	36.03 N	106.05 W
Chamah, Gunong ∧	114	5.13 N	101.33 E
Chamaicó	252	35.03 S	64.58 W
Chamal, Sierra ⋏	234	22.45 N	99.15 W
Chamama	154	12.55 S	33.43 E
Chamamat'urt	84	43.36 N	46.30 E
Chaman	120	30.55 N	66.27 E
Chamangonge	152	11.16 S	20.24 E
Chamao, Khao ∧	110	12.57 N	101.45 E
Chamarande	261	48.31 N	2.13 E
Chamar-Daban, chrebet ⋏	88	51.15 N	105.00 E
Chāmārpāra	272b	22.35 N	88.08 E
Chamaya ≐	248	5.44 S	78.39 W
Chamb ≐	60	49.13 N	12.42 E
Chamba, India	123	32.34 N	76.08 E
Chamba, Moç.	154	12.07 S	36.57 E
Chamba, Tan.	154	11.35 S	36.58 E
Chambal ≐	120	26.30 N	79.15 E
Chambaran, Plateau de ⋏[1]	62	45.15 N	5.15 E
Chambas	240p	22.12 N	78.55 W
Chambas ≐	240p	22.24 N	78.54 W
Chamberlain, Sk., Can.	184	50.50 N	105.34 W
Chamberlain, S.D., U.S.	198	43.48 N	99.19 W
Chamberlain ≐	164	15.08 S	128.06 E
Chamberlain Lake ⊜	186	46.17 N	69.20 W
Chamberlin, Mount ∧	180	69.16 N	144.55 W
Chamberry, Ruisseau ≐	275a	45.20 N	73.58 W
Chambers, Az., U.S.	200	35.11 N	109.25 W
Chambers, Ne., U.S.	198	42.12 N	98.44 W
Chambers, N.Y., U.S.	210	42.16 N	76.57 W
Chambers □[6]	222	29.42 N	94.40 W
Chambers Brook ≐	276	40.35 N	74.41 W
Chambersburg, Il., U.S.	219	39.49 N	90.39 W
Chambersburg, In., U.S.	218	38.31 N	86.24 W
Chambersburg, Pa., U.S.	208	39.56 N	77.39 W
Chambers Corner	285	40.01 N	74.44 W
Chambers Creek ≐	222	31.58 N	96.10 W
Chambers Creek, North Fork ≐	222	32.16 N	96.58 W
Chambers Creek, South Fork ≐	222	32.16 N	96.58 W
Chambers Island I	190	45.11 N	87.21 W
Chambéry	62	45.34 N	5.56 E
Chambeshi ≐	154	11.21 S	30.37 E
Chambi, Jebel ∧	148	35.11 N	8.42 E
Chambira ≐, Perú	246	4.28 S	74.50 W
Chambira ≐, Perú	246	3.55 S	73.45 W
Chamblee	192	33.53 N	84.17 W
Chambley-Bussières	56	49.03 N	5.54 E
Chambly, P.Q., Can.	206	45.27 N	73.17 W
Chambly, Fr.	50	49.10 N	2.15 E
Chambly □[6]	206	45.30 N	73.20 W
Chambly, Bassin de ⊜	206	45.27 N	73.17 W
Chambly, Canal de ≊	275a	45.25 N	73.15 W
Chambois	50	48.48 N	0.07 E
Chambon-sur-Dolore	62	45.30 N	3.37 E
Chambon-sur-Voueize	32	46.11 N	2.25 E
Chambord, Château de ⊥	50	47.37 N	1.31 E
Chambourcy	261	48.54 N	2.03 E
Chambri Lake ⊜	164	4.16 S	143.08 E
Chambry	261	49.00 N	2.54 E
Chamburi Kalāt	128	26.09 N	64.43 E
Chamdo → Qamdo	102	31.11 N	97.15 E
Chāme, Nepāl	124	28.33 N	84.15 E
Chame, Pan.	236	8.35 N	79.53 W
Chame, Punta ›	236	8.39 N	79.42 W
Chamela	234	19.32 N	105.05 W
Chamela, Bahía c	234	19.33 N	105.07 W
Chamelecón	236	15.24 N	88.01 W
Chamelecón ≐	236	15.51 N	87.49 W
Chamical	252	30.21 S	66.19 W
Chamizo	258	34.10 S	56.41 W
Chamizo, Arroyo ≐	258	34.15 S	56.44 W
Chamkanī	120	33.48 N	69.49 E
Chāmlūjā ≐	124	29.38 N	80.24 E
Chamo, Lake ⊜	144	5.50 N	37.33 E
Chamois, It.	62	45.50 N	7.37 E
Chamois, Mo., U.S.	219	38.40 N	91.46 W
Chamojie	89	49.25 N	124.45 E
Chamoli	124	30.24 N	79.21 E
Chamonix-Mont-Blanc	58	45.55 N	6.52 E
Chamousset	62	45.33 N	6.12 E
Chamoux-sur-Gelon	62	45.32 N	6.13 E
Chāmpa	124	22.03 N	82.39 E
Champagne, Yk., Can.	180	60.47 N	136.29 W
Champagne, Fr.	62	45.16 N	4.48 E
Champagne □[9]	32	49.00 N	4.30 E
Champagne Castle ∧	158	29.06 S	29.20 E
Champagne-en-Valromay	58	45.54 N	5.41 E
Champagner-Berg ∧[2]	264a	52.31 N	13.05 E
Champagne-sur-Seine	50	48.24 N	2.48 E
Champagney	58	47.42 N	6.41 E
Champagnole	58	46.45 N	5.55 E
Champagny	62	45.27 N	6.42 E
Chāmpāhāti	126	22.23 N	88.29 E
Champaign	194	40.06 N	88.14 W
Champaign □[6], Il., U.S.	216	40.07 N	88.12 W
Champaign □[6], Oh., U.S.	218	40.07 N	83.45 W
Champapur	126	24.02 N	86.31 E
Champaquí, Cerro ∧	252	31.59 S	64.56 W
Champasak	110	14.53 N	105.52 E
Champāwat	124	29.20 N	80.06 E
Champcueil	261	48.31 N	2.27 E
Champdāni	126	22.48 N	88.21 E
Champdeniers	32	46.29 N	0.24 W
Champdepraz	62	45.41 N	7.39 E
Champdeuil	261	48.37 N	2.44 E
Champdor	58	46.01 N	5.36 E
Champdoré, Lac ⊜	176	55.55 N	65.49 W
Champeaux	50	48.35 N	2.48 E
Champeix	32	45.36 N	3.08 E
Champerico	236	14.18 N	91.55 W
Champéry	58	46.10 N	6.52 E
Champex	58	46.02 N	7.07 E
Champier	62	45.27 N	5.17 E
Champigneulles	56	48.44 N	6.10 E
Champigny-sur-Marne	261	48.49 N	2.31 E
Champion, Ab., Can.	182	50.14 N	113.09 W
Champion, Mi., U.S.	190	46.30 N	87.57 W
Champion, Oh., U.S.	214	41.17 N	80.51 W
Champion, Pa., U.S.	214	40.05 N	79.21 W
Champions	222	29.59 N	95.31 W
Champlain	206	44.59 N	73.26 W
Champlain □[6]	206	46.45 N	72.35 W
Champlain ≐	206	46.27 N	72.17 W
Champlain, Lake ⊜	188	44.45 N	73.15 W
Champlain, Pont ◆[5]	206	45.28 N	73.32 W
Champlain Canal ≊	210	43.20 N	73.34 W
Champlan	261	48.43 N	2.16 E
Champlin Creek ≐	276	40.43 N	73.12 W
Champlitte-et-le-Prélot	58	47.37 N	5.31 E
Champlon	56	50.07 N	5.28 E
Champoluc	62	45.50 N	7.44 E
Champotón	232	19.21 N	90.43 W
Champrond-en-Gâtine	50	48.24 N	1.05 E
Champs	50	47.44 N	3.36 E
Champs-sur-Marne	261	48.51 N	2.36 E
Chāmpua	124	22.05 N	85.40 E
Champvans	58	47.06 N	5.26 E
Chāmrāil	272b	22.38 N	88.18 E
Chāmrājnagar Rāmasamudram	122	11.55 N	76.57 E
Chamrousse	62	45.08 N	5.52 E
Chamsara ≐	88	52.42 N	95.46 E
Chamusca	34	39.21 N	8.29 W
Chamza Chakimzada	85	40.26 N	71.30 E
Chana	110	6.55 N	100.44 E
Chanabadskij	85	40.49 N	72.58 E
Chanakyapuri □[9]	272a	28.36 N	77.11 E
Chañar	252	30.32 S	65.58 W
Chañaral	252	26.21 S	70.37 W
Chañaral, Isla I	252	29.02 S	71.35 W
Chanas	62	45.18 N	4.49 E
Chānasma	120	23.43 N	72.07 E
Chanbogd	102	43.12 N	107.10 E
Chancay	248	11.35 S	77.16 W
Chancay ≐	248	11.37 S	77.15 W
Chance	208	38.10 N	75.56 W
Chanceaux	58	47.31 N	4.42 E
Chanceaux-sur-Choisille	50	47.28 N	0.42 E
Chanch	88	51.30 N	100.40 E
Chan Chan ⊥	248	8.06 S	79.05 W
Chanchelulla Peak ∧	204	40.28 N	122.59 W
Chanchiang → Zhanjiang	102	21.16 N	110.28 E
Chanchöchij uul ⋏	88	49.30 N	94.30 E
Chanchongor	102	43.50 N	104.25 E
Chanco	252	35.44 S	72.32 W
Chancy	58	46.08 N	6.00 E
Chanda → Chandrapur, India	122	19.57 N	79.18 E
Chanda, S.S.S.R.	88	55.00 N	107.14 E
Chanda ≐	88	55.00 N	107.14 E
Chāndābila	126	22.05 N	87.00 E
Chandagajty	86	50.44 N	92.03 E
Chandalar	180	67.30 N	148.30 W
Chandalar ≐	180	66.36 N	145.48 W
Chandalar, East Fork ≐	180	67.05 N	147.16 W
Chandalar, Middle Fork ≐	180	67.10 N	148.19 W
Chandalar, North Fork ≐	180	67.10 N	148.19 W
Chandan Chauki	124	28.33 N	80.47 E
Chandankiāri	126	23.34 N	86.22 E
Chandannagar	126	22.51 N	88.21 E
Chandanpratāp	126	23.33 N	89.24 E
Chāndar	126	23.54 N	89.58 E
Chandausi	124	28.27 N	78.46 E
Chāndbāli	120	20.47 N	86.46 E
Chandeleur Islands II	194	29.48 N	88.51 W
Chandeleur Sound ⊔	194	29.55 N	89.10 W
Chanderi	124	24.43 N	78.08 E
Chandernagore → Chandannagar	126	22.51 N	88.21 E
Chandīgarh	123	30.44 N	76.55 E
Chandīgarh □[8]	123	30.45 N	76.50 E
Chāndil	124	22.58 N	86.03 E
Chandīpur	126	23.59 N	89.01 E
Chanditala	272b	22.41 N	88.16 E
Chandla	124	25.05 N	80.12 E
Chandler, P.Q., Can.	186	48.21 N	64.41 W
Chandler, Az., U.S.	200	33.18 N	111.50 W
Chandler, In., U.S.	194	38.02 N	87.22 W
Chandler, Ok., U.S.	196	35.42 N	96.52 W
Chandler, Tx., U.S.	222	32.18 N	95.29 W
Chandler ≐	180	69.27 N	151.30 W
Chandler, Mount ∧[2]	162	27.00 S	133.20 E
Chandler Lake ⊜	180	68.15 N	152.43 W
Chandler Park ♠	281	42.24 N	82.58 W
Chandler's Cross	260	51.40 N	0.27 W
Chandler's Ford	42	50.59 N	1.23 W
Chandlers Valley	214	41.56 N	79.18 W
Chandlerville	219	40.02 N	90.09 W
Chandless ≐	248	9.08 S	69.51 W
Chāndor Hills ⋏[2]	122	20.30 N	74.00 E
Chandos Lake ⊜	212	44.49 N	78.00 W
Chāndpara	126	22.58 N	88.47 E
Chāndpur, Bngl.	120	22.08 N	91.55 E
Chāndpur, Bngl.	124	23.13 N	90.39 E
Chāndpur, India	124	29.09 N	78.16 E
Chāndpur ◆[8]	272a	28.45 N	77.01 E
Chāndra	126	22.28 N	87.09 E
Chandrabhāga ≐	123	32.59 N	76.25 E
Chandra Dighalia	126	23.04 N	89.46 E
Chandrakona	126	22.44 N	87.31 E
Chandrakona Road	126	22.44 N	87.21 E
Chandrapur	122	19.57 N	79.18 E
Chāndvad	122	20.20 N	74.15 E
Chandyga	74	62.40 N	135.36 E
Chanfang	105	39.56 N	115.55 E
Chang (Yangtze) ≐, Zhg.	90	31.48 N	121.10 E
Chang ≐, Zhg.	100	28.59 N	116.42 E
Chang ≐, Zhg.	100	26.53 N	119.41 E
Chang, Ko I	110	12.05 N	102.20 E
Changa	84	44.27 N	50.36 E
Changaj	88	47.52 N	99.28 E
Changajn nuruu ⋏	90	47.30 N	100.00 E
Changal	88	49.19 N	104.24 E
Changalane	156	26.17 S	32.11 E
Changan → Xi'an, Zhg.	102	34.15 N	108.52 E
Chang'an, Zhg.	102	26.00 N	109.34 E
Changanācheri	122	9.28 N	76.33 E
Changane ≐	156	24.43 S	33.32 E
Chang'anzhen	106	30.28 N	120.27 E
Changara	154	16.54 S	33.14 E
Changarul'skij chrebet ⋏	88	51.10 N	103.00 E
Changbai	98	41.26 N	128.11 E
Changbai Shan ⋏	98	41.40 N	128.00 E
Changbu	100	23.48 N	115.26 E
Changcaocun	105	39.49 N	115.47 E
Changchaoling	106	31.00 N	119.40 E
Changcheng, Zhg.	100	31.49 N	116.54 E
Changcheng, Zhg.	110	19.24 N	108.42 E
Chang Cheng (Great Wall) ⊥	98	40.30 N	116.30 E
Chang Chenmo ≐	120	34.17 N	78.19 E
Changchiak'ou → Zhangjiakou	105	40.50 N	114.53 E
Ch'angchih → Changzhi	102	36.11 N	113.08 E
Changchou → Zhangzhou	100	24.33 N	117.39 E
Changchow → Changzhou	106	31.47 N	119.57 E
Changchun	89	43.53 N	125.19 E
Changchunling	89	45.22 N	125.28 E
Changdan	98	37.56 N	126.45 E
Changdang Hu ⊜	106	31.35 N	119.35 E
Changdao (Sihou)	98	37.56 N	120.42 E

≐ River	Fluß	Río	Rivière	Rio
≊ Canal	Kanal	Canal	Canal	Canal
ᒪ Waterfall, Rapids	Wasserfall, Stromschnellen	Cascada, Rápidos	Chute d'eau, Rapides	Cascata, Rápidos
⊔ Strait	Meeresstraße	Estrecho	Détroit	Estreito
c Bay, Gulf	Bucht, Golf	Bahía, Golfo	Baie, Golfe	Baía, Golfo
⊜ Lake, Lakes	See, Seen	Lago, Lagos	Lac, Lacs	Lago, Lagos
⋮ Swamp	Sumpf	Pantano	Marais	Pântano
⌂ Ice Features, Glacier	Eis- und Gletscherformen	Accidentes Glaciales	Formes glaciaires	Acidentes glaciares
⫫ Other Hydrographic Features	Andere Hydrographische Objekte	Otros Elementos Hidrográficos	Autres données hydrographiques	Outros acidentes hidrográficos

✣ Submarine Features	Untermeerische Objekte	Accidentes Submarinos	Formes de relief sous-marin	Acidentes submarinos
□ Political Unit	Politische Einheit	Unidad Politica	Entité politique	Unidade política
⚲ Cultural Institution	Kulturelle Institution	Institución Cultural	Institution culturelle	Instituição cultural
⊥ Historical Site	Historische Stätte	Sitio Histórico	Site historique	Sitio histórico
♠ Recreational Site	Erholungs- und Ferienort	Sitio de Recreo	Centre de loisirs	Area de Lazer
⊠ Airport	Flughafen	Aeropuerto	Aéroport	Aeroporto
■ Military Installation	Militäranlage	Instalación Militar	Installation militaire	Instalação militar
◆ Miscellaneous	Verschiedenes	Misceláneo	Divers	Diversos

Changde 102 29.02 N 111.41 E
Changdian 105 40.01 N 116.32 E
Ch'angdo 98 38.30 N 127.40 E
Ch'ang-dong 98 39.03 N 126.34 E
Change Islands 186 49.40 N 54.25 W
Changeon ≃ 50 47.16 N 0.05 E
Changfeng 100 32.27 N 117.09 E
Changgang 100 24.38 N 113.05 E
Changgangzi 104 41.26 N 122.41 E
Changge 100 34.15 N 113.50 E
Changgi-ap > 98 36.05 N 129.34 E
Changgi-li 271b 37.35 N 126.44 E
Changgi-ri 271b 37.38 N 126.41 E
Changgou 105 39.34 N 115.53 E
Changgouyu 105 39.44 N 115.52 E
Changguandian 100 32.58 N 115.16 E
Changguowei 100 29.15 N 121.56 E
Changgye-ri 98 34.33 N 126.49 E
Changgyong Palace ⊌ 271b 37.36 N 127.00 E
Changhai 98 39.18 N 122.35 E
Chang-hai
→ Shanghai 106 31.14 N 121.28 E
Changhang 98 36.01 N 126.40 E
Changhe 106 30.11 N 120.11 E
Changhowŏn 98 37.08 N 127.39 E
Chang Hu ⊜ 100 30.15 N 112.35 E
Changhua, T'aiwan 100 24.05 N 120.32 E
Changhua, Zhg. 100 30.11 N 119.13 E
Changhŭng 98 34.41 N 126.52 E
Changhŭng-ni 98 40.24 N 128.19 E
Changi 271c 1.23 N 103.59 E
Changi, Tanjong > 271c 1.23 N 104.00 E
Changi International Airport ⊠ 271c 1.22 N 103.59 E
Changi Prison ⊌ 271c 1.22 N 103.58 E
Changji 86 44.01 N 87.19 E
Changjiang, Zhg. 100 25.19 N 113.56 E
Changjiang, Zhg. 110 19.17 N 109.02 E
Changjiangbu 100 30.52 N 113.43 E
Changjiapuzi 104 40.51 N 123.43 E
Changjiazhuang 105 40.35 N 115.24 E
Changjie 100 29.16 N 121.40 E
Changjing 106 31.45 N 120.29 E
Changjin-gang ≃ 98 41.24 N 127.45 E
Changjin-ŭp 98 40.23 N 127.15 E
Changkai 100 28.04 N 116.18 E
Changkalajier 85 40.09 N 76.59 E
Changkeng 106 30.19 N 121.57 E
Changkiakow
→ Zhangjiakou 105 40.50 N 114.53 E
Changlapod Pass)(124 30.08 N 87.06 E
Changle, Zhg. 98 36.42 N 118.49 E
Changle, Zhg. 100 29.25 N 120.37 E
Changle, Zhg. 100 26.00 N 119.31 E
Changlejie 100 28.52 N 113.19 E
Changleqiao 106 30.21 N 119.51 E
Changlezhen 106 31.56 N 121.15 E
Changli, Zhg. 98 36.57 N 119.45 E
Changli, Zhg. 98 39.43 N 119.11 E
Changling 89 44.15 N 123.58 E
Changlingfeng 105 40.11 N 118.24 E
Changlingji 100 32.30 N 114.54 E
Changlingzi, Zhg. 98 39.33 N 121.19 E
Changlingzi, Zhg. 98 39.47 N 122.43 E
Changlinhe 100 31.40 N 117.29 E
Changlun 114 6.26 N 100.26 E
Changmar 120 34.15 N 79.45 E
Changmong-ni 98 34.58 N 128.41 E
Changning, Zhg. 102 26.19 N 112.21 E
Changning, Zhg. 102 24.55 N 99.35 E
Changning (Anningqiao), Zhg. 102 28.21 N 104.53 E
Changning, Zhg. 105 39.59 N 114.55 E
Ch'angnyŏng 98 35.33 N 128.29 E
Changnyŏn-ni 98 38.37 N 125.16 E
Changokurt 72 61.58 N 64.18 E
Ch'angpin 100 23.19 N 121.27 E
Changping 105 40.14 N 116.14 E
Changputong 102 28.05 N 98.29 E
Ch'angp'yŏng-dong 98 41.27 N 127.31 E
Changqiao, Zhg. 100 24.15 N 117.39 E
Changqiao, Zhg. 100 26.49 N 118.50 E
Changqing 98 36.34 N 116.43 E
Changsa 102 19.51 N 110.53 E
Changsan-got > 98 38.08 N 124.39 E
Changsha, Zhg. 100 28.12 N 112.58 E
Changsha, Zhg. 100 24.13 N 116.07 E
Changshaba Shuiku ⊜[1] 107 29.42 N 104.40 E
Changshageng 107 30.00 N 104.35 E
Changshan, Zhg. 98 36.54 N 117.50 E
Changshan, Zhg. 100 28.55 N 118.30 E
Changshan, Zhg. 107 29.30 N 104.13 E
Changshan ≃ 100 28.57 N 118.50 E
Changshan Qundao II 98 39.00 N 122.45 E
Changsheng 100 26.16 N 116.01 E
Changshengqiao 107 29.31 N 106.39 E
Changshitai 104 42.33 N 120.43 E
Changshitou 102 35.03 N 99.11 E
Changshou 102 29.51 N 107.06 E
Changshoudian 100 31.26 N 112.35 E
Changshoujie 100 28.44 N 113.57 E
Changshu 106 31.39 N 120.45 E
Changshui 102 34.21 N 111.29 E
Changsŏng 98 35.20 N 126.49 E
Changsŏng-ni 98 40.58 N 127.04 E
Changsu 98 35.40 N 127.32 E
Changtai, Zhg. 100 28.34 N 118.37 E
Changtai, Zhg. 100 24.40 N 117.46 E
Changtai, Zhg. 104 41.34 N 122.00 E
Changtancun 104 41.33 N 123.02 E
Ch'angte
→ Changde 102 29.02 N 111.41 E
Changteh
→ Anyang 98 36.06 N 114.21 E
Changting, Zhg. 89 44.32 N 128.47 E
Changting, Zhg. 100 25.52 N 116.20 E
Changtumiao 102 43.30 N 114.34 E
Changuinola ≃ 236 9.28 N 82.27 W
Changwu, Zhg. 89 46.00 N 125.36 E
Changwu, Zhg. 102 35.09 N 107.42 E
Changxindianzhen 105 39.49 N 116.12 E
Changxing 106 31.01 N 119.54 E
Changxing Dao I, Zhg. 98 39.34 N 121.23 E
Changxing Dao I, Zhg. 106 31.24 N 121.42 E
Changxingdian, Zhg. 104 41.33 N 123.23 E
Changxingdian, Zhg. 104 41.27 N 121.44 E
Changxingzhen 104 41.40 N 122.14 E
Changxuanling 100 31.08 N 114.20 E
Changyi 98 36.51 N 119.23 E
Changyŏn 98 38.15 N 125.06 E
Changyuan 98 35.13 N 114.39 E
Changyukou 105 40.46 N 115.08 E
Changzhi 102 36.11 N 113.08 E
Changzhou (Changchow) 106 31.47 N 119.57 E
Chanhanga 152 16.04 S 14.07 E
Chanh Hung 269c 10.44 N 106.41 E
Chani 88 57.05 N 120.58 E
Chani ≃ 88 57.02 N 120.59 E
Chanino 76 54.13 N 36.37 E
Chanka, ozero (Xingkai Hu) ⊜ 89 45.00 N 132.24 E
Chankiang
→ Zhanjiang 102 21.16 N 110.28 E
Chankou 102 35.52 N 104.27 E
Chanlar 84 40.34 N 46.20 E
Channagiri 122 14.02 N 75.56 E
Channahon 216 41.26 N 88.14 W
Channapatna 122 12.39 N 77.13 E
Channel Country ◆[1] 166 24.45 S 141.00 E
Channel Islands II, Europe 43b 49.20 N 2.20 W
Channel Islands II, Ca., U.S. 204 33.30 N 119.15 W
Channel Islands National Park ♠ 204 33.28 N 119.02 W
Channel Lake 216 42.29 N 88.08 W
Channel North Basin ⊂ 174h 2.49 S 171.43 W
Channel-Port-aux-Basques 186 47.34 N 59.09 W
Channelview 222 29.46 N 95.06 W
Channing, Mi., U.S. 190 46.08 N 88.05 W
Channing, Tx., U.S. 196 35.41 N 102.20 W
Chānpādānga 126 22.50 N 87.58 E
Chantada 34 42.37 N 7.46 W
Chantajskoje, ozero ⊜ 74 68.20 N 91.00 E
Chantajskoje vodochranilišče ⊜[1] 72 68.00 N 88.00 E
Chantang 100 33.41 N 117.37 E
Chantau 86 44.13 N 73.51 E
Chanteloup 261 48.51 N 2.44 E
Chanteloup-les-Vignes 261 48.59 N 2.02 E
Chantengo, Laguna ⊂ 234 16.37 N 99.07 W
Chanthaburi 110 12.36 N 102.09 E
Chantilly 50 49.12 N 2.28 E
Chantonnay 32 46.41 N 1.03 W
Chantraine 58 48.10 N 6.26 E
Chantrans 58 47.03 N 6.09 E
Chantrey Inlet ⊂ 176 67.48 N 96.20 W
Chanty-Mansijsk 74 61.00 N 69.06 E
Chanty-Mansijskij Nacional'nyj Okrug □[8] 86 60.15 N 70.45 E
Chanujn ≃ 88 49.22 N 102.22 E
Chanumla 110 8.19 N 93.05 E
Chanute 198 37.40 N 95.27 W
Chanute Air Force Base ■ 216 40.18 N 88.09 W
Chanuwāla 123 32.44 N 73.08 E
Chanžonkovo 83 48.06 N 38.06 E
Chao ≃ 105 40.36 N 117.08 E
Chao, Isla I 248 8.45 S 78.47 W
Chao'an 100 23.41 N 116.38 E
Chaobai ≃ 105 39.48 N 117.08 E
Chaobai Xinhe ≃ 105 39.37 N 117.26 E
Chaocheng 98 36.05 N 115.35 E
Ch'aochou 100 22.33 N 120.32 E
Ch'aochou
→ Chao'an 100 23.41 N 116.38 E
Chao Hu ⊜ 100 31.31 N 117.33 E
Chaomidian 105 39.04 N 117.01 E
Chao Phraya ≃ 110 13.32 N 100.36 E
Chaor ≃ 89 46.48 N 123.37 E
Chaoshui, Zhg. 89 49.44 N 127.21 E
Chaoshui, Zhg. 98 37.42 N 120.55 E
Chaouen 148 35.10 N 5.16 W
Chaouen □[4] 148 35.15 N 5.00 W
Chaource 50 48.04 N 4.08 E
Chaoxian 100 31.36 N 117.52 E
Chaoyang, Zhg. 89 44.34 N 126.20 E
Chaoyang, Zhg. 100 23.17 N 116.37 E
Chaoyang, Zhg. 104 41.35 N 120.28 E
Chaoyangchuan 98 42.54 N 129.21 E
Chaoyangcun 89 50.02 N 124.16 E
Chaoyanggou 104 42.07 N 121.04 E
Chaoyangpo 89 43.37 N 124.42 E
Chaoyangshan 89 43.02 N 125.40 E
Chaozhuang 98 34.18 N 114.56 E
Chapada dos Guimarães 248 15.26 S 55.45 W
Chapadinha 250 3.44 S 43.21 W
Chapala 234 20.18 N 103.12 W
Chapala, Lago de ⊜ 234 20.15 N 103.00 W
Chaparé ≃ 248 15.58 S 64.42 W
Chapareillan 62 45.28 N 5.58 E
Chāparmukh 120 26.12 N 92.32 E
Chaparra 240p 21.10 N 76.29 W
Chaparra, Bahía de ⊂ 240p 21.13 N 76.31 W
Chaparral 246 3.43 N 75.28 W
Chapčeranga 88 49.42 N 112.24 E
Chapeauroux 62 44.50 N 3.44 E
Chapecó 252 27.06 S 52.36 W
Chapel-en-le-Frith 262 53.20 N 1.54 W
Chapelfell Top ∧ 44 54.41 N 2.13 W
Chapelhall 46 55.50 N 3.56 W
Chapel Hill, De., U.S. 285 39.42 N 75.44 W
Chapel Hill, N.C., U.S. 192 35.54 N 79.03 W
Chapel Hill, Tn., U.S. 194 35.37 N 86.41 W
Chapel Hill Channel ʯ 276 40.32 N 74.02 W
Chapelle Creek ≃ 198 44.16 N 99.55 W
Chapellerie 261 49.02 N 2.26 E
Chapel Oaks 284c 38.54 N 76.55 W
Chapel Point > 42 50.16 N 4.46 W
Chapel Saint Leonards 44 53.13 N 0.19 E
Chapelton 241q 18.05 N 77.16 W
Chapeltown, Eng., U.K. 44 53.28 N 1.28 W
Chapeltown, Eng., U.K. 262 53.38 N 2.24 W
Chapet 261 48.58 N 1.56 E
Chapéu, Ribeirão do ≃ 256 23.14 S 45.18 W
Chapicuy 252 31.39 S 57.54 W
Chapimarca 248 13.58 S 73.04 W
Chapin 219 39.46 N 90.24 W
Chapin, Lake ⊜ 216 41.56 N 86.21 W
Chaplain, Lake ⊜[1] 224 47.57 N 121.51 W
Chapleau 190 47.50 N 83.24 W
Chapleau ≃ 190 48.29 N 82.57 W
Chapleau, Lac ⊜ 206 46.14 N 74.57 W
Chaplin, Sk., Can. 184 50.28 N 106.40 W
Chaplin, Ct., U.S. 207 41.47 N 72.07 W
Chaplin ≃ 194 37.50 N 85.11 W
Chaplin Lake ⊜ 184 50.18 N 106.35 W
Chapman, Ks., U.S. 198 38.58 N 97.01 W
Chapman, Ne., U.S. 198 41.01 N 98.09 W
Chapman, Pa., U.S. 208 40.46 N 75.24 W
Chapman, Cape > 176 69.12 N 88.59 W
Chapman, Mount ∧ 182 51.50 N 118.20 W
Chapman College ⊌[2] 280 33.47 N 117.51 W
Chapman Creek ≃ 198 38.58 N 97.00 W
Chapman Lake ⊜ 184 56.58 N 98.12 W
Chapman's (Okwa) ≃ 156 22.30 S 23.00 E
Chapmanville 188 37.58 N 82.01 W
Chapman Woods 280 34.08 N 118.05 W
Chapo 196 29.17 N 104.20 W
Chaponval 261 49.04 N 2.09 E
Chappaqua 210 41.09 N 73.45 W
Chappell 198 41.05 N 102.28 W
Chappell Hill 222 30.09 N 96.16 W
Chāpra 126 23.32 N 88.33 E
Chapry 83 47.14 N 39.31 E
Chaptico Bay ⊂ 208 38.21 N 76.49 W
Chapultepec, Méx. 204 31.50 N 116.38 W
Chapultepec, Méx. 204 32.22 N 115.05 W
Chapultepec ∧ 234 23.27 N 103.04 W
Chapultepec, Bosque de ♠ 286a 19.25 N 99.12 W
Chapultepec, Castillo de ⊥ 286a 19.25 N 99.11 W
Chá Pungana 152 13.44 S 18.39 E
Chaqui 248 19.36 S 65.32 W
Chaquiago 252 27.32 S 66.21 W
Char ≃ 42 50.44 N 2.53 W
Char ⍑[4] 148 21.31 N 12.51 W
Charaa ≃ 88 49.38 N 105.49 E
Charabali 80 47.24 N 47.16 E
Chara-Chužar 88 52.30 N 99.39 E
Charadai 252 27.38 S 59.54 W
Charagua 248 19.48 S 63.13 W
Charagun 88 51.36 N 111.05 E
Char-Ajrag 102 45.49 N 109.17 E
Charal 88 51.58 N 96.39 E
Charalá 246 6.17 N 73.10 W
Charām 128 30.45 N 50.44 E
Charaña 248 17.36 S 69.28 W
Charanor 88 50.05 N 116.40 E
Charanpur 126 23.45 N 87.02 E
Charapán 234 19.41 N 102.06 W
Charapucu, Ilha I 250 0.18 S 50.48 W
Charata 252 27.13 S 61.12 W
Charauz 88 52.16 N 106.17 E
Charavines-les-Bains 62 45.26 N 5.31 E
Charazani
→ Amarete 248 15.14 S 68.58 W
Charazargaj 88 52.57 N 104.41 E
Charbala 74 64.07 N 120.19 E
Char Bansi 126 22.59 N 90.43 E
Charbatovo 88 53.46 N 106.00 E
Charbon 170 32.54 S 149.58 E
Charcana 248 15.15 S 73.04 W
Charcas 234 23.08 N 101.07 W
Charco Azul, Bahía de ⊂ 236 8.15 N 82.45 W
Charco Hondo 240m 18.25 N 66.43 W
Charcos de Figueroa 232 27.45 N 102.11 W
Charcos de Risa 232 26.15 N 103.10 W
Charcot Island I 9 69.45 S 75.15 W
Charcyzsk 83 48.02 N 38.09 E
Chard 42 50.53 N 2.58 W
Chardon 214 41.36 N 81.08 W
Charduār 120 26.52 N 92.46 E
Chardzhou
→ Čardžou 128 39.06 N 63.34 E
Charef, Oued V 148 34.07 N 2.05 W
Charente □[5] 32 45.40 N 0.10 E
Charente ≃ 32 45.57 N 1.05 W
Charente-Maritime □[5] 32 45.30 N 0.45 W
Charenton-du-Cher 32 46.44 N 2.38 E
Charenton-le-Pont 261 48.49 N 2.25 E
Charentonne ≃ 50 49.07 N 0.44 E
Charest ≃ 206 46.36 N 72.14 W
Chārghāt 126 24.17 N 88.45 E
Char Hāim 126 23.04 N 90.38 E
Chari ≃ 146 12.58 N 14.31 E
Chariāl Canal ≊ 272b 22.28 N 88.11 E
Chari-Baguirmi □[5] 146 11.30 N 16.30 E
Charik 88 54.15 N 101.39 E
Chārīkār 120 35.01 N 69.11 E
Charing 42 51.13 N 0.48 E
Charing Cross 214 42.20 N 82.06 W
Charino, S.S.S.R. 76 59.57 N 43.44 E
Charino, S.S.S.R. 82 54.33 N 37.52 E
Charistvala 84 42.26 N 43.02 E
Chariton 190 41.00 N 93.18 W
Chariton ≃ 194 39.19 N 92.57 W
Chariton, Mussel Fork ≃ 194 39.24 N 92.55 W
Charitonovo, S.S.S.R. 24 61.27 N 47.28 E
Charitonovo, S.S.S.R. 82 56.52 N 36.44 E
Charity 246 7.24 N 58.36 W
Charkhāri 124 25.24 N 79.45 E
Charkhi Dādri 124 28.37 N 76.16 E
Char'kin 80 48.46 N 51.49 E
Charkop ◆[8] 272c 19.13 N 72.49 E
Char'kov (Kharkov) 78 50.00 N 36.15 E
Char'kov □[4] 83 49.42 N 37.10 E
Charkow
→ Char'kov 78 50.00 N 36.15 E
Char Lākhpur 126 24.04 N 90.40 E
Charland, Lac ⊜ 206 46.52 N 74.11 W
Charlbury 42 51.53 N 1.29 W
Charl Cilliers 158 26.39 S 29.12 E
Charlemagne 206 45.43 N 73.29 W
Charlemont 207 42.37 N 72.52 W
Charleroi, Bel. 50 50.25 N 4.26 E
Charleroi, Pa., U.S. 214 40.08 N 79.53 W
Charleroi à Bruxelles, Canal de ≊ 50 50.51 N 4.19 E
Charles □[6] 208 38.32 N 76.59 W
Charles ≃ 207 42.22 N 71.03 W
Charles, Cape > 208 37.08 N 75.58 W
Charles, Lake ⊜ 278 42.15 N 87.58 W
Charles, Peak ∧ 162 32.52 S 121.11 E
Charlesbourg 206 46.51 N 71.16 W
Charles Branch ≃ 284c 38.47 N 76.48 W
Charles City, Ia., U.S. 190 43.03 N 92.40 W
Charles City, Va., U.S. 208 37.20 N 77.04 W
Charles City □[6] 208 37.20 N 77.02 W
Charles de Gaulle, Aéroport ⊠ 50 49.01 N 2.33 E
Charles Island I 176 62.40 N 74.15 W
Charles Lee Tilden Regional Park ♠ 282 37.54 N 122.15 W
Charles Mill Lake ⊜[1] 214 40.45 N 82.22 W
Charles Mound ∧[2] 190 42.30 N 90.14 W
Charles Point > 164 12.23 S 130.36 E
Charles Sound ʯ 172 45.02 S 167.04 E
Charleston, Austl. 168b 34.55 S 138.54 E
Charleston, N.Z. 172 41.54 S 171.26 E
Charleston, Ar., U.S. 194 35.17 N 94.02 W
Charleston, Il., U.S. 194 39.29 N 88.10 W
Charleston, Ms., U.S. 194 34.00 N 90.03 W
Charleston, Mo., U.S. 194 36.55 N 89.21 W
Charleston, S.C., U.S. 192 32.46 N 79.55 W
Charleston, W.V., U.S. 188 38.20 N 81.37 W
Charleston Air Force Base ■ 192 32.55 N 80.03 W
Charleston Lake ⊜ 212 44.32 N 76.00 W
Charleston Peak ∧ 204 36.16 N 115.42 W
Charlestown, Austl. 170 32.58 S 151.42 E
Charlestown, Ire. 48 53.57 N 8.49 W
Charlestown, St. C.-N. 238 17.08 N 62.37 W
Charlestown, S. Afr. 158 27.30 S 29.55 E
Charlestown, In., U.S. 218 38.27 N 85.40 W
Charlestown, Md., U.S. 208 39.34 N 75.58 W
Charlestown, N.H., U.S. 188 43.14 N 72.25 W
Charlestown, Pa., U.S. 285 40.06 N 75.33 W
Charlestown, R.I., U.S. 207 41.22 N 71.38 W
Charles Town, W.V., U.S. 188 39.17 N 77.51 W
Charlestown ◆[8] 283 42.23 N 71.04 W
Charlestown of Aberlour 46 57.28 N 3.14 W
Charlesworth 262 53.26 N 1.59 W
Charleville 166 26.24 S 146.15 E
Charleville
→ Ráth Luirc 48 52.21 N 8.41 W
Charleville-Mézières 56 49.46 N 4.43 E
Charlevoix 190 45.19 N 85.15 W
Charlevoix, Lake ⊜ 190 45.15 N 85.08 W
Charley ≃ 180 65.20 N 142.49 W
Charlie Bluff 216 42.50 N 88.58 W
Charlie Creek ≃ 220 27.21 N 81.49 W
Charlie Lake 182 56.16 N 120.57 W
Charlieu 32 46.10 N 4.10 E
Charlotte, Mi., U.S. 216 42.33 N 84.50 W
Charlotte, N.C., U.S. 192 35.13 N 80.50 W
Charlotte, Tn., U.S. 194 36.10 N 87.20 W
Charlotte, Tx., U.S. 196 28.51 N 98.42 W
Charlotte □[6] 220 26.54 N 81.58 W
Charlotte Amalie 240m 18.21 N 64.56 W
Charlotte Court House 192 37.03 N 78.39 W
Charlotte Creek ≃ 210 42.27 N 75.01 W
Charlotte Harbor 220 26.57 N 82.04 W
Charlotte Harbor ⊂ 220 26.45 N 82.12 W
Charlotte Lake ⊜ 182 52.11 N 125.20 W
Charlottenberg 26 59.53 N 12.17 E
Charlottenburg 250 5.51 N 54.46 W
Charlottenburg ◆[8] 264a 52.31 N 13.16 E
Charlottenburg, Schloss ⊥ 264a 52.31 N 13.14 E
Charlottesburg Reservoir ⊜[1] 276 41.02 N 74.26 W
Charlottes Pass ♠ 171b 36.25 S 145.20 E
Charlottesville, In., U.S. 218 39.47 N 85.36 W
Charlottesville, Va., U.S. 192 38.01 N 78.28 W
Charlottetown, P.E., Can. 186 46.14 N 63.08 W
Charlotte Town (Gouyave), Gren. 241k 12.10 N 61.44 W
Charlotteville 210 42.33 N 74.40 W
Charlovka 24 68.47 N 37.15 E
Charlton, Austl. 166 36.16 S 143.21 E
Charlton, Ma., U.S. 207 42.08 N 71.58 W
Charlton ◆[8] 260 51.29 N 0.02 E
Charlton City 207 42.08 N 71.59 W
Charlton Island I 176 52.00 N 79.30 W
Charlton Kings 42 51.53 N 2.03 W
Charlu 24 61.48 N 30.52 E
Charly-sur-Marne 50 48.58 N 3.17 E
Charm 214 40.30 N 81.47 W
Charmentray 261 48.57 N 2.47 E
Charmes 58 48.22 N 6.17 E
Charmes-sur-Rhône 62 44.52 N 4.50 E
Charmey 58 46.38 N 7.10 E
Charminster 42 50.43 N 2.28 W
Charmois-l'Orgueilleux 58 48.06 N 6.16 E
Charmont-en-Beauce 50 48.14 N 2.06 E
Charmouth 42 50.45 N 2.55 W
Charnay-lès-Mâcon 58 46.18 N 4.47 E
Charneca 266c 38.44 N 9.27 W
Charneca ◆[8] 266c 38.47 N 9.08 W
Charnley ≃ 164 16.25 S 124.57 E
Charnock Richard 262 53.38 N 2.41 W
Char nuur ⊜, Mong. 88 48.20 N 96.05 E
Char nuur ⊜, Mong. 88 48.06 N 93.12 E
Charnwood Forest ◆[3] 42 52.43 N 1.15 W
Charny, P.Q., Can. 206 46.43 N 71.16 W
Charny, Fr. 50 47.53 N 3.06 E
Charny, Fr. 261 48.58 N 2.46 E
Charny-sur-Meuse 56 49.12 N 5.22 E
Charo 234 19.45 N 101.03 W
Charolles 32 46.26 N 4.17 E
Charouine 148 29.01 N 0.16 W
Charovsk 76 59.59 N 40.11 E
Charpi ≃ 89 49.40 N 136.10 E
Charquemont 58 47.13 N 6.49 E
Charred Oak Estates 284c 39.00 N 77.10 W
Charrette Creek ≃ 219 38.37 N 91.03 W
Charron Lake ⊜ 184 52.45 N 95.15 W
Charroux 32 46.09 N 0.24 E
Chars 50 49.10 N 1.56 E
Chārsadda 123 34.09 N 71.44 E
Charter Oak, Ca., U.S. 280 34.06 N 117.52 W
Charter Oak, Ia., U.S. 198 42.04 N 95.35 W
Charters Towers 166 20.05 S 146.16 E
Charterwood 279b 40.33 N 80.00 W
Chartiers Creek ≃ 214 40.28 N 80.03 W
Chartiers Run ≃, Pa., U.S. 279b 40.15 N 80.12 W
Chartiers Run ≃, Pa., U.S. 279b 40.36 N 79.43 W
Chartley 207 41.56 N 71.13 W
Chartres 50 48.27 N 1.30 E
Chartrettes 50 48.29 N 2.42 E
Chartridge 260 51.44 N 0.39 W
Chart Sutton 260 51.13 N 0.35 E
Chartwell ⊥ 260 51.14 N 0.05 E
Char Us nuur ⊜ 90 48.00 N 92.10 E
Charutajuvom 24 66.49 N 59.30 E
Chās 126 23.38 N 86.10 E
Chasav'urt 84 43.15 N 46.37 E
Chascomús 258 35.34 S 58.01 W
Chascomús, Laguna ⊜ 258 35.36 S 58.01 W
Chašdala 85 39.42 N 67.07 E
Chase, B.C., Can. 182 50.49 N 119.41 W
Chase, Ak., U.S. 180 62.27 N 150.07 W
Chase, Ks., U.S. 198 38.21 N 98.20 W
Chase, Md., U.S. 208 39.21 N 76.22 W
Chase, Mount ∧ 188 46.07 N 68.29 W
Chase Brook ≃ 283 42.48 N 71.27 W
Chase City 192 36.47 N 78.27 W
Chase Field Naval Air Station ■ 196 28.21 N 97.40 W
Chasefu 154 11.55 S 33.08 E
Chase Lake 212 43.46 N 75.19 W
Chase River 224 49.08 N 123.55 W
Chashma Barrage ◆[6] 123 32.26 N 71.23 E
Chasicó 254 40.18 S 68.58 W
Chasidaba 104 42.19 N 121.19 E
Chaska 190 44.47 N 93.36 W
Chaslands Mistake > 172 46.38 S 169.22 E
Chasŏng 98 41.27 N 126.37 E
Chasŏngganggu 98 41.34 N 126.36 E
Chassahowitzka 220 28.43 N 82.34 W
Chassahowitzka Bay ⊂ 220 28.41 N 82.40 W
Chassahowitzka Swamp ≡ 220 28.38 N 82.37 W
Chasseron, Mont ∧ 58 46.51 N 6.33 E
Chasse-sur-Rhône 62 45.34 N 4.49 E
Chassezac ≃ 62 44.26 N 4.19 E
Chašuri 84 42.00 N 43.36 E
Chasurta 88 52.17 N 108.52 E
Chasuta 248 6.35 S 76.11 W
Chāt 128 37.59 N 55.16 E
Chatanbulag 102 43.09 N 109.08 E
Chatanga 74 71.58 N 102.30 E
Chatanga ≃ 74 72.55 N 106.00 E
Chatangskij zaliv ⊂ 74 73.30 N 109.00 E
Chatanika 180 65.07 N 147.31 W
Chatanika ≃ 180 65.04 N 149.18 W
Château-Arnoux 62 44.06 N 6.00 E
Chateaubelair 241h 13.17 N 61.15 W
Chateaubelair Bay ⊂ 241h 13.17 N 61.15 W
Châteaubriant 32 47.43 N 1.23 W
Château-Chinon 32 47.04 N 3.56 E
Château d'Oex 58 46.28 N 7.08 E
Château-du-Loir 50 47.42 N 0.25 E
Châteaudun 50 48.05 N 1.20 E
Châteaufort 261 48.44 N 2.06 E
Chateaugay 206 44.55 N 74.04 W
Château-Gontier 32 47.50 N 0.42 W
Châteauguay 206 45.23 N 73.45 W
Châteauguay □[6] 206 45.15 N 73.45 W
Châteauguay ≃ 188 45.24 N 73.45 W
Châteauguay-Centre 206 45.21 N 73.45 W
Châteauguay Heights 275a 45.23 N 73.44 W
Château-Landon 50 48.09 N 2.42 E
Château-la-Vallière 50 47.33 N 0.19 E
Châteaulin 32 48.12 N 4.05 W
Châteaumeillant 32 46.34 N 2.12 E
Châteauneuf 62 43.23 N 5.10 E
Châteauneuf-de-Randon 62 44.39 N 3.40 E
Châteauneuf-du-Pape 62 44.03 N 4.50 E
Châteauneuf-du-Rhône 62 44.29 N 4.43 E
Châteauneuf-en-Thymerais 50 48.35 N 1.15 E
Châteauneuf-sur-Charente 32 45.36 N 0.03 W
Châteauneuf-sur-Loire 50 47.52 N 2.14 E
Châteauneuf-sur-Sarthe 32 47.41 N 0.30 W
Châteauneuf-Val-de-Bargis 50 47.17 N 3.14 E
Château-Porcien 50 49.32 N 4.15 E
Château-Queyras 62 44.45 N 6.47 E
Châteauredon 62 44.01 N 6.13 E
Châteaurenard, Fr. 50 47.56 N 2.56 E
Châteaurenard, Fr. 62 43.53 N 4.51 E
Château-Renault 50 47.35 N 0.55 E
Château-Richer 186 46.58 N 71.01 W
Châteauroux 32 46.49 N 1.42 E
Château-Salins 56 48.49 N 6.30 E
Château-Thierry 50 49.03 N 3.24 E
Châteauvillain 58 48.02 N 4.55 E
Châtel 58 46.17 N 6.50 E
Châtel-Censoir 50 47.31 N 3.38 E
Châtelet 50 50.24 N 4.31 E
Châtelineau 56 50.25 N 4.31 E
Châtellerault 32 46.49 N 0.33 E
Châtel-Saint-Denis 58 46.32 N 6.54 E
Châtel-sur-Moselle 58 48.18 N 6.24 E
Châtelus-Malvaleix 32 46.18 N 2.01 E
Châtenay-en-France 261 49.04 N 2.27 E
Châtenay-Malabry 261 48.46 N 2.17 E
Châtenois, Fr. 58 48.18 N 5.50 E
Châtenois, Fr. 58 48.16 N 7.24 E
Châtenois-les-Forges 58 47.34 N 6.51 E
Chatfield, Mn., U.S. 190 43.50 N 92.11 W
Chatfield, Oh., U.S. 214 40.57 N 82.56 W
Chatgal 88 50.26 N 100.09 E
Chatham, N.B., Can. 186 47.02 N 65.28 W
Chatham, On., Can. 214 42.24 N 82.11 W
Chatham, Eng., U.K. 42 51.23 N 0.32 E
Chatham, Il., U.S. 219 39.40 N 89.42 W
Chatham, La., U.S. 194 32.18 N 92.27 W
Chatham, Ma., U.S. 207 41.40 N 69.57 W
Chatham, N.J., U.S. 210 40.44 N 74.23 W
Chatham, N.Y., U.S. 210 42.21 N 73.35 W
Chatham, Oh., U.S. 214 41.06 N 82.01 W
Chatham, Pa., U.S. 208 39.51 N 75.49 W
Chatham, Va., U.S. 192 36.49 N 79.23 W
Chatham ◆[8] 278 41.45 N 87.37 W
Chatham ≃ 220 25.42 N 81.17 W
Chatham, Isla I 254 50.40 S 74.20 W
Chatham Head 186 47.00 N 65.33 W
Chatham Islands II 14 43.55 S 176.30 W
Chatham Rise ◆[3] 14 43.30 S 178.00 W
Chatham Sound ʯ 182 54.32 N 130.35 W
Chatham Strait ʯ 180 57.30 N 134.45 W
Chatian 100 27.54 N 118.58 E
Châtillon, Fr. 261 48.48 N 2.17 E
Châtillon, It. 62 45.45 N 7.37 E
Châtillon-Coligny 50 47.50 N 2.51 E
Châtillon-en-Bazois 32 47.03 N 3.40 E
Châtillon-en-Diois 62 44.41 N 5.28 E
Châtillon-la-Borde 261 48.33 N 2.49 E
Châtillon-sur-Chalaronne 58 46.07 N 4.58 E
Châtillon-sur-Indre 32 46.59 N 1.11 E
Châtillon-sur-Loire 50 47.35 N 2.45 E
Châtillon-sur-Marne 50 49.06 N 3.45 E
Châtillon-sur-Seine 58 47.51 N 4.33 E
Chating 106 31.21 N 119.25 E
Chātmohar 126 24.13 N 89.15 E
Chat Moss ◆[3] 262 53.27 N 2.27 W
Chato, Cerro ∧ 254 42.29 S 72.01 W
Chatom 194 31.27 N 88.15 W
Chatonville 261 48.33 N 1.52 E
Chatou 261 48.54 N 2.09 E
Chatpur ◆[8] 272b 22.36 N 88.22 E
Chatra, India 124 24.13 N 84.52 E
Chatra, India 272b 22.46 N 88.20 E
Châtres 261 48.43 N 2.49 E
Chats, Lac des ⊜ 212 45.28 N 76.23 W
Chatsquot Mountain ∧ 182 53.08 N 127.30 W
Chatswood 274a 33.48 S 151.12 E
Chatsworth, Austl. 166 21.58 S 140.19 E
Chatsworth, On., Can. 212 44.27 N 80.54 W
Chatsworth, Ga., U.S. 192 34.45 N 84.46 W
Chatsworth, Il., U.S. 216 40.45 N 88.17 W
Chatsworth, N.J., U.S. 208 39.49 N 74.32 W
Chatsworth, Zimb. 154 19.38 S 31.13 E
Chatsworth ◆[8] 280 34.15 N 118.36 W
Chatsworth Reservoir ⊜[1] 228 34.14 N 118.37 W
Chattahoochee 192 30.42 N 84.50 W
Chattahoochee ≃ 192 30.52 N 84.57 W
Chattanooga, Oh., U.S. 216 40.38 N 84.47 W
Chattanooga, Tn., U.S. 194 35.02 N 85.18 W
Chattaroy 192 37.42 N 82.16 W
Chattenden 260 51.25 N 0.32 E
Chatteris 42 52.27 N 0.03 E
Châttillon-de-Michaille 58 46.08 N 5.47 E
Chattolanee 284b 39.24 N 76.45 W
Chatton 44 55.33 N 1.55 W
Chatun' 82 55.00 N 37.50 E
Chaturat 110 15.34 N 101.51 E
Chatwood 208 39.58 N 75.35 W
Chatyrka 74 62.03 N 175.15 E
Chaubaria 126 22.59 N 88.40 E
Chaubourg, Mount ∧[2] 241f 14.02 N 60.57 W
Chauconin 261 48.58 N 2.51 E
Chaudes-Aigues 32 44.51 N 3.00 E
Chaudfontaine 56 50.35 N 5.38 E
Chaudière ≃ 186 46.45 N 71.17 W
Chau Doc 110 10.42 N 105.07 E
Chauekuktuli, Lake ⊜ 180 60.03 N 158.45 W
Chauffayer 62 44.45 N 6.01 E
Chaugācha, Bngl. 126 23.16 N 89.01 E
Chaugācha, Bngl. 126 23.16 N 89.01 E
Chauhtan 120 25.29 N 71.04 E
Chauk 110 20.54 N 94.50 E
Chaukhandi 272a 28.37 N 77.24 E
Chaullay 248 12.57 S 72.39 W
Chaulnes 50 49.49 N 2.48 E
Chaumergy 58 46.51 N 5.29 E
Chaumes-en-Brie 261 48.40 N 2.51 E
Chaumont, Fr. 58 48.07 N 5.08 E
Chaumont, N.Y., U.S. 212 44.04 N 76.07 W
Chaumont ≃ 212 44.04 N 76.08 W
Chaumont Bay ⊂ 212 44.02 N 76.13 W
Chaumont-en-Vexin 50 49.16 N 1.53 E
Chaumont-Porcien 50 49.39 N 4.15 E
Chaumont-sur-Aire 56 48.56 N 5.15 E
Chaumont-sur-Loire 50 47.29 N 1.11 E
Chaumont-sur-Tharonne 50 47.37 N 1.54 E
Chaumua 272b 22.39 N 88.33 E
Chauncey 188 39.23 N 82.07 W
Chaŭn-do I 98 34.53 N 126.03 E
Chaungwabyin 110 13.41 N 98.22 E
Chaungzon 110 16.22 N 97.32 E
Chauny 50 49.37 N 3.13 E
Chaupāran 124 24.23 N 85.15 E
Chaussin 58 46.58 N 5.25 E
Chausu-yama ∧ 94 35.14 N 137.39 E
Chausuyama-kofun ⊥ 94 36.25 N 139.50 E
Chautārā 124 27.46 N 85.42 E
Chautauqua 214 42.12 N 79.28 W
Chautauqua □[6] 214 42.15 N 79.30 W
Chautauqua Creek ≃ 214 42.20 N 79.36 W
Chautauqua Lake ⊜ 214 42.12 N 79.27 W
Chauvigny 32 46.34 N 0.39 E
Chauvin, Ab., Can. 184 52.42 N 110.07 W
Chauvin, La., U.S. 194 29.26 N 90.35 W
Chauvirey-le-Châtel 58 47.47 N 5.45 E
Chauvry 261 49.03 N 2.16 E
Chavakkad 122 10.32 N 76.06 E
Chaval 250 3.02 S 41.15 W
Chavanges 58 48.31 N 4.34 E
Chavannes, Lac ⊜ 190 46.51 N 77.10 W
Chavarría, Arg. 252 28.57 S 58.35 W
Chavarría, Perú 286d 12.01 S 77.05 W
Chavast 85 40.13 N 68.50 E
Chavenay 261 48.51 N 1.59 E
Chavenay-Villepreux, Aérodrome de ⊠ 261 48.51 N 1.58 E
Chavertovo 82 54.17 N 39.12 E
Chaves, Bra. 250 0.10 S 49.55 W
Chaves, Port. 34 41.44 N 7.28 W
Chaves, Ribeirão dos ≃ 256 21.24 S 44.29 W
Chaville 261 48.48 N 2.10 E
Chaviña 248 14.59 S 73.50 W
Chavinda 234 20.01 N 102.27 W
Cháviva 246 4.22 N 72.20 W
Chavki 82 54.20 N 38.13 E
Chavornay 58 46.43 N 6.34 E
Chavuma 152 13.05 S 22.40 E
Chawa'nanake 120 31.36 N 89.41 E
Chawang 110 8.25 N 99.30 E
Chawinda 123 32.21 N 74.42 E
Chay ≃ 110 21.39 N 105.12 E
Chayanta 248 18.27 S 66.30 W
Chayuan, Zhg. 100 29.20 N 121.34 E
Chayuan, Zhg. 100 27.40 N 112.57 E
Chayue 106 30.49 N 119.21 E
Chazay-d'Azergues 62 45.53 N 4.37 E
Chazelles-sur-Lyon 62 45.38 N 4.23 E
Chazratišoch, chrebet ⋏ 85 38.30 N 70.15 E
Chazumba 234 18.12 N 97.40 W
Chazy 188 44.53 N 73.26 W
Chbar ≃ 110 13.19 N 107.05 E
Cheadle, Eng., U.K. 42 52.59 N 1.59 W
Cheadle, Eng., U.K. 262 53.24 N 2.13 W
Cheadle Hulme 262 53.22 N 2.12 W
Cheaha Mountain ∧ 194 33.30 N 85.47 W
Cheakamus Indian Reserve ◆[4] 182 49.48 N 123.11 W
Cheam ◆[8] 260 51.21 N 0.13 W
Cheam View 224 49.15 N 121.41 W
Cheapside 222 29.17 N 97.24 W
Cheat ≃ 188 39.45 N 79.54 W
Cheat, Shavers Fork ≃ 188 39.06 N 79.33 W
Cheb 54 50.01 N 12.25 E
Chebacco Lake ⊜ 283 42.37 N 70.48 W
Chebanse 216 41.00 N 87.54 W
Chebba 148 35.14 N 10.02 E
Chebeigou 89 43.28 N 127.04 E
Chebogue Point > 186 43.45 N 66.07 W
Cheboksary
→ Čeboksary 80 56.09 N 47.15 E
Cheboygan 190 45.38 N 84.28 W
Chech, Erg ◆[2] 148 25.00 N 2.15 W
Ch'ech'eng 100 22.05 N 120.42 E
Chech'on 98 37.08 N 128.12 E
Chęciny 30 50.48 N 20.28 E
Checleset Bay ⊂ 182 50.03 N 127.40 W
Checoslovaquia
→ Czechoslovakia □[1] 30 49.30 N 17.00 E
Checotah 196 35.28 N 95.31 W
Chedabucto Bay ⊂ 186 45.23 N 61.10 W
Chedaoyu 105 40.22 N 117.57 E
Cheddar 42 51.17 N 2.46 W
Cheddleton 44 53.04 N 2.02 W
Cheduba Island I 110 18.48 N 93.38 E
Cheduba Strait ʯ 110 18.56 N 93.45 E
Chedun 100 24.09 N 117.19 E
Chée ≃ 56 48.45 N 4.39 E
Cheektowaga 210 42.55 N 78.46 W
Cheepie 166 26.39 S 145.01 E
Cheesequake 276 40.25 N 74.17 W
Cheesequake Creek ≃ 276 40.28 N 74.16 W
Cheesequake State Park ♠ 276 40.26 N 74.16 W
Cheetham Hill ◆[8] 262 53.31 N 2.15 W
Chefang, Zhg. 104 41.35 N 121.26 E
Chefang, Zhg. 106 31.15 N 120.45 E
Chef-Boutonne 32 46.07 N 0.04 W
Chefoo
→ Yantai 98 37.33 N 121.20 E
Chefornak 180 60.13 N 164.12 W
Chefumage ≃ 152 12.15 S 22.19 E
Chefuzwe 156 17.38 S 24.30 E
Chegar Perah 114 4.25 N 101.56 E
Chegga ⍑[4] 148 25.30 N 5.46 W
Chegutu 154 18.10 S 30.14 E
Chehalis 224 46.39 N 122.57 W
Chehalis ≃ 224 46.57 N 123.50 W
Chehalis, South Fork ≃ 224 46.40 N 123.15 W
Chehalis Indian Reservation ◆[4] 224 46.49 N 123.13 W
Chehe 102 25.00 N 107.38 E
Chehel Dokhtarān 128 35.06 N 62.19 E
Cheheqiao 105 40.21 N 118.16 E
Cheil, Ras el > 144 7.44 N 49.50 E
Cheine 54 52.52 N 11.04 E
Cheiron, Cime du ∧ 62 43.49 N 6.58 E
Chejiatun 104 41.57 N 123.01 E
Chejiawopeng 104 42.29 N 123.07 E
Cheju 90 33.31 N 126.32 E
Cheju-do I 90 33.20 N 126.30 E
Chekiang
→ Zhejiang □[4] 100 29.00 N 120.00 E
Chek Jawa, Tanjong > 271c 1.24 N 104.00 E
Chek Kang 271d 22.26 N 114.21 E
Chela, Serra da ∧ 152 16.00 S 13.10 E
Chelan 202 47.50 N 120.00 W
Chelan □[6] 224 47.56 N 120.52 W
Chelan, Lake ⊜ 202 48.05 N 120.30 W
Chelas ◆[8] 266c 38.45 N 9.07 W
Cheleiros 266c 38.53 N 9.20 W
Cheleiros, Ribeira de ≃ 266c 38.54 N 9.22 W
Chelelektu 144 6.00 N 38.09 E
Chelford 262 53.16 N 2.16 W
Chelforó 252 39.04 S 66.32 W
Chelghoum el Aïd 148 36.10 N 6.10 E
Chéliff, Oued ≃ 148 36.01 N 0.07 E
Chelīk-e Yās Khān 120 37.05 N 66.14 E
Chellaston 42 52.53 N 1.27 W
Chelles 50 48.53 N 2.36 E
Chelles-le-Pin, Aérodrome de ⊠ 261 48.55 N 2.35 E
Chełm 30 51.10 N 23.28 E
Chełm □[4] 30 51.20 N 23.20 E
Chelmer ≃ 260 51.48 N 0.40 E
Chelmer and Blackwater Navigation ≊ 260 51.44 N 0.43 E
Chełmno 30 53.22 N 18.26 E
Chelmorton 262 53.13 N 1.50 W
Chelmsford, On., Can. 190 46.35 N 81.12 W
Chelmsford, Eng., U.K. 260 51.44 N 0.28 E
Chelmsford, Ma., U.S. 207 42.35 N 71.21 W
Chelmsford □[8] 260 51.44 N 0.30 E
Chelmsford Dam ⊜[1] 158 28.02 S 29.52 E
Chełmża 30 53.12 N 18.37 E
Chelsea, Austl. 169 38.03 S 145.07 E
Chelsea, Ia., U.S. 190 41.55 N 92.23 W
Chelsea, Ma., U.S. 207 42.23 N 71.02 W
Chelsea, Mi., U.S. 216 42.19 N 84.01 W
Chelsea, Ok., U.S. 196 36.32 N 95.25 W
Chelsea, Pa., U.S. 285 39.52 N 75.28 W
Chelsea, Vt., U.S. 188 43.59 N 72.26 W
Chelsea Estates 208 39.41 N 75.36 W
Chelsea Park 224 47.28 N 122.21 W
Chelsfield ◆[8] 260 51.21 N 0.08 E
Cheltenham, Austl. 274a 33.46 S 151.05 E
Cheltenham, Austl. 274b 37.58 S 145.03 E
Cheltenham, Eng., U.K. 42 51.54 N 2.04 W
Cheltenham, Md., U.S. 208 38.44 N 76.49 W
Cheltenham, Pa., U.S. 208 40.03 N 75.05 W
Chel'ul'ja 26 61.44 N 30.41 E
Chelvand 128 38.18 N 48.50 E
Chelyabinsk
→ Čel'abinsk 86 55.10 N 61.24 E
Chelyāma 126 23.37 N 86.33 E
Chelyan 188 38.11 N 81.29 W
Chelyuskintsy Ice Tongue ⊓ 9 66.20 S 82.00 E
Chemaïa 148 32.05 N 8.37 W
Chemainus 224 48.55 N 123.43 W
Chemainus ⊜ 224 48.53 N 123.41 W
Chemaogang 106 31.33 N 121.52 E
Chemax 232 20.39 N 87.56 W
Chemba 154 17.08 S 34.52 E
Chembūr ◆[8] 272c 19.04 N 72.54 E
Chemchâm, Sebkhet ⊜ 148 21.05 N 12.05 W
Chemčik ≃ 86 51.47 N 92.00 E
Chemehuevi Indian Reservation ◆[4] 204 34.30 N 114.23 W
Chemillé 32 47.13 N 0.44 W
Chemin 58 46.59 N 5.19 E
Cheminis, Colline ∧[2] 190 48.08 N 79.31 W
Chemnitz
→ Karl-Marx-Stadt 54 50.50 N 12.55 E
Chemnitz ≃ 54 50.59 N 12.47 E
Chemor 114 4.43 N 101.07 E
Chemulpo
→ Inch'ŏn 98 37.28 N 126.38 E
Chemult 202 43.13 N 121.46 W
Chemung, Il., U.S. 216 42.25 N 88.40 W
Chemung, N.Y., U.S. 210 42.01 N 76.37 W

Symbols in the index entries represent the broad categories identified in the key at the right. Symbols with superior numbers (⋏[1]) identify subcategories (see complete key on page I · 1).

Symbole im Register stellen die rechts im Schlüssel erklärten Kategorien dar. Symbole mit hochgestellten Ziffern (⋏[1]) bezeichnen Unterabteilungen einer Kategorie (vgl. vollständiger Schlüssel auf Seite I · 1).

Los símbolos incluídos en el texto del índice representan las grandes categorias identificadas con la clave a la derecha. Los símbolos con numeros en su parte superior (⋏[1]) identifican las subcategorías (véase la clave completa en la página I · 1).

Les symboles de l'index représentent les catégories indiquées dans la légende à droite. Les symboles suivis d'un indice (⋏[1]) représentent des sous-catégories (voir légende complète à la page I · 1).

Os símbolos incluídos no texto do índice representam as grandes categorias identificadas com a chave à direita. Os símbolos com números em sua parte superior (⋏[1]) identificam as subcategorias (veja-se a chave completa à página I · 1).

∧ Mountain	Berg	Montaña	Montagne	Montanha
⋏ Mountains	Gebirge	Montañas	Montagnes	Montanhas
)(Pass	Paß	Paso	Col	Passo
V Valley, Canyon	Tal, Cañon	Valle, Cañón	Vallée, Canyon	Vale, Canhão
≃ Plain	Ebene	Llano	Plaine	Planície
> Cape	Kap	Cabo	Cap	Cabo
I Island	Insel	Isla	Île	Ilha
II Islands	Inseln	Islas	Îles	Ilhas
◆ Other Topographic Features	Andere Topographische Objekte	Otros Elementos Topográficos	Autres données topographiques	Outros acidentes topográficos

Chem-Chin I · 35

ESPAÑOL: Nombre | Página | Lat.°′ | Long.°′ W = Oeste

FRANÇAIS: Nom | Page | Lat.°′ | Long.°′ W = Ouest

PORTUGUÊS: Nome | Página | Lat.°′ | Long.°′ W = Oeste

Nombre / Nom / Nome	Página / Page	Lat.°′	Long.°′ W = Oeste
Chemung □[6]	210	42.06 N	76.49 W
Chemung ≃	210	41.55 N	76.31 W
Chemung County Airport ⊠	210	42.10 N	76.53 W
Chemung Lake ⊜	212	44.25 N	78.22 W
Chena, Cerro de ∧	286e	33.36 N	70.45 W
Chenāb ≃	123	29.23 N	71.02 E
Chenachane	148	26.00 N	4.15 W
Chenail Ecarté ≃[1]	214	42.28 N	82.29 W
Chenango □[6]	210	42.32 N	75.31 W
Chenango ≃	210	42.05 N	75.55 W
Chenango Bridge	210	42.10 N	75.51 W
Chenango Forks	210	42.14 N	75.50 W
Chenango Valley State Park ♠	210	42.14 N	75.50 W
Chenārān	128	36.39 N	59.06 E
Chenaut	258	34.15 S	59.13 W
Chen Barag Qi	89	49.21 N	119.31 E
Chenbofang	98	37.27 N	115.18 E
Chencai	100	29.37 N	120.22 E
Chenchiang → Zhenjiang	106	32.13 N	119.26 E
Chencun	100	22.58 N	113.13 E
Chendai	100	23.48 N	117.24 E
Chendauli ✶[8]	272c	19.07 N	72.54 E
Chenderiang	114	4.16 N	101.14 E
Chenderoh, Tasek ⊜	114	4.58 N	100.57 E
Chêne, Rivière du ≃, P.Q., Can.	206	46.34 N	72.00 W
Chêne, Rivière du ≃, P.Q., Can.	206	45.33 N	73.54 W
Chenele	152	12.54 S	23.54 E
Chenequa	216	43.06 N	88.23 W
Chénéville	206	45.53 N	75.03 W
Cheney, Ks., U.S.	198	37.37 N	97.46 W
Cheney, Wa., U.S.	202	47.29 N	117.34 W
Cheney Reservoir ⊜[1]	198	37.45 N	97.50 W
Cheneys Point	214	42.08 N	79.24 W
Cheneyville	194	31.00 N	92.17 W
Chenfang	100	28.01 N	117.32 E
Cheng'an	98	36.27 N	114.41 E
Chengannūr	122	9.20 N	76.38 E
Chengbu	102	26.18 N	110.13 E
Chengchow → Zhengzhou	102	34.48 N	113.39 E
Chengde (Xiabancheng), Zhg.	105	40.47 N	118.08 E
Chengde, Zhg.	105	40.58 N	117.53 E
Chengdu (Chengtu)	107	30.39 N	104.04 E
Chengele	120	28.47 N	96.16 E
Chenggang	100	26.32 N	115.26 E
Chenggu	102	33.10 N	107.22 E
Chenghai	100	23.30 N	116.46 E
Cheng Hu ⊜	106	31.13 N	120.49 E
Chenghuang	102	22.32 N	109.39 E
Chengjia	100	24.50 N	112.50 E
Chengjiahe	100	32.18 N	112.27 E
Chengjiang	102	24.45 N	102.54 E
Chengjiangzhen	107	29.52 N	106.23 E
Chengjiazhen	107	29.24 N	104.36 E
Chengkou	102	31.54 N	108.41 E
Chenglingji	100	29.26 N	113.09 E
Chenglong	100	24.51 N	114.41 E
Chengmai	110	19.48 N	110.02 E
Chengmao	106	31.10 N	120.53 E
Chengpu	100	25.46 N	118.48 E
Chengqian	98	35.21 N	117.21 E
Chengqianwei	100	28.09 N	116.13 E
Chengshan Jiao ≻	98	37.24 N	122.42 E
Chengteh → Chengde	105	40.58 N	117.53 E
Chengtu → Chengdu	107	30.39 N	104.04 E
Ch'engtzuliao	269d	25.06 N	121.27 E
Chengwu	98	34.58 N	115.52 E
Chengxian	102	33.43 N	105.41 E
Chengxi Hu ⊜	100	32.24 N	116.15 E
Chengyang, Zhg.	98	36.18 N	120.22 E
Chengyang, Zhg.	100	29.59 N	119.44 E
Chengzi, Zhg.	98	41.57 N	117.16 E
Chengzi, Zhg.	105	39.58 N	116.02 E
Chengzitan	98	39.30 N	122.30 E
Ch'enhsien → Chenxian	100	25.48 N	112.59 E
Chen Hu ⊜	100	30.29 N	113.22 E
Chenies	260	51.41 N	0.32 W
Chenil, Lac ⊜	186	51.51 N	59.41 W
Cheniménil	58	48.08 N	6.36 E
Chenji	100	33.50 N	119.11 E
Chenjiachang, Zhg.	107	29.35 N	104.52 E
Chenjiachang, Zhg.	107	30.04 N	105.15 E
Chenjiagang	98	34.25 N	119.49 E
Chenjiahe	102	29.28 N	109.59 E
Chenjiaji	100	30.42 N	114.21 E
Chenjiapang	106	31.14 N	119.42 E
Chenjiapu	105	40.31 N	115.37 E
Chenjiaqiao	106	31.27 N	121.16 E
Chenjiatun, Zhg.	104	42.20 N	124.06 E
Chenjiatun, Zhg.	104	40.57 N	121.01 E
Chenjiawan	106	31.02 N	120.35 E
Chenjiaxiang	100	31.29 N	113.45 E
Chenjiazhen	106	31.30 N	121.48 E
Chenjiazui	105	39.17 N	116.59 E
Chenkeng	100	25.06 N	116.15 E
Chenlingjiao	106	30.23 N	118.47 E
Chenliu	98	34.43 N	114.31 E
Chenlong	269b	31.17 N	121.25 E
Chennevières	261	49.00 N	2.07 E
Chennevières-lès-Lovres	261	49.03 N	2.33 E
Chenoa	216	40.44 N	88.43 W
Chenonceaux	50	47.20 N	1.04 E
Chenonceaux, Château de ⊥	50	47.20 N	1.04 E
Chenôve	58	47.17 N	5.00 E
Chenoweth	224	45.37 N	121.13 W
Chenqiao	98	34.58 N	114.32 E
Chenquingqiao	89	49.08 N	127.16 E
Chenshanzhuang	105	39.43 N	117.30 E
Chenshichang	107	29.17 N	106.00 E
Chens-sur-Léman	58	46.20 N	6.16 E
Chentang	102	23.54 N	110.39 E
Chentejn nuruu ⋏	88	48.30 N	108.30 E
Chentij	88	48.05 N	109.45 E
Chentij □[4]	88	48.00 N	110.30 E
Chenxi	102	27.51 N	109.59 E
Chenxian	100	25.48 N	112.59 E
Chenxiangtun	104	41.36 N	123.30 E
Chenyang, Zhg.	100	33.47 N	120.10 E
Chenyang → Shenyang, Zhg.	104	41.48 N	123.27 E
Cheonan → Ch'ŏnan	98	36.48 N	127.09 E
Cheongju → Ch'ŏngju	98	36.39 N	127.31 E
Cheo Reo	110	13.24 N	108.27 E
Chepachet	207	41.54 N	71.40 W
Chepaúa	152	12.58 S	22.43 E
Chepén	248	7.13 S	79.27 W
Chépénéhé	175f	20.47 S	167.09 E
Chepes	252	31.21 S	66.36 W
Chepkotet ∧	154	1.15 N	35.26 E
Chepo	246	9.10 N	79.06 W
Chepstow	42	51.39 N	2.41 W
Cheptainville	261	48.33 N	2.16 E
Cher □[5]	32	47.05 N	2.30 E
Cher ≃	32	47.21 N	0.29 E
Cheradi, Isole II	68	40.27 N	17.10 E
Cherain	56	50.11 N	5.52 E
Cherán	234	19.41 N	101.57 W
Chéran ≃	62	45.53 N	5.56 E
Cheranchi	150	12.40 N	7.42 E
Cherangany Hills ⋏[2]	154	1.15 N	35.27 E
Cherasco	62	44.39 N	7.51 E
Cherāt	123	33.49 N	71.53 E
Cheraw	192	34.41 N	79.53 W
Cheraw State Park ♠	192	34.36 N	79.55 W
Cherbaniani Reef ✦[2]	122	12.18 N	71.53 E
Cherbourg	32	49.39 N	1.39 W
Cherchell	148	36.36 N	2.12 E
Cheremkhovo → Čeremchovo	88	53.09 N	103.05 E
Chérence	261	49.05 N	1.41 E
Chereponi	150	10.09 N	0.17 E
Cherepovets → Čerepovec	76	59.08 N	37.54 E
Chergui, Chott ech ⊜	148	34.21 N	0.30 E
Chergui, Île I	148	34.44 N	11.14 E
Chergui, Zahrez ⊜	148	35.12 N	3.32 E
Cheribon → Cirebon	115a	6.44 S	108.34 E
Cherio ≃	64	45.46 N	9.55 E
Cherita. Sebkhet ⊜	36	35.21 N	10.19 E
Cheriton	208	37.17 N	75.58 W
Cheriyam Island I	122	10.09 N	73.40 E
Cherkassy → Čerkassy	78	49.26 N	32.04 E
Cherkessk → Čerkessk	84	44.14 N	42.04 E
Cherlen → Kerulen ≃	90	48.48 N	117.00 E
Chermside	171a	27.23 S	153.02 E
Chernigov → Černigov	78	51.30 N	31.18 E
Chernobyl → Černobyl'	78	51.16 N	30.14 E
Chernofski	180	53.24 N	167.33 W
Chernogorsk → Černogorsk	86	53.49 N	91.18 E
Chernovtsy → Černovcy	78	48.18 N	25.56 E
Chero ≃	62	44.58 N	9.51 E
Cherokee, Al., U.S.	194	34.45 N	87.58 W
Cherokee, Ia., U.S.	198	42.44 N	95.33 W
Cherokee, Ks., U.S.	198	37.20 N	94.48 W
Cherokee, Ok., U.S.	196	36.45 N	98.21 W
Cherokee, Tx., U.S.	196	30.59 N	98.43 W
Cherokee □[6]	222	31.48 N	95.10 W
Cherokee, Lake ⊜[1]	222	32.21 N	94.39 W
Cherokee Canal ≊	226	39.18 N	121.55 W
Cherokee Lake ⊜[1]	192	36.16 N	83.20 W
Cherokee Point ≻	192	26.16 N	77.03 W
Cherokee Ranch	208	40.25 N	75.55 W
Cherokees, Lake O' The ⊜[1]	194	36.39 N	94.49 W
Cherokee Sound	238	26.17 N	77.04 W
Cherokee Village	194	36.17 N	91.30 W
Chéroy	50	48.12 N	3.00 E
Cherpuči	89	53.01 N	138.52 E
Cherquenco	252	38.41 S	72.00 W
Cherrabun	162	18.29 S	125.19 E
Cherrapunji	120	25.18 N	91.42 E
Cherry Brook ≃, Ma., U.S.	283	42.23 N	71.17 W
Cherry Brook ≃, N.J., U.S.	276	41.01 N	74.00 W
Cherry City	279b	40.29 N	79.58 W
Cherry Creek, B.C., Can.	224	49.17 N	124.47 W
Cherry Creek, N.Y., U.S.	214	42.17 N	79.06 W
Cherry Creek ≃, Az., U.S.	200	33.41 N	110.49 W
Cherry Creek ≃, Ca., U.S.	226	37.53 N	119.58 W
Cherry Creek ≃, Co., U.S.	198	39.45 N	105.01 W
Cherry Creek ≃, Mt., U.S.	198	46.48 N	105.15 W
Cherry Creek ≃, N.D., U.S.	198	47.41 N	103.02 W
Cherry Creek ≃, S.D., U.S.	198	44.36 N	101.30 W
Cherry Creek ≃, Tx., U.S.	196	31.13 N	103.34 W
Cherry Creek, East Fork ≃	226	38.06 N	119.47 W
Cherry Creek, West Fork ≃	226	38.04 N	119.54 W
Cherry Fork	218	38.53 N	83.37 W
Cherry Grove, N.Y., U.S.	210	40.39 N	73.06 W
Cherry Grove, Or., U.S.	224	45.26 N	123.14 W
Cherry Hill, Il., U.S.	278	41.32 N	88.02 W
Cherry Hill, N.J., U.S.	208	39.56 N	75.01 W
Cherry Hill ✶[8]	284b	39.15 N	76.38 W
Cherry Hill Mall ✶[9]	285	39.56 N	75.02 W
Cherry Island I	285	39.43 N	75.31 W
Cherry Lake ⊜[1]	226	38.00 N	119.54 W
Cherryland	226	37.41 N	122.06 W
Cherry Lane	279b	40.34 N	79.33 W
Cherryplain	210	42.38 N	73.22 W
Cherry Point Marine Corps Air Station ■	192	34.54 N	76.54 W
Cherryvale	198	37.16 N	95.33 W
Cherry Valley, Ar., U.S.	194	35.24 N	90.45 W
Cherry Valley, Ca., U.S.	228	33.57 N	116.53 W
Cherry Valley, Il., U.S.	216	42.14 N	88.56 W
Cherry Valley, Ma., U.S.	207	42.14 N	71.52 W
Cherry Valley, N.Y., U.S.	210	42.47 N	74.45 W
Cherry Valley, Pa., U.S.	214	41.10 N	79.48 W
Cherry Valley Creek ≃	210	42.35 N	74.56 W
Cherryville, N.C., U.S.	192	35.22 N	81.22 W
Cherryville, Pa., U.S.	208	40.45 N	75.33 W
Cherrywood	275b	43.52 N	79.08 W
Cherson	78	46.38 N	32.35 E
Chersonesskij, mys ≻	78	44.35 N	33.23 E
Chertsey	260	51.24 N	0.30 W
Cherwell ≃	42	51.44 N	1.15 W
Chesaco Park	284b	39.19 N	76.30 W
Chesaning	190	43.11 N	84.06 W
Chesapeake	208	36.49 N	76.16 W
Chesapeake and Delaware Canal ≊	208	39.32 N	75.51 W
Chesapeake and Ohio Canal National Historical Park ♠	208	39.03 N	77.16 W
Chesapeake Bay ⊂	208	38.40 N	76.25 W
Chesapeake Bay Bridge-Tunnel ✶[5]	208	37.00 N	76.02 W
Chesapeake Beach	208	38.41 N	76.32 W
Chesapeake City	208	39.31 N	75.48 W
Chesaw	182	48.56 N	119.03 W
Chesdin, Lake ⊜[1]	208	37.15 N	77.33 W
Cheseaux	58	46.35 N	6.36 E
Chesham	260	51.43 N	0.38 W
Chesham Bois	260	51.41 N	0.37 W
Cheshire, Ct., U.S.	207	41.29 N	72.54 W
Cheshire, Ma., U.S.	207	42.33 N	73.09 W
Cheshire, N.Y., U.S.	210	42.49 N	77.20 W
Cheshire □[6], Eng., U.K.	44	53.23 N	2.30 W
Cheshire □[6], N.H., U.S.	207	42.50 N	72.15 W
Cheshire Plain ≚	44	53.17 N	2.40 W
Cheshire Reservoir ⊜[1]	207	42.32 N	73.11 W
Chesht-e Sharīf	128	34.21 N	63.44 E
Cheshunt	42	51.43 N	0.02 W
Chesil Beach ⏊[2]	42	50.38 N	2.33 W
Chesilhurst	285	39.43 N	74.52 W
Cheslatta Lake ⊜	182	53.44 N	125.18 W
Chesley	212	44.17 N	81.05 W
Chesnee	192	35.08 N	81.51 W
Chess ≃	260	51.38 N	0.27 W
Chessington ✶[8]	260	51.21 N	0.18 W
Chessy	261	48.53 N	2.46 E
Chest Creek ≃	214	40.53 N	78.44 W
Chester, Eng., U.K.	262	53.12 N	2.54 W
Chester, Ca., U.S.	204	40.18 N	121.13 W
Chester, Ct., U.S.	207	41.24 N	72.27 W
Chester, Il., U.S.	194	37.54 N	89.49 W
Chester, Md., U.S.	208	38.58 N	76.17 W
Chester, Ma., U.S.	207	42.16 N	72.58 W
Chester, Mt., U.S.	202	48.30 N	110.58 W
Chester, Ne., U.S.	198	40.00 N	97.37 W
Chester, N.J., U.S.	210	40.47 N	74.41 W
Chester, Ok., U.S.	196	36.12 N	98.55 W
Chester, Pa., U.S.	208	39.50 N	75.21 W
Chester, S.C., U.S.	192	34.42 N	81.12 W
Chester, Tx., U.S.	222	30.55 N	94.36 W
Chester, Vt., U.S.	188	43.15 N	72.35 W
Chester, Va., U.S.	208	37.21 N	77.26 W
Chester, W.V., U.S.	214	40.36 N	80.33 W
Chester □[6]	208	39.58 N	75.36 W
Chester □[8]	262	53.16 N	2.52 W
Chester ≃	208	39.00 N	76.10 W
Chester Basin	186	44.34 N	64.19 W
Chesterbrook	284c	38.55 N	77.09 W
Chester Brook ≃	283	42.23 N	71.14 W
Chesterbrook Woods	284c	38.56 N	77.08 W
Chester Creek ≃	208	39.50 N	75.22 W
Chester Creek, East Branch ≃	285	39.56 N	75.32 W
Chester Creek, West Branch ≃	285	39.54 N	75.27 W
Chesterfield, Eng., U.K.	44	53.15 N	1.25 W
Chesterfield, Ct., U.S.	207	41.24 N	72.11 W
Chesterfield, Il., U.S.	219	39.15 N	90.04 W
Chesterfield, In., U.S.	218	40.06 N	85.35 W
Chesterfield, Ma., U.S.	207	42.23 N	72.50 W
Chesterfield, S.C., U.S.	192	34.44 N	80.05 W
Chesterfield, Va., U.S.	192	37.22 N	77.30 W
Chesterfield □[6]	208	37.20 N	77.25 W
Chesterfield, Île I	157b	16.20 S	43.58 E
Chesterfield, Îles II	160	19.30 S	158.00 E
Chesterfield Inlet	176	63.21 N	90.42 W
Chesterfield Inlet ⊂	176	63.25 N	90.45 W
Chester Heights	285	39.53 N	75.28 W
Chester Hill, Austl.	274a	33.53 S	151.00 E
Chesterhill, Oh., U.S.	188	39.29 N	81.51 W
Chester Hill, Pa., U.S.	214	40.53 N	78.14 W
Chester Island I	285	39.50 N	75.21 W
Chesterland	214	41.31 N	81.21 W
Chester-le-Street	44	54.52 N	1.34 W
Chester Morse Lake ⊜[1]	224	47.23 N	121.42 W
Chesters	44	55.23 N	2.36 W
Chester Springs	285	40.06 N	75.37 W
Chesterton	216	41.36 N	87.03 W
Chesterton Range ⋏	166	25.30 S	147.27 E
Chestertown	208	39.12 N	76.04 W
Chesterville, On., Can.	212	45.06 N	75.14 W
Chesterville, Oh., U.S.	214	40.29 N	82.41 W
Chestnut	219	40.03 N	89.11 W
Chestnut Hill, Ma., U.S.	283	42.20 N	71.10 W
Chestnut Hill, Pa., U.S.	210	40.04 N	75.12 W
Chestnut Hill ✶[8]	285	40.04 N	75.13 W
Chestnut Hill ∧[2]	285	40.13 N	75.45 W
Chestnut Hill Estates	285	39.41 N	75.42 W
Chestnut Hill Reservoir ⊜[1]	283	42.20 N	71.10 W
Chestnut Ridge ∧	214	40.09 N	79.24 W
Chestnut Ridge Park ♠	284a	42.43 N	78.46 W
Chest Peak ∧	172	43.06 S	172.01 E
Chesuncook Lake ⊜	188	46.00 N	69.20 W
Cheswick	214	40.32 N	79.47 W
Cheswold	208	39.13 N	75.35 W
Chet ≃	42	52.33 N	1.32 E
Cheta ≃	74	71.54 N	102.06 E
Chetaibi	36	37.04 N	7.23 E
Chetco ≃	202	42.03 N	124.16 W
Chetek	190	45.18 N	91.39 W
Chéticamp	186	46.38 N	61.01 W
Chet Iter, Oued V	148	21.39 N	2.30 E
Chetopa	198	37.02 N	95.05 W
Chettlatt Island I	122	11.42 N	72.42 E
Chetumal	232	18.30 N	88.18 W
Chetumal Bay ⊂	232	18.20 N	88.05 W
Chetwynd	182	55.42 N	121.40 W
Cheung Chau I	271d	22.12 N	114.01 E
Cheung Shue Tan	271d	22.26 N	114.12 E
Chevak	180	61.39 N	165.17 W
Cheval-Blanc, Montagne du ⋏	62	44.07 N	6.26 E
Cheval Blanc, Pointe du ≻	238	19.41 N	73.27 W
Chevannes	261	48.32 N	2.27 E
Chevelon Creek ≃	200	34.57 N	110.31 W
Chevening	260	51.18 N	0.08 E
Chevenoz	58	46.20 N	6.39 E
Cheverly	284c	38.55 N	76.54 W
Cheverny	50	47.30 N	1.28 E
Chevillon	58	48.32 N	5.08 E
Chevilly-Larue	261	48.46 N	2.21 E
Cheviot, N.Z.	172	42.49 S	173.16 E
Cheviot, Oh., U.S.	218	39.09 N	84.36 W
Cheviot Hills ⋏[2]	44	55.22 N	2.22 W
Chevreuse	50	48.42 N	2.03 E
Chèvreville	261	49.07 N	2.51 E
Chevril, Lac du ⊜	62	45.29 N	6.56 E
Chevry-Cossigny	261	48.43 N	2.40 E
Chevy Chase	284c	38.58 N	77.04 W
Chevy Chase Heights	214	40.36 N	79.08 W
Chevy Chase View	284c	39.01 N	77.05 W
Chewaucan ≃	202	42.30 N	120.18 W
Chew Bahir (Lake Stefanie) ⊜	144	4.40 N	36.50 E
Chewelah	202	48.16 N	117.42 W
Chew Magna	42	51.22 N	2.35 W
Chew Reservoir ⊜[1]	262	53.31 N	1.56 W
Chews Landing	285	39.50 N	75.04 W
Chewton, Austl.	169	37.05 S	144.16 E
Chewton, Pa., U.S.	214	40.53 N	80.20 W
Chexbres	58	46.29 N	6.47 E
Cheyenne, Ok., U.S.	196	35.36 N	99.40 W
Cheyenne, Wy., U.S.	200	41.08 N	104.49 W
Cheyenne ≃	198	44.40 N	101.15 W
Cheyenne, Dry Fork ≃	198	43.25 N	105.23 W
Cheyenne River Indian Reservation ✶[4]	198	45.00 N	100.40 W
Cheyenne Wells	198	38.49 N	102.21 W
Cheyne Bay ⊂	162	34.35 S	118.50 E
Cheyne Point ≻	162	33.58 S	122.34 E
Cheyney	285	39.56 N	75.31 W
Cheyney University of Pennsylvania ʋ[2]	285	39.56 N	75.32 W
Chezhen	98	37.54 N	117.37 E
Chhabra	124	24.40 N	76.50 E
Chhachhrauli	124	30.15 N	77.22 E
Chhajārsi	272a	28.38 N	77.23 E
Chhalera Bāngar	272a	28.33 N	77.20 E
Chhanka	126	23.59 N	89.55 E
Chhapra	124	25.46 N	84.45 E
Chhātak	120	25.02 N	91.40 E
Chhatarpur, India	124	24.23 N	84.11 E
Chhatarpur, India	124	24.55 N	79.36 E
Chhātna	126	23.18 N	86.58 E
Chhatrapur	122	19.21 N	84.59 E
Chhattīsgarh ≚	122	21.15 N	82.00 E
Chhay Arêng ≃	110	11.31 N	103.25 E
Chhêb Kândal	110	13.45 N	105.24 E
Chhibrāmau	124	27.09 N	79.31 E
Chhināmor	272b	22.48 N	88.18 E
Chhindwāra	124	22.04 N	78.56 E
Chhiruti	126	24.01 N	88.11 E
Chhitauni	124	27.09 N	83.58 E
Chhlong ≃	110	12.15 N	105.58 E
Chhota Bāisdia	126	22.00 N	90.27 E
Chhota-Chhindwāra	124	23.03 N	79.29 E
Chhota Udepur	120	22.19 N	74.01 E
Chhukha Dzong	124	27.09 N	89.36 E
Chi ≃, Thai	110	15.18 N	103.31 E
Chi ≃, Thai	110	15.11 N	104.43 E
Chi ≃, Zhg.	100	32.51 N	117.59 E
Chía	246	4.52 N	74.04 W
Chiador	256	22.01 S	43.03 W
Chiador, Cachoeira do ⌞	256	22.03 S	43.02 W
Chiahsien	100	23.05 N	120.35 E
Chiahsing → Jiaxing	106	30.46 N	120.45 E
Chiai	100	23.29 N	120.27 E
Chialamberto	62	45.22 N	7.21 E
Chiali	100	23.10 N	120.10 E
Chiambala ≃	152	16.22 S	11.49 E
Chiampo	64	45.33 N	11.17 E
Chiampo ≃	64	45.20 N	11.16 E
Chiamussu → Jiamusi	89	46.50 N	130.21 E
Chian → Ji'an	100	27.07 N	114.58 E
Chiana, Val di V	66	43.15 N	11.50 E
Chianciano Terme	66	43.03 N	11.50 E
Chiang Dao	110	19.22 N	98.58 E
Chiange	152	15.45 S	13.48 E
Chiang Kham	110	19.32 N	100.18 E
Chiang Khan	110	17.52 N	101.36 E
Chiang Khian	110	19.37 N	100.00 E
Chiang Mai	110	18.47 N	98.59 E
Chiangmen → Jiangmen	100	22.35 N	113.05 E
Chiang Rai	110	19.54 N	99.50 E
Chiang Saen	110	20.16 N	100.05 E
Chiangtu → Yangzhou	100	32.24 N	119.26 E
Chiangyin → Jiangyin	106	31.55 N	120.16 E
Chiani ≃	66	42.52 N	12.14 E
Chianni	66	43.29 N	10.38 E
Chianti □[4]	66	43.22 N	11.23 E
Chianti ⋏[1]	66	43.25 N	11.20 E
Chianti, Monti del ⋏	66	43.32 N	11.25 E
Chiaohsi	100	24.49 N	121.46 E
Chiaohsien → Jiaoxian	98	36.18 N	119.58 E
Chiaopan	100	24.50 N	121.21 E
Chiaotso → Jiaozuo	102	35.15 N	113.13 E
Chiao-Tung Normal University ʋ[2]	269b	31.14 N	121.24 E
Chiapa	248	19.32 S	69.13 W
Chiapa de Corzo	234	16.42 N	93.00 W
Chiapaot'ai	100	24.11 N	121.00 E
Chiapas □[3]	232	16.30 N	92.30 W
Chiaramonte Gulfi	70	37.02 N	14.42 E
Chiaramonti	71	40.45 N	8.49 E
Chiaravalle	66	43.36 N	13.19 E
Chiaravalle Centrale	68	38.41 N	16.25 E
Chiareggio	64	46.19 N	9.47 E
Chiari	62	45.32 N	9.56 E
Chiaromonte	68	40.07 N	16.13 E
Chiasso	58	45.50 N	9.01 E
Chiautla de Tapia	234	18.17 N	98.36 W
Chiautzingo	234	19.12 N	98.28 W
Chiavari	62	44.19 N	9.19 E
Chiavenna	58	46.19 N	9.24 E
Chiawelo	273d	26.17 S	27.52 E
Chiba	94	35.36 N	140.07 E
Chiba □[5]	94	35.30 N	140.20 E
Chibabava	156	20.19 S	33.39 E
Chiba-kō ⊂	268	35.35 N	140.06 E
Chibakou	100	29.36 N	113.01 E
Chibango	152	13.38 S	21.56 E
Chiba University ʋ[2]	268	35.38 N	140.06 E
Chibemba	152	15.45 S	14.05 E
Chibi	154	20.19 S	30.30 E
Chibia	152	15.11 S	13.41 E
Chibouet ≃	206	45.47 N	72.52 W
Chibougamau	176	49.55 N	74.22 W
Chibuto	156	24.44 S	33.33 E
Chibuzhangchu Hu ⊜	120	33.25 N	90.15 E
Chibwe	154	14.12 S	28.31 E
Chica, Laguna ⊜	234	20.06 N	96.40 W
Chicago, Il., U.S.	216	41.51 N	87.39 W
Chicago, Il., U.S.	278	41.51 N	87.39 W
Chicago, North Branch ≃	216	41.53 N	87.38 W
Chicago, North Branch, West Fork ≃	278	42.03 N	87.54 W
Chicago, South Branch ≃	278	41.53 N	87.38 W
Chicago, University of ʋ[2]	278	41.47 N	87.36 W
Chicago Botanic Garden ♠	278	42.09 N	87.47 W
Chicago Harbor ⊂	278	41.53 N	87.37 W
Chicago Heights	216	41.30 N	87.38 W
Chicago-Hinsdale Airport ⊠	278	41.46 N	87.56 W
Chicago Lawn ✶[8]	278	41.47 N	87.41 W
Chicago-Midway Airport ⊠	216	41.47 N	87.45 W
Chicago-O'Hare International Airport ⊠	278	41.59 N	87.54 W
Chicago Park	226	39.09 N	120.58 W
Chicago Portage National Historic Site ⊥	278	41.48 N	87.49 W
Chicago Ridge	216	41.42 N	87.46 W
Chicago Sanitary and Ship Canal ≊	216	41.32 N	88.05 W
Chicago Stadium ♠	278	41.53 N	87.40 W
Chicama ≃	248	7.56 S	79.17 W
Chicamacomico ≃	208	38.26 N	75.59 W
Chicamba, Barragem de ✶[6]	156	19.08 S	33.00 E
Chicapa ≃	152	6.26 S	20.47 E
Chic-Chocs, Monts ⋏	186	48.55 N	66.00 W
Chichagof Island I	180	57.30 N	135.30 W
Chichas, Cordillera de ⋏	248	20.30 S	66.30 W
Chīchāwatni	123	30.32 N	72.42 E
Chiché ≃	250	8.15 S	53.30 W
Chicheng	98	40.54 N	115.46 E
Chichén Itzá	232	20.40 N	88.34 W
Chichén Itzá ⊥	232	20.40 N	88.35 W
Chichester, Eng., U.K.	42	50.50 N	0.48 W
Chichester, N.Y., U.S.	210	42.06 N	74.19 W
Chichester Range ⋏	162	22.00 S	118.50 E
Chichi	100	23.50 N	120.47 E
Chichibu	94	35.59 N	139.05 E
Chichibu-Tama-kokuritsu-kōen ♠	94	35.52 N	139.00 E
Chichica	236	8.22 N	81.40 W
Chichicastenango	236	14.56 N	91.07 W
Chichigalpa	236	12.34 N	87.02 W
Chichigapa	234	17.47 N	94.25 W
Ch'ich'ihaerh → Qiqihar	89	47.19 N	123.55 E
Chichihualco	234	17.41 N	99.39 W
Chichijima-rettō II	14	27.06 N	142.12 E
Chichimilá	232	20.37 N	88.13 W
Chichiriviche	246	10.56 N	68.16 W
Chicholi	124	22.01 N	77.40 E
Chichra	126	22.19 N	86.53 E
Chicicatiapa ≃	234	18.18 N	96.19 W
Chickahominy ≃	208	37.14 N	76.53 W
Chickaloon	180	61.48 N	148.28 W
Chickamauga	192	34.52 N	85.17 W
Chickamauga Lake ⊜[1]	192	35.22 N	85.02 W
Chickamin ≃	182	55.47 N	130.58 W
Chickasaw, Al., U.S.	194	30.45 N	88.04 W
Chickasaw, Oh., U.S.	216	40.26 N	84.30 W
Chickasaw Bogue ≃	194	32.17 N	87.55 W
Chickasawhatchie Creek ≃	192	31.19 N	84.29 W
Chickasawhay ≃	194	31.00 N	88.45 W
Chickasaw National Recreation Area ♠	196	34.25 N	96.59 W
Chickasha	196	35.03 N	97.56 W
Chicken	180	64.04 N	141.56 W
Chicken Brook ≃	283	42.08 N	71.25 W
Chickerell	42	50.37 N	2.30 W
Chickies Creek ≃	208	40.03 N	76.32 W
Chiclana de la Frontera	34	36.25 N	6.08 W
Chiclayo	248	6.46 S	79.51 W
Chico, Ca., U.S.	204	39.43 N	121.50 W
Chico, Tx., U.S.	196	33.17 N	97.47 W
Chico, Wa., U.S.	224	47.36 N	122.42 W
Chico ≃, Arg.	254	43.48 S	66.25 W
Chico ≃, Arg.	254	42.25 S	70.30 W
Chico ≃, Arg.	254	49.56 S	68.32 W
Chico ≃, Pan.	236	8.20 N	80.28 W
Chico ≃, Pil.	116	17.58 N	121.36 E
Chico ≃, S.A.	254	51.40 S	69.09 W
Chico, Arroyo ≃	286b	23.02 N	82.17 W
Chicoasen, Presa ⊜[1]	234	16.55 N	93.05 W
Chicobi, Lac ⊜	190	48.53 N	78.30 W
Chico Creek ≃	198	38.15 N	104.20 W
Chicolete Creek ≃	222	29.05 N	96.49 W
Chicomba	152	14.09 S	14.57 E
Chicomo	156	24.31 S	34.17 E
Chicomuselo	232	15.46 N	92.16 W
Chiconautla, Cerro ∧	286a	19.39 N	98.58 W
Chicono no	154	12.56 S	35.43 E
Chicontepec	234	20.58 N	98.10 W
Chicopee, Ga., U.S.	192	34.15 N	83.50 W
Chicopee, Ma., U.S.	207	42.08 N	72.36 W
Chicopee ≃	207	42.09 N	72.37 W
Chicora	214	40.56 N	79.44 W
Chicorato	232	26.02 N	107.54 W
Chicot, Lake ⊜	194	33.20 N	91.14 W
Chicot, Rivière du ≃	275a	45.35 N	73.51 W
Chicot State Park ♠	194	30.47 N	92.19 W
Chicoutimi	186	48.26 N	71.04 W
Chicoutimi ≃	186	48.26 N	71.05 W
Chicoutimi, Réserve ♠	186	48.30 N	70.15 W
Chicualoque	234	20.23 N	97.39 W
Chicuma	152	13.23 S	14.51 E
Chicxulub	232	21.08 N	89.31 W
Chidambaram	122	11.24 N	79.42 E
Chiddingfold	42	51.06 N	0.37 W
Chiddingstone Causeway	260	51.12 N	0.10 E
Chidenguele	156	24.54 S	34.13 E
Chidlow	168a	31.52 S	116.14 E
Chi-do I	98	35.04 N	126.13 E
Chidralada Palace ʋ	269a	13.46 N	100.32 E
Chief	222	32.33 N	96.10 W
Chief Justice William Cushing Memorial State Park ♠	283	42.10 N	70.45 W
Chiefland	192	29.28 N	82.51 W
Chiefs Point ≻	212	44.42 N	81.18 W
Chief's Point Indian Reserve ✶[4]	212	44.41 N	81.17 W
Chiehyang → Jieyang	100	23.35 N	116.21 E
Chiemgauer Alpen ⋏	64	47.40 N	12.30 E
Chiemsee ⊜	64	47.54 N	12.29 E
Chien, Bayou de ≃	194	36.35 N	89.11 W
Chienes (Kiens)	64	46.48 N	11.50 E
Chiengi	154	8.39 S	29.10 E
Chiengo	152	13.20 S	21.55 E
Chiens, Rivière aux ≃	275a	45.39 N	73.46 W
Chienti ≃	66	43.18 N	13.45 E
Chieo Lan Reservoir ⊜[1]	110	9.00 N	98.45 E
Chieri	62	45.01 N	7.49 E
Chiers ≃	56	49.39 N	5.00 E
Chiesa in Valmalenco	64	46.16 N	9.51 E
Chiese ≃	64	45.08 N	10.25 E
Chieti	66	42.21 N	14.10 E
Chieti □[4]	66	42.07 N	14.21 E
Chietla	234	18.31 N	98.35 W
Chieuti	68	41.51 N	15.10 E
Chieveley	42	51.27 N	1.19 W
Chièvres	50	50.35 N	3.48 E
Chifeng (Ulanhad)	98	42.18 N	119.00 E
Chigasaki	94	35.19 N	139.24 E
Chiginagak, Mount ∧	180	57.08 N	156.59 W
Chigmit Mountains ⋏	180	60.00 N	153.00 W
Chignahuapan	234	19.50 N	98.02 W
Chignall Saint James	260	51.46 N	0.25 E
Chignall Smealy	260	51.47 N	0.25 E
Chignecto, Cape ≻	186	45.20 N	64.57 W
Chignecto Bay ⊂	186	45.35 N	64.45 W
Chignik	180	56.18 N	158.23 W
Chignik Bay ⊂	180	56.22 N	158.15 W
Chignik Lagoon	180	56.21 N	158.31 W
Chignik Lake	180	56.15 N	158.45 W
Chignolo Po	62	45.09 N	9.29 E
Chigombe ≃	156	23.26 S	33.19 E
Chigorodó	246	7.41 N	76.42 W
Chigu	100	27.34 N	114.40 E
Chigubo	156	22.50 S	33.34 E
Chigu Co ⊜	120	28.40 N	91.45 E
Chigwell	260	51.38 N	0.05 E
Chigwell Row	260	51.37 N	0.07 E
Chigyŏng	98	39.51 N	127.26 E
Chihaya-akasaka	270	34.24 N	135.38 E
Chihaya Castle ⊥	270	34.24 N	135.40 E
Chihe	100	32.32 N	117.58 E
Ch'ihfeng → Chifeng	98	42.18 N	119.00 E
Chihli, Gulf of → Bo Hai ⊂	98	38.30 N	120.00 E
Chihpen	100	22.42 N	121.02 E
Ch'ihshang	100	23.07 N	121.12 E
Chihsi → Jixi	89	45.17 N	130.59 E
Ch'ihsing Shan ∧, T'aiwan	100	25.10 N	121.33 E
Ch'ihsing Shan ∧, T'aiwan	269d	25.10 N	121.33 E
Ch'ihsing Yen I	100	21.46 N	120.49 E
Chihtungtsun	100	22.44 N	120.14 E
Chihu	100	24.07 N	117.51 E
Chihuahua	232	28.38 N	106.05 W
Chihuahua □[3]	232	28.30 N	106.00 W
Chihuahuan Desert ✶[2]	16	35.00 N	106.00 W
Chii-san ∧	98	35.20 N	127.44 E
Chii-san Kukrip Kongwŏn ♠	98	35.20 N	127.39 E
Chiitola	26	61.16 N	29.38 E
Chikaskia ≃	196	36.37 N	97.15 W
Chik Ballāpur	122	13.28 N	77.44 E
Chikhli	122	20.21 N	76.15 E
Chikindzonot	232	20.20 N	88.29 W
Chikmagalūr	122	13.19 N	75.47 E
Chiknai ≃	126	24.06 N	89.17 E
Chiknāyakanhalli	122	13.26 N	76.37 E
Chikoa	154	13.24 S	32.07 E
Chikodi	122	16.26 N	74.36 E
Chikou	100	30.44 N	117.32 E
Chikrêng ≃	110	12.51 N	104.14 E
Ch'iku	100	23.08 N	120.07 E
Chikugo	96	33.12 N	130.30 E
Chikugo ≃	92	33.09 N	130.21 E
Chikujō-kichi, Kōkū-jieitai- ■	96	33.41 N	131.03 E
Chikuma ≃	94	36.59 N	138.35 E
Chikuminuk Lake ⊜	180	60.14 N	159.00 W
Chikura	94	34.57 N	139.57 E
Chikusa	96	35.09 N	134.26 E
Chikusa ≃	96	34.44 N	134.24 E
Chikushino	96	33.29 N	130.31 E
Chikwawa	154	16.03 S	34.48 E
Chi-kyaw	110	20.17 N	93.54 E
Chikyu-misaki ≻	92a	42.18 N	141.00 E
Chila, Ang.	152	12.04 S	14.29 E
Chila, Méx.	234	18.55 N	102.28 W
Chilacachapa	234	18.17 N	99.43 W
Chilakalūrupet	122	16.05 N	80.10 E
Chilako ≃	182	53.54 N	122.59 W
Chilam Chauki	123	35.03 N	75.07 E
Chilanga	154	15.34 S	28.17 E
Chilanko Forks	182	52.06 N	124.10 W
Chilapa de Alvarez	234	17.36 N	99.10 W
Chilapa de Díaz	234	17.31 N	97.41 W
Chilās	123	35.26 N	74.05 E
Chilaw	122	7.34 N	79.47 E
Chilca	248	12.32 S	76.44 W
Chilca, Cordillera de ⋏	248	15.30 S	71.50 W
Chilca, Punta ≻	248	12.27 S	76.48 W
Chilchota	234	19.51 N	102.08 W
Chilcotin ≃	182	51.45 N	122.24 W
Chilcott Island I	166	16.58 S	149.58 E
Childers	166	25.14 S	152.17 E
Childersburg	194	33.16 N	86.21 W
Childer Thornton	262	53.17 N	2.57 W
Childress	196	34.25 N	100.12 W
Childs	210	41.34 N	75.32 W
Chile □[1]	244	30.00 S	71.00 W
Chile, Hipódromo ♠	286e	33.24 S	70.41 W
Chile, Universidad de ʋ[2]	286e	33.27 S	70.40 W
Chile Basin ✦[1]	18	33.00 S	80.00 W
Chile Chico	254	46.33 S	71.44 W
Chilecito, Arg.	252	29.10 S	67.30 W
Chilecito, Arg.	252	33.53 S	69.03 W
Chilengue, Serra do ⋏	152	13.10 S	15.18 E
Chileno, Arroyo ≃, Ur.	258	33.55 S	58.08 W
Chileno, Arroyo ≃, Ur.	288	34.22 S	57.54 W
Chile Rise ✦[3]	18	40.00 S	90.00 W
Chilete	248	7.14 S	78.51 W
Chilham	42	51.15 N	0.57 E
Chilhowie	192	36.47 N	81.40 W
Chili	216	40.52 N	86.02 W
Chili → Chile □[1]	244	30.00 S	71.00 W
Chili ≃	248	16.23 S	71.46 W
Chili, Ouadi V	146	16.44 N	20.53 E
Chilia, Brațul ≃[1]	78	45.18 N	29.40 E
Chili Center	210	43.06 N	77.44 W
Chilika Lake ⊜	122	19.45 N	85.25 E
Chililabombwe (Bancroft)	154	12.18 S	27.43 E
Chilin → Jilin	89	43.51 N	126.33 E
Chilingchang	107	28.58 N	105.31 E
Chilivani	71	40.36 N	8.56 E
Chilkat Pass)(	180	59.43 N	136.35 W
Chilko ≃	182	52.08 N	123.30 W
Chilko Lake ⊜	182	51.20 N	124.05 W
Chilko Lake Indian Reserve ✶[4]	182	51.25 N	124.07 W
Chillagoe	166	17.09 S	144.32 E
Chillán	252	36.36 S	72.07 W
Chillar	252	37.18 S	59.59 W
Chilla Saroda ✶[8]	272a	28.36 N	77.18 E
Chillicothe, Il., U.S.	190	40.55 N	89.29 W
Chillicothe, Mo., U.S.	194	39.47 N	93.33 W
Chillicothe, Oh., U.S.	218	39.19 N	82.58 W
Chillicothe, Tx., U.S.	196	34.15 N	99.30 W
Chilliwack	224	49.10 N	121.57 W
Chilliwack ≃	224	49.05 N	121.57 W
Chilliwack Lake ⊜	224	49.03 N	121.25 W
Chillón	286d	11.55 S	77.05 W
Chillón ≃	248	11.57 S	77.09 W
Chillon, Château de ⊥	58	46.25 N	6.56 E
Chillum	284c	38.58 N	76.59 W
Chilly	84	39.25 N	49.05 E
Chilly-Mazarin	261	48.42 N	2.19 E
Chilmāri	124	25.33 N	89.43 E
Chilmark	207	41.20 N	70.44 W
Chilo	218	38.48 N	84.08 W
Chiloane, Ilha I	156	20.40 S	34.55 E
Chiloé, Isla de I	254	42.30 S	73.55 W
Chilok	88	51.21 N	110.28 E
Chilok ≃	88	51.19 N	106.59 E
Chilón	232	17.14 N	92.25 W
Chilonga	154	12.03 S	31.21 E
Chilongo	152	13.55 S	16.35 E
Chiloquin	202	42.34 N	121.51 W
Chilovo	76	57.46 N	29.23 E
Chilpancingo [de los Bravos]	234	17.33 N	99.30 W
Chilpi	124	22.15 N	81.33 E
Chilston Park ♠	260	51.12 N	0.42 E
Chiltern □[8]	260	51.40 N	0.37 W
Chiltern Hills ⋏[2]	42	51.42 N	0.48 W
Chilton, Eng., U.K.	44	54.39 N	1.33 W
Chilton, Tx., U.S.	222	31.16 N	97.03 W
Chilton, Wi., U.S.	190	44.01 N	88.09 W
Chiluage	152	9.30 S	21.47 E
Chilubula Mission	154	10.09 S	31.00 E
Chilumba	154	10.28 S	34.12 E
Chilung	100	25.08 N	121.44 E
Chilung ≃	269d	25.07 N	121.27 E
Chilung Kang ⊂	269d	25.09 N	121.45 E
Chilung Shih □[7]	269d	25.08 N	121.45 E
Chiluvya	154	12.18 S	34.01 E
Chilwa, Lake ⊜	154	15.12 S	35.50 E
Chilwell	169	38.10 S	144.21 E
Chimaco	152	15.12 S	21.56 E
Chimacum	224	48.00 N	122.46 W
Chimacum Creek ≃	224	48.03 N	122.45 W
Chimakela	152	15.24 S	16.58 E
Chimalhuacán □[7]	286a	19.24 N	99.00 W
Chimaltenango	236	14.40 N	90.49 W
Chimaltenango □[5]	236	14.40 N	90.55 W
Chimaltitán	234	21.46 N	103.50 W
Chimán	246	8.42 N	78.37 W
Chimanimani National Park ♠	154	19.48 S	33.56 E
Chimay	50	50.03 N	4.19 E
Chimayo	200	36.00 N	105.55 W
Chimbarongo	252	34.42 S	71.03 W
Chimbas	252	31.29 S	68.32 W
Chimborazo □[4]	246	2.00 S	78.40 W
Chimborazo ∧[1]	246	1.28 S	78.48 W
Chimbote	248	9.05 S	78.36 W
Chimbu □[5]	164	6.05 S	145.00 E
Chimbua	152	16.32 S	15.08 E
Ch'imei Yü I	100	23.13 N	119.26 E
Chimichagua	246	9.15 N	73.49 W
Chimkent → Čimkent	85	42.18 N	69.36 E
Chimki	82	55.54 N	37.26 E
Chimki-Chovrino ✶[8]	265b	55.51 N	37.30 E
Chimkinskoje vodochranilišče ⊜[1]	265b	55.51 N	37.28 E
Chimney Reservoir ⊜[1]	204	41.25 N	117.10 W
Chimney Rock National Historic Site ♠	198	41.39 N	103.20 W
Chimoio	156	19.08 S	33.29 E
Chimon Island I	276	41.04 N	73.23 W
Chimpay	252	39.10 S	66.09 W
Chimpembe	154	9.31 S	29.33 E
Chimpôro ≃	152	17.20 S	17.17 E
Chin □[8]	110	22.00 N	93.30 E
China, Méx.	232	25.42 N	99.14 W
Chinā, Nihon	174m	26.24 N	127.46 E
China (Zhongguo) □[1]	90	35.00 N	105.00 E
China, Tanjong ≻	271c	1.14 N	103.51 E
Chinácota	246	7.37 N	72.36 W
China Grove	192	35.34 N	80.34 W
China Lake ⊜	204	35.46 N	117.39 W
China Lake Naval Weapons Center ■	204	35.35 N	117.10 W
Chinameca	236	13.30 N	88.21 W
China Meridional, Mar de → South China Sea ⊤[2]	108	10.00 N	113.00 E
Chinan, Taehan	98	35.48 N	127.25 E
Chinan → Jinan, Zhg.	98	36.40 N	116.57 E
Chinandega	236	12.37 N	87.09 W
Chinandega □[5]	236	12.45 N	87.05 W
China Spring	222	31.39 N	97.18 W
Chinati Peak ∧	196	29.57 N	104.29 W
Chinatown ✶[8]	282	37.48 N	122.26 W
Chincha Alta	248	13.27 S	76.08 W
Chinchaga ≃	176	58.50 N	118.20 W
Chincheros	248	13.27 S	73.44 W
Chinchiang → Quanzhou	100	24.54 N	118.35 E
Chinchilla, Austl.	166	26.45 S	150.38 E

Symbol	English	Deutsch	Español	Français	Português
≃	River	Fluß	Río	Rivière	Rio
≊	Canal	Kanal	Canal	Canal	Canal
⌞	Waterfall, Rapids	Wasserfall, Stromschnellen	Cascada, Rápidos	Chute d'eau, Rapides	Cascata, Rápidos
ꭓ	Strait	Meeresstraße	Estrecho	Détroit	Estreito
⊂	Bay, Gulf	Bucht, Golf	Bahía, Golfo	Baie, Golfe	Baía, Golfo
⊜	Lake, Lakes	See, Seen	Lago, Lagos	Lac, Lacs	Lago, Lagos
≚	Swamp	Sumpf	Pantano	Marais	Pântano
⁂	Ice Features, Glacier	Eis- und Gletscherformen	Accidentes Glaciales	Formes glaciaires	Acidentes glaciares
⊤	Other Hydrographic Features	Andere Hydrographische Objekte	Otros Elementos Hidrográficos	Autres données hydrographiques	Outros acidentes hidrográficos

Symbol	English	Deutsch	Español	Français	Português
✦	Submarine Features	Untermeerische Objekte	Accidentes Submarinos	Formes de relief sous-marin	Acidentes submarinos
□	Political Unit	Politische Einheit	Unidad Política	Entité politique	Unidade política
ʋ	Cultural Institution	Kulturelle Institution	Institución Cultural	Institution culturelle	Instituição cultural
⊥	Historical Site	Historische Stätte	Sitio Histórico	Site historique	Sítio histórico
♠	Recreational Site	Erholungs- und Ferienort	Sitio de Recreo	Centre de loisirs	Área de Lazer
⊠	Airport	Flughafen	Aeropuerto	Aéroport	Aeroporto
■	Military Installation	Militäranlage	Instalación Militar	Installation militaire	Instalação militar
✶	Miscellaneous	Verschiedenes	Misceláneo	Divers	Diversos

I · 36 Chin-Chur

ENGLISH DEUTSCH

Name	Page	Lat. °′	Long. °′
Chinchilla, Pa., U.S.	210	41.28 N	75.41 W
Chinchiná	246	4.58 N	75.36 W
Chincholi	272c	19.10 N	73.08 E
Chinchón, Esp.	34	40.08 N	3.25 W
Chinch'ŏn, Taehan	98	36.52 N	127.26 E
Chinchorro, Banco ✢4	232	18.35 N	87.22 W
Chinchou → Jinzhou	104	41.07 N	121.08 E
Chincilla de Monte Aragón	34	38.55 N	1.43 W
Chincolco	252	32.13 S	70.50 W
Chincoteague	208	37.55 N	75.22 W
Chincoteague Bay ⊂	208	38.06 N	75.15 W
Chincoteague Inlet ⊂	208	37.53 N	75.25 W
Chinde	156	18.37 S	36.24 E
Chindo	98	34.28 N	126.15 E
Chin-do I	98	34.25 N	126.15 E
Chindong	98	35.07 N	128.29 E
Chindwinn ≃	110	21.26 N	95.15 E
Chine (la République populaire de) → China □1, Asia	90	35.00 N	105.00 E
Chine (nationaliste) → Taiwan □1, Asia	100	23.30 N	121.00 E
Chinen	174m	26.09 N	127.49 E
Chineni	123	33.02 N	75.17 E
Chine Orientale, Mer de → East China Sea ⊤2	90	30.00 N	126.00 E
Chinese Camp	226	37.52 N	120.26 W
Chinese Cemetery ◆	269f	14.38 N	120.59 E
Chinese University ʊ2	271d	22.26 N	114.12 E
Chingamba	152	12.49 S	18.20 E
Chingansk	89	49.07 N	131.11 E
Chingarora Creek ≃	276	40.27 N	74.12 W
Ch'ingchiang → Qingjiang	100	33.35 N	119.02 E
Chingford ◆8	260	51.38 N	0.01 E
Chingleput	122	12.42 N	79.59 E
Chingmei ◆8	269d	24.59 N	121.32 E
Chingola	154	12.32 S	27.52 E
Chingoni	157a	12.48 S	45.08 E
Chingoroi	152	13.37 S	14.01 E
Chingshih → Jinshi	102	29.39 N	111.52 E
Ch'ingtao → Qingdao	98	36.06 N	120.19 E
Chingtechen → Jingdezhen	100	29.16 N	117.11 E
Ch'ingt'ung	269d	25.02 N	121.43 E
Chinguar	152	12.36 S	16.20 E
Chinguetti	150	20.27 N	12.22 W
Chingune	156	20.38 S	34.55 E
Chinhae	98	35.09 N	128.40 E
Chinhae-man ⊂	98	35.01 N	128.34 E
Chin Hills ⋏2	110	22.30 N	93.30 E
Chinhoyi	154	17.22 S	30.12 E
Chinhsien → Jinxian	98	39.04 N	121.40 E
Chinhua → Jinhua	100	29.07 N	119.39 E
Ch'inhuangtao → Qinhuangdao	98	39.56 N	119.36 E
Chīni	120	31.32 N	78.15 E
Chiniak, Cape ≻	180	57.36 N	152.08 W
Chining → Jining, Zhg.	98	35.25 N	116.36 E
Chining → Jining, Zhg.	102	40.57 N	113.02 E
Chiniot	123	31.43 N	72.59 E
Chinit ≃	110	12.55 N	105.35 E
Chinitna Point ≻	180	59.43 N	153.02 W
Chinitos	232	25.01 N	107.54 W
Chiniziua	156	19.00 S	35.09 E
Chinjan	120	30.34 N	67.58 E
Chinju	98	35.11 N	128.05 E
Chinkiang → Zhenjiang	106	32.13 N	119.26 E
Chinko ≃	136	4.50 N	23.53 E
Chinkuashih	100	25.07 N	121.51 E
Chin Lakes ⊜	182	49.37 N	112.13 W
Chinle	200	36.09 N	109.33 W
Chinle Creek ≃	200	37.12 N	109.43 W
Chinle Wash V	200	36.54 N	109.45 W
Chinley	262	53.20 N	1.56 W
Chinley Churn ∧2	262	53.21 N	1.57 W
Chinmen	100	24.27 N	118.21 E
Chinmen Tao I	100	24.27 N	118.23 E
Chinnampo → Namp'o	98	38.45 N	125.23 E
Chinnor	42	51.43 N	0.56 W
Chino, Nihon	94	35.59 N	138.09 E
Chino, Ca., U.S.	228	34.00 N	117.41 W
Chino Airport ⊠	280	33.59 N	117.38 W
Chino Creek ≃	280	33.53 N	117.38 W
Chino Hills ⋏2	280	33.56 N	117.45 W
Chinon	50	47.10 N	0.15 E
Chinook, Ab., Can.	184	51.27 N	110.56 W
Chinook, Mt., U.S.	202	48.35 N	109.13 W
Chinook, Wa., U.S.	224	46.16 N	123.56 W
Chinook Cove	182	51.14 N	120.10 W
Chino Valley	200	34.45 N	112.27 W
Chinowths Corner	226	36.20 N	119.19 W
Chinpāi	126	23.50 N	87.28 E
Chinquapin	192	34.49 N	77.49 W
Chinsali	154	10.34 S	32.03 E
Chinshan	100	25.13 N	121.38 E
Chinshui	100	24.36 N	120.53 E
Chintāmani	122	13.24 N	78.04 E
Chintembwe	154	13.25 S	33.59 E
Chintheche	154	11.52 S	34.09 E
Chinú	246	9.06 N	75.24 W
Chinunje	154	11.19 S	37.19 E
Chinwangtao → Qinhuangdao	98	39.56 N	119.36 E
Chiny	56	49.44 N	5.20 E
Chinyama Litapi	152	13.31 S	22.21 E
Chioco	154	16.25 S	32.50 E
Chioggia	64	45.13 N	12.17 E
Chiomonte	62	45.07 N	6.59 E
Chios → Khíos	38	38.22 N	26.08 E
Chios → Khíos I	38	38.22 N	26.00 E
Chipao	248	14.15 S	73.57 W
Chipata (Fort Jameson)	154	13.39 S	32.40 E
Chipehua, Bahía ⊂	234	16.03 N	95.23 W
Chipei Tao I	100	23.45 N	119.37 E
Chipera	154	15.28 S	32.30 E
Chiperone ∧	154	16.28 S	35.12 E
Chipili	154	10.44 S	29.04 E
Chiping	98	36.37 N	116.16 E
Chipinge	154	20.12 S	32.38 E
Chip Lake ⊜	182	53.40 N	115.20 W
Chipley	194	30.46 N	85.32 W
Chiplūn	122	17.32 N	73.31 E
Chipman	186	46.11 N	65.53 W
Chipogolo	154	6.52 S	36.02 E
Chipoka	154	14.00 S	34.31 E
Chipola ≃	192	30.01 N	85.05 W
Chippawa ◆8	284a	43.04 N	79.03 W
Chippawa Channel ≃1	284a	43.04 N	79.01 W
Chippego Lake ⊜	212	44.34 N	76.49 W
Chippenham	42	51.28 N	2.07 W
Chipperfield	260	51.42 N	0.29 W
Chippewa ≃, Mi., U.S.	190	43.35 N	84.17 W
Chippewa ≃, Mn., U.S.	198	44.56 N	95.44 W
Chippewa ≃, Wi., U.S.	190	44.25 N	92.10 W
Chippewa, East Branch ≃	198	45.20 N	95.36 W
Chippewa, East Fork ≃	190	45.53 N	91.05 W
Chippewa, Lake ⊜	190	45.56 N	91.13 W
Chippewa Bay ⊂	212	44.27 N	75.47 W
Chippewa Creek ≃	212	44.27 N	75.46 W
Chippewa Falls	190	44.56 N	91.23 W
Chippewa Lake	214	41.04 N	81.54 W
Chippewanuck Creek ≃	216	41.07 N	86.12 W
Chipping Campden	42	52.03 N	1.46 W
Chipping Norton	42	51.56 N	1.32 W
Chipping Ongar	260	51.43 N	0.15 E
Chipping Sodbury	42	51.33 N	2.24 W
Chippis	58	46.17 N	7.33 E
Chippokes Plantation State Park ♠	208	37.08 N	76.44 W
Chipps Island I	282	38.03 N	121.55 W
Chipre → Cyprus □1	130	35.00 N	33.00 E
Chipstead, Eng., U.K.	260	51.17 N	0.09 E
Chipstead, Eng., U.K.	260	51.18 N	0.10 W
Chipuriro	154	16.39 S	30.42 E
Chiquelequele	152	16.40 S	19.06 E
Chiquián	248	10.09 S	77.11 W
Chiquihuitlán de Juárez	234	17.59 N	96.48 W
Chiquimula	236	14.48 N	89.33 W
Chiquimula □5	236	14.40 N	89.25 W
Chiquimulilla	236	14.05 N	90.23 W
Chiquinata, Bahía ⊂	248	20.20 S	70.10 W
Chiquinquirá	246	5.37 N	73.50 W
Chiquintirca	248	13.09 S	73.41 W
Chiquita	152	8.38 S	17.05 E
Chiquito Creek ≃	226	37.20 N	119.20 W
Chira ≃	246	4.54 S	81.08 W
Chira, Isla I	236	10.06 N	85.09 W
Chirad	272c	19.09 N	73.07 E
Chiradzulu	154	15.42 S	35.10 E
Chirāgh Delhi ◆8	272a	28.32 N	77.14 E
Chīrāla	122	15.49 N	80.21 E
Chiramba	154	16.55 S	34.39 E
Chirape	156	21.18 S	33.33 E
Chirāwa	120	28.15 N	75.38 E
Chirchik → Čirčik	85	41.29 N	69.35 E
Chire (Shire) ≃	154	17.42 S	35.19 E
Chiredzi	154	21.03 S	31.45 E
Chireno	194	31.30 N	94.21 W
Chirens	62	45.25 N	5.33 E
Chirfa	146	20.57 N	12.21 E
Chīrgaon	124	25.35 N	78.49 E
Chiricahua Mountains ⋏	200	31.50 N	109.15 W
Chiricahua National Monument ♠	200	32.02 N	109.19 W
Chiricahua Peak ∧	200	31.52 N	109.20 W
Chiriguaná	246	9.22 N	73.36 W
Chirikof Island I	180	55.50 N	155.35 W
Chirilagua	236	13.13 N	88.08 W
Chirinos	248	5.16 S	78.52 W
Chiriquí	236	8.24 N	82.19 W
Chiriquí □4	236	8.30 N	82.00 W
Chiriquí ≃	236	8.30 N	82.26 W
Chiriquí, Golfo de ⊂	246	8.00 N	82.20 W
Chiriquí, Laguna de ⊂	236	9.03 N	82.00 W
Chiriquí Grande	236	8.57 N	82.07 W
Chiriquí Viejo ≃	236	8.20 N	82.41 W
Chirk	42	52.56 N	3.03 W
Chirki	126	24.03 N	86.09 E
Chirle	272c	18.56 N	73.02 E
Chirmiri	124	23.12 N	82.21 E
Chirnside	46	55.48 N	2.13 W
Chiromo	154	16.33 S	35.08 E
Chirovo	76	58.56 N	33.24 E
Chirripó ≃	236	10.41 N	83.41 W
Chirripó, Cerro ∧	236	9.29 N	83.30 W
Chirsa	84	41.31 N	46.06 E
Chirundu	154	15.59 S	28.54 E
Chirvosti	265a	59.57 N	30.37 E
Chiryū	94	35.00 N	137.02 E
Chisago City	190	45.22 N	92.53 W
Chisamba	154	14.58 S	28.23 E
Chisana	180	62.09 N	142.10 W
Chisasibi	176	53.50 N	79.00 W
Chiscas	246	6.33 N	72.29 W
Chisec	236	15.49 N	90.17 W
Chiseldon	42	51.31 N	1.44 W
Chisenga	154	9.56 S	33.26 E
Chisep'o	98	34.50 N	128.42 E
Ch'ishan	100	22.53 N	120.28 E
Chishanji	98	36.56 N	122.23 E
Chishi	100	27.42 N	117.58 E
Chishisi	100	25.32 N	113.11 E
Chisholm, Al., U.S.	194	32.25 N	86.15 W
Chisholm, Me., U.S.	188	44.28 N	70.12 W
Chisholm, Mn., U.S.	190	47.29 N	92.53 W
Chisholm, Tx., U.S.	222	32.51 N	96.22 W
Chisholm Mills	182	54.55 N	114.08 W
Chishtiān Mandi	123	29.48 N	72.52 E
Chishui	102	28.29 N	105.38 E
Chishui ≃, Zhg.	102	28.53 N	105.48 E
Chishui ≃, Zhg.	107	28.49 N	105.50 E
Chishuihe	102	27.50 N	105.32 E
Chišig-Öndör	88	48.19 N	103.25 E
Chisimaio → Kismaayo	144	0.22 N	42.32 E
Chişinău → Kišin'ov	78	47.00 N	28.50 E
Chişineu-Criş	38	46.31 N	21.31 E
Chislaviči	76	54.11 N	32.10 E
Chislehurst ◆8	260	51.25 N	0.04 E
Chisone ≃	62	44.49 N	7.25 E
Chisone, Valle del V	62	45.01 N	7.07 E
Chisos Mountains ⋏	196	29.15 N	103.20 W
Chisseaux	50	47.20 N	1.05 E
Chissengue	152	9.14 S	20.42 E
Chissilo	152	13.34 S	16.30 E
Chist'akovo → Torez	83	48.01 N	38.37 E
Chistochina	180	62.34 N	144.40 W
Chistopol → Čistopol'	80	55.21 N	50.37 E
Chistyakovo → Torez	83	48.01 N	38.37 E
Chiswellgreen	260	51.44 N	0.22 W
Chiswick ◆8	260	51.29 N	0.16 W
Chita, Col.	246	6.11 N	72.28 W
Chita, Nihon	94	35.00 N	136.51 E
Chita → Čita	88	52.03 N	113.30 E
Chitado	152	17.20 S	13.54 E
Chitagá	246	7.09 N	72.40 W
Chita-hantō ≻1	94	34.50 N	136.53 E
Chitambo	154	12.55 S	30.39 E
Chitanda ≃	152	16.01 S	15.12 E
Chitarda	126	21.50 N	86.57 E
Chitata	152	13.47 S	15.43 E
Chitato	152	7.20 S	20.47 E
Chita-wan ⊂	94	34.47 N	136.58 E
Chitek ≃	184	54.06 N	108.16 W
Chitek Lake ⊜, Mb., Can.	184	52.26 N	99.25 W
Chitek Lake ⊜, Sk., Can.	184	53.44 N	107.47 W
Chitembo	152	13.34 S	16.40 E
Chitina	180	61.31 N	144.27 W
Chitina ≃	180	61.30 N	144.28 W
Chitipa	154	9.43 S	33.16 E
Chitokoloki	152	13.50 S	23.13 E
Chitose	92a	42.49 N	141.39 E
Chitose-chūtonchi, Rikujō-jieitai- ■	92a	42.46 N	141.40 E
Chitou Shan I	100	27.40 N	120.50 E
Chitra ≃1	126	22.53 N	89.40 E
Chitradurga	122	14.14 N	76.24 E
Chitrakūt Dham	124	25.11 N	80.52 E
Chitrāl	123	35.51 N	71.47 E
Chitrasāli	272b	22.52 N	88.09 E
Chitrāvati ≃	122	14.48 N	78.14 E
Chitré	236	7.58 N	80.26 W
Chittagong	120	22.20 N	91.50 E
Chittagong □5	120	23.00 N	91.00 E
Chīttāpur	122	17.07 N	77.05 E
Chittaranjan	126	23.52 N	86.52 E
Chittaurgarh	120	24.53 N	74.38 E
Chittenango	210	43.02 N	75.52 W
Chittenango Creek ≃	210	43.11 N	76.00 W
Chittenango Falls	210	42.59 N	75.50 W
Chittering	162	31.29 S	116.06 E
Chittoor	122	13.12 N	79.07 E
Chittūr	122	10.42 N	76.45 E
Chitu, Ityo.	144	8.36 N	37.59 E
Ch'itu, T'aiwan	269d	25.06 N	121.43 E
Chitungwiza	154	17.45 S	31.16 E
Chiuchiang → Jiujiang	100	29.44 N	115.59 E
Chíuchíu	252	22.21 S	68.39 W
Chiuduno	62	45.40 N	9.51 E
Chiumbe	152	12.29 S	16.08 E
Chiumbe ≃	152	7.00 S	21.12 E
Chiúme	152	15.03 S	21.14 E
Chiuppano	64	45.46 N	11.28 E
Chiuro	64	46.10 N	9.59 E
Chiusa (Klausen)	64	46.38 N	11.34 E
Chiusa di Pesio	62	44.19 N	7.40 E
Chiusa di San Michele	62	45.06 N	7.19 E
Chiusaforte	64	46.24 N	13.18 E
Chiusa Sclafani	70	37.41 N	13.16 E
Chiusella ≃	62	45.24 N	7.55 E
Chiusi	66	43.01 N	11.57 E
Chiusi, Lago di ⊜	66	43.03 N	11.58 E
Chiúta	154	15.34 S	33.17 E
Chiuta, Lake ⊜	154	14.55 S	35.50 E
Chiv	84	41.46 N	47.54 E
Chiva	72	41.24 N	60.22 E
Chivacoa	246	10.10 N	68.54 W
Chivapuri ≃	246	6.25 N	66.23 W
Chivasso	62	45.11 N	7.53 E
Chivato, Punta ≻	232	27.05 N	111.59 W
Chivay	248	15.40 S	71.35 W
Chivhu	154	19.01 S	30.53 E
Chivilcoy	252	34.53 S	60.01 W
Chivirira Falls ⌞	154	21.14 S	32.20 E
Chiwanda	154	11.22 S	34.54 E
Chiwawa ≃	224	47.47 N	120.40 W
Chixi	100	28.22 N	116.22 E
Chixoy ≃	236	16.03 N	90.27 W
Chiyoda, Nihon	94	36.12 N	139.26 E
Chiyoda, Nihon	94	36.11 N	140.14 E
Chiyoda, Nihon	96	34.41 N	132.32 E
Chiyoda ◆8	268	35.41 N	139.44 E
Chizarira National Park ♠	154	17.45 S	28.00 E
Chizhen	100	31.55 N	118.12 E
Chizizhen	100	32.22 N	115.11 E
Chizu	96	35.16 N	134.14 E
Chjargas	88	49.32 N	93.48 E
Chjargas nuur ⊜	88	49.12 N	93.24 E
Chkalov → Orenburg	86	51.54 N	55.06 E
Chlebnikovo, S.S.S.R.	80	56.38 N	49.56 E
Chlebnikovo, S.S.S.R.	265b	55.58 N	37.31 E
Chlebodarnyj	80	46.41 N	40.50 E
Chlebodarovka	83	47.29 N	37.23 E
Chlevnoje	76	52.12 N	39.05 E
Chloride	200	35.24 N	114.11 W
Chlum	60	48.52 N	13.55 E
Chlum ∧	61	48.42 N	14.04 E
Chmelevicy	80	57.45 N	46.22 E
Chmelevo	82	56.09 N	39.08 E
Chmelevoje	78	48.34 N	31.24 E
Chmelita	76	55.25 N	33.53 E
Chmel'nickij	78	49.25 N	27.00 E
Chmel'nik	78	49.33 N	27.57 E
Chmel'niki, S.S.S.R.	82	56.53 N	38.39 E
Chmel'niki, S.S.S.R.	82	56.52 N	38.13 E
Chmielnik	30	50.37 N	20.46 E
Chmost' ≃	76	54.45 N	32.34 E
Choa Chu Kang	271c	1.22 N	103.41 E
Choāli	272b	22.24 N	88.24 E
Chŏâm Khsant	110	14.13 N	104.56 E
Choapa ≃	252	31.38 S	71.34 W
Choapan	234	17.20 N	95.57 W
Choba	154	2.26 N	38.03 E
Chobe □5	156	18.30 S	25.00 E
Chobe ≃	156	17.50 S	25.05 E
Chobeju	24	64.53 N	60.10 E
Chobe National Park ♠	156	18.45 S	24.15 E
Chobham	260	51.21 N	0.36 W
Chobham Common ♠	260	51.23 N	0.37 W
Chobi	84	42.21 N	41.53 E
Chocamán	234	18.59 N	97.01 W
Choccolocco Creek ≃	194	33.33 N	86.11 W
Choceň	30	50.00 N	16.13 E
Chocenice	60	49.33 N	13.31 E
Chochis, Cerro ∧	248	18.04 S	60.03 W
Choch'iwŏn	98	36.37 N	127.18 E
Chochloma	80	56.58 N	43.54 E
Chöchmor't	88	47.21 N	94.33 E
Chochol'skij	78	51.34 N	38.45 E
Cho Chu	110	21.54 N	105.39 E
Chocianów	30	51.25 N	15.55 E
Chociwel	30	53.28 N	15.19 E
Chocó □5	246	6.00 N	77.00 W
Chocolate Bay ⊂	222	29.11 N	95.09 W
Chocolate Bayou ≃	222	29.13 N	95.13 W
Chocolate Mountains ⋏	204	33.20 N	115.15 W
Chocontá	246	5.09 N	73.41 W
Chocope	248	7.47 S	79.13 W
Choctawhatchee, East Fork ≃	194	31.21 N	85.33 W
Choctawhatchee, West Fork ≃	194	31.21 N	85.33 W
Choctawhatchee Bay ⊂	194	30.25 N	86.21 W
Choctaw Lake ⊜1	218	39.58 N	83.29 W
Chodarus	88	52.36 N	99.19 E
Chodavaram	122	17.50 N	82.57 E
Chodecz	30	52.24 N	19.01 E
Ch'o-do I, C.M.I.K.	98	38.32 N	124.50 E
Ch'o-do I, Taehan	98	34.14 N	127.15 E
Chodoi	114	2.50 N	101.27 E
Chodorov	78	49.24 N	24.17 E
Chodosy	76	53.56 N	31.29 E
Chodov	54	50.11 N	12.43 E
Chodovaja Griva	80	57.08 N	50.16 E
Chodovaricha	24	68.57 N	53.40 E
Chodz' ≃	84	44.43 N	40.45 E
Chodžaimetk	85	39.37 N	69.14 E
Chodžakala	128	38.43 N	56.20 E
Chodžejli	72	42.48 N	59.25 E
Chodzież	30	52.59 N	16.56 E
Choele-Choel	252	39.16 S	65.41 W
Chofombo	154	14.35 S	31.50 E
Chōfu	94	35.39 N	139.33 E
Chofu Airport ⊠	268	35.40 N	139.32 E
Chogo Lungma Glacier ⊓	123	35.52 N	75.19 E
Chogot	88	53.15 N	105.52 E
Choiceland	184	53.27 N	104.25 W
Choichuff, Laga ≃	154	1.34 N	39.24 E
Choire, Loch ⊜	46	58.13 N	4.21 W
Choisel	261	48.41 N	2.01 E
Choiseul	241f	13.47 N	61.03 W
Choiseul I	175e	7.05 S	157.00 E
Choiseul Sound Ʉ	254	51.57 S	58.35 W
Choisy	58	45.59 N	6.03 E
Choisy-le-Roi	261	48.46 N	2.25 E
Choix	232	26.43 N	108.17 W
Chojna	30	52.58 N	14.28 E
Chojnice	30	53.42 N	17.34 E
Chojniki	78	51.53 N	29.56 E
Chojnów	30	51.17 N	15.56 E
Chōkai-san ∧	92	39.06 N	140.03 E
Choke ⋏	144	10.45 N	37.35 E
Choke Canyon Lake ⊜1	196	28.30 N	98.20 W
Chokio	198	45.34 N	96.10 W
Chokoloskee	220	25.48 N	81.21 W
Chokwé	156	24.36 S	33.00 E
Cholame	226	35.43 N	120.17 W
Cholame Creek ≃	226	35.39 N	120.22 W
Cholame Hills ⋏2	226	35.45 N	120.30 W
Cholbon	88	51.53 N	116.15 E
Choldarkipčak	85	39.51 N	68.52 E
Cholet	32	47.04 N	0.53 W
Cholila	254	42.31 S	71.27 W
Chŏlla Namdo □4	98	34.45 N	127.00 E
Chŏlla Pukdo □4	98	35.45 N	127.15 E
Cholm	76	57.09 N	31.11 E
Cholmec, S.S.S.R.	76	56.21 N	33.21 E
Cholmeč', S.S.S.R.	78	52.09 N	30.37 E
Cholmogorovka	86	44.25 N	78.31 E
Cholmogorskaja	24	63.49 N	40.39 E
Cholmogory	24	64.15 N	41.40 E
Cholmsk	89	47.03 N	142.03 E
Cholmskij	78	44.52 N	38.24 E
Cholmy, S.S.S.R.	78	51.52 N	32.36 E
Cholmy, S.S.S.R.	82	54.56 N	38.33 E
Cholm-Žirkovskij	76	55.31 N	33.29 E
Cholodnaja Balka	83	48.02 N	38.04 E
Choloj ≃	88	53.12 N	112.47 E
Choloma	236	15.34 N	87.56 W
Chölönbujr	88	47.55 N	112.57 E
Cholopeniči	76	54.31 N	28.58 E
Ch'ŏlsan	98	39.46 N	124.40 E
Cholsey	42	51.34 N	1.10 W
Choltobino	82	54.11 N	38.28 E
Choltoson	88	50.20 N	103.20 E
Choluj, S.S.S.R.	80	56.34 N	41.53 E
Choluj, S.S.S.R.	80	56.04 N	42.08 E
Cholula [de Rivadabia]	234	19.04 N	98.18 W
Choluteca	236	13.18 N	87.12 W
Choluteca □5	236	13.20 N	87.10 W
Choluteca ≃	236	13.07 N	87.19 W
Choma	154	16.48 S	26.59 E
Chomedey ◆8	275a	45.32 N	73.44 W
Chomen Swamp ≡	144	9.25 N	37.20 E
Chomérac	62	44.42 N	4.39 E
Chomičev	80	48.11 N	45.01 E
Chomiomo ∧	124	28.01 N	88.31 E
Cho Moi, Viet.	110	10.33 N	105.24 E
Cho Moi, Viet.	269c	10.51 N	106.38 E
Chomo Lhāri ∧	124	27.50 N	89.15 E
Chom Thong	110	18.25 N	98.41 E
Chomūm	120	27.10 N	75.44 E
Chomutec	78	50.06 N	33.44 E
Chomutov	54	50.28 N	13.26 E
Chomutovka	78	51.56 N	34.33 E
Chomutovka ≃	54	50.11 N	13.37 E
Chomutovo, S.S.S.R.	76	52.51 N	37.27 E
Chomutovo, S.S.S.R.	88	52.28 N	104.25 E
Chomutovskaja	83	47.03 N	40.04 E
Chomutovskaja Step', zapovednik ♠	83	47.17 N	38.11 E
Chōnan, Nihon	94	35.24 N	140.14 E
Ch'ŏnan, Taehan	98	36.48 N	127.09 E
Chon'atino	82	55.11 N	38.07 E
Chon Buri	110	13.22 N	100.59 E
Chonchi	254	42.38 S	73.47 W
Choncholoj	88	51.08 N	108.14 E
Chon Daen	110	16.11 N	100.51 E
Chone	246	0.41 S	80.06 W
Chone ≃	246	0.35 S	80.25 W
Chong'an	100	27.45 N	118.02 E
Ch'ŏngch'ŏn-gang ≃	98	39.35 N	125.28 E
Ch'ŏngdan	98	37.58 N	125.56 E
Chongde	106	30.32 N	120.26 E
Ch'ŏngdo	98	35.38 N	128.43 E
Chonggu	106	31.12 N	121.10 E
Ch'ŏngha	98	36.13 N	129.20 E
Ch'onghak-ni	271b	37.43 N	127.05 E
Chonghe	89	44.43 N	127.45 E
Ch'ŏngjin	98	41.47 N	129.50 E
Chŏngju, C.M.I.K.	98	39.41 N	125.13 E
Ch'ŏngju, Taehan	98	36.39 N	127.31 E
Chŏng Kal	110	13.57 N	103.35 E
Chongkanzhen	107	30.09 N	105.37 E
Chongli (Xiwanzi)	98	40.54 N	115.16 E
Chongming	106	31.37 N	121.24 E
Chongming Dao I	106	31.36 N	121.33 E
Chongoene	156	25.00 S	33.47 E
Chongor	102	45.59 N	112.45 E
Chongos Bajo	248	12.07 S	75.16 W
Chongoyape	248	6.39 S	79.24 W
Chong Pang	271c	1.26 N	103.50 E
Chŏngp'yŏng-chŏsuji ⊜1	98	37.40 N	127.30 E
Chongqing, Zhg.	107	30.39 N	103.41 E
Chongqing (Chungking), Zhg.	107	29.34 N	106.35 E
Chongren, Zhg.	100	27.46 N	116.01 E
Chongren, Zhg.	100	29.37 N	120.43 E
Chongru	100	27.01 N	120.10 E
Ch'ŏngsan	98	36.22 N	127.46 E
Ch'ŏngsan-do I	98	34.11 N	126.54 E
Chongshi	100	25.24 N	115.28 E
Chŏngsŏn	98	37.22 N	128.38 E
Ch'ŏngsong	98	41.47 N	129.48 E
Chŏngŭp	98	35.36 N	126.51 E
Chongwe ≃	154	15.43 S	29.20 E
Chongwu	100	24.53 N	118.55 E
Chongxi	98	42.07 N	128.59 E
Chongxin	102	35.13 N	107.29 E
Ch'ŏngyang, Taehan	98	36.27 N	126.48 E
Chongyang, Zhg.	100	29.33 N	114.00 E
Chongyang ≃	100	27.18 N	118.08 E
Chongyi	100	25.44 N	114.18 E
Chongzuo	102	22.21 N	107.26 E
Chŏnju	98	35.49 N	127.08 E
Chonkham	120	27.48 N	96.02 E
Ch'ŏnma	98	40.03 N	125.01 E
Chonos, Archipiélago de los II	254	45.00 S	74.00 W
Ch'ŏnsu-ri	98	41.43 N	128.45 E
Chontaleña, Cordillera ⋏	236	11.50 N	84.50 W
Chontales □5	236	12.05 N	85.10 W
Chon Thanh	110	11.24 N	106.36 E
Chŏnŭi	98	36.42 N	127.11 E
Chonuu	74	66.27 N	143.06 E
Chonzie, Ben ∧	46	56.27 N	3.59 W
Cho Oyu → Chopu ∧	124	28.06 N	86.39 E
Chopda	120	21.15 N	75.18 E
Cho Phuoc Hai	110	10.26 N	107.18 E
Chopim ≃	252	25.35 S	53.05 W
Chopinzinho	252	25.51 S	52.30 W
Chopon	124	24.31 N	83.02 E
Chop'or ≃	80	49.36 N	42.19 E
Chop'orskij zapovednik ◆4	80	51.15 N	41.48 E
Choptank ≃	208	38.38 N	76.13 W
Chopu ∧	124	28.06 N	86.39 E
Chopwell	44	54.55 N	1.49 W
Chor	89	47.53 N	134.58 E
Chor ≃	89	47.48 N	134.43 E
Chora Saādatpur	272a	28.36 N	77.21 E
Chordil sar'dag ⋏	88	50.50 N	99.40 E
Chorejver	24	67.25 N	58.03 E
Chorges	62	44.33 N	6.17 E
Chori	84	41.37 N	45.59 E
Chorin ⊥	54	52.54 N	13.52 E
Chorina ≃	83	49.23 N	38.13 E
Chorinsk	88	52.10 N	109.46 E
Chorley	262	53.39 N	2.39 W
Chorley □8	262	53.38 N	2.33 W
Chorleywood	260	51.39 N	0.31 W
Chorlovo	82	55.20 N	38.49 E
Chorlton-cum-Hardy ◆8	262	53.27 N	2.17 W
Choro ≃	248	16.25 S	64.35 W
Chorog	120	37.31 N	71.33 E
Chorol, S.S.S.R.	78	49.47 N	33.17 E
Chorol', S.S.S.R.	89	44.25 N	132.04 E
Chorol ≃	78	49.28 N	33.47 E
Chorolque, Cerro ∧	248	20.56 S	66.01 W
Choros, Isla I	252	29.16 S	71.33 W
Chorošovo	82	55.08 N	38.47 E
Chorošovo ◆8	265b	55.47 N	37.28 E
Chorostkov	78	49.13 N	25.55 E
Choroszcz	30	53.09 N	22.59 E
Chorreras, Cerro ∧	232	26.02 N	106.21 W
Chorrillos	286d	12.10 S	77.02 W
Chorrochó	250	8.59 S	39.06 W
Chorro Creek ≃	226	35.20 N	120.50 W
Chort'ak, gora ∧	88	53.15 N	110.45 E
Ch'ŏrwŏn	98	38.16 N	127.12 E
Chorzele	30	53.16 N	20.55 E
Ch'osan	98	40.50 N	125.47 E
Chosanch'am	98	40.22 N	126.11 E
Chosedachard	24	67.02 N	59.22 E
Chosen	220	26.42 N	80.41 W
Chošeutovo	80	47.02 N	47.50 E
Chōshi	94	35.44 N	140.50 E
Choshi-ōhashi ◆5	94	35.44 N	140.50 E
Chōshi-zuka-kofun ⊥	94	34.42 N	137.50 E
Choshui ≃	100	24.03 N	120.24 E
Chosica	248	11.54 S	76.42 W
Chos Malal	252	37.23 S	70.16 W
Chosŏn Minjujuŭi In'min Konghwaguk → Korea, North □1	98	40.00 N	127.00 E
Chosrech	84	41.59 N	47.18 E
Chosta	84	43.33 N	39.53 E
Choszczno	30	53.10 N	15.26 E
Chota	248	6.33 S	78.39 W
Chotanāgpur Plateau ⋏1	124	23.30 N	84.30 E
Chotča ≃	82	56.54 N	37.35 E
Choteau	202	47.48 N	112.10 W
Choteau Creek ≃	198	42.51 N	98.09 W
Chotěboř	30	49.43 N	15.40 E
Choten'	78	51.07 N	34.46 E
Chotěšov, Česko.	60	49.39 N	13.12 E
Chotešov, S.S.S.R.	78	51.43 N	24.47 E
Chotila	120	22.25 N	71.11 E
Chotilovo	76	57.44 N	34.05 E
Chotimsk	76	53.26 N	32.35 E
Chotin	78	48.29 N	26.30 E
Chotisino	82	54.24 N	36.33 E
Chot'kovo, S.S.S.R.	76	53.46 N	35.14 E
Chot'kovo, S.S.S.R.	76	52.56 N	35.23 E
Chot'kovo, S.S.S.R.	82	56.15 N	38.00 E
Chotla, Cerro de ∧	234	17.55 N	101.31 W
Chotovn'a	76	53.17 N	30.32 E
Chotuš'	82	54.32 N	37.44 E
Chotynec	76	53.08 N	35.24 E
Chotyniči	76	52.38 N	26.18 E
Chouchiak'ou → Shangshui	100	33.33 N	114.34 E
Chouk'ou → Shangshui	100	33.33 N	114.34 E
Choûm	148	21.18 N	13.01 W
Chouteau	196	36.11 N	95.20 W
Chovaling	85	38.21 N	69.58 E
Chovd, Mong.	86	48.08 N	91.23 E
Chovd, Mong.	86	48.01 N	91.38 E
Chovd, Mong.	86	49.16 N	90.55 E
Chovd, Mong.	102	44.42 N	102.24 E
Chovd □4	86	48.00 N	91.30 E
Chovd ≃	90	48.06 N	92.11 E
Chövsgöl	102	43.36 N	109.39 E
Chövsgöl □4	88	50.00 N	100.00 E
Chövsgöl nuur ⊜	88	51.00 N	100.30 E
Chovu-Aksy	88	51.11 N	93.53 E
Chowan ≃	192	36.00 N	76.40 W
Chowchilla	226	37.07 N	120.15 W
Chowchilla ≃	226	37.07 N	120.32 W
Chowchilla, East Fork ≃	226	37.20 N	119.50 W
Chowchilla, West Fork ≃	226	37.20 N	119.50 W
Chowkay	123	34.41 N	70.56 E
Chown, Mount ∧	182	53.24 N	119.22 W
Ch'owŏn-ni	98	39.40 N	127.17 E
Choya	252	28.30 S	64.52 W
Choyak-to I	98	34.22 N	126.54 E
Chrapun'	78	51.42 N	27.29 E
Chr'aščevka	80	53.48 N	49.06 E
Chrást	60	49.48 N	13.29 E
Chrebtovo	82	56.35 N	38.16 E
Chrenovoje	80	51.07 N	40.17 E
Chreščatij	83	49.37 N	39.42 E
Chřibská	54	50.50 N	14.29 E
Chřič	60	49.57 N	13.39 E
Chriesman	222	30.36 N	96.46 W
Chrisman	194	39.48 N	87.40 W
Chrissiesmeer	158	26.16 S	30.13 E
Chrissiesmeer ⊜	158	26.19 S	30.13 E
Christanshåb (Qasigiannguit)	176	68.50 N	51.12 W
Christburg → Dzierzgoń	30	53.56 N	19.21 E
Christchurch, N.Z.	172	43.32 S	172.38 E
Christchurch, Eng., U.K.	42	50.44 N	1.45 W
Christ Church Cathedral ʊ1	273a	6.27 N	3.23 E
Christian □6	219	39.33 N	89.18 W
Christian ≃	180	66.36 N	145.49 W
Christian, Cape ≻	176	70.31 N	68.18 W
Christian, Point ≻	174e	25.04 S	130.07 W
Christiana, Jam.	241q	18.10 N	77.29 W
Christiana, S. Afr.	158	27.52 S	25.08 E
Christiana, De., U.S.	285	39.39 N	75.39 W
Christiana, Pa., U.S.	208	39.57 N	75.59 W
Christiana Creek ≃	216	41.41 N	85.59 W
Christianburg	218	38.17 N	85.06 W
Christian Channel Ʉ	212	44.47 N	80.08 W
Christian Island I	212	44.50 N	80.13 W
Christian Island Indian Reserve ◆4	212	44.50 N	80.10 W
Christiansburg, Oh., U.S.	218	40.03 N	84.01 W
Christiansburg, Va., U.S.	192	37.07 N	80.24 W
Christiansfeld	41	55.21 N	9.29 E
Christiansø I	26	55.19 N	15.12 E
Christian Sound Ʉ	180	55.56 N	134.40 W
Christiansted	241n	17.45 N	64.42 W
Christie, Mount ∧	180	63.01 N	129.40 W
Christie, Mount ∧2	216	42.53 N	83.20 W
Christie Bay ⊂	176	62.32 N	111.10 W
Christie Lake ⊜, Mb., Can.	184	56.54 N	96.56 W
Christie Lake ⊜, On., Can.	212	44.48 N	76.26 W
Christina ≃, Ab., Can.	184	56.40 N	111.03 W
Christina ≃, De., U.S.	285	39.43 N	75.31 W
Christina Lake ⊜, Ab., Can.	182	55.38 N	110.55 W
Christina Lake ⊜, B.C., Can.	182	49.05 N	118.14 W
Christinovka	78	48.49 N	29.58 E
Christišče	83	48.55 N	37.30 E
Christmas	220	28.32 N	81.01 W
Christmas Bay ⊂	222	29.03 N	95.11 W
Christmas Creek	162	18.53 S	125.55 E
Christmas Creek ≃	162	18.29 S	125.23 E
Christmas Island □2, Oc.	108	10.30 S	105.40 E
Christmas Island □2, Oc.	112	10.30 S	105.40 E
Christmas Island → Kiritimati I1	174o	1.52 N	157.20 W
Christmas Mountain ∧	180	64.34 N	160.34 W
Christmas Ridge ✢3	14	5.00 N	160.00 W
Christoforovka	78	47.59 N	33.05 E
Christoforovo	24	60.53 N	47.13 E
Christ of the Andes → Cristo Redentor ⊥	252	32.50 S	70.05 W
Christoph Columbus-Spitze → Cristóbal Colón, Pico ∧	246	10.50 N	73.41 W
Christopher	194	37.58 N	89.03 W
Christopher, Lake ⊜	162	24.49 S	127.42 E
Christoval	196	31.12 N	100.30 W
Chroma ≃	74	71.36 N	144.49 E
Chromtau	86	50.17 N	58.27 E
Chrudim	30	49.57 N	15.48 E
Chrustal'nyj	89	44.24 N	135.06 E
Chrzanów	30	50.09 N	19.24 E
Chu (Xam) ≃, Asia	110	19.53 N	105.45 E
Chu ≃, Zhg.	100	32.08 N	118.43 E
Chu ≃, Zhg.	106	32.15 N	119.03 E
Chuādanga	124	23.38 N	88.51 E
Chualar	226	36.34 N	121.31 W
Chuanbu	106	31.17 N	119.49 E
Chuanchang ≚	100	33.46 N	119.51 E
Chuanergu	105	39.20 N	117.43 E
Chuan'gang	106	31.57 N	121.04 E
Chuangjiapuzi	104	40.50 N	124.06 E
Chuanliao	100	28.17 N	120.13 E
Chuansha	106	31.12 N	121.42 E
Chuanshan	100	29.53 N	121.57 E
Chuanxindian	104	41.25 N	120.30 E
Chuanyao Gang ⊂	106	32.12 N	121.25 E
Chuathbaluk	180	61.40 N	159.15 W
Chubbuck	202	42.55 N	112.27 W
Chūbu-Sangaku-kokuritsu-kōen ♠	94	36.30 N	137.41 E
Chubut □4	254	44.00 S	69.00 W
Chubut ≃	254	43.20 S	65.03 W
Ch'üchiang → Shaoguan	100	24.50 N	113.37 E
Chuchi Lake ⊜	182	55.10 N	124.33 W
Chuchou → Zhuzhou	100	27.50 N	113.09 E
Chuchra	78	50.13 N	34.49 E
Chu Chua	182	51.21 N	120.10 W
Chuchuwayha Indian Reserve ◆4	182	49.21 N	120.06 W
Chuckatuck	208	36.52 N	76.35 W
Chučni	84	41.57 N	47.55 E
Chucuito	248	15.53 S	69.53 W
Chucun	100	33.04 N	116.32 E
Chucunaque ≃	246	8.09 N	77.44 W
Chudan ≃	88	52.08 N	109.40 E
Chudanskij chrebet ⋏	88	52.00 N	110.00 E
Chudat	84	41.38 N	48.42 E
Chudeč	60	49.58 N	13.05 E
Chudleigh	42	50.36 N	3.38 W
Chudojelan'	88	54.42 N	99.37 E
Chudzirt	86	47.05 N	91.10 E
Chuen Lung	271d	22.24 N	114.06 E
Chugach Islands II	180	59.06 N	151.42 W
Chugach Mountains ⋏	180	61.00 N	145.00 W
Chuginadak Island I	180	52.49 N	169.50 W
Chūgoku-sanchi ⋏	96	34.58 N	132.57 E
Chugwater	200	41.45 N	104.49 W
Chugwater Creek ≃	198	42.07 N	104.51 W
Chugyn-ri	271b	37.39 N	126.50 E
Chūhar Kāna	123	31.45 N	73.48 E
Chuhe	100	34.03 N	113.35 E
Chuhuichupa	232	29.38 N	108.22 W
Chuí	252	33.41 S	53.27 W
Chuius Mountain ∧	182	54.51 N	124.30 W
Chukai	114	4.15 N	103.25 E
Chukchi Sea ⊤2	16	69.00 N	171.00 W
Chuke Hu ⊜	120	31.40 N	88.00 E
Chukou	100	25.44 N	113.22 E
Chulalongkorn University ʊ2	269a	13.44 N	100.33 E
Chula Vista	228	32.38 N	117.05 W
Chuld	102	45.04 N	105.35 E
Chulga ≃	24	64.20 N	61.00 E
Chullora	274a	33.54 S	151.04 E
Chulmleigh	42	50.55 N	3.52 W
Chulo	84	41.41 N	42.18 E
Chulp'o	98	35.37 N	126.40 E
Chulucanas	248	5.06 S	80.10 W
Chulumani	248	16.24 S	67.31 W
Chuluota	220	28.38 N	81.10 W
Chuma	248	15.24 S	68.56 W
Chumalag	84	43.14 N	44.28 E
Chumbicha	252	28.52 S	66.14 W
Chummi, ozero ⊜	89	50.18 N	137.17 E
Chum Phae	110	16.32 N	102.06 E
Chumphon	110	10.30 N	99.10 E
Chumphon Buri	110	15.21 N	103.24 E
Chumpi	248	15.06 S	73.46 W
Chum Saeng	110	15.54 N	100.19 E
Chumunjin	98	37.54 N	128.49 E
Chunal	262	53.25 N	1.57 W
Chunan, T'aiwan	100	24.41 N	120.52 E
Chun'an, Zhg.	100	29.35 N	118.58 E
Chunār	124	25.08 N	82.54 E
Chuncheon → Ch'unch'ŏn	98	37.52 N	127.43 E
Chunchi, Ec.	246	2.17 S	78.55 W
Chunchi, Zhg.	100	27.22 N	119.20 E
Ch'unch'ŏn	98	37.52 N	127.43 E
Chunchula	194	30.55 N	88.12 W
Chūnd	123	31.26 N	72.16 E
Chung-ang University ʊ2	271b	37.30 N	126.58 E
Chungari ≃	89	50.04 N	136.55 E
Ch'ungch'ŏng Namdo □4	98	36.30 N	127.00 E
Ch'ungch'ŏng Pukdo □4	98	36.45 N	128.00 E
Chunggang-ni	98	40.52 N	127.20 E
Chung Hau	271d	22.16 N	114.00 E
Chungho	269d	25.00 N	121.30 E
Chung Hsing Bridge ◆5	269d	25.03 N	121.29 E
Chunghwa	98	38.52 N	125.47 E
Ch'ungju	98	36.58 N	127.58 E
Chungking → Chongqing	107	29.34 N	106.35 E
Chungli	100	24.57 N	121.13 E
Chungliao	100	22.41 N	121.28 E
Ch'ungmu	98	34.51 N	128.25 E
Chungp'u	100	23.25 N	120.31 E
Chungp'yŏngjang	98	41.11 N	128.03 E
Chungsam-ni	98	38.34 N	127.09 E
Chŭngsan	98	39.06 N	125.22 E
Chŭngsanha-ri ◆8	271b	37.35 N	126.54 E
Chungshan → Zhongshan	100	22.31 N	113.22 E
Chungshan Bridge ◆5	269d	25.05 N	121.31 E
Chunguj ≃	88	48.51 N	93.32 E
Chungyang Shanmo ⋏	100	23.30 N	121.00 E
Chunheji	100	32.12 N	115.22 E
Chunhua, Zhg.	102	34.50 N	108.31 E
Chunhua, Zhg.	106	31.56 N	118.56 E
Chunhuás	232	19.12 N	88.55 W
Chūniān	123	30.58 N	73.59 E
Chuntuquí	232	17.31 N	90.09 W
Chünüj ≃	88	48.48 N	102.00 E
Chunya	154	8.32 S	33.25 E
Ch'unyang, Taehan	98	36.56 N	128.54 E
Chunyang, Zhg.	89	43.43 N	129.28 E
Chunzach	84	42.33 N	46.43 E
Chūō	96	35.00 N	133.58 E
Chūō ◆8, Nihon	268	35.40 N	139.47 E
Chūō ◆8, Nihon	270	34.42 N	135.11 E
Chuŏr Phnum Krâvanh ⋏	110	12.00 N	103.15 E
Chuosijia	102	31.53 N	101.59 E
Chupaca	248	12.04 S	75.19 W
Chupadera Arroyo V	200	33.47 N	106.37 W
Chupadero, Cerro ∧	200	31.01 N	111.37 W
Chupaderos	234	23.50 N	102.20 W
Chupara Point ≻	241r	10.48 N	61.22 W
Chuquibamba	248	15.50 S	72.39 W
Chuquibambilla	248	14.07 S	72.43 W
Chuquicamata	252	22.19 S	68.56 W
Chuquisaca □5	248	20.00 S	64.20 W
Chuquitanta	286d	11.58 S	77.06 W
Chur	58	46.51 N	9.32 E
Churach ≃	88	48.37 N	110.42 E
Churāchāndpur	120	24.20 N	93.40 E
Churāmankāti	126	23.14 N	89.09 E
Churcampa	248	12.42 S	74.24 W
Church	262	53.45 N	2.24 W
Churchdown	42	51.53 N	2.10 W
Church Hill, Md., U.S.	208	39.08 N	75.59 W
Church Hill, Tn., U.S.	192	36.31 N	82.42 W
Churchill, Mb., Can.	176	58.46 N	94.10 W
Churchill, Oh., U.S.	214	41.09 N	80.39 W
Churchill, Pa., U.S.	279b	40.27 N	79.51 W
Churchill, Va., U.S.	284c	38.54 N	77.10 W
Churchill ≃, Can.	176	58.47 N	94.12 W

Symbols in the index entries represent the broad categories identified in the key at the right. Symbols with superior numbers (⋏1) identify subcategories (see complete key on page *I · 1*).

Symbole im Register stellen die rechts im Schlüssel erklärten Kategorien dar. Symbole mit hochgestellten Ziffern (⋏1) bezeichnen Unterabteilungen einer Kategorie (vgl. vollständiger Schlüssel auf Seite *I · 1*).

Los símbolos incluídos en el texto del índice representan las grandes categorias identificadas con la clave a la derecha. Los símbolos con numeros en su parte superior (⋏1) identifican las subcategorías (véase la clave completa en la página *I · 1*).

Les symboles de l'index représentent les catégories indiquées dans la légende à droite. Les symboles suivis d'un indice (⋏1) représentent des sous-catégories (voir légende complète à la page *I · 1*).

Os símbolos incluídos no texto do índice representam as grandes categorias identificadas com a chave à direita. Os símbolos com números em sua parte superior (⋏1) identificam as subcategorias (veja-se a chave completa à página *I · 1*).

∧ Mountain	Berg	Montaña	Montagne	Montanha
⋏ Mountains	Gebirge	Montañas	Montagnes	Montanhas
)(Pass	Paß	Paso	Col	Passo
V Valley, Canyon	Tal, Cañon	Valle, Cañón	Vallée, Canyon	Vale, Canhão
≚ Plain	Ebene	Llano	Plaine	Planície
≻ Cape	Kap	Cabo	Cap	Cabo
I Island	Insel	Isla	Île	Ilha
II Islands	Inseln	Islas	Îles	Ilhas
⊥ Other Topographic Features	Andere Topographische Objekte	Otros Elementos Topográficos	Autres données topographiques	Outros acidentes topográficos

Chur-Clea I · 37

ESPAÑOL

Nombre	Página	Lat.°′	Long.°′ W = Oeste
Churchill ≃, Nf., Can.	176	53.30 N	60.10 W
Churchill, Cape ≻	176	58.46 N	93.12 W
Churchill, Mount ∧, B.C., Can.	182	49.58 N	123.51 W
Churchill, Mount ∧, Ak., U.S.	180	61.25 N	141.43 W
Churchill Downs ♠	218	38.12 N	85.46 W
Churchill Falls ᒪ	176	53.35 N	64.27 W
Churchill Lake ⊜	184	55.55 N	108.20 W
Churchill National Park ♠	169	37.58 S	145.17 E
Church Point	194	30.24 N	92.12 W
Church Rock	200	35.32 N	108.35 W
Church Street	260	51.26 N	0.28 E
Church Stretton	42	52.32 N	2.49 W
Churchton	208	38.48 N	76.32 W
Churchtown, Eng., U.K.	262	53.40 N	2.58 W
Churchtown, Pa., U.S.	208	40.08 N	75.58 W
Church View	208	37.41 N	76.41 W
Churchville, On., Can.	275b	43.38 N	79.45 W
Churchville, Md., U.S.	208	39.33 N	76.14 W
Churchville, N.Y., U.S.	210	43.06 N	77.53 W
Churchville, Pa., U.S.	285	40.11 N	75.01 W
Churdan	198	42.09 N	94.28 W
Churen Himāl ∧	124	28.44 N	83.12 E
Chure Śringklā ⋏	124	27.40 N	83.40 E
Churfirsten ⋏	58	47.08 N	9.17 E
Churintzio	234	20.09 N	102.04 W
Chürmen	102	43.20 N	104.05 E
Churmuli	89	51.00 N	136.50 E
Churn ≃	42	51.38 N	1.53 W
Churn Creek ≃	182	51.30 N	122.17 W
Churnet ≃	42	52.55 N	1.50 W
Churni ≃[1]	126	23.08 N	88.30 E
Chursdorf	54	50.46 N	12.15 E
Chūru	120	28.18 N	74.57 E
Churubusco, In., U.S.	216	41.13 N	85.19 W
Churubusco, N.Y., U.S.	206	44.57 N	73.56 W
Churuguara	246	10.49 N	69.32 W
Churumuco	234	18.37 N	101.38 W
Churwalden	58	46.47 N	9.33 E
Chušenga	88	51.27 N	110.55 E
Chushan	100	23.45 N	120.40 E
Chushul	120	33.36 N	78.39 E
Chuska Mountains ⋏	200	36.15 N	108.50 W
Chuska Peak ∧	200	35.53 N	108.50 W
Chusovoy → Čusovoj	86	58.17 N	57.49 E
Chust	78	48.10 N	23.18 E
Chusuut uul ∧	88	47.45 N	105.45 E
Chūta	174m	26.32 N	127.58 E
Chutag	88	49.23 N	102.43 E
Chutag Uul	102	43.23 N	110.13 E
Chute-à-Blondeau	206	45.35 N	74.29 W
Chute-Panet	206	46.51 N	71.51 W
Chutorskoj	80	46.52 N	42.59 E
Chutu ≃	89	49.27 N	140.02 E
Chutung	100	24.44 N	121.05 E
Chuŭl	98	41.33 N	129.34 E
Chuwang	98	36.02 N	114.52 E
Chuwang-san Kukrip Kongwŏn ♠	98	36.26 N	129.10 E
Chuwei	269d	25.08 N	121.27 E
Chuxian	100	32.19 N	118.17 E
Chuxiong	102	25.02 N	101.30 E
Chuy	252	33.41 S	53.27 W
Chuzenji-ko ⊜	94	36.44 N	139.29 E
Chuzhai	100	33.22 N	113.37 E
Chužir	88	53.11 N	107.20 E
Chūzu	94	35.06 N	136.00 E
Chvalynsk	80	52.30 N	48.07 E
Chvančkara	84	42.34 N	43.01 E
Chvastoviči	76	53.28 N	35.06 E
Chvatovka	80	52.21 N	46.34 E
Chvojnaja	76	58.54 N	34.32 E
Chvorost'anka	80	52.36 N	48.59 E
Chvostovo	92a	46.08 N	142.14 E
Chwefru ≃	42	52.09 N	3.25 W
Ch'wiya-ri	98	38.03 N	125.32 E
Chypre → Cyprus □[1]	130	35.00 N	33.00 E
Chyrov	78	49.33 N	22.49 E
Ci ≃, Zhg.	98	38.19 N	115.23 E
Ci ≃, Zhg.	100	33.27 N	115.31 E
Ciago	64	46.12 N	12.46 E
Ciagola, Monte ∧	68	39.54 N	15.53 E
Ciales	240m	18.20 N	66.28 W
Ciamis	115a	7.20 S	108.21 E
Ciampino	66	41.48 N	12.36 E
Ciampino, Aeroporto di ⊠	267a	41.48 N	12.36 E
Cianciana	70	37.31 N	13.26 E
Ciandur	115a	6.24 S	105.59 E
Cianjur	115a	6.49 S	107.08 E
Ciano d'Enza	64	44.36 N	10.24 E
Cianorte	255	23.37 S	52.37 W
Çians, Gorges du V	62	43.57 N	6.59 E
Čiatura	84	42.17 N	43.17 E
Ciavolo	70	37.46 N	12.33 E
Ciawi, Indon.	115a	6.40 S	106.50 E
Ciawi, Indon.	115a	7.10 S	108.09 E
Ciawigebang	115a	6.58 S	108.34 E
Ciba	107	29.07 N	105.55 E
Cibadak	115a	6.53 S	106.46 E
Cibaliung	115a	6.46 S	105.51 E
Čibargata	85	41.08 N	69.48 E
Cibatu	115a	7.06 S	107.59 E
Cibeber	115a	6.56 S	107.07 E
Cibecue	200	34.02 N	110.29 W
Cibiana	64	46.23 N	12.17 E
Cibinong	115a	6.27 S	106.51 E
Čibisovka	78	50.47 N	40.05 E
Čibižek	86	54.27 N	93.40 E
Cibolo Creek ≃, Tx., U.S.	196	28.57 N	97.53 W
Cibolo Creek ≃, Tx., U.S.	196	29.34 N	104.24 W
Cibolo Creek ≃, Tx., U.S.	196	28.27 N	98.54 W
Cibuta	200	31.04 N	110.54 W
Cicagna	62	44.25 N	9.14 E
Cicala	68	39.01 N	16.29 E
Cicalengka	115a	6.59 S	107.50 E
Čićarija ⋏	36	45.30 N	13.54 E
Čičatka	89	54.03 N	121.18 E
Cicciano	68	40.58 N	14.32 E
Cicero, Il., U.S.	216	41.50 N	87.45 W
Cicero, In., U.S.	218	40.07 N	86.00 W
Cicero, N.Y., U.S.	210	43.10 N	76.07 W
Cicero Creek ≃	194	40.01 N	86.01 W
Cícero Dantas	250	10.36 S	38.23 W
Čichačovo, S.S.S.R.	76	57.17 N	29.54 E
Čichačovo, S.S.S.R.	89	51.50 N	141.07 E
Čichareši	84	42.48 N	43.03 E
Ciche, Sgurr na ∧	46	57.01 N	5.27 W
Cicheng	100	30.00 N	121.22 E
Čičikleja ≃	78	47.23 N	31.34 E
Čičkajul ≃	86	57.34 N	85.44 E
Cicladas, Islas de la → Kikládhes II	38	37.30 N	25.00 E
Cicolano ◆[1]	66	42.12 N	13.12 E
Cicurug	115a	6.47 S	106.47 E
Cidacos ≃	34	42.19 N	1.55 W
Cidade, Rio da ≃	256	22.25 S	43.09 W
Cidade Universitária ʊ[2], Bra.	287a	22.52 S	43.14 W
Cidade Universitária ʊ[2], Bra.	287b	23.33 S	46.43 W
Cide	130	41.54 N	33.00 E
Cidra	240m	18.11 N	66.10 W
Cidra, Lago de ⊜[1]	240m	18.12 N	66.08 W
Ciechanów	30	52.53 N	20.38 E
Ciechanów □[4]	30	53.00 N	20.20 E
Ciechanowiec	30	52.42 N	22.31 E
Ciechocinek	30	52.52 N	18.49 E
Ciego de Avila	240p	21.51 N	78.46 W
Ciego de Avila □[4]	240p	22.00 N	78.40 W
Ciempozuelos	34	40.10 N	3.37 W
Ciénaga	246	11.01 N	74.15 W

FRANÇAIS

Nom	Page	Lat.°′	Long.°′ W = Ouest
Ciénaga de Oro	246	8.53 N	75.37 W
Ciénega de Flores	196	25.57 N	100.11 W
Cienfuegos	240p	22.09 N	80.27 W
Cienfuegos □[4]	240p	22.10 N	80.25 W
Cienfuegos, Bahía de ᑕ	240p	22.07 N	80.29 W
Čierna [nad Tisou]	30	48.25 N	22.05 E
Čierny Balog	30	48.45 N	19.40 E
Cies, Islas II	34	42.13 N	8.54 W
Cieszanów	30	50.16 N	23.08 E
Cieszyn	30	49.45 N	18.38 E
Cieza	34	38.14 N	1.25 W
Çiftalan ◆[8]	267b	41.15 N	28.54 E
Çiftehan	130	37.31 N	34.46 E
Çifteler	130	39.22 N	31.03 E
Çiftlik	130	38.11 N	34.30 E
Cifuentes, Cuba	240p	22.39 N	80.03 W
Cifuentes, Esp.	34	40.47 N	2.37 W
Čiganak, S.S.S.R.	80	51.47 N	43.18 E
Čiganak, S.S.S.R.	86	45.06 N	73.58 E
Čiganaki	80	47.57 N	43.05 E
Čigirin	78	49.04 N	32.40 E
Cigliano	62	45.18 N	8.01 E
Čigorak	80	51.26 N	42.09 E
Cigou	100	33.51 N	113.35 E
Cigüela ≃	34	39.08 N	3.44 W
Cihanbeyli	130	38.40 N	32.56 E
Cihara	115a	6.52 S	106.06 E
Cihuatlán	234	19.14 N	104.35 W
Čiili	86	44.10 N	66.45 E
Cijara, Embalse de ⊜[1]	34	39.18 N	4.52 W
Čijen	85	43.08 N	75.55 E
Cijiawu	105	39.48 N	115.59 E
Čijirčik, pereval)(	85	40.15 N	73.20 E
Čijli ≃	85	40.17 N	72.38 E
Cijulang	115a	7.44 S	108.27 E
Čik	86	55.01 N	82.27 E
Cikajang	115a	7.22 S	107.47 E
Cikalong-kulon	115a	6.42 S	107.12 E
Cikampek	115a	6.24 S	107.27 E
Čikan	88	54.54 N	105.39 E
Cikarang	115a	6.15 S	107.09 E
Cikatomas	115a	7.37 S	108.15 E
Čikišl'ar	128	37.34 N	53.55 E
Čikoj	88	50.16 N	106.54 E
Čikoj ≃	88	51.02 N	106.39 E
Čikola	84	43.12 N	43.55 E
Cikou	100	29.42 N	114.46 E
Cıksı	130	38.30 N	40.55 E
Cilacap	115a	7.44 S	109.00 E
Cilamaya	115a	6.15 S	107.35 E
Cilavegna	62	45.19 N	8.44 E
Çıldır	84	41.08 N	43.07 E
Çıldır Gölü ⊜	84	41.04 N	43.15 E
Ciledug	115a	6.54 S	108.44 E
Cilegon	115a	6.01 S	106.03 E
Čilekovo	80	47.50 N	43.30 E
Cilento ⋏	68	40.17 N	15.19 E
Cilento ◆[1]	36	40.15 N	15.10 E
Čil'gazi	85	40.10 N	70.39 E
Cili	102	29.17 N	111.00 E
Cilicia □[9]	130	36.40 N	34.20 E
Čilik, S.S.S.R.	85	43.36 N	78.15 E
Čilik, S.S.S.R.	86	51.07 N	54.07 E
Čilik ≃	85	43.05 N	78.28 E
Cililin	115a	6.56 S	107.26 E
Cilimus	115a	6.52 S	108.29 E
Cilincing ◆[8]	269e	6.06 S	106.56 E
Cill Airne → Killarney	48	52.03 N	9.30 W
Cill Chainnigh → Kilkenny	48	52.39 N	7.15 W
Cilleruelo de Bezana	34	42.58 N	3.51 W
Cil'ma ≃	24	65.27 N	52.06 E
Cimabanche (Schluderbach)	64	46.37 N	12.11 E
Cima Gogna	64	46.31 N	12.28 E
Cimahi	115a	6.53 S	107.32 E
Cimalaka	115a	6.49 S	107.56 E
Cimalmotto	58	46.17 N	8.29 E
Cimarron, Ks., U.S.	198	37.48 N	100.20 W
Cimarron, N.M., U.S.	200	36.30 N	104.54 W
Cimarron ≃, U.S.	196	36.10 N	96.17 W
Cimarron ≃, N.M., U.S.	196	36.20 N	104.31 W
Cimarron, North Fork ≃	196	37.25 N	101.13 W
Čimbaj	86	42.57 N	59.47 E
Čimčinej, gora ∧[2]	180	63.37 N	178.04 E
Cimetière, Pointe du ≻	241o	15.58 N	61.19 W
Cimini, Monti ⋏	66	42.20 N	12.10 E
Ciminna	70	37.54 N	13.34 E
Cimino, Monte ∧	66	42.24 N	12.12 E
Čimion	85	40.16 N	71.31 E
Čimišlija	78	46.32 N	28.44 E
Cimitile	68	40.56 N	14.31 E
Čimkent	85	42.18 N	69.36 E
Čimkent □[4]	85	42.30 N	68.00 E
Čimkorgon	85	42.50 N	75.30 E
Cimla ≃	80	48.01 N	42.24 E
Ciml'ansk	80	47.38 N	42.04 E
Ciml'anskoje vodochranilišče ⊜[1]	80	48.00 N	43.00 E
Cimolais	64	46.17 N	12.26 E
Cimone, Monte ∧	64	44.12 N	10.42 E
Cîmpeni	38	46.22 N	23.03 E
Cîmpia Turzii	38	46.33 N	23.54 E
Cîmpina	38	45.08 N	25.44 E
Cimpu	112	3.25 S	120.22 E
Cîmpulung	38	45.16 N	25.03 E
Cîmpulung Moldovenesc	38	47.31 N	25.34 E
Čimtarga, gora ∧	85	39.12 N	68.10 E
Čina ≃	88	54.20 N	112.24 E
Cina, Tanjung ≻	112	5.56 S	104.45 E
Činabad	85	40.52 N	71.58 E
Činadijevo	78	48.30 N	22.50 E
Cinandali	84	41.53 N	45.34 E
Çınar	130	37.44 N	40.25 E
Çınarcık	130	40.39 N	29.06 E
Cinaruco ≃	246	6.41 N	67.07 W
Činaz	85	40.56 N	68.45 E
Cinca ≃	34	41.26 N	0.21 E
Cincar ∧	36	43.54 N	17.04 E
Cincinnati, Ia., U.S.	190	40.37 N	92.55 W
Cincinnati, Oh., U.S.	218	39.09 N	84.27 W
Cincinnatus	210	42.32 N	75.53 W
Cinco, Canal Numero ≅	252	37.35 S	57.20 W
Cinco Balas, Cayos II	240p	21.06 N	79.20 W
Cinco de Mayo	196	25.46 N	104.19 W
Cinco Palos, Sierra ⋏	234	22.40 N	99.36 W
Cinco Pinos	236	13.14 N	86.52 W
Cinco Saltos	252	38.49 S	68.04 W
Cinderella	273d	26.15 S	28.16 E
Cinderella Dam ⊜[1]	273d	26.15 S	28.14 E
Cinderford	42	51.50 N	2.29 W
Cinder Island I	276	40.36 N	73.36 W
Çine	130	37.36 N	28.04 E
Cinebar	224	46.36 N	122.32 W
Cinecittà ʊ[3]	267a	41.51 N	12.34 E
Cinema	182	53.14 N	122.27 W
Ciney	56	50.18 N	5.06 E
Cinfães	34	41.04 N	8.05 W
Cingaly	86	60.13 N	69.45 E
Čingis	86	54.08 N	81.41 E
Čingistaj	86	49.13 N	85.55 E
Cingoli	66	43.22 N	13.13 E
Cinigiano	66	42.53 N	11.24 E
Cinisello Balsamo	62	45.33 N	9.13 E
Činišeucy	78	47.42 N	28.52 E
Cinisi	70	38.09 N	13.06 E
Činja-Voryk	24	63.13 N	52.38 E
Cinkota ◆[8]	264c	47.31 N	19.14 E
Cinnaminson	285	40.00 N	74.59 W
Cínovec	54	50.43 N	13.45 E
Cinq, Lac des ⊜	206	46.51 N	72.59 W
Cinq Doigts, Lac ⊜	206	46.36 N	74.32 W
Cinquefrondi	68	38.25 N	16.06 E
Cinquemiglia, Piano delle ≚	66	41.50 N	14.00 E

PORTUGUÊS

Nome	Página	Lat.°′	Long.°′ W = Oeste
Cinqueterre □[9]	62	44.10 N	9.45 E
Cintalapa ≃	234	16.41 N	93.36 W
Cintalapa de Figueroa	234	16.44 N	93.43 W
Cinto, Monte ∧	36	42.23 N	8.56 E
Cinto Euganeo	64	45.16 N	11.40 E
Cintra → Sintra	34	38.48 N	9.23 W
Cintra, Golfe de ᑕ	148	23.00 N	16.20 W
Cinzas, Rio das ≃	252	22.56 S	50.32 W
Ciocănești	38	44.12 N	27.04 E
Ciociaria ◆[1]	66	41.45 N	13.15 E
Ciomas	115a	6.12 S	106.01 E
Čiovo, Otok I	36	43.30 N	16.20 E
Cipa ≃	88	55.23 N	115.55 E
Ciparay	115a	7.03 S	107.43 E
Cipatujah	115a	7.45 S	108.00 E
Cipikan	88	54.55 N	113.21 E
Cipikan ≃	88	55.14 N	113.05 E
Cipó	250	11.06 S	38.31 W
Cipó ≃	255	18.40 S	43.59 W
Cipolândia	255	20.08 S	55.24 W
Cipolletti	252	38.56 S	67.59 W
Ciqikou	107	29.35 N	106.26 E
Čir	80	48.29 N	43.10 E
Čir ≃	80	48.35 N	42.51 E
Ciraadhame	144	10.30 N	49.22 E
Čirachčaj ≃	84	41.40 N	48.11 E
Čiragidzor	84	40.27 N	46.19 E
Ciranjang	115a	6.49 S	107.14 E
Circeo, Monte ∧	66	41.14 N	13.03 E
Circeo, Parco Nazionale del ♠	66	41.17 N	13.05 E
Čirčik	85	41.29 N	69.35 E
Čirčik ≃	85	40.54 N	68.41 E
Çırçır	130	40.04 N	36.48 E
Circle, Ak., U.S.	180	65.50 N	144.04 W
Circle, Mt., U.S.	202	47.20 N	105.35 W
Circle Hot Springs	180	65.28 N	144.39 W
Circleville, N.Y., U.S.	210	41.31 N	75.23 W
Circleville, Oh., U.S.	218	39.36 N	82.56 W
Circleville, Pa., U.S.	279b	40.20 N	79.44 W
Circleville, Ut,. U.S.	200	38.10 N	112.16 W
Circleville Mountain ∧	200	38.12 N	112.24 W
Circular Reef ✦[2]	164	3.25 S	147.47 E
Circus World ♠	220	28.14 N	81.38 W
Cirebon	115a	6.44 S	108.34 E
Cireglio	66	43.59 N	10.51 E
Ciremay, Gunung ∧	115a	6.54 S	108.24 E
Cirencester	42	51.44 N	1.59 W
Cirey-sur-Vezouze	58	48.35 N	6.57 E
Čirgalandy	88	50.36 N	97.20 E
Ciriè	62	45.14 N	7.36 E
Cirigliano	68	40.24 N	16.10 E
Čirikovo	82	55.23 N	37.14 E
Ciriquiri ≃	248	8.05 S	65.18 W
Cirk, gora ∧	180	64.33 N	175.25 E
Cîrlibaba	38	47.35 N	25.07 E
Ciró	68	39.23 N	17.04 E
Ciró Marina	68	39.22 N	17.08 E
Čirpan	38	42.12 N	25.20 E
Ciruas	115a	6.06 S	106.13 E
Cisa, Passo della)(	64	44.28 N	9.55 E
Cisano	64	45.32 N	10.43 E
Cisarua	115a	6.40 S	106.59 E
Cisco, Il., U.S.	219	40.01 N	88.43 W
Cisco, Tx., U.S.	196	32.23 N	98.58 W
Cishan	98	36.37 N	114.07 E
Cishangang	106	30.55 N	119.31 E
Ciskei □[1], Afr.	138	32.50 S	27.00 E
Ciskei □[1], Afr.	158	32.50 S	27.00 E
Cislago	62	45.39 N	8.58 E
Cisliano	266b	45.27 N	8.59 E
Çismar	54	54.11 N	10.59 E
Čismena	82	56.02 N	36.13 E
Cismon ≃	64	46.55 N	11.43 E
Cismon del Grappa	64	45.55 N	11.44 E
Čišmy	86	54.35 N	55.20 E
Cisnădie	38	45.43 N	24.09 E
Cisne	194	38.31 N	88.26 W
Cisneros	246	6.33 N	75.04 W
Cisnes ≃	254	44.45 S	72.42 W
Cisolok	115a	6.57 S	106.26 E
Cison di Valmarino	64	45.58 N	12.10 E
Cispus ≃	224	46.25 N	122.10 W
Cisse ≃	50	47.25 N	0.47 E
Cissna Park	216	40.33 N	87.53 W
Čistá, Česko.	54	50.06 N	12.44 E
Čistá, Česko.	60	50.02 N	13.35 E
Cisterna di Latina	66	41.35 N	12.49 E
Cisternino	68	40.44 N	17.25 E
Cistern Point ≻	238	23.43 N	77.35 W
Cistierna	34	42.48 N	5.07 W
Čistoje	80	56.32 N	43.02 E
Čistooz'ornoje	86	54.43 N	76.33 E
Čistopol'	80	55.21 N	50.37 E
Čistopolje, S.S.S.R.	83	47.31 N	39.27 E
Čistopolje, S.S.S.R.	86	52.34 N	67.15 E
Čistovodovka	83	49.24 N	37.20 E
Čita	88	52.03 N	113.30 E
Čita □[4]	88	52.00 N	117.00 E
Čita ≃	88	52.00 N	113.30 E
Citac, Nevado ∧	248	12.50 S	75.15 W
Citaré ≃	250	1.11 N	54.41 W
Citeli-Ckaro	84	41.28 N	46.07 E
Cité Universitaire ʊ[2]	261	48.49 N	2.20 E
Citra	192	29.24 N	82.06 W
Citronelle	194	31.05 N	88.13 W
Citrus □[6]	220	28.52 N	82.28 W
Citrusdal	158	32.36 S	19.00 E
Citrus Heights	226	38.42 N	121.16 W
Citrus Springs	220	29.00 N	82.27 W
Citrus Tower ʊ	220	28.33 N	81.44 W
Cittadella	64	45.39 N	11.47 E
Città della Pieve	66	42.57 N	12.00 E
Città del Vaticano → Vatican City □[1]	66	41.54 N	12.27 E
Città di Castello	66	43.27 N	12.14 E
Cittaducale	66	42.23 N	12.57 E
Cittanova	68	38.21 N	16.05 E
Cittareale	66	42.37 N	13.10 E
Città Sant'Angelo	66	42.31 N	14.03 E
Città Universitaria ʊ[2]	267a	41.55 N	12.31 E
City Beach	168a	31.56 S	115.45 E
City Bell ◆[8]	258	34.52 S	58.05 W
City Island ◆[8]	276	40.51 N	73.47 W
City Mills	283	42.06 N	71.21 W
City of Hope National Medical Center ʊ	280	34.08 N	117.58 W
City Of Industry	280	34.01 N	117.57 W
City of London ◆[8]	260	51.31 N	0.05 W
City of Refuge → Pu'uhonua o Honaunau National Historic Site ♠	229d	19.25 N	155.54 W
City of Sunrise	220	26.08 N	80.14 W
City of Westminster ◆[8]	260	51.30 N	0.09 W
City Point	220	28.24 N	80.45 W
City University of New York Brooklyn College ʊ[2]	276	40.38 N	73.57 W
City University of New York City College ʊ[2]	276	40.49 N	73.57 W
City University of New York Queens College ʊ[2]	276	40.44 N	73.49 W
City University of New York York College ʊ[2]	276	40.42 N	73.48 W
Ciucaș, Vîrful ∧	38	45.31 N	25.55 E
Ciudad	234	23.44 N	105.42 W
Ciudad Acuña	232	29.18 N	100.55 W
Ciudad Altamirano	234	18.20 N	100.40 W
Ciudad Anáhuac	232	27.14 N	100.09 W
Ciudad Barrios	236	13.46 N	88.16 W
Ciudad Bolívar	246	8.08 N	63.33 W
Ciudad Bolivia	246	8.21 N	70.34 W
Ciudad Camargo, Méx.	232	27.40 N	105.10 W
Ciudad Camargo, Méx.	232	26.19 N	98.50 W
Ciudad Darío	236	12.43 N	86.08 W
Ciudad de Guayana → Ciudad Guayana	246	8.22 N	62.40 W
Ciudad de la Habana □[4]	240p	23.08 N	82.22 W
Ciudad del Cabo → Cape Town	158	33.55 S	18.22 E
Ciudad del Carmen	232	18.38 N	91.50 W
Ciudad del Maíz	234	22.24 N	99.36 W
Ciudad de los Deportes ♠	286a	19.23 N	99.11 W
Ciudad del Vaticano → Vatican City □[1]	66	41.54 N	12.27 E
Ciudad de México (Mexico City), Méx.	234	19.24 N	99.09 W
Ciudad de México (Mexico City), Méx.	286a	19.24 N	99.09 W
Ciudad de Naucalpan de Juárez	286a	19.28 N	99.14 W
Ciudad de Nutrias	246	8.05 N	69.18 W
Ciudad Deportiva ♠, Cuba	286b	23.07 N	82.22 W
Ciudad Deportiva ♠, Méx.	286a	19.24 N	99.06 W
Ciudad de Villaldama	232	26.30 N	100.26 W
Ciudadela, Parque de la ♠	266d	41.23 N	2.11 E
Ciudad General Belgrano	288	34.43 S	58.32 W
Ciudad Guayana	246	8.22 N	62.40 W
Ciudad Guerrero	232	28.33 N	107.30 W
Ciudad Guzmán	234	19.41 N	103.29 W
Ciudad Hidalgo, Méx.	234	19.41 N	100.34 W
Ciudad Hidalgo, Méx.	236	14.41 N	92.09 W
Ciudad Ixtepec	234	16.34 N	95.06 W
Ciudad Jiménez	232	27.08 N	104.55 W
Ciudad Juárez	232	31.44 N	106.29 W
Ciudad Lerdo	196	25.32 N	103.32 W
Ciudad Lineal ◆[8]	266a	40.27 N	3.40 W
Ciudad López Mateos	286a	19.33 N	99.15 W
Ciudad Madero	234	22.16 N	97.50 W
Ciudad Mante	234	22.44 N	98.57 W
Ciudad Manuel Doblado	234	20.44 N	101.56 W
Ciudad Melchor Múzquiz	232	27.53 N	101.31 W
Ciudad Mendoza	234	18.48 N	97.11 W
Ciudad Mier	232	26.26 N	99.09 W
Ciudad Miguel Alemán	232	26.23 N	99.01 W
Ciudad Morelos	232	32.38 N	114.52 W
Ciudad Obregón	232	27.29 N	109.56 W
Ciudad Ocampo	234	22.50 N	99.20 W
Ciudad Ojeda (Lagunillas)	246	10.12 N	71.19 W
Ciudad Piar	246	7.27 N	63.19 W
Ciudad Real	34	38.59 N	3.56 W
Ciudad Rodrigo	34	40.36 N	6.32 W
Ciudad Sahagún	234	19.47 N	98.33 W
Ciudad Santos	234	21.36 N	98.58 W
Ciudad Serdán	234	18.59 N	97.27 W
Ciudad Tecún Umán	236	14.40 N	92.09 W
Ciudad Trujillo → Santo Domingo	238	18.28 N	69.54 W
Ciudad Universitaria ◆[8]	266a	40.27 N	3.44 W
Ciudad Universitaria ʊ[2], Esp.	266a	40.27 N	3.43 W
Ciudad Universitaria ʊ[2], Méx.	286a	19.20 N	99.11 W
Ciudad Universitaria ʊ[2], Ven.	286c	10.29 N	66.53 W
Ciudad Valles	234	21.59 N	99.01 W
Ciudad Victoria, Méx.	204	32.20 N	115.06 W
Ciudad Victoria, Méx.	234	23.44 N	99.08 W
Ciudad Vieja	236	14.31 N	90.46 W
Ciuma	152	13.14 S	15.40 E
Ciutadella	34	40.02 N	3.50 E
Civa Burnu ≻	130	41.22 N	36.35 E
Civate	62	45.50 N	9.21 E
Civenna	58	45.56 N	9.16 E
Civetta, Monte ∧	64	46.23 N	12.03 E
Civezzano	64	46.05 N	11.11 E
Cividale del Friuli	64	46.06 N	13.25 E
Cividate al Piano	62	45.33 N	9.50 E
Cividate Camuno	64	45.57 N	10.17 E
Civil' ≃, S.S.S.R.	80	56.05 N	47.37 E
Civil' ≃, S.S.S.R.	80	56.08 N	47.35 E
Civil'sk	80	55.53 N	47.29 E
Civita	68	39.49 N	16.18 E
Civitacampomarano	66	41.47 N	14.41 E
Civita Castellana	66	42.17 N	12.25 E
Civita di Bagno	66	42.18 N	13.26 E
Civitanova Alta	66	43.19 N	13.40 E
Civitanova del Sannio	66	41.40 N	14.24 E
Civitanova Marche	66	43.18 N	13.44 E
Civitaquana	66	42.19 N	13.54 E
Civitavecchia	66	42.06 N	11.48 E
Civitella del Tronto	66	42.46 N	13.40 E
Civitella di Romagna	66	44.00 N	11.56 E
Civitella in Val di Chiana	66	43.25 N	11.43 E
Civitella Marittima	66	43.00 N	11.17 E
Civitella Roveto	66	41.54 N	13.25 E
Civray	32	46.09 N	0.18 E
Çivril	130	38.18 N	29.45 E
Ciwidey	115a	7.06 S	107.27 E
Cixerri ≃	71	39.17 N	8.59 E
Cixi	100	30.11 N	121.15 E
Cixian	98	36.22 N	114.23 E
Ciyutuo	104	41.31 N	122.53 E
Čiža	24	67.06 N	44.19 E
Čižapka ≃	86	59.01 N	79.36 E
Čiža Vtoraja	80	50.52 N	49.40 E
Cize	58	46.12 N	5.26 E
Cizhuping	107	29.11 N	103.36 E
Čižinskije razlivy ≡	80	50.25 N	49.40 E
Cizre	130	37.20 N	42.12 E
C.J. Strike Reservoir ⊜[1]	202	42.57 N	115.53 W
Čkalov → Orenburg	86	51.54 N	55.06 E
Čkalovo, S.S.S.R.	78	46.28 N	34.11 E
Čkalovo, S.S.S.R.	86	53.38 N	70.24 E
Čkalovsk, S.S.S.R.	80	56.46 N	43.16 E
Čkalovsk, S.S.S.R.	85	41.15 N	68.00 E
Čkalovsk, S.S.S.R.	85	40.13 N	69.50 E
Čkalovskij	265b	55.54 N	38.04 E
Ç K Creek ≃	202	47.36 N	108.29 W
Čkyně	60	49.07 N	13.49 E
Čl'a, ozero ⊜	89	53.27 N	140.03 E
Clachan	46	55.45 N	5.34 W
Clackamas	224	45.24 N	122.34 W
Clackamas □[6]	224	45.10 N	122.16 W
Clackamas ≃	224	45.22 N	122.36 W
Clackamas, Oak Grove Fork ≃	224	45.05 N	122.03 W
Clackamas Heights	224	45.23 N	122.34 W
Clackline	168a	31.43 S	116.31 E
Clackmannan	46	56.06 N	3.46 W
Clacton-on-Sea	42	51.48 N	1.09 E
Cladich	46	56.21 N	5.05 W
Claerwen ≃	42	52.16 N	3.35 W
Claerwen Reservoir ⊜[1]	42	52.17 N	3.43 W
Claflin	198	38.31 N	98.32 W
Claiborne	194	31.32 N	87.31 W
Clain ≃	32	46.47 N	0.32 E
Claire, Lake ⊜	176	58.35 N	112.05 W
Claire, Pointe ≻	275a	45.25 N	73.50 W
Clairefontaine-en-Yvelines	50	48.37 N	1.55 E
Clair Engle Lake ⊜[1]	204	40.52 N	122.43 W
Claireville	275b	43.45 N	79.38 W
Claireville Reservoir ⊜[1]	275b	43.44 N	79.39 W
Clairis ≃	50	48.07 N	2.45 E
Clairmarais	50	50.46 N	2.18 E
Clairmont	182	55.16 N	118.47 W
Clairton	214	40.17 N	79.52 W
Clairvaux-les-Lacs	58	46.34 N	5.45 E
Claix	62	45.07 N	5.40 E
Clallam □[6]	224	48.10 N	123.49 W
Clallam Bay	224	48.15 N	124.15 W
Clam ≃, Mi., U.S.	190	44.05 N	85.00 W
Clam ≃, Wi., U.S.	190	45.57 N	92.33 W
Clam, North Fork ≃	190	45.46 N	92.18 W
Clamart	261	48.48 N	2.16 E
Clamecy	50	47.27 N	3.31 E
Clam Gulch	180	60.15 N	151.22 W
Clam Lake ⊜	184	55.19 N	105.43 W
Clampton	162	29.56 S	119.06 E
Clan Alpine Mountains ⋏	204	39.40 N	117.55 W
Clandonald	182	53.34 N	110.44 W
Clandon Park ♠	260	51.15 N	0.30 W
Clandulla	170	32.55 S	149.57 E
Clane	48	53.18 N	6.41 W
Clans	62	44.00 N	7.09 E
Clanton	194	32.50 N	86.37 W
Clanwilliam	158	32.11 S	18.54 E
Claonaig	46	55.46 N	5.22 W
Clapham	42	52.09 N	0.29 W
Clapier, Mont ∧	62	44.07 N	7.25 E
Clapperton Island I	190	46.02 N	82.13 W
Clapp Farm	214	41.24 N	79.32 W
Clàr, Loch nan ⊜	46	58.17 N	4.08 W
Clara, Arg.	252	31.50 S	58.49 W
Clara, Ire.	48	53.20 N	7.36 W
Clara, Ms., U.S.	194	31.34 N	88.41 W
Clara ≃	166	18.30 S	141.18 E
Clara City	198	44.57 N	95.21 W
Clara Island I	110	10.54 N	97.55 E
Claraz	252	37.54 S	59.17 W
Clare, Austl.	166	33.25 S	143.55 E
Clare, Austl.	168b	33.50 S	138.36 E
Clare, Eng., U.K.	42	52.25 N	0.35 E
Clare, Mi., U.S.	190	43.49 N	84.46 W
Clare □[6]	48	52.50 N	9.00 W
Clare ≃, On., Can.	212	44.28 N	77.17 W
Clare ≃, Ire.	48	53.20 N	9.03 W
Clarecastle	48	52.49 N	8.57 W
Claregalway	48	53.21 N	8.57 W
Clare Island I	48	53.48 N	10.00 W
Claremont, On., Can.	212	43.58 N	79.07 W
Claremont, Eng., U.K.	260	51.21 N	0.22 W
Claremont, Ca., U.S.	228	34.05 N	117.43 W
Claremont, N.H., U.S.	188	43.22 N	72.20 W
Claremont, S.D., U.S.	198	45.40 N	98.00 W
Claremont, Va., U.S.	208	37.13 N	76.57 W
Claremont ∧	204	39.53 N	120.57 W
Claremore	196	36.18 N	95.36 W
Claremorris	48	53.44 N	9.00 W
Clarence, N.Z.	172	42.10 S	173.56 E
Clarence, Il., U.S.	216	40.28 N	87.58 W
Clarence, Ia., U.S.	190	41.53 N	91.03 W
Clarence, Mo., U.S.	219	39.44 N	92.15 W
Clarence, N.Y., U.S.	210	42.59 N	78.35 W
Clarence, Pa., U.S.	214	41.03 N	77.56 W
Clarence ≃, Austl.	166	29.25 S	153.22 E
Clarence ≃, N.Z.	172	42.10 S	173.57 E
Clarence, Isla I	254	54.10 S	71.50 W
Clarence, Port ᑕ	180	65.15 N	166.40 W
Clarence Cannon Dam ◆[6]	219	39.31 N	91.39 W
Clarence Center	210	43.00 N	78.35 W
Clarence Creek	206	45.30 N	75.13 W
Clarence Fahnestock Memorial State Park ♠	210	41.26 N	73.50 W
Clarence Island I	9	61.09 S	54.06 W
Clarence J. Brown Reservoir ⊜[1]	218	39.58 N	83.44 W
Clarence Strait ʮ, Austl.	164	12.00 S	131.00 E
Clarence Strait ʮ, Ak., U.S.	180	55.25 N	132.00 W
Clarence Town, Austl.	170	32.35 S	151.47 E
Clarence Town, Ba.	238	23.06 N	74.59 W
Clarenceville, P.Q., Can.	206	45.04 N	73.15 W
Clarenceville, Mi., U.S.	281	42.27 N	83.19 W
Clarendon, Austl.	168b	35.07 S	138.38 E
Clarendon, Ar., U.S.	194	34.41 N	91.18 W
Clarendon, N.Y., U.S.	210	43.11 N	78.04 W
Clarendon, Pa., U.S.	214	41.46 N	79.05 W
Clarendon, Tx., U.S.	196	34.56 N	100.53 W
Clarendon Hills	278	41.47 N	87.57 W
Clarens	158	28.30 S	28.29 E
Clarenville	186	48.10 N	53.58 W
Claresholm	182	50.02 N	113.35 W
Claret	62	43.52 N	3.54 E
Clarholz	52	51.54 N	8.11 E
Claridge	214	40.21 N	79.37 W
Clarie Coast ⍓[2]	9	66.30 S	133.00 E
Clarin	116	9.58 N	124.01 E
Clarinda	198	40.44 N	95.02 W
Clarines	246	9.56 N	65.10 W
Clarington	214	41.20 N	79.07 W
Clarion, Ia., U.S.	190	42.43 N	93.43 W
Clarion, Pa., U.S.	214	41.12 N	79.23 W
Clarion □[6]	214	41.13 N	79.24 W
Clarion ≃	214	41.07 N	79.41 W
Clarión, Isla I	232	18.22 N	114.44 W
Clarion, West Branch ≃	214	41.29 N	78.41 W
Clarion Fracture Zone ✦	16	18.00 N	122.00 W
Clarissa	198	46.07 N	94.56 W
Clark, N.J., U.S.	276	40.38 N	74.18 W
Clark, Oh., U.S.	214	40.27 N	81.54 W
Clark, S.D., U.S.	198	44.52 N	97.43 W
Clark, Tx., U.S.	222	30.23 N	94.46 W
Clark □[6], In., U.S.	218	38.17 N	85.44 W
Clark □[6], Oh., U.S.	218	39.56 N	83.49 W
Clark □[6], Wa., U.S.	224	45.48 N	122.31 W
Clark, Lake ⊜	180	60.15 N	154.15 W
Clark, Mount ∧	180	64.25 N	124.12 W
Clark, Point ≻	190	44.04 N	81.45 W
Clark Air Base (U.S.) ■	116	15.11 N	120.32 E
Clark Branch ≃	285	39.43 N	74.45 W
Clark Canyon Reservoir ⊜[1]	202	44.58 N	112.51 W
Clark Creek ≃	208	40.22 N	76.58 W
Clarkdale	200	34.46 N	112.03 W
Clarke ≃	166	19.12 S	145.30 E
Clarke City	186	50.12 N	66.38 W
Clarke Island I	166	40.33 S	148.10 E
Clarke Lake ⊜	184	54.25 N	106.51 W
Clarke Range ⋏	166	20.50 S	148.33 E
Clarkesville	192	34.36 N	83.31 W
Clarkfield	198	44.47 N	95.48 W
Clark Fork	202	48.08 N	116.10 W
Clark Fork ≃	202	48.09 N	116.15 W
Clark Hill	218	38.18 N	83.12 W
Clarklake	216	42.04 N	84.21 W
Clark Lake ⊜	216	42.07 N	84.19 W
Clark Mills	210	43.06 N	75.22 W
Clark Mountain ∧, Ca., U.S.	204	35.32 N	115.35 W
Clark Mountain ∧, Wa., U.S.	224	48.03 N	120.57 W
Clarks, La., U.S.	194	32.01 N	92.08 W
Clarks, Ne., U.S.	198	41.12 N	97.50 W
Clarks ≃	194	37.03 N	88.33 W
Clarks, West Fork ≃	194	36.59 N	88.31 W
Clarksboro	285	39.47 N	75.13 W
Clarksburg, On., Can.	212	44.43 N	80.27 W
Clarksburg, Ca., U.S.	226	38.25 N	121.32 W
Clarksburg, Il., U.S.	219	39.20 N	88.44 W
Clarksburg, In., U.S.	218	39.26 N	85.20 W
Clarksburg, Md., U.S.	208	39.14 N	77.16 W
Clarksburg, N.J., U.S.	208	40.11 N	74.26 W
Clarksburg, Oh., U.S.	218	39.30 N	83.09 W
Clarksburg, W.V., U.S.	188	39.16 N	80.20 W
Clarksburg State Park ♠	207	42.43 N	73.06 W
Clarks Creek ≃, Ks., U.S.	198	39.05 N	96.42 W
Clarks Creek ≃, Ky., U.S.	218	38.40 N	84.44 W
Clarksdale	194	34.12 N	90.34 W
Clarks Green	210	41.30 N	75.42 W
Clark's Harbour	186	43.26 N	65.38 W
Clarks Hill	216	40.14 N	86.43 W
Clarks Hill Lake ⊜[1]	192	33.50 N	82.20 W
Clarks Island I	283	42.01 N	70.38 W
Clarks Mills	214	41.24 N	80.11 W
Clarkson, On., Can.	275b	43.31 N	79.37 W
Clarkson, Ky., U.S.	194	37.29 N	86.13 W
Clarkson, Ne., U.S.	198	41.43 N	97.07 W
Clarkson, N.Y., U.S.	210	43.14 N	77.56 W
Clarks Point	180	58.51 N	158.30 W
Clarks Summit	210	41.29 N	75.42 W
Clarkston, Mi., U.S.	216	42.44 N	83.25 W
Clarkston, Wa., U.S.	202	46.24 N	117.02 W
Clark's Town	241q	18.25 N	77.34 W
Clarksville, Ar., U.S.	194	35.28 N	93.27 W
Clarksville, De., U.S.	208	38.32 N	75.08 W
Clarksville, In., U.S.	218	38.15 N	85.47 W
Clarksville, Ia., U.S.	190	42.47 N	92.40 W
Clarksville, Md., U.S.	208	39.12 N	76.56 W
Clarksville, Mi., U.S.	216	42.50 N	85.14 W
Clarksville, Mo., U.S.	219	39.22 N	90.54 W
Clarksville, N.Y., U.S.	210	42.35 N	73.58 W
Clarksville, Oh., U.S.	218	39.24 N	83.58 W
Clarksville, Tn., U.S.	194	36.31 N	87.21 W
Clarksville, Tx., U.S.	196	33.36 N	95.03 W
Clarksville, Va., U.S.	192	36.37 N	78.33 W
Clarksville City	222	32.32 N	94.34 W
Clarkton, Mo., U.S.	194	36.27 N	89.58 W
Clarkton, N.C., U.S.	192	34.29 N	78.39 W
Claro ≃, Bra.	255	15.28 S	51.43 W
Claro ≃, Bra.	255	19.06 S	47.52 W
Claro ≃, Bra.	255	19.08 S	50.40 W
Claro, Arroyo ≃	288	34.25 S	58.41 W
Claro, Ribeirão ≃	287b	23.40 S	46.17 W
Clary	50	50.05 N	3.24 E
Claryville	210	41.55 N	74.34 W
Clashmore	48	52.00 N	7.48 W
Clatskanie	224	46.06 N	123.12 W
Clatskanie ≃	224	46.08 N	123.14 W
Clatsop □[6]	224	46.01 N	123.41 W
Clatsop Spit ≻[2]	224	46.13 N	124.01 W
Clatteringshaws Lake ⊜	44	55.05 N	4.17 W
Claude	196	35.07 N	101.22 W
Claudy	48	54.54 N	7.09 W
Claughton	44	54.06 N	2.40 W
Claussnitz	54	50.56 N	12.53 E
Clausthal-Zellerfeld	52	51.48 N	10.20 E
Claver	116	9.35 N	125.44 E
Claverack	210	42.13 N	73.44 W
Claveria, Pil.	116	8.38 N	124.55 E
Claveria, Pil.	116	18.37 N	121.05 E
Clavet	184	52.00 N	106.23 W
Clavey ≃	226	37.52 N	120.07 W
Clawit, Mount ∧	116	16.58 N	120.58 E
Clawson, Mi., U.S.	281	42.32 N	83.08 W
Clawson, Tx., U.S.	222	31.24 N	94.47 W
Claxton	192	32.09 N	81.54 W
Clay, Ky., U.S.	194	37.28 N	87.49 W
Clay, Tx., U.S.	222	30.23 N	96.21 W
Clay, W.V., U.S.	188	38.27 N	81.05 W
Clay □[6]	219	38.45 N	88.40 W
Claybank Creek ≃	194	31.10 N	85.44 W
Clay Center, Ks., U.S.	198	39.22 N	97.07 W
Clay Center, Ne., U.S.	198	40.31 N	98.03 W
Clay Center, Oh., U.S.	214	41.33 N	83.21 W
Clay City, Il., U.S.	194	38.41 N	88.21 W
Clay City, In., U.S.	194	39.16 N	87.06 W
Clay City, Ky., U.S.	192	37.51 N	83.55 W
Clay Creek ≃	198	38.06 N	102.31 W
Clay Cross	44	53.10 N	1.24 W
Claydon	42	52.06 N	1.07 E
Claye-Souilly	50	48.57 N	2.42 E
Claygate	260	51.22 N	0.20 W
Claygate Cross	260	51.16 N	0.19 E
Clayhole Wash V	200	36.59 N	113.17 W
Clayhurst	182	56.15 N	120.01 W
Claymont	208	39.48 N	75.27 W
Clayoquot Sound ʮ	182	49.11 N	126.08 W
Claypole	288	34.48 S	58.20 W
Claypool, Az., U.S.	200	33.24 N	110.50 W
Claypool, In., U.S.	216	41.07 N	85.52 W
Claysburg	214	40.17 N	78.27 W
Clay Springs	200	34.21 N	110.17 W
Claysville	214	40.07 N	80.24 W
Clayton, Austl.	274b	37.56 S	145.07 E
Clayton, Eng., U.K.	262	53.47 N	1.52 W
Clayton, Al., U.S.	194	31.52 N	85.26 W
Clayton, Ca., U.S.	282	37.57 N	121.56 W
Clayton, De., U.S.	208	39.17 N	75.38 W
Clayton, Ga., U.S.	192	34.52 N	83.24 W
Clayton, Il., U.S.	219	40.01 N	90.57 W
Clayton, In., U.S.	218	39.41 N	86.31 W
Clayton, La., U.S.	194	31.43 N	91.32 W
Clayton, Mi., U.S.	216	41.52 N	84.14 W
Clayton, Mo., U.S.	219	38.38 N	90.19 W
Clayton, N.J., U.S.	208	39.39 N	75.05 W
Clayton, N.M., U.S.	196	36.27 N	103.11 W
Clayton, N.Y., U.S.	212	44.14 N	76.05 W
Clayton, N.C., U.S.	192	35.39 N	78.27 W
Clayton, Ok., U.S.	196	34.35 N	95.21 W
Clayton, Tx., U.S.	222	32.06 N	94.28 W
Clayton, Wa., U.S.	182	48.00 N	117.33 W
Clayton ≃	166	29.06 S	138.05 E
Claytonia	214	41.00 N	79.58 W
Clayton-le-Moors	262	53.47 N	2.23 W
Clayton-le-Woods	262	53.41 N	2.38 W
Clayton Park ♠	285	39.52 N	75.29 W
Clayton Valley V	282	37.58 N	121.58 W
Claytonville	216	40.34 N	87.49 W
Clay Village	218	38.11 N	85.07 W
Clayville	210	42.59 N	75.15 W
Clear ≃	182	56.11 N	119.42 W
Clear, Cape ≻, Ire.	48	51.24 N	9.30 W
Clear, Cape ≻, Ak., U.S.	180	59.48 N	147.54 W
Clear, Lake ⊜	212	45.26 N	77.12 W
Clear, Mount ∧	171b	35.52 S	149.04 E
Clear Boggy Creek ≃	196	34.03 N	95.47 W
Clearbrook, B.C., Can.	224	49.08 N	122.26 W
Clearbrook, Mn., U.S.	198	47.41 N	95.25 W
Clear Creek	218	39.07 N	86.32 W
Clear Creek ≃, Al., U.S.	194	34.00 N	87.19 W
Clear Creek ≃, Az., U.S.	200	34.59 N	110.38 W
Clear Creek ≃, Ca., U.S.	204	40.31 N	122.22 W
Clear Creek ≃, Ca., U.S.	280	34.17 N	118.12 W
Clear Creek ≃, Ca., U.S.	282	37.20 N	122.21 W
Clear Creek ≃, Ky., U.S.	218	38.10 N	85.17 W
Clear Creek ≃, Mo., U.S.	194	38.00 N	93.56 W
Clear Creek ≃, Mt., U.S.	202	48.46 N	109.25 W
Clear Creek ≃, Ne., U.S.	198	41.08 N	99.06 W
Clear Creek ≃, Oh., U.S.	218	39.33 N	84.20 W
Clear Creek ≃, Or., U.S.	224	45.23 N	122.29 W
Clear Creek ≃, Or., U.S.	224	45.09 N	121.31 W
Clear Creek ≃, Tn., U.S.	192	36.05 N	84.42 W
Clear Creek ≃, Tx., U.S.	196	33.16 N	97.03 W
Clear Creek ≃, Tx., U.S.	222	29.33 N	95.05 W
Clear Creek ≃, Tx., U.S.	222	29.09 N	97.23 W

Symbol	English	Deutsch	Español	Français	Português
≃	River	Fluß	Río	Rivière	Rio
≅	Canal	Kanal	Canal	Canal	Canal
ᒪ	Waterfall, Rapids	Wasserfall, Stromschnellen	Cascada, Rápidos	Chute d'eau, Rapides	Cascata, Rápidos
ʮ	Strait	Meeresstraße	Estrecho	Détroit	Estreito
ᑕ	Bay, Gulf	Bucht, Golf	Bahía, Golfo	Baie, Golfe	Baía, Golfo
⊜	Lake, Lakes	See, Seen	Lago, Lagos	Lac, Lacs	Lago, Lagos
≡	Swamp	Sumpf	Pantano	Marais	Pântano
⍓	Ice Features, Glacier	Eis- und Gletscherformen	Accidentes Glaciales	Formes glaciaires	Acidentes glaciares
⍑	Other Hydrographic Features	Andere Hydrographische Objekte	Otros Elementos Hidrográficos	Autres données hydrographiques	Outros acidentes hidrográficos
✦	Submarine Features	Untermeerische Objekte	Accidentes Submarinos	Formes de relief sous-marin	Acidentes submarinos
□	Political Unit	Politische Einheit	Unidad Politica	Entité politique	Unidade política
ʊ	Cultural Institution	Kulturelle Institution	Institución Cultural	Institution culturelle	Instituição cultural
⊥	Historical Site	Historische Stätte	Sitio Histórico	Site historique	Sitio histórico
♠	Recreational Site	Erholungs- und Ferienort	Sitio de Recreo	Centre de loisirs	Area de Lazer
⊠	Airport	Flughafen	Aeropuerto	Aéroport	Aeroporto
■	Military Installation	Militäranlage	Instalación Militar	Installation militaire	Instalação militar
◆	Miscellaneous	Verschiedenes	Misceláneo	Divers	Diversos

I · 38 **Clea-Cole**

ENGLISH — Name / Page / Lat.°′ / Long.°′
DEUTSCH — Name / Seite / Breite°′ / Länge°′ E = Ost

Clear Creek ≃, Wa., U.S. 224 46.07 N 122.00 W
Clear Creek ≃, Wy., U.S. 202 44.53 N 106.04 W
Clear Creek State Park ♦ 214 41.20 N 79.05 W
Clearfield, Ia., U.S. 198 40.48 N 94.28 W
Clearfield, Ky., U.S. 218 38.09 N 83.25 W
Clearfield, Pa., U.S. 214 41.01 N 78.26 W
Clearfield, Ut., U.S. 200 41.06 N 112.01 W
Clearfield □6 214 41.02 N 78.27 W
Clearfield Creek ≃ 214 41.02 N 78.24 W
Clear Fork Reservoir ⊜1 214 40.42 N 82.38 W
Clearing ✈8 278 41.47 N 87.47 W
Clear Island I 48 51.26 N 9.30 W
Clearlake, Ca., U.S. 226 38.57 N 122.38 W
Clear Lake, Ia., U.S. 190 43.08 N 93.22 W
Clear Lake, S.D., U.S. 198 44.44 N 96.40 W
Clearlake, Wa., U.S. 224 48.28 N 122.14 W
Clear Lake, Wi., U.S. 190 45.15 N 92.16 W
Clear Lake ⊜, Mb., Can. 184 50.42 N 100.00 W
Clear Lake ⊜, On., Can. 212 44.30 N 78.13 W
Clear Lake ⊜, On., Can. 212 45.14 N 79.57 W
Clear Lake ⊜, On., Can. 212 44.59 N 79.33 W
Clear Lake ⊜, In., U.S. 216 41.44 N 84.50 W
Clear Lake ⊜1, Ca., U.S. 204 39.02 N 122.50 W
Clear Lake ⊜1, La., U.S. 194 31.55 N 93.05 W
Clearlake Oaks 226 39.07 N 122.40 W
Clearlake Park 226 38.58 N 122.39 W
Clear Lake Reservoir ⊜1 204 41.52 N 121.08 W
Clear Lake Shores 222 29.33 N 95.02 W
Clearmont 202 44.38 N 106.22 W
Clear Run 214 41.08 N 78.45 W
Clear Site 180 64.19 N 149.11 W
Clearview, Oh., U.S. 214 41.25 N 82.10 W
Clearview, Wa., U.S. 224 47.45 N 122.06 W
Clearview, W.V., U.S. 214 40.09 N 80.41 W
Clearview Estates 279b 40.34 N 80.16 W
Clearwater, B.C., Can. 182 51.38 N 120.02 W
Clearwater, Mb., Can. 184 49.08 N 99.01 W
Clearwater, Fl., U.S. 220 27.57 N 82.48 W
Clearwater, Ks., U.S. 198 37.30 N 97.30 W
Clearwater, Ne., U.S. 198 42.10 N 98.11 W
Clearwater, S.C., U.S. 192 33.29 N 81.53 W
Clearwater, Wa., U.S. 224 47.34 N 124.17 W
Clearwater ≃, Can. 184 56.44 N 111.23 W
Clearwater ≃, Ab., Can. 182 52.23 N 114.50 W
Clearwater ≃, B.C., Can. 182 51.42 N 120.00 W
Clearwater ≃, Id., U.S. 202 46.25 N 117.02 W
Clearwater ≃, Mn., U.S. 198 47.54 N 96.16 W
Clearwater ≃, Mt., U.S. 202 46.58 N 113.23 W
Clearwater ≃, Wa., U.S. 224 47.33 N 124.21 W
Clearwater, Middle Fork ≃ 202 46.09 N 115.59 W
Clearwater, North Fork ≃ 202 46.30 N 116.19 W
Clearwater, South Fork ≃ 202 46.09 N 115.59 W
Clear Water Bay c 271d 22.17 N 114.18 E
Clearwater Beach Island I 220 27.59 N 82.49 W
Clearwater Lake ⊜, B.C., Can. 182 52.15 N 120.13 W
Clearwater Lake ⊜, Mb., Can. 184 54.05 N 101.00 W
Clearwater Lake Provincial Park ♦ 184 54.03 N 101.10 W
Clearwater Mountains ⋀ 202 46.00 N 115.30 W
Cleator Moor 44 54.31 N 3.30 W
Clebit 196 34.21 N 94.52 W
Cleburne 222 32.20 N 97.23 W
Cleckheaton 44 53.43 N 1.43 W
Cle Elum 224 47.11 N 120.56 W
Cle Elum ≃ 224 47.11 N 121.01 W
Cle Elum Lake ⊜1 224 47.18 N 121.06 W
Cleethorpes 44 53.34 N 0.02 W
Cleeve Cloud ∧2 42 51.34 N 2.00 W
Clefmont 58 48.06 N 5.31 E
Cleggan 48 53.33 N 10.09 W
Cleland Conservation Park ♦ 168b 34.59 S 138.44 E
Cleland Heights 285 39.44 N 75.34 W
Clelles 62 44.50 N 5.37 E
Clementon 285 39.48 N 74.59 W
Clementsport 186 44.40 N 65.37 W
Clemson 192 34.41 N 82.50 W
Clemville 222 29.00 N 96.08 W
Clendenin 188 38.29 N 81.20 W
Clendening Lake ⊜1 214 40.16 N 81.13 W
Clenze 54 52.56 N 10.58 E
Cleobury Mortimer 42 52.23 N 2.29 W
Cleona 208 40.20 N 76.28 W
Cléon-d'Andran 62 44.37 N 4.56 E
Cleopatra Needle ∧ 116 10.07 N 118.58 E
Clères 50 49.36 N 1.07 E
Clerke Rocks II1 244 55.01 S 34.41 W
Clermont, Austl. 166 22.49 S 147.39 E
Clermont, P.Q., Can. 186 47.41 N 70.14 W
Clermont, Fr. 50 49.23 N 2.24 E
Clermont, Fl., U.S. 220 28.32 N 81.46 W
Clermont, N.J., U.S. 285 39.59 N 74.48 W
Clermont, Pa., U.S. 214 41.41 N 78.29 W
Clermont □6 218 39.05 N 84.11 W
Clermont-en-Argonne 56 49.06 N 5.04 E
Clermont-Ferrand 32 45.47 N 3.05 E
Clermont State Park ♦ 210 42.05 N 73.55 W
Clerval 58 47.24 N 6.30 E
Clervaux 56 50.04 N 6.01 E
Cléry-Saint-André 50 47.49 N 1.45 E
Cles 64 46.22 N 11.02 E
Cleve 166 33.42 S 136.30 E
Clevedon 42 51.27 N 2.51 W
Cleveland, Austl. 171a 27.32 S 153.17 E
Cleveland, Al., U.S. 194 33.59 N 86.34 W
Cleveland, Fl., U.S. 220 26.57 N 82.00 W
Cleveland, Ga., U.S. 192 34.35 N 83.45 W
Cleveland, Ms., U.S. 194 33.44 N 90.43 W
Cleveland, N.Y., U.S. 210 43.14 N 75.53 W
Cleveland, N.C., U.S. 192 35.43 N 80.40 W
Cleveland, Oh., U.S. 214 41.29 N 81.41 W
Cleveland, Oh., U.S. 279a 41.29 N 81.41 W
Cleveland, Ok., U.S. 196 36.18 N 96.27 W
Cleveland, Tn., U.S. 194 35.09 N 84.52 W
Cleveland, Tx., U.S. 222 30.20 N 95.05 W
Cleveland, Va., U.S. 192 36.56 N 82.09 W
Cleveland □6 44 54.35 N 1.15 W
Cleveland, Cape ≻ 166 19.11 S 147.01 E
Cleveland, Mount ∧, Austl. 166 41.25 S 145.23 E
Cleveland, Mount ∧, Mt., U.S. 202 48.56 N 113.51 W
Cleveland Heights 214 41.31 N 81.33 W
Cleveland Hills ⋀2 44 54.23 N 1.05 W
Cleveland-Hopkins International Airport ⊠ 279a 41.25 N 81.51 W
Clevelândia 252 26.24 S 52.21 W
Clevelândia do Norte 250 3.49 N 51.52 W
Cleveland Museum of Art ʊ 279a 41.31 N 81.37 W
Cleveland National Forest ♦ 280 33.47 N 117.38 W
Cleveland Park ✈8 284c 38.56 N 77.04 W
Cleveland Peninsula ≻1 182 55.45 N 132.00 W
Cleveland Pond ⊜ 283 42.07 N 70.58 W
Cleveland State University ʊ2 279a 41.30 N 81.40 W
Cleveland Zoo ♦ 279a 41.27 N 81.43 W
Cleveleys 44 53.53 N 3.03 W
Cleversburg 208 40.02 N 77.28 W
Cleves → Kleve, B.R.D. 52 51.48 N 6.09 E
Cleves, Oh., U.S. 218 39.10 N 84.45 W
Clew Bay c 48 53.50 N 9.50 W
Clewer 158 25.55 S 29.07 E
Clewiston 220 26.45 N 80.56 W
Cley next the Sea 42 52.58 N 1.03 E
Clichy 50 48.54 N 2.18 E
Clichy-sous-Bois 261 48.55 N 2.33 E
Clifden 48 53.29 N 10.01 W
Clifden Bay c 48 53.28 N 10.05 W
Cliffdale Creek ≃ 166 16.56 S 138.48 E
Cliffdell 224 46.44 N 120.42 W
Cliffe 260 51.28 N 0.30 E
Cliffe Marshes ≋ 260 51.28 N 0.30 E
Cliffe Woods 260 51.26 N 0.30 E
Clifford, On., Can. 212 43.58 N 80.58 W
Clifford, S. Afr. 158 31.04 S 27.28 E
Clifford, In., U.S. 218 39.16 N 85.52 W
Clifford, Pa., U.S. 210 41.39 N 75.36 W
Clifford Park ♦ 274b 37.43 S 145.16 E
Cliffside 210 42.31 N 74.59 W
Cliffside Park 276 40.58 N 73.57 W
Cliffwood 276 40.26 N 74.14 W
Cliffwood Beach 276 40.26 N 74.13 W
Clifton, Austl. 171a 27.56 S 151.54 E
Clifton, Eng., U.K. 262 53.46 N 2.49 W
Clifton, Az., U.S. 200 33.03 N 109.17 W
Clifton, Il., U.S. 216 40.56 N 87.56 W
Clifton, Ks., U.S. 198 39.34 N 97.16 W
Clifton, N.J., U.S. 210 40.51 N 74.09 W
Clifton, N.Y., U.S. 210 43.03 N 77.49 W
Clifton, Or., U.S. 224 46.12 N 123.27 W
Clifton, Tn., U.S. 194 35.23 N 87.59 W
Clifton, Tx., U.S. 222 31.46 N 97.34 W
Clifton, Lake ⊜ 168a 32.49 S 115.41 E
Clifton Court Forebay ⊜1 226 37.50 N 121.35 W
Clifton Forge 192 37.48 N 79.49 W
Clifton Gorge V 42 51.28 N 2.37 W
Clifton Heights, N.Y., U.S. 284a 42.44 N 78.56 W
Clifton Heights, Pa., U.S. 285 39.55 N 75.17 W
Clifton Hills 166 26.52 S 138.50 E
Clifton Knolls 210 42.52 N 73.46 W
Clifton Park ♦ 284b 39.19 N 76.35 W
Clifton Point ≻ 240b 25.01 N 77.34 W
Clifton Springs 210 42.57 N 77.08 W
Clifty, Mount ∧ 224 47.07 N 121.10 W
Clifty Creek ≃ 218 39.09 N 85.54 W
Clifty Falls State Park ♦ 218 38.45 N 85.26 W
Clignon ≃ 50 49.07 N 3.04 E
Climax, Sk., Can. 184 49.13 N 108.23 W
Climax, Co., U.S. 200 39.22 N 106.10 W
Climax, Ga., U.S. 192 30.52 N 84.25 W
Climax, Mi., U.S. 216 42.14 N 85.20 W
Climax, Pa., U.S. 214 40.59 N 79.23 W
Clinch ≃ 192 35.53 N 84.29 W
Clinchco 192 37.09 N 82.21 W
Clingen 54 51.14 N 10.55 E
Clingmans Dome ∧ 192 35.35 N 83.30 W
Clinton, B.C., Can. 182 51.05 N 121.35 W
Clinton, On., Can. 190 43.37 N 81.32 W
Clinton, N.Z. 172 46.12 S 169.22 E
Clinton, Al., U.S. 194 32.55 N 88.00 W
Clinton, Ar., U.S. 194 35.35 N 92.27 W
Clinton, Ct., U.S. 207 41.16 N 72.31 W
Clinton, Il., U.S. 219 40.09 N 88.57 W
Clinton, In., U.S. 194 39.39 N 87.23 W
Clinton, Ia., U.S. 190 41.50 N 90.11 W
Clinton, Ky., U.S. 194 36.40 N 88.59 W
Clinton, La., U.S. 194 30.51 N 91.00 W
Clinton, Me., U.S. 188 44.38 N 69.30 W
Clinton, Md., U.S. 208 38.45 N 76.53 W
Clinton, Ma., U.S. 207 42.25 N 71.41 W
Clinton, Mi., U.S. 216 42.04 N 83.58 W
Clinton, Mn., U.S. 198 45.27 N 96.26 W
Clinton, Ms., U.S. 194 32.20 N 90.19 W
Clinton, Mo., U.S. 194 38.22 N 93.46 W
Clinton, N.J., U.S. 210 40.38 N 74.54 W
Clinton, N.Y., U.S. 210 43.02 N 75.22 W
Clinton, N.C., U.S. 192 34.59 N 78.19 W
Clinton, Oh., U.S. 214 40.56 N 81.42 W
Clinton, Ok., U.S. 196 35.30 N 98.58 W
Clinton, Pa., U.S. 214 40.29 N 80.18 W
Clinton, S.C., U.S. 192 34.28 N 81.52 W
Clinton, Tn., U.S. 192 36.06 N 84.07 W
Clinton, Tx., U.S. 222 33.06 N 96.14 W
Clinton, Wa., U.S. 224 47.58 N 122.21 W
Clinton, Wi., U.S. 216 42.33 N 88.51 W
Clinton □6, Il., U.S. 219 38.37 N 89.22 W
Clinton □6, In., U.S. 216 40.17 N 86.31 W
Clinton □6, Mi., U.S. 216 42.56 N 84.36 W
Clinton □6, N.Y., U.S. 206 44.57 N 73.42 W
Clinton □6, Oh., U.S. 218 39.27 N 83.50 W
Clinton □6, Pa., U.S. 210 41.08 N 71.26 W
Clinton ≃ 214 42.36 N 82.48 W
Clinton, Cape ≻ 166 22.32 S 150.47 E
Clinton, Lake ⊜1 194 40.10 N 88.50 W
Clinton, Middle Branch ≃ 281 42.36 N 82.54 W
Clinton, North Branch ≃ 214 42.36 N 82.54 W
Clinton-Colden Lake ⊜ 176 63.58 N 107.27 W
Clintondale 210 41.01 N 77.29 W
Clinton Lake ⊜1 198 38.55 N 95.25 W
Clinton Park 210 42.36 N 73.43 W
Clinton Reservoir ⊜1 276 41.05 N 74.27 W
Clinton Township 214 42.33 N 82.53 W
Clintonville, Mi., U.S. 281 42.43 N 83.22 W
Clintonville, Pa., U.S. 214 41.12 N 79.53 W
Clintonville, Wi., U.S. 190 44.37 N 88.45 W
Clintwood 192 37.09 N 82.27 W
Clio, Al., U.S. 194 31.42 N 85.36 W
Clio, Mi., U.S. 190 43.10 N 83.44 W
Clio, S.C., U.S. 192 34.34 N 79.32 W
Clipperton, Île I1 230 10.17 N 109.13 W
Clipperton Fracture Zone ✦ 16 10.00 N 115.00 W
Clisham ∧ 46 57.57 N 6.49 W
Clisson 32 47.05 N 1.17 W
Clitheroe 44 53.53 N 2.23 W
Clitunno ≃ 66 42.56 N 12.37 E
Clive 172 39.35 S 176.55 E
Cliza 248 17.36 S 65.56 W
Cloates, Point ≻ 162 22.43 S 113.40 E
Clock Face 262 53.25 N 2.43 W
Clocolan 158 29.00 S 27.30 E
Clodomira 252 27.35 S 64.08 W
Cloe 214 40.56 N 78.56 W
Cloete 196 27.55 N 101.10 W
Cloghan, Ire. 48 54.51 N 7.56 W
Cloghan, Ire. 48 53.13 N 7.53 W
Cloghane 48 52.13 N 10.12 W
Clogheen 48 52.16 N 8.00 W
Clogher 48 54.25 N 7.12 W
Clogher Head ≻ 48 53.48 N 6.12 W
Cloghjordan 48 52.57 N 8.02 W
Clonakilty 48 51.37 N 8.54 W
Clonakilty Bay c 48 51.35 N 8.50 W
Cloncurry 166 20.42 S 140.30 E
Cloncurry ≃ 166 18.37 S 140.40 E
Clondalkin 48 53.19 N 6.24 W
Clonee 48 53.25 N 6.26 W
Clones 48 54.11 N 7.15 W
Clonfert 48 53.14 N 8.05 W
Clonmacnois ⊥ 48 53.20 N 7.59 W
Clonmany 48 55.14 N 7.25 W
Clonmel 48 52.21 N 7.42 W
Clonroche 48 52.27 N 6.43 W
Clontarf 274a 33.48 S 151.16 E
Cloone 48 53.57 N 7.46 W
Clo-oose 224 48.40 N 124.49 W
Cloppenburg 52 52.50 N 8.02 E
Cloquallum Creek ≃ 224 46.58 N 123.24 W
Cloquet 190 46.43 N 92.27 W
Cloquet ≃ 190 46.52 N 92.35 W
Clorinda 252 25.17 S 57.43 W
Closter 276 40.58 N 73.57 W
Cloudcroft 200 32.57 N 105.44 W
Cloud Peak ∧, Ak., U.S. 180 68.24 N 148.26 W
Cloud Peak ∧, Wy., U.S. 202 44.25 N 107.10 W
Cloudy Bay c 172 41.27 S 174.10 E
Cloudy Mountain ∧ 180 63.11 N 156.05 W
Clough 48 54.18 N 5.50 W
Clough Foot 262 53.43 N 2.08 W
Clova 46 56.50 N 3.06 W
Clova, Glen V 46 56.49 N 3.04 W
Clove Lakes Park ♦ 276 40.37 N 74.07 W
Clovelly, Austl. 274a 33.55 S 151.16 E
Clovelly, Eng., U.K. 42 51.00 N 4.24 W
Clover 192 35.06 N 81.13 W
Clover Bank 210 42.45 N 78.53 W
Clover Creek ≃, Id., U.S. 202 43.00 N 115.11 W
Clover Creek ≃, Id., U.S. 202 42.34 N 115.38 W
Cloverdale, B.C., Can. 224 49.06 N 122.44 W
Cloverdale, Al., U.S. 194 34.56 N 87.46 W
Cloverdale, Ca., U.S. 204 38.48 N 123.00 W
Cloverdale, Il., U.S. 278 41.56 N 88.07 W
Cloverdale, In., U.S. 194 39.30 N 86.47 W
Cloverdale, Ky., U.S. 218 38.10 N 84.53 W
Cloverdale, Mi., U.S. 216 42.32 N 85.23 W
Cloverdale, Oh., U.S. 216 41.01 N 84.18 W
Cloverdale, Or., U.S. 224 45.12 N 123.53 W
Cloverdale Mall ✈9 275b 43.38 N 79.34 W
Cloverdene 273d 26.09 S 28.22 E
Cloverleaf 222 29.46 N 95.10 W
Clover Pass 182 55.28 N 131.47 W
Cloverport 194 37.50 N 86.37 W
Cloverville 216 43.11 N 86.10 W
Clovis, Ca., U.S. 226 36.49 N 119.42 W
Clovis, N.M., U.S. 196 34.24 N 103.12 W
Clowbridge Reservoir ⊜1 262 53.45 N 2.16 W
Clowne 44 53.18 N 1.16 W
Cloyes-sur-le-Loir 50 48.00 N 1.14 E
Cloyne 48 51.51 N 8.08 W
Cluain Meala → Clonmel 48 52.21 N 7.42 W
Cluanie, Loch ⊜ 46 57.07 N 5.05 W
Cluj-Napoca 38 46.47 N 23.36 E
Cluj-Napoca □6 38 46.45 N 23.45 E
Clun 42 52.26 N 3.00 W
Clun ≃ 42 52.22 N 2.53 W
Clune 214 40.34 N 79.18 W
Clunes 169 37.18 S 143.47 E
Clun Forest ✈3 42 52.28 N 3.07 W
Clunie Water ≃ 46 57.00 N 3.24 W
Cluny, Austl. 166 24.31 S 139.35 E
Cluny, Fr. 58 46.26 N 4.39 E
Cluses 58 46.04 N 6.36 E
Clusone 64 45.53 N 9.57 E
Clute 222 29.01 N 95.23 W
Clutha ≃ 172 46.21 S 169.48 E
Clwyd □6 44 53.05 N 3.20 W
Clwyd ≃ 44 53.20 N 3.30 W
Clwyd, Vale of V 44 53.12 N 3.24 W
Clwydian Range ⋀ 44 53.10 N 3.20 W
Clydach 42 51.43 N 3.50 W
Clyde, Austl. 274a 33.50 S 151.00 E
Clyde, Ab., Can. 182 54.09 N 113.39 W
Clyde, N.Z. 172 45.11 S 169.19 E
Clyde, Ca., U.S. 226 38.02 N 122.02 W
Clyde, Ks., U.S. 198 39.35 N 97.23 W
Clyde, Mi., U.S. 281 42.41 N 83.37 W
Clyde, N.Y., U.S. 210 43.05 N 76.52 W
Clyde, N.C., U.S. 192 35.32 N 82.54 W
Clyde, Oh., U.S. 214 41.18 N 82.58 W
Clyde, Tx., U.S. 196 32.24 N 99.30 W
Clyde ≃, Austl. 170 35.23 S 150.15 E
Clyde ≃, N.S., Can. 186 43.35 N 65.25 W
Clyde ≃, On., Can. 212 44.58 N 76.22 W
Clyde ≃, Dom. 240d 15.33 N 61.18 W
Clyde ≃, Scot., U.K. 46 55.56 N 4.29 W
Clyde ≃, N.Y., U.S. 210 43.04 N 77.00 W
Clyde ≃, Vt., U.S. 188 44.56 N 72.12 W
Clyde, Firth of c1 46 55.42 N 5.00 W
Clydebank 46 55.54 N 4.24 W
Clydegale Lake ⊜ 212 45.25 N 78.23 W
Clyde Lake ⊜ 182 55.18 N 111.28 W
Clyde No. 3 214 39.59 N 80.03 W
Clyde Park 202 45.53 N 110.36 W
Clyde Potts Reservoir ⊜1 276 40.48 N 74.35 W
Clyde River 176 70.25 N 68.30 W
Clydesdale 158 26.54 S 27.55 E
Clydesdale V 46 55.42 N 3.50 W
Clymer, N.Y., U.S. 214 42.01 N 79.37 W
Clymer, Pa., U.S. 214 40.40 N 79.00 W
Clynnog-fawr 44 53.01 N 4.23 W
Clywedog ≃ 42 52.27 N 3.32 W
Ćmielów 30 50.53 N 21.31 E
Cna ≃, S.S.S.R. 76 52.10 N 27.03 E
Cna ≃, S.S.S.R. 76 57.33 N 34.36 E
Cna ≃, S.S.S.R. 80 54.32 N 42.05 E
Cna ≃, S.S.S.R. 82 55.03 N 39.09 E
Côa ≃ 34 41.05 N 7.06 W
Coacalco □7 286a 19.37 N 99.06 W
Coacalco de Berriozábal 286a 19.37 N 9.05 W
Coachella 204 33.40 N 116.10 W
Coachella Canal ≊ 204 33.34 N 116.00 W
Coachford 48 51.53 N 8.48 W
Coacoyole 232 24.31 N 106.34 W
Coacuilco 234 21.07 N 98.35 W
Coahoma 196 32.18 N 101.18 W
Coahuayana 234 18.44 N 103.41 W
Coahuayana, Río de ≃ 234 18.41 N 103.45 W
Coahuayutla de Guerrero 234 18.19 N 101.49 W
Coahuila 200 32.12 N 114.59 W
Coahuila □3 232 27.20 N 102.00 W
Coal ≃ 180 59.39 N 126.57 W
Coalbrook 158 26.51 S 27.53 E
Coalbrookdale 42 52.38 N 2.30 W
Coalburg 214 41.11 N 80.36 W
Coalburn 46 55.36 N 3.54 W
Coal City 216 41.17 N 88.17 W
Coalcomán de Matamoros 234 18.47 N 103.09 W
Coal Creek 180 65.22 N 143.10 W
Coal Creek ≃, Co., U.S. 198 40.30 N 104.26 W
Coal Creek ≃, In., U.S. 194 39.57 N 87.25 W
Coal Creek ≃, Wa., U.S. 202 47.19 N 118.36 W
Coal Creek Flat 172 45.29 S 169.18 E
Coaldale, Ab., Can. 182 49.43 N 112.37 W
Coaldale, Pa., U.S. 210 40.49 N 75.54 W
Coal Fire Creek ≃ 194 33.15 N 88.18 W
Coal Fork 188 38.19 N 81.32 W
Coalgate, N.Z. 172 43.29 S 171.58 E
Coalgate, Ok., U.S. 196 34.32 N 96.13 W
Coal Grove 188 38.30 N 82.38 W
Coal Harbour 182 50.36 N 127.35 W
Coal Hill 194 35.26 N 93.40 W
Coal Hill Park ♦ 271a 39.56 N 116.23 E
Coalhurst 182 49.45 N 112.56 W
Coalinga 226 36.08 N 120.21 W
Coalisland 48 54.33 N 6.42 W
Coal Island I 172 46.07 S 166.38 E
Coalmont 182 49.31 N 120.41 W
Coalpit Heath 42 51.32 N 2.28 W
Coalport 214 40.44 N 78.32 W
Coal River 180 59.45 N 126.55 W
Coal Run ≃ 279b 40.21 N 80.07 W
Coalspur 182 53.11 N 117.01 W
Coalton 219 39.17 N 89.19 W
Coaltown 214 41.02 N 80.20 W
Coal Valley V 204 38.00 N 115.05 W
Coalville, S. Afr. 158 26.01 S 29.10 E
Coalville, Eng., U.K. 42 52.44 N 1.20 W
Coalville, Ut., U.S. 200 40.55 N 111.23 W
Coamo 240m 18.05 N 66.22 W
Coamo, Lago ⊜1 240m 18.01 N 66.23 W
Coapilla 234 17.08 N 93.10 W
Coaraci 255 14.38 S 39.32 W
Coari 246 4.05 S 63.08 W
Coari ≃ 246 4.30 S 63.33 W
Coari, Lago de ⊜ 246 4.15 S 63.22 W
Coarsegold 226 37.16 N 119.42 W
Coast □4 154 3.00 S 39.30 E
Coast Mountains ⋀ 176 55.00 N 129.00 W
Coast Ranges ⋀ 178 41.00 N 123.30 W
Coatán ≃ 236 14.48 N 92.31 W
Coatbridge 46 55.52 N 4.01 W
Coatepec 234 19.27 N 96.58 W
Coatepec de Harinas 234 18.54 N 99.43 W
Coatepeque 236 14.42 N 91.52 W
Coatepeque, Lago de ⊜ 236 13.52 N 89.33 W
Coatepetl, Cerro ∧ 234 18.25 N 97.35 W
Coates Creek ≃ 212 44.24 N 79.54 W
Coatesville 208 39.58 N 75.49 W
Coaticook 206 45.08 N 71.48 W
Coaticook ≃ 206 45.20 N 71.53 W
Coatsburg 219 40.02 N 91.10 W
Coats Island I 176 62.30 N 83.00 W
Coats Land ✈1 9 77.00 S 28.00 W
Coatzacoalcos 234 18.09 N 94.25 W
Coatzacoalcos ≃ 234 18.10 N 94.27 W
Coatzacoalcos, Bahía c 234 18.10 N 94.27 W
Coatzintla 234 20.29 N 97.27 W
Coayllo 248 12.44 S 76.28 W
Coazze 62 45.03 N 7.18 E
Cobá ⊥ 232 20.36 N 87.35 W
Cobadin 38 44.04 N 28.13 E
Coballo Cocha 246 3.54 S 70.32 W
Cobalt, On., Can. 190 47.24 N 79.41 W
Cobalt, Ct., U.S. 207 41.33 N 72.33 W
Cobán 236 15.29 N 90.19 W
Çobanlar 130 38.41 N 30.47 E
Cobar 166 31.30 S 145.49 E
Cobargo 166 36.23 S 149.53 E
Cobb 226 38.49 N 122.43 W
Cobb Creek ≃ 196 35.05 N 98.25 W
Cobberas, Mount ∧ 166 36.52 S 148.10 E
Cobbetts Pond ⊜ 283 42.48 N 71.17 W
Cobbin's Brook ≃ 260 51.41 N 0.01 W
Cobb Island 208 38.16 N 76.51 W
Cobb Island I, Md., U.S. 208 38.16 N 76.51 W
Cobb Island I, Va., U.S. 208 37.20 N 75.44 W
Cobbitty 274a 34.01 S 150.41 E
Cobbitty ∧2 274a 33.59 S 150.42 E
Cobble Hill 224 48.41 N 123.36 W
Cobble Mountain Reservoir ⊜1 207 42.08 N 72.55 W
Cobblestone Mountain ∧ 228 34.37 N 118.52 W
Cobb Neck ≻1 208 38.20 N 76.55 W
Cobbs Creek ≃ 285 39.54 N 75.15 W
Cobbs Creek Park ♦ 285 39.58 N 75.16 W
Cobb Seamount ✦3 16 46.46 N 130.49 W
Cobden, Austl. 169 38.20 S 143.05 E
Cobden, On., Can. 190 45.38 N 76.53 W
Cobden, Il., U.S. 194 37.31 N 89.15 W
Cobeña 266a 40.34 N 3.30 W
Cobequid Bay c 186 45.21 N 63.45 W
Cobequid Mountains ⋀ 186 45.31 N 64.05 W
Cobh 48 51.51 N 8.17 W
Cobham, Eng., U.K. 260 51.23 N 0.24 E
Cobham, Eng., U.K. 260 51.20 N 0.25 W
Cobham ≃ 184 53.15 N 93.58 W
Cobham Hall ⊥ 260 51.23 N 0.25 E
Cobija, Bol. 248 11.02 S 68.44 W
Cobija, Chile 252 22.33 S 70.16 W
Coblenz → Koblenz 56 50.21 N 7.35 E
Cobleskill 210 42.40 N 74.29 W
Cobleskill Creek ≃ 210 42.43 N 74.20 W
Coboconk 212 44.39 N 78.48 W
Cobo Hall ʊ 281 42.19 N 83.03 W
Cobolgo, gora ∧ 84 42.50 N 46.23 E
Coboto, Cerro ∧ 200 31.29 N 112.05 W
Čoboty 265b 55.39 N 37.21 E
Cobourg 212 43.58 N 78.10 W
Cobourg Peninsula ≻1 164 11.20 S 132.15 E
Cobquecura 252 36.08 S 72.47 W
Cobram 166 35.55 S 145.39 E
Cobras, Ilha das I 287a 22.54 S 43.10 W
Cobre ≃ 236 8.01 N 81.18 W
Cóbuè 154 12.04 S 34.50 E
Coburg, Austl. 169 37.45 S 144.58 E
Coburg, B.R.D. 56 50.15 N 10.58 E
Coburg Island I 176 76.00 N 79.25 W
Coburn 210 40.52 N 77.28 W
Coburn Mountain ∧ 188 45.28 N 70.06 W
Coca ≃ 246 0.29 S 76.58 W
Coca, Pizzo di ∧ 64 46.04 N 10.01 E
Coca, Punta ≻ 236 12.28 N 83.30 W
Cocachacra 248 17.06 S 71.46 W
Cocais ∧ 256 21.51 S 42.53 W
Cocais, Ribeirão dos ≃ 256 21.59 S 47.15 W
Cocal 250 3.28 S 41.34 W
Cocalico Creek ≃ 208 40.07 N 76.14 W
Coccaglio 64 45.34 N 9.58 E
Cocconato 62 45.05 N 8.02 E
Cocentaina 34 38.45 N 0.26 W
Cochabamba 248 17.24 S 66.09 W
Cochabamba □5 248 17.30 S 65.40 W
Cochagual 252 31.54 S 68.23 W
Čochatauri 84 42.01 N 42.15 E
Cochato ≃ 283 42.10 N 71.01 W
Coche, Isla I 246 10.45 N 63.55 W
Cochem 56 50.11 N 7.09 E
Cochesett 283 42.01 N 71.02 W
Cochetopa Creek ≃ 200 38.31 N 106.47 W
Cochichewick, Lake ⊜ 283 42.42 N 71.06 W
Cochin 122 9.58 N 76.14 E
Cochin China → Nam Phan □9 110 11.00 N 107.00 E
Cochinos, Bahía de (Bay of Pigs) c 240p 22.07 N 81.10 W
Cochinos, Cayos II 236 15.57 N 86.33 W
Cochise Head ∧ 200 32.03 N 109.18 W
Cochiti Indian Reservation ✈4 200 35.37 N 106.20 W
Cochituate 207 42.19 N 71.21 W
Cochituate, Lake ⊜ 283 42.17 N 71.22 W
Cochituate State Park ♦ 207 42.20 N 71.22 W
Cochran 192 32.23 N 83.21 W
Cochrane, Ab., Can. 182 51.11 N 114.28 W
Cochrane, On., Can. 176 49.04 N 81.01 W
Cochrane, Wi., U.S. 190 44.13 N 91.50 W
Cochrane ≃ 176 57.52 N 101.38 W
Cochrane, Lago (Lago Pueyrredón) ⊜ 254 47.20 S 72.00 W
Cochranton 214 41.31 N 80.02 W
Cochranville 208 39.53 N 75.55 W
Cochstedt 54 51.53 N 11.24 E
Cockatoo-Inseln → Buccaneer Archipelago II 160 16.17 S 123.20 E
Cock Bridge 46 57.09 N 3.14 W
Cockburn 166 32.05 S 141.00 E
Cockburn, Canal ʉ 254 54.20 S 71.30 W
Cockburn, Cape ≻ 164 11.20 S 132.52 E
Cockburn, Mount ∧ 162 22.46 S 130.36 E
Cockburn Island I 190 45.55 N 83.22 W
Cockburn Sound ʉ 168a 32.12 S 115.42 E
Cockburnspath 46 55.56 N 2.21 W
Cock Clarks 260 51.42 N 0.37 E
Cockenoe Island I 276 41.05 N 73.21 W
Cockenzie 46 55.58 N 2.58 W
Cocker ≃ 44 54.39 N 3.22 W
Cockerham 44 53.59 N 2.50 W
Cockermouth 44 54.40 N 3.21 W
Cockeysville 208 39.28 N 76.38 W
Cockfield 44 54.37 N 1.48 W
Cockfosters ✈8 260 51.39 N 0.09 W
Cocklebiddy 162 32.02 S 126.06 E
Cockpit Country ✈1 241q 18.18 N 77.43 W
Cockrell Hill 222 32.44 N 96.53 W
Cockroach Island I 240m 18.24 N 65.04 W
Cockscomb Point ≻ 174u 14.14 S 170.40 W
Coclé □4 236 8.30 N 80.15 W
Coclé del Norte ≃ 236 9.05 N 80.35 W
Coclois 50 48.28 N 4.20 E
Coco ≃ 236 15.00 N 83.10 W
Coco, Cayo I 240p 22.30 N 78.28 W
Coco, Isla del I 230 5.32 N 87.04 W
Côco, Rio do ≃ 250 9.27 S 50.02 W
Cocoa 220 28.23 N 80.44 W
Cocoa Beach 220 28.19 N 80.36 W
Cocobeach 152 0.59 N 9.36 E
Coco Channel ʉ 110 13.45 N 93.00 E
Cococi 250 6.25 S 40.30 W
Cocodrie Lake ⊜1 194 30.58 N 92.25 W
Coco Islands II 110 14.05 N 93.18 E
Coconino Plateau ⋀1 200 35.50 N 112.30 W
Cocorocuma, Cayos ✦2 236 15.45 N 83.00 W
Côcos 255 14.10 S 44.33 W
Cocos (Keeling) Islands □2 14 12.10 S 96.55 E
Cocos Bay c 241r 10.27 N 61.00 W
Cocos Island I 174p 13.14 N 144.39 E
Cocos Lagoon c 174p 13.14 N 144.38 E
Cocos Ridge ✦3 16 5.30 N 86.00 W
Cocotá ✈8 287a 22.49 S 43.11 W
Cocotitlán 234 19.14 N 98.52 W
Cocuiza ≃ 246 10.59 N 71.17 W
Cocula, Méx. 234 18.14 N 99.40 W
Cocula, Méx. 234 20.23 N 103.50 W
Cod ≃ 44 54.10 N 1.22 W
Cod, Cape ≻1 207 41.42 N 70.15 W
Codăești 38 46.52 N 27.46 E
Codajás 246 3.50 S 62.05 W
Codaruina 71 40.56 N 8.49 E
Coddenham 42 52.09 N 1.07 E
Codera, Cabo ≻ 246 10.35 N 66.05 W
Coderre 184 50.10 N 106.23 W
Coderre, Ruisseau ≃ 275a 45.43 N 73.19 W
Codesa 182 55.45 N 118.04 W
Codfish Island I 172 46.47 S 167.38 E
Codigoro 66 44.49 N 12.08 E
Cod Island I 176 57.45 N 61.50 W
Codlea 38 45.42 N 25.27 E
Codnor 44 53.03 N 1.23 W
Codó 250 4.29 S 43.53 W
Codogno 62 45.09 N 9.42 E
Codorus 208 39.48 N 76.52 W
Codorus Creek ≃ 208 40.03 N 76.38 W
Codorus State Park ♦ 208 39.48 N 76.54 W
Codòzinho 250 4.46 S 44.10 W
Çodpa 248 18.50 S 69.44 W
Čodro 86 50.50 N 88.34 E
Codroipo 64 45.58 N 12.59 E
Codrongianos 71 40.39 N 8.41 E
Codroy 186 47.53 N 59.24 W
Codroy Pond 186 48.04 N 58.52 W
Codru-Moma, Munții ⋀ 38 46.30 N 22.20 E
Codsall 42 52.38 N 2.12 W
Cody, Ne., U.S. 198 42.56 N 101.14 W
Cody, Wy., U.S. 202 44.31 N 109.03 W
Coeburn 192 36.56 N 82.27 W
Coelemu 252 36.29 S 72.42 W
Coelho da Rocha 256 22.47 S 43.23 W
Coelho Neto 250 4.15 S 43.00 W
Coemba 152 12.08 S 18.05 E
Coen 164 13.56 S 143.12 E
Coen ≃, Austl. 164 13.56 S 142.02 E
Coén ≃, C.R. 236 9.34 N 82.58 W
Coeneo [de la Libertad] 234 19.49 N 101.35 W
Coeroeni ≃ 250 3.21 N 57.31 W
Coesfeld 52 51.56 N 7.10 E
Coetivy Island I 138 7.08 S 56.16 E
Coeur d'Alene 202 47.40 N 116.46 W
Coeur d'Alene ≃ 202 47.28 N 116.48 W
Coeur d'Alene Indian Reservation ✈4 202 47.18 N 116.45 W
Coeur d'Alene Lake ⊜ 202 47.32 N 116.48 W
Coeur d'Alene Mountains ⋀ 202 47.50 N 116.05 W
Coevorden 52 52.40 N 6.45 E
Coeymans 210 42.28 N 73.48 W
Coffeen 219 39.05 N 89.24 W
Coffeen Lake ⊜1 219 39.03 N 89.20 W
Coffeeville 194 33.58 N 89.40 W
Coffeyville 198 37.02 N 95.36 W
Coffin Bay 162 34.37 S 135.29 E
Coffin Bay c 162 34.27 S 135.19 E
Coffin Bay Peninsula ≻1 162 34.32 S 135.15 E
Coffs Harbour 166 30.18 S 153.08 E
Cofimvaba 158 32.00 S 27.35 E
Cofradía 236 15.24 N 88.09 W
Cofre de Perote, Cerro (Nauhcampatépetl) ∧ 234 19.29 N 97.08 W
Cofre de Perote, Parque Nacional ♦ 234 19.32 N 97.10 W
Cofrents 34 39.14 N 1.04 W
Coggeshall 42 51.52 N 0.41 E
Coggiola 62 45.41 N 8.11 E
Coggon 190 42.16 N 91.31 W
Coghill, Mount ∧ 170 35.10 S 149.44 E
Coghinas ≃ 71 40.56 N 8.48 E
Coghinas, Lago del ⊜ 71 40.45 N 9.02 E
Coglians, Monte (Hohe Warte) ∧ 64 46.37 N 12.53 E
Cogliate 266b 45.39 N 9.05 E
Cognac 32 45.42 N 0.20 W
Cogne 62 45.37 N 7.21 E
Cognin 62 45.34 N 5.54 E
Cogo 152 1.05 N 9.42 E
Cogoleto 62 44.23 N 8.39 E
Cogolin 62 43.15 N 6.32 E
Cogollo del Cengio 64 45.47 N 11.25 E
Cogolludo 34 40.57 N 3.05 W
Cogolo 64 46.21 N 10.41 E
Çogoon ≃ 166 27.19 S 148.50 E
Čograjskoje vodochranilišče ⊜1 80 45.30 N 44.25 E
Cogswell 198 46.06 N 97.46 W
Cogswell Reservoir ⊜1 280 34.14 N 117.58 W
Cogt 102 45.20 N 96.38 E
Cogtoandman' 102 45.50 N 104.28 E
Cogton Bay c 116 9.51 N 124.33 E
Cogt-Ovoo 102 44.25 N 105.20 E
Çoğun 130 39.20 N 34.08 E
Čohansey ≃ 208 39.21 N 75.22 W
Cohasset 207 42.14 N 70.48 W
Cohasset Harbor c 283 42.15 N 70.47 W
Cohenga ≃ 248 10.17 S 73.57 W
Cohoctah 216 42.46 N 83.57 W
Cohocton 210 42.30 N 77.30 W
Cohocton ≃ 210 42.09 N 77.05 W
Cohoe 180 60.23 N 151.18 W
Cohoes 210 42.46 N 73.42 W
Cohoni 248 16.44 S 67.51 W
Cohoon, Lake ⊜1 208 36.45 N 76.38 W
Cohuna 166 35.49 S 144.13 E
Coiba, Isla de I 246 7.27 N 81.45 W
Coig ≃ 254 50.58 S 69.11 W
Coigeach, Rubha ≻ 46 58.06 N 5.26 W
Coignières 261 48.45 N 1.55 E
Coihaique 254 45.34 S 72.04 W
Coils Creek ≃ 204 39.32 N 116.16 W
Coimbatore 122 11.00 N 76.58 E
Coimbra, Bra. 248 19.55 S 57.47 W
Coimbra, Bra. 255 20.52 S 42.48 W
Coimbra, Port. 34 40.12 N 8.25 W
Coín, Esp. 34 36.40 N 4.45 W
Coin, Ia., U.S. 198 40.39 N 95.13 W
Coina ≃ 266c 38.38 N 9.03 W
Coipasa, Lago ⊜ 248 19.12 S 68.07 W
Coipasa, Salar de ≚ 248 19.26 S 68.09 W
Coire → Chur 58 46.51 N 9.32 E
Çoixtlahuaca 234 17.43 N 97.19 W
Čojbalsan, Mong. 88 48.25 N 114.52 E
Čojbalsan, Mong. 88 48.04 N 114.30 E
Čojbalsan uul ∧ 88 47.49 N 107.00 E
Cojedes 246 9.37 N 68.55 W
Cojedes □3 246 9.20 N 68.20 W
Cojímar ✈8 286b 23.10 N 82.18 W
Cojímar ≃ 286b 23.10 N 82.17 W
Cojudo Blanco, Cerro ∧ 254 47.05 S 69.20 W
Cojumatlán de Régules 234 20.07 N 102.50 W
Cojutepeque 236 13.43 N 88.56 W
Çokak 130 37.45 N 36.19 E
Čokato 190 45.04 N 94.11 W
Cokeburg 214 40.06 N 80.04 W
Coker 273a 6.29 N 3.20 E
Çokeville 200 42.04 N 110.57 W
Čoktal 85 42.36 N 76.44 E
Čokurdach 74 70.38 N 147.55 E
Colāba ✈8 272c 18.54 N 72.48 E
Colāba Point ≻ 272c 18.53 N 72.48 E
Colac 169 38.20 S 143.35 E
Colac, Lake ⊜ 169 38.18 S 143.35 E
Çolaklı 130 38.22 N 38.33 E
Čolalao del Valle 252 26.22 S 65.57 W
Colán Conhué 254 43.16 S 69.51 W
Colapsin Point ≻ 116 6.38 N 125.25 E
Colares, Bra. 250 0.56 S 48.17 W
Colares, Port. 266c 38.48 N 9.27 W
Colares, Ribeira de ≃ 266c 38.49 N 9.28 W
Colatina 255 19.32 S 40.37 W
Cölbe 56 50.51 N 8.48 E
Colbeck, Cape ≻ 9 77.06 S 157.48 W
Colberry Park 281 42.36 N 83.16 W
Colbert 196 33.51 N 96.30 W
Colbinabbin 166 36.35 S 144.49 E
Colbitz 54 52.19 N 11.36 E
Colbitz-Letzlinger Heide ✈3 54 52.27 N 11.35 E
Colborne, On., Can. 212 42.51 N 80.19 W
Colborne, On., Can. 212 44.00 N 77.53 W
Colbún 252 35.42 S 71.25 W
Colburn, Eng., U.K. 44 54.23 N 1.41 W
Colburn, In., U.S. 216 40.31 N 86.42 W
Colby, Ks., U.S. 198 39.23 N 101.03 W
Colby, Wi., U.S. 190 44.54 N 90.18 W
Colca 248 12.18 S 75.13 W
Colca ≃ 248 15.51 S 72.26 W
Colcamar 248 6.16 S 77.55 W
Colcapirhua 248 17.25 S 66.15 W
Colchester, On., Can. 214 41.59 N 82.56 W
Colchester, Eng., U.K. 42 51.54 N 0.54 E
Colchester, Ct., U.S. 207 41.34 N 72.19 W
Colchester, Il., U.S. 190 40.25 N 90.47 W
Coldbackie 46 58.31 N 4.23 W
Cold Bay 180 55.11 N 162.30 W
Cold Bay c 180 55.13 N 162.33 W
Coldblow ✈8 260 51.26 N 0.10 E
Cold Brook 210 43.15 N 75.03 W
Cold Creek ≃ 212 44.12 N 77.36 W
Colden 210 42.39 N 78.41 W
Cold Fell ∧ 44 54.54 N 2.36 W
Cold Harbor Battlefield ⊥ 208 37.36 N 77.20 W
Coldingham 46 55.53 N 2.10 W
Colditz 54 51.07 N 12.48 E
Cold Lake 184 54.27 N 110.10 W
Cold Lake ⊜ 184 54.33 N 110.05 W
Cold Lake, Canadian Forces Base ■ 184 54.25 N 110.17 W
Cold Lake Indian Reserve ✈4 184 54.33 N 110.10 W
Cold Norton 260 51.40 N 0.40 E
Coldrano 64 46.38 N 10.50 E
Cold Spring, Ky., U.S. 218 39.01 N 84.26 W
Cold Spring, Mn., U.S. 190 45.27 N 94.25 W
Cold Spring, N.J., U.S. 208 38.58 N 74.55 W
Cold Spring, N.Y., U.S. 210 41.25 N 73.57 W
Coldspring, Tx., U.S. 222 30.36 N 95.08 W
Cold Spring Harbor 276 40.52 N 73.27 W
Cold Spring Harbor c 276 40.53 N 73.28 W
Coldsprings, On., Can. 212 44.17 N 78.18 W
Cold Springs, N.Y., U.S. 210 43.08 N 76.15 W
Cold Spring Terrace 276 40.50 N 73.26 W
Coldstream, Austl. 169 37.44 S 145.23 E
Coldstream, Scot., U.K. 46 55.39 N 2.15 W
Cold Stream ≃ 226 39.35 N 120.22 W
Coldwater, On., Can. 212 44.42 N 79.40 W
Coldwater, Ks., U.S. 198 37.16 N 99.19 W
Coldwater, Mi., U.S. 216 41.56 N 85.00 W
Coldwater, Ms., U.S. 194 34.41 N 89.58 W
Coldwater, Oh., U.S. 216 40.28 N 84.37 W
Coldwater ≃, On., Can. 212 44.44 N 79.39 W
Coldwater ≃, Mi., U.S. 216 42.04 N 85.08 W
Coldwater ≃, Ms., U.S. 194 34.11 N 90.13 W
Coldwater Canyon V 280 34.14 N 117.44 W
Coldwater Creek ≃ 196 36.40 N 101.08 W
Coldwater Indian Reserve ✈4 182 50.04 N 120.48 W
Coldwater Lake ⊜ 216 41.49 N 84.58 W
Cole □6 219 38.30 N 92.13 W
Cole ≃, Ang. 152 9.07 S 15.50 E
Cole ≃, Eng., U.K. 42 51.42 N 1.42 W
Coleambally 166 34.49 S 145.52 E
Colebrook, N.H., U.S. 188 44.53 N 71.29 W
Colebrook, Oh., U.S. 214 41.32 N 80.46 W
Colebrook River Lake ⊜1 207 42.03 N 73.04 W
Cole Camp 194 38.27 N 93.12 W
Coledale 170 34.17 S 150.57 E
Coleen ≃ 180 67.05 N 142.31 W
Coleford, Eng., U.K. 42 51.48 N 2.36 W
Coleford, Eng., U.K. 42 51.14 N 2.27 W
Colégio, Morro do ∧ 287b 23.38 S 46.21 W
Coleman, Ab., Can. 182 49.38 N 114.30 W
Coleman, Fl., U.S. 220 28.47 N 82.04 W
Coleman, Md., U.S. 208 39.20 N 76.04 W
Coleman, Mi., U.S. 190 43.45 N 84.35 W
Coleman, Tx., U.S. 196 31.49 N 99.25 W
Coleman, Wi., U.S. 190 45.03 N 88.02 W
Coleman ≃ 164 15.06 S 141.38 E
Coleman, Lake ⊜1 196 32.02 N 99.30 W
Colembert 50 50.45 N 1.50 E
Colen Lakes ⊜ 184 54.33 N 95.25 W
Colenso 158 28.50 S 29.44 E
Colerain 214 40.07 N 80.49 W
Coleraine, Austl. 166 37.36 S 141.42 E
Coleraine, N. Ire., U.K. 48 55.08 N 6.40 W
Coleraine, Mn., U.S. 190 47.17 N 93.25 W
Coleridge 198 42.30 N 97.12 W
Coleridge, Lake ⊜ 172 43.17 S 171.30 E
Coles 194 31.16 N 91.01 W
Coles, Punta ≻ 248 17.42 S 71.23 W
Colesberg 158 30.45 S 25.05 E
Coles Brook ≃ 276 40.55 N 74.02 W
Coleshill, Eng., U.K. 42 52.30 N 1.42 W
Coleshill, Eng., U.K. 260 51.39 N 0.38 W
Coles Point 208 38.09 N 76.38 W
Colesville, Md., U.S. 284c 39.05 N 77.00 W

Symbols in the index entries represent the broad categories identified in the key at the right. Symbols with superior numbers (⋀1) identify subcategories (see complete key on page *I · 1*).

Symbole im Register stellen die rechts im Schlüssel erklärten Kategorien dar. Symbole mit hochgestellten Ziffern (⋀1) bezeichnen Unterabteilungen einer Kategorie (vgl. vollständiger Schlüssel auf Seite *I · 1*).

Los símbolos incluídos en el texto del índice representan las grandes categorías identificadas con la clave a la derecha. Los símbolos con numeros en su parte superior (⋀1) identifican las subcategorías (véase la clave completa en la página *I · 1*).

Les symboles de l'index représentent les catégories indiquées dans la légende à droite. Les symboles suivis d'un indice (⋀1) représentent des sous-catégories (voir légende complète à la page *I · 1*).

Os símbolos incluídos no texto do índice representam as grandes categorias identificadas com a chave à direita. Os símbolos com números em sua parte superior (⋀1) identificam as subcategorias (veja-se a chave completa à página *I · 1*).

∧ Mountain	Berg	Montaña	Montagne	Montanha
⋀ Mountains	Gebirge	Montañas	Montagnes	Montanhas
)(Pass	Paß	Paso	Col	Passo
V Valley, Canyon	Tal, Cañon	Valle, Cañón	Vallée, Canyon	Vale, Canhão
≚ Plain	Ebene	Llano	Plaine	Planície
≻ Cape	Kap	Cabo	Cap	Cabo
I Island	Insel	Isla	Île	Ilha
II Islands	Inseln	Islas	Îles	Ilhas
⊥ Other Topographic Features	Andere Topographische Objekte	Otros Elementos Topográficos	Autres données topographiques	Outros acidentes topográficos

ESPAÑOL — Nombre | Página | Lat.°′ | Long.°′ W = Oeste

FRANÇAIS — Nom | Page | Lat.°′ | Long.°′ W = Ouest

PORTUGUÊS — Nome | Página | Lat.°′ | Long.°′ W = Oeste

Nombre / Nom / Nome	Página / Page	Lat.°′	Long.°′
Colesville, N.J., U.S.	210	41.15 N	74.39 W
Coleto Creek ≃	196	28.41 N	97.01 W
Coleville, Sk., Can.	184	51.43 N	109.16 W
Coleville, Ca., U.S.	226	38.33 N	119.30 W
Colfax, Ca., U.S.	226	39.06 N	120.57 W
Colfax, Il., U.S.	216	40.34 N	88.36 W
Colfax, In., U.S.	194	40.11 N	86.40 W
Colfax, Ia., U.S.	190	41.40 N	93.14 W
Colfax, La., U.S.	194	31.31 N	92.42 W
Colfax, Wa., U.S.	202	46.52 N	117.21 W
Colfax, Wi., U.S.	190	44.59 N	91.43 W
Colfiorito	66	43.02 N	12.55 E
Colgate	216	43.12 N	88.12 W
Colgate Creek ≃	284b	39.15 N	76.32 W
Colgong	124	25.16 N	87.13 E
Colgrave Sound ꓴ	46a	60.37 N	0.58 W
Colhué Huapi, Lago ◎	254	45.30 S	68.48 W
Coliban ≃	169	36.56 S	144.33 E
Colibris, Pointe des ›, Guad.	241o	16.17 N	61.06 W
Colibris, Pointe des ›, Guad.	241o	16.15 N	61.11 W
Colico	58	46.08 N	9.22 E
Coligny, Fr.	58	46.23 N	5.21 E
Coligny, S. Afr.	158	26.17 S	26.15 E
Colijnsplaat	52	51.46 N	3.51 E
Colima, Méx.	200	32.25 N	115.05 W
Colima, Méx.	234	19.14 N	103.43 W
Colima □[3]	234	19.10 N	104.00 W
Colima, Nevado de ∧	234	19.33 N	103.38 W
Colimes ≃	246	1.32 S	80.00 W
Colin ≃	50	47.08 N	2.32 E
Colina	252	33.12 S	70.41 W
Colinas, Bra.	250	6.02 S	44.14 W
Colinas, Bra.	255	14.12 S	48.03 W
Colinet	186	47.13 N	53.33 W
Colinton, Austl.	171b	35.51 S	149.09 E
Colinton, Ab., Can.	182	54.37 N	113.15 W
Coll ▮	46	56.38 N	6.34 W
Colla	258	34.04 S	57.21 W
Colla, Arroyo ≃	258	34.19 S	57.20 W
Collagna	64	44.21 N	10.16 E
Collalbo (Klobenstein)	64	46.32 N	11.28 E
Collalto Sabino	66	42.08 N	13.02 E
Collamer	210	43.06 N	76.04 W
Collarenebri	166	29.33 S	148.35 E
Collarmele	66	42.03 N	13.38 E
Collaroy	274a	33.44 S	151.18 E
Collazzone	66	42.54 N	12.26 E
Collbran	200	39.14 N	107.57 W
Collecchio	64	44.45 N	10.13 E
Collecorvino	66	42.27 N	14.01 E
Colle di Tora	66	42.13 N	12.57 E
Colle di Val d'Elsa	66	43.25 N	11.07 E
Colleen Bawn	154	21.00 S	29.13 E
Colleferro	66	41.44 N	12.59 E
College	180	64.51 N	147.47 W
College City	226	39.00 N	122.00 W
College Corner	218	39.30 N	84.36 W
Collegedale	194	35.04 N	85.03 W
College Meadows	218	39.56 N	86.07 W
College Park, Ga., U.S.	192	33.39 N	84.26 W
College Park, Md., U.S.	208	38.58 N	76.56 W
College Park Airport ⊠	284c	38.58 N	76.55 W
College Place	202	46.02 N	118.23 W
College Point ◂[8]	276	40.47 N	73.51 W
College Station, Ar., U.S.	194	34.43 N	92.13 W
College Station, Tx., U.S.	222	30.37 N	96.20 W
Collegeville, In., U.S.	216	40.54 N	87.09 W
Collegeville, Pa., U.S.	208	40.11 N	75.27 W
Collégien	261	48.50 N	2.40 E
Collegno	62	45.05 N	7.34 E
Colle Isarco (Gossensass)	64	46.56 N	11.26 E
Collepardo	66	41.46 N	13.22 E
Collepasso	68	40.04 N	18.10 E
Collepietro	66	42.13 N	13.46 E
Collerina	166	29.41 S	146.38 E
Collesalvetti	66	43.35 N	10.28 E
Colle Sannita	68	41.22 N	14.50 E
Collesano	70	37.55 N	13.56 E
Colletorto	66	41.40 N	14.58 E
Colleymount	182	54.01 N	126.09 W
Colleyville	222	32.52 N	97.09 W
Colliano	68	40.43 N	15.17 E
Colli a Volturno	66	41.36 N	14.06 E
Colli del Tronto	66	42.52 N	13.44 E
Colli di Monte Bove	66	42.06 N	13.09 E
Collie	168a	33.21 S	116.09 E
Collie ≃	168a	33.18 S	115.44 E
Collie East ≃	168a	33.18 S	116.10 E
Collier □[6]	220	26.10 N	81.22 W
Collier Bay ⊂	160	16.10 S	124.15 E
Collier Bridge ◂[5]	220	26.57 N	82.04 W
Collier City	220	26.14 N	80.09 W
Collier Law ∧[2]	44	54.46 N	1.58 W
Collier Range ⋏	162	24.43 S	119.12 E
Collier Range National Park ♠	162	24.40 S	119.15 E
Collier Row ◂[8]	260	51.36 N	0.10 E
Colliers	214	40.22 N	80.32 W
Collier-Seminole State Park ♠	220	25.59 N	81.36 W
Colliersville	210	42.29 N	74.59 W
Collierville	194	35.02 N	89.39 W
Collie South ≃	168a	33.18 S	116.10 E
Collieston	46	57.21 N	1.56 W
Colliford Reservoir ◎[1]	42	50.32 N	4.33 W
Colligan ≃	48	52.06 N	7.38 W
Collin □[6]	222	33.07 N	96.35 W
Collina, Passo della)(	66	44.01 N	10.56 E
Collingbourne Kingston	42	51.18 N	1.13 W
Collingdale	208	39.54 N	75.16 W
Collingham	44	53.54 N	1.24 W
Collingswood	285	39.55 N	75.04 W
Collingwood, Austl.	274b	37.48 S	145.00 E
Collingwood, On., Can.	212	44.29 N	80.13 W
Collingwood, N.Z.	172	40.40 S	172.41 E
Collingwood Bay ⊂	164	9.20 S	149.30 E
Collins, Ga., U.S.	192	32.10 N	82.06 W
Collins, Ia., U.S.	190	41.54 N	93.18 W
Collins, Ms., U.S.	194	31.38 N	89.33 W
Collins, N.Y., U.S.	210	42.30 N	78.55 W
Collins, Oh., U.S.	214	41.16 N	82.30 W
Collins ≃	194	35.48 N	85.37 W
Collins, Mount ∧[2]	190	47.51 N	80.59 W
Collins Bay	212	44.15 N	76.36 W
Collinsburg	214	40.13 N	79.46 W
Collins Center	210	42.30 N	78.51 W
Collins Lake ◎	212	44.22 N	76.27 W
Collins Park	208	39.41 N	75.33 W
Collinston	194	32.41 N	91.52 W
Collinsville, Austl.	166	20.34 S	147.51 E
Collinsville, Al., U.S.	194	34.15 N	85.51 W
Collinsville, Ca., U.S.	282	38.05 N	121.51 W
Collinsville, Ct., U.S.	207	41.48 N	72.55 W
Collinsville, Il., U.S.	219	38.40 N	89.59 W
Collinsville, Ms., U.S.	194	32.29 N	88.50 W
Collinsville, N.J., U.S.	276	40.49 N	74.28 W
Collinsville, Ok., U.S.	196	36.21 N	95.50 W
Collinsville, Tx., U.S.	196	33.32 N	96.54 W
Collinwood	194	35.10 N	87.44 W
Collio	64	45.48 N	10.20 E
Collipulli	252	37.57 S	72.26 W
Collique Alto	286d	11.55 S	77.03 W
Collister	202	43.38 N	116.15 W
Collobrières	62	43.14 N	6.18 E
Collombey	58	46.16 N	6.57 E
Collomsville	210	41.09 N	77.09 W
Collon	48	53.47 N	6.29 W
Collonges	58	46.08 N	5.54 E
Collooney	48	54.11 N	8.29 W
Collserola, Serra de ⋏	266d	41.26 N	2.07 E
Colma	226	37.41 N	122.28 W
Colma Creek ≃	282	37.38 N	122.23 W
Colman	198	43.58 N	96.48 W
Colmar	58	48.05 N	7.22 E
Colmar Manor	284c	38.55 N	76.56 W
Colmars	62	44.11 N	6.38 E
Colmenar	34	36.54 N	4.20 W
Colmenar de Oreja	34	40.06 N	3.23 W
Colmenar Viejo	34	40.40 N	3.46 W
Colmeneros	234	18.06 N	101.40 W
Colmesneil	194	30.54 N	94.25 W
Colmnitz	54	50.54 N	13.31 E
Colmonell	44	55.08 N	4.55 W
Coln ≃	42	51.42 N	1.42 W
Colnbrook	260	51.29 N	0.31 W
Colne	44	53.52 N	2.09 W
Colne ≃, Eng., U.K.	42	51.48 N	1.01 E
Colne ≃, Eng., U.K.	260	51.26 N	0.30 W
Colney Heath	260	51.44 N	0.15 W
Colney Street	260	51.42 N	0.20 W
Colo	190	42.01 N	93.18 W
Colo ≃	170	33.26 S	150.53 E
Colobraro	68	40.11 N	16.25 E
Cologna Veneta	64	45.18 N	11.23 E
Cologne → Köln, B.R.D.	56	50.56 N	6.59 E
Cologne, Mn., U.S.	190	44.46 N	93.46 W
Cologne, N.J., U.S.	208	39.30 N	74.36 W
Cologno al Serio	62	45.37 N	9.42 E
Cologno Monzese	266b	45.32 N	9.17 E
Cololo, Nevado ∧	248	14.53 S	69.06 W
Coloma, Ca., U.S.	226	38.48 N	120.53 W
Coloma, Mi., U.S.	216	42.11 N	86.18 W
Coloma, Wi., U.S.	190	44.02 N	89.31 W
Coloma, Ensenada de la ⊂	240p	22.13 N	83.34 W
Colomb-Béchar → Béchar	148	31.37 N	2.13 W
Colombes	50	48.55 N	2.15 E
Colombey-les-Belles	58	48.32 N	5.54 E
Colombey-les-Deux-Eglises	58	48.13 N	4.53 E
Colômbia, Bra.	255	20.30 S	48.37 W
Colombia, Col.	246	3.24 N	74.49 W
Colombia, Méx.	196	27.42 N	99.45 W
Colombia □[1], S.A.	242	4.00 N	72.00 W
Colombia □[1], S.A.	246	4.00 N	72.00 W
Colombian Basin ✣[1]	16	13.00 N	76.00 W
Colombie → Colombia □[1]	246	4.00 N	72.00 W
Colombie-Britannique → British Columbia □[4]	182	54.00 N	125.00 W
Colombier	58	46.58 N	6.52 E
Colombo, Bra.	252	25.17 S	49.14 W
Colombo, S. Lan.	122	6.56 N	79.51 E
Colome	198	43.15 N	99.42 W
Colomiers	32	43.37 N	1.20 E
Colón, Arg.	252	32.13 S	58.08 W
Colón, Arg.	252	33.53 S	61.07 W
Colón, Cuba	240p	22.43 N	80.54 W
Colón, Pan.	236	9.22 N	79.54 W
Colon, Mi., U.S.	216	41.57 N	85.19 W
Colón, Ur.	252	33.53 S	54.43 W
Colón, Ur.	258	34.48 S	56.14 W
Colón □[4]	236	9.00 N	80.20 W
Colón □[5]	236	15.40 N	85.30 W
Colón, Archipiélago de (Galapagos Islands) ▮▮	246a	0.30 S	90.30 W
Colón, Cementerio ◂	286b	23.08 N	82.23 W
Colón, Isla ▮	236	9.24 N	82.17 W
Colón, Montañas de ⋏	236	14.55 N	84.45 W
Colón, Teatro ♠	288	34.36 S	58.23 W
Colona	162	31.38 S	132.05 E
Colonard-Corubert	50	48.25 N	0.39 E
Colonarie ≃	241h	13.14 N	61.06 W
Colonel Danforth Park ♠	275b	43.47 N	79.10 W
Colonelganj	124	27.08 N	81.42 E
Colonești	38	46.34 N	27.18 E
Colonet	204	31.05 N	116.10 W
Colonet, Cabo ›	204	30.58 N	116.19 W
Colongulac, Lake ◎	169	38.10 S	143.11 E
Colonia → Köln, B.R.D.	56	50.56 N	6.59 E
Colonia, T.T.P.I.	174q	9.31 N	138.08 E
Colonia, N.J., U.S.	210	40.34 N	74.18 W
Colonia □[5]	258	34.10 S	57.30 W
Colônia ≃	255	15.11 S	39.45 W
Colonia, Aeropuerto ⊠	258	34.28 S	57.49 W
Colonia, Cuchilla de la ⋏[2]	258	34.15 S	57.35 W
Colonia Agrícola de Turén	246	9.15 N	69.05 W
Colonia Alvear	252	35.00 S	67.40 W
Colonia Caroya	252	31.02 S	64.05 W
Colonia Cristóbal Obregón	234	16.20 N	93.30 W
Colonia del Sacramento	258	34.28 S	57.51 W
Colonia Dora	252	28.36 S	62.57 W
Colonia Elisa	252	26.56 S	59.32 W
Colonia Guadalupe	204	32.04 N	116.37 W
Colonia Hogar Ricardo Gutiérrez	288	34.51 S	58.51 W
Colonia José Mármol	252	26.59 S	60.44 W
Colonial Acres	208	39.31 N	76.20 W
Colonia Las Heras	254	46.33 S	68.57 W
Colonia Lavalleja	252	31.06 S	57.01 W
Colonial Beach	208	38.15 N	76.57 W
Colonial Crest	208	40.20 N	76.50 W
Colônia Leopoldina	250	8.57 S	35.39 W
Colonial Heights, Il., U.S.	278	41.05 N	88.01 W
Colonial Heights, Va., U.S.	208	37.14 N	77.24 W
Colonial Manor	285	39.51 N	75.09 W
Colonial National Historical Park ♠	208	37.12 N	76.45 W
Colonial Park	208	40.18 N	76.48 W
Colonial Village, N.Y., U.S.	210	43.08 N	78.58 W
Colonial Village, Pa., U.S.	285	40.04 N	75.24 W
Colonial Village Airport ⊠	284a	43.08 N	78.58 W
Colonial Williamsburg ⊥	208	37.16 N	76.42 W
Colonia Morelos	200	30.50 N	109.10 W
Colonia Nicolich	258	34.50 S	56.02 W
Colonia Progreso, Méx.	204	32.35 N	115.37 W
Colonia Progreso, Méx.	234	23.48 N	103.18 W
Colonia Providencia	240m	17.59 N	66.00 W
Colonias Unidas	252	26.42 S	59.38 W
Colonia Valdense	258	34.20 S	57.14 W
Colonia Villafañe	252	26.12 S	59.05 W
Colonie	210	42.43 N	73.50 W
Colon Koret	152	0.34 N	23.28 E
Colonna	267a	41.50 N	12.45 E
Colonna, Capo ›	68	39.02 N	17.11 E
Colonnata	64	44.05 N	10.10 E
Colón Ridge ✣[3]	18	2.00 N	96.00 W
Colonsay	184	51.59 N	105.53 W
Colonsay ▮	46	56.04 N	6.13 W
Colony	198	38.04 N	95.21 W
Colora	208	39.40 N	76.06 W
Colorada, Laguna ≋	254	44.50 S	68.15 W
Colorada, Punta ›	288	34.45 S	58.06 W
Coloradas, Lomas ⋏[2]	254	43.24 S	67.24 W
Colorado, C.R.	236	10.46 N	83.35 W
Colorado, Hond.	236	15.47 N	87.19 W
Colorado, Ak., U.S.	180	63.09 N	149.26 W
Colorado □[6]	222	29.40 N	96.30 W
Colorado □[3]	178	39.00 N	105.30 W
Colorado ≃, Arg.	244	39.50 S	62.08 W
Colorado ≃, Bra.	248	13.03 S	62.20 W
Colorado ≃, N.A.	200	31.54 N	114.57 W
Colorado ≃, Tx., U.S.	196	28.36 N	95.58 W
Colorado ≅	286a	19.24 N	98.59 W
Colorado, Cerro ∧, Arg.	254	45.02 S	69.38 W
Colorado, Cerro ∧, Chile	286e	33.24 S	70.45 W
Colorado, Cerro ∧, Méx.	232	31.31 N	115.31 W
Colorado, Cerro ∧, Perú	286d	12.07 S	76.55 W
Colorado, Williams Fork ≃	200	40.03 N	106.11 W
Colorado City, Az., U.S.	200	36.59 N	112.58 W
Colorado City, Co., U.S.	200	37.56 N	104.50 W
Colorado City, Tx., U.S.	196	32.23 N	100.51 W
Colorado de Abajo	196	26.28 N	99.54 W
Colorado National Monument ♠	200	39.04 N	108.25 W
Colorado Plateau ⋏[1]	200	36.30 N	108.00 W
Colorado River Aqueduct ≅[1]	204	33.50 N	117.23 W
Colorado River Indian Reservation ◂[4]	200	34.00 N	114.25 W
Colorados, Archipiélago de los ▮▮	240p	22.36 N	84.20 W
Colorado Springs	200	38.50 N	104.49 W
Colorines	234	19.07 N	100.12 W
Colorno	64	44.56 N	10.23 E
Colosimi	68	39.07 N	16.24 E
Colosseo ⊥	267a	41.54 N	12.29 E
Colotepec ≃	234	15.47 N	97.03 W
Colotlán	234	22.06 N	103.16 W
Colotlipa	234	17.25 N	99.09 W
Colo Vale	170	34.24 S	150.29 E
Čolpon	85	42.12 N	75.28 E
Čolpon-Ata	85	42.40 N	77.06 E
Colpoys Bay ⊂	212	44.47 N	81.05 W
Colquechaca	248	18.40 S	66.01 W
Colquencha	248	17.00 S	68.17 W
Colquiri	248	17.25 S	67.08 W
Colquitt	192	31.10 N	84.44 W
Colsterworth	42	52.48 N	0.37 W
Colstrip	202	45.53 N	106.37 W
Colt	194	35.07 N	90.48 W
Colta	248	15.10 S	73.18 W
Coltauco	252	34.18 S	71.06 W
Coltishall	42	52.44 N	1.22 E
Colton, Austl.	162	33.29 S	134.56 E
Colton, Ca., U.S.	228	34.04 N	117.18 W
Colton, Oh., U.S.	216	41.28 N	83.57 W
Colton, Or., U.S.	224	45.10 N	122.26 W
Colton, S.D., U.S.	198	43.47 N	96.55 W
Coltons Point	208	38.13 N	76.45 W
Colts Neck	208	40.17 N	74.10 W
Coltsville Center	214	41.05 N	80.34 W
Columbia, Al., U.S.	192	31.17 N	85.06 W
Columbia, Ca., U.S.	226	38.02 N	120.24 W
Columbia, Ct., U.S.	207	41.42 N	72.18 W
Columbia, Il., U.S.	219	38.26 N	90.12 W
Columbia, In., U.S.	218	39.35 N	85.12 W
Columbia, Ky., U.S.	194	37.06 N	85.18 W
Columbia, La., U.S.	194	32.06 N	92.04 W
Columbia, Md., U.S.	208	39.14 N	76.50 W
Columbia, Ms., U.S.	194	31.15 N	89.50 W
Columbia, Mo., U.S.	219	38.57 N	92.20 W
Columbia, N.J., U.S.	210	40.55 N	75.05 W
Columbia, N.C., U.S.	192	35.55 N	76.15 W
Columbia, Pa., U.S.	208	40.02 N	76.30 W
Columbia, S.C., U.S.	192	34.00 N	81.02 W
Columbia, Tn., U.S.	194	35.36 N	87.02 W
Columbia □[6], N.Y., U.S.	210	42.15 N	73.47 W
Columbia □[6], Or., U.S.	224	45.57 N	123.03 W
Columbia □[6], Pa., U.S.	210	41.00 N	76.28 W
Columbia ≃	176	46.15 N	124.05 W
Columbia, Cape ›	16	83.08 N	70.35 W
Columbia, Lake ◎[1]	216	42.05 N	84.18 W
Columbia, Mount ∧	182	52.09 N	117.25 W
Columbia Airport ⊠	279a	41.19 N	81.58 W
Columbia Basin ⊻[1]	202	46.45 N	119.05 W
Columbia Center	279a	41.19 N	81.56 W
Columbia City, In., U.S.	216	41.09 N	85.29 W
Columbia City, Or., U.S.	224	45.53 N	122.48 W
Columbia Cross Roads	210	41.50 N	76.48 W
Columbia Falls, Me., U.S.	188	44.39 N	67.43 W
Columbia Falls, Mt., U.S.	202	48.22 N	114.10 W
Columbia Heights	224	46.09 N	122.58 W
Columbia Hills	284b	39.15 N	76.50 W
Columbia Icefield ⊓	182	52.10 N	117.30 W
Columbia Lake ◎	182	50.15 N	115.57 W
Columbia Lake Indian Reserve ◂[4]	182	50.25 N	115.57 W
Columbia Mountains ⋏	182	52.00 N	119.00 W
Columbiana, Al., U.S.	194	33.10 N	86.36 W
Columbiana, Oh., U.S.	214	40.53 N	80.41 W
Columbiana □[6]	214	40.47 N	80.46 W
Columbia Plateau ⋏[1]	202	44.00 N	117.30 W
Columbia Regional Airport ⊠	219	38.50 N	92.13 W
Columbia Road Reservoir ◎[1]	198	45.45 N	98.15 W
Columbia State Historical Park ♠	226	38.02 N	120.25 W
Columbia Station	214	41.20 N	81.57 W
Columbia University ♉[2]	276	40.48 N	73.58 W
Columbiaville, Mi., U.S.	190	43.09 N	83.24 W
Columbiaville, N.Y., U.S.	210	42.19 N	73.45 W
Columbine, Cape ›	158	32.47 S	17.52 E
Columbrets, Illes ▮▮	34	39.52 N	0.40 E
Columbus, Ga., U.S.	192	32.29 N	84.59 W
Columbus, In., U.S.	218	39.12 N	85.55 W
Columbus, Ks., U.S.	198	37.10 N	94.50 W
Columbus, Ms., U.S.	194	33.29 N	88.25 W
Columbus, Mt., U.S.	202	45.38 N	109.15 W
Columbus, Ne., U.S.	198	41.25 N	97.22 W
Columbus, N.J., U.S.	208	40.04 N	74.43 W
Columbus, N.M., U.S.	200	31.49 N	107.38 W
Columbus, N.C., U.S.	192	35.15 N	82.11 W
Columbus, N.D., U.S.	198	48.54 N	102.46 W
Columbus, Oh., U.S.	214	39.57 N	82.59 W
Columbus, Pa., U.S.	214	41.56 N	79.35 W
Columbus, Tx., U.S.	222	29.42 N	96.32 W
Columbus, Wi., U.S.	190	43.20 N	89.00 W
Columbus Air Force Base ■	194	33.38 N	88.26 W
Columbus Grove	216	40.55 N	84.03 W
Columbus Junction	190	41.16 N	91.21 W
Columbus Lake ◎[1]	194	33.35 N	88.30 W
Columbus Park ♠	278	41.53 N	87.47 W
Columbus Point ›, Ba.	238	24.08 N	75.16 W
Columbus Point ›, Trin.	241r	11.08 N	60.48 W
Columbus Salt Marsh ≋	204	38.04 N	117.58 W
Coluna	255	18.14 S	42.50 W
Colusa	226	39.12 N	122.00 W
Colusa □[6]	226	39.13 N	122.01 W
Colusa Trough ≅	226	39.02 N	121.59 W
Colver	214	40.32 N	78.47 W
Colville, N.Z.	172	36.38 S	175.28 E
Colville, Wa., U.S.	202	48.32 N	117.54 W
Colville ≃, Ak., U.S.	180	70.25 N	150.30 W
Colville ≃, Wa., U.S.	202	48.37 N	118.05 W
Colville, Cape ›	172	36.28 S	175.21 E
Colville Channel ꓴ	172	36.23 S	175.24 E
Colville Indian Reservation ◂[4]	202	48.15 N	119.00 W
Colville Lake ◎	180	67.10 N	126.00 W
Colvin Run	284c	38.58 N	77.18 W
Colwell	44	55.04 N	2.04 W
Colwood	224	48.26 N	123.29 W
Colwyn	285	39.55 N	75.15 W
Colwyn Bay	44	53.18 N	3.43 W
Colyton, Austl.	274a	33.47 S	150.48 E
Colyton, Eng., U.K.	42	50.44 N	3.04 W
Comacchio	66	44.42 N	12.11 E
Comacchio, Valli di ⊂	66	44.38 N	12.06 E
Comal	115a	6.55 S	109.31 E
Comala	234	19.19 N	103.45 W
Comalapa, Guat.	236	14.44 N	90.53 W
Comalapa, Nic.	236	12.17 N	85.31 W
Comalcalco	234	18.16 N	93.13 W
Comales	232	26.10 N	98.56 W
Comalito, Cerro ∧	234	20.30 N	104.36 W
Comallo	254	40.40 S	63.30 W
Comallo, Arroyo ≃	254	40.29 S	70.12 W
Coman, Mount ∧	9	74.02 S	65.04 W
Comana	38	43.54 N	28.19 E
Comanche, Ok., U.S.	196	34.22 N	97.57 W
Comanche, Tx., U.S.	196	31.53 N	98.36 W
Comanche Creek ≃, Co., U.S.	198	39.53 N	104.19 W
Comanche Creek ≃, Tx., U.S.	196	31.06 N	102.24 W
Comandante Ferraz ♉[3]	9	62.05 S	58.23 W
Comandante Fontana	252	25.20 S	59.41 W
Comandante Leal	252	30.53 S	65.47 W
Comandante Luis Piedrabuena	254	49.59 S	68.54 W
Comandante Nicanor Otamendi	252	38.07 S	57.51 W
Comănești	38	46.25 N	26.26 E
Comanja de Corona	234	21.19 N	101.42 W
Comarapa	248	17.54 S	64.29 W
Comar Gambon	144	3.10 N	45.47 E
Comas, Perú	248	11.46 S	75.02 W
Comas, Perú	286d	11.57 S	77.04 W
Comayagua	236	14.25 N	87.37 W
Comayagua □[5]	236	14.30 N	87.40 W
Comayagua, Montañas de ⋏	236	14.23 N	87.26 W
Combahee ≃	192	32.30 N	80.31 W
Combarbalá	252	31.11 S	71.02 W
Combeaufontaine	58	47.43 N	5.53 E
Combe Martin	42	51.13 N	4.02 W
Comber, On., Can.	214	42.14 N	82.33 W
Comber, N. Ire., U.K.	48	54.33 N	5.45 W
Comberbach	262	53.17 N	2.32 W
Combermere Bay ⊂	110	19.37 N	93.34 E
Comberton	42	52.11 N	0.02 E
Combe Seamount ✣[3]	14	12.32 S	177.35 W
Combie, Lake ◎[1]	226	39.01 N	121.02 W
Comblain-au-Pont	56	50.28 N	5.35 E
Combles	50	50.01 N	2.52 E
Combloux	62	45.54 N	6.39 E
Combourg	32	48.25 N	1.45 W
Comboyne	166	31.36 S	152.29 E
Comboyuro Point ›	171a	27.04 S	153.24 E
Combres	50	48.19 N	1.04 E
Combronde	32	45.59 N	3.05 E
Combs	262	53.18 N	1.57 W
Combs-la-Ville	50	48.40 N	2.34 E
Combs Reservoir ◎[1]	262	53.19 N	1.57 W
Comburg ♉[1]	56	49.06 N	9.44 E
Comb Wash V	200	37.13 N	109.42 W
Come by Chance	186	47.51 N	53.58 W
Comeglians	64	46.31 N	12.52 E
Comelico Superiore	64	46.35 N	12.30 E
Comendador Gomes	255	19.41 S	49.05 W
Comer	192	34.03 N	83.07 W
Comercinho	255	16.19 S	41.47 W
Comerío	240m	18.13 N	66.14 W
Comet	166	23.37 S	148.33 E
Comet ≃	166	23.34 S	148.32 E
Cometela	156	21.51 S	34.29 E
Comfort, N.C., U.S.	192	35.00 N	77.30 W
Comfort, Tx., U.S.	196	29.58 N	98.54 W
Comfort, Cape ›	176	65.08 N	83.21 W
Comfort, Point ›	276	40.27 N	74.08 W
Comfrey	198	44.06 N	94.54 W
Comilla	124	23.27 N	91.12 E
Comines	50	50.46 N	3.01 E
Comino → Kemmuna ▮	36	36.00 N	14.20 E
Comino, Capo ›	71	40.32 N	9.49 E
Comiskey Park ♠	278	41.50 N	87.38 W
Comiso	70	36.56 N	14.36 E
Comitán [de Domínguez]	232	16.15 N	92.08 W
Comitini	70	37.24 N	13.39 E
Comloșu Mare	38	45.54 N	20.38 E
Commack	210	40.50 N	73.17 W
Commagene □[9]	130	37.50 N	38.00 E
Commencement Bay ⊂	224	47.17 N	122.28 W
Commentry	32	46.17 N	2.44 E
Commerce, Ga., U.S.	192	34.12 N	83.27 W
Commerce, Mi., U.S.	216	42.34 N	83.30 W
Commerce, Ok., U.S.	196	36.56 N	94.52 W
Commerce, Tx., U.S.	196	33.14 N	95.53 W
Commerce City	198	39.49 N	104.56 W
Commerciale Luigi Bocconi, Università ♉[2]	266b	45.26 N	9.11 E
Commercial Point	218	39.46 N	83.04 W
Commercy	56	48.45 N	5.35 E
Commewijne □[5]	250	5.30 N	55.00 W
Comminges ◂[1]	32	43.15 N	0.45 E
Committee Bay ⊂	176	68.30 N	86.30 W
Commodore	214	40.43 N	78.57 W
Commodore Barry Bridge ◂[5]	285	39.49 N	75.22 W
Commondale	158	27.20 S	30.56 E
Common Edge	262	53.47 N	3.02 W
Commonwealth Bay ⊂	9	66.54 S	142.40 E
Commonwealth Range ⋏	9	84.15 S	172.20 E
Commoron Creek ≃	166	28.22 S	150.08 E
Community Center	228	34.16 N	118.44 W
Como, Austl.	274a	34.00 S	151.04 E
Como, It.	62	45.47 N	9.05 E
Como, Ms., U.S.	194	34.30 N	89.56 W
Como, N.C., U.S.	208	36.30 N	77.00 W
Como, Tx., U.S.	222	33.03 N	95.28 W
Como, Wi., U.S.	216	42.37 N	88.28 W
Como □[4]	58	45.59 N	9.13 E
Como, Lago di ◎	58	46.00 N	9.20 E
Como, Lake ◎	216	42.36 N	88.29 W
Como, Mount ∧	226	39.02 N	119.28 W
Comodoro Py	252	35.19 S	60.31 W
Comodoro Rivadavia	254	45.52 S	67.30 W
Como Lake ◎	190	47.55 N	83.30 W
Comologno	58	46.12 N	8.34 E
Comondú	232	26.03 N	111.46 W
Comonfort	234	20.43 N	100.46 W
Comoras → Comoros □[1]	157a	12.10 S	44.15 E
Comores → Comoros □[1]	157a	12.10 S	44.15 E
Comores, Archipel des ▮▮	157a	12.10 S	44.15 E
Comorin, Cape ›	122	8.06 N	77.33 E
Comoros (Comores) □[1], Afr.	138	12.10 S	44.15 E
Comoros (Comores) □[1], Afr.	157a	12.10 S	44.15 E
Comox	182	49.40 N	124.55 W
Comox, Canadian Forces Base ■	182	49.43 N	124.54 W
Companhia Siderúrgica Nacional ♉[3]	256	22.31 S	44.07 W
Compans	261	49.00 N	2.40 E
Compatsch	58	46.58 N	10.25 E
Compiègne	50	49.25 N	2.50 E
Compo Cove ⊂	276	41.07 N	73.21 W
Compostela, Méx.	234	21.15 N	104.53 W
Compostela, Pil.	116	7.40 N	126.02 E
Comprida, Ilha ▮, Bra.	252	24.50 S	47.42 W
Comprida, Ilha ▮, Bra.	287a	23.02 S	43.12 W
Comps-sur-Artuby	62	43.43 N	6.30 E
Compstall	262	53.25 N	2.03 W
Compton, Eng., U.K.	260	51.13 N	0.38 W
Compton, Ca., U.S.	228	33.53 N	118.13 W
Compton, Il., U.S.	216	41.42 N	89.05 W
Compton □[6]	206	45.20 N	71.25 W
Compton Airport ⊠	280	33.53 N	118.15 W
Compton Creek ≃, Ca., U.S.	280	33.50 N	118.12 W
Compton Creek ≃, N.J., U.S.	276	40.26 N	74.05 W
Comptonville	273d	26.17 S	27.58 E
Comrie	46	56.22 N	4.00 W
Comstock, Mi., U.S.	216	42.17 N	85.30 W
Comstock, Ne., U.S.	198	41.33 N	99.15 W
Comstock, Tx., U.S.	196	29.41 N	101.11 W
Comstock Park	216	43.02 N	85.40 W
Comunanza	66	42.57 N	13.25 E
Con ≃, S.S.S.R.	76	52.54 N	36.00 E
Çon ≃, Viet.	110	19.02 N	104.58 E
Čona ≃, S.S.S.R.	74	62.54 N	111.06 E
Cona ≃, Scot., U.K.	46	56.46 N	5.14 W
Co Nag ◎	120	32.00 N	91.15 E
Conakry	150	9.31 N	13.43 W
Conambo ≃	246	2.07 S	76.03 W
Conanicut Island ▮	207	41.32 N	71.21 W
Cona Niyeo	254	41.53 S	67.00 W
Conara Junction	166	41.50 S	147.26 E
Conasauga ≃	192	34.33 N	84.55 W
Conaskonk Point ›	276	40.27 N	74.11 W
Conca ≃	66	43.58 N	12.43 E
Concarán	252	32.34 S	65.15 W
Concarneau	32	47.52 N	3.55 W
Conceição, Bra.	248	7.24 S	58.05 W
Conceição, Bra.	250	7.33 S	38.31 W
Conceição, Moç.	156	18.45 S	36.10 E
Conceição ≃	250	12.24 S	46.57 W
Conceição, Cachoeira ∟	248	9.34 S	64.22 W
Conceição, Ilha da ▮	287a	22.52 S	43.07 W
Conceição da Aparecida	255	21.06 S	46.12 W
Conceição da Barra	255	18.35 S	39.45 W
Conceição da Ibitipoca	256	21.43 S	43.55 W
Conceição da Pedra	256	22.09 S	45.27 W
Conceição das Alagoas	255	19.55 S	48.23 W
Conceição de Ipanema	255	19.55 S	41.41 W
Conceição de Jacareí	256	23.02 S	44.09 W
Conceição do Almeida	255	12.48 S	39.12 W
Conceição do Araguaia	250	8.15 S	49.17 W
Conceição do Canindé	250	7.54 S	41.34 W
Conceição do Coité	250	11.33 S	39.16 W
Conceição do Formoso	256	21.25 S	43.21 W
Conceição do Mato Dentro	255	19.01 S	43.25 W
Conceição do Maú	246	3.35 N	59.53 W
Conceição do Norte	255	12.13 S	47.18 W
Conceição do Rio Verde	256	21.53 S	45.05 W
Conceição dos Ouros	256	22.25 S	45.47 W
Concepción, Arg.	252	27.20 S	65.35 W
Concepción, Arg.	252	28.23 S	57.53 W
Concepción, Bol.	248	11.29 S	66.31 W
Concepción, Bol.	248	16.15 S	62.04 W
Concepción, Chile	252	36.50 S	73.03 W
Concepción, Col.	246	6.46 N	72.42 W
Concepción, Guat.	236	15.37 N	91.41 W
Concepción, Para.	252	23.25 S	57.17 W
Concepción, Perú	248	11.55 S	75.17 W
Concepcion, Pil.	116	10.42 N	123.03 E
Concepcion, Pil.	116	11.13 N	123.06 E
Concepcion, Pil.	116	15.19 N	120.39 E
Concepcion, Pil.	116	12.24 N	122.06 E
Concepción □[5]	252	23.00 S	57.00 W
Concepción, Bahía ⊂	232	26.39 N	111.48 W
Concepción, Estrecho del ꓴ	254	50.30 S	74.55 W
Concepción, Laguna ◎	248	17.29 S	61.25 W
Concepción, Río de la ≃	232	30.32 N	113.02 W
Concepción, Volcán ∧[1]	236	11.34 N	85.37 W
Concepcion Bay ⊂	116	11.15 N	123.07 E
Concepción de Ataco	236	13.52 N	89.51 W
Concepción de Buenos Aires	234	19.58 N	103.16 W
Concepción de la Sierra	252	27.59 S	55.31 W
Concepción de la Vega	238	19.13 N	70.31 W
Concepcíon del Oro	232	24.38 N	101.25 W
Concepción del Uruguay	252	32.29 S	58.14 W
Concepción Quezaltepeque	236	14.06 N	88.58 W
Conception, Point ›	204	34.27 N	120.27 W
Conception Bay ⊂, Nf., Can.	186	47.45 N	53.00 W
Conception Bay ⊂, Namibia	156	23.53 S	14.28 E
Concession	154	17.22 S	30.57 E
Conchagua	236	13.19 N	87.52 W
Conchagua, Volcán de ∧[1]	236	13.14 N	87.46 W
Conchal	256	22.20 S	47.10 W
Conchal, Ribeirão do ≃	256	22.20 S	47.10 W
Conchalí	286e	33.24 S	70.39 W
Conchas ≃	196	35.23 N	104.18 W
Conchas Dam	196	35.22 N	104.11 W
Conchas Lake ◎[1]	196	35.25 N	104.14 W
Conche	186	50.53 N	55.54 W
Conches-en-Ouche	50	48.58 N	0.56 E
Conchi	252	22.02 S	68.38 W
Conchillas	258	34.15 S	58.04 W
Conchitas, Arroyo ≃	288	34.45 S	58.09 W
Concho	200	34.28 N	109.36 W
Concho ≃	196	31.34 N	99.43 W
Conchos ≃, Méx.	232	29.35 N	104.25 W
Conchos ≃, Méx.	232	25.07 N	98.32 W
Concise	58	46.51 N	6.43 E
Conco	64	45.48 N	11.36 E
Concón	252	32.55 S	71.31 W
Conconongon Point ›	116	12.14 N	120.13 E
Conconully	182	48.33 N	119.44 W
Concord, Austl.	274a	33.52 S	151.06 E
Concord, On., Can.	275b	43.48 N	79.29 W
Concord, Ca., U.S.	226	37.58 N	122.01 W
Concord, Ga., U.S.	192	33.05 N	84.26 W
Concord, Il., U.S.	219	39.49 N	90.22 W
Concord, Ky., U.S.	218	38.41 N	83.29 W
Concord, Ma., U.S.	207	42.27 N	71.20 W
Concord, Mi., U.S.	216	42.10 N	84.38 W
Concord, Mo., U.S.	219	38.31 N	90.23 W
Concord, N.H., U.S.	188	43.12 N	71.32 W
Concord, N.C., U.S.	192	35.24 N	80.34 W
Concord, Pa., U.S.	214	40.15 N	77.42 W
Concord, Tx., U.S.	222	31.16 N	96.09 W
Concord ≃	283	42.39 N	71.18 W
Concord Battleground ⊥	283	42.28 N	71.21 W
Concordia, Arg.	252	31.24 S	58.02 W
Concórdia, Bra.	246	4.35 S	66.35 W
Concórdia, Bra.	252	27.14 S	52.01 W
Concordia, Méx.	232	25.47 N	103.07 W
Concordia, Méx.	234	23.17 N	106.04 W
Concordia, Perú	246	4.30 S	74.55 W
Concordia, Ks., U.S.	198	39.34 N	97.39 W
Concordia, Mo., U.S.	194	38.59 N	93.34 W
Concordia Gardens	216	41.09 N	85.08 W
Concordia Sagittaria ⊥	64	45.45 N	12.51 E
Concordia sulla Secchia	64	44.55 N	10.59 E
Concord Naval Weapons Station ■	282	38.03 N	122.02 W
Concordville	285	39.53 N	75.31 W
Concord West	274a	33.51 S	151.05 E
Concorezzo	62	45.35 N	9.20 E
Concrete	224	48.32 N	121.44 W
Con Cuong	110	19.02 N	104.54 E
Conda	152	11.06 S	14.20 E
Condamine	166	26.56 S	150.08 E
Condamine ≃	166	27.07 S	149.48 E
Condat-en-Féniers	32	45.21 N	2.46 E
Condé, Ang.	152	10.50 S	14.37 E
Conde, Bra.	255	11.49 S	37.37 W
Condé, Fr.	32	48.51 N	0.33 W
Conde, S.D., U.S.	198	45.09 N	98.05 W
Condécourt	261	49.02 N	1.57 E
Condé-en-Brie	50	49.00 N	3.33 E
Condega	236	13.21 N	86.24 W
Condeixa	250	0.54 S	48.36 W
Conderilla Señor	286d	12.02 S	77.05 W
Condé-sur-l'Escaut	50	50.27 N	3.35 E
Condè-sur-Vesgre	261	48.45 N	1.40 E
Condeúba	255	14.53 S	41.59 W
Condino	64	45.53 N	10.36 E
Condobolin	166	33.05 S	147.09 E
Condom	32	43.58 N	0.22 E
Condon	202	45.14 N	120.11 W
Condoto	246	5.06 N	76.37 W
Condove	62	45.07 N	7.18 E
Condrieu	62	45.27 N	4.46 E
Condroz □[9]	56	50.25 N	5.00 E
Cone	196	33.48 N	101.23 W
Conecuh ≃	194	30.58 N	87.14 W
Conegliano	64	45.53 N	12.18 E
Conejos	200	37.05 N	106.01 W
Conejos ≃	200	37.18 N	105.44 W
Conemaugh	214	40.24 N	78.52 W
Conemaugh ≃	214	40.28 N	79.27 W
Conemaugh River Lake ◎[1]	214	40.28 N	79.17 W
Cone Mountain ∧	180	66.12 N	156.03 W
Conero, Monte ∧	66	43.33 N	13.36 E
Conestoga	208	39.57 N	76.21 W
Conestoga Creek ≃	208	39.56 N	76.23 W
Conestogo	212	43.32 N	80.30 W
Conestogo ≃	212	43.32 N	80.29 W
Conestogo Lake ◎	212	43.44 N	80.44 W
Conesus	210	42.43 N	77.41 W
Conesus Lake ◎	210	42.47 N	77.43 W
Conesville	214	40.11 N	81.53 W
Conewago Creek ≃	208	40.07 N	76.42 W
Conewago Lake ◎	208	40.06 N	76.52 W
Conewango Creek ≃	214	41.50 N	79.09 W
Coney Island ◂[8]	276	40.34 N	74.00 W
Confederation Lake ◎	184	51.05 N	92.44 W
Configni	66	42.25 N	12.38 E
Conflans-en-Jarnisy	56	49.10 N	5.51 E
Conflans-Sainte-Honorine	50	48.59 N	2.06 E
Conflenti	68	39.04 N	16.17 E
Conflict Group ▮▮	164	10.45 S	151.45 E
Confluence	188	39.48 N	79.21 W
Confolens	32	46.01 N	0.41 E
Confraternidad, Parque ♠	286d	12.09 S	77.02 W
Confusion Bay ⊂	186	49.58 N	55.47 W
Confuso ≃	252	25.09 S	57.34 W
Cong	48	53.32 N	9.19 W
Congamond	207	42.01 N	72.46 W
Congaree ≃	192	33.45 N	80.37 W
Congelin	168a	32.50 S	116.54 E
Congers	210	41.09 N	73.56 W
Congers Lake ◎	276	41.09 N	73.57 W
Cong Hoa Stadium ♠	269c	10.45 N	106.40 E
Conghua	100	23.32 N	113.32 E
Congjiang	102	25.41 N	108.47 E
Congleton	44	53.10 N	2.13 W
Congo	250	7.48 S	36.40 W
Congo □[1], Afr.	138	1.00 S	15.00 E
Congo □[1], Afr.	152	1.00 S	15.00 E
Congo (Zaire) (Zaïre) ≃	138	6.04 S	12.24 E
Congo, Democratic Republic of the → Zaire □[1]	138	4.00 S	25.00 E
Congo, République démocratique du → Zaire □[1]	138	4.00 S	25.00 E
Congo, république du → Congo □[1]	152	1.00 S	15.00 E
Congo, Serra do ⋏	152	6.30 S	13.43 E
Congo Basin ⊻[1]	10	0.00	20.00 E
Congonhal	256	22.09 S	46.02 W
Congonhas, Aeroporto de ⊠	256	23.38 S	46.38 W
Congonhinhas	255	23.33 S	50.33 W
Congost ≃	266d	41.33 N	2.15 E
Congregación Cuauhtémoc	234	22.38 N	98.08 W
Congregación Ignacio Zaragoza	234	23.15 N	98.50 W
Congresbury	42	51.23 N	2.48 W
Congress, Sk., Can.	184	49.46 N	106.00 W
Congress, Oh., U.S.	214	40.55 N	82.03 W
Conie ≃	50	48.06 N	1.30 E
Conigli, Isola dei ▮	70a	35.30 N	12.33 E
Coningsby	44	53.07 N	0.10 W
Conisbrough	44	53.29 N	1.13 W
Coniston, On., Can.	190	46.29 N	80.51 W
Coniston, Eng., U.K.	44	54.22 N	3.05 W
Coniston Water ◎	44	54.20 N	3.04 W
Conitaca	232	24.10 N	106.43 W
Conjeeveram → Kānchipuram	122	12.50 N	79.43 E
Conjola	170	35.13 S	150.27 E
Çonjola Lake ⊂	170	35.16 S	150.27 E
Čon-Kemin ≃	85	42.42 N	75.54 E
Conklin, Ab., Can.	182	55.38 N	111.05 W
Conklin, N.Y., U.S.	210	42.02 N	75.48 W
Conklingville Dam ◂[6]	210	43.17 N	74.02 W
Conklin Point ›	276	40.41 N	73.17 W
Conkouati	152	4.00 S	11.13 E
Conliège	58	46.39 N	5.36 E
Conlin, Lake ◎	220	28.14 N	81.07 W
Conn, Lough ◎	48	54.04 N	9.20 W
Connah's Quay	44	53.13 N	3.03 W
Connaught □[9]	48	53.45 N	9.00 W
Connaughton	285	40.05 N	75.19 W
Connaughton, Mount ∧[2]	162	22.42 S	122.40 E
Connaught Place ♠	272a	28.38 N	77.12 E
Connaux	62	44.05 N	4.36 E
Conneaut	214	41.56 N	80.33 W
Conneaut Creek ≃	214	41.58 N	80.33 W
Conneaut Lake	214	41.36 N	80.19 W
Conneaut Lake ◎	214	41.37 N	80.18 W
Conneaut Outlet ≃	214	41.33 N	80.06 W
Conneautville	214	41.45 N	80.22 W
Connecticut □[3], U.S.	178	41.45 N	72.45 W
Connecticut □[3], U.S.	207	41.45 N	72.45 W
Connecticut ≃	188	41.17 N	72.21 W
Connell	202	46.39 N	118.51 W
Connell, Mount ∧	182	49.18 N	115.38 W
Connellsville	188	40.01 N	79.35 W
Connelly	210	41.55 N	73.59 W
Connel Park	44	55.23 N	4.12 W
Connemara	166	24.13 S	142.17 E
Connemara ◂[1]	48	53.25 N	9.45 W
Conner	116	17.48 N	121.19 E
Conner, Mount ∧	162	25.23 S	131.54 E
Connerré	50	48.03 N	0.30 E
Connersville, Fl., U.S.	220	27.54 N	81.47 W
Connersville, In., U.S.	218	39.38 N	85.08 W
Connetquot ≃	276	40.43 N	73.08 W
Connetquot Brook ≃	276	40.45 N	73.09 W
Connetquot River State Park ♠	210	40.46 N	73.09 W
Connewarre, Lake ◎	169	38.14 S	144.27 E
Conn Island ▮	284c	39.00 N	77.16 W

≃	River	Fluß	Río	Rivière	Rio	✣	Submarine Features	Untermeerische Objekte	Accidentes Submarinos	Formes de relief sous-marin	Acidentes submarinos
≅	Canal	Kanal	Canal	Canal	Canal	□	Political Unit	Politische Einheit	Unidad Politica	Entité politique	Unidade política
∟	Waterfall, Rapids	Wasserfall, Stromschnellen	Cascada, Rápidos	Chute d'eau, Rapides	Cascata, Rápidos	♉	Cultural Institution	Kulturelle Institution	Institución Cultural	Institution culturelle	Institução cultural
ꓴ	Strait	Meeresstraße	Estrecho	Détroit	Estreito	⊥	Historical Site	Historische Stätte	Sitio Histórico	Site historique	Sitio histórico
⊂	Bay, Gulf	Bucht, Golf	Bahía, Golfo	Baie, Golfe	Baía, Golfo	♠	Recreational Site	Erholungs- und Ferienort	Sitio de Recreo	Centre de loisirs	Area de Lazer
◎	Lake, Lakes	See, Seen	Lago, Lagos	Lac, Lacs	Lago, Lagos	⊠	Airport	Flughafen	Aeropuerto	Aéroport	Aeroporto
≋	Swamp	Sumpf	Pantano	Marais	Pântano	■	Military Installation	Militäranlage	Instalación Militar	Installation militaire	Instalação militar
⊓	Ice Features, Glacier	Eis- und Gletscherformen	Accidentes Glaciales	Formes glaciaires	Acidentes glaciares	◂	Miscellaneous	Verschiedenes	Misceláneo	Divers	Diversos
⍑	Other Hydrographic Features	Andere Hydrographische Objekte	Otros Elementos Hidrográficos	Autres données hydrographiques	Outros acidentes hidrográficos						

ENGLISH: Name | Page | Lat.°′ | Long.°′
DEUTSCH: Name | Seite | Breite°′ | Länge°′ E = Ost

Conn Lake ⊜ 176 70.34 N 73.30 W
Connoquenessing 214 40.49 N 80.59 W
Connoquenessing Creek ≃ 214 40.51 N 80.19 W
Connors Range ⋏ 166 21.40 S 149.10 E
Conodoguinet Creek ≃ 208 40.17 N 76.55 W
Conon ≃ 46 57.34 N 4.26 W
Cononaco ≃ 246 1.32 S 75.35 W
Cononbridge 46 57.34 N 4.26 W
Conorochite ≃ 246 2.41 N 67.29 W
Conotton Creek ≃ 214 40.34 N 81.23 W
Conover 192 35.42 N 81.13 W
Conowingo 208 39.40 N 76.09 W
Conowingo ⬥[6] 208 39.33 N 76.04 W
Conowingo Creek ≃ 208 39.41 N 76.12 W
Conowingo Dam ⬥[6] 208 39.39 N 76.10 W
Conquest 184 51.32 N 107.17 W
Conquista 255 19.56 S 47.33 W
Conquista, Ribeirão da ≃ 256 21.17 S 43.51 W
Conrad, Ia., U.S. 190 42.13 N 92.52 W
Conrad, Mt., U.S. 202 48.10 N 111.56 W
Conrado 256 22.32 S 43.33 W
Conroe 222 30.18 N 95.27 W
Conroe, Lake ⊜[1] 222 30.25 N 95.37 W
Consandolo 66 44.39 N 11.46 E
Con-Saryoj 85 42.37 N 76.53 E
Conscience Bay c 276 40.57 N 73.07 W
Consdorf 56 49.46 N 6.20 E
Consecon 212 44.00 N 77.31 W
Conselheiro Lafaiete 255 20.40 S 43.48 W
Conselheiro Paulino 256 22.13 S 42.31 W
Conselheiro Pena 255 19.10 S 41.30 W
Conselice 66 44.31 N 11.49 E
Conselve 64 45.14 N 11.52 E
Conservatória 256 22.18 S 43.57 W
Consett 44 54.51 N 1.49 W
Conshohocken 208 40.04 N 75.18 W
Consolação 256 22.33 S 45.55 W
Consolação ⬥[8] 287b 23.33 S 46.39 W
Consolación del Norte 240p 22.45 N 83.33 W
Consolación del Sur 240p 22.30 N 83.31 W
Consolidated Main Reef Mines ⬥[7] 273d 26.11 S 27.56 E
Con Son II 110 8.43 N 106.36 E
Consort 184 52.01 N 110.46 W
Constable 206 44.56 N 74.18 W
Constableville 212 43.34 N 75.25 W
Constance → Konstanz 58 47.40 N 9.10 E
Constance, Lake → Bodensee ⊜ 58 47.35 N 9.25 E
Constance Lake ⊜ 212 45.25 N 75.58 W
Constância 34 39.28 N 8.20 W
Constanța 38 44.11 N 28.39 E
Constanța □[6] 38 44.20 N 28.20 E
Constant Creek ≃ 212 45.17 N 76.46 W
Constantia 210 43.14 N 76.00 W
Constantina 34 37.52 N 5.37 W
Constantine → Qacentina 148 36.22 N 6.37 E
Constantine 216 41.50 N 85.40 W
Constantine, Cape › 180 58.25 N 158.50 W
Constantinople → İstanbul 130 41.01 N 28.58 E
Constant Lake ⊜ 212 45.24 N 77.00 W
Constitución, Chile 252 35.20 S 72.25 W
Constitución, Ur. 252 31.05 S 57.50 W
Constitución ⬥[8] 288 34.37 S 58.23 W
Constitución de 1857, Parque Nacional ♠ 204 32.05 N 115.55 W
Constitution, Mount ∧ 224 48.40 N 122.50 W
Consuegra 34 39.28 N 3.36 W
Consul 184 49.21 N 109.30 W
Consuma 66 43.47 N 11.35 E
Consuma, Passo della)(66 43.47 N 11.36 E
Contai 126 21.47 N 87.45 E
Contamana 248 7.15 S 74.54 W
Contarina 64 45.00 N 12.13 E
Contas, Rio de ≃ 255 14.17 S 39.01 W
Contee 208 39.05 N 76.52 W
Contendas do Sincorá 255 13.45 S 41.02 W
Contentnea Creek ≃ 192 35.21 N 77.23 W
Contes 62 43.49 N 7.19 E
Contessa Entellina 70 37.44 N 13.11 E
Contigliano 66 42.24 N 12.46 E
Continental 216 41.06 N 84.15 W
Continental Peak ∧ 200 42.16 N 108.43 W
Contoocook Lake ⊜ 207 42.47 N 72.01 W
Contraalmirante Cordero 252 38.44 S 68.10 W
Contra Costa □[6] 226 37.55 N 121.55 W
Contra Costa Canal ≅ 282 38.02 N 121.58 W
Contra Loma Reservoir ⊜[1] 282 37.58 N 121.49 W
Contramaestre 240p 20.18 N 76.15 W
Contramaestre ≃ 240p 20.31 N 76.18 W
Contratación 246 6.18 N 73.29 W
Contrecoeur 206 45.51 N 73.14 W
Contre Island ›[1] 276 40.54 N 73.32 W
Contreras □[7] 286a 19.16 N 99.16 W
Contreras, Embalse de ⊜[1] 34 39.32 N 1.30 W
Contres 50 47.25 N 1.26 E
Contrexéville 58 48.11 N 5.54 E
Contrisson 56 48.48 N 4.57 E
Controller Bay c 180 60.07 N 144.15 W
Contumazá 248 7.22 S 78.49 W
Contursi 68 40.39 N 15.14 E
Contwoyto Lake ⊜ 176 65.42 N 110.50 W
Conty 50 49.44 N 2.09 E
Contz-les-Bains 56 49.27 N 6.21 E
Convención 246 8.28 N 73.21 W
Convent 194 30.01 N 90.49 W
Convento 236 9.21 N 83.30 W
Convent Station 276 40.47 N 74.26 W
Conversano 68 40.58 N 17.08 E
Converse 216 40.34 N 85.52 W
Converse Lake ⊜ 276 41.08 N 73.39 W
Converse Pond Brook ≃ 276 41.03 N 73.40 W
Convoy 216 40.55 N 84.42 W
Conway, P.E., Can. 186 46.40 N 63.59 W
Conway, S. Afr. 158 31.43 S 25.16 E
Conway, Ar., U.S. 194 35.05 N 92.26 W
Conway, Fl., U.S. 220 28.30 N 81.19 W
Conway, Ma., U.S. 207 42.30 N 72.42 W
Conway, Mo., U.S. 194 37.30 N 92.49 W
Conway, N.H., U.S. 188 43.58 N 71.07 W
Conway, N.C., U.S. 192 36.26 N 77.13 W
Conway, Pa., U.S. 214 40.39 N 80.14 W
Conway, S.C., U.S. 192 33.50 N 79.02 W
Conway, Wa., U.S. 224 48.21 N 122.21 W
Conway, Cape › 166 20.32 S 148.56 E
Conway, Lake ⊜ 162 28.17 S 135.35 E
Conway, Lake ⊜[1] 194 35.00 N 92.25 W
Conway, Mount ∧ 162 23.45 S 133.25 E
Conway National Park ♠ 166 20.22 S 148.51 E
Conway Springs 198 37.23 N 97.38 W
Conwy 44 53.17 N 3.50 W
Conwy ≃ 44 53.17 N 3.50 W
Conwy, Vale of V 44 53.12 N 3.48 W
Conwy Bay c 44 53.18 N 3.55 W
Conyers 192 33.40 N 84.01 W
Conyngham 210 40.59 N 76.03 W
Coo 56 50.24 N 5.52 E
Coober Pedy 162 29.01 S 134.43 E
Coogee, Austl. 168a 32.07 S 115.46 E
Coogee, Austl. 274a 33.55 S 151.16 E
Coogee Bay c 274a 33.55 S 151.16 E
Cook, Austl. 162 30.37 S 130.25 E
Cook, In., U.S. 216 41.22 N 87.26 W
Cook, Mn., U.S. 190 47.51 N 92.41 W
Cook, Ne., U.S. 198 40.30 N 96.09 W
Cook, Wa., U.S. 224 45.43 N 121.40 W
Cook □[6] 216 41.53 N 87.45 W
Cook, Bahía c 254 55.10 S 70.10 W
Cook, Baie de c 174s 17.29 S 149.49 W
Cook, Cape › 182 50.08 N 127.55 W
Cook, Mount ∧ 172 43.36 S 170.10 E
Cook, Point › 274b 37.55 S 144.48 E
Cook, Récif de ✦[2] 175f 19.25 S 163.50 E
Cookardinia 171b 35.34 S 147.14 E
Cook Bay c 212 44.15 N 79.30 W
Cook Creek ≃ 224 47.17 N 124.05 W
Cooke, Mount ∧ 168a 32.25 S 116.18 E
Cookernup 168a 33.00 S 115.54 E
Cookes Peak ∧ 200 32.32 N 107.44 W
Cookeville 194 36.09 N 85.30 W
Cook Forest State Park ♠ 214 41.22 N 79.12 W
Cookham 42 51.34 N 0.43 W
Cookhouse 158 32.45 S 25.49 E
Cook Ice Shelf ⊓ 9 68.40 S 152.30 E
Cooking Lake ⊜ 182 53.25 N 113.02 W
Cook Inlet c 180 60.30 N 152.00 W
Cook-Inseln → Cook Islands □[2] 14 20.00 S 158.00 W
Cook Island I 174o 1.57 N 157.28 W
Cook Islands □[2] 14 20.00 S 158.00 W
Cooks ≃ 274a 33.56 S 151.10 E
Cooksburg 214 41.20 N 79.12 W
Cooks Falls 210 41.57 N 74.59 W
Cook's Harbour 186 51.36 N 55.52 W
Cookshire 206 45.25 N 71.38 W
Cooksmill Green 260 51.44 N 0.22 E
Cooks Mills 284a 43.00 N 79.11 W
Cookstown, On., Can. 212 44.11 N 79.42 W
Cookstown, N. Ire., U.K. 48 54.39 N 6.45 W
Cook Strait ʊ 172 41.15 S 174.30 E
Cooksville, Il., U.S. 216 40.33 N 88.43 W
Cooksville, Md., U.S. 208 39.19 N 77.01 W
Cooksville, Wi., U.S. 216 42.50 N 89.14 W
Cooksville Creek ≃ 275b 43.34 N 79.34 W
Cooktown 164 15.28 S 145.15 E
Cookville 222 33.11 N 94.51 W
Coolabah 166 31.02 S 146.43 E
Cooladdi 166 26.39 S 145.28 E
Coolah 166 31.50 S 149.42 E
Coolamon 166 34.49 S 147.12 E
Coolaney 48 54.11 N 8.29 W
Coolangatta 171a 28.10 S 153.32 E
Coolawanyah 162 21.47 S 117.48 E
Coole ≃ 50 48.56 N 4.21 E
Cooleemee 192 35.48 N 80.33 W
Cooley Lake ⊜ 281 42.37 N 83.27 W
Coolgardie 162 30.57 S 121.10 E
Coolidge, Az., U.S. 200 32.58 N 111.31 W
Coolidge, Ga., U.S. 192 31.00 N 83.51 W
Coolidge, Tx., U.S. 222 31.45 N 96.38 W
Coolidge, Mount ∧ 198 43.44 N 103.29 W
Coolidge Dam ⬥[6] 200 33.00 N 110.20 W
Coolidge Field ⊠ 240c 17.09 N 61.47 W
Coolidge Point › 283 42.34 N 70.44 W
Coolin 202 48.28 N 116.50 W
Cooling 260 51.27 N 0.32 E
Cooloola National Park ♠ 166 26.05 S 153.00 E
Cooloongup, Lake ⊜ 168a 32.18 S 115.47 E
Coolspring 214 41.02 N 79.05 W
Coolumburra Hill ∧ 170 35.01 S 150.10 E
Coolup 168a 32.44 S 115.53 E
Cooma 171b 36.14 S 149.08 E
Cooma Creek ≃ 171b 36.07 S 149.11 E
Coombe Cottage ⊥ 274b 37.43 S 145.23 E
Coomberdale 162 30.28 S 116.02 E
Coomera 171a 27.52 S 153.19 E
Coomera ≃ 171a 27.53 S 153.24 E
Coominya 171a 27.23 S 152.30 E
Coonabarabran 166 31.16 S 149.17 E
Coonalpyn 166 35.42 S 139.51 E
Coonamble 166 30.57 S 148.23 E
Coonana 162 31.01 S 123.07 E
Coon Creek ≃, Ca., U.S. 226 38.51 N 121.34 W
Coon Creek ≃, Il., U.S. 216 42.15 N 88.48 W
Coon Creek ≃, Tx., U.S. 222 31.59 N 95.52 W
Coon Creek Lake ⊜[1] 222 32.04 N 95.52 W
Coondambo 166 31.04 S 135.52 E
Coongan ≃ 162 20.53 S 119.47 E
Coonoor 122 11.21 N 76.49 E
Coon Rapids, Ia., U.S. 198 41.52 N 94.41 W
Coon Rapids, Mn., U.S. 190 45.10 N 93.19 W
Coontown 276 40.37 N 74.31 W
Coon Valley 190 43.42 N 91.00 W
Cooper 196 33.22 N 95.41 W
Cooper ≃, N.J., U.S. 285 39.57 N 75.07 W
Cooper ≃, Wa., U.S. 224 47.23 N 121.23 W
Cooper, Mount ∧, Austl. 162 26.11 S 127.56 E
Cooper, Mount ∧, B.C., Can. 182 50.11 N 117.12 W
Cooper, North Branch ≃ 285 39.55 N 75.02 W
Cooper Center 216 42.23 N 85.37 W
Cooper Creek ≃ 166 28.29 S 137.46 E
Cooper Island I 240m 18.22 N 64.30 W
Cooper Landing 180 60.29 N 149.51 W
Cooper Mountain ∧ 180 60.23 N 149.51 W
Cooper River Parkway ♠ 285 39.55 N 75.03 W
Cooper Road 194 32.26 N 93.48 W
Coopers 194 32.46 N 86.33 W
Coopersale Common 260 51.42 N 0.08 E
Coopersburg 208 40.30 N 75.23 W
Coopers Plains, Austl. 171a 27.34 S 153.02 E
Coopers Plains, N.Y., U.S. 210 42.11 N 77.08 W
Cooperstown, N.Y., U.S. 210 42.42 N 74.55 W
Cooperstown, N.D., U.S. 198 47.26 N 98.07 W
Cooperstown, Pa., U.S. 214 41.30 N 79.52 W
Cooperstown, Pa., U.S. 214 40.43 N 79.57 W
Coopersville 216 43.03 N 85.56 W
Coorabie 162 31.54 S 132.18 E
Cooranbong 170 33.04 S 151.27 E
Coorong National Park ♠ 166 36.01 S 139.32 E
Coorow 162 29.53 S 116.01 E
Cooroy 166 26.25 S 152.55 E
Coorparoo 171a 27.30 S 153.03 E
Coos □[6] 206 45.04 N 71.20 W
Coosa ≃ 194 32.30 N 86.16 W
Coosawhatchie ≃ 192 32.32 N 80.52 W
Coos Bay 202 43.22 N 124.12 W
Coos Bay c 202 43.23 N 124.16 W
Cootamundra 166 34.39 S 148.02 E
Cootehill 48 54.04 N 7.05 W
Cooyar 171a 26.59 S 151.50 E
Cooyar Creek ≃ 171a 27.24 S 152.03 E
Çooyar Mountain ∧ 171a 26.57 S 151.47 E
Čop 78 48.26 N 22.10 E
Copacabana, Arg. 252 28.12 S 67.29 W
Copacabana, Bol. 248 16.10 S 69.05 W
Copacabana ⬥[8] 287a 22.58 S 43.11 W
Copacabana, Forte de ⊥ 287a 22.59 S 43.11 W
Copainalá 234 17.05 N 93.12 W
Copake 210 42.06 N 73.33 W
Copake Falls 210 42.07 N 73.31 W
Copala 234 16.37 N 98.58 W
Copalillo 234 18.02 N 99.07 W
Copalis ≃ 224 47.07 N 124.13 W
Copalis Beach 224 47.06 N 124.10 W
Copalita ≃ 234 15.46 N 96.03 W
Copalquín 232 25.29 N 107.00 W
Copán, Hond. 236 14.50 N 89.09 W
Copan, Ok., U.S. 196 36.53 N 95.55 W
Copán □[5] 236 14.50 N 89.00 W
Copán ⊥ 236 14.50 N 89.09 W
Copanatoyac 234 17.15 N 98.45 W
Copándaro de Galeana 234 19.53 N 101.13 W
Copan Lake ⊜[1] 196 36.55 N 95.56 W
Copano Bay c 196 28.05 N 97.05 W
Copatana 246 2.48 S 67.04 W
Cope 198 39.39 N 102.51 W
Copeá, Paraná ≃[1] 246 3.52 S 63.20 W
Copeau ≃ 184 52.45 N 103.00 W
Copeland 220 25.57 N 81.21 W
Copeland Island I 48 54.41 N 5.32 W
Copenhagen → København, Dan. 41 55.40 N 12.35 E
Copenhagen, N.Y., U.S. 212 43.53 N 75.40 W
Copenhague → København 41 55.40 N 12.35 E
Copenhaver 284c 39.04 N 77.11 W
Copertino 68 40.16 N 18.03 E
Copetonas 252 38.43 S 60.27 W
Copeville 222 33.05 N 96.25 W
Copiague 210 40.40 N 73.24 W
Copiague Neck ›[1] 276 40.40 N 73.22 W
Copiapó 252 27.22 S 70.20 W
Copiapó ≃ 252 27.19 S 70.56 W
Copinsay I 46 58.54 N 2.40 W
Coplay 208 40.40 N 75.29 W
Copley, Austl. 166 30.32 S 138.25 E
Copley, Oh., U.S. 214 41.06 N 81.39 W
Copmanthorpe 44 53.55 N 1.08 W
Copoas, Mount ∧ 116 10.48 N 119.17 E
Copolo 152 10.22 S 14.07 E
Çoporito 246 8.56 N 62.00 W
Čopoviči 78 50.49 N 27.58 E
Copparo 64 44.54 N 11.49 E
Coppell 222 32.57 N 97.01 W
Coppename ≃ 250 5.48 N 55.55 W
Coppenbrügge 52 52.07 N 9.32 E
Copper ≃ 180 60.30 N 144.50 W
Copperas Cove 196 31.07 N 97.54 W
Copperas Mountain ∧ 276 41.02 N 74.28 W
Copperbelt □[4] 154 13.00 S 28.00 E
Copper Butte ∧ 202 48.42 N 118.28 W
Copper Center 180 61.58 N 145.19 W
Copper Cliff 190 46.28 N 81.04 W
Copper Creek ≃ 192 36.40 N 82.45 W
Copper Harbor 190 47.27 N 87.53 W
Coppermine 176 67.50 N 115.05 W
Coppermine ≃ 176 67.49 N 115.04 W
Copper Mine Point ›, Br. Vir. Is. 240m 18.26 N 64.25 W
Coppermine Point ›, On., Can. 190 46.59 N 84.47 W
Copper Mountain 182 49.20 N 120.33 W
Copper Mountain ∧, Ak., U.S. 182 55.14 N 132.36 W
Copper Mountain ∧, Wy., U.S. 200 43.27 N 107.57 W
Copperopolis 226 37.59 N 120.38 W
Coppet 58 46.19 N 6.12 E
Coppin State College ✥[2] 284b 39.19 N 76.40 W
Copplestone 42 50.49 N 3.45 W
Coppull 262 53.37 N 2.40 W
Copster Green 262 53.48 N 2.30 W
Coptic Museum ✥ 273c 30.00 N 31.13 E
Copton Creek ≃ 182 54.16 N 119.15 W
Copton Point › 116 10.00 N 123.22 E
Coqên 120 31.20 N 85.25 E
Coqueiro Grande, Serra do ∧ 256 21.40 S 42.55 W
Coquet ≃ 44 55.22 N 1.37 W
Coquet Dale V 44 55.16 N 1.50 W
Coquí 240m 17.59 N 66.14 W
Coquilhatville → Mbandaka 152 0.04 N 18.16 E
Coquille 202 43.10 N 124.11 W
Coquille ≃ 202 43.07 N 124.26 W
Coquille, East Fork ≃ 202 43.06 N 124.04 W
Coquille, Middle Fork ≃ 202 43.05 N 124.09 W
Coquille, South Fork ≃ 202 43.02 N 124.07 W
Coquimatlán 234 19.12 N 103.48 W
Coquimbo 252 29.58 S 71.21 W
Coquimbo □[4] 252 30.45 S 71.00 W
Coquina Key I 220 27.44 N 82.38 W
Corabia 38 43.46 N 24.30 E
Coração de Jesus 255 16.42 S 44.22 W
Coração de Maria 255 12.14 S 38.45 W
Corace ≃ 68 38.49 N 16.37 E
Coracora 248 15.02 S 73.47 W
Corail, Mer de → Coral Sea ⊤[2] 14 20.00 S 158.00 E
Coral 214 40.29 N 79.10 W
Coralaque ≃ 248 16.26 S 70.45 W
Coral Bay c, Pil. 116 8.25 N 117.20 E
Coral Bay c, Vir. Is., U.S. 240m 18.20 N 64.41 W
Coral Gables 220 25.43 N 80.16 W
Coral Harbour 176 64.08 N 83.10 W
Coral Hills 284c 38.52 N 76.55 W
Coral Sea ⊤[2] 14 20.00 S 158.00 E
Coral Sea Basin ✦[1] 14 14.00 S 152.00 E
Coral Sea Islands Territory □[8] 166 18.30 S 152.00 E
Coral Springs 220 26.16 N 80.13 W
Coralville 190 41.40 N 91.34 W
Coralville Lake ⊜[1] 190 41.47 N 91.48 W
Coram, Mt., U.S. 202 48.25 N 114.02 W
Coram, N.Y., U.S. 210 40.52 N 73.00 W
Corangamite, Lake ⊜ 169 38.10 S 143.25 E
Corantijn (Corentyne) ≃ 250 5.55 N 57.05 W
Coraopolis 214 40.31 N 80.10 W
Coraopolis Heights 279b 40.29 N 80.10 W
Corato 68 41.09 N 16.25 E
Corbara, Lago di ⊜[1] 66 42.43 N 12.15 E
Corbeil-Essonnes 50 48.36 N 2.29 E
Corbenay 58 47.54 N 6.20 E
Corbeny 50 49.28 N 3.49 E
Corbeolona 62 45.10 N 9.22 E
Corbera, Riera de ≃ 266d 41.27 N 1.59 E
Corberon 58 47.01 N 4.59 E
Corbeta Uruguay ✥[3] 9 59.27 S 27.15 W
Corbett 210 42.03 N 75.02 W
Corbetta 62 45.28 N 8.55 E
Corbett National Park ♠ 124 29.40 N 78.45 E
Corbettsville 210 42.01 N 75.48 W
Corbie 50 49.55 N 2.30 E
Corbière Point › 43b 49.11 N 2.15 W
Corbières ⋏ 32 42.55 N 2.38 E
Corbigny 50 47.15 N 3.40 E
Corbin 192 36.56 N 84.05 W
Corbion 56 49.48 N 5.00 E
Corbola 64 45.00 N 12.05 E
Corbones ≃ 34 37.36 N 5.39 W
Corbridge 44 54.58 N 2.01 W
Corbu 38 44.29 N 24.43 E
Corby 42 52.29 N 0.40 W
Corcaigh → Cork 48 51.54 N 8.28 W
Córcega 240m 18.19 N 67.15 W
Córcega, Isla de → Corse I 36 42.00 N 9.00 E
Corciano 66 43.08 N 12.17 E
Corcieux 58 48.10 N 6.53 E
Corcolle ⬥[8] 267a 41.55 N 12.46 E
Corcoran 226 36.05 N 119.33 W
Corcovado ∧ 287a 22.57 S 43.13 W
Corcovado, Golfo c 254 43.30 S 73.30 W
Corcovado, Volcán ∧[1] 254 43.12 S 72.48 W
Corcubión 34 42.57 N 9.11 W
Cordâ ≃ 250 6.26 S 48.17 W
Cordeaux Reservoir ⊜[1] 170 34.22 S 150.45 E
Cordeiro 255 22.02 S 42.22 W
Cordele, Ga., U.S. 192 31.57 N 83.46 W
Cordele, Tx., U.S. 222 29.08 N 96.38 W
Cordell 196 35.17 N 98.59 W
Cordell Hull Reservoir ⊜[1] 194 36.25 N 85.40 W
Cordenons 64 45.59 N 12.42 E
Corder 194 39.05 N 93.38 W
Cordes 32 44.04 N 1.57 E
Cordignano 64 45.57 N 12.25 E
Cordillera □[5] 252 25.15 S 57.00 W
Cordillo Downs 166 26.43 S 140.38 E
Cordisburgo 255 19.07 S 44.21 W
Córdoba, Arg. 252 31.24 S 64.11 W
Córdoba, Esp. 34 37.53 N 4.46 W
Córdoba, Méx. 234 18.53 N 96.56 W
Córdoba □[4] 252 32.00 S 64.00 W
Córdoba □[5] 246 8.20 N 75.40 W
Córdoba, Península ›[1] 254 53.20 S 72.50 W
Cordon 116 16.40 N 121.28 E
Cordova → Córdoba, Esp. 34 37.53 N 4.46 W
Córdova, Perú 248 14.04 S 75.03 W
Cordova, Al., U.S. 194 33.45 N 87.11 W
Cordova, Ak., U.S. 180 60.33 N 145.46 W
Cordova, Il., U.S. 190 41.41 N 90.19 W
Cordova, Md., U.S. 208 38.52 N 75.59 W
Cordova Bay c 182 54.55 N 132.35 W
Cordova Lake ⊜ 212 44.35 N 77.49 W
Cordova Peak ∧ 180 60.51 N 145.16 W
Corea, Estrecho de → Korea Strait ʊ 90 34.00 N 129.00 E
Corea del Norte → Korea, North □[1] 98 40.00 N 127.00 E
Corea del Sur → Korea, South □[1] 98 36.30 N 128.00 E
Coreaú 250 3.33 S 40.39 W
Coreaú ≃ 250 2.54 S 40.50 W
Core Creek ≃ 285 40.11 N 74.55 W
Corée, Détroit de → Korea Strait ʊ 90 34.00 N 129.00 E
Coree, Mount ∧ 171b 35.18 S 148.48 E
Corée du Nord → Korea, North □[1] 98 40.00 N 127.00 E
Corée du Sud → Korea, South □[1] 98 36.30 N 128.00 E
Coreglia Antelminelli 64 44.04 N 10.31 E
Coreinbob 171b 35.13 S 147.38 E
Coremas 250 7.01 S 37.58 W
Corentyne (Corantijn) ≃ 250 5.55 N 57.05 W
Corerepe 232 25.40 N 108.40 W
Corese Terra 66 42.10 N 12.42 E
Corey Lake ⊜ 216 41.55 N 85.45 W
Corfe Castle 42 50.38 N 2.04 W
Corfield 166 21.43 S 143.22 E
Corfu → Kérkira, Ellás 38 39.36 N 19.56 E
Corfu, N.Y., U.S. 210 42.57 N 78.24 W
Corfu → Kérkira I 38 39.40 N 19.42 E
Corhanwarrabul Creek ≃ 274b 37.55 S 145.12 E
Cori 66 41.39 N 12.55 E
Coria 34 39.59 N 6.32 W
Coria del Río 34 37.16 N 6.03 W
Coriaí ≃ 250 3.18 S 52.04 W
Coribe 255 13.50 S 44.28 W
Coricudgy, Mount ∧ 170 32.50 S 150.22 E
Corigliano Calabro 68 39.36 N 16.31 E
Corigliano d'Otranto 68 40.09 N 18.15 E
Corinaldo 66 43.39 N 13.03 E
Corinda 166 17.53 S 138.35 E
Corinne, Pa., U.S. 285 39.54 N 75.40 W
Corinne, Ut,. U.S. 200 41.33 N 112.06 W
Corinne, W.V., U.S. 192 37.34 N 81.21 W
Corinth → Kórinthos, Ellás 38 37.56 N 22.56 E
Corinth, Ky., U.S. 218 38.29 N 84.33 W
Corinth, Ms., U.S. 194 34.56 N 88.31 W
Corinth, N.Y., U.S. 210 43.14 N 73.49 W
Corinth, Gulf of → Korinthiakós Kólpos c 38 38.19 N 22.04 E
Corinth Canal → Korínthou, Dhiórix ≅ 38 37.57 N 22.56 E
Corinto, Bra. 255 18.21 S 44.27 W
Corinto, El Sal. 236 13.49 N 87.58 W
Corinto, Nic. 236 12.29 N 87.10 W
Corio 169 38.04 S 144.23 E
Corio Bay c 169 38.07 S 144.24 E
Coripata 248 16.18 S 67.36 W
Corire 248 16.14 S 72.28 W
Coris 248 9.50 S 77.45 W
Corisco, Isla de I 152 0.53 N 9.20 E
Corixao ≃ 248 18.22 S 57.23 W
Cork (Corcaigh) 48 51.54 N 8.28 W
Cork □[6] 48 51.58 N 8.35 W
Cork Airport ⊠ 48 51.51 N 8.29 W
Cork Harbour c 48 51.45 N 8.15 W
Corkscrew 220 26.28 N 81.33 W
Corkscrew Swamp ≡ 220 26.25 N 81.34 W
Čorku 85 39.58 N 70.33 E
Corlay 32 48.19 N 3.03 W
Corleone 70 37.49 N 13.18 E
Corleto Perticara 68 40.23 N 16.03 E
Çorlu 130 41.09 N 27.48 E
Cormainville 50 48.08 N 1.36 E
Cormano 266b 45.33 N 9.10 E
Cormatin 58 46.33 N 4.41 E
Cormeilles 50 49.15 N 0.23 E
Cormeilles-en-Parisis 50 48.59 N 2.12 E
Cormery 50 47.16 N 0.51 E
Cormons 64 45.58 N 13.28 E
Cormoran Reef ✦[2] 175b 7.50 N 134.32 E
Cormorant 184 54.14 N 100.35 W
Cormorant Lake ⊜ 184 54.13 N 100.47 W
Çorna 64 45.53 N 10.10 E
Çornaja, S.S.S.R. 24 68.35 N 56.30 E
Çornaja, S.S.S.R. 78 47.37 N 29.20 E
Çornaja, S.S.S.R. 82 55.45 N 38.04 E
Çornaja ≃, S.S.S.R. 265a 59.47 N 30.10 E
Çornaja ≃, S.S.S.R. 265a 59.50 N 30.00 E
Çornaja ≃, S.S.S.R. 265a 60.01 N 30.10 E
Çornaja ≃, S.S.S.R. 265a 59.55 N 30.59 E
Çornaja ≃, S.S.S.R. 265b 55.41 N 37.58 E
Çornaja Cholunica 86 58.51 N 51.42 E
Čornaja Gr'az', S.S.S.R. 82 54.31 N 35.52 E
Čornaja Gr'az', S.S.S.R. 82 54.58 N 36.48 E
Čornaja Gr'az', S.S.S.R. 265b 55.58 N 37.19 E
Çornaja Rečka 265a 59.56 N 30.58 E
Čornaja rečka ≃, S.S.S.R. 265a 59.46 N 30.45 E
Čornaja rečka ≃, S.S.S.R. 265a 59.55 N 30.22 E
Čornaja Sloboda 24 60.48 N 37.46 E
Cornaredo 266b 45.30 N 9.02 E
Cornas 62 44.58 N 4.51 E
Cornedo Vicentino 64 45.37 N 11.20 E
Cornelia, S. Afr. 158 27.13 S 28.52 E
Cornelia, Ga., U.S. 192 34.30 N 83.31 W
Cornélio Procópio 255 23.08 S 50.39 W
Cornelius, N.C., U.S. 192 35.29 N 80.51 W
Cornelius, Or., U.S. 224 45.31 N 123.03 W
Cornelius Grinnell Bay c 176 63.20 N 64.50 W
Cornell, Il., U.S. 216 41.00 N 88.44 W
Cornell, Wi., U.S. 190 45.10 N 91.08 W
Cornellà de Llobregat 266d 41.21 N 2.05 E
Corner Brook 186 48.57 N 57.57 W
Corner Inlet c 169 38.43 S 146.20 E
Corner Store 285 40.07 N 75.30 W
Cornersville 194 35.21 N 86.50 W
Cornes, Lac des ⊜ 206 46.43 N 75.09 W
Cornforth 44 54.42 N 1.31 W
Cornhill 46 57.36 N 2.42 W
Cornholme 262 53.44 N 2.08 W
Cornia ≃ 66 42.57 N 10.33 E
Corniglia 62 44.07 N 9.42 E
Corniglio 64 44.28 N 10.05 E
Corning, Ar., U.S. 194 36.24 N 90.34 W
Corning, Ca., U.S. 204 39.55 N 122.10 W
Corning, Ia., U.S. 198 40.59 N 94.44 W
Corning, Ks., U.S. 198 39.39 N 96.01 W
Corning, N.Y., U.S. 210 42.08 N 77.03 W
Corning, Oh., U.S. 188 39.36 N 82.05 W
Cornish 188 43.48 N 70.48 W
Cornish, Mount ∧ 162 20.13 S 126.28 E
Cornland 219 39.56 N 89.24 W
Çorno ≃ 66 42.49 N 12.55 E
Čornobajevka 78 46.42 N 32.32 E
Çorno Grande ∧ 66 42.28 N 13.34 E
Çornoje, S.S.S.R. 80 57.32 N 46.25 E
Čornoje, S.S.S.R. 86 51.44 N 77.34 E
Čornolesskoje 84 44.42 N 43.42 E
Čornomorskij 78 44.51 N 38.29 E
Čornomorskoje, S.S.S.R. 78 45.30 N 32.42 E
Čornomorskoje, S.S.S.R. 78 45.03 N 35.58 E
Čornoreck 86 52.45 N 76.40 E
Cornuda 64 45.50 N 12.00 E
Cornwall, On., Can. 206 45.02 N 74.44 W
Cornwall, N.Y., U.S. 210 41.26 N 74.01 W
Cornwall, Pa., U.S. 208 40.16 N 76.24 W
Cornwall □[6] 42 50.30 N 4.40 W
Cornwall Bridge 207 41.49 N 73.22 W
Cornwallis Island I 176 75.15 N 94.30 W
Cornwall on Hudson 210 41.27 N 74.00 W
Cornwell 220 27.23 N 81.05 W
Cornwells Heights 285 40.04 N 74.56 W
Čornyj Jar 80 48.04 N 46.08 E
Čornyj Mys, S.S.S.R. 24 68.20 N 38.37 E
Čornyj Mys, S.S.S.R. 86 55.33 N 80.04 E
Čornyj Ostrov 78 49.32 N 26.46 E
Čornyj Otrog 86 51.55 N 55.59 E
Čornyj Tašlyk ≃ 78 48.11 N 30.51 E
Corny Point 166 34.55 S 137.03 E
Coro 246 11.25 N 69.41 W
Coro, Golfete de c 241s 11.30 N 69.55 W
Coroaci 255 18.35 S 42.17 W
Coroa Grande 256 22.54 S 43.52 W
Coroatá 250 4.08 S 44.08 W
Çoroca ≃ 152 15.43 S 11.55 E
Čoroch (Çoruh) ≃ 130 41.36 N 41.35 E
Corocoro 248 17.12 S 68.29 W
Corocoro Island I 246 8.30 N 60.10 W
Coroico 248 16.10 S 67.44 W
Coroico ≃ 248 15.27 S 67.50 W
Coromandel, Bra. 255 18.28 S 47.13 W
Coromandel, N.Z. 172 36.46 S 175.30 E
Coromandel Coast ⊥[2] 122 13.30 N 80.30 E
Coromandel Peninsula ›[1] 172 36.50 S 175.35 E
Coromandel Range ⋏ 172 37.00 S 175.40 E
Coron 116 12.00 N 120.12 E
Corona, Ca., U.S. 228 33.52 N 117.33 W
Corona, N.M., U.S. 200 34.15 N 105.36 W
Corona ⬥[8] 276 40.45 N 73.52 W
Coronación, Golfo de la → Coronation Gulf c 176 68.25 N 110.00 W
Coronación, Isla de la → Coronation Island I 9 60.37 S 45.30 W
Corona del Mar ⬥[8] 228 33.36 N 117.52 W
Coronado, Méx. 234 22.55 N 100.56 W
Coronado, Ca., U.S. 228 32.41 N 117.10 W
Coronado, Bahía de c 236 9.00 N 83.50 W
Coronado National Memorial ♠ 200 31.10 N 110.29 W
Coronado Naval Amphibious Base ■ 228 32.40 N 117.10 W
Coronados, Golfo de los c 254 41.40 S 74.00 W
Coronation 182 52.05 N 111.27 W
Coronation Gardens ♠ 275b 43.41 N 79.29 W
Coronation Gulf c 176 68.25 N 110.00 W
Coronation Island I, B.A.T. 9 60.37 S 45.30 W
Coronation Island I, Ak., U.S. 180 55.52 N 134.15 W
Coronation Park ♠ 273d 26.06 S 27.47 E
Coron Bay c 116 11.54 N 120.08 E
Coronda 252 31.58 S 60.55 W
Coronel 252 37.01 S 73.08 W
Coronel Bogado 252 27.11 S 56.18 W
Coronel Brandsen 258 35.10 S 58.14 W
Coronel Dorrego 252 38.42 S 61.17 W
Coronel Du Graty 252 27.40 S 60.56 W
Coronel Eugenio del Busto 252 38.57 S 64.15 W
Coronel Fabriciano 255 19.31 S 42.38 W
Coronel Moldes, Arg. 252 33.38 S 64.36 W
Coronel Moldes, Arg. 252 25.16 S 65.29 W
Coronel Murta 255 16.37 S 42.11 W
Coronel Oviedo 252 25.25 S 56.27 W
Coronel Pacheco 256 21.35 S 43.16 W
Coronel Ponce 255 15.34 S 55.01 W
Coronel Pringles 252 37.58 S 61.22 W
Coronel Suárez 252 37.28 S 61.55 W
Coronel Vidal 252 37.27 S 57.43 W
Coronel Vivida 252 25.58 S 52.34 W
Corongo 248 8.35 S 77.55 W
Corongoros 234 19.17 N 102.48 W
Coronie □[5] 250 5.50 N 56.20 W
Coron Island I 116 11.55 N 120.14 E
Coronita 228 33.52 N 117.36 W
Coropuna, Nevado ∧ 248 15.31 S 72.42 W
Çorovodë 38 40.30 N 20.13 E
Corowa 166 36.02 S 146.23 E
Corozal, Belize 232 18.24 N 88.24 W
Corozal, Col. 246 9.19 N 75.18 W
Corozal, Hond. 236 15.48 N 86.43 W
Corozal, P.R. 240m 18.21 N 66.17 W
Corps 62 44.49 N 5.57 E
Corpus 252 27.07 S 55.31 W
Corpus Christi 196 27.48 N 97.23 W
Corpus Christi, Lake ⊜[1] 196 28.10 N 97.53 W
Corpus Christi Bay c 196 27.48 N 97.20 W
Corpus Christi Naval Air Station ■ 196 27.42 N 97.16 W
Corque 248 18.21 S 67.42 W
Corquín 236 14.34 N 88.52 W
Corral 254 39.52 S 73.26 W
Corral de Almaguer 34 39.46 N 3.11 W
Corral de Bustos 252 33.17 S 62.12 W
Corralillo 240p 22.59 N 80.35 W
Corralito 252 32.03 S 64.12 W
Corralito, Arroyo del ≃ 258 33.39 S 58.03 W
Corralito, Cuchilla del ⋏[2] 258 33.40 S 57.44 W
Corralitos, Méx. 196 26.57 N 104.39 W
Corralitos, Ca., U.S. 226 36.59 N 121.48 W
Corran 46 56.43 N 5.14 W
Corraun Peninsula ›[1] 48 53.54 N 9.53 W
Correas, Arroyo ≃ 288 34.24 S 58.32 W
Correboi, Arcu)(71 40.05 N 9.21 E
Correctionville 198 42.28 N 95.47 W
Corredor 287b 23.27 S 46.19 W
Correggio 64 44.46 N 10.47 E
Corregidor Island I 116 14.23 N 120.35 E
Córrego do Bom Jesus 256 22.38 S 46.02 W
Córrego do Ouro, Bra. 255 16.18 S 50.32 W
Córrego do Ouro, Bra. 256 21.22 S 45.47 W
Córrego Rico 255 15.14 S 47.48 W
Correia de Almeida 256 21.17 S 43.38 W
Corrente 250 10.27 S 45.10 W
Corrente ≃, Bra. 250 4.18 S 42.11 W
Corrente ≃, Bra. 255 19.19 S 50.50 W
Corrente ≃, Bra. 255 13.08 S 43.28 W
Correntes 250 9.08 S 36.19 W
Correntes ≃ 255 17.38 S 55.08 W
Correntes, Cabo das › 156 24.11 S 35.34 E
Correntezas 256 22.30 S 42.31 W
Correnti, Isola delle I 70 36.38 N 15.05 E
Correntina 255 13.20 S 44.39 W
Corrèze □[5] 32 45.20 N 1.50 E
Correzzana 266b 45.40 N 9.18 E
Corrib, Lough ⊜ 48 53.26 N 9.14 W
Corridonia 66 43.15 N 13.30 E
Corrientes 252 27.28 S 58.50 W
Corrientes □[4] 252 29.00 S 58.00 W
Corrientes ≃, Arg. 252 30.21 S 59.33 W
Corrientes ≃, S.A. 246 3.43 S 74.35 W
Corrientes, Cabo ›, Arg. 252 38.01 S 57.32 W
Corrientes, Cabo ›, Col. 246 5.30 N 77.34 W
Corrientes, Cabo ›, Cuba 240p 21.45 N 84.31 W
Corrientes, Cabo ›, Méx. 234 20.25 N 105.42 W
Corrientes, Ensenada de c 240p 21.51 N 84.36 W
Corrigan 222 30.59 N 94.49 W
Corrigin 162 32.21 S 117.52 E
Corrimal 170 34.22 S 150.54 E
Corringham 260 51.31 N 0.28 E
Corrofin 48 52.56 N 9.03 W
Corroios 266c 38.38 N 9.09 W
Corropoli 66 42.49 N 13.50 E
Corrumpa Creek ≃ 196 36.36 N 102.52 W
Corry 214 41.55 N 79.38 W
Corryong 171b 36.12 S 147.54 E
Corryong Creek ≃ 171b 36.06 S 147.59 E
Corryvreckan, Gulf of ʊ 46 56.09 N 5.44 W
Corsano 68 39.53 N 18.22 E
Corse (Corsica) I 36 42.00 N 9.00 E
Corse, Cap › 62 43.00 N 9.25 E
Corse-du-Sud □[5] 36 41.50 N 9.00 E
Corserine ∧ 44 55.09 N 4.22 W
Corsham 42 51.26 N 2.11 W
Corsica, Pa., U.S. 214 41.10 N 79.12 W
Corsica, S.D., U.S. 198 43.25 N 98.24 W
Corsica → Corse I 36 42.00 N 9.00 E
Corsicana 222 32.05 N 96.28 W
Corsica River c 208 39.05 N 76.08 W
Corsico 62 45.26 N 9.07 E
Corsock 44 55.04 N 3.57 W
Corson Inlet c 208 39.12 N 74.39 W
Cortaccia (Kurtatsch) 64 46.19 N 11.13 E
Cortachy 46 56.43 N 2.58 W
Cort Adelaer, Kap › 176 62.00 N 42.00 W
Cortaderas 252 32.30 S 65.00 W
Cortado, Rio do ≃ 287a 23.00 S 43.25 W
Cortale 68 38.50 N 16.25 E
Cortazar 234 20.29 N 100.56 W
Corte 36 42.18 N 9.08 E
Corte Alto 254 40.57 S 73.10 W
Cortegana 34 37.55 N 6.49 W
Corte Madera 226 37.55 N 122.31 W
Corte Madera Creek ≃ 282 37.23 N 122.14 W
Cortemaggiore 64 44.59 N 9.56 E
Cortemilia 62 44.35 N 8.12 E
Corteno Golgi 64 46.10 N 10.15 E
Cortes 116 9.17 N 126.11 E
Cortés □[5] 236 15.30 N 88.00 W
Cortes ✥ 266a 40.25 N 3.41 W
Cortés, Ensenada de c 240p 22.05 N 83.52 W
Cortez, Co., U.S. 200 37.20 N 108.35 W
Cortez, Fl., U.S. 220 27.28 N 82.41 W
Cortez, Sea of → California, Golfo de c 232 28.00 N 112.00 W
Cortez Mountains ⋏ 204 40.20 N 116.20 W
Cortina Creek ≃ 226 39.06 N 122.02 W
Cortina d'Ampezzo 64 46.32 N 12.08 E
Çortines 258 34.34 S 59.13 W
Čortkov 78 49.01 N 25.48 E
Cortland, Il., U.S. 216 41.55 N 88.41 W
Cortland, In., U.S. 218 38.58 N 85.58 W
Cortland, Ne., U.S. 198 40.30 N 96.42 W
Cortland, N.Y., U.S. 210 42.36 N 76.10 W
Cortland, Oh., U.S. 214 41.19 N 80.43 W
Cortland □[6] 210 42.36 N 76.11 W
Corton 42 52.32 N 1.44 E
Cortona 66 43.16 N 11.59 E
Çorubal (Koliba) ≃ 150 11.57 N 15.06 W
Čoruch-Dajron 85 40.24 N 69.40 E
Coruche 34 38.57 N 8.31 W
Çoruh (Čoroch) ≃ 130 41.36 N 41.35 E
Çorum, Tür. 130 39.14 N 28.27 E
Çorum, Tür. 130 40.33 N 34.58 E
Çorum □[4] 130 40.30 N 34.40 E
Corumbá 248 19.01 S 57.39 W
Corumbá ≃ 255 18.19 S 48.55 W
Corumbá de Goiás 255 15.55 S 48.48 W
Corumbaíba 255 18.09 S 48.34 W
Corumbataí ≃ 252 23.55 S 51.57 W
Corumbaú, Ponta de › 255 16.53 S 39.06 W
Corumbiara Antigo ≃ 248 13.13 S 62.06 W
Corumo ≃ 246 6.49 N 60.52 W
Corund 38 46.28 N 25.11 E
Corunna, On., Can. 214 42.53 N 82.26 W
Corunna → La Coruña, Esp. 34 43.22 N 8.23 W
Corunna, In., U.S. 216 41.26 N 85.08 W
Corunna, Mi., U.S. 216 42.58 N 84.07 W
Corunna Downs 162 21.28 S 119.51 E
Coruripe 250 10.08 S 36.10 W
Corvallis, Mt., U.S. 202 46.18 N 114.06 W
Corvallis, Or., U.S. 202 44.33 N 123.15 W
Corvara in Badia 64 46.33 N 11.52 E
Corve Dale V 42 52.30 N 2.40 W
Corvey, Kloster ✥[1] 52 51.46 N 9.25 E
Corviale ⬥[8] 267a 41.52 N 12.25 E
Corvo I 148a 39.42 N 31.06 W
Corwen 42 52.59 N 3.22 W
Corwin, Cape › 180 59.54 N 165.41 W
Corwith 190 42.59 N 93.57 W
Corydon, In., U.S. 218 38.12 N 86.07 W
Corydon, Ia., U.S. 190 40.45 N 93.19 W
Corydon, Ky., U.S. 194 37.44 N 87.42 W
Coryell 222 31.33 N 97.37 W
Coryell □[6] 222 31.25 N 97.40 W
Coryell Creek ≃ 222 31.23 N 97.35 W
Coryton 260 51.31 N 0.31 E
Coryville 214 41.53 N 78.24 W
Corzu 38 44.28 N 23.10 E
Corzuela 252 26.57 S 60.58 W
Cos → Kos I 38 36.50 N 27.10 E
Cosa (Ansedonia) ⊥ 66 42.25 N 11.18 E
Cosamaloapan [de Carpio] 232 18.22 N 95.48 W
Cosapa 248 18.11 S 68.40 W
Coscile ≃ 68 39.42 N 16.28 E
Cos Cob 276 41.02 N 73.36 W
Cos Cob Harbor c 276 41.01 N 73.36 W
Coscomatepec [de Bravo] 234 19.04 N 97.02 W
Cosel → Koźle 30 50.20 N 18.08 E
Coseley 42 52.33 N 2.06 W
Cosenza 68 39.17 N 16.15 E
Cosenza □[4] 68 39.28 N 16.25 E
Cosgroves Creek ≃ 274a 33.50 S 150.46 E
Coshocton 214 40.16 N 81.51 W
Coshocton □[6] 214 40.16 N 81.51 W
Cosigüina, Punta › 236 12.54 N 87.41 W
Cosigüina, Volcán ∧[1] 236 12.59 N 87.34 W
Coslada 266a 40.26 N 3.34 W
Cosmo ⬥[8] 256 22.54 S 43.37 W
Cosmoledo Island I 138 9.43 S 47.35 E
Cosmópolis, Bra. 256 22.38 S 47.12 W
Cosmopolis, Wa., U.S. 224 46.57 N 123.46 W
Cosmorama 255 20.28 S 49.47 W
Cosmos 198 44.56 N 94.41 W

Symbols in the index entries represent the broad categories identified in the key at the right. Symbols with superior numbers (⋏[1]) identify subcategories (see complete key on page *I · 1).*

Symbole im Register stellen die rechts im Schlüssel erklärten Kategorien dar. Symbole mit hochgestellten Ziffern (⋏[1]) bezeichnen Unterabteilungen einer Kategorie (vgl. vollständiger Schlüssel auf Seite *I · 1).*

Los símbolos incluídos en el texto del índice representan las grandes categorias identificadas con la clave a la derecha. Los símbolos con numeros en su parte superior (⋏[1]) identifican las subcategorías (véase la clave completa en la página *I · 1).*

Les symboles de l'index représentent les catégories indiquées dans la légende à droite. Les symboles suivis d'un indice (⋏[1]) représentent des sous-catégories (voir légende complète à la page *I · 1).*

Os símbolos incluídos no texto do índice representam as grandes categorias identificadas com a chave à direita. Os símbolos com números em sua parte superior (⋏[1]) identificam as subcategorias (veja-se a chave completa à página *I · 1).*

	English	Deutsch	Español	Français	Português
∧	Mountain	Berg	Montaña	Montagne	Montanha
⋏	Mountains	Gebirge	Montañas	Montagnes	Montanhas
)(	Pass	Paß	Paso	Col	Passo
V	Valley, Canyon	Tal, Cañon	Valle, Cañón	Vallée, Canyon	Vale, Canhão
≚	Plain	Ebene	Llano	Plaine	Planície
›	Cape	Kap	Cabo	Cap	Cabo
I	Island	Insel	Isla	Île	Ilha
II	Islands	Inseln	Islas	Îles	Ilhas
⊥	Other Topographic Features	Andere Topographische Objekte	Otros Elementos Topográficos	Autres données topographiques	Outros acidentes topográficos

ESPAÑOL Nombre / FRANÇAIS Nom / PORTUGUÊS Nome	Página / Page / Página	Lat.°′	Long.°′ W = Oeste / W = Ouest / W = Oeste
Cosmos ◆[8]	287a	22.55 S	44.37 W
Cosne-Cours-sur-Loire	50	47.24 N	2.55 E
Cosoleacaque	234	18.00 N	94.37 W
Cospán	248	7.26 S	78.33 W
Cosquín	252	31.15 S	64.29 W
Cossato	62	45.34 N	8.10 E
Cossatot ≃	194	33.48 N	94.09 W
Cossayuna	210	43.11 N	73.26 W
Cossayuna Lake ⊜	210	43.12 N	73.25 W
Cossebaude	54	51.05 N	13.38 E
Cossé-le-Vivien	28	47.57 N	0.55 W
Cossoine	71	40.27 N	8.43 E
Cosson ≃	50	47.30 N	1.15 E
Cossonay	58	46.37 N	6.31 E
Cost	222	29.26 N	97.32 W
Costa, Cayo I	220	26.41 N	82.15 W
Costa, Sierra de la → Coast Ranges ⋏	178	41.00 N	123.30 W
Costacciaro	66	43.21 N	12.42 E
Costa de Caparica	266c	38.38 N	9.14 W
Costa del Marfil → Ivory Coast □[1]	150	8.00 N	5.00 W
Costa de San José	258	33.51 S	56.53 W
Costa di Rovigo	64	45.03 N	11.42 E
Costa Mesa	228	33.38 N	117.55 W
Costanera, Cadena → Coast Mountains ⋏	176	55.00 N	129.00 W
Costanero, Canal de ≊	288	34.28 S	58.28 W
Costa Rica	232	28.55 N	111.36 W
Costa Rica □[1], N.A.	230	10.00 N	84.00 W
Costa Rica □[1], N.A.	236	10.00 N	84.00 W
Costaros	62	44.54 N	3.50 E
Costas	256	22.39 S	45.56 W
Costello	214	41.36 N	78.03 W
Costelloe	48	53.17 N	9.32 W
Costermansville → Bukavu	154	2.30 S	28.52 E
Costessey	42	52.40 N	1.11 E
Costești	38	44.40 N	24.53 E
Costiera, Catena ⋏	68	39.20 N	16.05 E
Costigan Lake ⊜	184	56.56 N	105.55 W
Costigliole d'Asti	62	44.47 N	8.11 E
Costigliole Saluzzo	62	44.34 N	7.29 E
Costilla	200	36.58 N	105.31 W
Costilla Creek ≃	200	36.59 N	105.43 W
Cosumnes ≃	226	38.16 N	121.26 W
Cosumnes, Middle Fork ≃	226	38.33 N	120.51 W
Cosumnes, North Fork ≃	226	38.33 N	120.51 W
Cosumnes, South Fork ≃	226	38.33 N	120.49 W
Coswig, D.D.R.	54	51.53 N	12.26 E
Coswig, D.D.R.	54	51.07 N	13.34 E
Cotabambas	248	13.45 S	72.21 W
Cotabato	116	7.13 N	124.15 E
Cotacajes ≃	248	16.00 S	67.01 W
Cotagaita	248	20.50 S	65.41 W
Cotagaita ≃	248	21.01 S	65.23 W
Cotahuasi	248	15.12 S	72.56 W
Cotão ∧[2]	266c	38.45 N	9.18 W
Cotati	226	38.20 N	122.42 W
Cotaxtla ≃	234	19.02 N	96.08 W
Coteau-Landing	206	45.15 N	74.13 W
Coteau-Station	206	45.17 N	74.14 W
Coteaux	238	18.12 N	74.02 W
Côte d'Ivoire → Ivory Coast □[1]	150	8.00 N	5.00 W
Côte-d'Or □[5]	50	47.30 N	4.50 E
Cotegipe	255	12.02 S	44.15 W
Cote Indian Reserve ◆[4]	184	51.38 N	101.53 W
Cotentin ›[1]	32	49.30 N	1.30 W
Côte-Saint-Luc	275a	45.28 N	73.40 W
Côtes-du-Nord □[5]	32	48.25 N	2.40 W
Côte Visitation ◆[8]	275a	45.33 N	73.36 W
Cothi ≃	42	51.52 N	4.10 W
Coti ≃	248	8.36 S	65.33 W
Cotia	256	23.37 S	46.56 W
Cotia □[7]	287b	23.38 S	46.56 W
Cotia ≃	256	23.31 S	46.51 W
Cotia, Represa de ⊜[1]	287b	23.44 S	46.57 W
Cotignac	62	43.32 N	6.09 E
Cotignola	66	44.23 N	11.56 E
Cotija de la Paz	234	19.49 N	102.43 W
Cotingo ≃	246	3.55 N	60.30 W
Cotis, Laguna ⊜	258	35.11 S	59.16 W
Cotmeana ≃	38	44.24 N	24.45 E
Cotoca	248	17.49 S	63.03 W
Cotonou	150	6.21 N	2.26 E
Cotopaxi □[4]	246	0.55 S	78.55 W
Cotopaxi ∧[1]	246	0.40 S	78.26 W
Cotorra, Isla I	241r	10.02 N	62.16 W
Cotovêlo, Cachoeira do ⌞	248	7.08 S	58.43 W
Cotronei	68	39.09 N	16.47 E
Cotswold Hills ⋏[2]	42	51.45 N	2.10 W
Cottage Grove, In., U.S.	218	39.36 N	84.52 W
Cottage Grove, Or., U.S.	202	43.47 N	123.03 W
Cottage Grove, Wi., U.S.	216	43.05 N	89.12 W
Cottage Hills	219	38.55 N	90.04 W
Cottageville	192	32.56 N	80.28 W
Cottam, On., Can.	214	42.08 N	82.45 W
Cottam, Eng., U.K.	262	53.47 N	2.46 W
Cottanello	66	42.24 N	12.41 E
Cottbus	54	51.45 N	14.19 E
Cottbus □[5]	54	51.45 N	14.00 E
Cottekill	210	41.51 N	74.06 W
Cottel Island I	186	48.51 N	53.42 W
Cottenham	42	52.18 N	0.09 E
Cotter	194	36.16 N	92.32 W
Cotter ≃	171b	35.19 S	148.57 E
Cottesloe	168a	31.59 S	115.45 E
Cottiennes, Alpes (Alpi Cozie) ⋏	62	44.45 N	7.00 E
Cottingham	44	53.47 N	0.24 W
Cottleville	219	38.44 N	90.39 W
Cottondale, Al., U.S.	194	33.11 N	87.27 W
Cottondale, Fl., U.S.	192	30.47 N	85.22 W
Cotton Lake ⊜, Mb., Can.	184	55.05 N	96.50 W
Cotton Lake ⊜, Tx., U.S.	222	29.48 N	94.48 W
Cotton Plant	194	35.00 N	91.15 W
Cottonport	194	30.59 N	92.03 W
Cotton Valley	194	32.49 N	93.25 W
Cottonwood, Az., U.S.	200	34.44 N	112.00 W
Cottonwood, Ca., U.S.	204	40.23 N	122.16 W
Cottonwood, Id., U.S.	202	46.02 N	116.20 W
Cottonwood, Mn., U.S.	198	44.36 N	95.40 W
Cottonwood ≃, Ks., U.S.	198	38.23 N	96.03 W
Cottonwood ≃, Mn., U.S.	198	44.17 N	94.25 W
Cottonwood Creek ≃, Ca., U.S.	226	36.27 N	119.20 W
Cottonwood Creek ≃, Ca., U.S.	226	36.52 N	120.12 W
Cottonwood Creek ≃, Mt., U.S.	202	48.33 N	107.45 W
Cottonwood Creek ≃, N.D., U.S.	198	46.16 N	98.15 W
Cottonwood Creek ≃, Ok., U.S.	196	35.54 N	97.27 W
Cottonwood Creek ≃, Or., U.S.	202	43.53 N	117.43 W
Cottonwood Creek ≃, Tx., U.S.	196	31.23 N	103.46 W
Cottonwood Creek ≃, Tx., U.S.	196	32.48 N	100.21 W
Cottonwood Creek ≃, Ut., U.S.	200	39.09 N	110.55 W
Cottonwood Creek ≃, Wy., U.S.	202	43.51 N	108.09 W
Cottonwood Creek, Middle Fork ≃	204	40.23 N	122.20 W
Cottonwood Creek, South Fork ≃	204	40.23 N	122.20 W
Cottonwood Falls	198	38.22 N	96.32 W
Cottonwood Wash ∨, Az., U.S.	200	35.00 N	110.39 W
Cottonwood Wash ∨, Az., U.S.	200	36.19 N	113.59 W
Cotubandê	287a	22.51 S	43.01 W
Cotuhé ≃	246	2.53 S	69.44 W
Cotuí	238	19.03 N	70.09 W
Cotuit	207	41.37 N	70.26 W
Cotulla	196	28.26 N	99.14 W
Cotunduba, Ilha de I	287a	22.58 S	43.09 W
Coubert	261	48.40 N	2.42 E
Coubre, Pointe de la ›	32	45.41 N	1.13 W
Coubron	261	48.55 N	2.35 E
Couches-les-Mines	58	46.52 N	4.34 E
Couchiching, Lake ⊜	212	44.40 N	79.23 W
Coucouron	62	44.48 N	3.58 E
Coucy-le-Château-Auffrique	50	49.31 N	3.19 E
Coudekerque-Branche	50	51.02 N	2.24 E
Coudersport	214	41.46 N	78.01 W
Coudres, Île aux I	186	47.24 N	70.23 W
Couesnon ≃	32	48.37 N	1.31 W
Cougar	224	46.03 N	122.17 W
Cougar Reservoir ⊜[1]	202	44.06 N	122.12 W
Couhé	32	46.18 N	0.11 E
Couillet	50	50.23 N	4.27 E
Couilly-Pont-aux-Dames	261	48.53 N	2.52 E
Coulanges-la-Vineuse	50	47.42 N	3.35 E
Coulanges-sur-Yonne	50	47.31 N	3.32 E
Coulee City	202	47.36 N	119.17 W
Coulee Dam	202	47.57 N	118.58 W
Coulee Dam National Recreation Area ♠	202	48.10 N	118.15 W
Coulihaut	240d	15.30 N	61.29 W
Coulman Island I	9	73.27 S	169.40 E
Coulmier-le-Sec	58	47.45 N	4.29 E
Coulogne	50	50.55 N	1.53 E
Coulomby	50	50.42 N	2.00 E
Coulommiers	50	48.49 N	3.05 E
Coulon ≃	62	43.51 N	5.00 E
Coulonge ≃	190	45.51 N	76.46 W
Coulonge Est ≃	190	46.06 N	76.44 W
Coulsdon ◆[8]	260	51.19 N	0.08 W
Coulta	166	34.23 S	135.29 E
Coulters	279b	40.18 N	79.48 W
Coulterville, Ca., U.S.	226	37.42 N	120.11 W
Coulterville, Il., U.S.	194	38.11 N	89.36 W
Counce	194	35.02 N	88.16 W
Council	202	44.44 N	116.26 W
Council Bluffs	198	41.15 N	95.51 W
Council Grove	198	38.39 N	96.29 W
Council Grove Lake ⊜[1]	198	38.42 N	96.31 W
Coundon	44	54.40 N	1.39 W
Countegany	171b	36.11 S	149.27 E
Countesthorpe	42	52.33 N	1.08 W
Country Campus	222	30.49 N	95.26 W
Country Club Estates	220	28.03 N	81.57 W
Country Club Hills	278	41.34 N	87.43 W
Country Club View	284c	38.49 N	77.19 W
Country Hills	279b	40.19 N	79.42 W
Country Homes	202	47.44 N	117.24 W
Country Ridge Estates	276	41.02 N	73.41 W
Countryside	278	41.46 N	87.52 W
Countryside Lake ⊜	278	42.15 N	88.03 W
Countryside Manor	278	42.18 N	87.56 W
Coupar Angus	46	56.33 N	3.17 W
Coupeville	224	48.13 N	122.41 W
Coupland	222	30.28 N	97.24 W
Coupon	214	40.32 N	78.31 W
Coupvray	261	48.54 N	2.48 E
Courbevoie	50	48.54 N	2.15 E
Courbons	62	44.06 N	6.12 E
Courçay	50	47.15 N	0.52 E
Courcelle	261	48.42 N	2.06 E
Courcelles, Bel.	50	50.28 N	4.22 E
Courcelles, Fr.	261	49.07 N	2.18 E
Courcelles-Chaussy	56	49.07 N	6.24 E
Courcelles-sur-Nied	56	49.04 N	6.18 E
Courchevel	62	45.25 N	6.38 E
Cour-Cheverny	50	47.30 N	1.27 E
Courcibo ≃	250	4.53 N	53.00 W
Courçon	32	46.15 N	0.49 W
Courcouronnes	261	48.37 N	2.24 E
Courdimanche	261	49.02 N	2.00 E
Cour-et-Buis	62	45.26 N	5.00 E
Courgent	261	48.54 N	1.40 E
Courland → Kurzeme □[9]	76	56.50 N	22.30 E
Courmayeur	62	45.47 N	6.58 E
Couronne, Cap ›	62	43.19 N	5.03 E
Couronnement, Île du → Coronation Island I	9	60.37 S	45.30 W
Courpière	62	45.45 N	3.33 E
Courquetaine	261	48.41 N	2.45 E
Course Brook ≃	283	42.17 N	71.22 W
Courseulles	28	49.20 N	0.27 W
Courson-les-Carrières	50	47.36 N	3.30 E
Court	58	47.14 N	7.20 E
Courtacon	50	48.42 N	3.17 E
Courtalain	50	48.05 N	1.09 E
Courtenay, B.C., Can.	182	49.41 N	125.00 W
Courtenay, Fr.	50	48.02 N	3.03 E
Courthézon	62	44.05 N	4.53 E
Courtice	212	43.55 N	78.46 W
Courtisols	56	48.59 N	4.31 E
Courtland, On., Can.	212	42.51 N	80.38 W
Courtland, Al., U.S.	194	34.40 N	87.18 W
Courtland, Ca., U.S.	226	38.20 N	121.34 W
Courtland, Va., U.S.	208	36.42 N	77.04 W
Courtleigh	284b	39.22 N	76.46 W
Courtmacsherry	48	51.38 N	8.43 W
Courtmacsherry Bay ⊂	48	51.35 N	8.40 W
Courtney, Pa., U.S.	279b	40.13 N	79.58 W
Courtney, Tx., U.S.	222	30.16 N	96.04 W
Courtney Creek ≃	196	31.16 N	102.50 W
Courtomer, Fr.	50	48.38 N	0.22 E
Courtomer, Fr.	261	48.39 N	2.54 E
Courtown	48	52.38 N	6.13 W
Courtrai → Kortrijk	50	50.50 N	3.16 E
Courtright	214	42.49 N	82.28 W
Courtry, Fr.	261	48.33 N	2.46 E
Courtry, Fr.	261	48.55 N	2.36 E
Court-Saint-Étienne	50	50.39 N	4.34 E
Courville-sur-Eure	50	48.27 N	1.15 E
Coushatta	194	32.00 N	93.20 W
Cousin ≃	50	47.15 N	4.04 E
Cousiño, Parque ♠	286e	33.28 S	70.40 W
Cousolre	50	50.15 N	4.09 E
Coussegrey	50	47.57 N	4.01 E
Coussey	58	48.25 N	5.41 E
Coustellet	62	43.53 N	5.11 E
Coutances	32	49.03 N	1.26 W
Coutevroult	261	48.52 N	2.51 E
Couto de Magalhães ≃	255	13.37 S	53.09 W
Couto Magalhães	250	8.17 S	49.16 W
Coutras	32	45.02 N	0.08 W
Coutts	182	49.00 N	111.57 W
Couture, Lac ⊜	176	60.07 N	75.20 W
Couture-sur-Loir	50	47.45 N	0.41 E
Couves, Ilha das I	256	23.25 S	44.52 W
Couvet	58	46.56 N	6.38 E
Couvin	50	50.03 N	4.29 E
Cova da Piedade	266c	38.40 N	9.10 W
Covane	156	21.22 S	33.56 E
Covasna	38	45.51 N	26.11 E
Covasna □[6]	38	46.00 N	26.00 E
Cove, Scot., U.K.	46	57.51 N	5.42 W
Cove, Or., U.S.	202	45.17 N	117.48 W
Cove Bay	46	57.06 N	2.04 W
Covedale	218	39.07 N	84.36 W
Cove Harbor ⊂	276	41.03 N	73.30 W
Cove Island I	190	45.17 N	81.44 W
Covelo, Ang.	152	12.06 S	13.55 E
Covelo, Ca., U.S.	204	39.47 N	123.14 W
Cove Neck	276	40.53 N	73.31 W
Cove Neck ›[1]	276	40.53 N	73.30 W
Coventry, Eng., U.K.	42	52.25 N	1.30 W
Coventry, Ct., U.S.	207	41.46 N	72.18 W
Coventry, De., U.S.	285	39.40 N	75.38 W
Coventry, R.I., U.S.	207	41.41 N	71.34 W
Coventry Cathedral ☉[1]	42	52.25 N	1.30 W
Coventryville	285	40.10 N	75.41 W
Cove Palisades State Park ♠	202	44.34 N	121.15 W
Cove Point	208	38.22 N	76.23 W
Cove Point ›	208	38.23 N	76.23 W
Cover ≃	44	54.17 N	1.46 W
Covered Wells	200	31.48 N	111.59 W
Covert	216	42.17 N	86.15 W
Covigliaio	66	44.08 N	11.18 E
Covilhã	34	40.17 N	7.30 W
Covina	228	34.05 N	117.53 W
Covington, Ga., U.S.	192	33.35 N	83.51 W
Covington, In., U.S.	194	40.08 N	87.23 W
Covington, Ky., U.S.	218	39.05 N	84.30 W
Covington, La., U.S.	194	30.28 N	90.06 W
Covington, Oh., U.S.	218	40.07 N	84.21 W
Covington, Ok., U.S.	196	36.18 N	97.35 W
Covington, Pa., U.S.	210	41.45 N	77.05 W
Covington, Tn., U.S.	194	35.33 N	89.38 W
Covington, Tx., U.S.	222	32.11 N	97.16 W
Covington, Va., U.S.	192	37.47 N	79.59 W
Covões	266c	38.50 N	9.20 W
Covunco, Arroyo ≃	252	38.29 S	69.32 W
Cow ≃	190	47.23 N	83.59 W
Cowal ›[1]	46	56.05 N	5.08 W
Cowal, Lake ⊜	166	33.35 S	147.25 E
Cowan, Ky., U.S.	218	38.24 N	83.54 W
Cowan, Tn., U.S.	194	35.09 N	86.00 W
Cowan, Lake ⊜	162	31.50 S	121.50 E
Cowan Creek ≃	274a	33.40 S	151.10 E
Cowanesque	210	41.56 N	77.30 W
Cowanesque ≃	210	42.00 N	77.07 W
Cowan Heights	280	33.47 N	117.47 W
Cowan Lake ⊜, Sk., Can.	184	54.00 N	107.15 W
Cowan Lake ⊜, Oh., U.S.	218	39.23 N	83.54 W
Cowan Lake State Park ♠	218	39.23 N	83.53 W
Cowansburg	279b	40.15 N	79.46 W
Cowanshannock Creek ≃	214	40.51 N	79.30 W
Cowansville, P.Q., Can.	206	45.12 N	72.45 W
Cowansville, Pa., U.S.	214	40.53 N	79.36 W
Cowaramup	162	33.52 S	115.05 E
Coward	192	33.58 N	79.44 W
Coward Springs	166	29.24 S	136.49 E
Cowarie	166	27.43 S	138.20 E
Cow Bayou ≃	222	31.19 N	97.00 W
Cowbridge	42	51.28 N	3.27 W
Cowburn Tunnel ◆[5]	262	53.21 N	1.52 W
Cow Canyon ∨	280	34.01 N	120.06 W
Cowcowing Lakes ⊜	162	31.01 S	117.18 E
Cow Creek ≃, Ks., U.S.	198	38.02 N	97.56 W
Cow Creek ≃, Mt., U.S.	202	47.47 N	108.56 W
Cow Creek ≃, Ok., U.S.	196	34.10 N	98.00 W
Cow Creek ≃, Or., U.S.	202	42.57 N	123.20 W
Cow Creek ≃, Wa., U.S.	202	46.45 N	118.09 W
Cowden, Il., U.S.	219	39.15 N	88.52 W
Cowden, Pa., U.S.	279b	40.19 N	80.13 W
Cowdenbeath	46	56.07 N	3.21 W
Coweeman ≃	224	46.06 N	122.52 W
Cowell	166	33.41 S	136.55 E
Cowen	188	38.24 N	80.33 W
Cowen, Mount ∧	202	45.23 N	110.29 W
Cowes, Austl.	169	38.27 S	145.14 E
Cowes, Eng., U.K.	42	50.45 N	1.18 W
Cowessess Indian Reserve ◆[4]	184	50.31 N	102.42 W
Coweta	196	35.57 N	95.39 W
Cow Green Reservoir ⊜[1]	44	54.40 N	2.18 W
Cow Gulch ≃	202	46.02 N	107.52 W
Cow Head	186	49.55 N	57.48 W
Cowhouse Creek ≃	222	31.10 N	97.35 W
Cowichan ≃	224	48.46 N	123.38 W
Cowichan Bay	224	48.44 N	123.40 W
Cowichan Lake ⊜	224	48.54 N	124.20 W
Cowiche Creek, North Fork ≃	224	46.38 N	120.41 W
Cowiche Creek, South Fork ≃	224	46.38 N	120.41 W
Cowie Water ≃	46	56.58 N	2.12 W
Cowles Dam ⊜[1]	273d	26.13 S	28.28 E
Cowlesville	210	42.51 N	78.28 W
Cowley, Austl.	166	26.54 S	144.49 E
Cowley, Ab., Can.	182	49.34 N	114.05 W
Cowley, Eng., U.K.	42	51.43 N	1.12 W
Cowley, Wy., U.S.	202	44.53 N	108.28 W
Cowley ◆[8]	260	51.32 N	0.29 W
Cowley, Mount ∧	169	38.33 S	143.52 E
Cowlitz □[6]	224	46.07 N	122.43 W
Cowlitz ≃	224	46.05 N	122.53 W
Cowm Reservoir ⊜[1]	262	53.40 N	2.11 W
Cow Palace ☉	282	37.42 N	122.25 W
Cowpasture ≃	188	37.48 N	79.45 W
Cowpens	192	35.01 N	81.48 W
Cowpens National Battlefield ♠	192	35.06 N	81.46 W
Cowra	166	33.50 S	148.41 E
Cox ≃	164	15.19 S	135.25 E
Cox, Mount ∧[2]	162	24.55 S	125.36 E
Coxá ≃	255	14.16 S	44.11 W
Cox Creek ≃	212	43.35 N	80.29 W
Coxheath	42	51.14 N	0.29 E
Coxim	255	18.30 S	54.45 W
Coxim ≃	255	18.34 S	54.46 W
Coxipi, Lac ⊜	186	51.33 N	58.25 W
Coxipó da Ponte	248	15.38 S	56.04 W
Coxquihui	234	20.11 N	97.35 W
Cox River Aboriginal Reserve ◆[4]	164	15.40 S	134.45 E
Coxs ≃	170	33.57 S	150.25 E
Coxsackie	210	42.21 N	73.48 W
Cox's Bāzār	120	21.26 N	91.59 E
Cox's Cove	186	49.07 N	58.05 W
Coyaguaima, Cerro ∧	252	22.55 S	66.35 W
Coyah	150	9.43 N	13.23 W
Coyame	232	29.28 N	105.06 W
Coyanosa Draw ∨	196	31.18 N	103.06 W
Coya Sur	252	22.25 S	69.38 W
Coyle, Water of ≃	44	55.28 N	4.32 W
Coyoacán □[7]	286a	19.19 N	99.11 W
Coyoacán ◆[8]	286a	19.20 N	99.10 W
Coyote	226	37.13 N	121.44 W
Coyote ≃	232	30.48 N	112.35 W
Coyote Creek ≃, Ca., U.S.	204	33.13 N	116.13 W
Coyote Creek ≃, Ca., U.S.	226	37.28 N	122.03 W
Coyote Creek ≃, Ca., U.S.	280	33.47 N	118.05 W
Coyote Creek, East Fork ≃	226	37.10 N	121.30 W
Coyote Creek, Middle Fork ≃	226	37.10 N	121.30 W
Coyote Hills ⋏[2]	282	37.33 N	122.05 W
Coyote Hills Regional Park ♠	282	37.33 N	122.06 W
Coyote Lake ⊜	204	35.04 N	116.45 W
Coyote Lake ⊜[1]	226	37.06 N	121.32 W
Coyotepec	234	19.46 N	99.12 W
Coyote Point ›	282	37.35 N	122.19 W
Coyote Wash ∨, Az., U.S.	200	32.40 N	114.08 W
Coyote Wash ∨, N.M., U.S.	200	36.11 N	108.33 W
Coy Pond ⊜	283	42.36 N	70.49 W
Coyuca de Benítez	234	17.02 N	100.04 W
Coyuca de Catalán	234	18.20 N	100.39 W
Coyutla	234	20.15 N	97.39 W
Cozad	198	40.51 N	99.59 W
Cozes	32	45.35 N	0.50 W
Cozie, Alpi (Alpes Cottiennes) ⋏	62	44.45 N	7.00 E
Cozoyoapan	234	16.46 N	98.15 W
Cozumel	232	20.31 N	86.55 W
Cozumel, Isla de I	232	20.25 N	86.55 W
Cozy Lake	276	41.01 N	74.30 W
Crab Alley Bay ⊂	208	38.55 N	76.17 W
Crab Creek ≃	202	46.49 N	119.55 W
Crab Hill	241g	13.19 N	59.38 W
Crab Meadow ☷	276	40.55 N	73.20 W
Crab Orchard, Ky., U.S.	192	37.27 N	84.30 W
Crab Orchard, Tn., U.S.	192	35.54 N	84.52 W
Crab Orchard Lake ⊜[1]	194	37.43 N	89.05 W
Crabtree	214	40.21 N	79.28 W
Crabtree Creek ≃	279b	40.21 N	79.30 W
Crabtree Mills	206	45.58 N	73.28 W
Craches	261	48.34 N	1.49 E
Crackenback ≃	171b	36.21 S	148.36 E
Craco	68	40.23 N	16.26 E
Cracovie → Kraków	30	50.03 N	19.58 E
Cradle Mountain-Lake Saint Clair National Park ♠	166	42.00 S	146.00 E
Cradock, Austl.	166	32.04 S	138.30 E
Cradock, S. Afr.	158	32.08 S	25.36 E
Cradock Channel ʮ	172	36.11 S	175.15 E
Crafers	168b	35.01 S	138.47 E
Crafton	214	40.26 N	80.03 W
Crafts Creek ≃	285	40.07 N	74.46 W
Cragg Vale	262	53.42 N	2.00 W
Cragsmoor	210	41.40 N	74.23 W
Crai	42	51.55 N	3.36 W
Craig, B.C., Can.	224	49.18 N	124.15 W
Craig, Ak., U.S.	182	55.29 N	133.09 W
Craig, Co., U.S.	200	40.30 N	107.32 W
Craig, Mo., U.S.	194	40.11 N	95.22 W
Craig, Ne., U.S.	198	41.47 N	96.21 W
Craig, Point ∧	162	26.51 S	126.19 E
Craigavon	48	54.27 N	6.24 W
Craig Beach	214	41.07 N	81.01 W
Craig Creek ≃	192	37.39 N	79.49 W
Craigellachie	182	50.59 N	118.43 W
Craighall ◆[8]	273d	26.07 S	28.02 E
Craighall Park ◆[8]	273d	26.08 S	28.01 E
Craighouse	46	55.51 N	5.57 W
Craigmont	202	46.14 N	116.27 W
Craigmyle	182	51.40 N	112.15 W
Craignish Point ›	46	56.07 N	5.37 W
Craignure	46	56.28 N	5.42 W
Craigsville, Pa., U.S.	214	40.51 N	79.39 W
Craigsville, Va., U.S.	192	38.04 N	79.23 W
Craigville	216	40.47 N	85.06 W
Craik	184	51.03 N	105.49 W
Crail	46	56.16 N	2.38 W
Crailsheim	56	49.08 N	10.04 E
Craiova	38	44.19 N	23.48 E
Crake ≃	44	54.14 N	3.03 W
Craley	208	39.57 N	76.31 W
Cramant	50	48.59 N	3.59 E
Cramlington	44	55.05 N	1.36 W
Cranage	262	53.12 N	2.22 W
Cranberry	214	41.21 N	79.43 W
Cranberry Brook ≃	283	42.11 N	71.01 W
Cranberry Creek	210	43.09 N	74.14 W
Cranberry Island I	212	44.44 N	81.18 W
Cranberry Lake	210	40.57 N	74.44 W
Cranberry Lake ⊜, On., Can.	212	44.26 N	76.19 W
Cranberry Lake ⊜, On., Can.	212	44.47 N	75.50 W
Cranberry Lake ⊜, N.Y., U.S.	188	44.10 N	74.50 W
Cranberry Lake ⊜, Wa., U.S.	224	47.17 N	123.05 W
Cranberry Mountain ∧	182	50.42 N	118.12 W
Cranberry Pond ⊜	276	41.08 N	74.12 W
Cranberry Portage	184	54.35 N	101.23 W
Cranborne Chase ◆[3]	42	50.55 N	2.05 W
Cranbourne	169	38.06 S	145.17 E
Cranbrook, Austl.	162	34.18 S	117.32 E
Cranbrook, B.C., Can.	182	49.31 N	115.46 W
Cranbrook, Eng., U.K.	42	51.06 N	0.33 E
Cranbrook Academy of Art ☉	281	42.34 N	83.14 W
Cranbury	276	40.18 N	74.30 W
Cranbury Brook ≃	276	40.19 N	74.37 W
Crandall	222	32.37 N	96.27 W
Crandon	190	45.34 N	88.54 W
Crandon Lakes	210	41.07 N	74.50 W
Crane, Az., U.S.	204	32.42 N	114.40 W
Crane, In., U.S.	194	38.53 N	86.54 W
Crane, Mo., U.S.	194	36.54 N	93.34 W
Crane, Tx., U.S.	196	31.23 N	102.20 W
Crane Beach ⊥[2]	283	42.41 N	70.46 W
Cranebrook	274a	33.43 S	150.42 E
Crane Creek ≃	190	43.01 N	91.58 W
Crane Lake ⊜, On., Can.	212	45.13 N	79.57 W
Crane Lake ⊜, Sk., Can.	184	50.06 N	109.06 W
Crane Mountain ∧	202	42.04 N	120.13 W
Crane Neck Point ›	210	40.58 N	73.10 W
Crane River Indian Reserve ◆[4]	184	51.30 N	99.14 W
Cranesville	214	41.54 N	80.21 W
Cranfield	42	52.05 N	0.35 W
Cranfills Gap	222	31.46 N	97.50 W
Cranford	210	40.39 N	74.19 W
Crange ◆[8]	263	51.32 N	7.11 E
Cran-Gévrier	58	45.54 N	6.06 E
Crank	262	53.29 N	2.45 W
Cranleigh	42	51.09 N	0.30 W
Crans	58	46.19 N	7.28 E
Cranston	207	41.46 N	71.26 W
Cranston Heights	285	39.38 N	75.38 W
Craolândia	250	7.57 S	47.15 W
Craon	32	47.51 N	0.57 W
Craonne	50	49.26 N	3.47 E
Craponne, Fr.	62	45.44 N	4.43 E
Craponne, Fr.	62	45.20 N	3.51 E
Craponne, Canal de ≊	62	43.40 N	4.39 E
Crary Mountains ⋏	9	76.48 S	117.40 W
Craryville	210	42.11 N	73.35 W
Crasna, Rom.	38	46.31 N	27.51 E
Crasna, Rom.	38	45.36 N	26.08 E
Crasna (Kraszna) ≃	38	48.09 N	22.20 E
Crassier	58	46.22 N	6.11 E
Crater Lake ⊜, St. Vin.	241h	13.20 N	61.11 W
Crater Lake ⊜, Or., U.S.	202	42.56 N	122.06 W
Crater Lake National Park ♠	202	42.49 N	122.08 W
Crater Mount ∧	164	6.30 S	145.10 E
Crater Point ›	164	5.22 S	152.09 E
Craters of the Moon National Monument ♠	202	43.20 N	113.35 W
Crateús	250	5.10 S	40.40 W
Crathie	46	57.02 N	3.12 W
Crati ⋏	68	39.43 N	16.31 E
Crato	250	7.14 S	39.23 W
Crau ◆[1]	62	43.36 N	4.50 E
Crauford, Cape ›	176	73.43 N	84.50 W
Craughwell	48	53.13 N	8.43 W
Cravant	50	47.41 N	3.41 E
Cravari ≃	248	12.06 S	58.03 W
Cravat	219	38.25 N	89.06 W
Craven	184	50.39 N	104.50 W
Craven Arms	42	52.26 N	2.50 W
Cravensville	171b	36.24 S	147.34 E
Cravo Norte	246	6.18 N	70.12 W
Cravo Norte ≃	246	6.18 N	70.12 W
Cravo Sur ≃	246	4.42 N	71.36 W
Crawfish ≃	216	43.00 N	88.49 W
Crawford, Scot., U.K.	44	55.28 N	3.40 W
Crawford, Co., U.S.	200	38.42 N	107.36 W
Crawford, Ms., U.S.	194	33.18 N	88.36 W
Crawford, Ne., U.S.	198	42.40 N	103.24 W
Crawford, Tx., U.S.	222	31.32 N	97.27 W
Crawford □[6], In., U.S.	218	38.20 N	86.28 W
Crawford □[6], Oh., U.S.	214	40.48 N	82.58 W
Crawford □[6], Pa., U.S.	214	41.39 N	80.10 W
Crawford Bay	182	49.42 N	116.48 W
Crawford Countryside	278	41.32 N	87.43 W
Crawford Notch State Park ♠	188	44.13 N	71.25 W
Crawfordsville, Ar., U.S.	194	35.13 N	90.19 W
Crawfordsville, In., U.S.	194	40.02 N	86.52 W
Crawfordville, Fl., U.S.	192	30.10 N	84.22 W
Crawfordville, Ga., U.S.	192	33.33 N	82.53 W
Crawinkel	54	50.47 N	10.47 E
Crawley	42	51.07 N	0.12 W
Crawshawbooth	262	53.43 N	2.17 W
Crayford ◆[8]	260	51.27 N	0.11 E
Crays Hill	260	51.36 N	0.28 E
Crazy Mountains ⋏	202	46.08 N	110.20 W
Crazy Peak ∧	202	46.01 N	110.16 W
Crazy Woman Creek ≃	202	44.29 N	106.08 W
Creagan	46	56.33 N	5.17 W
Creagorry	46	57.26 N	7.19 W
Creal Springs	194	37.37 N	88.50 W
Creamery	285	40.13 N	75.25 W
Crean Lake ⊜	184	54.05 N	106.10 W
Crêches-sur-Saône	58	46.15 N	4.47 E
Crécy, Forêt de ♠	261	48.48 N	2.53 E
Crécy-en-Brie	50	48.51 N	2.55 E
Crécy-en-Ponthieu	50	50.15 N	1.53 E
Crécy-sur-Serre	50	49.42 N	3.37 E
Credenhill	42	52.06 N	2.48 W
Credit ≃	212	43.33 N	79.35 W
Crediton	42	50.47 N	3.39 W
Cree ≃, Sk., Can.	176	59.00 N	105.47 W
Cree ≃, Scot., U.K.	44	54.52 N	4.20 W
Creede	200	37.50 N	106.55 W
Creedmoor	192	36.07 N	78.41 W
Creedmore	222	30.12 N	97.43 W
Creegh	48	52.44 N	9.26 W
Creek Brook ≃	283	42.47 N	71.08 W
Creek Locks	210	41.52 N	74.03 W
Creekmouth ◆[8]	260	51.31 N	0.06 E
Creekside	214	40.40 N	79.11 W
Creekwood	278	41.39 N	87.59 W
Creel	232	27.45 N	107.38 W
Cree Lake ⊜	176	57.30 N	106.30 W
Creemore	212	44.19 N	80.06 W
Creetown	44	54.54 N	4.23 W
Cregganbaun	48	53.42 N	9.51 W
Creglingen	56	49.28 N	10.01 E
Crégy-lès-Meaux	261	48.58 N	2.52 E
Créhange	56	49.03 N	6.35 E
Creighton, Sk., Can.	184	54.45 N	101.54 W
Creighton, S. Afr.	158	30.01 S	29.51 E
Creighton, Ne., U.S.	198	42.28 N	97.54 W
Creighton, Pa., U.S.	214	40.35 N	79.46 W
Creighton Mine	190	46.28 N	81.11 W
Creightons Creek ≃	169	36.43 S	145.22 E
Creil, Fr.	50	49.16 N	2.29 E
Creil, Ned.	52	52.45 N	5.40 E
Crema	62	45.22 N	9.41 E
Cremia	58	46.05 N	9.16 E
Crémieu	62	45.43 N	5.15 E
Cremlingen	54	52.15 N	10.39 E
Cremona, Ab., Can.	182	51.33 N	114.29 W
Cremona, It.	64	45.07 N	10.02 E
Cremona □[4]	64	45.12 N	10.00 E
Crenshaw, Ms., U.S.	194	34.30 N	90.12 W
Crenshaw, Pa., U.S.	214	41.15 N	78.46 W
Crep Nudo ∧	64	46.13 N	12.24 E
Crepori ≃	250	5.42 S	57.08 W
Crépy-en-Laonnois	50	49.36 N	3.31 E
Crépy-en-Valois	50	49.14 N	2.54 E
Créquy	50	50.29 N	2.03 E
Creran, Loch ⊜	46	56.31 N	5.20 W
Cres	36	44.58 N	14.25 E
Cres, Otok I	36	44.50 N	14.25 E
Cresaptown	188	39.35 N	78.50 W
Crescent, N.Y., U.S.	210	42.49 N	73.43 W
Crescent, Ok., U.S.	196	35.57 N	97.35 W
Crescent, Or., U.S.	202	43.27 N	121.41 W
Crescent, Lake ⊜	224	48.05 N	123.50 W
Crescent Beach, B.C., Can.	224	49.04 N	122.53 W
Crescent Beach, Fl., U.S.	220	27.15 N	82.32 W
Crescent City, Ca., U.S.	204	41.45 N	124.12 W
Crescent City, Fl., U.S.	192	29.25 N	81.30 W
Crescent City, Il., U.S.	216	40.46 N	87.51 W
Crescent Ditch ≊	226	36.29 N	120.07 W
Crescent Heights, N.J., U.S.	285	39.58 N	74.43 W
Crescent Heights, Tx., U.S.	222	32.11 N	95.56 W
Crescentino	62	45.11 N	8.06 E
Crescent Lake ⊜, Fl., U.S.	192	29.28 N	81.30 W
Crescent Lake ⊜, Or., U.S.	202	43.29 N	121.59 W
Crescent Lake Estates	281	42.38 N	83.25 W
Crescent Spur	182	53.35 N	120.41 W
Crescentville ◆[8]	285	40.02 N	75.05 W
Crescenzago ◆[8]	266b	45.30 N	9.15 E
Cresco, Ia., U.S.	190	43.22 N	92.06 W
Cresco, Pa., U.S.	210	41.09 N	75.17 W
Crespano del Grappa	64	45.49 N	11.50 E
Crespian	62	43.53 N	4.06 E
Crespières	261	48.53 N	1.55 E
Crespin	50	50.25 N	3.39 E
Crespino	64	44.59 N	11.53 E
Crespo	252	32.02 S	60.19 W
Cressbrook Creek ≃	171a	27.05 S	152.27 E
Cressely	261	48.43 N	2.05 E
Cressey	226	37.25 N	120.40 W
Cresskill	276	40.56 N	73.57 W
Cresskill Brook ≃	276	40.57 N	73.58 W
Cresson, Pa., U.S.	214	40.27 N	78.35 W
Cresson, Tx., U.S.	222	32.32 N	97.37 W
Cressona	208	40.37 N	76.11 W
Cressy	169	38.02 S	143.38 E
Crest	62	44.44 N	5.02 E
Cresta	58	46.28 N	9.31 E
Crested Butte	200	38.52 N	106.59 W
Cresthaven	220	26.03 N	80.08 W
Crest Hill	216	41.33 N	88.05 W
Crestline, Ca., U.S.	228	34.14 N	117.17 W
Crestline, Oh., U.S.	214	40.47 N	82.44 W
Creston, B.C., Can.	182	49.06 N	116.31 W
Creston, Nf., Can.	186	47.09 N	55.11 W
Creston, Ca., U.S.	226	35.31 N	120.31 W
Creston, Il., U.S.	216	41.56 N	88.58 W
Creston, Ia., U.S.	198	41.03 N	94.21 W
Creston, Oh., U.S.	214	40.59 N	81.53 W
Crestone Peak ∧	200	37.58 N	105.36 W
Crestview, Fl., U.S.	194	30.45 N	86.34 W
Crestview, Wi., U.S.	216	42.49 N	87.49 W
Crestview Heights	210	42.05 N	76.07 W
Crestwood, Il., U.S.	278	41.39 N	87.45 W
Crestwood, Ky., U.S.	218	38.19 N	85.28 W
Crestwood, Mo., U.S.	219	38.33 N	90.22 W
Crestwood Hills	192	35.56 N	84.05 W
Creswell, Eng., U.K.	44	53.16 N	1.12 W
Creswell, Or., U.S.	202	43.55 N	123.01 W
Creswell Bay ⊂	176	72.35 N	93.25 W
Creswell Creek ≃	162	18.10 S	135.11 E
Creswell Downs	162	17.57 S	135.55 E
Creswick	169	37.26 S	143.54 E
Creta, Isla de → Kríti I	38	35.29 N	24.42 E
Crete, Il., U.S.	216	41.27 N	87.38 W
Crete, Ne., U.S.	198	40.37 N	96.57 W
Crete → Kríti I	38	35.29 N	24.42 E
Crete, Sea of → Kritikón Pélagos ⍑[2]	38	35.46 N	23.54 E
Créteil	50	48.48 N	2.28 E
Crétéville	36	36.40 N	10.20 E
Cretin, Cape ›	164	6.40 S	147.52 E
Creus, Cap de ›	34	42.19 N	3.19 E
Creuse □[5]	32	46.05 N	2.00 E
Creuse ≃	32	47.00 N	0.34 E
Creussen	60	49.51 N	11.37 E
Creutzwald	56	49.12 N	6.41 E
Creuzburg	56	51.03 N	10.15 E
Crevacuore	62	45.41 N	8.15 E
Crevalcore	64	44.43 N	11.09 E
Creve Coeur, Il., U.S.	190	40.38 N	89.35 W
Creve Coeur, Mo., U.S.	219	38.39 N	90.25 W
Crèvecœur-en-Auge	50	49.07 N	0.01 E
Crèvecœur-en-Brie	261	48.45 N	2.55 E
Crèvecœur-le-Grand	50	49.36 N	2.05 E
Crevillent	34	38.15 N	0.48 W
Crevoladossola	58	46.09 N	8.18 E
Crewe, Eng., U.K.	44	53.05 N	2.27 W
Crewe, Va., U.S.	192	37.10 N	78.07 W
Crewkerne	42	50.53 N	2.48 W
Crews Lake ⊜	220	28.23 N	82.31 W
Crewsville	220	27.16 N	81.36 W
Crianlarich	46	56.23 N	4.36 W
Crib Point	169	38.22 S	145.12 E
Cricamola ≃	236	8.59 N	81.54 W
Criccieth	42	52.55 N	4.14 W
Crichi	68	38.57 N	16.38 E
Criciúma	252	28.40 S	49.23 W
Crick	42	52.21 N	1.07 W
Cricket	192	36.10 N	81.11 W
Crickhowell	42	51.53 N	3.07 W
Cricklade	42	51.39 N	1.51 W
Cridersville	216	40.39 N	84.09 W
Crieff	46	56.23 N	3.52 W
Criel-sur-Mer	50	50.01 N	1.19 E
Criffell ∧	44	54.57 N	3.38 W
Crikvenica	36	45.11 N	14.42 E
Crillon, Mount ∧	180	58.40 N	137.10 W
Crimea → Krymskij poluostrov ›[1]	78	45.00 N	34.00 E
Crimmitschau	54	50.49 N	12.23 E
Crimond	46	57.36 N	1.54 W
Crinan	46	56.05 N	5.35 W
Crîngeni	38	44.01 N	24.47 E
Cringila	170	34.28 S	150.53 E
Cripple Creek	200	38.44 N	105.10 W
Criquetot l'Esneval	50	49.39 N	0.16 E
Crirninoso, Monte ∧	256	21.32 S	43.25 W
Crisenoy	261	48.36 N	2.45 E
Crisfield	208	37.59 N	75.51 W
Crisólia	256	22.15 S	46.25 W
Crisóstomo, Ribeirão ≃	250	10.19 S	50.26 W
Crispiano	68	40.36 N	17.14 E
Criss Creek	182	51.03 N	120.44 W
Crissiumal	252	27.30 S	54.07 W
Cristal, Monts de ⋏	152	0.30 N	10.30 E
Cristal, Sierra del ⋏	240p	20.33 N	75.31 W
Cristalândia	250	10.36 S	49.11 W
Cristalina	255	16.45 S	47.36 W
Cristalino ≃	255	12.38 S	50.40 W
Cristallo ∧	64	46.34 N	12.12 E
Cristianópolis	255	17.13 S	48.45 W
Cristina	256	22.13 S	45.16 W
Cristinápolis	250	11.29 S	37.46 W
Cristino Castro	250	8.49 S	44.13 W
Cristóbal	236	9.21 N	79.55 W
Cristóbal, Punta de ›	240p	22.12 N	81.51 W
Cristóbal Colón, Pico ∧	246	10.50 N	73.41 W
Cristoforo Colombo, Aeroporto di ⊠	62	44.25 N	8.49 E
Cristo Redentor ⊥	252	32.50 S	70.05 W
Cristo Redentor, Estatua do ☉[1]	287a	22.57 S	43.13 W
Cristuru-Secuiesc	38	46.17 N	25.02 E
Crișul Alb ≃	38	46.42 N	21.17 E
Crișul Negru ≃	38	46.42 N	21.16 E
Crișul Repede (Sebes Körös) ≃	38	46.55 N	20.59 E
Crittenden	218	38.46 N	84.36 W
Crivitz, D.D.R.	54	53.35 N	11.38 E
Crivitz, Wi., U.S.	190	45.13 N	88.00 W
Crixalândia	255	15.18 S	47.15 W
Crixás	255	14.27 S	49.58 W
Crixás ≃	250	11.02 S	48.34 W
Crixás Açu ≃	255	13.19 S	50.36 W
Crixás Mirim ≃	255	13.30 S	50.30 W
Črna	61	46.28 N	14.51 E
Crna ≃	38	41.35 N	21.59 E
Crna Gora □[3]	38	42.30 N	19.18 E
Črni vrh ∧	61	46.29 N	15.14 E
Črnomelj	36	45.34 N	15.11 E
Croachy	46	57.19 N	4.14 W
Croagh Patrick ∧	48	53.46 N	9.40 W
Croajingolong National Park ♠	166	37.40 S	149.30 E
Croal ≃	262	53.33 N	2.23 W
Croatia → Hrvatska □[3]	36	45.10 N	15.30 E
Croce dello Scrivano, Passo)(	68	40.34 N	15.50 E
Croce Domini, Passo di)(	64	45.54 N	10.24 E
Crocefieschi	62	44.35 N	9.01 E
Crocetta del Montello	64	45.50 N	12.02 E
Crocheron	208	38.14 N	76.03 W
Crockenhill	260	51.23 N	0.10 E
Crocker	194	37.56 N	92.15 W
Crocker, Banjaran ⋏	112	5.40 N	116.14 E
Crockery Creek ≃	216	43.02 N	86.05 W
Crocketford	44	55.02 N	3.50 W
Crockett, Ca., U.S.	226	38.03 N	122.12 W
Crockett, Tx., U.S.	222	31.19 N	95.27 W
Crockham Hill	260	51.14 N	0.04 E
Crocus Hill → The Valley	238	18.13 N	63.04 W
Croft	262	53.26 N	2.33 W
Crofton, B.C., Can.	224	48.52 N	123.38 W
Crofton, Ky., U.S.	194	37.02 N	87.29 W
Crofton, Md., U.S.	208	39.00 N	76.41 W
Crofton, Ne., U.S.	198	42.43 N	97.29 W
Croft State Park ♠	192	34.49 N	81.52 W
Croggan	46	56.22 N	5.42 W
Croghan	212	43.53 N	75.23 W
Croglin	44	54.49 N	2.39 W
Croick	46	57.53 N	4.35 W
Croil Islands II	206	44.58 N	74.58 W
Croisette, Cap ›	62	43.13 N	5.20 E
Croisilles	50	50.12 N	2.53 E
Croissy-Beaubourg	261	48.50 N	2.40 E
Croissy-sur-Seine	261	48.53 N	2.09 E
Croix	50	50.40 N	3.09 E
Croix, Lac à la ⊜	186	51.16 N	70.13 W
Croix, Lac la ⊜	190	48.21 N	92.05 W
Croker, Cape ›, Austl.	164	10.58 S	132.35 E
Croker, Cape ›, On., Can.	212	44.58 N	80.59 W

	English	Deutsch	Español	Français	Português
≃	River	Fluß	Río	Rivière	Rio
≊	Canal	Kanal	Canal	Canal	Canal
⌞	Waterfall, Rapids	Wasserfall, Stromschnellen	Cascada, Rápidos	Chute d'eau, Rapides	Cascata, Rápidos
ʮ	Strait	Meeresstraße	Estrecho	Détroit	Estreito
⊂	Bay, Gulf	Bucht, Golf	Bahía, Golfo	Baie, Golfe	Baía, Golfo
⊜	Lake, Lakes	See, Seen	Lago, Lagos	Lac, Lacs	Lago, Lagos
☷	Swamp	Sumpf	Pantano	Marais	Pântano
⊓	Ice Features, Glacier	Eis- und Gletscherformen	Accidentes Glaciales	Formes glaciaires	Acidentes glaciares
⍑	Other Hydrographic Features	Andere Hydrographische Objekte	Otros Elementos Hidrográficos	Autres données hydrographiques	Outros acidentes hidrográficos
✤	Submarine Features	Untermeerische Objekte	Accidentes Submarinos	Formes de relief sous-marin	Acidentes submarinos
□	Political Unit	Politische Einheit	Unidad Política	Entité politique	Unidade política
☉	Cultural Institution	Kulturelle Institution	Institución Cultural	Institution culturelle	Instituição cultural
⊥	Historical Site	Historische Stätte	Sitio Histórico	Site historique	Sitio histórico
♠	Recreational Site	Erholungs- und Ferienort	Sitio de Recreo	Centre de loisirs	Area de Lazer
⊠	Airport	Flughafen	Aeropuerto	Aéroport	Aeroporto
■	Military Installation	Militäranlage	Instalación Militar	Installation militaire	Instalação militar
◆	Miscellaneous	Verschiedenes	Misceláneo	Divers	Diversos

I · 42 **Crok-Curu**

ENGLISH — DEUTSCH

Name	Page	Lat.°′	Long.°′
Croker Island I	164	11.12 S	132.32 E
Crolles	62	45.17 N	5.53 E
Cromarty	46	57.40 N	4.02 W
Cromarty Firth ⊂[1]	46	57.41 N	4.07 W
Cromby	285	40.09 N	75.32 W
Cromer, Austl.	274a	33.44 S	151.17 E
Cromer, Eng., U.K.	42	52.56 N	1.18 E
Cromford	44	53.06 N	1.34 W
Cromínia	255	17.17 S	49.21 W
Cromore	46	58.09 N	6.29 W
Crompton Point ›	240d	15.35 N	61.19 W
Cromwell, N.Z.	172	45.03 S	169.12 E
Cromwell, Al., U.S.	194	32.13 N	88.16 W
Cromwell, Ct., U.S.	207	41.35 N	72.38 W
Cromwell, In., U.S.	216	41.24 N	85.36 W
Cromwell Park ♠	279a	41.28 N	82.08 W
Cronadun	172	42.02 S	171.52 E
Cronenberg ◆[8]	263	51.12 N	7.08 E
Cronin, Mount ∧	182	54.54 N	126.52 W
Cronton	262	53.23 N	2.46 W
Cronulla	170	34.03 S	151.09 E
Cronulla Beach ⩲[2]	274a	34.02 S	151.11 E
Croob, Slieve ∧[2]	48	54.20 N	5.58 W
Crook, Eng., U.K.	44	54.43 N	1.44 W
Crook, Co., U.S.	198	40.51 N	102.48 W
Crooked ≐, B.C., Can.	182	54.50 N	122.54 W
Crooked ≐, Mo., U.S.	194	39.13 N	93.49 W
Crooked ≐, Or., U.S.	202	44.34 N	121.16 W
Crooked Creek	180	61.52 N	158.08 W
Crooked Creek ≐, U.S.	196	36.57 N	100.06 W
Crooked Creek ≐, Ar., U.S.	194	36.14 N	92.29 W
Crooked Creek ≐, Il., U.S.	219	38.30 N	89.25 W
Crooked Creek ≐, In., U.S.	216	40.45 N	86.30 W
Crooked Creek ≐, Mo., U.S.	219	39.34 N	91.55 W
Crooked Creek ≐, Pa., U.S.	210	41.55 N	77.08 W
Crooked Creek ≐, Pa., U.S.	214	40.45 N	79.33 W
Crooked Creek Lake ⊜[1]	214	40.42 N	79.30 W
Crooked Island I	238	22.45 N	74.13 W
Crooked Island Passage ⋃	238	22.55 N	74.35 W
Crooked Lake, In., U.S.	216	41.41 N	85.02 W
Crooked Lake, Mi., U.S.	216	42.29 N	85.25 W
Crooked Lake ⊜, Nf., Can.	186	48.24 N	56.17 W
Crooked Lake ⊜, Sk., Can.	184	50.36 N	102.45 W
Crooked Lake ⊜, N.A.	190	48.13 N	91.50 W
Crooked Lake ⊜, Fl., U.S.	220	27.48 N	81.35 W
Crooked Lake ⊜, In., U.S.	216	41.40 N	85.03 W
Crooked River	184	52.51 N	103.44 W
Crookes Point ›	276	40.32 N	74.08 W
Crookham	279b	40.12 N	79.59 W
Crookston	198	47.46 N	96.36 W
Crookstown	48	51.50 N	8.50 W
Crooksville	188	39.46 N	82.05 W
Crookwell	166	34.28 S	149.28 E
Croom	48	52.31 N	8.42 W
Cropalati	68	39.31 N	16.43 E
Cropani	68	38.58 N	16.47 E
Cropper	218	38.18 N	85.06 W
Crosby, Eng., U.K.	262	53.30 N	3.02 W
Crosby, Mn., U.S.	190	46.28 N	93.57 W
Crosby, Ms., U.S.	194	31.17 N	91.03 W
Crosby, N.D., U.S.	198	48.54 N	103.17 W
Crosby, Pa., U.S.	214	41.45 N	78.24 W
Crosby, Tx., U.S.	222	29.55 N	95.04 W
Crosby, Mount ∧	202	43.53 N	109.20 W
Crosby Lake ⊜	212	44.45 N	76.26 W
Crosbyton	196	33.39 N	101.14 W
Crosia	68	39.34 N	16.46 E
Crosne	261	48.43 N	2.28 E
Cross ≐	152	4.42 N	8.21 E
Cross Banks II	283	42.43 N	70.49 W
Cross Bay ⊂	184	53.15 N	99.25 W
Cross Bay Bridge ◆[5]	276	40.35 N	73.49 W
Crossbost	46	58.08 N	6.23 W
Cross City	192	29.38 N	83.07 W
Cross County Center ◆[9]	276	40.56 N	73.51 W
Cross Creek ≐, Ca., U.S.	226	36.08 N	119.38 W
Cross Creek ≐, Oh., U.S.	214	40.18 N	80.36 W
Crossen, D.D.R.	54	50.45 N	12.29 E
Crossen → Krosno Odrzańskie, Pol.	30	52.04 N	15.05 E
Crossens	262	53.41 N	2.57 W
Crossett	194	33.07 N	91.57 W
Cross Fell ∧	44	54.42 N	2.29 W
Crossfield	182	51.26 N	114.02 W
Crossgar	48	54.24 N	5.45 W
Cross Hands	42	51.48 N	4.04 W
Crosshaven	48	51.48 N	8.17 W
Crosshill	44	55.19 N	4.39 W
Crossinsee ⊜	264a	52.22 N	13.41 E
Cross Island I	272c	18.57 N	72.51 E
Cross Keys	285	39.42 N	75.01 W
Cross Keys Airfield ⊠	285	39.42 N	75.02 W
Cross Lake	184	54.37 N	97.47 W
Cross Lake ⊜, Mb., Can.	184	54.45 N	97.30 W
Cross Lake ⊜, On., Can.	190	46.53 N	79.57 W
Cross Lake ⊜, N.Y., U.S.	210	43.08 N	76.29 W
Crossley, Mount ∧	172	42.50 S	172.04 E
Crossmaglen	48	54.05 N	6.37 W
Crossman	168a	32.47 S	116.36 E
Crossman ≐	168a	32.47 S	116.32 E
Crossman Peak ∧	200	34.32 N	114.07 W
Crossmolina	48	54.06 N	9.20 W
Cross Plains, In., U.S.	218	38.57 N	85.12 W
Cross Plains, Tx., U.S.	196	32.08 N	99.11 W
Cross Plains, Wi., U.S.	190	43.06 N	89.39 W
Cross River □[3]	150	5.50 N	8.30 E
Cross Roads	222	32.03 N	95.58 W
Cross Sound ⋃	180	58.10 N	136.30 W
Crossville, Il., U.S.	194	38.09 N	88.03 W
Crossville, Tn., U.S.	194	35.56 N	85.01 W
Crosswicks	285	40.09 N	74.38 W
Crosswicks Creek ≐	208	40.09 N	74.43 W
Crostolo ≐	64	44.55 N	10.38 E
Croston, Eng., U.K.	44	53.39 N	2.46 W
Croston, Eng., U.K.	262	53.40 N	2.46 W
Croswell	190	43.16 N	82.37 W
Crotch Lake ⊜	212	44.55 N	76.48 W
Crotenay	58	46.45 N	5.49 E
Crothersville	218	38.48 N	85.50 W
Croton	214	40.14 N	82.41 W
Crotona Park ♠	276	40.50 N	73.54 W
Croton Creek ≐	196	33.18 N	100.25 W
Crotone	68	39.05 N	17.07 E
Croton Falls	210	41.21 N	73.40 W
Croton-on-Hudson	210	41.12 N	73.53 W
Croton Point ›	276	41.10 N	73.54 W
Crottendorf	54	50.30 N	12.56 E
Crouch ≐	42	51.37 N	0.57 E
Crouse Run ≐	279b	40.35 N	79.58 W
Crouy	50	49.24 N	3.22 E
Crow ≐	190	45.15 N	93.31 W
Crow, North Fork ≐	190	45.05 N	93.45 W
Crow, South Fork ≐	190	45.05 N	93.45 W
Crow Agency	202	45.36 N	107.27 W
Crowborough	42	51.03 N	0.09 E
Crow Creek ≐, U.S.	198	40.23 N	104.29 W
Crow Creek ≐, Ca., U.S.	282	37.42 N	122.03 W
Crow Creek ≐, Il., U.S.	194	40.56 N	89.27 W
Crow Creek ≐, Mt., U.S.	198	45.45 N	105.06 W
Crow Creek ≐, Mt., U.S.	202	46.11 N	111.29 W
Crow Creek ≐, S.D., U.S.	198	43.57 N	99.15 W
Crow Creek ≐, Wy., U.S.	202	43.19 N	109.09 W
Crow Creek Indian Reservation ◆[4]	198	44.11 N	99.30 W
Crowder, Ms., U.S.	194	34.10 N	90.08 W
Crowder, Ok., U.S.	196	35.07 N	95.40 W
Crowduck Lake ⊜	184	50.08 N	95.15 W
Crowdy Head ›	166	31.50 S	152.45 E
Crowe ≐	212	44.22 N	77.46 W
Crowe Lake ⊜	212	44.29 N	77.46 W
Crowell	196	33.59 N	99.43 W
Crowfoot, Mount ∧	172	45.33 S	167.03 E
Crow Hill ∧[2]	262	53.42 N	1.58 W
Crowhurst	260	51.12 N	0.01 W
Crow Indian Reservation ◆[4]	202	45.27 N	108.00 W
Crow Lake	184	49.12 N	93.57 W
Crow Lake ⊜	212	44.43 N	76.37 W
Crowland	42	52.41 N	0.11 W
Crowle	44	53.37 N	0.49 W
Crowley, Ca., U.S.	226	36.21 N	119.17 W
Crowley, La., U.S.	194	30.12 N	92.22 W
Crowley, Tx., U.S.	222	32.34 N	97.21 W
Crowley, Lake ⊜[1]	204	37.37 N	118.44 W
Crowleys Ridge ∧	194	35.45 N	90.45 W
Crowlin Islands II	46	57.20 N	5.44 W
Crown	214	41.23 N	79.16 W
Crown Hill	212	44.26 N	79.39 W
Crown Island I	164	5.05 S	146.55 E
Crown Memorial Beach ♠	282	37.46 N	122.16 W
Crown Mines ◆[7]	273d	26.13 S	28.00 E
Crown Mountain ∧	240m	18.21 N	64.58 W
Crown Point, In., U.S.	216	41.25 N	87.21 W
Crownpoint, N.M., U.S.	200	35.40 N	108.09 W
Crown Point, N.Y., U.S.	188	43.57 N	73.26 W
Crown Point State Park ♠	224	45.32 N	122.15 W
Crown Prince Frederik Island I	176	70.02 N	86.50 W
Crown Village	276	40.40 N	73.27 W
Crow Peak ∧	202	46.18 N	111.54 W
Crow Rock Creek ≐	202	47.06 N	106.15 W
Crows Fork Creek ≐	219	38.47 N	91.52 W
Crows Landing	226	37.24 N	121.04 W
Crows Nest, Austl.	171a	27.16 S	152.03 E
Crows Nest, Austl.	274a	33.50 S	151.12 E
Crowsnest, Ab., Can.	182	49.38 N	114.41 W
Crows Nest Falls National Park ♠	171a	27.16 S	152.08 E
Crowsnest Pass	182	49.36 N	114.26 W
Crowsnest Pass)(	182	49.39 N	114.45 W
Crows Nest Peak ∧	198	44.03 N	103.58 W
Crowthorne	42	51.23 N	0.49 W
Crowton	262	53.16 N	2.38 W
Crow Wing ≐	198	46.19 N	94.20 W
Croxley Green	260	51.39 N	0.27 W
Croxteth Park ♠	262	53.26 N	2.53 W
Croy	46	57.31 N	4.02 W
Croyde	42	51.07 N	4.13 W
Croydon, Austl.	166	18.12 S	142.14 E
Croydon, Austl.	169	37.48 S	145.17 E
Croydon, Austl.	274a	33.53 S	151.07 E
Croydon, Pa., U.S.	208	40.05 N	74.54 W
Croydon ◆[8]	260	51.23 N	0.06 W
Croydon Park	274a	33.54 S	151.07 E
Croydon Peak ∧	188	43.28 N	72.13 W
Croydon Station	182	53.05 N	119.44 W
Crozet	192	38.04 N	78.42 W
Crozet, Îles II	6	46.00 S	52.00 E
Crozet Basin ✦[1]	6	39.00 S	60.00 E
Crozon	32	48.15 N	4.29 W
Cruachan, Ben ∧	46	56.25 N	5.08 W
Cruas	62	44.39 N	4.46 E
Crucea	38	44.32 N	28.14 E
Crucero	248	14.21 S	70.00 W
Crucero, Cerro ∧	234	21.41 N	104.25 W
Cruces, Cuba	240p	22.21 N	80.16 W
Cruces, Méx.	232	29.26 N	107.24 W
Crucilândia	255	20.23 S	44.21 W
Crucoli	68	39.25 N	17.00 E
Cruden Bay	46	57.25 N	1.50 W
Crudgington	42	52.46 N	2.33 W
Crudine Creek ≐	170	33.05 S	149.40 E
Cruger	194	33.19 N	90.13 W
Cruillas	232	24.45 N	98.31 W
Crum Creek ≐	285	39.51 N	75.19 W
Crumhorn Mountain ∧	210	42.33 N	74.55 W
Crumlin, On., Can.	212	43.01 N	81.09 W
Crumlin, N. Ire., U.K.	48	54.37 N	6.14 W
Crum Lynne	285	39.52 N	75.20 W
Crummock Water ⊜	44	54.34 N	3.18 W
Crump Lake ⊜	202	42.17 N	119.50 W
Crumpton	208	39.14 N	75.55 W
Crumstown	216	41.38 N	86.25 W
Crupet	56	50.21 N	4.48 E
Cruseilles	58	46.02 N	6.07 E
Cruser Brook ≐	276	40.27 N	74.39 W
Crusheen	48	52.58 N	8.53 W
Crusnes	56	49.26 N	5.55 E
Crusnes ≐	56	49.27 N	5.36 E
Cruz, Arroyo de la ≐, Ca., U.S.	226	35.42 N	121.09 W
Cruz, Arroyo de la ≐, Ur.	258	34.00 S	56.08 W
Cruz, Cabo ›	240p	19.51 N	77.44 W
Cruz, Cañada de la ≐	258	34.09 S	58.58 W
Cruz, Cayo I	240p	22.15 N	77.49 W
Cruz, Pico de la ∧	148	28.44 N	17.52 W
Cruz Alta, Arg.	252	33.01 S	61.49 W
Cruz Alta, Bra.	252	28.39 S	53.36 W
Cruz Bay	240m	18.20 N	64.48 W
Cruz das Almas	256	22.44 S	46.51 W
Cruz de Elorza	234	23.49 N	100.29 W
Cruz del Eje	252	30.44 S	64.48 W
Cruz Descoberta	256	22.45 S	46.48 W
Cruzeiro	256	22.34 S	44.58 W
Cruzeiro do Oeste	255	23.46 S	53.04 W
Cruzeiro do Sul	248	7.38 S	72.36 W
Cruzeta	250	6.25 S	36.47 W
Cruz Grande, Chile	252	29.25 S	71.18 W
Cruz Grande, Méx.	234	16.44 N	99.08 W
Cruzília	256	21.50 S	44.48 W
Cruz Machado	252	26.01 S	51.21 W
Cruzy-le-Châtel	50	47.51 N	4.12 E
Crvenka	38	45.39 N	19.28 E
Crymych	42	51.59 N	4.40 W
Crynant	42	51.43 N	3.45 W
Crysler	188	45.13 N	75.09 W
Crystal, Mn., U.S.	190	45.01 N	93.21 W
Crystal, N.D., U.S.	198	48.35 N	97.40 W
Crystal ≐	200	39.25 N	107.14 W
Crystal Bay	226	39.13 N	120.00 W
Crystal Bay ⊂	220	28.55 N	82.43 W
Crystal Beach, On., Can.	284a	42.52 N	79.04 W
Crystal Beach, Fl., U.S.	220	28.05 N	82.46 W
Crystal Beach, Tx., U.S.	222	29.27 N	94.38 W
Crystal Brook	166	33.21 S	138.13 E
Crystal Cave ⩲[5]	208	40.32 N	75.51 W
Crystal City, Mb., Can.	184	49.09 N	98.56 W
Crystal City, Mo., U.S.	219	38.13 N	90.22 W
Crystal City, Tx., U.S.	196	28.40 N	99.49 W
Crystal Creek ≐	278	41.58 N	87.51 W
Crystal Falls	190	46.05 N	88.20 W
Crystal Gardens	216	42.14 N	88.23 W
Crystal Lake, Il., U.S.	216	42.14 N	88.18 W
Crystal Lake, N.Y., U.S.	210	42.31 N	74.12 W
Crystal Lake, N.Y., U.S.	210	42.28 N	78.20 W
Crystal Lake ⊜, On., Can.	212	44.45 N	78.30 W
Crystal Lake ⊜, Ma., U.S.	283	42.29 N	71.05 W
Crystal Lake ⊜, Ma., U.S.	283	42.48 N	71.09 W
Crystal Lake ⊜, Mi., U.S.	190	44.40 N	86.10 W
Crystal Lake ⊜, N.J., U.S.	276	41.02 N	74.15 W
Crystal Lakes	218	39.52 N	84.04 W
Crystal Lawns	216	41.34 N	88.09 W
Crystal Manor	216	42.14 N	88.17 W
Crystal Palace Stadium and Motor Race Track ♠	260	51.25 N	0.04 W
Crystal River	192	28.54 N	82.35 W
Crystal Spring Lake ⊜	285	39.43 N	75.01 W
Crystal Springs, Fl., U.S.	220	28.10 N	82.09 W
Crystal Springs, Ms., U.S.	194	31.59 N	90.21 W
Crystal Springs Dam ◆[6]	282	37.32 N	122.22 W
Crystal Vista	216	42.14 N	88.24 W
Csepel ◆[8]	264c	47.24 N	19.14 E
Csepel-sziget I	30	47.15 N	18.57 E
Csepreg	61	47.24 N	16.43 E
Cserhát ⩘	30	47.55 N	19.30 E
Cserta ≐	61	46.35 N	16.36 E
Csesznek ⊥	30	47.16 N	17.53 E
Csesztreg	61	46.43 N	16.31 E
Csobánka	264c	47.38 N	18.58 E
Csomád	264c	47.40 N	19.15 E
Csömödér	61	46.37 N	16.39 E
Csömör	264c	47.33 N	19.14 E
Csömöri-patak ≐	264c	47.36 N	19.07 E
Csongrád	30	46.43 N	20.09 E
Csongrád □[6]	30	46.25 N	20.15 E
Csorna	30	47.37 N	17.16 E
Csurgó	30	46.16 N	17.06 E
Ču	85	43.36 N	73.45 E
Ču ≐	86	45.00 N	67.44 E
Cúa	246	10.10 N	66.54 W
Cuacnopalan	234	18.49 N	97.30 W
Cuácua ≐	154	17.54 S	36.48 E
Cuadro Nacional	252	34.37 S	68.17 W
Cuajimalpa □[7]	286a	19.21 N	99.17 W
Cuajimalpa ◆[8]	286a	19.21 N	99.18 W
Cuajinicuilapa	234	16.28 N	98.25 W
Cuajone	248	17.00 S	70.43 W
Cuále	152	8.06 S	16.03 E
Cua Lo	110	18.49 N	105.43 E
Cuamato	152	17.05 S	15.09 E
Cuamba	154	14.49 S	36.33 E
Cuambog	116	7.20 N	125.52 E
Cuanavale ≐	152	15.07 S	19.14 E
Cuando	152	16.32 S	22.07 E
Cuando (Kwando) ≐	152	18.27 S	23.32 E
Cuando Cubango □[5]	152	16.00 S	20.00 E
Cuangar	152	17.36 S	18.39 E
Cuango, Ang.	152	14.30 S	18.59 E
Cuango, Ang.	152	9.10 S	17.58 E
Cuango, Ang.	152	6.17 S	16.41 E
Cuango (Kwango) ≐	152	3.14 S	17.23 E
Cuanza ≐	152	9.19 S	13.08 E
Cuanza Norte □[5]	152	8.50 S	14.30 E
Cuanza Sul □[5]	152	10.50 S	14.50 E
Cuao ≐	246	4.55 N	67.40 W
Cuapiaxtla	234	19.18 N	97.46 W
Cuaró	252	30.37 S	56.54 W
Cuartillo, Arroyo ≐	258	33.45 S	59.06 W
Cuarto ≐	252	33.25 S	63.02 W
Cuary ≐	246	1.30 N	68.11 W
Cuatir ≐	152	17.01 S	18.09 E
Cuatro Caminos	286b	22.54 N	82.23 W
Cuatro Ciénegas [de Carranza]	196	26.59 N	102.05 W
Cuatro Islands II	116	10.31 N	124.39 E
Cuauhtémoc, Méx.	232	28.25 N	106.52 W
Cuauhtémoc, Méx.	234	19.20 N	103.36 W
Cuautémoc □[7]	286a	19.26 N	99.09 W
Cuautepec [de Hinojosa]	234	20.02 N	98.18 W
Cuautepec el Alto ◆[8]	286a	19.34 N	99.08 W
Cuautitlán	234	19.26 N	104.23 W
Cuautitlán □[7]	286a	19.39 N	99.13 W
Cuautitlán ≐	286a	19.41 N	99.13 W
Cuautitlán [de Romero Rubio]	234	19.40 N	99.11 W
Cuautla	234	20.11 N	104.21 W
Cuautla Morelos	234	18.48 N	98.57 W
Cuautzin, Cerro ∧	286a	19.09 N	99.06 W
Cuba, Port.	34	38.10 N	7.53 W
Cuba, Al., U.S.	194	32.25 N	88.22 W
Cuba, Il., U.S.	190	40.29 N	90.11 W
Cuba, Ks., U.S.	198	39.48 N	97.27 W
Cuba, Mo., U.S.	194	38.03 N	91.24 W
Cuba, N.M., U.S.	200	36.01 N	106.57 W
Cuba, N.Y., U.S.	210	42.13 N	78.16 W
Cuba □[1], N.A.	230	21.30 N	80.00 W
Cuba □[1], N.A.	240p	21.30 N	80.00 W
Cubabi, Cerro ∧	200	31.42 N	112.46 W
Cubadak	112	0.19 N	100.00 E
Cubagua, Isla I	246	10.48 N	64.10 W
Cuba Island I	276	40.38 N	73.32 W
Cubal	152	13.02 S	14.19 E
Cubal ≐, Ang.	152	11.19 S	13.48 E
Cubal ≐, Ang.	152	12.42 S	13.56 E
Cubal ≐, Ang.	152	15.22 S	12.39 E
Cuba Lake ⊜	210	42.15 N	78.18 W
Cubanea	254	41.02 S	70.16 W
Cubango (Okavango) ≐	138	18.50 S	22.25 E
Cubangui ≐	152	14.22 S	19.58 E
Čubaricha	86	57.37 N	68.22 E
Čubarovo	82	55.12 N	36.56 E
Cubatão	256	23.53 S	46.25 W
Cubatão, Serra de ⩲[4]	256	23.52 S	46.28 W
Cubati	250	6.51 S	36.21 W
Cub Hills ⩘[2]	184	54.20 N	104.30 W
Cubia ≐	152	16.01 S	21.50 E
Čublas	24	64.44 N	45.00 E
Cub Run ≐	208	38.48 N	77.28 W
Çubuk	130	40.15 N	33.02 E
Čuc ≐	250	1.22 S	53.33 W
Cucamonga	228	34.06 N	117.35 W
Cucamonga Creek ≐	280	33.57 N	117.37 W
Cucamonga Peak ∧	228	34.14 N	117.36 W
Cuccaro Vetere	68	40.09 N	15.18 E
Cucco, Monte ∧	66	43.22 N	12.45 E
Čučeviči	76	52.35 N	26.52 E
Cuchara, Río de la ≐	234	16.37 N	97.41 W
Cucharas	234	22.52 N	105.19 W
Cucharas ≐	198	37.55 N	104.32 W
Cuchi	152	14.36 S	16.58 E
Cuchi ≐	152	15.28 S	17.21 E
Cuchibi ≐	152	15.00 S	20.45 E
Cuchilla Alta, Cerro ∧	236	15.10 N	88.12 W
Cuchilla Áquila, Cerro ∧	234	21.27 N	101.03 W
Cuchillo-Có	252	38.20 S	64.37 W
Cuchillo Negro Creek ≐	200	33.08 N	107.14 W
Cuchivero ≐	246	7.40 N	65.57 W
Čuchloma	76	58.45 N	42.41 E
Čuchlomskoje, ozero ⊜	76	58.46 N	42.35 E
Cuchumatanes, Sierra de los ⩘	236	15.35 N	91.25 W
Cuckels Brook ≐	276	40.33 N	74.33 W
Cuckfield	42	51.00 N	0.09 W
Cuckney	44	53.15 N	1.08 W
Cuckold Point ›	284b	39.14 N	76.24 W
Čučkovo, S.S.S.R.	76	59.36 N	41.14 E
Čučkovo, S.S.S.R.	80	54.17 N	41.26 E
Cucuí	246	1.12 N	66.50 W
Čučuleny	78	47.02 N	28.22 E
Cucumbi	152	10.17 S	19.05 E
Cucuron	62	43.47 N	5.26 E
Cucurpe	232	30.20 N	110.43 W
Cúcuta	246	7.54 N	72.31 W
Cudachar	84	42.21 N	47.11 E
Cudahy, Ca., U.S.	280	33.57 N	118.11 W
Cudahy, Wi., U.S.	216	42.57 N	87.51 W
Cuddalore	122	11.45 N	79.45 E
Cuddapah	122	14.28 N	78.49 E
Cuddeback Lake ⊜	228	35.18 N	117.28 W
Cuddebackville	210	41.28 N	74.36 W
Cuddia ≐	70	37.53 N	12.37 E
Cuddington, Eng., U.K.	44	53.14 N	2.36 W
Cuddington, Eng., U.K.	262	53.14 N	2.36 W
Cuddle Lake ⊜	184	55.25 N	95.47 W
Cuddy	279b	40.21 N	80.09 W
Cuddy Mountain ∧	202	44.46 N	116.47 W
Cudgegong	170	32.48 S	149.49 E
Cudgegong ≐	170	32.37 S	149.43 E
Cudgewa	171b	36.12 S	147.46 E
Cudgewa Creek ≐	171b	36.03 S	147.55 E
Cudham ◆[8]	260	51.19 N	0.05 E
Cudia Park ♠	275b	43.43 N	79.13 W
Čudin	76	52.44 N	26.59 E
Cudjoe Key I	220	24.40 N	81.30 W
Čudnov	78	50.04 N	28.06 E
Čudovo	76	59.07 N	31.41 E
Čudskoje ozero (Peipsi järv) ⊜	76	58.45 N	27.30 E
Cudworth, Sk., Can.	184	52.30 N	105.45 W
Cudworth, Eng., U.K.	44	53.35 N	1.25 W
Cue	162	27.25 S	117.54 E
Cuebe ≐	152	15.48 S	17.30 E
Cueio ≐, Ang.	152	15.27 S	21.21 E
Cueio ≐, Ang.	152	16.17 S	17.46 E
Cuelei ≐	152	15.33 S	17.21 E
Cuéllar	34	41.24 N	4.19 W
Cuenca, Ec.	246	2.53 S	78.59 W
Cuenca, Esp.	34	40.04 N	2.08 W
Cuencamé [de Ceniceros]	232	24.53 N	103.42 W
Cuerámaro	234	20.37 N	101.43 W
Cuernavaca	234	18.55 N	99.15 W
Cuero	222	29.05 N	97.17 W
Cuers	62	43.14 N	6.04 E
Cuervo, Laguna del ⊜	232	29.17 N	105.57 W
Cuervos	204	32.38 N	114.52 W
Cuesmes	50	50.26 N	3.55 E
Cuesta Pass)(	226	35.21 N	120.38 W
Cueto	240p	20.39 N	75.56 W
Cuetzala del Progreso	234	18.07 N	99.50 W
Cuetzalan del Progreso	234	20.02 N	97.31 W
Cuevas del Almanzora	34	37.18 N	1.53 W
Cuevo	248	20.27 S	63.32 W
Čufarovo	80	54.06 N	47.19 E
Cuffley	260	51.42 N	0.07 W
Cufra → Al-Kufrah ⊤[4]	146	24.20 N	23.15 E
Cufré	258	34.12 S	57.06 W
Cufré, Arroyo ≐	258	34.27 S	57.09 W
Cufré, Cuchilla ⩘[2]	258	34.20 S	57.10 W
Cuggiono	62	45.31 N	8.49 E
Cugir	38	45.50 N	23.22 E
Cuglieri	71	40.11 N	8.34 E
Cugo ≐	152	7.18 S	16.39 E
Čugujev	78	49.50 N	36.41 E
Čugujevka	89	44.08 N	133.53 E
Čugunaš	86	52.52 N	87.46 E
Čuguš, gora ∧	84	43.47 N	40.16 E
Cuiabá	248	15.35 S	56.05 W
Cuiabá ≐	248	17.05 S	56.36 W
Cuiari	246	1.30 N	68.11 W
Cuichapa	234	17.59 N	94.15 W
Cuieiras ≐	246	2.50 S	60.31 W
Cuigezhuang, Zhg.	105	40.01 N	116.28 E
Cuigezhuang, Zhg.	105	40.02 N	117.54 E
Cuihuangkou	105	39.32 N	117.11 E
Cuijiatun	104	40.57 N	121.09 E
Cuijiazhuang	104	40.57 N	122.44 E
Cuilapa	236	14.17 N	90.18 W
Cuilcagh ∧	48	54.10 N	7.48 W
Cuilco	236	15.24 N	91.58 W
Cuilco (San Miguel) ≐	236	15.56 N	92.10 W
Ču-Ilijskije gory ⩘	85	43.52 N	75.00 E
Cuillin Hills ⩘[2]	46	57.15 N	6.15 W
Cuilo (Kwilu) ≐, Afr.	152	3.22 S	17.22 E
Cuilo ≐, Afr.	152	5.52 S	16.35 E
Cuilo Futa	152	6.25 S	15.44 E
Cuimba	152	6.08 S	14.38 E
Cuio	152	12.58 S	12.58 E
Cuiqiao	98	34.12 N	114.36 E
Cuiseaux	58	46.30 N	5.24 E
Cuisery	58	46.33 N	5.00 E
Cuisy	261	49.01 N	2.46 E
Cuité	250	6.29 S	36.09 W
Cuitláhuac	234	18.49 N	96.43 W
Cuíto ≐	152	18.01 S	20.48 E
Cuíto-Cuanavale	152	15.10 S	19.10 E
Cuitzeo, Lago de ⊜	234	19.55 N	101.05 W
Cuitzeo del Porvenir	234	19.59 N	101.09 W
Cuitzmala	234	19.23 N	104.59 W
Cuiuni ≐	246	0.45 S	63.07 W
Cuivre ≐	219	38.56 N	90.42 W
Cuivre, North Fork ≐	219	39.02 N	90.59 W
Cuivre, West Fork ≐	219	39.02 N	90.59 W
Cuivre River State Park ♠	219	39.02 N	90.57 W
Čuja	88	59.12 N	112.25 E
Čuja ≐, S.S.S.R.	86	50.24 N	86.39 E
Čuja ≐, S.S.S.R.	88	59.17 N	112.24 E
Cují	286c	10.28 N	67.02 W
Cukas	112	0.25 S	104.18 E
Čukčagirskoje ozero ⊜	89	52.00 N	136.36 E
Čukotskij, mys ›	180	64.14 N	173.10 W
Čukotskij poluostrov ›[1]	180	66.00 N	175.00 W
Çukurca	128	37.15 N	43.37 E
Čukurčak	85	41.47 N	71.07 E
Cukurino	83	48.05 N	37.18 E
Culaba	116	11.40 N	124.32 E
Čulak-Kurgan	85	43.46 N	69.12 E
Culaman	116	5.58 N	125.40 E
Culari ≐	250	1.27 N	53.42 W
Culasi, Pil.	116	11.26 N	122.03 E
Culasi, Pil.	116	10.43 N	125.43 E
Culasian	116	8.51 N	117.29 E
Culasi Point ›	116	11.37 N	122.42 E
Culbertson, Mt., U.S.	198	48.08 N	104.30 W
Culbertson, Ne., U.S.	198	40.13 N	100.50 W
Culbertson Run ≐	285	40.03 N	75.45 W
Culbin	168a	33.10 S	116.50 E
Culburra	170	34.57 S	150.47 E
Culcairn	166	35.40 S	147.03 E
Culcheth	262	53.27 N	2.32 W
Culdaff	48	55.18 N	7.11 W
Culdaff Bay ⊂	48	55.17 N	7.10 W
Culebra, Isla de I	240m	18.19 N	65.17 W
Culebra, Laguna de la ⊜	234	22.28 N	98.20 W
Culebra, Sierra de la ⩘	34	41.54 N	6.20 W
Culebra Peak ∧	200	37.07 N	105.11 W
Culebrinos ≐	240m	18.24 N	67.11 W
Culebrita, Isla I	240m	18.19 N	65.14 W
Culebro, Arroyo del ≐	266a	40.19 N	3.34 W
Culemborg	52	51.56 N	5.13 E
Culgoa ≐	166	29.56 S	146.20 E
Culham Inlet ⊂	162	33.55 S	120.04 E
Culiacán	232	24.48 N	107.24 W
Culiacán ≐	232	24.31 N	107.41 W
Culiacán, Cerro ∧	234	20.20 N	100.58 W
Culiacancito	232	24.50 N	107.32 W
Culion	116	11.53 N	120.01 E
Culion Island I	116	11.50 N	119.55 E
Cúllar de Baza	34	37.35 N	2.34 W
Cull Creek ≐	282	37.42 N	122.03 W
Cullen, Scot., U.K.	46	57.41 N	2.49 W
Cullen, La., U.S.	194	32.58 N	93.27 W
Cullen Bullen	170	33.18 S	150.01 E
Cullen Point ›	164	11.57 S	141.54 E
Culleoka, Tn., U.S.	194	35.28 N	86.58 W
Culleoka, Tx., U.S.	222	33.08 N	96.29 W
Cullera	34	39.10 N	0.15 W
Cullicudden	46	57.39 N	4.13 W
Cullin, Lough ⊜	48	53.57 N	9.12 W
Cullinan	158	25.40 S	28.31 E
Cullman	194	34.10 N	86.50 W
Culloden Battlesite ⊥	46	57.28 N	4.05 W
Cullom	216	40.53 N	88.16 W
Cullompton	42	50.52 N	3.24 W
Cullowhee	192	35.18 N	83.10 W
Cully	58	46.29 N	6.44 E
Cullybackey	48	54.53 N	6.21 W
Culm ≐	42	50.46 N	3.31 W
Čul'man	74	56.52 N	124.52 E
Cülmen	130	37.19 N	38.48 E
Culmore	284c	38.51 N	77.08 W
Culoz	62	45.51 N	5.47 E
Culpeper	188	38.28 N	77.59 W
Culpina	248	20.50 S	64.58 W
Culrain	46	57.55 N	4.24 W
Cults	46	57.07 N	2.10 W
Cultus Lake	224	49.04 N	121.58 W
Cultus Lake ⊜	224	49.03 N	121.58 W
Cultus Lake Provincial Park ♠	224	49.03 N	121.58 W
Culú Culú, Arroyo ≐	258	35.19 S	58.57 W
Culú Culú, Laguna ⊜	258	35.20 S	58.59 W
Culuene ≐	255	12.56 S	52.51 W
Culukidze	84	42.20 N	42.25 E
Čuluunchoroot	88	49.41 N	114.15 E
Čuluut	102	45.48 N	107.05 E
Čuluutyn ≐	88	49.11 N	100.41 E
Culvain ∧	46	56.56 N	5.17 W
Culver, In., U.S.	216	41.13 N	86.25 W
Culver, Or., U.S.	202	44.31 N	121.12 W
Culver, Point ›	162	32.54 S	124.43 E
Culver City	228	34.01 N	118.23 W
Culverden	172	42.46 S	172.51 E
Culvers Lake	210	41.10 N	74.48 W
Culverstone Green	260	51.20 N	0.21 E
Čulym	86	55.06 N	80.58 E
Čulym ≐, S.S.S.R.	86	57.43 N	83.51 E
Čulym ≐, S.S.S.R.	86	54.38 N	78.16 E
Čulyšman ≐	86	51.20 N	87.45 E
Čum	24	67.06 N	63.07 E
Cuma	152	12.52 S	15.05 E
Cuma (Cumae) ⊥	68	40.50 N	14.06 E
Čumakovo	86	55.41 N	79.02 E
Cumalı	130	36.42 N	27.27 E
Cuman'	78	50.49 N	25.53 E
Cumaná	246	10.28 N	64.10 W
Cumanacoa	246	10.15 N	63.55 W
Cumanayagua	240p	22.09 N	80.12 W
Cumaovası	130	38.15 N	27.09 E
Cumare, Cerro ∧[2]	246	0.28 N	73.52 W
Cumari	255	18.16 S	48.11 W
Cumbal	246	0.54 N	77.47 W
Cumbal, Nevado de ∧	246	0.57 N	77.52 W
Cumbe	250	10.21 S	37.14 W
Cumbee	220	28.04 N	81.55 W
Cumberland, B.C., Can.	182	49.37 N	125.01 W
Cumberland, Ia., U.S.	198	41.16 N	94.52 W
Cumberland, Ky., U.S.	192	36.58 N	82.59 W
Cumberland, Md., U.S.	188	39.39 N	78.45 W
Cumberland, Va., U.S.	192	37.29 N	78.14 W
Cumberland, Wa., U.S.	224	47.16 N	121.55 W
Cumberland, Wi., U.S.	190	45.31 N	92.01 W
Cumberland □[6], N.J., U.S.	208	39.26 N	75.14 W
Cumberland □[6], Pa., U.S.	208	40.12 N	77.12 W
Cumberland ≐	178	37.09 N	88.25 W
Cumberland, Lake ⊜[1]	194	36.57 N	84.55 W
Cumberland, South Fork ≐	192	36.58 N	84.36 W
Cumberland Bay ⊂	241h	13.16 N	61.17 W
Cumberland City	194	36.23 N	87.38 W
Cumberland Falls State Resort Park ♠	192	36.50 N	84.20 W
Cumberland Gap)(	192	36.36 N	83.41 W
Cumberland Gap National Historical Park ♠	192	36.36 N	83.40 W
Cumberland Hill	207	41.58 N	71.27 W
Cumberland House	184	53.58 N	102.16 W
Cumberland Indian Reserve ◆[4]	184	53.04 N	104.50 W
Cumberland Island National Seashore ♠	192	30.50 N	81.27 W
Cumberland Islands II	166	20.40 S	149.09 E
Cumberland Lake ⊜	184	54.02 N	102.17 W
Cumberland Peninsula ›[1]	176	66.50 N	64.00 W
Cumberland Plateau ⩘[1]	192	36.20 N	84.30 W
Cumberland Sound ⋃	176	65.10 N	65.30 W
Cumbernauld	46	55.58 N	3.59 W
Cumborah	166	29.44 S	147.46 E
Cumbres de Monterrey, Parque Nacional ♠	232	25.31 N	100.18 W
Cumbria □[6]	44	54.30 N	3.00 W
Cumbrian Mountains ⩘	44	54.30 N	3.05 W
Čumbur-Kosa	83	46.57 N	38.53 E
Cumby	222	33.08 N	95.50 W
Cumeral Nuevo	200	30.54 N	110.51 W
Cumiana	62	44.59 N	7.22 E
Čumikan	89	54.42 N	135.19 E
Cuminá → Paru de Oeste ≐	250	1.30 S	56.00 W
Cuminapanema ≐	250	1.09 S	54.54 W
Cuminestown	46	57.32 N	2.20 W
Cumming	192	34.12 N	84.08 W
Cummings Mountain ∧	228	35.03 N	118.34 W
Cummington	207	42.27 N	72.53 W
Cummins	166	34.16 S	135.44 E
Cummins, Mount ∧	182	52.03 N	118.15 W
Cummins Creek ≐	222	29.43 N	96.31 W
Cummins Range ⩘	162	19.05 S	127.10 E
Cumnock	44	55.27 N	4.16 W
Cumnor	42	51.44 N	1.20 W
Cumpas	232	30.02 N	109.48 W
Çumra	130	37.34 N	32.48 E
Cumshewa Inlet ⊂	182	53.03 N	131.45 W
Cumuripa	232	28.08 N	109.53 W
Cumwhinton	44	54.52 N	2.51 W
Čumyš ≐	86	53.31 N	83.10 E
Čun'a ≐, S.S.S.R.	74	61.36 N	96.30 E
Čuna ≐, S.S.S.R.	88	57.47 N	95.26 E
Cunani	250	2.52 N	51.06 W
Cunauaru ≐	246	3.10 S	63.01 W
Cunaviche	246	7.22 N	67.25 W
Cunco	252	38.55 S	72.02 W
Cuncumén	252	31.53 S	70.38 W
Cundeelee Reserve ◆[4]	162	30.30 S	123.25 E
Cunderdin	162	31.39 S	117.15 E
Cundinamarca □[5]	246	5.00 N	74.00 W
Čundža	86	43.32 N	79.28 E
Cunene □[5]	152	16.30 S	15.30 E
Cunene (Kunene) ≐	152	17.20 S	11.50 E
Cuneo	62	44.23 N	7.32 E
Cuneo □[4]	62	44.31 N	7.34 E
Cunewalde	54	51.06 N	14.30 E
Cuney	222	32.02 N	95.25 W
Cung Hau, Cua ≐[1]	110	9.46 N	106.34 E
Cung Son	110	13.02 N	108.58 E
Çüngüş	130	38.13 N	39.17 E
Cunha	256	23.05 S	44.58 W
Cunhambebe	256	23.00 S	44.20 W
Cunha Porã	252	26.54 S	53.09 W
Cunhinga	152	12.11 S	16.47 E
Cunhinga ≐	152	10.38 S	16.48 E
Cunhuã, Igarapé ≐	248	5.46 S	64.36 W
Cunlhat	62	45.38 N	3.35 E
Cunliffe	168b	34.05 S	137.45 E
Cunnamulla	166	28.04 S	145.41 E
Cunningham, Austl.	171a	28.09 S	151.51 E
Cunningham, Ks., U.S.	198	37.38 N	98.25 W
Cunningham, Lake ⊜	240b	25.04 N	77.26 W
Cunninghame □[9]	46	55.40 N	4.30 W
Cunningham Falls State Park ♠	208	39.35 N	77.27 W
Cunningham Park ♠, Ma., U.S.	283	42.15 N	71.03 W
Cunningham Park ♠, N.Y., U.S.	276	40.44 N	73.46 W
Čunojar	88	57.27 N	97.18 E
Cunqian	100	28.30 N	115.10 E
Čunskij, S.S.S.R.	88	57.26 N	97.31 E
Čunskij, S.S.S.R.	88	56.05 N	99.41 E
Cuntan	107	29.37 N	106.36 E
Cunucunuma ≐	246	3.13 N	65.58 W
Čuny	76	59.39 N	36.04 E
Čuokkaraš'ša ∧	24	69.57 N	24.32 E
Cuorgnè	62	45.23 N	7.39 E
Čupa	24	66.16 N	33.00 E
Čupachovka	78	50.23 N	34.36 E
Čupalejka	80	55.11 N	42.33 E
Cupar, Sk., Can.	184	50.57 N	104.12 W
Cupar, Scot., U.K.	46	56.19 N	3.01 W
Cupecê, Ribeirão ≐	287b	23.37 S	46.42 W
Cupello	66	42.04 N	14.40 E
Cuperly	50	49.04 N	4.26 E
Cupertino	226	37.19 N	122.01 W
Cupica, Golfo de ⊂	246	6.35 N	77.25 W
Cupins	255	19.51 S	51.03 W
Cupra Marittima	66	43.01 N	13.51 E
Cupramontana	66	43.27 N	13.07 E
Ćuprija	38	43.56 N	21.23 E
Čuprovo	24	64.14 N	46.36 E
Cupsaw Lake ⊜	276	41.07 N	74.15 W
Cuqiao	107	30.36 N	103.59 E
Cuquema ≐	152	12.03 S	17.40 E
Cuquenán ≐	246	4.45 N	61.30 W
Cuquío	234	20.55 N	103.02 W
Čur	80	57.07 N	52.58 E
Curaçá	250	8.59 S	39.54 W
Curaçao I	241s	12.11 N	69.00 W
Curacautín	252	38.26 S	71.53 W
Curacaví	252	33.24 S	71.09 W
Čuračiki	80	55.44 N	47.26 E
Curacó ≐	252	38.49 S	64.57 W
Curaglia	58	46.41 N	8.51 E
Curahuara	248	17.40 S	68.02 W
Curanilahue	252	37.28 S	73.21 W
Curanipe	252	35.50 S	72.38 W
Curanja ≐	248	9.58 S	70.58 W
Čurapča	74	62.00 N	132.24 E
Curapi ≐	250	1.25 N	53.49 W
Curaray ≐	246	2.20 S	74.05 W
Čurbek	85	39.59 N	69.56 E
Curcani	38	44.12 N	26.35 E
Curdies ≐	169	38.30 S	142.55 E
Cure ≐	50	47.40 N	3.41 E
Curecanti National Recreation Area ♠	200	38.24 N	107.25 W
Curepipe	157c	20.19 S	57.31 E
Curepto	252	35.05 S	72.01 W
Curequetê ≐	248	8.20 S	65.40 W
Čureški prohod)(	38	42.47 N	23.49 E
Curiapo	246	8.33 N	61.00 W
Curib	84	42.14 N	46.49 E
Curicó	252	34.59 S	71.14 W
Curicuriari ≐	246	0.14 S	66.48 W
Curicuriari, Serra ∧[2]	246	0.20 S	66.50 W
Curières, Lac ⊜	206	46.41 N	74.51 W
Curimatá	250	10.02 S	44.17 W
Curimeo	234	20.01 N	101.42 W
Curinga	68	38.49 N	16.19 E
Curious, Mount ∧	162	27.28 S	114.20 E
Curisevo ≐	255	12.14 S	53.17 W
Curitiba	252	25.25 S	49.15 W
Curitibanos	252	27.18 S	50.36 W
Curiuaú ≐	246	1.51 S	61.14 W
Curiúva	255	24.02 S	50.27 W
Curl Curl	274a	33.46 S	151.18 E
Curlew	182	48.53 N	118.35 W
Curlewis	166	31.07 S	150.16 E
Curnamona	166	31.39 S	139.32 E
Curoca Norte	152	16.18 S	12.58 E
Curone ≐	62	45.03 N	8.54 E
Curon Venosta (Graun)	64	46.49 N	10.32 E
Čurovići	78	52.10 N	32.01 E
Currais Novos	250	6.15 S	36.31 W
Curralinho	250	1.48 S	49.47 W
Curramulka	168b	34.42 S	137.42 E
Curran	219	39.44 N	89.46 W
Currant Creek ≐, Co., U.S.	200	38.29 N	105.24 W
Currant Creek ≐, Mt., U.S.	202	46.22 N	108.39 W
Currant Mountain ∧	204	38.55 N	115.25 W
Currarong	170	35.01 S	150.49 E
Currency Creek	168b	35.28 S	138.46 E
Current ≐, On., Can.	190	48.27 N	89.11 W
Current ≐, U.S.	194	36.16 N	90.57 W
Current Islands II	192	25.22 N	76.49 W
Currie, Austl.	166	39.56 S	143.52 E
Currie, Scot., U.K.	46	55.54 N	3.20 W
Currie, Mn., U.S.	198	44.04 N	95.39 W
Currituck	192	36.26 N	76.00 W
Currituck □[6]	208	36.28 N	76.03 W
Currituck Seamount ✦[3]	14	30.00 S	173.30 W
Currituck Sound ⋃	192	36.20 N	75.52 W
Curry	180	62.37 N	150.01 W
Curry, Lake ⊜[1]	226	38.22 N	122.08 W
Curry Rivel	42	51.02 N	2.52 W
Curryville, Mo., U.S.	219	39.20 N	91.20 W
Curryville, Pa., U.S.	214	40.17 N	78.20 W
Cursi	68	40.09 N	18.18 E
Curslack ◆[8]	52	53.27 N	10.13 E
Curtarolo	64	45.31 N	11.50 E
Curtea de Argeș	38	45.08 N	24.41 E
Curtice	214	41.29 N	82.49 W
Curtina	252	32.09 S	56.07 W
Curtin Springs	162	25.20 S	131.45 E
Curtis, Esp.	34	43.07 N	8.03 W
Curtis, Ar., U.S.	194	33.59 N	93.06 W
Curtis, Ne., U.S.	198	40.37 N	100.30 W
Curtis, Port ⊤[3]	166	24.00 S	151.30 E
Curtis Bay ⊂	284b	39.13 N	76.35 W
Curtis Channel ⋃	166	23.30 S	151.45 E
Curtis Creek ⊂	284b	39.12 N	76.35 W
Curtis Island I, Austl.	166	23.38 S	151.09 E
Curtis Island I, N.Z.	14	30.30 S	178.34 W
Curtis Lake ⊜	176	66.38 N	89.02 W
Curtisville	214	40.38 N	79.51 W
Curu ≐	250	3.22 S	39.04 W
Curuá ≐, Bra.	250	5.23 S	54.22 W
Curuá ≐, Bra.	250	1.55 S	55.07 W
Curuá ≐, Bra.	255	13.51 S	51.38 W
Curuá, Ilha I	250	0.48 N	50.10 W
Curuá do Sul ≐	250	2.39 S	54.10 W
Curuaés ≐	250	7.30 S	54.45 W
Curuan	116	7.13 N	122.14 E

Symbols in the index entries represent the broad categories identified in the key at the right. Symbols with superior numbers (⩘[1]) identify subcategories (see complete key on page *I · 1*).

Symbole im Register stellen die rechts im Schlüssel erklärten Kategorien dar. Symbole mit hochgestellten Ziffern (⩘[1]) bezeichnen Unterabteilungen einer Kategorie (vgl. vollständiger Schlüssel auf Seite *I · 1*).

Los símbolos incluídos en el texto del índice representan las grandes categorias identificadas con la clave a la derecha. Los símbolos con numeros en su parte superior (⩘[1]) identifican las subcategorías (véase la clave completa en la página *I · 1*).

Les symboles de l'index représentent les catégories indiquées dans la légende à droite. Les symboles suivis d'un indice (⩘[1]) représentent des sous-catégories (voir légende complète à la page *I · 1*).

Os símbolos incluídos no texto do índice representam as grandes categorias identificadas com a chave à direita. Os símbolos com números em sua parte superior (⩘[1]) identificam as subcategorias (veja-se a chave completa à página *I · 1*).

∧ Mountain	Berg	Montaña	Montagne	Montanha
⩘ Mountains	Gebirge	Montañas	Montagnes	Montanhas
)(Pass	Paß	Paso	Col	Passo
V Valley, Canyon	Tal, Cañon	Valle, Cañón	Vallée, Canyon	Vale, Canhão
⩦ Plain	Ebene	Llano	Plaine	Planície
› Cape	Kap	Cabo	Cap	Cabo
I Island	Insel	Isla	Île	Ilha
II Islands	Inseln	Islas	Îles	Ilhas
⩲ Other Topographic Features	Andere Topographische Objekte	Otros Elementos Topográficos	Autres données topographiques	Outros acidentes topográficos

ESPAÑOL / FRANÇAIS / PORTUGUÊS			
Nombre / Nom / Nome	Página / Page	Lat.°'	Long.°' W=Oeste / W=Ouest

Column 1 (Español)

Nombre	Página	Lat.	Long.
Curuá Una ≃	250	2.24 S	54.05 W
Curubandé	236	10.43 N	85.26 W
Curuçá	250	0.43 S	47.50 W
Curuçá ↔[8]	287b	23.30 S	46.25 W
Curuçá ≃	246	4.27 S	71.23 W
Curuçambaba	250	2.08 S	49.18 W
Çurug, Indon.	115a	6.15 S	106.33 E
Çurug, Jugo.	38	45.29 N	20.04 E
Curuguaty	252	24.31 S	55.42 W
Curumo	286c	10.27 N	66.52 W
Curumu	250	1.01 S	51.03 W
Curunga	152	12.51 S	21.12 E
Curupá	112	3.28 S	102.22 E
Curupá	250	9.54 S	45.54 W
Curupayty, Riacho ≃	248	22.03 S	58.00 W
C'urupinsk	78	46.37 N	32.43 E
Curupira, Sierra de ⫝	246	1.25 N	64.30 W
Cururu ≃, Bra.	248	7.12 S	58.03 W
Cururu ≃, Bra.	250	0.39 S	50.11 W
Cururu-Açu ≃	250	8.58 S	57.13 W
Cururupu	250	1.50 S	44.52 W
Curutu ≃	246	5.05 N	63.28 W
Curuzú Cuatiá	252	29.47 S	58.03 W
Curva Grande	250	2.37 S	45.27 W
Curvelo	156	18.45 S	44.25 W
Curwensville	214	40.58 N	78.31 W
Curwensville Lake ⊜[1]	214	40.55 N	78.37 W
Curwensville State Park ♦	214	40.55 N	78.34 W
Cusago	266b	45.27 N	9.02 E
Cusano Milanino	62	45.33 N	9.11 E
Cusano Mutri	68	41.20 N	14.30 E
Cusapin	236	9.11 N	81.54 W
Cusco → Cuzco	248	3.31 S	71.59 W
Cuscuzeiro, Pico do ⋀	256	23.18 S	44.47 W
Cushabatay ≃	248	7.09 S	75.08 W
Cushendall	48	55.06 N	6.04 W
Cushendun	48	55.07 N	6.03 W
Cushina ≃	48	53.11 N	7.05 W
Cushing, Ok., U.S.	196	35.59 N	96.46 W
Cushing, Tx., U.S.	222	31.43 N	94.50 W
Cushing Memorial State Park ♦	283	42.10 N	70.45 W
Cushman	194	35.52 N	91.45 W
Cushman, Lake ⊜[1]	197	47.28 N	123.14 W
Cusiana ≃	246	4.33 N	71.51 W
Cusick	202	48.20 N	117.17 W
Cushuiriáchic	232	28.14 N	106.50 W
Çusna, Monte ⋀	64	44.17 N	10.23 E
Çusovaja ≃	86	58.13 N	56.22 E
Çusovoj	86	58.17 N	57.49 E
Cusset	32	46.08 N	3.28 E
Cusseta	192	32.18 N	84.46 W
Cussewago Creek ≃	214	41.38 N	80.11 W
Cussey-sur-l'Ognon	32	47.20 N	5.56 E
Cusso ≃	152	14.16 S	15.36 E
Çust, N.Z.	172	43.19 S	172.22 E
Çust, S.S.S.R.	85	41.00 N	71.15 E
Custar	216	41.17 N	83.51 W
Custer, Mi., U.S.	190	43.57 N	86.13 W
Custer, Mt., U.S.	202	46.07 N	107.33 W
Custer, Ok., U.S.	196	35.40 N	98.53 W
Custer, S.D., U.S.	198	43.46 N	103.35 W
Custer, Wa., U.S.	224	48.55 N	122.38 W
Custer Battlefield National Monument ♦	202	45.32 N	107.20 W
Custer City	214	41.54 N	78.39 W
Custer Creek ≃	198	46.42 N	105.29 W
Custer State Park ♦	198	43.43 N	103.23 W
Custines	32	48.48 N	6.09 E
Custódia	250	3.07 S	37.39 W
Cut, Nuhu I	164	5.35 S	133.00 E
Cutato ≃	152	10.33 S	16.48 E
Cut Bank	202	48.37 N	112.19 W
Cutbank ≃	188	54.44 N	118.37 W
Cut Bank Creek ≃, N.A.	198	48.35 N	100.52 W
Cut Bank Creek ≃, Mt., U.S.	202	48.29 N	112.14 W
Cut Beaver Lake ⊜	188	53.47 N	102.38 W
Cutejevo	80	55.16 N	47.47 E
Cutervo	248	6.22 S	78.51 W
Cuthand Creek ≃	194	33.23 N	94.57 W
Cuthbert	192	31.46 N	84.47 W
Cut Knife	184	52.44 N	109.01 W
Cutler, Ca., U.S.	184	36.31 N	119.17 W
Cutler, Me., U.S.	188	44.39 N	67.12 W
Cutler Ridge	220	25.34 N	80.20 W
Cutlerville	216	42.50 N	85.39 W
Cutovo	78	49.43 N	35.10 E
Cutral-Có	252	38.56 S	69.14 W
Cutro	68	39.02 N	16.59 E
Cutrofiano	68	40.07 N	18.12 E
Cuttack	120	20.30 N	85.50 E
Cuttyhunk Island I	207	41.25 N	70.56 W
Cutyr'	80	57.24 N	53.17 E
Cutzamalá ≃	234	18.22 N	100.39 W
Cutzamala de Pinzón	234	18.28 N	100.34 W
Cutzio	234	18.39 N	100.54 W
Çuvašskaja Avtonomnaja Sovetskaja Socialističeskaja Respublika □[3]	80	55.30 N	47.00 E
Cuvette □[5]	152	0.00	16.00 E
Cuvier, Cape ⟩	162	24.05 S	113.22 E
Cuvilly	50	49.33 N	2.42 E
Cuvo ≃	152	10.50 S	13.47 E
Cuxhaven	48	53.52 N	8.42 E
Cuxton	260	51.22 N	0.27 E
Cuyabá → Cuiabá	248	15.35 S	56.05 W
Cuyaguateje ≃	240p	22.05 N	83.58 W
Cuyahoga ≃	214	41.30 N	81.41 W
Cuyahoga □[6]	214	41.30 N	81.42 W
Cuyahoga County Airport ⊠	279a	41.24 N	81.29 W
Cuyahoga Falls	214	41.08 N	81.29 W
Cuyahoga Heights	279a	41.26 N	81.39 W
Cuyahoga Valley National Recreation Area ♦	214	41.20 N	81.35 W
Cuyama ≃	204	34.54 N	120.18 W
Cuyamaca Peak ⋀	204	32.57 N	116.36 W
Cuyamaca Rancho State Park ♦	204	32.58 N	116.32 W
Cuyamel	236	15.38 N	88.12 W
Cuyapo	116	15.46 N	120.40 E
Cuyk	52	51.44 N	5.52 E
Cuyler	210	42.44 N	75.57 W
Cuylerville	210	42.47 N	77.52 W
Cuyo	116	10.51 N	121.28 E
Cuyo East Pass ⟩	116	11.00 N	121.28 E
Cuyo Islands II	116	11.04 N	120.57 E
Cuyo West Pass ⟩	116	11.04 N	120.51 E
Cuyubini ≃	246	8.20 N	60.20 W
Cuyuni ≃	246	6.23 N	58.41 W
Cuyutlán, Laguna de ⪜	234	19.00 N	104.10 W
Cuzco	248	13.31 S	71.59 W
Cuzco □[5]	248	13.30 S	72.30 W
Cuzik	86	58.03 N	101.18 E
Cuzna ≃	34	38.04 N	4.41 W
Cuzzago	66	46.00 N	8.22 E
Cvetkovo	78	49.11 N	31.32 E
Cvetnoje	86	45.54 N	45.54 E
Cvetnye	78	53.42 N	61.58 E
Cvikov	54	50.48 N	14.40 E
Cwmbran	48	51.39 N	3.00 W
Cyangugu	154	2.29 S	28.54 E
Cybinka	30	52.12 N	14.48 E
Cybulev	78	49.06 N	29.50 E
Cyclades → Kikládhes II	38	37.30 N	25.00 E
Cyclone	214	41.50 N	78.35 W
Cygan	216	41.14 N	83.38 W
Cygnet Bay c	162	16.35 S	123.05 E

Column 2 (Français)

Nom	Page	Lat.	Long.
Cygnet Lake ⊜	184	56.47 N	94.54 W
Cygnet River	168b	35.42 S	137.31 E
Cylburn Park ♦	284b	39.21 N	76.39 W
Cynin ≃	42	51.48 N	4.29 W
Cynthiana, Ky., U.S.	218	38.23 N	84.17 W
Cynthiana, Oh., U.S.	218	39.10 N	83.21 W
Cynwyl Elfed	42	51.55 N	4.22 W
Cypern → Cyprus □[1]	130	35.00 N	33.00 E
Cypress, Ca., U.S.	280	33.49 N	118.02 W
Cypress, La., U.S.	194	31.36 N	93.02 W
Cypress, Tx., U.S.	222	29.58 N	95.42 W
Cypress Bayou ≃	194	33.05 N	91.42 W
Cypress Creek ≃, Fl., U.S.	220	28.05 N	82.24 W
Cypress Creek ≃, Tx., U.S.	194	30.19 N	93.45 W
Cypress Creek ≃, Tx., U.S.	222	30.02 N	95.19 W
Cypress Gardens ♦	220	28.00 N	81.42 W
Cypress Hills ⋌[2]	184	49.40 N	109.30 W
Cypress Hills Provincial Park ♦, Ab., Can.	184	49.39 N	110.10 W
Cypress Hills Provincial Park ♦, Sk., Can.	184	49.39 N	109.30 W
Cypress Island I	224	48.35 N	122.42 W
Cypress Lake ⊜, Sk., Can.	184	49.28 N	109.29 W
Cypress Lake ⊜, Fl., U.S.	220	28.05 N	81.19 W
Cypress Point ⟩	226	36.35 N	121.59 W
Cypress Quarters	220	27.15 N	80.48 W
Cypress River	184	49.34 N	99.05 W
Cypress Swamp ⪬	208	37.02 N	76.53 W
Cypress Swamp ⪬	208	38.30 N	75.17 W
Cyprus □[1], Asia	22	35.00 N	33.00 E
Cyprus □[1], Asia	130	35.00 N	33.00 E
Cyprus, North □[1]	22	35.15 N	33.40 E
Cyrenaica → Barqah □[9]	146	31.00 N	22.30 E
Cyrene	219	39.17 N	91.06 W
Cyrene ⊥	146	32.49 N	21.52 E
Cyril	196	34.53 N	98.12 W
Cyrildene ↔[8]	273d	26.11 S	28.06 E
Cyrus Field Bay c	176	62.50 N	64.55 W
Cysoing	50	50.34 N	3.13 E
Cythera → Kíthira I	38	36.20 N	22.58 E
Czaplinek	30	53.34 N	16.14 E
Czarna Białostocka	30	53.19 N	23.16 E
Czarna Woda	30	53.51 N	18.06 E
Czarne	30	53.42 N	16.57 E
Czarnków	30	52.55 N	16.34 E
Czechoslovakia (Československo) □[1], Europe	22	49.30 N	17.00 E
Czechoslovakia (Československo) □[1], Europe	30	49.30 N	17.00 E
Czempiń	30	52.10 N	16.47 E
Czerniejewo	30	52.26 N	17.30 E
Czernowitz → Černovcy	78	48.18 N	25.56 E
Czersk	30	53.48 N	18.00 E
Czerwieńsk	30	52.01 N	15.25 E
Czestochowa □[4]	30	50.49 N	19.06 E
Czestochowa	30	50.40 N	19.15 E
Człopa	30	53.06 N	16.08 E
Człuchów	30	53.41 N	17.21 E
Czudec	30	49.57 N	21.50 E

D

Nom	Page	Lat.	Long.
Da → Black ≃, Asia	110	21.15 N	105.20 E
Da ≃, Zhg.	100	28.10 N	120.14 E
Daaden	56	50.44 N	7.58 E
Da'an, Zhg.	89	45.28 N	124.18 E
Da'an, Zhg.	100	23.05 N	115.37 E
Da'an, Zhg.	107	29.23 N	106.11 E
Da'an, Zhg.	100	23.19 N	110.34 E
Daanbantayan	116	11.14 N	124.00 E
Daba	104	46.20 N	122.00 E
Dabāb, Jabal ad- ⋀	132	31.02 N	35.38 E
Dabagou	104	42.27 N	122.00 E
Dab'ah, Ra's ad- ⟩	140	31.05 N	28.26 E
Dabaila	150	8.22 N	4.26 W
Dabali	104	41.51 N	120.37 E
Daba Ling ⋀	100	24.28 N	113.17 E
Dabancheng	86	43.19 N	88.18 E
Dabangdan	100	31.37 N	113.41 E
Dabaozhuang	104	40.18 N	116.58 E
Dabaozi	105	31.55 N	109.05 E
Dabat	144	12.58 N	37.48 E
Dabayingzi	104	40.18 N	116.58 E
Dabbūriya	132	32.42 N	35.22 E
Dabeiba	246	7.01 N	76.16 W
Dabeiwa	104	42.05 N	118.36 E
Dabeiyingzi	104	40.29 N	122.08 E
Dabendorf	54	52.14 N	13.26 E
Daber → Dobra	30	53.35 N	15.18 E
Daberas	156	28.07 S	18.36 E
Dabhoi	120	22.11 N	73.26 E
Dabhol	120	17.36 N	73.10 E
Dąbie	54	52.11 N	14.40 E
Dąbie, Jezioro ⊜	54	53.27 N	14.40 E
Dabie Shan ⋀	100	31.20 N	115.20 E
Dabilda	146	12.46 N	14.34 E
Dāblān	130	34.52 N	40.34 E
Dabnou	150	14.09 N	5.22 E
Dabob Bay c	224	47.47 N	122.50 W
Dabola	150	10.45 N	11.07 W
Dabong	114	5.23 N	102.01 E
Dabou	150	5.19 N	4.23 W
Dabra	124	25.53 N	78.20 E
Dābri ↔[8]	272a	28.37 N	77.05 E
Dabrowa Białostocka	30	53.39 N	23.20 E
Dabrowa Tarnowska	30	50.11 N	21.00 E
Dabsan Hu ⊜	102	36.58 N	94.55 E
Dabu	100	24.20 N	116.43 E
Dacaitun	102	34.10 N	117.18 E
Dacangzhen	100	34.07 N	120.18 E
Dacaoyuan	150	10.48 N	35.10 E
Dacca → Dhaka	126	23.43 N	90.25 E
Dachang, Zhg.	104	32.14 N	119.40 E
Dachang, Zhg.	100	28.24 N	109.12 E
Dachang, Zhg.	107	31.45 N	118.18 E
Dachangshan Dao I	60	39.18 N	122.38 E
Dachau	56	48.15 N	11.27 E
Dachau-Moos ⪬	257	48.10 N	11.27 E
Dachengji	104	33.52 N	119.26 E
Dachen Dao I	106	28.27 N	121.56 E
Dachen Shan I	106	30.21 N	121.52 E

Column 3 (Portuguès)

Nome	Página	Lat.	Long.
Dachixu	100	25.10 N	116.46 E
Dachongqiao	105	40.23 N	117.41 E
Dachsberg ⋀[2]	263	51.30 N	6.30 E
Dachsteinhöhlen ⊥[5]	64	47.32 N	13.43 E
Dačice	61	49.05 N	15.26 E
Dac Lac, Cao Nguyen ⋌[1]	110	12.50 N	108.05 E
Dacoma	196	36.39 N	98.33 W
Dacorum □[8]	260	51.45 N	0.30 W
Dac To	110	14.42 N	107.51 E
Dacun, Zhg.	102	27.55 N	101.08 E
Dacun, Zhg.	106	31.12 N	119.40 E
Dadal	88	49.01 N	111.37 E
Dadanawa	246	2.50 N	59.30 W
Dadaolizhuang	105	39.59 N	116.59 E
Dadaotun	104	41.46 N	122.13 E
Dadar ↔[8]	272c	19.01 N	72.50 E
Daday	130	41.28 N	33.28 E
Dadayungou	104	41.23 N	123.25 E
Daddys Creek ≃	192	36.05 N	84.47 W
Dade □[6]	220	25.33 N	80.32 W
Dade Battlefield Historic Memorial ⊥	220	28.38 N	82.09 W
Dade City	220	28.21 N	82.11 W
Dadeldhurā	124	29.18 N	80.35 E
Dadeville	194	32.49 N	85.45 W
Dādhar	120	29.28 N	67.39 E
Dadian	100	33.36 N	117.16 E
Dadiangas → General Santos	116	6.07 N	125.11 E
Dadianzi	104	42.11 N	124.02 E
Dadinjiawopu	104	41.13 N	122.16 E
D'adino	88	55.44 N	105.45 E
Dadiya	146	9.37 N	11.26 E
Dadnah	128	25.33 N	56.21 E
Dadonggejiang	105	39.51 N	116.48 E
Dadongzhou	104	41.44 N	124.00 E
Dadou ≃	32	43.44 N	1.49 E
Dādpur, India	272b	22.42 N	88.33 E
Dādpur, India	272b	22.54 N	88.31 E
Dādra and Nagar Haveli □[8]	122	20.05 N	73.00 E
Dādu	120	26.44 N	67.47 E
Dadu ≃	102	29.33 N	103.45 E
Dadugang	102	22.23 N	100.55 E
Dadukou, Zhg.	100	25.44 N	119.05 E
Dadukou, Zhg.	107	28.45 N	105.13 E
Dadukou, Zhg.	107	29.28 N	106.29 E
Daegu → Taegu	98	35.52 N	128.35 E
Daejeon → Taejŏn	98	36.20 N	127.26 E
Daerhanwangfu	89	44.19 N	122.15 E
Da'erhao	98	41.45 N	116.01 E
Daet	116	14.05 N	122.55 E
Daf'	146	28.03 N	19.57 E
Dafan, Zhg.	100	29.41 N	114.40 E
Dafan, Zhg.	104	32.28 N	122.11 E
Dafang	100	27.04 N	105.31 E
Dafangshen, Zhg.	104	42.25 N	123.14 E
Dafangshen, Zhg.	104	42.34 N	123.28 E
Dafangshen, Zhg.	104	42.36 N	123.04 E
Dafanpuzi	104	41.37 N	122.50 E
Dafna	132	33.14 N	35.38 E
Dafoe	184	51.46 N	104.32 W
Dafoe ≃	184	55.55 N	94.48 W
Dafoe Lake ⊜	184	55.43 N	96.15 W
Da Fo Si (Great Buddha Temple) ⊻[1]	106	30.16 N	120.09 E
Dafu	100	29.55 N	115.58 E
Dafu	100	30.52 N	113.32 E
Dāfūr al-Janūbīyah □[4]	144	11.45 N	25.25 E
Dagā ≃	110	16.56 N	94.45 E
Daga Medo	144	7.59 N	43.01 E
Dagana	150	16.31 N	15.30 W
Dagang, Zhg.	105	38.52 N	117.26 E
Dagang, Zhg.	106	22.49 N	113.23 E
Dagang, Zhg.	100	33.12 N	120.07 E
Dagang, Zhg.	106	22.39 N	119.39 E
Dagangwanzhai	104	40.49 N	122.33 E
Dagango de Arriba	266a	40.33 N	3.27 W
Dagaokan	104	40.46 N	122.22 E
Dagaolitun	104	41.10 N	122.28 E
Dagaoyang	106	30.35 N	120.26 E
Daga Post	144	9.12 N	33.58 E
Dagardi	130	39.26 N	29.00 E
Dagash	140	19.22 N	33.24 E
Dagbeli	220	34.02 N	102.30 E
Dagcanglhamo	102	34.02 N	102.30 E
Dagda	76	56.06 N	27.32 E
Dagløkke	41	55.04 N	10.53 E
Dagemann ↔[8]	260	51.32 N	0.10 E

Column 4 (continuation)

Nome	Página	Lat.	Long.
Dahijuri	126	22.31 N	86.59 E
Da Hinggan Ling ⋀	90	49.00 N	122.00 E
Dahīrpur ↔[8]	272a	28.43 N	77.12 E
Dahl	56	51.18 N	7.31 E
Dahl ⋀	263	51.11 N	6.26 E
Dahlak Archipelago II	144	15.45 N	40.30 E
Dahlem	56	50.23 N	6.33 E
Dahlem ↔[8]	264a	52.28 N	13.17 E
Dahlem, Museum ⊻	264a	52.27 N	13.18 E
Dahlen	54	51.22 N	12.59 E
Dahlenburg	54	53.11 N	10.44 E
Dahlerau	263	51.13 N	7.19 E
Dahlewitz	54	52.19 N	13.26 E
Dahlgren, Il., U.S.	194	38.12 N	88.41 W
Dahlgren, Va., U.S.	208	38.19 N	77.03 W
Dahlhausen ↔[8]	54	53.03 N	12.20 E
Dahlia	148	18.35 S	27.08 E
Dahlonega	192	34.31 N	83.59 W
Dahlonega Plateau ⋌[1]	192	34.10 N	84.20 W
Dahlwitz-Hoppegarten	54	52.30 N	13.38 E
Dahmani	54	35.57 N	8.50 E
Dahmarū	142	28.41 N	30.49 E
Dahme, B.R.D.	54	54.13 N	11.04 E
Dahme, D.D.R.	54	51.52 N	13.25 E
Dahme ≃	54	52.25 N	13.35 E
Dāhod	120	22.50 N	74.16 E
Dahomey → Benin □[1]	150	9.30 N	2.15 E
Dahong	88	31.53 N	121.17 E
Dahongqi	104	41.52 N	122.36 E
Dahong Shan ⋌	100	31.30 N	113.00 E
Dahongtaizi	105	38.51 N	115.37 E
Dahoucun	105	38.51 N	115.37 E
Dahra	146	29.34 N	17.50 E
Dahra ⋌	34	36.25 N	1.00 E
Dahsah, Wādī ad- ⋎	132	27.19 N	31.26 E
Dahu, Zhg.	100	26.22 N	119.05 E
Dahu, Zhg.	100	26.04 N	117.19 E
Dahua	100	23.44 N	107.59 E
Dahuan	100	22.33 N	113.29 E
Dahuangdi	104	42.08 N	122.27 E
Dahuangqi	100	36.56 N	115.15 E
Dahuangpu	105	39.26 N	117.16 E
Dahuangshanpu	104	41.16 N	121.23 E
Dahuashan	105	40.17 N	117.04 E
Dahuasi	107	30.05 N	104.08 E
Dahujiang	104	26.10 N	114.57 E
Dahūk	130	37.00 N	43.00 E
Dahuni	164	10.31 S	149.55 E
Dahuofang Shuiku ⊜[1]	104	41.55 N	124.15 E
Dahy, Nafūd ad- ⋌	128	22.00 N	45.35 E
Dai I	175e	7.57 S	160.37 E
Dai, Pulau I	164	7.33 S	129.41 E
Daian	38	44.00 N	25.59 E
Daibosatsu-rei ⋀	94	35.05 N	138.33 E
Daibu, Zhg.	100	32.19 N	117.12 E
Daibu, Zhg.	106	31.18 N	119.30 E
Daien	94	35.19 N	139.32 E
Daiei	96	35.29 N	133.45 E
Daigo	94	36.46 N	140.21 E
Daigo	270	34.57 N	135.50 E
Daiguantun	105	39.57 N	117.50 E
Dai Hai ⊜	102	40.31 N	112.43 E
Daihaiyingzi	104	42.30 N	121.26 E
Daiji	100	33.48 N	115.03 E
Daijiagou	107	30.00 N	106.33 E
Daijin, Zhg.	100	32.56 N	120.10 E
Daikanbō ⋀	96	33.00 N	131.04 E
Daiku-u	110	17.47 N	96.40 E
Dā'il	132	32.45 N	36.06 E
Dailekh	124	28.50 N	81.44 E
Dailing	89	47.07 N	129.02 E
Daimanji-san ⋀	92	36.15 N	133.19 E
Daimiel	34	39.04 N	3.37 W
Daimon, Nihon	266	34.55 N	133.45 E
Daimon, Nihon	268	35.53 N	139.44 E
Daimukan-zan ⋀	94	32.43 N	120.06 E
Dainan	100	32.43 N	120.06 E
Daingean	48	53.18 N	7.17 W
Dainichiga-take ⋀	94	36.00 N	139.50 E
Dainippon-Tokyo ⋀	94	35.41 N	139.46 E
Dairago	62	45.35 N	8.52 E
Daireaux	252	36.36 S	61.45 W
Dairen → Dalian	98	38.53 N	121.35 E
Dairsie	46	56.20 N	2.56 W
Dairy	46	55.43 N	4.43 W
Dairy City	280	33.58 N	118.01 W
Dairy Creek, East Fork ≃	224	45.34 N	123.09 W
Dairy Creek, West Fork ≃	224	45.34 N	123.09 W
Dairyland	210	41.23 N	74.33 W
Dairyland Reservoir ⊜[1]	224	41.45 N	91.00 W
Dairy Valley → Cerritos	280	33.51 N	118.05 W
Dai-sen ⋀	96	35.22 N	133.33 E
Daisen-oki-kokuritsu-kōen ♦	92	35.20 N	133.20 E
Daisetsu-zan-kokuritsu-kōen ♦	92a	43.35 N	142.57 E
Daisetta	222	30.06 N	94.38 W
Daishan	106	30.16 N	122.15 E
Daishin	94	37.12 N	140.15 E
Daisie	96	34.18 N	130.56 E
Daitō, Nihon	270	34.42 N	135.38 E
Daitō, Nihon	270	34.42 N	135.38 E
Daiwa, Nihon	94	34.57 N	132.39 E
Daixi	106	30.40 N	120.07 E
Daiyang	94	36.53 N	140.13 E
Daixin ⋌	100	43.40 N	116.00 E
Daixi	106	30.40 N	120.07 E
Daiyun Shan ⋀	100	25.38 N	118.13 E
Dajabón	238	19.33 N	71.42 W
Dajal	122	29.33 N	70.23 E
Da Jānīyah, Jabal ad- ⋀	130	30.34 N	35.43 E
Dajarra	166	21.41 S	139.31 E
Dajian Shan ⋀	102	26.12 N	100.13 E
Dajin ≃	102	30.45 N	101.55 E
Dajing, Zhg.	102	37.26 N	102.55 E
Dajin Shan I	106	30.41 N	121.24 E
Dājkola	126	26.11 N	87.51 E
Dakanpu	104	41.32 N	121.06 E

Column 5 (continuation)

Nome	Página	Lat.	Long.
Dakanzi	104	40.52 N	122.53 E
Dakar	150	14.40 N	17.26 W
Dakar □[4]	150	14.45 N	17.25 W
Dākätia ≃[1]	126	22.57 N	90.42 E
Dakeng	100	26.18 N	115.32 E
Dakengkou	100	24.33 N	113.37 E
Daketa ≃	144	7.16 N	42.13 E
Dak Glei	110	15.11 N	107.48 E
Dakhal, Bi'r ad- ⋎[4]	140	28.40 N	32.24 E
Dakhal, Wādī ad- ⋎	142	28.49 N	32.45 E
Dākhilah, Al-Wāhāt ad- ⋌[4]	140	25.30 N	29.05 E
Dakhin Shāhbāzpur I	126	22.30 N	90.45 E
Dakhla	148	23.43 N	15.57 W
Dakhlet Nouādhibou □[4]	148	20.40 N	16.00 W
Dakingari	150	11.37 N	4.01 E
Dakka → Dhaka	110	23.43 N	90.25 E
Dākoānk	110	7.02 N	93.43 E
Dakongcheng	105	39.30 N	117.09 E
Dakongwan	104	40.51 N	122.19 E
Dakoro	150	14.31 N	6.46 E
Dakota City, Ia., U.S.	190	42.43 N	94.12 W
Dakota City, Ne., U.S.	198	42.24 N	96.25 W
Dakou	100	34.27 N	112.44 E
Dakoutou	100	39.35 N	117.14 E
Đakovica	38	42.23 N	20.25 E
Đakovo	38	45.19 N	18.25 E
Dakshin Gangotri ⊐[3]	5	70.05 S	12.00 E
Dakshingram	126	24.03 N	87.48 E
Dakumu	88	48.51 N	124.18 E
Dakunlun	90	33.30 N	113.00 E
Dákura, Laguna c	236	14.24 N	83.15 W
Dakwa	154	3.40 N	26.26 E
Dakwah, Tall ad- ⋌[2]	132	30.43 N	35.21 E
Dala, Ang.	152	8.05 S	15.50 E
Dala, Ang.	152	11.03 S	20.17 E
Dala, Sol.Is.	175e	8.35 S	160.40 E
Dalaas	58	47.07 N	10.00 E
Dalaba	150	10.42 N	12.15 W
Dalaban	105	10.28 N	9.27 W
Dala Cachibo	152	10.28 S	16.40 E
Dalad Qi	102	40.28 N	110.02 E
Dala-Floda	40	60.31 N	14.47 E
Dalaguete	116	9.46 N	123.32 E
Dalahan (Shiqizhan)	89	52.06 N	125.46 E
Dala-Husby	40	60.33 N	16.11 E
Dala-Järna	40	60.33 N	14.21 E
Dalaji	146	9.29 N	10.06 E
Dalälven ⊜	40	60.38 N	17.27 E
Dalama	100	37.47 N	28.04 E
Dalaman ≃	130	36.50 N	28.40 E
Dalandzadgad	88	43.35 N	104.25 E
Dalane □[1]	26	58.35 N	6.20 E
Dalangganem Islands II	116	11.52 N	30.28 E
Dalao	100	23.19 N	114.47 E
Dalarna □[9]	26	61.01 N	14.04 E
Dalarö	26	59.08 N	18.24 E
Dalat, Malay.	114	2.44 N	111.56 E
Da Lat, Viet.	110	11.56 N	108.26 E
Dalayacocu ≃	250	4.48 N	57.27 W
Dalbandin	128	28.53 N	64.25 E
Dälbandin	128	28.53 N	64.25 E
Dalbeattie	44	54.56 N	3.49 W
Dalby, Austl.	166	27.11 S	151.16 E
Dalby, Sve.	41	55.40 N	13.20 E
Dalby Söderskogs Nationalpark ♦	41	55.43 N	13.17 E
Dalcahue	254	42.23 S	73.40 W
Dalch ≃	42	50.52 N	3.47 W
Dale, Nor.	26	61.22 N	5.24 E
Dale, Nor.	26	60.35 N	5.49 E
Dale, Wales, U.K.	42	51.42 N	5.11 W
Dale, In., U.S.	194	38.10 N	86.59 W
Dale, Pa., U.S.	214	40.18 N	78.54 W
Dale, Tx., U.S.	222	29.59 N	97.34 W
Dale ≃	168a	32.10 S	116.49 E
Dale Hollow Lake ⊜[1]	192	36.35 N	85.18 W
Dale Lake ⊜	204	34.08 N	115.42 W
Dalen	26	59.27 N	8.00 E
Dalengtu	105	41.11 N	113.45 E
Dalešice, údolní nádrž ⊜[1]	61	49.06 N	16.05 E
Daly Bay c	176	64.33 N	89.40 W
Daly City	226	37.42 N	122.27 W
Daly River Aboriginal Reserve ♦[4]	164	14.20 S	130.00 E
Daly Waters	164	16.15 S	133.22 E

Column 6 (continuation)

Nome	Página	Lat.	Long.
Dallas, Or., U.S.	202	44.55 N	123.18 W
Dallas, Pa., U.S.	210	41.20 N	75.57 W
Dallas, Tx., U.S.	222	32.46 N	96.47 W
Dallas, Wi., U.S.	190	45.15 N	91.48 W
Dallas □[6]	222	32.17 N	96.47 W
Dallas Center	190	41.41 N	93.57 W
Dallas City	190	40.38 N	91.10 W
Dallas-Fort Worth Regional Airport ⊠	222	32.54 N	97.01 W
Dallas Naval Air Station ■	222	32.44 N	96.59 W
Dallastown	208	39.53 N	76.38 W
Dallgow	54	52.32 N	13.05 E
Dalli Rājhara	122	20.35 N	81.04 E
Dall Island I	182	54.50 N	132.55 W
Dalmā I	128	24.30 N	52.20 E
Dalmacija □[9]	36	43.00 N	17.00 E
Dalmatian Vélez Sarsfield	252	32.36 S	63.35 W
Dalmally	84	56.24 N	4.58 W
Dal'mamedli	84	40.43 N	46.54 E
Dalmatia	208	40.39 N	76.54 W
Dalmatia → Dalmacija □[9]	36	43.00 N	17.00 E
Dalmatovo	86	56.16 N	62.56 E
Dalmau	124	26.04 N	81.02 E
Dalmellington	44	55.19 N	4.24 W
Dalmeny	184	52.20 N	106.46 W
Dalmine	62	45.39 N	9.36 E
Dalmose	41	55.18 N	11.26 E
Dal'n'aja	89	45.56 N	142.04 E
Dal'n'aja Muja ⋀	88	54.21 N	103.37 E
Dalnaspidal	46	56.50 N	4.14 W
Dal'negorsk	89	44.35 N	135.35 E
Dal'nee → Konstantinovo		55.49 N	44.06 E
Dal'nerečensk	89	45.55 N	133.43 E
Dal'ne-Rusanovo	82	54.15 N	36.45 E
Dal'nik	78	46.28 N	30.34 E
Daloa	150	6.53 N	6.27 W
Dalongchang	105	39.50 N	116.06 E
Dalongtan	100	38.18 N	115.18 E
Dalongtian	100	24.14 N	115.44 E
Dalovice	54	50.11 N	12.55 E
Dalqū	140	20.07 N	30.37 E
Dalroy	182	51.07 N	113.39 W
Dalry, Scot., U.K.	44	55.07 N	4.10 W
Dalry, Scot., U.K.	46	55.43 N	4.44 W
Dalrymple	44	55.24 N	4.35 W
Dalrymple, Mount ⋀	166	21.02 S	148.38 E
Dalrymple Creek ≃	171a	27.59 S	151.46 E
Dalrymple Lake ⊜	212	44.38 N	79.07 W
Dalsbruk	26	60.02 N	22.31 E
Dalsingpara	126	26.47 N	89.22 E
Dalsing Sarai	124	25.40 N	85.50 E
Dalsjöfors	26	57.43 N	13.05 E
Dals-Långed	26	58.30 N	12.50 E
Dalsland □[9]	26	58.50 N	12.00 E
Dältengänj	124	24.02 N	84.04 E
Dalton, S. Afr.	158	29.20 S	30.40 E
Dalton, Eng., U.K.	262	53.34 N	2.46 W
Dalton, Ga., U.S.	192	34.47 N	84.58 W
Dalton, Ma., U.S.	207	42.28 N	73.10 W
Dalton, Oh., U.S.	214	40.47 N	81.41 W
Dalton, N.Y., U.S.	212	42.32 N	77.57 W
Dalton, Pa., U.S.	210	41.32 N	75.44 W
Dalton City	219	39.43 N	88.48 W
Dalton Gardens	202	47.43 N	116.45 W
Dalton Iceberg Tongue ⊻	9	66.15 S	121.30 E
Dalton-in-Furness	262	54.09 N	3.11 W
Dalu	104	24.23 N	123.19 E
Dalubeikou	105	38.59 N	117.12 E
Daludalu	114	1.05 N	100.15 E
Daluis, Gorges de ⋎	62	44.04 N	6.49 E
Dalum, B.R.D.	52	52.35 N	7.14 E
Dalum, Dan.	41	55.22 N	10.23 E
Daluojiazhuang	106	32.09 N	120.08 E
Daluotaozi	104	41.17 N	122.52 E
Daluoxi	100	25.14 N	118.36 E
Daluping	100	24.28 N	114.26 E
Dalupiri Island I, Pil.	116	19.05 N	121.14 E
Dalupiri Island I, Pil.	116	12.29 N	124.16 E
Daluxi	100	25.14 N	118.36 E
Dalview	273d	26.15 S	28.21 E
Dalvík	46	65.59 N	18.32 W
Dalwallinu	162	30.17 S	116.40 E
Dalwhinnie	46	56.56 N	4.14 W
Dalworthington Gardens	222	32.42 N	97.10 W
Daly ≃	164	13.20 S	130.19 E

ENGLISH — Name | Page | Lat.°′ | Long.°′
DEUTSCH — Name | Seite | Breite°′ | Länge°′ E = Ost

Damianópolis 255 14.33 S 46.10 W
Damianzhen 107 30.36 N 104.10 E
Damiao, Zhg. 98 42.26 N 118.22 E
Damiao, Zhg. 98 34.20 N 117.23 E
Damiao, Zhg. 102 37.18 N 104.39 E
Damiao, Zhg. 104 42.33 N 122.18 E
Damiaochang 107 29.39 N 106.05 E
Damiaogou 104 41.06 N 123.52 E
Damiaojiang 106 31.00 N 120.28 E
Damiaoshang 105 39.56 N 115.12 E
Dămienești 38 46.44 N 26.59 E
Damietta → Dumyāṭ 142 31.25 N 31.48 E
Damietta Branch → Dumyāṭ, Far' ≃ 142 31.32 N 31.51 E
Damietta Mouth → Dumyāṭ, Maṣabb ≃ [1] 142 31.32 N 31.51 E
Damin 100 28.56 N 120.29 E
Daming 98 36.19 N 115.06 E
Damingzhen 104 42.34 N 123.36 E
Damintun 104 41.52 N 122.56 E
Dāmiyā 132 32.06 N 35.33 E
Damlacık 130 37.56 N 38.39 E
Damm 263 51.40 N 6.48 E
Dammai Island I 116 5.47 N 120.25 E
Dammarie 50 48.21 N 1.30 E
Dammarie-lès-Lys 50 48.31 N 2.39 E
Dammartin-en-Goële 50 49.03 N 2.41 E
Dammartin-en-Serve 50 48.54 N 1.37 E
Dammastock ∧ 58 46.39 N 8.25 E
Damme, Bel. 50 51.15 N 3.17 E
Damme, B.R.D. 52 52.30 N 8.08 E
Damme, D.D.R. 54 53.17 N 14.01 E
Dammer Berge ⋀ [2] 52 52.32 N 8.10 E
Dāmodar ≃ 124 22.17 N 88.05 E
Dāmodar Main Canal ≚ 126 23.01 N 87.53 E
Damoh, India 118 23.50 N 79.27 E
Damoh, India 124 23.50 N 79.27 E
Damon 222 29.17 N 95.45 W
Damongo 150 9.05 N 1.49 W
Damotapāda 272c 19.03 N 73.04 E
Damous 34 36.33 N 1.42 E
Damozhuang 105 39.53 N 115.40 E
Dampar, Tasek ⊜ 114 3.02 N 102.43 E
Dampelas → Sabang 112 0.11 N 119.51 E
Dampier 162 20.39 S 116.45 E
Dampier, Cape ≻ 164 6.02 S 151.02 E
Dampier, Selat ⊔ 164 0.40 S 130.40 E
Dampier Archipelago II 162 20.35 S 116.35 E
Dampier Land ≻ [1] 162 17.30 S 122.55 E
Dampierre, Fr. 50 48.42 N 1.59 E
Dampierre, Fr. 58 47.09 N 5.45 E
Dampierre, Château de ⊥ 261 48.42 N 1.59 E
Dampierre-en-Burly 50 47.46 N 2.31 E
Dampierre-sur-Linotte 58 47.31 N 6.14 E
Dampierre-sur-Salon 58 47.33 N 5.41 E
Dampier Strait ⊔ 164 5.36 S 148.12 E
Dampit 115a 8.13 S 112.45 E
Dampmart 261 48.53 N 2.44 E
Damprichard 58 47.15 N 6.53 E
Dâmrei, Chuŏr Phnum ⋀ 110 11.00 N 104.05 E
Damují ≃ 240p 22.11 N 80.33 W
Damüls 58 47.17 N 9.53 E
Dāmurhuda 126 23.36 N 88.47 E
Damutougou 98 42.28 N 118.56 E
Damville 50 48.52 N 1.04 E
Damvillers 56 49.20 N 5.24 E
Damxung 120 30.31 N 91.08 E
Dan 132 33.14 N 35.39 E
Dan ≃, U.S. 192 36.42 N 78.45 W
Dan ≃, Zhg. 102 33.02 N 111.20 E
Dana, Cam. 146 10.14 N 15.18 E
Dana, In., U.S. 194 39.48 N 87.29 W
Dana, Mount ∧ 226 37.54 N 119.13 W
Dana, Pulau I 112 10.50 S 121.16 E
Danahu 102 42.28 N 93.32 E
Danai 112 0.29 N 103.26 E
Danajon Bank ◆ [4] 116 10.16 N 124.17 E
Danakil → Denakil ◆ [1] 144 13.00 N 41.00 E
Danakil National Park ♠ 144 10.50 N 40.45 E
Danané 150 7.16 N 8.09 W
Da Nang 110 16.04 N 108.13 E
Danan'gou 105 40.32 N 117.49 E
Danao, Pil. 116 10.32 N 124.02 E
Danao, Pil. 116 12.29 N 122.39 E
Dana Point 228 33.29 N 117.44 W
Dana Point ≻ 228 33.28 N 117.43 W
Dānāpur 124 25.38 N 85.03 E
Danba 102 31.00 N 101.50 E
Danboro 208 40.21 N 75.08 W
Danbury, Eng., U.K. 260 51.44 N 0.33 E
Danbury, Ct., U.S. 207 41.23 N 73.27 W
Danbury, Ia., U.S. 198 42.14 N 95.43 W
Danbury, Ne., U.S. 198 40.02 N 100.24 W
Danbury, N.C., U.S. 192 36.24 N 80.12 W
Danbury, Tx., U.S. 222 29.14 N 95.21 W
Danby Lake ⊜ 204 34.14 N 115.07 W
Dancheng 100 33.39 N 115.11 E
Danchengji 100 33.47 N 116.17 E
Dancug 144 10.58 N 49.04 E
Dand 120 31.37 N 65.41 E
Dandaragan 162 30.40 S 115.42 E
Dande ≃ 152 8.28 S 13.21 E
Dandeli 122 15.15 N 74.37 E
Dandenong 169 37.59 S 145.12 E
Dandenong, Mount ∧ 274b 37.50 S 145.21 E
Dandenong Creek ≃ 274b 38.01 S 145.05 E
Dandenong Ranges National Park ♠ 169 37.53 S 145.20 E
Danderyd 40 59.25 N 18.01 E
Dandīl 142 29.10 N 31.02 E
Dandong 98 40.08 N 124.20 E
Dandot 123 32.39 N 72.58 E
Dandridge 192 36.00 N 83.24 W
Dan Dume 150 11.27 N 7.10 E
Dane □ [6] 216 43.04 N 89.15 W
Dane ≃ 44 53.15 N 2.31 W
Dane County Regional Airport-Truax Field ⊠ 216 43.08 N 89.20 W
Dänemark → Denmark □ [1] 26 56.00 N 10.00 E
Dänemark-Strasse → Denmark Strait ⊔ 10 67.00 N 25.00 W
Danevang 222 29.03 N 96.13 W
Danewitz 264a 52.44 N 13.40 E
Danfeng 102 33.40 N 110.17 E
Danfengzhen 102 24.50 N 103.56 E
Danforth, Il., U.S. 216 40.49 N 87.59 W
Danforth, Me., U.S. 188 45.39 N 67.52 W
Danforth Hills ⋀ 200 40.15 N 108.00 W
Dang ≃ 102 40.30 N 94.42 E
Dānga, Bngl. 126 23.54 N 90.36 E
Dānga, India 272b 22.47 N 88.28 E
Danga ≃ 271c 1.27 N 103.43 E
Dangādiha 126 21.30 N 86.19 E
Dangan Liedao II 100 22.00 N 114.14 E
Dangara, S.S.S.R. 85 40.35 N 70.54 E
Dangara, S.S.S.R. 85 38.06 N 69.22 E
Dangba 98 40.46 N 118.32 E
Dangchang 102 34.03 N 104.23 E
Dangcheng 98 38.46 N 114.34 E
Dange, Ang. 152 7.56 S 15.02 E
Dange, Ang. 152 8.09 S 14.46 E
Dange, Nig. 150 12.52 N 5.21 E
Dange-lá-Menha 152 9.32 S 14.39 E
Danger, Point ≻ 171a 28.10 S 153.33 E
Danger Point ≻ 158 34.40 S 19.17 E
Danggali Conservation Park ♠ 166 33.20 S 140.40 E
Danghe Nanshan ⋀ 102 38.53 N 96.11 E
Danghui 105 40.03 N 117.04 E
Dangila 144 11.16 N 36.50 E
Dangkou 106 31.32 N 120.34 E
Dango 140 10.00 N 24.45 E
Dan Gora 150 11.30 N 8.09 E
Dāngori 120 27.40 N 95.32 E
Dangshan 98 34.26 N 116.21 E
Dangtu 100 31.34 N 118.30 E
Dan Gulbi 150 11.38 N 6.16 E
Dangyang 102 30.50 N 111.38 E
Dangyu 105 40.00 N 118.01 E
Dani 150 13.43 N 0.10 W
Dania 220 26.03 N 80.08 W
Daniel 200 42.51 N 110.04 W
Daniel, Mount ∧ 224 47.34 N 121.11 W
Daniel Boone Home ⊥ 219 38.39 N 90.52 W
Daniel Boone Homestead State Historic Site ⊥ 208 40.21 N 75.49 W
Daniel-Johnson, Barrage ◆ [6] 186 50.39 N 68.44 W
Daniels 284b 39.26 N 77.03 W
Daniel's Harbour 186 50.14 N 57.35 W
Danielskuil 158 28.11 S 23.33 E
Danielson 207 41.48 N 71.53 W
Daniels Pass)(200 40.18 N 111.15 W
Daniels Run ≃ 284c 38.51 N 77.17 W
Danielsville, Ga., U.S. 192 34.07 N 83.13 W
Danielsville, Pa., U.S. 208 40.48 N 75.32 W
Danilov 80 58.12 N 40.12 E
Danilovka, S.S.S.R. 80 50.21 N 44.06 E
Danilovka, S.S.S.R. 80 52.33 N 45.23 E
Danilovka, S.S.S.R. 86 52.23 N 70.39 E
Danilovo 82 55.40 N 38.46 E
Danilovskaja vozvyšennost' ⋀ [1] 80 58.12 N 40.16 E
Danilovskoje 82 56.48 N 35.45 E
Daning, Zhg. 102 24.39 N 111.51 E
Daning, Zhg. 102 36.33 N 110.38 E
Daningbashi 85 38.45 N 75.04 E
Dänisch Nienhof 54 54.28 N 10.07 E
Daniupucun 104 41.23 N 122.37 E
Danja 150 11.21 N 7.31 E
Danjiangkou Shuiku ⊜ [1] 102 32.37 N 111.30 E
Danjo-guntō II 92 32.02 N 128.23 E
Danjoutin 58 47.37 N 6.52 E
Ḑank 128 23.33 N 56.17 E
Dankama 150 13.20 N 7.44 E
Dankersen 52 52.17 N 8.58 E
Danki 82 54.55 N 37.34 E
Dankov 76 53.15 N 39.08 E
Dankova, Pik ∧ 85 41.05 N 77.38 E
Danleng, Zhg. 102 29.58 N 103.31 E
Danleng, Zhg. 102 29.18 N 103.10 E
Danleng, Zhg. 107 30.01 N 103.30 E
Danlí 236 14.00 N 86.35 W
Danmark → Denmark □ [1] 26 56.00 N 10.00 E
Dannebrog 198 41.07 N 98.32 W
Dannemare 41 54.45 N 11.12 E
Dannemarie 58 47.38 N 7.08 E
Dannemora, Sve. 40 60.11 N 17.49 E
Dannemora, N.Y., U.S. 188 44.43 N 73.43 W
Dannenberg 54 53.06 N 11.05 E
Dannenreich 264a 52.19 N 13.45 E
Dannenwalde 54 53.04 N 13.11 E
Dannevirke 172 40.12 S 176.07 E
Dannewerk 41 54.29 N 9.31 E
Dannhauser 158 28.04 S 30.04 E
Dano 150 11.09 N 3.04 W
Danompari 112 0.09 N 115.02 E
Dañoso, Cabo ≻ 254 48.50 S 67.13 W
Dan Ryan Woods ♠ 278 41.45 N 87.39 W
Dan Sai 110 17.17 N 101.09 E
Danshan 107 30.06 N 104.54 E
Danshui 100 22.49 N 114.27 E
Dansville, Mi., U.S. 216 42.34 N 84.18 W
Dansville, N.Y., U.S. 210 42.33 N 77.41 W
Dāntan 126 21.57 N 87.16 E
Dante 192 36.58 N 82.17 W
Dantewāra 122 18.54 N 81.21 E
Dantuzhen 106 32.12 N 119.31 E
Danube ≃ 22 45.20 N 29.40 E
Danube, Mouths of the ≃ [1] 38 45.10 N 29.50 E
Danubio → Danube ≃ 22 45.20 N 29.40 E
Danubyu 110 17.15 N 95.35 E
Danvers, Il., U.S. 190 40.31 N 89.10 W
Danvers, Ma., U.S. 207 42.34 N 70.55 W
Danvers ≃ 283 42.32 N 70.53 W
Danville, P.Q., Can. 206 45.47 N 72.01 W
Danville, Ar., U.S. 194 35.03 N 93.23 W
Danville, Ca., U.S. 226 37.49 N 121.59 W
Danville, Ga., U.S. 192 32.36 N 83.14 W
Danville, Il., U.S. 194 40.07 N 87.37 W
Danville, In., U.S. 218 39.45 N 86.31 W
Danville, Ky., U.S. 194 37.42 N 84.46 W
Danville, Mo., U.S. 219 38.54 N 91.32 W
Danville, Oh., U.S. 214 40.26 N 82.15 W
Danville, Pa., U.S. 210 40.57 N 76.36 W
Danville, Vt., U.S. 188 44.25 N 72.07 W
Danville, Va., U.S. 192 36.35 N 79.23 W
Danville, Wa., U.S. 182 48.59 N 118.30 W
Danxian (Nada) 110 19.35 N 109.17 E
Danyang, Zhg. 100 26.22 N 119.30 E
Danyang, Zhg. 106 32.00 N 119.35 E
Danzig → Gdańsk 30 54.23 N 18.40 E
Dao 116 10.31 N 121.57 E
Dâo ≃, Port. 34 40.20 N 8.11 W
Dao ≃, Zhg. 100 30.44 N 114.39 E
Daocheng 102 29.06 N 100.38 E
Daodemiao 89 43.41 N 120.19 E
Daodi 105 39.32 N 118.11 E
Daoguanhe 100 30.54 N 114.57 E
Daohu 100 29.42 N 117.29 E
Daolazui 105 40.06 N 115.06 E
Daoliban 104 41.52 N 121.37 E
Daolin 100 27.59 N 112.42 E
Daolinggang 98 34.02 N 114.34 E
Daoliupu 107 30.12 N 105.09 E
Daomaguan 98 39.07 N 114.38 E
Daosa 124 26.53 N 76.20 E
Daoshiwu 106 30.18 N 118.57 E
Daoshuqiao 106 31.51 N 119.41 E
Daotiandi 89 48.53 N 130.03 E
Dao Timmi 146 20.32 N 13.33 E
Daotou 98 37.14 N 120.20 E
Daoukro 150 7.03 N 3.58 W
Daoulas 32 48.22 N 4.15 W
Daoura, Oued V 148 28.15 N 3.30 W
Daoxian 102 25.35 N 111.27 E
Daozhen 102 28.42 N 107.56 E
Daozi 89 45.00 N 123.43 E
Dapa 116 9.46 N 126.03 E
Dapango 150 10.52 N 0.12 E
Dapanzhuang 98 37.20 N 115.28 E
Dapaozi 89 45.27 N 122.07 E
Dapchi 146 12.28 N 11.32 E
Dapdap 116 14.14 N 122.15 E
Dapeng 100 22.34 N 114.29 E
Daphne 194 30.36 N 87.54 W
Dapiak, Mount ∧ 116 8.15 N 123.28 E
Daping, Zhg. 100 23.11 N 115.49 E
Daping, Zhg. 100 24.24 N 115.58 E
Dapingshan 102 25.30 N 109.39 E
Dapishi 100 26.30 N 112.54 E
Dapitan 116 8.39 N 123.25 E
Dapitan ≃ 116 8.38 N 123.25 E
Dapitan Bay ⊂ 116 8.40 N 123.23 E
Dapto 170 34.30 S 150.47 E
Dapu, Zhg. 98 40.34 N 124.12 E
Dapu, Zhg. 100 23.16 N 113.32 E
Dapu, Zhg. 106 31.19 N 119.56 E
Dapujie 100 27.01 N 112.46 E
Da Qaidam 102 37.53 N 95.07 E
Da Qaidam Hu ⊜ 102 37.50 N 95.00 E
Daqian 106 30.55 N 120.11 E
Daqiangmen 106 31.29 N 120.27 E
Daqiangzi 104 42.21 N 120.29 E
Daqiao, Zhg. 100 24.56 N 113.09 E
Daqiao, Zhg. 100 29.39 N 121.26 E
Daqiao, Zhg. 100 26.38 N 118.54 E
Daqiao, Zhg. 100 28.11 N 114.16 E
Daqiao, Zhg. 100 32.21 N 119.41 E
Daqiao, Zhg. 106 30.59 N 121.14 E
Daqiao, Zhg. 107 28.52 N 105.40 E
Daqiaojie 106 30.46 N 119.14 E
Daqiaokou 100 27.06 N 113.38 E
Daqiaotou 106 30.47 N 120.52 E
Daqiaozhai 102 25.21 N 106.15 E
Daqing 98 39.13 N 118.51 E
Daqing ≃ 105 39.04 N 116.55 E
Daqinggou, Zhg. 98 41.16 N 114.10 E
Daqinggou, Zhg. 98 41.12 N 125.07 E
Daqing Shan ∧, Zhg. 89 45.35 N 127.51 E
Daqing Shan ∧, Zhg. 104 42.03 N 123.45 E
Daqing Shan ∧, Zhg. 104 41.47 N 121.15 E
Daqiu 100 25.24 N 119.39 E
Daqqāq 140 12.56 N 26.58 E
Daquan 102 41.21 N 95.17 E
Daquanshan 98 40.14 N 113.47 E
Daquantou 105 39.31 N 114.46 E
Daquanyan 104 42.37 N 123.32 E
Dāqūf 142 28.24 N 30.38 E
Daqu Shan I 100 30.27 N 122.20 E
Dara, Sén. 150 15.21 N 15.29 W
Dar'ā, Sūrīy. 132 32.37 N 36.06 E
Dar'ā □ [8] 132 33.00 N 36.10 E
Dārāb 128 28.45 N 54.34 E
Darāban 120 31.44 N 70.20 E
Darabani 38 48.11 N 26.35 E
Darāfisah 140 13.23 N 31.59 E
Daraga 116 11.54 N 123.52 E
Daragodleh 144 10.10 N 44.51 E
Daraina 157b 13.12 S 49.40 E
Darājīl 142 30.39 N 30.52 E
Daram Island I 116 11.38 N 124.47 E
Dārān 128 32.59 N 50.24 E
Daraoli ◆ [8] 272c 19.11 N 72.48 E
Darap 112 1.13 S 112.03 E
Dār as-Salām 273c 29.59 N 31.13 E
Darasun 88 51.40 N 114.00 E
Daraut-Kurgan 85 39.33 N 72.13 E
Darave 272c 19.02 N 73.01 E
Darāw 140 24.25 N 32.56 E
Darawah 142 30.13 N 31.06 E
Dārayyā 132 33.27 N 36.15 E
Darazo 146 11.00 N 10.24 E
Darb Al-Ḥājj 142 30.10 N 31.33 E
Darb al-Ḥajj, Jabal ∧ 132 30.05 N 35.26 E
Darband 123 34.20 N 72.52 E
Darbāsīyah 130 37.04 N 40.39 E
Darbaza 85 41.35 N 69.02 E
Darbėnai 76 56.01 N 21.15 E
Dar-Beni-Kriche-Bahri 34 35.30 N 5.20 W
Darbhanga 124 26.10 N 85.54 E
Darbod (Taikang) 89 46.52 N 124.27 E
D'Arbonne, Bayou ≃ 194 32.34 N 92.09 W
Darburruk 144 9.44 N 44.31 E
Darby, Mt., U.S. 202 46.01 N 114.10 W
Darby, Pa., U.S. 208 39.55 N 75.15 W
Darby, Cape ≻ 180 64.20 N 162.22 W
Darby Creek ≃ 285 39.52 N 75.18 W
Darbydale 218 39.51 N 83.11 W
Darčeli 84 42.27 N 41.42 E
Darchan 88 49.29 N 105.55 E
D'Archiac, Mount ∧ 172 43.28 S 170.35 E
D'Arcy 182 50.33 N 122.29 W
D'Arcy Island I 224 48.34 N 123.17 W
Darda 38 45.37 N 18.41 E
Dardadine 168a 33.14 S 116.50 E
Dardanelle, Ar., U.S. 194 35.13 N 93.09 W
Dardanelle, Ca., U.S. 226 38.20 N 119.50 W
Dardanelle Lake ⊜ [1] 194 35.25 N 93.20 W
Dardanelles → Çanakkale Boğazı ⊔ 130 40.15 N 26.25 E
Dardanup 168a 33.24 S 115.45 E
Dardara 34 35.08 N 5.15 W
Dardenelles Cone ∧ 226 38.25 N 119.53 W
Dardenne Creek ≃ 219 38.52 N 90.32 W
Dardesheim 54 51.59 N 10.49 E
Dardistān □ [9] 123 35.30 N 74.00 E
Dare 208 37.10 N 76.26 W
Darebin Creek ≃ 274b 37.47 S 145.02 E
Dareda 154 4.13 S 35.33 E
Dar-el-Beida → Casablanca 148 33.39 N 7.35 W
Darende 130 38.34 N 37.30 E
Darent ≃ 260 51.28 N 0.13 E
Daresbury 262 53.21 N 2.38 W
Dar es Salaam 154 6.48 S 39.17 E
Dar-Es-Salaam □ [4] 154 6.30 S 39.25 E
Daressalam → Dar es Salaam 154 6.48 S 39.17 E
Darfeld 52 52.01 N 7.16 E
Darfo 64 45.53 N 10.11 E
Dārfūr ash-Shamālīyah □ [4] 140 16.00 N 25.25 E
Dargai 123 34.30 N 71.54 E
Dargan-Ata 72 40.29 N 62.10 E
Dargaville 172 35.56 S 173.53 E
Dargeçit 130 37.33 N 41.44 E
Dargol 150 13.55 N 1.15 E
Dargol ≃ 150 13.53 N 1.33 E
Dargun 54 53.54 N 12.51 E
Darhan Muminggan Lianheqi 102 41.50 N 110.27 E
Dari 140 5.48 N 30.21 E
Dāriāpur 126 23.36 N 89.27 E
Darıca 130 40.45 N 29.23 E
Darie Hills ⋀ 144 8.21 N 47.16 E
Darién, Col. 246 3.56 N 76.31 W
Darien, Ct., U.S. 207 41.04 N 73.28 W
Darien, Ga., U.S. 192 31.22 N 81.26 W
Darien, Il., U.S. 278 41.45 N 87.58 W
Darien, N.Y., U.S. 210 42.54 N 78.21 W
Darien, Wi., U.S. 216 42.36 N 88.42 W
Darién, Serranía del ⋀ 246 8.20 N 77.22 W
Darien Center 210 42.54 N 78.23 W
Darien Lakes State Park ♠ 210 42.55 N 78.25 W
Dariense, Cordillera ⋀ 236 12.55 N 85.30 W
Dariganga 102 45.18 N 113.52 E
Darigayos Point ≻ 116 16.50 N 120.20 E
Dariv 88 46.57 N 93.38 E
Darjevka 83 47.42 N 39.41 E
Dārjiling 124 27.02 N 88.16 E
Darjinskij 86 49.04 N 72.56 E
Darjinskoje 80 51.20 N 51.44 E
Darkan 168a 33.20 S 116.44 E
Darke □ [6] 218 40.06 N 84.38 W
Darke Peak 166 33.28 S 136.12 E
Darkhāna 123 30.39 N 72.11 E
Dar Khazīneh 128 31.54 N 48.59 E
Dark Head ≻ 241h 13.17 N 61.16 W
Darkin ≃ 168a 32.00 S 116.14 E
Darkūsh 130 35.59 N 36.23 E
Darlag 102 33.48 N 99.52 E
Darlaston 42 52.34 N 2.02 W
Darley Woods 285 39.49 N 75.28 W
Darling, S. Afr. 158 33.23 S 18.23 E
Darling, Ms., U.S. 194 34.21 N 90.16 W
Darling ≃ 166 34.07 S 141.55 E
Darling, Lake ⊜ [1] 198 48.35 N 101.40 W
Darling Downs ◆ [1] 166 27.30 S 150.30 E
Darlingford 184 49.12 N 98.22 W
Darling Range ⋀ 162 31.25 S 116.00 E
Darlington, Austl. 169 38.00 S 143.03 E
Darlington, Eng., U.K. 44 54.31 N 1.34 W
Darlington, Md., U.S. 208 39.38 N 76.12 W
Darlington, Pa., U.S. 214 40.49 N 80.26 W
Darlington, Pa., U.S. 285 39.54 N 75.28 W
Darlington, S.C., U.S. 192 34.17 N 79.52 W
Darlington, Wi., U.S. 190 42.40 N 90.07 W
Darlington Brook ≃ 276 41.05 N 74.11 W
Darlington Corners 285 39.55 N 75.34 W
Darlington Range ⋀ 171a 27.50 S 153.15 E
Darlot, Lake ⊜ 162 27.48 S 121.35 E
Darłowo 30 54.26 N 16.23 E
Darmagī, Kūh-e ∧ 128 26.35 N 58.54 E
Darmstadt 56 49.53 N 8.40 E
Darmstadt □ [5] 56 49.45 N 8.40 E
Darnah 146 32.46 N 22.39 E
Darnall 158 29.23 S 31.18 E
Darnétal 50 49.27 N 1.09 E
Darney 58 48.05 N 6.03 E
Darnick 166 32.51 S 143.37 E
Darnley, Cape ≻ 9 67.43 S 69.30 E
Darnley Bay ⊂ 176 69.35 N 123.30 W
Daroca 34 41.07 N 1.25 W
Darodih 126 23.14 N 86.27 E
Daror 144 8.14 N 44.42 E
Dar-Ould-Zidouh 148 32.22 N 6.49 W
Darou Mousti 150 15.03 N 16.03 W
Darovoje 82 54.34 N 38.22 E
Darr ≃ 166 23.39 S 143.50 E
Darra 171a 27.34 S 152.58 E
Darragh 279b 40.16 N 79.41 W
Darrah, Mount ∧ 182 49.28 N 114.35 W
Darregueira 252 37.42 S 63.10 W
Darreh Gaz 128 37.27 N 59.07 E
Darrington 224 48.15 N 121.36 W
Darrouzett 196 36.27 N 100.20 W
Darryl Gardens 284b 39.25 N 76.25 W
Dārsana 126 23.32 N 88.52 E
Darscheid 56 50.12 N 6.53 E
Darss ≻ [1] 54 54.25 N 12.31 E
Darsser Ort ≻ 54 54.29 N 12.31 E
Dart ≃ 42 50.20 N 3.33 W
Dart, Cape ≻ 9 73.06 S 126.20 W
Dār Ta'izzah 130 36.17 N 36.51 E
Dartford 260 51.27 N 0.14 E
Dartford □ [8] 260 51.26 N 0.15 E
Dartford Tunnel ◆ [5] 260 51.28 N 0.16 E
Dartmoor 166 37.55 S 141.17 E
Dartmoor ◆ [3] 42 50.35 N 3.55 W
Dartmoor National Park ♠ 42 50.37 N 3.52 W
Dartmouth, N.S., Can. 186 44.40 N 63.34 W
Dartmouth, Eng., U.K. 42 50.21 N 3.35 W
Dartmouth ≃ 186 48.53 N 64.34 W
Dartmouth, Lake ⊜ 166 26.04 S 145.18 E
Dartmouth Woods 285 39.50 N 75.31 W
Darton 44 53.36 N 1.32 W
Daru, Pap. N. Gui. 164 9.04 S 143.21 E
Daru, S.L. 150 7.59 N 10.50 W
Daruvar 36 45.36 N 17.13 E
Darvaza 128 40.11 N 58.24 E
Darvazskij chrebet ⋀ 85 38.30 N 71.15 E
Darvel 46 55.37 N 4.18 W
Darvinskij Zapovednik ◆ [4] 76 58.50 N 37.40 E
Darwāzahgêy 120 31.48 N 67.44 E
Darwen 262 53.42 N 2.28 W
Darwen ≃ 262 53.45 N 2.41 W
Darwendale 154 17.43 S 30.33 E
Dārwha 122 20.19 N 77.46 E
Darwin, Arg. 254 39.12 S 65.46 W
Darwin, Austl. 164 12.28 S 130.50 E
Darwin, Bahía ⊂ 254 45.27 S 74.40 W
Darwin, Cordillera ⋀ 254 54.40 S 70.00 W
Darwin, Isla I 246a 1.39 N 92.00 W
Darwin, Volcán ∧ [1] 246a 0.10 S 91.18 W
Darwin River 164 12.49 S 130.58 E
Daryābād 124 26.53 N 81.33 E
Darya Khān 123 31.48 N 71.06 E
Daryāpur 120 20.56 N 77.20 E
Darzāb 120 35.58 N 65.22 E
Darzo 64 45.51 N 10.33 E
Dār Zubi 140 13.07 N 23.40 E
Dās 123 35.05 N 75.05 E
Dās I 128 25.09 N 52.53 E
Dasanjiazi 104 42.31 N 122.54 E
Dašava 78 49.16 N 24.01 E
Daš Balbar 88 49.31 N 114.21 E
Dasburg 56 50.03 N 6.07 E
Dase → Dese 144 11.05 N 39.41 E
Dašev 78 49.00 N 29.26 E
Dasha ≃ 98 38.20 N 115.22 E
Dashafa 105 39.19 N 116.19 E
Dashalitu 104 42.31 N 122.30 E
Dashan 98 38.02 N 117.39 E
Dashankou 105 40.17 N 115.49 E
Dashanpu 107 29.25 N 104.49 E
Dashaping 100 29.24 N 113.51 E
Dashengfenchang 106 31.53 N 121.34 E
Dashengpu 104 41.13 N 121.02 E
Dashentang 105 39.13 N 117.56 E
Dashetai 102 40.58 N 109.19 E
Dashi 107 30.39 N 105.37 E
Dashi ≃ 105 39.35 N 116.05 E
Dashields Dam ◆ [6] 214 40.33 N 80.12 W
Dashiqiao, Zhg. 100 33.57 N 113.53 E
Dashiqiao, Zhg. 104 41.52 N 123.17 E
Dashiqiao, Zhg. 107 30.07 N 106.12 E
Dashiqiao, Zhg. 107 30.28 N 106.29 E
Dashitou, Zhg. 89 43.19 N 128.28 E
Dashitou, Zhg. 102 42.49 N 95.19 E
Dashizhai 89 46.16 N 121.25 E
Dashlūṭ 142 27.34 N 30.42 E
Dash Point 224 47.19 N 122.26 W
Dasht ≃ 128 25.10 N 61.40 E
Dashu 106 31.13 N 120.56 E
Dashun 100 28.06 N 119.52 E
Dashutang 102 23.00 N 103.55 E
Dashuwan 105 40.37 N 117.19 E
Dasi (Huangfansi) 102 38.15 N 100.22 E
Dasiji 100 33.48 N 115.55 E
Dašinčilen 88 47.51 N 104.03 E
Dasing 60 48.23 N 11.03 E
Dasizhan 89 45.53 N 130.24 E
Daska 123 32.20 N 74.21 E
Daškesan 84 40.30 N 46.04 E
Daskop 158 33.44 S 22.43 E
Daškovka 76 53.44 N 30.13 E
Dasmina 126 22.17 N 90.35 E
Dasol 116 15.59 N 119.52 E
Dasol Bay ⊂ 116 15.53 N 119.51 E
Dassalan Island I 116 6.45 N 121.28 E
Dassel, B.R.D. 52 51.48 N 9.41 E
Dassel, Mn., U.S. 190 45.04 N 94.18 W
Dasseneiland I 158 33.26 S 18.04 E
Dasserat, Lac ⊜ 190 48.16 N 79.25 W
Dassiefontein 158 31.35 S 24.25 E
Dassow 54 53.50 N 10.59 E
Dasswang 60 49.09 N 11.40 E
Dastakert 84 39.23 N 46.02 E
Dastgardān 128 34.19 N 56.51 E
Daštidžum 85 38.01 N 70.12 E
Daštioburdon 85 39.24 N 69.04 E
Dastjerd 128 34.33 N 50.15 E
Dasūa 123 31.49 N 75.38 E
Dāsuria 126 24.07 N 89.08 E
Datachang 107 28.55 N 104.21 E
Datagenoyang 112 2.03 N 115.10 E
Datai 105 39.58 N 115.54 E
Dataizi 104 41.17 N 121.45 E
Datan, Zhg. 98 41.35 N 116.00 E
Datan, Zhg. 98 39.31 N 122.11 E
Datang, Zhg. 100 24.47 N 113.43 E
Datang, Zhg. 100 25.17 N 114.56 E
Datang, Zhg. 102 22.23 N 108.23 E
Datang, Zhg. 102 24.11 N 109.00 E
Datça 130 36.45 N 27.40 E
Datchet 260 51.29 N 0.34 W
Datchet Reservoir ⊜ [1] 260 51.29 N 0.33 W
Date 92a 42.27 N 140.51 E
Date Creek ≃ 200 34.13 N 113.29 W
Datia 124 25.40 N 78.28 E
Datian, Zhg. 100 25.42 N 117.49 E
Datian, Zhg. 100 24.06 N 116.19 E
Datian Ding ∧ 102 22.17 N 111.13 E
Datianwei 100 25.54 N 115.10 E
Dativli 272c 19.11 N 73.03 E
D'at'kovo 76 53.36 N 34.20 E
D'atlovići 76 52.20 N 26.50 E
D'atlovo, S.S.S.R. 76 53.28 N 25.24 E
D'atlovo, S.S.S.R. 82 56.14 N 36.16 E
Datong, Zhg. 89 46.03 N 124.50 E
Datong, Zhg. 100 30.48 N 117.45 E
Datong, Zhg. 100 32.50 N 118.52 E
Datong, Zhg. 102 37.03 N 101.45 E
Datong, Zhg. 102 40.05 N 113.18 E
Datong ≃ 102 36.20 N 102.55 E
Datong Shan ⋀ 102 38.00 N 99.30 E
Datongzhen 106 32.12 N 121.19 E
Datoushan 98 41.50 N 117.08 E
Dātra 272b 22.58 N 88.16 E
Datta 89 49.18 N 140.22 E
Dattapāra 126 23.01 N 90.53 E
Dattapukur 126 22.45 N 88.33 E
Dattapulia 126 23.14 N 88.43 E
Datteln 52 51.40 N 7.23 E
Datteln-Hamm-Kanal ≚ 263 51.39 N 7.21 E
Dattilo 70 37.58 N 12.39 E
Datu, Tanjung ≻ 112 2.05 N 109.39 E
Datuan 106 30.58 N 121.44 E
Datumakuta 112 2.32 N 117.51 E
Datun, Zhg. 89 43.49 N 125.12 E
Datun, Zhg. 98 40.37 N 119.57 E
Datun, Zhg. 104 40.59 N 122.55 E
Datuopu 100 28.03 N 112.58 E
Datu Piang 116 7.01 N 124.30 E
Daua (Dawa) ≃ 144 4.11 N 42.06 E
Daudkāndi 126 23.32 N 90.43 E
Dāud Khel 123 32.53 N 71.34 E
Daudnagar 124 25.02 N 84.24 E
Daugai 76 54.22 N 24.20 E
Daugård 41 55.44 N 9.43 E
Daugava (Zapadnaja Dvina) ≃ 76 57.04 N 24.03 E
Daugavpils 76 55.53 N 26.32 E
Dauin 116 9.12 N 123.16 E
Daulatabad 126 24.08 N 88.22 E
Daulatkhān 126 22.38 N 90.49 E
Daulatpur, Bngl. 126 23.58 N 89.50 E
Daulatpur, Bngl. 126 24.00 N 88.52 E
Daulatpur, Bngl. 126 22.53 N 89.31 E
Daulatpur, India 272b 22.26 N 88.18 E
Daulatpur, Pāk. 120 26.30 N 67.58 E
Daulatpur ◆ [8] 272a 28.44 N 77.06 E
Daule, Ec. 246 0.24 N 80.00 W
Daule, Ec. 246 1.50 S 79.56 W
Daule, India 272c 19.10 N 73.03 E
Daule ≃ 246 2.10 S 79.52 W
Daultāla 123 33.12 N 73.09 E
Daulton Creek ≃ 226 37.04 N 119.59 W
Daun 56 50.11 N 6.50 E
Daund 122 18.28 N 74.36 E
Daung Kyun I 110 12.14 N 98.05 E
Daunia, Monti della ⋀ 68 41.27 N 15.06 E
Dauphin, Mb., Can. 184 51.09 N 100.03 W
Dauphin, Pa., U.S. 208 40.22 N 76.55 W
Dauphin □ [6] 208 40.15 N 76.52 W
Dauphin ≃ 184 51.58 N 98.04 W
Dauphiné □ [9] 62 44.50 N 6.00 E
Dauphin Island 194 30.15 N 88.07 W
Dauphin Island I 194 30.14 N 88.12 W
Dauphin Lake ⊜ 184 51.17 N 99.48 W
Daura 150 13.02 N 8.21 E
Daurija 88 49.56 N 116.52 E
Daurskoje 86 55.14 N 92.05 E
Dausenau 56 50.20 N 7.45 E
D'Auteuil, Lac ⊜ 186 50.38 N 61.17 W
Dautphetal 56 50.51 N 8.32 E
Dāvangere 122 14.28 N 75.55 E
Davant 194 29.37 N 89.51 W
Davao 116 7.04 N 125.36 E
Davao □ [4] 116 7.40 N 125.50 E
Davao ≃ 116 7.04 N 125.37 E
Davao del Sur □ [4] 116 6.50 N 125.20 E
Davao Gulf ⊂ 116 6.40 N 125.55 E
Davao Oriental □ [4] 116 7.30 N 126.30 E
Dāvar Panāh 128 27.21 N 62.21 E
Dāvarzan 128 36.23 N 56.50 E
Davegoriale 144 8.45 N 44.50 E
Davel 158 26.24 S 29.40 E
Daveluyville 206 46.12 N 72.08 W
Davenda 88 53.33 N 119.18 E
Davenham 262 53.14 N 2.31 W
Davenport, Ca., U.S. 226 37.00 N 122.11 W
Davenport, Fl., U.S. 220 28.09 N 81.36 W
Davenport, Ia., U.S. 190 41.31 N 90.34 W
Davenport, Ne., U.S. 198 40.18 N 97.48 W
Davenport, N.Y., U.S. 210 42.28 N 74.51 W
Davenport, Ok., U.S. 196 35.42 N 96.45 W
Davenport, Wa., U.S. 202 47.39 N 118.08 W
Davenport, Mount ∧ 162 22.23 S 130.51 E
Davenport Downs 166 24.08 S 141.07 E
Davenport Range ⋀ 162 20.47 S 134.48 E
Daventry 42 52.16 N 1.09 W
Davey, Port ⊂ 166 43.19 S 145.55 E
Daveyton 273d 26.09 S 28.25 E
David 236 8.26 N 82.26 W
David City 198 41.15 N 97.07 W
David-Gorodok 78 52.03 N 27.14 E
Davido-Nikol'skoje 83 48.30 N 39.50 E
David Point ≻ 241k 12.14 N 61.39 W
Davids Island I 276 40.53 N 73.46 W
Davidson, Sk., Can. 184 51.16 N 105.59 W
Davidson, N.C., U.S. 192 35.29 N 80.50 W
Davidson, Ok., U.S. 196 34.14 N 99.04 W
Davidson, Mount ∧ 170 33.09 S 150.07 E
Davidson Creek ≃ 222 30.21 N 96.27 W
Davidson Heights 214 40.35 N 80.15 W
Davidson Lake ⊜ 184 53.47 N 99.37 W
Davidson Mountains ⋀ 180 68.45 N 142.10 W
Davidson Park ♠ 274a 33.45 S 151.12 E
Davidsville 214 40.14 N 78.56 W
Davie 220 26.03 N 80.13 W
Davies, Mount ∧ 162 26.14 S 129.16 E
Davignab 158 27.32 S 19.48 E
Davila 116 18.29 N 120.35 E
Davilla 222 30.47 N 97.17 W
Davington 44 55.18 N 3.12 W
Davin Lake ⊜ 184 56.50 N 103.40 W
Davinópolis 255 15.58 S 50.08 W
Daviot 46 57.25 N 4.08 W
Davis, Ca., U.S. 226 38.32 N 121.44 W
Davis, N.C., U.S. 192 34.47 N 76.27 W
Davis, Ok., U.S. 196 34.30 N 97.07 W
Davis, W.V., U.S. 188 39.07 N 79.27 W
Davis ≃ 162 21.42 S 121.05 E
Davis ⊽ [3] 9 68.35 S 77.58 E
Davis, Mount ∧ 188 39.47 N 79.10 W
Davis Bay ⊂ 9 66.08 S 134.05 E
Davisboro 192 32.58 N 82.36 W
Davisburg 216 42.45 N 83.33 W
Davis City 190 40.38 N 93.48 W
Davis Cove 186 47.40 N 54.18 W
Davis Creek ≃, Mi., U.S. 281 42.27 N 83.43 W
Davis Creek ≃, Mo., U.S. 219 39.12 N 91.53 W
Davis Dam 200 35.10 N 114.33 W
Davis Dam ◆ [6] 200 35.11 N 114.21 W
Davis Island I 279b 40.29 N 80.05 W
Davis Lake ⊜ 278 42.16 N 88.05 W
Davis-Monthan Air Force Base ■ 200 32.11 N 110.53 W
Davis Mountains ⋀ 196 30.35 N 104.00 W
Davison 216 43.02 N 83.31 W
Davis Park 210 40.42 N 72.59 W
Davis Point ≻ 282 38.03 N 122.15 W
Davis Sea ⊤ [2] 9 66.00 S 92.00 E
Davis Strait ⊔ 176 67.00 N 57.00 W
Davlekanovo 86 54.13 N 55.03 E
Davo ≃ 150 5.00 N 6.08 W
Davoli 68 38.39 N 16.29 E
Davos 58 46.48 N 9.50 E
Davron 261 48.52 N 1.57 E
Davst 86 50.36 N 92.28 E
Davulga 130 38.58 N 31.23 E
Davutlar 130 37.43 N 27.17 E
Davy 192 37.28 N 81.39 W
Davydkovo, S.S.S.R. 82 56.17 N 36.49 E
Davydkovo, S.S.S.R. 265b 55.35 N 37.12 E
Davydov, gora ∧ 88 52.34 N 107.25 E
Davydov Brod 78 47.14 N 33.12 E
Davydovka 78 51.10 N 39.25 E
Davydovo 82 55.37 N 38.52 E
Davydovskoje 82 55.52 N 36.48 E
Davyhulme 262 53.27 N 2.22 W
Dawa, Zhg. 104 41.00 N 122.03 E
Dawa, Zhg. 104 41.54 N 123.32 E
Dawa (Daua) ≃ 144 4.11 N 42.06 E
Dawaki 150 12.06 N 8.20 E
Dawan 102 23.52 N 109.29 E
Dawang 98 36.58 N 118.31 E
Dawangcun 106 30.45 N 118.59 E
Dawangdian 105 39.04 N 115.26 E
Dawangdong 105 38.53 N 116.21 E
Dawangjia Dao I 98 39.27 N 123.07 E
Dawangsangou 104 41.43 N 121.36 E
Dawangzhai 269b 31.22 N 121.25 E
Dawangzhuang, Zhg. 105 39.23 N 116.28 E
Dawangzhuang, Zhg. 105 38.59 N 115.56 E
Dawāsir, Wādī ad- V 144 20.24 N 46.29 E
Dawatun 104 41.05 N 121.01 E
Dawei (Tavoy) 110 14.05 N 98.12 E
Daweizhuang 105 39.34 N 116.53 E
Daweizigou 104 42.38 N 123.09 E
Dawen ≃ 98 35.38 N 116.24 E
Dawenkou 98 35.59 N 117.07 E
Dawera, Pulau I 164 7.44 S 130.00 E
Dawes Park ♠ 278 42.03 N 87.40 W
Dawlan 110 16.44 N 98.01 E
Dawlish 42 50.35 N 3.28 W
Dawn 208 37.50 N 77.22 W
Dawna Range ⋀ 110 16.50 N 98.15 E
Dawqah 144 19.36 N 40.54 E
Dawrah 140 12.22 N 24.19 E
Daws Heath 260 51.34 N 0.37 E
Dawson, Yk., Can. 180 64.04 N 139.25 W
Dawson, Ga., U.S. 192 31.46 N 84.26 W
Dawson, Il., U.S. 219 39.51 N 89.28 W
Dawson, Mn., U.S. 198 44.55 N 96.03 W
Dawson, Ne., U.S. 198 40.07 N 95.49 W
Dawson, Tx., U.S. 222 31.53 N 96.42 W
Dawson ≃ 166 23.38 S 149.46 E
Dawson, Isla I 254 53.55 S 70.45 W
Dawson, Mount ∧ 182 51.09 N 117.25 W
Dawson Bay ⊂ 184 52.55 N 100.50 W
Dawson Creek 182 55.46 N 120.14 W
Dawson Inlet ⊂ 176 61.50 N 93.25 W
Dawson-Lambton Glacier ⊓ 9 76.15 S 27.30 W
Dawson Range ⋀, Austl. 166 24.20 S 149.45 E
Dawson Range ⋀, Yk., Can. 180 62.40 N 139.00 W
Dawson Ridge 214 40.42 N 80.22 W
Dawson Springs 194 37.10 N 87.41 W
Dawsonville 192 34.25 N 84.07 W
Dawu, Zhg. 100 31.34 N 114.06 E
Dawu, Zhg. 102 31.07 N 101.08 E
Dawudapu 104 41.36 N 123.03 E
Dawuji 271a 39.51 N 116.30 E
Dawujiawopeng 104 41.55 N 122.29 E
Dawujiazi 104 42.16 N 121.52 E
Dawulaba 104 42.13 N 122.23 E
Dawulah 104 41.56 N 121.05 E
Dax 32 43.43 N 1.03 W
Daxian 102 31.18 N 107.30 E
Daxin, Zhg. 100 33.54 N 118.30 E
Daxin, Zhg. 102 22.50 N 107.26 E
Daxing, Zhg. 98 39.44 N 116.20 E
Daxing (Huangcun), Zhg. 105 39.44 N 116.20 E
Daxing, Zhg. 106 31.50 N 121.40 E
Daxingchang 107 30.17 N 103.26 E
Daxingcun 106 31.45 N 121.40 E
Daxingzhai 102 23.13 N 102.21 E
Daxinji 100 34.03 N 119.28 E
Daxinzhuang, Zhg. 105 40.23 N 116.44 E
Daxinzhuang, Zhg. 105 39.26 N 118.20 E
Daxiyang 106 30.21 N 121.58 E
Daxu, Zhg. 100 29.32 N 121.52 E
Daxu, Zhg. 102 25.09 N 110.21 E
Daxue Shan ⋀ 102 30.10 N 101.50 E
Daxujia 98 34.18 N 117.34 E
Dayakou 102 22.46 N 100.18 E
Dayanchi 102 27.41 N 101.55 E
Dayang, Zhg. 98 36.04 N 116.31 E
Dayang, Zhg. 100 25.56 N 118.48 E
Dayang ≃ 98 39.54 N 123.40 E
Dayang Bunting, Pulau I 114 6.14 N 99.48 E
Dayangcha 98 42.04 N 126.43 E
Dayanggou 104 41.14 N 123.51 E
Dayang Shan I 106 30.35 N 122.00 E
Dayangshu 89 49.45 N 124.35 E
Dayaniguas, Ensenada de ⊂ 240p 22.20 N 83.15 W
Dayao, Zhg. 100 27.59 N 113.42 E
Dayao, Zhg. 102 25.43 N 101.13 E
Dayaoshan 102 24.05 N 110.17 E
Daya Wan ⊂ 100 22.37 N 114.40 E
Dayboro 171a 27.11 S 152.50 E
Daye 100 30.06 N 114.57 E
Dayghar 272c 19.09 N 73.03 E
Day Heights 218 39.11 N 84.14 W
Dayi 107 30.37 N 103.31 E
Dayiji 100 32.32 N 119.14 E
Daying, Zhg. 98 34.27 N 113.59 E
Daying, Zhg. 98 37.19 N 115.43 E
Daying, Zhg. 98 39.53 N 123.07 E
Daying, Zhg. 98 39.19 N 113.46 E
Daying, Zhg. 100 33.59 N 112.51 E
Daying, Zhg. 105 39.05 N 116.06 E
Daying (Taping) ≃ 102 24.17 N 97.14 E
Dayingzi, Zhg. 98 41.19 N 118.19 E
Dayingzi, Zhg. 98 41.28 N 120.21 E
Dayingzi, Zhg. 104 41.08 N 122.50 E
Dayiqiao 106 31.44 N 120.45 E
Day Island 224 47.15 N 122.33 W
Day Lake ⊜ 224 48.23 N 121.58 W
Daylesford 169 37.21 S 144.09 E
Daymán ≃ 252 31.30 S 58.02 W
Daym Zubayr 140 7.43 N 26.13 E
Dayong, Zhg. 100 22.28 N 113.16 E
Dayong, Zhg. 102 29.06 N 110.29 E
Dayou 98 34.12 N 119.52 E
Dayr, Jabal ad- ∧ 140 12.27 N 30.42 E
Dayr Abū Sa'īd 132 32.30 N 35.41 E
Dayr al-Balaḥ 132 31.25 N 34.21 E
Dayr al-Ghuṣūn 132 32.21 N 35.05 E
Dayr 'Alī 132 33.17 N 36.18 E
Dayr 'Allā 132 32.12 N 35.37 E
Dayr 'Aṭīyah 130 34.06 N 36.46 E
Dayr az-Zawr 130 35.20 N 40.09 E
Dayr az-Zawr □ [8] 130 35.00 N 40.30 E
Dayr Dibwān 132 31.55 N 35.16 E
Dayr Ḥāfir 130 36.09 N 37.42 E
Dayr Jabal Aṭ-Ṭayr 142 28.17 N 30.45 E
Dayr Mawās 142 27.38 N 30.51 E
Dayr Qānūn 132 33.36 N 36.08 E
Dayr Sharaf 132 32.15 N 35.11 E
Dayrūṭ, Miṣr 142 27.33 N 30.49 E
Dayrūṭ, Miṣr 142 31.13 N 30.30 E
Dayrūṭ ash-Sharīf 142 27.35 N 30.49 E
Days Island I 284b 39.24 N 76.22 W
Daysland 182 52.52 N 112.15 W
Day Star Indian Reserve ◆ [4] 184 51.43 N 104.14 W
Dayton, Il., U.S. 216 41.23 N 88.47 W
Dayton, In., U.S. 216 40.22 N 86.46 W
Dayton, Ia., U.S. 190 42.15 N 94.04 W
Dayton, Ky., U.S. 218 39.06 N 84.28 W
Dayton, Mi., U.S. 216 41.48 N 86.26 W
Dayton, Nv., U.S. 226 39.14 N 119.35 W
Dayton, N.J., U.S. 276 40.22 N 74.30 W
Dayton, N.Y., U.S. 210 42.25 N 78.58 W
Dayton, Oh., U.S. 218 39.45 N 84.11 W
Dayton, Or., U.S. 224 45.13 N 123.04 W
Dayton, Pa., U.S. 214 40.52 N 79.14 W
Dayton, Tn., U.S. 194 35.29 N 85.00 W
Dayton, Tx., U.S. 222 30.02 N 94.53 W
Dayton, Va., U.S. 188 38.24 N 78.56 W
Dayton, Wa., U.S. 202 46.19 N 117.58 W
Dayton, Wy., U.S. 202 44.52 N 107.15 W
Daytona Beach 192 29.12 N 81.01 W
Dayton Municipal Airport ⊠ 218 39.54 N 84.13 W
Dayu, Indon. 112 1.59 S 115.04 E
Dayu, Zhg. 100 25.24 N 114.22 E

Symbols in the index entries represent the broad categories identified in the key at the right. Symbols with superior numbers (⋀ [1]) identify subcategories (see complete key on page I · 1).

Symbole im Register stellen die rechts im Schlüssel erklärten Kategorien dar. Symbole mit hochgestellten Ziffern (⋀ [1]) bezeichnen Unterabteilungen einer Kategorie (vgl. vollständiger Schlüssel auf Seite I · 1).

Los símbolos incluídos en el texto del índice representan las grandes categorias identificadas con la clave a la derecha. Los símbolos con numeros en su parte superior (⋀ [1]) identifican las subcategorías (véase la clave completa en la página I · 1).

Les symboles de l'index représentent les catégories indiquées dans la légende à droite. Les symboles suivis d'un indice (⋀ [1]) représentent des sous-catégories (voir légende complète à la page I · 1).

Os símbolos incluídos no texto do índice representam as grandes categorias identificadas com a chave à direita. Os símbolos com números em sua parte superior (⋀ [1]) identificam as subcategorias (veja-se a chave completa à página I · 1).

	English	Deutsch	Español	Français	Português
∧	Mountain	Berg	Montaña	Montagne	Montanha
⋀	Mountains	Gebirge	Montañas	Montagnes	Montanhas
)(	Pass	Paß	Paso	Col	Passo
V	Valley, Canyon	Tal, Cañon	Valle, Cañón	Vallée, Canyon	Vale, Canhão
≍	Plain	Ebene	Llano	Plaine	Planície
≻	Cape	Kap	Cabo	Cap	Cabo
I	Island	Insel	Isla	Île	Ilha
II	Islands	Inseln	Islas	Îles	Ilhas
◆	Other Topographic Features	Andere Topographische Objekte	Otros Elementos Topográficos	Autres données topographiques	Outros acidentes topográficos

ESPAÑOL — Nombre, Página, Lat.°′, Long.°′ W = Oeste · FRANÇAIS — Nom, Page, Lat.°′, Long.°′ W = Ouest · PORTUGUÊS — Nome, Página, Lat.°′, Long.°′ W = Oeste

Nombre	Página	Lat.°′	Long.°′ W = Oeste
Dayuba	107	29.15 N	103.34 E
Dayu Ling ⩘	100	25.20 N	114.16 E
Da Yunhe (Grand Canal) ≊	90	32.12 N	119.31 E
Dayu Shan I, Zhg.	100	26.57 N	120.21 E
Dayu Shan I, Zhg.	106	30.19 N	121.58 E
Dayushupu	104	41.32 N	121.24 E
Dayville, Ct., U.S.	207	41.50 N	71.53 W
Dayville, Or., U.S.	202	44.28 N	119.32 W
Dazaifu ⊥	96	33.31 N	130.31 E
Dazaoliyingzi	104	42.07 N	121.20 E
Dazaomiao	106	32.06 N	121.29 E
Dazhang ≃	100	25.56 N	119.12 E
Dazhangzi	98	40.38 N	118.07 E
Dazhaotai	104	41.14 N	123.03 E
Dazhengjiatun	98	39.37 N	122.52 E
Dazhengzhuangzi	105	39.16 N	116.46 E
Dazhi	100	34.29 N	113.17 E
Dazhiba	102	27.09 N	99.52 E
Dazhifang	104	41.21 N	123.12 E
Dazhou	100	28.53 N	118.58 E
Dazhu	102	30.48 N	107.12 E
Dazhuangke	105	40.32 N	115.42 E
Dazhubao	107	28.59 N	103.38 E
Dazhuyuan	100	23.43 N	115.57 E
Dazifangshen	104	42.27 N	124.12 E
Daziling	104	41.21 N	121.26 E
Daziying	104	41.42 N	123.36 E
Dazkırı	130	37.55 N	29.52 E
Dazu	107	29.43 N	105.42 E
Dazui	100	30.16 N	114.02 E
De Aar	158	30.39 S	24.00 E
Dead ≃, Me., U.S.	188	45.20 N	69.58 W
Dead ≃, Mi., U.S.	190	46.34 N	87.24 W
Dead ≃, N.J., U.S.	276	40.39 N	74.31 W
Deadhorse	180	70.11 N	148.27 W
Dead Horse Point State Park ♦	200	38.28 N	109.44 W
Deadman ≃	182	50.45 N	120.55 W
Deadman Brook ≃	276	41.08 N	73.22 W
Deadman Creek ≃	226	37.12 N	120.42 W
Deadman Hill ∧	162	23.48 S	119.25 E
Deadmans Cay	238	23.14 N	75.14 W
Deadmans Creek ≃	274a	33.58 S	151.00 E
Deadman's Creek Indian Reserve ◄[4]	182	50.49 N	121.00 W
Dead Run ≃	284c	38.57 N	77.11 W
Dead Sea (Al-Baḥr al-Mayyit) (Yam HaMelaḥ) ◎	132	31.30 N	35.30 E
Deadwood	198	44.22 N	103.43 W
Deadwood ≃	202	44.05 N	115.40 W
Deagan Island I	116	12.15 N	123.51 E
Deakin	162	30.46 S	128.58 E
Deakin, Mount ∧[2]	162	17.38 S	130.48 E
Deakin Bay ⊂	9	68.23 S	150.10 E
Deal, Eng., U.K.	42	51.14 N	1.24 E
Deal, N.J., U.S.	208	40.15 N	74.00 W
Deale	208	38.46 N	76.33 W
Dealesville	158	28.40 S	25.37 E
Deal Island	208	38.09 N	75.56 W
Deal Island I	208	38.09 N	75.56 W
Deam Lake ◎[1]	218	38.28 N	85.51 W
De'an	100	29.20 N	115.46 E
Dean ≃	182	52.50 N	126.57 W
Dean, Forest of ◄[3]	42	51.48 N	2.30 W
Dean Channel ʮ	182	52.33 N	127.13 W
Deane	262	53.34 N	2.28 W
Deán Funes	252	30.26 S	64.21 W
Dean Row	262	53.20 N	2.11 W
Deans	276	40.24 N	74.30 W
Deansboro	210	43.00 N	75.26 W
Deans Dundas Bay ⊂	176	72.15 N	118.25 W
Deanville	222	30.26 N	96.46 W
Dearborn	216	42.18 N	83.10 W
Dearborn □[6]	218	39.06 N	84.51 W
Dearborn ≃	202	47.07 N	111.55 W
Dearborn Heights, Il., U.S.	278	41.43 N	87.48 W
Dearborn Heights, Mi., U.S.	216	42.20 N	83.16 W
Dearg, Beinn ∧	46	57.47 N	4.56 W
Dearham	44	54.42 N	3.26 W
Dearne ≃	44	53.30 N	1.16 W
Dear Reservoir ◎[1]	44	55.20 N	3.37 W
Dease ≃	180	59.54 N	128.30 W
Dease Arm ⊂	180	66.52 N	119.37 W
Dease Lake ◎	180	58.35 N	130.02 W
Dease Strait ʮ	176	68.40 N	108.00 W
Death Valley	204	36.18 N	116.25 W
Death Valley V	204	36.30 N	117.00 W
Death Valley National Monument ♦	204	36.30 N	117.00 W
Deatsville	194	32.36 N	86.23 W
Deauville	50	49.22 N	0.04 E
Deba	146	10.20 N	11.54 E
Debagrām	126	23.41 N	88.18 E
Debal'cevo	83	48.20 N	38.24 E
Debānāndapur	272b	22.56 N	88.22 E
Debao	102	23.21 N	106.31 E
Debar	38	41.31 N	20.30 E
De Bary	220	28.52 N	81.18 W
Debauch Mountain ∧	180	64.31 N	159.52 W
Débé	241r	10.12 N	61.27 W
Debed ≃	84	41.22 N	44.58 E
Deben ≃	42	51.58 N	1.24 E
Debenham	42	52.13 N	1.11 E
De Beque	200	39.20 N	108.12 W
De Berry	194	32.18 N	94.10 W
Debesy	80	57.39 N	53.49 E
Debhāta	124	22.33 N	88.58 E
Dębica	30	50.04 N	21.24 E
De Bilt	52	52.06 N	5.10 E
Debipur	126	24.14 N	88.38 E
Debīr Char	126	22.24 N	90.41 E
Dęblin	30	51.35 N	21.50 E
Dębno	30	52.45 N	14.40 E
Débo, Lac ◎	150	15.18 N	4.09 W
Deborah, Mount ∧	180	63.38 N	147.15 W
Deborah West, Lake ◎	162	30.45 S	119.07 E
Deboyne Islands II	164	10.45 S	152.25 E
Debra	126	22.24 N	87.33 E
Debra Sina	144	9.51 N	39.50 E
Debre Birhan	144	9.40 N	39.33 E
Debrecen	30	47.32 N	21.38 E
Debre Markos	144	10.20 N	37.45 E
Debre May	144	11.19 N	37.30 E
Debre Tabor	144	11.50 N	38.05 E
Debre Zebit	144	11.50 N	38.40 E
Debre Zeyit	144	8.45 N	38.59 E
Debrzno	30	53.33 N	17.14 E
Debstedt	52	53.37 N	8.38 E
Decatur, Al., U.S.	194	34.36 N	86.59 W
Decatur, Ga., U.S.	192	33.46 N	84.17 W
Decatur, Il., U.S.	219	39.50 N	88.57 W
Decatur, In., U.S.	216	40.50 N	84.56 W
Decatur, Mi., U.S.	216	42.06 N	85.58 W
Decatur, Ms., U.S.	194	32.26 N	89.06 W
Decatur, Ne., U.S.	198	42.00 N	96.14 W
Decatur, Oh., U.S.	218	38.49 N	83.42 W
Decatur, Tn., U.S.	192	35.30 N	84.47 W
Decatur, Tx., U.S.	222	33.14 N	97.35 W
Decatur □[6]	218	39.20 N	85.29 W
Decatur, Lake ◎[1]	219	39.51 N	88.52 W
Decatur Island I	224	48.31 N	122.50 W
Decatur Municipal Airport ⊠	219	39.50 N	88.52 W
Decaturville	194	35.35 N	88.07 W
Decazeville	32	44.34 N	2.15 E
Deccan ⩘[1]	122	17.00 N	78.00 E
Decelles, Réservoir ◎[1]	190	47.42 N	78.08 W
Deception ≃	156	21.04 S	24.25 E
Deception, Mount ∧	224	47.49 N	123.14 W
Deception Bay ⊂	171a	27.07 S	153.05 E
Deception Island I	9	62.57 S	60.38 W
Deception Lake ◎	184	56.33 N	104.15 W
Deception Pass ≊	224	48.24 N	122.38 W
Deception Pass State Park ♦	224	48.24 N	122.39 W
Dechang	102	27.24 N	102.10 E
Dechêne, Lac ◎	186	51.15 N	67.51 W
Dechenhöhle ⏚[5]	263	51.22 N	7.39 E
Decherd	194	35.12 N	86.04 W
Dechhu	120	26.47 N	72.20 E
Déchy	50	50.21 N	3.07 E
Decimomannu	71	39.19 N	8.58 E
Decimoputzu	71	39.20 N	8.55 E
Děčín	54	50.48 N	14.13 E
Děčínské stěny ⩘	54	50.50 N	14.12 E
Decize	32	46.50 N	3.27 E
Decker Lake	182	54.17 N	125.50 W
Decker Lake ◎[1]	222	30.18 N	97.36 W
Deckers Point	214	40.46 N	78.59 W
Deckerville	190	43.31 N	82.44 W
De Cocksdorp	52	53.08 N	4.52 E
Decollatura	68	39.03 N	16.21 E
Decorah	190	43.18 N	91.47 W
Decs	30	46.17 N	18.46 E
Deda	38	46.57 N	24.53 E
Dedaye	110	16.24 N	95.53 E
Deddington	42	51.59 N	1.19 W
Dededo	174p	13.31 N	144.49 E
Dedegöl Dağları ⩘	130	37.47 N	31.13 E
Dedegöl Tepesi ∧	130	37.39 N	31.17 E
Dedeleben	54	52.03 N	10.25 E
Dedeli	84	39.11 N	43.05 E
Dedelow	54	53.22 N	13.48 E
Dedemsvaart	52	52.36 N	6.28 E
Dedenevo	82	56.15 N	37.31 E
Deder	144	9.22 N	41.26 E
Dedesdorf	52	53.27 N	8.30 E
Dedham	207	42.14 N	71.10 W
Dedilovskije Vyselki	82	54.20 N	38.03 E
Dedinovo	82	55.03 N	39.07 E
Dedo, Cerro ∧	254	44.49 S	71.52 W
Dedo de Deus ∧	256	22.30 S	43.03 W
De Doorns	158	33.28 S	19.41 E
Dédougou	150	12.28 N	3.28 W
Dedoviči	76	57.32 N	29.56 E
Dedovsk	82	55.52 N	37.07 E
Dedu	89	48.31 N	126.14 E
Deduru ≃	122	7.36 N	79.48 E
Dedza	154	14.22 S	34.20 E
Dee ≃, Ire.	48	53.52 N	6.21 W
Dee ≃, U.K.	44	53.20 N	3.12 W
Dee ≃, Eng., U.K.	44	54.18 N	2.32 W
Dee ≃, Scot., U.K.	44	54.50 N	4.03 W
Dee ≃, Scot., U.K.	46	57.09 N	2.07 W
Dee, Loch ◎	44	55.05 N	4.24 W
Deedsville	216	40.55 N	86.06 W
De Efteling ♦	52	51.39 N	5.02 E
Deeg	124	27.28 N	77.20 E
Deelfontein	158	30.59 S	23.48 E
Deelpan	158	26.19 S	25.36 E
Deenwood	192	31.14 N	82.23 W
Deep ≃, In., U.S.	216	41.34 N	87.17 W
Deep ≃, N.C., U.S.	192	35.36 N	79.03 W
Deepavaal Brook ≃	276	40.53 N	74.16 W
Deep Bay ⊂	184	56.25 N	103.00 W
Deep Brook ≃, Ma., U.S.	283	42.38 N	71.22 W
Deep Brook ≃, N.J., U.S.	276	40.58 N	74.09 W
Deep Creek ≃, Austl.	169	37.37 S	144.48 E
Deep Creek ≃, U.S.	200	41.44 N	113.00 W
Deep Creek ≃, Ca., U.S.	228	34.20 N	117.14 W
Deep Creek ≃, De., U.S.	208	38.38 N	75.37 W
Deep Creek ≃, Id., U.S.	202	42.15 N	116.40 W
Deep Creek ≃, Md., U.S.	284b	39.17 N	76.28 W
Deep Creek ≃, Tx., U.S.	196	32.45 N	99.10 W
Deep Creek ≃, Tx., U.S.	196	32.31 N	100.55 W
Deep Creek ≃, Ut,. U.S.	200	40.10 N	113.50 W
Deep Creek Conservation Park ♦	168b	35.39 S	138.12 E
Deep Creek Indian Reserve ◄[4]	182	52.16 N	122.07 W
Deeping Fen ≡	42	52.44 N	0.13 W
Deep Red Creek ≃	196	34.17 N	98.39 W
Deep River, On., Can.	190	46.06 N	77.30 W
Deep River, Ct., U.S.	207	41.23 N	72.26 W
Deep River, Ia., U.S.	190	41.34 N	92.22 W
Deep River, Wa., U.S.	224	46.21 N	123.41 W
Deep Run ≃, Md., U.S.	284b	39.13 N	76.42 W
Deep Run ≃, Md., U.S.	284b	39.25 N	76.40 W
Deep Run ≃, N.J., U.S.	276	40.26 N	74.22 W
Deep Run ≃, N.J., U.S.	285	39.44 N	74.41 W
Deepwater, Austl.	166	29.27 S	151.51 E
Deepwater, Mo., U.S.	194	38.15 N	93.46 W
Deep Water, N.J., U.S.	208	39.41 N	75.29 W
Deep Well	162	24.25 S	134.05 E
Deer ≃, N.Y., U.S.	188	44.55 N	74.43 W
Deer ≃, N.Y., U.S.	212	43.56 N	75.34 W
Deer Creek, In., U.S.	216	40.37 N	86.23 W
Deer Creek, Mn., U.S.	198	46.23 N	95.19 W
Deer Creek ≃, U.S.	208	39.37 N	76.09 W
Deer Creek ≃, Ca., U.S.	204	39.56 N	122.04 W
Deer Creek ≃, Ca., U.S.	226	35.56 N	119.28 W
Deer Creek ≃, Ca., U.S.	226	38.22 N	121.21 W
Deer Creek ≃, Ca., U.S.	226	39.13 N	121.17 W
Deer Creek ≃, Ca., U.S.	282	37.24 N	122.09 W
Deer Creek ≃, Il., U.S.	278	41.32 N	87.37 W
Deer Creek ≃, In., U.S.	216	40.34 N	86.41 W
Deer Creek ≃, Ks., U.S.	198	39.40 N	99.06 W
Deer Creek ≃, Ms., U.S.	194	32.33 N	90.47 W
Deer Creek ≃, Ne., U.S.	198	40.28 N	100.00 W
Deer Creek ≃, Oh., U.S.	218	39.27 N	83.00 W
Deer Creek ≃, Ok., U.S.	196	35.38 N	98.28 W
Deer Creek ≃, Or., U.S.	224	45.08 N	123.15 W
Deer Creek ≃, Pa., U.S.	279b	40.32 N	79.51 W
Deer Creek ≃, Wa., U.S.	224	48.16 N	121.55 W
Deer Creek ≃, Wy., U.S.	200	42.52 N	105.52 W
Deer Creek ≃, Wy., U.S.	202	43.09 N	107.42 W
Deer Creek Indian Reservation ◄[4]	190	47.50 N	93.25 W
Deer Creek Lake ◎[1]	218	39.40 N	83.15 W
Deerfield, Il., U.S.	216	42.10 N	87.50 W
Deerfield, In., U.S.	216	40.17 N	84.59 W
Deerfield, Ks., U.S.	198	37.58 N	101.07 W
Deerfield, Ma., U.S.	207	42.32 N	72.36 W
Deerfield, Mi., U.S.	216	41.53 N	83.46 W
Deerfield, Oh., U.S.	214	41.01 N	81.03 W
Deerfield, Wi., U.S.	216	43.03 N	89.04 W
Deerfield ≃	207	42.35 N	72.35 W
Deerfield Beach	220	26.19 N	80.06 W
Deerfield Manor	278	42.10 N	87.55 W
Deerfield Street	208	39.31 N	75.14 W
Deer Grove ♦	278	42.09 N	88.04 W
Deer Harbor	224	48.37 N	123.00 W
Deering	180	66.05 N	162.43 W
Deering, Mount ∧[2]	162	24.53 S	129.04 E
Deer Island ≻[1]	283	42.21 N	70.58 W
Deer Island I, N.B., Can.	186	45.00 N	66.57 W
Deer Island I, Ak., U.S.	180	54.53 N	162.25 W
Deer Island I, Or., U.S.	224	45.58 N	122.50 W
Deer Isle	188	44.13 N	68.40 W
Deer Lake, Nf., Can.	186	49.10 N	57.26 W
Deer Lake, Pa., U.S.	208	40.37 N	76.03 W
Deer Lake ◎, Nf., Can.	186	49.07 N	57.35 W
Deer Lake ◎, On., Can.	184	52.40 N	94.30 W
Deer Lakes Regional Park ♦	279b	40.38 N	79.49 W
Deerlijk	50	50.51 N	3.21 E
Deer Lodge	202	46.23 N	112.44 W
Deer Mountain ∧	188	45.01 N	70.56 W
Deer Park, Austl.	274b	37.47 S	144.47 E
Deer Park, Al., U.S.	194	31.13 N	88.19 W
Deer Park, Ca., U.S.	226	38.32 N	122.28 W
Deer Park, Il., U.S.	278	42.09 N	88.04 W
Deer Park, N.Y., U.S.	210	40.45 N	73.19 W
Deer Park, Oh., U.S.	218	39.12 N	84.23 W
Deer Park, Tx., U.S.	222	29.42 N	95.07 W
Deer Park, Wa., U.S.	202	47.57 N	117.28 W
Deer Park ♦	272a	28.33 N	77.11 E
Deer Park Airport ⊠	276	40.46 N	73.19 W
Deerpass Bay ⊂	180	65.56 N	122.25 W
Deer Pond ◎, Nf., Can.	186	48.30 N	54.45 W
Deer Pond ◎, N.J., U.S.	276	40.57 N	74.24 W
Deer River, Mn., U.S.	190	47.19 N	93.47 W
Deer River, N.Y., U.S.	212	43.56 N	75.36 W
Deer Sound ʮ	46	58.58 N	2.48 W
Deersville	214	40.19 N	81.11 W
Deer Trail	198	39.36 N	104.02 W
Deerwood	190	46.28 N	93.53 W
Dee Why	170	33.45 S	151.17 E
Dee Why Head ≻	274a	33.46 S	151.19 E
Dee Why Lagoon ⊂	274a	33.45 S	151.18 E
Deex Nugaaleed V	144	7.58 N	49.51 E
Defengzhuang	98	41.02 N	113.16 E
Defereggen V	64	46.55 N	12.25 E
Defereggen Alpen ⩘	64	46.52 N	12.20 E
Deferiet	212	44.02 N	75.41 W
Defiance, Ia., U.S.	198	41.49 N	95.20 W
Defiance, Oh., U.S.	216	41.17 N	84.21 W
Defiance, Pa., U.S.	214	40.10 N	78.14 W
Defiance □[6]	216	41.19 N	84.30 W
Defiance, Mount ∧	224	45.38 N	121.43 W
Defiance Plateau ⩘[1]	200	36.00 N	109.15 W
De Forest	190	43.14 N	89.20 W
De Forest Lake ◎	276	41.08 N	73.58 W
Defu	271c	1.21 N	103.54 E
De Funiak Springs	194	30.43 N	86.06 W
Deganga	126	22.40 N	88.39 E
Deganwy	44	53.18 N	3.47 W
Deganya	132	32.42 N	35.35 E
Dega Werabe	144	8.08 N	45.22 E
Dêgê	102	31.50 N	98.40 E
Degeberga	26	55.50 N	14.05 E
Degeh Bur	144	8.13 N	43.34 E
Dégelis (Sainte-Rose-du-Dégelis)	186	47.33 N	68.39 W
Degema	150	4.45 N	6.47 E
Degerby	26	60.02 N	20.23 E
Degeres	85	43.14 N	75.49 E
Degerfors	40	59.14 N	14.26 E
Degerhamn	26	56.21 N	16.24 E
Degerndorf	64	47.44 N	12.06 E
Deggendorf	60	48.51 N	12.59 E
Deggingen	56	48.36 N	9.43 E
Degh ≃	123	31.36 N	74.09 E
Değirmendere	130	38.07 N	27.09 E
Değirmenlik	130	35.15 N	33.29 E
Deglunden ◎	40	60.05 N	13.49 E
Dego	62	44.27 N	8.19 E
Degollado	234	20.28 N	102.09 W
Degoma	144	12.28 N	37.37 E
Degong	114	4.05 N	101.08 E
De Graafschap ◄[1]	52	52.00 N	6.30 E
De Graff	216	40.18 N	83.54 W
De Gray Lake ◎[1]	194	34.15 N	93.15 W
De Grey	162	20.10 S	119.12 E
De Grey ≃	162	20.12 S	119.11 E
Degt'ari	78	50.35 N	32.45 E
Degt'arka ≃	265a	59.57 N	30.52 E
Degt'arsk	86	56.42 N	60.06 E
Degunino ◄[8]	265b	55.52 N	37.33 E
De Haan	50	51.16 N	3.02 E
Dehak ≃	128	32.01 N	58.35 E
Dehalak Deset I	144	15.40 N	40.05 E
Deharda	126	21.40 N	87.25 E
De Hart Reservoir ◎[1]	208	40.28 N	76.45 W
Deh Bālā	123	34.04 N	70.29 E
Deh Bīd	128	30.38 N	53.13 E
Dehdez	128	31.43 N	50.17 E
Deh-e Salm	128	31.12 N	59.19 E
Dehgolān	128	35.17 N	47.25 E
Dehibat	148	32.01 N	10.42 E
Dehiwala-Mount Lavinia	122	6.51 N	79.52 E
Deh Kord	128	33.49 N	48.53 E
Dehlorān	128	32.41 N	47.16 E
De Hoek	158	32.57 S	18.46 E
Dehpehk I	174r	6.57 N	158.18 E
Dehra Dūn	124	30.19 N	78.02 E
Dehri	124	24.52 N	84.11 E
Dehrn	56	50.25 N	8.05 E
Dehu	122	18.35 N	73.51 E
Dehua	100	25.32 N	118.15 E
Dehuang	98	35.12 N	114.25 E
Dehui	89	44.34 N	125.43 E
Deidesheim	56	49.24 N	8.11 E
Deilbach ≃	263	51.23 N	7.05 E
Deilinghofen	56	51.22 N	7.47 E
Deining	60	49.13 N	11.32 E
Deinze	50	50.59 N	3.32 E
Deir el Asad	132	32.56 N	35.16 E
Deister ⩘	52	52.15 N	9.30 E
Deiva Marina	62	44.13 N	9.30 E
Dej	38	47.09 N	23.52 E
Deje	40	59.36 N	13.28 E
Dejima	94	36.05 N	140.20 E
Dejnau	128	39.15 N	63.11 E
De Jongs, Tanjong ≻	164	6.56 S	138.32 E
Deka ≃	154	18.04 S	26.42 E
De Kalb, Il., U.S.	216	41.55 N	88.45 W
De Kalb, Ms., U.S.	194	32.46 N	88.39 W
De Kalb, Tx., U.S.	194	33.30 N	94.36 W
De Kalb □[6], Il., U.S.	216	41.59 N	88.41 W
De Kalb □[6], In., U.S.	216	41.22 N	85.04 W
De Kalb Junction	212	44.30 N	75.16 W
Dekan, Hochland von → Deccan ⩘[1]	122	17.00 N	78.00 E
De-Kastri	89	51.28 N	140.47 E
Dekehtik I	174r	7.00 N	158.12 E
Dekemhare	144	15.05 N	39.02 E
Dekese	152	3.27 S	21.24 E
Deke Sokehs I	174r	6.59 N	158.11 E
Dekhgila Military Base ■	142	31.08 N	29.48 E
Dekina	150	7.39 N	7.02 E
Dékoa	152	6.19 N	19.04 E
De Koog	52	53.05 N	4.45 E
De Krim	52	52.38 N	6.38 E
De La Blanche, Lac ◎	186	50.05 N	69.29 W
Delabole	42	50.37 N	4.42 W
Delafield	216	43.03 N	88.24 W
Del Aire	280	33.55 N	118.21 W
Delamere, Austl.	164	15.45 S	131.33 E
Delamere, Austl.	168b	35.35 S	138.11 E
Delamere, Eng., U.K.	262	53.13 N	2.39 W
Delamere Forest ◄[3]	44	53.14 N	2.38 W
Delami Mayal, Jabal ∧	140	11.38 N	30.23 E
Del Amo Fashion Center ◄[9]	280	33.50 N	118.21 W
De Lancey, N.Y., U.S.	210	42.12 N	74.58 W
De Lancey, Pa., U.S.	214	40.59 N	78.58 W
Delanco	208	40.03 N	74.57 W
De Land	220	29.01 N	81.18 W
Delanggu	115a	7.37 S	110.41 E
Delano, Ca., U.S.	226	35.46 N	119.14 W
Delano, Mn., U.S.	190	45.02 N	93.47 W
Delano, Pa., U.S.	210	40.50 N	76.04 W
Delano Peak ∧	200	38.22 N	112.23 W
Delanson	210	42.44 N	74.11 W
Delaport Point ≻	240b	25.05 N	77.27 W
Delapu	120	31.35 N	90.35 E
Delārām	128	32.11 N	63.25 E
Delareyville	158	26.44 S	25.29 E
Delarof Islands II	181a	51.30 N	178.45 W
Delaronde Lake ◎	184	54.05 N	107.05 W
Del'atiči	76	53.47 N	25.59 E
Del'atin	78	48.32 N	24.37 E
Delatite ≃	169	37.10 S	146.00 E
Delavan, Il., U.S.	194	40.22 N	89.32 W
Delavan, Wi., U.S.	216	42.37 N	88.38 W
Delavan Lake	216	42.35 N	88.37 W
Delavan Lake ◎	216	42.37 N	88.38 W
Delaware, On., Can.	214	42.55 N	81.25 W
Delaware, N.J., U.S.	210	40.53 N	75.03 W
Delaware, Oh., U.S.	214	40.17 N	83.04 W
Delaware, Ok., U.S.	196	36.46 N	95.38 W
Delaware □[6], In., U.S.	216	40.18 N	85.23 W
Delaware □[6], N.Y., U.S.	210	42.17 N	74.55 W
Delaware □[6], Oh., U.S.	214	40.18 N	83.04 W
Delaware □[6], Pa., U.S.	208	39.55 N	75.23 W
Delaware □[3], U.S.	178	39.10 N	75.30 W
Delaware □[3], U.S.	208	39.10 N	75.30 W
Delaware ≃, U.S.	188	39.20 N	75.25 W
Delaware ≃, U.S.	196	32.02 N	104.01 W
Delaware ≃, Ks., U.S.	198	39.03 N	95.24 W
Delaware, East Branch ≃	210	41.55 N	75.17 W
Delaware, University of ʊ[2]	285	39.41 N	75.45 W
Delaware, West Branch ≃	210	41.56 N	75.17 W
Delaware and Raritan Canal ≊	208	40.29 N	74.26 W
Delaware Aqueduct ≊[1]	210	42.05 N	74.54 W
Delaware Bay ⊂	208	39.05 N	75.15 W
Delaware City	208	39.34 N	75.35 W
Delaware Lake ◎[1]	214	40.20 N	83.00 W
Delaware Memorial Bridge ◄[5]	285	40.07 N	74.50 W
Delaware Memorial Bridges ◄[5]	208	39.41 N	75.31 W
Delaware Mountains ⩘	196	31.35 N	104.40 W
Delaware Museum of Natural History ʊ	285	39.47 N	75.36 W
Delaware Park	210	40.43 N	75.11 W
Delaware Park ♦	284a	42.56 N	78.52 W
Delaware Park Race Track ♦	285	39.42 N	75.40 W
Delaware Seashore State Park ♦	208	38.38 N	75.04 W
Delaware State Park ♦	214	40.23 N	83.04 W
Delaware Water Gap	210	40.59 N	75.09 W
Delaware Water Gap National Recreation Area ♦	210	41.08 N	74.55 W
Delbrück	52	51.46 N	8.33 E
Delburne	182	52.12 N	113.14 W
Delcambre	194	29.57 N	91.59 W
Del Campillo	252	34.22 S	64.29 W
Del Carril	258	35.31 S	59.30 W
Del City	196	35.26 N	97.26 W
Delcommune, Lac ◎[1]	154	10.45 S	25.45 E
Del Dios	228	33.04 N	117.08 W
Delegate	166	37.03 S	148.58 E
Délembé	146	9.53 N	22.37 E
Delémont	58	47.22 N	7.21 E
De Leon	196	32.06 N	98.32 W
De Leon Springs	192	29.07 N	81.21 W
Delet ʮ	26	60.15 N	20.35 E
Delevan	210	42.29 N	78.28 W
Delfim Moreira	256	22.30 S	45.17 W
Delfinópolis	255	20.20 S	46.51 W
Delft	52	52.00 N	4.21 E
Delft Island I	122	9.30 N	79.42 E
Delfzijl	52	53.19 N	6.46 E
Delgada, Punta ≻	254	42.46 S	63.38 W
Delgado, Cabo ≻	154	10.40 S	40.35 E
Del Gallego	116	13.56 N	122.36 E
Delgany	48	53.08 N	6.05 W
Delger ≃	88	49.17 N	100.40 E
Delger chaan uul ∧	88	50.00 N	106.22 E
Delgerchangaj	102	45.15 N	104.50 E
Delgerchet	102	45.52 N	110.26 E
Delgercogt	102	46.08 N	106.23 E
Delgerech	102	45.48 N	111.12 E
Del Haven	208	39.03 N	74.56 W
Delhi, On., Can.	212	42.51 N	80.30 W
Delhi, India	124	28.40 N	77.13 E
Delhi, India	272a	28.40 N	77.13 E
Delhi, Ca., U.S.	226	37.26 N	120.46 W
Delhi, Il., U.S.	219	39.03 N	90.15 W
Delhi, Ia., U.S.	190	42.25 N	91.19 W
Delhi, La., U.S.	194	32.27 N	91.29 W
Delhi, N.Y., U.S.	210	42.16 N	74.54 W
Delhi □[8]	124	28.37 N	77.10 E
Delhi Cantonment	272a	28.36 N	77.08 E
Delhi Hills	218	39.05 N	84.36 W
Delhi Railroad Station ◄[5]	272a	28.40 N	77.13 E
Delhi Tail Distributary ≊	272a	28.41 N	77.10 E
Delhi University ʊ[2]	272a	28.42 N	77.13 E
Deli, Pulau I	115a	7.00 S	105.32 E
Delia, Ab., Can.	182	51.38 N	112.23 W
Delia, It.	70	37.21 N	13.55 E
Delia ≃	70	37.19 N	13.58 E
Delianuova	68	38.14 N	15.55 E
Deliblato	38	44.50 N	21.03 E
Delice	130	39.58 N	34.02 E
Delice ≃	130	40.28 N	34.10 E
Delices	240d	15.17 N	61.16 W
Deliceto	68	41.13 N	15.23 E
Delicias, Cuba	240p	21.11 N	76.34 W
Delicias, Méx.	232	28.13 N	105.28 W
De Lier	52	51.57 N	4.15 E
Delight	194	34.01 N	93.30 W
Delightful	214	41.18 N	80.57 W
Deliilyas	130	39.20 N	36.48 E
Delījān	128	33.59 N	50.40 E
Deliktaş	130	39.21 N	37.13 E
Delingde	74	70.08 N	114.00 E
Delingha	102	37.14 N	97.11 E
Dēliņkalns ∧[2]	76	57.30 N	26.58 E
Déli Pályaudvar ◄[5]	264c	47.30 N	19.01 E
Delisle	184	51.55 N	107.08 W
Delisle ≃	206	45.17 N	74.11 W
Delitua	114	3.30 N	98.41 E
Delitzsch	54	51.31 N	12.20 E
Delkern	228	35.21 N	119.01 W
Dell	46	58.30 N	6.20 W
Dellach	64	46.40 N	13.05 E
Dell City	200	31.56 N	105.12 W
Delle	58	47.30 N	7.00 E
Dellenbaugh, Mount ∧	200	36.07 N	113.32 W
Dellensjöarna ◎	26	61.54 N	16.41 E
Delles	148	36.55 N	3.55 E
Delligsen	52	51.57 N	9.48 E
Dello	64	45.25 N	10.04 E
Dell Rapids	198	43.50 N	96.43 W
Dellroy	214	40.33 N	81.11 W
Dellwig	263	51.29 N	7.41 E
Dellwig ◄[8]	263	51.29 N	6.56 E
Dellwood	219	38.44 N	90.17 W
Dellwood Highlands	278	41.34 N	88.03 W
Del Mar, Ca., U.S.	228	32.57 N	117.15 W
Delmar, De., U.S.	208	38.27 N	75.34 W
Delmar, Ia., U.S.	190	42.00 N	90.36 W
Delmar, Md., U.S.	208	38.27 N	75.34 W
Delmar, N.Y., U.S.	210	42.37 N	73.49 W
Del Mar Hills	196	27.37 N	99.26 W
Delmarva Peninsula ≻[1]	208	38.30 N	75.30 W
Del Mar Woods	278	42.12 N	87.51 W
Delmas, Sk., Can.	184	52.55 N	108.36 W
Delmas, S. Afr.	158	26.08 S	28.43 E
Delmas □[5]	273d	26.10 S	28.33 E
Delme	56	48.53 N	6.24 E
Delme ≃	52	53.05 N	8.40 E
Delmenhorst	52	53.03 N	8.38 E
Delmiro Gouveia	250	9.23 S	37.59 W
Delmont, N.J., U.S.	208	39.12 N	74.57 W
Delmont, Pa., U.S.	214	40.25 N	79.34 W
Delmont, S.D., U.S.	198	43.16 N	98.09 W
Del Monte Heights	226	36.36 N	121.50 W
Del Monte Park	226	36.36 N	121.56 W
Delnice	36	45.24 N	14.48 E
Del Norte	200	37.40 N	106.21 W
Del Norte Coast Redwood State Park ♦	204	41.38 N	124.05 W
De-Longa, ostrova II	74	76.30 N	153.00 E
De Long Mountains ⩘	180	68.20 N	162.00 W
De-Long-Strasse → Longa, proliv ʮ	74	70.20 N	178.00 E
Deloraine, Austl.	166	41.31 S	146.39 E
Deloraine, Mb., Can.	184	49.12 N	100.29 W
Delorme, Lac ◎	176	54.31 N	69.52 W
Deloro	212	44.31 N	77.37 W
Delos → Dhílos ⊥	38	37.26 N	25.16 E
Delph, Eng., U.K.	44	53.34 N	2.01 W
Delph, Eng., U.K.	262	53.34 N	2.01 W
Delphi	216	40.35 N	86.40 W
Delphi → Dhelfoí ⊥	38	38.30 N	22.29 E
Delphi Falls	210	42.53 N	75.55 W
Delphos, Ks., U.S.	198	39.16 N	97.46 W
Delphos, Oh., U.S.	216	40.50 N	84.20 W
Delph Reservoir ◎[1]	262	53.38 N	2.27 W
Delportshoop	158	28.22 S	24.20 E
Del Puerto Creek ≃	226	37.32 N	121.07 W
Delran	285	40.01 N	74.57 W
Delrath	263	51.08 N	6.47 E
Delray ◄[8]	281	42.18 N	83.08 W
Delray Beach	220	26.27 N	80.04 W
Del Rey	226	36.40 N	119.36 W
Del Rey Oaks	226	36.36 N	121.50 W
Del Rio, Fl., U.S.	220	28.03 N	82.26 W
Del Rio, Tx., U.S.	196	29.21 N	100.53 W
Del Rosa	228	34.08 N	117.15 W
Delsbo	26	61.48 N	16.35 E
Delson	206	45.22 N	73.33 W
Delstern ◄[8]	263	51.20 N	7.31 E
Delta, On., Can.	212	44.37 N	76.08 W
Delta, Méx.	200	32.22 N	115.12 W
Delta, Co., U.S.	200	38.44 N	108.04 W
Delta, Mo., U.S.	194	37.11 N	89.44 W
Delta, Oh., U.S.	216	41.34 N	84.00 W
Delta, Pa., U.S.	208	39.43 N	76.19 W
Delta, Ut,. U.S.	200	39.21 N	112.34 W
Delta □[9]	194	33.30 N	90.45 W
Delta ≃	180	64.09 N	146.18 W
Delta Amacuro □[8]	246	8.30 N	61.30 W
Delta Barrage ◄[6]	142	30.11 N	31.07 E
Delta Beach	184	50.11 N	98.19 W
Delta City	194	33.04 N	90.47 W
Delta Downs	166	17.00 S	141.18 E
Delta Junction	180	64.02 N	145.41 W
Delta Mendota Canal ≊	226	37.49 N	121.34 W
Delta Peak ∧	180	56.39 N	129.34 W
Delta Reservoir ◎[1]	210	43.17 N	75.26 W
Deltaville	208	37.33 N	76.20 W
Delton	216	42.29 N	85.24 W
Deltona	220	28.54 N	81.15 W
Delungra	166	29.39 S	150.50 E
Del'un-Uranskij chrebet ⩘	88	56.30 N	114.00 E
Delüün	86	47.42 N	90.59 E
De Luz Creek ≃	228	33.22 N	117.19 W
Del Valle	222	30.12 N	97.40 W
Del Valle, Lake ◎[1]	226	37.35 N	121.43 W
Del Verme Falls ⌊	144	5.27 N	40.17 E
Delvin	48	53.36 N	7.05 W
Delvinë	38	39.57 N	20.06 E
Del Viso	258	34.27 S	58.48 W
Delyn □[8]	262	53.16 N	3.11 W
Demak	115a	6.53 S	110.38 E
Demaki	80	58.26 N	51.43 E
Dem'ansk	76	57.38 N	32.28 E
Demarcation Point ≻	180	69.40 N	141.15 W
Demarest	276	40.57 N	73.57 W
Demarest Brook ≃	276	40.57 N	73.58 W
Demavend, Mount → Damāvand, Qolleh-ye ∧	128	35.56 N	52.08 E
Demba	152	5.30 S	22.16 E
Demba Chio	152	9.41 S	13.41 E
Dembecha	144	10.35 N	37.30 E
Dembéni	157a	11.50 S	43.24 E
Dembi	144	8.05 N	36.27 E
Dembia, Centraf.	154	5.07 N	24.25 E
Dembia, Zaïre	154	3.31 N	25.50 E
Dembi Dolo	144	8.32 N	34.48 E
Dembo	152	3.56 S	12.35 E
Dême ≃	50	47.43 N	0.29 E
Demer ≃	56	50.58 N	4.42 E
Demerara ≃	246	6.48 N	58.10 W
Demerthin	54	52.58 N	12.17 E
Demidov	76	55.16 N	31.31 E
Demidovka	78	50.25 N	25.20 E
Demidovo	76	59.17 N	38.17 E
Deming, N.M., U.S.	200	32.16 N	107.45 W
Deming, Wa., U.S.	224	48.49 N	122.12 W
Demini ≃	246	0.46 S	62.56 W
Demirci	130	39.03 N	28.40 E
Demir Kapija V	38	41.24 N	22.15 E
Demirköprü Barajı ◎[1]	130	38.40 N	28.20 E
Demirköy	130	41.49 N	27.45 E
Demirtaş	130	40.16 N	29.06 E
Demitz-Thumitz	54	51.09 N	14.14 E
Demjanka ≃	86	59.34 N	69.20 E
Demjanovo	24	60.22 N	47.03 E
Demjanskoje	86	59.36 N	69.18 E
Demjas	80	51.13 N	49.08 E
Demmeltrath ◄[8]	263	51.11 N	7.03 E
Demmin	54	53.54 N	13.02 E
Demmitt	182	55.26 N	119.54 W
Demnate	148	31.44 N	6.59 W
Democracy Monument ⊥	269a	13.45 N	100.30 E
Democrat Point ≻	276	40.37 N	73.18 W
Demoiselles, Grotte des ⏚[5]	62	43.55 N	3.45 E
Demone, Val ◄[1]	70	37.58 N	14.35 E
Demonte	62	44.19 N	7.17 E
De Montigny, Lac ◎	190	48.08 N	77.54 W
Demopolis	194	32.31 N	87.50 W
Demorest	192	34.33 N	83.32 W
De Mossville	218	38.48 N	84.25 W
Demotte	216	41.12 N	87.12 W
Dempo, Gunung ∧	112	4.02 S	103.09 E
Dempster, Point ≻	162	33.39 S	123.52 E
Demsa	146	9.32 N	13.14 E
Demta	164	2.20 S	140.08 E
Demurino	78	48.10 N	36.29 E
De Naauwte	158	30.08 S	21.42 E
Denain	50	50.20 N	3.23 E
Denair	226	37.32 N	120.47 W
Denakil ◄[1]	144	13.00 N	41.00 E
Denali	180	63.11 N	147.28 W
Denali National Park	180	63.44 N	148.54 W
Denali National Park ♦	180	63.15 N	150.30 W
Denan	144	6.30 N	43.30 E
Denare Beach	184	54.40 N	102.05 W
Denau	85	38.16 N	67.54 E
Denbigh, On., Can.	212	45.08 N	77.16 W
Denbigh, Wales, U.K.	44	53.11 N	3.25 W
Denbigh, Cape ≻	180	64.23 N	161.31 W
Den Burg	52	53.03 N	4.48 E
Denby Dale	44	53.35 N	1.38 W
Den Chai	110	17.59 N	100.04 E
Dendang	112	3.05 S	107.54 E
Dender (Dendre) ≃	50	51.02 N	4.06 E
Denderleeuw	50	50.53 N	4.04 E
Dendermonde	50	51.02 N	4.07 E
Dendre (Dender) ≃	50	51.02 N	4.06 E
Dendron, S. Afr.	156	23.25 S	29.11 E
Dendron, Va., U.S.	208	37.02 N	76.56 W
Dendy Park ♦	274b	37.56 S	145.00 E
Deneba	144	9.50 N	39.09 E
Denekamp	52	52.23 N	7.00 E
Denenchōfu ◄[8]	268	35.35 N	139.41 E
Deneysville	158	26.53 S	28.06 E
Deněžnikovo, S.S.S.R.	82	55.26 N	38.07 E
Deněžnikovo, S.S.S.R.	83	49.02 N	38.57 E
Dengcheng	100	33.41 N	114.27 E
Deng Deng	152	5.12 N	13.31 E
Denge	154	3.34 N	28.14 E
Denge Marsh ≡	42	50.57 N	0.55 E
Dengfeng	100	34.29 N	113.04 E
Denggongchang	107	30.24 N	103.49 E
Dengguanzhen	107	29.10 N	104.56 E
Dengkou	102	40.20 N	106.59 E
Denglongshu	98	41.20 N	115.15 E
Dengmingsi	98	37.53 N	116.42 E
Dêngqên	102	31.32 N	95.27 E
Dengshahe	98	39.13 N	122.04 E
Dengta	100	24.01 N	114.49 E
Denguiro	152	5.38 N	23.02 E
Dengxian	102	32.42 N	112.01 E
Dengyoufang	98	41.34 N	114.32 E
Den Haag → 's-Gravenhage	52	52.06 N	4.18 E
Denham, Austl.	162	25.55 S	113.32 E
Denham, Eng., U.K.	260	51.34 N	0.30 W
Denham, In., U.S.	216	41.09 N	86.43 W
Denham, Mount ∧	241q	18.13 N	77.32 W
Denham Aerodrome ⊠	260	51.36 N	0.31 W
Denham Island I	166	16.43 S	139.09 E
Denham Place ʊ	260	51.34 N	0.30 W
Denham Range ⩘	166	21.55 S	147.46 E
Denham Sound ʮ	162	25.40 S	113.15 E
Denham Springs	194	30.29 N	90.57 W
Den Helder	52	52.54 N	4.45 E
Denholme	262	53.48 N	1.54 W
Dénia	34	38.51 N	0.07 E
Denial Bay	162	32.06 S	133.32 E
Dénié	150	11.14 N	7.29 W
Deniliquin	166	35.32 S	144.58 E
Deniskoviči, S.S.S.R.	76	52.19 N	31.43 E
Deniskoviči, S.S.S.R.	76	52.44 N	26.41 E
Denison, Ia., U.S.	198	42.01 N	95.21 W
Denison, Tx., U.S.	196	33.45 N	96.32 W
Denison, Mount ∧	180	58.25 N	154.27 W
Denison Dam ◄[6]	196	33.50 N	96.34 W
Denisovka	24	66.14 N	55.20 E
Denisōvo	82	54.28 N	37.51 E
Denisy	261	48.33 N	1.56 E
Denizli	130	37.46 N	29.06 E
Denizli □[4]	130	37.40 N	29.15 E
Denkanikota	122	12.32 N	77.48 E
Denkendorf	60	48.56 N	11.27 E
Denkingen	58	47.53 N	9.19 E
Denklingen, B.R.D.	56	50.55 N	7.39 E
Denklingen, B.R.D.	58	47.55 N	10.51 E
Den'kovo	82	56.01 N	36.21 E
Denman Glacier ⍓	9	66.45 S	99.25 E
Denmark, Austl.	162	34.57 S	117.21 E
Denmark, S.C., U.S.	192	33.19 N	81.08 W
Denmark, Wi., U.S.	190	44.20 N	87.49 W
Denmark (Danmark) □[1], Europe	22	56.00 N	10.00 E
Denmark (Danmark) □[1], Europe	26	56.00 N	10.00 E
Denmark, Lake ◎	276	40.58 N	74.31 W
Denmark Bay ⊂	176	70.33 N	103.20 W
Denmark Strait ʮ	10	67.00 N	25.00 W
Denmead	42	50.54 N	1.04 W
Dennemont	261	49.01 N	1.42 E
Dennery	241f	13.55 N	60.54 W
Dennis	207	41.44 N	70.11 W
Dennis Head ≻	46	59.23 N	2.23 W
Dennison	214	40.23 N	81.20 W
Dennis Port	207	41.39 N	70.07 W
Denniston	172	41.44 S	171.48 E
Denniston Creek ≃	282	37.30 N	122.28 W
Dennisville	208	39.11 N	74.49 W
Denny	46	56.02 N	3.55 W
Den Oever	52	52.56 N	5.02 E
Denouval	261	48.58 N	2.03 E
Denpasar	115b	8.39 S	115.13 E
Denshaw	262	53.35 N	2.02 W
Dent Ditch ≊	279a	41.18 N	82.08 W
Denton, Eng., U.K.	262	53.27 N	2.07 W
Denton, Md., U.S.	208	38.53 N	75.49 W
Denton, Mi., U.S.	281	42.20 N	83.03 W
Denton, Mt., U.S.	202	47.19 N	109.56 W
Denton, N.C., U.S.	192	35.38 N	80.06 W
Denton, Tx., U.S.	222	33.12 N	97.07 W
Denton □[6]	222	33.07 N	97.10 W
Denton Creek ≃	196	32.58 N	96.57 W
Dentonia Park ♦	275b	43.42 N	79.17 W
D'Entrecasteaux, Point ≻	162	34.50 S	116.00 E
D'Entrecasteaux Islands II	164	9.30 S	150.40 E
D'Entrecasteaux National Park ♦	162	34.41 S	115.58 E
Dents du Midi ⩘	58	46.10 N	6.56 E
Denver, Co., U.S.	200	39.44 N	104.59 W
Denver, In., U.S.	216	40.51 N	86.04 W
Denver, Ia., U.S.	190	42.40 N	92.20 W
Denver, Pa., U.S.	208	40.13 N	76.08 W
Denver City	196	32.57 N	102.49 W
Denville	210	40.53 N	74.28 W
Denzlingen	58	48.04 N	7.52 E
Deoband	124	29.42 N	77.41 E
Deocha	126	24.03 N	87.35 E
Deodoro ◄[8]	287a	22.51 S	43.23 W
Deogarh, India	120	25.32 N	73.54 E
Deogarh, India	122	21.32 N	84.44 E
Deogarh, India	124	24.33 N	78.15 E
Deogarh ∧	124	23.32 N	82.16 E
Deogarh Hills ⩘[2]	124	23.35 N	82.30 E
Deoghar	124	24.29 N	86.42 E
Deogsu Palace ʊ	271b	37.35 N	126.58 E
Deolāli	122	19.57 N	73.50 E
Deoli	126	22.03 N	86.49 E
Deoli ◄[8]	272a	28.30 N	77.14 E
Deongwar, Mount ∧	171a	27.12 S	152.16 E
Deopāra	126	22.55 N	90.15 E
Deori, India	124	23.08 N	78.41 E
Deori, India	124	23.24 N	79.01 E
Deoria	124	26.31 N	83.47 E
Deosai Mountains ⩘	123	35.20 N	75.12 E
Deosil	124	23.42 N	82.15 E
Dep ≃	89	52.54 N	127.45 E
Depāl	126	21.44 N	87.33 E
De Panne	50	51.06 N	2.35 E
Depāra	272b	22.53 N	88.34 E
Departure Bay	224	49.12 N	123.58 W
DePaul University ʊ[2]	278	41.56 N	87.39 W
Depauville	212	44.08 N	76.04 W
Depauw	218	38.20 N	86.13 W
De Peel ≡	52	51.25 N	6.00 E
De Pere	190	44.26 N	88.03 W
Depew, N.Y., U.S.	210	42.54 N	78.41 W
Depew, Ok., U.S.	196	35.48 N	96.30 W
Deping	98	37.28 N	116.57 E
De Pinte	50	51.00 N	3.39 E
Depoe Bay	202	44.48 N	124.03 W
Depok	115a	6.24 S	106.50 E
Deport	196	33.32 N	95.19 W

Symbol	English	Deutsch	Español	Français	Português
≃	River	Fluß	Río	Rivière	Rio
≊	Canal	Kanal	Canal	Canal	Canal
⌊	Waterfall, Rapids	Wasserfall, Stromschnellen	Cascada, Rápidos	Chute d'eau, Rapides	Cascata, Rápidos
ʮ	Strait	Meeresstraße	Estrecho	Détroit	Estreito
⊂	Bay, Gulf	Bucht, Golf	Bahía, Golfo	Baie, Golfe	Baía, Golfo
◎	Lake, Lakes	See, Seen	Lago, Lagos	Lac, Lacs	Lago, Lagos
≡	Swamp	Sumpf	Pantano	Marais	Pântano
⍓	Ice Features, Glacier	Eis- und Gletscherformen	Accidentes Glaciales	Formes glaciaires	Acidentes glaciares
⍑	Other Hydrographic Features	Andere Hydrographische Objekte	Otros Elementos Hidrográficos	Autres données hydrographiques	Outros acidentes hidrográficos
✢	Submarine Features	Untermeerische Objekte	Accidentes Submarinos	Formes de relief sous-marin	Acidentes submarinos
□	Political Unit	Politische Einheit	Unidad Politica	Entité politique	Unidade política
ʊ	Cultural Institution	Kulturelle Institution	Institución Cultural	Institution culturelle	Instituição cultural
⊥	Historical Site	Historische Stätte	Sitio Histórico	Site historique	Sitio histórico
♦	Recreational Site	Erholungs- und Ferienort	Sitio de Recreo	Centre de loisirs	Area de Lazer
⊠	Airport	Flughafen	Aeropuerto	Aéroport	Aeroporto
■	Military Installation	Militäranlage	Instalación Militar	Installation militaire	Instalação militar
◄	Miscellaneous	Verschiedenes	Misceláneo	Divers	Diversos

ENGLISH — Name | Page | Lat.°′ | Long.°′ — DEUTSCH — Name | Seite | Breite°′ | Länge°′ E = Ost

Deposit 210 42.03 N 75.25 W
Depósito 246 3.12 N 60.35 W
Deptford 285 39.50 N 75.07 W
Deptford ◆[8] 260 51.28 N 0.02 W
Deptford Mall ◆[9] 285 39.50 N 75.06 W
Deptford Terrace 285 39.48 N 75.09 W
Depuch Island I 162 20.38 S 117.43 E
Depue 190 41.19 N 89.18 W
Deputy 218 38.48 N 85.39 W
Dêqên 102 28.38 N 98.52 E
Deqing, Zhg. 102 23.09 N 111.45 E
Deqing, Zhg. 106 30.33 N 120.05 E
De Queen 194 34.02 N 94.20 W
De Quincy 194 30.27 N 93.25 W
Dera ≃ 264c 47.39 N 19.05 E
Dera, Lach (Lak Dera) V 144 0.35 N 41.50 E
Dera Bugti 120 29.02 N 69.09 E
Derac 238 19.39 N 71.49 W
Dera Ghāzi Khān 123 30.03 N 70.38 E
Dera Gopipur 123 31.54 N 76.13 E
Dera Ismāīl Khān 123 31.50 N 70.54 E
Derakht-e Yahyá 120 31.50 N 68.08 E
Dera Nānak 123 32.02 N 75.01 E
Dera Nawāb 123 29.06 N 71.16 E
Derāwar Fort 123 28.46 N 71.20 E
Deražn'a 78 49.16 N 27.26 E
Derbent 84 42.03 N 48.18 E
Derbeškinskij 80 55.52 N 53.30 E
Derbetovka 80 45.48 N 43.05 E
Der Bodden ʉ 54 54.16 N 13.12 E
Derby, Austl. 162 17.18 S 123.38 E
Derby, Austl. 166 41.09 S 147.47 E
Derby, S. Afr. 158 25.55 S 27.02 E
Derby, Eng., U.K. 42 52.55 N 1.29 W
Derby, Ct., U.S. 207 41.19 N 73.05 W
Derby, Ks., U.S. 198 37.32 N 97.16 W
Derby, Me., U.S. 188 45.14 N 68.58 W
Derby, N.Y., U.S. 210 42.40 N 78.58 W
Derby, Oh., U.S. 218 39.46 N 83.12 W
Derby, Vt., U.S. 206 44.57 N 72.08 W
Derby Acres 226 35.15 N 119.35 W
Derby Line 206 45.00 N 72.05 W
Derbyshire □[6] 42 53.00 N 1.33 W
Der-Chantecoq, Lac du ⊜[1] 58 48.35 N 4.46 E
Derdepoort 156 24.42 S 26.20 E
Dere 130 39.00 N 39.18 E
Derecho ≃ 246 2.38 S 69.54 W
Dereĉin 76 53.15 N 24.55 E
Derecske 30 47.21 N 21.34 E
Dereköy, Tür. 130 41.56 N 27.21 E
Dereköy, Tür. 130 39.16 N 27.19 E
Dereköy, Tür. 130 40.08 N 37.47 E
Dereli 130 40.45 N 38.27 E
Derenburg 54 51.52 N 10.54 E
Derendorf ◆[8] 263 51.15 N 6.48 E
Derenwu 105 39.40 N 116.46 E
Dereseki ◆[8] 267b 41.08 N 29.08 E
Derev'anka 24 61.34 N 34.27 E
Derg ≃ 48 54.44 N 7.25 W
Derg, Lough ⊜, Ire. 48 54.36 N 7.53 W
Derg, Lough ⊜, Ire. 48 52.57 N 8.19 W
Dergači, S.S.S.R. 78 50.07 N 36.07 E
Dergači, S.S.S.R. 80 51.14 N 48.46 E
Dergaon 120 26.42 N 93.58 E
Der Grabow c 54 54.23 N 12.50 E
De Ridder 194 30.50 N 93.17 W
De Rijp 52 52.34 N 4.50 E
Derik 130 37.22 N 40.17 E
Derinkuyu 130 38.23 N 34.45 E
Der Kanal → English Channel ʉ 28 50.20 N 1.00 W
Derkul 80 51.16 N 51.18 E
Derkul ≃ 83 48.35 N 39.41 E
Dermbach 56 50.43 N 10.06 E
Dermott 194 33.31 N 91.26 W
Dermulo 64 46.20 N 11.04 E
Derne 263 51.35 N 7.41 E
Derne ◆[8] 263 51.34 N 7.31 E
Dernieres, Isles II 194 29.02 N 90.47 W
Dernoviči 78 51.36 N 29.43 E
Deroche 224 49.11 N 122.04 W
Dero Eri 144 9.01 N 46.43 E
Dêrong 102 28.47 N 99.14 E
Déroute, Passage de la ʉ 32 49.25 N 2.00 W
Derrame 196 26.19 N 104.23 W
Derravaragh, Lough ⊜ 48 53.40 N 7.24 W
Derre 154 16.56 S 36.11 E
Derrick City 214 41.58 N 78.34 W
Derrinallum 169 37.57 S 143.13 E
Derry → Londonderry, N. Ire., U.K. 48 54.59 N 7.20 W
Derry, N.H., U.S. 188 42.52 N 71.19 W
Derry, Pa., U.S. 214 40.20 N 79.18 W
Derrybrien 48 53.04 N 8.36 W
Derrykeighan 48 55.08 N 6.29 W
Derryveagh Mountains ⋏ 48 55.00 N 8.05 W
Derry West 275b 43.39 N 79.42 W
Der Sārāi ◆[8] 272a 28.33 N 77.11 E
Dersau 54 54.07 N 10.20 E
Dersingham 42 52.51 N 0.30 E
Derudeb 140 17.32 N 36.06 E
De Rust 158 33.30 S 22.32 E
Deruta 66 42.59 N 12.25 E
De Ruyter 210 42.45 N 75.53 W
DeRuyter Reservoir ⊜[1] 210 42.49 N 75.53 W
Der'uzino 82 56.18 N 38.16 E
Derval 32 47.40 N 1.40 W
Derventa 38 44.58 N 17.55 E
Derwent 182 53.39 N 110.58 W
Derwent ≃, Austl. 166 43.03 S 147.22 E
Derwent ≃, Eng., U.K. 44 53.45 N 0.57 W
Derwent ≃, Eng., U.K. 44 54.57 N 1.41 W
Derwent ≃, Eng., U.K. 44 54.38 N 3.34 W
Derwent ≃, Eng., U.K. 44 52.53 N 1.17 W
Derwent Bridge 166 42.08 S 146.13 E
Derwent Reservoir ⊜[1] 44 54.50 N 2.00 W
Derwent Water ⊜ 44 54.34 N 3.08 W
Deržavino 80 53.13 N 52.22 E
Deržavinsk 86 51.03 N 66.19 E
Desaguadero ≃, Arg. 252 34.13 S 66.47 W
Desaguadero ≃, Bol. 248 18.24 S 67.05 W
Dešt 130 39.10 N 39.22 E
Des Allemands 194 29.49 N 90.28 W
Désappointement, Îles du II 14 14.10 S 141.20 W
Des Arc 194 34.58 N 91.29 W
Desborough 42 52.27 N 0.49 W
Descabezado Grande, Volcán ∧[1] 252 35.36 S 70.45 W
Descanso, Bra. 252 26.50 S 53.35 W
Descanso, Ca., U.S. 204 32.51 N 116.37 W
Descanso, Punta > 204 32.16 N 117.03 W
Descanso Gardens ♦ 280 34.12 N 118.13 W
Descartes 32 46.58 N 0.42 E
Deschaillons 206 46.32 N 72.07 W
Deschambault 206 46.39 N 71.56 W
Deschambault Lake 184 54.55 N 103.22 W
Deschambault Lake ⊜ 184 54.40 N 103.35 W
Descharme Lake ⊜ 184 57.05 N 109.13 W
Deschênes 212 45.23 N 75.48 W
Deschênes, Lac ⊜ 212 45.22 N 75.51 W
Deschutes ≃, Or., U.S. 202 45.38 N 120.54 W
Deschutes ≃, Wa., U.S. 224 47.02 N 122.54 W
Descoberto 256 21.27 S 42.58 W
Descoberto, Serra do ⋏ 256 21.23 S 42.57 W
Dese 144 11.05 N 39.41 E
Deseado ≃ 254 47.45 S 65.54 W
Deseado, Cabo > 254 52.44 S 74.44 W
Desembarco de los 33 Orientales, Monumento ⊥ 258 33.48 S 58.25 W
Desengaño, Punta > 254 49.15 S 67.37 W
Desenzano del Garda 64 45.28 N 10.32 E
Desert Peak ∧ 200 40.28 N 112.38 W
Deseronto 212 44.12 N 77.03 W
Désert ≃ 190 46.23 N 75.58 W
Désert, Lac ⊜ 190 46.35 N 76.19 W
Desertas, Ilhas II 148 32.30 N 16.30 W
Desert Creek ≃ 226 38.48 N 119.19 W
Desert Hot Springs 204 33.57 N 116.30 W
Desert Lake ⊜, On., Can. 212 44.32 N 76.35 W
Desert Lake ⊜, Nv., U.S. 204 36.58 N 115.05 W
Desert Mountains ⋏ 226 39.16 N 119.00 W
Desert Peak ∧ 200 41.11 N 113.22 W
Desert Valley V 204 41.15 N 118.20 W
Desert View Highlands 228 34.37 N 118.13 W
Desfogue del Lago, Canal de ≃ 286a 19.26 N 99.03 W
Desford 42 52.39 N 1.17 W
Desha 194 35.44 N 91.40 W
Deshaies 241o 16.18 N 61.48 W
Desheng 102 24.45 N 108.28 E
Deshengchang 107 29.06 N 105.25 E
Deshengpo 102 26.58 N 103.59 E
Deshengtai 104 42.14 N 123.45 E
Deshengyingzi 104 41.44 N 123.14 E
Deshler, Ne., U.S. 198 40.08 N 97.43 W
Deshler, Oh., U.S. 216 41.12 N 83.53 W
Deshnok 120 27.48 N 73.21 E
Deshon Manor 214 40.52 N 79.57 W
Deshu 128 30.26 N 63.19 E
Deshun 106 31.58 N 120.29 E
Desiderio Tello 252 31.13 S 66.19 W
Desio 62 45.37 N 9.13 E
Des Lacs ≃ 198 48.17 N 101.25 W
Deslinde, Arroyo ≃ 258 33.44 S 58.52 W
Desloge 194 37.52 N 90.31 W
Desmarais 182 55.56 N 113.49 W
De Smet 198 44.23 N 97.33 W
De Smet, Lake ⊜[1] 202 44.28 N 106.45 W
Des Moines, Ia., U.S. 190 41.36 N 93.36 W
Des Moines, N.M., U.S. 196 36.45 N 103.50 W
Des Moines, Wa., U.S. 224 47.24 N 122.19 W
Des Moines ≃ 190 40.22 N 91.26 W
Des Moines, East Fork ≃ 198 42.41 N 94.12 W
Desmoronado, Cerro ∧ 234 20.21 N 104.59 W
Dešná, Česko. 61 48.58 N 15.33 E
Desna, S.S.S.R. 78 50.56 N 30.46 E
Desna ≃, S.S.S.R. 78 50.33 N 30.32 E
Desna ≃, S.S.S.R. 82 55.26 N 37.30 E
Desolación, Isla I 254 53.00 S 74.10 W
Désolation, Cap de la → Disappointment, Cape > 244 54.53 S 36.07 W
Desolation Point > 116 10.28 N 125.39 E
Desor, Mount ∧[2] 190 47.58 N 89.01 W
De Soto, Il., U.S. 194 37.49 N 89.13 W
De Soto, In., U.S. 216 40.15 N 85.17 W
De Soto, Mo., U.S. 194 38.08 N 90.33 W
De Soto, Tx., U.S. 222 32.35 N 96.51 W
De Soto □[6] 220 27.11 N 81.48 W
De Soto City 220 27.26 N 81.24 W
De Soto National Memorial ⊥ 220 27.31 N 82.40 W
De Soto State Park ♦ 194 34.28 N 85.36 W
Despatch 158 33.46 S 25.30 E
Despeñaperros, Desfiladero de ⋈ 34 38.24 N 3.30 W
Des Plaines 216 42.02 N 87.53 W
Des Plaines ≃ 216 41.24 N 88.16 W
Despotovac 38 44.05 N 21.33 E
Despujols 116 12.31 N 122.01 E
Desroches, Île I 138 5.41 S 53.41 E
Desruisseaux 241f 13.47 N 60.56 W
Dessau 54 51.50 N 12.14 E
Dessel 56 51.14 N 5.07 E
Destacado Island I 116 12.16 N 124.06 E
De Steeg 52 52.02 N 6.04 E
Destek 130 40.51 N 36.12 E
Destelbergen 50 51.03 N 3.48 E
Destêrro 250 7.17 S 37.06 W
Destin 194 30.23 N 86.29 W
Destruction, Mount ∧[2] 162 24.35 S 127.59 E
Destruction Bay 180 61.15 N 138.48 W
Destruction Island I 224 47.40 N 124.30 W
Desulo 71 40.01 N 9.14 E
Desvres 50 50.40 N 1.50 E
Deta 38 45.24 N 21.13 E
Detčino 82 54.49 N 36.19 E
Dete 154 18.58 S 26.50 E
Dethlingen 52 52.57 N 10.07 E
Detling 260 51.18 N 0.34 E
Detmold 52 51.56 N 8.52 E
Detmold □[5] 52 51.48 N 8.00 E
Detour, Point > 190 45.36 N 86.37 W
De Tour Village 190 46.00 N 83.54 W
Detrital Wash V 200 36.02 N 114.28 W
Detroit, Il., U.S. 219 39.37 N 90.40 W
Detroit, Mi., U.S. 216 42.20 N 83.03 W
Detroit, Mi., U.S. 281 42.20 N 83.03 W
Detroit, Or., U.S. 202 44.44 N 122.08 W
Detroit, Tx., U.S. 194 33.39 N 95.16 W
Detroit ≃ 214 42.06 N 83.08 W
Detroit, University of υ[2] 281 42.25 N 83.08 W
Detroit Beach 216 41.55 N 83.20 W
Detroit City Airport ⊠ 281 42.25 N 83.01 W
Detroit Institute of Arts ♦ 281 42.22 N 83.04 W
Detroit Lake ⊜[1] 202 44.42 N 122.10 W
Detroit Lakes 198 46.48 N 95.50 W
Detroit Metropolitan-Wayne County Airport ⊠ 281 42.13 N 83.22 W
Detroit Race Course ♦ 281 42.23 N 83.19 W
Detroit-Windsor Tunnel ◆[5] 281 42.20 N 83.02 W
Detroit Zoological Park ♦ 281 42.29 N 83.09 W
Detskosel'skij 265a 59.44 N 30.28 E
Dettelbach 56 49.48 N 10.09 E
Dettifoss ⌞ 24a 65.50 N 16.20 W
Dettingen an der Erms 58 48.32 N 9.20 E
Dettwiller 58 48.45 N 7.28 E
Det Udom 110 14.54 N 105.05 E
Detva 30 48.31 N 19.25 E
Deua National Park ♦ 166 36.00 S 149.45 E
Deuben 54 51.06 N 12.04 E
Deuels Corners 284a 42.49 N 78.45 W
Deuil-la-Barre 261 48.59 N 2.20 E
Deŭlgaon Rāja 122 20.01 N 76.02 E
Deulpur 272b 22.36 N 88.10 E
Deulti 126 22.26 N 87.56 E
Deurne, Bel. 50 51.13 N 4.28 E
Deurne, Ned. 52 51.28 N 5.47 E
Deusen ◆[8] 263 51.33 N 7.26 E
Deutsche Bucht c 30 54.30 N 7.30 E
Deutsche Demokratische Republik → German Democratic Republic □[1] 30 52.00 N 12.30 E
Deutsch Eylau → Iława 30 53.37 N 19.33 E
Deutschfeistritz 61 47.11 N 15.20 E
Deutschkreutz 61 47.36 N 16.38 E
Deutsch Krone → Wałcz 30 53.17 N 16.28 E
Deutschlandsberg 61 46.49 N 15.13 E
Deutsch-Neudorf 54 50.38 N 13.27 E
Deutsch Wagram 61 48.18 N 16.34 E
Deutsch Wusterhausen 264a 52.18 N 13.35 E
Deutzen 54 51.06 N 12.26 E
Deux-Montagnes 206 45.32 N 73.53 W
Deux-Montagnes □[6] 206 45.35 N 74.05 W
Deux Montagnes, Lac des ⊜ 206 45.28 N 73.59 W
Deux-Sèvres □[5] 32 46.30 N 0.20 W
Deva 38 45.53 N 22.55 E
Devakottai 122 9.57 N 78.49 E
De Valls Bluff 194 34.47 N 91.27 W
Devaprayāg 124 30.09 N 78.37 E
Dev'atern'a 80 56.12 N 53.24 E
Dev'atiny 24 60.56 N 36.46 E
Devault 285 40.05 N 75.32 W
Dévaványa 30 47.02 N 20.58 E
Devecikonağı 130 39.55 N 28.34 E
Devecser 30 47.06 N 17.26 E
Devedağı Tepesi ∧ 130 40.34 N 41.21 E
Devegeçidi Barajı ⊜[1] 130 38.05 N 39.55 E
Develi 130 38.23 N 35.30 E
Deventer 52 52.15 N 6.10 E
Deveron ≃ 46 57.40 N 2.31 W
Devers 222 30.02 N 94.36 W
Devers Canal, West Branch ≃ 222 29.57 N 94.46 W
Deversoir Military Base ■ 142 30.25 N 32.20 E
Devès, Monts du ⋏ 32 45.00 N 3.45 E
Devgadh Bāriya 120 22.42 N 73.54 E
De View, Bayou ≃ 194 34.48 N 91.18 W
Devīkot 120 26.42 N 71.12 E
Devil Lake ⊜ 212 44.35 N 76.27 W
Deville 56 49.53 N 4.42 E
Déville-lès-Rouen 50 49.28 N 1.02 E
Devil Peak ∧ 226 37.32 N 119.44 W
Devil River Peak ∧ 172 40.58 S 172.39 E
Devils ≃ 196 29.39 N 100.58 W
Devil's Bridge 42 52.23 N 3.51 W
Devils Brook ≃ 276 40.20 N 74.37 W
Devils Canyon V 280 34.16 N 117.58 W
Devil's Den State Park ♦ 194 35.46 N 94.16 W
Devils Hole Rapids ⌞ 284a 43.08 N 79.03 W
Devils Hopyard State Park ♦ 207 41.28 N 72.22 W
Devil's Island → Diable, Île du I 250 5.17 N 52.35 W
Devils Lake 198 48.06 N 98.51 W
Devils Lake ⊜, Mi., U.S. 216 41.58 N 84.17 W
Devils Lake ⊜, N.D., U.S. 198 48.01 N 98.52 W
Devils Lake State Park ♦ 190 43.24 N 89.44 W
Devils Marbles ♦ 162 20.30 S 134.14 E
Devils Paw ∧ 180 58.44 N 133.50 W
Devils Postpile National Monument ⊥ 226 37.37 N 119.05 W
Devils Tower ∧ 198 44.31 N 104.57 W
Devils Tower National Monument ⊥ 198 44.31 N 104.57 W
Devil's Water ≃ 44 54.58 N 2.02 W
Devin 38 41.45 N 24.24 E
Devine, B.C., Can. 182 50.32 N 122.30 W
Devine, Tx., U.S. 196 29.08 N 98.54 W
Devizes 42 51.22 N 1.59 W
Devladovo 78 48.07 N 33.45 E
Devli 120 25.45 N 75.23 E
De Voe Lake ⊜ 276 40.23 N 74.23 W
Devoll ≃ 38 40.49 N 19.51 E
Dévoluy ⋏ 62 44.39 N 5.53 E
Devon, Ab., Can. 182 53.22 N 113.44 W
Devon, S. Afr. 158 26.21 S 28.48 E
Devon, Pa., U.S. 285 40.02 N 75.25 W
Devon □[6] 42 50.45 N 3.50 W
Devon ≃, Eng., U.K. 42 53.04 N 0.43 W
Devon ≃, Scot., U.K. 46 56.07 N 3.51 W
Devon Island I 16 75.00 N 87.00 W
Devonport, Austl. 166 41.11 S 146.21 E
Devonport, N.Z. 172 36.49 S 174.48 E
Devonport, Eng., U.K. 42 50.22 N 4.10 W
Devonshire 285 39.49 N 75.32 W
Devonshire Plaza ◆[9] 281 42.17 N 83.00 W
Devore 228 34.13 N 117.25 W
Devoto 252 31.24 S 62.19 W
Devrek 130 41.13 N 31.57 E
Devrekâni 130 41.36 N 33.51 E
Devres ≃ 130 41.06 N 34.25 E
Devure ≃ 154 20.00 S 32.20 E
Dewa, Ujung > 114 2.55 N 95.48 E
Dewakang-lompo, Pulau I 112 5.24 S 118.25 E
Dewar 196 35.27 N 95.56 W
Dewart 210 41.07 N 76.53 W
Dewart Lake ⊜ 216 41.22 N 85.47 W
Dewās 120 22.58 N 76.04 E
Dewa-sanchi ⋏[2] 92 39.05 N 140.10 E
Dewdney 224 49.10 N 122.12 W
Dewetsdorp 158 29.33 S 26.34 E
Dewey, P.R. 240m 18.18 N 65.18 W
Dewey, Il., U.S. 216 40.19 N 88.17 W
Dewey, Ok., U.S. 196 36.47 N 95.56 W
Dewey, Wa., U.S. 224 48.25 N 122.37 W
Dewey Beach 208 38.41 N 75.04 W
Deweyville 194 30.18 N 93.45 W
De Witt, Ar., U.S. 194 34.17 N 91.20 W
Dewitt, Il., U.S. 219 40.11 N 88.47 W
De Witt, Ia., U.S. 190 41.49 N 90.32 W
De Witt, Mi., U.S. 216 42.50 N 84.34 W
De Witt, Ne., U.S. 198 40.23 N 96.55 W
De Witt, N.Y., U.S. 210 43.02 N 76.03 W
De Witt □[6], Il., U.S. 216 40.12 N 88.55 W
De Witt □[6], Tx., U.S. 222 29.07 N 97.20 W
Dewittville 214 42.14 N 79.27 W
Dewsbury 44 53.42 N 1.37 W
Dexing 100 28.54 N 117.36 E
Dexingjie 98 39.54 N 122.50 E
Dexter, Me., U.S. 188 45.01 N 69.17 W
Dexter, Mi., U.S. 216 42.20 N 83.53 W
Dexter, Mo., U.S. 194 36.47 N 89.57 W
Dexter, N.M., U.S. 196 33.11 N 104.22 W
Dexter, N.Y., U.S. 212 44.00 N 76.02 W
Dexterity Fiord c[2] 176 71.11 N 73.03 W
Deyang 102 31.14 N 104.22 E
Dey-Dey, Lake ⊜ 162 29.12 S 131.04 E
Deyhūk 128 33.17 N 57.30 E
Deyyer 128 27.50 N 51.55 E
Dez ≃ 128 31.39 N 48.52 E
Dezfūl 128 32.23 N 48.24 E
Dez Gerd 128 30.45 N 51.57 E
Dezhou 98 37.27 N 116.18 E
Dežneva, mys > 180 66.06 N 169.45 W
Dezong 120 32.09 N 90.20 E
Dezzo di Scalve 64 45.59 N 10.05 E
Dgâmcha, Sebkhet te-n- ⊜ 150 18.45 N 15.48 W
Dhabān Singh 123 31.44 N 73.34 E
Dhāding 124 27.52 N 84.55 E
Dhādkā 126 22.47 N 86.30 E
Dháfna ∧ 267c 38.07 N 23.38 E
Dháfni 38 37.48 N 22.01 E
Dhafnion Monastery υ[1] 267c 38.01 N 23.38 E
Dhahab 140 28.29 N 34.32 E
Dhahab, Wādī adh- V 132 32.44 N 35.54 E
Dhahran → Aẓ-Ẓahrān 128 26.18 N 50.08 E
Dhaka (Dacca), Bngl. 126 23.43 N 90.25 E
Dhāka, India 124 26.41 N 85.10 E
Dhaka □[5] 120 24.15 N 90.15 E
Dhākauli 124 24.45 N 77.51 E
Dhakuria Lake ⊜ 272b 22.31 N 88.22 E
Dhaleswari ≃ 126 23.32 N 90.34 E
Dháli 130 35.01 N 33.25 E
Dhamār 144 14.46 N 44.23 E
Dhāmpur 124 29.19 N 78.31 E
Dhāmrai 126 23.55 N 90.13 E
Dhamtari 122 20.41 N 81.34 E
Dhāmura 126 22.53 N 90.12 E
Dhanaula 123 30.17 N 75.35 E
Dhanaura 124 28.58 N 78.15 E
Dhanbād 126 23.48 N 86.27 E
Dhandhuka 120 22.22 N 71.59 E
Dhanera 120 24.31 N 72.02 E
Dhaneswargāti 126 23.25 N 89.20 E
Dhangadhī 124 28.41 N 80.36 E
Dhaniakhāli 126 22.58 N 88.06 E
D'Hanis 196 29.20 N 99.17 W
Dhankuṭa 124 26.59 N 87.20 E
Dhansar 272c 19.07 N 73.05 E
Dhānyahānā 272b 22.48 N 88.11 E
Dhār 120 22.36 N 75.18 E
Dharampur 122 20.32 N 73.11 E
Dharān 124 26.49 N 87.17 E
Dharangaon 120 21.01 N 75.16 E
Dhārāpuram 122 10.44 N 77.31 E
Dhāri 120 21.20 N 71.01 E
Dhārīwāl 123 31.57 N 75.19 E
Dharmābād 122 18.54 N 77.51 E
Dharmapuri 122 12.08 N 78.10 E
Dharmavaram 122 14.26 N 77.43 E
Dharmjaygarh 124 22.28 N 83.13 E
Dharmkot 123 30.57 N 75.14 E
Dharmshāla 123 32.13 N 76.19 E
Dharoor, Tog V 144 10.20 N 50.30 E
Dharug National Park ♦ 170 33.25 S 151.05 E
Dhasān ≃ 124 25.48 N 79.24 E
Dhātrigrām 126 23.15 N 88.20 E
Dhaulpur 124 26.42 N 77.54 E
Dhawalāgiri □[8] 124 28.30 N 83.30 E
Dhawalāgiri ∧ 124 28.42 N 83.30 E
Dhebar Lake ⊜ 120 24.16 N 74.00 E
Dhelfoí ⊥ 38 38.30 N 22.29 E
Dhenkānāl 120 20.40 N 85.36 E
Dherinia 130 35.03 N 33.57 E
Dhérmiu υ[1] 38 40.08 N 19.42 E
Dherue, Loch an ⊜ 46 58.25 N 4.27 W
Dheskáti 38 39.55 N 21.49 E
Dheune ≃ 58 46.54 N 5.00 E
Dhiavolítsion 38 37.18 N 21.58 E
Dhībān 132 31.30 N 35.47 E
Dhidhimótikhon 38 41.21 N 26.30 E
Dhiinsoor 144 2.24 N 42.59 E
Dhíkti ⋏ 38 35.08 N 25.22 E
Dhílos ⊥ 38 37.26 N 25.16 E
Dhimitsána 38 37.37 N 22.03 E
Dhiónisos 267c 38.06 N 23.53 E
Dhī Qār □[4] 128 31.00 N 46.15 E
Dhirāsrām 126 23.57 N 90.25 E
Dhirwah, Wādī adh- V 132 31.18 N 36.56 E
Dhodhekánisos (Dodecanese) II 38 36.30 N 27.00 E
Dhodhóni ⊥ 38 39.34 N 20.47 E
Dhofar → Ẓufār ◆[1] 118 17.00 N 54.10 E
Dhokra 272b 22.40 N 88.34 E
Dholka 120 22.43 N 72.28 E
Dhomhnuill, Sgurr ∧ 46 56.45 N 5.27 W
Dhone 122 15.25 N 77.53 E
Dhopākhola 126 23.08 N 89.10 E
Dhorāji 120 21.44 N 70.27 E
Dhosha 126 22.15 N 88.33 E
Dhowa 126 24.03 N 86.54 E
Dhoxáton 38 41.05 N 24.14 E
Dhrāngadhra 120 22.59 N 71.28 E
Dhrapetsóna 267c 37.57 N 23.37 E
Dhrol 120 22.34 N 70.25 E
Dhron ≃ 56 49.52 N 6.54 E
Dhubāb 144 12.56 N 43.25 E
Dhuburi 124 26.01 N 89.59 E
Dhudiāl 123 33.04 N 72.58 E
Dhulāgarh 272b 22.35 N 88.11 E
Dhule 120 20.54 N 74.47 E
Dhulia → Dhule 120 20.54 N 74.47 E
Dhuliān 124 24.41 N 87.58 E
Dhulikhel 124 27.37 N 85.33 E
Dhūlsiras ◆[8] 272a 28.33 N 77.02 E
Dhünn 56 51.06 N 7.16 E
Dhünn-Stausee ⊜[1] 263 51.05 N 7.16 E
Dhupgāri 124 26.36 N 89.01 E
Dhurbo 144 11.37 N 50.20 E
Dhūri 123 30.22 N 75.52 E
Dhurmukhar ≃ 272c 18.54 N 72.49 E
Dhuudo 144 9.20 N 50.12 E
Dhuudo V 144 9.14 N 50.39 E
Dhuusa Mareeb 144 5.31 N 46.24 E
Día I 38 35.27 N 25.13 E
Diabaig 46 57.34 N 5.40 W
Diabakania 150 10.38 N 10.58 W
Diable, Île du (Devil's Island) I 250 5.17 N 52.35 W
Diable, Lac du ⊜ 206 46.31 N 74.20 W
Diable, Morne au ∧ 240d 15.37 N 61.27 W
Diable, Pointe du > 240e 14.47 N 60.54 W
Diable, Rivière du ≃ 206 46.03 N 74.38 W
Diablo, Ca., U.S. 226 37.50 N 121.58 W
Diablo, Wa., U.S. 224 48.43 N 121.09 W
Diablo, Canyon V 200 35.18 N 110.59 W
Diablo, Isla del → Diable, Île du I 250 5.17 N 52.35 W
Diablo, Mount ∧ 226 37.53 N 121.55 W
Diablo, Sierra del ⋏ 196 27.20 N 104.05 W
Diablo Lake ⊜[1] 224 48.43 N 121.08 W
Diablo Plateau ⋏[1] 200 31.30 N 105.30 W
Diablo Range ⋏ 226 37.00 N 121.20 W
Diablotin, Morne ∧ 240d 15.30 N 61.24 W
Diabo 150 7.47 N 5.11 W
Diaca 154 11.30 S 39.59 E
Diadema 256 23.42 S 46.37 W
Diadema □[7] 287b 23.42 S 46.36 W
Diadema Argentina 254 45.46 S 67.40 W
Diafarabé 150 14.09 N 5.01 W
Diagonal 198 40.48 N 94.20 W
Diaka ≃[1] 150 15.13 N 4.14 W
Dialakoto 150 13.19 N 13.18 W
Dialassagou 150 13.45 N 3.37 W
Diamant, Pointe du > 240e 14.27 N 61.03 W
Diamante, Arg. 252 32.04 S 60.39 W
Diamante, It. 68 39.41 N 15.49 E
Diamante ≃ 252 34.31 S 66.56 W
Diamante, Punta del > 234 16.47 N 99.52 W
Diamante de Ubá 256 21.12 S 42.55 W
Diamantina 255 18.15 S 43.36 W
Diamantina ≃ 166 26.45 S 139.10 E
Diamantina Fracture Zone ✢ 14 36.00 S 105.00 E
Diamantina Lakes 166 23.46 S 141.09 E
Diamantino 248 14.25 S 56.27 W
Diamantino ≃ 255 16.08 S 52.28 W
Diamond, Il., U.S. 216 41.17 N 88.15 W
Diamond, Mo., U.S. 194 37.00 N 94.19 W
Diamond, Oh., U.S. 214 41.06 N 81.01 W
Diamond Bar 228 34.01 N 117.48 W
Diamond Brook ≃ 276 40.56 N 74.08 W
Diamond Creek 274b 37.41 S 145.09 E
Diamond Creek ≃ 169 37.44 S 145.09 E
Diamond Harbour 126 22.12 N 88.12 E
Diamond Head ±[6] 229c 21.16 N 157.49 W
Diamond Hill 207 41.59 N 71.24 W
Diamond Hill Reservoir ⊜[1] 283 42.00 N 71.24 W
Diamond Hill State Park ♦ 283 42.00 N 71.26 W
Diamond Islets II 166 17.25 S 150.53 E
Diamond Lake 216 42.15 N 88.00 W
Diamond Lake ⊜, On., Can. 212 45.04 N 78.02 W
Diamond Lake ⊜, Il., U.S. 278 42.15 N 88.00 W
Diamond Lake ⊜, Mi., U.S. 216 41.54 N 85.59 W
Diamond Lake ⊜, Or., U.S. 202 43.10 N 122.09 W
Diamond Peak ∧, Id., U.S. 202 44.09 N 113.05 W
Diamond Peak ∧, Or., U.S. 202 43.33 N 122.09 W
Diamond Peak ∧, Wa., U.S. 202 46.07 N 117.32 W
Diamond Springs 226 38.41 N 120.48 W
Diamondville 200 41.46 N 110.32 W
Diana 222 32.43 N 94.45 W
Diana Bay c 176 60.50 N 69.50 W
Dianalund 41 55.32 N 11.30 E
Dianbai 102 21.30 N 111.01 E
Dian Chi ⊜ 102 24.50 N 102.42 E
Diancun 105 39.55 N 116.14 E
Dianfangba 102 32.54 N 103.35 E
Diangounté Kamara 150 14.33 N 9.31 W
Dianhu 100 33.58 N 119.38 E
Dianji 98 36.32 N 120.27 E
Dianjiang 102 30.21 N 107.23 E
Diano, Vallo di V 68 40.21 N 15.36 E
Diano Marina 62 43.54 N 8.05 E
Dianópolis 250 11.38 S 46.50 W
Dianqianhe 100 30.44 N 116.02 E
Dianra 150 8.45 N 6.14 W
Dianshang 106 31.10 N 118.51 E
Dianshan Hu ⊜ 106 31.08 N 120.55 E
Diantou 100 27.18 N 120.11 E
Dianzi 104 41.37 N 122.05 E
Diaobingshan 104 42.28 N 123.33 E
Diao'ecun 105 40.43 N 115.49 E
Diaohetou 105 39.17 N 116.41 E
Diaopu 100 32.22 N 119.54 E
Diaoshuilouzi 104 40.59 N 122.22 E
Diaotai 100 29.40 N 119.39 E
Diaowo 105 39.30 N 116.04 E
Diapaga 150 12.04 N 1.47 E
Diapangou 150 12.07 N 0.11 E
Diapblo, Puntan > 174n 15.00 N 145.35 E
Dias 256 22.28 S 45.34 W
Diascund Creek Reservoir ⊜[1] 208 37.27 N 76.54 W
Diawala 150 10.07 N 5.28 W
Diaz 194 35.38 N 91.15 W
Diaz Point > 156 26.38 S 15.05 E
Dibai 124 28.13 N 78.15 E
Dibāng ≃ 120 27.50 N 95.32 E
Dibay → Dubayy 128 25.18 N 55.18 E
Dibaya 152 6.30 S 22.57 E
Dibbīn 132 32.26 N 36.34 E
Dibble Iceberg Tongue ⊓ 9 65.40 S 135.10 E
Dibeng 158 27.35 S 22.54 E
D'Iberville 194 30.25 N 88.53 W
Dibete 156 23.45 S 26.26 E
Dibi 144 4.13 N 41.56 E
Dibo 144 6.31 N 41.52 E
Diboll 222 31.11 N 94.46 W
Dibrugarh 120 27.29 N 94.54 E
Dibs 140 12.34 N 24.14 E
Dibs, Bi'r ╤[4] 140 22.12 N 29.32 E
Dichāon Kalān ◆[8] 272a 28.39 N 76.59 E
Dick, Mount ∧[2] 168a 31.35 S 116.42 E
Dickelsbach ≃ 263 51.24 N 6.45 E
Dickens 196 33.37 N 100.50 W
Dickerson 208 39.13 N 77.25 W
Dickey ≃ 224 47.55 N 124.37 W
Dickey Lake ⊜, On., Can. 212 44.47 N 77.44 W
Dickey Lake ⊜, Wa., U.S. 224 48.06 N 124.31 W
Dickinson, N.D., U.S. 198 46.52 N 102.47 W
Dickinson, Pa., U.S. 208 40.07 N 77.20 W
Dickinson, Tx., U.S. 222 29.27 N 95.03 W
Dickinson Bayou ≃ 222 29.28 N 94.58 W
Dickinson Island I 281 42.37 N 82.38 W
Dickins Seamount ✢[3] 16 54.30 N 137.00 W
Dicks 158 27.43 S 30.10 E
Dickson, Ok., U.S. 196 34.11 N 96.59 W
Dickson, Tn., U.S. 194 36.04 N 87.23 W
Dickson City 210 41.28 N 75.36 W
Dicle, Tür. 130 38.22 N 40.04 E
Dicle, Tür. 130 37.18 N 42.04 E
Dicle → Tigris ≃ 128 31.00 N 47.25 E
Dicomano 66 43.53 N 11.31 E
Diculom 116 7.54 N 122.14 E
Dicun 100 33.46 N 117.32 E
Didam 52 51.56 N 6.08 E
Didao 89 45.22 N 130.51 E
Didbiran 89 51.58 N 139.20 E
Didcot 42 51.37 N 1.15 W
Didesa ≃ 144 9.56 N 35.45 E
Didiéni 150 13.53 N 8.06 W
Didimbo 152 17.30 S 21.45 E
Didinga Hills ⋏ 154 4.20 N 33.35 E
Didsbury 182 51.40 N 114.08 W
Didsbury ◆[8] 262 53.25 N 2.14 W
Diduyon ≃ 116 16.36 N 121.42 E
Dīdwāna 120 27.24 N 74.34 E
Didy 157b 18.07 S 48.32 E
Die 62 44.45 N 5.22 E
Die Aue ◆[1] 263 51.40 N 6.35 E
Die Berg ∧ 156 25.12 S 30.09 E
Die Boss 158 31.59 S 19.44 E
Diébougou 150 10.58 N 3.15 W
Dieburg 56 49.54 N 8.50 E
Dieciocho de Julio 252 33.41 S 53.33 W
Dieciocho de Marzo 232 25.38 N 97.50 W
Diecke 150 7.21 N 8.58 W
Diedenhofen → Thionville 56 49.22 N 6.10 E
Diedersdorf 264a 52.20 N 13.21 E
Die Erpe ≃ 264a 52.27 N 13.38 E
Diefenbaker, Lake ⊜[1] 184 51.00 N 106.55 W
Diego de Almagro 252 26.23 S 70.03 W
Diego de Almagro, Isla I 254 51.25 S 75.10 W
Diego de Ocampo, Pico ∧ 238 19.35 N 70.45 W
Diego Garcia I 12 7.20 S 72.25 E
Diego Gaynor 258 34.17 S 59.14 W
Diego Ramírez, Islas II 244 56.30 S 68.44 W
Die Haard ◆[1] 263 51.41 N 7.15 E
Diekirch 56 49.53 N 6.10 E
Dieksee ⊜ 54 54.10 N 10.30 E
Dieleemu 86 46.22 N 88.43 E
Dielingen 52 52.26 N 8.20 E
Dielsdorf 58 47.29 N 8.27 E
Diéma 150 14.32 N 9.12 W
Diemansputs 158 29.54 S 21.33 E
Diembéring 150 12.28 N 16.47 W
Diemel ≃ 52 51.39 N 9.27 E
Diemel-Talsperre ◆[6] 56 51.22 N 8.43 E
Diemen 52 52.20 N 4.58 E
Diemuchuoke 120 32.42 N 79.29 E
Dien Bien Phu 110 21.23 N 103.01 E
Dien Khanh 110 12.15 N 109.06 E
Diepenau 52 52.25 N 8.44 E
Diepenbeek 56 50.54 N 5.24 E
Diepenheim 52 52.12 N 6.33 E
Diepensee 264a 52.22 N 13.31 E
Diepenveen 52 52.18 N 6.08 E
Diepholz 52 52.35 N 8.21 E
Diepoldsau 58 47.23 N 9.38 E
Dieppe, N.B., Can. 186 46.06 N 64.45 W
Dieppe, Fr. 50 49.56 N 1.05 E
Dierbao 98 40.20 N 114.32 E
Dierdorf 56 50.33 N 7.39 E
Dieren 52 52.03 N 6.06 E
Dierhagen 54 45.18 N 12.21 E
Dierks 194 34.07 N 94.00 W
Diersbach 60 48.25 N 13.34 E
Diersfordt 263 51.42 N 6.33 E
Di'er Songhua ≃ 89 45.26 N 124.39 E
Diesdorf 54 52.45 N 10.52 E
Dieskau 54 51.26 N 12.02 E
Diessem ◆[8] 263 51.20 N 6.35 E
Diessen 64 47.56 N 11.06 E
Diessenhofen 58 47.41 N 8.45 E
Diest 56 50.59 N 5.03 E
Dietenheim 58 48.12 N 10.04 E
Dietersburg 60 48.30 N 12.55 E
Dietersdorf 56 50.13 N 10.49 E
Dietfurt 56 48.57 N 10.56 E
Dietfurt an der Altmühl 60 49.02 N 11.35 E
Dietikon 58 47.24 N 8.24 E
Dietmannsried 58 47.49 N 10.17 E
Dietrich 202 42.54 N 114.15 W
Dietzenbach 56 50.01 N 8.47 E
Dietzhölztal 56 50.50 N 8.19 E
Dieue-sur-Meuse 56 49.04 N 5.25 E
Dieulefit 62 44.31 N 5.04 E
Dieulouard 56 48.51 N 6.04 E
Dieuze 56 48.49 N 6.43 E
Dieveniškės 76 54.12 N 25.37 E
Dievenow → Dziwnów 30 54.03 N 14.45 E
Diever 52 52.52 N 6.19 E
Die Ville ⋏[2] 56 50.40 N 6.55 E
Die Wurzen (Koren) ⋈ 64 46.31 N 13.45 E
Diez 56 50.22 N 8.01 E
Diez de Octubre 232 24.44 N 104.39 W
Dif 144 0.59 N 40.57 E
Difang 98 35.23 N 117.52 E
Diffa 146 13.19 N 12.37 E
Diffa □[5] 146 16.00 N 13.30 E
Differdange 56 49.32 N 5.52 E
Difficult Run ≃ 284c 38.58 N 77.14 W
Diffun 116 16.34 N 121.33 E
Difuri I 122 5.24 N 73.38 E
Digambar Jain Temple υ[1] 272b 22.36 N 88.23 E
Digambarpur 126 21.57 N 88.22 E
Digba 154 4.24 N 25.47 E
Digboi 120 27.23 N 95.38 E
Digby 186 44.37 N 65.46 W
Digby Neck >[1] 186 44.30 N 66.10 W
Dige 98 34.22 N 114.28 E
Digerberget ∧[2] 40 60.35 N 13.25 E
Digges Islands II 176 62.35 N 77.50 W
Diggle 262 53.34 N 1.59 W
Dighalia 126 23.07 N 89.39 E
Dighipāra 126 21.58 N 88.17 E
Dighode 272c 18.54 N 73.02 E
Dighra 272b 22.47 N 88.32 E
Dighton, Ks., U.S. 198 38.28 N 100.28 W
Dighton, Ma., U.S. 207 41.48 N 71.07 W
Di Giorgio 228 35.15 N 118.51 W
Dīglūr 122 18.33 N 77.36 E
Digmoor 262 53.32 N 2.45 W
Dīgnagar 126 23.27 N 87.41 E
Dignano 64 46.05 N 12.56 E
Digne 62 44.06 N 6.14 E
Digoin 32 46.29 N 3.59 E
Digomi 84 41.47 N 44.44 E
Digong 104 42.11 N 122.03 E
Digor 84 40.23 N 43.24 E
Digora 84 43.10 N 44.09 E
Digos 116 6.45 N 125.20 E
Digra 272b 22.50 N 88.20 E
Digras 122 20.07 N 77.43 E
Digri 120 25.10 N 69.07 E
Digui 152 5.28 N 20.50 E
Digul ≃ 164 7.07 S 138.42 E
Dihaer 86 42.35 N 89.49 E
Dihun 144 7.18 N 42.42 E
Diirmentobe 86 45.44 N 63.37 E
Dijag 24 65.48 N 57.39 E
Dijlah → Tigris ≃ 128 31.00 N 47.25 E
Dijlah, Wādī V 142 29.58 N 31.18 E
Dijle (Dyle) ≃ 56 50.53 N 4.42 E
Dijohan Point > 116 16.19 N 122.14 E
Dijon 58 47.19 N 5.01 E
Dik 146 9.58 N 17.31 E
Dikaja 76 59.15 N 39.30 E
Dikala 154 4.41 N 31.23 E
Dikan'ka 78 49.49 N 34.32 E
Dikbıyık 130 41.13 N 36.38 E
Dike 190 42.27 N 92.37 W
Dikhil 144 11.06 N 42.22 E
Dikili 130 39.04 N 26.53 E
Dikirnis 142 31.05 N 31.35 E
Dikli 76 57.35 N 25.06 E
Diklosmta, gora ∧ 84 42.29 N 45.47 E
Dikmen 130 39.53 N 32.50 E
Dikodougou 150 9.04 N 5.46 W
Diksmuide (Dixmude) 50 51.02 N 2.52 E
Dikson 74 73.30 N 80.35 E
Dikwa 146 12.02 N 13.56 E
Dila 144 6.21 N 38.17 E
Dilbeek 50 50.51 N 4.16 E
Dilektepe 130 38.04 N 41.49 E
Dile Point > 116 17.34 N 120.20 E
Dilerpur 272b 22.51 N 88.10 E
Dili 112 8.33 S 125.35 E
Dilia V 146 16.53 N 11.00 E
Diligent Strait ʉ 110 12.11 N 92.57 E
Di Linh 110 11.35 N 108.04 E
Diližan 84 40.45 N 44.52 E
Diližanskij zapovednik ♦ 84 40.40 N 45.00 E
Dill ≃ 56 50.33 N 8.29 E
Dill City 196 35.16 N 99.08 W
Dillenburg 56 50.44 N 8.17 E
Diller 198 40.06 N 96.56 W
Dilley, Or., U.S. 224 45.29 N 123.07 W
Dilley, Tx., U.S. 196 28.40 N 99.10 W
Dilling 140 12.03 N 29.39 E
Dillingen 56 49.21 N 6.44 E
Dillingen an der Donau 56 48.34 N 10.29 E
Dillingham 180 59.02 N 158.29 W
Dillon, Co., U.S. 200 39.37 N 106.02 W
Dillon, Mt., U.S. 202 45.12 N 112.38 W
Dillon, S.C., U.S. 192 34.24 N 79.22 W
Dillon ≃ 184 55.56 N 108.57 W
Dillon Cone ∧ 172 42.16 S 173.13 E
Dillon Lake ⊜ 184 55.45 N 109.30 W
Dillon Lake ⊜[1] 188 40.02 N 82.10 W
Dillon Mountain ∧ 200 33.51 N 108.48 W
Dillon Reservoir ⊜[1] 200 39.35 N 106.02 W
Dillon State Park ♦ 188 40.03 N 82.08 W
Dillonvale 214 40.11 N 80.46 W
Dillsboro 218 39.01 N 85.03 W
Dillsburg 208 40.06 N 77.02 W
Dilltown 214 40.29 N 79.00 W
Dillwyn 192 37.32 N 78.27 W
Dilly 150 15.01 N 7.40 W
Dilolo 152 10.42 S 22.20 E
Dilsen 56 51.02 N 5.44 E
Dilworth 198 46.52 N 96.42 W
Dilworthtown 285 39.54 N 75.34 W
Dima, Ang. 152 15.27 S 20.10 E
Dima, Indon. 114 1.20 N 97.20 E
Dimāpur 120 25.54 N 93.44 E
Dimaro 64 46.20 N 10.52 E
Dimasalang 116 12.12 N 123.51 E
Dimashq (Damascus) 132 33.30 N 36.18 E
Dimashq □[8] 132 33.30 N 37.00 E
Dimass, Rass > 36 35.37 N 11.03 E
Dimataling 116 7.32 N 123.22 E
Dimbelenge 152 5.33 S 23.07 E
Dimbokro 150 6.39 N 4.42 W
Dimboola 166 36.27 S 142.02 E
Dîmbovița □[6] 38 45.00 N 25.30 E
Dîmbovița ≃ 38 44.14 N 26.27 E
Dimbulah 166 17.09 S 145.07 E
Dime 144 6.16 N 36.20 E
Dime Box 222 30.21 N 96.50 W
Dimitrov 83 48.15 N 37.18 E
Dimitrovgrad, Blg. 38 42.03 N 25.36 E
Dimitrovgrad, Jugo. 38 43.01 N 22.47 E
Dimitrovgrad, S.S.S.R. 80 54.14 N 49.39 E
Dimitrovo → Pernik, Blg. 38 42.36 N 23.02 E
Dimitrovo, S.S.S.R. 78 48.36 N 33.01 E
Dimitrovskoje 85 40.16 N 69.03 E
Dimlang ∧ 146 8.24 N 11.47 E
Dimmitt 196 34.33 N 102.18 W
Dimo 154 5.19 N 29.10 E
Dimock 210 41.45 N 75.32 W
Dimona 132 31.04 N 35.02 E

Symbols in the index entries represent the broad categories identified in the key at the right. Symbols with superior numbers (⋏[1]) identify subcategories (see complete key on page *I · 1*).

Symbole im Register stellen die rechts im Schlüssel erklärten Kategorien dar. Symbole mit hochgestellten Ziffern (⋏[1]) bezeichnen Unterabteilungen einer Kategorie (vgl. vollständiger Schlüssel auf Seite *I · 1*).

Los símbolos incluídos en el texto del índice representan las grandes categorías identificadas con la clave a la derecha. Los símbolos con numeros en su parte superior (⋏[1]) identifican las subcategorías (véase la clave completa en la página *I · 1*).

Les symboles de l'index représentent les catégories indiquées dans la légende à droite. Les symboles suivis d'un indice (⋏[1]) représentent des sous-catégories (voir légende complète à la page *I · 1*).

Os símbolos incluídos no texto do índice representam as grandes categorias identificadas com a chave à direita. Os símbolos com números em sua parte superior (⋏[1]) identificam as subcategorias (veja-se a chave completa à página *I · 1*).

∧ Mountain	Berg	Montaña	Montagne	Montanha
⋏ Mountains	Gebirge	Montañas	Montagnes	Montanhas
⋈ Pass	Paß	Paso	Col	Passo
V Valley, Canyon	Tal, Cañon	Valle, Cañón	Vallée, Canyon	Vale, Canhão
≚ Plain	Ebene	Llano	Plaine	Planície
> Cape	Kap	Cabo	Cap	Cabo
I Island	Insel	Isla	Île	Ilha
II Islands	Inseln	Islas	Îles	Ilhas
± Other Topographic Features	Andere Topographische Objekte	Otros Elementos Topográficos	Autres données topographiques	Outros acidentes topográficos

ESPAÑOL: Nombre — Página — Lat.°′ — Long.°′ W = Oeste
FRANÇAIS: Nom — Page — Lat.°′ — Long.°′ W = Ouest
PORTUGUÊS: Nome — Página — Lat.°′ — Long.°′ W = Oeste

Nombre / Nom / Nome	Página / Page	Lat.°′	Long.°′
Dimondale	216	42.38 N	84.38 W
Dina	123	33.02 N	73.36 E
Dinach	144	9.15 N	50.37 E
Dinagat	116	9.59 N	125.35 E
Dinagat Island I	116	10.12 N	125.35 E
Dinagat Sound ʊ	116	9.59 N	125.50 E
Dinahican Point ≻	116	14.42 N	121.44 E
Dinājpur	124	25.38 N	88.38 E
Dinalupihan	116	14.52 N	120.28 E
Dinamarca → Denmark □[1]	26	56.00 N	10.00 E
Dinamarca, Estrecho de → Denmark Strait ʊ	10	67.00 N	25.00 W
Dinami	68	38.31 N	16.09 E
Dinamita	196	25.43 N	103.38 W
Dinamo	80	50.15 N	41.38 E
Dinan	32	48.27 N	2.02 W
Dīnānagar	123	32.09 N	75.28 E
Dinant	56	50.16 N	4.55 E
Dinar	130	38.04 N	30.10 E
Dinara ⋏	36	43.50 N	16.35 E
Dinard	32	48.38 N	2.04 W
Dinaric Alps → Dinara ⋏	36	43.50 N	16.35 E
Dinarische Alpen → Dinara ⋏	36	43.50 N	16.35 E
Dinas, Pil.	116	7.38 N	123.20 E
Dinas, Wales, U.K.	42	52.00 N	4.54 W
Dinas Head ≻	42	52.02 N	4.55 W
Dinas Powys	42	51.26 N	3.14 W
Dindanko	150	14.08 N	9.30 W
Dindar, Nahr ad- (Dinder) ≃	140	14.06 N	33.40 E
Dīndārpur ◆[8]	272a	28.36 N	76.59 E
Dinde	152	14.12 S	13.44 E
Dinder (Nahr ad-Dindar) ≃	140	14.06 N	33.40 E
Dinder National Park ♠	140	12.40 N	35.20 E
Dindi ≃	122	16.21 N	79.13 E
Dindigul	122	10.21 N	77.57 E
Dindima	150	10.18 N	10.12 E
Dindori	124	22.57 N	81.05 E
Dineksaray	130	37.23 N	32.37 E
Dinga, Pāk.	120	25.26 N	67.10 E
Dinga, Pāk.	123	32.38 N	73.43 E
Dinga, Zaïre	152	5.19 S	16.34 E
Dingalan Bay c	116	15.18 N	121.25 E
Ding'an	110	19.44 N	110.21 E
Dingba	154	3.24 N	27.55 E
Dingbian	102	37.40 N	107.41 E
Dingbianji	102	36.37 N	108.41 E
Dingbu	106	31.18 N	119.10 E
Dingden	52	51.46 N	6.37 E
Dinge	152	4.58 S	12.22 E
Dingelsdorf	58	47.44 N	9.09 E
Dingelstädt	54	51.18 N	10.19 E
Dingelstedt	54	51.58 N	10.58 E
Dingeryu	105	39.37 N	114.55 E
Dingfeng	106	31.20 N	121.45 E
Dinggou	100	32.34 N	119.39 E
Dinggyê	124	28.29 N	88.06 E
Dinghai	100	30.02 N	122.06 E
Dingila	154	3.39 N	26.22 E
Dingjia	107	29.24 N	106.09 E
Dingjiagou	104	40.40 N	122.35 E
Dingjiandian	106	32.06 N	120.52 E
Dingjiasuo	100	32.32 N	120.40 E
Dingjiazhuang	106	32.11 N	120.16 E
Dingkouzhen	102	39.55 N	106.40 E
Dingle	48	52.08 N	10.15 W
Dingle ◆[8]	262	53.23 N	2.57 W
Dingle Bay c	48	52.05 N	10.15 W
Dingley	274b	37.58 S	145.07 E
Dinglingen	58	48.20 N	7.50 E
Dingman Creek ≃	212	42.55 N	81.25 W
Dingmans Ferry	210	41.14 N	74.53 W
Dingnan	100	24.48 N	114.59 E
Dingnan ≃	100	24.28 N	115.26 E
Dingo	166	23.39 S	149.20 E
Dingolfing	60	48.38 N	12.31 E
Dingras	116	18.06 N	120.42 E
Dingshuzhen	106	31.17 N	119.50 E
Dingtao	98	35.04 N	115.34 E
Dingtuna	40	59.34 N	16.22 E
Dinguira	150	14.11 N	11.16 W
Dinguiraye	150	11.18 N	10.43 W
Dingwall, N.S., Can.	186	46.54 N	60.28 W
Dingwall, Scot., U.K.	46	57.35 N	4.29 W
Dingxi	102	35.33 N	104.32 E
Dingxian	98	38.32 N	114.59 E
Dingxiang	102	38.30 N	113.00 E
Dingxiao	102	25.13 N	105.07 E
Dingxing	105	39.17 N	115.46 E
Dingyan	100	32.23 N	120.45 E
Dingyuan	100	32.32 N	117.40 E
Dingzhouying	105	40.20 N	115.43 E
Dingzichang	107	28.54 N	106.08 E
Dingzi Gang c	98	36.37 N	120.50 E
Dinh, Mui ≻	110	11.22 N	109.01 E
Dinhāta	124	26.08 N	89.28 E
Dinh Ca	110	21.45 N	106.03 E
Dinh Lap	110	21.33 N	107.06 E
Dinin ≃	48	52.43 N	7.18 W
Dinkel ≃	52	52.30 N	6.58 E
Dinkelsbühl	56	49.04 N	10.19 E
Dinkelscherben	58	48.21 N	10.35 E
Dinkey Creek ≃	226	36.54 N	119.07 W
Dinklage	52	52.40 N	8.07 E
Dinnebito Wash V	200	35.29 N	111.14 W
Dinner Point ≻	220	28.28 N	82.41 W
Dinnet	46	57.03 N	2.54 W
Dinnington	44	53.22 N	1.12 W
Dinokwe	156	23.24 S	26.40 E
Dinorwic	184	49.41 N	92.30 W
Dinorwic Lake @	184	49.37 N	92.33 W
Dinosaur	200	40.14 N	109.00 W
Dinosaur Lake @[1]	182	55.57 N	122.07 W
Dinosaur National Monument ♠	200	40.32 N	108.58 W
Dinosaur Provincial Park ♠	182	50.45 N	111.30 W
Dinskaja	78	45.13 N	39.14 E
Dinslaken	52	51.34 N	6.44 E
Dinslakener Bruch	263	51.35 N	6.43 E
Dinslaken-Schwarze Heide, Flughafen ⊠	263	51.37 N	6.51 E
Dinsmore	184	51.20 N	107.26 W
Dintel ≃	52	51.39 N	4.22 E
Dinteloord	52	51.37 N	4.22 E
Dinuba	226	36.32 N	119.23 W
Dinwiddie, S. Afr.	273d	26.16 S	28.10 E
Dinwiddie, Va., U.S.	208	37.04 N	77.35 W
Dinwiddie □[6]	208	37.10 N	77.20 W
Dinxperlo	52	51.52 N	6.29 E
Diö	26	56.38 N	14.13 E
Diobo	152	2.16 N	20.29 E
Dioïla	150	12.29 N	6.48 W
Diois □[9]	62	44.40 N	5.20 E
Diomede	180	65.47 N	169.00 W
Dion ≃	150	10.12 N	8.39 W
Dionísio	255	19.49 S	42.45 W
Dionísio Cerqueira	252	26.15 S	53.38 W
Dionne, Lac @	186	49.26 N	67.55 W
Dions	62	43.56 N	4.19 E
Diorama	255	16.21 S	51.14 W
Dios	175e	5.33 S	154.58 E
Diósd	264c	47.25 N	18.57 E
Diouloulou	150	13.03 N	16.36 W
Dioumanténé	150	10.32 N	5.55 W
Dioundiou	150	12.37 N	3.33 E
Dioungani	150	14.19 N	2.44 W
Dioura	150	14.50 N	5.15 W
Diourbel	150	14.40 N	16.15 W
Diourbel □[4]	150	14.45 N	16.30 W
Dipaculao	116	15.51 N	121.32 E
Dipai	100	23.50 N	114.06 E
Dīpālpur	123	30.40 N	73.39 E
Dipignano	68	39.15 N	16.15 E
Dipilo, Pizzo ∧	70	37.57 N	13.59 E
Dipkarpaz	130	35.36 N	34.23 E
Diplo	120	24.28 N	69.35 E
Dipolog	116	8.35 N	123.20 E
Dippoldiswalde	54	50.54 N	13.40 E
Dipton	172	45.54 S	168.22 E
Dipu	106	30.38 N	119.41 E
Diqiyingzi	104	42.11 N	121.29 E
Dique Florentino Ameghino	254	43.40 S	66.25 W
Dīr	123	35.12 N	71.53 E
Dira, Djebel ∧	34	36.05 N	3.38 E
Diré	150	16.16 N	3.24 W
Direction, Cape ≻	164	12.51 S	143.32 E
Dire Dawa	144	9.37 N	41.52 E
Direkli	130	39.43 N	36.40 E
Diriamba	236	11.51 N	86.14 W
Dirico	152	17.58 S	20.47 E
Dirillo, Lago @	70	37.08 N	14.42 E
Diriomo	236	11.52 N	86.03 W
Dirj	146	30.09 N	10.26 E
Dirk Hartog Island I	162	25.48 S	113.00 E
Dirkiesdorp	158	27.10 S	30.25 E
Dirkou	146	19.01 N	12.53 E
Dirkshorn	52	52.45 N	4.45 E
Dirksland	52	51.44 N	4.06 E
Dirnaich	60	48.27 N	12.30 E
Dirrah	140	13.37 N	26.06 E
Dirranbandi	166	28.35 S	148.14 E
Dirri	144	4.20 N	46.37 E
Ḍirs	144	18.32 N	42.05 E
Dirschau → Tczew	30	54.06 N	18.47 E
Dirty Devil ≃	200	37.53 N	110.24 W
Dīsa	120	24.15 N	72.10 E
Dīsah	140	12.02 N	34.19 E
Disappointment, Cape ≻, Falk. Is.	244	54.53 S	36.07 W
Disappointment, Cape ≻, Wa., U.S.	224	46.18 N	124.03 W
Disappointment, Lake @	162	23.30 S	122.50 E
Disappointment, Mount ∧	169	37.25 S	145.18 E
Disappointment Creek ≃	200	38.01 N	108.51 W
Disaster Bay c	166	37.17 S	150.00 E
Disautel	182	48.22 N	119.14 W
Disbrow Drain ≋	281	42.06 N	83.27 W
Disco	214	42.41 N	83.02 W
Discovery	273d	26.10 S	27.54 E
Discovery Bay c, Austl.	166	38.12 S	141.07 E
Discovery Bay c, H.K.	271d	22.18 N	114.01 E
Discovery Bay c, Wa., U.S.	224	48.05 N	122.52 W
Discovery Island I	224	48.25 N	123.15 W
Discovery Passage ʊ	182	50.00 N	125.15 W
Discovery Tablemount ✣[3]	8	42.00 S	0.10 E
Disentis	58	46.43 N	8.51 E
Dishāshah	142	28.59 N	30.51 E
Dishergarh	126	23.41 N	86.50 E
Dishman	202	47.39 N	117.16 W
Dishnā	140	26.07 N	32.28 E
Dishna ≃	180	63.37 N	157.18 W
Disihao	89	50.28 N	124.35 E
Disko	216	41.00 N	85.57 W
Disko I	176	69.50 N	53.30 W
Disko Bugt c	176	69.15 N	52.00 W
Disley	262	53.21 N	2.02 W
Disley Tunnel ◆[5]	262	53.22 N	2.03 W
Dismal ≃	198	41.50 N	100.05 W
Dismal Lakes @	176	67.26 N	117.07 W
Dismal Swamp Canal ≋	208	36.45 N	76.20 W
Disna	76	55.33 N	28.10 E
Disna ≃	76	55.34 N	28.12 E
Disney	196	36.28 N	95.00 W
Disneyland ♠	228	33.48 N	117.55 W
Disneyworld ♠	220	28.27 N	81.28 W
Diso	68	40.00 N	18.23 E
Dispur	120	26.08 N	91.47 E
Disputanta	208	37.07 N	77.13 W
Disraeli	206	45.54 N	71.21 W
Diss	42	52.23 N	1.07 E
Dissen	52	52.07 N	8.12 E
Dissimieux, Lac @	186	49.51 N	69.48 W
Distant	214	40.58 N	79.21 W
Disteghil Sār ∧	123	36.19 N	75.12 E
Disteln	263	51.36 N	7.09 E
Distington	44	54.36 N	3.32 W
District Heights	284c	38.51 N	76.53 W
District of Columbia □[3]	208	38.54 N	77.01 W
Distrito Especial □[5]	246	4.15 N	74.15 W
Distrito Federal □[5], Arg.	258	34.36 S	58.26 W
Distrito Federal □[5], Bra.	255	15.45 S	47.45 W
Distrito Federal □[5], Méx.	234	19.15 N	99.10 W
Distrito Federal □[5], Ven.	246	10.30 N	66.55 W
Distroff	56	49.20 N	6.16 E
Disūq	142	31.08 N	30.39 E
Ditfurt	54	51.50 N	11.11 E
Dithmarschen ◆[1]	30	54.05 N	9.00 E
Dit Island I	116	11.15 N	120.56 E
Dittáino ≃	70	37.25 N	15.00 E
Ditton, Eng., U.K.	260	51.18 N	0.27 E
Ditton, Eng., U.K.	262	53.22 N	2.45 W
Ditton ≃	206	45.23 N	71.12 W
Ditton Priors	42	52.30 N	2.35 W
Ditzingen	56	48.49 N	9.03 E
Ditzum	52	53.18 N	7.16 E
Diu	120	20.42 N	70.59 E
Diu □[8]	120	20.42 N	70.59 E
Diuata Mountains ⋏	116	9.10 N	125.47 E
Diuata Point ≻	116	9.05 N	125.12 E
Dīva	272c	19.09 N	72.59 E
Divalá	236	8.25 N	82.43 W
Dīvāndarreh	128	35.55 N	47.02 E
Dívčice	61	49.06 N	14.19 E
Dive	272c	19.11 N	73.02 E
Divejevo	80	55.03 N	43.15 E
Divenié	152	2.41 S	12.05 E
Divenskaja	76	59.12 N	30.01 E
Diveria ≃	58	46.09 N	8.19 E
Divernon	219	39.33 N	89.39 W
Dives ≃	32	49.19 N	0.05 W
Diviči	84	41.12 N	48.59 E
Dividing Creek	208	39.16 N	75.06 W
Dividing Creek ≃	208	38.05 N	75.32 W
Dividing Ridge ∧	219	39.07 N	90.39 W
Divignano	266b	45.40 N	8.36 E
Divilacan Bay c	116	17.25 N	122.19 E
Divin	78	51.58 N	24.35 E
Divine Corners	210	41.48 N	74.40 W
Divinhe	156	20.40 S	34.49 E
Divino	255	20.37 S	42.09 W
Divinolândia	256	21.40 S	46.45 W
Divinópolis	255	20.09 S	44.54 W
Divion	50	50.28 N	2.30 E
Divi Point ≻	122	15.58 N	81.09 E
Divis ∧[2]	48	54.37 N	6.01 W
Divisa Nova	256	21.31 S	46.12 W
Divisões, Serra das ⋏[2]	255	17.00 S	51.00 W
Divisor, Serra do (Cordillera Ultraoriental) ⋏[1]	248	8.20 S	73.30 W
Divizija	78	45.57 N	29.59 E
Divnogorsk	86	55.58 N	92.22 E
Divnoje	80	45.55 N	43.22 E
Divo	150	5.50 N	5.22 W
Divodar	120	24.06 N	71.47 E
Divonne-les-Bains	58	46.22 N	6.08 E
Divriği	130	39.23 N	38.07 E
Dīwāl Qol	120	34.19 N	67.54 E
Dix, Il., U.S.	219	38.27 N	88.56 W
Dix, Ne., U.S.	198	41.14 N	103.29 W
Dix ≃	192	37.49 N	84.43 W
Dix, Lac des @	58	46.03 N	7.24 E
Dixboro	216	42.19 N	83.39 W
Dixfield	188	44.32 N	70.27 W
Dix Hills	276	40.49 N	73.22 W
Dixie	275b	43.36 N	79.36 W
Dixie Valley V	204	39.50 N	117.55 W
Dix Milles, Lac @	190	46.46 N	77.45 W
Dixmoor	278	41.38 N	87.40 W
Dixmude → Diksmuide	50	51.02 N	2.52 E
Dixon, Ca., U.S.	226	38.19 N	121.49 W
Dixon, Il., U.S.	190	41.50 N	89.28 W
Dixon, Ky., U.S.	194	37.31 N	87.41 W
Dixon, Mo., U.S.	194	37.59 N	92.05 W
Dixon, N.M., U.S.	200	36.11 N	105.53 W
Dixon, Oh., U.S.	216	40.57 N	84.48 W
Dixon Entrance ʊ	182	54.25 N	132.30 W
Dixons Mills	194	32.04 N	87.47 W
Dixons Pond @	276	40.56 N	74.27 W
Dixonville	214	40.42 N	79.00 W
Dixville	206	45.04 N	71.46 W
Diyā al-Kawm	142	30.38 N	31.05 E
Diyadin	84	39.33 N	43.41 E
Diyālā □[4]	128	34.00 N	45.00 E
Diyālā (Sīrvān) ≃	128	33.14 N	44.31 E
Diyanga	152	1.29 S	11.52 E
Diyarbakır	130	37.55 N	40.14 E
Diyarbakır □[4]	130	38.05 N	40.15 E
Diyarb Najm	142	30.45 N	31.26 E
Diyu al-Wasta	142	30.54 N	31.30 E
Dizangsi	104	41.26 N	120.57 E
Dizhou	102	23.00 N	106.20 E
Dizy	50	49.04 N	3.58 E
Dizzard Point ≻	42	50.45 N	4.38 W
Dja ≃	152	2.02 N	15.12 E
Dja, Réserve du ◆[4]	152	3.05 N	13.00 E
Djabalpur → Jabalpur	124	23.10 N	79.57 E
Djabir	152	0.32 N	24.05 E
Djadié ≃	152	0.46 N	12.58 E
Djado	146	21.01 N	12.18 E
Djado, Plateau du ⋏[1]	146	21.45 N	12.50 E
Djaipur → Jaipur	120	26.55 N	75.49 E
Djakarta → Jakarta	269e	6.10 S	106.48 E
Djakonovo	82	54.34 N	38.20 E
Djakovka	80	50.43 N	46.46 E
Djakovo	83	47.57 N	39.09 E
Djakovo ◆[8]	265b	55.39 N	37.40 E
Djamâa	148	33.32 N	6.00 E
Djamba, Ang.	152	16.46 S	13.59 E
Djamba, Zaïre	152	9.49 S	22.07 E
Djambala	152	2.33 S	14.45 E
Djamschedpur → Jamshedpur	126	22.48 N	86.11 E
Djanet	148	24.34 N	9.29 E
Djaouro Mbali	152	5.52 N	13.29 E
Djaret, Oued V	148	26.32 N	1.30 E
Djebobo ∧	150	8.20 N	0.35 E
Djébrène	146	11.14 N	19.01 E
Djédaa	146	13.31 N	18.34 E
Djedda → Jiddah	144	21.30 N	39.12 E
Djedi, Oued V	148	34.28 N	6.05 E
Djéké Djéké	146	8.25 N	18.12 E
Djelo-Binza	273b	4.23 S	15.16 E
Djema	140	6.03 N	25.19 E
Djember → Jember, Indon.	115a	8.10 S	113.42 E
Djember, Tchad	146	10.25 N	17.50 E
Djemila ⊥	34	36.25 N	5.44 E
Djénné	150	13.54 N	4.33 W
Djenoun, Garet el ∧	148	25.05 N	5.25 E
Djérem ≃	152	5.20 N	13.24 E
Djibasso	150	13.07 N	4.10 W
Djibo	150	14.06 N	1.38 W
Djibouti	144	11.36 N	43.09 E
Djibouti □[1], Afr.	136	11.30 N	43.00 E
Djibouti □[1], Afr.	144	11.30 N	43.00 E
Djibrouïa	150	13.13 N	11.14 W
Djiri	273b	4.08 S	15.19 E
Djiri ≃	273b	4.11 S	15.20 E
Djohong	152	6.50 N	14.42 E
Djokjakarta → Yogyakarta	115a	7.48 S	110.22 E
Djokoumatombi	152	0.47 N	15.22 E
Djokupunda	152	5.27 S	20.58 E
Djolu	152	0.37 N	22.21 E
Djombo	152	1.21 N	20.22 E
Djoua ≃	152	1.13 N	13.12 E
Djouari ≃	273b	4.13 S	15.08 E
Djoubissi	152	6.12 N	20.45 E
Djoué ≃	273b	4.19 S	15.14 E
Djougou	150	9.42 N	1.40 E
Djoum	152	2.40 N	12.40 E
Djouna	146	10.27 N	20.04 E
Djourab, Erg du ⊼[8]	146	16.40 N	18.50 E
Djugu	154	1.55 N	30.30 E
Djúpivogur	24a	64.40 N	14.10 W
Djura	40	60.37 N	15.00 E
Djurås	40	60.33 N	15.08 E
Djurmo	40	60.33 N	15.10 E
Djurö	40	59.19 N	18.41 E
Djurö I	26	58.52 N	13.28 E
Djursholm	40	59.24 N	18.05 E
Dlouhá Ves	60	49.12 N	13.31 E
Dmanisi	84	41.22 N	44.12 E
Dmitr'ašovka	76	52.09 N	39.04 E
Dmitrija Lapteva, proliv ʊ	74	73.00 N	142.00 E
Dmitrijevka, S.S.S.R.	76	52.53 N	40.47 E
Dmitrijevka, S.S.S.R.	78	50.56 N	32.58 E
Dmitrijevka, S.S.S.R.	83	48.55 N	39.10 E
Dmitrijevka, S.S.S.R.	83	47.56 N	38.56 E
Dmitrijevka, S.S.S.R.	85	43.30 N	77.02 E
Dmitrijevka, S.S.S.R.	86	55.10 N	75.36 E
Dmitrijev-L'govskij	78	52.08 N	35.05 E
Dmitrijevskij	86	49.08 N	57.50 E
Dmitrijevskoje, S.S.S.R.	80	45.48 N	41.54 E
Dmitrijevskoje, S.S.S.R.	82	54.40 N	37.38 E
Dmitrijev Usad, S.S.S.R.	76	54.08 N	43.08 E
Dmitrijev Usad, S.S.S.R.	80	54.14 N	43.18 E
Dmitrijevy Gory	80	55.12 N	41.47 E
Dmitrov	82	56.21 N	37.31 E
Dmitrovcy	82	55.16 N	38.55 E
Dmitroviči	76	53.59 N	29.06 E
Dmitrovka, S.S.S.R.	78	48.48 N	32.44 E
Dmitrovka, S.S.S.R.	78	45.29 N	35.04 E
Dmitrovka, S.S.S.R.	78	46.51 N	36.35 E
Dmitrovskij Pogost	76	55.19 N	39.49 E
Dmitrovsk-Orlovskij	76	52.30 N	35.09 E
Dmuchajlovka	78	49.03 N	34.46 E
Dnepr ≃	78	46.30 N	32.18 E
Dnepr'any	78	46.44 N	33.16 E
Dneprodzeržinsk	78	48.30 N	34.37 E
Dneprodzeržinskoje vodochranilšče @[1]	78	48.45 N	34.00 E
Dnepropetrovsk	78	48.27 N	34.59 E
Dneprovka	78	47.26 N	34.38 E
Dneprovskij liman c[1]	78	46.35 N	31.55 E
Dneprovsko-Bugskij kanal ≋	78	52.03 N	25.35 E
Dneprovskoje	76	55.40 N	33.55 E
Dnestr ≃	78	46.18 N	30.17 E
Dnestrovskij liman @	78	46.15 N	30.17 E
Dnieper → Dnepr ≃	78	46.30 N	32.18 E
Dniepropetrovsk → Dnepropetrovsk	78	48.27 N	34.59 E
Dniester → Dnestr ≃	78	46.18 N	30.17 E
Dno	76	57.50 N	29.59 E
Do, Lac @	150	15.54 N	2.45 W
Doa	154	16.44 S	34.32 E
Do Āb-e Mīkh-e Zarrīn	120	35.16 N	68.00 E
Doaktown	186	46.33 N	66.08 W
Doangdoangan-Besar, Pulau I	112	5.24 S	117.55 E
Doany	157b	14.22 S	49.31 E
Doba	146	8.39 N	16.51 E
Dobane	140	6.24 N	24.42 E
Dobbertin	54	53.37 N	12.04 E
Dobbiaco (Toblach)	64	46.44 N	12.14 E
Dobbin	222	30.22 N	95.46 W
Dobbins	226	39.22 N	121.12 W
Dobbins Air Force Base ■	192	33.54 N	84.31 W
Dobbs Ferry	210	41.00 N	73.52 W
Dobczyce	30	49.54 N	20.06 E
Dobel	56	48.48 N	8.29 E
Dobele	76	56.37 N	23.16 E
Döbeln	54	51.07 N	13.07 E
Doberai, Jazirah (Vogelkop) ≻[1]	164	1.30 S	132.30 E
Döberitz	264a	52.33 N	13.03 E
Doberlug-Kirchhain	54	51.38 N	13.34 E
Döbern	54	51.37 N	14.36 E
Dobiegniew	30	52.59 N	15.47 E
Döbling ◆[8]	264b	48.15 N	16.22 E
Dobo	164	5.46 S	134.13 E
Doboj	38	44.44 N	18.06 E
Dobra, Pol.	30	51.54 N	18.37 E
Dobra, Pol.	30	53.35 N	15.18 E
Dobra ≃	36	45.33 N	15.31 E
Dobr'anka, S.S.S.R.	78	52.04 N	31.11 E
Dobr'anka, S.S.S.R.	86	58.27 N	56.24 E
Dobr'ankka	78	48.21 N	30.54 E
Dobřany	60	49.40 N	13.18 E
Dobra Stausee @[1]	61	48.35 N	15.20 E
Dobre Miasto	30	53.59 N	20.25 E
Döbriach	64	46.47 N	13.39 E
Dobrich → Tolbuhin	38	43.34 N	27.50 E
Dobrinka, S.S.S.R.	80	52.09 N	40.29 E
Dobrinka, S.S.S.R.	80	50.49 N	41.51 E
Dobrinka, S.S.S.R.	80	48.49 N	42.58 E
Dobříš	30	49.47 N	14.11 E
Dobritz	54	52.01 N	12.13 E
Dobrodzień	30	50.44 N	18.27 E
Dobroje, S.S.S.R.	76	57.06 N	32.02 E
Dobroje, S.S.S.R.	76	52.52 N	39.48 E
Dobroměřice	54	50.23 N	13.46 E
Dobromil'	78	49.34 N	22.47 E
Dobropolje	78	48.28 N	37.05 E
Dobroslavka	76	52.24 N	26.15 E
Dobroteasa	38	44.47 N	24.23 E
Dobrotvor	78	50.14 N	24.22 E
Dobroveličkovka	78	48.23 N	31.11 E
Dobrovolje	78	48.41 N	36.37 E
Dobrovol'sk	76	54.46 N	22.31 E
Dobrudžansko plato ⋏[1]	38	43.32 N	27.50 E
Dobruja ◆[1]	38	44.00 N	28.00 E
Dobruš	76	52.25 N	31.19 E
Dobruška	30	50.17 N	16.10 E
Dobryn'	78	51.46 N	29.12 E
Dobrzany	30	53.22 N	15.25 E
Dobrzyń nad Wisłą	30	52.38 N	19.20 E
Dobšiná	30	48.49 N	20.23 E
Dobson	192	36.23 N	80.43 W
Dobzha	120	28.28 N	88.14 E
Doce ≃, Bra.	255	19.37 S	39.49 W
Doce ≃, Bra.	255	18.28 S	51.05 W
Doce de Octubre	196	25.38 N	97.47 W
Doce Leguas, Cayos de las II	240p	20.55 N	79.05 W
Dochart ≃	46	56.28 N	4.20 W
Döčin ≃	88	49.39 N	114.48 E
Docker River	162	24.52 S	129.05 E
Docking	42	52.55 N	0.38 E
Dock Junction	192	31.11 N	81.31 W
Dockton	224	47.22 N	122.27 W
Dockweiler	56	50.15 N	6.46 E
Dockweiler Beach State Park ♠	280	33.55 N	118.26 W
Doctor Arroyo	234	23.40 N	100.11 W
Doctor Cecilio Báez	252	25.03 S	56.19 W
Doctor Coss	196	25.55 N	99.11 W
Doctor Edmund A. Babler Memorial State Park ♠	219	38.36 N	90.43 W
Doctor González	232	25.52 N	99.57 W
Doctor Hicks Range ⋏	162	28.40 S	124.20 E
Doctor Pedro P. Peña	252	22.26 S	62.22 W
Doctors Creek ≃	208	40.11 N	74.41 W
Doda	123	33.08 N	75.34 E
Dod Ballāpur	122	13.18 N	77.32 E
Doddinghurst, Eng., U.K.	42	51.40 N	0.18 E
Doddinghurst, Eng., U.K.	260	51.40 N	0.18 E
Doddridge	194	33.05 N	93.54 W
Dodds Island I	219	38.35 N	91.59 W
Doddsville	194	33.39 N	90.31 W
Dodecanese → Dhodhekánisos II	38	36.30 N	27.00 E
Dodéo	152	7.29 N	12.04 E
Dodge, Ne., U.S.	198	41.43 N	96.52 W
Dodge, Tx., U.S.	222	30.45 N	95.24 W
Dodge □[6]	216	43.14 N	88.40 W
Dodge Brothers State Park Number 4 ♠, Mi., U.S.	281	42.37 N	83.22 W
Dodge Brothers State Park Number 8 ♠, Mi., U.S.	281	42.36 N	83.01 W
Dodge Center	190	44.01 N	92.51 W
Dodge City	198	37.45 N	100.01 W
Dodge Park	284c	38.56 N	76.53 W
Dodger Stadium ♠	280	34.04 N	118.14 W
Dodgeville	190	42.57 N	90.07 W
Dodman Point ≻	42	50.13 N	4.48 W
Dodo Goei	140	5.57 N	29.26 E
Dodola	144	7.02 N	39.07 E
Dodoma	154	6.11 S	35.45 E
Dodoma □[4]	154	6.00 S	36.00 E
Dodori ≃	154	1.52 S	41.02 E
Dodsland	184	51.48 N	108.49 W
Dodson, La., U.S.	194	32.04 N	92.39 W
Dodson, Mt., U.S.	202	48.23 N	108.14 W
Dodson, Tx., U.S.	196	34.46 N	100.02 W
Dodson Peninsula ≻[1]	9	75.46 S	62.50 W
Dodurga	130	39.48 N	29.55 E
Doe Lake @	212	45.32 N	79.25 W
Doe River	182	56.00 N	120.05 W
Doerun	192	31.19 N	83.55 W
Doesburg	52	52.01 N	6.09 E
Doetinchem	52	51.58 N	6.17 E
Dog ≃	190	48.51 N	89.37 W
Dogāchia	272b	22.58 N	88.31 E
Dogai Coring @	120	34.30 N	89.15 E
Dōga-mori ∧	96	33.09 N	132.53 E
Doğanbey, Tür.	130	37.37 N	27.11 E
Doğanbey, Tür.	130	38.04 N	26.53 E
Doğanbey, Tür.	130	37.48 N	31.54 E
Doğanca	130	37.49 N	42.20 E
Doğançay	130	40.37 N	30.20 E
Doganella	66	41.34 N	12.56 E
Doğanhisar	130	38.09 N	31.41 E
Doğankent, Tür.	130	40.48 N	38.56 E
Doğankent, Tür.	130	36.52 N	35.18 E
Doğanşehir	130	38.06 N	37.53 E
Doğanyol	130	38.19 N	39.03 E
Doğanyurt, Tür.	130	40.41 N	36.43 E
Doğanyurt, Tür.	130	42.00 N	33.27 E
Dog Creek	182	51.35 N	122.15 W
Dog Creek ≃, B.C., Can.	182	51.35 N	122.17 W
Dog Creek ≃, Mt., U.S.	202	47.44 N	109.36 W
Dog Creek ≃, Oh., U.S.	216	41.03 N	84.23 W
Dog Ear Creek ≃	198	43.42 N	99.59 W
Dog Island I	192	29.48 N	84.35 W
Dog Islands II	240m	18.29 N	64.28 W
Dog Lake @, Mb., Can.	184	51.02 N	98.30 W
Dog Lake @, On., Can.	190	48.18 N	84.10 W
Dog Lake @, On., Can.	190	48.46 N	89.32 W
Dog Lake @, On., Can.	212	44.27 N	76.20 W
Dogliani	62	44.32 N	7.56 E
Dogna	64	46.27 N	13.19 E
Dōgo I	92	36.15 N	133.16 E
Do Gonbadān	128	30.21 N	50.48 E
Dogondoutchi	150	13.38 N	4.02 E
Doğonşar	130	40.14 N	37.33 E
Dōgo-yama ∧	96	35.04 N	133.14 E
Dogpound Creek ≃	182	51.50 N	114.24 W
Dogs, Isle of I	260	51.29 N	0.01 W
D'ogtevo, S.S.S.R.	78	49.10 N	40.39 E
D'ogtevo, S.S.S.R.	80	49.11 N	40.39 E
Doğubayazıt	84	39.32 N	44.08 E
Doguéraoua	150	13.58 N	5.35 E
Doğu Karadeniz Dağları ⋏	130	40.30 N	40.30 E
Dogura	164	10.05 S	150.05 E
Doha → Ad-Dawḥah	128	25.17 N	51.32 E
Dohār	126	23.35 N	90.09 E
Dohhi	124	24.32 N	84.54 E
Dohna	54	50.57 N	13.51 E
Dohrgaul	263	51.06 N	7.27 E
Dohrīghāt	124	26.16 N	83.31 E
Doi	96	33.57 N	133.26 E
Doi, Kinh ≋	269c	10.43 N	106.37 E
Doilungdêqên	124	29.48 N	90.47 E
Doiran, Lake @	38	41.13 N	22.44 E
Doiras, Embalse de @[1]	34	43.10 N	6.45 W
Dois de Novembro, Cachoeira ∟	248	8.52 S	62.16 W
Dois Irmãos	250	9.16 S	49.05 W
Dois Irmãos, Pico ∧	287a	22.59 S	43.14 W
Dois Riachos	250	9.23 S	37.05 W
Doi Suthep-Pui National Park ♠	110	18.50 N	98.50 E
Dōjō	268	35.51 N	139.37 E
Dōjō ◆[8]	270	34.52 N	135.14 E
Doka, Indon.	164	6.39 S	134.15 E
Doka, Sūd.	140	13.31 N	35.46 E
Doki ≃	96	34.18 N	133.48 E
Dokka	26	60.50 N	10.05 E
Dokkum	52	53.19 N	6.00 E
Dökmetepe	130	40.19 N	36.18 E
Dokri	120	27.23 N	68.06 E
Dokšicy	76	54.54 N	27.46 E
Dokská pahorkatina ⋏[2]	54	50.30 N	14.45 E
Doksy	54	50.35 N	14.38 E
Dokučajevsk	83	47.44 N	37.40 E
Dol'a, S.S.S.R.	83	47.53 N	37.41 E
Dola, Oh., U.S.	216	40.47 N	83.42 W
Dolak ≃	164	7.48 S	139.00 E
Doland	198	44.53 N	98.06 W
Dolany	60	49.27 N	13.15 E
Dolavon	254	43.18 S	65.42 W
Dolayoba	267b	40.54 N	29.15 E
Dolbeau	176	48.53 N	72.14 W
Dolberg	52	51.42 N	7.55 E
Dolceacqua	62	43.51 N	7.37 E
Dolcedorme, Serra ∧	68	39.53 N	16.13 E
Dol-de-Bretagne	32	48.33 N	1.45 W
Dole	58	47.06 N	5.30 E
Dolega	236	8.34 N	82.25 W
Dolen	222	30.26 N	94.54 W
Dolgaja	86	55.49 N	64.15 E
Dolgaja, kosa ≻[2]	78	46.43 N	37.41 E
Dolgarrog	44	53.11 N	3.51 W
Dolgelin	54	52.29 N	14.24 E
Dolgellau	42	52.44 N	3.53 W
Dolgen'koje	83	49.01 N	37.19 E
Dolgeville	210	43.06 N	74.46 W
Dolgij, ostrov I	24	69.15 N	59.04 E
Dolgij Most	88	56.45 N	96.48 E
Dolginovo	76	54.39 N	27.29 E
Dolgoi Island I	180	55.10 N	161.45 W
Dolgoje	78	52.04 N	37.34 E
Dolgoprudnyj	82	55.56 N	37.31 E
Dolgorukovo	76	52.19 N	38.21 E
Dolgoščelje	24	66.03 N	43.24 E
Dolianova	71	39.22 N	9.10 E
Dolina, S.S.S.R.	78	48.58 N	24.01 E
Dolina, S.S.S.R.	83	48.59 N	37.27 E
Dolinnyj	80	51.16 N	52.11 E
Dolinovskoje	83	48.36 N	38.33 E
Dolinsk	89	47.21 N	142.48 E
Dolinskaja	78	48.07 N	32.44 E
Dolisie	152	4.12 S	12.41 E
Dolj □[6]	38	44.15 N	23.45 E
Döllach	64	46.58 N	12.54 E
Dollar	46	56.09 N	3.40 W
Dollard c	52	53.17 N	7.10 E
Dollard-des-Ormeaux	206	45.29 N	73.49 W
Dollar Law ∧	46	55.33 N	3.17 W
Döllbach	56	50.26 N	9.44 E
Dolle	54	52.25 N	11.37 E
Dollern	52	53.32 N	9.32 E
Dollerup	41	54.46 N	9.40 E
Döllnitz	54	51.24 N	12.01 E
Dollnstein	60	48.52 N	11.04 E
Döllstädt	54	51.05 N	10.49 E
Dolmabahce Palace ʋ	267b	41.02 N	29.00 E
Dolmatovka	78	46.13 N	32.26 E
Dolmatovskij	80	57.29 N	42.18 E
Dolni Dâbnik	38	43.24 N	24.26 E
Dolní Dvořiště	61	48.39 N	14.27 E
Dolní Jiřetín	54	50.35 N	13.33 E
Dolni Lom	38	43.31 N	22.47 E
Dolni Žandov	60	50.02 N	12.34 E
Dolný Kubín	30	49.12 N	19.17 E
Dolo	64	45.25 N	12.05 E
Dolohmwar ∧	174r	6.52 N	158.14 E
Dolokmerawan	114	3.10 N	99.08 E
Dolokparibuan	114	3.01 N	98.39 E
Dolomites → Dolomiti ⋏	64	46.25 N	11.50 E
Dolomiti (Dolomiten) ⋏	64	46.25 N	11.50 E
Dolon'	86	50.40 N	79.18 E
Dolon ≃	62	45.18 N	4.46 E
Dolon, pereval)(	85	41.52 N	75.45 E
Dolores, Arg.	252	36.20 S	57.40 W
Dolores, Col.	246	3.33 N	74.54 W
Dolores, Guat.	232	16.31 N	89.25 W
Dolores, Méx.	196	26.20 N	101.29 W
Dolores, Méx.	232	28.53 N	108.27 W
Dolores, Co., U.S.	200	37.28 N	108.30 W
Dolores, Ur.	252	33.33 S	58.13 W
Dolores, Ven.	246	8.18 N	69.34 W
Dolores ≃, Pil.	116	12.02 N	125.29 E
Dolores ≃, U.S.	200	38.49 N	109.17 W
Dolores, Mission ʋ[1]	282	37.46 N	122.26 W
Dolores Hidalgo	234	21.10 N	100.56 W
Dolphin, Cape ≻	254	51.15 S	58.57 W
Dolphin and Union Strait ʊ	176	69.05 N	114.45 W
Dolphin Head ∧	241q	18.22 N	78.10 W
Dölsach	64	46.49 N	12.51 E
Dolsk	30	52.00 N	17.03 E
Dol'skoje	82	54.47 N	36.26 E
Dolton, Eng., U.K.	42	50.53 N	4.01 W
Dolton, Il., U.S.	216	41.38 N	87.36 W
Dolwyddelan	44	53.03 N	3.53 W
Dolžak	78	48.41 N	26.32 E
Dolžanskaja, S.S.S.R.	78	46.37 N	37.48 E
Dolžanskaja, S.S.S.R.	83	48.03 N	39.39 E
Dolžicy, S.S.S.R.	76	58.00 N	29.51 E
Dolžicy, S.S.S.R.	76	58.31 N	29.08 E
Dolžik	78	50.13 N	35.55 E
Dom ∧	58	46.06 N	7.50 E
Dom, Gunung ∧	164	2.40 S	136.53 E
D'oma ≃	86	54.42 N	55.57 E
Domacha	76	52.28 N	34.58 E
Domačovo	78	51.44 N	23.37 E
Domadare	144	1.50 N	41.13 E
Domaine, Pointe du ≻	275a	45.23 N	73.54 W
Domanevka	78	47.37 N	30.58 E
Domaniči	76	53.02 N	33.25 E
Domanico	68	39.13 N	16.12 E
Dom Aquino	255	15.48 S	54.53 W
Domar, Enneri V	146	18.11 N	18.04 E
Domariāganj	124	27.13 N	82.40 E
Domart-en-Ponthieu	50	50.04 N	2.07 E
Domasi	154	15.18 S	35.20 E
Domaška	80	53.00 N	50.47 E
Domaso	58	46.09 N	9.19 E
Domat/Ems	58	46.50 N	9.28 E
Domažlice	60	49.27 N	12.56 E
Dombaj	84	43.17 N	41.37 E
Dombaj-Ul'gen, gora ∧	84	43.14 N	41.41 E
Dombarovskij	86	50.46 N	59.32 E
Dombås	26	62.05 N	9.08 E
Dombasle-sur-Meurthe	58	48.38 N	6.21 E
Dombe	156	19.59 S	33.25 E
Dombe Grande	152	12.58 S	13.11 E
Dombes ◆[1]	58	46.00 N	5.03 E
Dombóvár	30	46.23 N	18.08 E
Dombrád	30	48.14 N	21.56 E
Dombresson	58	47.04 N	6.58 E
Domburg	52	51.34 N	3.30 E
Dom Cavati	255	19.23 S	42.06 W
Dôme, Puy de ∧	32	45.47 N	2.58 E
Dome Creek	182	53.44 N	121.01 W
Domegge di Cadore	64	46.27 N	12.25 E
Domène	62	45.12 N	5.50 E
Dome Peak ∧, Pil.	116	5.37 N	125.20 E
Dome Peak ∧, Wa., U.S.	224	48.18 N	121.02 W
Domett	172	42.51 S	173.13 E
Domèvre-en-Haye	56	48.49 N	5.55 E
Domeyko	252	28.57 S	70.54 W
Domeyko, Cordillera ⋏	252	24.30 S	69.00 W
Domfront	32	48.36 N	0.39 W
Domiciano Ribeiro	255	16.56 S	47.46 W
Dominal, Parc ♠	62	44.52 N	6.32 E
Domíngo M. Irala	252	25.54 S	54.43 W
Domingos Martins	255	20.22 S	40.40 W
Dominguez	280	33.50 N	118.13 W
Dominguez Channel ʊ	280	38.47 N	118.15 W
Dominguez Hills ⋏[2]	280	33.52 N	118.14 W
Dominica □[1], N.A.	230	15.30 N	61.20 W
Dominica □[1], N.A.	240d	15.30 N	61.20 W
Dominica Channel ʊ	238	15.10 N	61.15 W
Dominicain (république) → Dominican Republic □[1]	238	19.00 N	70.40 W
Dominical	236	9.13 N	83.51 W
Dominicana, República → Dominican Republic □[1]	238	19.00 N	70.40 W
Dominican Republic (República Dominicana) □[1], N.A.	230	19.00 N	70.40 W
Dominican Republic (República Dominicana) □[1], N.A.	238	19.00 N	70.40 W
Dominikanische Republik → Dominican Republic □[1]	238	19.00 N	70.40 W
Dominion	186	46.13 N	60.01 W
Dominion, Cape ≻	176	66.13 N	74.28 W
Dominion Astrophysical Observatory ʋ[3]	224	48.31 N	123.25 W
Dominion City	184	49.08 N	97.09 W
Dominique → Dominica □[1]	240d	15.30 N	61.20 W
Domiongo	152	4.37 S	21.15 E
Domitilla, Catacombe di ⊥	267a	41.52 N	12.31 E
Dömitz	54	53.08 N	11.14 E
Dom Joaquim	255	18.57 S	43.16 W
Domleschg V	58	46.44 N	9.28 E
Dommartin-lès-Toul	58	48.40 N	5.54 E
Dommartin-Varimont	56	48.58 N	4.46 E
Dommary-Baroncourt	56	49.17 N	5.42 E
Dommel ≃	52	51.40 N	5.20 E
Dommitzsch	54	51.38 N	12.53 E
Domnarvet	40	60.30 N	15.27 E
Domnești	38	44.25 N	25.56 E
Domnino	82	54.10 N	38.11 E
Dom Noi ≃	110	15.17 N	105.28 E
Domo	144	7.54 N	46.52 E
Domodedovo	82	55.26 N	37.46 E
Domodossola	58	46.07 N	8.17 E
Domohani	124	26.35 N	88.48 E
Domoni	157a	12.15 S	44.32 E
Domont	261	49.02 N	2.20 E
Dompaire	58	48.13 N	6.13 E
Dom Pedrito	252	30.59 S	54.40 W
Dom Pedro	250	4.29 S	44.27 W
Dom Pedro II, Estação ◆[5]	287a	23.54 S	43.12 W
Dompu	115b	8.32 S	118.28 E
Domremy	184	52.47 N	105.44 W
Domrémy-la-Pucelle	58	48.27 N	5.41 E
Domselaar	258	35.04 S	58.18 W
Dom Silvério	255	20.09 S	42.58 W
Domsjö	26	63.15 N	18.43 E
Domus de Maria	71	38.57 N	8.52 E
Domusnovas	71	39.19 N	8.39 E
Domuyo, Volcán ∧[1]	252	36.38 S	70.26 W
Domvast	50	50.12 N	1.55 E
Dom Viçoso	256	22.13 S	45.09 W
Dom Yai ≃	110	15.18 N	105.10 E
Domzăle	36	46.08 N	14.36 E
Don ≃, On., Can.	212	43.39 N	79.21 W
Don ≃, India	122	16.17 N	76.27 E
Don ≃, Lao	110	15.07 N	105.48 E
Don ≃, S.S.S.R.	72	47.04 N	39.18 E
Don ≃, Eng., U.K.	44	53.39 N	0.59 W
Don ≃, Eng., U.K.	262	53.47 N	2.14 W
Don ≃, Scot., U.K.	46	57.08 N	2.05 W
Don, East Branch ≃, On., Can.	212	43.42 N	79.20 W
Don, East Branch ≃, On., Can.	275b	43.43 N	79.20 W
Don, West Branch ≃	275b	43.43 N	79.20 W
Dona Ana, Moç.	154	17.25 S	35.07 E
Dona Ana, N.M., U.S.	200	32.23 N	106.48 W
Donada	64	45.02 N	12.12 E
Donadeu	252	26.43 S	62.44 W
Dona Eusébia	256	21.18 S	42.48 W
Donaghadee	48	54.39 N	5.33 W
Donaghmore	48	54.32 N	6.49 W
Donahoe Creek ≃	222	30.49 N	97.12 W
Donald	166	36.22 S	143.00 E
Donalda	182	52.35 N	112.34 W
Donaldson, Ar., U.S.	194	34.14 N	92.55 W
Donaldson, In., U.S.	216	41.22 N	86.27 W
Donaldson, Pa., U.S.	208	40.38 N	76.24 W
Donaldson Crossroads	279b	40.16 N	80.07 W
Donaldson Dam @[1]	273d	26.17 S	27.41 E
Donaldsonville	194	30.06 N	90.59 W
Donalsonville	192	31.02 N	84.52 W
Doñana, Parque Nacional de ♠	34	37.00 N	6.30 W
Donard, Slieve ∧	48	54.11 N	5.55 W
Donau → Danube ≃	22	45.20 N	29.40 E
Donaueschingen	58	47.57 N	8.29 E
Donaufeld ◆[8]	264b	48.15 N	16.25 E
Donaukanal ≋	264b	48.10 N	16.30 E
Donaumoos ≣, B.R.D.	58	48.30 N	10.15 E
Donaumoos ≣, B.R.D.	60	48.40 N	11.15 E
Donaupark ♠	264b	48.14 N	16.25 E

Symbol	English	Deutsch	Español	Français	Português
≃	River	Fluß	Río	Rivière	Rio
≋	Canal	Kanal	Canal	Canal	Canal
∟	Waterfall, Rapids	Wasserfall, Stromschnellen	Cascada, Rápidos	Chute d'eau, Rapides	Cascata, Rápidos
ʊ	Strait	Meeresstraße	Estrecho	Détroit	Estreito
c	Bay, Gulf	Bucht, Golf	Bahía, Golfo	Baie, Golfe	Baía, Golfo
@	Lake, Lakes	See, Seen	Lago, Lagos	Lac, Lacs	Lago, Lagos
≣	Swamp	Sumpf	Pantano	Marais	Pântano
⊓	Ice Features, Glacier	Eis- und Gletscherformen	Accidentes Glaciales	Formes glaciaires	Acidentes glaciares
⫪	Other Hydrographic Features	Andere Hydrographische Objekte	Otros Elementos Hidrográficos	Autres données hydrographiques	Outros acidentes hidrográficos

Symbol	English	Deutsch	Español	Français	Português
✣	Submarine Features	Untermeerische Objekte	Accidentes Submarinos	Formes de relief sous-marin	Acidentes submarinos
□	Political Unit	Politische Einheit	Unidad Politica	Entité politique	Unidade política
ʋ	Cultural Institution	Kulturelle Institution	Institución Cultural	Institution culturelle	Instituição cultural
⊥	Historical Site	Historische Stätte	Sitio Histórico	Site historique	Sitio histórico
♠	Recreational Site	Erholungs- und Ferienort	Sitio de Recreo	Centre de loisirs	Area de Lazer
⊠	Airport	Flughafen	Aeropuerto	Aéroport	Aeroporto
■	Military Installation	Militäranlage	Instalación Militar	Installation militaire	Instalação militar
◆	Miscellaneous	Verschiedenes	Misceláneo	Divers	Diversos

Name	Page	Lat.	Long.
Donauried ←¹	56	48.35 N	10.40 E
Donaustadt ←⁸	264b	48.13 N	16.30 E
Donaustauf ʊ	60	49.02 N	12.13 E
Donauturm ʊ	264b	48.14 N	16.25 E
Donauwörth	56	48.43 N	10.46 E
Don Benito	34	38.57 N	5.52 W
Dönberg ←⁸	263	51.18 N	7.10 E
Don Bosco ←⁸	258	34.42 S	58.18 W
Doncaster, Austl.	274b	37.47 S	145.08 E
Doncaster, On., Can.	275b	43.48 N	79.25 W
Doncaster, Eng., U.K.	44	53.32 N	1.07 W
Doncaster ≃	206	45.58 N	74.06 W
Doncaster East	274b	37.47 S	145.10 E
Doncaster Indian Reserve ←⁴	206	46.09 N	74.07 W
Donchéry	56	49.42 N	4.52 E
Doncovka	83	49.35 N	39.16 E
Dondaicha	120	21.20 N	74.34 E
Dondo, Ang.	152	9.38 S	14.25 E
Dondo, Moç.	156	19.36 S	34.44 E
Dondo, Teluk c	112	0.55 N	120.30 E
Dondra Head c	122	5.55 N	80.35 E
Dond'ušany	78	48.15 N	27.37 E
Doneck, S.S.S.R.	83	48.21 N	40.02 E
Doneck, S.S.S.R.	83	48.00 N	37.48 E
Doneck ⊐	83	48.00 N	37.30 E
Doneckij kr'až ∧	83	48.15 N	38.45 E
Donegal, Ire.	48	54.39 N	8.07 W
Donegal, S. Afr.	158	26.10 S	23.58 E
Donegal, Pa., U.S.	214	40.07 N	79.23 W
Donegal Bay c	48	54.30 N	8.30 W
Doneraile, Ire.	48	52.13 N	8.35 W
Donetsk, S.C., U.S.	192	34.31 N	79.53 W
Dovetsk → Doneck	83	48.00 N	37.48 E
Dong ≃, Zhg.	100	23.06 N	114.00 E
Dong ≃, Zhg.	100	23.42 N	117.13 E
Dong ≃, Zhg.	100	25.00 N	118.27 E
Dong ≃, Zhg.	102	42.10 N	101.00 E
Donga ≃	146	8.19 N	9.58 E
Dong'an, Zhg.	89	47.20 N	134.10 E
Dongan → Mishan, Zhg.	89	45.33 N	131.52 E
Dong'an, Zhg.	100	33.24 N	114.24 E
Dong'an, Zhg.	102	26.17 N	111.07 E
Dong'an, Zhg.	106	30.30 N	118.48 E
Dongao	100	31.35 N	119.44 E
Dongao	100	29.23 N	121.25 E
Dongara	162	29.15 S	114.56 E
Dongargarh	120	21.12 N	80.44 E
Dongba ≃, Zhg.	100	39.58 N	116.32 E
Dongba, Zhg.	105	39.58 N	116.27 E
Dongba ≃	105	40.34 N	116.05 E
Dongbei	100	27.15 N	116.06 E
Dongbaimiao	105	40.34 N	116.05 E
Dongbeicha	98	41.43 N	127.23 E
Dongbeijipo	98	36.06 N	117.08 E
Dongchan	100	30.20 N	105.20 E
Dongchagjie	106	31.52 N	121.38 E
Dongchanghai	106	32.04 N	119.18 E
Dongcheng	106	28.56 N	121.16 E
Dongchong	100	26.35 N	119.52 E
Dongchuan	102	26.10 N	103.01 E
Dongcun	100	30.57 N	121.46 E
Dongdaoan	98	38.31 N	117.12 E
Dong Dian ⊞	105	39.03 N	116.35 E
Dongduluo	105	30.04 N	115.15 E
Dong'e (Tongcheng)	98	36.14 N	116.16 E
Dongen	52	51.37 N	4.56 E
Dong'ezhen	98	36.11 N	116.16 E
Dongfeng (Basuo)	110	19.05 N	108.39 E
Dongfeng, Zhg.	98	42.40 N	125.28 E
Dongfeng, Zhg.	105	27.20 N	118.53 E
Dongfengtai	105	39.34 N	117.45 E
Donggala	112	0.40 S	119.44 E
Donggang	105	32.28 N	120.50 E
Donggangzi	89	43.53 N	129.49 E
Donggi	112	1.33 S	122.15 E
Donggi Cona ⊜	102	37.10 N	96.55 E
Donggong Shan ⋌	100	27.36 N	119.26 E
Donggongsuo	106	32.07 N	121.36 E
Donggou, Zhg.	98	39.54 N	124.09 E
Donggou, Zhg.	100	33.38 N	119.40 E
Donggou, Zhg.	106	32.17 N	118.59 E
Donggu	100	26.46 N	115.22 E
Dongguan, Zhg.	100	27.49 N	116.25 E
Dongguan, Zhg.	100	23.03 N	113.46 E
Dongguang, Zhg.	98	30.22 N	119.28 E
Dongguang, Zhg.	107	30.40 N	106.16 E
Dongguang	98	37.53 N	116.30 E
Dongguanyingzi	106	31.13 N	120.43 E
Dongguanyingyizi	41	41.55 N	120.38 E
Dongguogang	105	39.16 N	116.56 E
Dong Hai, Viet.	110	12.34 N	109.14 E
Donghai (Niushan), Zhg.	98	34.30 N	118.47 E
Dong Hai → East China Sea	54		
Donghai Dao I	90	30.00 N	126.00 E
Dongheng ≅	102	21.02 N	110.25 E
Donghezhen	106	31.08 N	120.17 E
Dong Hoi	110	17.29 N	106.36 E
Dong Hu c	106	26.28 N	113.07 E
Donghuanggou	104	40.43 N	123.29 E
Dongji	112	2.02 S	121.28 E
Dongjia	58	46.27 N	8.58 E
Dongjiangkou	102	33.37 N	108.49 E
Dongjie	106	25.53 N	116.22 E
Dongjing	98	31.03 N	115.57 E
Dongjingcheng	89	44.07 N	129.09 E
Dongjingji	98	40.02 N	114.01 E
Dongjinling	104	41.18 N	123.35 E
Dongjug	98	29.58 N	94.53 E
Dongkaihecheng	104	41.04 N	122.38 E
Dongkalang	112	1.07 N	123.01 E
Dongkeng, Zhg.	100	27.48 N	119.42 E
Dongkeng, Zhg.	100	24.59 N	114.54 E
Dong Khe	102	22.26 N	106.27 E
Dongkou	98	35.29 N	115.20 E
Dongkou	102	27.08 N	110.35 E
Donglachuyu	104	42.28 N	124.17 E
Donglaojunpu	104	41.24 N	121.27 E
Dongli	100	20.50 N	110.20 E
Dongliang	104	42.00 N	121.25 E
Dongliangjia	98	36.02 N	118.23 E
Dongliao	98	42.54 N	125.00 E
Donglingmanzi	107	29.40 N	106.16 E
Dongling	104	41.50 N	123.35 E
Dongliu, Zhg.	100	30.14 N	116.53 E
Dongliu, Zhg.	98	32.06 N	116.58 E
Dongliujiazi	104	42.21 N	122.44 E
Donglong	98	39.21 N	116.47 E
Donglong	100	23.36 N	116.50 E
Donglucun	98	38.48 N	115.50 E
Dongmen	98	28.29 N	114.02 E
Dongming	98	35.18 N	115.08 E
Dong Nai ≃	110	10.45 N	106.46 E
Dongning	41	41.25 N	120.02 E
Dong Nhien, Rach ≃	269c	10.48 N	106.44 E
Dongning	89	44.04 N	131.07 E
Dongo, Ang.	152	14.36 S	15.48 E
Dongo, It.	58	46.07 N	9.17 E
Dongo, Zaïre	152	2.43 N	18.24 E
Dongobesh	154	4.37 S	35.23 E
Dongola → Dunqulah	140	19.10 N	30.29 E
Dongon Point ꜛ	116	12.44 N	120.48 E
Dongou	152	2.02 N	18.04 E
Dongping, Zhg.	100	22.26 N	111.43 E
Dongping, Zhg.	98	35.51 N	116.20 E
Dongping, Zhg.	102	21.43 N	111.15 E
Dongping Hu ⊜	98	35.58 N	116.10 E
Dongpu	100	30.03 N	120.34 E
Dongqian	106	30.52 N	121.63 E
Dongqing	98	31.12 N	121.48 E
Dongqingduizi	104	41.49 N	120.03 E
Dongsanjiazi	104	41.54 N	122.48 E

Name	Page	Lat.	Long.
Dongsanlintang	106	31.09 N	121.31 E
Dongsanpu	100	33.38 N	117.09 E
Dongsha ≅	104	41.07 N	121.50 E
Dongshaer	120	28.41 N	89.09 E
Dongshajiao	100	30.19 N	122.09 E
Dongshan, Zhg.	100	19.50 N	110.14 E
Dongshan, Zhg.	102	19.50 N	110.14 E
Dongshan Dao I	89	45.19 N	131.08 E
Dongshanqiao	106	31.52 N	118.46 E
Dongsheng	106	32.07 N	121.12 E
Dongsheng	102	39.49 N	109.59 E
Dongsheshanzi	104	42.15 N	123.09 E
Dongshi, Zhg.	106	24.42 N	118.27 E
Dongshi, Zhg.	100	24.43 N	115.59 E
Dongshi, Zhg.	271a	24.49 N	116.34 E
Dongshuiyan	105	39.15 N	115.23 E
Dongtai	100	32.51 N	120.20 E
Dongtai Hu c	106	31.05 N	120.30 E
Dongtaipingzhen	89	45.18 N	122.05 E
Dongtangou	105	39.23 N	118.22 E
Dongtianmu Shan ∧	106	30.22 N	119.31 E
Dongting ≅	106	30.51 N	120.06 E
Dongtinghu	98	38.29 N	115.08 E
Dongting Hu ⊜	102	29.20 N	112.54 E
Dongtingxi	100	28.34 N	110.36 E
Dongtou	100	27.50 N	121.09 E
Dongtou Shan I	106	27.50 N	121.08 E
Dong Trieu	110	21.05 N	106.31 E
Dongtuhulu	104	41.55 N	121.33 E
Dongtuozi	104	42.10 N	123.08 E
Dong Van	110	23.16 N	105.22 E
Dongwangfu	89	44.47 N	120.53 E
Dongwenzhuang	106	32.16 N	120.32 E
Dongwe ≃	152	13.58 S	23.53 E
Dongwuquan	105	39.20 N	115.43 E
Dongxi, Zhg.	106	31.57 N	121.42 E
Dongxi, Zhg.	102	29.16 N	120.14 E
Dongxi, Zhg.	106	30.52 N	120.34 E
Dongyang	98	35.56 N	113.58 E
Dongyian	105	39.22 N	115.46 E
Dongyin	98	39.09 N	117.43 E
Dongyou	100	27.10 N	118.37 E
Dongyuenhiao	106	30.52 N	119.14 E
Dongyuezhen	107	30.24 N	103.32 E
Dongzhang	100	25.44 N	119.17 E
Dongzhaozhuang	105	40.02 N	116.46 E
Dongzhi	100	30.07 N	116.59 E
Dongzhizhuang	105	40.34 N	115.42 E
Dongzhuangpu	105	38.30 N	116.44 E
Dongziya	105	38.50 N	116.44 E
Donie	222	31.29 N	96.13 W
Doninga	150	10.37 N	1.26 W
Donington	42	52.55 N	0.12 W
Doniphan, Mo., U.S.	194	36.37 N	90.49 W
Doniphan, Ne., U.S.	198	40.46 N	98.22 W
Don Islands ꞁꞁ	116	11.05 N	123.38 E
Donja Stubica	36	45.59 N	15.58 E
Donjek ≃	180	62.35 N	140.00 W
Donji Vakuf	36	44.09 N	17.25 E
Donk	52	51.33 N	5.37 E
Donkerpoort	158	30.32 S	25.30 E
Donkey Creek ≃	198	44.12 N	104.58 W
Donkey Town	260	51.20 N	0.39 W
Donmänick Islands ꞁꞁ	126	22.00 N	90.37 E
Don Martín	100	27.32 N	100.37 W
Don Matías	246	6.30 N	75.22 W
Don Mills ←⁸	275b	43.44 N	79.20 W
Don Mills Centre ←⁹	275b	43.44 N	79.21 W
Don Muang Airport ⊠	269a	13.56 N	100.37 E
Donna	196	26.10 N	98.03 W
Donna, Punta sa ∧	71	39.59 N	9.25 E
Donna Buang, Mount			
Donnaconna	206	46.40 N	71.47 W
Donnalucata	70	36.45 N	14.38 E
Donnaz	62	45.36 N	7.46 E
Donnell Lake ⊜¹	226	38.20 N	119.56 W
Donnellson	219	39.02 N	89.29 W
Donnelly, Ab., Can.	182	55.43 N	117.06 W
Donnelly, Ak., U.S.	180	63.40 N	145.54 W
Donnelly, Id., U.S.	202	44.43 N	116.04 W
Donnellys Crossing	172	35.43 S	173.37 E
Donnemarie-Dontilly	56	48.29 N	3.08 E
Donner	194	29.41 N	90.56 W
Donner Lake ⊜¹	226	39.20 N	120.16 W
Donner Memorial State Park ꜛ	226	39.18 N	120.16 W
Donner Pass ⤬	226	39.19 N	120.20 W
Donnersberg ∧	56	49.38 N	7.54 E
Donner und Blitzen ≃	202	43.17 N	118.49 W
Donnybrook, Austl.	162	33.35 S	115.49 E
Donnybrook, S. Afr.	158	30.00 S	29.48 E
Donora	214	40.10 N	79.51 W
Donostia (San Sebastián)	34	43.19 N	1.59 W
Donovan	48	51.57 N	8.45 W
Donovan	216	40.53 N	87.37 W
Don Pedro Reservoir ⊜¹	226	37.43 N	120.23 W
Don Peninsula ꜛ¹	182	52.30 N	128.10 W
Donque	152	15.28 S	14.06 E
Donskaja gr'ada ∧²	80	49.30 N	42.00 E
Donskoj, S.S.S.R.	76	53.58 N	38.20 E
Donskoj, S.S.S.R.	83	47.25 N	40.14 E
Donskoj, S.S.S.R.	76	52.37 N	39.00 E
Donskoje	83	45.10 N	41.33 E
Donskoje belogorje ∧²	76	50.30 N	39.45 E
Donsol	116	12.54 N	123.36 E
Don Torcuato	288	34.30 S	58.38 W
Don Torcuato, Aeródromo ⊠	288	34.30 S	58.36 W
Donuzlav, ozero ⊜	48	45.25 N	33.05 E
Donyztau ⤬	88	46.25 N	57.00 E
Donzdorf	56	48.41 N	9.48 E
Donzère	60	44.27 N	4.43 E
Donzy	56	47.22 N	3.08 E
Dood nuur ⊜	88	50.24 N	91.00 E
Doogort	48	54.01 N	10.01 W
Doolow	144	4.10 N	42.05 E
Doomadgee	166	17.56 S	138.49 E
Doomadgee Aboriginal Reserve ←⁴	166	17.43 S	138.36 E
Doon, Ia., Can.	212	43.03 N	96.13 W
Doon, On., Can.	283	43.22 N	80.25 W
Doon, Loch ⊜	44	55.15 N	4.22 W
Doonbeg ≃	48	52.44 N	9.34 W
Doon Doon Aboriginal Reserve ←⁴	164	16.15 S	128.15 E
Doonerak, Mount ∧	180	67.56 N	150.72 E
Doonside	274a	33.46 S	150.52 E
Doonloang	112	4.35 S	121.61 E
Doorn	52	52.02 N	5.20 E
Doornaba	158	28.03 S	21.03 E

Name	Page	Lat.	Long.
Doornik → Tournai	50	50.36 N	3.23 E
Door Peninsula ꜛ¹	190	44.55 N	87.20 W
Dopping Brook ≃	283	42.12 N	71.23 W
Do Qal'eh	128	32.18 N	61.31 E
Dor	132	32.37 N	34.55 E
Dora	194	33.43 N	87.05 W
Dora, Lake ⊜, Austl.	162	22.05 S	122.55 E
Dora, Lake ⊜, Fl., U.S.	220	29.00 N	81.37 W
Dora Baltea ≃	62	45.11 N	8.05 E
Dora di Rhêmes ≃	62	45.42 N	7.11 E
Dorado	240m	18.28 N	66.15 W
Doräha	123	30.49 N	76.01 E
Dorän Än ⤬	123	36.07 N	71.15 E
Dorain, Beinn ∧	46	56.30 N	4.42 W
Dorândia	256	22.27 S	43.57 W
Dora Riparia ≃	62	45.05 N	7.44 E
Doraville	192	33.53 N	84.17 W
Dorback Burn ≃	46	57.31 N	3.40 W
Dos Reyes, Punta ꜛ	252	24.33 S	70.35 W
Dorchester, N.B., Can.	186	45.54 N	64.31 W
Dorchester, On., Can.	212	42.59 N	81.04 W
Dorchester, Eng., U.K.	42	50.43 N	2.26 W
Dorchester, Eng., U.K.	42	51.39 N	1.10 W
Dorchester, Il., U.S.	219	39.05 N	89.53 W
Dorchester, Ne., U.S.	198	40.38 N	97.06 W
Dorchester, N.J., U.S.	208	39.16 N	74.58 W
Dorchester, Wi., U.S.	190	45.00 N	90.20 W
Dorchester ←⁸	208	38.34 N	76.04 W
Dorchester ←⁸	283	42.17 N	71.04 W
Dorchester, Cape ꜛ	176	65.29 N	77.30 W
Dorchester Bay c	283	42.19 N	71.02 W
Dorchester Crossing	186	46.10 N	64.34 W
Dorchester Estates	284c	38.47 N	76.55 W
Dorchester Heights National Historic Site ⊥	283	42.20 N	71.03 W
Dorchheim	56	50.30 N	8.04 E
Dordabis	156	22.52 S	17.38 E
Dordives	56	48.09 N	2.46 E
Dordogne ⊡⁵	32	45.10 N	0.45 E
Dordogne ≃	32	45.02 N	0.35 W
Dordon	42	52.36 N	1.37 W
Dordrecht, Ned.	52	51.49 N	4.40 E
Dordrecht, S. Afr.	158	31.20 S	27.03 E
Doré ≃, Sk., Can.	184	54.56 N	107.45 W
Doré Lake	62	45.50 S	8.25 E
Dore, ≃ Eng., U.K.	42	51.57 N	2.52 W
Dore, Monts ∧	32	45.30 N	2.45 E
Doreissou	146	10.33 N	15.08 E
Doré Lake	184	54.38 N	107.24 W
Doré Lake ⊜	184	54.46 N	107.17 W
Dorena	202	43.43 N	122.51 W
Dörentrup	52	52.03 N	8.59 E
Dorfen	56	48.16 N	12.09 E
Dorfgastein	64	47.15 N	13.06 E
Dorfmark	52	52.54 N	9.46 E
Dorgali	71	40.17 N	9.35 E
Dörgön nuur ⊜	88	47.40 N	93.30 E
Doring ≃	158	31.34 S	18.39 E
Doringkaip	158	31.48 S	18.15 E
Dorion → Tournai	206	45.23 N	74.01 W
Dorion-Vaudreuil	206	45.23 N	74.01 W
Dorje Läpka ∧	124	28.11 N	85.47 E
Dorloo	210	42.43 N	74.37 W
Dormaa Ahenkro	150	7.17 N	2.53 W
Dormans	56	49.04 N	3.38 E
Dormidontovka	89	47.45 N	134.57 E
Dormont	279b	40.23 N	80.02 W
Dormont	58	47.29 N	7.37 E
Dornach	58	47.29 N	7.37 E
Dornap ←⁸	263	51.15 N	7.04 E
Dornbach ←⁸	264b	48.14 N	16.18 E
Dornbirn	56	47.25 N	9.44 E
Dornburg	56	50.30 N	8.07 E
Dorndorf, D.D.R.	54	51.00 N	11.40 E
Dorndorf, D.D.R.	56	50.50 N	10.05 E
Dorney	260	51.30 N	0.41 W
Dornfeld ←⁸	56	48.21 N	8.30 E
Dornhan	58	48.17 N	8.30 E
Dornie	46	57.17 N	5.31 W
Dornoch	46	57.52 N	4.02 W
Dornoch Firth c¹	46	57.53 N	4.00 W
Dornod ⊡⁴	98	48.00 N	115.00 E
Dornogov' ⊡⁴	98	44.00 N	110.00 E
Dornsife	208	40.45 N	76.47 W
Dornstetten	58	48.28 N	8.30 E
Doro, Indon.	115a	7.02 S	109.41 E
Doro, Mali	150	16.09 N	0.51 W
Dorochovo	80	55.33 N	36.23 E
Dorog	60	47.43 N	18.44 E
Dorogobuž ꜛ	76	54.55 N	33.18 E
Dorohoi	38	47.57 N	26.24 E
Dorokempo	112	8.33 S	118.15 E
Doromata	115b	8.46 S	118.13 E
Doromo	152	3.49 N	26.17 E
Doroošata	88	57.21 N	51.08 E
Doroešata	26	64.16 N	26.24 E
Dorothy	208	39.24 N	74.49 W
Dorothy, Lake ⊜	224	47.34 N	121.22 W
Dorotockeys Run ≃	276	40.59 N	73.58 W
Dorpat → Tartu	76	58.23 N	26.43 E
Dörpen	52	52.57 N	7.20 E
Dorr	216	42.43 N	85.43 W
Dorrance	198	38.50 N	98.35 W
Dorre Island I	162	25.09 S	113.07 E
Dorrigo	163	30.21 S	152.43 E
Dorris	204	41.58 N	121.55 W
Dorset, Oh., U.S.	214	41.41 N	80.40 W
Dorset, Vt., U.S.	210	43.15 N	73.06 W
Dorset ⊡⁶	42	50.50 N	2.20 W
Dorset Peak ∧	210	43.27 N	73.02 W
Dorsey Run ≃	284	39.12 N	76.43 W
Dorseyville	279b	40.33 N	79.53 W
Dorsoduro ←⁸	59	45.25 N	12.19 E
Dort → Dordrecht	52	51.49 N	4.40 E
Dorsten	56	51.40 N	6.58 E
Dörtdivan	130	40.43 N	32.04 E
Dortmund, B.R.D.	56	51.31 N	7.28 E
Dortmund, B.R.D.	56	51.32 N	7.27 E
Dortmund-Ems-Kanal ꜛ	56	52.15 N	7.25 E
Dortmunder Rieselfelder ←¹	263	51.33 N	7.38 E
Dortmund-Wickede, Flughafen ⊠	263	51.32 N	7.35 E
Dörtyol	130	36.52 N	36.12 E
Dô Rüd ≃	128	33.28 N	48.08 E
Doruma	154	4.44 N	27.42 E
Dorval, Île ꞁ	275a	45.26 N	73.44 W
Dorval Gardens Centre ←⁹	275a	45.26 N	73.44 W
Dörverden	52	52.51 N	9.13 E
Dörzbach	56	49.23 N	9.42 E

Name	Page	Lat.	Long.
Dosatuj	88	50.23 N	118.38 E
Dos Bahías, Cabo ꜛ	254	44.55 S	65.32 W
Dos Bocas	240m	18.20 N	66.40 W
Dos Bocas, Lago ⊜¹	240m	18.19 N	66.40 W
Dosčatoje	80	55.23 N	42.07 E
Dösgemabh	130	37.04 N	30.36 E
Dosewallips ≃	224	47.42 N	122.53 W
Dos Hermanas	34	37.17 N	5.55 W
Dos Hermanas, Islas ꞁꞁ	258	34.05 S	58.17 W
Dōshi	94	35.32 N	139.02 E
Dōshi ≃	94	35.36 N	139.14 E
Doshisha University			
Dosi	270	35.02 N	135.46 E
Dösjebro	164	5.56 S	134.34 E
Do Son	110	20.42 N	106.47 E
Dosoris Island ꜛ¹	276	40.54 N	73.38 W
Dosoris Pond ⊜	276	40.54 N	73.38 W
Dos Palos	226	36.59 N	120.37 W
Dosse ≃	54	53.13 N	12.20 E
Dosséo, Bahr ≃	146	9.01 N	19.38 E
Dosso	150	13.03 N	3.12 E
Dosso ⊡⁵	150	13.00 N	3.00 E
Dossor	80	47.32 N	53.01 E
Doster	216	42.27 N	85.33 W
Doswell	208	37.51 N	77.27 W
Dothan	186	31.13 N	85.23 W
Doting Cove	186	49.27 N	53.57 W
Dot Lake	180	63.40 N	144.04 W
Dotnuva	76	55.21 N	23.54 E
Dotson	222	32.01 N	94.31 W
Döttingen	58	47.34 N	8.16 E
Doty	224	46.38 N	123.16 W
Dou ≃	39	39.13 N	118.03 E
Douai	50	50.22 N	3.04 E
Douf'noje	80	53.30 N	79.40 E
Douala-Edéa, Réserve de ←⁴	152	4.30 S	9.50 E
Douarnenez	32	48.06 N	4.20 W
Doubabougou	150	14.13 N	7.59 W
Double, Lac ⊜	158	50.46 N	70.23 W
Double, Pointe ꜛ	186	16.20 N	61.00 W
Double Bayou	222	29.41 N	94.39 W
Double Cone ∧	172	45.04 S	168.48 E
Double Island Point ꜛ	166	25.56 S	153.11 E
Double Mountain ∧	228	35.02 N	118.29 W
Double Point ꜛ	166	17.39 S	146.09 E
Double Springs	194	34.08 N	87.24 W
Doubletop Peak ∧	200	43.20 N	110.17 W
Doubs ⊡⁵	58	46.56 N	6.21 E
Doubs ≃	58	47.10 N	6.15 E
Doubs ⊡⁵, Fr.	58	47.10 N	6.25 E
Doubs ⊡⁵, Fr.	58	47.10 N	6.25 E
Doubs, Saut de ᴜ	58	46.54 N	5.02 E
Doubtful Sound c¹	172	45.15 S	166.51 E
Doubtless Bay c	172	34.55 S	173.25 E
Douchy	56	47.57 N	3.03 E
Douchy-les-Mines	50	50.18 N	3.23 E
Doudeville	50	49.43 N	0.48 E
Doudian	105	39.39 N	116.03 E
Doué-la-Fontaine	56	47.11 N	0.16 W
Douentza	150	15.00 N	2.57 W
Doué ≃	56	47.16 N	0.07 W
Dougga ⊥	68	36.25 N	9.13 E
Doughboy	170	35.15 S	149.39 E
Doughboy Bay c	172	47.02 S	167.41 E
Douglas, Austl.	164	16.29 S	145.28 E
Douglas, Mb., Can.	184	49.53 N	99.42 W
Douglas, S. Afr.	158	29.04 S	23.46 E
Douglas, Scot., U.K.	46	55.33 N	3.51 W
Douglas, Ak., U.S.	180	58.16 N	134.22 W
Douglas, Az., U.S.	200	31.20 N	109.32 W
Douglas, Ga., U.S.	192	31.30 N	82.51 W
Douglas, Mi., U.S.	216	42.38 N	86.12 W
Douglas, N.D., U.S.	198	48.21 N	101.30 W
Douglas, Wy., U.S.	200	42.45 N	105.22 W
Douglas ⊡⁶	226	38.55 N	119.39 W
Douglas Channel ꜛ	182	53.30 N	129.08 E
Douglas Creek ≃	200	40.05 N	108.46 W
Douglas Lake ⊜	192	36.00 N	83.22 W
Douglas Lake Indian Reserve ←⁴	182	50.10 N	120.40 W
Douglas Park	170	34.11 S	150.43 E
Douglas, Mount ∧	180	58.52 N	153.31 W
Douglass, Ks., U.S.	198	37.31 N	97.01 W
Douglass, Tx., U.S.	222	31.40 N	94.53 W
Douglass Run ≃	279b	40.15 N	79.44 W
Douglass Water ≃	46	55.39 N	3.51 W
Douglasville	192	33.45 N	84.44 W
Dougouzi, Zhg.	105	39.57 N	127.07 E
Dougouzi, Zhg.	98	36.55 N	121.15 E
Douhutun	98	42.06 N	124.52 E
Douigny	152	3.11 N	10.45 E
Doujiapu	98	40.22 N	116.56 E
Doukhane, Djebel ∧	68	35.23 N	8.06 E
Doulaincourt	56	48.19 N	5.12 E
Doulevant-le-Château	56	48.23 N	4.55 E
Doullens	50	50.09 N	2.21 E
Doumanga	152	2.53 S	11.53 E
Doumé, Cam.	152	4.14 N	13.27 E
Doumé, Cam.	152	5.32 N	12.15 E
Doumen, Zhg.	100	22.12 N	113.16 E
Doumen, Zhg.	98	37.43 N	115.53 E
Douna	150	12.40 N	6.00 W
Doune Castle ⊥	46	56.11 N	4.03 W
Doune ≃	152	2.00 S	16.05 E
Doupovské hory ⤬	54	50.16 N	13.08 E
Dour	52	50.24 N	3.47 E
Dourada, Serra ∧¹	256	14.05 S	49.14 W
Dourada, Serra ∧¹	256	16.05 S	50.15 W
Douradinho	256	21.45 S	45.46 W
Dourados ≃, Bra.	256	21.45 S	45.25 W
Dourados ≃, Bra.	256	21.43 S	54.48 W
Dourados	252	22.04 S	54.13 W
Douro (Duero) ≃	34	41.08 N	8.40 W
Doushanme	100	30.27 N	116.25 E
Doushi	98	30.59 N	115.03 E
Doutou	150	6.51 N	1.43 E
Douthat State Park ꜛ	192	37.54 N	79.50 W
Douvaine	62	46.19 N	6.18 E
Douvres → Dover	50	51.08 N	1.19 E
Douvres, Falaises de ⤬	273b	4.06 S	15.25 E

Name	Page	Lat.	Long.
Dove ≃, Eng., U.K.	44	54.12 N	0.54 W
Dove Creek	200	37.45 N	108.54 W
Dove Creek ≃, Tx., U.S.	196	31.20 N	100.36 W
Dove Creek ≃, Ut,. U.S.	200	41.37 N	113.15 W
Dove Holes	262	53.18 N	1.53 W
Dove Holes Tunnel ←⁵	262	53.18 N	1.53 W
Dover, Austl.	166	43.19 S	147.01 E
Dover, S. Afr.	158	27.02 S	27.46 E
Dover, Eng., U.K.	42	51.08 N	1.19 E
Dover, Ar., U.S.	194	35.24 N	93.06 W
Dover, De., U.S.	208	39.09 N	75.31 W
Dover, Fl., U.S.	220	27.59 N	82.13 W
Dover, Id., U.S.	202	48.15 N	116.36 W
Dover, Ky., U.S.	218	38.45 N	83.52 W
Dover, N.J., U.S.	210	40.53 N	74.34 W
Dover, N.H., U.S.	210	43.11 N	70.52 W
Dover, N.J., U.S.	208	40.53 N	74.34 W
Dover, Oh., U.S.	214	40.31 N	81.28 W
Dover, Ok., U.S.	196	35.58 N	97.54 W
Dover, Pa., U.S.	208	40.00 N	76.51 W
Dover, Tn., U.S.	194	36.29 N	87.50 W
Dover, Point ꜛ	162	32.32 S	125.32 E
Dover, Strait of (Pas de Calais) ᴜ	50	51.00 N	1.30 E
Dover Air Force Base ■	208	39.08 N	75.28 W
Dover-Foxcroft	188	45.11 N	69.13 W
Dover Heights	274a	33.53 S	151.17 E
Dover Hills	276	40.52 N	74.33 W
Dover Plains	210	41.44 N	73.35 W
Dovers Hills ⤬²	162	23.10 S	128.45 E
Dove Stone Reservoir ⊜¹	262	53.32 N	1.58 W
Doveton	274b	38.00 S	145.14 E
Dovey Valley V	42	52.35 N	3.50 W
Dovre	26	62.06 N	9.25 E
Dovrefjell ꜛ	26	61.59 N	9.15 E
Dovrefjell Nasjonalpark ꜛ	26	62.18 N	9.36 E
Dovsk	76	53.09 N	30.28 E
Dowa	154	13.40 S	33.58 E
Dowagiac	216	41.59 N	86.08 W
Dowagiac Creek ≃	216	41.59 N	86.10 W
Dowally	46	56.36 N	3.37 W
Dow City	198	41.55 N	95.29 W
Dowden Terrace	284c	38.50 N	77.08 W
Dowelltop ∧	208	38.20 N	76.27 W
Dowerin	162	31.12 S	117.02 E
Dowi, Tanjung ꜛ	114	1.31 N	97.25 E
Dowker, N.J.	275a	45.24 N	73.54 W
Dowlatābād, Afg.	120	36.26 N	64.55 E
Dowlatābād, Afg.	120	36.59 N	66.50 E
Dowlatābād, Īrān	128	28.18 N	56.40 E
Dowlat Yār	120	34.33 N	65.47 E
Dowling Lake ⊜	182	51.44 N	112.00 W
Downe ←⁸	260	51.20 N	0.03 E
Down East	260	51.20 N	0.03 E
Downers Grove	216	41.48 N	88.00 W
Downey, Ca., U.S.	228	33.56 N	118.07 W
Downey, Id., U.S.	202	42.25 N	112.07 W
Downham, Eng., U.K.	262	53.52 N	2.19 W
Downham Market	42	52.36 N	0.23 E
Down House ⊥	260	51.20 N	0.03 E
Downieville	226	39.33 N	120.49 W
Downing	194	40.29 N	92.22 W
Downingtown	208	40.00 N	75.42 W
Downingtown Airport ⊠	285	39.59 N	75.45 W
Downpatrick	48	54.20 N	5.43 W
Downpatrick Head ꜛ	48	54.20 N	9.20 W
Downs, Eng., U.K.	260	51.20 N	0.20 E
Downs, Ks., U.S.	198	39.30 N	98.32 W
Downs Mountain ∧	200	43.18 N	109.40 W
Downsview Dells Park ꜛ	275b	43.44 N	79.30 W
Downton	42	51.00 N	1.44 W
Downton, Mount ∧	182	52.42 N	124.51 W
Downwind Acres Airfield ⊠	281	39.08 N	83.34 W
Dows	190	42.39 N	93.30 W
Dowshī	120	35.37 N	68.41 E
Doygaab	144	3.59 N	43.32 E
Doyle	226	40.01 N	120.06 W
Doyles	186	47.50 N	59.12 W
Doylesburg	214	40.13 N	77.42 W
Doylestown, Oh., U.S.	214	40.58 N	81.41 W
Doylestown, Pa., U.S.	208	40.18 N	75.07 W
Doyline	194	32.32 N	93.24 W
Dōzen I	96	33.58 N	133.05 E
Dozier	194	31.30 N	86.22 W
Dozois, Réservoir ⊜¹	206	47.30 N	77.00 W
Dozza	59	44.22 N	11.37 E
Drâa, Cap ꜛ	148	28.44 N	11.09 W
Dra'a, Hamada du ⤬²	148	29.00 N	6.45 W
Drâa, Oued V	148	28.43 N	11.09 W
Dra el Mizan	68	36.32 N	3.50 E
Drable	182	52.12 N	114.58 W
Drabov	78	49.57 N	32.10 E
Drac ≃	62	45.13 N	5.41 E
Dracena	256	21.29 S	51.30 W
Drachenfels ⊥	56	50.40 N	7.12 E
Drachten	52	53.06 N	6.05 E
Dracut	210	42.40 N	71.18 W
Drag ≃	41	41.41 N	21.21 E
Drăgănesti-Olt	38	44.10 N	24.32 E
Drăgănesti-Vlasca	38	44.09 N	25.39 E
Drăgăsani	38	44.40 N	24.16 E
Drag Lake ⊜	212	44.55 N	78.22 W
Dragoe ≃	264a	45.44 N	21.18 E
Dragonera, Isla I	34	39.35 N	2.18 E
Dragon Mouth ᴜ	246	10.45 N	61.46 W
Dragon Swamp ≃	208	37.36 N	76.30 W
Draguignan	62	43.32 N	6.28 E
Drahičyn	76	52.11 N	25.09 E
Draille ≃	204	49.01 N	122.40 W
Drainville	288	34.50 S	58.33 W
Drake, N.D., U.S.	198	47.55 N	100.22 W
Drake Passage ᴜ	18	58.00 S	68.00 W
Drakenberg ⤬	56	51.15 N	9.00 E
Drakensberg ⤬	158	27.00 S	30.00 E
Drakes ≃	186	49.33 N	57.11 W
Drakes Branch	192	37.03 N	78.36 W
Drakes Brook ≃	186	48.32 N	57.56 W
Drakesboro	218	37.13 N	87.02 W
Drakino	214	54.52 N	37.17 E
Dráma ⊡⁴	38	41.09 N	24.08 E
Dramburg → Drawsko Pomorskie	54		
Drammen	26	59.44 N	10.15 E
Dranse ≃	62	46.17 N	6.25 E
Drau ≃	36		
Dransfeld	52	51.30 N	9.45 E
Dranske	54	54.38 N	13.14 E
Drap	62	43.45 N	7.19 E
Draper, N.C., U.S.	192	36.31 N	79.41 W
Draper, Ut., U.S.	200	40.31 N	111.51 W
Draperstown	48	54.48 N	6.47 W
Dräs	123	34.27 N	75.46 E
Drâs ≃	123	34.37 N	75.59 E
Drau (Drava) (Dráva) ≃	36	45.33 N	18.55 E
Drava (Drau) (Dráva) ≃	36	45.33 N	18.55 E
Draveil	50	48.41 N	2.25 E
Dravinja ≃	36	46.22 N	15.57 E
Dravograd	61	46.35 N	15.02 E
Dravosburg	279b	40.21 N	79.51 W
Drawno	30	53.13 N	15.45 E
Drawsko Pomorskie	30	53.32 N	15.48 E
Drayton, On., Can.	212	43.46 N	80.40 W
Drayton, Eng., U.K.	42	51.38 N	1.18 W
Drayton, N.D., U.S.	198	48.34 N	97.10 W
Drayton, S.C., U.S.	192	34.58 N	81.54 W
Drayton Plains	216	42.41 N	83.22 W
Drayton Valley	182	53.13 N	114.59 W
Draženov	60	49.28 N	12.52 E
Dream	36	36.41 N	7.46 E
Drebkau	54	51.39 N	14.13 E
Dreieich	56	50.01 N	8.41 E
Dreifelder Weiher ⊜	56	50.36 N	7.49 E
Dreihausen	56	50.43 N	8.50 E
Dreiherrnspitze (Picco dei Tre Signori) ∧	64	47.04 N	12.15 E
Dreik, N.C.	164	3.35 S	142.45 E
Drejo I	41	54.58 N	10.25 E
Dremsel, Mount ∧	164	2.10 S	146.55 E
Drena	64	45.58 N	10.56 E
Drenovec	38	43.42 N	22.59 E
Drensteinfurt	52	51.48 N	7.44 E
Dreschvitz	54	54.23 N	13.21 E
Dresden, On., Can.	214	42.35 N	82.11 W
Dresden, D.D.R.	54	51.03 N	13.44 E
Dresden, N.Y., U.S.	210	42.41 N	76.58 W
Dresden, Oh., U.S.	214	40.07 N	82.00 W
Dresden, Tn., U.S.	194	36.17 N	88.42 W
Dresden ⊡⁵	54	51.10 N	14.00 E
Dresher	285	40.09 N	75.10 W
Dretun	76	55.41 N	29.13 E
Dreux	50	48.44 N	1.22 E
Drevenack	263	51.40 N	6.45 E
Drew	194	33.48 N	90.31 W
Drewer	263	51.40 N	7.57 E
Drewitz, D.D.R.	54	52.22 N	13.07 E
Drewitz, D.D.R.	54	52.12 N	12.10 E
Drewitz ←⁸	264a	52.23 N	13.08 E
Drewryville	208	36.42 N	77.18 W
Drews Reservoir ⊜¹	202	42.10 N	120.40 W
Drew University ⊡¹	278	40.46 N	74.25 W
Drexel Gardens	218	39.44 N	86.15 W
Drexel Hill	285	39.56 N	75.17 W
Drexel University ⊡²	285	39.57 N	75.11 W
Drezdenko	30	52.51 N	15.50 E
Drezna	80	55.44 N	38.51 E
Dribin	76	54.08 N	31.06 E
Driebergen	52	52.03 N	5.16 E
Drienov	30	48.53 N	21.17 E
Driesen → Drezdenko	30		
Driffield	36	54.00 N	0.27 W
Driftless	210	41.00 N	75.34 W
Driftpile ←⁸	182	55.33 N	115.40 W
Drift Pile River Indian Reserve ←⁴	182	55.18 N	115.45 W
Driftwood, B.C., Can.	182	55.49 N	126.25 W
Driftwood ≃, B.C., Can.	182	55.49 N	126.25 W
Driftwood ≃, On., Can.	214	41.20 N	78.08 W
Driftwood ≃, In., U.S.	218	39.12 N	85.56 W
Driftwood Creek ≃	198	40.11 N	100.39 W
Driggs	202	43.43 N	111.06 W
Drimoleague	48	51.38 N	9.16 W
Drin ≃	38	41.45 N	19.34 E
Drina ≃	36	44.53 N	19.21 E
Drin, Gjiri i c	38	41.35 N	19.27 E
Drinjaca ≃	36	44.31 N	19.13 E
Driscoll	196	27.40 N	97.45 W
Driskill Mountain ∧²	194	32.25 N	92.54 W
Drissa	76	55.47 N	27.55 E
Driver	190	43.39 N	96.30 W
Drizzle Lake ⊜	212	46.48 N	79.09 W
Drljanovo	38	42.58 N	25.27 E
Dro	64	45.58 N	10.55 E
Drobeta-Turnu Severin	38	44.38 N	22.39 E
Drobkov	78	50.09 N	32.20 E
Drobolje	38	44.29 N	20.03 E
Drôme ⊡⁵	62	44.38 N	5.15 E
Drôme ≃	62	44.46 N	4.46 E
Drömling ꜛ	54	52.29 N	11.04 E
Dromod	48	53.54 N	7.55 W
Dromore	48	54.25 N	6.09 W
Dromore West	48	54.15 N	8.53 W
Dronfield	42	53.18 N	1.28 W
Drongen	52	51.03 N	3.40 E
Dronne ≃	60	45.02 N	0.09 W
Dronninglund	26	57.10 N	10.18 E
Dronrijp	52	53.11 N	5.38 E
Dronten	52	52.32 N	5.43 E
Dronville	280	35.22 N	119.10 W
Drøbak	26	59.39 N	10.39 E
Drogheda → Droichead Atha	48	53.43 N	6.21 W
Droichead Atha (Drogheda)	48	53.43 N	6.21 W
Droichead Nua	48	53.11 N	6.48 W
Droitwich	42	52.16 N	2.09 W
Dromana	169	38.21 S	144.58 E
Drôme	62	44.46 N	4.46 E
Droman	46	58.34 N	5.00 W
Dromdowney	48	52.14 N	8.54 W
Drumheller	182	51.28 N	112.42 W
Drummond	200	46.40 N	113.09 W
Drottningholm slott ⊥	40	59.19 N	17.53 E
Droué	56	48.02 N	1.05 E
Drouin	170	38.08 S	145.51 E
Drouwen	52	52.57 N	6.48 E
Drove-sur-Drouette	50	48.37 N	1.45 E
Drowned Lake ⊜	280	48.30 N	122.20 W
Droylsden	262	53.29 N	2.10 W
Droyßig	54	51.04 N	11.54 E
Dr. Petru Groza	38	46.31 N	22.28 E
Dru	26	59.17 N	6.00 E
Druid Hill Park ꜛ	284b	39.20 N	76.39 W
Druk-Yul → Bhutan ⊡¹	120	27.30 N	90.30 E
Drulingen	56	48.52 N	7.11 E
Drum ∧, Scot., U.K.	46	57.07 N	4.15 W
Drum ∧, Scot., U.K.	46	57.07 N	4.15 W
Drumcliff	48	54.20 N	8.30 W
Drumheller	182	51.28 N	112.42 W

ESPAÑOL: Nombre — Página — Lat.°′ — Long.°′ W = Oeste
FRANÇAIS: Nom — Page — Lat.°′ — Long.°′ W = Ouest
PORTUGUÊS: Nome — Página — Lat.°′ — Long.°′ W = Oeste

Nombre / Nom / Nome	Página / Page	Lat.°′	Long.°′
Drumcliff	48	54.20 N	8.30 W
Drumheller	182	51.28 N	112.42 W
Drumlish	48	53.48 N	7.46 W
Drummond, N.Z.	172	46.09 S	168.09 E
Drummond, Mt., U.S.	202	46.40 N	113.08 W
Drummond, Wi., U.S.	190	46.20 N	91.15 W
Drummond □[6]	206	45.50 N	72.20 W
Drummond, Lake ⊜	208	36.36 N	76.28 W
Drummond Island I	190	46.00 N	83.40 W
Drummond Range ⋏	166	23.30 S	147.15 E
Drummondville	206	45.53 N	72.29 W
Drummore	44	54.42 N	4.54 W
Drummoyne	274a	33.51 S	151.09 E
Drumquin	48	54.37 N	7.30 W
Drumright	196	35.59 N	96.36 W
Drumshanbo	48	54.02 N	8.02 W
Drunen	52	51.42 N	5.08 E
Drusenheim	56	48.46 N	7.57 E
Druskininkai	76	54.01 N	23.58 E
Drut' ≃	76	53.03 N	30.42 E
Druten	52	51.54 N	5.36 E
Druyes-les-Belles-Fontaines	50	47.33 N	3.25 E
Družba, S.S.S.R.	78	52.03 N	33.56 E
Družba, S.S.S.R.	86	45.15 N	82.26 E
Družba, S.S.S.R.	265b	55.53 N	37.45 E
Družina	74	68.14 N	145.18 E
Družkovka	83	48.37 N	37.33 E
Družnaja Gorka	76	59.17 N	30.08 E
Drvar	36	44.22 N	16.24 E
Drwęca ≃	30	53.00 N	18.42 E
Dry ≃	164	14.54 S	132.24 E
Dry Arm ⊂	202	47.45 N	106.20 W
Dry Bay ⊂	180	59.08 N	138.25 W
Dryberry Lake ⊜	184	49.33 N	93.53 W
Dryburgh Abbey ♉[1]	46	55.34 N	2.40 W
Dry Cimarron ≃	196	36.54 N	102.59 W
Dry Creek ≃, Ca., U.S.	204	38.35 N	122.51 W
Dry Creek ≃, Ca., U.S.	226	38.39 N	121.28 W
Dry Creek ≃, Ca., U.S.	226	37.27 N	120.37 W
Dry Creek ≃, Ca., U.S.	226	36.47 N	119.46 W
Dry Creek ≃, Ca., U.S.	226	38.22 N	122.18 W
Dry Creek ≃, Ca., U.S.	226	38.58 N	121.32 W
Dry Creek ≃, Ca., U.S.	226	39.13 N	121.25 W
Dry Creek ≃, Ca., U.S.	226	38.14 N	121.24 W
Dry Creek ≃, Ca., U.S.	226	36.58 N	120.13 W
Dry Creek ≃, Ca., U.S.	282	37.22 N	122.23 W
Dry Creek ≃, Or., U.S.	202	43.34 N	117.21 W
Dry Creek ≃, Or., U.S.	224	45.30 N	121.03 W
Dry Creek ≃, Tx., U.S.	222	32.46 N	95.28 W
Dry Creek ≃, Wy., U.S.	202	43.13 N	108.54 W
Dry Creek ≃, Wy., U.S.	202	44.30 N	108.03 W
Dry Creek Mountain ∧	204	41.22 N	116.22 W
Dryden, On., Can.	184	49.47 N	92.50 W
Dryden, N.Y., U.S.	210	42.29 N	76.17 W
Dryden, Wa., U.S.	224	47.32 N	120.33 W
Dry Devils ≃, Tx., U.S.	196	29.47 N	100.59 W
Dry Devils ≃, Tx., U.S.	196	30.20 N	100.57 W
Dryfe Water ≃	44	55.08 N	3.26 W
Dry Fork ≃	194	37.58 N	91.31 W
Dry Frio ≃	196	29.17 N	99.39 W
Drygalski Island I	9	65.45 S	92.30 E
Dry Lake ⊜	198	48.15 N	98.58 W
Drymen	46	56.04 N	4.27 W
Dry Prong	194	31.34 N	92.31 W
Dry Ridge	218	38.40 N	84.35 W
Dry Run	214	40.10 N	77.45 W
Drysdale	169	38.11 S	144.34 E
Drysdale ≃	164	13.59 S	126.51 E
Drysdale River National Park ♠	164	15.00 S	127.00 E
Dry Tortugas II	220	24.38 N	82.55 W
Drzewica	30	51.27 N	20.28 E
Drzewice	54	52.38 N	14.38 E
Dschang	152	5.27 N	10.04 E
Dschidda → Jiddah	144	21.30 N	39.12 E
Dschuba → Jubba ≃	144	0.15 S	42.38 E
Du	150	10.30 N	0.59 W
Du ≃	102	32.48 N	110.38 E
Dua ≃	152	3.20 N	20.53 E
Duabo	150	5.40 N	8.05 W
Duāigaon	126	24.14 N	90.51 E
Duala → Douala	152	4.03 N	9.42 E
Dualchi	71	40.13 N	8.54 E
Du'an	102	24.06 N	108.10 E
Duancun	105	38.52 N	115.56 E
Duane L. Bliss State Park ♠	226	38.59 N	120.06 W
Duanesburg	210	42.46 N	74.08 W
Duanjialing	105	39.59 N	117.09 E
Duaringa	166	23.43 S	149.40 E
Duarte	228	34.08 N	117.58 W
Duarte, Pico ∧	238	19.02 N	70.59 W
Duartina	255	22.24 S	49.25 W
Duas Barras	256	22.02 S	42.32 W
Duayaw Nkwanta	150	7.10 N	2.06 W
Ḍubā, Ar. Su.	128	27.21 N	35.40 E
Dubá, Česko.	54	50.34 N	14.33 E
Dubach	194	32.41 N	92.39 W
Dubai → Dubayy	128	25.18 N	55.18 E
Dubawnt ≃	176	64.33 N	100.06 W
Dubawnt Lake ⊜	176	63.08 N	101.30 W
Dubayy	128	25.18 N	55.18 E
Dubbeldam	52	51.47 N	4.42 E
Dubbo	166	32.15 S	148.36 E
Dube ≃	150	5.45 N	8.00 W
Dubele	154	2.54 N	29.33 E
Dübendorf	58	47.25 N	8.38 E
Dübener Heide ◆[3]	54	51.40 N	12.40 E
Dubenskij	86	51.27 N	56.38 E
Dubh Artach II[1]	46	56.08 N	6.40 W
Dubí	54	50.42 N	13.45 E
Dubi Bheri	272b	22.53 N	88.17 E
Dubica	36	45.11 N	16.48 E
Dubie	154	8.33 S	28.32 E
Dubinino	82	56.09 N	37.01 E
Dubino	58	46.09 N	9.27 E
Dubjazy	80	56.08 N	49.13 E
Dubki, S.S.S.R.	265a	60.00 N	30.00 E
Dubki, S.S.S.R.	265b	55.41 N	37.14 E
Dublin, Austl.	168b	34.27 S	138.21 E
Dublin, On., Can.	212	43.31 N	81.17 W
Dublin (Baile Átha Cliath), Ire.	48	53.20 N	6.15 W
Dublin, Ca., U.S.	226	37.42 N	121.56 W
Dublin, Ga., U.S.	192	32.32 N	82.54 W
Dublin, In., U.S.	218	39.48 N	85.12 W
Dublin, Md., U.S.	208	39.39 N	76.16 W
Dublin, Oh., U.S.	214	40.06 N	83.07 W
Dublin, Pa., U.S.	208	40.22 N	75.12 W
Dublin, Tx., U.S.	196	32.05 N	98.20 W
Dublin, Va., U.S.	192	37.06 N	80.41 W
Dublin □[6]	48	53.20 N	6.15 W
Dublin (Collinstown) Airport ⊠	48	53.26 N	6.15 W
Dublin Bay ⊂	48	53.20 N	6.06 W
Dublin Canyon V	282	37.42 N	121.59 W
Dublon I	175c	7.23 N	151.53 E
Dubna, S.S.S.R.	82	54.09 N	36.58 E
Dubna, S.S.S.R.	82	56.44 N	37.10 E
Dubna ≃, S.S.S.R.	76	56.22 N	26.10 E
Dubna ≃, S.S.S.R.	82	56.47 N	37.15 E
Dubňany	30	48.55 N	17.06 E
Dubnevo	82	55.06 N	38.08 E
Dubnica nad Váhom	30	48.58 N	18.09 E
Dubno	78	50.26 N	25.44 E
Dubois, Id., U.S.	202	44.10 N	112.13 W
Dubois, Il., U.S.	219	38.13 N	89.13 W
Dubois, In., U.S.	194	38.26 N	86.48 W
Du Bois, Ne., U.S.	198	40.02 N	96.02 W
Du Bois, Pa., U.S.	214	41.07 N	78.45 W
Dubois, Wy., U.S.	200	43.32 N	109.37 W
Du Bois Reservoir ⊜[1]	214	41.06 N	78.38 W
Duboistown	210	41.13 N	77.02 W
Dub'onki	80	54.27 N	46.18 E
Dubossarskoje vodochranilišče ⊜[1]	78	47.35 N	29.00 E
Dubossary	78	47.16 N	29.08 E
Dubovaja Rošča	76	53.11 N	36.04 E
Dubov'azovka	78	51.08 N	33.22 E
Duboviči	78	51.38 N	33.35 E
Dubovka, S.S.S.R.	78	51.26 N	41.25 E
Dubovka, S.S.S.R.	80	49.03 N	44.50 E
Dubovoje	76	53.08 N	40.05 E
Dubovskij	80	56.21 N	46.48 E
Dubovskoje	80	47.25 N	42.46 E
Dubovyj Ovrag	80	48.20 N	44.37 E
Dubovyj Umet	80	52.59 N	50.17 E
Duboweitun	89	50.42 N	120.14 E
Dubra	126	23.32 N	86.31 E
Dubrājpur	126	23.48 N	87.23 E
Dubréka	150	9.48 N	13.31 W
Dubrova, S.S.S.R.	76	52.25 N	29.58 E
Dubrova, S.S.S.R.	78	51.47 N	28.13 E
Dubrova, S.S.S.R.	80	56.59 N	54.33 E
Dubrova, S.S.S.R.	80	57.42 N	55.01 E
Dubrovica	78	51.34 N	26.34 E
Dubroviči	80	54.39 N	39.56 E
Dubrovicy	82	56.46 N	39.10 E
Dubrovino	86	55.28 N	83.17 E
Dubrovka, S.S.S.R.	76	53.42 N	33.30 E
Dubrovka, S.S.S.R.	76	59.51 N	30.56 E
Dubrovka, S.S.S.R.	76	59.13 N	36.13 E
Dubrovka, S.S.S.R.	82	54.44 N	36.21 E
Dubrovka, S.S.S.R.	83	47.54 N	39.02 E
Dubrovki	80	53.49 N	43.19 E
Dubrovnik	38	42.38 N	18.07 E
Dubrovno	76	54.35 N	30.41 E
Dubrovnoje, S.S.S.R.	86	57.58 N	69.25 E
Dubrovnoje, S.S.S.R.	86	54.49 N	68.06 E
Dubrovo	76	59.51 N	33.34 E
Dubrovskoje	88	58.45 N	111.10 E
Dubunskaja	86	43.46 N	80.13 E
Dubuque	190	42.30 N	90.39 W
Dubysa ≃	76	55.05 N	23.26 E
Duchana	85	38.02 N	68.13 E
Duchang	100	29.15 N	116.13 E
Duchcov	54	50.37 N	13.45 E
Ducherow	54	53.46 N	13.46 E
Duchesne	200	40.09 N	110.24 W
Duchesne ≃	200	40.05 N	109.41 W
Duchess	166	21.22 S	139.52 E
Duchovnickoje	80	52.28 N	48.15 E
Duchovščina	76	55.12 N	32.25 E
Duck ≃, Austl.	274a	33.50 S	151.02 E
Duck ≃, Tn., U.S.	194	36.02 N	87.52 W
Duckabush ≃	224	47.38 N	122.56 W
Duck Bay	184	52.10 N	100.09 W
Duck Creek ≃, On., Can.	281	42.18 N	82.41 W
Duck Creek ≃, Ca., U.S.	226	37.55 N	121.16 W
Duck Creek ≃, In., U.S.	218	40.08 N	85.57 W
Duck Creek ≃, Nv., U.S.	204	40.06 N	114.43 W
Duck Creek ≃, N.D., U.S.	198	46.03 N	102.14 W
Duck Creek ≃, Tx., U.S.	196	33.14 N	100.42 W
Duck Creek ≃, Tx., U.S.	222	32.48 N	96.31 W
Duck Creek ≃, Tx., U.S.	222	31.06 N	96.17 W
Duck Creek ≃, Wi., U.S.	190	44.33 N	88.02 W
Duck Hill	194	33.37 N	89.42 W
Duck Island Harbor ⊂	276	40.55 N	73.23 W
Duck Key I	220	24.46 N	80.56 W
Duck Lake, Sk., Can.	184	52.47 N	106.13 W
Duck Lake, Mi., U.S.	216	42.24 N	84.47 W
Duck Lake ⊜, Mb., Can.	184	54.52 N	98.11 W
Duck Lake ⊜, Mi., U.S.	216	42.23 N	84.47 W
Duck Lake ⊜, Mi., U.S.	281	42.40 N	83.35 W
Duck Mountain ∧	184	51.35 N	101.00 W
Duck Mountain Provincial Park ♠, Mb., Can.	184	51.36 N	100.55 W
Duck Mountain Provincial Park ♠, Sk., Can.	184	51.38 N	101.53 W
Duck Valley Indian Reservation ◆[4]	204	42.00 N	116.10 W
Duckwall Mountain ∧	226	37.58 N	120.07 W
Duclair	50	49.29 N	0.53 E
Ducos	240e	14.34 N	60.58 W
Du Couedic, Cape ›	166	36.04 S	136.42 E
Ducun	106	31.07 N	120.27 E
Duda ≃	246	2.33 N	74.02 W
Dudačkino	76	59.57 N	32.53 E
Dudčany	78	47.12 N	33.46 E
Duddington	42	52.36 N	0.32 W
Duddon ≃	44	54.15 N	3.13 W
Dudelange	56	49.28 N	6.05 E
Dudergofka ≃	265a	59.52 N	30.12 E
Duderstadt	52	51.31 N	10.16 E
Dūdhi	124	24.13 N	83.15 E
Dudhkośī ≃	124	27.08 N	86.26 E
Dudhnai	124	25.59 N	90.44 E
Dudinka	74	69.25 N	86.15 E
Dudkin	78	47.53 N	40.32 E
Dudley, Eng., U.K.	42	52.30 N	2.05 W
Dudley, Eng., U.K.	44	55.03 N	1.35 W
Dudley, Ma., U.S.	207	42.02 N	71.55 W
Dudley, Pa., U.S.	214	40.12 N	78.10 W
Dudley Pond ⊜	283	42.20 N	71.22 W
Dudleyville	200	32.58 N	110.47 W
Dudna ≃	122	19.07 N	76.54 E
Dudorovskij	76	53.40 N	35.22 E
Ḍūḍuwā Śriṅgklā ⋏	124	27.45 N	82.30 E
Dudwa National Park ♠	124	28.30 N	80.40 E
Dudweiler	56	49.17 N	7.02 E
Dudzele	50	51.17 N	3.14 E
Due	89	50.50 N	142.06 E
Duékoué	150	6.45 N	7.21 W
Dueré	250	11.20 S	49.17 W
Duerji	89	45.39 N	121.49 E
Duerna ≃	34	42.19 N	5.54 W
Duero (Douro) ≃	34	41.08 N	8.40 W
Dueville	64	45.38 N	11.32 E
Due West	192	34.20 N	82.23 W
Dufault, Lac ⊜	190	48.19 N	79.00 W
Duff Dunbar	123	32.15 N	77.12 E
Duffel	50	51.06 N	4.31 E
Dufferin □[6]	212	44.05 N	80.15 W
Duffer Peak ∧	204	41.40 N	118.44 W
Duffield, Austl.	162	25.50 S	134.40 E
Duffield, Eng., U.K.	44	52.58 N	1.29 W
Duffins Creek ≃	212	43.49 N	79.02 W
Dufftown	46	57.26 N	3.08 W
Dufourspitze ∧	58	45.55 N	7.52 E
Dufresne ≃	206	46.16 N	73.59 W
Dufur	224	45.27 N	121.07 W
Dugadda	124	29.48 N	78.37 E
Duga Resa	36	45.27 N	15.30 E
Duga-Zapadnaja, mys ›	74	59.09 N	145.59 E
Dugdemona ≃	194	31.47 N	92.22 W
Dugede	120	30.54 N	90.48 E
Dugger	194	39.04 N	87.16 W
Dugino	83	47.09 N	39.27 E
Dugi Otok I	36	44.00 N	15.04 E
Dugna	82	54.25 N	36.51 E
Dugny-sur-Meuse	56	49.06 N	5.23 E
Dug Pond ⊜	283	42.17 N	71.22 W
Du Gué ≃	176	57.21 N	70.45 W
Dugui Qarag	102	39.38 N	108.40 E
Dugway Proving Ground ■	200	40.10 N	113.15 W
Duhernal Lake ⊜	276	40.24 N	74.22 W
Duhi	140	7.07 N	28.45 E
Duhnen	52	53.53 N	8.38 E
Duhu	100	22.04 N	112.56 E
Ḍuhūr ash-Shuwayr	132	33.55 N	35.43 E
Duich, Loch ⊂	46	57.14 N	5.30 W
Duida, Cerro ∧	246	3.25 N	65.40 W
Duifken Point ›	164	12.33 S	141.38 E
Duingen	52	52.00 N	9.42 E
Duingt	62	45.50 N	6.12 E
Duino	64	45.46 N	13.36 E
Duirinish	46	57.19 N	5.41 W
Duisburg, B.R.D.	56	51.25 N	6.46 E
Duisburg, B.R.D.	263	51.25 N	6.46 E
Duissern ◆[8]	263	51.26 N	6.47 E
Duitama	246	5.50 N	73.02 W
Duiveland I	52	51.38 N	4.00 E
Duiwelskloof	156	23.42 S	30.06 E
Duji, Zhg.	98	34.11 N	115.48 E
Duji, Zhg.	98	37.44 N	116.50 E
Dujiahang	106	31.03 N	121.29 E
Dujuuma	144	1.15 N	42.34 E
Dukambiya	144	14.47 N	37.28 E
Dukana ⊤[4]	154	3.59 N	37.16 E
Dukazi	120	30.54 N	92.52 E
Duke	196	34.39 N	99.34 W
Duke Center	214	41.57 N	78.28 W
Duke Island I	182	54.56 N	131.20 W
Duke of York Bay ⊂	176	65.25 N	84.50 W
Duke of York Island I	164	4.10 S	152.26 E
Dukes □[6]	207	41.23 N	70.31 W
Dukes Brook ≃	276	40.33 N	74.37 W
Duk Fadiat	140	7.45 N	31.25 E
Duk Faiwil	140	7.30 N	31.29 E
Dukhān	128	25.25 N	50.48 E
Dukhmays	142	31.07 N	31.04 E
Duki	120	30.09 N	68.34 E
Dukinfield	262	53.29 N	2.05 W
Dukla	30	49.34 N	21.41 E
Dukla Pass)(	30	49.25 N	21.43 E
Dukou	102	26.40 N	101.39 E
Dūkštas	76	55.32 N	26.20 E
Duku, Nig.	146	10.49 N	10.46 E
Duku, Nig.	150	11.10 N	4.55 E
Dula	152	4.41 N	20.22 E
Dūlāb ◆[8]	267d	35.39 N	51.27 E
Dulag	116	10.57 N	125.02 E
Dulāi	124	23.57 N	89.31 E
Dulais ≃	42	51.41 N	3.47 W
Dulan (Chahanwusu)	102	36.16 N	98.28 E
Dul'apino	80	57.15 N	40.49 E
Dulas ≃	42	52.36 N	3.50 W
Dulas Bay ⊂	44	53.23 N	4.15 W
Dulata	86	43.26 N	80.50 E
Dulayb, Khawr V	140	11.45 N	32.47 E
Dulaym	146	25.58 N	14.03 E
Dulce	200	36.56 N	106.59 W
Dulce ≃	252	30.31 S	62.32 W
Dulce, Arroyo ≃	258	35.28 S	57.41 W
Dulce, Bahía ⊂	234	16.33 N	98.50 W
Dulce, Golfo ⊂	236	8.32 N	83.14 W
Dulce Grande	234	22.59 N	102.14 W
Dulce Nombre de Culmí	236	15.09 N	85.37 W
Dul'durga	88	50.41 N	113.36 E
Duleek	48	53.39 N	6.25 W
Dulgalach ≃	74	67.44 N	133.12 E
Dulin	98	38.22 N	116.43 E
Duliu, Zhg.	105	39.13 N	116.16 E
Duliu, Zhg.	105	39.01 N	116.54 E
Duliu Jianhe ≃	105	38.51 N	117.20 E
Duljo Point ›	116	9.35 N	123.43 E
Dulkaninna	166	29.01 S	138.27 E
Dülken	56	51.15 N	6.20 E
Dulles International Airport ⊠	208	38.58 N	77.28 W
Dullstroom	156	25.27 S	30.07 E
Dülmen	52	51.51 N	7.16 E
Dulnain Bridge	46	57.16 N	3.41 W
Dulnan ≃	46	57.18 N	3.40 W
Dulovka	76	57.32 N	28.20 E
Dulovo	38	43.49 N	27.09 E
Dulq Maghār	130	36.22 N	38.39 E
D'ul'tydag, gora ∧	84	41.58 N	46.56 E
Dulung ≃	126	22.08 N	87.05 E
Dulunguin Point ›	116	7.45 N	122.05 E
Duluth, Ga., U.S.	192	34.00 N	84.08 W
Duluth, Mn., U.S.	190	46.45 N	92.07 W
Dulverton	42	51.03 N	3.33 W
Dulwich ◆[8]	260	51.26 N	0.05 W
Duma, Bots.	156	18.45 S	22.46 E
Dūmā, Lubnān	130	34.12 N	35.50 E
Dūmā, Sūrīy.	132	33.35 N	36.24 E
Duma, Zaïre	154	4.57 N	27.19 E
Dumaguete	116	9.18 N	123.18 E
Dumai	114	1.41 N	101.27 E
Dumalag	116	11.18 N	122.37 E
Dumalinao	116	7.49 N	123.23 E
Dumali Point ›	116	13.07 N	121.33 E
Dumanjug	116	10.04 N	123.26 E
Dumanlıdağ ∧	84	40.31 N	43.25 E
Dumanquilas Bay ⊂	116	7.34 N	123.04 E
Dumaran Channel ⊍	116	10.25 N	119.45 E
Dumaran Island I	116	10.33 N	119.51 E
Dumaresq ≃	166	28.40 S	150.28 E
Dumaring	112	1.36 N	118.12 E
Dumas, Ar., U.S.	194	33.53 N	91.29 W
Dumas, Tx., U.S.	196	35.51 N	101.58 W
Ḍumayr	132	33.38 N	36.40 E
Dumbarton	46	55.57 N	4.35 W
Dumbarton Bridge ◆[5]	282	37.31 N	122.07 W
Dumbarton Point ›	282	37.30 N	122.06 W
Ďumbier ∧	30	48.57 N	19.37 E
Dumbleyung	162	33.19 S	117.44 E
Dumbo	152	14.06 S	17.24 E
Dumboa	146	11.10 N	12.45 E
Dumbrăveni	38	46.14 N	24.35 E
Dum Dum	126	22.35 N	88.24 E
Dum Dum International Airport ⊠	126	22.38 N	88.25 E
Dume, Point ›	228	34.00 N	118.48 W
Dumei	100	24.47 N	117.21 E
Dumfries, Scot., U.K.	44	55.04 N	3.37 W
Dumfries, Va., U.S.	208	38.34 N	77.19 W
Dumfries and Galloway □[4]	44	55.00 N	4.00 W
Duminiči	76	53.55 N	35.06 E
Dumjor	272b	22.38 N	88.13 E
Dumka	126	24.16 N	87.15 E
Dumlupınar	130	38.52 N	30.00 E
Dummar	132	33.32 N	36.14 E
Dümmer ⊜	52	52.31 N	8.19 E
Dummer Range ⋏	162	20.11 S	125.59 E
Dumoga-Bone National Park ♠	112	0.30 N	123.25 E
Dumoga Kecil	112	0.31 N	123.55 E
Dumoine ≃	190	46.13 N	77.51 W
Dumoine, Lac ⊜	190	46.53 N	77.54 W
Dumont, Ia., U.S.	190	42.45 N	92.58 W
Dumont, N.J., U.S.	210	40.56 N	73.59 W
Dumont, Lac ⊜	190	46.04 N	76.27 W
Dumont d'Urville ♉[3]	9	66.35 S	140.00 E
Dümpelfeld	56	50.27 N	6.56 E
Dümpten ◆[8]	263	51.27 N	6.54 E
Dumpu	164	5.50 S	145.45 E
Dumra	124	26.34 N	85.31 E
Dumraon	124	25.33 N	84.09 E
Dumuria, Bngl.	126	22.47 N	89.26 E
Dumuriā, India	126	22.11 N	86.20 E
Dumyāṭ (Damietta)	142	31.25 N	31.48 E
Dumyāṭ □[4]	142	31.20 N	31.45 E
Dumyāṭ, Far' (Damietta Branch) ≃	142	31.32 N	31.51 E
Dumyāṭ, Maṣabb (Damietta Mouth) ≃[1]	142	31.32 N	31.51 E
Dün ∧	54	51.21 N	10.30 E
Duna → Danube ≃	22	45.20 N	29.40 E
Dünaburg → Daugavpils	76	55.53 N	26.32 E
Dunaff Head ›	48	55.17 N	7.33 W
Dunaföldvár	30	46.48 N	18.55 E
Dunaharaszti	30	47.21 N	19.05 E
Dunaj, S.S.S.R.	89	42.52 N	132.22 E
Dunaj, S.S.S.R.	265a	59.58 N	30.56 E
Dunaj → Danube ≃	22	45.20 N	29.40 E
Dunaj, ostrova II	74	73.52 N	124.29 E
Dunajec ≃	30	50.14 N	20.44 E
Dunajevcy	78	48.54 N	26.51 E
Dunajevo	88	52.05 N	117.02 E
Dunajská Streda	30	48.01 N	17.35 E
Dunakeszi	30	47.38 N	19.08 E
Dunany Point ›	48	53.52 N	6.14 W
Dunărea → Danube ≃	22	45.20 N	29.40 E
Dunărea Veche, Braţul ≃	38	45.17 N	28.02 E
Duna-Tisza-csatorna ≊	264c	47.21 N	19.05 E
Dunaújváros	30	46.58 N	18.57 E
Dunav → Danube ≃	22	45.20 N	29.40 E
Dunavăţu-de-Sus	38	44.59 N	29.13 E
Duna-Völgyi-főcsatorna ≊	30	46.12 N	18.56 E
Dunback	172	45.23 S	170.38 E
Dunbar, Scot., U.K.	46	56.00 N	2.31 W
Dunbar, W.V., U.S.	188	38.21 N	81.44 W
Dunbarton	275b	43.49 N	79.06 W
Dunbeath	46	58.15 N	3.25 W
Dunblane, Sk., Can.	184	51.11 N	106.52 W
Dunblane, Scot., U.K.	46	56.12 N	3.59 W
Dunboyne	48	53.24 N	6.28 W
Duncan, B.C., Can.	224	48.47 N	123.42 W
Duncan, Az., U.S.	200	32.43 N	109.06 W
Duncan, Ms., U.S.	194	34.02 N	90.44 W
Duncan, Ok., U.S.	196	34.30 N	97.57 W
Duncan ≃	182	50.11 N	116.57 W
Duncan Lake ⊜[1]	182	50.20 N	117.00 W
Duncannon	208	40.23 N	77.01 W
Duncan Passage ⊍	110	11.00 N	92.30 E
Duncans	241q	18.28 N	77.32 W
Duncansby Head ›	46	58.39 N	3.02 W
Duncans Creek ≃	274a	33.53 S	150.39 E
Duncansville	214	40.25 N	78.26 W
Duncanville	222	32.39 N	96.54 W
Dunchurch	42	52.20 N	1.16 W
Duncormick	48	52.14 N	6.39 W
Dundaga	76	57.31 N	22.21 E
Dundāhera	272a	28.38 N	77.26 E
Dundalk, On., Can.	212	44.10 N	80.24 W
Dundalk (Dún Dealgan), Ire.	48	54.01 N	6.25 W
Dundalk, Md., U.S.	208	39.15 N	76.31 W
Dundalk Bay ⊂	48	53.57 N	6.17 W
Dundas, Austl.	274a	33.48 S	151.02 E
Dundas, On., Can.	212	43.16 N	79.58 W
Dundas, Mn., U.S.	190	44.25 N	93.12 W
Dundas, Cape ›	212	44.57 N	81.07 W
Dundas, Lake ⊜	162	32.35 S	121.50 E
Dundas Island I	182	54.33 N	130.55 W
Dundas Peninsula ›[1]	176	74.50 N	111.30 W
Dundas Strait ⊍	164	11.20 S	131.35 E
Dún Dealgan → Dundalk	48	54.01 N	6.25 W
Dundee, S. Afr.	158	28.12 S	30.16 E
Dundee, Scot., U.K.	46	56.28 N	2.58 W
Dundee, Fl., U.S.	220	28.01 N	81.37 W
Dundee, Il., U.S.	216	42.06 N	88.17 W
Dundee, Mi., U.S.	216	41.57 N	83.39 W
Dundee, Ms., U.S.	194	34.31 N	90.27 W
Dundee, N.Y., U.S.	210	42.31 N	76.58 W
Dundee, Oh., U.S.	214	40.35 N	81.37 W
Dundee, Or., U.S.	224	45.16 N	123.00 W
Dundee Creek ⊂	284b	39.21 N	76.22 W
Dundgov' □[4]	102	45.30 N	106.30 E
Dundīṭ	142	30.41 N	31.18 E
Dundonald	46	55.34 N	4.35 W
Dundoo	166	27.39 S	144.39 E
Dundrum, Ire.	48	52.33 N	8.03 W
Dundrum, N. Ire., U.K.	48	54.16 N	5.51 W
Dundrum Bay ⊂	48	54.13 N	5.45 W
Dundurn	184	51.49 N	106.30 W
Duneaton Water ≃	46	55.32 N	3.42 W
Dunedin, N.Z.	172	45.52 S	170.30 E
Dunedin, Fl., U.S.	220	28.01 N	82.46 W
Dunedoo	166	32.01 S	149.24 E
Duneland Beach	216	41.35 N	86.50 W
Dunellen	276	40.35 N	74.28 W
Dunewood	276	40.38 N	73.11 W
Dunfanaghy	48	55.11 N	7.59 W
Dunfermline	46	56.04 N	3.29 W
Du Ngae, Khao ∧	110	15.10 N	98.47 E
Dungannon, N. Ire., U.K.	48	54.31 N	6.46 W
Dungannon, Va., U.S.	192	36.49 N	82.28 W
Dūngarpur	120	23.50 N	73.43 E
Dungarvan	48	52.05 N	7.37 W
Dungarvan Harbour ⊂	48	52.10 N	7.35 W
Dungas	150	13.04 N	9.20 E
Dungau ◆[1]	60	48.50 N	12.40 E
Dungeness ›	42	50.55 N	0.58 E
Dungeness ≃	224	48.08 N	123.06 W
Dungeness, Punta ›	254	52.23 S	68.25 W
Dungeness Bay ⊂	224	48.10 N	123.07 W
Dungeness Spit ›[2]	224	48.10 N	123.09 W
Dungiven	48	54.55 N	6.55 W
Dunglow	48	54.57 N	8.22 W
Dungo, Lagoa do ⊜	152	17.20 S	18.58 E
Dungog	166	32.24 S	151.46 E
Dungu	154	3.37 N	28.34 E
Dungu ≃	154	3.37 N	28.34 E
Dungun	114	4.47 N	103.26 E
Dungun ≃	114	4.47 N	103.23 E
Dunham	206	45.08 N	72.48 W
Dunham Lake ⊜	281	42.39 N	83.41 W
Dunham-on-the-Hill	262	53.15 N	2.47 W
Dunham Park ♠	262	53.23 N	2.24 W
Dunham Town	262	53.23 N	2.24 W
Dunheved, Austl.	274a	33.45 S	150.47 E
Dunheved → Launceston, Eng., U.K.	42	50.38 N	4.21 W
Dunholme	44	53.18 N	0.28 W
Dunhou	100	27.02 N	114.58 E
Dunhua	89	43.21 N	128.13 E
Dunhuang	102	40.12 N	94.41 E
Dunières	62	45.13 N	4.20 E
Dunilovo, S.S.S.R.	76	57.46 N	38.55 E
Dunilovo, S.S.S.R.	80	57.00 N	41.27 E
Dunkeld	46	56.34 N	3.35 W
Dunkeld ◆[8]	273d	26.09 S	28.03 E
Dunkellin ≃	48	53.12 N	8.54 W
Dunkelsteinerwald ◆[3]	61	48.15 N	15.29 E
Dunkern ⊜	40	59.09 N	16.52 E
Dunker Pond ⊜	276	41.05 N	74.28 W
Dunkerque	50	51.03 N	2.22 E
Dunkerrin	48	52.55 N	7.55 W
Dunkery Hill ∧[2]	42	51.11 N	3.35 W
Dunkineely	48	54.38 N	8.23 W
Dunkinsville	218	38.51 N	83.30 W
Dunkirk → Dunkerque, Fr.	50	51.03 N	2.22 E
Dunkirk, Eng., U.K.	42	51.17 N	0.59 E
Dunkirk, In., U.S.	216	40.22 N	85.12 W
Dunkirk, N.Y., U.S.	214	42.28 N	79.20 W
Dunkirk, Oh., U.S.	216	40.47 N	83.38 W
Dunk's Green	260	51.15 N	0.19 E
Dunkuj	140	12.50 N	32.49 E
Dunkwa, Ghana	150	5.58 N	1.46 W
Dunkwa, Ghana	150	5.22 N	1.12 W
Dún Laoghaire	48	53.17 N	6.08 W
Dunlap, In., U.S.	216	41.38 N	85.55 W
Dunlap, Ia., U.S.	198	41.51 N	95.36 W
Dunlap, Tn., U.S.	194	35.22 N	85.23 W
Dunlap Acres	228	34.03 N	117.06 W
Dunlavin	48	53.02 N	6.41 W
Dunleary → Dún Laoghaire	48	53.17 N	6.08 W
Dunleer	48	53.50 N	6.24 W
Dunleith	285	39.42 N	75.33 W
Dun-le-Palestel	32	46.18 N	1.40 E
Dunlo	214	40.17 N	78.43 W
Dunlop	46	55.43 N	4.32 W
Dunloy	48	55.01 N	6.25 W
Dunmanus Bay ⊂	48	51.35 N	9.45 W
Dunmanway	48	51.43 N	9.06 W
Dunmarra	164	16.42 S	133.25 E
Dunmore, Ire.	48	53.36 N	8.46 W
Dunmore, Pa., U.S.	210	41.25 N	75.37 W
Dunmore Cave ⌓[5]	48	52.44 N	7.15 W
Dunmore East	48	52.09 N	7.00 W
Dunmore Town	238	25.30 N	76.39 W
Dunmurry	48	54.33 N	6.01 W
Dunn	192	35.18 N	78.36 W
Dunnamanagh	48	54.52 N	7.18 W
Dünnbach ≃	56	50.10 N	7.18 E
Dunnellon	220	29.02 N	82.27 W
Dunnet	46	58.31 N	3.20 W
Dunnet Bay ⊂	46	58.37 N	3.24 W
Dunnet Head ›	46	58.40 N	3.24 W
Dunnigan	226	38.53 N	121.58 W
Dunning	198	41.49 N	100.06 W
Dunning Creek ≃	214	40.02 N	78.28 W
Dunnington	44	53.57 N	0.59 W
Dunningtown	279b	40.25 N	79.35 W
Dunn Loring	284c	38.53 N	77.14 W
Dunn Loring Woods	284c	38.52 N	77.14 W
Dunnockshaw	262	53.45 N	2.17 W
Dunnottar Castle ⊥	46	56.57 N	2.11 W
Dunns Bridge	216	41.13 N	86.59 W
Dunnville	212	42.54 N	79.36 W
Dunolly	169	36.52 S	143.44 E
Dunoon	46	55.57 N	4.56 W
Dunqul ⊤[4]	140	23.26 N	31.37 E
Dunqulah	140	19.10 N	30.29 E
Dunqulah al-Qadīmah	140	18.13 N	30.45 E
Dunqunāb	140	21.06 N	37.05 E
Dunqunāb, Khalīj ⊂	140	21.05 N	37.08 E
Dunrea	184	49.25 N	99.44 W
Dun Rig ∧	46	55.34 N	3.10 W
Duns	46	55.47 N	2.20 W
Dunsandel	172	43.40 S	172.11 E
Dunsborough	162	33.36 S	115.06 E
Dunseith	198	48.48 N	100.03 W
Dunsford	42	50.41 N	3.40 W
Dunsmuir	204	41.13 N	122.16 W
Dunstable, Eng., U.K.	42	51.53 N	0.32 W
Dunstable, Ma., U.S.	207	42.40 N	71.29 W
Dunstaffnage Castle ⊥	46	56.26 N	5.32 W
Dunstan Mountains ⋏	172	44.57 S	169.32 E
Dunster, B.C., Can.	182	53.08 N	119.50 W
Dunster, Eng., U.K.	42	51.12 N	3.27 W
Dun-sur-Auron	32	46.53 N	2.34 E
Dun-sur-Meuse	56	49.23 N	5.11 E
Duntelchaig, Loch ⊜	46	57.20 N	4.18 W
Dunton Green	260	51.18 N	0.11 E
Dunton Wayletts	260	51.35 N	0.24 E
Duntou	100	29.21 N	119.46 E
Duntroon	172	44.52 S	170.41 E
Dunvegan, S. Afr.	273d	26.09 S	28.09 E
Dunvegan, Scot., U.K.	46	57.26 N	6.35 W
Dunvegan, Loch ⊂	46	57.28 N	6.40 W
Dunvegan Castle ⊥	46	57.26 N	6.35 W
Dunvegan Head ›	46	57.31 N	6.43 W
Dunville	186	47.16 N	53.54 W
Dunwich	171a	27.31 S	153.23 E
Dunyāpur	123	29.48 N	71.44 E
Duobukur ≃	89	49.56 N	125.12 E
Duogu'nao	102	31.32 N	103.14 E
Duojundian	105	39.22 N	117.31 E
Duolun (Dolonnur)	98	42.15 N	116.18 E
Duolundabohuer	120	33.25 N	93.54 E
Duomo ♉[1]	266b	45.27 N	9.11 E
Duomula	120	34.07 N	82.30 E
Duoyuezhen	107	30.11 N	103.42 E
Duozhu	100	22.59 N	114.43 E
Duozhuang	98	35.35 N	118.12 E
Du Page □[6]	216	41.52 N	88.06 W
Du Page ≃	216	41.25 N	88.14 W
Du Page, East Branch ≃	278	41.42 N	88.09 W
Dupang Ling ⋏	102	25.32 N	111.11 E
Duparquet, Lac ⊜	190	48.28 N	79.16 W
Dupax	116	16.17 N	121.05 E
Duping	102	27.11 N	108.20 E
Dupl'atka	80	51.07 N	42.20 E
Dupli	82	54.21 N	36.54 E
Dupo	219	38.31 N	90.13 W
Dupont, In., U.S.	218	38.53 N	85.31 W
Dupont, Oh., U.S.	216	41.03 N	84.18 W
Dupont, Pa., U.S.	210	41.19 N	75.44 W
Du Pont, Wa., U.S.	224	47.05 N	122.37 W
Dupont Research Center ♉[3]	285	39.46 N	75.34 W
Düppel, Berliner Forst ◆[3]	264a	52.25 N	13.08 E
Dupree	198	45.02 N	101.36 W
Duque Bacelar	250	4.09 S	42.57 W
Duque de Caxias	256	22.47 S	43.18 W
Duque de Caxias □[7]	287a	22.45 S	43.16 W
Duque de York, Isla I	254	50.40 S	75.20 W
Duquesne	214	40.22 N	79.51 W
Duquesne University ♉[2]	279b	40.26 N	79.59 W
DuQuoin	194	37.59 N	89.15 W
Dūrā	132	31.30 N	35.02 E
Durack ≃	164	15.33 S	127.52 E
Durack Ranges ⋏	160	17.00 S	128.00 E
Durağan	130	41.25 N	35.04 E
Durak	130	39.42 N	28.17 E
Durak Dağı ∧	84	39.47 N	43.42 E
Dural	170	33.41 S	151.02 E
Duran	200	34.28 N	105.23 W
Durance ≃	62	43.55 N	4.44 E
Durand, Il., U.S.	190	42.26 N	89.19 W
Durand, Mi., U.S.	216	42.54 N	83.59 W
Durand, Wi., U.S.	190	44.37 N	91.57 W
Durand Reef ✦[2]	175f	22.03 S	168.39 E
Duran Durat I	271c	1.15 N	103.51 E
Durango, Esp.	34	43.10 N	2.37 W
Durango, Méx.	234	24.02 N	104.40 W
Durango, Co., U.S.	200	37.16 N	107.52 W
Durango □[3]	232	24.50 N	104.50 W
Duranillin	168a	33.31 S	116.48 E
Durant, Ia., U.S.	190	41.35 N	90.54 W
Durant, Ms., U.S.	194	33.04 N	89.51 W
Durant, Ok., U.S.	196	33.59 N	96.22 W
Duras	32	44.41 N	0.11 E
Duratón ≃	34	41.37 N	4.07 W
Duraur V	144	10.33 N	49.07 E
Durazno	252	33.22 S	56.31 W
Durazno, Arroyo ≃	258	34.41 S	58.52 W
Durazzo → Durrës	38	41.19 N	19.26 E
Durbādānga	126	22.57 N	89.15 E
Durban	158	29.55 S	30.56 E
Durban Roodepoort Deep Gold Mines ◆[7]	273d	26.10 S	27.51 E
Durbanville	158	33.50 S	18.39 E
Durbe	76	56.35 N	21.21 E
D'urbel'džin	85	41.16 N	74.57 E
Durbet-Daba, pereval)(	86	49.37 N	89.25 E
Durbin	188	38.32 N	79.49 W
Durbuy	56	50.21 N	5.28 E
Durchholz	263	51.23 N	7.17 E
Durdent ≃	50	49.51 N	0.36 E
Đurđevac	36	46.03 N	17.04 E
Durdur V	144	10.34 N	43.58 E
Dureji	120	25.53 N	67.18 E
Düren	56	50.48 N	6.28 E
Durg	120	21.11 N	81.17 E
Durgāpur	126	23.29 N	87.20 E
Durham, On., Can.	212	44.10 N	80.49 W
Durham, Eng., U.K.	44	54.47 N	1.34 W
Durham, Ca., U.S.	204	39.38 N	121.47 W
Durham, Ct., U.S.	207	41.28 N	72.40 W
Durham, Mo., U.S.	219	39.58 N	91.40 W
Durham, N.H., U.S.	188	43.08 N	70.55 W
Durham, N.C., U.S.	192	35.59 N	78.53 W
Durham, Or., U.S.	224	45.25 N	122.46 W
Durham □[6], On., Can.	212	43.56 N	78.53 W
Durham □[6], Eng., U.K.	44	54.45 N	1.45 W
Durham Cathedral ♉[1]	44	54.46 N	1.36 W
Durham Downs	166	27.05 S	141.54 E
Durham Heights ∧	176	71.08 N	122.56 W
Durham Pond ⊜	276	41.00 N	74.27 W
Durhamville	210	43.07 N	75.40 W
Durian ≃	115a	6.01 S	106.24 E
Durian, Selat ⊍	114	0.42 N	103.42 E
Duriansebatang	112	0.47 S	109.56 E
Durian Tipus	114	3.07 N	102.13 E
D'urinskije razlivy ≣	80	50.25 N	50.20 E
Durlabhpur	272b	22.47 N	88.29 E
Durlach ◆[8]	56	49.00 N	8.28 E
Durlešty	78	47.02 N	28.45 E
Durmersheim	56	48.56 N	8.16 E
Durmitor ∧	38	43.08 N	19.01 E
Durness	46	58.33 N	4.45 W
Durness, Kyle of ⊂	46	58.34 N	4.49 W
Durneva, ostrova II	80	45.25 N	52.50 E
Durnikino	80	51.39 N	42.49 E
Dürnkrut	61	48.28 N	16.51 E
Dürnstein ⊥	61	48.24 N	15.32 E
Duro ∧	144	5.31 N	37.12 E
Durón	34	40.38 N	2.43 W
Duross Heights	285	39.40 N	75.37 W
Dürre Liesing ≃	264b	48.08 N	16.16 E
Durrell	186	49.40 N	54.44 W
Dürrenboden	58	46.57 N	8.50 E
Durrës	38	41.19 N	19.26 E
Durrie	166	25.38 S	140.16 E
Durrington	42	51.13 N	1.45 W
Dürröhrsdorf	54	51.01 N	14.00 E
Durrow	48	52.50 N	7.22 W
Durrus	48	51.36 N	9.31 W
Dursey Head ›	48	51.35 N	10.14 W
Dursey Island I	48	51.36 N	10.12 W
Dursley	42	51.42 N	2.21 W
Dursunbey	130	39.35 N	28.38 E
D'urt'uli	86	55.29 N	54.52 E
Duru	154	4.14 N	28.45 E
Duru Gölü ⊜	130	41.20 N	28.35 E
Durulova	130	38.17 N	38.01 E
Durunkah	142	27.08 N	31.10 E
Durūz, Jabal ad- ⋏	132	32.40 N	36.44 E
D'Urville, Tanjung ›	164	1.28 S	137.54 E
D'Urville Island I	172	40.50 S	173.52 E
Duryea	210	41.20 N	75.44 W
Dury Voe ⊂	46a	60.20 N	1.08 W
Dušak	128	37.13 N	60.02 E
Dušanbe	85	38.35 N	68.48 E
Dušanbe □[4]	85	38.40 N	69.40 E
Dušekan	74	60.39 N	109.03 E
Dušeti	84	42.06 N	44.42 E
Dusetos	76	55.45 N	25.51 E
Dushan, Zhg.	100	31.36 N	116.14 E
Dushan, Zhg.	102	25.53 N	107.30 E
Du Shan ∧	98	40.30 N	118.45 E
Dushanbe → Dušanbe	85	38.35 N	68.48 E
Dushan Hu ⊜	98	35.06 N	116.52 E
Dushantou	106	30.46 N	119.47 E
Dushanzi	86	44.20 N	84.51 E
Dusheng	98	38.23 N	116.33 E
Dushichang	107	29.10 N	106.31 E
Dushikou	98	41.17 N	115.38 E
Dushore	210	41.31 N	76.24 W
Düshorn	52	52.49 N	9.37 E
Dushu	100	33.21 N	113.09 E
Dushu Hu ⊜	106	31.17 N	120.42 E
Dusios ežeras ⊜	76	54.18 N	23.42 E
Dusky Sound ⊍	172	45.47 S	166.28 E
Dušocha, gora ∧	85	39.10 N	70.01 E
Duson	194	30.14 N	92.11 W
Dušonovo	82	56.04 N	38.18 E
Düssel	263	51.16 N	7.03 E
Düssel ≃	263	51.13 N	6.45 E
Düsseldorf, B.R.D.	56	51.12 N	6.47 E
Düsseldorf, B.R.D.	263	51.12 N	6.47 E
Düsseldorf □[5]	52	51.15 N	7.00 E
Düsseldorf, Flughafen ⊠	56	51.17 N	6.47 E
Düsseldorf, Universität ♉[2]	263	51.12 N	6.48 E
Dusslingen	58	48.27 N	9.03 E
Dussnang	58	47.26 N	8.58 E
Dustin	196	35.16 N	96.01 W
Dutch Creek ≃, B.C., Can.	182	50.20 N	115.52 W
Dutch Creek ≃, Ar., U.S.	194	35.03 N	93.24 W
Dutchess □[6]	210	41.42 N	73.56 W
Dutch Harbor	180	53.53 N	166.32 W
Dutch John	200	40.55 N	109.23 W
Dutchman Creek ≃	226	37.11 N	120.28 W
Dutianjie	102	24.38 N	101.31 E
Dutluca	130	39.09 N	38.37 E
Dutlwe	156	23.55 S	23.47 E
Dutoitspiek ∧	158	33.46 S	19.12 E
Dutou, Zhg.	100	22.54 N	115.12 E
Dutou, Zhg.	106	31.19 N	120.54 E
Dutovlje	64	45.46 N	13.50 E
Dutovo	24	63.47 N	56.35 E
Dutsen Wai	150	10.50 N	8.12 E
Dutton, Austl.	168b	34.22 S	139.08 E
Dutton, On., Can.	214	42.39 N	81.30 W
Dutton, Eng., U.K.	262	53.19 N	2.38 W
Dutton, Mi., U.S.	216	42.50 N	85.35 W
Dutton, Mt., U.S.	202	47.50 N	111.42 W
Dutton ≃	166	20.45 S	143.12 E
Dutton, Mount ∧, Ak., U.S.	180	55.10 N	162.15 W
Dutton, Mount ∧, Ut., U.S.	200	38.01 N	112.13 W
Dutun	105	39.46 N	117.02 E
Dutzow	219	38.37 N	90.59 W
Duut	86	47.30 N	91.40 E
Duval, Lac ⊜	190	46.19 N	76.55 W
Duvall	224	47.44 N	121.59 W
Duvan	86	55.42 N	57.54 E
Duvanka ≃	83	49.35 N	38.10 E
Duved	26	63.24 N	12.52 E
Duvernay ◆[8]	275a	45.35 N	73.40 W
Duvno	36	43.43 N	17.14 E
Duwamish	224	47.32 N	122.19 W
Duwaydār, Bi'r ad- ⊤[4]	142	30.55 N	32.31 E
Duxbury	207	42.02 N	70.40 W
Duxbury Bay ⊂	207	42.02 N	70.39 W
Duxbury Beach ⌓[2]	283	42.03 N	70.38 W
Duxun	100	23.55 N	117.37 E
Duyagan Point ›	116	12.36 N	121.33 E
Duyun	102	26.12 N	107.31 E
Düzce	130	40.50 N	31.10 E
Duze	100	29.07 N	118.56 E
Dve Mogili	38	43.36 N	25.52 E
Dvina Occidental → Zapadnaja Dvina ≃	76	57.04 N	24.03 E
Dvina Setentrional → Severnaja Dvina ≃	24	64.32 N	40.30 E
Dvinje, ozero ⊜	76	56.08 N	31.12 E
Dvinsk → Daugavpils	76	55.53 N	26.32 E
Dvinskaja guba ⊂	24	65.00 N	39.45 E
Dvojnovskij	80	51.03 N	42.27 E
Dvorcy	82	54.37 N	36.00 E

Symbol	English	Deutsch	Español	Français	Português
≃	River	Fluß	Río	Rivière	Rio
≊	Canal	Kanal	Canal	Canal	Canal
∟	Waterfall, Rapids	Wasserfall, Stromschnellen	Cascada, Rápidos	Chute d'eau, Rapides	Cascata, Rápidos
⊍	Strait	Meeresstraße	Estrecho	Détroit	Estreito
⊂	Bay, Gulf	Bucht, Golf	Bahía, Golfo	Baie, Golfe	Baía, Golfo
⊜	Lake, Lakes	See, Seen	Lago, Lagos	Lac, Lacs	Lago, Lagos
≣	Swamp	Sumpf	Pantano	Marais	Pântano
⍓	Ice Features, Glacier	Eis- und Gletscherformen	Accidentes Glaciales	Formes glaciaires	Acidentes glaciares
⊤	Other Hydrographic Features	Andere Hydrographische Objekte	Otros Elementos Hidrográficos	Autres données hydrographiques	Outros acidentes hidrográficos
✦	Submarine Features	Untermeerische Objekte	Accidentes Submarinos	Formes de relief sous-marin	Acidentes submarinos
□	Political Unit	Politische Einheit	Unidad Política	Entité politique	Unidade política
♉	Cultural Institution	Kulturelle Institution	Institución Cultural	Institution culturelle	Institução cultural
⊥	Historical Site	Historische Stätte	Sitio Histórico	Site historique	Sitio histórico
♠	Recreational Site	Erholungs- und Ferienort	Sitio de Recreo	Centre de loisirs	Area de Lazer
⊠	Airport	Flughafen	Aeropuerto	Aéroport	Aeroporto
■	Military Installation	Militäranlage	Instalación Militar	Installation militaire	Instalação militar
◆	Miscellaneous	Verschiedenes	Misceláneo	Divers	Diversos

I · 50 **Dvor-Eccl**

ENGLISH Name / Page / Lat.°′ / Long.°′ — **DEUTSCH** Name / Seite / Breite°′ / Länge°′ E = Ost

Name	Page	Lat.°′	Long.°′
Dvorec	**88**	58.23 N	99.56 E
Dvoriši	**76**	58.12 N	35.13 E
Dvornikovo	**82**	55.30 N	38.38 E
Dvuch Cirkov, gora ∧	**74**	67.35 N	168.07 E
Dvugorbaja, gora ∧	**180**	68.30 N	179.20 E
Dvulučnoje	**78**	50.02 N	38.02 E
Dvurečnaja	**78**	49.52 N	37.40 E
Dvůr Králové [nad Labem]	**30**	50.26 N	15.48 E
Dwangwa ≃	**154**	12.33 S	34.12 E
Dwarbasini	**272b**	22.59 N	88.14 E
Dwārka	**120**	22.14 N	68.58 E
Dwārka ≃	**126**	23.44 N	88.11 E
Dwārkeswar ≃	**126**	23.06 N	87.21 E
Dwarli	**272c**	19.12 N	73.08 E
Dwars Kill ≃	**276**	40.58 N	73.58 W
Dwellingup	**168a**	32.43 S	116.02 E
D.W. Field Park ♠	**283**	42.06 N	71.03 W
Dwight	**216**	41.05 N	88.25 W
Dwight D. Eisenhower Lock ◆[5]	**206**	45.00 N	74.45 W
Dwina-Bucht → Dvinskaja guba ⊂	**24**	65.00 N	39.45 E
Dwingeloo	**52**	52.50 N	6.21 E
Dworshak Reservoir ⊜[1]	**202**	46.40 N	116.00 W
Dwyfor ≃	**42**	52.55 N	4.17 W
Dwyka	**158**	33.02 S	21.30 E
Dwyka ≃	**158**	33.18 S	21.39 E
Dyaul Island I	**164**	2.56 S	150.55 E
Dybbøl	**41**	54.55 N	9.45 E
Dyberry Creek ≃	**210**	41.35 N	75.15 W
Dyce	**46**	57.12 N	2.11 W
Dyche Stadium ♠	**278**	42.04 N	87.41 W
Dychtau, gora ∧	**84**	43.03 N	43.08 E
Dyck, Schloss ⊥	**263**	51.09 N	6.34 E
Dyer, In., U.S.	**216**	41.29 N	87.31 W
Dyer, Tn., U.S.	**194**	36.04 N	88.59 W
Dyer, Cape ›	**176**	66.37 N	61.18 W
Dyer Bay ⊂	**212**	45.10 N	81.18 W
Dyer Island I	**158**	34.41 S	19.25 E
Dyero	**150**	12.50 N	6.30 W
Dyersburg	**194**	36.02 N	89.23 W
Dyersville	**190**	42.29 N	91.07 W
Dyess Air Force Base ■	**196**	32.25 N	99.51 W
Dyfed □[6]	**42**	52.00 N	4.30 W
Dyfi ≃	**42**	52.32 N	4.03 W
Dyje (Thaya) ≃	**61**	48.37 N	16.56 E
Dyke	**46**	57.36 N	3.41 W
Dyke Ackland Bay ⊂	**164**	9.00 S	148.45 E
Dyken Pond ⊜	**210**	42.43 N	73.26 W
Dykes Pond ⊜	**283**	42.36 N	70.44 W
Dyle (Dijle) ≃	**56**	51.04 N	4.25 E
Dyleň ∧	**60**	49.58 N	12.30 E
Dylym	**84**	43.04 N	46.38 E
Dymchurch	**42**	51.02 N	1.00 E
Dyment	**184**	49.37 N	92.19 W
Dymer	**78**	50.47 N	30.18 E
Dymock	**42**	51.59 N	2.26 W
Dynamo Stadium ♠	**265b**	55.48 N	37.34 E
Dynów	**30**	49.49 N	22.14 E
Dyreborg	**41**	55.04 N	10.13 E
Dyrnesvågen	**26**	63.26 N	7.51 E
Dyrotz	**264a**	52.33 N	12.58 E
Dysart, Austl.	**166**	22.27 S	148.20 E
Dysart, Sk., Can.	**184**	50.56 N	104.02 W
Dysart, Scot., U.K.	**46**	56.08 N	3.08 W
Dysart, Ia., U.S.	**190**	42.10 N	92.18 W
Dysart, Pa., U.S.	**214**	40.36 N	78.31 W
Dýšina	**60**	49.46 N	13.29 E
Dysnų ežeras ⊜	**76**	55.29 N	26.20 E
Dysselsdorp	**158**	33.34 S	22.28 E
Dysynni ≃	**42**	52.36 N	4.05 W
Dzaamar	**88**	48.10 N	104.50 E
Dzaamaryn uul ∧	**88**	48.10 N	104.30 E
Džabžur	**84**	40.54 N	43.58 E
Dzachuj	**102**	44.59 N	96.37 E
Džagdy, chrebet ⋏	**89**	53.40 N	131.00 E
Džalagaš	**86**	45.05 N	64.40 E
Džalal-Abad	**85**	40.56 N	73.00 E
Džalinda	**89**	53.29 N	123.54 E
Džamantau, gory ⋏	**85**	40.55 N	74.40 E
Džamašuj	**85**	40.52 N	71.28 E
Džambejty	**80**	50.16 N	52.35 E
Džambul, S.S.S.R.	**80**	47.34 N	50.12 E
Džambul, S.S.S.R.	**85**	42.54 N	71.22 E
Džambul, S.S.S.R.	**86**	47.12 N	71.42 E
Džambul □[4]	**86**	44.00 N	72.00 E
Džambul, gora ∧	**86**	44.46 N	73.08 E
Džanga	**128**	40.00 N	53.03 E
Džangi-Džol	**85**	41.36 N	72.08 E
Džankoj	**78**	45.43 N	34.24 E
Džansugurov	**86**	45.24 N	79.29 E
Džanybek	**80**	49.25 N	46.51 E
Dzaoudzi	**157a**	12.47 S	45.17 E
Džardžan	**74**	68.43 N	124.02 E
Džargalant → Chovd, Mong.	**86**	48.01 N	91.39 E
Džargalant, Mong.	**88**	48.40 N	100.43 E
Džargalant, Mong.	**88**	46.57 N	115.15 E
Džargalant, Mong.	**88**	48.33 N	99.20 E
Džargaltchaan	**88**	47.28 N	109.30 E
Džarylgačkij, ostrov I	**78**	46.02 N	32.55 E
Džarylgačskij zaliv ⊂	**78**	46.05 N	32.50 E
Dzaudzhikau → Ordžonikidze	**84**	43.03 N	44.40 E
Džaur	**89**	50.02 N	138.30 E
Džava	**84**	42.24 N	43.54 E
Dzavchan	**88**	48.48 N	93.07 E
Dzavchan □[4]	**88**	48.00 N	96.00 E
Dzavchan ≃	**88**	48.54 N	93.23 E
Dzavchan Mandal	**88**	48.19 N	95.07 E
Džavchlant → Uliastaj	**88**	47.45 N	96.49 E
Džazator	**86**	49.45 N	87.23 E
Džbán ∧	**54**	50.12 N	13.45 E
Džebel	**128**	39.38 N	54.14 E
Džebrail	**84**	39.23 N	47.02 E
Dzegamčaj ≃	**84**	41.00 N	45.59 E
Dzelter ≃	**88**	50.30 N	105.06 E
Dzemul	**232**	21.12 N	89.18 W
Dzeng	**152**	3.45 N	12.00 E
Dženretlen, mys ›	**180**	67.07 N	173.45 W
Džergetal	**85**	41.30 N	75.47 E
Džermuk	**84**	39.51 N	45.41 E
Dzerzhinsk → Dzeržinsk	**80**	56.15 N	43.24 E
Dzeržinsk, S.S.S.R.	**76**	53.41 N	27.08 E
Dzeržinsk, S.S.S.R.	**78**	50.09 N	27.56 E
Dzeržinsk, S.S.S.R.	**80**	56.15 N	43.24 E
Dzeržinsk, S.S.S.R.	**83**	48.26 N	37.50 E
Dzeržinskaja, gora ∧[2]	**76**	53.51 N	27.03 E
Dzeržinskij, S.S.S.R.	**78**	48.02 N	39.26 E
Dzeržinskij, S.S.S.R.	**82**	55.38 N	37.50 E
Dzeržinskij ◆[8]	**83**	48.02 N	39.26 E
Dzeržinskoje, S.S.S.R.	**86**	56.49 N	95.18 E
Dzeržinskoje, S.S.S.R.	**86**	45.50 N	81.07 E
Džetim, chrebet ⋏	**85**	41.35 N	77.05 E
Džetygara	**86**	52.11 N	61.12 E
Džetyoguz	**85**	42.27 N	78.14 E
Džetyoguzskij zapovednik ♠	**85**	42.15 N	78.20 E
Džetysaj	**85**	40.47 N	68.16 E
Džezdy	**86**	48.04 N	67.05 E
Džezkazgan, S.S.S.R.	**86**	47.53 N	67.27 E
Džezkazgan, S.S.S.R.	**86**	47.47 N	67.46 E
Džezkazgan □[4]	**86**	47.20 N	69.00 E
Dzhalilabad	**84**	39.14 N	48.31 E
Dzhambul → Džambul	**85**	42.54 N	71.22 E
Działdowo	**30**	53.15 N	20.10 E
Działoszyce	**30**	50.22 N	20.21 E
Dzibalchén	**232**	19.31 N	89.45 W
Dzibilchaltun ⊥	**232**	21.05 N	89.36 W
Džida ≃	**88**	50.37 N	106.14 E
Džidinskij chrebet ⋏	**88**	50.10 N	102.00 E
Dzierzgoń	**30**	53.56 N	19.21 E
Dzierżoniów (Reichenbach)	**30**	50.44 N	16.39 E
Dzilam González	**232**	21.17 N	88.56 W
Džilav	**85**	39.19 N	67.45 E
Džilga	**85**	41.43 N	69.01 E
Džinst	**102**	45.24 N	100.35 E
Dzioua	**148**	33.14 N	5.14 E
Džirgatal'	**85**	39.13 N	71.12 E
Dzitás	**232**	20.51 N	88.31 W
Dzitbalché	**232**	20.19 N	90.03 W
Dziwna ≃[1]	**54**	54.01 N	14.44 E
Dziwnów	**30**	54.03 N	14.45 E
Džizak	**85**	40.06 N	67.50 E
Džizak □[4]	**85**	40.35 N	67.40 E
Dzodze	**150**	6.14 N	1.00 E
Džubga	**78**	44.20 N	38.43 E
Džugdžur, chrebet ⋏	**74**	58.00 N	136.00 E
Džūkste	**76**	56.47 N	23.15 E
Džul'fa	**84**	38.58 N	45.38 E
Džumabazar	**85**	39.31 N	67.13 E
Džumgoltau, chrebet ⋏	**85**	42.18 N	74.32 E
Dzungarian Basin → Junggar Pendi ⊻[1]	**86**	45.00 N	88.00 E
Dzungarian Gate (Džungarskije vorota))(	**86**	45.25 N	82.25 E
Džungarskij Alatau, chrebet ⋏	**86**	45.00 N	81.00 E
Džungarskije vorota → Dzungarian Gate)(	**86**	45.25 N	82.25 E
Džurak-Sal ≃	**80**	47.18 N	43.36 E
Dzürch	**88**	48.55 N	100.10 E
Džurin	**78**	48.41 N	28.18 E
Džurun	**86**	49.15 N	57.37 E
Džusaly	**86**	45.28 N	64.05 E
Dzüün Changaj	**88**	49.17 N	95.14 E
Dzüün Charaa	**88**	48.52 N	106.28 E
Dzüün Gov	**88**	49.55 N	93.47 E
Dzuunmod	**88**	47.45 N	106.55 E
Džvari	**84**	42.43 N	42.04 E
Dzygovka	**78**	48.22 N	28.19 E

E

Name	Page	Lat.°′	Long.°′
Eads	**198**	38.28 N	102.46 W
Eagar	**200**	34.06 N	109.17 W
Eagle, Ak., U.S.	**180**	64.46 N	141.16 W
Eagle, Co., U.S.	**200**	39.39 N	106.49 W
Eagle, N.Y., U.S.	**210**	42.33 N	78.18 W
Eagle, Wi., U.S.	**216**	42.52 N	88.28 W
Eagle ≃, Nf., Can.	**176**	53.35 N	57.25 W
Eagle ≃, Yk., Can.	**180**	67.20 N	137.10 W
Eagle ≃, Co., U.S.	**200**	39.39 N	107.04 W
Eagle, Mount ∧	**241n**	17.46 N	64.49 W
Eagle Bay	**182**	50.56 N	119.12 W
Eagle Bend	**198**	46.09 N	95.02 W
Eagle Bridge	**210**	42.57 N	73.24 W
Eagle Butte	**198**	45.00 N	101.14 W
Eagle Chief Creek ≃	**196**	36.22 N	98.27 W
Eagle Creek	**224**	45.21 N	122.21 W
Eagle Creek ≃, Sk., Can.	**184**	52.22 N	107.24 W
Eagle Creek ≃, Az., U.S.	**200**	32.58 N	109.25 W
Eagle Creek ≃, In., U.S.	**218**	39.43 N	86.12 W
Eagle Creek ≃, Ky., U.S.	**218**	38.36 N	85.04 W
Eagle Creek ≃, Mt., U.S.	**202**	48.12 N	111.11 W
Eagle Creek ≃, N.M., U.S.	**196**	32.47 N	104.20 W
Eagle Creek ≃, Oh., U.S.	**214**	41.18 N	80.53 W
Eagle Creek ≃, Oh., U.S.	**218**	38.43 N	83.51 W
Eagle Creek ≃, Or., U.S.	**202**	44.45 N	117.10 W
Eagle Creek ≃, Or., U.S.	**224**	45.21 N	122.23 W
Eagle Creek, East Fork ≃	**218**	38.47 N	83.43 W
Eagle Creek, West Fork ≃	**218**	38.47 N	83.43 W
Eagle Creek Reservoir ⊜[1]	**218**	39.50 N	86.18 W
Eagledale	**224**	47.37 N	122.32 W
Eagle Grove	**190**	42.39 N	93.54 W
Eagle Harbor	**210**	43.15 N	78.15 W
Eaglehawk	**169**	36.43 S	144.15 E
Eagle Hill ≃	**283**	42.42 N	70.49 W
Eagle Key I	**220**	25.09 N	80.36 W
Eagle Lake, Fl., U.S.	**220**	27.59 N	81.45 W
Eagle Lake, Me., U.S.	**186**	47.02 N	68.35 W
Eagle Lake, Mi., U.S.	**216**	41.48 N	86.02 W
Eagle Lake, Tx., U.S.	**222**	29.35 N	96.20 W
Eagle Lake ⊜, B.C., Can.	**182**	51.55 N	124.25 W
Eagle Lake ⊜, On., Can.	**184**	50.39 N	94.54 W
Eagle Lake ⊜, On., Can.	**184**	49.42 N	93.13 W
Eagle Lake ⊜, On., Can.	**212**	44.41 N	76.43 W
Eagle Lake ⊜, On., Can.	**212**	45.08 N	78.29 W
Eagle Lake ⊜, Ca., U.S.	**204**	40.39 N	120.44 W
Eagle Lake ⊜, Me., U.S.	**186**	46.20 N	69.20 W
Eagle Lake ⊜, Mi., U.S.	**216**	41.48 N	86.02 W
Eagle Lake ⊜, Tx., U.S.	**222**	29.34 N	96.21 W
Eagle Lake ⊜, Wi., U.S.	**216**	42.42 N	88.07 W
Eagle Mountain, Ca., U.S.	**204**	33.49 N	115.27 W
Eagle Mountain, Tx., U.S.	**222**	32.52 N	97.30 W
Eagle Mountain ∧	**202**	46.20 N	115.07 W
Eagle Mountain ∧[2]	**190**	47.54 N	90.33 W
Eagle Mountain Lake ⊜[1]	**222**	32.55 N	97.30 W
Eagle Nest Butte ∧	**198**	43.27 N	101.39 W
Eagle Nest Lake ⊜	**222**	29.13 N	95.37 W
Eagle Pass	**196**	28.42 N	100.29 W
Eagle Peak ∧, Ca., U.S.	**204**	41.17 N	120.12 W
Eagle Peak ∧, Ca., U.S.	**228**	35.15 N	118.28 W
Eagle Peak ∧, Ca., U.S.	**282**	37.54 N	121.54 W
Eagle River, Mi., U.S.	**190**	47.24 N	88.18 W
Eagle River, Wi., U.S.	**190**	45.55 N	89.14 W
Eagle Rock	**192**	37.38 N	79.48 W
Eagle Rock ◆[8]	**280**	34.09 N	118.12 W
Eagle Rock Reservation ♠	**276**	40.49 N	74.14 W
Eaglesfield	**44**	55.03 N	3.12 W
Eaglesham, Ab., Can.	**182**	55.47 N	117.53 W
Eaglesham, Scot., U.K.	**46**	55.44 N	4.18 W
Eagles Mere	**210**	41.25 N	76.35 W
Eagleton Village	**192**	35.46 N	83.56 W
Eagletown	**194**	34.02 N	94.34 W
Eagle Village	**180**	64.47 N	141.07 W
Eagleville, Ct., U.S.	**207**	41.47 N	72.16 W
Eagleville, Pa., U.S.	**285**	40.10 N	75.24 W
Eagleville, Wi., U.S.	**216**	42.52 N	88.26 W
Ealing ◆[8]	**260**	51.31 N	0.20 W
Eamont ≃	**44**	54.40 N	2.39 W
Earaheedy	**162**	25.34 S	121.39 E
Earby	**44**	53.56 N	2.08 W
Earcroft	**262**	53.43 N	2.29 W
Eardisley	**42**	52.08 N	2.59 W
Eardley Lake ⊜	**184**	52.32 N	96.05 W
Ear Falls	**184**	50.38 N	93.13 W
Earle	**194**	35.16 N	90.28 W
Earlestown	**262**	53.27 N	2.39 W
Earl Grey	**184**	50.56 N	104.45 W
Earlham	**194**	41.29 N	94.07 W
Earlimart	**226**	35.53 N	119.16 W
Earlington	**194**	37.16 N	87.30 W
Earlish	**46**	57.34 N	6.23 W
Earl Park	**216**	40.40 N	87.24 W
Earl Rowe Provincial Park ♠	**212**	44.10 N	79.54 W
Earls Barton	**42**	52.15 N	0.45 W
Earls Colne	**42**	51.56 N	0.42 E
Earl Shilton	**42**	52.35 N	1.20 W
Earl Soham	**42**	52.14 N	1.16 E
Earlston	**46**	55.39 N	2.40 W
Earlton	**210**	42.21 N	73.54 W
Earlville, Il., U.S.	**216**	41.35 N	88.55 W
Earlville, N.Y., U.S.	**210**	42.44 N	75.33 W
Earlville, Pa., U.S.	**208**	40.19 N	75.44 W
Earlwood	**274a**	33.56 S	151.08 E
Early, Ia., U.S.	**198**	42.27 N	95.09 W
Early, Tx., U.S.	**196**	31.45 N	98.54 W
Early Winters Creek ≃	**224**	48.35 N	120.35 W
Earn ≃	**46**	56.21 N	3.19 W
Earn, Loch ⊜	**46**	56.23 N	4.14 W
Earnslaw, Mount ∧	**172**	44.37 S	168.24 E
Earth	**196**	34.14 N	102.24 W
Eas	**175f**	16.22 S	168.12 E
Easington, Eng., U.K.	**44**	53.40 N	0.07 E
Easington, Eng., U.K.	**44**	54.47 N	1.19 W
Easingwold	**44**	54.07 N	1.11 W
Easky	**48**	54.18 N	8.58 W
Easley	**192**	34.49 N	82.36 W
East ≃, On., Can.	**190**	45.20 N	79.17 W
East ≃, Co., U.S.	**200**	38.40 N	106.51 W
East ≃, N.Y., U.S.	**276**	40.48 N	73.48 W
East, University of the ⊍[2]	**269f**	14.36 N	120.59 E
East Acton	**283**	42.28 N	71.24 W
East Allen ≃	**44**	54.55 N	2.19 W
East Alliance	**214**	40.55 N	81.04 W
East Alligator ≃	**164**	12.08 S	132.42 E
East Alton	**219**	38.52 N	90.06 W
East Amherst	**210**	43.01 N	78.42 W
East-Angus	**206**	45.29 N	71.40 W
East Arlington	**210**	43.03 N	73.08 W
East Atlantic Beach	**276**	40.35 N	73.43 W
East Aurora	**210**	42.46 N	78.36 W
East Avon	**210**	42.55 N	77.42 W
East Baines ≃	**164**	15.38 S	129.58 E
East Bangor	**210**	40.52 N	75.11 W
East Barming	**260**	51.16 N	0.28 E
East Barnet ◆[8]	**260**	51.38 N	0.09 W
East Basin ⊂	**279a**	41.32 N	81.40 W
East Bay ⊂, Fl., U.S.	**194**	30.05 N	85.32 W
East Bay ⊂, N.Y., U.S.	**210**	40.38 N	73.32 W
East Bay ⊂, Tx., U.S.	**222**	29.30 N	94.35 W
East Bedfont ◆[8]	**260**	51.27 N	0.26 W
East Bend	**192**	36.12 N	80.30 W
East Berbice-Corentyne □[5]	**246**	4.00 N	58.15 W
East Berkshire	**206**	44.56 N	72.42 W
East-Berlin → Berlin (Ost), D.D.R.	**264a**	52.30 N	13.25 E
East Berlin, Ct., U.S.	**207**	41.37 N	72.42 W
East Berlin, N.J., U.S.	**285**	39.48 N	74.55 W
East Berlin, Pa., U.S.	**208**	39.56 N	76.58 W
East Bernard	**222**	29.32 N	96.04 W
East Bernstadt	**192**	37.11 N	84.07 W
East Berwick	**210**	41.03 N	76.13 W
East Bethany	**210**	42.56 N	78.06 W
East Bhāgīrath Plain ⊻	**126**	23.30 N	88.30 E
East Bijou Creek ≃	**198**	39.51 N	104.08 W
East Billerica	**283**	42.34 N	71.14 W
East Blackstone	**207**	42.02 N	71.31 W
East Bloomfield	**210**	42.54 N	77.26 W
East Boston ◆[8]	**283**	42.23 N	71.02 W
Eastbourne, N.Z.	**172**	41.18 S	174.54 E
Eastbourne, Eng., U.K.	**42**	50.46 N	0.17 E
East Brady	**214**	40.59 N	79.36 W
East Braintree	**184**	49.37 N	95.38 W
East Branch	**210**	41.59 N	75.08 W
East Branch Lake ⊜[1]	**214**	41.35 N	78.35 W
East Brewster	**207**	41.46 N	70.03 W
East Brewton	**194**	31.05 N	87.03 W
East Bridgewater	**207**	42.02 N	70.58 W
East Brimfield Lake ⊜[1]	**207**	42.06 N	72.10 W
East Brookfield	**207**	42.13 N	72.02 W
East Brooklyn	**207**	41.47 N	71.53 W
East Brother I	**271d**	22.20 N	113.58 E
East Brunswick	**208**	40.25 N	74.23 W
East Bucas Island I	**116**	9.43 N	126.02 E
East Burwood	**274b**	37.51 S	145.09 E
Eastbury	**260**	51.37 N	0.25 W
East Butler	**214**	40.53 N	79.51 W
East Cache Creek ≃	**196**	34.08 N	98.16 W
East Caicos I	**238**	21.41 N	71.30 W
East Calder	**46**	55.54 N	3.27 W
East Canaan	**207**	42.00 N	73.17 W
East Canada Creek ≃	**210**	43.00 N	74.45 W
East Canton	**214**	40.47 N	81.17 W
East Cape ›, N.Z.	**172**	37.41 S	178.33 E
East Cape ›, Ak., U.S.	**181a**	51.21 N	179.29 E
East Cape ›, Fl., U.S.	**220**	25.07 N	81.05 W
East Carancahua Creek ≃	**222**	28.51 N	96.19 W
East Carbon	**200**	39.32 N	110.24 W
East Carlisle	**214**	41.19 N	82.05 W
East Caroline Basin ✣[1]	**14**	4.00 N	146.45 E
East Castor ≃	**212**	45.16 N	75.17 W
East Catfish Creek ≃	**212**	42.47 N	81.04 W
East Channel ≃[1]	**180**	69.20 N	134.00 W
East Chatham	**210**	42.25 N	73.32 W
East Chelmsford	**207**	42.36 N	71.18 W
Eastchester	**210**	40.57 N	73.49 W
Eastchester Bay ⊂	**276**	40.51 N	73.48 W
East Chicago	**216**	41.38 N	87.27 W
East Chicago Heights	**278**	41.30 N	87.35 W
East China Sea ⊤[2]	**90**	30.00 N	126.00 E
Eastchurch	**42**	51.25 N	0.52 E
East Clandon	**260**	51.15 N	0.29 W
East Claridon	**214**	41.32 N	81.07 W
East Cleddau ≃	**42**	51.46 N	4.52 W
East Cleveland	**214**	41.31 N	81.34 W
East Coast Bays	**172**	36.45 S	174.46 E
East Concord	**210**	42.33 N	78.38 W
Eastcote ◆[8]	**260**	51.35 N	0.24 W
East Cote Blanche Bay ⊂	**194**	29.35 N	91.40 W
East Coulee	**182**	51.20 N	112.29 W
East Creek ≃	**276**	40.27 N	74.09 W
East Cross Creek ≃	**212**	44.17 N	78.44 W
East Dean	**42**	50.45 N	0.12 E
East Delaware Aqueduct ≋[1]	**210**	41.52 N	74.31 W
East Demerara-West Coast Berbice □[5]	**246**	6.20 N	58.00 W
East Dennis	**207**	41.44 N	70.09 W
East Dereham	**42**	52.41 N	0.56 E
East Detroit	**214**	42.28 N	82.57 W
East Dismal Swamp ≣	**192**	35.45 N	76.35 W
East Ditch ≋	**276**	40.56 N	74.19 W
East Douglas	**207**	42.04 N	71.42 W
East Dublin	**192**	32.32 N	82.52 W
East Dubuque	**190**	42.29 N	90.38 W
East Dundee	**216**	42.06 N	88.16 W
East Durham	**210**	42.22 N	74.06 W
East Ely	**204**	39.15 N	114.53 W
Eastend, Sk., Can.	**184**	49.31 N	108.48 W
East End, Vir. Is., U.S.	**240m**	18.21 N	64.40 W
East End Point ›	**240b**	25.03 N	77.16 W
East Enterprise	**218**	38.52 N	84.59 W
Easter Island → Pascua, Isla de I	**174z**	27.07 S	109.22 W
Easterly	**222**	31.06 N	96.23 W
Eastern □[4], Ghana	**150**	6.30 N	0.30 W
Eastern □[4], Kenya	**154**	0.05 N	38.00 E
Eastern □[4], S.L.	**150**	8.15 N	11.00 W
Eastern □[4], Zam.	**154**	13.00 S	32.15 E
Eastern □[5]	**154**	1.25 N	33.50 E
Eastern Bay ⊂	**208**	38.51 N	76.19 W
Eastern Channel → Tsushima-kaikyō ⋓	**92**	34.00 N	129.00 E
Eastern Cherokee Indian Reservation ◆[4]	**192**	35.25 N	83.24 W
Eastern Cove ⊂	**168b**	35.46 S	137.50 E
Eastern Creek ≃, Austl.	**166**	20.10 S	141.08 E
Eastern Creek ≃, Austl.	**274a**	33.39 S	150.51 E
Eastern Division □[5]	**175g**	19.00 S	180.00 E
Eastern Fields ✣[2]	**164**	10.20 S	145.45 E
Eastern Ghāts ⋏	**122**	14.00 N	78.50 E
Eastern Highlands □[5]	**164**	6.30 S	145.15 E
Eastern Island I	**174g**	28.12 N	177.20 W
Eastern Isles II	**42a**	49.57 N	6.15 W
Eastern Michigan University ⊍[2]	**281**	42.15 N	83.37 W
Eastern Neck Island I	**208**	39.02 N	76.13 W
Eastern Point ›	**283**	42.35 N	70.40 W
Eastern Samar □[4]	**116**	12.00 N	125.00 E
Eastern Sayans → Vostočnyj Sajan ⋏	**88**	53.00 N	97.00 E
Eastern Shore ◆[1]	**208**	38.40 N	75.50 W
Eastern Yamuna Canal ≋	**272a**	28.40 N	77.15 E
East Falkland I	**254**	51.55 S	59.00 W
East Falls ◆[8]	**285**	40.01 N	75.11 W
East Falmouth	**207**	41.34 N	70.33 W
East Farleigh	**260**	51.15 N	0.29 E
East Farmingdale	**276**	40.44 N	73.26 W
East Faxon	**210**	41.15 N	76.58 W
East Fayetteville	**192**	35.05 N	78.51 W
Eastfield	**44**	54.14 N	0.24 W
East Flat Rock	**192**	35.16 N	82.25 W
Eastford	**207**	41.54 N	72.04 W
East Foxboro	**283**	42.03 N	71.12 W
East Freedom	**214**	40.21 N	78.26 W
East Freetown	**207**	41.46 N	70.57 W
East Frisian Islands → Ostfriesische Inseln II	**52**	53.44 N	7.25 E
East Gaffney	**192**	35.04 N	81.37 W
East Gallatin ≃	**202**	45.53 N	111.20 W
Eastgate	**224**	47.34 N	122.09 W
East Germany → German Democratic Republic □[1]	**30**	52.00 N	12.30 E
East Ghor Canal → Ghawr ash-Sharqīyah, Qanāt al- ≋	**132**	32.41 N	35.38 E
East Glacier Park	**202**	48.26 N	113.13 W
East Glenville	**210**	42.53 N	73.55 W
East Granby	**207**	41.56 N	72.43 W
East Grand Forks	**198**	47.55 N	97.01 W
East Grand Rapids	**216**	42.56 N	85.36 W
East Greenbush	**210**	42.35 N	73.42 W
East Greenville, Oh., U.S.	**214**	40.48 N	81.36 W
East Greenville, Pa., U.S.	**208**	40.24 N	75.30 W
East Greenwich, N.Y., U.S.	**210**	43.09 N	73.24 W
East Greenwich, R.I., U.S.	**207**	41.39 N	71.27 W
East Grinstead	**42**	51.08 N	0.01 W
East Gwillimbury	**212**	44.08 N	79.25 W
East Haddam	**207**	41.27 N	72.27 W
East Half Hollow Hills	**276**	40.57 N	72.11 W
Eastham, Eng., U.K.	**262**	53.19 N	2.58 W
Eastham, Ma., U.S.	**207**	41.49 N	69.58 W
East Ham ◆[8]	**260**	51.32 N	0.03 E
East Hampton, Ct., U.S.	**207**	41.34 N	72.30 W
Easthampton, Ma., U.S.	**207**	42.16 N	72.40 W
East Hampton, N.Y., U.S.	**207**	40.57 N	72.11 W
East Hanningfield	**260**	51.41 N	0.34 E
East Hanover	**276**	40.48 N	74.22 W
East Harbor State Park ♠	**214**	41.32 N	82.49 W
East Harling	**42**	52.26 N	0.55 E
East Hartford	**207**	41.46 N	72.36 W
East Hartland	**207**	41.59 N	72.54 W
East Harwich	**207**	41.43 N	70.02 W
East Haven	**207**	41.16 N	72.52 W
East Hazel Crest	**278**	41.35 N	87.39 W
East Helena	**202**	46.35 N	111.54 W
East Hemet	**228**	33.45 N	116.57 W
East Herkimer	**210**	43.02 N	74.58 W
East Hertfordshire □[8]	**260**	51.46 N	0.02 W
East Hickory	**214**	41.35 N	79.24 W
East Highland Park	**208**	37.36 N	77.25 W
East Hills, Austl.	**274a**	33.58 S	150.59 E
East Hills, N.Y., U.S.	**276**	40.47 N	73.37 W
East Hoathly	**42**	50.55 N	0.10 E
East Horsley	**42**	51.15 N	0.26 W
East Humber ≃	**212**	43.47 N	79.35 W
East Huntington	**276**	40.52 N	73.24 W
East Ilsley	**42**	51.32 N	1.17 W
East Irvington	**276**	41.03 N	73.51 W
East Island ›[1]	**276**	40.54 N	73.38 W
East Islip	**276**	40.43 N	73.11 W
East Jewett	**210**	42.14 N	74.09 W
East Jordan	**190**	45.09 N	85.07 W
East Keansburg	**276**	40.26 N	74.07 W
East Kelowna	**182**	49.51 N	119.25 W
East Kilbride	**46**	55.46 N	4.10 W
East Killingly	**207**	41.50 N	71.49 W
East Kingston	**210**	41.57 N	73.58 W
Eastlake, Mi., U.S.	**190**	44.15 N	86.18 W
Eastlake, Oh., U.S.	**214**	41.39 N	81.27 W
East Lake ⊜, On., Can.	**184**	53.42 N	93.10 W
East Lake ⊜, On., Can.	**212**	43.55 N	77.12 W
East Lake ⊜, N.J., U.S.	**276**	40.58 N	74.21 W
East Lake Tohopekaliga ⊜	**220**	28.18 N	81.17 W
East Lamma Channel ⋓	**271d**	22.14 N	114.09 E
Eastland	**196**	32.24 N	98.49 W
Eastland Center ◆[9]	**281**	42.27 N	82.56 W
Eastland Shopping Plaza ◆[9]	**279b**	40.22 N	79.50 W
East Lansdowne	**285**	39.56 N	75.16 W
East Lansing	**216**	42.44 N	84.29 W
East Laurinburg	**192**	34.46 N	79.26 W
East Leake	**42**	52.49 N	1.10 W
Eastleigh	**42**	50.58 N	1.22 W
East Lewistown	**214**	40.57 N	80.42 W
East Liberty	**216**	40.19 N	83.34 W
East Liberty ◆[8]	**279b**	40.27 N	79.55 W
East Licking Creek ≃	**208**	40.32 N	77.24 W
East Lindfield	**274a**	33.46 S	151.11 E
East Linton	**46**	55.59 N	2.39 W
East Liverpool	**214**	40.37 N	80.34 W
East London (Oos-Londen)	**158**	33.00 S	27.55 E
East Longmeadow	**207**	42.03 N	72.30 W
East Los Angeles	**228**	34.01 N	118.10 W
East Lyme	**207**	41.22 N	72.13 W
East Lynn	**216**	40.28 N	87.48 W
East Lynn Lake ⊜[1]	**188**	38.05 N	82.20 W
Eastmain	**176**	52.15 N	78.30 W
Eastmain ≃	**176**	52.15 N	78.35 W
Eastmain-Opinaca, Réservoir ⊜[1]	**176**	52.25 N	76.35 W
East Malling	**260**	51.17 N	0.26 E
Eastman, P.Q., Can.	**206**	45.18 N	72.19 W
Eastman, Ga., U.S.	**192**	32.11 N	83.10 W
Eastman Lake ⊜[1]	**226**	37.14 N	119.58 W
East Mansfield	**283**	42.01 N	71.10 W
East Mariana Basin ✣[1]	**14**	12.00 N	153.00 E
East Marin Island I	**282**	37.58 N	122.27 W
East Markham	**44**	53.15 N	0.54 W
East McKeesport	**279b**	40.23 N	79.48 W
East Meadow	**210**	40.43 N	73.33 W
East Meadow ≃	**283**	42.47 N	71.02 W
East Meadow Brook ≃	**276**	40.39 N	73.34 W
East Meadowview	**216**	41.08 N	87.52 W
East Mecca	**214**	41.24 N	80.45 W
East Meredith	**210**	42.25 N	74.53 W
East Midlands Airport ⊠	**42**	52.50 N	1.20 W
East Millbury	**207**	42.13 N	71.44 W
East Mill Creek ≃	**222**	29.55 N	96.17 W
East Millinocket	**188**	45.37 N	68.34 W
East Millstone	**276**	40.30 N	74.35 W
East Missoula	**202**	46.52 N	113.58 W
East Molesey	**260**	51.24 N	0.21 W
East Moline	**190**	41.30 N	90.26 W
East Monongahela	**279b**	40.12 N	79.55 W
East Mountain	**222**	32.35 N	94.51 W
East Mustang Creek ≃	**222**	29.03 N	96.27 W
East Naples	**220**	26.06 N	81.44 W
East Nassau	**210**	42.30 N	73.30 W
East Newark	**276**	40.48 N	73.59 W
East New Britain □[5]	**164**	6.00 S	152.00 E
East New Market	**208**	38.35 N	75.55 W
East New York ◆[8]	**276**	40.40 N	73.53 W
East Nishnabotna ≃	**198**	40.39 N	95.37 W
East Nodaway ≃	**194**	40.38 N	95.01 W
East Norriton	**208**	40.09 N	75.18 W
East Northfield	**207**	42.43 N	72.27 W
East Northport	**210**	40.52 N	73.19 W
East Norwich	**210**	40.50 N	73.32 W
East Novaya Zemlya Trough ✣[1]	**12**	73.30 N	61.00 E
East Olympia	**224**	46.58 N	122.50 W
Easton, Eng., U.K.	**42**	50.32 N	2.26 W
Easton, Ca., U.S.	**226**	36.39 N	119.47 W
Easton, Ct., U.S.	**207**	41.15 N	73.17 W
Easton, Il., U.S.	**219**	40.14 N	89.50 W
Easton, Md., U.S.	**208**	38.46 N	76.04 W
Easton, Ma., U.S.	**283**	42.02 N	71.06 W
Easton, Pa., U.S.	**208**	40.41 N	75.13 W
Easton, Tx., U.S.	**222**	32.23 N	94.35 W
Easton, Wa., U.S.	**224**	47.14 N	121.10 W
Eastondale	**283**	42.02 N	71.04 W
Easton Reservoir ⊜[1]	**207**	41.16 N	73.16 W
East Orange	**210**	40.46 N	74.12 W
East Orleans	**207**	41.47 N	69.58 W
East Otto	**210**	42.23 N	78.45 W
Eastover	**192**	33.52 N	80.41 W
East Pacific Rise ✣[3]	**6**	20.00 S	115.00 W
East Pakistan → Bangladesh □[1]	**118**	24.00 N	90.00 E
East Palatka	**192**	29.39 N	81.35 W
East Palestine	**214**	40.50 N	80.32 W
East Palo Alto	**226**	37.28 N	122.08 W
East Park Reservoir ⊜[1]	**226**	39.21 N	122.30 W
East Parkrose	**224**	45.33 N	122.32 W
East Peak ∧	**116**	11.13 N	119.29 E
East Peckham	**260**	51.15 N	0.23 E
East Pecos	**200**	35.34 N	105.39 W
East Pembroke, Ma., U.S.	**283**	42.05 N	70.46 W
East Pembroke, N.Y., U.S.	**210**	42.59 N	78.18 W
East Peoria	**190**	40.39 N	89.34 W
East Pepperell	**207**	42.39 N	71.34 W
East Petersburg	**208**	40.06 N	76.21 W
East Pharsalia	**210**	42.34 N	75.43 W
East Pine	**182**	55.43 N	121.13 W
East Pines	**284c**	38.57 N	76.55 W
East Pittsburgh	**279b**	40.23 N	79.50 W
Eastpoint, Fl., U.S.	**192**	29.44 N	84.52 W
East Point, Ga., U.S.	**192**	33.40 N	84.26 W
East Point ›, P.E., Can.	**186**	46.27 N	61.58 W
East Point ›, Ma., U.S.	**207**	42.25 N	70.54 W
East Point ›, Vir. Is., U.S.	**241n**	17.45 N	64.34 W
Eastpoint ◆[9]	**284b**	39.18 N	76.31 W
Eastport, Nf., Can.	**186**	48.39 N	53.45 W
Eastport, Id., U.S.	**202**	49.00 N	116.10 W
Eastport, Me., U.S.	**188**	44.54 N	66.59 W
Eastport, N.Y., U.S.	**207**	40.49 N	72.44 W
East Porterville	**204**	36.04 N	118.56 W
East Potomac Park ♠	**284c**	38.52 N	77.01 W
East Prairie	**194**	36.46 N	89.23 W
East Prairie ≃	**182**	55.34 N	116.25 W
East Prospect	**208**	39.58 N	76.31 W
East Providence	**207**	41.48 N	71.22 W
East Pryor Mountain ∧	**202**	45.11 N	108.20 W
East Quogue	**207**	40.51 N	72.35 W
East Rājasthān Uplands ⋏[1]	**124**	26.40 N	76.35 E
East Randolph	**210**	42.10 N	78.56 W
East Retford	**44**	53.19 N	0.56 W
East Richmond	**226**	37.57 N	122.19 W
Eastridge Center ◆[9]	**282**	37.20 N	121.49 W
East Rigaud ≃	**206**	45.27 N	74.22 W
Eastriggs	**44**	54.59 N	3.10 W
East River ⊂	**208**	37.24 N	76.21 W
East Rochester, N.Y., U.S.	**210**	43.06 N	77.29 W
East Rochester, Oh., U.S.	**214**	40.45 N	81.02 W
East Rockaway	**276**	40.38 N	73.40 W
East Rockingham	**192**	34.55 N	79.45 W
East Rockwood	**216**	42.03 N	83.13 W
East Rosebud Creek ≃	**202**	45.29 N	109.27 W
East Rudolf National Park ♠	**154**	3.55 N	36.20 E
East Rutherford	**276**	40.50 N	74.05 W
Eastry	**42**	51.15 N	1.18 E
East Saint Louis	**219**	38.38 N	90.09 W
East Salem	**208**	40.37 N	77.14 W
East Salt Creek ≃	**200**	39.13 N	108.54 W
East Sandwich	**207**	41.44 N	70.27 W
East Sandy Creek ≃	**214**	41.22 N	79.51 W
East Schodack	**210**	42.34 N	73.38 W
East Scotia Basin ✣[1]	**9**	57.00 S	35.00 W
East Sepik □[5]	**164**	4.00 S	143.30 E
East Setauket	**210**	40.57 N	73.06 W
East Shoal Lake ⊜	**184**	50.23 N	97.37 W
East Siberian Sea → Vostočno-Sibirskoje more ⊤[2]	**12**	74.00 N	166.00 E
East Side	**210**	41.04 N	75.46 W
Eastside Bypass ≋	**226**	37.05 N	120.28 W
East Side Canal ≋, Ca., U.S.	**226**	37.21 N	120.55 W
East Side Canal ≋, Ca., U.S.	**226**	35.33 N	119.33 W
East Sixteen Mile Creek ≃	**275b**	43.28 N	79.48 W
East Smethport	**214**	41.49 N	78.26 W
East Smithfield	**210**	41.52 N	76.38 W
East Sooke	**224**	48.22 N	123.43 W
Eastsound	**224**	48.41 N	122.54 W
East Sound ⋓	**224**	48.39 N	122.53 W
East Sparta	**214**	40.40 N	81.21 W
East Spencer	**192**	35.40 N	80.25 W
East Springbrook	**284c**	39.04 N	77.00 W
East Springfield, Oh., U.S.	**214**	40.27 N	80.52 W
East Springfield, Pa., U.S.	**214**	41.57 N	80.28 W
East Stony Creek ≃	**210**	43.15 N	74.12 W
East Stour ≃	**42**	51.08 N	0.53 E
East Stroudsburg	**210**	40.59 N	75.10 W
East Sudbury	**283**	42.24 N	71.24 W
East Sussex □[6]	**42**	50.55 N	0.15 E
East Syracuse	**210**	43.04 N	76.05 W
East Tawas	**190**	44.16 N	83.29 W
East Templeton	**207**	42.33 N	72.02 W
East Texas	**210**	40.33 N	75.33 W
East Thompson	**207**	42.00 N	71.48 W
East Tilbury	**260**	51.28 N	0.26 E
East Troy	**216**	42.47 N	88.24 W
East Tustin	**280**	33.46 N	117.49 W
Eastvale	**214**	40.46 N	80.19 W
East Vandergrift	**214**	40.36 N	79.34 W
Eastview	**218**	40.19 N	80.38 W
Eastville	**208**	37.21 N	75.56 W
East Walker ≃	**204**	38.53 N	119.10 W
East Walpole	**207**	42.09 N	71.12 W
East Wareham	**207**	41.45 N	70.40 W
East Washington	**214**	40.10 N	80.14 W
East Waterford	**208**	40.22 N	77.36 W
East Wemyss	**46**	56.09 N	3.04 W
East Wenatchee	**202**	47.24 N	120.17 W
East Wenonah	**285**	39.47 N	75.08 W
East White Plains	**276**	41.03 N	73.47 W
Eastwick ◆[8]	**285**	39.55 N	75.14 W
East Wickham ◆[8]	**260**	51.28 N	0.07 E
East Williamson	**210**	43.14 N	77.09 W
East Williston	**276**	40.46 N	73.38 W
East Wilmington	**192**	34.13 N	77.53 W
East Wittering	**42**	50.41 N	0.53 W
Eastwood, Austl.	**274a**	33.48 S	151.05 E
Eastwood, Eng., U.K.	**44**	53.01 N	1.18 W
Eastwood, Eng., U.K.	**260**	51.34 N	0.40 E
Eastwood, Eng., U.K.	**262**	53.43 N	2.03 W
Eastwood, Mi., U.S.	**216**	42.18 N	85.33 W
Eastwood, Pa., U.S.	**279b**	40.17 N	79.31 W
East Worcester	**210**	42.37 N	74.40 W
East Yegua Creek ≃	**222**	30.19 N	96.45 W
East Yellow Creek ≃	**194**	39.38 N	93.04 W
East York, On., Can.	**212**	43.41 N	79.20 W
East York, Pa., U.S.	**208**	39.58 N	76.43 W
Eaton, Austl.	**168a**	33.19 S	115.43 E
Eaton, Co., U.S.	**200**	40.31 N	104.42 W
Eaton, In., U.S.	**216**	40.20 N	85.21 W
Eaton, N.Y., U.S.	**210**	42.51 N	75.37 W
Eaton, Oh., U.S.	**218**	39.44 N	84.38 W
Eaton ≃	**206**	45.28 N	71.39 W
Eaton Estates	**214**	41.19 N	82.01 W
Eatonia	**184**	51.13 N	109.23 W
Eaton Nord ≃	**206**	45.24 N	71.35 W
Eaton Park	**220**	28.00 N	81.54 W
Eaton Rapids	**216**	42.30 N	84.39 W
Eatons Neck	**276**	40.56 N	73.24 W
Eatons Neck ›[1]	**276**	40.57 N	73.23 W
Eatons Neck Point ›	**210**	40.57 N	73.24 W
Eaton Socon	**42**	52.13 N	0.18 W
Eatonton	**192**	33.19 N	83.23 W
Eatontown	**208**	40.17 N	74.03 W
Eatonville	**224**	46.52 N	122.15 W
Eaton Wash V	**280**	34.04 N	118.03 W
Eaton Wash Dam ◆[6]	**280**	34.10 N	118.06 W
Eau ≃	**44**	53.31 N	0.44 W
Eaubonne	**261**	49.00 N	2.17 E
Eau Claire, Mi., U.S.	**216**	41.59 N	86.17 W
Eau Claire, Pa., U.S.	**214**	41.08 N	79.48 W
Eau Claire, Wi., U.S.	**190**	44.48 N	91.29 W
Eau Claire ≃, Wi., U.S.	**190**	44.49 N	91.31 W
Eau Claire ≃, Wi., U.S.	**190**	44.55 N	89.37 W
Eau Claire, Lac à l' ⊜, P.Q., Can.	**176**	56.10 N	74.25 W
Eau Claire, Lac à l' ⊜, P.Q., Can.	**206**	46.33 N	73.04 W
Eau d'Heure ≃	**56**	50.18 N	4.24 E
Eau Galle ≃	**190**	44.37 N	92.00 W
Eau Gallie	**220**	28.08 N	80.38 W
Eaulne ≃	**50**	49.54 N	1.07 E
Eauripik I[1]	**108**	6.42 N	143.03 E
Eauripik Rise ✣[3]	**14**	3.00 N	142.00 E
Eauze	**32**	43.52 N	0.06 E
Ebabaka	**152**	2.30 S	18.19 E
Eban	**150**	9.44 N	4.56 E
Ebanga	**152**	12.44 S	14.44 E
Ebangalakata	**152**	0.29 S	21.29 E
Ebano	**234**	22.13 N	98.22 W
Ebb and Flow Indian Reserve ◆[4]	**184**	51.05 N	99.05 W
Ebb and Flow Lake ⊜	**184**	51.05 N	98.56 W
Ebbegebirge ⋏	**56**	51.08 N	7.46 E
Ebben Creek ≃	**283**	42.38 N	70.45 W
Ebberup	**41**	55.15 N	9.59 E
Ebbetts Pass)(	**226**	38.33 N	119.48 W
Ebbs	**64**	47.38 N	12.13 E
Ebbw ≃	**42**	51.33 N	2.59 W
Ebbw Vale	**42**	51.47 N	3.12 W
Ebebiyín	**152**	2.09 N	11.20 E
Ebeji (El Beïd) ≃	**146**	12.32 N	14.11 E
Ebejty, ozero ⊜	**86**	54.38 N	71.44 E
Ebeleben	**54**	51.17 N	10.43 E
Ebeltoft	**41**	56.12 N	10.41 E
Ebeltoft Vig ⊂	**41**	56.10 N	10.36 E
Ebenau	**64**	47.47 N	13.11 E
Ebendorf	**54**	52.11 N	11.34 E
Ebene Reichenau	**64**	46.51 N	13.54 E
Ebenezer	**275b**	43.46 N	79.40 W
Ebenezer Ridge ∧	**218**	39.06 N	84.55 W
Eben Junction	**190**	46.21 N	86.58 W
Ebensburg	**214**	40.29 N	78.43 W
Ebensee	**64**	47.48 N	13.46 E
Ebensfeld	**56**	50.04 N	10.58 E
Eberbach	**56**	49.28 N	8.59 E
Ebergassing	**264b**	48.03 N	16.31 E
Eber Gölü ⊜	**130**	38.38 N	31.12 E
Ebergötzen	**52**	51.34 N	10.06 E
Ebermannstadt	**60**	49.43 N	11.13 E
Ebern	**56**	50.05 N	10.47 E
Eberndorf	**61**	46.35 N	14.38 E
Ebersbach, B.R.D.	**56**	48.43 N	9.31 E
Ebersbach, D.D.R.	**54**	51.00 N	14.35 E
Ebersberg	**60**	48.05 N	11.58 E
Eberschwang	**60**	48.09 N	13.34 E
Ebersdorf	**52**	53.31 N	9.03 E
Ebersdorf bei Coburg	**56**	50.13 N	11.04 E
Eberstein	**61**	46.48 N	14.34 E
Eberswalde	**54**	52.50 N	13.49 E
Ebetsu	**92a**	43.07 N	141.34 E
Ebian	**102**	29.10 N	103.20 E
Ebina	**94**	35.26 N	139.25 E
Ebingen	**58**	48.13 N	9.01 E
Ebino	**92**	32.03 N	130.50 E
Ebinur Hu ⊜	**86**	44.55 N	82.55 E
Ebi-Sekigahara-Yōrō-kokutei-kōen ♠	**94**	35.30 N	136.30 E
Ebnat	**58**	47.15 N	9.08 E
Ebo	**152**	11.02 S	14.41 E
Ebola ≃	**152**	3.20 N	20.57 E
Eboli	**68**	40.37 N	15.04 E
Ebolowa	**152**	2.54 N	11.09 E
Ebon I[1]	**14**	4.35 N	168.44 E
Ebonda	**152**	2.12 N	22.21 E
Ebony	**156**	22.05 S	15.15 E
Eboshi-yama ∧	**96**	35.04 N	133.04 E
Eboué Stadium ♠	**273b**	4.17 S	15.18 E
Ebrach	**56**	49.50 N	10.29 E
Ebre, Delta de l' ⊻[2]	**34**	40.43 N	0.54 E
Ebreichsdorf	**61**	47.58 N	16.24 E
Ébrié, Lagune ⊂	**150**	5.14 N	4.26 W
Ebro (Ebre) ≃	**34**	40.43 N	0.54 E
Ebro, Embalse del ⊜[1]	**34**	43.00 N	3.58 W
Ebstorf	**52**	53.01 N	10.25 E
Ebute-Ikorodu	**273a**	6.37 N	3.30 E
Ebute-Metta ◆[8]	**273a**	6.29 N	3.23 E
Ecatepec □[7]	**286a**	19.36 N	99.04 W
Ecatepec de Morelos	**286a**	19.35 N	99.04 W
Écaussinnes-d'Enghen	**50**	50.34 N	4.10 E
Ecclefechan	**44**	55.03 N	3.17 W
Eccles, Eng., U.K.	**260**	51.19 N	0.29 E

Symbols in the index entries represent the broad categories identified in the key at the right. Symbols with superior numbers (⋏[1]) identify subcategories (see complete key on page *I* · *1*).

Symbole im Register stellen die rechts im Schlüssel erklärten Kategorien dar. Symbole mit hochgestellten Ziffern (⋏[1]) bezeichnen Unterabteilungen einer Kategorie (vgl. vollständiger Schlüssel auf Seite *I* · *1*).

Los símbolos incluídos en el texto del índice representan las grandes categorias identificadas con la clave a la derecha. Los símbolos con numeros en su parte superior (⋏[1]) identifican las subcategorías (véase la clave completa en la página *I* · *1*).

Les symboles de l'index représentent les catégories indiquées dans la légende à droite. Les symboles suivis d'un indice (⋏[1]) représentent des sous-catégories (voir légende complète à la page *I* · *1*).

Os símbolos incluídos no texto do índice representam as grandes categorias identificadas com a chave à direita. Os símbolos com números em sua parte superior (⋏[1]) identificam as subcategorias (veja-se a chave completa à página *I* · *1*).

	English	Deutsch	Español	Français	Português
∧	Mountain	Berg	Montaña	Montagne	Montanha
⋏	Mountains	Gebirge	Montañas	Montagnes	Montanhas
)(	Pass	Paß	Paso	Col	Passo
V	Valley, Canyon	Tal, Cañon	Valle, Cañón	Vallée, Canyon	Vale, Canhão
⊻	Plain	Ebene	Llano	Plaine	Planície
›	Cape	Kap	Cabo	Cap	Cabo
I	Island	Insel	Isla	Île	Ilha
II	Islands	Inseln	Islas	Îles	Ilhas
✣	Other Topographic Features	Andere Topographische Objekte	Otros Elementos Topográficos	Autres données topographiques	Outros acidentes topográficos

Eccl-Eldi *I* · 51

ESPAÑOL / **FRANÇAIS** / **PORTUGUÊS**

Nombre	Página	Lat.°′	Long.°′ W = Oeste
Eccles, Eng., U.K.	262	53.29 N	2.21 W
Eccles, W.V., U.S.	192	37.46 N	81.15 W
Eccleshall	42	52.52 N	2.15 W
Eccleston, Eng., U.K.	44	53.38 N	2.43 W
Eccleston, Eng., U.K.	262	53.39 N	2.44 W
Eccleston, Eng., U.K.	262	53.27 N	2.47 W
Eccleston, Md., U.S.	284b	39.24 N	76.44 W
Eceabat	130	40.11 N	26.21 E
Echabi	89	53.30 N	142.59 E
Echague	116	16.42 N	121.40 E
Echallens	58	46.38 N	6.38 E
Echaporã	255	22.26 S	50.12 W
Echarcon	261	48.34 N	2.24 E
Échauffour	50	48.44 N	0.23 E
Ech Cheliff (Orléansville)	148	36.10 N	1.20 E
Ech Cheliff □[5]	148	36.20 N	1.50 E
Echeconnee Creek ≃	192	32.39 N	83.36 W
Echelon Mall ◆[9]	285	39.51 N	75.00 W
Echeng	100	30.24 N	114.51 E
Échenoz-la-Méline	58	47.36 N	6.08 E
Echi ≃	94	35.13 N	136.07 E
Echigawa	94	35.10 N	136.12 E
Echigo-sammyaku ⋏	92	37.50 N	139.50 E
Echimamish ≃	184	54.20 N	97.27 W
Eching	60	48.18 N	11.37 E
Echizen	94	35.54 N	136.00 E
Echizen-Kaga-kaigan-kokutei-kōen ♠	94	36.08 N	136.05 E
Echizen-misaki ≻	94	35.59 N	135.57 E
Echo	198	44.37 N	95.25 W
Echo Bay	176	66.05 N	118.02 W
Echo Bay c	276	40.54 N	73.46 W
Echoing ≃	184	55.51 N	92.05 W
Echoing Lake ⊜	184	54.31 N	92.15 W
Echo Lake ⊜, Il., U.S.	278	42.13 N	88.05 W
Echo Lake ⊜, N.J., U.S.	276	41.04 N	74.25 W
Echo Summit ∧	226	38.50 N	120.02 W
Echouani, Lac ⊜	190	47.46 N	75.42 W
Echt, Ned.	52	51.06 N	5.52 E
Echt, Scot., U.K.	46	57.08 N	2.26 W
Echternach	56	49.48 N	6.26 E
Echternacherbrück	56	49.49 N	6.25 E
Echuca	166	36.08 S	144.46 E
Echunga	168b	35.07 S	138.48 E
Écija	34	37.32 N	5.05 W
Ecilda Paullier	258	34.22 S	57.04 W
Eck, Loch ⊜	46	56.05 N	5.00 W
Eckartsberga	54	51.07 N	11.34 E
Eckbolsheim	58	48.35 N	7.41 E
Eckernförde	41	54.28 N	9.50 E
Eckernförder Bucht c	41	54.30 N	10.02 E
Eckerö I	26	60.14 N	19.35 E
Eckington	44	53.19 N	1.21 W
Eckley	210	40.59 N	75.51 W
Eckville	182	52.21 N	114.22 W
Eckwarderhörne	52	53.31 N	8.14 E
Eclectic	194	32.38 N	86.02 W
Ecleto	222	29.03 N	97.45 W
Ecleto Creek ≃	196	28.52 N	97.45 W
Eclipse Sound ʮ	176	72.38 N	79.00 W
Ečmiadzin	84	40.10 N	44.18 E
Ecola State Park ♠	224	45.57 N	123.58 W
École ≃	261	48.32 N	2.33 E
Écommoy	50	47.50 N	0.16 E
Econfina ≃	192	30.02 N	83.55 W
Econlockhatchee ≃	220	28.42 N	81.02 W
Economy, In., U.S.	218	39.58 N	85.05 W
Economy, Pa., U.S.	214	40.39 N	80.14 W
Economy Park ♠	279b	40.37 N	80.12 W
Écorce, Lac de l' ⊜[1]	190	47.05 N	76.24 W
Écorces, Lac des ⊜	206	46.00 N	74.32 W
Ecorse	216	42.14 N	83.08 W
Ecorse ≃	281	42.14 N	83.09 W
Ecorse, South Branch ≃	281	42.14 N	83.09 W
Écos	50	49.10 N	1.39 E
Écosse → Scotland □[8]	28	57.00 N	4.00 W
Écouen	50	49.01 N	2.23 E
Écouen, Château d' ⊥	261	49.01 N	2.23 E
Écouis	50	49.19 N	1.26 E
Ecoute, Ru d' ≃	261	48.39 N	2.26 E
Ecquevilly	261	48.57 N	1.55 E
Écrins, Barre des ∧	62	44.55 N	6.22 E
Écrins, Massif des ⋏[1]	62	44.55 N	6.20 E
Écrins, Parc National des ♠	62	44.50 N	6.15 E
Écrosnes	261	48.33 N	1.44 E
Ecru	194	34.21 N	89.01 W
Ecser	264c	47.27 N	19.20 E
Ecstall ≃	182	54.09 N	129.56 W
Ecuador □[1], S.A.	242	2.00 S	77.30 W
Ecuador □[1], S.A.	246	2.00 S	77.30 W
Ecuandureo	234	20.10 N	102.11 W
Écueillé	32	47.05 N	1.21 E
Écuisses	58	46.45 N	4.32 E
Ecum Secum	186	44.58 N	62.08 W
Écury-sur-Coole	50	48.54 N	4.20 E
Ed, Ityo.	144	13.52 N	41.40 E
Ed, Sve.	26	58.55 N	11.55 E
Eda ◆[8]	268	35.34 N	139.34 E
Edah	162	28.17 S	117.10 E
Edam, Sk., Can.	184	53.12 N	108.46 W
Edam, Ned.	52	52.31 N	5.03 E
Eday I	46	59.11 N	2.47 W
Edderton	46	57.50 N	4.10 W
Eddington Gardens	285	40.06 N	74.57 W
Eddleston	46	55.43 N	3.13 W
Eddrachillis Bay c	46	58.18 N	5.15 W
Eddy	222	31.18 N	97.15 W
Eddystone	208	39.51 N	75.20 W
Eddystone Point ≻	166	41.00 S	148.21 E
Eddystone Rocks II[1]	42	50.12 N	4.15 W
Eddyville, Ia., U.S.	190	41.09 N	92.38 W
Eddyville, Ky., U.S.	194	37.05 N	88.04 W
Eddyville, N.Y., U.S.	210	41.54 N	74.02 W
Ede, Ned.	52	52.03 N	5.40 E
Ede, Nig.	150	7.44 N	4.27 E
Edéa	152	3.48 N	10.08 E
Edebäck	40	60.04 N	13.33 E
Edebo	40	60.01 N	18.34 E
Edegem	52	51.09 N	4.27 E
Edehon Lake ⊜	176	60.25 N	97.15 W
Edéia	255	17.18 S	49.55 W
Edelény	30	48.18 N	20.44 E
Edelsfeld	60	49.34 N	11.42 E
Edelshausen	60	48.37 N	11.17 E
Edelweiss	273d	26.16 S	28.28 E
Edelweiss Spitze ∧	64	47.07 N	12.50 E
Edemissen	52	52.23 N	10.16 E
Eden, Austl.	166	37.04 S	149.54 E
Éden, Bra.	287a	22.48 S	43.24 W
Eden, N. Ire., U.K.	48	54.44 N	5.47 W
Eden, Mi., U.S.	216	42.32 N	84.26 W
Eden, Ms., U.S.	194	32.59 N	90.19 W
Eden, N.Y., U.S.	210	42.39 N	78.53 W
Eden, Tx., U.S.	196	31.12 N	99.50 W
Eden, Wy., U.S.	200	42.03 N	109.26 W
Eden ≃, Eng., U.K.	42	51.10 N	0.11 E
Eden ≃, Eng., U.K.	44	54.57 N	3.01 W
Eden ≃, Scot., U.K.	46	56.22 N	2.50 W
Eden ≃, Wales, U.K.	42	52.48 N	3.53 W
Edenbridge	260	51.12 N	0.04 E
Edenburg	158	29.45 S	25.56 E
Eden Canyon V	282	37.42 N	122.01 W
Edendale, N.Z.	172	46.19 S	168.47 E
Edendale, S. Afr.	158	29.39 S	30.18 E
Edendale, S. Afr.	273d	26.09 S	28.09 E
Edenderry	48	53.20 N	7.03 W
Edenfield	262	53.40 N	2.18 W
Eden Hill ∧[2]	207	41.20 N	73.19 W
Edenkoben	56	49.17 N	8.07 E
Eden Lake ⊜	184	56.38 N	100.15 W
Eden Mills	212	43.35 N	80.09 W
Eden Park ◆[8]	260	51.23 N	0.02 W
Edenside V	44	54.40 N	2.35 W
Edenton	192	36.03 N	76.36 W
Edenvale	273d	26.08 S	28.09 E
Eden Valley, Austl.	168b	34.39 S	139.06 E

Nom	Page	Lat.°′	Long.°′ W = Ouest
Eden Valley, Mn., U.S.	190	45.19 N	94.32 W
Edenville	158	27.37 S	27.34 E
Edeowie	166	31.27 S	138.27 E
Eder ≃	56	51.13 N	9.27 E
Ederkopf ∧	56	50.56 N	8.12 E
Ederny	48	54.32 N	7.39 W
Edersee ⊜[1]	56	51.11 N	9.00 E
Eder-Talsperre ◆[6]	56	51.11 N	9.02 E
Edesheim	56	49.16 N	8.08 E
Edessa → Édhessa	38	40.48 N	22.03 E
Edewecht	52	53.07 N	8.02 E
Edfu → Idfū	140	24.58 N	32.52 E
Edgar, Ne., U.S.	198	40.22 N	97.58 W
Edgar, Wi., U.S.	190	44.55 N	89.57 W
Edgard	194	30.03 N	90.34 W
Edgar Ranges ⋏	162	18.43 S	123.25 E
Edgars Creek ≃	274b	37.44 S	144.58 E
Edgartown	207	41.23 N	70.30 W
Edgartown Harbor c	207	41.24 N	70.30 W
Edgecliff	222	32.39 N	97.22 W
Edgecumbe	172	37.59 S	176.50 E
Edgefield	192	33.47 N	81.55 W
Edge Hill ◆[8]	262	53.24 N	2.57 W
Edge Hill ∧[2]	42	52.08 N	1.27 W
Edgeley, On., Can.	275b	43.48 N	79.31 W
Edgeley, N.D., U.S.	198	46.21 N	98.42 W
Edgely	285	40.07 N	74.50 W
Edgemere	208	39.14 N	76.26 W
Edgemont, Ca., U.S.	228	33.53 N	117.18 W
Edgemont, Pa., U.S.	285	39.57 N	75.27 W
Edgemont, S.D., U.S.	198	43.18 N	103.49 W
Edgemont Park	216	42.44 N	84.36 W
Edgemoor	285	39.45 N	75.30 W
Edge Mountain ∧	180	58.12 N	152.06 W
Edgeøya I	12	77.45 N	22.30 E
Edgeroi	166	30.07 S	149.48 E
Edgerton, Ab., Can.	184	52.45 N	110.27 W
Edgerton, In., U.S.	216	41.05 N	84.49 W
Edgerton, Mn., U.S.	198	43.52 N	96.07 W
Edgerton, Oh., U.S.	216	41.26 N	84.44 W
Edgerton, Wi., U.S.	216	42.50 N	89.04 W
Edgerton, Wy., U.S.	200	43.24 N	106.14 W
Edgewater, Al., U.S.	194	33.31 N	86.57 W
Edgewater, Fl., U.S.	220	28.59 N	80.54 W
Edgewater, N.J., U.S.	276	40.50 N	73.58 W
Edgewater Park	285	40.04 N	74.54 W
Edgewater Park ♠	279a	41.29 N	81.43 W
Edgewater Point ≻	276	40.55 N	73.44 W
Edgewood, B.C., Can.	182	49.47 N	118.08 W
Edgewood, Fl., U.S.	220	28.29 N	81.22 W
Edgewood, Il., U.S.	219	38.55 N	88.40 W
Edgewood, In., U.S.	218	40.06 N	85.44 W
Edgewood, Ia., U.S.	190	42.38 N	91.24 W
Edgewood, Md., U.S.	208	39.25 N	76.17 W
Edgewood, Oh., U.S.	214	41.52 N	80.46 W
Edgewood, Pa., U.S.	279b	40.25 N	79.52 W
Edgewood, Tx., U.S.	222	32.42 N	95.53 W
Edgeworth	214	40.33 N	80.11 W
Edgeworthstown → Mostrim	48	53.42 N	7.36 W
Edgware ◆[8]	260	51.37 N	0.17 W
Edgworth	262	53.39 N	2.24 W
Édhessa	38	40.48 N	22.03 E
Ediger	56	50.06 N	7.09 E
Edimbourg → Edinburgh	46	55.57 N	3.13 W
Edimburgo → Edinburgh	46	55.57 N	3.13 W
Edina, Liber.	150	6.01 N	10.10 W
Edina, Mn., U.S.	190	44.53 N	93.20 W
Edina, Mo., U.S.	219	40.10 N	92.10 W
Edinboro	214	41.52 N	80.07 W
Edinboro Lake ⊜	214	41.53 N	80.08 W
Edinburg, Il., U.S.	219	39.39 N	89.23 W
Edinburg, In., U.S.	218	39.21 N	85.58 W
Edinburg, Ms., U.S.	194	32.47 N	89.20 W
Edinburg, N.Y., U.S.	210	43.13 N	74.07 W
Edinburg, N.D., U.S.	198	48.29 N	97.51 W
Edinburg, Oh., U.S.	214	41.06 N	81.09 W
Edinburg, Tx., U.S.	196	26.18 N	98.09 W
Edinburg, Va., U.S.	188	38.49 N	78.33 W
Edinburgh	46	55.57 N	3.13 W
Edinburgh (Turnhouse) Airport ⊠	46	55.57 N	3.21 W
Edinburgh Castle ⊥	46	55.56 N	3.14 W
Edinburgh Channel ʮ	236	14.45 N	82.40 W
Edinburgh Mountain ∧	224	48.38 N	124.24 W
Edinburgh Reef ⊤[2]	236	14.50 N	82.39 W
Edincik	130	40.20 N	27.51 E
Edingen → Enghien	50	50.42 N	4.02 E
Edirne	130	41.40 N	26.34 E
Edirne □[4]	130	41.20 N	26.40 E
Edison, Ga., U.S.	192	31.33 N	84.44 W
Edison, N.J., U.S.	210	40.27 N	74.18 W
Edison, Oh., U.S.	214	40.33 N	82.51 W
Edison, Pa., U.S.	208	40.17 N	75.07 W
Edison Bridge ◆[5]	214	41.27 N	82.49 W
Edison National Historic Site ⊥	276	40.47 N	74.14 W
Edison Park ◆[8]	278	42.01 N	87.49 W
Edisseja	84	44.03 N	44.33 E
Edisto ≃	192	32.39 N	80.24 W
Edisto, North Fork ≃	192	33.16 N	80.53 W
Edisto, South Fork ≃	192	33.16 N	80.53 W
Edisto Island I	192	32.35 N	80.20 W
Edith	170	33.48 S	149.55 E
Edith, Mount ∧	202	46.26 N	111.11 W
Edithburgh	168b	35.06 S	137.44 E
Edith Cavell, Mount ∧	182	52.40 N	118.03 W
Edith River	164	14.11 S	132.02 E
Edithvale	274b	38.02 S	145.07 E
Edith Weston	42	52.37 N	0.37 W
Edjejou, Oued i-n- V	148	22.46 N	4.05 E
Edjeleh	148	27.38 N	9.50 E
Edjerir ≃	150	18.06 N	0.50 E
Edjudina	162	29.48 S	122.23 E
Edmeston	210	42.41 N	75.14 W
Edmond	196	35.39 N	97.28 W
Edmondbyers	44	54.51 N	1.58 W
Edmonds	224	47.48 N	122.22 W
Edmondson Heights	284b	39.18 N	76.43 W
Edmonston	284c	38.57 N	76.56 W
Edmonton, Austl.	166	17.01 S	145.45 E
Edmonton, Ab., Can.	182	53.33 N	113.28 W
Edmonton, Ky., U.S.	194	36.58 N	85.36 W
Edmonton ◆[8]	260	51.37 N	0.04 W
Edmore, Mi., U.S.	190	43.24 N	85.02 W
Edmore, N.D., U.S.	198	48.24 N	98.27 W
Edmund	162	23.46 S	116.02 E
Edmund Lake ⊜	184	54.45 N	93.15 W
Edmundson Acres	228	35.14 N	118.49 W
Edmundston	186	47.22 N	68.20 W
Edna, Ks., U.S.	198	37.03 N	95.21 W
Edna, Pa., U.S.	279b	40.19 N	79.39 W
Edna, Tx., U.S.	222	28.58 N	96.38 W
Edna Bay	180	55.57 N	133.40 W
Ednor	208	39.09 N	76.59 W
Edo ≃	94	35.37 N	139.53 E
Edogawa ◆[8]	268	35.42 N	139.52 E
Edolo	64	46.11 N	10.20 E
Edom	222	32.22 N	95.37 W
Edon	216	41.33 N	84.46 W
Edosaki	94	35.57 N	140.19 E
Edremit	130	39.35 N	27.01 E
Edremit Körfezi c	130	39.30 N	26.45 E
Edrengijn nuruu ⋏	102	44.15 N	97.45 E
Edsall Park	284c	38.48 N	77.11 W
Edsbro	40	59.54 N	18.29 E
Edsbruk	26	58.02 N	16.28 E
Edsbyn	26	61.23 N	15.49 E
Edsgatan	40	59.26 N	13.33 E
Edson	182	53.35 N	116.26 W
Edson Butte ∧	202	42.52 N	124.20 W
Eduardo Castex	252	35.54 S	64.18 W

Nome	Página	Lat.°′	Long.°′ W = Oeste
Eduardo VII, Península → Edward VII Peninsula ≻[1]	9	77.40 S	155.00 W
Eduni, Mount ∧	180	64.15 N	128.04 W
Edward ≃, Austl.	164	14.44 S	141.35 E
Edward ≃, Austl.	166	35.33 S	144.58 E
Edward, Lake ⊜	154	0.25 S	29.30 E
Edward, Mount ∧	162	23.22 S	131.55 E
Edwardes Park ♠	274b	37.43 S	145.00 E
Edward Island I	190	48.24 N	88.36 W
Edward River Aboriginal Reserve ◆[4]	164	14.30 S	141.45 E
Edwards, Ca., U.S.	228	34.54 N	117.53 W
Edwards, Ms., U.S.	194	32.19 N	90.36 W
Edwards, N.Y., U.S.	212	44.19 N	75.15 W
Edwards ≃	190	41.09 N	90.59 W
Edwards Air Force Base ■	228	34.54 N	117.52 W
Edwards Airport ⊠	276	40.45 N	73.03 W
Edwardsburg	216	41.47 N	86.04 W
Edwards Butte ∧	224	45.23 N	123.41 W
Edwards Gardens ♠	275b	43.44 N	79.22 W
Edwards Plateau ⋏[1]	196	31.20 N	101.00 W
Edwards Point ≻	169	38.13 S	144.42 E
Edwards Run ≃	285	39.48 N	75.12 W
Edwardsville, Il., U.S.	219	38.48 N	89.57 W
Edwardsville, In., U.S.	218	38.16 N	85.55 W
Edwardsville, Pa., U.S.	210	41.16 N	75.55 W
Edward VIII Bay c	9	66.50 S	57.00 E
Edward VII Peninsula ≻[1]	9	77.40 S	155.00 W
Edwinstowe	44	53.12 N	1.04 W
Edzell	46	56.48 N	2.39 W
Edziza, Mount ∧	180	57.40 N	130.36 W
Eede	52	51.15 N	3.28 E
Eefde	52	52.10 N	6.14 E
Eek	180	60.12 N	162.15 W
Eek ≃	180	60.12 N	162.15 W
Eeklo	50	51.11 N	3.34 E
Eel ≃, Ca., U.S.	204	40.40 N	124.20 W
Eel ≃, In., U.S.	194	39.07 N	86.57 W
Eel ≃, In., U.S.	216	40.45 N	86.22 W
Eel, Middle Fork ≃	204	39.42 N	123.21 W
Eel, North Fork ≃	204	39.57 N	123.26 W
Eel, South Fork ≃	204	40.22 N	123.55 W
Eel Bay c	212	44.19 N	76.02 W
Eelde	52	53.07 N	6.35 E
Eels Creek ≃	212	44.35 N	78.03 W
Eels Lake ⊜	212	44.54 N	78.08 W
Eemskanaal ≅	52	53.15 N	6.45 E
Eerbeek	52	52.07 N	6.04 E
Eersel	52	51.22 N	5.19 E
Eexta	52	53.10 N	6.59 E
Efate □[8]	175f	17.45 S	168.20 E
Éfaté I	175f	17.40 S	168.25 E
Eferding	61	48.18 N	14.02 E
Efes (Ephesus) ⊥	130	37.55 N	27.17 E
Effigy Mounds National Monument ♠	190	43.06 N	91.13 W
Effingham, Eng., U.K.	260	51.16 N	0.24 W
Effingham, Il., U.S.	194	39.07 N	88.32 W
Effingham, Ks., U.S.	198	39.31 N	95.24 W
Effingham □[6]	219	39.07 N	88.33 W
Effingham Lake ⊜	212	44.59 N	77.22 W
Effort	210	40.56 N	75.26 W
Efiduasi	150	6.51 N	1.24 W
Efkere	130	38.47 N	35.40 E
Eflâni	130	41.26 N	32.57 E
Eforie Nord	38	44.06 N	28.38 E
Eforie Sud	38	44.03 N	28.38 E
Efringen-Kirchen	58	47.49 N	7.35 E
Ega ≃	34	42.19 N	1.55 W
Egadi, Isole II	70	37.58 N	12.16 E
Egan	222	32.28 N	97.17 W
Egaña	252	36.59 S	59.06 W
Egan Range ⋏	204	39.10 N	114.55 W
Eganville	190	45.32 N	77.06 W
Egau ≃	58	48.36 N	10.34 E
Egba □[8]	273a	6.41 N	3.23 E
Egbe, Nig.	150	8.16 N	5.31 E
Egbe, Nig.	273a	6.33 N	3.17 E
Egbunda	154	2.44 N	27.12 E
Egedesminde (Aasiaat)	176	68.42 N	52.45 W
Égée, Mer → Aegean Sea ⊤[2]	38	38.30 N	25.00 E
Egegik	180	58.13 N	157.22 W
Egeln	54	51.56 N	11.25 E
Egeo, Mar → Aegean Sea ⊤[2]	38	38.30 N	25.00 E
Eger → Cheb, Česko.	54	50.01 N	12.25 E
Eger, Magy.	30	47.54 N	20.23 E
Eger ≃, B.R.D.	56	48.50 N	10.37 E
Eger (Ohře) ≃, Europe	54	50.32 N	14.08 E
Egeria Mountain ∧	182	53.55 N	130.22 W
Egernsund	41	54.54 N	9.37 E
Egerpohl	263	51.07 N	7.27 E
Egersund	26	58.27 N	6.00 E
Egerton	262	53.38 N	2.26 W
Egerton, Mount ∧	9	80.50 S	158.50 E
Egeskov ⊥	41	55.10 N	10.30 E
Egestorf	52	53.11 N	10.04 E
Egestorf [am Süntel]	52	52.17 N	9.31 E
Egg	58	47.26 N	9.54 E
Egg Creek ≃	198	48.22 N	100.47 W
Egge ⋏	52	51.40 N	8.55 E
Eggebek	41	54.37 N	9.22 E
Eggelsberg	60	48.05 N	13.00 E
Eggenberg, Schloss ⊥	61	47.05 N	15.25 E
Eggenburg	61	48.39 N	15.50 E
Eggenfelden	60	48.25 N	12.46 E
Eggenstein-Leopoldshafen	56	49.04 N	8.23 E
Eggerscheid	263	51.19 N	6.53 E
Eggersdorf	54	52.32 N	13.49 E
Eggesin	54	53.41 N	14.05 E
Egg Harbor City	208	39.31 N	74.38 W
Egg Island Point ≻	208	39.11 N	75.08 W
Egg Lagoon	166	39.39 S	143.58 E
Egg Lake ⊜, Mb., Can.	184	54.21 N	101.26 W
Egg Lake ⊜, Sk., Can.	184	55.05 N	105.30 W
Egglestone Abbey ʊ[1]	44	54.32 N	1.54 W
Egglham	60	48.32 N	13.04 E
Egglkofen	60	48.24 N	12.27 E
Eggmühl	60	48.51 N	12.11 E
Egham	260	51.26 N	0.34 W
Egherta	144	2.04 N	43.11 E
Éghezée	56	50.36 N	4.54 E
Egijn ≃	88	49.24 N	103.36 E
Eğil	130	38.15 N	40.05 E
Egilsay I	46	59.09 N	2.56 W
Egilsstaðir	24a	65.16 N	14.18 W
Eging	60	48.43 N	13.16 E
Egipto → Egypt □[1]	140	27.00 N	30.00 E
Égletons	32	45.24 N	2.03 E
Eglin Air Force Base ■	194	30.29 N	86.30 W
Eglinton	48	55.02 N	7.11 W
Eglisau	58	47.34 N	8.32 E
Egloskerry	42	50.39 N	4.27 W
Égly	261	48.35 N	2.13 E
Egmond aan Zee	52	52.36 N	4.37 E
Egmond-Binnen	52	52.35 N	4.39 E
Egmont, Cape ≻	172	39.17 S	173.45 E
Egmont, Mount → Taranaki, Mount ∧	172	39.18 S	174.04 E
Egmont Bay c	186	46.35 N	64.12 W
Egmont Channel ʮ	220	27.36 N	82.45 W
Egmont Key I	220	27.35 N	82.46 W
Egmont National Park ♠	172	39.15 S	174.05 E

Egna (Neumarkt)	64	46.19 N	11.16 E
Egnach	58	47.33 N	9.23 E
Egnazia ⊥	68	40.53 N	17.24 E
Egoryevsk → Jegorjevsk	82	55.23 N	39.02 E
Egota ◆[8]	268	35.43 N	139.40 E
Egra	126	21.54 N	87.32 E
Egremont, Ab., Can.	182	54.02 N	113.08 W
Egremont, Eng., U.K.	44	54.29 N	3.33 W
Égreville	50	48.10 N	2.52 E
Eğridir	130	37.52 N	30.51 E
Eğridir Gölü ⊜	130	38.02 N	30.53 E
Eğriköy	130	38.44 N	27.21 E
Egrisskij chrebet ⋏	84	42.49 N	42.24 E
Egton	44	54.26 N	0.45 W
Egtved	41	55.37 N	9.18 E
Éguas, Rio das ≃	255	13.26 S	44.14 W
Éguilles	62	43.34 N	5.22 E
Eguisheim	58	48.03 N	7.18 E
Egum Atoll I[1]	164	9.25 S	151.55 E
Egvekinot	180	66.19 N	179.10 W
Egyházasrádóc	61	47.05 N	16.37 E
Egypt, Ma., U.S.	207	42.12 N	70.45 W
Egypt, Pa., U.S.	208	40.41 N	75.32 W
Egypt, Tx., U.S.	222	29.24 N	96.14 W
Egypt (Miṣr) □[1], Afr.	136	27.00 N	30.00 E
Egypt (Miṣr) □[1], Afr.	140	27.00 N	30.00 E
Egypt, Lake of ⊜[1]	194	37.35 N	88.55 W
Égypte → Egypt □[1]	140	27.00 N	30.00 E
Egyptian Museum ʊ	273c	30.03 N	31.14 E
Eha-Amufu	150	6.40 N	7.46 E
Ehekirchen	60	48.38 N	11.06 E
Ehen ≃	44	54.25 N	3.30 W
Ehime □[5]	96	33.40 N	132.50 E
Ehingen	58	48.17 N	9.43 E
Ehingen ◆[8]	263	51.22 N	6.42 E
Ehle ≃	54	52.12 N	11.44 E
Ehmen	54	52.24 N	10.41 E
Ehra-Lessien	54	52.34 N	10.46 E
Ehrang	56	49.49 N	6.41 E
Ehrenberg	200	33.36 N	114.31 W
Ehrenberg Range ⋏	162	23.18 S	130.20 E
Ehrenbreitstein, Feste ⊥	56	50.21 N	7.37 E
Ehrenburg ⊥	56	50.12 N	7.27 E
Ehrenfeld	214	40.22 N	78.46 W
Ehrenfriedersdorf	54	50.38 N	12.58 E
Ehrenhausen	61	46.43 N	15.35 E
Ehreshoven	56	50.58 N	7.20 E
Ehrhardt	192	33.05 N	81.00 W
Ehrhorn	52	53.10 N	9.53 E
Ehringhausen	263	51.11 N	7.33 E
Ehringhausen ◆[8]	263	51.09 N	7.11 E
Ehrwald	58	47.24 N	10.55 E
Ehwa Women's University ʊ[2]	271b	37.34 N	126.56 E
Ei	92	31.12 N	130.30 E
Eibar	34	43.11 N	2.28 W
Eibau	54	50.58 N	14.40 E
Eibelstadt	56	49.43 N	10.00 E
Eibenstock	54	50.29 N	12.35 E
Eibergen	52	52.06 N	6.39 E
Eibiswald	61	46.41 N	15.15 E
Eibsee ⊜	64	47.27 N	10.58 E
Eicha	54	50.21 N	10.34 E
Eich-Berg ∧[2]	264a	52.39 N	13.50 E
Eiche, D.D.R.	264a	52.34 N	13.36 E
Eiche, D.D.R.	264a	52.25 N	12.58 E
Eichenbarleben	54	52.10 N	11.24 E
Eichenbrandt	264a	52.38 N	13.51 E
Eichendorf	60	48.38 N	12.51 E
Eichgraben	61	48.10 N	15.59 E
Eichlinghofen ◆[8]	263	51.29 N	7.24 E
Eichsfeld ◆[1]	56	51.25 N	10.20 E
Eichstädt	264a	52.42 N	13.07 E
Eichstätt	60	48.54 N	11.12 E
Eichstetten	58	48.05 N	7.44 E
Eichtersheim	56	49.14 N	8.46 E
Eichwalde	54	52.22 N	13.37 E
Eickelborn	52	51.39 N	8.13 E
Eicken ◆[8]	263	51.13 N	6.26 E
Eickerend	263	51.13 N	6.34 E
Eickerkopf ∧[2]	263	51.21 N	7.42 E
Eicklingen	52	52.33 N	10.10 E
Eide	26	62.55 N	7.26 E
Eidelstedt ◆[8]	52	53.36 N	9.53 E
Eider ≃	41	54.19 N	8.58 E
Eiderstedt ≻[1]	41	54.22 N	8.50 E
Eidfjord	26	60.28 N	7.05 E
Eidsvåg, Nor.	26	62.47 N	8.03 E
Eidsvåg, Nor.	26	60.27 N	5.21 E
Eidsvold	166	25.22 S	151.07 E
Eidsvoll	26	60.19 N	11.14 E
Eifa	56	50.58 N	8.34 E
Eifel ⋏	56	50.15 N	6.45 E
Eiffel, Tour ⊥	261	48.51 N	2.18 E
Eiffel Flats	154	18.15 S	29.59 E
Eifgenbach ≃	263	51.05 N	7.09 E
Eige, Carn ∧	46	57.17 N	5.07 W
Eigen ◆[8]	263	51.33 N	6.57 E
Eigenji	94	35.04 N	136.18 E
Eigenrieden	54	51.11 N	10.22 E
Eiger ∧	58	46.35 N	8.00 E
Eigg I	46	56.54 N	6.10 W
Eigg, Sound of ʮ	46	56.51 N	6.13 W
Eight Degree Channel ʮ	122	8.00 N	73.00 E
Eighteenmile Creek ≃, N.Y., U.S.	210	43.21 N	78.43 W
Eighteenmile Creek ≃, N.Y., U.S.	210	42.43 N	78.58 W
Eight Mile Creek ≃, On., Can.	284a	43.14 N	79.11 W
Eightmile Creek ≃, In., U.S.	216	40.57 N	85.22 W
Eightmile Creek ≃, Or., U.S.	224	45.36 N	121.05 W
Eights Coast ⊻[2]	9	73.30 S	93.00 W
Eighty Four	279b	40.11 N	80.08 W
Eighty Mile Beach ⊻[2]	162	19.45 S	121.00 E
Eiheiji	94	36.05 N	136.20 E
Eijerlandsche Gat c	52	53.12 N	4.50 E
Eijsden	56	50.47 N	5.43 E
Eikeren ⊜	26	59.38 N	9.58 E
Eikisdalsvatnet ⊜	26	62.34 N	8.11 E
Eildon	169	37.14 S	145.56 E
Eildon, Lake ⊜[1]	169	37.11 S	145.55 E
Eilean Gowan Island I	212	45.02 N	79.25 W
Eileen	216	41.17 N	88.15 W
Eilenburg	54	51.27 N	12.37 E
Eil Malk I	175b	7.09 N	134.22 E
Eilpe ◆[8]	263	51.21 N	7.29 E
Eilsleben	54	52.09 N	11.13 E
Eimbeckhausen	52	52.14 N	9.25 E
Eimke	52	52.58 N	10.19 E
Eina	26	60.38 N	10.36 E
Einasleigh	166	18.31 S	144.05 E
Einasleigh ≃	166	17.30 S	142.17 E
Einbeck	52	51.49 N	9.52 E
Eindhoven	52	51.26 N	5.28 E
Eine	50	50.52 N	3.37 E
Einme	110	16.54 N	95.11 E
Einöd	56	49.16 N	7.19 E
Einödriegel ∧	60	48.56 N	13.02 E
Einruhr	56	50.35 N	6.22 E
Einsiedel	54	50.46 N	12.58 E
Einsiedeln	58	47.08 N	8.45 E
Einville-au-Jard	58	48.39 N	6.30 E
Eirauli	272c	19.10 N	72.59 E
Éire → Ireland □[1]	48	53.00 N	8.00 W
Eiru ≃	248	6.42 S	69.52 W
Eirunepé	248	6.40 S	69.52 W
Eisbach ≃	56	49.38 N	8.22 E
Eisch ≃	56	49.45 N	6.07 E
Eiseb ≃	156	20.33 S	20.59 E
Eisenach	54	50.59 N	10.19 E
Eisenberg, B.R.D.	56	49.38 N	8.05 E
Eisenberg, D.D.R.	54	50.58 N	11.53 E
Eisenberg ∧[2]	61	47.12 N	16.24 E
Eisenerz	61	47.33 N	14.53 E
Eisenerzer Alpen ⋏	61	47.28 N	14.45 E

Eisenhower Center ʊ	198	38.54 N	97.12 W
Eisenhower Memorial Park ♠	276	40.44 N	73.34 W
Eisenhüttenstadt	54	52.10 N	14.39 E
Eisenkappel	61	46.29 N	14.35 E
Eisenschmitt	56	50.03 N	6.43 E
Eisenstadt	61	47.51 N	16.32 E
Eisfeld	54	50.26 N	10.54 E
Eisgarn	61	48.54 N	15.06 E
Eishken	46	58.01 N	6.32 W
Eishort, Loch c	46	57.10 N	5.59 W
Eišiškės	76	54.10 N	25.00 E
Eisk → Jejsk	78	46.42 N	38.16 E
Eisleben	54	51.31 N	11.32 E
Eislingen	56	48.42 N	9.42 E
Eisriesenwelt ⊻[5]	64	47.32 N	13.10 E
Eita	174t	1.21 N	173.05 E
Eitorf	56	50.46 N	7.26 E
Eivissa	34	38.54 N	1.26 E
Eivissa (Ibiza) I	34	39.00 N	1.25 E
Ejasi → Eyasi, Lake ⊜	154	3.40 S	35.05 E
Ejby, Dan.	41	55.30 N	12.07 E
Ejby, Dan.	41	55.26 N	9.57 E
Ejea de los Caballeros	34	42.08 N	1.08 W
Ejeda	157b	24.20 S	44.31 E
Ejido	246	8.33 N	71.14 W
Ejigbo	273a	6.33 N	3.18 E
Ejin Horo Qi	102	39.27 N	109.40 E
Ejin Qi	102	41.50 N	100.50 E
Ejstrup	41	55.59 N	9.17 E
Ejura	150	7.23 N	1.22 W
Ejutla de Crespo	234	16.34 N	96.44 W
Ekalaka	198	45.53 N	104.33 W
Ekáli	267c	38.07 N	23.50 E
Ekanga	152	2.23 S	23.14 E
Ekas	115b	8.53 S	116.27 E
Ekaterinburg → Sverdlovsk	86	56.51 N	60.36 E
Ekaterinodar → Krasnodar	78	45.02 N	39.00 E
Ekaterinoslav → Dnepropetrovsk	78	48.27 N	34.59 E
Ekeby	41	56.00 N	12.58 E
Ekenäs (Taamisaari)	26	59.58 N	23.26 E
Ekenässjön	26	57.30 N	15.00 E
Ekerö I	40	59.18 N	17.43 E
Eket, Nig.	150	4.39 N	7.56 E
Eket, Sve.	41	56.15 N	13.11 E
Eketahuna	172	40.39 S	175.42 E
Ekhínos	38	41.17 N	24.59 E
Ekiatapskij chrebet ⋏	74	68.30 N	179.00 E
Ekibastuz	86	51.42 N	75.22 E
Ekimčan	89	53.04 N	132.58 E
Ekitykskij chrebet ⋏	180	67.45 N	179.00 E
Eko → Lagos	150	6.27 N	3.24 E
Ekoli	152	0.23 S	24.16 E
Ekoln ⊜	40	59.45 N	17.37 E
Ekolsund	40	59.37 N	17.22 E
Ekolsundsviken c	40	59.35 N	17.24 E
Ekombe	152	1.16 N	21.36 E
Ekonda	74	65.47 N	105.17 E
Ekoungounou	152	0.33 S	15.38 E
Ekovamou	152	0.07 N	16.31 E
Ekpoma	150	6.46 N	6.08 E
Eksāra	272b	22.38 N	88.17 E
Eksel	56	51.09 N	5.23 E
Eksjö	26	57.40 N	14.57 E
Ekuk	180	58.49 N	158.34 W
Ekuku	152	0.42 S	21.38 E
Ekuta	152	2.59 N	18.42 E
Ekwan ≃	176	53.14 N	82.13 W
Ekwata	152	0.13 S	9.18 E
Ekwendeni	154	11.23 S	33.50 E
Ekwok	180	59.22 N	157.30 W
El- → Ad-, Al-, An-, Ar-, As-, Ash-, At-, Az-			
Ela	110	19.37 N	96.13 E
El Aaiún (La'youn)	148	27.09 N	13.12 W
El Abiadh Sidi Cheikh	148	32.56 N	0.42 E
El 'Açâba □[4]	150	16.10 N	11.30 W
El 'Açâba ⋏[1]	150	16.00 N	12.00 W
El-Adde	144	2.35 N	46.09 E
El Adeb Larache	148	27.22 N	8.52 E
El Adelanto	236	14.10 N	89.50 W
El Affroun	34	36.30 N	2.38 E
El Agreb	148	30.48 N	5.30 E
El Aguacate	286c	10.28 N	66.59 W
El Aguilar	252	23.12 S	65.42 W
Elaía	38	39.35 N	20.20 E
Elaine	194	34.18 N	90.51 W
El Alamein → Al-'Alamayn	140	30.49 N	28.57 E
El Álamo, Méx.	196	26.29 N	99.46 W
El Álamo, Méx.	196	27.32 N	100.52 W
El Álamo, Méx.	204	31.34 N	116.02 W
El Alia	36	37.10 N	10.03 E
El Alto, Chile	286e	33.30 S	70.43 W
El Alto, Perú	246	4.18 S	81.07 W
Elam	285	39.51 N	75.32 W
Elamanchili	122	17.33 N	82.52 E
El Amparo de Apure	246	7.06 N	70.45 W
Elan ≃	38	46.07 N	28.04 E
Élancourt	261	48.47 N	1.58 E
Elands ≃, S. Afr.	156	25.10 S	29.10 E
Elands ≃, S. Afr.	158	25.31 S	26.39 E
Elandsbaai	158	32.19 S	18.21 E
Elandsfontein	273d	26.10 S	28.12 E
Elandsvlei	158	32.19 S	19.33 E
El Angel	246	0.37 N	77.56 W
Elanora Heights	274a	33.42 S	151.17 E
El Aouinet	36	35.52 N	7.54 E
El Arahal	34	37.16 N	5.33 W
El Arba	34	36.37 N	3.13 E
El Arco	232	28.00 N	113.25 W
El Arenal	234	20.47 N	103.42 W
El Aricha	148	34.09 N	1.10 W
El Aroussa	36	36.22 N	9.28 E
El Arrayán	286e	33.21 S	70.28 W
Elassón	38	39.54 N	22.11 E
Elat	132	29.33 N	34.57 E
Elat, Gulf of → Aqaba, Gulf of c	128	29.00 N	34.40 E
Elat, Sede Te'Ufa ⊠	132	29.34 N	34.55 E
El Avagi	144	3.36 N	46.57 E
El Avila, Cerro ∧	286c	10.33 N	66.52 W
El Ávila, Parque Nacional ♠	246	10.35 N	66.48 W
El Avión	232	24.08 N	106.59 W
Elazığ	130	38.41 N	39.14 E
Elazığ □[4]	130	38.35 N	39.30 E
El Azúcar, Presa de ⊜[1]	196	26.10 N	99.00 W
El Azul, Sierra ⋏	234	23.25 N	100.30 W
Elba, Al., U.S.	194	31.24 N	86.04 W
Elba, Mi., U.S.	216	43.02 N	83.26 W
Elba, N.Y., U.S.	210	43.04 N	78.11 W
Elba → Elbe ≃	30	53.50 N	9.00 E
Elba, Isola d' I	66	42.46 N	10.17 E
El'ban	89	50.06 N	136.31 E
El Banco	246	9.00 N	73.58 W
El Barco de Avila	34	40.21 N	5.31 W
El Barco de Valdeorras	34	42.25 N	6.59 W
El Barreal	200	31.17 N	107.10 W
El Barril	234	23.02 N	102.08 W
El Barrio	234	16.48 N	95.15 W
Elbasan	38	41.06 N	20.05 E
Elbaşı	130	38.41 N	35.59 E
El Baúl	246	8.57 N	68.17 W
Elbe	224	46.45 N	121.49 W
Elbe (Labe) ≃	30	53.50 N	9.00 E
Elbe, Île d' → Elba, Isola di I	66	42.46 N	10.17 E
Elbe-Havel-Kanal ≅	54	52.24 N	12.23 E
El Beïd (Ebeji) ≃	146	12.32 N	14.11 E

El-Beida → Al-Bayḍā'	146	32.46 N	21.43 E
Elbe-Lübeck-Kanal ≅	54	53.50 N	10.36 E
Elberfeld ◆[8]	263	51.16 N	7.08 E
Elbert	198	39.13 N	104.32 W
Elbert, Mount ∧	200	39.07 N	106.27 W
Elberta	190	44.37 N	86.13 W
Elberton	192	34.06 N	82.52 W
Elbeuf	50	49.17 N	1.00 E
Elbeyli	130	36.41 N	37.26 E
El Beyyadh	148	33.40 N	1.01 E
Elbing → Elbląg	30	54.10 N	19.25 E
Elbingerode	54	51.45 N	10.46 E
Elbistan	130	38.13 N	37.12 E
Elbląg (Elbing)	30	54.10 N	19.25 E
Elbląg □[4]	30	54.00 N	19.30 E
El Bluff	236	11.59 N	83.40 W
El Bolsón	254	41.58 S	71.31 W
El Bonillo	34	38.57 N	2.32 W
El Bordo	246	2.06 N	76.58 W
El-Borj	34	35.43 N	5.40 W
El-Borouj	148	32.30 N	7.10 W
El Bosque	234	17.04 N	92.44 W
El Bosque, Aeropuerto ⊠	286e	33.34 S	70.42 W
El Boulaïda	148	36.28 N	2.50 E
El Boulaïda □[5]	148	36.20 N	2.20 E
Elbow	184	51.07 N	106.35 W
Elbow ≃	182	51.03 N	114.02 W
Elbow Cay I	238	23.57 N	80.29 W
Elbow Lake	198	45.59 N	95.58 W
Elbow Lake ⊜	184	54.50 N	100.53 W
Elbridge	210	43.02 N	76.27 W
El'brus, gora (Mount Elbrus) ∧	84	43.21 N	42.26 E
Elbrus, Mount → El'brus, gora ∧	84	43.21 N	42.26 E
El'brusskij	84	43.38 N	42.10 E
Elbsandsteingebirge ⋏	54	50.50 N	14.20 E
Elburg	52	52.26 N	5.50 E
El Burgo de Osma	34	41.35 N	3.04 W
Elburn	216	41.53 N	88.28 W
Elburz Mountains → Alborz, Reshteh-ye Kūhhā-ye ⋏	128	36.00 N	53.00 E
El'buzd	83	46.53 N	39.41 E
El'buzd ≃	83	46.53 N	39.43 E
El Caburé	252	26.01 S	62.22 W
El Cajon	228	32.47 N	116.57 W
El Callao	246	7.21 N	61.49 W
El Calvario	246	4.22 N	73.40 W
El Calvario ◆[8]	286b	23.05 N	82.20 W
El Calverio	246	8.59 N	67.00 W
El Campamento	240m	18.22 N	66.28 W
El Campamento ◆[8]	266a	40.24 N	3.46 W
El Campo	222	29.11 N	96.16 W
El Capitan ∧, Ca., U.S.	226	37.43 N	119.38 W
El Capitan ∧, Mt., U.S.	202	46.01 N	114.23 W
El Capomo	234	21.17 N	105.13 W
El Caribe	286c	10.37 N	66.50 W
El Carmen, Arg.	252	24.23 S	65.16 W
El Carmen, Bol.	248	18.49 S	58.33 W
El Carmen, Chile	286e	33.21 S	70.43 W
El Carmen, Col.	246	8.30 N	73.27 W
El Carmen, Méx.	234	15.35 N	93.05 W
El Carmen, Méx.	234	19.19 N	97.40 W
El Carmen, Perú	248	13.30 S	76.04 W
El Carmen, Ven.	286c	10.24 N	66.50 W
El Carmen, Ven.	286c	10.24 N	67.01 W
El Carmen, Canal ≅	286e	33.18 S	70.41 W
El Carmen de Bolívar	246	9.43 N	75.08 W
El Carricito	232	28.24 N	103.23 W
El Carril	252	25.05 S	65.28 W
El Carrizal	234	23.00 N	97.50 W
El Carrizo	232	29.58 N	105.16 W
El Casco	196	25.34 N	104.35 W
El Castillo	236	11.01 N	84.24 W
El Cedral	236	16.26 N	90.03 W
El Cedrito	232	29.11 N	101.59 W
El Cenajo, Embalse de ⊜[1]	34	38.25 N	2.00 W
El Centinela	204	32.38 N	115.40 W
El Centinela, Cerro ∧	234	19.13 N	104.17 W
El Centro	204	32.47 N	115.33 W
El Cerrito, Col.	246	3.42 N	76.19 W
El Cerrito, Ca., U.S.	226	37.54 N	122.18 W
El Cerrito, Ca., U.S.	228	37.54 N	122.18 W
El Cerro, Bol.	248	17.31 S	61.34 W
El Cerro, Ur.	258	34.00 S	58.15 W
El Cerro Del Aripo ∧	241r	10.43 N	61.15 W
El Chamal	234	23.56 N	97.54 W
El Chante	234	19.41 N	104.10 W
El Charco Largo	232	24.10 N	97.58 W
Elche → Elx	34	38.15 N	0.42 W
Elche de la Sierra	34	38.27 N	2.03 W
El Chimborazo, Cerro ∧	236	13.05 N	85.58 W
El'chkakvun ≃	180	68.42 N	171.00 E
Elcho	190	45.26 N	89.11 W
Elcho Island I	164	11.55 S	135.45 E
El Cholar	252	37.25 S	70.39 W
El Chorrillo	252	33.18 S	66.16 W
El Ciprés	204	31.50 N	116.38 W
El Coacoyul	234	17.37 N	101.26 W
El Cobre	240p	20.03 N	75.57 W
El Cocuy	246	6.25 N	72.27 W
El Cojo	286c	10.37 N	66.53 W
El Cojo, Quebrada ≃	286c	10.37 N	66.53 W
El Colorado	252	26.18 S	59.22 W
El Colorado, Canal de ≅	286e	33.34 S	70.32 W
El Cóndor, Cerro ∧	252	26.38 S	68.22 W
El Congo	236	13.54 N	89.30 W
El Consuelo	232	31.02 N	111.53 W
El Corazón	246	1.12 S	79.06 W
El Corcovado	254	43.32 S	71.36 W
El Corozo	286c	10.35 N	66.58 W
El Corpus	236	13.16 N	87.03 W
El Corte de Madera Creek ≃	282	37.19 N	122.20 W
El Cortijo	286e	33.22 S	70.42 W
El Coto	240m	18.28 N	66.44 W
El Cotorro ◆[8]	286b	23.03 N	82.16 W
El Coyote	200	30.50 N	112.40 W
El Coyote, Laguna ⊜	196	27.14 N	103.18 W
El Cozón	232	31.18 N	112.29 W
El Cristo	240p	20.07 N	75.45 W
El Cubo → Casigua	246	8.46 N	72.30 W
El Cuco	236	13.10 N	88.07 W
El Cuidado	234	22.20 N	103.07 W
El Cuy	254	39.56 S	68.20 W
Elda	34	38.29 N	0.47 W
Eldagsen	52	52.10 N	9.40 E
El Dambahaddo	144	3.17 N	46.40 E
El Dátil	232	30.07 N	112.15 W
Elde ≃	54	53.14 N	11.27 E
Eldekanal ≅	54	53.24 N	11.36 E
Eldena, D.D.R.	54	53.13 N	11.25 E
Eldena, D.D.R.	54	54.05 N	13.26 E
El Depósito	234	17.44 N	94.23 W
El Der V	144	8.49 N	47.28 E
El Dere	144	5.07 N	43.10 E
Elder Island I	276	40.38 N	73.23 W
Elder Mills	275b	43.49 N	79.38 W
Eldersville	214	40.21 N	80.29 W
Elderton	214	40.42 N	79.21 W
El Descanso	204	32.12 N	116.55 W
El Desemboque, Méx.	232	29.30 N	112.27 W
El Desemboque, Méx.	232	30.30 N	112.59 W
Eldforsen	40	60.26 N	14.13 E
El'dikan	74	60.48 N	135.11 E
Eldingen	52	52.41 N	10.21 E
Eld Inlet c	224	47.04 N	123.01 W
Eldivan	130	40.32 N	33.31 E

≃ River	Fluß	Río	Rivière	Rio
≅ Canal	Kanal	Canal	Canal	Canal
Waterfall, Rapids	Wasserfall, Stromschnellen	Cascada, Rápidos	Chute d'eau, Rapides	Cascata, Rápidos
ʮ Strait	Meeresstraße	Estrecho	Détroit	Estreito
c Bay, Gulf	Bucht, Golf	Bahía, Golfo	Baie, Golfe	Baía, Golfo
⊜ Lake, Lakes	See, Seen	Lago, Lagos	Lac, Lacs	Lago, Lagos
Swamp	Sumpf	Pantano	Marais	Pântano
Ice Features, Glacier	Eis- und Gletscherformen	Accidentes glaciares	Formes glaciaires	Acidentes glaciares
Other Hydrographic Features	Andere Hydrographische Objekte	Otros Elementos Hidrográficos	Autres données hydrographiques	Outros acidentes hidrográficos

⊤ Submarine Features	Untermeerische Objekte	Accidentes Submarinos	Formes de relief sous-marin	Acidentes submarinos
□ Political Unit	Politische Einheit	Unidad Política	Entité politique	Unidade política
ʊ Cultural Institution	Kulturelle Institution	Institución Cultural	Institution culturelle	Instituição cultural
⊥ Historical Site	Historische Stätte	Sitio Histórico	Site historique	Sitio histórico
♠ Recreational Site	Erholungs- und Ferienort	Sitio de Recreo	Centre de loisirs	Area de Lazer
⊠ Airport	Flughafen	Aeropuerto	Aéroport	Aeroporto
■ Military Installation	Militäranlage	Instalación Militar	Installation militaire	Instalação militar
◆ Miscellaneous	Verschiedenes	Misceláneo	Divers	Diversos

ENGLISH — Name | Page | Lat.°′ | Long.°′

DEUTSCH — Name | Seite | Breite°′ | Länge°′ E = Ost

Name	Page	Lat.°′	Long.°′
El Diviso	**246**	1.22 N	78.14 W
El Djazaïr (Algiers)	**148**	36.47 N	3.03 E
El Djazaïr □[5]	**148**	36.50 N	3.00 E
El Djelfa	**148**	34.40 N	3.15 E
El Djelfa □[5]	**148**	35.20 N	3.50 E
Eldon, Ia., U.S.	**190**	40.55 N	92.13 W
Eldon, Mo., U.S.	**194**	38.20 N	92.34 W
Eldon Hazlet State Park ♦	**219**	38.39 N	89.22 W
Eldora, Ia., U.S.	**190**	42.21 N	93.05 W
Eldora, Pa., U.S.	**279b**	40.10 N	79.53 W
Eldorado, Arg.	**252**	26.24 S	54.38 W
Eldorado, Bra.	**252**	24.32 S	48.06 W
El Dorado, Méx.	**232**	24.17 N	107.21 W
El Dorado, Ar., U.S.	**194**	33.12 N	92.39 W
El Dorado, Ca., U.S.	**226**	38.41 N	120.51 W
Eldorado, Il., U.S.	**194**	37.48 N	88.26 W
El Dorado, Ks., U.S.	**198**	37.49 N	96.51 W
Eldorado, Oh., U.S.	**218**	39.54 N	84.40 W
Eldorado, Ok., U.S.	**196**	34.28 N	99.38 W
Eldorado, Tx., U.S.	**196**	30.51 N	100.36 W
El Dorado, Ven.	**246**	6.44 N	61.38 W
El Dorado □[6]	**226**	38.43 N	120.48 W
Eldorado Hills	**226**	38.37 N	120.27 W
Eldoradopark	**273d**	26.18 S	27.53 E
El Dorado Park ♦	**280**	33.49 N	118.05 W
Eldorado Peak ∧	**224**	48.32 N	121.08 W
El Dorado Springs	**194**	37.52 N	94.01 W
Eldoret	**154**	0.31 N	35.17 E
Eldred, Il., U.S.	**219**	39.17 N	90.33 W
Eldred, N.Y., U.S.	**210**	41.32 N	74.53 W
Eldred, Pa., U.S.	**214**	41.57 N	78.23 W
Eldridge	**190**	41.39 N	90.35 W
Eldridge, Mount ∧	**180**	64.46 N	141.48 W
Eldridges Hill	**285**	39.40 N	75.18 W
El Dudu	**144**	2.37 N	41.46 E
Eleanor	**188**	38.32 N	81.55 W
Eleanor, Lake ⊜[1]	**226**	37.59 N	119.51 W
Eleasar	**158**	26.40 S	26.53 E
Electra	**196**	34.01 N	98.55 W
Electric City	**202**	47.56 N	119.02 W
Eleele	**229b**	21.55 N	159.35 W
Elefante, Isla del → Elephant Island I	**9**	61.10 S	55.14 W
Elefantes, Fiordo ⊂[2]	**254**	46.10 S	73.41 W
Elefantes, Rio dos (Olifants) ≏	**156**	24.10 S	32.40 E
Elegest ≏	**88**	51.32 N	94.05 E
El Eglab ⬌[2]	**148**	26.25 N	5.00 W
Elei, Wādī V	**140**	22.04 N	34.27 E
Eleja	**76**	56.26 N	23.42 E
Elektrogorsk	**82**	55.53 N	38.47 E
Elektrostal'	**82**	55.47 N	38.28 E
Elektrougli	**82**	55.43 N	38.13 E
Elektrozavod	**80**	52.34 N	54.01 E
Elele	**150**	5.07 N	6.48 E
Elena	**38**	42.56 N	25.53 E
El Encantado	**286c**	10.27 N	66.47 W
El Encanto, Col.	**246**	1.37 S	73.14 W
El Encanto, Guat.	**232**	17.17 N	89.34 W
Elend	**54**	51.44 N	10.41 E
Elepete	**273a**	6.41 N	3.28 E
Elephant, Mount ∧[2]	**169**	37.58 S	143.12 E
Elephanta Caves ⏏[5]	**272c**	18.58 N	72.56 E
Elephanta Island (Ghārāpuri) I	**272c**	18.57 N	72.55 E
Elephant Butte Lake State Park ♦	**200**	33.11 N	107.14 W
Elephant Butte Reservoir ⊜[1]	**200**	33.19 N	107.10 W
Elephant Island I	**9**	61.10 S	55.14 W
Elephant Lake ⊜	**212**	45.08 N	78.07 W
Elephant Mountain ∧	**188**	44.46 N	70.46 W
Elesbão Veloso	**250**	6.13 S	42.08 W
Eleşkirt	**130**	39.48 N	42.42 E
El Estor	**236**	15.32 N	89.21 W
El Estribo	**234**	22.26 N	99.17 W
Elets → Jelec	**76**	52.37 N	38.30 E
El Eulma	**148**	36.08 N	5.40 E
Eleusis → Elevsís	**38**	38.02 N	23.32 E
Eleutério	**256**	22.19 S	46.43 W
Eleutero ≏	**70**	38.06 N	13.29 E
Eleuthera I	**238**	25.10 N	76.14 W
Eleuthera Point ›	**238**	24.40 N	76.11 W
Eleva	**190**	44.34 N	91.28 W
Eleven Point ≏	**194**	36.09 N	91.05 W
Elevsínos, Kólpos ⊂	**267c**	38.02 N	23.34 E
Elevsís	**38**	38.02 N	23.32 E
Elevtheroúpolis	**38**	40.55 N	24.16 E
El Fahs	**36**	36.22 N	9.55 E
El Faro, It.	**71**	40.36 N	8.13 E
El Faro, P.R.	**240m**	18.00 N	66.47 W
Elfenbeinküste → Ivory Coast □[1]	**150**	8.00 N	5.00 W
El Ferrol del Caudillo	**34**	43.29 N	8.14 W
Elfers	**220**	28.13 N	82.43 W
Elfgen	**263**	51.05 N	6.32 E
Elfin Cove	**180**	58.12 N	136.20 W
Elfrida	**200**	31.41 N	109.41 W
Elfros	**184**	51.43 N	103.52 W
El Fud	**144**	7.20 N	42.50 E
El Fuerte	**232**	26.25 N	108.39 W
El Galpón	**252**	25.23 S	64.38 W
Elgershausen	**56**	51.16 N	9.22 E
El Ghazawet	**148**	35.06 N	1.51 W
Elgin, Austl.	**168a**	33.31 S	115.37 E
Elgin, On., Can.	**212**	44.36 N	76.13 W
Elgin, Scot., U.K.	**46**	57.39 N	3.20 W
Elgin, Il., U.S.	**216**	42.02 N	88.16 W
Elgin, Ia., U.S.	**190**	42.57 N	91.37 W
Elgin, Mn., U.S.	**190**	44.07 N	92.15 W
Elgin, Ne., U.S.	**198**	41.59 N	98.05 W
Elgin, N.D., U.S.	**198**	46.24 N	101.50 W
Elgin, Oh., U.S.	**216**	40.44 N	84.28 W
Elgin, Ok., U.S.	**196**	34.46 N	98.17 W
Elgin, Or., U.S.	**202**	45.33 N	117.54 W
Elgin, Pa., U.S.	**214**	41.54 N	79.45 W
Elgin, Tx., U.S.	**222**	30.20 N	97.22 W
Elgin □[6]	**214**	42.42 N	81.15 W
Elgin, Lake ⊜	**206**	45.45 N	71.20 W
El Gogorrón, Parque Nacional ♦	**234**	21.48 N	100.48 W
Elgol	**46**	57.09 N	6.06 W
El Golfete ⊜	**236**	15.44 N	88.53 W
El Golfo de Santa Clara	**232**	31.42 N	114.30 W
El Goloso ⬌[8]	**266a**	40.33 N	3.42 W
Elgon, Mount ∧	**154**	1.08 N	34.33 E
Elgoras, gora ∧	**24**	68.06 N	31.30 E
El Granada	**226**	37.30 N	122.28 W
El Grara	**148**	32.46 N	4.34 E
El Grove	**34**	42.30 N	8.52 W
El Grullo	**234**	19.48 N	104.13 W
El Guaje	**232**	27.52 N	103.18 W
El Guamo	**246**	10.02 N	74.59 W
El Guanábano	**286c**	10.24 N	67.01 W
El Guapo	**246**	10.09 N	65.58 W
El Guarapo	**286c**	10.36 N	66.58 W
El Guayabo	**246**	8.37 N	72.20 W
El'gygytgyn, ozero ⊜	**180**	67.30 N	172.00 E
El Hadjar	**36**	36.48 N	7.45 E
Elham	**42**	51.10 N	1.07 E
El Ḥammâmi ⬌[1]	**148**	23.03 N	11.30 W
El Hank ⏏[4]	**148**	24.30 N	7.00 W
El Haouaria	**36**	37.03 N	11.02 E
El Hatillo	**286c**	10.26 N	66.49 W
El Hatillo, Quebrada ≏	**286c**	10.27 N	66.47 W
El Havre → Le Havre	**50**	49.30 N	0.08 E
El Higo	**234**	21.46 N	98.28 W
Elhovo	**38**	42.10 N	26.34 E
El Huecú	**252**	37.37 S	70.36 W
Eliase	**164**	8.21 S	130.47 E
Elías Piña	**238**	18.53 N	71.42 W
Elías Romero	**258**	34.46 S	58.52 W
Eliasville	**196**	32.57 N	98.46 W
Elida, N.M., U.S.	**196**	33.56 N	103.39 W
Elida, Oh., U.S.	**216**	40.47 N	84.12 W
El Idrissia	**148**	34.30 N	2.37 E
Elila	**154**	2.43 S	25.53 E
Elila ≏	**154**	2.45 S	25.53 E
Elim, Namibia	**156**	17.48 S	15.31 E
Elim, S. Afr.	**158**	34.35 S	19.45 E
Elim, Ak., U.S.	**180**	64.37 N	162.15 W
Elimsport	**210**	41.08 N	77.02 W
Elingampangu	**152**	2.03 S	24.02 E
Elin Pelin	**38**	42.40 N	23.36 E
Eliot	**188**	43.09 N	70.48 W
Elipa	**152**	0.53 S	24.34 E
Elisabeth-Sophien-Koog	**41**	54.30 N	8.53 E
Élisabethville	**261**	48.58 N	1.51 E
Élisabethville → Lubumbashi	**154**	11.40 S	27.28 E
Elisenvaara	**24**	61.25 N	29.46 E
Eliseu Martins	**250**	8.13 S	43.42 W
Elista	**80**	46.16 N	44.14 E
Elizabeth, Austl.	**168b**	34.43 S	138.40 E
Elizabeth, Co., U.S.	**200**	39.21 N	104.35 W
Elizabeth, Il., U.S.	**190**	42.19 N	90.13 W
Elizabeth, La., U.S.	**194**	30.52 N	92.47 W
Elizabeth, N.J., U.S.	**210**	40.39 N	74.12 W
Elizabeth, Pa., U.S.	**214**	40.16 N	79.53 W
Elizabeth, W.V., U.S.	**188**	39.03 N	81.23 W
Elizabeth ≏, N.J., U.S.	**276**	40.38 N	74.12 W
Elizabeth ≏, Va., U.S.	**208**	36.54 N	76.20 W
Elizabeth, Cape ›	**224**	47.22 N	124.22 W
Elizabeth, Lake ⊜[1]	**282**	37.33 N	121.58 W
Elizabeth, West Branch ≏	**276**	40.42 N	74.14 W
Elizabeth Bay ⊂	**156**	27.04 S	15.11 E
Elizabeth City	**192**	36.18 N	76.13 W
Elizabeth Creek ≏	**222**	33.02 N	97.14 W
Elizabeth Islands II	**207**	41.27 N	70.47 W
Elizabeth Lake ⊜	**281**	42.38 N	83.23 W
Elizabeth Lake Estates	**281**	42.38 N	83.22 W
Elizabeth Park ♦	**281**	42.07 N	83.11 W
Elizabeth Reef I[1]	**160**	29.56 S	159.04 E
Elizabethton	**192**	36.20 N	82.12 W
Elizabethtown, Il., U.S.	**194**	37.26 N	88.18 W
Elizabethtown, In., U.S.	**218**	39.08 N	85.48 W
Elizabethtown, Ky., U.S.	**194**	37.41 N	85.51 W
Elizabethtown, N.Y., U.S.	**188**	44.12 N	73.35 W
Elizabethtown, N.C., U.S.	**192**	34.37 N	78.36 W
Elizabethtown, Pa., U.S.	**208**	40.09 N	76.36 W
Elizabethville	**208**	40.32 N	76.48 W
Eliza Howell Park ♦	**281**	42.24 N	83.16 W
Elizaville, In., U.S.	**218**	40.08 N	86.24 W
Elizaville, N.Y., U.S.	**210**	42.03 N	73.48 W
El-Jadida (Mazagan)	**148**	33.16 N	8.30 W
El-Jadida □[4]	**148**	33.00 N	8.40 W
El Jaralito	**232**	26.07 N	104.10 W
El Jebel	**200**	39.23 N	107.05 W
El-Jebha	**34**	35.13 N	4.38 W
El Jem	**148**	35.18 N	10.43 E
El Jícaro	**236**	13.43 N	86.08 W
El Jícaro ≏	**236**	13.31 N	86.00 W
El Jobean	**220**	26.58 N	82.13 W
Ełk	**30**	53.50 N	22.22 E
Elk □[6]	**214**	41.26 N	78.43 W
Elk ≏, Ab., Can.	**182**	52.55 N	115.40 W
Elk ≏, B.C., Can.	**182**	49.10 N	115.14 W
Ełk ≏, Pol.	**30**	53.31 N	22.47 E
Elk ≏, U.S.	**194**	34.46 N	87.16 W
Elk ≏, Co., U.S.	**200**	40.29 N	106.58 W
Elk ≏, Ks., U.S.	**198**	37.15 N	95.41 W
Elk ≏, Mn., U.S.	**190**	45.18 N	93.34 W
Elk ≏, Mo., U.S.	**194**	36.38 N	94.38 W
Elk ≏, W.V., U.S.	**188**	38.21 N	81.38 W
Elk ≏, Wi., U.S.	**190**	45.42 N	90.37 W
Elkader	**190**	42.51 N	91.24 W
El Kantara	**148**	33.41 N	10.55 E
El-Karafab	**140**	18.10 N	31.36 E
Elk Bayou ≏	**226**	36.06 N	119.24 W
Elk City	**196**	35.24 N	99.24 W
Elk City Lake ⊜[1]	**198**	37.15 N	95.55 W
Elk Creek	**204**	39.36 N	122.32 W
Elk Creek ≏, Ok., U.S.	**196**	34.48 N	99.09 W
Elk Creek ≏, Or., U.S.	**202**	43.38 N	123.34 W
Elk Creek ≏, Pa., U.S.	**214**	42.01 N	80.22 W
Elk Creek ≏, S.D., U.S.	**198**	44.15 N	102.22 W
Elk Creek ≏, Wa., U.S.	**224**	46.38 N	123.17 W
Elkedra ≏	**162**	21.08 S	136.22 E
El Kef	**148**	36.11 N	8.43 E
El Kef □[8]	**148**	36.00 N	9.00 E
El-Kelâa-des-Srarhna	**148**	32.02 N	7.23 W
El-Kelâa-des-Srarhna □[4]	**148**	32.05 N	7.30 W
El Kere	**144**	5.51 N	42.06 E
El Kerma	**34**	35.36 N	0.35 W
Elk Grove	**226**	38.24 N	121.22 W
Elk Grove Village	**278**	42.00 N	87.58 W
Elkhart, Il., U.S.	**219**	40.01 N	89.29 W
Elkhart, In., U.S.	**216**	41.40 N	85.58 W
Elkhart, Ks., U.S.	**198**	37.00 N	101.53 W
Elkhart, Tx., U.S.	**222**	31.38 N	95.35 W
Elkhart □[6]	**216**	41.35 N	85.50 W
Elkhart ≏	**216**	41.41 N	85.58 W
Elkhart Lake	**190**	43.50 N	88.01 W
El Khaṭṭ ⏏[4]	**148**	22.40 N	10.05 W
Elkhead Creek ≏	**200**	40.31 N	107.26 W
Elkhead Mountains ⋏	**200**	40.50 N	107.05 W
Elk Hills ⋏[2]	**226**	35.15 N	119.25 W
El Khnâchîch ⏏[4]	**148**	21.50 N	3.45 W
Elkhorn, Mb., Can.	**184**	49.58 N	101.14 W
Elk Horn, Ia., U.S.	**198**	41.35 N	95.03 W
Elkhorn, Wi., U.S.	**216**	42.40 N	88.32 W
Elkhorn ≏	**198**	41.07 N	96.19 W
Elkhorn City	**192**	37.18 N	82.21 W
Elkhorn Creek ≏, Ky., U.S.	**218**	38.19 N	84.52 W
Elkhorn Creek ≏, Mo., U.S.	**219**	39.05 N	91.20 W
Elkhorn Mountain ∧	**182**	49.48 N	125.50 W
Elkin	**192**	36.14 N	80.50 W
Elkins	**188**	38.55 N	79.50 W
Elkins Park	**208**	40.04 N	75.07 W
Elk Island I	**184**	50.45 N	96.32 W
Elk Island National Park ♦	**182**	53.37 N	112.45 W
Elkland	**210**	41.59 N	77.18 W
Elk Mills	**208**	39.39 N	75.49 W
Elk Mountain	**200**	41.41 N	106.24 W
Elk Mountain ∧, Wa., U.S.	**224**	46.08 N	122.28 W
Elk Mountain ∧, Wy., U.S.	**200**	41.38 N	106.32 W
Elk Neck ›[1]	**208**	39.35 N	75.55 W
Elk Neck State Park ♦	**208**	39.30 N	75.58 W
Elko, B.C., Can.	**182**	49.18 N	115.07 W
Elko, Nv., U.S.	**204**	40.49 N	115.45 W
El Kouif	**36**	35.29 N	8.19 E
Elk Peak ∧	**202**	46.27 N	110.46 W
Elk Plain	**224**	47.04 N	122.24 W
Elk Point, Ab., Can.	**182**	53.54 N	110.54 W
Elk Point, S.D., U.S.	**198**	42.41 N	96.41 W
Elk Rapids	**190**	44.53 N	85.24 W
El Krib	**36**	36.19 N	9.09 E
Elkridge	**284b**	39.12 N	76.42 W
Elk River, Id., U.S.	**202**	46.47 N	116.10 W
Elk River, Mn., U.S.	**190**	45.18 N	93.35 W
Elk River ⊂	**208**	39.31 N	75.55 W
El Kseur	**34**	36.46 N	4.49 E
Elk State Park ♦	**214**	41.38 N	78.34 W
Elkton, Ky., U.S.	**194**	36.48 N	87.09 W
Elkton, Md., U.S.	**208**	39.36 N	75.50 W
Elkton, Mi., U.S.	**190**	43.49 N	83.10 W
Elkton, Oh., U.S.	**214**	40.46 N	80.42 W
Elkton, S.D., U.S.	**198**	44.14 N	96.28 W
Elkton, Va., U.S.	**188**	38.24 N	78.37 W
El Kure	**144**	5.41 N	42.21 E
Elkville	**194**	37.54 N	89.14 W
Ell, Lake ⊜	**162**	29.13 S	127.46 E
Ellamar	**180**	60.54 N	146.42 W
Elland	**262**	53.41 N	1.50 W
Ellard Lake ⊜	**184**	54.33 N	91.55 W
Ellás → Greece □[1]	**38**	39.00 N	22.00 E
Ellavalla	**162**	25.05 S	114.22 E
Ellaville	**192**	32.14 N	84.18 W
Ellefeld	**54**	50.29 N	12.23 E
Ellef Ringnes Island I	**16**	78.30 N	104.00 W
El Leh	**144**	3.48 N	39.48 E
Elleker	**162**	35.00 S	117.43 E
Ellemandsbjerg ∧[2]	**41**	56.07 N	10.32 E
Ellen ≏	**44**	54.43 N	3.30 W
Ellen, Mount ∧	**200**	38.07 N	110.49 W
Ellen Brook ≏	**168a**	31.48 S	116.00 E
Ellendale, Austl.	**162**	17.56 S	124.48 E
Ellendale, De., U.S.	**208**	38.48 N	75.25 W
Ellendale, Mn., U.S.	**190**	43.52 N	93.18 W
Ellendale, N.D., U.S.	**198**	46.00 N	98.31 W
Ellensburg	**202**	46.59 N	120.32 W
Ellenton, Fl., U.S.	**220**	27.31 N	82.31 W
Ellenton, Ga., U.S.	**192**	31.10 N	83.35 W
Ellenville	**210**	41.43 N	74.23 W
Eller ⬌[8]	**263**	51.12 N	6.51 E
Ellerbe	**192**	35.04 N	79.46 W
Ellero ≏	**62**	44.27 N	7.54 E
Ellerspring ∧[2]	**56**	49.55 N	7.37 E
Ellès	**36**	35.57 N	9.06 E
Ellesmere	**42**	52.54 N	2.54 W
Ellesmere, Lake ⊂	**172**	43.48 S	172.25 E
Ellesmere Island I	**16**	81.00 N	80.00 W
Ellesmere Park	**262**	53.29 N	2.20 W
Ellesmere Port	**262**	53.17 N	2.54 W
Ellesmere Port □[8]	**262**	53.18 N	2.47 W
Ellettsville	**194**	39.14 N	86.37 W
Ellewoutsdijk	**52**	51.24 N	3.49 E
Ellezelles	**50**	50.44 N	3.41 E
Ellice ≏	**176**	68.02 N	103.26 W
Ellice Islands → Tuvalu □[1]	**14**	8.00 S	178.00 E
Ellichpur → Achalpur	**120**	21.16 N	77.31 E
Ellicott City	**208**	39.16 N	76.47 W
Ellicott Creek ≏	**210**	43.01 N	78.53 W
Ellicott Creek Park ♦	**284a**	43.01 N	78.50 W
Ellicottville	**210**	42.16 N	78.40 W
Ellijay	**192**	34.41 N	84.28 W
El Limón, Méx.	**234**	18.05 N	101.59 W
El Limón, Méx.	**234**	19.49 N	104.11 W
El Limoncito	**286c**	10.29 N	66.47 W
El Limón de Talleaché	**232**	24.16 N	107.04 W
Ellingen	**56**	49.04 N	10.58 E
Ellinger	**222**	29.50 N	96.44 W
Ellinghorst ⬌[8]	**263**	51.34 N	6.57 E
Ellington, Eng., U.K.	**44**	55.13 N	1.34 W
Ellington, Ct., U.S.	**207**	41.54 N	72.28 W
Ellington, Mo., U.S.	**194**	37.14 N	90.58 W
Ellington, N.Y., U.S.	**214**	42.13 N	79.07 W
Elliniko International Airport ⊠	**267c**	37.54 N	23.44 E
Ellinikón	**267c**	37.53 N	23.44 E
Ellinwood	**198**	38.21 N	98.34 W
Elliot	**158**	31.18 S	27.50 E
Elliot, Mount ∧	**166**	19.29 S	146.58 E
Elliotdale	**158**	31.55 S	28.38 E
Elliotganj	**126**	23.31 N	90.52 E
Elliot Lake	**190**	46.23 N	82.39 W
Elliot Lake ⊜	**184**	52.55 N	95.20 W
Elliott, Austl.	**162**	17.33 S	133.32 E
Elliott, Il., U.S.	**216**	40.28 N	88.16 W
Elliott, Ia., U.S.	**198**	41.09 N	95.10 W
Elliott, Ms., U.S.	**194**	33.36 N	89.45 W
Elliott □[6]	**218**	38.13 N	83.10 W
Elliott, Mount ∧	**162**	20.29 S	126.37 E
Elliott Bay ⊂	**224**	47.36 N	122.22 W
Elliott Key I	**220**	25.27 N	80.11 W
Elliottville	**218**	38.11 N	83.16 W
Ellis	**198**	38.56 N	99.33 W
Ellis □[6]	**222**	32.20 N	96.48 W
Ellisburg	**212**	43.44 N	76.08 W
Ellis Island I	**276**	40.42 N	74.02 W
Ellis Mountain ∧	**224**	48.10 N	124.19 W
Ellison Creek Reservoir ⊜[1]	**222**	32.56 N	94.43 W
Ellisport	**224**	47.25 N	122.26 W
Ellisras	**156**	23.40 S	27.46 E
Elliston, Austl.	**162**	33.39 S	134.55 E
Elliston, Nf., Can.	**186**	48.38 N	53.03 W
Elliston, Mt., U.S.	**202**	46.33 N	112.25 W
Ellisville, Ms., U.S.	**194**	31.36 N	89.11 W
Ellisville, Mo., U.S.	**219**	38.35 N	90.35 W
Ellmau	**64**	47.31 N	12.18 E
Ellmauer Halt ∧	**64**	47.34 N	12.18 E
Ellon	**46**	57.22 N	2.05 W
Ellora	**122**	20.01 N	75.10 E
Ellore → Elūru	**122**	16.42 N	81.06 E
Elloree	**192**	33.31 N	80.34 W
Ellport	**214**	40.51 N	80.15 W
Ellrich	**54**	51.35 N	10.40 E
Ellsworth, Il., U.S.	**216**	40.27 N	88.43 W
Ellsworth, Ks., U.S.	**198**	38.43 N	98.13 W
Ellsworth, Me., U.S.	**188**	44.32 N	68.25 W
Ellsworth, Mi., U.S.	**190**	45.09 N	85.14 W
Ellsworth, Mn., U.S.	**198**	43.31 N	96.01 W
Ellsworth, Oh., U.S.	**214**	41.01 N	80.52 W
Ellsworth, Pa., U.S.	**214**	40.06 N	80.01 W
Ellsworth, Wa., U.S.	**224**	45.37 N	122.36 W
Ellsworth, Wi., U.S.	**190**	44.43 N	92.29 W
Ellsworth Air Force Base ■	**198**	44.08 N	103.05 W
Ellsworth Land ⬌[1]	**9**	75.30 S	80.00 W
Ellsworth Mountains ⋏	**9**	79.00 S	85.00 W
El Lucero	**196**	25.53 N	103.25 W
Ellwangen	**56**	48.57 N	10.07 E
Ellwanger Berge ⋏[2]	**56**	49.00 N	10.15 E
Ellwood City	**214**	40.51 N	80.17 W
Elm, B.R.D.	**52**	53.31 N	9.12 E
Elm, Schw.	**58**	46.55 N	9.11 E
Elm, Eng., U.K.	**42**	52.38 N	0.10 E
Elm ∧	**64**	47.40 N	13.57 E
Elm ⋏[2]	**54**	52.09 N	10.53 E
Elm ≏, U.S.	**198**	45.36 N	98.19 W
Elm ≏, Il., U.S.	**194**	38.24 N	88.14 W
Elm ≏, N.D., U.S.	**198**	47.15 N	96.50 W
Elma, Ia., U.S.	**190**	43.14 N	92.26 W
Elma, N.Y., U.S.	**210**	42.51 N	78.38 W
Elma, Wa., U.S.	**224**	47.00 N	123.24 W
El Macero	**226**	38.33 N	121.41 W
El Machorro, Punta ›	**200**	31.03 N	114.51 W
Elmadağ (Küçükyozgat)	**130**	39.55 N	33.15 E
Elmadağ ∧	**130**	39.49 N	33.00 E
El Mahia ⬌[1]	**148**	22.30 N	2.30 W
El Maitén	**254**	42.03 S	71.10 W
El Malah	**34**	35.24 N	1.05 W
Elmalı	**130**	36.44 N	29.56 E
Elmalı Bendi ⬌[6]	**267b**	41.04 N	29.06 E
El Manchón	**236**	14.23 N	92.02 W
El Maneadero	**232**	31.45 N	116.35 W
El Manteco	**246**	7.27 N	62.32 W
El Marsa el Kebir	**148**	35.45 N	0.43 W
Elmas	**71**	39.16 N	9.03 E
Elmas, Aeroporto di ⊠	**71**	39.14 N	9.03 E
Elmas Burnu ›	**267b**	41.13 N	29.13 E
El Masnou	**266d**	41.29 N	2.19 E
Elmaton	**222**	28.53 N	96.09 W
El Mayoco	**254**	42.39 S	70.59 W
Elmbridge □[8]	**260**	51.22 N	0.23 W
Elm Brook ≏	**283**	42.29 N	71.16 W
Elm City	**192**	35.48 N	77.51 W
Elm Creek, Mb., Can.	**184**	49.41 N	98.00 W
Elm Creek, Ne., U.S.	**198**	40.43 N	99.22 W
Elm Creek ≏, Mn., U.S.	**198**	43.45 N	94.11 W
Elm Creek ≏, S.D., U.S.	**198**	44.21 N	102.42 W
Elm Creek ≏, Tx., U.S.	**196**	33.12 N	98.50 W
Elm Creek ≏, Tx., U.S.	**196**	28.54 N	100.12 W
Elm Creek ≏, Tx., U.S.	**196**	32.40 N	99.41 W
Elm Creek ≏, Tx., U.S.	**222**	29.15 N	97.32 W
El Meco	**234**	22.35 N	99.20 W
El Médano	**232**	24.25 N	111.30 W
El Melón, Sierra ⋏	**234**	23.56 N	99.39 W
Elmen	**58**	47.20 N	10.32 E
El Menia	**148**	30.30 N	2.50 E
Elmer	**208**	39.35 N	75.10 W
El Mghayyar	**148**	33.55 N	5.58 E
Elm Grove	**216**	43.02 N	88.04 W
Elmhurst, Austl.	**169**	37.11 S	143.15 E
Elmhurst, Il., U.S.	**216**	41.53 N	87.56 W
Elmhurst, Pa., U.S.	**210**	41.22 N	75.32 W
Elmhurst ⬌[8]	**276**	40.44 N	73.53 W
El Mijao	**286c**	10.23 N	66.48 W
El Milagro	**252**	31.01 S	65.59 W
El Miliyya	**148**	36.48 N	6.14 E
El Mimbre	**196**	25.40 N	102.20 W
Elmina	**150**	5.05 N	1.21 W
El Minao	**240m**	18.22 N	66.05 W
Elmira, On., Can.	**212**	43.36 N	80.33 W
Elmira, P.E., Can.	**186**	46.27 N	62.04 W
Elmira, Ca., U.S.	**226**	38.21 N	121.55 W
Elmira, N.Y., U.S.	**210**	42.05 N	76.48 W
El Mirage	**200**	33.36 N	112.19 W
El Mirage Lake ⊜	**228**	34.38 N	117.35 W
Elmira Heights	**210**	42.07 N	76.49 W
Elm Mott	**222**	31.40 N	97.06 W
Elmo, Mt., U.S.	**182**	47.49 N	114.20 W
Elmo, Tx., U.S.	**222**	32.43 N	96.10 W
El Mohammadia	**148**	35.33 N	0.03 E
El Molinillo	**34**	39.28 N	4.13 W
El Molinito	**286a**	19.27 N	99.15 W
Elmont, N.Y., U.S.	**276**	40.42 N	73.42 W
Elmont, Va., U.S.	**208**	37.42 N	77.29 W
El Monte, Chile	**252**	33.41 S	71.01 W
El Monte, Ca., U.S.	**228**	34.04 N	118.01 W
El Monte Airport ⊠	**280**	34.06 N	118.02 W
Elmora	**214**	40.36 N	78.45 W
El Moral	**196**	28.51 N	100.39 W
Elmore, Austl.	**166**	36.30 S	144.37 E
Elmore, Mn., U.S.	**190**	43.30 N	94.05 W
Elmore, Oh., U.S.	**214**	41.28 N	83.17 W
Elmore City	**196**	34.37 N	97.23 W
El Morro ⊥	**240m**	18.28 N	66.07 W
El Morro National Monument ♦	**200**	35.05 N	108.22 W
Elm Point ›	**276**	40.49 N	73.46 W
Elmpt	**56**	51.13 N	6.10 E
El Mreiti ⊤[4]	**148**	23.29 N	7.52 W
El Mreyyé ⬌[1]	**150**	19.30 N	7.00 W
Elmschenhagen ⬌[8]	**54**	54.18 N	10.12 E
Elmsdale	**186**	44.58 N	63.30 W
Elmsford	**210**	41.03 N	73.49 W
Elmshorn	**52**	53.45 N	9.39 E
Elm Springs	**194**	36.12 N	94.14 W
Elmsta	**26**	59.58 N	18.48 E
Elmstein	**56**	49.21 N	7.56 E
Elmswell	**42**	52.15 N	0.53 E
El Mulato	**196**	29.22 N	104.10 W
Elmvale	**212**	44.35 N	79.52 W
Elmville	**218**	38.20 N	84.46 W
Elmwood, On., Can.	**212**	44.14 N	81.03 W
Elmwood, Il., U.S.	**190**	40.46 N	89.57 W
Elmwood, Md., U.S.	**284b**	39.21 N	76.32 W
Elmwood, Ma., U.S.	**283**	42.00 N	70.57 W
Elmwood, Ne., U.S.	**198**	40.50 N	96.17 W
Elmwood, Wi., U.S.	**190**	44.46 N	92.08 W
Elmwood ⬌[8]	**285**	39.56 N	75.14 W
Elmwood Park, Il., U.S.	**216**	41.55 N	87.48 W
Elmwood Park, N.J., U.S.	**276**	40.54 N	74.07 W
Elmwood Park, Wi., U.S.	**216**	42.41 N	87.50 W
Elmwood Park ♦	**285**	40.08 N	75.21 W
El Naranjo, Arg.	**252**	25.44 S	64.59 W
El Naranjo, Méx.	**234**	22.30 N	98.33 W
Elne	**32**	42.36 N	2.53 E
El Negralejo	**266a**	40.24 N	3.31 W
El Negrito	**236**	15.16 N	87.41 W
El Nevado, Cerro ∧	**252**	35.35 S	68.30 W
El Nido, Pil.	**116**	11.11 N	119.23 E
El Nido, Ca., U.S.	**226**	37.08 N	120.29 W
El Nihuil	**252**	35.02 S	68.40 W
El Niybo	**144**	4.32 N	39.59 E
Elnora, Ab., Can.	**182**	51.59 N	113.12 W
Elnora, In., U.S.	**194**	38.52 N	87.05 W
El Oasis	**286c**	10.35 N	66.59 W
El-Obeid → Al-Ubayyiḍ	**140**	13.11 N	30.13 E
Elobey, Islas II	**152**	0.59 N	9.30 E
Elogbatindi	**152**	3.27 N	10.08 E
Eloida, Lake ⊜	**212**	44.40 N	75.58 W
Elói Mendes	**256**	21.37 S	45.34 W
Eloise	**220**	27.59 N	81.44 W
Elora, On., Can.	**212**	43.41 N	80.26 W
Elora, Tn., U.S.	**194**	35.00 N	86.21 W
El Oro □[4]	**246**	3.30 S	79.50 W
Elortondo	**252**	33.42 S	61.37 W
Elorza	**246**	7.03 N	69.31 W
El Oso	**246**	4.59 N	65.25 W
El Otro Lado	**286c**	10.24 N	66.49 W
Eloy	**200**	32.45 N	111.33 W
Éloyes	**58**	48.06 N	6.37 E
El Pacayal	**232**	15.37 N	92.02 W
El Palmar, Bol.	**248**	21.54 S	63.39 W
El Palmar, Ven.	**246**	7.58 N	61.53 W
El Palmar, Ven.	**286c**	10.38 N	66.52 W
El Palomar	**288**	34.36 S	58.36 W
El Palomar, Base Aérea Militar ■	**288**	34.37 S	58.37 W
El Palqui	**252**	30.45 S	70.59 W
El Pantanoso, Arroyo ≏	**288**	34.47 S	58.40 W
El Pao, Ven.	**246**	8.01 N	62.38 W
El Pao, Ven.	**246**	9.38 N	68.08 W
El Papiol	**266d**	41.26 N	2.01 E
El Paradero	**246**	10.38 N	69.32 W
El Paraíso, Hond.	**236**	13.51 N	86.34 W
El Paraíso, Méx.	**234**	17.25 N	100.15 W
El Paraíso □[5]	**236**	14.10 N	86.30 W
El Pardo ⬌[8]	**266a**	40.31 N	3.47 W
El Pardo, Embalse de ⊜[1]	**266a**	40.33 N	3.48 W
El Pardo, Monte de ⋏[2]	**266a**	40.33 N	3.48 W
El Paso, Il., U.S.	**216**	40.44 N	89.00 W
El Paso, Tx., U.S.	**200**	31.45 N	106.29 W
El Paso Creek ≏	**228**	35.02 N	118.51 W
El Paso de Robles → Paso Robles	**226**	35.38 N	120.41 W
El Paso Peaks ⋏	**204**	35.28 N	117.43 W
El Pato	**246**	2.50 N	74.48 W
El Paují	**286c**	10.26 N	66.49 W
El Pedregal ⬌[8]	**286c**	10.30 N	66.51 W
El Peñuelo	**232**	24.34 N	100.46 W
El Peral	**286e**	33.35 S	70.34 W
El Perú	**246**	7.19 N	61.49 W
El Pescado, Arroyo ≏	**258**	34.54 S	57.47 W
Elphin	**48**	53.51 N	8.12 W
Elphinstone	**184**	50.33 N	100.19 W
El Picacho, Cerro ∧	**234**	20.40 N	100.43 W
El Pilar	**246**	10.32 N	63.09 W
El Pinar, Parque Nacional ♦	**286c**	10.29 N	66.56 W
El Piñón	**246**	10.24 N	74.50 W
El Pintado	**252**	24.38 S	61.27 W
El Piojo, Arroyo ≏	**288**	34.50 S	58.45 W
El Piquete	**252**	24.13 S	64.39 W
El Placer	**234**	23.33 N	106.10 W
El Plantío ⬌[8]	**266a**	40.28 N	3.49 W
El Platanillo	**234**	18.28 N	101.52 W
El Plomo	**200**	31.15 N	112.04 W
El Polvorín	**240m**	18.26 N	66.17 W
El Pont de Segur	**34**	42.24 N	0.45 E
El Porcal	**266a**	40.18 N	3.32 W
El Portal, Ca., U.S.	**226**	37.40 N	119.46 W
El Portal, Fl., U.S.	**220**	25.51 N	80.11 W
El Port de Pollença	**34**	39.55 N	3.05 E
El Porvenir, Méx.	**196**	27.33 N	104.57 W
El Porvenir, Méx.	**204**	32.05 N	116.38 W
El Porvenir, Méx.	**232**	31.15 N	105.51 W
El Porvenir, Méx.	**234**	15.44 N	93.22 W
El Potosí	**232**	24.51 N	100.19 W
El Potosí, Parque Nacional ♦	**234**	22.00 N	99.58 W
El Potrero	**196**	26.23 N	100.27 W
El Potro, Cerro ∧	**252**	28.24 S	69.39 W
El Prat de Llobregat	**34**	41.20 N	2.06 E
El Progreso, Ec.	**246a**	0.54 S	89.33 W
El Progreso, Guat.	**236**	14.51 N	90.04 W
El Progreso, Guat.	**236**	14.21 N	89.51 W
El Progreso, Hond.	**236**	15.21 N	87.49 W
El Progreso □[5]	**236**	14.50 N	90.00 W
El Puente del Arzobispo	**34**	39.48 N	5.10 W
El Puerto de Santa María	**34**	36.36 N	6.13 W
El Puesto	**252**	27.57 S	67.38 W
El Qala	**148**	36.50 N	8.30 E
El Qoll	**148**	37.00 N	6.34 E
El Quebrachal	**252**	25.17 S	64.04 W
El Quelite	**234**	23.32 N	106.28 W
Elquera Bushland ♦	**274a**	33.42 S	150.04 E
Elqui ≏	**252**	29.54 S	71.17 W
Elrama	**214**	40.15 N	79.55 W
El Ranchito	**234**	18.40 N	103.41 W
El Rastro	**246**	9.03 N	67.27 W
El Real de Santa María	**246**	8.08 N	77.43 W
El Recreo ⬌[8]	**286c**	10.30 N	66.53 W
El Remolino, Méx.	**196**	28.44 N	101.07 W
El Remolino, Méx.	**234**	17.39 N	94.13 W
El Reno	**196**	35.31 N	97.57 W
El Rio	**228**	34.13 N	119.10 W
El Rito	**200**	36.20 N	106.11 W
El Rito ≏	**200**	36.12 N	106.14 W
El Roba	**154**	3.57 N	40.01 E
El Roble	**234**	23.32 N	106.14 W
El Rom	**132**	33.11 N	35.46 E
Elrose	**184**	51.13 N	108.01 W
Elroy	**190**	43.44 N	90.16 W
El Rucio	**234**	23.23 N	102.05 W
Elsa, Yk., Can.	**180**	63.55 N	135.28 W
Elsa, Tx., U.S.	**196**	26.17 N	97.59 W
Elsa ≏	**66**	43.43 N	10.52 E
Elsah	**219**	38.57 N	90.22 W
El Sahuaro	**200**	31.05 N	112.55 W
El Salado	**252**	26.25 S	70.19 W
El Salto, Chile	**286e**	33.23 S	70.38 W
El Salto, Méx.	**234**	23.47 N	105.22 W
El Salto, Méx.	**234**	20.32 N	103.11 W
El Salvador	**116**	8.34 N	124.32 E
El Salvador □[1], N.A.	**230**	13.50 N	88.55 W
El Salvador □[1], N.A.	**236**	13.50 N	88.55 W
El Samán de Apure	**246**	7.55 N	68.44 W
El Santo	**240p**	22.42 N	79.41 W
Elsass → Alsace □[9]	**32**	48.30 N	7.30 E
El Sauce	**236**	12.53 N	86.32 W
El Sauce, Laguna ⊜	**258**	35.20 S	58.16 W
El Sauz	**232**	29.02 N	106.16 W
El Sauzal	**232**	31.54 N	116.41 W
Elsberry	**219**	39.10 N	90.46 W
Elsbethen	**64**	47.45 N	13.05 E
Elsburg	**273d**	26.15 S	28.12 E
Elsdorf, B.R.D.	**52**	53.14 N	9.20 E
Elsdorf, B.R.D.	**56**	50.54 N	6.34 E
El Seco, Laguna ⊜	**258**	35.31 S	58.42 W
El Segundo	**228**	33.55 N	118.24 W
Elsen	**52**	51.44 N	8.39 E
Elsenham	**42**	51.55 N	0.14 E
Elsen Nur ⊜	**120**	35.11 N	92.15 E
Elsenz ≏	**56**	49.24 N	8.48 E
Elsey	**263**	51.22 N	7.34 E
Elsfleth	**52**	53.14 N	8.28 E
El Siasgo, Arroyo ≏	**258**	35.33 S	58.33 W
Elsie, Mi., U.S.	**216**	43.05 N	84.23 W
Elsie, Or., U.S.	**224**	45.52 N	123.35 W
Elsinore → Helsingør, Dan.	**41**	56.02 N	12.37 E
Elsinore, Ut,. U.S.	**200**	38.40 N	112.08 W
Elsinore, Lake ⊜[1]	**228**	33.39 N	117.21 W
El Sitio	**286c**	10.28 N	66.46 W
Elsmere, De., U.S.	**208**	39.44 N	75.35 W
Elsmere, Ky., U.S.	**218**	39.00 N	84.36 W
Elsmere, N.Y., U.S.	**210**	42.37 N	73.49 W
El Sobrante	**226**	37.58 N	122.17 W
El Socorro	**246**	8.59 N	65.44 W
El Sombrero	**246**	9.23 N	67.03 W
Elspark	**273d**	26.16 S	28.14 E
Elspeet	**52**	52.17 N	5.46 E
Elst	**52**	51.55 N	5.50 E
Elstal	**54**	52.32 N	12.59 E
Elstead	**42**	51.11 N	0.43 W
Elster	**54**	51.50 N	12.49 E
Elsterberg	**54**	50.36 N	12.10 E
Elstergebirge ⋏	**54**	50.15 N	12.20 E
Elsterwerda	**54**	51.28 N	13.31 E
Elston, In., U.S.	**216**	40.22 N	86.55 W
Elston, Mo., U.S.	**219**	38.37 N	92.19 W
Elstra	**54**	51.13 N	14.08 E
Elstree	**42**	51.39 N	0.16 W
Elstree Aerodrome ⊠	**260**	51.39 N	0.19 W
El Sueco	**232**	29.54 N	106.24 W
El Tajín ⊥	**234**	20.27 N	97.23 W
El Tala	**252**	26.07 S	65.17 W
El Talar	**258**	34.27 S	58.39 W
El Tamarindo	**236**	13.11 N	87.54 W
El Tambo	**246**	1.26 N	77.23 W
El Tanque	**196**	26.28 N	99.38 W
El Tapextle	**234**	23.52 N	105.33 W
El Tarf	**36**	36.45 N	8.20 E
Elten	**52**	51.52 N	6.10 E
El Tepozteco, Parque Nacional ♦	**234**	19.00 N	99.00 W
El Terrero	**234**	18.58 N	102.28 W
Eltham, Austl.	**169**	37.44 S	145.09 E
Eltham, N.Z.	**172**	39.26 S	174.18 E
Eltham ⬌[8]	**260**	51.27 N	0.04 E
Eltham Palace ✝	**260**	51.27 N	0.03 E
El Tigre, Col.	**246**	2.28 N	68.15 W
El Tigre, Ven.	**246**	8.55 N	64.15 W
El Tigre, Isla I	**236**	13.16 N	87.38 W
El Tigrito → San José de Guanipa	**246**	8.54 N	64.09 W
El Timbiriche	**234**	18.38 N	101.31 W
El Tisey, Cerro ∧	**236**	12.59 N	86.22 W
Eltmann	**56**	49.58 N	10.40 E
El Tocuyo	**246**	9.47 N	69.48 W
El Tofo	**252**	29.27 S	71.15 W
El'ton, S.S.S.R.	**80**	49.08 N	46.50 E
Elton, Eng., U.K.	**262**	53.16 N	2.49 W
Elton, La., U.S.	**194**	30.28 N	92.41 W
Elton, Pa., U.S.	**214**	40.17 N	78.48 W
El'ton, ozero ⊜	**80**	49.16 N	46.35 E
El Toreo ♦	**286a**	19.27 N	99.13 W
El Toro	**228**	33.37 N	117.41 W
El Toro ∧	**240m**	18.16 N	65.49 W
El Toro I	**234**	21.26 N	97.31 W
El Toro Marine Corps Air Station ■	**228**	33.41 N	117.44 W
El Tranco, Embalse de ⊜[1]	**34**	38.10 N	2.45 W
El Tránsito, Chile	**252**	28.52 S	70.17 W
El Tránsito, El Sal.	**236**	13.22 N	88.21 W
El Trapiche	**246**	3.03 N	77.33 W
El Trébol	**252**	32.12 S	61.42 W
El Triunfo, Hond.	**236**	13.06 N	87.00 W
El Triunfo, Hond.	**236**	15.46 N	87.26 W
El Triunfo, Méx.	**232**	23.47 N	110.08 W
El Tuito	**234**	20.19 N	105.22 W
El Tunal	**252**	24.48 S	65.45 W
El Turbio	**254**	51.41 S	72.05 W
Eltville	**56**	50.02 N	8.07 E
Eltz, Burg ⊥	**56**	50.12 N	7.20 E
El-Uarre	**144**	3.41 N	45.20 E
Elura → Ellora	**122**	20.01 N	75.10 E
Elūru	**122**	16.42 N	81.06 E
Elva	**76**	58.13 N	26.25 E
El Valle	**236**	8.36 N	80.08 W
El Valle ⬌[8]	**286c**	10.27 N	66.55 W
Elvas	**34**	38.53 N	7.10 W
Elvas ≏	**256**	21.12 S	44.08 W
Elven	**32**	47.44 N	2.35 W
El Venado, Isla I	**236**	11.57 N	83.44 W
El Vendrell	**34**	41.13 N	1.32 E
El Verano	**226**	38.18 N	122.29 W
El Verde	**234**	23.21 N	106.09 W
Elverdissen	**52**	52.05 N	8.38 E
Elverlingsen	**263**	51.17 N	7.42 E
Elverta	**226**	38.43 N	121.28 W
Elverum	**26**	60.53 N	11.34 E
El Viejo	**236**	12.40 N	87.10 W
El Vigía	**246**	8.38 N	71.39 W
El Vigía, Cerro ∧	**234**	21.19 N	104.03 W
Elvins	**194**	37.50 N	90.31 W
Elvira	**258**	35.14 S	59.29 W
Elvo ≏	**62**	45.23 N	8.21 E
El Volcán, Arg.	**252**	33.15 S	66.12 W
El Volcán, Chile	**252**	33.49 S	70.11 W
El Wad	**148**	33.20 N	6.58 E
El Wak	**154**	2.49 N	40.56 E
El Wanza	**148**	35.57 N	8.04 E
Elwell, Lake ⊜[1]	**202**	48.22 N	111.17 W
Elwha ≏	**224**	48.10 N	123.35 W
Elwood, Austl.	**274b**	37.53 S	144.59 E
Elwood, Il., U.S.	**216**	41.24 N	88.07 W
Elwood, In., U.S.	**216**	40.16 N	85.50 W
Elwood, Ks., U.S.	**198**	39.45 N	94.52 W
Elwood, Ne., U.S.	**198**	40.35 N	99.51 W
Elwood, N.J., U.S.	**208**	39.35 N	74.43 W
Elwood, N.Y., U.S.	**207**	40.50 N	73.20 W
Elwood Park, Fl., U.S.	**220**	27.28 N	82.30 W
Elwood Park, Pa., U.S.	**279b**	40.10 N	80.17 W
Elwy ≏	**44**	53.16 N	3.26 W
Elwyn	**285**	39.54 N	75.24 W
Elx	**34**	38.15 N	0.42 W
Elxleben	**54**	51.02 N	10.56 E
Ely, Eng., U.K.	**42**	52.24 N	0.16 E
Ely, Mn., U.S.	**190**	47.54 N	91.52 W
Ely, Mo., U.S.	**219**	39.41 N	91.39 W
Ely, Nv., U.S.	**204**	39.14 N	114.53 W
Ely, Isle of ⬌[1]	**42**	52.24 N	0.10 E
El Yagual	**246**	7.29 N	68.25 W
Ely Cathedral ✝[1]	**42**	52.24 N	0.16 E
Elyria	**214**	41.22 N	82.06 W
Elyria Airport ⊠	**279a**	41.20 N	82.06 W
Elysburg	**210**	40.51 N	76.33 W
Elysian Park ♦	**280**	34.05 N	118.14 W
El Yunque ∧	**240m**	18.19 N	65.48 W
Elywood Park ♦	**279a**	41.23 N	82.06 W
Elz	**56**	50.25 N	8.02 E
Elz ≏	**58**	48.21 N	7.45 E
Elzach	**58**	48.10 N	8.04 E
El Zamural	**286c**	10.27 N	67.00 W
El Zapotal	**234**	15.27 N	93.10 W
El Zapotán	**234**	18.41 N	103.39 W
El Zapote de Calabacillas	**232**	25.42 N	106.32 W
Elzbach ≏	**56**	50.12 N	7.22 E
Elze, B.R.D.	**52**	52.35 N	9.44 E
Elze, B.R.D.	**52**	52.07 N	9.44 E
El Zig-Zag	**286c**	10.33 N	66.58 W
Émaé I	**175f**	17.04 S	168.24 E
Emajõgi ≏	**76**	58.26 N	27.15 E
Emali	**154**	2.05 S	37.38 E
Emam Khomeyni Mosque ✝[1]	**267d**	35.40 N	51.25 E
Emāmshahr (Shāhrūd)	**128**	36.25 N	55.01 E
Emån ≏	**26**	57.08 N	16.30 E
Émancé	**261**	48.35 N	1.44 E
Emas, Parque Nacional das ♦	**255**	18.08 S	52.48 W
Emba	**86**	48.50 N	58.08 E
Emba ≏	**80**	46.38 N	53.14 E
Embarcación	**252**	23.13 S	64.06 W
Embarras ≏, Ab., Can.	**182**	53.27 N	116.37 W
Embarras ≏, Il., U.S.	**194**	38.39 N	87.37 W
Embarras, North Fork ≏	**194**	38.55 N	87.59 W
Embarrass	**190**	44.39 N	88.42 W
Embarrass ≏, Mn., U.S.	**190**	47.24 N	92.25 W
Embarrass ≏, Wi., U.S.	**190**	44.23 N	88.45 W
Embetsu	**92a**	44.44 N	141.47 E
Embid	**34**	40.58 N	1.43 W
Embira ≏	**248**	7.19 S	70.15 W
Embleton	**44**	55.30 N	1.37 W
Embo	**46**	57.54 N	3.59 W
Emboabas	**256**	21.18 S	44.08 W
Embondo	**152**	0.15 N	19.38 E
Embrach	**58**	47.30 N	8.36 E
Embreeville, Pa., U.S.	**285**	39.56 N	75.44 W
Embreeville, Tn., U.S.	**192**	36.10 N	82.27 W
Embro	**212**	43.09 N	80.54 W
Embrun, On., Can.	**212**	45.16 N	75.17 W
Embrun, Fr.	**62**	44.34 N	6.30 E
Embry	**50**	50.29 N	1.58 E
Embsay	**44**	53.58 N	1.59 W
Embu, Bra.	**256**	23.39 S	46.51 W
Embu, Kenya	**154**	0.32 S	37.27 E
Embu □[7]	**287b**	23.40 S	46.50 W
Embu-Guaçu	**256**	23.49 S	46.48 W
Embu-Guacu □[7]	**287b**	23.48 S	46.48 W
Embu-Mirim ≏	**287b**	23.39 S	46.51 W
Emden, B.R.D.	**52**	53.22 N	7.12 E
Emden, Il., U.S.	**194**	40.18 N	89.29 W
Emden, Mo., U.S.	**219**	39.48 N	91.52 W
Emei	**107**	29.36 N	103.31 E
Emeigh	**214**	40.42 N	78.47 W
Emel' (Emin) ≏	**86**	46.20 N	81.46 E
Emelle	**194**	32.43 N	88.18 W
Emerado	**198**	47.55 N	97.21 W
Émerainville	**261**	48.49 N	2.37 E
Emerald, Austl.	**166**	23.32 S	148.10 E
Emerald, Austl.	**169**	37.56 S	145.26 E
Emerald Bay State Park ♦	**226**	38.57 N	120.05 W
Emerald Lake	**226**	37.28 N	122.16 W
Emero ≏	**248**	13.19 S	67.17 W
Emerson, Mb., Can.	**184**	49.00 N	97.12 W
Emerson, Ar., U.S.	**194**	33.05 N	93.11 W
Emerson, Ga., U.S.	**192**	34.07 N	84.45 W
Emerson, Ia., U.S.	**198**	41.01 N	95.24 W
Emerson, Mo., U.S.	**219**	39.53 N	91.42 W
Emerson, Ne., U.S.	**198**	42.17 N	96.44 W
Emerson, N.J., U.S.	**276**	40.58 N	74.01 W
Emery, S.D., U.S.	**198**	43.36 N	97.37 W
Emery, Ut,. U.S.	**200**	38.55 N	111.14 W
Emeryville, On., Can.	**214**	42.18 N	82.45 W
Emeryville, Ca., U.S.	**226**	37.50 N	122.17 W
Emet	**130**	39.20 N	29.15 E
Emgayet	**146**	29.04 N	12.58 E
Emhouse	**222**	32.09 N	96.35 W
Emi	**88**	50.36 N	97.49 E
Emigrant Gap	**226**	39.17 N	120.40 W
Emigrant Gap)(	**226**	39.18 N	120.40 W
Emigsville	**208**	40.01 N	76.44 W
Emiliano Zapata, Méx.	**232**	17.45 N	91.46 W
Emiliano Zapata, Méx.	**234**	16.10 N	94.01 W
Emilia-Romagna □[4]	**66**	44.35 N	11.00 E
Emílio de Carvalho	**152**	5.55 S	12.57 E
Emily Provincial Park ♦	**212**	44.21 N	78.31 W
Emin	**86**	46.32 N	83.39 E
Emin (Emel') ≏	**86**	46.20 N	81.46 E
Eminābād	**123**	32.02 N	74.16 E
Emine, nos ›	**38**	42.42 N	27.51 E
Eminence, Ky., U.S.	**218**	38.22 N	85.10 W

Symbols in the index entries represent the broad categories identified in the key at the right. Symbols with superior numbers (⋏[1]) identify subcategories (see complete key on page *I · 1).*

Symbole im Register stellen die rechts im Schlüssel erklärten Kategorien dar. Symbole mit hochgestellten Ziffern (⋏[1]) bezeichnen Unterabteilungen einer Kategorie (vgl. vollständiger Schlüssel auf Seite *I · 1).*

Los símbolos incluídos en el texto del índice representan las grandes categorias identificadas con la clave a la derecha. Los símbolos con numeros en su parte superior (⋏[1]) identifican las subcategorías (véase la clave completa en la página *I · 1).*

Les symboles de l'index représentent les catégories indiquées dans la légende à droite. Les symboles suivis d'un indice (⋏[1]) représentent des sous-catégories (voir légende complète à la page *I · 1).*

Os símbolos incluídos no texto do índice representam as grandes categorias identificadas com a chave à direita. Os símbolos com números em sua parte superior (⋏[1]) identificam as subcategorias (veja-se a chave completa à página *I · 1).*

	English	Deutsch	Español	Français	Português
∧	Mountain	Berg	Montaña	Montagne	Montanha
⋏	Mountains	Gebirge	Montañas	Montagnes	Montanhas
)(	Pass	Paß	Paso	Col	Passo
V	Valley, Canyon	Tal, Cañon	Valle, Cañón	Vallée, Canyon	Vale, Canhão
≍	Plain	Ebene	Llano	Plaine	Planície
›	Cape	Kap	Cabo	Cap	Cabo
I	Island	Insel	Isla	Île	Ilha
II	Islands	Inseln	Islas	Îles	Ilhas
⏏	Other Topographic Features	Andere Topographische Objekte	Otros Elementos Topográficos	Autres données topographiques	Outros acidentes topográficos

Emin-Espa I · 53

ESPAÑOL — Nombre | Página | Lat.°′ | Long.°′ W = Oeste
FRANÇAIS — Nom | Page | Lat.°′ | Long.°′ W = Ouest
PORTUGUÊS — Nome | Página | Lat.°′ | Long.°′ W = Oeste

Eminence, Mo., U.S.	194	37.09 N	91.21 W
Emiralem	130	38.36 N	27.09 E
Emiratos Arabes Unidos → United Arab Emirates □[1]	128	24.00 N	54.00 E
Emirau Island I	164	1.40 S	150.00 E
Emirdağ	130	39.01 N	31.10 E
Emır Dağları ⋏	130	38.50 N	31.15 E
Emirhan	130	39.42 N	37.46 E
Emir Pasha Gulf c	154	2.32 S	31.52 E
Emissi, Tarso ∧	146	21.13 N	18.32 E
Emita	166	40.00 S	147.54 E
Emlembe ∧	158	25.57 S	31.11 E
Emlenton	214	41.11 N	79.43 W
Emlichheim	52	52.36 N	6.50 E
Emmaån ≃	40	58.44 N	15.35 E
Emmaboda	26	56.38 N	15.32 E
Emmaste	76	58.42 N	22.36 E
Emmaus, S.S.S.R.	82	56.47 N	36.07 E
Emmaus, Pa., U.S.	208	40.32 N	75.29 W
Emmaville	166	29.26 S	151.36 E
Emme ≃	58	47.13 N	7.34 E
Emmeline Lake ⊜	184	55.00 N	106.22 W
Emmeloord	52	52.43 N	5.45 E
Emmen	52	52.47 N	6.54 E
Emmenbrücke	58	47.04 N	8.17 E
Emmendingen	58	48.07 N	7.50 E
Emmental V	58	46.56 N	7.45 E
Emmer ≃	52	52.03 N	9.23 E
Emmer-Compascuum	52	52.48 N	7.02 E
Emmer-Erfscheidenveen	52	52.48 N	7.01 E
Emmerich	52	51.50 N	6.15 E
Emmerstedt	54	52.15 N	10.58 E
Emmerthal	52	52.03 N	9.23 E
Emmet, Austl.	166	24.40 S	144.28 E
Emmet, Ar., U.S.	194	33.43 N	93.28 W
Emmetsburg	198	43.06 N	94.40 W
Emmett, Id., U.S.	202	43.52 N	116.29 W
Emmett, Mi., U.S.	214	42.59 N	82.45 W
Emmiganūru	122	15.44 N	77.29 E
Emmitsburg	208	39.42 N	77.20 W
Emmonak	180	62.46 N	164.30 W
Emneth	42	52.38 N	0.11 E
Emo	190	48.38 N	93.50 W
Emőd	30	47.56 N	20.49 E
Emory	222	32.52 N	95.46 W
Emory ≃	192	35.56 N	84.29 W
Emory Peak ∧	196	29.13 N	103.17 W
Empalme	232	27.58 N	110.51 W
Empalme Escobedo	234	20.41 N	100.44 W
Empalme Purísima	234	23.55 N	105.05 W
Empalme San Vicente	258	34.58 S	58.22 W
Empangeni	158	28.50 S	31.48 E
Empedrado, Arg.	252	27.57 S	58.48 W
Empedrado, Chile	252	35.36 S	72.17 W
Emperor Jimmu, Tomb of ⊥	270	34.29 N	135.47 E
Emperor Nintoku, Tomb of ⊥	270	34.34 N	135.29 E
Emperor Range ⋏	175e	5.45 S	154.55 E
Emperor Seamounts ✦[3]	6	42.00 N	170.00 E
Emperor Tenchi, Tomb of ⊥	270	34.59 N	135.48 E
Empfingen	58	48.24 N	8.42 E
Empire, Ca., U.S.	226	37.38 N	120.54 W
Empire, La., U.S.	194	29.23 N	89.35 W
Empire, Nv., U.S.	204	40.34 N	119.20 W
Empire, Oh., U.S.	214	40.30 N	80.37 W
Empoli	66	43.43 N	10.57 E
Emporia, Ks., U.S.	198	38.24 N	96.10 W
Emporia, Va., U.S.	208	36.41 N	77.32 W
Emporium	214	41.30 N	78.14 W
Empress	184	50.57 N	110.00 W
Empress Augusta Bay c	175e	6.25 S	155.05 E
Emptinne	56	50.19 N	5.07 E
Ems ≃	52	53.30 N	7.00 E
Emscher ≃	263	51.34 N	6.42 E
Emscherbruch ◆[1]	263	51.34 N	7.09 E
Emsdetten	52	52.10 N	7.31 E
Ems-Jade-Kanal ≊	52	53.19 N	7.10 E
Emskirchen	56	49.33 N	10.43 E
Emsland ◆[1]	52	52.50 N	7.20 E
Emst ◆[8]	263	51.21 N	7.30 E
Emstek	52	52.50 N	8.09 E
Emsworth, Eng., U.K.	42	50.51 N	0.56 W
Emsworth, Pa., U.S.	214	40.30 N	80.05 W
Emu	89	43.45 N	128.10 E
Emu, Mount ∧[2]	169	37.35 S	143.27 E
Emu Creek ≃	171a	26.56 S	152.19 E
Emu Downs	168b	33.54 S	138.59 E
Emukae	92	33.18 N	129.38 E
Emu Park	166	23.15 S	150.50 E
Emu Plains	274a	33.45 S	150.41 E
Emur ≃	89	53.24 N	124.00 E
Emuren	273a	6.40 N	3.31 E
Emyvale	48	54.20 N	6.59 W
En (Inn) ≃, Europe	32	48.35 N	13.28 E
En ≃, Zhg.	100	27.12 N	115.08 E
Ena	94	35.27 N	137.25 E
Enana	156	17.29 S	16.19 E
Enånger	26	61.32 N	17.00 E
Enard Bay c	46	58.05 N	5.20 W
Enarotali	164	3.55 S	136.21 E
Ena-san ∧	94	35.26 N	137.36 E
Ena-san Tunnel ◆[5]	94	35.30 N	137.40 E
Enbacka	40	60.25 N	15.36 E
Enborne ≃	42	51.24 N	1.06 W
Encampment	200	41.12 N	106.47 W
Encampment ≃	200	41.18 N	106.43 W
Encantado	252	29.15 S	51.53 W
Encantado ◆[8]	287a	22.54 S	43.18 W
Encanto, Cape ›	116	15.44 N	121.37 E
Encarnação ◆[8]	266c	38.47 N	9.06 W
Encarnación	252	27.20 S	55.54 W
Encarnación de Díaz	234	21.31 N	102.14 W
Encha	98	37.25 N	115.42 E
Enchenberg	56	49.01 N	7.20 E
Enchi	150	5.49 N	2.49 W
Enchilayas	200	30.50 N	112.50 W
Enchovas, Enseada das c	256	23.57 S	45.18 W
Enciastraia, Monte ∧	62	44.22 N	6.53 E
Encinal	196	28.02 N	99.21 W
Encinitas	228	33.02 N	117.17 W
Encino, N.M., U.S.	200	34.39 N	105.27 W
Encino, Tx., U.S.	196	26.57 N	98.08 W
Encino ◆[8]	280	34.09 N	118.30 W
Encino Reservoir ⊜[1]	280	34.05 N	118.31 W
Encontrados	246	9.03 N	72.14 W
Encounter Bay c	168b	35.35 S	138.44 E
Encrucijada, Cuba	240p	22.37 N	79.52 W
Encrucijada, Méx.	234	18.18 N	93.29 W
Encruzilhada	255	15.31 S	40.54 W
Encruzilhada do Sul	252	30.32 S	52.31 W
Encs	30	48.20 N	21.08 E
Endako	182	54.05 N	125.02 W
Endako ≃	182	54.05 N	124.55 W
Endau ≃	114	2.39 N	103.38 E
Ende	115b	8.50 S	121.39 E
Ende, Pulau I	115b	8.53 S	121.32 E
Ende, Teluk c	115b	8.52 S	121.30 E
Endeavor, Pa., U.S.	214	41.35 N	79.23 W
Endeavor, Wi., U.S.	190	43.42 N	89.27 W
Endeavour	184	52.08 N	102.40 W
Endeavour Strait ⅄	164	10.50 S	142.15 E
Endelave I	41	55.46 N	10.17 E
Enderbury I[1]	14	3.08 S	171.05 W
Enderby, B.C., Can.	182	50.33 N	119.08 W
Enderby, Eng., U.K.	42	52.36 N	1.12 W
Enderby Land ◆[1]	9	67.30 S	53.00 E
Enderlin	198	46.37 N	97.36 W
Endicott, N.Y., U.S.	210	42.05 N	76.02 W
Endicott, Wa., U.S.	202	46.55 N	117.40 W
Endicott Mountains ⋏	180	67.50 N	152.00 W
Endimari ≃	248	8.46 S	66.07 W
Endine	64	45.46 N	9.59 E
Endine Gaiano	64	45.48 N	9.59 E
Endingen	58	48.09 N	7.42 E
Endja, Oued ≃	34	36.31 N	6.15 E
Endō	268	35.23 N	139.27 E
Endola	156	17.37 S	15.50 E
ʻEn Dor	132	32.39 N	35.25 E
Endorf in Oberbayern	64	47.54 N	12.18 E
Endre ≃	62	43.28 N	6.36 E
Endrick ∧	170	35.12 S	150.12 E
Endrick ≃	170	35.01 S	150.03 E
Endwell	210	42.06 N	76.01 W
Ene ≃	248	11.09 S	74.19 W
Eneabba	162	29.50 S	115.20 E
Enemonzo	64	46.25 N	12.53 E
Enewetak I[1]	14	11.30 N	162.15 E
Enez	130	40.44 N	26.04 E
Enfer, Pointe d' ›	240e	14.24 N	60.52 W
Enfida	36	36.07 N	10.23 E
Enfield, Austl.	168b	34.53 S	138.35 E
Enfield, Austl.	274a	33.53 S	151.06 E
Enfield, N.Z.	172	45.03 S	170.52 E
Enfield, Ct., U.S.	207	41.58 N	72.35 W
Enfield, N.H., U.S.	188	43.38 N	72.08 W
Enfield, N.C., U.S.	192	36.10 N	77.40 W
Enfield, Va., U.S.	208	37.43 N	77.12 W
Enfield ◆[8]	260	51.40 N	0.05 W
Enga □[5]	164	5.30 S	143.30 E
Engadine	170	34.04 S	151.01 E
Engaño, Cabo ›	238	18.37 N	68.20 W
Engaru	92a	44.03 N	143.31 E
Engažimo	88	57.51 N	114.56 E
Engcobo	158	31.37 S	28.00 E
ʻEn Gedi	132	31.27 N	35.23 E
Engelberg	58	46.49 N	8.25 E
Engelhard	192	35.30 N	75.59 W
Engelhartszell	60	48.31 N	13.44 E
Engel's	80	51.30 N	46.07 E
Engelsdorf	54	51.20 N	12.29 E
Engelskirchen	56	50.59 N	7.24 E
Engelsmanplaat I	52	53.28 N	6.02 E
Engel's'ovo	83	48.22 N	39.23 E
Engen, B.R.D.	58	47.51 N	8.46 E
Engen, B.C., Can.	182	54.02 N	124.18 W
Engenheiro Passos	256	22.30 S	44.41 W
Engenheiro Paulo de Frontin	256	22.33 S	43.41 W
Engenho	248	15.10 S	56.25 W
Engenho, Ilha do I	287a	22.50 S	43.07 W
Engenho de Dentro ◆[8]	287a	22.54 S	43.18 W
Engenho do Mato	287a	22.52 S	43.01 W
Engenho Nôvo	256	21.49 S	43.00 W
Engenho Nôvo ◆[8]	287a	22.55 S	43.17 W
Enger	52	52.08 N	8.34 E
Engestofte	41	54.46 N	11.34 E
Engesvang	41	56.10 N	9.21 E
ʻEn Gev	132	32.47 N	35.38 E
Enggano, Pulau I	112	5.24 S	102.16 E
Enghershatu ∧	144	16.40 N	38.20 E
Enghien (Edingen)	50	50.42 N	4.02 E
Enghien-les-Bains	261	48.58 N	2.19 E
Enghien-Moisselles, Aéroport d' ⊠	261	49.02 N	2.21 E
Engiadina Bassa V	58	46.50 N	10.20 E
Engis	56	50.35 N	5.25 E
Engizek Dağı ∧	130	37.50 N	37.10 E
Engjan	26	63.09 N	8.32 E
England	194	34.32 N	91.58 W
England □[8]	28	52.30 N	1.30 W
England Air Force Base ■	194	31.20 N	92.33 W
Englebright Lake ⊜[1]	226	39.15 N	121.15 W
Englee	186	50.44 N	56.06 W
Englefield, Cape ›	176	69.51 N	85.39 W
Englefield Green	260	51.26 N	0.35 W
Englefontaine	50	50.11 N	3.39 E
Englehart	190	47.49 N	79.52 W
Englehart ≃	190	47.51 N	79.50 W
Engleside	208	38.43 N	77.05 W
Englewood, B.C., Can.	182	50.33 N	126.53 W
Englewood, Co., U.S.	200	39.38 N	104.59 W
Englewood, Fl., U.S.	220	26.57 N	82.21 W
Englewood, In., U.S.	218	38.50 N	86.31 W
Englewood, Ks., U.S.	198	37.02 N	99.58 W
Englewood, N.J., U.S.	210	40.53 N	73.58 W
Englewood, Oh., U.S.	218	39.52 N	84.18 W
Englewood, Tn., U.S.	192	35.25 N	84.29 W
Englewood ◆[8]	278	41.47 N	87.39 W
Englewood Cliffs	276	40.53 N	73.57 W
Englewood Dam ◆[6]	218	39.52 N	84.17 W
English, In., U.S.	218	38.20 N	86.27 W
English, Ky., U.S.	218	38.37 N	85.08 W
English ≃, On., Can.	176	50.12 N	95.00 W
English (Rivière des Anglais) ≃, N.A.	206	45.13 N	73.50 W
English ≃, Ia., U.S.	190	41.29 N	91.30 W
English Bay	180	59.22 N	151.55 W
English Bāzār → Ingrāj Bāzār	124	25.00 N	88.09 E
English Center	210	41.26 N	77.17 W
English Channel (La Manche) ⅄	28	50.20 N	1.00 W
English Coast ✻[2]	9	73.45 S	73.00 W
English Harbour West	186	47.28 N	55.29 W
Englishman ≃	224	49.22 N	124.18 W
Englishtown	208	40.17 N	74.21 W
Engong	152	0.36 N	10.06 E
Engter	52	52.23 N	8.04 E
Énguera	34	38.59 N	0.41 W
Engum	41	55.44 N	9.40 E
Engure	76	57.10 N	23.13 E
Engures ezers ⊜	76	57.16 N	23.06 E
Engwilen	58	47.37 N	9.05 E
ʻEn Ḥarod	132	32.33 N	35.23 E
ʻEn HaShofét	132	32.35 N	35.06 E
Enid	196	36.23 N	97.52 W
Enid Lake ⊜[1]	194	34.10 N	89.50 W
Enilda	182	55.25 N	116.18 W
Eningen unter Achalm	58	48.29 N	9.16 E
Eniwa	92a	42.45 N	141.33 E
Eniwetok → Enewetak I[1]	14	11.30 N	162.15 E
eNjesuthi ∧	158	29.09 S	29.23 E
Enka	192	35.32 N	82.39 W
Enkenbach	56	49.29 N	7.54 E
Enkhuizen	52	52.42 N	5.17 E
Enkirch	56	49.59 N	7.07 E
Enköping	40	59.38 N	17.04 E
Enle	102	24.00 N	101.07 E
Enmedio	196	29.04 N	103.29 W
Enmelen	180	65.01 N	175.54 W
Enmore	246	6.46 N	57.59 W
Enna	70	37.34 N	14.16 E
Enna □[4]	70	37.35 N	14.26 E
Ennadai Lake ⊜	176	60.53 N	101.15 W
Enné, Ouadi V	146	14.24 N	18.45 E
Ennedi ⋏[1]	146	17.15 N	22.00 E
Ennell, Lough ⊜	48	53.28 N	7.24 W
Ennenda	58	47.01 N	9.05 E
Ennepe ≃	263	51.22 N	7.27 E
Ennepestausee ⊜[1]	263	51.14 N	7.25 E
Ennepetal	56	51.18 N	7.22 E
Ennerdale Water ⊜	44	54.31 N	3.23 W
Ennery	261	49.05 N	2.06 E
Enngonia	166	29.19 S	145.51 E
Enniger	52	51.50 N	7.56 E
Ennigerloh	52	51.50 N	8.02 E
Ennigloh	52	52.12 N	8.34 E
Ennis, Ire.	48	52.50 N	8.59 W
Ennis, Mt., U.S.	202	45.20 N	111.43 W
Ennis, Tx., U.S.	222	32.19 N	96.37 W
Enniscorthy	48	52.30 N	6.34 W
Enniskillen	48	54.21 N	7.38 W
Ennis Lake ⊜[1]	202	45.26 N	111.41 W
Ennistimon	48	52.57 N	9.15 W
Enns	61	48.13 N	14.29 E
Enns ≃	30	48.14 N	14.32 E
Ennstaler Alpen ⋏	61	47.37 N	14.35 E
Eno	26	62.48 N	30.09 E
Enø I	41	55.10 N	11.40 E
Eno ≃	96	34.53 N	132.41 E
Enochs	196	33.52 N	102.46 W
Enogera Military Camp ■	171a	27.25 S	152.58 E
Enola	208	40.17 N	76.56 W
Enon	218	39.53 N	83.56 W
Enontekiö	24	68.23 N	23.38 E
Enon Valley	214	40.51 N	80.28 W
Enoree ≃	192	34.26 N	81.25 W
Enosburg Falls	188	44.54 N	72.48 W
Eno-shima I	94	35.18 N	139.29 E
Enping	102	22.11 N	112.17 E
Enrekang	112	3.34 S	119.47 E
Enrile	116	17.34 N	121.42 E
Enrique Fynn	258	34.50 S	59.08 W
Enrique Urien	252	27.34 S	60.32 W
Enriquillo	238	17.54 N	71.14 W
Enriquillo, Lago ⊜	238	18.27 N	71.39 W
Ens	52	52.38 N	5.50 E
Ensay I	46	57.46 N	7.05 W
Enschede	52	52.12 N	6.53 E
Ensdorf	60	49.21 N	11.56 E
Enseada	256	23.29 S	45.05 W
Ensenada, Arg.	258	34.51 S	57.55 W
Ensenada, Méx.	232	31.52 N	116.37 W
Ensenada, P.R.	240m	17.58 N	66.56 W
Ensenada □[5]	288	34.50 S	58.00 W
Enshi	102	30.17 N	109.19 E
Enshū-nada ⊤[2]	92	34.27 N	137.38 E
Ensisheim	58	47.52 N	7.21 E
Enstaberga	40	58.45 N	16.51 E
Entebbe	154	0.04 N	32.28 E
Entenbühl ∧	60	49.46 N	12.24 E
Enter	52	52.18 N	6.34 E
Enterprise, Guy.	246	6.56 N	58.24 W
Enterprise, Al., U.S.	194	31.18 N	85.51 W
Enterprise, Ca., U.S.	204	39.32 N	121.22 W
Enterprise, Ks., U.S.	198	38.54 N	97.07 W
Enterprise, Ms., U.S.	194	32.10 N	88.49 W
Enterprise, Or., U.S.	202	45.25 N	117.16 W
Enterprise, Ut,. U.S.	200	37.34 N	113.43 W
Entiat ≃	202	47.40 N	120.14 W
Entiat, Lake ⊜[1]	202	47.40 N	120.12 W
Entiat Mountains ⋏	224	48.00 N	120.42 W
Entinas, Punta de las ›	34	36.41 N	2.46 W
Entlebuch	58	47.00 N	8.04 E
Entlebuch V	58	46.58 N	8.00 E
Entracque	62	44.14 N	7.24 E
Entraigues-sur-Sorgue	62	44.00 N	4.55 E
Entrains-sur-Nohain	50	47.27 N	3.15 E
Entrance, Cape ›	164	2.21 S	150.12 E
Entraunes	62	44.11 N	6.45 E
Entraygues	32	44.39 N	2.34 E
Entrechaux	62	44.13 N	5.08 E
Entrée, Île d' I	186	47.17 N	61.42 W
Entremont-le-Vieux	62	45.26 N	5.53 E
Entrepeñas, Embalse de ⊜[1]	34	40.34 N	2.42 W
Entre Ríos, Bol.	248	21.32 S	64.12 W
Entre Rios, Bra.	255	11.56 S	38.05 W
Entre Ríos □[4]	252	32.00 S	59.00 W
Entre Ríos, Cordillera ⋏	236	14.19 N	85.26 W
Entre Rios de Minas	255	20.41 S	44.04 W
Entrevaux	62	43.57 N	6.49 E
Entrèves	62	45.49 N	6.57 E
Entriken	214	40.20 N	78.12 W
Entroncamento	34	39.28 N	8.28 W
Entupido	256	22.30 S	44.51 W
Entwistle	182	53.36 N	115.00 W
Enu, Pulau I	164	7.05 S	134.30 E
Enugu	150	6.27 N	7.27 E
Enumclaw	224	47.12 N	121.59 W
Enurmino	180	66.57 N	171.49 W
Envalira, Port d')(	34	42.35 N	1.45 E
Envermeu	50	49.54 N	1.16 E
Envies, Rivière des ≃	206	46.37 N	72.24 W
Envigado	246	6.10 N	75.35 W
Envira	248	7.18 S	70.13 W
ʻEn Yahav	132	30.38 N	35.11 E
Enyamba	154	3.40 S	24.58 E
Enyang	102	31.48 N	106.31 E
Enyellé	152	2.49 N	18.06 E
Enys, Mount ∧	172	43.14 S	171.38 E
Enz ≃	56	49.01 N	9.07 E
Enza ≃	64	44.54 N	10.31 E
Enzan	94	35.42 N	138.44 E
Enzbach ≃	56	49.54 N	6.25 E
Enzenkirchen	60	48.23 N	13.39 E
Enzesfeld	61	47.55 N	16.10 E
Enzklösterle	56	48.40 N	8.28 E
Eo ≃	34	43.28 N	7.03 W
Eolia	219	39.14 N	91.00 W
Eolie o Lipari, Isole II	70	38.30 N	14.50 E
Epanomí	38	40.26 N	22.56 E
Épars, Bois de l' ♠	261	48.45 N	1.45 E
Epazote, Cerro ∧	232	24.35 N	105.07 W
Epe, B.R.D.	52	52.11 N	7.02 E
Epe, Ned.	52	52.21 N	6.00 E
Epe, Nig.	150	6.37 N	3.59 E
Epecuén, Lago ⊜	252	37.10 S	62.54 W
Épéhy	50	50.02 N	3.10 E
Epéna	152	1.22 N	17.29 E
Épernay	50	49.03 N	3.57 E
Épernon	50	48.37 N	1.41 E
Epes	194	32.41 N	88.07 W
Ephesus → Efes ⊥	130	37.55 N	27.17 E
Ephraim	200	39.21 N	111.35 W
Ephrata, Pa., U.S.	208	40.10 N	76.10 W
Ephrata, Wa., U.S.	202	47.19 N	119.33 W
Ephrata Cloister ⊥	208	40.12 N	76.09 W
Ephratah	210	43.00 N	74.32 W
Epi □[8]	175f	16.42 S	168.15 E
Épi I	175f	16.43 S	168.15 E
Épiais-lès-Louvres	261	49.02 N	2.33 E
Épila	34	41.36 N	1.17 W
Épinac-Les-Mines	58	46.59 N	4.31 E
Épinal	58	48.11 N	6.27 E
Épinay-sous-Sénart	261	48.42 N	2.31 E
Épinay-sur-Orge	261	48.40 N	2.20 E
Épinay-sur-Seine	261	48.57 N	2.19 E
Epirus → Ípeiros □[9]	38	39.40 N	20.50 E
Episcopia	68	40.04 N	16.06 E
Episkopí	130	34.40 N	32.54 E
Époisses	50	47.30 N	4.10 E
Epokiro	156	21.41 S	19.08 E
Epomeo, Monte ∧	68	40.44 N	13.54 E
Épône	261	48.57 N	1.49 E
Eport, Loch c	46	57.33 N	7.11 W
Eppalock, Lake ⊜[1]	169	36.52 S	144.31 E
Eppelborn	56	49.24 N	6.58 E
Eppendorf ◆[8]	263	51.27 N	7.11 E
Eppenhausen ◆[8]	263	51.21 N	7.31 E
Eppeville	50	49.44 N	3.03 E
Epping, Austl.	169	37.39 S	145.02 E
Epping, Austl.	274a	33.46 S	151.05 E
Epping, Eng., U.K.	260	51.43 N	0.07 E
Epping, N.H., U.S.	188	43.02 N	71.04 W
Eppingen	56	49.08 N	8.54 E
Epping Forest □[8]	260	51.43 N	0.10 E
Epping Forest ◆[3]	260	51.40 N	0.03 E
Epping Green, Eng., U.K.	260	51.44 N	0.05 E
Epping Green, Eng., U.K.	260	51.45 N	0.07 W
Epping Upland	260	51.43 N	0.06 E
Epsom	260	51.20 N	0.16 W
Epsom and Ewell □[8]	260	51.20 N	0.16 W
Epsom Downs Race Course ♠	260	51.19 N	0.15 W
Epte ≃	50	49.04 N	1.37 E
Épuisay	50	47.54 N	0.56 E
Epukiro ≃	156	20.45 S	21.05 E
Epupa Falls ∟	152	16.55 S	13.10 E
Epuyén	254	42.14 S	71.21 W
Epworth	44	53.32 N	0.49 W
Eqlīd	128	30.55 N	52.39 E
Equality	194	37.44 N	88.20 W
Équateur □[4]	152	1.00 N	20.30 E
Équateur → Ecuador □[1]	246	2.00 S	77.30 W
Equatorial Guinea (Guinea Ecuatorial) □[1]	152	2.00 N	9.00 E
Équihen-Plage	50	50.41 N	1.34 E
Equimina ≃	152	13.11 S	12.47 E
Equinox Mountain ∧	210	43.10 N	73.08 W
Equinunk	210	41.51 N	75.14 W
Equi Terme	64	44.09 N	10.10 E
Era ≃, It.	66	43.40 N	10.38 E
Era ≃, Pap. N. Gui.	164	7.35 S	144.41 E
Erac Creek ≃	166	26.56 S	145.48 E
Eraclea	64	45.35 N	12.40 E
Eraclea ⊥	68	40.13 N	16.40 E
Eraclea Minoa ⊥	70	37.23 N	13.17 E
Eradu	162	28.41 S	115.02 E
Éragny	261	49.01 N	2.06 E
Eramosa ≃	212	43.32 N	80.14 W
Eran Bay c	116	9.06 N	117.43 E
Eranga	152	1.52 S	18.56 E
Erangal ◆[8]	272c	19.10 N	72.47 E
Erap	164	6.35 S	146.40 E
Erath	194	29.57 N	92.02 W
Erave	164	6.40 S	143.50 E
Erave ≃	164	6.40 S	143.55 E
Erba	62	45.48 N	9.15 E
Erba, Jabal ∧, Sūd.	140	19.04 N	36.46 E
Erba, Jabal ∧, Sūd.	140	20.45 N	36.50 E
Erbaa	130	40.42 N	36.36 E
Erbach, B.R.D.	56	49.40 N	8.59 E
Erbach, B.R.D.	58	48.20 N	9.53 E
Erbendorf	60	49.50 N	12.03 E
Erbeskopf ∧	56	49.44 N	7.05 E
Erchie	68	40.26 N	17.44 E
Erciş	84	39.02 N	43.22 E
Erciyes Dağı ∧	130	38.32 N	35.28 E
Ercolano	68	40.48 N	14.21 E
Ercolano (Herculaneum) ⊥	68	40.46 N	14.20 E
Érd	30	47.23 N	18.56 E
Erdao ≃, Zhg.	98	42.39 N	127.35 E
Erdao ≃, Zhg.	104	42.16 N	122.20 E
Erdao Bai ≃	98	42.34 N	128.08 E
Erdaobaihe	98	42.22 N	128.07 E
Erdaofang, Zhg.	104	41.54 N	123.57 E
Erdaofang, Zhg.	104	41.37 N	122.34 E
Erdaofangshen	104	42.09 N	123.17 E
Erdaogangzi, Zhg.	104	41.57 N	122.09 E
Erdaogangzi, Zhg.	104	42.04 N	123.06 E
Erdaohe	89	43.37 N	127.35 E
Erdaohezi, Zhg.	89	45.07 N	127.16 E
Erdaohezi, Zhg.	89	45.08 N	129.39 E
Erdaojingzi	104	41.49 N	122.20 E
Erdaoliangzi, Zhg.	98	40.50 N	119.04 E
Erdaoliangzi, Zhg.	105	40.31 N	118.03 E
Erdaowan	89	47.58 N	124.33 E
Erdek	130	40.24 N	27.48 E
Erdemli	130	36.37 N	34.18 E
Erdene, Mong.	88	47.48 N	107.55 E
Erdene, Mong.	102	44.15 N	111.14 E
Erdene, Mong.	102	45.08 N	97.45 E
Erdene Bulgan	88	50.07 N	101.35 E
Erdene-Büren	86	48.26 N	91.27 E
Erdenedalaj	102	46.02 N	104.55 E
Erdene Mandal	88	48.30 N	101.21 E
Erdenheim	285	40.05 N	75.12 W
Erdevik	38	45.07 N	19.25 E
Erdiao	106	32.12 N	121.12 E
Erding	60	48.18 N	11.54 E
Erdinger Moos ≡	60	48.22 N	11.52 E
Erdnijevskij	80	46.52 N	46.17 E
Erebato ≃	246	5.54 N	64.16 W
Erebus, Mount ∧	9	77.32 S	167.09 E
Erechim	252	27.38 S	52.17 W
Ereğli, Tür.	130	41.17 N	31.25 E
Ereğli, Tür.	130	37.31 N	34.04 E
Eregun	273a	6.36 N	3.22 E
Erei, Monti ⋏	70	37.27 N	14.19 E
Eremita	256	21.35 S	45.04 W
Erenas	116	12.25 N	124.19 E
Erenhot	102	43.46 N	112.05 E
Erenköy ◆[8]	267b	40.58 N	29.04 E
Erepecu, Lago do ⊜	250	1.20 S	56.35 W
Eresma ≃	34	41.26 N	4.45 W
Eressós	38	39.18 N	25.51 E
Erétria	38	38.24 N	23.48 E
Erez	132	31.34 N	34.34 E
Érezée	56	50.18 N	5.33 E
Erfa ≃	56	49.40 N	9.23 E
Erfde	41	54.19 N	9.19 E
Erfelek	130	41.53 N	34.55 E
Erfenisdam ⊜[1]	158	28.33 S	26.50 E
Erfoud	148	31.28 N	4.10 W
Erft ≃	56	51.11 N	6.44 E
Erftstadt	56	50.48 N	6.46 E
Erfurt	54	50.58 N	11.01 E
Erfurt □[5]	54	51.10 N	10.45 E
Ergak-Targak-Tajga, chrebet ⋏	88	53.25 N	95.30 E
Ergani	130	38.17 N	39.46 E
Ergene ≃	130	41.01 N	26.22 E
Ergenzingen	58	48.29 N	8.48 E
Erges (Erjas) ≃	34	39.40 N	7.01 W
Ērgļi	76	56.54 N	25.38 E
Ergolding	60	48.35 N	12.10 E
Ergoldsbach	60	48.41 N	12.12 E
Ergste	56	51.25 N	7.34 E
Erguig, Bahr ≃	146	11.22 N	15.24 E
Ergun (Argun') ≃	74	53.20 N	121.28 E
Ergun Youqi	89	50.14 N	120.10 E
Ergun Zuoqi	89	50.47 N	121.31 E
Erguvejem ≃	180	65.20 N	176.00 W
Er Hai ⊜	102	25.48 N	100.11 E
Erhlin	100	23.54 N	120.22 E
Erhshui	100	23.49 N	120.36 E
Erhulai	98	41.23 N	125.08 E
Eria ≃	34	42.03 N	5.44 W
Erial	208	39.46 N	75.00 W
Eriba	140	16.37 N	36.04 E
Eriboll	46	58.28 N	4.41 W
Eriboll, Loch c	46	58.31 N	4.41 W
Erica, Austl.	169	37.59 S	146.22 E
Erica, Ned.	52	52.43 N	6.55 E
Erice	70	38.02 N	12.35 E
Ericeira	34	38.59 N	9.25 W
Erichsen Lake ⊜	176	70.38 N	80.21 W
Erichshagen	52	52.40 N	9.14 E
Ericht, Loch ⊜	46	56.48 N	4.24 W
Erick	196	35.12 N	99.51 W
Erickson, B.C., Can.	182	49.05 N	116.28 W
Erickson, Mb., Can.	184	50.30 N	99.55 W
Ericson	198	41.46 N	98.40 W
Erie, Co., U.S.	200	40.03 N	105.03 W
Erie, Il., U.S.	190	41.39 N	90.04 W
Erie, Ks., U.S.	198	37.34 N	95.14 W
Erie, Mi., U.S.	216	41.47 N	83.29 W
Erie, Pa., U.S.	214	42.07 N	80.05 W
Erie □[6], N.Y., U.S.	210	42.54 N	78.53 W
Erie □[6], Oh., U.S.	214	41.27 N	82.42 W
Erie □[6], Pa., U.S.	214	42.08 N	80.04 W
Erie, Lake ⊜	214	42.15 N	81.00 W
Erieau	214	42.16 N	81.56 W
Erie Basin c	276	40.40 N	74.01 W
Erie Beach, On., Can.	214	42.16 N	82.00 W
Erie Beach, On., Can.	284a	42.53 N	78.57 W
Erie Canal → New York State Barge Canal ≊	210	43.05 N	78.43 W
Erie County Fairgrounds ♠	284a	42.45 N	78.49 W
Erie International Airport ⊠	214	42.05 N	80.11 W
Eriksberg ⊥	40	58.56 N	16.22 E
Eriksdale	184	50.52 N	98.06 W
Erímanthos ∧	38	37.59 N	21.51 E
Erimo	92a	42.01 N	143.09 E
Erimo-misaki ›	92a	41.55 N	143.15 E
Erin, On., Can.	212	43.45 N	80.07 W
Erin, N.Y., U.S.	210	42.11 N	76.40 W
Erin, Tn., U.S.	194	36.19 N	87.41 W
Erindale	275b	43.32 N	79.39 W
Ering	60	48.18 N	13.09 E
Eriskay I	46	57.04 N	7.18 W
Erisort, Loch c	46	58.07 N	6.24 W
Eriswil	58	47.05 N	7.51 E
Erith ◆[8]	260	51.29 N	0.10 E
Erithraí	38	38.13 N	23.19 E
Eritrea □[9]	144	15.20 N	39.00 E
Erivan → Jerevan	84	40.11 N	44.30 E
Erjas (Erges) ≃	34	39.40 N	7.01 W
Erjiazhen	106	32.02 N	121.13 E
Erkelenz	56	51.05 N	6.19 E
Erken ⊜	40	59.51 N	18.34 E
Erken-Jurt	84	44.27 N	41.54 E
Erkheim	58	48.02 N	10.20 E
Erkilet	130	38.49 N	35.27 E
Erkina ≃	48	52.51 N	7.23 W
Erkner	54	52.25 N	13.45 E
Erkner, Forst ◆[3]	264a	52.22 N	13.47 E
Erkowit	140	18.46 N	37.07 E
Erkrath	56	51.13 N	6.55 E
Erl	64	47.41 N	12.11 E
Erlach, Öst.	61	47.43 N	16.13 E
Erlach, Schw.	58	47.03 N	7.06 E
Erlands Point	224	47.36 N	122.42 W
Erlangen	60	49.36 N	11.01 E
Erlanger	218	39.01 N	84.36 W
Erlanghe	100	30.19 N	116.04 E
Erlangmiao	100	33.46 N	112.23 E
Erlau ≃	60	48.34 N	13.36 E
Erlauf ≃	61	48.12 N	15.11 E
Erlbach	54	50.18 N	12.22 E
Erldunda	162	25.14 S	133.12 E
Erle ◆[8]	263	51.33 N	7.05 E
Erli	62	44.08 N	8.06 E
Erling	106	31.53 N	119.36 E
Erling, Lake ⊜[1]	194	33.05 N	93.35 W
Erlistoun	162	28.20 S	122.08 E
Erlongshan, Zhg.	89	47.20 N	132.28 E
Erlongshan, Zhg.	89	50.04 N	126.47 E
Erlongshantun	89	48.28 N	126.31 E
Erlsbach	64	46.55 N	12.15 E
Erma	208	38.58 N	74.54 W
Ermana, chrebet ⋏	88	50.00 N	113.30 E
Ermatingen	58	47.41 N	9.06 E
Erme ≃	42	50.18 N	3.56 W
Ermelindo Matarazo ◆[8]	287b	23.29 S	46.29 W
Ermelo, Ned.	52	52.17 N	5.37 E
Ermelo, S. Afr.	158	26.34 S	29.58 E
Ermendegou	104	42.02 N	121.56 E
Ermenek	130	36.38 N	32.54 E
Ermenek ≃	130	36.35 N	33.23 E
Ermenonville	50	49.08 N	2.42 E
Ermidas	34	38.00 N	8.23 W
Ermil Post	140	13.37 N	27.36 E
Ermineskin Indian Reserve ◆[4]	182	52.52 N	113.30 W
Ermington	274a	33.48 S	151.04 E
Ermita de los Correa	234	22.54 N	103.01 W
Ermont	50	48.59 N	2.16 E
Ermoúpolis	38	37.26 N	24.56 E
Ermsleben	54	51.44 N	11.21 E
Ernaballa	162	26.17 S	132.07 E
Erndtebrück	56	50.59 N	8.15 E
Erne ≃	48	54.30 N	8.16 W
Erne, Lower Lough ⊜	48	54.26 N	7.46 W
Erne, Upper Lough ⊜	48	54.14 N	7.32 W
Ernée	32	48.18 N	0.56 W
Ernest	214	40.41 N	79.10 W
Ernestina	258	35.16 S	59.34 W
Ernest Sound ⅄	182	55.52 N	132.10 W
Ernici, Monti ⋏	66	41.48 N	13.22 E
Ernstbrunn	61	48.32 N	16.22 E
Ernst Thälmann, Pioneerpark ♠	264a	52.28 N	13.33 E
Ernst-Thälmann-Stadion ♠	264a	52.23 N	13.05 E
Erode	122	11.21 N	77.44 E
Eromanga	166	26.40 S	143.16 E
Erongo	156	21.44 S	15.53 E
Erongo ⋏	156	21.45 S	15.37 E
Erota	144	16.14 N	37.55 E
Erp	56	50.46 N	6.43 E
Erpuzi	105	40.29 N	115.33 E
Erquelinnes	50	50.18 N	4.07 E
Err, Piz d' ∧	58	46.33 N	9.41 E
Errabiddy	162	25.28 S	117.07 E
Er-Rachidia	148	31.58 N	4.25 W
Er-Rachidia □[4]	148	31.15 N	4.05 W
Errego	154	16.02 S	37.14 E
Errer ≃	144	7.32 N	42.05 E
Er-Riad → Ar-Riyāḍ	128	24.38 N	46.43 E
Errigal Mountain ∧	48	55.02 N	8.07 W
Errington	224	49.17 N	124.22 W
Erris Head ›	48	54.19 N	10.00 W
Errochty, Loch ⊜	46	56.45 N	4.12 W
Errogie	46	57.16 N	4.22 W
Errol Heights	224	45.28 N	122.36 W
Erromango I	175f	18.45 S	169.05 E
Ersekë	38	40.20 N	20.41 E
Ershijiazi	104	41.17 N	120.32 E
Ershilipu	105	40.07 N	117.24 E
Ershiqizhan	89	53.23 N	123.16 E
Ershiwuzhan	89	53.22 N	123.55 E
Erskine	198	47.40 N	96.00 W
Erskine, Lake ⊜	276	41.06 N	74.15 W
Erskine Inlet c	176	76.15 N	102.20 W
Erskine Park	274a	33.49 S	150.47 E
Erstein	58	48.26 N	7.40 E
Erste Wiener Hochquellenleitung ≊[1]	61	48.10 N	16.17 E
Erstfeld	58	46.49 N	8.39 E
Ertai, Zhg.	86	46.07 N	90.06 E
Ertai, Zhg.	86	44.14 N	80.52 E
Ertaizi, Zhg.	104	42.05 N	123.35 E
Ertaizi, Zhg.	104	41.52 N	121.56 E
Ertaizi, Zhg.	104	42.35 N	124.00 E
Ertaizi, Zhg.	104	40.47 N	120.54 E
Ertil'	78	51.51 N	40.49 E
Ertingen	58	48.06 N	9.28 E
Ertix (Irtyš) ≃	74	61.04 N	68.52 E
Erto	64	46.16 N	12.22 E
Ertra □[4]	144	15.20 N	39.00 E
Ertuğrul	130	39.34 N	27.43 E
Ertvelde	50	51.11 N	3.45 E
Eruar	126	23.28 N	87.52 E
Erudina	166	31.28 S	139.23 E
Eruh	130	37.46 N	42.11 E
Erundu	156	20.36 S	16.25 E
Erunkan	273a	6.37 N	3.24 E
Erva, Ponta da ›	266c	38.50 N	8.58 W
Erval	252	32.02 S	53.24 W
Ervalla	40	59.22 N	15.15 E
Erving	207	42.36 N	72.23 W
Ervy-le-Châtel	50	48.02 N	3.55 E
Erwin, N.C., U.S.	192	35.19 N	78.40 W
Erwin, Tn., U.S.	192	36.08 N	82.25 W
Erwitte	52	51.37 N	8.20 E
Erwood	184	52.50 N	102.10 W
Erxleben	54	52.13 N	11.14 E
Érythrée → Eritrea □[9]	144	15.20 N	39.00 E
Eryuan	102	26.06 N	99.55 E
Erzaohang	106	31.05 N	121.49 E
Erzberg ◆[7]	61	47.32 N	14.54 E
Erzgebirge (Krušné hory) ⋏	54	50.30 N	13.10 E
Erzhan	89	43.58 N	128.44 E
Erzhuang	105	39.24 N	117.22 E
Erzin	88	50.15 N	95.10 E
Erzincan	130	39.44 N	39.29 E
Erzincan □[4]	130	39.40 N	39.30 E
Erzingen	58	47.39 N	8.25 E
Erzurum	130	39.55 N	41.17 E
Erzurum □[4]	130	40.00 N	41.30 E
Esa'ala	164	9.44 S	150.49 E
Esambo	152	3.40 S	23.24 E
Esan-misaki ›	92a	41.49 N	141.11 E
Esashi, Nihon	92	39.12 N	141.09 E
Esashi, Nihon	92	41.52 N	140.07 E
Esashi, Nihon	92a	44.56 N	142.35 E
Esbiye	130	40.57 N	38.44 E
Esbjerg	26	55.28 N	8.27 E
Esbly	261	48.54 N	2.49 E
Esbo → Espoo	26	60.13 N	24.40 E
Esborn	263	51.23 N	7.20 E
Esca ≃	34	42.37 N	1.03 W
Escada	250	8.22 S	35.14 W
Escalada	258	34.10 S	59.07 W
Escalante, Pil.	116	10.50 N	123.33 E
Escalante, Ut,. U.S.	200	37.46 N	111.36 W
Escalante ≃, Ut,. U.S.	200	37.17 N	110.53 W
Escalante ≃, Ven.	246	9.15 N	71.50 W
Escalante Desert ◆[2]	200	37.50 N	113.30 W
Escalaplano	71	39.37 N	9.21 E
Escalón, Méx.	232	26.45 N	104.20 W
Escalon, Ca., U.S.	226	37.47 N	120.59 W
Escalona	34	40.10 N	4.24 W
Escambia ≃	194	30.32 N	87.11 W
Escanaba	190	45.44 N	87.04 W
Escanaba ≃	190	45.47 N	87.04 W
Escandón, Puerto)(	34	40.17 N	1.00 W
Escárcega de Matamoros	232	18.37 N	90.43 W
Escarpada Point ›	116	18.31 N	122.13 E
Escarpado Peak ∧	116	8.36 N	117.22 E
Escarpment	284a	43.10 N	79.00 W
Escatawpa ≃	194	30.25 N	88.35 W
Escaudain	50	50.20 N	3.21 E
Escaut (Schelde) ≃	50	51.22 N	4.15 E
Esch ≃	56	48.54 N	6.04 E
Eschach	58	47.44 N	9.36 E
Eschau	58	48.29 N	7.43 E
Eschebrügge	52	52.37 N	6.46 E
Eschede	52	52.44 N	10.14 E
Eschen	58	47.13 N	9.31 E
Eschenau	60	49.34 N	11.12 E
Eschenbach	60	49.45 N	11.49 E
Eschenburg	56	50.49 N	8.20 E
Eschenlohe	64	47.36 N	11.11 E
Eschershausen	52	51.56 N	9.38 E
Eschlkam	60	49.18 N	12.55 E
Escholzmatt	58	46.55 N	7.56 E
Eschscholtz Bay c	180	66.18 N	161.25 W
Esch-sur-Alzette	56	49.30 N	5.59 E
Esch-sur-Sûre	56	49.55 N	5.55 E
Eschwege	56	51.11 N	10.04 E
Eschweiler	56	50.49 N	6.16 E
Esclave, Grand Lac de l' → Great Slave Lake ⊜	176	61.30 N	114.00 W
Esclavo, Gran Lago del → Great Slave Lake ⊜	176	61.30 N	114.00 W
Escobal	236	9.09 N	79.58 W
Escobar □[5]	288	34.23 S	58.46 W
Escobar, Arroyo ≃	288	34.21 S	58.44 W
Escobedo	196	27.13 N	101.21 W
Escocesa, Bahía c	238	19.25 N	69.45 W
Escoheag	207	41.36 N	71.45 W
Escondido	228	33.07 N	117.05 W
Escondido ≃, Méx.	196	28.39 N	100.34 W
Escondido ≃, Nic.	236	12.04 N	83.45 W
Escondido Creek ≃	228	33.01 N	117.15 W
Escorial → San Lorenzo de El Escorial	34	40.35 N	4.09 W
Escoutay ≃	62	44.29 N	4.42 E
Escravos ≃[1]	150	5.35 N	5.10 E
Escrick	44	53.53 N	1.02 W
Escuadrón 201 ◆[8]	286a	19.22 N	99.06 W
Escudero, Arroyo ≃	258	34.20 S	57.05 W
Escudo de Veraguas, Isla I	236	9.06 N	81.33 W
Escuinapa [de Hidalgo]	234	22.51 N	105.48 W
Escuintla, Guat.	236	14.18 N	90.47 W
Escuintla, Méx.	232	15.20 N	92.38 W
Escuintla □[5]	236	14.10 N	91.00 W
Escuminac, Point ›	186	47.04 N	64.46 W
Escurial, Serra do ∧	250	10.04 S	41.05 W
Esebi	154	2.57 N	30.39 E
Eséka	152	3.39 N	10.46 E
Eşen	130	36.27 N	29.16 E
Eşen ≃	130	36.16 N	29.15 E
Esenler ◆[8]	267b	41.02 N	28.51 E
Esens	52	53.39 N	7.37 E
Esera ≃	34	42.06 N	0.15 E
Esesi	130	39.49 N	39.19 E
Eṣfahān (Isfahan)	128	32.40 N	51.38 E
Eṣfahān □[4]	128	33.00 N	52.00 E
Esfandaqeh	128	28.38 N	57.12 E
Esfarāyen	128	37.02 N	57.27 E
Esgueva ≃	34	41.40 N	4.43 W
Eshan	102	24.11 N	102.22 E
Esher ◆[8]	260	51.23 N	0.22 W
Eshkāshem	123	36.42 N	71.34 E
Eshowe	158	28.58 S	31.29 E
Esh-Sham → Dimashq	132	33.30 N	36.18 E
Eshta'ol	132	31.47 N	35.00 E
Esh Winning	44	54.47 N	1.43 W
Esiama	150	4.56 N	2.21 W
Esigodini	154	20.18 S	28.56 E
Esine	64	45.55 N	10.15 E
Esino ≃	66	43.39 N	13.22 E
Esira	157b	24.20 S	46.42 E
Esk	171a	27.15 S	152.25 E
Esk ≃, N.Z.	172	43.06 S	171.57 E
Esk ≃, U.K.	44	54.58 N	3.04 W
Esk ≃, Eng., U.K.	44	54.29 N	0.37 W
Esk ≃, Eng., U.K.	44	54.21 N	3.23 W
Esk ≃, Scot., U.K.	46	55.57 N	3.03 W
Eskdale, N.Z.	172	39.24 S	176.50 E
Eskdale, W.V., U.S.	188	38.05 N	81.26 W
Eskdale V	44	55.10 N	3.00 W
Eske, Lough ⊜	48	54.41 N	8.03 W
Eski Dzhumaya → Târgovište	38	43.15 N	26.34 E
Eskifjörður	24a	65.04 N	13.59 W
Eskiikan	85	43.12 N	68.31 E
Eskilstrup	41	54.51 N	11.54 E
Eskilstuna	40	59.22 N	16.30 E
Eskimalatya	130	38.26 N	38.23 E
Eskimo Lakes ⊜	180	69.15 N	132.17 W
Eskimo Point	176	61.07 N	94.03 W
Eskipazar	130	40.58 N	32.33 E
Eskişehir	130	39.46 N	30.32 E
Eskişehir □[4]	130	39.35 N	31.10 E
Eskridge	198	38.51 N	96.06 W
Esla ≃	34	41.29 N	6.03 W
Eslāmābād	128	34.06 N	46.31 E
Eslām Qalʻeh	128	34.40 N	61.04 E
Eslāmshahr	128	35.40 N	51.10 E
Eslarn	60	49.35 N	12.32 E
Eslohe	56	51.15 N	8.09 E
Eslöv	41	55.50 N	13.20 E
Eşme	130	38.24 N	28.59 E
Esmeralda, Austl.	166	18.50 S	142.34 E
Esmeralda, Cuba	240p	21.51 N	78.07 W
Esmeralda, Méx.	196	25.40 N	103.30 W
Esmeralda, Isla I	254	48.57 S	75.25 W
Esmeraldas	246	0.59 N	79.42 W
Esmeraldas □[4]	246	0.40 N	79.30 W
Esmeraldas ≃	246	0.58 N	79.38 W
Esmirna → İzmir	130	38.25 N	27.09 E
Esmond, N.D., U.S.	198	48.02 N	99.45 W
Esmond, R.I., U.S.	207	41.52 N	71.29 W
Esnagi Lake ⊜	190	48.38 N	84.32 W
Esneux	56	50.32 N	5.34 E
Esong	152	2.09 N	10.58 E
Esopus Creek ≃	210	42.04 N	73.56 W
Espada, Punta ›	246	12.05 N	71.07 W
Espagne → Spain □[1]	34	40.00 N	4.00 W
Espalion	32	44.31 N	2.46 E
Espaly-Saint-Marcel	62	45.03 N	3.52 E
España → Spain □[1]	34	40.00 N	4.00 W

≃ River	Fluß	Río	Rivière	Rio
≊ Canal	Kanal	Canal	Canal	Canal
∟ Waterfall, Rapids	Wasserfall, Stromschnellen	Cascada, Rápidos	Chute d'eau, Rapides	Cascata, Rápidos
⅄ Strait	Meeresstraße	Estrecho	Détroit	Estreito
c Bay, Gulf	Bucht, Golf	Bahía, Golfo	Baie, Golfe	Baía, Golfo
⊜ Lake, Lakes	See, Seen	Lago, Lagos	Lac, Lacs	Lago, Lagos
≡ Swamp	Sumpf	Pantano	Marais	Pântano
✻ Ice Features, Glacier	Eis- und Gletscherformen	Accidentes Glaciales	Formes glaciaires	Acidentes glaciares
⊤ Other Hydrographic Features	Andere Hydrographische Objekte	Otros Elementos Hidrográficos	Autres données hydrographiques	Outros acidentes hidrográficos
✦ Submarine Features	Untermeerische Objekte	Accidentes Submarinos	Formes de relief sous-marin	Acidentes submarinos
□ Political Unit	Politische Einheit	Unidad Politica	Entité politique	Unidade política
ʊ Cultural Institution	Kulturelle Institution	Institución Cultural	Institution culturelle	Instituição cultural
⊥ Historical Site	Historische Stätte	Sitio Histórico	Site historique	Sitio histórico
♠ Recreational Site	Erholungs- und Ferienort	Sitio de Recreo	Centre de loisirs	Area de Lazer
⊠ Airport	Flughafen	Aeropuerto	Aéroport	Aeroporto
■ Military Installation	Militäranlage	Instalación Militar	Installation militaire	Instalação militar
◆ Miscellaneous	Verschiedenes	Misceláneo	Divers	Diversos

ENGLISH — Name, Page, Lat.°′, Long.°′ · **DEUTSCH** — Name, Seite, Breite°′, Länge°′ E = Ost

Name	Page	Lat.°′	Long.°′
Espanola, On., Can.	190	46.15 N	81.46 W
Espanola, N.M., U.S.	200	35.59 N	106.04 W
Española, Isla I	246a	1.25 S	89.42 W
Esparta	236	9.59 N	84.40 W
Esparto	226	38.41 N	122.00 W
Espasingen	58	47.49 N	9.00 E
Espe, Dan.	41	55.12 N	10.25 E
Espe, S.S.S.R.	85	43.52 N	74.10 E
Espejo	34	37.41 N	4.33 W
Espejo, Canal de ≌	286e	33.32 S	70.43 W
Espelkamp	52	52.25 N	8.36 E
Espenberg, Cape ›	180	66.33 N	163.36 W
Espenhain	54	51.11 N	12.29 E
Espera, Arroyo ≃[1]	288	34.24 S	58.36 W
Espera Feliz	255	20.39 S	41.55 W
Esperança, Bra.	246	4.24 S	69.52 W
Esperança, Bra.	250	7.01 S	35.51 W
Esperance, Austl.	162	33.51 S	121.53 E
Esperance, N.Y., U.S.	210	42.46 N	74.15 W
Esperance Bay ⊂	162	33.51 S	121.53 E
Esperantina	250	3.54 S	42.14 W
Esperantinópolis	250	4.53 S	44.53 W
Esperanza, Arg.	252	31.27 S	60.56 W
Esperanza, Méx.	232	27.35 N	109.56 W
Esperanza, Méx.	234	18.52 N	97.24 W
Esperanza, Pil.	116	11.44 N	124.03 E
Esperanza, Pil.	116	8.43 N	125.36 E
Esperanza, P.R.	240m	18.06 N	65.28 W
Esperanza, S. Afr.	158	30.21 S	30.40 E
Esperanza ʊ[3]	9	63.24 S	56.59 W
Esperanza Inlet ⊂	182	49.48 N	126.50 W
Espergærde	41	56.00 N	12.34 E
Esperia	66	41.23 N	13.41 E
Esperito, Arroyo ≃[1]	288	34.23 S	58.36 W
Espevær	26	59.36 N	5.10 E
Espichel, Cabo ›	34	38.25 N	9.13 W
Espinal, Col.	246	4.09 N	74.53 W
Espinal, Méx.	234	16.29 N	95.03 W
Espinar	248	14.47 S	71.29 W
Espinazo	196	26.16 N	101.06 W
Espinazo, Sierra del → Espinhaço, Serra do ⋀	255	17.30 S	43.30 W
Espinazo del Diablo, Sierra ⋀	234	23.55 N	106.00 W
Espingarda ≃	250	10.03 S	47.13 W
Espinhaço, Serra do ⋀	255	17.30 S	43.30 W
Espinho	34	41.00 N	8.39 W
Espinillo	252	24.58 S	58.34 W
Espinillo, Arroyo ≃	258	34.59 S	57.36 W
Espinillo, Punta ›	258	34.50 S	56.26 W
Espino	246	8.34 N	66.01 W
Espinosa	255	14.56 S	42.50 W
Espinos de Judio	234	19.52 N	104.35 W
Espírito Santo → Vila Velha	250	3.13 N	51.13 W
Espírito Santo □[3]	255	19.30 S	40.30 W
Espírito Santo do Dourado	256	22.03 S	45.58 W
Espiritu Santo I	175f	15.15 S	166.50 E
Espíritu Santo, Bahía del ⊂	232	19.20 N	87.35 W
Espíritu Santo, Isla del I	232	24.30 N	110.22 W
Espita	232	21.01 N	88.19 W
Esplanada	255	11.47 S	37.57 W
Espoir, Bay d' ⊂	186	47.50 N	55.51 W
Espoo (Esbo)	26	60.13 N	24.40 E
Esposende	34	41.32 N	8.47 W
Esposizione Universale di Roma ♠	267a	41.50 N	12.28 E
Espugues de Llobregat	266d	41.22 N	2.05 E
Espumoso	252	28.44 S	52.51 W
Espungabera	156	20.29 S	32.48 E
Espy	210	41.00 N	76.24 W
Espyville Station	214	41.36 N	80.29 W
Esquatzel Coulee ∨	202	46.17 N	119.07 W
Esquel	254	42.54 S	71.19 W
Esquimalt	224	48.26 N	123.24 W
Esquina	252	30.01 S	59.32 W
Esquina Negra	258	35.02 S	58.03 W
Esquipulas, Guat.	236	14.34 N	89.21 W
Esquipulas, Nic.	236	12.40 N	85.47 W
Esquiú	252	29.23 S	65.17 W
Esrum Sø ⊜	41	56.00 N	12.24 E
Essa ≃	76	54.53 N	28.40 E
Essaoui Mellene, Oued ∨	148	27.26 N	6.40 E
Essaouira (Mogador)	148	31.30 N	9.47 W
Essaouira □[4]	148	31.25 N	9.30 W
Essarts	261	48.30 N	1.46 E
Essé	152	4.05 N	11.53 E
Esse ≃	66	43.16 N	11.54 E
Esseg → Osijek	38	45.33 N	18.41 E
Es-Sekhira	148	34.17 N	10.06 E
Essen, Bel.	50	51.28 N	4.28 E
Essen, B.R.D.	52	52.43 N	7.57 E
Essen, B.R.D.	56	51.28 N	7.01 E
Essen, B.R.D.	263	51.28 N	7.01 E
Essenbach	60	48.37 N	12.13 E
Essenberg ⬥[8]	263	51.26 N	6.42 E
Essendon, Austl.	169	37.46 S	144.55 E
Essendon, Eng., U.K.	260	51.46 N	0.09 W
Essendon, Mount ∧	162	24.59 S	120.28 E
Essendon Airport ⊠	169	37.43 S	144.53 E
Essen-Mülheim, Flughafen ⊠	263	51.24 N	6.58 E
Essentuki → Jessentuki	84	44.03 N	42.51 E
Essequibo ≃	246	6.59 N	58.23 W
Es Sers	36	36.04 N	9.02 E
Essex, On., Can.	214	42.10 N	82.49 W
Essex, Ct., U.S.	207	41.21 N	72.23 W
Essex, Il., U.S.	216	41.11 N	88.11 W
Essex, Ia., U.S.	198	40.50 N	95.18 W
Essex, Md., U.S.	208	39.18 N	76.28 W
Essex, Ma., U.S.	207	42.37 N	70.47 W
Essex, Mo., U.S.	194	36.48 N	89.51 W
Essex, Mt., U.S.	182	48.16 N	113.36 W
Essex □[6], On., Can.	214	42.10 N	82.50 W
Essex □[6], Eng., U.K.	42	51.48 N	0.40 E
Essex □[6], Ma., U.S.	207	42.40 N	70.55 W
Essex □[6], N.J., U.S.	210	40.48 N	74.12 W
Essex □[6], Vt., U.S.	206	44.57 N	71.43 W
Essex □[6], Va., U.S.	208	37.55 N	76.55 W
Essex ≃	283	42.39 N	70.46 W
Essex Bay ⊂	283	42.39 N	70.44 W
Essex Fells	276	40.49 N	74.17 W
Essex Junction	188	44.29 N	73.06 W
Essex Skypark ⊠	284b	39.18 N	76.28 W
Essexville	190	43.36 N	83.50 W
Essing	60	48.56 N	11.47 E
Essington	285	39.52 N	75.18 W
Essling ⬥[8]	264b	48.13 N	16.32 E
Esslingen	56	48.45 N	9.16 E
Es Smala es Souassi	36	35.21 N	10.33 E
Esson Lake ⊜	212	45.02 N	78.16 W
Essonne □[5]	50	48.36 N	2.20 E
Essonne ≃	50	48.37 N	2.29 E
Essoyes	58	48.04 N	4.32 E
Es-Suki	140	13.20 N	33.54 E
Essvik	26	62.19 N	17.24 E
Est □[4]	152	4.00 N	14.00 E
Est, Canal de l' ≌	58	48.45 N	5.35 E
Est, Cap ›	157b	15.16 S	50.29 E
Est, Gare ⬥[5]	261	48.53 N	2.22 E
Est, Île de l' I	186	47.37 N	61.26 W
Est, Pointe de l' ›	186	49.08 N	61.41 W
Estacada	224	45.17 N	122.19 W
Estaca de Bares, Punta de la ›	34	43.46 N	7.42 W
Estacado, Llano ≚	196	33.30 N	102.40 W
Estado, Parque do ♠	287b	23.39 S	46.37 W
Estados, Isla de los (Staten Island) I	254	54.47 S	64.15 W
Estados Unidos → United States □[1]	178	38.00 N	97.00 W
Eṣṭahbān	128	29.08 N	54.04 E
Estaires	50	50.38 N	2.43 E
Estambul → İstanbul	130	41.01 N	28.58 E
Estância, Bra.	250	11.16 S	37.26 W
Estancia, Pil.	116	11.28 N	123.09 E
Estancia, S. Afr.	158	26.17 S	29.52 E
Estancia, N.M., U.S.	200	34.45 N	106.03 W
Estancia de los López	234	20.53 N	104.31 W
Estandarte	250	1.26 S	45.32 W
Estanislao del Campo	252	25.03 S	60.06 W
Estanzuelas	236	13.38 N	88.30 W
Estarreja	34	40.45 N	8.34 W
Estats, Pique d' ∧	34	42.40 N	1.24 E
Estavayer-le-Lac	58	46.51 N	6.50 E
Estcourt	158	29.01 S	29.52 E
Este	64	45.14 N	11.39 E
Este ≃	52	53.32 N	9.47 E
Este, Parque Nacional del ♠	286c	10.30 N	66.50 W
Este, Punta ›	240m	18.08 N	65.16 W
Esteban Echeverría	258	34.50 S	58.28 W
Esteban Echeverría □[5]	288	34.51 S	58.32 W
Estefanía, Lago → Stefanie, Lake ⊜	144	4.40 N	36.50 E
Esteio	252	29.51 S	51.10 W
Estelí	236	13.05 N	86.23 W
Estelí □[5]	236	13.10 N	86.20 W
Estella	34	42.40 N	2.02 W
Estelline, S.D., U.S.	198	44.34 N	96.54 W
Estelline, Tx., U.S.	196	34.33 N	100.26 W
Estell Manor	208	39.24 N	74.44 W
Estèng	62	44.14 N	6.45 E
Estepa	34	37.18 N	4.54 W
Estepas de Kirguises → Kirgizskij chrebet ⋀	85	42.30 N	74.00 E
Estepona	34	36.26 N	5.08 W
Ester	180	64.51 N	148.01 W
Esterel ⋀	62	43.30 N	6.50 E
Esterhazy	184	50.40 N	102.08 W
Esterhazy, Schloss ⊥	61	47.51 N	16.32 E
Estérias, Cap ›	152	0.37 N	9.20 E
Esternay	50	48.44 N	3.34 E
Estero	220	26.26 N	81.49 W
Estero Bay ⊂, Ca., U.S.	226	35.24 N	120.53 W
Estero Bay ⊂, Fl., U.S.	220	26.25 N	81.52 W
Estero Island I	220	26.26 N	81.56 W
Estéron ≃	62	43.49 N	7.11 E
Esteros	252	26.37 S	63.39 W
Esterwegen	52	52.59 N	7.38 E
Estes Park	200	40.22 N	105.31 W
Este Sudeste, Cayos del II	236	12.26 N	81.27 W
Estevan	184	49.08 N	102.59 W
Estevan Group II	182	53.05 N	129.40 W
Estevan Point	182	49.23 N	126.33 W
Esther Island I	180	60.50 N	148.05 W
Estherville	198	43.24 N	94.49 W
Estí ≃	236	8.28 N	82.16 W
Estill	192	32.45 N	81.14 W
Estissac	50	48.16 N	3.49 E
Estiva	256	22.28 S	46.02 W
Estiva, Ribeirão da ≃	287b	23.44 S	46.23 W
Estling, Lake ⊜	276	40.53 N	74.30 W
Estocolmo → Stockholm	40	59.20 N	18.03 E
Eston, Sk., Can.	184	51.10 N	108.46 W
Eston, Eng., U.K.	44	54.34 N	1.07 W
Estonia → Estonskaja Sovetskaja Socialističeskaja Respublika □[3]	76	59.00 N	26.00 E
Estonskaja Sovetskaja Socialističeskaja Respublika □[3]	76	59.00 N	26.00 E
Estoril	34	38.42 N	9.23 W
Estrasburgo → Strasbourg	58	48.35 N	7.45 E
Estrées-Saint-Denis	50	49.26 N	2.39 E
Estrêla	252	29.29 S	51.58 W
Estrela ∧	34	40.19 N	7.37 W
Estrêla ≃	287a	22.43 S	43.13 W
Estrela, Serra da ⋀	34	40.20 N	7.38 W
Estrêla do Indaiá	255	19.31 S	45.47 W
Estrêla do Leste	255	16.17 S	53.34 W
Estrêla do Norte	255	13.49 S	49.04 W
Estrêla do Sul	255	18.46 S	47.42 W
Estrella ≃	226	35.45 N	120.41 W
Estrella, Cerro de la ∧	286a	19.20 N	99.05 W
Estrella, Punta ›	232	30.55 N	114.43 W
Estremadura □[9]	34	39.15 N	9.10 W
Estremoz	34	38.51 N	7.35 W
Estrondo, Serra do ⋀[1]	250	9.00 S	48.45 W
Estuaire □[4]	152	0.15 N	10.00 E
Estuary	184	50.56 N	109.46 W
Esumba, Île I	152	2.00 N	21.12 E
Eszék → Osijek	38	45.33 N	18.41 E
Esztergom	30	47.48 N	18.45 E
Étables	32	48.38 N	2.50 W
Etadunna	166	28.43 S	138.38 E
Etah, India	124	27.38 N	78.40 E
Etah, Kal. Nun.	16	78.19 N	72.38 W
Étain	56	49.13 N	5.38 E
Etajima	96	34.15 N	132.30 E
Eta-jima I	96	34.15 N	132.28 E
Étalle	56	49.41 N	5.36 E
Étamaniou ≃	186	50.17 N	59.58 W
Étampes	50	48.26 N	2.09 E
Etamunbanie, Lake ⊜	166	26.15 S	139.44 E
Étaples	50	50.31 N	1.39 E
États-Unis → United States □[1]	178	38.00 N	97.00 W
Etāwah	124	26.46 N	79.02 E
Etchemin ≃	186	46.46 N	71.14 W
Etchojoa	232	26.55 N	109.38 W
Etchoropo	232	26.41 N	109.40 W
Etéké	152	1.29 S	11.35 E
Etembue	152	1.17 N	9.25 E
Eten	248	6.54 S	79.52 W
Etendard, Pic de l' ∧	62	45.09 N	6.09 E
Eternity Range ⋀	9	69.46 S	64.34 W
Ethan	198	43.32 N	97.59 W
Ethel	194	33.07 N	89.27 W
Ethel ≃	162	24.09 S	118.26 E
Ethel, Mount ∧	200	40.39 N	106.41 W
Ethelbert	184	51.31 N	100.22 W
Ethel Creek	162	22.54 S	120.09 E
Ethel Lake ⊜	180	63.21 N	136.00 W
Etherow ≃	262	53.24 N	2.03 W
Ethiopia (Ityopiya) □[1], Afr.	136	9.00 N	39.00 E
Ethiopia (Ityopiya) □[1], Afr.	144	9.00 N	39.00 E
Ethiopian Plateau ⋀[1]	144	9.00 N	38.00 E
Ethiopie → Ethiopia □[1]	144	9.00 N	39.00 E
Ethridge, Mt., U.S.	202	48.33 N	112.07 W
Ethridge, Tn., U.S.	194	35.19 N	87.18 W
Eticoga	150	11.09 N	16.08 W
Eticuera Creek ≃	226	38.41 N	122.16 W
Etigo-heiya ≚	92	37.45 N	139.00 E
Etili	130	39.59 N	26.54 E
Étiolles	261	48.38 N	2.29 E
Etiopía → Ethiopia □[1]	144	9.00 N	39.00 E
Etive, Loch ⊜	46	56.29 N	5.09 W
Etiwanda	228	34.08 N	117.31 W
Etjo ∧	156	21.09 S	16.30 E
Etna, Ca., U.S.	204	41.27 N	122.53 W
Etna, N.Y., U.S.	210	42.29 N	76.23 W
Etna, Pa., U.S.	214	40.30 N	79.56 W
Etna, Wy., U.S.	200	43.02 N	111.00 W
Etna, Monte (Mongibello) ∧[1]	70	37.46 N	15.00 E
Etna Green	216	41.17 N	86.03 W
Etne	26	59.40 N	5.56 E
Etobicoke	212	43.42 N	79.32 W
Etobicoke Creek ≃	212	43.35 N	79.32 W
Etoile	154	11.38 S	27.34 E
Étoile, Chaîne de l' ⋀	62	43.22 N	5.30 E
Etoka	152	0.10 N	23.23 E
Etolin Island I	180	56.08 N	132.26 W
Etolin Strait ⊔	180	60.20 N	165.15 W
Etomami ≃	184	52.48 N	102.33 W
Eton, Austl.	166	21.16 S	148.58 E
Eton, Eng., U.K.	260	51.31 N	0.37 W
Eton College ʊ[2]	260	51.30 N	0.36 W
Etondo	152	7.46 S	23.36 E
Etorofu-tō → Iturup, ostrov I	92a	44.54 N	147.30 E
Etosha National Park ♠	156	19.00 S	15.50 E
Etosha Pan ≚	156	18.45 S	16.15 E
Etoumbi	152	0.01 S	14.57 E
Etowah	192	35.19 N	84.31 W
Etowah ≃	192	34.15 N	85.11 W
Étréchy	50	48.30 N	2.12 E
Étrépagny	50	49.18 N	1.37 E
Étretat	50	49.42 N	0.12 E
Etrotroka	157b	22.53 S	47.36 E
Etroubles	62	45.49 N	7.14 E
Etrusca, Necropoli ⊥	66	42.15 N	11.47 E
Etsch → Adige ≃	64	45.10 N	12.20 E
Ettal	64	47.34 N	11.05 E
Ettalong	170	33.31 S	151.21 E
Ettelbruck	56	49.52 N	6.05 E
Ettenheim	58	48.15 N	7.49 E
Etten-Leur	52	51.34 N	4.38 E
Etterbeek	56	50.50 N	4.23 E
Etters	208	40.09 N	76.45 W
Et Tîdra I	150	19.44 N	16.24 W
Ettington	42	52.09 N	1.36 W
Ettlingen	56	48.56 N	8.24 E
Ettrema Creek ≃	170	34.50 S	150.22 E
Ettrick	208	37.14 N	77.25 W
Ettrick Forest ⬥[3]	46	55.30 N	3.00 W
Ettrick Pen ∧	44	55.22 N	3.16 W
Ettrick Water ≃	46	55.31 N	2.55 W
Ettringen, B.R.D.	56	50.21 N	7.13 E
Ettringen, B.R.D.	58	48.06 N	10.39 E
Etuku	154	3.43 S	25.44 E
Etyka	88	51.00 N	116.50 E
Etzatlán	234	20.46 N	104.05 W
Etzikom Coulee ≃	184	49.25 N	111.10 W
Etzná-Tixmucuy ⊥	232	19.35 N	90.15 W
Eu	50	50.03 N	1.25 E
Eua I	14	21.22 S	174.56 W
Eua Iki I	174w	21.07 S	174.59 W
Eubank Acres	222	30.23 N	97.42 W
Eubanque	256	21.33 S	43.30 W
Euboea → Évvoia I	38	38.34 N	23.50 E
Eucalyptus Hills	228	32.56 N	116.56 W
Euchiniko ≃	182	53.14 N	123.30 W
Eucla	162	31.43 S	128.52 E
Euclid, Oh., U.S.	214	41.35 N	81.31 W
Euclid, Pa., U.S.	214	41.00 N	79.56 W
Euclid Center	216	42.08 N	86.24 W
Euclid Creek ≃	279a	41.35 N	81.35 W
Euclid Creek Reservation ♠	279a	41.33 N	81.32 W
Euclides da Cunha	250	10.31 S	39.01 W
Eucumbene	171b	36.07 S	148.38 E
Eucumbene ≃	171b	36.21 S	148.38 E
Eucumbene, Lake ⊜[1]	171b	36.05 S	148.45 E
Eucumbene Dam ⬥[5]	171b	36.07 S	148.40 E
Eudistes, Lac des ⊜	186	50.30 N	65.15 W
Eudora, Ar., U.S.	194	33.06 N	91.15 W
Eudora, Ks., U.S.	198	38.56 N	95.05 W
Eudunda	168b	34.11 S	139.04 E
Eufaula, Al., U.S.	194	31.53 N	85.08 W
Eufaula, Ok., U.S.	196	35.17 N	95.34 W
Eufaula Lake ⊜[1]	196	35.17 N	95.31 W
Eufrates → Euphrates ≃	128	31.00 N	47.25 E
Euganei, Colli ⋀[2]	64	45.19 N	11.40 E
Eugendorf	64	47.52 N	13.07 E
Eugene	202	44.03 N	123.05 W
Eugenia, Punta ›	232	27.50 N	115.05 W
Eugenia Lake ⊜	212	44.20 N	80.30 W
Eugenio Bustos	252	33.46 S	69.04 W
Eugênio de Melo	256	23.09 S	45.47 W
Eugenópolis	255	21.06 S	42.11 W
Eugmo I	26	63.49 N	22.45 E
Eugowra	166	33.26 S	148.23 E
Euijeongbu → Ŭijŏngbu	98	37.44 N	127.03 E
Euless	222	32.50 N	97.04 W
Eulo	166	28.10 S	145.03 E
Eulogio Sánchez Errázuriz, Aeropuerto ⊠	286e	33.27 S	70.33 W
Eume ≃	34	43.25 N	8.08 W
Eumemmerring Creek ≃	274b	38.03 S	145.10 E
Eumungerie	166	31.57 S	148.37 E
Eungella National Park ♠	166	21.00 S	148.30 E
Eunice, La., U.S.	194	30.29 N	92.25 W
Eunice, N.M., U.S.	196	32.26 N	103.09 W
Eupen	56	50.38 N	6.02 E
Euphrat → Euphrates ≃	128	31.00 N	47.25 E
Euphrates (Fırat) (Nahr al-Furāt) ≃	128	31.00 N	47.25 E
Eupora	194	33.32 N	89.16 W
Eure	208	36.25 N	76.51 W
Eure □[5]	50	49.10 N	1.00 E
Eure ≃	50	49.18 N	1.12 E
Eure-et-Loir □[5]	50	48.30 N	1.30 E
Eureka, Ak., U.S.	180	61.56 N	147.10 W
Eureka, Ca., U.S.	204	40.48 N	124.09 W
Eureka, Il., U.S.	190	40.43 N	89.16 W
Eureka, Ks., U.S.	198	37.49 N	96.17 W
Eureka, Mo., U.S.	219	38.30 N	90.37 W
Eureka, Mt., U.S.	202	48.52 N	115.03 W
Eureka, Nv., U.S.	204	39.30 N	115.57 W
Eureka, Pa., U.S.	214	40.15 N	78.46 W
Eureka, S.C., U.S.	192	34.42 N	81.11 W
Eureka, S.D., U.S.	198	45.46 N	99.37 W
Eureka, Tx., U.S.	222	32.01 N	96.18 W
Eureka, Ut,. U.S.	200	39.57 N	112.07 W
Eureka, Mount ∧	162	26.34 S	121.32 E
Eureka Springs	194	36.24 N	93.44 W
Eurialo, Castello ⊥	70	37.06 N	15.14 E
Eurinilla Creek ≃	166	30.50 S	140.01 E
Euroa	169	36.45 S	145.35 E
Europa, Île I	138	22.20 S	40.22 E
Europa, Picos de ⋀	34	43.12 N	4.48 W
Europabrücke ⬥[5]	64	47.11 N	11.23 E
Europa Point ›	34	36.10 N	5.22 W
Europe ⩡[1]	4	50.00 N	28.00 E
Europe ⩡[1]	10	50.00 N	28.00 E
Europoort ⬥[5]	52	51.58 N	4.00 E
Eursinge	52	52.46 N	6.28 E
Eurville	58	48.35 N	5.02 E
Euseigne	58	46.10 N	7.25 E
Euskal Herriko □[4]	34	43.00 N	2.30 W
Euskirchen	56	50.39 N	6.47 E
Eustace	222	32.18 N	96.01 W
Eustis, Fl., U.S.	220	28.51 N	81.41 W
Eustis, Ne., U.S.	198	40.39 N	100.09 W
Eustis, Lake ⊜	220	28.50 N	81.44 W
Euston	166	34.35 S	142.44 E
Euston Station ⬥[5]	260	51.32 N	0.08 W
Eutaw	194	32.50 N	87.53 W
Eutin	54	54.08 N	10.37 E
Eutingen	56	48.28 N	8.44 E
Eutsuk Lake ⊜	182	53.20 N	126.44 W
Eutzsch	54	51.49 N	12.38 E
Euxton, Eng., U.K.	44	53.39 N	2.40 W
Euxton, Eng., U.K.	262	53.40 N	2.41 W
Euzet-les-Bains	62	44.04 N	4.14 E
Eva	194	34.20 N	86.46 W
Evadale	194	30.21 N	94.04 W
Eva Downs	162	18.01 S	134.52 E
Evale	152	16.33 S	15.44 E
Evällen ⊜	40	60.03 N	18.20 E
Evançon ≃	62	45.40 N	7.41 E
Evandale	166	41.34 S	147.14 E
Evans	200	40.22 N	104.41 W
Evans, Lac ⊜	176	50.55 N	77.00 W
Evans, Mount ∧	200	39.35 N	105.38 W
Evansburg, Ab., Can.	182	53.36 N	115.01 W
Evansburg, Pa., U.S.	285	40.11 N	75.26 W
Evans Center	210	42.39 N	79.02 W
Evans City	214	40.46 N	80.03 W
Evans Creek ≃	202	42.25 N	123.11 W
Evansdale	190	42.28 N	92.16 W
Evans Head ›	166	29.07 S	153.26 E
Evans Mills	212	44.05 N	75.48 W
Evansport	216	41.25 N	84.24 W
Evans Strait ⊔	176	63.15 N	82.00 W
Evanston, Il., U.S.	216	42.02 N	87.41 W
Evanston, Pa., U.S.	279b	40.16 N	79.41 W
Evanston, Wy., U.S.	200	41.16 N	110.57 W
Evansville, Il., U.S.	194	38.05 N	89.56 W
Evansville, In., U.S.	194	37.58 N	87.33 W
Evansville, Mn., U.S.	198	46.00 N	95.40 W
Evansville, Wi., U.S.	216	42.46 N	89.17 W
Evansville, Wy., U.S.	200	42.51 N	106.16 W
Evant	196	31.29 N	98.09 W
Evanton	46	57.40 N	4.20 W
Eva Perón → La Plata	258	34.55 S	57.57 W
Evart	190	43.54 N	85.15 W
Evarts	192	36.51 N	83.11 W
Evaz	128	27.46 N	53.59 E
Ève	261	49.05 N	2.42 E
Evecquemont	261	49.02 N	1.57 E
Eveking	263	51.14 N	7.44 E
Eveleth	190	47.27 N	92.32 W
Evelyn, Mount ∧[2]	164	13.36 S	132.53 E
Evening Shade	194	36.04 N	91.37 W
Evenkamp	263	51.40 N	7.39 E
Evenkijskij Nacionalnyj Okrug □[8]	88	59.15 N	104.00 E
Evenlode ≃	42	51.47 N	1.21 W
Evensk	74	61.57 N	159.14 E
Evenwood	44	54.37 N	1.46 W
Even Yehuda	132	32.16 N	34.53 E
Everard, Lake ⊜	162	31.25 S	135.05 E
Everard, Mount ∧, Austl.	162	26.16 S	132.04 E
Everard, Mount ∧, B.C., Can.	182	51.05 N	125.45 W
Everard Ranges ⋀	162	27.05 S	132.28 E
Evercreech	42	51.09 N	2.30 W
Evere	56	50.52 N	4.24 E
Everest	198	39.40 N	95.25 W
Everest, Mount (Qomolangma Feng) ∧	124	27.59 N	86.56 E
Everett, On., Can.	212	44.11 N	79.57 W
Everett, Ma., U.S.	207	42.24 N	71.03 W
Everett, N.J., U.S.	276	40.21 N	74.09 W
Everett, Pa., U.S.	188	40.00 N	78.22 W
Everett, Wa., U.S.	224	47.58 N	122.12 W
Everett, Mount ∧	207	42.06 N	73.25 W
Evergem	50	51.07 N	3.42 E
Everglades City	220	25.52 N	81.23 W
Everglades National Park ♠	220	25.27 N	80.53 W
Evergreen, Al., U.S.	194	31.26 N	86.57 W
Evergreen, Ca., U.S.	204	35.54 N	120.26 W
Evergreen, Mt., U.S.	202	48.13 N	114.18 W
Evergreen, Tx., U.S.	222	30.33 N	95.14 W
Evergreen Lake ⊜[1]	216	40.40 N	89.02 W
Evergreen Park	216	41.43 N	87.42 W
Evergreen Plaza ⬥[9]	278	41.43 N	87.41 W
Everly	198	43.09 N	95.19 W
Everman	222	32.37 N	97.17 W
Everöd	26	55.54 N	14.06 E
Eversael	263	51.33 N	6.39 E
Eversberg	56	51.21 N	8.20 E
Eversen	52	52.45 N	10.02 E
Everson, Pa., U.S.	214	40.05 N	79.35 W
Everson, Wa., U.S.	224	48.55 N	122.20 W
Everswinkel	52	51.55 N	7.50 E
Everton	218	39.34 N	85.05 W
Everton ⬥[8]	262	53.25 N	2.58 W
Everton Football Ground ♠	262	53.26 N	2.58 W
Evesen	52	52.17 N	8.59 E
Evesham, Sk., Can.	184	52.24 N	109.50 W
Evesham, Eng., U.K.	42	52.06 N	1.56 W
Evesham, Vale of ∨	42	52.06 N	1.50 W
Évian-les-Bains	58	46.23 N	6.35 E
Evijärvi	26	63.22 N	23.29 E
Evinayong	152	1.27 N	10.34 E
Eving ⬥[8]	263	51.33 N	7.29 E
Evingsen	263	51.18 N	7.44 E
Evionnaz	58	46.11 N	7.01 E
Evisa	36	42.15 N	8.47 E
Evje	26	58.36 N	7.51 E
Evolène	58	46.07 N	7.30 E
Évora	34	38.34 N	7.54 W
Evoron, ozero ⊜	89	51.28 N	136.30 E
Evpatoria → Jevpatorija	78	45.12 N	33.22 E
Évrange	56	49.30 N	6.12 E
Évreux	50	49.01 N	1.09 E
Evrieu	62	45.35 N	5.34 E
'Evron	132	32.59 N	35.06 E
Évros (Marica) (Meriç) ≃	38	40.52 N	26.12 E
Evrótas ≃	38	36.48 N	22.40 E
Évry	50	48.38 N	2.27 E
Évry-les-Châteaux	261	48.39 N	2.38 E
E. V. Spence Reservoir ⊜[1]	196	31.55 N	100.35 W
Evungu	154	4.27 S	25.12 E
Évvoia I	38	38.34 N	23.50 E
Évzonos ∧	267c	37.57 N	23.49 E
Ewa	229c	21.20 N	158.02 W
Ewa Beach	229c	21.18 N	158.00 W
Ewan	285	39.42 N	75.11 W
Ewaninga	162	23.58 S	133.53 E
Ewan Lake ⊜	285	39.42 N	75.11 W
Ewansville	285	39.59 N	74.44 W
Ewarton	241q	18.11 N	77.05 W
Ewbank	158	26.14 S	23.35 E
Ewe, Loch ⊂	46	57.48 N	5.40 W
Ewell, Eng., U.K.	260	51.21 N	0.15 W
Ewell, Md., U.S.	208	37.59 N	76.02 W
Ewen	190	46.32 N	89.16 W
Ewenkiku Zizhiqi	89	49.07 N	119.40 E
Ewes Water ≃	44	55.08 N	3.00 W
Ewing, Ky., U.S.	218	38.25 N	83.51 W
Ewing, Mo., U.S.	219	40.00 N	91.42 W
Ewing, Ne., U.S.	198	42.15 N	98.20 W
Ewing, Va., U.S.	192	36.38 N	83.25 W
Ewingsville	279b	40.24 N	80.06 W
Ewing Township	208	40.16 N	74.46 W
Ewo	152	0.53 S	14.49 E
Ewu	273a	6.33 N	3.19 E
Exaltación	248	13.16 S	65.15 W
Excelda	158	32.16 S	22.08 E
Excello	218	39.29 N	84.25 W
Excelsior	158	28.56 S	27.06 E
Excelsior Mountain ∧	226	38.02 N	119.18 W
Excelsior Park ♠	274a	33.45 S	151.01 E
Excelsior Springs	194	39.20 N	94.13 W
Excenevex	58	46.21 N	6.21 E
Exchange	210	41.07 N	76.41 W
Exchange Station ⬥[5]	262	53.29 N	2.15 W
Excursion Inlet	180	58.25 N	135.27 W
Exe ≃	42	50.37 N	3.25 W
Executive Committee Range ⋀	9	76.50 S	126.00 W
Exeter, Austl.	170	34.38 S	150.19 E
Exeter, On., Can.	190	43.21 N	81.29 W
Exeter, Eng., U.K.	42	50.43 N	3.31 W
Exeter, Ca., U.S.	226	36.17 N	119.08 W
Exeter, Ne., U.S.	198	40.38 N	97.27 W
Exeter, N.H., U.S.	188	42.58 N	70.56 W
Exeter, Pa., U.S.	210	41.19 N	75.49 W
Exeter, R.I., U.S.	207	41.34 N	71.32 W
Exeter ≃	188	43.02 N	70.55 W
Exeter Sound ⊔	176	66.14 N	62.00 W
Exford	42	51.08 N	3.38 W
Exhibition of Economic Achievements ʊ	265b	55.50 N	37.37 E
Exhibition Park ♠	275b	43.38 N	79.25 W
Exhibition Stadium ♠	275b	43.38 N	79.25 W
Exincourt	58	47.30 N	6.50 E
Exira	198	41.35 N	94.52 W
Exline Slough ≃	216	41.05 N	87.47 W
Exloërmond	52	52.54 N	6.57 E
Exmes	50	48.46 N	0.11 E
Exminster	42	50.41 N	3.29 W
Exmoor ⋀[1]	42	51.10 N	3.45 W
Exmoor National Park ♠	42	51.12 N	3.46 W
Exmore	208	37.31 N	75.49 W
Exmouth, Austl.	162	21.56 S	114.07 E
Exmouth, Eng., U.K.	42	50.37 N	3.25 W
Exmouth Gulf ⊂	162	22.00 S	114.20 E
Exmouth Plateau ⊹[3]	14	19.00 S	114.00 E
Exning	42	52.16 N	0.21 E
Expedition Range ⋀	166	24.30 S	149.05 E
Experiment	192	33.15 N	84.16 W
Exploits ≃	186	49.05 N	55.20 W
Exploits, Bay of ⊂	186	49.24 N	55.00 W
Exploits Dam ⬥[6]	186	48.45 N	56.30 W
Expo Memorial Park ♠	270	34.48 N	135.32 E
Export	214	40.25 N	79.37 W
Exposition Park ♠	280	34.01 N	118.17 W
Exshaw	182	51.03 N	115.09 W
Extension	224	49.06 N	123.57 W
Exter	52	52.08 N	8.46 E
Externsteine ⊥	52	51.52 N	8.55 E
Extertal	52	52.04 N	9.07 E
Exton	208	40.02 N	75.37 W
Extorás ≃	234	21.06 N	99.23 W
Extrema	256	22.51 S	46.19 W
Extremadura □[4]	34	39.15 N	6.15 W
Exu	250	7.31 S	39.43 W
Exuma Cays II	238	24.15 N	76.30 W
Exuma Sound ⊔	238	24.15 N	76.00 W
Eyak	180	60.32 N	145.36 W
Eyam	44	53.17 N	1.41 W
Eyasi, Lake ⊜	154	3.40 S	35.05 E
Eydehavn	26	58.31 N	8.53 E
Eye, Eng., U.K.	42	52.19 N	1.09 E
Eye, Eng., U.K.	42	52.35 N	0.10 W
Eyebrow	184	50.47 N	106.09 W
Eyehill Creek ≃	184	52.40 N	109.39 W
Eyemouth	46	55.52 N	2.06 W
Eye Peninsula ›[1]	46	58.13 N	6.13 W
Eyers Grove	210	41.05 N	76.31 W
Eye Water ≃	46	55.53 N	2.06 W
Eygalières	62	43.45 N	4.57 E
Eyguières	62	43.42 N	5.02 E
Eyhorne Street	260	51.16 N	0.38 E
Eyjafjörður ⊂[2]	24a	65.54 N	18.15 W
Eyl	144	7.59 N	49.49 E
Eylar Mountain ∧	204	37.28 N	121.33 W
Eymet	32	44.40 N	0.24 E
Eymir	130	40.02 N	35.14 E
Eymoutiers	32	45.44 N	1.44 E
Eynesil	130	41.03 N	39.08 E
Eynhallow Sound ⊔	46	59.08 N	3.06 W
Eynort, Loch ⊂	46	57.13 N	7.18 W
Eynsford	260	51.22 N	0.13 E
Eynsham	42	51.48 N	1.22 W
Eyota	190	43.59 N	92.13 W
Eyrarbakki	24a	63.53 N	21.05 W
Eyre	162	32.15 S	126.18 E
Eyrecourt	48	53.11 N	8.07 W
Eyre Creek ≃	166	26.40 S	139.00 E
Eyre Mountains ⋀	172	45.20 S	168.30 E
Eyre North, Lake ⊜	166	28.40 S	137.10 E
Eyre Peninsula ›[1]	162	34.00 S	135.45 E
Eyre South, Lake ⊜	166	29.30 S	137.20 E
Eyrieux ≃	62	44.48 N	4.48 E
Eystrup	52	52.46 N	9.13 E
Eythorne	42	51.11 N	1.17 E
Eythra	54	51.14 N	12.17 E
Eyüp ⬥[8]	267b	41.03 N	28.55 E
Eyvānekey	128	35.20 N	52.04 E
Ézanville	261	49.02 N	2.22 E
Ezbekīyah ⬥[8]	273c	30.03 N	31.15 E
Ezeiza	258	34.51 S	58.32 W
Ezeiza, Aeropuerto Internacional de ⊠	288	34.49 S	58.32 W
Ezequiel Ramos Mexía, Embalse ⊜[1]	254	39.30 S	69.00 W
Ezere	76	56.26 N	22.22 E
Ežerėlis	76	54.53 N	23.37 E
Ezeriș	38	45.24 N	21.53 E
Ezine	130	39.47 N	26.20 E
Ezinepazarı	130	40.34 N	36.09 E
Ezop, chrebet ⋀	89	52.36 N	133.37 E
Ezpeleta	258	34.46 S	58.15 W
Ežva	24	61.47 N	50.40 E
Ézy-sur-Eure	50	48.52 N	1.25 E
Ezzell	222	29.17 N	96.58 W
F			
Faaa Airport ⊠	174s	17.33 S	149.36 W
Faafaxdhuun	144	2.13 N	41.37 E
Faal	174q	9.37 N	138.10 E
Faaone	174s	17.40 S	149.18 W
Fabala	150	9.44 N	9.05 W
Fabbrico	64	44.52 N	10.50 E
Fabens	200	31.30 N	106.09 W
Fåberg	26	61.10 N	10.24 E
Faber Lake ⊜	176	63.56 N	117.15 W
Fabert Seamount ⊹[3]	14	24.07 S	158.33 W
Fabius	210	42.50 N	75.59 W
Fåborg	41	55.06 N	10.15 E
Fábrega, Cerro ∧	236	9.07 N	82.52 W
Fabrègues	62	43.33 N	3.46 E
Fabreville ⬥[8]	275a	45.34 N	73.50 W
Fabriano	66	43.20 N	12.54 E
Fabrica di Roma	66	42.20 N	12.18 E
Fabričnyj	85	43.11 N	76.24 E
Fabrizia	68	38.29 N	16.18 E
Facatativá	246	4.49 N	74.22 W
Facha	146	29.27 N	17.18 E
Faches-Thumesnil	50	50.35 N	3.04 E
Fachi	146	18.06 N	11.34 E
Facpi Point ›	174p	13.20 N	144.38 E
Factoryville	210	41.34 N	75.47 W
Facundo	254	45.18 S	69.58 W
Fada	146	17.14 N	21.33 E
Fada, Lochan ⊜	46	57.41 N	5.18 W
Fadalto	64	46.05 N	12.20 E
Fada Ngourma	150	12.04 N	0.21 E
Fadd	30	46.28 N	18.50 E
Faddeja, zaliv ⊂	74	76.40 N	107.20 E
Faddejevskij, ostrov I	74	75.30 N	144.00 E
Faddoi	140	8.07 N	32.07 E
Fadian Point ›	174p	13.26 N	144.49 E
Fadiffolu Atoll I[1]	122	5.25 N	73.30 E
Fadit	140	9.58 N	32.13 E
Faedis	64	46.10 N	13.20 E
Fænø I	41	55.29 N	9.42 E
Faenza	66	44.17 N	11.53 E
Faeroe Islands □[2]	22	62.00 N	7.00 W
Faeröerne → Faeroe Islands □[2]	22	62.00 N	7.00 W
Faete, Monte ∧	267a	41.45 N	12.44 E
Fafa	150	15.20 N	0.43 E
Fafa ≃	152	7.18 N	18.16 E
Fafakourou	150	13.04 N	14.34 W
Fafe	34	41.27 N	8.10 W
Fafen ≃	144	5.59 N	44.25 E
Faga ≃	150	13.15 N	0.55 E
Fagaitua	174u	14.16 S	170.37 W
Fagamalo	175a	13.25 S	172.21 W
Făgăraș	38	45.51 N	24.58 E
Făgărașului, Munții ⋀	38	45.35 N	25.00 E
Fagasa	174u	14.17 S	170.43 W
Fagatogo	174u	14.17 S	170.41 W
Fagel	41	54.27 N	9.31 E
Fagernes	26	60.59 N	9.15 E
Fagersta	40	60.00 N	15.47 E
Fagertärn ⬥[4]	40	58.46 N	14.42 E
Fagerviken	40	60.33 N	17.45 E
Făget	38	45.51 N	22.10 E
Faggen Bach ≃	64	47.05 N	10.40 E
Faggo	150	11.23 N	9.57 E
Fagnano, Lago ⊜	254	54.35 S	68.00 W
Fagnano Castello	68	39.34 N	16.03 E
Fagnano Olona	62	45.40 N	8.52 E
Fagnières	50	48.58 N	4.19 E
Faguibine, Lac ⊜	150	16.45 N	3.54 W
Fagundes ≃	256	22.12 S	43.11 W
Fagurhólsmýri	24a	63.54 N	16.38 W
Fagwir	140	9.33 N	30.25 E
Fahan	48	55.05 N	7.28 W
Fahl, Oued el ∨	148	31.15 N	4.41 E
Fahraj	128	28.58 N	58.52 E
Fährdorf	54	53.58 N	11.28 E
Fahrland	54	52.28 N	13.01 E
Fahrlander See ⊜	264a	52.27 N	13.01 E
Fahrn → Varna	64	46.44 N	11.38 E
Fahrnau	58	47.39 N	7.50 E
Fahuaqiao	106	30.52 N	121.25 E
Faial I	148a	38.34 N	28.42 W
Faichuk II	175c	7.23 N	151.40 E
Fā'id	142	30.19 N	32.19 E
Fā'id Military Base ■	142	30.20 N	32.16 E
Faido	58	46.29 N	8.48 E
Faillon, Lac ⊜	190	48.21 N	76.38 W
Failsworth	262	53.31 N	2.09 W
Fains-les-Sources	56	48.47 N	5.08 E
Fairbairn Airport ⊠	171b	35.18 S	149.15 E
Fairbairn Park ♠	274b	37.47 S	144.55 E
Fairbairn Reservoir ⊜[1]	166	23.45 S	148.00 E
Fairbank	190	42.38 N	92.02 W
Fairbanks, Ak., U.S.	180	64.51 N	147.43 W
Fairbanks, La., U.S.	194	30.00 N	92.02 W
Fair Bluff	192	34.18 N	79.02 W
Fairborn	218	39.49 N	84.01 W
Fairbourne	42	52.41 N	4.03 W
Fairburn	192	33.34 N	84.34 W
Fairbury, Il., U.S.	216	40.44 N	88.30 W
Fairbury, Ne., U.S.	198	40.08 N	97.10 W
Fairchance	188	39.49 N	79.45 W
Fairchild	190	44.36 N	90.57 W
Fairchild Air Force Base ■	202	47.38 N	117.38 W
Fairchild Creek ≃	212	43.07 N	80.07 W
Fairdale	216	42.06 N	88.56 W
Faire	116	17.53 N	121.34 E
Fairfax, Al., U.S.	194	32.47 N	85.11 W
Fairfax, Ca., U.S.	226	37.59 N	122.35 W
Fairfax, De., U.S.	285	39.47 N	75.32 W
Fairfax, Mn., U.S.	198	44.31 N	94.43 W
Fairfax, Mo., U.S.	194	40.20 N	95.23 W
Fairfax, Ok., U.S.	196	36.34 N	96.42 W
Fairfax, S.C., U.S.	192	32.57 N	81.14 W
Fairfax, S.D., U.S.	198	43.01 N	98.53 W
Fairfax, Vt., U.S.	188	44.39 N	73.00 W
Fairfax, Va., U.S.	208	38.50 N	77.18 W
Fairfax □[6]	208	38.45 N	77.15 W
Fairfax Forest	284c	38.52 N	77.15 W
Fairfax Park	284c	38.47 N	77.14 W
Fairfax State Recreation Area ♠	218	39.02 N	86.29 W
Fairfax Station	284c	38.48 N	77.19 W
Fairfield, Austl.	170	33.52 S	150.57 E
Fairfield, Al., U.S.	194	33.33 N	86.47 W
Fairfield, Ca., U.S.	226	38.14 N	122.02 W
Fairfield, Ct., U.S.	210	41.08 N	73.15 W
Fairfield, Id., U.S.	202	43.20 N	114.47 W
Fairfield, Il., U.S.	194	38.22 N	88.21 W
Fairfield, Ia., U.S.	190	41.00 N	91.57 W
Fairfield, Me., U.S.	188	44.35 N	69.35 W
Fairfield, Mt., U.S.	202	47.36 N	111.58 W
Fairfield, Ne., U.S.	198	40.25 N	98.06 W
Fairfield, N.J., U.S.	276	40.53 N	74.16 W
Fairfield, N.Y., U.S.	210	43.08 N	74.55 W
Fairfield, Oh., U.S.	218	39.20 N	84.33 W
Fairfield, Pa., U.S.	214	39.47 N	77.22 W
Fairfield, Tx., U.S.	222	31.43 N	96.09 W
Fairfield □[6]	207	41.15 N	73.20 W
Fairfield Lake ⊜[1]	222	31.50 N	96.05 W
Fairfield University ʊ[2]	276	41.09 N	73.15 W
Fairford	42	51.44 N	1.47 W
Fairgrove	190	43.31 N	83.32 W
Fair Harbor	210	40.38 N	73.11 W
Fairhaven, Ma., U.S.	207	41.38 N	70.54 W
Fair Haven, Mi., U.S.	214	42.40 N	82.39 W
Fair Haven, N.J., U.S.	208	40.21 N	74.02 W
Fair Haven, N.Y., U.S.	210	43.18 N	76.42 W
Fairhaven, Oh., U.S.	218	39.38 N	84.47 W
Fair Haven, Vt., U.S.	188	43.35 N	73.15 W
Fair Haven, Va., U.S.	284c	38.47 N	77.05 W
Fairhaven Bay ⊜	283	42.26 N	71.21 W
Fair Haven Beach State Park ♠, N.Y., U.S.	210	43.21 N	76.41 W
Fair Haven Beach State Park ♠, N.Y., U.S.	212	43.21 N	76.41 W
Fair Head ›	48	55.13 N	6.09 W
Fairhope, Al., U.S.	194	30.31 N	87.54 W
Fairhope, Oh., U.S.	214	40.51 N	81.19 W
Fairhope, Pa., U.S.	214	40.07 N	79.50 W
Fair Isle I	46	59.32 N	1.39 W
Fairknoll	284c	39.05 N	76.59 W
Fairland, In., U.S.	218	39.35 N	85.51 W
Fairland, Md., U.S.	284c	39.05 N	76.58 W
Fairland, Ok., U.S.	196	36.45 N	94.50 W
Fairlane Town Center ⬥[9]	281	42.19 N	83.13 W
Fair Lawn, N.J., U.S.	210	40.56 N	74.07 W
Fairlawn, Oh., U.S.	214	41.07 N	81.36 W
Fairlee	284c	38.52 N	77.16 W
Fairleigh Dickinson University ʊ[2], N.J., U.S.	276	40.50 N	74.07 W
Fairleigh Dickinson University (Florham-Madison) ʊ[2], N.J., U.S.	276	40.46 N	74.26 W
Fairleigh Dickinson University (Teaneck) ʊ[2], N.J., U.S.	276	40.53 N	74.02 W
Fairless Hills	208	40.10 N	74.51 W
Fairlie, N.Z.	172	44.06 S	170.50 E
Fairlie, Scot., U.K.	46	55.46 N	4.51 W
Fairlight	42	50.53 N	0.40 E
Fairmont, Il., U.S.	216	41.33 N	88.03 W
Fairmont, Mn., U.S.	198	43.39 N	94.27 W
Fairmont, Ne., U.S.	198	40.38 N	97.35 W
Fairmont, N.C., U.S.	192	34.29 N	79.06 W
Fairmont, Pa., U.S.	279b	40.19 N	79.43 W
Fairmont, Wa., U.S.	224	48.54 N	122.16 W
Fairmont, W.V., U.S.	188	39.29 N	80.08 W
Fairmont City	219	38.40 N	90.06 W
Fairmont Hot Springs	182	50.19 N	115.53 W
Fairmont Reservoir ⊜[1]	228	34.43 N	118.26 W
Fairmont Terrace	282	37.43 N	122.07 W
Fairmount, Ga., U.S.	192	34.26 N	84.42 W
Fairmount, Il., U.S.	194	40.03 N	87.56 W
Fairmount, In., U.S.	216	40.24 N	85.39 W
Fairmount, N.Y., U.S.	210	43.02 N	76.14 W
Fairmount, N.D., U.S.	198	46.03 N	96.36 W
Fairmount City	214	41.01 N	79.19 W
Fairmount Heights	208	38.54 N	76.54 W
Fairmount Park ♠	285	40.00 N	75.12 W
Fair Ness ›	176	63.24 N	72.05 W
Fair Oaks, Ca., U.S.	226	38.38 N	121.16 W
Fair Oaks, Ga., U.S.	192	33.54 N	84.32 W
Fair Oaks, In., U.S.	216	41.05 N	87.16 W

Symbols in the index entries represent the broad categories identified in the key at the right. Symbols with superior numbers (⋀[1]) identify subcategories (see complete key on page *I · 1).*

Symbole im Register stellen die rechts im Schlüssel erklärten Kategorien dar. Symbole mit hochgestellten Ziffern (⋀[1]) bezeichnen Unterabteilungen einer Kategorie (vgl. vollständiger Schlüssel auf Seite *I · 1).*

Los símbolos incluídos en el texto del índice representan las grandes categorias identificadas con la clave a la derecha. Los símbolos con numeros en su parte superior (⋀[1]) identifican las subcategorías (véase la clave completa en la página *I · 1).*

Les symboles de l'index représentent les catégories indiquées dans la légende à droite. Les symboles suivis d'un indice (⋀[1]) représentent des sous-catégories (voir légende complète à la page *I · 1).*

Os símbolos incluídos no texto do índice representam as grandes categorias identificadas com a chave à direita. Os símbolos com números em sua parte superior (⋀[1]) identificam as subcategorias (veja-se a chave completa à página *I · 1).*

∧ Mountain	Berg	Montaña	Montagne	Montanha
⋀ Mountains	Gebirge	Montañas	Montagnes	Montanhas
)(Pass	Paß	Paso	Col	Passo
∨ Valley, Canyon	Tal, Cañon	Valle, Cañón	Vallée, Canyon	Vale, Canhão
≚ Plain	Ebene	Llano	Plaine	Planície
› Cape	Kap	Cabo	Cap	Cabo
I Island	Insel	Isla	Île	Ilha
II Islands	Inseln	Islas	Îles	Ilhas
⩡ Other Topographic Features	Andere Topographische Objekte	Otros Elementos Topográficos	Autres données topographiques	Outros acidentes topográficos

ESPAÑOL Nombre / FRANÇAIS Nom / PORTUGUÊS Nome	Página / Page	Lat.°′	Long.°′ W = Oeste / W = Ouest
Fairoaks, Pa., U.S.	279b	40.34 N	80.13 W
Fairoaks Airport ⊠	260	51.21 N	0.32 W
Fair Plain	216	42.05 N	86.27 W
Fairplains	192	36.13 N	81.10 W
Fairplay	200	39.13 N	106.00 W
Fairpoint	214	40.07 N	80.55 W
Fairport, On., Can.	275b	43.49 N	79.05 W
Fairport, N.Y., U.S.	210	43.05 N	77.26 W
Fairport Beach	275b	43.48 N	79.06 W
Fairport Harbor	214	41.44 N	81.16 W
Fairseat	260	51.20 N	0.20 E
Fairton	208	39.22 N	75.13 W
Fairview, Austl.	164	15.33 S	144.19 E
Fairview, Ab., Can.	182	56.04 N	118.23 W
Fairview, Ga., U.S.	192	34.56 N	85.17 W
Fairview, Il., U.S.	190	40.38 N	90.10 W
Fairview, In., U.S.	216	40.18 N	85.11 W
Fairview, Ks., U.S.	198	39.50 N	95.43 W
Fairview, Md., U.S.	208	39.09 N	76.29 W
Fairview, Mi., U.S.	190	44.43 N	84.03 W
Fairview, Mt., U.S.	198	47.51 N	104.02 W
Fairview, N.J., U.S.	276	40.51 N	73.58 W
Fairview, N.Y., U.S.	210	41.43 N	73.55 W
Fairview, Oh., U.S.	214	40.03 N	81.14 W
Fairview, Ok., U.S.	196	36.16 N	98.28 W
Fairview, Pa., U.S.	214	42.01 N	80.15 W
Fairview, Tn., U.S.	194	35.58 N	87.07 W
Fairview, Ut,. U.S.	200	39.37 N	111.26 W
Fairview, W.V., U.S.	188	39.35 N	80.14 W
Fairview Heights	219	38.10 N	90.00 W
Fairview Lanes	214	41.23 N	82.40 W
Fairview Mall ◆[9]	275b	43.47 N	79.21 W
Fairview Park, In., U.S.	194	39.40 N	87.25 W
Fairview Park, Oh., U.S.	214	41.26 N	81.51 W
Fairview Park, Pa., U.S.	210	41.10 N	75.53 W
Fairview Peak ʌ, Nv., U.S.	204	39.14 N	118.08 W
Fairview Peak ʌ, Or., U.S.	202	43.35 N	122.39 W
Fairview Pointe Claire Centre ◆[9]	275a	45.28 N	73.50 W
Fairview Shores	220	28.35 N	81.23 W
Fairview Village	285	40.10 N	75.23 W
Fairvilla	220	28.35 N	81.24 W
Fairville	285	39.51 N	75.38 W
Fairweather Mountain ʌ	180	58.54 N	137.32 W
Fairy Lake ⊜	212	45.20 N	79.11 W
Fairy Meadow	170	34.23 S	150.54 E
Fairy Stone State Park ♦	192	36.48 N	80.06 W
Fairy Water ≃	48	54.37 N	7.20 W
Fais I	108	9.46 N	140.31 E
Faisalabad (Lyallpur)	123	31.25 N	73.05 E
Faison	192	35.06 N	78.08 W
Faistós ⊥	38	35.01 N	24.48 E
Faith	198	45.01 N	102.02 W
Faiyum → Al-Fayyūm	142	29.19 N	30.50 E
Faizābād	124	26.47 N	82.08 E
Fajansovyj	76	54.04 N	34.24 E
Fajardo	240m	18.20 N	65.39 W
Fajou, Îlet à I	241o	16.21 N	61.35 W
Fajr, Wādī ∨	128	30.06 N	38.18 E
Fajzabad	85	38.34 N	69.19 E
Fakahatchee Strand ⠿	220	39.35 N	89.25 W
Fakaofo I[1]	14	9.22 S	171.14 W
Fakarava I[1]	14	16.20 S	145.37 W
Fakejev	80	48.57 N	49.56 E
Fakel	80	57.38 N	53.02 E
Fakenham	42	52.50 N	0.51 E
Fakfak	164	2.55 S	132.18 E
Fakılı	130	39.13 N	35.00 E
Fakīrganj	124	25.58 N	90.02 E
Fakī Ṣādiq	140	12.08 N	23.55 E
Fakrinkotti	140	18.01 N	31.20 E
Fakse	41	55.15 N	12.08 E
Fakse Bugt ⊂	41	55.10 N	12.15 E
Fakse Ladeplads	41	55.13 N	12.11 E
Faku	104	42.30 N	123.24 E
Fal ≃	42	50.08 N	5.02 W
Falaba	150	9.51 N	11.19 W
Faladyé	150	13.08 N	8.20 W
Falaise	32	48.54 N	0.12 W
Fālākāta	124	26.32 N	89.12 E
Falam	110	22.55 N	93.40 E
Falāvarjān	128	32.33 N	51.30 E
Falcade	64	46.21 N	11.51 E
Falcão	256	22.17 S	44.16 W
Fălciu	38	46.18 N	28.08 E
Falck	56	49.14 N	6.38 E
Falcognana di Sotto ◆[8]	267a	41.45 N	12.33 E
Falcón □[3]	246	11.00 N	69.50 W
Falcon, Cap ›	34	35.46 N	0.48 W
Falcon, Cape ›	224	45.46 N	123.59 W
Falcón, Presa (Falcon Reservoir) ⊜[1]	196	26.37 N	99.11 W
Falconara Albanese	68	39.16 N	16.05 E
Falconara Alta	66	43.37 N	13.24 E
Falconara Marittima	66	43.37 N	13.24 E
Falconbridge	190	46.35 N	80.48 W
Falconcrest	285	39.58 N	75.33 W
Falcone	70	38.07 N	15.05 E
Falcone, Capo del ›	71	40.58 N	8.12 E
Falconer	214	42.07 N	79.11 W
Falcon Heights	202	42.08 N	121.45 W
Falcon Reservoir (Presa Falcón) ⊜[1]	196	26.37 N	99.11 W
Falconwood	210	43.00 N	78.57 W
Faldsled	41	55.09 N	10.09 E
Faléa	150	12.16 N	11.17 W
Faleasao	174y	14.13 S	169.32 W
Falelatai	175a	13.55 S	171.59 W
Falelima	175a	13.32 S	172.41 W
Falémé ≃	150	14.46 N	12.14 W
Falenki	80	58.22 N	51.35 E
Falerii Novi ⊥	66	42.16 N	12.20 E
Falerna	68	39.00 N	16.10 E
Falerone	66	43.06 N	13.28 E
Falešty	78	47.34 N	27.43 E
Falfurrias	196	27.13 N	98.08 W
Falher	182	55.44 N	117.12 W
Falicon	62	43.45 N	7.17 E
Fálirou, Órmos ⊂	267c	37.56 N	23.40 E
Falkenberg, B.R.D.	60	49.52 N	12.14 E
Falkenberg, B.R.D.	60	48.28 N	12.43 E
Falkenberg, D.D.R.	54	51.35 N	13.14 E
Falkenberg, D.D.R.	54	52.48 N	13.58 E
Falkenberg → Niemodlin, Pol.	30	50.39 N	17.37 E
Falkenberg, Sve.	26	56.54 N	12.28 E
Falkenberg ◆[8]	264a	52.34 N	13.33 E
Falkenburg → Złocieniec	30	53.33 N	16.01 E
Falkenhagen, D.D.R.	54	52.26 N	14.19 E
Falkenhagen, D.D.R.	54	53.12 N	12.12 E
Falkenhagener See ⊜	264a	52.34 N	13.08 E
Falkenrehde	264a	52.30 N	12.56 E
Falkensee	54	52.33 N	13.04 E
Falkenstein	54	50.29 N	12.22 E
Falkenthal	54	52.54 N	13.17 E
Falkirk	46	56.00 N	3.48 W
Falkland, B.C., Can.	182	50.30 N	119.33 W
Falkland, Scot., U.K.	46	56.15 N	3.12 W
Falkland-Inseln → Falkland Islands (Islas Malvinas) □[2]	254	51.45 S	59.00 W
Falkland Islands □[2], S.A.	244	51.45 S	59.00 W
Falkland Islands (Islas Malvinas) □[2], S.A.	254	51.45 S	59.00 W
Falkland Plateau ✦[3]	18	51.00 S	50.00 W
Falkland Sound ʊ	254	51.45 S	59.25 W
Falköping	26	58.10 N	13.31 E
Falkville	194	34.22 N	86.54 W
Fall ≃, On., Can.	212	44.59 N	76.22 W
Fall ≃, Ks., U.S.	198	37.24 N	95.40 W
Fall ≃, Wa., U.S.	224	46.47 N	123.30 W
Falla	40	58.41 N	15.45 E
Fallais	56	50.37 N	5.10 E
Fallbach	61	48.39 N	16.25 E
Fallbrook	228	33.22 N	117.15 W
Fallbrook Square ◆[9]	280	34.12 N	118.38 W
Fall City	224	47.34 N	121.53 W
Fall Creek	190	44.45 N	91.16 W
Fall Creek ≃, In., U.S.	218	39.47 N	86.11 W
Fall Creek ≃, N.Y., U.S.	210	42.28 N	76.31 W
Fall Creek Falls State Park ♦, Tn., U.S.	192	35.39 N	85.25 W
Fall Creek Falls State Park ♦, Tn., U.S.	194	35.39 N	85.25 W
Fallen Jerusalem I	240m	18.25 N	64.27 W
Fallen Leaf	226	38.53 N	120.04 W
Fallen Leaf Reservoir ⊜[1]	226	38.54 N	120.03 W
Fallentimber	214	40.41 N	78.30 W
Fallentimber Creek ≃	182	51.45 N	114.39 W
Fallen Timbers State Memorial ⊥	216	41.33 N	83.42 W
Fallersleben	54	52.25 N	10.43 E
Fallin	46	56.06 N	3.52 W
Falling ≃	192	37.01 N	78.55 W
Fallingbostel	52	52.52 N	9.41 E
Falling Creek ≃	208	37.26 N	77.26 W
Fallon, Mt., U.S.	198	46.50 N	105.07 W
Fallon, Nv., U.S.	204	39.28 N	118.46 W
Fall River, Ks., U.S.	198	37.36 N	96.01 W
Fall River, Ma., U.S.	207	41.42 N	71.09 W
Fall River, Wi., U.S.	190	43.23 N	89.02 W
Fall River Lake ⊜[1]	198	37.42 N	96.08 W
Fall River Mills	204	41.00 N	121.26 W
Falls	210	41.28 N	75.51 W
Falls □[6]	222	31.17 N	96.55 W
Fallsburg	210	41.44 N	74.36 W
Falls Church	208	38.53 N	77.11 W
Falls City, Ne., U.S.	198	40.03 N	95.36 W
Falls City, Or., U.S.	202	44.51 N	123.26 W
Falls Creek, Austl.	170	34.59 S	150.36 E
Falls Creek, Pa., U.S.	214	41.09 N	78.48 W
Falls Creek ≃	226	37.57 N	119.46 W
Fallsington	208	40.12 N	74.48 W
Falls Lake ⊜[1]	192	36.00 N	78.45 W
Falls Pond ⊜	283	41.58 N	71.20 W
Falls Run ≃	284b	39.22 N	76.52 W
Fallston	208	39.31 N	76.25 W
Falls Village	207	41.57 N	73.21 W
Falmer	42	50.51 N	0.04 W
Falmey	150	12.36 N	2.51 E
Falmouth, Jam.	241q	18.30 N	77.39 W
Falmouth, Eng., U.K.	42	50.08 N	5.04 W
Falmouth, Ky., U.S.	218	38.40 N	84.19 W
Falmouth, Me., U.S.	188	43.43 N	70.14 W
Falmouth, Ma., U.S.	207	41.33 N	70.36 W
Falmouth, Va., U.S.	208	38.19 N	77.28 W
Falmouth Bay ⊂	42	50.05 N	5.01 W
Falmouth Heights	207	41.33 N	70.36 W
Falsa Chipana, Punta ›	248	21.20 S	70.06 W
False Cape ›, Fl., U.S.	220	28.35 N	80.34 W
False Cape ›, Va., U.S.	208	36.39 N	76.51 W
False Divi Point ›	122	15.43 N	80.49 E
False Ducks Islands II	212	43.57 N	76.49 W
False Pass	180	54.52 N	163.24 W
Falset	34	41.08 N	0.49 E
Falsino ≃	250	0.56 N	51.35 W
Fal'šivyj Gelendžik	78	44.31 N	38.09 E
Falso, Cabo ›, Hond.	236	15.12 N	83.20 W
Falso, Cabo ›, Rep. Dom.	238	17.47 N	71.41 W
Falso Cabo de Hornos ›	254	55.43 S	68.05 W
Falster I	41	54.48 N	11.58 E
Falsterbo	41	55.24 N	12.50 E
Falstone	44	55.11 N	2.25 W
Falterona, Monte ʌ	66	43.52 N	11.42 E
Fălticeni	38	47.28 N	26.18 E
Falun, Sve.	40	60.36 N	15.38 E
Falun, Zhg.	107	29.58 N	104.29 E
Falzarego, Passo di)(	64	46.31 N	12.00 E
Fam, Kepulauan II	164	0.40 S	130.15 E
Fama, Ouadi ∨	146	15.22 N	20.34 E
Famagusta → Gazimağusa	130	35.07 N	33.57 E
Famaillá	252	27.03 S	65.24 W
Famatina	252	28.55 S	67.31 W
Famatina, Sierra de ⋏	252	29.00 S	67.51 W
Fambach	54	50.44 N	10.22 E
Fameck	56	49.18 N	6.07 E
Famenne ◆[1]	56	50.10 N	5.15 E
Familleureux	50	50.31 N	4.12 E
Family Lake ⊜	184	51.54 N	95.30 W
Fan ≃	104	42.16 N	123.40 E
Fana	150	12.47 N	6.57 W
Fanaco, Lago ⊜	70	37.39 N	13.33 E
Fanad Head ›	48	55.16 N	7.38 W
Fanado ≃	255	17.10 S	42.40 W
Fanambana	157b	13.34 S	50.00 E
Fanan I	175c	7.11 N	151.59 E
Fanano	64	44.12 N	10.47 E
Fanārah	142	30.17 N	32.21 E
Fanchang	100	31.07 N	118.12 E
Fanch'eng → Xiangfan	102	32.03 N	112.01 E
Fancher, Il., U.S.	219	39.16 N	88.47 W
Fancher, N.Y., U.S.	210	43.15 N	66.06 W
Fanchuan	100	32.40 N	119.42 E
Fancy	241h	13.22 N	61.11 W
Fancy Creek ≃	198	39.28 N	96.45 W
Fancy Prairie	219	39.59 N	89.36 W
Fandriana	157b	20.14 S	47.23 E
Fane ≃	48	53.57 N	6.22 W
Fanepura	123	31.29 N	72.54 E
Faneromenis Monastery ʋ[1]	267c	37.59 N	23.26 E
Fang	110	19.55 N	99.13 E
Fangaga ʌ	144	17.30 N	38.01 E
Fangak	140	9.04 N	30.53 E
Fangbian	106	31.42 N	119.06 E
Fangcheng, Zhg.	100	33.16 N	112.59 E
Fangcheng, Zhg.	102	21.49 N	108.22 E
Fangcheng, Zhg.	105	39.16 N	115.28 E
Fangcun, Zhg.	100	29.04 N	118.36 E
Fangcun, Zhg.	100	26.50 N	118.15 E
Fangdao	100	27.01 N	118.06 E
Fängersee ⊜	264a	52.35 N	13.50 E
Fangguan	105	39.20 N	115.58 E
Fangji	100	31.54 N	115.35 E
Fangjiachang	107	30.05 N	104.16 E
Fangjiazhuang	106	30.45 N	119.53 E
Fangliao	100	22.22 N	120.35 E
Fangmutun	98	42.34 N	124.34 E
Fangniu	102	27.40 N	100.25 E
Fangshan, T'aiwan	100	22.16 N	120.39 E
Fangshan, Zhg.	98	39.42 N	115.58 E
Fang Shan ʌ	106	31.40 N	119.16 E
Fang Shan ʌ[2]	106	31.29 N	119.09 E
Fangshanzhen	104	41.54 N	122.05 E
Fangshen	104	42.02 N	124.04 E
Fangshengpu	107	30.20 N	104.54 E
Fangsi	98	36.56 N	116.29 E
Fangtai	106	31.19 N	121.12 E
Fangxi	100	28.23 N	114.38 E
Fangxian	102	32.02 N	110.45 E
Fangxianzhen	106	32.00 N	119.44 E
Fangzheng	89	45.50 N	128.50 E
Fangzi	98	36.36 N	119.07 E
Fanhões	266c	38.53 N	9.09 W
Fanipol'	76	53.45 N	27.20 E
Fanjakana	157b	21.10 S	46.53 E
Fanjiadai	106	32.04 N	120.15 E
Fanjiadian	104	41.41 N	121.50 E
Fanjiatun	89	43.43 N	125.06 E
Fanjiazhuang	105	39.12 N	117.20 E
Fannaråki ʌ	26	61.31 N	7.55 E
Fannettsburg	214	40.04 N	77.50 W
Fannich, Loch ⊜	46	57.38 N	5.00 W
Fannrem	26	63.16 N	9.50 E
Fanny, Mount ʌ	202	45.20 N	117.41 W
Fanny Bay	182	49.30 N	124.50 W
Fano	66	43.50 N	13.01 E
Fanø I	26	55.25 N	8.25 E
Fanqiao	100	28.48 N	121.10 E
Fans, Col des)(	62	44.56 N	4.47 E
Fanshan, Zhg.	100	27.21 N	120.24 E
Fanshan, Zhg.	105	40.13 N	115.25 E
Fanshang	106	31.40 N	120.01 E
Fanshawe Lake ⊜	212	43.05 N	81.10 W
Fansher Creek ≃	214	42.37 N	82.01 W
Fanshui	100	33.07 N	119.25 E
Fan Si Pan ʌ	110	22.15 N	103.46 E
Fantasy Island ♦	284a	43.02 N	78.58 W
Fanthyttan	40	59.40 N	15.06 E
Fanwood	276	40.38 N	74.23 W
Fanxian	98	35.57 N	115.38 E
Fanzhen	98	36.14 N	117.21 E
Faoileann, Bàgh nam ⊂	46	57.23 N	7.17 W
Faqīrah, Wādī ∨	142	28.52 N	30.57 E
Faqqūʻah	132	32.30 N	35.24 E
Fāqūs	142	30.44 N	31.48 E
Farab	85	39.14 N	67.28 E
Faraday ʋ[3]	9	65.15 S	64.16 W
Faraday, Mount ʌ	172	42.02 S	171.34 E
Faradje	154	3.44 N	29.43 E
Faradofay	157b	25.02 S	47.00 E
Farafangana	157b	22.49 S	47.50 E
Farāfirah, Al-Wāḥat al- ⊤[4]	140	27.15 N	28.10 E
Farāh	128	32.22 N	62.07 E
Farāh □[4]	128	33.00 N	62.30 E
Farāh ≃	128	31.29 N	61.24 E
Farahābād	267d	35.42 N	51.30 E
Farahalana	157b	14.26 S	50.10 E
Farā'id, Jabal al- ʌ	140	23.31 N	35.20 E
Fara in Sabina	66	42.12 N	12.43 E
Farallon de Medinilla I	108	16.01 N	146.04 E
Farallon de Pajaros I	108	20.32 N	144.54 E
Farallon Islands II	204	37.43 N	123.03 W
Faramana	150	12.03 N	4.40 W
Faranah	150	10.02 N	10.44 W
Farángi Samariás (Samaria Gorge) ∨	38	35.18 N	24.00 E
Fara Novarese	62	45.33 N	8.27 E
Farasān, Jazā'ir II	144	16.48 N	41.54 E
Farasān al-Kabīr I	144	16.42 N	42.00 E
Faratsiho	157b	19.24 S	46.57 E
Faraulep I[1]	108	8.36 N	144.33 E
Farber	219	39.16 N	91.34 W
Farbovano	78	50.09 N	31.51 E
Farcău, Vîrful ʌ	38	47.56 N	24.27 E
Farchant	64	47.32 N	11.06 E
Farcy	261	48.31 N	2.37 E
Fardes ≃	34	37.35 N	3.00 W
Fare ≃	50	47.39 N	0.14 E
Fareara, Pointe ›	174s	17.52 S	149.39 W
Fareham	42	50.51 N	1.10 W
Fårevejle	41	55.48 N	11.27 E
Farewell	180	62.31 N	153.53 W
Farewell, Cape ›	172	40.30 S	172.41 E
Farewell Spit ›[2]	172	40.31 S	172.52 E
Färgelanda	26	58.34 N	11.59 E
Fargniers	50	49.39 N	3.19 E
Fargo	198	46.52 N	96.47 W
Far Hills	276	40.41 N	74.38 W
Faria ≃	287a	22.53 S	43.15 W
Fāriʻah, Wādī al- ∨	132	32.06 N	35.31 E
Faribault	190	44.17 N	93.16 W
Faribault, Lac ⊜	176	59.00 N	72.00 W
Farīdābad	124	28.26 N	77.19 E
Farīdganj	126	23.08 N	90.45 E
Farīdkot	123	30.40 N	74.45 E
Farīdnagar	124	28.46 N	77.37 E
Farīdpur, Bngl.	126	24.10 N	89.26 E
Farīdpur, Bngl.	126	23.36 N	89.50 E
Farīdpur, India	124	28.13 N	79.33 E
Farié Haoussa	150	13.48 N	1.38 E
Fārigh, Wādī al- ∨	146	29.59 N	19.25 E
Färila	26	61.48 N	15.51 E
Farilhões II	34	39.28 N	9.34 W
Farim	150	12.27 N	15.17 W
Farīmān	128	35.43 N	59.53 E
Farina	219	38.50 N	88.46 W
Faringdon	42	51.40 N	1.35 W
Farington	262	53.43 N	2.42 W
Farinha ≃	250	6.51 S	47.30 W
Farini d'Olmo	62	44.43 N	9.34 E
Fariš	85	40.35 N	66.52 E
Fariske	130	36.37 N	32.38 E
Fāriskūr	142	31.20 N	31.43 E
Farit, Amba ʌ	144	10.56 N	38.58 E
Färjestaden	26	56.39 N	16.27 E
Farkwa	154	5.24 S	35.36 E
Farleigh	260	51.19 N	0.02 W
Farley	190	42.26 N	91.00 W
Farley Green	260	51.12 N	0.29 W
Farmahīn	128	34.30 N	49.41 E
Farmer City	216	40.14 N	88.38 W
Farmers Branch	222	32.55 N	96.53 W
Farmersburg	194	39.14 N	87.22 W
Farmers Fork	208	38.02 N	76.45 W
Farmer's Museum ʋ	210	42.42 N	74.57 W
Farmers Retreat	218	38.58 N	85.06 W
Farmersville, Ca., U.S.	226	36.17 N	119.12 W
Farmersville, Il., U.S.	219	39.26 N	89.39 W
Farmersville, Pa., U.S.	208	40.08 N	76.10 W
Farmersville, Tx., U.S.	222	33.09 N	96.21 W
Farmersville Station	210	42.26 N	78.22 W
Farmerville	194	32.46 N	92.24 W
Farmingdale, N.J., U.S.	208	40.11 N	74.10 W
Farmingdale, N.Y., U.S.	276	40.43 N	73.26 W
Farmington, Ca., U.S.	226	37.56 N	120.59 W
Farmington, Ct., U.S.	207	41.43 N	72.49 W
Farmington, De., U.S.	208	38.52 N	75.34 W
Farmington, Il., U.S.	190	40.41 N	90.00 W
Farmington, Ia., U.S.	190	40.38 N	91.44 W
Farmington, Me., U.S.	188	44.40 N	70.09 W
Farmington, Mi., U.S.	216	42.27 N	83.22 W
Farmington, Mn., U.S.	190	44.38 N	93.08 W
Farmington, Mo., U.S.	194	37.47 N	90.25 W
Farmington, Mt., U.S.	182	47.54 N	112.11 W
Farmington, N.H., U.S.	188	43.23 N	71.03 W
Farmington, N.M., U.S.	200	36.43 N	108.13 W
Farmington, Ut,. U.S.	200	40.58 N	111.53 W
Farmington ≃	207	41.51 N	72.38 W
Farmington, West Branch ≃	207	41.52 N	72.57 W
Farmington Flood Control Basin ⊜[1]	226	37.55 N	120.55 W
Farmington Hills	281	42.28 N	83.23 W
Farmingville	210	40.49 N	73.01 W
Farmland	218	40.11 N	85.07 W
Far Mountain ʌ	182	52.46 N	125.17 W
Farm Pond ⊜, Ma., U.S.	283	42.17 N	71.26 W
Farm Pond ⊜, Ma., U.S.	283	42.14 N	71.21 W
Farmville, N.C., U.S.	192	35.35 N	77.35 W
Farmville, Va., U.S.	192	37.18 N	78.23 W
Färna	40	59.47 N	15.51 E
Farnam	198	40.42 N	100.12 W
Farnawā	142	30.59 N	30.39 E
Farnborough	42	51.17 N	0.46 W
Farnborough ◆[8]	260	51.21 N	0.04 E
Farncombe	260	51.12 N	0.36 W
Farndon	44	53.05 N	0.51 W
Färnebofjärden ⊜	40	60.14 N	16.47 E
Farne Islands II	44	55.38 N	1.38 W
Farnham, P.Q., Can.	206	45.17 N	72.59 W
Farnham, Eng., U.K.	42	51.13 N	0.49 W
Farnham, N.Y., U.S.	214	42.36 N	79.05 W
Farnham, Va., U.S.	208	37.53 N	76.37 W
Farnham, Mount ʌ	182	50.29 N	116.30 W
Farnham Common	260	51.33 N	0.37 W
Farnham Royal	260	51.32 N	0.37 W
Farnhamville	198	42.16 N	94.24 W
Farningham	260	51.23 N	0.13 E
Farnroda	54	50.56 N	10.23 E
Farnworth	262	53.33 N	2.24 W
Faro, Bra.	250	2.11 S	56.44 W
Faro, Port.	34	37.01 N	7.56 W
Faro □[5]	34	37.15 N	8.00 W
Faro ≃	146	9.21 N	12.55 E
Faro, Punta ›	246	11.07 N	74.51 W
Faro, Punta del ›	70	38.16 N	15.39 E
Faro, Réserve du ◆[4]	146	8.10 N	12.35 E
Färöer → Faeroe Islands □[2]	22	62.00 N	7.00 W
Fårön I	26	57.56 N	19.08 E
Fårösund	26	57.52 N	19.03 E
Farquhar, Cape ›	162	23.37 S	113.37 E
Farquhar Group II	138	10.10 S	51.10 E
Farr	46	57.21 N	4.12 W
Farra d'Isonzo	64	45.56 N	12.31 E
Farragut	198	40.43 N	95.28 W
Farragut State Recreation Area ♦	202	47.55 N	116.35 W
Farrandsville	210	41.10 N	77.31 W
Farrar ≃	46	57.24 N	4.50 W
Farrar Pond ⊜	283	42.25 N	71.21 W
Farrars Creek ≃	166	25.35 S	140.43 E
Farrāshband	128	28.53 N	52.06 E
Farrell	214	41.12 N	80.29 W
Farrell Flat	168b	33.50 S	138.47 E
Farrer Park ♦	271c	1.19 N	103.51 E
Farrington Lake ⊜	276	40.26 N	74.28 W
Farrington Lake Heights	276	40.26 N	74.27 W
Far Rockaway ◆[8]	276	40.36 N	73.45 W
Farrukhābād	124	27.24 N	79.34 E
Farrukhnagar, India	124	28.27 N	76.49 E
Farrukhnagar, India	272a	28.43 N	77.23 E
Fārs □[4]	128	29.00 N	53.00 E
Fársala	38	39.18 N	22.23 E
Farschviller	56	49.06 N	6.54 E
Fārsī	128	33.47 N	63.15 E
Fārsī, Jazīreh-ye I	128	27.58 N	50.11 E
Farsīs	142	30.40 N	31.14 E
Farsø	26	56.47 N	9.21 E
Farsta	40	59.14 N	18.04 E
Farsund	26	58.05 N	6.48 E
Fartak, Ra's ›	118	15.38 N	52.15 E
Fartura, Rio da ≃	256	21.37 S	46.55 W
Farukolu I	122	6.12 N	73.16 E
Farum	41	55.48 N	12.22 E
Fårvang	41	56.16 N	9.44 E
Farvel, Kap ›	176	59.45 N	44.00 W
Farwell, Mi., U.S.	190	43.50 N	84.52 W
Farwell, Tx., U.S.	196	30.15 N	103.15 W
Fāryāb □[4]	128	36.00 N	65.00 E
Fasā	128	28.56 N	53.42 E
Fasano	68	40.50 N	17.22 E
Faščovka	83	48.16 N	38.37 E
Fashkhah, 'Ayn ⊤[4]	132	31.43 N	35.27 E
Fåsjön ⊜	40	59.36 N	14.58 E
Fasmund ›[1]	41	54.32 N	13.35 E
Fassa	150	13.26 N	8.15 W
Fassberg	52	52.54 N	10.10 E
Fasterholt	41	56.01 N	9.07 E
Fastnet Rock I[2]	48	51.24 N	9.35 W
Fastov	78	50.06 N	29.55 E
Fastoveckaja	78	45.56 N	40.09 E
Fatagar Tuting, Tanjung ›	164	2.46 S	131.57 E
Fataki	154	4.46 S	28.11 E
Fatala ≃	150	10.13 N	14.00 W
Fat Deer Key I	220	24.44 N	81.00 W
Fate	222	32.56 N	96.23 W
Fatehābād, India	123	29.31 N	75.27 E
Fatehābād, India	124	27.01 N	78.19 E
Fatehgarh, India	124	27.22 N	79.38 E
Fatehgarh, India	124	24.48 N	76.58 E
Fatehgarh Chūriān	123	31.52 N	74.58 E
Fatehjang	123	33.34 N	72.39 E
Fatehpur, India	120	27.59 N	74.57 E
Fatehpur, India	124	27.10 N	81.13 E
Fatehpur, India	124	25.56 N	80.48 E
Fatehpur, India	126	24.05 N	87.44 E
Fatehpur, India	126	22.17 N	88.14 E
Fatehpur, Pāk.	123	31.09 N	71.13 E
Fatehpur Sīkri	124	27.06 N	77.40 E
Fathai	140	8.05 N	31.48 E
Fathom Five National Marine Park ♦	190	45.15 N	81.40 W
Fatick	150	14.20 N	16.25 W
Fatick □[4]	150	14.00 N	16.30 W
Fatigue, Mount ʌ	169	38.34 S	146.18 E
Fatima, Arg.	258	34.26 S	59.00 W
Fátima, Bra.	248	16.11 S	54.58 W
Fátima, Port.	34	39.37 N	8.39 W
Fāṭimah, Wādī ∨	144	21.27 N	39.09 E
Fatoto	150	13.26 N	13.52 W
Fat'ož	78	52.07 N	35.52 E
Fatsa	130	41.02 N	37.31 E
Fatshan → Foshan	100	23.03 N	113.09 E
Fat Tong Point ›	271d	22.16 N	114.15 E
Fatu-Berlio	112	8.56 S	125.52 E
Fatulla	126	23.38 N	90.29 E
Fatumu	174w	21.13 S	175.07 W
Fatunda	152	4.08 S	17.13 E
Fatwā	124	25.31 N	85.19 E
Fauabu	175e	8.34 S	160.43 E
Faucigny	58	46.07 N	6.22 E
Faucille, Col de la)(	58	46.22 N	6.02 E
Faucilles, Monts ⋏	58	48.07 N	6.16 E
Faucogney	58	47.51 N	6.34 E
Faucon-de-Barcelonnette	62	44.24 N	6.41 E
Fauglia	66	43.34 N	10.31 E
Fauldhouse	46	55.50 N	3.37 W
Faulkton	198	45.02 N	99.07 W
Faulquemont	56	49.03 N	6.36 E
Fauquembergues	50	50.36 N	2.05 E
Fauquier	182	49.53 N	118.05 W
Fauquier □[6]	208	38.35 N	77.35 W
Făurei	38	45.06 N	27.14 E
Faure Island I	162	25.51 S	113.52 E
Fauresmith	158	29.42 S	25.21 E
Fauro Island I	175e	6.55 S	156.04 E
Fauske	24	67.15 N	15.24 E
Faust	182	55.19 N	115.38 W
Faustovo	82	55.26 N	38.29 E
Fauville-en-Caux	50	49.39 N	0.35 E
Fauvillers	56	49.51 N	5.40 E
Faux-Cap	157b	25.33 S	45.32 E
Fåvang	26	61.27 N	10.11 E
Favara	70	37.19 N	13.39 E
Faverges	62	45.45 N	6.18 E
Faverney	58	47.46 N	6.06 E
Faversham	42	51.20 N	0.53 E
Favières	261	48.46 N	2.47 E
Favignana	70	37.56 N	12.20 E
Favignana, Isola I	70	37.56 N	12.19 E
Favoriten ◆[8]	264b	48.11 N	16.23 E
Favourable Lake ⊜	184	52.53 N	93.56 W
Favrieux	261	48.57 N	1.39 E
Fawcett	182	54.32 N	114.05 W
Fawcett Lake ⊜	182	55.19 N	113.57 W
Fawkham Green	260	51.22 N	0.17 E
Fawkner	274b	37.43 S	144.58 E
Fawkner Park ♦	274b	37.50 S	144.59 E
Fawley	42	50.49 N	1.20 W
Fawn ≃, On., Can.	176	55.22 N	88.20 W
Fawn ≃, U.S.	216	41.51 N	85.40 W
Fawn Grove	208	39.44 N	76.27 W
Fawnie Nose ʌ	182	53.16 N	125.08 W
Fawnie Range ⋏	182	53.10 N	125.00 W
Fawsett Farms	284c	38.59 N	77.14 W
Faxaflói ⊂	24a	64.25 N	23.00 W
Faxälven ≃	26	63.13 N	17.13 E
Faxinal	255	23.59 S	51.22 W
Faxinal do Soturno	252	29.37 S	53.26 W
Faxon	210	41.15 N	76.58 W
Faya	146	17.55 N	19.07 E
Fayd	128	27.07 N	42.27 E
Fayence	62	43.37 N	6.41 E
Fayerweather Island I	276	41.08 N	73.13 W
Fayette, Al., U.S.	194	33.41 N	87.49 W
Fayette, Ia., U.S.	190	42.50 N	91.48 W
Fayette, Ms., U.S.	194	31.42 N	91.03 W
Fayette, Mo., U.S.	194	39.08 N	92.41 W
Fayette, N.Y., U.S.	210	42.49 N	76.49 W
Fayette, Oh., U.S.	216	41.40 N	84.19 W
Fayette □[6], Il., U.S.	219	38.58 N	89.06 W
Fayette □[6], In., U.S.	218	39.39 N	85.08 W
Fayette □[6], Ky., U.S.	218	38.07 N	84.30 W
Fayette □[6], Oh., U.S.	218	39.32 N	83.26 W
Fayette □[6], Pa., U.S.	214	40.05 N	79.39 W
Fayette □[6], Tx., U.S.	222	29.50 N	96.57 W
Fayette, Lake ⊜[1]	222	29.56 N	96.44 W
Fayette City	214	40.06 N	79.50 W
Fayetteville, Ar., U.S.	194	36.03 N	94.09 W
Fayetteville, Ga., U.S.	192	33.26 N	84.27 W
Fayetteville, Il., U.S.	219	38.22 N	89.48 W
Fayetteville, N.Y., U.S.	210	43.02 N	76.00 W
Fayetteville, N.C., U.S.	192	35.03 N	78.52 W
Fayetteville, Oh., U.S.	218	39.11 N	83.55 W
Fayetteville, Pa., U.S.	208	39.54 N	77.33 W
Fayetteville, Tn., U.S.	194	35.09 N	86.34 W
Fayetteville, Tx., U.S.	222	29.54 N	96.41 W
Fayetteville, W.V., U.S.	188	38.03 N	81.06 W
Faylakah I	128	29.27 N	48.20 E
Fayl-Billot	58	47.47 N	5.36 E
Fayrā	144	13.17 N	43.25 E
Fay-sur-Lignon	62	44.59 N	4.14 E
Fayville	207	42.17 N	71.30 W
Fayyum → Al-Fayyūm	142	29.19 N	30.50 E
Fažana	64	44.55 N	13.49 E
Fazao	150	8.42 N	0.46 E
Fazao, Parc National du ♦	150	8.40 N	0.42 E
Fazeley	42	52.37 N	1.42 W
Fazenda de Cima	248	15.56 S	56.37 W
Fazenda Libongo	152	8.24 S	13.24 E
Fazenda Nova	255	16.11 S	50.48 W
Fāzilka	123	30.24 N	74.02 E
Fāzilpur	120	29.18 N	70.27 E
Fazzān (Fezzan) □[9]	146	26.00 N	14.00 E
Fdérik	148	22.41 N	12.43 W
Feale ≃	48	52.28 N	9.40 W
Fear, Cape ›	192	33.50 N	77.58 W
Fearnhead	262	53.25 N	2.33 W
Feasterville	208	40.08 N	75.00 W
Feather ≃	204	38.47 N	121.36 W
Feather, Middle Fork ≃	204	39.34 N	121.26 W
Feather, North Fork ≃	204	39.34 N	121.28 W
Feather, North Fork, East Branch ≃	204	40.01 N	121.13 W
Feather, South Fork ≃	204	39.33 N	121.28 W
Featherbed Top ʌ	262	53.26 N	1.52 W
Featherly Regional Park ♦	280	33.52 N	117.42 W
Featherston	172	41.07 S	175.20 E
Featherstone, Eng., U.K.	44	53.41 N	1.21 W
Featherstone, Zimb.	154	18.42 S	30.49 E
Feathertop, Mount ʌ	166	36.54 S	147.08 E
Fécamp	50	49.45 N	0.22 E
Fedala → Mohammedia	148	33.44 N	7.24 W
Fedderwardergroden	52	53.35 N	8.05 E
Feddet ›[1]	41	55.09 N	12.07 E
Federación	252	31.00 S	57.54 W
Federal, Arg.	252	30.57 S	58.48 W
Federal, Pa., U.S.	279b	40.23 N	80.09 W
Federal Capital Territory □[3]	150	9.00 N	7.15 E
Federalsburg	208	38.41 N	75.46 W
Federal Territory □[8]	273a	6.29 N	3.25 E
Federal Way	224	47.19 N	122.18 W
Federation Forest State Park ♦	224	47.09 N	121.40 W
Federsee ⊜	58	48.05 N	9.38 E
Fedeshk	128	32.45 N	58.50 E
Fedje	26	60.47 N	4.42 E
Fedons Camp ʌ	241k	12.07 N	61.42 W
Fedorino	82	55.08 N	36.06 E
Fedosejevka	80	46.53 N	44.00 E
Fedosejevskaja	24	62.07 N	40.42 E
Fedosicha	86	54.47 N	81.54 E
Fedosjino	82	55.08 N	38.30 E
Fedotovo	82	55.41 N	39.12 E
Feeagh, Lough ⊜	48	53.55 N	9.36 W
Feeding Hills	207	42.04 N	72.40 W
Feehanville	278	42.05 N	87.54 W
Feerfeer	144	8.30 N	47.55 E
Feesburg	218	38.52 N	83.58 W
Fefan I	175c	7.21 N	151.51 E
Fehérgyarmat	30	47.58 N	22.32 E
Fehmarn I	54	54.28 N	11.08 E
Fehmarnbelt (Femer Bælt) ʊ	41	54.35 N	11.15 E
Fehmarnsund ʊ	54	54.24 N	11.07 E
Fehrbellin	54	52.49 N	12.46 E
Fehring	61	46.56 N	16.01 E
Feia, Lagoa ⊂	255	22.00 S	41.20 W
Feicheng	98	36.15 N	116.46 E
Feichten	58	47.02 N	10.44 E
Feidong	100	31.52 N	117.29 E
Feignies	50	50.18 N	3.55 E
Feigumfossen ∟	26	61.23 N	7.26 E
Feiheji	100	33.36 N	115.36 E
Fei Huang ≃	100	33.35 N	119.02 E
Feijó	248	8.09 S	70.21 W
Feiketu	89	45.46 N	127.09 E
Feilding	172	40.13 S	175.34 E
Feiler ʌ	58	47.07 N	10.52 E
Feiliqiao	106	31.05 N	119.05 E
Feilitzsch	54	50.22 N	11.56 E
Feilong, Zhg.	107	30.25 N	106.20 E
Feilong, Zhg.	107	30.36 N	105.54 E
Feilongguan	107	28.57 N	105.05 E
Feiluan	100	26.35 N	119.35 E
Feio ≃	255	21.03 S	51.47 W
Feira	154	15.37 S	30.25 E
Feira de Santana	255	12.15 S	38.57 W
Feistritz ≃	61	47.01 N	16.08 E
Feistritz an der Gail	64	46.34 N	13.36 E
Feistritzer Spitze ʌ	61	46.31 N	14.45 E
Feixi	100	31.42 N	117.10 E
Feixian	98	35.18 N	117.57 E
Feixiang	98	36.34 N	114.49 E
Feiyun ≃	100	27.48 N	120.36 E
Fejaj, Chott ⠿	148	33.55 N	9.10 E
Fejér □[6]	30	47.10 N	18.35 E
Fejø I	41	54.57 N	11.26 E
Feke	130	37.53 N	35.58 E
Feklistova, ostrov I	89	55.02 N	136.55 E
Felâhiye	130	39.06 N	35.35 E
Felanitx	34	39.28 N	3.08 E
Felbertauren-Tunnel ◆[5]	64	47.08 N	12.31 E
Felda	220	26.33 N	81.26 W
Felda ≃, B.R.D.	56	50.42 N	9.03 E
Felda ≃, D.D.R.	56	50.51 N	10.05 E
Feldafing	64	47.57 N	11.17 E
Feldaist ≃	61	48.19 N	14.34 E
Feld am See	64	46.47 N	13.45 E
Feldbach	61	46.57 N	15.54 E
Feldberg, B.R.D.	58	47.51 N	8.02 E
Feldberg, D.D.R.	54	53.20 N	13.26 E
Feldberg ʌ	58	47.52 N	8.00 E
Felderbach ≃	263	51.22 N	7.08 E
Feldhausen ◆[8]	263	51.37 N	6.59 E
Feldis	58	46.48 N	9.26 E
Feldkirch	58	47.14 N	9.36 E
Feldkirchen an der Donau	61	48.21 N	14.03 E
Feldkirchen bei Graz	61	47.01 N	15.27 E
Feldkirchen in Kärnten	61	46.43 N	14.05 E
Feldmark	263	51.41 N	6.38 E
Feldstetten	58	48.28 N	9.37 E
Felhit	144	16.43 N	38.02 E
Feliciano	240m	18.28 N	67.08 W
Feliciano, Arroyo ≃	252	31.06 S	59.54 W
Felicity	218	38.50 N	84.05 W
Felino	64	44.42 N	10.15 E
Felipe Carrillo Puerto	232	19.35 N	88.03 W
Felix, Cape ›	176	69.54 N	97.50 W
Felix, Rio ≃	196	33.08 N	104.19 W
Felixburg	154	19.29 S	30.51 E
Felixdorf	61	47.53 N	16.15 E
Félix Gómez	232	29.50 N	111.30 W
Felixlândia	255	18.47 S	44.55 W
Felixstowe	42	51.58 N	1.20 E
Felixton	158	28.50 S	31.53 E
Félix U. Gómez	232	30.35 N	105.50 W
Felizzano	62	44.54 N	8.26 E
Fella ≃	64	46.21 N	13.07 E
Fellbach	56	48.48 N	9.15 E
Felletin	32	45.53 N	2.10 E
Felling	44	54.57 N	1.33 W
Fellingsbro	40	59.26 N	15.35 E
Fellows	226	35.11 N	119.32 W
Fellows Creek ≃	281	42.17 N	83.26 W
Fellowship	285	39.55 N	74.58 W
Fellsburg	214	40.11 N	79.49 W
Fellsmere	220	27.46 N	80.36 W
Fellwick	285	40.08 N	75.11 W
Felpham	42	50.47 N	0.39 W
Felsberg	56	51.08 N	9.25 E
Felső-Válicka ≃	61	46.52 N	16.53 E
Feltham ◆[8]	260	51.27 N	0.24 W
Felt Lake ⊜	282	37.23 N	122.11 W
Felton, Ca., U.S.	226	37.03 N	122.04 W
Felton, De., U.S.	208	39.00 N	75.34 W
Felton, Pa., U.S.	208	39.51 N	76.34 W
Feltre	64	46.01 N	11.54 E
Felts Mills	212	44.01 N	75.46 W
Feltwell	42	52.29 N	0.32 E
Fêmeas, Rio das ≃	255	12.27 S	45.12 W
Femer Bælt (Fehmarnbelt) ʊ	41	54.35 N	11.15 E
Femme Osage Creek ≃	219	38.39 N	90.44 W
Femmøller	41	56.14 N	10.35 E
Femø I	41	54.58 N	11.33 E
Femund ⊜	26	62.12 N	11.52 E
Femundsenden	26	61.55 N	11.55 E
Femundsmarka Nasjonalpark ♦	26	62.20 N	12.07 E
Fen ≃	102	35.36 N	110.42 E
Fena Valley Reservoir ⊜[1]	174p	13.21 N	144.42 E
Fendaozi	104	41.35 N	120.51 E
Fenelon Falls	212	44.32 N	78.45 W
Fenelton	214	40.52 N	79.44 W
Fener ◆[8]	267b	41.02 N	28.56 E
Fenerbahce Stadium ♦	267b	40.59 N	29.02 E
Fener Burnu ›	130	41.07 N	39.25 E
Fener Tepesi ʌ[2]	267b	41.09 N	28.47 E
Fenestrelle	62	45.02 N	7.03 E
Fénétrange	56	48.51 N	7.01 E
Feng ≃	105	39.25 N	116.57 E
Fengcheng, Zhg.	98	40.27 N	124.02 E
Fengcheng, Zhg.	100	28.10 N	115.46 E
Fengcheng, Zhg.	102	38.32 N	101.50 E
Fengcheng, Zhg.	106	30.55 N	121.38 E
Fengdengwu	105	39.42 N	117.55 E
Fengdian	107	30.41 N	104.51 E
Fengdu	102	29.58 N	107.41 E
Fengfeng	98	36.28 N	114.14 E
Fenggang, Zhg.	100	28.34 N	116.34 E
Fenggang, Zhg.	102	27.58 N	107.47 E
Fenggaopu	107	29.24 N	105.41 E
Fenghua	100	29.40 N	121.24 E
Fenghuang, Zhg.	100	23.58 N	116.44 E
Fenghuang, Zhg.	102	24.25 N	107.17 E
Fenghuang, Zhg.	102	27.58 N	109.19 E
Fenghuang, Zhg.	106	31.21 N	121.44 E
Fenghuangchang	107	29.44 N	106.19 E
Fenghuang Shan ʌ	107	28.54 N	106.35 E
Fenghuanjing	100	31.11 N	117.49 E
Fenghui	100	29.56 N	120.58 E
Fengjia, Zhg.	98	37.03 N	121.42 E
Fengjia, Zhg.	104	42.35 N	122.30 E
Fengjiabao	102	36.12 N	104.49 E
Fengjiakou	98	38.11 N	116.44 E
Fengjianjiao	106	30.41 N	120.51 E
Fengjiatun	104	41.14 N	122.00 E
Fengjiawopeng	104	42.19 N	123.40 E
Fengjiaxiang	106	30.56 N	121.06 E
Fengjie	102	31.03 N	109.31 E
Fengjing	106	30.53 N	121.01 E
Fengkou	100	30.05 N	113.18 E
Fengle, Zhg.	89	45.47 N	125.26 E
Fengle, Zhg.	100	27.13 N	118.11 E
Fenglezhen	98	36.14 N	114.18 E
Fengliang	100	23.59 N	116.14 E
Fenglin, T'aiwan	100	23.45 N	121.26 E
Fenglin, Zhg.	100	28.19 N	120.46 E
Fengling Guan)(	100	28.14 N	118.29 E
Fenglingtou	100	28.26 N	117.50 E
Fengman	89	43.46 N	126.41 E
Fengnan (Xugezhuang)	105	39.34 N	118.06 E
Fengning (Dagezhen)	98	41.12 N	116.32 E
Fengpin	100	23.36 N	121.31 E
Fengpingzi	102	32.46 N	105.12 E
Fengqiao, Zhg.	100	29.46 N	120.26 E
Fengqiao, Zhg.	106	31.19 N	120.33 E
Fengqing	102	24.46 N	99.52 E
Fengqiu	98	35.05 N	114.25 E
Fengrun	105	39.50 N	118.07 E
Fengshan, Zhg.	89	46.22 N	128.30 E
Fengshan, Zhg.	98	41.14 N	117.05 E
Fengshan, Zhg.	102	22.01 N	109.59 E
Fengshi	100	24.42 N	116.34 E
Fengshun	100	23.48 N	116.11 E
Fengtai, Zhg.	100	32.44 N	116.43 E
Fengtai, Zhg.	105	39.51 N	116.16 E
Fengtian, Zhg.	100	25.46 N	115.30 E
Fengtian, Zhg.	100	27.24 N	114.43 E
Fengtien → Shenyang	104	41.48 N	123.27 E
Fengting	100	25.16 N	118.54 E
Fengwan	100	24.48 N	113.50 E
Fengxi	102	31.48 N	109.50 E
Fengxian, Zhg.	98	34.42 N	116.34 E
Fengxian, Zhg.	102	33.57 N	106.44 E
Fengxian, Zhg.	106	30.55 N	121.27 E
Fengxiang	102	34.29 N	107.29 E
Fengxin	100	28.43 N	115.23 E
Fengyang, Zhg.	100	32.52 N	117.34 E
Fengyang, Zhg.	100	24.49 N	117.53 E
Fengyi	102	31.44 N	103.53 E
Fengyu	100	26.31 N	119.18 E
Fengyüan	100	24.15 N	120.43 E
Fengzhen	102	40.24 N	113.09 E
Fengzhou	100	25.41 N	113.52 E
Fengzhuangtou	106	31.00 N	118.39 E
Fenholloway ≃	192	29.59 N	83.47 W
Fen Hu ⊜	106	31.00 N	120.47 E
Feni	124	23.00 N	91.24 E
Fenicia Moncata ⊥	70	37.33 N	14.57 E
Feni Islands II	14	4.05 S	153.42 E
Fenimore Pass ʊ	180	52.00 N	175.35 W
Fenino	265b	55.44 N	37.57 E
Fenis	62	45.44 N	7.29 E
Feniscowles	262	53.43 N	2.32 W
Fenjie	106	32.17 N	120.20 E
Fennimore	190	42.59 N	90.39 W
Fennville	216	42.35 N	86.06 W
Fenny Compton	42	52.09 N	1.20 W
Fenny Stratford	42	52.00 N	0.43 W
Feno, Capo di ›, Fr.	36	41.57 N	8.36 E
Feno, Capo di ›, Fr.	71	41.23 N	9.06 E

Symbol	English	Deutsch	Español	Français	Português
≃	River	Fluß	Río	Rivière	Rio
≚	Canal	Kanal	Canal	Canal	Canal
∟	Waterfall, Rapids	Wasserfall, Stromschnellen	Cascada, Rápidos	Chute d'eau, Rapides	Cascata, Rápidos
ʊ	Strait	Meeresstraße	Estrecho	Détroit	Estreito
⊂	Bay, Gulf	Bucht, Golf	Bahía, Golfo	Baie, Golfe	Baía, Golfo
⊜	Lake, Lakes	See, Seen	Lago, Lagos	Lac, Lacs	Lago, Lagos
⠿	Swamp	Sumpf	Pantano	Marais	Pântano
⊓	Ice Features, Glacier	Eis- und Gletscherformen	Accidentes Glaciales	Formes glaciaires	Acidentes glaciares
⊤	Other Hydrographic Features	Andere Hydrographische Objekte	Otros Elementos Hidrográficos	Autres données hydrographiques	Outros acidentes hidrográficos
✦	Submarine Features	Untermeerische Objekte	Accidentes Submarinos	Formes de relief sous-marin	Acidentes submarinos
□	Political Unit	Politische Einheit	Unidad Politica	Entité politique	Unidade política
ʋ	Cultural Institution	Kulturelle Institution	Institución Cultural	Institution culturelle	Instituição cultural
⊥	Historical Site	Historische Stätte	Sitio Histórico	Site historique	Sitio histórico
♦	Recreational Site	Erholungs- und Ferienort	Sitio de Recreo	Centre de loisirs	Area de Lazer
⊠	Airport	Flughafen	Aeropuerto	Aéroport	Aeroporto
■	Military Installation	Militäranlage	Instalación Militar	Installation militaire	Instalação militar
◆	Miscellaneous	Verschiedenes	Misceláneo	Divers	Diversos

Fenoarivo, Madag. 157b 18.26 S 46.34 E
Fenoarivo, Madag. 157b 21.43 S 46.24 E
Fenoarivo, Madag. 157b 20.52 S 46.53 E
Fenoarivo Atsinanana 157b 17.22 S 49.25 E
Fensfjorden c[2] 26 60.51 N 4.50 E
Fenshui 104 40.41 N 122.32 E
Fenshui ≃ 100 29.49 N 119.41 E
Fenshui'ao 100 25.20 N 114.43 E
Fenshuidunshen 106 31.30 N 120.01 E
Fenshuiling, Zhg. 107 28.51 N 105.35 E
Fenshuiling, Zhg. 107 30.20 N 105.15 E
Fenshuipu 107 30.05 N 104.05 E
Fenshuizhen 107 29.44 N 103.55 E
Fenshuizui 100 30.35 N 113.38 E
Fensmark 41 55.17 N 11.49 E
Fenstanton 42 52.18 N 0.04 W
Fenton, Mi., U.S. 216 42.47 N 83.42 W
Fenton, Mo., U.S. 219 38.32 N 90.22 W
Fenton, Lake ⊜ 216 42.50 N 83.43 W
Fentou 105 38.53 N 116.32 E
Fentress 222 29.45 N 97.47 W
Fenway Park ♠ 283 42.21 N 71.06 W
Fenwick 188 38.13 N 80.34 W
Fenwick Island ›[1] 208 38.25 N 75.03 W
Fenyang 102 37.17 N 111.48 E
Fenyi 100 27.47 N 114.42 E
Feodosija 78 45.02 N 35.23 E
Feodosijskij zaliv c 78 45.05 N 35.35 E
Fépin 56 50.01 N 4.44 E
Fer, Cap de › 148 37.05 N 7.10 E
Ferbane 48 53.15 N 7.49 W
Ferbitz 264a 52.30 N 13.01 E
Ferch 264a 52.19 N 12.56 E
Fercher Berge ∧[2] 264a 52.19 N 12.57 E
Ferchland 54 52.26 N 12.00 E
Ferdig 182 48.45 N 111.46 W
Ferdinand 194 38.13 N 86.51 W
Ferdinandshof 54 53.39 N 13.53 E
Ferdows 128 34.00 N 58.09 E
Fère-Champenoise 50 48.45 N 3.59 E
Fère-en-Tardenois 50 49.12 N 3.31 E
Ferencváros ✦[8] 264c 47.28 N 19.06 E
Ferentillo 66 42.37 N 12.47 E
Ferentino 66 41.42 N 13.15 E
Fergana 85 40.23 N 71.46 E
Fergana □[4] 85 40.30 N 71.20 E
Ferganskaja dolina V 85 40.50 N 71.30 E
Ferganskij chrebet ⋀ 85 41.00 N 74.00 E
Fergus 212 43.42 N 80.22 W
Fergus Falls 198 46.16 N 96.04 W
Ferguson, Austl. 168a 33.26 S 115.51 E
Ferguson, B.C., Can. 182 50.41 N 117.28 W
Ferguson, Ky., U.S. 192 37.04 N 84.36 W
Ferguson, Mo., U.S. 219 38.44 N 90.18 W
Ferguson ≃ 168a 33.21 S 115.40 E
Fergusonville 285 40.07 N 74.54 W
Fergusson Island I 164 9.30 S 150.40 E
Fériana 148 34.57 N 8.34 E
Ferihegyi Airport ⊠ 264c 47.26 N 19.15 E
Ferkéssédougou 150 9.36 N 5.12 W
Ferla 70 37.07 N 14.56 E
Ferlach 61 46.31 N 14.18 E
Ferleiten 64 47.10 N 12.49 E
Ferlo ✦[1] 150 0.15 N 0.14 W
Ferlo, Vallée du V 150 15.42 N 15.30 W
Fermiers, Île aux I 275a 45.40 N 73.27 W
Fermignano 66 43.40 N 12.39 E
Fermin, Point › 228 33.42 N 118.18 W
Fermi National Accelerator Laboratory ❦[3] 216 41.50 N 88.15 W
Fermo 66 43.09 N 13.43 E
Fermont 176 52.47 N 67.05 W
Fermoselle 34 41.19 N 6.23 W
Fermoy 48 52.08 N 8.16 W
Fernandes Belo 250 1.07 S 46.19 W
Fernández 252 27.55 S 63.54 W
Fernández Leal 200 30.51 N 108.17 W
Fernandina, Isla I 246a 0.25 S 91.30 W
Fernandina Beach 192 30.40 N 81.27 W
Fernando de la Mora 252 25.19 S 57.36 W
Fernando de Noronha □[3] 250 3.51 S 32.25 W
Fernando de Noronha, Ilha I 250 3.51 S 32.25 W
Fernandópolis 255 20.16 S 50.14 W
Fernando Póo → Bioko I 152 3.30 N 8.40 E
Fernán-Núñez 34 37.40 N 4.43 W
Fernão Veloso, Baía de c 154 14.20 S 40.45 E
Ferndale, S. Afr. 273d 26.05 S 27.59 E
Ferndale, Ca., U.S. 204 40.34 N 124.15 W
Ferndale, Fl., U.S. 220 28.37 N 81.42 W
Ferndale, Md., U.S. 208 39.10 N 76.38 W
Ferndale, Mi., U.S. 216 42.27 N 83.08 W
Ferndale, N.Y., U.S. 210 41.46 N 74.44 W
Ferndale, Pa., U.S. 214 40.17 N 78.54 W
Ferndale, Wa., U.S. 202 48.50 N 122.35 W
Ferndale Lake ⊜ 222 32.57 N 95.05 W
Ferndown 42 50.48 N 1.55 W
Ferney-Voltaire 58 46.15 N 6.07 E
Fern Glen 210 40.57 N 76.10 W
Fernhatten ⋀[2] 41 56.15 N 10.48 E
Fernhill Heath 42 52.14 N 2.12 W
Fernie 182 49.30 N 115.03 W
Fernilee 262 53.18 N 1.58 W
Fernilee Reservoir ⊜[1] 262 53.17 N 1.59 W
Fernley 204 39.36 N 119.15 W
Ferno 62 45.37 N 8.45 E
Fernow, Mount ∧ 224 47.45 N 121.14 W
Fern Park 220 28.41 N 81.20 W
Fernpass)(58 47.22 N 10.50 E
Fern Ridge Lake ⊜[1] 202 44.05 N 123.18 W
Ferns 48 52.35 N 6.31 W
Fernvale 171a 27.27 S 152.39 E
Fernway, Il., U.S. 278 41.36 N 87.50 W
Fernway, Pa., U.S. 214 40.41 N 80.07 W
Fernwood, Id., U.S. 202 47.06 N 116.23 W
Fernwood, N.Y., U.S. 210 43.16 N 73.40 W
Fernwood, Pa., U.S. 285 39.57 N 75.15 W
Ferny Creek 274b 37.53 S 145.21 E
Feroé, Islas → Faeroe Islands □[2] 22 62.00 N 7.00 W
Feroës → Faeroe Islands □[2] 22 62.00 N 7.00 W
Ferokh 122 11.11 N 75.51 E
Feroleto Antico 68 38.58 N 16.23 E
Feroleto della Chiesa 68 38.28 N 16.04 E
Ferolle Point › 186 51.05 N 57.07 W
Ferozepore → Fīrozpur 123 30.55 N 74.36 E
Ferrandina 68 40.29 N 16.28 E
Ferrara 64 44.50 N 11.35 E
Ferrara □[4] 64 44.48 N 11.50 E
Ferrat, Cap › 34 35.54 N 0.23 W
Ferrato, Capo › 71 39.18 N 9.38 E
Ferraz de Vasconcelos 256 23.32 S 46.22 W
Ferraz de Vasconcelos □[7] 287b 23.33 S 46.21 W
Ferrazzano 66 41.32 N 14.40 E
Ferré, Cap › 240e 14.28 N 60.49 W
Ferreira, Ang. 152 12.53 S 22.48 E
Ferreira, S. Afr. 158 29.13 S 26.10 E
Ferreira, Riacho ≃ 250 10.06 S 42.13 W
Ferreira do Alentejo 34 38.03 N 8.07 W
Ferreira Gomes 250 0.48 N 51.08 W
Ferreiros 256 22.25 S 43.34 W
Ferrell 285 39.41 N 75.12 W
Ferrell's Bridge Dam ✦[6] 222 32.45 N 94.30 W
Ferreñafe 248 6.38 S 79.45 W
Ferrera Erbognone 62 45.07 N 8.52 E
Ferret 58 45.55 N 7.06 E
Ferret, Cap › 32 44.37 N 1.15 W
Ferreyra 252 31.28 S 64.08 W
Ferriday 194 31.37 N 91.33 W
Ferriere 62 44.38 N 9.30 E
Ferrière-la-Grande 50 50.15 N 4.00 E
Ferrières 50 48.05 N 2.47 E
Ferrières-en-Brie 50 48.49 N 2.43 E
Ferris 222 32.32 N 96.39 W
Ferritslev 41 55.18 N 10.36 E
Ferro ≃ 255 12.27 S 54.31 W
Ferrol → El Ferrol del Caudillo 34 43.29 N 8.14 W
Ferrol, Península de ›[1] 248 9.10 S 78.37 W
Ferron 200 39.05 N 111.08 W
Ferron Creek ≃ 200 39.09 N 110.55 W
Ferros 255 19.14 S 43.02 W
Ferru, Monte ∧ 71 39.44 N 9.38 E
Ferruzzano 68 38.02 N 16.05 E
Ferry, Pointe › 241o 16.17 N 61.49 W
Ferryhill 44 54.41 N 1.33 W
Ferryland 186 47.02 N 52.53 W
Ferry Point Park ♠ 276 40.49 N 73.50 W
Ferrysburg 216 43.05 N 86.13 W
Ferry Village 284a 43.58 N 78.57 W
Ferryville → Menzel Bourguiba 148 37.10 N 9.48 E
Feršampenuaz 86 53.32 N 59.51 E
Fertile 198 47.32 N 96.16 W
Fertilia, Aeroporto di ⊠ 71 40.37 N 8.15 E
Fertő (Neusiedler See) ⊜ 61 47.50 N 16.45 E
Fertőd ⊥ 61 47.37 N 16.53 E
Fertőrákos 61 47.43 N 16.39 E
Fertőújlak 61 47.40 N 16.51 E
Ferulargiu, Monte ∧ 71 40.31 N 9.34 E
Ferzikovo 82 54.32 N 36.45 E
Fès 148 34.05 N 4.57 W
Fès □[4] 148 33.55 N 4.57 W
Feshi 152 6.07 S 18.10 E
Feshie ≃ 46 57.08 N 3.55 W
Fessenden 198 47.38 N 99.37 W
Festenberg → Twardogóra 30 51.22 N 17.28 E
Festus 219 38.13 N 90.23 W
Fetcham 260 51.17 N 0.22 W
Fet Dom, Tanjung › 164 1.53 S 129.43 E
Fété Bowé 150 14.56 N 13.30 W
Fetești 38 44.23 N 27.50 E
Fethaland, Point of › 46a 60.38 N 1.18 W
Fethard 48 52.27 N 7.41 W
Fethiye 130 36.37 N 29.07 E
Fethiye Körfezi c 130 36.40 N 29.00 E
Fetisovo 72 42.46 N 52.38 E
Fetlar I 46a 60.37 N 0.52 W
Fetsund 26 59.56 N 11.10 E
Fetterangus 46 57.33 N 2.01 W
Fettercairn 46 56.51 N 2.34 W
Feucherolles 261 48.52 N 1.58 E
Feucht 60 49.22 N 11.13 E
Feuchtwangen 56 49.10 N 10.20 E
Feudingen 56 50.56 N 8.19 E
Feuerland → Tierra del Fuego, Isla Grande de I 254 54.00 S 69.00 W
Feuet 146 24.57 N 10.04 E
Feuilles, Baie aux c 176 58.55 N 69.20 W
Feuilles, Rivière aux ≃ 176 58.47 N 70.04 W
Feuquières-en-Vimeu 50 50.04 N 1.36 E
Feura Bush 210 42.35 N 73.53 W
Feurs 62 45.45 N 4.14 E
Fevik 26 58.23 N 8.42 E
Fevzipaşa 130 37.07 N 36.37 E
Féy 56 49.02 N 6.06 E
Feyẕābād, Afg. 120 37.06 N 70.34 E
Feyẕābād, Īrān 128 35.01 N 58.46 E
Feyzin 62 45.40 N 4.51 E
Fez → Fès 148 34.05 N 4.57 W
Fezzan → Fazzān □[9] 146 26.00 N 14.00 E
Ffestiniog 42 52.58 N 3.55 W
Fforest Fawr ✦[1] 42 51.52 N 3.36 W
F. Gilbert Hills State Forest ♠ 283 42.03 N 71.17 W
Fhada, Beinn ∧ 46 57.13 N 5.18 W
Fiambalá 252 27.41 S 67.38 W
Fiamignano 66 42.16 N 13.07 E
Fian 150 10.23 N 2.29 W
Fianarantsoa 157b 21.26 S 47.05 E
Fianarantsoa □[4] 157b 22.00 S 47.00 E
Fianga 146 9.55 N 15.09 E
Fiano 62 45.13 N 7.31 E
Fiantsonana 157b 19.09 S 46.12 E
Fiastra, Abbazia di ❦[1] 66 43.13 N 13.25 E
Fiavè 64 46.00 N 10.50 E
Ficarazzi 70 38.05 N 13.28 E
Ficarolo 64 44.57 N 11.26 E
Ficarra 70 38.06 N 14.50 E
Fiche 144 9.52 N 38.46 E
Fichtelberg 60 50.01 N 11.51 E
Fichtelberg ∧ 54 50.26 N 12.57 E
Fichtelgebirge ⋀ 30 50.00 N 11.55 E
Fichtenau 264a 52.27 N 13.42 E
Ficksburg 158 28.57 S 27.50 E
Ficulle 66 42.50 N 12.04 E
Ficuzza ≃ 70 37.00 N 14.20 E
Fidalgo ≃ 250 7.28 S 42.32 W
Fidalgo Island I 224 48.25 N 122.35 W
Fidān, Wādī al- V 132 30.46 N 35.18 E
Fiddlers Hamlet 260 51.41 N 0.08 E
Fiddletown 226 38.30 N 120.46 W
Fiddyment Creek ≃ 278 41.36 N 88.03 W
Fidelity 219 39.09 N 90.10 W
Fidenza 64 44.52 N 10.03 E
Fidīmīn 142 29.23 N 30.46 E
Fiditi 150 7.45 N 3.53 E
Fidji → Fiji □[1] 175g 18.00 S 178.00 E
Fidler Lake ⊜ 184 57.11 N 96.57 W
Fidschi → Fiji □[1] 175g 18.00 S 178.00 E
Fiè (Völs) 64 46.31 N 11.30 E
Fieberbrunn 64 47.29 N 12.33 E
Field 182 51.24 N 116.29 W
Fieldale 192 36.42 N 79.56 W
Field Museum ❦ 278 41.53 N 87.37 W
Fieldon 219 39.07 N 90.30 W
Fieldsboro 285 40.08 N 74.43 W
Fieldstone 276 40.44 N 74.33 W
Fiemme, Val di V 64 46.24 N 11.25 E
Fiener Bruch ≡ 54 52.19 N 12.10 E
Fienvillers 50 50.07 N 2.14 E
Fier 38 40.43 N 19.34 E
Fier ≃ 58 45.56 N 5.50 E
Fiéra Campionaria ♦ 266b 45.28 N 9.09 E
Fiera di Primiero 64 46.10 N 11.49 E
Fierenana 157b 18.29 S 48.24 E
Fiery Creek ≃, Austl. 166 18.23 S 139.52 E
Fiery Creek ≃, Austl. 169 37.44 S 142.56 E
Fiery Range ⋀ 171b 35.30 S 148.40 E
Fierzës, Liqeni i ⊜[1] 38 42.10 N 20.15 E
Fiesch 58 46.20 N 8.10 E
Fiesole 66 43.48 N 11.17 E
Fiesso d'Artico 64 45.24 N 12.02 E
Fiesso Umbertiano 64 44.56 N 11.36 E
Fife 224 47.14 N 122.22 W
Fife □[4] 46 56.13 N 3.02 W
Fife Lake, Sk., Can. 184 49.12 N 105.43 W
Fife Lake, Mi., U.S. 190 44.34 N 85.21 W
Fife Lake ⊜ 184 49.14 N 105.53 W
Fife Ness › 46 56.17 N 2.36 W
Fifield 190 45.52 N 90.25 W
Fifteenmile Creek ≃, Or., U.S. 224 45.37 N 121.07 W
Fifteenmile Creek ≃, Wy., U.S. 202 44.01 N 108.01 W
Fifth Cataract → Khāmis, Ash-Shallāl al- ∟ 140 18.23 N 33.47 E
Fifth Depot Lake ⊜ 212 44.36 N 76.52 W
Figeac 32 44.37 N 2.02 E
Figeholm 26 57.22 N 16.33 E
Fig Garden 226 36.48 N 119.47 W
Fighting Island I 281 42.13 N 83.07 W
Figline Valdarno 66 43.37 N 11.28 E
Figtree 154 20.24 S 28.21 E
Figueira → Governador Valadares, Bra. 255 18.51 S 41.56 W
Figueira, Bra. 287a 22.42 S 43.27 W
Figueira, Cachoeira ∟ 250 9.49 S 58.13 W
Figueira da Foz 34 40.09 N 8.52 W
Figueres 34 42.16 N 2.58 E
Figuig 148 32.10 N 1.15 W
Figuig □[4] 148 32.40 N 2.15 W
Fihaonana 157b 18.36 S 47.12 E
Fiherenana ≃ 157b 23.19 S 43.37 E
Fiji □[1], Oc. 14 18.00 S 178.00 E
Fiji □[1], Oc. 175g 18.00 S 178.00 E
Fiji Islands II 14 18.00 S 178.00 E
Fijnaart 52 51.37 N 4.31 E
Fik 144 8.10 N 42.18 E
Fika 146 11.17 N 11.18 E
Fiktūriyā, Bi'r ⊤[4] 142 30.24 N 30.36 E
Filabusi 154 20.34 S 29.20 E
Filadélfia, Bra. 250 7.21 S 47.30 W
Filadelfia, C.R. 236 10.26 N 85.34 W
Filadelfia, It. 68 38.48 N 16.18 E
Filadelfia → Philadelphia, Pa., U.S. 208 39.57 N 75.07 W
Fil'akovo 30 48.17 N 19.51 E
Filandari 68 38.37 N 16.02 E
Filatova Gora 76 57.40 N 28.10 E
Filchner Ice Shelf ⊓ 9 79.00 S 40.00 W
Filderstadt 56 48.41 N 9.13 E
File Lake ⊜ 184 54.53 N 100.20 W
Filettino 66 41.53 N 13.19 E
Filey 44 54.12 N 0.17 W
Filey Bay c 44 54.12 N 0.16 W
Fili ✦[8] 265b 55.45 N 37.31 E
Filí ⊥ 38 38.10 N 23.40 E
Filiano 68 40.49 N 15.42 E
Filiași 38 44.33 N 23.31 E
Filiatrá 38 37.10 N 21.35 E
Filicudi, Isola I 70 38.34 N 14.34 E
Filimonovo 86 56.12 N 95.28 E
Filingué 150 14.21 N 3.19 E
Filipinas → Philippines □[1] 116 13.00 N 122.00 E
Filipinas, Mar de → Philippine Sea ⊤[2] 14 20.00 N 135.00 E
Filipino Cemetery and Memorial ✦ 269f 14.31 N 121.02 E
Fílippoi ⊥ 38 41.00 N 24.16 E
Filippovka 80 53.59 N 49.46 E
Filippovo 80 58.18 N 50.30 E
Filippovskoje, S.S.S.R. 82 56.06 N 38.37 E
Filippovskoje, S.S.S.R. 82 56.48 N 39.07 E
Filipstad 40 59.43 N 14.10 E
Filisola 234 17.50 N 94.19 W
Fillmore, Sk., Can. 184 49.50 N 103.25 W
Fillmore, Ca., U.S. 228 34.23 N 118.55 W
Fillmore, Il., U.S. 219 39.07 N 89.17 W
Fillmore, N.Y., U.S. 210 42.27 N 78.06 W
Fillmore, Ut,. U.S. 200 38.58 N 112.19 W
Fillmore Glen State Park ♠ 210 42.42 N 76.20 W
Filogaso 68 38.41 N 16.14 E
Filomeno Mata 234 20.12 N 97.42 W
Filonovskaja 80 50.34 N 42.46 E
Filottrano 66 43.26 N 13.21 E
Fils ≃ 56 48.42 N 9.25 E
Filskov 41 55.48 N 9.02 E
Filton 42 51.31 N 2.35 W
Filtu 144 5.07 N 40.39 E
Filzbach 58 47.07 N 9.08 E
Fimi ≃ 152 3.01 S 16.58 E
Fina, Réserve de ✦[4] 150 12.50 N 8.30 W
Finale Emilia 64 44.50 N 11.17 E
Finale Ligure 62 44.10 N 8.20 E
Finarwa 144 13.06 N 39.01 E
Finca El Rey, Parque Nacional ♠ 252 25.00 S 64.40 W
Fincastle 192 37.29 N 79.52 W
Finch 206 45.11 N 75.07 W
Fincham 42 52.37 N 0.30 E
Finchley ✦[8] 260 51.36 N 0.10 W
Finderne 276 40.34 N 74.35 W
Findhorn 46 57.39 N 3.36 W
Findhorn ≃ 46 57.38 N 3.38 W
Fındık 130 37.31 N 41.58 E
Findlay, Il., U.S. 219 39.31 N 88.45 W
Findlay, Oh., U.S. 216 41.02 N 83.39 W
Findlay, Mount ∧ 182 50.04 N 116.28 W
Findley Lake 214 42.07 N 79.44 W
Findley Lake ⊜ 214 42.06 N 79.43 W
Findochty 46 57.41 N 2.54 W
Fine Arts, Museum of ❦ 283 42.20 N 71.06 W
Finedon 42 52.20 N 0.39 W
Finejevo 82 56.02 N 38.53 E
Finesville 210 40.36 N 75.10 W
Fingal, On., Can. 214 42.43 N 81.19 W
Fingal, N.D., U.S. 198 46.45 N 97.47 W
Finger Lake ⊜ 184 53.09 N 93.30 W
Fíngoè 154 15.12 S 31.50 E
Finike 130 36.18 N 30.09 E
Finike Körfezi c 130 36.17 N 30.16 E
Finisk ≃ 48 52.07 N 7.50 W
Finistère □[5] 32 48.20 N 4.00 W
Finisterre 196 25.59 N 103.15 W
Finisterre → Land's End › 42 50.03 N 5.44 W
Finisterre, Cabo de › 34 42.53 N 9.16 W
Finisterre Range ⋀ 164 5.50 S 146.05 E
Finja 41 56.10 N 13.41 E
Finjasjön ⊜ 41 56.08 N 13.42 E
Finke 162 25.34 S 134.35 E
Finke ≃ 162 26.20 S 136.00 E
Finke, Mount ∧[2] 162 30.55 S 134.02 E
Finke Gorge National Park ♠ 162 23.15 S 132.50 E
Finkenkrug 264a 52.34 N 13.03 E
Finkenwerder ✦[8] 52 53.31 N 9.52 E
Finksburg 208 39.29 N 76.53 W
Finland (Suomi) □[1], Europe 22 64.00 N 26.00 E
Finland (Suomi) □[1], Europe 24 64.00 N 26.00 E
Finland, Gulf of (Suomenlahti) (Finskij zaliv) c 26 60.00 N 27.00 E
Finlande → Finland □[1] 24 64.00 N 26.00 E
Finlandia → Finland □[1] 24 64.00 N 26.00 E
Finlandia, Golfo de → Finland, Gulf of c 26 60.00 N 27.00 E
Finland Station ✦[5] 265a 59.57 N 30.22 E
Finlas, Loch ⊜ 44 55.15 N 4.25 W
Finlay ≃ 176 56.54 N 124.57 W
Finley, Austl. 166 35.39 S 145.35 E
Finley, N.D., U.S. 198 47.30 N 97.50 W
Finley Creek ≃ 194 36.58 N 93.22 W
Finleyville, Pa., U.S. 214 40.09 N 78.11 W
Finleyville, Pa., U.S. 214 40.15 N 80.00 W
Finleyville Airport ⊠ 279b 40.15 N 80.01 W
Finmoore 182 53.59 N 123.37 W
Finn ≃ 48 54.50 N 7.29 W
Finne ✦[1] 54 51.13 N 11.19 E
Finnegan 182 51.07 N 112.04 W
Finnentrop 56 51.09 N 7.58 E
Finnerödja 40 58.56 N 14.26 E
Finney Creek ≃ 224 48.31 N 121.51 W
Finnhamn 40 59.28 N 18.50 E
Finnigan, Mount ∧ 164 15.49 S 145.17 E
Finnis, Cape › 162 33.38 S 134.51 E
Finnischer Meerbusen → Finland, Gulf of c 26 60.00 N 27.00 E
Finniss 168b 35.24 S 138.49 E
Finniss ≃ 168b 35.30 S 138.53 E
Finnland → Finland □[1] 24 64.00 N 26.00 E
Finnmark □[6] 24 70.00 N 25.00 E
Finn Mountain ∧ 180 60.37 N 157.11 W
Finno ∧[2] 154 3.27 N 41.32 E
Finnskogen ✦[3] 26 60.40 N 12.40 E
Finnsnes 24 69.14 N 17.59 E
Finocchio ✦[8] 267a 41.53 N 12.41 E
Finow 54 52.50 N 13.43 E
Finowfurt 54 52.51 N 13.41 E
Finowkanal ≋ 54 52.51 N 13.24 E
Fins, Fr. 50 50.02 N 3.03 E
Fins, 'Umān 128 22.56 N 59.13 E
Finsbury 273d 26.13 S 27.39 E
Finschhafen 164 6.35 S 147.50 E
Finse 26 60.36 N 7.30 E
Finskij zaliv → Finland, Gulf of c 26 60.00 N 27.00 E
Finspång 40 58.43 N 15.47 E
Finsta 40 59.44 N 18.30 E
Finsteraarhorn ∧ 58 46.32 N 8.08 E
Finsterwalde 54 51.38 N 13.42 E
Finsterwolde 52 53.12 N 7.04 E
Fintel 52 53.10 N 9.40 E
Fintona 48 54.30 N 7.19 W
Fintown 48 54.52 N 8.08 W
Finvoy 48 55.00 N 6.30 W
Fionn Loch ⊜ 46 57.46 N 5.29 W
Fiora ≃ 66 42.20 N 11.34 E
Fiorano Modenese 64 44.32 N 10.49 E
Fiordland National Park ♠ 172 45.30 S 167.20 E
Fiorenzuola d'Arda 62 44.56 N 9.55 E
Fiorenzuola di Focara 66 43.57 N 12.48 E
Fiorito ✦[8] 288 34.42 S 58.27 W
Fīq 132 32.47 N 35.42 E
Fırat → Euphrates ≃ 128 31.00 N 47.25 E
Firavitoba 246 5.40 N 73.00 W
Fircrest 224 47.14 N 122.30 W
Fire ≃ 190 48.52 N 83.21 W
Firebaugh 226 36.51 N 120.27 W
Firebrick 218 38.41 N 83.03 W
Fire Island I 210 40.42 N 73.00 W
Fire Island Inlet c 276 40.38 N 73.16 W
Fire Island National Seashore ♠ 188 40.38 N 73.08 W
Fire Island Pines 276 40.40 N 73.04 W
Fire Islands II 276 40.40 N 73.11 W
Firenze (Florence) 66 43.46 N 11.15 E
Firenze □[4] 66 43.50 N 11.20 E
Firenzuola 66 44.07 N 11.23 E
Firesteel Creek ≃ 198 43.43 N 97.58 W
Firgrove 262 53.37 N 2.08 W
Firmat 252 33.27 S 61.29 W
Firminópolis 255 16.40 S 50.19 W
Firminy 62 45.23 N 4.18 E
Firmo 68 39.43 N 16.10 E
Firovo 76 57.29 N 33.40 E
Fīrozābād 124 27.09 N 78.25 E
Fīrozpur 123 30.55 N 74.36 E
Firozpur Jhirka 124 27.48 N 76.57 E
Firsanovka 265b 55.57 N 37.15 E
Firsovo 88 52.20 N 118.06 E
First Broad ≃ 192 35.11 N 81.37 W
First Cataract → Awwal, Ash-Shallāl al- ∟ 140 24.01 N 32.52 E
First Cliff ⫠[4] 283 42.12 N 70.43 W
First Connecticut Lake ⊜ 206 45.05 N 71.15 W
First Han-gang Bridge ✦[5] 271b 37.32 N 126.56 E
First Herring Brook ≃ 283 42.11 N 70.45 W
First Watchung Mountain ∧ 276 40.55 N 74.10 W
Firth 198 40.31 N 96.36 W
Firth ≃ 180 69.32 N 139.22 W
Fir'uza 128 37.56 N 58.04 E
Fīrūzābād 128 28.50 N 52.36 E
Fīrūz Kūh 128 35.45 N 52.47 E
Fischa ≃ 264b 48.04 N 16.35 E
Fischamend 61 48.07 N 16.37 E
Fischbach, B.R.D. 56 49.44 N 7.23 E
Fischbach, B.R.D. 60 49.25 N 11.12 E
Fischbachau 64 47.43 N 11.57 E
Fischbacher Alpen ⋀ 61 47.28 N 15.30 E
Fischbeck, B.R.D. 52 52.09 N 9.17 E
Fischbeck, D.D.R. 54 52.32 N 12.01 E
Fischeln ✦[8] 263 51.18 N 6.35 E
Fischen 58 47.28 N 10.16 E
Fischhausen → Primorsk 76 54.44 N 20.01 E
Fischland ⫠[2] 54 54.22 N 12.25 E
Fish ≃, Austl. 170 33.29 S 149.37 E
Fish (Vis) ≃, Namibia 156 28.07 S 17.45 E
Fish ≃, Al., U.S. 194 30.25 N 87.50 W
Fish ≃, Me., U.S. 186 47.15 N 68.36 W
Fishbourne 42 50.44 N 1.12 W
Fish Brook ≃, Ma., U.S. 283 42.42 N 71.13 W
Fish Brook ≃, Ma., U.S. 283 42.38 N 70.58 W
Fish Camp 226 37.29 N 119.38 W
Fish Canyon V 280 34.11 N 117.55 W
Fish Creek ≃, On., Can. 212 43.13 N 81.13 W
Fish Creek ≃, U.S. 216 41.28 N 84.45 W
Fish Creek ≃, Mi., U.S. 190 43.04 N 84.51 W
Fish Creek ≃, Mt., U.S. 202 46.17 N 109.13 W
Fish Creek ≃, N.Y., U.S. 212 43.12 N 75.43 W
Fish Creek ≃, Or., U.S. 224 45.09 N 122.09 W
Fish Creek, East Branch ≃ 212 43.16 N 75.38 W
Fish Creek, West Branch ≃ 212 43.16 N 75.38 W
Fish Creek Mountain ∧ 224 45.05 N 122.08 W
Fisheating Creek ≃ 220 26.57 N 81.07 W
Fisher, Austl. 162 30.33 S 130.58 E
Fisher, Ar., U.S. 194 35.29 N 90.58 W
Fisher, Il., U.S. 216 40.18 N 88.21 W
Fisher, La., U.S. 194 31.29 N 93.27 W
Fisher, Pa., U.S. 214 41.16 N 79.15 W
Fisher ≃, Mb., Can. 184 51.26 N 97.18 W
Fisher ≃, Mt., U.S. 202 48.22 N 115.19 W
Fisher Bay c, Mb., Can. 184 51.30 N 97.16 W
Fisher Bay c, Mi., U.S. 281 42.36 N 82.39 W
Fisher Branch 184 51.05 N 97.37 W
Fisher Channel ʯ 182 52.10 N 127.42 W
Fisher Glacier ⊓ 9 73.15 S 66.00 E
Fisher Heights 279b 40.10 N 79.54 W
Fishermans Island I 208 37.06 N 75.58 W
Fisherman's Wharf ✦ 282 37.48 N 122.25 W
Fisher Peak ∧ 192 36.33 N 80.50 W
Fisher River Indian Reserve ✦[4] 184 51.26 N 97.20 W
Fishers, In., U.S. 218 39.57 N 86.00 W
Fishers, N.Y., U.S. 210 43.00 N 77.28 W
Fishers Island I 207 41.16 N 72.02 W
Fishers Peak ∧ 196 37.06 N 104.28 W
Fisher Strait ʯ 176 63.15 N 83.30 W
Fishertown 214 40.08 N 78.35 W
Fisherville 275b 43.47 N 79.28 W
Fishguard 42 51.59 N 4.59 W
Fishhook 219 39.48 N 90.53 W
Fish House 210 43.08 N 74.08 W
Fishing Bay c 208 38.18 N 76.01 W
Fishing Creek 208 38.20 N 76.14 W

ENGLISH			
Name	Page	Lat.°′	Long.°′

Fishing Creek ≃, Ky., U.S. 192 37.06 N 84.41 W
Fishing Creek ≃, N.C., U.S. 192 35.57 N 77.31 W
Fishing Creek ≃, Pa., U.S. 210 41.07 N 77.29 W
Fishing Creek ≃, Pa., U.S. 210 40.58 N 76.28 W
Fishing Creek ≃, S.C., U.S. 192 34.36 N 80.54 W
Fishing Islands II 212 44.45 N 81.20 W
Fishing Lake ⊜, Mb., Can. 184 52.07 N 95.25 W
Fishing Lake ⊜, Sk., Can. 184 51.50 N 103.32 W
Fishkill 210 41.32 N 73.53 W
Fishkill Creek ≃ 210 41.29 N 73.59 W
Fish Lake 216 41.34 N 86.33 W
Fish Lake ⊜, On., Can. 212 44.06 N 77.11 W
Fish Lake ⊜, Mi., U.S. 216 42.03 N 85.52 W
Fish Lake ⊜, Wa., U.S. 224 47.50 N 120.42 W
Fishmoor Reservoir ⊜[1] 262 53.44 N 2.28 W
Fish Point › 214 41.43 N 82.40 W
Fishpool 262 53.35 N 2.17 W
Fish River 166 17.55 S 137.45 E
Fishs Eddy 210 41.58 N 75.10 W
Fisk 194 36.46 N 90.12 W
Fiskárdhon 38 38.27 N 20.35 E
Fiskdale 207 42.06 N 72.06 W
Fiskebäckskil 26 58.15 N 11.27 E
Fismes 50 49.18 N 3.41 E
Fišt, gora ∧ 84 43.58 N 39.54 E
Fitchburg, Ma., U.S. 207 42.35 N 71.48 W
Fitchburg, Wi., U.S. 216 42.57 N 89.28 W
Fitchville, Ct., U.S. 207 41.33 N 72.09 W
Fitchville, Oh., U.S. 214 41.06 N 82.29 W
Fitful Head › 46a 59.54 N 1.23 W
Fitiuta 174y 14.13 S 169.27 W
Fito, Mount ∧ 175a 13.55 S 171.44 W
Fitri, Lac ⊜ 146 12.50 N 17.28 E
Fittja 40 59.15 N 17.52 E
Fittleworth 42 50.58 N 0.35 W
Fitzgerald 192 31.42 N 83.15 W
Fitzgerald River National Park ♠ 162 34.00 S 119.30 E
Fitz Henry 279b 40.10 N 79.45 W
Fitz Hugh Sound ʯ 182 51.40 N 127.57 W
Fitzmaurice ≃ 164 14.50 S 129.44 E
Fitz Roy, Arg. 254 47.02 S 67.15 W
Fitzroy, Austl. 274b 37.48 S 144.59 E
Fitzroy ≃, Austl. 162 17.31 S 123.35 E
Fitzroy ≃, Austl. 166 23.32 S 150.52 E
Fitzroy, Monte (Cerro Chaltel) ∧ 254 49.17 S 73.05 W
Fitzroy Crossing 162 18.11 S 125.35 E
Fitzroy Falls Reservoir ⊜[1] 170 34.38 S 150.30 E
Fitzwilliam 207 42.46 N 72.08 W
Fitzwilliam Island I 190 45.30 N 81.45 W
Fiuggi 66 41.48 N 13.13 E
Fiumalbo 64 44.11 N 10.39 E
Fiume → Rijeka 36 45.20 N 14.27 E
Fiumedinisi 70 38.02 N 15.23 E
Fiumefreddo Bruzio 68 39.14 N 16.04 E
Fiumefreddo di Sicilia 70 37.47 N 15.12 E
Fiumesino 66 43.38 N 13.22 E
Fiume Veneto 64 45.56 N 12.44 E
Fiumicino 36 41.46 N 12.14 E
Fiumicino ✦[8] 66 41.46 N 12.14 E
Five Corners 283 42.01 N 71.07 W
Five Cowrie Creek ≃[1] 273a 6.27 N 3.27 E
Five Dock 274a 33.52 S 151.08 E
Five Forks 284c 38.47 N 77.16 W
Five Islands 186 45.25 N 64.02 W
Five Islands Harbour c 240c 17.06 N 61.54 W
Fivemile ≃ 276 41.03 N 73.27 W
Fivemile Creek ≃, N.Y., U.S. 210 42.22 N 77.22 W
Fivemile Creek ≃, Or., U.S. 224 45.36 N 121.05 W
Fivemile Creek ≃, Wy., U.S. 202 43.14 N 108.12 W
Fivemile Point 210 42.06 N 75.48 W
Fivemiletown 48 54.23 N 7.18 W
Five Penny Borve 46 58.25 N 6.25 W
Five Points, Ca., U.S. 226 36.26 N 120.06 W
Five Points, In., U.S. 218 39.35 N 86.20 W
Five Points, N.M., U.S. 200 35.03 N 106.39 W
Five Points, Oh., U.S. 218 39.41 N 83.12 W
Five Points, Pa., U.S. 214 40.34 N 80.15 W
Five Points, Pa., U.S. 285 39.50 N 75.42 W
Fivizzano 64 44.14 N 10.08 E
Fiwila Mission 154 13.58 S 29.36 E
Fixin 58 47.15 N 4.58 E
Fix-Saint-Geneys 62 45.08 N 3.40 E
Fizi 154 4.18 S 28.57 E
Fizuli 84 39.37 N 47.08 E
Fjællebroen 41 55.03 N 10.24 E
Fjærlandsfjorden c[2] 26 61.17 N 6.40 E
Fjällåsen 24 67.29 N 20.10 E
Fjällbacka 26 58.36 N 11.17 E
Fjällsjöälven ≃ 26 63.29 N 16.50 E
Fjärdhundra 40 59.47 N 16.56 E
Fjärdhundra □[9] 40 59.47 N 16.55 E
Fjenneslev 41 55.26 N 11.40 E
Fjerritslev 26 57.05 N 9.16 E
Fjugesta 40 59.10 N 14.52 E
Fkih-Ben-Salah 148 32.32 N 6.40 W
Flacksta 40 59.23 N 16.27 E
Fladnitz im Raabtal 61 46.59 N 15.47 E
Fladså ≃ 41 55.19 N 8.54 E
Fladungen 56 50.31 N 10.08 E
Flag Creek ≃ 278 41.43 N 87.55 W
Flagler 198 39.17 N 103.04 W
Flagler Beach 192 29.28 N 81.07 W
Flagstaff, Transkei 158 31.05 S 29.29 E
Flagstaff, Az., U.S. 200 35.11 N 111.39 W
Flagstaff Lake ⊜[1] 188 45.10 N 70.15 W
Flagtown 276 40.31 N 74.41 W
Flaken-See ⊜ 264a 52.25 N 13.46 E
Flåm 26 60.50 N 7.07 E
Flambeau ≃ 190 45.18 N 91.15 W
Flambeau, South Fork ≃ 190 45.39 N 90.48 W
Flamborough, On., Can. 212 43.20 N 79.53 W
Flamborough, Eng., U.K. 44 54.06 N 0.07 W
Flamborough Head › 44 54.07 N 0.04 W
Fläming ✦[1] 54 52.00 N 12.30 E
Flaming Gorge National Recreation Area ♠ 200 41.30 N 109.30 W
Flaming Gorge Reservoir ⊜[1] 200 41.15 N 109.30 W
Flamingo 220 25.09 N 80.56 W
Flamingo, Teluk c 164 5.33 S 138.00 E
Flanagan 216 40.52 N 88.51 W
Flanagan ≃ 184 52.50 N 93.28 W
Flanagan Passage ʯ 240m 18.18 N 64.39 W
Flanders, On., Can. 190 48.44 N 92.05 W
Flanders, N.J., U.S. 276 40.50 N 74.41 W
Flanders, N.Y., U.S. 207 40.49 N 72.36 W
Flanders (Flandre) (Vlaanderen) □[9] 50 51.00 N 3.00 E
Flanders Airport ⊠ 276 40.50 N 74.41 W
Flandes 246 4.18 N 74.49 W
Flandorf 264b 48.21 N 16.23 E
Flandre → Flanders □[9] 50 51.00 N 3.00 E
Flandreau 198 44.02 N 96.35 W
Flannan Islands II 46 58.18 N 7.36 W
Flåren ⊜ 26 57.02 N 14.06 E
Flasher 198 46.27 N 101.13 W
Flåsjön ⊜ 26 64.06 N 15.51 E

DEUTSCH			
Name	Seite	Breite°′	Länge°′ E = Ost

Flat, Ak., U.S. 180 62.27 N 158.01 W
Flat, Tx., U.S. 222 31.19 N 97.38 W
Flat ≃, N.T., Can. 180 61.33 N 125.18 W
Flat ≃, Mi., U.S. 190 42.56 N 85.20 W
Flat ≃, N.C., U.S. 192 36.05 N 78.49 W
Flat Bay 186 48.24 N 58.36 W
Flat Branch ≃ 219 39.33 N 89.16 W
Flatbush ✦[8] 276 40.39 N 73.56 W
Flat Creek ≃, Ky., U.S. 218 38.17 N 83.48 W
Flat Creek ≃, Mo., U.S. 194 36.45 N 93.31 W
Flat Creek ≃, Mt., U.S. 202 47.43 N 109.50 W
Flat Creek ≃, N.J., U.S. 276 40.27 N 74.10 W
Flat Creek Reservoir ⊜[1] 222 32.14 N 95.45 W
Flatey 24a 65.19 N 23.07 W
Flateyri 24a 65.59 N 23.42 W
Flathead ≃ 202 47.22 N 114.47 W
Flathead, Middle Fork ≃ 202 48.28 N 114.04 W
Flathead, North Fork ≃ 202 48.28 N 114.04 W
Flathead, South Fork ≃ 202 48.23 N 114.04 W
Flathead Indian Reservation ✦[4] 202 47.30 N 114.25 W
Flathead Lake ⊜ 202 47.52 N 114.08 W
Flat Holm I 42 51.23 N 3.08 W
Flat Lake ⊜ 182 54.39 N 112.55 W
Flat Lick 192 36.49 N 83.46 W
Flatonia 222 29.41 N 97.06 W
Flatow, D.D.R. 264a 52.44 N 12.57 E
Flatow → Złotów, Pol. 30 53.22 N 17.02 E
Flat River, P.E., Can. 186 46.01 N 62.52 W
Flat River, Mo., U.S. 194 37.51 N 90.31 W
Flat River Reservoir ⊜[1] 207 41.42 N 71.37 W
Flat Rock, Al., U.S. 194 34.46 N 85.42 W
Flat Rock, Il., U.S. 194 38.54 N 87.40 W
Flat Rock, In., U.S. 218 39.22 N 85.50 W
Flat Rock, Mi., U.S. 216 42.05 N 83.17 W
Flat Rock, Oh., U.S. 214 41.14 N 82.51 W
Flatrock ≃ 218 39.12 N 85.56 W
Flatrock Creek ≃ 216 41.10 N 84.27 W
Flatrock Lake ⊜ 184 55.37 N 100.47 W
Flatruet ⋀[2] 26 62.45 N 12.50 E
Flats 222 32.50 N 95.53 W
Flattery, Cape ›, Austl. 164 14.58 S 145.21 E
Flattery, Cape ›, Wa., U.S. 224 48.23 N 124.43 W
Flatts 240a 32.19 N 64.44 W
Flatwillow Creek ≃ 202 46.56 N 107.55 W
Flatwood 194 32.27 N 86.15 W
Flatwoods 188 38.31 N 82.43 W
Flaugherty Run ≃ 279b 40.33 N 80.13 W
Flaunden 260 51.42 N 0.32 W
Flavigny-sur-Moselle 58 48.34 N 6.11 E
Flavigny-sur-Ozerain 58 47.30 N 4.32 E
Flavy-le-Martel 50 49.43 N 3.12 E
Flawil 58 47.24 N 9.12 E
Flaxcombe 184 51.29 N 109.36 W
Flaxman Island I 180 70.13 N 146.00 W
Flax Pond ⊜, Ma., U.S. 283 42.29 N 70.57 W
Flax Pond ⊜, N.Y., U.S. 276 40.58 N 73.08 W
Flaxton 198 48.53 N 102.23 W
Flaxville 198 48.48 N 105.10 W
Flechas Point › 116 10.22 N 119.34 E
Flechtingen 54 52.20 N 11.14 E
Fleckeby 41 54.29 N 9.41 E
Flecken Zechlin 54 53.09 N 12.46 E
Fleesensee ⊜ 54 53.30 N 12.29 E
Fleet 42 51.16 N 0.50 W
Fleet ≃ 46 57.57 N 4.05 W
Fleets Bay c 208 37.40 N 76.19 W
Fleetville 210 41.36 N 75.43 W
Fleetwing Estates 285 40.07 N 74.51 W
Fleetwood, Eng., U.K. 44 53.56 N 3.01 W
Fleetwood, Pa., U.S. 208 40.27 N 75.49 W
Flehe ✦[8] 263 51.12 N 6.47 E
Flehingen 56 49.05 N 8.46 E
Fleischmanns 210 42.09 N 74.31 W
Fleischman Village 284c 38.51 N 76.57 W
Flekkefjord 26 58.17 N 6.41 E
Fleming, Co., U.S. 198 40.40 N 102.50 W
Fleming, Pa., U.S. 214 40.55 N 77.52 W
Fleming □[6] 218 38.21 N 83.42 W
Fleming Creek ≃, On., Can. 214 42.38 N 81.47 W
Fleming Creek ≃, Ky., U.S. 218 38.22 N 83.57 W
Fleming Creek ≃, Mi., U.S. 281 42.16 N 83.40 W
Fleming-Neon 192 37.11 N 82.42 W
Flemingsburg 218 38.25 N 83.44 W
Flemington, N.J., U.S. 210 40.30 N 74.51 W
Flemington, Pa., U.S. 210 41.07 N 77.28 W
Flemington Racecourse ♦ 274b 37.47 S 144.55 E
Flemish Cap ✧[4] 16 47.00 N 45.00 W
Flemsdorf 54 53.02 N 14.10 E
Flen 40 59.04 N 16.35 E
Flensburg 41 54.47 N 9.26 E
Flensburger Förde c 41 54.49 N 9.45 E
Fleres (Boden) 64 46.58 N 11.21 E
Flers 32 48.45 N 0.34 W
Flers-sur-Noye 50 49.44 N 2.15 E
Flesherton 212 44.16 N 80.33 W
Flesko, Tanjung › 112 0.29 N 124.30 E
Fletcher, On., Can. 214 42.18 N 82.18 W
Fletcher, N.C., U.S. 192 35.25 N 82.30 W
Fletcher, Oh., U.S. 218 40.08 N 84.06 W
Fletcher, Ok., U.S. 196 34.49 N 98.14 W
Fletcher Islands II 9 72.40 S 94.10 W
Fletcher Moss Museum ❦ 262 53.25 N 2.14 W
Fletcher Pond ⊜[1] 190 44.58 N 83.52 W
Fletchers Creek ≃ 275b 43.38 N 79.42 W
Fleurance 32 43.50 N 0.40 E
Fleur-de-Lys 186 50.07 N 56.08 W
Fleurier 58 46.54 N 6.35 E
Fleurieu Peninsula ›[1] 168b 35.30 S 138.30 E
Fleurus 56 50.29 N 4.33 E
Fleurville 58 46.27 N 4.53 E
Fleury-les-Aubrais 50 47.56 N 1.55 E
Fleury-Mérogis 261 48.38 N 2.22 E
Fleury-sur-Andelle 50 49.22 N 1.22 E
Fleuth ≃ 263 51.32 N 6.26 E
Flevoland □[4] 52 52.30 N 5.30 E
Flexanville 261 48.51 N 1.44 E
Flexenpass)(58 47.09 N 10.10 E
Fley ✦[8] 263 51.23 N 7.30 E
Flieden 56 50.25 N 9.33 E
Flierich 263 51.35 N 7.48 E
Flight Locks ❦[3] 284a 43.08 N 79.12 W
Flimby 44 54.41 N 3.31 W
Flims 58 46.50 N 9.17 E
Flinders 169 38.28 S 145.01 E
Flinders ≃ 166 17.36 S 140.36 E
Flinders Bay c 162 34.23 S 115.19 E
Flinders Chase National Park ♠ 166 36.00 S 136.45 E
Flinders Island I, Austl. 162 33.44 S 134.31 E
Flinders Island I, Austl. 166 40.00 S 148.00 E
Flinders Peak ∧ 171a 27.49 S 152.49 E
Flinders Peak ∧[2] 169 37.51 S 144.24 E
Flinders Ranges National Park ♠ 166 31.20 S 138.45 E
Flinders Reefs ✧[2] 166 17.37 S 148.31 E
Flinders Street Station ✦[5] 274b 37.49 S 144.58 E
Flinesjön ⊜ 40 60.23 N 16.06 E
Flines-lèz-Râches 50 50.25 N 3.11 E

Symbols in the index entries represent the broad categories identified in the key at the right. Symbols with superior numbers (⋀[1]) identify subcategories (see complete key on page *I · 1).*

Symbole im Register stellen die rechts im Schlüssel erklärten Kategorien dar. Symbole mit hochgestellten Ziffern (⋀[1]) bezeichnen Unterabteilungen einer Kategorie (vgl. vollständiger Schlüssel auf Seite *I · 1).*

Los símbolos incluídos en el texto del índice representan las grandes categorias identificadas con la clave a la derecha. Los símbolos con numeros en su parte superior (⋀[1]) identifican las subcategorías (véase la clave completa en la página *I · 1).*

Les symboles de l'index représentent les catégories indiquées dans la légende à droite. Les symboles suivis d'un indice (⋀[1]) représentent des sous-catégories (voir légende complète à la page *I · 1).*

Os símbolos incluídos no texto do índice representam as grandes categorias identificadas com a chave à direita. Os símbolos com números em sua parte superior (⋀[1]) identificam as subcategorias (veja-se a chave completa à página *I · 1).*

∧ Mountain	Berg	Montaña	Montagne	Montanha
⋀ Mountains	Gebirge	Montañas	Montagnes	Montanhas
)(Pass	Paß	Paso	Col	Passo
V Valley, Canyon	Tal, Cañon	Valle, Cañón	Vallée, Canyon	Vale, Canhão
≚ Plain	Ebene	Llano	Plaine	Planície
› Cape	Kap	Cabo	Cap	Cabo
I Island	Insel	Isla	Île	Ilha
II Islands	Inseln	Islas	Îles	Ilhas
⫠ Other Topographic Features	Andere Topographische Objekte	Otros Elementos Topográficos	Autres données topographiques	Outros acidentes topográficos

Flin-Fort I · 57

ESPAÑOL
Nombre | Página | Lat.°′ | Long.°′ W = Oeste

Flin Flon 184 54.46 N 101.53 W
Flingern ◆⁸ 263 51.14 N 6.49 E
Flins-sur-Seine 261 48.58 N 1.52 E
Flint, Wales, U.K. 44 53.15 N 3.07 W
Flint, Mi., U.S. 216 43.00 N 83.41 W
Flint, Tx., U.S. 222 32.12 N 95.21 W
Flint I 14 11.26 S 151.48 W
Flint ≃, U.S. 194 34.30 N 86.31 W
Flint ≃, Ga., U.S. 192 30.52 N 84.38 W
Flint ≃, Mi., U.S. 190 43.21 N 84.03 W
Flint, South Branch ≃ 216 43.10 N 83.23 W
Flint Castle ⊥ 262 53.16 N 3.07 W
Flint Creek ≃, Al., U.S. 194 34.30 N 86.57 W
Flint Creek ≃, Mt., U.S. 202 46.39 N 113.08 W
Flint Creek ≃, N.Y., U.S. 210 42.57 N 77.03 W
Flint Creek Range ⋏ 202 46.20 N 113.05 W
Flinthill 219 38.53 N 90.52 W
Flint Hills ⋏² 198 37.50 N 96.40 W
Flint Lake ◎, N.T., Can. 176 69.10 N 74.20 W
Flint Lake ◎, In., U.S. 216 41.31 N 87.03 W
Flinton, Austl. 166 27.54 S 149.34 E
Flinton, Pa., U.S. 214 40.43 N 78.31 W
Flint Peak ∧ 280 34.10 N 118.12 W
Flint Pond ◎ 283 42.40 N 71.26 W
Flinträsnan ≬ 41 55.34 N 12.50 E
Flintridge 228 34.11 N 118.11 W
Flintville 194 35.03 N 86.25 W
Flipper Point › 174a 19.18 N 166.35 E
Flippin 194 36.16 N 92.35 W
Flirey 56 48.53 N 5.50 E
Flirsch 58 47.09 N 10.24 E
Flisa 26 60.34 N 12.06 E
Flitwick 42 52.00 N 0.29 W
Flix, Pantà de ◎¹ 34 41.15 N 0.25 E
Flixecourt 50 50.01 N 2.05 E
Flize 56 49.42 N 4.46 E
Flobecq (Vloesberg) 50 50.44 N 3.44 E
Floby 26 58.08 N 13.20 E
Floda, Sve. 26 57.48 N 12.22 E
Floda, Sve. 40 59.04 N 16.21 E
Flodden 44 55.38 N 2.10 W
Flodden Field Battlesite ⊥ 44 55.38 N 2.13 W
Flogny 50 47.57 N 3.52 E
Flöha 54 50.51 N 13.04 E
Flöha ≃ 54 50.51 N 13.04 E
Floing 56 49.43 N 4.56 E
Flomaton 194 31.00 N 87.15 W
Flomborn 56 49.41 N 8.08 E
Flomot 196 34.14 N 100.59 W
Floodwood 190 46.55 N 92.55 W
Flora, Il., U.S. 194 38.40 N 88.29 W
Flora, In., U.S. 216 40.32 N 86.31 W
Flora, Ms., U.S. 194 32.32 N 90.18 W
Florac 32 44.19 N 3.36 E
Florala 194 31.00 N 86.19 W
Floral City 220 28.45 N 82.17 W
Floral Park, Mt., U.S. 202 45.57 N 112.26 W
Floral Park, N.Y., U.S. 210 40.43 N 73.42 W
Florange 56 49.20 N 6.07 E
Florânia 250 6.08 S 36.49 W
Flora Vista 200 36.47 N 108.04 W
Flore, Piton ∧ 241f 3.58 N 60.57 W
Floreffe 56 50.26 N 4.45 E
Florence → Firenze, It. 66 43.46 N 11.15 E
Florence, Al., U.S. 194 34.47 N 87.40 W
Florence, Az., U.S. 200 33.02 N 111.23 W
Florence, Ca., U.S. 228 33.58 N 118.14 W
Florence, Co., U.S. 200 38.23 N 105.07 W
Florence, Ks., U.S. 198 38.14 N 96.55 W
Florence, Ky., U.S. 218 38.59 N 84.37 W
Florence, N.J., U.S. 285 40.07 N 74.49 W
Florence, Or., U.S. 202 43.58 N 124.05 W
Florence, Pa., U.S. 214 40.26 N 80.26 W
Florence, S.C., U.S. 192 34.11 N 79.45 W
Florence, Tx., U.S. 222 30.51 N 97.48 W
Florence, Wi., U.S. 190 45.55 N 88.15 W
Florencia, Col. 246 1.36 N 75.36 W
Florencia → Firenze, It. 66 43.46 N 11.15 E
Florencio Sánchez 258 33.53 S 57.24 W
Florencio Varela 258 34.49 S 58.17 W
Florencio Varela □⁵ 288 34.52 S 58.15 W
Florennes 56 50.15 N 4.37 E
Florentia 273d 26.16 S 28.08 E
Florentino Ameghino, Embalse ◎¹ 254 43.55 S 66.20 W
Florenville 56 49.42 N 5.18 E
Florenz → Firenze 66 43.46 N 11.15 E
Flores, Bra. 250 7.51 S 37.59 W
Flores, Perú 286d 12.01 S 77.01 W
Flores □⁵ 258 33.48 S 56.50 W
Flores ◆⁸ 288 34.38 S 58.28 W
Flores I, Indon. 115b 8.30 S 121.00 E
Flores I, Port. 148a 39.26 N 31.13 W
Flores, Cachoeira das ᒐ 255 14.19 S 53.32 W
Flores, Laut (Flores Sea) ⚲² 112 8.00 S 120.00 E
Flores, Rio das ≃ 256 22.05 S 43.34 W
Flores, Selat ≬ 115b 8.25 S 122.55 E
Flores Chica, Laguna ◎ 258 35.30 S 59.01 W
Flores da Cunha 252 29.02 S 51.11 W
Flôres de Goiás 255 14.34 S 47.04 W
Flores Grande, Laguna ◎ 258 35.34 S 59.02 W
Flores Island I 182 49.20 N 126.10 W
Flores Sea → Flores, Laut ⚲² 112 8.00 S 120.00 E
Floresta, Bra. 250 8.36 S 38.34 W
Floresta, It. 70 37.59 N 14.55 E
Floresta ◆⁸ 288 34.38 S 58.29 W
Floresta Azul 255 14.51 S 39.41 W
Florestal de Monsanto, Parque ♦ 266c 38.43 N 9.11 W
Florestina 255 18.29 S 48.01 W
Florešty 78 47.53 N 28.17 E
Floresville 196 29.08 N 98.09 W
Florham Park 210 40.47 N 74.23 W
Floriano, Bra. 250 6.47 S 43.01 W
Floriano, Bra. 256 22.27 S 44.18 W
Floriano Peixoto, Bra. 248 9.03 S 67.24 W
Floriano Peixoto, Bra. 250 9.32 S 35.36 W
Florianópolis 252 27.35 S 48.34 W
Florida, Col. 246 3.21 N 76.15 W
Florida, Cuba 240p 21.32 N 78.14 W
Florida, Hond. 236 15.01 N 88.50 W
Florida, Perú 248 5.50 S 77.55 W
Florida, P.R. 240m 18.22 N 66.34 W
Florida, P.R. 240m 18.14 N 65.47 W
Florida, S. Afr. 273d 26.11 S 27.55 E
Florida, In., U.S. 218 40.10 N 85.42 W
Florida, N.Y., U.S. 210 41.19 N 74.21 W
Florida, Oh., U.S. 216 41.20 N 84.12 W
Florida, Ur. 258 34.06 S 56.13 W
Florida □⁵ 258 34.00 S 56.15 W
Florida ◆⁸ 288 34.31 S 58.30 W
Florida □³, U.S. 178 28.00 N 82.00 W
Florida □³, U.S. 192 28.00 N 82.00 W
Florida ≃ 200 37.03 N 107.52 W
Florida, Cape › 220 25.40 N 80.09 W
Florida, Cerro la ∧ 234 23.13 N 99.15 W
Florida, Straits of ≬ 238 25.00 N 79.45 W
Florida Bay ⊂ 220 25.00 N 80.45 W
Floridablanca 246 7.04 N 73.06 W
Florida Caverns State Park ♦ 192 30.50 N 85.18 W
Florida City 220 25.26 N 80.28 W
Florida Islands II 175e 9.00 S 160.10 E
Florida Keys II 220 24.45 N 81.00 W
Florida Lake ◎¹ 273d 26.11 S 27.54 E
Florida Ridge 220 27.35 N 80.23 W
Floridia 70 37.05 N 15.09 E

FRANÇAIS
Nom | Page | Lat.°′ | Long.°′ W = Ouest

Florido ≃ 232 27.43 N 105.10 W
Floridsdorf ◆⁸ 264b 48.16 N 16.24 E
Floridsdorfer Brücke ◆⁵ 264b 48.14 N 16.23 E
Florien 194 31.26 N 93.27 W
Florin 226 38.29 N 121.24 W
Flórina 38 40.47 N 21.24 E
Florisbad 158 28.46 S 26.06 E
Florissant 219 38.47 N 90.19 W
Florissant Fossil Beds National Monument ♦ 200 38.54 N 105.16 W
Floriston 226 39.24 N 120.01 W
Florø 26 61.36 N 5.00 E
Flörsheim 56 50.01 N 8.26 E
Florvåg 26 60.25 N 5.14 E
Flosaille 62 45.39 N 5.18 E
Floss 60 49.44 N 12.17 E
Flossach ≃, B.R.D. 58 48.24 N 10.25 E
Flossach ≃, B.R.D. 64 48.13 N 10.30 E
Flossenbürg 60 49.44 N 12.21 E
Flossmoor 216 41.32 N 87.41 W
Flotantes, Jardínes ♦ 286a 19.16 N 99.06 W
Flöthbach ≃ 263 51.17 N 6.26 E
Flotta I 46 58.50 N 3.07 W
Flotte, Cap de › 175f 21.10 S 167.25 E
Flotten Lake ◎ 184 54.38 N 108.30 W
Flourtown 285 40.06 N 75.12 W
Flowerfield 278 41.52 N 88.02 W
Flower Hill 276 40.48 N 73.40 W
Flower Mound 222 33.02 N 97.04 W
Flower's Cove 186 51.18 N 56.44 W
Flowery Branch 192 34.11 N 83.55 W
Floyd, N.M., U.S. 196 34.13 N 103.35 W
Floyd, Tx., U.S. 222 33.09 N 96.15 W
Floyd, Va., U.S. 192 36.54 N 80.19 W
Floyd □⁶ 218 38.18 N 85.49 W
Floyd ≃ 198 42.29 N 96.23 W
Floydada 196 33.59 N 101.20 W
Floyds Fork ≃ 194 38.00 N 85.41 W
Fluchthorn ∧ 58 46.53 N 10.13 E
Flüela Pass)(58 46.45 N 9.57 E
Flüelen 58 46.54 N 8.38 E
Fluessen ◎ 52 52.57 N 5.30 E
Flughafen Wien-Schwechat ⊠ 61 48.07 N 16.33 E
Flühli 58 46.53 N 8.01 E
Flumen ≃ 34 41.43 N 0.09 W
Flumendosa ≃ 71 39.26 N 9.37 E
Flumendosa, Lago Alto del ◎ 71 39.56 N 9.26 E
Flumeri 68 41.05 N 15.09 E
Flumet 62 45.49 N 6.30 E
Fluminimaggiore 71 39.26 N 8.30 E
Flums 58 47.05 N 9.20 E
Flüren 263 51.41 N 6.33 E
Flushing → Vlissingen, Ned. 52 51.26 N 3.35 E
Flushing, Mi., U.S. 216 43.03 N 83.51 W
Flushing, Oh., U.S. 214 40.08 N 81.03 W
Flushing ◆⁸ 276 40.45 N 73.49 W
Flushing Airport ⊠ 276 40.47 N 73.50 W
Flushing Bay ⊂ 276 40.47 N 73.51 W
Flushing Meadow-Corona Park ♦ 276 40.45 N 73.51 W
Fluvanna, N.Y., U.S. 214 42.07 N 79.18 W
Fluvanna, Tx., U.S. 196 32.53 N 101.09 W
Fluvià ≃ 34 42.12 N 3.07 E
Fly ≃ 164 8.30 S 143.41 E
Fly Creek 210 42.43 N 74.59 W
Fly Creek ≃ 202 45.59 N 107.59 W
Flyinge 41 55.45 N 13.21 E
Flying Fish Cove 112 10.25 S 105.43 E
Flynn 222 31.09 N 96.08 W
Foam Lake 184 51.39 N 103.33 W
Fobbing 260 51.32 N 0.29 E
Fobello 62 45.53 N 8.10 E
Foča, Jugo. 38 43.31 N 18.46 E
Foça, Tür. 130 38.39 N 26.46 E
Focene ◆⁸ 267a 41.48 N 12.14 E
Fochabers 46 57.37 N 3.05 W
Fochville 158 26.30 S 27.30 E
Fockbek 41 54.18 N 9.36 E
Focșani 38 45.41 N 27.11 E
Fodda, Oued ≃ 34 35.14 N 1.28 E
Fodé 152 5.29 N 23.18 E
Fodécontea 150 10.50 N 14.22 W
Foding Shan ∧ 102 27.08 N 108.02 E
F'odorovka, S.S.S.R. 78 49.23 N 35.07 E
F'odorovka, S.S.S.R. 78 47.33 N 36.33 E
F'odorovka, S.S.S.R. 80 53.28 N 49.38 E
F'odorovka, S.S.S.R. 80 51.09 N 51.59 E
F'odorovka, S.S.S.R. 80 52.21 N 52.55 E
F'odorovka, S.S.S.R. 82 56.15 N 37.14 E
F'odorovka, S.S.S.R. 83 47.20 N 38.23 E
F'odorovka, S.S.S.R. 86 56.05 N 78.49 E
F'odorovka, S.S.S.R. 86 53.11 N 55.11 E
F'odorovka, S.S.S.R. 86 53.38 N 62.42 E
F'odorovka, S.S.S.R. 86 53.22 N 76.18 E
F'odorovskoje, S.S.S.R. 82 56.08 N 38.04 E
F'odorovskoje, S.S.S.R. 82 56.44 N 36.58 E
F'odorovskoje, S.S.S.R. 82 56.07 N 38.52 E
Foëcy 50 47.10 N 2.10 E
Foelsche ≃ 164 16.03 S 136.50 E
Foeni 38 45.30 N 20.53 E
Fogang (Shijiao) 100 23.52 N 113.32 E
Fogdön ›¹ 40 59.25 N 16.52 E
Fogelevo 85 42.03 N 69.32 E
Fogelsville 208 40.35 N 75.38 W
Foggaret el Arab 148 27.03 N 2.59 E
Foggaret ez Zoua 148 27.20 N 3.00 E
Foggia 68 41.27 N 15.34 E
Foggia □⁴ 68 41.30 N 15.30 E
Foggy Island Bay ⊂ 180 70.15 N 147.30 W
Foglia ≃ 66 43.55 N 12.54 E
Foglianise 68 41.10 N 14.40 E
Fogliano, Lago di ⊂ 66 41.24 N 12.54 E
Foglizzo 62 45.16 N 7.49 E
Fogo 186 49.43 N 54.17 W
Fogo I 150a 14.55 N 24.25 W
Fogo, Cape › 186 49.39 N 54.00 W
Fogo Island I 186 49.40 N 54.13 W
Fogolawa 150 12.19 N 8.41 E
Fogueteiro 266c 38.37 N 9.07 W
Fohnsdorf 61 47.13 N 14.41 E
Föhr I 30 54.43 N 8.30 E
Foia ∧ 34 37.19 N 8.36 W
Foiano della Chiana 66 43.15 N 11.49 E
Foiano di Val Fortore 68 41.21 N 14.59 E
Foinaven ∧ 46 58.25 N 4.53 W
Foins, Lac aux ◎ 190 47.05 N 78.11 W
Foivre ≃ 56 49.30 N 4.32 E
Foix 32 42.58 N 1.36 E
Foix □⁹ 32 43.00 N 1.40 E
Fojnica 36 43.58 N 17.54 E
Foki 80 56.42 N 54.21 E
Fokino 76 53.27 N 34.24 E
Fokku 150 11.40 N 4.31 E
Folakara 157b 18.20 S 45.02 E
Folamasi 104 41.56 N 121.27 E
Folarskardnuten ∧ 26 60.37 N 7.45 E
Folcroft 208 39.53 N 75.17 W
Folda ⊂² 24 67.36 N 14.50 E
Foldingbro 41 55.26 N 9.01 E
Folembray 50 49.33 N 3.17 E
Foley, Al., U.S. 194 30.24 N 87.41 W
Foley, Mn., U.S. 190 45.39 N 93.54 W
Foley, Mo., U.S. 219 39.02 N 90.44 W
Foleyet 190 48.15 N 82.27 W
Foley Island I 176 68.35 N 75.10 W
Folgaria 64 45.55 N 11.10 E
Folgefonni ⊓ 26 60.00 N 6.20 E
Folger Hill ∧² 207 41.17 N 70.01 W
Foligno 66 42.57 N 12.42 E
Folk 219 38.26 N 92.06 W
Folkärna 40 60.09 N 16.19 E
Folkestone 42 51.05 N 1.11 E
Folkingham 42 52.54 N 0.24 W
Folkston 192 30.49 N 82.00 W
Folkwangmuseum ᵾ 263 51.27 N 7.00 E

PORTUGUÊS
Nome | Página | Lat.°′ | Long.°′ W = Oeste

Follafoss 26 63.59 N 11.06 E
Follainville-Dennemont 261 49.01 N 1.43 E
Follansbee 214 40.19 N 80.35 W
Folldal 26 62.08 N 10.03 E
Folle Anse, Pointe de › 241o 15.57 N 61.20 W
Follebu 26 61.14 N 10.17 E
Follets Island I 222 29.02 N 95.10 W
Follett 196 36.26 N 100.08 W
Follina 64 45.57 N 12.07 E
Föllinge 26 63.40 N 14.37 E
Follonica 66 42.55 N 10.45 E
Follonica, Golfo di ⊂ 66 42.54 N 10.43 E
Folly Branch ≃ 284b 38.56 N 76.49 W
Folmhusen 52 53.10 N 7.28 E
Folschviller 56 49.04 N 6.41 E
Folsom, Ca., U.S. 226 38.40 N 121.10 W
Folsom, N.J., U.S. 208 39.36 N 74.50 W
Folsom, Pa., U.S. 285 39.53 N 75.19 W
Folsom Lake ◎¹ 226 38.43 N 121.08 W
Folsom Lake State Recreation Area ♦ 226 38.46 N 121.06 W
Fomboni 157a 12.16 S 43.45 E
Fomento, Cuba 240p 22.06 N 79.43 W
Fomento, Ur. 258 34.26 S 57.14 W
Fomin 80 46.58 N 43.38 E
Fominiči 76 54.07 N 34.41 E
Fominki 80 55.57 N 42.22 E
Fominskaja 24 61.17 N 48.40 E
Fominskoje, S.S.S.R. 24 59.43 N 42.05 E
Fominskoje, S.S.S.R. 76 58.59 N 39.06 E
Fomkino 80 54.25 N 50.30 E
Foncine-le-Bas 58 46.38 N 6.03 E
Fonda, Ia., U.S. 198 42.34 N 94.50 W
Fonda, N.Y., U.S. 210 42.57 N 74.22 W
Fondachelli 70 37.58 N 15.11 E
Fond d'Or Bay ⊂ 241f 13.56 N 60.54 W
Fond du Lac, Sk., Can. 176 59.19 N 107.10 W
Fond du Lac, Wi., U.S. 190 43.46 N 88.26 W
Fond du Lac ≃ 176 59.17 N 106.00 W
Fond du Lac Indian Reservation ◆⁴ 190 46.45 N 92.37 W
Fondi 66 41.21 N 13.25 E
Fondi, Lago di ⊂ 66 41.19 N 13.20 E
Fondo 64 46.26 N 11.08 E
Fondouk el Aouareb 36 35.34 N 9.46 E
Fongfong 140 12.56 N 23.14 E
Fonni 71 40.07 N 9.15 E
Fonsagrada 34 43.08 N 7.04 W
Fonseca 246 10.54 N 72.51 W
Fonseca, Golfo de ⊂ 236 13.10 N 87.40 W
Fons-Outre-Gardon 62 43.54 N 4.11 E
Font ≃ 44 55.10 N 1.44 W
Fontaine, Fr. 58 47.40 N 7.00 E
Fontaine, Fr. 62 45.11 N 5.40 E
Fontainebleau, Fr. 50 48.24 N 2.42 E
Fontainebleau, S. Afr. 273d 26.07 S 27.59 E
Fontaine-Française 58 47.31 N 5.22 E
Fontaine-le-Dun 50 49.49 N 0.51 E
Fontaine-lès-Dijon 58 47.21 N 5.01 E
Fontaine-lès-Grès 50 48.25 N 3.54 E
Fontaine-lès-Luxeuil 58 47.51 N 6.20 E
Fontaines 58 46.51 N 4.46 E
Fontaines-sur-Saône 62 45.50 N 4.51 E
Fontan 62 44.00 N 7.33 E
Fontana, Arg. 252 27.25 S 59.02 W
Fontana, Ca., U.S. 228 34.05 N 117.26 W
Fontana, Wi., U.S. 216 42.33 N 88.34 W
Fontana, Lago ◎ 254 44.56 S 71.30 W
Fontanafredda 64 45.58 N 12.34 E
Fontana Lake ◎¹ 192 35.26 N 83.38 W
Fontanarosa 68 41.01 N 15.01 E
Fontanarossa, Aeroporto di ⊠ 70 37.29 N 15.03 E
Fontanelas 266c 38.51 N 9.26 W
Fontanelice 66 44.15 N 11.33 E
Fontanella 64 45.27 N 9.48 E
Fontanellato 64 44.53 N 10.10 E
Fontanelle 198 41.17 N 94.33 W
Fontanetto Po 62 45.12 N 8.11 E
Fontanigorda 62 44.33 N 9.19 E
Fontarabie, Lac ◎ 186 51.10 N 66.25 W
Fontas ≃ 176 58.20 N 121.50 W
Fonte, Bra. 287b 23.25 S 46.21 W
Fonte, It. 64 45.47 N 11.53 E
Fonte, It. 66 41.46 N 13.13 E
Fonte Avellana, Monastero di ᵾ¹ 66 43.29 N 12.45 E
Fonte Blanda 66 42.34 N 11.10 E
Fonte Boa 246 2.32 S 66.01 W
Fonte Colombo, Convento di ᵾ¹ 66 42.23 N 12.50 E
Fontenay, Abbaye de ᵾ¹ 50 47.39 N 4.24 E
Fontenay-aux-Roses 261 48.47 N 2.17 E
Fontenay-en-Parisis 261 49.03 N 2.27 E
Fontenay-le-Comte 32 46.28 N 0.48 W
Fontenay-le-Fleury 261 48.49 N 2.03 E
Fontenay-lès-Briis 261 48.37 N 2.09 E
Fontenay-le-Vicomte 261 48.33 N 2.24 E
Fontenay-Saint-Père 261 49.02 N 1.45 E
Fontenay-sous-Bois 261 48.51 N 2.29 E
Fontenay-Trésigny 50 48.42 N 2.52 E
Fonteneau, Lac ◎ 186 51.55 N 61.30 W
Fontenelle 186 48.53 N 64.33 W
Fontenelle Creek ≃ 200 42.05 N 110.08 W
Fontenelle Reservoir ◎¹ 200 42.05 N 110.06 W
Fontespina 66 43.17 N 13.45 E
Fontevivo 64 44.51 N 10.10 E
Font Hill Manor 284b 39.17 N 76.52 W
Fontibón 246 4.40 N 74.09 W
Fonti del Clitunno ⚲⁴ 66 42.49 N 12.46 E
Fontoy 56 49.21 N 6.00 E
Fontur › 24a 66.23 N 14.30 W
Fontvieille 62 43.43 N 4.43 E
Fonyód 30 46.44 N 17.34 E
Fonzaso 64 46.01 N 11.48 E
Foochow → Fuzhou 100 26.06 N 119.17 E
Foot Creek ≃ 198 45.26 N 98.29 W
Foothill Farms 226 38.40 N 121.20 W
Foothills 182 53.04 N 116.48 W
Footprint Lake ◎ 184 55.47 N 98.53 W
Footscray 169 37.48 S 144.54 E
Footville 216 42.40 N 89.12 W
Foping 102 33.21 N 107.59 E
Foppolo 64 46.03 N 9.45 E
Fora, Ponta de › 287a 22.57 S 43.07 W
Foraker, Mount ∧ 180 62.56 N 151.26 W
Forari 175f 17.39 S 168.32 E
Forbach, B.R.D. 56 48.41 N 8.21 E
Forbach, Fr. 56 49.11 N 6.54 E
Forbes 166 33.23 S 148.01 E
Forbes, Lac ◎ 206 46.31 N 74.12 W
Forbes, Mount ∧ 182 51.52 N 116.56 W
Forbes Field ♦ 279b 40.27 N 79.57 W
Forbesganj 124 26.18 N 87.15 E
Forbes Reef 158 26.10 S 31.05 E
Forbes Road 214 40.21 N 79.32 W
Forbestown 226 39.31 N 121.16 W
Forcados 150 5.22 N 5.24 E
Forcados ≃¹ 150 5.25 N 5.19 E
Forcalquier 62 43.58 N 5.47 E
Force 214 41.15 N 78.30 W
Forchheim, B.R.D. 60 49.43 N 11.04 E
Forchheim, D.D.R. 54 50.43 N 13.16 E
Forclaz, Col de la)(58 46.04 N 7.00 E
Ford, Scot., U.K. 46 56.10 N 5.26 W
Ford, Ks., U.S. 198 37.38 N 99.45 W
Ford □⁶ 216 40.27 N 88.06 W
Ford ≃ 190 45.40 N 87.09 W
Ford, Cape › 164 13.26 S 129.52 E
Ford City, Ca., U.S. 226 35.09 N 119.27 W
Ford City, Pa., U.S. 214 40.46 N 79.31 W
Ford City ◆⁹ 278 41.46 N 87.44 W
Ford Cliff 214 40.45 N 79.32 W
Ford Dam ◆⁶ 281 42.13 N 83.33 W
Ford Dry Lake ◎ 204 33.38 N 115.00 W
Førde, Nor. 26 59.36 N 5.29 E

Førde, Nor. 26 61.27 N 5.52 E
Førdefjorden ⊂² 26 61.28 N 5.39 E
Forden 42 52.36 N 3.08 W
Förderstedt 54 51.54 N 11.38 E
Fordham University ᵾ² 276 40.51 N 73.53 W
Fordingbridge 42 50.56 N 1.47 W
Ford Lake ◎ 281 42.13 N 83.36 W
Ford Mansion ⊥ 276 40.48 N 74.28 W
Ford Motor Company (River Rouge Plant) ᵾ³ 281 42.18 N 83.10 W
Ford Museum ᵾ 281 42.18 N 83.14 W
Fordongianus 71 39.59 N 8.48 E
Ford Ranges ⋏ 9 77.00 S 145.00 W
Fords 276 40.31 N 74.18 W
Fords Bridge 166 29.45 S 145.26 E
Fordsburg ◆⁸ 273d 26.13 S 28.02 E
Fords Prairie 224 46.44 N 122.59 W
Fordsville 194 37.38 N 86.43 W
Fordville 198 48.13 N 97.47 W
Fordyce 194 33.48 N 92.24 W
Fordyce Lake ◎¹ 226 39.23 N 120.28 W
Foré 150 13.08 N 10.42 W
Forécariah 150 9.26 N 13.06 W
Forel, Mont ∧ 176 67.00 N 37.00 W
Foreland Point › 42 51.16 N 3.47 W
Foreman 194 33.43 N 94.23 W
Foremost 184 49.29 N 111.25 W
Forenza 68 40.51 N 15.51 E
Forepaugh Airport ⊠ 279a 41.21 N 81.30 W
Foresman 216 40.52 N 87.18 W
Forest, Bel. 50 50.48 N 4.19 E
Forest, On., Can. 190 43.06 N 82.00 W
Forest, In., U.S. 216 40.22 N 86.19 W
Forest, Ms., U.S. 194 32.21 N 89.28 W
Forest, Oh., U.S. 216 40.48 N 83.30 W
Forest □⁶ 214 41.29 N 79.27 W
Forest, Middle Branch ≃ 198 48.13 N 97.48 W
Forest Acres 192 34.01 N 80.59 W
Forestburg 182 52.35 N 112.04 W
Forest City, Ia., U.S. 190 43.15 N 93.38 W
Forest City, N.C., U.S. 192 35.20 N 81.51 W
Forest City, Pa., U.S. 210 41.39 N 75.28 W
Forest Creek ≃ 226 38.23 N 120.28 W
Forest Gate ◆⁸ 260 51.33 N 0.02 E
Forest Glade 222 31.39 N 96.31 W
Forest Grove, B.C., Can. 182 51.46 N 121.06 W
Forest Grove, Or., U.S. 224 45.31 N 123.06 W
Forest Grove, Pa., U.S. 279b 40.18 N 75.04 W
Forest Heights 284c 38.49 N 77.00 W
Forest Hill, Austl. 171a 27.35 S 152.22 E
Forest Hill, Austl. 171b 35.09 S 147.27 E
Forest Hill, Austl. 274b 37.50 S 145.11 E
Foresthill, Ca., U.S. 226 39.01 N 120.49 W
Forest Hill, Md., U.S. 208 39.35 N 76.23 W
Forest Hill, Tx., U.S. 222 32.40 N 97.16 W
Forest Hill ◆⁸ 275b 43.42 N 79.24 W
Forest Hill Park ♦ 279a 41.31 N 81.35 W
Forest Hill Parkway ♦ 279a 41.33 N 81.36 W
Forest Hills 279b 40.25 N 79.51 W
Forest Hills ◆⁸ 276 40.42 N 73.51 W
Forest Home 194 31.52 N 86.50 W
Forestier Peninsula ›¹ 166 42.57 S 147.55 E
Forest Knolls 284c 39.02 N 77.01 W
Forest Lake, Il., U.S. 216 42.13 N 88.03 W
Forest Lake, Mn., U.S. 190 45.16 N 92.59 W
Forest Lake ◎, Il., U.S. 278 42.13 N 88.03 W
Forest Lake ◎, Ma., U.S. 283 42.43 N 71.15 W
Forest Lawn Memorial Park ◆ 280 34.09 N 118.19 W
Forest Manor 284c 38.50 N 76.53 W
Forest Park, Ga., U.S. 192 33.37 N 84.22 W
Forest Park, Il., U.S. 278 41.52 N 87.48 W
Forest Park, Oh., U.S. 218 39.16 N 84.34 W
Forest Park ◆⁸ 284b 39.19 N 76.41 W
Forest Park ♦ 276 40.42 N 73.51 W
Forest River 278 42.05 N 87.54 W
Forest Row 42 51.06 N 0.02 E
Forest View 278 41.49 N 87.47 W
Forestville, Austl. 274a 33.46 S 151.13 E
Forestville, P.Q., Can. 186 48.45 N 69.06 W
Forestville, Md., U.S. 284c 38.50 N 76.52 W
Forestville, N.Y., U.S. 214 42.28 N 79.10 W
Forestville, Pa., U.S. 214 41.06 N 80.00 W
Forestville, Wi., U.S. 190 44.41 N 87.28 W
Forêt l'Orient, Lac de la ◎¹ 50 48.17 N 4.20 E
Forêt-Noire → Schwarzwald ⋏ 58 48.00 N 8.15 E
Forez, Monts du ⋏ 32 45.35 N 3.48 E
Forfar 46 56.38 N 2.54 W
Forfry 261 49.03 N 2.51 E
Forgan 196 36.54 N 100.32 W
Forgaria 64 46.13 N 12.58 E
Forge Acres 284b 39.25 N 76.27 W
Forge Heights 284b 39.25 N 76.25 W
Forges-les-Bains 261 48.38 N 2.06 E
Forges-les-Eaux 50 49.37 N 1.33 E
Forget, Pointe › 275a 45.27 N 73.58 W
Forge Village 207 42.34 N 71.29 W
Forggensee ◎ 58 47.36 N 10.44 E
Forillon, Parc National de ♦ 186 48.55 N 64.12 W
Forino 68 40.52 N 14.44 E
Foristell 219 38.49 N 90.57 W
Fork 208 39.28 N 76.27 W
Forked Creek ≃ 216 41.19 N 88.09 W
Forked Deer ≃ 194 35.56 N 89.35 W
Forked Deer, Middle Fork ≃ 194 36.01 N 89.13 W
Forked Deer, North Fork ≃ 194 36.00 N 89.26 W
Forked Deer, South Fork ≃ 194 36.00 N 89.26 W
Forked River 208 39.50 N 74.11 W
Forks 224 47.57 N 124.23 W
Forkston 210 41.31 N 76.07 W
Forksville 210 41.29 N 76.36 W
Forleti, Arroyo ≃ 288 34.35 S 58.41 W
Forlì 66 44.13 N 12.03 E
Forlì □⁴ 64 44.05 N 12.02 E
Forlimpopoli 66 44.11 N 12.07 E
Forman 198 46.06 N 97.38 W
Formazza 58 46.22 N 8.26 E
Formby 262 53.34 N 3.05 W
Formby Hills ⋏² 262 53.34 N 3.06 W
Formby Point › 262 53.33 N 3.06 W
Formentera I 34 38.42 N 1.28 E
Formentor, Cap de › 34 39.58 N 3.12 E
Formerie 50 49.39 N 1.44 E
Formia 66 41.15 N 13.37 E
Formiga 255 20.27 S 45.25 W
Formiga ≃ 256 22.18 S 42.52 W
Formigine 64 44.34 N 10.51 E
Formignana 64 44.50 N 11.51 E
Formosa, Arg. 252 26.11 S 58.11 W
Formosa, Bra. 255 15.32 S 47.20 W
Formosa □⁴ 252 25.00 S 60.00 W
Formosa → Taiwan □¹ 100 23.30 N 121.00 E
Formosa, Ilha I 150 11.29 N 15.58 W
Formosa, Serra ⋏¹ 250 12.00 S 55.00 W
Formosa Strait → Taiwan Strait ≬ 100 24.00 N 119.00 E
Formoso ≃, Bra. 250 10.34 S 49.56 W
Formoso ≃, Bra. 255 17.25 S 44.57 W
Formoso ≃, Bra. 255 13.26 S 44.14 W
Formoso ≃, Bra. 255 18.25 S 52.28 W
Formoso ≃, Bra. 256 21.20 S 43.10 W
Forncelle 66 43.55 N 11.06 E
Fornelli 71 41.00 N 8.14 E

Forney 222 32.44 N 96.28 W
Forni Avoltri 64 46.35 N 12.46 E
Forni di sopra 64 46.25 N 12.35 E
Forni di sotto 64 46.23 N 12.40 E
Forni di Val d'Astico 64 45.51 N 11.22 E
Forno 64 46.21 N 11.37 E
Forno Alpi Graie 62 45.22 N 7.13 E
Forno di Zoldo 64 46.21 N 12.11 E
Fornosovo 76 59.35 N 30.35 E
Fornovo di Taro 64 44.42 N 10.06 E
Foro Romano ⊥ 267a 41.54 N 12.29 E
Føroyar → Faeroe Islands □² 22 62.00 N 7.00 W
Forpost 86 56.47 N 72.10 E
Forres, Arg. 252 27.53 S 63.58 W
Forres, Scot., U.K. 46 57.37 N 3.38 W
Forrest, Austl. 162 30.51 S 128.06 E
Forrest, Austl. 169 38.31 S 143.43 E
Forrest, Il., U.S. 216 40.45 N 88.24 W
Forrest ≃ 164 15.18 S 128.04 E
Forrest, Mount ∧ 162 24.48 S 127.45 E
Forrestal Research Center ᵾ³ 276 40.21 N 74.37 W
Forrest City 194 35.00 N 90.47 W
Forrester Island I 182 54.48 N 133.32 W
Forrest Lakes ◎ 162 29.12 S 128.46 E
Forreston, Il., U.S. 190 42.07 N 89.34 W
Forreston, Tx., U.S. 222 32.16 N 96.52 W
Forrest River Aboriginal Reserve ◆⁴ 164 15.00 S 127.40 E
Fors 40 60.13 N 16.18 E
Forsan 196 32.07 N 101.22 W
Forsayth 166 18.35 S 143.36 E
Forsbacka 40 60.37 N 16.53 E
Forsby 26 60.30 N 25.56 E
Forserum 26 57.42 N 14.28 E
Forshaga 40 59.32 N 13.28 E
Forsmark 40 60.22 N 18.09 E
Forssa 26 60.49 N 23.38 E
Forst 54 51.44 N 14.39 E
Förste 52 51.44 N 10.10 E
Forster 166 32.11 S 152.31 E
Forstwald ◆⁸ 263 51.18 N 6.30 E
Forsyth, Ga., U.S. 192 33.02 N 83.56 W
Forsyth, Il., U.S. 219 39.56 N 88.57 W
Forsyth, Mo., U.S. 194 36.41 N 93.07 W
Forsyth, Mt., U.S. 202 46.15 N 106.40 W
Forsyth Island I 164 16.50 S 139.06 E
Forsyth Range ⋏ 166 22.45 S 143.15 E
Fort ◆⁸ 272c 18.56 N 72.50 E
Fort Abbās 123 29.12 N 72.52 E
Fort Adams 194 31.05 N 91.32 W
Fort Albany 176 52.15 N 81.37 W
Fort Alexander Indian Reserve ◆⁴ 184 50.27 N 96.15 W
Fortaleza 250 3.43 S 38.30 W
Fortaleza ≃ 248 10.40 S 77.52 W
Fortaleza de Santa Teresa ♦ 252 33.59 S 53.32 W
Fortaleza do Ituxi 248 7.29 S 66.20 W
Fortaleza dos Nogueiras 250 6.54 S 46.09 W
Fort Allen ■ 240m 18.01 N 66.30 W
Fort Amherst National Historic Park ♦ 186 46.12 N 63.09 W
Fort Ancient State Memorial ⊥ 218 39.24 N 84.06 W
Fort Anne National Historic Park ♦ 186 44.44 N 65.26 W
Fort Apache Indian Reservation ◆⁴ 200 34.01 N 110.28 W
Fort-Archambault → Sarh 146 9.09 N 18.23 E
Fort Assiniboine 182 54.20 N 114.46 W
Fort Atkinson 216 42.55 N 88.50 W
Fort Augusta ⊥ 210 40.53 N 76.46 W
Fort Augustus 46 57.09 N 4.41 W
Fort Baker ■ 282 37.50 N 122.29 W
Fort Battleford National Historic Park ♦ 184 52.42 N 108.15 W
Fort Bayard → Zhanjiang 102 21.16 N 110.28 E
Fort Beaufort 158 32.46 S 26.40 E
Fort Beauséjour National Historic Park ♦ 186 45.51 N 64.18 W
Fort Belknap Agency 202 48.28 N 108.45 W
Fort Belknap Indian Reservation ◆⁴ 202 48.16 N 108.38 W
Fort Belvoir ■ 208 38.44 N 77.10 W
Fort Bend □⁶ 222 29.32 N 95.47 W
Fort Benjamin Harrison ■ 218 39.52 N 86.01 W
Fort Benning ■ 192 32.22 N 84.50 W
Fort Benton 202 47.49 N 110.40 W
Fort Berthold Indian Reservation ◆⁴ 198 47.40 N 102.25 W
Fort Bidwell 204 41.51 N 120.09 W
Fort Bliss ■ 200 32.15 N 106.00 W
Fort Bowie National Historic Site ⊥ 200 32.09 N 109.24 W
Fort Bragg 204 39.26 N 123.48 W
Fort Bragg ■ 192 35.09 N 78.59 W
Fort Branch 194 38.15 N 87.34 W
Fort Bridger 200 41.19 N 110.23 W
Fort Calhoun 198 41.27 N 96.01 W
Fort Campbell ■ 194 36.39 N 87.29 W
Fort Canby State Park ♦ 224 46.17 N 124.04 W
Fort-Carnot 157b 21.53 S 47.28 E
Fort Caroline National Memorial ⊥ 192 30.20 N 81.30 W
Fort Carson ■ 200 38.44 N 104.48 W
Fort Casey Historical State Park ♦ 224 48.10 N 122.40 W
Fort Chambly National Historic Park ♦ 206 45.27 N 73.17 W
Fort Chipewyan 176 58.42 N 111.08 W
Fort Churchill Historic State Monument ⊥ 226 39.18 N 119.17 W
Fort Clatsop National Memorial ⊥ 224 46.08 N 123.54 W
Fort Cobb 196 35.05 N 98.26 W
Fort Cobb Reservoir ◎¹ 196 35.12 N 98.29 W
Fort Collins 200 40.35 N 105.05 W
Fort Columbia Historical State Park ♦ 224 46.15 N 123.56 W
Fort Constantine 166 20.28 S 140.37 E
Fort-Coulonge 188 45.51 N 76.44 W
Fort Covington 206 44.59 N 74.29 W
Fort Custer State Recreation Area ♦ 216 42.18 N 85.20 W
Fort Davis, Al., U.S. 194 32.14 N 85.42 W
Fort Davis, Tx., U.S. 196 30.35 N 103.53 W
Fort Davis National Historic Site ⊥ 196 30.33 N 103.53 W
Fort de Douaumont ⊥ 56 49.13 N 5.25 E
Fort Defiance 200 35.44 N 109.04 W
Fort-de-France 240e 14.36 N 61.05 W
Fort-de-France, Baie de ⊂ 240e 14.34 N 61.04 W
Fort-de-France-Lamentin, Aérodrome de ⊠ 240e 14.35 N 61.00 W
Fort Deposit 194 31.59 N 86.34 W
Fort Detrick ■ 208 39.27 N 77.26 W
Fort de Vaux ⊥ 56 49.12 N 5.28 E
Fort Devens ■ 207 42.32 N 71.37 W
Fort Dix ■ 208 40.00 N 74.33 W
Fort Dodge 190 42.29 N 94.10 W
Fort Donelson National Military Park ♦ 194 36.26 N 87.49 W
Fort Duchesne 200 40.17 N 109.51 W
Fort Dupont Park ♦ 284c 38.53 N 76.57 W
Forte, Monte ∧ 71 40.43 N 8.15 E

Forteau 186 51.28 N 56.58 W
Forte dei Marmi 64 43.57 N 10.10 E
Forte de Magoito 266c 38.52 N 9.27 W
Fort Edward 210 43.16 N 73.35 W
Forte República 152 7.45 S 16.23 E
Fort Erie 212 42.54 N 78.56 W
Fort Erie Race Track ♦ 284a 42.55 N 78.56 W
Fortescue ≃ 162 21.00 S 116.06 E
Fort Eustis ■ 208 37.09 N 76.35 W
Fortevoit 46 56.20 N 3.32 W
Fortezza (Franzensfeste) 64 46.47 N 11.37 E
Fort Fairfield 186 46.46 N 67.50 W
Fort Fitzgerald 176 59.53 N 111.37 W
Fort Foote Village 284c 38.46 N 77.01 W
Fort-Foureau 146 12.05 N 15.02 E
Fort Frances 190 48.36 N 93.24 W
Fort Franklin 180 65.11 N 123.46 W
Fort Fraser 182 54.04 N 124.33 W
Fort Frederica National Monument ♦ 192 31.12 N 81.26 W
Fort Gaines 192 31.36 N 85.02 W
Fort Garland 200 37.25 N 105.26 W
Fort Gay 188 38.06 N 82.35 W
Fort George ⊥ 284a 43.15 N 79.04 W
Fort George G. Meade ■ 208 39.05 N 76.50 W
Fort Gibson 196 35.47 N 95.15 W
Fort Gibson Lake ◎¹ 196 36.00 N 95.18 W
Fort Good Hope 180 66.15 N 128.38 W
Fort Gordon ■ 192 33.25 N 82.11 W
Fort-Gourand → Fdérik 148 22.41 N 12.43 W
Fort Green 220 27.36 N 81.56 W
Forth 46 55.47 N 3.41 W
Forth ≃ 46 56.03 N 3.44 W
Forth, Carse of V 46 56.08 N 4.05 W
Forth, Firth of ⊂ 46 56.10 N 2.45 W
Förtha 56 50.56 N 10.14 E
Fort Hall 202 43.02 N 112.26 W
Fort Hall Indian Reservation ◆⁴ 202 43.10 N 112.10 W
Fort Hamilton ■ 276 40.37 N 74.02 W
Forth Bridge ◆⁵ 46 56.00 N 3.25 W
Fort Hertz → Putao 102 27.21 N 97.24 E
Fort Hill → Chitipa 154 9.43 S 33.16 E
Fort Hill ■ 188 38.04 N 77.19 W
Fort Hill State Memorial ⊥ 218 39.07 N 83.25 W
Fort Hood ■ 222 31.08 N 97.46 W
Fort Howard 208 39.12 N 76.27 W
Fort Huachuca ■ 200 31.33 N 110.20 W
Fort Hunter 210 42.57 N 74.17 W
Fort Hunter Liggett ■ 226 35.55 N 121.15 W
Fortierville 206 46.29 N 72.02 W
Fortin, Lac ◎ 186 50.50 N 67.46 W
Fortín Ayacucho 248 19.58 S 59.47 W
Fortín Coroneles Sanchez 248 19.20 S 59.58 W
Fortín de las Flores 234 18.54 N 97.00 W
Fortine 182 48.45 N 114.54 W
Fortín Florida 248 20.45 S 59.17 W
Fortín Garrapatal 248 21.27 S 61.30 W
Fortín Teniente Montanía 252 22.04 S 59.57 W
Fortín Uno 252 38.51 S 65.17 W
Fort Jackson ■ 192 34.01 N 80.57 W
Fort Jameson → Chipata 154 13.39 S 32.40 E
Fort Jefferson National Monument ♦ 220 24.37 N 82.54 W
Fort Jennings 216 40.54 N 84.17 W
Fort Jeudy, Point of › 241k 12.00 N 61.42 W
Fort Johnson 210 42.57 N 74.14 W
Fort Johnston → Mangochi 154 14.28 S 35.16 E
Fort Jones 204 41.36 N 122.50 W
Fort Kent 186 47.15 N 68.35 W
Fort Klamath 202 42.42 N 121.59 W
Fort Knox ■ 194 37.54 N 85.57 W
Fort-Lamy → N'Djamena 146 12.07 N 15.03 E
Fort Langley 224 49.10 N 122.35 W
Fort Langley National Historic Park ♦ 224 49.10 N 122.35 W
Fort Laramie 200 42.12 N 104.31 W
Fort Laramie National Historic Site ♦ 198 42.09 N 104.41 W
Fort Larned National Historic Site ⊥ 198 38.10 N 99.12 W
Fort Lauderdale 220 26.07 N 80.08 W
Fort Lauderdale-Hollywood International Airport ⊠ 220 26.04 N 80.09 W
Fort Laurens State Memorial ⊥ 214 40.38 N 81.27 W
Fort Leavenworth ■ 198 39.21 N 94.55 W
Fort Le Boeuf ⊥ 214 41.56 N 79.59 W
Fort Lee 210 40.51 N 73.58 W
Fort Lee ■ 208 37.14 N 77.20 W
Fort Lennox National Historic Park ♦ 206 45.06 N 73.16 W
Fort Leonard Wood ■ 194 37.45 N 92.07 W
Fort Lewis ■ 224 47.05 N 122.37 W
Fort Liard 176 60.15 N 123.28 W
Fort Lincoln State Park ♦ 198 46.45 N 100.52 W
Fort Littleton 214 40.04 N 77.58 W
Fort Loramie 216 40.21 N 84.22 W
Fort Loudoun Lake ◎¹ 192 35.45 N 84.10 W
Fort Lupton 200 40.05 N 104.48 W
Fort Lyon Canal ≋ 198 38.11 N 102.31 W
Fort Macleod 182 49.43 N 113.25 W
Fort Madison 190 40.37 N 91.18 W
Fort-Mahon-Plage 50 50.21 N 1.34 E
Fort Malden National Historic Park ♦ 281 42.06 N 83.07 W
Fort Matanzas National Monument ♦ 192 29.40 N 81.18 W
Fort McClellan ■ 194 33.43 N 85.47 W
Fort McDermitt Indian Reservation ◆⁴ 202 42.00 N 117.32 W
Fort McDowell Indian Reservation ◆⁴ 200 33.38 N 111.41 W
Fort McHenry National Monument and Historic Shrine ♦ 208 39.16 N 76.35 W
Fort Mckinley 218 39.47 N 84.15 W
Fort McMurray 184 56.44 N 111.23 W
Fort McNair ■ 284c 38.52 N 77.04 W
Fort McPherson 180 67.27 N 134.53 W
Fort Meade 220 27.45 N 81.48 W
Fort Mill 192 35.00 N 80.56 W
Fort Miller 210 43.10 N 73.35 W
Fort Mitchell, Al., U.S. 192 32.21 N 85.01 W
Fort Mitchell, Ky., U.S. 218 39.03 N 84.32 W
Fort Mojave Indian Reservation ◆⁴ 200 34.55 N 114.35 W
Fort Monmouth ■ 208 40.19 N 74.02 W
Fort Monroe ■ 208 37.00 N 76.18 W
Fort Montgomery 210 41.20 N 73.59 W
Fort Morgan 198 40.15 N 103.47 W
Fort Myer ■ 284c 38.53 N 77.05 W
Fort Myers 220 26.38 N 81.52 W
Fort Myers Beach 220 26.27 N 81.56 W
Fort Myers Shores 220 26.43 N 81.45 W
Fort Myers Villas 220 26.34 N 81.52 W
Fort Necessity National Battlefield ⊥ 188 39.47 N 79.39 W
Fort Neck ›¹ 276 40.39 N 73.28 W
Fort Nelson 176 58.49 N 122.43 W

≃ River | Fluß | Río | Rivière | Rio
≋ Canal | Kanal | Canal | Canal | Canal
ᒐ Waterfall, Rapids | Wasserfall, Stromschnellen | Cascada, Rápidos | Chute d'eau, Rapides | Cascata, Rápidos
≬ Strait | Meeresstraße | Estrecho | Détroit | Estreito
⊂ Bay, Gulf | Bucht, Golf | Bahía, Golfo | Baie, Golfe | Baía, Golfo
◎ Lake, Lakes | See, Seen | Lago, Lagos | Lac, Lacs | Lago, Lagos
☷ Swamp | Sumpf | Pantano | Marais | Pântano
⊓ Ice Features, Glacier | Eis- und Gletscherformen | Accidentes Glaciales | Formes glaciaires | Acidentes glaciares
⚲ Other Hydrographic Features | Andere Hydrographische Objekte | Otros Elementos Hidrográficos | Autres données hydrographiques | Outros acidentes hidrográficos

✣ Submarine Features | Untermeerische Objekte | Accidentes Submarinos | Formes de relief sous-marin | Acidentes submarinos
□ Political Unit | Politische Einheit | Unidad Política | Entité politique | Unidade política
ᵾ Cultural Institution | Kulturelle Institution | Institución Cultural | Institution culturelle | Instituição cultural
⊥ Historical Site | Historische Stätte | Sitio Histórico | Site historique | Sitio histórico
♦ Recreational Site | Erholungs- und Ferienort | Sitio de Recreo | Centre de loisirs | Area de Lazer
⊠ Airport | Flughafen | Aeropuerto | Aéroport | Aeroporto
■ Military Installation | Militäranlage | Instalación Militar | Installation militaire | Instalação militar
◆ Miscellaneous | Verschiedenes | Misceláneo | Divers | Diversos

Fort Nelson ≐ 176 59.30 N 124.00 W
Fort Niagara Beach 284a 43.16 N 79.03 W
Fort Niagara State Park ♠, N.Y., U.S. 210 43.16 N 79.03 W
Fort Niagara State Park ♠, N.Y., U.S. 284a 43.16 N 79.03 W
Fort Nonsense ⊥ 276 40.48 N 74.29 W
Fort Norman 180 64.54 N 125.34 W
Fort Nottingham 158 29.25 S 29.55 E
Fort Ogden 220 27.05 N 81.57 W
Fort Ord ■ 226 36.40 N 121.48 W
Fortore ≐ 68 41.55 N 15.17 E
Fort Parker State Park ♠ 222 31.36 N 96.33 W
Fort Payne 194 34.26 N 85.43 W
Fort Peck 202 48.00 N 106.26 W
Fort Peck Dam ◆[6] 202 47.52 N 106.38 W
Fort Peck Indian Reservation ◆[4] 202 48.22 N 105.40 W
Fort Peck Lake ⊜[1] 202 47.45 N 106.50 W
Fort Pierce 220 27.26 N 80.19 W
Fort Pierce Inlet c 220 27.28 N 80.18 W
Fort Pierre 198 44.21 N 100.22 W
Fort Pitt Tunnels ◆[5] 279b 40.25 N 80.00 W
Fort Plain 210 42.55 N 74.37 W
Fort Point National Historical Site ⊥ 282 37.48 N 122.28 W
Fort Polk ■ 194 31.04 N 93.11 W
Fort Portal 154 0.40 N 30.17 E
Fort Providence 176 61.21 N 117.39 W
Fort Pulaski National Monument ♠ 192 32.01 N 80.59 W
Fort Qu'Appelle 184 50.46 N 103.48 W
Fort Raleigh National Historic Site ⊥ 192 35.55 N 75.40 W
Fort Randall Dam ◆[6] 198 42.48 N 98.35 W
Fort Recovery 216 40.24 N 84.46 W
Fort Resolution 176 61.10 N 113.40 W
Fortress Mountain ∧ 202 44.20 N 109.47 W
Fortress of Louisbourg National Historic Park ♠ 186 45.56 N 59.57 W
Fort Riley ■ 198 39.04 N 96.47 W
Fort Ritchie ■ 208 39.43 N 77.30 W
Fort Rixon 154 20.01 S 29.18 E
Fort Robinson State Park ♠ 198 42.41 N 103.30 W
Fort Rodd Hill National Historic Park ♠ 224 48.26 N 123.28 W
Fortrose, N.Z. 172 46.34 S 168.48 E
Fortrose, Scot., U.K. 46 57.34 N 4.09 W
Fort Rosebery → Mansa 154 11.12 S 28.53 E
Fort Rucker ■ 194 31.20 N 85.42 W
Fort Saint James 182 54.26 N 124.15 W
Fort Saint John 182 56.15 N 120.51 W
Fort Salonga 276 40.55 N 73.18 W
Fort Sam Houston ■ 196 29.27 N 98.27 W
Fort Saskatchewan 182 53.43 N 113.13 W
Fort Scott 198 37.50 N 94.42 W
Fort Seneca 214 41.13 N 83.10 W
Fort-Ševčenko 84 44.31 N 50.16 E
Fort Severn 176 56.00 N 87.38 W
Fort Shawnee 216 40.41 N 84.08 W
Fort Sheridan ■ 216 42.13 N 87.48 W
Fort Sill ■ 196 34.40 N 98.25 W
Fort Simcoe Historical State Park ♠ 224 46.21 N 120.50 W
Fort Simpson 176 61.52 N 121.23 W
Fort Sisseton State Park ♠ 198 45.39 N 97.32 W
Fort Smith, N.T., Can. 176 60.00 N 111.53 W
Fort Smith, Ar., U.S. 194 35.23 N 94.23 W
Fort Steele 182 49.37 N 115.38 W
Fort Stevens State Park ♠ 224 46.10 N 124.00 W
Fort Stewart ■ 192 31.52 N 81.37 W
Fort Stockton 196 30.53 N 102.52 W
Fort Sumner 196 34.28 N 104.14 W
Fort Sumter National Monument ♠ 192 32.44 N 79.46 W
Fort Supply 196 36.34 N 99.34 W
Fort Tejon State Historical Park ♠ 228 34.52 N 118.53 W
Fort Thomas, Az., U.S. 200 33.02 N 109.57 W
Fort Thomas, Ky., U.S. 218 39.04 N 84.26 W
Fort Thompson 198 44.04 N 99.26 W
Fort Tilden ■ 276 40.33 N 73.53 W
Fort Totten 198 47.58 N 98.59 W
Fort Totten Indian Reservation ◆[4] 198 47.53 N 98.50 W
Fort Totten Park ♠ 284c 38.57 N 77.00 W
Fort Towson 196 34.01 N 95.15 W
Fort-Trinquet → Bîr Mogreïn 148 25.14 N 11.35 W
Fortuna, Arg. 252 35.07 S 65.23 W
Fortuna, Ca., U.S. 204 40.35 N 124.09 W
Fortuna, Río de la ≐ 248 16.36 S 58.46 W
Fortuna Ledge (Marshall) 180 61.53 N 162.05 W
Fortune 186 47.04 N 55.50 W
Fortune Bay c 186 47.25 N 55.25 W
Fortune Ditch ≋ 279a 41.20 N 82.03 W
Fortune Harbour 186 49.31 N 55.15 W
Fortuneswell 42 50.34 N 2.27 W
Fort Union National Monument ♠ 200 35.55 N 105.01 W
Fort Union Trading Post National Historical Site ⊥ 198 48.00 N 104.03 W
Fort Valley 192 32.33 N 83.53 W
Fort Vancouver National Historic Site ⊥ 224 45.38 N 122.37 W
Fort Vermilion 176 58.24 N 116.00 W
Fortville 218 39.55 N 85.50 W
Fort Wadsworth ■ 276 40.36 N 74.04 W
Fort Walton Beach 194 30.24 N 86.37 W
Fort Washakie 200 43.00 N 108.52 W
Fort Washington 208 40.08 N 75.12 W
Fort Washington Forest 208 38.43 N 76.59 W
Fort Washington State Park ♠ 285 40.07 N 75.14 W
Fort Wayne 216 41.07 N 85.07 W
Fort Wayne Military Museum ♥ 281 42.18 N 83.06 W
Fort Wellington 246 6.24 N 57.36 W
Fort Wellington National Historic Park ♠ 212 44.44 N 75.31 W
Fort White 192 29.55 N 82.42 W
Fort William → Thunder Bay, On., Can. 190 48.23 N 89.15 W
Fort William, Scot., U.K. 46 56.49 N 5.07 W
Fort Worth 222 32.43 N 97.19 W
Fort Yates 198 46.05 N 100.37 W
Forty Foot Drain ≋ 42 52.28 N 0.05 W
Forty Fort 210 41.16 N 75.52 W
Fortymile ≐ 180 64.26 N 140.32 W
Fort Yukon 180 66.34 N 145.17 W
Fort Yuma Indian Reservation ◆[4] 204 32.48 N 114.34 W
Forum ♠, P.Q., Can. 275a 45.29 N 73.35 W
Forum ♠, Ca., U.S. 280 33.57 N 118.20 W
Forūr, Jazīreh-ye I 128 26.17 N 54.32 E
Forza d'Agrò 70 37.55 N 15.20 E
Foscagno, Passo di)(64 46.30 N 10.08 E
Fosdinovo 64 44.08 N 10.01 E
Fosforescénte, Bahía c 240m 17.59 N 67.01 W
Fosforitnyj 82 55.19 N 38.54 E
Foshan 100 23.03 N 113.09 E
Fosna >[1] 24 64.00 N 10.30 E
Fosnavåg 26 62.21 N 5.39 E
Foso 150 5.42 N 1.17 W
Foss 46 56.41 N 3.58 W
Foss ≐, Eng., U.K. 44 53.57 N 1.06 W
Foss ≐, Wa., U.S. 224 47.43 N 121.18 W
Fossacesia 66 42.15 N 14.29 E
Fossacesia Marina 66 42.15 N 14.30 E
Fossa Eugeniana ≋ 263 51.33 N 6.36 E
Fossano 62 44.33 N 7.43 E
Fossanova, Abbazia di ♥[1] 66 41.29 N 13.13 E
Fossato, Colle di)(66 43.19 N 12.47 E
Fossato di Vico 66 43.18 N 12.46 E
Fossé 56 49.27 N 5.00 E
Fosse-Martin 261 49.05 N 2.54 E
Fosses 261 49.06 N 2.29 E
Fosses-la-Ville 56 50.24 N 4.42 E
Fossil 202 44.59 N 120.12 W
Fossil Butte National Monument ♠ 202 41.50 N 110.40 W
Fossil Downs 162 18.08 S 125.38 E
Fossil Lake ⊜ 202 43.18 N 120.15 W
Fossombrone 66 43.41 N 12.48 E
Fosston 198 47.34 N 95.45 W
Fos-sur-Mer 62 43.26 N 4.57 E
Foster, Austl. 169 38.39 S 146.12 E
Foster, Ky., U.S. 218 38.47 N 84.12 W
Foster, R.I., U.S. 207 41.51 N 71.45 W
Foster ≐ 184 55.47 N 105.49 W
Foster, Mount ∧ 180 59.48 N 135.29 W
Foster Brook 214 41.59 N 78.37 W
Foster City 226 37.33 N 122.16 W
Foster Creek ≐ 198 44.34 N 98.12 W
Fosterdale 210 41.42 N 74.58 W
Foster Joseph Sayers Reservoir ⊜[1] 214 41.02 N 77.40 W
Foster Park 228 34.21 N 119.18 W
Fosters 194 33.05 N 87.41 W
Fosters Pond ⊜ 283 42.37 N 71.08 W
Foster Street 260 51.46 N 0.09 E
Foster Village 229c 21.21 N 157.55 W
Fostoria 214 41.09 N 83.25 W
Fót 264c 47.37 N 19.12 E
Fotadrevo 157b 24.03 S 45.01 E
Fotan 100 24.12 N 117.53 E
Fóti-Somlyó ∧[2] 264c 47.38 N 19.13 E
Foucarmont 50 49.51 N 1.34 E
Fou-Chouen → Fushun 104 41.52 N 123.53 E
Fouesnant 32 47.54 N 4.01 W
Foug 56 48.41 N 5.47 E
Fougamou 152 1.13 S 10.36 E
Fougères 32 48.21 N 1.12 W
Fougères-sur-Bièvre 50 47.27 N 1.21 E
Fougerolles 58 47.53 N 6.24 E
Fouhsin → Fuxin 104 42.03 N 121.46 E
Fouju 261 48.35 N 2.47 E
Fouke 194 33.16 N 93.53 W
Foula I 46a 60.08 N 2.05 W
Foulain 58 48.02 N 5.13 E
Foulalaba 150 10.41 N 7.22 W
Foula Mori 150 12.10 N 13.51 W
Foulatari 146 13.41 N 12.03 E
Foul Bay c 140 23.30 N 35.39 E
Fouling → Fuling 102 29.42 N 107.21 E
Foulness ≐ 44 53.47 N 0.43 W
Foulness Island I 42 51.36 N 0.55 E
Foulness Point > 42 51.38 N 0.57 E
Foulpointe 157b 17.41 S 49.31 E
Foulsham 42 52.48 N 1.01 E
Foulwind, Cape > 172 41.45 S 171.28 E
Foumban 152 5.43 N 10.55 E
Foumbot 152 5.30 N 10.38 E
Foumbouni 157a 11.50 S 43.30 E
Foum-el-Hisn 148 28.59 N 8.55 W
Foum-Zguid 148 30.04 N 6.54 W
Foundiougne 150 14.08 N 16.28 W
Fountain, Co., U.S. 198 38.40 N 104.42 W
Fountain, Fl., U.S. 192 30.09 N 85.38 W
Fountain □[6] 216 40.17 N 87.13 W
Fountain City, In., U.S. 218 39.57 N 84.55 W
Fountain City, Wi., U.S. 190 44.07 N 91.43 W
Fountain Creek ≐, Co., U.S. 198 38.15 N 104.35 W
Fountain Creek ≐, Il., U.S. 219 38.20 N 90.22 W
Fountain Green 200 39.37 N 111.38 W
Fountain Hill 208 40.36 N 75.23 W
Fountain Inn 192 34.41 N 82.11 W
Fountain Park 216 41.50 N 84.32 W
Fountain Peak ∧ 204 34.57 N 115.32 W
Fountain Place 194 30.31 N 91.09 W
Fountains Abbey ♥[1] 44 54.07 N 1.34 W
Fountains Creek ≐ 208 36.33 N 77.21 W
Fountaintown 218 39.41 N 85.46 W
Fountain Valley 228 33.42 N 117.57 W
Fourche LaFave ≐ 194 34.58 N 92.35 W
Fourche Maline ≐ 194 34.55 N 94.55 W
Fourchu 186 45.43 N 60.15 W
Four Corners 202 44.55 N 122.58 W
Four Elms 260 51.13 N 0.06 E
Four Hole Swamp ≐ 192 33.03 N 80.24 W
Fouriesburg 158 28.38 S 28.14 E
Fourmies 50 50.00 N 4.03 E
Four Mile Creek ≐, On., Can. 284a 43.15 N 79.08 W
Fourmile Creek ≐, N.Y., U.S. 284a 43.17 N 79.00 W
Four Mile Creek ≐, Oh., U.S. 218 39.26 N 84.32 W
Four Mile Creek State Park ♠ 284a 43.16 N 79.00 W
Fourmile Draw V 196 32.40 N 104.18 W
Four Mile Lake ⊜ 212 44.40 N 78.44 W
Four Mile Run ≐ 284c 38.50 N 77.02 W
Four Mountains, Islands of II 180 52.50 N 170.00 W
Fournaise, Piton de la ∧ 157c 21.14 S 55.43 E
Fourneau, Pointe à > 275a 45.22 N 73.51 W
Fourneaux, Fr. 50 47.53 N 1.48 E
Fourneaux, Fr. 62 45.11 N 6.39 E
Fournier, Lac ⊜ 186 51.33 N 65.25 W
Fournière, Lac ⊜ 190 48.04 N 78.03 W
Foúrnoi I 38 37.34 N 26.30 E
Four Oaks 192 35.26 N 78.25 W
Fourqueux 261 48.53 N 2.04 E
Fours 32 46.49 N 3.43 E
Fourteenmile Creek ≐ 218 38.26 N 85.37 W
Fourth Cataract → Rābiʿ, Ash-Shallāl ar- ∟ 140 18.47 N 32.03 E
Fourth Cliff ≛[4] 283 42.09 N 70.42 W
Four Towns 281 42.37 N 83.25 W
Fous, Pointe des > 240d 15.12 N 61.20 W
Foussard ≐ 50 48.16 N 1.17 E
Fouta Djalon ◆[1] 150 11.30 N 12.30 W
Fou-Tcheou → Fuzhou 100 26.06 N 119.17 E
Fouyang → Fuyang 100 32.54 N 115.49 E
Fouzon ≐ 50 47.16 N 1.27 E
Foveaux Strait ⊔ 172 46.35 S 168.00 E
Foveran 46 57.18 N 2.02 W
Fowey 42 50.20 N 4.38 W
Fowler, Ca., U.S. 226 36.37 N 119.40 W
Fowler, Co., U.S. 198 38.07 N 104.01 W
Fowler, In., U.S. 216 40.37 N 87.19 W
Fowler, Ks., U.S. 198 37.23 N 100.11 W
Fowler, Mi., U.S. 216 43.00 N 84.44 W
Fowler, Oh., U.S. 214 41.19 N 80.40 W
Fowler, Lake ⊜ 168b 35.06 S 137.37 E
Fowler, Point > 162 32.02 S 132.29 E
Fowler Creek ≐ 281 42.17 N 83.30 W
Fowlers Bay 162 31.59 S 132.27 E
Fowlerton 196 28.28 N 98.48 W
Fowlerville 216 42.39 N 84.04 W
Fowliang → Jingdezhen 100 29.16 N 117.11 E
Fowman 128 37.13 N 49.19 E
Fox 180 64.51 N 147.46 W
Fox ≐, Mb., Can. 184 56.03 N 93.18 W
Fox ≐, U.S. 194 40.18 N 91.30 W
Fox ≐, U.S. 216 41.21 N 88.50 W
Fox ≐, Il., U.S. 194 38.32 N 88.08 W
Fox ≐, Wi., U.S. 190 44.32 N 88.01 W
Fox, Cape > 182 54.47 N 130.51 W
Foxboro, On., Can. 212 44.15 N 77.26 W
Foxboro, Ma., U.S. 207 42.03 N 71.15 W
Foxboro Raceway ♠ 283 42.06 N 71.16 W
Fox Brook ≐ 276 41.03 N 74.13 W
Foxburg 214 41.09 N 79.41 W
Fox Chapel 279b 40.30 N 79.55 W
Fox Chase ◆[8] 285 40.04 N 75.05 W
Fox Chase Manor 285 40.05 N 75.06 W
Fox Creek ≐, Ky., U.S. 218 38.16 N 83.41 W
Fox Creek ≐, N.Y., U.S. 210 42.41 N 74.18 W
Foxe Basin c 176 68.25 N 77.00 W
Foxe-Becken → Foxe Basin c 176 68.25 N 77.00 W
Foxe Channel ⊔ 176 64.30 N 80.00 W
Foxen ⊜ 26 59.23 N 11.52 E
Foxe Peninsula >[1] 176 65.00 N 76.00 W
Foxford 48 53.58 N 9.08 W
Fox Glacier 172 43.28 S 170.00 E
Foxhall 284c 39.04 N 77.03 W
Fox Harbour 186 47.19 N 53.55 W
Fox Hills 284c 39.02 N 77.11 W
Foxhole 42 50.21 N 4.52 W
Foxholes 44 54.08 N 0.28 W
Fox Hollow Lake ⊜ 276 41.02 N 74.40 W
Fox Island I, On., Can. 212 44.28 N 78.24 W
Fox Island I, Wa., U.S. 224 47.16 N 122.37 W
Fox Islands II 180 53.30 N 168.00 W
Fox Lake, Il., U.S. 216 42.23 N 88.11 W
Fox Lake, Wi., U.S. 190 43.33 N 88.54 W
Fox Lake ⊜ 216 42.25 N 88.09 W
Fox Mountain ∧ 180 61.55 N 133.22 W
Foxpark 200 41.05 N 106.09 W
Fox Point 216 43.09 N 87.54 W
Fox Point > 276 40.54 N 73.35 W
Fox River Estates 216 41.58 N 88.20 W
Fox River Grove 216 42.12 N 88.12 W
Foxton 172 40.28 S 175.18 E
Foxton Beach 172 40.28 S 175.13 E
Foxvale 283 42.02 N 71.14 W
Fox Valley, Austl. 274a 33.45 S 151.06 E
Fox Valley, Sk., Can. 184 50.29 N 109.28 W
Foxwells 208 37.38 N 76.18 W
Foxwist Green 262 53.12 N 2.34 W
Foxworth 194 31.14 N 89.52 W
Foyedong 98 40.41 N 119.12 E
Foyers 46 57.14 N 4.29 W
Foyle ≐ 48 54.59 N 7.18 W
Foyle, Lough c 48 55.06 N 7.08 W
Foynes 48 52.37 N 9.06 W
Foza 64 45.54 N 11.38 E
Foz do Cunene 152 17.16 S 11.50 E
Foz do Iguaçu 252 25.33 S 54.35 W
Foz do Jordão 248 9.23 S 71.56 W
Foz Giraldo 34 40.00 N 7.43 E
Foziling 100 31.20 N 116.17 E
Frabosa Soprana 62 44.17 N 7.48 E
Fracción del Refugio 234 21.57 N 100.02 W
Frackville 208 40.47 N 76.13 W
Fraction Run ≐ 278 41.34 N 88.04 W
Fraga, Arg. 252 33.30 S 65.48 W
Fraga, Esp. 34 41.31 N 0.21 E
Fragagnano 68 40.26 N 17.28 E
Fragneto Monforte 68 41.15 N 14.46 E
Fragoso, Cayo I 240p 22.44 N 79.30 W
Fragrant Hills Park ♠ 271a 39.59 N 116.11 E
Fragua, Sierra de la ⋏ 196 26.41 N 102.13 W
Fraile Muerto 252 32.31 S 54.32 W
Fraïn, Chott el ⊜ 34 35.57 N 5.38 E
Fraire 50 50.16 N 4.30 E
Fraisans 58 47.09 N 5.46 E
Fraisse 62 45.23 N 4.15 E
Fraize 58 48.11 N 7.00 E
Fram 61 46.27 N 15.38 E
Frameries 50 50.24 N 3.54 E
Framingham 207 42.16 N 71.25 W
Framingham State College ♥[2] 283 42.18 N 71.26 W
Framlingham 42 52.13 N 1.21 E
Frammersbach 56 50.04 N 9.28 E
Framnes Mountains ⋏ 9 67.50 S 62.35 E
Frampol 30 50.41 N 22.40 E
Frampton Cotterell 42 51.32 N 2.29 W
Frampton on Severn 42 51.46 N 2.22 W
França, Bra. 250 11.34 S 40.36 W
Franca, Bra. 255 20.32 S 47.24 W
Franca-Iosifa, Zemľa (Franz Josef Land) II 12 81.00 N 55.00 E
Français, Récif des ✣[2] 175f 19.40 S 163.20 E
Francavilla al Mare 66 42.25 N 14.17 E
Francavilla Angitola 68 38.46 N 16.16 E
Francavilla d'Ete 66 43.11 N 13.32 E
Francavilla di Sicilia 70 37.54 N 15.08 E
Francavilla Fontana 68 40.31 N 17.35 E
Francavilla in Sinni 68 40.05 N 16.12 E
Francavilla Marittima 68 39.49 N 16.23 E
France □[1], Europe 22 46.00 N 2.00 E
France □[1], Europe 32 46.00 N 2.00 E
Frances ≐ 180 60.12 N 129.02 W
Francés, Cabo > 240p 21.54 N 84.02 W
Francés, Punta > 240p 21.38 N 83.12 W
Frances Creek 164 13.35 S 131.52 E
Francês dos Carvalhos 256 22.05 S 44.29 W
Frances Lake ⊜ 180 61.25 N 129.30 W
Francés Viejo, Cabo > 238 19.39 N 69.55 W
Francesville 216 40.59 N 86.52 W
Franceville 152 1.38 S 13.35 E
Francfort-sur-Main → Frankfurt am Main 56 50.07 N 8.40 E
Franche-Comté □[9] 58 47.00 N 6.00 E
Franchère, Lac ⊜ 206 46.47 N 74.58 W
Franches-Montagnes ⋏ 58 47.12 N 7.00 E
Francia 252 32.33 S 56.37 W
Francia → France □[1] 32 46.00 N 2.00 E
Francia, Estación de ◆[5] 266d 41.23 N 2.11 E
Francia, Peña de ∧ 34 42.35 N 8.02 W
Francis 184 50.05 N 103.55 W
Francis, Lake ⊜ 206 45.02 N 71.20 W
Francisca, Punta > 232 21.34 N 87.21 W
Francis Case, Lake ⊜[1] 198 43.15 N 99.00 W
Francisco A. Berra 258 35.23 S 58.51 W
Francisco Alvarez 258 34.38 S 58.52 W
Francisco Beltrão 252 26.05 S 53.04 W
Francisco González Villarreal 232 25.22 N 97.53 W
Francisco I. Madero, Méx. 232 25.45 N 103.21 W
Francisco I. Madero, Méx. 232 24.32 N 104.22 W
Francisco I. Madero, Méx. 234 16.50 N 93.50 W
Francisco I. Madero, Méx. 234 21.36 N 104.49 W
Francisco José, Tierra → Franca-Iosifa, Zemľa II 12 81.00 N 55.00 E
Francisco Morato 256 23.16 S 46.45 W
Francisco Morazán □[5] 236 14.15 N 87.15 W
Francisco Perito Moreno, Parque Nacional ♠ 254 47.50 S 72.08 W
Francisco Primo Verdad 234 21.48 N 101.55 W
Francisco Sá 255 16.28 S 43.30 W
Francisco Zarco 204 32.06 N 116.30 W
Francis E. Warren Air Force Base ■ 198 41.09 N 104.52 W
Francistown 156 21.11 S 27.32 E
Francitas 222 28.52 N 96.20 W
Franco da Rocha 256 23.20 S 46.43 W
Francofonte 70 37.14 N 14.53 E
François 186 47.35 N 56.45 W
François, Lacs à ⊜ 186 51.40 N 65.49 W
François-Joseph, Îles du → Frnca-Iosifa, Zemľa II 12 81.00 N 55.00 E
François Lake 182 54.04 N 125.44 W
François Lake ⊜ 182 54.00 N 125.40 W
Francolise 68 41.11 N 14.03 E
Franconia Notch State Park ♠ 188 44.06 N 71.43 W
Franconville 261 48.59 N 2.14 E
Francs Peak ∧ 202 43.58 N 109.20 W
Francueil 50 47.19 N 1.05 E
Franeker 52 53.11 N 5.32 E
Frangy 58 46.01 N 5.56 E
Frank 279b 40.16 N 79.48 W
Frank and Poet Drain ≋ 281 42.06 N 83.12 W
Frankby 262 53.22 N 3.08 W
Frankel City 196 32.23 N 102.47 W
Franken □[9] 30 50.00 N 10.00 E
Frankenau 56 51.05 N 8.56 E
Frankenbach 56 50.40 N 8.34 E
Frankenberg 54 50.54 N 13.01 E
Frankenberg-Eder 56 51.03 N 8.48 E
Frankenburg 60 48.05 N 13.30 E
Frankenheim 56 50.32 N 10.04 E
Frankenhöhe ⋏ 56 49.15 N 10.15 E
Frankenmarkt 64 47.59 N 13.25 E
Frankenmuth 190 43.19 N 83.44 W
Frankenstein 56 49.26 N 7.58 E
Frankenstein → Ząbkowice Śląskie 30 50.36 N 16.53 E
Frankenthal 56 49.32 N 8.21 E
Frankenwald ⋏ 54 50.18 N 11.36 E
Frankfield 241q 18.09 N 77.22 W
Frankford, On., Can. 212 44.12 N 77.36 W
Frankford, De., U.S. 208 38.31 N 75.14 W
Frankford, Mo., U.S. 219 39.29 N 91.19 W
Frankford ◆[8] 285 40.01 N 75.05 W
Frankford Arsenal ■ 285 40.00 N 75.04 W
Frankfort, S. Afr. 158 32.44 S 27.28 E
Frankfort, S. Afr. 158 27.17 S 28.30 E
Frankfort, Il., U.S. 216 41.29 N 87.50 W
Frankfort, In., U.S. 216 40.16 N 86.30 W
Frankfort, Ks., U.S. 198 39.42 N 96.25 W
Frankfort, Ky., U.S. 218 38.12 N 84.52 W
Frankfort, Mi., U.S. 190 44.38 N 86.14 W
Frankfort, N.Y., U.S. 210 43.02 N 75.04 W
Frankfort, Oh., U.S. 218 39.24 N 83.10 W
Frankfort, S.D., U.S. 198 44.52 N 98.18 W
Frankfort Springs 214 40.30 N 80.25 W
Frankfurt □[5] 54 52.30 N 14.00 E
Frankfurt am Main 56 50.07 N 8.40 E
Frankfurt am Main, Flughafen ⊠ 56 50.02 N 8.33 E
Frankfurt an der Oder 54 52.20 N 14.33 E
Frank G. Bonelli Regional County Park ♠ 280 34.05 N 117.49 W
Frank Hann National Park ♠ 162 32.50 S 120.25 E
Fränkische Alb ⋏[2] 60 49.20 N 11.30 E
Fränkische Rezat ≐ 56 49.11 N 11.01 E
Fränkische Saale ≐ 56 50.03 N 9.42 E
Fränkische Schweiz ◆[1] 60 49.45 N 11.25 E
Frank Key I 220 25.07 N 80.54 W
Frankland ≐ 162 34.58 S 116.49 E
Frankleben 54 51.18 N 11.56 E
Franklin, S. Afr. 158 30.18 S 29.30 E
Franklin, Az., U.S. 200 32.40 N 109.04 W
Franklin, Ga., U.S. 192 33.16 N 85.05 W
Franklin, Id., U.S. 202 42.00 N 111.48 W
Franklin, Il., U.S. 219 39.37 N 90.03 W
Franklin, In., U.S. 218 39.28 N 86.03 W
Franklin, Ky., U.S. 194 36.43 N 86.34 W
Franklin, La., U.S. 194 29.47 N 91.30 W
Franklin, Me., U.S. 188 44.35 N 68.13 W
Franklin, Ma., U.S. 207 42.05 N 71.23 W
Franklin, Mi., U.S. 281 42.31 N 83.18 W
Franklin, Mn., U.S. 198 44.31 N 94.52 W
Franklin, Ne., U.S. 198 40.05 N 98.57 W
Franklin, N.H., U.S. 188 43.26 N 71.38 W
Franklin, N.J., U.S. 210 41.07 N 74.34 W
Franklin, N.Y., U.S. 210 42.20 N 75.09 W
Franklin, N.C., U.S. 192 35.10 N 83.22 W
Franklin, Oh., U.S. 218 39.33 N 84.18 W
Franklin, Pa., U.S. 214 41.24 N 79.50 W
Franklin, Tn., U.S. 194 35.55 N 86.52 W
Franklin, Tx., U.S. 222 31.01 N 96.29 W
Franklin, Vt., U.S. 206 44.58 N 72.55 W
Franklin, Va., U.S. 208 36.40 N 76.55 W
Franklin, W.V., U.S. 188 38.39 N 79.20 W
Franklin, Wi., U.S. 216 42.54 N 88.03 W
Franklin □[5] 176 72.00 N 100.00 W
Franklin □[6], In., U.S. 218 39.25 N 85.01 W
Franklin □[6], Ky., U.S. 218 38.14 N 84.52 W
Franklin □[6], Ma., U.S. 207 42.36 N 72.36 W
Franklin □[6], Mo., U.S. 219 38.25 N 91.03 W
Franklin □[6], N.Y., U.S. 206 44.57 N 74.18 W
Franklin □[6], Oh., U.S. 218 39.57 N 83.00 W
Franklin □[6], Pa., U.S. 208 39.56 N 77.40 W
Franklin □[6], Tx., U.S. 222 33.07 N 95.13 W
Franklin □[6], Vt., U.S. 206 44.57 N 72.52 W
Franklin, Mount ∧ 171b 35.29 S 148.47 E
Franklin, Point > 180 70.54 N 158.48 W
Franklin Bay c 176 69.45 N 126.00 W
Franklin Canyon Reservoir ⊜[1] 280 34.06 N 118.25 W
Franklin Delano Roosevelt, Parque Nacional ♠ 258 34.52 S 56.03 W
Franklin Delano Roosevelt National Historic Site ⊥ 210 41.46 N 73.56 W
Franklin Delano Roosevelt Park ♠ 285 39.54 N 75.11 W
Franklin D. Roosevelt Lake ⊜[1] 202 48.20 N 118.10 W
Franklin Farms 279b 40.10 N 80.16 W
Franklin Grove 190 41.50 N 89.18 W
Franklin Harbor c 166 33.42 S 136.56 E
Franklin Institute ♥ 285 39.57 N 75.11 W
Franklin Island I 212 45.24 N 80.20 W
Franklin Lake ⊜, N.T., Can. 176 66.56 N 96.03 W
Franklin Lake ⊜, Nv., U.S. 204 40.24 N 115.12 W
Franklin Lake ⊜, N.J., U.S. 276 40.59 N 74.13 W
Franklin Lakes 276 41.01 N 74.12 W
Franklin-Lower Gordon Wild Rivers National Park ♠ 166 42.46 S 145.45 E
Franklin Mountains ⋏, N.T., Can. 180 63.00 N 123.50 W
Franklin Mountains ⋏, N.Z. 172 44.55 S 167.45 E
Franklin Park, Il., U.S. 216 41.56 N 87.51 W
Franklin Park, Md., U.S. 284c 39.03 N 77.06 W
Franklin Park, N.J., U.S. 276 40.26 N 74.32 W
Franklin Park, N.Y., U.S. 210 43.05 N 76.05 W
Franklin Park, Pa., U.S. 279b 40.35 N 80.06 W
Franklin Park, Va., U.S. 284c 38.55 N 77.09 W
Franklin Park ♠ 283 42.18 N 71.06 W
Franklin Pond ⊜ 276 41.06 N 74.35 W
Franklin Ridge ∧ 282 38.00 N 122.10 W
Franklin River 224 49.06 N 124.49 W
Franklin Roosevelt Park ◆[8] 273d 26.09 S 27.59 E
Franklin Springs 210 43.02 N 75.24 W
Franklin Square 210 40.42 N 73.40 W
Franklin State Forest ♠ 283 42.04 N 71.26 W
Franklin Strait ⊔ 176 72.00 N 96.00 W
Franklinton, La., U.S. 194 30.50 N 90.09 W
Franklinton, N.C., U.S. 192 36.06 N 78.27 W
Franklintown 208 40.05 N 77.02 W
Franklinville, N.J., U.S. 208 39.37 N 75.04 W
Franklinville, N.Y., U.S. 210 42.20 N 78.27 W
Frankreich → France □[1] 32 46.00 N 2.00 E
Frankston, Austl. 169 38.08 S 145.07 E
Frankston, Tx., U.S. 222 32.03 N 95.30 W
Franksville 216 42.45 N 87.54 W
Frankton 216 40.13 N 85.46 W
Frankville 194 31.38 N 88.08 W
Frånö 26 62.54 N 17.50 E
Fr'anovo 82 56.08 N 38.27 E
Franschhoek 158 33.55 S 19.09 E
Fransfontein 156 20.12 S 15.01 E
Fränsta 26 62.30 N 16.09 E
Františkovy Lázně 54 50.04 N 12.21 E
Franvillers 50 49.58 N 2.30 E
Franzburg 54 54.11 N 12.52 E
Franzensburg ⊥ 264b 48.04 N 16.22 E
Franzensfeste → Fortezza 64 46.47 N 11.37 E
Franz Josef 172 43.24 S 170.11 E
Franz Josef Land → Franca Iosifa, Zemľa II 12 81.00 N 55.00 E
Franz-Josefs-Bahnhof ◆[5] 264b 48.13 N 16.21 E
Franz-Josefs-Höhe ♠ 64 47.04 N 12.45 E
Französische Süd- und Antarktis-Gebiete → French Southern and Antarctic Territories □[2] 6 49.30 S 69.30 E
Französisch-Polynesien → French Polynesia □[2] 14 15.00 S 140.00 W
Frasca, Capo della > 71 39.46 N 8.27 E
Frascati 66 41.48 N 12.41 E
Frascineto 68 39.50 N 16.16 E
Frasdorf 64 47.48 N 12.16 E
Fraser, Co., U.S. 200 39.56 N 105.49 W
Fraser, Mi., U.S. 281 42.32 N 82.56 W
Fraser ≐, B.C., Can. 182 49.09 N 123.12 W
Fraser ≐, Nf., Can. 176 56.35 N 61.55 W
Fraser ≐, Co., U.S. 200 40.06 N 105.58 W
Fraser, Mount ∧ 162 25.39 S 118.23 E
Fraserburg 158 31.55 S 21.30 E
Fraserburgh 46 57.42 N 2.00 W
Fraser Island I 166 25.15 S 153.10 E
Fraser Lake 182 54.04 N 124.51 W
Fraser Lake ⊜ 182 54.05 N 124.35 W
Fraser Mills 224 49.14 N 122.52 W
Fraser National Park ♠ 169 37.10 S 145.50 E
Fraser Plateau ⋏[1] 182 52.00 N 123.00 W
Fraser Range 162 32.03 S 122.48 E
Frasertown 172 38.58 S 177.24 E
Frasne 58 46.51 N 6.10 E
Frasnes-lez-Anvaing 50 50.40 N 3.36 E
Frassine ≐ 64 45.18 N 11.37 E
Frassinoro 64 44.18 N 10.34 E
Frati, Monte dei ∧ 66 43.40 N 12.10 E
Fratres 61 48.59 N 15.21 E
Frattamaggiore 68 40.57 N 14.16 E
Frattócchie 267a 41.46 N 12.37 E
Frauenburg → Frombork 30 54.22 N 19.41 E
Frauenfeld 58 47.34 N 8.54 E
Frauenkirchen 61 47.50 N 16.56 E
Frauenstein 54 50.48 N 13.32 E
Frauental an der Lassnitz 61 46.48 N 15.14 E
Frauenwald 54 50.35 N 10.51 E
Fray Bentos 252 33.08 S 58.18 W
Fray Luis Beltrán 252 39.19 S 65.46 W
Fray Marcos 252 34.11 S 55.44 W
Frazee 198 46.43 N 95.42 W
Frazer, Mt., U.S. 202 48.03 N 106.02 W
Frazer, Pa., U.S. 208 40.02 N 75.33 W
Frazeysburg 214 40.07 N 82.07 W
Frazier Mountain ∧ 228 34.47 N 118.58 W
Frazier Park 228 34.49 N 118.56 W
Fr'azino 82 55.58 N 38.04 E
Frazzanò 70 38.04 N 14.44 E
Frecheiras 250 2.51 S 42.05 W
Frecheirinha 250 3.46 S 40.48 W
Frechen 56 50.54 N 6.49 E
Frechilla 34 42.08 N 4.50 W
Freckenhorst 52 51.55 N 7.58 E
Freckleton 262 53.45 N 2.52 W
Freddo ≐ 70 38.01 N 12.54 E
Fredeburg 56 51.11 N 8.18 E
Freden 52 51.56 N 9.54 E
Fredensborg 41 55.58 N 12.24 E
Fredensborg ⊥ 41 55.58 N 12.23 E
Frederic 190 45.39 N 92.28 W
Frederica 208 39.00 N 75.27 W
Fredericia 41 55.35 N 9.46 E
Frederick, Il., U.S. 219 40.04 N 90.26 W
Frederick, Md., U.S. 208 39.24 N 77.24 W
Frederick, Ok., U.S. 196 34.23 N 99.01 W
Frederick, S.D., U.S. 198 45.49 N 98.30 W
Frederick □[6] 208 39.25 N 77.25 W
Frederick Hills ⋏[2] 164 12.41 S 136.00 E
Frederick House ≐ 190 49.06 N 81.10 W
Frederick House Lake ⊜ 190 48.40 N 80.55 W
Frederick Island I 162 34.04 S 122.00 E
Frederick Reef ✣[2] 166 20.58 S 154.23 E
Fredericksburg, In., U.S. 218 38.26 N 86.11 W
Fredericksburg, Ia., U.S. 190 42.57 N 92.11 W
Fredericksburg, Oh., U.S. 214 40.40 N 81.52 W
Fredericksburg, Pa., U.S. 214 40.27 N 76.26 W
Fredericksburg, Tx., U.S. 196 30.16 N 98.52 W
Fredericksburg, Va., U.S. 208 38.18 N 77.27 W
Fredericksburg Battlefield ⊥ 208 38.17 N 77.28 W
Frederick Sound ⊔ 180 57.00 N 133.00 W
Fredericktown, Mo., U.S. 194 37.33 N 90.17 W
Fredericktown, Oh., U.S. 214 40.28 N 82.32 W
Frederico Westphalen 252 27.22 S 53.24 W
Fredericton 186 45.58 N 66.39 W
Fredericton Junction 186 45.40 N 66.37 W
Frederik Hendrikeiland → Yos Sudarso, Pulau I 164 7.50 S 138.30 E
Frederiksberg, Dan. 41 55.41 N 12.32 E
Frederiksberg, Dan. 41 55.25 N 11.34 E
Frederiksborg □[6] 41 55.56 N 12.18 E
Frederiksborg Slot ⊥ 41 55.56 N 12.19 E
Frederikshåb (Paamiut) 176 62.00 N 49.43 W
Frederikshavn 26 57.26 N 10.32 E
Frederikssund 41 55.50 N 12.04 E
Frederiksted 241n 17.43 N 64.53 W
Frederiksværk 41 55.58 N 12.02 E
Frederik Willem IV Vallen ∟ 250 3.28 N 57.37 W
Fredersdorf bei Berlin 54 52.31 N 13.44 E
Fredonia, Col. 246 5.55 N 75.41 W
Fredonia, Az., U.S. 200 36.03 N 112.08 W
Fredonia, Ks., U.S. 198 37.32 N 95.49 W
Fredonia, N.Y., U.S. 214 42.26 N 79.19 W
Fredonia, N.D., U.S. 198 46.19 N 99.05 W
Fredonia, Pa., U.S. 214 41.20 N 80.14 W
Fredrika 26 64.05 N 18.24 E
Fredriksberg 40 60.08 N 14.23 E
Fredrikstad 26 59.13 N 10.57 E
Freeburg, Il., U.S. 219 38.25 N 89.54 W
Freeburg, Mo., U.S. 219 38.18 N 91.55 W
Freeburg, Pa., U.S. 208 40.46 N 76.57 W
Freedom, Ca., U.S. 226 36.56 N 121.46 W
Freedom, Pa., U.S. 214 40.40 N 80.14 W
Freehold, N.J., U.S. 208 40.15 N 74.16 W
Freehold, N.Y., U.S. 210 42.22 N 74.03 W
Freeland, Mi., U.S. 190 43.31 N 84.07 W
Freeland, Pa., U.S. 210 41.01 N 75.53 W
Freeland, Wa., U.S. 224 48.01 N 122.32 W
Freeland Park 216 40.37 N 87.30 W
Freeling, Mount ∧ 162 22.35 S 133.06 E
Freel Peak ∧ 226 38.52 N 119.54 W
Freels, Cape >, Nf., Can. 186 49.15 N 53.28 W
Freels, Cape >, Nf., Can. 186 46.37 N 53.33 W
Freeman 198 43.21 N 97.26 W
Freeman ≐ 182 54.20 N 114.47 W
Freeman, Lake ⊜ 216 40.42 N 86.45 W
Freemansburg 210 40.37 N 75.20 W
Freemount 48 52.16 N 8.53 W
Freeport, Ba. 238 26.30 N 78.45 W
Freeport, N.S., Can. 186 44.17 N 66.19 W
Freeport, On., Can. 212 43.25 N 80.25 W
Freeport, Fl., U.S. 194 30.29 N 86.08 W
Freeport, Il., U.S. 190 42.17 N 89.37 W
Freeport, Me., U.S. 188 43.51 N 70.06 W
Freeport, Mi., U.S. 216 42.45 N 85.18 W
Freeport, N.Y., U.S. 210 40.39 N 73.35 W
Freeport, Oh., U.S. 214 40.12 N 81.15 W
Freeport, Pa., U.S. 210 40.40 N 79.41 W
Freeport, Tx., U.S. 222 28.57 N 95.21 W
Freer 196 27.52 N 98.37 W
Freest 54 54.08 N 13.43 E
Freeston 222 31.32 N 96.15 W
Freestone 171a 28.08 S 152.08 E
Freestone □[6] 222 31.44 N 96.10 W
Freetown, Antig. 240c 17.03 N 61.42 W
Freetown, S.L. 150 8.30 N 13.15 W
Freetown, In., U.S. 218 38.58 N 86.07 W
Freetown, N.Y., U.S. 207 40.58 N 72.11 W
Freeville 210 42.30 N 76.20 W
Freewood Acres 208 40.10 N 74.15 W
Freezeout Lake ⊜ 202 47.40 N 112.03 W
Fregenal de la Sierra 34 38.10 N 6.39 W
Fregene ◆[8] 66 41.51 N 12.12 E
Freiberg 54 50.54 N 13.20 E
Freiberger Mulde ≐ 54 51.10 N 12.48 E
Freiburg → Świebodzice 30 50.52 N 16.19 E
Freiburg → Fribourg 58 46.48 N 7.09 E
Freiburg □[5] 58 48.00 N 8.25 E
Freiburg an der Elbe 52 53.49 N 9.17 E
Freiburger Mulde ≐ 54 51.10 N 12.48 E
Freiburg im Breisgau 58 47.59 N 7.51 E
Freienbach 58 47.12 N 8.45 E
Freienhufen 54 51.35 N 13.58 E
Freienwalde in Pommern → Chociwel 30 53.28 N 15.19 E
Freie Universität ♥[2] 264a 52.26 N 13.16 E
Freigericht 56 50.08 N 9.07 E
Freihung 60 49.37 N 11.55 E
Freiland 61 47.58 N 15.34 E
Freilassing 64 47.50 N 12.59 E
Freilingen 56 50.33 N 7.50 E
Freinberg 60 48.34 N 13.31 E
Freinsheim 56 49.30 N 8.13 E
Freirina 252 28.30 S 71.06 W
Freisen 56 49.33 N 7.14 E
Freisenbruch ◆[8] 263 51.27 N 7.06 E
Freising 60 48.23 N 11.44 E
Freistadt, Öst. 61 48.31 N 14.31 E
Freistadt → Kożuchów, Pol. 30 51.45 N 15.35 E
Freital 54 51.00 N 13.39 E
Freiwaldau → Gozdnica 30 51.26 N 15.06 E
Freiwalde 54 51.58 N 13.44 E
Freixial 266c 38.54 N 9.09 W
Fréjus 62 43.26 N 6.44 E
Fréjus, Tunnel du ◆[5] 62 45.08 N 6.40 E
Frémainville 261 49.04 N 1.52 E
Fremantle 168a 32.03 S 115.45 E
Fremdingen 56 48.58 N 10.27 E
Fremington 42 51.04 N 4.07 W
Fremont, Ca., U.S. 226 37.32 N 121.59 W
Fremont, In., U.S. 216 41.43 N 84.55 W
Fremont, Ia., U.S. 190 41.12 N 92.26 W
Fremont, Mi., U.S. 190 43.28 N 85.56 W
Fremont, Ne., U.S. 198 41.26 N 96.29 W
Fremont, N.C., U.S. 192 35.32 N 77.58 W
Fremont, Oh., U.S. 214 41.21 N 83.07 W
Fremont, Wi., U.S. 190 44.15 N 88.51 W
Fremont ≐ 200 38.24 N 110.42 W
Fremont Canyon V 280 33.48 N 117.42 W
Fremont Island I 200 41.09 N 112.20 W
Fremont Lake ⊜ 202 42.57 N 109.49 W
Fremont Peak ∧, Ca., U.S. 226 36.46 N 121.30 W
Fremont Peak ∧, Ca., U.S. 228 35.12 N 117.27 W
Fremont Valley V 228 35.10 N 118.00 W
French ≐ 190 45.56 N 80.54 W
French Broad ≐ 192 35.57 N 83.51 W
Frenchburg 192 37.57 N 83.37 W
French Camp 226 37.53 N 121.16 W
Frenchcap Cay I 240m 18.14 N 64.51 W
French Creek ≐, Mb., Can. 184 57.02 N 92.12 W
French Creek ≐, U.S. 214 41.25 N 79.50 W
French Creek ≐, Oh., U.S. 279a 41.27 N 82.07 W
French Creek ≐, Pa., U.S. 208 40.08 N 75.31 W
French Creek ≐, S.D., U.S. 198 43.38 N 102.55 W
French Creek, South Branch ≐, Pa., U.S. 214 41.54 N 79.54 W
French Creek, South Branch ≐, Pa., U.S. 285 40.10 N 75.42 W
French Creek, West Branch ≐ 214 41.58 N 79.52 W
French Creek State Park ♠ 208 40.13 N 75.47 W
French Frigate Shoals ✣[2] 14 23.45 N 166.10 W
French Guiana (Guyane français) □[2], S.A. 242 4.00 N 53.00 W
French Guiana (Guyane français) □[2], S.A. 250 4.00 N 53.00 W
French Island I 169 38.21 S 145.21 E
French Lick 194 38.32 N 86.37 W
Frenchman (Frenchman Creek) ≐ 202 48.24 N 107.05 W
Frenchman Bay c 188 44.25 N 68.10 W
Frenchman Butte 184 53.35 N 109.38 W

Symbols in the index entries represent the broad categories identified in the key at the right. Symbols with superior numbers (⋏[1]) identify subcategories (see complete key on page *I · 1).*

Symbole im Register stellen die rechts im Schlüssel erklärten Kategorien dar. Symbole mit hochgestellten Ziffern (⋏[1]) bezeichnen Unterabteilungen einer Kategorie (vgl. vollständiger Schlüssel auf Seite *I · 1).*

Los símbolos incluídos en el texto del índice representan las grandes categorias identificadas con la clave a la derecha. Los símbolos con numeros en su parte superior (⋏[1]) identifican las subcategorías (véase la clave completa en la página *I · 1).*

Les symboles de l'index représentent les catégories indiquées dans la légende à droite. Les symboles suivis d'un indice (⋏[1]) représentent des sous-catégories (voir légende complète à la page *I · 1).*

Os símbolos incluídos no texto do índice representam as grandes categorias identificadas com a chave à direita. Os símbolos com números em sua parte superior (⋏[1]) identificam as subcategorias (veja-se a chave completa à página *I · 1).*

	English	Deutsch	Español	Français	Português
∧	Mountain	Berg	Montaña	Montagne	Montanha
⋏	Mountains	Gebirge	Montañas	Montagnes	Montanhas
)(	Pass	Paß	Paso	Col	Passo
V	Valley, Canyon	Tal, Cañon	Valle, Cañón	Vallée, Canyon	Vale, Canhão
≚	Plain	Ebene	Llano	Plaine	Planície
>	Cape	Kap	Cabo	Cap	Cabo
I	Island	Insel	Isla	Île	Ilha
II	Islands	Inseln	Islas	Îles	Ilhas
≛	Other Topographic Features	Andere Topographische Objekte	Otros Elementos Topográficos	Autres données topographiques	Outros acidentes topográficos

ESPAÑOL — FRANÇAIS — PORTUGUÊS

Nombre / Nom / Nome	Página / Page / Página	Lat.°′	Long.°′ W = Oeste / W = Ouest / W = Oeste
Frenchman Creek (Frenchman) ≃, N.A.	202	48.24 N	107.05 W
Frenchman Creek ≃, U.S.	198	40.13 N	100.50 W
Frenchman Lake ⊜	204	36.48 N	116.56 W
Frenchman Point ≻	212	44.35 N	81.18 W
Frenchman's Bay ⊂	275b	43.49 N	79.05 W
Frenchmans Cap ∧	166	42.16 S	145.50 E
Frenchman's Creek ≃, On., Can.	284a	42.56 N	78.56 W
Frenchmans Creek ≃, Ca., U.S.	282	37.29 N	122.27 W
French Meadows Reservoir ⊜[1]	226	39.07 N	120.25 W
Frenchpark	48	53.52 N	8.26 W
French Pass	172	40.56 S	173.50 E
French Polynesia □[2]	14	15.00 S	140.00 W
Frenchs Forest	274a	33.45 S	151.14 E
French Southern and Antarctic Territories □[2]	6	49.30 S	69.30 E
French Stream ≃	283	42.07 N	70.53 W
Frenchtown	210	40.31 N	75.03 W
Frenda	148	35.02 N	1.01 E
Freneuse	261	49.03 N	1.36 E
Frensdorferhaar	52	52.25 N	7.03 E
Frenštát pod Radhoštěm	30	49.33 N	18.14 E
Frentani, Monti dei ⌃	66	41.54 N	14.37 E
Frépillon	261	49.03 N	2.12 E
Frere	158	28.52 S	29.47 E
Freren	52	52.29 N	7.32 E
Fresco	150	5.05 N	5.34 W
Fresco ≃	250	6.39 S	51.59 W
Freshfield	262	53.34 N	3.04 W
Freshfield, Mount ∧	182	51.44 N	116.57 W
Freshford	48	52.43 N	7.24 W
Fresh Meadows ⧫[8]	276	40.44 N	73.48 W
Fresh Pond ⊜, Ma., U.S.	283	42.23 N	71.09 W
Fresh Pond ⊜, N.Y., U.S.	276	40.55 N	73.18 W
Freshwater	42	50.40 N	1.30 W
Freshwater Creek ≃	226	39.12 N	122.04 W
Fresia	254	41.09 S	73.27 W
Fresnes	261	48.45 N	2.19 E
Fresne-Saint-Mamès	58	47.33 N	5.52 E
Fresnes-en-Woëvre	56	49.08 N	5.39 E
Fresnes-sur-Escaut	50	50.26 N	3.35 E
Fresnes-sur-Marne	261	48.56 N	2.45 E
Fresnillo	234	23.10 N	102.53 W
Fresno, Col.	246	5.09 N	75.01 W
Fresno, Ca., U.S.	226	36.44 N	119.46 W
Fresno, Oh., U.S.	214	40.20 N	81.44 W
Fresno, Tx., U.S.	222	29.32 N	95.27 W
Fresno □[6]	226	36.38 N	119.45 W
Fresno ≃	226	37.05 N	120.33 W
Fresno, Lewis Fork ≃	226	37.20 N	119.39 W
Fresno Air Terminal ⊠	226	36.46 N	119.43 W
Fresno Reservoir ⊜[1]	202	48.41 N	109.57 W
Fresno Slough ≃	226	36.47 N	120.22 W
Fresnoy-Folny	50	49.53 N	1.26 E
Fresnoy-le-Grand	50	49.57 N	3.25 E
Fressenneville	50	50.04 N	1.34 E
Fressin	50	50.27 N	2.03 E
Freswick	46	58.35 N	3.05 W
Fréteval	50	47.53 N	1.13 E
Frétigney-et-Velloreille	58	47.29 N	5.56 E
Fretin	50	50.33 N	3.08 E
Frettes	58	47.41 N	5.34 E
Freu, Cap des ≻	34	39.45 N	3.27 E
Freudenberg, B.R.D.	56	49.44 N	9.19 E
Freudenberg, B.R.D.	56	50.54 N	7.52 E
Freudenberg, D.D.R.	264a	52.42 N	13.49 E
Freudenstadt	58	48.28 N	8.25 E
Frévent	50	50.16 N	2.17 E
Frew ≃	162	20.00 S	135.38 E
Frewena	162	19.25 S	135.25 E
Frewsburg	214	42.03 N	79.09 W
Freyburg	54	51.13 N	11.46 E
Freycinet, Cape ≻	162	34.06 S	114.59 E
Freycinet Estuary ⊂[1]	162	26.25 S	113.45 E
Freycinet National Park ♠	166	42.10 S	148.20 E
Freycinet Peninsula ≻[1]	166	42.13 S	148.18 E
Freyenstein	54	53.17 N	12.20 E
Freyming-Merlebach	56	49.09 N	6.48 E
Freyre	252	31.10 S	62.06 W
Freystadt	60	49.12 N	11.20 E
Freyung	60	48.48 N	13.33 E
Fria	150	10.05 N	13.32 W
Fria, Cape ≻	152	18.30 S	12.01 E
Friant	226	36.59 N	119.42 W
Friant Dam ⧫[6]	226	37.00 N	119.43 W
Friant-Kern Canal ≍	226	35.22 N	119.06 W
Friars Point	194	34.22 N	90.38 W
Frías, Arg.	252	28.39 S	65.09 W
Frías, Perú	248	4.52 S	79.57 W
Fribourg (Freiburg)	58	46.48 N	7.09 E
Fribourg (Freiburg) □[3]	58	46.45 N	7.05 E
Frick	58	47.31 N	8.01 E
Frick Park ♠	279b	40.26 N	79.54 W
Friday	222	31.07 N	95.15 W
Friday Harbor	224	48.32 N	123.00 W
Fridaythorpe	44	54.01 N	0.40 W
Fridingen an der Donau	58	48.01 N	8.56 E
Fridley	190	45.05 N	93.15 W
Fridolfing	60	48.00 N	12.49 E
Fridtjof Nansen, Mount ∧	9	85.21 S	167.33 W
Friedberg, B.R.D.	56	50.20 N	8.45 E
Friedberg, B.R.D.	58	48.21 N	10.58 E
Friedberg, Öst.	61	47.27 N	16.03 E
Friedeberg in der Neumark → Strzelce Krajeńskie	30	52.53 N	15.32 E
Friedeburg	54	51.37 N	11.44 E
Friedenau ⧫[8]	264a	52.28 N	13.20 E
Friedens	214	40.03 N	79.00 W
Friedensburg	208	40.36 N	76.14 W
Friedersdorf, D.D.R.	54	51.01 N	14.34 E
Friedersdorf, D.D.R.	54	52.17 N	13.47 E
Friedersdorf, D.D.R.	54	51.39 N	12.21 E
Friedesheim	158	27.55 S	26.43 E
Friedland, B.R.D.	56	51.25 N	9.55 E
Friedland, D.D.R.	54	53.40 N	13.33 E
Friedland, D.D.R.	54	52.06 N	14.16 E
Friedland → Mieroszów, Pol.	30	50.41 N	16.10 E
Friedrich-Ebert-Brücke ⧫[5]	263	51.28 N	6.43 E
Friedrich Krupp-Aktiengesellschaft ♡[3]	263	51.28 N	7.00 E
Friedrichroda	54	50.52 N	10.34 E
Friedrichsbrunn	54	51.41 N	11.02 E
Friedrichsdorf	56	50.15 N	8.38 E
Friedrichsfeld	263	51.38 N	6.39 E
Friedrichsfelde ⧫[8]	264a	52.31 N	13.31 E
Friedrichshafen	58	47.39 N	9.28 E
Friedrichshagen ⧫[8]	264a	52.27 N	13.38 E
Friedrichshof	264a	52.19 N	13.46 E
Friedrichsort ⧫[8]	54	54.24 N	10.11 E
Friedrichsruh, Schloss ⊥	52	53.32 N	10.20 E
Friedrichsruhe	54	53.31 N	11.45 E
Friedrichstadt	41	54.22 N	9.05 E
Friedrichsthal, B.R.D.	56	49.19 N	7.06 E
Friedrichsthal, D.D.R.	54	52.48 N	13.16 E
Friedrichstrasse, Bahnhof ⧫[5]	264a	52.31 N	13.24 E
Friedrichswalde	54	53.02 N	13.42 E
Frielas	266c	38.49 N	9.09 W
Frielendorf	56	50.58 N	9.19 E
Friemersheim ⧫[8]	263	51.23 N	6.42 E
Friend, Ne., U.S.	198	40.39 N	97.17 W
Friend, Or., U.S.	224	45.21 N	121.16 W
Friends Colony ⧫[8]	272a	28.34 N	77.16 E
Friendship, N.Y., U.S.	210	42.12 N	78.08 W
Friendship, Tn., U.S.	194	35.54 N	89.14 W
Friendship, Wi., U.S.	190	43.58 N	89.49 W
Friendship Creek ≃	285	39.55 N	74.43 W
Friendship Shoal ✣[2]	112	5.58 N	112.31 E
Friends Meeting House State Memorial ⊥	214	40.09 N	80.47 W
Friendswood	222	29.31 N	95.12 W
Friern Barnet ⧫[8]	260	51.37 N	0.10 W
Fries	192	36.42 N	80.58 W
Friesach	61	46.57 N	14.24 E
Friesack	54	52.44 N	12.34 E
Friesenheim	58	48.22 N	7.53 E
Friesenhofen	58	47.45 N	10.04 E
Friesenried	58	47.52 N	10.31 E
Friesland □[4]	52	53.03 N	5.45 E
Friesland □[9]	30	53.00 N	5.40 E
Fries Mills	285	39.39 N	75.03 W
Friesoythe	52	53.01 N	7.51 E
Frigate Point ≻	174g	28.11 N	177.24 W
Frigento	68	41.01 N	15.06 E
Frignano	68	41.00 N	14.10 E
Frignano ⧫[1]	64	44.20 N	10.51 E
Friguia	150	12.03 N	10.56 W
Friitala	26	61.26 N	21.52 E
Frillendorf ⧫[8]	263	51.28 N	7.05 E
Frindsbury	260	51.24 N	0.30 E
Frinsted	260	51.17 N	0.43 E
Frinton-on-Sea	42	51.50 N	1.14 E
Frintrop ⧫[8]	263	51.29 N	6.55 E
Frío ≃, N.A.	236	11.08 N	84.46 W
Frio ≃, Tx., U.S.	196	28.30 N	98.10 W
Frio, Cabo ≻	255	22.53 S	42.00 W
Friockheim	46	56.38 N	2.38 W
Frio Draw V	196	34.50 N	102.19 W
Friona	196	34.38 N	102.43 W
Frisa, Loch ⊜	46	56.34 N	6.05 W
Frisange	56	49.32 N	6.12 E
Frisches Haff → Vislinskij zaliv ⊂	30	54.27 N	19.40 E
Frisco, Pa., U.S.	214	40.51 N	80.16 W
Frisco, Tx., U.S.	222	33.09 N	96.49 W
Frisco City	194	31.26 N	87.24 W
Frisco Creek ≃	196	36.34 N	101.23 W
Frisian Islands II	30	53.35 N	6.40 E
Friskney	44	53.04 N	0.11 E
Fristad	26	57.50 N	13.01 E
Fritch	196	35.38 N	101.36 W
Fritsla	26	57.33 N	12.47 E
Fritzlar	56	51.08 N	9.16 E
Friuli □[9]	64	46.00 N	13.00 E
Friuli-Venezia Giulia □[4]	64	46.00 N	13.00 E
Friza, proliv ų	74	45.30 N	149.10 E
Frizington	44	54.32 N	3.30 W
Frobisher	184	49.12 N	102.26 W
Frobisher Bay ⊂	176	62.30 N	66.00 W
Frobisher Lake ⊜	184	56.25 N	108.20 W
Frodsham	262	53.18 N	2.44 W
Frog Lake ⊜	184	53.55 N	110.18 W
Frohavet ų	24	63.52 N	9.26 E
Frohburg	54	51.03 N	12.33 E
Frohlinde ⧫[8]	263	51.32 N	7.21 E
Frohnau ⧫[8]	264a	52.38 N	13.18 E
Frohnhausen	263	51.29 N	7.48 E
Frohnhausen ⧫[8]	263	51.27 N	6.58 E
Frohnleiten	61	47.16 N	15.20 E
Frohse	54	52.02 N	11.43 E
Froid	198	48.20 N	104.30 W
Froid, Lac ⊜	206	46.40 N	74.32 W
Froid, Ruisseau ≃	206	46.23 N	74.46 W
Froidmont-Cohartille	50	49.41 N	3.42 E
Froidos	56	49.03 N	5.07 E
Froissy	50	49.34 N	2.13 E
Froitzheim	56	50.42 N	6.34 E
Frolišči, S.S.S.R.	80	56.25 N	42.39 E
Frolišči, S.S.S.R.	82	56.18 N	39.13 E
Frolovo	80	49.47 N	43.39 E
Froman Run ≃	279b	40.12 N	80.00 W
Fromberg	202	45.23 N	108.54 W
Frombork	30	54.22 N	19.41 E
Frome	42	51.14 N	2.20 W
Frome ≃, Austl.	166	29.06 S	137.52 E
Frome ≃, Eng., U.K.	42	52.03 N	2.38 W
Frome ≃, Eng., U.K.	42	50.41 N	2.04 W
Frome, Lake ⊜	166	30.48 S	139.48 E
Frome Downs	166	31.13 S	139.46 E
Fromelennes	56	50.08 N	4.52 E
Fromentières	50	48.54 N	3.43 E
Frömern	263	51.30 N	7.44 E
Frommern	58	48.15 N	8.52 E
Fröndenberg	56	51.28 N	7.46 E
Frönsberg	263	51.21 N	7.46 E
Fronteiras	250	7.05 S	40.37 W
Frontenac, Fl., U.S.	220	28.27 N	80.46 W
Frontenac, Ks., U.S.	198	37.27 N	94.41 W
Frontenac □[6], On., Can.	212	44.40 N	76.45 W
Frontenac □[6], P.Q., Can.	206	45.42 N	71.15 W
Frontenard	58	46.55 N	5.10 E
Frontenex-Villard-Rosset	62	45.38 N	6.19 E
Frontera	234	18.32 N	92.38 W
Frontera, Punta ≻	234	18.36 N	92.42 W
Fronteras	200	30.56 N	109.31 W
Frontier, Sk., Can.	184	49.12 N	108.34 W
Frontier, Mi., U.S.	216	41.47 N	84.36 W
Frontier, Wy., U.S.	200	41.48 N	110.32 W
Frontignan	62	43.27 N	3.45 E
Frontino	246	6.46 N	76.08 W
Frontino, Páramo ∧	246	6.28 N	76.04 W
Frontón, Isla I	286d	12.07 S	77.11 W
Front Range ⌃, Leso.	158	29.05 S	28.20 E
Front Range ⌃, Co., U.S.	200	39.45 N	105.45 W
Front Royal	188	38.55 N	78.11 W
Frose	54	51.48 N	11.23 E
Frosinone	66	41.38 N	13.19 E
Frosinone □[4]	66	41.37 N	13.27 E
Frosna ≻[1]	26	63.45 N	10.25 E
Frosolone	66	41.36 N	14.27 E
Frösön	26	63.11 N	14.32 E
Frost	222	32.05 N	96.48 W
Frostavallen	41	55.58 N	13.30 E
Frostburg	188	39.39 N	78.55 W
Frost Creek ≃	276	40.54 N	73.37 W
Frostproof	220	27.44 N	81.31 W
Frotheim	52	52.21 N	8.40 E
Frouard	56	48.46 N	6.08 E
Frövi	40	59.28 N	15.22 E
Frøya I	24	63.43 N	8.42 E
Fruges	50	50.31 N	2.08 E
Fruita	200	39.09 N	108.43 W
Fruitdale, Al., U.S.	194	31.20 N	88.24 W
Fruitdale, Or., U.S.	202	42.24 N	123.20 W
Fruithurst	194	33.43 N	85.26 W
Fruitland, Id., U.S.	202	44.00 N	116.54 W
Fruitland, Md., U.S.	208	38.19 N	75.37 W
Fruitland Park	220	28.51 N	81.54 W
Fruitport	216	43.07 N	86.09 W
Fruitvale, B.C., Can.	182	49.07 N	117.33 W
Fruitvale, Tx., U.S.	222	32.41 N	95.48 W
Fruitvale, Wa., U.S.	202	46.37 N	120.33 W
Fruitville	192	27.19 N	82.27 W
Frumușita	38	45.40 N	28.04 E
Frunze, S.S.S.R.	78	46.16 N	34.52 E
Frunze, S.S.S.R.	83	48.40 N	38.45 E
Frunze, S.S.S.R.	85	40.07 N	71.44 E
Frunze, S.S.S.R.	85	42.54 N	74.36 E
Frunze □[4]	85	42.30 N	74.00 E
Frunzovka	78	47.20 N	29.44 E
Frutal	255	20.02 S	48.55 W
Frutigen	58	46.35 N	7.39 E
Frutillar	254	41.07 S	73.03 W
Fryburg	214	41.21 N	79.26 W
Frýdek-Místek	30	49.41 N	18.22 E
Frýdlant	30	50.56 N	15.05 E
Frye	279b	40.11 N	79.56 W
Fryeburg	188	44.00 N	70.58 W
Fryerning	260	51.41 N	0.22 E
Fryingpan ≃	200	39.22 N	107.02 W
Fu ≃, Zhg.	100	28.36 N	116.04 E
Fu ≃, Zhg.	100	29.52 N	115.28 E
Fu ≃, Zhg.	102	29.59 N	106.16 E
Fua'amotu	174w	21.16 S	175.08 W
Fua'amotu International Airport ⊠	174w	21.17 S	175.08 W
Fu'an, Zhg.	100	27.08 N	119.40 E
Fu'an, Zhg.	100	32.41 N	120.41 E
Fuanjie	100	25.29 N	117.53 E
Fubao	107	28.47 N	106.05 E
Fubine	62	44.58 N	8.26 E
Fucecchio	66	43.44 N	10.48 E
Fuchang	100	30.06 N	113.08 E
Fucheng	98	37.52 N	116.07 E
Fuchikou	100	29.51 N	115.27 E
Fuchow → Fuzhou	100	28.01 N	116.20 E
Fuchs-Berg ∧[2]	264a	52.27 N	13.51 E
Fuchskaute ∧	56	50.27 N	7.52 E
Füchtorf	52	52.03 N	8.02 E
Fuchū, Nihon	94	35.40 N	139.29 E
Fuchū, Nihon	94	36.39 N	137.10 E
Fuchū, Nihon	96	34.24 N	132.30 E
Fuchū, Nihon	96	34.34 N	133.14 E
Fuchun ≃	106	30.10 N	120.09 E
Fucine	64	46.18 N	10.44 E
Fucino, Conca del ≚	66	42.01 N	13.31 E
Fudan University ♡[2]	269b	31.17 N	121.29 E
Fuday I	46	57.03 N	7.23 W
Fuding	100	27.21 N	120.12 E
Fudu ≃	107	29.52 N	106.10 E
Fuefuki ≃	94	35.33 N	138.28 E
Fuelbeckestausee ⊜[1]	263	51.15 N	7.40 E
Fuencaliente	34	38.24 N	4.18 W
Fuencarral ⧫[8]	266a	40.30 N	3.41 W
Fuenlabrada	266a	40.17 N	3.48 W
Fuensalida	34	40.03 N	4.12 W
Fuensanta, Embalse de ⊜[1]	34	38.23 N	2.13 W
Fuente	196	28.40 N	100.32 W
Fuente de Cantos	34	38.15 N	6.18 W
Fuente de Oro	246	3.28 N	73.37 W
Fuenteobejuna	34	38.16 N	5.25 W
Fuentesaúco	34	41.14 N	5.30 W
Fuentes de Ebro	34	41.31 N	0.38 W
Fuerli	105	39.40 N	116.41 E
Fuerte ≃	232	25.54 N	109.22 W
Fuerte Olimpo	248	21.02 S	57.54 W
Fuerteventura I	148	28.20 N	14.00 W
Fuerza, Castillo de la ⊥	286b	23.09 N	82.21 W
Fufeng	102	34.20 N	107.51 E
Fuga Island I	116	18.52 N	121.22 E
Fugama, Wādī V	140	14.43 N	24.36 E
Fügen	64	47.21 N	11.51 E
Fuglebjerg	41	55.18 N	11.34 E
Fugløysund ų	24	70.12 N	20.20 E
Fugong	102	27.09 N	98.52 E
Fugou	98	34.04 N	114.24 E
Fuhai	86	47.06 N	87.23 E
Fuhe	100	23.22 N	113.37 E
Fuhlenbrock ⧫[8]	263	51.32 N	6.54 E
Fuhrberg	52	52.34 N	9.50 E
Fuhse ≃	52	52.37 N	10.03 E
Fuhsien → Fuxian	98	39.37 N	122.01 E
Fuhu	100	29.11 N	118.04 E
Fuji, Nihon	94	35.09 N	138.39 E
Fuji, Zhg.	98	34.24 N	114.48 E
Fuji, Zhg.	107	29.09 N	105.23 E
Fuji ≃	94	35.07 N	138.39 E
Fuji, Mount → Fuji-san ∧[1]	94	35.22 N	138.44 E
Fujiafeng	105	39.11 N	117.32 E
Fujian (Fukien) □[4]	100	26.00 N	118.00 E
Fujiatun	104	41.42 N	123.44 E
Fujiawopu	104	40.58 N	122.14 E
Fujiazhen	107	29.57 N	104.18 E
Fujiazhuangcun	104	41.15 N	122.20 E
Fujie	106	31.09 N	119.27 E
Fujieda	94	34.52 N	138.16 E
Fuji-Hakone-Izu-kokuritsu-kōen ♠	94	35.21 N	138.44 E
Fujiidera	96	34.34 N	135.36 E
Fujikawa	94	35.08 N	138.37 E
Fujikubo	268	35.50 N	139.32 E
Fujimi, Nihon	94	36.27 N	139.05 E
Fujimi, Nihon	94	35.55 N	138.15 E
Fujimi, Nihon	94	35.51 N	139.33 E
Fujin	89	47.14 N	132.00 E
Fujino	94	35.37 N	139.10 E
Fujinomiya	94	35.12 N	138.38 E
Fujioka, Nihon	94	35.12 N	137.12 E
Fujioka, Nihon	94	36.15 N	139.05 E
Fujioka, Nihon	94	36.15 N	139.39 E
Fuji-san ∧[1]	94	35.22 N	138.44 E
Fujisawa	94	35.21 N	139.29 E
Fujishiro	94	35.55 N	140.07 E
Fujiwara, Nihon	94	36.51 N	139.44 E
Fujiwara, Nihon	94	35.09 N	136.30 E
Fujiwara-dam ⧫[6]	94	36.49 N	139.02 E
Fujiyama → Fuji-san ∧[1]	94	35.22 N	138.44 E
Fuji-yoshida	94	35.29 N	138.48 E
Fukagawa	92a	43.43 N	142.03 E
Fukagawa ⧫[8]	268	35.40 N	139.48 E
Fukami	268	35.28 N	139.28 E
Fukane I	174w	21.05 S	175.02 W
Fukang	86	44.10 N	87.59 E
Fukasaka-tunnel ⧫[5]	94	35.35 N	136.10 E
Fuka Shan ∧	89	47.55 N	120.53 E
Fukaya	94	36.12 N	139.17 E
Fukiage	94	36.06 N	139.27 E
Fukiai ⧫[8]	270	34.42 N	135.12 E
Fukien → Fujian □[4]	100	26.00 N	118.00 E
Fukou, Zhg.	100	26.28 N	117.40 E
Fukou, Zhg.	100	25.45 N	118.28 E
Fukube	96	35.33 N	134.18 E
Fukuchiyama	96	35.18 N	135.07 E
Fukude	94	34.40 N	137.53 E
Fukue	92	32.41 N	128.50 E
Fukuei Chiao ≻	100	25.18 N	121.32 E
Fukue-jima I	92	32.40 N	128.45 E
Fukui, Nihon	94	36.04 N	136.13 E
Fukui, Nihon	270	34.51 N	135.34 E
Fukui □[5]	92	36.00 N	136.15 E
Fukuma	96	33.46 N	130.28 E
Fukumitsu	94	36.33 N	136.52 E
Fukuno	94	36.35 N	136.55 E
Fukuoka, Nihon	94	35.34 N	137.27 E
Fukuoka, Nihon	94	36.42 N	136.56 E
Fukuoka, Nihon	96	33.35 N	130.24 E
Fukuoka □[5]	96	33.45 N	130.30 E
Fukuoka-chūtonchi, Rikujō-jieitai- ■	96	33.32 N	130.28 E
Fukuroda-no-taki ⌞	94	36.46 N	140.25 E
Fukuroi	94	34.45 N	137.55 E
Fukushima, Nihon	92	37.45 N	140.28 E
Fukushima, Nihon	92a	41.29 N	140.15 E
Fukushima □[5]	94	37.08 N	140.00 E
Fukushima ⧫[8]	270	34.42 N	135.29 E
Fukusumi	270	34.37 N	135.56 E
Fukutani ⧫[8]	270	34.43 N	135.02 E
Fukuyama	96	34.29 N	133.22 E
Fukuzaki	96	34.57 N	134.45 E
Fulacunda	150	11.44 N	15.03 W
Fūlādī, Kūh-e ∧	120	34.38 N	67.32 E
Fūlād Maḥalleh	128	36.02 N	53.44 E
Fulanga Island I	175g	19.08 S	178.34 W
Fulanga Passage ų	175g	19.00 S	178.40 W
Fulbourn	42	52.11 N	0.13 E
Fulda, B.R.D.	56	50.33 N	9.41 E
Fulda, Mn., U.S.	198	43.52 N	95.36 W
Fulda ≃	30	51.25 N	9.39 E
Fuldatal	56	51.22 N	9.31 E
Fuldera	58	46.37 N	10.22 E
Fule	102	25.27 N	104.19 E
Fulerum ⧫[8]	263	51.26 N	6.57 E
Fulford Harbour	224	48.46 N	123.27 W
Fulgatore	70	37.57 N	12.42 E
Fulham ⧫[8]	260	51.29 N	0.12 W
Fuli	100	23.11 N	121.14 E
Fuliji	100	33.46 N	116.58 E
Fuling	102	29.42 N	107.21 E
Fulitun	89	46.42 N	131.10 E
Fullarton ≃	166	20.15 S	141.10 E
Fullen ⊜	40	60.31 N	16.09 E
Fuller Springs	222	31.18 N	94.41 W
Fullerton, Ca., U.S.	228	33.52 N	117.55 W
Fullerton, Ky., U.S.	218	38.43 N	82.58 W
Fullerton, Md., U.S.	284b	39.22 N	76.31 W
Fullerton, Ne., U.S.	198	41.21 N	97.58 W
Fullerton, Pa., U.S.	208	40.38 N	75.28 W
Fullerton Municipal Airport ⊠	280	33.52 N	117.59 W
Fullerton Point ≻	240c	17.06 N	61.54 W
Fulmer	260	51.33 N	0.34 W
Fulong	102	22.57 N	107.41 E
Fulongchang	107	30.03 N	103.38 E
Fulongquan	89	44.22 N	124.36 E
Fulpmes	64	47.10 N	11.21 E
Fulshear	222	29.41 N	95.54 W
Fulton, Al., U.S.	194	31.47 N	87.43 W
Fulton, Ar., U.S.	194	33.36 N	93.48 W
Fulton, Il., U.S.	190	41.52 N	90.09 W
Fulton, In., U.S.	216	40.56 N	86.15 W
Fulton, Ks., U.S.	198	38.00 N	94.43 W
Fulton, Ky., U.S.	194	36.30 N	88.52 W
Fulton, Md., U.S.	208	39.09 N	76.55 W
Fulton, Mi., U.S.	216	47.17 N	88.21 W
Fulton, Ms., U.S.	194	34.16 N	88.24 W
Fulton, Mo., U.S.	219	38.50 N	91.56 W
Fulton, N.Y., U.S.	210	43.19 N	76.25 W
Fulton, Oh., U.S.	214	40.27 N	82.49 W
Fulton, Tx., U.S.	196	28.04 N	97.02 W
Fulton □[6], Il., U.S.	219	40.13 N	90.17 W
Fulton □[6], In., U.S.	216	41.04 N	86.13 W
Fulton □[6], N.Y., U.S.	210	43.00 N	74.22 W
Fulton □[6], Oh., U.S.	216	41.33 N	84.09 W
Fulton □[6], Pa., U.S.	214	40.06 N	78.04 W
Fulton ≃	182	54.48 N	126.07 W
Fultondale	194	33.36 N	86.47 W
Fultonham	210	42.31 N	75.03 W
Fultonville	210	42.57 N	74.22 W
Fuluchang	107	29.38 N	106.08 E
Fulufjället ∧	26	61.33 N	12.43 E
Fuluzhen	107	29.18 N	103.40 E
Fulwood	262	53.47 N	2.41 W
Fumaça	256	22.17 S	44.19 W
Fumahashi	94	36.42 N	137.19 E
Fumane	156	24.29 S	33.58 E
Fumay	56	49.59 N	4.42 E
Fumel	32	44.29 N	0.57 E
Fumin, Zhg.	102	25.16 N	102.26 E
Fumin, Zhg.	106	31.54 N	121.10 E
Fumintun	98	42.29 N	126.22 E
Fuminzhen	106	31.37 N	121.39 E
Funa ≃	273b	4.23 S	15.19 E
Funabashi	94	35.42 N	139.59 E
Funafuti I	14	8.31 S	179.13 E
Funagawa → Oga	92	39.53 N	139.51 E
Funakuyā	175d	24.30 N	124.17 E
Funan	100	32.39 N	115.32 E
Funan Gaba	144	4.25 N	37.57 E
Funaoka	96	35.23 N	134.14 E
Funasaka	270	34.48 N	135.17 E
Funäsdalen	26	62.32 N	12.33 E
Funchal	148	32.38 N	16.54 W
Funchal □[5]	148	32.40 N	16.55 W
Fundación	246	10.31 N	74.11 W
Fundão, Bra.	255	19.55 S	40.24 W
Fundão, Port.	34	40.08 N	7.30 W
Fundão, Ilha do I	287a	22.51 S	43.14 W
Funde	272c	18.54 N	72.58 E
Fundición de Avalos	232	28.35 N	106.00 W
Fundo ≃	250	10.12 S	44.39 W
Fundo, Arroio ≃	287a	22.58 S	43.22 W
Fundo, Córrego ≃	287b	23.46 S	46.47 W
Fundy, Bay of ⊂	186	45.00 N	66.00 W
Fundy National Park ♠	186	45.38 N	65.00 W
Fünfkirchen → Pécs	30	46.05 N	18.13 E
Funhalouro	156	23.03 S	34.25 E
Funil, Ribeirão do ≃	256	22.02 S	43.46 W
Funil, Rio do ≃	256	22.58 S	44.34 W
Funing, Zhg.	98	39.54 N	119.14 E
Funing, Zhg.	100	33.47 N	119.48 E
Funing, Zhg.	102	23.33 N	105.35 E
Funiuchang	107	29.03 N	106.33 E
Funiu Shan ⌃	100	33.40 N	112.30 E
Funk Island I	186	49.46 N	53.10 W
Funks Creek ≃	226	39.19 N	122.11 W
Funkturm ♡	264a	52.31 N	13.16 E
Funne ≃	263	51.42 N	7.36 E
Funnel Creek ≃	166	22.18 S	148.57 E
Funnel Hill ∧[2]	272c	18.54 N	73.07 E
Funo	96	34.53 N	132.47 E
Funshinagh, Lough ⊜	48	53.31 N	8.07 W
Funsi	150	10.17 N	1.58 W
Funtana Coberta ⊥	71	39.34 N	9.21 E
Funtua	150	11.31 N	7.17 E
Fuorn, Pass dal (Ofenpass))(	58	46.37 N	10.15 E
Fuping	102	34.47 N	109.07 E
Fuqiao	106	31.36 N	121.12 E
Fuqikou	100	29.44 N	117.48 E
Fuqing	100	25.44 N	119.22 E
Fuquay-Varina	192	35.35 N	78.48 W
Füramoos	58	48.00 N	9.53 E
Furancungo	154	14.55 S	33.35 E
Furano	92a	43.21 N	142.24 E
Furāt, Nahr al- → Euphrates ≃	128	31.00 N	47.25 E
Furci Siculo	70	37.57 N	15.23 E
Furculești	38	43.52 N	25.09 E
Fures	62	45.19 N	5.30 E
Fūrg	128	28.18 N	55.13 E
Furkapass)(	58	46.34 N	8.25 E
Furka-Tunnel ⧫[5]	58	46.33 N	8.26 E
Furlong	208	40.18 N	75.05 W
Furmanov	80	57.15 N	41.07 E
Furmanovka	86	44.17 N	72.57 E
Furmanovo	80	49.42 N	49.28 E
Furn, Wādī al- V	142	30.13 N	31.40 E
Furnace	46	56.09 N	5.10 W
Furnace Brook ≃	283	42.06 N	70.43 W
Furnace Creek ≃	284b	39.11 N	76.35 W
Furnace Pond ⊜	283	42.03 N	70.49 W
Furnari	70	38.07 N	15.08 E
Furnas, Represa de ⊜[1]	255	20.45 S	46.00 W
Furn ash-Shubbāk	132	33.52 N	35.31 E
Furneaux Group II	166	40.10 S	148.05 E
Furnes → Veurne	50	51.04 N	2.40 E
Furness Abbey ♡[1]	44	54.07 N	3.12 W
Furness Fells ⌃[2]	44	54.18 N	3.07 W
Furong Shan ∧	100	27.30 N	115.52 E
Furqlus	130	34.36 N	37.05 E
Fürstenau, B.R.D.	52	51.50 N	9.19 E
Fürstenau, B.R.D.	52	52.31 N	7.40 E
Fürstenberg, B.R.D.	52	51.44 N	9.24 E
Fürstenberg, D.D.R.	54	52.09 N	14.40 E
Fürstenberg/Havel	54	53.11 N	13.08 E
Fürstenfeld	61	47.03 N	16.05 E
Fürstenfeldbruck	60	48.10 N	11.15 E
Fürstenfelde → Boleszkowice	30	52.44 N	14.36 E
Fürstenhagen	56	51.12 N	9.41 E
Fürstenstein	60	48.43 N	13.20 E
Fürstenwalde	54	52.21 N	14.04 E
Fürstenwerder	54	53.24 N	13.34 E
Fürstenzell	60	48.32 N	13.19 E
Furtei	71	39.34 N	8.57 E
Fürth, B.R.D.	56	49.28 N	10.59 E
Fürth, B.R.D.	56	49.39 N	8.47 E
Furth im Wald	60	49.18 N	12.51 E
Furtwangen	58	48.03 N	8.12 E
Furuba ≃	256	23.21 S	44.57 W
Furubō-san ∧[2]	270	34.53 N	135.19 E
Furudal	26	61.10 N	15.08 E
Furudono	94	37.05 N	140.34 E
Furukawa, Nihon	92	38.34 N	140.58 E
Furukawa, Nihon	94	36.14 N	137.11 E
Furulund	41	55.46 N	13.04 E
Furusund	40	59.40 N	18.55 E
Furu-tone ≃	94	35.48 N	139.51 E
Furuvik	40	60.39 N	17.20 E
Furuyakami	268	35.55 N	139.32 E
Fürwiggestausee ⊜[1]	263	51.09 N	7.41 E
Fury and Hecla Strait ų	176	69.56 N	84.00 W
Fusagasugá	246	4.21 N	74.22 W
Fusain ≃	50	48.09 N	2.45 E
Fusan → Pusan	98	35.06 N	129.03 E
Fuscaldo	68	39.25 N	16.02 E
Fusch	64	47.13 N	12.49 E
Fuschl am See	64	47.48 N	13.18 E
Fuschun → Fushun	104	41.52 N	123.53 E
Fuse → Higashiōsaka, Nihon	96	34.39 N	135.35 E
Fuse, Nihon	268	35.53 N	140.00 E
Fushan, Zhg.	98	37.29 N	121.16 E
Fushan, Zhg.	102	35.58 N	111.51 E
Fushan, Zhg.	106	31.49 N	120.46 E
Fushimi ⧫[8]	270	34.55 N	135.46 E
Fushino ≃	96	34.03 N	131.24 E
Fushuigang	100	31.21 N	113.40 E
Fushun (Funan), Zhg.	104	41.52 N	123.53 E
Fushun, Zhg.	107	29.11 N	105.00 E
Fushuncheng	104	41.53 N	123.51 E
Fusignano	66	44.28 N	11.57 E
Fusilier	184	51.51 N	109.46 W
Fusin → Fuxin	104	42.03 N	121.46 E
Fusine in Valromana	64	46.30 N	13.39 E
Fusio	58	46.27 N	8.40 E
Fusō	94	35.21 N	136.55 E
Fusong	98	42.18 N	127.20 E
Fussa	94	35.45 N	139.20 E
Füssen	64	47.34 N	10.42 E
Fuste, Picacho del ∧	196	27.35 N	102.47 W
Fusui	102	22.32 N	107.56 E
Futa, Passo della)(	66	44.05 N	11.17 E
Futaba	94	35.41 N	138.30 E
Futago-san ∧	96	33.35 N	131.36 E
Futamata → Tenryū	94	34.52 N	137.49 E
Futamatagawa ⧫[8]	268	35.28 N	139.33 E
Futami, Nihon	94	34.30 N	136.47 E
Futami, Nihon	96	33.41 N	132.38 E
Futang, Zhg.	102	24.26 N	112.09 E
Futang, Zhg.	106	30.40 N	119.35 E
Futaoi-jima I	96	34.06 N	130.47 E
Futatabi-yama ∧	270	34.43 N	135.11 E
Futatsubashi ⧫[8]	268	35.28 N	139.30 E
Futatsu-ne I[2]	174f	24.46 N	141.18 E
Fu Tau Pun Chau I	271d	22.21 N	114.22 E
Futian	100	27.26 N	114.56 E
Futianhe	100	31.30 N	115.05 E
Futianpu	100	27.22 N	112.47 E
Futjāni ≃	126	24.06 N	90.09 E
Futschou → Fuzhou	100	26.06 N	119.17 E
Futtsu, Nihon	94	35.13 N	139.52 E
Futtsu, Nihon	94	35.19 N	139.49 E
Futtsu-misaki ≻	268	35.19 N	139.46 E
Futun ≃	100	26.51 N	117.46 E
Futuna I	175f	19.32 S	170.14 E
Futuna, Île I	14	14.15 S	178.09 W
Futuyu	105	39.18 N	114.50 E
Fuveau	62	43.27 N	5.34 E
Fuwah	142	31.12 N	30.33 E
Fuwen	86	47.13 N	89.39 E
Fuxi, Zhg.	100	27.14 N	119.50 E
Fuxi, Zhg.	100	25.14 N	113.52 E
Fuxi ≃	107	29.09 N	104.57 E
Fuxian (Wafangdian), Zhg.	98	39.37 N	122.01 E
Fuxian, Zhg.	102	36.02 N	109.13 E
Fuxian Hu ⊜	102	24.30 N	102.55 E
Fuxin, Zhg.	104	42.08 N	121.45 E
Fuxin, Zhg.	104	42.03 N	121.46 E
Fuxing, Zhg.	107	30.27 N	106.04 E
Fuxing, Zhg.	107	30.24 N	104.53 E
Fuxing, Zhg.	107	29.54 N	105.43 E
Fuxingchang	107	29.40 N	105.13 E
Fuxing Dao I	269b	31.17 N	121.23 E
Fuxinghao	104	42.35 N	120.32 E
Fuyang, Zhg.	100	23.36 N	116.37 E
Fuyang, Zhg.	100	32.54 N	115.49 E
Fuyang, Zhg.	100	30.03 N	119.57 E
Fuyang ≃	98	38.14 N	116.05 E
Fuyouertuo Shan ∧	89	45.52 N	119.48 E
Fuyu, Zhg.	89	47.49 N	124.27 E
Fuyu, Zhg.	89	45.10 N	124.50 E
Fuyuan, Zhg.	89	48.21 N	134.18 E
Fuyuan, Zhg.	102	25.39 N	104.12 E
Fuzhai	100	29.32 N	120.02 E
Fuzhong	102	24.28 N	111.22 E
Fuzhou, Zhg.	100	28.01 N	116.20 E
Fuzhou (Foochow), Zhg.	100	26.06 N	119.17 E
Fuzhoucheng	98	39.45 N	121.47 E
Fuzhuang	98	34.57 N	118.17 E
Fuzhuangyi	98	38.02 N	116.08 E
Fyfield	260	51.45 N	0.16 E
Fylde □[8]	262	53.46 N	2.53 W
Fylde ≻[1]	262	53.47 N	2.56 W
Fylland ≻[1]	41	56.00 N	9.15 E
Fyn □[6]	41	55.20 N	10.25 E
Fyn I	41	55.20 N	10.30 E
Fyne, Loch ⊂	46	56.00 N	5.24 W
Fyns Hoved ≻	41	55.37 N	10.36 E
Fyresvatn ⊜	26	59.06 N	8.12 E
Fyrisån ≃	40	59.47 N	17.39 E
Fysingen ⊜	40	59.34 N	17.55 E
Fyvie	46	57.25 N	2.23 W
Fzâra, Gara'et ⊜	36	36.47 N	7.30 E
G			
Ga	150	9.47 N	2.30 W
Gaaden	264b	48.03 N	16.12 E
Gaalkacyo	144	6.47 N	47.26 E
Gaanderen	52	51.56 N	6.21 E
Gabah	144	8.08 N	50.02 E
Gabai	146	11.05 N	11.39 E
Gabaldon	116	15.28 N	121.19 E
Gabare	38	43.19 N	23.55 E
Gabarus	186	45.50 N	60.09 W
Gabarus Bay ⊂	186	45.51 N	60.07 W
Gabas ≃	32	43.46 N	0.42 W
Gabbs	204	38.52 N	117.55 W
Gabby Heights	214	40.09 N	80.15 W
Gabela	152	10.48 S	14.20 E
Gaberones → Gaborone	156	24.45 S	25.55 E
Gabès	148	33.53 N	10.07 E
Gabès □[8]	148	33.15 N	9.00 E
Gabès, Golfe de ⊂	148	34.00 N	10.25 E
Gabia	152	4.34 S	17.07 E
Gabiarra	255	16.15 S	39.41 W
Gabicce Mare	66	43.58 N	12.46 E
Gabii ⊥	267a	41.54 N	12.43 E
Gabil	146	11.09 N	18.12 E
Gabilan Creek ≃	226	36.41 N	121.38 W
Gabilan Range ⌃	226	36.30 N	121.15 W
Gąbin	30	52.25 N	19.44 E
Gabir	140	8.35 N	24.40 E
Gable Mountain ∧	182	54.30 N	121.40 W
Gablenz	54	51.41 N	14.31 E
Gablingen	58	48.27 N	10.49 E
Gablitz	61	48.14 N	16.09 E
Gablonz → Jablonec nad Nisou	30	50.44 N	15.10 E
Gabon □[1], Afr.	138	1.00 S	11.45 E
Gabon □[1], Afr.	152	1.00 S	11.45 E
Gabon, Estuaire du ⊂[1]	152	0.25 N	9.20 E
Gaborone	156	24.45 S	25.55 E
Gabras	140	10.16 N	26.14 E
Gabria	64	45.52 N	13.34 E
Gabriel	250	11.14 S	41.53 W
Gabriel Strait ų	176	61.45 N	65.30 W
Gabriel y Galan, Embalse de ⊜[1]	34	40.15 N	6.15 W
Gabriel Zamora	234	19.05 N	102.05 W
Gābrīk	128	25.44 N	58.28 E
Gabriola	224	49.12 N	123.50 W
Gabriola Island I	224	49.10 N	123.47 W
Gabrovo	38	42.52 N	25.19 E
Gabun → Gabon □[1]	152	1.00 S	11.45 E
Gaby	62	45.43 N	7.53 E
Gacé	50	48.48 N	0.18 E
Gachetá	246	4.49 N	73.36 W
Gachpar	174q	9.33 N	138.10 E
Gachsārān	128	30.12 N	50.47 E
Gackle	198	46.37 N	99.08 W
Gacko	38	43.10 N	18.32 E
Gad'ač	78	50.22 N	34.00 E
Gadag	122	15.25 N	75.37 E
Gadamai	140	17.09 N	36.06 E
Gādarwāra	124	22.55 N	78.47 E
Gadbjerg	41	55.46 N	9.20 E
Gäddede	26	64.30 N	14.09 E
Gadderbaum	52	52.00 N	8.31 E
Gade ≃	260	51.38 N	0.28 W
Gadebusch	54	53.42 N	11.07 E
Gadein	140	8.11 N	28.44 E
Gadera ≃	64	46.47 N	11.54 E
Gadevang	41	55.58 N	12.18 E
Gadiloviči	76	53.05 N	30.16 E
Gadis ≃	114	1.03 N	98.55 E
Gadmen	58	46.44 N	8.21 E
Gado Bravo, Ilha do I	250	10.54 S	42.52 W
Gádor	34	36.57 N	2.29 W
Gadra	120	25.40 N	70.37 E
Gadrut	84	39.32 N	47.02 E
Gadsden, Al., U.S.	194	34.00 N	86.00 W
Gadsden, Az., U.S.	200	32.33 N	114.47 W
Gadwāl	122	16.14 N	77.48 E
Gadzi	152	4.47 N	16.42 E
Gaerwen	44	53.13 N	4.16 W
Găești	38	44.43 N	25.19 E
Gaeta	66	41.12 N	13.35 E
Gaeta, Golfo di ⊂	66	41.06 N	13.30 E
Gaferut I	108	9.14 N	145.23 E
Gaffney	192	35.04 N	81.39 W
Gafour	36	36.18 N	9.19 E
Gafsa	148	34.25 N	8.48 E
Gafsa □[8]	148	34.15 N	8.25 E
Gafurov	85	40.14 N	69.44 E
Gag, Pulau I	164	0.27 S	129.52 E
Gagal	146	9.01 N	15.08 E
Gagarawa	150	12.25 N	9.32 E
Gagarin	76	55.33 N	35.00 E
Gage	196	36.18 N	99.45 W
Gagere ≃	150	13.21 N	6.23 E
Gages Lake	278	42.21 N	87.59 W
Gages Lake ⊜	278	42.21 N	88.00 W
Gagetown	186	45.47 N	66.09 W
Gagetown, Canadian Forces Base ■	186	45.43 N	66.15 W
Gaggenau	56	48.48 N	8.19 E
Gaggi	70	37.51 N	15.13 E
Gaggiano	62	45.24 N	9.02 E
Gaghamni	140	11.41 N	28.19 E
Gagil Tamil I	174q	9.32 N	138.10 E
Gagino	80	55.14 N	45.02 E
Gagliano Castelferrato	70	37.43 N	14.32 E
Gagliano del Capo	68	39.50 N	18.22 E
Gagnef	40	60.35 N	15.04 E
Gagnia	152	1.28 S	16.02 E
Gagnoa	150	6.08 N	5.56 W
Gagnon	176	51.53 N	68.10 W
Gagnon, Lac ⊜	206	46.07 N	75.07 W
Gagny	261	48.53 N	2.32 E
Gagra	84	43.20 N	40.15 E
Gagret	123	31.40 N	76.04 E
Gahanna	218	40.01 N	82.52 W
Gahlen	52	51.40 N	6.52 E
Gaiarine	64	45.52 N	12.29 E
Gaibandha	124	25.19 N	89.33 E
Gaichtpass)(	58	47.27 N	10.37 E
Gaigalava	76	56.40 N	27.18 E
Gaighāta	126	22.56 N	88.44 E
Gaijiatun	104	40.50 N	122.37 E
Gail	196	32.46 N	101.27 W
Gail ≃	64	46.36 N	13.53 E
Gailberg Sattel)(	64	46.43 N	12.58 E
Gail Creek ≃	222	31.07 N	95.23 W
Gaildorf	56	49.00 N	9.46 E
Gaillac	32	43.54 N	1.55 E
Gaillard, Château ⊥	50	48.09 N	1.54 E
Gaillard, Lac ⊜	186	50.06 N	68.47 W
Gaillard, Lake ⊜	207	41.21 N	72.46 W
Gaillefontaine	50	49.39 N	1.37 E
Gaillimh → Galway	48	53.16 N	9.03 W
Gaillon, Fr.	50	49.10 N	1.20 E
Gaillon, Fr.	261	49.02 N	1.54 E
Gailtaler Alpen ⌃	64	46.42 N	13.00 E
Gaima	164	8.20 S	142.55 E
Gaimán	254	43.17 S	65.29 W
Gaimersheim	60	48.49 N	11.22 E
Gaines, Mi., U.S.	216	42.52 N	83.54 W
Gaines, Pa., U.S.	210	41.45 N	77.34 W
Gainesboro	194	36.21 N	85.39 W
Gainesville, Fl., U.S.	192	29.39 N	82.19 W
Gainesville, Ga., U.S.	192	34.17 N	83.49 W
Gainesville, Mo., U.S.	194	36.36 N	92.25 W
Gainesville, N.Y., U.S.	210	42.38 N	78.08 W
Gainesville, Tx., U.S.	196	33.37 N	97.07 W
Gainford	44	54.32 N	1.44 W
Gainsborough, Sk., Can.	184	49.10 N	101.26 W
Gainsborough, Eng., U.K.	44	53.24 N	0.46 W
Gainsborough Creek ≃	184	49.10 N	101.02 W
Gaiole in Chianti	66	43.28 N	11.26 E
Gairatganj	124	23.24 N	78.13 E
Gairdner ≃	162	34.17 S	119.28 E
Gairdner, Lake ⊜	162	31.35 S	136.00 E
Gairloch	46	57.42 N	5.40 W
Gairloch, Loch ⊂	46	57.44 N	5.44 W
Gairn ≃	46	57.03 N	3.05 W
Gais, It.	64	46.50 N	11.57 E
Gais, Schw.	58	47.22 N	9.27 E
Gaisberg ∧	64	47.48 N	13.07 E
Gaisbeuren	58	47.54 N	9.43 E
Gaital, Cerro ∧	236	8.37 N	80.07 W
Gaither	208	39.21 N	76.59 W
Gaithersburg	208	39.08 N	77.12 W
Gaixian	98	40.24 N	122.22 E
Gaiziņa kalns ∧[2]	76	56.52 N	25.57 E
Gaj, Jugo.	36	45.29 N	17.02 E
Gaj, S.S.S.R.	86	51.27 N	58.27 E
Gajā	272b	22.52 N	88.10 E
Gajahmungkur, Waduk ⊜[1]	115a	7.55 S	110.55 E
Gajčur ≃	78	47.57 N	36.11 E
Gajendragarh	122	15.44 N	75.59 E
Gajiram	146	12.30 N	13.12 E
Gajny	24	60.15 N	54.15 E
Gājol	124	25.13 N	88.12 E
Gajsin	78	48.48 N	29.24 E
Gajsinghpur	123	29.40 N	73.27 E
Gajuapara ≃	250	4.17 S	47.25 W
Gajutino	76	58.42 N	38.32 E
Gajvoron	78	48.22 N	29.52 E
Gakarosa ∧	158	27.54 S	23.33 E
Gakona	180	62.18 N	145.18 W
Gākuch	123	36.10 N	73.45 E
Gakugsa	24	61.34 N	36.26 E
Gāla, Bngl.	126	24.18 N	89.54 E

Symbol	English	Deutsch	Español	Français	Português
≃	River	Fluß	Río	Rivière	Rio
≍	Canal	Kanal	Canal	Canal	Canal
⌞	Waterfall, Rapids	Wasserfall, Stromschnellen	Cascada, Rápidos	Chute d'eau, Rapides	Cascata, Rápidos
ų	Strait	Meeresstraße	Estrecho	Détroit	Estreito
⊂	Bay, Gulf	Bucht, Golf	Bahía, Golfo	Baie, Golfe	Baía, Golfo
⊜	Lake, Lakes	See, Seen	Lago, Lagos	Lac, Lacs	Lago, Lagos
≚	Swamp	Sumpf	Pantano	Marais	Pântano
⧖	Ice Features, Glacier	Eis- und Gletscherformen	Accidentes Glaciales	Formes glaciaires	Acidentes glaciares
≑	Other Hydrographic Features	Andere Hydrographische Objekte	Otros Elementos Hidrográficos	Autres données hydrographiques	Outros acidentes hidrográficos
✣	Submarine Features	Untermeerische Objekte	Accidentes Submarinos	Formes de relief sous-marin	Acidentes submarinos
□	Political Unit	Politische Einheit	Unidad Politica	Entité politique	Unidade política
♡	Cultural Institution	Kulturelle Institution	Institución Cultural	Institution culturelle	Instituição cultural
⊥	Historical Site	Historische Stätte	Sitio Histórico	Site historique	Sitio histórico
♠	Recreational Site	Erholungs- und Ferienort	Sitio de Recreo	Centre de loisirs	Area de Lazer
⊠	Airport	Flughafen	Aeropuerto	Aéroport	Aeroporto
■	Military Installation	Militäranlage	Instalación Militar	Installation militaire	Instalação militar
⧫	Miscellaneous	Verschiedenes	Misceláneo	Divers	Diversos

I · 60 **Gala-Gasp**

Name	Page	Lat. °′	Long. °′
Gala, Zhg.	124	28.16 N	89.23 E
Galaassija	128	39.52 N	64.27 E
Galāchipa	126	22.10 N	90.25 E
Galahad	182	52.31 N	111.56 W
Galamares	266c	38.48 N	9.25 W
Galán, Cerro ∧	252	25.55 S	66.52 W
Galana ≃	154	3.09 S	40.08 E
Galangue	152	13.48 S	16.09 E
Galanovo	80	56.09 N	54.07 E
Galanta	30	48.12 N	17.43 E
Galápagos □[4]	246a	0.30 S	90.30 W
Galapagos Islands → Colón, Archipiélago de II	246a	0.30 S	90.30 W
Galaroza	34	37.55 N	6.42 W
Galas ≃	114	5.31 N	102.12 E
Galashiels	46	55.37 N	2.49 W
Galata ◆[8]	267b	41.01 N	28.58 E
Galata Köprüsü ◆[5]	267b	41.00 N	28.57 E
Galata Tower ʋ	267b	41.01 N	28.58 E
Galatea	172	38.25 S	176.45 E
Galați	38	45.26 N	28.03 E
Galați □[6]	38	45.45 N	27.45 E
Galatia	194	37.50 N	88.36 W
Galatia □[9]	130	39.30 N	32.40 E
Galatina	68	40.10 N	18.10 E
Galatone	68	40.09 N	18.04 E
Galatro	68	38.28 N	16.06 E
Galátsion	267c	38.01 N	23.45 E
Galatz → Galați	38	45.26 N	28.03 E
Galaure ≃	62	45.11 N	4.49 E
Gala Water ≃	46	55.37 N	2.48 W
Galax	192	36.39 N	80.55 W
Galaxídhion	38	38.22 N	22.23 E
Galbyn gov' ◆[2]	102	42.30 N	107.00 E
Galdhøpiggen ∧	26	61.37 N	8.17 E
Gale, Lac ⊜	190	46.46 N	76.51 W
Galeairy Lake ⊜	212	45.29 N	78.17 W
Galeana, Méx.	232	30.07 N	107.38 W
Galeana, Méx.	232	24.50 N	100.04 W
Galeão, Aeroporto do ⊠	256	22.50 S	43.15 W
Galeata	66	44.00 N	11.55 E
Galegu	140	12.36 N	35.02 E
Galeh Dār	128	27.38 N	52.42 E
Galela	108	1.50 N	127.50 E
Galena, Austl.	162	27.50 S	114.41 E
Galena, Ak., U.S.	180	64.44 N	156.57 W
Galena, Il., U.S.	190	42.25 N	90.25 W
Galena, In., U.S.	218	38.21 N	85.56 W
Galena, Ks., U.S.	198	37.04 N	94.38 W
Galena, Md., U.S.	208	39.20 N	75.52 W
Galena, Mo., U.S.	194	36.48 N	93.27 W
Galena, Oh., U.S.	214	40.12 N	82.52 W
Galena Park	222	29.43 N	95.13 W
Galenbecker See ⊜	54	53.38 N	13.43 E
Galeota Point ›	241r	10.08 N	60.59 W
Galera ≃	248	14.25 S	60.07 W
Galera, Punta ›, Chile	254	39.59 S	73.43 W
Galera, Punta ›, Ec.	246	0.49 N	80.03 W
Galera, Punta de ›	34	39.10 N	1.05 E
Galera Point ›	241r	10.49 N	60.55 W
Galeria ⊥	267a	42.02 N	12.18 E
Galeria, Fosso la ≃	267a	41.48 N	12.21 E
Galesburg, Il., U.S.	190	40.56 N	90.22 W
Galesburg, Mi., U.S.	216	42.17 N	85.25 W
Gales Creek	224	45.35 N	123.12 W
Gales Creek ≃	224	45.29 N	123.06 W
Gales Ferry	207	41.25 N	72.04 W
Gales Point ›	283	42.33 N	70.47 W
Galesville, Md., U.S.	208	38.50 N	76.32 W
Galesville, Wi., U.S.	190	44.04 N	91.20 W
Galeton	214	41.43 N	77.38 W
Galeville	210	43.05 N	76.10 W
Galgasc	144	0.11 N	41.38 E
Galgate	44	54.00 N	2.47 W
Galguduud □[4]	144	5.00 N	46.30 E
Galheirão ≃	255	12.23 S	45.05 W
Galheiros	255	13.18 S	46.25 W
Gali	84	42.38 N	41.44 E
Gali, Torrente de ≃	266d	41.28 N	2.00 E
Galiano	224	48.52 N	123.21 W
Galiano Island I	224	48.56 N	123.29 W
Galibier, Col du)(	62	45.04 N	6.24 E
Galič, S.S.S.R.	78	49.08 N	24.43 E
Galič, S.S.S.R.	80	58.23 N	42.21 E
Galicia □[4]	34	42.45 N	8.00 W
Galicia □[9]	22	49.00 N	22.00 E
Galičskaja vozvyšennost' ⋏[2]	24	58.25 N	42.20 E
Galičskoje, ozero ⊜	80	58.24 N	42.18 E
Galien	216	41.47 N	86.29 W
Galien ≃	216	41.48 N	86.45 W
Galilee	207	41.22 N	71.30 W
Galilee → HaGalil □[9]	132	32.54 N	35.20 E
Galilee, Lake ⊜	166	22.21 S	145.48 E
Galilee, Sea of → Kinneret, Yam ⊜	132	32.48 N	35.35 E
Galiléia	255	19.00 S	41.33 W
Galim	152	7.06 N	12.29 E
Galina Point ›	241q	18.24 N	76.53 W
Galindo Creek ≃	282	37.58 N	122.02 W
Galion	214	40.44 N	82.47 W
Galion, Baie du ⊂	240e	14.44 N	60.57 W
Galion, Rivière du ≃	240e	14.44 N	60.57 W
Galis	115a	7.08 S	113.33 E
Galisteo Creek ≃	200	35.31 N	106.22 W
Galite, Canal de la ʊ	36	37.20 N	9.00 E
Galiuro Mountains ⋏	200	32.40 N	110.20 W
Galiwinku	164	12.02 S	135.34 E
Galižana	64	44.56 N	13.52 E
Galka'yo	144	6.47 N	47.26 E
Galkhausen	263	51.05 N	6.58 E
Galkino, S.S.S.R.	82	54.46 N	35.49 E
Galkino, S.S.S.R.	86	55.36 N	62.55 E
Galkino, S.S.S.R.	86	52.14 N	78.20 E
Gall'aaral	85	40.02 N	67.35 E
Gallan Head ›	46	58.14 N	7.03 W
Gallarate	62	45.40 N	8.47 E
Gallardon	50	48.32 N	1.42 E
Gallatin, Mo., U.S.	194	39.54 N	93.57 W
Gallatin, Pa., U.S.	279b	40.12 N	79.53 W
Gallatin, Tn., U.S.	194	36.23 N	86.26 W
Gallatin, Tx., U.S.	222	31.54 N	95.09 W
Gallatin □[6]	218	38.45 N	84.51 W
Gallatin ≃	202	45.56 N	111.29 W
Gallatin Range ⋏	202	45.15 N	111.05 W
Galle	122	6.02 N	80.13 E
Gállego ≃	34	41.39 N	0.51 W
Gallegos ≃	254	51.36 S	68.59 W
Galles → Wales □[8]	28	52.30 N	3.30 W
Galleyend	260	51.42 N	0.29 E
Galley Head ›	48	51.30 N	8.57 W
Galleywood	260	51.42 N	0.28 E
Galliano	194	29.26 N	90.17 W
Galliate	62	45.29 N	8.42 E
Gallicano	64	44.04 N	10.26 E
Gallicano nel Lazio	267a	41.52 N	12.49 E
Gallicchio	68	40.17 N	16.08 E
Gallico	68	38.10 N	15.41 E
Galliera Veneta	64	45.39 N	11.49 E
Gallinara I	62	44.02 N	8.14 E
Gallinas ≃	196	35.10 N	104.55 W
Gallinas, Punta ›	246	12.28 N	71.40 W
Gallinas Creek ≃	282	38.01 N	122.30 W
Gallinas Peak ∧	200	34.13 N	105.45 W
Gallio	64	45.53 N	11.33 E
Gallipoli, Austl.	166	19.10 S	137.55 E
Gallipoli, It.	68	40.03 N	17.58 E
Gallipoli → Gelibolu, Tür.	130	40.24 N	26.40 E
Gallipoli Peninsula → Gelibolu Yarımadası ›[1]	130	40.20 N	26.30 E
Gallipolis	188	38.48 N	82.12 W
Gallitzin	214	40.28 N	78.33 W
Gallivaggio	58	46.21 N	9.21 E
Gällivare	24	67.07 N	20.45 E
Gallneukirchen	61	48.21 N	14.25 E
Gällö	26	62.55 N	15.14 E
Gallo, Capo ›	70	38.13 N	13.19 E
Gallo, Lago del ⊜[1]	64	46.07 N	10.10 E
Gallo, Lago di ⊜[1]	58	46.37 N	10.10 E
Gallo, Laguna ⊜	258	35.30 S	58.28 W
Gallo Arroyo V	200	33.55 N	105.00 W
Galloo Island I	212	43.54 N	76.25 W
Galloupes Point ›	283	42.28 N	70.53 W
Galloway □[9]	44	55.00 N	4.25 W
Galloway, Mull of ›	44	54.38 N	4.50 W
Galloway Creek ≃, Md., U.S.	284b	39.18 N	76.23 W
Galloway Creek ≃, Mi., U.S.	281	42.39 N	83.12 W
Galluis	261	48.48 N	1.48 E
Gallup	200	35.31 N	108.44 W
Gallupville	210	42.40 N	74.14 W
Gallur	34	41.52 N	1.19 W
Gallura ◆[1]	71	41.00 N	9.13 E
Gally, Ru de ≃	261	48.53 N	1.53 E
Gälnan ʊ	40	59.31 N	18.45 E
Gålö I	40	59.05 N	18.17 E
Galop Island I	212	44.46 N	75.24 W
Galoppo, Ippodromo del ♠	266b	45.28 N	9.07 E
Galougo	150	13.50 N	11.04 W
Galsi	126	23.20 N	87.42 E
Galston	46	55.36 N	4.24 W
Galt, Mong.	88	48.46 N	99.53 E
Galt, Ca., U.S.	226	38.15 N	121.17 W
Gal Tardo	144	3.34 N	45.58 E
Galtat Zemmour	148	25.15 N	12.20 W
Galtelli	71	40.23 N	9.37 E
Galten	41	56.09 N	9.55 E
Galten ⊂	40	59.27 N	16.09 E
Galtür	58	46.58 N	10.11 E
Galtymore Mountain ∧	48	52.22 N	8.10 W
Galty Mountains ⋏	48	52.25 N	8.10 W
Galūgāh-e Āsīyeh	128	34.01 N	59.55 E
Galugur	114	2.34 N	99.39 E
Galula	154	8.36 S	33.02 E
Galunggung, Gunung ∧	115a	7.15 S	108.03 E
Galuut	88	48.33 N	113.12 E
Galva, Il., U.S.	190	41.10 N	90.02 W
Galva, Ia., U.S.	198	42.30 N	95.25 W
Galva, Ks., U.S.	198	38.22 N	97.32 W
Galvarino	252	38.24 S	72.47 W
Galveston, In., U.S.	216	40.34 N	86.11 W
Galveston, Tx., U.S.	222	29.17 N	94.47 W
Galveston □[6]	222	29.20 N	94.53 W
Galveston Bay ⊂	222	29.36 N	94.57 W
Galveston Island I	222	29.13 N	94.55 W
Gálvez	252	32.02 S	61.13 W
Galvin, Austl.	274b	37.51 S	144.49 E
Galvin, Wa., U.S.	224	46.44 N	123.01 W
Galway (Gaillimh), Ire.	48	53.16 N	9.03 W
Galway, N.Y., U.S.	210	43.01 N	74.02 W
Galway □[6]	48	53.20 N	9.00 W
Galway Bay ⊂	48	53.10 N	9.15 W
Gam (Jin) ≃	110	21.55 N	105.12 E
Gam, Pulau I	164	0.27 S	130.36 E
Gama, Isla I	254	40.29 S	62.12 W
Gamaches	50	49.59 N	1.33 E
Gamagōri	94	34.50 N	137.14 E
Gamalejevka	80	52.16 N	53.26 E
Gamaliel	194	36.38 N	85.47 W
Ga-Mankoeng	156	23.57 S	29.42 E
Gamare, Lake ⊜	144	11.30 N	41.40 E
Gamarra	246	8.20 N	73.45 W
Gamawa	146	12.08 N	10.32 E
Gamay	116	12.23 N	125.18 E
Gamay Bay ⊂	116	12.21 N	125.21 E
Gamba	120	28.17 N	88.32 E
Gambach	56	50.28 N	8.44 E
Gambaga	150	10.32 N	0.26 W
Gambais	261	48.46 N	1.40 E
Gambaiseuil	261	48.45 N	1.44 E
Gambang	114	3.43 N	103.06 E
Gambara, It.	64	45.15 N	10.18 E
Gámbara, Méx.	234	18.55 N	102.05 W
Gambarie	68	38.10 N	15.50 E
Gambassi	66	43.32 N	10.57 E
Gambatesa	66	41.30 N	14.54 E
Gambela	144	8.18 N	34.37 E
Gambell	180	63.46 N	171.46 W
Gambellara	64	45.28 N	11.20 E
Gamber	208	39.27 N	76.56 W
Gambia □[1], Afr.	134	13.30 N	15.30 W
Gambia □[1], Afr.	150	13.30 N	15.30 W
Gambia (Gambie) ≃	150	13.28 N	16.34 W
Gambi Aṭrash	140	10.03 N	33.47 E
Gambie → Gambia □[1]	150	13.30 N	15.30 W
Gambie (Gambia) ≃	150	13.28 N	16.34 W
Gambier	214	40.22 N	82.23 W
Gambier, Îles II	6	21.20 S	136.30 W
Gamble Mansion State Historic Site ⊥	220	27.32 N	82.32 W
Gambo, Nf., Can.	186	48.46 N	54.14 W
Gambo, Centraf.	152	4.39 N	22.16 E
Gamboa	236	9.07 N	79.42 W
Gamboli	120	29.50 N	68.26 E
Gambolò	62	45.15 N	8.51 E
Gamboma	152	1.53 S	15.51 E
Gamboula	152	4.08 N	15.09 E
Gambrill State Park ♠	208	39.30 N	77.30 W
Gamchab ≃	156	28.15 S	17.26 E
Gamé	150	6.44 N	1.11 E
Game Creek ≃	285	39.41 N	75.28 W
Gamen-See ⊜	264a	52.40 N	13.51 E
Gaming	61	47.56 N	15.06 E
Gamka ≃	158	33.18 S	21.39 E
Gamlakarleby → Kokkola	26	63.50 N	23.07 E
Gamla Uppsala	40	59.54 N	17.38 E
Gamleby	26	57.54 N	16.24 E
Gamlitz	61	46.43 N	15.33 E
Gammel Estrup ⊥	26	56.26 N	10.21 E
Gammelstad ʋ[1]	26	65.38 N	22.01 E
Gammertingen	58	48.15 N	9.13 E
Gammon ≃	184	51.07 N	95.09 W
Gammon, Point ›	207	41.36 N	70.16 W
Gammon Ranges National Park ♠	166	30.29 S	139.10 E
Gamō, Nihon	94	35.03 N	136.11 E
Gamō, Nihon	268	35.52 N	139.48 E
Gamoep	158	29.55 S	18.25 E
Ga-Mogara ≃	158	27.07 S	22.57 E
Gamo Gofa □[4]	144	5.45 N	37.00 E
Gamon	150	13.20 N	12.55 W
Gamova, mys ›	89	42.35 N	131.12 E
Gamph, Slieve ⋏	48	54.05 N	9.00 W
Gampoko	273b	4.16 S	15.10 E
Gampola	122	7.10 N	80.34 E
Gampongbatak	114	4.48 N	97.39 E
Gampoui	273b	4.08 S	15.22 E
Gams	58	47.12 N	9.28 E
Gamsfeld ∧	64	47.37 N	13.29 E
Gamtoos ≃	158	33.58 S	25.01 E
Gamud ∧	144	4.05 N	38.03 E
G'amyš, gora ∧	84	40.18 N	46.23 E
Gan ≃, Zhg.	89	49.12 N	125.14 E
Gan ≃, Zhg.	100	29.12 N	116.00 E
Ganado, Az., U.S.	200	35.42 N	109.32 W
Ganado, Tx., U.S.	222	29.02 N	96.31 W
Ganano ≃	116	16.45 N	121.44 E
Gananoque	212	44.20 N	76.10 W
Gananoque ≃	212	44.19 N	76.09 W
Gananoque Lake ⊜	212	44.27 N	76.09 W
Ganaraska ≃	212	43.57 N	78.18 W
Ganargua Creek ≃	210	43.04 N	77.00 W
Ganassi	116	7.49 N	124.06 E
Ganāveh	128	29.34 N	50.31 E
Gancevičі	76	52.45 N	26.26 E
Ganchangba	107	28.52 N	103.41 E
Ganči	85	39.58 N	69.08 E
Gand → Gent	50	51.03 N	3.43 E
Ganda, Ang.	152	13.02 S	14.40 E
Ganda, Zaïre	152	4.05 N	23.32 E
Gandadiwata, Bulu ∧	112	2.42 S	119.27 E
Gandajika	152	6.45 S	23.57 E
Gandak (Nārāyaṇi) ≃	124	25.39 N	85.13 E
Gaṇḍakī □[8]	124	28.15 N	84.15 E
Gandara	258	35.26 S	58.06 W
Ganda Singhwāla	123	31.02 N	74.31 E
Gandāva	120	28.37 N	67.29 E
Gandavaroyi Falls ʟ	154	17.17 S	29.07 E
Gānde	126	24.10 N	86.26 E
Gander	186	48.57 N	54.37 W
Gander ≃	186	49.15 N	54.30 W
Gander Bay	186	49.18 N	54.29 W
Gander Bay ⊂	186	49.25 N	54.28 W
Ganderkesee	52	53.02 N	8.32 E
Gander Lake ⊜	186	48.55 N	54.40 W
Gandesa	34	41.03 N	0.26 E
Gandevi	120	20.49 N	72.59 E
Gāndhinagar	120	23.12 N	72.40 E
Gāndhi Sāgar ⊜[1]	120	24.18 N	75.21 E
Gandi	150	12.55 N	5.49 E
Gandi, Wādī V	140	11.23 N	24.31 E
Gandia	34	38.58 N	0.11 W
Gandino	62	45.49 N	9.54 E
Gando	152	12.30 S	17.25 E
Gandole	146	8.26 N	11.34 E
Gandou	152	2.24 N	17.27 E
Gandrange	56	49.16 N	6.08 E
Gandria	58	46.01 N	9.00 E
Gandu	255	13.45 S	39.30 W
Gandy Bridge ◆[5]	220	27.53 N	82.34 W
G'andžačaj ≃	84	40.54 N	46.28 E
Gandzha → Kirovabad	84	40.40 N	46.22 E
Ganfang	100	28.40 N	114.51 E
Ganfosi	107	29.36 N	104.03 E
Ganga → Ganges ≃	124	23.22 N	90.32 E
Gangādharpur	272b	22.36 N	88.11 E
Gangafani	150	14.23 N	2.24 W
Gangājalghāti	126	23.25 N	87.07 E
Gangala-Na-Bodio	154	3.41 N	29.08 E
Gangalingolo	273b	4.20 S	15.09 E
Gan Gan	254	42.30 S	68.16 W
Gangānagar	123	29.55 N	73.53 E
Gangāpur, India	120	25.13 N	74.16 E
Gangāpur, India	122	19.41 N	75.01 E
Gangāpur, India	124	26.29 N	76.43 E
Gangara, Niger	150	14.36 N	8.30 E
Gangara, Niger	150	13.33 N	7.14 E
Gāngārāmpur	124	25.24 N	88.31 E
Ganga Sāgar	126	21.38 N	88.05 E
Gangaw	110	22.11 N	94.07 E
Gangāwati	122	15.26 N	76.32 E
Gangaw Range ⋏	110	24.50 N	96.40 E
Ganga-Yamuna Doāb ⋏[1]	124	26.40 N	79.30 E
Gangcheng	98	35.52 N	116.52 E
Gangdaba, Tchabal ∧	152	7.44 N	12.45 E
Gangdhār	120	23.57 N	75.37 E
Gangdisê Shan ⋏	120	31.00 N	82.00 E
Gangelt	56	50.59 N	5.59 E
Ganges, B.C., Can.	224	48.51 N	123.30 W
Ganges, Fr.	62	43.56 N	3.42 E
Ganges (Ganga) (Padma) ≃	124	23.22 N	90.32 E
Ganges, Mouths of the ≃[1]	120	22.00 N	89.00 E
Ganges Delta ≚[2]	124	23.00 N	89.00 E
Ganghu	120	32.05 N	86.45 E
Gangi	70	37.49 N	14.13 E
Gangkofen	60	48.26 N	12.34 E
Gangkou, Zhg.	100	29.12 N	113.19 E
Gangkou, Zhg.	100	29.45 N	115.44 E
Gangkou, Zhg.	100	29.21 N	117.58 E
Gangkou, Zhg.	100	22.38 N	113.22 E
Gangkou, Zhg.	100	22.36 N	114.54 E
Gangkou, Zhg.	106	30.44 N	118.54 E
Gangkouzhen	106	31.45 N	120.40 E
Gangmar Co ⊜	120	33.46 N	84.15 E
Gang Mills	210	42.08 N	77.06 W
Gāngnāpur	126	23.09 N	88.38 E
Gangneung → Kangnŭng	98	37.45 N	128.54 E
Gango ≃	152	9.48 S	15.40 E
Gangoa	102	37.15 N	100.28 E
Gangoh	124	29.46 N	77.15 E
Gangotri, India	120	30.56 N	79.02 E
Gangotri, India	120	31.01 N	78.27 E
Gangou	98	40.30 N	119.27 E
Gangoumen	98	41.40 N	116.35 E
Gangouyi	102	36.01 N	105.03 E
Gangqiao	107	30.13 N	105.22 E
Gang Ranch	182	51.33 N	122.20 W
Gangshangji	100	28.06 N	116.30 E
Gangtok	124	27.20 N	88.37 E
Gangtou	98	38.04 N	113.56 E
Gangtouli	106	31.42 N	119.02 E
Gangu	102	34.45 N	105.20 E
Gangwa, Zaïre	152	3.30 S	20.55 E
Gangwa, Zhg.	105	39.48 N	116.10 E
Gangwei	100	24.20 N	118.01 E
Ganhezi	86	44.08 N	88.32 E
Ganhu	102	44.33 N	94.09 E
Gani	164	0.47 S	128.13 E
Ganišob	85	39.03 N	70.47 E
Ganj Dundwara	124	27.44 N	78.57 E
Ganjiang	107	29.42 N	103.38 E
Ganlan Shan ∧	124	29.54 N	90.02 E
Ganlu	106	31.32 N	120.35 E
Ganluchang	107	29.54 N	104.47 E
Ganluo	102	29.03 N	102.59 E
Gannahoek	158	26.44 S	24.08 E
Gannan	89	47.54 N	123.30 E
Gannano, Lago di ⊜	68	40.19 N	16.26 E
Gannapan	158	30.23 S	22.12 E
Gannat	32	46.06 N	3.12 E
Gannett Peak ∧	200	43.11 N	109.39 W
Gannovka	83	48.33 N	38.35 E
Gannvalley	198	44.02 N	98.59 W
Ganpingsi	102	35.13 N	102.30 E
Ganpu	106	30.24 N	120.53 E
Ganq	120	37.25 N	92.15 E
Ganquan	102	36.25 N	109.16 E
Gansbaai	158	34.35 S	19.22 E
Gänsbrunnen	58	47.16 N	7.28 E
Gänserndorf	61	48.20 N	16.43 E
Gansevoort	210	43.12 N	73.39 W
Ganso Azul	248	8.51 S	74.44 W
Ganspan	158	27.57 S	24.47 E
Gansu (Kansu) □[4]	102	37.00 N	103.00 E
Ganta	150	7.15 N	8.59 W
Gantan	100	29.37 N	119.34 E
Gantang, Zhg.	100	26.56 N	119.40 E
Gantang, Zhg.	102	22.58 N	109.00 E
Gantao ≃	98	38.01 N	114.07 E
Gante → Gent	50	51.03 N	3.43 E
Gantheaume, Cape ›	166	36.05 S	137.27 E
Gantheaume Bay ⊂	162	27.44 S	114.07 E
Gantheaume Point ›	162	17.59 S	122.10 E
Gantiadi	84	43.24 N	40.06 E
Gantian	100	27.30 N	113.10 E
Gantt	194	31.24 N	86.29 W
Gantung	112	2.58 S	108.09 E
Gantung, Mount ∧	116	8.57 N	117.48 E
Gan'uškino	80	46.36 N	49.16 E
Ganwo	150	11.13 N	4.42 E
Ganxi, Zhg.	100	28.08 N	118.06 E
Ganxi, Zhg.	102	29.02 N	109.32 E
Ganyanchi	102	36.39 N	105.18 E
Ganyesa	158	26.35 S	24.10 E
Ganyu (Qing Kou)	98	34.52 N	119.10 E
Ganzê	102	31.40 N	100.01 E
Ganzhenyi	100	30.33 N	113.21 E
Ganzhou, Zhg.	100	25.54 N	114.55 E
Ganzhou, Zhg.	100	28.49 N	115.25 E
Ganzhou → Zhangye, Zhg.	102	38.56 N	100.27 E
Ganzhuermiao	88	48.24 N	118.08 E
Ganzlin	54	53.23 N	12.15 E
Gao	150	16.16 N	0.03 W
Gao □[4]	150	18.00 N	1.30 E
Gao'an	100	28.25 N	115.22 E
Gaobaita	271a	39.53 N	116.30 E
Gaobei	100	26.37 N	114.38 E
Gaobeidian	271a	39.54 N	116.33 E
Gaobu	100	27.48 N	117.01 E
Gaochang	107	28.49 N	104.24 E
Gaocheng, Zhg.	98	38.04 N	114.49 E
Gaocheng, Zhg.	100	31.57 N	113.25 E
Gaocheng, Zhg.	106	31.28 N	119.48 E
Gaochengzhai	104	41.24 N	123.43 E
Gaochun	106	31.20 N	118.52 E
Gaocun	98	37.05 N	122.12 E
Gaodianzi	102	30.40 N	110.01 E
Gao Feng ∧	106	30.34 N	118.40 E
Gaogongmiao	100	33.25 N	115.53 E
Gaogou	100	34.03 N	119.15 E
Gaohe	100	22.47 N	112.57 E
Gaohebu	100	30.44 N	116.50 E
Gaoil, Sliabh ∧	46	55.55 N	5.28 W
Gaojiabu	102	38.30 N	110.11 E
Gaojiadi	98	41.33 N	114.58 E
Gaojiadian	98	42.40 N	124.28 E
Gaojian	100	29.04 N	121.14 E
Gaojiapuzi	104	41.22 N	123.36 E
Gaojiaqiao	106	30.43 N	120.38 E
Gaojiatun	104	41.06 N	121.19 E
Gaojiawopeng	104	41.28 N	122.10 E
Gaojiawopu	104	41.50 N	122.47 E
Gaojiazhai	269b	31.23 N	121.33 E
Gaojiazhen	102	30.05 N	107.51 E
Gaokan	104	40.46 N	122.23 E
Gaokeng	100	27.40 N	113.58 E
Gaolan	102	36.25 N	103.56 E
Gaolan Dao I	100	21.55 N	113.15 E
Gaolao	104	41.54 N	120.59 E
Gaoli	105	39.17 N	115.38 E
Gaoliang	107	29.45 N	105.15 E
Gaoliban	104	41.39 N	121.58 E
Gaolifangshen	104	42.27 N	123.21 E
Gaolimen	98	40.22 N	124.02 E
Gaoling	105	40.32 N	117.01 E
Gaolinying	105	39.06 N	115.38 E
Gaoliying	105	40.10 N	116.29 E
Gaoliyingzi	104	41.56 N	124.17 E
Gaolong	100	26.56 N	113.45 E
Gaolou	105	39.59 N	116.50 E
Gaolouchang, Zhg.	107	29.51 N	104.41 E
Gaolouchang, Zhg.	107	30.03 N	105.58 E
Gaoluo	98	37.27 N	113.55 E
Gaomi	98	36.23 N	119.44 E
Gaona	252	25.12 S	64.05 W
Gaopi	100	24.14 N	116.39 E
Gaoping, Zhg.	102	35.48 N	112.52 E
Gaoping, Zhg.	107	30.28 N	105.45 E
Gaopingba	107	30.47 N	106.06 E
Gaoqiao, Zhg.	100	30.08 N	119.56 E
Gaoqiao, Zhg.	100	26.36 N	117.46 E
Gaoqiao, Zhg.	102	28.06 N	106.36 E
Gaoqiao, Zhg.	106	32.14 N	119.38 E
Gaoqiao, Zhg.	106	31.21 N	121.34 E
Gaoqiaomen	106	32.01 N	118.51 E
Gaoqiaozhen	104	40.55 N	121.00 E
Gaoqing (Tianzhen)	98	37.11 N	117.47 E
Gaoqipu	104	41.32 N	121.40 E
Gaosha	100	26.27 N	117.56 E
Gaoshaling	105	38.51 N	117.36 E
Gaoshan, Zhg.	100	25.29 N	119.34 E
Gaoshan, Zhg.	107	29.26 N	104.28 E
Gaoshanbao	105	40.40 N	117.29 E
Gaoshangbao	98	39.11 N	118.30 E
Gaoshanpu	102	27.10 N	105.14 E
Gaoshantai	104	42.22 N	122.28 E
Gaoshanzi	104	41.34 N	122.02 E
Gaoshengchang	107	29.59 N	105.31 E
Gaoshengzhen	104	41.20 N	122.12 E
Gaoshi	107	29.36 N	104.44 E
Gaoshikan	107	29.12 N	105.04 E
Gaosichang	107	30.17 N	104.52 E
Gaotai	102	39.20 N	99.58 E
Gaotaishan	104	42.02 N	122.52 E
Gaotan, Zhg.	100	30.23 N	117.23 E
Gaotan, Zhg.	100	23.12 N	115.22 E
Gaotan, Zhg.	102	32.22 N	108.36 E
Gaotang	98	36.54 N	116.14 E
Gaotangji	100	32.24 N	116.01 E
Gaotingsi	100	26.05 N	112.53 E
Gaotuozi	104	41.08 N	122.40 E
Gaoua	150	10.20 N	3.11 W
Gaoual	150	11.45 N	13.12 W
Gaoxian	102	28.20 N	104.38 E
Gaoxingru	100	26.28 N	115.14 E
Gaoxinji	98	34.11 N	115.33 E
Gaoya	98	36.22 N	118.49 E
Gaoyang	98	34.30 N	114.40 E
Gaoyapu	107	29.14 N	106.19 E
Gaoyi	98	37.36 N	114.36 E
Gaoyou, Zhg.	100	32.47 N	119.27 E
Gaoyou, Zhg.	100	28.25 N	115.31 E
Gaoyou Hu ⊜	100	32.50 N	119.20 E
Gaozhangjia	102	36.06 N	107.18 E
Gaozhou	102	21.55 N	110.50 E
Gaozi	106	32.11 N	119.18 E
Gaoziba	107	29.01 N	106.00 E
Gaozuo	100	33.57 N	118.03 E
Gap, Fr.	62	44.34 N	6.05 E
Gap, Pa., U.S.	208	39.59 N	76.01 W
Gapālnagar	272b	22.49 N	88.08 E
Gapan	116	15.19 N	120.57 E
Gapeau ≃	62	43.07 N	6.11 E
Gapern ⊜	40	59.31 N	13.40 E
Gar	120	32.11 N	79.59 E
Gar ≃	120	32.28 N	79.44 E
Gara, Lough ⊜	48	53.55 N	8.25 W
Garacad	144	6.57 N	49.19 E
Garachiné	246	8.04 N	78.22 W
Garachiné, Punta ›	246	8.06 N	78.25 W
Garadag	144	9.26 N	46.52 E
Gārādāha	126	24.14 N	89.34 E
Garagoa	246	5.05 N	73.21 W
Garaguso	68	40.33 N	16.14 E
Garah	166	29.04 S	149.38 E
Garai ≃[1]	126	23.32 N	89.31 E
Garaina	164	7.50 S	147.10 E
Gārākhola Madhukhāli	126	23.33 N	89.38 E
Garamba ≃	154	3.53 N	29.12 E
Garamba, Parc National de la ♠	154	4.10 N	29.30 E
Gara Muleta ∧	144	9.17 N	41.47 E
Garānberia	272b	22.24 N	88.34 E
Garancières	261	48.49 N	1.46 E
Garango	150	11.48 N	0.34 W
Garanhuns	250	8.54 S	36.29 W
Garapan	174n	15.12 N	145.43 E
Garara	164	8.37 S	148.17 E
Garautha	124	25.34 N	79.18 E
Garba	146	9.12 N	20.30 E
Garbagna	266b	45.23 N	8.39 E
Garbagnate Milanese	266b	45.35 N	9.05 E
Garbahaarey	144	3.19 N	42.13 E
Garbatella ◆[8]	267a	41.52 N	12.29 E
Garba Tula	154	0.32 N	38.31 E
Garber	196	36.26 N	97.35 W
Garberville	204	40.06 N	123.47 W
Garbokaraj	88	54.09 N	99.52 E
Garboldisham	42	52.24 N	0.56 E
Garbsen	52	52.25 N	9.34 E
Garça	255	22.14 S	49.37 W
Garças, Rio das ≃	255	15.54 S	52.16 W
Garcevo	76	52.45 N	32.59 E
Garches	261	48.51 N	2.11 E
Garching	60	48.15 N	11.39 E
Garching an der Alz	60	48.08 N	12.34 E
Garchitorena	116	13.52 N	123.40 E
García	232	29.59 N	108.20 W
García, Laguna ⊜	288	34.58 S	58.09 W
García de la Cadena	234	21.09 N	103.28 W
García de Sola, Embalse de ⊜[1]	34	39.15 N	5.05 W
Garcia Hernandez	116	9.37 N	124.18 E
Garcias	255	20.34 S	52.13 W
Garcitas Creek ≃	222	28.51 N	96.46 W
Gard □[5]	62	44.00 N	4.00 E
Gard ≃	62	43.51 N	4.37 E
Gard, Pont du ◆[5]	62	43.56 N	4.36 E

ENGLISH

Name	Page	Lat. °′	Long. °′
Garda	64	45.34 N	10.42 E
Garda, Lago di ⊜	64	45.40 N	10.41 E
Gardabani	84	41.28 N	45.06 E
Gardanne	62	43.27 N	5.28 E
Garde, Lac la ⊜	190	46.46 N	78.14 W
Gardelegen	54	52.31 N	11.23 E
Garden ≃	190	46.32 N	84.09 W
Gardena	228	33.53 N	118.18 W
Gardena, Val V	64	46.35 N	11.35 E
Garden Acres	226	37.58 N	121.13 W
Garden City, Ga., U.S.	192	32.06 N	81.09 W
Garden City, Ks., U.S.	198	37.58 N	100.52 W
Garden City, Mi., U.S.	216	42.19 N	83.19 W
Garden City, Mo., U.S.	194	38.33 N	94.11 W
Garden City, N.Y., U.S.	210	40.43 N	73.38 W
Garden City, Tx., U.S.	196	31.52 N	101.29 W
Garden City → Qasr al-Dubārā ◆[8]	273c	30.02 N	31.14 E
Garden City Park	276	40.44 N	73.39 W
Garden City Raceway ♠	284a	43.09 N	79.11 W
Gardendale	194	33.39 N	86.48 W
Garden Farms	226	35.24 N	120.07 W
Garden Gate Village	282	37.20 N	122.02 W
Garden Grove, Ca., U.S.	228	33.46 N	117.56 W
Garden Grove, Ia., U.S.	190	40.50 N	93.36 W
Garden Home	224	45.27 N	122.45 W
Garden Island I, Austl.	168a	32.13 S	115.41 E
Garden Island I, Mi., U.S.	190	45.49 N	85.30 W
Garden Lakes	192	34.17 N	85.16 W
Garden Peninsula ›[1]	190	45.45 N	86.35 W
Garden Plain	198	37.39 N	97.41 W
Garden Prairie	216	42.15 N	88.44 W
Garden Reach	126	22.33 N	88.17 E
Gardenside	218	38.03 N	84.33 W
Garden State Arts Center ʋ	276	40.24 N	74.11 W
Garden State Plaza ◆[9]	276	40.55 N	74.05 W
Gardenton	184	49.05 N	96.40 W
Garden Valley	226	38.51 N	120.51 W
Garden View	210	41.16 N	77.03 W
Gardenville	208	40.22 N	75.07 W
Gardermoen	26	60.13 N	11.06 E
Gardey	252	37.17 S	59.21 W
Gardeyz	120	33.37 N	69.07 E
Gardinas → Grodno	76	53.41 N	23.50 E
Gardiner, Me., U.S.	188	44.13 N	69.46 W
Gardiner, Mt., U.S.	202	45.01 N	110.42 W
Gardiner, N.Y., U.S.	210	41.41 N	74.09 W
Gardiner, Or., U.S.	202	43.43 N	124.06 W
Gardiner, Wa., U.S.	224	48.03 N	122.55 W
Gardiner Dam ◆[6]	184	51.17 N	106.51 W
Gardiner Range ⋏	162	23.50 S	131.46 E
Gardiners Bay ⊂	207	41.08 N	72.10 W
Gardiners Creek ≃	274b	37.50 S	145.02 E
Gardiners Island I	207	41.05 N	72.07 W
Garding	41	54.20 N	8.46 E
Gardner, Il., U.S.	216	41.11 N	88.18 W
Gardner, Ks., U.S.	198	38.48 N	94.55 W
Gardner, Ma., U.S.	207	42.34 N	71.59 W
Gardner Canal ⊂	182	53.28 N	128.15 W
Gardner Lake ⊜	207	41.31 N	72.13 W
Gardner Pinnacles II[1]	14	25.00 N	167.55 W
Gardnersville	218	38.46 N	84.30 W
Gardnertown	210	41.32 N	74.04 W
Gardnerville	226	38.56 N	119.44 W
Gardno	54	53.15 N	14.38 E
Gardolo	64	46.07 N	11.05 E
Gardon d'Alès ≃	62	44.02 N	4.08 E
Gardon d'Anduze ≃	62	44.02 N	4.08 E
Gardone Riviera	64	45.37 N	10.34 E
Gardone Val Trompia	64	45.41 N	10.11 E
Gårdsjö	40	58.52 N	14.19 E
Gårdskär	40	60.37 N	17.35 E
Gare Loch ⊂	46	56.01 N	4.48 W
Garelochhead	46	56.05 N	4.50 W
Gareloi Island I	181a	51.47 N	178.48 W
Garenfeld ◆[8]	263	51.24 N	7.31 E
Garenin	46	58.21 N	6.50 W
Gare Simon	273b	4.15 S	15.11 E
Garešnica	36	45.35 N	16.56 E
Garessio	62	44.12 N	8.02 E
Garet, Mont ∧[1]	175f	14.16 S	167.30 E
Garfield, Ks., U.S.	198	38.04 N	99.14 W
Garfield, N.J., U.S.	210	40.52 N	74.06 W
Garfield, N.M., U.S.	200	32.45 N	107.15 W
Garfield, Wa., U.S.	202	47.00 N	117.08 W
Garfield Heights	214	41.25 N	81.36 W
Garfield Mountain ∧	202	44.31 N	112.37 W
Garfield Park	285	39.42 N	75.33 W
Garfield Park ♠, Il., U.S.	278	41.53 N	87.43 W
Garfield Park ♠, Oh., U.S.	279a	41.26 N	81.36 W
Garfield Peak ∧	200	42.47 N	107.18 W
Garforth	44	53.48 N	1.22 W
Garga	88	54.26 N	110.33 E
Gargaliánoi	38	37.04 N	21.39 E
Gargano, Promontorio del ›	68	41.50 N	16.00 E
Gargano, Testa del ›	68	41.49 N	16.12 E
Gargantua, Cape ›	190	47.36 N	85.02 W
Garga Sarali	152	5.11 N	14.00 E
Gargazzone (Gargazon)	64	46.35 N	11.12 E
Gargellen	58	46.58 N	9.56 E
Gargenville	261	49.00 N	1.49 E
Garges-lès-Gonesse	261	48.58 N	2.25 E
Gargnano	64	45.41 N	10.40 E
Gargouna	150	15.56 N	0.13 E
Gargrave	44	53.59 N	2.06 W
Gargždai	76	55.43 N	21.24 E
Garhākota	124	23.46 N	79.09 E
Garhbeta	126	22.51 N	87.19 E
Garhdīwāla	123	31.44 N	75.45 E
Garhi Habībullāh Khān	123	34.24 N	73.23 E
Garhi Jasaya	272a	28.46 N	77.16 E
Garhi Katiya	272a	28.45 N	77.16 E
Garhi Khairo	120	28.04 N	67.59 E
Garhi Malehra	124	25.02 N	79.40 E
Garhjāt Hills ⋏[2]	126	21.47 N	86.20 E
Garhmuktesar	124	28.48 N	78.06 E
Garhshankar	123	31.13 N	76.08 E
Garhwa	124	24.11 N	83.49 E
Gari	86	59.26 N	62.21 E
Garibaldi, Bra.	252	29.15 S	51.32 W
Garibaldi, B.C., Can.	182	49.58 N	123.09 W
Garibaldi, Or., U.S.	224	45.34 N	123.55 W
Garibaldi, Casa di ⊥	71	41.13 N	9.27 E
Garibaldi, Mount ∧	182	49.51 N	123.01 W
Garibaldi Provincial Park ♠	182	50.00 N	122.50 W
Garies	158	30.30 S	18.00 E
Garigliano ≃	68	41.13 N	13.45 E
Gariglione, Monte ∧	68	39.09 N	16.41 E
Garín	258	34.26 S	58.44 W
Garín, Arroyo ≃	288	34.23 S	58.43 W
Garin Regional Park ♠	282	37.38 N	122.03 W
Garipçe Burnu ›	267b	41.13 N	29.07 E
Garissa	154	0.28 S	39.38 E
Garita Palmera	236	13.44 N	90.05 W
Gariya	272b	22.28 N	88.23 E
Gārji	272b	22.51 N	88.19 E
Garkida	146	10.25 N	12.36 E
Garko	150	11.38 N	8.48 E
Garland, Al., U.S.	194	31.33 N	86.49 W
Garland, Md., U.S.	284b	39.11 N	76.39 W
Garland, Pa., U.S.	214	41.49 N	79.27 W

DEUTSCH

Name	Seite	Breite °′	Länge °′ E = Ost
Garland, Tx., U.S.	222	32.54 N	96.38 W
Garland, Ut,. U.S.	200	41.44 N	112.09 W
Garland Park ♠	275b	43.44 N	79.35 W
Garland Peak ∧	224	48.01 N	120.43 W
Garlasco	62	45.12 N	8.55 E
Garlate	62	45.49 N	9.23 E
Garlate, Lago di ⊜	58	45.49 N	9.24 E
Garliava	76	54.49 N	23.52 E
Garlieston	44	54.48 N	4.22 W
Garlin	32	43.34 N	0.15 W
Garm	85	39.02 N	70.22 E
Garm Āb	120	32.14 N	65.01 E
Garmal	144	8.35 N	50.19 E
Gärmersdorf	60	49.26 N	11.54 E
Garmī	128	39.01 N	48.03 E
Garmisch-Partenkirchen	64	47.29 N	11.05 E
Garmouth	46	57.40 N	3.07 W
Garmsār	128	35.20 N	52.13 E
Garnavillo	190	42.52 N	91.14 W
Garne	261	48.41 N	1.58 E
Garner, Ia., U.S.	190	43.06 N	93.36 W
Garner, N.C., U.S.	192	35.42 N	78.36 W
Garnet Range ⋏	202	46.45 N	113.15 W
Garnett	198	38.16 N	95.14 W
Garnijskij zapovednik ♠	84	40.00 N	44.55 E
Garnish	186	47.14 N	55.22 W
Garnock ≃	46	55.38 N	4.42 W
Garnpung, Lake ⊜	166	33.30 S	143.12 E
Gāro Hills ⋏[2]	124	25.30 N	90.30 E
Garona → Garonne ≃	32	45.02 N	0.36 W
Garonne ≃	32	45.02 N	0.36 W
Garoowe	144	8.24 N	48.29 E
Garou, Lac ⊜	150	16.04 N	2.45 W
Garoua, Cam.	146	9.18 N	13.24 E
Garoua, Niger	146	13.53 N	13.11 E
Garoua Boulaï	152	5.53 N	14.33 E
Garove Island I	164	4.40 S	149.30 E
Garpenberg	40	60.19 N	16.12 E
Garphyttan	40	59.19 N	14.56 E
Garphyttans Nationalpark ♠	40	59.17 N	14.51 E
Garqu Yan, Zhg.	118	34.29 N	92.35 E
Garqu Yan, Zhg.	120	33.50 N	92.28 E
Garraf, Costa de ⊥[2]	266d	41.16 N	2.02 E
Garrattsville	210	42.39 N	75.10 W
Garrel	52	52.57 N	8.01 E
Garret Mountain Reservation ♠	276	40.54 N	74.11 W
Garretson	198	43.43 N	96.30 W
Garrett, In., U.S.	216	41.20 N	85.08 W
Garrett, Ky., U.S.	192	37.28 N	82.49 W
Garrett Creek ≃	222	32.57 N	95.44 W
Garrett Park	208	39.02 N	77.05 W
Garrett Park Estates	284c	39.02 N	77.06 W
Garrettsville	214	41.17 N	81.06 W
Garrison, N. Ire., U.K.	48	54.25 N	8.05 W
Garrison, Ky., U.S.	218	38.36 N	83.10 W
Garrison, Md., U.S.	208	39.24 N	76.45 W
Garrison, Mt., U.S.	202	46.31 N	112.48 W
Garrison, N.Y., U.S.	210	41.23 N	73.56 W
Garrison, N.D., U.S.	198	47.39 N	101.24 W
Garrison, Tx., U.S.	222	31.49 N	94.30 W
Garrison Dam ◆[6]	198	47.22 N	101.25 W
Garron Point ›	48	55.03 N	5.57 W
Garros	46	57.37 N	6.11 W
Garrovillas	34	39.43 N	6.33 W
Garry ≃	46	56.43 N	3.47 W
Garry, Loch ⊜	206	45.15 N	74.43 W
Garry Bay ⊂	176	68.55 N	85.05 W
Garry Lake ⊜	176	66.00 N	100.00 W
Gars am Kamp	61	48.36 N	15.40 E
Garsdale Head	44	54.19 N	2.20 W
Garsen	154	2.16 S	40.07 E
Garskolk	158	30.41 S	22.02 E
Gårslev	41	55.38 N	9.43 E
Garson	190	46.34 N	80.52 W
Garson Lake ⊜	184	56.19 N	110.02 W
Garstang	44	53.55 N	2.47 W
Garstedt	52	53.41 N	9.58 E
Garsten	61	48.01 N	14.24 E
Garston	260	51.41 N	0.23 W
Garston ◆[8]	262	53.21 N	2.53 W
Garswood	262	53.29 N	2.40 W
Gartempe ≃	32	46.48 N	0.50 E
Gartenstadt ◆[8]	263	51.30 N	7.26 E
Garthby Station (Beaulac)	206	45.50 N	71.23 W
Gartow	54	53.02 N	11.29 E
Gartrop-Bühl	263	51.40 N	6.49 E
Gartz	54	53.12 N	14.23 E
Garu	150	10.51 N	0.11 W
Garub	156	26.33 S	16.00 E
Garubhāsa	124	26.33 N	90.22 E
Gārulia	126	22.49 N	88.22 E
Garut	115a	7.13 S	107.54 E
Garve	46	57.37 N	4.42 W
Garvellachs II	46	56.14 N	5.47 W
Garvey Reservoir ⊜[1]	280	34.13 N	118.07 W
Garvie Mountains ⋏	172	45.30 S	168.50 E
Garwin	190	42.05 N	92.40 W
Garwolin	30	51.54 N	21.37 E
Garwood, N.J., U.S.	276	40.39 N	74.19 W
Garwood, Tx., U.S.	222	29.27 N	96.24 W
Gary, In., U.S.	216	41.35 N	87.20 W
Gary, S.D., U.S.	198	44.47 N	96.27 W
Gary, Tx., U.S.	194	32.07 N	94.22 W
Gary, W.V., U.S.	192	37.21 N	81.33 W
Garyarsa	120	31.44 N	80.21 E
Gary Harbor ⊂	278	41.38 N	87.20 W
Garyi	102	30.54 N	98.56 E
Gary Municipal Airport ⊠	278	41.37 N	87.25 W
Garysburg	208	36.27 N	77.33 W
Garz	54	54.19 N	13.20 E
Garza	252	28.09 S	63.32 W
Garza Ayala	196	26.29 N	100.02 W
Garza García	196	25.40 N	100.24 W
Garzas Creek ≃	226	37.13 N	120.57 W
Garzeno	58	46.08 N	9.15 E
Garzón, Col.	246	2.12 N	75.38 W
Garzón, Ur.	252	34.36 S	54.33 W
Gas	261	48.34 N	1.40 E
Gasan	116	13.19 N	121.51 E
Gasan-Kuli	128	37.27 N	53.59 E
Gas City	216	40.29 N	85.36 W
Gascogne □[9]	32	44.00 N	0.05 E
Gascogne, Golfe de → Biscay, Bay of ⊂	32	44.00 N	4.00 W
Gasconade	219	38.40 N	91.33 W
Gasconade □[6]	219	38.27 N	91.30 W
Gasconade ≃	194	38.40 N	91.33 W
Gasconade, Osage Fork ≃	194	37.45 N	92.26 W
Gascoyne ≃	162	24.52 S	113.37 E
Gascoyne, Mount ∧	162	24.58 S	116.38 E
Gascoyne Junction	162	25.03 S	115.12 E
Gash (Nahr al-Qāsh) ≃	140	16.48 N	35.51 E
Gashaka	146	7.21 N	11.27 E
Gasherbrum I ∧	123	35.43 N	76.43 E
Gas Hu ⊜	120	38.10 N	90.42 E
Gashua	146	12.54 N	11.00 E
Gasline	284a	42.53 N	79.11 W
Gasny	50	49.05 N	1.36 E
Gaspar	252	26.56 S	48.58 W
Gaspard Creek ≃	182	51.34 N	122.17 W
Gasparilla Island I	220	26.46 N	82.16 W
Gasparilla Sound ʊ	220	26.48 N	82.15 W
Gaspé	186	48.50 N	64.29 W
Gaspé, Baie de ⊂	186	48.46 N	64.17 W
Gaspé, Cap ›	186	48.45 N	64.10 W
Gaspé Peninsula → Gaspésie, Péninsule de la ›[1]	186	48.30 N	65.00 W
Gaspereau Lake ⊜	186	44.57 N	64.34 W
Gasperina	68	38.44 N	16.30 E
Gaspésie, Parc Provincial de la ♠	186	48.55 N	66.00 W

Symbols in the index entries represent the broad categories identified in the key at the right. Symbols with superior numbers (⋏[1]) identify subcategories (see complete key on page *I · 1).*

Symbole im Register stellen die rechts im Schlüssel erklärten Kategorien dar. Symbole mit hochgestellten Ziffern (⋏[1]) bezeichnen Unterabteilungen einer Kategorie (vgl. vollständiger Schlüssel auf Seite *I · 1).*

Los símbolos incluídos en el texto del índice representan las grandes categorias identificadas con la clave a la derecha. Los símbolos con numeros en su parte superior (⋏[1]) identifican las subcategorías (véase la clave completa en la página *I · 1).*

Les symboles de l'index représentent les catégories indiquées dans la légende à droite. Les symboles suivis d'un indice (⋏[1]) représentent des sous-catégories (voir légende complète à la page *I · 1).*

Os símbolos incluídos no texto do índice representam as grandes categorias identificadas com a chave à direita. Os símbolos com números em sua parte superior (⋏[1]) identificam as subcategorias (veja-se a chave completa à página *I · 1).*

∧ Mountain	Berg	Montaña	Montagne	Montanha
⋏ Mountains	Gebirge	Montañas	Montagnes	Montanhas
)(Pass	Paß	Paso	Col	Passo
V Valley, Canyon	Tal, Cañon	Valle, Cañón	Vallée, Canyon	Vale, Canhão
≚ Plain	Ebene	Llano	Plaine	Planície
› Cape	Kap	Cabo	Cap	Cabo
I Island	Insel	Isla	Île	Ilha
II Islands	Inseln	Islas	Îles	Ilhas
⊥ Other Topographic Features	Andere Topographische Objekte	Otros Elementos Topográficos	Autres données topographiques	Outros acidentes topográficos

ESPAÑOL Nombre	Página	Lat.°′	Long.°′ W = Oeste
FRANÇAIS Nom	Page	Lat.°′	Long.°′ W = Ouest
PORTUGUÊS Nome	Página	Lat.°′	Long.°′ W = Oeste

Legend (footer)

Symbol	English	Français	Deutsch	Español	Português
≃	River	Rivière	Fluß	Río	Rio
≡	Canal	Canal	Kanal	Canal	Canal
⌐	Waterfall, Rapids	Chute d'eau, Rapides	Wasserfall, Stromschnellen	Cascada, Rápidos	Cascata, Rápidos
ᴜ	Strait	Détroit	Meeresstraße	Estrecho	Estreito
c	Bay, Gulf	Baie, Golfe	Bucht, Golf	Bahía, Golfo	Baía, Golfo
⊕	Lake, Lakes	Lac, Lacs	See, Seen	Lago, Lagos	Lago, Lagos
⊠	Swamp	Marais	Sumpf	Pantano	Pântano
⊟	Ice Features, Glacier	Formes glaciaires	Eis- und Gletscherformen	Accidentes Glaciales	Formas glaciares
∓	Other Hydrographic Features	Autres données hydrographiques	Andere Hydrographische Objekte	Otros Elementos Hidrográficos	Outros acidentes hidrográficos
⊹	Submarine Features	Accidents sous-marin	Untermeerische Objekte	Accidentes Submarinos	Acidentes submarinos
□	Political Unit	Entité politique	Politische Einheit	Unidad Política	Unidade política
⋲	Cultural Institution	Institution culturelle	Kulturelle Institution	Institución Cultural	Instituição cultural
⊥	Historical Site	Site historique	Historische Stätte	Sitio Histórico	Sítio histórico
♦	Recreational Site	Centre de loisirs	Erholungs- und Ferienort	Sitio de Recreo	Área de Lazer
⊠	Airport	Aéroport	Flughafen	Aeropuerto	Aeroporto
⌂	Military Installation	Installation militaire	Militäranlage	Instalación Militar	Instalação militar
◆	Miscellaneous	Divers	Verschiedenes	Misceláneo	Diversos

Gerthe ◆[8] 263 51.31 N 7.17 E
Gerufa 156 19.17 S 26.02 E
Gervais 224 45.06 N 122.53 W
Gerwisch 54 52.10 N 11.44 E
Gerza 142 29.26 N 31.11 E
Gerze, Tür. 130 41.48 N 35.12 E
Gêrzê, Zhg. 120 32.16 N 84.12 E
Gerzen 60 48.31 N 12.25 E
Gerzensee 58 46.51 N 7.33 E
Gescher 52 51.57 N 6.59 E
Geschriebenstein (Írottkő) ∧ 61 47.21 N 16.26 E
Geschwenda 54 50.44 N 10.49 E
Gesees 60 49.54 N 11.32 E
Geseke 52 51.38 N 8.31 E
Geser 164 3.53 S 130.54 E
Gesher HaZiw 132 33.02 N 35.06 E
Gesi 115a 7.20 S 111.01 E
Gesoa 164 8.25 S 143.35 E
Gespunsart 56 49.49 N 4.50 E
Gessertshausen 58 48.20 N 10.44 E
Gesso ≃ 62 44.24 N 7.33 E
Gessopalena 66 42.03 N 14.16 E
Gesten 41 55.31 N 9.12 E
Gesualdo 68 41.00 N 15.04 E
Geta 26 60.23 N 19.50 E
Getafe 34 40.18 N 3.43 W
Getafe, Aeropuerto ⊠ 266a 40.18 N 3.43 W
Gete ≃ 56 50.57 N 5.07 E
Gethaoli 272c 19.08 N 73.01 E
Geti 154 1.13 N 30.12 E
Getinge 26 56.49 N 12.44 E
Gettorf 41 54.24 N 9.58 E
Gettysburg, Oh., U.S. 218 40.06 N 84.29 W
Gettysburg, Pa., U.S. 208 39.49 N 77.13 W
Gettysburg, S.D., U.S. 198 45.00 N 99.57 W
Gettysburg National Military Park ♠ 208 39.49 N 77.15 W
Getulândia 256 22.40 S 44.06 W
Getulina 255 21.49 S 49.55 W
Getulio 116 10.45 N 122.40 E
Getúlio Vargas 252 27.50 S 52.16 W
Getz Ice Shelf ⊓ 9 75.00 S 129.00 W
Getzville 210 43.01 N 78.46 W
Geumpang 114 4.48 N 96.09 E
Geureudong, Gunung ∧ 114 4.48 N 96.48 E
Gevān 128 26.03 N 57.17 E
Gevaş 128 38.16 N 43.07 E
Gevelsberg 56 51.19 N 7.20 E
Gevgelija 38 41.08 N 22.30 E
Gévora ≃ 34 38.53 N 6.57 W
Gevrey-Chambertin 58 47.14 N 4.57 E
Gewane 144 10.10 N 40.39 E
Geweke ◆[8] 263 51.22 N 7.25 E
Gex 58 46.20 N 6.04 E
Geyer 54 50.37 N 12.55 E
Geyer Ditch ≋ 216 41.36 N 86.25 W
Geyikli 130 39.48 N 26.12 E
Geysdorp 158 26.32 S 25.18 E
Geyser 202 47.15 N 110.29 W
Geyserville 204 38.42 N 122.54 W
Geyshtasar, Kūh-e ∧ 84 38.51 N 47.14 E
Geyuan 100 28.31 N 117.44 E
Geyve 130 40.30 N 30.18 E
Gézenti 146 21.41 N 18.18 E
Gezer 132 31.52 N 34.55 E
Gföhl 61 48.31 N 15.30 E
Ghaapplato ⋏[1] 158 27.30 S 24.00 E
Ghabāghib 132 33.10 N 36.13 E
Ghābat al-ʿArab 140 9.02 N 29.29 E
Ghadaf, Wādī al- V 132 31.46 N 36.50 E
Ghadāmis 146 30.08 N 9.30 E
Ghaddūwah 146 26.26 N 14.18 E
Ghafe 272c 19.05 N 73.07 E
Ghagghar ≃ 123 29.30 N 74.53 E
Ghāghara ≃ 124 25.47 N 84.37 E
Ghaghar Reservoir ⊜[1] 124 24.38 N 83.11 E
Ghāghra 124 23.17 N 84.33 E
Ghakhar 123 32.18 N 74.09 E
Ghallah, Wādī al- V 140 10.25 N 27.32 E
Ghammāzah al-Kubrā 142 29.43 N 31.18 E
Ghamrīn 142 30.30 N 30.55 E
Ghana □[1], Afr. 134 8.00 N 1.00 W
Ghana □[1], Afr. 150 8.00 N 1.00 W
Ghansoli 272c 19.08 N 72.59 E
Ghanzi 156 21.38 S 21.45 E
Ghanzi □[5] 156 22.00 S 23.00 E
Ghārāpuri 272c 18.54 N 72.56 E
Gharaunda 124 29.33 N 76.58 E
Gharbah, Wādī V 142 29.40 N 31.58 E
Gharbi, Chott ⊜ 148 33.50 N 1.30 W
Gharbi, Oued el V 148 31.50 N 0.51 E
Gharbīyah, Aṣ-Ṣaḥrā' al- (Western Desert) ◆[2] 140 27.00 N 27.00 E
Ghardaïa 148 32.31 N 3.37 E
Ghardimaou 36 36.26 N 8.27 E
Gharghoda 124 22.10 N 83.21 E
Gharībwāl 123 32.41 N 73.10 E
Gharīfah 132 33.38 N 35.33 E
Gharig 140 10.47 N 27.33 E
Ghārīyat al-Gharbīyah 132 32.41 N 36.13 E
Ghārīyat ash-Sharqīyah 132 32.40 N 36.16 E
Gharo 120 24.44 N 67.35 E
Gharrāf, Shaṭṭ al- ≃ 128 32.30 N 45.48 E
Gharroli ◆[8] 272a 28.37 N 77.20 E
Gharsa, Chott el ⊜ 148 34.06 N 7.50 E
Gharw, Jazīrat I 142 31.21 N 30.06 E
Gharyān 146 32.10 N 13.01 E
Ghaṣm 132 32.33 N 36.22 E
Ghāt 146 24.58 N 10.11 E
Ghātāl 126 22.40 N 87.43 E
Ghatampur 272b 22.54 N 88.10 E
Ghatere, Mount ∧ 175e 7.49 S 158.54 E
Ghātkopar ◆[8] 272c 19.05 N 72.54 E
Ghātprabha ≃ 122 16.20 N 75.48 E
Ghātsīla 126 22.36 N 86.29 E
Ghats Occidentales → Western Ghāts ⋏ 122 14.00 N 75.00 E
Ghats Orientales → Eastern Ghāts ⋏ 122 14.00 N 78.50 E
Għawdex (Gozo) I 36 36.03 N 14.15 E
Ghawr ash-Sharqīyah, Qanāt al- (East Ghor Canal) ≋ 132 32.41 N 35.38 E
Ghaylah ∧[1] 132 33.11 N 37.05 E
Ghayl Bā Wazīr 144 14.48 N 49.21 E
Ghayl Bin Yumayn ╤[4] 144 15.33 N 49.23 E
Ghayth, Wādī V 132 30.59 N 36.00 E
Ghazāl, Baḥr al- ≃ 140 9.31 N 30.25 E
Ghazal, Bahr el V 146 13.01 N 15.28 E
Ghazālat al-Khīs 142 30.34 N 31.34 E
Ghāziābād 123 28.40 N 77.26 E
Ghāzīpur, India 124 25.35 N 83.34 E
Ghazipur, India 272b 22.36 N 88.34 E
Ghāzipur ◆[8] 272a 28.38 N 77.19 E
Ghazīr 130 34.01 N 35.40 E
Ghazlūna 120 31.24 N 67.49 E
Ghaznī 120 33.33 N 68.26 E
Ghaznī □[4] 120 33.15 N 67.45 E
Ghaznī ≃ 120 32.35 N 67.58 E
Ghazni Khel 123 32.33 N 70.44 E
Ghazzah (Gaza), Isr. Occ 132 31.30 N 34.28 E
Ghazzah, Lubnān 132 33.40 N 35.49 E
Gheā ≃ 272b 22.52 N 88.19 E
Ghedi 64 45.24 N 10.16 E
Ghemme 62 45.37 N 8.25 E
Ghennes Heights 279b 40.09 N 79.56 W
Ghent → Gent, Bel. 50 51.03 N 3.43 E
Ghent, Ky., U.S. 218 38.44 N 85.03 W
Ghent, N.Y., U.S. 210 42.19 N 73.36 W
Ghent, Oh., U.S. 214 41.09 N 81.38 W
Gheora ◆[8] 272a 28.42 N 77.01 E
Gheorghe Gheorghiu-Dej 38 46.14 N 26.44 E
Gheorgheni 38 46.43 N 25.36 E
Gherla 38 47.02 N 23.55 E
Ghesar 272c 19.09 N 73.05 E
Ghigo 62 44.53 N 7.03 E
Ghilarza 71 40.07 N 8.50 E
Ghilizane 148 35.44 N 0.30 E
Ghīn, Tall ∧ 132 32.39 N 36.43 E
Ghior 126 23.54 N 89.53 E
Ghislenghien, Bel. 50 50.39 N 3.52 E
Ghislenghien (Gellingen), Bel. 50 50.39 N 3.52 E
Ghisonaccia 36 42.00 N 9.25 E
Ghizar ≃ 123 36.15 N 73.25 E
Ghizunabeana Islands II 175e 7.31 S 158.42 E
Ghlin 50 50.28 N 3.53 E
Ghlò, Beinn a' ∧ 46 56.50 N 3.43 W
Ghogha 120 21.41 N 72.17 E
Gholson 222 31.43 N 97.12 W
Ghonda ◆[8] 272a 28.41 N 77.16 E
Ghondi ◆[8] 272a 28.42 N 77.16 E
Ghorāsahan 124 26.50 N 85.08 E
Ghoshpur, Bngl. 126 23.27 N 89.39 E
Ghoshpur, India 272b 22.23 N 88.29 E
Ghotki 120 28.01 N 69.19 E
Ghowr □[4] 128 34.00 N 65.00 E
Ghubaysh 140 12.09 N 27.21 E
Ghudāf, Wādī al- V 128 32.56 N 43.30 E
Ghulayfiqah 144 14.27 N 43.02 E
Ghunthur 130 34.23 N 37.09 E
Ghurāb, Jabal ∧[2] 142 28.58 N 31.16 E
Ghurayrah 144 18.37 N 42.41 E
Ghūrīān 128 34.21 N 61.30 E
Ghushuri 272b 22.37 N 88.22 E
Ghuwaybah, Wādī V 142 29.36 N 32.20 E
Ghuwayr, ʿAyn al- ╤[4] 132 31.37 N 35.25 E
Ghuzzayil, Sabkhat ⊜ 146 29.50 N 19.35 E
Giaginskaja 78 44.53 N 40.05 E
Gianh ≃ 110 17.40 N 106.30 E
Giannutri, Isola di I 66 42.15 N 11.06 E
Giano, Monte ∧ 66 42.25 N 13.06 E
Giano dell'Umbria 66 42.50 N 12.35 E
Giant City State Park ♠ 194 37.39 N 89.12 W
Giant Mountain ∧ 188 44.10 N 73.44 W
Giant's Castle ∧ 158 29.21 S 29.27 E
Giant's Castle Game Reserve ◆[4] 158 29.16 S 29.30 E
Giant's Causeway ♠ 48 55.14 N 6.30 W
Giants Neck 207 41.18 N 72.13 W
Giants Tomb Island I 212 44.55 N 80.00 W
Gianyar 115b 8.32 S 115.20 E
Gia Rai 110 9.14 N 105.28 E
Giardinello 70 38.05 N 13.09 E
Giardinetto 68 41.19 N 15.24 E
Giardini 70 37.50 N 15.17 E
Giarratana 70 37.03 N 14.48 E
Giarre 70 37.43 N 15.11 E
Giaveno 62 45.02 N 7.21 E
Giazza 64 45.39 N 11.07 E
Giba 71 39.04 N 8.38 E
Gibara 240p 21.07 N 76.08 W
Gibbon, Mn., U.S. 190 44.32 N 94.31 W
Gibbon, Ne., U.S. 198 40.44 N 98.50 W
Gibbons 182 53.50 N 113.20 W
Gibbonsville 202 45.33 N 113.55 W
Gibb River 164 15.39 S 126.38 E
Gibbs, Mount ∧ 162 32.55 S 120.00 E
Gibbsboro 285 39.50 N 74.58 W
Gibbstown 208 39.49 N 75.17 W
Gibellina 70 37.47 N 12.58 E
Gibeon 156 25.09 S 17.43 E
Gibilmanna, Santuario di ʋ[1] 70 37.59 N 14.02 E
Gibraleón 34 37.23 N 6.58 W
Gibraltar, Gib. 34 36.08 N 5.21 W
Gibraltar, Mi., U.S. 216 42.06 N 83.12 W
Gibraltar, Pa., U.S. 208 40.17 N 75.52 W
Gibraltar □[2], Europe 22 36.08 N 5.21 W
Gibraltar □[2], Europe 34 36.08 N 5.21 W
Gibraltar, Strait of (Estrecho de Gibraltar) ⊔ 34 35.57 N 5.36 W
Gibraltar Point ›, On., Can. 275b 43.36 N 79.23 W
Gibraltar Point ›, Eng., U.K. 44 53.05 N 0.19 E
Gibsland 194 32.32 N 93.03 W
Gibson, Austl. 162 33.39 S 121.48 E
Gibson, Ga., U.S. 192 33.14 N 82.35 W
Gibson, N.Y., U.S. 210 42.08 N 76.59 W
Gibson, Pa., U.S. 210 41.44 N 75.38 W
Gibson ≃ 212 44.58 N 79.51 W
Gibson, Lake ⊜[1] 284a 43.06 N 79.14 W
Gibsonburg 214 41.23 N 83.19 W
Gibson City 216 40.27 N 88.22 W
Gibson Desert ◆[2] 162 24.30 S 126.00 E
Gibson Hill ∧[2] 214 41.51 N 80.10 W
Gibsonia, Fl., U.S. 220 28.06 N 81.58 W
Gibsonia, Pa., U.S. 214 40.38 N 79.59 W
Gibson Indian Reserve ◆[4] 212 45.01 N 79.44 W
Gibson Island I 208 39.05 N 76.26 W
Gibsons 182 49.24 N 123.30 W
Gibsonton 220 27.51 N 82.22 W
Gidajevo 24 59.57 N 52.22 E
Gidami 144 9.58 N 34.37 E
Gidda 144 9.34 N 35.23 E
Giddalūr 122 15.21 N 78.55 E
Giddarbāha 123 30.12 N 74.40 E
Giddings 222 30.10 N 96.56 W
Gideälven ≃ 26 63.20 N 19.08 E
Gidea Park ◆[8] 260 51.35 N 0.12 E
Gideåvallen 26 63.29 N 18.58 E
Gideon 194 36.27 N 89.55 W
Gidgee 162 27.16 S 119.22 E
Gidgi, Lake ⊜ 162 29.16 S 126.03 E
Gidhni 126 22.29 N 86.51 E
Gidole 144 5.38 N 37.30 E
Gidrotorf 80 56.28 N 43.33 E
Gidžaki, gora ∧ 84 40.25 N 49.01 E
Giebelstadt 56 49.39 N 9.56 E
Gieboldehausen 52 51.36 N 10.13 E
Giedraičiai 76 55.05 N 25.15 E
Gielow 54 53.42 N 12.44 E
Gielsdorf 264a 52.36 N 13.52 E
Gien 50 47.42 N 2.38 E
Giengen 56 48.37 N 10.14 E
Giens 62 43.02 N 6.08 E
Gier ≃ 62 45.35 N 4.46 E
Gierath 263 51.07 N 6.33 E
Gierle 56 51.16 N 4.51 E
Giesebitz → Izbica 30 54.42 N 17.26 E
Gieselwerder 52 51.36 N 9.33 E
Giesenkirchen ◆[8] 263 51.09 N 6.30 E
Giesing ◆[8] 64 48.06 N 11.35 E
Giessbachfälle ∟ 58 46.42 N 8.03 E
Giessen 56 50.35 N 8.40 E
Giessen □[5] 56 50.40 N 8.40 E
Gieten 52 53.00 N 6.46 E
Giethoorn 52 52.43 N 6.05 E
Gièvres 50 47.16 N 1.40 E
Giez 62 45.45 N 6.15 E
Giffone 68 38.27 N 16.10 E
Giffoni Valle Piana 68 40.44 N 14.56 E
Gifford, Scot., U.K. 46 55.54 N 2.45 W
Gifford, Fl., U.S. 220 27.40 N 80.24 W
Gifford, Il., U.S. 216 40.18 N 88.01 W
Gifford, In., U.S. 216 41.06 N 87.01 W
Gifford, Pa., U.S. 214 41.51 N 78.36 W
Gifford ≃ 176 70.21 N 83.05 W
Gifford Creek 162 24.05 S 116.11 E
Gifford Pinchot State Park ♠ 208 40.04 N 76.53 W
Giffre ≃ 58 46.05 N 6.30 E
Gifhorn 52 52.29 N 10.33 E
Giflitz 56 51.09 N 9.07 E
Gif-sur-Yvette 261 48.42 N 2.08 E
Gifu 94 35.25 N 136.45 E
Gifu □[5] 94 35.45 N 137.00 E
Gigant 80 46.30 N 41.20 E
Giganta, Cerro ∧ 232 26.07 N 111.36 W
Giganta, Sierra de la ⋏ 232 25.30 N 111.15 W
Gigante 246 2.23 N 75.33 W
Gigante Islands II 116 11.36 N 123.20 E
Gigen 38 43.42 N 24.29 E
Gigena → Alcira 252 32.45 S 64.20 W
Giggleswick 44 54.04 N 2.17 W
Gigha, Sound of ⊔ 46 55.41 N 5.42 W
Gigha Island I 46 55.41 N 5.46 W
Gig Harbor 224 47.19 N 122.34 W
Giglio, Isola del I 66 42.21 N 10.54 E
Giglio Castello 66 42.22 N 10.54 E
Gigliola 66 44.51 N 12.14 E
Giglio Porto 66 42.22 N 10.55 E
Gigmoto 116 13.47 N 124.23 E
Gignod 62 45.46 N 7.17 E
Gihu → Gifu 94 35.25 N 136.45 E
Gijón 34 43.32 N 5.40 W
Gikongoro 154 2.29 S 29.34 E
Gila ≃ 200 32.43 N 114.33 W
Gila, Middle Fork ≃ 200 33.14 N 108.14 W
Gila Bend 200 32.56 N 112.42 W
Gila Bend Indian Reservation ◆[4] 200 33.00 N 112.46 W
Gila Bend Mountains ⋏ 200 33.10 N 113.10 W
Gila Cliff Dwellings National Monument ♠ 200 33.02 N 108.16 W
Gila Mountains ⋏ 200 33.05 N 109.50 W
Gīlān □[4] 128 37.15 N 49.30 E
Gīlān-e Gharb 128 34.08 N 45.55 E
Gila River Indian Reservation ◆[4] 200 33.12 N 112.00 W
Gilātala 126 22.36 N 89.41 E
Gilberdyke 44 53.45 N 0.44 W
Gilbert, La., U.S. 194 32.02 N 91.39 W
Gilbert, Mn., U.S. 190 47.29 N 92.27 W
Gilbert ≃, Austl. 166 16.35 S 141.15 E
Gilbert ≃, Austl. 168b 34.22 S 138.40 E
Gilbert, Mount ∧ 182 50.51 N 124.20 W
Gilbert Airport ⊠ 279a 41.22 N 81.58 W
Gilbert Island I 219 39.35 N 91.11 W
Gilbert Islands → Kiribati □[1] 14 5.00 S 170.00 W
Gilbert Lake ⊜ 281 42.34 N 83.17 W
Gilbert Lake State Park ♠ 210 42.36 N 75.08 W
Gilberton 210 40.48 N 76.13 W
Gilbertown 194 31.52 N 88.19 W
Gilbert Peak ∧ 224 46.30 N 121.25 W
Gilbert Plains 184 51.09 N 100.29 W
Gilbert River 166 18.09 S 142.52 E
Gilberts 216 42.06 N 88.23 W
Gilbert Seamount ◆[3] 16 52.50 N 150.10 W
Gilbertsville, N.Y., U.S. 210 42.28 N 75.19 W
Gilbertsville, Pa., U.S. 208 40.19 N 75.37 W
Gilbertville 207 42.18 N 72.12 W
Gilbjerg Hoved › 41 56.08 N 12.17 E
Gilboa 216 41.01 N 83.55 W
Gilboaʿ, Haré ⋏[2] 132 32.30 N 35.23 E
Gilbués 250 9.50 S 45.21 W
Gilching 60 48.07 N 11.17 E
Gildehaus 52 52.18 N 7.06 E
Gildford 202 48.34 N 110.17 W
Gilead 216 41.48 N 85.09 W
Giles, Arroyo de ≃ 258 34.20 S 59.23 W
Giles Meteorological Station ʋ[3] 162 25.02 S 128.18 E
Giles Point › 168b 35.03 S 137.45 E
Gilette 62 43.51 N 7.10 E
Gilford 48 54.23 N 6.22 W
Gilford Island I 182 50.45 N 126.25 W
Gilford Park 208 39.58 N 74.08 W
Gilgai 162 31.15 S 119.56 E
Gilgandra 166 31.42 S 148.39 E
Gilgil 154 0.30 S 36.19 E
Gil Gil Creek ≃ 166 29.10 S 148.51 E
Gilgit 123 35.55 N 74.18 E
Gilgit ≃ 123 35.44 N 74.38 E
Gilgo Island I 276 40.38 N 73.25 W
Gilgo State Park ♠ 276 40.38 N 73.22 W
Gilima 154 3.55 N 28.22 E
Gilimanuk 115a 8.10 S 114.26 E
Gilirang 112 3.55 S 120.09 E
Gil Island I 182 53.13 N 129.15 W
Gill, Lough ⊜ 48 54.16 N 8.24 W
Gillam 184 56.21 N 94.43 W
Gilleland Creek ≃ 222 30.13 N 97.32 W
Gilleleje 41 56.07 N 12.19 E
Gillen, Lake ⊜ 162 26.11 S 124.38 E
Gilles, Lake ⊜ 166 32.50 S 136.45 E
Gillespie 219 39.07 N 89.49 W
Gillespies Point › 172 43.24 S 169.50 E
Gillett, Ar., U.S. 194 34.07 N 91.22 W
Gillett, Pa., U.S. 210 41.57 N 76.48 W
Gillett, Wi., U.S. 190 44.53 N 88.18 W
Gillette, N.J., U.S. 276 40.41 N 74.28 W
Gillette, Wy., U.S. 198 44.17 N 105.30 W
Gillette Castle State Park ♠ 207 41.26 N 72.25 W
Gillian, Lake ⊜ 176 69.32 N 75.23 W
Gillingham, Eng., U.K. 42 51.02 N 2.17 W
Gillingham, Eng., U.K. 260 51.24 N 0.33 E
Gillingham □[8] 260 51.22 N 0.35 E
Gills Rock 190 45.17 N 87.01 W
Gilman, Ct., U.S. 207 41.34 N 72.11 W
Gilman, Il., U.S. 216 40.46 N 87.59 W
Gilman, Ia., U.S. 190 41.52 N 92.47 W
Gilman, Wi., U.S. 190 45.10 N 90.48 W
Gilman Hot Springs 228 33.50 N 116.59 W
Gilman Lake 285 39.41 N 75.11 W
Gilmer, Il., U.S. 278 42.14 N 88.02 W
Gilmer, Tx., U.S. 222 32.43 N 94.56 W
Gilmer Park 216 41.36 N 86.15 W
Gilmore 171b 35.20 S 148.11 E
Gilmore City 198 42.44 N 94.27 W
Gilmore Creek ≃ 171b 35.18 S 148.13 E
Gilo ≃ 144 8.10 N 33.15 E
Gilroy 226 37.00 N 121.34 W
Gilserberg 56 50.57 N 9.04 E
Gilsizer Slough ≃ 226 38.58 N 121.44 W
Gilston Park ♠ 260 51.48 N 0.04 E
Giltner 198 40.46 N 98.09 W
Gil'uj ≃ 89 53.58 N 127.30 E
Giluwe, Mount ∧ 164 6.05 S 143.50 E
Gilwern 42 51.51 N 3.06 W
Gilze 52 51.33 N 4.57 E
Gimån ≃ 26 62.28 N 16.20 E
Gimbi 144 9.10 N 35.42 E
Gimcheon → Kimch'ŏn 98 36.07 N 128.05 E
Gimie, Mount ∧ 241f 13.52 N 61.01 W
Gimigliano 68 38.58 N 16.32 E
Gimlet 218 38.13 N 83.09 W
Gimli 184 50.38 N 96.59 W
Gimo 40 60.11 N 18.11 E
Gimoly 24 63.03 N 32.19 E
Gimone ≃ 32 44.00 N 1.06 E
Gimont 32 43.38 N 0.53 E
Gimpu 112 1.36 S 120.02 E
Ginderich 263 51.39 N 6.32 E
Ginebra → Genève 58 46.12 N 6.09 E
Gineste, Col de la)(62 43.15 N 5.27 E
Gingell 216 42.43 N 83.17 W
Gingera, Mount ∧ 171b 35.35 S 148.47 E
Ginger Hill 279b 40.12 N 80.00 W
Ginger Island I 240m 18.24 N 64.28 W
Gingin, Austl. 162 31.21 S 115.42 E
Gin Gin, Austl. 166 25.00 S 151.58 E
Gingindlovu 158 29.02 S 31.30 E
Gingoog 116 8.50 N 125.07 E
Gingoog Bay ⊂ 116 8.59 N 125.05 E
Gingst 54 54.27 N 13.16 E
Ginir 144 7.07 N 40.46 E
Ginkakuji Temple ʋ[1] 270 35.03 N 135.47 E
Ginkgo State Park ♠ 202 46.59 N 120.01 W
Ginnosar 132 32.51 N 35.31 E
Ginosa 68 40.35 N 16.46 E
Ginostra 70 38.47 N 15.11 E
Ginowan 174m 26.17 N 127.46 E
Ginoza 174m 26.28 N 127.57 E
Ginter 214 40.46 N 78.23 W
Ginza ◆[8] 268 35.40 N 139.47 E
Gioi 68 40.17 N 15.13 E
Gioia, Golfo di ⊂ 68 38.30 N 15.45 E
Gioia dei Marsi 66 41.57 N 13.42 E
Gioia del Colle 68 40.48 N 16.56 E
Gioia Tauro 68 38.26 N 15.54 E
Gioia Vecchio 66 41.54 N 13.44 E
Gioiosa Ionica 68 38.20 N 16.18 E
Gioiosa Marea 70 38.10 N 14.54 E
Giong Rieng 110 9.55 N 105.19 E
Giornico 58 46.24 N 8.52 E
Giovi, Passo dei)(62 44.33 N 8.57 E
Giovinazzo 68 41.11 N 16.40 E
Giporlos 116 11.07 N 125.27 E
Gipping ≃ 42 52.04 N 1.10 E
Gipsy 214 40.48 N 78.53 W
Gipuzkoako □[4] 34 43.10 N 2.10 W
Giraglia, Île de la I 62 43.02 N 9.24 E
Giralia 162 22.41 S 114.21 E
Giraltovce 30 49.07 N 21.31 E
Girard, Il., U.S. 219 39.26 N 89.46 W
Girard, Ks., U.S. 198 37.30 N 94.50 W
Girard, Mi., U.S. 216 42.02 N 85.00 W
Girard, Oh., U.S. 214 41.09 N 80.42 W
Girard, Pa., U.S. 214 42.00 N 80.19 W
Girard, Tx., U.S. 196 33.22 N 100.40 W
Girardot 246 4.18 N 74.48 W
Girardville 208 40.47 N 76.17 W
Giraud, Pointe › 240d 15.19 N 61.15 W
Giraul ≃ 152 15.04 S 12.08 E
Giraumont 56 49.10 N 5.55 E
Girbovu 38 44.44 N 23.21 E
Girdletree 208 38.05 N 75.23 W
Giresun 130 40.55 N 38.24 E
Giresun □[4] 130 40.30 N 38.30 E
Giresun Dağları ⋏ 130 40.30 N 39.00 E
Girgarre 166 36.24 S 144.59 E
Girgaum ◆[8] 272c 18.57 N 72.48 E
Girgenti → Agrigento 70 37.18 N 13.35 E
Girgir, Cape › 164 3.50 S 144.34 E
Giri ≃ 152 0.28 N 17.59 E
Girīdīh 126 24.11 N 86.18 E
Girifalco 68 38.49 N 16.25 E
Girilambone 166 31.15 S 146.54 E
Girmeli 130 37.07 N 41.26 E
Girna ≃ 122 21.08 N 75.19 E
Gir National Park ♠ 120 21.00 N 70.50 E
Girne (Kyrenia) 130 35.20 N 33.19 E
Giro, Nig. 150 11.06 N 4.46 E
Giro, Zaïre 154 3.08 N 29.15 E
Giromagny 58 47.45 N 6.50 E
Girón, Ec. 246 3.10 S 79.08 W
Giron, Fr. 58 46.14 N 5.46 E
Girona 34 41.59 N 2.49 E
Gironde □[5] 32 44.45 N 0.35 W
Gironde ⊂[1] 32 45.20 N 0.45 W
Gironville-sous-les-Côtes 56 48.48 N 5.40 E
Girou ≃ 32 43.46 N 1.23 E
Girouxville 182 55.45 N 117.20 W
Gīr Range ⋏ 120 21.18 N 71.00 E
Girton 42 52.14 N 0.05 E
Girtys Run ≃ 279b 40.28 N 79.58 W
Giru 166 19.31 S 147.06 E
Giruá 252 28.02 S 54.21 W
Girvan 44 55.15 N 4.51 W
Girvan, Water of ≃ 44 55.15 N 4.51 W
Girvas 24 62.30 N 33.40 E
Gisborne, Austl. 169 37.29 S 144.35 E
Gisborne, N.Z. 172 38.40 S 178.01 E
Gisborne Lake ⊜ 186 47.48 N 54.50 W
Giscome 182 54.04 N 122.22 W
Gisenyi 154 1.42 S 29.15 E
Gishyita 154 2.11 S 29.18 E
Gislaved 26 57.18 N 13.32 E
Gislev 41 55.13 N 10.37 E
Gislinge 41 55.44 N 11.33 E
Gislövs läge 41 55.21 N 13.14 E
Gisors 50 49.17 N 1.47 E
Gissar 85 38.33 N 68.35 E
Gissarskij chrebet ⋏ 85 39.00 N 68.40 E
Gisselfeld 41 55.18 N 11.59 E
Gissi 66 42.01 N 14.33 E
Gisslarbo 40 59.38 N 15.49 E
Gistel 50 51.10 N 2.57 E
Giswil 58 46.50 N 8.11 E
Gitambo 154 4.21 N 24.45 E
Gitarama 154 2.07 S 29.45 E
Gitega 154 3.26 S 29.56 E
Gittelde 52 51.48 N 10.10 E
Giuba, Isole II 144 0.45 S 42.19 E
Giudicarie, Valli V 64 45.58 N 10.45 E
Giugliano in Campania 68 40.56 N 14.12 E
Giuliana 70 37.40 N 13.14 E
Giulianova 66 42.45 N 13.57 E
Giulie, Alpi → Julian Alps ⋏ 36 46.00 N 14.00 E
Giumbo → Jumboo 144 0.15 S 42.38 E
Giurgiu 38 43.53 N 25.57 E
Giurgiu □[6] 38 44.10 N 26.00 E
Giussano 62 45.42 N 9.14 E
Giuvala, Pasul)(38 45.26 N 25.17 E
Givʿatayim 132 32.04 N 34.48 E
Givʿat Brenner 132 31.52 N 34.48 E
Give 41 55.51 N 9.15 E
Giverny 50 49.04 N 1.32 E
Givet 56 50.08 N 4.50 E
Givors 62 45.35 N 4.46 E
Givrine, Col de la)(58 46.27 N 6.05 E
Givry 58 46.47 N 4.45 E
Givry-en-Argonne 56 48.57 N 4.53 E
Givry Island I 175c 7.07 N 151.53 E
Giyon 144 8.30 N 38.00 E
Giza → Al-Jīzah 142 30.01 N 31.13 E
Gīzāb 120 33.23 N 66.16 E
Giżduvan 128 40.06 N 64.41 E
Gizen 140 10.49 N 34.48 E
Gizeux 50 47.24 N 0.12 E
Gižiga 74 62.03 N 160.30 E
Gižiginskaja guba ⊂ 74 61.30 N 158.00 E
Gizo 175e 8.06 S 156.51 E
Gizo Island I 175e 8.04 S 156.48 E
Giżycko 30 54.03 N 21.47 E
Gizzeria 68 38.59 N 16.12 E
Gjedved 41 55.56 N 9.51 E
Gjern 41 56.14 N 9.45 E
Gjirokastër 38 40.05 N 20.10 E
Gjoa Haven 176 68.38 N 95.57 W
Gjøvik 26 60.48 N 10.42 E
Gjuesevo 38 42.14 N 22.28 E
Gjuhëzës, Kep i › 38 40.25 N 19.18 E
Glace Bay 186 46.12 N 59.57 W
Glacier, B.C., Can. 182 51.16 N 117.31 W
Glacier, Wa., U.S. 224 48.53 N 121.56 W
Glacier Bay ⊂ 180 58.40 N 136.00 W
Glacier Bay National Park ♠ 180 58.45 N 136.30 W
Glacier Hills 276 40.51 N 74.28 W
Glacier National Park ♠, B.C., Can. 182 51.15 N 117.35 W
Glacier National Park ♠, Mt., U.S. 202 48.35 N 113.40 W
Glacier Peak ∧ 224 48.07 N 121.07 W
Glad' 76 59.07 N 32.06 E
Gl'ad'anskoje 86 54.54 N 65.06 E
Gladbach → Mönchengladbach 56 51.12 N 6.28 E
Gladbeck 52 51.34 N 6.59 E
Gladbrook 190 42.11 N 92.42 W
Gladden 279b 40.21 N 80.11 W
Gladden Heights 279b 40.22 N 80.15 W
Glade Creek ≃ 202 45.54 N 119.42 W
Gladenbach 56 50.46 N 8.34 E
Glades □[6] 220 26.59 N 81.12 W
Glade Spring 192 36.47 N 81.46 W
Gladesville 274a 33.50 S 151.08 E
Gladewater 222 32.32 N 94.56 W
Gladewater, Lake ⊜[1] 222 32.35 N 94.57 W
Gladkovka 78 46.23 N 32.36 E
Gladsakse 41 55.44 N 12.29 E
Gladstone, Austl. 166 23.51 S 151.16 E
Gladstone, Austl. 166 33.17 S 138.22 E
Gladstone, Mb., Can. 184 50.13 N 98.57 W
Gladstone, Mi., U.S. 190 45.51 N 87.01 W
Gladstone, Mo., U.S. 194 39.12 N 94.33 W
Gladstone, N.J., U.S. 210 40.43 N 74.39 W
Gladstone, Or., U.S. 224 45.22 N 122.35 W
Gladstone Brook ≃ 276 40.43 N 74.40 W
Gladwin 190 43.58 N 84.29 W
Gladwyne 285 40.02 N 75.17 W
Gladys Lake ⊜ 180 59.55 N 132.55 W
Glænø I 41 55.12 N 11.28 E
Glafsfjorden ⊜ 26 59.34 N 12.37 E
Gláma ∧ 24a 65.47 N 23.00 W
Glåma ≃ 26 59.12 N 10.57 E
Glamis 46 56.36 N 3.00 W
Glamis Castle ⊥ 46 56.37 N 3.00 W
Glamoč 36 44.03 N 16.51 E
Glamor Lake ⊜ 212 44.58 N 78.23 W
Glamsbjerg 41 55.16 N 10.07 E
Glan 116 5.49 N 125.10 E
Glan ⊜ 40 58.37 N 15.58 E
Glan ≃, B.R.D. 56 49.47 N 7.43 E
Glan ≃, Öst. 61 46.36 N 14.25 E
Glan ≃, Pil. 116 5.50 N 125.12 E
Glanamman 42 51.48 N 3.54 W
Gland 58 46.26 N 6.16 E
Gland ≃ 50 49.55 N 4.05 E
Glandon, Col du)(62 45.14 N 6.11 E
Glandorf, B.R.D. 52 52.05 N 7.59 E
Glandorf, Oh., U.S. 216 41.01 N 84.04 W
Glâne ≃ 58 46.47 N 7.08 E
Glanegg 61 46.44 N 14.11 E
Glanerbrug 52 52.13 N 6.58 E
Glanmire 48 51.55 N 8.24 W
Glanshammar 40 59.19 N 15.24 E
Glanum ⊥ 62 43.49 N 4.47 E
Glan-y-Don 262 53.19 N 3.15 W
Glaris → Glarus 58 47.02 N 9.04 E
Glarner Alpen ⋏ 58 46.55 N 9.00 E
Glärnisch ⋏ 58 47.00 N 9.00 E
Glarus 58 47.02 N 9.04 E
Glarus □[3] 58 47.00 N 9.03 E
Glascarnoch, Loch ⊜ 46 57.40 N 4.50 W
Glasco, Ks., U.S. 198 39.21 N 97.50 W
Glasco, N.Y., U.S. 210 42.02 N 73.56 W
Glasgow, Scot., U.K. 46 55.53 N 4.15 W
Glasgow, Il., U.S. 219 39.33 N 90.29 W
Glasgow, Ky., U.S. 194 36.59 N 85.54 W
Glasgow, Mo., U.S. 194 39.13 N 92.50 W
Glasgow, Mt., U.S. 202 48.11 N 106.38 W
Glasgow, Pa., U.S. 214 40.42 N 78.27 W
Glasgow, Va., U.S. 192 37.38 N 79.27 W
Glasgow (Abbotsinch) Airport ⊠ 46 55.52 N 4.26 W
Glashütte, B.R.D. 52 53.41 N 10.02 E
Glashütte, D.D.R. 54 50.51 N 13.47 E
Glashütte ◆[8] 263 51.13 N 6.52 E
Glaslyn 184 53.21 N 108.22 W
Glaslyn ≃ 42 52.56 N 4.06 W
Glas Maol ∧ 46 56.52 N 3.22 W
Glasow 54 52.20 N 13.28 E
Glass, Loch ⊜ 46 57.43 N 4.30 W
Glassan 48 53.28 N 7.52 W
Glassboro 208 39.42 N 75.06 W
Glassboro State College ʋ[2] 285 39.42 N 75.07 W
Glass House Mountains 171a 26.53 S 152.58 E
Glassmanor 284c 38.49 N 76.59 W
Glass Mountains ⋏ 196 30.25 N 103.15 W
Glassport 214 40.19 N 79.53 W
Glastonbury, Eng., U.K. 42 51.06 N 2.43 W
Glastonbury, Ct., U.S. 207 41.42 N 72.36 W
Glatt ≃ 58 47.34 N 8.28 E
Glatten 58 48.26 N 8.31 E
Glattfelden 58 47.33 N 8.30 E
Glatz → Kłodzko 30 50.27 N 16.39 E
Glaubitz 54 51.19 N 13.22 E
Glauchau 54 50.49 N 12.32 E
Glaven ≃ 42 52.58 N 1.03 E
Glaze Brook ≃ 262 53.25 N 2.27 W
Glazebury 262 53.28 N 2.30 W
Glaževo 76 59.41 N 32.05 E
Glazok 80 53.06 N 40.42 E
Glazov 80 58.09 N 52.40 E
Glazovo, S.S.S.R. 82 54.57 N 37.22 E
Glazovo, S.S.S.R. 82 54.47 N 37.34 E
Glazovo, S.S.S.R. 82 55.38 N 35.46 E
Glazunovka 76 52.30 N 36.19 E
Glazunovskaja 80 49.50 N 42.51 E
Gleason 194 36.12 N 88.36 W
Glebovka 78 46.38 N 39.59 E
Glebovo, S.S.S.R. 82 56.54 N 37.43 E
Glebovo, S.S.S.R. 82 56.39 N 38.42 E
Gleed 224 46.40 N 120.37 W
Glehn 263 51.10 N 6.35 E
Gleichen 182 50.52 N 113.03 W
Gleidingen 52 52.16 N 9.50 E
Gleinalpe ⋏ 61 47.15 N 15.03 E
Gleisdorf 61 47.06 N 15.44 E
Gleiwitz → Gliwice 30 50.17 N 18.40 E
Glejbjerg 41 55.33 N 8.50 E
Glemsford 42 52.06 N 0.41 E
Glen ≃, Ire. 48 54.38 N 8.40 W
Glen ≃, Eng., U.K. 42 52.51 N 0.06 W
Glen Acres 285 39.58 N 75.34 W
Glen Afton 172 37.37 S 175.02 E
Glen Alice 170 33.02 S 150.13 E
Glen Allen 208 37.39 N 77.30 W
Glen Alpine 192 35.43 N 81.46 W
Glenamoy 48 54.14 N 9.42 W
Glenarchy 275b 43.29 N 79.46 W
Glenarden 208 38.56 N 76.52 W
Glenarm, N. Ire., U.K. 48 54.58 N 5.57 W
Glen Arm, Md., U.S. 284b 39.27 N 76.30 W
Glen Ashton Farms 285 40.06 N 74.55 W
Glen Aubrey 210 42.15 N 76.01 W
Glenavon, Sk., Can. 184 50.10 N 103.10 W
Glen Avon, S. Afr. 158 31.43 S 26.12 E
Glen Avon, Ca., U.S. 228 34.01 N 117.29 W
Glenavy, N.Z. 172 44.55 S 171.06 E
Glenavy, N. Ire., U.K. 48 54.36 N 6.13 W
Glenboro 184 49.32 N 99.15 W
Glenbrook 170 33.46 S 150.37 E
Glenbrook Heights 226 39.15 N 121.02 W
Glenburn, N.D., U.S. 198 48.30 N 101.13 W
Glenburn, Pa., U.S. 210 41.31 N 75.44 W
Glen Burnie 208 39.09 N 76.37 W
Glen Burnie Park 208 39.09 N 76.38 W
Glen Campbell 214 40.49 N 78.50 W
Glen Canyon V 200 37.10 N 110.50 W
Glen Canyon Dam ◆[6] 200 36.48 N 111.13 W
Glen Canyon National Recreation Area ♠ 200 37.00 N 111.20 W
Glen Carbon 219 38.44 N 89.58 W
Glencoe, Austl. 166 37.42 S 140.37 E
Glencoe, On., Can. 214 42.45 N 81.43 W
Glencoe, S. Afr. 158 28.12 S 30.07 E
Glencoe, Al., U.S. 194 33.57 N 85.55 W
Glencoe, Il., U.S. 216 42.08 N 87.45 W
Glencoe, Ky., U.S. 218 38.42 N 84.49 W
Glencoe, Md., U.S. 208 39.32 N 76.38 W
Glencoe, Mn., U.S. 190 44.46 N 94.09 W
Glencolumbkille 48 54.43 N 8.45 W
Glencoul, Loch ⊂ 46 58.14 N 4.58 W
Glencova 154 19.59 S 31.26 E
Glen Cove 210 40.51 N 73.38 W
Glendale, Az., U.S. 200 33.32 N 112.11 W
Glendale, Ca., U.S. 228 34.08 N 118.15 W
Glendale, Ma., U.S. 207 42.17 N 73.20 W
Glendale, Ms., U.S. 194 31.21 N 89.18 W
Glendale, Mo., U.S. 219 38.35 N 90.22 W
Glendale, Or., U.S. 202 42.44 N 123.25 W
Glendale, R.I., U.S. 207 41.58 N 71.37 W
Glendale, Tx., U.S. 222 31.01 N 95.18 W
Glendale, Ut,. U.S. 200 37.19 N 112.35 W
Glendale, Wi., U.S. 216 43.08 N 87.56 W
Glendale, Zimb. 154 17.21 S 31.04 E
Glendale Heights, Il., U.S. 278 41.54 N 88.04 W
Glendale Heights, Md., U.S. 284c 38.59 N 76.49 W
Glendale Lake ⊜ 214 40.41 N 78.32 W
Glendalough ⊥ 48 53.01 N 6.26 W
Glen Davis 170 33.08 S 150.17 E
Glendive 198 47.06 N 104.42 W
Glendo 200 42.30 N 105.01 W
Glendoe Forest ◆[3] 46 57.06 N 4.37 W
Glendon, Ab., Can. 182 54.15 N 111.10 W
Glendon, Pa., U.S. 208 40.40 N 75.14 W
Glendora, Ca., U.S. 228 34.08 N 117.51 W
Glendora, N.J., U.S. 285 39.50 N 75.04 W
Glendo Reservoir ⊜[1] 198 42.31 N 104.58 W
Glendo State Park ♠ 198 42.33 N 104.58 W
Glendowan 48 54.58 N 7.57 W
Glen Eagle, Austl. 168a 32.17 S 116.11 E
Gleneagle, Austl. 171a 27.57 S 152.59 E
Glen Echo 284c 38.58 N 77.08 W
Glen Echo Amusement Park ♠ 284c 38.58 N 77.08 W
Glen Echo Heights 284c 38.58 N 77.08 W
Gleneden Beach 202 44.53 N 124.02 W
Glen Elder 198 39.29 N 98.18 W
Glenelg, Austl. 168b 34.59 S 138.31 E
Glenelg, Scot., U.K. 46 57.13 N 5.38 W
Glenelg ≃ 166 38.03 S 141.00 E
Glen Ellen 226 38.22 N 122.31 W
Glenelly ≃ 48 54.44 N 7.18 W
Glen Ellyn 278 41.52 N 88.04 W
Glen Ellyn Countryside 278 41.55 N 88.04 W
Glenfarg 46 56.16 N 3.24 W
Glenfarne 48 54.17 N 7.59 W
Glenfield, Austl. 274a 33.58 S 150.54 E
Glenfield, Eng., U.K. 42 52.39 N 1.12 W
Glenfield, N.Y., U.S. 212 43.43 N 75.24 W
Glenfield, Pa., U.S. 279b 40.31 N 80.08 W
Glenfinnan 46 56.52 N 5.27 W
Glen Flora 222 29.21 N 96.12 W
Glen Florrie 162 22.55 S 115.59 E
Glenford 210 42.00 N 74.07 W
Glen Forest 168a 31.54 S 116.06 E
Glengallan Creek ≃ 171a 28.09 S 151.53 E
Glen Gardner 210 40.41 N 74.56 W
Glengarriff 48 51.45 N 9.33 W
Glengarry Range ⋏ 162 26.13 S 118.59 E
Glengyle 166 24.48 S 139.37 E
Glenham 210 41.31 N 73.55 W
Glenhaven 274a 33.42 S 151.00 E
Glen Head 276 40.50 N 73.37 W
Glen Helen 162 23.43 S 132.40 E
Glen Hills 208 39.04 N 77.12 W
Glenhope 172 41.39 S 172.39 E
Glenhuntly 274b 37.54 S 145.03 E
Glen Innes 166 29.44 S 151.44 E
Glen Island I 276 40.53 N 73.47 W
Glen Lake 224 48.26 N 123.31 W
Glenluce 44 54.53 N 4.49 W
Glenluce Abbey ʋ[1] 44 54.53 N 4.50 W
Glen Lyon 210 41.10 N 76.04 W
Glen Miller 212 44.08 N 77.35 W
Glen Mills 285 39.55 N 75.30 W
Glenmont, N.Y., U.S. 210 42.36 N 73.46 W
Glenmont, Oh., U.S. 214 40.31 N 82.06 W
Glenmoor 214 40.40 N 80.37 W
Glen Moore, Pa., U.S. 208 40.03 N 76.18 W
Glenmoore, Pa., U.S. 208 40.05 N 75.46 W
Glenmora 194 30.58 N 92.35 W
Glenmore 284b 39.11 N 76.36 W
Glenmorgan 166 27.15 S 149.41 E
Glenn, Ca., U.S. 226 39.31 N 122.01 W
Glenn, Mi., U.S. 216 42.31 N 86.13 W
Glenn □[6] 226 39.29 N 122.18 W
Glennallen 180 62.07 N 145.33 W
Glennamaddy 48 53.37 N 8.35 W
Glenn-Colusa Canal ≋ 226 39.07 N 122.08 W
Glenn Dale 284c 38.59 N 76.49 W
Glenns Creek ≃ 218 38.09 N 84.52 W
Glenns Ferry 202 42.57 N 115.18 W
Glenn Shoals, Lake ⊜[1] 219 39.13 N 89.28 W
Glennville 192 31.56 N 81.55 W
Glen Oak 278 41.53 N 88.02 W
Glenolden 285 39.54 N 75.17 W
Glenoma 224 46.30 N 122.09 W
Glenorchy 172 44.51 S 168.23 E
Glenore Grove 171a 27.32 S 152.24 E
Glenorie 170 33.33 S 151.00 E
Glenormiston 166 22.55 S 138.48 E
Glen Park 212 44.00 N 75.57 W
Glenreagh 166 30.03 S 152.59 E
Glen Richey 214 40.57 N 78.29 W
Glen Riddle 285 39.54 N 75.26 W
Glenridge, Ma., U.S. 283 42.14 N 71.19 W
Glen Ridge, N.J., U.S. 276 40.48 N 74.12 W
Glen Robertson 206 45.21 N 74.30 W
Glen Rock, N.J., U.S. 276 40.57 N 74.08 W
Glen Rock, Pa., U.S. 208 39.47 N 76.43 W
Glenrock, Wy., U.S. 200 42.52 N 105.52 W
Glen Rose 222 32.14 N 97.45 W
Glen Ross 212 44.16 N 77.36 W
Glenrothes 46 56.12 N 3.10 W
Glenroy, Austl. 162 17.22 S 126.06 E
Glenroy, Austl. 162 21.46 S 114.49 E
Glenroy, Austl. 274b 37.42 S 144.55 E
Glenroy ≃ 172 42.00 S 172.20 E
Glens Falls 210 43.18 N 73.38 W
Glenshaw 214 40.31 N 79.58 W
Glenshee V 46 56.48 N 3.30 W
Glenside, S. Afr. 158 29.25 S 30.47 E
Glenside, N.J., U.S. 208 39.40 N 75.29 W
Glenside, Pa., U.S. 208 40.06 N 75.09 W
Glen Spey 210 41.29 N 74.49 W
Glen Stewart Park ♠ 275b 43.41 N 79.18 W
Glenties 48 54.47 N 8.17 W
Glen Ullin 198 46.48 N 101.49 W
Glenview 216 42.04 N 87.47 W
Glenview Countryside 278 42.04 N 87.50 W
Glenview Naval Air Station ■ 216 42.05 N 87.50 W
Glenville, Ire. 48 52.03 N 8.26 W
Glenville, Mn., U.S. 190 43.34 N 93.16 W
Glenville, N.Y., U.S. 276 41.04 N 73.50 W
Glenville, W.V., U.S. 188 38.56 N 80.50 W
Glenvista 273d 26.17 S 28.13 E
Glen Waverley 274b 37.53 S 145.10 E
Glen White 192 37.43 N 81.16 W
Glen Wild 210 41.29 N 74.49 W
Glen Wild Lake ⊜ 276 41.02 N 74.20 W
Glenwillard 214 40.34 N 80.13 W
Glen Williams 212 43.40 N 79.55 W
Glenwillow 214 41.22 N 81.28 W
Glenwood, Ab., Can. 182 49.22 N 113.31 W
Glenwood, Nf., Can. 186 48.59 N 54.52 W
Glenwood, Al., U.S. 194 31.39 N 86.10 W
Glenwood, Ar., U.S. 194 34.19 N 93.33 W
Glenwood, Ga., U.S. 192 32.10 N 82.40 W
Glenwood, Il., U.S. 278 41.32 N 87.36 W
Glenwood, In., U.S. 218 39.37 N 85.18 W
Glenwood, Ia., U.S. 198 41.02 N 95.44 W
Glenwood, Mn., U.S. 198 45.39 N 95.23 W
Glenwood, N.J., U.S. 210 41.15 N 74.29 W
Glenwood, N.M., U.S. 200 33.19 N 108.52 W
Glenwood, N.Y., U.S. 210 42.37 N 78.39 W
Glenwood, Or., U.S. 224 45.38 N 123.16 W
Glenwood, Tx., U.S. 222 32.39 N 94.51 W
Glenwood, Ut,. U.S. 200 38.45 N 111.59 W

Symbols in the index entries represent the broad categories identified in the key at the right. Symbols with superior numbers (⋏[1]) identify subcategories (see complete key on page *I · 1).*

Symbole im Register stellen die rechts im Schlüssel erklärten Kategorien dar. Symbole mit hochgestellten Ziffern (⋏[1]) bezeichnen Unterabteilungen einer Kategorie (vgl. vollständiger Schlüssel auf Seite *I · 1).*

Los símbolos incluídos en el texto del índice representan las grandes categorias identificadas con la clave a la derecha. Los símbolos con numeros en su parte superior (⋏[1]) identifican las subcategorías (véase la clave completa en la página *I · 1).*

Les symboles de l'index représentent les catégories indiquées dans la légende à droite. Les symboles suivis d'un indice (⋏[1]) représentent des sous-catégories (voir légende complète à la page *I · 1).*

Os símbolos incluídos no texto do índice representam as grandes categorias identificadas com a chave à direita. Os símbolos com números em sua parte superior (⋏[1]) identificam as subcategorias (veja-se a chave completa à página *I · 1).*

∧ Mountain	Berg	Montaña	Montagne	Montanha
⋏ Mountains	Gebirge	Montañas	Montagnes	Montanhas
)(Pass	Paß	Paso	Col	Passo
V Valley, Canyon	Tal, Cañon	Valle, Cañón	Vallée, Canyon	Vale, Canhão
≃ Plain	Ebene	Llano	Plaine	Planície
› Cape	Kap	Cabo	Cap	Cabo
I Island	Insel	Isla	Île	Ilha
II Islands	Inseln	Islas	Îles	Ilhas
⊥ Other Topographic Features	Andere Topographische Objekte	Otros Elementos Topográficos	Autres données topographiques	Outros acidentes topográficos

ESPAÑOL — Nombre | Página | Lat.°′ | Long.°′ W = Oeste

FRANÇAIS — Nom | Page | Lat.°′ | Long.°′ W = Ouest

PORTUGUÊS — Nome | Página | Lat.°′ | Long.°′ W = Oeste

Nombre / Nom / Nome	Página / Page / Página	Lat.°′	Long.°′ W = Oeste / W = Ouest / W = Oeste
Glenwood, Va., U.S.	**192**	36.35 N	79.21 W
Glenwood, Wa., U.S.	**224**	46.01 N	121.17 W
Glenwood City	**190**	45.03 N	92.10 W
Glenwood Landing	**276**	40.50 N	73.39 W
Glenwood Park	**284c**	38.58 N	76.50 W
Glenwood Springs	**200**	39.33 N	107.19 W
Gleschendorf	**54**	54.02 N	10.40 E
Glesien	**54**	51.27 N	12.13 E
Gletsch	**58**	46.34 N	8.22 E
Glew	**258**	34.53 S	58.23 W
Glidden, Ia., U.S.	**198**	42.03 N	94.43 W
Glidden, Tx., U.S.	**222**	29.42 N	96.35 W
Glidden, Wi., U.S.	**190**	46.08 N	90.34 W
Glide	**202**	43.18 N	123.06 W
Gliener Berg ʌ [2]	**264a**	52.42 N	13.00 E
Glienicke, D.D.R.	**54**	52.37 N	13.19 E
Glienicke, D.D.R.	**54**	52.13 N	14.05 E
Glífa	**38**	38.57 N	22.58 E
Glifádha	**267c**	37.52 N	23.45 E
Glimåkra	**26**	56.18 N	14.08 E
Glimmingehus	**26**	55.30 N	14.13 E
Glin	**48**	52.34 N	9.17 W
Glina	**36**	45.20 N	16.06 E
Glina ≃	**36**	45.26 N	16.07 E
Glin'any	**78**	49.49 N	24.30 E
Glinde	**52**	53.32 N	10.13 E
Glindow	**54**	52.21 N	12.54 E
Glindowsee ⊜	**264a**	52.21 N	12.56 E
Glinka	**76**	54.39 N	32.52 E
Glinkovo	**85**	42.55 N	69.40 E
Glittertinden ʌ	**26**	61.39 N	8.33 E
Gliwice (Gleiwitz)	**30**	50.17 N	18.40 E
G. L. Martin State Airport ⊠	**284b**	39.20 N	76.25 W
Globe, Az., U.S.	**200**	33.23 N	110.47 W
Globe, Ky., U.S.	**218**	38.17 N	83.14 W
Globino	**78**	49.23 N	33.17 E
Glod'any	**78**	47.47 N	27.31 E
Glodeanu-Siliștea	**38**	44.50 N	26.48 E
Glodok ◆ [8]	**269e**	6.08 S	106.48 E
Glogau → Głogów	**30**	51.40 N	16.05 E
Gloggnitz	**61**	47.40 N	15.57 E
Glogn ≃	**58**	46.46 N	9.12 E
Głogów, Pol.	**30**	51.40 N	16.05 E
Głogów, Pol.	**30**	50.10 N	21.58 E
Głogówek	**30**	50.22 N	17.51 E
Glommersträsk	**26**	65.16 N	19.38 E
Glonn	**64**	47.59 N	11.52 E
Glonn ≃	**60**	48.26 N	11.36 E
Glorenza (Glurns)	**64**	46.40 N	10.33 E
Glória	**250**	9.11 S	38.18 W
Gloria, Bahía de la ⊂	**240p**	21.50 N	77.40 W
Glória de Dourados	**255**	22.21 S	54.13 W
Gloria Glens Park	**214**	41.03 N	81.54 W
Glorieta	**200**	35.34 N	105.46 W
Glorieuses, Îles II	**138**	11.30 S	47.20 E
Glörstausee ⊜ [1]	**263**	51.14 N	7.29 E
Glos-la-Ferrière	**50**	48.51 N	0.36 E
Glossop	**262**	53.27 N	1.57 W
Glossopteris, Mount ʌ	**9**	84.44 S	113.51 W
Gloster	**194**	31.11 N	91.01 W
Glostrup	**41**	55.40 N	12.24 E
Glotovka	**80**	53.57 N	46.42 E
Glotovo	**24**	63.30 N	49.23 E
Gloucester, Austl.	**166**	31.59 S	151.58 E
Gloucester, On., Can.	**212**	45.22 N	75.35 W
Gloucester, Eng., U.K.	**42**	51.53 N	2.14 W
Gloucester, Ma., U.S.	**207**	42.36 N	70.39 W
Gloucester, Va., U.S.	**208**	37.24 N	76.31 W
Gloucester □ [6], N.J., U.S.	**208**	39.50 N	75.10 W
Gloucester □ [6], Va., U.S.	**208**	37.25 N	76.30 W
Gloucester, Cape ›	**164**	5.27 S	148.25 E
Gloucester, Vale of V	**42**	51.55 N	2.10 W
Gloucester City	**285**	39.53 N	75.07 W
Gloucester Fisherman ⊥	**283**	42.36 N	70.40 W
Gloucester Harbor ⊂	**207**	42.36 N	70.40 W
Gloucester Island I	**166**	20.01 S	148.27 E
Gloucester Point	**208**	37.15 N	76.29 W
Gloucester Pool ⊜	**212**	44.51 N	79.43 W
Gloucestershire □ [6]	**42**	51.47 N	2.15 W
Glouster	**188**	39.30 N	82.05 W
Glover-Archbold Park ♠	**284c**	38.55 N	77.05 W
Glover Creek ≃	**194**	34.02 N	94.56 W
Glover Island I	**186**	48.44 N	57.45 W
Glovers Reef ✦ [2]	**232**	16.49 N	87.48 W
Gloversville	**210**	43.03 N	74.20 W
Glovertown	**186**	48.41 N	54.02 W
Glowe	**54**	54.35 N	13.28 E
Glöwen	**54**	52.55 N	12.05 E
Głowno	**30**	51.58 N	19.44 E
Głubczyce	**30**	50.13 N	17.49 E
Glubokij, S.S.S.R.	**78**	48.31 N	40.19 E
Glubokij, S.S.S.R.	**80**	47.01 N	42.47 E
Glubokij, S.S.S.R.	**89**	52.53 N	129.44 E
Glubokoje, S.S.S.R.	**76**	55.08 N	27.41 E
Glubokoje, S.S.S.R.	**82**	54.32 N	38.32 E
Glubokoje, S.S.S.R.	**86**	50.06 N	82.19 E
Głuchołazy	**30**	50.20 N	17.22 E
Gluchov	**78**	51.41 N	33.53 E
Gluchovo	**265b**	55.46 N	37.16 E
Glückauf-Kampfbahn ♠	**263**	51.32 N	7.05 E
Glücksburg	**41**	54.50 N	9.33 E
Glückstadt, B.R.D.	**52**	53.47 N	9.25 E
Gluckstadt, S. Afr.	**158**	27.57 S	31.02 E
Glucomanka, gora ʌ	**89**	45.10 N	135.48 E
Glud	**41**	55.49 N	10.00 E
Glumslöv	**41**	55.56 N	12.48 E
Glumsø	**41**	55.21 N	11.42 E
Gluša	**76**	53.05 N	28.52 E
Glusburn	**44**	53.54 N	1.59 W
Glusk	**76**	52.54 N	28.41 E
Gluškeviči	**78**	51.34 N	27.47 E
Gluškovo	**78**	51.22 N	34.38 E
Glybokaja	**78**	48.07 N	25.56 E
Glyde ≃, Austl.	**164**	12.15 S	135.03 E
Glyde ≃, Ire.	**48**	53.52 N	6.21 W
Glyder Fawr ʌ	**44**	53.06 N	4.01 W
Glyme ≃	**42**	51.49 N	1.22 W
Glyndebourne	**50**	50.52 N	0.04 E
Glyndon, Md., U.S.	**208**	39.28 N	76.48 W
Glyndon, Mn., U.S.	**198**	46.52 N	96.34 W
Glyngøre	**26**	56.46 N	8.52 E
Glyn-Neath	**42**	51.46 N	3.38 W
Gmelinka	**80**	50.24 N	46.54 E
Gmünd, Öst.	**61**	48.47 N	15.00 E
Gmünd, Öst.	**64**	46.54 N	13.32 E
Gmund am Tegernsee	**64**	47.45 N	11.44 E
Gmunden	**64**	47.55 N	13.48 E
Gnadenhutten	**214**	40.21 N	81.26 W
Gnadenhutten Monument ⊥	**214**	40.21 N	81.25 W
Gnalta	**166**	31.03 S	142.20 E
Gnaraloo	**162**	23.51 S	113.31 E
Gnarp	**26**	62.03 N	17.16 E
Gnarpurt, Lake ⊜	**169**	38.03 S	143.24 E
Gnarrenburg	**52**	53.22 N	9.00 E
Gnaw Bone	**218**	39.12 N	86.09 W
Gnesen → Gniezno	**30**	52.31 N	17.37 E
Gnesta	**40**	59.03 N	17.18 E
Gnezdovo	**76**	54.47 N	31.47 E
Gniben ›	**41**	56.01 N	11.18 E
Gniew	**30**	53.51 N	18.49 E
Gniewkowo	**30**	52.54 N	18.25 E
Gniezno	**30**	52.31 N	17.37 E
Gnilaja Lipa ≃	**78**	49.07 N	24.44 E
Gnilec	**76**	52.22 N	36.01 E
Gniloj Jelanec ≃	**78**	47.20 N	31.44 E
Gniloj Tikič ≃	**78**	48.47 N	30.53 E
Gnivan'	**78**	49.06 N	28.20 E
Gnjilane	**38**	42.28 N	21.29 E
Gnoien	**54**	53.58 N	12.42 E
Gnosall	**42**	52.47 N	2.15 W
Gnosjö	**26**	57.22 N	13.44 E
Gnowangerup	**162**	33.56 S	117.59 E
Gō ≃	**96**	35.02 N	132.13 E
Goa	**116**	13.42 N	123.29 E
Goa □ [3]	**122**	15.20 N	74.00 E
Goageb	**156**	26.44 S	17.15 E
Goalen Head ›	**166**	36.40 S	150.05 E
Goāliar ≃	**126**	24.07 N	90.18 E
Goālpāra	**124**	26.11 N	90.37 E
Goāltor	**126**	22.43 N	87.10 E
Goan	**150**	13.14 N	5.09 W
Goascorán	**236**	13.36 N	87.45 W
Goascorán ≃	**236**	13.25 N	87.48 W
Goat Fell ʌ	**46**	55.38 N	5.12 W
Goathland	**44**	54.23 N	0.44 W
Goat Island I	**284a**	43.05 N	79.04 W
Goat Mountain ʌ	**202**	47.21 N	113.21 W
Goat Peak ʌ	**224**	46.56 N	121.16 W
Goba, Ityo.	**144**	7.02 N	40.00 E
Goba, Moç.	**156**	26.12 S	32.08 E
Gobabis	**156**	22.30 S	18.58 E
Gobabis □ [5]	**156**	22.30 S	19.00 E
Gobai ≃	**126**	23.37 N	86.28 E
Gobardānga	**126**	22.53 N	88.45 E
Göbel	**130**	40.00 N	28.09 E
Gobernador Andonaegui	**258**	34.10 S	59.19 W
Gobernador Costa	**254**	44.04 S	70.35 W
Gobernador Gregores	**254**	48.46 S	70.15 W
Gobernador Ingeniero Valentín Virasoro	**252**	28.03 S	56.02 W
Gobernador Juan E. Martínez	**252**	28.55 S	58.56 W
Gobernador Monteverde	**288**	34.48 S	58.16 W
Gobernador Racedo	**252**	31.34 S	60.04 W
Gobernador Udaondo	**258**	35.18 S	58.36 W
Gobi ◆ [2]	**102**	43.00 N	105.00 E
Gobindapur, India	**126**	23.16 N	87.58 E
Gobindapur, India	**272b**	22.23 N	88.25 E
Gobindapur, India	**272b**	22.55 N	88.12 E
Gobindgarh	**123**	30.41 N	76.18 E
Gobindpur	**126**	23.50 N	86.31 E
Göblberg ʌ	**60**	48.06 N	13.32 E
Gobles	**216**	42.21 N	85.52 W
Gobō	**96**	33.53 N	135.10 E
Gobowen	**42**	52.53 N	3.02 W
Gobra	**126**	23.45 N	89.12 E
Gobur	**154**	4.20 N	31.04 E
Gobustan	**84**	40.06 N	49.24 E
Gobza ≃	**76**	55.16 N	31.31 E
Göçbeyli	**130**	39.13 N	27.25 E
Goceano, Catena del ⋏	**71**	40.28 N	9.02 E
Goce Delčev	**38**	41.34 N	23.44 E
Goch	**52**	51.41 N	6.10 E
Gochas	**156**	24.55 S	18.55 E
Gochsheim	**56**	50.01 N	10.16 E
Go Cong	**269c**	10.50 N	106.50 E
Göcsej ⋏ [2]	**61**	46.43 N	16.42 E
Gođafoss ⌞	**24a**	65.40 N	17.30 W
Godalming	**42**	51.11 N	0.37 W
Godalo	**144**	4.28 N	43.24 E
Godar	**128**	28.10 N	63.14 E
Godāvari ≃	**122**	17.00 N	81.45 E
Godāvari, Mouths of the ≃ [1]	**122**	16.25 N	82.00 E
Godbout	**186**	49.19 N	67.37 W
Godbout ≃	**186**	49.19 N	67.36 W
Godda	**124**	24.50 N	87.13 E
Goddard	**218**	38.22 N	83.37 W
Goddard Space Flight Center ʊ	**284c**	39.00 N	76.52 W
Godeffroy	**210**	41.27 N	74.37 W
Godega di Sant'Urbano	**64**	45.56 N	12.24 E
Godegård	**40**	58.44 N	15.09 E
Godelheim	**52**	51.44 N	9.22 E
Godere	**144**	5.05 N	43.50 E
Goderich	**190**	43.45 N	81.43 W
Goderville	**50**	49.39 N	0.22 E
Godfrey	**219**	38.57 N	90.11 W
Godhavn (Qeqertarsuaq)	**176**	69.15 N	53.33 W
Godhra	**120**	22.45 N	73.38 E
Godinlabe	**144**	5.54 N	46.38 E
Godinne	**56**	50.21 N	4.52 E
Godley	**222**	32.27 N	97.32 W
Godmanchester	**42**	52.19 N	0.11 W
Godo, Indon.	**115b**	8.33 S	118.40 E
Gōdo, Nihon	**94**	35.25 N	136.36 E
Gōdo, Nihon	**268**	35.51 N	139.44 E
Gödöllő	**264c**	47.36 N	19.22 E
Gödöllői Dombság ⋏ [2]	**264c**	47.37 N	19.16 E
Godong	**115a**	7.02 S	110.46 E
Godoy Cruz	**252**	32.55 S	68.50 W
Godramstein	**56**	49.12 N	8.05 E
Godrano	**70**	37.54 N	13.26 E
Gods ≃	**184**	56.22 N	92.51 W
Godshill	**42**	50.38 N	1.14 W
Godshorn	**52**	52.26 N	9.43 E
Gods Lake	**184**	54.40 N	94.09 W
Gods Lake ⊜	**184**	54.40 N	94.20 W
Gods Mercy, Bay of ⊂	**176**	63.30 N	86.10 W
Godstone	**260**	51.15 N	0.04 W
Godthåb (Nuuk)	**176**	64.11 N	51.44 W
Godunovo	**82**	56.29 N	39.02 E
Godwin Austen → K2 ʌ	**123**	35.53 N	76.30 E
Goéland, Lac au ⊜	**176**	49.47 N	76.48 W
Goélands, Lac aux ⊜	**176**	55.27 N	64.17 W
Goeree I	**52**	51.50 N	3.55 E
Goes	**52**	51.30 N	3.54 E
Goetzenbruck	**56**	48.59 N	7.23 E
Goff, Som.	**144**	2.39 N	41.00 E
Goff, Ks., U.S.	**198**	39.39 N	95.55 W
Goff Creek ≃	**196**	36.43 N	101.29 W
Goffle Brook ≃	**276**	40.56 N	74.08 W
Goff's Oak	**260**	51.43 N	0.05 W
Goffstown	**188**	43.01 N	71.36 W
Gogama	**190**	47.40 N	81.43 W
Gogebic, Lake ⊜	**190**	46.30 N	89.35 W
Gogebic Range ⋏ [2]	**190**	46.30 N	90.10 W
Göggingen	**58**	48.20 N	10.52 E
Gogland, ostrov I	**76**	60.04 N	27.00 E
Goglio	**58**	46.18 N	8.16 E
Gogoi	**156**	20.17 S	33.08 E
Gogolevo	**78**	49.56 N	33.48 E
Gogonou	**150**	10.50 N	2.50 E
Gogo-shima I	**96**	33.54 N	132.41 E
Gogrial	**140**	8.32 N	28.07 E
Gohad	**124**	26.26 N	78.27 E
Gohāla	**126**	23.15 N	89.59 E
Gohāla ≃	**126**	24.08 N	89.35 E
Gohāna	**124**	29.08 N	76.42 E
Gohfeld	**52**	52.12 N	8.45 E
Gohitafla	**150**	7.30 N	5.53 W
Göhl	**54**	54.17 N	10.56 E
Gohoku	**96**	33.39 N	133.21 E
Go Home Lake ⊜	**212**	45.00 N	79.51 W
Gohpur	**120**	26.53 N	93.38 E
Gohr	**263**	51.06 N	6.43 E
Göhrde	**54**	53.08 N	10.52 E
Göhren	**54**	54.20 N	13.44 E
Goiana, Bra.	**250**	7.33 S	34.59 W
Goianá, Bra.	**256**	21.32 S	43.12 W
Goianápolis	**255**	16.30 S	49.01 W
Goiandira	**255**	18.08 S	48.06 W
Goianésia	**255**	15.18 S	49.07 W
Goiânia	**255**	16.40 S	49.16 W
Goianinha	**250**	6.16 S	35.12 W
Goianira	**255**	16.30 S	49.26 W
Goianorte	**250**	8.35 S	48.56 W
Goiás	**255**	15.56 S	50.08 W
Goiás □ [3]	**255**	15.00 S	49.00 W
Goiatuba	**255**	18.01 S	49.22 W
Goichran	**120**	31.04 N	78.07 E
Goil, Loch ⊂	**46**	56.08 N	4.52 W
Goio-Erê	**252**	24.12 S	53.01 W
Goio-Erê ≃	**252**	24.14 S	53.21 W
Goirle	**52**	51.32 N	5.04 E
Góis, Bra.	**256**	22.33 S	46.18 W
Góis, Port.	**34**	40.09 N	8.07 W
Goito	**64**	45.15 N	10.40 E
Gojam □ [4]	**144**	11.00 N	37.00 E
Gojeb ≃	**144**	7.20 N	37.21 E
Gojō	**96**	34.21 N	135.42 E
Gojōme	**92**	39.56 N	140.07 E
Gojra	**123**	31.09 N	72.41 E
Gojtchskij, pereval)(	**84**	44.18 N	39.18 E
Gök ≃	**130**	41.24 N	35.08 E
Gokāk	**122**	16.10 N	74.50 E
Gokarna	**126**	24.03 N	88.07 E
Gokase ≃	**92**	32.35 N	131.42 E
Gökçeada I	**130**	40.10 N	25.50 E
Gökçebey	**130**	41.19 N	32.08 E
Gökçedağ	**130**	39.33 N	28.56 E
Gökçekent	**130**	40.19 N	38.07 E
Gökçeli	**130**	40.35 N	36.44 E
Gökçen	**130**	38.07 N	27.53 E
Gökçesu	**130**	40.54 N	31.58 E
Gökdere, Tür.	**130**	40.29 N	36.47 E
Gökdere, Tür.	**130**	38.44 N	40.13 E
Gōkōmutsumi	**268**	35.48 N	139.59 E
Gökova Körfezi ⊂	**130**	36.50 N	28.00 E
Göksholm	**40**	59.16 N	15.33 E
Göksu ≃, Tür.	**84**	39.19 N	42.17 E
Göksu ≃, Tür.	**130**	36.19 N	34.02 E
Göksu ≃, Tür.	**130**	37.37 N	35.35 E
Göksu ≃, Tür.	**267b**	41.06 N	29.03 E
Göksun	**130**	38.03 N	36.30 E
Göktaş	**130**	41.17 N	41.46 E
Göktepe	**130**	37.15 N	28.36 E
Göktürk ◆ [8]	**267b**	41.11 N	28.53 E
Gokwe	**154**	18.07 S	28.58 E
Gol	**26**	60.42 N	8.57 E
Gol, Khawr V	**140**	6.55 N	30.16 E
Golabāri	**272b**	22.36 N	88.20 E
Golāghāt	**120**	26.31 N	93.58 E
Gola Gokarannāth	**124**	28.05 N	80.28 E
Gola Island I	**48**	55.05 N	8.22 W
Golaja Pristan'	**78**	46.31 N	32.31 E
Gołańcz	**30**	52.57 N	17.18 E
Golan Heights ♠ [4]	**132**	32.55 N	35.42 E
Golāshkerd	**128**	27.59 N	57.16 E
Golbāf	**128**	29.51 N	57.44 E
Gölbası, Tür.	**130**	37.50 N	37.40 E
Gölbaşı, Tür.	**130**	39.48 N	32.49 E
Golborne	**262**	53.29 N	2.36 W
Golcar	**262**	53.39 N	1.51 W
Gol'čicha	**74**	71.43 N	83.36 E
Golconda, Il., U.S.	**194**	37.22 N	88.29 W
Golconda, Nv., U.S.	**204**	40.57 N	117.29 W
Gölcük, Tür.	**130**	39.18 N	27.59 E
Gölcük, Tür.	**130**	40.44 N	29.48 E
Golczewo	**54**	53.49 N	14.59 E
Gołdap	**30**	54.19 N	22.19 E
Goldau	**58**	47.03 N	8.33 E
Gold Bar	**224**	47.51 N	121.41 W
Gold Beach	**202**	42.24 N	124.25 W
Goldbeck	**54**	52.43 N	11.52 E
Goldberg, D.D.R.	**54**	53.35 N	12.05 E
Goldberg → Złotoryja, Pol.	**30**	51.08 N	15.55 E
Goldberger See ⊜	**54**	53.36 N	12.07 E
Goldbergtunnel ◆ [5]	**263**	51.01 N	7.28 E
Goldbey	**58**	48.12 N	6.26 E
Goldboro	**186**	45.11 N	61.39 W
Gold Bridge	**182**	50.51 N	122.50 W
Gold Coast → Southport	**171a**	27.58 S	153.25 E
Gold Coast ♠ [2]	**150**	5.20 N	0.45 W
Gold Creek	**180**	62.46 N	149.41 W
Gold Creek ≃	**182**	49.04 N	115.12 W
Golden, B.C., Can.	**182**	51.18 N	116.58 W
Golden, Ire.	**48**	52.29 N	7.58 W
Golden, Co., U.S.	**200**	39.45 N	105.13 W
Golden, Il., U.S.	**219**	40.07 N	91.01 W
Golden Bay ⊂	**172**	40.40 S	172.50 E
Golden Beach	**220**	25.57 N	80.07 W
Golden Brook ≃	**283**	42.44 N	71.19 W
Golden City	**194**	37.23 N	94.05 W
Goldendale	**224**	45.49 N	120.49 W
Golden Ears Provincial Park ♠	**182**	49.30 N	122.25 W
Goldene Aue V	**54**	51.25 N	11.00 E
Golden Gate	**220**	26.09 N	81.43 W
Golden Gate ⊻	**226**	37.49 N	122.29 W
Golden Gate Bridge ◆ [5]	**282**	37.49 N	122.28 W
Golden Gate Fields Race Track ♠	**282**	37.53 N	122.19 W
Golden Gate Highlands National Park ♠	**158**	28.30 S	28.40 E
Golden Gate National Recreation Area ♠	**282**	37.49 N	122.31 W
Golden Gate Park ♠	**282**	37.46 N	122.28 W
Golden Green	**260**	51.12 N	0.21 E
Golden Hill Creek ≃	**210**	43.22 N	78.28 W
Golden Hinde ʌ	**182**	49.40 N	125.45 W
Golden Horn → Haliç ⊂	**267b**	41.02 N	28.58 E
Golden Lake ⊜	**190**	45.35 N	77.20 W
Golden Meadow	**194**	29.22 N	90.15 W
Golden Prairie	**184**	50.14 N	109.38 W
Golden Ring Mall ◆ [9]	**284b**	39.20 N	76.29 W
Golden Rock	**122**	10.48 N	78.44 E
Goldenrod	**220**	28.37 N	81.18 W
Golden Spike National Historic Site ⊥	**202**	41.38 N	112.35 W
Goldenstedt	**52**	52.48 N	8.25 E
Golden Valley V	**42**	52.02 N	2.56 W
Golders Green ◆ [8]	**260**	51.35 N	0.12 W
Goldfield, Ia., U.S.	**190**	42.44 N	93.55 W
Goldfield, Nv., U.S.	**204**	37.42 N	117.14 W
Gold Lake ⊜	**212**	44.43 N	78.17 W
Goldlauter	**54**	50.38 N	10.44 E
Gold Mountain ʌ	**204**	37.15 N	117.18 W
Goldney	**258**	34.37 S	59.18 W
Goldonna	**194**	32.01 N	92.54 W
Goldpan Peak ʌ	**180**	61.12 N	153.22 W
Gold River	**182**	49.41 N	126.08 W
Gold Rock	**184**	49.27 N	92.43 W
Gold Run	**226**	39.10 N	120.52 W
Goldsand Lake ⊜	**184**	57.02 N	101.08 W
Goldsboro, Md., U.S.	**208**	39.02 N	75.47 W
Goldsboro, N.C., U.S.	**192**	35.23 N	77.59 W
Goldsmith, In., U.S.	**216**	40.17 N	86.08 W
Goldsmith, Tx., U.S.	**196**	31.58 N	102.36 W
Goldsmith, Lake ⊜	**169**	37.32 S	143.21 E
Goldston	**192**	35.35 N	79.19 W
Goldstone Lake ⊜	**228**	35.22 N	116.54 W
Goldstream Provincial Park ♠	**224**	48.29 N	123.33 W
Goldsworthy	**162**	20.20 S	119.30 E
Goldsworthy, Mount ʌ [2]	**162**	20.21 S	119.32 E
Goldthwaite	**196**	31.26 N	98.34 W
Göle	**130**	40.48 N	42.36 E
Golec, gora ʌ	**88**	58.39 N	94.10 E
Goleen	**48**	51.28 N	9.43 W
Golela	**158**	27.20 S	31.55 E
Goleniów	**30**	53.36 N	14.50 E
Golestan Palace ʊ	**267d**	35.41 N	51.25 E
Goleta	**204**	34.26 N	119.49 W
Goleta, Cerro ʌ	**234**	18.38 N	100.04 W
Golf, Fl., U.S.	**220**	26.31 N	80.06 W
Golf, Il., U.S.	**278**	42.03 N	87.48 W
Golfcrest	**216**	41.57 N	83.22 W
Golfe-Juan	**62**	43.34 N	7.05 E
Golfito	**236**	8.38 N	83.11 W
Golf Manor	**285**	39.42 N	75.28 W
Golf Mill ◆ [9]	**278**	42.03 N	87.50 W
Golfo Aranci	**71**	40.59 N	9.38 E
Golfside	**281**	42.15 N	83.41 W
Golf View	**208**	39.43 N	75.28 W
Golfview Hills	**278**	41.47 N	87.56 W
Gölhisar	**130**	37.10 N	29.30 E
Goliad	**196**	28.40 N	97.23 W
Goliad □ [6]	**222**	28.52 N	97.22 W
Golicyno, S.S.S.R.	**80**	53.38 N	44.07 E
Golicyno, S.S.S.R.	**80**	55.58 N	40.26 E
Golicyno, S.S.S.R.	**82**	55.37 N	36.59 E
Golina	**30**	52.16 N	18.05 E
Golin Baixing	**89**	44.53 N	121.58 E
Golinda	**222**	31.25 N	97.05 W
Goljama Kamčija ≃	**38**	43.03 N	27.29 E
Goljam Perelik ʌ	**38**	41.36 N	24.34 E
Goljanovo ◆ [8]	**265b**	55.49 N	37.48 E
Goljevo	**265b**	55.48 N	37.19 E
Gölköy	**130**	40.42 N	37.38 E
Gollach ≃	**56**	49.31 N	10.00 E
Göllersbach ≃	**61**	48.22 N	16.11 E
Göllet	**130**	40.45 N	42.18 E
Golling an der Salzach	**64**	47.36 N	13.10 E
Gollnow → Goleniów	**30**	53.36 N	14.50 E
Golm	**264a**	52.24 N	12.57 E
Gölmarmara	**130**	38.42 N	27.56 E
Golmberg ʌ [2]	**54**	52.01 N	13.21 E
Gol'movskij	**83**	48.25 N	38.05 E
Golmud	**102**	36.22 N	94.55 E
Golmud ≃	**102**	36.54 N	95.11 E
Golo ≃	**32**	42.31 N	9.32 E
Goloby	**78**	51.06 N	24.59 E
Golodnaja Guba, ozero ⊜	**24**	67.52 N	52.48 E
Gologory ⋏	**78**	49.45 N	24.35 E
Golo Island I	**116**	13.40 N	120.22 E
Golok (Kolok) ≃	**114**	6.15 N	102.05 E
Golongoso	**146**	9.00 N	19.09 E
Gölören	**130**	37.48 N	33.52 E
Gölova	**130**	40.04 N	38.37 E
Golovačovka	**85**	42.52 N	71.13 E
Golovanevsk	**78**	48.23 N	30.28 E
Golovanovo	**80**	54.55 N	40.27 E
Golovčin	**76**	54.04 N	29.55 E
Golovčino	**78**	50.32 N	35.47 E
Golovin	**180**	64.33 N	163.02 W
Golovinka	**84**	43.48 N	39.28 E
Golovino, S.S.S.R.	**76**	55.58 N	40.26 E
Golovino, S.S.S.R.	**82**	56.01 N	39.11 E
Golovinščino	**80**	53.18 N	43.59 E
Golovinskaja	**88**	53.26 N	102.43 E
Golovnino	**82**	54.23 N	36.10 E
Golovno	**78**	51.21 N	24.04 E
Golovskoje	**88**	55.30 N	105.32 E
Golpāyegān	**128**	33.27 N	50.18 E
Gölpazarı	**130**	40.15 N	30.19 E
Golra	**123**	33.42 N	72.58 E
Golrān	**128**	35.06 N	61.41 E
Gols	**61**	47.54 N	16.55 E
Gol'šany	**76**	54.15 N	26.01 E
Gölsdorf	**54**	51.59 N	12.39 E
Golspie, Austl.	**170**	34.17 S	149.40 E
Golspie, Scot., U.K.	**46**	57.58 N	3.58 W
Golssen	**54**	51.58 N	13.36 E
Gol't'ajevo	**82**	55.13 N	36.02 E
Gol't'avino	**88**	58.26 N	98.27 E
Golub-Dobrzyń	**30**	53.08 N	19.02 E
Golubi	**76**	59.28 N	41.39 E
Golubinskij	**80**	48.52 N	43.34 E
Golubovka, S.S.S.R.	**78**	48.53 N	35.19 E
Golubovka, S.S.S.R.	**86**	53.09 N	74.12 E
Golubovka ◆ [8]	**83**	48.38 N	38.39 E
Golumet'	**88**	53.03 N	102.21 E
Golungo Alto	**152**	9.08 S	14.46 E
Golva	**198**	46.44 N	103.59 W
Golweyn	**144**	1.40 N	44.35 E
Gölyaka	**130**	40.47 N	30.59 E
Golynki	**76**	54.52 N	31.23 E
Golyšmanovo, S.S.S.R.	**86**	56.28 N	68.38 E
Golyšmanovo, S.S.S.R.	**86**	56.23 N	68.23 E
Golzheim ◆ [8]	**263**	51.15 N	6.46 E
Golzow, D.D.R.	**54**	52.16 N	12.36 E
Golzow, D.D.R.	**54**	52.34 N	14.29 E
Goma	**154**	1.41 S	29.14 E
Gomadan-zan ʌ	**96**	34.03 N	135.34 E
Gomagoi	**64**	46.35 N	10.32 E
Gomang Co ⊜	**120**	31.15 N	89.15 E
Gomaringen	**58**	48.27 N	9.05 E
Gomas, Sierra de ⋏	**196**	26.23 N	100.32 W
Gomati ≃	**124**	25.32 N	83.10 E
Gomati Plain ≚	**124**	26.30 N	81.10 E
Goma Tsétsé	**273b**	4.14 S	15.08 E
Gombari	**154**	2.43 N	29.04 E
Gombe, Nig.	**146**	10.19 N	11.02 E
Gombe, Zaïre	**152**	0.42 S	17.35 E
Gombe Stream National Park ♠	**154**	4.30 S	29.42 E
Gombi	**146**	10.10 N	12.45 E
Gomboro	**150**	13.29 N	2.46 W
Gomel'	**76**	52.25 N	31.00 E
Gomel' □ [4]	**78**	52.00 N	29.00 E
Gomer	**216**	40.51 N	84.11 W
Gomera I	**148**	28.06 N	17.08 W
Gometra I	**46**	56.29 N	6.17 W
Gometz-la-Ville	**261**	48.40 N	2.08 E
Gometz-le-Châtel	**261**	48.41 N	2.08 E
Gomez	**220**	27.06 N	80.09 W
Gómez Farías, Méx.	**232**	29.18 N	107.40 W
Gómez Farías, Méx.	**234**	19.47 N	103.29 W
Gómez Palacio	**232**	25.34 N	103.30 W
Gómez Plata	**246**	6.41 N	75.12 W
Gomīshān	**128**	37.04 N	54.06 E
Gommécourt	**261**	49.05 N	1.36 E
Gommern	**54**	52.04 N	11.50 E
Gomo Co ⊜	**120**	33.47 N	85.30 E
Gomogomo	**164**	6.40 S	134.43 E
Gomoh	**126**	23.52 N	86.10 E
Gompa	**123**	35.02 N	77.20 E
Goms V	**58**	46.27 N	8.15 E
Gomshall	**260**	51.13 N	0.27 W
Gomumu, Pulau I	**164**	1.49 S	127.38 E
Gonābād	**128**	34.20 N	58.42 E
Gonaïves	**238**	19.27 N	72.41 W
Gonaka	**152**	2.56 S	13.14 E
Gonam	**74**	57.21 N	131.12 E
Gonam ≃	**74**	57.21 N	131.14 E
Gonarezhou National Park ♠	**154**	21.30 S	32.00 E
Gonars	**64**	45.53 N	13.13 E
Gonäs	**40**	60.09 N	15.06 E
Gonâve, Golfe de la ⊂	**238**	19.00 N	73.30 W
Gonâve, Île de la I	**238**	18.51 N	73.03 W
Gonbad-e Qābūs	**128**	37.17 N	55.17 E
Gonçalves	**256**	22.40 S	45.51 W
Gonçalves Dias	**250**	4.57 S	44.14 W
Gončarovka	**78**	50.32 N	39.28 E
Goncelin	**62**	45.20 N	5.59 E
Gonda	**124**	27.08 N	81.56 E
Gondal	**120**	21.58 N	70.48 E
Gondang	**115a**	7.24 S	111.06 E
Gondar → Gonder	**144**	12.40 N	37.30 E
Gondarbal	**123**	34.14 N	74.47 E
Gonder	**144**	12.40 N	37.30 E
Gonder □ [4]	**144**	13.10 N	37.00 E
Gondey	**146**	9.09 N	19.19 E
Gondia	**120**	21.27 N	80.12 E
Gondola	**156**	19.10 S	33.40 E
Gondomar	**34**	41.09 N	8.32 W
Gondrecourt-le-Château	**58**	48.31 N	5.30 E
Gondreville	**58**	48.42 N	5.58 E
Gondrexange, Étang de ⊜	**58**	48.42 N	6.54 E
Goneāna	**123**	30.19 N	74.54 E
Gönen, Tür.	**130**	40.06 N	27.39 E
Gonén, Yis.	**132**	33.08 N	35.39 E
Gonesse	**50**	48.59 N	2.27 E
Gonfaron	**62**	43.19 N	6.17 E
Gong ≃	**100**	26.00 N	115.22 E
Gong'an	**102**	30.02 N	112.04 E
Gonganbao	**86**	44.59 N	86.18 E
Gonganpucun	**104**	41.19 N	123.27 E
Gongbuchang	**105**	40.17 N	116.15 E
Gongchangling	**104**	41.06 N	123.30 E
Gongcheng	**102**	24.49 N	110.46 E
Gongchenqiao	**106**	30.20 N	120.08 E
Gongchuan, Zhg.	**100**	26.06 N	117.24 E
Gongchuan, Zhg.	**102**	23.40 N	107.50 E
Gongcun	**105**	39.28 N	116.10 E
Gongdaoqiao	**100**	32.36 N	119.22 E
Gongdian	**100**	28.06 N	116.56 E
Gongen-yama ʌ	**94**	35.40 N	139.01 E
Gongfang	**100**	27.36 N	115.34 E
Gonggar	**120**	29.17 N	90.46 E
Gongga Shan (Minya Konka) ʌ	**102**	29.35 N	101.51 E
Gonghe	**102**	36.20 N	100.48 E
Gonghui	**98**	41.12 N	114.37 E
Gongjialu	**106**	31.17 N	121.40 E
Gongjiatun	**104**	40.55 N	120.37 E
Gongjiazhai	**104**	41.57 N	124.01 E
Gongjing	**107**	29.21 N	104.43 E
Gongjingying	**105**	39.12 N	116.11 E
Gongkou	**98**	35.38 N	119.47 E
Gongli	**98**	35.55 N	117.24 E
Gongling	**100**	26.18 N	119.40 E
Gongliu	**86**	43.30 N	82.15 E
Gonglu Shan ʌ	**106**	30.39 N	119.18 E
Gongo	**146**	9.00 N	18.56 E
Gongogi	**255**	14.19 S	39.29 W
Gongola □ [3]	**146**	9.00 N	11.40 E
Gongola ≃	**146**	9.30 N	12.04 E
Gongoué	**152**	0.32 S	9.12 E
Gongo-Yembe	**152**	1.58 S	18.40 E
Gongpengzi	**89**	45.09 N	125.39 E
Gongping	**100**	23.05 N	115.24 E
Gongpingxu	**100**	26.12 N	112.51 E
Gongshan	**102**	25.50 N	103.13 E
Gongshiya	**120**	31.25 N	84.37 E
Gongsizhen	**106**	31.41 N	121.48 E
Gongtangtou	**106**	31.48 N	118.42 E
Gongxi	**100**	27.38 N	115.52 E
Gongxian	**102**	34.48 N	113.03 E
Gongyefu	**98**	42.16 N	118.32 E
Gongyemiao	**89**	43.40 N	121.06 E
Gongyingzi	**98**	40.54 N	119.41 E
Gongzhutun	**104**	42.10 N	123.00 E
Gongzui	**107**	29.19 N	103.28 E
Goni, It.	**71**	39.34 N	9.17 E
Goñi, Ur.	**252**	33.31 S	56.24 W
Goniądz	**30**	53.30 N	22.45 E
Gonini ≃	**250**	4.10 N	54.24 W
Goniri	**146**	11.30 N	12.20 E
Gonjo	**102**	30.43 N	98.19 E
Gonnesa	**71**	39.16 N	8.28 E
Gonnesa, Golfo di ⊂	**71**	39.17 N	8.23 E
Gonnosfanadiga	**71**	39.29 N	8.39 E
Gonnostramatza	**71**	39.41 N	8.50 E
Gonochovo	**86**	52.57 N	81.20 E
Gōnoura	**92**	33.45 N	129.41 E
Gonubie Mouth	**158**	32.57 S	28.01 E
Gonža	**89**	53.36 N	125.19 E
Gonzaga, It.	**64**	44.57 N	10.49 E
Gonzaga, Pil.	**116**	18.16 N	122.00 E
Gonzales, Ca., U.S.	**226**	36.30 N	121.26 W
Gonzales, La., U.S.	**194**	30.14 N	90.55 W
Gonzales, Tx., U.S.	**222**	29.30 N	97.27 W
Gonzales □ [6]	**222**	29.28 N	97.30 W
González	**258**	34.14 S	56.52 W
González, Riacho ≃	**252**	22.48 S	57.54 W
González Catán	**258**	34.46 S	58.39 W
González Chaves	**252**	38.02 S	60.06 W
González Moreno	**252**	35.33 S	63.22 W
González Ortega	**204**	32.40 N	115.23 W
González Risos	**258**	34.52 S	59.13 W
Gonzanamá	**246**	4.15 S	79.27 W
Goobarragandra ≃	**171b**	35.20 S	148.15 E
Goochland	**192**	37.41 N	77.53 W
Good Easter	**260**	51.47 N	0.21 E
Goodells	**214**	42.59 N	82.40 W
Goode Mountain ʌ	**224**	48.29 N	120.55 W
Goodenough, Mount ʌ	**180**	67.56 N	135.31 W
Goodenough Bay ⊂	**164**	9.55 S	150.00 E
Goodenough Island I	**164**	9.20 S	150.15 E
Gooderham	**212**	44.54 N	78.23 W
Goodeve	**184**	51.04 N	103.10 W
Goodfellow Air Force Base ■	**196**	31.26 N	100.25 W
Good Hope, S. Afr.	**158**	31.51 S	21.55 E
Good Hope, Oh., U.S.	**218**	39.26 N	83.21 W
Good Hope, Cape of (Kaap die Gooie Hoop) ›	**158**	34.24 S	18.30 E
Goodhope Bay ⊂	**180**	66.10 N	163.45 W
Good Hope Mountain ʌ	**182**	51.09 N	124.10 W
Goodhouse	**158**	28.57 S	18.13 E
Goodhue	**190**	44.24 N	92.37 W
Gooding	**202**	42.56 N	114.42 W
Goodison	**214**	42.44 N	83.10 W
Goodland, Fl., U.S.	**220**	25.55 N	81.38 W
Goodland, In., U.S.	**216**	40.45 N	87.17 W
Goodland, Ks., U.S.	**198**	39.21 N	101.42 W
Goodlands	**184**	49.05 N	100.35 W
Goodlow Park	**222**	32.07 N	96.14 W
Goodman, Ms., U.S.	**194**	32.58 N	89.54 W
Goodman, Wi., U.S.	**190**	45.37 N	88.21 W
Goodman Bay ⊂	**240b**	25.05 N	77.24 W
Goodna	**171a**	27.37 S	152.54 E
Goodnews Bay	**180**	59.07 N	161.35 W
Goodnight	**200**	38.14 N	104.43 W
Goodooga	**166**	29.07 S	147.27 E
Goodradigbee ≃	**171b**	35.08 S	148.41 E
Goodrich, Mi., U.S.	**216**	42.55 N	83.30 W
Goodrich, N.D., U.S.	**198**	47.28 N	100.07 W
Goodrich, Tx., U.S.	**222**	30.36 N	94.57 W
Good Spirit Lake ⊜	**184**	51.34 N	102.40 W
Good Spirit Lake Provincial Park ♠	**184**	51.36 N	102.45 W
Good Thunder	**190**	44.00 N	94.03 W
Goodview	**190**	44.03 N	91.41 W
Goodville	**208**	40.08 N	76.00 W
Goodwater	**194**	33.03 N	86.03 W
Goodwell	**196**	36.35 N	101.38 W
Goodwick	**42**	52.00 N	5.00 W
Goodwin, Lake ⊜	**224**	48.08 N	122.18 W
Goodwives ≃	**276**	41.04 N	73.28 W
Goodwood	**212**	44.02 N	79.12 W
Goodyear	**200**	33.26 N	112.21 W
Goof, Webi ≃	**144**	1.10 N	43.43 E
Googong Reservoir ⊜ [1]	**171b**	35.27 S	149.16 E
Gooie Hoop, Kaap die → Good Hope, Cape of ›	**158**	34.24 S	18.30 E
Goole	**44**	53.42 N	0.52 W
Goolgowi	**166**	33.59 S	145.42 E
Goolwa	**168b**	35.31 S	138.47 E
Goomalling	**162**	31.19 S	116.49 E
Goombalie	**166**	29.59 S	145.23 E
Goombungee	**171a**	27.18 S	151.51 E
Goomburra	**171a**	28.03 S	152.07 E
Goonda	**156**	19.51 S	34.00 E
Goondiwindi	**166**	28.32 S	150.19 E
Goongarrie	**162**	30.03 S	121.09 E
Goongarrie National Park ♠	**162**	29.58 S	121.34 E
Goonyella	**166**	21.45 S	147.55 E
Goor	**52**	52.14 N	6.35 E
Goose ≃, Ab., Can.	**182**	54.58 N	117.11 W
Goose ≃, N.D., U.S.	**198**	47.28 N	96.52 W
Goose Bay → Happy Valley-Goose Bay	**176**	53.20 N	60.25 W
Goose Bay ⊂	**281**	42.35 N	82.41 W
Gooseberry Creek ≃	**202**	43.55 N	108.04 W
Goose Creek	**192**	32.58 N	80.01 W
Goose Creek ≃, U.S.	**202**	42.33 N	113.46 W
Goose Creek ≃, Ne., U.S.	**198**	42.02 N	100.03 W
Goose Creek ≃, N.Y., U.S.	**214**	42.06 N	79.22 W
Goose Creek ≃, Va., U.S.	**208**	39.06 N	77.29 W
Goose Island I	**182**	51.55 N	128.25 W
Goose Lake ⊜, Mb., Can.	**184**	54.26 N	101.30 W
Goose Lake ⊜, On., Can.	**184**	51.46 N	93.00 W
Goose Lake ⊜, On., Can.	**212**	44.25 N	78.52 W
Goose Lake ⊜, On., Can.	**214**	42.31 N	82.31 W
Goose Lake ⊜, Sk., Can.	**184**	51.45 N	107.23 W
Goose Lake ⊜, U.S.	**204**	41.57 N	120.25 W
Goose Lake Canal ≊	**226**	35.50 N	119.37 W
Goose Lake Prairie State Park ♠	**216**	41.21 N	88.18 W
Gooseprairie	**224**	46.54 N	121.15 W
Goostrey	**262**	53.13 N	2.20 W
Gooty	**122**	15.07 N	77.38 E
Gopālganj, Bngl.	**124**	23.01 N	89.50 E
Gopālganj, India	**124**	26.28 N	84.26 E
Gopālnagar, India	**126**	23.03 N	88.45 E
Gopālnagar, India	**272b**	22.50 N	88.14 E
Gopālpur, Bngl.	**124**	24.33 N	89.56 E
Gopālpur, India	**272b**	22.38 N	88.27 E
Gopeng	**114**	4.28 N	101.10 E
Göpfritz an der Wild	**61**	48.43 N	15.24 E
Gopiballabhpur	**126**	22.13 N	86.54 E
Gopichettipālaiyam	**122**	11.28 N	77.27 E
Gopinagar	**272b**	22.50 N	88.07 E
Goppenstein	**58**	46.22 N	7.45 E
Göppingen	**56**	48.42 N	9.40 E
Goqên	**102**	29.15 N	96.59 E
Go Quao	**110**	9.43 N	105.17 E
Gor	**123**	35.32 N	74.31 E
Góra, Pol.	**30**	51.40 N	16.33 E
Gora, S.S.S.R.	**76**	60.02 N	41.43 E
Gor'ačegorsk	**86**	55.24 N	88.55 E
Gor'ačij Kl'uč	**84**	44.37 N	39.07 E
Gor'ačinsk	**88**	52.59 N	108.18 E
Goradit	**144**	11.25 N	38.25 E
Goradiz	**84**	39.27 N	47.20 E
Góra Kalwaria	**30**	51.59 N	21.12 E
Gorakhpur	**124**	26.45 N	83.22 E
Gor'any	**76**	55.25 N	29.02 E
Goras	**124**	25.32 N	76.56 E
Goražde	**38**	43.40 N	18.56 E
Gorbačevo Michajlovka	**83**	47.50 N	38.00 E
Gorbatov	**80**	56.08 N	43.04 E
Gorbatovka	**80**	56.15 N	43.45 E
Gorbica	**88**	53.06 N	119.13 E
Gorboviči	**76**	53.49 N	30.41 E
Gorčucha	**80**	57.43 N	43.43 E
Gorda, Punta ›, Chile	**248**	19.18 S	70.18 W
Gorda, Punta ›, Cuba	**240p**	22.24 N	82.10 W
Gorda, Punta ›, Méx.	**234**	19.14 N	96.11 W
Gorda, Punta ›, Nic.	**236**	11.26 N	83.48 W
Gorda, Punta ›, Nic.	**236**	14.21 N	83.12 W
Gordejevka	**76**	52.59 N	31.58 E
Gordes, Fr.	**62**	43.54 N	5.12 E
Gördes, Tür.	**130**	38.54 N	28.18 E
Gordil	**146**	9.44 N	21.35 E
Gørding	**41**	55.29 N	8.48 E
Gordion ⊥	**130**	39.41 N	32.01 E
Gordo	**194**	33.19 N	87.54 W
Gordo, Cerro ʌ	**234**	20.46 N	102.35 W
Gordola	**58**	46.11 N	8.52 E
Gordon, Scot., U.K.	**46**	55.41 N	2.34 W
Gordon, Ga., U.S.	**192**	32.52 N	83.19 W
Gordon, Ne., U.S.	**198**	42.48 N	102.12 W
Gordon, Oh., U.S.	**218**	39.56 N	84.31 W
Gordon, Pa., U.S.	**208**	40.45 N	76.21 W
Gordon, Wi., U.S.	**190**	46.14 N	91.47 W
Gordon ≃	**224**	48.35 N	124.24 W
Gordon, Isla I	**254**	54.58 S	69.35 W
Gordon, Lake ⊜ [1]	**166**	42.42 S	146.12 E
Gordon Creek ≃	**198**	42.49 N	100.40 W
Gordon Downs	**162**	18.44 S	128.35 E
Gordon Heights	**207**	40.51 N	72.58 W
Gordon Horne Peak ʌ	**182**	51.46 N	118.50 W
Gordon Indian Reserve ◆ [4]	**184**	51.16 N	104.16 W
Gordon Lake ⊜, Ab., Can.	**184**	56.30 N	110.25 W
Gordon Lake ⊜, Sk., Can.	**184**	55.50 N	106.26 W
Gordon Lakes	**276**	41.03 N	74.22 W
Gordon Pass ⊂	**220**	26.06 N	81.48 W
Gordon River	**224**	48.47 N	124.21 W
Gordon's Bay	**158**	34.10 S	18.52 E
Gordonsville	**188**	38.08 N	78.11 W
Gordonton	**172**	37.40 S	175.18 E
Gordonvale	**166**	17.05 S	145.47 E
Gordonville	**220**	27.57 N	81.49 W
Gore, Austl.	**166**	28.17 S	151.29 E
Gore, N.S., Can.	**186**	45.07 N	63.43 W
Gore, Ityo.	**144**	8.08 N	35.33 E
Gore, N.Z.	**172**	46.06 S	168.58 E
Goré, Tchad	**146**	7.53 N	16.40 E
Gore Bay	**190**	45.55 N	82.28 W
Gorebridge	**46**	55.51 N	3.02 W
Goreda	**164**	3.39 S	134.58 E
Goree	**196**	33.28 N	99.31 W
Gore Hill	**274a**	33.49 S	151.11 E
Görele	**130**	41.02 N	39.00 E
Gorelki	**82**	54.15 N	37.37 E
Goreloje	**80**	52.57 N	41.28 E
Gorelovo	**265a**	59.47 N	30.08 E
Gorelovo Airport ⊠	**265a**	59.47 N	30.05 E
Gorelyj ≃	**265a**	59.58 N	30.28 E
Göreme Milli Parkı ♠	**130**	38.26 N	34.54 E
Gore Mountain ʌ	**188**	44.55 N	71.48 W
Gorenki	**265b**	55.48 N	37.55 E
Gore Point ›, Austl.	**166**	17.38 S	139.56 E
Gore Point ›, Ak., U.S.	**180**	59.12 N	151.00 W
Gore Range ⋏	**200**	40.00 N	106.30 W
Goretovka ≃	**265b**	55.56 N	37.20 E
Goreville	**194**	37.33 N	88.58 W
Gorey, Ire.	**48**	52.40 N	6.18 W
Gorey, Jersey	**43b**	49.12 N	2.02 W
Gorfoundurei	**144**	4.30 N	46.41 E
Gorgān	**128**	36.50 N	54.29 E
Gorgān ≃	**128**	36.59 N	54.00 E
Gorgany ⋏	**78**	48.30 N	24.00 E
Gorge Lake ⊜ [1]	**224**	48.42 N	121.13 W
Görgeshausen	**56**	50.24 N	7.56 E
Gorgoglione	**68**	40.23 N	16.09 E
Gorgol □ [4]	**150**	16.00 N	13.00 W
Gorgol el Abiod ≃	**150**	16.14 N	12.58 W
Gorgol el Akhdar ≃	**150**	16.13 N	12.58 W
Gorgona, Isla I	**246**	2.59 N	78.12 W
Gorgonzola	**62**	45.32 N	9.24 E
Gorgor	**248**	10.35 S	77.02 W
Gorgora	**144**	12.13 N	37.16 E
Gorgoram	**146**	12.38 N	10.43 E
Gorgota	**38**	44.47 N	26.05 E
Gorgova	**38**	45.11 N	29.10 E
Gorham, Me., U.S.	**188**	43.40 N	70.26 W
Gorham, N.H., U.S.	**188**	44.23 N	71.10 W
Gorham, N.Y., U.S.	**210**	42.47 N	77.07 W
Gorhambury House ⊥	**260**	51.47 N	0.24 W
Gori	**84**	41.58 N	44.07 E
Goria	**272b**	22.24 N	88.29 E
Gorica → Gorizia	**64**	45.57 N	13.38 E
Goričan	**61**	46.23 N	16.41 E
Goricy	**76**	57.09 N	36.44 E
Gorinchem	**52**	51.50 N	5.00 E
Goring	**42**	51.32 N	1.09 W
Goring-by-Sea	**42**	50.49 N	0.25 W
Goring Gap V	**42**	51.32 N	1.08 W
Goris	**84**	39.31 N	46.23 E
Göritz	**54**	53.24 N	13.54 E
Göritzhain	**54**	50.58 N	12.47 E
Gorizia	**64**	45.57 N	13.38 E
Gorizia □ [4]	**64**	45.55 N	13.30 E
Gorj □ [6]	**38**	45.00 N	23.20 E
Gorjani	**38**	45.24 N	18.21 E
Gor'kaja Balka	**84**	44.17 N	43.59 E
Gor'kaja balka V	**84**	44.38 N	45.00 E
Görke	**54**	53.51 N	13.38 E
Gorkhā	**124**	28.00 N	84.37 E
Gorki, S.S.S.R.	**76**	54.17 N	30.59 E

Symbol	English	Deutsch	Español	Français	Português
≃	River	Fluß	Río	Rivière	Rio
≊	Canal	Kanal	Canal	Canal	Canal
⌞	Waterfall, Rapids	Wasserfall, Stromschnellen	Cascada, Rápidos	Chute d'eau, Rapides	Cascata, Rápidos
⊻	Strait	Meeresstraße	Estrecho	Détroit	Estreito
⊂	Bay, Gulf	Bucht, Golf	Bahía, Golfo	Baie, Golfe	Baía, Golfo
⊜	Lake, Lakes	See, Seen	Lago, Lagos	Lac, Lacs	Lago, Lagos
≡	Swamp	Sumpf	Pantano	Marais	Pântano
⌂	Ice Features, Glacier	Eis- und Gletscherformen	Accidentes Glaciales	Formes glaciaires	Acidentes glaciares
⚲	Other Hydrographic Features	Andere Hydrographische Objekte	Otros Elementos Hidrográficos	Autres données hydrographiques	Outros acidentes hidrográficos
✦	Submarine Features	Untermeerische Objekte	Accidentes Submarinos	Formes de relief sous-marin	Acidentes submarinos
□	Political Unit	Politische Einheit	Unidad Politica	Entité politique	Unidade política
ʊ	Cultural Institution	Kulturelle Institution	Institución Cultural	Institution culturelle	Instituição cultural
⊥	Historical Site	Historische Stätte	Sitio Histórico	Site historique	Sitio histórico
♠	Recreational Site	Erholungs- und Ferienort	Sitio de Recreo	Centre de loisirs	Area de Lazer
⊠	Airport	Flughafen	Aeropuerto	Aéroport	Aeroporto
■	Military Installation	Militäranlage	Instalación Militar	Installation militaire	Instalação militar
◆	Miscellaneous	Verschiedenes	Misceláneo	Divers	Diversos

ENGLISH: Name | Page | Lat.°′ | Long.°′
DEUTSCH: Name | Seite | Breite°′ | Länge°′ E = Ost

Gorki → Gor'kij, S.S.S.R. 80 56.20 N 44.00 E
Gorki, S.S.S.R. 80 57.38 N 45.05 E
Gorki, S.S.S.R. 82 54.18 N 36.08 E
Gorki, S.S.S.R. 82 55.32 N 37.45 E
Gorki, S.S.S.R. 82 56.54 N 38.51 E
Gorki, S.S.S.R. 265b 55.57 N 37.55 E
Gor'kij (Gorky) 80 56.20 N 44.00 E
Gorki Park → Central'nyj park imeni Gor'kogo ♦ 265b 55.44 N 37.36 E
Gorki Vtoryje 265b 55.44 N 37.11 E
Gor'kiy → Gor'kij 80 56.20 N 44.00 E
Gor'koje, ozero ⊜ 86 52.30 N 81.20 E
Gor'kovskoje 86 55.22 N 74.24 E
Gor'kovskoje vodochranilišče ⊜[1] 80 57.00 N 43.10 E
Gorky → Gor'kij 80 56.20 N 44.00 E
Gorlago 62 45.40 N 9.49 E
Gorla Maggiore 266b 45.40 N 8.53 E
Gorla Minore 266b 45.39 N 8.54 E
Gorleston on Sea 42 52.36 N 1.43 E
Gørlev 41 55.32 N 11.14 E
Gorlice 30 49.40 N 21.10 E
Görlitz 54 51.09 N 14.59 E
Gorlosen 54 53.11 N 11.27 E
Gorlovka, S.S.S.R. 83 48.18 N 38.03 E
Gorlovka, S.S.S.R. 84 41.14 N 43.42 E
Gorlovo 76 53.50 N 39.02 E
Gorm, Loch ⊜ 46 55.48 N 6.25 W
Gorman, Ca., U.S. 228 34.48 N 118.51 W
Gorman, Tx., U.S. 196 32.12 N 98.40 W
Gorman Creek ≃ 228 34.38 N 118.45 W
Görmin 54 53.59 N 13.16 E
Gorn'ackij, S.S.S.R. 24 67.32 N 64.03 E
Gorn'ackij, S.S.S.R. 78 48.17 N 40.55 E
Gorn'ackoje 78 47.42 N 34.08 E
Gorna Dzhumaya → Blagoevgrad 38 42.01 N 23.06 E
Gornaja Prolejka 80 49.24 N 44.59 E
Gorn'ak, S.S.S.R. 76 53.36 N 39.29 E
Gorn'ak, S.S.S.R. 78 50.20 N 24.10 E
Gorn'ak, S.S.S.R. 83 48.04 N 37.24 E
Gorn'ak, S.S.S.R. 86 51.00 N 81.29 E
Gornalunga ≃ 70 37.24 N 15.03 E
Gorna Orjahovica 38 43.07 N 25.41 E
Gornergrat ♦ 58 45.59 N 7.47 E
Gornja Radgona 61 46.41 N 16.00 E
Gornji Grad 36 46.18 N 14.49 E
Gornji Milanovac 38 44.01 N 20.27 E
Gornji Vakuf 36 43.56 N 17.35 E
Gorno-Altajsk 86 51.58 N 85.58 E
Gorno-Altajskaja Avtonomnaja Oblast' □[8] 86 51.00 N 86.00 E
Gorno-Badachšanskaja Avtonomnaja Oblast' □[4] 85 38.30 N 73.00 E
Gornoje 86 48.29 N 85.00 E
Gorno-Lesnoj zapovednik ♦ 85 41.10 N 69.55 E
Gornopravdinsk 86 60.07 N 69.54 E
Gornostajevka 78 47.01 N 33.44 E
Gorno-Vod'anoje 80 49.16 N 44.56 E
Gornovodnoje 89 43.42 N 134.44 E
Gornozavodsk, S.S.S.R. 86 58.20 N 58.32 E
Gornozavodsk, S.S.S.R. 89 46.34 N 141.49 E
Gornyj, S.S.S.R. 80 51.46 N 48.34 E
Gornyj, S.S.S.R. 89 50.48 N 136.29 E
Gornyj, S.S.S.R. 89 44.57 N 133.59 E
Gornyj Balyklej 80 49.34 N 45.04 E
Gornyje Kľuči 89 45.12 N 133.31 E
Gornyj Tikič ≃ 78 48.47 N 30.53 E
Goro, Ityo. 144 6.56 N 40.32 E
Goro, N. Cal. 175f 22.16 S 167.02 E
Gorochan ʌ 144 9.22 N 37.04 E
Gorochov 78 50.30 N 24.45 E
Gorochovatka 83 49.21 N 37.31 E
Gorochovec 80 56.12 N 42.40 E
Gorochovje 76 56.31 N 30.29 E
Gorodec, S.S.S.R. 76 52.12 N 24.40 E
Gorodec, S.S.S.R. 76 58.32 N 29.47 E
Gorodec, S.S.S.R. 76 52.58 N 30.21 E
Gorodec, S.S.S.R. 76 53.33 N 30.02 E
Gorodec, S.S.S.R. 78 51.17 N 26.19 E
Gorodec, S.S.S.R. 80 56.38 N 43.30 E
Gorodeja 76 53.19 N 26.32 E
Gorodenka 38 48.41 N 25.29 E
Gorodišče, S.S.S.R. 76 53.44 N 29.48 E
Gorodišče, S.S.S.R. 76 59.38 N 32.08 E
Gorodišče, S.S.S.R. 76 53.19 N 26.00 E
Gorodišče, S.S.S.R. 78 51.09 N 38.04 E
Gorodišče, S.S.S.R. 78 49.17 N 31.27 E
Gorodišče, S.S.S.R. 80 53.17 N 45.42 E
Gorodišče, S.S.S.R. 80 48.48 N 44.29 E
Gorodišče, S.S.S.R. 82 54.53 N 38.13 E
Gorodišče, S.S.S.R. 82 56.47 N 38.52 E
Gorodišče, S.S.S.R. 83 49.03 N 39.38 E
Gorodišče, S.S.S.R. 83 48.19 N 38.39 E
Gorodišči 82 55.52 N 39.05 E
Gorodkovka 78 48.23 N 28.42 E
Gorodn'a, S.S.S.R. 78 51.53 N 31.36 E
Gorodn'a, S.S.S.R. 82 54.57 N 38.49 E
Gorodn'a, S.S.S.R. 82 56.43 N 36.19 E
Gorodn'a ≃ 265b 55.38 N 37.48 E
Gorodnica 78 50.48 N 27.20 E
Gorodno 76 57.32 N 29.35 E
Gorodok, S.S.S.R. 76 55.28 N 29.59 E
Gorodok, S.S.S.R. 78 49.47 N 23.39 E
Gorodok, S.S.S.R. 78 49.10 N 26.34 E
Gorod'onka 78 48.41 N 25.29 E
Goroka 164 6.05 S 145.25 E
Gorokan 170 33.16 S 151.30 E
Gorom-Gorom 150 14.26 N 0.14 W
Gorong, Pulau I 164 3.59 S 131.25 E
Gorongosa, Parque Nacional da ♦ 156 18.45 S 34.15 E
Gorongosa, Serra da ʌ 154 18.30 S 34.03 E
Gorongose ≃ 156 20.30 S 34.40 E
Gorontalo 112 0.33 N 123.03 E
Goronyo 150 13.29 N 5.39 E
Goroubi ≃ 150 12.54 N 2.23 E
Gorouol ≃ 150 14.42 N 0.53 E
Górowo Iławeckie 30 54.17 N 20.30 E
Gorple Reservoirs ⊜[1] 262 53.47 N 2.06 W
Gorran ⊜ 40 59.43 N 17.32 E
Gorredijk 52 53.00 N 6.05 E
Gorron 28 48.25 N 0.49 W
Görsdorf 54 51.54 N 13.29 E
Goršečnoje 78 51.32 N 38.02 E
Gorsedd 262 53.17 N 3.16 W
Gorseinon 42 51.40 N 4.02 W
Gorskaja 265a 60.03 N 29.59 E
Gorskoje 83 48.46 N 38.30 E
Gorškovo 82 54.26 N 37.59 E
Gorst 224 47.32 N 122.42 W
Gort 48 53.04 N 8.50 W
Gortahork 48 55.08 N 8.09 W
Gorton ◆[8] 262 53.27 N 2.10 W
Görtschitz ≃ 61 46.45 N 14.32 E
Goru, Vîrful ʌ 38 45.48 N 26.25 E
Görükle 130 40.14 N 28.50 E
Gorumna Island I 48 53.14 N 9.40 W
Gor'un ≃ 89 50.45 N 137.50 E
Gorutuba ≃ 255 14.57 S 43.33 W
Görwihl 58 47.39 N 8.04 E
Gory, S.S.S.R. 76 54.16 N 31.13 E
Gory, S.S.S.R. 80 48.38 N 51.46 E
Goryn' ≃ 78 52.08 N 27.17 E
Görz → Gorizia 64 45.57 N 13.38 E
Gorzano, Monte ʌ 66 42.37 N 13.24 E
Gorze 56 49.03 N 6.00 E
Görzig 54 51.40 N 12.00 E
Görzke 54 52.10 N 12.22 E
Górzno 30 53.13 N 19.38 E
Gorzów Śląski 30 51.02 N 18.24 E
Gorzów Wielkopolski (Landsberg an der Warthe) 30 52.44 N 15.15 E
Gorzów Wielkopolski □[4] 30 52.45 N 15.20 E
Górzyca 54 52.29 N 14.40 E
Gosāba 126 22.10 N 88.48 E
Gosairhāt 126 23.05 N 90.26 E
Gosaldo 64 46.13 N 11.58 E
Gosau 64 47.34 N 13.31 E
Gosauseen ⊜ 64 47.32 N 13.31 E
Gosberton 42 52.51 N 0.09 W
Gošča 78 50.36 N 26.41 E
Göschenen 58 46.40 N 8.35 E
Goschen Strait ⊔ 164 10.09 S 150.56 E
Gose 96 34.27 N 135.44 E
Gosen, D.D.R. 264a 52.24 N 13.43 E
Gosen, Nihon 92 37.44 N 139.11 E
Gosford 170 33.26 S 151.21 E
Gosforth, Eng., U.K. 44 55.01 N 1.37 W
Gosforth, Eng., U.K. 44 54.26 N 3.27 W
Gosforth Park ♦ 273d 26.14 S 28.10 E
Gosforth Park Race Course ♦ 273d 26.14 S 28.08 E
Goshabi 140 17.58 N 31.06 E
Goshen, N.S., Can. 186 45.23 N 61.59 W
Goshen, Ca., U.S. 226 36.21 N 119.25 W
Goshen, Ct., U.S. 207 41.49 N 73.13 W
Goshen, In., U.S. 216 41.34 N 85.50 W
Goshen, Ma., U.S. 207 42.26 N 72.48 W
Goshen, N.J., U.S. 208 39.08 N 74.51 W
Goshen, N.Y., U.S. 210 41.24 N 74.19 W
Goshen, Oh., U.S. 218 39.14 N 84.10 W
Goshiki 96 34.24 N 134.47 E
Goshogawara 92 40.48 N 140.27 E
Goshute Indian Reservation ◆[4] 200 39.53 N 114.08 W
Goshute Lake ⊜ 204 40.08 N 114.38 W
Goshute Valley V 204 40.30 N 114.30 W
Goslar 52 51.54 N 10.25 E
Gosnells 168a 32.04 S 116.00 E
Gospić 36 44.33 N 15.23 E
Gosport, Eng., U.K. 42 50.48 N 1.08 W
Gosport, In., U.S. 194 39.21 N 86.40 W
Gossa 54 51.40 N 12.26 E
Gossas 150 14.30 N 16.04 W
Gossau 58 47.25 N 9.15 E
Gosse ◆[8] 263 51.08 N 7.01 E
Gosse Bluff ʌ 162 23.49 S 132.19 E
Gosselies 56 50.28 N 4.25 E
Gössenheim 56 50.01 N 9.46 E
Gossensass → Colle Isarco 64 46.56 N 11.26 E
Gosser Hill 279b 40.37 N 79.37 W
Gossi 150 15.49 N 1.17 W
Gossinga 140 8.39 N 25.59 E
Gössnitz 54 50.53 N 12.26 E
Gossolengo 62 44.59 N 9.37 E
Gössweinstein 60 49.46 N 11.20 E
Gostagajevskaja 78 45.01 N 37.30 E
Gostilovo 82 55.18 N 38.36 E
Gostiščevo 78 50.47 N 36.39 E
Gostivar 38 41.47 N 20.54 E
Göstling an der Ybbs 61 47.48 N 14.55 E
Gostyń 30 51.53 N 17.00 E
Gostynin 30 52.26 N 19.29 E
Gosudarev Bajrak 83 48.21 N 38.26 E
Göta älv ≃ 26 57.42 N 11.52 E
Göta kanal ≋ 40 58.50 N 13.58 E
Gotchen Creek ≃ 224 46.00 N 121.30 W
Got Creek ≃ 284a 43.03 N 78.42 W
Gotebo 196 35.04 N 98.52 W
Göteborg (Gothenburg) 26 57.43 N 11.58 E
Göteborgs Och Bohus län □[6] 26 58.30 N 11.30 E
Gotel Mountains ⋀ 152 6.55 N 11.15 E
Gotemba 94 35.18 N 138.56 E
Götene 26 58.32 N 13.29 E
Gotešty 78 46.09 N 28.10 E
Gotha, D.D.R. 54 50.57 N 10.41 E
Gotha, Fl., U.S. 220 28.32 N 81.31 W
Gothem 26 57.35 N 18.43 E
Gothenburg → Göteborg, Sve. 26 57.43 N 11.58 E
Gothenburg, Ne., U.S. 198 40.55 N 100.09 W
Gothèye 150 13.52 N 1.34 E
Gotland I 26 57.30 N 18.33 E
Gotlands Län □[6] 26 57.30 N 18.30 E
Gotoputovo 86 56.46 N 70.10 E
Gotō-rettō II 92 32.50 N 129.00 E
Gotska Sandön I 26 58.23 N 19.16 E
Gōtsu 96 35.00 N 132.14 E
Gottenheim 58 48.03 N 7.44 E
Götterswickerhamm 263 51.35 N 6.40 E
Gottesbrücke 264a 52.25 N 13.49 E
Gotthard Tunnel ◆[5] 58 46.35 N 8.35 E
Göttin 264a 52.27 N 12.54 E
Göttingen, B.R.D. 52 51.32 N 9.55 E
Göttingen, B.R.D. 56 50.52 N 8.46 E
Göttin See ⊜ 264a 52.28 N 12.54 E
Gottmadingen 58 47.44 N 8.47 E
Gottolengo 64 45.17 N 10.16 E
Gottorf, Schloss ⊥ 41 54.30 N 9.32 E
Gottsbüren 52 51.35 N 9.30 E
Gottvaterkapelle ⌂[1] 60 49.42 N 11.41 E
Gottwaldov 30 49.13 N 17.41 E
Gotval'd 78 49.40 N 36.19 E
Götzendorf 264b 48.01 N 16.35 E
Götzis 58 47.20 N 9.38 E
Gouarec 32 48.13 N 3.11 W
Goubangzi 104 41.22 N 121.46 E
Goubone 146 20.43 N 17.08 E
Gouda, Ned. 52 52.01 N 4.43 E
Gouda, S. Afr. 158 33.19 S 19.04 E
Goudet 62 44.53 N 3.55 E
Goudge 252 34.40 S 68.08 W
Goudhurst 42 51.07 N 0.28 E
Goudiry 150 14.11 N 12.43 W
Goudoumaria 146 13.42 N 11.10 E
Goudswaard 52 51.47 N 4.16 E
Gouéké 150 8.02 N 8.43 W
Goûfi, Djebel el ʌ 34 36.57 N 6.27 E
Gougezhuang 105 38.53 N 116.11 E
Gough Island I 10 40.20 S 10.00 W
Gough Lake ⊜ 182 52.02 N 112.28 W
Gouin, Réservoir ⊜[1] 176 48.38 N 74.54 W
Goujiaozhen 107 30.36 N 106.33 E
Goukou 89 48.39 N 122.06 E
Goulais ≃ 190 46.43 N 84.27 W
Goulburn 170 34.45 S 149.43 E
Goulburn ≃ 169 36.41 S 145.12 E
Goulburn Islands II 164 11.33 S 133.26 E
Goulburn Weir ⊜[1] 169 36.45 S 145.08 E
Gould 194 33.59 N 91.33 W
Gould City 190 46.05 N 85.41 W
Gould Park 214 40.04 N 82.53 W
Goulds 220 25.33 N 80.22 W
Gouldsboro 210 41.44 N 75.28 W
Gouldsboro State Park ♦ 210 41.13 N 75.28 W
Goulet Lake ⊜ 184 55.23 N 96.18 W
Goulia 150 10.01 N 7.11 W
Goulicun 106 31.40 N 120.00 E
Goulimime 148 28.56 N 10.04 W
Goulimine □[4] 148 28.30 N 9.45 W
Goulmima 148 31.02 N 5.00 W
Goumbati ʌ[2] 150 13.08 N 12.06 W
Goumbou 150 14.59 N 7.27 W
Gouménissa 38 40.57 N 22.27 E
Goumois 58 47.16 N 6.57 E
Gouna 146 8.32 N 13.34 E
Gounda ≃ 146 9.25 N 20.57 E
Goundam 150 16.25 N 3.40 W
Goundi 146 9.22 N 17.22 E
Gounou-Gaya 146 9.38 N 15.31 E
Gouougang, Mount ʌ 170 33.53 S 150.07 E
Goupillières 261 48.53 N 1.46 E
Gouraya 34 36.34 N 1.55 E
Gourbassi 150 13.24 N 11.38 W
Gourbeyre 241o 16.00 N 61.42 W
Gourcy 150 13.13 N 2.21 W
Gourdhead Run ≃ 279b 40.33 N 79.57 W
Gourdon, Fr. 32 44.44 N 1.23 E
Gourdon, Fr. 62 43.43 N 6.59 E
Gouré 150 13.58 N 10.18 E
Gouri ⊥ 124 24.53 N 88.07 E
Gourin 32 48.08 N 3.36 W
Gouripur 124 24.46 N 90.34 E
Gourits ≃ 158 34.21 S 21.52 E
Gourlay Lake ⊜ 190 48.52 N 84.54 W
Gourma Rharous 150 16.53 N 1.55 W
Gournay-en-Bray 50 49.29 N 1.44 E
Gournay-sur-Marne 261 48.52 N 2.34 E
Gouro 146 19.33 N 19.33 E
Gourock 46 55.58 N 4.49 W
Goussainville 50 49.01 N 2.28 E
Goussonville 261 48.55 N 1.46 E
Goutou 105 39.49 N 117.11 E
Gouvêa 255 18.27 S 43.44 W
Gouveia 266c 38.50 N 9.26 W
Gouverneur 212 44.20 N 75.27 W
Gouyadong 100 25.10 N 112.55 E
Gov'altaj □[4] 102 45.30 N 96.00 E
Govan 184 51.18 N 105.00 W
Go Vap 269c 10.49 N 106.41 E
Govardhan 124 27.30 N 77.28 E
Gove 198 38.57 N 100.29 W
Govea ≃ 286b 22.56 N 82.30 W
Govena, mys > 74 59.48 N 166.06 E
Govenlock 184 49.15 N 109.48 W
Gove Peninsula >[1] 164 12.20 S 136.50 E
Goverla, gora ʌ 78 48.10 N 24.32 E
Governador, Ilha do I 287a 22.48 S 43.12 W
Governador Portela 256 22.29 S 43.30 W
Governador Valadares 255 18.51 S 41.56 W
Government Camp 224 45.18 N 121.45 W
Governor Bond Lake ⊜[1] 219 38.56 N 89.23 W
Governor Dodge State Park ♦ 190 43.00 N 90.07 W
Governor Generoso 116 6.39 N 126.05 E
Governor Head > 170 35.07 S 150.46 E
Governor Nice Memorial Bridge ◆[5] 208 38.22 N 77.00 W
Governor Printz Park ♦ 285 39.52 N 75.18 W
Governors Harbour 238 25.10 N 76.14 W
Governors Island I 276 40.41 N 74.01 W
Govind Ballabh Pant Sāgar ⊜[1] 124 24.05 N 82.50 E
Govindgarh 124 24.23 N 81.18 E
Govind Sāgar ⊜[1] 123 31.20 N 76.45 E
Gov'-Ugtaal 102 46.04 N 107.30 E
Gowan ≃ 184 55.49 N 94.08 W
Gowanda 210 42.27 N 78.56 W
Gowan Range ⋀ 166 25.00 S 145.00 E
Gowen City 208 40.45 N 76.32 W
Gower 194 39.36 N 94.35 W
Gower >[1] 42 51.36 N 4.10 W
Gowerton 42 51.39 N 4.01 W
Gowienica ≃ 54 53.40 N 14.38 E
Gowmal (Gumal) ≃ 120 31.56 N 70.22 E
Gowmal Kalay 120 32.29 N 68.55 E
Gowna, Lough ⊜ 48 53.51 N 7.34 W
Gowrie 198 42.16 N 94.17 W
Gowy ≃ 262 53.17 N 2.51 W
Goya 252 29.08 S 59.16 W
Goyania → Goiânia 255 16.40 S 49.16 W
Goyatz 54 52.01 N 14.09 E
Goyave 241o 16.08 N 61.34 W
Goyaves, Grande Rivière à ≃ 241o 16.18 N 61.37 W
Goyaves, Îlets à II 241o 16.10 N 61.48 W
Goyder ≃ 164 12.38 S 135.11 E
Goyder Creek ≃ 162 25.39 S 134.47 E
Goyelle, Lac ⊜ 186 50.47 N 60.45 W
Goyeneche 258 35.20 S 58.43 W
Goyer, Île I 275a 45.29 N 73.17 W
Goyerkāta 124 26.42 N 89.02 E
Göynücek 130 40.24 N 35.32 E
Göynük, Tür. 130 39.08 N 40.53 E
Göynük, Tür. 130 40.24 N 30.47 E
Göynük ≃, Tür. 130 38.53 N 40.34 E
Göynük ≃, Tür. 130 40.20 N 30.05 E
Goyt ≃ 262 53.24 N 2.09 W
Goz-Beïda 146 12.13 N 21.25 E
Gozdnica 30 51.26 N 15.06 E
Gozdowice 54 52.45 N 14.18 E
Göze Dağı ʌ 130 41.24 N 42.30 E
Gözeli 130 38.25 N 39.04 E
Gozen-yama 94 36.32 N 140.20 E
Gozha Co ⊜ 120 34.59 N 81.06 E
Gözne 130 36.59 N 34.34 E
Gozo → Għawdex I 36 36.03 N 14.15 E
Göz Tepe ʌ[2] 267b 41.06 N 29.06 E
Gozzano 62 45.45 N 8.26 E
Graaff-Reinet 158 32.14 S 24.32 E
Graafwater 158 32.00 S 18.37 E
Graauw 52 51.20 N 4.05 E
Grabc'ovo 82 54.34 N 36.22 E
Graben-Neudorf 56 49.09 N 8.29 E
Grabenstätt 64 47.51 N 12.32 E
Grabill 216 41.12 N 84.58 W
Grabo 150 4.55 N 7.30 W
Grabouw 158 34.09 S 19.02 E
Grabovaja Balka, les ♦ 83 48.09 N 38.37 E
Grabovo 86 53.07 N 74.52 E
Grabow 54 53.16 N 11.34 E
Grabowiec 30 50.50 N 23.33 E
Grabów nad Prosną 30 51.31 N 18.06 E
Gračac 36 44.18 N 15.51 E
Gračanica 38 44.42 N 18.19 E
Gračanica, Manastir ⌂[1] 38 42.36 N 21.09 E
Graçay 50 47.08 N 1.51 E
Grace 202 42.34 N 111.43 W
Gracefield 188 46.06 N 76.03 W
Graceham 208 39.36 N 77.22 W
Graceton 214 40.30 N 79.10 W
Graceville, Fl., U.S. 192 30.57 N 85.31 W
Graceville, Mn., U.S. 198 45.34 N 96.26 W
Gračevka 82 55.06 N 36.49 E
Grächen 58 46.12 N 7.50 E
Grachovo 80 56.04 N 51.58 E
Grači 80 49.49 N 43.33 E
Gracia ◆[8] 266d 41.23 N 2.09 E
Gracias 236 14.35 N 88.35 W
Gracias a Dios □[5] 236 15.10 N 84.20 W
Gracias a Dios, Cabo > 236 15.00 N 83.10 W
Gračiki ≃ 83 48.30 N 39.52 E
Graciosa I 148a 39.04 N 28.00 W
Graciosa, Isla I 148 29.15 N 13.30 W
Gračov 80 49.26 N 41.32 E
Gračovka, S.S.S.R. 80 52.57 N 52.52 E
Gračovka, S.S.S.R. 80 52.07 N 40.01 E
Gračov Kust 80 51.59 N 49.50 E
Gradačac 38 44.53 N 18.26 E
Gradara 66 43.57 N 12.46 E
Gradaús 250 7.43 S 51.11 W
Gradaús, Serra dos ⋀[1] 250 8.00 S 50.45 W
Gr'adcy 76 56.24 N 31.55 E
Gräddö 40 59.46 N 19.02 E
Gradisca d'Isonzo 64 45.53 N 13.30 E
Gradižsk 78 49.13 N 33.07 E
Grado, Esp. 34 43.23 N 6.04 W
Grado, It. 64 45.40 N 13.23 E
Grado, Laguna di ⊂ 64 45.43 N 13.20 E
Gradoli 66 42.39 N 11.51 E
Grady, Ar., U.S. 194 34.04 N 91.42 W
Grady, N.M., U.S. 196 34.49 N 103.19 W
Gradyville 285 39.57 N 75.28 W
Graemsay I 46 58.56 N 3.17 W
Græsted 41 56.04 N 12.17 E
Graettinger 198 43.14 N 94.45 W
Gräfelfing 60 48.07 N 11.25 E
Grafenau 60 48.52 N 13.25 E
Gräfenberg 60 49.39 N 11.15 E
Grafenberg ◆[8] 263 51.14 N 6.50 E
Gräfenhainichen 54 51.44 N 12.27 E
Gräfenroda 54 50.45 N 10.48 E
Gräfenthal 54 50.31 N 11.18 E
Gräfentonna 54 51.05 N 10.44 E
Grafenwöhr 60 49.43 N 11.54 E
Graffignano 66 42.34 N 12.12 E
Grafham Water ⊜ 42 52.17 N 0.20 W
Gräfinau-Angstedt 54 50.42 N 11.01 E
Grafing bei München 60 48.02 N 11.59 E
Gråfjell ʌ 26 60.16 N 9.29 E
Graford 196 32.56 N 98.14 W
Gräfrath ◆[8] 263 51.13 N 7.04 E
Grafschaft Bentheim □[9] 52 52.30 N 7.00 E
Grafton, Austl. 166 29.41 S 152.56 E
Grafton, On., Can. 212 44.00 N 78.01 W
Grafton, Il., U.S. 219 38.58 N 90.25 W
Grafton, Ma., U.S. 207 42.12 N 71.41 W
Grafton, N.Y., U.S. 210 42.46 N 73.27 W
Grafton, N.D., U.S. 198 48.24 N 97.24 W
Grafton, Oh., U.S. 214 41.16 N 82.03 W
Grafton, W.V., U.S. 188 39.20 N 80.01 W
Grafton, Wi., U.S. 190 43.19 N 87.57 W
Grafton, Cape > 164 16.52 S 145.55 E
Grafton Lakes State Park ♦ 210 42.48 N 73.28 W
Grafty Green 260 51.12 N 0.41 E
Graglia 62 45.33 N 7.59 E
Gragnano 68 40.41 N 14.31 E
Gragnano Trebbiense 62 45.01 N 9.34 E
Graham, Ca., U.S. 280 34.15 N 118.31 W
Graham, N.C., U.S. 192 36.04 N 79.24 W
Graham, Tx., U.S. 196 33.06 N 98.35 W
Graham, Wa., U.S. 224 47.03 N 122.17 W
Graham, Mount ʌ 200 32.42 N 109.52 W
Graham Cave State Park ♦ 219 38.55 N 91.32 W
Graham Creek ≃ 218 38.49 N 85.39 W
Graham Island I 182 53.40 N 132.30 W
Graham Lake ⊜, On., Can. 212 44.34 N 75.53 W
Graham Lake ⊜, Me., U.S. 188 44.40 N 68.25 W
Graham Land ◆[1] 9 66.00 S 63.30 W
Graham Memorial Park ♦ 284b 39.25 N 76.30 W
Graham Moore, Cape > 176 72.52 N 76.04 W
Graham Moore Bay ⊂ 176 75.26 N 101.25 W
Grahamstad → Grahamstown 158 33.19 S 26.31 E
Grahamstown 158 33.19 S 26.31 E
Grahamsville 210 41.51 N 74.33 W
Grahn 218 38.17 N 83.04 W
Graie, Alpi (Alpes Grées) ⋀ 62 45.30 N 7.10 E
Graiguenarmanagh 48 52.32 N 6.57 W
Grain 260 51.28 N 0.43 E
Grain, Isle of I 42 51.27 N 0.41 E
Grain Coast ±[2] 150 5.00 N 9.00 W
Grainfield 198 39.06 N 100.27 W
Grajagan 115a 8.35 S 114.13 E
Grajagan, Teluk ⊂ 115a 8.40 S 114.18 E
Grajaú 250 5.49 S 46.08 W
Grajaú ≃ 250 3.41 S 44.48 W
Grajewo 30 53.39 N 22.27 E
Grajvoron 78 50.28 N 35.39 E
Gram 41 55.17 N 9.04 E
Gramacho 287a 22.44 S 43.18 W
Gramada 38 43.50 N 22.39 E
Gramado 252 29.24 S 50.54 W
Gramalote 246 7.53 N 72.48 W
Gramastetten 61 48.23 N 14.12 E
Gramat 32 44.47 N 1.43 E
Gramatneusiedl 264b 48.02 N 16.29 E
Grambling 194 32.31 N 92.42 W
Gramilla 252 27.18 S 64.37 W
Gramínea 256 22.10 S 46.38 W
Graminha, Represa da ⊜[1] 256 21.40 S 46.35 W
Grammer 218 39.09 N 85.43 W
Grammichele 70 37.13 N 14.38 E
Grammont → Geraardsbergen 50 50.46 N 3.52 E
Gramoteino 86 54.31 N 86.22 E
Grampian 214 40.57 N 78.36 W
Grampian □[4] 46 57.15 N 2.45 W
Grampian Mountains ⋀ 46 56.55 N 4.00 W
Grampians National Park ♦ 166 37.20 S 142.30 E
Gramschatz 56 49.56 N 9.58 E
Gramsh 38 40.52 N 20.11 E
Gramzow 54 53.12 N 14.00 E
Gran → Esztergom 30 47.48 N 18.45 E
Grana ≃ 62 44.25 N 7.27 E
Granaatboskolk 158 30.02 S 19.51 E
Granada, Col. 246 3.34 N 73.45 W
Granada, Esp. 34 37.13 N 3.41 W
Granada, Nic. 236 11.56 N 85.57 W
Granada, Pil. 116 10.40 N 123.02 E
Granada, Co., U.S. 198 38.03 N 102.18 W
Granada, Mn., U.S. 190 43.41 N 94.20 W
Granada □[5] 236 11.50 N 86.00 W
Granada → Grenada □[1] 241k 12.07 N 61.40 W
Granada Hills ◆[8] 280 34.16 N 118.31 W
Granado 286d 12.04 S 76.57 W
Granaglione 66 44.07 N 10.58 E
Gran Altiplanicie Central ⋀[1] 254 48.55 S 69.25 W
Granard 48 53.47 N 7.30 W
Granarolo dell'Emilia 64 44.33 N 11.27 E
Granatello 70 37.53 N 12.32 E
Gran Bahía Australiana → Great Australian Bight ⊂[3] 162 35.00 S 135.00 E
Gran Bajo de San Julián V 254 49.30 S 68.30 W
Gran Barrera de Arrecifes → Great Barrier Reef ✦[2] 160 18.00 S 145.50 E
Granbergsdal 40 59.24 N 14.35 E
Granbury 222 32.26 N 97.47 W
Granbury, Lake ⊜[1] 222 32.25 N 97.45 W
Granby, P.Q., Can. 206 45.24 N 72.44 W
Granby, Co., U.S. 200 40.05 N 105.56 W
Granby, Ct., U.S. 207 41.57 N 72.47 W
Granby, Ma., U.S. 207 42.15 N 72.31 W
Granby, Mo., U.S. 194 36.55 N 94.15 W
Granby ≃ 182 49.03 N 118.25 W
Granby, Lake ⊜[1] 200 40.09 N 105.50 W
Gran Canal del Desagüe ≋ 286a 19.29 N 99.05 W
Gran Canaria I 148 28.00 N 15.36 W
Grancey-le-Château 58 47.40 N 5.02 E
Gran Chaco ≚ 18 23.00 S 60.00 W
Grand 58 48.23 N 5.29 E
Grand ≃, On., Can. 212 42.51 N 79.34 W
Grand ≃, U.S. 194 39.23 N 93.06 W
Grand ≃, Mi., U.S. 216 43.04 N 86.15 W
Grand ≃, Oh., U.S. 214 41.46 N 81.17 W
Grand ≃, S.D., U.S. 198 45.40 N 100.32 W
Grand ≃, Wi., U.S. 190 43.45 N 89.16 W
Grand, East Fork ≃ 194 40.12 N 94.21 W
Grand, Lac ⊜ 190 47.10 N 76.57 W
Grand, North Fork ≃ 198 45.47 N 102.16 W
Grand, South Fork ≃ 198 45.43 N 102.17 W
Grandas 34 43.13 N 6.52 W
Grand Bahama I 238 26.38 N 78.25 W
Grand Ballon ʌ 58 47.55 N 7.08 E
Grand Bank 186 47.06 N 55.46 W
Grand Banks of Newfoundland ✦[4] 16 45.00 N 53.00 W
Grand-Bassam 150 5.12 N 3.44 W
Grand Bay, N.B., Can. 186 45.18 N 66.12 W
Grand Bay, Al., U.S. 194 30.28 N 88.20 W
Grand Bay ⊂ 240d 15.14 N 61.19 W
Grand Beach 184 50.35 N 96.40 W
Grand Bend 190 43.15 N 81.45 W
Grand Béréby 150 4.38 N 6.55 W
Grand Blanc 216 42.55 N 83.37 W
Grand-Bourg 241o 15.53 N 61.19 W
Grand Bruit 186 47.41 N 58.13 W
Grand Caille Point > 241f 13.52 N 61.05 W
Grand Calumet ≃ 278 41.38 N 87.34 W
Grand Calumet, Île du I 190 45.44 N 76.41 W
Grand Canal ≋ 48 53.21 N 6.14 W
Grand Canal → Da Yunhe ≋ 90 32.12 N 119.31 E
Grand Cane 194 32.05 N 93.48 W
Grand Cañon du Verdon ♦ 62 43.47 N 6.27 E
Grand Canyon 200 36.03 N 112.08 W
Grand Canyon V 200 36.10 N 112.45 W
Grand Canyon National Park ♦ 200 36.15 N 112.58 W
Grand Canyon of Pennsylvania ♦ 210 41.43 N 77.28 W
Grand Cayman I 238 19.20 N 81.15 W
Grand Central Terminal ◆[5] 276 40.45 N 73.59 W
Grand Centre 184 54.25 N 110.13 W
Grand Cess 150 4.36 N 8.10 W
Grandchamp, Fr. 58 47.43 N 5.27 E
Grandchamp, Fr. 261 48.43 N 1.37 E
Grand-Charmont 58 47.32 N 6.50 E
Grand Chenier 194 29.46 N 92.58 W
Grand Combin ʌ 58 45.56 N 7.18 E
Grand Coulee 202 47.56 N 119.00 W
Grand Coulee V 202 47.45 N 119.15 W
Grand Coulee Dam ◆[6] 202 47.57 N 118.59 W
Grand-Couronne 50 49.21 N 1.00 E
Grand Cul-de-Sac Marin ⊂ 241o 16.20 N 61.35 W
Grande ≃, Arg. 252 24.12 S 64.42 W
Grande ≃, Arg. 252 36.52 S 69.45 W
Grande ≃, Bol. 248 15.51 S 64.39 W
Grande ≃, Bra. 242 11.05 S 43.09 W
Grande ≃, Bra. 255 20.06 S 51.04 W
Grande ≃, Bra. 287a 22.55 S 43.25 W
Grande ≃, Bra. 287b 23.45 S 46.22 W
Grande ≃, Chile 252 30.35 S 71.11 W
Grande ≃, Esp. 34 39.07 N 0.44 W
Grande ≃, It. 70 37.55 N 13.13 E
Grande ≃, Méx. 234 16.47 N 95.52 W
Grande ≃, Méx. 234 17.13 N 100.55 W
Grande ≃, Méx. 234 17.43 N 96.56 W
Grande ≃, Pan. 236 8.18 N 80.24 W
Grande ≃, Perú 248 14.59 S 75.29 W
Grande ≃, S.A. 254 53.48 S 67.40 W
Grande, Arroyo ≃, Arg. 258 34.37 S 59.25 W
Grande, Arroyo ≃, Arg. 288 34.45 S 58.08 W
Grande, Arroyo ≃, Méx. 234 23.55 N 98.44 W
Grande, Arroyo ≃, Ur. 252 33.08 S 57.09 W
Grande, Arroyo ≃, Ur. 258 33.37 S 57.09 W
Grande, Bahía ⊂[3] 254 50.45 S 68.45 W
Grande, Boca ⊂ 220 26.43 N 82.16 W
Grande, Boca ≃[1] 246 8.38 N 60.30 W
Grande, Cañada ≃, Arg. 258 35.15 S 59.23 W
Grande, Cañada ≃, Arg. 258 35.19 S 57.48 W
Grande, Cayo I 240p 20.59 N 79.09 W
Grande, Cerro ʌ, Méx. 234 23.39 N 100.51 W
Grande, Cerro ʌ, Méx. 234 21.45 N 103.05 W
Grande, Cerro ʌ, Méx. 234 20.30 N 103.02 W
Grande, Cerro ʌ, Méx. 234 20.43 N 101.12 W
Grande, Corixa (Curiche Grande) ⩸ 248 17.10 S 58.20 W
Grande, Cuchilla ʌ 252 33.15 S 55.07 W
Grande, Curiche (Corixa Grande) ⩸ 248 17.10 S 58.20 W
Grande, Igarapé ≃ 250 3.37 S 48.53 W
Grande, Ilha I, Bra. 252 23.45 S 54.03 W
Grande, Ilha I, Bra. 256 23.09 S 44.14 W
Grande, Isola I 70 37.53 N 12.26 E
Grande, Lago ⊜, Arg. 254 47.44 S 68.04 W
Grande, Lago ⊜, Bra. 250 2.16 S 54.17 W
Grande, Laguna ⊂ 286b 23.05 N 82.30 W
Grande, Laguna ⊜ 258 34.14 S 58.53 W
Grande, Mare (Taranto) ⊂ 68 40.27 N 17.12 E
Grande, Naviglio ≋ 266b 45.35 N 8.42 E
Grande, Ponta > 255 16.22 S 39.01 W
Grande, Praia ±[2] 256 24.05 S 46.30 W
Grande, Punta > 252 25.06 S 70.30 W
Grande, Ribeirão ≃ 256 22.11 S 43.19 W
Grande, Rio (Bravo del Norte) ≃ 178 25.55 N 97.09 W
Grande, Salina ⩸ 68 40.26 N 17.18 E
Grande, Serra ⋀ 250 6.00 S 40.52 W
Grande, Serra → Geral, Serra ±[4] 250 11.15 S 46.30 W
Grande, Sierra ⋀ 196 29.40 N 104.55 W
Grande, Volcán ʌ[1] 234 20.06 N 101.38 W
Grande-Anse, N.B., Can. 186 47.48 N 65.11 W
Grande Anse, Guad. 241o 16.18 N 61.04 W
Grande Anse, La ⊂ 275a 45.23 N 73.53 W
Grande Anse Bay ⊂ 241k 12.02 N 61.45 W
Grande Baie, La ⊂ 275a 45.29 N 74.00 W
Grande Cache 182 53.53 N 119.08 W
Grande Casse, Pointe de la ʌ 62 45.24 N 6.50 E
Grande Cayemite I 238 18.37 N 73.45 W
Grande Chartreuse, Couvent de la ⌂[1] 62 45.22 N 5.50 E
Grande da Botija, Ilha I 246 3.58 S 62.53 W
Grande de Añasco ≃ 240m 18.16 N 67.11 W
Grande de Arecibo ≃ 240m 18.29 N 66.42 W
Grande de Jutaí, Ilha I 250 3.15 S 49.37 W
Grande de Lipez ≃ 248 20.47 S 67.14 W
Grande de Loíza ≃ 240m 18.27 N 65.53 W
Grande de Manacapuru, Lago ⊜ 246 3.04 S 61.25 W
Grande de Manatí ≃ 240m 18.29 N 66.32 W
Grande de Matagalpa ≃ 236 12.54 N 83.32 W
Grande de Santa Marta, Ciénaga ⊂ 246 10.50 N 74.25 W
Grande de Santiago ≃ 234 21.36 N 105.26 W
Grande de Tarija ≃ 248 22.53 S 64.21 W
Grande de Térraba ≃ 236 9.03 N 83.40 W
Grande do Curuaí, Lago ⊜ 250 2.15 S 55.20 W
Grande do Gurupá, Ilha I 250 1.00 S 51.30 W
Grande do Tapará, Ilha I 250 2.14 S 54.39 W
Grande Île de Criques I 273b 4.20 S 15.25 E
Grande Inferior, Cuchilla ⋀[2] 258 33.50 S 56.27 W
Grand-Entrée 186 47.33 N 61.34 W
Grande Pointe > 241o 15.58 N 61.38 W
Grande-Prairie 182 55.10 N 118.48 W
Grand Erg de Bilma ◆[2] 146 18.30 N 14.00 E
Grand Erg Occidental ◆[2] 148 30.30 N 0.30 E
Grand Erg Oriental ◆[2] 148 30.30 N 7.00 E
Grande-Rivière 186 48.24 N 64.30 W
Grande Rivière, La ≃ 176 53.50 N 79.00 W
Grande Ronde ≃ 202 46.05 N 116.59 W
Grandes, Salinas ≚, Arg. 252 30.05 S 65.05 W
Grandes, Salinas ≚, Arg. 252 23.43 S 66.00 W
Grandes Antillas, Islas → Greater Antilles II 238 20.00 N 74.00 W
Grandes Antilles, Îles → Greater Antilles II 238 20.00 N 74.00 W
Grande Sassière, Aiguille de la ʌ 62 45.30 N 7.00 E
Grande Sauldre ≃ 50 47.22 N 1.55 E
Gran Desierto de Arena → Great Sandy Desert ◆[2] 162 21.30 S 125.00 E
Gran Desierto Victoria → Great Victoria Desert ◆[2] 162 28.30 S 127.45 E
Grandes-Piles 206 46.41 N 72.44 W
Grande-Synthe 50 51.01 N 2.19 E
Grand-Étang 186 46.33 N 61.02 W
Grande-Terre I 241o 16.20 N 61.25 W
Grande Vigie, Pointe de la > 241o 16.31 N 61.28 W
Grand Eyvia ≃ 62 45.42 N 7.14 E
Grand Falls, N.B., Can. 186 47.03 N 67.44 W
Grand Falls, Nf., Can. 186 48.56 N 55.40 W
Grandfalls, Tx., U.S. 196 31.20 N 102.51 W
Grandfather Mountain ʌ 192 36.07 N 81.48 W
Grandfield 196 34.13 N 98.41 W
Grand Forks, B.C., Can. 182 49.02 N 118.27 W
Grand Forks, N.D., U.S. 198 47.55 N 97.01 W
Grand Forks Air Force Base ■ 198 47.57 N 97.25 W
Grand-Fort-Philippe 50 51.00 N 2.06 E
Grand-Fougeray 32 47.44 N 1.44 W
Grand-Gallargues 62 43.43 N 4.10 E
Grand Gorge 210 42.21 N 74.29 W
Grand-Halleux 56 50.19 N 5.54 E
Grand Haven 216 43.03 N 86.13 W
Grand Haven State Park ♦ 216 43.02 N 86.13 W
Grand Hers ≃ 32 43.47 N 1.20 E
Grandiči 76 53.43 N 23.49 E
Grandin, Lac ⊜ 176 63.59 N 119.00 W
Grandioznyj, pik ʌ 88 53.50 N 96.11 E
Grand Island, Fl., U.S. 220 28.53 N 81.44 W
Grand Island, Ne., U.S. 198 40.55 N 98.20 W
Grand Island, N.Y., U.S. 212 43.01 N 78.58 W
Grand Island I, On., Can. 212 44.34 N 78.50 W
Grand Island I, Mi., U.S. 190 46.30 N 86.40 W
Grand Island I, N.Y., U.S. 210 43.02 N 78.58 W
Grand Isle 194 29.14 N 89.59 W
Grand Isle □[6] 206 44.57 N 73.17 W
Grand Junction, Co., U.S. 200 39.03 N 108.33 W
Grand Junction, Ia., U.S. 198 42.01 N 94.14 W
Grand Junction, Mi., U.S. 216 42.24 N 86.04 W
Grand Junction, Tn., U.S. 194 35.02 N 89.11 W
Grand Lac Salé → Great Salt Lake ⊜ 200 41.10 N 112.30 W
Grand lac Victoria ⊜ 190 47.31 N 77.30 W
Grand-Lahou 150 5.08 N 5.01 W
Grand Lake 200 40.15 N 105.49 W
Grand Lake ⊜, N.B., Can. 186 45.55 N 66.05 W
Grand Lake ⊜, Nf., Can. 186 49.00 N 57.25 W
Grand Lake ⊜, N.A. 186 45.43 N 67.50 W
Grand Lake ⊜, La., U.S. 194 29.55 N 91.25 W
Grand Lake ⊜, La., U.S. 194 29.55 N 92.47 W
Grand Lake ⊜, Mi., U.S. 190 45.18 N 83.30 W
Grand Lake ⊜, Oh., U.S. 216 40.30 N 84.32 W
Grand Lake Saint Marys State Park ♦ 216 40.33 N 84.27 W
Grand Ledge 216 42.45 N 84.44 W
Grand Lieu, Lac de ⊜ 32 47.06 N 1.40 W
Grand'Maison, Barrage de ◆[6] 62 45.12 N 6.07 E
Grand Manan Channel ⊔ 186 44.45 N 66.52 W
Grand Manan Island I 186 44.40 N 66.50 W
Grand Marais, Mi., U.S. 190 46.40 N 85.59 W
Grand Marais, Mn., U.S. 190 47.45 N 90.20 W
Grand Meadow 190 43.42 N 92.34 W
Grand-Mère 206 46.37 N 72.41 W
Grand Mesa ʌ 200 39.00 N 108.00 W
Grandmesnil, Lac ⊜ 186 51.19 N 67.33 W
Grand Morin ≃ 50 48.54 N 2.50 E
Grand Muveran ʌ 58 46.14 N 7.08 E
Grandola, It. 58 46.02 N 9.13 E
Grândola, Port. 34 38.10 N 8.34 W
Grand Pabos, Rivière du ≃ 186 48.21 N 64.43 W
Grand Palace ⌂ 269a 13.45 N 100.30 E
Grand Passage ⊔ 175f 18.45 S 163.10 E
Grand-Popo 150 6.17 N 1.50 E
Grand Portage 190 47.57 N 89.41 W
Grand Portage Indian Reservation ◆[4] 190 47.55 N 89.45 W
Grand Portage National Monument ♦ 190 48.02 N 89.38 W
Grand Prairie 222 32.44 N 96.59 W
Grandpré 56 49.20 N 4.52 E
Grand Pré National Historic Park ♦ 186 45.08 N 64.18 W
Grand Prix Airport ⊠ 281 42.33 N 83.11 W
Grand Rapids, Mb., Can. 184 53.08 N 99.20 W
Grand Rapids, Mi., U.S. 216 42.58 N 85.40 W
Grand Rapids, Mn., U.S. 190 47.14 N 93.31 W
Grand Rapids, Oh., U.S. 216 41.24 N 83.51 W
Grand Rhône ≃ 62 43.20 N 4.50 E
Grand Ridge 216 41.14 N 88.50 W
Grandrieu, Bel. 50 50.12 N 4.10 E
Grandrieu, Fr. 62 44.47 N 3.38 E
Grand River 214 41.44 N 81.17 W
Grand' Rivière 240e 14.52 N 61.11 W
Grand Ronde 224 45.03 N 123.36 W
Grand Roy 241k 12.08 N 61.45 W
Grand Ruisseau, Le ≃ 275a 45.39 N 73.12 W
Grand-Saint-Bernard, Col du)(58 45.50 N 7.10 E
Grand-Saint-Bernard, Tunnel du ◆[5] 58 45.51 N 7.11 E
Grand Saline 222 32.40 N 95.42 W
Grand Saline Creek ≃ 222 32.41 N 95.36 W
Grandson 58 46.49 N 6.38 E
Grand Terrace 228 34.02 N 117.18 W
Grand Teton ʌ 202 43.44 N 110.48 W
Grand Teton National Park ♦ 202 43.30 N 110.45 W
Grand Tower 194 37.37 N 89.29 W

Symbols in the index entries represent the broad categories identified in the key at the right. Symbols with superior numbers (⋀[1]) identify subcategories (see complete key on page *I · 1).*

Symbole im Register stellen die rechts im Schlüssel erklärten Kategorien dar. Symbole mit hochgestellten Ziffern (⋀[1]) bezeichnen Unterabteilungen einer Kategorie (vgl. vollständiger Schlüssel auf Seite *I · 1).*

Los símbolos incluídos en el texto del índice representan las grandes categorias identificadas con la clave a la derecha. Los símbolos con numeros en su parte superior (⋀[1]) identifican las subcategorías (véase la clave completa en la página *I · 1).*

Les symboles de l'index représentent les catégories indiquées dans la légende à droite. Les symboles suivis d'un indice (⋀[1]) représentent des sous-catégories (voir légende complète à la page *I · 1).*

Os símbolos incluídos no texto do índice representam as grandes categorias identificadas com a chave à direita. Os símbolos com números em sua parte superior (⋀[1]) identificam as subcategorias (veja-se a chave completa à página *I · 1).*

ʌ Mountain	Berg	Montaña	Montagne	Montanha
⋀ Mountains	Gebirge	Montañas	Montagnes	Montanhas
)(Pass	Paß	Paso	Col	Passo
V Valley, Canyon	Tal, Cañon	Valle, Cañón	Vallée, Canyon	Vale, Canhão
≚ Plain	Ebene	Llano	Plaine	Planície
> Cape	Kap	Cabo	Cap	Cabo
I Island	Insel	Isla	Île	Ilha
II Islands	Inseln	Islas	Îles	Ilhas
± Other Topographic Features	Andere Topographische Objekte	Otros Elementos Topográficos	Autres données topographiques	Outros acidentes topográficos

ESPAÑOL				FRANÇAIS				PORTUGUÊS			
Nombre	Página	Lat.°′	Long.°′ W = Oeste	Nom	Page	Lat.°′	Long.°′ W = Ouest	Nome	Página	Lat.°′	Long.°′ W = Oeste

Column 1 (ESPAÑOL)

Nombre	Página	Lat.°′	Long.°′ W = Oeste
Grand Traverse Bay c	190	45.02 N	85.30 W
Grand Traverse Bay, East Arm c	190	44.52 N	85.28 W
Grand Traverse Bay, West Arm c	190	44.52 N	85.35 W
Grandtully	46	56.39 N	3.46 W
Grand Turk	238	21.28 N	71.08 W
Grand Union Canal ≖	260	51.30 N	0.02 W
Grand Valley, On., Can.	212	43.54 N	80.19 W
Grand Valley, Pa., U.S.	214	41.43 N	79.32 W
Grandview, Mb., Can.	184	51.10 N	100.42 W
Grandview, Il., U.S.	219	42.06 N	89.50 W
Grandview, Mo., U.S.	194	38.53 N	94.31 W
Grandview, Pa., U.S.	279b	40.10 N	79.52 W
Grandview, Tx., U.S.	222	32.16 N	97.11 W
Grandview, Wa., U.S.	202	46.15 N	119.54 W
Grand View, Wi., U.S.	190	46.30 N	91.06 W
Grandview Beach	216	41.50 N	83.24 W
Grandview Heights, Oh., U.S.	218	39.58 N	83.02 W
Grandview Heights, Pa., U.S.	208	40.03 N	76.17 W
Grandview Homes	216	40.44 N	84.04 W
Grand View-on-Hudson	276	41.44 N	73.55 W
Grandvillars	58	47.33 N	6.58 E
Grandville	216	42.54 N	85.45 W
Grandvilliers	50	49.40 N	1.56 E
Grand Wash Cliffs ⊥	200	35.40 N	113.50 W
Grand Winterberg ʌ	56	48.59 N	7.37 E
Grandyle Village	210	43.00 N	78.57 W
Grâne	62	44.44 N	4.55 E
Grañén	34	41.56 N	0.22 W
Graneros	252	54.04 S	70.44 W
Granetalsperre ≖ ⁶	52	51.48 N	10.27 E
Graney, Lough ◎	48	52.59 N	8.40 W
Grangärde	40	60.16 N	14.59 E
Grange, Austl.	168b	34.54 S	138.30 E
Grange, Eng., U.K.	262	53.23 N	3.09 W
Grange, Bois de la ♦	261	48.45 N	2.30 E
Grange-Bléneau, Château du la ⊥	50	48.41 N	2.55 E
Grange Hill	260	51.37 N	0.05 E
Grangemouth	46	56.02 N	3.45 W
Grängen ◎	40	59.45 N	14.47 E
Grangent, Lac de @ ¹	62	45.25 N	4.15 E
Grange-over-Sands	44	54.12 N	2.55 W
Granger, Tx., U.S.	222	30.43 N	97.26 W
Granger, Wa., U.S.	202	46.20 N	120.11 W
Granger, Wy., U.S.	200	41.35 N	109.58 W
Granger Draw V	196	30.20 N	100.57 W
Granger Lake @ ¹	222	30.42 N	97.22 W
Granges — Grenchen	58	47.11 N	7.24 E
Granges-sur-Vologne	58	48.09 N	6.47 E
Grangeville, Id., U.S.	202	45.55 N	116.07 W
Grangeville, Pa., U.S.	208	39.47 N	76.58 W
Grangousier Hill ʌ²	190	47.35 N	84.56 W
Gran Guardia	252	25.52 S	58.53 W
Granite, Md., U.S.	284b	39.21 N	76.51 W
Granite, Ok., U.S.	196	34.57 N	99.22 W
Granite City	219	38.42 N	90.08 W
Granite Creek	224	48.43 N	120.55 W
Granite Dome ʌ	226	38.13 N	119.44 W
Granite Downs	162	26.57 S	133.30 E
Granite Falls, Mn., U.S.	198	44.48 N	95.32 W
Granite Falls, N.C., U.S.	215	35.47 N	81.25 W
Granite Falls, Wa., U.S.	224	48.05 N	121.58 W
Granite Lake @	186	48.08 N	57.05 W
Granite Mountain ʌ, Austl.	171b	35.44 S	148.13 E
Granite Mountain ʌ, Ak., U.S.	180	65.26 N	161.14 W
Granite Mountain ʌ, Ak., U.S.	182	55.30 N	132.35 W
Granite Mountains ⟋	202	42.35 N	107.30 W
Granite Pass x	202	44.38 N	107.30 W
Granite Peak	162	25.38 S	121.21 E
Granite Peak ʌ, Mt., U.S.	202	45.10 N	109.48 W
Granite Peak ʌ, Mt., U.S.	202	45.34 N	112.02 W
Granite Peak ʌ, Nv., U.S.	204	41.40 N	117.35 W
Granite Peak ʌ, Nv., U.S.	204	40.48 N	119.25 W
Granite Range ⟋	204	41.00 N	119.35 W
Graniteville, Ma., U.S.	207	42.31 N	71.27 W
Graniteville, S.C., U.S.	215	33.33 N	81.48 W
Graniteville, Vt., U.S.	188	44.09 N	72.29 W
Granitnoje	83	47.27 N	37.52 E
Granito	250	7.43 S	39.36 W
Granitogorsk	85	42.44 N	73.27 E
Granitola, Capo ⟩	70	37.34 N	12.41 E
Granitola Torretta	70	37.34 N	12.40 E
Granity	172	41.38 S	171.51 E
Granitzenbach ≖	61	47.11 N	14.46 E
Granja, Bra.	250	3.06 S	40.50 W
Granja, Port.	266c	38.51 N	9.06 W
Gran Khingan — Da Hinggan Ling ⟋	90	49.00 N	122.00 E
Granki	76	54.51 N	31.27 E
Grankulla (Kauniainen)	26	60.13 N	24.45 E
Gran Lago Salado — Great Salt Lake @		41.10 N	112.30 W
Gran Laguna Salada @	254	44.24 S	67.23 W
Granma ◻⁴	240p	21.20 N	76.50 W
Gränna	26	58.01 N	14.28 E
Grannoch, Loch @	44	55.00 N	4.17 W
Granollers	34	41.37 N	2.18 E
Granón	26	64.15 N	19.19 E
Granov	78	48.52 N	29.34 E
Gran Pajonal ⟋	248	10.45 S	74.30 W
Gran Paradiso ʌ	62	45.32 N	7.16 E
Gran Paradiso, Parco Nazionale del ♦	62	45.34 N	7.18 E
Gran Piedra ʌ	240p	20.01 N	75.38 W
Gran Pilastro (Hochfeiler) ʌ	64	46.58 N	11.44 E
Gran Rio ≖	250	4.01 N	55.31 W
Gran Sasso d'Italia ⟋	66	42.27 N	13.42 E
Gransee	54	53.00 N	13.09 E
Grant, Fl., U.S.	220	27.55 N	80.31 W
Grant, Mi., U.S.	190	43.20 N	85.48 W
Grant, Ne., U.S.	198	40.50 N	101.43 W
Grant ◻ ⁶, In., U.S.	216	40.33 N	85.40 W
Grant ◻ ⁶, Ky., U.S.	218	38.39 N	84.39 W
Grant ◻ ⁶	202	42.40 N	90.45 W
Grant, Lake ☰	218	39.00 N	80.45 W
Grant, Mount ʌ	204	38.34 N	118.48 W
Grant, Point ⟩	168b	38.31 S	145.07 E
Granta ≖	42	52.10 N	0.06 E
Grant Birthplace ⊥	218	38.54 N	84.14 W
Grant City	194	40.29 N	94.24 W
Grantham, Eng., U.K.	171a	27.34 S	152.12 E
Grantham, Eng., U.K.	42	52.55 N	0.39 W
Grant-Kohrs Ranch National Historic Site ⊥	202	46.25 N	112.40 W
Grant Lake @	226	37.50 N	119.07 W
Grant Mills	283	41.57 N	71.26 W
Granton	46	55.59 N	3.14 W
Granton-on-Spey	46	57.20 N	3.36 W
Grant Park	216	41.14 N	87.39 W
Grant Park ♦	278	41.52 N	87.37 W
Grant Point ⟩	176	68.19 N	98.53 W

Column 2 (FRANÇAIS)

Nom	Page	Lat.°′	Long.°′ W = Ouest
Grant Range ⟋	204	38.25 N	115.30 W
Grants	200	35.09 N	107.50 W
Grantsburg, In., U.S.	218	38.17 N	86.28 W
Grantsburg, Wi., U.S.	190	45.46 N	92.40 W
Grantshouse	46	55.53 N	2.19 W
Grants Pass	202	42.26 N	123.19 W
Grants Patch	162	30.27 S	121.07 E
Grant-Suttie Bay c	176	69.47 N	77.15 W
Grantsville, Ut., U.S.	200	40.36 N	112.27 W
Grantsville, W.V., U.S.	188	38.55 N	81.05 W
Grantville, Ga., U.S.	192	33.14 N	84.50 W
Grantville, Pa., U.S.	208	40.23 N	76.39 W
Granum	182	49.52 N	113.30 W
Granville, Austl.	274a	33.50 S	151.01 E
Granville, Fr.	32	48.50 N	1.36 W
Granville, Il., U.S.	190	41.15 N	89.13 W
Granville, Ma., U.S.	207	42.04 N	72.51 W
Granville, Mo., U.S.	219	39.34 N	92.06 W
Granville, N.Y., U.S.	188	43.24 N	73.15 W
Granville, N.D., U.S.	198	48.16 N	100.50 W
Granville, Oh., U.S.	214	40.04 N	82.31 W
Granville, Pa., U.S.	208	40.33 N	77.38 W
Granville, W.V., U.S.	188	39.38 N	79.59 W
Granville Lake @	184	56.18 N	100.30 W
Granvin	26	60.33 N	6.43 E
Granzin, D.D.R.	54	53.30 N	11.56 E
Granzin, D.D.R.	54	53.25 N	12.53 E
Grão Mogol	255	16.34 S	42.54 W
Grão Mogol, Ribeirão ≖	256	21.46 S	43.40 W
Grape Creek ≖	200	38.26 N	105.16 W
Grape Island I	283	42.16 N	70.55 W
Grapeview	222	31.29 N	95.28 W
Grapevine	224	47.19 N	122.50 W
Grapeville	214	40.19 N	79.36 W
Grapevine	222	32.56 N	97.04 W
Grapevine Lake @ ¹	222	32.59 N	97.06 W
Grapevine Peak ʌ	204	36.57 N	117.09 W
Grappa, Monte ʌ	64	45.52 N	11.48 E
Grappenhall	262	53.22 N	2.32 W
Grarem	34	36.31 N	6.19 E
Gras, Lac de @	176	64.30 N	110.30 W
Grasbult	158	30.52 S	21.47 E
Grasdorf	52	52.06 N	10.09 E
Graskelen	156	24.58 S	30.49 E
Graskelen	54	52.18 N	11.01 E
Grasmere, S. Afr.	158	26.26 S	27.52 E
Grasmere, Eng., U.K.	44	54.28 N	3.02 W
Grasmere Lake @	276	40.36 N	74.05 W
Gräsö I	40	60.21 N	18.28 E
Gräsö I	40	60.24 N	18.25 E
Grasonville	208	38.57 N	76.12 W
Grass ≖, Mb., Can.	184	56.03 N	96.33 W
Grass ≖, N.Y., U.S.	188	44.59 N	74.46 W
Grass, North Branch ≖	188	44.25 N	75.06 W
Grass, South Branch ≖	188	44.25 N	75.05 W
Grassano	68	40.38 N	16.18 E
Grassau	64	47.47 N	12.27 E
Grass Creek ≖	223	43.56 N	108.39 W
Grass Creek ≖	223	43.52 N	108.22 W
Grasscroft	262	53.32 N	2.01 W
Grasse	62	43.40 N	6.55 E
Grassendale ◻ ⁸	262	53.21 N	2.54 W
Grassflat	214	41.00 N	78.07 W
Grass Hassock Channel ʊ	276	40.36 N	73.48 W
Grasshopper Creek ≖	202	45.06 N	112.47 W
Grass Island I	276	40.39 N	73.18 W
Grässjön @	40	59.52 N	13.43 E
Grass Lake ≖	216	42.15 N	84.13 W
Grass Lake @	216	42.20 N	88.10 W
Grassmere, Lake @ ¹	172	41.44 S	174.10 E
Grass Patch	162	33.14 S	121.43 E
Grass Range	202	47.01 N	108.48 W
Grassridge Dam @ ¹	158	31.45 S	25.29 E
Grass River			
Provincial Park ♦	184	54.40 N	100.50 W
Grass Valley, Austl.	168a	31.38 S	116.48 E
Grass Valley, Ca., U.S.	226	39.13 N	121.03 W
Grass Valley, Or., U.S.	224	45.21 N	120.47 W
Grassy	166	40.03 S	144.04 E
Grassy Bay c	190	48.22 N	81.27 W
Grassy Brook ≖	276	40.38 N	73.48 W
Grassy Creek ≖, In., U.S.	216	40.55 N	86.30 W
Grassy Creek ≖, Mo., U.S.	219	39.54 N	91.37 W
Grassy Hill ʌ	271d	22.25 N	114.09 E
Grassy Island Lake @	184	51.50 N	110.20 W
Grassy Key I	220	24.46 N	80.57 W
Grassy Lake	182	49.49 N	111.43 W
Grassy Lake @	220	27.13 N	81.20 W
Grassy Plains	182	53.57 N	125.54 W
Grassy Sprain Reservoir @ ¹	276	40.58 N	73.51 W
Graston	41	54.55 N	9.36 E
Grästorp	26	58.20 N	12.40 E
Graterford	285	40.13 N	75.27 W
Graterford State Correctional Institution ♦	285	40.14 N	75.26 W
Grates Point ⟩	186	48.10 N	52.57 W
Gratis	218	39.38 N	84.31 W
Gratkorn	61	47.07 N	15.21 E
Gratwein	61	47.07 N	15.19 E
Gratz, Ky., U.S.	218	38.26 N	84.57 W
Gratz, Pa., U.S.	208	40.37 N	76.43 W
Gratztown	279b	40.14 N	79.47 W
Graubünden (Grischun) ◻ ³	58	46.45 N	9.30 E
Graudenz — Grudziadz	30	53.29 N	18.45 E
Graue Hörner ʌ	58	46.57 N	9.23 E
Graukogel ʌ	64	47.06 N	13.10 E
Graulhet	32	43.46 N	2.00 E
Graulinster	58	49.45 N	6.18 E
Graun — Curon Venosta	64	46.49 N	10.32 E
Graupa	54	51.00 N	13.54 E
Gravatá	250	8.12 S	35.34 W
Gravataí	255	16.53 S	42.10 W
Grave	52	51.45 N	5.44 E
Grave Creek ≖	202	42.39 N	123.35 W
Gravedona	58	46.09 N	9.18 E
Gravelbourg	184	49.53 N	106.34 W
Gravelines	50	50.59 N	2.07 E
Gravellona-Toce	58	45.50 N	8.26 E
Gravell Point ⟩	176	67.16 N	76.43 W
Gravelly Bay c	284a	42.52 N	79.15 W
Gravelly Brook ≖	276	40.25 N	74.30 W
Gravelly Point ♦	283	42.36 N	70.48 W
Gravelotte, Fr.	56	49.07 N	6.01 E
Gravelotte, S. Afr.	156	23.56 S	30.34 E
Gravenhurst	212	44.55 N	79.22 W
Grävenwiesbach	56	50.23 N	8.27 E
Grave Peak ʌ	202	46.24 N	114.44 W
Gravesend, Austl.	166	29.35 S	150.19 E
Gravesend, Eng., U.K.	260	51.27 N	0.24 E
Gravesend Bay c	276	40.36 N	74.01 W
Gravesham ◻ ⁸	260	51.25 N	0.24 E
Graviny	50	49.03 N	1.10 E
Gravina	70	37.34 N	15.03 E
Gravina di Matera ≖	68	40.33 N	16.49 E
Gravina in Puglia	68	40.49 N	16.25 E
Gravina Island I	182	55.17 N	131.45 W
Gray, Fr.	58	47.27 N	5.35 E
Gray, Ga., U.S.	192	33.00 N	83.32 W
Gray, Ky., U.S.	192	36.56 N	84.00 W
Gray, Pa., U.S.	214	40.08 N	79.05 W
Grayback Mountain ʌ, Ak., U.S.	182	57.08 N	153.54 W

Column 3 (PORTUGUÊS)

Nome	Página	Lat.°′	Long.°′ W = Oeste
Grayback Mountain ʌ, Or., U.S.	202	42.07 N	123.18 W
Grayland	224	46.48 N	124.05 W
Grayling, Ak., U.S.	180	62.57 N	160.03 W
Grayling, Mi., U.S.	190	44.39 N	84.42 W
Graylyn Crest	285	39.48 N	75.31 W
Grays	42	51.29 N	0.20 E
Grays ≖	224	46.18 N	123.41 W
Grays Harbor ◻ ⁶	224	47.09 N	123.45 W
Grays Harbor c	224	46.56 N	124.05 W
Grayshott	42	51.11 N	0.45 W
Grayslake	216	42.21 N	88.03 W
Grays Lake ☰	202	43.04 N	111.26 W
Grays Lake Outlet ≖	202	43.22 N	111.46 W
Grayson, Sk., Can.	184	50.44 N	102.40 W
Grayson, Ca., U.S.	226	37.34 N	121.10 W
Grayson, Ky., U.S.	218	38.19 N	82.56 W
Grayson Lake @ ¹	218	38.13 N	83.00 W
Grayson Lake State Park ♦	218	38.13 N	83.02 W
Grays Peak ʌ	200	39.37 N	105.45 W
Grays Point	274a	34.04 S	151.07 E
Grays River	224	46.21 N	123.36 W
Gray Summit	219	38.29 N	90.49 W
Graysville	194	35.26 N	85.05 W
Graytown	214	41.33 N	83.16 W
Grayville	194	37.57 N	88.10 W
Gray Wolf ʌ	224	47.55 N	123.07 W
Graz	61	47.05 N	15.27 E
Grazalema	34	36.46 N	5.22 W
Grdzadanka ≖ ⁸	265a	60.00 N	30.24 E
Gr'azeva ≖	265b	55.51 N	37.08 E
Gr'azi	80	52.29 N	39.57 E
Graziervelle	214	40.40 N	78.16 W
Gr'aznoje	82	54.02 N	39.07 E
Gr'aznovo, S.S.S.R.	82	54.18 N	36.49 E
Gr'aznovo, S.S.S.R.	265b	55.57 N	37.34 E
Gr'aznyj Irtek	80	51.56 N	53.11 E
Gr'azovec	76	58.53 N	40.14 E
Grdelica	38	42.54 N	22.04 E
Greåker	26	59.16 N	11.02 E
Greasby	262	53.23 N	3.07 W
Great Abaco I	238	26.28 N	77.05 W
Great Adventure ♦	208	40.09 N	74.27 W
Great Altcar	262	53.33 N	3.01 W
Great America ♦	282	37.24 N	121.59 W
Great Amwell	260	51.48 N	0.01 W
Great Artesian Basin ≖¹	166	25.00 S	143.00 E
Great Australian Bight c³	162	35.00 S	130.00 E
Great Ayton	44	54.30 N	1.08 W
Great Bacolet Point ⟩	241k	12.04 N	61.37 W
Great Baddow	260	51.43 N	0.29 E
Great Bahama Bank ≖⁴	238	23.15 N	78.00 W
Great Barford	42	52.09 N	0.21 W
Great Barrier Island I	172	36.10 S	175.25 E
Great Barrier Reef Marine Park ♦	166	21.00 S	151.00 E
Great Barrington	207	42.11 N	73.21 W
Great Barrow	262	53.12 N	2.48 W
Great Basin ≖¹	178	40.00 N	117.00 W
Great Basin National Park ♦	204	38.55 N	114.14 W
Great Bay c	208	39.30 N	74.23 W
Great Bear ≖	180	64.54 N	125.35 W
Great Bear Lake @	176	66.00 N	120.00 W
Great Beaver Lake @	182	54.25 N	123.45 W
Great Belt — Storebælt ʊ	41	55.30 N	11.00 E
Great Bend, Ks., U.S.	198	38.21 N	98.45 W
Great Bend, N.Y., U.S.	212	44.02 N	75.43 W
Great Bend, Pa., U.S.	210	41.58 N	75.44 W
Great Bitter Lake — Murrah al-Kubrā, Al-Buhayrah al-☰	142	30.20 N	32.23 E
Great Blasket Island I	48	52.05 N	10.32 W
Great Blue Hill ʌ²	283	42.13 N	71.07 W
Great Bookham	260	51.16 N	0.22 W
Great Braxted	260	51.49 N	0.41 E
Great Brewster Island I	283	42.20 N	70.53 W
Great Britain I	22	54.00 N	2.00 W
Great Brook ≖	276	40.42 N	74.31 W
Great Buddha ʌ ¹	268	35.19 N	139.32 E
Great Budworth	262	53.18 N	2.30 W
Great Burnt Lake @	186	48.20 N	56.13 W
Great Burso Bank ≖⁴			
Great Burstead	260	51.36 N	0.25 E
Great Camanoe I	240m	18.29 N	64.32 W
Great Captain Island I	276	40.59 N	73.38 W
Great Central	182	49.19 N	124.59 W
Great Central Lake @	182	49.27 N	125.12 W
Great Channel ʊ	110	6.25 N	94.20 E
Great Chazy ≖	188	44.58 N	73.23 W
Great Clifton	44	54.40 N	3.29 W
Great Coco Island I	110	14.05 N	93.24 E
Great Coharie Creek ≖	192	34.50 N	78.22 W
Great Cove ♦	276	40.43 N	74.14 W
Great Crosby	262	53.29 N	3.01 W
Great Crossing	218	38.08 N	84.38 W
Great Cumbrae Island I	46	55.46 N	4.55 W
Great Dismal Swamp ≖	192	36.30 N	76.30 W
Great Ditch ≖	276	40.54 N	74.07 W
Great Divide Basin ≖¹	202	42.00 N	108.10 W
Great Dividing Range ⟋	160	25.00 S	147.00 E
Great Driffield	44	54.00 N	0.27 W
Great Duck Island I	190	45.40 N	82.58 W
Great Dunmow	42	51.53 N	0.22 E
Great Eau ≖	44	53.25 N	0.13 E
Great Egg Harbor ≖	208	39.18 N	74.40 W
Great Egg Harbor Bay c	208	39.18 N	74.37 W
Great Egg Harbor Inlet c	208	39.20 N	74.34 W
Greater Antilles II	238	20.00 N	74.00 W
Greater Buffalo International Airport ☀	210	42.56 N	78.44 W
Greater Cincinnati Airport ☀	218	39.03 N	84.40 W
Greater Khingan Range — Da Hinggan Ling ⟋	90	49.00 N	122.00 E
Greater London ◻ ⁶	260	51.30 N	0.10 W
Greater Manchester ◻ ⁶	44	53.30 N	2.20 W
Greater Pittsburgh International Airport ☀	214	40.29 N	80.14 W
Greater Sunda Islands II	108	2.00 S	110.00 E
Greater Wilmington Airport ☀	208	39.41 N	75.36 W
Greater Wollongong — Wollongong	170	34.25 S	150.54 E
Great Escape ♦	210	43.22 N	73.42 W
Great Exuma I	238	23.32 N	75.50 W
Great Falls, Mb., Can.		50.27 N	96.02 W
Great Falls, Mt., U.S.	202	47.30 N	111.17 W
Great Falls, S.C., U.S.	192	34.34 N	80.54 W
Great Falls, Va., U.S.	284c	39.00 N	77.17 W
Great Falls Park ♦	284c	39.00 N	77.15 W

Column 4

Great Fish Point ⟩	158	33.30 S	27.10 E
Great Gable ʌ	44	54.28 N	3.12 W
Great Gaddesden	260	51.47 N	0.30 W
Great Grimsby — Grimsby	44	53.35 N	0.05 W
Great Guana Cay I	238	24.00 N	76.20 W
Great Hameldon ʌ ²	262	53.45 N	2.19 W
Great Harwood	262	53.48 N	2.24 W
Great Haywood	42	52.48 N	2.00 W
Greathead Bay c	241h	13.08 N	61.14 W
Great Himalaya Range ⟋	120	29.00 N	83.00 E
Greathouse Peak ʌ	202	46.46 N	109.21 W
Great Inagua I	238	21.05 N	73.18 W
Great Indian Desert (Thar Desert) ≖ ²	120	27.00 N	71.00 E
Great Island I, Ire.	48	51.52 N	8.17 W
Great Island I, N.Y., U.S.	276	40.38 N	73.30 W
Great Island I, N.Y., U.S.	276	41.05 N	73.44 W
Great Karroo (Groot Karroo) ≖¹	158	32.25 S	22.40 E
Great Kills	276	40.33 N	74.10 W
Great Kills Harbor c	276	40.32 N	74.08 W
Great Kills Park ♦	276	40.33 N	74.08 W
Great La Cloche Island I	190	46.01 N	81.52 W
Great Lake @	166	41.52 S	146.45 E
Great Lakes Naval Training Center ♦	216	42.18 N	87.50 W
Great Lakes Steel Works ♦	281	42.15 N	83.08 W
Great Machipongo ≖	208	37.22 N	75.43 W
Great Malvern	42	52.07 N	2.19 W
Great Marsh ≖	208	36.32 N	75.57 W
Great Marton	262	53.48 N	3.02 W
Great Massingham	42	52.46 N	0.40 E
Great Meadows	210	40.52 N	74.54 W
Great Meadows National Wildlife Refuge ♦ ⁴	283	42.29 N	71.20 W
Great Mercury Island I	172	36.37 S	175.48 E
Great Meteor Tablemount ♦ ³	18	30.00 N	28.30 W
Great Miami ≖	188	39.06 N	84.49 W
Great Mills	208	38.14 N	76.30 W
Great Misery Island I	283	42.33 N	70.48 W
Great Missenden	42	51.43 N	0.43 W
Great Mis Tor ʌ	42	50.34 N	4.01 W
Great Mosque ♦ ¹	146	32.46 N	22.40 E
Great Namaqualand ◻ ⁹	156	25.00 S	17.00 E
Great Neck ⟩, Ma., U.S.	276	40.48 N	73.43 W
Great Neck ⟩ ¹, N.Y., U.S.	283	42.42 N	70.48 W
Great Neck ⟩ ¹, N.Y., U.S.	276	40.50 N	73.45 W
Great Neck Estates	276	40.47 N	73.44 W
Great Nicobar I	110	7.00 N	93.50 E
Great North East Channel ʊ	164	9.30 S	143.25 E
Great Notch Reservoir @ ¹	276	40.53 N	74.12 W
Great Ormes Head ⟩	44	53.21 N	3.52 W
Great Ouse ≖	42	52.47 N	0.22 E
Great Oxney Green	260	51.44 N	0.25 E
Great Palm Island I	166	18.43 S	146.37 E
Great Pardnon	260	51.45 N	0.05 E
Great Patchogue Lake @	276	40.46 N	73.01 W
Great Peconic Bay c	207	40.56 N	72.30 W
Great Pee Dee ≖	192	33.21 N	79.16 W
Great Point ⟩	207	41.23 N	70.03 W
Great Pubnico Lake @	186	43.42 N	65.43 W
Great Quittacas Pond @	207	41.48 N	70.54 W
Great Ruaha ≖	154	7.56 S	37.52 E
Great Sacandaga Lake @	210	43.08 N	74.10 W
Great Saint Bernard Pass — Grand-Saint-Bernard, Col du x	58	45.50 N	7.10 E
Great Sale Cay I	192	27.00 N	78.12 W
Great Salt Lake @	200	41.10 N	112.30 W
Great Salt Lake Desert ≖ ²	200	40.40 N	113.30 W
Great Salt Plains Lake @ ¹	196	36.44 N	98.12 W
Great Sand Dunes National Monument ♦	200	37.43 N	105.36 W
Great Sandy Desert ≖ ²	162	21.30 S	125.00 E
Great Sandy National Park ♦	166	24.59 S	153.17 E
Great Sankey	262	53.24 N	2.37 W
Great Santa Cruz Island I	116	6.52 N	122.03 E
Great Scarcies (Kolenté) ≖	150	8.55 N	13.08 W
Great Sea Reef ♦ ²	175a	16.15 S	179.00 E
Great Seneca Creek ≖	208	39.08 N	77.20 W
Great Shelford	42	52.09 N	0.09 E
Great Sitkin Island I	180	52.03 N	176.07 W
Great Slave Lake @	176	61.30 N	114.00 W
Great Smoky Mountains ⟋	192	35.35 N	83.30 W
Great Smoky Mountains National Park ♦	192	35.39 N	83.30 W
Great Sound ʊ, Ber.	240a	32.17 N	64.51 W
Great Sound ʊ, N.J., U.S.	208	39.06 N	74.47 W
Great Stour ≖	42	51.19 N	1.15 E
Great Sutton	262	53.17 N	2.56 W
Great Swamp National Wildlife Refuge ♦ ⁴	276	40.43 N	74.28 W
Great Tenasserim ≖	110	12.16 N	99.03 E
Great Thatch Island I	240m	18.23 N	64.43 W
Great Tobago I	240m	18.27 N	64.48 W
Great Torrington	42	50.57 N	4.08 W
Great Totham	260	51.47 N	0.40 E
Great Usutu (Maputo) (Lusutfu) ≖	158	26.11 S	32.42 E
Great Valley	210	42.13 N	78.38 W
Great Victoria Desert ≖ ²	162	28.30 S	127.45 E
Great Wall — Chang Cheng ⊥	90	40.30 N	116.30 E
Great Waltham	260	51.48 N	0.25 E
Great Warley	260	51.35 N	0.17 E
Great Whernside ʌ	44	54.09 N	1.59 W
Great Wicomico ≖	208	37.48 N	76.18 W
Great Yarmouth	42	52.41 N	1.44 E
Great Zab (Büyükzap) (Az-Zāb al-Kabīr) ≖	128	36.00 N	43.21 E
Great Zimbabwe Ruins National ⊥	154	20.17 S	30.57 E
Grebbestad	26	58.42 N	11.15 E
Grebenstein	52	51.27 N	9.25 E
Grebin	52	54.07 N	10.27 E
Grebenstein	56	50.07 N	9.24 E
Greco ◻⁵	265b	55.58 N	38.05 E
Greb'onki	78	49.57 N	30.12 E

Column 5

Gréboun ʌ	150	20.00 N	8.35 E
Grèce — Greece ◻ ¹	38	39.00 N	22.00 E
Grecia	236	10.05 N	84.18 W
Grècia — Greece ◻ ¹	38	39.00 N	22.00 E
Grečiškino	83	48.52 N	38.54 E
Grecken ◎	40	59.35 N	14.44 E
Greco	252	32.48 S	57.03 W
Greco ◻ ⁸	266b	45.30 N	9.13 E
Greco, Monte ʌ	66	41.48 N	14.00 E
Greding	52	49.03 N	11.21 E
Gredos, Sierra de ⟋	34	40.18 N	5.05 W
Gredstedbro	41	55.24 N	8.45 E
Greece	210	43.12 N	77.41 W
Greece (Ellás) ◻ ¹, Europe	22	39.00 N	22.00 E
Greece (Ellás) ◻ ¹, Europe	38	39.00 N	22.00 E
Greeley, Co., U.S.	200	40.25 N	104.42 W
Greeley, Ks., U.S.	198	38.19 N	95.26 W
Greeley, Ne., U.S.	198	41.33 N	98.32 W
Greeley ◻ ⁶	198	41.25 N	79.00 W
Greeleyville	192	33.34 N	79.59 W
Green ◻ ⁶	216	42.48 N	89.25 W
Green ≖, N.B., Can.	186	47.18 N	68.09 W
Green ≖, U.S.	207	42.35 N	72.36 W
Green ≖, U.S.	207	42.10 N	73.22 W
Green ≖, Il., U.S.	190	41.28 N	90.23 W
Green ≖, In., U.S.	216	41.46 N	89.10 W
Green ≖, Ky., U.S.	194	37.55 N	87.30 W
Green ≖, N.D., U.S.	198	46.52 N	102.35 W
Green ≖, Vt., U.S.	213	43.06 N	73.13 W
Green ≖, Wa., U.S.	224	47.27 N	122.20 W
Green ≖, Wa., U.S.	224	46.20 N	122.34 W
Greenacres c, U.S.	226	35.23 N	119.07 W
Greenacres ≖, U.S.	276	40.40 N	73.43 W
Greenacres City	220	26.37 N	80.07 W
Greenbackville	208	38.00 N	75.23 W
Greenbank	224	48.06 N	122.34 W
Green Bay c, Nf., Can.	186	49.43 N	55.58 W
Green Bay c, On., Can.	212	44.38 N	76.36 W
Green Bay c, U.S.	190	45.00 N	87.30 W
Greenbelt	284c	39.00 N	76.52 W
Greenbelt Park ♦	284c	38.59 N	76.54 W
Greenbo Lake @	218	38.29 N	82.54 W
Greenbo Lake State Resort Park ♦	218	38.29 N	82.54 W
Greenbooth Reservoir @ ¹	262	53.38 N	2.13 W
Greenbrier, Ar., U.S.	194	35.14 N	92.23 W
Greenbrier, Tn., U.S.	194	36.25 N	86.48 W
Greenbrier ≖	192	37.39 N	80.53 W
Greenbrier State Park ♦	208	39.33 N	77.38 W
Green Brook	276	40.36 N	74.27 W
Green Brook ≖	276	40.36 N	74.32 W
Greenburg	214	40.18 N	79.33 W
Greenbush, Ma., U.S.	207	42.11 N	70.45 W
Greenbush, Va., U.S.	208	38.42 N	96.10 W
Greenbushes	162	33.51 S	116.03 E
Green Camp	214	40.31 N	83.12 W
Green Cape ⟩	168b	37.15 S	150.03 E
Green City	188	39.47 N	77.43 W
Green Cove Springs	192	29.59 N	81.40 W
Green Creek	208	39.02 N	74.54 W
Green Creek ≖, Oh., U.S.	214	41.26 N	83.01 W
Greencrest Park	281	39.53 N	75.28 W
Greendale, Austl.	274a	33.55 S	150.39 E
Greendale, In., U.S.	218	39.06 N	84.51 W
Greendale, Wi., U.S.	218	42.56 N	87.59 W
Greene, B.R.D.	52	51.52 N	9.56 E
Greene, Ia., U.S.	190	42.54 N	92.48 W
Greene, N.Y., U.S.	210	42.19 N	75.46 W
Greene, R.I., U.S.	207	41.41 N	71.44 W
Greene ◻ ⁶, Il., U.S.	219	39.18 N	90.24 W
Greene ◻ ⁶, Oh., U.S.	218	39.41 N	83.56 W
Greeneville	192	36.09 N	82.49 W
Greenfield, Eng., U.K.	44	53.18 N	3.13 W
Greenfield, Wales, U.K.	44	53.16 N	4.04 W
Greenfield, Ca., U.S.	226	36.19 N	121.14 W
Greenfield, In., U.S.	216	39.47 N	85.46 W
Greenfield, Ma., U.S.	207	42.35 N	72.36 W
Greenfield, Mo., U.S.	194	37.24 N	93.50 W
Greenfield, Oh., U.S.	218	39.21 N	83.22 W
Greenfield, Tn., U.S.	194	36.09 N	88.48 W
Greenfield Park, P.Q., Can.	275a	45.28 N	73.28 W
Greenfield Park, N.Y., U.S.	210	41.44 N	74.29 W
Greenfield Village	285	75.10 N	83.14 W
Greenford	260	51.32 N	0.21 W
Green Forest	194	36.20 N	93.25 W
Green Harbor	207	42.05 N	70.39 W
Green Head ⟩	283	35.51 S	114.58 E
Green Hill	207	41.21 N	71.37 W
Greenhill ≖	158	28.16 S	27.40 E
Greenhills, S. Afr.	273d	26.14 S	27.48 E
Greenhills, Oh., U.S.	218	39.16 N	84.31 W
Greenhorn Creek ≖	202	44.07 N	118.30 W
Greenhurst	214	42.10 N	79.19 W
Green Hut Park	276	40.53 N	73.42 W
Greenisland, N. Ire., U.K.	44	54.42 N	5.52 W
Green Island ≖	210	42.44 N	73.41 W
Green Island, Austl.	241k	12.01 N	61.35 W
Green Island Bay c	116	10.12 N	119.22 E
Green Islands II	14	4.30 S	154.10 E
Green Knoll	276	40.36 N	74.40 W
Green Lake, Wi., U.S.	184	54.17 N	107.47 W
Green Lake, Wi., U.S.	190	43.50 N	88.57 W
Green Lake @, B.C., Can.	182	51.24 N	121.13 W
Green Lake @, Sk., Can.	184	54.10 N	107.46 W
Green Lake @, Mi., U.S.	216	42.36 N	83.55 W
Green Lake @, N.Y., U.S.	281	42.36 N	73.57 W
Green Lakes State Park ♦	212	43.03 N	75.58 W

Column 6

Greenland-Iceland Rise ♦ ³	10	67.00 N	27.00 W
Greenlands	158	27.07 S	27.40 E
Greenland Sea ≖ ²	16	77.00 N	1.00 W
Green Lane	208	40.20 N	75.28 W
Green Lane Reservoir @ ¹	208	40.22 N	75.29 W
Greenlaw	46	55.43 N	2.28 W
Greenlawn	276	40.52 N	73.21 W
Greenlawn Park	285	40.07 N	74.51 W
Greenleaf	198	39.43 N	96.58 W
Green Lookout Mountain ʌ	224	45.52 N	122.08 W
Green Manorville	207	40.20 N	72.32 W
Green Meadows	284c	38.58 N	76.57 W
Greenmount, Austl.	171a	27.47 S	151.54 E
Greenmount, Eng., U.K.	262	53.37 N	2.20 W
Greenmount, Md., U.S.	208		
Green Mountains ⟋	188	43.45 N	72.45 W
Green Oak Lake @	281	42.27 N	83.43 W
Green Oaks	278	42.18 N	87.55 W
Greenock, Austl.	168b	34.27 S	138.55 E
Greenock, Scot., U.K.	46	55.57 N	4.45 W
Greenock, Pa., U.S.	279b	40.19 N	79.48 W
Greenodd	44	54.14 N	3.04 W
Greenore Point ⟩	48	52.15 N	6.18 W
Greenough	162	28.57 S	114.44 E
Greenough, Mount ʌ	180	69.10 N	141.35 W
Green Park	208	40.23 N	77.19 W
Green Peter Lake @ ¹	224	44.28 N	122.30 W
Green Point ⟩	276	40.43 N	73.06 W
Green Pond, Al., U.S.	194	33.13 N	87.07 W
Green Pond, N.J., U.S.	276	41.01 N	74.29 W
Green Pond @	276	41.00 N	74.30 W
Green Pond Brook ≖	276	40.53 N	74.34 W
Greenport	207	41.06 N	72.21 W
Green Ridge	285	39.51 N	75.25 W
Green River, Pap. N. Gui.	164	3.55 S	141.10 E
Green River, Ut., U.S.	200	38.59 N	110.09 W
Green River, Wy., U.S.	200	41.31 N	109.27 W
Green River Lake @ ¹	194	37.15 N	85.15 W
Greensboro, Al., U.S.	194	32.42 N	87.35 W
Greensboro, Ga., U.S.	192	30.34 N	84.44 W
Greensboro, Ga., U.S.	192	33.34 N	83.10 W
Greensboro, Md., U.S.	208	38.58 N	75.48 W
Greensboro, N.C., U.S.	192	36.04 N	79.47 W
Greensborough	274b	37.42 S	145.06 E
Greensburg, In., U.S.	218	39.20 N	85.29 W
Greensburg, Ky., U.S.	198	37.36 N	99.17 W
Greensburg, Ks., U.S.	194	37.15 N	85.29 W
Greensburg, Oh., U.S.	214	40.56 N	81.28 W
Greensburg, Pa., U.S.	214	40.18 N	79.32 W
Greens Farms	276	40.07 N	73.19 W
Greens Fork	218	39.53 N	85.02 W
Greenside ≖ ⁸	273d	26.09 S	28.01 E
Greens Peak ʌ	200	34.07 N	109.35 W
Greenspond	186	49.04 N	53.34 W
Green Springs	214	41.15 N	83.03 W
Greenstead	260	51.53 N	0.14 E
Greenstone	208	39.45 N	77.27 W
Greenstone Point ⟩	46	57.55 N	5.38 W
Green Street	260	51.40 N	0.16 W
Green Street Green ≖ ⁸	260	51.21 N	0.04 E
Greensville ◻ ⁶	208	36.40 N	77.30 W
Green Swamp ≖, Fl., U.S.	220	28.20 N	81.48 W
Green Swamp ≖, N.C., U.S.	192	34.10 N	78.20 W
Greentown, In., U.S.	216	40.28 N	85.58 W
Greentown, Oh., U.S.	214	40.56 N	81.28 W
Greentown, Pa., U.S.	210	41.19 N	75.18 W
Green Tree	279b	40.24 N	80.02 W
Greenup, Il., U.S.	194	39.14 N	88.09 W
Greenup, Ky., U.S.	218	38.34 N	82.49 W
Greenup ◻ ⁶	218	38.39 N	82.52 W
Greenup Dam ♦ ⁶	218	38.38 N	82.52 W
Greenvale, Austl.	166	18.59 S	145.07 E
Greenvale, N.Y., U.S.	276	40.49 N	73.38 W
Green Valley, On., Can.	206	45.16 N	74.36 W
Green Valley, Az., U.S.	200	31.52 N	110.59 W
Green Valley, Il., U.S.	190	40.24 N	89.44 W
Green Valley Creek ≖	226	38.13 N	122.08 W
Greenview	219	40.04 N	89.44 W
Green Village, N.J., U.S.	276	40.44 N	74.27 W
Greenville, Liber.	150	5.01 N	9.03 W
Greenville, Al., U.S.	194	31.49 N	86.37 W
Greenville, Ca., U.S.	204	40.08 N	120.57 W
Greenville, Fl., U.S.	192	30.28 N	83.37 W
Greenville, Ga., U.S.	192	33.03 N	84.13 W
Greenville, Il., U.S.	219	38.53 N	89.24 W
Greenville, Ky., U.S.	194	37.12 N	87.10 W
Greenville, Me., U.S.	188	45.28 N	69.35 W
Greenville, Mi., U.S.	190	43.10 N	85.15 W
Greenville, Ms., U.S.	194	33.24 N	91.03 W
Greenville, N.H., U.S.	207	42.46 N	71.48 W
Greenville, N.Y., U.S.	210	42.25 N	74.01 W
Greenville, N.C., U.S.	192	35.36 N	77.22 W
Greenville, Oh., U.S.	214	40.06 N	84.37 W
Greenville, Pa., U.S.	214	41.24 N	80.23 W
Greenville, R.I., U.S.	207	41.52 N	71.33 W
Greenville, S.C., U.S.	192	34.51 N	82.23 W
Greenville, Tx., U.S.	222	33.08 N	96.06 W
Greenville ◻ ⁶	192	34.52 N	82.21 W
Green Village ♦	276	40.44 N	74.00 W
Greenwater			
Provincial Park ♦	184	52.33 N	103.33 W
Greenwell Point	168b	34.55 S	150.46 E
Greenwich, Austl.	274a	33.50 S	151.11 E
Greenwich, Eng., U.K.	207	41.01 N	73.37 W
Greenwich, Ct., U.S.	276	40.59 N	73.36 W
Greenwich, N.Y., U.S.	188	43.05 N	73.30 W
Greenwich, Oh., U.S.	214	41.02 N	82.31 W
Greenwich Village ≖ ⁸	276	40.44 N	74.00 W
Greenwood, B.C., Can.	182	49.05 N	118.41 W
Greenwood, N.S., Can.	186	44.58 N	64.56 W
Greenwood, Ca., U.S.	226	38.54 N	120.55 W
Greenwood, In., U.S.	216	39.37 N	86.06 W
Greenwood, Ma., U.S.	283	42.29 N	71.04 W

Column 1

Greenwood, N.Y., U.S. 210 42.08 N 77.38 W
Greenwood, Pa., U.S. 214 40.32 N 78.21 W
Greenwood, S.C., U.S. 192 34.11 N 82.09 W
Greenwood, Wi., U.S. 190 44.46 N 90.35 W
Greenwood, Lake ⍩¹ 192 34.15 N 82.02 W
Greenwood Cemetery ⊕ 276 40.39 N 73.59 W
Greenwood Lake 210 41.13 N 74.17 W
Greenwood Lake ⍩, U.S. 210 41.11 N 74.19 W
Greenwood Lake ⍩, Ma., U.S. 283 42.00 N 71.17 W
Greenwood Race Track ✦ 275b 43.40 N 79.19 W
Greer, Oh., U.S. 214 40.31 N 82.13 W
Greer, S.C., U.S. 192 34.56 N 82.13 W
Greers Ferry Lake ⍩¹ 194 35.30 N 92.10 W
Greerton 172 37.43 S 176.08 E
Grées, Alpes (Alpi Graie) ⚲ 45.30 N 7.10 E
Greeson, Lake ⍩¹ 194 34.10 N 93.45 W
Greetland 262 53.41 N 1.52 W
Greetsiel 52 53.30 N 7.05 E
Greffiers 261 48.37 N 1.51 E
Grefrath, B.R.D. 56 51.20 N 6.20 E
Grefrath, B.R.D. 263 51.10 N 6.38 E
Gregadoo 171b 35.14 S 147.27 E
Gregbe 150 6.48 N 6.43 W
Gregg 279b 40.24 N 80.10 W
Gregg ◻⁶ 222 32.30 N 94.50 W
Greggio 62 45.27 N 8.23 E
Greg Greg 171b 36.03 S 148.02 E
Gregoire Lake Indian Reserve ◻⁴ 184 56.28 N 111.10 W
Gregorio ≃ 248 6.50 S 70.46 W
Gregory, Mi., U.S. 216 42.27 N 84.05 W
Gregory, S.D., U.S. 198 43.13 N 99.25 W
Gregory, Tx., U.S. 196 27.55 N 97.17 W
Gregory ≃ 166 17.53 S 139.17 E
Gregory, Lake ⍩, Austl. 162 25.38 S 119.58 E
Gregory, Lake ⍩, Austl. 162 20.10 S 127.20 E
Gregory, Lake ⍩, Austl. 166 28.55 S 139.00 E
Gregory National Park ✦ 166 16.30 S 130.30 E
Gregory Range ⚲ 166 19.00 S 143.05 E
Grégy-sur-Yerre 261 48.40 N 2.37 E
Greifenberg → Gryfice 30 53.56 N 15.12 E
Greifenburg 64 46.45 N 13.11 E
Greifendorf 54 51.01 N 13.06 E
Greifenhagen → Gryfino 30 53.16 N 14.30 E
Greifensee 58 47.22 N 8.41 E
Greifensee ⍩ 58 47.21 N 8.41 E
Greifenstein 264b 48.21 N 15.25 E
Greifenberg 54 53.03 N 13.58 E
Greiffenburg ⊥ 263 51.20 N 6.38 E
Greifswald 54 54.05 N 13.23 E
Greifswalder Bodden ⊂ 54 54.15 N 13.35 E
Greifswalder Oie I 54 54.15 N 13.55 E
Greim ⚲ 61 47.15 N 14.09 E
Grein 61 48.14 N 14.51 E
Greiz 54 50.39 N 12.12 E
Grejdernoje 80 46.53 N 45.01 E
Grejsdal 41 55.45 N 9.32 E
Grekov 80 47.24 N 43.41 E
Grekovo 83 48.54 N 40.14 E
Grem'ačevo 83 54.36 N 36.15 E
Grem'ačii 88 57.01 N 108.12 E
Grem'ačinsk, S.S.S.R. 86 58.34 N 57.51 E
Grem'ačinsk, S.S.S.R. 88 52.48 N 107.57 E
Grem'ačje 78 51.29 N 39.00 E
Gremersdorf 54 54.20 N 10.55 E
Gremicha 24 68.03 N 39.27 E
Grenå 26 56.25 N 10.53 E
Grenada ◻¹ 230 12.07 N 61.40 W
Grenada ◻¹, N.A. 230 12.07 N 61.40 W
Grenada ◻¹, N.A. 194 33.50 N 89.40 W
Grenade → Grenada ◻¹ 241k 12.07 N 61.40 W
Grenadier Island I 212 44.01 N 76.22 W
Grenadier Pond ⍩ 275b 43.38 N 79.28 W
Grenadine Islands II 238 12.40 N 61.15 W
Grenagh 48 52.00 N 8.37 W
Grenay 50 50.27 N 2.44 E
Grenchen 57 47.11 N 7.24 E
Grenell 92 44.49 N 76.04 W
Grenen ⚲², Dan. 26 57.44 N 10.40 E
Grenen ⚲², Dan. 26 57.44 N 10.40 E
Grenfell, Austl. 163 33.54 S 148.10 E
Grenfell, Sk., Can. 184 50.25 N 102.56 W
Grenloch 285 39.47 N 75.03 W
Grenoble 62 45.10 N 5.43 E
Grenola 198 37.20 N 96.27 W
Grenora 198 48.37 N 103.56 W
Grenville, P.Q., Can. 206 45.37 N 74.36 W
Grenville, Gren. 241k 12.07 N 61.37 W
Grenville, Cape ⚲ 164 11.58 S 143.14 E
Grenville Bay ⊂ 241k 12.07 N 61.36 W
Grenville Bay ⊂ 241k 12.07 N 61.36 W
Grenville Channel ☰ 182 53.40 N 129.40 W
Grenzau ⍩ 52 52.39 N 6.45 E
Grenz-Berge ⚲² 264a 52.27 N 13.44 E
Grenzlandring ✦ 56 51.11 N 6.17 E
Gréolières 62 43.48 N 6.57 E
Gréoux-les-Bains 62 43.45 N 5.53 E
Greppin 52 51.39 N 12.18 E
Gresenhorst 54 54.17 N 12.26 E
Gresham 192 45.29 N 122.25 W
Gresham Park 192 33.42 N 84.19 W
Gresik, Indon. 112 2.18 S 103.57 E
Gresik, Indon. 115a 7.09 S 112.38 E
Gressåmoen Nasjonalpark ✦ 26 64.15 N 13.08 E
Gressoney, Val di V 62 45.47 N 7.49 E
Gressitt 58 37.29 N 76.43 W
Gressit 208 37.29 N 76.43 W
Gressoney, Val di V 62 45.47 N 7.49 E
Gressoney-la-Trinité 62 45.49 N 7.52 E
Gressoney-Saint-Jean 62 45.47 N 7.49 E
Gressy 261 48.58 N 2.41 E
Gresten 61 47.59 N 15.02 E
Grésy-sur-Aix 62 45.43 N 5.57 E
Grésy-sur-Isère 62 45.36 N 6.15 E
Greta 170 32.41 S 151.24 E
Greta ≃, Eng., U.K. 44 54.09 N 1.53 W
Greta ≃, Eng., U.K. 44 54.36 N 3.10 W
Gretna, Mb., Can. 184 49.02 N 97.35 W
Gretna, Scot., U.K. 44 54.59 N 3.04 W
Gretna, La., U.S. 194 29.54 N 90.03 W
Gretna, Va., U.S. 192 36.57 N 79.21 W
Gretz-Armainvilliers 261 48.45 N 2.44 E
Greußen 54 51.14 N 10.57 E
Greussen 54 51.14 N 10.57 E
Greve, Dan. 41 55.36 N 12.18 E
Greve ⚲ 41 55.35 N 11.19 E
Greve ≃ 66 43.35 N 11.19 E
Grevelingen ⊂ 52 51.40 N 4.10 E
Grevelingendam ⚲⁵ 52 51.40 N 4.10 E
Greven 52 52.05 N 7.36 E
Grevená 34 40.05 N 21.25 E
Grevenbroich 56 51.05 N 6.35 E
Greven-Granzin 54 53.29 N 10.28 E
Grevenmacher 52 49.42 N 6.20 E
Grevesmühlen 54 53.52 N 11.10 E
Greve Strand 41 55.35 N 12.14 E
Greville Bay ⊂ 186 45.12 N 64.38 W
Grevinge 41 55.46 N 11.38 E
Grey ◻⁶ 212 44.20 N 80.45 W
Grey ≃, Nf., Can. 188 47.38 N 57.01 W
Grey ≃, N.Z. 172 42.27 S 171.12 E
Grey, Cape ⚲ 166 13.00 S 136.40 E

Column 2

Grey, Point ⚲, Austl. 169 38.34 S 143.59 E
Grey, Point ⚲, B.C., Can. 224 49.16 N 123.16 W
Greyabbey 48 54.32 N 5.33 W
Greybull 202 44.29 N 108.03 W
Greybull ⍩ 202 44.28 N 108.03 W
Grey Eagle 190 45.49 N 94.44 W
Grey Islands II 186 50.50 N 55.37 W
Greylingstad 158 26.44 S 28.45 E
Greylock, Mount ⚲ 207 42.38 N 73.10 W
Greymouth 172 42.28 S 171.12 E
Grey Range ⚲ 166 27.00 S 143.35 E
Grey River 186 47.35 N 57.06 W
Greys ⍩ 202 43.10 N 111.00 W
Greystanes 274a 33.49 S 150.55 E
Greystoke 44 54.40 N 2.52 W
Greystones 48 53.09 N 6.04 W
Greyton 158 34.04 S 19.38 E
Greytown 172 41.05 S 175.27 E
Greytown → San Juan del Norte, Nic. 236 10.55 N 83.42 W
Greytown, S. Afr. 158 29.04 S 30.30 E
Grez-Doiceau 56 50.44 N 4.42 E
Grez-sur-Loing 62 48.19 N 2.42 E
Grezzana 64 45.31 N 11.01 E
Gribanovskij 182 53.25 N 129.00 W
Gribb Bank ⚲⁴ 9 61.30 S 88.00 E
Gribbin Head ⚲ 42 50.19 N 4.40 W
Gribingui ◻⁵ 152 7.00 N 19.15 E
Gribingui ≃ 146 8.33 N 19.05 E
Gribingui-Bamingui, Réserve de Faune du ◻⁴ 146 8.00 N 19.10 E
Gribohm 52 54.19 N 38.27 E
Gricev 78 49.58 N 27.14 E
Gridley, Ca., U.S. 226 39.21 N 121.41 W
Gridley, Il., U.S. 216 40.44 N 88.52 W
Griebnitz See 264a 52.24 N 13.06 E
Griechenland → Greece ◻¹ 38 39.00 N 22.00 E
Griede 52 51.23 N 3.30 E
Grien ≃, S. Afr. 158 30.40 S 23.17 E
Groen ≃, S. Afr. 158 29.00 S 22.10 E
Grier City 210 40.50 N 76.04 W
Gries am Brenner 64 47.03 N 11.29 E
Griesbach im Rottal 64 48.28 N 13.11 E
Griesen 64 47.29 N 10.56 E
Griesheim 56 49.50 N 8.34 E
Gries im Sellrain 64 47.12 N 11.09 E
Grieskirchen 60 48.14 N 13.50 E
Griessem 52 52.00 N 9.12 E
Griesspitzen ⚲ 64 47.22 N 10.58 E
Griffen 61 46.42 N 14.44 E
Griffith, Austl. 163 34.17 S 146.03 E
Griffith, In., U.S. 216 41.31 N 84.15 W
Griffith, Lake ⍩ 220 28.52 N 81.51 W
Griffith Bay ⊂ 224 48.30 N 122.58 W
Griffiss Air Force Base ✦ 210 43.14 N 75.26 W
Griffith Island I, On., Can. 212 44.51 N 80.54 W
Griffith Park ✦ 280 34.09 N 118.17 W
Grifton 192 35.22 N 77.26 W
Griggs Drain ≃ 281 42.11 N 83.26 W
Griggs Reservoir ⍩¹ 214 40.03 N 83.06 W
Griggstown 276 40.26 N 74.36 W
Griggsville 219 39.42 N 90.43 W
Grignan 62 44.25 N 4.54 E
Grignasco 62 45.41 N 8.20 E
Grigno 64 46.01 N 11.38 E
Grignols 32 44.23 N 0.03 W
Grignon 261 48.51 N 1.57 E
Grigny, Fr. 62 45.37 N 4.47 E
Grigny, Fr. 261 48.40 N 2.24 E
Grigoriopol' 78 47.10 N 29.18 E
Grigorjevka, S.S.S.R. 78 46.17 N 33.44 E
Grigorjevka, S.S.S.R. 84 47.27 N 38.23 E
Grigorjevka, S.S.S.R. 85 42.43 N 77.30 E
Grigorjevskoje, S.S.S.R. 82 54.49 N 37.59 E
Grigorjevskoje, S.S.S.R. 82 54.48 N 39.15 E
Grigorovka, S.S.S.R. 78 51.03 N 32.51 E
Grigorovka, S.S.S.R. 78 50.05 N 30.39 E
Grigoryevka, S.S.S.R. 84 50.13 N 36.20 E
Grigorovo 82 56.42 N 37.35 E
Grigorovskoje 82 54.17 N 36.21 E
Grijalva ≃ 232 18.36 N 92.39 W
Grijpskerk 52 53.15 N 6.18 E
Grillbach ≃ 263 51.11 N 6.44 E
Grillby 41 59.37 N 17.15 E
Grillenburg 54 50.57 N 13.28 E
Grim, Cape ⚲ 152 3.59 N 17.06 E
Grimailov 78 49.20 N 26.01 E
Grimaldi 68 39.08 N 16.14 E
Grimari 152 5.44 N 20.03 E
Grimbergen 50 50.56 N 4.23 E
Grimeford Village 262 53.36 N 2.34 W
Grimes 226 39.04 N 121.54 W
Grimes ◻⁶ 222 30.35 N 96.00 W
Grimlinghausen 263 51.10 N 6.43 E
Grimmen 54 54.07 N 13.02 E
Grimmenstein 61 47.38 N 16.06 E
Grimnitzsee ⍩ 54 52.58 N 13.47 E
Grimsby, Austl. 212 43.12 N 79.34 W
Grimsby, On., Can. 212 43.12 N 79.34 W
Grimsby, Eng., U.K. 44 53.35 N 0.05 W
Grimselpass ⚲ 58 46.34 N 8.21 E
Grimsey I 24a 66.33 N 18.00 W
Grimshaw 184 56.11 N 117.36 W
Grimstad 26 58.20 N 8.36 E
Grimstead 208 37.30 N 76.18 W
Grimsvötn ⚲¹ 24a 64.24 N 17.22 W
Grin 24 47.59 N 24.49 E
Grindavik 24a 63.50 N 22.26 W
Grindelwald 58 46.37 N 8.02 E
Grindsted 41 55.45 N 8.56 E
Grindstone Island → Cap-aux-Meules 186 47.23 N 61.52 W
Grindstone Island ⍩ 186 76.07 N
Grinnell 190 41.45 N 92.43 W
Grinnell, Lake ⍩ 276 41.06 N 74.38 W
Grinnell Peninsula ⚲¹ 176 76.40 N 95.00 W
Grin'ovo 76 52.35 N 33.04 E
Grintavec ⚲ 64 46.21 N 14.33 E
Grintz ⚲⁸ 264b 48.15 N 16.21 E
Grip 26 63.14 N 7.37 E
Gripsholm slott ⊥ 40 59.15 N 17.13 E
Gripsholmslän ⚲ 40 59.17 N 17.20 E
Griqualand East ◻⁹ 158 30.30 S 29.00 E
Griqualand West ◻⁹ 158 28.30 S 23.30 E
Grira 224 45.22 N 123.37 W
Grisea 66 43.35 N 11.19 E
→ Gresik 115a 7.09 S 112.38 E
Grišino ⚲ 88 51.00 N 37.40 E
Griškovcy 78 50.06 N 28.29 E
Gris-Nez, Cap ⚲ 50 50.52 N 1.35 E
Grisola 68 39.43 N 15.51 E
Grisslehamn → Graubünden ◻³ 40 60.06 N 18.50 E
Grissom Air Force Base ✦ 216 40.39 N 86.09 W
Griston 45 52.34 N 0.51 E
Griswold, Mb., Can. 184 49.40 N 100.25 W
Griswold, Ia., U.S. 198 41.14 N 95.08 W
Griswold Creek ≃ 279a 42.39 N 72.42 W
Grivaï Pamia 152 7.03 N 19.26 E
Grivenskaja 84 45.35 N 38.34 E

Column 3

Grizzana 64 44.15 N 11.09 E
Grizzly Bay ⊂ 226 38.07 N 122.01 W
Grizzly Bear Mountain ⚲ 176 65.22 N 121.00 W
Grizzly Bear's Head and Lead Man Indian Reserve ◻⁴ 184 52.33 N 108.16 W
Grizzly Creek ≃ 282 37.52 N 122.06 W
Grizzly Flats 226 38.38 N 120.31 W
Grizzly Island I 282 38.08 N 121.58 W
Grizzly Mountain ⚲, Id., U.S. 202 47.43 N 116.06 W
Grizzly Mountain ⚲, Or., U.S. 202 44.26 N 120.57 W
Grizzly Mountain ⚲, Wa., U.S. 202 48.05 N 118.30 W
Grizzly Slough ≃ 282 38.06 N 121.53 W
Grmeč ⚲ 36 44.40 N 16.30 E
Groairas 250 3.53 S 40.23 W
Groais Island I 186 50.57 N 55.35 W
Grobbendonk 56 51.12 N 4.43 E
Gröben 264a 52.17 N 13.10 E
Gröbner-See ⍩ 264a 52.11 N 13.18 E
Gröbenzell 60 48.11 N 11.22 E
Grobina 76 56.33 N 21.10 E
Groblersdal 156 25.15 S 29.25 E
Groblershoop 158 28.55 S 20.59 E
Gröbming 64 47.26 N 13.54 E
Grobogan 182 53.25 N 129.00 W
Grodekovo 85 42.49 N 71.29 E
Gródig 64 47.44 N 13.02 E
Gröditsch 54 52.03 N 13.59 E
Gröditz 54 51.24 N 13.27 E
Gródków 30 50.43 N 17.22 E
Grodno 76 53.41 N 23.50 E
Grodno ◻⁹ 76 54.00 N 25.30 E
Grodovka 83 48.15 N 37.23 E
Grodz'anka 76 53.23 N 28.45 E
Grodzisk Mazowiecki 30 52.07 N 20.37 E
Grodzisk [Wielkopolski] 30 52.14 N 16.22 E
Groede 52 51.23 N 3.30 E
Groen ≃, S. Afr. 158 30.40 S 23.17 E
Groen ≃, S. Afr. 158 29.00 S 22.10 E
Grönland → Greenland ◻² 16 70.00 N 40.00 W
Groenlandia → Greenland ◻² 16 70.00 N 40.00 W
Groenlo 52 52.03 N 6.38 E
Groenvlei 158 27.27 S 30.13 E
Groesbeck, Oh., U.S. 218 39.13 N 84.35 W
Groesbeck, Tx., U.S. 222 31.31 N 96.32 W
Groesbeek 52 51.47 N 5.55 E
Grögl, gora ⚲ 78 48.37 N 23.56 E
Grogol, Kali ≃ 269e 6.10 S 106.47 E
Grogol-Hilir ⚲⁸ 269e 6.13 S 106.47 E
Grohnde 52 52.01 N 9.25 E
Groitzsch 54 51.09 N 12.16 E
Groix 32 47.38 N 3.28 W
Groix, Île de I 32 47.38 N 3.27 W
Grojec 30 51.52 N 20.52 E
Grokgak 115a 8.11 S 114.47 E
Grolley 58 46.50 N 7.05 E
Grombalia 148 36.36 N 10.30 E
Grömitz 54 54.09 N 10.58 E
Gromo 64 45.58 N 9.56 E
Gromoklea ≃ 78 47.21 N 32.14 E
Gromoslavka 78 48.12 N 43.37 E
Gromovka 78 46.19 N 34.06 E
Gronau, B.R.D. 52 52.05 N 9.46 E
Gronau, B.R.D. 52 52.13 N 7.02 E
Grondines (Saint-Charles-des-Grondines) 206 46.36 N 72.03 W
Grondneus 158 28.06 S 20.48 E
Grone 52 51.32 N 9.53 E
Grönenbach 60 47.52 N 10.13 E
Grong 24 64.28 N 12.18 E
Groningen, D.D.R. 54 51.56 N 11.13 E
Groningen, Ned. 52 53.13 N 6.33 E
Groningen, Sur. 250 5.48 N 55.28 W
Groningen ◻⁴ 52 53.15 N 6.45 E
Grønland → Greenland ◻² 16 70.00 N 40.00 W
Grönlid 184 53.06 N 104.28 W
Grønsund ⫟ 41 54.53 N 12.08 E
Grönwohld 54 53.39 N 10.25 E
Groom 196 35.12 N 101.06 W
Groom Lake ⍩ 204 37.15 N 115.48 W
Groot ≃, S. Afr. 158 33.45 S 24.36 E
Groot ≃, S. Afr. 158 33.54 S 21.39 E
Groot-Berg ≃ 158 32.47 S 18.08 E
Groot-Brakrivier 158 34.02 S 22.14 E
Grootdraaidam ⚲¹ 158 26.56 S 29.20 E
Grootebroek 52 52.43 N 5.13 E
Groote Eylandt I 164 14.00 S 136.40 E
Groote Eylandt Aboriginal Reserve ◻⁴ 164 14.00 S 136.40 E
Grootfontein 156 19.32 S 18.05 E
Groot Karasberge ⚲ 158 27.20 S 18.40 E
Groot Karroo → Great Karroo ⚲¹ 158 32.25 S 22.40 E
Groot-Kei ≃ 158 32.41 S 28.22 E
Groot Laagte ≃ 156 20.37 S 21.37 E
Groot-Letaba ≃ 158 23.58 S 31.50 E
Groot-Marico 158 25.37 S 26.26 E
Grootpan 158 25.58 S 26.33 E
Groot-Swartberge ⚲ 158 33.22 S 22.20 E
Groot-Vis ≃ 158 33.30 S 27.08 E
Grootvlei 158 26.44 S 28.32 E
Grootvloer ≃ 158 30.00 S 20.40 E
Gröpelingen ⚲⁸ 52 53.07 N 8.46 E
Grorud 40 59.58 N 10.53 E
Gros Morne ⚲ 240e 18.05 N 72.34 W
Gros Morne National Park ✦ 186 49.36 N 57.48 W
Grosne ≃ 62 46.42 N 4.56 E
Grosnez Point ⚲ 43b 49.15 N 2.15 W
Grosotto 64 46.20 N 10.16 E
Gros Piton ⚲ 241l 13.49 N 61.04 W
Grosrouvre 261 48.48 N 1.46 E
Grossa, Ponta ⚲, Bra. 256 23.35 S 45.13 W
Grossa, Ponta ⚲, Bra. 287a 22.47 S 43.11 W
Grossache (Tiroler Ache) ≃ 60 47.51 N 12.30 E
Grossalmerode 52 51.15 N 9.46 E
Grossalsleben 54 51.50 N 11.13 E
Gross Ammensleben 52 52.14 N 11.31 E
Grossarl 61 47.14 N 13.12 E
Gross Berkel 52 52.04 N 9.18 E
Grossbodungen 54 51.28 N 10.28 E
Gross Börnecke 54 51.52 N 11.28 E
Grossbottwar 56 49.00 N 9.17 E
Grossbreitenbach 54 50.35 N 11.02 E
Grossdubrau 54 51.15 N 14.28 E
Grosse ≃ 52 52.06 N 10.01 E
Grosse Antillen → Greater Antilles II 238 20.00 N 74.00 W
Grosse Aue ≃ 52 52.37 N 9.10 E
Grosse Australische Bucht → Great Australian Bight ⊂ 162 35.00 S 135.00 E
Grossebersdorf 264b 48.21 N 16.29 E

Column 4

Grosse Ebene → Great Plains ≃ 16 42.00 N 100.00 W
Grossefehn 52 53.24 N 7.36 E
Grosse Herrenwiese ⚲ 264a 52.17 N 13.20 E
Grosse Ile 216 42.08 N 83.09 W
Grosse Ile ⍩ 216 42.08 N 83.09 W
Grosse Ile, La ⍩ 186 47.37 N 61.31 W
Grosse Laber ≃ 60 48.56 N 12.30 E
Grosse Mühl ≃ 61 48.25 N 13.59 E
Grossenbaum ⚲⁸ 263 51.22 N 6.47 E
Grossenbrode 54 54.22 N 11.05 E
Grossengottern 54 51.09 N 10.34 E
Grossengstingen 56 48.23 N 9.17 E
Grossenhain 54 51.17 N 13.31 E
Grossenheidorn 52 52.27 N 9.23 E
Grossenkneten 52 52.56 N 8.16 E
Grossen-Linden 56 50.31 N 8.39 E
Grossenlüder 56 50.35 N 9.32 E
Grossenwiehe 41 54.43 N 9.15 E
Gross-Enzersdorf 64 48.12 N 16.33 E
Grosse Pointe ⚲ 214 42.23 N 82.54 W
Grosse Pointe 210 41.16 N 81.16 W
Grosse Pointe Farms 214 42.25 N 82.53 W
Grosse Pointe Park 214 42.22 N 82.56 W
Grosse Pointe Shores 214 42.26 N 82.53 W
Grosse Pointe Woods 214 42.26 N 82.54 W
Grosser Arber ⚲ 60 49.07 N 13.07 E
Grosser Bären-See ⍩ → Great Bear Lake ⍩ 176 66.00 N 120.00 W
Grosser Beerberg ⚲ 54 50.37 N 10.44 E
Grosser Bösenstein ⚲ 61 47.26 N 14.24 E
Grosser Buchstein ⚲ 61 47.36 N 14.35 E
Grosser Chingan → Da Hinggan Ling ⚲ 90 49.00 N 122.00 E
Grosser Feldberg ⚲ 56 50.14 N 8.26 E
Grosser Galtenberg ⚲ 64 47.20 N 11.58 E
Grosser Gleichberg ⚲ 54 50.23 N 10.35 E
Grosser Heuberg ⚲¹ 58 48.06 N 8.55 E
Grosser Jasmunder Bodden ⊂ 54 54.31 N 13.29 E
Grosser Knallstein ⚲ 61 47.19 N 13.58 E
Grosser Königstuhl ⚲ 64 46.57 N 13.47 E
Grosser Müggelsee ⍩ 54 52.26 N 13.39 E
Grosse Röder ≃ 54 51.30 N 13.25 E
Grosser oder Kaiser-Kanal → Da Yunhe ⚲ 90 32.12 N 119.31 E
Grosser Rodl ≃ 61 48.20 N 14.09 E
Grosser Peilstein ⚲ 64 48.18 N 15.06 E
Grosser Plessower See ⍩ 264a 52.23 N 12.54 E
Grosser Plöner See ⍩ 54 54.06 N 10.25 E
Grosser Priel ⚲ 61 47.43 N 14.04 E
Grosser Rachel ⚲ 60 48.59 N 13.24 E
Grosser Ravens-Berg ⚲² 264a 52.21 N 13.04 E
Grosser Riedelstein ⚲ 60 49.10 N 12.59 E
Grosser Salz-See → Great Salt Lake ⍩ 200 41.10 N 112.30 W
Grosser Seddiner See ⍩ 264a 52.17 N 13.02 E
Grosser Selchower See ⍩ 264a 52.13 N 13.53 E
Grosser Sklaven-See → Great Slave Lake ⍩ 176 61.30 N 114.00 W
Grosser Speikkogel ⚲ 61 46.47 N 14.58 E
Grosser Walfisch-Fluss → Baleine, Grande rivière de la ≃ 176 55.16 N 77.47 W
Grosser Wannsee ⍩ 264a 52.26 N 13.11 E
Grosser Winterberg ⚲² 54 50.54 N 14.16 E
Grosser Zern-See ⍩ 264a 52.24 N 12.56 E
Grosse Sandspitze ⚲ 64 46.46 N 12.49 E
Grosse Sandwüste → Great Sandy Desert ⚲² 162 21.30 S 125.00 E
Grosses Barrier-Riff → Great Barrier Reef ⚲² 160 18.00 S 145.50 E
Grosses Meer ⍩ 52 53.25 N 7.17 E
Grosses Moor ⚲³, B.R.D. 52 52.35 N 8.45 E
Grosses Moor ⚲³, B.R.D. 52 52.13 N 7.00 E
Grosses Schulerloch ⊡ 60 48.55 N 11.43 E
Grosse Sundainseln → Greater Sunda Islands II 108 2.00 S 110.00 E
Grosses Walsertal V 64 47.14 N 9.53 E
Grosse Syrte → Surt, Khalij ⊂ 146 31.30 N 18.00 E
Grosseto 66 42.46 N 11.08 E
Grosse Tulln ≃ 61 48.20 N 16.02 E
Grosseviči 89 49.55 N 139.33 E
Gross-Gerungs 61 48.34 N 14.57 E
Gross-Gerungs 61 48.34 N 14.57 E
Gross-Vis ⚲ 158 33.30 S 27.08 E
Gross Glienicke 264a 52.28 N 13.08 E
Gross-Glienicke See ⍩ 264a 52.28 N 13.08 E
Grossglockner ⚲ 64 47.04 N 12.42 E
Grossgmain 61 47.42 N 12.56 E
Gross-Gräschen 54 51.13 N 12.11 E
Grossgörschen 54 51.15 N 12.11 E
Grosslibenstein ⚲⁸ 261 48.49 N 2.32 E
Grosshansdorf 52 53.40 N 10.17 E
Grosshartmannsdorf 54 50.51 N 13.20 E
Gross-Hehlen 52 52.39 N 10.03 E
Grossheide 52 53.33 N 7.20 E
Grossennersdorf 52 52.39 N 7.38 E
Grosshöchstetten 58 46.55 N 7.38 E
Grossholzleute 58 47.36 N 10.08 E
Grosskjedersdorf ⚲⁸ 264b 48.17 N 16.26 E
Gross-Kollmar 52 53.55 N 9.28 E
Gross-Kollmar 52 53.55 N 9.28 E
Gross Köris 54 52.08 N 13.39 E
Grosskreutz 54 52.24 N 12.46 E
Grosskrotzenburg 56 50.05 N 8.58 E
Grosskrut 264b 48.38 N 16.43 E
Grosskühnau 54 51.52 N 12.10 E
Grosse Leine ≃ 52 52.01 N 9.47 E
Grossmachnow 54 52.16 N 13.26 E
Grossmehring 60 48.47 N 11.33 E
Grossmonra 54 51.12 N 11.08 E
Grossmugl 264b 48.30 N 16.14 E
Grossörner 54 51.37 N 11.28 E
Grosspetersdorf 61 47.14 N 16.23 E
Grosspetrowitz → Zielona Góra, Pol. 30 51.56 N 15.31 E
Grosspriel 264a 52.28 N 13.16 E
Grossquenstedt 54 51.55 N 11.01 E
Gross-Rakow ⚲⁸ 264b 48.16 N 16.39 E
Grosse Rhüden 52 51.57 N 10.08 E
Grossröhrsdorf 54 51.08 N 14.01 E
Grossröcketitz 54 51.00 N 11.06 E
Gross-Sarau 52 53.46 N 10.44 E
Grossschirma 54 50.59 N 13.18 E
Gross Schönau 52 52.00 N 7.20 E
Grossschönau 54 50.55 N 14.40 E
Gross Siel 52 53.39 N 8.34 E
Grossschwechat ≃ 264b 48.07 N 16.32 E
Gross Schönebeck 54 52.54 N 13.35 E

Column 5

Gross-Schulzendorf 264a 52.16 N 13.21 E
Gross-Siegharts 61 48.48 N 15.24 E
Grossödlk 64 47.25 N 13.58 E
Gross Strehlitz → Strzelce Opolskie 30 50.31 N 18.19 E
Grosstimmern 56 49.52 N 8.50 E
Gross-Umstadt 56 49.52 N 8.55 E
Grossvenediger ⚲ 64 47.06 N 12.21 E
Grosswardein → Sycòw 30 51.19 N 17.43 E
Grossweil 64 47.41 N 11.18 E
Grossweissenbach 61 48.33 N 15.10 E
Gross Wingällten ⚲ 58 46.49 N 8.44 E
Gross Ziethen, D.D.R. 41 52.26 N 7.08 E
Gross Ziethen, D.D.R. 264a 52.24 N 13.27 E
Gross-Zimmern 56 49.52 N 8.50 E
Grosuplje 56 45.58 N 14.38 E
Grosvenor, Lake ⍩ 180 58.40 N 155.15 W
Grosvenor Dale 207 41.58 N 71.53 W
Gros Ventre ≃ 202 43.33 N 110.46 W
Grote Nete ≃ 56 51.07 N 4.34 E
Groton, Ct., U.S. 207 41.21 N 72.04 W
Groton, Ma., U.S. 207 42.36 N 71.34 W
Groton, N.Y., U.S. 210 42.35 N 76.22 W
Groton, S.D., U.S. 198 45.26 N 98.05 W
Grottaferrata 66 41.47 N 12.40 E
Grottaglie 68 40.32 N 17.26 E
Grottaminarda 68 41.04 N 15.02 E
Grottammare 66 42.59 N 13.52 E
Grotte 70 37.24 N 13.42 E
Grotte di Castro 66 42.40 N 11.52 E
Grotteria 68 38.22 N 16.16 E
Grottkau → Grodków 30 50.43 N 17.22 E
Grottoes 188 38.16 N 78.49 W
Grottole 68 40.36 N 16.23 E
Grou, Oued V 148 33.56 N 6.45 W
Grouard Mission 182 55.31 N 116.09 W
Groundbirch 182 55.47 N 120.55 W
Groundhog ≃ 176 49.43 N 81.58 W
Grouse Creek ≃, Ks., U.S. 198 37.00 N 96.55 W
Grouse Creek Mountain ⚲ 202 44.22 N 113.54 W
Grouw 52 53.05 N 5.45 E
Grove, Eng., U.K. 42 51.36 N 1.25 W
Grove, Ok., U.S. 196 36.35 N 94.46 W
Grove, Pa., U.S. 285 40.01 N 75.38 W
Grove City, Fl., U.S. 220 26.54 N 82.19 W
Grove City, Mn., U.S. 198 45.09 N 94.40 W
Grove City, Oh., U.S. 218 39.52 N 83.05 W
Grove City, Pa., U.S. 214 41.09 N 80.05 W
Grove Hill 194 31.42 N 87.46 W
Groveland, Fl., U.S. 220 28.33 N 81.51 W
Groveland, Ma., U.S. 207 42.45 N 71.01 W
Groveland, N.Y., U.S. 210 42.39 N 77.46 W
Grovely Ridge ⚲ 42 51.08 N 2.04 W
Grove Mountains ⚲ 9 72.53 S 74.53 E
Groveport 218 39.52 N 82.53 W
Grover 210 41.37 N 76.52 W
Grover City 204 35.07 N 120.37 W
Grover Cleveland Birthplace ⊥ 276 40.50 N 74.16 W
Grover Cleveland Park ✦ 284a 42.57 N 78.49 W
Grover Hill 216 41.01 N 84.28 W
Grovers Mills 276 40.19 N 74.37 W
Groves 222 29.56 N 93.55 W
Groveton, N.H., U.S. 188 44.35 N 71.30 W
Groveton, Tx., U.S. 279b 40.30 N 80.06 W
Groveton, Va., U.S. 222 31.03 N 95.07 W
Groveton, Va., U.S. 284c 38.46 N 77.05 W
Grovetown 192 33.27 N 82.11 W
Groveville 208 40.10 N 74.40 W
Growa Point ⚲ 150 4.21 N 7.37 W
Growler Peak ⚲ 204 32.36 N 113.30 W
Growler Wash V 204 32.35 N 113.30 W
Groznoje 88 52.46 N 71.12 E
Groznyj 84 43.20 N 45.42 E
Groznyj → Groznyj 84 43.20 N 45.42 E
Grube, B.R.D. 54 54.14 N 11.02 E
Grube, D.D.R. 264a 52.26 N 12.57 E
Grubišno Polje 36 45.42 N 17.10 E
Grubweg 60 48.35 N 13.29 E
Grudovo 38 42.21 N 27.10 E
Grudziądz 30 53.29 N 18.45 E
Gruesas, Punta ⚲ 248 20.19 S 70.11 W
Gruetli-Laager 193 35.22 N 85.40 W
Grugapark ✦ 263 51.26 N 7.00 E
Grugliasco 62 45.04 N 7.34 E
Gruia 36 44.16 N 22.42 E
Gruinard Bay ⊂ 46 57.53 N 5.31 W
Gruinart, Loch ⊂ 46 55.52 N 6.20 W
Gruiten 263 51.14 N 7.01 E
Gruitrode 56 51.05 N 5.36 E
Grumello del Monte 64 45.39 N 9.52 E
Grumento Nova 68 40.17 N 15.53 E
Grumentum ⊥ 68 40.17 N 15.55 E
Grumman-Bethpage Airport ⚲ 276 40.45 N 73.29 W
Grumman Corporation ⚲³ 276 40.45 N 73.29 W
Grumo Appula 68 41.01 N 16.42 E
Grums 26 59.21 N 13.06 E
Grünau, B.R.D. 56 50.56 N 8.58 E
Grünau im Almtal 61 47.51 N 13.57 E
Grünbach 54 50.24 N 12.22 E
Grünbach, B.R.D. 54 50.35 N 8.58 E
Grünberg → Zielona Góra, Pol. 30 51.56 N 15.31 E
Grünburg 61 47.58 N 14.15 E
Gründlsee 61 47.38 N 13.50 E
Gründlsee ⍩ 61 47.37 N 13.51 E
Grundy 192 37.16 N 82.06 W
Grundy ◻⁶ 216 42.22 N 88.26 W
Grundy Center 198 42.21 N 92.46 W
Grundy Lake Provincial Park ✦ 190 45.48 N 80.34 W
Grünefeld 264a 52.41 N 13.04 E
Grünenplan 52 51.57 N 9.44 E
Grünewald 54 51.26 N 13.45 E
Grünewald, D.D.R. 54 51.26 N 14.00 E
Grunewald ⚲⁸ 264a 52.28 N 13.15 E
Grunewald, Berliner Forst ⚲ 264a 52.28 N 13.15 E
Grunewald, Jagdschloss ⊥ 264a 52.28 N 13.16 E
Grünhainichen 54 50.47 N 13.16 E
Grünheide 264a 52.26 N 13.50 E
Gruniki ⚲ 115a 7.09 S 112.38 E
Grünkraut 58 47.43 N 9.35 E
Gruñidora 234 24.10 N 101.42 W
Grünkrainach 263 51.14 N 6.13 E
Grünstadt 56 49.34 N 8.10 E
Gruvdal 40 59.50 N 18.23 E
Gruyère, Lac de la ⍩ 58 46.38 N 7.06 E
Gruyères 58 46.35 N 7.04 E
Gruž";ivka 88 50.12 N 92.53 E
Gruž 84 50.38 N 36.15 E
Grušev 78 47.42 N 30.30 E
Gruszka 38 45.13 N 21.58 E
Gruver 196 36.16 N 101.24 W
Gruvér ⍩ 196 36.16 N 101.24 W
Gruvön 40 59.21 N 13.08 E
Gružinskaja → Sovetskaja Socialističeskaja Respublika ◻³ 84 42.00 N 44.00 E
Gruznovka 88 55.09 N 105.12 E
Gruzskaja Balka 78 46.25 N 40.19 E
Gruzskij Jelančik ≃ 83 47.07 N 38.04 E
Gruzskoje 83 48.33 N 37.18 E
Gruzsko-Zor'anskoje 83 47.56 N 38.06 E
Grybów 30 49.38 N 20.56 E
Grycken ⍩ 40 60.27 N 16.13 E
Gryfice 30 53.56 N 15.12 E
Gryfino 30 53.12 N 14.30 E
Grytgöl 58 58.48 N 15.33 E
Grythyttan 40 59.42 N 14.32 E
Grzybowa ⚲ 78 47.03 N 11.22 E
Gschnitt, Pass ⚲ 64 47.35 N 13.30 E
Gschwend 56 48.57 N 9.44 E
Gstaad 58 46.28 N 7.17 E
Gsteig 58 46.23 N 7.16 E
Gu ≃ 100 27.02 N 115.03 E
Guabara ≃¹ 126 22.12 N 85.23 E
Guabito 536 48.59 N 80.37 W
Guabu 106 32.16 N 118.53 E

Column 6

Guacanayabo, Golfo de ⊂ 240p 20.28 N 77.30 W
Guacara 246 10.14 N 67.53 W
Guaçu 246 3.46 N 76.20 W
Guachinango 234 20.32 N 104.24 W
Guachochic 232 26.51 N 107.05 W
Guaçui 255 20.46 S 41.41 W
Guadajoz ≃ 34 37.50 N 4.51 W
Guadalajara, Méx. 234 20.40 N 103.20 W
Guadalajara, Esp. 34 40.38 N 3.10 W
Guadalcanal, Esp. 34 38.06 N 5.49 W
Guadalcanal ◻⁶ 175e 9.50 S 160.00 E
Guadalcanal I 175e 9.32 S 160.12 E
Guadalcázar 234 22.37 N 100.24 W
Guadalén ≃ 34 38.05 N 3.32 W
Guadalén, Embalse de ⍩¹ 34 38.25 N 3.15 W
Guadalentin ≃ 34 37.59 N 1.04 W
Guadalete ≃ 34 36.35 N 6.13 W
Guadalhorce ≃ 34 36.41 N 4.27 W
Guadalimar ≃ 34 38.05 N 3.06 W
Guadalope ≃ 34 41.15 N 0.03 W
Guadalquivir ≃ 34 36.47 N 6.22 W
Guadalupe, Bol. 248 18.33 S 64.25 W
Guadalupe, Col. 246 2.01 N 75.45 W
Guadalupe, C.R. 236 9.57 N 84.03 W
Guadalupe, Méx. 236 28.09 N 100.36 W
Guadalupe, Méx. 232 25.41 N 100.15 W
Guadalupe, Méx. 234 22.45 N 102.31 W
Guadalupe, Méx. 234 22.45 N 102.31 W
Guadalupe, Perú 248 7.15 S 79.29 W
Guadalupe, Ca., U.S. 204 34.58 N 120.34 W
Guadalupe ≃ 222 28.27 N 96.47 W
Guadalupe → Guadeloupe ◻² 287a 16.15 N 61.35 W
Guadalupe ≃, Ca., U.S. 282 37.25 N 121.58 W
Guadalupe ≃, Tx., U.S. 196 28.30 N 96.53 W
Guadalupe, Basilica de ⊥ 286a 19.29 N 99.07 W
Guadalupe, Isla I 178 29.00 N 118.16 W
Guadalupe, Presa de ⍩¹ 286a 19.37 N 99.16 W
Guadalupe, Sierra de ⚲ 34 39.26 N 5.25 W
Guadalupe, Sierra de ⚲, Méx. 286a 19.35 N 99.08 W
Guadalupe [Bravos] 232 31.23 N 106.07 W
Guadalupe del Norte 234 19.01 N 99.01 W
Guadalupe de Ramírez 234 17.45 N 98.10 W
Guadalupe Garzarón 232 24.35 N 101.15 W
Guadalupe Mountains ⚲ 196 32.20 N 105.00 W
Guadalupe Mountains National Park ✦ 196 31.55 N 104.55 W
Guadalupe Peak ⚲ 196 31.50 N 104.52 W
Guadalupe Seamount ⚲⁴³ 14 27.50 N 168.45 E
Guadalupe Slough ≃ 282 37.27 N 122.02 W
Guadalupe Victoria, Méx. 196 27.47 N 101.04 W
Guadalupe Victoria, Méx. 232 24.27 N 104.07 W
Guadalupe Victoria, Méx. 234 19.17 N 97.21 W
Guadalupe Victoria, Méx. 200 36.08 N 105.14 W
Guadalupita 196 36.07 N 105.14 W
Guadarrama, Sierra de ⚲ 34 40.43 N 4.10 W
Guadarranque ≃ 34 40.00 N 5.15 W
Guadeloupe ◻², N.A. 241o 16.15 N 61.35 W
Guadeloupe Passage ⫟ 238 16.45 N 61.30 W
Guadiana ≃ 34 37.14 N 7.22 W
Guadiana, Bahía de ⊂ 240p 22.11 N 84.24 W
Guadiana, Ensenada de ⊂ 240p 22.15 N 84.24 W
Guadiana Menor ≃ 34 37.56 N 3.15 W
Guadiaro ≃ 34 36.17 N 5.17 W
Guadiato ≃ 34 37.48 N 5.17 W
Guadix 34 37.18 N 3.08 W
Guafo, Isla I 252 43.36 S 74.43 W
Guagua 116 14.58 N 120.38 E
Guaíba 258 30.07 S 51.19 W
Guaíba ≃ 258 30.13 S 51.01 W
Guaicaipuro ◻⁵ 286c 10.26 N 66.57 W
Guaiçara 256 21.37 S 49.48 W
Guaicurus 246 2.00 S 56.08 W
Guaimaca 236 14.32 N 86.51 W
Guaimoreto, Laguna de ⊂ 236 15.58 N 85.55 W
Guaimú 98 41.31 N 125.26 E
Guainía ◻⁵ 246 2.00 N 69.00 W
Guainía ≃ 246 2.01 N 67.07 W
Guaíra, Bra. 258 24.05 S 54.15 W
Guaíra, Bra. 256 20.19 S 48.18 W
Guaíra ◻⁵ 258 24.05 S 54.15 W
Guaiuba 250 4.02 S 38.38 W
Guajaba, Cayo I 240p 21.50 N 77.36 W
Guajará ≃ 246 1.26 S 50.18 W
Guajará-Mirim 248 10.48 S 65.22 W
Guajataca, Lago de ⍩¹ 240m 18.23 N 66.55 W
Gualaca 538 8.32 N 82.17 W
Gualala 204 38.45 N 123.31 W
Gualán 236 15.08 N 89.22 W
Gualaceo 246 2.54 S 78.47 W
Gualdo Tadino 66 43.14 N 12.47 E

ESPAÑOL — FRANÇAIS — PORTUGUÊS

Nombre / Nom / Nome	Página / Page / Página	Lat.°′	Long.°′ W = Oeste / W = Ouest / W = Oeste
Gualeguay	252	33.09 S	59.20 W
Gualeguay ≃	252	33.19 S	59.39 W
Gualeguaychú	252	33.01 S	58.31 W
Gualicho, Salina del ≃	254	40.24 S	65.15 W
Gualjaina	254	42.42 S	70.30 W
Gualtieri	64	44.54 N	10.38 E
Guam □[2], Oc.	14	13.28 N	144.47 E
Guam □[2], Oc.	174p	13.28 N	144.47 E
Guamá ≃, Bra.	250	1.29 S	48.30 W
Guamá ≃, Cuba	240p	22.11 N	83.41 W
Guamal, Col.	246	9.09 N	74.14 W
Guamal, Col.	246	3.52 N	73.44 W
Guamal, Quebrada ≃	286c	10.31 N	66.59 W
Guamblin, Isla I	254	44.51 S	75.05 W
Guaminí	252	37.02 S	62.25 W
Guam International Airport ⊠	174p	13.29 N	144.48 E
Guamo	246	4.02 N	74.58 W
Guamo Embarcadero	240p	20.37 N	76.58 W
Guamote	246	1.56 S	78.43 W
Guamúchil, Méx.	232	25.28 N	108.06 W
Guamúchil, Méx.	234	23.55 N	106.05 W
Guamués ≃	246	0.32 N	76.33 W
Gua Musang	114	4.53 N	101.58 E
Gu'an	105	39.26 N	116.18 E
Guan ≃, Zhg.	100	32.16 N	115.42 E
Guan ≃, Zhg.	100	34.29 N	119.49 E
Guanábana	240m	18.01 N	67.07 W
Guanabara, Baía de c	287a	22.50 S	43.10 W
Guanabara, Palácio de ⛫	287a	22.56 S	43.11 W
Guanacaste □[4]	236	10.30 N	85.15 W
Guanacaste, Cordillera de ⋏	236	10.45 N	85.05 W
Guanacaure, Cerro ∧	236	13.14 N	87.07 W
Guanaceví	232	25.56 N	105.57 W
Guanache ≃	248	5.53 S	74.21 W
Guanahacabibes, Golfo de c	240p	22.08 N	84.35 W
Guanahacabibes, Península de ›[1]	240p	21.57 N	84.35 W
Guana Island I	240m	18.29 N	64.34 W
Guanaja	236	16.27 N	85.54 W
Guanaja, Isla de I	236	16.30 N	85.55 W
Guanajay	240p	22.55 N	82.42 W
Guanajibo ≃	240m	18.10 N	67.11 W
Guanajibo, Punta ›	240m	18.10 N	67.11 W
Guanajuato	234	21.01 N	101.15 W
Guanajuato □[3]	234	21.00 N	101.00 W
Guanambi	255	14.13 S	42.47 W
Guañape, Isla I	248	8.33 S	78.57 W
Guanare	246	9.03 N	69.45 W
Guanare ≃	246	8.13 N	67.46 W
Guanare Viejo ≃	246	8.19 N	68.10 W
Guanarito	246	8.42 N	69.12 W
Guanay	248	15.28 S	67.52 W
Guanay, Cerro ∧	246	5.51 N	66.18 W
Guanay, Cerro ∧[2]	286d	12.07 S	77.13 W
Guanbuqiao	100	29.56 N	114.21 E
Guanchao	100	26.41 N	114.58 E
Guancheng, Zhg.	100	30.11 N	121.25 E
Guancheng, Zhg.	107	30.01 N	103.54 E
Guancun	106	31.30 N	119.43 E
Guandacol	252	29.31 S	68.32 W
Guandanghu	100	30.06 N	113.37 E
Guandi, Zhg.	98	41.48 N	116.52 E
Guandi, Zhg.	98	42.37 N	118.27 E
Guandian	100	32.40 N	118.04 E
Guandu, Zhg.	100	24.17 N	113.53 E
Guandu, Zhg.	107	30.04 N	106.25 E
Guane	240p	22.12 N	84.05 W
Guang'an	107	30.28 N	106.39 E
Guang'anmen Station ⬥[5]	271a	39.53 N	116.20 E
Guangchang	100	26.50 N	116.14 E
Guangde	106	30.54 N	119.26 E
Guangdong (Kwangtung) □[4]	90	23.00 N	113.00 E
Guangfeng	100	28.25 N	118.11 E
Guangfu, Zhg.	106	31.18 N	120.23 E
Guangfu, Zhg.	107	30.13 N	104.41 E
Guangfu, Zhg.	269b	31.21 N	121.19 E
Guangfuyingzi	104	42.14 N	120.58 E
Guanghua	102	32.25 N	111.36 E
Guangji	100	29.52 N	115.34 E
Guangling, Zhg.	98	39.47 N	114.17 E
Guangling, Zhg.	106	32.06 N	120.13 E
Guanglu Dao I	98	39.09 N	122.21 E
Guangmao Shan ∧	102	27.02 N	100.58 E
Guangming Ding ∧	100	30.07 N	118.10 E
Guangnan	102	24.10 N	105.06 E
Guangningsi, Zhg.	98	40.27 N	118.31 E
Guangningsi, Zhg.	98	39.08 N	121.45 E
Guangping	98	36.30 N	114.57 E
Guangrao	98	37.02 N	118.25 E
Guangsbunchang	107	29.22 N	105.31 E
Guangshan	100	32.02 N	114.52 E
Guangshui	100	31.40 N	114.00 E
Guangxing	107	29.04 N	106.33 E
Guangxi Zhuangzu Zizhiqu (Kwangsi Chuang) □[4]	102	24.00 N	109.00 E
Guangyuan	102	32.26 N	105.52 E
Guangyuanzhen	107	30.37 N	104.47 E
Guangze	100	27.32 N	117.20 E
Guangzhen	106	30.45 N	121.07 E
Guangzhou (Canton)	100	23.06 N	113.16 E
Guangzong	98	37.06 N	115.08 E
Guanhães	255	18.46 S	42.53 W
Guanhu	98	34.26 N	117.59 E
Guánica	240m	17.58 N	66.55 W
Guánica, Laguna de ⊜	240m	18.00 N	66.56 W
Guaniguanico, Cordillera de ⋏	240p	22.35 N	83.45 W
Guanipa ≃	246	9.56 N	62.26 W
Guanjian	107	29.59 N	105.59 E
Guanjian ≃	107	30.00 N	106.01 E
Guankou, Zhg.	100	30.35 N	115.20 E
Guankou, Zhg.	107	30.39 N	103.26 E
Guanlin	106	31.32 N	119.42 E
Guanling	102	25.57 N	105.29 E
Guanlipu	104	41.37 N	123.18 E
Guanmenshan	89	47.23 N	122.20 E
Guannan (Xin'anzhen)	98	34.07 N	119.23 E
Guano	246	1.35 S	78.38 W
Guano Creek ≃	202	42.12 N	119.31 W
Guanpata	236	15.01 N	85.02 W
Guanputou	105	38.58 N	117.04 E
Guanqian, Zhg.	100	30.42 N	117.39 E
Guanqian, Zhg.	100	27.48 N	118.31 E
Guanqian, Zhg.	100	25.57 N	116.33 E
Guanqian, Zhg.	100	25.12 N	117.57 E
Guanqiao, Zhg.	98	34.58 N	117.14 E
Guanqiao, Zhg.	100	25.03 N	118.06 E
Guanqiaopu	100	31.08 N	112.54 E
Guanshanchang	107	28.46 N	103.42 E
Guanshi	100	25.43 N	112.53 E
Guanshui	98	40.55 N	124.33 E
Guanta	246	10.14 N	64.36 W
Guantánamo	240p	20.08 N	75.12 W
Guantánamo □[4]	240p	20.20 N	75.00 W
Guantánamo ≃	240p	19.55 N	75.12 W
Guantánamo, Bahía de c	240p	20.00 N	75.08 W
Guantanamo Bay Naval Station ■	240p	19.55 N	75.10 W
Guantang	106	31.37 N	119.06 E
Guantangqiao	106	32.09 N	119.27 E
Guantao (Nanguantao)	98	36.35 N	115.19 E
Guanting, Zhg.	100	34.19 N	113.47 E
Guanting, Zhg.	105	40.13 N	115.37 E
Guanting Shuiku ⊜[1]	105	40.20 N	115.38 E
Guantou, Zhg.	100	28.03 N	120.41 E
Guantou, Zhg.	100	26.08 N	119.33 E
Guantunpu	98	40.28 N	113.24 E
Guanxian, Zhg.	98	36.30 N	115.27 E
Guanxian, Zhg.	102	31.00 N	103.40 E
Guanxun	100	24.19 N	117.45 E
Guanyin	107	30.16 N	103.51 E
Guanyinchang, Zhg.	107	29.15 N	104.02 E
Guanyinchang, Zhg.	107	30.28 N	105.16 E
Guanyingzicun	104	41.52 N	121.53 E
Guanyinpu	107	28.58 N	104.53 E
Guanyinqiao, Zhg.	107	29.46 N	104.12 E
Guanyinqiao, Zhg.	107	29.05 N	104.46 E
Guanyinshan	106	32.01 N	120.58 E
Guanyinsi	106	31.48 N	118.57 E
Guanyintan	107	29.35 N	105.14 E
Guanyintang, Zhg.	100	31.01 N	112.35 E
Guanyintang, Zhg.	105	39.52 N	116.31 E
Guanyintang, Zhg.	106	32.09 N	121.09 E
Guanyinzhen	107	29.06 N	104.24 E
Guanyinzhou	100	29.30 N	113.09 E
Guanyun (Dayishan)	98	34.20 N	119.17 E
Guanzhuang, Zhg.	98	37.12 N	114.30 E
Guanzhuang, Zhg.	100	32.49 N	114.16 E
Guanzhuang, Zhg.	100	28.58 N	117.24 E
Guapí	246	2.36 N	77.54 W
Guapiaçu ≃	256	22.40 S	42.55 W
Guapiara	255	24.10 S	48.32 W
Guápiles	236	10.13 N	83.46 W
Guapimirim	256	22.32 S	42.59 W
Guapimirim ≃	256	22.40 S	42.58 W
Guapó	255	16.49 S	49.32 W
Guapo Bay c	241r	10.12 N	61.40 W
Guaporé	252	28.51 S	51.54 W
Guaporé ≃, Bra.	252	29.10 S	51.54 W
Guaporé (Iténez) ≃, S.A.	248	11.54 S	65.01 W
Guaqui	248	16.35 S	68.51 W
Guará ≃	255	12.59 S	44.49 W
Guara, Sierra de ⋏	34	42.17 N	0.10 W
Guarabira	250	6.51 S	35.29 W
Guaraçaí	255	21.02 S	51.11 W
Guaracarumbo	286c	10.34 N	66.59 W
Guaraci, Bra.	255	20.29 S	48.57 W
Guaraci, Bra.	255	22.57 S	51.40 W
Guaraciaba do Norte	250	4.10 S	40.46 W
Guaraciama	255	17.03 S	43.41 W
Guaraguara, Punta ›	241r	10.31 N	62.19 W
Guaraí ≃	287a	22.42 S	43.02 W
Guaramirim	252	26.27 S	49.00 W
Guaranda	246	1.36 S	79.00 W
Guaranésia	256	21.18 S	46.48 W
Guarani	256	21.22 S	43.03 W
Guaraniaçu	252	25.06 S	52.52 W
Guarani das Missões	252	28.08 S	54.34 W
Guarani de Goiás	255	13.59 S	46.31 W
Guarapari	255	20.40 S	40.30 W
Guarapiranga, Barragem do ⬥[6]	287b	23.41 S	46.43 W
Guarapiranga, Reservatório de ⊜[1]	256	23.44 S	46.44 W
Guarapuava	252	25.23 S	51.27 W
Guaraqueçaba	252	25.17 S	48.21 W
Guarará	256	21.43 S	43.02 W
Guarará ≃	287b	23.39 S	46.30 W
Guararé	246	7.49 N	80.17 W
Guararema	256	23.25 S	46.02 W
Guaratiba, Morro de ∧	287a	23.04 S	43.33 W
Guaratinguetá	256	22.49 S	45.13 W
Guaratinguetá, Ribeirão de ≃	256	22.49 S	45.13 W
Guaratuba	252	25.54 S	48.34 W
Guar Chempedak	114	5.52 N	100.28 E
Guarcino	66	41.48 N	13.19 E
Guarda	34	40.32 N	7.16 W
Guardado de Abajo	196	26.22 N	98.57 W
Guardafui, Cape → Caseyr ›	144	11.49 N	51.15 E
Guardavalle	68	38.30 N	16.30 E
Guardea	66	42.37 N	12.18 E
Guardia Escolta	252	28.59 S	62.08 W
Guardiagrele	66	42.11 N	14.13 E
Guardia Lombardi	68	40.57 N	15.12 E
Guardia Mitre	254	40.26 S	63.41 W
Guardia Sanframondi	68	41.15 N	14.36 E
Guardia Vieja, Arroyo de la ≃	258	33.37 S	57.07 W
Guardo	34	42.47 N	4.50 W
Guareí ≃	255	22.40 S	53.34 W
Guareim (Quaraí) ≃	252	30.12 S	57.36 W
Guareña	34	38.51 N	6.06 W
Guareña ≃	34	41.29 N	5.23 W
Guarenas	246	10.28 N	66.37 W
Guarenas ≃	286c	10.30 N	66.45 W
Guariba ≃	248	7.41 S	60.18 W
Guarico	246	9.32 N	69.48 W
Guárico □[3]	246	8.40 N	66.35 W
Guárico ≃	246	7.55 N	67.23 W
Guárico, Embalse del ⊜[1]	246	9.05 N	67.25 W
Guarico, Punta ›	240p	20.37 N	74.44 W
Guariquito ≃	246	7.40 N	66.18 W
Guarizama	236	14.55 N	86.20 W
Guarujá	256	24.00 S	46.16 W
Guarulhos	256	23.28 S	46.32 W
Guarulhos □[7]	287b	23.26 S	46.29 W
Guasare ≃	246	11.03 N	72.02 W
Guasave	232	25.34 N	108.27 W
Guasdualito	246	7.15 N	70.44 W
Guasila	71	39.34 N	9.03 E
Guasipati	246	7.28 N	61.54 W
Guastalla	64	44.55 N	10.39 E
Guāsuba ≃[1]	126	21.38 N	88.53 E
Guatajiagua	236	13.40 N	88.13 W
Guatemala	236	14.38 N	90.31 W
Guatemala □[5]	236	14.40 N	90.30 W
Guatemala □[1], N.A.	230	15.30 N	90.15 W
Guatemala □[1], N.A.	236	15.30 N	90.15 W
Guatemala Basin ✣[1]	16	11.00 N	95.00 W
Guateque	246	5.00 N	73.28 W
Guatimozín	252	33.27 S	62.27 W
Guatire	246	10.28 N	66.32 W
Guatopo, Parque Nacional ♠	246	10.05 N	66.25 W
Guatraché	252	37.40 S	63.32 W
Guaugurina	164	10.37 S	150.28 E
Guavi ≃	164	7.49 S	143.15 E
Guaviare □[8]	246	2.00 N	72.00 W
Guaviare ≃	246	4.03 N	67.44 W
Guaxindiba ≃	287a	22.44 S	43.02 W
Guaxupé	256	21.18 S	46.42 W
Guayabal, Cuba	240p	20.42 N	77.36 W
Guayabal, Ven.	246	8.00 N	67.24 W
Guayabal, Lago ⊜[1]	240m	18.06 N	66.30 W
Guayabero ≃	246	2.36 N	72.47 W
Guayabo	232	26.00 N	107.26 W
Guayabo Colorado	234	19.02 N	101.35 W
Guayacán	252	29.58 S	71.22 W
Guayaguayare	241r	10.08 N	61.02 W
Guayama	240m	17.59 N	66.07 W
Guayambre ≃	236	14.26 N	86.02 W
Guayameo	234	18.12 N	101.19 W
Guayana → Ciudad Guayana	246	8.22 N	62.40 W
Guayana → Guyana □[1]	246	5.00 N	59.00 W
Guayaneco, Archipiélago II	254	47.45 S	75.10 W
Guayanés, Punta ›	240m	18.04 N	65.48 W
Guayanilla	240m	18.01 N	66.47 W
Guayanilla, Bahía de c	240m	18.00 N	66.46 W
Guayape	236	14.45 N	86.52 W
Guayape ≃	236	14.26 N	85.58 W
Guayapo ≃	246	4.30 N	67.35 W
Guayaquil	246	2.10 S	79.50 W
Guayaquil, Golfo de c	246	3.00 S	80.30 W
Guayaramerín	248	10.48 S	65.23 W
Guayas □[4]	246	2.00 S	80.00 W
Guayas ≃, Col.	246	1.23 N	74.50 W
Guayas ≃, Ec.	246	2.36 S	79.52 W
Guayatayoc, Laguna de ⊜	252	23.25 S	65.51 W
Guaycora	232	28.50 N	109.21 W
Guaycurú, Arroyo ≃	258	34.00 S	56.50 W
Guaymas	232	27.56 N	110.54 W
Guaynabo	240m	18.22 N	66.07 W
Guayquiraró ≃	252	30.10 S	58.34 W
Guayuriba ≃	246	3.55 N	73.05 W
Guazacapán	236	14.04 N	90.25 W
Guazapares	232	27.22 N	108.15 W
Guazárachic	232	26.57 N	106.43 W
Guazhou	106	32.15 N	119.23 E
Guazunamby, Arroyo ≃	288	34.24 S	58.38 W
Guba, Ityo.	144	10.16 N	35.17 E
Guba, Zaïre	154	10.40 S	26.26 E
Gubacha	86	58.52 N	57.36 E
Gubam	164	8.40 S	141.55 E
Gubany	76	56.37 N	30.40 E
Gubari	80	51.32 N	42.33 E
Gubat	116	12.55 N	124.07 E
Gubavica ⌊	36	43.26 N	16.54 E
Gubbi	122	13.19 N	76.56 E
Gubbio	66	43.21 N	12.35 E
Gubeikou	105	40.42 N	117.09 E
Gubentaoligai	104	42.16 N	122.13 E
Gubin	30	51.56 N	14.45 E
Gubinicha	78	48.48 N	35.15 E
Gubino, S.S.S.R.	80	53.19 N	48.44 E
Gubino, S.S.S.R.	82	55.42 N	39.07 E
Gubio	146	12.29 N	12.48 E
Gubkin	78	51.18 N	37.32 E
Gubug	115a	7.03 S	110.40 E
Gucheng (Zhengjiakou), Zhg.	98	37.22 N	115.56 E
Gucheng, Zhg.	100	32.46 N	118.32 E
Gucheng, Zhg.	100	33.59 N	117.29 E
Gucheng, Zhg.	100	25.53 N	116.11 E
Gucheng, Zhg.	102	32.18 N	111.35 E
Gucheng, Zhg.	105	40.32 N	116.02 E
Gucheng, Zhg.	105	39.08 N	115.42 E
Gucheng, Zhg.	106	30.29 N	119.46 E
Guchengcang	100	32.34 N	115.20 E
Gucheng Hu ⊜	106	31.17 N	118.54 E
Guchengzi, Zhg.	104	42.33 N	123.45 E
Guchengzi, Zhg.	104	40.58 N	122.36 E
Guchengzi, Zhg.	104	40.40 N	120.31 E
Guchengzi, Zhg.	104	41.44 N	123.35 E
Gučin-Us	102	45.27 N	102.25 E
Gücük	130	38.12 N	37.29 E
Gūdalūr	122	9.41 N	77.16 E
Gúdar, Sierra de ⋏	34	40.27 N	0.42 W
Gudauta	84	43.06 N	40.37 E
Gudbrandsdalen V	26	61.30 N	10.00 E
Gudenå ≃	26	56.29 N	10.13 E
Gudensberg	56	51.10 N	9.22 E
Gudermes	84	43.20 N	46.08 E
Guderup	41	54.59 N	9.53 E
Gudgenby ≃	171b	35.39 S	149.04 E
Gudhjem	26	55.13 N	14.59 E
Gudianzi	100	31.49 N	116.05 E
Gudivāda	122	16.27 N	80.59 E
Gudiyāttam	122	12.57 N	78.52 E
Gudme	41	55.09 N	10.43 E
Gudow	54	53.33 N	10.46 E
Güdül	130	40.13 N	32.15 E
Gūdūr	122	14.08 N	79.51 E
Gudvangen	26	60.52 N	6.50 E
Guebwiller (Gebweiler)	58	47.55 N	7.12 E
Guéckédou	150	8.33 N	10.09 W
Gué-de-Longroi	261	48.30 N	1.43 E
Gué-d'Hossus	50	49.57 N	4.32 E
Guédi, Mont ∧	146	12.14 N	18.58 E
Guéguen, Lac ⊜	190	48.06 N	77.13 W
Guéherville	261	48.32 N	1.53 E
Güéjar ≃	246	2.55 N	73.14 W
Guélendeng	146	10.56 N	15.32 E
Guelma	148	36.28 N	7.26 E
Guelma □[5]	148	36.10 N	7.50 E
Guelph	212	43.33 N	80.15 W
Guéméné-sur-Scorff	32	48.04 N	3.12 W
Güemes	234	23.56 N	99.00 W
Guemes Island I	224	48.33 N	122.37 W
Guené	150	11.44 N	3.13 E
Guenguel ≃	254	45.41 S	70.20 W
Guer	32	47.54 N	2.07 W
Guéra □[5]	146	11.30 N	18.30 E
Guéra, Massif de ∧	146	11.55 N	18.12 E
Guérande	32	47.20 N	2.26 W
Guercif	148	34.15 N	3.21 W
Guerdjoumane, Djebel ∧	34	36.25 N	2.51 E
Güere ≃	246	9.50 N	65.08 W
Guéréda	146	14.31 N	22.05 E
Guéret	32	46.10 N	1.52 E
Guérin Kouka	150	9.41 N	0.37 E
Guerla Mandata Shan ∧	120	30.26 N	81.20 E
Guermantes	261	48.51 N	2.42 E
Guerne	214	40.46 N	81.54 W
Guernes	261	49.01 N	1.38 E
Guerneville	204	38.30 N	123.00 W
Guernica	258	34.56 S	58.25 W
Guernica → Gernika-Lumo	34	43.19 N	2.41 W
Guernsey	200	42.16 N	104.44 W
Guernsey □[6]	214	40.08 N	81.30 W
Guernsey □[2], Europe	22	49.28 N	2.35 W
Guernsey □[2], Europe	43b	49.28 N	2.35 W
Guernsey Reservoir ⊜[1]	198	42.19 N	104.48 W
Guernsey State Park ♠	198	42.20 N	104.50 W
Guerrero	196	28.20 N	100.23 W
Guerrero □[3]	234	17.40 N	100.00 W
Guerville	261	48.57 N	1.44 E
Guerzim	148	29.45 N	1.47 W
Guesle ≃	261	48.36 N	1.40 E
Guessou-Sud	150	10.03 N	2.38 E
Guest Peninsula ›[1]	9	76.18 S	148.00 W
Gueydan	194	30.01 N	92.30 W
Guéyo	150	5.49 N	6.36 W
Gufang	100	29.04 N	119.32 E
Guffin Bay c	212	44.01 N	76.09 W
Guga	89	52.43 N	137.35 E
Gugang	100	28.17 N	113.46 E
Guge ∧	144	6.10 N	37.26 E
Gugera	123	30.58 N	73.19 E
Gugging	264b	48.19 N	16.15 E
Güglia, Pass dal)(	58	46.28 N	9.44 E
Güglingen	56	49.04 N	9.00 E
Guglionesi	66	41.55 N	14.55 E
Gugu ∧	144	8.12 N	39.58 E
Guguan	102	40.27 N	99.13 E
Guguan I	108	17.19 N	145.51 E
Guhe	100	31.54 N	117.58 E
Guhrau → Góra	30	51.40 N	16.33 E
Gui ≃	102	23.28 N	111.18 E
Guia	248	15.22 S	56.14 W
Guia de Pacobaíba	256	22.43 S	43.10 W
Guialana, Cerro ∧	234	16.52 N	96.30 W
Guia Lopes da Laguna	248	21.26 S	56.07 W
Guiana Basin ✣[1]	18	11.00 N	52.00 W
Guiana Island I	240c	17.07 N	61.44 W
Guibéroua	150	6.14 N	6.10 W
Guibes	156	26.41 S	16.42 E
Güicán	246	6.28 N	72.25 W
Guichen	32	47.58 N	1.48 W
Guichi	100	30.40 N	117.28 E
Guichicovi	234	16.58 N	95.06 W
Guichón	252	32.21 S	57.12 W
Guicun	100	33.37 N	114.11 E
Guidan Roumji	150	13.40 N	6.42 E
Guidari	146	9.17 N	16.40 E
Guide	102	36.03 N	101.28 E
Guide, Mount ∧[2]	162	22.36 S	136.54 E
Guide Post	44	55.10 N	1.35 W
Guider	146	9.56 N	13.57 E
Guide Rock	198	40.04 N	98.19 W
Guidexiang	107	29.51 N	104.47 E
Guidigri	146	13.40 N	9.51 E
Guidimaka □[4]	150	15.30 N	12.10 W
Guidimouni	150	13.42 N	9.30 E
Guiding	102	26.34 N	107.14 E
Guidizzolo	64	45.19 N	10.35 E
Guidong	100	26.05 N	113.57 E
Guidonia	66	42.01 N	12.45 E
Guidouma	152	1.37 S	10.41 E
Guiers ≃	62	45.37 N	5.37 E
Guiers, Lac de ⊜	150	16.12 N	15.50 W
Guifujie	100	27.20 N	120.01 E
Guiglia	64	44.26 N	10.58 E
Guiglo	150	6.33 N	7.29 W
Guignes-Rabutin	50	48.38 N	2.48 E
Guihuayuan	107	30.37 N	105.25 E
Guihulngan	116	10.07 N	123.16 E
Güija, Lago de ⊜	236	14.17 N	89.31 W
Guijalo	116	13.44 N	123.52 E
Guiji	100	32.51 N	116.33 E
Guijingqiao	106	31.21 N	119.40 E
Guijuelo	34	40.33 N	5.40 W
Guil ≃	62	44.40 N	6.36 E
Guilarte, Monte ∧	240m	18.09 N	66.46 W
Guilderland	210	42.42 N	73.54 W
Guildford, Austl.	274a	33.51 S	150.59 E
Guildford, Eng., U.K.	260	51.14 N	0.35 W
Guildford □[8]	260	51.16 N	0.32 W
Guildford Cathedral ⛫[1]	260	51.14 N	0.35 W
Guildhall	188	44.33 N	71.33 W
Guildtown	46	56.28 N	3.24 W
Guiler	89	46.11 N	121.45 E
Guilford, Ct., U.S.	207	41.17 N	72.40 W
Guilford, In., U.S.	218	39.10 N	84.55 W
Guilford, Me., U.S.	188	45.10 N	69.23 W
Guilford, N.Y., U.S.	210	42.24 N	75.29 W
Guilford Courthouse National Military Park ♠	192	36.01 N	79.45 W
Guilherand	62	44.56 N	4.52 E
Guilin (Kweilin)	102	25.17 N	110.17 E
Guilinchang	107	30.13 N	105.50 E
Guilinzhen	107	30.15 N	104.53 E
Guillaume-Delisle, Lac ⊜	176	56.15 N	76.17 W
Guillaumes	62	44.05 N	6.51 E
Guillermo E. Hudson	288	34.47 S	58.10 W
Guillestre	62	44.40 N	6.39 E
Guillon	50	47.31 N	4.06 E
Guilsfield	42	52.42 N	3.09 W
Guilvinec	32	47.47 N	4.17 W
Guimarães, Bra.	250	2.08 S	44.36 W
Guimarães, Port.	34	41.27 N	8.18 W
Guimaras Island I	116	10.35 N	122.37 E
Guimaras Strait ⋓	116	10.30 N	122.44 E
Guimba	116	15.40 N	120.46 E
Guimbal	116	10.40 N	122.19 E
Guimeishan	100	24.44 N	114.52 E
Guimu Zhang ∧	100	24.40 N	116.48 E
Guin	194	33.57 N	87.54 W
Guinan	102	35.24 N	100.57 E
Guinayang	269f	14.42 N	121.08 E
Guinayangan	116	13.54 N	122.27 E
Guinda	226	38.50 N	122.12 W
Guindulman	116	9.46 N	124.29 E
Guindulman Bay c	116	9.44 N	124.29 E
Guiné → Guinea-Bissau □[1]	150	12.00 N	15.00 W
Guinea	208	38.08 N	77.26 W
Guinea (Guinée) □[1], Afr.	134	11.00 N	10.00 W
Guinea (Guinée) □[1], Afr.	150	11.00 N	10.00 W
Guinea, Gulf of c	10	2.00 N	2.30 E
Guinea Basin ✣[1]	10	0.00	5.00 W
Guinea-Bissau (Guiné-Bissau) □[1], Afr.	134	12.00 N	15.00 W
Guinea-Bissau (Guiné-Bissau) □[1], Afr.	150	12.00 N	15.00 W
Guineacor Creek ≃	170	34.21 S	150.05 E
Guinea Ecuatorial → Equatorial Guinea □[1]	152	2.00 N	9.00 E
Guinea Rise ✣[3]	10	8.00 S	0.00
Guiné-Bissau → Guinea-Bissau □[1]	150	12.00 N	15.00 W
Guinecourt, Lac ⊜	186	50.55 N	69.16 W
Guinée → Guinea □[1]	150	11.00 N	10.00 W
Guinée-Bissau → Guinea-Bissau □[1]	150	12.00 N	15.00 W
Guinée équitoriale → Equatorial Guinea □[1]	152	2.00 N	9.00 E
Güines, Cuba	240p	22.50 N	82.02 W
Guînes, Fr.	50	50.52 N	1.52 E
Guingamp	32	48.33 N	3.11 W
Guinguinéo	150	14.16 N	15.57 W
Guinobatan	116	13.11 N	123.36 E
Güinope	236	13.51 N	86.55 W
Guintacan Island I	116	11.19 N	123.54 E
Guintinguintin, Mount ∧	116	12.25 N	122.24 E
Guintinua Island I	116	14.26 N	122.51 E
Guiones, Punta ›	236	9.54 N	85.41 W
Guiong	116	6.25 N	122.01 E
Guiperreux	261	48.40 N	1.42 E
Guiperreux, Étang de ⊜	261	48.40 N	1.43 E
Guiping	102	23.20 N	110.09 E
Guir, Hammada du ⬥[2]	148	30.45 N	3.15 W
Guir, Oued V	148	30.29 N	2.17 W
Güira de Melena	240p	22.48 N	82.30 W
Guiratinga	255	16.21 S	53.45 W
Guiren	100	33.42 N	118.12 E
Güiria	246	10.34 N	62.18 W
Guiricema	255	21.00 S	42.43 W
Guisachan Forest ⬥[3]	46	57.17 N	4.55 W
Guisanbourg	250	4.25 N	51.56 W
Guisborough	44	54.32 N	1.04 W
Guiscard	50	49.39 N	3.03 E
Guise	50	49.54 N	3.38 E
Guiseley	44	53.53 N	1.42 W
Guisijan	116	11.05 N	122.03 E
Güisisil, Cerro ∧	236	12.37 N	86.13 W
Guist Creek ≃	218	38.09 N	85.13 W
Guitiriz	34	43.11 N	7.54 W
Guitou	100	24.58 N	113.25 E
Guitrancourt	261	49.01 N	1.47 E
Guîtres	32	45.03 N	0.11 W
Guitry	150	5.31 N	5.14 W
Guiuan	116	11.02 N	125.43 E
Guixi	100	28.16 N	117.10 E
Guixian	102	23.06 N	109.39 E
Guiyang, Zhg.	100	25.46 N	112.43 E
Guiyang (Kweiyang), Zhg.	102	26.35 N	106.43 E
Güiza ≃	246	1.22 N	78.36 W
Guizhou (Kweichow) □[4]	102	27.00 N	107.00 E
Gujarāt □[3]	118	22.00 N	72.00 E
Gūjar Khān	123	33.16 N	73.19 E
Gujba	146	11.30 N	11.55 E
Gujiabeng	106	30.45 N	120.59 E
Gujiang	100	27.11 N	114.49 E
Gujiatun	104	40.39 N	124.08 E
Gujiatuo	107	29.14 N	106.12 E
Gujiazhai	269b	31.22 N	121.28 E
Gujiazi, Zhg.	104	42.02 N	123.01 E
Gujiazi, Zhg.	104	41.44 N	124.11 E
Gujrānwāla	123	32.09 N	74.11 E
Gujrāt	123	32.34 N	74.05 E
Gukas'an	84	41.03 N	43.52 E
Gukou	100	26.27 N	118.38 E
Gukovo	83	48.03 N	39.56 E
Gul, Tanjong ›	271c	1.17 N	103.39 E
Gul'a	88	54.41 N	121.01 E
Gul'aj-Borisovka	78	46.38 N	40.13 E
Gul'ajevskije Koški, ostrova II	24	68.55 N	55.10 E
Gul'ajpole	78	47.38 N	36.16 E
Gulang	102	37.36 N	102.58 E
Gulaothi	124	28.36 N	77.47 E
Gulargambone	166	31.20 S	148.28 E
Gulbarga	122	17.20 N	76.50 E
Gulbene	76	57.11 N	26.45 E
Gul'ča	85	40.19 N	73.26 E
Gul'ča ≃	85	40.20 N	73.26 E
Guldasteh	267d	35.36 N	51.16 E
Guldborg	41	54.52 N	11.45 E
Guldborg Sund ⋓	41	54.48 N	11.48 E
Guldsmedshyttan	40	59.42 N	15.06 E
Güldüzü	130	36.52 N	37.07 E
Gülebağdı	130	39.52 N	39.50 E
Guledagudda	122	16.03 N	75.48 E
Guleitou	100	23.47 N	117.36 E
Gülek Boğazı)(	130	37.16 N	34.48 E
Gulf □[5]	164	7.00 S	145.00 E
Gulf Gate Estates	220	27.15 N	82.31 W
Gulf Hammock	192	29.15 N	82.43 W
Gulf Harbors	220	28.14 N	82.45 W
Gulf Islands National Seashore ♠	194	30.14 N	88.42 W
Gulf of Alaska Seamount Province ✣	16	56.00 N	147.00 W
Gulfport, Fl., U.S.	220	27.45 N	82.40 W
Gulfport, Ms., U.S.	194	30.22 N	89.05 W
Gulf Shores	194	30.14 N	87.42 W
Gulf State Park ♠	194	30.16 N	87.40 W
Gulf Stream ≃	212	43.51 N	75.56 W
Gulgong	166	32.22 S	149.32 E
Guli	106	31.38 N	120.50 E
Gulian	89	52.55 N	122.19 E
Gulicun	106	31.52 N	118.41 E
Gul Imām	123	32.16 N	70.32 E
Gulistān, Pāk.	120	30.36 N	66.35 E
Gulistan, S.S.S.R.	85	40.30 N	68.46 E
Guliya Shan ∧	89	49.48 N	122.25 E
Guljanci	38	43.38 N	24.42 E
Gulkana	180	62.16 N	145.23 W
Gull ≃	212	44.37 N	78.49 W
Gulland Rock II[1]	42	50.34 N	4.59 W
Gullane	46	56.02 N	2.50 W
Gullfoss ⌊	24a	64.24 N	20.08 W
Gullholmen	26	58.11 N	11.24 E
Gullion, Slieve ∧[2]	48	54.08 N	6.27 W
Gull Island I	281	42.32 N	82.41 W
Gullivan Bay c	220	25.52 N	81.38 W
Gull Lake	184	50.08 N	108.27 W
Gull Lake ⊜, Ab., Can.	182	52.35 N	114.00 W
Gull Lake ⊜, On., Can.	184	51.18 N	91.58 W
Gull Lake ⊜, On., Can.	212	44.51 N	78.47 W
Gull Lake ⊜, Mi., U.S.	216	42.24 N	85.25 W
Gull Lake ⊜, Mn., U.S.	190	46.25 N	94.20 W
Gullrock Lake ⊜	184	50.58 N	93.40 W
Gullspång	40	58.59 N	14.06 E
Güllük	130	37.14 N	27.36 E
Güllük Körfezi c	130	37.12 N	27.20 E
Gulmarg	123	34.03 N	74.23 E
Gulnam	140	6.55 N	29.30 E
Gülnar	130	36.20 N	33.25 E
Gulong	89	45.51 N	124.14 E
Gulpen	56	50.48 N	5.54 E
Gülper See ⊜	54	52.44 N	12.14 E
Gulph Mills	285	40.04 N	75.21 W
Gülpınar	130	39.32 N	26.07 E
Gul'ripš	84	42.57 N	41.06 E
Gul'šad	86	46.39 N	74.24 E
Gülşehir	130	38.45 N	34.38 E
Gulshan	126	23.49 N	90.27 E
Gulsvik	26	60.23 N	9.35 E
Gulu, Ug.	154	2.47 N	32.18 E
Gulu, Zhg.	120	28.06 N	89.17 E
Gulukguluk	115a	7.04 S	113.40 E
Guluogongba	120	34.20 N	84.50 E
Guluy	144	14.44 N	36.43 E
Gulwe	154	6.30 S	36.29 E
Gumaca	116	13.55 N	122.06 E
Gumahang	116	12.35 N	123.16 E
Gumal (Gowmal) ≃	120	31.56 N	70.22 E
Gumare	156	19.21 S	22.12 E
Gumba, Ang.	152	11.40 S	16.34 E
Gumba, Zaïre	152	2.57 N	21.26 E
Gumbinnen → Gusev	76	54.36 N	22.12 E
Gumbiro	154	10.16 S	35.39 E
Gumel	150	12.39 N	9.22 E
Gumeracha	168b	34.49 S	138.53 E
Gumiao	100	32.26 N	113.16 E
Gumieńce ⬥[8]	54	53.51 N	14.30 E
Gumistskij zapovednik ♠	84	43.15 N	41.05 E
Gumla	124	23.03 N	84.33 E
Gumma □[5]	94	36.30 N	139.00 E
Gummersbach	56	51.02 N	7.34 E
Gummi	150	12.09 N	5.09 E
Gumpas Pond ⊜	283	42.44 N	71.22 W
Gumpas Pond Brook ≃	283	42.42 N	71.21 W
Gumpoldskirchen	264b	48.03 N	16.17 E
Gum Swamp Creek ≃	192	32.08 N	82.55 W
Gumti ≃	126	23.32 N	90.43 E
Gümüşçay	130	40.16 N	27.17 E
Gümüşhacıköy	130	40.53 N	35.14 E
Gümüşhane	130	40.27 N	39.29 E
Gümüşhane □[4]	130	40.15 N	39.45 E
Gümüşkent	130	38.50 N	34.32 E
Gümüşköy ⬥[8]	267b	41.14 N	28.58 E
Gümüşova	130	40.51 N	30.57 E
Gümüşsü	130	38.14 N	30.01 E
Gun ≃	216	42.28 N	85.40 W
Guna, India	124	24.39 N	77.19 E
Guna, Ityo.	144	8.19 N	39.51 E
Guna ∧	144	11.42 N	38.12 E
Gunbar	166	34.01 S	145.25 E
Gun Barrel City	222	32.20 N	96.10 W
Gun Creek ≃	284a	43.03 N	78.55 W
Gunda	88	52.47 N	111.44 E
Gundagai	166	35.04 S	148.07 E
Gundelfingen, B.R.D.	56	48.33 N	10.22 E
Gundelfingen, B.R.D.	58	48.03 N	7.52 E
Gundelsheim	56	49.17 N	9.09 E
Gundik	115a	7.12 S	110.54 E
Gundji	152	2.05 N	21.27 E
Gundlakamma ≃	122	15.32 N	80.14 E
Gundlupet	122	11.48 N	76.41 E
Gündoğdu	130	40.15 N	27.07 E
Gündoğmuş	130	36.48 N	32.01 E
Guneh Ghar ∧	123	35.19 N	71.47 E
Güney	130	38.09 N	29.05 E
Gungartan ∧	171b	36.18 S	148.24 E
Gungi	152	6.21 S	19.15 E
Gungo	152	11.48 S	14.08 E
Güngören ⬥[8]	267b	41.01 N	28.53 E
Gungu	152	5.44 S	19.19 E
Gunib	84	42.25 N	46.57 E
Gunisao ≃	184	53.54 N	97.58 W
Gunisao Lake ⊜	184	53.33 N	96.15 W
Gunjrauliya	124	26.35 N	84.34 E
Gun Lake ⊜	216	42.37 N	85.32 W
Gunma	94	36.24 N	139.00 E
Gunnar	176	59.23 N	108.53 W
Günnarijn	102	45.38 N	102.01 E
Gunnarn	26	65.00 N	17.40 E
Gunnbjørn Fjeld ∧	16	68.55 N	29.53 W
Gunnebo	26	57.43 N	16.32 E
Gunnedah	166	30.59 S	150.15 E
Gunning Island I	276	40.22 N	73.59 W
Gunnislake	42	50.31 N	4.12 W
Gunnison, Co., U.S.	200	38.32 N	106.55 W
Gunnison, Ut,. U.S.	200	39.09 N	111.49 W
Gunnison ≃	200	39.03 N	108.35 W
Gunnison, Lake Fork ≃	200	38.28 N	107.19 W
Gunnison, North Fork ≃	200	38.47 N	107.50 W
Gunn Peak ∧	224	47.49 N	121.27 W
Gunong Mulu National Park ♠	112	4.10 N	114.55 E
Gunpowder Creek ≃, Austl.	166	19.14 S	139.58 E
Gunpowder Creek ≃, Ky., U.S.	218	38.53 N	84.47 W
Gunpowder Falls ≃	208	39.24 N	76.22 W
Gunpowder Falls State Park ♠	208	39.37 N	76.40 W
Gunpowder River c	208	39.22 N	76.22 W
Gunsan → Kunsan	98	35.58 N	126.41 E
Gunskirchen	60	48.08 N	13.57 E
Gunston Cove c	208	38.40 N	77.09 W
Guntakal	122	15.10 N	77.23 E
Güntersberge	54	51.38 N	10.59 E
Guntersblum	56	49.47 N	8.21 E
Guntersdorf	61	48.39 N	16.03 E
Guntersville	194	34.21 N	86.17 W
Guntersville Dam ⬥[6]	194	34.13 N	86.23 W
Guntersville Lake ⊜[1]	194	34.45 N	86.03 W
Guntingsaga	114	2.33 N	99.39 E
Guntramsdorf, Öst.	61	48.03 N	16.19 E
Guntramsdorf, Öst.	264b	48.03 N	16.19 E
Guntung	114	1.38 N	101.34 E
Guntūr	122	16.18 N	80.27 E
Gunungkencana	115a	6.34 S	106.04 E
Gunungmegang	112	3.27 S	103.52 E
Gunungsahilan	112	0.06 N	101.18 E
Gunungsitoli	114	1.17 N	97.37 E
Gunungtua	114	1.30 N	99.37 E
Gunupur	122	19.05 N	83.49 E
Gunyidi	162	30.08 S	116.04 E
Günyüzü	130	39.24 N	31.50 E
Günz ≃	58	48.27 N	10.16 E
Gunza ≃	152	11.10 S	13.50 E
Günzburg	58	48.27 N	10.16 E
Gunzenhausen	56	49.07 N	10.45 E
Gunzigou	104	41.31 N	123.58 E
Guo ≃	100	32.57 N	117.14 E
Guobei	107	29.33 N	105.08 E
Guodian	106	30.27 N	120.33 E
Guoji	100	32.59 N	113.06 E
Guojiadian	104	41.51 N	121.30 E
Guojiajiang	106	32.17 N	120.50 E
Guojiatun, Zhg.	98	41.31 N	117.02 E
Guojiatun, Zhg.	104	42.00 N	122.51 E
Guojiatun, Zhg.	104	40.52 N	122.04 E
Guojiawopeng	104	42.03 N	122.46 E
Guojiayao	105	40.37 N	115.39 E
Guojiayuan	106	32.10 N	120.35 E
Guojiga	86	43.47 N	80.48 E
Guoleizhuang	98	40.44 N	114.36 E
Guolutan	100	32.04 N	115.40 E
Guosu	98	38.24 N	114.00 E
Guoyang	100	33.32 N	116.12 E
Guoyangzhen	102	38.54 N	112.50 E
Guozhuang	98	35.25 N	117.10 E
Guozhuangmiao	106	31.49 N	119.01 E
Gupei	98	34.09 N	117.54 E
Gupis	123	36.14 N	73.26 E
Gura	80	57.18 N	51.25 E
Gura, Wādī V	140	17.28 N	35.10 E
Gurabo	240m	18.16 N	65.58 W
Guraferda	144	6.51 N	35.04 E
Gura-Galbena	78	46.43 N	28.42 E
Gurage ∧	144	8.24 N	38.24 E
Gurahonț	38	46.16 N	22.21 E
Gura Humorului	38	47.33 N	25.54 E
Gurais	123	34.38 N	74.50 E
Guran	88	54.46 N	100.38 E
Gurara ≃	150	8.12 N	6.41 E
Gurban Anggir	102	37.45 N	97.30 E
Gurban Obo	102	43.14 N	112.28 E
Gurdāspur	123	32.02 N	75.31 E
Gurdon	194	33.55 N	93.09 W
Gurdžaani	84	41.43 N	45.48 E
Güre	130	38.39 N	29.10 E
Gurejev	80	47.21 N	43.16 E
G'urg'an	84	40.23 N	50.19 E
Gurgaon	124	28.28 N	77.02 E
Gurgei, Jabal ∧	140	13.50 N	24.19 E
Gurghiului, Munții ⋏	38	46.41 N	25.12 E
Gurgó ∧[2]	61	46.31 N	16.50 E
Gurguéia ≃	250	6.50 S	43.24 W
Gurgur	144	7.48 N	41.32 E
Gurha	120	25.11 N	71.40 E
Guri	144	7.27 N	40.36 E
Guri, Embalse ⊜[1]	246	7.30 N	62.50 W
Gurig National Park ♠	164	11.25 S	132.15 E
Gurjev	80	47.07 N	51.56 E
Gurjev □[4]	86	47.10 N	54.00 E
Gurjevo	82	54.42 N	36.28 E
Gurjevsk, S.S.S.R.	76	54.47 N	20.38 E
Gurjevsk, S.S.S.R.	86	54.17 N	85.56 E
Gurk	61	46.52 N	14.18 E
Gurk ≃	61	46.36 N	14.31 E
Gurk ⛫[1]	61	46.52 N	14.15 E
Gurktaler Alpen ⋏	64	46.55 N	14.00 E
Gūr Kūh ∧	128	26.06 N	58.28 E
Gurla Mandhata → Guerla Mandata Shan ∧	120	30.26 N	81.20 E
Gurlevo	76	59.28 N	28.54 E
Gurnee	216	42.22 N	87.54 W
Gurnet Point ›	283	42.01 N	70.34 W
Gurnley Football Ground ♠	262	53.47 N	2.14 W
Gürpınar	128	38.18 N	43.25 E
Gurror	174q	9.27 N	138.04 E
Gursarai	124	25.37 N	79.11 E
Gurskoje	89	50.21 N	138.12 E
Gurskøy I	26	62.15 N	5.41 E
Gürsu	130	40.13 N	29.12 E
Gurué	154	15.25 S	36.58 E
Guru Har Sahāi	123	30.43 N	74.25 E
Gurumeti ≃	154	2.05 S	33.57 E
Gurun, Malay.	114	5.49 N	100.29 E
Gürün, Tür.	130	38.43 N	37.17 E
Gurupá	250	1.25 S	51.39 W
Gurupi	250	11.43 S	49.04 W
Gurupi ≃	250	1.13 S	46.06 W
Guru Sikhar ∧	120	24.39 N	72.46 E
Gurvanbulag	88	47.38 N	103.31 E
Gurvansajchan	102	45.32 N	107.00 E
Gurvan Sajchan uul ⋏	102	43.50 N	103.30 E
Gurvantes	102	43.26 N	101.36 E
Gurzuf	78	44.33 N	34.17 E
Gus' ≃	80	55.00 N	41.11 E
Gusar	85	39.28 N	67.50 E
Gušari	85	38.55 N	68.51 E
Gusarka	78	47.23 N	36.31 E
Gus'atin	78	49.05 N	26.11 E
Gusau	150	12.12 N	6.40 E
Gus'-Chrustal'nyj	80	55.37 N	40.40 E
Guselka	80	50.27 N	45.09 E
Güsen	54	52.21 N	11.59 E
Gusen ≃	61	48.15 N	14.30 E
Gusev, S.S.S.R.	76	54.36 N	22.12 E
Gusev, S.S.S.R.	78	48.27 N	40.32 E
Gusevo	76	56.06 N	33.21 E
Gusevskij	80	55.40 N	40.34 E
Gushan, Zhg.	98	39.53 N	123.36 E
Gushan, Zhg.	98	36.30 N	116.53 E
Gushan, Zhg.	106	31.44 N	120.33 E
Gu Shan ∧, Zhg.	100	26.05 N	119.22 E
Gu Shan ∧, Zhg.	104	41.18 N	120.35 E
Gushanbeizifu	104	42.10 N	120.30 E
Gushankou	105	39.38 N	115.49 E
Gushantun	89	48.18 N	123.47 E
Gushanzi, Zhg.	98	40.22 N	120.03 E
Gushanzi, Zhg.	104	41.03 N	123.03 E
Gushi, Zhg.	100	28.34 N	119.24 E
Gushi, Zhg.	100	32.12 N	115.41 E
Gushiago	150	9.55 N	0.12 W
Gushikami	174m	26.07 N	127.45 E
Gushikawa	174m	26.21 N	127.52 E
Gushu, Zhg.	104	42.36 N	123.26 E
Gushu, Zhg.	105	39.55 N	117.35 E
Gushuji	98	34.15 N	115.48 E
Gusi	112	6.07 N	117.08 E
Gusino	76	54.44 N	31.22 E
Gusinoje, ozero ⊜	88	51.12 N	106.24 E
Gusinoje Ozero	88	51.09 N	106.10 E
Gusinoozersk	88	51.17 N	106.30 E
Guskef	85	39.02 N	69.20 E
Guskhara	126	23.30 N	87.45 E

Symbol	English	Deutsch	Español	Français	Português
≃	River	Fluß	Río	Rivière	Rio
≊	Canal	Kanal	Canal	Canal	Canal
⌊	Waterfall, Rapids	Wasserfall, Stromschnellen	Cascada, Rápidos	Chute d'eau, Rapides	Cascata, Rápidos
⋓	Strait	Meeresstraße	Estrecho	Détroit	Estreito
c	Bay, Gulf	Bucht, Golf	Bahía, Golfo	Baie, Golfe	Baía, Golfo
⊜	Lake, Lakes	See, Seen	Lago, Lagos	Lac, Lacs	Lago, Lagos
≡	Swamp	Sumpf	Pantano	Marais	Pântano
⌂	Ice Features, Glacier	Eis- und Gletscherformen	Accidentes Glaciales	Formes glaciaires	Acidentes glaciares
⍑	Other Hydrographic Features	Andere Hydrographische Objekte	Otros Elementos Hidrográficos	Autres données hydrographiques	Outros acidentes hidrográficos
✣	Submarine Features	Untermeerische Objekte	Accidentes Submarinos	Formes de relief sous-marin	Acidentes submarinos
□	Political Unit	Politische Einheit	Unidad Politica	Entité politique	Unidade política
⛫	Cultural Institution	Kulturelle Institution	Institución Cultural	Institution culturelle	Institução cultural
⊥	Historical Site	Historische Stätte	Sitio Histórico	Site historique	Sitio histórico
♠	Recreational Site	Erholungs- und Ferienort	Sitio de Recreo	Centre de loisirs	Area de Lazer
⊠	Airport	Flughafen	Aeropuerto	Aéroport	Aeroporto
■	Military Installation	Militäranlage	Instalación Militar	Installation militaire	Instalação militar
⬥	Miscellaneous	Verschiedenes	Misceláneo	Divers	Diversos

ENGLISH Name	Page	Lat.°′	Long.°′	DEUTSCH Name	Seite	Breite°′	Länge°′ E = Ost
Haiyang Dao **I**	98	39.02 N	123.14 E	Halhūl	132	31.35 N	35.07 E
Haiyuan	102	36.35 N	105.40 E	Hali **≃** [4]	142	18.42 N	41.20 E
Haizhou, Zhg.	98	34.34 N	119.11 E	Haliburton	212	45.03 N	78.31 W
Haizhou, Zhg.	100	22.40 N	113.10 E	Haliburton **□** [6]	212	44.10 N	78.30 W
Haizhoumiao	102	42.00 N	121.39 E	Haliburton Lake **⊜**	212	45.12 N	78.24 W

(Right-hand English/Deutsch cross-reference index — full data table, abbreviated here for legibility)

Column 1

Gus′-Khrustal′nyy → Gus′-Chrustal′nyj 80 55.37 N 40.40 E
Guskube 175d 24.45 N 125.26 E
Gusong 102 28.18 N 105.14 E
Gusgoni 71 39.32 N 8.37 E
Gussago 64 45.35 N 10.09 E
Gusselby 40 59.39 N 15.14 E
Güssing 61 47.04 N 16.20 E
Gussola 64 45.00 N 10.20 E
Gusswerk 61 47.45 N 15.18 E
Gustav Holm, Kap ► 176 67.00 N 34.00 W
Gustavo A. Madero □ [7]
Gustavo A. Madero 286a 19.29 N 99.08 W
Gustavo A. Madero ◆ [8] 286a 19.29 N 99.07 W
Gustavsberg 40 59.19 N 18.23 E
Gustavus 180 58.25 N 135.44 W
Güsten 54 51.49 N 11.35 E
Gustia 272b 22.59 N 88.26 E
Gustine, Ca., U.S. 226 37.15 N 120.59 W
Gustine, Tx., U.S. 196 31.51 N 98.24 W
Gustorf 56 51.04 N 6.34 E
Güstrow 54 53.48 N 12.10 E
Gusum 26 58.16 N 16.29 E
Gus′-Železnyj 80 55.03 N 41.10 E
Gutach 88 48.15 N 8.13 E
Gutaj 88 49.59 N 108.12 E
Gutanggou 104 42.02 N 124.10 E
Gutara **≃** 88 54.50 N 97.23 E
Gutarskij chrebet **⋌** 88 54.30 N 97.40 E
Gutau 61 48.25 N 14.37 E
Gutcher 46 60.40 N 1.00 W
Gutenfels, Burg **⊥** 56 50.07 N 7.46 E
Guten Hoffnung, Kap der → Good Hope, Cape of ► 158 34.24 S 18.30 E
Güterfelde 264a 52.22 N 13.12 E
Gütersloh 52 51.54 N 8.23 E
Guthrie, In., U.S. 218 38.59 N 86.31 W
Guthrie, Ky., U.S. 194 36.38 N 87.09 W
Guthrie, Ok., U.S. 196 35.52 N 97.25 W
Guthrie, Tx., U.S. 196 33.37 N 100.19 W
Guthrie Center 198 41.40 N 94.30 W
Guthrie Lake **⊜** 184 55.17 N 100.38 W
Gutian, Zhg. 100 25.43 N 116.57 E
Gutian, Zhg. 100 26.36 N 118.46 E
Gutian, Zhg. 100 25.15 N 116.46 E
Gutian **≃** 100 26.22 N 118.42 E
Gutiérrez 248 19.25 S 63.34 W
Gutiérrez Zamora 234 20.27 N 97.05 W
Gutland ◆ [1] 56 49.40 N 6.10 E
Gutob Bay **C** 116 12.09 N 119.54 E
Guton, gora **▲** 84 41.51 N 46.45 E
Gutorfölde 61 46.39 N 16.44 E
Guttannen 58 46.39 N 8.18 E
Guttau 54 51.15 N 14.34 E
Guttenberg, Ia., U.S. 190 42.47 N 91.05 W
Guttenberg, N.J., U.S. 276 40.47 N 74.00 W
Guttentag → Dobrodzień
Guttstadt → Dobre Miasto 30 53.59 N 20.25 E
Gutu 158 19.38 S 31.10 E
Gutujevskij, ostrov **I** 265a 59.54 N 30.14 E
Gutulia Nasjonalpark ◆
Guty 78 50.08 N 35.21 E
Gützkow 54 53.56 N 13.24 E
Güvem 130 40.36 N 32.40 E
Guwähäti 120 26.10 N 91.45 E
Guxhagen 56 51.12 N 9.28 E
Guxi 107 25.09 N 118.08 E
Guxian, Zhg. 98 37.35 N 121.09 E
Guxian, Zhg. 102 32.26 N 113.37 E
Guxian, Zhg. 102 27.09 N 115.31 E
Guxiandu 100 29.06 N 116.50 E
Guxiansi 100 32.01 N 116.20 E
Guxiong 104 31.55 N 118.38 E
Guy 222 29.21 N 95.47 W
Guyana □ [1], S.A. 242 5.00 N 59.00 W
Guyana □ [1], S.A. 246 5.00 N 59.00 W
Guyancourt 261 48.46 N 2.04 E
Guyancourt, Aéroport de **☒** 261 48.45 N 2.05 E
Guyandotte **≃** 188 38.26 N 82.23 W
Guyane → Guyana □ [1] 246 5.00 N 59.00 W
Guyane française → French Guiana □ [2] 250 4.00 N 53.00 W
Guyang, Zhg. 100 34.58 N 114.58 E
Guyang, Zhg. 102 41.03 N 110.03 E
Guye 105 39.44 N 118.25 E
Guy Fawkes River National Park ◆ 166 30.02 S 152.18 E
Guyi, Zhg. 100 25.38 N 118.47 E
Guyi, Zhg. 107 30.22 N 118.32 E
Guyin 102 23.58 N 105.47 E
Guymon 196 36.40 N 101.28 W
Guyonne, Ruisseau la **≃** 261 48.49 N 1.52 E
Guyra 166 30.12 S 151.40 E
Guysborough 186 45.23 N 61.30 W
Guys Mills 214 41.38 N 79.59 W
Guyton 222 32.20 N 81.23 W
Guyuan (Pingdingbu), Zhg. 98 41.40 N 115.41 E
Guyuan, Zhg. 102 36.01 N 106.17 E
Guzar 72 38.36 N 66.15 E
Güzel **▲** 84 34.43 N 42.51 E
Güzelbahçe 130 38.21 N 26.54 E
Güzelsu 130 37.05 N 30.32 E
Güzelyurt, Kıbrıs 130 35.12 N 32.59 E
Güzelyurt, Tür. 130 38.17 N 34.23 E
Güzelyurt Körfezi **C** 130 35.10 N 32.50 E
Guzhang 102 28.31 N 109.57 E
Guzhen, Zhg. 100 22.37 N 113.11 E
Guzhen, Zhg. 100 33.19 N 117.21 E
Guzhu 100 30.32 N 119.39 E
Guzmán, Méx. 232 31.13 N 107.27 W
Guzmán → Ciudad Guzmán, Méx. 234 19.41 N 103.29 W
Guzmán, Laguna de **⊜** 232 31.20 N 107.30 W
Gvardejsk 78 54.39 N 21.05 E
Gvardejskoje, S.S.S.R. 78 48.44 N 35.19 E
Gvardejskoje, S.S.S.R. 78 49.20 N 26.42 E
Gvardejskoje, S.S.S.R. 78 45.07 N 34.01 E
Gvozdec 78 48.36 N 25.17 E
Gwa 110 17.36 N 94.35 E
Gwabegar 166 30.36 S 148.58 E
Gwadabawa 150 13.20 N 5.15 E
Gwädar 150 25.07 N 62.19 E
Gwagwada 150 10.15 N 7.15 E
Gwai 154 19.15 S 27.42 E
Gwai **≃** 154 17.59 S 26.52 E
Gwalangu **≃** 152 2.19 N 18.11 E
Gwaldam 120 30.00 N 79.34 E
Gwäl Haidarzai 128 30.44 N 68.48 E
Gwalia 162 28.55 S 121.20 E
Gwalior 120 26.13 N 78.10 E
Gwambygine 168a 31.59 S 116.48 E
Gwanda 154 20.57 S 29.00 E
Gwandu 150 12.30 N 4.41 E
Gwane 152 4.43 N 25.50 E
Gwangjang Bridge ◆ [5] 271b 37.33 N 127.05 E
Gwangju → Kwangju 98 35.09 N 126.54 E
Gwasaro 110 11.56 N 7.56 E
Gwasero 150 9.29 N 7.30 E
Gwash **≃** 42 52.39 N 0.39 W
Gwätar Bay **C** 128 25.04 N 61.36 E
Gwatt 58 46.43 N 7.38 E

Column 2

Gwaun **≃** 42 52.00 N 4.58 W
Gwda **≃** 30 53.04 N 16.44 E
Gweebarra **≃** 48 54.50 N 8.20 W
Gweebarra Bay **C** 48 54.52 N 8.20 W
Gweedore 48 55.03 N 8.14 W
Gweesalia 48 54.07 N 9.54 W
Gwelo **≃** 154 18.45 S 28.36 E
Gwembe 154 16.30 S 27.35 E
Gwendraeth Fâch **≃** 42 51.44 N 4.18 W
Gwendraeth Fawr **≃** 42 51.43 N 4.18 W
Gwent □ [6] 42 51.43 N 2.57 W
Gweru 154 19.27 S 29.49 E
Gweta 156 20.10 S 25.18 E
Gwinhurst 285 39.47 N 75.29 W
Gwinn 190 46.16 N 87.26 W
Gwinner 198 46.13 N 97.39 W
Gwobu 154 2.37 N 26.13 E
Gwongorella National Park ◆ 171a 28.10 S 153.17 E
Gwydir **≃** 166 29.27 S 149.48 E
Gwynedd 285 40.12 N 75.15 W
Gwynedd □ [6] 28 53.00 N 4.00 W
Gwynedd Square 285 40.13 N 75.18 W
Gwynedd Valley 285 40.13 N 75.15 W
Gwynneville 218 39.39 N 85.38 W
Gwynn Island **I** 208 37.30 N 76.17 W
Gwynn Oak Amusement Park ◆ 284b 39.20 N 76.43 W
Gwynns Falls **≃** 284b 39.16 N 76.41 W
Gwynns Falls Park ◆ 284b 39.18 N 76.41 W
Gyál 264c 47.23 N 19.14 E
Gya La **⋊** 124 28.44 N 84.40 E
Gyáli-patak **≃** 264c 47.24 N 19.07 E
Gyangtse → Gyangzê 120 28.57 N 89.35 E
Gyangzê 120 28.57 N 89.35 E
Gyaring Co **⊜** 120 31.10 N 88.15 E
Gyaring Hu **⊜** 102 34.53 N 97.58 E
Gybdan 80 56.33 N 51.39 E
Gyda 74 70.52 N 78.30 E
Gydanskaja guba **C** 74 71.20 N 76.30 E
Gydanskij poluostrov **⊁** 74 70.50 N 79.00 E
Gyêbu 124 3.03 S 133.51 E
Gyemo Chen **▲** 124 27.20 N 88.52 E
Gyeongbog Palace **⊻** 271b 37.36 N 126.57 E
Gyeongju → Kyŏngju 120 35.51 N 129.14 E
Gyirong, Zhg. 120 28.29 N 85.20 E
Gyirong, Zhg. 120 28.57 N 85.15 E
Gyldenløves Fjord **C** [2] 176 64.30 N 41.30 W
Gyldenløveshøj **▲** [2] 41 55.33 N 11.52 E
Gylling 41 55.53 N 10.11 E
Gymea Bay 274a 34.02 S 151.07 E
Gym Peak **▲** 196 32.05 N 107.35 W
Gympie 166 26.11 S 152.40 E
Gyóngyáosgauk 110 18.13 N 95.39 E
Gyóda 94 36.08 N 139.28 E
Gyoma 30 46.56 N 20.50 E
Gyöngyös 30 47.47 N 19.56 E
Gyöngyös **≃** 61 47.16 N 16.55 E
Györ 30 47.42 N 17.38 E
Gyôr-Sopron □ [6] 30 47.35 N 17.15 E
Gypsey Race **≃** 44 54.05 N 0.12 W
Gypsum, Co., U.S. 200 39.38 N 106.57 W
Gypsum, Ks., U.S. 198 38.42 N 97.25 W
Gypsum, Oh., U.S. 214 41.29 N 82.52 W
Gypsum Creek **≃**, U.S. 200 37.09 N 109.52 W
Gypsum Creek **≃**, Ks., U.S. 198 38.51 N 97.25 W
Gypsum Hills **⋌** [2] 196 36.25 N 99.20 W
Gypsum Point ► 176 61.53 N 114.35 W
Gypsumville 184 51.45 N 98.35 W
Gyrbovec 78 46.40 N 29.21 E
Gysinge 40 60.17 N 16.53 E
Gyttorp 40 59.31 N 14.58 E
Gyula 30 46.39 N 21.17 E
Gyulafehérvár → Alba-Iulia 38 46.04 N 23.35 E
Gyzylsu 82 55.56 N 34.33 E
Gžatsk 82 55.42 N 78.11 E
Gžel 82 55.36 N 38.24 E
Gžatsk → Gagarin 76 55.33 N 35.00 E

H

Haag → 's-Gravenhage, Ned. 52 52.06 N 4.18 E
Haag, Öst. 61 48.07 N 14.34 E
Haag am Hausruck 61 48.11 N 13.38 E
Hagen 52 47.38 N 7.40 E
Haag in Oberbayern 58 48.10 N 12.11 E
Haaksbergen 52 52.09 N 6.44 E
Haalenberg 156 26.52 S 15.30 E
Haaltert 52 50.54 N 4.00 E
Haamstede 52 51.11 N 7.00 E
Haapajärvi 26 63.45 N 25.20 E
Haapajärvi 26 63.33 N 27.00 E
Haapamäki 26 62.15 N 24.28 E
Haapavesi 26 64.08 N 25.22 E
Haapiti 174s 17.34 S 149.52 W
Haapsalu 76 58.56 N 23.33 E
Haar 58 48.06 N 11.44 E
Haar **▲** 263 51.26 N 7.13 E
Ha'Arava (Wādī al-Jayb) **V**, Asia 132 30.58 N 35.24 E
Ha'Arava (Wādī al-'Arabah) **V**, Asia 132 30.10 N 35.10 E
Haardt ► 56 49.15 N 8.00 E
Haaren, B.R.D. 52 51.34 N 8.44 E
Haaren, Ned. 52 51.36 N 5.12 E
Haarlem, Ned. 52 52.23 N 4.38 E
Haarlem, S. Afr. 158 33.46 S 23.23 E
Haarlemmermeer ◆ [1] 52 52.18 N 4.40 E
Haarstrang **≃** [1] 52 51.35 N 8.10 E
Haarzopf ◆ [8] 263 51.25 N 6.58 E
Haast 172 43.53 S 169.03 E
Haast **≃** 172 43.50 S 169.02 E
Haast Bluff 162 23.30 S 131.50 E
Haast Pass **⋊** 172 44.06 S 169.21 E
Haasts Bluff Reserve ◆ [4] 162 23.30 S 131.50 E
Haatinao, Pointe ► 174x 9.47 S 138.51 W
Haava, Canal **⋊** 174s 9.53 S 139.04 W
Hab **≃** 128 24.52 N 66.41 E
Habahe 86 46.51 N 86.15 E
Habaqi, Zhg. 102 42.36 N 122.52 E
Habartov 54 50.11 N 12.35 E
Habay, Harrach ► [9] 144 16.40 N 49.40 E
Habaswein 154 1.00 N 39.29 E
Habay-la-Neuve 52 49.44 N 5.39 E
Habbānīyah, Hawr al- **⊜** 128 33.17 N 43.30 E
Habbūsh 132 33.24 N 35.29 E
Hab Chauki 128 24.53 N 66.53 E
Haberschwerdt → Bystrzyca Kłodzka 30 50.18 N 16.38 E
Habère-Poche 58 46.16 N 6.29 E
Haberfield 274a 33.53 S 151.08 E
Habermehl Peak **▲** 9 71.49 S 6.38 E
Habib, Wādī **V** 140 19.36 N 39.01 E
Habiganj 120 24.23 N 91.25 E
Habikino 94 34.33 N 135.36 E
Hablah 140 18.54 N 42.33 E
Habo 40 57.55 N 14.04 E
Habob, Wādī **V** 140 18.07 N 35.01 E

Column 3

Habomai-shotō → Malaja Kuril′skaja Gr′ada **II** 92a 43.30 N 146.10 E
Haboro 92a 44.22 N 141.42 E
Häbra 126 22.50 N 88.38 E
Habsburg **⊥** 58 47.28 N 8.13 E
Habsheim 58 47.44 N 7.25 E
Habu 270 34.27 N 135.24 E
Habur (Nahr al-Khābūr) **≃** 130 35.08 N 40.26 E
Habutaki 270 34.25 N 135.26 E
Hache, Lac la **⊜** 182 51.50 N 121.30 W
Hachen 56 51.22 N 7.59 E
Hachenburg 56 50.39 N 7.50 E
Hachi 120 27.46 N 94.01 E
Hachijō 270 34.37 N 135.48 E
Hachijō-jima **I** 93 33.05 N 139.48 E
Hachiman 94 35.45 N 136.57 E
Hachiman → Ōmi-hachiman 94 35.08 N 136.06 E
Hachiman-misaki ► 94 35.08 N 140.19 E
Hachinohe 92a 40.30 N 141.29 E
Hachiōji 94 35.39 N 139.20 E
Hachmühlen 52 52.10 N 9.28 E
Hachuekbektas 130 38.57 N 34.35 E
Hacienda Heights 228 34.00 N 117.57 W
Hacienda Miravalles 236 10.41 N 85.14 W
Hachamza 130 41.05 N 34.28 E
Hacilar 130 38.39 N 35.27 E
Hack, Mount **▲** 164 30.46 S 138.48 E
Hacks 26 62.56 N 14.31 E
Hackberry, Az., U.S. 200 35.22 N 113.43 W
Hackberry, La., U.S. 194 29.59 N 93.20 W
Hackberry Creek **≃**, Ks., U.S. 198 38.48 N 100.03 W
Hackberry Creek **≃**, U.S. 222 31.53 N 97.12 W
Hackensack 210 40.53 N 74.02 W
Hackensack **≃** 276 40.43 N 74.06 W
Hackettstown 48 52.52 N 6.33 W
Hackett, Ar., U.S. 194 35.11 N 94.24 W
Hackett, Pa., U.S. 279b 40.15 N 80.01 W
Hacketts 260 51.45 N 0.05 W
Hackettstown 210 40.52 N 74.48 W
Hacking **≃** 274a 34.04 S 151.08 E
Hacking, Port **C** 274a 34.05 S 151.09 E
Hackney **≃** 194 34.16 N 87.49 W
Hackney 260 51.33 N 0.03 W
Hack Point 208 39.27 N 75.52 W
Häckren **≃** 26 63.22 N 14.00 E
Haco 152 10.12 S 15.44 E
Hacreş Dağları **≃** 130 38.38 N 41.37 E
Hadāli 123 32.18 N 72.12 E
Hadaliya 140 16.10 N 36.06 E
Hadan, Harrat **≃** [9] 144 21.30 N 41.23 E
HaDarom □ [5] 132 30.40 N 34.50 E
Hadbat, Ra's al- ► 140 22.04 N 36.54 E
HaDarom □ [5] 132 30.40 N 34.50 E
Haddeb 88 49.40 N 119.40 E
Hadayingzi 104 42.22 N 121.40 E
Hadd, Ra's al- ► 146 22.32 N 59.48 E
Haddad, Ouadi **V** 146 14.40 N 18.46 E
Haddādīn, Qārat al- ◆ 142 30.04 N 30.58 E
Haddam, Ct., U.S. 207 41.28 N 72.30 W
Haddam, Ks., U.S. 198 39.51 N 97.18 W
Haddenham, Eng., U.K. 42 51.46 N 0.56 W
Haddenham, Eng., U.K. 42 52.22 N 0.09 E
Haddock 55 55.58 N 2.47 W
Haddock 192 33.01 N 83.25 W
Haddon Downs 166 26.21 S 140.50 E
Haddonfield 208 39.53 N 75.02 W
Haddon Heights 208 39.52 N 75.03 W
Haddon Hills 285 39.54 N 75.03 W
Hadejia 150 12.30 N 9.59 E
Hadejia **≃** 134 12.50 N 10.51 E
Haden, Land □ [1] 52 53.45 N 8.45 E
Hadera 132 32.26 N 34.55 E
Hadera **≃** 132 32.27 N 34.53 E
Hadersdorf □ [8] 264b 48.13 N 16.14 E
Hadersfeld 264b 48.20 N 16.15 E
Haderslev 41 55.15 N 9.30 E
Haderslev Fjord **C** 41 55.17 N 9.40 E
Hadfield, Austl. 274b 37.42 S 144.58 E
Hadfield, Eng., U.K. 262 53.28 N 1.58 W
Hadībū 118 12.38 N 54.02 E
Hadim 130 36.59 N 32.28 E
Hadjout 142 36.31 N 2.25 E
Hadleigh, Eng., U.K. 42 51.33 N 0.36 E
Hadleigh, Eng., U.K. 42 52.03 N 0.57 E
Hadley Castle **⊥** 260 51.33 N 0.36 E
Hadley, Eng., U.K. 42 52.42 N 2.29 W
Hadley, Ma., U.S. 207 42.20 N 72.35 W
Hadley, Mi., U.S. 216 42.57 N 83.24 W
Hadley, N.Y., U.S. 210 43.19 N 73.50 W
Hadley, Pa., U.S. 214 41.25 N 80.14 W
Hadley Bay **C** 176 72.30 N 107.45 W
Hadley Creek **≃** 219 39.37 N 91.12 W
Hadlock 208 38.01 N 122.45 W
Hadlow 260 51.14 N 0.20 E
Hadlyme 207 41.25 N 72.24 W
Hadong, Taehan 98 35.05 N 127.44 E
Ha Dong, Viet. 110 20.58 N 105.46 E
Hadramawt ◆ [1] 144 17.34 N 49.52 E
Hadrian's Wall ◆ [1] 144 55.00 N 2.30 W
Hadsten 41 56.20 N 10.03 E
Hadsund 41 56.43 N 10.07 E
Hadyai → Hat Yai 110 7.01 N 100.28 E
Haeju 98 38.02 N 125.42 E
Haengyon-ni ◆ [8] 271b 37.35 N 126.49 E
Haena 229b 22.14 N 159.34 W
Haena Point ► 229b 22.14 N 159.34 W
Haenertsburg 156 24.00 S 29.50 E
Haenam 98 34.34 N 126.35 E
Haenao 102 42.23 N 122.52 E
Hafeïra, Oued el **V** 148 25.18 N 10.48 W
Hafelekarspitze **▲** 64 47.19 N 11.23 E
Haffen-Mehr 52 51.44 N 6.28 E
Haffouz 184 52.43 S 107.21 W
Hafik 130 39.52 N 37.24 E
Hafira, Qā' al- **⊜** 132 30.16 N 36.14 E
Häfirat al-'Ayda 128 26.26 N 39.10 E
Hafit, Jabal **▲** 146 24.03 N 55.46 E
Hāfiz, Bi'r **⊤** [4] 128 30.51 N 29.40 E
Häflong 120 25.10 N 93.01 E
Hafnarfjördur 24a 64.03 N 21.56 W
Haft Gel 128 31.27 N 49.27 E
Hafun, Ras ► 144 10.27 N 51.24 E
Haga, Nihon 94 36.32 N 140.04 E
Haga, Nihon 95 35.09 N 134.33 E
Hagachi-zaki ► 94 34.31 N 138.45 E
Hagal 132 32.46 N 34.59 E
HaGalil (Galilee) □ [9] 132 32.47 N 35.32 E
Hagan 192 32.08 N 81.56 W
Hagari **≃** 122 15.30 N 76.44 E
Hagar Shores 216 42.13 N 86.22 W
Hagarstown 219 39.01 N 89.10 W
Hagari **≃** 122 15.30 N 76.44 E
Hagberg ◆ [2] 54 52.08 N 12.32 E
Hagelberg **▲** 55 52.08 N 12.32 E
Hagemeister Island **I** 180 58.40 N 161.00 W
Hagen, B.R.D. 52 51.21 N 7.28 E
Hagen, B.R.D. 56 51.22 N 7.28 E
Hagen-Gebirge **≃** 64 47.32 N 13.07 E
Hagenow 54 53.26 N 11.11 E
Hagenwerder 54 51.04 N 14.58 E

Column 4

Hagere Hiywet 144 8.59 N 37.51 E
Hagere Selam 144 6.29 N 38.31 E
Hagerman, Id., U.S. 202 42.48 N 114.53 W
Hagerman, N.M., U.S. 196 33.06 N 104.19 W
Hagerstown, In., U.S. 218 39.54 N 85.09 W
Hagerstown, Md., U.S. 188 39.38 N 77.43 W
Hagersville 212 42.58 N 80.03 W
Hagfors 32 43.40 N 0.35 W
Hagfors 40 60.02 N 13.42 E
Haggen **≃** 40 60.06 N 15.13 E
Haggetts Pond **⊜** 283 42.39 N 71.12 W
Haggin, Mount **▲** 202 46.05 N 113.05 W
Hagi 126 34.24 N 131.25 E
Ha Giang 110 22.50 N 104.59 E
Hagitani 270 34.54 N 135.35 E
Hagiwara 94 35.45 N 136.57 E
Hagley 42 52.26 N 2.08 W
Hagley Museum **⊻** 285 39.46 N 75.35 W
Hagondange 56 49.15 N 6.10 E
HaGosherim 132 33.14 N 35.37 E
Hagudo-do 98 34.17 N 126.03 E
Hague, Sk., Can. 184 52.30 N 106.25 W
Hague, N.D., U.S. 198 46.01 N 99.59 W
Hague, Cap de la **⊁** 32 49.43 N 1.57 W
Haguenau 56 48.49 N 7.47 E
Hagues Peak **▲** 200 40.29 N 105.38 W
Hahaïa 157a 11.33 S 43.17 E
Hahajima-rettō **II** 26 26.37 N 142.10 E
Haharro, Uebi **≃** 144 1.37 N 44.13 E
Hähipur 272b 22.47 N 88.10 E
Hahira 192 30.59 N 83.22 W
Hahlen 52 52.18 N 8.50 E
Hahn am See 56 50.31 N 7.53 E
Hahndorf 60 49.37 N 10.40 E
Hahnenberg 52 51.13 N 7.00 E
Hahnbach 168b 35.03 S 138.49 E
Hahnenkamm ▲ 64 47.25 N 12.22 E
Hahnenklee-Bockswiese 52 51.51 N 10.20 E
Hahnerberg 263 51.13 N 7.09 E
Hahnstätten 56 50.18 N 8.04 E
Hahntown 279b 40.19 N 79.44 W
Haho **≃** 150 6.17 N 1.23 E
Hahyŏn-ni 98 38.43 N 127.57 E
Hai **≃** 105 39.00 N 117.43 E
Hai'an 100 32.34 N 120.28 E
Haian Shanmo **≃** 100 23.25 N 121.25 E
Haibara, Nihon 94 34.44 N 138.13 E
Haibara, Nihon 94 34.30 N 135.57 E
Haibatpur 272a 28.37 N 77.26 E
Haibei 89 47.39 N 126.51 E
Haicheng, Zhg. 100 24.25 N 117.51 E
Haicheng, Zhg. 104 40.52 N 122.45 E
Haidargarh 124 26.37 N 81.22 E
Haidärpur **≃** [1] 272a 28.43 N 77.09 E
Haidenaab **≃** 60 49.36 N 12.08 E
Haiderabad → Hyderäbäd, India 122 17.23 N 78.29 E
Haiderabad → Hyderäbäd, Päk. 120 25.22 N 68.22 E
Haidershofen 61 48.05 N 14.28 E
Haidian 105 39.59 N 116.18 E
Haidinge 60 49.13 N 13.46 E
Haidmühle 60 48.48 N 13.32 E
Haidra 36 35.34 N 8.27 E
Haidstein ▲ 60 49.13 N 12.48 E
Haidun 100 26.23 N 121.49 E
Hai Duong 110 20.56 N 106.19 E
Haifa → Hefa 132 32.50 N 35.00 E
Haifa, Bay of → Hefa, Mifraz **C** 132 32.50 N 35.03 E
Haifeng 100 22.59 N 115.21 E
Haifuzhen 106 31.53 N 121.46 E
Haig 162 30.59 S 126.06 E
Haig, Mount **▲** 182 49.17 N 114.29 W
Haigerloch 60 49.28 N 8.04 E
Haigerloch 58 48.22 N 8.48 E
Haigh 262 53.35 N 2.36 W
Haighton Green 262 53.49 N 2.38 W
Haigler 198 40.01 N 101.56 W
Haikang 100 20.55 N 110.04 E
Haikou, Zhg. 102 20.03 N 110.19 E
Haikou, Zhg. 100 24.54 N 102.32 E
Haikou, Zhg. 102 28.20 N 120.06 E
Hai'il 128 27.33 N 41.42 E
Hailäkändi 120 24.41 N 92.34 E
Hailakändi 120 24.41 N 92.34 E
Hailar **≃** 88 49.30 N 117.55 E
Haile 192 48.13 N 121.00 E
Hailey, Id., U.S. 202 43.31 N 114.18 W
Hailey, N.D., U.S. 219 39.37 N 91.12 W
Haileybury 186 47.27 N 79.38 W
Hailin 98 44.35 S 129.22 E
Hailing Dao **I** 102 21.37 N 111.55 E
Hailong (Meihekou) 98 42.32 N 125.38 E
Hailsham 42 50.52 N 0.16 E
Hailun 88 47.28 N 126.58 E
Hailuoto 26 65.02 N 24.42 E
Hailuoto **I** 26 65.02 N 24.42 E
Haiman Tepesi ▲ 267b 41.27 N 29.10 E
Haimen, Zhg. 100 28.41 N 121.27 E
Haimen, Zhg. 106 31.55 N 121.10 E
Haimen Wan **C** 100 23.15 N 116.34 E
Haimhausen 58 48.19 N 11.34 E
Haiming 94 37.13 N 119.51 E
Haina 56 51.02 N 8.58 E
Hainan 110 19.00 N 109.30 E
Hainan → Hainan Dao **I** 110 19.00 N 109.30 E
Hainan Dao **I** 110 19.00 N 109.30 E
Hainault □ [8] 260 51.36 N 0.06 E
Hainaut □ [6] 52 50.30 N 3.50 E
Hainaut □ [8] 52 50.30 N 3.50 E
Hainburg an der Donau 61 48.09 N 16.57 E
Haines, Ak., U.S. 180 59.14 N 135.27 W
Haines, Or., U.S. 202 44.54 N 117.56 W
Haines City 192 28.06 N 81.37 W
Haines Junction 180 60.45 N 137.30 W
Hainesville 208 39.59 N 74.49 W
Hainewalde 54 50.55 N 14.42 E
Hainfeld 61 48.02 N 15.46 E
Hainich ◆ 54 51.05 N 10.27 E
Hainichen 54 50.58 N 13.08 E
Hainleite **⋌** 54 51.20 N 10.58 E
Hainsberg 54 50.59 N 13.38 E
Haiphong 110 20.52 N 106.41 E
Hai Phong 110 20.52 N 106.41 E
Haiqiao 100 31.47 N 121.19 E
Haiqing 98 43.53 N 132.10 E
Haitan Dao **I** 100 25.37 N 119.48 E
Haitangkou 102 22.05 N 110.52 E
Haitan Xia **⋊** 100 25.27 N 119.38 E
Haiti (Haiti) □ [1], N.A. 230 19.00 N 72.25 W
Haiti (Haiti) □ [1], N.A. 238 19.00 N 72.25 W
Haitou, Zhg. 102 19.51 N 109.13 E
Haitou, Zhg. 107 24.57 N 118.45 E
Haiwee Reservoirs **⊜[1]** 204 36.10 N 117.57 W
Haixing 100 38.15 N 117.30 E
Haiyan, Zhg. 100 30.31 N 120.55 E
Haiyan, Zhg. 102 36.54 N 100.59 E
Haiyang, Zhg. 98 36.46 N 121.10 E
Haiyang (Dongcun) 98 36.46 N 121.10 E
Halgān **≃** 40 60.16 N 13.27 E

Column 5 (Deutsch)

Halhül 132 31.35 N 35.07 E
Hali **≃** [4] 142 18.42 N 41.20 E
Haliburton 212 45.03 N 78.31 W
Haliburton □ [6] 212 44.10 N 78.30 W
Haliburton Lake **⊜** 212 45.12 N 78.24 W
Halibut Point ► 283 42.42 N 70.38 W
Halic (Golden Horn) **C** 267b 41.02 N 28.58 E
Halicarnassus **⊥** 130 37.03 N 27.23 E
Halidmand 212 42.56 N 79.51 W
Halifax, Austl. 166 18.33 S 146.18 E
Halifax, N.S., Can. 186 44.39 N 63.36 W
Halifax, Eng., U.K. 44 53.44 N 1.52 W
Halifax, Ma., U.S. 207 41.59 N 70.51 W
Halifax, N.C., U.S. 192 36.19 N 77.35 W
Halifax, Pa., U.S. 208 40.28 N 76.55 W
Halifax, Va., U.S. 208 36.46 N 78.56 W
Halifax, Canadian Forces Base ◆ 186 44.43 N 63.38 W
Halifax Citadel National Historic Park ◆ 186 44.35 N 63.39 W
Halifax Harbour **C** 186 44.35 N 63.31 W
Halimaile 229a 20.52 N 156.20 W
Hall □ [8] 128 27.28 N 58.44 E
Halimatazi 104 42.37 N 122.35 E
Halim Perdanakusuma Airport **☒** 96 6.16 S 106.54 E
Halitnam, Gunung **▲** 115a 6.42 S 106.26 E
Haljaspan 263 51.27 N 7.44 E
Hälleberga 26 56.42 N 15.48 E
Hällabrottet 40 59.07 N 15.12 E
Halladale **≃** 46 58.33 N 3.55 W
Halland 274b 38.01 S 145.06 E
Halland □ [9] 26 57.00 N 12.40 E
Hallandale 26 25.58 N 80.08 W
Hallands Väderö **I** 26 56.26 N 12.33 E
Hallau 58 47.42 N 8.27 E
Hällbybrunn 40 59.19 N 16.36 E
Hällefors 40 59.24 N 16.25 E
Hällbymagasinet **⊜** [1] 265b 59.23 N 15.06 E
Halle, Bel. 52 50.44 N 4.13 E
Halle, B.R.D. 52 52.04 N 8.22 E
Halle, B.R.D. 52 51.59 N 9.33 E
Halle, D.D.R. 54 51.29 N 11.58 E
Halle □ [3] 54 51.30 N 11.45 E
Halleberg **▲** [2] 40 59.47 N 14.30 E
Hällefors 40 59.47 N 14.30 E
Hälleforsnäs 40 59.10 N 16.30 E
Hällekis 26 58.38 N 13.25 E
Hallein 64 47.41 N 13.06 E
Hällena 26 63.11 N 14.05 E
Halle-Neustadt 54 51.29 N 11.56 E
Halletts, Cape ► 9 72.19 S 170.18 E
Hallettsville 194 29.26 N 96.56 W
Halleaula 198 47.21 N 102.20 W
Hälleviken ◆ [2] 26 58.05 N 14.45 E
Halligen **II** 30 54.35 N 8.35 E
Halling 95 35.21 N 0.27 E
Hällingsälvi **≃** [5] 26 60.24 N 9.35 E
Hallingskarvet **▲** 26 64.20 N 14.22 E
Halll in Tirol 60 47.17 N 11.31 E
Hall Island **I** 180 60.40 N 173.05 W
Hall Islands **II** 14 8.37 N 152.00 E
Hall Lake **⊜** 176 58.31 N 25.03 E
Hallandale 76 58.31 N 25.03 E
Hall Meadow Brook Reservoir **⊜** [1] 207 41.52 N 73.10 W
Hall Mountain ▲ 202 48.49 N 117.15 W
Hällnäs 26 64.19 N 19.38 E
Hallock 198 48.46 N 96.56 W
Hallowell 186 44.17 N 69.47 W
Hall Peninsula ► [1] 176 63.30 N 66.00 W
Halls Bayou **≃** 222 29.52 N 95.07 W
Hallsberg 40 59.04 N 15.07 E
Halls Creek 162 18.16 S 127.46 E
Halls Creek **≃** 162 18.16 S 127.40 E
Hallshuk 26 57.39 N 18.45 E
Hallstadt 60 49.55 N 10.54 E
Hallstahammar **≃** 40 59.37 N 16.14 E
Hallstadt 60 49.55 N 10.54 E
Hallstätter See **⊜** 64 47.33 N 13.39 E
Hallstavik 40 60.03 N 18.36 E
Hallstead 210 41.57 N 75.44 W
Hällsta 40 59.50 N 16.27 E
Hallsville, Mo., U.S. 219 39.07 N 92.13 W
Hallsville, Tx., U.S. 222 32.30 N 94.34 W
Hallviken 26 63.38 N 15.44 E
Hallwil, See **⊜** 58 47.18 N 8.13 E
Hallwood 208 37.52 N 75.35 W
Halma 26 50.05 N 5.09 E
Halmahera **I** 108 1.00 N 128.00 E
Halmahera, Laut (Halmahera Sea) **≃** [2] 108 1.00 S 129.00 E
Halmeu 38 47.59 N 23.01 E
Halmstad 26 56.39 N 12.50 E
Halom 276 40.56 N 74.04 W
Halpine Village 284c 39.04 N 77.07 W
Hals 41 56.59 N 10.19 E
Hälsafjorden **C** [2] 26 57.00 N 10.53 E
Halstad 198 47.21 N 96.50 W
Halsinger 198 47.21 N 96.50 W
Halsted, Eng., U.K. 42 51.57 N 0.38 E
Halsted, Eng., U.K. 42 52.01 N 2.33 W
Halstenbek 52 53.38 N 9.51 E
Halsteren 52 51.32 N 4.16 E
Halstead, Eng., U.K. 260 51.33 N 1.30 E
Halstead, Ks., U.S. 198 38.00 N 97.30 W
Halstead Green 262 53.14 N 2.41 W
Halstenbek 52 53.38 N 9.51 E
Halstow Marshes **⊜** 260 51.26 N 0.35 E
Haltern 52 51.44 N 7.11 E
Haltiatunturi **▲** 24 69.18 N 21.16 E
Halton City 222 32.48 N 97.16 W
Halton, Eng., U.K. 262 53.20 N 2.42 W
Halton, Eng., U.K. 44 54.04 N 2.44 W
Haltwhistle 262 54.58 N 2.27 W
Halul **I** 128 25.40 N 52.25 E
Halver 263 51.11 N 7.30 E
Halvorson, Mount ▲ 182 53.15 N 120.30 W
Halwell 50 50.30 N 3.43 W
Ham, Fr. 56 49.45 N 3.04 E
Ham, Tchad 146 11.39 N 15.51 E
Ham □ [4] 146 11.45 N 15.51 E
Halalajes ◆ 158 13.50 S 28.31 E
Hamab 156 28.05 S 19.31 E
Hamad, Oued el **≃** 35 35.42 N 10.50 E
Hamadan 128 34.48 N 48.30 E
Hamadãn □ [4] 128 34.40 N 48.30 E
Hamada 96 34.54 N 132.05 E

Hajar, Tall al- **▲** [2] 132 33.21 N 37.03 E
Hajdú-Bihar □ [6] 30 47.25 N 21.30 E
Hajdúböszörmény 30 47.41 N 21.30 E
Hajdúnánás 30 47.51 N 21.26 E
Hajdúszoboszló 30 47.21 N 21.24 E
Hajeb el Ayoun 36 35.24 N 9.33 E
Hăjigani 126 41.32 N 117.10 E
Hăjigani 272b 22.56 N 88.28 E
Hajipur, India 124 25.41 N 85.13 E
Hajipur, India 126 22.49 N 87.38 E
Hajipur, India 272b 22.57 N 88.25 E
Hajj, Wādī al- **≃** 142 30.03 N 32.45 E
Hajnówka 30 52.45 N 23.36 E
Hajr, Wādī **V** 144 14.04 N 48.40 E
Hajūl, Wādī **V** 142 29.42 N 32.22 E
Hakata 96 33.12 N 133.07 E
Hakata-jima **I** 96 34.12 N 133.00 E
Hakatárama 172 44.44 S 170.29 E
Hakendover 52 50.48 N 4.59 E
Hakha 110 22.39 N 93.37 E
Hakï 96 33.20 N 130.50 E
Hakīm, Abyār al- **⊤** [4] 146 31.36 N 23.29 E
Hakkāri 128 37.34 N 43.45 E
Hakkäri □ [4] 128 37.30 N 43.45 E
Hakkali **≃** [8] 267b 41.02 N 28.57 E
Hakapanar 130 37.25 N 34.13 E
Hakkett, Cape ► 180 70.49 N 152.12 W
Hakīrk 46 58.30 N 3.30 W
Hakyn 262 53.14 N 3.11 W
Halkyn Mountain **▲** 262 53.14 N 3.13 W
Hall, Austl. 171b 35.10 S 149.04 E
Hall, In., U.S. 218 39.33 N 86.32 W
Hall, N.Y., U.S. 210 42.49 N 77.04 W
Hällabrottet 40 59.07 N 15.12 E
Haksberg 40 60.11 N 15.12 E
Hakskeenpan **≃** 158 26.48 S 20.12 E
Haktanir 130 36.51 N 38.50 E
Halden 26 59.07 N 11.23 E
Haktanir 130 36.51 N 38.50 E
Hakuba 94 36.42 N 137.52 E
Hakui 94 36.53 N 136.47 E
Hakupu 174v 19.06 S 169.50 W
Haku-san ▲ 94 34.38 N 136.21 E
Haku-san ▲ 94 36.09 N 136.46 E
Haku-san-kokuritsu-kōen ◆ 94 36.12 N 136.47 E
Hakushū 94 35.48 N 138.20 E
Hakuta 96 35.21 N 133.17 E
Hala 120 25.49 N 68.25 E
Halaaobao 102 41.21 N 107.20 E
Halab (Aleppo) 130 36.12 N 37.10 E
Halab □ [8] 130 36.07 N 37.30 E
Halabjah 128 35.11 N 45.59 E
Halaberje 232 20.29 N 90.05 W
Halaga 242 24.34 N 122.11 E
Halageti 102 42.34 N 122.40 E
Halahi 89 41.30 N 125.07 E
Halahushao 140 22.11 N 121.44 E
Halä'ib 140 22.13 N 36.38 E
Halali Lake **⊜** 229b 21.52 N 160.11 W
Halalamutai 86 46.10 N 84.52 E
Halangingie Point ► 174v 19.03 S 169.57 W
Halasa 140 14.26 N 30.39 E
Halas-patak **≃** 264c 47.24 N 19.20 E
Halataojie 140 42.30 N 122.06 E
Halatieke Shan **≃** 85 39.30 N 77.05 E
Halawa 229b 21.10 N 158.01 W
Halawa ◆ 26 58.05 N 14.45 E
Halāvenden **≃** 26 58.48 N 15.18 E
Halawa, Cape ► 229a 21.10 N 156.43 W
Halawa Bay **C** 229a 21.10 N 156.44 W
Halawa Heights 229c 21.22 N 157.55 W
Halba 132 34.33 N 36.04 E
Halbach ◆ [8] 263 51.12 N 7.12 E
Halba Deset **⊜** 38 44.12 N 22.55 E
Halbau → Iłowa 30 51.29 N 15.12 E
Halbe 54 52.06 N 13.42 E
Halberstadt 54 51.54 N 11.02 E
Halbert, Lake **⊜** [1] 222 32.04 N 96.25 W
Halberton 50 50.55 N 3.25 W
Halbrite 184 49.31 N 103.29 W
Halbury 168b 34.05 S 138.31 E
Halcombe 172 40.09 S 175.30 E
Halcon, Mount ▲ 116 13.16 N 121.00 E
Halcottsville 210 42.16 N 74.39 W
Halden 26 59.08 N 11.23 E
Haldensleben 54 52.17 N 11.24 E
Halberg 54 51.33 N 7.31 E
Haldi **≃** 126 22.06 N 88.05 E
Haldia 120 22.02 N 88.06 E
Haldibāri 124 26.20 N 88.46 E
Haldibunia 272b 21.59 N 89.23 E
Haldimand-Norfolk □ 212 42.48 N 80.10 W
Hale, U.K. 262 53.20 N 2.48 W
Hale, Eng., U.K. 262 53.22 N 2.18 W
Hale, Eng., U.K. 262 53.20 N 2.29 W
Hale, Mi., U.S. 216 44.23 N 83.49 W
Hale, Mo., U.S. 219 39.36 N 93.20 W
Hale **≃** 162 24.56 S 135.53 E
Hale ◆ 162 24.56 S 135.53 E
Haleakala Crater ◆ [6] 229a 20.43 N 156.13 W
Haleakala National Park ◆ 229a 20.44 N 156.13 W
Halab → Halab 130 36.12 N 37.10 E
Hale Center 196 34.04 N 101.50 W
Hale Creek **≃** 276 37.33 N 122.06 W
Haledon 276 40.56 N 74.11 W
Haleion Reservoir **⊜** 276 40.56 N 74.11 W
Halekii-Pihana Heiaus State Monument ⊥ 229a 20.54 N 156.29 W
Halenkov 54 49.19 N 18.09 E
Hales Corners 216 42.56 N 88.03 W
Halesowen 42 52.26 N 2.03 W
Hale Street 260 51.13 N 0.24 E
Halesworth 42 52.21 N 1.30 E
Halethorpe 284b 39.14 N 76.40 W
Halewood 262 53.21 N 2.50 W
Haleyville 194 34.13 N 87.37 W
Halfa al Jadida 140 15.03 N 35.35 E
Half Assini 150 5.03 N 2.53 W
Halfa → Wādi Halfa 140 21.56 N 31.20 E
Halfāyah, Naqb al- (Halfaya Pass) **⋊** 140 25.11 N 29.53 E
Halfaya Pass → Halfāyah, Naqb al- 140 25.11 N 29.53 E
Half Day 216 42.11 N 87.57 W
Halfeti 130 37.15 N 37.52 E
Half Hollow Hills 276 40.48 N 73.21 W
Halfmoon Bay, B.C., Can. 182 49.31 N 123.54 W
Halfmoon Bay, N.Z. 172 46.54 S 168.08 E
Half Moon Bay, Ca., U.S. 204 37.27 N 122.26 W
Half Moon Bay Airport **☒** 282 37.31 N 122.30 W
Half Moon Bay State Beach ◆ 282 37.29 N 122.27 W
Halfway, Md., U.S. 208 39.37 N 77.45 W
Halfway, Or., U.S. 202 44.52 N 117.06 W
Halfway **≃** 182 56.12 N 121.32 W
Halfway Lake **⊜** 212 44.48 N 80.37 W

ESPAÑOL / FRANÇAIS / PORTUGUÊS

Nombre / Nom / Nome	Página / Page / Página	Lat.°′	Long.°′ W = Oeste / W = Ouest / W = Oeste
Hamadān	128	34.48 N	48.30 E
Hamadān □[4]	128	35.00 N	48.40 E
Ḥamāh	130	35.08 N	36.45 E
Ḥamāh □[8]	130	35.10 N	37.00 E
Hamahika-jima I	174m	26.19 N	127.57 E
Hamakeza	89	47.05 N	120.52 E
Hamakita	94	34.48 N	137.47 E
Hamale	150	10.59 N	2.44 W
Hamamatsu	94	34.42 N	137.44 E
Hamamatsukita-kichi, Kōkū-jieitai- ■	94	34.45 N	137.42 E
Hamamözü	130	40.48 N	35.02 E
Haman	98	35.15 N	128.24 E
Hamanaka	92a	43.05 N	145.10 E
Hamana-ko ⊜	94	34.45 N	137.34 E
Hamano	268	35.33 N	140.08 E
Hamaoka	94	34.39 N	138.08 E
Hamar	26	60.48 N	11.06 E
Hamasaka	96	35.37 N	134.27 E
Ḥamāṭah, Jabal ∧	140	24.12 N	35.00 E
Hamatang	98	40.12 N	124.20 E
Hama-tombetsu	92a	45.07 N	142.23 E
Hambach	56	49.04 N	7.02 E
Hambaek-san ∧	98	37.09 N	128.55 E
Hambantota	122	6.07 N	81.07 E
Hambergen	52	53.18 N	8.49 E
Hamber Provincial Park ♠	182	52.25 N	117.40 W
Hamble	42	50.52 N	1.19 W
Hambledon	42	50.56 N	1.04 W
Hambleton	44	53.52 N	2.57 W
Hambleton Hills ⋏[2]	44	54.16 N	1.12 W
Hamborn ◆[8]	263	51.29 N	6.46 E
Hambourg → Hamburg	52	53.33 N	9.59 E
Hamburg, B.R.D.	52	53.33 N	9.59 E
Hamburg, Ciskei	158	33.17 S	27.28 E
Hamburg, Ar., U.S.	194	33.13 N	91.47 W
Hamburg, Ct., U.S.	207	41.23 N	72.21 W
Hamburg, Il., U.S.	219	39.14 N	90.43 W
Hamburg, Ia., U.S.	198	40.36 N	95.39 W
Hamburg, Mi., U.S.	216	42.27 N	83.48 W
Hamburg, N.J., U.S.	210	41.09 N	74.34 W
Hamburg, N.Y., U.S.	210	42.42 N	78.49 W
Hamburg, Pa., U.S.	208	40.33 N	75.58 W
Hamburg □[3]	52	53.35 N	10.00 E
Hamburg, Flughafen ⊠	52	53.38 N	10.00 E
Hamburg Airport ⊠	284a	42.42 N	78.55 W
Hamburg Ditch ≅	208	36.31 N	76.33 W
Hamburger Hallig ≻[1]	41	54.36 N	8.49 E
Hamburg Mountains ⋏	276	41.08 N	74.32 W
Hamburgo → Hamburg	52	53.33 N	9.59 E
Hamburgsund	26	58.33 N	11.16 E
Ḥamḍ, Wādī al- ∨	128	25.54 N	36.38 E
Ḥamḍah	144	19.02 N	43.36 E
Hamdallay Timbou	150	12.03 N	10.37 W
Hamdam Āb, Dasht-e ⌣	128	34.45 N	61.30 E
Ḥamdānah	144	19.58 N	40.35 E
Hamden, Ct., U.S.	207	41.23 N	72.53 W
Hamden, N.Y., U.S.	210	42.12 N	75.00 W
Hamden, Oh., U.S.	188	39.09 N	82.31 W
Hamdibey	130	39.50 N	27.15 E
Häme ◆[1]	26	61.30 N	24.30 E
Hämeenkangas ◆[3]	26	61.45 N	22.40 E
Hämeenkylä	26	60.16 N	24.47 E
Hämeen lääni □[4]	26	61.30 N	24.30 E
Hämeenlinna	26	61.00 N	24.27 E
Hamel	168a	32.52 S	115.55 E
HaMelah, Yam → Dead Sea ⊜	132	31.30 N	35.30 E
Hämelerwald	52	52.22 N	10.05 E
Hamelin	162	26.26 S	114.11 E
Hamelin Pool ⊂	162	26.15 S	114.05 E
Hameln	52	52.06 N	9.21 E
HaMerkaz □[5]	132	32.05 N	34.55 E
Hamer Koke	144	5.12 N	36.45 E
Hamero Hadad	144	7.34 N	42.18 E
Hamersleben	54	52.04 N	11.05 E
Hamersley Range ⋏	162	21.53 S	116.46 E
Hamersley Range National Park ♠	162	22.40 S	118.15 E
Hamersville	218	38.55 N	83.59 W
Hames Creek ≃	226	35.53 N	120.50 W
Hamgyŏng Namdo □[4]	98	40.00 N	127.30 E
Hamgyŏng Pukdo □[4]	98	41.45 N	129.50 E
Hamgyŏng-sanmaek ⋏	98	41.00 N	128.30 E
Ham House ⊥	260	51.27 N	0.19 W
Hamhŭng	98	39.54 N	127.32 E
Hami (Kumul)	102	42.48 N	93.27 E
Hamidiye	130	41.09 N	26.40 E
Hamiguitan, Mount ∧	116	6.44 N	126.11 E
Hamilton, Austl.	166	37.45 S	142.02 E
Hamilton, Ber.	240a	32.17 N	64.46 W
Hamilton, On., Can.	212	43.15 N	79.51 W
Hamilton, N.Z.	172	37.47 S	175.17 E
Hamilton, Scot., U.K.	46	55.47 N	4.03 W
Hamilton, Al., U.S.	194	34.08 N	87.59 W
Hamilton, Ak., U.S.	180	62.54 N	163.53 W
Hamilton, Ga., U.S.	192	32.45 N	84.52 W
Hamilton, Il., U.S.	190	40.23 N	91.20 W
Hamilton, In., U.S.	216	41.32 N	84.54 W
Hamilton, Ks., U.S.	198	37.58 N	96.09 W
Hamilton, Ma., U.S.	207	42.37 N	70.52 W
Hamilton, Mi., U.S.	216	42.40 N	86.00 W
Hamilton, Mo., U.S.	194	39.44 N	93.59 W
Hamilton, Mt., U.S.	202	46.14 N	114.09 W
Hamilton, N.Y., U.S.	210	42.49 N	75.32 W
Hamilton, N.C., U.S.	192	35.56 N	77.12 W
Hamilton, Oh., U.S.	218	39.23 N	84.33 W
Hamilton, R.I., U.S.	207	41.32 N	71.26 W
Hamilton, Tx., U.S.	196	31.42 N	98.07 W
Hamilton, Wa., U.S.	224	48.31 N	121.59 W
Hamilton □[6], In., U.S.	218	40.03 N	86.01 W
Hamilton □[6], N.Y., U.S.	210	43.24 N	74.25 W
Hamilton □[6], Oh., U.S.	218	39.06 N	84.31 W
Hamilton ◆[8]	284b	39.21 N	76.33 W
Hamilton ≃	166	23.30 S	139.47 E
Hamilton, Lake ⊜	220	28.03 N	81.39 W
Hamilton, Lake ⊜[1]	194	34.30 N	93.05 W
Hamilton, Mount ∧, Ak., U.S.	180	61.10 N	159.46 W
Hamilton, Mount ∧, Ca., U.S.	226	37.21 N	121.38 W
Hamilton, Mount ∧, Nv., U.S.	204	39.14 N	115.32 W
Hamilton Acres	180	64.51 N	147.40 W
Hamilton Air Force Base ■	282	38.03 N	122.31 W
Hamilton City	204	39.44 N	122.00 W
Hamilton Creek ≃	162	26.40 S	135.19 E
Hamilton Creek Indian Reserve ◆[4]	182	50.11 N	120.30 W
Hamilton Dome	200	43.46 N	108.34 W
Hamilton Harbour ⊂	212	43.17 N	79.50 W
Hamilton Hill	168a	32.05 S	115.46 E
Hamilton Hotel	166	22.50 S	140.35 E
Hamilton Inlet ⊂	176	54.00 N	57.30 W
Hamilton Lake ⊜	216	41.33 N	84.55 W
Hamilton Mountain ∧	188	43.25 N	74.22 W
Hamilton Park, In., U.S.	216	40.17 N	85.19 W
Hamilton Park, Pa., U.S.	208	40.02 N	76.20 W
Hamilton Sound ʊ	186	49.30 N	54.30 W
Hamilton Square	285	40.13 N	74.39 W
Hamilton-Wentworth □[6]	212	43.15 N	80.00 W
Ḥamīm, Wādī al- ∨	146	30.10 N	21.32 E
Hamina	26	60.34 N	27.12 E
Hamiota	184	50.11 N	100.36 W
Ḥāmir, Wādī ∨	128	31.37 N	42.12 E
Hamīrpur, India	123	31.41 N	76.31 E
Hamīrpur, India	124	25.57 N	80.09 E
Hamjong-ni	98	38.59 N	125.17 E
Hamler	216	41.13 N	84.02 W
Hamlet, In., U.S.	216	41.32 N	86.34 W
Hamlet, N.C., U.S.	192	34.53 N	79.41 W
Hamlet, Oh., U.S.	218	39.01 N	84.12 W
Hamlet, Mount ∧	180	68.47 N	165.57 W
Hamley Bridge	168b	34.21 S	138.41 E
Hamlin, N.Y., U.S.	210	43.18 N	77.55 W
Hamlin, Pa., U.S.	210	41.24 N	75.24 W
Hamlin, Tx., U.S.	196	32.53 N	100.08 W
Hamlin, W.V., U.S.	188	38.16 N	82.06 W
Hamlin Beach State Park ♠	210	43.22 N	77.58 W
Hamlin Lake ⊜	190	44.03 N	86.27 W
Hamlin Valley Wash ∨	200	38.53 N	114.01 W
Hamm	52	51.41 N	7.49 E
Hamm ◆[8], B.R.D.	263	51.15 N	6.25 E
Hamm ◆[8], B.R.D.	263	51.12 N	6.44 E
Hamm ◆[8], B.R.D.	263	51.23 N	7.03 E
Ḥammād, Wādī ∨	142	29.45 N	32.24 E
Hamma Hamma ≃	224	47.33 N	123.03 W
Håmmålfjell ∧	26	62.27 N	11.17 E
Ḥammām at-Turkumān	130	36.32 N	39.03 E
Hammamet, Alg.	36	35.27 N	7.58 E
Hammamet, Tun.	148	36.24 N	10.37 E
Hammamet, Golfe de ⊂	36	36.05 N	10.40 E
Hammam Lif	148	36.44 N	10.20 E
Ḥammānā	132	33.49 N	35.44 E
Hammar	40	58.49 N	14.57 E
Ḥammār, Hawr al- ⊜	128	30.50 N	47.10 E
Hammarby	40	60.33 N	16.34 E
Hammarn	40	59.45 N	14.30 E
Hammarö	40	59.20 N	13.31 E
Hammarön I	40	59.19 N	13.31 E
Hammarstrand	26	63.06 N	16.21 E
Hamme	50	51.06 N	4.08 E
Hamme ≃	52	53.10 N	8.44 E
Hammel	41	56.15 N	9.52 E
Hammelburg	56	50.07 N	9.53 E
Hamme-Mille	56	50.47 N	4.43 E
Hammerdal	26	63.36 N	15.21 E
Hammerfest	24	70.40 N	23.42 E
Hammermühle → Kepice	30	54.15 N	16.52 E
Hämmern	263	51.08 N	7.21 E
Hammershus ⊥	26	55.16 N	14.45 E
Hammersley Inlet ⊂	224	47.12 N	123.00 W
Hammersmith ◆[8]	260	51.30 N	0.14 W
Hammerstein → Czarne	30	53.42 N	16.57 E
Hammerum	41	56.08 N	9.04 E
Hamminkeln	52	51.44 N	6.35 E
Hammon	196	35.37 N	99.22 W
Hammonasset ≃	207	41.16 N	72.33 W
Hammond, In., U.S.	216	41.35 N	87.30 W
Hammond, La., U.S.	194	30.30 N	90.27 W
Hammond, N.Y., U.S.	212	44.26 N	75.41 W
Hammond, Or., U.S.	224	46.12 N	123.57 W
Hammond, Wi., U.S.	190	44.58 N	92.26 W
Hammond Island I, Austl.	164	10.35 S	142.13 E
Hammond Island I, Ca., U.S.	282	38.06 N	121.57 W
Hammond Pond Park ♠	283	42.19 N	71.11 W
Hammondsport	210	42.24 N	77.13 W
Hammondsville	214	40.33 N	80.43 W
Hammondville	274a	33.57 S	150.57 E
Hammonia	158	28.43 S	27.49 E
Hammonton	208	39.38 N	74.48 W
Hamningberg	24	70.31 N	30.37 E
Ham-Nord	206	45.54 N	71.39 W
Hamoir	56	50.26 N	5.32 E
Hamont	56	51.15 N	5.33 E
HaMore, Giv'at ∧	132	32.37 N	35.21 E
Hamorton	285	39.52 N	75.39 W
Hamoyet, Jabal ∧	144	17.33 N	38.02 E
Hampden, Austl.	168b	34.09 S	139.03 E
Hampden, Nf., Can.	186	49.33 N	56.51 W
Hampden, N.Z.	172	45.19 S	170.49 E
Hampden, Me., U.S.	188	44.44 N	68.50 W
Hampden, Ma., U.S.	207	42.03 N	72.24 W
Hampden, N.D., U.S.	198	48.32 N	98.39 W
Hampden □[6]	207	42.07 N	72.36 W
Hampden Sydney	192	37.15 N	78.29 W
Hampetorp	40	59.09 N	15.40 E
Hampi	122	15.24 N	76.37 E
Hampshire	216	42.05 N	88.31 W
Hampshire □[6], Eng., U.K.	42	51.05 N	1.15 W
Hampshire □[6], Ma., U.S.	207	42.19 N	72.38 W
Hampshire Downs ⋏[1]	42	51.15 N	1.17 W
Hampshire Heights	279b	40.20 N	79.33 W
Hampstead, P.Q., Can.	275a	45.29 N	73.38 W
Hampstead, Md., U.S.	208	39.36 N	76.51 W
Hampstead, N.C., U.S.	192	34.22 N	77.42 W
Hampstead ◆[8]	260	51.33 N	0.11 W
Hampstead Heath ♠	260	51.34 N	0.10 W
Hampton, Austl.	274b	37.56 S	145.00 E
Hampton, N.B., Can.	186	45.32 N	65.51 W
Hampton, On., Can.	212	43.58 N	78.45 W
Hampton, Ar., U.S.	194	33.32 N	92.28 W
Hampton, Ct., U.S.	207	41.47 N	72.03 W
Hampton, Fl., U.S.	192	29.51 N	82.07 W
Hampton, Ga., U.S.	192	33.23 N	84.16 W
Hampton, Ia., U.S.	190	42.44 N	93.12 W
Hampton, Ne., U.S.	198	40.52 N	97.53 W
Hampton, N.H., U.S.	188	42.56 N	70.50 W
Hampton, N.J., U.S.	210	40.42 N	74.57 W
Hampton, Pa., U.S.	208	39.56 N	77.04 W
Hampton, S.C., U.S.	192	32.52 N	81.06 W
Hampton, Tn., U.S.	192	36.17 N	82.10 W
Hampton, Va., U.S.	208	37.01 N	76.20 W
Hampton ◆[8]	260	51.25 N	0.22 W
Hampton Bays	207	40.52 N	72.31 W
Hampton Butte ∧	202	43.46 N	120.17 W
Hampton Court Palace ∪	260	51.24 N	0.20 W
Hampton Harbour ⊂	162	20.40 S	116.30 E
Hampton National Historic Site ⊥	284b	39.25 N	76.35 W
Hampton Park	274b	38.02 S	145.15 E
Hampton Roads ⊤[3]	208	36.58 N	76.20 W
Hampton Roads Bridge-Tunnel ◆[5]	208	37.00 N	76.18 W
Hampton Tableland ⋏[1]	162	32.10 S	126.10 E
Hamp'yŏng	98	35.05 N	126.30 E
Hamr	54	50.35 N	13.35 E
Hamra	26	61.39 N	15.00 E
Ḥamrā', Al-Ḥamādah al- ◆[2]	146	30.00 N	12.00 E
Hamra, As Saquia al ∨	148	27.15 N	13.21 W
Hamra, Ouadi ∨	146	12.52 N	21.15 E
Ḥamrah, Jabal al- ∧	132	29.39 N	34.47 E
Ḥamran, Har ∧	132	30.41 N	34.34 E
Hamra Nationalpark ♠	26	61.45 N	14.55 E
Ḥamrat ash-Shaykh	140	14.35 N	27.58 E
Hams Bluff ±[4]	241n	17.46 N	64.52 W
Hams Fork ≃	200	41.35 N	109.59 W
Hamstreet	42	51.04 N	0.51 E
Ham-Sud	206	45.46 N	71.36 W
Ham Tan	110	10.40 N	107.46 E
Hamtramck	216	42.23 N	83.02 W
Hāmūn, Daryācheh-ye ⊜	128	30.50 N	61.07 E
Hamur	84	39.36 N	42.59 E
Hamura	94	35.45 N	139.19 E
Hamyang	98	35.32 N	127.42 E
Hamzalı	130	38.19 N	41.09 E
Han	150	10.41 N	2.27 W
Han ≃, Zhg.	100	23.41 N	116.38 E
Han ≃, Zhg.	102	30.35 N	114.17 E
Han, Grottes de ±[5]	56	50.08 N	5.15 E
Han, Nong ⊜	110	17.12 N	104.11 E
Hana	229a	20.45 N	155.59 W
Hanábana ≃	240p	22.23 N	80.58 W
Hanahan	192	32.55 N	80.01 W
Hanailike	85	39.16 N	76.26 E
Ḥanak	128	25.33 N	36.56 E
Hanakaoo Point ≻	229a	20.55 N	156.42 W
Hanalei	229b	22.12 N	159.30 W
Hanalei Bay ⊂	229b	22.13 N	159.31 W
Hanamaki	92	39.23 N	141.07 E
Hanamaulu	229b	21.59 N	159.21 W
Hanamenu, Baie ⊂	174x	9.46 S	139.08 W
Hanam-ni	98	38.23 N	126.43 E
Hanang ∧	154	4.26 S	35.24 E
Hanapepe	229b	21.54 N	159.35 W
Hānār Char	126	23.08 N	90.38 E
Hanataka-sen ∧	96	35.24 N	132.45 E
Hanateio	174x	9.59 S	139.06 W
Hanatetena	174x	9.58 S	139.04 W
Hanau	56	50.08 N	8.55 E
Hanaui	174x	9.45 S	139.05 W
Hanawa, Nihon	94	36.57 N	140.25 E
Hanawa, Nihon	268	35.13 N	139.53 E
Hanbury ≃	176	63.37 N	104.33 W
Hanceville, B.C., Can.	182	51.55 N	123.03 W
Hanceville, Al., U.S.	194	34.03 N	86.46 W
Hanchang	107	30.26 N	103.43 E
Hancheng, Zhg.	102	35.28 N	110.29 E
Hancheng, Zhg.	105	39.39 N	118.02 E
Hanches	261	48.36 N	1.39 E
Hanchō	270	34.49 N	135.27 E
Han-ch'ŏn ≃	271b	37.33 N	127.02 E
Hanchuan	100	30.39 N	113.48 E
Hanchung → Hanzhong	102	33.08 N	107.02 E
Hancock, Md., U.S.	188	39.41 N	78.10 W
Hancock, Mi., U.S.	190	47.07 N	88.34 W
Hancock, Mn., U.S.	198	45.29 N	95.47 W
Hancock, N.Y., U.S.	210	41.57 N	75.17 W
Hancock, Wi., U.S.	190	44.08 N	89.31 W
Hancock □[6], Il., U.S.	219	40.13 N	91.15 W
Hancock □[6], In., U.S.	218	39.47 N	85.46 W
Hancock □[6], Oh., U.S.	216	41.02 N	83.39 W
Hancock □[6], W.V., U.S.	214	40.30 N	80.33 W
Hancock, Lake ⊜	220	27.58 N	81.50 W
Hancocks Bridge	208	39.30 N	75.27 W
Hancun	105	39.24 N	116.36 E
Handa, Nihon	94	34.53 N	136.56 E
Handa, Nihon	96	34.02 N	134.02 E
Handa, Som.	144	10.40 N	51.07 E
Handa I	46	58.22 N	5.12 W
Handan	98	36.37 N	114.29 E
Handaokou	98	34.16 N	116.24 E
Handawor	123	34.24 N	74.17 E
Handen	40	59.10 N	18.08 E
Handeni	154	5.26 S	38.01 E
Handforth	262	53.21 N	2.13 W
Handlová	30	48.44 N	18.46 E
Handöl	26	63.16 N	12.26 E
Handorf	52	51.59 N	7.41 E
Handsworth	184	49.48 N	103.00 W
Handub	140	19.14 N	37.16 E
Handzame	50	51.02 N	3.00 E
Haneda Airport ⊠	268	35.33 N	139.46 E
HaNegev (Negev Desert) ◆[1]	132	30.30 N	34.55 E
Haney	224	49.13 N	122.36 W
Hane-yama ∧	96	33.14 N	131.08 E
Hane-zaki ≻	96	33.22 N	134.02 E
Hanford	226	36.19 N	119.38 W
Hanford Site ∪[3]	202	46.35 N	119.30 W
Han'gang	98	34.39 N	114.38 E
Han-gang ≃	98	37.45 N	126.11 E
Hanga Roa	174z	27.09 S	109.26 W
Hangatiki	172	38.15 S	175.10 E
Hangbu	100	28.53 N	118.49 E
Hangchow → Hangzhou	106	30.15 N	120.10 E
Hangchow Bay → Hangzhou Wan ⊂	100	30.25 N	121.00 E
Hanger ≃	144	9.35 N	36.02 E
Hanggai	106	30.35 N	119.23 E
Hanggin Houqi	102	40.55 N	107.15 E
Hanggin Qi	102	39.56 N	108.54 E
Hang Hau Town	271d	22.19 N	114.16 E
Hanging Gardens ♠	272c	18.58 N	72.48 E
Hanging Rock State Park ♠	192	36.25 N	80.15 W
Hangingstone Hill ∧[2]	42	50.39 N	3.57 W
Hanging Woman Creek ≃	202	45.19 N	106.31 W
Hangklip, Kaap ≻	158	34.26 S	18.48 E
Hangkou	100	29.03 N	114.27 E
Hangman Creek ≃	202	47.38 N	117.27 W
Hangö (Hanko)	26	59.50 N	22.57 E
Hangou	105	39.18 N	117.07 E
Hang-Tcheou → Hangzhou	106	30.15 N	120.10 E
Hangtou	106	31.01 N	121.35 E
Hangtschou → Hangzhou	106	30.15 N	120.10 E
Hangu, Pāk.	123	33.32 N	71.04 E
Hangu, Zhg.	105	39.15 N	117.47 E
Hangu, Zhg.	107	28.58 N	104.30 E
Hanguang	100	24.16 N	113.08 E
Hanguchang	107	29.32 N	106.21 E
Hangugang	105	39.15 N	116.56 E
Hangzhou (Hangchow)	106	30.15 N	120.10 E
Hangzhou Wan (Hangchow Bay) ⊂	100	30.25 N	121.00 E
Hani	130	38.24 N	40.24 E
Hänigsen	52	52.29 N	10.05 E
Hanimadu I	122	6.45 N	73.09 E
Ḥanīsh II	144	13.45 N	42.45 E
Ḥanīsh al-Kabīr, Jazīrat al- I	144	13.43 N	42.45 E
Ḥanita	132	33.05 N	35.10 E
Hanjalipan	112	2.15 S	112.47 E
Hanjiagou	104	40.42 N	120.47 E
Hanjiang	100	25.30 N	119.06 E
Hanjiapuzi	104	40.48 N	123.14 E
Hanjiashu	105	39.11 N	117.04 E
Hanjiawa	106	31.16 N	119.18 E
Hankamer	222	29.51 N	94.38 W
Hankasalmi	26	62.23 N	26.26 E
Hanke	26	59.12 N	10.47 E
Hankendi	130	38.35 N	39.04 E
Hankensbüttel	54	52.44 N	10.36 E
Hankey	158	33.50 S	24.53 E
Hankins	210	41.49 N	75.05 W
Hankinson	198	46.04 N	96.54 W
Hanko → Hangö	26	59.50 N	22.57 E
Hankow → Wuhan	100	30.36 N	114.17 E
Hanks Pond ⊜	276	41.05 N	74.26 W
Hanku → Hangu	105	39.15 N	117.47 E
Hānle	120	32.48 N	79.00 E
Hanley	184	51.37 N	106.27 W
Hanmer	190	46.39 N	80.56 W
Hanmer Springs	172	42.31 S	172.49 E
Hanmiao	89	44.33 N	119.59 E
Hann ≃	164	17.10 S	126.10 E
Hann, Mount ∧	164	15.51 S	125.48 E
Hanna, Ab., Can.	182	51.38 N	111.54 W
Hanna, In., U.S.	216	41.24 N	86.46 W
Hanna, Ok., U.S.	196	35.12 N	95.53 W
Hanna, Wy., U.S.	200	41.52 N	106.33 W
Hanna City	190	40.41 N	89.47 W
Hannaford	198	47.18 N	98.11 W
Hannah	198	48.58 N	98.41 W
Hannah Bay ⊂	176	51.05 N	79.45 W
Hannastown	214	40.21 N	79.30 W
Hannibal, Mo., U.S.	219	39.42 N	91.21 W
Hannibal, N.Y., U.S.	210	43.19 N	76.34 W
Hanningfield Reservoir ⊜[1]	260	51.39 N	0.31 E
Hannō	94	35.51 N	139.19 E
Hannover	52	52.24 N	9.44 E
Hannover □[6]	52	52.30 N	9.00 E
Hannover, Flughafen ⊠	52	52.27 N	9.42 E
Hannut	56	50.40 N	5.05 E
Hanö I	26	56.00 N	14.50 E
Hanobası	130	38.35 N	33.50 E
Hanöbukten ⊂	26	55.45 N	14.30 E
Ha Noi	110	21.02 N	105.51 E
Hanönü	130	41.38 N	34.28 E
Hanoura	96	33.57 N	134.38 E
Hanover → Hannover, B.R.D.	52	52.24 N	9.44 E
Hanover, On., Can.	212	44.09 N	81.02 W
Hanover, S. Afr.	158	31.04 S	24.29 E
Hanover, Ct., U.S.	207	41.38 N	72.03 W
Hanover, Il., U.S.	190	42.15 N	90.16 W
Hanover, In., U.S.	218	38.42 N	85.28 W
Hanover, Ks., U.S.	198	39.53 N	96.52 W
Hanover, Ma., U.S.	207	42.06 N	70.48 W
Hanover, Mi., U.S.	216	42.06 N	84.33 W
Hanover, N.H., U.S.	188	43.42 N	72.17 W
Hanover, N.M., U.S.	200	32.48 N	108.05 W
Hanover, Oh., U.S.	214	40.04 N	82.15 W
Hanover, Pa., U.S.	208	39.48 N	76.59 W
Hanover, Va., U.S.	208	37.45 N	77.22 W
Hanover, Wi., U.S.	216	42.38 N	89.10 W
Hanover □[6]	208	37.42 N	77.20 W
Hanover, Isla I	254	51.00 S	74.40 W
Hanover Airport ⊠	276	40.50 N	74.21 W
Hanover Center	283	42.07 N	70.50 W
Hanover Park	216	42.00 N	88.09 W
Hanover Road	158	30.58 S	24.33 E
Hanoverton	214	40.45 N	80.56 W
Hanovre → Hannover	52	52.24 N	9.44 E
Hanpan, Cape ≻	175e	5.01 S	154.37 E
Hanryeosudo Kukrip Kongwŏn ♠	98	34.46 N	128.30 E
Hansanjiazi	104	41.44 N	122.57 E
Hansard	182	54.05 N	121.52 W
Hanscom Air Force Base ■	207	42.28 N	71.17 W
Hans Creek ≃	210	43.06 N	74.08 W
Hansdiha	124	24.36 N	87.05 E
Hansen Dam ◆[6]	280	34.16 N	118.23 W
Hansen Flood Control Basin ⌣[1]	228	34.16 N	118.23 W
Hanshan	100	31.44 N	118.08 E
Hansharo ⊥	94	35.02 N	138.56 E
Hansi, India	120	32.27 N	77.50 E
Hānsi, India	123	29.06 N	75.58 E
Hansia	272b	22.48 N	88.24 E
Hanska	198	44.08 N	94.29 W
Hānskhāli	126	23.21 N	88.37 E
Hans Lollik Island I	240m	18.24 N	64.55 W
Hanslope	42	52.06 N	0.49 W
Hans Meyer Range ⋏	164	4.20 S	152.55 E
Hanson	207	42.04 N	70.52 W
Hanson ≃	162	20.15 S	133.25 E
Hanson Lake ⊜	184	54.42 N	102.49 W
Hanstholm	26	57.07 N	8.38 E
Han-sur-Lesse	56	50.08 N	5.11 E
Han-sur-Nied	56	48.59 N	6.26 E
Hansville	224	47.55 N	122.33 W
Hansweert	52	51.26 N	4.00 E
Hantaj	88	49.31 N	103.13 E
Hāntālbunia	126	22.44 N	89.31 E
Hantamsberg ⋏	158	31.22 S	19.45 E
Hantan → Handan	98	36.37 N	114.29 E
Hantes ≃	50	50.19 N	4.11 E
Hant's Harbour	186	48.01 N	53.16 W
Hantsport	186	45.04 N	64.11 W
Hantu, Pulau I	271c	1.14 N	103.45 E
Hantu, Tanjong ≻	114	4.18 N	100.34 E
Hantzsch ≃	176	67.32 N	72.25 W
Hanumangarh	123	29.35 N	74.19 E
Hanumān Nagar	124	26.30 N	86.51 E
Hanušovce nad Topl'ou	30	49.02 N	21.30 E
Hanušovice	30	50.05 N	16.55 E
Hanveden ⋏[2]	40	59.07 N	18.00 E
Hanwood	166	34.20 S	146.03 E
Hanworth ◆[8]	260	51.26 N	0.23 W
Hanxinzhuang	105	40.16 N	116.44 E
Hanyang	107	29.44 N	103.44 E
Hanyangping	102	32.41 N	108.34 E
Hanyin	102	32.42 N	108.50 E
Hanyū	94	36.10 N	139.32 E
Hanyuan	102	29.22 N	102.38 E
Hanyuangai	102	29.30 N	102.31 E
Hanzan	96	34.16 N	133.51 E
Hanzhong	102	33.08 N	107.02 E
Hanzhuang	98	34.38 N	117.24 E
Hao I[1]	14	18.15 S	140.54 W
Hao ≃	100	28.27 N	119.56 E
Haohekou	100	28.38 N	112.49 E
Haojiadian	100	31.47 N	113.44 E
Haoli → Hegang	89	47.24 N	130.17 E
Haoluqi	106	30.38 N	119.34 E
HaOn	132	32.43 N	35.38 E
Hāora	126	22.35 N	88.20 E
Hāora Bridge ◆[5]	272b	22.35 N	88.21 E
Hāora Railroad Station ◆[5]	272b	22.35 N	88.21 E
Haouach, Ouadi ∨	146	16.45 N	19.35 E
Haoxue	102	30.00 N	112.20 E
Haozhikou	107	29.36 N	105.02 E
Haparanda	26	65.50 N	24.10 E
Hapatoni, Baie ⊂	174x	9.58 S	139.07 W
Hapert	52	51.23 N	5.15 E
Hapeville	192	33.39 N	84.24 W
Happ'o-ri	98	40.40 N	127.49 E
Happy	196	34.45 N	101.52 W
Happy Camp	204	41.47 N	123.22 W
Happy Jack	200	34.45 N	111.11 W
Happy Valley-Goose Bay	176	53.20 N	60.25 W
Happy Valley Race Course ♠	271d	22.16 N	114.10 E
Hapsford	262	53.16 N	2.48 W
Hapsu	98	41.13 N	128.51 E
Hapton	262	53.47 N	2.19 W
Hāpur	124	28.43 N	77.47 E
Ḥaql	128	29.18 N	34.57 E
Haquira	248	14.13 S	72.11 W
Har	164	5.20 S	133.10 E
Har, Laga ≃	154	1.40 N	39.36 E
Hara, Nihon	94	35.58 N	138.14 E
Hara, Nihon	268	35.50 N	139.46 E
Ḥaraḍ, Ar. Su.	128	24.08 N	49.05 E
Härad, Sve.	40	59.23 N	16.55 E
Ḥaraḍ, Yaman	144	16.28 N	43.04 E
Ḥaraḍ, Jabal al- ∧	132	29.40 N	35.49 E
Haraiki I[1]	14	17.28 S	143.27 W
Harajuku	268	35.54 N	139.21 E
Haraldsted	41	55.30 N	11.47 E
Haramachi	92	37.38 N	140.58 E
Haramachida	268	35.33 N	139.27 E
Haramosh ∧	123	35.50 N	74.54 E
Haramosh Range ⋏	123	35.40 N	75.22 E
Harappa	123	30.38 N	72.52 E
Harappa Road	123	30.36 N	72.55 E
Harar → Harer	144	9.18 N	42.08 E
Harare (Salisbury)	154	17.50 S	31.03 E
Ḥarash, Bi'r al- ⊤[4]	146	25.30 N	22.12 E
Ḥarastā al-Baṣal	132	33.34 N	36.22 E
Hārāt	272b	22.53 N	88.11 E
Haraz-Djombo	146	13.57 N	19.26 E
Haraze-Mangueigne	146	9.55 N	20.48 E
Harbāti	272b	22.55 N	88.33 E
Harbert	216	41.52 N	86.38 W
Harbeson	208	38.43 N	75.17 W
Harbin	89	45.45 N	126.41 E
Harbiye	130	36.11 N	36.05 E
Harbke	54	52.12 N	11.03 E
Harbo	40	60.06 N	17.12 E
Harbonnières	50	49.51 N	2.40 E
Harboør	26	56.37 N	8.12 E
Harbor	202	42.03 N	124.15 W
Harbor Beach	190	43.50 N	82.39 W
Harbor City ◆[8]	280	33.48 N	118.17 W
Harborcreek	214	42.10 N	79.57 W
Harbord	170	33.45 S	151.26 E
Harbor Isle	276	40.36 N	73.40 W
Harbor Side	228	32.37 N	117.05 W
Harbor Springs	190	45.25 N	84.59 W
Harborton	208	37.39 N	75.49 W
Harbor Tunnel ◆[5]	284b	39.15 N	76.34 W
Harbor View	214	41.42 N	83.27 W
Harbour Breton	186	47.29 N	55.48 W
Harbour Buffett	186	47.31 N	54.05 W
Harbour Deep	186	50.22 N	56.31 W
Harbour Grace	186	47.42 N	53.13 W
Harbours, Bay of ⊂	254	52.15 S	59.15 W
Harbourville	186	45.09 N	64.49 W
Harburg	56	48.47 N	10.41 E
Harburg ◆[8]	52	53.28 N	9.59 E
Hårby	41	55.13 N	10.07 E
Harchies	50	50.29 N	3.41 E
Harcourt, Austl.	169	37.00 S	144.15 E
Harcourt, Fr.	50	49.10 N	0.48 E
Harcuvar Mountains ⋏	200	34.00 N	113.30 W
Hard	58	47.29 N	9.41 E
Harda	124	22.20 N	77.06 E
Hardangerfjorden ⊂[2]	26	60.10 N	6.00 E
Hardangerjøkulen ⊓	26	60.33 N	7.26 E
Hardangervidda ⋏[1]	26	60.20 N	7.30 E
Hardangervidda Nasjonalpark ♠	26	60.15 N	7.05 E
Hardapdam ⊜[1]	156	24.28 S	17.48 E
Hardee □[6]	220	27.29 N	81.48 W
Hardeeville	192	32.17 N	81.04 W
Hardegarijp	52	53.13 N	5.56 E
Hardegsen	52	51.39 N	9.49 E
Hardelot-Plage	50	50.38 N	1.35 E
Hardenberg	52	52.34 N	6.37 E
Harderwijk	52	52.21 N	5.36 E
Hardesty	196	36.36 N	101.11 W
Hardey ≃	162	22.45 S	116.07 E
Hardgrave, Mount ∧[2]	171a	27.30 S	153.29 E
Hardheim	56	49.36 N	9.28 E
Hardin, Il., U.S.	219	39.09 N	90.37 W
Hardin, Mt., U.S.	202	45.43 N	107.36 W
Hardin, Tx., U.S.	222	30.09 N	94.44 W
Hardin □[6], Oh., U.S.	216	40.39 N	83.36 W
Hardin □[6], Tx., U.S.	222	30.20 N	94.35 W
Harding, S. Afr.	158	30.34 S	29.58 E
Harding, Il., U.S.	216	41.31 N	88.51 W
Harding, Ma., U.S.	283	42.12 N	71.27 W
Harding, Lake ⊜[1]	192	32.40 N	85.06 W
Harding Lake ⊜	184	56.13 N	98.23 W
Harding Lakes	208	39.27 N	74.45 W
Hardinsburg, In., U.S.	218	38.27 N	86.16 W
Hardinsburg, Ky., U.S.	194	37.46 N	86.27 W
Hardisty	182	52.40 N	111.18 W
Hardisty Lake ⊜	176	64.30 N	117.45 W
Hardoi	124	27.25 N	80.07 E
Hardoi Branch ≅	124	28.41 N	80.08 E
Hardricourt	261	49.01 N	1.54 E
Hardscrabble Wash ∨	200	34.39 N	109.28 W
Hardt	263	51.07 N	6.58 E
Hardtner	198	37.00 N	98.38 W
Hardwick, Ga., U.S.	192	33.04 N	83.13 W
Hardwick, Ma., U.S.	207	42.21 N	72.12 W
Hardwick, Vt., U.S.	188	44.30 N	72.22 W
Hardwood	194	30.49 N	91.23 W
Hardwood Ridge ∧	210	41.15 N	75.23 W
Hardy, Ar., U.S.	194	36.18 N	91.28 W
Hardy, Ne., U.S.	198	40.00 N	97.55 W
Hardy, Península ≻[1]	254	55.25 S	68.30 W
Hardy Bay ⊂	176	75.02 N	115.16 W
Hardy Creek ≃	214	42.52 N	81.52 W
Hardy Lake ⊜[1]	218	38.47 N	85.42 W
Hardy Lake State Recreation Area ♠	218	38.44 N	86.26 W
Hardys Pond ⊜	283	42.25 N	71.15 W
Hare, Mount ∧	180	66.38 N	136.12 W
Hare Bay	186	48.51 N	54.01 W
Hare Bay ⊂	186	51.18 N	55.50 W
Harefield ◆[8]	260	51.36 N	0.29 W
Hareid	26	62.22 N	6.02 E
Hare Indian ≃	180	66.18 N	128.38 W
Harelbeke	50	50.51 N	3.18 E
Haren, B.R.D.	52	52.47 N	7.14 E
Haren, Ned.	52	53.10 N	6.35 E
Hareøen I	176	70.25 N	54.50 W
Harer	144	9.18 N	42.08 E
Harerge □[4]	144	8.00 N	43.00 E
Hareskov	41	55.46 N	12.25 E
Hareto	144	9.20 N	37.06 E
Harewa	144	9.55 N	41.59 E
Harewood	172	43.29 S	172.35 E
Harewood Park	284b	39.23 N	76.22 W
Harfaz	130	38.01 N	41.19 E
Harfleur	50	49.30 N	0.12 E
Harford, N.Y., U.S.	210	42.26 N	76.14 W
Harford, Pa., U.S.	210	41.47 N	75.42 W
Harford □[6]	208	39.32 N	76.21 W
Harford Heights	279b	40.22 N	79.46 W
Harford Mills	210	42.25 N	76.12 W
Harg, Sve.	40	59.49 N	18.57 E
Harg, Sve.	40	60.11 N	18.24 E
Hargele	144	5.20 N	42.05 E
Hargeville	261	48.53 N	1.45 E
Hargeysa	144	9.35 N	44.04 E
Harghita □[6]	38	46.35 N	25.30 E
Harghita, Munții ⋏	38	46.15 N	25.45 E
Hargrave ≃	184	54.24 N	98.48 W
Hargrave Lake ⊜	184	54.29 N	99.40 W
Hargshamn	40	60.10 N	18.28 E
Har Hu (Heihai) ⊜	102	38.15 N	97.40 E
Hāriabhānga ≃[1]	126	21.43 N	89.05 E
Hariāna	123	31.38 N	75.51 E
Hariarapitu	114	2.33 N	98.35 E
Ḥarīb	144	14.57 N	45.30 E
Haribes	156	24.20 S	17.40 E
Ḥaricha, Ḥamâda el ◆[2]	148	22.36 N	3.31 W
Haridwār	124	29.58 N	78.10 E
Harigabessho	270	34.37 N	135.58 E
Harihar	122	14.31 N	75.48 E
Harihari	172	43.09 S	170.33 E
Hariharpāra	126	24.02 N	88.27 E
Harīke	123	31.10 N	74.57 E
Hārim	130	36.12 N	36.31 E
Ḥarim, Jabal al- ∧	128	25.58 N	56.14 E
Harima	96	34.42 N	134.53 E
Harima-nada ⊤[2]	96	34.29 N	134.35 E
Harinagar	124	27.09 N	84.19 E
Harinākunda	126	23.39 N	89.03 E
Haringey ◆[8]	260	51.35 N	0.07 W
Hāringhāta ≃[1]	126	21.54 N	89.57 E
Haringvliet ʊ	52	51.47 N	4.10 E
Haringvlietbrug ◆[5]	52	51.43 N	4.20 E
Haringvlietdam ◆[5]	52	51.50 N	4.03 E
Haripāl	272b	22.49 N	88.07 E
Haripur, India	126	24.18 N	87.05 E
Haripur, India	272b	22.56 N	88.14 E
Harīpur, Pāk.	123	33.59 N	72.56 E
Harirāmpur	126	23.42 N	89.57 E
Harīrūd (Tedžen) ≃	128	37.24 N	60.38 E
Harischandra Range ⋏	122	19.15 N	74.05 E
Hārithān	130	36.16 N	37.05 E
Hariyo	144	5.00 N	47.23 E
Harjavalta	26	61.19 N	22.08 E
Härjedalen □[9]	26	62.20 N	13.00 E
Harkaway	274b	38.00 S	145.21 E
Härkeberga	40	59.42 N	17.11 E
Harkema-Opeinde	52	53.11 N	6.08 E
Harker Heights	222	31.05 N	97.40 W
Harkers Island	192	34.41 N	76.33 W
Harker Village	285	39.51 N	75.09 W
Harkness Memorial State Park ♠	207	41.18 N	72.07 W
Harkortsee ⊜	263	51.24 N	7.25 E
Harlaching ◆[8]	60	48.06 N	11.33 E
Harlan, In., U.S.	216	41.11 N	84.55 W
Harlan, Ia., U.S.	198	41.39 N	95.19 W
Harlan, Ky., U.S.	192	36.50 N	83.19 W
Harlan County Lake ⊜[1]	198	40.04 N	99.16 W
Harlech	42	52.52 N	4.07 W
Harlem, Fl., U.S.	220	26.44 N	80.57 W
Harlem, Ga., U.S.	192	33.24 N	82.18 W
Harlem, Mt., U.S.	202	48.32 N	108.47 W
Harlem ◆[8]	276	40.49 N	73.56 W
Harlem River ʊ	276	40.48 N	73.54 W
Harlem Springs	214	40.31 N	81.02 W
Harlesden ◆[8]	260	51.32 N	0.15 W
Harlesiel	52	53.43 N	7.49 E
Harleston	42	52.24 N	1.18 E
Harleton	222	32.41 N	94.35 W
Hårlev	41	55.21 N	12.15 E
Harleysville	208	40.17 N	75.23 W
Harlin	171a	26.59 S	152.22 E
Harlingen, Ned.	52	53.10 N	5.24 E
Harlingen, Tx., U.S.	196	26.11 N	97.41 W
Harlinger Land ◆[1]	52	53.40 N	7.30 E
Harlingerode	54	51.54 N	10.31 E
Harlington ◆[8]	260	51.29 N	0.26 W
Harlösa	41	55.43 N	13.32 E
Harlow	260	51.47 N	0.08 E
Harlow □[8]	260	51.44 N	0.07 E
Harlowton	202	46.26 N	109.50 W
Harlpur	272b	22.42 N	88.10 E
Harman	188	38.55 N	79.31 W
Harmancık	130	39.41 N	29.10 E
Harmånger	26	61.56 N	17.13 E
Harmanli, Blg.	38	41.56 N	25.54 E
Harmanlı, Tür.	130	37.51 N	37.45 E
Harmanschlag	61	48.39 N	14.47 E
Harmar Heights	279b	40.33 N	79.49 W
Harmarville	279b	40.32 N	79.51 W
Hármashatár-hegy ∧	264c	47.33 N	19.00 E
Harmelen	52	52.05 N	4.58 E
Harmil I	144	16.31 N	40.09 E
Harmonsburg	214	41.40 N	80.19 W
Harmonville	285	40.06 N	75.17 W
Harmony, Ca., U.S.	226	35.35 N	121.01 W
Harmony, In., U.S.	194	39.32 N	87.06 W
Harmony, Mn., U.S.	190	43.33 N	92.00 W
Harmony, N.J., U.S.	210	40.44 N	75.08 W
Harmony, Pa., U.S.	214	40.48 N	80.07 W
Harmony, R.I., U.S.	207	41.53 N	71.35 W
Harmony Brook ≃	276	40.48 N	74.34 W
Harmony Heights	220	27.29 N	80.21 W
Harmony Hills	285	39.42 N	75.41 W
Harmonyville	285	40.11 N	75.43 W
Harnai, India	122	17.48 N	73.06 E
Harnai, Pāk.	120	30.06 N	67.56 E
Harnäs	40	60.39 N	17.22 E
Harnātānr	124	27.19 N	84.01 E
Harndrup	41	55.28 N	10.02 E
Harnes	50	50.27 N	2.54 E
Härnevi	40	59.44 N	17.05 E
Harney ≃	220	25.25 N	81.10 W
Harney, Lake ⊜	220	28.45 N	81.03 W
Harney Basin ⌣[1]	202	43.15 N	119.00 W
Harney Lake ⊜	202	43.14 N	119.07 W
Harney Peak ∧	198	43.51 N	103.31 W
Harney Pond Canal ≅	220	27.00 N	81.04 W
Härnösand	26	62.38 N	17.56 E
Haro, Esp.	34	42.35 N	2.51 W
Haro, Ityo.	144	8.28 N	38.37 E
Ḥarod ≃	132	32.31 N	35.33 E
Harola	272a	28.36 N	77.19 E
Harold Hill ◆[8]	260	51.36 N	0.13 E
Harold Parker State Forest ♠	283	42.37 N	71.05 W
Haroldswick	46a	60.41 N	0.50 W
Harold Wood ◆[8]	260	51.36 N	0.14 E
Haro Strait ʊ	224	48.30 N	123.15 W
Haroué	58	48.28 N	6.11 E
Harpālpur	124	25.17 N	79.20 E
Harpanahalli	122	14.48 N	75.59 E
Harpen ◆[8]	263	51.29 N	7.16 E
Harpenden	42	51.49 N	0.22 W
Harper, Liber.	150	4.25 N	7.43 W
Harper, Ks., U.S.	198	37.17 N	98.01 W
Harper, Tx., U.S.	196	30.18 N	99.15 W
Harper, Wa., U.S.	224	47.31 N	122.31 W
Harper, Mount ∧	180	64.14 N	143.50 W
Harper Lake ⊜	228	35.02 N	117.17 W
Harpers Ferry National Historical Park ♠	188	39.13 N	77.45 W
Harpersfield	210	42.26 N	74.41 W
Harper Town	44	54.55 N	2.31 W
Harper Woods	214	42.25 N	82.55 W
Harpille ∧	62	43.50 N	6.48 E
Harpstedt	52	52.54 N	8.35 E
Harpster	214	40.44 N	83.15 W
Harpsund ∪	40	59.06 N	16.29 E
Harpurhey ◆[8]	262	53.31 N	2.13 W
Harpur Hill	262	53.14 N	1.54 W
Harpursville	210	42.11 N	75.38 W
Harqin	98	41.08 N	119.38 E
Harqin Qi (Jinshan)	98	41.56 N	118.36 E
Harquahala Mountain ∧	200	33.49 N	113.21 W
Ḥarrah	144	14.57 N	50.19 E
Ḥārrah, Jabal al- ∧	132	33.04 N	35.59 E
Harrai	124	22.37 N	79.13 E
Harran	130	36.51 N	39.00 E
Ḥarrān al-'Awāmīd	132	33.27 N	36.34 E
Harray, Loch of ⊜	46	59.01 N	3.13 W
Harrell	194	33.30 N	92.23 W
Harricana ≃	176	51.15 N	79.45 W
Harrietfield	46	56.25 N	3.39 W
Harrietsham	260	51.15 N	0.41 E
Harriman, N.Y., U.S.	210	41.18 N	74.09 W
Harriman, Tn., U.S.	192	35.56 N	84.33 W
Harriman Reservoir ⊜[1]	207	42.50 N	72.53 W
Harriman State Park ♠	210	41.14 N	74.09 W
Harrington, Eng., U.K.	44	54.37 N	3.34 W
Harrington, De., U.S.	208	38.55 N	75.34 W
Harrington, Me., U.S.	188	44.37 N	67.48 W
Harrington, Wa., U.S.	202	47.28 N	118.15 W
Harrington Creek ≃	282	37.19 N	122.18 W
Harrington Drain ≅	281	42.36 N	82.54 W
Harrington Park	276	40.59 N	73.58 W
Harris, Sk., Can.	184	51.44 N	107.35 W
Harris, Scot., U.K.	46	56.59 N	6.20 W
Harris, Mn., U.S.	190	45.35 N	92.58 W
Harris, N.Y., U.S.	210	41.43 N	74.44 W
Harris, R.I., U.S.	207	41.43 N	71.31 W
Harris □[6]	222	29.50 N	95.22 W
Harris ≃	168a	33.18 S	116.09 E
Harris ◆[1]	46	57.55 N	6.50 W
Harris, Lake ⊜, Austl.	162	31.08 S	135.14 E
Harris, Lake ⊜, Fl., U.S.	220	28.46 N	81.49 W
Harris, Sound of ʊ	46	57.45 N	7.10 W
Harris Bay ⊂	212	45.23 N	77.50 W
Harris Brook ≃	283	42.44 N	71.13 W
Harrisburg, Ar., U.S.	194	35.33 N	90.43 W
Harrisburg, Il., U.S.	194	37.44 N	88.32 W
Harrisburg, In., U.S.	218	39.41 N	85.11 W
Harrisburg, Ne., U.S.	198	41.33 N	103.44 W
Harrisburg, Oh., U.S.	214	40.53 N	81.13 W
Harrisburg, Or., U.S.	202	44.16 N	123.10 W
Harrisburg, Pa., U.S.	208	40.16 N	76.53 W
Harrisburg International Airport ⊠	208	40.12 N	76.45 W
Harris Creek ⊂	208	38.45 N	76.18 W
Harris Creek ≃, Austl.	274a	33.57 S	150.57 E
Harris Creek ≃, Tx., U.S.	222	32.33 N	95.08 W
Harrisfield	274b	37.57 S	145.11 E
Harris Hill	210	42.58 N	78.40 W
Harrislee	41	54.48 N	9.22 E
Harrismith, Austl.	162	32.56 S	117.52 E
Harrismith, S. Afr.	158	28.18 S	29.03 E
Harrison, Ar., U.S.	194	36.13 N	93.06 W
Harrison, Id., U.S.	202	47.27 N	116.47 W
Harrison, Il., U.S.	216	42.25 N	89.11 W
Harrison, Mi., U.S.	190	44.01 N	84.47 W
Harrison, Ne., U.S.	198	42.41 N	103.53 W
Harrison, N.J., U.S.	276	40.44 N	74.09 W

Symbol	English	Deutsch	Español	Français	Português
≃	River	Fluß	Río	Rivière	Rio
≅	Canal	Kanal	Canal	Canal	Canal
⌞	Waterfall, Rapids	Wasserfall, Stromschnellen	Cascada, Rápidos	Chute d'eau, Rapides	Cascata, Rápidos
ʊ	Strait	Meeresstraße	Estrecho	Détroit	Estreito
⊂	Bay, Gulf	Bucht, Golf	Bahía, Golfo	Baie, Golfe	Baía, Golfo
⊜	Lake, Lakes	See, Seen	Lago, Lagos	Lac, Lacs	Lago, Lagos
⊞	Swamp	Sumpf	Pantano	Marais	Pântano
⊓	Ice Features, Glacier	Eis- und Gletscherformen	Accidentes Glaciales	Formes glaciaires	Acidentes glaciares
⊤	Other Hydrographic Features	Andere Hydrographische Objekte	Otros Elementos Hidrográficos	Autres données hydrographiques	Outros acidentes hidrográficos
✢	Submarine Features	Untermeerische Objekte	Accidentes Submarinos	Formes de relief sous-marin	Acidentes submarinos
□	Political Unit	Politische Einheit	Unidad Politica	Entité politique	Unidade política
∪	Cultural Institution	Kulturelle Institution	Institución Cultural	Institution culturelle	Institução cultural
⊥	Historical Site	Historische Stätte	Sitio Histórico	Site historique	Sitio histórico
♠	Recreational Site	Erholungs- und Ferienort	Sitio de Recreo	Centre de loisirs	Area de Lazer
⊠	Airport	Flughafen	Aeropuerto	Aéroport	Aeroporto
■	Military Installation	Militäranlage	Instalación Militar	Installation militaire	Instalação militar
◆	Miscellaneous	Verschiedenes	Misceláneo	Divers	Diversos

Harrison, N.Y., U.S. 210 40.58 N 73.43 W
Harrison, Oh., U.S. 218 39.15 N 84.49 W
Harrison □[6], In., U.S. 218 38.17 N 86.07 W
Harrison □[6], Ky., U.S. 218 38.25 N 84.19 W
Harrison □[6], Oh., U.S. 214 40.16 N 81.05 W
Harrison □[6], Tx., U.S. 222 32.35 N 94.35 W
Harrison ≃ 224 49.14 N 121.57 W
Harrison, Cape ≻ 176 54.55 N 57.55 W
Harrison Bay ⊂ 180 70.30 N 151.30 W
Harrisonburg, La., U.S. 194 31.46 N 91.49 W
Harrisonburg, Va., U.S. 188 38.26 N 78.52 W
Harrison City 279b 40.21 N 79.39 W
Harrison Hot Springs 224 49.18 N 121.47 W
Harrison Islands II 176 69.13 N 90.30 W
Harrison Lake ⊜ 182 49.30 N 121.50 W
Harrison Mills 224 49.14 N 121.57 W
Harrisons Brook ≃ 276 40.38 N 74.34 W
Harrison Tomb State Memorial ⊥ 218 39.09 N 84.46 W
Harrison Valley 214 41.57 N 77.39 W
Harrisonville, Md., U.S. 284b 39.23 N 77.50 W
Harrisonville, Mo., U.S. 194 38.39 N 94.20 W
Harrisonville, N.J., U.S. 285 39.41 N 75.15 W
Harris Park 274a 33.49 S 151.01 E
Harris Pond ⊜ 283 42.45 N 71.16 W
Harris Reservoir ⊜[1] 222 29.14 N 95.33 W
Harriston, On., Can. 212 43.54 N 80.53 W
Harriston, Ms., U.S. 194 31.43 N 91.01 W
Harristown 219 39.51 N 89.05 W
Harrisville, Austl. 171a 27.49 S 152.40 E
Harrisville, Mi., U.S. 190 44.39 N 83.17 W
Harrisville, N.Y., U.S. 212 44.09 N 75.19 W
Harrisville, Oh., U.S. 214 40.11 N 80.53 W
Harrisville, Pa., U.S. 214 41.08 N 80.00 W
Harrisville, R.I., U.S. 207 41.57 N 71.40 W
Harrisville, W.V., U.S. 188 39.12 N 81.03 W
Harrod 216 40.42 N 83.55 W
Harrodsburg 194 37.45 N 84.50 W
Harrods Creek ≃ 218 38.20 N 85.38 W
Harrogate 44 54.00 N 1.33 W
Harrold 196 34.05 N 99.02 W
Harrop Lake ⊜ 184 52.38 N 95.58 W
Harrow 214 42.02 N 82.55 W
Harrow ✦[8] 260 51.35 N 0.21 W
Harrow on the Hill ✦[8] 260 51.34 N 0.20 W
Harrow School ʋ[2] 260 51.34 N 0.20 W
Harrowsmith 212 44.24 N 76.40 W
Harry S. Truman Reservoir ⊜[1] 194 38.10 N 93.45 W
Harry Truman Field ⊠ 240m 18.21 N 64.59 W
Har Sai Shan ∧ 102 35.28 N 97.55 E
Harsefeld 52 53.27 N 9.30 E
Harsens Island 214 42.34 N 82.34 W
Harsens Island I 281 42.35 N 82.38 W
Harsewinkel 52 51.58 N 8.13 E
Harsīn 128 34.16 N 47.35 E
Harşit ≃ 130 41.01 N 38.52 E
Harskamp 52 52.07 N 5.45 E
Harsleben 54 51.52 N 11.05 E
Harstad 24 68.46 N 16.30 E
Harstena 26 58.16 N 17.01 E
Har Su 89 48.09 N 122.25 E
Harsūd 124 22.06 N 76.44 E
Harsum 52 52.12 N 9.57 E
Hart, Mi., U.S. 190 43.41 N 86.21 W
Hart, Tx., U.S. 196 34.23 N 102.07 W
Hart ≃ 180 65.51 N 136.22 W
Hart, Lake ⊜, Austl. 166 31.08 S 136.24 E
Hart, Lake ⊜, Fl., U.S. 220 28.22 N 81.13 W
Ḩartā 132 32.42 N 35.51 E
Hartbees ≃ 158 28.45 S 20.32 E
Hartbeesfontein 158 26.42 S 26.26 E
Hartbeespoort 158 25.44 S 27.52 E
Hartberg 61 47.17 N 15.59 E
Hartenholm 52 53.54 N 10.03 E
Hartenstein 54 50.39 N 12.40 E
Hart Fell ∧ 44 55.25 N 3.25 W
Hartfield 208 37.34 N 76.30 W
Hartford, Eng., U.K. 262 53.15 N 2.33 W
Hartford, Al., U.S. 194 31.06 N 85.41 W
Hartford, Ar., U.S. 194 35.01 N 94.22 W
Hartford, Ct., U.S. 207 41.46 N 72.41 W
Hartford, Il., U.S. 219 38.50 N 90.05 W
Hartford, In., U.S. 218 38.59 N 84.57 W
Hartford, Ks., U.S. 198 38.18 N 95.57 W
Hartford, Ky., U.S. 194 37.27 N 86.54 W
Hartford, Mi., U.S. 216 42.12 N 86.10 W
Hartford, N.J., U.S. 285 39.58 N 74.53 W
Hartford, N.Y., U.S. 210 43.21 N 73.22 W
Hartford, Oh., U.S. 214 41.19 N 80.34 W
Hartford, S.D., U.S. 198 43.37 N 96.56 W
Hartford, Wi., U.S. 190 43.19 N 88.22 W
Hartford □[6] 207 41.46 N 72.41 W
Hartford City 216 40.27 N 85.22 W
Hartha 54 51.05 N 12.58 E
Hartington 198 42.37 N 97.15 W
Hart Island I 276 40.51 N 73.46 W
Hart Lake ⊜ 202 42.24 N 119.51 W
Hartland, N.B., Can. 186 46.18 N 67.32 W
Hartland, Eng., U.K. 42 50.59 N 4.29 W
Hartland, Il., U.S. 216 42.22 N 88.31 W
Hartland, Me., U.S. 188 44.53 N 69.26 W
Hartland, Mi., U.S. 216 42.39 N 83.45 W
Hartland, N.Y., U.S. 210 43.14 N 78.35 W
Hartland, Wi., U.S. 216 43.06 N 88.20 W
Hartland Point ≻ 42 51.02 N 4.31 W
Hartlepool 44 54.42 N 1.11 W
Hartleton 210 40.54 N 77.10 W
Hartley, Austl. 170 33.33 S 150.11 E
Hartley, Eng., U.K. 260 51.23 N 0.19 E
Hartley, Ia., U.S. 198 43.10 N 95.28 W
Hartley, Tx., U.S. 196 35.53 N 102.24 W
Hartley Bay 182 53.25 N 129.15 W
Hartlip 260 51.21 N 0.39 E
Hart Lot 210 43.01 N 76.28 W
Hartly 208 39.10 N 75.42 W
Hartmannsdorf 54 50.53 N 12.48 E
Hartmannshain 56 50.28 N 9.16 E
Hart-Miller Island I 208 39.15 N 76.23 W
Hart Mountain ∧ 184 52.29 N 101.25 W
Hartney 184 49.28 N 100.30 W
Hartola 26 61.35 N 26.01 E
Harts ≃ 158 28.24 S 24.17 E
Hartsburg 219 38.41 N 92.18 W
Hartsdale 210 41.01 N 73.47 W
Hartselle 194 34.26 N 86.56 W
Härtsfeld ✦[1] 56 48.50 N 10.15 E
Hartshill 42 52.37 N 1.32 W
Hartshorne 196 34.50 N 95.33 W
Harts Range 162 23.00 S 134.55 E
Hartstene Island I 224 47.14 N 122.53 W
Hartstown 214 41.33 N 80.23 W
Hartsville, In., U.S. 218 39.16 N 85.41 W
Hartsville, Pa., U.S. 285 40.14 N 75.05 W
Hartsville, S.C., U.S. 192 34.22 N 80.04 W
Hartsville, Tn., U.S. 194 36.23 N 86.10 W
Hartswater 158 27.34 S 24.43 E
Hartville, Mo., U.S. 194 37.15 N 92.30 W
Hartville, Oh., U.S. 214 40.57 N 81.19 W
Hartwell 192 34.21 N 82.55 W
Hartwell Lake ⊜[1] 192 34.30 N 82.55 W
Hartwick 210 42.39 N 75.02 W
Hartwick Pines State Park ♦ 190 44.47 N 84.41 W
Hartz Mountains National Park ♦ 166 43.15 S 146.50 E
Harue 94 36.08 N 136.14 E
Haruki 270 34.29 N 135.23 E
Haruku, Pulau I 164 3.34 S 128.29 E
Hārūn 140 11.20 N 25.43 E
Haruna 94 36.23 N 138.53 E
Hārūnābād 123 29.37 N 73.08 E
Haruna-san ∧ 94 36.28 N 138.52 E
Haruniye 130 37.17 N 36.27 E
Haruno, Nihon 94 34.57 N 137.53 E
Haruno, Nihon 96 33.30 N 133.30 E
Harūr 122 12.04 N 78.30 E
Hārūt ≃ 128 31.35 N 61.18 E
Harvard, Il., U.S. 216 42.25 N 88.36 W
Harvard, Ma., U.S. 207 42.30 N 71.35 W
Harvard, Ne., U.S. 198 40.37 N 98.05 W
Harvard University ʋ[2] 283 42.22 N 71.07 W
Harvel, Eng., U.K. 260 51.21 N 0.22 E
Harvel, Il., U.S. 219 39.21 N 89.32 W
Harvest, Mount ∧[2] 162 25.54 S 126.28 E
Harvey, Austl. 168a 33.05 S 115.54 E
Harvey, N.B., Can. 186 45.43 N 64.43 W
Harvey, Il., U.S. 216 41.36 N 87.38 W
Harvey, N.D., U.S. 198 47.46 N 99.56 W
Harvey ≃ 168a 32.46 S 115.43 E
Harvey Estuary ⊂[1] 168a 32.43 S 115.42 E
Harvey Mountain ∧ 207 42.18 N 73.25 W
Harvey Reservoir ⊜[1] 168a 33.05 S 115.58 E
Harveysburg 218 39.30 N 84.00 W
Harveys Lake 210 41.23 N 76.02 W
Harwell 42 51.37 N 1.18 W
Harwich, Eng., U.K. 42 51.57 N 1.17 E
Harwich, Ma., U.S. 207 41.41 N 70.04 W
Harwich Port 207 41.40 N 70.04 W
Harwick 279b 40.34 N 79.48 W
Harwinton 207 41.46 N 73.03 W
Harwood, Eng., U.K. 262 53.35 N 2.23 W
Harwood, Tx., U.S. 222 29.40 N 97.30 W
Harwood Heights 278 41.58 N 87.48 W
Harwood Mines 210 40.57 N 76.01 W
Harwood Park 284b 39.12 N 76.44 W
Haryāna □[3] 120 29.20 N 76.20 E
Harz ⋀ 54 51.45 N 10.30 E
Harzgerode 54 51.38 N 11.08 E
Ḩaşā, Bi'r al- ⊤[4] 140 22.58 N 35.40 E
Ḩasā, Wādī al- V 132 31.05 N 35.27 E
Hasafen 86 45.14 N 90.20 E
Ḩaşāh, Wādī al- V 132 30.38 N 37.09 E
Hasaki 94 35.44 N 140.50 E
Hasalbag 120 37.54 N 76.44 E
Ḩasanābād 267d 35.44 N 51.19 E
Ḩasanābād-e Khāleşeh 267d 35.37 N 51.12 E
Hasan Abdāl 123 33.49 N 72.41 E
Hasançelebi 130 38.58 N 37.54 E
Hasan Dağı ∧ 130 38.08 N 34.12 E
Hasankale → Pasinler 130 39.59 N 41.41 E
Hasankeyf 130 37.43 N 41.25 E
Ḩasan Kīādeh 128 37.24 N 49.58 E
Hasanpur 124 28.43 N 78.17 E
Hasayaz 130 40.15 N 33.20 E
Ḩāşbānī, Nahr al- ≃ 132 33.11 N 35.37 E
Ḩāşbayyā 132 33.24 N 35.41 E
Hasbek 130 39.33 N 35.33 E
Hasbergen, B.R.D. 52 52.14 N 7.57 E
Hasbergen, B.R.D. 52 53.05 N 8.40 E
Hasbrouck Heights 276 40.51 N 74.04 W
Hascosay I 46a 60.37 N 0.59 W
Hasdo ≃ 120 21.44 N 82.44 E
Hasdo-Rāmpur Basin ≚[1] 124 22.50 N 82.35 E
Hase, Nihon 94 35.47 N 138.06 E
Hase, Nihon 270 34.32 N 135.54 E
Hase ≃, B.R.D. 52 52.41 N 7.18 E
Hase ≃, Nihon 270 34.34 N 135.38 E
Hasel ≃ 54 50.32 N 10.27 E
Häselgehr 58 47.19 N 10.30 E
Haselhorst ✦[8] 264a 52.33 N 13.15 E
Haselünne 52 52.40 N 7.29 E
Hasenkamp 252 31.31 S 59.51 W
Ḩashā', Jabal al- ∧ 144 13.45 N 44.30 E
HaShefela ✦[1] 132 31.40 N 34.55 E
Hashima 94 35.19 N 136.42 E
Hashimoto, Nihon 96 34.19 N 135.37 E
Hashimoto, Nihon 270 34.26 N 135.23 E
Hashira-jima I 96 34.01 N 132.25 E
Hashiri-jima I 96 34.21 N 133.27 E
Hashitai 89 49.24 N 125.18 E
Hasht Sāl ✦[8] 272a 28.38 N 77.03 E
Hasil, Pulau I 164 1.06 S 128.24 E
Hāsilpur 123 29.43 N 72.33 E
Ḩāsīn-e Bozorg 84 39.23 N 44.42 E
Haskayne 262 53.34 N 2.58 W
Haskeir Islands II 46 57.42 N 7.41 W
Haskell, Ok., U.S. 196 35.49 N 95.40 W
Haskell, Tx., U.S. 196 33.09 N 99.44 W
Haskell Pond ⊜ 283 42.37 N 70.44 W
Hasketh Bank 262 53.43 N 2.51 W
Haskins 216 41.27 N 83.42 W
Haskovo 38 41.56 N 25.33 E
Haskovo □[4] 130 41.50 N 25.50 E
Hasköy, Tür. 130 41.38 N 26.41 E
Hasköy, Tür. 130 40.59 N 42.52 E
Hasköy ✦[8] 267b 41.02 N 28.58 E
Haslach im Kinzigtal 58 48.16 N 8.06 E
Hasle, Dan. 41 55.11 N 14.43 E
Hasle, Schw. 58 47.01 N 7.39 E
Haslemere 42 51.06 N 0.43 W
Haslett 216 42.44 N 84.24 W
Haslev 41 55.20 N 11.58 E
Haslingden 262 53.43 N 2.18 W
Haslingden Grane 262 53.42 N 2.21 W
Haslington 44 53.06 N 2.24 W
Haslital V 58 46.42 N 8.10 E
Haslum 26 59.50 N 10.22 E
Hasmark 41 55.33 N 10.28 E
Ḩasmat 'Umar, Bi'r ⊤[4] 140 21.46 N 34.00 E
Hāsnābād 126 22.35 N 88.55 E
Hasnācha 272b 22.26 N 88.09 E
Haspe ✦[8] 263 51.21 N 7.26 E
Hasperos Canyon V 200 33.50 N 105.02 W
Hasper-Stausee ⊜[1] 263 51.18 N 7.25 E
Haspres 50 50.15 N 3.25 E
Ḩaşş, Jabal al- ∧[2] 130 35.52 N 37.22 E
Hassa 130 36.50 N 36.29 E
Hassan 122 13.00 N 76.05 E
Hassard 219 39.39 N 91.40 W
Hassayampa ≃ 200 33.20 N 112.43 W
Hassberge ⋀[2] 56 50.12 N 10.29 E
Hassbergen 52 52.44 N 9.13 E
Hassel, B.R.D. 52 52.48 N 9.11 E
Hassel, B.R.D. 263 51.39 N 7.30 E
Hassel ✦[8] 263 51.36 N 7.03 E
Hasselbeck-Schwarzbach 263 51.16 N 6.53 E
Hasselfelde 54 51.41 N 10.51 E
Hasselfors 40 59.05 N 14.39 E
Hassels ✦[8] 263 51.10 N 6.53 E
Hasselt, Bel. 56 50.56 N 5.20 E
Hasselt, Ned. 52 52.35 N 6.05 E
Hassfurt 56 50.02 N 10.31 E
Hassi Bel Guebbour 148 28.46 N 6.27 E
Hassi el Ghella 34 35.28 N 1.03 W
Hassi Mameche 34 35.52 N 0.04 E
Hassi Messaoud 148 31.43 N 5.59 E
Hassi Zehana 34 35.01 N 0.53 W
Hassleben 54 53.13 N 13.41 E
Hässleholm 41 56.09 N 13.46 E
Hasslinghausen 56 51.20 N 7.17 E
Hassloch 56 49.22 N 8.16 E
Hasson Heights 214 41.26 N 79.41 W
Hästbo 40 60.27 N 16.27 E
Hasten ✦[8], B.R.D. 263 51.12 N 7.09 E
Hästen ✦[8], B.R.D. 263 51.09 N 7.06 E
Hastière-Lavaux 56 50.13 N 4.50 E
Hastings, Austl. 169 38.18 S 145.11 E
Hastings, Barb. 241g 13.04 N 59.35 W
Hastings, On., Can. 212 44.18 N 77.57 W
Hastings, N.Z. 172 39.38 S 176.51 E
Hastings, Eng., U.K. 42 50.51 N 0.36 E
Hastings, Fl., U.S. 192 29.43 N 81.30 W
Hastings, Il., U.S. 278 41.41 N 87.58 W
Hastings, Mi., U.S. 216 42.39 N 85.17 W
Hastings, Mn., U.S. 190 44.44 N 92.51 W
Hastings, Ne., U.S. 198 40.35 N 98.23 W
Hastings, N.Y., U.S. 210 43.22 N 76.09 W
Hastings, Pa., U.S. 214 40.39 N 78.42 W
Hastings □[6] 212 44.45 N 77.40 W
Hastings Battlesite ⊥ 42 50.53 N 0.31 E
Hastings-on-Hudson 276 40.59 N 73.52 W
Hastingwood 260 51.45 N 0.09 E
Hastrup 41 55.26 N 12.11 E
Hasty 198 38.06 N 102.57 W
Hasuda 94 35.59 N 139.40 E
Hasumi 96 34.52 N 132.37 E
Haswell 198 38.27 N 103.09 W
Hata 94 36.11 N 137.51 E
Hat'ae-do I 98 34.32 N 126.03 E
Ha Tan 110 18.30 N 105.20 E
Hatanagi-dam ✦[6] 94 35.18 N 138.12 E
Hatashō 94 35.10 N 136.15 E
Hatay □[4] 130 36.30 N 36.15 E
Hatboro 208 40.10 N 75.06 W
Hatch, N.M., U.S. 200 32.39 N 107.09 W
Hatch, Ut., U.S. 200 37.38 N 112.26 W
Hat Chao Mai National Park ♦ 110 7.40 N 99.35 E
Hatches Creek 162 20.56 S 135.12 E
Hatchet Creek ≃ 194 32.52 N 86.20 W
Hatchet Lake 186 44.35 N 63.40 W
Hatchie ≃ 194 35.35 N 89.53 W
Hatchineha, Lake ⊜ 220 28.02 N 81.25 W
Hatchlands ⊥ 260 51.15 N 0.28 W
Hatchmere 262 53.15 N 2.40 W
Hatchville 207 41.37 N 70.33 W
Hatch Wash V 200 38.32 N 109.36 W
Hat Creek ≃, U.S. 198 43.16 N 103.36 W
Hat Creek ≃, Ca., U.S. 204 40.59 N 121.33 W
Haţeg 38 45.37 N 22.57 E
Hateruma-shima I 175d 24.03 N 123.47 E
Hatfield, Austl. 166 33.52 S 143.45 E
Hatfield, Eng., U.K. 44 53.34 N 1.00 W
Hatfield, Eng., U.K. 260 51.46 N 0.13 W
Hatfield, Ar., U.S. 194 34.29 N 94.22 W
Hatfield, Ma., U.S. 207 42.22 N 72.35 W
Hatfield Aerodrome ⊠ 260 51.46 N 0.16 W
Hatfield House ⊥ 260 51.46 N 0.13 W
Hatfield Peverel 260 51.47 N 0.35 E
Hatfield Swamp ⁝⁝ 276 40.50 N 74.20 W
Hathāla 123 32.03 N 70.34 E
Hathaway Pines 226 38.07 N 120.28 W
Hatherleigh 42 50.49 N 4.04 W
Hathersage 44 53.19 N 1.38 W
Hāthras 124 27.36 N 78.03 E
Hātia µ 124 22.30 N 91.15 E
Ḩāţibah, Ra's ≻ 144 21.55 N 38.58 E
Ha Tien 110 10.23 N 104.29 E
Hatillo 240m 18.29 N 66.49 W
Ha Tinh 110 18.20 N 105.54 E
Hatinoe → Hachinohe 92 40.30 N 141.29 E
Hatiozi → Hachiōji 94 35.39 N 139.20 E
Hatip 130 37.46 N 32.25 E
Hātisāla 272b 22.33 N 88.32 E
Hato 241s 12.12 N 68.57 W
Hato, Bocht van ⊂ 241s 12.13 N 68.58 W
Hato del Volcán 236 8.46 N 82.38 W
Hatogaya 94 35.50 N 139.44 E
Hato Mayor [del Rey] 238 18.46 N 69.15 W
Hato Rey 240m 18.25 N 66.03 W
Hatoyama 94 35.59 N 139.20 E
Hāt Pīplia 124 22.46 N 76.18 E
Hatsukaichi 96 34.21 N 132.20 E
Hatsu-shima I 94 35.02 N 139.10 E
Hatsutomi 268 35.46 N 140.01 E
Hatta 124 24.07 N 79.36 E
Hattab, Oued el V 36 35.23 N 9.32 E
Hattah-Kulkyne National Park ♦ 166 34.40 S 142.30 E
Hattem 52 52.28 N 6.04 E
Hatten, B.R.D. 52 53.02 N 8.22 E
Hatten, Fr. 56 48.54 N 7.59 E
Hattenhofen 60 48.13 N 11.07 E
Hatteras 192 35.13 N 75.41 W
Hatteras, Cape ≻ 192 35.13 N 75.32 W
Hatteras Island I 192 35.25 N 75.30 W
Hattiesburg 194 31.19 N 89.17 W
Hatting 41 55.51 N 9.46 E
Hattingen 56 51.23 N 7.10 E
Hattingspruit 158 28.09 S 30.11 E
Hatton, Eng., U.K. 262 53.20 N 2.36 W
Hatton, Scot., U.K. 46 57.25 N 1.54 W
Hatton, Al., U.S. 194 34.33 N 87.24 W
Hatton, N.D., U.S. 198 47.38 N 97.27 W
Hatton ✦[8] 260 51.28 N 0.25 W
Hatton Fields 226 36.33 N 121.54 W
Hattorf [am Harz] 52 51.39 N 10.14 E
Hattori, Nihon 270 34.46 N 135.27 E
Hattori, Nihon 270 34.52 N 135.36 E
Hattstatt 58 48.01 N 7.17 E
Hattstedt 41 54.31 N 9.01 E
Hatunsaray 130 37.35 N 32.21 E
Hatvan 30 47.40 N 19.41 E
Hat Yai 110 7.01 N 100.28 E
Hatzfeld ✦[8] 263 51.17 N 7.11 E
Hatzic 224 49.09 N 122.15 W
Hatzic Lake ⊜ 224 49.10 N 122.14 W
Haubourdin 50 50.36 N 2.59 E
Haubstadt 194 38.12 N 87.34 W
Hāudullāpur 272b 22.25 N 88.33 E
Hauge 26 58.18 N 6.15 E
Haugesund 26 59.25 N 5.18 E
Haugh of Urr 44 54.58 N 3.52 W
Haughton Green 262 53.27 N 2.06 W
Haugsdorf 61 48.42 N 16.05 E
Hau Hoi Wan ⊂ 100 22.28 N 113.56 E
Hauhungaroa Range ⋀ 172 38.50 S 175.34 E
Haukeligrend 26 59.45 N 7.31 E
Haukipudas 26 65.11 N 25.21 E
Haukivesi ⊜ 26 62.06 N 28.28 E
Haukivuori 26 62.01 N 27.13 E
Hauldres, Ru des ≃ 261 48.37 N 2.28 E
Haulerwijk 52 53.04 N 6.20 E
Haultain ≃ 184 55.51 N 106.46 W
Haune ≃ 56 50.52 N 9.43 E
Haunersdorf 60 48.36 N 12.43 E
Haunstetten 58 48.18 N 10.54 E
Haunts Creek µ 276 40.37 N 73.31 W
Hauppauge 210 40.49 N 73.12 W
Hauptsrus 158 26.33 S 26.18 E
Hauraki Gulf ⊂ 172 36.20 S 175.05 E
Hauroko, Lake ⊜ 172 46.00 S 167.20 E
Hauru, Pointe ≻ 174s 17.29 S 149.55 W
Haus 64 47.25 N 13.49 E
Hausa 273a 6.37 N 3.21 E
Hausach 58 48.17 N 8.10 E
Hausham 64 47.45 N 11.50 E
Hausruck ⋀ 60 48.07 N 13.35 E
Haussee ⊜ 264a 52.38 N 13.41 E
Haussömmern 54 51.11 N 10.49 E
Haut, Isle au I 188 44.03 N 68.38 W
Haut Atlas ⋀ 148 31.30 N 6.00 W
Haut-Bout 261 48.32 N 1.55 E
Haute Colme, Canal de la ≊ 50 50.50 N 2.12 E
Hautecombe, Abbaye de ʋ[1] 62 45.45 N 5.50 E
Haute-Corse □[5] 36 42.30 N 9.00 E
Haute-Garonne □[5] 32 43.25 N 1.30 E
Haute-Kotto □[5] 152 7.00 N 23.00 E
Haute-Loire □[5] 32 45.05 N 3.50 E
Hauteluce 62 45.45 N 6.35 E
Haute-Marne □[5] 58 48.05 N 5.10 E
Hauterive 186 49.12 N 68.16 W
Hauterives 62 45.15 N 5.02 E
Hautes-Alpes □[5] 62 44.40 N 6.30 E
Haute-Sangha □[5] 152 4.30 N 16.00 E
Haute-Saône □[5] 58 47.40 N 6.10 E
Haute-Savoie □[5] 32 46.00 N 6.20 E
Haute Seine, Canal de la ≊ 50 48.34 N 3.43 E
Hautes Fagnes ⋀ 56 50.30 N 6.05 E
Hautes-Pyrénées □[5] 32 43.00 N 0.10 E
Haute Sûre, Lac de la ⊜[1] 56 49.52 N 5.52 E
Haute-Vienne □[5] 32 45.50 N 1.15 E
Hauteville-Lompnes 58 45.58 N 5.36 E
Haute Volta → Burkina Faso □[1] 150 13.00 N 1.30 W
Haut-Folin ∧ 32 47.00 N 4.02 E
Haut-Kœnigsbourg, Château du ⊥ 58 48.14 N 7.22 E
Haut-Mbomou □[5] 140 6.00 N 26.00 E
Hautmont 50 50.15 N 3.56 E
Haut-Ogooué □[4] 152 1.00 S 13.50 E
Haut-Rhin □[5] 58 47.53 N 7.13 E
Hauts-de-Seine □[5] 261 48.50 N 2.11 E
Hautvillers 50 49.05 N 3.57 E
Haut-Zaïre □[4] 154 2.20 N 27.00 E
Hauula 229c 21.36 N 157.54 W
Hauzenberg 60 48.39 N 13.38 E
Hauz Rāni ✦[8] 272a 28.32 N 77.13 E
Havana → La Habana, Cuba 240p 23.08 N 82.22 W
Havana, Ar., U.S. 194 35.06 N 93.31 W
Havana, Fl., U.S. 192 30.37 N 84.24 W
Havana, Il., U.S. 194 40.18 N 90.03 W
Havana, N.D., U.S. 198 45.57 N 97.37 W
Havane, La → La Habana 240p 23.08 N 82.22 W
Havannah, Canal de la µ 175f 22.22 S 167.01 E
Havant 42 50.51 N 0.59 W
Havasu, Lake ⊜[1] 200 34.30 N 114.20 W
Havasu Creek ≃ 200 36.19 N 112.46 W
Havasupai Indian Reservation ✦[4] 200 36.13 N 112.40 W
Havdrup 41 55.32 N 12.08 E
Havel ≃ 54 52.53 N 11.58 E
Havelange 56 50.23 N 5.14 E
Havelberg 54 52.50 N 12.04 E
Havelberg ∧[2] 264a 52.28 N 13.12 E
Haveli 123 30.27 N 73.42 E
Haveliān 123 34.03 N 73.10 E
Havel-Kanal ≊ 264a 52.36 N 13.12 E
Havelland ✦[1] 54 52.25 N 12.45 E
Havelländischer Grosser Hauptkanal ≊ 264a 52.37 N 13.03 E
Havelländisches Luch ⁝⁝ 54 52.40 N 12.40 E
Havelock, On., Can. 212 44.26 N 77.53 W
Havelock, N.Z. 172 41.17 S 173.46 E
Havelock, N.C., U.S. 192 34.52 N 76.54 W
Havelock Island I 110 11.58 N 93.00 E
Havelock North 172 39.40 S 176.53 E
Haven 198 37.53 N 97.46 W
Haverford 285 40.00 N 75.17 W
Haverford College ʋ[2] 285 40.00 N 75.18 W
Haverfordwest 42 51.49 N 4.58 W
Haverhill, Eng., U.K. 42 52.05 N 0.26 E
Haverhill, Ma., U.S. 207 42.46 N 71.04 W
Haverhill Airport ⊠ 283 42.48 N 71.04 W
Haverhill-Riverside Airport ⊠ 283 42.46 N 71.02 W
Hāveri 122 14.48 N 75.24 E
Haverigg 44 54.11 N 3.17 W
Havering ✦[8] 260 51.34 N 0.14 E
Havering-atte-Bower ✦[8] 260 51.37 N 0.11 E
Havering's Grove 260 51.38 N 0.23 E
Havern ⊜ 26 62.17 N 15.07 E
Haverö 26 62.24 N 15.05 E
Haverstraw 210 41.11 N 73.57 W
Havertown 208 39.58 N 75.18 W
Haviland, Ks., U.S. 198 37.37 N 99.06 W
Haviland, Oh., U.S. 216 41.01 N 84.35 W
Haviland Brook ≃ 276 41.07 N 73.33 W
Ḩavīq 128 38.10 N 48.54 E
Havířov 30 49.47 N 18.27 E
Havixbeck 52 51.58 N 7.25 E
Hävla 40 58.55 N 15.52 E
Havlíčkův Brod 30 49.36 N 15.35 E
Havnbjerg 41 55.02 N 9.48 E
Havnsø 41 55.45 N 11.20 E
Havran 130 39.33 N 27.06 E
Havré, Bel. 50 50.28 N 4.02 E
Havre → Le Havre, Fr. 50 49.30 N 0.08 E
Havre, Mt., U.S. 202 48.32 N 109.40 W
Havre-Aubert 186 47.14 N 61.51 W
Havre Aubert, Île du I 186 47.14 N 61.57 W
Havre aux Maisons, Île du I 186 47.25 N 61.47 W
Havre de Grace 208 39.32 N 76.05 W
Havre de Grace Heights 208 39.35 N 76.07 W
Havre North 202 48.36 N 109.41 W
Havre-Saint-Pierre 186 50.14 N 63.36 W
Havsa 130 41.33 N 26.49 E
Havza 130 40.58 N 35.41 E
Haw ≃ 192 35.36 N 79.03 W
Hawaii □[3] 229d 20.00 N 157.45 W
Hawaii I 229d 19.30 N 155.30 W
Hawaiian Gardens 280 33.49 N 118.04 W
Hawaiian Islands II 229d 20.30 N 157.30 W
Hawaiian Ridge ✦[3] 14 24.00 N 165.00 W
Hawaii Volcanoes National Park ♦ 229d 19.23 N 155.17 W
Hawal ≃ 146 10.00 N 12.05 E
Hawarden, Sk., Can. 184 51.23 N 106.36 W
Hawarden, N.Z. 172 42.56 S 172.38 E
Hawarden, Wales, U.K. 44 53.11 N 3.02 W
Hawarden, Ia., U.S. 198 42.59 N 96.29 W
Ḩawashīyah, Wādī V 140 28.31 N 32.58 E
Haw Creek ≃ 218 39.11 N 85.55 W
Hawea, Lake ⊜ 172 44.30 S 169.17 E
Hawera 172 39.35 S 174.17 E
Hawes 44 54.18 N 2.12 W
Hawesville 194 37.54 N 86.45 W
Haweswater Reservoir ⊜ 44 54.32 N 2.48 W
Ḩawf, Jabal ⋀[2] 273c 29.55 N 31.21 E
Ḩawf, Wādī V 142 29.53 N 31.18 E
Hawi 229d 20.14 N 155.50 W
Hawick 44 55.25 N 2.47 W
Hawk Creek ≃ 198 44.44 N 95.25 W
Hawkdun Range ⋀ 172 44.46 S 170.00 E
Hawke, Cape ≻ 166 32.13 S 152.34 E
Hawke Bay ⊂ 172 39.20 S 177.30 E
Hawker 166 31.53 S 138.25 E
Hawkes, Mount ∧ 9 83.56 S 55.45 W
Hawkes Brook ≃ 283 42.45 N 71.08 W
Hawkesbury 206 45.36 N 74.37 W
Hawkesbury ≃ 170 33.30 S 151.10 E
Hawkesbury Island I 182 53.38 N 129.00 W
Hawkes Pond ⊜ 283 42.30 N 71.02 W
Hawkeye 190 42.56 N 91.57 W
Hawkhurst 42 51.02 N 0.30 E
Hawking 42 51.06 N 1.10 E
Hawkins, Tx., U.S. 222 32.35 N 95.12 W
Hawkins, Wi., U.S. 190 45.30 N 90.43 W
Hawkins, Lake ⊜[1] 222 32.38 N 95.15 W
Hawkins Island I 180 60.30 N 146.00 W
Hawkinsville 192 32.17 N 83.28 W
Hawk Junction 190 48.05 N 84.34 W
Hawk Lake 184 49.48 N 93.59 W
Haw Knob ∧ 192 35.19 N 84.02 W
Hawk Point 219 38.58 N 91.07 W
Hawk Run 214 40.55 N 78.12 W
Hawksbill ∧ 188 38.33 N 78.23 W
Hawksbill Creek ⊂ 192 26.32 N 78.43 W
Hawks Nest Point ≻ 238 24.09 N 75.32 W
Hawkwell 260 51.36 N 0.40 E
Hawkwood 166 25.47 S 150.50 E
Hawley, Eng., U.K. 260 51.25 N 0.14 E
Hawley, Mn., U.S. 198 46.52 N 96.18 W
Hawley, Pa., U.S. 210 41.28 N 75.10 W
Hawleyton 210 42.01 N 75.55 W
Hawleyville 207 41.25 N 73.21 W
Haworth 276 40.57 N 73.59 W
Haw Par Villa ʋ 271c 1.16 N 103.47 E
Hawr 142 27.52 N 30.44 E
Ḩawrān, Wādī V 128 33.58 N 42.34 E
Ḩawsh 'Īsā 142 30.55 N 30.17 E
Hawthorn, Austl. 274b 37.49 S 145.02 E
Hawthorn, Pa., U.S. 214 41.01 N 79.17 W
Hawthorne, Ca., U.S. 228 33.54 N 118.21 W
Hawthorne, Fl., U.S. 192 29.35 N 82.05 W
Hawthorne, Nv., U.S. 204 38.31 N 118.37 W
Hawthorne, N.J., U.S. 210 40.56 N 74.09 W
Hawthorne, N.Y., U.S. 210 41.06 N 73.47 W
Hawthorne Lake ⊜ 276 41.03 N 74.35 W
Hawthorne Municipal Airport ⊠ 280 33.55 N 118.20 W
Hawthorne Race Course ♦ 278 41.50 N 87.45 W
Hawthorn Woods 278 42.13 N 88.03 W
Ḩawwārah 132 32.32 N 35.54 E
Hawwārat 'Adlān 142 29.12 N 30.58 E
Hawwārat al-Maqṭa' 142 29.15 N 30.54 E
Hawza 148 27.06 N 10.55 W
Hawzen 144 13.56 N 39.28 E
Haxby 44 54.01 N 1.04 W
Haxey 44 53.29 N 0.50 W
Haxtun 198 40.38 N 102.37 W
Hay 166 34.30 S 144.51 E
Hay ≃, Austl. 166 25.14 S 138.00 E
Hay ≃, Can. 176 60.52 N 115.44 W
Hay ≃, Wi., U.S. 190 44.59 N 91.51 W
Hay, Cape ≻ 176 74.25 N 113.00 W
Hay, Mount ∧, Austl. 162 23.28 S 133.05 E
Hay, Mount ∧, Austl. 170 33.37 S 150.26 E
Hay, Mount ∧, N.A. 180 59.15 N 137.37 W
Hay, South Fork ≃ 190 45.03 N 91.57 W
Haya 164 3.27 S 129.33 E
Haya ≃, Nihon 94 35.25 N 138.27 E
Haya ≃, Nihon 94 35.14 N 139.09 E
Hayachine-san ∧ 92 39.34 N 141.29 E
Hayakawa 94 35.25 N 138.22 E
Hayama, Nihon 94 35.16 N 139.35 E
Hayama, Nihon 96 33.26 N 133.13 E
Hayang 98 35.55 N 128.47 E
Hayange 56 49.20 N 6.03 E
HaYarden → Jordan ≃ 132 31.46 N 35.33 E
Hayashima 96 34.36 N 133.50 E
Hayasui-seto µ 96 33.18 N 131.59 E
Haybān 140 11.13 N 30.31 E
Haybān, Jabal ∧ 140 11.15 N 30.31 E
Hay Bay ⊂ 212 44.10 N 76.55 W
Haybes 56 50.00 N 4.43 E
Haydān, Wādī al- V 132 31.27 N 35.36 E
Haydarlı 130 38.16 N 30.23 E
Hayden, Az., U.S. 200 33.00 N 110.47 W
Hayden, Co., U.S. 200 40.29 N 107.15 W
Hayden, In., U.S. 218 38.58 N 85.44 W
Hayden Peak ∧ 202 42.59 N 116.39 W
Haydenville, Ma., U.S. 207 42.22 N 72.42 W
Haydenville, Oh., U.S. 188 39.28 N 82.19 W
Haydock 262 53.28 N 2.39 W
Haydock Park Race Course ♦ 262 53.29 N 2.37 W
Haydon Bridge 44 54.58 N 2.14 W
Haye, La → 's-Gravenhage 52 52.06 N 4.18 E
Hayes 194 30.06 N 92.55 W
Hayes ✦[8], Eng., U.K. 260 51.31 N 0.25 W
Hayes ✦[8], Eng., U.K. 260 51.23 N 0.01 E
Hayes ≃, Mb., Can. 184 57.03 N 92.09 W
Hayes ≃, N.T., Can. 176 67.18 N 95.02 W
Hayes, Mount ∧ 180 63.37 N 146.43 W
Hayes Center 198 40.30 N 101.01 W
Hayes State Memorial ⊥ 214 41.21 N 83.08 W
Hayesville, N.C., U.S. 192 35.02 N 83.49 W
Hayesville, Oh., U.S. 214 40.46 N 82.15 W
Hayesville, Or., U.S. 224 44.59 N 122.58 W
Hayfield, Eng., U.K. 262 53.23 N 1.57 W
Hayfield, Mn., U.S. 190 43.53 N 92.50 W
Hayford Peak ∧ 204 36.40 N 115.11 W
Hayfork 204 40.33 N 123.10 W
Hayfork Bally ∧ 204 40.39 N 123.13 W
Hayfork Creek ≃ 204 40.37 N 123.26 W
Hay Island I 212 44.53 N 80.58 W
Hayk, Lake ⊜ 144 11.21 N 39.43 E
Haykota 144 15.10 N 37.03 E
Hay Lake ⊜ 212 45.23 N 78.11 W
Hay Lakes 182 53.13 N 113.03 W
Hayle 42 50.11 N 5.23 W
Haymakers Run ≃ 279b 40.25 N 79.43 W
Haymana 130 39.27 N 32.30 E
Haynau → Chojnów 30 51.17 N 15.56 E
Haynes 194 34.53 N 90.47 W
Haynes Creek ≃ 285 39.53 N 74.50 W
Haynesville, La., U.S. 194 32.57 N 93.08 W
Haynesville, Va., U.S. 208 37.57 N 76.40 W
Hayneville 194 32.11 N 86.34 W
Haynin 144 15.50 N 48.19 E
Hay-on-Wye 42 52.04 N 3.07 W
Hay Point ≻ 166 21.17 S 149.18 E
Hayrabolu 130 41.12 N 27.06 E
Hay River 176 60.51 N 115.40 W
Hays, Ab., Can. 182 50.06 N 111.48 W
Hays, Ks., U.S. 198 38.52 N 99.19 W
Hays, Mt., U.S. 202 47.59 N 108.41 W
Hays □[6] 222 30.02 N 97.45 W
Hays ✦[8] 279b 40.23 N 79.56 W
Hayshah, Sabkhat al- ⁝⁝ 146 31.45 N 15.20 E
Hays Mill Creek ≃ 285 39.44 N 74.50 W
Hay Springs 198 42.41 N 102.41 W
Haystack Mountain ∧ 204 41.39 N 115.38 W
Haysville, Ks., U.S. 198 37.33 N 97.21 W
Haysville, Pa., U.S. 279b 40.32 N 80.09 W
Hayti, Mo., U.S. 194 36.14 N 89.44 W
Hayti, Pa., U.S. 208 39.59 N 75.51 W
Hayti, S.D., U.S. 198 44.39 N 97.12 W
Hayward, Ca., U.S. 226 37.40 N 122.04 W
Hayward, Wi., U.S. 190 46.00 N 91.29 W
Hayward Brook ≃ 283 42.22 N 71.20 W
Hayward Municipal Airport ⊠ 282 37.40 N 122.08 W
Haywards Heath 42 51.00 N 0.06 W
Haywood 184 49.40 N 98.12 W
Ḩayy, Jabal al- ∧ 142 29.43 N 31.35 E
HaẔafon □[5] 132 32.50 N 35.20 E
Hazār, Kūh-e ∧ 128 29.30 N 57.18 E
Hazard 192 37.14 N 83.11 W
Hazardville 207 41.59 N 72.32 W
Hazar Gölü ⊜ 130 38.30 N 39.25 E
Hazārībāg 124 23.59 N 85.21 E
Hazārībāg Plateau ⋀[1] 124 24.00 N 85.10 E
Haze, Cape ≻ 220 26.46 N 82.10 W
Hazebrouck 50 50.43 N 2.32 E
Hazel ≃ 188 38.33 N 77.51 W
Hazelbrook 170 33.44 S 150.27 E
Hazel Crest 278 41.34 N 87.41 W
Hazel Dell 224 45.40 N 122.39 W
Hazel Green, Il., U.S. 278 41.41 N 87.45 W
Hazel Green, Wi., U.S. 190 42.31 N 90.26 W
Hazelgrove, Austl. 170 33.40 S 149.52 E
Hazel Grove, Eng., U.K. 262 53.23 N 2.08 W
Hazel Hurst 214 41.42 N 78.35 W
Hazel Kirk 279b 40.11 N 79.57 W
Hazel Park 216 42.27 N 83.06 W
Hazel Park Race Track ♦ 281 42.29 N 83.05 W
Hazelton, B.C., Can. 182 55.15 N 127.40 W
Hazelton, Id., U.S. 202 42.35 N 114.08 W
Hazelton, N.D., U.S. 198 46.29 N 100.16 W
Hazelton Mountains ⋀ 182 54.30 N 128.20 W
Hazelton Peak ∧ 202 44.06 N 107.03 W
Hazelwood, Mo., U.S. 219 38.46 N 90.22 W
Hazelwood, N.C., U.S. 192 35.28 N 83.00 W
Hazelwood ✦[8] 279b 40.25 N 79.56 W
Hazen, Ar., U.S. 194 34.46 N 91.34 W
Hazen, Nv., U.S. 226 39.33 N 119.02 W
Hazen, N.D., U.S. 198 47.17 N 101.37 W
Hazen, Pa., U.S. 214 41.12 N 78.58 W
Hazen Bay ⊂ 180 61.00 N 165.10 W
Hazerim 132 31.14 N 34.43 E
Hazlehurst, Ga., U.S. 192 31.52 N 82.35 W
Hazlehurst, Ms., U.S. 194 31.51 N 90.23 W
Hazlet, Sk., Can. 184 50.25 N 108.36 W
Hazlet, N.J., U.S. 208 40.26 N 74.13 W
Hazleton, Ia., U.S. 190 42.37 N 91.54 W
Hazleton, Pa., U.S. 210 40.57 N 75.58 W
Hazlett, Lake ⊜ 162 21.30 S 128.48 E
Ḩazor HaGelilit 132 32.59 N 35.33 E
Hazro, Pāk. 123 33.54 N 72.29 E
Hazro, Tür. 130 38.15 N 40.47 E
Hazu 94 34.47 N 137.08 E
He ≃, Zhg. 100 27.05 N 114.59 E
He ≃, Zhg. 102 23.26 N 111.30 E
Heacham 42 52.55 N 0.30 E
Head ≃ 212 44.44 N 79.15 W
Head Bay d'Espoir 186 47.56 N 55.45 W
Headcorn 42 51.11 N 0.37 E
Headford 48 53.28 N 9.05 W
Head Lake ⊜ 212 44.45 N 78.55 W
Headland 194 31.21 N 85.20 W
Headlands 154 18.14 S 32.03 E
Headley, Eng., U.K. 42 51.07 N 0.50 W
Headley, Eng., U.K. 260 51.17 N 0.16 W
Headley, Mount ∧ 202 47.44 N 115.15 W
Head of the Harbor 276 40.54 N 73.10 W
Heald Green 262 53.22 N 2.14 W
Heald Moor ✦[3] 262 53.44 N 2.10 W
Healdsburg 204 38.36 N 122.52 W
Healdton 196 34.13 N 97.29 W
Healesville 169 37.40 S 145.31 E
Healing 44 53.34 N 0.10 W
Healy, Ak., U.S. 180 63.52 N 148.58 W
Healy, Ks., U.S. 198 38.36 N 100.37 W
Healy, Mount ∧ 180 63.46 N 149.01 W
Healy Lake ⊜ 212 45.10 N 79.55 W
Heani, Mont ∧ 174x 9.47 S 139.04 W
Heanna 174m 26.19 N 127.54 E
Heanor 44 53.01 N 1.22 W
Heany Junction 154 20.06 S 28.54 E
Heard Island I 6 53.06 S 73.30 E
Heard Pond ⊜ 283 42.21 N 71.22 W
Hearne 222 30.52 N 96.35 W
Hearst 176 49.41 N 83.40 W
Hearst Island I 9 69.25 S 62.10 W
Hearst San Simeon State Historical Park ♦ 226 35.42 N 121.10 W
Heart ≃, Ab., Can. 182 56.14 N 117.17 W
Heart ≃, N.D., U.S. 198 46.47 N 100.51 W
Heart Lake ⊜, Ab., Can. 182 55.02 N 111.30 W
Heart Lake ⊜, On., Can. 275b 43.44 N 79.48 W
Heart Lake Indian Reserve ✦[4] 182 55.02 N 111.30 W
Heart Pond ⊜ 283 42.34 N 71.23 W
Heart's Content 186 47.53 N 53.22 W
Heath, Ma., U.S. 207 42.40 N 72.49 W
Heath, Oh., U.S. 214 40.02 N 82.28 W
Heath, Tx., U.S. 222 32.50 N 96.29 W
Heath ≃ 248 12.31 S 68.38 W
Heath, Pointe ≻ 186 49.05 N 61.42 W
Heathcote, Austl. 169 36.55 S 144.42 E
Heathcote, Austl. 274a 34.05 S 151.01 E
Heathcote Brook ≃ 276 40.23 N 74.37 W
Heath End 42 51.22 N 1.09 W
Heatherton 274b 37.58 S 145.06 E
Heathfield 42 50.59 N 0.17 E
Heathmont 274b 37.49 S 145.15 E
Heath Springs 192 34.35 N 80.40 W
Heathsville 208 37.55 N 76.28 W
Heatley 262 53.24 N 2.27 W
Heaton Hall ⊥ 262 53.32 N 2.15 W
Heaton Moor 262 53.25 N 2.11 W
Heaven, Temple of ʋ[1] 271a 39.53 N 116.25 E
Heavener 194 34.53 N 94.36 W
Heaverham 260 51.18 N 0.15 E
Heaviley 262 53.24 N 2.09 W
Hebaochang 107 29.33 N 105.32 E
Hebao Dao I 100 21.52 N 113.09 E
Hebbronville 196 27.18 N 98.40 W
Hebburn 44 54.59 N 1.30 W
Hebbville 284b 39.20 N 77.46 W
Hebden Bridge 262 53.45 N 2.00 W
Hebden Water ≃ 262 53.44 N 2.00 W
Hebei, Zhg. 104 41.01 N 123.51 E
Hebei, Zhg. 104 40.43 N 122.12 E
Hebei (Hopeh) □[4] 98 38.00 N 116.00 E
Hebeitun 105 39.35 N 117.07 E
Hebel 166 28.59 S 147.48 E
Heber, Az., U.S. 200 34.25 N 110.35 W
Heber, Ca., U.S. 204 32.44 N 115.32 W
Heber City 200 40.30 N 111.24 W
Heber Springs 194 35.29 N 92.01 W
Hebgen Lake ⊜[1] 202 44.47 N 111.14 W
Hebi 98 35.59 N 114.11 E
Hebian 107 30.29 N 105.08 E
Hebo, Or., U.S. 224 45.13 N 123.51 W
Hebo, Zhg. 102 31.29 N 98.58 E
Hebo, Mount ∧ 224 45.12 N 123.45 W
Hébridas, Islas → Hebrides II 46 57.00 N 6.30 W
Hebrides II 46 57.00 N 6.30 W
Hebrides, Sea of the ⊤[2] 46 57.07 N 6.55 W
Hebron, Nf., Can. 176 58.12 N 62.38 W
Hebron → Al-Khalīl, Isr. Occ 132 31.32 N 35.06 E
Hebron, Ct., U.S. 207 41.39 N 72.21 W
Hebron, Il., U.S. 216 42.28 N 88.25 W
Hebron, In., U.S. 216 41.19 N 87.12 W
Hebron, Ky., U.S. 218 39.03 N 84.42 W
Hebron, Md., U.S. 208 38.25 N 75.41 W
Hebron, Ne., U.S. 198 40.09 N 97.35 W
Hebron, N.D., U.S. 198 46.54 N 102.02 W
Hebron, Pa., U.S. 208 40.21 N 76.24 W
Hebron, Tx., U.S. 222 33.01 N 96.52 W
Hebron, Wi., U.S. 216 42.56 N 88.42 W
Hebu 100 27.50 N 115.22 E
Hebutu 104 42.19 N 122.20 E
Heby 40 59.56 N 16.53 E
Hecao 105 40.21 N 116.47 E
Hecate Strait µ 182 53.00 N 131.00 W
Hecelchakán 232 20.10 N 90.08 W
Heceta Island I 180 55.45 N 133.35 W
Hechi 102 24.42 N 108.02 E
Hechiceros 196 28.33 N 103.38 W
Hechingen 58 48.21 N 8.58 E
Hechtel 56 51.08 N 5.21 E
Hechthausen 52 53.38 N 9.14 E
Hechuan 107 30.00 N 106.16 E
Heckelberg 54 52.44 N 13.50 E
Hecker 219 38.18 N 90.00 W
Heckington 42 52.59 N 0.18 W
Hecklingen 54 51.51 N 11.32 E
Heckscher State Park ♦ 210 40.43 N 73.10 W
Hecla, Mb., Can. 184 51.08 N 96.40 W
Hecla, S.D., U.S. 198 45.52 N 98.09 W
Hecla Island I 184 51.08 N 96.45 W
Hecla Provincial Park ♦ 184 51.12 N 96.35 W
Hectanooga 186 44.06 N 66.02 W
Hector, N.Z. 172 41.36 S 171.53 E
Hector, Mn., U.S. 198 44.44 N 94.42 W
Hector, Mount ∧ 172 40.57 S 175.17 E
Heda 94 34.58 N 138.46 E
Hedal 26 60.37 N 9.42 E
Hedaru 154 4.30 S 37.54 E
Heddal ʋ[1] 26 59.35 N 9.11 E
Hedding 285 40.06 N 74.44 W
Hédé, Fr. 32 48.18 N 1.48 W
Hede, Sve. 26 62.25 N 13.30 E
Hedehusene 41 55.39 N 12.12 E
Hedel 52 51.45 N 5.15 E
Hedemora 40 60.17 N 15.59 E
Hedemünden 56 51.23 N 9.46 E
Hedensted 41 55.46 N 9.42 E
Hedersleben 54 51.51 N 11.15 E
Hedesunda 40 60.24 N 16.59 E

Symbols in the index entries represent the broad categories identified in the key at the right. Symbols with superior numbers (⋀[1]) identify subcategories (see complete key on page *I · 1)*.

Symbole im Register stellen die rechts im Schlüssel erklärten Kategorien dar. Symbole mit hochgestellten Ziffern (⋀[1]) bezeichnen Unterabteilungen einer Kategorie (vgl. vollständiger Schlüssel auf Seite *I · 1)*.

Los símbolos incluídos en el texto del índice representan las grandes categorias identificadas con la clave a la derecha. Los símbolos con numeros en su parte superior (⋀[1]) identifican las subcategorías (véase la clave completa en la página *I · 1)*.

Les symboles de l'index représentent les catégories indiquées dans la légende à droite. Les symboles suivis d'un indice (⋀[1]) représentent des sous-catégories (voir légende complète à la page *I · 1)*.

Os símbolos incluídos no texto do índice representam as grandes categorias identificadas com a chave à direita. Os símbolos com números em sua parte superior (⋀[1]) identificam as subcategorias (veja-se a chave completa à página *I · 1)*.

	English	Deutsch	Español	Français	Português
∧	Mountain	Berg	Montaña	Montagne	Montanha
⋀	Mountains	Gebirge	Montañas	Montagnes	Montanhas
)(	Pass	Paß	Paso	Col	Passo
V	Valley, Canyon	Tal, Cañon	Valle, Cañón	Vallée, Canyon	Vale, Canhão
≚	Plain	Ebene	Llano	Plaine	Planície
≻	Cape	Kap	Cabo	Cap	Cabo
I	Island	Insel	Isla	Île	Ilha
II	Islands	Inseln	Islas	Îles	Ilhas
⊥	Other Topographic Features	Andere Topographische Objekte	Otros Elementos Topográficos	Autres données topographiques	Outros acidentes topográficos

ESPAÑOL Nombre	Página	Lat.°′	Long.°′ W = Oeste
Hedesundafjärdarna �container	40	60.20 N	17.00 E
He Devil ▲	202	45.21 N	116.33 W
Hedge End	42	50.54 N	1.18 W
Hedgerley	260	51.35 N	0.36 W
Hedian	100	32.45 N	114.18 E
Hedley, B.C., Can.	182	49.21 N	120.04 W
Hedley, Tx., U.S.	196	34.52 N	100.39 W
Hedmark □⁶	26	61.30 N	11.45 E
Hednesford	42	52.43 N	2.00 W
Hedo	174m	26.51 N	128.16 E
Hedo-misaki ➤	174m	26.52 N	128.16 E
Hedon	44	53.44 N	0.12 W
Hedrick	190	41.10 N	92.18 W
Hedströmmen ≃	40	59.28 N	16.04 E
Hedutne	272c	19.10 N	73.06 E
Hedwig Village	222	29.47 N	95.27 W
Heek	52	52.07 N	7.06 E
Heel	52	51.11 N	5.53 E
Heel Point ➤	174a	19.19 N	166.37 E
Heemskerk	52	31.41 N	4.40 E
Heemstede	52	52.21 N	4.37 E
Heepen	52	52.01 N	8.35 E
Heer, Bel.	56	50.10 N	4.50 E
Heer, Ned.	56	50.50 N	5.44 E
Heerde	52	52.23 N	6.03 E
Heerdt ➤⁸	263	51.13 N	6.43 E
Heerenveen	52	52.57 N	5.55 E
Heeren-Werve	52	51.35 N	7.43 E
Heerhugowaard	52	52.40 N	4.50 E
Heerkan	107	29.32 N	103.56 E
Heerlen	56	50.54 N	5.59 E
Heesch	52	51.44 N	5.32 E
Heeslingen	52	53.19 N	9.20 E
Heessen	52	51.42 N	7.50 E
Heeze	52	51.24 N	5.35 E
Hefa (Haifa)	132	32.50 N	35.00 E
Hefa □⁵	132	32.35 N	35.00 E
Hefa, Mifraz c	132	32.52 N	35.03 E
Hefa, Sede-Teʿufa ≃	132	32.49 N	35.02 E
Hefei	100	31.51 N	117.17 E
Hefengchang	107	30.26 N	104.43 E
Heffron Park ♦	274a	33.57 S	151.15 E
Heflin	194	33.38 N	85.35 W
Hegang	89	47.24 N	130.22 E
Hegau ↙¹	58	47.50 N	8.45 E
Hégenheim	58	47.34 N	7.32 E
Hegewisch ➤⁸	278	41.40 N	87.33 W
Hegins	208	40.39 N	76.29 W
Hegra	26	63.28 N	11.07 E
Hegura-jima I	92	37.51 N	136.55 E
Heguri	270	34.38 N	135.42 E
Hegyeshalom	61	47.55 N	17.10 E
Hehlen	52	51.59 N	9.28 E
Heho	110	20.43 N	96.49 E
Hehou	100	28.40 N	114.28 E
Hei ≃, Zhg.	102	40.18 N	99.26 E
Hei ≃, Zhg.	105	40.44 N	116.27 E
Heicheng (Karakhoto)			
	102	41.47 N	101.03 E
Heichengzhen	102	36.16 N	106.06 E
Heichengzi	104	42.10 N	121.01 E
Heidayingzi	98	40.52 N	116.12 E
Heidberg ▲²	263	51.15 N	7.21 E
Heide	30	54.12 N	9.06 E
Heide ➤⁸, B.R.D.	263	51.31 N	7.01 E
Heide ➤⁸, B.R.D.	263	51.26 N	7.01 E
Heideck	58	49.08 N	11.07 E
Heidelberg, Austl.	169	37.45 S	145.04 E
Heidelberg, B.R.D.	56	49.25 N	8.43 E
Heidelberg, On., Can.	212	43.31 N	80.37 W
Heidelberg, S. Afr.	158	26.32 S	28.18 E
Heidelberg, S. Afr.	158	34.06 S	20.59 E
Heidelberg, Ms., U.S.	194	31.53 N	88.59 W
Heidelberg, Pa., U.S.	279b	40.23 N	80.05 W
Heidelberg □⁵	273d	26.19 S	28.16 E
Heidelsheim	58	49.24 N	8.42 E
Heidelsheim	58	49.06 N	8.38 E
Heiden, B.R.D.	52	51.59 N	8.50 E
Heiden, Schw.	58	47.27 N	9.33 E
Heiden, Port c	180	56.55 N	158.45 W
Heidenau, B.R.D.	52	53.19 N	9.39 E
Heidenau, B.R.D.	56	49.01 N	10.44 E
Heidenheim an der Brenz	56	48.40 N	10.08 E
Heidenheimer	222	31.01 N	97.18 W
Heidenoldendorf	52	51.57 N	8.50 E
Heidenreichstein	61	48.52 N	15.07 E
Heider Ditch ≃¹	279a	41.31 N	82.01 W
Heiderscheid	56	49.53 N	5.54 E
Heidhausen ➤⁸	263	51.23 N	7.01 E
Heidhof ➤⁸	263	51.11 N	7.11 E
Heidlersburg	208	39.57 N	77.09 W
Heidouwo	105	39.42 N	117.15 E
Heigenbrücken	56	50.02 N	9.23 E
Heigoutaicun	104	41.30 N	123.01 E
Heigun-tō I	96	33.47 N	132.14 E
Heihai			
→ Har Hu @	102	38.15 N	97.40 E
Heihe	89	50.16 N	127.28 E
Heiji			
→ Pʻyŏngyang	98	39.01 N	125.45 E
Heikega-dake ▲	96	34.19 N	131.54 E
Heikendorf	54	54.22 N	10.12 E
Heil	263	51.38 N	7.35 E
Heilangkou	105	39.37 N	117.24 E
Heilbron	158	27.21 S	27.58 E
Heilbronn	56	-9.08 N	9.13 E
Heilenbecker-Stausee @¹	263	51.15 N	7.22 E
Heiligenberg	58	+7.49 N	9.19 E
Heiligenblut	61	+7.02 N	12.50 E
Heiligendamm	54	54.08 N	11.50 E
Heiligenhafen	54	54.22 N	10.58 E
Heiligenhaus	52	51.19 N	6.59 E
Heiligensee ➤⁸	264a	52.36 N	13.13 E
Heiligenstadt, B.R.D.	60	49.51 N	11.12 E
Heiligenstadt, D.D.R.	56	51.23 N	10.09 E
Heilin	98	45.01 N	118.58 E
Hei Ling Chau I	271d	22.15 N	114.02 E
Heilong (Amur) ≃	89	52.56 N	141.10 E
Heilongguan	102	36.19 N	111.11 E
Heilongjiang ≃¹	89	48.00 N	128.00 E
Heilongtan, Zhg.	105	40.00 N	116.11 E
Heilongtan, Zhg.	105	40.02 N	116.11 E
Heilongtan Shuiku @¹	107	30.03 N	104.02 E
Heiloo	52	52.36 N	4.43 E
Heilsberg			
→ Lidzbark			
Warmiński	30	54.09 N	20.35 E
Heilsbronn	56	49.20 N	10.47 E
Heiltz-le-Maurupt	58	48.48 N	4.49 E
Heilungkiang			
→ Heilongjiang □⁴	89	48.00 N	128.00 E
Heilwood	214	40.37 N	78.54 W
Heimahe	102	36.40 N	99.52 E
Heimbach	56	50.38 N	6.28 E
Heimbuchenthal	56	49.55 N	9.17 E
Heimburg	52	51.50 N	10.57 E
Heimdal	26	63.21 N	10.22 E
Heimenkirch	58	47.37 N	9.53 E
Heimsheim	58	48.48 N	8.51 E
Heinävesi	28	62.26 N	28.36 E
Heinersdorf, D.D.R.	264a	52.23 N	13.20 E
Heinersdorf, D.D.R.	264a	52.34 N	13.27 E
Heiniuyingzi	98	41.07 N	120.19 E
Heinola	28	61.13 N	26.02 E
Heinrichshorst	54	53.09 N	11.42 E
Heinsberg	56	51.03 N	6.06 E
Heiquan	102	39.32 N	99.42 E
Heirnkut	110	25.14 N	94.45 E
Heistelde	52	51.29 N	4.43 E
Heishan	104	41.41 N	122.07 E
Heishanguan	98	33.33 N	114.41 E
Heishantou, Zhg.	98	50.13 N	119.28 E
Heishantou, Zhg.	104	42.09 N	118.28 E
Heishuisi	102	36.30 N	108.42 E
Heisingen ➤⁸	263	51.25 N	7.04 E

FRANÇAIS Nom	Page	Lat.°′	Long.°′ W = Ouest
Heisler	182	52.41 N	112.13 W
Heislerville	208	39.13 N	74.59 W
Heissen ➤⁸	263	51.26 N	6.56 E
Heist-aan-Zee	50	51.21 N	3.15 E
Heist-op-den-Berg	56	51.05 N	4.43 E
Heitang	102	26.29 N	105.09 E
Heitersheim	58	47.53 N	7.40 E
Heiwa	94	35.12 N	136.44 E
Heiyanghebao	105	39.07 N	118.15 E
Heiyantang	102	27.28 N	101.11 E
Heiyanzi	105	39.13 N	118.08 E
Hejaz			
→ Al-Ḥijāz ⬦¹	118	24.30 N	38.30 E
Hejiachang	107	29.24 N	104.56 E
Hejian, Zhg.	98	38.26 N	116.05 E
Hejian, Zhg.	105	39.25 N	116.25 E
Hejiang	102	28.49 N	105.50 E
Hejiaqiao	107	29.16 N	104.16 E
Hejiaqiao	107	27.24 N	113.21 E
Hejiawoqeng	104	43.32 N	122.07 E
Hejiaying	105	39.55 N	118.19 E
Hejiazhen	107	29.52 N	104.26 E
Hejin	102	35.39 N	110.40 E
Hejlsminde	41	55.23 N	9.37 E
Hejnsvig	41	55.41 N	8.59 E
Hekelgem	50	50.54 N	4.06 E
Hekill Point ➤	229a	20.48 N	156.37 W
Hekimhan	130	38.49 N	37.56 E
Hekinan	94	34.51 N	136.58 E
Hekla ▲¹	24a	64.00 N	19.39 W
Hekou, Zhg.	98	31.22 N	114.26 E
Hekou, Zhg.	102	36.09 N	103.22 E
Hekou, Zhg.	102	28.22 N	108.14 E
Hekou, Zhg.	102	29.57 N	111.04 E
Hekou, Zhg.	102	22.38 N	103.56 E
Hekouchang	107	29.21 N	104.21 E
Hekouji	102	32.09 N	116.04 E
Hekouqi	102	26.31 N	100.39 E
Hekpoort	158	25.55 S	27.38 E
Hel	30	54.37 N	18.48 E
Helagsfjället ▲	26	62.55 N	12.27 E
Helaluo	102	33.56 N	102.10 E
Helangou	104	41.00 N	123.25 E
Helan Shan ↗	102	38.40 N	105.57 E
Helbe ≃	54	51.13 N	11.06 E
Helbra	54	51.33 N	11.29 E
Helchteren	56	51.03 N	5.22 E
Heldburg	54	50.17 N	10.44 E
Helden	56	51.07 N	7.56 E
Helden, In., U.S.	218	39.40 N	85.31 W
Helden, Ky., U.S.	194	37.50 N	87.35 W
Heldrungen	54	51.17 N	11.13 E
Helechos, Cañada de los ≃	286a	19.22 N	99.12 W
Helemano Stream ≃	229c	21.35 N	158.06 W
Helen, Mount ▲	166	21.34 S	141.13 E
Helena, Ar., U.S.	194	34.31 N	90.35 W
Helena, Mt., U.S.	202	46.35 N	112.02 W
Helena, N.Y., U.S.	206	44.55 N	74.44 W
Helena, Ok., U.S.	196	36.32 N	98.16 W
Helena River ≃	168a	31.54 S	116.00 E
Helendale	234	34.45 N	117.18 W
Helenenberg	56	49.51 N	6.32 E
Helenental ≃¹	264b	48.01 N	16.11 E
Helen Island I	108	2.58 N	131.49 E
Helensburgh, Austl.	168	34.11 S	150.59 E
Helensburgh, Scot., U.K.	46	56.01 N	4.44 W
Helen Springs	162	18.26 S	133.52 E
Helensville	172	36.40 S	174.28 E
Helenville	216	43.01 N	88.41 W
Helenwood	192	36.25 N	84.32 W
Helez	132	31.35 N	34.40 E
Helfenberg	61	48.32 N	14.08 E
Helfenstein	208	40.45 N	76.27 W
Helffta	54	51.30 N	11.34 E
Helgå ≃	26	55.53 N	14.08 E
Helgenæs I	41	56.08 N	10.32 E
Helgoland I	30	54.12 N	7.53 E
Helgoländer Bucht c	30	54.10 N	8.04 E
Heli	89	47.05 N	130.16 E
Helicoïde ⬦⁹	286c	10.29 N	66.55 W
Helidon	171a	27.33 S	152.08 E
Heliodora	256	22.04 S	45.32 W
Héliopolis	122	30.06 N	31.20 E
Héliopolis	122	30.08 N	31.17 E
Héliopolis			
→ Miṣr al-Jadīdah	122	30.06 N	31.20 E
Héliopolis Aerodrome	142	30.08 N	31.17 E
Héliopolis Racing Club ♦	273c	30.06 N	31.19 E
Heliuji	100	33.02 N	116.57 E
Hell	26	63.26 N	10.54 E
Hellam	208	40.00 N	76.36 W
Hellberge ↗²	54	52.34 N	11.17 E
Hellbrunn, Schloss ⌂	64	47.46 N	13.04 E
Hellebæk	41	56.04 N	12.34 E
Hellen Blazes, Lake @	128	29.10 N	50.40 E
Hellendoorn	52	52.24 N	6.26 E
Hellenthal	56	50.29 N	6.26 E
Hellerau ➤⁸	52	51.07 N	13.44 E
Hellern ➤⁸	52	52.15 N	7.58 E
Hellern	52	51.12 N	7.39 E
Hellertown	208	40.34 N	75.20 W
Hellesylt	26	62.05 N	6.54 E
Hellevad	41	55.05 N	9.13 E
Hellevoetsluis	52	51.49 N	4.08 E
Hell Gate Ladit ≃	276	40.47 N	73.56 W
Hellie	@	226	39.04 N	120.22 W
Hellifield	44	54.01 N	2.12 W
Hell In Ness I	34	58.11 N	1.41 W
Hell Ness ➤	46a	60.02 N	1.10 W
Hellmonsödt	61	48.26 N	14.18 E
Hell Point ➤	188	44.16 N	64.15 W
Hells Canyon I	202	45.15 N	116.40 W
Hellsee @	264a	52.45 N	13.35 E
Hell's Gate V	157	51.32 N	7.47 E
Hell-Ville	157	13.25 S	48.16 E
Hellweg ↙¹	52	51.32 N	8.20 E
Helm	226	36.31 N	120.05 W
Helmand ≃	128	31.00 N	64.00 E
Helmand □⁴	128	31.12 N	61.34 E
Helmbrechts	54	50.14 N	11.43 E
Helmcken Falls L	182	51.57 N	120.11 W
Helme ≃	54	51.27 N	11.09 E
Helmeringhausen	158	25.54 S	16.57 E
Helmetta	276	40.23 N	74.25 W
Helmetta Pond @	276	40.23 N	74.26 W
Helmond	52	51.29 N	5.40 E
Helmsdale	46	58.07 N	3.40 W
Helmsdale ≃	46	58.07 N	3.40 W
Helmshore	262	53.41 N	2.20 W
Helmsley	44	54.14 N	1.04 W
Helmstedt	54	52.13 N	11.00 E
Helnæs I	41	55.08 N	10.02 E
Helong	98	42.31 N	128.59 E
Helper	200	39.41 N	110.51 W
Helpter Berg ▲²	54	53.30 N	13.36 E
Helsby	262	53.16 N	2.46 W
Helsby Hill ▲	262	53.16 N	2.44 W
Helsingborg	40	56.03 N	12.42 E
Helsinge	41	56.01 N	12.12 E
Helsingfors			
→ Helsinki	26	60.10 N	24.58 E
Helsingør (Elsinore)	41	56.02 N	12.37 E
Helsinki (Helsingfors)	26	60.10 N	24.58 E
Helska, Mierzeja ➤²	30	54.45 N	18.40 E
Heltonville	218	38.55 N	86.22 W
Helvecia	252	31.06 S	60.05 W
Helvellyn ▲	44	54.31 N	3.01 W
Helvick Head ➤	48	52.03 N	7.33 W
Helvoirt	52	51.38 N	5.13 E

PORTUGUÊS Nome	Página	Lat.°′	Long.°′ W = Oeste
Hem ≃	50	50.51 N	2.06 E
Hemar, Naḥal V	132	31.08 N	35.22 E
Hemau	60	49.03 N	11.47 E
Hemāvati ≃	122	12.31 N	76.27 E
Hembe	152	1.54 N	22.42 E
Hemel Hempstead	260	51.46 N	0.28 W
Hemelingen ➤⁸	52	53.03 N	8.53 E
Hemeln	52	51.30 N	9.36 E
Hemer	56	51.23 N	7.46 E
Hemet	228	33.44 N	116.58 W
Hemfjärden c	40	59.17 N	15.20 E
Hemford	186	44.30 N	64.47 W
Hemfurth-Edersee	56	51.10 N	9.02 E
Hemiksem	50	51.09 N	4.21 E
Héming	58	48.42 N	6.57 E
Hemingford	198	42.19 N	103.04 W
Hemingway	192	33.45 N	79.26 W
Hemlock, In., U.S.	216	40.25 N	86.03 W
Hemlock, N.Y., U.S.	210	42.47 N	77.36 W
Hemlock Lake @	210	42.43 N	77.37 W
Hemmerde	52	51.33 N	7.48 E
Hemmerden	263	51.07 N	6.36 E
Hemmingen-Westerfeld	52	52.19 N	9.45 E
Hemmoor	52	53.41 N	9.08 E
Hemphill	194	31.20 N	93.50 W
Hempnall	42	52.30 N	1.19 E
Hempstead, N.Y., U.S.	210	40.42 N	73.37 W
Hempstead, Tx., U.S.	222	30.05 N	96.04 W
Hempstead Harbor c	276	40.50 N	73.39 W
Hempstead Lake State Park ♦	276	40.41 N	73.38 W
Hemsby	42	52.41 N	1.42 E
Hemse	26	57.14 N	18.22 E
Hemsedal	26	60.52 N	8.34 E
Hemsedal ≃	26	60.49 N	9.06 E
Hemstreet Park	210	42.54 N	73.41 W
Hemsworth	44	53.38 N	1.21 W
Hemujing	98	37.54 N	115.22 E
Henan	102	34.35 N	101.34 E
Henan (Honan) □⁴	90	34.00 N	114.00 E
Hen and Chickens II	172	35.55 S	174.45 E
Henares ≃	34	40.24 N	3.30 W
Henbury, Austl.	162	24.35 S	133.15 E
Henbury, Eng., U.K.	262	53.15 N	2.11 W
Hendek	130	40.48 N	30.45 E
Henderson, Arg.	252	36.18 S	61.43 W
Henderson, In., U.S.	218	39.40 N	85.31 W
Henderson, Ky., U.S.	194	37.50 N	87.35 W
Henderson, Mn., U.S.	198	44.31 N	93.54 W
Henderson, Ne., U.S.	198	40.46 N	97.48 W
Henderson, Nv., U.S.	204	36.02 N	114.58 W
Henderson, N.Y., U.S.	210	43.51 N	76.11 W
Henderson, N.C., U.S.	192	36.19 N	78.23 W
Henderson, Tn., U.S.	194	35.26 N	88.38 W
Henderson, Tx., U.S.	222	32.09 N	94.47 W
Henderson □⁶	222	32.13 N	95.50 W
Henderson Bay c, N.Y., U.S.		43.54 N	76.10 W
Henderson Bay c, Wa., U.S.	224	47.18 N	122.42 W
Henderson Creek ≃	190	40.52 N	91.02 W
Henderson Island I	6	24.22 S	128.19 W
Hendersonville, Pa., U.S.	279b	40.16 N	80.14 W
Hendersonville, Tn., U.S.	194	36.18 N	86.37 W
Hendijān	128	30.14 N	49.43 E
Hendon ➤⁸	260	51.35 N	0.14 W
Hendorābī, Jazīreh-ye I		26.40 N	53.37 E
Hendricks, Mn., U.S.	198	44.30 N	96.25 W
Hendricks, W.V., U.S.	208	39.04 N	79.37 W
Hendrik Verwoerddam @¹	218	39.46 N	86.26 W
	158	30.40 S	25.40 E
Hendrina	158	26.11 S	29.45 E
Hendry □⁶	220	26.36 N	81.13 W
Hendrysburg	214	40.04 N	81.10 W
Hendy	42	51.43 N	4.04 W
Henefer	200	41.01 N	111.29 W
Heng ≃, Zhg.	102	28.40 N	104.25 E
Heng ≃, Zhg.	107	28.57 N	105.22 E
Hengām, Jazīreh-ye I	128	26.39 N	55.53 E
Henganofi	164	6.15 S	145.35 E
Hengchow → Hengyang	100	26.54 N	112.36 E
Hengdaochuan	98	41.15 N	125.31 E
Hengdaohe	104	41.23 N	123.51 E
Hengdaohezi	89	44.51 N	129.09 E
Hengdong	100	27.03 N	112.57 E
Hengelo	52	52.15 N	6.45 E
Hengersberg	60	48.47 N	13.03 E
Hengfan	105	40.20 N	119.45 E
Henggang	107	29.32 N	115.27 E
Henggouzi	89	43.23 N	124.07 E
Hengjie	105	31.13 N	119.30 E
Hengjiezhen	105	31.13 N	119.30 E
Hengjinghong	100	30.34 N	120.50 E
Hengkou	102	32.50 N	108.56 E
Hengli	100	22.59 N	113.41 E
Hengnan	100	26.54 N	112.36 E
Hengning	98	37.43 N	115.40 E
Hengqi ≃¹	105	30.58 N	119.34 E
Hengshan, Zhg.	102	37.56 N	109.14 E
Hengshan, Zhg.	100	27.15 N	112.51 E
Hengshan ▲, Zhg.	102	37.56 N	108.53 E
Hengshan ▲, Zhg.	100	32.02 N	109.03 E
Hengshanchang	107	30.18 N	118.44 E
Hengshanqiao	105	31.45 N	120.05 E
Hengshi, Zhg.	100	30.05 N	115.33 E
Hengshi, Zhg.	100	24.25 N	113.08 E
Hengshui	98	37.43 N	115.40 E
Hengsteysee @¹	263	51.23 N	7.28 E
Hengtangshi	100	31.41 N	121.02 E
Hengtangxi	107	29.05 N	105.03 E
Hengxi, Zhg.	100	31.43 N	118.46 E
Hengxi, Zhg.	100	29.21 N	121.23 E
Hengxian	100	22.41 N	109.16 E
Hengyang	100	26.54 N	112.36 E
Héngyang	100	26.54 N	112.36 E
Hénin-Beaumont	50	50.25 N	2.57 E
Henley Beach	168b	34.55 S	138.30 E
Henley-in-Arden	42	52.17 N	1.46 W
Henley-on-Thames	42	51.32 N	0.56 W
Henlopen, Cape ➤	208	38.48 N	75.05 W
Henlow	260	52.02 N	0.17 W
Hennan ≃	26	62.06 N	15.46 E
Hennaya	34	34.58 N	1.22 W
Henneberg	54	50.28 N	10.21 E
Hennebont	32	47.48 N	3.17 W
Hennef	56	50.46 N	7.16 E
Hennenman	158	27.59 S	27.01 E
Hennepin	190	41.15 N	89.21 W
Hennepin, Point ➤	281	42.17 N	82.10 W
Hennersdorf	264b	48.06 N	16.22 E
Hennessey	196	36.06 N	97.53 W
Hennessey, Lake @¹	226	38.29 N	122.22 W
Henniker	206	43.10 N	71.49 W
Henning, Il., U.S.	216	40.18 N	87.42 W
Henning, Mn., U.S.	198	46.19 N	95.26 W
Henning, Tn., U.S.	194	35.40 N	89.34 W
Henri ≃	206	46.30 N	71.47 W
Henri, Cap ➤	186	49.48 N	64.23 W
Henri-Chapelle	56	50.40 N	5.56 E
Henrichemont	50	47.18 N	2.32 E
Henrichenburg	263	51.35 N	7.19 E
Henrietta, N.Y., U.S.	210	43.03 N	77.36 W
Henrietta, N.C., U.S.	192	35.15 N	81.47 W
Henrietta, Tx., U.S.	196	33.49 N	98.11 W
Henrietta Maria, Cape ➤	178	55.09 N	82.20 W
Henry, Il., U.S.	190	41.06 N	89.21 W
Henry, S.D., U.S.	198	44.53 N	97.27 W
Henry ≃⁶, In., U.S.	218	39.55 N	85.22 W
Henry ≃⁶, Ky., U.S.	218	38.26 N	85.09 W
Henry ≃⁶, Oh., U.S.	216	41.20 N	84.04 W
Henry ≃	162	22.40 S	115.40 E
Henry, Cape ➤	208	36.55 N	76.01 W
Henry, Mount ▲¹	202	48.58 N	114.55 W
Henry, Mount ▲²	274a	33.50 S	150.38 E
Henry, Point ➤	162	34.29 S	119.23 E
Henry Cowell Redwoods State Park ♦	226	37.02 N	122.03 W
Henryetta	196	35.26 N	95.58 W
Henry Island I	182	48.35 N	123.11 W
Henry Kater, Cape ➤	176	69.05 N	66.44 W
Henry Mountains ↗	200	38.00 N	110.50 W
Henry Pittier, Parque Nacional ♦	246	10.25 N	67.43 W
Henrys Bend	214	41.28 N	79.37 W
Henrys Fork ≃, U.S.	200	41.00 N	109.39 W
Henrys Fork ≃, Id., U.S.	202	43.45 N	111.56 W
Henryville, P.Q., Can.	206	45.08 N	73.11 W
Henryville, In., U.S.	218	38.32 N	85.46 W
Henry W. Coe State Park ♦	226	37.12 N	121.30 W
Hensall	190	43.26 N	81.30 W
Henshaw, Lake @¹	228	33.15 N	116.45 W
Hensley	194	34.30 N	92.12 W
Hensley Lake @¹	226	37.07 N	119.53 W
Henslow, Cape ➤	175e	9.56 S	160.38 E
Henson Creek ≃	284b	38.46 N	77.00 W
Hentesville	210	42.17 N	74.13 W
Henstedt-Ulzburg	52	53.47 N	9.58 E
Henstridge	42	50.59 N	2.24 W
Hentiesbaai	156	22.08 S	14.18 E
Henty	166	35.31 S	147.02 E
Henzada	110	17.38 N	95.28 E
Hepburn, Fl., U.S.	220	30.59 N	81.39 W
Hepburn Springs	169	37.19 S	144.09 E
Hephzibah	192	33.18 N	82.05 W
Heping, Zhg.	100	27.10 N	117.18 E
Heping, Zhg.	102	22.01 N	112.59 E
Heping, Zhg.	100	23.17 N	116.29 E
Heping, Zhg.	100	24.28 N	114.58 E
Heppenheim	56	49.39 N	8.38 E
Heppner	202	45.21 N	119.33 W
Heptonstall	262	53.45 N	2.01 W
Heptonstall Moor ↙³	262	53.46 N	2.05 W
Hepu (Lianzhou)	102	21.39 N	109.11 E
Hepworth	212	44.37 N	81.09 W
Hepworth	100	32.55 N	118.22 E
Heqiao, Zhg.	106	33.10 N	119.53 E
Heqiao, Zhg.	100	31.37 N	119.53 E
Heqing	102	26.34 N	100.12 E
Hequ	102	39.26 N	111.08 E
Héradsflói c	24a	65.45 N	14.10 W
Hera Lacinia, Tempio ⌂¹	68	39.01 N	17.13 E
Herāt	128	34.20 N	62.12 E
Herāt □⁴	128	34.30 N	62.00 E
Hérault □⁵	32	43.40 N	3.30 E
Hérault ≃	32	43.17 N	3.26 E
Herbasse ≃	62	45.07 N	4.57 E
Herbignac	50	47.27 N	2.19 W
Herbitzheim	58	49.01 N	7.09 E
Herborn	56	50.41 N	8.19 E
Herbrechtingen	58	48.37 N	10.11 E
Herby	30	50.46 N	18.48 E
Herceg-Novi	66	42.27 N	18.32 E
Herculaneum	219	38.16 N	90.23 W
Hercules	228	38.01 N	122.17 W
Herdecke	263	51.24 N	7.26 E
Herdorf	56	50.46 N	7.56 E
Herdubreid ▲	24a	65.10 N	16.18 W
Heredia	236	10.00 N	84.07 W
Hereford, Eng., U.K.	42	52.04 N	2.43 W
Hereford, Az., U.S.	200	31.26 N	110.05 W
Hereford, Md., U.S.	208	39.35 N	76.39 W
Hereford, Tx., U.S.	196	34.48 N	102.23 W
Hereford and Worcester □⁶	42	52.10 N	2.30 W
Hereford Mountain ▲	206	45.05 N	71.36 W
Hereke	130	40.48 N	29.39 E
Herekino	172	35.17 S	173.13 E
Herent	56	50.54 N	4.40 E
Herentals	56	51.11 N	4.50 E
Herford	52	52.07 N	8.40 E
Herford □⁶	52	52.08 N	8.41 E
Herfølge	41	55.26 N	12.10 E
Herington	190	38.40 N	96.56 W
Herisau	58	47.23 N	9.17 E
Hérisson	62	46.31 N	2.42 E
Heritage Range ↗	7	79.30 S	84.00 W
Herk-de-Stad	56	50.56 N	5.10 E
Herkimer	210	43.01 N	74.59 W
Herkimer □⁶	210	43.25 N	74.59 W
Herlen ≃			
→ Kerulen ≃	90	48.48 N	117.00 E
Herlev	41	55.44 N	12.27 E
Herm I	48	49.28 N	2.27 W
Herma Ness ➤	46a	60.50 N	0.55 W
Hermann	219	38.42 N	91.26 W
Hermannsburg, Austl.	162	23.57 S	132.45 E
Hermannsburg, B.R.D.	52	52.50 N	10.05 E
Hermannsburg Aboriginal Reserve ↙⁴	162	24.00 S	132.45 E
Hermanns-Denkmal ⌂	52	51.55 N	8.50 E
Hermannskogel ▲	264b	48.16 N	16.18 E
Hermannstadt → Sibiu	85	45.48 N	24.09 E
Hermano Peak ▲	200	37.13 N	108.48 W
Hermanverk	26	61.11 N	6.51 E
Hermansville	190	45.42 N	87.36 W
Hermanus	158	34.25 S	19.16 E
Hermanville	194	31.57 N	90.50 W
Hermeray	261	48.38 N	1.41 E
Hermes ≃⁶	56	49.22 N	2.15 E
Hermeskeil	56	49.39 N	6.56 E
Hermidale	166	31.33 S	146.43 E
Hermies	50	50.07 N	3.02 E
Herminie	244	39.05 N	77.04 W
Hermiston	202	45.50 N	119.17 W
Hermitage, Nf., Can.	186	47.33 N	55.56 W
Hermitage, Eng., U.K.	42	51.27 N	1.16 W
Hermitage, Ar., U.S.	194	33.26 N	92.10 W
Hermitage, Mo., U.S.	190	37.56 N	93.18 W
Hermitage Bay c	186	47.35 N	56.05 W
Hermitage Park	284c	39.05 N	77.04 W
Hermit Islands II	164	1.30 S	145.05 E
Hermitleigh	196	32.38 N	100.46 W
Hermon, S. Afr.	158	33.27 S	18.59 E
Hermon, Mount → Shaykh, Jabal ash- ▲	132	33.26 N	35.51 E
Hermosa Beach	280	33.51 N	118.23 W
Hermosillo, Méx.	200	32.30 N	114.59 W
Hermosillo, Méx.	232	29.04 N	110.58 W
Hermoso, Cerro ▲	246	1.10 S	78.12 W
Hermsdorf ➤⁸	54	50.54 N	11.52 E
Hermsdorf ➤⁸	264a	52.37 N	13.18 E
Hermyingyi	110	14.15 N	98.21 E
Hernád ≃	30	47.56 N	21.08 E
Hernals ➤⁸	264b	48.13 N	16.20 E
Hernandarias	252	25.22 S	54.45 W
Hernandez	234	23.01 N	102.01 W
Hernandez Reservoir @¹	226	36.22 N	120.49 W
Hernando, Arg.	252	32.25 S	63.44 W
Hernando, Fl., U.S.	220	28.54 N	82.22 W
Hernando, Ms., U.S.	194	34.49 N	89.59 W
Hernando □⁶	220	28.34 N	82.22 W
Hernani	116	11.20 N	125.37 E
Herndon, Ca., U.S.	226	36.49 N	119.54 W
Herndon, Ks., U.S.	198	39.54 N	100.47 W
Herndon, Pa., U.S.	210	40.42 N	76.50 W
Herndon, Va., U.S.	208	38.58 N	77.23 W
Herndon Canal ≃	226	36.46 N	119.46 W
Herne	56	51.32 N	7.13 E
Herne Bay	42	51.23 N	1.08 E
Herne Hill	168a	31.50 S	116.01 E
Herning	41	56.08 N	8.59 E
Hernwood Heights	284b	39.22 N	76.47 W
Heroica Caborca	232	30.37 N	112.06 W
Herongate	260	51.36 N	0.21 E
Herongen	263	51.26 N	6.15 E
Heron Island I	166	23.26 S	151.55 E
Heron Lake	198	43.47 N	95.19 W
Hérons, Île aux I	275a	45.25 N	73.35 W
Héronsgate	260	51.38 N	0.31 W
Hérouville	261	49.06 N	2.08 E
Hérouville-Saint-Clair	32	49.13 N	0.18 W
Herpf	54	50.34 N	10.20 E
Herradura	252	26.29 S	58.18 W
Herräng	40	60.08 N	18.39 E
Herrenalb	58	48.50 N	8.26 E
Herrenberg	58	48.35 N	8.52 E
Herrenchiemsee, Schloss ⌂	64	47.52 N	12.23 E
Herrera, N.Z.	166	18.32 S	146.17 E
Herrera, Mount ▲	236	7.54 N	80.38 W
Herrera del Duque	34	39.10 N	5.03 W
Herrera de Pisuerga	34	42.36 N	4.20 W
Herrick, Austl.	166	41.06 S	147.52 E
Herrick, Il., U.S.	219	39.13 N	88.59 W
Herrick Creek ≃	182	54.20 N	121.30 W
Herrick Grove	212	44.04 N	76.12 W
Herricks	276	40.45 N	73.40 W
Herrieden	56	49.14 N	10.30 E
Herrin	194	37.48 N	89.01 W
Herring Bay c	208	38.44 N	76.33 W
Herring Brook ≃	272	42.10 N	70.44 W
Herring Cove, N.S., Can.	186	44.34 N	63.34 W
Herring Cove, Ak., U.S.	182	55.21 N	131.41 W
Herring Creek ≃	208	37.49 N	77.07 W
Herring Run ≃	284b	39.18 N	76.31 W
Herring Run Park ♦	284b	39.19 N	76.33 W
Herritsvold	41	55.42 N	11.41 E
Herrljunga	40	58.05 N	13.02 E
Herrnhut	54	51.01 N	14.45 E
Herrnsdorf	60	49.53 N	10.45 E
Herrsching am Ammersee	58	48.00 N	11.10 E
Herrsking	279b	42.09 N	71.14 W
Herry	50	47.13 N	2.53 E
Hersbruck	54	49.30 N	11.26 E
Herschbach	56	50.34 N	7.44 E
Herscher	216	41.03 N	88.06 W
Herschel, Sk., Can.	184	51.38 N	108.22 W
Herschel, S. Afr.	158	30.37 S	27.12 E
Herschel Island I	180	69.36 N	139.05 W
Herselt	50	51.03 N	4.53 E
Herserange	58	49.31 N	5.47 E
Hershey, Ne., U.S.	198	41.09 N	100.59 W
Hershey, Pa., U.S.	208	40.17 N	76.39 W
Herstal	56	50.40 N	5.38 E
Herstmonceux	42	50.53 N	0.20 E
Hertel	226	39.56 N	122.30 W
Herten	52	51.36 N	7.08 E
Hertford, Eng., U.K.	42	51.48 N	0.05 W
Hertford, N.C., U.S.	192	36.11 N	76.27 W
Hertford □⁶	42	51.50 N	0.03 W
Hertfordshire □⁶	42	51.50 N	0.10 W
Hertingsburg	54	51.49 N	11.16 E
Hertogenwald ↙³	56	50.35 N	6.05 E
Herton	276	40.46 N	73.41 W
Hertzogville	158	28.08 S	25.33 E
Heruncun	98	37.58 N	115.44 E
Hervás	34	40.16 N	5.51 W
Hervé d'Oeste	252	27.11 S	51.30 W
Hervey Bay ☰	166	25.00 S	153.00 E
Herxheim	58	49.09 N	8.13 E
Héry, Fr.	58	47.54 N	3.54 E
Héry, Fr.	50	47.38 N	3.39 E
Herzberg am Harz	54	51.39 N	10.20 E
Herzebrock	52	51.53 N	8.14 E
Herzegovina ▸¹	66	43.20 N	18.00 E
Herzele	50	50.53 N	3.53 E
Herzliyya	132	32.10 N	34.51 E
Herzogenbuchsee	58	47.11 N	7.41 E
Herzogenrath	56	50.52 N	6.06 E
Hesarak	267d	35.47 N	51.19 E
Hesdin	50	50.22 N	2.02 E
Hesel	52	53.18 N	7.35 E
Hesepe	52	52.26 N	7.58 E
Heshachang	107	30.37 N	105.40 E
Heshan	110	23.52 N	108.52 E
Heshangqiao	100	34.15 N	113.47 E
Heshengqiao	100	30.00 N	114.22 E
Heshi, Zhg.	100	25.04 N	118.37 E
Heshi, Zhg.	107	29.10 N	104.22 E
Heshui, Zhg.	100	24.24 N	114.56 E
Heshui, Zhg.	102	22.48 N	112.29 E
Heshuijian	100	30.33 N	116.05 E
Heshun, Zhg.	100	27.30 N	117.24 E
Heshun, Zhg.	102	37.21 N	113.35 E
Hesketh Bank	262	53.42 N	2.51 W
Hesketh Out Marsh ≃	262	53.43 N	2.55 W
Heskin Green	262	53.38 N	2.42 W
Hesler	216	38.28 N	84.47 W
Hesperange	56	49.34 N	6.09 E
Hesperia, Ca., U.S.	198	37.33 N	117.18 W
Hesperia, Mi., U.S.	190	43.34 N	86.02 W
Hesperus Mountain ▲	200	37.27 N	108.05 W
Hessle	180	63.34 N	133.57 W
Hesselager	41	55.10 N	10.45 E
Hesselberg ▲	56	49.04 N	10.31 E
Hesselte	52	52.25 N	7.22 E
Hessen □³	56	50.30 N	9.15 E
Hessen □³	30	50.30 N	9.15 E
Hessen Cassal	216	41.00 N	85.05 W
Hessenthal	56	49.55 N	9.17 E
Hessisch Lichtenau	56	51.12 N	9.43 E
Hessisch Oldendorf	52	52.10 N	9.15 E
Hessle	44	53.44 N	0.26 W
Hesso	166	32.08 S	137.27 E
Hess Tablemount ➤³	14	17.50 N	174.15 W
Hesston, Ks., U.S.	198	38.08 N	97.25 W
Hesston, Pa., U.S.	214	40.26 N	78.07 W
Heston ➤⁸	260	51.29 N	0.22 W
Het ≃	110	20.49 N	104.01 E
Hetang, Zhg.	102	22.03 N	112.19 E
Hetang, Zhg.	100	26.40 N	119.09 E
Hetang, Zhg.	107	31.43 N	120.27 E
Hetang, Zhg.	107	28.58 N	106.03 E
Hetauṇḍā	124	27.25 N	85.02 E
Hetch Hetchy Aqueduct ≃¹	226	37.29 N	122.19 W
Hetch Hetchy Reservoir @¹	226	37.57 N	119.43 W
Hettersett	42	52.36 N	1.11 E
Hetian, Zhg.	102	25.41 N	116.26 E
Hetian, Zhg.	100	25.03 N	115.38 E
Het Loo, Paleis ⌂	52	52.14 N	5.56 E
Hetou	100	24.18 N	113.29 E
Hetoudian	98	37.02 N	120.35 E
Hettange-Grande	56	49.24 N	6.09 E
Hettenleidelheim	56	49.32 N	8.04 E
Hettick	219	39.21 N	90.02 W
Hettinger	198	46.00 N	102.38 W
Hettstedt	54	51.39 N	11.30 E
Hetupu	100	30.50 N	116.03 E
Hetzendorf ➤⁸	264b	48.10 N	16.18 E
Het Zoute	50	51.21 N	3.18 E
Heubach	56	48.48 N	9.56 E
Heudeber	54	51.54 N	10.50 E
Heule	50	50.50 N	3.14 E
Heuningspruit	158	27.26 S	27.28 E
Heusden	52	51.44 N	5.08 E
Heustreu	56	50.21 N	10.15 E
Heusweiler	56	49.20 N	6.55 E
Heuvelton	212	44.37 N	75.24 W
Hève, Cap de la ➤	32	49.31 N	0.04 E
Heves	30	47.36 N	20.17 E
Heves □⁶	30	47.50 N	20.15 E
Hevlín	61	48.45 N	16.23 E
Hewett, Naḥal V	132	31.15 N	34.50 E
Hewitt, N.J., U.S.	210	41.08 N	74.18 W
Hewitt, Tx., U.S.	222	31.27 N	97.11 W
Hewittsville	219	39.32 N	89.19 W
Hewlett, N.Y., U.S.	276	40.38 N	73.41 W
Hewlett, Va., U.S.	208	37.55 N	77.35 W
Hewlett Bay Park	276	40.37 N	73.42 W
Hewlett Harbor	276	40.38 N	73.42 W
Hewlett Neck	276	40.37 N	73.42 W
Hewlett Point ➤	276	40.49 N	73.45 W
Hexham, Austl.	166	32.49 S	151.41 E
Hexham, Eng., U.K.	262	54.58 N	2.06 W
Hexi, Zhg.	102	24.09 N	102.36 E
Hexi, Zhg.	100	24.29 N	114.56 E
Hexi, Zhg.	100	31.03 N	119.49 E
Hexian	100	31.42 N	118.21 E
Hexian	100	24.25 N	111.43 E
Hexiang	105	40.02 N	116.11 E
Hexigten Qi (Jingpeng)	98	43.15 N	117.34 E
Hexingjie	105	31.03 N	120.36 E
Hexinzhuang	105	39.38 N	116.58 E
Hexi Zoulang ↙¹	102	38.30 N	101.00 E
Hextable	260	51.25 N	0.10 E
Heyan	104	41.48 N	123.07 E
Heyang, Zhg.	102	35.27 N	110.33 E
Heyang, Zhg.	105	30.55 N	121.18 E
Heybeli Ada I	130	40.52 N	29.05 E
Heybeli Ada I	267b	40.52 N	29.05 E
Heybridge	260	51.44 N	0.41 E
Heyderbreck → Kedzierzyn	30	50.20 N	18.12 E
Heyerode	54	51.10 N	10.25 E
Heyersum	52	52.07 N	9.50 E
Heyin	56	34.02 N	108.57 E
Heytesbury	42	51.11 N	2.06 W
Heywood, Austl.	166	38.08 S	141.38 E
Heywood, Eng., U.K.	262	53.36 N	2.13 W
Heyworth	216	40.19 N	88.59 W
Hezhang	102	27.00 N	104.37 E
Hezheng	102	35.25 N	103.18 E
Hezhou	89	39.57 N	90.44 E
Hezuo	102	34.58 N	102.58 E
Hiʿala	132	33.16 N	35.20 E
Hialeah	220	25.51 N	80.17 W
Hialeah Park Race Track ♦	220	25.51 N	80.17 W
Hialeah	234	31.21 N	114.02 W
Hiawassee	192	34.57 N	83.45 W
Hiawatha, Ks., U.S.	190	39.51 N	95.32 W
Hiawatha, Ut., U.S.	200	39.29 N	111.00 W
Hibaru-Dōgo-Onsen-kokuritsu-kōen ♦	96	35.07 N	133.08 E
Hibbing	190	47.25 N	92.56 W
Hibbs, Point ➤	166	42.38 S	145.15 E
Hibernia Reef ➤²	162	12.00 S	123.23 E
Hibi ➤⁸	270	34.44 N	133.55 E
Hibiki-nada ☰	96	34.00 N	130.35 E
Hiburi-shima I	96	33.10 N	132.22 E
Hickam Air Force Base ☒	229c	21.20 N	157.57 W
Hickey, Mount ▲	182	51.11 N	125.31 W
Hickman, Ky., U.S.	194	36.34 N	89.11 W
Hickman, Ne., U.S.	190	40.37 N	96.37 W
Hickman's Harbour	186	48.06 N	53.44 W
Hickory, Ms., U.S.	194	32.19 N	89.01 W
Hickory, N.C., U.S.	192	35.44 N	81.21 W
Hickory, Pa., U.S.	214	40.18 N	80.18 W

Hickory Corners 216 42.26 N 85.22 W
Hickory Creek ≃, Il., U.S. 278 41.30 N 88.06 W
Hickory Creek ≃, Mi., U.S. 216 42.05 N 86.29 W
Hickory Creek ≃, Tx., U.S. 222 31.29 N 95.07 W
Hickory Flat 194 34.36 N 89.11 W
Hickory Hills 216 41.43 N 87.49 W
Hickory Run State Park ♦ 210 41.02 N 75.41 W
Hickory Township 214 41.15 N 80.27 W
Hicks, Point ⟩ 166 37.48 S 149.17 E
Hicks Bay 172 37.36 S 178.18 E
Hickson Lake ⊘ 184 56.17 N 104.25 W
Hicksville, N.Y., U.S. 210 40.46 N 73.31 W
Hicksville, Oh., U.S. 214 41.17 N 84.45 W
Hico 196 31.58 N 98.02 W
Hicpochee, Lake ⊘ 220 26.50 N 81.10 W
Hida → Hita 96 33.19 N 130.56 E
Hidaka, Nihon 96 35.26 N 137.03 E
Hidaka, Nihon 96 35.54 N 139.21 E
Hidaka, Nihon 96 35.28 N 134.47 E
Hidaka, Nihon 96 33.55 N 135.09 E
Hidaka ≃ 96 33.52 N 135.09 E
Hida-sammyaku ⋌ 92a 42.35 N 142.45 E
Hida-Kiso-gawa-kokutei-kōen ♦ 94 35.37 N 137.15 E
Hida-kōchi ⋌¹ 94 36.16 N 137.05 E
Hidalgo, Méx. 232 27.47 N 99.52 W
Hidalgo, Méx. 232 25.59 N 100.27 W
Hidalgo, Méx. 232 24.15 N 99.26 W
Hidalgo, Méx. 234 23.10 N 103.13 W
Hidalgo □³ 234 20.30 N 99.00 W
Hidalgo del Parral 234 26.56 N 105.40 W
Hidalgo Yalalag 234 17.11 N 96.11 W
Hida-sammyaku ⋌ 94 35.17 N 137.40 E
Hiddenhausen 52 52.08 N 8.38 E
Hidden Hills 228 34.09 N 118.43 W
Hiddensee ⦈ 54 54.33 N 13.07 E
Hidden Valley, Ca., U.S. 226 38.46 N 121.09 W
Hidden Valley, Tx., U.S. 222 29.54 N 95.25 W
Hiddensen 52 51.55 N 8.50 E
Hiddinghausen 263 51.22 N 7.17 E
Hidrbaba 130 38.47 N 39.00 E
Hidrolândia 255 16.58 S 49.14 W
Hidrolina 255 14.37 S 49.25 W
Hieflau 61 47.36 N 14.44 E
Hienghène 175f 20.41 S 164.56 E
Hierapolis → Pamukkale ⊥ 130 37.56 N 29.19 E
Hierges 56 50.06 N 4.44 E
Hierro (Ferro) ⦈ 148 27.45 N 18.00 W
Hiesfeld 263 51.33 N 6.46 E
Hietzing ⫽⁸ 264b 48.11 N 16.18 E
Higashi 174m 26.38 N 128.09 E
Higashi ◂⊸⁸ 270 34.41 N 135.31 E
Higashibetsuin 270 34.56 N 135.31 E
Higashifuji-enshūjō ♦ 94 34.26 N 132.42 E
Higashiichiki 96 31.40 N 130.20 E
Higashiiyama 96 33.52 N 133.54 E
Higashiizu 94 34.48 N 139.04 E
Higashi-jima ⦈ 174f 24.47 N 141.23 E
Higashikurume 268 35.45 N 139.32 E
Higashimatsuyama 96 36.02 N 139.24 E
Higashimonzen 268 35.56 N 139.40 E
Higashimurayama 94 35.46 N 139.29 E
Higashinada ◂⊸⁸ 270 34.43 N 135.16 E
Higashinakano 268 35.38 N 139.25 E
Higashinari ◂⊸⁸ 270 34.40 N 135.33 E
Higashine 92 38.26 N 140.24 E
Higashinose 94 34.55 N 135.30 E
Higashiōizumi ◂⊸⁸ 268 34.55 N 139.36 E
Higashiōsaka 96 34.39 N 135.35 E
Higashishirakawa 96 35.39 N 137.19 E
Higashisumiyoshi ◂⊸⁸ 270 34.37 N 135.31 E
Higashitokonoo-san ⋌ 96 35.25 N 134.55 E
Higashitsuno 96 33.23 N 133.02 E
Higashiura, Nihon 94 34.59 N 136.58 E
Higashiura, Nihon 270 34.33 N 135.00 E
Higashiyama ◂⊸⁸ 270 35.00 N 135.48 E
Higashiyamato 268 35.44 N 139.26 E
Higashiyodogawa ◂⊸⁸ 270 34.44 N 135.31 E
Higashiyoshino 94 34.24 N 135.58 E
Higbee 194 39.18 N 92.30 W
Higganum 207 41.29 N 72.33 W
Higgins 196 36.07 N 100.02 W
Higgins, Mount ⋌ 222 48.19 N 121.45 W
Higgins Lake ⊘ 190 44.30 N 84.45 W
Higginsport 218 38.47 N 83.58 W
Higginsville, Austl. 162 31.45 S 121.43 E
Higginsville, Mo., U.S. 194 39.04 N 93.43 W
Higgs' Hope 158 29.19 S 23.16 E
Higham Ferrers 42 52.18 N 0.36 W
Higham Upshire 260 51.26 N 0.28 E
Highbank 222 31.10 N 96.50 W
High Bank Creek ≃ 202 42.37 N 85.11 W
High Bar Indian Reserve ◂⁸ 182 51.06 N 122.00 W
High Beach 226 51.39 N 0.02 E
High Bentham 44 54.08 N 2.30 W
High Bluff Island ⦈ 212 43.58 N 77.45 W
Highbridge, Eng., U.K. 42 51.13 N 2.49 W
High Bridge, N.J., U.S. 210 40.40 N 74.53 W
Highbury 164 16.25 S 143.09 E
Highcliff 279b 40.32 N 80.03 W
Higher Ballam 232 53.46 N 2.59 W
Higher Broughton ◂⊸⁸ 246 53.30 N 2.15 W
Higher Hogshead ⋌² 262 53.42 N 2.09 W
Higher Penwortham 262 53.45 N 2.44 W
Higher Walton, Eng., U.K. 44 53.44 N 2.39 W
Higher Walton, Eng., U.K. 262 53.22 N 2.37 W
Higher Whitley 262 53.45 N 2.38 W
Highett 274b 37.57 S 145.03 E
High Falls 210 41.50 N 74.08 W
High Falls 212 46.55 N 75.23 W
High Force ⌣ 44 54.38 N 2.13 W
Highgate 214 30.30 N 81.49 W
Highgate Center 206 44.56 N 73.02 W
Highgate Springs 206 44.58 N 73.06 W
Highgrove 228 33.59 N 117.20 W
High Halstow 260 51.27 N 0.34 E
High Hesket 44 54.48 N 2.48 W
High Hill 219 38.52 N 91.23 W
High Hill ⋌ 276 40.49 N 73.25 W
High Hill ≃, Can. 184 56.45 N 110.30 W
High Hill ≃, Mb., Can. 184 55.52 N 94.42 W
High Hill Lake ⊘ 219 38.52 N 91.25 W
High Island, H.K. 271d 22.22 N 114.21 E
High Island ⦈, Mi., U.S. 190 45.42 N 85.40 W
High Island Creek ≃ 202 44.35 N 93.54 W
High Island Reservoir ⊘¹ 271d 22.22 N 114.21 E
Highland, Ca., U.S. 228 34.07 N 117.12 W
Highland, Il., U.S. 218 38.44 N 89.40 W
Highland, In., U.S. 216 41.33 N 87.27 W
Highland, Ks., U.S. 198 39.51 N 95.16 W
Highland, Md., U.S. 284c 39.11 N 76.57 W
Highland, Mi., U.S. 281 42.38 N 83.37 W
Highland, N.Y., U.S. 210 41.43 N 73.58 W
Highland ◂⊸⁸ 218 39.21 N 83.36 W
Highland □⁶ 42 57.40 N 5.00 W
Highland Beach 220 26.25 N 80.04 W
Highland City 220 27.58 N 81.53 W
Highland, On., Can. 275b 43.46 N 79.08 W

Highland Creek ≃, Ca., U.S. 226 38.24 N 121.14 W
Highland Falls 210 41.22 N 73.58 W
Highland Heights, Ky., U.S. 218 39.04 N 84.27 W
Highland Heights, Oh., U.S. 214 41.33 N 81.28 W
Highland Hills 278 41.52 N 88.01 W
Highland Home 194 31.57 N 86.18 W
Highland Lake ⊘, Il., U.S. 278 42.21 N 88.04 W
Highland Lake ⊘, Ma., U.S. 283 42.41 N 72.37 W
Highland Lake ⊘, N.Y., U.S. 210 41.32 N 74.51 W
Highland Lake ⊘, Ct., U.S. 207 41.54 N 73.06 W
Highland Lake ⊘, Il., U.S. 278 42.22 N 88.04 W
Highland Lake ⊘, N.J., U.S. 276 41.10 N 74.28 W
Highland Lakes 210 41.10 N 74.28 W
Highland-on-the-Lake 284a 42.42 N 79.59 W
Highland Park ⦈, U.S. 182 42.10 N 87.48 W
Highland Park, Md., U.S. 284c 38.54 N 76.54 W
Highland Park, Mi., U.S. 216 42.24 N 83.05 W
Highland Park, N.J., U.S. 210 40.29 N 74.25 W
Highland Park, Pa., U.S. 210 40.38 N 77.35 W
Highland Park, Tx., U.S. 222 32.50 N 96.48 W
Highland Park ◂⊸⁸ 280 34.07 N 118.13 W
Highland Park ♦, Ma., U.S. 283 42.30 N 70.55 W
Highland Peak ⋌ 226 39.06 N 79.55 W
Highland Point ⟩ 220 25.30 N 81.12 W
Highlands, N.J., U.S. 208 40.24 N 73.59 W
Highlands, N.C., U.S. 192 35.03 N 83.11 W
Highlands, Tx., U.S. 222 29.49 N 95.03 W
Highlands □⁶ 220 27.20 N 81.16 W
Highlands Hammock State Park ♦ 220 27.28 N 81.33 W
Highland Silver Lake ⊘¹ 219 38.47 N 89.39 W
Highlands North ◂⊸⁸ 273d 26.09 S 28.05 E
Highlands Springs 208 37.32 N 77.19 W
Highlands Reservoir ⊘¹ 222 29.50 N 95.02 W
Highland State Recreation Area ♦ 216 42.39 N 83.33 W
Highlandtown ◂⊸⁸ 284b 39.17 N 76.33 W
High Lane 260 51.45 N 0.13 E
High Legh 262 53.21 N 2.27 W
Highley 42 52.27 N 2.23 W
Highmore 198 44.31 N 99.26 W
High Ongar 260 51.43 N 0.16 E
High Park ♦ 275b 43.39 N 79.28 W
High Peak □⁸ 262 53.23 N 1.55 W
High Peak ⋌, Pil. 116 15.29 N 120.07 E
High Peak ⋌, N.Y., U.S. 210 42.09 N 74.05 W
High Peak ⋌ 44 53.22 N 1.50 W
High Point, Fl., U.S. 220 27.55 N 82.42 W
High Point, N.C., U.S. 192 35.57 N 80.00 W
Highpoint, Oh., U.S. 218 39.14 N 84.24 W
High Point ⋌, N.J., U.S. 210 41.19 N 74.40 W
High Point ⋌, Wy., U.S. 202 41.37 N 107.47 W
High Point State Park ♦ 210 41.18 N 74.41 W
High Prairie 182 55.26 N 116.29 W
High Ridge 219 38.27 N 90.32 W
High River 182 50.35 N 113.52 W
High Rock 226 26.36 N 76.18 W
High Rock 188 39.33 N 79.06 W
Highrock Indian Reserve ⊘, Mb., Can. 184 55.54 N 100.30 W
Highrock Lake ⊘, Sk., Can. 184 57.04 N 105.30 W
High Rock Lake ⊘¹ 192 35.40 N 80.17 W
High Seat ⋌ 44 54.24 N 2.18 W
High Spire 208 40.12 N 76.47 W
High Springs 220 29.49 N 82.35 W
High Street ⋌ 44 54.30 N 2.52 W
Hightown, Eng., U.K. 44 53.31 N 3.03 W
Hightown, Eng., U.K. 262 53.32 N 3.04 W
Hightstown 208 40.16 N 74.31 W
High View 210 41.33 N 74.27 W
Highway City 226 36.49 N 119.54 W
High Willhays ⋌ 42 50.40 N 3.59 W
Highwood, Il., U.S. 216 42.11 N 87.48 W
Highwood, Mt., U.S. 182 50.49 N 113.47 W
Highwood ≃ 182 50.49 N 113.47 W
Highwood Baldy ⋌ 202 47.40 N 110.00 W
Highwood Creek ≃ 202 47.40 N 111.00 W
Highwood Mountains ⋌ 202 47.25 N 110.30 W
Highworth 42 51.38 N 1.43 W
High Wycombe 42 51.38 N 0.46 W
Higlet 154 1.04 S 40.19 E
Higuera Blanca 232 20.46 N 105.27 W
Higuera de Zaragoza 232 25.59 N 109.16 W
Higuera Gorda 234 22.04 N 104.29 W
Higueras 196 25.58 N 100.01 W
Higüero, Punta ⟩ 240m 18.22 N 67.16 W
Higuerote 236 10.29 N 66.06 W
Higuito 238 14.43 N 88.40 W
Hihetro 150 7.32 N 1.06 E
Hihyā 142 30.40 N 31.36 E
Hii ◂⊸⁸ 96 35.26 N 132.54 E
Hiidenportin kansallispuisto ♦ 36 63.34 N 28.59 E
Hiiraan □³ 144 4.00 N 45.30 E
Hiiumaa ⦈ 76 58.52 N 22.40 E
Hiiänah, Buhayrat al- ⊘ 132 33.18 N 36.36 E
Hijar 34 41.10 N 0.27 W
Hiji 96 33.22 N 131.32 E
Hiji 96 35.30 N 132.29 E
Hijikawa 96 33.27 N 132.41 E
Hijiri-dake ⋌ 94 35.39 N 138.10 E
Hikami 96 35.10 N 135.02 E
Hikami, Nihon 96 35.10 N 135.02 E
Hikari, Nihon 96 33.58 N 131.56 E
Hikarigaoka 268 35.50 N 139.58 E
Hikawa 96 35.00 N 133.37 E
Hikawa Shrine ⫧¹ 268 35.54 N 139.38 E
Hiketa 96 34.13 N 134.24 E
Hiki ◂⊸⁸ 96 34.13 N 135.27 E
Hikigawa 96 33.35 N 135.27 E
Hikimi 96 34.37 N 131.48 E
Hikiura 96 35.15 N 136.15 E
Hikone 94 35.15 N 136.15 E
Hikone-jō ⊥ 94 35.17 N 136.15 E
Hiko-san ⋌ 96 33.28 N 130.54 E
Hikurangi 14 17.36 S 142.37 W
Hikurangi 172 35.36 S 174.18 E
Hikurangi ⋌ 172 37.55 S 178.04 E
Hikutaia 172 37.12 S 175.35 E
Hikutavake 114v 18.55 S 169.53 W
Hila 114 7.35 S 127.24 E
Hilaban Island ⦈ 116 10.03 N 125.34 E
Hilal, Jabal ⋌ 132 30.40 N 34.00 E
Hilāl, Ra's al- ⟩ 146 32.57 N 22.00 E
Hilbersdorf 56 50.55 N 13.23 E
Hilbringen 56 49.27 N 6.33 E
Hilchenbach 56 50.59 N 8.06 E
Hilda 184 50.28 N 110.03 W
Hildburghausen 56 50.26 N 10.44 E
Hilden 56 51.10 N 6.56 E

Hildenborough 260 51.13 N 0.15 E
Hilders 56 50.34 N 10.00 E
Hildesheim 52 52.09 N 9.57 E
Hildreth 198 40.20 N 99.02 W
Hilgen 263 51.06 N 7.09 E
Hilialawa 114 0.41 N 97.53 E
Hiligeo 114 1.22 N 97.10 E
Hiloluwa 114 0.44 N 97.53 E
Hilo ◂⊸⁸ 222 32.02 N 97.10 W
Hillaby, Mount ⋌ 241g 13.12 N 59.35 W
Hill Air Force Base ◾ 202 41.05 N 111.58 W
Hillandale, S. Afr. 158 33.06 S 20.36 E
Hillandale, Md., U.S. 284c 39.01 N 76.58 W
Hillandale Heights 232 17.35 N 88.42 W
Hillbank 210 44.08 N 74.10 W
Hill City, Ks., U.S. 198 39.21 N 99.50 W
Hill City, Mn., U.S. 202 46.59 N 93.35 W
Hill City, S.D., U.S. 198 43.56 N 103.34 W
Hill Creek ≃ 202 39.20 N 109.40 W
Hillcrest, Il., U.S. 216 41.57 N 89.04 W
Hillcrest, N.Y., U.S. 210 41.07 N 74.02 W
Hillcrest, N.Y., U.S. 210 42.09 N 75.53 W
Hillcrest Center 228 35.23 N 118.57 W
Hillcrest Heights 284c 38.49 N 76.57 W
Hillcrest Mines 182 49.34 N 114.23 W
Hillcrest Park 226 41.51 N 83.29 W
Hill Cumorah ⊥ 210 43.01 N 77.15 W
Hille, B.R.D. 52 52.20 N 8.44 E
Hille, Sve. 40 60.44 N 17.11 E
Hillegom 52 52.18 N 4.35 E
Hillegossen 52 51.59 N 8.37 E
Hillerød 41 55.56 N 12.19 E
Hillers Creek ≃ 219 38.38 N 91.54 W
Hillesheim 56 50.18 N 6.38 E
Hilli 124 25.17 N 89.01 E
Hilliard, Fl., U.S. 192 30.41 N 81.55 W
Hilliard, Oh., U.S. 218 40.02 N 83.09 W
Hilliards 214 41.05 N 79.50 W
Hillingdon ◂⊸⁸ 260 51.32 N 0.27 W
Hillisburg 216 40.17 N 86.20 W
Hill Island Lake ⊘ 176 60.29 N 109.50 W
Hillister 194 30.40 N 94.23 W
Hillman 190 34.40 N 84.55 W
Hillman ≃ 168a 33.26 S 116.48 E
Hillmersdorf 54 51.42 N 13.29 E
Hillof Fearn 46 57.45 N 3.49 W
Hills 198 43.31 N 96.21 W
Hills and Dales 214 39.42 N 84.13 W
Hillsboro, Il., U.S. 219 39.09 N 89.29 W
Hillsboro, Ks., U.S. 198 38.21 N 97.12 W
Hillsboro, Md., U.S. 218 38.55 N 75.56 W
Hillsboro, Mo., U.S. 219 38.13 N 90.33 W
Hillsboro, N.H., U.S. 188 43.06 N 71.53 W
Hillsboro, N.M., U.S. 200 32.55 N 107.33 W
Hillsboro, N.D., U.S. 198 47.24 N 97.03 W
Hillsboro, Oh., U.S. 218 39.12 N 83.36 W
Hillsboro, Or., U.S. 224 45.31 N 122.59 W
Hillsboro, Tx., U.S. 222 32.00 N 97.07 W
Hillsboro Beach 220 26.19 N 80.05 W
Hillsboro Canal ≃ 220 26.19 N 80.05 W
Hillsborough, N.B., Can. 186 45.56 N 64.39 W
Hillsborough, N. Ire., U.K. 48 54.28 N 6.05 W
Hillsborough, Ca., U.S. 237 37.34 N 122.22 W
Hillsborough, N.C., U.S. 192 36.04 N 79.06 W
Hillsborough □⁶, Fl., U.S. 220 27.55 N 82.15 W
Hillsborough □⁶, N.H., U.S. 220 42.49 N 71.41 W
Hillsborough, Cape ⟩ 166 20.54 S 149.03 E
Hillsborough Bay ⊂, P.E., Can. 186 46.10 N 63.05 W
Hillsborough Bay ⊂, Fl., U.S. 220 27.52 N 82.27 W
Hillsborough River State Park ♦ 220 28.09 N 82.14 W
Hillsburgh 213 43.47 N 80.09 W
Hills Creek Lake ⊘¹ 202 43.40 N 122.26 W
Hillsdale, Mi., U.S. 216 41.55 N 84.37 W
Hillsdale, N.J., U.S. 276 41.00 N 74.02 W
Hillsdale, N.Y., U.S. 210 42.13 N 73.31 W
Hillsdale, Pa., U.S. 214 41.53 N 78.17 W
Hillsdale □⁶ 216 41.53 N 84.36 W
Hillsdale ◂⊸⁹ 282 37.32 N 122.18 W
Hillsdale Lake ⊘ 198 38.38 N 94.55 W
Hills Flat 226 39.13 N 121.03 W
Hillsgrove 210 41.27 N 76.39 W
Hillside, Austl. 162 21.44 S 119.23 E
Hillside, Scot., U.K. 46 56.44 N 2.29 W
Hillside, Md., U.S. 284c 38.52 N 76.55 W
Hillside, N.J., U.S. 276 40.42 N 74.13 W
Hillside Gardens 285 39.41 N 75.34 W
Hillside Heights 285 39.41 N 75.41 W
Hillside Lake 210 41.36 N 73.50 W
Hillston 214 33.29 S 145.32 E
Hillsville, Pa., U.S. 214 41.00 N 80.30 W
Hillsville, Va., U.S. 192 36.45 N 80.44 W
Hillswick 46a 60.28 N 1.30 W
Hilltop 283 39.49 N 75.04 W
Hilltop Center ◂⊸⁹ 282 39.22 N 122.19 W
Hilltown, N. Ire., U.K. 48 54.12 N 6.07 W
Hilltown, Pa., U.S. 208 40.20 N 75.14 W
Hillview 226 40.20 N 122.22 W
Hillview Reservoir ⊘¹ 276 40.55 N 73.52 W
Hillwood 284c 38.52 N 77.10 W
Hilo 229d 19.43 N 155.05 W
Hilo Bay ⊂ 229d 19.44 N 155.04 W
Hilonghilong, Mount ⋌ 116 9.06 N 125.44 E
Hilongos 116 10.23 N 124.45 E
Hilpoltstein 60 49.12 N 11.11 E
Hilpsford Point ⟩ 44 54.03 N 3.12 W
Hilsa 124 25.19 N 85.17 E
Hilshire Village 222 29.48 N 95.26 W
Hiltaba, Mount ⋌ 164 32.09 S 135.03 E
Hilter 52 52.08 N 8.08 E
Hilton, N.Y., U.S. 210 43.17 N 77.47 W
Hilton, Pa., U.S. 284 40.00 N 76.49 W
Hilton Head Island ⦈ 192 32.10 N 80.45 W
Hiltpoltstein 60 49.40 N 11.19 E
Hiltrop ◂⊸⁸ 263 51.30 N 7.15 E
Hiltrup 52 51.54 N 7.38 E
Hilvarenbeek 52 51.29 N 5.09 E
Hilversum 52 52.13 N 5.11 E
Hima 192 37.07 N 83.46 W
Himachal Pradesh □³ 120 28.00 N 77.00 E
Himal Chuli ⋌ 124 28.26 N 84.38 E
Himamaylan 116 10.06 N 122.52 E
Himanka 26 64.04 N 23.39 E
Himarë 24 40.06 N 19.44 E
Himatnagar 120 23.36 N 72.57 E
Himberg 61 48.05 N 16.26 E
Hime 94 48.05 N 16.26 E
Himeji 94 34.49 N 134.42 E
Hime-shima ⦈ 96 33.43 N 131.39 E
Himeville 158 29.44 S 29.31 E
Himi 94 36.51 N 136.59 E
Himki (Himki) 130 55.54 N 37.26 E
Himmelberget ⋌² 41 56.06 N 9.42 E
Himmelgeist ◂⊸⁸ 263 51.11 N 6.49 E
Himmelpforten 52 53.36 N 9.18 E
Himmelsthür ◂⊸⁸ 56 52.08 N 9.55 E
Himmerfjärden ⊂² 41 59.00 N 17.43 E
Himmerland ⫽¹ 41 56.48 N 9.45 E
Himrod 210 42.34 N 76.58 W
Hims (Homs) 130 34.44 N 36.43 E
Hims □⁴ 130 34.45 N 37.15 E
Himsä ≃ 130 34.44 N 36.43 E
Hinako, Kepulauan ⦈⦈ 114 0.52 N 97.21 E

Hinase 96 34.44 N 134.16 E
Hinatuan 116 8.23 N 126.20 E
Hinatuan Island ⦈ 116 9.47 N 125.43 E
Hinatuan Passage ⊔ 116 9.45 N 125.47 E
Hinche 238 19.09 N 72.01 W
Hinchinbrook Entrance ⊔ 180 60.25 N 146.50 W
Hinchinbrook Island ⦈, Austl. 166 18.23 S 146.17 E
Hinchinbrook Island ⦈, Ak., U.S. 180 60.22 N 146.30 W
Hinchinbrook Island National Park ♦ 166 18.20 S 146.20 E
Hinckley, Eng., U.K. 42 52.33 N 1.21 W
Hinckley, Il., U.S. 216 41.46 N 88.38 W
Hinckley, Mn., U.S. 190 46.00 N 92.56 W
Hinckley, Oh., U.S. 214 41.14 N 81.45 W
Hinckley, Ut., U.S. 200 39.19 N 112.40 W
Hinckley Reservoir ⊘ 210 43.20 N 75.05 W
Hindang 116 10.26 N 124.44 E
Hindau 124 26.43 N 77.01 E
Hindelang 58 47.30 N 10.22 E
Hindelbank 58 47.03 N 7.32 E
Hindeloopen 52 52.56 N 5.24 E
Hindenburg → Zabrze 30 50.18 N 18.46 E
Hindhead 42 51.07 N 0.44 W
Hindley 262 53.32 N 2.35 W
Hindley Green 262 53.31 N 2.32 W
Hindman 192 37.20 N 82.58 W
Hindmarsh Island ⦈ 168b 35.32 S 138.52 E
Hindmarsh Valley 168b 35.30 S 138.38 E
Hindon 42 51.06 N 2.08 W
Hindsboru 41 55.33 N 10.40 E
Hinds Lake ⊘ 186 48.57 N 57.00 W
Hindu Kush ⋌ 120 36.00 N 71.30 E
Hindnalkot 123 30.09 N 73.55 E
Hindupur 122 13.49 N 77.29 E
Hi-Nella 285 39.50 N 75.01 W
Hines, Or., U.S. 202 43.33 N 119.04 W
Hines Creek 182 56.15 N 118.36 W
Hines Creek ≃ 182 56.14 N 118.37 W
Hines Peak ⋌ 228 34.31 N 119.05 W
Hinesville 192 31.50 N 81.35 W
Hinganghāt 122 20.34 N 78.50 E
Hingatungan 116 10.35 N 125.11 E
Hingham, Eng., U.K. 42 52.35 N 0.59 E
Hingham, Ma., U.S. 207 42.14 N 70.53 W
Hingham Bay ⊂ 283 42.16 N 70.53 W
Hingham Harbor ⊂ 283 42.15 N 70.53 W
Hingol ≃ 120 25.23 N 65.28 E
Hingoli 122 19.43 N 77.09 E
Hiniganan 116 10.17 N 122.51 E
Hinis 130 39.18 N 42.12 E
Hinkley 228 34.56 N 117.11 W
Hinkson Creek ≃ 219 38.56 N 92.23 W
Hinkston Creek ≃ 188 38.18 N 84.14 W
Hinnerjoki 26 61.00 N 22.00 E
Hinnerup 41 56.16 N 10.04 E
Hinojosa del Duque 32 38.30 N 5.09 W
Hinokage 92 32.39 N 131.24 E
Hinomi-saki ⟩, Nihon 96 33.53 N 135.04 E
Hinomi-saki ⟩, Nihon 96 35.26 N 132.38 E
Hinsbeck 56 51.21 N 6.17 E
Hinsdale, Il., U.S. 216 41.48 N 87.56 W
Hinsdale, Ma., U.S. 226 42.26 N 73.07 W
Hinsdale, N.H., U.S. 207 42.47 N 72.29 W
Hinsdale, N.Y., U.S. 210 42.10 N 78.23 W
Hinsel ◂⊸⁸ 263 51.26 N 7.05 E
Hinson 40 60.39 N 16.05 E
Hinte 52 53.25 N 7.11 E
Hinterbichl 61 47.01 N 12.20 E
Hinterbrühl 61 48.05 N 16.15 E
Hinterhermsdorf 54 50.55 N 14.22 E
Hinterrhein ≃ 58 46.43 N 9.12 E
Hinterrhein ⫽ 264b 48.18 N 16.13 E
Hinterstoder 61 47.42 N 14.09 E
Hintertux 61 47.07 N 11.41 E
Hinterweidenthal 56 49.13 N 7.45 E
Hinterzarten 58 47.54 N 8.06 E
Hintlesham 260 52.04 N 0.59 E
Hinton, Ab., Can. 182 53.25 N 117.34 W
Hinton, Mo., U.S. 219 39.03 N 92.21 W
Hinton, Ok., U.S. 196 35.10 N 98.21 W
Hinton, W.V., U.S. 192 37.40 N 80.53 W
Hi-numa ⊘ 94 36.16 N 140.30 E
Hinwil 58 47.18 N 8.51 E
Hinzik 84 40.08 N 40.58 E
Hípico, Club ♦ 236e 10.26 N 66.49 W
Hipólito 232 25.41 N 101.26 W
Hipólito Yrigoyen 252 22.45 S 66.20 W
Hippolytushoef 52 52.54 N 4.57 E
Hirado 96 33.22 N 129.33 E
Hirado-shima ⦈ 96 33.20 N 129.30 E
Hiraiwa-hana ⟩ 174f 24.48 N 141.18 E
Hiraizumi 92 38.59 N 141.07 E
Hirakata, Nihon 94 34.48 N 135.38 E
Hirakata, Nihon 96 35.14 N 139.37 E
Hirākud 122 21.31 N 83.57 E
Hirākud Reservoir ⊘¹ 122 21.35 N 83.50 E
Hiram, Me., U.S. 207 43.53 N 70.48 W
Hiram, Oh., U.S. 214 41.18 N 81.08 W
Hirano ◂⊸⁸ 270 34.37 N 135.34 E
Hirano 175d 24.55 N 124.19 E
Hirao 96 33.56 N 132.04 E
Hirao-dai ⊥ 96 33.45 N 130.52 E
Hiraoka 96 34.17 N 135.03 E
Hiraoka → Higashiōsaka 96 34.39 N 135.34 E
Hirara 175d 24.48 N 125.17 E
Hirata, Nihon 96 35.25 N 132.49 E
Hirata, Nihon 94 37.00 N 140.39 E
Hiratsuka 94 35.19 N 139.21 E
Hirfanlı Barajı ⊘¹ 130 39.08 N 33.32 E
Hirhafok 148 23.49 N 5.45 E
Hiriyūr 122 13.58 N 76.36 E
Hîrlăul 26 47.26 N 26.54 E
Hirna 154 9.13 N 41.05 E
Hirochö 94 36.18 N 139.51 E
Hirose → Hiroshima 96 34.24 N 132.27 E
Hirose 96 35.18 N 133.10 E
Hirosaki 92 40.35 N 140.28 E
Hiroshima → Hiroshima 96 34.24 N 132.27 E
Hiroshima 96 34.24 N 132.27 E
Hiro-shima ⦈ 96 34.16 N 132.54 E
Hiroshima-wan ⊂ 96 34.06 N 132.20 E
Hiroo 92 42.17 N 143.19 E
Hirooka 94 36.13 N 137.58 E
Hirosama ⫽¹ 92a 42.20 N 142.40 E
Hirschaid 56 49.49 N 10.59 E
Hirschau 54 49.33 N 11.57 E
Hirschberg, B.R.D. 54 50.33 N 11.44 E
Hirschberg, D.D.R. 54 51.08 N 11.49 E

Hirschberg, → Jelenia Góra, Pol. 30 50.55 N 15.46 E
Hirschfeld 54 51.23 N 13.37 E
Hirschfelde, D.D.R. 54 50.57 N 14.53 E
Hirschfelde, D.D.R. 264a 52.38 N 13.48 E
Hirschhorn 56 49.27 N 8.53 E
Hirschstetten ◂⊸⁸ 264b 48.14 N 16.29 E
Hirshfeld Brook ≃ 276 40.57 N 74.02 W
Hirsingue 57 47.35 N 7.15 E
Hîrşova 38 44.41 N 27.57 E
Hirsts Hill ⋌ 171a 27.13 S 152.06 E
Hirtshals 26 57.36 N 9.58 E
Hirtzfelden 58 47.55 N 7.27 E
Hirukawa 94 35.31 N 137.23 E
Hiru-zen ⋌ 96 35.19 N 133.40 E
Hirwaun 42 51.45 N 3.30 W
Hisai, Nihon 94 34.40 N 136.28 E
Hisai, Nihon 270 34.25 N 135.28 E
Hisār 123 29.10 N 75.43 E
Hisarönü 130 41.33 N 32.02 E
Hisbān 132 31.48 N 35.48 E
Hisn al-'Abr 144 16.05 N 48.25 E
Hisn al-Qarn 144 15.11 N 49.05 E
Hispaniola ⦈ 238 19.00 N 71.00 W
Hispar Glacier ⦂ 123 36.05 N 75.20 E
Histon 42 52.15 N 0.06 E
Hisua 124 24.50 N 85.25 E
Hisyah 130 34.24 N 36.45 E
Hita 96 33.19 N 130.56 E
Hitachi 94 36.36 N 140.39 E
Hitachi-ōta 96 36.32 N 140.31 E
Hitati → Hitachi 94 36.36 N 140.39 E
Hitchcock 222 29.20 N 95.00 W
Hitchin 42 51.57 N 0.17 W
Hitchins 218 38.16 N 82.55 W
Hither Green ◂⊸⁸ 260 51.27 N 0.01 W
Hitra ⦈ 26 63.33 N 8.45 E
Hittarp 41 56.06 N 12.38 E
Hitzacker 54 53.09 N 11.02 E
Hitze-Berge ⋌² 264a 52.35 N 13.02 E
Hiu 175f 13.10 S 166.35 E
Hiuchiga-take ⋌ 94 36.57 N 139.17 E
Hiuchi-nada ≃² 96 34.05 N 133.20 E
Hiuchinukui Pătan ⋌ 124 28.00 N 82.30 E
Hiva Oa ⦈ 174x 9.45 S 139.00 W
Hi Vista 228 34.44 N 117.47 W
Hiwa 96 34.59 N 132.59 E
Hiwannee 194 31.48 N 88.41 W
Hiwasa 96 33.44 N 134.32 E
Hiwassee ≃ 192 35.10 N 84.47 W
Hiwassee Lake ⊘¹ 192 35.10 N 84.05 W
Hixon 182 53.26 N 122.36 W
Hixson 192 35.09 N 85.14 W
Hiyoshi, Nihon 96 35.53 N 137.45 E
Hiyoshi, Nihon 96 33.20 N 132.48 E
Hiyoshi, Nihon 96 35.12 N 135.33 E
Hiyon, Nahal V 132 30.12 N 35.07 E
Hizaonna 174m 26.24 N 127.50 E
Hjälmare kanal ⊠ 40 59.24 N 15.56 E
Hjälmaren ⊘ 40 59.15 N 15.45 E
Hjälmarsund ⊔ 40 59.15 N 16.06 E
Hjarråker 41 56.46 N 12.38 E
Hjellestad 41 60.16 N 5.13 E
Hjelteifjorden ⊂² 26 60.40 N 4.55 E
Hjembæk 41 55.42 N 11.25 E
Hjellund 41 56.05 N 9.25 E
Hjo 41 58.18 N 14.17 E
Hjordkær 41 55.01 N 9.18 E
Hjørring 26 57.28 N 9.59 E
Hjort Basin ⁺¹ 58 58.00 S 157.30 E
Hjortkvarn 41 59.01 N 15.25 E
Hjorthagen ◂⊸⁷ 281 59.21 N 18.06 E
Hkakabo Razi ⋌ 102 28.20 N 97.32 E
Hkok (Kok) ≃ 110 20.14 N 100.09 E
Hlabisa 158 28.08 S 31.52 E
Hlaingbwe 110 17.08 N 97.50 E
Hlatikulu 158 26.58 S 31.19 E
Hlegu 110 17.06 N 96.12 E
Hlinsko 56 49.46 N 15.55 E
Hlobane 158 27.42 S 31.00 E
Hluboká 56 49.03 N 14.27 E
Hluboká nad Vltavou 56 49.03 N 14.27 E
Hlučín 56 49.54 N 18.12 E
Hluhluwe 158 28.01 S 32.15 E
Hluhluwe Game Reserve ◂⁴ 158 28.05 S 32.04 E
Hluti 158 27.13 S 31.35 E
Hlwabi 158 17.06 N 96.02 E
H. Neely Henry Lake ⊘¹ 194 33.55 N 86.05 W
Hoa Binh 110 20.50 N 105.20 E
Hoa Da 110 11.11 N 108.33 E
Hoagland 216 40.55 N 84.08 W
Hoagland Ditch ≃ 262 41.08 N 86.20 W
Hoanib ≃ 158 19.27 S 12.46 E
Hoare Bay ⊂ 176 65.20 N 62.30 W
Hoarusib ≃ 158 19.03 S 12.36 E
Hoa Thoi 110 10.44 N 106.35 E
Hobart, Austl. 166 42.53 S 147.19 E
Hobart, N.Y., U.S. 210 42.22 N 74.40 W
Hobart, Ok., U.S. 196 35.01 N 99.05 W
Hobart, Wi., U.S. 202 44.30 N 88.08 W
Hobbs, N.M., U.S. 196 32.42 N 103.08 W
Hobbs Coast ⋌² 5 74.45 S 131.00 W
Hobe Sound 220 27.04 N 80.08 W
Hobol 96 36.35 N 129.23 E
Hoboken, Bel. 51 51.10 N 4.21 E
Hoboken, N.J., U.S. 276 40.45 N 74.02 W
Hobøl 41 59.37 N 10.58 E
Hobro 41 56.38 N 9.48 E
Hobson 202 46.59 N 109.52 W
Hobsonville 172 36.50 S 174.38 E
Hobro 41 56.38 N 9.48 E
Hobson ≃ 158 29.30 S 31.08 E
Hobucken 192 35.15 N 76.34 W
Hochbirg ⋌ 60 49.39 N 11.56 E
Hochblauen ⋌ 58 47.45 N 7.42 E

Hochheim, Tx., U.S. 222 29.19 N 97.17 W
Hochiss ⋌ 64 47.27 N 11.46 E
Hochkirch 54 51.09 N 14.34 E
Hochkönig ⋌ 64 47.25 N 13.04 E
Hochkreuz ◂⊸⁸ 263 46.49 N 13.04 E
Hochlar ◂⊸⁸ 263 51.36 N 7.10 E
Hochneukirch 56 51.06 N 6.26 E
Hochobir ⋌ 61 46.30 N 14.29 E
Hochreichhart ⋌ 61 47.22 N 14.41 E
Hochries ⋌ 64 47.45 N 12.14 E
Hochschwab ⋌ 61 47.37 N 15.09 E
Hochschwab ⋌¹ 61 47.37 N 15.05 E
Hochsimmer ⋌ 56 56.21 N 7.12 E
Hochspeyer 56 49.26 N 7.54 E
Höchst, B.R.D. 56 49.48 N 8.59 E
Höchst, Öst. 58 47.28 N 9.38 E
Höchst ◂⊸⁸ 56 50.07 N 8.33 E
Höchstadt an der Aisch 56 49.42 N 10.44 E
Höchstädt an der Donau 58 48.36 N 10.34 E
Höchsten ⋌ 263 51.27 N 7.29 E
Höchstenbach 56 50.38 N 7.44 E
Hochstuhl (Veliki Stol) ⋌ 61 46.26 N 14.10 E
Hochtor ✕ 64 47.05 N 12.51 E
Hoch'uan → Hechuan 107 30.00 N 106.16 E
Hochvogel ⋌ 64 47.23 N 10.26 E
Hochwildstelle ⋌ 64 47.20 N 13.50 E
Hockenheim 58 49.19 N 8.33 E
Hockeroda 54 50.35 N 11.26 E
Hockessin 285 39.47 N 75.41 W
Hocking ◂⊸⁸ 188 39.12 N 81.45 W
Hocking Hills State Park ♦ 188 39.30 N 82.32 W
Hockley, Eng., U.K. 260 51.37 N 0.40 E
Hockley, Tx., U.S. 222 30.02 N 95.51 W
Hockomock Swamp ⊏ 283 41.59 N 71.05 W
Höd ◂⁷¹ 150 16.10 N 8.40 W
Hodal 124 27.54 N 77.22 E
Hōdatsu-san ⋌ 94 36.47 N 136.49 E
Hodder ≃ 44 53.50 N 2.25 W
Hoddesdon 260 51.46 N 0.01 W
Hoddlesden 262 53.42 N 2.26 W
Hodeida → Al-Hudaydah 144 14.48 N 42.57 E
Hodenhagen 52 52.46 N 9.35 E
Hodge 194 32.16 N 92.43 W
Hodges, Lake ⊘¹ 228 33.03 N 117.05 W
Hodges Brook ≃ 283 41.58 N 71.14 W
Hodges Hill ⋌² 186 49.04 N 55.53 W
Hodgeville 184 50.08 N 106.58 W
Hodgkins 278 41.46 N 87.51 W
Hodgson 184 51.13 N 97.34 W
Hodgson ≃ 184 51.13 N 97.34 W
Hodgson, Mount ⋌² 162 22.26 S 121.10 E
Hodh ech Chargui □⁴ 150 16.30 N 10.00 W
Hodh el Gharbi □⁴ 150 16.30 N 10.00 W
Hódmezővásárhely 30 46.25 N 20.20 E
Hodna, Chott el ⊘ 148 35.25 N 4.45 E
Hodna, Monts du ⋌ 34 35.38 N 4.30 E
Hodna, Plaine du ⊏ 34 35.38 N 4.30 E
Hodnet 42 52.51 N 2.35 W
Hodonín 56 48.51 N 17.08 E
Hodošš 61 46.49 N 16.20 E
Hodzana ≃ 180 66.16 N 149.58 W
Hoe ⁻¹ 41 56.19 N 10.49 E
Hoedekenskerke 52 51.25 N 3.55 E
Hoehne 198 37.16 N 104.22 W
Hoeksche Waard ⦈ 52 51.49 N 4.09 E
Hoek van Holland 52 51.59 N 4.09 E
Hoenderloo 263 52.06 N 5.46 E
Hoensbroek 52 50.55 N 5.55 E
Hoerdt 58 48.42 N 7.47 E
Hoerstgen 263 51.30 N 6.27 E
Hoeryöng 98 42.27 N 129.44 E
Hoeyang 98 38.43 N 127.36 E
Hof, B.R.D. 54 50.18 N 11.55 E
Hof, Island 24a 64.34 N 14.29 W
Hofburg ◂⊸⁸ 264b 48.12 N 16.22 E
Höfdakaupstadur 24a 65.50 N 20.19 W
Hofei → Hefei 100 31.51 N 117.17 E
Hoffman, Il., U.S. 219 38.32 N 89.16 W
Hoffman, Mn., U.S. 198 45.50 N 95.47 W
Hoffman Estates 216 42.03 N 88.08 W
Hoffman Island ⦈ 276 40.35 N 74.03 W
Hoffnungsthal ◂⊸⁸ 263 50.55 N 7.10 E
Hoffman Station 285 39.51 N 75.13 W
Hoffnung 263 51.07 N 7.13 E
Hofgeismar 52 51.30 N 9.23 E
Hofheim 56 50.07 N 8.26 E
Hofheim in Unterfranken 56 50.08 N 10.31 E
Hofkirchen an der Trattnac 61 48.13 N 13.44 E
Höflein an der Donau 264b 48.08 N 16.17 E
Hofmeyr 158 31.39 S 25.50 E
Hofn 24 64.17 N 15.10 W
Hofors 40 60.33 N 16.17 E
Höfdajökull ⦂ 24a 64.48 N 18.50 W
Hofstade 51 51.01 N 4.31 E
Hofstede ◂⊸⁸ 263 51.30 N 7.13 E
Hofstra University ⫽² 276 40.43 N 73.36 W
Hofuf → Al-Hufūf 128 25.22 N 49.34 E
Hofweier 58 48.20 N 7.51 E
Hog, Tanjong ⟩ 110 5.18 N 119.16 E
Hogaland ≃ 158 21.28 S 23.01 E
Hogan ≃ 150 15.52 N 12.33 E
Hogan Lake ⊘ 200 35.12 N 112.30 W
Hogansville 192 33.10 N 84.54 W
Hogatza ≃ 180 66.13 N 156.00 W
Hogback Mountain ⋌, Ne., U.S. 198 41.40 N 103.44 W
Hogback Mountain ⋌, Vt., U.S. 207 42.43 N 72.20 W
Hogbacks ⋌ 202 44.54 N 112.07 W
Hog Creek ≃ 222 31.32 N 97.18 W
Hoge Veluwe, Nationale Park de ⁺ 52 52.02 N 5.55 E
Högfors 40 59.59 N 15.01 E
Hoggar → Ahaggar ⋌ 148 23.10 N 6.20 E
Hoghton 262 53.44 N 2.35 W
Hoghton Tower ⊥ 262 53.44 N 2.34 W
Hog Island ⦈, Mi., U.S. 190 45.48 N 85.22 W
Hog Island ⦈, Va., U.S. 206 44.57 N 73.13 W
Hog Island Bay ⊂ 208 37.25 N 75.46 W
Hogo 96 34.43 N 135.19 E
Hog Point ⟩ 208 38.17 N 76.31 W
Hogs Back ⋌⁴ 260 51.13 N 0.40 W
Högsäter 41 58.36 N 12.02 E
Högsby 41 57.10 N 16.02 E
Hogsty Reef ⊶ 238 21.41 N 73.48 W

Symbols in the index entries represent the broad categories identified in the key at the right. Symbols with superior numbers (⋌¹) identify subcategories (see complete key on page *I · 1*).

Symbole im Register stellen die rechts im Schlüssel erklärten Kategorien dar. Symbole mit hochgestellten Ziffern (⋌¹) bezeichnen Unterteilungen einer Kategorie (vgl. vollständigen Schlüssel auf Seite *I · 1*).

Los símbolos incluidos en el texto del índice representan las grandes categorías identificadas en la clave a la derecha. Los símbolos con números en su parte superior (⋌¹) identifican las subcategorías (véase la clave completa en la página *I · 1*).

Os símbolos incluídos no texto do índice representam as grandes categorias identificadas com o chave à direita. Os símbolos com números em sua parte superior (⋌¹) identificam as subcategorias (veja-se a chave completa à página *I · 1*).

Les symboles de l'index représentent les catégories indiquées dans la légende à droite. Les symboles suivis d'un indice (⋌¹) représentent des sous-catégories (voir légende complète à la page *I · 1*).

⋌ Mountain	Berg	Montaña	Montagne	Montanha
⋌ Mountains	Gebirge	Montañas	Montagnes	Montanhas
✕ Pass	Paß	Paso	Col	Passo
V Valley, Canyon	Tal, Cañon	Valle, Cañón	Vallée, Canyon	Vale, Canhão
⊏ Plain	Ebene	Llano	Plaine	Planície
⟩ Cape	Kap	Cabo	Cap	Cabo
⦈ Island	Insel	Isla	Île	Ilha
⦈⦈ Islands	Inseln	Islas	Îles	Ilhas
⊥ Other Topographic Features	Andere Topographische Objekte	Otros Elementos Topográficos	Autres données topographiques	Outros acidentes topográficos

Hohe-Horn I · 73

ESPAÑOL — Nombre | Página | Lat. °′ | Long. °′ W = Oeste

FRANÇAIS — Nom | Page | Lat. °′ | Long. °′ W = Ouest

PORTUGUÊS — Nome | Página | Lat. °′ | Long. °′ W = Oeste

Nombre	Página	Lat. °′	Long. °′ W = Oeste
Hohegeiss	54	51.40 N	10.40 E
Hohenau	252	27.05 S	55.45 W
Hohenau an der March	61	48.36 N	16.55 E
Höhenberg	61	48.46 N	14.53 E
Hohenbrunn	60	48.03 N	11.42 E
Hohenbucko	54	51.46 N	13.28 E
Hohenbudberg ➛[8]	263	51.23 N	6.40 E
Hohenburg	60	49.16 N	11.30 E
Hohendorf	54	54.01 N	13.44 E
Hohenebra	54	51.18 N	10.49 E
Hohenems	58	47.22 N	9.41 E
Hohenfels	60	49.12 N	11.51 E
Hohenfurch	58	47.51 N	10.54 E
Hohengüstow	54	53.14 N	13.59 E
Hohenhameln	52	52.15 N	10.03 E
Hohenheide	263	51.29 N	7.47 E
Hohenkammer	60	48.25 N	11.32 E
Hohenkirchen, B.R.D.	52	53.39 N	7.55 E
Hohenkirchen, B.R.D.	56	51.23 N	9.29 E
Hohenkirchen, D.D.R.	54	53.51 N	11.17 E
Hohenkirchen, D.D.R.	54	50.51 N	10.41 E
Hohenleipisch	54	51.30 N	13.34 E
Hohenleuben	54	50.43 N	12.03 E
Hohenlimburg	56	51.21 N	7.35 E
Hohenlimburg, Schloss ⊥	263	51.21 N	7.34 E
Hohenlinden	60	48.09 N	12.00 E
Hohenmölsen	54	51.09 N	12.06 E
Hohen Neuendorf	54	52.40 N	13.16 E
Hohenpolding	60	48.23 N	12.08 E
Hohensalza → Inowrocław	30	52.48 N	18.15 E
Hohenschönhausen ➛[8]	264a	52.33 N	13.30 E
Hohenseeden	54	52.19 N	12.01 E
Hohenseefeld	54	51.53 N	13.18 E
Hohenstaufen	56	48.44 N	9.43 E
Hohenstein → Olsztynek	30	53.36 N	20.17 E
Hohenstein-Ernstthal	54	50.48 N	12.42 E
Hohensyburg ⊥	56	51.25 N	7.29 E
Hohentauern	61	47.26 N	14.29 E
Hohenthurm	54	51.31 N	12.05 E
Hohenthurn	64	46.33 N	13.40 E
Hohentwiel ∧	58	47.46 N	8.49 E
Hohenwald	194	35.32 N	87.33 W
Hohenwart	60	48.36 N	11.23 E
Hohenwarte-Stausee ⊜[1]	54	50.32 N	11.30 E
Hohenwarthe	54	52.13 N	11.42 E
Hohenwutzen	54	52.51 N	14.07 E
Hohenzethen	54	53.03 N	10.49 E
Hohenzollern, Burg ⊥	58	48.19 N	8.58 E
Hohenzollernkanal ≅	264a	52.32 N	13.20 E
Hoher Bogen ∧	60	49.15 N	12.55 E
Hoher Dachstein ∧	64	47.28 N	13.35 E
Hoher Freschen ∧	58	47.18 N	9.46 E
Hohe Rhön ⋏	56	50.30 N	10.00 E
Hoher Ifen ∧	58	47.21 N	10.05 E
Hoherlehme	264a	52.19 N	13.37 E
Hoher Mechtin ∧[2]	54	53.03 N	10.55 E
Hoher Riffler ∧	58	47.07 N	10.22 E
Hoher Sonnblick ∧	64	47.03 N	12.57 E
Hoher Zinken ∧	64	47.40 N	13.20 E
Hohe Tauern ⋏	64	47.10 N	12.45 E
Hohe Warte (Monte Coglians) ∧	64	46.37 N	12.53 E
Hoh Head ›	224	47.46 N	124.29 W
Hohhot	102	40.51 N	111.40 E
Höhn	56	50.37 N	8.00 E
Hohndorf	54	50.45 N	12.40 E
Hohne	52	52.35 N	10.22 E
Hohneck, Le ∧	58	48.02 N	7.01 E
Hohnstein	54	50.59 N	14.10 E
Hohoe	150	7.09 N	0.28 E
Hōhoku	96	34.17 N	130.57 E
Ho-Ho-Kus	276	40.59 N	74.06 W
Hohokus Brook ≃	276	40.57 N	74.06 W
Hoholitna ≃	180	61.31 N	157.00 W
Hoh Sai Hu ⊜	120	35.43 N	92.45 E
Höhscheid ➛[8]	263	51.09 N	7.04 E
Hohultslätt	26	56.58 N	15.39 E
Hohwacht	54	54.19 N	10.41 E
Hohwachter Bucht ⊂	41	54.20 N	10.45 E
Hoh Xil Hu ⊜	120	35.35 N	91.06 E
Hoh Xil Shan ⋏	120	35.20 N	90.00 E
Hoi An	110	15.52 N	108.19 E
Hoihow → Haikou	102	20.03 N	110.19 E
Hoima	154	1.26 N	31.21 E
Hoisdorf	52	53.39 N	10.20 E
Hoisington	198	38.31 N	98.46 W
Hoisten	263	51.08 N	6.42 E
Hoi Xuan	110	20.22 N	105.07 E
Hojāi	120	26.00 N	92.51 E
Højby, Dan.	41	55.20 N	10.27 E
Højby, Dan.	41	55.55 N	11.37 E
Höje	40	59.54 N	13.33 E
Højer	26	54.58 N	8.43 E
Højerup	41	55.17 N	12.27 E
Hōjō → Kasai, Nihon	96	34.56 N	134.50 E
Hōjō, Nihon	96	34.54 N	134.56 E
Hōjō, Nihon	96	33.58 N	132.46 E
Hokah	190	43.45 N	91.20 W
Hokang → Hegang	89	47.24 N	130.17 E
Hökåsen	40	59.40 N	16.35 E
Hokendauqua	208	40.39 N	75.29 W
Hökensås ⋏[2]	26	58.11 N	14.08 E
Hokes Bluff	194	33.59 N	85.51 W
Hōki ≃	94	36.47 N	140.08 E
Hokianga Harbour ⊂	172	35.32 S	173.22 E
Hokitika	172	42.43 S	170.58 E
Hokkaidō □[5]	92a	44.00 N	143.00 E
Hokkaidō I	92a	44.00 N	143.00 E
Hokksund	26	59.47 N	9.59 E
Hoko ≃	224	48.17 N	124.22 W
Hōkōji	270	34.52 N	135.07 E
Hököpinge	41	55.30 N	13.00 E
Hokota	94	36.09 N	140.31 E
Hok So Wan	271d	22.13 N	114.14 E
Hokubo	96	34.57 N	133.38 E
Hokudan	96	34.32 N	134.56 E
Hokura ≃	94	37.10 N	138.16 E
Hokuriku-tunnel ➛[5]	94	35.42 N	136.10 E
Hokusei	94	35.09 N	136.31 E
Hola	154	1.29 S	40.02 E
Holalkere	122	14.02 N	76.11 E
Holanda → Netherlands □[1]	30	52.15 N	5.30 E
Holbæk	41	55.43 N	11.43 E
Holbeach	42	52.49 N	0.01 E
Holbeach Marsh ≡	42	52.52 N	0.05 E
Holberg	182	50.39 N	128.00 W
Holborn ➛[8]	260	51.31 N	0.07 W
Holbrook, Austl.	171b	35.44 S	147.19 E
Holbrook, Az., U.S.	200	34.54 N	110.09 W
Holbrook, Il., U.S.	278	41.32 N	87.38 W
Holbrook, Md., U.S.	284b	39.24 N	76.51 W
Holbrook, Ma., U.S.	207	42.09 N	71.00 W
Holbrook, Ne., U.S.	198	40.18 N	100.00 W
Holbrook, N.Y., U.S.	210	40.48 N	73.04 W
Holbrook, Lake ⊜[1]	222	32.42 N	95.33 W
Holbrook Mountain ∧[2]	212	44.25 N	77.51 W
Holckenhavn	41	55.17 N	10.47 E
Holcomb, Il., U.S.	216	42.04 N	89.06 W
Holcomb, N.Y., U.S.	210	42.54 N	77.25 W
Holcomb Creek ≃	228	34.17 N	117.08 W
Holden, Ab., Can.	182	53.14 N	112.14 W
Holden, Ma., U.S.	207	42.21 N	71.51 W
Holden, Mo., U.S.	194	38.42 N	93.59 W
Holden, Ut,. U.S.	200	39.05 N	112.16 W
Holden, W.V., U.S.	188	37.49 N	82.03 W
Holden, Mount ∧[2]	216	41.40 N	87.03 W
Holdenstedt	52	52.55 N	10.31 E
Holden Village	224	48.12 N	120.47 W
Holdenville	196	35.04 N	96.23 W
Holder	220	28.58 N	82.25 W
Holderness ›[1]	44	53.47 N	0.10 W
Holdfast	184	50.58 N	105.25 W
Holdich	254	45.57 S	68.13 W
Holdingford	190	45.43 N	94.28 W
Holdorf	52	52.35 N	8.07 E
Holdrege	198	40.26 N	99.22 W
Holeby	41	54.43 N	11.28 E
Hole in the Mountain Peak ∧	204	40.55 N	115.05 W
Hole Narsipur	122	12.47 N	76.15 E
Holešov	30	49.20 N	17.35 E
Holetown	241g	13.11 N	59.39 W
Holgate, S. Afr.	158	33.59 S	22.21 E
Holgate, Oh., U.S.	216	41.14 N	84.07 W
Holguín	240p	20.53 N	76.15 W
Holguín □[4]	240p	20.55 N	75.50 W
Hol-Hol	144	11.19 N	42.57 E
Holíč	30	48.49 N	17.10 E
Holice	30	50.04 N	15.59 E
Holiday Beach Provincial Park ♠	214	42.02 N	83.05 W
Holiday Hills	216	42.18 N	88.13 W
Holiday Lake Amusement Park ♠	285	40.02 N	74.56 W
Holiday Shores	219	38.55 N	89.56 W
Holitna ≃	180	61.40 N	157.12 W
Höljes	26	60.54 N	12.36 E
Hollabrunn	61	48.34 N	16.05 E
Holladay	200	40.40 N	111.49 W
Holland, Mb., Can.	184	49.36 N	98.53 W
Holland, Mi., U.S.	216	42.47 N	86.06 W
Holland, N.Y., U.S.	210	42.38 N	78.32 W
Holland, Oh., U.S.	216	41.37 N	83.42 W
Holland, Pa., U.S.	285	40.10 N	74.59 W
Holland, Tx., U.S.	222	30.53 N	97.24 W
Holland, Va., U.S.	208	36.41 N	76.47 W
Holland □[9]	52	52.20 N	4.45 E
Holland → Netherlands □[1]	30	52.15 N	5.30 E
Holland ≃	212	44.12 N	79.31 W
Holland, Mount ∧[2]	162	32.12 S	119.44 E
Hollandale	194	33.10 N	90.51 W
Holland Creek ≃	169	36.43 S	146.06 E
Hollande, Étangs de ⊜	261	48.44 N	1.48 E
Holland Fen ≡	42	53.00 N	0.10 W
Hollandia → Jayapura	164	2.32 S	140.42 E
Holland Landing	212	44.06 N	79.29 W
Holland Park	171a	27.31 S	153.03 E
Holland Patent	210	43.14 N	75.15 W
Holland Point ›	208	38.43 N	76.32 W
Holland Pond State Park ♠	207	42.04 N	72.09 W
Hollandsbird Island I	156	24.45 S	14.34 E
Hollandsch Diep ʯ	52	51.42 N	4.30 E
Hollandstoun	46	59.21 N	2.16 W
Holland Straits ʯ	208	38.08 N	76.02 W
Holland Tunnel ➛[5]	276	40.44 N	74.02 W
Hollansburg	218	39.59 N	84.47 W
Holleben	54	51.26 N	11.53 E
Hollenfels, Château ⊥	56	49.43 N	6.03 E
Höllengebirge ⋏	64	47.48 N	13.39 E
Hollenstedt	52	53.22 N	9.43 E
Hollenstein an der Ybbs	61	47.48 N	14.46 E
Höllensteinberg ∧	264b	48.06 N	16.11 E
Höllental V	61	47.45 N	15.47 E
Hollern	52	53.36 N	9.32 E
Holleton	162	31.57 S	119.02 E
Holley	210	43.13 N	78.01 W
Hollfeld	60	49.56 N	11.18 E
Hollick-Kenyon Plateau ⋏[1]	9	79.00 S	97.00 W
Holliday, Mo., U.S.	219	39.29 N	92.07 W
Holliday, Tx., U.S.	196	33.49 N	98.42 W
Holliday Creek ≃	196	33.55 N	98.28 W
Holliday Park ♠	281	42.21 N	83.24 W
Hollidaysburg	214	40.25 N	78.23 W
Hollingbourne	260	51.16 N	0.38 E
Hollingstedt	41	54.27 N	9.19 E
Hollingworth	262	53.28 N	1.59 W
Hollingworth Lake ⊜	262	53.38 N	2.06 W
Hollins, Eng., U.K.	262	53.34 N	2.17 W
Hollins, Va., U.S.	192	37.20 N	79.56 W
Hollins Green	262	53.25 N	2.27 W
Hollinswood	284c	38.55 N	77.13 W
Hollis, N.H., U.S.	207	42.44 N	71.35 W
Hollis, Ok., U.S.	196	34.41 N	99.54 W
Hollis ➛[8]	276	40.43 N	73.46 W
Hollister	226	36.51 N	121.24 W
Hollister, Mount ∧[2]	162	22.08 S	114.01 E
Holliston	207	42.12 N	71.25 W
Hollman, Cape ›	164	4.59 S	150.06 E
Holloman Air Force Base ■	200	32.51 N	106.05 W
Holloway	214	40.10 N	81.08 W
Holloway Terrace	285	39.42 N	75.32 W
Hollow Rock	194	36.02 N	88.16 W
Hollowville	210	42.13 N	73.42 W
Hollsopple	214	40.13 N	78.56 W
Hollum	52	53.26 N	5.37 E
Höllviken ⊂	41	55.26 N	12.54 E
Höllviksnäs	41	55.25 N	12.57 E
Holly, Co., U.S.	198	38.03 N	102.07 W
Holly, Mi., U.S.	216	42.47 N	83.37 W
Holly, Wa., U.S.	224	47.34 N	122.58 W
Holly, Mount ∧[2]	285	40.00 N	74.47 W
Holly Brook	285	39.59 N	74.48 W
Holly Grove	194	34.35 N	91.11 W
Holly Hill, Fl., U.S.	192	29.14 N	81.02 W
Holly Hill, S.C., U.S.	192	33.19 N	80.24 W
Holly Park, N.J., U.S.	208	39.53 N	74.10 W
Holly Park, Va., U.S.	284c	38.50 N	77.17 W
Holly Pond ⊜	276	41.03 N	73.30 W
Holly River State Park ♠	188	38.40 N	80.21 W
Holly Run ≃	285	39.47 N	75.03 W
Holly Springs	194	34.46 N	89.26 W
Holly State Recreation Area ♠	216	42.49 N	83.32 W
Hollywood, Ire.	48	53.06 N	6.35 W
Hollywood, Fl., U.S.	220	26.00 N	80.08 W
Hollywood, Md., U.S.	208	38.20 N	76.34 W
Hollywood, Pa., U.S.	285	40.05 N	75.06 W
Hollywood ➛[8]	228	34.06 N	118.21 W
Hollywood, Mount ∧	280	34.08 N	118.18 W
Hollywood Bowl ♠	280	34.07 N	118.20 W
Hollywood-Burbank Airport ⊠	228	34.12 N	118.21 W
Hollywood Heights	219	38.39 N	89.59 W
Hollywood Indian Reservation ➛[4]	220	26.02 N	80.13 W
Hollywood Park Race Track ♠	280	33.57 N	118.20 W
Hollywood Reservoir ⊜[1]	280	34.07 N	118.20 W
Holman	176	70.43 N	117.43 W
Hólmavík	24a	65.43 N	21.43 W
Holmdel	208	40.20 N	74.11 W
Holme, Dan.	41	56.07 N	10.11 E
Holme, Eng., U.K.	262	53.33 N	1.50 W
Holme ≃	44	53.41 N	1.43 W
Holme Chapel	262	53.45 N	2.11 W
Holmen, Nor.	26	60.40 N	10.22 E
Holmen, Wi., U.S.	190	43.57 N	91.15 W
Holme-on-Spaulding-Moor	44	53.50 N	0.46 W
Holmes, N.Y., U.S.	210	41.31 N	73.39 W
Holmes, Pa., U.S.	285	39.54 N	75.19 W
Holmes □[6]	214	40.33 N	81.55 W
Holmes, Mount ∧	202	44.49 N	110.51 W
Holmes Beach	220	27.31 N	82.43 W
Holmesburg ➛[8]	285	40.02 N	75.03 W
Holmes Chapel	44	53.12 N	2.22 W
Holmes Creek ≃	194	30.30 N	85.47 W
Holmesglen	274b	37.53 S	145.06 E
Holmes Harbor ⊂	224	48.04 N	122.32 W
Holmes Lake ⊜	184	57.05 N	96.45 W
Holmes Reef ✣[2]	164	16.27 S	148.00 E
Holmes Run ≃	284c	38.48 N	77.07 W
Holmes Run Acres	284c	38.51 N	77.13 W
Holmestrand	26	59.29 N	10.18 E
Holmesville, N.Y., U.S.	210	42.31 N	75.24 W
Holmesville, Oh., U.S.	214	40.37 N	81.55 W
Holmeswood	262	53.39 N	2.52 W
Holmfirth	44	53.35 N	1.46 W
Holmia	246	4.58 N	59.35 W
Holmön I	26	63.47 N	20.53 E
Holmsbu	26	59.33 N	10.27 E
Holmsjön ⊜, Sve.	26	62.41 N	16.33 E
Holmsjön ⊜, Sve.	26	62.25 N	15.20 E
Holmsund	26	63.42 N	20.21 E
Hölö	40	59.01 N	17.35 E
Holod	38	46.47 N	22.08 E
Holoit, Punta ›	232	21.37 N	88.08 W
Holon	132	32.01 N	34.46 E
Holoog	156	27.22 S	17.55 E
Holopaw	220	28.08 N	81.04 W
Holroyd	274a	33.50 S	150.58 E
Holroyd ≃	164	14.10 S	141.36 E
Holsloot	52	52.44 N	6.48 E
Holstebro	26	56.21 N	8.38 E
Holsted	41	55.30 N	8.55 E
Holstein	198	42.29 N	95.32 W
Holsteinborg ⊥	41	55.13 N	11.28 E
Holsteinische Schweiz ➛[1]	54	54.11 N	10.36 E
Holsteinsborg (Sisimiut)	176	66.55 N	53.40 W
Holsterhausen	263	51.41 N	6.57 E
Holston ≃	192	35.57 N	83.51 W
Holston, North Fork ≃	192	36.33 N	82.36 W
Holston High Knob ∧	192	36.27 N	82.05 W
Holsworthy	42	50.49 N	4.21 W
Holt, Eng., U.K.	42	52.55 N	1.05 E
Holt, Wales, U.K.	44	53.05 N	2.53 W
Holt, Al., U.S.	194	33.14 N	87.29 W
Holt, Ca., U.S.	226	37.56 N	121.26 W
Holt, Fl., U.S.	194	30.42 N	86.44 W
Holt, Mi., U.S.	216	42.38 N	84.30 W
Holt Creek ≃	198	42.28 N	98.50 W
Holte	41	55.49 N	12.28 E
Holtemme ≃	54	51.57 N	11.10 E
Holten	52	52.17 N	6.25 E
Holten ➛[8]	263	51.31 N	6.48 E
Holtenau ➛[8]	54	54.22 N	10.08 E
Holter Lake ⊜[1]	202	46.55 N	111.57 W
Holthausen, B.R.D.	52	52.33 N	7.17 E
Holthausen, B.R.D.	263	51.23 N	7.13 E
Holthausen ➛[8]	263	51.34 N	7.26 E
Holthusen	52	53.08 N	7.18 E
Holton, In., U.S.	218	39.04 N	85.23 W
Holton, Ks., U.S.	198	39.27 N	95.44 W
Holtorf	52	52.40 N	9.13 E
Holts Summit	219	38.39 N	92.07 W
Holtsville	210	40.49 N	73.02 W
Holtug	41	55.21 N	12.25 E
Holtville	204	32.48 N	115.22 W
Holtwick	52	52.00 N	7.05 E
Holtwood	208	39.50 N	76.19 W
Holwerd	52	53.22 N	5.54 E
Holycross, Ire.	48	52.38 N	7.52 W
Holy Cross, Ak., U.S.	180	62.12 N	159.47 W
Holy Cross Mountain ∧	182	53.47 N	120.47 W
Holyhead	44	53.19 N	4.38 W
Holyhead Bay ⊂	44	53.23 N	4.37 W
Holy Island I, Eng., U.K.	44	55.41 N	1.48 W
Holy Island I, Scot., U.K.	46	55.32 N	5.04 W
Holy Island I, Wales, U.K.	44	53.18 N	4.37 W
Holy Island I, Ma., U.S.	283	42.43 N	70.50 W
Holyoke, Co., U.S.	198	40.35 N	102.18 W
Holyoke, Ma., U.S.	207	42.12 N	72.37 W
Holyrood	198	38.35 N	98.24 W
Holyrood Palace ʊ	46	55.56 N	3.12 W
Holýšov	60	49.36 N	13.05 E
Holywell	44	53.17 N	3.13 W
Holywell Green	262	53.41 N	1.52 W
Holywood	48	54.38 N	5.50 W
Holzbüttgen	263	51.12 N	6.37 E
Holzen	56	51.26 N	7.31 E
Holzgau	58	47.16 N	10.21 E
Holzgerlingen	56	48.38 N	9.00 E
Holzhausen, B.R.D.	52	52.17 N	8.32 E
Holzhausen, B.R.D.	52	52.13 N	8.01 E
Holzhausen, B.R.D.	52	52.01 N	8.44 E
Holzhausen, D.D.R.	54	51.18 N	12.28 E
Holzhausen an der Haide	56	50.13 N	7.55 E
Holzheim	56	51.09 N	6.39 E
Holzkirchen	64	47.52 N	11.42 E
Holzminden	52	51.50 N	9.27 E
Holzweissig	54	51.36 N	12.18 E
Holzwickede	52	51.30 N	7.36 E
Hom ≃	158	28.51 S	18.37 E
Homa Bay	154	0.31 S	34.27 E
Homalin	110	24.52 N	94.55 E
Homathko ≃	182	50.55 N	124.50 W
Homathko Icefield ⊓	182	51.05 N	124.30 W
Homberg, B.R.D.	56	50.43 N	8.59 E
Homberg, B.R.D.	56	51.02 N	9.24 E
Homberg, B.R.D.	56	51.28 N	6.43 E
Homberg, B.R.D.	263	51.18 N	6.56 E
Hombori	150	15.17 N	1.42 W
Hombori Tondo ∧	150	15.16 N	1.40 W
Hombourg-Haut	56	49.08 N	6.46 E
Hombre Muerto, Salar del ≡	252	25.23 S	67.06 W
Hombruch ➛[8]	263	51.29 N	7.26 E
Homburg → Bad Homburg vor der Höhe, B.R.D.	56	50.13 N	8.37 E
Homburg, B.R.D.	56	49.19 N	7.20 E
Home, Pa., U.S.	214	40.44 N	79.06 W
Home, Wa., U.S.	224	47.17 N	122.46 W
Homeacre	214	40.51 N	79.55 W
Home Bay ⊂, N.T., Can.	176	68.45 N	67.10 W
Home Bay ⊂, Kiribati	174d	0.53 S	169.35 E
Homebush Bay ⊂	274a	33.50 S	151.05 E
Home Corner	216	40.31 N	85.38 W
Homécourt	56	49.14 N	5.59 E
Home Creek ≃	196	31.29 N	99.14 W
Homedale, Id., U.S.	202	43.37 N	116.55 W
Homedale, Oh., U.S.	214	40.04 N	83.02 W
Home Gardens	228	33.52 N	117.31 W
Home Hill	166	19.40 S	147.25 E
Homeland, Ca., U.S.	228	33.44 N	117.07 W
Homeland, Fl., U.S.	220	27.49 N	81.49 W
Homeland Canal ≅	226	35.57 N	119.27 W
Homeland Park	192	34.27 N	82.41 W
Home Place	218	39.56 N	86.08 W
Homer, Ak., U.S.	180	59.39 N	151.33 W
Homer, Ga., U.S.	192	34.20 N	83.29 W
Homer, La., U.S.	194	32.47 N	93.03 W
Homer, Mi., U.S.	216	42.08 N	84.48 W
Homer, Ne., U.S.	198	42.19 N	96.29 W
Homer, N.Y., U.S.	210	42.38 N	76.10 W
Homer, Oh., U.S.	214	40.15 N	82.31 W
Homer, Tx., U.S.	222	31.18 N	94.36 W
Homer City	214	40.32 N	79.09 W
Homert ∧[2]	263	51.11 N	7.39 E
Homer Tunnel ➛[5]	172	44.45 S	168.00 E
Homerville, Ga., U.S.	192	31.02 N	82.44 W
Homerville, Oh., U.S.	214	41.02 N	82.08 W
Homer Wash V	204	34.20 N	115.02 W
Homer Youngs Peak ∧	202	45.19 N	113.41 W
Home Seamount ✣[3]	14	12.55 S	175.37 W
Homestead, Austl.	166	20.22 S	145.39 E
Homestead, Fl., U.S.	220	25.28 N	80.28 W
Homestead, Pa., U.S.	279b	40.24 N	79.54 W
Homestead Air Force Base ■	220	25.29 N	80.23 W
Homestead National Monument of America ♠	198	40.14 N	96.54 W
Homestead Valley	282	37.54 N	122.32 W
Hometown, Il., U.S.	278	41.44 N	87.43 W
Hometown, Pa., U.S.	210	40.49 N	75.59 W
Homewood, Al., U.S.	194	33.28 N	86.48 W
Homewood, Ca., U.S.	226	39.05 N	120.09 W
Homewood, Il., U.S.	216	41.33 N	87.39 W
Homewood, Oh., U.S.	218	39.23 N	84.33 W
Homewood ➛[8]	279b	40.27 N	79.54 W
Homewood Acres	278	41.34 N	87.43 W
Homeworth	214	40.50 N	81.03 W
Hominy	196	36.24 N	96.23 W
Hominy Creek ≃	196	36.20 N	96.00 W
Hommersåk	26	58.58 N	5.42 E
Hommura	92	34.22 N	139.15 E
Homnābād	122	17.46 N	77.08 E
Homochitto ≃	194	31.09 N	91.31 W
Homoíne	156	23.52 S	35.09 E
Homonhon Island I	116	10.44 N	125.43 E
Homosassa	220	28.46 N	82.36 W
Homosassa Bay ⊂	220	28.45 N	82.43 W
Homosassa Springs	220	28.48 N	82.35 W
Homs → Al-Khums	146	32.39 N	14.16 E
Homs → Ḥimṣ	130	34.44 N	36.43 E
Honai	96	33.30 N	132.25 E
Honaker	192	37.00 N	81.58 W
Honami	96	33.36 N	130.42 E
Honan → Luoyang	102	34.41 N	112.28 E
Honan → Henan □[4]	90	34.00 N	114.00 E
Honāvar	122	14.17 N	74.27 E
Honaz	130	37.45 N	29.17 E
Honbetsu	92a	43.07 N	143.37 E
Hon Chong	110	10.10 N	104.37 E
Honda	246	5.12 N	74.45 W
Honda, Bahía ⊂, Col.	246	12.21 N	71.47 W
Honda, Bahía ⊂, Cuba	240p	22.57 N	83.10 W
Honda, Cañada ≃	258	33.57 S	59.21 W
Honda Bay ⊂	116	9.53 N	118.49 E
Honddu ≃, U.K.	42	51.54 N	2.58 W
Honddu ≃, Wales, U.K.	42	51.57 N	3.23 W
Hondeklipbaai	156	30.20 S	17.18 E
Honderfontein	158	32.12 S	21.22 E
Hon Dien, Nui ∧	110	11.33 N	108.38 E
Hondo, Ab., Can.	182	55.04 N	114.02 W
Hondo, Nihon	92	32.27 N	130.12 E
Hondo, N.M., U.S.	200	33.23 N	105.16 W
Hondo, Tx., U.S.	196	29.20 N	99.08 W
Hondo ≃, Cuba	286b	22.55 N	82.16 W
Hondo ≃, Méx.	286a	19.26 N	99.15 W
Hondo ≃, N.A.	232	18.29 N	88.19 W
Hondo, Arroyo ≃	226	37.28 N	121.47 W
Hondo, Rio ≃, Ca., U.S.	280	33.55 N	118.10 W
Hondo, Rio ≃, N.M., U.S.	196	33.22 N	104.24 W
Hondo Creek ≃	196	28.45 N	99.11 W
Hondoji Temple ʊ[1]	268	35.51 N	139.56 E
Hondschoote	50	50.59 N	2.35 E
Hondsrug ⋏[2]	52	52.55 N	6.50 E
Honduras □[1], N.A.	230	15.00 N	86.30 W
Honduras □[1], N.A.	236	15.00 N	86.30 W
Honduras, Cabo de ›	236	16.01 N	86.02 W
Honduras, Gulf of ⊂	230	16.10 N	87.50 W
Honduras, Port ⊂	236	16.13 N	88.41 W
Honea Path	192	34.26 N	82.23 W
Hönebach	56	50.56 N	9.56 E
Hønefoss	26	60.10 N	10.18 E
Honeoye	210	42.47 N	77.31 W
Honeoye Creek ≃	210	42.58 N	77.43 W
Honeoye Falls	210	42.57 N	77.35 W
Honeoye Lake ⊜	210	42.45 N	77.31 W
Honesdale	210	41.34 N	75.15 W
Honey Brook	208	40.05 N	75.54 W
Honey Creek	216	42.44 N	88.18 W
Honey Creek ≃, Ia., U.S.	190	42.09 N	93.03 W
Honey Creek ≃, Mo., U.S.	194	39.53 N	93.34 W
Honey Creek ≃, Oh., U.S.	214	41.05 N	83.12 W
Honey Creek ≃, Pa., U.S.	208	40.36 N	77.35 W
Honey Creek ≃, Wi., U.S.	216	42.41 N	88.17 W
Honeydew	273d	26.05 S	27.55 E
Honeygo Run ≃	284b	39.22 N	76.25 W
Honey Grove	196	33.35 N	95.54 W
Honey Lake ⊜	204	40.16 N	120.19 W
Honeymoon Bay	224	48.49 N	124.10 W
Honeyville	200	41.38 N	112.04 W
Honfleur	50	49.25 N	0.14 E
Høng	41	55.31 N	11.18 E
Hong → Red ≃	110	20.17 N	106.34 E
Hong ≃	100	32.25 N	115.35 E
Honga	152	15.09 S	15.12 E
Hon Gai	110	20.57 N	107.05 E
Hong'an	100	31.18 N	114.37 E
Honga River ⊂	208	38.19 N	76.10 W
Hongawa	96	33.43 N	133.19 E
Hongchang	100	34.05 N	113.20 E
Hongch'ŏn	98	37.42 N	127.52 E
Hongchoudai	100	29.03 N	121.11 E
Hongcun, Zhg.	100	27.10 N	116.48 E
Hongcun, Zhg.	106	31.01 N	119.15 E
Höngen	56	51.02 N	5.56 E
Honggun	98	40.46 N	128.27 E
Honghai Wan ⊂	100	22.40 N	115.10 E
Honghe	102	23.23 N	102.35 E
Honghu	100	29.48 N	113.27 E
Hong Hu ⊜	100	29.52 N	113.23 E
Honghuaerji	89	48.15 N	120.01 E
Honghuaji	100	33.52 N	114.26 E
Honghualiangzi	89	48.06 N	123.12 E
Honghuamu	89	48.33 N	125.39 E
Hongjiang, Zhg.	100	26.49 N	120.03 E
Hongjiang, Zhg.	102	27.07 N	109.56 E
Hong Kong → Victoria	271d	22.17 N	114.09 E
Hong Kong □[2], Asia	90	22.15 N	114.10 E
Hong Kong □[2], Asia	100	22.15 N	114.10 E
Hong Kong I	271d	22.15 N	114.11 E
Hong Kong, University of ʊ[2]	271d	22.17 N	114.08 E
Hongkou Park ♠	269b	31.16 N	121.28 E
Honglai	100	25.08 N	118.32 E
Honglanbu	106	31.37 N	118.57 E
Honglinqiao	106	30.59 N	118.59 E
Hongliutai	85	39.48 N	77.26 E
Hongliuyuan	102	41.04 N	95.26 E
Honglongdian	106	30.30 N	119.00 E
Honglongtang	105	40.41 N	117.37 E
Honglu	100	25.44 N	119.20 E
Hongluan	100	28.31 N	117.01 E
Hongluo Shan ∧	104	40.56 N	120.42 E
Hongluoxian	104	41.01 N	120.53 E
Hongmeichang	105	39.50 N	115.51 E
Hongmendu	102	26.10 N	102.37 E
Hongmenkou	102	27.22 N	100.30 E
Hongmenpu	107	30.37 N	104.08 E
Hongmiaozi	107	28.47 N	104.02 E
Hong Ngu	110	10.48 N	105.21 E
Hongō, Nihon	96	34.24 N	132.59 E
Hongō, Nihon	96	34.17 N	132.02 E
Hongō ➛[8]	268	35.42 N	139.47 E
Hongpailou	107	30.38 N	104.01 E
Hongqi	89	44.23 N	126.32 E
Hongqiao, Zhg.	100	28.14 N	121.01 E
Hongqiao, Zhg.	105	39.50 N	117.44 E
Hongqiao, Zhg.	106	31.29 N	121.49 E
Hongqiao, Zhg.	269b	31.12 N	121.22 E
Hongqiao Ji Chang ⊠	106	31.12 N	121.20 E
Hongrie → Hungary □[1]	30	47.00 N	20.00 E
Hongshan, Zhg.	89	48.02 N	129.00 E
Hongshan, Zhg.	98	36.37 N	118.00 E
Hongshanzi	98	42.34 N	117.14 E
Hongshi, Zhg.	89	43.00 N	127.04 E
Hongshi, Zhg.	98	41.21 N	119.32 E
Hongshidou	104	41.52 N	122.11 E
Hongshili	98	40.41 N	125.03 E
Hongshui	102	37.24 N	104.00 E
Hongshui ≃	102	23.45 N	109.30 E
Hongshuichuan	105	40.06 N	117.55 E
Hongshuyangzi	105	40.36 N	116.36 E
Hongsŏng	98	36.36 N	126.39 E
Hongtang	100	26.06 N	119.14 E
Hongtian	100	25.52 N	117.15 E
Hongtong	102	36.19 N	111.39 E
Hongtuwan	98	41.03 N	113.39 E
Hongtu Zhang ∧	100	23.46 N	115.56 E
Honguedo, Détroit d' ʯ	186	49.15 N	64.00 W
Hongwŏn	98	40.02 N	127.57 E
Hongxin	100	32.43 N	117.47 E
Hongxing	105	39.48 N	116.27 E
Hongxingqiao	106	30.55 N	119.52 E
Hongyang, Zhg.	100	26.32 N	119.27 E
Hongyang, Zhg.	100	23.28 N	116.13 E
Hongyanzi	104	40.38 N	120.31 E
Hongyōtoku	268	35.41 N	139.55 E
Hongze	100	33.19 N	118.53 E
Hongze Hu ⊜	100	33.16 N	118.34 E
Honiara	175e	9.26 S	159.57 E
Honiton	42	50.48 N	3.13 W
Hon-jima I	96	34.23 N	133.47 E
Honjō, Nihon	92	39.23 N	140.03 E
Honjō, Nihon	94	36.24 N	138.01 E
Honjō, Nihon	94	36.14 N	139.11 E
Honkamäki ∧[2]	26	62.58 N	27.05 E
Hon-kawane	94	35.07 N	138.09 E
Honker Bay ⊂	282	38.04 N	121.56 W
Hönne ≃	263	51.28 N	7.46 E
Honnecourt-sur-Escaut	50	50.02 N	3.12 E
Honningsvåg	24	70.59 N	25.59 E
Hönö	26	57.42 N	11.39 E
Honokaa	229d	20.04 N	155.28 W
Honokahua	229a	21.00 N	156.39 W
Honokawai	229a	20.57 N	156.41 W
Honolulu	229c	21.18 N	157.51 W
Honolulu □[6]	229c	21.19 N	157.52 W
Honolulu International Airport ⊠	229c	21.20 N	157.55 W
Honomu	229d	19.52 N	155.07 W
Honouliuli	229c	21.22 N	158.02 W
Hönow	54	52.32 N	13.38 E
Hon Quan	110	11.39 N	106.36 E
Honshū I	92	36.00 N	138.00 E
Hontoon Island State Park ♠	220	28.59 N	81.22 W
Höntrop ➛[8]	263	51.27 N	7.08 E
Honuapo Bay ⊂	229d	19.05 N	155.33 W
Hoo	260	51.25 N	0.34 E
Hood	226	38.22 N	121.31 W
Hood □[6]	222	32.25 N	97.45 W
Hood ≃, N.T., Can.	176	67.26 N	108.53 W
Hood ≃, Or., U.S.	224	45.42 N	121.30 W
Hood, East Fork ≃	224	45.36 N	121.38 W
Hood, Mount ∧	224	45.23 N	121.41 W
Hood, West Fork ≃	224	45.36 N	121.38 W
Hood Canal ⊂	224	47.35 N	123.00 W
Hood Canal Floating Bridge ➛[5]	224	47.52 N	122.38 W
Hoodoo Peak ∧	202	48.15 N	120.19 W
Hood Point ›, Austl.	162	34.23 S	119.34 E
Hood Point ›, Pap. N. Gui.	164	10.05 S	147.45 E
Hood Pond ⊜	283	42.40 N	70.57 W
Hood River	224	45.42 N	121.31 W
Hoodsport	224	47.24 N	123.08 W
Hoods Range ⋏	166	28.35 S	144.30 E
Hoof	56	51.17 N	9.20 E
Hoogerheide	52	51.25 N	4.20 E
Hoogeveen	52	52.43 N	6.29 E
Hoogeveense Vaart ≃	52	52.42 N	6.11 E
Hoogezand-Sappemeer	52	53.09 N	6.47 E
Hoogkerk	52	53.13 N	6.30 E
Hooglede	50	50.59 N	3.05 E
Hoogstede	52	52.34 N	6.56 E
Hoogstraten	56	51.24 N	4.46 E
Hoogte	158	27.28 S	28.03 E
Hoogvliet	52	51.52 N	4.21 E
Hook	42	51.17 N	0.58 W
Hook ➛[8]	260	51.22 N	0.18 W
Hooker	196	36.51 N	101.12 W
Hooker, Bi'r ⊤[4]	142	30.23 N	30.20 E
Hooker Creek	162	18.20 S	130.40 E
Hooker Creek Aboriginal Reserve ➛[4]	162	18.10 S	130.25 E
Hook Head ›	48	52.07 N	6.55 W
Hookina	166	31.45 S	138.20 E
Hook Island I	166	20.08 S	148.55 E
Hook Mountain State Park ♠	276	41.09 N	73.55 W
Hook Norton	42	51.59 N	1.29 W
Hook Point ›	166	25.48 S	153.05 E
Hooks	194	33.28 N	94.15 W
Hooksiel	52	53.38 N	8.01 E
Hoolehua	229a	21.10 N	157.04 W
Hoonah	180	58.07 N	135.26 W
Hoopa	204	41.03 N	123.40 W
Hoopa Valley Indian Reservation ➛[4]	204	41.08 N	123.40 W
Hooper	198	41.36 N	96.32 W
Hooper Bay	180	61.31 N	166.06 W
Hooper Islands II	208	38.20 N	76.13 W
Hooper Strait ʯ	208	38.12 N	76.03 W
Hoopersville	208	38.15 N	76.10 W
Hoopes Reservoir ⊜[1]	285	39.47 N	75.37 W
Hoopeston	216	40.28 N	87.40 W
Hooping Harbour	186	50.37 N	56.17 W
Hoople	198	48.32 N	97.38 W
Hoopstad	158	27.54 S	25.58 E
Hoopstick Brook ≃	276	40.39 N	74.41 W
Höör	41	55.56 N	13.32 E
Hoorn	52	52.38 N	5.04 E
Hoorn, Kap → Hornos. Cabo de ›	254	55.59 S	67.16 W
Hoosac Range ⋏	207	42.45 N	73.02 W
Hoosac Tunnel ➛[5]	207	42.41 N	73.03 W
Hoosic ≃	210	42.54 N	73.39 W
Hoosick	210	42.52 N	73.20 W
Hoosick Falls	210	42.54 N	73.21 W
Hooton	262	53.18 N	2.57 W
Hoot Owl Estates	285	39.53 N	74.50 W
Hoover Dam ➛[6]	200	36.00 N	114.27 W
Hoover Reservoir ⊜[1]	214	40.08 N	82.53 W
Hooversville	214	40.08 N	78.54 W
Hopa	130	41.25 N	41.24 E
Hopatcong	210	40.55 N	74.39 W
Hopatcong, Lake ⊜	210	40.57 N	74.38 W
Hopatcong State Park ♠	276	40.55 N	74.40 W
Hop Bottom	210	41.42 N	75.46 W
Hop Brook ≃	276	40.19 N	74.08 W
Hope, B.C., Can.	182	49.23 N	121.26 W
Hope, Ak., U.S.	180	60.55 N	149.38 W
Hope, Ar., U.S.	194	33.40 N	93.35 W
Hope, In., U.S.	218	39.18 N	85.46 W
Hope, N.J., U.S.	210	40.54 N	74.58 W
Hope, N.D., U.S.	198	47.19 N	97.43 W
Hope, R.I., U.S.	207	41.44 N	71.33 W
Hope, Ben ∧	46	58.24 N	4.37 W
Hope, Loch ⊜	46	58.27 N	4.39 W
Hope, Point ›	180	68.21 N	166.50 W
Hope Bay ⊂	212	44.55 N	81.08 W
Hopedale, Nf., Can.	176	55.28 N	60.13 W
Hopedale, Il., U.S.	194	40.25 N	89.24 W
Hopedale, La., U.S.	194	29.49 N	89.39 W
Hopedale, Ma., U.S.	207	42.07 N	71.32 W
Hopedale, Oh., U.S.	214	40.19 N	80.54 W
Hope Farm	210	41.44 N	73.40 W
Hopefield	158	33.04 S	18.22 E
Hopeh → Hebei □[4]	98	38.00 N	116.00 E
Hope Island I, B.C., Can.	182	50.55 N	127.53 W
Hope Island I, On., Can.	212	44.55 N	80.12 W
Hopeland	208	40.14 N	76.16 W
Hopelawn	276	40.31 N	74.17 W
Hopelchén	232	19.46 N	89.51 W
Hopeman	46	57.42 N	3.25 W
Hope Mills	192	34.58 N	78.56 W
Hopes Advance, Cap ›	176	61.04 N	69.34 W
Hopetoun, Austl.	162	33.57 S	120.07 E
Hopetoun, Austl.	166	35.44 S	142.22 E
Hopetown	158	29.34 S	24.03 E
Hope Vale Aboriginal Reserve ➛[4]	164	15.10 S	145.15 E
Hope Valley, Austl.	168b	34.50 S	138.44 E
Hope Valley, R.I., U.S.	207	41.30 N	71.43 W
Hopewell, N.J., U.S.	208	40.23 N	74.45 W
Hopewell, Pa., U.S.	214	40.08 N	78.16 W
Hopewell, Va., U.S.	208	37.18 N	77.17 W
Hopewell Islands II	176	58.25 N	78.00 W
Hopewell Junction	210	41.35 N	73.48 W
Hopewell Village National Historic Site ⊥	208	40.12 N	75.46 W
Hopfgarten	64	47.27 N	12.10 E
Hopfgarten in Defereggen	64	46.55 N	12.31 E
Hopi → Hebi	98	35.59 N	114.11 E
Hopi Buttes ∧	200	35.20 N	110.15 W
Hopi Indian Reservation ➛[4]	200	35.45 N	110.35 W
Hopkins, Mi., U.S.	216	42.37 N	85.45 W
Hopkins, Mo., U.S.	194	40.33 N	94.49 W
Hopkins □[6]	222	33.07 N	95.35 W
Hopkins ≃	166	38.24 S	142.31 E
Hopkins, Lake ⊜	162	24.15 S	128.50 E
Hopkins Creek ≃	284a	43.17 N	78.46 W
Hopkinsville	194	36.51 N	87.29 W
Hopkinton, Ia., U.S.	190	42.20 N	91.14 W
Hopkinton, Ma., U.S.	207	42.13 N	71.31 W
Hopkinton, R.I., U.S.	207	41.27 N	71.46 W
Hopland	204	38.58 N	123.06 W
Hoppegarten	264a	52.31 N	13.40 E
Hoppenrade	264a	52.32 N	12.56 E
Hoppo → Hepu	102	21.39 N	109.11 E
Hopsten	52	52.23 N	7.36 E
Hoptrup	41	55.11 N	9.28 E
Ho Pui	271d	22.25 N	114.03 E
Hopwood, Mount ∧	166	21.49 S	144.26 E
Hoque	152	14.39 S	13.54 E
Hoquiam	224	46.58 N	123.53 W
Hoquiam, East Fork ≃	224	46.58 N	123.54 W
Hora Califo	144	8.49 N	43.07 E
Horace Mountain ∧	180	67.40 N	149.06 W
Horado	94	35.36 N	136.50 E
Hōrai	94	34.56 N	137.34 E
Horancia	144	6.31 N	38.44 E
Horasan	130	40.03 N	42.11 E
Horatio	194	33.56 N	94.21 W
Horatio Gardens	278	42.10 N	87.57 W
Horažd'ovice	60	49.20 N	13.43 E
Horb am Neckar	58	48.26 N	8.41 E
Horbelev	41	54.49 N	12.04 E
Horbourg	58	48.05 N	7.23 E
Hörby	41	55.51 N	13.39 E
Horconcitos	236	8.19 N	82.10 W
Hordaland □[6]	26	60.15 N	6.30 E
Hörde ➛[8]	263	51.29 N	7.30 E
Horden	44	54.46 N	1.18 W
Horden ≃	164	3.50 S	141.25 E
Horezu	38	45.08 N	23.59 E
Horgen	58	47.15 N	8.36 E
Hořice	30	50.22 N	15.38 E
Horicon	190	43.27 N	88.37 W
Horigane	268	35.50 N	139.27 E
Horine	219	38.16 N	90.25 W
Horinger	102	40.23 N	111.53 E
Horinouchi	94	37.14 N	138.56 E
Horinouchi ➛[8]	268	35.41 N	139.40 E
Horizon Tablemount ✣[3]	14	19.40 N	168.30 W
Horizontina	252	27.37 S	54.19 W
Horka	54	51.16 N	14.56 E
Hörken	40	60.02 N	14.56 E
Horley	42	51.11 N	0.11 W
Horlick Mountains ⋏	9	85.23 S	121.00 W
Horloff ≃	56	50.20 N	8.52 E
Hormigueros	240m	18.09 N	67.08 W
Hormoz, Jazīreh-ye I	128	27.04 N	56.28 E
Hormozgān □[4]	128	27.50 N	56.00 E
Hormuz, Strait of ʯ	128	26.34 N	56.15 E
Horn, B.R.D.	52	51.52 N	8.56 E
Horn, Öst.	61	48.40 N	15.40 E
Horn ➛[8]	52	53.38 N	10.05 E
Horn ›	24a	66.28 N	22.28 W
Horn ≃, N.T., Can.	176	61.30 N	118.01 W
Horn ≃, Europe	56	49.15 N	7.20 E
Horn, Ben ∧[2]	46	58.01 N	4.02 W
Horn, Cape → Hornos, Cabo de ›	254	55.59 S	67.16 W
Hornaday ≃	180	69.22 N	123.50 W
Hornafjörður ⊂	24a	64.17 N	15.16 W
Hornavan ⊜	24	66.10 N	17.30 E
Hornbach	56	49.11 N	7.22 E
Hornbæk	41	56.05 N	12.28 E
Hornbeak	194	36.19 N	89.17 W
Hornbeck	194	31.19 N	93.23 W
Hornberg	58	48.13 N	8.13 E
Hornbrook	204	41.55 N	122.33 W
Hornburg	54	52.01 N	10.36 E
Hornby, On., Can.	275b	43.34 N	79.50 W
Hornby, N.Z.	172	43.33 S	172.32 E
Hornby Bay ⊂	176	66.35 N	117.50 W
Horncastle	44	53.13 N	0.07 W
Hornchurch ➛[8]	260	51.34 N	0.12 E
Horndal	40	60.18 N	16.25 E
Horndean	42	50.55 N	1.00 W
Horndon on the Hill	260	51.31 N	0.25 E
Horne	41	55.06 N	10.11 E
Horne, Îles de II	14	14.16 S	178.05 W
Hornebach ≃	263	51.39 N	7.38 E
Horneburg, B.R.D.	52	53.30 N	9.34 E
Horneburg, B.R.D.	263	51.38 N	7.18 E
Hörnefors	26	63.38 N	19.54 E
Hornell	210	42.19 N	77.39 W
Hornepayne	176	49.13 N	84.47 W
Hornerstown	208	40.06 N	74.30 W
Hornhausen	54	52.02 N	11.10 E
Horn Head ›	48	55.14 N	7.59 W
Horn Hill	260	51.37 N	0.32 W
Horní Jiřetín	54	50.35 N	13.32 E
Hornindal	26	61.58 N	6.31 E
Hornindalsvatnet ⊜	26	61.56 N	6.22 E
Hørning	41	56.05 N	10.03 E
Hörningsholm	40	59.03 N	17.40 E
Horní Počernice	54	50.06 N	14.38 E
Hornisgrinde ∧	56	48.36 N	8.12 E
Horn Island I, Austl.	164	10.37 S	142.17 E
Horn Island I, Ms., U.S.	194	30.13 N	88.38 W
Horní Slavkov	54	50.07 N	12.46 E
Horní Stropnice	61	48.46 N	14.44 E
Hornito, Cerro ∧	236	8.42 N	82.06 W
Hornitos	226	37.30 N	120.14 W
Horní Vltavice	60	48.57 N	13.46 E
Horn Lake	194	34.58 N	90.02 W
Horn Lake ⊜	212	45.24 N	79.36 W
Hornos, Cabo de (Cape Horn) ›	254	55.59 S	67.16 W
Hornos, Isla I	254	55.57 S	67.17 W
Hornos, Islas de II	288	34.25 S	57.55 W
Hornow	54	51.38 N	14.31 E
Hornoy	50	49.51 N	1.54 E
Horn Plateau ⋏[1]	176	62.15 N	119.15 W
Horn Pond ⊜	283	42.28 N	71.09 W
Hornsby, Austl.	170	33.42 S	150.06 E
Hornsby, Il., U.S.	219	39.10 N	89.45 W
Hornsbyville	208	37.11 N	76.28 W

≃ River	Fluß	Río	Rivière	Rio
≅ Canal	Kanal	Canal	Canal	Canal
ʟ Waterfall, Rapids	Wasserfall, Stromschnellen	Cascada, Rápidos	Chute d'eau, Rapides	Cascata, Rápidos
ʯ Strait	Meeresstraße	Estrecho	Détroit	Estreito
⊂ Bay, Gulf	Bucht, Golf	Bahía, Golfo	Baie, Golfe	Baía, Golfo
⊜ Lake, Lakes	See, Seen	Lago, Lagos	Lac, Lacs	Lago, Lagos
≡ Swamp	Sumpf	Pantano	Marais	Pântano
⊓ Ice Features, Glacier	Eis- und Gletscherformen	Accidentes Glaciales	Formes glaciaires	Acidentes glaciares
⊤ Other Hydrographic Features	Andere Hydrographische Objekte	Otros Elementos Hidrográficos	Autres données hydrographiques	Outros acidentes hidrográficos

✣ Submarine Features	Untermeerische Objekte	Accidentes Submarinos	Formes de relief sous-marin	Acidentes submarinos
□ Political Unit	Politische Einheit	Unidad Politica	Entité politique	Unidade política
ʊ Cultural Institution	Kulturelle Institution	Institución Cultural	Institution culturelle	Instituição cultural
⊥ Historical Site	Historische Stätte	Sitio Histórico	Site historique	Sitio histórico
♠ Recreational Site	Erholungs- und Ferienort	Sitio de Recreo	Centre de loisirs	Area de Lazer
⊠ Airport	Flughafen	Aeropuerto	Aéroport	Aeroporto
■ Military Installation	Militäranlage	Instalación Militar	Installation militaire	Instalação militar
➛ Miscellaneous	Verschiedenes	Misceláneo	Divers	Diversos

I · 74 Horn-Huic

ENGLISH — Name Page Lat.°′ Long.°′ / DEUTSCH — Name Seite Breite°′ Länge°′ E = Ost

Hornsea 44 53.55 N 0.10 W
Hornsey ◆[8] 260 51.35 N 0.07 W
Hornslet 41 56.19 N 10.20 E
Hornstorf 54 53.54 N 11.32 E
Hornsyld 41 55.45 N 9.51 E
Horntown 208 37.58 N 75.28 W
Hornu 50 50.26 N 3.49 E
Horoshiri-dake ∧ 92a 42.43 N 142.41 E
Horotiu 172 37.43 S 175.12 E
Hořovice 60 49.50 N 13.54 E
Horqin Youyi Qianqi (Ulan Hot) 89 46.05 N 122.05 E
Horqin Youyi Zhongqi 89 45.09 N 121.24 E
Horqin Zuoyi Houqi 89 42.58 N 122.20 E
Horqin Zuoyi Zhongqi 89 44.07 N 123.18 E
Horqueta 252 23.24 S 56.53 W
Horrabridge 42 50.31 N 4.05 W
Horrelville 172 43.20 S 172.20 E
Horrem 263 51.06 N 6.48 E
Hörsching 61 48.14 N 14.11 E
Horse ≃ 184 56.43 N 111.23 W
Horseback Knob ∧[2] 218 39.14 N 83.06 W
Horse Cave 194 37.10 N 85.54 W
Horse Creek 200 41.25 N 105.11 W
Horse Creek ≃, U.S. 198 41.57 N 103.58 W
Horse Creek ≃, Co., U.S. 198 38.05 N 103.19 W
Horse Creek ≃, Fl., U.S. 220 27.06 N 81.58 W
Horse Creek ≃, Il., U.S. 219 39.45 N 89.34 W
Horse Creek ≃, Mo., U.S. 194 37.46 N 93.53 W
Horsefly 182 52.20 N 121.24 W
Horsefly Lake ⊜ 182 52.25 N 121.00 W
Horsehead Creek ≃ 198 43.17 N 103.22 W
Horsehead Lake ⊜ 198 47.02 N 99.47 W
Horseheads 210 42.10 N 76.49 W
Horse Islands II 186 50.13 N 55.45 W
Horsell 260 51.19 N 0.34 W
Horseneck Brook ≃ 276 41.01 N 73.38 W
Horsens 41 55.52 N 9.52 E
Horsens Fjord ⊂ 41 55.50 N 10.05 E
Horseshoe Bend, Ar., U.S. 194 36.15 N 91.43 W
Horseshoe Bend, Id., U.S. 202 43.55 N 116.12 W
Horseshoe Bend National Military Park ♦ 194 33.00 N 85.46 W
Horseshoe Cove ⊂ 276 40.27 N 74.00 W
Horseshoe Creek ≃ 198 42.27 N 104.58 W
Horseshoe Falls L 284a 43.05 N 79.04 W
Horseshoe Lake ⊜, Mb., Can. 184 52.12 N 95.50 W
Horseshoe Lake ⊜, Mi., U.S. 281 42.24 N 83.45 W
Horseshoe Lake ⊜, N.J., U.S. 276 40.52 N 74.38 W
Horse Shoe Reef ✦[2] 240m 18.40 N 64.12 W
Horsfjärden ⊂ 40 59.04 N 18.09 E
Horsford 42 52.41 N 1.15 E
Horsforth 44 53.51 N 1.39 W
Horsham, Austl. 166 36.43 S 142.13 E
Horsham, Eng., U.K. 42 51.04 N 0.21 W
Horsham, Pa., U.S. 208 40.10 N 75.07 W
Hørsholm 41 55.53 N 12.30 E
Hörsingen 54 52.16 N 11.09 E
Horsley, Austl. 274a 33.51 S 150.51 E
Horsley, Eng., U.K. 260 51.16 N 0.26 W
Horslunde 41 54.54 N 11.14 E
Horšovský Týn 60 49.32 N 12.56 E
Horst, B.R.D. 52 53.48 N 9.37 E
Horst, D.D.R. 54 53.22 N 10.37 E
Horst, Ned. 52 51.27 N 6.04 E
Horst ◆[8] 263 51.32 N 7.02 E
Horsted Keynes 42 51.02 N 0.01 W
Hörstel 52 52.18 N 7.35 E
Horstmar, B.R.D. 52 52.05 N 7.17 E
Horstmar, B.R.D. 263 51.36 N 7.33 E
Horsunlu 130 37.55 N 28.36 E
Horta 148a 38.32 N 28.38 W
Horta □[5] 148a 38.30 N 29.00 W
Horta ◆[8] 266d 41.26 N 2.00 E
Hortaleza ◆[8] 266a 40.28 N 3.39 W
Horten 26 59.25 N 10.30 E
Hortobágy ◆[1] 30 47.35 N 21.00 E
Horton, Eng., U.K. 260 51.28 N 0.32 W
Horton, In., U.S. 218 40.05 N 86.09 W
Horton, Ks., U.S. 198 39.39 N 95.31 W
Horton, Mi., U.S. 216 42.09 N 84.31 W
Horton ≃ 180 70.00 N 126.53 W
Horton in Ribblesdale 44 54.09 N 2.17 W
Horton Kirby 260 51.23 N 0.15 E
Horton Lake ⊜ 180 67.29 N 122.31 W
Hortonville, N.Y., U.S. 210 41.46 N 75.02 W
Hortonville, Wi., U.S. 190 44.20 N 88.38 W
Horumersiel 52 53.41 N 8.00 E
Hørup 41 54.56 N 9.55 E
Hørve 41 55.45 N 11.28 E
Horw 58 47.01 N 8.18 E
Horwich 262 53.37 N 2.33 W
Horwood Lake ⊜ 190 48.03 N 82.20 W
Hory Matky Boží 60 49.16 N 13.27 E
Hōryūji Temple ʋ[1] 270 34.36 N 135.44 E
Hosaina 144 7.38 N 37.52 E
Hösbach 56 50.00 N 9.12 E
Hosei University ʋ[2] 268 35.42 N 139.44 E
Hösel 56 51.19 N 6.54 E
Hosena 54 51.27 N 14.01 E
Hoséré Vokré ∧ 146 8.20 N 13.15 E
Hoseynābād 128 35.33 N 47.08 E
Hoseynīyeh-ye Khodā-Dād 128 32.42 N 48.14 E
Hosford 192 30.23 N 84.47 W
Hoshāb 128 26.01 N 63.56 E
Hoshangābād 124 22.45 N 77.43 E
Hoshangābād Plain ≚ 124 22.35 N 77.25 E
Hoshiārpur, India 123 31.32 N 75.54 E
Hoshiarpur, India 272a 28.35 N 77.22 E
Hoshigajō ∧ 96 34.31 N 134.19 E
Hosingen 56 50.01 N 6.05 E
Hosjö 40 60.35 N 15.46 E
Hoskins 164 5.27 S 150.30 E
Hosmer, B.C., Can. 182 49.35 N 114.57 W
Hosmer, S.D., U.S. 198 45.34 N 99.28 W
Hosoe 94 34.49 N 137.39 E
Hospental 58 46.37 N 8.34 E
Hospers 198 43.04 N 95.54 W
Hospet 122 15.16 N 76.24 E
Hospital 48 52.29 N 8.25 W
Hospital de Orbigo 34 42.28 N 5.53 W
Hossegor 32 43.40 N 1.27 W
Hosston 194 32.53 N 93.52 W
Hosta Butte ∧ 200 35.35 N 108.12 W
Hoste, Isla I 254 55.15 S 69.00 W
Hostěradice 61 48.57 N 16.15 E
Hostetter 214 40.16 N 79.24 W
Hostigrām 272b 22.26 N 88.31 E
Hostivař ◆[8] 54 50.01 N 14.32 E
Hostivice 54 50.04 N 14.15 E
Hošt'ka 54 50.30 N 14.20 E
Hostomice 54 50.35 N 13.46 E
Hostotipaquillo 234 21.04 N 104.04 W
Hostouň 60 49.34 N 12.46 E
Hosūr 122 12.43 N 77.49 E
Hot 110 18.06 N 98.36 E
Hota 268 35.08 N 139.51 E
Hotagen 26 63.59 N 14.15 E
Hotagen ⊜ 26 63.53 N 14.29 E
Hotagsfjällen ∧ 26 64.20 N 14.30 E
Hotaka 94 36.20 N 137.53 E
Hotaka-dake ∧ 94 36.17 N 137.39 E
Hotamış 130 37.36 N 33.13 E
Hotan 120 37.08 N 79.54 E
Hotan ≃ 90 40.30 N 80.45 E
Hotarele 38 44.10 N 26.22 E
Hotazel 158 27.15 S 23.00 E
Hotchkiss 200 38.47 N 107.43 W
Hotchkissville 207 41.34 N 73.13 W
Hot Creek Range ⋏ 204 38.30 N 116.25 W
Hötensleben 54 52.08 N 11.01 E
Hotevilla 200 35.55 N 110.40 W
Hotham ≃ 168a 32.58 S 116.22 E
Hotham Inlet ⊂ 180 66.45 N 162.00 W
Hotham Peak ∧ 180 66.48 N 160.42 W
Hoting 26 64.07 N 16.10 E
Hot Springs, Mt., U.S. 202 47.36 N 114.40 W
Hot Springs → Truth or Consequences, N.M., U.S. 200 33.08 N 107.15 W
Hot Springs, N.C., U.S. 192 35.53 N 82.49 W
Hot Springs, S.D., U.S. 198 43.25 N 103.28 W
Hot Springs, Va., U.S. 192 37.59 N 79.49 W
Hot Springs National Park 194 34.30 N 93.04 W
Hot Springs Peak ∧, Ca., U.S. 204 40.22 N 120.07 W
Hot Springs Peak ∧, Nv., U.S. 204 41.22 N 117.26 W
Hot Springs State Park ♦ 202 43.40 N 108.10 W
Hot Sulphur Springs 200 40.04 N 106.06 W
Hottah Lake ⊜ 176 65.04 N 118.29 W
Hotte, Massif de la ⋏ 238 18.25 N 73.55 W
Hottentotbaai ⊂ 156 26.05 S 14.58 E
Hottentotskloof 158 33.15 S 19.40 E
Hotton 56 50.16 N 5.27 E
Hötzum 54 52.13 N 10.37 E
Houaïlou 175f 21.17 S 165.38 E
Houamuang 110 20.09 N 103.38 E
Houbaishu 106 31.49 N 119.10 E
Houbao 98 41.54 N 125.14 E
Houcheng 106 31.55 N 120.26 E
Houdahepao 104 41.49 N 123.01 E
Houdain 50 50.27 N 2.32 E
Houdan 50 48.47 N 1.36 E
Houdelaincourt 58 48.33 N 5.28 E
Houdeng-Aimeries 50 50.29 N 4.08 E
Houeillès 32 44.12 N 0.02 E
Houffalize 56 50.08 N 5.47 E
Hougang 271c 1.22 N 103.54 E
Hough Green 262 53.23 N 2.47 W
Houghton, Mi., U.S. 190 47.07 N 88.34 W
Houghton, N.Y., U.S. 210 42.25 N 78.09 W
Houghton, Wa., U.S. 224 47.40 N 122.12 W
Houghton Estates ◆[8] 273d 26.10 S 28.04 E
Houghton Green 262 53.25 N 2.34 W
Houghton Lake 190 44.18 N 84.45 W
Houghton Lake ⊜, Sk., Can. 184 52.23 N 105.08 W
Houghton Lake ⊜, Mi., U.S. 190 44.20 N 84.45 W
Houghton-le-Spring 44 54.51 N 1.28 W
Houghton Regis 42 51.55 N 0.31 W
Houguangzhengtai 104 41.13 N 122.07 E
Hougujiazi 104 42.21 N 123.22 E
Houhuangtukan 104 41.02 N 122.29 E
Houille ≃ 56 50.08 N 4.49 E
Houillères de la Sarre, Canal des ≖ 56 48.42 N 6.55 E
Houilles 261 48.56 N 2.11 E
Houjiangfushan 105 40.03 N 117.09 E
Houjiaping 107 30.02 N 104.38 E
Houjiaying 105 39.51 N 117.15 E
Houjie 100 22.58 N 113.39 E
Houjiumen 104 42.38 N 123.18 E
Houkou 98 37.34 N 115.09 E
Houliujia 104 40.47 N 122.19 E
Houlka 194 34.02 N 89.01 W
Houlton 188 46.07 N 67.50 W
Houluan 105 39.13 N 116.32 E
Houma, Tonga 174w 21.09 S 175.19 W
Houma, La., U.S. 194 29.35 N 90.43 W
Houma, Zhg. 102 35.36 N 111.21 E
Houmanzhoutun 104 42.29 N 123.14 E
Houmen 100 22.51 N 115.09 E
Houmet Essouq 148 33.59 N 10.51 E
Houmont Park 222 29.50 N 95.13 W
Hound Creek ≃ 202 47.13 N 111.23 W
Houndé 150 11.30 N 3.31 W
Hounslow ◆[8] 260 51.29 N 0.22 W
Houplines 50 50.42 N 2.55 E
Houqianjiayu 104 40.50 N 120.41 E
Houqiao 105 40.04 N 116.39 E
Hourn, Loch ⊂ 46 57.08 N 5.36 W
Housatonic 207 42.15 N 73.22 W
Housatonic ≃ 207 41.10 N 73.07 W
House 196 34.38 N 103.54 W
House ≃ 184 56.13 N 112.31 W
House of Seven Gables ⊥ 283 42.32 N 70.53 W
Houserville 214 40.50 N 77.50 W
House Springs 219 38.24 N 90.34 W
Houshan 106 31.03 N 120.21 E
Houston, B.C., Can. 182 54.24 N 126.38 W
Houston, De., U.S. 208 38.55 N 75.30 W
Houston, Mn., U.S. 190 43.45 N 91.34 W
Houston, Ms., U.S. 194 33.53 N 88.59 W
Houston, Mo., U.S. 194 37.19 N 91.57 W
Houston, Oh., U.S. 216 40.15 N 84.20 W
Houston, Pa., U.S. 214 40.14 N 80.12 W
Houston, Tx., U.S. 222 29.45 N 95.21 W
Houston □[6] 222 31.20 N 95.20 W
Houston ≃ 194 30.16 N 93.13 W
Houston, Lake ⊜[1] 222 29.58 N 95.07 W
Houston County Lake ⊜[1] 222 31.25 N 95.35 W
Houston Creek ≃ 218 38.13 N 84.15 W
Houston Intercontinental Airport ⊠ 222 29.59 N 95.27 W
Houston Ship Channel ≖ 222 29.21 N 94.47 W
Hout ≃ 156 23.04 S 29.36 E
Houtbaai 158 34.03 S 18.21 E
Houthalen 56 51.02 N 5.22 E
Houthulst 50 50.59 N 2.57 E
Houtkop 158 26.36 S 27.52 E
Houtkraal 158 30.23 S 24.05 E
Houtman Abrolhos II 162 28.43 S 113.48 E
Houtskär I 26 60.12 N 21.22 E
Houtzdale 214 40.49 N 78.21 W
Houwuliangdian 104 41.31 N 121.55 E
Houwutaigou 104 41.46 N 121.42 E
Houx 261 48.34 N 1.37 E
Houxijie 100 28.46 N 118.49 E
Houxinlitun 104 41.05 N 122.33 E
Houxinqiu 104 42.34 N 122.43 E
Houyatai 104 41.26 N 121.49 E
Houying 105 39.42 N 118.18 E
Houyingzi 98 40.24 N 123.50 E
Houzhangcun 105 40.08 N 116.11 E
Houzhou 106 31.35 N 119.22 E
Houzitun 104 41.04 N 121.18 E
Hov 41 55.55 N 10.16 E
Hova 40 58.52 N 14.13 E
Hovborg 41 55.36 N 8.57 E
Høve, Dan. 41 55.50 N 11.30 E
Hove, Eng., U.K. 42 50.49 N 0.10 W
Hovedgård 41 55.57 N 9.58 E
Hövelhof 52 51.49 N 8.40 E
Hoven, Dan. 41 55.51 N 8.46 E
Hoven, S.D., U.S. 198 45.14 N 99.46 W
Hovenweep National Monument ♦ 200 37.25 N 109.04 W
Hovmantorp 26 56.47 N 15.08 E
Hovran ⊜ 40 60.16 N 16.03 E
Hovsta 40 59.21 N 15.13 E
Howa, Ouadi (Wādī Howar) V 140 17.30 N 27.08 E
Howakil I 144 15.10 N 40.16 E
Howar, Wādī (Ouadi Howa) V 140 17.30 N 27.08 E
Howard, Austl. 166 25.19 S 152.34 E
Howard, Ks., U.S. 198 37.28 N 96.15 W
Howard, Oh., U.S. 214 40.24 N 82.19 W
Howard, Pa., U.S. 214 41.00 N 77.39 W
Howard, S.D., U.S. 198 44.00 N 97.31 W
Howard, Wi., U.S. 190 44.32 N 88.05 W
Howard □[6], In., U.S. 216 40.29 N 86.08 W
Howard □[6], Md., U.S. 208 39.16 N 76.48 W
Howard Beach ◆[8] 276 40.40 N 73.51 W
Howard City 190 43.23 N 85.28 W
Howard Draw V 196 30.08 N 101.35 W
Howard Hanson Reservoir ⊜[1] 224 47.15 N 121.45 W
Howard Heights 284b 39.17 N 76.50 W
Howardian Hills ⋏[2] 44 54.07 N 1.00 W
Howard Island I 164 12.10 S 135.24 E
Howard Lake 190 45.03 N 94.04 W
Howard Prairie Lake ⊜[1] 202 42.15 N 122.20 W
Howard University ʋ[2] 284c 38.55 N 77.01 W
Howden 44 53.45 N 0.52 W
Howe, In., U.S. 216 41.43 N 85.25 W
Howe, Tx., U.S. 196 33.30 N 96.37 W
Howe, Cape › 166 37.31 S 149.59 E
Howe Caverns ⩢[5] 210 42.42 N 74.25 W
Howe Green 260 51.42 N 0.32 E
Howe Island I 212 44.17 N 76.15 W
Howeke 150 4.50 N 7.45 W
Howell 216 42.36 N 83.55 W
Howell Airport ⊠ 278 41.39 N 87.45 W
Howell Island I 219 38.40 N 90.42 W
Howells 198 41.43 N 97.00 W
Howells Pond ⊜ 276 41.03 N 74.42 W
Howes Cave 210 42.41 N 74.23 W
Howe Sound ʯ 182 49.22 N 123.18 W
Howe's Range ⋏ 170 33.08 S 150.47 E
Howes Valley 170 32.50 S 150.51 E
Howey In The Hills 220 28.43 N 81.47 W
Howick, P.Q., Can. 206 45.11 N 73.51 W
Howick, S. Afr. 158 29.28 S 30.14 E
Howitt, Mount ∧ 166 37.10 S 146.40 E
Howland 188 45.14 N 68.39 W
Howland Island I 14 0.48 N 176.38 W
Howley 186 49.10 N 57.07 W
Howley, Mount ∧ 186 48.17 N 58.26 W
Howmore 46 57.18 N 7.23 W
Howqua ≃ 169 37.14 S 146.08 E
Howrah → Hāora 126 22.35 N 88.20 E
Howse Peak ∧ 182 51.49 N 116.41 W
Howser 182 50.18 N 116.57 W
Howson Peak ∧ 182 54.25 N 127.44 W
Howth 48 53.23 N 6.04 W
Howth Head › 48 53.22 N 6.03 W
Ho Xa 110 17.04 N 107.02 E
Hoxie, Ar., U.S. 194 36.03 N 90.58 W
Hoxie, Ks., U.S. 198 39.21 N 100.26 W
Höxter 52 51.46 N 9.23 E
Hoxtolgay 86 46.35 N 86.01 E
Hoxton Park 274a 33.55 S 150.51 E
Hoxton Park Aerodrome ⊠ 274a 33.54 S 150.50 E
Hoy I 46 58.51 N 3.18 W
Hoya, B.R.D. 52 52.48 N 9.08 E
Hōya, Nihon 94 35.43 N 139.34 E
Høyanger 26 61.13 N 6.05 E
Hoyerswerda 54 51.26 N 14.14 E
Hoylake 262 53.23 N 3.11 W
Hoyleton, Austl. 168b 34.01 S 138.33 E
Hoyleton, Il., U.S. 219 38.27 N 89.16 W
Hoym 54 51.47 N 11.19 E
Hoyos 34 40.10 N 6.43 W
Hōyo-shotō II 96 33.52 N 132.18 E
Höytiäinen ⊜ 26 62.48 N 29.39 E
Hoyt Lakes 190 47.31 N 92.08 W
Hoytville, Mi., U.S. 216 42.45 N 84.53 W
Hoytville, Oh., U.S. 216 41.11 N 83.47 W
Hozain ≃ 50 48.16 N 4.06 E
Hozat 130 39.07 N 39.14 E
Hozumi 94 35.24 N 136.41 E
Hpru-so 110 19.25 N 97.08 E
Hracholusky, údolní nádrž ⊜[1] 60 49.47 N 13.07 E
Hradec Králové 30 50.12 N 15.50 E
Hrádek 61 48.46 N 16.16 E
Hrádek nad Nisou 54 50.48 N 14.51 E
Hradiště ∧ 54 50.13 N 13.08 E
Hranice, Česko. 30 49.33 N 17.44 E
Hranice, Česko. 54 50.15 N 12.10 E
Hrdlovka 54 50.36 N 13.40 E
Hřensko 54 50.50 N 14.14 E
Hriňová 30 48.36 N 19.31 E
Hrob 54 50.39 N 13.44 E
Hron ≃ 30 47.49 N 18.45 E
Hronov 30 50.29 N 16.12 E
Hrotovice 61 49.06 N 16.07 E
Hrubieszów 30 50.49 N 23.55 E
Hrubý Jeseník ⋏ 30 50.00 N 17.20 E
Hrušovany 61 48.50 N 16.23 E
Hrvatska (Croatia) □[3] 36 45.10 N 15.30 E
Hsenwi 110 23.18 N 97.58 E
Hsiakuan → Xiaguan 102 25.34 N 100.14 E
Hsiamen → Xiamen 100 24.28 N 118.07 E
Hsian → Xi'an 102 34.15 N 108.52 E
Hsiangt'an → Xiangtan 100 27.51 N 112.54 E
Hsiangyang → Xiangfan 102 32.03 N 112.01 E
Hsiaohungt'ou Yü I 100 21.57 N 121.36 E
Hsichih 269d 25.04 N 121.39 E
Hsichi Yü I 100 23.15 N 119.37 E
Hsich'üan Tao I 100 25.59 N 119.56 E
Hsientung 269d 25.09 N 121.44 E
Hsienyang → Xianyang 102 34.22 N 108.42 E
Hsi-hseng 110 20.09 N 97.15 E
Hsihu 100 23.58 N 120.28 E
Hsilo 100 23.48 N 120.27 E
Hsilo ≃ 100 23.50 N 120.15 E
Hsim ≃ 110 20.48 N 98.31 E
Hsinch'eng 100 24.08 N 121.39 E
Hsinchu 100 24.48 N 120.58 E
Hsinchuang 100 25.02 N 121.27 E
Hsinghua → Xinghua 100 32.57 N 119.50 E
Hsingt'ai → Xingtai 98 37.04 N 114.29 E
Hsinhailien → Lianyungang 98 34.39 N 119.16 E
Hsinhsiang → Xinxiang 98 35.20 N 113.51 E
Hsinhua 100 23.02 N 120.18 E
Hsining → Xining 102 36.38 N 101.55 E
Hsinking → Changchun 89 43.53 N 125.19 E
Hsinpeit'ou ◆[8] 269d 25.09 N 121.30 E
Hsinp'u → Lianyungang 98 34.39 N 119.16 E
Hsinshih 100 23.05 N 120.17 E
Hsintien 100 24.57 N 121.32 E
Hsintien ≃ 269d 25.02 N 121.29 E
Hsinyang → Xinyang 100 32.08 N 114.04 E
Hsipaw 110 22.37 N 97.18 E
Hsiukuluan ≃ 100 23.28 N 121.30 E
Hsiyü 100 23.36 N 119.30 E
Hsüanhua → Xuanhua 105 40.37 N 115.03 E
Hsüch'ang → Xuchang 100 34.03 N 113.49 E
Hsüchou → Xuzhou 98 34.16 N 117.11 E
Hsüehchia 100 23.14 N 120.10 E
Hsüeh Shan ∧ 100 24.23 N 121.13 E
Hsuphāng 110 20.18 N 98.42 E
Hua'an 100 25.02 N 117.34 E
Huab ≃ 156 20.52 S 13.25 E
Huabu 100 29.00 N 118.20 E
Huaca Juliana ⊥ 286d 12.07 S 77.02 W
Huacaña 248 14.02 S 74.02 W
Huacao 269b 31.14 N 121.19 E
Huacaraje 248 13.33 S 63.45 W
Huachacalla 248 18.45 S 68.17 W
Huacheng 100 24.04 N 115.38 E
Huachi 102 36.43 N 107.52 E
Huachi, Laguna ⊜ 248 14.11 S 63.30 W
Huachipa 286d 12.00 S 76.56 W
Huacho 248 11.07 S 77.37 W
Huachón 248 10.40 S 75.57 W
Huachos 248 13.12 S 75.31 W
Huachuca City 200 31.37 N 110.20 W
Huaco 252 30.09 S 68.31 W
Huacrachuco 248 8.39 S 77.05 W
Huade 98 41.46 N 114.16 E
Huadian 89 42.58 N 126.43 E
Huading Shan ∧ 100 29.15 N 121.05 E
Huafeng 106 32.14 N 121.16 E
Huagutang 106 30.55 N 119.18 E
Hua Hin 110 12.34 N 99.58 E
Huai ≃, Zhg. 98 37.28 N 114.55 E
Huai ≃, Zhg. 100 32.58 N 118.17 E
Huaiá-Miçu ≃ 250 10.52 S 53.15 W
Huai'an (Chaigoubu), Zhg. 98 40.39 N 114.27 E
Huai'an, Zhg. 100 33.32 N 119.10 E
Huaibin 100 32.28 N 115.24 E
Huaide 89 43.32 N 124.50 E
Huaidezhen, Zhg. 89 43.54 N 124.47 E
Huaidezhen, Zhg. 107 28.59 N 105.15 E
Huaihuazhenshi 106 31.05 N 119.41 E
Huaiji 102 24.01 N 112.18 E
Huailai (Shacheng) 105 40.23 N 115.33 E
Huailin 100 31.26 N 117.36 E
Huaillati 248 14.05 S 72.31 W
Huainan 100 32.40 N 117.00 E
Huaining 100 30.25 N 116.38 E
Huairou 105 40.19 N 116.37 E
Huaite → Huaide 89 43.32 N 124.50 E
Huaiyang 100 33.44 N 114.53 E
Huai Yot 110 7.45 N 99.37 E
Huaiyuan 100 32.57 N 117.12 E
Huaiyu Shan ⋏ 100 28.50 N 117.50 E
Huaji 100 32.46 N 115.20 E
Huajiang 102 25.50 N 110.21 E
Huajianzi 104 40.48 N 122.12 E
Huajiapuzi 104 40.52 N 123.14 E
Huajiayingzi 104 42.20 N 121.00 E
Huajimic 234 21.42 N 104.20 W
Huajintepec 234 16.36 N 98.14 W
Huajuapan de León 234 17.48 N 97.46 W
Huakou 100 25.13 N 117.35 E
Hualahuises 232 24.53 N 99.41 W
Hualalai ∧[1] 229d 19.42 N 155.52 W
Hualañé 252 34.59 S 71.49 W
Hualapai Indian Reservation ◆[4] 200 35.38 N 113.30 W
Hualapai Mountains ⋏ 200 34.50 N 113.55 W
Hualapai Peak ∧ 200 35.04 N 113.54 W
Hualfín 252 27.14 S 66.50 W
Hualgayoc 248 6.46 S 78.37 W
Hualien 100 23.59 N 121.36 E
Hualien ≃ 100 23.57 N 121.36 E
Hualingpuzi 104 41.31 N 123.54 E
Hualla 248 13.44 S 73.55 W
Huallaga ≃ 248 5.10 S 75.32 W
Huallanca, Perú 248 8.49 S 77.52 W
Huallanca, Perú 248 9.51 S 76.56 W
Hualong 102 36.05 N 102.36 E
Huamachuco 248 7.48 S 78.04 W
Huamanquiquia 248 13.44 S 74.15 W
Huamantla 234 19.19 N 97.56 W
Huambo (Nova Lisboa), Ang. 152 12.44 S 15.47 E
Huambo, Perú 248 15.44 S 72.07 W
Huambo □[5] 152 12.30 S 15.40 E
Huambo ≃ 248 7.04 S 77.10 W
Huambos 248 6.28 S 78.58 W
Huameiao 100 26.32 N 115.47 E
Huamei Shan ∧ 100 25.28 N 113.58 E
Huamuxtitlán 234 17.49 N 98.34 W
Huan ≃ 100 30.40 N 114.05 E
Huanan 89 46.13 N 130.32 E
Huancabamba, Perú 248 10.21 S 75.32 W
Huancabamba, Perú 248 5.14 S 79.28 W
Huancané 248 15.12 S 69.46 W
Huancapi 248 13.41 S 74.04 W
Huancarama 248 13.39 S 73.05 W
Huancarqui 248 16.06 S 72.29 W
Huancavelica 248 12.46 S 75.02 W
Huancavelica □[5] 248 13.00 S 75.00 W
Huancaybamba 248 9.05 S 76.50 W
Huancayo 248 12.04 S 75.14 W
Huanchaca 248 20.20 S 66.39 W
Huanchaca, Serranía de ⋏ 248 14.30 S 60.39 W
Huandacareo 234 19.59 N 101.17 W
Huando 248 12.29 S 74.58 W
Huang ≃, Asia 110 17.49 N 101.33 E
Huang ≃, T'aiwan 269d 25.14 N 121.37 E
Huang (Yellow) ≃, Zhg. 90 37.32 N 118.19 E
Huang'aicun 106 31.43 N 118.40 E
Huang'an 98 35.28 N 115.42 E
Huang'anshi 100 29.06 N 113.34 E
Huangbai 98 41.17 N 126.21 E
Huangbaozi 102 39.54 N 99.26 E
Huangbeipu 104 42.21 N 123.25 E
Huangcaoping 100 25.42 N 113.27 E
Huangchong 100 22.18 N 113.03 E
Huangchuan 100 32.09 N 115.03 E
Huangcun 105 39.56 N 116.11 E
Huangdaizhen 106 31.26 N 120.33 E
Huangdan 107 29.10 N 103.44 E
Huangda Yang ʯ 100 30.03 N 122.26 E
Huangdi, Zhg. 98 40.14 N 120.15 E
Huangdi, Zhg. 105 40.57 N 118.24 E
Huangdu, Zhg. 106 30.47 N 118.51 E
Huangdu, Zhg. 106 31.16 N 121.13 E
Huangduqiao 100 29.18 N 120.55 E
Huanggai Hu ⊜ 100 29.44 N 113.23 E
Huanggang 100 30.27 N 114.52 E
Huanggangji 98 34.39 N 116.03 E
Huanggangkou 100 28.32 N 114.33 E
Huanggang Shan ∧ 100 27.50 N 117.45 E
Huanggangshi 100 33.09 N 115.55 E
Huangguayingzi 104 41.46 N 120.46 E
Huangguoshu 102 26.02 N 105.32 E
Huang Hai → Yellow Sea ⊤[2] 90 36.00 N 123.00 E
Huanghe Kou ≃[1] 98 37.54 N 118.48 E
Huangho → Huang ≃ 90 37.32 N 118.19 E
Huanghu 106 30.27 N 119.48 E
Huanghua 98 38.22 N 117.21 E
Huanghuadianzi 104 41.44 N 122.48 E
Huanghuashi 100 28.14 N 113.14 E
Huangjialing 104 42.12 N 122.55 E
Huangjialu 106 31.00 N 121.45 E
Huangjiatun 104 41.11 N 122.54 E
Huangjiazhai 106 32.01 N 121.36 E
Huangjinbu 100 28.27 N 116.47 E
Huangjing 106 31.39 N 121.06 E
Huangjinggou 107 29.37 N 104.35 E
Huangjinjing 107 29.44 N 104.38 E
Huangjinzi 89 50.02 N 127.20 E
Huangjuezhen 107 29.50 N 106.27 E
Huangkan 105 40.22 N 116.28 E
Huangkeng 100 27.35 N 117.39 E
Huangkou 102 42.46 N 93.58 E
Huanglaomen 100 29.30 N 115.49 E
Huangli 106 31.39 N 119.42 E
Huanglian 107 29.17 N 106.18 E
Huangling 102 35.41 N 109.09 E
Huanglingji 100 30.25 N 114.03 E
Huanglong, Zhg. 100 31.58 N 112.28 E
Huanglong, Zhg. 102 35.45 N 109.42 E
Huanglongxi 107 30.19 N 103.58 E
Huangmao 100 28.07 N 114.04 E
Huangmapi 100 23.30 N 114.33 E
Huangmei 100 30.04 N 115.56 E
Huangnihe, Zhg. 89 43.32 N 127.59 E
Huangnihe, Zhg. 100 31.06 N 117.22 E
Huangpi, Zhg. 100 30.53 N 114.22 E
Huangpi, Zhg. 100 26.39 N 115.51 E
Huangpu ≃ 106 31.24 N 121.31 E
Huangqi 100 26.21 N 119.54 E
Huangqiao 106 32.15 N 120.13 E
Huangqiao ≃ 106 32.00 N 120.20 E
Huangshahe 102 26.03 N 110.58 E
Huangshajie 100 29.03 N 113.08 E
Huangshan 98 36.57 N 122.18 E
Huangshanguan 98 37.32 N 120.16 E
Huangshapu, Zhg. 100 26.50 N 113.26 E
Huangshapu, Zhg. 100 25.08 N 112.44 E
Huangshaqiao 100 28.56 N 114.40 E
Huangshatuo 104 41.12 N 122.31 E
Huangshi, Zhg. 100 30.13 N 115.05 E
Huangshi, Zhg. 100 25.23 N 119.04 E
Huangshi, Zhg. 102 29.00 N 111.02 E
Huangshidu 100 27.44 N 116.44 E
Huangshiguan 100 26.15 N 115.54 E
Huangshui 107 30.32 N 103.55 E
Huangtan, Zhg. 100 27.44 N 119.58 E
Huangtan, Zhg. 100 26.41 N 117.17 E
Huangtan ≃ 100 24.48 N 116.31 E
Huangtang, Zhg. 100 23.44 N 114.58 E
Huangtang, Zhg. 106 31.47 N 119.40 E
Huangtang, Zhg. 106 31.46 N 120.21 E
Huangtang Hu ⊜ 100 30.00 N 114.12 E
Huangtankou 100 28.50 N 118.53 E
Huangtantuan 100 30.53 N 113.33 E
Huangtian 100 23.52 N 114.58 E
Huangtianfan 100 29.10 N 120.08 E
Huangtu, Zhg. 100 27.36 N 118.00 E
Huangtu, Zhg. 106 31.52 N 120.03 E
Huangtuchang 107 30.41 N 104.18 E
Huangtugang 100 31.25 N 115.05 E
Huangtukan 104 41.21 N 122.45 E
Huangtuliangzi 98 41.14 N 118.39 E
Huangtuling 100 27.18 N 113.30 E
Huangtupo 105 39.47 N 116.16 E
Huanguelén 252 37.02 S 61.57 W
Huangwan 106 30.22 N 120.48 E
Huangxian 98 37.38 N 120.29 E
Huangxu 106 32.06 N 119.37 E
Huangyaguan 105 40.14 N 117.26 E
Huangyan 100 28.39 N 121.15 E
Huangyang Shan ⋏ 105 40.20 N 115.00 E
Huangyanzhuang 105 40.01 N 118.21 E
Huangyuan 102 36.40 N 101.12 E
Huangyuzeng 104 42.05 N 124.11 E
Huangze 100 29.35 N 120.55 E
Huangze Yang ʯ 100 30.36 N 122.28 E
Huangzhai 100 29.27 N 120.00 E
Huangzhong 102 36.31 N 101.40 E
Huangzhu 110 19.29 N 110.24 E
Huangzhuang, Zhg. 100 34.05 N 112.15 E
Huangzhuang, Zhg. 105 39.29 N 117.31 E
Huangzhuang, Zhg. 105 39.53 N 117.05 E
Huangzhuang Wa ⊜ 105 39.33 N 117.33 E
Huaning 102 24.14 N 102.56 E
Huaniqueo [de Morales] 234 19.54 N 101.26 W
Huaniugouzi 104 41.34 N 122.35 E
Huaniupuzi 104 41.23 N 123.31 E
Huanjiang 102 24.54 N 108.21 E
Huanren 98 41.14 N 125.21 E
Huanta 248 12.56 S 74.15 W
Huantai (Suozhen) 98 36.59 N 118.06 E
Huantan 100 31.49 N 113.04 E
Huántar 248 9.26 S 77.15 W
Huánuco 248 9.55 S 76.14 W
Huánuco □[5] 248 9.30 S 75.50 W
Huanuni 248 18.16 S 66.51 W
Huanxi 100 26.34 N 113.36 E
Huanxian 102 36.39 N 107.18 E
Huanxiang ≃ 105 39.34 N 117.45 E
Huanxiling 104 41.17 N 123.54 E
Huanzo, Cordillera de ⋏ 248 14.30 S 73.20 W
Huapí, Serranía ⋏ 236 12.30 N 85.00 W
Huap'ing Yü I 100 25.26 N 121.56 E
Huaqiao, Zhg. 100 29.32 N 117.11 E
Huaqiao, Zhg. 100 28.56 N 121.27 E
Huaqiao, Zhg. 102 27.28 N 110.02 E
Huaqiao, Zhg. 107 30.28 N 103.52 E
Huaqiaozhen 107 30.47 N 106.41 E
Huaqiying 106 32.10 N 118.38 E
Huara 248 19.59 S 69.47 W
Huaral 248 11.30 S 77.12 W
Huaraz 248 9.32 S 77.32 W
Huari, Bol. 248 19.00 S 66.48 W
Huari, Perú 248 9.20 S 77.14 W
Huariaca 248 10.27 S 76.07 W
Huaribamba 248 12.16 S 74.57 W
Huarina 248 16.12 S 68.38 W
Huarmey 248 10.04 S 78.10 W
Huarochirí 248 12.09 S 76.14 W
Huarocondo 248 13.25 S 72.13 W
Huarong 100 29.30 N 112.34 E
Huásabas 232 29.47 N 109.18 W
Huasaga ≃ 246 3.42 S 76.26 W
Hua Sai 110 8.02 N 100.18 E
Huasamota 234 22.30 N 104.30 W
Huascarán, Nevado ∧ 248 9.07 S 77.37 W
Huasco 252 28.28 S 71.14 W
Huasco ≃ 252 28.27 S 71.13 W
Huashan 98 34.39 N 116.44 E
Huashaoying 98 40.12 N 114.36 E
Huashi 106 31.50 N 120.28 E
Huatabampo 232 26.50 N 109.38 W
Huatangpu 100 25.48 N 112.52 E
Huating 102 35.09 N 106.38 E
Huatong, Zhg. 98 40.03 N 121.56 E
Huatong, Zhg. 102 23.01 N 106.36 E
Huatunas, Lagunas ⊜ 248 13.06 S 66.15 W
Huatusco de Chicuellar 234 19.09 N 96.57 W
Huauchinango 234 20.11 N 98.03 W
Huaura 248 11.04 S 77.36 W
Huaura ≃ 248 11.06 S 77.39 W
Huautla 234 21.02 N 98.17 W
Huautla de Jiménez 234 18.08 N 96.51 W
Huaxian (Daokou), Zhg. 98 35.37 N 114.32 E
Huaxian, Zhg. 100 23.22 N 113.12 E
Huaxian, Zhg. 102 34.30 N 109.40 E
Huayan 107 30.01 N 105.02 E
Huayang 107 30.32 N 104.04 E
Huayangzhen 102 33.25 N 107.44 E
Huaying Shan ∧ 107 30.10 N 106.42 E
Huayingtai 104 40.43 N 122.19 E
Huayllay 248 11.01 S 76.21 W
Huayna Potosí, Nevado ∧ 248 16.16 S 68.11 W
Huaytará 248 13.36 S 75.22 W
Hua Yü I 100 23.24 N 119.19 E
Huayuan, Zhg. 98 42.17 N 127.07 E
Huayuan, Zhg. 100 31.16 N 113.58 E
Huayuan, Zhg. 102 28.34 N 109.13 E
Huayuanzui 100 33.00 N 118.16 E
Huayunca, Nevado ∧ 248 14.39 S 72.28 W
Huayuri, Pampa de ≚ 248 14.30 S 75.30 W
Huazhou 102 21.40 N 110.33 E
Huazi 104 41.25 N 123.29 E
Huazigou 104 41.50 N 121.01 E
Huazikou 106 32.13 N 118.57 E
Huazolotitlán 234 16.17 N 97.56 W
Ḥubārah, Wādī V 142 27.21 N 31.39 E
Ḥubaytah, Bi'r ⊤[4] 142 30.27 N 32.27 E
Hubbard, Ia., U.S. 190 42.18 N 93.18 W
Hubbard, Oh., U.S. 214 41.09 N 80.34 W
Hubbard, Or., U.S. 224 45.10 N 122.48 W
Hubbard, Tx., U.S. 222 31.50 N 96.47 W
Hubbard Creek ≃ 196 32.54 N 98.53 W
Hubbard Creek Reservoir ⊜[1] 196 32.45 N 99.00 W
Hubbard Lake ⊜ 190 44.49 N 83.34 W
Hubbards 186 44.38 N 64.04 W
Hubbardston 207 42.28 N 72.00 W
Hubbard Woods 278 42.06 N 87.44 W
Hubbell 190 47.10 N 88.25 W
Hubbell Trading Post National Historical Site ⊥ 200 35.43 N 109.33 W
Hubbelrath ◆[8] 263 51.16 N 6.55 E
Hubei (Hupeh) □[4] 90 31.00 N 112.00 E
Huben, Öst. 64 47.03 N 10.58 E
Huben, Öst. 64 46.56 N 12.34 E
Huberdeau 206 45.58 N 74.38 W
Huber Heights 218 39.50 N 84.07 W
Hublersburg 210 40.58 N 77.37 W
Hubli-Dhārwār 122 15.21 N 75.10 E
Hubuleng 102 41.19 N 111.08 E
Hucaogang 106 32.00 N 120.29 E
Hucclecote 42 51.51 N 2.11 W
Huch'ang 98 41.25 N 127.03 E
Hucheng 100 25.26 N 118.27 E
Huchi 100 31.08 N 117.40 E
Huchow → Huzhou 106 30.52 N 120.06 E
Huckarde ◆[8] 263 51.32 N 7.24 E
Hückelhoven 56 51.04 N 6.10 E
Hückeswagen 56 51.08 N 7.20 E
Hucking 260 51.18 N 0.39 E
Huckingen ◆[8] 263 51.22 N 6.43 E
Huckitta Creek ≃ 162 22.38 S 135.30 E
Huckleberry Island I 276 40.53 N 73.45 W
Huckleberry Mountain ∧ 202 43.51 N 122.19 W
Huckleberry Mountain ∧[2] 212 44.28 N 75.28 W
Hucknall 42 53.02 N 1.11 W
Hucqueliers 50 50.34 N 1.54 E
Hucun 105 39.02 N 115.56 E
Hudangtou 106 30.48 N 121.22 E
Huddart Park ♦ 282 37.26 N 122.19 W
Hudderfield Narrow Canal ≖ 262 53.29 N 2.06 W
Huddersfield 262 53.39 N 1.47 W
Huddinge 40 59.14 N 17.59 E
Huddle Park Municipal Golf Course ♦ 273d 26.09 S 28.07 E
Huddunge 40 60.03 N 16.59 E
Hude 52 53.07 N 8.27 E
Huder 89 50.00 N 121.37 E
Hudgin Creek ≃ 194 33.40 N 91.59 W
Hūdī 140 17.42 N 34.17 E
Hudiksvall 26 61.44 N 17.07 E
Hudong 100 22.51 N 115.56 E
Hudson, P.Q., Can. 206 45.27 N 74.09 W
Hudson, Il., U.S. 216 40.36 N 88.59 W
Hudson, In., U.S. 216 41.31 N 85.04 W
Hudson, Ia., U.S. 190 42.24 N 92.27 W
Hudson, Md., U.S. 208 38.35 N 76.15 W
Hudson, Ma., U.S. 207 42.23 N 71.34 W
Hudson, Mi., U.S. 216 41.51 N 84.21 W
Hudson, N.H., U.S. 207 42.45 N 71.26 W
Hudson, N.Y., U.S. 210 42.15 N 73.47 W
Hudson, N.C., U.S. 192 35.50 N 81.29 W
Hudson, Oh., U.S. 214 41.14 N 81.26 W
Hudson, S.D., U.S. 198 43.07 N 96.27 W
Hudson, Tx., U.S. 222 31.19 N 94.50 W
Hudson, Wi., U.S. 190 44.58 N 92.45 W
Hudson, Wy., U.S. 200 42.54 N 108.34 W
Hudson □[6] 276 40.44 N 74.02 W
Hudson ≃, U.S. 188 40.42 N 74.02 W
Hudson ≃, Ga., U.S. 192 34.14 N 83.10 W
Hudson, Lake ⊜[1] 194 36.20 N 95.05 W
Hudson Bay 184 52.52 N 102.25 W
Hudson Bay ⊂ 176 60.00 N 86.00 W
Hudson-Bayonet Point 220 28.21 N 82.41 W
Hudson Falls 210 43.18 N 73.35 W
Hudson Highlands State Park ♦ 210 41.26 N 73.58 W
Hudson Hope 182 56.02 N 121.55 W
Hudson Lake 216 41.42 N 86.32 W
Hudson Mountains ⋏ 9 74.32 S 99.20 W
Hudsons Peak ∧ 171b 36.26 S 149.10 E
Hudson Strait ʯ 176 62.30 N 72.00 W
Hudsonville 216 42.52 N 85.51 W
Hudwin Lake ⊜ 184 53.12 N 95.42 W
Hue 110 16.28 N 107.36 E
Huebra ≃ 34 41.02 N 6.48 W
Huechucuicui, Punta › 254 41.47 S 74.02 W
Huechulafquén, Lago ⊜ 254 39.46 S 71.28 W
Huedin 38 46.52 N 23.02 E
Huehuetán 236 15.01 N 92.22 W
Huehuetenango 236 15.20 N 91.28 W
Huehuetenango □[5] 236 15.40 N 91.35 W
Huehuetlán el Chico 234 18.21 N 98.42 W
Huejúcar 234 22.21 N 103.13 W
Huejuquilla el Alto 234 22.36 N 103.52 W
Huejutla de Reyes 234 21.08 N 98.25 W
Huelgoat 32 48.22 N 3.45 W
Huelma 34 37.39 N 3.27 W
Huelva 34 37.16 N 6.57 W
Huelva, Río de ≃ 34 37.27 N 6.00 W
Huenque ≃ 248 16.12 S 69.44 W
Huentelauquén 252 31.35 S 71.32 W
Huércal-Overa 34 37.23 N 1.57 W
Huerfano ≃ 198 38.14 N 104.15 W
Huerfano Mountain ∧ 200 36.26 N 107.51 W
Huerhuero Creek ≃ 226 35.40 N 120.42 W
Huerlumada 120 32.45 N 90.00 E
Huerva ≃ 34 41.39 N 0.52 W
Huesca 34 42.08 N 0.25 W
Huéscar 34 37.49 N 2.32 W
Hueston Woods State Park ♦ 218 39.34 N 84.44 W
Huetamo de Núñez 234 18.35 N 100.53 W
Huete 34 40.08 N 2.41 W
Huey 219 38.36 N 89.17 W
Hueyapan 234 18.52 N 98.40 W
Hueyapan de Ocampo 234 18.07 N 95.09 W
Hueytown 194 33.27 N 86.59 W
Hufengzhen 107 29.43 N 106.07 E
Hüffenhardt 56 49.18 N 9.04 E
Huffman 222 30.01 N 95.05 W
Huffman Dam ◆[6] 218 39.48 N 84.05 W
Hüfingen 58 47.55 N 8.29 E
Ḥufrat an-Naḥās 140 9.45 N 24.19 E
Hufu 106 31.16 N 119.47 E
Hügel, Villa ʋ 263 51.25 N 7.01 E
Huggins, Mount ∧ 9 78.17 S 162.28 E
Hugh ≃ 162 25.01 S 134.01 E
Hugh Butler Lake ⊜[1] 198 40.22 N 100.42 W
Hughenden 166 20.51 S 144.12 E
Hughes, Austl. 162 30.42 S 129.31 E
Hughes, Ak., U.S. 180 66.03 N 154.16 W
Hughes, Ar., U.S. 194 34.56 N 90.28 W
Hughes ≃ 184 56.46 N 100.01 W
Hughes, South Fork ≃ 188 39.08 N 81.20 W
Hughes Airport ⊠ 280 33.58 N 118.25 W
Hughes Creek ≃ 169 36.53 S 145.08 E
Hughes Springs 222 33.05 N 94.38 W
Hughesville, Md., U.S. 208 38.31 N 76.47 W
Hughesville, Pa., U.S. 210 41.14 N 76.43 W
Hugh Keenleyside Dam ◆[6] 182 49.20 N 117.49 W
Hughson 226 37.36 N 120.52 W
Hughsonville 210 41.35 N 73.56 W
Hugh Town 42a 49.55 N 6.17 W
Hugli ≃ 126 21.55 N 88.05 E
Hugli-Chinsurah 126 22.54 N 88.24 E
Hugo, Co., U.S. 198 39.08 N 103.28 W
Hugo, Ok., U.S. 196 34.00 N 95.30 W
Hugo Lake ⊜[1] 196 34.05 N 95.25 W
Hugoton 198 37.10 N 101.20 W
Hugou 100 33.23 N 117.08 E
Huguenot 210 41.25 N 74.38 W
Huguenot Lake ⊜ 276 40.56 N 73.47 W
Huhehot → Hohhot 102 40.51 N 111.40 E
Huhsi 100 23.35 N 119.39 E
Hui'an, Zhg. 100 25.04 N 118.47 E
Huian, Zhg. 106 31.47 N 121.45 E
Huiarau Range ⋏ 172 38.45 S 177.00 E
Huib-Hoch Plateau ⋏[1] 156 27.00 S 16.45 E
Huibie Yang ʯ 100 30.08 N 121.44 E
Huibu 100 28.18 N 115.15 E
Huichang, Zhg. 100 25.34 N 115.49 E
Huichang, Zhg. 105 39.04 N 115.04 E
Huichapan 234 20.23 N 99.39 W
Hüich'ŏn 98 40.10 N 126.17 E

Symbols in the index entries represent the broad categories identified in the key at the right. Symbols with superior numbers (⋏[1]) identify subcategories (see complete key on page *I · 1)*.

Symbole im Register stellen die rechts im Schlüssel erklärten Kategorien dar. Symbole mit hochgestellten Ziffern (⋏[1]) bezeichnen Unterabteilungen einer Kategorie (vgl. vollständiger Schlüssel auf Seite *I · 1)*.

Los símbolos incluídos en el texto del índice representan las grandes categorias identificadas con la clave a la derecha. Los símbolos con numeros en su parte superior (⋏[1]) identifican las subcategorías (véase la clave completa en la página *I · 1)*.

Les symboles de l'index représentent les catégories indiquées dans la légende à droite. Les symboles suivis d'un indice (⋏[1]) représentent des sous-catégories (voir légende complète à la page *I · 1)*.

Os símbolos incluídos no texto do índice representam as grandes categorias identificadas com a chave à direita. Os símbolos com números em sua parte superior (⋏[1]) identificam as subcategorias (veja-se a chave completa à página *I · 1)*.

	English	Deutsch	Español	Français	Português
∧	Mountain	Berg	Montaña	Montagne	Montanha
⋏	Mountains	Gebirge	Montañas	Montagnes	Montanhas
)(	Pass	Paß	Paso	Col	Passo
V	Valley, Canyon	Tal, Cañon	Valle, Cañón	Vallée, Canyon	Vale, Canhão
≚	Plain	Ebene	Llano	Plaine	Planície
›	Cape	Kap	Cabo	Cap	Cabo
I	Island	Insel	Isla	Île	Ilha
II	Islands	Inseln	Islas	Îles	Ilhas
⩢	Other Topographic Features	Andere Topographische Objekte	Otros Elementos Topográficos	Autres données topographiques	Outros acidentes topográficos

ESPAÑOL			FRANÇAIS			PORTUGUÊS		
Nombre	Página	Lat.°′ / W = Oeste	Nom	Page	Lat.°′ / W = Ouest	Nome	Página	Lat.°′ / W = Oeste

ESPAÑOL

Nombre	Página	Lat.	Long.
Huichou → Huizhou	100	23.05 N	114.24 E
Huichuan	102	35.11 N	104.02 E
Huicungo	248	7.17 S	76.48 W
Huidong	102	26.41 N	102.36 E
Huidui	105	39.24 N	117.16 E
Huihe, Zhg.	89	48.12 N	119.17 E
Huihe, Zhg.	106	31.45 N	121.43 E
Huiji ≃	100	33.53 N	115.36 E
Huila	152	15.04 S	13.32 E
Huila □⁵, Ang.	152	15.00 S	15.00 E
Huila □⁵, Col.	246	2.30 N	75.45 W
Huila, Nevado del ▲	246	3.00 N	76.00 W
Huilai	100	23.04 N	116.18 E
Huili	102	26.43 N	102.10 E
Huiluji	100	32.50 N	115.58 E
Huillapima	252	28.44 S	65.59 W
Huilong, Zhg.	100	27.30 N	118.24 E
Huilong, Zhg.	100	25.22 N	116.24 E
Huilong, Zhg.	100	24.09 N	113.58 E
Huilong, Zhg.	107	30.28 N	105.26 E
Huilong, Zhg.	107	30.35 N	105.49 E
Huiliongchang, Zhg.	107	30.18 N	103.39 E
Huilongchang, Zhg.	107	29.41 N	104.17 E
Huilongchang, Zhg.	107	30.41 N	106.34 E
Huilongchang, Zhg.	107	29.7 N	105.01 E
Huimanguillo	234	17.51 N	93.23 W
Huimin	98	37.29 N	117.29 E
Huinan (Chaoyang)	98	42.40 N	126.00 E
Huinca Renancó	252	34.50 S	64.23 W
Huinghausen	263	51.11 N	7.48 E
Huining	102	35.41 N	105.08 E
Huisachal	196	26.41 N	101.07 W
Huisduinen	52	52.56 N	4.44 E
Huishan	106	31.35 N	120.16 E
Huishui	102	26.07 N	106.24 E
Huismes	50	47.14 N	0.15 E
Huisne ≃	50	47.59 N	0.11 E
Huissen	52	51.57 N	5.56 E
Huistepec	234	16.39 N	98.20 W
Huiten Nur ⊜	120	35.30 N	92.00 E
Huiting	98	34.05 N	116.04 E
Huitingan	234	17.13 N	92.39 W
Huitong	102	26.54 N	109.31 E
Huitongqiao	102	24.43 N	98.56 E
Huitupan	234	17.13 N	92.39 W
Huittinen (Lauttakylä)	26	61.11 N	22.42 E
Huitzilán	234	19.58 N	97.41 W
Huitzuco de los Figueroa	234	18.18 N	99.21 W
Huixian	102	33.47 N	106.16 E
Huixquilucan □⁷	286a	19.24 N	99.18 W
Huixtla	232	15.09 N	92.28 W
Huiyang → Huizhou	100	23.05 N	114.24 E
Huiyang	100	27.16 N	118.05 E
Huizache	234	22.55 N	100.25 W
Huize	102	26.27 N	103.09 E
Huizen	52	52.17 N	5.14 E
Huizhou	100	23.05 N	114.24 E
Hujia, Zhg.	104	41.20 N	121.52 E
Hujia, Zhg.	106	31.25 N	121.37 E
Hujiadian	107	29.41 N	104.07 E
Hujiajie	104	41.06 N	122.10 E
Hujiasi	107	29.16 N	105.13 E
Hujiayu	105	39.24 N	122.11 E
Hujiazhuang, Zhg.	105	39.51 N	117.07 E
Hujiazhuang, Zhg.	269b	21.21 N	121.25 E
Hujie	102	24.56 N	100.32 E
Hukeng	100	27.29 N	114.18 E
Hukou	100	29.45 N	116.13 E
Hŭksan-chedo II	98	34.30 N	125.20 E
Hukul → Fukui	94	36.04 N	136.13 E
Hukŭmah	140	13.52 N	36.07 E
Hukuntsi	156	24.02 S	21.48 E
Hukuoka → Fukuoka	96	33.35 N	130.24 E
Hukusima → Fukushima	92	37.45 N	140.28 E
Hukuyama → Fukuyama	96	34.29 N	133.22 E
Hula, 'Emeq ≃¹	132	33.08 N	35.37 E
Hulahula ≃	180	70.00 N	144.01 W
Hulan	89	46.00 N	126.38 E
Hulan ≃	89	45.55 N	126.41 E
Hulan Ergi	89	47.13 N	123.39 E
Hulbert, Mi., U.S.	190	46.21 N	85.09 W
Hulbert, Ok., U.S.	194	35.55 N	95.08 W
Hulberton	210	43.15 N	78.04 W
Hulda	132	31.50 N	34.53 E
Huldrefossen L	26	61.28 N	5.58 E
Hulei	100	24.50 N	116.48 E
Huleia Stream ≃	229b	21.57 N	159.22 W
Hulett	198	44.40 N	104.36 W
Hulín, Česko.	30	49.19 N	17.28 E
Hulin, Zhg.	89	45.46 N	132.59 E
Hulin ≃, Zhg.	89	45.19 N	124.06 E
Huliu ≃	98	40.10 N	114.33 E
Hull, P.Q., Can.	212	45.26 N	75.43 W
Hull → Kingston upon Hull, Eng., U.K.	44	53.45 N	0.20 W
Hull, Il., U.S.	219	39.43 N	91.13 W
Hull, Ia., U.S.	198	43.11 N	96.08 W
Hull, Ma., U.S.	207	42.18 N	70.54 W
Hull, Tx., U.S.	202	30.09 N	94.39 W
Hull □⁶	212	45.40 N	75.35 W
Hull ≃	44	53.44 N	0.19 W
Hullavington	42	51.33 N	2.09 W
Hull Bay ⊂	283	42.18 N	70.53 W
Hullbridge	260	51.37 N	0.38 E
Hull Glacier ⁊	79	75.05 S	137.15 W
Hullo	76	59.00 N	23.14 E
Hulmeville	285	40.08 N	74.55 W
Hüls, B.R.D.	56	51.22 N	6.30 E
Hüls, B.R.D.	263	51.40 N	7.08 E
Hülscheid	56	51.16 N	7.34 E
Hülser Berg ▲²	263	51.24 N	6.33 E
Hülser Berg ▲²	263	51.23 N	6.33 E
Hulst	52	51.17 N	4.03 E
Hultsfred	26	57.29 N	15.50 E
Huludao	104	40.43 N	121.00 E
Hulun → Hailar	105	49.12 N	116.02 E
Hulun Nur ⊜	88	49.01 N	117.32 E
Huluyu	105	40.14 N	116.53 E
Hulwân	142	29.51 N	31.20 E
Hulwan Observatory ▲³	142	29.52 N	31.21 E
Huma, Tonga	174w	21.19 S	175.57 W
Huma, Zhg.	89	51.43 N	126.38 E
Huma ≃	89	51.43 N	126.44 E
Humacao	240m	13.09 N	65.50 W
Humahuaca	252	23.12 S	65.21 W
Humaitá, Bra.	248	7.31 S	63.02 W
Humaitá, Para.	252	27.03 S	58.33 W
Humaitá ≃	248	3.58 S	72.44 W
Humansdorp	156	34.02 S	24.46 E
Humansville	194	37.47 N	93.34 W
Humara, Jabal al- ▲	140	16.16 N	30.59 E
Humarock	283	42.08 N	70.41 W
Humaydah	140	14.22 N	33.56 E
Humayingzi	105	41.06 N	116.48 E
Humayun's Tomb ⊾	278a	28.36 N	77.15 E
Humbe	156	16.40 S	14.55 E
Humbe, Serra do ▲	152	12.13 S	15.25 E
Humbeek	50	50.58 N	4.23 E
Humber ≃, On., Can.	212	43.55 N	79.30 W
Humber ≃, Eng., U.K.	44	53.40 N	0.10 W
Humber, Mouth of the ≃¹	44	53.32 N	0.08 E
Humber Bay ⊂	275b	43.38 N	79.27 W
Humber Bridge ↗⁵	44	53.43 N	0.27 W
Humberside □⁶	44	53.55 N	0.40 W
Humberston	44	53.33 N	0.02 W
Humberto de Campos	250	2.37 S	43.27 W
Humberto Primo	252	30.52 S	61.22 W

FRANÇAIS

Nom	Page	Lat.	Long.
Humber Valley Park ♦	275b	43.39 N	79.30 W
Humbird	190	44.31 N	90.53 W
Humble, Dan.	41	54.50 N	10.42 E
Humble, Tx., U.S.	222	29.59 N	95.15 W
Humboldt, Sk., Can.	184	52.12 N	105.07 W
Humboldt, Az., U.S.	200	34.30 N	112.14 W
Humboldt, Il., U.S.	194	39.36 N	88.19 W
Humboldt, Ia., U.S.	198	42.43 N	94.12 W
Humboldt, Ks., U.S.	198	37.48 N	95.26 W
Humboldt, Ne., U.S.	198	40.09 N	95.56 W
Humboldt, S.D., U.S.	198	43.39 N	97.04 W
Humboldt, Tn., U.S.	194	35.49 N	88.54 W
Humboldt □⁵	175l	21.53 S	166.25 E
Humboldt ≃	204	40.02 N	118.31 W
Humboldt, North Fork ≃	204	40.56 N	115.32 W
Humboldt, Parque ♦	286c	10.28 N	66.54 W
Humboldt, Planetario ⛬	286c	10.30 N	66.50 W
Humboldt, South Fork ≃	204	40.47 N	115.53 W
Humboldt Bay ⊂	204	40.47 N	124.11 W
Humboldt Lake ⊜	204	39.58 N	118.38 W
Humboldt Mountains ⱥ	9	71.45 S	11.30 E
Humboldt Park ♦	278	41.54 N	87.42 W
Humboldt Redwoods State Park ♦	204	40.19 N	124.00 W
Humboldt Salt Marsh ⫶	204	39.50 N	117.55 W
Hume, Ca., U.S.	204	36.47 N	118.55 W
Hume, N.Y., U.S.	210	42.29 N	78.08 W
Hume, Lake ⊜¹	166	36.06 S	147.05 E
Hume and Hovell Lookout ♦	169	37.15 S	144.59 E
Hume and Hovell Memorial ⱥ	170	34.10 S	150.47 E
Humelum	166	27.24 S	145.14 E
Hümecän	128	25.24 N	59.39 E
Hu Men ⊂¹	100	22.44 N	113.40 E
Humera	266a	40.26 N	3.47 W
Humeston	190	40.51 N	93.29 W
Humlá Karnâlî ≃	124	29.38 N	81.52 E
Humlebæk	41	55.58 N	12.33 E
Hummelstown	208	40.16 N	76.43 W
Hummels Wharf	210	40.49 N	76.50 W
Hümmling ≃	42	52.52 N	7.31 E
Húmos, Isla I	254	45.58 S	73.56 W
Humpata	152	15.02 S	13.24 E
Hümpfershausen	56	50.40 N	10.13 E
Humphrey, Ar., U.S.	194	34.25 N	91.42 W
Humphrey, Ne., U.S.	198	41.41 N	97.29 W
Humphreys, Mount ▲	204	37.17 N	118.40 W
Humphreys Peak ▲	200	35.20 N	111.40 W
Humpolec	30	49.32 N	15.22 E
Humppila	26	60.56 N	23.22 E
Humptulips	224	47.13 N	123.57 W
Humptulips ≃	224	47.03 N	124.03 W
Humptulips, East Fork ≃	224	47.15 N	123.54 W
Humptulips, West Fork ≃	224	47.15 N	123.54 W
Humptulips Ridge ⱥ	224	47.20 N	123.45 W
Humpty Doo	164	12.38 S	131.15 E
Humula	174	35.29 S	147.45 E
Humuya ≃	236	15.13 N	87.57 W
Hün ≃	146	29.07 N	15.56 E
Hun ≃, Zhg.	98	41.01 N	122.27 E
Hun ≃, Zhg.	98	40.52 N	125.42 E
Hunabasi → Funabashi	94	35.42 N	139.59 E
Húnaflói ⊂	24a	65.50 N	20.50 W
Hunan □⁴	102	28.00 N	111.00 E
Hunaynshāt, Ghurd al- ⫿²	142	30.07 N	29.47 E
Hunchun	98	42.54 N	130.22 E
Hundelaft	54	51.58 N	12.20 E
Hundested	41	55.58 N	11.52 E
Hundewäli	123	31.55 N	72.38 E
Hundorp	26	61.33 N	9.54 E
Hundred End	188	39.41 N	80.27 W
Hundslund	41	55.55 N	10.04 E
Hundstein ▲	64	47.20 N	12.54 E
Hundwil	58	47.22 N	9.19 E
Hunedoara	38	45.45 N	22.54 E
Hunedoara □⁶	38	45.45 N	22.54 E
Hünfeld	56	50.40 N	9.46 E
Hungary (Magyarország) □¹, Europe	22	47.00 N	20.00 E
Hungary (Magyarország) □¹, Europe	30	47.00 N	20.00 E
Hungcheng → Hongjiang	102	27.07 N	109.56 E
Hungen	56	50.28 N	8.54 E
Hungerford, Austl.	166	29.00 S	144.25 E
Hungerford, Eng., U.K.	42	51.26 N	1.30 W
Hungerford, Tx., U.S.	222	29.24 N	96.05 W
Húngho-ri	98	37.14 N	127.44 E
Hung Long	110	19.35 N	105.30 E
Hungnam	98	39.03 N	127.38 E
Hungngan	269c	10.40 N	106.39 E
Hungngan	100	24.55 N	120.58 E
Hungman	98	39.50 N	127.38 E
Hungria → Hungary □¹	30	47.00 N	20.00 E
Hungry Hill ▲	48	51.41 N	9.48 W
Hungry Horse	202	48.23 N	114.03 W
Hungry Horse Dam ⸋⁶	202	48.14 N	114.04 W
Hungry Horse Reservoir ⊜¹	202	48.20 N	114.16 W
Hungry Lake ⊜	212	44.48 N	76.53 W
Hungry Lake ▲²	144	55.21 N	2.24 W
Hung Yen	110	20.39 N	106.04 E
Hunhe ≃	89	41.45 N	122.42 E
Huningue	62	47.36 N	7.35 E
Hunish, Rubha ⊱	46	57.41 N	6.21 W
Huni Valley	154	5.35 N	1.55 W
Hunjiang (Badaojiang)	98	41.56 N	126.29 E
Hunjiang ≃	98	40.12 N	125.30 E
Hunker	211b	40.10 N	79.38 W
Hunkurák, Ra's ⊱	140	24.34 N	35.10 E
Hunlen Falls L	182	52.17 N	125.47 W
Hunmanby	44	54.10 N	0.19 W
Hunn ≃	204	58.51 N	15.57 E
Hunneberg ▲²	26	58.21 N	12.29 E
Hunnebostrand	26	58.27 N	11.18 E
Hunnewell	219	39.40 N	91.51 W
Hunnewell Lake ⊜	219	39.42 N	91.52 W
Hunnsberge ⱥ	156	27.45 S	17.12 E
Hunseby	41	54.48 N	11.32 E
Hunspach	56	48.57 N	7.57 E
Hünsrück ⱥ	56	49.56 N	7.20 E
Hunstanton	42	52.57 N	0.30 E
Hunstein Range ⱥ	164	4.30 S	142.40 E
Hunt ≃	180	64.20 N	155.30 W
Hunt, Cape ⊱	164	13.57 S	129.05 E
Hundalssjøen ⊜	42	52.57 N	0.30 E
Huntdorf	62	53.16 N	8.22 E
Huntenburg	219	40.12 N	92.41 W
Hunter ≃, N.S.W., Austl.	170	32.50 S	151.42 E
Hunter ≃, N.D., U.S.	198	47.11 N	97.12 W
Hunter ≃, Austl.	170	32.50 S	151.42 E
Hunter, N.Z.	176	44.31 S	169.40 E
Hunter, Île I	14	22.24 S	172.03 E
Hunter, Mount ▲	183	62.56 N	151.06 W
Hunter, Port ⊂	164	4.05 S	152.20 E
Hunter ≃	208	40.31 N	74.52 W
Hunter Island I	182	51.55 N	128.05 W
Hunter Island I, B.C., Can.	182	51.55 N	128.05 W
Hunter Island I, N.Y., U.S.	285	40.53 N	73.47 W
Hunter Mountain ▲	172	35.42 S	167.25 E
Hunter Range ▲²	14	22.30 S	174.50 E
Hunter River	182	46.21 N	63.21 W
Hunters	182	48.07 N	118.12 W

PORTUGUÊS

Nome	Página	Lat.	Long.
Hunters Bay ⊂	110	19.57 N	93.19 E
Hunters Creek Village	222	29.46 N	95.24 W
Huntersfield Mountain ▲	210	42.21 N	74.21 W
Hunters Hill	274a	33.50 S	151.09 E
Hunters Point ⊱	282	37.43 N	122.22 W
Hunter's Quay	46	55.58 N	4.55 W
Hunters Road	154	19.09 S	29.48 E
Hunters Run	208	40.05 N	77.11 W
Huntersville	192	35.25 N	80.50 W
Huntertown	216	41.13 N	85.10 W
Hunterville	172	39.56 S	175.34 E
Hunter Wash V	200	36.17 N	108.34 W
Huntingburg	194	38.17 N	86.57 W
Huntingdon, B.C., Can.	224	49.00 N	122.16 W
Huntingdon, P.Q., Can.	206	45.05 N	74.10 W
Huntingdon, Eng., U.K.	42	52.20 N	0.12 W
Huntingdon, Pa., U.S.	214	40.29 N	78.00 W
Huntingdon, Tn., U.S.	194	36.00 N	88.25 W
Huntingdon □⁶, P.Q., Can.	206	45.05 N	74.00 W
Huntingdon □⁶, Pa., U.S.	214	40.29 N	78.01 W
Huntingdon Valley	285	40.07 N	75.03 W
Huntingdon Valley Creek ≃	285	40.07 N	75.04 W
Hunting Island State Park ♦	192	32.20 N	80.30 W
Hunting Ridge	284c	38.55 N	77.12 W
Huntington, Eng., U.K.	44	54.01 N	1.04 W
Huntington, In., U.S.	216	40.52 N	85.29 W
Huntington, Ma., U.S.	207	42.14 N	72.52 W
Huntington, N.Y., U.S.	210	40.51 N	73.25 W
Huntington, Or., U.S.	202	44.21 N	117.15 W
Huntington, Tx., U.S.	222	31.16 N	94.34 W
Huntington, Ut., U.S.	200	39.19 N	110.57 W
Huntington, Va., U.S.	284c	38.48 N	77.11 W
Huntington, W.V., U.S.	188	38.25 N	82.26 W
Huntington □⁶	216	40.53 N	85.30 W
Huntington Bay	276	40.53 N	73.24 W
Huntington Bay ⊂	276	40.55 N	73.25 W
Huntington Lake ⊜¹, Ca., U.S.	226	37.14 N	119.12 W
Huntington Lake ⊜¹, In., U.S.	216	40.50 N	85.25 W
Huntington Library ⱥ³	280	34.08 N	118.07 W
Huntington Mills	208	41.11 N	76.14 W
Huntington Park	228	33.58 N	118.13 W
Huntington Park	279a	41.29 N	81.56 W
Huntington Station	210	40.51 N	73.24 W
Huntington Woods	281	42.28 N	83.10 W
Huntingtown	208	38.36 N	76.36 W
Hunting Valley	279a	41.31 N	81.23 W
Huntingville	206	45.20 N	71.51 W
Huntland	194	35.03 N	86.16 W
Huntley, Il., U.S.	216	42.10 N	88.25 W
Huntley, Mt., U.S.	202	45.53 N	108.18 W
Huntly, N.Z.	172	37.33 S	175.10 E
Huntly, Scot., U.K.	46	57.27 N	2.47 W
Hunt Mountain ▲	202	44.44 N	107.45 W
Hunton	260	51.13 N	0.28 E
Hutayni, Harrat ▲⁹	128	26.15 N	40.20 E
Hutberg ▲²	54	52.09 N	14.33 E
Hutchins	222	32.39 N	96.43 W
Hutchinson, S. Afr.	158	31.30 S	23.09 E
Hutchinson, Ks., U.S.	198	38.03 N	97.55 W
Hutchinson, Mn., U.S.	190	44.53 N	94.22 W
Hutchinson, Pa., U.S.	214	40.13 N	79.44 W
Hutchinson Island I	220	27.25 N	80.17 W
Hutch Mountain ▲	200	34.47 N	111.22 W
Huthwaite	44	53.09 N	1.17 W
Huttrop ≃⁸	263	51.27 N	7.03 E
Huttrop	263	51.27 N	7.03 E
Huttwil	58	47.07 N	7.51 E
Hutubi	86	44.07 N	86.57 E
Hutuo ≃	98	38.04 N	116.05 E
Hutwisch ▲	61	47.28 N	16.13 E
Huu	115b	8.48 S	118.25 E
Huvaa Forest ⱥ³	174v	19.00 S	169.51 W
Huuvaune ≃	62	43.08 N	5.54 E
Huvadhá Kanal ⪼	130	0.30 N	73.15 E
Hvalfjörður ⊂	24a	64.15 N	21.40 W
Hvammstangi	24a	65.24 N	20.57 W
Hvannadalshnúkur ▲	24a	64.01 N	16.41 W
Hvar	36	43.09 N	16.39 E
Hvar, Otok I	36	43.09 N	16.45 E
Hvarski Kanal ⪼	36	43.18 N	16.28 E
Hveragerdi	24a	64.00 N	21.11 W
Hvide Sande	41	56.00 N	8.08 E
Hvittingfoss	26	59.29 N	10.00 E
Hvolsvöllur	24a	63.45 N	20.13 W
Hwach'on	98	38.06 N	127.42 E
Hwach'on-chósuji ⊜¹	98	38.07 N	127.45 E
Hwado	98	37.55 N	126.40 E
Hwain-gai	110	20.51 N	106.40 E
Hwainan → Huainan	100	32.40 N	117.00 E
Hwaksan	98	40.36 N	125.50 E
Hwang → Huang ≃	90	37.32 N	118.19 E
Hwangju	98	38.42 N	125.46 E
Hwangshih → Huangshi	100	30.13 N	115.05 E
Hyak	224	47.23 N	121.23 W
Hyakuna	174m	26.08 N	127.48 E
Hyakuri-ga-dake ▲	94	35.23 N	135.49 E
Hyakuri-kichi, Kōkū-jieitai- ⛬	94	36.11 N	140.25 E
Hyannis, Ma., U.S.	207	41.39 N	70.17 W
Hyannis, Ne., U.S.	198	42.00 N	101.45 W
Hyannis Port	207	41.38 N	70.18 W
Hyattsville	208	38.57 N	76.56 W
Hyattville	202	44.14 N	107.36 W
Hybla Valley	208	38.45 N	77.05 W
Hyco ≃	192	36.40 N	78.45 W
Hyco Lake ⊜¹	192	36.30 N	79.05 W
Hyda ≃	26	60.30 N	15.05 E
Hyde, N.Z.	172	45.18 S	170.15 E
Hyde, Eng., U.K.	262	53.27 N	2.04 W
Hyde, Pa., U.S.	214	41.00 N	78.28 W
Hyden, Austl.	162	32.27 S	118.53 E
Hyden, Ky., U.S.	192	37.10 N	83.22 W
Hyde Park, Guy.	246	6.30 N	58.16 W
Hyde Park, N.Y., U.S.	210	41.47 N	73.56 W
Hyde Park, Vt., U.S.	188	44.35 N	72.37 W
Hyde Park ⊞⁸, Ma., U.S.	278	41.48 N	87.36 W
Hyde Park ♦, Austl.	274a	33.53 S	151.13 E
Hyde Park ♦, Eng., U.K.	260	51.20 N	0.10 W
Hyde Park ♦, N.Y., U.S.	284a	43.06 N	79.01 W
Hyder	182	55.55 N	130.01 W
Hyderābād, India	122	17.23 N	78.29 E
Hyderābād, Pāk.	120	25.22 N	68.22 E
Hydetown	214	41.40 N	79.44 W
Hydra → Ídhra I	38	37.20 N	23.32 E
Hydraulic	182	52.36 N	121.42 W
Hydro	196	35.21 N	98.22 W
Hydrographers Passage ⫶	166	20.45 S	150.15 E
Hyères	62	43.07 N	6.07 E
Hyères, Îles d' II	62	43.00 N	6.20 E
Hyères-Plage	62	43.06 N	6.10 E
Hyesan	98	41.23 N	128.12 E
Hyland ≃	180	59.50 N	128.10 W
Hylestad	26	59.05 N	7.32 E
Hyllekrog I	41	54.36 N	11.30 E
Hyllinge, Dan.	41	55.06 N	11.37 E
Hyllinge, Sve.	41	56.06 N	12.51 E
Hyllstofta	41	56.08 N	13.16 E
Hyltebruk	26	57.00 N	13.14 E
Hymera	194	39.11 N	87.18 W
Hyndburn ≃⁸	262	53.45 N	2.23 W
Hyndman	188	39.49 N	78.43 W
Hyndman Peak ▲	204	43.45 N	114.08 W
Hyne Field ⋋²	281	42.34 N	83.47 W
Hynish Bay ⊂	46	56.28 N	6.50 W
Hyōgo ⊞⁵	96	35.00 N	135.00 E
Hyōgo □⁵	270	34.39 N	135.10 E
Hyŏn-ni	98	37.57 N	128.20 E
Hyōno-sen ▲	96	35.21 N	134.31 E
Hyōnosen-Ushiroyama-Nagisan-kokutei-kōen ♦	96	35.15 N	134.30 E
Hyōpch'on → Hyrum	200	41.38 N	111.51 W
Hyrynsalmi	26	64.40 N	28.32 E
Hysham	202	46.17 N	107.14 W
Hythe, Ab., Can.	182	55.20 N	119.33 W
Hythe, Eng., U.K.	42	51.05 N	1.05 E
Hythe, Eng., U.K.	42	50.51 N	1.24 W
Hythe End	260	51.27 N	0.32 W
Hyūga	96	32.25 N	131.38 E
Hyūga-nada ⊤²	92	32.00 N	131.35 E
Hyvinge → Hyvinkää	26	60.38 N	24.52 E
Hyvinkää	26	60.38 N	24.52 E

I

Nome	Página	Lat.	Long.
Iacanga	255	21.54 S	49.01 W
Iaciara	255	14.09 S	46.40 W
Iaco (Yaco) ≃	248	9.03 S	68.34 W
Iaeger	192	37.27 N	81.48 W
Iago	222	29.15 N	95.58 W
Iakora	157c	23.06 S	46.40 E
Ialomita □⁶	38	44.40 N	27.20 E
Ialomita ≃	38	44.42 N	27.51 E
Ialomita, Balta ⫷	38	44.30 N	28.00 E
Ialomita, Braţul ≃¹	38	44.38 N	29.10 E
Ianaivo ▲	157c	22.56 S	46.54 E
Ianakafy	157c	24.34 S	46.24 E
Ianapera ≃	157c	23.09 S	45.10 E
Iancanga ≃	255	21.50 S	50.01 W
Iapó, Monte ▲	287b	24.46 S	50.24 W
Iapó ≃	287b	24.46 S	50.24 W
Iaşi	38	47.10 N	27.35 E
Iaşi □⁶	38	47.20 N	27.20 E
Ib ≃	124	21.57 N	83.55 E
Iba	115a	15.20 N	119.59 E
Ibadan	154	7.17 N	3.30 E
Ibagué	246	4.27 N	75.14 W
Ibaiti	255	23.51 S	50.11 W
Ibajay	115a	11.49 N	122.10 E
Ibănesti	38	46.22 N	27.27 E
Ibapah	200	40.02 N	113.59 W
Ibaraki, Ōsaka, Nihon	270	34.49 N	135.34 E
Ibaraki, Ibaraki, Nihon	94	36.17 N	140.24 E
Ibaraki □⁵	94	36.10 N	140.25 E
Ibaraki-daimon	94	36.17 N	140.21 E
Ibarra	248	0.21 N	78.07 W
Ibatuba	255	19.30 S	42.39 W
Ibb	140	14.01 N	44.11 E
Ibba	148	4.48 N	29.06 E
Ibba ≃	148	7.08 N	28.01 E
Ibbenbüren	56	52.16 N	7.43 E
Ibembo	148	2.38 N	23.37 E
Ibenga ≃	152	1.45 N	17.41 E
Iberá, Esteros del ⫶	252	28.30 S	57.09 W
Ibérica, Cordillera ⱥ	34	41.00 N	2.30 W
Iberia, La., Perú	248	14.20 S	75.30 W
Iberia, La., S.S.S.R.	76	56.52 N	26.59 E
Ibestad	24	68.48 N	17.10 E
Ibeto	154	10.29 N	5.09 E
Ibi	150	8.12 N	9.45 E
Ibi ≃	94	35.03 N	136.42 E
Ibiá	255	19.29 S	46.32 W
Ibiapaba, Serra da ⱥ	250	4.00 S	41.00 W
Ibiapina	250	3.55 S	40.54 W
Ibiara	250	7.30 S	38.25 W
Ibicaraí	255	14.51 S	39.36 W
Ibicuí	255	14.51 S	39.59 W
Ibicuí ≃	252	29.25 S	56.47 W
Ibicuicito, Arroyo ≃	258	33.49 S	58.49 W
Ibicuy	258	33.44 S	59.10 W
Ibigawa	94	35.29 N	136.34 E
Ibipetuba	250	11.00 S	44.32 W
Ibipira	250	6.31 S	44.38 W
Ibiquera	255	12.38 S	40.57 W
Ibiraci	255	20.28 S	47.08 W
Ibiraçu	255	19.50 S	40.22 W
Ibirama	252	27.04 S	49.31 W
Ibirapuã	255	17.39 S	40.07 W
Ibirapuera ⬥⁸	287b	23.37 S	46.40 W
Ibirapuera, Parque ♦	287b	23.35 S	46.39 W
Ibirapuitã ≃	252	29.22 S	55.57 W
Ibirataia	255	14.04 S	39.38 W
Ibiri	154	4.56 S	32.33 E
Ibirubá	252	28.38 S	53.06 W
Ibitiara	255	12.39 S	42.13 W
Ibitiguaia	255	21.57 S	43.25 W
Ibitinga	255	21.45 S	48.49 W
Ibitiúra De Minas	256	22.04 S	46.26 W
Ibituporanga	256	22.45 S	43.47 W
Ibiúna	256	23.39 S	47.13 W
Ibiza → Eivissa I	34	39.00 N	1.25 E
Iblei, Monti ⱥ	70	37.10 N	14.50 E
Ibnahs	142	30.34 N	31.07 E
Ibn Hâni', Ra's ⊱	130	35.35 N	35.43 E
Ibn Sarrār, Bi'r ⊤⁴	144	19.30 N	42.41 E
Ibo	154	12.20 S	40.35 E
Ibo ≃	96	34.46 N	134.35 E
Iboando	154	2.38 S	32.40 E
Ibonma	164	3.28 S	133.28 E
Ibor ≃	34	39.49 N	5.33 W
Ibotirama	255	12.11 S	43.13 W
Iboundji, Mont ▲	152	1.08 S	11.48 E
Ibrah, Wādī V	140	10.36 N	24.58 E
Ibrahimiyah, Qārah al- ⱥ	142	29.10 N	31.10 E
Ibresi	80	55.18 N	47.03 E
'Ibrī	128	23.14 N	56.30 E
İbriktepe	130	41.00 N	26.30 E
Ibshān	142	31.19 N	30.41 E
Ibshawāy	142	29.22 N	30.41 E
Ibstock	42	52.42 N	1.23 W
Ibta'	132	32.47 N	36.09 E
Ibu	174m	26.45 N	128.19 E
Ibuki	96	34.08 N	133.32 E
Ibuki-jima I	96	34.08 N	133.38 E
Ibuki-sanchi ⱥ	94	35.35 N	136.18 E
Ibuki-yama ▲	94	35.25 N	136.24 E
Iburg	52	52.09 N	8.02 E
Ibusuki	92	31.16 N	130.39 E
Ibwe Munyama	154	16.09 S	28.34 E
Ibychen, gora ▲	89	49.48 N	129.38 E
Ica	248	14.04 S	75.42 W
Ica ≃	248	14.25 S	75.30 W
Ica □⁵, Perú	248	14.20 S	75.30 W
Içá (Putumayo) ≃, S.A.	248	3.07 S	67.58 W
Icabarú	246	4.45 N	62.15 W
Icadambanauan Island I	116	10.49 N	119.38 E
Icamaquã ≃	252	28.34 S	56.00 W
Içana	246	0.21 N	67.19 W
Içana (Isana) ≃	246	0.26 N	67.19 W
Icaño, Arg.	252	28.54 S	65.19 W
Icaño, Arg.	252	28.41 S	62.54 W
Icatu	250	2.46 S	44.04 W
Icatuaçu	256	23.44 S	46.24 W
Iceberg Pass ⌙	196	40.25 N	105.45 W
Ice House Reservoir ⊜¹	226	38.49 N	120.23 W
İçel (Mersin)	130	36.48 N	34.38 E
İçel □⁴	130	36.45 N	34.00 E
Iceland (Ísland) □¹, Europe	22	65.00 N	18.00 W
Iceland (Ísland) □¹, Europe	24a	65.00 N	18.00 W
Iceland Basin ⫽¹	10	62.00 N	19.00 W
Ice Mountain ▲	182	54.25 N	121.08 W
Ibera	88	58.32 N	109.47 E
Ichaikaronji	122	16.42 N	74.28 E
Ichāmati ≃, Asia	126	22.40 N	88.57 E
Ichāmati ≃, Bngl.	126	24.00 N	89.15 E
Ichang → Yichang	102	30.42 N	111.17 E
Ichawaynochaway Creek ≃	192	31.10 N	84.28 W
Ichchāpuram	124	19.07 N	84.42 E
Ichenbuig	56	50.49 N	11.50 E
Ichibusa-yama ▲	96	32.20 N	131.05 E
Ichihara	270	35.31 N	140.05 E
Ichikai	94	36.32 N	140.06 E
Ichikawa, Hyōgo, Nihon	96	35.00 N	134.49 E
Ichikawa, Chiba, Nihon	270	35.44 N	139.55 E
Ichikawa-daimon	94	35.34 N	138.33 E
Ichilo ≃	248	15.57 S	64.42 W
Ichinohe	92	40.13 N	141.17 E
Ichinomiya, Nihon	94	34.18 N	131.32 E
Ichinomiya, Nihon	94	35.18 N	136.48 E
Ichinomiya, Nihon	94	35.22 N	140.22 E
Ichinoseki	92	38.55 N	141.08 E
Ichinotani	96	34.39 N	135.09 E
Ich'ŏn, C.M.I.K.	98	38.28 N	127.14 E
Ich'ŏn, Taehan	98	37.17 N	127.27 E
Ichŏngdŏk	98	37.40 N	127.32 E
Ich'ŏngni	98	38.47 N	125.28 E
Ich'on-si	98	37.14 N	127.27 E
Ichtegem	50	51.05 N	3.00 E
Ichtershausen	56	50.52 N	10.58 E
İçmeler	130	36.49 N	28.56 E
Icó	250	6.24 S	38.51 W
Icoca ≃	152	6.11 S	16.19 E
Icoaraci	250	1.18 S	48.28 W

ENGLISH — Name | Page | Lat.°′ | Long.°′ · DEUTSCH — Name | Seite | Breite°′ | Länge°′ E = Ost

Name	Page	Lat.°′	Long.°′
Icy Bay ⊂	**180**	60.00 N	141.15 W
Icy Cape ›	**180**	70.20 N	161.52 W
Icy Strait ⋈	**180**	58.18 N	135.30 W
Ida	**216**	41.54 N	83.34 W
Ida, Mount ∧, Austl.	**162**	29.14 S	120.25 E
Ida, Mount ∧, Jam.	**241q**	17.58 N	77.43 W
Idabel	**194**	33.53 N	94.49 W
Idaga Hamus	**144**	14.12 N	39.48 E
Ida Grove	**198**	42.20 N	95.28 W
Idah	**150**	7.07 N	6.43 E
Idaho □3, U.S.	**178**	45.00 N	115.00 W
Idaho □3, U.S.	**202**	45.00 N	115.00 W
Idaho City	**202**	43.49 N	115.50 W
Idaho Falls	**202**	43.28 N	112.02 W
Idaho National Engineering Laboratory ☉3	**202**	43.40 N	112.45 W
Idaho Springs	**200**	39.44 N	105.00 W
Idalou	**196**	33.39 N	101.40 W
Idanha-a-Nova	**34**	39.55 N	7.14 W
Idāppādi	**122**	11.35 N	77.51 E
Idar	**120**	23.50 N	73.00 E
Idarkopf ∧	**56**	49.51 N	7.16 E
Idar-Oberstein	**56**	49.42 N	7.19 E
Idarwald ⊸3	**56**	49.20 N	7.15 E
Idaville, In., U.S.	**216**	40.45 N	86.38 W
Idaville, Or., U.S.	**224**	45.30 N	123.51 W
Iddo ⊸8	**273a**	6.28 N	3.23 E
Ide	**96**	34.47 N	135.49 E
Idel'	**24**	64.08 N	34.14 E
Idelès	**148**	23.58 N	5.53 E
Idemba	**152**	2.38 S	11.38 E
Iden	**54**	52.46 N	11.55 E
Ider	**88**	48.13 N	97.23 E
Iderijn ≃	**88**	49.16 N	100.41 E
Idermeg	**88**	47.40 N	111.05 E
Idfīnā	**142**	31.18 N	30.31 E
Idfū	**140**	24.58 N	32.52 E
Ídhi Óros ∧	**38**	35.18 N	24.43 E
Ídhra	**38**	37.20 N	23.29 E
Ídhra I	**38**	37.20 N	23.32 E
Idi	**114**	4.57 N	97.46 E
Idice ≃	**64**	44.35 N	11.49 E
Idi-cut	**114**	4.59 N	97.42 E
Ididole	**144**	5.53 N	43.36 E
Idifina Barrage ⊸6	**142**	31.17 N	30.31 E
İdil	**130**	37.21 N	41.54 E
Idimu	**273a**	6.35 N	3.17 E
Idio	**116**	11.37 N	122.06 E
Idiofa	**152**	5.02 S	19.36 E
Iditarod ≃	**180**	63.02 N	158.58 W
Idjwi, Île I	**154**	2.09 S	29.04 E
Idkerberget	**40**	60.23 N	15.14 E
Idkū	**142**	31.18 N	30.18 E
Idkū, Buḥayrat ⊜	**142**	31.16 N	30.17 E
Idle Hill	**260**	51.15 N	0.08 E
Idlib	**130**	35.55 N	36.38 E
Idlib □8	**130**	35.50 N	36.40 E
Idmū	**142**	28.09 N	30.41 E
Idnah	**132**	31.34 N	34.59 E
Idodi	**154**	7.47 S	35.11 E
Ídolo, Isla del I	**234**	21.25 N	97.27 W
Idomogu	**273a**	6.43 N	3.30 E
Idracowra	**162**	25.00 S	133.47 E
Idre	**26**	61.52 N	12.43 E
Idria	**226**	36.25 N	120.40 W
Idrica	**76**	56.21 N	28.53 E
Idrigill Point ›	**46**	57.20 N	6.35 W
Idrija	**36**	46.00 N	14.01 E
Idrijca ≃	**64**	46.09 N	13.45 E
Idrinskoje	**86**	54.21 N	92.07 E
Idro	**64**	45.44 N	10.29 E
Idro, Lago d' ⊜	**64**	45.47 N	10.30 E
Idroscalo ⊜	**266b**	45.28 N	9.18 E
Idstedt	**41**	54.35 N	9.31 E
Idstein	**56**	50.13 N	8.16 E
Idutywa	**158**	32.02 S	28.16 E
Idyllwild	**204**	33.45 N	116.43 W
Idylside	**216**	41.31 N	88.07 W
Idylwood	**284c**	38.54 N	77.12 W
Idževan	**84**	40.53 N	45.07 E
Ie	**174m**	26.42 N	127.48 E
Iecava	**76**	56.36 N	24.12 E
Iecava ≃	**76**	56.41 N	23.42 E
Ielsi	**66**	41.30 N	14.48 E
Ienne	**66**	41.53 N	13.10 E
Iepê	**255**	22.40 S	51.05 W
Ieper (Ypres)	**50**	50.51 N	2.53 E
Ierápetra	**38**	35.00 N	25.45 E
Ierisós	**38**	40.24 N	23.52 E
Ierzu	**71**	39.47 N	9.31 E
Ieshima	**96**	34.40 N	134.32 E
Ie-shima I	**174m**	26.43 N	127.47 E
Ieshima-shotō II	**96**	34.40 N	134.32 E
Iesolo	**64**	45.32 N	12.38 E
Ie-suidō ⋈	**174m**	26.42 N	127.51 E
If, Château d' ⊥	**62**	43.17 N	5.19 E
Ifakara	**154**	8.08 S	36.41 E
Ifako	**273a**	6.39 N	3.20 E
Ifalik I1	**108**	7.15 N	144.27 E
Ifanadiana	**157b**	21.19 S	47.39 E
Ife	**150**	7.30 N	4.30 E
Iferouâne	**150**	19.04 N	8.24 E
Iferten → Yverdon	**58**	46.47 N	6.39 E
Iffezheim	**56**	48.49 N	8.08 E
Ifni □9	**148**	29.15 N	10.08 W
Ifôghas, Adrar des ⋏	**150**	20.00 N	2.00 E
Ifon	**150**	6.58 N	5.45 E
Ifould Lake ⊜	**162**	30.53 S	132.09 E
Ifrane	**148**	33.32 N	5.06 W
Ifrane □4	**148**	33.15 N	5.05 W
Ifta	**56**	51.04 N	10.11 E
Ifugao □4	**116**	16.45 N	121.15 E
Iga	**94**	34.49 N	136.13 E
Iga ≃	**94**	34.45 N	136.01 E
Igaci	**250**	9.33 S	36.38 W
Igal	**30**	46.31 N	17.55 E
Igalula, Tan.	**154**	5.14 S	33.00 E
Igalula, Tan.	**154**	5.38 S	32.38 E
Igan	**112**	2.49 N	111.43 E
Igan ≃	**112**	2.51 N	111.39 E
Iganga	**154**	0.37 N	33.29 E
Iganmu ⊸8	**273a**	6.29 N	3.22 E
Iganna	**150**	7.59 N	3.14 E
Igaporã	**255**	13.46 S	42.43 W
Igara	**250**	10.24 S	40.07 W
Igaraí	**256**	21.25 S	46.49 W
Igara Paraná ≃	**246**	2.09 S	71.47 W
Igarapé-Açu	**250**	1.07 S	47.37 W
Igarapé Grande	**250**	4.41 S	44.58 W
Igarapé-Mirí	**250**	1.59 S	48.58 W
Igaratá	**256**	23.12 S	46.07 W
Igarka	**74**	67.28 N	86.35 E
Igarra	**150**	7.18 N	6.07 E
Igarukiro	**154**	3.08 S	33.31 E
Igatpuri	**122**	19.42 N	73.33 E
Igaun	**273a**	6.42 N	3.23 E
Igawa	**154**	8.35 S	34.28 E
Igbaja	**150**	8.23 N	4.52 E
Igbobi	**273a**	6.32 N	3.22 E
Igboho	**150**	8.51 N	3.45 E
Igbologun	**273a**	6.25 N	3.20 E
Igbo-Ora	**150**	7.26 N	3.17 E
Igbor	**150**	7.27 N	8.34 E
Igdir, Īrān	**84**	39.20 N	47.30 E
Iğdır, Tür.	**84**	39.55 N	44.02 E
Iğdır, Tür.	**130**	40.16 N	35.38 E
Iğdır, Tür.	**130**	41.14 N	33.07 E
Igdy	**128**	39.54 N	56.54 E
Igea Marina	**66**	44.08 N	12.29 E
Igel	**56**	49.42 N	6.32 E
Igelfors	**40**	58.51 N	15.41 E
Igelsberg	**58**	48.32 N	8.26 E
Igel'vejem ≃	**180**	65.40 N	172.50 W
Igersheim	**56**	49.29 N	9.49 E
Iggensbach	**60**	48.44 N	13.08 E
Iggesund	**26**	61.38 N	17.04 E
Igharghar, Oued V, Afr.	**148**	20.25 N	6.10 E
Igharghar, Oued V, Alg.	**148**	28.03 N	6.15 E
Ightham	**260**	51.17 N	0.17 E
Ightham Mote ⊥	**260**	51.15 N	0.16 E
Igikpak, Mount ∧	**180**	67.25 N	154.58 W
Igirma	**88**	56.59 N	103.37 E
Igiugig	**180**	59.20 N	155.55 W
Iglau → Jihlava	**30**	49.24 N	15.36 E
Iglesia	**252**	30.24 S	69.13 W
Iglesias	**71**	39.19 N	8.32 E
Iglesiente ⊸1	**71**	39.18 N	8.40 E
Igli	**148**	30.25 N	2.12 W
Iglino	**86**	54.50 N	56.26 E
Igloolik	**176**	69.24 N	81.49 W
Iglovo	**82**	55.47 N	36.40 E
Igls	**64**	47.14 N	11.25 E
Ignacej	**78**	47.41 N	28.40 E
Ignacio, Ca., U.S.	**226**	38.05 N	122.32 W
Ignacio, Co., U.S.	**200**	37.06 N	107.37 W
Ignacio de la Llave	**234**	18.43 N	95.59 W
Ignacio Zaragoza, Méx.	**232**	29.35 N	107.30 W
Ignacio Zaragoza, Méx.	**234**	23.55 N	103.42 W
Ignalina	**76**	55.21 N	26.10 E
Ignašino	**89**	53.28 N	122.24 E
Ignatjevcy	**80**	57.32 N	51.39 E
Ignatovka	**80**	53.57 N	47.38 E
Ignatovo	**82**	56.10 N	37.32 E
İğneada	**130**	41.52 N	27.58 E
İğneada Burnu ›	**130**	41.54 N	28.03 E
Igney	**58**	48.17 N	6.24 E
Ignon ≃	**58**	47.31 N	5.10 E
Igny	**261**	48.45 N	2.14 E
Igodovo	**80**	58.01 N	42.21 E
Igombe ≃	**154**	4.38 S	31.40 E
Igoumenítsa	**38**	39.30 N	20.16 E
Igra	**80**	57.33 N	53.04 E
Igreja Nova	**250**	10.07 S	36.39 W
Iguaçu ≃, Bra.	**287a**	22.45 S	43.14 W
Iguaçu ≃, S.A.	**252**	25.36 S	54.36 W
Iguaçu, Saltos do ⌞	**252**	25.41 S	54.26 W
Iguaí	**255**	14.45 S	40.04 W
Iguala	**234**	18.21 N	99.32 W
Igualada	**34**	41.35 N	1.38 E
Iguana ≃	**246**	7.54 N	65.46 W
Iguape	**252**	24.43 S	47.33 W
Iguará ≃	**250**	3.28 S	43.55 W
Iguaraçu	**255**	23.11 S	51.50 W
Iguassu Falls → Iguaçu, Saltos do ⌞	**252**	25.41 S	54.26 W
Iguatemi	**255**	23.40 S	54.34 W
Iguatemi ≃	**255**	23.55 S	54.10 W
Iguatu	**250**	6.22 S	39.18 W
Iguazú (Iguaçu), Parque Nacional ♦	**252**	25.35 S	54.20 W
Iguéla	**152**	1.55 S	9.19 E
Iguéla, Lagune ⊂	**152**	1.55 S	9.25 E
Iguetti, Sebkhet ≚	**148**	25.05 N	9.50 W
Iguîdi, 'Erg ⍊8	**148**	26.35 N	5.40 W
Iguig	**116**	17.45 N	121.44 E
Igumale	**150**	6.49 N	7.59 E
Igumnovo	**82**	55.37 N	38.18 E
Igvak, Cape ›	**180**	57.26 N	156.00 W
Igžej	**88**	53.59 N	103.10 E
Ihavandiffulu Atoll I1	**122**	7.00 N	72.55 E
Iheya-shima I	**93b**	27.04 N	127.58 E
Ihiala	**150**	5.51 N	6.51 E
Ihirène, Oued V	**148**	20.25 N	4.35 E
Ihle ≃	**54**	52.17 N	11.52 E
Ihlienworth	**52**	53.44 N	8.55 E
Ihlow	**52**	53.25 N	7.27 E
Ihmert	**56**	51.20 N	7.44 E
Ihnāsiyat al-Madīnah	**142**	29.05 N	30.56 E
Ihorombe	**157b**	23.00 S	47.33 E
Ihosy	**157b**	22.24 S	46.08 E
Ihosy ≃	**157b**	21.44 S	45.53 E
Ihotry, Lac ⊜	**157b**	21.56 S	43.41 E
Ihringen	**58**	48.02 N	7.39 E
Ihrlerstein	**60**	48.56 N	11.52 E
İhsangazi	**130**	41.11 N	33.33 E
Ih Tal	**89**	43.13 N	122.15 E
Ihtiman	**38**	42.26 N	23.49 E
Ihu	**164**	7.55 S	145.25 E
Ihugh	**150**	7.02 N	9.00 E
Ihwah	**142**	29.03 N	31.00 E
Ii	**26**	65.19 N	25.22 E
Iida	**94**	35.31 N	137.50 E
Iidaan	**144**	6.06 N	48.59 E
Iijima	**94**	35.40 N	137.56 E
Iijoki ≃	**24**	65.20 N	25.17 E
Iiktu, gora ∧	**86**	49.51 N	87.40 E
Iinan	**94**	34.27 N	136.24 E
Iinashi ≃	**96**	35.27 N	133.13 E
Iioka	**94**	35.42 N	140.43 E
Iisaku	**76**	59.06 N	27.19 E
Iisalmi	**26**	63.34 N	27.11 E
Iisvesi	**26**	62.40 N	27.02 E
Iitaka	**94**	34.26 N	136.21 E
Iittala	**26**	61.04 N	24.10 E
Iivaara ∧2	**26**	65.47 N	29.40 E
Iiyama	**94**	36.51 N	138.22 E
Iizuka	**96**	33.38 N	130.41 E
Ij ≃	**88**	52.34 N	96.10 E
Ija ≃	**88**	55.05 N	101.05 E
Ijâfene ⊸2	**134**	20.30 N	8.00 W
Ijaiye	**273a**	6.40 N	3.18 E
Ijaji	**144**	8.59 N	37.13 E
Ijara	**154**	1.36 S	40.31 E
Ijebu-Igbo	**150**	6.56 N	4.01 E
Ijebu-Ode	**150**	6.50 N	3.56 E
Ijesa-Tedo	**273a**	6.30 N	3.19 E
Ijin	**98**	42.05 N	130.08 E
Ijira	**94**	35.31 N	136.44 E
IJmuiden	**52**	52.27 N	4.36 E
IJssel ≃	**52**	52.35 N	5.50 E
IJsselmeer (Zuiderzee) ⍑2	**52**	52.45 N	5.25 E
IJsselmuiden	**52**	52.34 N	5.56 E
IJsselstein	**52**	52.02 N	5.03 E
Ijuí	**252**	28.23 S	53.55 W
Ijuí ≃	**252**	27.58 S	55.20 W
Iju Junction	**273a**	6.40 N	3.19 E
Ijuw	**174b**	0.30 S	166.57 E
Iju Water Works ☉3	**273a**	6.40 N	3.20 E
IJzendijke	**52**	51.19 N	3.38 E
IJzer (Yser) ≃	**50**	51.09 N	2.43 E
Ik ≃	**80**	55.55 N	52.36 E
Ika	**88**	59.18 N	106.12 E
Ikaalinen	**26**	61.46 N	23.03 E
Ikaho	**94**	36.30 N	138.55 E
Ikalamavony	**157b**	21.09 S	46.35 E
Ikali	**152**	2.02 S	21.02 E
Ikalou	**152**	4.03 S	11.48 E
Ikamatua	**172**	42.16 S	171.41 E
Ikamba	**273b**	4.22 S	15.16 E
Ikang	**150**	4.50 N	8.32 E
Ikara	**150**	11.12 N	8.15 E
Ikare	**150**	7.32 N	5.45 E
Ikaría I	**38**	37.41 N	26.20 E
Ikari-dam ⊸6	**94**	36.52 N	139.42 E
Ikari-ko ⊜	**94**	36.56 N	139.41 E
Ikaruga	**96**	34.36 N	135.44 E
Ikast	**41**	56.08 N	9.10 E
Ikatan	**180**	54.45 N	163.19 W
Ikatskij chrebet ⋏	**88**	54.00 N	111.00 E
Ikawa	**94**	35.13 N	138.15 E
Ikawa-dam ⊸6	**94**	35.12 N	138.13 E
Ikawhenua Range ⋏	**172**	38.20 S	176.56 E
Ikazaki	**96**	33.32 N	132.39 E
Ikeda, Nihon	**92a**	42.55 N	143.27 E
Ikeda, Nihon	**94**	35.53 N	136.21 E
Ikeda, Nihon	**94**	35.26 N	136.34 E
Ikeda, Nihon	**94**	36.25 N	137.53 E
Ikeda, Nihon	**96**	34.49 N	135.25 E
Ikeda, Nihon	**96**	34.01 N	133.48 E
Ikegawa	**96**	33.36 N	133.11 E
Ikej	**88**	54.12 N	100.04 E
Ikeja	**150**	6.36 N	3.21 E
Ikeja □8	**273a**	6.30 N	3.25 E
Ikela	**152**	1.11 S	23.16 E
Ikélemba	**152**	1.14 N	16.31 E
Ikelemba ≃	**152**	0.07 N	18.17 E
Ikema-jima I	**175d**	24.56 N	125.16 E
Ikerre	**150**	7.31 N	5.14 E
Ike-shima I	**174m**	26.23 N	128.00 E
Ikeura	**270**	34.30 N	135.25 E
Iki I	**92**	33.47 N	129.43 E
Iki-Burul	**80**	45.49 N	44.39 E
Ikimba, Lake ⊜	**154**	1.28 S	31.30 E
Īkinjī Maryūt	**142**	31.00 N	29.45 E
Ikire	**150**	7.23 N	4.12 E
Ikirun	**150**	7.55 N	4.41 E
İkizce	**130**	39.36 N	32.40 E
İkizdere, Tür.	**84**	40.47 N	40.33 E
İkizdere, Tür.	**130**	40.47 N	40.33 E
Iko	**152**	0.35 S	16.01 E
Ikole	**150**	7.49 N	5.30 E
Ikolik, Cape ›	**180**	57.17 N	154.48 W
Ikom	**150**	5.58 N	8.42 E
Ikoma, Nihon	**96**	34.41 N	135.42 E
Ikoma, Tan.	**154**	2.04 S	34.37 E
Ikoma-sanchi ⋏	**270**	34.40 N	135.40 E
Ikoma-tunnel ⊸5	**270**	34.41 N	135.41 E
Ikoma-yama ∧	**270**	34.40 N	135.41 E
Ikon-Chal'	**84**	44.18 N	41.55 E
Ikopa ≃	**157b**	17.01 S	46.45 E
Ikorec ≃	**78**	50.58 N	39.45 E
Ikorodu	**150**	6.37 N	3.31 E
Ikot Ekpene	**150**	5.12 N	7.40 E
Ikoy ≃	**152**	0.53 S	10.36 E
Ikoyi ⊸8	**273a**	6.27 N	3.26 E
Ikoyi Island I	**273a**	6.27 N	3.26 E
Ikoyi Prison ☉	**273a**	6.25 N	3.25 E
Ikozi	**154**	2.32 S	27.37 E
Ikpikpuk ≃	**180**	70.50 N	154.25 W
Ikra	**126**	23.42 N	87.07 E
Ikr'anoje	**80**	46.06 N	47.45 E
Ikrāsh	**142**	30.45 N	31.30 E
Ikša	**82**	56.10 N	37.31 E
Iksa ≃	**86**	57.48 N	82.36 E
Ikti, Cape ›	**180**	56.00 N	158.30 W
Ikuata	**273a**	6.25 N	3.22 E
Ikuchi-shima I	**96**	34.17 N	133.07 E
Ikuji-hana ›	**94**	36.54 N	137.25 E
Ikuktlitlig Mountain ∧	**180**	59.16 N	161.27 W
Ikungu	**154**	1.34 S	33.40 E
Ikuno	**96**	35.10 N	134.48 E
Ikuno ⊸8	**270**	34.39 N	135.34 E
Ikurangi, Mount ∧2	**174k**	21.13 S	159.45 W
Ikusaka	**94**	36.25 N	137.56 E
Ikusu ≃	**273b**	4.24 S	15.14 E
Ikuta	**268**	35.36 N	139.32 E
Ikva ≃, Magy.	**61**	47.42 N	16.58 E
Ikva ≃, S.S.S.R.	**78**	50.33 N	25.24 E
Ikwah	**142**	30.41 N	31.28 E
Ila, Nig.	**150**	8.01 N	4.55 E
Ila, Zaïre	**152**	2.53 S	21.05 E
Ilabaya	**248**	17.25 S	70.31 W
Ilacaon Point ›	**116**	11.00 N	123.12 E
Ilagala	**154**	5.12 S	29.50 E
Ilagan	**116**	17.10 N	121.54 E
Ilagan ≃	**116**	17.09 N	121.54 E
Ilaiyānkudi	**122**	9.38 N	78.38 E
Ilaka, Madag.	**157b**	19.33 S	48.52 E
Ilaka, Madag.	**157b**	20.20 S	47.09 E
Īlām, Īrān	**128**	33.38 N	46.26 E
Ilām, Nepāl	**124**	26.55 N	87.56 E
Īlām □4	**128**	33.15 N	46.45 E
Ilam → Sri Lanka □1	**122**	7.00 N	81.00 E
Ilām Bāzār	**126**	23.38 N	87.32 E
Ilan	**100**	24.46 N	121.45 E
Ilan ≃	**100**	24.43 N	121.49 E
Ilanskij	**88**	56.14 N	96.03 E
Ilanz	**58**	46.46 N	9.12 E
Ilara	**273a**	6.42 N	3.27 E
Ilaro	**150**	6.53 N	3.03 E
Ilasco	**219**	39.40 N	91.18 W
Iława	**30**	53.37 N	19.33 E
Ilawe-Ekiti	**150**	7.37 N	5.06 E
Ilay	**58**	46.37 N	5.53 E
Ilbenge	**74**	62.49 N	124.24 E
Ilberstedt	**54**	51.48 N	11.40 E
Il Catalano	**71**	39.53 N	8.17 E
Ilchester, Eng., U.K.	**42**	51.01 N	2.41 W
Ilchester, Md., U.S.	**284b**	39.15 N	76.45 W
Ildefonso, Islas II	**254**	55.44 S	69.26 W
Île-à-la-Crosse	**184**	55.27 N	107.53 W
Île-à-la-Crosse, Lac ⊜	**184**	55.40 N	107.45 W
Ilebo (Port-Francqui)	**152**	4.19 S	20.35 E
Île-Cadieux	**275a**	45.25 N	74.01 W
Île-de-France □9	**50**	49.00 N	2.20 E
Île-de-Montréal □6	**206**	45.30 N	73.40 W
Île-Jésus □6	**206**	45.35 N	73.45 W
Ilek	**80**	51.30 N	53.22 E
Ilek ≃	**72**	51.30 N	53.20 E
Ilen ≃	**48**	51.33 N	9.19 W
Île-Perrot	**206**	45.23 N	73.57 W
Ileret	**154**	4.19 N	36.13 E
Îles, Grand lac des ⊜	**206**	46.43 N	73.30 W
Îles, Lac des ⊜, P.Q., Can.	**206**	46.06 N	74.02 W
Îles, Lac des ⊜, Sk., Can.	**184**	54.26 N	109.25 W
Ilesha	**150**	7.38 N	4.45 E
Ilesha Ibarida	**150**	8.56 N	3.25 E
Ilet' ≃	**80**	55.56 N	48.14 E
Ilevskij Pogost	**24**	60.41 N	43.46 E
Ileza	**24**	60.43 N	43.54 E
Ilfeld	**54**	51.34 N	10.47 E
Ilford, Austl.	**170**	32.58 S	149.51 E
Ilford, Mb., Can.	**184**	56.04 N	95.35 W
Ilford ⊸8	**260**	51.33 N	0.05 E
Ilfov □6	**38**	44.30 N	26.15 E
Ilfracombe, Austl.	**166**	23.30 S	144.30 E
Ilfracombe, Eng., U.K.	**42**	51.13 N	4.08 W
Il Fuorn	**58**	46.40 N	10.12 E
Ilga ≃	**88**	55.00 N	105.04 E
Ilgaz	**130**	40.56 N	33.38 E
Ilgaz Dağları ⋏	**130**	41.00 N	33.35 E
Ilgın	**130**	38.17 N	31.55 E
Ilha ⊸8	**256**	23.00 S	43.33 W
Ilhabela	**256**	23.47 S	45.21 W
Ilha das Flôres	**250**	10.27 S	36.33 W
Ilha Grande	**246**	0.27 S	65.02 W
Ilha Grande, Baía da ⊂	**256**	23.09 S	44.30 W
Ilhas, Cachoeira das ⌞	**250**	1.03 S	57.33 W
Ilhavo	**34**	40.36 N	8.40 W
Ilhea Point ›	**156**	23.25 S	14.27 E
Ilhéos → Ilhéus	**255**	14.49 S	39.02 W
Ilhéus	**255**	14.49 S	39.02 W
Ili ≃	**86**	45.24 N	74.02 E
Ilia	**38**	45.56 N	22.39 E
Iliamna	**180**	59.45 N	154.54 W
Iliamna Lake ⊜	**180**	59.30 N	155.00 W
Ilian, Mount ∧	**116**	10.26 N	119.33 E
Iliatenco	**234**	16.58 N	98.40 W
İliç	**130**	39.28 N	38.34 E
Ilıca, Tür.	**130**	39.52 N	27.46 E
Ilıca, Tür.	**130**	39.57 N	41.07 E
Ilicínea	**255**	20.56 S	45.50 W
Iliff	**198**	40.45 N	103.03 W
Iliff, Lake ⊜	**276**	41.02 N	74.43 W
Iligan	**116**	8.14 N	124.14 E
Iligan Bay ⊂	**116**	8.25 N	124.05 E
Ilijan	**116**	13.38 N	121.04 E
Ilijsk	**85**	43.53 N	77.10 E
Ilim ≃	**88**	57.38 N	102.34 E
Ilimsk	**88**	56.46 N	103.52 E
Ilin	**116**	12.15 N	121.02 E
Ilinge	**158**	31.59 S	27.02 E
Ilin Island I	**116**	12.14 N	121.05 E
Ilinka	**82**	54.04 N	38.12 E
Ilion	**210**	43.00 N	75.02 W
Ilio Point ›	**229a**	21.13 N	157.15 W
Ilioúpolis	**267c**	37.56 N	23.45 E
Ilir	**88**	55.13 N	100.40 E
Ilirska Bistrica	**36**	45.34 N	14.15 E
Ilisós ≃	**267c**	37.57 N	23.41 E
Ilizi	**148**	26.29 N	8.28 E
Ilja	**76**	54.25 N	27.18 E
Iljak	**86**	60.11 N	77.59 E
Iljič	**85**	40.50 N	68.27 E
Iljičevsk	**84**	39.33 N	44.58 E
Iljičovsk	**78**	46.18 N	30.39 E
Iljincy	**78**	49.07 N	29.12 E
Iljinka	**80**	48.32 N	41.05 E
Iljino	**76**	55.57 N	31.40 E
Iljinskij, S.S.S.R.	**24**	61.02 N	32.41 E
Iljinskij, S.S.S.R.	**86**	58.35 N	55.41 E
Iljinskij, S.S.S.R.	**88**	52.05 N	114.10 E
Iljinskij, S.S.S.R.	**89**	47.58 N	142.12 E
Iljinskij, S.S.S.R.	**265b**	55.37 N	38.06 E
Iljinskij Pogost	**82**	55.28 N	38.54 E
Iljinskoje, S.S.S.R.	**76**	56.58 N	37.11 E
Iljinskoje, S.S.S.R.	**76**	58.47 N	44.36 E
Iljinskoje, S.S.S.R.	**76**	53.14 N	35.26 E
Iljinskoje, S.S.S.R.	**76**	57.19 N	38.32 E
Iljinskoje, S.S.S.R.	**80**	56.29 N	52.49 E
Iljinskoje, S.S.S.R.	**82**	54.59 N	36.11 E
Iljinskoje, S.S.S.R.	**82**	56.34 N	35.57 E
Iljinskoje, S.S.S.R.	**265b**	55.46 N	37.15 E
Iljinskoje-Chovanskoje	**80**	56.58 N	39.46 E
Iljinsko-Podomskoje	**24**	61.08 N	47.56 E
Iljinsko-Zaborskoje	**80**	57.16 N	44.23 E
Iljiny gory ⋏2	**76**	56.34 N	34.12 E
Il'ka	**88**	51.43 N	108.32 E
Ilkal	**122**	15.58 N	76.08 E
Ilkeston	**42**	52.59 N	1.18 W
Il'kino	**80**	55.13 N	41.36 E
Ilkley	**44**	53.55 N	1.50 W
Ill ≃, Fr.	**58**	48.40 N	7.53 E
Ill ≃, Öst.	**58**	47.17 N	9.33 E
Illabot Creek ≃	**224**	48.29 N	121.30 W
Illampu, Nevado ∧	**248**	15.50 S	68.34 W
Illana Bay ⊂	**116**	7.25 N	123.45 E
Illapel	**252**	31.38 S	71.10 W
Illarionovo	**78**	48.25 N	35.16 E
Illasi	**64**	45.28 N	11.10 E
Illawarra, Lake ⊂	**170**	34.32 S	150.50 E
Illbillee, Mount ∧	**162**	27.02 S	132.30 E
Ille-et-Vilaine □5	**32**	48.10 N	1.30 W
Illéla	**150**	14.28 N	5.15 E
Iller ≃	**58**	48.23 N	9.58 E
Illertissen	**58**	48.13 N	10.06 E
Illescas, Esp.	**34**	40.07 N	3.50 W
Illescas, Méx.	**234**	23.13 N	102.07 W
Illfurth	**58**	47.40 N	7.16 E
Illhaeusern	**58**	48.11 N	7.26 E
Illi, Ba ≃	**146**	10.44 N	15.21 E
Illiers	**50**	48.18 N	1.15 E
Illimani, Nevado ∧	**248**	16.39 S	67.48 W
Illimo	**248**	6.28 S	79.51 W
Illingen	**56**	48.57 N	8.55 E
Illingworth	**262**	53.45 N	1.54 W
Illiniza ∧	**246**	0.40 S	78.42 W
Illinois □3, U.S.	**178**	40.00 N	89.00 W
Illinois □3, U.S.	**194**	40.00 N	89.00 W
Illinois ≃, U.S.	**194**	35.30 N	95.06 W
Illinois ≃, Co., U.S.	**200**	40.45 N	106.18 W
Illinois ≃, Il., U.S.	**194**	38.58 N	90.27 W
Illinois ≃, Or., U.S.	**202**	42.33 N	124.03 W
Illinois and Michigan Canal ≅	**278**	41.32 N	88.05 W
Illinois at Chicago, University of ☉2	**278**	41.52 N	87.39 W
Illinois Beach State Park ♦	**216**	42.26 N	87.48 W
Illinois Institute of Technology ☉2	**278**	41.50 N	87.38 W
Illinois Peak ∧	**202**	47.02 N	115.04 W
Illiopolis	**219**	39.51 N	89.14 W
Illkirch-Graffenstaden	**58**	48.32 N	7.43 E
Illminster	**42**	50.56 N	2.55 W
Illo ⊸	**150**	11.33 N	3.42 E
Illovo, S. Afr.	**158**	30.05 S	30.50 E
Illovo, S. Afr.	**273d**	26.08 S	28.03 E
Illzach	**58**	47.47 N	7.20 E
Ilm ≃, B.R.D.	**60**	48.49 N	11.45 E
Ilm ≃, D.D.R.	**54**	51.07 N	11.40 E
Ilmajoki	**26**	62.44 N	22.34 E
Il'men', ozero ⊜	**76**	58.17 N	31.20 E
Ilmenau	**54**	50.41 N	10.55 E
Ilmenau ≃	**54**	53.23 N	10.10 E
Il'menskij zapovednik ♦	**86**	55.16 N	60.17 E
Il'mino	**80**	53.47 N	45.40 E
Ilo	**248**	17.38 S	71.20 W
Ilobasco	**236**	13.51 N	88.51 W
Ilobu	**150**	7.51 N	4.30 E
Iloc Island I	**116**	11.18 N	119.41 E
Ilocos Norte □4	**116**	18.10 N	120.45 E
Ilocos Sur □4	**116**	17.05 N	120.35 E
Iloilo	**116**	10.42 N	122.34 E
Iloilo □4	**116**	11.00 N	122.35 E
Iloilo Strait ⋈	**116**	10.43 N	122.36 E
Ilomantsi	**26**	62.40 N	30.55 E
Ilondola Mission	**154**	10.42 S	31.47 E
Ilongero	**154**	4.40 S	34.52 E
Ilop	**164**	2.54 S	141.13 E
Ilopango, Lago de ⊜	**236**	13.40 N	89.03 W
Ilora	**150**	7.45 N	3.50 E
Ilorin	**150**	8.30 N	4.32 E
Iloron, Cerro ∧	**234**	20.57 N	104.22 W
Ilovajsk	**83**	47.56 N	38.13 E
Ilovatka	**80**	50.31 N	45.55 E
Ilovka	**78**	50.43 N	38.38 E
Ilovl'a	**80**	49.18 N	43.59 E
Ilovl'a ≃	**80**	49.14 N	43.54 E
Iłowa	**30**	51.30 N	15.12 E
Il Palone ∧	**64**	46.02 N	11.04 E
Il'pyrskij	**74**	59.56 N	164.10 E
Ilsan-ni	**271b**	37.41 N	126.46 E
Ilse ≃	**54**	52.06 N	10.35 E
Ilshofen	**56**	49.10 N	9.55 E
Il'skij	**78**	44.51 N	38.35 E
Ilskov	**41**	56.14 N	9.06 E
Il Telegrafo ∧	**66**	42.22 N	11.10 E
Ilten	**52**	52.21 N	9.55 E
Ilu	**152**	4.12 N	23.02 E
Ilubabor □4	**144**	7.50 N	35.00 E
Iluhār	**126**	22.48 N	90.06 E
Ilūkste	**76**	55.58 N	26.18 E
Ilverich	**263**	51.17 N	6.42 E
Ilwaco	**224**	46.19 N	124.03 W
Ilwaki	**112**	7.56 S	126.26 E
Ilwŏl-san ∧	**98**	36.50 N	129.06 E
İlyasbey	**130**	40.13 N	29.52 E
Ilz	**61**	47.05 N	15.55 E
Ilz ≃	**60**	48.35 N	13.29 E
Iłża	**30**	51.11 N	21.14 E
Ima	**88**	55.13 N	115.55 E
Ima ≃	**96**	33.45 N	131.01 E
Imabari	**96**	34.03 N	133.00 E
Imabu ≃	**250**	0.44 S	57.22 W
Imadomi	**268**	35.28 N	140.06 E
Imaichi	**94**	36.43 N	139.41 E
Imajō	**94**	35.46 N	136.12 E
Imajuku	**268**	35.58 N	139.21 E
Imajuku ⊸8	**268**	35.29 N	139.32 E
Imaki	**270**	34.24 N	135.46 E
Imaloto ≃	**157b**	23.27 S	45.13 E
Imambara ☉1	**272b**	22.54 N	88.25 E
Imanbaj ⊥	**86**	43.13 N	60.25 E
Imandan-Makit, gora ∧, S.S.S.R.	**88**	54.15 N	117.38 E
Imandan-Makit, gora ∧, S.S.S.R.	**89**	54.06 N	117.50 E
Imandra, ozero ⊜	**24**	67.30 N	33.00 E
Imanombo	**157b**	24.26 S	45.49 E
Imantau	**86**	52.58 N	68.22 E
Imari	**92**	33.16 N	129.53 E
Imaruí	**252**	28.21 S	48.49 W
Imaruí, Lagoa ⊂	**252**	28.21 S	48.52 W
Imasa	**140**	18.01 N	36.12 E
Imatra	**26**	61.10 N	28.46 E
Imavere	**76**	58.44 N	25.48 E
Imaza ≃	**248**	5.05 S	78.19 W
Imazu	**94**	35.24 N	136.02 E
Imbābah ⊸8	**142**	30.04 N	31.13 E
Imbabura □4	**246**	0.22 N	78.25 W
Imba-numa ⊜	**94**	35.45 N	140.12 E
Imbariê	**256**	22.39 S	43.13 W
Imbituba	**252**	28.14 S	48.40 W
Imbituva	**252**	25.12 S	50.35 W
Imboassu, Canal ≅	**287a**	22.48 S	43.04 W
Imboden	**194**	36.12 N	91.10 W
Imbonga	**152**	0.43 S	19.46 E
Imbundi	**152**	5.44 S	16.16 E
Ime, Beinn ∧	**46**	56.14 N	4.49 W
Imeni 26 Bakinskich Komissarov	**84**	39.19 N	49.12 E
Imeni Abaja	**86**	50.44 N	69.30 E
Imeni Babuškina	**76**	59.45 N	43.07 E
Imeni Čapajeva	**85**	43.28 N	76.50 E
Imeni C'urupy	**82**	55.30 N	38.39 E
Imeni Džambula, S.S.S.R.	**86**	45.26 N	74.24 E
Imeni Džambula, S.S.S.R.	**86**	47.43 N	74.09 E
Imeni Frunze	**86**	46.23 N	77.20 E
Imeni Il-Go Okt'abr'a	**88**	55.54 N	119.36 E
Imeni Kalinina, S.S.S.R.	**80**	51.51 N	52.43 E
Imeni Kalinina, S.S.S.R.	**85**	41.28 N	76.22 E
Imeni Kalinina, S.S.S.R.	**85**	43.16 N	74.03 E
Imeni Kalinina, S.S.S.R.	**86**	43.40 N	59.07 E
Imeni Karla Libknechta	**78**	51.37 N	35.27 E
Imeni Kirova, S.S.S.R.	**74**	59.42 N	128.12 E
Imeni Kirova, S.S.S.R.	**86**	46.27 N	77.13 E
Imeni Leninskogo Komsomola	**86**	50.45 N	66.44 E
Imeni Marta	**86**	46.57 N	58.58 E
Imeni Michajla Ivanoviča Kalinina	**80**	57.59 N	45.07 E
Imeni Molodogvardejcev	**86**	54.03 N	70.44 E
Imeni Panfilova	**85**	43.23 N	77.07 E
Imeni Poliny Osipenko	**89**	52.25 N	136.28 E
Imeni Sardarova Karachana	**85**	38.26 N	68.46 E
Imeni Šeredy	**83**	46.52 N	40.03 E
Imeni Ševčenko	**86**	45.58 N	61.04 E
Imeni Stepana Razina	**80**	54.54 N	44.18 E
Imeni Tel'mana	**89**	48.36 N	134.59 E
Imeni Timir'azeva	**86**	53.39 N	65.31 E
Imeni Vladimira Iljiča Lenina	**80**	53.36 N	46.58 E
Imeni Vorovskogo, S.S.S.R.	**80**	55.43 N	41.06 E
Imeni Vorovskogo, S.S.S.R.	**82**	55.43 N	38.20 E
Imeni XXI Partsjezda	**86**	50.43 N	67.50 E
Imeni Žel'abova	**76**	58.57 N	36.36 E
Imera ⊥	**70**	37.59 N	13.49 E
Imerimandroso	**157b**	17.23 S	48.38 E
Imese	**152**	2.07 N	18.06 E
Imgenbroich	**56**	50.34 N	6.16 E
Imi	**144**	6.28 N	42.18 E
Imías	**240p**	20.04 N	74.38 W
Imilac	**252**	24.14 S	68.53 W
Imilili ⍑4	**148**	23.18 N	15.54 W
Imi-n'Tanout	**148**	31.10 N	8.50 W
Imišli	**84**	39.52 N	48.04 E
Imittós	**267c**	37.57 N	23.45 E
Imittós Óros ∧	**267c**	37.55 N	23.47 E
Imja-do I	**98**	35.05 N	126.05 E
Imjin-gang ≃	**98**	37.47 N	126.40 E
Imlay	**204**	40.39 N	118.08 W
Imlay City	**190**	43.01 N	83.04 W
Imlaystown	**208**	40.10 N	74.31 W
Imler	**214**	40.12 N	78.31 W
Immarna	**162**	30.30 S	132.09 E
Immendingen	**58**	47.56 N	8.44 E
Immenhausen	**56**	51.25 N	9.28 E
Immensen	**52**	52.23 N	10.04 E
Immenstaad	**58**	47.40 N	9.22 E
Immenstadt	**58**	47.33 N	10.13 E
Immigrath	**263**	51.06 N	6.57 E
Immingham	**44**	53.36 N	0.13 W
Immokalee	**220**	26.25 N	81.25 W
Imnaha ≃	**202**	45.49 N	116.46 W
Imo □3	**150**	5.30 N	7.25 E
Imo ≃	**150**	4.36 N	7.35 E
Imogiri	**115a**	7.55 S	110.23 E
Imokt'an	**98**	38.50 N	126.41 E
Imola	**66**	44.21 N	11.42 E
Imonda	**164**	3.20 S	141.10 E
Imore	**273a**	6.26 N	3.17 E
Imoro	**273a**	6.43 N	3.30 E
Im Ostholz ⊸8	**263**	51.26 N	7.12 E
Imotski	**36**	43.27 N	17.13 E
Imp'a	**98**	35.59 N	126.49 E
Impasugong	**116**	8.19 N	125.00 E
Impe	**152**	2.44 S	15.17 E
Impendle	**158**	29.37 S	29.55 E
Imperatore, Campo ≚	**66**	42.25 N	13.40 E
Imperatriz	**250**	5.32 S	47.29 W
Imperia	**62**	43.53 N	8.03 E
Imperia □4	**62**	43.58 N	7.47 E
Imperial, Sk., Can.	**184**	51.22 N	105.27 W
Imperial, Perú	**248**	13.04 S	76.21 W
Imperial, Ca., U.S.	**204**	32.50 N	115.34 W
Imperial, Mo., U.S.	**219**	38.22 N	90.22 W
Imperial, Ne., U.S.	**198**	40.31 N	101.38 W
Imperial, Pa., U.S.	**214**	40.26 N	80.14 W
Imperial, Tx., U.S.	**196**	31.16 N	102.41 W
Imperial ≃	**254**	38.48 S	73.24 W
Imperial Beach	**228**	32.35 N	117.06 W
Imperial Dam ⊸6	**204**	32.55 N	114.30 W
Imperial de Aragón, Canal ≅	**34**	42.02 N	1.33 W
Imperiale	**68**	40.07 N	16.35 E
Imperial Mills	**182**	55.00 N	111.44 W
Imperial Palace ☉	**268**	35.41 N	139.45 E
Imperial Valley V	**204**	32.50 N	115.30 W
Impflingen	**56**	49.10 N	8.07 E
Impfondo	**152**	1.37 N	18.04 E
Imphāl	**120**	24.49 N	93.57 E
Impilachti	**24**	61.40 N	31.04 E
Imprensa, Gruta da ⍊6	**287a**	23.00 S	43.15 W
Impruneta	**66**	43.41 N	11.15 E
Impulo	**152**	13.53 S	13.39 E
İmralı Adası I	**130**	40.32 N	28.32 E
İmranlı	**130**	39.54 N	38.07 E
Imroz	**130**	40.11 N	25.55 E
Imsil	**98**	35.37 N	127.15 E
Imst	**58**	47.14 N	10.44 E
Imtān	**132**	32.24 N	36.49 E
Imuris	**232**	30.47 N	110.52 W
Imuruan Bay ⊂	**116**	10.40 N	119.16 E
Imuruk Basin ⊜	**180**	65.06 N	165.36 W
Imuruk Lake ⊜	**180**	65.36 N	163.10 W
Imute	**273a**	6.42 N	3.29 E
Imwŏn-ni	**98**	37.15 N	129.20 E
Ina, Nihon	**94**	35.50 N	137.57 E
Ina, Nihon	**94**	37.10 N	139.32 E
Ina, Nihon	**94**	35.59 N	140.03 E
Ina, Nihon	**268**	35.59 N	139.38 E
In'a, S.S.S.R.	**74**	59.24 N	144.48 E
In'a, S.S.S.R.	**86**	53.31 N	82.40 E
In'a, S.S.S.R.	**86**	50.48 N	86.37 E
Ina, Il., U.S.	**194**	38.09 N	88.54 W
Ina ≃, Nihon	**94**	37.16 N	139.33 E
Ina ≃, Nihon	**96**	34.43 N	135.28 E
Ina ≃, Pol.	**54**	53.32 N	14.38 E
In'a ≃, S.S.S.R.	**74**	59.23 N	144.54 E
In'a ≃, S.S.S.R.	**86**	54.59 N	82.59 E
Inaba	**270**	34.26 N	135.27 E
Inabe	**94**	35.07 N	136.33 E
Ina-bonchi ≚1	**94**	35.45 N	137.57 E
Inabu	**94**	35.13 N	137.30 E
Inaccessible Island I	**10**	37.17 S	12.45 W
Inada	**270**	34.54 N	135.08 E
I Naftan, Puntan ›	**174n**	15.05 N	145.45 E
Inagawa	**96**	34.53 N	135.22 E
Inagawan	**116**	9.33 N	118.39 E
Inage	**268**	35.38 N	140.05 E
Inagi	**94**	35.38 N	139.30 E
Inajá	**250**	8.54 S	37.49 W
Inajá ≃	**250**	8.53 S	49.44 W
In'akino	**80**	54.26 N	41.07 E
Inakona	**175e**	9.49 S	160.02 E
Inala	**171a**	27.35 S	152.58 E
Inamangando ≃	**152**	14.03 S	12.23 E
Inambari ≃	**248**	12.41 S	69.44 W
In Amguel	**148**	23.40 N	5.10 E
Inami, Nihon	**94**	36.33 N	136.58 E
Inami, Nihon	**96**	34.45 N	134.54 E
Inami, Nihon	**96**	33.48 N	135.13 E
In Amnas	**148**	28.05 N	9.30 E
Inampulugan Island I	**116**	10.28 N	122.42 E
Inamuragasaki Point ⊥	**268**	35.18 N	139.32 E
Inanda	**273d**	26.07 S	28.03 E
Inangahua Junction	**172**	41.51 S	171.57 E
Inanwatan	**164**	2.08 S	132.10 E
Iñapari	**248**	10.57 S	69.35 W
Inaporok	**164**	8.15 S	141.55 E
In'aptuk, gora ∧	**88**	56.22 N	110.11 E
Inari	**24**	68.54 N	27.01 E
Inarigda	**74**	63.14 N	107.27 E
Inarijärvi ⊜	**24**	69.00 N	28.00 E
Inas, Gunong ∧	**114**	5.15 N	100.56 E
Inasa	**94**	34.50 N	137.40 E
Inatsuki	**96**	33.36 N	130.43 E
Inauini ≃	**248**	8.30 S	67.24 W
Inawaia	**164**	8.40 S	146.35 E
Inawashiro-ko ⊜	**92**	37.29 N	140.06 E
I-n-Azaoua ⍑4	**148**	20.49 N	7.30 E
Inazawa	**94**	35.15 N	136.47 E
Inba	**94**	35.46 N	140.14 E
Inba-numa ⊜	**94**	35.46 N	140.12 E
In Belbel	**148**	27.54 N	1.10 E
Inca	**34**	39.43 N	2.54 E
Inca de Oro	**252**	26.45 S	69.54 W
Incaguasi	**252**	29.13 S	71.03 W
Ince	**262**	53.17 N	2.49 W
Ince Blundell	**262**	53.31 N	3.02 W
İnce Burun ›	**130**	42.06 N	34.56 E
Ince-in-Makerfield	**262**	53.32 N	2.37 W
İncekum Burnu ›	**130**	36.13 N	33.58 E
İncesu	**130**	38.38 N	35.11 E
Inch	**48**	52.08 N	9.59 W
I-n-Chaouag ≃	**150**	16.23 N	0.10 E
Inchard, Loch ⊂	**46**	58.27 N	5.04 W
Inchas Military Base ■	**142**	30.20 N	31.27 E
Inchbare	**46**	56.47 N	2.38 W
Inchcape I2	**46**	56.26 N	2.23 W
Inchelium	**182**	48.17 N	118.11 W
Inchiri □4	**150**	19.50 N	15.00 W
Inchmarnock I	**46**	55.47 N	5.09 W
Inchnadamph	**46**	58.09 N	4.59 W
Inch'ŏn	**98**	37.28 N	126.38 E
Inch'ŏn □4	**98**	37.28 N	126.38 E
Inchture	**46**	56.26 N	3.10 W
Inchwagh Lake ⊜	**281**	42.27 N	83.41 W
İncirliova	**130**	37.50 N	27.43 E
Incisa in Val d'Arno	**66**	43.40 N	11.27 E
Incline Village	**226**	39.16 N	119.56 W
Incomáti (Komati) ≃	**156**	25.46 S	32.43 E
Inconfidência	**256**	22.16 S	43.13 W
Inconfidentes	**256**	22.20 S	46.20 W
Inčoun	**180**	66.18 N	170.17 W
Incudine	**64**	46.14 N	10.22 E
Incudine, Monte ∧	**36**	41.51 N	9.12 E
Incy	**24**	65.48 N	40.26 E
Indaal, Loch ⊂	**46**	55.45 N	6.21 W
Indaiá ≃	**255**	18.27 S	45.22 W
Indaiatuba	**256**	23.05 S	47.14 W
Indalsälven ≃	**26**	62.31 N	17.27 E
Indanan	**116**	5.58 N	120.59 E
Indaparapeo	**234**	19.47 N	100.58 W
Inda Silase	**144**	14.05 N	38.20 E
Indaw	**110**	23.40 N	94.46 E
Indawgyi Lake ⊜	**110**	25.10 N	96.19 E
Indé	**232**	25.54 N	105.13 W
Inde → India □1	**118**	20.00 N	77.00 E
Inde ≃	**56**	50.54 N	6.21 E
Indemini	**58**	46.06 N	8.50 E
Independence, Ca., U.S.	**204**	36.48 N	118.11 W
Independence, In., U.S.	**216**	40.20 N	87.10 W
Independence, Ia., U.S.	**190**	42.28 N	91.53 W
Independence, Ks., U.S.	**198**	37.13 N	95.42 W
Independence, Ky., U.S.	**218**	38.56 N	84.32 W
Independence, La., U.S.	**194**	30.38 N	90.30 W
Independence, Mo., U.S.	**194**	39.05 N	94.24 W
Independence, Oh., U.S.	**279a**	41.23 N	81.38 W
Independence, Or., U.S.	**202**	44.51 N	123.11 W
Independence, Pa., U.S.	**214**	40.15 N	80.31 W
Independence, Tx., U.S.	**222**	30.19 N	96.21 W
Independence, Va., U.S.	**192**	36.37 N	81.09 W
Independence, Wi., U.S.	**190**	44.21 N	91.25 W
Independence ≃	**188**	43.45 N	75.20 W
Independence Creek ≃	**196**	30.27 N	101.44 W
Independence Hall ⊥	**285**	39.57 N	75.09 W
Independence Lake ⊜1	**226**	39.26 N	120.18 W
Independence Mountains ⋏	**204**	41.15 N	115.55 W
Independencia, Bol.	**248**	17.07 S	66.53 W
Independência, Bra.	**250**	5.23 S	40.19 W
Independencia, Isla I	**248**	14.15 S	76.12 W
Independența	**38**	43.58 N	28.05 E
Inder, ozero ⊜	**80**	48.27 N	51.54 E
Inderborskij	**80**	48.33 N	51.44 E
In der Bredde	**263**	51.20 N	7.23 E
İnderesi	**130**	37.50 N	35.40 E
Index	**224**	47.49 N	121.33 W
Index, Mount ∧	**224**	47.46 N	121.35 W
Indi	**122**	17.10 N	75.58 E
India (Bhārat) □1	**118**	20.00 N	77.00 E
India Brook ≃	**276**	40.47 N	74.37 W
India Gate ⊥	**272a**	28.37 N	77.18 E
Indialantic	**220**	28.05 N	80.34 W
Indian ≃, On., Can.	**212**	45.16 N	76.14 W
Indian ≃, On., Can.	**212**	44.13 N	78.08 W
Indian ≃, De., U.S.	**208**	38.36 N	75.10 W
Indian ≃, Ma., U.S.	**283**	42.47 N	70.58 W
Indian ≃, Mi., U.S.	**190**	45.59 N	86.15 W
Indian ≃, N.Y., U.S.	**212**	44.24 N	75.39 W
Indiana	**214**	40.37 N	79.09 W
Indiana □6	**214**	40.37 N	79.09 W
Indiana □3, U.S.	**178**	40.00 N	86.15 W
Indiana □3, U.S.	**194**	40.00 N	86.15 W
Indiana Dunes National Lakeshore ♦	**216**	41.40 N	87.00 W
Indiana Dunes State Park ♦	**216**	41.40 N	87.02 W
Indian Agricultural Research Institute ☉3	**272a**	28.38 N	77.10 E
Indiana Harbor ⊂	**278**	41.40 N	87.27 W
Indiana Harbor Canal ≅	**278**	41.40 N	87.27 W
Indianapolis	**218**	39.46 N	86.09 W
Indianapolis International Airport ⊠	**218**	39.43 N	86.16 W
Indianapolis Motor Speedway ♦	**218**	39.48 N	86.14 W
Indian Bayou ≃	**194**	34.14 N	91.52 W
Indian Brook	**186**	46.23 N	60.32 W
Indian Caverns ⍊5	**214**	40.38 N	78.05 W
Indian Church	**232**	17.45 N	88.40 W

Symbols in the index entries represent the broad categories identified in the key at the right. Symbols with superior numbers (⋏1) identify subcategories (see complete key on page *I · 1*).

Symbole im Register stellen die rechts im Schlüssel erklärten Kategorien dar. Symbole mit hochgestellten Ziffern (⋏1) bezeichnen Unterabteilungen einer Kategorie (vgl. vollständiger Schlüssel auf Seite *I · 1*).

Los símbolos incluídos en el texto del índice representan las grandes categorias identificadas con la clave a la derecha. Los símbolos con numeros en su parte superior (⋏1) identifican las subcategorías (véase la clave completa en la página *I · 1*).

Les symboles de l'index représentent les catégories indiquées dans la légende à droite. Les symboles suivis d'un indice (⋏1) représentent des sous-catégories (voir légende complète à la page *I · 1*).

Os símbolos incluídos no texto do índice representam as grandes categorias identificadas com a chave à direita. Os símbolos com números em sua parte superior (⋏1) identificam as subcategorias (veja-se a chave completa à página *I · 1*).

∧	Mountain	Berg	Montaña	Montagne	Montanha
⋏	Mountains	Gebirge	Montañas	Montagnes	Montanhas
)(	Pass	Paß	Paso	Col	Passo
V	Valley, Canyon	Tal, Cañon	Valle, Cañón	Vallée, Canyon	Vale, Canhão
≚	Plain	Ebene	Llano	Plaine	Planície
›	Cape	Kap	Cabo	Cap	Cabo
I	Island	Insel	Isla	Île	Ilha
II	Islands	Inseln	Islas	Îles	Ilhas
⍊	Other Topographic Features	Andere Topographische Objekte	Otros Elementos Topográficos	Autres données topographiques	Outros acidentes topográficos

ESPAÑOL

Nombre	Página	Lat.°′	Long.°′ W = Oeste
Indian Creek	278	42.14 N	87.59 W
Indian Creek ≃, U.S.	218	39.19 N	84.38 W
Indian Creek ≃, Ca., U.S.	228	35.18 N	118.26 W
Indian Creek ≃, Il., U.S.	216	41.26 N	88.46 W
Indian Creek ≃, Il., U.S.	219	39.56 N	90.32 W
Indian Creek ≃, Il., U.S.	278	42.11 N	87.55 W
Indian Creek ≃, In., U.S.	216	40.55 N	86.42 W
Indian Creek ≃, In., U.S.	218	38.43 N	85.06 W
Indian Creek ≃, In., U.S.	218	39.23 N	86.29 W
Indian Creek ≃, In., U.S.	218	38.10 N	86.14 W
Indian Creek ≃, Md., U.S.	284c	38.59 N	76.55 W
Indian Creek ≃, Mo., U.S.	194	36.33 N	94.29 W
Indian Creek ≃, Mo., U.S.	219	39.10 N	91.11 W
Indian Creek ≃, N.M., U.S.	200	36.11 N	108.23 W
Indian Creek ≃, N.Y., U.S.	276	40.43 N	73.06 W
Indian Creek ≃, Oh., U.S.	218	39.19 N	84.38 W
Indian Creek ≃, Oh., U.S.	279a	41.17 N	81.31 W
Indian Creek ≃, S.D., U.S.	198	44.39 N	103.19 W
Indian Creek ≃, Tn., U.S.	194	35.13 N	88.08 W
Indian Creek Lake ⊜[1]	222	31.44 N	95.58 W
Indianford	216	42.49 N	88.35 W
Indian Grave Mountain ∧[2]	192	32.59 N	84.21 W
Indian Harbour Beach	220	28.08 N	80.35 W
Indian Head, Sk., Can.	184	50.32 N	103.40 W
Indian Head, Md., U.S.	208	38.36 N	77.09 W
Indian Head ≃	283	42.04 N	70.52 W
Indian Head Park	278	41.47 N	87.54 W
Indian Head Pond ⊜	283	42.03 N	70.51 W
Indian Heights	216	40.25 N	86.07 W
Indian Island I	224	48.04 N	122.43 W
Indian Kentuck Creek ≃	218	38.43 N	85.16 W
Indian Lake, Mi., U.S.	216	41.59 N	86.12 W
Indian Lake, N.Y., U.S.	188	43.46 N	74.16 W
Indian Lake ⊜, On., Can.	190	47.08 N	82.08 W
Indian Lake ⊜, Mi., U.S.	190	45.59 N	86.20 W
Indian Lake ⊜, Mi., U.S.	216	42.09 N	85.29 W
Indian Lake ⊜, Mi., U.S.	216	42.00 N	86.13 W
Indian Lake ⊜, N.J., U.S.	276	40.53 N	74.29 W
Indian Lake ⊜, Oh., U.S.	216	40.29 N	83.53 W
Indian Lake Estates	220	27.48 N	81.19 W
Indian Lakes ⊜	216	41.33 N	85.25 W
Indian Lake State Park ♠	216	40.29 N	83.52 W
Indian Mills Brook ≃	285	39.47 N	74.44 W
Indian Mills Lake ⊜	285	39.48 N	74.44 W
Indian Neck	207	41.15 N	72.48 W
Indian Ocean ⊤[1]	4	10.00 S	70.00 E
Indian Ocean ⊤[1]	6	10.00 S	70.00 E
Indianola, Ia., U.S.	190	41.21 N	93.33 W
Indianola, Ms., U.S.	194	33.27 N	90.39 W
Indianola, Ne., U.S.	198	40.14 N	100.25 W
Indianola, Pa., U.S.	279b	40.34 N	79.51 W
Indianola, Wa., U.S.	224	47.45 N	122.31 W
Indianópolis	255	19.02 S	47.55 W
Indianópolis ◆[8]	287b	23.36 S	46.38 W
Indian Peak ∧, Ut,. U.S.	200	38.16 N	113.53 W
Indian Peak ∧, Wy., U.S.	202	44.47 N	109.51 W
Indian Point ›	212	44.37 N	78.49 W
Indian Prairie Canal ≡	220	27.02 N	80.57 W
Indian Queen Estates	284c	38.46 N	77.02 W
Indian River	190	45.24 N	84.36 W
Indian River □[6]	220	27.43 N	80.36 W
Indian River ⊂	220	28.00 N	80.30 W
Indian River Bay ⊂	208	38.36 N	75.05 W
Indian River Inlet ⊂	208	38.37 N	75.03 W
Indian Rock ∧	224	45.59 N	120.49 W
Indian Rock Dam ◆[6]	208	39.57 N	76.45 W
Indian Rock Paintings ⊥	224	46.38 N	120.31 W
Indian Rocks Beach	220	27.52 N	82.51 W
Indian Springs, Nv., U.S.	204	36.34 N	115.40 W
Indian Springs, Va., U.S.	284c	38.49 N	77.10 W
Indian Stream ≃	206	45.03 N	71.26 W
Indiantown	220	27.01 N	80.29 W
Indian Town Point ›	240c	17.06 N	61.40 W
Indian Valley Reservoir ⊜[1]	226	39.07 N	122.32 W
Indian Village, In., U.S.	218	40.10 N	85.22 W
Indian Village, N.Y., U.S.	210	42.57 N	76.10 W
Indiaporã	255	19.57 S	50.17 W
Indiaroba	250	11.32 S	37.31 W
Indibir	144	8.05 N	37.58 E
Indico, Océano → Indian Ocean ⊤[1]	6	10.00 S	70.00 E
Indien → India □[1]	118	20.00 N	77.00 E
Indien, Océan → Indian Ocean ⊤[1]	6	10.00 S	70.00 E
Indien, territoires britanniques de l'Ocean → British Indian Ocean Territory □[2]	12	7.00 S	72.00 E
Indiera Alta	240m	18.09 N	66.53 W
Indiga	24	67.41 N	49.00 E
Indigirka ≃	74	70.48 N	148.54 E
Indija	38	45.03 N	20.05 E
Indin	120	20.16 N	92.57 E
Indio	204	33.43 N	116.12 W
Indio ≃, Nic.	236	10.57 N	83.44 W
Indio ≃, Pan.	236	9.12 N	80.11 W
Indio, Punta ›	258	35.16 S	57.13 W
Indira Gandhi Canal ≡	120	31.10 N	75.00 E
Indira Gandhi International Airport ⊠	272a	28.35 N	77.07 E
Indischer Ozean → Indian Ocean ⊤[1]	6	10.00 S	70.00 E
Indispensable Reefs ✦[2]	160	12.40 S	160.25 E
Indispensable Strait Ц	175e	9.00 S	160.30 E
Indo → Indus ≃	120	24.20 N	67.47 E
Indochina ◆[1]	12	16.00 N	107.00 E
Indom	24	64.36 N	55.22 E
Indonesia □[1]	108	5.00 S	120.00 E
Indonesia, University of ℧[2]	269e	6.12 S	106.51 E
Indonesia in Miniature ♠	269e	6.08 S	106.49 E
Indonesian Culture, Museum of ℧[3]	269e	6.09 N	106.49 E
Indonésie → Indonesia □[1]	108	5.00 S	120.00 E

FRANÇAIS

Nom	Page	Lat.°′	Long.°′ W = Ouest
Indonesien → Indonesia □[1]	108	5.00 S	120.00 E
Indooroopilly	171a	27.30 S	152.58 E
Indore	120	22.43 N	75.50 E
Indpur	126	23.10 N	86.56 E
Indragiri ≃	112	0.22 S	103.26 E
Indramayu	115a	6.20 S	108.19 E
Indramayu, Ujung ›	115a	6.14 S	108.17 E
Indrapuri	114	5.26 N	95.27 E
Indrāvati ≃	122	18.44 N	80.16 E
Indre □[5]	32	46.45 N	1.30 E
Indre ≃	32	47.16 N	0.19 E
Indre-et-Loire □[5]	32	47.15 N	0.45 E
Indrois ≃	50	47.13 N	0.56 E
Indungo	152	14.48 S	16.17 E
Induno Olona	62	45.52 N	8.51 E
Indur → Indore	120	22.43 N	75.50 E
Indura	76	53.27 N	23.53 E
Indus ≃	120	24.20 N	67.47 E
Industry, Il., U.S.	194	40.20 N	90.36 W
Industry, Pa., U.S.	214	40.39 N	80.25 W
Industry, Tx., U.S.	222	29.58 N	96.30 W
Indwe	158	31.27 S	27.23 E
Indwe ≃	158	32.01 S	27.21 E
Ine	96	35.39 N	135.17 E
İnebolu	130	41.58 N	33.46 E
İnece	130	41.41 N	27.04 E
İnecik	130	40.56 N	27.16 E
In Ecker	148	24.09 N	5.03 E
İnegöl	130	40.05 N	29.31 E
Inerie, Gunung ∧	115b	8.52 S	120.56 E
Inés, Monte ∧	254	48.29 S	69.40 W
Ineu	38	46.26 N	21.49 E
Inez, Ky., U.S.	192	37.51 N	82.32 W
Inez, Tx., U.S.	222	28.54 N	96.47 W
Inez, Lake ⊜	276	41.01 N	74.17 W
Infanta, Pil.	116	15.50 N	119.55 E
Infanta, Pil.	116	14.45 N	121.39 E
Infantas	286d	11.57 S	77.04 W
Infante, Kaap ›	158	34.29 S	20.51 E
Inferior, Laguna ⊂	234	16.20 N	94.40 W
Inferno, Cachoeira do ∟	250	1.00 S	56.04 W
Infiernillo, Canal del Ц	232	29.09 N	112.15 W
Infiernillo, Presa del ⊜[1]	234	18.35 N	101.45 W
Infiesto	34	43.21 N	5.22 W
Infreschi, Ponta degli ›	68	39.59 N	15.25 E
Ing ≃	110	20.13 N	100.27 E
Ingá	250	7.17 S	35.36 W
Ingabu	110	17.49 N	95.16 E
Ingaí	256	21.24 S	44.55 W
Ingaí ≃	256	21.23 S	44.52 W
Ingal	150	16.47 N	6.56 E
Ingalls	218	39.57 N	85.48 W
Ingalls Creek ≃	224	47.28 N	120.39 W
Ingalls Park	216	41.32 N	88.03 W
Inganda	152	0.05 S	20.57 E
Inganno ≃	70	38.04 N	14.37 E
Ingarö I	40	59.16 N	18.28 E
Ingatestone	42	51.41 N	0.22 E
Ingatestone Hall ⊥	260	51.39 N	0.23 E
Ingelfingen	56	49.18 N	9.39 E
Ingelheim	56	49.59 N	8.05 E
Ingelmunster	50	50.55 N	3.15 E
Ingelstad	26	56.45 N	14.55 E
Ingende	152	0.15 S	18.57 E
Ingeniero Budge ◆[8]	288	34.43 S	58.28 W
Ingeniero Jacobacci	254	41.18 S	69.35 W
Ingeniero Juan Allan	258	34.53 S	58.11 W
Ingeniero Luiggi	252	35.25 S	64.29 W
Ingeniero Luis A. Huergo	252	39.05 S	67.14 W
Ingeniero Maschwitz	258	34.23 S	58.44 W
Ingeniero Romulo Otamendi	258	34.13 S	58.54 W
Ingeniero White	252	38.47 S	62.16 W
Ingeniero Williams	258	34.54 S	59.22 W
Ingenio La Esperanza	252	24.13 S	64.51 W
Ingenio Santa Ana	252	27.28 S	65.41 W
Ingeringbach ≃	61	47.12 N	14.49 E
Ingersheim	58	48.06 N	7.18 E
Ingersoll	212	43.02 N	80.53 W
Ingham	166	18.39 S	146.10 E
Ingham □[6]	216	42.37 N	84.22 W
Ingička	85	39.52 N	67.20 E
Ingleborough ∧	44	54.11 N	2.23 W
Ingleburn	170	34.00 S	150.52 E
Inglesa, Costa → English Coast ⊡[2]	9	73.45 S	73.00 W
Ingleside, Austl.	274a	33.41 S	151.13 E
Ingleside, On., Can.	206	45.00 N	75.00 W
Ingleside, Il., U.S.	216	42.23 N	88.09 W
Ingleside, Tx., U.S.	196	27.52 N	97.12 W
Ingleside ◆[8]	282	37.43 N	122.28 W
Ingleton	44	54.10 N	2.27 W
Inglewood, Austl.	166	28.25 S	151.05 E
Inglewood, Austl.	166	36.34 S	143.52 E
Inglewood, On., Can.	212	43.47 N	79.56 W
Inglewood, N.Z.	172	39.09 S	174.12 E
Inglewood, Ca., U.S.	228	33.57 N	118.21 W
Inglewood, Wa., U.S.	224	47.44 N	122.15 W
Inglewood Forest ◆[3]	44	54.45 N	2.50 W
Inglis, Mb., Can.	184	50.57 N	101.15 W
Inglis, Fl., U.S.	220	29.02 N	82.40 W
Inglis Lock ◆[5]	220	29.02 N	82.37 W
Ingoda ≃	88	51.42 N	115.48 E
Ingogo	158	27.32 S	29.56 E
Ingoldmells	44	53.11 N	0.20 E
Ingolstadt	60	48.46 N	11.27 E
Ingomar	279b	40.35 N	80.05 W
Ingonish	186	46.42 N	60.22 W
Ingornachoix Bay ⊂	186	50.38 N	57.20 W
Ingraham, Lake ⊜	220	25.09 N	81.08 W
Ingrāj Bāzār	124	25.00 N	88.09 E
Ingram, Pa., U.S.	279b	40.26 N	80.04 W
Ingram, Tx., U.S.	196	30.04 N	99.14 W
Ingram Bay ⊂	208	37.48 N	76.17 W
Ingrave	260	51.36 N	0.21 E
Ingrid Christensen Coast ⊡[2]	9	69.30 S	76.00 E
In Guezzam	150	19.32 N	5.42 E
Ingul ≃	78	47.00 N	31.59 E
Ingulec	78	47.43 N	33.14 E
Ingulec ≃	78	46.41 N	32.48 E
Ingulo-Kamenka	78	48.17 N	32.30 E
Inguri ≃	84	42.24 N	41.33 E
Inguzet	86	58.50 N	83.52 E
Ingvallsbenning	40	60.15 N	15.53 E
Ingwavuma	158	27.09 S	32.00 E
Ingwe	154	13.02 S	26.25 E
Ingwiller	56	48.52 N	7.29 E
Inhaca, Ilha da I	158	26.03 S	32.57 E
Inhafenga	156	20.35 S	33.53 E
Inhambane	156	23.51 S	35.29 E
Inhambane □[5]	156	23.00 S	34.30 E
Inhambane, Baía de ⊂	156	23.58 S	35.51 E
Inhambupe	255	11.47 S	38.21 W
Inhaminga	156	18.24 S	35.00 E
Inhapim	255	19.33 S	42.07 W
Inharrime	156	24.29 S	35.01 E
Inharrime ≃	156	24.29 S	35.01 E
Inhassoro	156	21.33 S	35.11 E
Inhaúma	255	19.29 S	44.22 W
Inhaúma ◆[8]	287a	22.52 S	43.17 W
İnhisar	130	40.03 N	30.23 E
Inhoaíba ◆[8]	256	22.54 S	43.36 W
Inhobi ≃	255	23.45 S	54.40 W
Inhomirim	256	22.35 S	43.10 W
Inhuma	250	6.40 S	41.42 W
Inhumas	255	16.22 S	49.30 W
Ini ≃	146	9.30 N	12.20 E
Iniesta	34	39.26 N	1.45 W
Inimutaba	255	18.45 S	44.22 W
Ining → Yining	86	43.54 N	81.21 E
Inini ≃	250	3.39 N	54.00 W
Inírida ≃	246	3.55 N	67.52 W
Inisa	150	7.52 N	4.20 E

PORTUGUÊS

Nome	Página	Lat.°′	Long.°′ W = Oeste
Inishbofin I, Ire.	48	53.37 N	10.15 W
Inishbofin I, Ire.	48	55.09 N	8.11 W
Inishcrone	48	54.12 N	9.06 W
Inisheer I	48	53.02 N	9.26 W
Inishkea North I	48	54.08 N	10.12 W
Inishkea South I	48	54.07 N	10.13 W
Inishmaan I	48	53.05 N	9.32 W
Inishmore I	48	53.07 N	9.45 W
Inishmurray I	48	54.26 N	8.40 W
Inishowen ›[1]	48	55.12 N	7.20 W
Inishowen Head ›,	48	55.14 N	6.56 W
Inishshark I	48	53.37 N	10.18 W
Inishtrahull I	48	55.26 N	7.14 W
Inishturk I	48	53.43 N	10.08 W
Inistioge	48	52.29 N	7.04 W
Initao	116	8.30 N	124.18 E
Inje	98	38.05 N	128.09 E
Injibara	144	11.00 N	36.59 E
Injune	166	25.51 S	148.34 E
Inkeroinen	26	60.42 N	26.51 E
Inketete	152	2.37 S	21.53 E
Inkisi (Zadi) ≃	152	4.46 S	14.52 E
Inkom	202	42.47 N	112.15 W
Inkster, Mi., U.S.	216	42.17 N	83.18 W
Inkster, N.D., U.S.	198	48.09 N	97.38 W
Inland Kaikoura Range ⋀	172	42.00 S	173.40 E
Inland Lake ⊜, Mb., Can.	184	52.17 N	99.42 W
Inland Lake ⊜, Ak., U.S.	180	66.27 N	159.47 W
Inland Sea → Seto-naikai ⊤[2]	96	34.20 N	133.30 E
Inle Lake ⊜	110	20.32 N	96.55 E
Inmaculadita	232	29.55 N	111.48 W
Inman, Ks., U.S.	198	38.13 N	97.46 W
Inman, S.C., U.S.	192	35.02 N	82.05 W
Inman Mills	192	35.02 N	82.06 W
Inman Valley	168b	35.30 S	138.28 E
Inn (En) ≃	32	48.35 N	13.28 E
Innamincka	166	27.45 S	140.44 E
Innbach ≃	61	48.18 N	14.07 E
Innellan	46	55.54 N	4.57 W
Inner Bay ⊂	214	42.37 N	80.24 W
Innerbraz	58	47.09 N	9.55 E
Innerferrera	58	46.31 N	9.28 E
Innerfragant	64	46.58 N	13.04 E
Inner Harbor ⊂	276	40.52 N	73.28 W
Inner Hebrides II	46	56.30 N	6.00 W
Innerkip	212	43.13 N	80.42 W
Innerleithen	46	55.38 N	3.05 W
Inner Mongolia → Nei Monggol Zizhiqu □[4]	90	43.00 N	115.00 E
Inner Sister Island I	166	39.42 S	147.55 E
Inner Sound Ц	46	57.25 N	5.56 W
Innerste ≃	52	52.15 N	9.50 E
Innerstetalsperre ◆[6]	52	51.55 N	10.17 E
Innerthal	58	47.06 N	8.56 E
Innertkirchen	58	46.42 N	8.14 E
Innervillgraten	64	46.48 N	12.23 E
Innichen → San Candido	64	46.44 N	12.17 E
Inning	60	48.05 N	11.09 E
Innisfail, Austl.	166	17.32 S	146.02 E
Innisfail, Ab., Can.	182	52.02 N	113.57 W
Innisfil Creek ≃	212	44.08 N	79.49 W
Innisfree	182	53.22 N	111.32 W
Innisplain	171a	28.10 S	152.55 E
Innokentjevka	89	49.42 N	136.57 E
Innokentjevskij	89	48.37 N	140.10 E
Innoko ≃	180	62.14 N	159.45 W
Innolovo	265a	59.47 N	29.59 E
Innoshima	96	34.17 N	133.11 E
Inno-shima I	96	34.19 N	133.10 E
Innsbruck	64	47.16 N	11.24 E
Innviertel ◆[1]	60	48.10 N	13.15 E
Inny ≃, Ire.	48	53.33 N	7.48 W
Inny ≃, Eng., U.K.	42	50.35 N	4.17 W
Ino, Nihon	96	33.33 N	133.26 E
Ino, Va., U.S.	208	37.46 N	76.48 W
Inoã	256	22.55 S	42.57 W
Inobonto	112	0.52 N	123.57 E
Inocência	255	19.47 S	51.48 W
Inokashira Park ♠	268	35.42 N	139.34 E
Inokovka	80	52.33 N	42.34 E
Inola	196	36.09 N	95.30 W
Ino-misaki ›	96	33.01 N	133.06 E
Inongo	152	1.57 S	18.16 E
Inoni	152	3.04 S	15.39 E
İnönü	130	39.48 N	30.09 E
Inoue	270	34.48 N	135.03 E
Inowrocław	30	52.48 N	18.15 E
Inozemcevo	84	44.06 N	43.06 E
Inp'ung-dong	98	41.25 N	126.34 E
Inrath ◆[8]	263	51.21 N	6.32 E
In Rhar	148	27.10 N	1.59 E
Ins	58	47.00 N	7.06 E
In Salah	148	27.12 N	2.28 E
Insan-ni	98	41.01 N	127.21 E
Insar	80	53.52 N	44.21 E
Insar ≃	80	54.43 N	45.18 E
Insch	46	57.21 N	2.37 W
Inscription, Cape ›	162	25.29 S	112.59 E
Inscription Point ›	274a	34.00 S	151.13 E
Insel Man → Isle of Man □[2]	44	54.15 N	4.30 W
Inshar	150	8.49 N	9.40 E
Inshāṣ ar-Raml	142	30.23 N	31.27 E
Insjön	26	60.41 N	15.05 E
Ińsko	30	53.27 N	15.33 E
In Sokki, Oued V	148	29.37 N	4.13 E
Inspiration	200	33.24 N	110.52 W
Insterburg → Černʼachovsk	76	54.38 N	21.49 E
Instow	184	49.44 N	108.16 W
Insurgente José María Morelos, Parque Nacional ♠	234	19.51 N	101.18 W
Inta	24	66.02 N	60.08 E
Intendente Alvear	252	35.14 S	63.35 W
İntepe	130	40.00 N	26.20 E
Intercession City	220	28.15 N	81.30 W
Intercourse	208	40.02 N	76.06 W
Interlagos ◆[8]	287b	23.42 S	46.42 W
Interlaken, Schw.	58	46.41 N	7.51 E
Interlaken, Ma., U.S.	210	42.18 N	73.19 W
Interlaken, N.J., U.S.	208	40.14 N	74.01 W
Interlaken, N.Y., U.S.	210	42.37 N	76.43 W
Interlândia	255	16.12 S	49.02 W
International Amphitheatre ℧	278	41.49 N	87.39 W
International Falls	190	48.36 N	93.24 W
International Peace Garden ♠	198	49.00 N	100.04 W
International Trade Fair ♠	267d	35.47 N	51.24 E
Interstate State Park ♠	190	45.23 N	92.40 W
Inthanon, Doi ∧	110	18.35 N	98.29 E
Intibucá	236	14.16 N	88.10 W
Intibucá □[5]	236	14.20 N	88.15 W
Intipucá	236	13.12 N	88.04 W
Intiyaco	252	28.39 S	60.05 W
Intracoastal Waterway ≡, U.S.	192	24.33 N	81.46 W
Intracoastal Waterway ≡, U.S.	196	26.04 N	97.12 W
Intragna	58	46.10 N	8.42 E
Intrånget	40	60.20 N	16.09 E
Introbio	58	45.57 N	9.27 E
Introdacqua	66	42.00 N	13.54 E
Intschön → Inch'ŏn	98	37.28 N	126.38 E
Intu	112	0.15 S	115.21 E
Intuto	246	3.39 S	74.44 W
Inubō-saki ›	94	35.42 N	140.53 E
Inukai	96	33.04 N	131.38 E
Inukjuak	176	58.27 N	78.06 W
Inútil, Bahía ⊂	254	53.30 S	69.50 W
Inuvik	180	68.25 N	133.30 W
Inuya ≃	248	10.41 S	73.30 W
Inuyama	94	35.23 N	136.56 E
In'va ≃	86	58.59 N	55.40 E
Inver	46	57.49 N	3.55 W
Inverallochy	46	57.40 N	1.55 W
Inveralochy	170	34.57 S	149.39 E
Inveraray	46	56.13 N	5.05 W
Inverarity	46	56.35 N	2.53 W
Inverbervie	46	56.51 N	2.17 W
Invercargill	172	46.24 S	168.21 E
Inverdruie	46	57.10 N	3.48 W
Inverell	166	29.47 S	151.07 E
Invergarry	46	57.02 N	4.47 W
Invergordon	46	57.42 N	4.10 W
Inverkeilor	46	56.38 N	2.32 W
Inverkeithing	46	56.02 N	3.25 W
Inverkeithny	46	57.30 N	2.37 W
Inverleigh	169	38.06 S	144.03 E
Inverloch	169	38.38 S	145.43 E
Invermay	184	51.48 N	103.09 W
Invermere	182	50.30 N	116.02 W
Invermoriston	46	57.13 N	4.38 W
Inverness, N.S., Can.	186	46.14 N	61.18 W
Inverness, P.Q., Can.	206	46.15 N	71.31 W
Inverness, Scot., U.K.	46	57.27 N	4.15 W
Inverness, Ca., U.S.	204	38.06 N	122.51 W
Inverness, Fl., U.S.	220	28.50 N	82.19 W
Inverness, Il., U.S.	216	42.07 N	88.05 W
Inverness, Ms., U.S.	194	33.21 N	90.35 W
Inveruglas	46	56.15 N	4.43 W
Inveruno	62	45.31 N	8.51 E
Inverurie	46	57.17 N	2.23 W
Inverway	162	17.50 S	129.38 E
Investigator Group II	162	33.45 S	134.30 E
Investigator Shoal ✦[2]	108	8.09 N	114.44 E
Investigator Strait Ц	166	35.25 S	137.10 E
Inwood, Mb., Can.	184	50.30 N	97.30 W
Inwood, On., Can.	214	42.49 N	81.59 W
Inwood, Fl., U.S.	220	28.02 N	81.45 W
Inwood, In., U.S.	216	41.19 N	86.12 W
Inwood, Ia., U.S.	198	43.18 N	96.25 W
Inwood, N.Y., U.S.	276	40.37 N	73.44 W
Inwood Hill Park ♠	276	40.52 N	73.56 W
Inyanga	154	18.13 S	32.46 E
Inyanga Mountains ⋀	154	18.00 S	33.00 E
Inyangani ∧	154	18.20 S	32.50 E
Inyan Kara Mountain ∧	198	44.13 N	104.21 W
Inyantue	154	18.32 S	26.41 E
Inyati	154	19.39 S	28.54 E
Inyo, Mount ∧	204	36.44 N	117.59 W
Inyokern	204	35.38 N	117.48 W
Inyo Mountains ⋀	204	36.40 N	118.10 W
Inyonga	154	6.43 S	32.04 E
Inywa	110	23.56 N	96.17 E
Inza	80	53.51 N	46.21 E
Inza ≃	80	53.54 N	45.44 E
Inzago	62	45.32 N	9.29 E
Inzai	94	35.50 N	140.09 E
Inzana Lake ⊜	182	54.58 N	124.40 W
Inžavino	80	52.19 N	42.30 E
Inzell	64	47.46 N	12.44 E
Inzer	86	54.14 N	57.34 E
Inzer ≃	86	54.30 N	56.28 E
Inzersdorf ◆[8]	264b	48.09 N	16.21 E
Inzia ≃	152	3.45 S	17.57 E
Ioanna, gora ∧	180	64.50 N	178.08 E
Ioánnina	38	39.40 N	20.50 E
Ioco	224	49.18 N	122.52 W
Iō-jima (Iwo Jima) I	174f	24.47 N	141.20 E
Iokanga ≃	24	68.00 N	39.43 E
Iola, Ks., U.S.	198	37.55 N	95.23 W
Iola, Pa., U.S.	210	45.08 N	76.32 W
Iola, Tx., U.S.	222	30.46 N	96.05 W
Iola, Wi., U.S.	190	44.30 N	89.07 W
Iolgo, chrebet ⋀	86	51.30 N	86.25 E
Iolotan'	72	37.18 N	62.21 E
Ioma	164	8.20 S	147.50 E
Iôna, Ang.	152	16.50 S	12.20 E
Iona, N.S., Can.	186	45.58 N	60.48 W
Iona, Id., U.S.	202	43.31 N	111.55 W
Iona I	46	56.19 N	6.25 W
Iôna, Parque Nacional do ♠	152	16.30 S	12.00 E
Iona, Sound of Ц	46	56.19 N	6.24 W
Iona College ℧[2]	276	40.56 N	73.47 W
Ione, Ca., U.S.	226	38.21 N	120.55 W
Ione, Or., U.S.	202	45.30 N	119.50 W
Ione, Wa., U.S.	202	48.44 N	117.24 W
Ionia, Mi., U.S.	216	42.59 N	85.04 W
Ionia, N.Y., U.S.	210	42.56 N	77.30 W
Ionia □[6]	216	42.56 N	85.04 W
Ionian Islands → Iónioi Nísoi II	38	38.30 N	20.30 E
Ionian Sea ⊤[2]	22	39.00 N	19.00 E
Ionia State Recreation Area ♠	216	42.58 N	85.36 W
Ionico, Mare → Ionian Sea ⊤[2]	22	39.00 N	19.00 E
Ionienne, Mer → Ionian Sea ⊤[2]	22	39.00 N	19.00 E
Iónioi Nísoi II	38	38.30 N	20.30 E
Ionisches Meer → Ionian Sea ⊤[2]	22	39.00 N	19.00 E
Ionivejem ≃	180	66.12 N	174.00 W
Iony, ostrov I	74	56.26 N	143.25 E
Ioppolo	68	38.35 N	15.53 E
Ioppolo Giancaxio	70	37.23 N	13.33 E
Iordan	85	39.58 N	71.46 E
Iori ≃	84	41.03 N	46.17 E
Iorskoje ploskogorje ⋀[1]	84	41.20 N	46.00 E
Iory	85	39.30 N	67.53 E
Íos	38	36.44 N	25.17 E
Íos I	38	36.42 N	25.24 E
Ioscoe, Lake ⊜	276	41.02 N	74.19 W
Iosegun ≃	182	54.44 N	117.11 W
Iosegun Lake	182	54.29 N	116.50 W
Iō-shima I	93b	30.48 N	130.18 E
Iota	194	30.19 N	92.29 W
Iovlevo	82	56.10 N	38.20 E
Iowa	194	30.14 N	93.00 W
Iowa □[3]	178	42.15 N	93.15 W
Iowa ≃	190	41.10 N	91.02 W
Iowa, South Fork ≃	190	42.18 N	93.04 W
Iowa City	190	41.39 N	91.31 W
Iowa Falls	190	42.31 N	93.15 W
Iowa Park	196	33.57 N	98.40 W
Iō-zen ∧	94	36.31 N	136.48 E
Ipa ≃	76	52.13 N	29.08 E
Ipala	154	4.30 S	32.53 E
Ipameri	255	17.43 S	48.09 W
Ipanema ◆[8]	256	22.59 S	43.12 W
Ipanema ≃	250	9.53 S	37.15 W
Ipanguaçu	250	5.30 S	36.52 W
Ipat	24	66.13 N	56.33 E
Ipatinga	255	19.30 S	42.32 W
Ipatovo	80	45.43 N	42.53 E
Ipaumirim	250	6.47 S	38.43 W
Ipava	194	40.21 N	90.19 W
Ípeiros □[9]	38	39.40 N	20.50 E
Ipel'(Ipoly) ≃	30	47.49 N	18.52 E
Iperu	150	6.52 N	3.38 E
Iphigenia Bay ⊂	180	55.40 N	133.55 W
Iphofen	56	49.42 N	10.15 E
Ipiabas	256	22.23 S	43.53 W
Ipiales	246	0.50 N	77.37 W
Ipiaú	255	14.08 S	39.44 W
Ipiíba	256	22.52 S	42.57 W
Ipil	116	7.47 N	122.35 E
Ipin → Yibin	107	28.47 N	104.38 E
Ipirá	255	12.10 S	39.44 W
Ipiranga, Bra.	246	3.12 S	66.01 W
Ipiranga, Bra.	252	25.01 S	50.35 W
Ipiranga, Bra.	287a	22.43 S	43.12 W
Ipiranga ◆[8]	287b	23.36 S	46.35 W
Ipiranga ≃, Bra.	256	23.21 S	45.10 W
Ipiranga ≃, Bra.	287a	22.48 S	43.37 W
Ipiranga, Canal ≡	287a	22.46 S	43.37 W
Ipiranga, Museu do ℧	287b	23.35 S	46.36 W
Ipitá	248	19.20 S	63.32 W
Ipitinga ≃	250	0.02 N	53.01 W
Ipixuna	250	4.22 S	44.34 W
Ipixuna ≃, Bra.	248	7.11 S	71.51 W
Ipixuna ≃, Bra.	248	5.45 S	63.02 W
Ipixuna ≃, Bra.	248	6.16 S	61.52 W
Ipixuna, Igarapé ≃	250	4.32 S	52.40 W
Ipoh	114	4.35 N	101.05 E
Ipojuca	250	8.24 S	35.04 W
Ipojuca ≃	250	8.25 S	34.58 W
Ipokera	154	8.03 S	35.41 E
Ipole	154	5.47 S	32.44 E
Ipoly (Ipel') ≃	30	47.49 N	18.52 E
Iporá, Bra.	255	16.28 S	51.07 W
Iporã, Bra.	255	23.59 S	53.37 W
Ipota	175f	18.48 S	169.16 E
Ippari ≃	70	36.52 N	14.26 E
Ippinghausen	56	51.17 N	9.08 E
Ipplepen	42	50.29 N	3.38 W
Ippy	152	6.15 N	21.12 E
Ipsala	130	40.55 N	26.23 E
Ipswich, Austl.	171a	27.36 S	152.46 E
Ipswich, Eng., U.K.	42	52.04 N	1.10 E
Ipswich, Ma., U.S.	207	42.40 N	70.50 W
Ipswich, S.D., U.S.	198	45.26 N	99.01 W
Ipswich ≃	207	42.42 N	70.48 W
Ipswich Bay ⊂	207	42.41 N	70.42 W
Ipu	250	4.20 S	40.42 W
Ipubi	250	7.39 S	40.07 W
Ipueiras	250	4.33 S	40.43 W
Ipuh	112	3.00 S	101.30 E
Ipuiúna	256	22.06 S	46.11 W
Ipun, Isla I	254	44.37 S	74.46 W
Ipupiara	255	11.49 S	42.37 W
Iput' ≃	76	52.26 N	31.02 E
Iqaluit	176	63.44 N	68.28 W
Iqe ≃	102	38.14 N	94.18 E
Iqfahṣ	142	28.47 N	30.49 E
Iquique	248	20.13 S	70.10 W
Iquitos	246	3.46 S	73.15 W
Ira	196	32.35 N	101.00 W
Iraan, Pil.	116	9.04 N	117.42 E
Iraan, Tx., U.S.	196	30.54 N	101.53 W
Ira Banda	152	5.57 N	22.04 E
Irabu	175d	24.50 N	125.09 E
Irabu-jima I	175d	24.50 N	125.10 E
Iracema	250	5.48 S	38.18 W
Iracoubo	250	5.29 N	53.13 W
Irago-misaki ›	94	34.35 N	137.01 E
Irago-suidō Ц	94	34.35 N	137.00 E
Iraí	252	27.11 S	53.15 W
Irajá ◆[8]	287a	22.51 S	43.19 W
Irajá ≃	287a	22.49 S	43.17 W
Irajol'	24	64.27 N	55.08 E
Irak → Iraq □[1]	128	33.00 N	44.00 E
Iráklion, Ellás	38	35.20 N	25.09 E
Iráklion, Ellás	267c	38.04 N	23.46 E
Irámuco	234	19.57 N	100.55 W
Iran (Īrān) □[1], Asia	118	32.00 N	53.00 E
Iran (Īrān) □[1], Asia	128	32.00 N	53.00 E
Iran, Pegunungan ⋀	112	2.05 N	114.55 E
Iran National Arts Museum ℧	267d	35.41 N	51.27 E
Īrānshahr	128	27.13 N	60.41 E
Irapa	246	10.34 N	62.35 W
Irapuato	234	20.41 N	101.21 W
Iraq (Al-ʿIrāq) □[1], Asia	118	33.00 N	44.00 E
Iraq (Al-ʿĪrāq) □[1], Asia	128	33.00 N	44.00 E
Irará	255	12.02 S	38.46 W
Iratapuru ≃	250	0.36 S	52.35 W
Irati	252	25.27 S	50.39 W
Irati ≃	34	42.35 N	1.16 W
Irauçuba	250	3.45 S	39.47 W
Irazú, Volcán ∧[1]	236	9.58 N	83.53 W
Irba	88	58.07 N	99.00 E
Irbejskoje	88	55.39 N	95.28 E
Irbeni väin (Irves šaurums) Ц	76	57.48 N	22.05 E
Irbid	132	32.33 N	35.51 E
Irbid □[8]	132	32.30 N	35.45 E
Irbīl	128	36.11 N	44.01 E
Irbīl □[4]	128	36.10 N	44.00 E
Irbit	86	57.41 N	63.03 E
Irby	262	53.21 N	3.07 W
Irchester	42	52.16 N	0.38 W
Irdning	61	47.33 N	14.01 E
Irdyn'	78	49.23 N	31.44 E
Ire, Mount ∧	175e	9.10 S	161.05 E
Irebu	152	0.37 S	17.45 E
Irecê	250	11.18 S	41.52 W
Iregua ≃	34	42.27 N	2.24 W
Ireland (Eire) □[1], Europe	22	53.00 N	8.00 W
Ireland (Eire) □[1], Europe	48	53.00 N	8.00 W
Ireland Brook ≃	276	40.25 N	74.29 W
Ireland Island I	240a	32.19 N	64.50 W
Iren' ≃	86	57.27 N	56.56 E
Irene, S. Afr.	158	25.53 S	28.13 E
Irene, S.D., U.S.	198	43.05 N	97.10 W
Irene, Tx., U.S.	222	31.59 N	96.52 W
Irene, Mount ∧	172	45.10 S	167.22 E
Ireng (Maú) ≃	246	3.33 N	59.51 W
Iresick Brook ≃	276	40.24 N	74.22 W
Ireton	198	42.58 N	96.19 W
Irfon ≃	42	52.09 N	3.24 W
Irgakly	84	44.22 N	44.45 E
Irgiz	86	48.37 N	61.16 E
Irgiz ≃	86	48.13 N	62.08 E
Iri	98	35.56 N	126.57 E
Irian Jaya □[4]	164	5.00 S	138.00 E
Iriba	146	15.07 N	22.15 E
Irié	150	8.17 N	9.11 W
Iriga	116	13.25 N	123.25 E
Irigny	62	45.40 N	4.49 E
Irîgui ◆[1]	150	16.43 N	5.30 W
Iriklinskij	86	51.39 N	58.38 E
Iringa	154	7.46 S	35.42 E
Iringa □[4]	154	9.00 S	35.00 E
Irinjālakuda	122	10.20 N	76.14 E
Iriomote-jima I	175d	24.20 N	123.50 E
Iriona	236	15.57 N	85.11 W
Iriri ≃, Bra.	250	3.52 S	52.37 W
Iriri ≃, Bra.	287a	22.41 S	43.05 W
Iriri Novo ≃	250	8.46 S	53.22 W
Irische See → Irish Sea ⊤[2]	28	53.30 N	5.20 W
Irish, Mount ∧	204	37.38 N	115.24 W
Irish Sea ⊤[2]	28	53.30 N	5.20 W
Irishtown	166	40.55 S	145.08 E
Irituia	250	1.46 S	47.26 W
Iriyamazu	268	35.16 N	139.39 E
Irkās, Wādī V	142	28.57 N	32.00 E
Irkeštam	85	39.41 N	73.55 E
Irkinejeva ≃	88	58.30 N	96.48 E
Irkinejevo	88	58.30 N	96.49 E
Irklijev	78	49.32 N	32.18 E
Irklijevskaja	78	45.51 N	39.39 E
Irkoutsk → Irkutsk	88	52.16 N	104.20 E
Irkut ≃	88	52.18 N	104.15 E
Irkutsk	88	52.16 N	104.20 E
Irkutsk □[4]	88	56.00 N	106.00 E
Irlam	44	53.28 N	2.25 W
Irland → Ireland □[1]	48	53.00 N	8.00 W
Irlanda, Mar de → Irish Sea ⊤[2]	28	53.30 N	5.20 W
Irlande → Ireland □[1]	48	53.00 N	8.00 W
Irlande, Mer d' → Irish Sea ⊤[2]	28	53.30 N	5.20 W
Irma	182	52.55 N	111.14 W
Irmauw	164	7.25 S	131.42 E
Irminger Basin ✦[1]	10	61.00 N	35.00 W
Irminio ≃	70	36.46 N	14.36 E
Irmino ◆[8]	83	48.36 N	38.36 E
Irnijärvi ⊜	26	65.36 N	29.05 E
Irnsum	52	53.05 N	5.47 E
Iro, Lac ⊜	146	10.06 N	19.25 E
Iroise ⊂	32	48.15 N	4.55 W
Iron Baron	166	32.59 S	137.09 E
Iron Belt	190	46.24 N	90.19 W
Iron Bottom Sound Ц	175e	9.15 S	160.00 E
Iron Bridge, On., Can.	190	46.17 N	83.14 W
Iron Bridge, Eng., U.K.	42	52.38 N	2.29 W
Iron Bridge Dam ◆[6]	222	32.50 N	95.54 W
Iron City	194	35.01 N	87.34 W
Iron Cove ⊂	274a	33.52 S	151.10 E
Iron Creek ≃	182	52.43 N	111.14 W
Irondale, Al., U.S.	194	33.32 N	86.42 W
Irondale, Mo., U.S.	194	37.49 N	90.40 W
Irondale, Oh., U.S.	214	40.34 N	80.43 W
Irondale ≃	212	44.49 N	78.37 W
Irondequoit	210	43.12 N	77.36 W
Irondequoit Bay ⊂	210	43.12 N	77.32 W
Iron Gate V	38	44.41 N	22.31 E
Iron Gate Reservoir ⊜[1]	38	44.30 N	22.00 E
Ironia	276	40.49 N	74.37 W
Iron Knob	166	32.44 S	137.08 E
Iron Mountain	190	45.49 N	88.03 W
Iron Mountain ∧, Az., U.S.	200	33.27 N	111.10 W
Iron Mountain ∧, Ca., U.S.	280	34.17 N	117.43 W
Iron Mountains ⋀	192	36.30 N	81.50 W
Iron Range	164	12.42 S	143.18 E
Iron Range National Park ♠	164	12.44 S	143.16 E
Iron River, Mi., U.S.	190	46.05 N	88.38 W
Iron River, Wi., U.S.	190	46.33 N	91.24 W
Iron Springs	208	39.46 N	77.25 W
Ironton, Mn., U.S.	190	46.28 N	93.58 W
Ironton, Mo., U.S.	194	37.35 N	90.37 W
Ironton, Oh., U.S.	188	38.32 N	82.40 W
Ironwood	190	46.27 N	90.10 W
Ironworks Creek ≃	285	40.10 N	74.59 W
Iroquois, On., Can.	212	44.51 N	75.19 W
Iroquois, Il., U.S.	216	40.50 N	87.35 W
Iroquois, S.D., U.S.	198	44.22 N	97.51 W
Iroquois □[6]	216	40.47 N	87.44 W
Iroquois ≃	216	41.05 N	87.49 W
Iroquois Falls	190	48.46 N	80.41 W
Iroquois Lock and Dam ◆[5]	212	44.45 N	75.23 W
Irosin	116	12.42 N	124.02 E
Írottko (Geschriebenstein) ∧	61	47.21 N	16.26 E
Irō-zaki ›	94	34.36 N	138.51 E
Irpen'	78	50.31 N	30.15 E
Irpen' ≃	78	50.34 N	30.16 E
Irrawaddy → Ayeyarwady ≃	110	20.32 N	96.55 E
Irrawaddy, Mouths of the ≃[1]	110	15.45 N	94.50 E
Irregully Creek ≃	162	23.06 S	116.21 E
Irrel	56	49.51 N	6.28 E
Irricana	182	51.19 N	113.37 W
Irrigon	202	45.53 N	119.29 W
Irša ≃	78	50.45 N	29.30 E
Iršava	78	48.20 N	23.03 E
Irschenberg	64	47.50 N	11.55 E
Irsee	58	47.54 N	10.34 E
Irsina	68	40.45 N	16.15 E
Irt ≃	44	54.22 N	3.26 W
Irtek ≃	80	51.28 N	52.39 E
Irthing ≃	44	54.55 N	2.50 W
Irthlingborough	42	52.20 N	0.37 W
Irtyš	86	54.29 N	74.22 E
Irtyš (Ertix) ≃	74	61.04 N	68.52 E
Irtysch → Irtyš ≃	72	61.04 N	68.52 E
Irtysh → Irtyš ≃	72	61.04 N	68.52 E
Irtyšsk	86	53.21 N	75.27 E
Irubaj	80	50.11 N	51.21 E
Iruma	94	35.50 N	139.24 E
Iruma ≃	94	35.57 N	139.30 E
Iruma Air Base ■	268	35.50 N	139.24 E
Iruma-kichi, Kaijō-jieitai- ■	94	35.50 N	139.24 E
Irumu	154	1.27 N	29.52 E
Irún	34	43.21 N	1.47 W
Irupana	248	16.28 S	67.28 W
Irurzun	34	42.55 N	1.50 W
Irú Tepuy ∧	246	5.25 N	61.02 W
Irves šaurums (Irbeni väin) Ц	76	57.48 N	22.05 E
Irvine, Ab., Can.	184	49.57 N	110.16 W
Irvine, Scot., U.K.	46	55.37 N	4.40 W
Irvine, Ca., U.S.	228	33.40 N	117.49 W
Irvine, Ky., U.S.	192	37.42 N	83.58 W
Irvine, Pa., U.S.	214	41.50 N	79.17 W
Irvine ≃	46	55.37 N	4.41 W
Irvine, Mount ∧	210	42.03 N	78.40 W
Irvine Creek ≃	212	43.41 N	80.25 W
Irvine Park ♠	280	33.48 N	117.45 W
Irvines Landing	182	49.38 N	124.03 W
Irvinestown	48	54.28 N	7.38 W
Irving, Il., U.S.	219	39.12 N	89.24 W
Irving, N.Y., U.S.	214	42.34 N	79.07 W
Irving, Tx., U.S.	222	32.48 N	96.56 W
Irving Park ◆[8]	278	41.57 N	87.43 W
Irvington, Il., U.S.	219	38.26 N	89.10 W
Irvington, Ky., U.S.	194	37.52 N	86.17 W
Irvington, N.J., U.S.	210	40.43 N	74.13 W
Irvington, N.Y., U.S.	210	41.02 N	73.51 W
Irvington, Oh., U.S.	218	39.51 N	84.15 W
Irvington, Va., U.S.	208	37.39 N	76.25 W
Irvington ◆[8]	284b	39.17 N	76.41 W
Irvona	214	40.46 N	78.33 W
Irwell ≃	44	53.27 N	2.17 W
Irwin, Austl.	162	29.12 S	115.04 E
Irwin, Oh., U.S.	218	40.07 N	83.29 W
Irwin, Pa., U.S.	279b	40.19 N	79.42 W
Irwin ≃	162	29.15 S	114.56 E
Irwin, Point ›	162	35.04 S	116.56 E
Irwindale	280	34.06 N	117.56 W
Irwinton	192	32.48 N	83.10 W
Is	86	58.48 N	59.43 E
Is, Jabal ∧	140	21.49 N	35.39 E
Isa	150	13.14 N	6.24 E
ʿĪsā, Ra's ›	144	15.11 N	42.39 E
Isaac ≃	166	22.52 S	149.20 E
Isaac Lake ⊜, B.C., Can.	182	53.10 N	120.50 W
Isaac Lake ⊜, On., Can.	212	44.47 N	81.14 W
Isaba	34	42.52 N	0.55 W
Isabel, Pil.	116	10.56 N	124.26 E
Isabel, S.D., U.S.	198	45.23 N	101.25 W
Isabel □[4]	175e	7.55 S	159.10 E
Isabel, Bahía ⊂	246a	0.38 S	91.27 W
Isabela, Pil.	116	10.12 N	122.59 E
Isabela (Basilan), Pil.	116	6.42 N	121.58 E
Isabela, P.R.	240m	18.30 N	67.01 W
Isabela □[4]	116	17.00 N	122.00 E
Isabela, Cabo ›	238	19.56 N	71.01 W
Isabela, Canal Ц	246a	0.20 S	90.55 W
Isabela, Isla I, Ec.	246a	0.30 S	91.06 W
Isabela, Isla I, Méx.	234	21.51 N	105.55 W
Isabelia, Cordillera ⋀	236	13.45 N	85.15 W
Isabella Indian Reservation ◆[4]	190	43.41 N	84.48 W
Isabella Lake ⊜	212	45.24 N	79.49 W
Isabella Lake ⊜[1]	204	35.40 N	118.26 W
Isabelle ≃	190	47.50 N	91.41 W
Isábena ≃	34	42.11 N	0.21 E
Isaccea	38	45.16 N	28.28 E
Ísafjarðardjúp ⊂[2]	24a	66.10 N	23.00 W
Ísafjörður	24a	66.08 N	23.13 W
Isāgarh	124	24.50 N	77.53 E
Isagatedo	273a	6.32 N	3.20 E
Isahaya	92	32.50 N	130.03 E
Isak	114	4.28 N	96.55 E
Isaka, Tan.	154	3.54 S	32.56 E
Isaka, Zaïre	152	2.35 S	18.48 E
Isaka-Buku	152	3.55 S	22.03 E
Īsa Khel	123	32.41 N	71.17 E
Isakly	80	54.08 N	51.32 E
Isakovka	86	55.45 N	74.24 E
Isakovo, S.S.S.R.	76	55.11 N	34.40 E

≃ River	Fluß	Río	Rivière	Rio
≡ Canal	Kanal	Canal	Canal	Canal
∟ Waterfall, Rapids	Wasserfall, Stromschnellen	Cascada, Rápidos	Chute d'eau, Rapides	Cascata, Rápidos
Ц Strait	Meeresstraße	Estrecho	Détroit	Estreito
⊂ Bay, Gulf	Bucht, Golf	Bahía, Golfo	Baie, Golfe	Baía, Golfo
⊜ Lake, Lakes	See, Seen	Lago, Lagos	Lac, Lacs	Lago, Lagos
☷ Swamp	Sumpf	Pantano	Marais	Pântano
⊡ Ice Features, Glacier	Eis- und Gletscherformen	Accidentes Glaciales	Formes glaciaires	Acidentes glaciares
⊤ Other Hydrographic Features	Andere Hydrographische Objekte	Otros Elementos Hidrográficos	Autres données hydrographiques	Outros acidentes hidrográficos

✦ Submarine Features	Untermeerische Objekte	Accidentes Submarinos	Formes de relief sous-marin	Acidentes submarinos
□ Political Unit	Politische Einheit	Unidad Politica	Entité politique	Unidade política
℧ Cultural Institution	Kulturelle Institution	Institución Cultural	Institution culturelle	Institução cultural
⊥ Historical Site	Historische Stätte	Sitio Histórico	Site historique	Sitio histórico
♠ Recreational Site	Erholungs- und Ferienort	Sitio de Recreo	Centre de loisirs	Area de Lazer
⊠ Airport	Flughafen	Aeropuerto	Aéroport	Aeroporto
■ Military Installation	Militäranlage	Instalación Militar	Installation militaire	Instalação militar
◆ Miscellaneous	Verschiedenes	Misceláneo	Divers	Diversos

Name	Page	Lat.°′	Long.°′
Isakovo, S.S.S.R.	76	60.30 N	41.13 E
Isakovo, S.S.S.R.	82	54.36 N	37.02 E
Isakovo, S.S.S.R.	265b	55.59 N	37.23 E
Işalniţa	38	44.24 N	23.44 E
Isalo, Massif de l' ⋀	157b	22.45 S	45.15 E
Isalo, Parc National de l' ♠	157b	22.45 S	45.15 E
Isana (Içana) ≏	246	0.26 N	67.19 W
Īsānagar	124	27.54 N	81.13 E
Isandhlwana ⊥	158	28.21 S	30.39 E
Isandja Etat	152	2.59 S	22.00 E
Isando	273d	26.09 S	28.12 E
Isanga	152	1.26 S	22.18 E
Isangano National Park ♠	154	11.10 S	30.40 E
Isangel	175f	19.32 S	169.16 E
Isangi	152	0.46 N	24.15 E
Is'angulovo	86	52.12 N	56.36 E
Isanlu Makutu	150	8.17 N	5.46 E
Isan-ni	98	40.46 N	128.55 E
Isanti	190	45.29 N	93.14 W
Isar ≏	30	48.49 N	12.58 E
Isara	150	6.59 N	3.41 E
Isarco (Eisack) ≏	64	46.27 N	11.18 E
Isarco, Valle V	64	46.45 N	11.37 E
Isarog, Mount ∧	116	13.39 N	123.23 E
Isasi	273a	6.40 N	3.23 E
Isawa	94	35.39 N	138.38 E
Isbergues	50	50.37 N	2.27 E
Isbister	46a	60.36 N	1.19 W
İscehisar	130	38.51 N	30.45 E
Iščeino	76	52.57 N	38.50 E
Iščerskaja	84	43.43 N	45.08 E
Ischgl	58	47.01 N	10.17 E
Ischia	68	40.44 N	13.57 E
Ischia, Isola d' I	68	40.43 N	13.54 E
Ischia di Castro	66	42.33 N	11.45 E
Ischim → Išim ≏	86	57.45 N	71.12 E
Ischitella	68	41.54 N	15.54 E
Ischma → Ižma ≏	24	65.19 N	52.54 E
Ischodnaja, gora ∧	180	64.50 N	173.26 W
Ischua	210	42.15 N	78.24 W
Ischua Creek ≏	210	42.10 N	78.23 W
Iscuandé ≏	246	2.38 N	78.04 W
Isdell ≏	162	16.27 S	124.51 E
Isdes	50	47.40 N	2.15 E
Ise (Uji-yamada)	94	34.29 N	136.42 E
Ise ≏	54	52.30 N	10.33 E
Isefjord c	41	55.52 N	11.49 E
Isehara	94	35.24 N	139.18 E
Išejevka	80	54.25 N	48.16 E
Iseke	154	6.25 S	35.01 E
Isel ≏	64	46.50 N	12.47 E
Iselin, N.J., U.S.	210	40.34 N	74.19 W
Iselin, Pa., U.S.	214	40.33 N	79.23 W
Iselle	58	46.12 N	8.12 E
Iseltwald	58	46.43 N	7.58 E
Isen	60	48.13 N	12.04 E
Isen ≏	60	48.15 N	12.40 E
Isenbajevo	80	56.03 N	53.25 E
Isenbüttel	52	52.26 N	10.34 E
Isenyela	154	8.36 S	33.30 E
Iseo	64	45.39 N	10.03 E
Iseo, Lago d' ⊜	64	45.43 N	10.04 E
Iseramagazi	154	4.40 S	32.09 E
Iseran, Col de l')(	62	45.25 N	7.02 E
Isère □[5]	62	45.10 N	5.50 E
Isère ≏	62	44.59 N	4.51 E
Iseri	273a	6.39 N	3.23 E
Iseri-Oke	273a	6.38 N	3.23 E
Iseri-Osun	273a	6.31 N	3.17 E
Iserlohn	56	51.22 N	7.41 E
Isernhagen	52	52.26 N	9.51 E
Isernia	66	41.36 N	14.14 E
Isernia □[4]	66	41.40 N	14.15 E
Isesaki	94	36.19 N	139.12 E
Ise-Shima-kokuritsu-kōen ♠	92	34.23 N	136.48 E
Iset' ≏	86	56.36 N	66.24 E
Isetskoje	86	56.29 N	65.21 E
Ise-wan c	94	34.43 N	136.43 E
Iseyin	150	7.58 N	3.36 E
Isezaki → Isesaki	92	36.19 N	139.12 E
Isfahan → Eşfahān	128	32.40 N	51.38 E
Isfana	85	39.50 N	69.31 E
Isfana ≏	85	40.13 N	69.26 E
Isfara	85	40.07 N	70.38 E
'Isfiyā	132	32.43 N	35.04 E
Ishenga Oswe	152	3.46 S	22.34 E
Isheri-Olofin	273a	6.35 N	3.17 E
Isherton	246	2.19 N	59.22 W
Ishi ≏	270	34.35 N	135.38 E
Ishibashi	94	36.26 N	139.52 E
Ishibe	94	35.00 N	136.04 E
Ishigaki	175d	24.20 N	124.09 E
Ishigaki-shima I	175d	24.24 N	124.12 E
Ishige	94	36.07 N	139.58 E
Ishii	96	34.04 N	134.26 E
Ishikari ≏	92a	43.15 N	141.23 E
Ishikari-dake ∧	92a	43.33 N	143.02 E
Ishikari-heiya ≌	92a	43.15 N	141.23 E
Ishikari-sanchi ⋀	92a	43.35 N	143.00 E
Ishikari-wan c	92a	43.25 N	141.01 E
Ishikawa, Nihon	94	37.09 N	140.27 E
Ishikawa, Nihon	174m	26.25 N	127.50 E
Ishikawa □[5]	94	36.45 N	136.45 E
Ishiki	94	34.48 N	137.01 E
Ishikiri	270	34.41 N	135.39 E
I-shima I	96	33.51 N	134.49 E
Ishinomaki	92	38.25 N	141.18 E
Ishinomaki-wan c	92	38.18 N	141.18 E
Ishioka	94	36.11 N	140.16 E
Ishiyama	270	34.58 N	135.55 E
Ishizuchi-san ∧	96	33.46 N	133.07 E
Ishkumān	123	36.32 N	73.49 E
Ishmant	142	29.12 N	31.11 E
Ishpeming	190	46.29 N	87.40 W
Ishuizu ≏	270	34.33 N	135.27 E
Ishurdi	124	24.08 N	89.05 E
Isidro Casanova	288	34.42 S	58.35 W
Isigny	32	49.19 N	1.06 W
Işık Dağı ∧	130	38.21 N	36.32 E
Işıklı	130	38.19 N	29.51 E
Işıklı Burnu ›	267b	41.14 N	29.15 E
Isili	71	39.44 N	9.06 E
Isil'kul'	86	54.55 N	71.16 E
Išim	86	56.09 N	69.27 E
Išim ≏	86	57.45 N	71.12 E
Išimbaj	86	53.28 N	56.02 E
Išimka	86	51.24 N	67.08 E
Išimskaja step' ≌	86	55.00 N	70.00 E
Isimu	112	0.40 N	122.51 E
Isinga	88	52.55 N	112.00 E
Isiolo	154	0.21 N	37.35 E
Isiolo Game Reserve ✦[4]	154	0.32 N	37.34 E
Isipingo	158	29.59 S	30.56 E
Isipingo Beach	158	29.59 S	30.57 E
Isiro (Paulis)	154	2.47 N	27.37 E
Isis	166	25.12 S	152.13 E
Isisford	166	24.16 S	144.26 E
Iskandar	85	41.36 N	69.43 E
Iskâr ≏	38	43.44 N	24.27 E
Iskâr, jazovir ⊜[1]	38	42.28 N	23.35 E
Iškašim	123	36.44 N	71.37 E
Iskaten', chrebet ⋀	180	66.30 N	179.00 W
Iškejevo	80	55.51 N	50.56 E
İskele	130	35.17 N	33.52 E
İskenderun	130	36.37 N	36.07 E
İskenderun Körfezi (Gulf of Alexandretta) c	130	36.30 N	35.40 E
Iske-R'az'ap	80	54.36 N	49.42 E
İskilip	130	40.45 N	34.29 E
Iski-Naukat	85	40.16 N	72.36 E
Iskininskij	80	47.13 N	52.41 E
Iskitim	86	54.38 N	83.18 E
Iskona ≏	82	55.34 N	36.05 E
Iskushuban	144	10.17 N	50.14 E
Iskut ≏	180	56.42 N	131.45 W
Isla	234	18.01 N	95.30 W
Isla ≏	46	57.30 N	2.47 W
Isla, Salar de la ≌	252	25.49 S	68.53 W
Isla Cristina	34	37.12 N	7.19 W
Isla de Maipo	252	33.45 S	70.54 W
İslâhiye	130	37.03 N	36.36 E
Islāmābād → Anantnāg, India	123	33.44 N	75.09 E
Islāmābād, Pāk.	123	33.42 N	73.10 E
Isla Mala	258	34.12 S	56.21 W
Islāmkot	120	24.42 N	70.11 E
Islamorada	220	24.55 N	80.37 W
Islāmpur, India	122	17.03 N	74.16 E
Islāmpur, India	124	25.09 N	85.12 E
Islāmpur, India	124	26.16 N	88.12 E
Islāmpur, India	126	21.43 N	87.39 E
Islāmpur, India	126	24.09 N	88.28 E
Isla Mujeres	232	21.12 N	86.43 W
Island	194	37.26 N	87.08 W
Island □[6]	224	48.07 N	122.36 W
Island → Iceland □[1]	24a	65.00 N	18.00 W
Island ≏	262	53.44 N	2.51 W
Island Bay c	116	9.06 N	118.10 E
Island Beach State Park ♠	208	39.50 N	74.06 W
Island Bend	171b	36.19 S	148.29 E
Island Creek	283	42.00 N	70.43 W
Island Falls, Sk., Can.	184	55.32 N	102.21 W
Island Falls, Me., U.S.	188	46.00 N	68.16 W
Island Heights	208	39.56 N	74.09 W
Islandia → Iceland □[1]	24a	65.00 N	18.00 W
Island Lagoon ⊜	166	31.30 S	136.40 E
Island Lake, Mb., Can.	184	53.58 N	94.47 W
Island Lake, Il., U.S.	216	42.17 N	88.12 W
Island Lake, Mi., U.S.	281	42.31 N	83.44 W
Island Lake ⊜	184	53.47 N	94.25 W
Island Lake State Recreation Area ♠	216	42.30 N	83.43 W
Island Park, Id., U.S.	202	44.24 N	111.19 W
Island Park, N.Y., U.S.	276	40.36 N	73.39 W
Island Park, R.I., U.S.	207	41.37 N	71.13 W
Island Park Reservoir ⊜[1]	202	44.25 N	111.29 W
Island Point ›	162	30.20 S	115.02 E
Island Pond	188	44.48 N	71.52 W
Island Pond ⊜	186	48.25 N	56.23 W
Islands, Bay of c, Nf., Can.	186	49.10 N	58.15 W
Islands, Bay of c, N.Z.	172	35.12 S	174.10 E
Island View	216	40.31 N	83.53 W
Isla Patrulla	252	32.59 S	54.35 W
Islas de la Bahía □[5]	236	16.20 N	86.30 W
Islas Malvinas → Falkland Islands □[2]	254	51.45 S	59.00 W
Isla Verde	252	33.14 S	62.24 W
Isla Vista	204	34.25 N	119.50 W
Islay I	46	55.46 N	6.10 W
Islay, Punta ›	248	17.01 S	72.07 W
Islay, Rhinns of ›[1]	46	55.45 N	6.25 W
Islay, Sound of ꭒ	46	55.50 N	6.01 W
Isle	190	46.08 N	93.28 W
Isle ≏, Fr.	32	44.55 N	0.15 W
Isle ≏, Eng., U.K.	42	50.59 N	2.53 W
Isle-Adam, Forêt de l' ♠	261	49.05 N	2.15 E
Isle-aux-Morts	186	47.35 N	58.59 W
Isle of Hope	192	31.58 N	81.05 W
Isle of Man □[2], Europe	22	54.15 N	4.30 W
Isle of Man □[2], Europe	44	54.15 N	4.30 W
Isle of Man (Ronaldsway) Airport ⊠	44	54.06 N	4.36 W
Isle of Palms	192	32.47 N	79.48 W
Isle of Wight	208	36.54 N	76.42 W
Isle of Wight □[6], Eng., U.K.	42	50.40 N	1.20 W
Isle of Wight □[6], Va., U.S.	208	36.50 N	76.42 W
Isle of Wight Bay c	208	38.22 N	75.06 W
Isle Royale National Park ♠	190	48.00 N	89.00 W
Isles, Lake of the ⊜	212	44.19 N	75.59 W
Isle Saint George	214	41.43 N	82.49 W
Islesboro Island I	188	44.20 N	68.53 W
Isleta	200	34.54 N	106.41 W
Isleta Indian Reservation ✦[4]	200	34.55 N	106.45 W
Isleton	226	38.09 N	121.36 W
Islets-Caribou	186	49.30 N	67.14 W
Isleworth ✦[8]	260	51.28 N	0.20 W
Islington	207	42.13 N	71.11 W
Islington ✦[8], On., Can.	275b	43.39 N	79.32 W
Islington ✦[8], Eng., U.K.	42	51.34 N	0.06 W
Islip, Eng., U.K.	42	51.50 N	1.14 W
Islip, N.Y., U.S.	276	40.43 N	73.12 W
Islip Terrace	276	40.44 N	73.11 W
Islivig	46	58.05 N	7.11 W
Isloč' ≏	76	53.55 N	26.13 E
Islón	252	29.54 S	71.12 W
Ismael Cortinas (Arroyo Grande)	258	33.58 S	57.06 W
Ismailia → Al-Ismā'īlīyah	142	30.35 N	32.16 E
Ismā'īlīyah ✦[8]	273c	30.03 N	31.14 E
Ismā'īlīyah, Tur'at al- ≖	142	30.04 N	31.16 E
İsmailli	130	38.56 N	27.13 E
Ismailly	84	40.47 N	48.09 E
Ismailovo	80	55.34 N	54.39 E
Ismaning	60	48.14 N	11.41 E
Isnā	140	25.18 N	32.33 E
Isny	58	47.41 N	10.02 E
Isoanala	157b	23.50 S	45.44 E
Isobe	94	34.22 N	136.49 E
Isogo ✦[8]	268	35.23 N	139.37 E
Isojoki	26	62.07 N	21.58 E
Isoka	154	10.10 S	32.35 E
Isokyrö	26	63.00 N	22.19 E
Isola, Fr.	62	44.11 N	7.03 E
Isola, Ms., U.S.	194	33.15 N	90.35 W
Isola, Monte ∧	64	45.42 N	10.05 E
Isola d'Asti	62	44.50 N	8.11 E
Isola del Cantone	62	44.39 N	8.57 E
Isola del Gran Sasso d'Italia	66	42.30 N	13.40 E
Isola della Scala	64	45.16 N	11.00 E
Isola del Liri	66	41.41 N	13.34 E
Isola di Capo Rizzuto	68	38.58 N	17.06 E
Isola Dovarese	64	45.10 N	10.18 E
Isola Farnese ✦[8]	66	42.01 N	12.23 E
Isola Vicentina	64	45.38 N	11.25 E
Isoletta	66	41.30 N	13.34 E
Isolillock Peak ∧	224	49.18 N	121.27 W
Isolo	273a	6.32 N	3.19 E
Isone	58	46.08 N	8.59 E
Isonzo (Soča) ≏	64	45.47 N	13.32 E
Isorella	64	45.18 N	10.19 E
Iso-Syöte ∧[2]	26	65.37 N	27.35 E
Iso-zaki ›	94	36.23 N	140.38 E
Ispani	68	40.08 N	15.34 E
Isparta	130	37.46 N	30.33 E
Isparta □[4]	130	38.00 N	31.00 E
Isperih	38	43.43 N	26.50 E
Ispica	70	36.47 N	14.55 E
Ispica, Cava d' ⫠[5]	70	36.51 N	14.51 E
Ispikān	128	26.14 N	62.12 E
İspir	130	40.29 N	41.00 E
Ispra	62	45.49 N	8.37 E
Ispringen	56	48.55 N	8.40 E
Israel (Yisra'el) □[1], Asia	118	31.30 N	35.00 E
Israel (Yisra'el) □[1], Asia	132	31.30 N	35.00 E
Israel ≏	188	44.29 N	71.35 W
Issa	80	53.52 N	44.51 E
Issa ≏	76	56.58 N	28.47 E
Issano	246	5.49 N	59.25 W
Issaquah	224	47.31 N	122.01 W
Issaran, Ra's ›	142	28.48 N	32.47 E
Issel (Oude IJssel) ≏	52	52.00 N	6.10 E
Isselburg	52	51.51 N	6.28 E
Isselhorst	52	51.57 N	8.24 E
Isser, Oued ≏, Alg.	34	35.08 N	1.28 W
Isser, Oued ≏, Alg.	34	36.52 N	3.48 E
Issia	150	6.29 N	6.35 W
Issigeac	32	44.44 N	0.36 E
Issime	62	45.41 N	7.51 E
Issogne	62	45.39 N	7.41 E
Issoire	32	45.33 N	3.15 E
Issole ≏	62	43.27 N	6.12 E
Issou	261	48.59 N	1.48 E
Issoudun	32	46.57 N	2.00 E
Issum	52	51.32 N	6.25 E
Issuna	154	5.23 S	34.46 E
Is-sur-Tille	58	47.31 N	5.06 E
Issy	50	48.49 N	2.17 E
Issyk	85	43.22 N	77.28 E
Issyk-Kul', ozero ⊜	85	42.25 N	77.15 E
Issy-les-Moulineaux	261	48.49 N	2.17 E
Īstādeh-ye Moqor, Āb-e ⊜	120	32.32 N	67.57 E
Istana Presidential Palace ʋ	269e	6.10 S	106.49 E
İstanbul, Tür.	130	41.01 N	28.58 E
İstanbul, Tür.	267b	41.01 N	28.58 E
İstanbul □[4]	130	41.10 N	28.45 E
Istanbul (Yeşilköy) International Airport ⊠	267b	40.58 N	28.49 E
İstanbul Boğazı (Bosporus) ꭒ	130	41.06 N	29.04 E
Istanbul University ʋ[2]	267b	41.00 N	28.58 E
Iṣṭanhā	142	30.28 N	31.07 E
Istead Rise	260	51.24 N	0.22 E
Isteren ⊜	26	61.58 N	11.48 E
Isthmus Bay c	212	45.00 N	81.15 W
Istiaía	38	38.57 N	23.09 E
İstinye ✦[8]	267b	41.06 N	29.03 E
Istisu	84	39.57 N	45.59 E
Istmina	246	5.10 N	76.39 W
Isto, Mount ∧	180	69.12 N	143.48 W
Istobensk	80	58.25 N	48.48 E
Istobnoje, S.S.S.R.	78	51.08 N	37.21 E
Istobnoje, S.S.S.R.	78	51.16 N	38.39 E
Istok	38	42.47 N	20.29 E
Istokpoga, Lake ⊜	220	27.22 N	81.17 W
Istra	82	55.55 N	36.52 E
Istra ›[1]	36	45.15 N	14.00 E
Istra ≏	82	55.44 N	37.08 E
Istrana	64	45.41 N	12.07 E
Istres	62	43.31 N	4.59 E
Istria → Istra ›[1]	36	45.15 N	14.00 E
Istrinskoje vodochranilišče ⊜[1]	82	56.04 N	36.49 E
Isulan	116	6.34 N	124.37 E
Isumi	94	35.17 N	140.19 E
Isumi ≏	94	35.18 N	140.25 E
Isumrud Strait ꭒ	164	4.45 S	145.50 E
Isunba	273a	6.27 N	3.17 E
Iswarīpur	126	22.19 N	89.07 E
Iswepe	158	26.50 S	30.31 E
Itá	252	25.29 S	57.21 W
Itabaiana, Bra.	250	7.20 S	35.20 W
Itabaiana, Bra.	250	10.41 S	37.26 W
Itabaiana, Bra.	250	11.16 S	37.47 W
Itabapoana	255	21.18 S	40.58 W
Itabashi ✦[8]	268	35.45 N	139.43 E
Itaberá	255	23.51 S	49.09 W
Itaberaba	255	12.32 S	40.18 W
Itaberaí	255	16.02 S	49.48 W
Itabi	250	10.08 S	37.06 W
Itabira	255	19.37 S	43.13 W
Itaboca	256	22.03 S	44.05 W
Itaboraí	256	22.45 S	42.52 W
Itaboraí □[7]	287a	22.43 S	43.00 W
Itabuna	255	14.48 S	39.16 W
Itacaiunas ≏	250	5.21 S	49.08 W
Itacajá	250	8.19 S	47.46 W
Itacambiruçu ≏	255	16.44 S	42.45 W
Itacaré	255	14.18 S	39.00 W
Itacoatiara	250	3.08 S	58.25 W
Itacoatiara, Ponta de ›	287a	22.59 S	43.02 W
Itacuaí ≏	246	4.20 S	70.12 W
Itacurubí del Rosario	252	24.29 S	56.41 W
Itacuruça, Ilha de I	256	22.56 S	43.53 W
Itacurussá	256	22.55 S	43.55 W
Itaetê	255	12.59 S	40.58 W
Itagacaba ≏	256	22.34 S	44.56 W
Itagi	255	14.10 S	40.01 W
Itaguaçu	255	19.48 S	40.51 W
Itaguaí	256	22.52 S	43.47 W
Itaguajé	255	22.37 S	51.59 W
Itaguara	255	20.23 S	44.29 W
Itaguaré, Pico do ∧	256	22.30 S	45.10 W
Ítaguari ≏	255	14.11 S	44.40 W
Itaguaru	255	15.44 S	49.37 W
Itaguatins	250	5.47 S	47.29 W
Itagüí	246	6.10 N	75.36 W
Itaí	255	23.24 S	49.06 W
Itá-Ibaté	252	27.26 S	57.20 W
Itaiçaba	250	4.40 S	37.51 W
Itaim	256	22.24 S	45.53 W
Itaim ≏, Bra.	250	7.02 S	42.02 W
Itaim ≏, Bra.	256	23.07 S	45.08 W
Itaim ≏, Bra.	256	22.19 S	45.51 W
Itainópolis	250	7.24 S	41.31 W
Itaiópolis	252	26.20 S	49.56 W
Itaipava	256	22.23 S	43.08 W
Itaipu, Bra.	256	22.58 S	43.02 W
Itaipu, Bra.	287a	22.44 S	43.26 W
Itaipu, Lagoa de c	287a	22.58 S	43.02 W
Itaipu, Ponta de ›	287a	22.59 S	43.03 W
Itäisen Suomenlahden kansallispuisto ♠	26	60.15 N	27.00 E
Itaituba	250	4.17 S	55.59 W
Itajá	255	19.07 S	51.37 W
Itajaí	252	26.53 S	48.39 W
Itajaí do Sul ≏	252	27.12 S	49.39 W
Itajubá	256	22.26 S	45.27 W
Itaju do Colônia	255	15.09 S	39.44 W
Itajuípe	255	14.41 S	39.22 W
Itaka, S.S.S.R.	88	53.53 N	118.42 E
Itaka, Tan.	154	8.52 S	32.47 E
Itaki	273a	6.43 N	3.17 E
Itako	94	35.56 N	140.33 E
Itakura, Nihon	94	36.13 N	139.36 E
Itakura, Nihon	94	37.03 N	138.18 E
Itala Game Reserve ✦[4]	158	27.31 S	31.19 E
Italia → Italy □[1]	36	42.50 N	12.50 E
Itálica ⊥	34	37.30 N	6.05 W
Italie → Italy □[1]	36	42.50 N	12.50 E
Italien → Italy □[1]	36	42.50 N	12.50 E
Italy	222	32.11 N	96.53 W
Italy (Italia) □[1], Europe	22	42.50 N	12.50 E
Italy (Italia) □[1], Europe	36	42.50 N	12.50 E
Itamaraju	255	17.05 S	39.31 W
Itamarandiba	255	17.51 S	42.51 W
Itamarandiba ≏	255	17.18 S	42.48 W
Itamarati	256	21.25 S	42.49 W
Itamari	255	13.47 S	39.37 W
Itamataré	250	2.16 S	46.24 W
Itambacuri	255	18.01 S	41.42 W
Itambé	255	15.15 S	40.37 W
Itambi	256	22.44 S	42.58 W
Itami	96	34.46 N	135.25 E
Itami, Camp ■	270	34.47 N	135.24 E
Itamonte	256	22.17 S	44.53 W
Itampolo	157b	24.41 S	43.57 E
Itānagar	120	27.09 N	93.33 E
Itandéua, Lago ⊜	250	2.01 S	55.10 W
Itandrano	157b	21.47 S	45.17 E
Itanhaém	255	24.11 S	46.47 W
Itanhandu	256	22.18 S	44.57 W
Itanhauã ≏	248	4.45 S	63.48 W
Itanhém	255	17.09 S	40.20 W
Itanhém ≏	255	17.32 S	39.12 W
Itanhomi	255	19.10 S	41.52 W
Itano	96	34.07 N	134.28 E
Itany (Litani) ≏	250	3.40 N	54.00 W
Itaobim	255	16.34 S	41.30 W
Itaocaia	287a	22.58 S	43.01 W
Itapaci	255	14.57 S	49.34 W
Itapagé	250	3.41 S	39.34 W
Itapagipe	255	19.54 S	49.22 W
Itapanhaú ≏	256	23.51 S	46.10 W
Itaparaná ≏	248	5.47 S	63.03 W
Itaparica, Ilha de I	255	13.00 S	38.42 W
Itapaya	248	17.34 S	66.21 W
Itapé	255	14.54 S	39.26 W
Itapebi	255	15.56 S	39.32 W
Itapecerica	255	20.28 S	45.07 W
Itapecerica da Serra	256	23.43 S	46.50 W
Itapecerica da Serra □[7]	287b	23.44 S	46.52 W
Itapechinga	256	22.58 S	46.35 W
Itapecuru ≏	250	2.52 S	44.12 W
Itapecuru-Mirim	250	3.24 S	44.20 W
Itapemirim	255	21.01 S	40.50 W
Itapera	250	2.32 S	43.47 W
Itaperina, Pointe ›	157b	24.59 S	47.06 E
Itaperuna	255	21.12 S	41.54 W
Itapeteiú	256	22.54 S	42.47 W
Itapetim	250	7.22 S	37.11 W
Itapetinga	255	15.15 S	40.15 W
Itapetininga	255	23.36 S	48.03 W
Itapetininga ≏	255	23.35 S	48.27 W
Itapeva, Bra.	255	23.58 S	48.52 W
Itapeva, Bra.	256	22.46 S	46.13 W
Itapevi	256	23.33 S	46.56 W
Itapevi □[7]	287b	23.31 S	46.55 W
Itapicuru	250	11.19 S	38.15 W
Itapicuru ≏	250	11.47 S	37.32 W
Itapipoca	250	3.30 S	39.35 W
Itapira	256	22.26 S	46.50 W
Itapiranga, Bra.	250	2.45 S	58.01 W
Itapiranga, Bra.	252	27.08 S	53.43 W
Itapirapuã	255	15.52 S	50.36 W
Itapitanga	255	14.26 S	39.34 W
Itapiúna	250	4.33 S	38.57 W
Itápolis	255	21.35 S	48.46 W
Itaporã	255	22.01 S	54.54 W
Itaporã de Goiás	250	8.02 S	48.39 W
Itaporanga, Bra.	250	7.18 S	38.10 W
Itaporanga, Bra.	255	23.42 S	49.29 W
Itaporanga d'Ajuda	250	10.59 S	37.18 W
Itapúa □[5]	252	26.50 S	55.50 W
Itapuranga	255	15.35 S	49.59 W
Itaquaciara	287b	23.47 S	46.51 W
Itaquaquecetuba	256	23.29 S	46.21 W
Itaquaquecetuba □[7]	287b	23.28 S	46.20 W
Itaquara	255	13.27 S	39.57 W
Itaquari	255	20.20 S	40.22 W
Itaquera ✦[8]	256	23.32 S	46.27 W
Itaquera, Ribeirão ≏	287b	23.28 S	46.26 W
Itaqui	252	29.08 S	56.33 W
Itaqui, Serra do ∧	287b	23.28 S	46.55 W
Itaquyry	252	24.56 S	55.13 W
Itarantim	255	15.39 S	40.03 W
Itararé	255	24.07 S	49.20 W
Itararé ≏	252	23.10 S	49.42 W
Itārsi	124	22.37 N	77.45 E
Itarumã	255	18.42 S	51.25 W
Itasca, Il., U.S.	278	41.58 N	88.00 W
Itasca, Tx., U.S.	222	32.09 N	97.08 W
Itasca, Lake ⊜	198	47.11 N	95.12 W
Itasca State Park ♠	198	47.18 N	95.18 W
Itatá ≏, Bra.	250	3.28 S	51.57 W
Itata ≏, Chile	252	36.23 S	72.52 W
Itatí	252	27.16 S	58.15 W
Itatiaia	256	22.30 S	44.34 W
Itatiaia, Parque Nacional do ♠	256	22.28 S	44.37 W
Itatiba	256	23.00 S	46.51 W
Itatinga	255	23.07 S	48.36 W
Itatira	250	4.30 S	39.37 W
Itatka	86	56.49 N	85.37 E
Itatolo	273b	4.09 S	15.15 E
Itatskij	86	56.04 N	89.05 E
Itatupã	250	0.37 S	51.12 W
Itaú	250	5.50 S	37.59 W
Itauaiuri, Serra ∧[2]	250	1.47 S	54.06 W
Itauçu	255	16.13 S	49.37 W
Itaueira	250	7.36 S	43.02 W
Itaueiras ≏	250	6.41 S	42.55 W
Itaúna	255	20.04 S	44.34 W
Itaúna, Morro do ∧[2]	287a	22.46 S	43.02 W
Itāwa	124	25.32 N	76.22 E
Itazuke-kūkō ⊠	96	33.35 N	130.28 E
Itbayat Island I	108	20.46 N	121.50 E
Ité ≏	246	7.00 N	74.15 W
Itéa	38	38.26 N	22.24 E
Iténez (Guaporé) ≏	248	11.54 S	65.01 W
Ith ∧	52	52.05 N	9.35 E
Ithaca, Mi., U.S.	190	43.17 N	84.36 W
Ithaca, N.Y., U.S.	210	42.26 N	76.29 W
Itháki	38	38.23 N	20.42 E
Itháki I	38	38.24 N	20.42 E
Ithan Creek ≏	285	40.00 N	75.21 W
Ithnayn	142	30.41 N	32.21 E
Ithon ≏	42	52.12 N	3.27 W
Itigi	154	5.42 S	34.29 E
Itikawa → Ichikawa	94	35.44 N	139.55 E
Itimādpur	124	27.15 N	78.12 E
Itimbiri ≏	152	2.02 N	22.44 E
Itinga	255	16.36 S	41.47 W
Itinga ≏	255	16.35 S	41.45 W
Itinomiya → Ichinomiya	94	35.18 N	136.48 E
Itipo	152	0.50 S	18.35 E
Itiquira	255	17.12 S	54.07 W
Itiquira ≏	248	17.18 S	56.44 W
Itirapina	255	22.15 S	47.49 W
Itire	273a	6.31 N	3.21 E
Itiruçu	255	13.31 S	40.09 W
Itiúba	250	10.43 S	39.51 W
Itkillik ≏	180	70.08 N	150.57 W
Itlar'	82	56.51 N	39.17 E
Itlīdim	142	27.52 N	30.48 E
Itmīdah	142	30.46 N	31.20 E
Itmuryn, ozero ⊜	80	49.30 N	52.22 E
Itō	94	34.58 N	139.05 E
Itobi	256	21.44 S	46.58 W
Itobo	154	4.10 S	33.01 E
Itóca, Ilha de I	287a	22.46 S	43.04 W
Itoculo	154	14.42 S	40.18 E
Itoigawa	94	37.02 N	137.51 E
Itoko	152	1.00 S	21.45 E
Itomamo, Lac ⊜	186	49.11 N	70.28 W
Itoman	174m	26.08 N	127.40 E
Iton ≏	50	49.09 N	1.12 E
Itonamas ≏	248	12.28 S	64.24 W
Itororó	255	15.07 S	40.06 W
Itri	66	41.17 N	13.32 E
Itsā	142	29.15 N	30.48 E
Itsukaichi, Nihon	94	35.44 N	139.13 E
Itsukaichi, Nihon	96	34.24 N	132.22 E
Itsuki	92	32.24 N	130.50 E
Itsuku-shima I	96	34.16 N	132.19 E
Itsuwa	92	32.30 N	130.10 E
Itta Bena	194	33.29 N	90.19 W
Ittel, Oued V	148	34.19 N	6.01 E
Itter ≏	263	51.09 N	6.52 E
Ittersum	52	52.28 N	6.07 E
Itteville	261	48.31 N	2.21 E
Ittiri	71	40.36 N	8.34 E
Itu	255	23.16 S	47.19 W
Itu ≏	252	29.25 S	55.51 W
Ituaçu	255	13.49 S	41.18 W
Ituango	246	7.04 N	75.45 W
Ituberá	255	13.44 S	39.09 W
Itucumã ≏	248	6.59 S	69.48 W
Itueta	255	19.23 S	41.11 W
Ituí	256	21.32 S	42.55 W
Ituí ≏	246	4.38 S	70.19 W
Ituim ≏	252	28.35 S	51.20 W
Ituiutaba	255	18.58 S	49.28 W
Itula	154	3.29 S	27.52 E
Itumbiara	255	18.25 S	49.13 W
Itumirim	256	21.19 S	44.53 W
Itum-Kale	84	42.43 N	45.35 E
Ituna	184	51.10 N	103.30 W
Itungi Port	154	9.35 S	33.56 E
Ituni	246	5.30 N	58.14 W
Itupeva	256	23.09 S	47.04 W
Itupeva ≏	256	22.03 S	47.15 W
Itupiranga	250	5.09 S	49.20 W
Ituporanga	252	27.25 S	49.36 W
Iturama	255	19.44 S	50.11 W
Iturbe	252	26.01 S	56.30 W
Iturbide	232	19.40 N	89.37 W
Ituri ≏	154	1.40 N	27.01 E
Iturup, ostrov (Etorofu-tō) I	92a	44.54 N	147.30 E
Itutinga	256	21.18 S	44.40 W
Ituverava	255	20.20 S	47.47 W
Ituxi ≏	248	7.18 S	64.51 W
Ituzaingó, Arg.	252	27.36 S	56.41 W
Ituzaingó, Arg.	258	34.40 S	58.40 W
Ituzaingó, Ur.	258	34.25 S	56.26 W
Itwa	124	27.20 N	82.42 E
Ityāy al-Bārūd	142	30.53 N	30.40 E
Ityopiya → Ethiopia □[1]	144	9.00 N	39.00 E
Itz ≏	56	49.58 N	10.52 E
Itzehoe	52	53.55 N	9.31 E
Iubundha ≏	126	24.06 N	90.20 E
Iuka, Il., U.S.	219	38.37 N	88.47 W
Iuka, Ms., U.S.	194	34.48 N	88.11 W
Iul'tin	180	67.50 N	178.48 W
Iul'tin, gora ∧	180	67.50 N	178.25 W
Iúna	255	20.21 S	41.32 W
Iupeba	256	23.41 S	46.22 W
Iva	192	34.18 N	82.39 W
Ivacevičí	76	52.43 N	25.21 E
Ivačovo	76	60.32 N	36.22 E
Ivahona	157b	23.27 S	46.10 E
Ivaí ≏	255	23.18 S	53.42 W
Ivaiporã	252	24.15 S	51.45 W
Ivajlovgrad	38	41.32 N	26.08 E
Ivakoany, Massif de l' ⋀	157b	23.50 S	46.25 E
Ivalo	24	68.42 N	27.30 E
Ivalojoki ≏	24	68.43 N	27.36 E
Ivancevo	82	55.58 N	36.07 E
Ivančice	61	49.06 N	16.23 E
Ivancovo	82	56.39 N	35.50 E
Ivanec	36	46.13 N	16.08 E
Ivane-Puste	78	48.39 N	26.11 E
Ivangorod	76	59.24 N	28.10 E
Ivangrad	38	42.50 N	19.52 E
Ivanhoe, Austl.	166	32.54 S	144.18 E
Ivanhoe, Austl.	274b	37.46 S	145.03 E
Ivanhoe, Ca., U.S.	226	36.23 N	119.13 W
Ivanhoe, Il., U.S.	278	42.17 N	88.02 W
Ivanhoe, Mn., U.S.	198	44.27 N	96.14 W
Ivanhoe, Va., U.S.	192	36.50 N	80.58 W
Ivanhoe ≏	190	48.40 N	82.11 W
Ivanhoe Lake ⊜	190	48.05 N	82.38 W
Ivanica	78	50.47 N	32.36 E
Ivanić Grad	36	45.42 N	16.24 E
Ivaniči	78	50.39 N	24.20 E
Ivanišči, S.S.S.R.	76	56.36 N	35.13 E
Ivanišči, S.S.S.R.	80	55.46 N	40.26 E
Ivanjci	61	46.38 N	15.54 E
Ivanjica	38	43.35 N	20.14 E
Ivankov	78	50.56 N	29.54 E
Ivankovcy	89	49.06 N	134.28 E
Ivan'kovo	82	54.44 N	37.57 E
Ivan'kovskij	80	56.39 N	40.05 E
Ivan'kovskoje vodochranilišče ⊜[1]	82	56.37 N	36.32 E
Ivanof Bay	180	55.54 N	159.29 W
Ivano-Frankovo	78	49.55 N	23.43 E
Ivano-Frankovsk	78	48.55 N	24.43 E
Ivanopol'	78	49.52 N	28.12 E
Ivanopolje	83	48.28 N	37.46 E
Ivano-Šamševo	83	46.52 N	39.54 E
Ivanov	78	49.28 N	28.21 E
Ivanovka, S.S.S.R.	78	46.43 N	34.33 E
Ivanovka, S.S.S.R.	78	46.58 N	30.28 E
Ivanovka, S.S.S.R.	80	52.51 N	53.48 E
Ivanovka, S.S.S.R.	80	51.54 N	43.46 E
Ivanovka, S.S.S.R.	80	52.15 N	41.35 E
Ivanovka, S.S.S.R.	83	48.14 N	38.58 E
Ivanovka, S.S.S.R.	83	47.35 N	37.19 E
Ivanovka, S.S.S.R.	85	42.54 N	75.05 E
Ivanovka, S.S.S.R.	89	50.22 N	128.02 E
Ivanovka, S.S.S.R.	89	43.58 N	132.30 E
Ivanovo, S.S.S.R.	78	52.09 N	25.32 E
Ivanovo, S.S.S.R.	80	57.00 N	40.59 E
Ivanovo-Voznesensk → Ivanovo	80	57.00 N	40.59 E
Ivanovskaja, S.S.S.R.	24	60.48 N	55.52 E
Ivanovskaja, S.S.S.R.	78	45.17 N	38.29 E
Ivanovskoje, S.S.S.R.	76	59.17 N	28.49 E
Ivanovskoje, S.S.S.R.	78	51.37 N	34.57 E
Ivanovskoje, S.S.S.R.	82	54.55 N	36.50 E
Ivanovskoje, S.S.S.R.	82	55.05 N	37.50 E
Ivanovskoje, S.S.S.R.	82	55.52 N	36.55 E
Ivanovskoje, S.S.S.R.	82	56.23 N	37.07 E
Ivanovskoje, S.S.S.R.	265a	59.46 N	30.47 E
Ivan-Ozero	82	54.04 N	38.20 E
Ivan-Ozero, ozero ⊜	82	54.07 N	38.17 E
Ivanpah Lake ⊜	204	35.35 N	115.25 W
Ivantejevka, S.S.S.R.	80	52.16 N	49.07 E
Ivantejevka, S.S.S.R.	82	55.58 N	37.55 E
Ivantejevo	76	57.48 N	33.09 E
Ivato	157b	20.37 S	47.12 E
Ivatuva	255	23.37 S	52.13 W
Ivdel'	72	60.42 N	60.24 E
Ivenec	76	53.53 N	26.45 E
Iver	260	51.31 N	0.30 W
Iver Heath	260	51.32 N	0.31 W
Iverny	261	49.00 N	2.47 E
Ivigtut	176	61.12 N	48.10 W
Ivindo ≏	152	0.09 S	12.09 E
Ivinghoe	42	51.50 N	0.37 W
Ivinheima ≏	255	23.14 S	53.42 W
Ivje	76	53.56 N	25.46 E
Ivn'a	78	51.04 N	36.08 E
Ivnica	78	50.09 N	29.03 E
Ivo	248	20.27 S	63.26 W
Ivohibe	157b	22.29 S	46.52 E
Ivolginsk	88	51.45 N	107.14 E
Ivon ≏	248	11.06 S	66.08 W
Ivondro	157b	24.47 S	46.52 E
Ivor	208	36.54 N	76.54 W
Ivorogbo	150	5.30 N	6.21 E
Ivory Coast (Côte d'Ivoire) □[1], Afr.	134	8.00 N	5.00 W
Ivory Coast (Côte d'Ivoire) □[1], Afr.	150	8.00 N	5.00 W
Ivory Coast ⫠[2]	150	5.10 N	5.00 W
Ivoryton	207	41.20 N	72.26 W
Ivösjön ⊜	26	56.06 N	14.27 E
Ivot, S.S.S.R.	76	53.42 N	34.12 E
Ivot, S.S.S.R.	78	51.58 N	33.28 E
Ivotka ≏	78	51.57 N	33.22 E
Ivrea	62	45.28 N	7.52 E
İvrindi	130	39.34 N	27.29 E
Ivry-la-Bataille	50	48.53 N	1.28 E
Ivry [-sur-Seine]	50	48.49 N	2.23 E
Ivujivik	176	62.24 N	77.55 W
Ivybridge	42	50.23 N	3.56 W
Ivy Hatch	260	51.16 N	0.16 E
Ivyland	285	40.12 N	75.04 W
Iwade	96	34.15 N	135.19 E
Iwafune, Nihon	94	36.19 N	139.40 E
Iwafune, Nihon	270	34.44 N	135.54 E
Iwagi	96	34.15 N	133.09 E
Iwai	94	36.03 N	139.54 E
Iwai-shima I	96	33.47 N	131.58 E
Iwaizumi	92	39.50 N	141.48 E
Iwaki (Taira)	94	37.03 N	140.55 E
Iwaki ≏	92	41.01 N	140.22 E
Iwaki-san ∧	92	40.39 N	140.18 E
Iwakuni	96	34.09 N	132.11 E
Iwakuni Marine Corps Air Station ■	96	34.08 N	132.14 E
Iwakura	94	35.17 N	136.52 E
Iwama	94	36.18 N	140.16 E
Iwami, Nihon	96	34.53 N	132.26 E
Iwami, Nihon	96	35.35 N	134.20 E
Iwami-kōgen ⋀[1]	96	35.00 N	132.30 E
Iwami-kokubun-ji ʋ[1]	96	34.56 N	132.08 E
Iwamizawa	92a	43.12 N	141.46 E
Iwamura	94	35.22 N	137.26 E
Iwanai	92a	42.58 N	140.30 E
Iwanowo → Ivanovo	80	57.00 N	40.59 E
Iwanuma	92	38.06 N	140.52 E
Iwaoka ✦[8]	270	34.44 N	134.58 E
Iwase, Nihon	94	36.21 N	140.06 E
Iwase, Nihon	268	35.17 N	139.52 E
Iwata	94	34.42 N	137.48 E
Iwataki	96	35.34 N	135.09 E
Iwate □[5]	92	39.37 N	141.22 E
Iwate-san ∧	92	39.51 N	141.00 E
Iwatsuki	94	35.57 N	139.42 E
Iwaya → Awaji, Nihon	96	34.35 N	135.01 E
Iwaya, Nihon	270	34.35 N	135.02 E
Iwayama	270	34.52 N	135.52 E
Iwazono	270	34.45 N	135.19 E
Iwo	150	7.38 N	4.11 E
Iwo Jima → Iō-jima I	174f	24.47 N	141.20 E
Iwŏn	98	40.19 N	128.39 E
Iwuy	50	50.14 N	3.19 E
Ixcán ≏	236	16.07 N	91.05 W
Ixchiguán	236	15.12 N	91.53 W
Ixcuintepec ≏	234	17.21 N	95.24 W
Ixelles	50	50.50 N	4.22 E
Ixhuatlán del Café	234	19.04 N	96.59 W
Ixiamas	248	13.45 S	68.09 W
Iximché ⊥	236	14.44 N	90.59 W
Ixmiquilpan	234	20.29 N	99.14 W
Ixonia	216	43.09 N	88.36 W
Ixopo	158	30.08 S	30.00 E
Ixtacalco □[7]	286a	19.24 N	99.06 W
Ixtacalco ✦[8]	286a	19.23 N	99.07 W
Ixtacihuatl y Popocatépetl, Parques Nacionales ♠	234	19.10 N	98.38 W
Ixtaltepec	234	16.30 N	95.03 W
Ixtapa, Punta ›	234	17.39 N	101.40 W
Ixtapalapa □[7]	286a	19.21 N	99.04 W
Ixtapalapa ✦[8]	286a	19.21 N	99.06 W
Ixtapan de la Sal	234	18.50 N	99.41 W
Ixtlahuacán del Río	234	20.52 N	103.15 W
Ixtlán	234	20.11 N	102.24 W
Ixtlán de Juárez	234	17.20 N	96.29 W
Ixtlán del Río	234	21.02 N	104.22 W
Ixworth	42	52.18 N	0.50 E
Iya ≏	96	33.58 N	133.47 E
'Iyādh	144	14.59 N	46.51 E
'Iyāl Bakhīt	140	13.25 N	28.41 E
Iyang, Taehan	98	34.53 N	127.01 E
Iyang → Yiyang, Zhg.	102	28.36 N	112.20 E
Iyang, Gili I	115a	6.59 S	114.10 E
Iyo	96	33.46 N	132.42 E
Iyo-mishima	96	33.58 N	133.33 E
Iyo-nada ⫧[2]	96	33.40 N	132.20 E
Iž ≏	80	55.58 N	52.38 E
Izabal	236	15.24 N	89.08 W
Izabal □[5]	236	15.30 N	89.00 W
Izabal, Lago de ⊜	236	15.30 N	89.10 W
'Izab al-Başāriţah	142	31.23 N	31.47 E
Īzad Khvāst	128	31.31 N	52.07 E
Izalco	236	13.45 N	89.40 W
'Izam, Jabal al- ∧	132	30.51 N	35.46 E
Izapa ⊥	232	14.55 N	92.10 W
Iz'aslav	78	50.07 N	26.51 E
'Izbat Abū Şuql	132	31.09 N	33.49 E
Izberbaš	84	42.33 N	47.52 E
Izbica, Pol.	30	50.54 N	23.09 E
Izbica, Pol.	30	54.42 N	17.26 E
Izd'oškovo	76	55.08 N	33.37 E
Izegem	50	50.55 N	3.12 E
Īzeh	128	31.50 N	49.50 E
Izena-shima I	174m	26.56 N	127.56 E
Izendy	86	45.48 N	59.28 E
Izernore	58	46.13 N	5.33 E
Iževsk	80	56.51 N	53.14 E
Iževskoje	80	54.34 N	40.53 E
Izkī	128	22.56 N	57.46 E
Ižma	24	65.02 N	53.55 E
Ižma ≏	24	65.19 N	52.54 E
Izmail	78	45.21 N	28.50 E
Izmajlovo	80	53.43 N	47.14 E
Izmajlovo ✦[8]	265b	55.48 N	37.46 E
Izmajlovskij park ♠	265b	55.46 N	37.47 E
Izmalkovo	76	52.41 N	37.58 E
İzmir	130	38.25 N	27.09 E
İzmir □[4]	130	38.30 N	27.15 E
İzmir Körfezi c	130	38.30 N	26.50 E
İzmit (Kocaeli)	130	40.46 N	29.55 E
İzmit Körfezi c	130	40.45 N	29.35 E
Ižmorskij	86	56.11 N	86.38 E
Iznajar, Embalse de ⊜[1]	34	37.15 N	4.30 W
Iznalloz	34	37.23 N	3.31 W
İznik	130	40.26 N	29.43 E
İznik Gölü ⊜	130	40.26 N	29.30 E
Iznoski	76	54.59 N	35.19 E
Izola	64	45.32 N	13.40 E
Izoplit	82	56.38 N	36.12 E
Izopo, Punta ›	236	15.48 N	87.23 W
Ižora ≏	265a	59.48 N	30.36 E
Izozog, Bañados de ∷	248	18.48 S	62.10 W
Izra'	132	32.51 N	36.15 E
Izsák	30	46.48 N	19.22 E
Iztaccíhuatl ∧[1]	234	19.11 N	98.39 W
Iztapa	236	13.56 N	90.43 W
Izúcar de Matamoros	234	18.36 N	98.28 W
Izu-hantō ›[1]	94	34.45 N	139.00 E
Izuhara	92	34.12 N	129.17 E
Iz'um	83	49.12 N	37.19 E
Izumi, Nihon	92	38.20 N	140.53 E
Izumi, Nihon	92	32.05 N	130.22 E
Izumi, Nihon	94	35.54 N	136.40 E
Izumi, Nihon	96	34.55 N	134.55 E
Izumi, Nihon	96	34.29 N	135.26 E
Izumi ✦[8]	268	35.25 N	139.30 E
Izumi-ōtsu	96	34.30 N	135.24 E
Izumi-sano	96	34.25 N	135.19 E
Izumizaki	94	37.09 N	140.17 E
Izumo	96	35.22 N	132.46 E
Izumo ≏	94	34.38 N	136.33 E
Izumo-kokubun-ji ʋ[1]	96	35.26 N	133.06 E
Izumrud	86	57.05 N	61.23 E
Izu-nagaoka	94	35.02 N	138.56 E
Izushi	96	35.28 N	134.52 E
Izu-shotō II	6	32.00 N	140.00 E
Izu Trench ✦[1]	6	31.00 N	142.00 E
Izuwara	270	34.53 N	135.32 E
Izvarino	83	48.17 N	39.52 E
Izvestij CIK, ostrova II	74	75.55 N	82.30 E
Izvestkovyj	89	48.59 N	131.33 E
Izvorul Muntelui, Lacul ⊜[1]	38	47.00 N	26.00 E
Izynžul'	86	52.24 N	90.13 E

J

Name	Page	Lat.°′	Long.°′
Ja'ār, Birkat al- ⊜	142	30.28 N	30.10 E
Jääsjärvi ⊜	26	61.36 N	26.07 E

Symbols in the index entries represent the broad categories identified in the key at the right. Symbols with superior numbers (⋀[1]) identify subcategories (see complete key on page *I · 1).*

Symbole im Register stellen die rechts im Schlüssel erklärten Kategorien dar. Symbole mit hochgestellten Ziffern (⋀[1]) bezeichnen Unterabteilungen einer Kategorie (vgl. vollständiger Schlüssel auf Seite *I · 1).*

Los símbolos incluídos en el texto del índice representan las grandes categorias identificadas con la clave a la derecha. Los símbolos con numeros en su parte superior (⋀[1]) identifican las subcategorías (véase la clave completa en la página *I · 1).*

Les symboles de l'index représentent les catégories indiquées dans la légende à droite. Les symboles suivis d'un indice (⋀[1]) représentent des sous-catégories (voir légende complète à la page *I · 1).*

Os símbolos incluídos no texto do índice representam as grandes categorias identificadas com a chave à direita. Os símbolos com números em sua parte superior (⋀[1]) identificam as subcategorias (veja-se a chave completa à página *I · 1).*

English	Deutsch	Español	Français	Português
∧ Mountain	Berg	Montaña	Montagne	Montanha
⋀ Mountains	Gebirge	Montañas	Montagnes	Montanhas
)(Pass	Paß	Paso	Col	Passo
V Valley, Canyon	Tal, Cañon	Valle, Cañón	Vallée, Canyon	Vale, Canhão
≌ Plain	Ebene	Llano	Plaine	Planície
› Cape	Kap	Cabo	Cap	Cabo
I Island	Insel	Isla	Île	Ilha
II Islands	Inseln	Islas	Îles	Ilhas
⫠ Other Topographic Features	Andere Topographische Objekte	Otros Elementos Topográficos	Autres données topographiques	Outros acidentes topográficos

ESPAÑOL

Nombre — Página — Lat.°′ — Long.°′ W = Oeste

Jaba, Ityo. 144 6.17 N 35.12 E
Jaba, Pap. N. Gui. 175e 6.32 S 155.12 E
Jabā, Sūrīy. 132 33.10 N 35.56 E
Jabal, Baḥr al- → Mountain Nile ≃ 136 9.30 N 30.30 E
Jabal Abyad Plateau ⋏ [1] 140 19.00 N 29.00 E
Jabal al-Awliyā' 140 15.14 N 32.30 E
Jabal al-Awliyā', Khazzān (White Nile Dam) ◆ [6] 140 15.14 N 32.29 E
Jabalambre ∧ 34 40.06 N 1.03 W
Jabal an-Nūr 142 28.57 N 31.02 E
Jabal Aṭ-Ṭayr 142 28.14 N 30.45 E
Jabal Dūd 140 13.25 N 33.09 E
Jabal Lubnān □ [4] 132 33.50 N 35.40 E
Jabalón ≃ 34 38.53 N 4.05 W
Jabal os Sarāj 120 35.07 N 69.14 E
Jabalpur 124 23.10 N 79.57 E
Jabal Qerri 140 16.15 N 32.48 E
Jabal 'Uwaybid 142 30.09 N 32.12 E
Jabālyah 132 31.32 N 34.29 E
Jabal Zuqar, Jazīrat I 144 14.00 N 42.45 E
Jabbān, Arḍ al- ◆ [1] 132 32.08 N 36.35 E
Jabbeke 50 51.11 N 3.05 E
Jabbi 123 32.24 N 72.06 E
Jabbū, Qā' ≡ 132 29.35 N 36.13 E
Jabbūl, Sabkhat al- ⊜ 130 36.03 N 37.39 E
Jabel 54 53.32 N 12.32 E
Jabi 114 2.32 N 102.48 E
Jabiru 164 12.40 S 132.53 E
Jabjabah, Wādī V 140 22.37 N 33.17 E
Jablah 130 35.21 N 35.55 E
Jablanac 36 44.42 N 14.54 E
Jablanica 36 43.39 N 17.45 E
Jablanica ≃ 38 43.07 N 21.57 E
Jablaničko Jezero ⊜ [1] 36 43.40 N 17.50 E
Jablines 261 48.55 N 2.46 E
Jabločnoje 78 50.18 N 35.14 E
Jabločnyj 89 47.10 N 142.04 E
Jablonec nad Nisou 30 50.44 N 15.10 E
Jablonica 30 48.37 N 17.25 E
Jabłonka 30 49.29 N 19.41 E
Jablonné v Podještědí 54 50.48 N 14.47 E
Jablonoj → Jablonovyj chrebet ⋏ 88 53.30 N 115.00 E
Jablonov 78 48.24 N 24.57 E
Jablonovo 88 51.51 N 112.49 E
Jablonovyj chrebet ⋏ 88 53.30 N 115.00 E
Jabłonowo 30 53.24 N 19.09 E
Jablonowy-Gebirge → Jablonovyj chrebet ⋏ 88 53.30 N 115.00 E
Jablunkov 30 49.35 N 18.47 E
Jaboatão 250 8.07 S 35.01 W
Jaboncillos 232 28.57 N 102.39 W
Jaboncillos Creek ≃ 196 27.23 N 97.45 W
Jabonga 116 9.20 N 125.32 E
Jaborandi 255 20.40 S 48.25 W
Jaboticabal 255 21.16 S 48.19 W
Jabrat Sa'īd ⍑ [4] 140 16.06 N 31.50 E
Jabron ≃ 62 44.33 N 4.45 E
Jabron, Torrent le ≃ 62 44.09 N 5.57 E
Jabung 115a 5.29 S 105.40 E
Jabung, Tanjung > 112 1.01 S 104.22 E
Jaca 34 42.34 N 0.33 W
Jacala de Ledesma 234 21.01 N 99.11 W
Jacaleapa 236 14.00 N 86.40 W
Jacaltenango 236 15.40 N 91.44 W
Jacana 274b 37.42 S 144.55 E
Jacaraci 255 14.51 S 42.26 W
Jacaré 256 21.20 S 42.51 W
Jacaré ≃, Bra. 248 5.49 S 63.35 W
Jacaré ≃, Bra. 250 10.03 S 42.13 W
Jacaré ≃, Bra. 255 13.50 S 40.42 W
Jacaré ≃, Bra. 287a 22.56 S 43.04 W
Jacareí 256 23.19 S 45.58 W
Jacareí ≃ 256 22.54 S 46.28 W
Jacarepaguá ◆ [8] 256 22.56 S 43.20 W
Jacarepaguá, Lagoa de ⊂ 256 22.59 S 43.24 W
Jacarèzinho 255 23.09 S 49.59 W
Jaceel V 144 10.25 N 51.01 E
Jaceruba 256 22.35 S 43.34 W
Jáchal ≃ 252 30.44 S 68.08 W
Jachenau 64 47.36 N 11.25 E
Jachniki 78 50.26 N 33.10 E
Jachroma 82 56.17 N 37.30 E
Jachroma ≃ 82 56.31 N 37.07 E
Jáchymov 54 50.20 N 12.55 E
Jaciara 255 15.59 S 54.57 W
Jacinto 255 16.10 S 40.17 W
Jacinto Aráuz 252 38.04 S 63.26 W
Jacinto City 222 29.46 N 95.14 W
Jacinto Machado 252 29.00 S 49.46 W
Jaci Paraná 248 9.15 S 64.23 W
Jaciparaná ≃ 248 9.22 S 64.22 W
Jackass Creek ≃ 226 37.22 N 119.23 W
Jack Creek ≃ 202 42.59 N 121.32 W
Jackfish Lake ⊜ 184 53.05 N 108.25 W
Jackhead Harbour 184 51.52 N 97.16 W
Jack Lake ⊜ 212 44.42 N 78.03 W
Jack London State Historical Park ♠ 226 38.21 N 122.32 W
Jackman 188 45.38 N 70.15 W
Jackman Creek ≃ 224 48.30 N 121.43 W
Jack Mountain ∧, Mt., U.S. 202 46.21 N 112.18 W
Jack Mountain ∧, Wa., U.S. 224 48.47 N 120.57 W
Jackpot 204 41.59 N 114.40 W
Jacksboro, Tn., U.S. 192 36.19 N 84.11 W
Jacksboro, Tx., U.S. 196 33.13 N 98.09 W
Jacks Creek ≃ 208 40.35 N 77.33 W
Jacks Fork ≃ 194 37.12 N 91.17 W
Jacks Island I 279b 40.37 N 79.43 W
Jacks Mountain ∧ 210 40.45 N 77.30 W
Jackson, Al., U.S. 194 31.30 N 87.53 W
Jackson, Ca., U.S. 226 38.20 N 120.46 W
Jackson, Ga., U.S. 192 33.17 N 83.57 W
Jackson, Ky., U.S. 192 37.33 N 83.23 W
Jackson, La., U.S. 194 30.50 N 91.13 W
Jackson, Mi., U.S. 216 42.14 N 84.24 W
Jackson, Mn., U.S. 198 43.37 N 94.59 W
Jackson, Ms., U.S. 194 32.17 N 90.11 W
Jackson, Mo., U.S. 194 37.22 N 89.39 W
Jackson, N.J., U.S. 208 40.08 N 74.19 W
Jackson, N.C., U.S. 192 36.23 N 77.25 W
Jackson, Oh., U.S. 188 39.03 N 82.38 W
Jackson, Pa., U.S. 210 41.50 N 75.36 W
Jackson, S.C., U.S. 192 33.19 N 81.47 W
Jackson, Tn., U.S. 194 35.36 N 88.48 W
Jackson, Wy., U.S. 200 43.28 N 110.45 W
Jackson □ [6], In., U.S. 218 38.53 N 86.03 W
Jackson □ [6], Mi., U.S. 216 42.15 N 84.24 W
Jackson □ [6], Tx., U.S. 222 29.00 N 96.35 W
Jackson ≃ 188 37.47 N 79.46 W
Jackson, Cape > 172 41.00 S 174.18 E
Jackson, Lake ⊜, Fl., U.S. 192 30.30 N 84.17 W
Jackson, Lake ⊜, Fl., U.S. 220 27.55 N 81.10 W
Jackson, Lake ⊜, Fl., U.S. 220 27.29 N 81.28 W
Jackson, Mount ∧, Ant. 9 71.23 S 63.22 W
Jackson, Mount ∧, Austl. 162 30.15 S 119.16 E
Jackson, Port ⊂ 170 33.50 S 151.16 E
Jackson Bay ⊂ 172 43.58 S 168.42 E
Jackson Brook ≃ 276 40.53 N 74.34 W
Jackson Butte ∧ 226 38.20 N 120.43 W
Jackson Center, Oh., U.S. 216 40.27 N 84.02 W
Jackson Center, Pa., U.S. 214 41.16 N 80.09 W
Jackson Creek ≃, Can. 184 49.18 N 100.50 W
Jackson Creek ≃, Ca., U.S. 226 38.18 N 121.01 W

FRANÇAIS

Nom — Page — Lat.°′ — Long.°′ W = Ouest

Jackson Creek ≃, Il., U.S. 216 41.26 N 88.10 W
Jackson Head > 172 43.58 S 168.37 E
Jackson Heights ◆ [8] 276 40.45 N 73.53 W
Jackson Lake ⊜ 202 43.55 N 110.40 W
Jackson Lake ⊜ [1] 192 33.22 N 83.52 W
Jackson Meadows Reservoir ⊜ [1] 226 39.29 N 120.32 W
Jackson Mountain ∧ 188 44.46 N 70.32 W
Jackson Park ♠, On., Can. 281 42.17 N 83.01 W
Jackson Park ♠, Il., U.S. 278 41.47 N 87.35 W
Jackson's Arm 186 49.52 N 56.47 W
Jacksons Creek ≃ 169 37.40 S 144.48 E
Jacksonville, Al., U.S. 194 33.48 N 85.45 W
Jacksonville, Ar., U.S. 194 34.51 N 92.06 W
Jacksonville, Fl., U.S. 192 30.19 N 81.39 W
Jacksonville, Il., U.S. 219 39.44 N 90.13 W
Jacksonville, N.J., U.S. 285 40.03 N 74.46 W
Jacksonville, N.Y., U.S. 210 42.31 N 76.37 W
Jacksonville, N.C., U.S. 192 34.45 N 77.25 W
Jacksonville, Or., U.S. 202 42.18 N 122.57 W
Jacksonville, Tx., U.S. 222 31.57 N 95.16 W
Jacksonville, Vt., U.S. 207 42.47 N 72.49 W
Jacksonville, Lake ⊜ [1] 222 31.55 N 95.17 W
Jacksonville Beach 192 30.17 N 81.23 W
Jacksonville Naval Air Station ■ 192 30.14 N 81.41 W
Jacks Reef 210 43.06 N 76.25 W
Jacks Run ≃ 279b 40.13 N 79.35 W
Jacktown Acres 279b 40.19 N 79.45 W
Jacmel 238 18.14 N 72.32 W
Jacob, Morne ∧ 240e 14.46 N 61.06 W
Jacobābād 120 28.17 N 68.26 E
Jacobina 250 11.11 S 40.31 W
Jacob Island I 212 44.28 N 78.28 W
Jacob Riis Park ♠ 276 40.34 N 73.52 W
Jacobs Creek ≃ 214 40.07 N 79.44 W
Jacobsdal 158 29.13 S 24.41 E
Jacobus 208 39.53 N 76.43 W
Jacona de Plancarte 234 19.57 N 102.16 W
Jacques, Lac à ⊜ 180 66.10 N 127.25 W
Jacques-Cartier 275a 45.31 N 73.29 W
Jacques-Cartier ≃ 206 46.40 N 71.45 W
Jacques-Cartier, Détroit de ⊔ 186 50.00 N 63.30 W
Jacques-Cartier, Mont ∧ 186 48.59 N 65.57 W
Jacques-Cartier, Pont ◆ [5] 275a 45.31 N 73.32 W
Jacquet River 186 47.55 N 66.00 W
Jacqueville 150 5.12 N 4.25 W
Jacquinot Bay ⊂ 164 5.35 S 151.30 E
Jacu ≃, Bra. 250 6.13 S 35.09 W
Jacú ≃, Bra. 256 23.05 S 45.08 W
Jacu, Rio do ≃ 287b 23.29 S 46.27 W
Jacuba ≃ 255 18.25 S 52.28 W
Jacuecanga 256 23.01 S 44.13 W
Jacuí ≃ 252 30.02 S 51.15 W
Jacuípe 255 12.29 S 38.38 W
Jacuípe ≃ 255 12.30 S 39.05 W
Jacumba 204 32.37 N 116.11 W
Jacundá 250 4.33 S 49.28 W
Jacundá ≃ 250 1.57 S 50.26 W
Jacupiranga 252 24.42 S 48.00 W
Jacuriaí ≃ 250 10.57 S 39.35 W
Jacutinga 256 22.17 S 46.37 W
Jada 146 8.46 N 12.09 E
Jada'ah, Jabal ∧ [2] 142 29.58 N 30.40 E
Jādabpur 126 22.29 N 88.23 E
Jaddi, Rās > 128 25.14 N 63.31 E
Jade 52 53.20 N 8.14 E
Jade Buddha, Temple of the ♉ [1] 269b 31.14 N 121.26 E
Jadebusen ⊂ 52 53.30 N 8.10 E
Jäder 40 59.25 N 16.41 E
Jäderfors 40 60.41 N 16.40 E
Jade Run ≃ 285 39.56 N 74.45 W
Jadīdah 128 34.01 N 42.28 E
Jadito Wash V 200 35.22 N 110.50 W
J.A.D. Jensens Nunatakker ∧ 176 62.45 N 48.00 W
Jadotville → Likasi 154 10.59 S 26.44 E
Jadraque 34 40.55 N 2.55 W
Jadrin 80 55.56 N 46.12 E
Jadromino 82 55.57 N 36.36 E
Jādū 146 31.57 N 12.01 E
Jaduty 78 51.22 N 32.19 E
Jægerspris 41 55.51 N 11.59 E
Jaeger Summit ∧ 154 2.52 S 35.47 E
Jaén, Esp. 34 37.46 N 3.47 W
Jaén, Perú 248 5.42 S 78.47 W
Jæren ◆ [1] 26 58.45 N 5.45 E
Jāfarābād, India 120 20.52 N 71.22 E
Ja'farābād, Īrān 128 35.43 N 50.43 E
Jāfarpur 126 22.29 N 89.06 E
Jāfarpur ◆ [8] 272a 28.40 N 77.01 E
Jaffa, Cape > 166 36.58 S 139.40 E
Jaffa, Tel Aviv- → Tel Aviv-Yafo 132 32.04 N 34.46 E
Jaffna 122 9.40 N 80.00 E
Jaffna Lagoon ⊂ 122 9.35 N 80.15 E
Jaffrey 207 42.48 N 72.01 W
Jafr, Qā' al- ≡ [7] 132 30.17 N 36.20 E
Jagādhri 124 30.10 N 77.18 E
Jägala ≃ 76 59.29 N 25.09 E
Jagalūr 122 14.32 N 76.21 E
Jāgan 120 28.05 N 68.30 E
Jagannāthganj Ghāt 124 24.45 N 89.49 E
Jagannāthpūr 272b 22.43 N 88.19 E
Jagati 126 23.54 N 89.06 E
Jagatnagar 272b 22.47 N 88.13 E
Jagatpur ◆ [8] 272a 28.44 N 77.14 E
Jagatsingpur 120 20.16 N 86.10 E
Jagdalpur 122 19.04 N 82.02 E
Jagdīspur 124 25.29 N 84.25 E
Jagel 41 54.27 N 9.32 E
Jagel'urta, gora ∧ [2] 24 67.33 N 38.02 E
Jagenbach 61 48.38 N 15.02 E
Jägerndorf → Krnov 30 50.05 N 17.41 E
Jagersfontein 158 29.44 S 25.29 E
Jaggayyapeta 122 16.54 N 80.06 E
Jagged Mountain ∧ 180 58.38 N 162.02 W
Jagīn ≃ 128 25.35 N 58.18 E
Jagnob ≃ 85 39.15 N 68.35 E
Jagny-sous-Bois 261 49.05 N 2.27 E
Jagodnoje, S.S.S.R. 74 62.33 N 149.40 E
Jagodnoje, S.S.S.R. 80 53.36 N 49.04 E
Jagodnyj 86 59.44 N 65.04 E
Jagorlyckij zaliv ⊂ 78 46.24 N 31.50 E
Jagotin 78 50.17 N 31.46 E
Jagraon 123 30.47 N 75.29 E
Jagst ≃ 56 49.14 N 9.11 E
Jagsthausen 56 49.19 N 9.28 E
Jagstzell 56 49.02 N 10.05 E
Jagtiāl 122 18.48 N 78.56 E
Jaguaquara 255 13.32 S 39.58 W
Jaguarão 252 32.34 S 53.23 W
Jaguarão (Yaguarón) ≃ 252 32.39 S 53.12 W
Jaguarari 250 10.16 S 40.12 W
Jaguaretama 250 5.37 S 38.46 W
Jaguari 252 29.30 S 54.41 W
Jaguari ≃, Bra. 256 22.41 S 47.17 W
Jaguari ≃, Bra. 256 23.10 S 45.55 W
Jaguariaíva 252 24.15 S 49.42 W
Jaguaribara 250 5.40 S 38.37 W
Jaguaribe 250 5.53 S 38.37 W
Jaguaribe ≃ 250 4.25 S 37.45 W
Jaguari-Mirim ≃ 256 21.59 S 47.17 W
Jaguaripe 255 13.06 S 38.53 W
Jaguariúna 256 22.41 S 46.59 W
Jaguaruana 250 4.50 S 37.47 W
Jaguaruna 252 28.36 S 49.02 W

PORTUGUÊS

Nome — Página — Lat.°′ — Long.°′ W = Oeste

Jagüé 252 28.38 S 68.24 W
Jagüey Grande 240p 22.32 N 81.08 W
Jāguli 126 22.56 N 88.32 E
Jāgulia 272b 22.44 N 88.32 E
Jagungal, Mount ∧ 171b 36.09 S 148.23 E
Jagunovskij 86 55.17 N 85.59 E
Jahānābād, India 124 25.13 N 84.59 E
Jahānābād, Pāk. 123 32.11 N 72.29 E
Jahāngīra 123 33.58 N 72.13 E
Jahāngīrābād 124 28.25 N 78.06 E
Jahangirpur ◆ [8] 272a 28.44 N 77.13 E
Jahānia 123 30.02 N 71.49 E
Jahannam, Qārat ∧ [2] 142 29.19 N 30.09 E
Jahdānīyah, Wādī al- V 132 30.12 N 36.22 E
Jahnsdorf 54 50.44 N 12.51 E
Jahrom 128 28.31 N 53.33 E
Jahú → Jaú 255 22.18 S 48.33 W
Jai ≃ 250 3.58 N 54.49 W
Jaicós 250 7.21 S 41.08 W
Jaidak 120 31.58 N 66.43 E
Jaihti ≃ 126 24.08 N 86.48 E
Jaijon 123 31.21 N 76.09 E
Jailolo 108 1.05 N 127.30 E
Jaimanitas ≃ 286b 23.05 N 82.29 W
Jainca 102 35.59 N 102.02 E
Jainti 124 26.42 N 89.36 E
Jaintiāpur 120 25.08 N 92.07 E
Jaipur 120 26.55 N 75.49 E
Jaipur Hāt 124 25.06 N 89.01 E
Jais 124 26.15 N 81.32 E
Jaisalmer 120 26.55 N 70.54 E
Jaito 123 30.28 N 74.53 E
Jaja 86 56.12 N 86.26 E
Jaja ≃ 86 56.58 N 86.23 E
Jājapur 120 20.51 N 86.20 E
Jājarkoṭ 124 28.42 N 82.12 E
Jājarm 128 36.58 N 56.27 E
Jajce 36 44.21 N 17.16 E
Jajichi 174m 26.47 N 128.13 E
Jajjha 123 28.45 N 70.34 E
Jajl'u 86 51.48 N 87.36 E
Jajpan 85 40.23 N 70.48 E
Jajsan 86 50.51 N 56.14 E
Jajva 86 59.20 N 57.15 E
Jajva ≃ 86 59.13 N 56.40 E
Ják 61 47.08 N 16.35 E
Jakarta, Indon. 115a 6.10 S 106.48 E
Jakarta, Indon. 269e 6.10 S 106.48 E
Jakarta, Teluk ⊂ 115a 6.05 S 106.48 E
Jakarta Kota Station ◆ [5] 269e 6.08 S 106.49 E
Jakarta Raya □ [4] 115a 6.10 S 106.45 E
Jakdūl ⊜ 140 17.39 N 32.59 E
Jake Creek Mountain ∧ 204 41.13 N 116.54 W
Jakenan 115a 6.45 S 111.11 E
Jākhal 123 29.48 N 75.50 E
Jakhāu 120 23.13 N 68.43 E
Jakkonen 24 66.33 N 29.52 E
Jakobsberg 40 59.26 N 17.50 E
Jakobsdalsberget ∧ [2] 40 58.41 N 16.07 E
Jakobshagen → Dobrzany 30 53.22 N 15.25 E
Jakobshavn (Ilulissat) 176 69.13 N 51.06 W
Jakobstad (Pietarsaari) 26 63.40 N 22.42 E
Jakovleviči 76 54.20 N 30.31 E
Jakovlevka 89 44.26 N 133.28 E
Jakovlevo, S.S.S.R. 78 50.51 N 36.27 E
Jakovlevo, S.S.S.R. 82 54.48 N 37.26 E
Jakša 24 61.48 N 56.49 E
Jakšanga 80 58.23 N 45.56 E
Jakšur-Bodja 80 57.11 N 53.09 E
Jakupica ⋏ 38 41.43 N 21.26 E
Jakutsk 74 62.00 N 129.40 E
Jakutskaja Avtonomnaja Sovetskaja Socialističeskaja Respublika □ [8] 88 58.00 N 121.00 E
Jal 196 32.06 N 103.11 W
Jala 234 21.05 N 104.26 W
Jalacingo 234 19.48 N 97.18 W
Jalaid Qi 89 46.40 N 122.55 E
Jalājil 128 25.41 N 45.28 E
Jalālābād, Afg. 120 34.26 N 70.28 E
Jalālābād, India 123 30.37 N 74.15 E
Jalālābād, India 124 27.43 N 79.40 E
Jalālah al-Baḥrīyah, Jabal ⋏ [1] 142 29.20 N 32.00 E
Jalālat al-Qiblīyah, Jabal al- ⋏ 142 28.42 N 32.22 E
Jalālpur, India 124 26.19 N 82.44 E
Jalālpur, Pāk. 123 32.38 N 74.12 E
Jalālpur Pīrwāla 123 29.30 N 71.13 E
Jalama 84 41.44 N 48.34 E
Jalan' 86 58.21 N 91.53 E
Jalán ≃ 236 14.39 N 86.12 W
Jalan Besar Stadium ♠ 271c 1.18 N 103.52 E
Jalandhar 123 31.19 N 75.34 E
Jalangi 126 24.08 N 88.42 E
Jalangi ≃ 126 23.25 N 88.22 E
Jalan Kayu 271c 1.24 N 103.52 E
Jalapa, Guat. 236 14.38 N 89.59 W
Jalapa, Méx. 234 19.32 N 96.55 W
Jalapa, Méx. 234 17.43 N 92.49 W
Jalapa, Nic. 236 13.55 N 86.08 W
Jalapa □ [5] 236 14.35 N 89.55 W
Jalapa de Díaz 234 18.04 N 96.32 W
Jalasjärvi 26 62.30 N 22.45 E
Jalaud ≃ 116 10.45 N 122.40 E
Jālaun 124 26.09 N 79.21 E
Jal'čiki 80 55.09 N 48.01 E
Jalcocotán 234 21.28 N 105.07 W
Jalcomulco ≃ 234 19.20 N 96.33 W
Jalda 126 21.56 N 87.30 E
Jalea de Catalán 234 17.26 N 99.51 W
Jalesar 124 27.29 N 78.19 E
Jaleshwar 126 21.49 N 87.13 E
Jaleśwar 124 26.38 N 85.48 E
Jālgaon, India 122 21.03 N 76.32 E
Jālgaon, India 122 21.01 N 75.34 E
Jal'gelevo 265a 59.44 N 29.57 E
Jalhay 56 50.34 N 5.58 E
Jalingo 146 8.53 N 11.22 E
Jalirpār 126 23.13 N 89.58 E
Jalisco 234 21.27 N 104.54 W
Jalisco □ [3] 234 20.20 N 103.40 W
Jallas ≃ 34 42.54 N 9.08 W
Jallieu 62 45.35 N 5.16 E
Jālna 122 19.50 N 75.53 E
Jalón ≃ 34 41.47 N 1.04 W
Jālor 120 25.21 N 72.37 E
Jalostotitlán 234 21.12 N 102.28 W
Jalpa 234 21.38 N 102.58 W
Jalpa de Méndez 234 18.08 N 93.05 W
Jalpāiguri 124 26.31 N 88.44 E
Jalpan 234 21.14 N 99.29 W
Jalpug ≃ 78 45.41 N 28.35 E
Jalpug, ozero ⊜ 78 45.25 N 28.37 E
Jalta (Yalta), S.S.S.R. 78 44.30 N 34.10 E
Jalta, S.S.S.R. 83 46.58 N 37.16 E
Jaltenango de la Paz 234 15.55 N 92.43 W
Jaltepec ≃ 234 17.26 N 94.59 W
Jáltipan 234 17.58 N 94.42 W
Jaltocán 234 21.09 N 98.32 W
Jaltuškov 78 48.58 N 27.30 E
Jaluit II [1] 14 6.00 N 169.35 E
Jalūlā' 128 34.16 N 45.10 E
Jalutorovsk 86 56.40 N 66.18 E
Jam, S.S.S.R. 82 55.29 N 37.45 E
Jam, S.S.S.R. 85 40.07 N 68.11 E
Jām ≃ 128 35.10 N 61.06 E
Jama 83 48.52 N 38.06 E
Jamaame (Margherita) 144 0.04 N 42.45 E
Jamaare ≃ 146 12.06 N 10.14 E
Jāmāibāti 272b 22.51 N 88.08 E
Jamaica 240p 20.12 N 75.09 W
Jamaica ◆ [8] 276 40.42 N 73.47 W
Jamaica □ [1], N.A. 230 18.15 N 77.30 W
Jamaica □ [1], N.A. 241q 18.15 N 77.30 W
Jamaica Bay ⊂ 210 40.36 N 73.51 W
Jamaica Channel ⊔ 238 18.00 N 75.30 W
Jamaica Plain ◆ [8] 283 42.19 N 71.06 W
Jamaika → Jamaica □ [1] 241q 18.15 N 77.30 W
Jamaïque → Jamaica □ [1] 241q 18.15 N 77.30 W
Jamal, poluostrov > [1] 74 70.00 N 70.00 E
Jam-Alin', chrebet ⋏ 89 53.00 N 134.36 E
Jamālīyah ◆ [8] 273c 30.03 N 31.16 E
Jamalo-neneckij Nacional'nyj Okrug □ [8] 24 66.30 N 64.00 E
Jamālpur, Bngl. 124 24.55 N 89.56 E
Jamālpur, India 124 25.18 N 86.30 E
Jamālpurganj 126 23.04 N 87.59 E
Jamanari ≃ 246 2.58 S 68.53 W
Jamanchalinka 80 47.40 N 51.35 E
Jamantau, gora ∧ 86 54.15 N 58.06 E
Jamanxim ≃ 250 4.43 S 56.18 W
Jamapará 256 21.55 S 42.43 W
Jamari ≃ 248 8.27 S 63.30 W
Jamari, Lago ⊜ 250 1.26 S 56.35 W
Jamarovka 88 50.38 N 110.16 E
Jamašurma 80 55.58 N 49.36 E
Jamay 234 20.18 N 102.43 W
Jamba 152 13.50 S 15.30 E
Jāmbād 126 22.42 N 86.35 E
Jambeiro 256 23.16 S 45.41 W
Jambeiro, Serra do ⋏ [2] 256 23.13 S 45.38 W
Jambelí, Canal de ⊔ 246 3.00 S 80.00 W
Jamberoo 170 34.39 S 150.47 E
Jambes 56 50.28 N 4.52 E
Jambi 112 1.36 S 103.37 E
Jambi □ [4] 112 1.30 S 103.00 E
Jambin 166 24.12 S 150.22 E
Jamboaye ≃ 114 5.16 N 97.29 E
Jambol 38 42.29 N 26.30 E
Jambongan, Pulau I 116 6.40 N 117.27 E
Jambuair, Tanjung > 114 5.16 N 97.30 E
Jambusar 120 22.03 N 72.48 E
James ≃, Austl. 166 20.36 S 137.41 E
James ≃, Ab., Can. 182 51.55 N 114.34 W
James ≃, U.S. 198 42.52 N 97.18 W
James ≃, Mo., U.S. 194 36.45 N 93.30 W
James ≃, Va., U.S. 192 36.57 N 76.26 W
James, Isla I 254 44.57 S 74.07 W
James, Lake ⊜ 216 41.42 N 85.02 W
James, Lake ⊜ [1] 192 35.45 N 81.55 W
James Bay ⊂ 176 53.30 N 80.30 W
Jamesburg 208 40.21 N 74.26 W
James Bypass ≊ 226 36.41 N 120.16 W
James City, N.C., U.S. 192 35.05 N 77.02 W
James City, Pa., U.S. 214 41.37 N 78.50 W
James City □ [6] 208 37.17 N 76.48 W
James Craik 252 32.09 S 63.28 W
James Creek 214 40.23 N 78.10 W
James Gardens ♠ 275b 43.40 N 79.31 W
James Island, B.C., Can. 224 48.37 N 123.22 W
James Island, S.C., U.S. 192 32.44 N 79.57 W
James Island I 208 38.31 N 76.20 W
Jameson Raid Memorial ⊥ 273d 26.11 S 27.49 E
James Point > 192 25.21 N 76.24 W
Jamesport 194 39.58 N 93.48 W
James Price Point > 162 17.30 S 122.08 E
James Ranges ⋏ 162 24.06 S 132.30 E
James River Bridge ◆ [5] 208 37.00 N 76.30 W
James Ross, Cape > 176 74.40 N 114.25 W
James Ross Island I 9 64.15 S 57.45 W
James Ross Strait ⊔ 176 69.40 N 95.30 W
James Smith Indian Reserve ◆ [4] 184 53.08 N 104.52 W
Jamestown, Austl. 166 33.12 S 138.36 E
Jamestown, Ire. 48 53.55 N 8.02 W
Jamestown, S. Afr. 158 31.06 S 26.45 E
Jamestown, Ca., U.S. 226 37.57 N 120.25 W
Jamestown, Ks., U.S. 198 39.35 N 97.51 W
Jamestown, Ky., U.S. 194 36.59 N 85.03 W
Jamestown, Mi., U.S. 216 42.50 N 85.51 W
Jamestown, N.Y., U.S. 214 42.05 N 79.14 W
Jamestown, N.C., U.S. 192 35.59 N 79.56 W
Jamestown, N.D., U.S. 198 46.54 N 98.42 W
Jamestown, Oh., U.S. 218 39.39 N 83.44 W
Jamestown, Pa., U.S. 214 41.29 N 80.26 W
Jamestown, R.I., U.S. 207 41.29 N 71.22 W
Jamestown, Tn., U.S. 194 36.25 N 84.55 W
Jamestown ⊥ 208 37.12 N 76.46 W
Jamestown Festival Park ♠ 208 37.14 N 76.48 W
Jamestown Island I 208 37.12 N 76.46 W
Jamestown Reservoir ⊜ [1] 198 47.15 N 98.40 W
Jamesville, N.Y., U.S. 210 42.59 N 76.04 W
Jamesville, Va., U.S. 208 37.30 N 75.55 W
Jamet, Lac ⊜ 206 46.34 N 74.30 W
Jametz 56 49.26 N 5.23 E
Jamieson ≃ 169 37.18 S 146.08 E
Jamiltepec 234 16.17 N 97.49 W
Jaminauá ≃ 248 9.20 S 70.59 W
Jaminsk 76 52.46 N 28.16 E
Jaminskij 80 50.21 N 42.14 E
Jāmira ≃ 126 21.45 N 87.02 E
Jamira ≃ [1] 126 21.35 N 88.28 E
Jamison 208 40.16 N 75.05 W
Jamison City 210 41.18 N 76.22 W
Jamison Town 274a 33.46 S 150.41 E
Jam-Ižora 265a 59.42 N 30.36 E
Jām Jodhpur 120 21.54 N 70.01 E
Jamkhandi 122 16.31 N 75.18 E
Jamki 86 59.33 N 66.47 E
Jamkino 82 55.55 N 38.24 E
Jamm 76 58.26 N 28.03 E
Jammalamadugu 122 14.50 N 78.24 E
Jammerbugten ⊂ 26 57.20 N 9.30 E
Jammerland Bugt ⊂ 41 55.35 N 11.05 E
Jammu 123 32.42 N 74.52 E
Jammu Airport ⊠ 123 32.42 N 74.51 E
Jammu and Kashmīr □ [2] 120 34.00 N 76.00 E
Jamnagar 120 22.28 N 70.04 E
Jamoigne 56 49.42 N 5.25 E
Jamor ≃ 266c 38.42 N 9.15 W
Jampang-kulon 115a 7.16 S 106.37 E
Jampol', S.S.S.R. 78 49.58 N 26.14 E
Jampol', S.S.S.R. 78 51.57 N 33.46 E
Jampol', S.S.S.R. 78 48.16 N 28.17 E
Jampol', S.S.S.R. 83 48.56 N 37.58 E
Jāmpur, India 272b 22.56 N 88.12 E
Jāmpur, Pāk. 123 29.39 N 70.36 E
Jämsä 26 61.52 N 25.12 E
Jamsah 140 27.38 N 33.35 E
Jämsänkoski 26 61.55 N 25.11 E
Jamshedpur 126 22.48 N 86.11 E
Jamsk 74 59.35 N 154.10 E
Jamskaja Sloboda 82 55.29 N 36.01 E
Jāmtāra 126 23.57 N 86.48 E
Jämtland □ [9] 26 63.30 N 14.00 E
Jämtlands Län □ [6] 24 63.00 N 14.40 E
Jamuāni 126 21.57 N 86.14 E
Jamuga 82 56.24 N 36.40 E
Jamūi 124 24.55 N 86.13 E
Jamuna ≃, Bngl. 124 23.51 N 89.45 E
Jamuna ≃, India 272b 22.57 N 88.35 E
Jamundí 246 3.15 N 76.32 W
Jāmuria 126 23.44 N 87.02 E
Jāmurki 126 24.09 N 90.02 E
Jana ≃ 74 71.31 N 136.32 E
Janāi 272b 22.43 N 88.16 E
Janāj 142 31.00 N 30.46 E
Janajkino 80 50.43 N 51.06 E
Janakpur 124 26.39 N 85.55 E
Janakpur □ [8] 124 27.15 N 86.00 E
Janas 266c 38.49 N 9.26 W
Janauacá, Lago ⊜ 246 3.28 S 60.17 W
Janaúba 255 15.48 S 43.19 W
Janaucu, Ilha I 250 0.30 N 50.10 W
Janaul 86 56.16 N 54.56 E
Jand 123 33.26 N 72.01 E
Janda, Laguna de la ⊜ 34 36.15 N 5.51 W
Jandaia 255 17.06 S 50.07 W
Jandaia do Sul 255 23.36 S 51.39 W
Jandaíra 250 11.34 S 37.47 W
Jandalī, Wādī al- V 142 30.05 N 31.52 E
Jandaq 128 34.02 N 54.26 E
Jandelsbrunn 60 48.44 N 13.42 E
Jandiāla 123 31.36 N 75.03 E
Jandiatuba ≃ 246 3.28 S 68.42 W
Jandira 256 23.31 S 46.54 W
Jandira □ [7] 287b 23.32 S 46.54 W
Jandowae 166 26.47 S 151.06 E
Jandrakinot 180 64.54 N 172.32 W
Jándula ≃ 34 38.03 N 4.06 W
Jándula, Embalse de ⊜ [1] 34 38.30 N 4.00 W
Janeiro, Rio de ≃ 250 11.51 S 45.09 W
Jane Peak ∧ 172 45.20 S 168.19 E
Janes Island I 208 38.00 N 75.52 W
Janes Island State Park ♠ 208 38.00 N 75.52 W
Janesville, Ca., U.S. 204 40.17 N 120.31 W
Janesville, Mn., U.S. 190 44.06 N 93.42 W
Janesville, Wi., U.S. 216 42.40 N 89.01 W
Jangal Bādhāl 126 23.07 N 89.21 E
Jangamo 156 24.06 S 35.21 E
Jangany 157b 23.14 S 45.27 E
Jangarej 24 68.46 N 61.25 E
Jangel'skij 86 53.08 N 58.59 E
Jangeru 112 2.20 S 116.29 E
Jangiabad 85 41.08 N 70.05 E
Jangi-Bazar 85 41.40 N 70.53 E
Jangijer 85 40.17 N 68.50 E
Jangijul' 85 41.07 N 69.03 E
Jangikišlak 85 40.25 N 67.10 E
Jangikurgan, S.S.S.R. 85 40.34 N 71.09 E
Jangikurgan, S.S.S.R. 85 41.12 N 71.44 E
Jangipāra 126 22.45 N 88.04 E
Jangīpur 124 24.28 N 88.04 E
Jangong 114 4.23 N 96.48 E
Jangoon 122 17.43 N 79.11 E
Jangulovo 80 56.26 N 50.25 E
Janikowo 30 52.45 N 18.07 E
Janīn 132 32.28 N 35.18 E
Janina → Ioánnina 38 39.40 N 20.50 E
Janino 265a 59.56 N 30.36 E
Janisjarvi, ozero ⊜ 24 61.59 N 30.57 E
Janiuay 116 10.58 N 122.30 E
Janja 38 44.40 N 19.15 E
Janjina, Jugo. 36 42.56 N 17.26 E
Janjina, Madag. 157b 20.30 S 45.50 E
Janka 126 21.52 N 87.56 E
Jankan, chrebet ⋏ 88 55.45 N 118.00 E
Jankāpur 126 21.54 N 87.23 E
Jan Kempdorp (Andalusia) 158 27.55 S 24.51 E
Jan Lake ⊜ 184 54.55 N 102.55 W
Janlohong 112 2.15 N 117.03 E
Jan Mayen I 12 71.00 N 8.20 W
Jan Mayen Ridge ✢ [3] 10 69.00 N 8.00 W
Jannaale 144 1.48 N 44.42 E
Jannali 274a 34.01 S 151.04 E
Jannali Park ♠ 274a 34.01 S 151.03 E
Janos 232 30.54 N 108.10 W
Janos, Río de ≃ 232 30.56 N 108.08 W
Jánoshalma 30 46.18 N 19.20 E
Jánosháza 30 47.08 N 17.10 E
János-hegy ∧ 264c 47.31 N 18.58 E
Jánossomorja 61 47.47 N 17.08 E
Janoviči 76 55.17 N 30.42 E
Janowiec Wielkopolski 30 52.46 N 17.31 E
Janów Lubelski 30 50.43 N 22.24 E
Jānsath 124 29.20 N 77.51 E
Jansen 184 51.47 N 104.43 W
Jansenville 158 32.56 S 24.40 E
Janskij 74 68.28 N 134.48 E
Janskij zaliv ⊂ 74 71.50 N 136.00 E
Jantarnyj 76 54.52 N 19.57 E
Jantetelco 234 18.42 N 98.46 W
Jantikovo 80 55.32 N 47.48 E
Jantra ≃ 38 43.38 N 25.34 E
Januária 255 15.29 S 44.22 W
Januário Cicco 250 6.09 S 35.35 W
Jan Van Riebeeck Park ♠ 273d 26.10 S 27.59 E
Janvarcevo 80 51.26 N 52.15 E
Janville 50 48.12 N 1.53 E
Janville-sur-Juine 261 48.31 N 2.16 E
Janvry 261 48.39 N 2.09 E
Jany-Kurgan 85 43.55 N 67.15 E
Janzé 32 47.58 N 1.30 W
Janzūr 142 30.41 N 31.02 E
Jaora 120 23.38 N 75.08 E
Japan (Nihon) □ [1], Asia 90 36.00 N 138.00 E
Japan (Nihon) □ [1], Asia 92 36.00 N 138.00 E
Japan, Sea of ⍑ [2] 90 40.00 N 135.00 E
Japan Basin ✢ [1] 12 40.00 N 135.00 E
Japanisches Meer → Japan, Sea of ⍑ [2] 90 40.00 N 135.00 E
Japan Trench ✢ [1] 6 37.00 N 143.00 E
Japaratinga 250 9.05 S 35.15 W
Japaratuba 250 10.35 S 36.57 W
Japeri 256 22.39 S 43.40 W
Japi 250 6.27 S 35.56 W
Japichaua, Ilha I 250 0.55 S 50.35 W
Japiim 248 7.37 S 72.54 W
Japla 124 24.33 N 84.01 E
Japoatã 250 10.20 S 36.48 W
Japon → Japan □ [1] 92 36.00 N 138.00 E
Japón, Mar del → Japan, Sea of ⍑ [2] 90 40.00 N 135.00 E
Japtiksal'a 74 69.21 N 72.32 E
Japuíba 256 22.35 S 42.42 W
Japurá 246 1.48 S 66.30 W
Japurá (Caquetá) ≃ 246 3.08 S 64.46 W
Jaqué 246 7.31 N 78.10 W
Jaqui 248 15.30 S 74.26 W
Jar 80 58.15 N 52.06 E
Jār, Jabal ∧ 128 24.34 N 38.18 E
Jarābulus 130 36.49 N 38.01 E
Jarad 144 18.59 N 41.24 E
Jaradū 142 29.18 N 30.42 E
Jaraguá 255 15.45 S 49.20 W
Jaraguá ◆ [8] 287b 23.27 S 46.44 W
Jaraguá, Pico do ∧ 287b 23.26 S 46.46 W
Jaraguá do Sul 252 26.29 S 49.04 W
Jaraicejo 34 39.40 N 5.49 W
Jaraiz de la Vera 34 40.04 N 5.45 W
Jaral del Progreso 234 20.22 N 101.04 W
Jarales 200 34.36 N 106.45 W
Jarama ≃ 34 40.02 N 3.39 W
Jarama, Canal del ≊ 266a 40.18 N 3.32 W
Jaramānah 132 33.29 N 36.21 E
Jaramillo 254 47.11 S 67.09 W
Jaramor 80 56.07 N 48.44 E
Jaran' ≃ 80 57.35 N 48.14 E
Jarandilla 34 40.08 N 5.39 W
Jaransk 80 57.19 N 47.54 E
Jarānwāla 123 31.20 N 73.26 E
Jarash 132 32.17 N 35.54 E
Jaraucu ≃ 250 1.48 S 52.22 W
Jarawī, Wādī V 142 29.47 N 31.19 E
Jarbah, Jabal al- ∧ 142 30.16 N 32.03 E
Jarbah, Wāḥat ⍑ [4] 140 29.21 N 25.20 E
Jarbidge ≃ 202 42.19 N 115.39 W
Järbo 40 60.43 N 16.36 E
Jarcevo 76 55.04 N 32.41 E
Jardas al-'Abīd 146 32.19 N 20.56 E
Jardim, Bra. 248 21.28 S 56.09 W
Jardim, Bra. 250 7.35 S 39.16 W
Jardim América ◆ [8] 287b 23.34 S 46.41 W
Jardim de Angicos 250 5.39 S 35.59 W
Jardim de Piranhas 250 6.22 S 37.20 W
Jardim do Seridó 250 6.35 S 36.46 W
Jardim Paulista ◆ [8] 287b 23.35 S 46.40 W
Jardín América 252 27.03 S 55.14 W
Jardine ≃ 164 10.55 S 142.13 E
Jardine River National Park ♠ 164 11.20 S 142.40 E
Jardines de la Reina, Archipiélago de los II 240p 20.50 N 78.55 W
Jardinópolis 255 21.02 S 47.46 W
Jardymly 84 38.55 N 48.15 E
Jaredi 150 12.46 N 5.05 E
Jaremča 78 48.27 N 24.33 E
Jarenga, S.S.S.R. 24 62.43 N 49.30 E
Jaren'ga, S.S.S.R. 24 63.27 N 53.26 E
Jarensk 24 62.11 N 49.02 E
Järfälla 40 59.24 N 17.50 E
Jargalang 89 43.06 N 122.54 E
Jargara 78 46.27 N 28.27 E
Jargeau 50 47.52 N 2.07 E
Jari ≃, Bra. 248 5.07 S 62.21 W
Jari ≃, Bra. 250 1.09 S 51.54 W
Jari, Lago ⊜ 246 5.00 S 62.19 W
Jāria Jhānjail 124 25.02 N 90.39 E
Jaridih 124 23.38 N 86.04 E
Jarinu 256 23.06 S 46.44 W
Jarīr, Wādī al- V 128 25.38 N 42.30 E
Jarkino 88 59.08 N 99.23 E
Jarkovo 86 57.24 N 67.05 E
Jarkul'-Mat'uškino 86 55.51 N 76.06 E
Järlåsa 40 59.53 N 17.12 E
Jarmen 54 53.55 N 13.20 E
Jarmolincy 78 49.12 N 26.50 E
Järna 40 59.06 N 17.34 E
Jarnac 32 45.41 N 0.10 W
Jarny 56 49.09 N 5.53 E
Jaro 116 11.11 N 124.47 E
Jarochta 88 58.58 N 98.58 E
Jarocin 30 51.59 N 17.31 E
Jaroměř 30 50.21 N 15.55 E
Jaroměřice 61 49.05 N 15.53 E
Jaropolec 82 56.08 N 35.49 E
Jaroslavec 78 51.33 N 33.40 E
Jaroslavl' 80 57.37 N 39.52 E
Jaroslavl' □ [4] 82 56.45 N 38.45 E
Jaroslavl' Station ◆ [5] 265b 55.47 N 37.39 E
Jaroslavskaja 84 44.36 N 40.27 E
Jaroslavskij 89 44.10 N 132.13 E
Jarosław 30 50.02 N 22.42 E
Jarovaja 83 49.03 N 37.37 E
Järpen 26 63.21 N 13.29 E
Jarrahdale 168a 32.21 S 116.04 E
Jarratt 208 36.48 N 77.28 W
Jarreau 194 30.39 N 91.29 W
Jarrell 222 30.49 N 97.36 W
Jarrettsville 208 39.36 N 76.28 W
Jarrīs 142 27.55 N 30.46 E
Jarrow 44 54.59 N 1.29 W
Jarry, Parc ♠ 275a 45.32 N 73.38 W
Jar-Sale 74 66.50 N 70.50 E
Jarsomovy 86 60.15 N 73.38 E
Jartai Yanchi ⊜ 102 39.43 N 105.41 E
Jaru 248 10.26 S 62.27 W
Jaru ≃ 248 10.05 S 61.59 W
Jarud Qi 89 44.37 N 120.58 E
Jaruu 88 48.08 N 96.45 E
Järva-Jaani 76 59.02 N 25.53 E
Järvakandi 76 58.47 N 24.49 E
Järvelä 26 60.52 N 25.17 E
Järvenpää 26 60.28 N 25.06 E
Jarvie 182 54.27 N 113.59 W
Jarville-la-Malgrange 58 48.40 N 6.13 E
Jarvis 212 42.53 N 80.06 W
Jarvisburg 192 36.12 N 75.52 W
Jarvis Island I 14 0.23 S 160.02 W
Järvsö 26 61.43 N 16.10 E
Jarwa 124 27.39 N 82.31 E
Jasaan 116 8.39 N 124.45 E
Jasai 272c 18.56 N 73.01 E
Jašalta 80 46.20 N 42.17 E
Jasašnaja Tašla 80 53.55 N 48.16 E
Jaša Tomić 38 45.27 N 20.51 E
Jasdan 120 22.02 N 71.12 E
Jasel'da ≃ 76 52.07 N 26.28 E
Jasenevo ◆ [8] 265b 55.36 N 37.33 E
Jasenki 78 51.32 N 38.12 E
Jasenovoje 82 54.10 N 36.47 E
Jasenovskij 83 48.10 N 39.10 E
Jasenskaja 78 46.22 N 38.16 E
Jashpurnagar 124 22.54 N 84.09 E
Jāshpur Pāts ◆ [1] 124 22.55 N 84.00 E
Jasidih 124 24.31 N 86.39 E
Jasień 30 51.46 N 15.01 E
Jasienica 54 53.37 N 14.32 E
Jasikan 150 7.24 N 0.28 E
Jašil'kul', ozero ⊜ 120 37.45 N 72.55 E
Jasin 114 2.19 N 102.26 E
Jasin'a 78 48.16 N 24.20 E
Jasinga 115a 6.29 S 106.27 E
Jasinovataja 83 48.08 N 37.51 E
Jasinovka 83 48.08 N 37.57 E
Jāsk 128 25.38 N 57.46 E
Jaskhar 272c 18.54 N 72.59 E
Jaškino, S.S.S.R. 80 52.41 N 53.26 E
Jaškino, S.S.S.R. 86 55.54 N 85.26 E
Jaskino, S.S.S.R. 265b 55.40 N 37.16 E
Jaškul' 80 46.11 N 45.21 E
Jaškul' ≃ 80 46.15 N 45.05 E
Jasło 30 49.45 N 21.29 E
Jasmine Estates 220 28.17 N 82.42 W
Jasmund > [1] 54 54.32 N 13.35 E
Jasnaja Pol'ana ⊥ 82 54.05 N 37.32 E
Jasnogorka 83 48.47 N 37.33 E
Jasnogorsk 82 54.29 N 37.42 E
Jasnomorskij 89 46.45 N 141.54 E
Jasnyj, S.S.S.R. 86 51.04 N 59.58 E
Jasnyj, S.S.S.R. 89 53.17 N 127.59 E
Jason Islands II 254 51.05 S 61.00 W
Jason Peninsula > [1] 9 66.10 S 61.00 W
Jasonville 194 39.09 N 87.11 W
Jasper, Ab., Can. 182 52.53 N 118.05 W
Jasper, Al., U.S. 194 33.49 N 87.16 W
Jasper, Ar., U.S. 194 36.00 N 93.11 W
Jasper, Fl., U.S. 192 30.31 N 82.56 W
Jasper, Ga., U.S. 192 34.28 N 84.25 W
Jasper, In., U.S. 194 38.23 N 86.55 W
Jasper, Mi., U.S. 216 41.48 N 84.02 W
Jasper, Mn., U.S. 198 43.51 N 96.23 W
Jasper, Mo., U.S. 194 37.20 N 94.18 W
Jasper, N.Y., U.S. 210 42.07 N 77.30 W
Jasper, Tn., U.S. 194 35.04 N 85.37 W
Jasper, Tx., U.S. 194 30.55 N 93.59 W
Jasper □ [6] 216 40.57 N 87.09 W
Jasper Lake ⊜ 182 53.07 N 118.00 W
Jasper National Park ♠ 182 52.53 N 118.03 W
Jaspur 124 29.17 N 78.49 E
Jasra 124 25.17 N 81.48 E
Jassans-Riottier 58 45.59 N 4.45 E
Jassar 123 32.06 N 74.57 E
Jassy → Iași 38 47.10 N 27.35 E
Jassy ≃ 85 40.46 N 73.05 E
Jastarnia 30 54.43 N 18.40 E
Jastrebarsko 36 45.40 N 15.39 E
Jastrebovka, S.S.S.R. 78 51.27 N 37.32 E
Jastrebovka, S.S.S.R. 82 54.36 N 36.24 E
Jastrow → Jastrowie 30 53.26 N 16.49 E
Jastrowie 30 53.26 N 16.49 E
Jaswantnagar 124 26.53 N 78.55 E
Jászapáti 30 47.31 N 20.09 E

Symbol	English	Deutsch	Español	Français	Português
≃	River	Fluß	Río	Rivière	Rio
≊	Canal	Kanal	Canal	Canal	Canal
⌞	Waterfall, Rapids	Wasserfall, Stromschnellen	Cascada, Rápidos	Chute d'eau, Rapides	Cascata, Rápidos
⊔	Strait	Meeresstraße	Estrecho	Détroit	Estreito
⊂	Bay, Gulf	Bucht, Golf	Bahía, Golfo	Baie, Golfe	Baía, Golfo
⊜	Lake, Lakes	See, Seen	Lago, Lagos	Lac, Lacs	Lago, Lagos
≡	Swamp	Sumpf	Pantano	Marais	Pântano
⌂	Ice Features, Glacier	Eis- und Gletscherformen	Accidentes Glaciales	Formes glaciaires	Acidentes glaciares
⍑	Other Hydrographic Features	Andere Hydrographische Objekte	Otros Elementos Hidrográficos	Autres données hydrographiques	Outros acidentes hidrográficos
✢	Submarine Features	Untermeerische Objekte	Accidentes Submarinos	Formes de relief sous-marin	Acidentes submarinos
□	Political Unit	Politische Einheit	Unidad Politica	Entité politique	Unidade política
♉	Cultural Institution	Kulturelle Institution	Institución Cultural	Institution culturelle	Institução cultural
⊥	Historical Site	Historische Stätte	Sitio Histórico	Site historique	Sitio histórico
♠	Recreational Site	Erholungs- und Ferienort	Sitio de Recreo	Centre de loisirs	Area de Lazer
⊠	Airport	Flughafen	Aeropuerto	Aéroport	Aeroporto
■	Military Installation	Militäranlage	Instalación Militar	Installation militaire	Instalação militar
◆	Miscellaneous	Verschiedenes	Misceláneo	Divers	Diversos

Name	Page	Lat.°′	Long.°′
Jászberény	**30**	47.30 N	19.55 E
Jataí	**255**	17.53 S	51.43 W
Jatapu ≃	**246**	2.13 S	58.17 W
Jatatè ≃	**236**	16.15 N	91.17 W
Jati, Bra.	**250**	7.41 S	39.01 W
Jāti, Pāk.	**120**	24.21 N	68.16 E
Jatibarang	**115a**	6.28 S	108.17 E
Jatibonico	**240p**	21.56 N	79.10 W
Jatibonico del Sur ≃	**240p**	21.33 N	79.09 W
Jatilawang	**115a**	7.32 S	109.06 E
Jatiluhur, Waduk ⊜[1]	**115a**	6.35 S	107.20 E
Jatinegara ✦[8]	**269e**	6.13 S	106.52 E
Jatiroto	**115a**	8.07 S	113.21 E
Jatisrono	**115a**	7.49 S	111.07 E
Jatiwangi	**115a**	6.44 S	108.15 E
Jatni	**120**	20.10 N	85.42 E
Jatniel	**273d**	26.07 S	28.19 E
Jatobá ≃	**255**	12.23 S	54.07 W
Jatoi Janūbi	**123**	29.31 N	70.51 E
Jātrāpur	**126**	22.44 N	89.45 E
Jatt (Tel Gat)	**132**	32.24 N	35.02 E
Jatznick	**54**	53.35 N	13.56 E
Jáu, Ang.	**152**	15.12 S	13.31 E
Jaú, Bra.	**255**	22.18 S	48.33 W
Jaú ≃	**246**	1.54 S	61.26 W
Jauaperi ≃	**246**	1.26 S	61.35 W
Jauer → Jawor	**30**	51.03 N	16.11 E
Jauerling ʌ	**61**	48.20 N	15.20 E
Jaugrām	**126**	23.06 N	88.05 E
Jauja	**248**	11.48 S	75.30 W
Jauli	**272a**	28.44 N	77.21 E
Jaumave	**234**	23.25 N	99.23 W
Jaúna ≃	**248**	6.24 S	59.57 W
Jaunde → Yaoundé	**152**	3.52 N	11.31 E
Jaune, Mer → Yellow Sea ⊽[2]	**90**	36.00 N	123.00 E
Jaungulbene	**76**	57.04 N	26.36 E
Jaunjelgava	**76**	56.37 N	25.05 E
Jaunpass)(	**58**	46.36 N	7.20 E
Jaunpiebalga	**76**	57.11 N	26.03 E
Jaunpils	**76**	56.44 N	23.01 E
Jaunpur	**124**	25.44 N	82.41 E
Jaupaci	**255**	16.18 S	50.54 W
Jauquara ≃	**248**	15.06 S	57.06 W
Jáuregui	**258**	34.36 S	59.10 W
Jauru ≃, Bra.	**248**	16.22 S	57.46 W
Jauru ≃, Bra.	**255**	18.40 S	54.36 W
Jausiers	**62**	44.25 N	6.44 E
Jauza ≃, S.S.S.R.	**82**	56.25 N	36.05 E
Jauza ≃, S.S.S.R.	**265b**	55.45 N	37.38 E
Java	**198**	45.30 N	99.53 W
Java → Jawa I	**115a**	7.30 S	110.00 E
Java Center	**210**	42.39 N	78.23 W
Javādi Hills ⩘[2]	**122**	12.35 N	78.50 E
Javan	**85**	38.19 N	69.02 E
Javari (Yavarí) ≃	**242**	4.21 S	70.02 W
Javas	**80**	54.26 N	42.51 E
Java Sea → Jawa, Laut ⊽[2]	**112**	5.00 S	110.00 E
Java Trench ✧[1]	**12**	10.30 S	110.00 E
Java Village	**210**	42.40 N	78.26 W
Jävenitz	**54**	52.31 N	11.30 E
Javier, Isla I	**254**	47.06 S	74.24 W
Javkino	**78**	47.16 N	32.37 E
Javlenka	**86**	54.21 N	68.27 E
Javor ⩘	**38**	44.05 N	18.55 E
Javořice ʌ	**61**	49.14 N	15.20 E
Javorie ʌ	**30**	48.27 N	19.18 E
Javorná	**60**	49.13 N	13.18 E
Javorník	**30**	50.23 N	17.00 E
Javorov	**78**	49.56 N	23.23 E
Javorová skála ʌ	**30**	49.31 N	14.30 E
Javr ≃	**24**	68.09 N	30.06 E
Jävre	**26**	65.09 N	21.59 E
Jawa (Java) I	**115a**	7.30 S	110.00 E
Jawa, Laut (Java Sea) ⊽[2]	**112**	5.00 S	110.00 E
Jawa Barat □[4]	**115a**	7.00 S	107.00 E
Jaw'āīyāt, Jabal al- ʌ	**132**	31.26 N	36.26 E
Jawāla Mukhi	**123**	31.53 N	76.19 E
Jawa Tengah □[4]	**115a**	7.30 S	110.00 E
Jawa Timur □[4]	**115a**	8.00 S	113.00 E
Jawbar	**132**	33.31 N	36.19 E
Jawf, Wādī V	**144**	15.50 N	45.30 E
Jawi	**112**	0.48 S	109.16 E
Jawor	**30**	51.03 N	16.11 E
Jaworzno	**30**	50.13 N	19.15 E
Jay, Fl., U.S.	**194**	30.57 N	87.09 W
Jay, Ok., U.S.	**196**	36.25 N	94.47 W
Jay □[6]	**216**	40.26 N	84.59 W
Jaya, Puncak ʌ	**164**	4.05 S	137.11 E
Jayanca	**248**	6.24 S	79.50 W
Jayapura (Sukarnapura)	**164**	2.32 S	140.42 E
Jayb, Wādī al- (Ha'Arava) V	**132**	30.58 N	35.24 E
Jay Cooke State Park ♠	**190**	46.41 N	92.23 W
Jay Creek Aboriginal Reserve ✦[4]	**162**	23.45 S	133.35 E
Jaydebpur	**124**	24.00 N	90.26 E
Jaynagar	**126**	22.36 N	90.42 E
Jaynagar Majilpur	**126**	22.11 N	88.25 E
Jaynes	**200**	32.16 N	111.01 W
Jay Peak ʌ	**188**	44.55 N	72.32 W
Jaypur, India	**122**	18.51 N	82.35 E
Jaypur, India	**126**	23.03 N	87.27 E
Jayrūd	**130**	33.49 N	36.44 E
Jayton	**196**	33.15 N	100.34 W
Jayuya	**240m**	18.13 N	66.36 W
Jaywick	**42**	51.47 N	1.08 E
Jaz	**80**	54.54 N	45.13 E
Jaželbicy	**76**	58.02 N	32.58 E
Jazevec	**24**	65.43 N	46.30 E
Jazgulem ≃	**85**	38.12 N	71.21 E
Jazīrat Muḥammad	**273c**	30.07 N	31.12 E
Jazjavan	**85**	40.39 N	71.44 E
Jažma	**24**	66.56 N	44.29 E
Jaz Mūrīān, Hāmūn-e ⊜	**128**	27.20 N	58.55 E
Jazovaja	**86**	49.27 N	85.20 E
Jazykovo	**80**	54.18 N	47.24 E
Jazzīn	**132**	33.32 N	35.34 E
Jbā'	**132**	33.29 N	35.31 E
J.B. Thomas, Lake ⊜[1]	**196**	32.35 N	101.10 W
J. C. Murphey Lake ⊜	**216**	40.58 N	87.30 W
Jdiouia	**34**	35.57 N	0.50 E
Jeanerette	**194**	29.54 N	91.39 W
Jeanesville	**210**	40.56 N	75.58 W
Jeannette	**214**	40.19 N	79.36 W
Jebba	**150**	9.08 N	4.50 E
Jebel	**38**	45.33 N	21.14 E
Jebeniana	**148**	35.02 N	10.55 E
Jeber-Bergfrieden	**54**	51.59 N	12.20 E
Jeberos	**248**	5.17 S	76.13 W
Jebri	**120**	27.18 N	65.44 E
Jebus	**112**	1.44 S	105.29 E
Jechegnadzor	**84**	39.46 N	45.21 E
Jéci, Serra ʌ	**154**	12.48 S	35.12 E
Jedane, Oued ti-n- V	**148**	24.55 N	6.30 E
Jedarma	**88**	58.44 N	102.36 E
Jedburgh	**44**	55.29 N	2.34 W
Jedburgh Abbey ᵿ[1]	**44**	55.27 N	2.34 W
Jeddore Lake ⊜[1]	**186**	48.03 N	55.55 W
Jedelevo	**80**	53.24 N	47.45 E
Jedepo	**150**	5.16 N	8.20 W
Jedincy	**78**	48.10 N	27.19 E
Jedisa	**84**	42.31 N	44.16 E
Jedlesee ✦[8]	**264b**	48.16 N	16.23 E
Jednevo	**82**	56.06 N	36.14 E
Jedogon	**88**	54.15 N	100.15 E
Jedrovo	**76**	57.55 N	33.38 E
Jędrzejów	**30**	50.39 N	20.18 E
Jedwabne	**30**	53.17 N	22.19 E
Jed Water ≃	**46**	55.32 N	2.33 W
Jeetzel (Jeetze) ≃	**54**	53.09 N	11.04 E
Jefawa	**140**	10.57 N	23.48 E
Jeffara (Al-Jifārah) ≚	**146**	32.30 N	11.45 E
Jeffers	**198**	44.03 N	95.11 W
Jefferson, Ga., U.S.	**192**	34.07 N	83.34 W
Jefferson, In., U.S.	**216**	40.17 N	86.36 W
Jefferson, Ia., U.S.	**198**	42.00 N	94.22 W
Jefferson, Md., U.S.	**208**	39.21 N	77.31 W
Jefferson, Ma., U.S.	**207**	42.21 N	71.52 W
Jefferson, N.J., U.S.	**285**	39.45 N	75.13 W
Jefferson, N.Y., U.S.	**210**	42.14 N	73.54 W
Jefferson, N.Y., U.S.	**210**	42.29 N	74.37 W
Jefferson, N.C., U.S.	**192**	36.25 N	81.28 W
Jefferson, Oh., U.S.	**214**	41.44 N	80.46 W
Jefferson, Or., U.S.	**202**	44.43 N	123.00 W
Jefferson, Pa., U.S.	**279b**	40.18 N	80.03 W
Jefferson, S.C., U.S.	**192**	34.39 N	80.23 W
Jefferson, S.D., U.S.	**198**	42.36 N	96.33 W
Jefferson, Tx., U.S.	**194**	32.45 N	94.20 W
Jefferson, Wi., U.S.	**216**	43.00 N	88.48 W
Jefferson □[6], Il., U.S.	**219**	38.19 N	88.55 W
Jefferson □[6], In., U.S.	**218**	38.44 N	85.23 W
Jefferson □[6], Ky., U.S.	**218**	38.14 N	85.10 W
Jefferson □[6], Mo., U.S.	**219**	38.20 N	90.34 W
Jefferson □[6], N.Y., U.S.	**212**	43.59 N	75.55 W
Jefferson □[6], Oh., U.S.	**214**	40.22 N	80.37 W
Jefferson □[6], Pa., U.S.	**214**	41.09 N	79.05 W
Jefferson □[6], Wa., U.S.	**224**	47.50 N	122.36 W
Jefferson □[6], Wi., U.S.	**216**	43.02 N	88.46 W
Jefferson ≃	**202**	45.56 N	111.30 W
Jefferson, Mount ʌ, U.S.	**202**	44.34 N	111.30 W
Jefferson, Mount ʌ, Nv., U.S.	**204**	38.46 N	116.55 W
Jefferson, Mount ʌ, Or., U.S.	**202**	44.40 N	121.47 W
Jefferson City, Mo., U.S.	**219**	38.34 N	92.10 W
Jefferson City, Tn., U.S.	**192**	36.07 N	83.29 W
Jefferson Farms	**285**	39.40 N	75.34 W
Jefferson Manor	**284c**	38.47 N	77.04 W
Jefferson Park ✦[8]	**278**	41.59 N	87.46 W
Jefferson Proving Ground ■	**218**	38.50 N	85.25 W
Jeffersonton	**188**	38.38 N	77.55 W
Jeffersontown	**218**	38.11 N	85.33 W
Jefferson Village	**284c**	38.52 N	77.10 W
Jeffersonville, Ga., U.S.	**192**	32.41 N	83.20 W
Jeffersonville, In., U.S.	**218**	38.16 N	85.44 W
Jeffersonville, N.Y., U.S.	**210**	41.46 N	74.56 W
Jeffersonville, Oh., U.S.	**218**	39.39 N	83.33 W
Jeffrey City	**200**	42.29 N	107.49 W
Jeffreys Bay	**158**	34.02 S	24.54 E
Jeffries Creek ≃	**192**	34.05 N	79.32 W
Jefimovka	**80**	52.13 N	52.03 E
Jefimovskij	**76**	59.30 N	35.02 E
Jefremov	**76**	53.09 N	38.07 E
Jefremova	**82**	56.13 N	38.59 E
Jefremovka	**83**	47.19 N	38.29 E
Jefremovo-Stepanovka	**78**	48.43 N	40.50 E
Jefremovskaja	**82**	55.25 N	38.59 E
Jega	**150**	12.15 N	4.23 E
Jegenstorf	**58**	47.03 N	7.30 E
Jegindybulak, S.S.S.R.	**86**	49.45 N	76.23 E
Jegindybulak, S.S.S.R.	**86**	48.42 N	81.48 E
Jegizkara, gora ʌ	**86**	46.24 N	64.09 E
Jegorjevka	**89**	50.42 N	127.42 E
Jegorjevsk	**82**	55.23 N	39.02 E
Jegorlyk ≃	**80**	46.33 N	41.52 E
Jehol → Chengde	**105**	40.58 N	117.53 E
Jeja ≃	**78**	46.41 N	38.36 E
Jejsk	**78**	46.42 N	38.16 E
Jejskij liman ⊂	**78**	46.42 N	38.25 E
Jeju → Cheju	**90**	33.31 N	126.32 E
Jejur	**272b**	22.53 N	88.08 E
Jēkabpils	**76**	56.29 N	25.51 E
Jekaterinburg → Sverdlovsk	**86**	56.51 N	60.36 E
Jekaterinino	**76**	55.49 N	33.58 E
Jekaterininskoje	**86**	56.53 N	74.34 E
Jekaterinoslav → Dnepropetrovsk	**78**	48.27 N	34.59 E
Jekaterinoslavka	**89**	50.23 N	129.08 E
Jekaterinovka, S.S.S.R.	**78**	46.42 N	38.46 E
Jekaterinovka, S.S.S.R.	**80**	53.04 N	49.28 E
Jekaterinovka, S.S.S.R.	**80**	46.32 N	41.42 E
Jekaterinovka, S.S.S.R.	**80**	52.03 N	44.21 E
Jekaterinovka, S.S.S.R.	**83**	47.33 N	38.23 E
Jekaterinovka, S.S.S.R.	**86**	54.36 N	70.58 E
Jekaterinovka ✦[8]	**265b**	55.46 N	37.23 E
Jekaterinovskaja	**78**	46.20 N	39.58 E
Jekateriny, proliv ⊔, S.S.S.R.	**74**	44.30 N	146.45 E
Jekateriny, proliv ⊔, S.S.S.R.	**92a**	44.25 N	146.40 E
Jekimoviči	**76**	54.07 N	33.18 E
Jekpindykurylys	**80**	47.49 N	47.17 E
Jekyll Island I	**192**	31.04 N	81.25 W
Jekyll Island State Park ♠	**192**	31.02 N	81.25 W
Jelabuga	**80**	55.47 N	52.04 E
Jelai ≃, Indon.	**112**	2.59 S	110.45 E
Jelai ≃, Malay.	**114**	4.04 N	102.20 E
Jelan', S.S.S.R.	**80**	52.13 N	44.11 E
Jelan', S.S.S.R.	**80**	50.57 N	43.44 E
Jelan', S.S.S.R.	**83**	48.41 N	39.47 E
Jelan', S.S.S.R.	**86**	57.39 N	63.42 E
Jelan' ≃, S.S.S.R.	**78**	51.07 N	41.25 E
Jelan' ≃, S.S.S.R.	**80**	50.57 N	43.44 E
Jelan' ≃, S.S.S.R.	**80**	51.07 N	41.26 E
Jelancy	**88**	52.49 N	106.25 E
Jelanec	**78**	47.42 N	31.51 E
Jelanka	**86**	55.37 N	75.18 E
Jelan'-Koleno	**78**	51.09 N	41.14 E
Jelan'-Kolenovskij	**78**	51.10 N	41.10 E
Jelat'ma	**80**	54.58 N	41.45 E
Jelaur, S.S.S.R.	**80**	54.34 N	50.21 E
Jelaur, S.S.S.R.	**80**	53.50 N	48.48 E
Jelchovka	**80**	53.51 N	50.18 E
Jel'covka	**86**	53.15 N	86.15 E
Jel'cy, S.S.S.R.	**76**	56.40 N	33.51 E
Jel'cy, S.S.S.R.	**82**	56.11 N	38.46 E
Jelec	**76**	52.37 N	38.30 E
Jeleckij	**24**	67.03 N	64.10 E
Jelenia Góra (Hirschberg)	**30**	50.55 N	15.46 E
Jelenia Góra □[4]	**30**	51.10 N	15.30 E
Jelenskij	**76**	53.29 N	35.23 E
Jelep La Pass)(	**124**	27.23 N	88.51 E
Jelgava	**76**	56.39 N	23.42 E
Jelgavkrasti	**76**	57.28 N	24.26 E
Jelisejevka	**78**	47.02 N	36.24 E
Jelizarovo, S.S.S.R.	**78**	48.12 N	34.33 E
Jelizarovo, S.S.S.R.	**80**	58.33 N	44.50 E
Jelizavetgradka	**78**	48.48 N	32.24 E
Jelizavetinka	**86**	51.28 N	71.12 E
Jelizavetopol'skoje	**86**	52.51 N	60.36 E
Jelizavetovka	**78**	46.39 N	38.53 E
Jelizavety, mys ›	**89**	54.26 N	142.42 E
Jelizovo	**76**	53.24 N	29.01 E
Jelli	**154**	5.22 N	31.48 E
Jellico	**192**	36.35 N	84.07 W
Jelling	**41**	55.45 N	9.26 E
Jelloway	**214**	40.33 N	82.18 W
Jelm Mountain ʌ	**200**	41.06 N	105.58 W
Jel'n'a	**76**	54.35 N	33.11 E
Jelnat'	**80**	57.20 N	42.49 E
Jel'niki	**80**	54.37 N	43.53 E
Jeloguj ≃	**74**	63.13 N	87.45 E
Jel'onovka, S.S.S.R.	**83**	47.50 N	37.40 E
Jel'onovka, S.S.S.R.	**83**	48.39 N	38.01 E
Jelošnoje	**86**	55.27 N	66.44 E
Jelovo	**80**	57.03 N	54.54 E
Jels	**41**	55.21 N	9.12 E
Jelšanka, S.S.S.R.	**80**	51.49 N	46.23 E
Jelšanka, S.S.S.R.	**80**	52.35 N	47.59 E
Jelšanka Pervaja	**80**	52.53 N	52.02 E
Jelšava	**30**	48.39 N	20.14 E
Jel'sk	**78**	51.48 N	29.09 E
Jema ≃	**144**	10.09 N	38.20 E
Jemaa	**150**	9.27 N	8.23 E
Jemaja, Pulau I	**112**	2.55 N	105.45 E
Jemaluang	**114**	2.17 N	103.52 E
Jemantajevo	**80**	53.34 N	53.50 E
Jemanželinsk	**86**	54.45 N	61.20 E
Jemappes	**50**	50.27 N	3.53 E
Jember	**115a**	8.10 S	113.42 E
Jemca	**24**	63.04 N	40.20 E
Jemca ≃	**24**	63.15 N	41.20 E
Jemeljanovka	**78**	45.32 N	34.53 E
Jemeljanovo	**86**	56.11 N	92.40 E
Jemel'stan	**24**	61.13 N	52.29 E
Jemen → Yemen □[1]	**144**	15.00 N	44.00 E
Jemen, Volksrepublik → Yemen □[1]	**144**	15.00 N	47.00 E
Jemez ≃	**200**	35.22 N	106.31 W
Jemez Canyon Reservoir ⊜[1]	**200**	35.28 N	106.39 W
Jemez Indian Reservation ✦[4]	**200**	35.35 N	106.45 W
Jemez Springs	**200**	35.46 N	106.41 W
Jemgum	**52**	53.16 N	7.23 E
Jemil'čino	**78**	50.52 N	27.48 E
Jeminary	**86**	47.32 N	85.38 E
Jemmal	**148**	35.38 N	10.46 E
Jemnice	**61**	49.01 N	15.35 E
Jempang, Kenohan ⊜	**112**	0.26 S	116.12 E
Jena, D.D.R.	**54**	50.56 N	11.35 E
Jena, La., U.S.	**194**	31.40 N	92.08 W
Jenakijevo	**83**	48.14 N	38.13 E
Jenašimskij Polkan, gora ʌ	**74**	59.50 N	92.52 E
Jenaz	**58**	46.55 N	9.45 E
Jenbach	**64**	47.24 N	11.47 E
Jenbek	**86**	48.53 N	77.12 E
Jendarata	**114**	3.55 N	100.57 E
Jendongin	**88**	53.27 N	113.01 E
Jendouba (Souk el Arba)	**148**	36.30 N	8.47 E
Jendouba □[8]	**148**	36.30 N	8.45 E
Jeneponto	**112**	5.41 S	119.42 E
Jenera	**216**	40.54 N	83.44 W
Jeniang	**114**	5.49 N	100.38 E
Jenisej (Yenisey) ≃	**72**	71.50 N	82.40 E
Jenisejsk	**86**	58.27 N	92.10 E
Jenisejskij kr'až ⩘	**74**	59.00 N	93.00 E
Jenisejskij zaliv ⊂	**74**	72.30 N	80.00 E
Jenison	**216**	42.54 N	85.47 W
Jenkins, Ky., U.S.	**192**	37.10 N	82.37 W
Jenkins, Tx., U.S.	**222**	32.59 N	94.44 W
Jenkins, Mount ʌ	**162**	25.36 S	129.41 E
Jenkinson Lake ⊜[1]	**226**	38.44 N	120.33 W
Jenkinsville	**192**	34.16 N	81.17 W
Jenkintown	**208**	40.05 N	75.07 W
Jenks	**196**	36.01 N	95.58 W
Jenli	**100**	23.15 N	120.08 E
Jenners	**214**	40.08 N	79.02 W
Jennersdorf	**61**	46.57 N	16.08 E
Jennerstown	**214**	40.10 N	79.04 W
Jennifer Branch ≃	**284b**	39.25 N	76.30 W
Jennings, Fl., U.S.	**192**	30.36 N	83.05 W
Jennings, La., U.S.	**194**	30.13 N	92.39 W
Jennings, Mo., U.S.	**219**	38.43 N	90.15 W
Jennings □[6]	**218**	38.59 N	85.36 W
Jennings Creek ≃	**216**	40.53 N	84.17 W
Jennings Lodge	**224**	45.23 N	122.36 W
Jenotajevka	**80**	47.15 N	47.03 E
Jenpeg Dam ✦[6]	**184**	54.33 N	98.02 W
Jensen	**200**	40.22 N	109.20 W
Jensen Beach	**220**	27.15 N	80.13 W
Jens Munk Island I	**176**	69.42 N	79.30 W
Jens Munks Ø I	**176**	64.40 N	40.30 W
Jenu	**112**	0.36 S	109.52 E
Jen'uka	**88**	57.58 N	121.42 E
Jeonju → Chŏnju	**98**	35.49 N	127.08 E
Jepač	**24**	66.58 N	61.22 E
Jepara	**115a**	6.35 S	110.39 E
Jeparit	**166**	36.09 S	141.59 E
Jepelacio	**248**	6.07 S	76.57 W
Jepichin	**80**	48.16 N	45.14 E
Jepifan'	**76**	53.49 N	38.33 E
Jeppener	**258**	35.17 S	58.12 W
Jeptha Knob ʌ[2]	**218**	38.11 N	85.07 W
Jepua (Jeppo)	**26**	63.24 N	22.37 E
Jequeri	**255**	20.27 S	42.40 W
Jequetepeque ≃	**248**	7.21 S	79.36 W
Jequié	**255**	13.51 S	40.05 W
Jequitaí	**255**	17.15 S	44.28 W
Jequitinhonha	**255**	16.26 S	41.00 W
Jequitinhonha ≃	**255**	15.51 S	38.53 W
Jerachtur	**80**	54.43 N	41.09 E
Jerada	**148**	34.17 N	2.13 W
Jeradou	**36**	36.15 N	10.23 E
Jerangle	**171b**	35.52 S	149.22 E
Jeransang	**114**	3.52 N	102.22 E
Jerantut	**114**	3.56 N	102.22 E
Jerba, Île de I	**148**	33.48 N	10.54 E
Jerbar	**140**	5.39 N	31.05 E
Jerbent	**128**	39.19 N	58.36 E
Jerbogačon	**74**	61.16 N	108.00 E
Jercevo	**24**	60.48 N	40.05 E
Jerdenevo	**82**	54.55 N	36.27 E
Jerécuaro	**234**	20.09 N	100.31 W
Jeremejevka	**83**	46.58 N	39.33 E
Jeremejevo	**82**	55.57 N	37.01 E
Jérémie	**238**	18.39 N	74.07 W
Jeremino	**82**	56.27 N	37.58 E
Jeremoabo	**250**	10.04 S	38.21 W
Jeremy Hill ʌ[2]	**207**	42.45 N	71.21 W
Jeremy Point ›	**207**	41.53 N	70.04 W
Jerevan	**84**	40.11 N	44.30 E
Jerez ≃	**234**	22.15 N	103.11 W
Jerez, Punta ›	**234**	22.54 N	97.46 W
Jerez de García Salinas	**234**	22.39 N	103.00 W
Jerez de la Frontera	**34**	36.41 N	6.08 W
Jerez de los Caballeros	**34**	38.19 N	6.46 W
Jergač	**86**	57.28 N	56.39 E
Jergeni ⩘[2]	**80**	47.00 N	44.00 E
Jergeninskij	**80**	47.07 N	44.28 E
Jericho, Austl.	**166**	23.36 S	146.08 E
Jericho → Arīḥā, Isr. Occ	**132**	31.52 N	35.27 E
Jericho, N.J., U.S.	**285**	39.48 N	75.09 W
Jericho, N.Y., U.S.	**210**	40.47 N	73.32 W
Jericho Dam ⊜[1]	**158**	26.39 S	30.28 E
Jerichow	**54**	52.30 N	12.01 E
Jericó, Bra.	**250**	6.33 S	37.48 W
Jericó, Col.	**246**	5.47 N	75.47 W
Jerid, Chott ≡	**148**	33.42 N	8.26 E
Jerik ≃	**83**	48.59 N	38.30 E
Jerilderie	**166**	35.22 S	145.44 E
Jerimoth Hill ʌ[2]	**207**	41.52 N	71.47 W
Jerki	**78**	48.59 N	31.00 E
Jermak	**86**	52.02 N	76.55 E
Jermakovo	**80**	53.11 N	49.38 E
Jermakovskaja	**80**	48.03 N	41.17 E
Jermakovskoje	**86**	53.16 N	92.24 E
Jermekejevo	**80**	54.05 N	53.40 E
Jermentau	**86**	51.38 N	73.10 E
Jermentau ⩘	**86**	51.10 N	73.10 E
Jermica	**24**	66.56 N	52.15 E
Jermilovka	**86**	57.40 N	72.55 E
Jermiš'	**80**	54.46 N	42.16 E
Jermolajevo, S.S.S.R.	**86**	52.43 N	55.48 E
Jermolajevo, S.S.S.R.	**86**	55.13 N	92.10 E
Jermolino, S.S.S.R.	**82**	56.48 N	37.49 E
Jermolino, S.S.S.R.	**82**	55.12 N	36.36 E
Jermolino, S.S.S.R.	**82**	55.57 N	36.54 E
Jermolino, S.S.S.R.	**86**	57.20 N	64.43 E
Jermyn	**210**	41.31 N	75.32 W
Jernhatten ʌ[2]	**41**	56.15 N	10.48 E
Jernih	**114**	4.25 N	97.43 E
Jeroaquara	**255**	15.23 S	50.25 W
Jerofej Pavlovič	**89**	53.58 N	122.01 E
Jerome, Az., U.S.	**200**	34.44 N	112.06 W
Jerome, Id., U.S.	**202**	42.43 N	114.31 W
Jerome, Il., U.S.	**219**	39.46 N	89.41 W
Jerome, Mi., U.S.	**216**	42.01 N	84.28 W
Jerome, Pa., U.S.	**214**	40.12 N	78.59 W
Jeromesville	**214**	40.48 N	82.11 W
Jer'omino	**86**	58.35 N	79.25 E
Jerônimo Monteiro	**255**	20.47 S	41.24 W
Jerónimos, Mosteiro dos ᵿ[1]	**266c**	38.42 N	9.12 W
Jeröö	**88**	49.45 N	106.40 E
Jeröö ≃	**88**	49.54 N	106.08 E
Jeropol	**74**	65.15 N	168.40 E
Jerpoint Abbey ⊥	**48**	53.29 N	7.08 W
Jerry City	**216**	41.15 N	83.36 W
Jerry Slough ≃	**226**	35.33 N	119.31 W
Jersey	**214**	40.03 N	82.46 W
Jersey □[6]	**219**	39.07 N	90.20 W
Jersey □[2], Europe	**22**	49.15 N	2.10 W
Jersey □[2], Europe	**43b**	49.15 N	2.10 W
Jersey City	**210**	40.43 N	74.04 W
Jersey City State College ᵿ[2]	**276**	40.43 N	74.05 W
Jersey Mountain ʌ	**202**	45.29 N	115.34 W
Jersey Shore	**210**	41.12 N	77.16 W
Jersey Village	**222**	29.52 N	95.35 W
Jerseyville	**219**	39.07 N	90.19 W
Jerši	**76**	54.24 N	34.12 E
Jeršiči	**76**	53.40 N	32.44 E
Jeršov	**80**	51.20 N	48.17 E
Jeršovka	**86**	54.07 N	64.59 E
Jeršovo	**82**	55.46 N	36.52 E
Jeršovskij	**86**	52.29 N	59.08 E
Jertarskij	**86**	56.47 N	64.18 E
Jerte ≃	**34**	39.58 N	6.17 W
Jerteh	**114**	5.45 N	102.30 E
Jertoma	**24**	63.32 N	47.48 E
Jerumenha	**250**	7.05 S	43.30 W
Jerusalem → Yerushalayim	**132**	31.46 N	35.14 E
Jerusalem Airport ⊠	**132**	31.52 N	35.12 E
Jerusalim (Talusan)	**116**	7.26 N	122.49 E
Jeruslan ≃	**80**	50.15 N	45.42 E
Jervaulx Abbey ᵿ[1]	**44**	54.16 N	1.43 W
Jervis, Cape ›	**168b**	35.38 S	138.06 E
Jervis Bay	**170**	35.08 S	150.42 E
Jervis Bay ⊂	**170**	35.05 S	150.44 E
Jervis Inlet ⊂	**182**	49.46 N	124.10 W
Jervois Range ⩘	**162**	22.38 S	136.05 E
Jerxheim	**54**	52.05 N	10.54 E
Jerykly	**80**	55.11 N	51.26 E
Jerzens	**58**	47.10 N	10.45 E
Jesaulovka	**83**	48.03 N	39.02 E
Jesenankaty ≃	**80**	50.32 N	51.47 E
Jesenice, Česko.	**54**	50.04 N	13.29 E
Jesenice, Jugo.	**61**	46.27 N	14.04 E
Jesenice, údolní nádrž ⊜[1]	**60**	50.04 N	12.27 E
Jeseník	**30**	50.14 N	17.13 E
Jesenoviči	**76**	57.17 N	34.14 E
Jesensaj	**80**	49.54 N	51.28 E
Ješera	**84**	43.04 N	40.55 E
Jeserig bei Wiesenburg	**54**	52.05 N	12.27 E
Jesi	**66**	43.31 N	13.14 E
Jesil'	**86**	51.58 N	66.24 E
Jes'ki	**76**	57.56 N	36.23 E
Jesönbulag → Altaj	**90**	46.20 N	96.18 E
Jessej	**74**	68.29 N	102.10 E
Jesselton → Kota Kinabalu	**112**	5.59 N	116.04 E
Jessen	**54**	51.47 N	12.58 E
Jessentuki	**84**	44.03 N	42.51 E
Jesser Point ›	**158**	27.32 S	32.40 E
Jessheim	**26**	60.09 N	11.11 E
Jessnitz	**54**	51.41 N	12.17 E
Jessore	**124**	23.10 N	89.13 E
Jessup, Md., U.S.	**208**	39.08 N	76.46 W
Jessup, Pa., U.S.	**210**	41.28 N	75.33 W
Jessup Park ♠	**280**	34.15 N	118.24 W
Jestetten	**58**	47.39 N	8.34 E
Jestřebí	**54**	50.38 N	14.36 E
Jesuânia	**256**	22.00 S	45.18 W
Jésuite, Lac du ⊜	**206**	46.53 N	72.36 W
Jesup, Ga., U.S.	**192**	31.36 N	81.53 W
Jesup, Ia., U.S.	**190**	42.28 N	92.03 W
Jesup, Lake ⊜	**220**	28.43 N	81.14 W
Jesús	**252**	27.03 S	55.47 W
Jésus, Île I	**206**	45.35 N	73.45 W
Jesús Carranza	**234**	17.26 N	95.02 W
Jesús del Monte ✦[8]	**286b**	23.06 N	82.22 W
Jesús de Otoro	**236**	14.26 N	87.59 W
Jesús María, Arg.	**252**	30.59 S	64.06 W
Jesús María, Méx.	**232**	25.06 N	107.28 W
Jesús María, Méx.	**234**	21.58 N	102.21 W
Jesús María, Perú	**286d**	12.04 S	77.04 W
Jesús María ≃	**234**	21.51 N	104.42 W
Jesús María, Punta ›	**258**	34.39 S	56.55 W
Jet	**196**	36.39 N	98.10 W
Jeta, Ilha de I	**150**	11.53 N	16.15 W
Jetafe	**116**	10.09 N	124.09 E
Jetmore	**198**	38.05 N	99.53 W
Jet Propulsion Laboratory ᵿ[3]	**280**	34.12 N	118.11 W
Jetpur	**120**	21.44 N	70.37 E
Jetřichovice	**54**	50.49 N	14.25 E
Jett	**218**	38.11 N	84.49 W
Jette	**50**	50.52 N	4.20 E
Jettingen	**58**	48.23 N	10.26 E
Jeumont	**50**	50.18 N	4.06 E
Jeune Landing	**182**	50.27 N	127.30 W
Jeunieb	**114**	5.10 N	96.29 E
Jeuram	**114**	4.14 N	96.18 E
Jever	**52**	53.34 N	7.54 E
Jeverland ✦[1]	**52**	53.35 N	8.00 E
Jevgaščino	**86**	56.26 N	74.41 E
Jevgenjevka	**85**	43.31 N	77.40 E
Jevíčko	**30**	49.38 N	16.43 E
Jevišovice	**61**	48.59 N	16.00 E
Jevišovka ≃	**61**	48.49 N	16.28 E
Jevlach	**84**	40.36 N	47.09 E
Jevlaš'ovo	**80**	53.07 N	46.51 E
Jevnaker	**26**	60.15 N	10.28 E
Jevpatorija	**78**	45.12 N	33.22 E
Jevra	**86**	59.56 N	64.27 E
Jevrejskaja Avtonomnaja Oblast' □[8]	**89**	48.30 N	132.00 E
Jevsug	**83**	49.13 N	39.18 E
Jevsug ≃	**83**	48.47 N	39.19 E
Jewel Cave National Monument ♠	**198**	43.42 N	103.50 W
Jewell, Ia., U.S.	**190**	42.18 N	93.38 W
Jewell, Ks., U.S.	**198**	39.40 N	98.09 W
Jewell, N.Y., U.S.	**210**	43.13 N	75.48 W
Jewell, Oh., U.S.	**216**	41.20 N	84.17 W
Jewell, Or., U.S.	**224**	45.56 N	123.30 W
Jewell Ridge	**192**	37.11 N	81.47 W
Jewell Village	**218**	39.10 N	85.51 W
Jewett, Il., U.S.	**194**	39.13 N	88.15 W
Jewett, Oh., U.S.	**214**	40.22 N	81.00 W
Jewett, Tx., U.S.	**222**	31.22 N	96.09 W
Jewett City	**207**	41.36 N	71.58 W
Jewett Creek ≃	**212**	44.22 N	75.45 W
Jewett Lake ⊜	**184**	56.09 N	104.40 W
Jewettville	**284a**	42.43 N	78.52 W
Jey ✦[8]	**267d**	35.41 N	51.21 E
Jeyretān	**120**	37.10 N	67.20 E
Jezerce ʌ	**38**	42.26 N	19.49 E
Jezerišče	**76**	55.50 N	29.59 E
Jezerní hora ʌ	**60**	49.10 N	13.11 E
Ježicha	**80**	58.06 N	47.40 E
Jeziorany	**30**	53.58 N	20.46 E
Ježovo	**80**	58.02 N	52.14 E
Jezreel, Valley of → Yizre'el, 'Émeq ≚	**132**	32.36 N	35.14 E
J. G. Strijdomdam ⊜[1]	**158**	27.25 S	32.05 E
Jhābua	**120**	22.46 N	74.36 E
Jhāhtipahāri	**126**	23.22 N	86.54 E
Jha Jha	**124**	24.46 N	86.22 E
Jhajjar	**124**	28.37 N	76.39 E
Jhal	**120**	28.17 N	67.27 E
Jhālakāti	**124**	22.39 N	90.12 E
Jhālārāpātan	**124**	24.33 N	76.10 E
Jhālāwār	**124**	24.36 N	76.09 E
Jhalida	**124**	23.22 N	85.58 E
Jhal Jhao	**120**	26.18 N	65.35 E
Jhālod	**120**	23.06 N	74.09 E
Jhang Sadar	**123**	31.16 N	72.19 E
Jhānsi	**124**	25.26 N	78.35 E
Jhānsi Post	**123**	33.52 N	71.24 E
Jhāpā	**124**	26.29 N	87.51 E
Jhārgrām	**126**	22.27 N	86.59 E
Jharia	**126**	23.45 N	86.24 E
Jhārpokhariā	**126**	22.10 N	86.38 E
Jhārsuguda	**120**	21.51 N	84.02 E
Jhawāriān	**123**	32.22 N	72.38 E
Jhelum	**123**	32.56 N	73.44 E
Jhelum ≃	**123**	31.12 N	72.08 E
Jhenida	**124**	23.33 N	89.10 E
Jhenkāri	**272b**	22.46 N	88.18 E
Jhikergacha	**126**	23.07 N	89.07 E
Jhikra	**126**	22.37 N	87.55 E
Jhilimili	**126**	22.49 N	86.37 E
Jhil Kuranga ✦[8]	**272a**	28.40 N	77.17 E
Jhilla ≃[1]	**126**	21.58 N	88.56 E
Jhinkpāni	**124**	22.25 N	85.47 E
Jhok Rind	**120**	31.27 N	70.26 E
Jhumra	**123**	31.34 N	73.11 E
Jhunjhunūn	**120**	28.08 N	75.24 E
Jiaban, Zhg.	**102**	25.10 N	107.03 E
Jiaban, Zhg.	**102**	25.38 N	107.07 E
Jiabong	**116**	11.46 N	124.57 E
Jiacha	**120**	29.11 N	92.44 E
Jiading	**106**	31.23 N	121.15 E
Jiāganj	**126**	24.14 N	88.16 E
Jiagedan	**89**	51.35 N	120.55 E
Jiahashitai	**89**	46.25 N	122.17 E
Jiahe	**102**	25.43 N	112.05 E
Jiajiachang, Zhg.	**107**	29.44 N	105.06 E
Jiajiachang, Zhg.	**107**	30.26 N	104.21 E
Jiajiagou, Zhg.	**104**	41.44 N	120.58 E
Jiajiagou, Zhg.	**104**	42.20 N	121.46 E
Jiajiang	**107**	29.45 N	103.34 E
Jiajiayuan	**106**	32.18 N	120.55 E
Jiakou	**100**	30.10 N	119.03 E
Jiakou Wa ≡	**105**	38.58 N	116.50 E
Jiali	**120**	30.47 N	93.24 E
Jialing ≃	**102**	29.34 N	106.35 E
Jialou	**100**	32.54 N	113.26 E
Jialu	**106**	30.26 N	118.50 E
Jialu ≃	**100**	33.38 N	114.36 E
Jiamingzhen	**107**	29.16 N	105.20 E
Jiamusi (Kiamusze)	**89**	46.50 N	130.21 E
Jiamuyingzi	**104**	41.56 N	121.43 E
Ji'an, Zhg.	**98**	41.06 N	126.08 E
Ji'an, Zhg.	**100**	27.07 N	114.58 E
Jian ≃, Zhg.	**100**	26.38 N	118.12 E
Jian ≃, Zhg.	**104**	40.59 N	121.51 E
Jian'an	**89**	43.04 N	125.03 E
Jianba	**106**	31.59 N	120.35 E
Jianbi	**106**	32.11 N	119.35 E
Jianchang, Zhg.	**98**	40.51 N	119.46 E
Jianchang, Zhg.	**98**	39.58 N	122.35 E
Jianchang, Zhg.	**98**	41.16 N	124.29 E
Ji'anchang, Zhg.	**107**	30.31 N	106.02 E
Jianchangying	**98**	40.06 N	118.49 E
Jianchapu	**105**	39.06 N	116.31 E
Jianchaxi, Zhg.	**102**	28.08 N	108.04 E
Jianchaxi, Zhg.	**107**	30.22 N	104.03 E
Jianchuan	**102**	26.34 N	99.53 E
Jiande	**100**	29.29 N	119.16 E
Jiang'an	**107**	28.44 N	105.05 E
Jiangba	**100**	33.08 N	118.45 E
Jiangbei (Lianglukou)	**107**	29.44 N	106.38 E
Jiangbeixu	**100**	26.20 N	115.26 E
Jiangbian	**102**	24.03 N	103.37 E
Jiangbianzhai	**102**	23.49 N	100.11 E
Jiangcheng, Zhg.	**102**	22.40 N	101.48 E
Jiangcheng, Zhg.	**105**	38.52 N	115.22 E
Jiangcun	**100**	28.17 N	117.49 E
Jiangdi	**102**	25.08 N	104.45 E
Jiangdihe	**102**	25.55 N	101.31 E
Jiangdu	**100**	32.26 N	119.34 E
Jiangduo	**100**	32.22 N	120.15 E
Jiange	**102**	32.06 N	105.29 E
Jianggezhuang	**98**	39.27 N	119.09 E
Jianghua (Shuikou)	**102**	24.58 N	111.38 E
Jianghuaqiao	**106**	32.05 N	120.00 E
Jiangji	**100**	32.19 N	115.44 E
Jiangjia, Zhg.	**106**	31.40 N	121.09 E
Jiangjia, Zhg.	**106**	31.58 N	121.28 E
Jiangjiadian	**104**	41.41 N	121.03 E
Jiangjiagou	**104**	41.44 N	121.44 E
Jiangjiaji	**100**	31.59 N	115.16 E
Jiangjiatun, Zhg.	**104**	41.42 N	122.02 E
Jiangjiatun, Zhg.	**104**	41.42 N	122.25 E
Jiangjin	**107**	29.17 N	106.15 E
Jiangjing	**100**	25.34 N	119.25 E
Jiangjunmiao	**86**	44.43 N	90.05 E
Jiangjunqiao	**102**	31.18 N	100.55 E
Jiangkou, Zhg.	**100**	27.27 N	118.03 E
Jiangkou, Zhg.	**100**	29.43 N	121.25 E
Jiangkou, Zhg.	**100**	27.44 N	114.49 E
Jiangkou, Zhg.	**100**	25.29 N	119.12 E
Jiangkou, Zhg.	**100**	27.21 N	115.31 E
Jiangkou, Zhg.	**102**	23.31 N	110.17 E
Jiangkou, Zhg.	**102**	27.37 N	108.48 E
Jiangkou, Zhg.	**102**	30.26 N	111.42 E
Jiangkou, Zhg.	**102**	33.39 N	107.12 E
Jiangkou, Zhg.	**102**	29.38 N	110.20 E
Jiangkou, Zhg.	**107**	30.14 N	103.55 E
Jiangkouji	**100**	32.50 N	116.16 E
Jiangkoutang	**100**	27.30 N	112.44 E
Jiangle	**100**	26.42 N	117.25 E
Jiangliadian	**98**	42.33 N	117.27 E
Jiangling	**102**	30.20 N	112.06 E
Jianglingxi	**102**	31.28 N	107.13 E
Jiangmen	**100**	22.35 N	113.05 E
Jiangmifeng	**89**	43.58 N	126.45 E
Jiangning	**106**	31.58 N	118.50 E
Jiangpu	**100**	32.04 N	118.37 E
Jiangqiao	**89**	46.48 N	123.45 E
Jiangqiaotou	**106**	30.37 N	120.38 E
Jiangshan	**100**	28.45 N	118.37 E
Jiangshan ≃	**100**	28.57 N	118.50 E
Jiangshe	**106**	31.34 N	120.08 E
Jiangshui	**98**	37.13 N	113.59 E
Jiangsu (Kiangsu) □[4]	**90**	33.00 N	120.00 E
Jiangtian	**100**	25.52 N	119.34 E
Jiangtun, Zhg.	**102**	23.41 N	112.37 E
Jiangtun, Zhg.	**104**	41.37 N	122.22 E
Jiangwakou	**105**	39.31 N	117.42 E
Jiangwan, Zhg.	**100**	29.25 N	118.02 E
Jiangwan, Zhg.	**106**	31.18 N	121.29 E
Jiangwan Airport ⊠	**269b**	31.20 N	121.30 E
Jiangxi	**102**	22.51 N	101.50 E
Jiangxi (Kiangsi) □[4]	**100**	28.00 N	116.00 E
Jiangxiacun	**106**	31.44 N	121.50 E
Jiangxiang	**100**	32.16 N	117.37 E
Jiangxikou	**100**	27.36 N	118.23 E
Jiangya	**102**	29.17 N	110.39 E
Jiangyi	**100**	29.12 N	115.46 E
Jiangyin	**106**	31.55 N	120.16 E
Jiangyou	**102**	31.47 N	104.45 E
Jiangyu, Zhg.	**98**	36.16 N	118.40 E
Jiangyu, Zhg.	**100**	27.50 N	112.46 E
Jiangyuanzhen	**107**	30.35 N	103.48 E
Jiangzaogang	**106**	32.01 N	121.03 E
Jiangzhasiji	**120**	30.28 N	88.55 E
Jiangzhong	**120**	29.10 N	93.32 E
Jianhe, Zhg.	**102**	26.27 N	108.33 E
Jianhe, Zhg.	**105**	39.14 N	118.03 E
Jianhu	**100**	33.28 N	119.50 E
Jianli	**100**	29.49 N	112.53 E
Jianling	**100**	32.45 N	113.12 E
Jianning	**100**	26.50 N	116.49 E
Jian'ou	**100**	27.03 N	118.19 E
Jianping (Yebaishou)	**98**	41.24 N	119.37 E
Jianqiao	**106**	30.20 N	120.12 E
Jianqigou	**104**	40.54 N	123.17 E
Jianshan, Zhg.	**100**	29.14 N	120.44 E
Jianshan, Zhg.	**100**	29.58 N	120.16 E
Jian Shan ʌ	**104**	41.49 N	121.44 E
Jianshi	**102**	30.36 N	109.38 E
Jianshui	**102**	23.38 N	102.49 E
Jiantiao	**100**	29.04 N	121.36 E
Jiantou	**105**	39.26 N	115.41 E
Jiantouji	**98**	34.35 N	117.34 E
Jianyang, Zhg.	**100**	27.22 N	118.04 E
Jianyang, Zhg.	**100**	33.27 N	119.40 E
Jianyang, Zhg.	**107**	30.24 N	104.32 E
Jiao ≃	**100**	26.48 N	119.42 E
Jiaocheng	**102**	37.33 N	112.02 E
Jiaodao	**105**	39.39 N	116.06 E
Jiaodianzi	**104**	41.32 N	121.49 E
Jiaodonggou	**104**	40.50 N	123.58 E
Jiaohe, Zhg.	**89**	43.42 N	127.19 E
Jiaohe, Zhg.	**98**	38.01 N	116.17 E
Jiaojiapuzi	**104**	40.47 N	123.48 E
Jiaolai ≃, Zhg.	**89**	43.43 N	123.05 E
Jiaolai ≃, Zhg.	**98**	42.47 N	120.44 E
Jiaolai ≃, Zhg.	**98**	37.07 N	119.35 E
Jiaoling	**100**	24.41 N	116.10 E
Jiaomei	**100**	24.32 N	117.54 E
Jiaonan (Wanggezhuang)	**98**	35.51 N	119.59 E
Jiao Shan I	**106**	31.21 N	120.06 E
Jiaoshanhe	**100**	29.38 N	112.33 E
Jiaoxi	**106**	31.49 N	120.10 E
Jiaoxian	**98**	36.18 N	119.58 E
Jiaoyang	**100**	27.56 N	119.16 E
Jiaozhou Wan ⊂	**98**	36.10 N	120.15 E
Jiaozhuang	**100**	33.14 N	114.02 E
Jiaozuo	**102**	35.15 N	113.13 E
Jiapu	**106**	31.06 N	119.56 E
Jiashan, Zhg.	**100**	32.47 N	118.00 E
Jiashan, Zhg.	**106**	30.51 N	120.54 E
Jiashi	**85**	39.28 N	76.45 E
Jiashun Hu ⊜	**120**	34.35 N	86.05 E
Jiasi	**107**	29.06 N	106.24 E
Jiatan	**107**	30.12 N	106.29 E
Jiatanchang	**107**	29.09 N	106.16 E
Jiawang	**98**	34.27 N	117.27 E
Jiaxian, Zhg.	**100**	33.58 N	113.13 E
Jiaxian, Zhg.	**102**	38.01 N	110.31 E
Jiaxiang	**98**	35.25 N	116.21 E
Jiaxing	**106**	30.46 N	120.45 E
Jiayin	**89**	48.53 N	130.24 E
Jiayu	**100**	29.58 N	113.55 E
Jiayun Hu ⊜	**120**	35.02 N	85.40 E
Jiaze	**106**	31.42 N	119.47 E
Jiazhai	**98**	34.33 N	115.48 E
Jiazhuang	**105**	39.19 N	117.22 E
Jiazi	**100**	22.55 N	116.04 E
Jiazier	**85**	38.40 N	76.33 E
Jibacoa ≃	**240p**	20.15 N	77.12 W
Jibagalle	**144**	8.04 N	48.39 E
Jibalei	**144**	10.09 N	50.53 E
Jibannagar	**126**	23.25 N	88.50 E
Jíbaro, Arroyo ≃	**286b**	23.03 N	82.23 W
Jibat ʌ	**144**	8.45 N	37.29 E
Jibiya	**150**	13.05 N	7.12 E
Jiboa ≃	**236**	13.22 N	89.04 W
Jibóia, Ilha da I	**256**	23.03 S	44.22 W
Jibuti → Djibouti	**144**	11.36 N	43.09 E
Jicamarca, Quebrada V	**286d**	12.02 S	76.57 W
Jicarilla Apache Indian Reservation ✦[4]	**200**	36.40 N	107.00 W
Jicarón, Isla I	**246**	7.16 N	81.47 W
Jicatuyo ≃	**236**	14.43 N	88.39 W
Jicheng	**105**	39.23 N	116.17 E
Jičín	**30**	50.26 N	15.21 E
Jicotea ≃	**286b**	23.01 N	82.14 W
Jidād	**140**	11.05 N	24.44 E
Jiddah	**144**	21.30 N	39.12 E
Jidingxilin	**120**	32.52 N	92.21 E
Jidy, Wādī al- V	**142**	30.13 N	32.46 E
Jiebu	**100**	28.15 N	115.02 E
Jiedong	**100**	26.02 N	113.00 E
Jiegou	**100**	33.21 N	117.55 E
Jiehe	**98**	35.16 N	117.04 E
Jieji	**100**	33.33 N	118.24 E
Jiejiang	**106**	31.58 N	120.43 E
Jiejinkou	**89**	47.57 N	132.50 E
Jielingkou	**98**	40.09 N	119.15 E
Jielongchang	**107**	29.13 N	106.32 E
Jiemian	**100**	25.56 N	118.02 E
Jiepai, Zhg.	**100**	26.41 N	112.46 E
Jiepai, Zhg.	**100**	29.34 N	115.06 E
Jiepai, Zhg.	**106**	30.55 N	119.32 E
Jiepai, Zhg.	**107**	29.28 N	104.43 E
Jiepaiji	**100**	32.15 N	117.50 E
Jiesheng	**100**	22.45 N	115.25 E
Jieshi, Zhg.	**100**	22.51 N	115.49 E
Jieshi, Zhg.	**107**	29.27 N	105.17 E
Jieshi Wan ⊂	**100**	22.46 N	115.40 E
Jieshou, Zhg.	**100**	33.18 N	115.20 E
Jieshou, Zhg.	**100**	27.22 N	117.40 E
Jieshou, Zhg.	**100**	33.00 N	119.27 E
Jiexi	**100**	23.28 N	115.56 E
Jiexiu	**102**	37.05 N	111.51 E
Jieyang	**100**	23.35 N	116.21 E
Jiezhongdian	**100**	32.41 N	112.29 E
Jieznas	**76**	54.36 N	24.10 E
Jifjāfah, Bi'r ⊽[4]	**140**	30.27 N	33.11 E
Jiftūn, Jazā'ir II	**140**	27.13 N	33.56 E
Jiggalong	**162**	23.25 S	120.47 E
Jiggalong Creek ≃	**162**	22.53 S	120.14 E
Jigongying	**102**	26.18 N	104.48 E
Jigongzhen	**98**	34.02 N	115.32 E
Jiguaní	**240p**	20.22 N	76.26 W
Jiguanshan, Zhg.	**98**	40.32 N	123.55 E
Jiguanshan, Zhg.	**104**	42.08 N	124.15 E
Jiguanshan, Zhg.	**104**	41.18 N	123.36 E
Jigüey, Bahía de ⊂	**240p**	22.08 N	78.05 W
Jigzhi	**102**	33.28 N	101.29 E
Jihe	**100**	32.15 N	112.48 E
Jiheier	**85**	38.11 N	75.46 E
Jihlava	**30**	49.24 N	15.36 E
Jihlava ≃	**61**	48.55 N	16.37 E
Jihočeský Kraj □[4]	**30**	49.05 N	14.30 E
Jihomoravský Kraj □[4]	**30**	49.10 N	16.40 E
Jiiqley	**144**	4.25 N	45.22 E
Jijel	**148**	36.48 N	5.46 E
Jijel □[5]	**148**	36.45 N	6.00 E
Jijia ≃	**38**	46.54 N	28.05 E
Jijiadianzi	**98**	35.31 N	118.59 E
Jijiamiao	**107**	29.18 N	104.06 E
Jijiapuzi	**104**	41.16 N	124.12 E
Jijiashi	**106**	32.08 N	120.18 E
Jijiaying	**105**	40.20 N	115.24 E
Jijiga	**144**	9.22 N	42.47 E
Jikawo	**144**	8.22 N	33.46 E
Jikawo ≃	**144**	8.22 N	33.47 E
Jike	**102**	31.00 N	99.41 E
Jilalin	**89**	51.19 N	119.55 E
Jilantai	**102**	39.47 N	105.45 E
Jilbānah, Bi'r al- ⊽[4]	**142**	30.55 N	32.29 E
Jilemutu	**89**	52.14 N	120.47 E
Jilib	**144**	0.29 N	42.46 E
Jilibulake	**120**	33.05 N	93.10 E
Jili Hu ⊜	**86**	46.57 N	87.27 E
Jilin (Kirin)	**89**	43.51 N	126.33 E
Jilin (Kirin) □[4]	**90**	44.00 N	126.00 E
Jiliu ≃	**89**	52.04 N	120.48 E
Jill, Kediet ej ʌ	**148**	22.38 N	12.33 W

Symbols in the index entries represent the broad categories identified in the key at the right. Symbols with superior numbers (⩘[1]) identify subcategories (see complete key on page *I · 1).*

Symbole im Register stellen die rechts im Schlüssel erklärten Kategorien dar. Symbole mit hochgestellten Ziffern (⩘[1]) bezeichnen Unterabteilungen einer Kategorie (vgl. vollständiger Schlüssel auf Seite *I · 1).*

Los símbolos incluídos en el texto del índice representan las grandes categorias identificadas con la clave a la derecha. Los símbolos con numeros en su parte superior (⩘[1]) identifican las subcategorías (véase la clave completa en la página *I · 1).*

Les symboles de l'index représentent les catégories indiquées dans la légende à droite. Les symboles suivis d'un indice (⩘[1]) représentent des sous-catégories (voir légende complète à la page *I · 1).*

Os símbolos incluídos no texto do índice representam as grandes categorias identificadas com a chave à direita. Os símbolos com números em sua parte superior (⩘[1]) identificam as subcategorias (veja-se a chave completa à página *I · 1).*

	English	Deutsch	Español	Français	Português
ʌ	Mountain	Berg	Montaña	Montagne	Montanha
⩘	Mountains	Gebirge	Montañas	Montagnes	Montanhas
)(	Pass	Paß	Paso	Col	Passo
V	Valley, Canyon	Tal, Cañon	Valle, Cañón	Vallée, Canyon	Vale, Canhão
≚	Plain	Ebene	Llano	Plaine	Planície
›	Cape	Kap	Cabo	Cap	Cabo
I	Island	Insel	Isla	Île	Ilha
II	Islands	Inseln	Islas	Îles	Ilhas
⊥	Other Topographic Features	Andere Topographische Objekte	Otros Elementos Topográficos	Autres données topographiques	Outros acidentes topográficos

ESPAÑOL — Nombre | Página | Lat.°′ | Long.°′ W = Oeste
FRANÇAIS — Nom | Page | Lat.°′ | Long.°′ W = Ouest
PORTUGUÊS — Nome | Página | Lat.°′ | Long.°′ W = Oeste

Nombre	Página	Lat.°′	Long.°′ W = Oeste
Jill, Sebkhet ej ⊜	148	22.47 N	12.53 W
Jilliby Creek ≃	170	33.16 S	151.24 E
Jiloca ≃	34	41.21 N	1.39 W
Jilotepec de Abasolo	234	19.58 N	99.32 W
Jilotlán de los Dolores	234	19.14 N	102.59 W
Jílové	54	50.46 N	14.07 E
Jima	144	7.36 N	36.50 E
Jimbaran	115b	8.46 S	115.11 E
Jimbolia	38	45.47 N	20.43 E
Jimboomba	171a	27.50 S	153.02 E
Jimei	100	24.37 N	118.07 E
Jimena de la Frontera	34	36.26 N	5.27 W
Jiménez, Méx.	232	29.02 N	100.41 W
Jimenez, Pil.	116	8.20 N	123.50 E
Jiménez, Arroyo ≃	288	34.44 S	58.13 W
Jiménez, Laguna de ⊜	258	35.26 S	59.01 W
Jiménez del Teúl	234	23.10 N	104.05 W
Jimeta	146	9.16 N	12.27 E
Jimi ≃	164	5.20 S	144.20 E
Jimingcun	105	39.19 N	116.09 E
Jiminghe	100	30.36 N	115.32 E
Jim Ned Creek ≃	196	31.50 N	99.07 W
Jimo	98	36.23 N	120.27 E
Jimsar	86	44.00 N	89.04 E
Jim Thorpe	210	40.52 N	75.43 W
Jimuganayaji	85	38.36 N	75.39 E
Jin (Gam) ≃, Asia	110	21.55 N	105.12 E
Jin ≃, Zhg.	100	24.54 N	118.35 E
Jin ≃, Zhg.	100	28.24 N	115.49 E
Jin ≃, Zhg.	100	26.51 N	117.46 E
Jināḥ	140	25.20 N	30.31 E
Jinan (Tsinan), Zhg.	98	36.40 N	116.57 E
Jin'an, Zhg.	100	28.38 N	119.18 E
Jinbang	100	25.01 N	118.01 E
Jinbo ≃	107	28.54 N	103.40 E
Jincang	89	43.20 N	130.30 E
Jince	60	49.47 N	13.59 E
Jinchanggouliang	98	41.56 N	120.19 E
Jincheng, Zhg.	102	35.30 N	112.50 E
Jincheng, Zhg.	104	41.12 N	121.25 E
Jinchengshai	102	26.43 N	111.00 E
Jincheng Shan ʌ	107	30.47 N	106.32 E
Jinchuan	102	31.25 N	102.08 E
Jinchuanqiao	102	27.18 N	101.48 E
Jincun	106	31.08 N	119.49 E
Jīnd	123	29.19 N	76.19 E
Jindabyne	171b	36.25 S	148.38 E
Jindabyne, Lake ⊜[1]	171b	36.22 S	148.37 E
Jindaichang	107	29.43 N	104.49 E
Jindālī, Bi'r ╤[4]	142	29.55 N	31.40 E
Jindřichovice	54	50.15 N	12.37 E
Jindřichův Hradec	30	49.09 N	15.00 E
Jinfeng	100	26.01 N	119.36 E
Jinfosi	102	39.29 N	99.00 E
Jing ≃, Zhg.	86	44.52 N	82.50 E
Jing ≃, Zhg.	102	34.28 N	109.00 E
Jing'an	100	28.52 N	115.20 E
Jin'gangpo	107	29.38 N	106.25 E
Jingangtou	100	27.54 N	113.40 E
Jingangtuo	107	29.10 N	106.07 E
Jing'anji	98	34.30 N	116.55 E
Jingbian	102	37.25 N	108.21 E
Jingbohu ⊜	89	43.54 N	128.54 E
Jingcheng	100	24.36 N	117.30 E
Jingde	100	30.19 N	118.31 E
Jingdezhen (Kingtechen)	100	29.16 N	117.11 E
Jingdong	102	24.28 N	100.52 E
Jingellic	171b	35.56 S	147.42 E
Jingeryu	105	39.43 N	115.36 E
Jinggang	100	28.28 N	112.46 E
Jinggangshan	100	26.36 N	114.05 E
Jinggongqiao	100	29.45 N	117.11 E
Jinggu	102	23.32 N	100.41 E
Jingguanzhen	107	29.55 N	106.33 E
Jinghai, Zhg.	100	23.03 N	116.31 E
Jinghai, Zhg.	105	38.56 N	116.55 E
Jinghaiwei	98	36.52 N	122.13 E
Jinghe	86	44.39 N	82.50 E
Jinghong	102	22.01 N	100.49 E
Jinghuiling	105	40.22 N	117.27 E
Jingjiang, Zhg.	102	26.19 N	100.33 E
Jingjiang, Zhg.	106	32.01 N	120.15 E
Jingjiayu	104	41.40 N	123.51 E
Jingle	102	38.24 N	111.54 E
Jinglou	100	32.39 N	112.56 E
Jingmen	102	31.00 N	112.09 E
Jingning, Zhg.	100	27.59 N	119.38 E
Jingning, Zhg.	102	35.25 N	105.56 E
Jingou	104	41.38 N	120.35 E
Jingoutun	98	41.03 N	117.27 E
Jingshan	100	31.02 N	113.05 E
Jingtai	102	37.17 N	104.09 E
Jingu	100	25.13 N	118.07 E
Jingxi	102	23.08 N	106.29 E
Jingxian, Zhg.	98	37.42 N	116.16 E
Jingxian, Zhg.	100	30.42 N	118.24 E
Jingxian, Zhg.	102	26.40 N	109.25 E
Jingxin	100	24.14 N	115.56 E
Jingxing, Zhg.	89	47.04 N	123.01 E
Jingxing, Zhg.	98	38.02 N	114.08 E
Jingyan	107	29.40 N	104.04 E
Jingyu	98	42.22 N	126.50 E
Jingyuan, Zhg.	102	36.38 N	104.37 E
Jingyuan, Zhg.	102	35.30 N	106.48 E
Jingzhi	98	36.19 N	119.23 E
Jingzichang	107	29.00 N	104.41 E
Jinhae → Chinhae	98	35.09 N	128.40 E
Jinhu	100	33.00 N	119.02 E
Jinhua	100	29.07 N	119.39 E
Jinhua ≃	100	29.06 N	119.39 E
Jinhui	106	30.59 N	121.29 E
Jining, Zhg.	98	35.25 N	116.36 E
Jining, Zhg.	102	40.57 N	113.02 E
Jinja	154	0.26 N	33.12 E
Jinjiadian	98	41.39 N	118.18 E
Jinjiang, Zhg.	100	24.50 N	118.35 E
Jinjiang, Zhg.	110	26.19 N	100.33 E
Jinjiawopeng	104	41.38 N	122.16 E
Jinjiawopu	104	42.32 N	122.10 E
Jinjiazhen	89	42.49 N	123.40 E
Jinjing, Zhg.	100	24.37 N	118.36 E
Jinjing, Zhg.	100	28.31 N	113.25 E
Jinjini	150	7.26 N	2.39 W
Jinju → Chinju	98	35.11 N	128.05 E
Jinkeng	100	27.15 N	117.14 E
Jinkichi-mori ʌ	96	33.41 N	134.07 E
Jinkou, Zhg.	98	36.35 N	120.46 E
Jinkou, Zhg.	100	29.18 N	115.15 E
Jinkou, Zhg.	100	30.22 N	114.10 E
Jinkuang	102	28.20 N	101.54 E
Jinlijing	107	29.48 N	104.45 E
Jinlingsi	104	41.42 N	120.49 E
Jinlingyu	105	40.06 N	117.32 E
Jinlingzhen	98	36.49 N	118.11 E
Jinlonggou	89	51.45 N	125.51 E
Jinmachi-chūtonchi, Rikujō-jieitai- ■	92	38.25 N	140.27 E
Jinmu Jiao ›	110	18.09 N	109.34 E
Jinnah Barrage ◆[6]	123	32.57 N	71.30 E
Jinning	102	24.41 N	102.35 E
Jinniu, Zhg.	100	29.59 N	114.38 E
Jinniu, Zhg.	100	31.24 N	117.12 E
Jinotega	236	13.06 N	86.00 W
Jinotega □[5]	236	14.00 N	85.25 W
Jinotepe	236	11.51 N	86.12 W
Jinping, Zhg.	102	26.38 N	109.03 E
Jinping, Zhg.	102	22.50 N	103.10 E
Jinpingchang	107	28.54 N	104.43 E
Jinpo	105	39.18 N	115.15 E
Jinqian ≃	102	32.52 N	110.01 E
Jinqiao	100	31.46 N	116.50 E
Jinrui	100	27.57 N	114.12 E
Jinseki	96	34.48 N	133.11 E
Jinsen → Inch'ŏn	98	37.28 N	126.38 E
Jinsha, Zhg.	100	26.12 N	118.39 E
Jinsha, Zhg.	102	27.18 N	106.10 E
Jinsha, Zhg.	106	32.06 N	121.05 E
Jinsha (Yangtze) ≃	102	28.50 N	104.36 E
Jinshan, Zhg.	89	51.51 N	126.30 E
Jinshan, Zhg.	106	30.54 N	121.09 E
Jinshanwei	106	30.44 N	121.19 E
Jinshanxiang	107	30.35 N	104.52 E
Jinshanzui	106	30.44 N	121.22 E
Jinshi	102	29.39 N	111.52 E
Jinshijing	107	29.23 N	104.08 E
Jinshuzhen	106	31.23 N	120.24 E
Jinsiniangqiao	106	30.43 N	121.15 E
Jinta	102	40.03 N	98.53 E
Jintan	106	31.45 N	119.34 E
Jintang, Zhg.	102	30.54 N	104.19 E
Jintang, Zhg.	102	30.19 N	102.19 E
Jintian	100	27.10 N	114.27 E
Jintotolo Channel ʉ	116	11.48 N	123.05 E
Jintotolo Island I	116	11.51 N	123.08 E
Jinxi, Zhg.	100	27.54 N	116.43 E
Jinxi, Zhg.	104	40.45 N	120.50 E
Jinxian, Zhg.	98	38.02 N	115.02 E
Jinxian, Zhg.	98	39.04 N	121.40 E
Jinxian, Zhg.	100	28.22 N	116.14 E
Jinxian (Dalinghe), Zhg.	104	41.11 N	121.22 E
Jinxiang, Zhg.	98	35.05 N	116.18 E
Jinxiang, Zhg.	100	27.26 N	120.35 E
Jin-ya ⊥	94	36.06 N	137.15 E
Jinyun	100	28.40 N	120.03 E
Jinz, Qā' al- ≃	132	30.45 N	36.04 E
Jinze	106	31.02 N	120.56 E
Jinzhai	100	31.44 N	115.54 E
Jinzhaizhen	100	31.32 N	115.46 E
Jinzhen	100	33.39 N	118.17 E
Jinzhong ≃	105	39.08 N	117.42 E
Jinzhou (Chinchou)	104	41.07 N	121.08 E
Jinzisi	107	29.09 N	106.22 E
Jinzū ≃	94	36.46 N	137.13 E
Jiō	270	34.58 N	135.28 E
Jiparaná ≃	248	8.03 S	62.52 W
Jipijapa	246	1.20 S	80.35 W
Jipioca, Ilha I	250	1.53 N	50.12 W
Jiquilisco	236	13.19 N	88.35 W
Jiquilisco, Bahía de ᑕ	236	13.10 N	88.28 W
Jiquilpan de Juárez	234	19.59 N	102.43 W
Jiquipilas	234	16.40 N	93.39 W
Jiquipilco	234	19.32 N	99.36 W
Jiquiriçá	255	13.14 S	39.36 W
Jiquiriçá ≃	255	13.12 S	38.57 W
Jirāfī, Wādī al- (Naḥal Paran) V	132	30.24 N	35.10 E
Jirbān	140	11.03 N	30.36 E
Jiřetín	54	50.50 N	14.35 E
Jiri ≃	120	24.42 N	93.06 E
Jiřikov	54	50.59 N	13.35 E
Jirjā	140	26.20 N	31.53 E
Jirkov	54	50.30 N	13.27 E
Jīroft	128	28.40 N	57.46 E
Jīsh (Gush Ḥalav)	132	33.02 N	35.27 E
Jishou	102	28.17 N	109.29 E
Jishui, Zhg.	100	27.14 N	115.06 E
Jishui, Zhg.	100	33.46 N	115.24 E
Jisr ash-Shughūr	130	35.48 N	36.19 E
Jitan	100	24.56 N	115.43 E
Jitarning	162	32.48 S	117.59 E
Jitaúna	255	14.01 S	39.57 W
Jitianzhen	107	30.19 N	104.01 E
Jitotol	234	17.02 N	92.52 W
Jitra	114	6.16 N	100.25 E
Jituo	120	34.15 N	82.05 E
Jiu ≃	38	43.47 N	23.48 E
Jiubao	100	25.57 N	115.48 E
Jiubingtai	104	41.39 N	124.07 E
Jiucheng, Zhg.	98	38.12 N	117.18 E
Jiucheng, Zhg.	105	39.23 N	116.44 E
Jiuchuchang	107	29.55 N	104.38 E
Jiudaoliang	102	31.35 N	110.12 E
Jiudhara	126	22.24 N	89.44 E
Jiudian	106	32.10 N	120.57 E
Jiudongle	102	38.49 N	101.05 E
Jiudu	106	30.31 N	119.53 E
Jiufanxian	98	35.51 N	115.41 E
Jiufeng, Zhg.	100	24.20 N	117.02 E
Jiufeng, Zhg.	100	25.33 N	119.08 E
Jiugang	105	39.03 N	116.12 E
Jiugongan	102	29.52 N	112.00 E
Jiugongkou	105	39.50 N	114.43 E
Jiugong Shan ʌ	100	29.26 N	114.42 E
Jiuguan, Zhg.	98	37.26 N	121.53 E
Jiuguan, Zhg.	106	30.51 N	120.16 E
Jiuguantao	98	36.40 N	115.25 E
Jiuhe	100	23.32 N	115.04 E
Jiuhongshui	102	37.14 N	103.57 E
Jiuhu	98	37.03 N	117.36 E
Jiuhuai'an	98	40.24 N	114.31 E
Jiuhuajie	100	30.25 N	117.51 E
Jiuhuaxian	100	23.30 N	113.16 E
Jiuhuinan	98	42.37 N	126.14 E
Jiujiang, Zhg.	100	22.51 N	113.02 E
Jiujiang, Zhg.	100	29.36 N	115.52 E
Jiujiang, Zhg.	100	29.44 N	115.59 E
Jiujiawopeng	104	40.59 N	121.22 E
Jiujiji	98	35.09 N	114.48 E
Jiujing	107	29.05 N	103.54 E
Jiukou	100	30.52 N	112.38 E
Jiuli	107	29.32 N	103.32 E
Jiulian Shan ⩘	100	24.40 N	114.46 E
Jiuliguan	100	31.50 N	114.14 E
Jiuling Shan ⩘	100	28.46 N	114.45 E
Jiulong → Kowloon, H.K.	271d	22.18 N	114.10 E
Jiulong, Zhg.	100	24.08 N	112.55 E
Jiulong, Zhg.	102	29.00 N	101.50 E
Jiulong ≃, Zhg.	100	24.28 N	117.48 E
Jiulong ≃, Zhg.	100	25.59 N	117.18 E
Jiulongchang	107	29.32 N	106.05 E
Jiulonggang	100	32.38 N	117.03 E
Jiulongpo	107	29.29 N	106.32 E
Jiulongzhen	106	31.54 N	121.34 E
Jiumen	98	40.42 N	120.27 E
Jiumianyang	100	30.16 N	113.13 E
Jiumiao	104	42.24 N	121.36 E
Jiumu	100	28.11 N	118.27 E
Jiuninghe	105	39.28 N	117.46 E
Jiuningyang	100	25.38 N	117.21 E
Jiupu, Zhg.	100	32.50 N	118.45 E
Jiupu, Zhg.	105	40.21 N	115.18 E
Jiuquan (Suzhou)	102	39.45 N	98.34 E
Jiurongcheng	98	37.21 N	122.32 E
Jiushangshui	100	33.32 N	114.32 E
Jiushan Liedao II	100	29.26 N	122.12 E
Jiushenqiu	100	33.11 N	115.08 E
Jiusiyang	100	33.41 N	118.39 E
Jiusongyu	105	40.27 N	116.58 E
Jiutai	89	44.08 N	125.50 E
Jiuwuqing	105	39.31 N	116.52 E
Jiuxian, Zhg.	98	37.53 N	117.06 E
Jiuxian, Zhg.	100	31.11 N	118.04 E
Jiuxian, Zhg.	100	25.54 N	113.22 E
Jiuxian, Zhg.	100	33.15 N	115.35 E
Jiuxian, Zhg.	100	25.14 N	116.31 E
Jiuxian, Zhg.	100	33.32 N	113.17 E
Jiuxian, Zhg.	107	30.27 N	103.51 E
Jiuxian, Zhg.	107	29.51 N	106.13 E
Jiuxian ≃	100	25.07 N	116.24 E
Jiuxiangcheng	100	33.13 N	114.49 E
Jiuyingkou	105	39.42 N	114.44 E
Jiuyingzi	104	42.03 N	121.38 E
Jiuyuanqu	102	35.09 N	111.51 E
Jiuyuhang	106	30.17 N	119.56 E
Jiuyunjie	86	44.12 N	88.05 E
Jiuzhan	89	43.57 N	126.29 E
Jiuzhen	100	24.05 N	117.42 E
Jiuzhou	105	39.30 N	116.33 E
Jiuzhuangwo	105	40.11 N	115.36 E
Jiwangmiao	269b	31.14 N	121.17 E
Jiwangtun	104	41.02 N	122.58 E
Jīwani	128	25.03 N	61.45 E
Jiwen	89	50.32 N	123.15 E
Jixi, Zhg.	89	45.17 N	130.59 E
Jixi, Zhg.	100	30.06 N	118.35 E
Jixian, Zhg.	98	35.26 N	114.05 E
Jixian, Zhg.	98	37.36 N	115.31 E
Jixian, Zhg.	105	40.03 N	117.24 E
Jixiangsi	107	30.39 N	105.32 E
Jixiashi	100	28.22 N	118.44 E
Jixingji	100	32.55 N	116.46 E
Jiyang, Zhg.	98	36.59 N	117.11 E
Jiyang, Zhg.	100	27.10 N	118.07 E
Jiyang, Zhg.	105	39.38 N	115.59 E
Jiyi	102	35.50 N	110.23 E
Jiyuan	102	35.08 N	112.35 E
Jiyun ≃	105	39.07 N	117.43 E
Jiz', Wādī al- V	144	16.19 N	52.00 E
Jīzah, Ahrāmāt al- (Pyramids of Giza) ⊥	142	29.59 N	31.08 E
Jīzah, Tur'at al- ≊	273c	29.50 N	31.16 E
Jīzān	144	16.54 N	42.29 E
Jizayy	142	30.28 N	30.51 E
Jize	98	36.54 N	114.52 E
Jizera ≃	54	50.10 N	14.43 E
Jizl, Wādī al- V	128	25.38 N	38.21 E
Jizō-dake ʌ	94	36.36 N	139.28 E
Jizō-zaki ›	96	35.34 N	133.20 E
Joaçaba	252	27.10 S	51.30 W
Joachimsthal → Jáchymov, Česko.	54	50.20 N	12.55 E
Joachimsthal, D.D.R.	54	52.58 N	13.44 E
Joaíma	255	16.39 S	41.02 W
Joal Fadiout	150	14.10 N	16.51 W
Joana Coeli	250	1.58 S	49.23 W
Joana Peres	250	3.18 S	49.42 W
Joanes	250	0.51 S	48.31 W
Joanésia	255	19.12 S	42.40 W
Joanicó	258	34.36 S	56.15 W
Joanna	192	34.24 N	81.48 W
Joanópolis	256	22.56 S	46.17 W
João, Lago ⊜	250	3.16 S	42.15 W
João Alfredo	250	7.52 S	35.35 W
João Câmara	250	5.32 S	35.48 W
João de Tiba ≃	255	16.16 S	39.01 W
João Mendes ≃	287a	22.57 S	43.03 W
João Neiva	255	19.45 S	40.24 W
João Pessoa	250	7.07 S	34.52 W
João Pinheiro	255	17.45 S	46.10 W
Joaquim Távora	255	23.30 S	49.58 W
Joaquin	194	31.58 N	94.03 W
Joaquín Gorina ◆[8]	258	34.54 S	58.02 W
Joaquin Miller Park ♦	282	37.49 N	122.11 W
Joaquín Suárez	258	34.44 S	56.02 W
Joaquín V. González	252	25.05 S	64.11 W
Job	62	45.37 N	3.45 E
Jobabo	240p	20.54 N	77.17 W
Jobat	120	22.25 N	74.34 E
Jobo Point ›	116	8.42 N	126.15 E
Jobos	240m	17.58 N	66.10 W
Jobos, Bahía de ᑕ	240m	17.56 N	66.13 W
Job Peak ʌ	204	39.35 N	118.14 W
Jobstown	285	40.02 N	74.41 W
Jochberg	64	47.23 N	12.24 E
Jock ≃	212	45.16 N	75.43 W
Jocketa	54	50.33 N	12.10 E
Jockgrim	56	49.06 N	8.17 E
Jocko ≃	202	47.20 N	114.17 W
Jocolí	252	32.35 S	68.41 W
Jo Co Marsh ⸬	276	40.37 N	73.47 W
Jocón	236	15.17 N	86.58 W
Jocoro	236	13.37 N	88.01 W
Jocotán	236	14.49 N	89.23 W
Jocotepec	234	20.18 N	103.26 W
Jocotitlán	234	19.42 N	99.48 W
Jocuixtita	232	24.15 N	106.16 W
Jódar	34	37.50 N	3.21 W
Jodhpur	120	26.17 N	73.02 E
Jodiya	120	22.42 N	70.18 E
Jodoigne	56	50.43 N	4.52 E
Jodrell Bank Radio Telescope ʋ[3]	262	53.14 N	2.18 W
Joe ≃	220	25.17 N	81.05 W
Joe Batt's Arm	186	49.44 N	54.10 W
Joel	158	28.42 S	28.21 E
Joensuu	26	62.36 N	29.46 E
Joetsu	94	37.06 N	138.15 E
Jœuf	56	49.14 N	6.01 E
Jofane	156	21.17 S	34.16 E
Joffre, Mount ʌ	182	50.32 N	115.13 W
Jōganzi ≃	94	36.46 N	137.18 E
Jōga-shima I	94	35.08 N	139.37 E
Jōgawara	268	35.42 N	139.22 E
Jōge	96	34.42 N	133.07 E
Jogeshvari ◆[8]	272c	19.08 N	72.51 E
Jogeshvari Cave ⊥[5]	272c	19.08 N	72.51 E
Jõgeva	76	58.45 N	26.24 E
Jog Falls ∟	122	14.13 N	74.45 E
Joggins	186	45.42 N	64.27 W
Joghatāy	128	36.36 N	57.01 E
Jogindarnagar	123	31.59 N	76.46 E
Jogjakarta → Yogyakarta	115a	7.48 S	110.22 E
Jōhana	94	36.31 N	136.54 E
Johannesburg, S. Afr.	158	26.12 S	28.05 E
Johannesburg, S. Afr.	273d	26.12 S	28.05 E
Johannesburg, Ca., U.S.	228	35.22 N	117.38 W
Johannesburg □[5]	273d	26.13 S	28.02 E
Johannesburg (Jan Smuts) Airport ⊠	273d	26.08 S	28.14 E
Johanngeorgenstadt	54	50.26 N	12.43 E
Johannisburg → Pisz	30	53.38 N	21.49 E
Johanniskreuz	56	49.20 N	7.49 E
Johannisthal ◆[8]	264a	52.26 N	13.30 E
Jōhen	92	32.57 N	132.35 E
Johi	120	26.41 N	67.37 E
Johilla ≃	124	23.37 N	81.14 E
John ≃	180	66.55 N	151.35 W
John Boyd Thacher State Park ♦	210	42.38 N	74.01 W
John Carroll University ʋ[2]	279a	41.29 N	81.32 W
John Day	202	44.24 N	118.57 W
John Day ≃	202	45.44 N	120.39 W
John Day, Middle Fork ≃	202	44.55 N	119.18 W
John Day, North Fork ≃	202	44.45 N	119.38 W
John Day, South Fork ≃	202	44.28 N	119.31 W
John Day Dam ◆[6]	224	45.43 N	120.41 W
John Day Fossil Beds National Monument ♦	202	44.34 N	119.39 W
John Fitzgerald Kennedy Stadium ♦	285	39.54 N	75.10 W
John F. Kennedy International Airport ⊠	210	40.38 N	73.47 W
John F. Kennedy National Historical Site ⊥	283	42.21 N	71.08 W
John F. Kennedy Space Center ʋ[3]	220	28.40 N	80.40 W
John Forrest National Park ♦	168a	31.53 S	116.06 E
John Hancock Center ʋ	278	41.55 N	87.37 W
John H. Kerr Reservoir ⊜[1]	192	36.35 N	78.35 W
John J. Duffy Preserve ♦	278	41.39 N	87.55 W
John Martin Reservoir ⊜[1]	198	38.05 N	103.02 W
John McLaren Park ♦	282	37.43 N	122.25 W
John Muir National Historical Site ⊥	282	37.59 N	122.08 W
Johnny Run ≃	216	41.17 N	88.21 W
John o'Groats	46	58.38 N	3.05 W
John Pennekamp Coral Reef State Park ♦	220	25.11 N	80.15 W
John Redmond Reservoir ⊜[1]	198	38.18 N	95.55 W
Johns ≃	224	46.54 N	124.01 W
Johns Creek ≃	192	37.30 N	80.06 W
Johnshaven	46	56.47 N	2.20 W
Johns Hopkins University ʋ[2]	284b	39.20 N	76.37 W
Johns Island I	192	32.40 N	80.05 W
Johnson, Ar., U.S.	194	36.07 N	94.09 W
Johnson, Ks., U.S.	198	37.34 N	101.45 W
Johnson, Ne., U.S.	198	40.24 N	95.59 W
Johnson, N.Y., U.S.	210	41.22 N	74.30 W
Johnson, Vt., U.S.	188	44.38 N	72.40 W
Johnson □[6], In., U.S.	218	39.29 N	86.03 W
Johnson □[6], Tx., U.S.	222	32.20 N	97.20 W
Johnson, Mount ʌ	226	36.37 N	121.19 W
Johnson Bay ᑕ	208	38.03 N	75.20 W
Johnsonburg, N.J., U.S.	210	40.58 N	74.53 W
Johnsonburg, N.Y., U.S.	210	42.44 N	78.18 W
Johnsonburg, Pa., U.S.	214	41.29 N	78.40 W
Johnson City, N.Y., U.S.	210	42.06 N	75.57 W
Johnson City, Tn., U.S.	192	36.18 N	82.21 W
Johnson City, Tx., U.S.	196	30.16 N	98.24 W
Johnson Creek, N.Y., U.S.	210	43.15 N	78.31 W
Johnson Creek, Wi., U.S.	216	43.04 N	88.46 W
Johnson Creek ≃, Id., U.S.	202	44.58 N	115.30 W
Johnson Creek ≃, Ky., U.S.	218	38.27 N	84.04 W
Johnson Creek ≃, N.Y., U.S.	210	43.22 N	78.16 W
Johnson Creek ≃, Tx., U.S.	222	32.02 N	94.59 W
Johnson Creek ≃, Wa., U.S.	224	46.35 N	121.42 W
Johnsondale	204	35.58 N	118.32 W
Johnson Drain ≊	281	42.26 N	83.28 W
Johnson Draw V, Tx., U.S.	196	31.58 N	101.41 W
Johnson Draw V, Tx., U.S.	196	30.08 N	101.07 W
Johnson Hall State Historic Site ⊥	210	43.01 N	74.23 W
Johnson Park ♦	276	40.30 N	74.27 W
Johnson Point ›	241h	13.07 N	61.12 W
Johnsons Crossing	180	60.29 N	133.16 W
Johnsons Point ›	240c	17.02 N	61.53 W
Johnsons Pond ⊜	283	42.44 N	71.03 W
Johnsons Station	222	32.42 N	97.08 W
Johnsonville, N.Z.	172	41.14 S	174.47 E
Johnsonville, N.Y., U.S.	210	42.55 N	73.31 W
Johnsonville, S.C., U.S.	192	33.49 N	79.26 W
Johnston, Wales, U.K.	42	51.46 N	5.00 W
Johnston, Ia., U.S.	190	41.40 N	93.41 W
Johnston, R.I., U.S.	207	41.46 N	71.21 W
Johnston, S.C., U.S.	192	33.49 N	81.48 W
Johnston, Lake ⊜	162	32.25 S	120.30 E
Johnston Atoll I[1]	14	16.45 N	169.32 W
Johnston City	194	37.49 N	88.55 W
Johnstone	46	55.50 N	4.31 W
Johnstone Peak ʌ	280	34.10 N	117.48 W
Johnstone Strait ʉ	182	50.25 N	126.00 W
Johnston Falls ∟	154	10.35 S	28.40 E
Johnstown, Co., U.S.	200	40.20 N	104.54 W
Johnstown, N.Y., U.S.	210	43.00 N	74.22 W
Johnstown, Oh., U.S.	214	40.09 N	82.41 W
Johnstown, Pa., U.S.	214	40.19 N	78.55 W
Johnstown Center	216	42.42 N	88.50 W
Johnstown Flood National Memorial ⊥	214	40.21 N	78.47 W
John Tyler Arboretum ♦	285	39.56 N	75.26 W
Jōhoku	94	36.28 N	140.22 E
Johol	114	2.36 N	102.16 E
Johor □[3]	114	2.00 N	103.30 E
Johor ≃	114	1.27 N	104.02 E
Johor, Selat ʉ	271c	1.28 N	103.48 E
Johor Baharu	114	1.28 N	103.45 E
Jöhstadt	54	50.30 N	13.05 E
Joice Island I	282	38.08 N	122.02 W
Joigny	50	47.59 N	3.24 E
Joiner	194	35.30 N	90.08 W
Joinerville	222	32.11 N	94.55 W
Joinvile	252	26.18 S	48.50 W
Joinville	58	48.27 N	5.08 E
Joinville, Lac ⊜	206	46.18 N	75.12 W
Joinville Island I	9	63.15 S	55.45 W
Joinville-le-Pont	261	48.49 N	2.28 E
Jōjima	96	33.15 N	130.26 E
Jojogan	115a	6.58 S	111.46 E
Jojutla	234	18.37 N	99.11 W
Joka	272b	22.27 N	88.18 E
Jokau	140	8.24 N	33.49 E
Jokioinen	26	60.49 N	23.28 E
Jokkmokk	24	66.37 N	19.50 E
Jökulsá á Brú ≃	24a	65.41 N	14.13 W
Jökulsárgljúfur National Park ♦	24a	66.00 N	16.20 W
Jolārpettai	122	12.34 N	78.35 E
Jolfā	84	38.57 N	45.38 E
Joliet, Il., U.S.	216	41.31 N	88.04 W
Joliet, Mt., U.S.	202	45.29 N	108.58 W
Joliet Correctional Center ʋ	278	41.33 N	88.04 W
Joliett	208	40.37 N	76.27 W
Joliette	206	46.01 N	73.27 W
Joliette □[6]	206	46.25 N	74.00 W
Jolietville	218	40.03 N	86.15 W
Jöllenbeck	52	52.11 N	8.45 E
Jollyville	222	30.27 N	97.47 W
Jolo	116	6.03 N	121.00 E
Jolo Group II	116	6.00 N	121.09 E
Jolo Island I	116	5.58 N	121.06 E
Jølstravatnet ⊜	26	61.32 N	6.13 E
Jomalig Island I	116	14.42 N	122.22 E
Jomba	102	31.27 N	98.15 E
Jombang	115a	7.33 S	112.14 E
Jombo ≃	152	10.36 S	17.32 E
Jona	58	47.14 N	8.52 E
Jonacatepec	234	18.41 N	98.48 W
Jonah	222	30.38 N	97.32 W
Jönåker	40	58.44 N	16.40 E
Jonathan Dickinson State Park ♦	220	27.01 N	80.08 W
Jonava	76	55.05 N	24.17 E
Jones, Pil.	116	16.33 N	121.42 E
Jones, Mi., U.S.	216	41.54 N	85.48 W
Jones, Ok., U.S.	196	35.33 N	97.17 W
Jones ≃	283	42.00 N	70.42 W
Jones and Laughlin Steel Corporation ʋ[3], Pa., U.S.	279b	40.26 N	79.58 W
Jones and Laughlin Steel Corporation ʋ[3], Pa., U.S.	279b	40.37 N	80.14 W
Jones Beach State Park ♦	210	40.35 N	73.31 W
Jonesboro, Ar., U.S.	194	35.50 N	90.42 W
Jonesboro, Ga., U.S.	192	33.31 N	84.21 W
Jonesboro, Il., U.S.	194	37.27 N	89.16 W
Jonesboro, In., U.S.	216	40.28 N	85.37 W
Jonesboro, La., U.S.	194	32.14 N	92.42 W
Jonesboro, Tn., U.S.	192	36.17 N	82.28 W
Jonesburg	219	38.51 N	91.18 W
Jones Creek	222	28.58 N	95.27 W
Jones Creek ≃, On., Can.	212	44.30 N	75.49 W
Jones Creek ≃, Tx., U.S.	222	29.08 N	96.03 W
Jones Falls ≃	284b	39.18 N	76.37 W
Jones Falls, North Branch ≃	284b	39.25 N	76.42 W
Jones Inlet ᑕ	210	40.35 N	73.34 W
Jones Mill	194	34.27 N	92.50 W
Jones Mountains ⩘	9	73.32 S	94.00 W
Jonesport	188	44.31 N	67.35 W
Jones Sound ʉ	176	76.00 N	85.00 W
Jonestown	194	34.19 N	90.27 W
Jonesville, In., U.S.	218	39.04 N	85.53 W
Jonesville, La., U.S.	194	31.37 N	91.49 W
Jonesville, Mi., U.S.	216	41.59 N	84.40 W
Jonesville, N.Y., U.S.	210	42.55 N	73.49 W
Jonesville, N.C., U.S.	192	36.14 N	80.50 W
Jonesville, S.C., U.S.	192	34.50 N	81.40 W
Jonesville, Va., U.S.	192	36.41 N	83.06 W
Jong ≃	150	7.32 N	12.23 W
Jongunjärvi ⊜	26	65.17 N	27.15 E
Jónico, Mar → Ionian Sea ╤[2]	22	39.00 N	19.00 E
Joniškėlis	76	56.02 N	24.10 E
Joniškis	76	56.14 N	23.37 E
Jonkersberg	158	33.55 S	22.15 E
Jönköping	26	57.47 N	14.11 E
Jönköpings Län □[6]	26	57.30 N	14.30 E
Jonquière	186	48.24 N	71.15 W
Jonquières	62	44.07 N	4.54 E
Jonsdorf	54	50.51 N	14.43 E
Jonstorp	41	56.14 N	12.40 E
Jonuta	232	18.05 N	92.08 W
Jonvilliers	261	48.34 N	1.42 E
Jonzac	32	45.27 N	0.26 W
Joondalup, Lake ⊜	168a	31.45 S	115.47 E
Joplin, Mo., U.S.	194	37.05 N	94.30 W
Joplin, Mt., U.S.	202	48.33 N	110.46 W
Joppa, Il., U.S.	194	37.12 N	88.50 W
Joppa, Md., U.S.	208	39.26 N	76.21 W
Jóquei Clube ♦	287b	23.35 S	46.41 W
Joquicingo	234	19.03 N	99.33 W
Jora	124	26.20 N	77.49 E
Jordan, Pil.	116	10.40 N	122.35 E
Jordan, Mn., U.S.	190	44.40 N	93.37 W
Jordan, Mt., U.S.	202	47.19 N	106.54 W
Jordan, N.Y., U.S.	210	43.03 N	76.28 W
Jordan (Al-Urdunn) □[1], Asia	118	31.00 N	36.00 E
Jordan (Al-Urdun) □[1], Asia	128	31.00 N	36.00 E
Jordan (Nahr al-Urdunn) (HaYarden) ≃, Asia	132	31.46 N	35.33 E
Jordan ≃, B.C., Can.	224	48.26 N	124.08 W
Jordan ≃, Ut,. U.S.	200	40.49 N	112.08 W
Jordan Creek ≃	202	42.52 N	117.38 W
Jordânia	255	15.54 S	40.11 W
Jordania → Jordan □[1]	128	31.00 N	36.00 E
Jordanie → Jordan □[1]	128	31.00 N	36.00 E
Jordanien → Jordan □[1]	128	31.00 N	36.00 E
Jordan Lake ⊜	216	42.46 N	85.09 W
Jordanów	30	49.40 N	19.50 E
Jordans	260	51.37 N	0.36 W
Jordan Valley	202	42.58 N	117.03 W
Jordanville	210	42.55 N	74.57 W
Jordão ≃	252	25.46 S	52.07 W
Jordbro	40	59.09 N	18.07 E
Jördenstorf	54	53.52 N	12.37 E
Jordet	26	61.25 N	12.09 E
Jorge Grego, Ilha I	256	23.13 S	44.09 W
Jorge Montt, Isla I	254	51.20 S	74.45 W
Jorge Montt, Ventisquero ⊓	254	48.17 S	73.30 W
Jorge V, Costade → George V Coast ⊥[2]	9	68.30 S	147.30 E
Jorge VI, Estrecho de → George VI Sound ʉ	9	71.00 S	68.00 W
Jorhāt	120	26.46 N	94.13 E
Jork	52	53.32 N	9.41 E
Jörlfeld	41	54.38 N	9.15 E
Jorm	120	36.52 N	70.51 E
Jörn	26	65.04 N	20.02 E
Jornado del Muerto ◆[2]	200	33.20 N	106.50 W
Joroinen	26	62.11 N	27.50 E
Jorong	112	3.58 S	114.56 E
Jørpeland	26	59.01 N	6.03 E
J'orzovka	80	48.56 N	44.33 E
Jos	150	9.55 N	8.53 E
Jose Abad Santos	116	5.38 N	125.27 E
José Batlle y Ordóñez	252	33.28 S	55.07 W
José Bonifácio	255	21.03 S	49.41 W
José Cardel	234	19.22 N	96.22 W
José C. Paz	258	34.30 S	58.45 W
José de Freitas	250	4.45 S	42.35 W
José de San Martín	254	44.02 S	70.29 W
José Enrique Rodó (Drabble)	258	33.41 S	57.34 W
José Francisco Vergara	252	22.28 S	69.38 W
Joselândia	248	16.32 S	56.12 W
José María Blanco (Tres Lomas)	252	36.27 S	62.51 W
José Martí, Aeropuerto Internacional ⊠	286b	23.00 N	82.24 W
Jose Panganiban	116	14.17 N	122.41 E
José Pedro Varela	252	33.27 S	54.32 W
Joseph	202	45.21 N	117.13 W
Joseph, Lac ⊜	176	52.45 N	65.15 W
Joseph, Lake ⊜	212	45.10 N	79.44 W
Joseph Bonaparte Gulf ᑕ	164	14.15 S	128.30 E
Joseph City	200	34.57 N	110.20 W
Joseph Creek ≃	202	46.03 N	117.01 W
Joseph Davis State Park ♦	284a	43.13 N	79.03 W
Josephine, Pa., U.S.	214	40.29 N	79.11 W
Josephine, Tx., U.S.	222	33.04 N	96.19 W
Josephine, Lake ⊜	220	27.24 N	81.26 W
Josephine Peak ʌ	280	34.17 N	118.09 W
Josephstaal	164	4.44 S	145.01 E
José Santos Arévalo	258	35.10 S	59.14 W
Joshīmath	120	30.34 N	79.34 E
Jōshin-Etsu-kōgen-kokuritsu-kōen ♦	94	36.46 N	138.40 E
Joshua	222	32.28 N	97.23 W
Joshuas Creek ≃	275b	43.29 N	79.37 W
Joshua Tree	204	34.08 N	116.18 W
Joshua Tree National Monument ♦	204	33.55 N	116.00 W
Joshua Trees State Park ♦	228	34.41 N	117.47 W
Joškar-Ola	80	56.38 N	47.52 E
Jos Plateau ⩘[1]	150	9.30 N	9.00 E
Jossa	56	50.14 N	9.35 E
Josselin	32	47.57 N	2.33 W
Jossigny	50	48.50 N	2.45 E
Jostedalsbreen ⊓	26	61.40 N	7.00 E
Jost Van Dyke I	240m	18.28 N	64.45 W
Jōtō ◆[8]	270	34.42 N	135.34 E
Jotunheimen ⩘	26	61.38 N	8.18 E
Jotunheimen Nasjonalpark ♦	26	61.35 N	8.30 E
Jouarre	50	48.56 N	3.08 E
Jouars-Pontchartrain	261	48.47 N	1.54 E
Joubertina	158	33.50 S	23.51 E
Joué-lès-Tours	50	47.21 N	0.40 E
Jougne	58	46.46 N	6.24 E
Jouques	62	43.38 N	5.38 E
Jourdanton	196	28.55 N	98.32 W
Joure	52	52.57 N	5.47 E
Joutsa	26	61.44 N	26.07 E
Joutseno	26	61.06 N	28.30 E
Joutsijärvi	24	66.40 N	28.00 E
Joux, Lac de ⊜	58	46.38 N	6.18 E
Joux, Vallée de V	58	46.35 N	6.15 E
Jouy	50	48.31 N	1.33 E
Jouy-en-Josas	261	48.46 N	2.10 E
Jouy-le-Moutier	261	49.01 N	2.03 E
Jouy-le-Potier	50	47.45 N	1.49 E
Jovellanos	240p	22.48 N	81.12 W
Jovellar	116	13.04 N	123.36 E
Jovet, Mont ʌ	62	45.30 N	6.39 E
Joveyn ≃	128	36.48 N	56.28 E
Joviânia	255	17.49 S	49.30 W
Jowai	120	25.27 N	92.12 E
Jowhar	144	2.46 N	45.31 E
Jowlaenga, Mount ʌ	162	17.21 S	122.56 E
Jowzjān □[4]	120	36.30 N	66.00 E
Joy	190	41.12 N	90.55 W
Joy, Mount ʌ	180	63.46 N	132.55 W
Joya, Laguna de la ᑕ	234	15.55 N	93.40 W
Joyce	194	31.56 N	92.35 W
Joyeuse	62	44.29 N	4.14 E
Jōyō	96	34.51 N	135.47 E
Joyous Pavilion Park ♦	271a	39.52 N	116.22 E
Joyuda	240m	18.07 N	67.11 W
Józefów	30	52.09 N	21.12 E
J. Percy Priest Lake ⊜[1]	194	36.05 N	86.30 W
Ju ≃, Zhg.	100	30.38 N	114.51 E
Ju ≃, Zhg.	105	39.45 N	117.35 E
Juaba	250	2.23 S	49.33 W
Juagdan	116	10.00 N	124.35 E
Juami ≃	246	1.45 S	67.30 W
Juanacatlán	234	20.31 N	103.10 W
Juana Díaz	240m	18.03 N	66.31 W
Juan Aldama	232	24.19 N	103.21 W
Juan Anchorena ◆[8]	288	34.29 S	58.30 W
Juana Ramírez, Isla I	234	21.50 N	97.40 W
Juan Atucha	258	35.32 S	59.21 W
Juan B. Arruabarrena	252	30.20 S	58.19 W
Juan Blanco, Arroyo ≃	258	35.05 S	57.26 W
Juancheng	98	35.35 N	115.29 E
Juan de Fuca, Strait of ʉ	224	48.18 N	124.00 W
Juan de Garay	254	38.52 S	64.34 W
Juan de Mena	252	24.55 S	56.44 W
Juan de Nova, Île I	138	17.03 S	42.45 E
Juan Díaz Covarrubias	234	18.07 N	95.09 W
Juan E. Barra	252	37.48 S	60.29 W
Juan Eugenio	232	25.10 N	103.20 W
Juan Fernández, Archipiélago II, Chile	18	33.00 S	80.00 W
Juan Fernández, Archipiélago II, Chile	244	33.00 S	80.00 W
Juan González Grande, Arroyo ≃	258	34.00 S	58.14 W
Juan González Romero ◆[8]	286a	19.30 N	99.04 W
Juangriego	246	11.05 N	63.57 W
Juan Gualberto Gómez	240p	22.52 N	81.33 W
Juan Guerra	248	6.35 S	76.21 W
Juanita, Méx.	234	17.47 N	95.09 W
Juanita, Wa., U.S.	224	47.42 N	122.13 W
Juan Jorba	252	33.37 S	65.16 W
Juan José Castelli	252	25.57 S	60.37 W
Juanjuí	248	7.11 S	76.45 W
Juankoski	26	63.04 N	28.21 E
Juan-les-Pins	62	43.34 N	7.06 E
Juan L. Lacaze	258	34.26 S	57.27 W
Juan N. Fernández	252	38.00 S	59.16 W
Juan Perez Sound ʉ	182	52.30 N	131.18 W
Juan Rodríguez Clara	234	18.00 N	95.25 W
Juan Tronconi	258	35.30 S	59.15 W
Juan Viñas	236	9.54 N	83.45 W
Juárez, Arg.	252	37.40 S	59.48 W
Juárez → Ciudad Juárez, Méx.	232	31.44 N	106.29 W
Juárez, Méx.	232	27.37 N	100.44 W
Juárez, Méx.	234	17.39 N	93.10 W
Juárez, Cerro ʌ	234	20.37 N	99.17 W
Juárez, Sierra de ⩘	232	32.00 N	115.50 W
Juarzon	150	5.20 N	8.52 W
Juatinga, Ponta de ›	256	23.17 S	44.30 W
Juàzeirinho	250	7.04 S	36.35 W
Juàzeiro	250	9.25 S	40.30 W
Juàzeiro do Norte	250	7.12 S	39.20 W
Jūbā	154	4.51 N	31.37 E
Juba ≃	248	14.59 S	57.44 W
Jubachstausee ⊜[1]	263	51.10 N	7.37 E
Jūbāl, Maḍīq ʉ	140	27.40 N	33.55 E
Jubal, Strait of → Jūbāl, Maḍīq ʉ	140	27.40 N	33.55 E
Jubayl (Byblos)	130	34.07 N	35.39 E
Jubaysho	144	5.48 N	37.22 E
Jubayt	140	18.57 N	36.50 E
Jubba (Genale) ≃	144	0.15 S	42.38 E
Jubbada Dhexe □[4]	144	1.00 N	43.00 E
Jubbada Hoose □[4]	144	0.00	42.00 E
Jubbah	128	28.02 N	40.56 E
Jubb al-Jarrāḥ	130	34.49 N	37.19 E
Jubbātā al-Khashab	132	33.13 N	35.49 E
Jubb Jannīn	132	33.37 N	35.47 E
Jubbulpore → Jabalpur	124	23.10 N	79.57 E
Jubilee Downs	162	18.22 S	125.17 E
Jubilee Lake ⊜, Austl.	162	29.12 S	126.38 E
Jubilee Lake ⊜, Nf., Can.	186	48.04 N	55.11 W
Jubones ≃	246	3.13 S	79.57 W
Jūbu-san ʌ	270	34.50 N	135.55 E
Juby, Cap ›	148	27.58 N	12.55 W
Jucá ≃	250	6.22 S	40.08 W
Júcar (Xúquer) ≃	34	39.09 N	0.14 W
Juçara	255	15.53 S	50.51 W
Júcaro	240p	21.37 N	78.51 W
Jucás	250	6.32 S	39.32 W
Jüchen	56	51.06 N	6.30 E
Juchhöh	54	50.24 N	11.52 E
Juchipila	234	21.25 N	103.07 W
Juchipila ≃	234	21.03 N	103.25 W
Juchitán [de Zaragoza]	234	16.26 N	95.01 W
Juchitepec	234	19.06 N	98.53 W
Juchitlán	234	20.05 N	104.07 W
Juchnov	76	54.45 N	35.14 E
Juchoviči	76	56.02 N	28.39 E
Jucuapa	236	13.31 N	88.24 W
Jucurucu ≃	255	17.21 S	39.13 W
Jucurutu	250	6.02 S	37.01 W
Judaea □[9]	132	31.35 N	35.00 E
Judas, Punta ›	236	9.31 N	84.32 W
Judaydat al-Khās	132	33.24 N	36.33 E
Judaydat 'Arṭūz	132	33.26 N	36.10 E
Juddah → Jiddah	144	21.30 N	39.12 E
Jude Island I	186	47.15 N	54.49 W
Judenau	61	48.17 N	16.00 E
Judenburg	61	47.10 N	14.40 E
Judges Hill ʌ[2]	283	42.12 N	70.49 W
Judian	102	27.20 N	99.36 E
Judinki, S.S.S.R.	82	54.37 N	37.17 E
Judinki, S.S.S.R.	82	55.27 N	35.48 E
Judino, S.S.S.R.	76	58.43 N	39.17 E
Judino, S.S.S.R.	80	55.51 N	48.55 E
Judino, S.S.S.R.	82	54.09 N	38.19 E
Judino, S.S.S.R.	265b	55.40 N	37.12 E
Judío, Rambla del ≃	34	38.15 N	1.27 W
Judique	186	45.52 N	61.30 W
Judith ≃	202	47.44 N	109.38 W
Judith, Point ›	207	41.22 N	71.29 W
Judith Gap	202	46.40 N	109.45 W
Judith Mountains ⩘	202	47.12 N	109.15 W
Judith Peak ʌ	202	47.13 N	109.13 W
Judoma ≃	74	59.08 N	135.06 E
Judson, S.C., U.S.	192	34.50 N	82.27 W
Judson, Tx., U.S.	222	32.35 N	94.45 W
Judsonia	194	35.16 N	91.38 W
Jue ≃	100	31.42 N	113.20 E
Juehedian	105	39.26 N	117.06 E
Juelsminde	41	55.43 N	10.01 E
Juexi	100	29.27 N	121.57 E
Juexizhen	107	28.55 N	104.16 E
Jufari ≃	246	1.13 S	62.00 W

Symbol	English	Deutsch	Español	Français	Português
≃	River	Fluß	Río	Rivière	Rio
≊	Canal	Kanal	Canal	Canal	Canal
∟	Waterfall, Rapids	Wasserfall, Stromschnellen	Cascada, Rápidos	Chute d'eau, Rapides	Cascata, Rápidos
ʉ	Strait	Meeresstraße	Estrecho	Détroit	Estreito
ᑕ	Bay, Gulf	Bucht, Golf	Bahía, Golfo	Baie, Golfe	Baía, Golfo
⊜	Lake, Lakes	See, Seen	Lago, Lagos	Lac, Lacs	Lago, Lagos
⸬	Swamp	Sumpf	Pantano	Marais	Pântano
⊓	Ice Features, Glacier	Eis- und Gletscherformen	Accidentes Glaciales	Formes glaciaires	Acidentes glaciares
╤	Other Hydrographic Features	Andere Hydrographische Objekte	Otros Elementos Hidrográficos	Autres données hydrographiques	Outros acidentes hidrográficos
✢	Submarine Features	Untermeerische Objekte	Accidentes Submarinos	Formes de relief sous-marin	Acidentes submarinos
□	Political Unit	Politische Einheit	Unidad Politica	Entité politique	Unidade política
ʋ	Cultural Institution	Kulturelle Institution	Institución Cultural	Institution culturelle	Instituição cultural
⊥	Historical Site	Historische Stätte	Sitio Histórico	Site historique	Sitio histórico
♦	Recreational Site	Erholungs- und Ferienort	Sitio de Recreo	Centre de loisirs	Area de Lazer
⊠	Airport	Flughafen	Aeropuerto	Aéroport	Aeroporto
■	Military Installation	Militäranlage	Instalación Militar	Installation militaire	Instalação militar
◆	Miscellaneous	Verschiedenes	Misceláneo	Divers	Diversos

ENGLISH

Name	Page	Lat.°′	Long.°′
Jufayr, Bi'r al- ⍑[4]	**142**	30.49 N	32.40 E
Jufrah, Wādī al- V	**142**	30.24 N	31.35 E
Jug	**86**	57.43 N	56.10 E
Jug ≃	**24**	60.45 N	46.20 E
Jughna	**140**	12.24 N	25.06 E
Jugo-Kamskij	**86**	57.42 N	55.35 E
Jugon	**32**	48.25 N	2.20 W
Jugo-Osetinskaja Avtonomnaja Oblast' □[8]	**84**	42.20 N	44.00 E
Jugoslavija → Yugoslavia □[1]	**22**	44.00 N	19.00 E
Jugoslawien → Yugoslavia □[1]	**22**	44.00 N	19.00 E
Jugo-Zapad ◆[8]	**265b**	55.40 N	37.32 E
Juḥā	**144**	16.41 N	42.54 E
Jühnsdorf	**264a**	52.18 N	13.23 E
Jühnsdorfer Heide ◆[3]	**264a**	52.19 N	13.24 E
Juhu ◆[8]	**272c**	19.07 N	72.49 E
Juhua Dao I	**98**	40.29 N	120.47 E
Juhu Airport ⊠	**272c**	19.06 N	72.50 E
Jui	**272c**	19.01 N	73.05 E
Juidongshan	**100**	23.46 N	117.31 E
Juigalpa	**236**	12.05 N	85.24 W
Juile	**234**	17.45 N	94.59 W
Juillac	**32**	45.19 N	1.19 E
Juilly	**261**	49.01 N	2.42 E
Juiná ≃	**248**	12.36 S	58.57 W
Juine ≃	**50**	48.32 N	2.23 E
Juist	**52**	53.40 N	6.59 E
Juist I	**52**	53.40 N	7.00 E
Juisui	**100**	23.30 N	121.21 E
Juiz de Fora	**256**	21.45 S	43.20 W
Jūjō Base ■	**268**	35.45 N	139.43 E
Jujurieux	**58**	46.02 N	5.25 E
Jujuy → San Salvador de Jujuy	**252**	24.11 S	65.18 W
Jujuy □[4]	**252**	23.00 S	66.00 W
Jukagirskoje ploskogorje ⋀[1]	**74**	66.00 N	155.00 E
Jukamenskoje	**80**	57.53 N	52.15 E
Jukonda ≃	**86**	59.38 N	67.26 E
Juksa	**86**	56.55 N	85.10 E
Juksejevo	**24**	59.52 N	54.19 E
Jukskei ≃	**273d**	26.06 S	28.06 E
Jukta	**74**	63.23 N	105.41 E
Jula ≃	**24**	63.49 N	44.44 E
Julāna	**124**	29.08 N	76.25 E
Julayfah, Bi'r al- ⍑[4]	**142**	30.43 N	29.35 E
Julbach	**60**	48.40 N	13.52 E
Juldybajevo	**86**	52.20 N	57.52 E
Julebu	**98**	40.09 N	113.36 E
Julesburg	**198**	40.59 N	102.15 W
Juli	**248**	16.13 S	69.27 W
Juliaca	**248**	15.30 S	70.08 W
Julia Creek	**166**	20.39 S	141.45 E
Julia Creek ≃	**166**	20.00 S	141.11 E
Julian	**214**	40.52 N	77.56 W
Juliana, Lake ⊜	**220**	28.07 N	81.48 W
Julianakanaal ≡	**56**	51.05 N	5.50 E
Julian Alps ⋀	**36**	46.00 N	14.00 E
Juliana Top ∧	**250**	3.41 N	56.32 W
Julianehåb (Qaqortoq)	**176**	60.43 N	46.01 W
Julia Pfeiffer Burns State Park ♦	**226**	36.10 N	120.40 W
Jülich	**56**	50.55 N	6.21 E
Juliénas	**58**	46.14 N	4.43 E
Juliette, Lake ⊜[1]	**192**	33.05 N	83.50 W
Julijske Alpe → Julian Alps ⋀	**36**	46.00 N	14.00 E
Julimes	**232**	28.25 N	105.27 W
Júlio de Castilhos	**252**	29.14 S	53.41 W
Julio Prestes, Estação ◆[5]	**287b**	23.32 S	46.38 W
Julita ʋ	**40**	59.09 N	16.02 E
Juliuhe	**104**	42.03 N	122.55 E
Juliustown	**285**	40.00 N	74.40 W
Julu	**98**	37.13 N	115.01 E
Juma	**24**	65.07 N	33.16 E
Juma ≃, Bra.	**248**	4.57 S	64.31 W
Juma ≃, Zhg.	**98**	39.34 N	115.42 E
Jumaguzino	**86**	52.54 N	56.23 E
Jumapolo	**115a**	7.42 S	111.00 E
Jumaševo	**80**	54.59 N	54.25 E
Jumay, Volcán ∧[1]	**236**	14.41 N	89.59 W
Jumbilla	**248**	5.54 S	77.45 W
Jumbo	**154**	17.28 S	30.55 E
Jumbo, Raas ≻	**144**	1.39 S	41.36 E
Jumboo	**144**	0.15 S	42.38 E
Jumbo Peak ∧	**204**	36.12 N	114.11 W
Jumeauville	**261**	48.55 N	1.47 E
Jumentos Cays II	**238**	22.42 N	75.55 W
Jumet	**50**	50.26 N	4.25 E
Jumhūrīyat al-Yaman ad-Dīmuqrāṭīyah ash-Sha'bīyah → Yemen	**144**	15.00 N	47.00 E
Jumièges	**50**	49.26 N	0.49 E
Jumilla	**34**	38.29 N	1.17 W
Jumlā	**124**	29.17 N	82.10 E
Jummayzat Banī 'Amr	**142**	30.48 N	31.32 E
Jump ≃	**190**	45.17 N	91.05 W
Jump, North Fork ≃	**190**	45.25 N	90.40 W
Jump, South Fork ≃	**190**	45.25 N	90.40 W
Jumt uul ∧	**102**	44.29 N	97.10 E
Jūn	**132**	33.35 N	35.27 E
Jun ≃	**100**	25.57 N	118.03 E
Jūnāgadh	**120**	21.31 N	70.28 E
Junan (Shizilu)	**98**	35.11 N	118.51 E
Junayfah	**142**	30.12 N	32.25 E
Junaynah, Ra's al- ∧	**140**	29.01 N	33.58 E
Juncal, Isla I	**258**	33.58 S	58.24 W
Juncal, Serra do ∧	**256**	22.45 S	45.55 W
Juncal do Norte ⩩	**266c**	38.52 N	8.59 W
Juncal do Sul ⩩	**266c**	38.51 N	8.58 W
Juncheng	**98**	38.57 N	114.41 E
Juncos	**240m**	18.14 N	65.55 W
Junction, Tx., U.S.	**196**	30.29 N	99.46 W
Junction, Ut,. U.S.	**200**	38.14 N	112.13 W
Junction City, Ar., U.S.	**194**	33.00 N	92.43 W
Junction City, Il., U.S.	**219**	38.34 N	89.07 W
Junction City, Ks., U.S.	**198**	39.01 N	96.49 W
Junction City, Ky., U.S.	**194**	37.35 N	84.47 W
Junction City, Or., U.S.	**202**	44.13 N	123.12 W
Junction City, Wa., U.S.	**224**	46.58 N	123.46 W
Jundah	**166**	24.50 S	143.04 E
Jundiaí	**256**	23.11 S	46.52 W
Jundiaí ≃, Bra.	**256**	23.32 S	46.15 W
Jundiaí ≃, Bra.	**256**	23.11 S	47.16 W
Jundiaí do Sul	**255**	23.27 S	50.17 W
Jundiaí-Mirim ≃	**256**	23.10 S	46.56 W
Jundiapeba	**256**	23.33 S	46.15 W
Jundu Shan ⋀	**105**	40.30 N	116.05 E
Juneau, Ak., U.S.	**180**	58.20 N	134.27 W
Juneau, Wi., U.S.	**190**	43.24 N	88.42 W
Junee	**166**	34.52 S	147.35 E
June in Winter, Lake ⊜	**220**	27.18 N	81.24 W
June Lake	**226**	37.46 N	119.04 W
June Park	**220**	28.04 N	80.41 W
Jungapeo	**234**	19.27 N	100.29 W
Jungar Qi	**102**	39.49 N	111.10 E
Jungbluth Ditch ≡	**279a**	41.27 N	82.07 W
Jungfernheide ◆[3]	**264a**	52.34 N	13.17 E
Jungfern-Inseln → Virgin Islands □[2]	**240m**	18.20 N	64.50 W
Jungfern-See ⊜	**264a**	52.25 N	13.05 E
Jungfrau ∧	**58**	46.32 N	7.58 E
Jungfraujoch ◆[5]	**58**	46.33 N	7.58 E
Junggar Pendi (Dzungarian Basin) ≚[1]	**86**	45.00 N	88.00 E
Jungle Habitat ♦	**276**	41.08 N	74.21 W
Junglinster	**56**	49.43 N	6.15 E
Jungshāhi	**120**	24.51 N	67.46 E
Juniata	**198**	40.35 N	98.30 W
Juniata □[6]	**208**	40.34 N	77.24 W
Juniata ◆[8]	**285**	40.01 N	75.07 W
Juniata ≃	**188**	40.24 N	77.01 W
Juniata, Frankstown Branch ≃	**214**	40.34 N	78.03 W
Juniata, Raystown Branch ≃	**214**	40.25 N	77.58 W
Juniata Gap	**214**	40.33 N	78.26 W
Juniata Terrace	**208**	40.35 N	77.34 W
Junín, Arg.	**252**	34.35 S	60.57 W
Junín, Ec.	**246**	0.56 S	80.13 W
Junín, Perú	**248**	11.10 S	76.00 W
Junín □[5]	**248**	11.30 S	75.00 W
Junín, Lago ⊜	**248**	11.02 S	76.06 W
Junín de los Andes	**254**	39.56 S	71.05 W
Junior	**188**	38.59 N	79.57 W
Juniper	**186**	46.33 N	67.13 W
Junipero Serra Peak ∧	**226**	36.08 N	121.25 W
Juniville	**50**	49.24 N	4.23 E
Jūniyah	**130**	33.59 N	35.38 E
Junk Bay ⊂	**271d**	22.17 N	114.15 E
Jun Kharchanai	**123**	36.52 N	75.01 E
Junk Island I	**271d**	22.17 N	114.16 E
Junkou	**100**	26.42 N	116.49 E
Junlian	**102**	28.08 N	104.35 E
Junliangcheng	**105**	39.04 N	117.27 E
Junling	**100**	28.17 N	116.28 E
Junnar	**122**	19.12 N	73.53 E
Juno Beach	**220**	26.52 N	80.04 W
Junokommunarskoje ◆[8]	**83**	48.13 N	38.18 E
Junqalī □[4]	**140**	7.30 N	32.20 E
Junqueiro	**250**	9.56 S	36.29 W
Junqueirópolis	**255**	21.32 S	51.26 W
Junsele	**26**	63.41 N	16.54 E
Jun Ul Shan ⋀	**102**	37.30 N	97.00 E
Junxian	**102**	32.31 N	111.30 E
Jūō	**94**	36.40 N	140.41 E
Juodkrantė	**76**	55.33 N	21.08 E
Juodupė	**76**	56.05 N	25.37 E
Juojärvi ⊜	**26**	62.43 N	28.33 E
Juparanã, Lagoa ⊜	**255**	19.35 S	40.18 W
Jupilingo ≃	**236**	14.48 N	89.14 W
Jupille	**56**	50.39 N	5.38 E
Jupiter	**220**	26.56 N	80.05 W
Jupiter ≃	**186**	49.29 N	63.37 W
Jupiter Inlet ⊂	**220**	26.57 N	80.04 W
Jupiter Island I	**220**	27.04 N	80.07 W
Juqueri ≃	**256**	23.24 S	46.52 W
Juqueri-Mirim	**256**	23.21 S	46.37 W
Juqueriquerê, Serra do ⋀	**256**	23.43 S	45.37 W
Juquiá	**252**	24.19 S	47.38 W
Juquiá ≃	**256**	23.56 S	47.09 W
Juquiá-Guaçu ≃	**256**	24.00 S	47.16 W
Juquila	**234**	16.14 N	97.18 W
Juquitiba	**256**	23.57 S	47.03 W
Jur, Česko.	**30**	48.15 N	17.13 E
Jur, S.S.S.R.	**74**	59.52 N	137.39 E
Jur ≃	**140**	8.39 N	29.18 E
Jura □[3]	**58**	47.20 N	7.15 E
Jura □[5]	**58**	46.50 N	5.50 E
Jura ⋀	**58**	46.45 N	6.30 E
Jura I	**46**	56.00 N	5.50 W
Jūra ≃	**76**	55.03 N	22.09 E
Jura, Sound of ⊔	**46**	55.57 N	5.48 W
Juramento	**255**	16.50 S	43.35 W
Juratiški	**76**	54.02 N	25.54 E
Jurayrah, Jabal al- ∧	**128**	24.06 N	39.16 E
Jurays wa 'Izbatuhā	**142**	30.19 N	30.55 E
Jurbarkas	**76**	55.05 N	22.48 E
Jurcevo	**76**	60.02 N	32.36 E
Juréia	**256**	21.17 S	46.22 W
Jurenino	**76**	59.24 N	42.47 E
Jurevič̌i	**78**	51.57 N	29.32 E
Jurf ad-Darāwīsh	**132**	30.42 N	35.52 E
Jurga	**86**	55.42 N	84.51 E
Jurgamyš	**86**	55.21 N	64.28 E
Jurgenson Woods ♦	**278**	41.34 N	87.36 W
Jurien	**162**	30.19 S	115.02 E
Juriesfontein	**158**	31.40 S	22.08 E
Juring	**164**	6.26 S	134.20 E
Jurino	**80**	56.18 N	46.18 E
Jurja	**24**	59.03 N	49.14 E
Jurjev → Tartu	**76**	58.23 N	26.43 E
Jurjevec	**80**	57.18 N	43.06 E
Jurjevka, S.S.S.R.	**78**	48.44 N	36.02 E
Jurjevka, S.S.S.R.	**83**	48.30 N	39.00 E
Jurjev-Pol'skij	**80**	56.30 N	39.41 E
Jurjevskoje	**82**	55.05 N	36.13 E
Jurla	**86**	59.17 N	54.19 E
Jurlovo, S.S.S.R.	**82**	55.19 N	35.52 E
Jurlovo, S.S.S.R.	**82**	55.54 N	37.16 E
Jūrmala	**76**	56.58 N	23.42 E
Jurong, Sing.	**271c**	1.19 N	103.43 E
Jurong, Zhg.	**106**	31.57 N	119.10 E
Jurong ≃	**271c**	1.18 N	103.44 E
Jurong, Selat ⊔	**271c**	1.18 N	103.42 E
Jurovo, S.S.S.R.	**78**	51.22 N	27.50 E
Jurovo, S.S.S.R.	**80**	57.30 N	43.50 E
Jurovo, S.S.S.R.	**82**	55.30 N	38.22 E
Jurovskoje	**86**	59.29 N	69.02 E
Jursla	**40**	58.40 N	16.11 E
Jurty	**88**	56.03 N	97.37 E
Juruá	**246**	3.27 S	66.03 W
Juruá ≃	**242**	2.37 S	65.44 W
Juruaia	**256**	21.15 S	46.35 W
Juruá Mirim ≃	**248**	8.08 S	72.48 W
Juruena ≃	**248**	7.20 S	58.03 W
Jurujuba, Enseada de ⊂	**287a**	22.56 S	43.07 W
Jurumkuvejem ≃	**180**	66.14 N	173.35 E
Jurupari ≃	**248**	7.45 S	70.10 W
Jurupari, Arquipélago do II	**250**	0.07 N	50.30 W
Jurupari, Ilha I	**250**	0.20 N	50.07 W
Juruti	**250**	2.09 S	56.04 W
Jur'uzan'	**86**	54.52 N	58.26 E
Jur'uzan' ≃	**86**	55.42 N	57.00 E
Jurva	**26**	62.41 N	21.59 E
Jušala	**86**	57.04 N	64.17 E
Juscelândia	**255**	15.20 S	51.19 W
Jusepín	**246**	9.45 N	63.31 W
Jushiguan	**102**	24.47 N	97.38 E
Jūshiyama	**94**	35.06 N	136.46 E
Juskatla	**182**	53.37 N	132.18 W
Jus'ki	**80**	56.39 N	53.05 E
Juškovo	**76**	59.46 N	45.11 E
Juškozero	**24**	64.44 N	32.06 E
Jūsō ◆[8]	**270**	34.43 N	135.28 E
Jussey	**58**	47.49 N	5.54 E
Justa	**80**	47.07 N	46.18 E
Justice	**278**	41.44 N	87.50 W
Justin	**222**	33.05 N	97.18 W
Justineberg ∧[2]	**40**	58.43 N	15.04 E
Justiniano Posse	**252**	32.53 S	62.40 W
Justo Daract	**252**	33.52 S	65.11 W
Justus	**214**	40.42 N	81.35 W
Jušut ≃	**80**	56.12 N	48.23 E
Jus'va	**24**	58.56 N	54.57 E
Jutaí	**248**	5.11 S	68.54 W
Jutaí ≃	**242**	2.43 S	66.57 W
Jutaza	**80**	54.35 N	53.16 E
Jütchendorf	**264a**	52.16 N	13.10 E
Jüterbog	**54**	51.59 N	13.04 E
Juththah, Jabal al- ∧	**132**	30.12 N	35.36 E
Juti	**255**	22.52 S	54.37 W
Jutiapa	**236**	14.17 N	89.54 W
Jutiapa □[5]	**236**	14.10 N	89.50 W
Juticalpa	**236**	14.42 N	86.15 W
Jutiquile	**236**	14.45 N	86.08 W
Jutland → Jylland ◆[1]	**26**	56.00 N	9.15 E
Jutogh	**123**	31.06 N	77.07 E
Jutrosin	**30**	51.40 N	17.10 E
Juupajoki	**26**	61.47 N	24.27 E
Juuru	**76**	59.04 N	24.59 E
Juva	**26**	61.54 N	27.51 E
Juventud, Isla de la (Isla de Pinos) I	**240p**	21.40 N	82.50 W
Juvisy-sur-Orge	**50**	48.41 N	2.23 E
Juvuln ⊜	**26**	63.43 N	13.09 E
Juwana	**115a**	6.42 S	111.09 E
Juwangi	**115a**	7.10 S	110.45 E
Juxi	**100**	27.30 N	119.08 E
Juxian	**98**	35.37 N	118.54 E
Juxing	**106**	31.56 N	121.33 E
Juxtlahuaca	**234**	17.20 N	98.01 W
Juyanhai → Gaxun Nur ⊜	**102**	42.22 N	100.34 E
Juye	**98**	35.23 N	116.06 E
Jūyom	**128**	28.34 N	53.56 E
Juyongguan	**105**	40.18 N	116.04 E
Juža	**80**	56.35 N	42.01 E
Juzennecourt	**58**	48.11 N	4.59 E
Juzi ≃	**98**	40.18 N	123.35 E
Juziers	**261**	49.00 N	1.51 E
Južna Morava ≃	**38**	43.41 N	21.24 E
Južno-Aleksandrovka	**88**	55.51 N	96.10 E
Južno-Aličurskij chrebet ⋀	**120**	37.30 N	73.20 E
Južno-Golodnostepskij kanal ≡	**85**	40.15 N	69.08 E
Južno-Jenisejskij	**86**	58.48 N	94.39 E
Južno-Mujskij chrebet ⋀	**88**	55.40 N	114.00 E
Južno-Sachalinsk	**89**	46.58 N	142.42 E
Južno-Suchokumsk	**84**	44.37 N	45.34 E
Južno-Ural'sk	**86**	54.26 N	61.15 E
Južnyj, S.S.S.R.	**80**	56.08 N	44.09 E
Južnyj, S.S.S.R.	**80**	47.20 N	41.51 E
Južnyj, S.S.S.R.	**86**	53.14 N	83.42 E
Južnyj, S.S.S.R.	**86**	53.33 N	60.02 E
Južnyj, S.S.S.R.	**86**	49.21 N	73.01 E
Južnyj, mys ≻	**74**	57.45 N	156.45 E
Južnyj-Alamyšik	**85**	40.46 N	72.38 E
Južnyj Bug ≃	**78**	46.59 N	31.58 E
Južnyj Prijut	**84**	43.12 N	41.55 E
Južnyj Ural ⋀	**86**	54.00 N	58.30 E
Juzovka → Doneck	**83**	48.00 N	37.48 E
Jwālahari ◆[8]	**272a**	28.40 N	77.06 E
Jwayyā	**132**	33.14 N	35.19 E
Jyderup	**41**	55.40 N	11.26 E
Jylland (Jutland) ◆[1]	**26**	56.00 N	9.15 E
Jyllinge	**41**	55.45 N	12.07 E
Jyväskylä	**26**	62.14 N	25.44 E
K			
K2 (Qogir Feng) ∧	**123**	35.53 N	76.30 E
Ka ≃	**150**	11.40 N	4.10 E
Kaaawa	**229c**	21.33 N	157.51 W
Kaabong	**154**	3.31 N	34.08 E
Kaachka	**128**	37.21 N	59.36 E
Kaala ∧	**229c**	21.31 N	158.09 W
Kaalaea	**229c**	21.28 N	157.51 W
Kaala-Gomén	**175f**	20.40 S	164.25 E
Kaalspruit	**158**	29.15 S	26.10 E
Kaapahu Bay ⊂	**229a**	20.39 N	156.05 W
Kaapmuiden	**156**	25.33 S	31.20 E
Kaappunt ≻	**158**	34.21 S	18.30 E
Kaapstad → Cape Town	**158**	33.55 S	18.22 E
Kaarli	**76**	59.24 N	26.27 E
Kaarssen	**54**	53.12 N	11.02 E
Kaarst	**56**	51.14 N	6.37 E
Kaaterskill Creek ≃	**210**	42.13 N	73.53 W
Kaatoan, Mount ∧	**116**	8.07 N	124.55 E
Kaatsheuvel	**52**	51.40 N	5.02 E
Kaavi	**26**	62.59 N	28.30 E
Kaba	**150**	10.09 N	11.40 W
Kaba ≃	**86**	47.53 N	86.12 E
Kaba, Goulbin V	**150**	13.42 N	6.19 E
Kabacan	**116**	7.08 N	124.49 E
Kabacan ≃	**116**	7.08 N	124.50 E
Kabadak	**126**	22.13 N	89.19 E
Kabadak ≃[1]	**126**	22.13 N	89.18 E
Kabadüz	**130**	40.53 N	37.56 E
Kabaena, Pulau I	**112**	5.15 S	121.55 E
Kabaena, Selat ⊔	**112**	5.00 S	122.00 E
Kabah ⊥	**232**	20.07 N	89.29 W
Kabala	**150**	9.35 N	11.33 W
Kabale	**154**	1.15 S	29.59 E
Kabalega Falls ∟	**154**	2.17 N	31.41 E
Kabalega Falls National Park ♦	**154**	2.15 N	31.50 E
Kabali, Indon.	**112**	1.42 S	121.54 E
Kabalı, Tür.	**130**	41.52 N	35.05 E
Kabalo	**154**	6.03 S	26.55 E
Kabambare	**154**	4.42 S	27.43 E
Kaban'	**86**	54.39 N	66.28 E
Kabangu Kuta	**154**	14.00 S	24.03 E
Kabanjahe	**114**	3.06 N	98.30 E
Kabanje	**83**	49.13 N	38.12 E
Kabankalan	**116**	9.59 N	122.49 E
Kabanovka	**80**	53.39 N	51.18 E
Kabanovo	**86**	55.20 N	70.52 E
Kabansk	**88**	52.03 N	106.39 E
Kabardinka	**78**	44.39 N	37.57 E
Kabardino-Balkarskaja Avtonomnaja Sovetskaja Socialističeskaja Respublika □[3]	**84**	43.30 N	43.30 E
Kabasalan	**116**	7.48 N	122.45 E
Kabayan	**116**	16.37 N	120.51 E
Kabba	**150**	7.50 N	6.03 E
Kabbani ≃	**122**	12.13 N	76.54 E
Kåbdalis	**24**	66.10 N	20.00 E
Kabd aṣ-Ṣārim ◆[1]	**130**	34.34 N	39.33 E
Kabd Warqah ◆[1]	**130**	34.20 N	39.37 E
Kabel ◆[8]	**263**	51.24 N	7.29 E
Kabenung Lake ⊜	**190**	48.16 N	85.00 W
Kabetogama Lake ⊜	**190**	48.28 N	92.59 W
Kabeya	**154**	5.40 S	27.58 E
Kab-hegy ∧	**30**	47.03 N	17.39 E
Kabia ≃	**146**	9.54 N	15.10 E
Kabid, Wādī V	**132**	30.08 N	36.31 E
Kabinakagami Lake ⊜	**190**	48.54 N	84.25 W
Kabin Buri	**110**	13.59 N	101.43 E
Kabinda	**152**	6.08 S	24.29 E
Kabinu	**112**	4.00 N	116.05 E
Kabir	**112**	8.17 S	124.13 E
Kabira	**175d**	24.27 N	124.08 E
Kabīr Kili	**123**	33.11 N	71.19 E
Kabīr Kūh ⋀	**128**	33.25 N	46.45 E
Kabīrwāla	**123**	30.24 N	71.52 E
Kabkābīyah	**140**	13.39 N	24.05 E
Kablow	**264a**	52.18 N	13.44 E
Kablower Ziegelei	**264a**	52.19 N	13.43 E
Kablukovo, S.S.S.R.	**82**	56.50 N	36.12 E
Kablukovo, S.S.S.R.	**82**	56.02 N	38.10 E
Kablumgu, Cape ≻	**164**	6.20 S	150.00 E
Kabna	**140**	19.10 N	32.41 E
Kabo	**152**	7.39 N	18.37 E
Kabobo	**154**	5.07 S	29.03 E
Kaboe ≃	**158**	28.55 S	19.17 E
Kābol	**120**	34.31 N	69.12 E
Kābol □[4]	**120**	34.30 N	69.15 E
Kābol ≃	**120**	33.55 N	72.14 E
Kabompo	**154**	13.36 S	24.12 E
Kabompo ≃	**138**	14.10 S	23.11 E
Kabondo-Dianda	**154**	8.53 S	25.40 E
Kabongo, Zaïre	**154**	7.19 S	25.35 E
Kabongo, Zaïre	**154**	8.43 S	28.11 E
Kabongo-Lunda, Chutes ∟	**152**	7.34 S	17.17 E
Kaboro	**152**	6.59 N	17.33 E
Kabot	**150**	10.48 N	14.57 W
Kabotshome	**154**	3.46 S	26.54 E
Kabou, Centraf.	**152**	5.20 N	21.43 E
Kabou, Togo	**150**	9.27 N	0.49 E
Kaboudia, Rass ≻	**148**	35.14 N	11.10 E
Kaboul → Kābol	**120**	34.31 N	69.12 E
Kabr	**140**	10.54 N	26.50 E
Kabri	**132**	33.01 N	35.09 E
Kabūdarāhang	**128**	35.12 N	48.44 E
Kabūd Gonbad	**128**	37.00 N	59.45 E
Kābul → Kābol	**120**	34.31 N	69.12 E
Kabunda	**154**	12.25 S	29.22 E
Kabunga	**154**	1.42 S	28.08 E
Kabura ≃	**94**	36.17 N	139.04 E
Kaburuang, Pulau I	**108**	3.48 N	126.48 E
Kabūshīyah	**140**	16.53 N	33.42 E
Kabwanga	**152**	7.01 S	22.37 E
Kabwe (Broken Hill)	**154**	14.27 S	28.27 E
Kabwe-Katanda	**152**	7.59 S	24.29 E
Kabyčovka	**83**	49.28 N	39.45 E
Kabylie ◆[1]	**34**	36.30 N	4.30 E
Kača	**78**	44.47 N	33.32 E
Kačalinskaja	**80**	49.07 N	44.03 E
Kačanik	**38**	42.13 N	21.14 E
Kačanovo	**76**	57.28 N	27.46 E
Kacbachskij	**86**	52.58 N	59.40 E
Kačerginė	**76**	54.56 N	23.44 E
Kacha ≃[1]	**126**	22.23 N	89.54 E
Kachagalau ∧	**154**	2.19 N	35.03 E
Kach'ang-ni	**98**	38.24 N	126.11 E
Kachati	**84**	42.30 N	41.46 E
Kachchh, Gulf of ⊂	**120**	22.36 N	69.30 E
Kachemak Bay ⊂	**180**	59.35 N	151.30 W
Kachess Lake ⊜[1]	**224**	47.20 N	121.14 W
Kachhwa	**124**	25.13 N	82.43 E
Kachi	**84**	41.26 N	46.56 E
Kachia	**150**	9.53 N	7.58 E
Kachib	**84**	42.25 N	46.36 E
Kachin □[3]	**102**	26.00 N	97.30 E
Kach'i-ri	**98**	34.27 N	126.08 E
Kachisi	**144**	9.39 N	37.50 E
Kachovka	**78**	46.47 N	33.30 E
Kachovskoje vodochranilišče ⊜[1]	**78**	47.25 N	34.10 E
Kachowka-Stausee → Kachovskoje vodochranilišče ⊜[1]	**78**	47.25 N	34.10 E
K'achta	**88**	50.26 N	106.25 E
Kachua, Bngl.	**126**	23.21 N	90.54 E
Kachua, Bngl.	**126**	22.39 N	89.53 E
Kačiry	**86**	53.05 N	76.07 E
Kačkanar	**86**	58.42 N	59.38 E
Kačkanar, gora ∧	**86**	58.47 N	59.23 E
Kaçkar Dağı ∧	**130**	40.50 N	41.10 E
Kačkarovka	**78**	47.06 N	33.44 E
Kačug	**88**	53.58 N	105.52 E
Kada ≃	**88**	55.03 N	102.04 E
Kadada ≃	**80**	53.09 N	46.01 E
Kadaingti	**110**	17.37 N	97.32 E
Kadaiyanallūr	**122**	9.05 N	77.21 E
Kadamatt Island I	**122**	11.14 N	72.47 E
Kadaň	**54**	50.20 N	13.15 E
Kadanai (Kadaney) ≃	**120**	31.02 N	66.09 E
Kadaney (Kadanai) ≃	**120**	31.02 N	66.09 E
Kadan Kyun I	**110**	12.30 N	98.22 E
Kadapongan, Pulau I	**112**	4.43 S	115.44 E
Kadassa ≃	**115b**	9.24 S	120.02 E
Kaddam ⊜[1]	**122**	19.07 N	78.46 E
Kade	**150**	6.05 N	0.50 W
Kadéï ≃	**152**	3.31 N	16.05 E
Kadena	**174m**	26.22 N	127.45 E
Kadena Airfield ⊠	**174m**	26.22 N	127.45 E
Kadeshiki	**80**	58.08 N	49.11 E
Kadetrenden (Kadet Rinne) ⊔	**41**	54.30 N	12.15 E
Kadgo, Lake ⊜	**162**	26.42 S	127.18 E
Kadi	**120**	23.18 N	72.20 E
Kadiana	**150**	10.45 N	6.30 W
Kadıköy	**130**	40.46 N	26.46 E
Kadina	**168b**	33.58 S	137.43 E
Kading ≃	**110**	18.19 N	104.00 E
Kadınhanı	**130**	38.15 N	32.14 E
Kadiolo	**150**	10.33 N	5.46 W
Kadipaten	**115a**	6.46 S	108.10 E
Kādīpur	**124**	26.10 N	82.23 E
Kadiri	**122**	14.07 N	78.10 E
Kadirli	**130**	37.23 N	36.05 E
Kadışehri	**130**	40.00 N	35.49 E
Kadiyevka → Stachanov	**83**	48.34 N	38.40 E
Kadja, Ouadi (Wādī Kaja) V	**146**	12.02 N	22.28 E
Kadkan	**128**	35.35 N	58.50 E
Kadnikov	**76**	59.30 N	40.20 E
Kadnikovskij	**76**	60.19 N	40.15 E
Kado	**150**	7.39 N	9.44 E
Ka-do I	**98**	39.33 N	124.40 E
Kadodo	**140**	11.04 N	29.31 E
Kadogawa	**92**	32.28 N	131.39 E
Kadoka	**198**	43.50 N	101.30 W
Kadom	**80**	54.34 N	42.30 E
Kadoma, Nihon	**270**	34.44 N	135.35 E
Kadoma, Zimb.	**154**	18.21 S	29.55 E
Kadoškino	**80**	54.01 N	44.25 E
Kadov	**60**	49.24 N	13.47 E
Kaduj	**76**	59.12 N	37.09 E
Kadumbul ≃	**115b**	9.42 S	120.32 E
Kaduna	**150**	10.33 N	7.27 E
Kaduna □[3]	**150**	10.30 N	7.45 E
Kaduna ≃	**150**	8.45 N	5.45 E
Kāduqlī	**140**	11.01 N	29.43 E
Kadūr	**122**	13.34 N	76.01 E
Kadyj	**80**	57.47 N	43.11 E
Kadykčan	**74**	63.02 N	146.50 E
Kadyšovo	**80**	54.20 N	46.45 E
Kadžerom	**24**	64.41 N	55.54 E
Kadži-Saj	**85**	42.08 N	77.10 E
Kaech'ŏn	**98**	39.42 N	125.53 E
Kaédi	**150**	16.09 N	13.30 W
Kaedo-ri	**98**	34.35 N	127.39 E
Kaegudeck Lake ⊜	**186**	48.07 N	55.11 W
Kaélé	**146**	10.07 N	14.27 E
Kaena Point ≻	**229c**	21.35 N	158.17 W
Kaeo	**172**	35.06 S	173.47 E
Kaesŏng	**98**	37.59 N	126.33 E
Kāf	**128**	31.24 N	37.24 E
Kafakumba	**152**	9.41 S	23.44 E
Kafan, S.S.S.R.	**84**	39.11 N	46.08 E
Kafan, S.S.S.R.	**84**	39.13 N	46.24 E
Kafanchan	**150**	9.36 N	8.17 E
Kaffraria □[9]	**158**	31.30 S	28.30 E
Kaffrine	**150**	14.06 N	15.33 W
Kafia Kingi	**140**	9.16 N	24.25 E
Kafin	**150**	9.30 N	7.04 E
Kafinda	**154**	12.39 S	30.20 E
Kafin Madaki	**150**	10.41 N	9.46 E
Kafirévs, Ákra ≻	**38**	38.09 N	24.36 E
Kafirnigan ≃	**120**	36.58 N	68.02 E
Kafo ≃	**154**	1.08 N	31.05 E
Kafr ad-Dawwār	**142**	31.08 N	30.07 E
Kafr ad-Difrāwī	**142**	31.03 N	30.40 E
Kafr al-'Ā'id	**142**	30.27 N	31.35 E
Kafr al-Baṭṭīkh	**142**	31.24 N	31.44 E
Kafr al-Jarā'idah	**142**	31.13 N	31.16 E
Kafr ash-Shaykh	**142**	31.07 N	30.56 E
Kafr ash-Shaykh □[4]	**142**	31.15 N	30.50 E
Kafrat Ṭā'il Mūsā	**142**	30.53 N	29.44 E
Kafr at-Tamīmī	**142**	30.37 N	31.21 E
Kafr az-Zayyāt	**142**	30.49 N	30.49 E
Kafr Diyamā	**142**	30.48 N	30.52 E
Kafr el-Zaiyat → Kafr az-Zayyāt	**142**	30.49 N	30.49 E
Kafr Ḥakīm	**273c**	30.05 N	31.07 E
Kafr Ḥūnah	**132**	33.29 N	35.35 E
Kafr Kanna	**132**	32.45 N	35.20 E
Kafr Kilā al-Bāb	**142**	30.41 N	31.09 E
Kafr Nabrakh	**132**	33.42 N	35.38 E
Kafr Naffākh	**132**	33.04 N	35.44 E
Kafr Nāsij	**132**	33.09 N	36.03 E
Kafr Rabī'	**142**	30.42 N	30.50 E
Kafr Sa'd	**142**	31.19 N	31.39 E
Kafr Salīm	**142**	31.09 N	30.06 E
Kafr Ṣaqr	**142**	30.48 N	31.37 E
Kafr Shanawān	**142**	30.30 N	31.01 E
Kafr Shibīn	**142**	30.18 N	31.18 E
Kafr Shīmā	**132**	33.49 N	35.32 E
Kafr Shukr	**142**	30.33 N	31.16 E
Kafr Sūsah	**132**	33.29 N	36.16 E
Kafr Takhārīm	**130**	36.07 N	36.31 E
Kafr Ṭarkhān al-Gharbī	**142**	29.29 N	31.13 E
Kafr Yasif	**132**	32.57 N	35.10 E
Kafue	**154**	15.47 S	28.11 E
Kafue ≃	**154**	15.56 S	28.55 E
Kafue Flats ≚	**154**	15.40 S	27.25 E
Kafue Gorge V	**154**	15.54 S	28.34 E
Kafue National Park ♦	**154**	15.00 S	25.45 E
Kafulwe Mission	**154**	9.00 S	29.02 E
Kafumba	**152**	5.23 S	18.55 E
Kafwira	**154**	12.10 S	27.33 E
Kaga	**94**	36.18 N	136.18 E
Kaga Bandoro	**152**	6.59 N	19.11 E
Kagalaska Island I	**180**	51.47 N	176.23 W
Kagal'nickaja	**83**	46.53 N	40.09 E
Kagal'nik	**83**	47.05 N	39.19 E
Kagal'nik ≃	**83**	47.04 N	39.18 E
Kagami	**96**	33.37 N	133.26 E
Kagamigahara	**94**	35.24 N	136.54 E
Kagamil Island I	**180**	53.00 N	169.43 W
Kagamino	**96**	35.05 N	133.56 E
Kāgān, Pāk.	**123**	34.47 N	73.32 E
Kagan, S.S.S.R.	**128**	39.43 N	64.33 E
Kagan Valley V	**123**	34.25 N	73.17 E
Kagarko	**150**	9.29 N	7.41 E
Kagarlyk	**78**	49.51 N	30.50 E
Kagawa	**96**	34.15 N	134.02 E
Kagawa □[5]	**96**	34.15 N	134.00 E
Kagawong, Lake ⊜	**190**	45.49 N	82.18 W
Kagaznagar	**122**	19.18 N	79.50 E
Kåge	**26**	64.50 N	20.59 E
Kagelike	**120**	37.20 N	87.02 E
Kagera (Akagera) ≃	**154**	0.57 S	31.47 E
Kågeröd	**41**	56.01 N	13.06 E
Kâgheṭ ◆[1]	**148**	24.00 N	7.30 W
Kâğıthane ◆[8]	**267b**	41.04 N	28.58 E
Kagitumba	**154**	1.04 S	30.27 E
Kağızman	**84**	40.09 N	43.08 E
Käglan ⋀[2]	**40**	59.23 N	15.31 E
Kagmar	**140**	14.24 N	30.25 E
Kagopal	**146**	8.17 S	16.27 E
Kagoshima	**92**	31.36 N	130.33 E
Kagoshima □[5]	**93b**	29.00 N	129.30 E
Kagoshima-wan ⊂	**92**	31.25 N	130.38 E
Kagran ◆[8]	**264b**	48.15 N	16.27 E
Kagul	**78**	45.54 N	28.11 E
Kagulu	**154**	1.15 N	33.18 E
Kagyo-ri	**98**	34.25 N	126.48 E
Kahalīya, Jabal ∧	**142**	29.55 N	32.09 E
Kahaluu	**229c**	21.27 N	157.50 W
Kahama	**154**	3.50 S	32.36 E
Kahana Bay ⊂	**229c**	21.34 N	157.52 W
Kahayan ≃	**112**	3.20 S	114.04 E
Kahe	**154**	3.30 S	37.26 E
Kahemba	**152**	7.17 S	19.00 E
Kahia	**154**	6.21 S	28.24 E
Kahiu Point ⊂	**229a**	21.13 N	156.58 W
Kaḥk	**142**	29.25 N	30.38 E
Kahl ≃	**56**	50.04 N	9.00 E
Kahla	**54**	50.48 N	11.35 E
Kahl am Main	**56**	50.04 N	9.00 E
Kahlenberg ∧	**264b**	48.16 N	16.21 E
Kahler Asten ∧	**56**	51.11 N	8.29 E
Kahlersberg ∧	**64**	47.32 N	13.02 E
Kāhna	**123**	31.22 N	74.22 E
Kahnūj	**128**	27.58 N	57.45 E
Kahoka	**194**	40.25 N	91.43 W
Kahoku, Nihon	**96**	33.39 N	133.47 E
Kahoku, Nihon	**96**	33.06 N	130.41 E
Kahoku-gata ⊜	**94**	36.40 N	136.41 E
Kahoolawe I	**229a**	20.33 N	156.37 W
Kahouanne, Îlet à I	**241o**	16.22 N	61.47 W
Kahoué, Mont ∧	**150**	7.06 N	7.15 W
Kahramanmaraş	**130**	37.36 N	36.55 E
Kahraman Maraş □[4]	**130**	38.00 N	37.05 E
Kahror Pakka	**123**	29.37 N	71.55 E
Kahshe Lake ⊜	**212**	44.52 N	79.16 W
Kâhta	**130**	37.46 N	38.36 E
Kahuku	**229c**	21.40 N	157.57 W
Kahuku Point ≻	**229c**	21.43 N	157.59 W
Kahului	**229a**	20.54 N	156.28 W
Kahului Airport ⊠	**229a**	20.54 N	156.26 W
Kahului Bay ⊂	**229a**	20.54 N	156.28 W
Kahurangi Point ≻	**172**	40.47 S	172.13 E
Kahūta	**123**	33.35 N	73.23 E
Kahuzi-Biega, Parc National de ♦	**154**	1.50 N	28.40 E
Kahyŏn-bong ∧	**271b**	37.38 N	126.39 E
Kahyŏn-ni	**271b**	37.32 N	126.44 E
Kai	**164**	2.15 S	136.32 E
Kai, Kepulauan II	**164**	5.35 S	132.45 E
Kai, Tanjung ≻	**112**	2.52 S	118.45 E
Kaia, Wādī V	**140**	11.31 N	24.15 E
Kaiai, Jabal ∧	**140**	19.54 N	36.48 E
Kaiama	**150**	9.37 N	3.58 E
Kaiapit	**164**	6.15 S	146.15 E
Kaiapoi	**172**	43.23 S	172.40 E
Kaibab Indian Reservation ◆[4]	**200**	36.55 N	112.40 W
Kaibab Plateau ⋀[1]	**200**	36.30 N	112.15 W
Kaibara	**96**	35.08 N	135.05 E
Kai Beab	**164**	7.29 S	139.40 E
Kaibing	**61**	47.12 N	15.50 E
Kaibito Plateau ⋀[1]	**200**	36.40 N	111.20 W
Kaichengqiao	**100**	31.18 N	117.44 E
Kaida	**94**	35.56 N	137.36 E
Kaidori	**268**	35.37 N	139.27 E
Kaidu ≃	**90**	41.55 N	86.38 E
Kaiedin	**140**	9.45 N	32.11 E
Kaieteur Fall ∟	**246**	5.10 N	59.28 W
Kaifeng	**98**	34.51 N	114.21 E
Kaifu	**96**	33.35 N	134.21 E
Kaifu ≃	**96**	33.35 N	134.22 E
Kaihe	**98**	35.42 N	116.20 E
Kaihu	**172**	35.46 S	173.42 E
Kaihua	**100**	29.09 N	118.23 E
Kai Iwi	**172**	39.51 S	174.56 E
Kaijian	**102**	23.42 N	111.48 E
Kaijiang	**102**	31.05 N	107.55 E
Kaijo → Kaesŏng	**98**	37.59 N	126.33 E
Kai Kecil I	**164**	5.45 S	132.40 E
Kaikohe	**172**	35.25 S	173.48 E
Kaikoura	**172**	42.25 S	173.41 E
Kaikoura Peninsula ≻[1]	**172**	42.26 S	173.42 E
Kaikukang	**89**	53.07 N	124.46 E
Kailahun	**150**	8.17 N	10.34 W
Kailāshahar	**120**	24.20 N	92.01 E
Kaili	**102**	26.35 N	107.55 E
Kailu	**89**	43.36 N	121.14 E
Kailua	**229c**	21.24 N	157.44 W
Kailua Bay ⊂	**229c**	21.25 N	157.44 W
Kailua Kona	**229d**	19.22 N	155.59 W
Kaim ≃	**164**	6.40 S	141.45 E
Kaimai Range ⋀	**172**	37.45 S	175.55 E
Kaïmaktsalán ∧	**38**	40.58 N	21.48 E
Kaimana	**164**	3.39 S	133.45 E
Kaimanawa Mountains ⋀	**172**	39.15 S	175.54 E
Kaiman-Inseln → Cayman Islands □[2]	**238**	19.30 N	80.40 W
Kaimenshan	**104**	41.03 N	123.08 E
Kaimganj	**124**	27.34 N	79.21 E
Kaimon-dake ∧	**92**	31.11 N	130.32 E
Kain	**50**	50.38 N	3.22 E
Käina	**76**	58.50 N	22.45 E
Kainab ≃	**158**	28.31 S	19.35 E
Kainach ≃	**61**	46.54 N	15.31 E
Kainan, Nihon	**96**	34.09 N	135.12 E
Kainan, Nihon	**96**	33.36 N	134.22 E
Kainantu	**164**	6.15 S	145.55 E
Kainda	**85**	42.50 N	73.41 E
Kai-Ndunda	**152**	5.42 S	12.42 E
Kaingan ≃	**115a**	7.44 S	107.54 E
Kainji Lake ⊜[1]	**150**	10.30 N	4.35 E
Kaioba	**112**	5.20 S	122.37 E
Kaipara Harbour ⊂	**172**	36.25 S	174.13 E
Kaiparowits Plateau ⋀[1]	**200**	37.20 N	111.15 W

DEUTSCH

Name	Seite	Breite°′	Länge°′ E = Ost
Kaiping, Zhg.	**102**	22.23 N	112.35 E
Kaiping, Zhg.	**105**	39.41 N	118.16 E
Kaipuri, Pulau I	**164**	1.51 S	137.01 E
Kairābani	**126**	24.08 N	87.02 E
Kairaku-en ♦	**94**	36.22 N	140.27 E
Kairāna	**124**	29.24 N	77.12 E
Kairatu	**164**	3.21 S	128.22 E
Kairiru Island I	**164**	3.20 S	143.35 E
Kairo → Al-Qāhirah	**142**	30.03 N	31.15 E
Kairouan	**148**	35.41 N	10.07 E
Kairouan □[8]	**148**	35.30 N	9.55 E
Kairuku	**164**	8.50 S	146.35 E
Kairy	**78**	46.57 N	33.43 E
Kaisarganj	**124**	27.15 N	81.33 E
Kaisariani	**267c**	37.58 N	23.47 E
Kaisariani Monastery ʋ[1]	**267c**	37.58 N	23.47 E
Kaisergebirge ⋀	**64**	47.36 N	12.20 E
Kaisermühlen ◆[8]	**264b**	48.14 N	16.26 E
Kaiser Pass)(	**226**	37.17 N	119.06 W
Kaisersesch	**56**	50.14 N	7.08 E
Kaiserslautern	**56**	49.26 N	7.46 E
Kaiserstuhl ⋀[2]	**58**	48.06 N	7.40 E
Kaiserswerth ◆[8]	**263**	51.18 N	6.44 E
Kaiser-Wilhelm-Museum ʋ	**263**	51.20 N	6.34 E
Kaishantun	**98**	42.43 N	129.43 E
Kaisheim	**56**	48.46 N	10.48 E
Kaišiadorys	**76**	54.52 N	24.27 E
Kait, Tanjung ≻	**112**	3.14 S	106.05 E
Kaita	**96**	34.20 N	132.32 E
Kaitaia	**172**	35.07 S	173.16 E
Kaitaichi-chūtonchi, Rikujō-jieitai- ■	**96**	34.21 N	132.32 E
Kai Tak Airport ⊠	**271d**	22.20 N	114.12 E
Kaitangata	**172**	46.18 S	169.51 E
Kaitersberg ⋀	**60**	49.11 N	12.57 E
Kaithal	**124**	29.48 N	76.23 E
Kaituma ≃	**246**	8.11 N	59.41 W
Kaiwaka	**172**	36.10 S	174.27 E
Kaiwatu	**164**	8.07 S	127.49 E
Kaiwi Channel ⊔	**229b**	21.15 N	157.30 W
Kaixian	**102**	31.13 N	108.25 E
Kaiyang	**102**	26.58 N	106.40 E
Kaiyuan, Zhg.	**102**	23.44 N	103.11 E
Kaiyuan, Zhg.	**104**	42.32 N	124.01 E
Kaiyuancheng	**98**	42.37 N	124.04 E
Kaiyuh Mountains ⋀	**180**	64.00 N	158.00 W
Kaizhou	**104**	41.22 N	121.19 E
Kaizu	**94**	35.13 N	136.38 E
Kaizuka	**96**	34.27 N	135.21 E
Kaja, Wādī (Ouadi Kadja) V	**146**	12.02 N	22.28 E
Kajaani	**26**	64.14 N	27.41 E
Kajabbi	**166**	20.02 S	140.02 E
Kajakī, Band-e ⊜[1]	**128**	32.22 N	65.16 E
Kajang, Indon.	**112**	5.20 S	120.21 E
Kajang, Malay.	**114**	2.59 N	101.47 E
Kajang, Gunong ∧	**114**	2.46 N	104.09 E
Kajasan	**86**	55.12 N	62.16 E
Kajasula	**84**	44.19 N	44.59 E
Kajen	**115a**	7.02 S	109.34 E
Kajgy	**86**	50.55 N	64.43 E
Kajiado	**154**	1.51 S	36.47 E
Kajikazawa	**94**	35.33 N	138.27 E
Kajiki	**92**	31.44 N	130.40 E
Kājlāgarh	**126**	22.02 N	87.47 E
Kajmanačicha	**86**	53.32 N	75.11 E
Kajmonovo	**88**	56.50 N	104.54 E
Kajmysovy	**86**	59.48 N	76.31 E
Kajnar	**86**	49.12 N	77.25 E
Kajo Kaji	**154**	3.53 N	31.40 E
Kajrakkum	**85**	40.16 N	69.49 E
Kajrakkumskoje vodochranilišce ⊜[1]	**85**	40.20 N	70.10 E
Kajrakty	**86**	48.31 N	73.14 E
Kajsackoje	**80**	49.44 N	46.51 E
Kājū ≃	**128**	25.34 N	61.13 E
Kājulia	**126**	23.01 N	89.57 E
Kajuru	**150**	10.21 N	7.40 E
Kaka, Centraf.	**140**	6.01 N	26.30 E
Kākā, Sūd.	**140**	10.36 N	32.11 E
Kaka, Lae o ≻	**229a**	20.31 N	156.33 W
Kakabeka Falls ∟	**190**	48.24 N	89.37 W
Kakabia, Pulau I	**112**	6.54 S	122.13 E
Kakadu National Park ♦	**164**	13.00 S	132.45 E
Kakagi Lake ⊜	**184**	49.13 N	93.52 W
Kakamas	**158**	28.45 S	20.33 E
Kakamega	**154**	0.17 N	34.45 E
Kakamigahara	**94**	35.24 N	136.54 E
Kakana	**110**	9.07 N	92.49 E
Kakanui Mountains ⋀	**172**	45.09 S	170.26 E
Kaka Point	**172**	46.23 S	169.47 E
Kakaramea	**172**	39.43 S	174.27 E
Kakasa	**164**	9.20 S	148.45 E
Kakata	**150**	6.35 N	10.19 W
Kakatahi	**172**	39.41 S	175.20 E
Kākdwīp	**126**	21.53 N	88.11 E
Kake, Nihon	**96**	34.36 N	132.19 E
Kake, Ak., U.S.	**180**	56.58 N	133.56 W
Kakegawa	**94**	34.46 N	138.01 E
Kakehashi ≃	**94**	36.25 N	136.25 E
Kakelwe	**154**	4.49 S	29.00 E
Kakenge	**152**	4.51 S	21.55 E
Kakeya	**96**	35.11 N	132.49 E
Kakhonak	**180**	59.26 N	154.51 W
Kakhra	**126**	21.38 N	87.27 E
Kākī	**128**	28.19 N	51.34 E
Kākināda	**122**	16.56 N	82.13 E
Kakino	**80**	55.12 N	44.53 E
Kakinoki	**96**	34.26 N	131.52 E
Kakisa Lake ⊜	**176**	60.55 N	117.40 W
Kakizaki	**92**	37.15 N	138.25 E
Kako ≃, Guy.	**246**	5.46 N	60.35 W
Kako ≃, Nihon	**96**	34.44 N	134.49 E
Kakoaka	**156**	18.40 S	24.22 E
Kakogawa	**96**	34.46 N	134.51 E
Kakrāla	**272a**	28.33 N	77.25 E
Kāksa	**126**	23.28 N	87.28 E
Kaktovik	**180**	70.08 N	143.37 W
Kakuda	**92**	37.58 N	140.47 E
Kakui-shima I	**96**	34.43 N	134.19 E
Kakuma	**154**	3.43 N	34.52 E
Kakunodate	**92**	39.35 N	140.34 E
Kakus ≃	**112**	2.46 N	113.01 E
Kakwa ≃	**182**	54.36 N	118.28 W
Kala	**146**	12.05 N	14.27 E
Kala ≃	**122**	8.18 N	79.50 E
Kalaa Kebira	**148**	35.52 N	10.32 E
Kalaallit Nunaat → Greenland □[2]	**16**	70.00 N	40.00 W
Kalaa Sghira	**36**	35.49 N	10.33 E
Kālābāgh	**123**	32.58 N	71.34 E
Kalabahi	**112**	8.13 S	124.31 E
Kalabáka	**38**	39.42 N	21.43 E
Kalabakan	**112**	4.25 N	117.29 E
Kalabo	**152**	14.57 S	22.40 E
Kalabula	**86**	43.24 N	83.06 E
Kalač	**78**	50.25 N	41.01 E
Kalačinsk	**86**	55.03 N	74.34 E
Kalač-Kurtlak	**80**	49.00 N	42.26 E
Kalač-na-Donu	**80**	48.43 N	43.31 E
Kalačskaja vozvyšennost' ⋀[1]	**80**	50.30 N	41.30 E
Kaladan ≃	**110**	20.09 N	92.57 E
Kaladar	**212**	44.39 N	77.07 W
Kalae	**229a**	21.10 N	157.00 W
Ka Lae ≻	**229d**	18.55 N	155.41 W
Kalaena ≃	**112**	2.40 S	120.53 E
Kalagan	**89**	50.30 N	119.55 E
Kalagwe	**110**	22.31 N	96.31 E
Kalahari Desert ◆[2]	**156**	24.00 S	21.30 E
Kalahari Gemsbok National Park ♦	**156**	25.30 S	20.30 E
Kalaheo	**229b**	21.55 N	159.31 W
Kālaia	**126**	22.23 N	90.36 E
Kalai-Chumb	**85**	38.28 N	70.46 E
Kalai-Mor	**128**	35.39 N	62.33 E

Symbols in the index entries represent the broad categories identified in the key at the right. Symbols with superior numbers (⋀[1]) identify subcategories (see complete key on page *I · 1).*

Symbole im Register stellen die rechts im Schlüssel erklärten Kategorien dar. Symbole mit hochgestellten Ziffern (⋀[1]) bezeichnen Unterabteilungen einer Kategorie (vgl. vollständiger Schlüssel auf Seite *I · 1).*

Los símbolos incluídos en el texto del índice representan las grandes categorias identificadas con la clave a la derecha. Los símbolos con numeros en su parte superior (⋀[1]) identifican las subcategorías (véase la clave completa en la página *I · 1).*

Les symboles de l'index représentent les catégories indiquées dans la légende à droite. Les symboles suivis d'un indice (⋀[1]) représentent des sous-catégories (voir légende complète à la page *I · 1).*

Os símbolos incluídos no texto do índice representam as grandes categorias identificadas com a chave à direita. Os símbolos com números em sua parte superior (⋀[1]) identificam as subcategorias (veja-se a chave completa à página *I · 1).*

	English	Deutsch	Español	Français	Português
∧	Mountain	Berg	Montaña	Montagne	Montanha
⋀	Mountains	Gebirge	Montañas	Montagnes	Montanhas
)(	Pass	Paß	Paso	Col	Passo
V	Valley, Canyon	Tal, Cañon	Valle, Cañón	Vallée, Canyon	Vale, Canhão
≚	Plain	Ebene	Llano	Plaine	Planície
≻	Cape	Kap	Cabo	Cap	Cabo
I	Island	Insel	Isla	Île	Ilha
II	Islands	Inseln	Islas	Îles	Ilhas
◆	Other Topographic Features	Andere Topographische Objekte	Otros Elementos Topográficos	Autres données topographiques	Outros acidentes topográficos

ESPAÑOL	FRANÇAIS	PORTUGUÊS
Nombre · Página · Lat.°' · Long.°'/W=Oeste	Nom · Page · Lat.°' · Long.°'/W=Ouest	Nome · Página · Lat.°' · Long.°'/W=Oeste

Columna 1

Nombre	Pág.	Lat.	Long.
Kalais	80	52.38 N	42.38 E
Kalaiyā	124	27.02 N	85.00 E
Kalajka	88	58.28 N	111.46 E
Kalajoki	26	64.15 N	23.57 E
Kalajoki ≈	26	64.17 N	23.55 E
Kalakarnate	156	20.39 S	27.21 E
Kalakan	88	55.08 N	116.45 E
Kalakan ≈	88	55.07 N	116.46 E
Kalakepen	114	2.45 N	97.50 E
Kalām	123	35.32 N	72.35 E
Kalama, Wa., U.S.	224	46.00 N	122.50 W
Kalama, Zaïre	154	2.55 S	28.33 E
Kalama ≈	224	46.02 N	122.52 W
Kalama, Pulau I	112	3.15 N	125.28 E
Kalamai	38	37.04 N	22.07 E
Kalamákion	267c	37.55 N	23.43 E
Kalamalka Lake ⊜	182	50.09 N	119.22 W
Kalamariá	38	40.35 N	22.58 E
Kalamazoo	216	42.17 N	85.35 W
Kalamazoo ≈⁶	216	42.14 N	85.32 W
Kalamazoo □⁶	216	42.40 N	86.10 W
Kalamazoo, North Branch ≈	216	42.14 N	84.44 W
Kalamazoo, South Branch ≈	216	42.14 N	84.44 W
Kalamazoo Lake c	216	42.39 N	86.13 W
Kalamb	122	19.03 N	73.57 E
Kalamba	152	0.26 S	18.17 E
Kalambau, Pulau I	112	4.55 S	115.39 E
Kalambo Falls ∟	154	8.36 S	31.14 E
Kalamboli	272c	19.01 N	73.06 E
Kalamitskij zaliv c	78	45.05 N	33.23 E
Kalamo	216	42.32 N	85.01 W
Kalampáka	38	39.42 N	21.39 E
Kalampising	112	3.44 N	116.42 E
Kalamunda	168a	31.57 S	116.03 E
Kalamunda National Park ♦	168a	31.59 S	116.04 E
Kalana	150	10.47 N	8.12 W
Kalančak	78	46.16 N	33.17 E
Kalandula	152	9.06 S	15.57 E
Kalange-Bushimaie ≈	152	7.55 S	23.11 E
Kalanguj	88	51.01 N	116.31 E
Kalankalan	150	1.07 N	8.54 W
Kalannie	162	30.21 S	117.04 E
Kalanshiyū ar-Ramlī al-Kabīr, Sarīr ±⁸	146	28.00 N	23.00 E
Kalao, Pulau I	112	7.18 S	120.58 E
Kalaong	116	6.04 N	124.28 E
Kalaotoa, Pulau I	112	7.22 S	121.47 E
Kalapana	229d	19.21 N	154.58 W
Kalāpāra	126	21.59 N	90.14 E
Kalar ≈	88	55.23 N	116.18 E
Kalar, Küh-e ∧	132	47.16 N	28.19 E
Kalarash	78	47.16 N	28.19 E
Kālärne	26	62.59 N	16.05 E
Käläroa	26	22.52 N	89.02 E
Kalasarv	84	39.11 N	48.03 E
Kalasi	86	48.43 N	86.59 E
Kalasin, Indon.	112	0.12 N	114.16 E
Kalasin, Thai	110	16.29 N	103.30 E
Kalašnikovo	76	57.17 N	35.13 E
Kalāt	120	29.02 N	66.35 E
Kalatungan Mountain ∧	116	7.58 N	124.47 E
Kalaupapa National Historical Park ♦	229a	21.11 N	156.59 W
Kalaupapa Peninsula ⊁¹	229a	21.12 N	156.58 W
Kalauri	84	41.49 N	45.42 E
Kalaus ≈	80	45.43 N	44.07 E
Kalaus-Kr'akovka	83	48.46 N	38.52 E
Kalävárdha	38	36.20 N	27.57 E
Kalávrita	38	38.01 N	22.06 E
Kalaw	110	20.38 N	96.34 E
Kalawao ⊙⁸	229a	21.12 N	156.58 W
Kal'azin	76	57.15 N	37.52 E
Kalb, Nahr al- ≈	132	33.57 N	35.35 E
Kalb, Ra's al- ⊁	144	14.02 N	48.41 E
Kalbā'	128	25.03 N	56.21 E
Kalbar	171a	27.56 S	152.37 E
Kalbarri	162	27.42 S	114.09 E
Kalbarri National Park ♦	162	27.45 S	114.25 E
Kalbe	54	52.40 N	11.25 E
Kalbinskij chrebet ∧	86	49.10 N	83.00 E
Kalchãs	29	29.21 N	69.42 E
Kal'čik ≈	83	47.07 N	37.36 E
Kaldırım ≈	267b	41.10 N	29.12 E
Kaldygaity ≈	80	49.20 N	52.38 E
Kale, Tür.	130	36.14 N	29.59 E
Kale, Tür.	130	37.26 N	28.51 E
Kalecik, Tür.	130	40.23 N	39.39 E
Kalecik, Tür.	130	37.17 N	39.02 E
Kaleden	182	49.23 N	119.35 W
Kaledupa, Pulau I	112	5.32 S	123.47 E
Kalegauk Island I	110	15.32 N	97.40 E
Kalehe	154	2.06 S	28.55 E
Kaleindaung c	110	18.50 N	94.00 E
Kalema, Tan.	154	.12 S	31.50 E
Kalema, Zaïre	152	4.08 S	24.15 E
Kalemie (Albertville)	154	5.56 S	29.12 E
Kalemyo	120	23.12 N	94.10 E
Kalene Hill	152	1.11 S	24.10 E
Kaleščatcha	89	49.35 N	39.55 E
Kaletwa	110	22.45 N	92.48 E
Kalety	30	50.34 N	18.54 E
Kalevala	24	65.13 N	31.08 E
Kale Water ≈	46	55.32 N	2.28 W
Kaleybar	84	38.47 N	47.02 E
Kalfafell	24	63.58 N	17.40 W
Kalgačicha	24	63.20 N	36.44 E
Kalgan (→ Zhangjiakou, Zhg.)	162	34.53 S	118.01 E
Kalgin Island I	228	40.50 N	151.55 W
Kalgoorlie	162	30.45 S	121.28 E
Kalhe	272c	18.52 N	73.06 E
Kāli	150	12.10 N	11.29 W
Kāli ≈¹	126	23.40 N	89.12 E
Kāliā	126	23.03 N	89.38 E
Kāliāganj	124	25.38 N	88.19 E
Kāliāghaj ≈	124	21.50 N	87.50 E
Kāliāganj	126	24.05 N	90.14 E
Kaliakra, nos ⊁	38	43.21 N	28.27 E
Kalianda	115a	5.45 S	105.38 E
Kalianget	115a	7.03 S	113.56 E
Kalibok, ozero ⊜	86	52.54 N	70.40 E
Kālibhīt Hills ∧²	124	22.10 N	77.30 E
Kalida	216	40.59 N	84.12 W
Kalifornien, Golf von de c	232	28.00 N	112.00 W
Kāli Gandakī ≈	124	27.42 N	84.25 E
Kāliganj, Bngl.	126	23.43 N	90.15 E
Kāliganj, Bngl.	126	23.25 N	89.38 E
Kāliganj, Bngl.	126	22.58 N	88.19 E
Kāliganj, India	124	23.44 N	88.14 E
Kalihiwai ≈	229b	22.13 N	159.26 W
Kālijati	115a	6.32 S	107.40 E
Kālīkāpur, Bngl.	124	22.43 N	89.27 E
Kālīkāpur, Bngl.	126	23.46 N	89.55 E
Kālīkāpur, India	272b	22.39 N	88.32 E
Kalikino, S.S.S.R.	76	52.57 N	39.08 E
Kalikino, S.S.S.R.	80	52.55 N	54.05 E
Kalima, Zhg.	104	41.32 N	122.40 E
Kalimantan (→ Borneo) □⁴	112	0.30 N	114.00 E
Kalimantan Barat □⁴	112	0.30 N	110.00 E
Kalimantan Selatan □⁴	112	2.30 S	115.30 E
Kalimantan Tengah □⁴	112	2.00 S	113.30 E

Columna 2

Nom	Page	Lat.	Long.
Kalimantan Timur □⁴	112	1.30 N	116.30 E
Kálimnos	38	36.57 N	26.59 E
Kálimnos I	38	37.00 N	27.00 E
Kálimpang	124	27.04 N	88.29 E
Kalina, Pointe de ⊳	273b	4.18 S	15.16 E
Kālinadi ≈	122	14.50 N	74.08 E
Kālinagar	126	22.26 N	88.51 E
Kalinga-Apayao □⁴	116	17.50 N	121.10 E
Kalinga Bil ⊜	272b	22.33 N	88.33 E
Kalinin, S.S.S.R.	80	47.11 N	42.10 E
Kalinin, S.S.S.R.	82	56.52 N	35.55 E
Kalinin □⁴	82	56.45 N	36.30 E
Kalininabad	85	39.45 N	69.08 E
Kaliningrad (Königsberg), S.S.S.R.	82	54.43 N	20.30 E
Kaliningrad, S.S.S.R.	82	55.55 N	37.49 E
Kalinino, S.S.S.R.	78	45.07 N	39.00 E
Kalinino, S.S.S.R.	80	46.21 N	48.53 E
Kalinino, S.S.S.R.	83	47.07 N	37.28 E
Kalinino, S.S.S.R.	84	41.07 N	44.17 E
Kalinino, S.S.S.R.	86	57.20 N	56.20 E
Kalinino, S.S.S.R.	89	49.24 N	129.20 E
Kalininsk, S.S.S.R.	80	51.30 N	44.28 E
Kalininsk, S.S.S.R.	85	42.29 N	72.06 E
Kalininskaja, S.S.S.R.	78	45.29 N	38.40 E
Kalininskaja, S.S.S.R.	80	47.52 N	42.15 E
Kalininskij	83	48.01 N	39.36 E
Kalininskoje, S.S.S.R.	78	47.07 N	32.59 E
Kalininskoje, S.S.S.R.	78	42.50 N	73.49 E
Kalinkoviči	78	52.08 N	29.21 E
Kalino	154	11.12 S	33.12 E
Kalinovik	38	43.31 N	18.26 E
Kalinovka, S.S.S.R.	78	50.14 N	30.14 E
Kalinovka, S.S.S.R.	78	51.54 N	34.28 E
Kalinovka, S.S.S.R.	78	49.27 N	28.32 E
Kalinovo	82	54.58 N	55.22 E
Kalinovo, S.S.S.R.	83	48.34 N	38.31 E
Kālipur	272b	22.41 N	88.17 E
Kaliro	154	0.54 N	33.30 E
Kalis	144	8.23 N	49.05 E
Kalisat	115a	8.08 S	113.48 E
→ Kalisz	30	51.46 N	18.06 E
Kāli Sindh ≈	124	25.32 N	76.17 E
Kalispell	202	48.11 N	114.18 W
Kalistraticha	86	52.59 N	83.35 E
Kalisz	30	51.46 N	18.06 E
Kalisz Pomorski	30	53.19 N	15.54 E
Kalitva ≈	78	48.10 N	40.46 E
Kaliua	154	5.04 S	31.48 E
Kaliveli Tank ⊜¹	122	12.05 N	79.50 E
Kaliwiro	115a	7.27 S	109.51 E
Kalivunguv	115a	6.57 S	110.14 E
Kalix	26	65.51 N	23.08 E
Kalixälven ≈	24	65.50 N	23.11 E
Kâlka	123	30.50 N	76.56 E
Kalkåji ◆⁸	272a	28.33 N	77.16 E
Kalkaman	86	51.58 N	76.02 E
Kalkar	130	36.15 N	29.24 E
Kalkar	52	50.36 N	6.46 E
Kalkaska	190	44.44 N	85.10 W
Kalkfeld	156	20.53 S	16.11 E
Kalkfontein	156	22.08 S	20.53 E
Kalkfonteindam ⊜¹	156	29.30 S	25.15 E
Kalkhorst	54	53.58 N	11.02 E
Kalkim	130	39.48 N	27.13 E
Kālkini	126	23.06 N	90.16 E
Kalkmond	158	28.40 N	20.26 E
Kalkranc	156	24.03 N	17.33 E
Kalkrodung ◆⁸	264b	48.08 N	16.15 E
Kalksee	264a	52.26 N	13.46 E
Kalkstaise	158	30.00 S	18.55 E
Kalkum ◆⁸	263	51.18 N	6.46 E
→ Calcutta	126	22.32 N	88.22 E
Kallakkurichichi	122	11.44 N	78.58 E
Kallakoopah Creek ≈	166	27.29 S	138.15 E
Kållandsö I	26	58.40 N	13.09 E
Kallang	271c	1.19 N	103.52 E
Kallar Kahär	123	32.47 N	72.42 E
Kallaste	76	58.39 N	27.09 E
Kallavesi ⊜	26	62.50 N	27.45 E
Kalletal	52	52.06 N	8.54 E
Källfallet	40	59.50 N	15.31 E
Kallhäll	40	59.27 N	17.48 E
Kalliecahoolie Lake ⊜	184	54.14 N	95.29 W
→ Kalisz Pomorski	30	53.19 N	15.54 E
Kallinge	26	56.15 N	15.17 E
Kallithéa	274b	37.53 S	145.22 E
Kallithéa	267c	37.57 N	23.42 E
Kallmünz	60	49.09 N	11.58 E
Kalloch	58	47.01 N	7.14 E
Kalisjön ◆	40	59.33 N	13.00 E
Kalmakkora	86	46.58 N	78.44 E
Kalmakkyrgan ≈	86	46.58 N	64.32 E
Kalmar	26	56.40 N	16.22 E
Kalmar Län □⁶	26	57.20 N	16.02 E
Kalmarsund ⊔	26	56.40 N	16.25 E
Kalmit ∧	58	49.19 N	8.05 E
Kal'mius ≈	83	47.05 N	37.34 E
Kalmthout	50	51.23 N	4.28 E
Kalmyckaja Avtonomnaja Sovetskaja Socialističeskaja Respublika □³	80	46.00 N	46.00 E
Kalmyckie Mysy	80	51.53 N	82.16 E
Kalmykov	80	49.01 N	42.49 E
Kalmykovka, S.S.S.R.	83	49.17 N	38.39 E
Kalmytskij	80	49.03 N	51.47 E
Kalmünz ≈	54	53.48 N	13.42 E
Kaľnibolotis	78	46.01 N	40.28 E
Kalničko Gorje ∧	36	46.10 N	16.24 E
Kalo	164	10.00 S	147.45 E
Kalócfa	60	46.45 N	16.34 E
Kalodnaje ≈	84	38.40 N	48.39 E
Kalofer	38	42.37 N	24.59 E
Kalohi Channel ⊔	229a	21.00 N	156.56 W
Kalol, India	126	6.47 S	25.48 E
Kalol, India	124	23.15 N	72.29 E
Kalol, India	124	22.36 N	73.27 E
Kaloli Point ⊁	229d	19.38 N	154.57 W
Kalomo	154	17.02 S	26.24 E
Kalona	190	41.29 N	91.42 W
Kalone Peak ∧	182	52.38 N	126.37 W
Kalorama	274b	37.49 S	145.22 E
Kaloe Vig c	41	56.15 N	10.25 E
Kalol	85	34.49 N	73.21 E
Kalpi	124	26.07 N	79.44 E
Kal Qal'eh	128	31.39 N	72.33 E
Kalsdorf bei Graz	180	46.59 N	15.28 E
Kalsūbai ∧	122	19.36 N	73.43 E
Kaltan	86	53.30 N	87.17 E
Kalte Herberge ∧	56	50.03 N	7.59 E
Kaltenhouse	56	51.19 N	10.08 E
Kaltenkirchen	56	53.50 N	9.58 E
Kaltenleutgeben	264b	48.07 N	16.08 E
Kaltennordheim	56	50.38 N	10.00 E
Kaltensundheim	56	50.38 N	10.03 E
Kalter Gang ⊔	264b	48.02 N	16.25 E

Columna 3

Nome	Pág.	Lat.	Long.
Kalthof	263	51.26 N	7.40 E
Kal'tino	265a	59.58 N	30.40 E
Kaltungo	146	9.50 N	11.19 E
Kaluga	82	54.31 N	36.16 E
Kaluga □⁴	82	54.45 N	36.30 E
Kalugino, S.S.S.R.	80	48.22 N	51.33 E
Kalugino, S.S.S.R.	82	54.59 N	37.11 E
Kalukalukuang, Pulau I	112	5.14 S	117.38 E
Kālu Khuhar	120	25.08 N	67.46 E
Kalulushi	154	12.50 S	28.03 E
Kalumba, Mount ∧	166	31.49 S	146.22 E
Kalumburu	164	14.18 S	126.39 E
Kalumburu Aboriginal Reserve ♦	164	14.15 S	126.50 E
Kalundborg	41	55.41 N	11.06 E
Kalundborg Fjord c	41	55.41 N	11.00 E
Kālundri	272c	18.59 N	73.08 E
Kalundu, Zaïre	154	3.26 S	29.08 E
Kalundu, Zam.	154	10.16 S	29.24 E
Kalungwishi ≈	154	9.01 S	28.57 E
Kalūr Kot	123	32.09 N	71.16 E
Kaluš	78	49.03 N	24.23 E
Kalutara	122	6.35 N	79.58 E
Kalvåg	26	61.46 N	4.53 E
Kalvarija	76	54.21 N	23.14 E
Kalvaz	84	38.39 N	48.18 E
Kalvehave	41	55.00 N	12.10 E
Kälviä	26	63.52 N	23.26 E
Kalwa	272c	19.12 N	72.59 E
Kalwang	61	47.26 N	14.46 E
Kalwaria Zebrzydowska	30	49.52 N	19.41 E
Kalyān	122	19.15 N	73.09 E
Kalyāndurg	122	14.33 N	77.06 E
Kam ≈	146	8.15 N	11.00 E
Kama, Mya.	110	19.02 N	95.06 E
Kama, S.S.S.R.	86	56.19 N	54.06 E
Kama, S.S.S.R.	86	60.08 N	62.10 E
Kama, Zaïre	154	3.32 S	27.07 E
Kama ≈, S.S.S.R.	72	55.45 N	52.00 E
Kama ≈, S.S.S.R.	86	55.35 N	76.54 E
Kamachumu	154	1.35 S	31.37 E
Kamado-zaki ⊁	96	33.03 N	132.02 E
Kamae	92	32.48 N	131.56 E
Kamagaya	94	35.45 N	140.01 E
Kamaki Point ⊁	229a	20.46 N	156.50 W
Kamaishi	92	39.16 N	141.53 E
Kama-iwa I	174f	24.47 N	141.17 E
Kamajai	76	55.49 N	25.30 E
Kamakou ∧	229a	21.07 N	156.52 W
Kamakura	94	35.19 N	139.33 E
Kamakwie	150	9.30 N	12.14 W
Kamal	115a	7.10 S	112.42 E
Kamālia	123	30.44 N	72.39 E
Kamamaung	110	17.29 N	97.40 E
Kāman, India	124	27.39 N	77.16 E
Kaman, Tür.	130	39.22 N	33.44 E
Kamanashi ≈	94	35.33 N	138.28 E
Kamango	154	.39 N	29.53 E
Kamaniskeg Lake ⊜	212	45.25 N	77.42 W
Kamanjab	156	19.35 S	14.51 E
Kamapanda	152	12.00 S	24.10 E
Kamara Forest ♦	152	11.26 N	19.00 E
Kamaran I	144	15.21 N	42.35 E
Kamaran, Hadjer ∧	146	12.41 N	21.46 E
Kamarang ≈	246	5.53 N	60.35 W
Kāmāreddi	122	18.19 N	78.21 E
Kāmārhāti	272b	22.40 N	88.22 E
Kāmārkhāli Ghāt	126	23.32 N	89.33 E
Kāmārkunda	272b	22.49 N	88.31 E
Kamas	200	40.38 N	111.16 W
Kamata ◆⁸	268	35.33 N	139.43 E
Kamatsi Lake ⊜	184	56.10 N	102.15 W
Kamay	196	33.51 N	98.48 W
Kamba	150	11.53 N	3.36 E
Kamba Kota	152	7.10 N	17.54 E
Kambalda	162	31.12 S	121.40 E
Kambam	122	9.44 N	77.18 E
Kambanga	112	1.42 S	100.42 E
Kambar	120	27.36 N	68.00 E
Kambara	94	35.07 N	138.36 E
Kambara Island I	175g	18.57 S	178.57 W
Kambara-tunnel ≈⁵	94	35.02 N	138.31 E
Kambarka	86	56.17 N	54.12 E
Kambia	150	9.07 N	12.55 W
Kamboké	152	8.45 N	1.36 E
Kambolé Mission	154	10.52 S	26.38 E
Kambu	115b	8.23 S	118.20 E
Kambuta	152	7.18 S	22.50 E
Kamčatka ≈	94	56.15 N	162.30 E
Kamčatka, poluostrov (Kamchatka) ⊁¹	74	56.00 N	160.00 E
Kamčatskij poluostrov ⊁¹	74	56.15 N	163.00 E
Kamčatskij zaliv c	74	55.35 N	162.21 E
Kamchatka → Kamčatka, poluostrov ⊁¹	74	56.00 N	160.00 E
Kâmchay Méa	110	11.35 N	105.40 E
Kāmdebpur, India	272b	22.54 N	88.20 E
Kāmdebpur, India	272b	22.47 N	88.30 E
Kâmdeysh	123	35.24 N	71.20 E
Kameari	268	35.46 N	139.51 E
Kameda	92	37.52 N	139.07 E
Kamei	158	26.38 S	24.58 E
Kamegamori ∧	96	33.47 N	133.12 E
Kameido ◆⁸	268	35.42 N	139.49 E
Kamelik ≈	80	52.06 N	49.30 E
Kamen, B.R.D.	54	51.35 N	7.39 E
Kamen', S.S.S.R.	78	55.01 N	28.53 E
Kamen', gora ∧	74	69.06 N	94.48 E
Kamenec	76	52.28 N	26.20 E
Kamenec-Podol'skij	76	48.41 N	26.36 E
Kamenický Šenov	56	50.45 N	14.29 E
Kamenjak, Rt ⊁	36	44.47 N	13.55 E
Kamenka, S.S.S.R.	78	48.03 N	26.42 E
Kamenka, S.S.S.R.	78	50.07 N	39.25 E
Kamenka, S.S.S.R.	78	45.22 N	28.42 E
Kamenka, S.S.S.R.	80	53.11 N	44.05 E
Kamenka, S.S.S.R.	80	50.56 N	45.30 E
Kamenka, S.S.S.R.	80	51.19 N	42.46 E
Kamennogorsk	76	60.58 N	30.40 E
Kamenniyovskij	80	54.31 N	36.58 E
Kamen'-na-Obi	86	53.47 N	81.20 E
Kamennomostskij	84	44.18 N	40.12 E

Columna 4

Nome	Pág.	Lat.	Long.
Kamennye Mogily, zapovednik ♦	78	47.18 N	37.04 E
Kamennyj Brod, S.S.S.R.	78	50.25 N	27.49 E
Kamennyj Brod, S.S.S.R.	83	47.26 N	39.51 E
Kamennyj Jar	80	48.27 N	45.34 E
Kamen'-Rybolov	89	44.46 N	132.02 E
Kamensk	88	51.58 N	106.36 E
Kamenskij	80	50.53 N	45.29 E
Kamenskoje, S.S.S.R.	74	62.30 N	166.12 E
Kamenskoje, S.S.S.R.	82	55.49 N	29.16 E
Kamenskoje, S.S.S.R.	82	55.16 N	36.50 E
Kamensk-Šachtinskij	83	48.21 N	40.19 E
Kamensk-Ural'skij	86	56.28 N	61.54 E
Kamenz	54	51.16 N	14.06 E
Kamerik	96	35.00 N	135.35 E
Kamerik	52	52.06 N	4.54 E
Kamerun → Cameroon □¹	134	6.00 N	12.00 E
Kamerun Mountain → Cameroon Mountain ∧	152	4.12 N	9.11 E
Kames	46	55.54 N	5.15 W
Kameškovo	86	56.21 N	41.00 E
Kāmet ∧	120	30.54 N	79.37 E
Kameur, Bahr ≈	146	9.26 N	20.50 E
Kameyama	94	34.51 N	136.27 E
Kami, Nihon	94	34.41 N	137.42 E
Kami, Nihon	96	35.05 N	134.53 E
Kamiah	202	46.13 N	116.01 W
Kamiak Butte ∧	202	46.52 N	117.10 W
Kamiasō	268	34.56 S	135.23 E
Kami-Ina □³	94	35.33 N	137.32 E
Kamienna ≈	30	51.06 N	21.47 E
Kamienna Góra	30	50.47 N	16.01 E
Kamień Pomorski	30	53.58 N	14.46 E
Kamieński	30	51.12 N	19.30 E
Kamieskroon	156	30.09 S	17.56 E
Kamifukuoka	94	35.52 N	139.32 E
Kamigōri	96	34.52 N	134.22 E
Kamigyō ◆⁸	270	35.02 N	135.45 E
Kamiichi	94	36.42 N	137.22 E
Kamiishihara	268	35.39 N	139.32 E
Kamiiso	92a	41.49 N	140.39 E
Kamiita	96	34.07 N	134.24 E
Kamikawa, Nihon	94	34.33 N	136.59 E
Kamikamagari-jima I	96	34.11 N	132.44 E
Kamikatsu	96	33.53 N	134.24 E
Kamikawa, Nihon	92a	43.51 N	142.46 E
Kamikawa, Nihon	96	36.13 N	137.07 E
Kamikitazawa ◆⁸	268	35.40 N	139.38 E
Kamikume	268	34.55 N	135.03 E
Kamikuishiki	94	35.30 N	138.33 E
Kamilukuak Lake ⊜	176	62.22 N	101.40 W
Kamimaki	270	34.34 N	135.43 E
Kamimizo	268	35.33 N	139.22 E
Kamina	154	8.44 S	25.00 E
Kaminaka, Nihon	96	33.28 N	134.23 E
Kaminaka, Nihon	176	62.10 N	95.00 W
Kaminaljuyú ⌂	236	14.38 N	90.33 W
Kaminokuni	92a	41.48 N	140.06 E
Kaminoseki	96	33.49 N	132.07 E
Kaminoyama	92	38.09 N	140.17 E
Kaminuriak Lake ⊜	176	63.00 N	95.40 W
Kamioka	94	36.18 N	137.18 E
Kamioyamada	268	35.35 N	139.24 E
Kamisato	94	36.15 N	139.09 E
Kamishihi Bay c	96	36.04 N	136.24 E
Kamishihinden	270	34.49 N	135.30 E
Kamisunagawa	92a	43.30 N	142.00 E
Kamitaira	94	36.24 N	136.54 E
Kamitakara	270	34.57 N	134.59 E
Kamitomi	268	35.49 N	139.31 E
Kamitonda	96	33.43 N	135.27 E
Kamitsuma	268	35.31 N	139.33 E
Kamitsushima	96	34.50 N	129.28 E
Kamituga	154	3.04 S	28.11 E
Kamiura	96	35.14 N	132.29 E
Kamiyahagi	94	35.18 N	137.29 E
Kamiyama	96	33.58 N	134.23 E
Kamiyama-jima I	174m	26.15 N	127.35 E
Kamiyamoto	268	35.35 N	139.29 E
Kamizima	268	38.58 N	47.44 E
Kamkhat Muhaywir ∧²	132	31.08 N	36.30 E
Kamku	120	27.30 N	96.30 E
Kamla (Kamlā) ≈	124	25.37 N	86.40 E
Kamlach ≈	58	48.30 N	10.32 E
Kamloops	182	50.40 N	120.20 W
Kamloops Indian Reserve ♦	182	50.42 N	120.20 W
Kamnik	36	46.13 N	14.37 E
Kamniokan	88	56.17 N	111.57 E
Kamo, N.Z.	172	35.41 S	174.19 E
Kamo, Nihon	94	34.49 N	135.52 E
Kamo, Nihon	270	34.54 N	135.42 E
Kamo ≈, Nihon	270	34.56 N	135.38 E
Kamoda-misaki ⊁	96	33.50 N	134.45 E
Kamogata	96	34.32 N	133.35 E
Kamogawa, Nihon	94	35.06 N	140.06 E
Kamojima	96	34.04 N	134.21 E
Kamono	96	33.51 N	131.03 E
Kamoshida ◆⁸	268	35.32 N	139.29 E
Kamoto	92	32.58 N	130.46 E
Kamp ≈	60	48.23 N	15.43 E
Kampala	154	0.19 N	32.25 E
Kampar	114	4.18 N	101.09 E
Kampar ≈	114	0.30 N	103.08 E
Kamparkalns ∧²	76	57.10 N	22.37 E
Kampar Kanan ≈	114	0.20 N	100.41 E
Kampe, Lake ⊜	276	41.02 N	74.21 W
Kampen	50	52.33 N	5.54 E
Kamphaeng, Khao ∧	110	14.37 N	99.58 E
Kamphaeng Phet	110	16.30 N	99.32 E
Kampinoski Park Narodowy ♦	30	52.20 N	20.35 E
Kampire-Dior, Tanjona ⊁	156	12.33 S	48.39 E
Kampli	122	15.24 N	76.36 E
Kampong Benta	114	4.03 N	102.01 E
Kampong Chom	110	12.00 N	105.27 E
Kampóng Chhnāng	110	12.15 N	104.40 E
Kampong Dong	114	3.54 N	101.58 E
Kampong Guchil	114	5.00 N	102.31 E
Kampong Jabor	114	3.57 N	103.02 E

Columna 5

Nome	Pág.	Lat.	Long.
Kampong Jerangau	114	4.51 N	103.12 E
Kampong Kandang	114	2.11 N	102.18 E
Kampong Kāntuót	110	11.26 N	104.49 E
Kampong Kenyam	114	4.31 N	102.28 E
Kampong Kuala Kemaman	114	4.14 N	103.27 E
Kampong Lamir	114	3.36 N	103.21 E
Kampong Lawa	114	5.40 N	101.42 E
Kampong Mengkarak	114	3.19 N	102.27 E
Kampong Merang	114	5.32 N	102.57 E
Kampong Nuri	114	5.02 N	102.23 E
Kampong Penarek	114	5.37 N	102.48 E
Kampong Raja	114	5.48 N	102.35 E
Kampong Renggong	114	4.33 N	102.35 E
Kampong Saôm, S.S.S.R.	110	10.38 N	103.30 E
Kampong Saôm, Chhâk c	110	10.50 N	103.32 E
Kampong Sebuyau	112	1.31 N	110.55 E
Kampong Sekendi	114	3.43 N	100.55 E
Kampong Surau	114	5.49 N	100.54 E
Kampong Tanjong Batu	114	3.12 N	103.27 E
Kampong Tebing Runtoh	271c	1.26 N	103.40 E
Kâmpóng Thum	110	12.42 N	104.54 E
Kâmpóng Trâlach	110	11.54 N	104.47 E
Kampong Ulu	110	10.03 N	98.33 E
Kampong Ulu Chalok	114	5.26 N	102.50 E
Kâmpôt	110	10.37 N	104.11 E
Kampsville	194	39.18 N	90.37 W
Kampti	150	10.08 N	3.27 W
Kâmpúchéa → Cambodia □¹	110	13.00 N	105.00 E
Kampung ≈	164	5.44 S	138.24 E
Kampungbaru	112	1.12 S	102.57 E
Kampville	219	38.51 N	90.33 W
Kamrau, Teluk c	164	3.32 S	133.37 E
Kamsack	184	51.34 N	101.54 W
Kamsdorf	54	50.38 N	11.28 E
Kamskij	24	60.04 N	53.13 E
Kamskoje Ustje	80	55.13 N	49.16 E
Kamskoje vodochraniliščе ⊜¹	86	58.52 N	56.15 E
Kamsvības, ozero ⊜	76	56.12 N	61.48 E
Kamsu-ri ◆⁸	98	38.03 N	125.54 E
Kamsuuma	144	0.15 N	42.47 E
Kam Tin	271d	22.27 N	114.03 E
Kamuchawie Lake ⊜	184	56.18 N	101.56 W
Kamuela	154	7.42 S	27.11 E
Kamuela (Waimea)	229d	20.01 N	155.40 W
Kamui-misaki ⊁	92a	43.20 N	140.21 E
Kámuk, Cerro ∧	236	9.17 N	83.04 W
Kamuli	154	0.57 N	33.07 E
Kamutumaebe ≈	152	7.17 S	23.41 E
Kamwanbu	152	6.04 S	22.42 E
Kamyšet	88	55.32 N	98.42 E
Kamyšev, S.S.S.R.	80	46.39 N	42.38 E
Kamyšev, S.S.S.R.	83	46.43 N	42.31 E
Kamyševacha, S.S.S.R.	78	47.43 N	35.32 E
Kamyševacha, S.S.S.R.	83	48.42 N	38.23 E
Kamyševskaja	78	46.25 N	37.57 E
Kamyšin	80	50.06 N	45.24 E
Kamyškurgon	85	40.34 N	70.24 E
Kamyšlov	86	56.52 N	62.43 E
Kamyšlybas	86	46.11 N	61.57 E
Kamyšnaja ≈	83	48.55 N	39.55 E
Kamyšnoje	86	51.58 N	61.47 E
Kamyšovoj	80	46.26 N	45.12 E
Kamyš-Samarskich Ozer, razlivy ⊜	80	50.50 E	
Kamyz'ak	80	46.00 N	48.05 E
Kan, Irán	128	35.48 N	51.16 E
Kan, Irán	128	35.51 N	51.16 E
Kan, Süd.	146	9.01 N	31.47 E
Kan ≈	88	56.31 N	93.47 E
Kana ≈	154	18.30 S	27.22 E
Kanaaupscow ≈	176	53.39 N	77.09 W
Kanab	200	37.02 N	112.31 W
Kanab Creek ≈	200	36.24 N	112.38 W
Kanab Plateau ⊼¹	200	36.40 N	112.45 W
Kanada → Canada □¹	176	60.00 N	95.00 W
Kanadej	80	53.10 N	47.32 E
Kanafis	146	9.48 N	25.62 E
Kanaga Island I	180	51.45 N	177.10 W
Kanaga Volcano ∧¹	180	51.55 N	177.09 W
Kanagawa □³	94	35.20 N	139.20 E
Kanagisukuuq	176	61.36 N	71.58 W
Kanagisujuaq	176	61.36 N	71.58 W
Kanagjin	98	35.00 N	100.00 W
Kangar Lenggor ≈	114	2.16 N	103.44 E
Kangar Teberau ≈	114	1.39 N	103.53 E
Kangley	216	41.09 N	88.53 W
Kanguro	85	40.07 N	67.54 E
Kanguo Zhuang	98	39.30 N	114.55 E
Kanguo'p o	98	41.07 N	127.31 E
Kanggye	98	40.58 N	126.36 E
Kanghwa	98	37.45 N	126.28 E
Kanghwa-do I	98	37.40 N	126.25 E
Kanghwa-man c	98	37.40 N	126.25 E
Kangiqsualujjuaq	176	58.41 N	65.57 W
Kangiqsujuaq	176	61.36 N	71.58 W
Kangirsuk	176	60.01 N	70.01 W
Kangjin	98	34.35 N	126.47 E
Kangkar Lenggor	114	2.16 N	103.44 E
Kanglong	104	26.03 N	119.40 E
Kangnŭng	98	37.45 N	128.54 E
Kangping	104	42.44 N	123.20 E
Kangrinboqê Feng ∧, Zhg.	90	31.04 N	81.18 E
Kangrinboqê Feng ∧, Zhg.	120	31.29 N	80.45 E
Kangshan	100	22.48 N	120.18 E
Kāngsŏ	98	38.58 N	125.28 E
Kangtog	120	32.08 N	88.13 E
Kangtoqu'un ≈	88	54.41 N	122.40 E
Kanhangad	122	12.19 N	75.05 E
Kani, C. Iv.	150	8.29 N	6.36 W
Kani, Mya.	120	22.26 N	94.52 E
Kani ≈	96	35.25 N	136.57 E
Kaniama	152	7.31 S	24.11 E
Kaniba	154	2.05 S	26.33 E
Kanibadam	85	40.17 N	70.25 E
Kanibongan	116	6.24 N	117.08 E
Kanice	56	50.05 N	16.42 E
Kaniere	172	42.51 S	171.02 E
Kaniet Islands II	162	0.53 S	145.30 E
Kaniflu	146	15.20 N	7.31 W
Kanigiri	122	15.24 N	79.31 E
Kanigoro	115a	8.10 S	112.15 E
Kanin, poluostrov ⊁¹	24	68.00 N	45.00 E
Kaningo	154	0.29 S	37.31 E
Kanin-Kamen' ∧	24	67.30 N	45.00 E
Kanin Nos	24	68.39 N	43.14 E

Columna 6

Nome	Pág.	Lat.	Long.
Kanda-Kanda	152	6.56 S	23.36 E
Kandala	152	6.02 S	19.24 E
Kandalakša	24	67.09 N	32.21 E
Kandalakšskaja guba c	24	66.55 N	32.45 E
Kandalakšskij zapovednik ♦	24	68.50 N	37.30 E
Kandang	114	3.03 N	97.20 E
Kandangan	112	2.47 S	115.16 E
Kandanghaur	115a	6.21 S	108.06 E
Kandat	86	57.08 N	89.02 E
Kandava	76	57.05 N	22.49 E
Kandavu Island I	175g	19.03 S	178.13 E
Kandavu Passage ⊔	175g	18.45 S	178.00 E
Kandé	150	9.57 N	1.03 E
Kandel	56	49.04 N	8.01 E
Kandel ∧	58	48.04 N	8.01 E
Kander ≈	58	46.43 N	7.38 E
Kandern	58	47.43 N	7.40 E
Kandersteg	58	46.30 N	7.40 E
Kândhkot	120	28.14 N	69.11 E
Kândhla	124	29.19 N	77.16 E
Kandi, Bénin	150	11.08 N	2.56 E
Kandi, India	126	23.57 N	88.02 E
Kandi, Tanjung ⊁	112	1.19 N	121.28 E
Kandia	123	35.28 N	73.18 E
Kandiãro	120	27.04 N	68.13 E
Kandik ≈	180	65.24 N	142.34 W
Kandili ◆⁸	267b	41.04 N	29.03 E
Kandira	130	41.04 N	30.09 E
Kandivli ◆⁸	272c	19.12 N	72.51 E
Kando ≈	96	35.22 N	132.40 E
Kandor, Ouadi ≈	146	17.13 N	20.52 E
Kandos	170	32.52 S	149.58 E
Kândra	126	23.44 N	87.58 E
Kândrāch	120	25.29 N	65.29 E
Kândreho	157b	17.29 S	46.06 E
Kandrian	164	6.15 S	149.35 E
Kandsack	184	54.34 N	54.07 E
Kanduri	122	7.05 N	72.48 E
Kandute I	122	6.20 N	72.57 E
Kandy	122	7.18 N	80.38 E
Kane, II., U.S.	219	39.11 N	90.21 W
Kane, Pa., U.S.	214	41.39 N	78.48 W
Kane ☆⁸	216	41.53 N	88.18 W
Kaneksa	268	35.28 N	139.22 E
Kaneilio Point ⊁	229c	21.27 N	158.12 W
Kanektok ≈	180	59.45 N	161.55 W
Kanem □⁵	146	15.00 N	16.00 E
Kanemi	116	6.55 N	123.58 E
Kaneohe Bay c	229c	21.25 N	157.48 W
Kaneohe Bay Marine Corps Air Station ■	229c	21.27 N	157.46 W
Kaneville	216	41.50 N	88.31 W
Kaneyama	94	35.28 N	137.06 E
Kanfanar	64	45.07 N	13.51 E
Kang	156	23.41 S	22.50 E
Kangaba	150	11.56 N	8.25 W
Kangal	130	39.15 N	37.24 E
Kangalassy	74	62.23 N	129.59 E
Kangan	128	27.50 N	52.03 E
Kangānpur	123	30.46 N	74.08 E
Kangar	114	6.26 N	100.12 E
Kangaré	150	11.35 N	8.10 W
Kangaría	168b	35.09 S	138.40 E
Kangaroo ≈	170	34.46 S	150.18 E
Kangaroo Creek Reservoir ⊜¹	168b	34.52 S	138.46 E
Kangaroo Flat	168b	34.33 S	138.40 E
Kangaroo Ground	274b	37.41 S	145.13 E
Kangaroo Island I	166	35.50 S	137.06 E
Kangaroo Valley	170	34.44 S	150.32 E
Kangarooma ≈	26	61.24 N	24.05 E
Kangasniemi	26	61.59 N	26.38 E
Kangávar	128	34.30 N	47.58 E
Kangaz	78	46.07 N	28.33 E
Kangdong	98	39.09 N	126.05 E
Kangean, Kepulauan II	112	6.54 S	115.20 E
Kangean, Pulau I	112	6.54 S	115.20 E
Kangerdlugssuatsiaq c	176	66.47 N	33.45 W
Kangge-zhuang	105	38.40 N	117.00 E
Kanggu'o	98	41.07 N	127.31 E
Kangdong	98	39.09 N	126.05 E
Kani Nos ⊁	24	68.38 N	43.20 E

Español	Alemán	Portugués	Francés	—
≈ River	Fluß	Río	Rivière	Rio
☰ Canal	Kanal	Canal	Canal	Canal
∟ Waterfall, Rapids	Wasserfall, Stromschnellen	Cascada, Rápidos	Chute d'eau, Rapides	Cascata, Rápidos
⊔ Strait	Meeresstraße	Estrecho	Détroit	Estreito
c Bay, Gulf	Bucht, Golf	Bahía, Golfo	Baie, Golfe	Baía, Golfo
⊜ Lake, Lakes	See, Seen	Lago, Lagos	Lac, Lacs	Lago, Lagos
⧗ Swamp	Sumpf	Pantano	Marais	Pântano
⊠ Ice Features, Glacier	Eis- und Gletscherformen	Accidentes Glaciales	Formes glaciaires	Geleiras
⊽ Other Hydrographic Features	Andere Hydrographische Objekte	Otros Elementos Hidrográficos	Autres données hydrographiques	Outros acidentes hidrográficos
♯ Submarine Features	Untermeerische Objekte	Accidentes Submarinos	Formes de relief sous-marin	Acidentes submarinos
◘ Political Unit	Politische Einheit	Unidad Política	Entité politique	Unidade política
✴ Cultural Institution	Kulturelle Institution	Institución Cultural	Institution culturelle	Instituição cultural
⌂ Historical Site	Historische Stätte	Sitio Histórico	Site historique	Sítio Histórico
♦ Recreational Site	Erholungs- und Ferienort	Sitio de Recreo	Centre de loisirs	Área de Lazer
✈ Airport	Flughafen	Aeropuerto	Aéroport	Aeroporto
■ Military Installation	Militäranlage	Instalación Militar	Installation militaire	Instalação militar
◆ Miscellaneous	Verschiedenes	Misceláneo	Divers	Diversos

ENGLISH / DEUTSCH

Symbols in the index entries represent the broad categories identified in the key at the right. Symbols with superior numbers (⋀[1]) identify subcategories (see complete key on page *I · 1).*

Symbole im Register stellen die rechts im Schlüssel erklärten Kategorien dar. Symbole mit hochgestellten Ziffern (⋀[1]) bezeichnen Unterabteilungen einer Kategorie (vgl. vollständiger Schlüssel auf Seite *I · 1).*

Los símbolos incluídos en el texto del índice representan las grandes categorias identificadas con la clave a la derecha. Los símbolos con numeros en su parte superior (⋀[1]) identifican las subcategorias (véase la clave completa en la página *I · 1).*

Les symboles de l'index représentent les catégories indiquées dans la légende à droite. Les symboles suivis d'un indice (⋀[1]) représentent des sous-catégories (voir légende complète à la page *I · 1).*

Os símbolos incluídos no texto do índice representam as grandes categorias identificadas com a chave à direita. Os símbolos com números em sua parte superior (⋀[1]) identificam as subcategorias (veja-se a chave completa à página *I · 1).*

∧ Mountain	Berg	Montaña	Montagne	Montanha
⋀ Mountains	Gebirge	Montañas	Montagnes	Montanhas
)(Pass	Paß	Paso	Col	Passo
V Valley, Canyon	Tal, Cañon	Valle, Cañón	Vallée, Canyon	Vale, Canhão
≚ Plain	Ebene	Llano	Plaine	Planície
› Cape	Kap	Cabo	Cap	Cabo
I Island	Insel	Isla	Île	Ilha
II Islands	Inseln	Islas	Îles	Ilhas
⊥ Other Topographic Features	Andere Topographische Objekte	Otros Elementos Topográficos	Autres données topographiques	Outros acidentes topográficos

ESPAÑOL				FRANÇAIS				PORTUGUÊS			
Nombre	Página	Lat.°′	Long.°′ W=Oeste	Nom	Page	Lat.°′	Long.°′ W=Ouest	Nome	Página	Lat.°′	Long.°′ W=Oeste

Kaskaskia, North Fork ≃ 219 38.46 N 89.09 W
Kaskattama ≃ 176 57.03 N 90.07 W
Kaskelen 85 43.12 N 76.37 E
Kaskelen ≃ 85 43.53 N 77.08 E
Kaskinen
→ Kaskö 26 62.23 N 21.13 E
Kaskö (Kaskinen) 26 62.23 N 21.13 E
Kašlagač ≃ 83 47.45 N 37.16 E
Kaslätu ʌ 124 23.58 N 84.54 E
Kasli 86 55.53 N 60.46 E
Kaslo 182 49.55 N 116.55 W
Käsmark
→ Kežmarok 30 49.08 N 20.25 E
Kasn'a 76 55.24 N 34.20 E
Kasn'a ≃ 76 55.51 N 34.25 E
Kaso ≃ 115a 7.25 S 106.40 E
Kasongo 154 4.27 S 26.40 E
Kasongo-Lunda 152 6.28 S 16.49 E
Kásos I 38 35.22 N 26.56 E
Kasota 190 44.18 N 93.57 W
Kašperovka 78 49.26 N 29.41 E
Kaspi 84 41.57 N 44.25 E
Kaspijsk 84 42.52 N 47.38 E
Kaspijskij 22 45.22 N 47.24 E
Kaspijskoje more
→ Caspian Sea ≈² 72 42.00 N 50.30 E
Kaspiskaja Senke
→ Prikaspijskaja nizmennost' ≃ 80 48.00 N 52.00 E
Kaspisches Meer
→ Caspian Sea ≈² 72 42.00 N 50.30 E
Kaspl'a 76 55.00 N 31.38 E
Kaspl'a ≃ 76 55.24 N 30.43 E
Kasr, Ra's ‣ 140 18.02 N 38.35 E
Kasrik 130 38.13 N 41.54 E
Kassa
→ Košice 30 48.43 N 21.15 E
Kassab 130 35.56 N 35.59 E
Kassai
→ Cassai (Kasai) ≃ 152 3.02 S 16.57 E
Kassalá 140 15.28 N 36.24 E
Kassalá □⁴ 140 15.00 N 35.00 E
Kassándra ‣¹ 38 40.06 N 23.22 E
Kassándras, Kólpos ⌣ 38 40.06 N 23.30 E
Kassel 56 51.19 N 9.29 E
Kassel □⁵ 56 51.10 N 9.20 E
Kasserine 148 35.11 N 8.48 E
Kasserine □⁸ 148 35.00 N 8.45 E
Kasshabog Lake ⌷ 212 44.38 N 77.58 W
Kassikaityu ≃ 246 1.49 N 58.32 W
Kassinger 140 18.45 N 31.54 E
Kassīr, Sabkhat al- ⌷ 130 35.03 N 41.07 E
Kasslerfeld ‣⁸ 263 51.26 N 6.45 E
Kasson 190 44.01 N 92.45 W
Kassou 150 11.35 N 2.03 W
Kastamonu 130 13.05 N 3.18 W
Kastamonu □⁴ 130 41.42 N 33.47 E
Kastamonu 130 41.40 N 33.45 E
Kastanéai 38 41.38 N 26.28 E
Kastelholm 26 60.14 N 20.04 E
Kastellaun 56 50.04 N 7.26 E
Kastelhorizon I 130 36.08 N 29.34 E
Kasterlee 56 51.15 N 4.57 E
Kastiyou, Puntan ‣ 174n 14.57 N 145.40 E
Kastl, B.R.D. 60 49.50 N 11.54 E
Kastl, B.R.D. 60 49.22 N 11.42 E
Kastorf 52 53.44 N 10.34 E
Kastoriás, Límni ⌷ 38 40.31 N 21.15 E
Kastornoje 78 51.50 N 38.06 E
Kastrávion, Teknití Límni ⌷¹ 38 38.50 N 21.20 E
Kastrup Lufthavn ≈ 41 55.38 N 12.39 E
Kasuga, Nihon 94 35.28 N 136.29 E
Kasuga, Nihon 96 35.10 N 135.06 E
Kasuga, Nihon 96 33.32 N 130.27 E
Kasugai, Nihon 95 35.14 N 136.58 E
Kasugai, Nihon 94 35.13 N 138.39 E
Kasuga-kōkūkichi, Kaijō-jieitai- ≈ 96 33.31 N 130.28 E
Kasuga Shrine ‣¹ 270 34.41 N 135.51 E
Kasuka 158 33.40 S 26.41 E
Kasukabe 94 35.58 N 139.45 E
Kasulu 94 36.24 N 139.13 E
Kasulu 154 4.34 S 30.06 E
Kasumi 94 35.38 N 134.38 E
Kasumiga-ura ⌷ 94 36.00 N 140.25 E
Kasum-Ismailov 84 40.36 N 46.47 E
Kasumkent 84 41.41 N 48.07 E
Kasungan 112 1.58 S 113.24 E
Kasungu 13 13.01 S 33.30 E
Kasungu National Park ♦ 154 12.55 S 33.15 E
Kasupe 154 15.10 S 35.15 E
Kaszuby ≃¹ 30 54.10 N 18.15 E
Kata 88 58.46 N 102.40 E
Kataba 154 16.05 S 25.10 E
Kataeregi 150 9.22 N 6.17 E
Katagum 146 12.17 N 10.21 E
Kataḥdin, Mount ʌ 188 45.55 N 68.55 W
Katai 272c 19.10 N 73.05 E
Katajevo 88 50.57 N 108.41 E
Katajsk 86 56.18 N 62.35 E
Katako-Kombe 152 3.24 S 24.25 E
Katakura 270 34.29 N 135.31 E
Katakwi 154 1.55 N 33.57 E
Katale 154 4.59 S 31.03 E
Katalla 180 60.12 N 144.31 W
Katanga 138 5.50 S 29.22 E
Katanga ⌷⁹ 138 11.00 S 26.00 E
Katangi 84 60.08 N 102.13 E
Katangi 124 23.27 N 79.47 E
Katanglad Mountains ʌ 116 30.06 N 124.54 E
Katangli 89 51.42 N 143.14 E
Katanimara 126 22.17 N 87.11 E
Katanning 158 33.42 S 117.33 E
Katano 270 34.47 N 135.40 E
Katano-hana ‣ 174f 24.49 N 141.20 E
Kataoka 152 2.18 S 27.08 E
Kataoka 270 35.03 N 135.58 E
Katapakishi 152 8.15 S 22.49 E
Katar
→ Qatar □¹ 128 25.00 N 51.10 E
Katara, Depresión de
Qattārah, Munkhafaḍ al- ≃⁷ 140 30.00 N 27.30 E
Katrimân Ghāt 124 28.20 N 81.29 E
Katase 268 35.19 N 139.29 E
Katashina 94 36.46 N 139.14 E
Katav-Ivanovsk 86 54.45 N 58.12 E
Katayama 268 35.46 N 139.34 E
Katchall Island I 110 7.57 N 93.22 E
Katchewanooka Lake ⌷ 212 44.27 N 78.16 W
Katchin-wan c 174m 26.18 N 127.53 E
Katchirga 150 14.03 N 0.06 E
Katchungo 152 1.39 S 28.00 E
Katech 84 41.21 N 46.34 E
Kateel ≃ 180 65.28 N 157.35 W
Katélé 150 10.38 N 5.37 W
Katena-wan c 174m 26.22 N 128.05 E
Katepwa Beach 184 50.42 N 103.38 W
Katerini 38 40.16 N 22.30 E
Katerinopol' 78 49.00 N 30.58 E
Katerloch ≈ 61 47.16 N 15.32 E
Katernberg ≈⁸, B.R.D. 263 51.16 N 7.06 E
Katernberg ≈⁸, B.R.D. 263 51.29 N 7.04 E
Katesbridge 48 54.18 N 6.09 W
Kates Needle ʌ 180 57.02 N 132.04 W
Kateševo 82 54.58 N 46.19 E
Katete, Malawi 154 12.17 S 33.39 E
Katete, Zam. 154 14.05 S 32.07 W
Katghora 124 22.30 N 82.33 E
Katha 110 24.11 N 96.21 E

Kathangor, Jabal ʌ 140 5.45 N 33.59 E
Katherine 164 14.28 S 132.16 E
Katherine ≃ 164 14.39 S 131.42 E
Katherine Creek ≃ 166 23.48 S 143.62 E
Katherine Gorge National Park ♦ 164 14.10 S 132.30 E
Käthgodām 26 29.16 N 79.32 E
Kathiār 120 25.32 N 87.35 E
Käthiāwār Peninsula
‣¹ 120 22.00 N 71.00 E
Kathīti. Ra's ‣ 144 14.55 N 42.53 E
Kathla 123 31.59 N 76.47 E
Kathleen 220 28.07 N 82.01 W
Kathleen Valley 162 27.23 S 120.38 E
Kathlow ⌣ 54 51.43 N 14.29 E
Käthmāndāu 124 27.43 N 85.19 E
Kathor 120 21.18 N 72.56 E
Kathrabbā 132 31.08 N 35.37 E
Kathua 123 32.21 N 75.31 E
Kāthuli 126 23.52 N 88.40 E
Kati 150 12.44 N 8.04 W
Kātiādi 126 24.15 N 90.48 E
Katibas ≃ 112 2.01 N 112.33 E
Katihār 124 25.32 N 87.35 E
Katikati 172 37.33 S 175.55 E
Katima Mulilo 152 17.27 S 24.14 E
Katimik Lake ⌷ 184 52.54 N 99.22 W
Katiola 150 8.08 N 5.06 W
Katipunan 116 8.31 N 123.17 E
Katiti Aboriginal Land Reserve ♦⁴ 162 25.10 S 131.15 E
Kätlang 123 34.22 N 72.05 E
Katlehong 273d 26.19 S 28.09 E
Katlenburg-Duhm 52 51.41 N 10.06 E
Katmai, Mount ʌ 180 58.17 N 154.56 W
Katmai National Park ♦ 180 58.30 N 155.00 W
Kätmāndu
→ Käthmāndāu 124 27.43 N 85.19 E
Katni
→ Murwāra, India 124 23.51 N 80.24 E
Káto Akhaïa 38 38.09 N 21.32 E
Kátol 120 21.16 N 78.35 E
Katompi 154 6.11 S 26.20 E
Katonah 210 41.16 N 73.41 W
Katonga ≃ 154 0.34 N 31.52 E
Katon-Karagaj 86 49.11 N 85.57 E
Katoomba 170 33.42 S 150.18 E
Katopa 154 2.45 S 25.06 E
Katori-jingū ‣¹ 94 35.52 N 140.30 E
Katoúna 38 38.47 N 21.07 E
Katovice 60 49.16 N 13.49 E
Katowice □ 30 50.15 N 19.00 E
Katowice □⁴ 30 50.15 N 19.00 E
Katra 123 32.59 N 74.57 E
Kätrās 126 23.48 N 86.17 E
Katriček 80 49.23 N 45.33 E
Katrine, Loch ⌷ 46 56.15 N 4.31 W
Katrineholm 40 59.00 N 16.12 E
Katsch, Golf von
→ Kutch, Gulf of c 120 22.36 N 69.30 E
Katschbach ≃ 61 47.08 N 14.17 E
Katschberg ⌣ 64 47.03 N 13.37 E
Katscher
→ Kietrz 30 50.05 N 18.01 E
Katsepe 157b 15.45 S 46.15 E
Katshurgu 154 2.27 S 27.23 E
Katsina 150 13.00 N 7.32 E
Katsina □³ 150 12.20 N 7.45 E
Katsina Ala 150 7.10 N 9.17 E
Katsina Ala ≃ 152 7.48 N 8.52 E
Katsunuma 94 35.39 N 138.44 E
Katsura ≈⁸ 270 34.59 N 135.42 E
Katsura ≃, Nihon 94 34.53 N 135.42 E
Katsura ≃, Nihon 95 35.36 N 139.15 E
Katsuura, Nihon 96 33.58 N 134.35 E
Katsuura, Nihon 94 35.08 N 140.18 E
Katsuyama, Nihon 94 36.03 N 136.30 E
Katsuyama, Nihon 96 35.05 N 133.41 E
Kattakurgan 72 39.55 N 66.15 E
Kattara-Senke
→ Qaṭṭārah, Munkhafaḍ al- ≃⁷ 140 30.00 N 27.30 E
Kattaqurghan
→ Kattakurgan 72 39.55 N 66.15 E
Kattavia 38 35.57 N 27.46 E
Katta-Taldyk ⌣ 85 40.19 N 73.12 E
Kattaviá 38 35.57 N 27.46 E
Katternberg ≈⁸ 263 51.09 N 7.02 E
Katthammarsvik 26 57.26 N 18.50 E
Kattowitz
→ Katowice 30 50.15 N 19.00 E
Kāttuppūttūr 122 10.50 N 78.14 E
Katul, Jabal ʌ 140 14.16 N 29.23 E
Katuma ≃ 154 6.10 S 30.34 E
Katumba 154 7.45 S 25.18 E
Katun' ≃ 88 50.25 N 85.05 E
Katunki 86 56.50 N 43.14 E
Kātūria 124 24.44 N 86.43 E
Katu Shan ‣ 114 30.05 N 122.30 E
Katusice 54 50.40 N 14.50 E
Kātwa 126 23.39 N 88.08 E
Katwijk aan de Rijn 56 52.11 N 4.26 E
Katwijk aan Zee 56 52.12 N 4.24 E
Katy 222 29.47 N 95.49 W
Katy Wrocławskie 30 51.02 N 16.46 E
Katzenbuckel ʌ 56 49.28 N 9.02 E
Katzenelnbogen 56 50.17 N 8.01 E
Katzenfurt 56 50.37 N 8.21 E
Kātzhütte 54 50.37 N 11.04 E
Kaua ⌷ 156 19.24 S 22.03 E
Kauai I 229b 22.00 N 159.22 W
Kauai Channel ⌣ 229b 21.45 N 158.50 W
Kaub 56 50.05 N 7.46 E
Kau Desert ≈² 229d 19.21 N 155.19 W
Kaufbeuren 58 47.53 N 10.37 E
Kaufering 58 48.05 N 10.52 E
Kauffung
→ Wojcieszów 30 50.58 N 15.56 E
Kaufman 222 32.35 N 96.18 W
Kaufman ⌷⁴ 222 32.01 N 81.15 E
Kaufungen 56 51.17 N 9.38 E
Kaufungen, B.R.D. 56 51.11 N 9.38 E
Kaufungen, B.R.D. 56 51.17 N 9.38 E
Kaugama 150 12.28 N 9.44 E
Kauhajoki 26 62.26 N 22.11 E
Kauhanevan-Pohjankankaan kansallispuisto ♦ 26 63.08 N 22.25 E
Kauhava 26 63.06 N 23.05 E
Kauiki Head ‣ 229a 20.45 N 155.58 W
Kaukapakapa 172 36.37 S 174.30 E
Kaukau Veld ≃¹ 156 19.30 S 20.30 E
Kaukhali 126 22.38 N 90.04 E
Kaula I ‣¹ 229b 21.40 N 160.32 W
Kaulakahi Channel ⌣ 229b 22.05 N 159.50 W
Kaulille 56 51.11 N 5.31 E
Kaulranta 26 66.28 N 23.40 E
Kaūl-li 26 37.58 N 124.37 E
Kaulsdorf 54 50.38 N 11.25 E
Kaulsdorf-Süd ≈⁸ 264a 52.31 N 13.33 E
Kaumalapau 229a 20.47 N 156.59 W
Kaunakakai 229a 21.05 N 157.01 W
Kaunas 76 54.54 N 23.54 E
Kaunenga Lake ⌷ 154 14.41 S 24.50 W
Kauner Tal V 58 47.01 N 10.44 E

Kaunghein 110 25.40 N 95.26 E
Kauniainen
→ Grankulla 26 60.13 N 24.45 E
Kaununui ‣ 229b 21.56 N 160.10 W
Kaup 164 3.50 S 144.00 E
Kaupanger 26 61.11 N 7.14 E
Kaura Namoda 150 12.35 N 6.35 E
Kauriyāla Ghāt 124 28.23 N 81.02 E
Kauru 150 10.33 N 8.12 E
Kausa 272c 19.10 N 73.02 E
Kau Sai Chau I 271d 22.22 N 114.18 E
Kausala 26 60.54 N 26.22 E
Kaušany 78 46.38 N 29.25 E
Kaustinen 26 63.32 N 23.42 E
Kauswagan 116 8.11 N 124.05 E
Kautokeino 24 69.00 N 23.02 E
Kauttua 26 61.06 N 22.10 E
Kau-ye Kyun I 110 11.01 N 98.32 E
Kavača 74 60.16 N 169.51 E
Kavaca 130 39.40 N 28.30 E
Kavadarci 38 41.26 N 22.00 E
Kavajë 38 41.11 N 19.33 E
Kavak, Tür. 130 38.24 N 39.26 E
Kavak, Tür. 130 41.05 N 36.03 E
Kavak, Tür. 130 39.18 N 37.30 E
Kavakbaşı 130 38.29 N 41.49 E
Kavaklıdere 130 37.26 N 28.22 E
Kavála 38 40.56 N 24.25 E
Kavalerovo 89 44.15 N 135.04 E
Kávali 122 14.55 N 79.59 E
Kavango ≃⁵ 156 18.30 S 20.15 E
Kavaratti 122 10.34 N 72.39 E
Kavaratti Island I 122 10.33 N 72.38 E
Kavarna 38 43.25 N 28.20 E
Kavendou, Mont ʌ 150 10.41 N 12.12 W
Kāveri ≃ 122 11.09 N 79.52 E
Kāveri Falls ⌊ 122 12.18 N 77.17 E
Kaverino, S.S.S.R. 80 54.10 N 41.47 E
Kaverino, S.S.S.R. 82 56.11 N 36.15 E
Kavieng 156 2.35 S 150.50 E
Kavimba 156 18.02 S 24.38 E
Kavīr, Dasht-e ≈² 128 34.40 N 54.30 E
Kävlinge 41 55.48 N 13.06 E
Kävlingeån ≃ 41 55.47 N 13.06 E
Kavungo 152 11.31 S 23.03 E
Kavuu ≃ 154 7.40 S 31.46 E
Kavyücü-Gazimurskije 88 51.22 N 118.10 E
Kaw, Guy. fr. 250 4.29 N 52.02 W
Kaw, Ok., U.S. 196 36.46 N 96.50 W
Kawa 110 17.05 N 96.28 E
Kawabe, Nihon 94 36.41 N 139.07 E
Kawabe, Nihon 96 35.29 N 137.04 E
Kawachi, Nihon 94 33.55 N 135.11 E
Kawachi, Nihon 94 36.24 N 136.38 E
Kawachi, Nihon 96 36.37 N 139.56 E
Kawachi-nagano 96 34.27 N 135.34 E
Kawagama Lake ⌷ 212 45.18 N 78.45 W
Kawagoe 94 35.55 N 139.29 E
Kawaguchi 94 35.48 N 139.43 E
Kawaguchiko 96 35.30 N 138.46 E
Kawaguchi-ko ⌷ 94 35.31 N 138.45 E
Kawahara 96 35.24 N 134.12 E
Kawai, Nihon 96 36.18 N 137.07 E
Kawaihoa ‣ 229b 21.46 N 160.15 W
Kawaikini ʌ 229b 22.05 N 159.29 W
Kawailoa Beach 229c 21.37 N 158.04 W
Kawajiri 96 34.14 N 132.42 E
Kawakami, Nihon 94 35.58 N 138.35 E
Kawakami, Nihon 96 34.44 N 133.29 E
Kawakami, Nihon 96 35.17 N 133.39 E
Kawakawa 172 35.23 S 174.04 E
Kawakubo 270 34.44 N 135.38 E
Kawali 115a 7.11 S 108.22 E
Kawama Mission 154 10.04 S 28.37 E
Kawamata 92 37.39 N 140.36 E
Kawambwa 154 9.47 S 29.05 E
Kawamoto, Nihon 94 36.09 N 139.17 E
Kawamoto, Nihon 96 34.59 N 132.30 E
Kawane 94 34.57 N 138.05 E
Kawanishi, Nihon 96 34.49 N 135.24 E
Kawanishi, Nihon 94 34.40 N 135.17 E
Kawara, Nihon 96 33.40 N 130.51 E
Kawara, Nihon 96 33.40 N 130.51 E
Kawara Débé 150 12.20 N 3.26 E
Kawardha 124 22.01 N 81.15 E
Kawardha Park 124 22.00 N 78.12 W
Kawasaki, Nihon 96 33.32 N 130.49 E
Kawasaki, Nihon 94 33.35 N 130.49 E
Kawasaki-kō c 268 35.32 N 139.43 E
Kawasaki Stadium ♦ 268 35.32 N 139.43 E
Kawashima, Nihon 94 35.59 N 136.56 E
Kawashima, Nihon 96 35.59 N 130.30 E
Kawashima ≈⁸ 268 35.28 N 139.35 E
Kawashiri-misaki ‣ 96 34.26 N 130.58 E
Kawau Island I 172 36.25 S 174.51 E
Kawaw 268 35.39 N 139.33 E
Kawayan 116 11.41 N 124.21 E
Kawbein 110 16.33 N 97.52 E
Kawdut 110 15.31 N 97.47 E
Kawe, Pulau I 164 0.03 S 130.07 E
Kaweenakumik Lake ⌷ 184 52.52 N 99.30 W
Kaweka Range ʌ 172 39.17 S 176.23 E
Kawerau 172 38.03 S 176.43 E
Kawhia 172 38.04 S 174.50 E
Kawhia Harbour c 172 38.05 S 174.47 E
Kawich Peak ʌ 204 37.48 N 116.26 W
Kawich Range ʌ 204 37.30 N 116.26 W
Kawm 140 2.45 S 150.45 E
Kawm al-Farā'in ‣ 142 31.11 N 30.45 E
Kawm ar-Rāhib 142 28.20 N 30.37 E
Kawm Birah 273c 30.05 N 31.08 E
Kawm Dafanah (Daphnae) ‣ 142 30.52 N 32.11 E
Kawm Ḥamādah 142 30.46 N 30.42 E
Kawm Ishū 142 30.38 N 31.15 E
Kawm Ishū 142 31.07 N 30.40 E
Kawm Umbū 140 24.28 N 32.57 E
Kawnglanghpu 110 27.04 N 98.21 E
Kawnipi Lake ⌷ 190 48.30 N 91.14 W
Kawthaung 110 9.59 N 98.33 E
Kaxgar
→ Kaxgar ≃ 85 39.40 N 78.00 E
Kaxgar 85 39.29 N 75.59 E
Kaxgar ≃ 85 39.40 N 78.00 E
Kaxil Kiuic ‣¹ 236 20.07 N 89.33 W
Kaya, Burkina 96 13.05 N 1.05 W
Kaya, Nihon 96 35.36 N 135.06 E
Kayadibi, Tür. 130 37.58 N 124.37 E
Kayadibi, Tür. 130 37.58 N 124.37 E
Kayak Island I 180 59.52 N 144.30 W
Kayalpattinam 122 8.34 N 78.07 E
Kāyamkulam 122 9.11 N 76.30 E
Kayan ≃ 112 2.55 N 117.35 E
Kayangel Islands II 108 8.04 N 134.43 E

Kayang-san ʌ² 271b 37.33 N 126.43 E
Kāyamkulam 122 9.11 N 76.30 E
Kayapa 116 16.22 N 120.53 E
Kayapınar 130 37.34 N 41.10 E
Kayas 130 39.56 N 32.58 E
Kaya-san ʌ 98 35.49 N 128.07 E
Kaya-san Kukrip Kongwŏn ♦ 98 35.47 N 128.06 E
Kaycee 200 43.42 N 106.38 W
Kayeli 146 3.23 S 127.06 E
Kayembe-Mukulu 152 9.03 S 23.57 E
Kayen 115a 6.54 S 110.59 E
Kayenta 200 36.43 N 110.15 W
Kayes, Congo 152 4.25 S 11.41 E
Kayes, Mali 150 14.27 N 11.26 W
Kayes □⁴ 150 14.00 N 11.00 W
Kay Gardens 285 39.45 N 75.25 W
Kayima 150 8.53 N 11.10 W
Kayin □³ 110 17.30 N 97.45 E
Kayış Dağı ʌ 267b 40.59 N 29.10 E
Kaymakçı 150 38.10 N 28.08 E
Kaymaz, Tür. 130 40.55 N 30.18 E
Kaymaz, Tür. 130 39.31 N 31.11 E
Kayna 54 50.59 N 12.14 E
Kaynar 130 38.55 N 36.28 E
Kayō, Nihon 96 34.51 N 133.42 E
Kayō, Nihon 174m 26.33 N 128.07 E
Kayoa, Pulau I 164 0.05 S 127.25 E
Kayombo 154 9.36 S 25.37 E
Kaypak 130 37.08 N 36.27 E
Kay Point ‣ 180 69.18 N 138.22 W
Kayser Gebergte ʌ 250 3.03 N 56.35 W
Kayseri 130 38.43 N 35.30 E
Kayseri □⁴ 130 38.30 N 35.55 E
Kaysersberg 58 48.08 N 7.15 E
Kaysville 200 41.02 N 111.56 W
Kayuadi, Pulau I 112 6.49 S 120.47 E
Kayuagung 112 3.24 S 104.50 E
Kayumas 115a 7.50 S 114.08 E
Kayuta Lake ⌷ 210 43.25 N 75.12 W
Kayuyu 154 3.39 S 26.21 E
Kazačka ≃ 84 41.06 N 45.22 E
Kazachskaja Sovetskaja Socialističeskaja Respublika (Kazakhstan) □³ 72 48.00 N 68.00 E
Kazačij melkosopočnik ≈² 86 49.00 N 72.00 E
Kazadži 83 46.58 N 40.03 E
Kazačinskoje, S.S.S.R. 86 57.49 N 93.17 E
Kazačinskoje, S.S.S.R. 88 56.16 N 107.36 E
Kazačje 78 50.21 N 36.11 E
Kazačje Lopan' 78 70.44 N 136.13 E
Kazači Lageri 84 46.42 N 32.59 E
Kazačka ≃ 80 51.28 N 43.56 E
Kazakdarja 86 49.20 N 58.31 E
Kazakdarja 86 51.18 N 33.29 E
Kazakević′evo 89 43.27 N 59.46 E
Kazakstan 89 48.17 N 134.46 E
→ Kazachskaja Sovetskaja Socialističeskaja Respublika □³ 72 48.00 N 68.00 E
Kazaki 76 52.38 N 38.16 E
Kazalija 78 45.46 N 62.07 E
Kazan' ≃, S.S.S.R. 86 59.18 N 80.30 E
Kazalinsk 86 45.46 N 62.07 E
Kazan', Nihon 270 34.35 N 135.45 E
Kazan' 176 64.02 N 95.30 W
Kazanbulak 84 40.36 N 46.41 E
Kazancı 130 36.30 N 32.53 E
Kazanka, S.S.S.R. 78 47.50 N 32.49 E
Kazanka, S.S.S.R. 82 55.48 N 49.01 E
Kazanlăk 38 42.38 N 25.21 E
Kazan Lake ⌷ 184 55.33 N 108.21 W
Kazanlı 130 36.50 N 34.45 E
Kazan-rettō (Volcano Islands) II 14 25.00 N 141.00 E
Kazanskaja 83 49.48 N 41.09 E
Kazanskoje, S.S.S.R. 86 54.59 N 37.39 E
Kazanskoje, S.S.S.R. 86 55.39 N 69.14 E
Kazan' Station ≈⁵ 265b 55.46 N 37.40 E
Kazarman, mys ‣ 86 55.26 N 35.51 E
Kazatin 78 49.44 N 28.50 E
Kazbegi 84 42.40 N 44.38 E
Kazbek, gora ʌ 84 42.42 N 44.31 E
Kaz Dağı ʌ 130 39.42 N 26.50 E
Kazembe 154 12.11 S 32.37 E
Kazerne 154 12.11 S 32.37 E
Kāzerūn 128 29.37 N 51.38 E
Kazi-Magomed 84 40.03 N 49.00 E
Kazimierz Wielka 30 50.16 N 20.30 E
Kazimierz Dolny 30 51.20 N 21.57 E
Kazincbarcika 30 48.15 N 20.38 E
Kazinka ≃ 78 51.26 N 39.42 E
Kazinka, S.S.S.R. 76 52.40 N 38.57 E
Kazipāra 272b 22.43 N 88.31 E
Kazlu Rūda 76 54.45 N 23.30 E
Kazl'y minskoje 86 40.28 N 57.04 E
Kaznačejevo 76 48.35 N 41.41 E
Kazo 94 36.07 N 139.36 E
Kaz'onnyj Torec ≃ 78 48.40 N 37.45 E
Kaztalovka 80 49.46 N 48.42 E
Kazumba 152 8.15 S 25.33 E
Kazungula 154 17.48 S 25.16 E
Kazy 92 40.11 N 140.47 E
→ Qazvīn 128 36.16 N 50.00 E
Kazym ≃ 74 63.54 N 65.50 E
Kazym ≃ 74 63.54 N 65.50 E
Kazymskij Mys 74 63.14 N 66.16 E
Kbal Dâmrei 110 13.48 N 106.00 E
Kbelnico 60 49.05 N 13.45 E
→ Sŏul 98 37.34 N 126.58 E
Kcynia 30 52.59 N 17.30 E
Kéa I 38 37.36 N 24.19 E
Kéa 38 37.38 N 24.21 E
Keaau 229d 19.37 N 155.02 W
Keady 48 54.15 N 6.42 W
Keahole Point ‣ 229d 19.44 N 156.04 W
Keal, Loch na ⌷ 46 56.28 N 6.04 W
Kealaikahiki, Lae o ‣ 229a 20.36 N 157.04 W
Kealaikahiki Channel ⌣ 229a 20.37 N 156.50 W
Kealakekua Bay c 229d 19.29 N 155.56 W
Keams Canyon 200 35.48 N 110.11 W
Keanae 229a 20.52 N 156.08 W
Keane College of New Jersey ♦ 276 40.41 N 74.14 W
Kéané 150 14.54 N 6.04 W
Kearney, Mo., U.S. 194 39.22 N 94.21 W
Kearney, Ne., U.S. 210 40.42 N 99.04 W
Kearney, N.J., U.S. 276 40.46 N 74.09 W
Kearns 204 40.39 N 111.59 W
Kearny, N.J., U.S. 276 40.46 N 74.09 W
Kearsarge 211 43.22 N 71.52 W
Kearsley Creek ≃ 216 43.00 N 83.40 W
Kéa Strait ⌣ 38 37.40 N 24.20 E
Keasbey 276 40.31 N 74.19 W
Kebajoran ≈⁸ 269e 6.15 S 106.46 E
Keban 130 38.48 N 38.58 E

Keban Barajı ⌷¹ 130 38.50 N 39.20 E
Kebanyartimur 115a 7.09 S 112.52 E
Kébara 152 2.27 S 14.25 E
Kebbi 150 12.08 N 4.44 E
Kebeiti 120 36.47 N 79.29 E
Kébémer 150 15.22 N 16.27 W
Kébi, Mayo ≃ 146 9.18 N 13.33 E
Kebili 148 33.42 N 8.58 E
Kebīr, Oued el ≃ 34 36.50 N 6.07 E
Kebnekaise ʌ 24 67.53 N 18.33 E
Kebock Head ‣ 46 58.01 N 6.20 W
Kebri Dehar 144 6.47 N 44.17 E
Kebumen 115a 7.40 S 109.39 E
Keç 85 45.50 N 44.14 E
Kečel 30 46.32 N 19.16 E
Kech ≃ 128 26.00 N 62.44 E
Kechika ≃ 176 36.39 N 127.05 W
Keçiborlu 130 37.57 N 30.18 E
Kecskemét 30 46.54 N 19.42 E
Kedah □³ 114 6.00 N 100.40 E
Kedainiai 76 55.17 N 24.00 E
Kedārpur 126 23.18 N 90.27 E
Kedge Strait ⌣ 208 38.03 N 76.02 W
Kédganj 154 9.36 S 25.37 E
Kédhrion ‣ 38 39.13 N 22.03 E
Kedian 100 31.23 N 112.51 E
Kediri 115a 7.49 S 112.01 E
Kedjebi 150 8.12 N 0.25 E
Kedon 74 64.08 N 159.14 E
Kedong 89 48.02 N 126.15 E
Kédougou 150 12.33 N 12.11 W
Kedrasju 86 54.36 N 60.24 E
Kedrovka 86 55.32 N 86.03 E
Kedu 102 26.33 N 104.21 E
Kedugrup 115a 7.06 S 113.15 E
Kedul 148 36.51 N 11.06 E
Kedungwuni 115a 6.58 S 109.39 E
Kedvavom 24 64.15 N 53.27 E
Kędzierzyn Kozle 30 50.20 N 18.12 E
Keechuus Lake ⌷ 224 47.22 N 121.22 W
Keefer 218 38.32 N 84.38 W
Keefers 182 50.02 N 121.33 W
Keego Harbor 216 42.36 N 83.20 W
Keelby 44 53.34 N 0.15 W
Keele 42 53.00 N 2.17 W
Keele ≃ 180 64.24 N 124.50 W
Keele Peak ʌ 180 63.26 N 130.19 W
Keeley Lake ⌷ 184 54.54 N 108.08 W
Keeling Islands
→ Cocos Islands II 12 12.10 S 96.55 E
Keels 48 48.36 N 53.24 W
Keelung
→ Chilung 100 25.08 N 121.44 E
Keene, Mount ʌ 46 56.58 N 2.54 W
Keene, Ont., Can. 212 44.15 N 78.10 W
Keene, Ca., U.S. 228 35.13 N 118.33 W
Keene, N.Y., U.S. 192 37.56 N 84.38 W
Keene, Tx., U.S. 222 32.23 N 97.19 W
Keene, N.H., U.S. 188 42.56 N 72.16 W
Keene, Oh., U.S. 218 40.19 N 81.37 W
Keene Valley 210 44.11 N 73.47 W
Keenesburg 200 40.06 N 104.31 W
Keeney Knob ʌ 192 37.47 N 80.42 W
Keeneyville 278 41.59 N 88.07 W
Keep River National Park ♦ 164 15.38 S 129.02 E
Keer-Weer, Cape ‣ 164 13.58 S 141.30 E
Keeseg ʌ 56 46.58 N 12.14 E
Keeseville 188 44.30 N 73.28 W
Keesler Air Force Base ≈ 194 30.26 N 88.55 W
Keetmanshoop 156 26.36 S 18.08 E
Keetmanshoop □⁵ 156 26.30 S 19.00 E
Keewatin, Mn., U.S. 190 47.23 N 93.04 W
Keewatin, Ont., Can. 184 49.46 N 94.34 W
Kefa □⁴ 144 6.30 N 36.30 E
Kefallinía I 38 38.15 N 20.35 E
Kétalos 38 36.45 N 27.07 E
Kefamenanu 112 9.27 S 124.29 E
Kefar 'Azza 132 31.29 N 34.32 E
Kefar Blum 132 33.10 N 35.36 E
Kefar 'Ezyon 132 31.39 N 35.07 E
Kefar Naḥum (Capernaum) ‣ 132 32.53 N 35.34 E
Kefar Sava 132 32.10 N 34.54 E
Kefar Shammay 132 32.57 N 35.27 E
Kefar Szold 132 33.11 N 35.39 E
Kefar Warburg 132 31.43 N 34.44 E
Kefar Yona 132 32.19 N 34.56 E
Kefermarkt 61 48.26 N 14.32 E
Keffi 150 8.51 N 7.52 E
Keffin Hausa 150 12.05 N 9.54 E
Kefken 130 41.11 N 30.14 E
Keftya 144 13.53 N 37.10 E
Kega 154 6.55 N 36.07 E
Ke Ga, Mui ‣, Viet. 110 10.42 N 107.58 E
Ke Ga, Mui ‣, Viet. 110 15.38 N 108.43 E
Kegashka, Lac ⌷ 189 50.09 N 61.17 W
Kegaska 189 50.12 N 61.18 W
Kégashka, Lac ⌷ 189 50.09 N 61.17 W
Kegegovka 85 49.17 N 35.42 E
Kegnæs ‣¹ 41 54.50 N 9.56 E
Kegonsa, Lake ⌷ 206 42.58 N 89.15 W
Kegon-taki ⌊ 94 36.44 N 139.30 E
Kegonsa Hatch 260 35.38 N 77.35 W
Kegums 76 56.45 N 24.42 E
Kegworth 44 52.50 N 1.17 W
Kehlen, Land ≈¹ 56 52.03 N 10.46 E
Kehlstein, Luxembourg ≈¹ 56 49.41 N 6.01 E
Kehl 58 48.34 N 7.49 E
Kehlen 56 49.41 N 6.01 E
Kehra 86 59.20 N 25.19 E
Kehrigk ≈⁸ 264c 52.15 N 13.56 E
Ke-hsi Mānsām 110 21.56 N 97.50 E
Kehya 86 59.58 N 28.41 E
Keighley 44 53.52 N 1.54 W
Keila 86 59.18 N 24.26 E
Keilor 169 37.43 N 144.50 E
Keimoes 156 28.43 S 21.00 E
Keinton Mandeville 50 51.04 N 2.33 W
Keiskammahoek 158 32.42 S 27.07 E
Keitele ⌷ 26 63.00 N 26.30 E
Keith, S. Austl. 168 36.06 S 140.21 E
Keith, Scot., U.K. 46 57.32 N 2.57 W
Keithsburg 206 41.06 N 90.56 W
Keizer 224 44.59 N 123.01 W
Kejimkujik National Park ♦ 186 44.25 N 65.14 W

Kekeyaer 85 38.02 N 75.05 E
Kek Lok Si ‣¹ 114 5.23 N 100.14 E
Kekpära 126 22.27 N 86.35 E
Kekri 120 25.58 N 75.09 E
Kekurnoi, Cape ‣ 180 57.44 N 155.15 W
Kelafo 144 5.40 N 44.20 E
Kelang 112 2.10 N 102.50 E
Kelan 102 38.43 N 111.32 E
Kelanang 114 2.48 N 101.26 E
Kelang 114 3.02 N 101.27 E
Kelang, Pulau I, Indon. 164 3.12 S 127.44 E
Kelang, Pulau I, Malay. 114 3.00 N 101.18 E
Kelani ≃ 122 6.58 N 79.52 E
Kelantan 114 0.51 N 101.40 E
Kelantan ≃ 114 5.20 N 102.00 E
Kelantan □³ 114 6.11 N 102.15 E
Kelapa 112 1.52 S 105.42 E
Kelasuri 83 43.08 N 41.13 E
Kelat 218 38.32 N 84.19 W
Kelayres 210 40.54 N 76.00 W
Kelb, Ouadi ⩗ 146 15.19 N 18.51 E
Keld 44 54.24 N 2.11 W
Keld Ula ʌ 86 43.20 N 85.25 E
Kel'd'ušov ‣ 80 55.01 N 44.59 E
Keleft 128 37.21 N 66.15 E
Kélégou 88 41.57 N 118.11 E
Kélékélé 273b 4.20 S 15.08 E
Kelem 144 4.48 N 35.58 E
Kelenföld ≈⁸ 264c 47.28 N 19.03 E
Kelenken, gora ʌ 180 66.07 N 170.52 W
Keles, S.S.S.R. 85 41.29 N 69.12 E
Keles, Tür. 130 39.55 N 29.14 E
Keles ≃ 85 41.02 N 68.42 E
Keleti-főcsatorna ≈ 30 48.01 N 21.20 E
Keleti Pályaudvar ≈⁵ 264c 47.30 N 19.06 E
Kelheim 60 48.55 N 11.52 E
Kelibia 148 36.51 N 11.06 E
Kelkheim 56 50.08 N 8.26 E
Kelkit 130 40.09 N 39.27 E
Kelkit ≃ 130 40.46 N 36.32 E
Kell 219 38.30 N 88.54 W
Kellé 152 0.06 S 14.33 E
Kellen 52 51.48 N 6.10 E
Kellenhusen 54 54.11 N 11.03 E
Keller, Tx., U.S. 222 32.56 N 97.15 W
Keller, Va., U.S. 208 37.37 N 75.45 W
Keller, Wa., U.S. 182 48.04 N 118.41 W
Kellerberg 64 46.40 N 13.42 E
Kellerberrin 64 31.38 S 117.43 E
Kellerjoch ʌ 64 47.19 N 11.46 E
Keller Lake ⌷, N.T., Can. 176 64.00 N 121.30 W
Keller Lake ⌷, Sk., Can. 184 56.04 N 106.46 W
Kellerovka 86 53.50 N 69.17 E
Keller Peak ʌ 228 34.12 N 117.03 W
Kellett, Cape ‣ 176 71.59 N 125.34 W
Kellettville 214 41.33 N 79.16 W
Kelleys Island 214 41.36 N 82.42 W
Kelleys Island I 214 41.36 N 82.42 W
Kelliher 184 51.15 N 103.44 W
Kellinghusen 52 53.57 N 9.43 E
Kellmünz 58 48.07 N 10.08 E
Kelloe 44 54.43 N 1.28 W
Kellogg, Id., U.S. 182 47.32 N 116.07 W
Kellogg, Ia., U.S. 190 41.43 N 92.54 W
Kellogg, Mn., U.S. 190 44.18 N 92.00 W
Kellogg Marsh 224 48.05 N 122.07 W
Kelloggsville 214 41.52 N 80.36 W
Kellojärvi ⌷ 26 64.16 N 29.03 E
Kelloselkä 26 66.56 N 28.50 E
Kells
→ Ceanannus Mór, Ire. 48 53.44 N 6.53 W
Kells, N. Ire., U.K. 48 54.48 N 6.13 W
Kells, N. Ire., U.K. 48 54.48 N 6.13 W
Kelly Air Force Base ≈ 196 29.24 N 98.35 W
Kelly Lake ⌷ 180 65.30 N 126.10 W
Kelly Run ≃, Pa., U.S. 279b 40.15 N 79.55 W
Kelly Run ≃, Pa., U.S. 279b 40.15 N 79.55 W
Kellyville, Austl. 274a 33.43 S 150.57 E
Kellyville, Ok., U.S. 196 35.56 N 96.12 W
Kelme 76 55.38 N 22.56 E
Kel'mency 78 48.30 N 26.50 E
Kelmis 56 50.43 N 6.01 E
Kelmscott 162 32.07 S 116.01 E
Kelo 146 9.19 N 15.48 E
Kelolokan 112 1.08 N 117.54 E
Kelottijärvi 24 68.36 N 22.06 E
Kelowna 182 49.53 N 119.29 W
Kelsall 44 53.13 N 2.43 W
Kelsey Bay 182 50.24 N 125.57 W
Kelsey Head ‣ 50 50.24 N 5.09 W
Kelseyville 228 38.59 N 122.50 W
Kelso, Scot., U.K. 46 55.36 N 2.25 W
Kelso, Wa., U.S. 224 46.09 N 122.54 W
Kelsterbach 58 50.04 N 8.32 E
Keltern 58 48.57 N 8.39 E
Keluang, Tanjung ‣ 112 3.56 S 111.10 E
Kelud, Gunung ʌ 115a 7.56 S 112.18 E
Keluo ≃ 89 49.22 N 125.12 E
Kelvdon 44 51.51 N 0.43 E
Kelvedon Hatch 260 51.39 N 0.16 E
Kelvin 60 51.24 N 4.23 E
Kelvin Seamount ≈⁴ 14 38.50 N 64.00 W
Kelyehxeed 144 9.19 N 42.12 E
Kem' 24 64.57 N 34.36 E
Kem' ≃ 24 64.57 N 34.36 E
Kema 112 1.22 N 125.04 E
Kemano 182 53.34 N 128.07 W
Kemayoran Airport ≈ 269e 6.09 S 106.51 E
Kembé 146 4.37 N 21.55 E
Kemberg 54 51.46 N 12.38 E
Kembolcha 144 11.05 N 39.44 E
Kemer, Tür. 130 36.35 N 30.33 E
Kemer, Tür. 130 37.25 N 27.00 E
Kemer, Tür. 130 36.24 N 29.16 E
Kémerovo 86 55.20 N 86.05 E
Kemerovo □⁴ 86 55.00 N 87.00 E
Kém'evo 82 57.14 N 46.22 E
Kemi 24 65.49 N 24.32 E
Kemi ≃ 24 65.47 N 24.30 E
Kémijärvi 24 66.40 N 27.25 E
Kémijärvi ⌷ 24 66.36 N 27.24 E
Kemi River
→ Kemi ≃ 24 65.47 N 24.30 E
Kéminmaa 26 65.48 N 24.33 E
Kemiö 26 60.10 N 22.45 E
Kémli 82 56.30 N 45.44 E
Kemmel 56 50.47 N 2.49 E

ENGLISH / **DEUTSCH**

Name / Name	Page / Seite	Lat.°′ / Breite°′	Long.°′ / Länge°′ E = Ost
Kemmelberg ∧ 2	50	50.47 N	2.50 E
Kemmerer	200	41.47 N	110.32 W
Kemminghausen ◆ 8	263	51.34 N	7.29 E
Kemmuna (Comino) I	36	36.00 N	14.20 E
Kemnader See ⊜	263	51.25 N	7.15 E
Kemnath	60	49.52 N	11.54 E
Kemnay	46	57.14 N	2.27 W
Kemnitz	54	54.04 N	13.31 E
Kémo-Gribingui □ 5	152	6.00 N	19.00 E
Kemp	222	32.26 N	96.13 W
Kemp, Lake ⊜ 1	196	33.45 N	99.13 W
Kemparana	150	12.50 N	4.56 W
Kemp Coast ⩡ 2	9	67.10 S	58.00 E
Kempele	26	64.55 N	25.30 E
Kempen	56	51.22 N	6.25 E
Kempen □ 9	56	51.10 N	5.20 E
Kempener Land ◆ 1	263	51.19 N	6.29 E
Kempenfelt Bay c	212	44.23 N	79.36 W
Kempenich	56	50.25 N	7.07 E
Kemper → Quimper	32	48.00 N	4.06 W
Kempisch Kanaal ≊	56	51.10 N	4.49 E
Kemp Mill	284c	39.02 N	77.01 W
Kempner	196	31.05 N	98.00 W
Kemp Peninsula ≻ 1	9	73.08 S	60.15 W
Kemps Bay	238	24.02 N	77.33 W
Kemps Creek ≃	274a	33.51 S	150.46 E
Kempsey, Austl.	166	31.05 S	152.50 E
Kempsey, Eng., U.K.	42	52.08 N	2.12 W
Kempston	42	52.07 N	0.30 W
Kempt, Lac ⊜	176	47.25 N	74.22 W
Kempten (Allgäu)	58	47.43 N	10.19 E
Kempton, Il., U.S.	216	40.56 N	88.14 W
Kempton, In., U.S.	216	40.17 N	86.13 W
Kempton Park	158	26.06 S	28.14 E
Kempton Park □ 5	273d	26.06 S	28.14 E
Kempton Park Race Course ♠	260	51.25 N	0.23 W
Kemptville	212	45.01 N	75.38 W
Kemptville Creek ≃	212	45.03 N	75.39 W
Kemsing	260	51.18 N	0.14 E
Kemubu	114	5.18 N	102.01 E
Kemujan, Pulau I	115a	5.48 S	110.28 E
Kemul, Kong ∧	112	1.52 N	116.11 E
Ken ≃	124	25.46 N	80.31 E
Ken, Loch ⊜	44	55.02 N	4.02 W
Ken, Water of ≃	44	55.04 N	4.08 W
Kena ≃	24	62.05 N	39.06 E
Kenai	180	60.33 N	151.15 W
Kenai Fjords National Park ♠	180	59.45 N	150.00 W
Kenai Mountains ⋏	180	60.00 N	150.00 W
Kenai Peninsula ≻ 1	180	60.10 N	150.00 W
Kenamuke Swamp ⩨	140	6.15 N	33.48 E
Kenansville, Fl., U.S.	220	27.52 N	80.59 W
Kenansville, N.C., U.S.	192	34.57 N	77.57 W
Kenaral	85	42.32 N	72.08 E
Kenašči	80	50.32 N	53.20 E
Kenashiga-sen ∧	96	35.14 N	133.31 E
Kenaston	184	51.30 N	106.18 W
Kenberma	283	42.17 N	70.52 W
Kenbridge	192	36.57 N	78.07 W
Kenda	126	23.12 N	86.32 E
Kendai	124	22.45 N	82.37 E
Kendal, Sk., Can.	184	50.15 N	103.37 W
Kendal, Indon.	115a	6.55 S	110.12 E
Kendal, S. Afr.	158	26.04 S	28.58 E
Kendal, Eng., U.K.	44	54.20 N	2.45 W
Kendall, Austl.	166	31.38 S	152.43 E
Kendall, Fl., U.S.	220	25.40 N	80.19 W
Kendall, Mi., U.S.	216	42.22 N	85.49 W
Kendall, N.Y., U.S.	210	43.20 N	78.02 W
Kendall, Wi., U.S.	190	43.47 N	90.22 W
Kendall □ 6	216	41.38 N	88.27 W
Kendall, Cape ≻	176	63.36 N	87.09 W
Kendall, Mount ∧	172	41.22 S	172.24 E
Kendall Park	208	40.31 N	74.24 W
Kendallville	216	41.26 N	85.15 W
Kendari	112	3.57 S	122.35 E
Kendari, Teluk c	112	3.57 S	122.38 E
Kendawangan	112	2.32 S	110.12 E
Kende	150	11.30 N	4.12 E
Kendenup	162	34.29 S	117.39 E
Kendghāta	126	24.05 N	87.10 E
Kendikolu I	122	5.57 N	73.24 E
Kendiktas ⋏	85	43.35 N	74.45 E
Kendleton	222	29.27 N	96.00 W
Kendrāparha	120	20.30 N	86.25 E
Kendrew	158	32.31 S	24.30 E
Kendrick, Fl., U.S.	192	29.22 N	82.12 W
Kendrick, Id., U.S.	202	46.36 N	116.38 W
Kendrick Creek ≃	226	38.00 N	119.50 W
Kendua	272b	22.34 N	88.10 E
Kendu Bay	154	0.22 S	34.39 E
Kendujhargarh	120	21.38 N	85.35 E
Kendyrlik	86	47.30 N	85.12 E
Kenedy	196	28.49 N	97.50 W
Kenefick	222	30.07 N	94.51 W
Kenema	150	7.52 N	11.12 W
Kenes, S.S.S.R.	85	43.41 N	67.49 E
Kenes, S.S.S.R.	85	43.59 N	73.35 E
Kenesaw	198	40.37 N	98.39 W
Kenga	86	57.27 N	80.57 E
Kenga ≃	86	58.05 N	80.37 E
Kenge	152	4.52 S	16.59 E
Kengeja	154	5.25 S	39.44 E
Kēng Hkam, Mya.	110	21.01 N	98.29 E
Keng Hkam, Mya.	110	21.27 N	97.03 E
Kengkou, Zhg.	100	29.48 N	117.22 E
Kengkou, Zhg.	100	28.27 N	120.26 E
Kengtian	100	25.54 N	119.26 E
Kēng Tung	110	21.17 N	99.36 E
Kengun-chūtonchi, Rikujō-jieitai- ■	92	32.46 N	130.45 E
Kenhardt	158	29.19 S	21.12 E
Kenhorst	208	40.18 N	75.57 W
Kenia	152	2.43 S	17.04 E
Kenia → Kenya □ 1	154	1.00 N	38.00 E
Kenia → Kirinyaga ∧	154	0.10 S	37.20 E
Kéniéba	150	12.50 N	11.14 W
Kenilworth, Eng., U.K.	42	52.21 N	1.34 W
Kenilworth, Il., U.S.	278	42.05 N	87.43 W
Kenilworth, N.J., U.S.	276	40.40 N	74.17 W
Kenilworth, Pa., U.S.	208	40.14 N	75.38 W
Kenilworth, Ut., U.S.	200	39.41 N	110.48 W
Kenilworth Castle ⊥	42	52.21 N	1.34 W
Keningau	112	5.20 N	116.10 E
Kenitra	148	34.16 N	6.40 W
Kenitra □ 4	148	34.30 N	6.00 W
Kenley ◆ 8	260	51.19 N	0.06 W
Kenli (Xishuanghe)	98	37.40 N	118.35 E
Kenly	192	35.35 N	78.07 W
Kenmare, Ire.	48	51.53 N	9.35 W
Kenmare, N.D., U.S.	198	48.40 N	102.04 W
Kenmare River ≃	48	51.45 N	10.00 W
Kenmawr	279b	40.28 N	80.06 W
Kenmore, Scot., U.K.	46	56.34 N	3.59 W
Kenmore, N.Y., U.S.	210	42.57 N	78.52 W
Kenmore, Wa., U.S.	224	47.45 N	122.14 W
Kennard, In., U.S.	218	39.54 N	85.31 W
Kennard, Pa., U.S.	214	41.28 N	80.20 W
Kennard, Tx., U.S.	222	31.22 N	95.11 W
Kennebec	198	43.54 N	99.51 W
Kennebec ≃	188	44.00 N	69.50 W
Kennebecasis Bay c	186	45.25 N	66.00 W
Kennebec Lake ⊜	212	44.43 N	77.00 W
Kennebunk	188	43.23 N	70.32 W
Kennedale	222	32.38 N	97.13 W
Kennedy, Al., U.S.	194	33.35 N	87.59 W
Kennedy, N.Y., U.S.	214	42.09 N	79.06 W
Kennedy, Zimb.	154	18.52 S	27.10 E
Kennedy, Cape → Canaveral, Cape ≻	220	28.27 N	80.32 W
Kennedy, Mount ∧, B.C., Can.	182	50.49 N	125.33 W
Kennedy, Mount ∧, Yk., Can.	180	60.30 N	139.00 W
Kennedy Entrance ⋓	180	59.00 N	152.00 W
Kennedy Lake ⊜	182	49.05 N	125.40 W
Kennedy Peak ∧	110	23.19 N	93.45 E
Kennedy Range ⋏	162	24.30 S	115.00 E
Kennedyville	208	39.18 N	75.59 W
Kennemerduinen, Nationale Park de ♠	52	52.25 N	4.35 E
Kenner	194	29.59 N	90.14 W
Kennerdell	214	41.16 N	79.51 W
Kennet ≃, Eng., U.K.	42	52.26 N	0.28 E
Kennet ≃, Eng., U.K.	42	51.28 N	0.57 W
Kennetcook	186	45.11 N	63.44 W
Kenneth City	220	27.49 N	82.44 W
Kennett	194	36.14 N	90.03 W
Kennett Square	208	39.50 N	75.42 W
Kennewick	202	46.12 N	119.08 W
Kenney	219	40.06 N	89.05 W
Kenney Dam ◆ 6	182	53.37 N	124.58 W
Kennington, Eng., U.K.	42	51.10 N	0.54 E
Kennington, Eng., U.K.	42	51.43 N	1.15 W
Kennisis Lake ⊜	212	45.13 N	78.39 W
Kenn Reef ✦ 2	160	21.12 S	155.46 E
Kenny	222	30.03 N	96.20 W
Kennydale	224	47.31 N	122.12 W
Kennywood Park ♠	279b	40.23 N	79.52 W
Kénogami	186	48.26 N	71.14 W
Kenogami ≃	176	51.06 N	84.28 W
Kénogami, Lac ⊜	186	48.20 N	71.23 W
Kenogamissi Lake ⊜	190	48.15 N	81.31 W
Keno Hill	180	63.55 N	135.18 W
Kenora	184	49.47 N	94.29 W
Kenosha	216	42.35 N	87.49 W
Kenosha □ 6	216	42.35 N	88.03 W
Kenova	188	38.23 N	82.34 W
Kenoza Lake	210	41.44 N	74.57 W
Kenoza Lake ⊜	283	42.47 N	71.03 W
Kenozero, ozero ⊜	24	62.03 N	38.14 E
Ken Rock	216	42.15 N	89.03 W
Kensal	198	47.18 N	98.43 W
Kense	86	46.49 N	68.20 E
Kensett	194	35.13 N	91.40 W
Kensico Lake ⊜	276	41.07 N	73.45 W
Kensico Reservoir ⊜ 1	210	41.05 N	73.46 W
Kensington, Austl.	274a	33.55 S	151.14 E
Kensington, P.E., Can.	186	46.26 N	63.38 W
Kensington, Ca., U.S.	226	37.54 N	122.16 W
Kensington, Ct., U.S.	207	41.38 N	72.46 W
Kensington, Ks., U.S.	198	39.46 N	99.01 W
Kensington, Md., U.S.	284c	39.01 N	77.04 W
Kensington, Oh., U.S.	214	40.44 N	80.57 W
Kensington ◆ 8, S. Afr.	273d	26.12 S	28.06 E
Kensington ◆ 8, N.Y., U.S.	276	40.39 N	73.58 W
Kensington ◆ 8, Pa., U.S.	285	39.58 N	75.08 W
Kensington and Chelsea ◆ 8	260	51.29 N	0.11 W
Kensington Estates	284c	39.02 N	77.05 W
Kensington Metropolitan Park ♠	281	42.32 N	83.39 W
Kensington Park	220	27.22 N	82.31 W
Kent, S.L.	150	8.10 N	13.10 W
Kent, Ct., U.S.	207	41.43 N	73.28 W
Kent, N.Y., U.S.	210	43.20 N	78.08 W
Kent, Oh., U.S.	214	41.09 N	81.21 W
Kent, Or., U.S.	224	45.11 N	120.41 W
Kent, Wa., U.S.	224	47.22 N	122.14 W
Kent □ 6, On., Can.	214	42.25 N	82.10 W
Kent □ 6, Eng., U.K.	42	51.15 N	0.40 E
Kent □ 6, De., U.S.	208	39.10 N	75.32 W
Kent □ 6, Md., U.S.	208	39.13 N	76.04 W
Kent □ 6, Mi., U.S.	216	42.56 N	85.33 W
Kent □ 6, R.I., U.S.	207	41.40 N	71.38 W
Kent ≃	44	54.15 N	2.48 W
Kent, Vale of V	42	51.10 N	0.30 E
Kent Acres	208	39.07 N	75.31 W
Kentallen	46	56.39 N	5.15 W
Kentani	158	32.31 S	28.19 E
Kentau	85	43.36 N	68.36 E
Kent Bridge	214	42.31 N	82.04 W
Kent County Airport ⊠	216	42.54 N	85.39 W
Kentfield	282	37.57 N	122.33 W
Kent Group II	166	39.27 S	147.20 E
Kenthurst	274a	33.40 S	151.00 E
Kent Island I	208	38.55 N	76.20 W
Kent Lake ⊜	216	42.32 N	83.40 W
Kentland, In., U.S.	216	40.46 N	87.26 W
Kentland, Md., U.S.	284c	38.55 N	76.53 W
Kenton, Eng., U.K.	42	50.38 N	3.28 W
Kenton, De., U.S.	208	39.13 N	75.39 W
Kenton, Mi., U.S.	190	46.29 N	88.53 W
Kenton, Oh., U.S.	216	40.38 N	83.36 W
Kenton, Tn., U.S.	194	36.12 N	89.00 W
Kenton □ 6	218	38.56 N	84.33 W
Kent Park	283	42.06 N	70.41 W
Kent Park ♠	273d	26.08 S	28.04 E
Kent Peninsula ≻ 1	176	68.30 N	107.00 W
Kent Point ≻	208	38.50 N	76.22 W
Kentucky □ 3	178	37.30 N	85.15 W
Kentucky ≃	218	38.41 N	85.11 W
Kentucky, Middle Fork ≃	192	37.35 N	83.40 W
Kentucky, North Fork ≃	192	37.34 N	83.42 W
Kentucky, South Fork ≃	192	37.34 N	83.42 W
Kentucky Horse Park ♠	218	38.08 N	84.31 W
Kentucky Lake ⊜ 1	194	36.25 N	88.05 W
Kent Village	284c	38.55 N	76.53 W
Kentville	186	45.05 N	64.30 W
Kentwood, La., U.S.	194	30.56 N	90.30 W
Kentwood, Mi., U.S.	216	42.52 N	85.38 W
Kent Woodlands	282	37.57 N	122.34 W
Kenvil	276	40.52 N	74.37 W
Kenwick	168a	32.02 S	115.58 E
Kenwood, Ca., U.S.	226	38.25 N	122.33 W
Kenwood, Md., U.S.	284b	39.21 N	76.31 W
Kenwood, Oh., U.S.	218	39.12 N	84.22 W
Kenwood ◆ 8	278	41.49 N	87.36 W
Kenwood ⊥	260	51.34 N	0.10 W
Kenya □ 1	154	1.00 N	38.00 E
Kenya, Mount → Kirinyaga ∧	154	0.10 S	37.20 E
Kenyon, Eng., U.K.	262	53.27 N	2.34 W
Kenyon, Mn., U.S.	190	44.16 N	92.59 W
Kenyon, R.I., U.S.	207	41.26 N	71.37 W
Ken-zaki ≻	268	35.08 N	139.41 E
Kenzingen	58	48.11 N	7.46 E
Kenzou	152	4.10 N	15.02 E
Keokea	229a	20.42 N	156.21 W
Keokuk	190	40.23 N	91.23 W
Keoladeo National Park ♠	124	27.10 N	77.20 E
Keonchi	124	22.38 N	81.47 E
Keo Neua, Col de)(	110	18.23 N	105.09 E
Keon Park	274b	37.42 S	145.01 E
Keosauqua	190	40.43 N	91.57 W
Keota, Ia., U.S.	190	41.21 N	91.57 W
Keota, Ok., U.S.	196	35.15 N	94.55 W
Keowee, Lake ⊜ 1	192	34.45 N	82.55 W
Kepa (Mittagskogel) ∧	61	46.31 N	13.57 E
Kepala Batas	114	5.31 N	100.26 E
Kepanjen	115a	8.07 S	112.34 E
Kepi	164	6.32 S	139.19 E
Kępice	30	54.15 N	16.52 E
Kepina	24	65.24 N	41.50 E
Keping Shan ⋏	85	40.00 N	77.10 E
Kępno	30	51.17 N	17.59 E
Kepo	112	2.56 S	106.33 E
Keppel Bay c	166	23.21 S	150.55 E
Keppel Harbour c	271c	1.16 N	103.50 E
Kepsut	130	39.41 N	28.09 E
Keptown	219	39.05 N	88.40 W
Kequan	98	36.04 N	114.00 E
Kerala □ 3	122	10.00 N	76.30 E
Keram ≃	164	4.07 S	144.07 E
Keramian, Pulau I	112	5.04 S	114.36 E
Kerandin	112	0.12 S	104.46 E
Kerang	166	35.44 S	143.55 E
Keranyo	144	5.04 N	38.18 E
Keratéa	38	37.48 N	23.59 E
Keratsínion	267c	37.58 N	23.37 E
Keraudren, Cape ≻	162	19.57 S	119.45 E
Kerava	26	60.24 N	25.07 E
Keravat	164	4.19 S	152.01 E
Kerbat ≃	114	5.01 N	102.51 E
Kerbela → Karbalā'	128	32.36 N	44.02 E
Kerbi ≃	89	52.28 N	136.25 E
Kerby	202	42.11 N	123.39 W
Kerč'	78	45.22 N	36.27 E
Kerčel'	86	59.18 N	64.46 E
Kerčemja	24	61.28 N	53.50 E
Kerčenskij poluostrov ≻ 1	78	45.15 N	36.00 E
Kerčenskij proliv ⋓	78	45.22 N	36.38 E
Kerčevskij	24	59.55 N	56.17 E
Kerch → Kerč'	78	45.22 N	36.27 E
Kerckhoff Lake ⊜ 1	226	37.09 N	119.31 W
Kéré	154	5.16 N	26.11 E
Kéré ≃	140	5.19 N	25.40 E
Kerec, mys ≻	24	65.20 N	39.40 E
Kerej, ozero ⊜	86	50.08 N	68.45 E
Kerema	164	8.00 S	145.45 E
Keremeos	182	49.12 N	119.50 W
Kerem Maharal	132	32.39 N	34.59 E
Kerempe Burnu ≻	130	42.01 N	33.21 E
Keren	144	15.46 N	38.28 E
Kerend	128	34.16 N	46.15 E
Kerens	222	32.07 N	96.13 W
Kerepes	264c	47.34 N	19.18 E
Keret'	24	66.16 N	33.34 E
Keret', ozero ⊜	24	65.55 N	32.56 E
Kerewan	150	13.29 N	16.10 W
Kerga	24	62.39 N	46.00 E
Kergez	84	40.18 N	49.38 E
Kerguélen, Îles II	6	49.15 S	69.10 E
Kerguelen Plateau ✦ 3	6	55.00 S	75.00 E
Kerhonkson	210	41.46 N	74.17 W
Kerian ≃	114	5.10 N	100.26 E
Kericho	154	0.22 S	35.17 E
Keri Kera	140	12.21 N	32.46 E
Kerikeri	172	35.13 S	173.58 E
Kerimäki	26	61.55 N	29.17 E
Kerinci, Gunung ∧	112	1.42 S	101.16 E
Kerio ≃	154	2.59 N	36.07 E
Keríon	38	37.40 N	20.48 E
Keritang	112	0.51 S	102.39 E
Keriya ≃	120	38.30 N	82.10 E
Kerka ≃	61	46.28 N	16.36 E
Kerkafalva	61	46.46 N	16.30 E
Kerkdriel	52	51.46 N	5.20 E
Kerkebet	144	16.18 N	37.24 E
Kerken	56	51.27 N	6.22 E
Kerkenna, Îles II	148	34.44 N	11.12 E
Kerkhove	50	50.48 N	3.30 E
Kerkhoven	198	45.11 N	95.19 W
Kerki, S.S.S.R.	24	63.43 N	54.05 E
Kerki, S.S.S.R.	128	37.50 N	65.12 E
Kérkira (Corfu)	38	39.36 N	19.56 E
Kérkira I	38	39.40 N	19.42 E
Kerkrade [-Holz]	56	50.52 N	6.04 E
Kerling	114	3.35 N	101.36 E
Kermadec Islands II	14	29.16 S	177.55 W
Kermadec Ridge ✦ 3	14	30.30 S	178.30 W
Kermadec Trench ✦ 1	14	30.00 S	177.00 W
Kermajärvi ⊜	26	62.28 N	28.40 E
Kermān, Īrān	128	30.17 N	57.05 E
Kerman, Ca., U.S.	226	36.43 N	120.04 W
Kermān □ 4	128	29.00 N	57.30 E
Kermit	196	31.51 N	103.05 W
Kermit Roosevelt Seamount ✦ 3	16	39.35 N	146.00 W
Kermode, Mount ∧	182	52.57 N	131.51 W
Kern □ 6	228	35.20 N	118.55 W
Kern ≃	204	35.13 N	119.17 W
Kern, South Fork ≃	204	35.40 N	118.27 W
Kern City	228	35.18 N	119.05 W
Kernersville	192	36.07 N	80.04 W
Kernforschungszentrum ⊌ 3	56	49.07 N	8.26 E
Kernhof	61	47.49 N	15.32 E
Kern Island Canal ≊	228	35.22 N	119.01 W
Kern Lake Bed ⊜	228	35.10 N	119.05 W
Kern River Channel ≃ 1	226	35.49 N	119.40 W
Kernville	204	35.45 N	118.25 W
Keroh	114	5.43 N	101.00 E
Keros	24	60.44 N	52.50 E
Kérou	150	10.50 N	2.06 E
Kérouané	150	9.16 N	9.01 W
Kerowagi	164	5.50 S	144.50 E
Kerpen	56	50.52 N	6.41 E
Kerpinen'	78	46.47 N	28.22 E
Kerr	214	41.03 N	78.25 W
Kerrera I	46	56.23 N	5.34 W
Kerridge	262	53.17 N	2.06 W
Kerridge Hill ∧ 2	262	53.17 N	2.06 W
Kerrobert	184	51.55 N	109.08 W
Kerrtown	214	41.38 N	80.10 W
Kerruish Park ♠	279a	41.26 N	81.34 W
Kerrville	196	30.02 N	99.08 W
Kerry	42	52.30 N	3.16 W
Kerry □ 6	48	52.10 N	9.30 W
Kerry Head ≻	48	52.25 N	9.57 W
Kersa	144	9.28 N	41.53 E
Kersbrook	168b	34.47 S	138.51 E
Kersey	214	41.21 N	78.35 W
Kershaw	192	34.33 N	80.35 W
Kersinyane	150	15.24 N	10.10 W
Kersley	182	52.49 N	122.25 W
Kerspestausee ⊜ 1	263	51.08 N	7.30 E
Kerstenhausen	56	51.04 N	9.13 E
Kert, Oued ≃	34	35.15 N	3.15 W
Kertamulia	112	0.23 S	109.09 E
Kerteh	114	4.31 N	103.27 E
Kerteminde	41	55.27 N	10.40 E
Kertosono	115a	7.35 S	112.06 E
Kerulen (Cherlen) (Herlen) ≃	90	48.48 N	117.00 E
Kerva	80	55.37 N	39.35 E
Kerzaz	148	29.30 N	1.37 W
Kerzendorf	264a	52.16 N	13.17 E
Keržanec	80	56.28 N	44.26 E
Keržanec ≃	80	56.05 N	45.03 E
Kerzers	58	46.58 N	7.12 E
Kesabpur	126	22.55 N	89.13 E
Ke Sach	110	9.46 N	105.59 E
Kesagami Lake ⊜	176	50.23 N	80.15 W
Kesälahti	26	61.54 N	29.50 E
Keşan	130	40.51 N	26.37 E
Keşap	130	40.55 N	38.31 E
Kesbern	263	51.20 N	7.42 E
Kesch, Piz ∧	58	46.38 N	9.52 E
Kesem ≃	144	9.14 N	40.06 E
Kesennuma	92	38.54 N	141.35 E
Kesh	48	54.32 N	7.43 W
Keshan	89	48.02 N	125.51 E
Keshena	190	44.53 N	88.38 W
Keshendeh	120	36.05 N	66.51 E
Keshequa Creek ≃	210	42.43 N	77.50 W
Keshod	120	21.18 N	70.15 E
Keşiş Dağları ⋏	130	39.50 N	39.45 E
Keskastel	56	48.58 N	7.02 E
Keskin	130	39.41 N	33.37 E
Keski-Suomen lääni □ 4	26	62.30 N	25.30 E
Keskozero	24	61.24 N	33.12 E
Keskuvejem, gora ∧	180	66.12 N	177.40 W
Kes'ma	76	58.27 N	37.04 E
Kesova Gora	76	57.35 N	37.17 E
Kespur	126	22.35 N	87.29 E
Kesra	36	35.49 N	9.22 E
Kessebüren	263	51.31 N	7.43 E
Kessel	56	51.08 N	4.37 E
Kesselsdorf	54	51.02 N	13.35 E
Kessingland	42	52.25 N	1.42 E
Kesswil	58	47.36 N	9.20 E
Kestel Gölü ⊜	130	37.24 N	30.28 E
Kestell	158	28.19 S	28.38 E
Kesten'ga	24	65.55 N	31.47 E
Kestilä	26	64.21 N	26.17 E
Keston ◆ 8	260	51.22 N	0.02 E
Keswick, On., Can.	212	44.15 N	79.28 W
Keswick, Eng., U.K.	44	54.37 N	3.08 W
Keszthely	30	46.46 N	17.15 E
Ket' ≃	86	58.55 N	81.32 E
Keta	150	5.55 N	1.00 E
Keta ≃	94	34.56 N	137.50 E
Keta, ozero ⊜	74	68.44 N	90.00 E
Ketaka	96	35.30 N	134.03 E
Keta Lagoon c	150	5.54 N	0.56 E
Ketam, Pulau I	271c	1.24 N	103.57 E
Ketama	34	34.50 N	4.37 W
Ketang	100	22.58 N	115.28 E
Ketapang, Indon.	112	1.52 S	109.59 E
Ketapang, Indon.	115a	6.54 S	113.17 E
Ketapang, Indon.	115a	5.44 S	105.48 E
Ketaun	112	3.23 S	101.49 E
Ketchikan	182	55.21 N	131.35 W
Ketchum	202	43.40 N	114.21 W
Kete Krachi	150	7.46 N	0.03 W
Ketelmeer ⊜	52	52.35 N	5.45 E
Keti Bandar	120	24.08 N	67.27 E
Ketingwan ∧	154	0.40 N	35.50 E
Ketoj, ostrov I	74	47.20 N	152.28 E
Kétou	150	7.22 N	2.36 E
Ketovo	86	55.21 N	65.18 E
Kętrzyn (Rastenburg)	30	54.06 N	21.23 E
Ketsch	56	49.22 N	8.31 E
Ketta	152	1.28 N	15.56 E
Kettering, Eng., U.K.	42	52.24 N	0.44 W
Kettering, Md., U.S.	284c	38.53 N	76.49 W
Kettering, Oh., U.S.	218	39.41 N	84.10 W
Kettinge	41	54.42 N	11.45 E
Kettle ≃, Mb., Can.	184	56.23 N	94.34 W
Kettle ≃, N.A.	182	48.42 N	118.07 W
Kettle ≃, Mn., U.S.	190	45.52 N	92.45 W
Kettle Creek ≃, On., Can.	212	42.40 N	81.13 W
Kettle Creek ≃, Pa., U.S.	210	41.18 N	77.51 W
Kettle Creek State Park ♠	214	41.23 N	77.56 W
Kettle Falls	202	48.36 N	118.03 W
Kettleman City	226	36.00 N	119.57 W
Kettleman Hills ⋏ 2	226	36.00 N	120.00 W
Kettle Rapids Dam ◆ 6	184	56.23 N	94.38 W
Kettlersville	216	40.22 N	84.16 W
Kettleshulme	262	53.19 N	2.01 W
Kettlewell	44	54.09 N	2.02 W
Kettwig	56	51.22 N	6.56 E
Kęty	30	49.53 N	19.13 E
Ketzin	54	52.28 N	12.50 E
Keudemane	114	5.15 N	96.55 E
Keudepasi	114	4.18 N	95.56 E
Keudeteunom	114	4.27 N	95.48 E
Keudeunga	114	5.01 N	95.22 E
Keuka Lake ⊜	210	42.27 N	77.10 W
Keuka Lake, West Branch c	210	42.33 N	77.09 W
Keuka Park	210	42.37 N	77.06 W
Keukenhof ♠	52	52.16 N	4.33 E
Keul'	88	58.25 N	102.49 E
Keula	54	51.20 N	10.31 E
Keum ≃	86	59.32 N	70.35 E
Keurboomsrivier	158	34.00 S	23.24 E
Keurusselkä ⊜	26	62.10 N	24.40 E
Keuruu	26	62.16 N	24.42 E
Kevdo-Mel'sitovo	80	53.09 N	43.54 E
Kevelaer	52	51.35 N	6.15 E
Kevin	202	48.44 N	111.57 W
Kevsala	80	45.48 N	42.41 E
Kew, Austl.	169	37.49 S	145.02 E
Kew, T./C. Is.	238	21.54 N	72.02 W
Kewanee	190	41.14 N	89.55 W
Kewanna	216	41.01 N	86.25 W
Kewaunee	190	44.27 N	87.30 W
Keweenaw Bay c	190	46.56 N	88.23 W
Keweenaw Peninsula ≻ 1	190	47.12 N	88.25 W
Keweenaw Point ≻	190	47.30 N	87.50 W
Kew Gardens ♠, On., Can.	275b	43.40 N	79.18 W
Kew Gardens ♠, Eng., U.K.	260	51.28 N	0.18 W
Keyala	154	4.27 N	32.52 E
Keyangkeer Shan ∧	120	31.20 N	87.13 E
Keya Paha ≃	198	42.54 N	99.00 W
Key Biscayne	220	25.42 N	80.10 W
Keyes, Ca., U.S.	226	37.33 N	120.54 W
Keyes, Ok., U.S.	196	36.48 N	102.15 W
Keyesport	219	38.44 N	89.17 W
Keyhole Reservoir ⊜ 1	198	44.21 N	104.51 W
Keyhole State Park ♠	198	44.19 N	104.48 W
Keyihe	89	50.40 N	122.27 E
Keyingham	44	53.42 N	0.07 W
Key Largo	220	25.04 N	80.28 W
Key Largo I	220	25.16 N	80.19 W
Keymer	42	50.55 N	0.08 W
Keynes Hill ∧ 2	168b	34.37 S	139.06 E
Keyneton	168b	34.34 S	139.08 E
Keynsham	42	51.26 N	2.30 W
Keynshamburg	154	19.15 S	29.39 E
Keyport, N.J., U.S.	276	40.25 N	74.12 W
Keyport, Wa., U.S.	224	47.42 N	122.38 W
Keyport Harbor c	276	40.26 N	74.12 W
Keysborough	274b	38.00 S	145.10 E
Keysbrook	168a	32.26 S	115.59 E
Keyser	188	39.26 N	78.58 W
Keystone, In., U.S.	216	40.36 N	85.16 W
Keystone, Ia., U.S.	190	41.59 N	92.11 W
Keystone, S.D., U.S.	198	43.53 N	103.25 W
Keystone, W.V., U.S.	192	37.24 N	81.27 W
Keystone Lake ⊜ 1, Ok., U.S.	196	36.15 N	96.25 W
Keystone Lake ⊜ 1, Pa., U.S.	214	40.45 N	79.15 W
Keystone Peak ∧	200	31.53 N	111.13 W
Keystone Race Track ♠	285	40.07 N	74.57 W
Keystone State Park ♠	214	40.23 N	79.24 W
Keysville, Fl., U.S.	220	27.52 N	82.06 W
Keysville, Va., U.S.	192	37.02 N	78.29 W
Keytesville	194	39.26 N	92.56 W
Key West	220	24.33 N	81.46 W
Key West Island I	220	24.33 N	81.47 W
Key West Naval Air Station ■	220	24.34 N	81.41 W
Keyworth	42	52.52 N	1.05 W
Kez	80	57.53 N	53.43 E
Kezar Stadium ♠	282	37.46 N	122.27 W
Kezi	154	20.58 S	28.32 E
Kezilesu Zizhizhou □ 8	85	40.00 N	75.30 E
Kežma	88	58.59 N	101.09 E
Kežmarok	30	49.08 N	20.25 E
Kgalagadi □ 5	156	25.00 S	22.00 E
Kgatleng □ 5	156	24.28 S	26.05 E
Kgokgole ≃	158	26.44 S	22.28 E
Kgun Lake ⊜	180	61.32 N	163.45 W
Khaanziir, Ras ≻	144	10.55 N	45.47 E
Khabab	132	33.00 N	36.16 E
Khabīr, Kūh-e ∧	128	28.48 N	56.26 E
Khābūr, Nahr al- (Habur) ≃	130	35.08 N	40.26 E
Khādar	272a	28.33 N	77.22 E
Khadari, Wādī al- V	140	10.29 N	26.15 E
Khadaungnge Taung ∧	110	18.57 N	94.37 E
Khadki (Kirkee)	122	18.34 N	73.52 E
Khadra	34	36.15 N	0.35 E
Khafūrī, Wādī V	142	29.37 N	32.04 E
Khagaria	124	25.30 N	86.29 E
Khagdon ≃ 1	126	22.09 N	90.05 E
Khāgrāmuri	272b	22.26 N	88.14 E
Khaïdhárion	267c	37.33 N	22.53 E
Khair	124	27.57 N	77.50 E
Khairābād	124	27.32 N	80.45 E
Khairāgarh	120	21.25 N	80.58 E
Khairbani	126	24.14 N	87.05 E
Khairna	272c	19.06 N	73.01 E
Khairpur, Pāk.	120	27.32 N	68.46 E
Khairpur, Pāk.	123	29.35 N	72.14 E
Khairwāra	120	23.59 N	73.35 E
Khajrāho	120	24.50 N	79.58 E
Khajuri	126	21.52 N	87.58 E
Khajuri ◆ 8	272a	28.43 N	77.16 E
Kha Khaeng ≃	110	14.55 N	99.07 E
Khakhea	156	24.51 S	23.20 E
Khalándrion	267c	38.01 N	23.48 E
Khalatse	123	34.20 N	76.49 E
Khālidī, Khirbat al- ⊥	132	29.39 N	35.14 E
Khalkhāl	128	37.37 N	48.32 E
Khalkhalah	132	33.04 N	36.32 E
Khálki I	130	36.17 N	27.35 E
Khalkidhikí □ 9	38	40.25 N	23.27 E
Khalkís	38	38.28 N	23.36 E
Khālsar	120	34.31 N	77.41 E
Khambhāliya	120	22.12 N	69.39 E
Khambhāt	120	22.18 N	72.37 E
Khambhāt, Gulf of c	122	21.00 N	72.30 E
Khāmgaon	122	20.41 N	76.34 E
Khamir	144	16.05 N	43.55 E
Khāmis, Ash-Shallāl al- (Fifth Cataract) ∟	140	18.23 N	33.47 E
Khamīs Mushayṭ	144	18.18 N	42.44 E
Khamkeut	110	18.15 N	104.43 E
Khamma	70	36.47 N	12.02 E
Khammam	122	17.15 N	80.09 E
Khamsah	142	30.25 N	32.23 E
Khan ≃, Lao	110	19.54 N	102.09 E
Khan ≃, Namibia	156	22.37 S	14.56 E
Khāna	126	23.20 N	87.44 E
Khānābād	120	36.41 N	69.07 E
Khān Abū Shāmāt	132	33.40 N	36.54 E
Khānākul	126	22.43 N	87.51 E
Khān al-Baghdādī	128	33.51 N	42.33 E
Khānaqīn	128	34.21 N	45.22 E
Khān Arnabah	132	33.11 N	35.53 E
Khancoban	171b	36.12 S	148.05 E
Khandaghosh	126	23.13 N	87.41 E
Khandela	120	27.36 N	75.30 E
Khandwa	124	21.50 N	76.20 E
Khān-e Chahār Bāgh, Afg.	120	35.58 N	69.38 E
Khān-e Chahār Bāgh, Afg.	128	37.00 N	65.14 E
Khāneh Khvodī	128	36.02 N	55.59 E
Khānewāl	123	30.18 N	71.56 E
Khāngāh Dogrān	123	31.50 N	73.37 E
Khāngarh, Pāk.	120	28.22 N	71.43 E
Khāngarh, Pāk.	123	29.55 N	71.10 E
Khangkhai	110	19.28 N	103.15 E
Khaniá	38	35.31 N	24.02 E
Khaníon, Kólpos c	38	35.34 N	23.48 E
Khānkurda	126	22.00 N	87.25 E
Khanna	123	30.42 N	76.13 E
Khannā, Qā' ≚	132	32.04 N	36.26 E
Khānozai	120	30.37 N	67.19 E
Khānpur, India	272b	22.40 N	88.16 E
Khānpur, Pāk.	123	28.39 N	70.39 E
Khānpur ◆ 8, India	272a	28.34 N	77.01 E
Khānpur ◆ 8, India	272a	28.31 N	77.14 E
Khān Shaykhūn	130	35.26 N	36.38 E
Khanty-Mansiysk → Chanty-Mansijsk	74	61.00 N	69.06 E
Khān Yūnus	132	31.21 N	34.19 E
Khao Laem Reservoir ⊜ 1	110	14.50 N	98.30 E
Khao Saming	110	12.21 N	102.27 E
Khao Sok National Park ♠	110	8.55 N	98.35 E
Khao Yoi	110	13.14 N	99.50 E
Khapalu	123	35.10 N	76.20 E
Khaptad National Park ♠	124	29.28 N	81.10 E
Kharab, Ghoubet al c	144	11.30 N	42.35 E
Kharabā	132	32.34 N	36.27 E
Kharagdiha	124	24.25 N	86.10 E
Kharagpur, India	124	25.07 N	86.33 E
Kharagpur, India	126	22.20 N	87.20 E
Kharak	123	33.07 N	71.06 E
Khārān	120	28.35 N	65.25 E
Kharānoq	128	32.20 N	54.39 E
Kharar, India	123	30.45 N	76.39 E
Kharar, India	126	22.42 N	87.41 E
Khāravli ∧ 2	272c	18.54 N	72.55 E
Kharāyij, Sabkhat al- ⊜	130	35.40 N	37.20 E
Kharaz, Jabal ∧	144	12.44 N	44.09 E
Kharbatā	132	31.57 N	35.04 E
Kharbine → Harbin	89	45.45 N	126.41 E
Khardaha	126	22.44 N	88.22 E
Khārghar	272c	19.03 N	73.04 E
Kharg Island → Khārk, Jazīreh-ye I	128	29.15 N	50.20 E
Khargon	120	21.49 N	75.36 E
Khāriān Cantonment	123	32.49 N	73.52 E
Khariār Road	122	20.54 N	82.31 E
Khārijah, Al-Wāḥāt al- ⊤ 4	140	25.20 N	30.35 E
Kharīm, Jabal ∧	132	30.17 N	33.58 E
Kharīṭ, Wādī al- V	140	24.26 N	33.03 E
Khārk, Jazīreh-ye (Kharg Island) I	128	29.15 N	50.20 E
Kharkov → Char'kov	78	50.00 N	36.15 E
Kharmān, Kūh-e ∧	128	29.13 N	53.35 E
Kharri	272b	22.55 N	88.14 E
Kharsāwān	124	22.48 N	85.50 E
Kharsia	124	21.58 N	83.07 E
Khartoum → Al-Kharṭūm	140	15.36 N	32.32 E
Khartoum North → Al-Kharṭūm Baḥrī	140	15.38 N	32.33 E
Khartum → Al-Kharṭūm	140	15.36 N	32.32 E
Kharumwa	154	3.12 S	32.39 E
Khāsbāti	272b	22.55 N	88.25 E
Khasebake	156	20.41 S	24.29 E
Khāsh, Afg.	128	31.31 N	62.52 E
Khāsh, Īrān	128	28.14 N	61.14 E
Khāsh ≃	128	31.11 N	62.05 E
Khāsh, Dasht-e ◆ 2	128	31.50 N	62.30 E
Khashab, Jabal al- ∧ 2	142	29.56 N	31.01 E
Khashm al-Qirbah	140	14.58 N	35.55 E
Khashm al-Qirbah, Khazzān ⊜ 1	140	14.40 N	35.55 E
Khashshab, Tur'at al- ≊	273c	29.53 N	31.17 E
Khashum	140	12.27 N	28.02 E
Khāş Konar	120	34.39 N	70.54 E
Khaskovo → Haskovo	38	41.56 N	25.33 E
Khatauli	124	29.17 N	77.43 E
Khātegaon	124	22.36 N	76.55 E
Khātra	126	22.59 N	86.51 E
Khatt, Oued al V	148	26.45 N	13.03 W
Khaur	123	33.16 N	72.28 E
Khāvda	120	23.51 N	69.43 E
Khawrah	144	14.26 N	46.09 E
Khawsa	110	15.03 N	97.50 E
Khayāla ◆ 8	272a	28.40 N	77.06 E
Khaybar, Ḥarrat ⩡ 9	128	25.30 N	39.45 E
Khayerpur	272b	22.35 N	88.33 E
Khayl, Kathīb al- ⩡ 8	142	30.33 N	32.28 E
Khayra Bil ⊜	272b	22.52 N	88.29 E
Khayrasole	126	23.48 N	87.16 E
Khayung ≃	110	15.07 N	104.42 E
Kheardaha	272b	22.29 N	88.28 E
Khe Bo	110	19.08 N	104.41 E
Khed	122	17.43 N	73.23 E
Khefapur	272a	28.30 N	77.05 E
Khejurdaha	272b	22.59 N	88.10 E
Khemis	148	36.16 N	2.13 E
Khemis el Khechna	34	36.39 N	3.20 E
Khemisset	148	33.50 N	6.03 W
Khemisset □ 4	148	33.50 N	6.05 W
Khem Karan	123	31.09 N	74.34 E
Khemmarat	110	16.03 N	105.13 E
Khenchla	148	35.28 N	7.11 E
Khenifra	148	33.00 N	5.40 W
Khenifra □ 4	148	32.35 N	5.10 W
Khenjān	120	35.36 N	70.59 E
Khenyen	272b	22.59 N	88.19 E
Khera ◆ 8	272a	28.46 N	77.08 E
Kheri	124	27.54 N	80.48 E
Kheri Branch ≊	124	28.11 N	80.25 E
Kherli	124	27.12 N	77.02 E
Kherrata	148	36.31 N	5.26 E
Khersān ≃	128	31.33 N	50.22 E
Kherson → Cherson	78	46.38 N	32.35 E
Khetia	120	21.40 N	74.35 E
Khevāj	120	38.13 N	71.02 E
Khewāri	120	26.36 N	68.52 E
Khewra	123	32.39 N	73.01 E
Kheyr Khāneh	128	34.57 N	63.37 E
Khichīwāra Plateau ⋏ 1	124	24.25 N	77.30 E
Khichripur ◆ 8	272a	28.37 N	77.19 E
Khilchipur	124	24.02 N	76.34 E
Khilkāpur	272b	22.46 N	88.29 E
Khimki → Chimki	82	55.54 N	37.26 E
Khíos	38	38.22 N	26.08 E
Khíos I	38	38.22 N	26.00 E
Khipro	120	25.50 N	69.22 E
Khirbat al-Ghazālah	132	32.44 N	36.12 E
Khirbat 'Awwād	132	32.19 N	36.43 E
Khirbat Qanāfār	132	33.38 N	35.43 E
Khirbat Umm as-Surab	132	32.26 N	36.19 E
Khirbitā	142	30.45 N	30.40 E
Khiri Mat	110	16.50 N	99.48 E
Khirpai	126	22.42 N	87.37 E
Khirr, Wādī al- V	128	31.51 N	44.29 E
Khisfīn	132	32.51 N	35.49 E
Khiuri Khala ∧	124	29.58 N	81.18 E
Khiva → Chiva	72	41.24 N	60.22 E
Khlong Khlung	110	16.12 N	99.43 E
Khlong Thom	110	7.56 N	99.09 E
Khlong Yai	110	11.46 N	102.54 E
Khlung	110	12.27 N	102.14 E
Khmel'nitskiy → Chmel'nickij	78	49.25 N	27.00 E
Khoai, Hon I	110	8.26 N	104.50 E
Khogali	140	6.08 N	27.47 E
Khojāng ∧	124	28.41 N	85.09 E
Khok Kloi	110	8.17 N	98.19 E
Khok Pho	110	6.43 N	101.06 E
Khoksa	126	23.48 N	89.17 E
Khok Samrong	110	15.04 N	100.44 E
Kholargós	267c	38.00 N	23.48 E
Kholm	120	36.42 N	67.41 E
Kholombidzo Falls ∟	154	15.54 S	34.44 E
Khomām	128	37.22 N	49.40 E
Khomas Hochland ⋏ 1	156	22.30 S	16.30 E
Khomeyn	128	33.38 N	50.04 E
Khomeynīshahr	128	32.41 N	51.31 E
Khomodimo	156	22.46 S	23.52 E
Khondmāl Hills ⋏ 2	122	20.20 N	84.00 E
Khong → Mekong ≃	12	10.33 N	105.24 E
Khoni	272c	19.10 N	73.07 E
Khon Kaen	110	16.26 N	102.50 E
Khóra	38	37.04 N	21.43 E
Khorāsān □ 4	128	35.00 N	58.00 E
Khóra Sfakíon	38	35.12 N	24.09 E
Khordha	120	20.11 N	85.37 E
Khorel	272b	22.42 N	88.19 E
Khorramābād	128	33.30 N	48.20 E
Khorram Daraq	128	36.26 N	48.36 E
Khorramshahr	128	30.25 N	48.11 E
Khoru	272b	22.51 N	88.31 E
Khossanto	150	13.08 N	11.58 W
Khouribga	148	32.54 N	6.57 W
Khouribga □ 4	148	32.50 N	6.30 W
Khowai	120	24.06 N	91.38 E
Khowāng	120	27.16 N	94.53 E
Khowst	120	33.22 N	69.57 E
Khrisokhoús, Kólpos c	130	35.06 N	32.25 E
Khrisoúpolis	38	40.58 N	24.42 E
Khudiān	123	30.59 N	74.17 E
Khuff	128	24.57 N	44.42 E
Khugaung	110	26.07 N	98.18 E
Khūgīānī Sānī	120	31.31 N	66.12 E
Khuis	156	26.37 S	21.45 E
Khuīyāla	120	27.14 N	70.30 E
Khu Khan	110	14.42 N	104.12 E
Khulna	124	22.48 N	89.33 E
Khulna □ 5	126	22.45 N	89.30 E
Khŭm Bathéay	110	11.59 N	104.57 E
Khumbur Khūlē Ghar ∧	120	32.49 N	68.47 E
Khungdugang ∧	124	27.31 N	89.02 E
Khūnjerāb Pass)(	123	36.52 N	75.27 E
Khun Tan, Doi ∧	110	18.30 N	99.20 E
Khunti	124	23.05 N	85.17 E
Khūr	128	32.57 N	58.26 E
Khurai	124	24.03 N	78.19 E
Khuralji Khās ◆ 8	272a	28.39 N	77.17 E
Khuria Tank ⊜ 1	124	22.25 N	81.36 E
Khurigāchi	272b	22.49 N	88.20 E
Khurīyā Murīyā, Jazā'ir II	118	17.30 N	56.00 E
Khurja	124	28.15 N	77.51 E
Khurli	120	28.59 N	65.52 E
Khurramshahr → Khorramshahr	128	30.25 N	48.11 E
Khūsf	128	32.46 N	58.53 E
Khushāb	123	32.18 N	72.21 E
Khushālgarh	123	33.30 N	71.54 E
Khushk Khurd ◆ 8	272a	28.46 N	77.10 E
Khutubi ≃	86	44.45 N	86.25 E
Khuwayy	140	13.05 N	29.14 E
Khuzdār	120	27.48 N	66.37 E
Khūzestān □ 4	128	31.00 N	49.00 E
Khvāf	128	34.33 N	60.08 E
Khvājeh Moḥammad, Kūh-e ⋏	120	36.22 N	70.17 E
Khvājeh Ra'ūf	120	33.19 N	64.43 E
Khvor	128	33.47 N	55.03 E
Khvormūj	128	28.39 N	51.23 E
Khvoy	128	38.33 N	44.58 E
Khwae Noi ≃	110	14.01 N	99.32 E
Khyber Pass)(	123	34.05 N	71.10 E
Kia	175e	7.33 S	158.26 E
Kialwe	154	9.22 S	27.08 E
Kiama, Austl.	170	34.41 S	150.51 E
Kiama, Zaïre	152	7.15 S	17.44 E
Kiamba	116	5.59 N	124.37 E
Kiambi	154	7.20 S	28.01 E
Kiamboni, Kap → Jumbo, Raas ≻	144	1.39 S	41.36 E
Kiambu	154	1.10 S	36.50 E
Kiamesha Lake	210	41.41 N	74.40 W
Kiamichi ≃	194	33.57 N	95.14 W
Kiamika ≃	206	46.38 N	75.15 W
Kiamika, Barrage ◆ 6	206	46.37 N	75.08 W
Kiamika, Réservoir ⊜ 1	206	46.40 N	75.05 W
Kiamusze → Jiamusi	89	46.50 N	130.21 E
Kian → Ji'an	100	27.07 N	114.58 E
Kiana	180	66.59 N	160.25 W
Kiandra	171b	35.53 S	148.30 E
Kiangara	157b	17.58 S	47.02 E
Kiangarow, Mount ∧	166	26.49 S	151.33 E
Kiangsi → Jiangxi □ 4	100	28.00 N	116.00 E
Kiangsu → Jiangsu □ 4	90	33.00 N	120.00 E
Kiantajärvi ⊜	26	65.03 N	29.07 E

Symbols in the index entries represent the broad categories identified in the key at the right. Symbols with superior numbers (⋏ 1) identify subcategories (see complete key on page *I · 1)*.

Symbole im Register stellen die rechts im Schlüssel erklärten Kategorien dar. Symbole mit hochgestellten Ziffern (⋏ 1) bezeichnen Unterabteilungen einer Kategorie (vgl. vollständiger Schlüssel auf Seite *I · 1)*.

Los símbolos incluídos en el texto del índice representan las grandes categorias identificadas con la clave a la derecha. Los símbolos con numeros en su parte superior (⋏ 1) identifican las subcategorías (véase la clave completa en la página *I · 1)*.

Les symboles de l'index représentent les catégories indiquées dans la légende à droite. Les symboles suivis d'un indice (⋏ 1) représentent des sous-catégories (voir légende complète à la page *I · 1)*.

Os símbolos incluídos no texto do índice representam as grandes categorias identificadas com a chave à direita. Os símbolos com números em sua parte superior (⋏ 1) identificam as subcategorias (veja-se a chave completa à página *I · 1)*.

∧	Mountain	Berg	Montaña	Montagne	Montanha
⋏	Mountains	Gebirge	Montañas	Montagnes	Montanhas
)(	Pass	Paß	Paso	Col	Passo
V	Valley, Canyon	Tal, Cañon	Valle, Cañón	Vallée, Canyon	Vale, Canhão
≚	Plain	Ebene	Llano	Plaine	Planície
≻	Cape	Kap	Cabo	Cap	Cabo
I	Island	Insel	Isla	Île	Ilha
II	Islands	Inseln	Islas	Îles	Ilhas
⩡	Other Topographic Features	Andere Topographische Objekte	Otros Elementos Topográficos	Autres données topographiques	Outros acidentes topográficos

ESPAÑOL Nombre	FRANÇAIS Nom	PORTUGUÊS Nome	Página/Page	Lat. °′	Long. °′ W=Oeste/Ouest

Column 1

Nombre	Página	Lat.	Long.
Kiaohsien → Jiaoxian	98	36.18 N	119.58 E
Kibæk	41	56.02 N	8.51 E
Kibaha	154	6.46 S	38.55 E
Kibali ≃	154	3.37 N	28.34 E
Kibali-Sturi Game Reserve ◆4	154	2.45 N	29.33 E
Kibamba	154	4.53 S	26.33 E
Kibanga Port	154	0.11 N	32.52 E
Kibangou	152	3.27 S	12.21 E
Kibanseke	273b	4.26 S	15.23 E
Kibar	120	32.20 N	78.01 E
Kibara	154	2.09 S	33.27 E
Kibāsī	128	30.34 N	47.50 E
Kibau Iyayi	154	8.52 S	34.32 E
Kibawe	116	7.34 N	125.00 E
Kibaya	154	5.18 S	36.34 E
Kibenga	152	7.55 S	17.35 E
Kibeni	164	7.25 S	143.48 E
Kiberashi	154	5.23 S	37.26 E
Kiberege	154	7.57 S	36.62 E
Kibi	150	6.10 N	0.33 W
Kibi-kögen ⚊1	46	34.45 N	133.15 E
Kibila	154	8.14 S	26.23 E
Kibiti	154	7.44 S	38.57 E
Kibler Park	273d	26.18 S	28.00 E
Kiboga	154	1.02 N	30.58 E
Kiboko	154	2.15 S	37.42 E
Kibombo	154	3.54 S	25.55 E
Kibondo	154	3.35 S	30.42 E

[Page contains an extensive multilingual gazetteer index with hundreds of place-name entries arranged in six columns (Español / Français / Português headings), each giving name, page, latitude and longitude. Full entry-by-entry transcription omitted for brevity.]

I · 88 **Kire-Kock**

ENGLISH — Name | Page | Lat.°′ | Long.°′
DEUTSCH — Name | Seite | Breite°′ | Länge°′ E = Ost

Name	Page	Lat.°′	Long.°′
Kireç	130	39.33 N	28.22 E
Kirej ≃	88	54.12 N	100.40 E
Kirejevo	80	50.01 N	44.29 E
Kirejevsk	76	53.56 N	37.56 E
Kirejkovo	76	53.38 N	35.49 E
Kirenga ≃	88	57.47 N	108.07 E
Kirensk	88	57.46 N	108.08 E
Kirghizia → Kirgizskaja Sovetskaja Socialističeskaja Respublika □[3]	85	41.30 N	75.00 E
Kirgili	85	40.24 N	71.43 E
Kirgiz-Mijaki	86	53.38 N	54.47 E
Kirgizskaja Sovetskaja Socialističeskaja Respublika □[3]	85	41.30 N	75.00 E
Kirgizskij chrebet ⋀	85	42.30 N	74.00 E
Kiri	152	1.27 S	19.00 E
Kiribati □[1]	14	5.00 S	170.00 W
Kiribati II	14	0.30 S	174.00 E
Kiries West	158	26.34 S	19.00 E
Kiriga-mine ∧	94	36.06 N	138.12 E
Kırıkhan, Tür.	130	39.32 N	41.20 E
Kırıkhan, Tür.	130	36.32 N	36.19 E
Kirikiri Prisons ⚑	273a	6.27 N	3.19 E
Kırıkkale	130	39.50 N	33.31 E
Kirikovka	78	50.22 N	35.07 E
Kirillov	76	59.52 N	38.23 E
Kirillovka	265b	55.57 N	37.20 E
Kirillovo, S.S.S.R.	80	57.07 N	45.27 E
Kirillovo, S.S.S.R.	80	53.47 N	42.40 E
Kirillovskoje	76	60.28 N	29.17 E
Kirin → Jilin	89	43.51 N	126.33 E
Kirin → Jilin □[4]	90	44.00 N	126.00 E
Kirinyaga (Mount Kenya) ∧	154	0.10 S	37.20 E
Kirishima-Yaku-kokuritsu-kōen ♦	92	31.55 N	130.51 E
Kirishima-yama ∧	92	31.56 N	130.52 E
Kiriši	76	59.27 N	32.02 E
Kiritimati (Christmas Island) I[1]	174o	1.52 N	157.20 W
Kiriwina Island I	164	8.35 S	151.05 E
Kiriwina Islands II	164	8.35 S	151.05 E
Kirizume-tōge ∧[2]	270	34.56 N	135.16 E
Kirjanovskaja Kontora	88	58.18 N	104.13 E
Kirka	130	39.17 N	30.33 E
Kirkabister	46a	60.07 N	1.08 W
Kırkağaç	130	39.06 N	27.40 E
Kirkbride	44	54.54 N	3.12 W
Kirkburton	44	53.37 N	1.42 W
Kirkby ✦[8]	44	53.29 N	2.54 W
Kirkby in Ashfield	44	53.06 N	1.15 W
Kirkby Lonsdale	44	54.13 N	2.36 W
Kirkby Malzeard	44	54.11 N	1.38 W
Kirkbymoorside	44	54.16 N	0.55 W
Kirkby Stephen	44	54.28 N	2.20 W
Kirkcaldy	46	56.07 N	3.10 W
Kirkcolm	44	54.58 N	5.05 W
Kirkconnel	44	55.23 N	4.00 W
Kirkcudbright	44	54.50 N	4.03 W
Kirkcudbright Bay ⊂	44	54.48 N	4.04 W
Kirkdale ✦[8]	262	53.26 N	2.59 W
Kirkeby	41	56.09 N	9.27 E
Kirkee → Khadki	122	18.34 N	73.52 E
Kirkenær	26	60.28 N	12.03 E
Kirkenes	24	69.40 N	30.03 E
Kirke Stillinge	41	55.26 N	11.15 E
Kirkham	44	53.47 N	2.53 W
Kirkhill	46	57.28 N	4.26 W
Kirkintilloch	46	55.57 N	4.10 W
Kirkjubæjarklaustur	24a	63.47 N	18.04 W
Kirkkonummi → Kyrkslätt	26	60.07 N	24.26 E
Kirkland, P.Q., Can.	275a	45.27 N	73.52 W
Kirkland, Il., U.S.	216	42.05 N	88.51 W
Kirkland, Tx., U.S.	196	34.23 N	100.04 W
Kirkland, Wa., U.S.	224	47.40 N	122.12 W
Kirkland Creek ≃	200	34.32 N	113.00 W
Kirkland Lake	190	48.09 N	80.02 W
Kırklar Dağı ∧	130	40.32 N	40.35 E
Kırklareli	130	41.44 N	27.12 E
Kırklareli □[4]	130	41.40 N	27.30 E
Kirklees □[8]	262	53.36 N	1.52 W
Kirkleyditch	262	53.18 N	2.12 W
Kirklin	194	40.11 N	86.21 W
Kirkliston	46	55.58 N	3.25 W
Kirk Michael, I. of Man	44	54.17 N	4.35 W
Kirkmichael, Scot., U.K.	46	56.43 N	3.29 W
Kirkmuirhill	46	55.40 N	3.55 W
Kirkness Lake ⊜	184	51.32 N	93.56 W
Kirkpatrick, Mount ∧	9	84.20 S	166.19 E
Kirkpatrick Lake ⊜	182	51.52 N	111.18 W
Kirk Sandall	44	53.33 N	1.04 W
Kirksville, Il., U.S.	219	39.34 N	88.40 W
Kirksville, Mo., U.S.	194	40.11 N	92.34 W
Kirkton of Culsalmond	46	57.23 N	2.34 W
Kirkton of Glenisla	46	56.44 N	3.17 W
Kirktown of Auchterless	46	57.27 N	2.28 W
Kirkūk	128	35.28 N	44.28 E
Kirkville	210	43.05 N	75.57 W
Kirkwall	46	58.59 N	2.58 W
Kirkwood, S. Afr.	158	33.24 S	25.26 E
Kirkwood, De., U.S.	208	39.34 N	75.41 W
Kirkwood, Il., U.S.	190	40.51 N	90.44 W
Kirkwood, Mo., U.S.	219	38.35 N	90.24 W
Kirkwood, N.J., U.S.	285	39.50 N	75.01 W
Kirkwood, N.Y., U.S.	210	42.02 N	75.48 W
Kirmir ≃	130	40.07 N	31.43 E
Kirn	56	49.47 N	7.28 E
Kirnāhar	126	23.45 N	87.52 E
Kirotshe	154	1.37 S	29.02 E
Kirov, S.S.S.R.	76	54.05 N	34.20 E
Kirov, S.S.S.R.	80	58.38 N	49.42 E
Kirova, zaliv ⊂	84	39.09 N	49.03 E
Kirovabad	84	40.40 N	46.22 E
Kirovakan	84	40.48 N	44.30 E
Kirovgrad	86	57.26 N	60.04 E
Kirovka	86	47.07 N	82.00 E
Kirovo, S.S.S.R.	78	47.41 N	35.46 E
Kirovo, S.S.S.R.	78	51.29 N	29.24 E
Kirovo, S.S.S.R.	83	48.50 N	38.03 E
Kirovo, S.S.S.R.	83	48.23 N	37.55 E
Kirovo, S.S.S.R.	85	40.26 N	70.34 E
Kirovo, S.S.S.R.	86	55.33 N	63.46 E
Kirovo-Čepeck	80	58.33 N	50.01 E
Kirovograd	78	48.30 N	32.18 E
Kirovograd □[4]	38	48.10 N	30.20 E
Kirovsk, S.S.S.R.	24	67.37 N	33.35 E
Kirovsk, S.S.S.R.	76	53.16 N	29.29 E
Kirovsk, S.S.S.R.	83	49.01 N	37.56 E
Kirovsk, S.S.S.R.	83	48.38 N	38.39 E
Kirovsk, S.S.S.R.	84	38.48 N	48.43 E
Kirovsk, S.S.S.R.	128	37.42 N	60.23 E
Kirovsk, S.S.S.R.	265a	59.52 N	31.00 E
Kirovskij, S.S.S.R.	74	54.18 N	155.47 E
Kirovskij, S.S.S.R.	80	45.51 N	48.07 E
Kirovskij, S.S.S.R.	84	40.26 N	49.51 E
Kirovskij, S.S.S.R.	86	44.52 N	78.12 E
Kirovskij, S.S.S.R.	89	54.26 N	126.55 E
Kirovskij, S.S.S.R.	89	45.07 N	133.30 E
Kirovskije ostrova II	265a	59.58 N	30.15 E
Kirovskoje, S.S.S.R.	78	48.33 N	34.53 E
Kirovskoje, S.S.S.R.	78	45.14 N	35.13 E
Kirovskoje, S.S.S.R.	83	48.09 N	38.21 E
Kirovskoje, S.S.S.R.	85	42.39 N	71.35 E
Kirov Stadium ♦	265a	59.58 N	30.14 E
Kirov Theatre ⚑	265a	59.55 N	30.18 E
Kirpičnyj Zavod	265a	60.01 N	30.48 E
Kirpil'skaja	78	45.23 N	39.43 E
Kirriemuir	46	56.41 N	3.01 W
Kirs	86	59.21 N	52.14 E
Kirsanov	80	52.38 N	42.43 E
Kirsanovka	80	52.30 N	52.53 E
Kirschau	54	51.04 N	14.27 E
Kırşehir	130	39.09 N	34.10 E
Kırşehir □[4]	130	39.20 N	34.10 E
Kīrthar National Park ♦	120	25.50 N	67.40 E
Kīrthar Range ⋀	120	27.00 N	67.10 E
Kirtland, N.M., U.S.	200	36.44 N	108.21 W
Kirtland, Oh., U.S.	214	41.37 N	81.21 W
Kirtland Air Force Base ■	200	35.02 N	106.37 W
Kirtland Hills	214	41.37 N	81.24 W
Kirtle Water ≃	44	54.58 N	3.05 W
Kirton	42	52.56 N	0.04 W
Kirton in Lindsey	44	53.28 N	0.36 W
Kirton of Largo	46	56.13 N	2.55 W
Kirtorf	56	50.46 N	9.06 E
Kiruna	24	67.51 N	20.16 E
Kirundu	154	0.44 S	25.32 E
Kirurumo	154	5.53 S	34.11 E
Kirvin	222	31.46 N	96.20 W
Kirwan Heights	279b	40.22 N	80.06 W
Kirwee	172	43.30 S	172.13 E
Kirwin	198	39.40 N	99.07 W
Kirwin Reservoir ⊜[1]	198	39.39 N	99.10 W
Kiryandongo	154	1.53 N	32.03 E
Kiryū	94	36.24 N	139.20 E
Kirza	86	54.14 N	81.40 E
Kirżač	82	56.09 N	38.52 E
Kirżač ≃	82	55.52 N	39.04 E
Kisa, Nihon	96	34.43 N	132.59 E
Kisa, Sve.	26	57.59 N	15.37 E
Kisai	94	36.06 N	139.35 E
Kisaichi	270	34.46 N	135.42 E
Kisakata	92	39.13 N	139.54 E
Kisaki	154	7.28 S	37.36 E
Kišaly	76	54.23 N	43.12 E
Kisambo	152	6.25 S	18.14 E
Kisanga	154	2.29 N	26.35 E
Kisangani (Stanleyville)	154	0.30 S	25.12 E
Kisantu	152	5.07 S	15.05 E
Kisar, Pulau I	112	8.05 S	127.10 E
Kisaralik ≃	180	60.51 N	161.16 W
Kisaran	114	2.59 N	99.37 E
Kisarawe	154	6.54 S	39.04 E
Kisarazu	94	35.23 N	139.55 E
Kisarazu-Kichi, Kōkū-jieitai ■	94	35.24 N	139.55 E
Kisawa	96	33.49 N	134.18 E
K.I. Sawyer Air Force Base ■	190	46.21 N	87.25 W
Kisbér	30	47.30 N	18.02 E
Kisbey	184	49.38 N	102.41 W
Kise ≃	94	35.06 N	138.53 E
Kiselevsk → Kisel'ovsk	86	54.00 N	86.39 E
Kisel'ovka	80	47.18 N	44.07 E
Kisel'ovsk	86	54.00 N	86.39 E
Kisengwa	154	6.00 S	25.50 E
Kisen-yama ∧[2]	270	34.54 N	135.51 E
Kiser Lake ⊜	218	40.11 N	83.58 W
Kīsh, Jazīreh-ye I	128	26.32 N	53.56 E
Kishanda	154	1.42 S	31.34 E
Kishanganga ≃	123	34.22 N	73.30 E
Kishanganj	124	26.07 N	87.56 E
Kishangarh	120	27.52 N	70.34 E
Kishangarh ✦[8]	272a	28.31 N	77.08 E
Kishangarh Bās	120	26.34 N	74.52 E
Kishb, Ḥarrat al- ⊥[9]	144	23.00 N	41.25 E
Kishi, Nig.	150	9.05 N	3.52 E
Kishi, Zaïre	154	10.04 S	26.26 E
Kishida ≃	96	35.38 N	134.27 E
Kishigawa	96	34.13 N	135.20 E
Kishikas ≃	184	52.45 N	91.43 W
Kishimoto	96	35.23 N	133.25 E
Kishinev → Kišin'ov	78	47.00 N	28.50 E
Kishiwada	96	34.28 N	135.22 E
Kishorganj	124	24.26 N	90.46 E
Kishorn, Loch ⊂	46	57.21 N	5.41 W
Kishtwār	123	33.19 N	75.46 E
Kishwaukee ≃	216	42.11 N	89.08 W
Kishwaukee, South Branch ≃	216	42.12 N	88.59 W
Kisia	152	4.35 S	18.22 E
Kisigo ≃	154	7.03 S	35.50 E
Kisii	154	0.41 S	34.46 E
Kisiju	154	7.24 S	39.20 E
Kiši-Karoj, ozero ⊜	86	54.03 N	71.20 E
Kisika-zaki ›	93b	30.50 N	131.04 E
Kısıklı ✦[8]	267b	41.01 N	29.03 E
Kišin	78	51.08 N	27.41 E
Kišin'ov (Kishinev)	78	47.00 N	28.50 E
Kısır Dağı ∧	84	40.58 N	43.04 E
Kısırkaya ✦[8]	267b	41.14 N	28.58 E
Kısırmandıra ✦[8]	267b	41.14 N	28.49 E
Kisiwada → Kishiwada	96	34.28 N	135.22 E
Kisiwani	154	4.08 S	37.57 E
Kisizi	154	1.00 S	29.56 E
Kiska Island I	181a	52.00 N	177.30 E
Kiskatinaw ≃	182	56.06 N	120.08 W
Kiska Volcano ∧[1]	181a	52.07 N	177.36 E
Kis-Kevély ∧[2]	264c	47.38 N	18.59 E
Kiski Lake ⊜	184	54.46 N	98.55 W
Kiskimere	279b	40.37 N	79.35 W
Kiskiminetas ≃	214	40.41 N	79.40 W
Kiskittogisu Lake ⊜	184	54.13 N	98.20 W
Kiskitto Lake ⊜	184	54.16 N	98.34 W
Kiskörei-víztároló ⊜[1]	30	47.35 N	20.40 E
Kiskőrös	30	46.38 N	19.17 E
Kiskunfélegyháza	30	46.43 N	19.52 E
Kiskunhalas	30	46.26 N	19.30 E
Kiskunmajsa	30	46.30 N	19.45 E
Kisl'akovka	78	46.44 N	31.59 E
Kisl'akovskaja	78	46.27 N	39.40 E
Kislovka	83	49.38 N	37.53 E
Kislovo	80	49.54 N	45.25 E
Kislovodsk	84	43.55 N	42.44 E
Kismaayo	144	0.22 S	42.32 E
Kismet	276	40.38 N	73.12 W
Kisnema	76	60.20 N	37.39 E
Kiso, Nihon	94	35.56 N	137.47 E
Kiso, Nihon	268	35.34 N	139.26 E
Kiso ≃	94	35.02 N	136.45 E
Kisofukushima	94	35.51 N	137.42 E
Kisogawa	94	35.20 N	136.47 E
Kisoripur	126	22.05 N	88.34 E
Kisoro	154	1.17 S	29.41 E
Kiso-sammyaku ⋀	94	35.43 N	137.50 E
Kisozaki	94	35.04 N	136.44 E
Kispest ✦[8]	264c	47.27 N	19.08 E
Kispiox	182	55.21 N	127.41 W
Kispiox ≃	182	55.16 N	127.41 W
Kispiox Mountain ∧	182	55.25 N	127.57 W
Kissamos	38	35.30 N	23.38 E
Kissena Park ♦	276	40.45 N	73.49 W
Kisseynew Lake ⊜	184	54.58 N	101.35 W
Kissidougou	150	9.11 N	10.06 W
Kissimmee	220	28.17 N	81.24 W
Kissimmee ≃	220	27.10 N	80.53 W
Kissimmee, Lake ⊜	220	27.55 N	81.16 W
Kissing	60	48.18 N	10.59 E
Kississing	184	55.07 N	101.07 W
Kississing Lake ⊜	184	55.10 N	101.20 W
Kisslegg	58	47.47 N	9.53 E
Kissū, Jabal ∧	140	21.35 N	25.09 E
Kista	80	46.05 N	43.06 E
Kistanje	36	43.59 N	15.58 E
Kistarcsa	264c	47.33 N	19.16 E
Kistendej	80	52.08 N	43.39 E
Kistigan Lake ⊜	184	54.38 N	92.37 W
Kistler	214	40.22 N	77.51 W
Kisújszállás	30	47.13 N	20.46 E
Kisuki	96	35.17 N	132.54 E
Kisumu	154	0.06 S	34.45 E
Kisvárda	30	48.13 N	22.05 E
Kiswere	154	9.26 S	39.33 E
Kita	150	13.03 N	9.29 W
Kita ✦[8], Nihon	268	35.45 N	139.44 E
Kita ✦[8], Nihon	270	34.42 N	135.30 E
Kita ✦[8], Nihon	270	34.45 N	135.08 E
Kita ✦[8], Nihon	270	35.03 N	135.45 E
Kitaaiki	94	36.04 N	138.34 E
Kita-Daitō-jima I	90	25.57 N	131.18 E
Kitafuji-enshūjō ■	94	35.25 N	138.48 E
Kitagata	94	35.26 N	136.41 E
Kitagawa	96	33.27 N	134.03 E
Kitagi-shima I	96	34.23 N	133.32 E
Kitaibaraki	94	36.48 N	140.45 E
Kitain Temple ⚑[1]	268	35.54 N	139.30 E
Kita-Iō-jima I	14	25.26 N	141.17 E
Kitairiso	268	35.50 N	139.26 E
Kitajima	96	34.05 N	134.35 E
Kitakami	92	39.18 N	141.07 E
Kitakami ≃	92	38.25 N	141.19 E
Kitakami-kōchi ⋀	92	39.30 N	141.30 E
Kitakata	92	37.39 N	139.52 E
Kitakyuschu → Kitakyūshū	96	33.53 N	130.50 E
Kitakyūshū	96	33.53 N	130.50 E
Kitakyushu-kokutei-kōen ♦	96	33.45 N	130.50 E
Kitale	154	1.01 N	35.00 E
Kitamachi ✦[8]	268	35.46 N	139.39 E
Kitamba ✦[8]	273b	4.19 S	15.14 E
Kitami	92a	43.48 N	143.54 E
Kitami-sanchi ⋀	92a	44.22 N	142.43 E
Kitamoto	94	36.02 N	139.32 E
Kita-Nagato-kaigan-kokutei-kōen ♦	96	34.24 N	131.16 E
Kitanakagusuku	174m	26.21 N	127.51 E
Kitanda, Zaïre	154	9.59 S	27.28 E
Kitanda, Zaïre	154	6.36 S	26.27 E
Kitangari	154	10.39 S	39.20 E
Kitangiri, Lake ⊜	154	4.05 S	34.19 E
Kitangua	152	6.17 S	20.22 E
Kitano, Nihon	96	33.20 N	130.35 E
Kitano, Nihon	268	35.47 N	139.26 E
Kitanoshinden	268	35.48 N	139.26 E
Kitatachibana	94	36.29 N	139.03 E
Kitatajima	268	35.56 N	139.30 E
Kitatawara	270	34.44 N	135.42 E
Kitaura	94	36.04 N	140.32 E
Kita-ura ⊜	94	36.00 N	140.34 E
Kitava Island I	164	8.40 S	151.20 E
Kitaya	154	10.39 S	40.10 E
Kit Carson, Ca., U.S.	226	38.41 N	120.07 W
Kit Carson, Co., U.S.	198	38.45 N	102.47 W
Kitchener, Austl.	162	31.02 S	124.11 E
Kitchener, On., Can.	212	43.27 N	80.29 W
Kitee	26	62.06 N	30.09 E
Kitega → Gitega	154	3.26 S	29.56 E
Kiteiyab	140	17.12 N	33.43 E
Kitenda	152	6.53 S	17.21 E
Kitenevo	82	56.21 N	36.13 E
Kitengo	152	7.26 S	24.08 E
Kitéssa	154	5.20 N	25.20 E
Kitgum	154	3.18 N	32.53 E
Kíthira	38	36.09 N	23.00 E
Kíthira I	38	36.20 N	22.58 E
Kíthnos	38	37.26 N	24.26 E
Kíthnos I	38	37.25 N	24.28 E
Kitimat	182	54.03 N	128.33 W
Kitimat ≃	182	54.06 N	128.38 W
Kitimat Ranges ⋀	182	53.30 N	128.50 W
Kitinen ≃	24	67.08 N	27.29 E
Kitíou, Akrotírion ›	130	34.48 N	33.36 E
Kitlope ≃	182	53.10 N	127.45 W
Kitlope Lake ⊜	182	53.07 N	127.47 W
Kitō, Nihon	94	34.42 N	138.03 E
Kitō, Nihon	96	33.46 N	134.12 E
Kitoj ≃	88	52.39 N	103.56 E
Kitridge Point ›	241g	13.09 N	59.25 W
Kitsap □[6]	224	47.41 N	122.44 W
Kitscoty	184	53.20 N	110.20 W
Kit's Coty House ⚑	260	51.19 N	0.30 E
Kitshua-Nseke	152	4.26 S	19.36 E
Kitsuki	92	33.25 N	131.37 E
Kitsuregawa	94	36.43 N	140.01 E
Kittanning	214	40.48 N	79.31 W
Kittatinny Mountain ∧	210	41.10 N	74.55 W
Kittatinny Tunnel ✦[5]	214	40.09 N	77.41 W
Kittendorf	54	53.37 N	12.54 E
Kittery	188	43.05 N	70.44 W
Kitt Green	262	53.33 N	2.41 W
Kittilä	24	67.40 N	24.54 E
Kittitas	202	46.59 N	120.24 W
Kittitas □[6]	224	47.13 N	121.01 W
Kitt Peak National Observatory ⚑[3]	200	31.58 N	111.36 W
Kittsee	61	48.05 N	17.04 E
Kitu	154	7.38 S	27.42 E
Kitui	154	1.22 S	38.01 E
Kitumbeine ∧[1]	154	2.44 S	36.16 E
Kitunda	154	6.48 S	33.13 E
Kitutu	154	3.17 S	28.05 E
Kitwanga	182	55.06 N	128.03 W
Kitwangar Indian Reserve ✦[4]	182	55.06 N	128.04 W
Kitwe	154	12.49 S	28.13 E
Kitwitwi	156	17.25 S	18.25 E
Kityang → Jieyang	100	23.35 N	116.21 E
Kitzbühel	64	47.27 N	12.23 E
Kitzbüheler Alpen ⋀	64	47.20 N	12.20 E
Kitzingen	56	49.44 N	10.09 E
Kitzscher	54	51.09 N	12.33 E
Kiukiang → Jiujiang	100	29.44 N	115.59 E
Kiukiu, Pointe ›	174x	9.47 S	139.09 W
Kiul	124	25.09 N	86.06 E
Kiunga, Kenya	154	1.45 S	41.29 E
Kiunga, Pap. N. Gui.	164	6.10 S	141.15 E
Kiuruvesi	26	63.39 N	26.37 E
Kiuschu → Kyūshū I	92	33.00 N	131.00 E
Kivak	180	64.16 N	172.57 W
Kivalina	180	67.44 N	164.33 W
Kivercy	78	50.50 N	25.27 E
Kiveriči	76	57.22 N	36.36 E
Kivijärvi	26	63.04 N	25.03 E
Kivijärvi ⊜	26	63.10 N	25.09 E
Kivik	26	55.41 N	14.15 E
Kiviõli	76	59.21 N	26.57 E
Kivu □[4]	154	2.30 S	27.00 E
Kivu, Lac ⊜	154	2.00 S	29.10 E
Kiwaba N'zogi	152	8.57 S	16.32 E
Kiwai Island I	164	8.30 S	143.25 E
Kiwalik	180	66.02 N	161.50 W
Kiwanis Lake	214	41.28 N	81.09 W
Kiyama	96	33.25 N	130.32 E
Kīyāmakī Dāgh ∧	84	38.47 N	45.51 E
Kiyan	174m	26.05 N	127.40 E
Kiyan-zaki ›	174m	26.05 N	127.39 E
Kıyıköy	130	41.38 N	28.05 E
Kiyiu Lake ⊜	184	51.38 N	108.55 W
Kiyl ≃	86	49.25 N	54.50 E
Kiyokawa	94	35.29 N	139.17 E
Kiyomi	94	36.07 N	137.11 E
Kiyosawa	94	35.03 N	138.15 E
Kiyose	94	35.47 N	139.32 E
Kiyosu	94	35.13 N	136.50 E
Kiyosumi-yama ∧	94	35.09 N	140.09 E
Kiyotani	270	34.52 N	134.59 E
Kiyotsu ≃	94	37.03 N	138.41 E
Kizel	86	59.03 N	57.40 E
Kizevatovo	80	53.13 N	45.18 E
Kızıl ≃	130	41.44 N	35.58 E
Kızıl Adalar II	130	40.52 N	29.05 E
Kızılcabölük	130	37.37 N	29.01 E
Kızılcadağ	130	37.01 N	29.58 E
Kızılcahamam	130	40.28 N	32.39 E
Kızılçakçak	84	40.46 N	43.37 E
Kızıldağ Milli Parkı ♦	130	37.58 N	31.28 E
Kızıldikme	130	39.05 N	37.01 E
Kızılhisar	130	37.33 N	29.18 E
Kızılırmak	130	40.21 N	33.59 E
Kızılören	130	37.52 N	32.07 E
Kizil'skoje	86	52.44 N	58.54 E
Kızılsu	130	37.28 N	42.13 E
Kiziltašskij liman ⊂	78	45.07 N	37.05 E
Kızıltepe	130	37.12 N	40.36 E
Kızıltoprak ✦[8]	267b	40.58 N	29.03 E
Kizil'unt	84	43.12 N	46.53 E
Kızılyaka	130	37.09 N	32.54 E
Kižimiz, gora ∧	24	63.12 N	58.48 E
Kizimkazi	154	6.27 S	39.28 E
Kižinga	88	51.51 N	109.55 E
Kizir ≃	86	53.51 N	93.06 E
Kızkalesi ⊥	130	36.28 N	34.04 E
Kızkulesi ✦[5]	267b	41.01 N	29.00 E
Kizl'ar	84	43.50 N	46.40 E
Kizl'arskij zaliv ⊂	84	44.33 N	46.55 E
Kizner	80	56.17 N	51.31 E
Kiz'oma	24	61.08 N	44.50 E
Kizu	96	34.44 N	135.49 E
Kizu ≃	94	34.53 N	135.42 E
Kizuki	268	35.34 N	139.40 E
Kizuri	270	34.39 N	135.34 E
Kizyl-Ajak	128	37.40 N	65.23 E
Kizyl-Arvat	128	38.58 N	56.15 E
Kizyl-Atrek	128	37.36 N	54.46 E
Kizyl-Su	128	39.48 N	53.01 E
Kjellerup	41	56.17 N	9.26 E
Kjøbenhavn → København	41	55.40 N	12.35 E
Kjustendil	38	42.17 N	22.41 E
Klaarstroom	158	33.20 S	22.32 E
Klaaswaal	52	51.46 N	4.26 E
Klabat, Gunung ∧	112	1.28 N	125.02 E
Kladanj	38	44.13 N	18.41 E
Kladbišči	80	55.32 N	45.33 E
Kläden	54	52.38 N	11.39 E
Kladkovo	82	55.24 N	38.51 E
Kladno	54	50.08 N	14.05 E
Kladovo	38	44.37 N	22.37 E
Kladow ✦[8]	264a	52.27 N	13.09 E
Kladruby	60	49.43 N	12.59 E
Klaeng	110	12.47 N	101.39 E
Klagan	112	5.58 N	117.27 E
Klagenfurt	61	46.37 N	14.18 E
Klågerup	41	55.36 N	13.15 E
Klagshamn	41	55.32 N	12.55 E
Klagstorp	41	55.24 N	13.22 E
Klahoose Indian Reserve ✦[4]	182	50.31 N	124.19 W
Klaipėda (Memel)	76	55.43 N	21.07 E
Klakah	115a	7.59 S	113.15 E
Klamath	204	41.31 N	124.02 W
Klamath ≃	204	41.33 N	124.04 W
Klamath Falls	202	42.13 N	121.46 W
Klamath Marsh ≋	202	42.54 N	121.44 W
Klamath Mountains ⋀	204	41.40 N	123.20 W
K. Lamido	146	9.21 N	11.12 E
Klämmingen ⊜	40	59.07 N	17.15 E
Klammpass)(	64	47.17 N	13.05 E
Klamono	164	1.08 S	131.30 E
Klang → Kelang	114	3.02 N	101.27 E
Klangenan	115a	6.42 S	108.26 E
Klangpi	110	22.59 N	93.20 E
Klarälven (Trysilelva) ≃	26	59.23 N	13.32 E
Kl'as'ma	265b	55.59 N	37.50 E
Klášterec	54	50.24 N	13.10 E
Kl'asticy	76	55.53 N	28.36 E
Klaten	115a	7.42 S	110.35 E
Klatovy	60	49.24 N	13.18 E
Klausdorf, B.R.D.	54	54.18 N	10.15 E
Klausdorf, D.D.R.	54	54.20 N	13.01 E
Klausenburg → Cluj-Napoca	38	46.47 N	23.36 E
Klausenpass)(	58	46.52 N	8.51 E
Kl'avlino	80	54.17 N	52.01 E
Klawer	158	31.44 S	18.36 E
Klawock	182	55.33 N	133.06 W
Klazienaveen	52	52.44 N	7.00 E
Kl'az'ma	82	55.58 N	37.27 E
Kl'az'ma ≃	80	56.10 N	42.58 E
Kl'az'minskoje vodochranilišče ⊜[1]	265b	55.59 N	37.35 E
Kleberg	222	32.40 N	96.37 W
Kleck	76	53.04 N	26.38 E
Kłecko	30	52.38 N	17.26 E
Kleczew	30	52.23 N	18.10 E
Kledering ✦[8]	264b	48.08 N	16.26 E
Kleef	263	51.11 N	6.56 E
Kleena Kleene	182	51.57 N	124.50 W
Kleinasien → Asia Minor □[9]	22	39.00 N	32.00 E
Kleinbeeren	264a	52.22 N	13.20 E
Kleinbegin	158	28.50 S	21.36 E
Klein-Blesboksspruit ≃	273d	26.16 S	28.29 E
Kleinbodungen	54	51.28 N	10.32 E
Klein Bonaire I	241s	12.10 N	68.18 W
Klein Bünzow	54	53.53 N	13.48 E
Kleinburg	275b	43.50 N	79.38 W
Klein Curaçao I	241s	12.00 N	68.40 W
Kleine Elster ≃	54	51.32 N	13.23 E
Kleine Emme ≃	58	47.04 N	8.17 E
Kleine Emscher ≃	263	51.31 N	6.43 E
Kleine Erlauf ≃	61	48.07 N	15.08 E
Kleineichen	263	51.08 N	7.21 E
Kleine Laber ≃	60	48.55 N	12.31 E
Kleinenberg	52	51.35 N	8.58 E
Kleinenbroich	263	51.12 N	6.35 E
Kleinengstingen	58	48.23 N	9.18 E
Kleiner Jasmunder Bodden ⊂	54	54.28 N	13.32 E
Kleiner Ravens-Berg ∧[2]	264a	52.22 N	13.04 E
Kleiner Wannsee ⊜	264a	52.25 N	13.10 E
Kleiner Zern-See ⊜	264a	52.26 N	12.55 E
Kleine Spree ≃	54	51.31 N	14.24 E
Kleines Walsertal V	64	47.23 N	10.12 E
Kleinfeltersville	208	40.18 N	76.15 W
Kleinglödnitz	61	46.51 N	14.08 E
Kleinhammer	263	51.14 N	7.46 E
Klein-Jukskei ≃	273d	26.08 S	27.56 E
Klein-Karas	156	27.32 S	18.06 E
Klein Karroo → Little Karroo ⋀[1]	158	33.45 S	21.30 E
Klein Kienitz	264a	52.18 N	13.29 E
Kleinlützel	58	47.26 N	7.25 E
Kleinmachnow	54	52.24 N	13.15 E
Klein Marzehns	54	52.01 N	12.37 E
Kleinmond	158	34.21 S	19.03 E
Klein-Olifants ≃	158	25.41 S	29.19 E
Kleinschönebeck	264a	52.29 N	13.43 E
Klein-Soutpan	158	30.26 S	22.26 E
Klein Stöckheim	54	52.12 N	10.31 E
Klein-Vis ≃	158	33.05 S	26.00 E
Klein Wanzleben	54	52.04 N	11.21 E
Klein Ziethen	264a	52.23 N	13.27 E
Klein Ziethener-Berge ∧[2]	264a	52.22 N	13.26 E
Klekovača ∧	36	44.26 N	16.31 E
Klementjevka	86	50.16 N	80.56 E
Klementjevo	82	55.38 N	36.01 E
Klemme	190	43.00 N	93.36 W
Klemtu	182	52.36 N	128.31 W
Klenovka	80	57.45 N	54.19 E
Klenovo	82	55.19 N	37.21 E
Klerksdorp	158	26.58 S	26.39 E
Klerkskraal	158	26.15 S	27.10 E
Klesov	78	51.19 N	26.54 E
Klésso	150	10.57 N	3.59 W
Klet' ∧	61	48.52 N	14.17 E
Kletn'a	76	53.23 N	33.12 E
Kletskij	80	49.19 N	43.04 E
Kletsko-Počtovskij	80	49.36 N	43.03 E
Klettgau ✦[1]	58	47.40 N	8.25 E
Klettwitz	54	51.32 N	13.53 E
Klevan'	78	50.44 N	26.02 E
Kleve	52	51.48 N	6.09 E
Klevenka	80	52.07 N	49.33 E
Kley ✦[8]	263	51.30 N	7.22 E
Klibreck, Ben ∧	46	58.14 N	4.22 W
Kličev	76	53.29 N	29.21 E
Klička	88	50.26 N	118.00 E
Klickitat	224	45.49 N	121.09 W
Klickitat □[6]	224	45.50 N	121.07 W
Klickitat ≃	224	45.42 N	121.17 W
Kliedbruch ✦[1]	263	51.22 N	6.33 E
Klietz	54	52.40 N	12.04 E
Klimino	88	58.39 N	98.42 E
Klimoviči	76	53.37 N	31.58 E
Klimovo, S.S.S.R.	76	52.23 N	32.11 E
Klimovo, S.S.S.R.	82	55.22 N	38.52 E
Klimovsk	82	55.22 N	37.32 E
Klimovskoje	82	54.42 N	37.48 E
Klimov Zavod	76	54.50 N	34.55 E
Klimpfjäll	24	65.04 N	14.52 E
Klin, S.S.S.R.	82	56.20 N	36.44 E
Klin, S.S.S.R.	82	55.19 N	36.20 E
Klinaklini ≃	182	51.05 N	125.36 W
Klin-Bel'din	82	54.45 N	39.13 E
Klincovka	80	51.41 N	49.11 E
Klincy	76	52.47 N	32.14 E
Kline Ditch ≍	279a	41.28 N	82.04 W
Kling	116	5.58 N	124.42 E
Klingbach ≃	56	50.17 N	9.22 E
Klingenberg	54	50.55 N	13.31 E
Klingenberg am Main	56	49.47 N	9.11 E
Klingenmünster	56	49.08 N	8.01 E
Klingenthal	54	50.21 N	12.28 E
Klinger Lake ⊜	216	41.47 N	85.33 W
Klingerstown	208	40.40 N	76.41 W
Klinghardtberge ∧	156	27.18 S	15.48 E
Klingnau	58	47.35 N	8.15 E
Klink	54	53.29 N	12.37 E
Klinkino	83	47.17 N	38.15 E
Klínovec ∧	54	50.24 N	12.58 E
Klinsko-Dmitrovskaja gr'ada ∧	82	56.15 N	37.30 E
Klintehamn	26	57.24 N	18.12 E
Klintsy → Klincy	76	52.47 N	32.14 E
Klip ≃, S. Afr.	158	27.03 S	29.03 E
Klip ≃, S. Afr.	273d	26.19 S	27.53 E
Klipbakken	158	28.50 S	21.21 E
Klipdale	158	34.19 S	19.57 E
Klipdam	158	27.35 S	19.56 E
Kliplev	41	54.56 N	9.25 E
Klippan	41	56.08 N	13.06 E
Klipplaat	158	33.02 S	24.21 E
Klippoortjie	273d	26.13 S	28.10 E
Klipriviersberg ⋀	273d	26.17 S	28.02 E
Kliptown	273d	26.17 S	27.53 E
Klipwerf	158	31.09 S	19.52 E
Kliškovcy	78	48.26 N	26.15 E
Klisura	38	42.42 N	24.27 E
Klitmøller	26	57.02 N	8.31 E
Klitten	54	51.20 N	14.36 E
Klixbüll	41	54.48 N	8.53 E
Ključ	36	44.32 N	16.47 E
Klobbicke	264a	52.46 N	13.48 E
Klobouky	61	49.00 N	16.52 E
Kłobuck	30	50.55 N	18.57 E
Klobuticy	76	58.35 N	29.35 E
Kłodawa	30	52.16 N	18.55 E
Kłodzko	30	50.27 N	16.39 E
Kløfta	26	60.04 N	11.09 E
Kłomnice	30	50.56 N	19.21 E
Klondike	216	40.28 N	86.57 W
Klondike □[9]	180	63.30 N	139.00 W
Klondike ≃	180	64.05 N	139.26 W
Klöntaler See ⊜	58	47.02 N	8.58 E
Klooga	76	59.19 N	24.16 E
Kloosterveen	52	52.59 N	6.33 E
Kloosterzande	52	51.22 N	4.02 E
Kloster	54	54.35 N	13.06 E
Klosterfelde	54	52.48 N	13.28 E
Klosterhardt ✦[8]	263	51.31 N	6.53 E
Klösterle	58	47.08 N	10.05 E
Klostermansfeld	54	51.35 N	11.29 E
Klosterneuburg	264b	48.18 N	16.20 E
Kloster Oesede	52	52.12 N	8.07 E
Klosters	58	46.54 N	9.53 E
Klostertal V	58	47.08 N	9.59 E
Kloster Zinna	54	52.01 N	13.07 E
Kloten, Schw.	58	47.27 N	8.35 E
Kloten, Sve.	40	59.54 N	15.17 E
Klotz, Lac ⊜	176	60.32 N	73.40 W
Klötze	54	52.38 N	11.10 E
Kloulklubed	175b	7.02 N	134.15 E
Klouto	150	6.57 N	0.34 E
Kluane ≃	180	61.53 N	139.43 W
Kluane Lake ⊜	180	61.15 N	138.40 W
Kluane National Park ♦	180	60.45 N	139.30 W
Kluang	112	2.41 S	103.54 E
Kl'učevaja	24	65.16 N	41.32 E
Kl'učevskaja Sopka, vulkan ∧[1]	74	56.04 N	160.38 E
Kl'učevskij	88	53.33 N	119.26 E
Kluchorskij, pereval)(	84	43.15 N	41.54 E
Kl'uči, S.S.S.R.	74	56.18 N	160.51 E
Kl'uči, S.S.S.R.	80	51.59 N	46.31 E
Kl'uči, S.S.S.R.	80	51.26 N	45.11 E
Kl'uči, S.S.S.R.	86	52.16 N	79.10 E
Kl'učovka, S.S.S.R.	85	42.34 N	71.48 E
Kl'učovka, S.S.S.R.	86	51.22 N	55.48 E
Kluczbork	30	50.59 N	18.13 E
Kluess	54	53.46 N	12.14 E
Kluet ≃	114	3.04 N	97.20 E
Kl'ukvenka	86	58.34 N	85.55 E
Klukwan	180	59.24 N	135.54 W
Klundert	52	51.40 N	4.32 E
Klungkung	115b	8.32 S	115.24 E
Klüppelberg	56	51.06 N	7.28 E
Klüterthöhle ⊥[5]	52	51.18 N	7.21 E
Klutina Lake ⊜	180	61.37 N	146.55 W
Klütz	54	53.58 N	11.10 E
Knaben gruver	26	58.39 N	7.04 E
Knaddah	130	35.45 N	36.12 E
Kn'aginino	80	55.49 N	45.03 E
Knaik ≃	46	56.14 N	3.52 W
Knapdaar	158	30.43 S	26.09 E
Knapdale ✦[1]	46	55.55 N	5.30 W
Knaphill	260	51.19 N	0.37 W
Knapp	190	44.57 N	92.04 W
Knapp Creek	210	42.00 N	78.30 W
Knappenberg	61	46.56 N	14.35 E
Knäred	26	56.32 N	13.19 E
Knaresborough	44	54.00 N	1.27 W
Knargram	126	24.01 N	87.59 E
Knauertown	285	40.10 N	75.44 W
Knauthain ✦[8]	54	51.16 N	12.18 E
Kn'ažaja Bajgora	76	52.23 N	40.02 E
Kn'azevka	86	57.35 N	74.10 E
Kn'ažji Gory	76	56.05 N	35.14 E
Kn'ažovo	76	59.40 N	43.54 E
Knebel	41	56.13 N	10.30 E
Knebworth	42	51.52 N	0.12 W
Kneehills Creek ≃	182	51.30 N	112.50 W
Knee Lake ⊜, Mb., Can.	184	55.03 N	94.40 W
Knee Lake ⊜, Sk., Can.	184	55.51 N	107.00 W
Knesebeck	54	52.41 N	10.42 E
Knesselare	50	51.08 N	3.25 E
Knetzgau	56	50.00 N	10.33 E
Knevicy	76	57.56 N	32.14 E
Kneža	38	43.30 N	24.05 E
Knić	38	43.55 N	20.43 E
Knickerbocker	196	31.16 N	100.38 W
Kniebis	58	48.28 N	8.17 E
Knife ≃	198	47.20 N	101.23 W
Knife Lake ⊜	184	53.47 N	91.20 W
Knife River Indian Villages National Historical Site ⊥	198	47.21 N	101.23 W
Knight Inlet ⊂	182	50.41 N	125.40 W
Knight Island I	180	60.20 N	147.45 W
Knighton	42	52.21 N	3.03 W
Knightsen	226	37.58 N	121.40 W
Knights Landing	226	38.47 N	121.43 W
Knightstown	218	39.47 N	85.31 W
Knightville Dam ✦[6]	207	42.17 N	72.52 W
Knik Arm ⊂	180	61.25 N	149.45 W
Knin	36	44.02 N	16.12 E
Knippa	196	29.18 N	99.38 W
Knislinge	26	56.11 N	14.05 E
Knittelfeld	61	47.14 N	14.50 E
Knittlingen	56	49.01 N	8.45 E
Knivsbjerg ∧[2]	41	55.08 N	9.27 E
Knivsta	40	59.43 N	17.48 E
Knjaževac	38	43.34 N	22.16 E
Knob, Cape ›	162	34.32 S	119.16 E
Knobby Head ›	162	29.40 S	114.58 E
Knob Noster	194	38.45 N	93.33 W
Knob Peak ∧	116	12.28 N	121.21 E
Knoc	48	52.38 N	9.20 W
Knock	46	57.33 N	2.45 W
Knockholt	260	51.18 N	0.06 E
Knockholt Pound	260	51.19 N	0.08 E
Knocklayd ∧	48	55.09 N	6.15 W
Knocklong	48	52.26 N	8.24 W
Knockmealdown Mountains ⋀	48	52.10 N	8.00 W
Knokke	50	51.21 N	3.17 E
Knole ⊥	260	51.16 N	0.12 E
Knolls Green	262	53.19 N	2.18 W
Knollwood, Ct., U.S.	207	41.16 N	72.23 W
Knollwood, Il., U.S.	278	42.17 N	87.53 W
Knollwood, Md., U.S.	284c	39.02 N	76.58 W
Knollwood Park	216	42.14 N	84.22 W
Knon ⊜	40	60.12 N	13.40 E
Knossós ⊥	38	35.20 N	25.10 E
Knottingley	44	53.43 N	1.14 W
Knott's Berry Farm ♦	280	33.50 N	118.00 W
Knotts Island	208	36.31 N	75.56 W
Knotty Ash ✦[8]	262	53.25 N	2.54 W
Knotty Green	260	51.37 N	0.39 W
Knowland State Arboretum and Park ♦	282	37.45 N	122.09 W
Knowle	42	52.23 N	1.43 W
Knowlesville	210	43.14 N	78.19 W
Knowlton Lake ⊜	212	44.28 N	76.41 W
Knowltonwood	285	39.53 N	75.24 W
Knowsley ✦[8], Eng., U.K.	262	53.27 N	2.50 W
Knowsley ✦[8], Eng., U.K.	262	53.27 N	2.51 W
Knowsley Hall ⚑	262	53.26 N	2.50 W
Knowsley Park ♦	262	53.27 N	2.49 W
Knox, In., U.S.	216	41.17 N	86.37 W
Knox, N.Y., U.S.	210	42.40 N	74.07 W
Knox, Pa., U.S.	214	41.14 N	79.32 W
Knox □[6], Mo., U.S.	219	40.08 N	92.09 W
Knox □[6], Oh., U.S.	214	40.23 N	82.29 W
Knox, Cape ›	182	54.11 N	133.04 W
Knoxboro	210	42.58 N	75.36 W
Knox City, Mo., U.S.	219	40.08 N	92.00 W
Knox City, Tx., U.S.	196	33.25 N	99.49 W
Knox Coast ⊥[2]	9	66.30 S	105.00 E
Knox Dale	214	41.05 N	79.02 W
Knoxfield	274b	37.53 S	145.15 E
Knox Lake ⊜[1]	214	40.31 N	82.30 W
Knoxville, Ga., U.S.	192	32.43 N	83.59 W
Knoxville, Il., U.S.	190	40.54 N	90.17 W
Knoxville, Ia., U.S.	190	41.19 N	93.06 W
Knoxville, Pa., U.S.	210	41.57 N	77.26 W
Knoxville, Tn., U.S.	192	35.57 N	83.55 W
Knuckles ∧	122	7.24 N	80.48 E
Knudshoved Odde ›[1]	41	55.03 N	11.45 E
Knüll ∧	56	50.53 N	9.24 E
Knutby	40	59.55 N	18.15 E
Knuthenborg	41	54.50 N	11.30 E
Knutsford	44	53.19 N	2.22 W
Knysna	158	34.02 S	23.02 E
Knyszyn	30	53.19 N	22.55 E
Koala Sanctuary ✦[4]	274a	33.40 S	151.10 E
Koani	154	6.08 S	39.17 E
Kob'	88	55.25 N	101.24 E
Koba	112	2.29 S	106.24 E
Kob'aj	74	63.34 N	126.30 E
Kőbánya ✦[8]	264c	47.29 N	19.10 E
Kobarid	36	46.15 N	13.35 E
Kobar Sink ⊥[7]	144	13.35 N	40.50 E
Kobayashi	92	31.59 N	130.59 E
Kōbe, Nihon	96	34.41 N	135.10 E
Kōbe, Nihon	270	34.41 N	135.10 E
Kōbe-kō ⊂	270	34.40 N	135.12 E
Kobel'aki	78	49.09 N	34.12 E
København (Copenhagen)	41	55.40 N	12.35 E
København □[6]	41	55.45 N	12.25 E
Kōbe University ⚑[2]	270	34.43 N	135.14 E
Kobi	84	42.33 N	44.32 E
Koblenz, B.R.D.	56	50.21 N	7.35 E
Koblenz, Schw.	58	47.37 N	8.14 E
Koblenz □[5]	56	50.10 N	7.30 E
Kobo, Ityo.	144	12.11 N	39.33 E
Kobo, Zaïre	152	4.54 S	17.09 E
Ko-boke ♦	96	33.50 N	133.46 E
Koboko	154	3.25 N	30.58 E
Koboldo	89	52.58 N	132.42 E
Kobona	76	60.01 N	31.36 E
Kobou ≃	152	6.13 N	23.19 E
Kobowen Swamp ≋	144	5.38 N	33.54 E
Koboža	76	58.49 N	35.01 E
Koboža ≃	76	58.52 N	36.17 E
Kobra	24	60.03 N	50.44 E
Kobrin	76	52.13 N	24.21 E
Kobrinskoje	76	59.25 N	30.07 E
Kobroor, Pulau I	164	6.12 S	134.32 E
Kobuchizawa	94	35.52 N	138.19 E
Kobuga-hara ♦	94	36.40 N	139.35 E
Kobuk	180	66.54 N	156.52 W
Kobuk ≃	180	66.45 N	161.00 W
Kobuk Valley National Park ♦	180	67.20 N	159.00 W
Kobuleti	84	41.50 N	41.47 E
Kobushiga-take ∧	94	35.54 N	138.44 E
Kobylanka	54	53.19 N	14.50 E
Kobylin	30	51.43 N	17.13 E
Kobyl'nik	76	54.56 N	26.41 E
Kobyžča	78	50.49 N	31.30 E
Kocaali	130	41.03 N	30.52 E
Kocaaliler	130	37.19 N	30.44 E
Kocaavşar ≃	130	40.08 N	27.57 E
Kocaeli → İzmit	130	40.46 N	29.55 E
Kocaeli □[4]	130	40.55 N	29.55 E
Koçali	130	37.55 N	38.15 E
Kočani	38	41.55 N	22.25 E
Koçarlı	130	37.45 N	27.42 E
Kocasinan ✦[8]	267b	41.01 N	28.50 E
Koçbaşı Tepe ∧	84	39.25 N	43.21 E
Kočečum ≃	74	64.17 N	101.10 E
Kočelajevo	80	54.01 N	44.02 E
Kočemary	80	54.50 N	40.58 E
Kočen'ajevka	80	53.52 N	46.59 E
Kočen'ga, S.S.S.R.	76	60.09 N	43.33 E
Kočenga, S.S.S.R.	88	55.55 N	104.06 E
Kočenga ≃	88	55.55 N	104.06 E
Kočerdyk	86	54.35 N	62.58 E
Kočerga	88	55.15 N	103.46 E
Kočerov	78	50.21 N	29.21 E
Kočetovka, S.S.S.R.	80	55.16 N	46.07 E
Kočetovka, S.S.S.R.	80	52.58 N	40.29 E
Kočevar	76	60.26 N	42.11 E
Kočevje	36	45.38 N	14.52 E
Kočevo	86	59.36 N	54.18 E
Koch'am-ni	98	41.06 N	129.23 E
Kŏch'ang, Taehan	98	35.41 N	127.55 E
Kŏch'ang, Taehan	98	35.26 N	126.42 E
Kochanoviči	76	55.52 N	28.08 E
Kochanovo	76	54.28 N	30.01 E
Koch Bihār	124	26.19 N	89.26 E
Kochel	64	47.39 N	11.22 E
Kochelsee ⊜	64	47.38 N	11.20 E
Kochena	158	27.00 S	18.50 E
Kocher ≃	56	49.14 N	9.12 E
Kōchi, Nihon	96	34.28 N	132.53 E
Kōchi, Nihon	96	33.33 N	133.33 E
Kōchi □[5]	96	33.40 N	133.30 E
Kōchi-dani ♦	94	34.34 N	136.10 E
Kochinda	174m	26.08 N	127.43 E
Koch Island I	176	69.38 N	78.15 W
Kochiu → Gejiu	90	23.22 N	103.06 E
Kochma	80	56.56 N	41.06 E
Koch Peak ∧	202	45.02 N	111.28 W
Kochugaon	124	26.34 N	90.04 E
Kock	30	51.39 N	22.27 E
Kočki, S.S.S.R.	86	52.24 N	80.40 E
Kočki, S.S.S.R.	86	54.20 N	80.29 E
Kočkor-Ata	85	41.04 N	72.29 E
Kočkorka	85	42.14 N	75.45 E

Symbols in the index entries represent the broad categories identified in the key at the right. Symbols with superior numbers (⋀[1]) identify subcategories (see complete key on page *I · 1).*

Symbole im Register stellen die rechts im Schlüssel erklärten Kategorien dar. Symbole mit hochgestellten Ziffern (⋀[1]) bezeichnen Unterabteilungen einer Kategorie (vgl. vollständiger Schlüssel auf Seite *I · 1).*

Los símbolos incluídos en el texto del índice representan las grandes categorias identificadas con la clave a la derecha. Los símbolos con numeros en su parte superior (⋀[1]) identifican las subcategorías (véase la clave completa en la página *I · 1).*

Les symboles de l'index représentent les catégories indiquées dans la légende à droite. Les symboles suivis d'un indice (⋀[1]) représentent des sous-catégories (voir légende complète à la page *I · 1).*

Os símbolos incluídos no texto do índice representam as grandes categorias identificadas com a chave à direita. Os símbolos com números em sua parte superior (⋀[1]) identificam as subcategorias (veja-se a chave completa à página *I · 1).*

	English	Deutsch	Español	Français	Português
∧	Mountain	Berg	Montaña	Montagne	Montanha
⋀	Mountains	Gebirge	Montañas	Montagnes	Montanhas
)(	Pass	Paß	Paso	Col	Passo
V	Valley, Canyon	Tal, Cañon	Valle, Cañón	Vallée, Canyon	Vale, Canhão
≚	Plain	Ebene	Llano	Plaine	Planície
›	Cape	Kap	Cabo	Cap	Cabo
I	Island	Insel	Isla	Île	Ilha
II	Islands	Inseln	Islas	Îles	Ilhas
⊥	Other Topographic Features	Andere Topographische Objekte	Otros Elementos Topográficos	Autres données topographiques	Outros acidentes topográficos

ESPAÑOL

Nombre	Página	Lat.°′	Long.°′ W = Oeste
Kocksoord	273d	26.13 S	27.39 E
Kočkurovo	80	54.02 N	45.26 E
Kočmes	24	66.12 N	60.44 E
Kočon'ovo	86	55.02 N	82.12 E
Kočov	60	49.49 N	12.44 E
Kočubej	84	44.24 N	46.33 E
Kočubejevskoje	84	44.41 N	41.41 E
Kōda, Nihon	94	34.52 N	137.10 E
Kōda, Nihon	96	34.42 N	132.45 E
Kodačdikost	24	63.11 N	55.49 E
Kodaikānal	122	10.14 N	77.29 E
Kodaira	94	35.44 N	139.29 E
Kodama	94	36.11 N	139.08 E
Kodar, chrebet ⋏	88	57.15 N	118.10 E
Kodāri	124	27.56 N	85.56 E
Kodarma	124	24.28 N	85.36 E
Kodera ◆[8]	270	34.41 N	135.04 E
Kodersdorf	54	51.15 N	14.53 E
Kodi	152	3.34 S	22.12 E
Kodiak	180	57.48 N	152.23 W
Kodiak Island I	180	57.30 N	153.30 W
Kodiang	114	6.24 N	100.18 E
Kodinār	120	20.47 N	70.42 E
Kodino	24	63.43 N	39.41 E
Kodo ≏	152	7.05 N	19.10 E
Kodo, Jabal ∧	140	12.26 N	23.38 E
Kodok	140	9.53 N	32.07 E
Kodori ≏	84	42.47 N	41.10 E
Kodorskij chrebet ⋏	84	43.00 N	42.00 E
Kodra	78	50.36 N	29.34 E
Kodry ⋏[2]	78	47.10 N	28.25 E
Kodyma	78	48.07 N	29.07 E
Kodyma ≏	78	48.01 N	30.48 E
Kodžori	84	41.40 N	44.41 E
Koegas	158	29.16 S	22.20 E
Koehn Lake ⊜	228	35.20 N	117.53 W
Koekelare	50	51.05 N	2.58 E
Koekenaap	158	31.30 S	18.18 E
Koeltztown	219	38.19 N	92.03 W
Koenigsmacker	56	49.24 N	6.17 E
Koersel	56	51.04 N	5.16 E
Koes	156	25.59 S	19.08 E
Kofa Mountains ⋏	200	33.20 N	114.00 W
Kofçaz	130	41.58 N	27.12 E
Kofeld	58	47.44 N	9.41 E
Köfering	60	48.56 N	12.12 E
Koffiefontein	158	29.30 S	25.00 E
Kofiau, Pulau I	164	1.11 S	129.50 E
Köflach	61	47.04 N	15.05 E
Koforidua	150	6.03 N	0.17 W
Kōfu, Nihon	94	35.39 N	138.35 E
Kōfu, Nihon	96	35.17 N	133.30 E
Koga, Nihon	94	36.11 N	139.43 E
Koga, Nihon	96	33.40 N	130.30 E
Koga, Tan.	154	6.14 S	32.25 E
Kogaluc ≏	176	59.40 N	77.35 W
Kogaluc, Baie ⊂	176	59.20 N	77.50 W
Kogaluk ≏	176	56.12 N	61.44 W
Kogan	166	27.03 S	150.46 E
Kogane	268	35.50 N	139.56 E
Koganei	94	35.42 N	139.32 E
Kogarah	274a	33.58 S	151.08 E
Kogarah Bay ⊂	274a	33.59 S	151.07 E
Køge, Dan.	41	55.27 N	12.11 E
Kōge, Nihon	96	35.24 N	134.15 E
Køge Bugt ⊂, Dan.	41	55.30 N	12.20 E
Køge Bugt ⊂, Kal. Nun.	176	65.00 N	40.30 W
Kogil'nik ≏	78	45.51 N	29.38 E
Kogin Baba	146	7.55 N	11.30 E
Koglhof	61	47.19 N	15.40 E
Kogon ≏	150	11.09 N	14.42 W
Kogoni	150	14.44 N	6.02 W
Kŏgŭm-do I	98	34.27 N	127.11 E
Kohak	128	25.44 N	62.33 E
Kohala Mountains ⋏	229d	20.05 N	155.45 W
Kohama-shima I	175d	24.19 N	123.59 E
Kohāt	123	33.35 N	71.26 E
Kohāt ≏	123	33.24 N	71.48 E
Kohatk Wash V	200	32.38 N	111.55 W
Kohila	76	59.10 N	24.45 E
Kohīma	120	25.40 N	94.07 E
Kohistān □[9]	123	35.03 N	72.52 W
Kohlberg ∧[2]	263	51.18 N	7.46 E
Kohler	190	43.44 N	87.46 W
Kohlfurt → Węgliniec	30	51.17 N	15.13 E
Kohlstädt	52	51.50 N	8.52 E
Kohoku	94	35.26 N	136.15 E
Kōhoku ◆[8]	268	35.31 N	139.38 E
Kohren-Sahlis	54	51.01 N	12.36 E
Kohsān	128	34.39 N	61.12 E
Kohtla-Järve	76	59.24 N	27.15 E
Kohu → Kōfu	94	35.39 N	138.35 E
Kohukohu	172	35.21 S	173.32 E
Kohŭng	98	34.37 N	127.16 E
Kohuratahi	172	39.06 S	174.46 E
Koide	94	37.13 N	138.57 E
Koidern	180	61.58 N	140.25 W
Koidu	150	8.38 N	10.59 W
Koigi	76	58.50 N	25.45 E
Koihoa	110	8.12 N	93.29 E
Koil-Aligarh → Alīgarh	124	27.53 N	78.05 E
Koimbani	157a	11.37 S	43.23 E
Koindu	150	8.26 N	10.19 W
Koin-ni	98	40.28 N	126.22 E
Koitere ⊜	26	62.58 N	30.45 E
Koito ≏	94	35.21 N	139.52 E
Kojandy	86	49.51 N	75.40 E
Kojda	24	66.23 N	42.31 E
Kŏje-do I	98	34.52 N	128.37 E
Kojetín	30	49.21 N	17.18 E
Kojgorodok	24	60.26 N	50.58 E
Ko-jima I	92a	41.22 N	139.48 E
Kojima-ko ⊜[1]	96	34.37 N	134.00 E
Kojō	98	38.57 N	127.51 E
Kojonup	162	33.50 S	117.09 E
Kojsary	85	42.33 N	78.10 E
Kojsug	83	47.07 N	39.41 E
Kojtaš, S.S.S.R.	85	40.11 N	67.19 E
Kojtas, S.S.S.R.	86	51.32 N	76.15 E
Kok (Hkok) ≏	110	20.14 N	100.09 E
Kōka	94	34.54 N	136.13 E
Koka, Lake ⊜[1]	144	8.23 N	39.05 E
Kokai ≏	94	35.52 N	140.08 E
K'okajgyr	85	40.43 N	75.37 E
Kokalaat	86	49.47 N	64.15 E
Kokand	85	40.33 N	70.57 E
Kokanee Glacier Provincial Park ♠	182	49.47 N	117.10 W
Kokankišlak	85	40.56 N	72.30 E
Kökar I	26	59.56 N	20.55 E
Kokaral, ostrov I	86	46.12 N	60.30 E
Kokas	164	2.42 S	132.26 E
Kokašice	60	49.53 N	12.57 E
Kokava nad Rimavicou	30	48.34 N	19.50 E
Kokawa	96	34.16 N	135.24 E
K'okbel'	85	40.17 N	72.55 E
Kokčetav	86	53.17 N	69.25 E
Kokčetavskaja vozvyšennost' ⋏[1]	86	52.50 N	69.00 E
Kokee State Park ♠	229b	22.08 N	159.40 W
Kokemäenjoki ≏	26	61.33 N	21.42 E
Kokemäki	26	61.15 N	22.21 E
Kokenau	164	4.43 S	136.26 E
Ko Kha	110	18.11 N	99.24 E
Kokhav HaYarden (Belvoir) ⊥	132	32.36 N	35.31 E
Kókhi, Ákra >	267c	37.53 N	23.27 E
Koki	150	15.30 N	15.59 W
Kokinu	268	35.59 N	139.59 E
Kokiu → Gejiu	102	23.22 N	103.06 E
Kok-Jangak	85	41.02 N	73.12 E
Kokka	140	20.00 N	30.35 E
Kokkilai Lagoon ⊂	122	9.00 N	80.56 E
Kokkola (Karleby)	26	63.50 N	23.07 E
Kokku	98	40.22 N	128.44 E
Koknese	76	56.39 N	25.29 E
Koko	150	11.26 N	4.32 E

FRANÇAIS

Nom	Page	Lat.°′	Long.°′ W = Ouest
Kokoda	164	8.52 S	147.45 E
Koko Head >	229c	21.16 N	157.42 W
Kokola	154	0.47 N	29.36 E
Kokole Point >	229b	21.59 N	159.46 W
Kokolik ≏	180	69.46 N	163.00 W
Kokolopozo	150	5.08 N	6.05 W
K'ok'omeren ≏	85	41.43 N	73.54 E
Kokomo, Hi., U.S.	229a	20.52 N	156.18 W
Kokomo, In., U.S.	216	40.29 N	86.08 W
Kokomo, Ms., U.S.	194	31.11 N	90.00 W
Kokong	156	24.27 S	23.03 E
Kokonoe	96	33.10 N	131.10 E
Koko Nor → Qinghai Hu ⊜	102	36.50 N	100.20 E
Kokopo	164	4.20 S	152.15 E
Kokorevka	76	52.35 N	34.16 E
Kokosing ≏	214	40.22 N	82.12 W
Kokos-Inseln → Cocos (Keeling) Islands □[2]	14	12.10 S	96.55 E
Kokoškino	265b	55.38 N	37.11 E
Kokpāra Narsinghgarh	126	22.31 N	86.33 E
Kokpaš	86	51.12 N	87.45 E
Kokpekty	86	48.45 N	82.24 E
Kokrājhār	124	26.24 N	90.16 E
Kokrines	180	64.56 N	154.42 W
Kokrines Hills ⋏[2]	180	65.15 N	154.00 W
Koksa ≏	86	50.16 N	85.36 E
Kokšaalatau, chrebet ⋏	72	41.00 N	78.00 E
Koksan	98	38.46 N	126.40 E
Koksaraj	85	42.40 N	68.08 E
Kokšekol', ozero ⊜	86	46.05 N	62.00 E
Koksijde	50	51.07 N	2.38 E
Koksilah	224	48.40 N	123.38 W
Koksilah ≏	224	48.45 N	123.39 W
Koksoak ≏	176	58.32 N	68.10 W
Koksŏng	98	35.17 N	127.17 E
Koksovyj	78	48.12 N	40.39 E
Kokstad	158	30.32 S	29.29 E
Koksu, S.S.S.R.	85	41.27 N	68.01 E
Koksu, S.S.S.R.	86	44.59 N	77.56 E
Koktal	86	44.09 N	79.48 E
Kok-Taš, S.S.S.R.	85	41.12 N	72.25 E
Koktas, S.S.S.R.	86	45.59 N	73.32 E
Koktas, S.S.S.R.	86	47.33 N	70.55 E
Kokterek	80	49.25 N	49.15 E
Koktubek	86	48.07 N	56.51 E
Kokubu, Nihon	92	31.44 N	130.46 E
Kokubu, Nihon	96	34.56 N	132.07 E
Kokubunji, Nihon	94	36.22 N	139.51 E
Kokubunji, Nihon	96	34.18 N	133.58 E
Kokubunji, Nihon	268	35.42 N	139.29 E
Kokubunji Temple ☗[1]	268	35.44 N	139.55 E
Kokufu	96	35.28 N	134.16 E
Kokuj	88	52.13 N	117.33 E
Kokujbel' ≏	85	38.21 N	72.46 E
Kokžar	86	49.01 N	60.10 E
Kol ≏	128	26.59 N	55.47 E
Kola, Indon.	164	5.26 S	134.29 E
Kola, S.S.S.R.	24	68.53 N	33.01 E
Kola ≏	24	68.53 N	33.02 E
Kolachel	122	8.10 N	77.15 E
Kolāchi ≏	120	27.08 N	67.02 E
Kol'adovka	83	49.05 N	39.12 E
Kolageran	84	40.58 N	44.37 E
Kolahun	150	8.24 N	10.02 W
Kolaka	112	4.03 S	121.36 E
Kolambo	152	7.34 S	21.58 E
Kolambugan	116	8.07 N	123.55 E
Kolangār	120	34.02 N	69.01 E
Kola Peninsula → Kol'skij poluostrov >[1]	24	67.30 N	37.00 E
Kolār	122	13.08 N	78.08 E
Kolāras	124	25.14 N	77.36 E
Kolār Gold Fields	122	12.55 N	78.17 E
Kolari	24	67.20 N	23.48 E
Kolarovgrad → Šumen	38	43.16 N	26.55 E
Kolárovo	30	47.52 N	18.02 E
Kolašin	38	42.49 N	19.31 E
Kolāyat	120	27.50 N	72.57 E
Kolbači	89	54.22 N	123.02 E
Kolbäck	40	59.34 N	16.15 E
Kolbäcksån ≏	40	59.32 N	16.16 E
Kol'baj, gora ∧[2]	86	43.43 N	53.57 E
Kolbano	112	10.02 S	124.31 E
Kolbasna	78	47.47 N	29.13 E
Kolbča	76	53.39 N	29.14 E
Kolberg → Kołobrzeg	30	54.12 N	15.33 E
Kolbermoor	64	47.51 N	12.04 E
Kolbio	144	1.10 S	41.15 E
Kolbnitz	64	46.52 N	13.19 E
Kolbotn	26	59.49 N	10.48 E
Kolbuszowa	30	50.15 N	21.47 E
Kolby Kås	41	55.48 N	10.33 E
Kolchida ⩩	84	42.15 N	42.00 E
Kolchozabad	120	37.27 N	68.31 E
Kol'covo	82	54.27 N	36.40 E
Kol'čuga	82	55.43 N	37.12 E
Kol'čugino	80	56.18 N	39.23 E
Kołczewo	54	53.58 N	14.38 E
Kolda	150	12.53 N	14.57 W
Kolda □[4]	150	12.50 N	14.50 W
Kolding	41	55.31 N	9.29 E
Kolding Fjord ⊂	41	55.30 N	9.35 E
Kole, Zaïre	152	3.27 S	22.29 E
Kole, Zaïre	154	2.07 N	25.26 E
Kolea	34	36.38 N	2.46 E
Kolebīra	124	22.43 N	84.42 E
Kole Kalyan ◆[8]	272c	19.06 N	72.51 E
Kolenfeld	52	52.24 N	9.27 E
Koleno	80	51.52 N	44.07 E
Kolenté	150	10.06 N	12.37 W
Kolenté (Great Scarcies) ≏	150	8.55 N	13.08 W
Kolga	76	59.32 N	25.42 E
Kolgujev, ostrov I	24	69.05 N	49.15 E
Kolhāpur, India	122	16.06 N	78.16 E
Kolhāpur, India	122	16.42 N	74.13 E
Kolho	26	62.08 N	24.31 E
Koli	76	59.30 N	34.30 E
Koli ∧[2]	26	63.06 N	29.48 E
Koli, Jabal ∧	140	14.05 N	25.31 E
Kolia	150	9.46 N	6.28 W
Koliba (Corubal) ≏	150	11.57 N	15.06 W
Koliganek	180	59.48 N	157.25 W
Kolima ⊜	26	63.16 N	25.50 E
Kolimbine ≏	150	14.26 N	11.23 W
Kolín	30	50.01 N	15.13 E
Kolka	76	57.45 N	22.35 E
Kølkær	41	56.04 N	9.06 E
Kolkasrags >	76	57.47 N	22.36 E
Kolki, S.S.S.R.	78	51.37 N	26.37 E
Kolki, S.S.S.R.	78	51.07 N	25.41 E
Kolkwitz	54	51.45 N	14.15 E
Kollbach ≏	60	48.36 N	12.58 E
Kölleda	54	51.11 N	11.15 E
Kollegāl	122	12.09 N	77.07 E
Kolleru Lake ⊜	122	16.39 N	81.13 E
Kollum	52	53.16 N	6.09 E
Kollund	41	54.51 N	9.27 E
Kolmanskop	156	26.40 S	15.12 E
Kolmården	40	58.40 N	16.23 E
Kolmården ⋏[2]	40	58.41 N	16.35 E
Kolmårdens Djurpark ♠	40	58.40 N	16.29 E
Kolmogorovo	86	59.15 N	91.20 E
Köln (Cologne)	56	50.56 N	6.59 E
Köln □[5]	56	50.55 N	6.40 E
Köln-Bonn, Flughafen ⊠	56	50.50 N	7.10 E
Kolno	30	53.25 N	21.56 E
Kolo, Niger	150	13.14 N	2.20 E
Koło, Pol.	30	52.12 N	18.38 E
Kolo, Tan.	154	4.44 S	35.50 E
Koloa	229b	21.54 N	159.28 W
Kolobovo	80	56.42 N	41.21 E
Kołobrzeg	30	54.12 N	15.33 E
Koloč' ≏	82	55.34 N	35.52 E

PORTUGUÊS

Nome	Página	Lat.°′	Long.°′ W = Oeste
Kolochau	54	51.44 N	13.16 E
Kolodn'a	76	54.48 N	32.09 E
Kologriv	76	58.51 N	44.17 E
Kologrivovka	80	51.44 N	45.20 E
Kolojar	80	52.34 N	46.58 E
Kolok (Golok) ≏	114	6.15 N	102.05 E
Kolokani	150	13.35 N	8.02 W
Koloko	150	11.05 N	5.19 W
Kolokol'covka, S.S.S.R.	80	52.36 N	49.48 E
Kolokol'covka, S.S.S.R.	80	51.12 N	44.36 E
Kololo	144	7.29 N	41.58 E
Kolom'agi ◆[8]	265a	60.00 N	30.17 E
Kolom'agi Airport ⊠	265a	60.01 N	30.17 E
Kolomak	78	49.50 N	35.18 E
Kolombangara Island I	175e	8.00 S	157.05 E
Kolomea → Kolomyja	78	48.32 N	25.04 E
Kolomenka ≏	82	55.06 N	38.46 E
Kolomenskaja Sloboda	82	54.22 N	38.15 E
Kolomenskoje ◆[8]	265b	55.40 N	37.41 E
Kolomna	82	55.05 N	38.49 E
Kolomyja	78	48.32 N	25.04 E
Kolondiéba	150	11.05 N	6.54 W
Kolonga	174w	21.08 S	175.04 W
Kolonia	174r	6.58 N	158.13 E
Kolonie Stolp	264a	52.28 N	13.46 E
Kolono	112	4.18 S	122.41 E
Kolonodale	112	2.00 S	121.19 E
Kolora	272b	22.55 N	88.22 E
Kolosib	120	24.14 N	92.42 E
Kol'osnoje	78	46.02 N	29.56 E
Kolosovka	86	56.28 N	73.36 E
Kolovai	174w	21.06 S	175.20 W
Kolovertnoje	80	50.36 N	51.06 E
Kolowana Watobo, Teluk ⊂	112	5.00 S	123.06 E
Kolozsvár → Cluj-Napoca	38	46.47 N	23.36 E
Kolp' ≏	76	59.20 N	36.49 E
Kolpaševo	86	58.20 N	82.50 E
Kolpino	76	59.45 N	30.36 E
Kölpinsee ⊜	54	53.30 N	12.34 E
Kolpny	76	52.15 N	37.02 E
Kölsa	54	51.28 N	12.13 E
Kol'skij poluostrov (Kola Peninsula) >[1]	24	67.30 N	37.00 E
Kolsnaren ⊜	40	59.02 N	16.01 E
Kolsva	40	59.36 N	15.50 E
Kol'togan	85	43.51 N	67.25 E
Koltovskaja	80	52.47 N	44.16 E
Koltubanovskij	80	52.57 N	52.02 E
Koltuši	265a	59.56 N	30.40 E
Kol'ubakino	82	55.40 N	36.32 E
Kolubara ≏	38	44.40 N	20.15 E
Kol'učinskaja guba ⊂	180	66.40 N	174.30 W
Koluel Kayke	254	46.43 S	68.14 W
Kolumbien → Colombia □[1]	246	4.00 N	72.00 W
Kol'upanovo	82	54.26 N	36.14 E
Koluškino	78	48.39 N	40.56 E
Koluszki	30	51.44 N	19.49 E
Koluton	86	51.43 N	69.25 E
Koluton ≏	86	51.42 N	69.10 E
Kolva ≏	24	65.55 N	57.15 E
Kolvereid	24	64.51 N	11.32 E
Kølvrå	41	56.18 N	9.08 E
Kolwezi	154	10.43 S	25.28 E
Kolyberovo	82	55.16 N	38.44 E
Kolyčevo	82	55.30 N	37.52 E
Kolyma ≏	74	69.30 N	161.00 E
Kolymskaja	74	68.44 N	158.44 E
Kolymskaja nizmennost' ⩩	74	68.30 N	154.00 E
Kolyšlej	80	52.42 N	44.32 E
Kolyšovo	82	54.54 N	36.57 E
Kolyvan', S.S.S.R.	86	51.18 N	82.34 E
Kolyvan', S.S.S.R.	86	55.18 N	82.45 E
Kom → Qom	128	34.39 N	50.54 E
Kom ∧	38	43.10 N	23.03 E
Kom ≏	152	2.18 N	11.40 E
Koma, Ityo.	144	8.27 N	36.52 E
Koma, Mya.	110	15.39 N	98.12 E
Koma, S.S.S.R.	86	55.02 N	91.19 E
Koma ≏	94	35.59 N	139.26 E
Komadougou Yobé (Komadugu Yobe) ≏	146	13.43 N	13.20 E
Komadugu Gana ≏	146	13.05 N	12.24 E
Komadugu Yobe (Komadougou Yobé) ≏	146	13.43 N	13.20 E
Komae	94	35.38 N	139.35 E
Komagane	94	35.43 N	137.55 E
Komaga-take ∧, Nihon	92a	42.04 N	140.41 E
Komaga-take ∧, Nihon	94	35.45 N	138.14 E
Komaga-take ∧, Nihon	94	35.47 N	137.48 E
Komagome ◆[8]	268	35.44 N	139.45 E
Komaki	94	35.17 N	136.55 E
Komandorskije ostrova II	74	55.00 N	167.00 E
Komandorski Village	226	37.43 N	121.54 W
Komariči	76	52.27 N	34.47 E
Komarin	78	51.26 N	30.31 E
Komarniki	78	49.00 N	23.04 E
Komárno, Česko.	30	47.45 N	18.09 E
Komarno, S.S.S.R.	78	49.38 N	23.42 E
Komárom	30	47.44 N	18.08 E
Komárom □[6]	30	47.40 N	18.15 E
Komarovka	78	51.14 N	32.07 E
Komarovo	76	58.39 N	33.26 E
Komarovy	86	60.26 N	75.50 E
Komati (Incomáti) ≏	156	25.46 S	32.43 E
Komatipoort	156	25.25 S	31.55 E
Komatsu, Nihon	94	36.24 N	136.27 E
Komatsu, Nihon	96	33.53 N	133.07 E
Komatsu-kūkō ⊠	94	36.24 N	136.26 E
Komatsushima	96	34.00 N	134.35 E
Kombissiri	150	12.04 N	1.20 W
Kombone	152	4.37 N	9.19 E
Komdhārā	272b	22.53 N	88.14 E
Kome Island I	154	0.06 S	32.45 E
Komen	64	45.49 N	13.44 E
Komenda	150	5.03 N	1.29 W
Komenoi	268	35.55 N	140.01 E
Komering ≏	112	2.59 S	104.50 E
Komeshia	154	8.01 S	27.07 E
Komfane	164	5.39 S	134.44 E
Komga	158	32.35 S	27.55 E
Kominato → Amatsu-kominato	94	35.07 N	140.10 E
Kominternovskoje	78	46.49 N	30.56 E
Komin Yanga	150	11.42 N	0.08 E
Komi-Perm'ackij Nacional'nyj Okrug □[8]	24	60.00 N	54.30 E
Komissarovka, S.S.S.R.	83	48.23 N	38.32 E
Komissarovka, S.S.S.R.	83	48.07 N	40.09 E
Komissarovo	89	44.59 N	131.46 E
Komissarovskij	80	47.29 N	42.59 E
Komkans	158	31.16 S	18.09 E
Komló	30	46.12 N	18.16 E
Kommadagga	158	33.09 S	25.55 E
Kommandodrif	158	27.30 S	26.14 E
Kommandokraal	158	33.06 S	22.51 E
Kommetjie	158	34.08 S	18.21 E
Kommunal'naja	88	52.03 N	115.06 E
Kommunar, S.S.S.R.	80	58.10 N	43.33 E
Kommunar, S.S.S.R.	86	54.20 N	89.18 E
Kommunarka	265b	55.34 N	37.29 E
Kommunarsk	83	48.30 N	38.47 E
Kommunary	26	60.54 N	29.47 E
Kommunizma, pik ∧	85	38.57 N	72.01 E
Komo ≏	152	0.09 N	9.50 E
Komodo	115b	8.35 S	119.30 E
Komodo, Pulau I	115b	8.36 S	119.30 E
Komoé ≏	150	5.12 N	3.44 W
Komoé, Parc National de la ♠	150	9.00 N	3.30 W
Komoka	214	42.57 N	81.26 W
Komono, Congo	152	3.15 S	13.14 E
Komono, Nihon	94	35.00 N	136.31 E
Komoran, Pulau I	164	8.18 S	138.45 E
Komoren → Comoros □[1]	157a	12.10 S	44.10 E
Komorin, Kap → Comorin, Cape >	122	8.04 N	77.34 E
Komorn → Komárno	30	47.45 N	18.09 E
Komoro	94	36.19 N	138.26 E
Komotau → Chomutov	54	50.28 N	13.26 E
Komotiní	38	41.08 N	25.25 E
Kompanejevka	78	48.15 N	32.12 E
Kompasberg ∧	158	31.45 S	24.32 E
Kompiam	164	5.20 S	143.55 E
Kompot	112	0.24 N	124.10 E
Komrat	78	46.18 N	28.38 E
Komsomolabad	85	38.52 N	69.57 E
Komsomolec	86	53.45 N	62.02 E
Komsomolec, ostrov I	74	80.30 N	95.00 E
Komsomolec, zaliv ⊂	72	45.30 N	52.45 E
Komsomol'sk, S.S.S.R.	80	57.02 N	40.21 E
Komsomol'sk, S.S.S.R.	86	55.38 N	88.11 E
Komsomol'sk, S.S.S.R.	86	57.27 N	86.02 E
Komsomol'sk, S.S.S.R.	128	39.02 N	63.36 E
Komsomol'skij, S.S.S.R.	80	54.27 N	45.49 E
Komsomol'skij, S.S.S.R.	83	47.40 N	37.26 E
Komsomol'skij, S.S.S.R.	86	51.40 N	66.39 E
Komsomol'skij, S.S.S.R.	86	47.20 N	53.42 E
Komsomol'skij, S.S.S.R.	89	50.22 N	142.10 E
Komsomol'sk-na-Amure	89	50.35 N	137.02 E
Komsomol'sk-na-Ust'urte	86	44.03 N	58.20 E
Komsomol'skoje, S.S.S.R.	78	49.35 N	36.30 E
Komsomol'skoje, S.S.S.R.	78	49.43 N	28.40 E
Komsomol'skoje, S.S.S.R.	80	55.16 N	47.33 E
Komsomol'skoje, S.S.S.R.	80	50.46 N	47.03 E
Komsomol'skoje, S.S.S.R.	83	47.40 N	38.05 E
Komsomol'skoje, S.S.S.R.	88	52.29 N	111.06 E
Komsomol'skoj Pravdy, ostrova II	74	77.20 N	107.40 E
Kŏmun-do I	98	34.02 N	127.19 E
Kömürcüpınar ◆[8]	267b	41.15 N	28.51 E
Komusan	98	42.08 N	129.41 E
Komyšn'a	78	50.12 N	33.41 E
Kona, India	272b	22.37 N	88.18 E
Kona, Mali	150	14.57 N	3.53 W
Kona Coast ⊥[2]	229d	19.25 N	155.55 W
Konagkend	84	41.04 N	48.37 E
Konakovo	82	56.42 N	36.46 E
Konakpınar, Tür.	130	38.53 N	37.22 E
Konakpınar, Tür.	130	39.26 N	27.53 E
Konan → Hŭngnam, C.M.I.K.	98	39.50 N	127.38 E
Konan, C. Iv.	150	8.21 N	8.00 W
Kōnan, Nihon	94	35.20 N	136.53 E
Kōnan, Nihon	94	34.56 N	136.11 E
Kōnan ◆[8]	268	35.22 N	139.35 E
Konar (Kunar) ≏	123	34.25 N	70.32 E
Konārak	120	19.54 N	86.07 E
Konār Dam ◆[6]	124	23.58 N	85.45 E
Konarhā □[4]	120	35.15 N	71.00 E
Konawa	196	34.57 N	96.45 W
Končanskoje-Suvorovskoje	76	58.39 N	34.04 E
Konceba	78	48.07 N	29.56 E
Konch	124	25.59 N	79.09 E
Konda	74	61.20 N	63.58 E
Konda ≏, S.S.S.R.	86	60.40 N	69.46 E
Konda ≏, S.S.S.R.	88	53.30 N	113.32 E
Kondagaon	122	19.36 N	81.40 E
Konde	154	4.57 S	39.45 E
Kondega	76	60.14 N	33.30 E
Kondiaronk, Lac ⊜	190	46.56 N	76.45 W
Kondinin	162	32.30 S	118.16 E
Kondinskoje	86	59.40 N	67.22 E
Kondli ◆[8]	272a	28.37 N	77.19 E
Kondoa	154	4.54 S	35.47 E
Kondol'	80	52.49 N	45.03 E
Kondolole	154	1.20 N	25.58 E
Kondopoga	24	62.12 N	34.17 E
Kondorfa	61	46.54 N	16.24 E
Kondratjevo, S.S.S.R.	76	60.38 N	28.08 E
Kondratjevo, S.S.S.R.	88	57.21 N	98.11 E
Kondrovka	80	54.36 N	43.17 E
Kondrovo	82	54.48 N	35.56 E
Konduga	146	11.39 N	13.24 E
Kondukūr	122	15.13 N	79.55 E
Kondurča ≏	80	53.31 N	50.24 E
Kondūz	120	37.45 N	68.51 E
Kondūz □[4]	120	36.45 N	68.30 E
Koné	175f	21.04 S	164.52 E
Koné, Passe de ʉ	175f	21.08 S	164.41 E
Konecbor	24	64.52 N	57.44 E
Konergino	180	65.54 N	178.50 W
Konfara	150	11.55 N	8.50 W
Kong, C. Iv.	150	9.09 N	4.37 W
Køng, Dan.	41	55.07 N	11.50 E
Kông ≏	110	13.32 N	105.58 E
Kông, Kaôh I	110	11.20 N	103.00 E
Kongakut ≏	180	69.48 N	141.50 W
Kongbo	152	4.44 N	21.23 E
Kongcheng	100	31.02 N	117.05 E
Kongeå ≏	41	55.23 N	8.40 E
Kongens Lyngby	41	55.46 N	12.31 E
Kongfang	100	27.58 N	116.53 E
Kongiganak	180	59.58 N	162.45 W
Konginkangas	26	62.46 N	25.48 E
Kongjiamatou	105	39.07 N	116.10 E
Kongjiatun	104	40.42 N	124.04 E
Kongjiawopeng	89	43.58 N	122.41 E
Kongjiazhuang	105	40.47 N	114.48 E
Kongju	98	36.27 N	127.07 E
Konglong	100	29.56 N	115.54 E
Konglongshan	105	40.33 N	117.17 E
Konglu	102	27.16 N	97.56 E
Kongmoon → Jiangmen	100	22.35 N	113.05 E
Kongo → Congo ≏	138	6.04 S	12.24 E
Kongo, Republik → Zaire □[1]	138	4.00 S	25.00 E
Kongō-Ikoma-kokutei-kōen ♠	96	34.28 N	135.40 E
Kongolo, Zaïre	154	5.23 S	27.00 E
Kongolo, Zaïre	154	5.26 S	24.49 E
Kongor	140	7.10 N	31.21 E
Kongō-sanchi ⋏	270	34.27 N	135.41 E
Kongoussi	150	13.19 N	1.32 W
Kongō-zan ∧	96	34.25 N	135.41 E
Kongsberg	26	59.39 N	9.39 E
Kongsvinger	26	60.12 N	12.00 E
Kongsvoll	26	62.18 N	9.37 E
Kongtan	107	29.10 N	104.42 E
Kongur Shan ∧	85	38.37 N	75.20 E
Kongwa	154	6.12 S	36.25 E
Kongyangcun	106	31.23 N	118.54 E
Kongzhen	106	31.29 N	119.00 E
Koni	154	10.42 S	27.15 E
Koni ≏	150	13.05 N	5.37 W
Koniakari	150	14.34 N	10.54 W
Konice	30	49.35 N	16.53 E
Koniecpol	30	50.48 N	19.41 E
Königgrätz → Hradec Králové	30	50.12 N	15.50 E
Königheim	56	49.37 N	9.35 E
Königin Alexandra-Kette → Queen Alexandra Range ⋏	9	84.00 S	168.00 E
Königin Fabiola-Gebirge → Queen Fabiola Mountains ⋏	9	71.30 S	35.40 E
Königin Mary-Küste → Queen Mary Coast ⊥[2]	9	67.00 S	96.00 E
Königin Maud-Land → Queen Maud Land ◆[1]	9	72.30 S	12.00 E
König-Otto-Höhle ⊥[5]	60	49.15 N	11.42 E
Königsbach	56	48.58 N	8.36 E
Königsberg, B.R.D.	56	50.05 N	10.34 E
Königsberg → Chojna, Pol.	30	52.58 N	14.28 E
Königsberg → Kaliningrad, S.S.S.R.	76	54.43 N	20.30 E
Königsborn	263	51.33 N	7.41 E
Königsbrück	54	51.16 N	13.54 E
Königsbrunn, B.R.D.	58	48.16 N	10.53 E
Königsbrunn, Öst.	264b	48.21 N	16.25 E
Königsdorf	64	47.49 N	11.28 E
Königsee	54	50.39 N	11.05 E
Königsfelden ☗[1]	58	47.29 N	8.14 E
Königsfeld im Schwarzwald	58	48.08 N	8.25 E
Königshain	54	51.11 N	14.52 E
Königshardt ◆[8]	263	51.33 N	6.51 E
Königsheim	58	48.06 N	8.51 E
Königslutter	54	52.15 N	10.49 E
Königsmoor ◆[3]	52	53.15 N	9.40 E
Königssee	64	47.33 N	12.58 E
Königssee ⊜	64	47.36 N	12.59 E
Königsstuhl ⊥[4]	54	54.34 N	13.40 E
Königstein, B.R.D.	56	50.11 N	8.29 E
Königstein, B.R.D.	60	49.37 N	11.38 E
Königstein, D.D.R.	54	50.55 N	14.04 E
Königstetten	264b	48.18 N	16.09 E
Königswalde	54	50.33 N	13.02 E
Königswartha	54	51.18 N	14.20 E
Königswiesen	61	48.24 N	14.50 E
Königswinter	56	50.40 N	7.11 E
Königs Wusterhausen	54	52.18 N	13.37 E
Konin	30	52.13 N	18.16 E
Konin □[4]	30	52.20 N	18.20 E
Konispol	38	39.39 N	20.10 E
Kónitsa	38	40.02 N	20.45 E
Köniz	58	46.56 N	7.25 E
Konjic	38	43.39 N	17.57 E
Konka ≏	78	47.40 N	35.22 E
Könkämäälven ≏	24	68.29 N	22.17 E
Konkapot ≏	210	42.03 N	73.20 W
Konkiep ≏	156	28.03 S	17.21 E
Konkō	96	34.32 N	133.37 E
Kon'-Kolodez'	76	52.08 N	39.11 E
Konkouré ≏	150	9.58 N	13.42 W
Kon'kovo	83	47.20 N	38.10 E
Konkudera	88	57.33 N	112.30 E
Konkug University ☗[2]	271b	37.32 N	127.05 E
Konnagar	126	22.42 N	88.22 E
Könnern	54	51.40 N	11.46 E
Konnevesi ⊜	26	62.40 N	26.35 E
Konnur	122	16.12 N	74.45 E
Kōno	94	35.49 N	136.04 E
Konobejevo	82	55.24 N	38.40 E
Konohana ◆[8]	270	34.41 N	135.26 E
Kōnoike	270	34.42 N	135.37 E
Konolfingen	58	46.53 N	7.38 E
Konongo	150	6.37 N	1.11 W
Konoša	24	60.58 N	40.15 E
Kōno-shima I	96	34.28 N	133.31 E
Kōnosu	94	36.03 N	139.31 E
Konotop	78	51.14 N	33.12 E
Konovalovka	80	53.06 N	51.34 E
Kon'ovo, S.S.S.R.	24	62.08 N	39.16 E
Kon'ovo, S.S.S.R.	86	56.18 N	70.43 E
Konqi ≏	90	40.40 N	90.10 E
Konradshöhe ◆[8]	264a	52.35 N	13.14 E
Konradsreuth	54	50.16 N	11.50 E
Konsankoro	150	9.02 N	9.00 W
Konsen-daichi ⋏[1]	92a	43.25 N	144.52 E
Końskie	30	51.12 N	20.26 E
Konstabel	158	33.16 S	20.17 E
Konstadt → Wołczyn	30	51.01 N	18.03 E
Konstantinopel → İstanbul	130	41.01 N	28.58 E
Konstantinovka, S.S.S.R.	78	49.57 N	35.07 E
Konstantinovka, S.S.S.R.	78	47.51 N	31.09 E
Konstantinovka, S.S.S.R.	80	56.41 N	50.53 E
Konstantinovka, S.S.S.R.	83	48.32 N	37.43 E
Konstantinovka, S.S.S.R.	83	47.52 N	37.24 E
Konstantinovka, S.S.S.R.	265a	59.47 N	30.08 E
Konstantinovo	82	56.33 N	38.02 E
Konstantinovsk	80	47.35 N	41.06 E
Konstantinovskij	76	57.50 N	39.36 E
Konstantinovskije Porogi	76	60.34 N	37.04 E
Konstantynów Łódzki	30	51.45 N	19.20 E
Konstanz	58	47.40 N	9.10 E
Kontagora	150	10.24 N	5.28 E
Kontcha	152	7.58 N	12.14 E
Kontejevo	80	58.26 N	41.21 E
Kontha	110	19.30 N	96.03 E
Kontich	50	51.08 N	4.27 E
Kontiolahti	26	62.46 N	29.51 E
Kontiomäki	26	64.21 N	28.09 E
Kon Tum	110	14.21 N	108.00 E
Kontum, Plateau du ⋏[1]	110	13.55 N	108.05 E
Kōnu	96	34.42 N	133.05 E
Kon'uchovo	86	55.08 N	70.38 E
Konus, gora ∧	180	67.34 N	178.10 E
Konya	130	37.52 N	32.31 E
Konya □[4]	130	38.00 N	33.00 E
Konyr	80	50.25 N	53.25 E
Konyrat	80	49.36 N	47.01 E
Konyrolen	86	44.16 N	79.19 E
Konyševka	78	51.51 N	35.18 E
Konystanu	80	48.51 N	53.20 E
Konz	56	49.42 N	6.34 E
Konza	154	1.45 S	37.07 E
Konžakovskij Kamen', gora ∧	86	59.38 N	59.08 E
Konzell	60	49.04 N	12.43 E
Koocanusa, Lake ⊜[1]	202	49.00 N	115.10 W
Koog [aan de Zaan]	52	52.27 N	4.49 E
Kookynie	162	29.20 S	121.29 E
Koolamarra	166	20.12 S	140.14 E
Koolatah	164	15.53 S	142.27 E
Koolau Range ⋏	229c	21.35 N	158.00 W
Kooloonong	166	34.53 S	143.09 E
Koolskamp	50	51.00 N	3.12 E
Koolyanobbing	162	30.50 S	119.35 E
Koolywurtie	168b	34.38 S	137.37 E
Koombana Bay ⊂	168a	33.18 S	115.36 E
Koonap ≏	158	33.03 S	26.39 E
Koondrook	166	35.39 S	144.08 E
Koonga	76	58.35 N	24.12 E
Koonibba	162	31.58 S	133.27 E
Koontz Lake	216	41.25 N	86.29 W
Koontz Lake ⊜	216	41.25 N	86.28 W
Koopan-Noord	158	26.53 S	20.41 E
Koopan-Suid	158	27.15 S	20.22 E
Koopmansfontein	158	28.14 S	24.01 E
Koorawatha	166	34.02 S	148.33 E
Koorda	162	30.50 S	117.29 E
Koosa	76	58.33 N	27.07 E
Koosfontein	158	27.22 S	25.27 E
Koosharem	200	38.30 N	111.52 W
Kooskia	202	46.08 N	115.58 W
Koossa	150	9.32 N	8.32 W
Kootenai (Kootenay) ≏	182	49.15 N	117.39 W
Kootenay (Kootenai) ≏	182	49.15 N	117.39 W
Kootenay Indian Reserve ◆[4]	182	49.37 N	115.45 W
Kootenay Lake ⊜	182	49.35 N	116.50 W
Kootenay National Park ♠	182	51.00 N	116.00 W
Kootjieskolk	158	31.15 S	20.21 E
Kootwijk	52	52.12 N	5.45 E
Koo-wee-rup	169	38.12 S	145.30 E
Kopa	85	43.32 N	75.50 E
Kopa ≏	85	43.40 N	76.15 E
Kopāganj	124	26.01 N	83.34 E
Kopāi ≏	126	23.48 N	87.47 E
Kopajgorod	78	48.51 N	27.48 E
Kopanbulak	86	48.56 N	80.52 E
Kopang	115b	8.39 S	116.21 E
Kopanovka	80	47.27 N	46.48 E
Kopanskaja	78	46.17 N	38.29 E
Kopapan	80	50.20 N	50.26 E
Kopargaon	122	19.53 N	74.29 E
Koparkhairna	272c	19.06 N	72.59 E
Koparpāda	272c	19.02 N	73.04 E
Kópasker	24a	66.20 N	16.24 W
Kopatkeviči	76	52.19 N	28.49 E
Kópavogur	24a	64.06 N	21.50 W
Kopcevičí	78	52.14 N	28.19 E
Kopé, Mont ∧[2]	150	4.59 N	7.27 W
Kopejsk	86	55.07 N	61.37 E
Kopenhagen → København	41	55.40 N	12.35 E
Köpenick ◆[8]	54	52.27 N	13.34 E
Köpenick, Schloss ☗	264a	52.27 N	13.34 E
Koper	36	45.33 N	13.44 E
Köpernitz	54	53.04 N	12.56 E
Kopervik	26	59.17 N	5.18 E
Kopetdag, chrebet ⋏	128	37.50 N	58.00 E
Kopeysk → Kopejsk	86	55.07 N	61.37 E
Kop Geçidi)(	130	40.03 N	40.33 E
Kopice	54	53.44 N	14.32 E
Köping	40	59.31 N	16.00 E
Kopisty	54	50.34 N	13.35 E
Kopjevo	86	55.03 N	89.50 E
Koplik	38	42.13 N	19.26 E
Köpmanholmen	26	63.10 N	18.34 E
Kopnino	82	56.53 N	38.29 E
Kopondei, Tanjung >	115b	8.04 S	122.52 E
Koporje	76	59.44 N	29.01 E
Koporskaja guba ⊂	76	59.52 N	28.55 E
Koppal	122	15.21 N	76.09 E
Koppang	26	61.34 N	11.04 E
Koppány ≏	30	46.35 N	18.26 E
Kopparberg	40	59.52 N	14.59 E
Kopparbergs Län □[6]	26	61.00 N	14.30 E
Koppel	214	40.50 N	80.19 W
Kopperå	26	63.24 N	11.51 E
Kopperby	41	54.38 N	9.56 E
Kopperl	222	32.04 N	97.30 W
Koppi	89	48.32 N	140.07 E
Koppi ≏	89	48.33 N	140.08 E
Koppies	158	27.20 S	27.30 E
Koppom	26	59.43 N	12.09 E
Kopri	272c	19.11 N	72.58 E
Koprivnica	36	46.10 N	16.50 E
Köprü ≏	130	36.50 N	31.10 E
Köprülü Kanyon Milli Parkı ♠	130	37.20 N	31.18 E
Köprüören	130	39.30 N	29.47 E
Kopt'ovo	80	56.43 N	40.31 E
Kopyčincy	78	49.06 N	25.55 E
Kopyl'	76	53.09 N	27.05 E
Kopylovka	86	58.40 N	82.22 E
Kopylovo, S.S.S.R.	24	60.35 N	45.02 E
Kopylovo, S.S.S.R.	82	56.26 N	36.25 E
Kopys'	76	54.19 N	30.18 E
Kor ≏	128	29.36 N	53.18 E
Kōra	94	35.12 N	136.15 E
Koraa Shiir	144	3.18 N	46.16 E
Korab ⋏	38	41.47 N	20.34 E
Kor Aban	144	3.58 N	42.44 E
Korablino	80	53.55 N	40.01 E
Korahe	144	6.35 N	44.23 E
Kor'akovka	86	52.24 N	77.08 E
Kor'akskaja Sopka, vulkan ∧[1]	74	53.20 N	158.43 E
Kor'akskoje nagorje ⋏	74	62.30 N	172.00 E
Kōrakuen ♠	96	34.38 N	133.53 E
Korakuen Stadium ♠	268	35.43 N	139.45 E
Korallenmeer → Coral Sea ⍑[2]	14	20.00 S	158.00 E
Koralpe ⋏	61	46.50 N	14.58 E
Korannaberg ⋏	158	27.25 S	22.32 E
Korapun	164	5.25 S	152.00 E
Korāput	122	18.49 N	82.43 E
Korarou, Lac ⊜	150	15.15 N	3.16 W
Korat → Nakhon Ratchasima	110	14.58 N	102.07 E
Koratla	122	18.49 N	78.43 E
Kor'ažma	24	61.18 N	47.06 E
Korba, India	124	22.21 N	82.41 E
Korba, Tun.	36	36.35 N	10.52 E
Korbach	56	51.16 N	8.52 E
Korbeta	144	13.03 N	39.43 E
Korbol	146	10.01 N	17.43 E
Korbous	36	36.49 N	10.35 E
Korbu, Gunong ∧	114	4.43 N	101.17 E
Korçë	38	40.37 N	20.46 E
Korcovo	76	58.52 N	42.13 E
Korčula	36	42.58 N	17.08 E
Korčula, Otok I	36	42.57 N	16.50 E
Korčulanski Kanal ʉ	36	43.03 N	16.40 E
Kordestān □[4]	128	35.30 N	47.00 E
Kord Kūy	128	36.48 N	54.07 E
Kordovo	86	54.06 N	93.17 E
Korea, North □[1], Asia	90	40.00 N	127.00 E
Korea, North □[1], Asia	98	40.00 N	127.00 E
Korea, South □[1], Asia	90	36.30 N	128.00 E
Korea, South □[1], Asia	98	36.30 N	128.00 E
Korea Bay ⊂	98	39.00 N	124.00 E
Korea Strait ʉ	90	34.00 N	129.00 E
Korea University ☗[2]	271b	37.36 N	127.02 E
Korec	78	50.37 N	27.09 E
Korekozevo	82	54.20 N	36.11 E
Korelakša	24	65.33 N	32.22 E
Koreliči	76	53.34 N	26.08 E
Korem	144	12.30 N	39.30 E
Koré Mayroua	150	13.18 N	3.55 E
Koren (Die Wurzen))(	64	46.31 N	13.45 E
Korenkovo	78	45.07 N	36.24 E
Koren'ovo, S.S.S.R.	78	51.25 N	34.55 E
Koren'ovo, S.S.S.R.	265b	55.40 N	38.00 E
Korenovsk	78	45.29 N	39.28 E
Korf	74	60.19 N	165.50 E
Korfovskij	89	48.13 N	135.03 E
Korga	158	30.12 S	20.28 E
Korgan	130	40.44 N	37.13 E
Korgašino	82	54.45 N	37.41 E
Kõrgessaare	76	58.59 N	22.28 E
Korgonskij chrebet ⋏	86	50.45 N	84.30 E
Korgus	140	19.13 N	33.29 E
Korhogo	150	9.27 N	5.38 W
Kōri	270	34.47 N	135.39 E
Koridhallós	267c	37.59 N	23.39 E
Korido	164	0.50 S	135.35 E
Koriella	169	37.10 S	145.39 E
Korienzé	150	15.24 N	3.47 W

≏	River	Fluß	Río	Rivière	Rio
≚	Canal	Kanal	Canal	Canal	Canal
˪	Waterfall, Rapids	Wasserfall, Stromschnellen	Cascada, Rápidos	Chute d'eau, Rapides	Cascata, Rápidos
ʉ	Strait	Meeresstraße	Estrecho	Détroit	Estreito
⊂	Bay, Gulf	Bucht, Golf	Bahía, Golfo	Baie, Golfe	Baía, Golfo
⊜	Lake, Lakes	See, Seen	Lago, Lagos	Lac, Lacs	Lago, Lagos
⩩	Swamp	Sumpf	Pantano	Marais	Pântano
⊓	Ice Features, Glacier	Eis- und Gletscherformen	Accidentes Glaciales	Formes glaciaires	Acidentes glaciares
⍑	Other Hydrographic Features	Andere Hydrographische Objekte	Otros Elementos Hidrográficos	Autres données hydrographiques	Outros acidentes hidrográficos
✦	Submarine Features	Untermeerische Objekte	Accidentes Submarinos	Formes de relief sous-marin	Acidentes submarinos
□	Political Unit	Politische Einheit	Unidad Politica	Entité politique	Unidade política
☗	Cultural Institution	Kulturelle Institution	Institución Cultural	Institution culturelle	Instituição cultural
⊥	Historical Site	Historische Stätte	Sitio Histórico	Site historique	Sitio histórico
♠	Recreational Site	Erholungs- und Ferienort	Sitio de Recreo	Centre de loisirs	Area de Lazer
⊠	Airport	Flughafen	Aeropuerto	Aéroport	Aeroporto
■	Military Installation	Militäranlage	Instalación Militar	Installation militaire	Instalação militar
◆	Miscellaneous	Verschiedenes	Misceláneo	Divers	Diversos

ENGLISH — Name / Page / Lat.°′ / Long.°′

DEUTSCH — Name / Seite / Breite°′ / Länge°′ E = Ost

Name	Page	Lat.°′	Long.°′
Korim	164	0.54 S	136.02 E
Korima, Oued el V	148	33.51 N	0.23 W
Koringberg	158	33.01 S	18.40 E
Koringplaas	158	32.48 S	20.58 E
Korinth	41	55.08 N	10.21 E
Korinthiakós Kólpos ⊂	38	38.19 N	22.04 E
Kórinthos (Corinth)	38	37.56 N	22.56 E
Korínthou, Dhiórix ≍	38	37.57 N	22.56 E
Kőris-hegy ʌ	30	47.18 N	17.45 E
Koritsa → Korçë	38	40.37 N	20.46 E
Köritz	54	52.51 N	12.27 E
Kōriyama	92	37.24 N	140.23 E
Kōriyama → Yamato-kōriyama	96	34.38 N	135.47 E
Korizo, Passe de)(	146	22.28 N	15.27 E
Korkino, S.S.S.R.	86	54.54 N	61.23 E
Korkino, S.S.S.R.	88	54.23 N	105.14 E
Korkinskoje, ozero ⊜	265a	59.55 N	30.44 E
Korkuteli	130	37.04 N	30.13 E
Korla	90	41.44 N	86.09 E
Korl'aki	80	57.06 N	46.57 E
Korliki	74	61.31 N	82.22 E
Körlin → Karlino	30	54.03 N	15.51 E
Korma, S.S.S.R.	76	53.08 N	30.48 E
Korma, S.S.S.R.	76	52.21 N	31.31 E
Körmend	61	47.01 N	16.37 E
Kormilovka	86	55.00 N	74.06 E
Kormovoje	80	46.17 N	43.30 E
Kornat, Otok I	36	43.50 N	15.16 E
Körnebach ≃	263	51.35 N	7.38 E
Kornejevka, S.S.S.R.	80	51.45 N	48.46 E
Kornejevka, S.S.S.R.	86	54.01 N	68.27 E
Kornejevka, S.S.S.R.	86	50.12 N	74.19 E
Kornelimünster	56	50.43 N	6.11 E
Körner, D.D.R.	54	51.13 N	10.35 E
Korner, Mt., U.S.	182	48.59 N	112.15 W
Kornešty	78	47.22 N	27.59 E
Korneuburg	264b	48.21 N	16.20 E
Kórnik	30	52.17 N	17.04 E
Kornilovo	86	53.32 N	81.05 E
Kornin	78	50.06 N	29.32 E
Kornouchovo	80	55.33 N	49.53 E
Korn'ovo	265a	60.03 N	30.45 E
Kornsjø	26	58.57 N	11.39 E
Kornwestheim	56	48.52 N	9.11 E
Koro, C. Iv.	150	8.34 N	7.28 W
Koro, Mali	150	14.04 N	3.05 W
Koro I	175g	17.19 S	179.23 E
Koroba	164	5.40 S	142.45 E
Koroča	78	50.48 N	37.11 E
Korodougou Markala	150	12.26 N	6.17 W
Köroğlu Tepesi ʌ	130	40.31 N	31.53 E
Korogwe	154	5.09 S	38.29 E
Koroit	166	38.17 S	142.22 E
Korolenko, gora ʌ	88	58.15 N	115.01 E
Korolevskij Belok, gora ʌ	86	51.00 N	83.43 E
Korol'ovo	78	48.09 N	23.08 E
Korol'ovščina	76	55.49 N	31.45 E
Korom, Bahr ≃	146	10.35 N	19.45 E
Koromba ʌ	175g	17.53 S	177.34 E
Koromiri I	174k	21.15 S	159.43 W
Koromo → Toyota	94	35.05 N	137.09 E
Koronadal	116	6.30 N	124.51 E
Koróni	38	36.48 N	21.56 E
Korónia, Límni ⊜	38	40.41 N	23.05 E
Koronowo	30	53.19 N	17.57 E
Korop	78	51.34 N	32.56 E
Koropélé	152	4.44 N	17.11 E
Koropíon	38	37.54 N	23.53 E
Koror	175b	7.20 N	134.29 E
Koror I	175b	7.20 N	134.30 E
Kororoit Creek ≃	274b	37.52 S	144.52 E
Körös ≃	30	46.43 N	20.12 E
Koro Sea ⊤ [2]	175g	18.00 S	179.50 E
Korosten'	78	50.57 N	28.39 E
Korostyšev	78	50.19 N	29.03 E
Korotkova	88	56.43 N	107.55 E
Korotojak	78	50.59 N	39.10 E
Koro Toro	146	16.05 N	18.30 E
Korotovo	76	58.57 N	37.28 E
Korotyš	76	52.22 N	37.27 E
Korovincy	78	50.48 N	33.45 E
Korovin Island I	180	55.25 N	160.15 W
Korovino, S.S.S.R.	78	51.25 N	36.45 E
Korovino, S.S.S.R.	80	53.49 N	53.03 E
Korovin Volcano ʌ [1]	180	52.22 N	174.10 W
Korovou	175g	17.57 S	178.21 E
Koroyanitu ʌ	175g	17.40 S	177.35 E
Korožečna ≃	76	57.32 N	38.18 E
Korpilahti	26	62.01 N	25.33 E
Korpo (Korppoo)	26	60.10 N	21.34 E
Korså	40	60.38 N	16.08 E
Korsakov	89	46.38 N	142.46 E
Korsakovo	76	53.16 N	37.21 E
Korschen → Korsze	30	54.10 N	21.09 E
Korschenbroich	56	51.11 N	6.31 E
Korselbränna	26	64.27 N	15.35 E
Korševo	78	51.11 N	40.07 E
Korsika → Corse I	36	42.00 N	9.00 E
Korsnäs, Suomi	26	62.47 N	21.12 E
Korsnäs, Sve.	40	60.35 N	15.43 E
Korsør	41	55.20 N	11.09 E
Korsør Nor ⊂	41	55.20 N	11.11 E
Korsun'	83	48.12 N	38.05 E
Koršunovo	88	58.37 N	110.10 E
Korsun'-Ševčenkovskij	78	49.26 N	31.16 E
Korsze	30	54.10 N	21.09 E
Kortgene	52	51.34 N	3.48 E
Kortilisy	78	51.51 N	24.25 E
Kortkeros	24	61.49 N	51.28 E
Kortrijk (Courtrai)	50	50.50 N	3.16 E
Kortuz, gora ʌ	86	54.33 N	91.56 E
Koruçam Burnu >	130	35.24 N	32.56 E
Korucu	130	39.28 N	27.22 E
Kor'ukovka	78	51.46 N	32.14 E
Korumburra	169	38.26 S	145.49 E
Korwai	124	24.08 N	78.03 E
Kōryō	96	34.33 N	135.45 E
Koryŏng	98	35.44 N	128.15 E
Koryst'	78	50.35 N	27.01 E
Koryta	60	49.24 N	13.13 E
Korženevskoj, pik ʌ	85	39.04 N	72.00 E
Koržeuc'	78	48.13 N	27.02 E
Korževka	80	54.12 N	46.22 E
Kos	38	36.53 N	27.18 E
Kos I	38	36.50 N	27.10 E
Kosa, Ityo.	144	7.51 N	36.51 E
Kosa, S.S.S.R.	24	59.56 N	54.55 E
Kosa, S.S.S.R.	88	54.47 N	108.52 E
Kosa ≃, S.S.S.R.	24	60.11 N	55.10 E
Kosa ≃, S.S.S.R.	80	58.26 N	51.15 E
Kosa ⊥	150	15.50 N	7.00 W
Koš-Agač	86	50.00 N	88.40 E
Kosai	94	34.43 N	137.33 E
Kosaja, šivera ∟	88	58.24 N	97.48 E
Kosaja Gora	82	54.07 N	37.33 E
Kosaka	92	40.19 N	140.44 E
Kosan	98	38.52 N	127.24 E
Košankol'	80	49.56 N	48.11 E
Koščagyl	86	46.51 N	53.48 E
Kösching	60	48.49 N	11.30 E
Kościan	30	52.06 N	16.38 E
Kościerzyna	30	54.08 N	18.00 E
Kosciusko	194	33.03 N	89.35 W
Kosciusko □ [6]	216	41.14 N	85.51 W
Kosciusko, Mount ʌ	171b	36.27 S	148.16 E
Kosciusko National Park ♦	166	36.10 S	148.15 E
Kös Dağı ʌ	130	40.59 N	34.25 E
Kosdaulet, peski ◆ [2]	80	47.45 N	49.30 E
Kose, Nihon	270	34.25 N	135.46 E
Kose, S.S.S.R.	76	59.11 N	25.10 E
Köse, Tür.	130	40.13 N	39.39 E
Kösedağı ʌ	130	39.54 N	42.39 E
Kösefakılı	130	39.36 N	34.09 E
Koševelka	82	55.09 N	38.05 E
Koševelicha	80	55.02 N	43.33 E
Koševerovo	82	55.38 N	38.22 E
Koserow	54	54.03 N	13.59 E
Kosha	140	20.49 N	30.32 E
Koshien Stadium ♦	270	34.42 N	135.22 E
Koshigaya	94	35.54 N	139.48 E
Koshigoe	268	35.18 N	139.30 E
Koshikijima-rettō II	92	31.45 N	129.49 E
Koshino	94	36.02 N	136.01 E
Koshk-e Kohneh	128	34.52 N	62.31 E
Koshkonong	194	36.35 N	91.38 W
Koshkonong, Lake ⊜	216	42.52 N	88.58 W
Koshkonong Creek ≃	216	42.53 N	88.59 W
Koshlong Lake ⊜	212	44.58 N	78.29 W
Kōshoku	94	36.32 N	138.06 E
Koshu → Kwangju	98	35.09 N	126.54 E
Kosī □ [8]	124	27.15 N	87.15 E
Kosi ≃	124	25.26 N	87.22 E
Košice	30	48.43 N	21.15 E
Kosigi	122	15.51 N	77.16 E
Kosi Kalan	124	27.48 N	77.26 E
Kosikovo	76	59.52 N	43.23 E
Kosimeer ⊜	158	26.55 S	32.52 E
Kosino, S.S.S.R.	80	58.23 N	51.17 E
Kosino, S.S.S.R.	82	55.43 N	37.52 E
Kosju	24	65.38 N	59.03 E
Kosju ≃	24	66.18 N	59.53 E
Kosjuvom	24	66.17 N	59.50 E
Köşk	130	37.51 N	28.03 E
Koskaecodde Lake ⊜	186	48.00 N	55.20 W
Koškar	80	47.27 N	53.29 E
Koški, S.S.S.R.	80	54.12 N	50.28 E
Koski, Suomi	26	60.39 N	23.09 E
Koškino	80	56.20 N	50.49 E
Koskol'	86	49.31 N	67.05 E
Koskuduk	86	44.06 N	77.22 E
Koskullskulle	24	67.12 N	20.50 E
Koslan	24	63.28 N	48.52 E
Köslin → Koszalin	30	54.12 N	16.09 E
Kosmonosy	54	50.26 N	15.00 E
Kosmynino	80	57.35 N	40.46 E
Kosoba, gora ʌ	86	48.15 N	79.40 E
Kosogor	80	57.07 N	47.34 E
Kosoj, porog ∟, S.S.S.R.	86	57.30 N	95.30 E
Kosoj, porog ∟, S.S.S.R.	88	57.44 N	96.20 E
Kosolapovo	80	56.57 N	49.37 E
Kosŏng, C.M.I.K.	98	38.40 N	128.19 E
Kosŏng, Taehan	98	34.58 N	128.18 E
Kosov	78	48.19 N	25.05 E
Kosovo-Metohija □ [4]	38	42.35 N	21.00 E
Kosový potok ≃	60	49.46 N	12.48 E
Kosrae I	14	5.19 N	162.59 E
Kösreli	130	37.11 N	35.59 E
Kossdorf	54	51.29 N	13.14 E
Kosse	222	31.18 N	96.38 W
Kössen	64	47.40 N	12.24 E
Kossindi	152	3.51 N	16.19 E
Kösslarn	60	48.22 N	13.07 E
Kossol Passage ʮ	175b	7.52 N	134.36 E
Kossol Reef ✣ [2]	175b	7.57 N	134.41 E
Kossou, Lac de ⊜ [1]	150	7.25 N	5.45 W
Kossovo	76	52.45 N	25.09 E
Kossuth	214	41.17 N	79.35 W
Kosta	26	56.51 N	15.23 E
Košťahy	54	50.39 N	13.45 E
Kostajnica	36	45.14 N	16.33 E
Koš-Tegirmen	85	42.47 N	73.53 E
Kostelec nad Labem	54	50.11 N	14.35 E
Kostenec	38	42.16 N	23.49 E
Koster	158	25.57 S	26.42 E
Kosterevo	80	55.56 N	39.37 E
Kosteröarna I	26	58.54 N	11.02 E
Kostešty	78	46.52 N	28.44 E
Kostešty-Stynka, vodochranilišče (Lacul Stînca-Costeşti) ⊜ [1]	38	47.55 N	27.10 E
Koštice	54	50.24 N	13.55 E
Kostino, S.S.S.R.	80	52.11 N	51.20 E
Kostino, S.S.S.R.	80	52.24 N	51.39 E
Kostino, S.S.S.R.	82	56.18 N	37.43 E
Kostino, S.S.S.R.	265b	55.55 N	37.51 E
Kostino-Otdelec	78	51.33 N	41.26 E
Kost'kovo	76	60.02 N	33.14 E
Košt'ob'o	85	41.06 N	74.15 E
Kostomukša	24	64.41 N	30.49 E
Kostonjärvi ⊜	26	65.47 N	28.27 E
Kostopol'	78	50.53 N	26.26 E
Kostriževka	78	48.38 N	25.41 E
Kostroma	76	57.46 N	40.55 E
Kostroma ≃	24	57.47 N	40.55 E
Kostrovo	82	55.53 N	36.42 E
Kostrzyn	30	52.37 N	14.39 E
Kost'ukoviči	76	53.20 N	32.03 E
Kost'ukovka	76	52.32 N	30.56 E
Kosugaya ◆ [8]	268	35.22 N	139.33 E
Kosuge	94	35.45 N	138.57 E
Kosugi	94	36.43 N	137.06 E
Kosum Phisai	110	16.13 N	103.01 E
Koszalin (Köslin)	30	54.12 N	16.09 E
Koszalin □ [4]	30	54.00 N	16.00 E
Kőszeg	61	47.23 N	16.33 E
Koszyce	30	50.11 N	20.35 E
Kota, India	120	25.11 N	75.50 E
Kota, India	124	22.18 N	82.02 E
Kota, Malay.	114	2.31 N	102.10 E
Kota, Malay.	114	5.35 N	100.23 E
Kotaagung	112	5.30 S	104.38 E
Kotabaharu, Indon.	112	0.48 S	111.33 E
Kota Baharu, Malay.	114	6.08 N	102.15 E
Kotabangun	112	0.16 S	116.35 E
Kotabaru, Indon.	112	3.14 S	116.13 E
Kotabaru, Indon.	112	1.08 S	101.43 E
Kotabaru → Jayapura, Indon.	164	2.32 S	140.42 E
Kota Belud	112	6.25 N	116.31 E
Kotabumi	112	4.50 S	104.54 E
Kotabunan	112	0.49 N	124.38 E
Kotadabok	112	0.30 S	104.33 E
Kot Addu	123	30.28 N	70.58 E
Kotagiri	122	11.26 N	76.53 E
Kot'ajevka	80	46.33 N	48.46 E
Kotake	96	33.41 N	130.43 E
Kota Kinabalu (Jesselton)	112	5.59 N	116.04 E
Kota Kota → Nkhotakota	154	12.57 S	34.17 E
Kotālpur	126	23.02 N	87.36 E
Kotamobagu	112	0.46 N	124.19 E
Kotanemel', gora ʌ	86	47.43 N	77.18 E
Kotapinang	114	1.53 N	100.05 E
Kotari ⋏	36	44.05 N	15.30 E
Kotaringin	114	0.53 N	102.03 E
Kota Sarang Semut	114	5.59 N	100.24 E
Kotatengah	114	1.05 N	100.33 E
Kota Tinggi	114	1.44 N	103.54 E
Kotawaringin	112	2.29 S	111.25 E
Kotchāndpur	124	23.24 N	89.01 E
Kotcho Lake ⊜	176	59.05 N	121.10 W
Kot Chutta	123	29.53 N	70.39 E
Kotdwāra	124	29.45 N	78.32 E
Kotel	38	42.53 N	26.27 E
Kotel'nič	80	58.18 N	48.20 E
Kotel'niki	82	55.39 N	37.52 E
Kotel'nikovo	80	47.38 N	43.09 E
Kotel'nyj, ostrov I	74	75.45 N	138.44 E
Kotel'va	78	50.05 N	34.45 E
Kot Fateh	123	30.07 N	75.05 E
Köthen	54	51.45 N	11.58 E
Koti → Kōchi	96	33.33 N	133.33 E
Kotido	154	3.00 N	34.06 E
Kotikovo	89	49.08 N	144.13 E
Kotka	26	60.28 N	26.55 E
Kot Kapūra	123	30.35 N	74.54 E
Kotkino	24	67.02 N	51.03 E
Kotla	123	32.15 N	76.02 E
Kotl'akovo	82	56.17 N	35.49 E
Kotlas	24	61.16 N	46.35 E
Kotli	123	33.31 N	73.55 E
Kotlik	180	63.02 N	163.33 W
Kotlin, ostrov I	76	60.00 N	29.46 E
Kotly	76	59.36 N	28.45 E
Kot Mūmin	123	32.11 N	73.02 E
Kotō	94	35.08 N	136.14 E
Kōtō ◆ [8]	268	35.41 N	139.48 E
Koto ≃, Nihon	96	33.58 N	131.13 E
Kotō ≃, Nihon	96	34.21 N	134.02 E
Kotobiki-san ʌ	96	35.03 N	132.47 E
Kotohira	96	34.11 N	133.49 E
Kotohira-gu ʊ [1]	96	34.11 N	133.49 E
Kotohira-yama ʌ	96	34.11 N	133.48 E
Kotonami	96	34.10 N	133.56 E
Koton-Karifi	150	8.08 N	6.48 E
Kotonkoro	150	11.02 N	5.58 E
Kotor	38	42.25 N	18.46 E
Kotoriba	36	46.21 N	16.49 E
Kotorovo	80	54.54 N	41.35 E
Kotor Varoš	36	44.37 N	17.23 E
Kotouba	150	8.41 N	3.12 W
Kotovka	78	49.08 N	34.57 E
Kotovo	80	50.18 N	44.50 E
Kotovsk, S.S.S.R.	78	47.45 N	29.33 E
Kotovsk, S.S.S.R.	78	46.49 N	28.34 E
Kotovsk, S.S.S.R.	80	52.36 N	41.32 E
Kot Pūtli	124	27.43 N	76.12 E
Kotra, India	120	24.22 N	73.10 E
Kotra, India	272b	22.46 N	88.34 E
Kot Rādha Kishan	123	31.10 N	74.06 E
Kotri	120	25.22 N	68.18 E
Kotri Allāhrakhio	120	24.24 N	67.50 E
Kotrung → Uttarpara-Kotrung	272b	22.40 N	88.21 E
Kötschach	64	46.40 N	13.00 E
Kot Sultān	123	30.46 N	70.56 E
Kōtsu-zan ʌ	96	34.01 N	134.12 E
Kottagūdem	122	17.33 N	80.38 E
Kottas Mountains ⋏	9	74.20 S	12.00 W
Kottayam	122	9.35 N	76.31 E
Kotte → Sri Jayawardenepura	122	6.54 N	79.54 E
Kottingbrunn	61	47.57 N	16.14 E
Kotto ≃	136	4.14 N	22.02 E
Kotton	144	9.35 N	50.28 E
Kottūru	122	14.49 N	76.13 E
Kotuj ≃	74	71.55 N	102.05 E
Kot'užen'	78	47.51 N	28.36 E
Kotwālīpāra	126	22.59 N	89.59 E
Kotzebue	180	66.53 N	162.39 W
Kotzebue Sound ʮ	180	66.20 N	163.00 W
Kotzenau → Chocianów	30	51.25 N	15.55 E
Kötzting	60	49.11 N	12.52 E
Koualé	150	11.24 N	7.01 W
Kou'an	106	32.19 N	119.52 E
Kouandé	150	10.20 N	1.42 E
Kouango	152	4.58 N	19.59 E
Kouassi-Datékro	150	7.49 N	3.31 W
Koubansaki	273b	4.22 S	15.09 E
Koubia	150	11.35 N	11.54 W
Kouchibouguac National Park ♦	186	46.50 N	65.00 W
Koudougou	150	12.15 N	2.22 W
Kouéré	150	10.27 N	3.59 W
Kouffo ≃	150	6.35 N	1.59 E
Kouga	146	9.56 N	21.03 E
Kouga ≃	158	33.37 S	22.14 E
Kougaberge ⋏	158	33.40 S	23.50 E
Kougarok Mountain ʌ	180	65.41 N	165.13 W
K'ouhu	100	23.35 N	120.11 E
Kouilou □ [5]	152	4.30 S	12.00 E
Kouilou ≃	152	4.28 S	11.41 E
Koukdjuak ≃	176	66.45 N	73.09 W
Kouki	152	7.10 N	17.18 E
Koúklia	130	34.42 N	32.34 E
Koukourou ≃	152	7.32 N	19.42 E
Koukourou-Bamingui, Réserve de Faune du ◆ [4]	152	7.20 N	20.00 E
Koula ≃	229b	21.54 N	159.36 W
Koulamoutou	152	1.08 S	12.29 E
Koulikoro	150	12.53 N	7.33 W
Koulikoro □ [4]	150	13.00 N	8.00 W
Koulouguidi	150	13.27 N	11.03 W
Koulountou ≃	150	13.15 N	13.37 W
Koumac	175f	20.33 S	164.17 E
Koumac, Grand Récif de ✣ [2]	175f	20.32 S	164.04 E
Koumala	166	21.37 S	149.15 E
Koumaméyong	152	0.11 N	11.51 E
Koumankou	150	12.06 N	6.08 W
Koumbakara	150	12.42 N	14.29 W
Koumbal	146	9.26 N	22.39 E
Koumbala ≃	146	9.14 N	20.42 E
Koumbia, Burkina	150	11.14 N	3.42 W
Koumbia, Guinée	150	11.48 N	13.30 W
Koumbisaleh ⊥	150	15.46 N	7.59 W
Koumbouma	150	10.24 N	12.56 W
Koumi	94	36.05 N	138.29 E
Koumpentoum	150	13.59 N	14.34 W
Koumra	146	8.55 N	17.33 E
Koundara	150	12.29 N	13.18 W
Koundé	152	6.07 N	14.38 E
Koundian ⊥	150	13.10 N	10.41 W
Koundougou	150	11.44 N	4.31 W
Koun-Fao	150	7.29 N	3.15 W
Koungheul	150	13.59 N	14.48 W
Koungoulou	152	3.32 S	13.20 E
Kouniohou	150	7.40 N	0.48 E
Kounradskij	86	46.59 N	75.00 E
Kountze	194	30.22 N	94.18 W
Koupé, Mont ʌ	152	4.47 N	9.43 E
Koupéla	150	12.11 N	0.21 W
Kouragué	150	12.18 N	10.02 W
Kourak	86	54.50 N	84.40 E
Kouriles, Détroit des → Pervyj Kuril'skij proliv ʮ	74	50.50 N	156.36 E
Kouri-shima I	174m	26.42 N	128.01 E
Kourou	250	5.09 N	52.39 W
Kouroukoto	150	12.35 N	10.05 W
Kourouma	150	11.37 N	4.48 W
Kourouninkoto	150	13.52 N	9.35 W
Kouroussa	150	10.39 N	9.53 W
Koury	150	12.11 N	4.48 W
Koussanar	150	13.52 N	14.05 W
Koussané, Mali	150	14.53 N	11.14 W
Koussane, Sén.	150	14.08 N	12.26 W
Kousser, Massif de ʌ	148	32.02 N	5.59 W
Koussi, Emi ʌ	146	19.50 N	18.30 E
Koussili	150	13.30 N	11.38 W
Koutia Ba	150	14.11 N	14.28 W
Koutiala	150	12.23 N	5.28 W
Kouto	150	9.53 N	6.25 W
Koutou	98	38.35 N	114.24 E
Koutoumo, Île I	175f	22.40 S	167.33 E
Kouts	216	41.19 N	87.01 W
Kouvola	26	60.52 N	26.42 E
Kouya ≃	150	10.09 N	9.45 W
Kouyou ≃	152	0.45 S	16.38 E
Kova	88	58.18 N	100.21 E
Kova ≃	88	58.18 N	100.18 E
Kovada Milli Parkı ♦	130	37.32 N	30.53 E
Kovaksa	80	55.31 N	43.30 E
Koval'ovka	78	47.16 N	31.43 E
Kovarskas	76	55.26 N	24.55 E
Kovarzino	76	60.09 N	38.33 E
Kovdor	24	67.34 N	30.22 E
Kovdozero, ozero ⊜	24	66.47 N	32.00 E
Kovel'	78	51.14 N	24.41 E
Kovernino	80	57.07 N	43.49 E
Kovilpatti	122	9.10 N	77.52 E
Kovin	38	44.45 N	20.59 E
Kovno → Kaunas	76	54.54 N	23.54 E
Kovpyta	78	51.23 N	30.50 E
Kovrina Vtoraja	80	47.01 N	41.44 E
Kovrov	80	56.22 N	41.18 E
Kovševata	78	49.29 N	30.38 E
Kovsug ≃	83	48.48 N	39.17 E
Kovūr	122	14.29 N	79.59 E
Kovvur	122	17.01 N	81.44 E
Kovylkin	80	48.16 N	41.28 E
Kovylkino	80	54.02 N	43.56 E
Kovža	24	61.09 N	38.58 E
Kovžinskij Zavod	76	60.24 N	37.04 E
Kowal	30	52.32 N	19.09 E
Kowalewo Pomorskie	30	53.10 N	18.53 E
Kowangge	115b	8.16 S	118.32 E
Kowanyama	164	15.28 S	141.44 E
Kowanyama Aboriginal Reserve ◆ [4]	164	15.15 S	141.45 E
Kowār	126	24.13 N	86.11 E
Koweït → Kuwait □ [1]	128	29.30 N	47.45 E
Kowel → Kovel'	78	51.14 N	24.41 E
Kowghān ≃	128	34.15 N	62.57 E
Kowhitirangi	172	42.52 S	171.01 E
Kowie → Port Alfred	158	33.36 S	26.55 E
Kowkcheh ≃	120	37.10 N	69.23 E
Kowloon (Jiulong)	271d	22.18 N	114.10 E
Kowloon City	271d	22.19 N	114.11 E
Kowloon Peak ʌ	271d	22.21 N	114.13 E
Kowmung ≃	170	33.52 S	150.16 E
Kowŏn	98	39.26 N	127.14 E
Kowt-e 'Ashrow	120	34.27 N	68.48 E
Koxtag	120	37.23 N	78.05 E
Kōya	96	34.12 N	135.35 E
Koyadaira	96	33.56 N	134.13 E
Kōyaguchi	96	34.18 N	135.33 E
Koyama ◆ [8]	268	35.37 N	139.43 E
Koyama-ike ⊜	96	35.30 N	134.09 E
Kōyama-misaki >	96	34.40 N	131.36 E
Koyambattur → Coimbatore	122	11.00 N	76.58 E
Koyang-ni	98	37.42 N	126.56 E
Kōya-Ryūjin-kokutei-kōen ♦	96	34.10 N	135.35 E
Köyceğiz	130	36.57 N	28.41 E
Köyceğiz Gölü ⊜	130	36.55 N	28.40 E
Koyna Reservoir ⊜ [1]	122	17.25 N	73.45 E
Koyra ≃ [1]	126	22.27 N	89.16 E
Koyuk	180	64.56 N	161.08 W
Koyuk ≃	180	64.55 N	161.12 W
Koyukuk	180	64.53 N	157.43 W
Koyukuk ≃	180	64.56 N	157.30 W
Koyukuk, Middle Fork ≃	180	67.03 N	151.04 W
Koyukuk, North Fork ≃	180	67.03 N	151.04 W
Koyukuk, South Fork ≃	180	66.35 N	151.57 W
Koyulhisar	130	40.18 N	37.51 E
Koža	80	57.47 N	48.57 E
Kozakai	94	34.48 N	137.22 E
Kōzaki	94	35.54 N	140.24 E
Kō-zaki >	92	34.05 N	129.13 E
Kozaklı	130	39.14 N	34.49 E
Kōzan, Nihon	96	34.35 N	133.03 E
Kozan, Tür.	130	37.27 N	35.49 E
Kozáni	38	40.18 N	21.47 E
Kožanka	78	49.58 N	29.46 E
Kožany, S.S.S.R.	76	52.48 N	31.44 E
Koz'any, S.S.S.R.	76	55.18 N	26.52 E
Kozara ⋏	36	45.00 N	16.50 E
Kozarac	36	44.58 N	16.51 E
Kozdinga	24	63.43 N	47.32 E
Kozelec	78	50.55 N	31.08 E
Kozel'ščina	78	49.13 N	33.51 E
Kozel'sk	82	54.02 N	35.48 E
Koževnikovo	86	56.16 N	84.00 E
Kozhikode → Calicut	122	11.15 N	75.46 E
Koziegłowy	30	50.36 N	19.09 E
Kozienice	30	51.35 N	21.33 E
Kožim	24	65.48 N	59.28 E
Kozin	78	50.14 N	30.39 E
Kozino	265b	55.54 N	37.11 E
Kozjak (Possruck) ⋏	61	46.37 N	15.28 E
Kozlov	78	49.33 N	25.20 E
Kozlov Bereg	76	58.57 N	27.44 E
Kozlovka, S.S.S.R.	78	51.39 N	41.16 E
Kozlovka, S.S.S.R.	78	50.52 N	40.27 E
Kozlovka, S.S.S.R.	80	55.52 N	48.14 E
Kozlovka, S.S.S.R.	80	52.33 N	45.41 E
Kozlovo, S.S.S.R.	76	57.34 N	35.29 E
Kozlovo, S.S.S.R.	82	56.31 N	36.16 E
Kozlovščina	76	53.19 N	25.18 E
Kozlu, Tür.	130	40.37 N	36.30 E
Kozlu, Tür.	130	41.26 N	31.46 E
Kozluk	130	38.11 N	41.29 E
Koźmin	30	51.50 N	17.28 E
Koz'mino	24	61.56 N	48.19 E
Koz'modemjansk	80	56.20 N	46.36 E
Koz'mogorodskoje	24	65.32 N	44.55 E
Kozova	78	49.26 N	25.09 E
Kožpos'olok	24	63.10 N	38.06 E
Kožuchovo	265b	55.43 N	37.54 E
Kożuchów	30	51.45 N	15.35 E
Kozuka	268	35.09 N	139.57 E
Kōzuki	96	34.59 N	134.20 E
Kozukue ◆ [8]	268	35.30 N	139.36 E
Kozul'ka	86	56.10 N	91.24 E
Kožurla	86	55.21 N	79.02 E
Kōzu-shima I	92	34.13 N	139.10 E
Kozuya	270	34.52 N	135.45 E
Kpandae	150	8.28 N	0.01 W
Kpandu	150	7.00 N	0.18 E
Kpong	150	6.09 N	0.04 E
Kpo Range ⋏	150	7.15 N	10.15 W
Kra, Isthmus of ⊥ [3]	110	10.20 N	99.00 E
Kraai ≃	158	30.40 S	26.45 E
Kraaifontein	158	33.50 S	18.43 E
Kraal	158	26.34 S	28.26 E
Kraankuil	158	29.52 S	24.10 E
Krabbendijke	52	51.26 N	4.07 E
Krabi	110	8.04 N	98.55 E
Krâchéh	110	12.29 N	106.01 E
Krackow	54	53.20 N	14.16 E
Kraftsdorf	54	50.52 N	11.55 E
Kragan	115a	6.42 S	111.37 E
Kragenæs	41	54.55 N	11.22 E
Kragerø	26	58.52 N	9.25 E
Kraghave	41	54.48 N	11.53 E
Kragujevac	38	44.01 N	20.55 E
Krahenhöhe ◆ [8]	263	51.10 N	7.06 E
Kraiburg	60	48.10 N	12.26 E
Kraichgau □ [9]	56	49.10 N	8.50 E
Krainburg → Kranj	36	46.15 N	14.21 E
Krainka	82	54.07 N	36.21 E
Krai-Russkije	80	57.23 N	46.50 E
Krajčikovo	86	56.16 N	73.20 E
Krajenka	30	53.19 N	17.00 E
Krajeva	89	44.54 N	131.08 E
Krajneje	80	47.29 N	46.01 E
Krajnik Dolny	54	53.05 N	14.25 E
Krajnovka	84	43.57 N	47.24 E
Krakatau ʌ [1]	115a	6.07 S	105.24 E
Krakatoa → Krakatau ʌ [1]	115a	6.07 S	105.24 E
Krakau → Kraków	30	50.03 N	19.58 E
Krâkôr	110	12.32 N	104.12 E
Krakovec	78	49.57 N	23.07 E
Krakovo	80	53.36 N	50.51 E
Krakow, D.D.R.	54	53.39 N	12.13 E
Kraków, Pol.	30	50.03 N	19.58 E
Kraków □ [4]	30	49.50 N	20.00 E
Krakower See ⊜	54	53.37 N	12.17 E
Kraksaan	115a	7.46 S	113.25 E
Kraksdorf	54	54.18 N	11.04 E
Kralendijk	241s	12.10 N	68.17 W
Kralice	61	49.11 N	16.12 E
Kraljevica	36	45.16 N	14.34 E
Kraljevo	38	43.43 N	20.41 E
Kralovice	60	49.59 N	13.29 E
Královské Vinohrady ◆ [8]	54	50.01 N	14.29 E
Kralupy nad Vltavou	54	50.11 N	14.18 E
Kralupy u Chomutova	54	50.25 N	13.20 E
Králův Dvůr	60	49.56 N	14.02 E
Kramatorsk	83	48.43 N	37.32 E
Kramer	216	40.20 N	87.17 W
Kramfors	26	62.56 N	17.47 E
Krammer ʮ	52	51.38 N	4.15 E
Krampen	61	47.40 N	15.32 E
Krampnitz	264a	52.28 N	13.04 E
Krampnitzsee ⊜	264a	52.27 N	13.03 E
Kramsach	64	47.27 N	11.52 E
Kranebitten, Flughafen ⊠	64	47.16 N	11.20 E
Kranenburg	52	51.47 N	6.03 E
Krångede	26	63.09 N	16.05 E
Kranichfeld	54	50.51 N	11.12 E
Kranídhion	38	37.22 N	23.10 E
Kranj	36	46.15 N	14.21 E
Kranji, Sing.	271c	1.26 N	103.46 E
Kranji, Sing.	271c	1.26 N	103.45 E
Kranji ≃	271c	1.26 N	103.45 E
Kranji Reservoir ⊜ [1]	271c	1.26 N	103.45 E
Kranji War Memorial ⊥	271c	1.26 N	103.45 E
Kranjska Gora	64	46.29 N	13.47 E
Kransaja Pol'ana	84	43.41 N	40.13 E
Kranskop	158	29.00 S	30.47 E
Kranskop ʌ	158	27.43 S	29.41 E
Kranzberg	156	21.55 S	15.43 E
Krapina	36	46.10 N	15.52 E
Krapivinskij	86	55.00 N	86.49 E
Krapivna	76	53.38 N	35.31 E
Krapkowice	30	50.29 N	17.56 E
Krapperup	41	56.16 N	12.31 E
Krappitz → Krapkowice	30	50.29 N	17.56 E
Krapuh	114	3.39 N	98.10 E
Kras ⋏ [1]	64	45.48 N	14.00 E
Krasavino	24	60.58 N	46.26 E
Krasavka	80	51.11 N	43.24 E
Krasieo ≃	110	14.49 N	100.05 E
Krasilov	78	49.39 N	26.59 E
Krasino	72	70.45 N	54.27 E
Krasivaja Meča ≃	76	52.55 N	39.03 E
Krasivka	80	52.16 N	42.31 E
Krasivoje	86	51.54 N	66.46 E
Kraskino	89	42.44 N	130.48 E
Kraskovo	265b	55.39 N	37.59 E
Krāslava	76	55.54 N	27.10 E
Kraslice	54	50.18 N	12.31 E
Krasnaja ≃	83	49.01 N	38.15 E
Krasnaja Gora, S.S.S.R.	76	53.01 N	31.37 E
Krasnaja Gora, S.S.S.R.	76	60.16 N	35.42 E
Krasnaja Gorbatka	80	55.52 N	41.46 E
Krasnaja Gorka	80	56.12 N	43.04 E
Krasnaja Jaranga	180	65.40 N	172.50 W
Krasnaja Jaruga	78	50.48 N	35.39 E
Krasnaja Pachra	82	55.27 N	37.17 E
Krasnaja Pol'ana, S.S.S.R.	78	47.33 N	37.05 E
Krasnaja Pol'ana, S.S.S.R.	80	46.06 N	41.30 E
Krasnaja Pol'ana, S.S.S.R.	80	56.15 N	51.09 E
Krasnaja Pol'ana, S.S.S.R.	80	52.13 N	53.38 E
Krasnaja Popovka	83	49.08 N	38.09 E
Krasnaja Sloboda, S.S.S.R.	76	52.51 N	27.10 E
Krasnaja Sloboda, S.S.S.R.	84	41.24 N	48.31 E
Krasnaja Talovka	83	48.51 N	39.51 E
Krasnaja Vol'a	76	52.23 N	27.04 E
Krasnaja Zar'a	76	52.47 N	37.41 E
Krásná Lípa	54	50.54 N	14.31 E
Krasn'anka	80	51.04 N	47.56 E
Krasneno	180	64.38 N	174.48 E
Kraśnik	30	50.56 N	22.13 E
Krasnoarmejsk, S.S.S.R.	80	51.02 N	45.42 E
Krasnoarmejsk, S.S.S.R.	82	56.08 N	38.08 E
Krasnoarmejsk, S.S.S.R.	83	48.17 N	37.11 E
Krasnoarmejsk, S.S.S.R.	86	53.50 N	69.42 E
Krasnoarmejskaja	78	45.23 N	38.12 E
Krasnoarmejskij, S.S.S.R.	74	69.35 N	172.00 E
Krasnoarmejskij, S.S.S.R.	80	47.01 N	42.12 E
Krasnoarmejskoje, S.S.S.R.	80	55.46 N	47.11 E
Krasnoarmejskoje, S.S.S.R.	80	52.44 N	50.02 E
Krasnoarmejskoje, S.S.S.R.	83	47.14 N	37.56 E
Krasnoborsk, S.S.S.R.	24	61.34 N	45.53 E
Krasnoborsk, S.S.S.R.	80	53.46 N	48.04 E
Krasnobród	30	50.33 N	23.13 E
Krasnobrodskij	86	54.10 N	86.28 E
Krasnodar	78	45.02 N	39.00 E
Krasnodar □ [8], S.S.S.R.	78	45.00 N	39.00 E
Krasnodar □ [8], S.S.S.R.	80	44.10 N	40.30 E
Krasnodarskij	83	48.15 N	39.51 E
Krasnodarskoje vodochranilišče ⊜ [1]	78	45.06 N	39.31 E
Krasnodon	83	48.17 N	39.48 E
Krasnofarfornyj	76	59.08 N	31.51 E
Krasnoflotskoje	80	50.04 N	41.14 E
Krasnogorka	85	43.15 N	75.10 E
Krasnogorodskoje	76	56.50 N	28.17 E
Krasnogorovka	83	48.00 N	37.31 E
Krasnogorsk, S.S.S.R.	82	55.50 N	37.20 E
Krasnogorsk, S.S.S.R.	89	48.24 N	142.06 E
Krasnogorskij, S.S.S.R.	80	56.09 N	48.20 E
Krasnogorskij, S.S.S.R.	85	41.09 N	69.39 E
Krasnogorskij, S.S.S.R.	86	54.36 N	61.15 E
Krasnogorskoje, S.S.S.R.	80	57.42 N	52.30 E
Krasnogorskoje, S.S.S.R.	86	52.18 N	86.12 E
Krasnogovardejskij	86	57.22 N	62.20 E
Krasnograd	78	49.22 N	35.27 E
Krasnogvardejsk	85	39.46 N	67.16 E
Krasnogvardejskij	82	54.04 N	37.46 E
Krasnogvardejskoje, S.S.S.R.	78	50.39 N	38.24 E
Krasnogvardejskoje, S.S.S.R.	78	45.29 N	34.17 E
Krasnogvardejskoje, S.S.S.R.	80	45.51 N	41.31 E
Krasnogvardejskoje, S.S.S.R.	86	51.24 N	69.18 E
Krasnoil'sk	78	48.01 N	25.34 E
Krasnojar	80	48.54 N	51.46 E
Krasnojarka, S.S.S.R.	86	55.20 N	73.04 E
Krasnojarka, S.S.S.R.	86	59.26 N	60.30 E
Krasnoj Armii, proliv ʮ	74	80.00 N	94.35 E
Krasnojarovo	89	51.27 N	128.28 E
Krasnojarsk	86	56.01 N	92.50 E
Krasnojarsk □ [7]	88	56.00 N	94.00 E
Krasnojarskij	86	51.58 N	59.55 E
Krasnojarskoje vodochranilišče ⊜ [1]	86	55.00 N	92.00 E
Krasnoje, S.S.S.R.	24	59.12 N	47.49 E
Krasnoje, S.S.S.R.	76	54.14 N	27.05 E
Krasnoje, S.S.S.R.	76	53.06 N	33.55 E
Krasnoje, S.S.S.R.	76	52.51 N	38.47 E
Krasnoje, S.S.S.R.	78	50.21 N	38.50 E
Krasnoje, S.S.S.R.	78	50.56 N	38.41 E
Krasnoje, S.S.S.R.	78	46.44 N	39.34 E
Krasnoje, S.S.S.R.	78	46.38 N	29.50 E
Krasnoje, S.S.S.R.	82	54.26 N	38.38 E
Krasnoje, S.S.S.R.	83	48.23 N	39.31 E
Krasnoje, S.S.S.R.	83	48.25 N	37.19 E
Krasnoje, S.S.S.R.	86	54.37 N	85.23 E
Krasnoje, ozero ⊜	74	64.30 N	174.24 E
Krasnoje Echo	80	55.48 N	40.42 E
Krasnoje Gorodišče	82	54.04 N	38.44 E
Krasnoje-na-Volge	80	57.31 N	41.14 E
Krasnoje Selo, S.S.S.R.	80	48.02 N	45.13 E
Krasnoje Selo, S.S.S.R.	80	48.46 N	42.20 E
Krasnoje Selo, S.S.S.R.	265a	59.44 N	30.05 E
Krasnoje Znam'a, S.S.S.R.	76	57.26 N	35.13 E
Krasnoje Znam'a, S.S.S.R.	128	36.58 N	62.30 E
Krasnokamsk	86	58.04 N	55.48 E
Krasnokutsk, S.S.S.R.	78	50.06 N	35.09 E
Krasnokutsk, S.S.S.R.	86	53.01 N	75.59 E
Krasnolesje	76	54.24 N	22.23 E
Krasnolesnyj	78	51.53 N	39.35 E
Krasnoluki	76	54.37 N	28.50 E
Krasnomajskij	76	57.37 N	34.22 E
Krasnookt'abr'skij, S.S.S.R.	80	56.40 N	47.45 E
Krasnookt'abr'skij, S.S.S.R.	80	48.53 N	44.45 E
Krasnookt'abr'skij, S.S.S.R.	85	42.50 N	74.18 E
Krasnooskol'skoje vodochranilišče ⊜ [1]	83	49.17 N	37.37 E
Krasnoostrovskij	76	60.18 N	28.40 E
Krasnopavlovka	78	49.08 N	36.19 E
Krasnoperekopsk	78	45.57 N	33.47 E
Krasnopolje, S.S.S.R.	76	53.20 N	31.24 E
Krasnopolje, S.S.S.R.	78	50.46 N	35.16 E
Krasnorečenskij	89	44.41 N	135.14 E
Krasnoščelje	24	67.21 N	37.02 E
Krasnoščokovo	86	51.40 N	82.45 E
Krasnosel'kup	74	65.41 N	82.28 E
Krasnosel'sk	84	40.36 N	45.21 E
Krasnosel'skoje	78	45.25 N	32.42 E
Krasnosielc	30	53.03 N	21.10 E
Krasnoslobodsk, S.S.S.R.	80	48.42 N	44.34 E
Krasnoslobodsk, S.S.S.R.	80	54.26 N	43.48 E
Krasnotorka	83	48.41 N	37.31 E
Krasnoturansk	86	54.16 N	91.29 E
Krasnoturjinsk	86	59.46 N	60.12 E
Krasnoufimsk	86	56.37 N	57.46 E
Krasnoural'sk	86	58.21 N	60.03 E
Krasnousol'skij	86	53.54 N	56.27 E
Krasnovidovo	80	55.21 N	49.04 E
Krasnovišersk	24	60.23 N	56.59 E
Krasnovka, S.S.S.R.	83	48.47 N	40.07 E
Krasnovka, S.S.S.R.	83	47.24 N	37.26 E
Krasnovodsk	128	40.00 N	53.00 E
Krasnovodsk □ [4]	128	39.30 N	55.00 E
Krasnovodskij poluostrov > [1]	128	40.30 N	53.15 E
Krasnovodskij zaliv ⊂	128	39.55 N	53.15 E
Krasnoyarsk → Krasnojarsk	86	56.01 N	92.50 E
Krasnozatonskij	24	61.41 N	50.58 E
Krasnozavodsk	82	56.27 N	38.13 E
Krasnoznamensk	76	54.57 N	22.30 E
Krasnoznamenskij	86	51.03 N	69.30 E
Krasnoz'orskoje	86	53.59 N	79.14 E
Krásný Dvůr	54	50.10 N	13.24 E
Krasnyj, S.S.S.R.	76	54.34 N	31.26 E
Krasnyj, S.S.S.R.	92a	46.15 N	141.15 E
Krasnyj Aul	86	51.03 N	81.02 E
Krasnyj Bazar	84	39.41 N	46.58 E
Krasnyj Bogatyr'	80	56.02 N	41.08 E
Krasnyj Bor, S.S.S.R.	80	55.17 N	43.59 E
Krasnyj Bor, S.S.S.R.	80	55.53 N	53.06 E
Krasnyj Bor, S.S.S.R.	265a	59.41 N	30.41 E
Krasnyj Cholm, S.S.S.R.	76	58.03 N	37.07 E
Krasnyj Cholm, S.S.S.R.	80	54.11 N	40.42 E
Krasnyj Cholm, S.S.S.R.	86	51.35 N	54.09 E
Krasnyj Čhuduk	80	46.18 N	46.56 E
Krasnyj Čikoj	88	50.22 N	108.15 E
Krasnyje Baki	80	57.08 N	45.10 E
Krasnyje Barrikady	80	46.14 N	47.53 E
Krasnyje Četai	80	55.42 N	46.09 E
Krasnyje Gory	76	58.57 N	29.29 E
Krasnyje Okny	78	47.32 N	29.27 E
Krasnyje Partizany	78	50.57 N	31.47 E
Krasnyje Tkači	80	57.30 N	39.45 E
Krasnyj Gorodok	76	57.11 N	33.44 E
Krasnyj Gul'aj	80	54.01 N	48.22 E
Krasnyj Jar, S.S.S.R.	80	46.33 N	48.21 E
Krasnyj Jar, S.S.S.R.	80	53.30 N	50.22 E
Krasnyj Jar, S.S.S.R.	80	51.38 N	46.25 E
Krasnyj Jar, S.S.S.R.	80	50.37 N	45.47 E
Krasnyj Jar, S.S.S.R.	80	50.42 N	44.46 E
Krasnyj Jar, S.S.S.R.	86	55.54 N	86.57 E
Krasnyj Jar, S.S.S.R.	86	55.14 N	72.56 E
Krasnyj Jar, S.S.S.R.	86	57.07 N	84.33 E
Krasnyj Jar, S.S.S.R.	86	53.20 N	69.14 E
Krasnyj Kl'ič	86	55.26 N	56.12 E
Krasnyj Kut, S.S.S.R.	80	50.57 N	46.58 E
Krasnyj Kut, S.S.S.R.	83	48.12 N	38.48 E
Krasnyj Liman, S.S.S.R.	78	51.32 N	39.50 E
Krasnyj Liman, S.S.S.R.	83	48.59 N	37.49 E
Krasnyj Log	78	51.23 N	39.46 E
Krasnyj Luč, S.S.S.R.	76	57.04 N	30.05 E
Krasnyj Luč, S.S.S.R.	83	48.08 N	38.56 E
Krasnyj Majak	80	56.03 N	41.23 E
Krasnyj Manyč, S.S.S.R.	80	46.33 N	42.10 E
Krasnyj Manyč, S.S.S.R.	80	45.31 N	44.42 E
Krasnyj Manyč, S.S.S.R.	80	46.59 N	41.07 E
Krasnyj Meliorator	80	50.02 N	46.06 E
Krasnyj Okt'abr', S.S.S.R.	80	56.06 N	41.23 E
Krasnyj Okt'abr', S.S.S.R.	80	51.33 N	45.42 E
Krasnyj Okt'abr', S.S.S.R.	82	56.07 N	38.53 E
Krasnyj Okt'abr', S.S.S.R.	82	55.37 N	36.30 E
Krasnyj Okt'abr', S.S.S.R.	83	48.15 N	38.12 E
Krasnyj Okt'abr', S.S.S.R.	83	48.56 N	39.23 E
Krasnyj Okt'abr', S.S.S.R.	86	55.37 N	64.48 E
Krasnyj Okt'abr', S.S.S.R.	86	46.50 N	75.59 E
Krasnyj Oskol	83	49.11 N	37.26 E
Krasnyj Partizan	80	46.20 N	43.10 E
Krasnyj Perekop	78	46.41 N	33.46 E
Krasnyj Profintern	80	57.45 N	40.27 E
Krasnyj Rog	76	52.57 N	33.45 E
Krasnyj Steklovar	80	56.13 N	48.47 E
Krasnyj Stroitel' ◆ [8]	265b	55.35 N	37.37 E
Krasnyj Sulin	83	47.54 N	40.03 E
Krasnyj Tekstil'ščik	80	51.23 N	45.50 E
Krasnyj Tkač	82	55.28 N	39.05 E
Krasnystaw	30	50.59 N	23.10 E
Krasnyy Luch → Krasnyj Luč	83	48.08 N	38.56 E
Krasucha	76	57.23 N	33.12 E
Kras'ukovskaja	83	47.31 N	40.06 E
Kraszna (Crasna) ≃	38	48.09 N	22.20 E
Kratovo	38	42.05 N	22.11 E

Symbols in the index entries represent the broad categories identified in the key at the right. Symbols with superior numbers (⋏[1]) identify subcategories (see complete key on page *I · 1).*

Symbole im Register stellen die rechts im Schlüssel erklärten Kategorien dar. Symbole mit hochgestellten Ziffern (⋏[1]) bezeichnen Unterabteilungen einer Kategorie (vgl. vollständiger Schlüssel auf Seite *I · 1).*

Los símbolos incluídos en el texto del índice representan las grandes categorias identificadas con la clave a la derecha. Los símbolos con numeros en su parte superior (⋏[1]) identifican las subcategorías (véase la clave completa en la página *I · 1).*

Les symboles de l'index représentent les catégories indiquées dans la légende à droite. Les symboles suivis d'un indice (⋏[1]) représentent des sous-catégories (voir légende complète à la page *I · 1).*

Os símbolos incluídos no texto do índice representam as grandes categorias identificadas com a chave à direita. Os símbolos com números em sua parte superior (⋏[1]) identificam as subcategorias (veja-se a chave completa à página *I · 1).*

ʌ	Mountain	Berg	Montaña	Montagne	Montanha
⋏	Mountains	Gebirge	Montañas	Montagnes	Montanhas
)(	Pass	Paß	Paso	Col	Passo
V	Valley, Canyon	Tal, Cañon	Valle, Cañón	Vallée, Canyon	Vale, Canhão
≚	Plain	Ebene	Llano	Plaine	Planície
>	Cape	Kap	Cabo	Cap	Cabo
I	Island	Insel	Isla	Île	Ilha
II	Islands	Inseln	Islas	Îles	Ilhas
⊥	Other Topographic Features	Andere Topographische Objekte	Otros Elementos Topográficos	Autres données topographiques	Outros acidentes topográficos

ESPAÑOL / FRANÇAIS / PORTUGUÊS

Nombre / Nom / Nome	Página / Page / Página	Lat.°′	Long.°′ W = Oeste / W = Ouest / W = Oeste
Krauchenwies	58	48.01 N	9.14 E
Kraul Mountains ✗	9	73.10 S	14.10 W
Krauschwitz	54	51.31 N	14.41 E
Kräuterin ✗	61	47.41 N	15.05 E
Krautheim	56	49.23 N	9.38 E
Kravaře, Česko.	30	49.56 N	18.01 E
Kravaře, Česko.	54	50.38 N	14.23 E
Kray ◆ [8]	263	51.28 N	7.05 E
Kražiai	76	55.36 N	22.40 E
Krbava ◆ [1]	36	44.40 N	15.35 E
Kreamer Island ▮	220	26.46 N	80.44 W
Kreba	54	51.20 N	14.40 E
Krebs	196	34.55 N	95.42 W
Krečetovo	24	60.56 N	38.30 E
Krečevicy	76	58.37 N	31.21 E
Krefeld	56	51.20 N	6.34 E
Kregme	41	55.57 N	12.04 E
Kreiensen	52	51.51 N	9.58 E
Kreischa	54	50.56 N	13.45 E
Kreitzer Glacier ⊓	9	70.25 S	72.30 E
Kremastón, Tekhnití Límni ⊜ [1]	38	38.55 N	21.30 E
Kremenčug	78	49.04 N	33.25 E
Kremenčugskoje vodochranilišče ⊜ [1]	78	49.20 N	32.30 E
Kremenec	78	50.07 N	25.45 E
Kremennaja	83	49.03 N	38.14 E
Kremen'ovka	83	47.20 N	37.29 E
Kremenskoj	80	47.49 N	41.08 E
Kremenskoje	82	55.06 N	35.57 E
Kremlin ᴥ	265b	55.45 N	37.37 E
Kremmen	54	52.45 N	13.01 E
Kremmling	200	40.03 N	106.23 W
Kremnica	30	48.43 N	18.54 E
Krempe	52	53.50 N	9.29 E
Krems ≃, Öst.	61	48.14 N	14.19 E
Krems ≃, Öst.	61	48.25 N	15.36 E
Krems an der Donau	61	48.25 N	15.36 E
Kremsbrücke	64	46.57 N	13.37 E
Kremsmünster	61	48.03 N	14.08 E
Krenitzin Islands ▮▮	180	54.08 N	166.00 W
Krensitz	54	51.29 N	12.27 E
Krepenskij	83	48.06 N	39.03 E
Krepkaja ≃	83	47.35 N	39.23 E
Krepoljin	38	44.16 N	21.37 E
Krešchonka	86	55.52 N	80.06 E
Kresgeville	210	40.54 N	75.30 W
Kress	196	34.22 N	101.45 W
Kressbronn	58	47.35 N	9.36 E
Kressey Lake ⊜	285	39.44 N	75.07 W
Kresta, zaliv ⊂	180	66.00 N	179.15 W
Krestcy, S.S.S.R.	76	58.15 N	32.31 E
Krestcy, S.S.S.R.	76	58.23 N	39.00 E
Krestjanskij	85	40.32 N	69.02 E
Krestjanskoje	80	45.34 N	42.56 E
Krest-Major	74	67.37 N	144.45 E
Krestovaja Guba	72	74.07 N	55.33 E
Krestovo-Gorodišče	80	54.10 N	48.36 E
Krestovyj, pereval ⋈	84	42.32 N	44.28 E
Kresty	82	55.16 N	37.06 E
Kreta → Kríti ▮	38	35.29 N	24.42 E
Kretek	115a	7.59 S	110.19 E
Kretinga	76	55.53 N	21.13 E
Kreuth	64	47.38 N	11.44 E
Kreuz an der Ostbahn → Krzyż	30	52.54 N	16.01 E
Kreuzau	56	50.45 N	6.29 E
Kreuzberg	263	51.09 N	7.27 E
Kreuzberg ◆ [8]	264a	52.30 N	13.23 E
Kreuzberg ∧	56	50.22 N	9.58 E
Kreuzburg → Kluczbork	30	50.59 N	18.13 E
Kreuzeck-Gruppe ✗	64	46.51 N	13.06 E
Kreuzen	64	46.40 N	13.35 E
Kreuzlingen	58	47.39 N	9.11 E
Kreuznach → Bad Kreuznach	56	49.52 N	7.51 E
Kreuztal	56	50.58 N	7.59 E
Krevo	76	54.19 N	26.17 E
Kreyenhagen	54	52.55 N	10.52 E
Krian	115a	7.24 S	112.35 E
Kría Vrísi	38	40.41 N	22.18 E
Kribi	152	2.57 N	9.55 E
Kričov	76	53.42 N	31.43 E
Kriebstein, Burg ⊥	54	51.02 N	13.00 E
Krieglach	61	47.33 N	15.34 E
Kriel	158	26.16 S	29.14 E
Kriens	58	47.02 N	8.17 E
Krigujgun, mys ≻	180	65.30 N	171.05 W
Kriljon, mys ≻	89	45.53 N	142.05 E
Krim → Krymskij poluostrov ≻ [1]	78	45.00 N	34.00 E
Křimice	60	49.46 N	13.15 E
Krim-Krim	146	8.58 N	15.48 E
Krimmler Wasserfälle ∟	64	47.12 N	12.10 E
Krimnicksee ⊜	264a	52.18 N	13.39 E
Krimpen aan de IJssel	52	51.54 N	4.35 E
Krimskij	80	47.39 N	40.44 E
Kriničćno-Lugskoje	83	47.45 N	39.12 E
Krinički	78	48.22 N	34.27 E
Kriničnaja	83	48.08 N	38.02 E
Kriničnoje	78	45.32 N	28.40 E
Krishna ≃	122	15.57 N	80.59 E
Krishna, Mouths of the ≃ [1]	122	15.43 N	80.55 E
Krishnachaadrapur	126	21.50 N	86.49 E
Krishnagiri	122	12.32 N	78.14 E
Krishnamāti	272b	22.40 N	88.32 E
Krishnanagar, India	126	23.24 N	88.30 E
Krishnanagar, India	126	23.13 N	87.33 E
Krishnapur, Bngl.	126	23.30 N	89.56 E
Krishnapur, India	272b	22.36 N	88.26 E
Krishnarāja Sāgara ⊜ [1]	122	12.30 N	76.26 E
Krishnarājpet	122	12.40 N	76.30 E
Krishnarāmpur	126	22.43 N	88.14 E
Kristdala	26	57.24 N	16.11 E
Kristiania → Oslo	26	59.55 N	10.45 E
Kristianopel	26	56.15 N	16.02 E
Kristiansand	26	58.10 N	8.00 E
Kristianstad	26	56.02 N	14.08 E
Kristianstads Län □ [6]	26	56.15 N	14.00 E
Kristiansund	26	63.07 N	7.45 E
Kristiinankaupunki → Kristinestad	26	62.17 N	21.23 E
Kristineberg	26	65.04 N	18.35 E
Kristinehamn	40	59.20 N	14.07 E
Kristinestad (Kristiinankau-Punki)	26	62.17 N	21.23 E
Kríti (Crete) ▮	38	35.29 N	24.42 E
Kritikón Pélagos (Sea of Crete) ⫧ [2]	38	35.46 N	23.54 E
Kritzendorf	264b	48.20 N	16.18 E
Kriul'any	78	47.13 N	29.09 E
Kriuša	82	54.28 N	36.24 E
Kriv'ačka	80	58.40 N	45.27 E
Krivaja ≃	38	44.27 N	18.09 E
Krivaja, kosa ≻ [2]	83	47.02 N	38.06 E
Krivaja Ruda	78	49.31 N	32.59 E
Kriv'anskaja	83	47.24 N	40.10 E
Kriva Palanka	38	42.12 N	22.20 E
Krivcy	82	55.28 N	38.12 E
Kriviči	76	54.43 N	27.17 E
Krivinka	86	51.08 N	78.10 E
Krivodol	38	43.23 N	23.29 E
Krivoj Buzan	80	46.31 N	48.33 E
Krivoje Ozero	78	47.56 N	30.21 E
Krivoj Rog	78	47.55 N	33.21 E
Krivoj Torec ≃	83	48.39 N	37.32 E
Křivoklát	60	50.02 N	13.54 E
Krivonosovo	78	49.55 N	39.16 E
Krivorožje, S.S.S.R.	78	48.51 N	40.45 E
Krivorožje, S.S.S.R.	78	48.31 N	38.40 E
Krivorožje, S.S.S.R.	83	48.31 N	38.40 E
Krivošeino	86	57.20 N	83.57 E
Krivošin	76	52.52 N	26.08 E
Krivoy Rog → Krivoj Rog	78	47.55 N	33.21 E
Kriwoi-Rog → Krivoj Rog	78	47.55 N	33.21 E
Križevci	36	46.02 N	16.33 E
Krizskoje	83	49.28 N	39.38 E
Krk, Otok ▮	36	45.05 N	14.35 E
Krkonošský národní park ♠	30	50.45 N	15.35 E
Krn ∧	64	46.16 N	13.40 E
Krnov	30	50.05 N	17.41 E
Krobia	30	51.47 N	16.58 E
Krøderen ⊜	26	60.15 N	9.38 E
Krogager	41	55.42 N	8.51 E
Krögis	54	51.07 N	13.22 E
Krojanke → Krajenka	30	53.19 N	17.00 E
Krokek	40	58.40 N	16.24 E
Kroken	24	65.22 N	14.20 E
Krokodil ≃, S. Afr.	156	24.12 S	26.52 E
Krokodil ≃, S. Afr.	156	25.26 S	31.58 E
Krokom	26	63.19 N	14.30 E
Krokowa	30	54.48 N	18.11 E
Krolevec	78	51.33 N	33.23 E
Kröller-Müller, Rijksmuseum ᴥ	52	52.05 N	5.50 E
Krölpa	54	50.41 N	11.32 E
Krom ≃	158	30.53 S	19.01 E
Krombi Pits	156	19.30 S	25.02 E
Kroměříž	30	49.18 N	17.24 E
Krommenie	52	52.29 N	4.45 E
Krompachy	30	48.56 N	20.52 E
Kromy	76	52.43 N	35.46 E
Kronach	54	50.14 N	11.20 E
Kronberg	56	50.10 N	8.30 E
Kronborg ⊥	41	56.02 N	12.38 E
Krone	263	51.27 N	7.20 E
Krong Ana ⊜ [1]	110	12.30 N	108.00 E
Krông Kaôh Kông	110	11.37 N	102.59 E
Krông Kêb	110	10.29 N	104.19 E
Kronobergs Län □ [6]	26	56.40 N	14.40 E
Kronoby (Kruunupyy)	26	63.43 N	23.02 E
Kronockij zaliv ⊂	74	54.12 N	160.36 E
Kronocki	74	54.36 N	161.10 E
Kronshagen	41	54.20 N	10.05 E
Kronstadt → Brașov, Rom.	38	45.39 N	25.37 E
Kronštadt, S.S.S.R.	76	59.59 N	29.45 E
Kronwa	110	15.25 N	98.26 E
Kroondal	158	25.45 S	27.19 E
Kroonstad	158	27.46 S	27.12 E
Kröpelin	54	54.04 N	11.48 E
Kropotkin, S.S.S.R.	72	45.26 N	40.34 E
Kropotkin, S.S.S.R.	88	58.30 N	115.17 E
Kropotkina, gora ∧	88	53.43 N	117.32 E
Kropp	41	54.24 N	9.31 E
Kroppefjäll ∧ [2]	26	58.40 N	12.13 E
Kroppenstedt	54	51.56 N	11.18 E
Kropstädt	54	51.58 N	12.44 E
Kropufino	76	60.23 N	39.10 E
Krościenko	30	49.27 N	20.26 E
Kröslin	54	54.07 N	13.45 E
Krošn'a	78	50.18 N	28.39 E
Krośniewice	30	52.16 N	19.10 E
Krosno	30	49.42 N	21.46 E
Krosno □ [4]	30	49.30 N	22.00 E
Krosno Odrzańskie	30	52.04 N	15.05 E
Krossen	54	50.58 N	11.59 E
Krostitz	54	51.28 N	12.27 E
Krotoszyn	30	51.42 N	17.26 E
Krotovka	80	53.18 N	51.12 E
Krotovo	86	56.57 N	69.20 E
Krotz Springs	194	30.32 N	91.45 W
Kröv	56	49.59 N	7.05 E
Kroya	115a	7.38 S	109.14 E
Krško	36	45.58 N	15.29 E
Krsy	60	49.54 N	13.03 E
Kr'učkov	80	48.01 N	45.40 E
Kr'učkovo	76	57.03 N	35.34 E
Kruckow	54	53.54 N	13.14 E
Krudenburg	263	51.39 N	6.45 E
Kruenggeukueh	114	5.15 N	97.02 E
Kruengluak	114	2.50 N	97.45 E
Kruft	56	50.23 N	7.20 E
Kruger National Park ♠	156	24.00 S	31.40 E
Krugersdorp	158	26.05 S	27.35 E
Krugersdorp □ [5]	273d	26.05 S	27.35 E
Krugersdorp Race Course ♠	273d	26.08 S	27.45 E
Krugersdorp West	273d	26.06 S	27.45 E
Krugloje, S.S.S.R.	76	54.15 N	29.48 E
Krugloje, S.S.S.R.	83	47.01 N	39.15 E
Kruglooz'ornoje	86	55.13 N	79.01 E
Kruglooz'ornyj	80	51.06 N	51.17 E
Kruglyži	80	58.31 N	47.42 E
Krugzell	58	47.47 N	10.16 E
Krui	112	5.11 S	103.56 E
Kruidfontein	158	32.51 S	21.57 E
Kruiningen	52	51.27 N	4.02 E
Kruis, Kaap ≻	156	21.49 S	13.57 E
Kruisfontein	158	34.00 S	24.43 E
Kruishoutem	50	50.54 N	3.31 E
Kruisland	52	51.34 N	4.24 E
Kruisrivier	158	33.26 S	21.55 E
Kruisvallei	158	33.53 S	23.10 E
Krujë	38	41.30 N	19.48 E
Kr'ukov	80	47.24 N	42.28 E
Kr'ukovo, S.S.S.R.	74	66.30 N	159.31 E
Kr'ukovo, S.S.S.R.	82	55.59 N	37.10 E
Kr'ukovo, S.S.S.R.	82	55.28 N	36.32 E
Kr'ukovo, S.S.S.R.	83	47.40 N	39.13 E
Krukut, Kali ≃	269e	6.12 S	106.48 E
Krulevščina	76	55.02 N	27.45 E
Krumasye	164	1.40 S	133.09 E
Krumbach, B.R.D.	58	48.14 N	10.22 E
Krumbach, B.R.D.	58	47.58 N	9.02 E
Krumme Lanke ⊜	264a	52.27 N	13.14 E
Krummendammer Heide ◆ [3]	264a	52.28 N	13.39 E
Krummenerl	263	51.05 N	7.45 E
Krummensee	264a	52.36 N	13.42 E
Krumme Steyrling ≃	61	47.54 N	14.14 E
Krummhörn	52	53.26 N	7.06 E
Krummhörn ◆ [1]	52	53.25 N	7.10 E
Krumovgrad	38	41.28 N	25.39 E
Krumroy	214	39.58 N	81.24 W
Krün	64	47.30 N	11.16 E
Krung Thep (Bangkok), Thai	110	13.45 N	100.31 E
Krung Thep (Bangkok), Thai	269a	13.45 N	100.31 E
Krung Thep Mahanakhon □ [4]	269a	13.47 N	100.43 E
Krung Thon Bridge ◆ [5]	269a	13.47 N	100.30 E
Krupá	54	50.08 N	13.41 E
Krupec	78	51.38 N	34.21 E
Krüpel-See ⊜	264a	52.18 N	13.42 E
Krupka	54	50.43 N	13.46 E
Krupki	76	54.19 N	29.08 E
Kruså	41	54.50 N	9.25 E
Kruščica jezero ⊜ [1]	36	44.39 N	15.19 E
Krusenstern, Cape ≻	180	67.07 N	163.43 W
Kruševac	38	43.35 N	21.20 E
Kruševo	38	41.22 N	21.14 E
Krušinovka	76	53.14 N	29.50 E
Krušné hory (Erzgebirge) ✗	54	50.30 N	13.15 E
Kruszwica	30	52.41 N	18.19 E
Krutaja, S.S.S.R.	24	63.02 N	54.38 E
Krutaja, S.S.S.R.	86	57.24 N	76.27 E
Krutaja Gorka	86	55.25 N	73.15 E
Krutcy	76	57.10 N	29.23 E
Krutec, S.S.S.R.	76	60.17 N	39.25 E
Krutec, S.S.S.R.	82	56.10 N	38.33 E
Kruticha, S.S.S.R.	86	53.58 N	81.14 E
Kruticha, S.S.S.R.	86	56.49 N	77.10 E
Krutinka	86	56.01 N	71.31 E
Krutoje	76	52.26 N	37.28 E
Krutoj Log	86	57.53 N	58.14 E
Krutoj Majdan	80	55.35 N	44.04 E
Krutyje Verchi	82	54.19 N	36.26 E
Kruunupyy → Kronoby	26	63.43 N	23.02 E
Kruzenšterna, proliv ʊ	74	48.30 N	153.50 E
Kruzof Island ▮	180	57.10 N	135.40 W
Krydor	184	52.47 N	107.03 W
Krylatskoje ◆ [8]	265b	55.45 N	37.26 E
Krylbo	40	60.08 N	16.13 E
Krylovskaja	78	46.07 N	39.19 E
Krym	83	47.19 N	39.31 E
Krymsk	78	44.56 N	37.59 E
Krymskaja Oblast' □ [4]	78	45.00 N	34.00 E
Krymskij	78	47.40 N	40.46 E
Krymskije gory ✗	78	44.45 N	34.25 E
Krymskij poluostrov (Crimea) ≻ [1]	78	45.00 N	34.00 E
Krymskij Zapovednik ◆ [4]	78	44.42 N	34.12 E
Krymskoje	83	48.45 N	38.48 E
Krynica	30	49.25 N	20.56 E
Krynka ≃	83	47.36 N	38.47 E
Kryžina, chrebet ✗	88	54.00 N	95.00 E
Kryžopol'	78	48.23 N	28.52 E
Krzepice	30	50.58 N	18.44 E
Krzeszowice	30	50.09 N	19.39 E
Krzeszyce	54	52.36 N	15.01 E
Krzna ≃	30	52.08 N	23.31 E
Krzywiń	30	51.58 N	16.49 E
Krzyż	30	52.54 N	16.01 E
Ksar Chellala	148	35.13 N	2.18 E
Ksar el Barka	150	18.24 N	12.13 W
Ksar-el-Kebir	148	35.01 N	5.54 W
Ksar-el-Seghir	34	35.50 N	5.32 W
Ksar Hellal	36	35.39 N	10.54 E
Ksaverovka	78	50.03 N	30.12 E
Ksel, Djebel ∧	148	33.44 N	1.10 E
Kšen' ≃	76	52.23 N	37.44 E
Ksenjevka	88	53.34 N	118.44 E
Ksenofontova	24	60.58 N	56.12 E
Kšenskij	78	51.52 N	37.43 E
Książ Wielkopolski	30	52.05 N	17.14 E
Ksob, Oued ≃	36	35.49 N	7.53 E
Ksour, Monts des ✗	148	32.45 N	0.30 W
Ksour Essaf	148	35.25 N	11.00 E
Kstovo	80	56.11 N	44.11 E
Kū', Wādī al- ∨	140	13.37 N	25.15 E
Kuah	114	6.19 N	99.51 E
Kuai ≃	100	33.09 N	117.32 E
Kuala, Indon.	112	2.55 N	105.48 E
Kuala, Indon.	114	3.32 N	98.24 E
Kualabee	114	4.24 N	96.03 E
Kuala Berang	114	5.04 N	103.01 E
Kualacenako	112	0.28 S	102.40 E
Kuala Kangsar	114	4.46 N	100.56 E
Kualakapuas	112	3.01 S	114.21 E
Kuala Kedah	114	6.06 N	100.18 E
Kuala Kelawang	114	2.56 N	102.05 E
Kuala Kerai	114	5.32 N	102.12 E
Kuala Kerau	114	3.43 N	102.22 E
Kualakeriau	112	0.50 N	113.20 E
Kuala Ketil	114	5.36 N	100.39 E
Kuala Kubu Baharu	114	3.34 N	101.39 E
Kuala Kurau	114	5.01 N	100.26 E
Kualakurun	112	1.07 S	113.53 E
Kualalangsa	114	4.32 N	98.01 E
Kuala Lipis	114	4.11 N	102.03 E
Kuala Lumpur	114	3.10 N	101.42 E
Kuala Lumpur □ [3]	114	3.10 N	101.42 E
Kualamanjual	112	1.25 S	112.00 E
Kuala Nerang	114	6.15 N	100.36 E
Kualapesaguan	112	2.01 S	110.08 E
Kuala Pilah	114	2.44 N	102.15 E
Kualapuu	229a	21.09 N	157.02 W
Kuala Selangor	114	3.21 N	101.15 E
Kualasimpang	114	4.17 N	98.03 E
Kuala Terengganu	114	5.20 N	103.08 E
Kualu ≃	114	2.45 N	100.00 E
Kuamut	112	5.13 N	117.30 E
Kuamut ≃	112	5.13 N	117.32 E
Kuanbang	98	40.29 N	120.04 E
Kuancheng, Zhg.	98	40.37 N	118.31 E
Kuancheng, Zhg.	105	40.38 N	118.27 E
Kuandang	112	0.52 N	122.55 E
Kuandian	98	40.43 N	124.44 E
Kuando → Cuando ≃	152	18.27 S	23.32 E
Kuanhsi	100	24.48 N	121.10 E
Kuanmiao	100	22.58 N	120.19 E
Kuanshan	100	23.03 N	121.09 E
Kuan Shan ∧	100	23.14 N	120.54 E
Kuantan	114	3.48 N	103.20 E
Kuantan ≃	114	3.50 N	103.17 E
Kuanyin	100	25.02 N	121.04 E
Kuanyün → Guanyun	98	34.20 N	119.17 E
Kuanza → Cuanza ≃	152	9.19 S	13.08 E
Kuba	84	41.22 N	48.31 E
Kuba → Cuba □ [1]	240p	21.30 N	80.00 W
Kuban' ≃	72	45.20 N	37.30 E
Kubatly	84	39.22 N	46.34 E
Kubbī	140	11.08 N	25.14 E
Kubbum	140	11.47 N	23.47 E
Kubena ≃	76	59.36 N	39.39 E
Kubenskoje	76	59.26 N	39.40 E
Kubenskoje, ozero ⊜	76	59.40 N	39.25 E
Kubiki	94	37.11 N	138.20 E
Kubinka	82	55.35 N	36.43 E
Kubitzer Bodden ⊂	54	54.24 N	13.12 E
Küblis	58	46.55 N	9.47 E
Kubn'a ≃	80	55.31 N	48.27 E
Kubokawa	96	33.12 N	133.08 E
Kubor, Mount ∧	164	6.05 S	144.45 E
Kubr' ≃	82	56.52 N	38.17 E
Kubrat	38	43.48 N	26.30 E
Kubu	115b	8.16 S	115.35 E
Kubuchaj	88	50.30 N	114.48 E
Kubu Gajah	114	5.10 N	100.41 E
Kubumesaai	112	1.31 N	115.06 E
Kubutambahan	115b	8.05 S	115.10 E
Kučema	24	65.37 N	42.28 E
Kučen'ajevo	80	54.44 N	46.24 E
Kučevo	38	44.27 N	21.44 E
Kuchaiburi	126	22.16 N	86.10 E
Kuchāman	120	27.09 N	74.52 E
Kuch'ang-ni	98	40.09 N	124.46 E
Kuchelebai	154	1.29 N	35.01 E
Kuchen Spitze ∧	58	47.03 N	10.14 E
Kuchinarai	110	16.32 N	104.04 E
Kuching	112	1.33 N	110.20 E
Kuchinoerabu-jima ▮	93b	30.28 N	130.12 E
Kuchino-shima ▮	93b	29.57 N	129.57 E
Kuchiwa	96	34.53 N	132.55 E
Kuchl	64	47.37 N	13.09 E
Kūchnay Darweyshān	128	30.59 N	64.11 E
Kuchterin Lug	89	52.25 N	128.05 E
Kuchtinka	82	54.29 N	38.10 E
Kučino	265b	55.45 N	37.58 E
Kučkak	85	40.15 N	70.20 E
Kučki	80	53.01 N	44.29 E
Kuçovë → Stalin	38	40.48 N	19.54 E
Küçük Ağrı Dağı ∧	84	39.40 N	44.25 E
Küçükbahçe	130	38.33 N	26.24 E
Küçükbakkal ◆ [8]	267b	40.58 N	29.06 E
Küçükçekmece ◆ [8]	267b	40.59 N	28.46 E
Küçükçekmece Gölü ⊜	267b	41.00 N	28.46 E
Küçükköy ◆ [8]	267b	41.04 N	28.54 E
Küçükkuyu	130	39.32 N	26.36 E
Kučukskoje, ozero ⊜	86	52.42 N	79.46 E
Kucur, Tanjung ≻	115a	8.39 S	114.34 E
Kučurgan ≃	78	46.43 N	29.53 E
Kūd	123	33.05 N	75.17 E
Kuda ≃	88	52.25 N	104.08 E
Kudaka-jima ▮	174m	26.09 N	127.54 E
Kudamatsu	96	34.00 N	131.52 E
Kudanggou	104	41.06 N	124.00 E
Kudap	114	1.17 N	102.26 E
Kudara, S.S.S.R.	85	38.25 N	72.41 E
Kudara, S.S.S.R.	88	52.13 N	106.39 E
Kudara ≃	85	38.19 N	72.28 E
Kudara-Somon	88	50.10 N	107.25 E
Kudat	112	6.53 N	116.50 E
Kudbrooke ◆ [8]	260	51.28 N	0.03 E
Kudejevskij	86	54.52 N	56.46 E
Kudene	164	6.14 S	134.39 E
Kudever'	76	56.47 N	29.23 E
Kudinovo	82	55.45 N	38.12 E
Kudirkos Naumiestis	76	54.46 N	22.53 E
Kudongho	98	35.31 N	126.29 E
Kudoyama	96	34.17 N	135.34 E
Kudremukh ∧	122	13.08 N	75.16 E
Kudrovo	265a	59.54 N	30.31 E
Kudus	115a	6.48 S	110.50 E
Kudyat al-Islām	142	27.32 N	30.45 E
Kudymkar	86	59.01 N	54.37 E
Kuee Ruins ⊥	229d	19.21 N	155.23 W
Kueishan Tao ▮	100	24.51 N	121.57 E
Kueisui → Hohhot	102	40.51 N	111.40 E
Kueiyang → Guiyang	102	26.35 N	106.43 E
Kuekvun' ≃	180	69.14 N	179.25 E
Kuënlun → Kunlun Shan ✗	120	36.30 N	88.00 E
Kuerbin	89	49.25 N	128.59 E
K'uerhlo → Korla	90	41.44 N	86.09 E
Kufayr az-Zayt	132	33.26 N	35.44 E
Kufayr Yābūs	132	33.42 N	36.01 E
Kufrinjah	132	32.18 N	35.42 E
Kufstein	64	47.35 N	12.10 E
Kufūr Bilshāy	142	30.51 N	30.48 E
Kufūr Najm	142	30.44 N	31.35 E
Kuga, Nihon	96	34.05 N	132.05 E
Kuga, Nihon	96	33.56 N	132.16 E
Kuga, Zhg.	90	41.43 N	82.54 E
Kugaluk ≃	180	69.10 N	131.00 W
Kugaly	86	44.29 N	78.40 E
Kugarčino	80	55.33 N	50.29 E
Kugart ≃	85	40.52 N	72.53 E
Kugas	85	38.21 N	70.48 E
Kugej	83	46.53 N	39.19 E
Kugesi	80	56.02 N	47.18 E
Kugmallit Bay ⊂	180	69.33 N	133.25 W
Kugojeja ≃	78	46.34 N	39.38 E
Kuguno	94	36.03 N	137.16 E
Kuḥaylī	140	19.25 N	32.50 E
Kühbach	60	48.29 N	11.11 E
Kūhdasht	128	33.32 N	47.36 E
Kūh Lab, Ra's-e ≻	128	25.17 N	60.28 E
Kuḥlīyah, Wādī ∨	142	30.05 N	31.58 E
Kühlungsborn	54	54.09 N	11.43 E
Kuhmo	26	64.08 N	29.31 E
Kuhmoinen	26	61.34 N	25.11 E
Kühnhausen	54	51.02 N	10.58 E
Kühnsdorf	61	46.37 N	14.37 E
Kūhpāyeh	128	32.43 N	52.26 E
Kühren	54	51.20 N	12.50 E
Kuhstedt	52	53.23 N	8.58 E
Kui	164	7.30 S	147.15 E
Kuibyschew → Kujbyšev	80	53.12 N	50.09 E
Kuidesu	98	41.46 N	119.29 E
Kuidou	100	25.10 N	118.11 E
Kuikkol', ozero ⊜	86	50.57 N	64.30 E
Kuikui, Lae o ≻	229a	20.36 N	156.35 W
Kuilāpāl	126	22.50 N	86.38 E
Kuinre	52	52.47 N	5.50 E
Kuiseb ≃	156	22.59 S	14.31 E
Kuishi-yama ∧, Nihon	96	33.51 N	133.35 E
Kuishi-yama ∧, Nihon	96	33.40 N	133.31 E
Kuitan	100	23.05 N	115.58 E
Kuito	152	12.22 S	16.56 E
Kuiu Island ▮	180	56.45 N	134.10 W
Kuivaniemi	26	65.35 N	25.11 E
Kuivastu	76	58.35 N	23.22 E
Kuja, S.S.S.R.	24	65.05 N	40.06 E
Kuja, S.S.S.R.	24	67.46 N	53.10 E
Kujal'nickij liman ⊜	78	46.40 N	30.42 E
Kujang	98	39.52 N	126.01 E
Kujani Game Reserve ◆ [4]	150	7.10 N	0.50 W
Kujawy ◆ [1]	30	52.45 N	18.30 E
Kujbyšev, S.S.S.R.	80	53.12 N	50.09 E
Kujbyšev, S.S.S.R.	80	54.57 N	49.05 E
Kujbyšev, S.S.S.R.	86	55.27 N	78.19 E
Kujbyševka	78	47.37 N	31.42 E
Kujbyševo, S.S.S.R.	78	44.38 N	33.52 E
Kujbyševo, S.S.S.R.	78	47.22 N	36.39 E
Kujbyševo, S.S.S.R.	83	47.49 N	38.55 E
Kujbyševo, S.S.S.R.	85	40.22 N	71.17 E
Kujbyševskij, S.S.S.R.	72	37.52 N	68.44 E
Kujbyševskij, S.S.S.R.	86	53.15 N	66.51 E
Kujbyševskij Zaton	80	55.09 N	49.12 E
Kujbyševskoje vodochranilišče ⊜ [1]	80	54.30 N	48.30 E
Kujeda	86	56.26 N	55.35 E
Kujgan	86	45.25 N	74.10 E
Kujgenkol'	80	49.17 N	47.59 E
Kuji	92	40.11 N	141.46 E
Kuji ≃	94	36.29 N	140.37 E
Kujirai	268	35.56 N	139.27 E
Kujl'uk	85	41.15 N	69.20 E
Kujman'	76	52.52 N	39.16 E
Kujŏng-ni	98	37.53 N	125.54 E
Kujtun	88	54.21 N	101.29 E
Kujū	96	33.01 N	131.18 E
Kujūkuri	94	35.32 N	140.25 E
Kujūkuri-hama ≗ [2]	94	35.35 N	140.30 E
Kujū-san ∧	96	33.05 N	131.15 E
Kuk ∧	64	46.16 N	13.45 E
Kuk ≃	180	70.36 N	160.00 W
Kukaklek Lake ⊜	180	59.09 N	155.20 W
Kukalaya ≃	236	13.39 N	83.37 W
Kukan	89	49.12 N	133.28 E
Kukarino	82	55.31 N	35.59 E
Kukawa	146	12.56 N	13.35 E
Kukerin	162	33.11 S	118.05 E
Kukës	38	42.05 N	20.24 E
Kuke Shan ✗	85	40.00 N	75.00 E
Kuki	94	36.04 N	139.40 E
Kukipi	164	8.10 S	146.05 E
Kukkola	26	65.59 N	24.04 E
Kukmirn	61	47.04 N	16.13 E
Kukmor	80	56.13 N	50.54 E
Kukoboj	76	58.42 N	39.54 E
Kukol'	76	59.52 N	32.35 E
Kükong → Shaoguan	100	24.50 N	113.37 E
Kukpowruk ≃	180	69.35 N	163.00 W
Kukpuk ≃	180	68.23 N	166.20 W
Kukshi	120	22.12 N	74.45 E
Kukuj	76	59.21 N	32.33 E
Kuku-Nor → Qinghai Hu ⊜	102	36.50 N	100.20 E
Kukup	114	1.19 N	103.27 E
Kuku Point ≻	174a	19.18 N	166.34 E
Kukuri Mukuri Char ▮	126	21.56 N	90.39 E
Kukuštan	86	57.38 N	56.30 E
Kula, Blg.	38	43.53 N	22.31 E
Kula, Jugo.	38	45.36 N	19.32 E
Kula, Tür.	130	38.32 N	28.40 E
Kula, Hi., U.S.	229a	20.52 N	156.40 W
Kul'ab	120	37.55 N	69.46 E
Kulāchi	123	31.56 N	70.27 E
Kulagi	76	52.56 N	32.24 E
Kula Gulf ʊ	175e	8.05 S	157.18 E
Kulai	114	1.40 N	103.36 E
Kulaj	86	57.42 N	75.15 E
Kula Kangri ∧	124	28.03 N	90.27 E
Kulākh	144	21.18 N	40.41 E
Kulakovo, S.S.S.R.	82	55.06 N	37.28 E
Kulakovo, S.S.S.R.	86	58.06 N	93.57 E
Kulakši	86	47.12 N	55.24 E
Kulal, Mount ∧	154	2.43 N	36.56 E
Kulanak	85	41.22 N	75.31 E
Kulandy	86	46.08 N	59.31 E
Kular	74	70.41 N	134.22 E
Kulassein Island ▮	116	6.25 N	120.41 E
Kulaura	120	24.32 N	92.03 E
Kulautuva	76	54.58 N	23.38 E
Kulaykilī	140	11.21 N	25.36 E
Kul'či	89	53.33 N	139.36 E
Kuldīga	76	56.58 N	21.59 E
Kuldja → Yining	86	43.54 N	81.21 E
Kul'dur	89	49.13 N	131.38 E
Kule	156	23.05 S	20.05 E
Kulebaki	80	55.24 N	42.32 E
Kulejevo	86	59.40 N	80.59 E
Kulen Vakuf	36	44.34 N	16.06 E
Kulešovka	83	47.05 N	39.33 E
Kulevčinskij	86	53.12 N	61.26 E
Kulgām	123	33.39 N	75.01 E
Kulgera	162	25.50 S	133.18 E
Kulgunino	86	53.35 N	56.56 E
Kuligi	80	58.11 N	53.46 E
Kulikov	78	49.58 N	24.04 E
Kulikovka, S.S.S.R.	78	51.23 N	31.37 E
Kulikovka, S.S.S.R.	80	52.14 N	47.36 E
Kulikovo	76	52.14 N	39.35 E
Kulikovskij	80	50.51 N	42.34 E
Kulim	114	5.22 N	100.34 E
Kulin	162	32.40 S	118.10 E
Kuliushucun	105	40.07 N	116.34 E
Kulju	26	61.23 N	23.46 E
Kulkyne Creek ≃	166	30.16 S	144.12 E
Kullaberg ✗ [2]	41	56.18 N	12.30 E
Kullamaa	76	58.53 N	24.05 E
Küllenhahn ◆ [8]	263	51.14 N	7.08 E
Küllstedt	56	51.16 N	10.17 E
Kullu	123	31.58 N	77.06 E
Kulm	198	46.18 N	98.57 W
Kulmbach	54	50.06 N	11.27 E
Kulnura	170	33.14 S	151.13 E
Kuloj, S.S.S.R.	24	64.58 N	43.28 E
Kuloj, S.S.S.R.	24	61.02 N	42.29 E
Kuloj ≃, S.S.S.R.	24	66.03 N	43.22 E
Kuloj ≃, S.S.S.R.	76	60.25 N	42.30 E
Kuloli	85	39.22 N	68.03 E
Kulongshan	98	41.43 N	116.54 E
Kulongshanpuzi	104	41.16 N	123.59 E
Kulotino	76	58.27 N	33.21 E
Kulp	130	38.30 N	41.02 E
Kulpahar	124	25.19 N	79.39 E
Kulpara	168b	34.04 S	138.02 E
Kulpawn ≃	150	10.21 N	1.05 W
Kulpi	126	22.06 N	88.15 E
Kul'pino	82	56.18 N	37.09 E
Kulpmont	208	40.47 N	76.28 W
Kulpsville	285	40.15 N	75.20 W
Kul'sary	86	46.59 N	54.01 E
Kulsbjerge ✗ [2]	41	55.01 N	12.01 E
Külsheim	56	49.40 N	9.31 E
Kültepe ⊥	130	38.44 N	35.34 E
Kulti	126	23.44 N	86.51 E
Kultikri	126	22.10 N	87.09 E
Kultuk	88	51.44 N	103.42 E
Kulu	130	39.06 N	33.05 E
Kuluha, Jabal ∧	140	15.31 N	23.25 E
Kulumadau	164	9.03 S	152.43 E
Kulunda	86	52.35 N	78.57 E
Kulunda ≃	86	52.59 N	79.48 E
Kulundinskaja step' ≍	86	53.00 N	79.00 E
Kulundinskoje, ozero ⊜	86	53.00 N	79.36 E
Kuluqi	89	50.23 N	124.13 E
Kulwin	166	35.02 S	142.33 E
Kum ≃	130	38.38 N	27.32 E
Kuma	96	33.39 N	132.54 E
Kuma ≃, Nihon	92	32.30 N	130.34 E
Kuma ≃, S.S.S.R.	72	44.56 N	47.00 E
Kuma ≃, S.S.S.R.	86	59.32 N	66.45 E
Kumagaya	94	36.08 N	139.23 E
Kumai, Indon.	112	3.23 S	112.33 E
Kumai, Indon.	112	2.44 S	111.43 E
Kumai, Teluk ⊂	112	3.00 S	111.43 E
Kumaishi	92a	42.08 N	139.59 E
Kumakanda	88	52.44 N	116.55 E
Kumalarang	116	7.44 N	123.08 E
Kumamba, Kepulauan ▮▮	164	1.36 S	138.45 E
Kumamoto	92	32.48 N	130.43 E
Kumamoto □ [5]	96	32.58 N	130.55 E
Kumano, Nihon	92	33.54 N	136.05 E
Kumano, Nihon	96	34.20 N	132.34 E
Kumano ≃	92	33.44 N	136.01 E
Kumano-nada ⫧ [2]	92	33.47 N	136.20 E
Kumanovo	38	42.08 N	21.43 E
Kumār ≃ [1], Bngl.	126	23.31 N	89.28 E
Kumār ≃ [1], Bngl.	126	23.11 N	90.10 E
Kumara, N.Z.	172	42.38 S	171.11 E
Kumara, S.S.S.R.	89	51.37 N	126.47 E
Kumārapālaiyam	122	11.28 N	77.43 E
Kumardhubi	126	23.48 N	86.43 E
Kumarganj	126	22.59 N	87.44 E
Kumārghāt	120	24.04 N	92.04 E
Kumārgrām	124	26.37 N	89.50 E
Kumāri ≃	126	22.57 N	86.48 E
Kumārkhāli	124	23.51 N	89.15 E
Kumarl	162	32.47 S	121.33 E
Kumasi	150	6.41 N	1.35 W
Kumatori	270	34.24 N	135.22 E
Kumawa, Pegunungan ✗	164	3.50 S	132.50 E
Kumba	152	4.38 N	9.25 E
Kumbakonam	122	10.58 N	79.23 E
Kumba Pits	156	18.45 S	24.45 E
Kumbar	140	12.03 N	30.16 E
Kumbarilla	166	27.19 S	150.53 E
Kumbe	164	8.21 S	140.13 E
Kumbel'	85	42.30 N	73.11 E
Kŭmch'ŏn	98	38.10 N	126.29 E
Kum-Dag	128	39.16 N	54.35 E
Kumdah ⫧ [4]	144	20.23 N	45.05 E
Kumdan ∧	123	35.09 N	77.35 E
Kumdanlı	130	38.19 N	30.59 E
Kume	96	35.03 N	133.54 E
Kume-jima ▮	93b	26.20 N	126.47 E
Kumenan	96	34.56 N	133.58 E
Kumeny	80	58.07 N	49.56 E
Kumertau	86	52.46 N	55.47 E
Kŭm-gang ≃	98	36.00 N	126.40 E
Kŭmgang-san ∧	98	38.35 N	128.10 E
Kŭmhwa	98	38.17 N	127.28 E
Kumi	154	1.29 N	33.56 E
Kumihama	96	35.36 N	134.55 E
Kuminovskoje	86	57.48 N	64.07 E
Kuminskij	86	58.40 N	66.04 E
Kumiyama	270	34.53 N	135.45 E
Kumizawa ◆ [8]	268	35.23 N	139.31 E
Kumköy ◆ [8]	267b	41.15 N	29.02 E
Kumla	40	59.08 N	15.08 E
Kumli	84	43.58 N	46.04 E
Kumlinge ▮	26	60.16 N	20.47 E
Kumluca, Tür.	130	36.22 N	30.18 E
Kumluca, Tür.	130	41.27 N	32.28 E
Kummelnäs	40	59.21 N	18.17 E
Kummerow	54	54.17 N	12.53 E
Kummerower See ⊜	54	53.49 N	12.52 E
Kümmersbruck	60	49.25 N	11.53 E
Kumo	146	10.03 N	11.13 E
Kŭmŏ-do ▮	98	34.31 N	127.45 E
Kumon Range ✗	102	26.30 N	97.15 E
Kumora	88	55.53 N	111.13 E
Kumosō-yama ∧	96	33.54 N	134.18 E
Kumotori-yama ∧	94	35.51 N	138.57 E
Kumphawapi	110	17.07 N	103.01 E
Kumrābād	126	24.10 N	87.16 E
Kumru	130	40.53 N	37.17 E
Kŭmsan	98	36.07 N	127.30 E
Kŭmsan-ni	98	37.55 N	125.41 E
Kumsenga	154	3.47 S	30.25 E
Kumta	122	14.25 N	74.24 E
Kumu	154	3.04 N	25.09 E
Kumu ≃	114	1.24 N	100.43 E
Kumuch	84	42.11 N	47.07 E
Kumukahi, Cape ≻	229d	19.31 N	154.49 W
Kumukuli	120	37.33 N	88.50 E
Kumusi ≃	164	8.35 S	148.00 E
Kümüx	86	42.14 N	88.11 E
Kumzār	128	26.20 N	56.25 E
Kuna	202	43.29 N	116.25 W
Kunar (Konar) ≃	123	34.25 N	70.32 E
Kunašak	86	55.43 N	61.36 E
Kunashiri-tō → Kunašir, ostrov ▮	92a	44.10 N	146.00 E
Kunašir, ostrov (Kunashiri-tō) ▮	92a	44.10 N	146.00 E
Kun'batar	84	44.17 N	45.34 E
Kuncheng Hu ⊜	106	31.35 N	120.45 E
Kunchhā	124	28.08 N	84.20 E
Kunc'ovo ◆ [8]	265b	55.44 N	37.26 E
Kunda, S.S.S.R.	76	59.29 N	26.32 E
Kunda, Zaïre	154	3.57 S	26.35 E
Kunda Hills ✗ [2]	122	11.10 N	76.30 E
Kundahit	126	23.58 N	87.10 E
Kundam	124	23.13 N	80.21 E
Kundāpura	122	13.38 N	74.42 E
Kundar ≃	120	31.56 N	69.19 E
Kundat	86	55.14 N	87.51 E
Kundelungu, Parc National de ♠	154	10.30 S	27.45 E
Kunderu ≃	122	14.38 N	78.42 E
Kundi	154	1.08 S	40.41 E
Kundiān	123	32.27 N	71.28 E
Kundiawa	164	6.00 S	145.00 E
Kundima	164	4.14 S	143.52 E
Kundl	64	47.28 N	11.59 E
Kundla	120	21.20 N	71.18 E
Kundr'učje ≃	83	47.52 N	40.15 E
Kundur, Pulau ▮	112	0.45 N	103.26 E
Kunene (Cunene) ≃	152	17.20 S	11.50 E
Kunersdorf, Forst ◆ [3]	264a	52.17 N	12.59 E
Kunes	24	70.21 N	26.31 E
Künes ≃	86	43.55 N	80.55 E
Kunga ≃ [1]	126	21.45 N	89.30 E
Kungälv	26	57.52 N	11.58 E
Kungana	146	7.50 N	10.42 E
Kungchuling → Huaide	89	43.32 N	124.50 E
Kungej-Alatau, chrebet ✗	85	42.50 N	77.00 E
Kunggyü Yumco ⊜	124	30.35 N	82.09 E
Kunghit Island ▮	182	52.06 N	131.04 W
Kunghsi	100	24.37 N	121.16 E
Kung-pei-tien	269d	25.06 N	121.38 E
Kungrad	86	43.06 N	58.54 E
Kungsängen	40	59.29 N	17.45 E
Kungsängen flygplats ⊠	40	58.36 N	16.15 E
Kungsbacka	26	57.29 N	12.04 E
Kungsgården	40	60.36 N	16.37 E
Kungshamn	26	58.22 N	11.15 E
Kungsör	40	59.25 N	16.05 E
Kungu	152	2.47 N	19.12 E
Kungur	86	57.25 N	56.57 E
Kunhār ≃	123	34.17 N	73.29 E
Kunhegyes	30	47.22 N	20.38 E
Kunhing	110	21.18 N	98.26 E
Kuni	94	36.35 N	138.38 E
Kunia	229c	21.29 N	158.07 W
Kunigami	174m	26.45 N	128.10 E
Kunimi	96	33.41 N	131.36 E
Kuningan	115a	6.59 S	108.29 E
Kunisaki	96	33.33 N	131.45 E
Kunisaki-hantō ≻ [1]	96	33.30 N	131.40 E
Kunitachi	268	35.41 N	139.26 E
Kuni Vyselki	82	54.18 N	38.41 E
Kunja	76	56.18 N	30.59 E
Kunja ≃, S.S.S.R.	76	57.09 N	31.10 E
Kunja ≃, S.S.S.R.	82	56.31 N	38.12 E
Kunjāh	123	32.32 N	73.59 E
Kunje	83	49.23 N	37.15 E
Kunkle	216	41.38 N	84.30 W
Kunkletown	210	40.51 N	75.27 W
Kunkuri	124	22.45 N	83.57 E
Kunlong	110	23.25 N	98.39 E
Kunlun Shan ✗	120	36.30 N	88.00 E
Kunming	102	25.05 N	102.40 E
Kunming Hu ⊜	271a	39.59 N	116.15 E
Kunmunya Aboriginal Reserve ◆ [4]	164	15.45 S	124.45 E
Kunnamkulam	122	10.39 N	76.05 E
Kunost'	76	60.01 N	37.38 E
Kunovice	30	49.03 N	17.29 E
Kunow	54	53.00 N	12.07 E
Kunowice	54	52.20 N	14.50 E
Kunrau	54	52.35 N	11.01 E
Kunsan	98	35.58 N	126.41 E
Kunshan	106	31.23 N	120.57 E
Kunszentmárton	30	46.51 N	20.18 E
Kuntair	150	13.32 N	16.13 W
Kuntaur	150	13.40 N	14.48 W
Kuntiki	86	58.29 N	76.24 E
Kunting	100	29.48 N	121.56 E
Kuntshankoie	152	3.20 S	23.34 E
Kuntuolun	102	45.13 N	115.21 E
Kununurra	164	15.47 S	128.44 E
Kunwi	98	36.15 N	128.34 E
Kunya	150	12.14 N	8.34 E
Kunyo	144	6.17 N	42.33 E
Kunžak	61	49.07 N	15.11 E
Künzell	56	50.33 N	9.42 E
Künzelsau	56	49.16 N	9.41 E
Künzing	60	48.40 N	13.05 E
Kunzulu	152	3.29 S	16.09 E
Kuocang Shan ✗	100	28.36 N	120.30 E
Kuohsing	100	24.02 N	120.51 E
Kuokegan	120	37.30 N	89.55 E
Kuolajarvi	24	66.58 N	29.12 E
Kuop ▮ [1]	175c	7.03 N	151.56 E
Kuopio	26	62.54 N	27.41 E
Kuopion lääni □ [4]	26	63.00 N	27.30 E
Kuortane	26	62.48 N	23.30 E
Kupa ≃	36	45.28 N	16.24 E
Kup'abal	271b	37.37 N	126.54 E
Kupang	112	10.10 S	123.35 E
Kupang, Teluk ⊂	112	10.04 S	123.40 E
Kup'ansk	83	49.42 N	37.38 E
Kupanskoje	82	56.51 N	38.43 E
Kup'ansk-Uzlovoj	83	49.39 N	37.39 E
Kuparuk ≃	180	70.25 N	148.55 W
Kupava	80	51.07 N	42.57 E
Kupavna	265b	55.45 N	38.08 E
Kuper Island ▮	224	48.58 N	123.39 W
Kupferberg	263	51.09 N	7.27 E
Kupferdreh ◆ [8]	263	51.23 N	7.05 E
Kupfermühle	41	54.50 N	9.24 E
Kupferzell	56	49.14 N	9.41 E
Kupiano	164	10.05 S	148.11 E
Kupičev	78	51.00 N	24.44 E
Kupino	86	54.22 N	77.18 E
Kupiškis	76	55.50 N	24.58 E
Küplü, Tür.	130	41.07 N	26.21 E
Küplü, Tür.	130	40.06 N	30.00 E
Kupol, gora ∧	180	68.38 N	174.45 E
Kuppenheim	56	48.49 N	8.15 E
Kupper Airport ⊠	276	40.31 N	74.36 W
Kupreanof	180	56.49 N	132.57 W
Kupreanof Island ▮	180	56.50 N	133.30 W
Kupreanof Point ≻	180	55.34 N	159.35 W
Kupres	36	44.00 N	17.17 E
Küps	54	50.11 N	11.16 E
Kupuri	89	54.44 N	130.30 E
Kur ≃	89	48.44 N	134.14 E
Kur, Pulau ▮	164	5.20 S	132.00 E
Kura (Kuruçay) ≃	84	39.24 N	49.19 E
Kura ≃	84	44.06 N	44.57 E
Kurabuchi	94	36.25 N	138.48 E
Kur'ačeje	83	48.10 N	39.37 E
Kur'ačevka, S.S.S.R.	83	49.39 N	38.42 E
Kur'ačevka, S.S.S.R.	83	49.22 N	39.36 E
Kurach	84	41.36 N	47.46 E
Kurach ≃	84	41.40 N	48.11 E
Kurachovka	83	48.02 N	37.23 E
Kurachovo	83	47.59 N	37.16 E
Kuragaty	85	43.06 N	72.59 E
Kuragaty ≃	85	43.57 N	73.34 E
Kuragino	86	53.53 N	92.40 E
Kurahashi	96	34.06 N	132.30 E
Kurahashi-jima ▮	96	34.08 N	132.31 E
Kuraj	86	56.42 N	95.29 E
Kurajlysaj	80	50.07 N	51.51 E
Kurakaki	270	34.59 N	135.28 E
Kurakino, S.S.S.R.	80	52.33 N	44.03 E

≃	River	Fluß	Río	Rivière	Rio	✣	Submarine Features	Untermeerische Objekte	Accidentes Submarinos	Formes de relief sous-marin	Acidentes submarinos
≍	Canal	Kanal	Canal	Canal	Canal	□	Political Unit	Politische Einheit	Unidad Politica	Entité politique	Unidade política
∟	Waterfall, Rapids	Wasserfall, Stromschnellen	Cascada, Rápidos	Chute d'eau, Rapides	Cascata, Rápidos	ᴥ	Cultural Institution	Kulturelle Institution	Institución Cultural	Institution culturelle	Instituição cultural
ʊ	Strait	Meeresstraße	Estrecho	Détroit	Estreito	⊥	Historical Site	Historische Stätte	Sitio Histórico	Site historique	Sitio histórico
⊂	Bay, Gulf	Bucht, Golf	Bahía, Golfo	Baie, Golfe	Baía, Golfo	♠	Recreational Site	Erholungs- und Ferienort	Sitio de Recreo	Centre de loisirs	Area de Lazer
⊜	Lake, Lakes	See, Seen	Lago, Lagos	Lac, Lacs	Lago, Lagos	⊠	Airport	Flughafen	Aeropuerto	Aéroport	Aeroporto
≣	Swamp	Sumpf	Pantano	Marais	Pântano	■	Military Installation	Militäranlage	Instalación Militar	Installation militaire	Instalação militar
⊓	Ice Features, Glacier	Eis- und Gletscherformen	Accidentes Glaciales	Formes glaciaires	Acidentes glaciares	◆	Miscellaneous	Verschiedenes	Misceláneo	Divers	Diversos
⫧	Other Hydrographic Features	Andere Hydrographische Objekte	Otros Elementos Hidrográficos	Autres données hydrographiques	Outros acidentes hidrográficos						

Kurakino, S.S.S.R. 82 54.30 N 35.48 E
Kurakovo 82 54.05 N 37.14 E
Kūrāli 123 30.50 N 76.35 E
Kuram 85 43.33 N 78.08 E
Kuramā', Ḥarrat ⊥[9] 128 24.30 N 40.15 E
Kurama-yama ∧ 96 35.07 N 135.46 E
Kuraminskij chrebet ⋏ 85 40.45 N 70.10 E
Kuramo Waters C 273a 6.26 N 3.26 E
Kuranami 268 35.27 N 140.00 E
Kuraon 124 24.59 N 82.05 E
Kurar ◆[8] 272c 19.11 N 72.52 E
Kurašasaj 86 50.18 N 56.55 E
Kurashiki 96 34.35 N 133.46 E
Kurasiki
→ Kurashiki 96 34.35 N 133.46 E
Kurate 96 33.47 N 130.41 E
Kurauli 124 27.24 N 78.59 E
Kuraymah 140 18.33 N 31.51 E
Kurayoshi 96 35.26 N 133.49 E
Kurayyimah 132 32.16 N 35.36 E
Kurba 80 57.34 N 39.32 E
Kurba ≃ 88 52.02 N 108.30 E
Kurbağa Gölü ⊜ 130 38.21 N 35.17 E
Kurbağalı ≃ 267b 40.59 N 29.02 E
Kurbatovo 86 55.34 N 91.10 E
Kurbulik 88 53.45 N 108.57 E
Kurčaloj 84 43.12 N 46.05 E
Kurchatov 78 51.39 N 35.36 E
Kur-Čilik ≃ 85 43.50 N 78.06 E
Kurčum 86 48.37 N 83.40 E
Kurdaj 85 43.21 N 74.59 E
K'urdamir 84 40.21 N 48.08 E
Kurdgelauri 84 41.58 N 45.32 E
Kurdistan □[9] 128 37.00 N 45.00 E
Kurdufān al-Janūbīyah □[4] 140 11.00 N 30.00 E
Kurdufān ash-Shamālīyah □[4] 140 14.00 N 29.45 E
Kurd'umovka 83 48.28 N 37.59 E
Kurduvādi 122 18.05 N 75.26 E
Kure, Austl. 164 15.27 S 124.33 E
Kure, Nihon 96 34.14 N 132.34 E
Küre, Tür. 130 41.48 N 33.43 E
Kure Atoll I[1] 14 28.25 N 178.25 W
Küre Dağları ⋏ 130 41.45 N 34.00 E
Kurejka ≃ 74 66.30 N 87.12 E
Kurejskaja 88 58.56 N 111.20 E
Kuren' 78 51.09 N 32.44 E
Kurenalus 26 65.21 N 26.59 E
Kurenec 76 54.33 N 26.57 E
Kuressaare 76 58.15 N 22.28 E
Kurgal'džinskij 86 50.36 N 70.01 E
Kurgan 86 55.26 N 65.18 E
Kurgan Mečetnyj, gora ∧[2] 83 48.06 N 39.21 E
Kurgan-T'ube 120 37.50 N 68.48 E
Kurgasyn 86 49.15 N 66.43 E
Kurgatej 88 54.23 N 99.27 E
Kurgolovo 76 59.46 N 28.06 E
Kuria I 14 0.14 N 173.25 E
Kuria Muria Islands → Khurīyā Murīyā, Jazā'ir II 118 17.30 N 56.00 E
Kuriasol 126 22.06 N 86.39 E
Kuridala 166 21.17 S 140.30 E
Kurīgrām 124 25.49 N 89.39 E
Kurihama 268 35.13 N 139.43 E
Kurihashi 94 36.08 N 139.42 E
Kurikka 26 62.37 N 22.25 E
Kurilen → Kuril'skije ostrova II 74 46.10 N 152.00 E
Kurilen-Strasse → Pervyj Kuril'skij proliv ⊻ 74 50.50 N 156.36 E
Kuriles, Islas → Kuril'skije ostrova II 74 46.10 N 152.00 E
Kuril Islands → Kuril'skije ostrova II 74 46.10 N 152.00 E
Kurilovka 80 50.44 N 48.02 E
Kuril'sk 74 45.14 N 147.53 E
Kuril'skije ostrova (Kuril Islands) II 74 46.10 N 152.00 E
Kuril Strait → Pervyj Kuril'skij proliv ⊻ 74 50.50 N 156.36 E
Kuril Trench ◆[1] 6 47.00 N 155.00 E
Kuřim 30 49.18 N 16.32 E
Kurimoto 94 35.49 N 140.30 E
Ku-Ring-Gai Chase National Park ♦ 170 33.38 S 151.15 E
Kurinjippadi 122 11.34 N 79.36 E
Kurinskaja kosa ≻[2] 84 39.03 N 49.13 E
Kurinwás ≃ 236 12.49 N 83.41 W
Kuripapango 172 39.23 S 176.21 E
Kuriyama, Nihon 92a 43.03 N 141.47 E
Kuriyama, Nihon 94 36.52 N 139.37 E
Kurja, S.S.S.R. 24 61.42 N 57.09 E
Kurja, S.S.S.R. 86 51.36 N 82.19 E
Kurjanovskaja 76 60.19 N 41.33 E
Kurkijoki 26 61.18 N 29.54 E
Kurkino, S.S.S.R. 76 53.26 N 38.40 E
Kurkino, S.S.S.R. 265b 55.53 N 37.23 E
Kurkliai 76 55.25 N 25.03 E
Kurl ◆[8] 263 51.35 N 7.35 E
Kurla ◆[8] 272c 19.05 N 72.53 E
Kurlackoje 83 47.21 N 39.03 E
Kurleja 88 52.11 N 119.11 E
Kurlin 80 51.48 N 51.00 E
Kurlovskij 80 55.27 N 40.36 E
Kurmanajevka, S.S.S.R. 80 49.53 N 42.36 E
Kurmanajevka, S.S.S.R. 80 52.31 N 52.06 E
Kurmani 126 22.47 N 89.53 E
Kurmankol' 80 49.09 N 48.27 E
Kurmenty 85 42.48 N 78.15 E
Kurmuk 140 10.33 N 34.17 E
Kurnell 274a 34.01 S 151.13 E
Kurnell Peninsula ≻[1] 274a 34.02 S 15.11 E
Kurnool 122 15.50 N 78.03 E
Kurobane 94 36.51 N 140.07 E
Kurobe 94 36.51 N 137.26 E
Kurobe ≃ 94 36.55 N 137.25 E
Kurobe-dam ◆[6] 94 36.36 N 137.38 E
Kurodashō 96 35.01 N 135.00 E
Kurogi 96 33.12 N 130.40 E
Kurohone 94 36.30 N 139.17 E
Kuroishi 92 40.38 N 140.36 E
Kuroiso 94 36.58 N 140.03 E
Kuroo-tōge)(96 35.11 N 134.12 E
Kuropatkino, S.S.S.R. 80 46.32 N 45.20 E
Kuropatkino, S.S.S.R. 85 39.57 N 67.27 E
Kurort-Darasun 88 51.12 N 113.44 E
Kurose 96 34.19 N 132.40 E
Kurose ≃ 96 34.13 N 132.36 E
Kuro-shima I, Nihon 93b 30.50 N 129.57 E
Kuro-shima I, Nihon 175d 24.19 N 124.05 E
Kurosu 268 35.51 N 139.23 E
Kurovo 82 55.49 N 36.00 E
Kurovskoje 82 55.34 N 38.55 E
Kurow 172 44.44 S 170.28 E
Kuroya 268 35.55 N 139.44 E
Kurrajong 170 33.33 S 150.40 E
Kurram 120 30.06 N 66.31 E
Kurram ≃ 123 32.36 N 71.20 E
Kurri Kurri 170 32.49 S 151.29 E
Kuršab ≃ 85 40.46 N 73.06 E
Kursavka 84 44.28 N 42.31 E
Kursela 124 25.27 N 87.15 E
Kuršėnai 76 56.00 N 22.56 E
Kurseong 120 26.53 N 88.17 E
Kursk 78 51.42 N 36.12 E
Kursk □[4] 76 52.14 N 35.30 E
Kurskaja 84 44.03 N 44.27 E
Kurskaja kosa ≻[2] 76 55.18 N 21.00 E
Kurskij zaliv C 76 55.00 N 21.00 E
Kursk Station ◆[5] 265b 55.46 N 37.40 E
Kuršumlija 38 43.08 N 21.17 E
Kurşunlu, Tür. 130 40.51 N 33.16 E
Kurşunlu, Tür. 130 38.40 N 37.51 E
Kurtalan 130 37.57 N 41.42 E
Kurtamyš 86 54.55 N 64.27 E
Kurtatsch → Cortaccia 64 46.19 N 11.13 E
Kürten, B.R.D. 56 51.03 N 7.16 E
Kurten, Tx., U.S. 222 30.47 N 96.16 W
Kurthasanlı 130 38.20 N 32.11 E
Kurth Lake ⊜ 222 31.26 N 94.42 W
Kūrtī 140 18.07 N 31.33 E
Kurtino 82 54.59 N 38.17 E
Kurtinskoje vodochranilišče ⊜[1] 85 43.50 N 76.20 E
Kurtistown 229d 19.36 N 155.03 W
Kurtoğlu Burnu ≻ 130 36.35 N 28.50 E
Kurtušibinskij chrebet ⋏ 88 52.10 N 93.30 E
Kurty ≃ 85 44.05 N 76.20 E
Kurtz 218 38.58 N 86.12 W
Kuru, Sūd. 140 7.43 N 26.31 E
Kuru, Suomi 26 61.52 N 23.44 E
Kuru ≃ 140 9.08 N 26.57 E
Kurucaşile 130 41.50 N 32.43 E
Kuruçay 130 39.39 N 38.29 E
Kuruçay (Kura) ≃ 84 39.24 N 49.19 E
Kuruçeşme ◆[8] 267b 41.03 N 29.02 E
Kuruktag ⋏ 90 41.30 N 90.00 E
Kurum 164 4.45 S 145.55 E
Kuruman 158 27.28 S 23.28 E
Kuruman ≃ 158 26.56 S 20.39 E
Kurumanheuwels ⋏[2] 158 27.40 S 23.25 E
Kurumdy, gora ∧ 85 39.28 N 73.32 E
Kurume 96 33.19 N 130.31 E
Kurumkan 88 54.18 N 110.18 E
Kurun ≃ 144 5.30 N 34.17 E
Kurunegala 122 7.29 N 80.22 E
Kurungbaja, Tanjung ≻ 115b 8.15 S 120.35 E
Kurung Tank ⊜[1] 124 22.19 N 82.14 E
Kurunzulaj 88 51.00 N 117.10 E
Kuruqi 89 48.58 N 123.50 E
Kurur, Jabal ∧ 140 20.31 N 31.32 E
Kurusaj 85 40.35 N 69.24 E
Kurushima-kaikyo ⊻ 96 34.07 N 133.00 E
Kuruson-zan ∧ 96 34.12 N 130.58 E
Kurylys 86 48.38 N 60.47 E
Kuryongp'o 98 35.59 N 129.32 E
Kurzeme □[9] 76 56.50 N 22.30 E
Kusa 86 55.20 N 59.29 E
Kusabe 270 34.31 N 135.29 E
Kuşadası 130 37.51 N 27.15 E
Kuşadası Körfezi C 130 37.50 N 27.08 E
Kusak ≃ 86 47.50 N 75.45 E
Kušalino 76 57.07 N 36.05 E
Kusan-ni, Taehan 98 37.43 N 128.49 E
Kusan-ni, Taehan 271b 37.29 N 126.45 E
Kusatsu, Nihon 94 36.37 N 138.36 E
Kusatsu, Nihon 94 35.00 N 135.57 E
Kusawa Lake ⊜ 180 60.20 N 136.15 W
Kusaybah, Bi'r ⊤[4] 140 22.41 N 29.55 E
Kuščovskaja 78 46.33 N 39.37 E
Kuse 96 35.04 N 133.45 E
Kusel 56 49.32 N 7.24 E
Kušen'ki 78 48.53 N 34.07 E
Kusey 54 52.36 N 11.05 E
Kuş Gölü ⊜ 130 40.10 N 27.57 E
Kuş Gölü Milli Parkı ♦ 130 40.15 N 27.55 E
Kushaka 150 10.32 N 6.48 E
Kushālgarh 120 23.10 N 74.27 E
Kusheriki 150 10.33 N 6.28 E
Kushi 174m 26.33 N 128.06 E
Kushida ≃ 94 34.36 N 136.34 E
Kushigata 94 35.36 N 138.28 E
Kushihiki 268 35.55 N 139.36 E
Kushikino 92 31.44 N 130.16 E
Kushima 92 31.29 N 131.14 E
Kushimoto 92 33.28 N 135.47 E
Kushira 270 34.28 N 135.43 E
Kushiro 92a 42.58 N 144.23 E
Kushog Lake ⊜ 212 45.05 N 78.48 W
Kushtia 124 23.55 N 89.07 E
Kushui 102 42.11 N 94.25 E
Kusiro → Kushiro 92a 42.58 N 144.23 E
Kusiyāra ≃ 120 24.36 N 91.44 E
Kuška 128 35.16 N 62.20 E
Kuška ≃ 128 36.00 N 62.40 E
Kuskokwim ≃ 180 60.17 N 162.27 W
Kuskokwim, North Fork ≃ 180 63.06 N 154.37 W
Kuskokwim, South Fork ≃ 180 63.06 N 154.37 W
Kuskokwim Bay C 180 59.45 N 162.25 W
Kuskokwim Mountains ⋏ 180 62.30 N 156.00 W
Kuskovo ◆[8] 265b 55.44 N 37.49 E
Kuškušara 24 64.58 N 40.21 E
Kuśmā 124 28.14 N 83.41 E
Kušmurun 86 52.27 N 64.36 E
Kušmurun, ozero ⊜ 86 52.40 N 64.48 E
Küsnacht 58 47.19 N 8.35 E
Kušnarenkovo 86 55.06 N 55.22 E
Kušnica 78 48.27 N 23.14 E
Kusŏng 98 39.59 N 125.15 E
Kusria 272b 22.58 N 88.14 E
Kussharo-ko ⊜ 92a 43.38 N 144.21 E
Küssnacht am Rigi 58 47.05 N 8.27 E
Kustanaj 86 53.10 N 63.35 E
Kustanajskaja □[4] 86 52.20 N 63.40 E
Kustar'ovka 80 54.16 N 42.16 E
Küsten-Gebirge → Coast Mountains ⋏ 176 55.00 N 129.00 W
Küstenkanal ☰ 52 52.57 N 7.18 E
Küsten-Ketten → Coast Ranges ⋏ 178 41.00 N 123.30 W
Kusthalia 126 23.29 N 87.03 E
Kūstī 140 13.10 N 32.40 E
Küstrin → Kostrzyn 30 52.37 N 14.39 E
Kusu, Nihon 94 34.55 N 136.38 E
Kusu, Nihon 96 33.16 N 131.09 E
Kušugum 78 47.42 N 35.14 E
Kušum ≃ 80 48.54 N 50.32 E
Kusumba 272b 22.27 N 88.24 E
Kusumbāni ∧ 126 21.57 N 86.26 E
Kušumskij 80 51.38 N 48.21 E
Kusung 98 36.18 N 128.55 E
Kusunoki 96 34.03 N 131.15 E
K'us'ur 74 70.39 N 127.15 E
Kušva 86 58.18 N 59.45 E
Kut, Ko I 110 11.40 N 102.35 E
Kuta 150 9.52 N 6.43 E
Kuta ≃ 88 56.46 N 105.40 E
Kutabaru 112 0.44 S 102.56 E
Kutabuloh 114 3.28 N 97.04 E
Kutacane 114 3.30 N 97.48 E
Kütahya 130 39.25 N 29.59 E
Kütahya □[4] 130 39.20 N 29.30 E
Kutais 78 44.32 N 39.18 E
Kutaisi 84 42.15 N 42.40 E
Kutāmat al-Ghābah 142 30.55 N 30.54 E
Kutanibong 114 3.53 N 96.22 E
Kutaradja → Banda Aceh 114 5.34 N 95.20 E
Kutarere 172 38.03 S 177.09 E
Kutasawang 114 5.08 N 96.54 E
Kutch, Rann of (Rann of Kachchh) ◆[1] 120 24.05 N 70.10 E
Kutchan 92a 42.54 N 140.45 E
Kutcharo-ko ⊜ 92a 45.09 N 142.19 E
Kutejnikovo, S.S.S.R. 83 47.49 N 38.18 E
Kutejnikovo, S.S.S.R. 83 47.34 N 39.46 E
Kutenholz 52 53.29 N 9.19 E
Kutima 88 57.10 N 108.16 E
Kutima ≃ 88 57.08 N 108.14 E
Kutina 36 45.29 N 16.46 E
Kutiyāna 120 21.38 N 69.59 E
Kutkai 110 23.27 N 97.56 E
Kutkašen 84 40.59 N 47.50 E
Kutluškino 80 55.14 N 50.24 E
Kutná Hora 30 49.57 N 15.16 E
Kutno 30 52.15 N 19.23 E
Kutoarjo 115a 7.43 S 109.54 E
Kutomara 88 51.06 N 118.49 E
Kutse Game Reserve ◆[4] 156 23.30 S 24.05 E
Kutsuki 94 35.21 N 135.55 E
Küttigen 58 47.25 N 8.03 E
Kuttura 24 68.24 N 26.28 E
Kuttusoja 24 67.46 N 28.50 E
Kuttuzi 265a 59.45 N 30.04 E
Kutu 152 2.44 S 18.09 E
Kutubdia Island I 120 21.50 N 91.52 E
Kutubu, Lake ⊜ 164 6.23 S 143.18 E
Kutukovo 80 54.26 N 40.31 E
Kutulik 88 53.21 N 102.48 E
Kutulo, Lagh ≃ 154 2.08 N 40.56 E
Kutuluk ≃ 80 53.19 N 51.09 E
Kutum 140 14.12 N 24.40 E
Kutu-Moke 152 3.12 S 17.21 E
Kúty, Česko. 30 48.40 N 17.03 E
Kuty, S.S.S.R. 78 48.16 N 25.10 E
Kutztown 210 40.31 N 75.46 W
Kuujjuaq 176 58.06 N 68.25 W
Kuuli-Majak 128 40.14 N 52.42 E
Kuurne 50 50.51 N 3.17 E
Kuusamo 26 65.58 N 29.11 E
Kuusankoski 26 60.54 N 26.38 E
Kuva 85 40.32 N 72.05 E
Kuvak-Nikol'skoje 80 53.37 N 43.30 E
Kuvandyk 86 51.28 N 57.21 E
Kuvango 152 14.28 S 16.20 E
Kuvasaj 85 40.18 N 71.58 E
Kuvet ≃ 180 69.14 N 175.00 E
Kuvšinovo 76 57.02 N 34.10 E
Kuwabara 270 34.53 N 135.15 E
Kuwait → Al-Kuwayt 128 29.20 N 47.59 E
Kuwait (Al-Kuwayt) □[1], Asia 118 29.30 N 47.45 E
Kuwait (Al-Kuwayt) □[1], Asia 128 29.30 N 47.45 E
Kuwait Bay → Kuwayt, Jūn al- C 128 29.30 N 48.00 E
Kuwana 94 35.04 N 136.42 E
Kuwayt, Jūn al- (Kuwait Bay) C 128 29.30 N 48.00 E
Kuyāli 126 22.31 N 86.11 E
Kuybyshev → Kujbyšev 80 53.12 N 50.09 E
Kuye ≃ 102 38.30 N 110.44 E
Kūysanjaq 128 36.05 N 44.38 E
Kuyucak, Tür. 130 37.51 N 38.21 E
Kuyucak, Tür. 130 37.55 N 28.28 E
Kuyuwini ≃ 246 2.16 N 58.16 W
Kuyuyukak, Cape ≻ 180 56.54 N 156.50 W
Kuzaranda 24 62.22 N 35.37 E
Kuze 94 35.33 N 136.30 E
Kuze ◆[8] 270 34.57 N 135.43 E
Kuzedejevo 86 53.20 N 87.10 E
Kuzemin 78 50.09 N 34.39 E
Kuzemovka 83 49.31 N 37.59 E
Kužener 80 56.48 N 48.56 E
Kuženkino 76 57.44 N 33.59 E
Kuzitrin ≃ 180 65.10 N 165.28 W
Kuzkejevo 80 55.46 N 52.48 E
Kuz'miniči 76 54.16 N 33.42 E
Kuz'minka ≃ 265a 59.48 N 30.31 E
Kuz'minki ◆[8] 265b 55.42 N 37.48 E
Kuz'mino, S.S.S.R. 82 55.09 N 37.53 E
Kuz'mino, S.S.S.R. 82 56.36 N 37.55 E
Kuzmiščevo 82 54.46 N 37.12 E
Kuz'movka 74 62.19 N 92.02 E
Kuznečicha 80 54.43 N 49.38 E
Kuznečikovo 82 56.13 N 36.35 E
Kuzneck, S.S.S.R. 80 53.07 N 46.36 E
Kuzneck → Novokuzneck, S.S.S.R. 86 53.45 N 87.06 E
Kuzneckij Alatau ⋏ 86 54.45 N 88.00 E
Kuznečnoje 26 61.09 N 29.52 E
Kuznecova 89 46.16 N 138.03 E
Kuznecovka 76 56.18 N 28.33 E
Kuznecovo, S.S.S.R. 82 55.30 N 38.21 E
Kuznecovo, S.S.S.R. 82 55.27 N 36.57 E
Kuznecovo, S.S.S.R. 86 59.15 N 63.28 E
Kuznecovo-Michajlovka 83 47.27 N 38.13 E
Kuznecovskij 80 47.25 N 40.57 E
Kuznecy 82 55.51 N 38.40 E
Kuznetsk → Kuzneck 80 53.07 N 46.36 E
Kuznetsovsk 78 51.22 N 25.53 E
Kuzomen', S.S.S.R. 24 66.17 N 36.54 E
Kuzomen', S.S.S.R. 24 64.17 N 42.53 E
Kuzovatovo 80 53.33 N 47.41 E
Kuzucubelen 130 36.51 N 34.27 E
Kuzuha 270 34.52 N 135.41 E
Kuzuryū ≃ 94 36.13 N 136.08 E
Kuzuu 94 36.24 N 139.37 E
Kuzyaka 130 41.14 N 33.44 E
Kvænangen C[2] 24 70.05 N 21.13 E
Kværndrup 41 55.10 N 10.32 E
Kvaisi 84 42.31 N 43.40 E
Kvaløy I 24 69.40 N 18.30 E
Kvaløya I 24 70.37 N 23.52 E
Kvam 26 61.40 N 9.42 E
Kvanløse 41 55.39 N 11.41 E
Kvanndal 26 60.29 N 6.36 E
Kvareli 84 41.56 N 45.54 E
Kvarner C 36 44.45 N 14.15 E
Kvarnerić ⊻ 36 44.45 N 14.35 E
Kvarnsveden 40 60.31 N 15.24 E
Kvarntorp 40 59.08 N 15.15 E
Kvarsa 80 56.58 N 53.57 E
Kvarsebo 40 58.39 N 16.39 E
Kvašenki 82 56.48 N 37.33 E
Kvenna ≃ 26 60.01 N 7.56 E
Kverkfjöll ∧ 24a 64.43 N 16.38 W
Kvichak Bay C 180 58.48 N 157.30 W
Kvicksund 40 59.27 N 16.19 E
Kvidinge 41 56.08 N 13.04 E
Kvien ⊜ 40 60.24 N 13.48 E
Kvikkjokk 24 66.55 N 17.50 E
Kvilda 60 49.01 N 13.35 E
Kvina ≃ 26 58.17 N 6.56 E
Kvismare kanal ☰ 40 59.12 N 15.11 E
Kvissleby 26 62.17 N 17.21 E
Kvistbro 40 59.09 N 14.49 E
Kvistgård 41 55.59 N 12.30 E
Kvitok 88 56.03 N 98.30 E
Kwa ≃ 152 3.10 S 16.11 E
Kwachaga 154 5.38 S 38.08 E
Kwada 164 6.09 S 141.53 E
Kwahae-ri ◆[8] 271b 37.33 N 126.50 E
Kwahu Plateau ⋏[1] 150 6.30 N 0.30 W
Kwai → Khwae Noi ≃ 110 14.00 N 99.33 E
Kwajalein I[1] 14 9.05 N 167.20 E
Kwajok 140 8.19 N 28.00 E
Kwakoegron 250 5.15 N 55.20 W
Kwale, Kenya 154 4.11 S 39.27 E
Kwale, Nig. 150 5.46 N 6.26 E
Kwambilo ≃ 273b 4.26 S 15.20 E
Kwa-Mbonambi 158 28.36 S 32.05 E
Kwamisa ∧ 150 7.08 N 1.53 W
Kwamouth 152 3.10 S 16.12 E
Kwa Mtoro 154 5.14 S 35.26 E
Kwanak-san ∧ 271b 37.27 N 126.58 E
Kwando (Cuando) ≃ 152 18.27 S 23.32 E
Kwangchow → Guangzhou 100 23.06 N 113.16 E
Kwangju 98 35.09 N 126.54 E
Kwangju □[4] 98 35.09 N 126.55 E
Kwango (Cuango) ≃ 152 3.14 S 17.23 E
Kwangsi Chuang Autonomous Region → Guangxi Zhuangzu Zizhiqu □[4] 102 24.00 N 109.00 E
Kwangtung → Guangdong □[4] 90 23.00 N 113.00 E
Kwangwazi 154 7.47 S 38.15 E
Kwangyang 98 34.59 N 127.34 E
Kwania, Lake ⊜ 154 1.45 N 32.45 E
Kwanmo-bong ∧ 98 41.42 N 129.13 E
Kwansan-ni 271b 37.43 N 126.51 E
Kwanto Plain → Kantō-heiya ≚ 94 36.00 N 139.30 E
Kwara □[3] 150 8.45 N 5.00 E
Kware 150 13.12 N 5.14 E
Kwa-Thema 273d 26.18 S 28.23 E
Kwatisore 164 3.15 S 134.57 E
Kweichow → Guizhou □[4] 102 27.00 N 107.00 E
Kweihwa → Hohhot 102 40.51 N 111.40 E
Kweijang → Guiyang 102 26.35 N 106.43 E
Kweilin → Guilin 102 25.17 N 110.17 E
Kweisui → Hohhot 102 40.51 N 111.40 E
Kweiyang → Guiyang 102 26.35 N 106.43 E
Kwekwe 154 18.55 S 29.49 E
Kweneng □[5] 156 24.00 S 24.00 E
Kwenge (Caengo) ≃ 152 4.50 S 18.42 E
Kwesimintim 150 4.54 N 1.47 W
Kwethluk 180 60.49 N 161.27 W
Kwethluk ≃ 180 60.46 N 161.26 W
Kwidzyn 30 53.45 N 18.56 E
Kwigillingok 180 59.51 N 163.08 W
Kwiguk 180 62.45 N 164.28 W
Kwiha 144 13.31 N 39.32 E
Kwikila 164 9.48 S 147.41 E
Kwilu (Cuilo) ≃ 152 3.22 S 17.22 E
Kwinana 168a 32.15 S 115.48 E
Kwitaro ≃ 246 3.19 N 58.47 W
Kwobrup 162 33.37 S 117.46 E
Kwoka, Gunung ∧ 164 0.31 S 132.27 E
Kwolla 150 9.00 N 9.15 E
Kwun Tong 271d 22.19 N 114.12 E
Kyabé 146 9.27 N 18.57 E
Kyabra 166 26.18 S 143.10 E
Kyabra Creek ≃ 166 25.36 S 142.55 E
Kyabram 166 36.19 S 145.03 E
Kyaikkami 110 16.04 N 97.34 E
Kyaiklat 110 16.26 N 95.44 E
Kyaikto 110 17.18 N 97.01 E
Kya-in 110 16.02 N 98.08 E
Kyaka 154 1.16 S 31.25 E
Kyalite 166 34.57 S 143.29 E
Kyancutta 166 33.08 S 135.34 E
Ky Anh 110 18.05 N 106.18 E
Kyat-aw 110 12.29 N 98.19 E
Kyaukhnyat 110 18.15 N 97.31 E
Kyaukkyi 110 18.19 N 96.46 E
Kyaukme 110 22.32 N 97.02 E
Kyaukpa 110 13.05 N 98.59 E
Kyaukpyu, Mya. 110 19.05 N 93.52 E
Kyaukpyu, Mya. 110 19.26 N 93.33 E
Kyaukse 110 21.36 N 96.08 E
Kyauktaw 110 20.51 N 92.59 E
Kyaunggon 110 17.06 N 95.11 E
Kybartai 76 54.39 N 22.45 E
Kybean 171b 36.22 S 149.25 E
Kybeyan Range ⋏ 171b 36.10 S 149.30 E
Kyburz 226 38.47 N 120.18 W
Kydra 171b 36.27 S 149.23 E
Kyeamba 171b 35.26 S 147.37 E
Kyeamba Creek ≃ 171b 35.06 S 147.29 E
Kyebang-san ∧ 98 37.43 N 128.29 E
Kyegegwa 154 0.29 N 31.03 E
Kyeikdon 110 16.00 N 98.24 E
Kyeintali 110 18.00 N 94.29 E
Kyenjojo 154 0.37 N 30.38 E
Kyeryong-san Kukrip Kongwŏn ♦ 98 36.21 N 127.13 E
Kyes Peak ∧ 224 47.57 N 121.19 W
Kyffhäuser-Denkmal ⊥ 54 51.23 N 11.06 E
Kyffhäuser Gebirge ⋏ 54 51.23 N 11.05 E
Kyidaunggan 110 19.53 N 96.12 E
Kyindwe 110 20.58 N 93.51 E
Kyje ◆[8] 54 50.04 N 14.32 E
Kyjov 30 49.01 N 17.08 E
Kykladen → Kikládhes II 38 37.30 N 25.00 E
Kykotsmovi Village 200 35.52 N 110.37 W
Kykva 80 57.22 N 53.50 E
Kylās ∧ 124 25.18 N 90.45 E
Kyle, Sk., Can. 184 50.50 N 108.02 W
Kyle, S.D., U.S. 198 43.25 N 102.10 W
Kyle, Tx., U.S. 196 29.59 N 97.52 W
Kyle □[9] 44 55.29 N 4.24 W
Kyle, Lake ⊜[1] 154 20.14 S 31.00 E
Kyleakin 46 57.16 N 5.44 W
Kyle of Lochalsh 46 57.17 N 5.43 W
Kylerhea 46 57.14 N 5.41 W
Kylertown 214 41.00 N 78.10 W
Kylestrome 46 58.16 N 5.02 W
Kyll ≃ 56 49.48 N 6.42 E
Kyllburg 56 50.02 N 6.35 E
Kym ≃ 42 52.14 N 0.17 W
Kymen lääni □[4] 26 61.00 N 28.00 E
Kymijoki ≃ 26 60.30 N 26.52 E
Kyn 86 57.52 N 58.38 E
Kyndby 41 55.48 N 11.56 E
Kyneton 169 37.15 S 144.27 E
Kynnefjäll ∧[2] 26 58.42 N 11.41 E
Kynšperk nad Ohří 54 50.04 N 12.32 E
Kynuna 166 21.35 S 141.55 E
Kyodong-do I 98 37.45 N 126.16 E
Kyoga, Lake ⊜ 154 1.30 N 33.00 E
Kyōga-misaki ≻ 96 35.46 N 135.13 E
Kyogle 166 28.37 S 153.00 E
Kyoha-ri 271b 37.46 N 126.46 E
Kyohyŏn-ni 271b 37.43 N 126.58 E
Kyom ≃ 140 8.58 N 28.13 E
Kyŏmip'o → Songnim 98 38.44 N 125.38 E
Kyonan 94 35.07 N 139.50 E
Kyondo 110 16.35 N 98.03 E
Kyŏnggi Do □[4] 98 37.30 N 127.15 E
Kyŏnggi-man C 98 37.25 N 126.00 E
Kyŏngju 98 35.51 N 129.14 E
Kyŏngju Kukrip Kongwŏn ♦ 98 35.47 N 129.15 E
Kyŏngsan 98 35.48 N 128.43 E
Kyŏngsang Namdo □[4] 98 35.15 N 128.30 E
Kyŏngsang Pukdo □[4] 98 36.15 N 128.45 E
Kyŏngsŏng, C.M.I.K. 98 41.35 N 129.36 E
Kyŏngsŏng → Sŏul, Taehan 98 37.33 N 126.58 E
Kyŏngwŏn 98 42.48 N 130.09 E
Kyônkadun 110 16.04 N 95.38 E
Kyonmange 110 16.30 N 95.50 E
Kyonpyaw 110 17.18 N 95.12 E
Kyotera 154 0.33 S 31.19 E
Kyōto, Nihon 94 35.00 N 135.45 E
Kyōto, Nihon 270 35.00 N 135.45 E
Kyōto □[5] 94 35.05 N 135.45 E
Kyōto-bonchi ⋏ 270 35.03 N 135.45 E
Kyōto Race Track ♦ 270 34.54 N 135.44 E
Kyōto University ◆[2] 270 35.02 N 135.46 E
Kyōwa 94 36.19 N 140.03 E
Kyōyomi-dake ∧ 96 33.31 N 131.02 E
Kypšak, ozero ⊜ 86 50.09 N 68.28 E
Kyra 88 49.36 N 111.58 E
Kyra ≃ 88 49.24 N 112.19 E
Kyrčany 80 57.37 N 50.10 E
Kyren 88 51.41 N 102.08 E
Kyrenia → Girne 130 35.20 N 33.19 E
Kyritz 54 52.56 N 12.23 E
Kyrkheden 40 60.10 N 13.29 E
Kyrkkazyk 85 42.30 N 72.20 E
Kyrksæterøra 26 63.17 N 9.06 E
Kyrkslätt (Kirkkonummi) 26 60.07 N 24.26 E
Kyrö 26 60.42 N 22.45 E
Kyrönjoki ≃ 26 63.14 N 21.45 E
Kyrösjärvi ⊜ 26 61.45 N 23.10 E

ENGLISH
Name | Page | Lat.°′ | Long.°′

Kyröskoski 26 61.40 N 23.11 E
Kyrta 24 64.04 N 57.42 E
Kyrykkuduk 80 49.51 N 51.54 E
Ky Son 110 19.24 N 104.08 E
Kyštovka 86 56.33 N 76.38 E
Kyštym 86 55.42 N 60.34 E
Kysykkamys 80 49.14 N 50.19 E
Kyte ≃ 190 42.00 N 89.19 W
Kytlym 86 59.30 N 59.12 E
Kytmanovo 86 53.28 N 85.28 E
Kyūhōji 270 34.38 N 135.35 E
Kyunchaung 110 15.33 N 98.15 E
Kyundon 110 20.31 N 95.44 E
Kyungyi I 110 15.04 N 97.44 E
Kyunhla 110 23.21 N 95.18 E
Kyuquot 182 50.02 N 127.23 W
Kyuquot Sound ⊻ 182 50.05 N 127.15 W
Kyūroku-jima I 92 40.32 N 139.29 E
Kyū-shizudani-gakkō ⊥ 96 34.45 N 134.13 E
Kyūshū I 92 33.00 N 131.00 E
Kyushu-Palau Ridge ◆[3] 14 20.00 N 136.00 E
Kyūshū-sanchi ⋏ 92 32.35 N 131.17 E
Kywebwe 110 18.42 N 96.25 E
Kywong 166 34.59 S 146.44 E
Kyyjärvi 26 63.02 N 24.34 E
Kyyvesi ⊜ 26 61.58 N 27.07 E
Kyzas 86 52.20 N 89.20 E
Kyzyl 88 51.42 N 94.27 E
Kyzylagadžskij zapovednik ◆[4] 84 39.10 N 49.00 E
Kyzylagaš 86 45.54 N 81.37 E
Kyzylaryk 85 43.57 N 70.42 E
Kyzylbejit 85 41.30 N 72.24 E
Kyzyl-Chaja 86 50.03 N 89.54 E
Kyzyl-Chem (Šišchid) ≃ 88 51.21 N 96.58 E
Kyzyl-Džar 85 41.17 N 72.02 E
Kyzylemgek 85 41.57 N 74.56 E
Kyzylespe 86 47.27 N 73.53 E
Kyzylkak, ozero ⊜ 86 53.25 N 73.48 E
Kyzyl-Kija 85 40.16 N 72.08 E
Kyzyl-Kommuna 86 48.44 N 67.32 E
Kyzylkum ◆[2] 72 42.00 N 64.00 E
Kyzylkup 128 40.38 N 53.58 E
Kyzyl-Mažalyk 86 51.10 N 90.32 E
Kyzylmazar 85 39.39 N 68.25 E
Kyzyloba 80 49.37 N 50.38 E
Kyzylsu ≃ 85 39.17 N 71.23 E
Kyzyltas, gory ⋏ 86 48.30 N 74.50 E
Kyzyltau 86 47.53 N 72.05 E
Kyzylt'ob'o 85 42.13 N 75.16 E
Kyzyltu, S.S.S.R. 85 42.11 N 76.40 E
Kyzyltu, S.S.S.R. 86 47.46 N 59.08 E
Kyzyltu, S.S.S.R. 86 47.43 N 75.42 E
Kyzyluj 86 48.07 N 65.28 E
Kyzylžar 86 48.17 N 69.39 E
Kzyl-Kuga 80 48.28 N 53.01 E
Kzyl-Orda 86 44.48 N 65.28 E
Kzyl-Orda □[4] 85 43.30 N 67.00 E
Kzyltu 86 53.38 N 72.20 E

L

La'a 102 29.44 N 101.26 E
Laa an der Thaya 61 48.43 N 16.23 E
Laaben 61 48.06 N 15.52 E
Laaber 60 49.04 N 11.53 E
Laaberberg 60 48.46 N 12.01 E
Laab im Walde 264b 48.09 N 16.11 E
Laacher See ⊜ 56 50.25 N 7.16 E
Laaerberg ∧[2] 264b 48.09 N 16.24 E
Laage 54 53.56 N 12.20 E
La Aguada, Zanjón de ≃ 286e 33.30 S 70.47 W
La Aguja, Cabo de ≻ 246 11.18 N 74.12 W
Laakajärvi ⊜ 26 63.50 N 27.55 E
Laaken ◆[8] 263 51.15 N 7.15 E
Laakirchen 64 47.58 N 13.49 E
La Albuera 34 38.43 N 6.49 W
La Alcarria ◆[1] 34 40.45 N 2.45 W
La Aldea 234 20.54 N 101.29 W
La Aldehuela 266a 40.18 N 3.36 W
La Algaba 34 37.28 N 6.01 W
La Almarcha 34 39.41 N 2.22 W
La Almunia de Doña Godina 34 41.29 N 1.22 W
Laanecoorie Reservoir ⊜[1] 169 36.52 S 143.53 E
La Antigua, Salina ≚ 252 30.00 S 66.06 W
La Antorcha, Cerro ∧ 234 21.43 N 102.45 W
Laar ◆[8] 263 51.28 N 6.43 E
La Araucanía □[4] 252 38.45 S 72.30 W
La Arena 236 7.58 N 80.28 W
Laas → Lasa 64 46.37 N 10.42 E
Laas Caanood 144 8.28 N 47.21 E
Laas Dawaco 144 10.28 N 49.05 E
Laas Dhaareed 144 10.10 N 45.59 E
Laase 54 53.04 N 11.18 E
Laas Qoray 144 11.10 N 48.13 E
La Asunción 246 11.02 N 63.53 W
Laatzen 52 52.19 N 9.47 E
Laau Point ≻ 229a 21.06 N 157.19 W
La Aurora 286e 33.36 S 70.38 W
La Azufrosa 196 28.14 N 100.50 W
Laba ≃ 78 45.11 N 39.42 E
La Babia 232 28.34 N 102.04 W
L'Abacou, Pointe ≻ 238 18.03 N 73.47 W
Labadie 219 38.31 N 90.51 W
Labadieville 194 29.50 N 90.57 W
La Baie 186 48.19 N 70.53 W
La Balme-de-Sillingy 58 45.58 N 6.02 E
La Balme-les-Grottes 62 45.51 N 5.20 E
Laban 208 37.24 N 76.17 W
La Banda 252 27.44 S 64.15 W
La Bandera 286e 33.34 S 70.39 W
La Bañeza 34 42.18 N 5.54 W
La Barca 234 20.17 N 102.34 W
La Barceloneta ◆[8] 266d 41.22 N 2.11 E
La Barge 200 42.15 N 110.11 W
La Barge Creek ≃ 200 42.14 N 110.10 W
La Barre-en-Ouche 50 48.57 N 0.40 E
La Barr Meadows 226 39.11 N 121.02 W
Labason 116 8.04 N 122.31 E
La Bassée 50 50.32 N 2.48 E
Labastide-Murat 32 44.39 N 1.34 E
La Bastide-Puylaurent 62 44.36 N 3.54 E
La Bâte 261 48.35 N 2.01 E
La Baule-Escoublac 32 47.17 N 2.24 W
La Bazoche-Gouet 50 48.08 N 0.59 E
L'Abbé 261 48.34 N 1.50 E
Labdah (Leptis Magna) ⊥ 146 32.38 N 14.18 E
Labé 150 11.19 N 12.17 W
Labe (Elbe) ≃ 30 53.50 N 9.00 E
Labégude 62 44.39 N 4.22 E
La Bégude-Blanche 62 43.55 N 6.08 E
La Bégude-de-Mazenc 62 44.32 N 4.56 E
Labelle, P.Q., Can. 206 46.16 N 74.44 W
La Belle, Fl., U.S. 220 26.45 N 81.26 W
La Belle, Mo., U.S. 219 40.07 N 91.54 W
Labelle □[6] 206 46.20 N 75.00 W
Labelle, Lac ⊜, P.Q., Can. 206 46.13 N 74.52 W
La Belle, Lac ⊜, Wi., U.S. 216 43.08 N 88.31 W
Labengke, Pulau I 112 3.27 S 122.25 E
La Bérarde 62 44.56 N 6.18 E
Laberge, Lake ⊜ 180 61.11 N 135.12 W
Laberinto de las Doce Leguas II 240p 20.35 N 78.30 W
La Berra ∧ 58 46.41 N 7.11 E
Laberweinting 60 48.48 N 12.19 E
Labes → Łobez 30 53.39 N 15.36 E
La Besace 56 49.34 N 4.58 E
Labette Creek ≃ 198 37.03 N 95.05 W

DEUTSCH
Name | Seite | Breite°′ | Länge°′ E = Ost

Labi 112 4.25 N 114.22 E
La Biche ≃ 182 55.01 N 112.44 W
Labico 66 41.47 N 12.53 E
Labin 36 45.05 N 14.07 E
Labinsk 84 44.38 N 40.44 E
Labis 114 2.23 N 103.02 E
La Bisbal 34 41.57 N 3.03 E
Łabiszyn 30 52.57 N 17.55 E
Lablābah, Wādī al- ∨ 273c 30.02 N 31.19 E
La Blanca 286e 33.31 S 70.41 W
Labná ⊥ 232 20.11 N 89.34 W
Labo 116 14.09 N 122.51 E
Labo ≃ 116 14.11 N 122.56 E
Labo, Mount ∧ 116 14.01 N 122.48 E
La Boca 234 23.56 N 99.17 W
Laboe 54 54.24 N 10.15 E
La Boissière 261 48.46 N 1.59 E
La Boissière-Ecole 261 48.41 N 1.39 E
La Bollène-Vésubie 62 43.59 N 7.20 E
La Bonneville-sur-Iton 50 49.00 N 1.02 E
Laboratory 214 40.09 N 80.13 W
Laborde, Arg. 252 33.09 S 62.51 W
La Borde, Fr. 261 48.32 N 2.50 E
Laborec ≃ 30 48.36 N 22.00 E
Laborie 241f 13.45 N 61.00 W
Laborie Bay C 241f 13.45 N 61.01 W
Labouchere, Mount ∧ 162 25.12 S 118.18 E
Labouheyre 32 44.13 N 0.55 W
Laboulaye 252 34.07 S 63.24 W
La Bouverie 50 50.24 N 3.52 E
La Boyera, Ven. 286c 10.23 N 66.57 W
La Boyera, Ven. 286c 10.25 N 66.50 W
Lābpur 126 23.50 N 87.49 E
Labrador ◆[1] 176 54.00 N 62.00 W
Labrador Basin ◆[1] 16 53.00 N 48.00 W
Labrador City 176 52.57 N 66.55 W
Labrador Sea ⊤[2] 176 57.00 N 53.00 W
Lábrea, Bra. 248 7.16 S 64.47 W
La Brea, Trin. 241r 10.15 N 61.37 W
Labrède 32 44.41 N 0.31 W
La Bresse 58 48.00 N 6.53 E
La Brévine 58 46.59 N 6.36 E
Labrieville, Réserve ♦ 186 49.20 N 69.40 W
La Brigue 62 44.04 N 7.37 E
La Brillanne 62 43.55 N 5.53 E
Labrit 32 44.07 N 0.33 W
La Broquerie 184 49.28 N 96.27 W
Labroye 50 50.17 N 1.59 E
Labry 56 49.10 N 5.52 E
Labuan, Pulau I 112 5.21 N 115.13 E
Labuha 164 0.37 S 127.29 E
Labuhan 115a 6.22 S 105.50 E
Labuhanbajo 115b 8.29 S 119.54 E
Labuhanbatu 114 2.12 N 100.12 E
Labuhanbilik 114 2.31 N 100.10 E
Labuhandeli 114 3.45 N 98.41 E
Labuhanhaji, Indon. 114 3.33 N 97.00 E
Labuhanhaji, Indon. 115b 8.42 S 116.34 E
Labuhanmarege 112 7.06 S 120.40 E
Labuhanmaringgai 115a 5.21 S 105.48 E
Labuhanruku 114 3.13 N 99.35 E
Labuk ≃ 112 5.54 N 117.30 E
Labuk, Telukan C 116 6.07 N 117.46 E
Labu Kananga 115b 8.08 S 117.47 E
Labutta 110 16.09 N 94.46 E
Labytnangi 72 66.39 N 66.21 E
Laç, Shq. 38 41.38 N 19.43 E
Lač, S.S.S.R. 24 63.18 N 54.28 E
Lac □[5] 146 13.30 N 14.15 E
Lača, ozero ⊜ 24 61.20 N 38.48 E
La Cadena 196 25.53 N 104.12 W
L'Acadie 275a 45.19 N 73.21 W
L'Acadie ≃ 206 45.29 N 73.16 W
La Cadière-d'Azur 62 43.12 N 5.46 E
Lacadivas, Islas → Lakshadweep II 122 10.00 N 73.00 E
Laca Jahuira ≃ 248 19.21 S 67.54 W
La Cal ≃ 248 17.27 S 58.15 W
Lac-à-la-Tortue 206 46.37 N 72.38 W
La Calera, Chile 252 32.47 S 71.12 W
La Calera, Perú 286d 12.12 S 76.54 W
Lac-Allard 186 50.33 N 63.25 W
Lacamas Creek ≃ 224 46.20 N 122.55 W
Lacamas Lake ⊜ 224 45.37 N 122.26 W
La Campana, Esp. 34 37.34 N 5.26 W
La Campana, Méx. 234 22.45 N 105.35 W
La Cañada 234 20.37 N 100.19 W
La Canada Flintridge 228 34.12 N 118.12 W
La Canada Verde Creek ≃ 280 33.52 N 118.02 W
Lacanau 32 44.59 N 1.05 W
Lacanau, Lac de C 32 44.58 N 1.07 W
La Candelaria, Arg. 252 26.06 S 65.06 W
La Candelaria, Méx. 200 31.07 N 106.29 W
La Cañiza 34 42.13 N 8.16 W
La Canourgue 32 44.26 N 3.13 E
Lacantum ≃ 232 16.36 N 90.39 W
La Capelle-en-Thiérache 50 49.58 N 3.55 E
La Capelle-lès-Boulogne 50 50.44 N 1.42 E
Lacapelle-Marival 32 44.44 N 1.54 E
La Capilla, Méx. 234 23.59 N 98.25 W
La Capilla, Méx. 234 18.30 N 96.40 W
La Carlota, Arg. 252 33.26 S 63.18 W
La Carlota, Pil. 116 10.25 N 122.55 E
La Carlota, Aeropuerto ⊠ 286c 10.29 N 66.50 W
Lacarne 214 41.31 N 83.03 W
La Carolina 34 38.15 N 3.37 W
La Casita 234 23.43 N 104.46 W
La Castellana 116 10.20 N 123.03 E
La Castrina, Aeropuerto ⊠ 286e 33.31 S 70.38 W
Lacaune 32 43.43 N 2.42 E
Lac-Bellemare 206 46.34 N 72.55 W
Lac-Brome 206 45.13 N 72.31 W
Laccadive, Minicoy, and Amīndīvi → Lakshadweep □[3] 122 10.00 N 73.00 E
Laccadive Islands → Lakshadweep II 122 10.00 N 73.00 E
Laccadive Sea ⊤[2] 12 7.00 N 76.00 E
Lacchiarella 62 45.19 N 9.08 E
Lacco Ameno 68 40.45 N 13.54 E
Lac Courte Oreilles Indian Reservation ◆[4] 190 45.55 N 91.19 W
Lac du Flambeau 190 45.59 N 89.51 W
Lac du Flambeau Indian Reservation ◆[4] 190 45.59 N 89.53 W
Laceby 44 53.32 N 0.10 W
Lacedonia 68 41.03 N 15.25 E
La Ceiba, Hond. 236 15.47 N 86.50 W
La Ceiba, Ven. 246 9.28 N 71.04 W
La Celle-les-Bordes 261 48.38 N 1.57 E
La Celle-Saint-Cloud 261 48.51 N 2.08 E
La Celle-Saint-Cyr 50 47.58 N 3.18 E
La Center, Ky., U.S. 194 37.04 N 88.58 W
La Center, Wa., U.S. 224 45.52 N 122.40 W
Lacepede Bay C 166 36.47 S 139.45 E
Lacerdónia 156 18.01 S 35.30 E
Laces (Latsch) 64 46.37 N 10.52 E
Lac-Etchemin 186 46.24 N 70.30 W
Lacey 224 47.02 N 122.49 W
Lacey Creek ≃ 278 41.50 N 88.03 W
Laceyville 210 41.39 N 76.10 W
Lac-Frontière 186 46.42 N 70.00 W
La Chaise-Dieu 62 45.19 N 3.42 E
La Chambre 62 45.22 N 6.18 E
La Chapelle-d'Angillon 50 47.22 N 2.26 E
La Chapelle-en-Vercors 62 44.58 N 5.25 E
La Chapelle-Gauthier 261 48.33 N 2.54 E
La Chapelle-la-Reine 50 48.19 N 2.35 E
La Chapelle-Saint-Luc 50 48.20 N 4.03 E
La Chapelle-Vendômoise 50 47.40 N 1.15 E
La Charité-sur-Loire 50 47.11 N 3.01 E

Symbols in the index entries represent the broad categories identified in the key at the right. Symbols with superior numbers (⋏[1]) identify subcategories (see complete key on page *I · 1).*

Symbole im Register stellen die rechts im Schlüssel erklärten Kategorien dar. Symbole mit hochgestellten Ziffern (⋏[1]) bezeichnen Unterabteilungen einer Kategorie (vgl. vollständiger Schlüssel auf Seite *I · 1).*

Los símbolos incluídos en el texto del índice representan las grandes categorias identificadas con la clave a la derecha. Los símbolos con numeros en su parte superior (⋏[1]) identifican las subcategorías (véase la clave completa en la página *I · 1).*

Les symboles de l'index représentent les catégories indiquées dans la légende à droite. Les symboles suivis d'un indice (⋏[1]) représentent des sous-catégories (voir légende complète à la page *I · 1).*

Os símbolos incluídos no texto do índice representam as grandes categorias identificadas com a chave à direita. Os símbolos com números em sua parte superior (⋏[1]) identificam as subcategorias (veja-se a chave completa à página *I · 1).*

∧ Mountain	Berg	Montaña	Montagne	Montanha
⋏ Mountains	Gebirge	Montañas	Montagnes	Montanhas
)(Pass	Paß	Paso	Col	Passo
∨ Valley, Canyon	Tal, Cañon	Valle, Cañón	Vallée, Canyon	Vale, Canhão
≚ Plain	Ebene	Llano	Plaine	Planície
≻ Cape	Kap	Cabo	Cap	Cabo
I Island	Insel	Isla	Île	Ilha
II Islands	Inseln	Islas	Îles	Ilhas
⊥ Other Topographic Features	Andere Topographische Objekte	Otros Elementos Topográficos	Autres données topographiques	Outros acidentes topográficos

Lach-Lake *I* · 93

ESPAÑOL — Nombre | Página | Lat. °′ | Long. °′ W = Oeste
FRANÇAIS — Nom | Page | Lat. °′ | Long. °′ W = Ouest
PORTUGUÊS — Nome | Página | Lat. °′ | Long. °′ W = Oeste

Nombre	Página	Lat. °′	Long. °′ W = Oeste
La Chartre-sur-le-Loir	50	47.44 N	0.35 E
La Châtaigneraie	32	46.39 N	0.44 W
La Châtre	32	46.35 N	1.59 E
Lachaussée, Étang de ⊜	56	49.02 N	5.48 E
La Chaux-de-Fonds	58	47.06 N	6.50 E
Lachay, Punta ›	248	11.18 S	77.39 W
Lach Dennis	262	53.15 N	2.26 W
Lachdenpochja	24	61.31 N	30.08 E
Lachen	58	47.12 N	8.51 E
Lachenaie	275a	45.42 N	73.34 W
Lachendorf	52	52.37 N	10.14 E
Lachhmangarh Sīkar	120	27.49 N	75.02 E
L'achi	80	55.20 N	41.56 E
Lachine	206	45.26 N	73.40 W
Lachine, Canal de ≍	275a	45.26 N	73.40 W
Lachine, Rapides de ʟ	275a	45.25 N	73.36 W
La Chira, Punta ›	286d	12.13 S	77.03 W
La Chivera	286c	10.37 N	66.54 W
Lachkaltsap Indian Reserve ◆[4]	182	55.03 N	129.34 W
Lachlan ≃	166	34.21 S	143.57 E
La Chorrera, Col.	246	0.44 S	73.01 W
La Chorrera, Pan.	236	8.53 N	79.47 W
L'achoviči, S.S.S.R.	76	53.02 N	26.16 E
L'achoviči, S.S.S.R.	76	52.23 N	27.55 E
L'achovskije ostrova II	74	73.30 N	141.00 E
La Choza	258	34.47 S	59.07 W
La Choza, Arroyo ≃	258	34.40 S	58.58 W
Lachta ◆[8]	265a	60.00 N	30.09 E
Lachtinskij Razliv, ozero ⊜	265a	60.00 N	30.11 E
Lachute	206	45.38 N	74.20 W
Lachva	78	52.13 N	27.04 E
La Ciénaga	252	27.30 S	66.57 W
La Ciénega	234	16.54 N	96.46 W
Lâçin	130	40.47 N	34.54 E
La Cinta Creek ≃	196	35.24 N	104.06 W
La Ciotat	62	43.10 N	5.36 E
La Cisterna	286e	33.33 S	70.41 W
La Citadelle ⊥	238	19.35 N	72.14 W
La Ciudad, Parque Nacional ♠	234	23.55 N	105.35 W
Lack	48	54.33 N	7.35 W
Lackawanna	210	42.49 N	78.49 W
Lackawanna □[6]	210	41.24 N	75.40 W
Lackawanna ≃	210	41.21 N	75.47 W
Lackawanna, Lake ⊜	276	40.57 N	74.42 W
Lackawanna State Park ♠	210	41.33 N	75.44 W
Lackawaxen	210	41.29 N	74.59 W
Lackawaxen ≃	210	41.29 N	74.59 W
Lackey	208	37.14 N	76.33 W
Lackland Air Force Base ■	196	29.27 N	98.37 W
Läckö	26	58.41 N	13.13 E
Lackoje	76	58.05 N	38.08 E
Lac La Belle	216	43.09 N	88.32 W
Lac la Biche	182	54.46 N	111.58 W
Lac la Hache	182	51.49 N	121.28 W
Lac la Ronge Provincial Park ♠	184	55.15 N	104.55 W
La Clayette	32	46.18 N	4.19 E
Laclede, Id., U.S.	182	48.10 N	116.45 W
La Clede, Il., U.S.	219	38.53 N	88.43 W
Laclede, Mo., U.S.	194	39.47 N	93.09 W
La Clotilde	252	27.08 S	60.40 W
La Clusaz	58	45.54 N	6.25 E
La Cluse	58	46.10 N	5.34 E
La Cluse-et-Mijoux	58	46.53 N	6.23 E
Lacmalac	171b	35.19 S	148.19 E
Lac-Masson	206	46.02 N	74.04 W
Lac-Mégantic	188	45.36 N	70.53 W
Lacob ti-duyong, Mount ∧	116	17.35 N	121.09 E
La Cocha	252	27.47 S	65.34 W
Lacolle	206	45.05 N	73.22 W
Lacolle ≃	206	45.04 N	73.20 W
La Colle-sur-Loup	62	43.41 N	7.06 E
La Colmena	286a	19.36 N	99.18 W
La Colorada	232	28.41 N	110.25 W
La Columna → Bolívar, Pico ∧	246	8.30 N	71.02 W
Lacombe, Ab., Can.	182	52.28 N	113.44 W
Lacombe, La., U.S.	194	30.18 N	89.56 W
Lacon	190	41.01 N	89.24 W
Lacona, Ia., U.S.	190	41.11 N	93.22 W
Lacona, N.Y., U.S.	212	43.38 N	76.04 W
La Concepción, Méx.	234	18.15 N	102.27 W
La Concepción, Pan.	236	8.31 N	82.37 W
La Concepción, Ven.	246	10.38 N	71.50 W
La Condamine-Châtelard	62	44.27 N	6.45 E
Laconi	71	39.51 N	9.03 E
Laconia	188	43.31 N	71.28 W
La Conner	224	48.23 N	122.29 W
La Consulta	252	33.44 S	69.07 W
Lacoochee	220	28.27 N	82.10 W
La Coruña	34	43.22 N	8.23 W
Lacoste, Fr.	62	43.50 N	5.18 E
La Coste, Tx., U.S.	196	29.19 N	98.49 W
La Côte-Saint-André	62	45.23 N	5.15 E
La Courneuve	261	48.56 N	2.23 E
La Couronne	62	43.20 N	5.03 E
La Courtine	32	45.42 N	2.16 E
Lac qui Parle ≃	198	45.01 N	95.53 W
Lac qui Parle, West Branch ≃	198	44.55 N	96.02 W
La Crau	62	43.09 N	6.04 E
Lacre Punt ›	241s	12.02 N	68.15 W
La Crescent	190	43.49 N	91.18 W
La Crescenta	228	34.13 N	118.14 W
La Croft	214	40.39 N	80.35 W
Lacroix-Saint-Ouen	50	49.21 N	2.47 E
La Crosse, In., U.S.	216	41.19 N	86.53 W
La Crosse, Ks., U.S.	198	38.31 N	99.18 W
La Crosse, Va., U.S.	192	36.41 N	78.05 W
Lacrosse, Wa., U.S.	202	46.49 N	117.53 W
La Crosse, Wi., U.S.	190	43.48 N	91.14 W
La Crosse ≃	190	43.49 N	91.16 W
La Cruz, Arg.	252	29.10 S	56.38 W
La Cruz, Col.	246	1.35 N	76.58 W
La Cruz, C.R.	236	11.04 N	85.39 W
La Cruz, Méx.	196	28.33 N	100.48 W
La Cruz, Ur.	258	33.56 S	56.15 W
La Cruz de Río Grande	236	13.06 N	84.10 W
Lac-Saguay	206	46.30 N	75.09 W
Lac Seul	184	50.20 N	92.16 W
Lac Seul Indian Reserve ◆[4]	184	50.15 N	92.10 W
La Cuchilla	234	18.54 N	103.19 W
La Cuesta, C.R.	236	8.30 N	82.50 W
La Cuesta, Méx.	234	20.10 N	104.51 W
La Cuesta, P.R.	240m	18.25 N	66.49 W
La Cumbre, Arg.	252	30.58 S	64.30 W
La Cumbre, Ven.	286c	10.32 N	66.57 W
La Cumbre, Volcán ∧[1]	246a	0.20 S	91.30 W
La Cure	58	46.28 N	6.05 E
Lacy Fork ≃	222	32.24 N	96.08 W
La Cygne	198	38.21 N	94.45 W
Lacy-Lakeview	222	31.37 N	97.06 W
Lada, Teluk c	115a	6.29 S	105.44 E
Ladainha	255	17.39 S	41.44 W
Ladākh □[9]	120	35.10 N	76.10 E
Ladākh Range ⋏	120	34.00 N	78.00 E
Ladan	78	50.31 N	32.35 E
La Dang, Ko I	114	6.33 N	99.18 E
Ladang Jagor	114	4.42 N	101.35 E
Ladara	114	1.28 N	97.28 E
Ladário	248	19.01 S	57.35 W
Ladbergen	52	52.08 N	7.44 E
Ladby	41	55.26 N	10.38 E
Ladd	190	41.22 N	89.13 W
Ladder Creek ≃	198	38.48 N	100.52 W
Laddingford	260	51.12 N	0.25 E
Laddonia	219	39.14 N	91.38 W
Ladeburg	264a	52.42 N	13.35 E
La Défense ʊ	261	48.53 N	2.15 E
La Dehesa	286e	33.22 S	70.33 W
La Dent d'Oche ∧	58	46.21 N	6.44 E
Ladera Heights	280	33.59 N	118.22 W
La Désirade I	241o	16.19 N	61.03 W
Ládhi	38	41.27 N	26.17 E
Ladhurka	126	23.22 N	86.32 E
La Digue I	138	4.21 S	55.50 E
Lâdik	130	40.55 N	35.55 E
Ladinger Spitze ∧	61	46.51 N	14.39 E
L'adiny	24	61.33 N	38.20 E
Ladismith	158	33.30 S	21.16 E
Ladispoli	66	41.56 N	12.05 E
Lādīz	128	28.56 N	61.19 E
Ladner	224	49.05 N	123.05 W
Lādnūn	120	27.39 N	74.23 E
Ladoga	194	39.54 N	86.48 W
Ladoga, Lake → Ladožskoje ozero ⊜	24	61.00 N	31.30 E
La Dolorita	286c	10.29 N	66.47 W
Ladon	50	48.00 N	2.32 E
Ladonia	196	33.25 N	95.56 W
La Dorada	246	5.27 N	74.40 W
La Dormida	252	33.21 S	67.55 W
Lado Sarāi ◆[8]	272a	28.32 N	77.12 E
L'adova ≃	78	48.28 N	27.37 E
Ladovskaja Balka	80	45.38 N	41.25 E
Ladožskaja	78	45.19 N	39.54 E
Ladožskoje Ozero	76	60.08 N	31.04 E
Ladožskoje ozero (Lake Ladoga) ⊜	24	61.00 N	31.30 E
Lādpur ◆[8]	272a	28.44 N	76.59 E
Ladrillero, Golfo c	254	49.20 S	75.37 W
Ladson	192	32.59 N	80.06 W
Ladue	219	38.38 N	90.23 W
Ladue ≃	180	63.09 N	140.25 W
Laduozong	102	31.27 N	97.19 E
Laduškin	76	54.36 N	20.11 E
Ladva	24	61.21 N	34.34 E
Ladva-Vetka	24	61.21 N	34.27 E
Lādwa	124	29.59 N	77.03 E
Lady, Fr.	261	48.35 N	2.54 E
L'ady, S.S.S.R.	76	58.38 N	28.47 E
L'ady, S.S.S.R.	76	54.36 N	31.10 E
Lady Ann Strait ʯ	176	75.40 N	79.50 W
Ladybank	46	56.16 N	3.08 W
Lady Barron	166	40.12 S	148.14 E
Ladybower Reservoir ⊜[1]	44	53.20 N	1.45 W
Ladybrand	158	29.19 S	27.25 E
Lady Elliot Island I	166	24.07 S	152.42 E
Lady Evelyn Lake ⊜	190	47.20 N	80.10 W
Lady Frere	158	31.44 S	27.16 E
Lady Grey	158	30.45 S	27.13 E
Lady Lake	220	28.55 N	81.55 W
Ladysmith, Austl.	171b	35.12 S	147.31 E
Ladysmith, B.C., Can.	182	48.58 N	123.49 W
Ladysmith, S. Afr.	158	28.34 S	29.45 E
Ladysmith, Wi., U.S.	190	45.27 N	91.06 W
Ladyženka	86	51.00 N	68.42 E
Ladyžin	78	48.41 N	29.15 E
Ladžanurges	84	42.37 N	42.50 E
Lae	164	6.45 S	147.00 E
Lae I[1]	14	8.56 N	166.14 E
Laem, Khao ∧	110	14.27 N	101.30 E
Laem Ngop	110	12.10 N	102.26 E
La Encantada, Cerro de ∧	232	31.00 N	115.24 W
La Encarnacion	234	23.23 N	98.01 W
Laer	52	52.03 N	7.21 E
Laer ◆[8]	263	51.28 N	7.16 E
Lærdalsøyri	26	61.06 N	7.29 E
La Escondida, Méx.	196	26.17 N	99.46 W
La Escondida, Méx.	232	25.40 N	98.18 W
La Esmeralda, Méx.	232	27.17 N	103.39 W
La Esmeralda, Para.	252	22.13 S	62.38 W
La Esmeralda, Ven.	246	3.10 N	65.33 W
Læsø I	26	57.16 N	11.01 E
La Esperanza, Cuba	240p	22.27 N	80.06 W
La Esperanza, Cuba	240p	22.46 N	83.44 W
La Esperanza, Hond.	236	14.20 N	88.10 W
La Esperanza, Méx.	196	26.46 N	104.00 W
La Esperanza, Méx.	200	32.06 N	114.47 W
La Esperanza, P.R.	240m	18.22 N	66.07 W
La Esperanza ◆[8]	286b	23.03 N	82.22 W
La Estación ◆[8]	266a	40.27 N	3.48 W
La Estancia	234	18.05 N	101.25 W
La Estrada	34	42.41 N	8.29 W
La Estrella, Bol.	248	16.30 S	63.45 W
La Estrella, Ven.	286c	10.25 N	66.48 W
Lafa	89	43.50 N	127.19 E
La Falda	252	31.05 S	64.30 W
La Farge	190	43.34 N	90.38 W
LaFargeville	212	44.11 N	75.57 W
Lafayette, Fr.	62	45.35 N	5.04 E
Lafayette, Al., U.S.	194	32.53 N	85.24 W
Lafayette, Ca., U.S.	226	37.53 N	122.07 W
Lafayette, Co., U.S.	198	39.59 N	105.05 W
Lafayette, Ga., U.S.	192	34.42 N	85.16 W
Lafayette, In., U.S.	216	40.25 N	86.52 W
Lafayette, La., U.S.	194	30.13 N	92.01 W
Lafayette, Mn., U.S.	190	44.26 N	94.23 W
Lafayette, N.J., U.S.	210	41.05 N	74.41 W
La Fayette, N.Y., U.S.	210	42.54 N	76.06 W
Lafayette, Oh., U.S.	216	40.46 N	83.57 W
Lafayette, Or., U.S.	224	45.14 N	123.06 W
La Fayette, R.I., U.S.	207	41.34 N	71.28 W
Lafayette, Tn., U.S.	194	36.31 N	86.01 W
La Fayette, Tx., U.S.	222	32.54 N	94.51 W
Lafayette, Mount ∧	188	44.10 N	71.38 W
Lafayette Hill	285	40.05 N	75.15 W
Lafayette Reservoir ⊜[1]	282	37.53 N	122.08 W
Lafayette Water Tunnel ◆[5]	282	37.54 N	122.12 W
La Fère	50	49.40 N	3.22 E
La Feria	196	26.09 N	97.49 W
Laferrere	288	34.45 S	58.35 W
La Ferrière-sur-Risle	50	48.59 N	0.48 E
La Ferté-Alais	50	48.29 N	2.21 E
La Ferté-Bernard	50	48.11 N	0.40 E
La Ferté-Frênel	50	48.50 N	0.30 E
La Ferté-Gaucher	50	48.47 N	3.18 E
La Ferté-Imbault	50	47.23 N	1.58 E
La Ferté-Macé	32	48.36 N	0.22 W
La Ferté-Milon	50	49.10 N	3.07 E
La Ferté-Saint-Aubin	50	47.43 N	1.56 E
La Ferté-sous-Jouarre	50	48.57 N	3.08 E
Laferté-sur-Amance	58	47.50 N	5.42 E
La Ferté-Vidame	50	48.37 N	0.55 E
La Ferté-Villeneuil	50	47.59 N	1.21 E
Lafferty	214	40.06 N	81.01 W
Laffrey	62	45.02 N	5.46 E
Lafia	150	8.30 N	8.30 E
Lafiagi	150	8.52 N	5.25 E
Laflamme ≃	190	48.56 N	77.18 W
Laflèche, P.Q., Can.	275a	45.30 N	73.28 W
Lafleche, Sk., Can.	184	49.43 N	106.35 W
La Flèche, Fr.	32	47.42 N	0.05 W
La Floresta	266d	41.27 N	2.04 E
La Florida, Chile	286e	33.33 S	70.34 W
La Florida, Esp.	266d	41.31 N	2.12 E
La Florida, Guat.	232	16.33 N	90.27 W
Lafnitz ≃	61	46.57 N	16.16 E
La Foa	175f	21.43 S	165.50 E
La Foce	62	44.08 N	9.47 E
La Follette	192	36.22 N	84.07 W
Lafon	154	5.02 N	32.27 E
Lafontaine, P.Q., Can.	206	45.48 N	74.01 W
La Fontaine, In., U.S.	216	40.40 N	85.43 W
Lafontaine, Parc ♠	275a	45.32 N	73.34 W
La Fortuna	236	10.30 N	84.35 W
Lafourche, Bayou ≃	194	29.05 N	90.14 W
La Foux, Fr.	62	43.16 N	6.35 E
La Foux, Fr.	62	44.17 N	6.34 E
La Fragua	252	26.05 S	64.20 W
La Francia	252	31.24 S	62.38 W
La Fregeneda	34	40.59 N	6.52 W
La Frette-sur-Seine	261	48.58 N	2.11 E
La Fría	246	8.13 N	72.15 W
Lafrimbolle	58	48.36 N	7.01 E
La Fuente de San Esteban	34	40.48 N	6.15 W
Laga, Monti della ⋏	66	42.37 N	13.24 E
La Gacilly	28	47.46 N	2.09 W
Lagaip ≃	164	5.05 S	142.40 E
La Galite I	36	37.32 N	8.56 E
La Gallareta	252	29.34 S	60.23 W
La Gallega	34	41.54 N	3.16 W
Lagan	26	56.55 N	13.59 E
Lagan ≃, Sve.	26	56.33 N	12.56 E
Lagan ≃, N. Ire., U.K.	44	54.37 N	5.53 W
Lagan ≃, N. Ire., U.K.	48	54.37 N	5.53 W
Lagangzong	120	28.05 N	91.04 E
Lagantu	102	42.20 N	108.22 E
La Garde	62	43.07 N	6.01 E
La Garde-Freinet	62	43.19 N	6.28 E
La Garenne-Colombes	261	48.55 N	2.15 E
Lagarina, Val V	64	45.50 N	11.10 E
La Garita	234	19.43 N	103.10 W
Lagarto, Bra.	250	10.54 S	37.41 W
Lagarto, C.R.	236	10.07 N	84.56 W
Lagarto Creek ≃	196	28.08 N	97.56 W
Lagawe	116	16.49 N	121.06 E
Lagay	116	14.06 N	122.12 E
Lagayan	116	17.43 N	120.42 E
Lage, B.R.D.	52	51.59 N	8.48 E
Lage, Esp.	34	43.13 N	9.00 W
Lage, Zhg.	120	29.26 N	85.51 E
Lagedu	102	26.24 N	101.11 E
Lågen ≃, Nor.	26	59.03 N	10.05 E
Lågen ≃, Nor.	26	61.08 N	10.25 E
Lägerdorf	52	53.53 N	9.34 E
Lageuen	114	4.44 N	95.31 E
Lage Zwaluwe	52	51.43 N	4.41 E
Laggan	46	57.02 N	4.16 W
Laggan, Loch ⊜[1]	46	56.57 N	4.28 W
Laggan Bay c	46	55.41 N	6.19 W
Lagginhorn ∧	58	46.11 N	8.01 E
Laghmān □[4]	120	35.00 N	70.15 E
Laghouat	148	33.50 N	2.59 E
Laghouat □[5]	148	32.00 N	3.30 E
Laghy	48	54.37 N	8.05 W
Lagič	84	40.51 N	48.24 E
La Giettaz	62	45.52 N	6.30 E
La Giustiniana ◆[8]	267a	41.59 N	12.24 E
La Gleize	56	50.25 N	5.51 E
La Gloria	246	8.37 N	73.48 W
Lagnieu	58	45.54 N	5.21 E
Lagny	50	48.52 N	2.43 E
Lagny-le-Sac	261	49.05 N	2.45 E
Lago	68	39.10 N	16.09 E
Lago, Mount ∧	224	48.51 N	120.32 W
Lagoa	256	23.18 S	45.36 W
Lagoa Branca	256	21.54 S	47.02 W
Lagoa da Prata	255	20.01 S	45.33 W
Lagoa Dourada	255	20.55 S	44.05 W
Lagoa Formosa	255	18.47 S	46.24 W
Lago Argentino → Calafate	254	50.20 S	72.18 W
Lagoa Santa	255	19.38 S	43.53 W
Lagoa Vermelha	252	28.13 S	51.32 W
Lago Blanco	254	45.55 S	71.15 W
Lago da Pedra	250	4.20 S	45.10 W
Lago de Camécuaro, Parque Nacional ♠	234	19.51 N	102.18 W
Lagodechi	84	41.49 N	46.18 E
Lagodechskij zapovednik ♠	84	41.53 N	46.22 E
Lago Futalaufquen	254	42.53 S	71.37 W
Lagoinha	256	23.06 S	45.11 W
Lagolândia	255	15.37 S	49.02 W
Lagolovo	265a	59.42 N	30.00 E
La Gomera	236	14.05 N	91.03 W
Lagonegro	68	40.07 N	15.46 E
Lagonglong	116	8.48 N	124.47 E
Lagonoy	116	13.44 N	123.31 E
Lagonoy Gulf c	116	13.35 N	123.45 E
Lagopesole, Castel di ⊥	68	40.48 N	15.45 E
Lago Posadas	254	47.32 S	71.45 W
Lagorai, Catena del ⋏	64	46.18 N	11.35 E
Lago Ranco	254	40.20 S	72.38 W
La Gorgue	50	50.38 N	2.42 E
Lagos, Ang.	152	16.04 S	17.03 E
Lagos, Nig.	150	6.27 N	3.24 E
Lagos, Nig.	273a	6.27 N	3.24 E
Lagos, Port.	34	37.06 N	8.40 W
Lagos □[3]	150	6.30 N	3.30 E
Lagos (Ikeja) Airport ⊠	273a	6.35 N	3.20 E
Lagos, University of ʊ[2]	273a	6.32 N	3.24 E
Lagosanto	66	44.46 N	12.08 E
Lagos de Moreno	234	21.21 N	101.55 W
Lagos Harbour c	273a	6.26 N	3.24 E
Lagos Island I	273a	6.27 N	3.26 E
Lagos Lagoon c	273a	6.30 N	3.26 E
Lagos Terminus ◆[5]	273a	6.28 N	3.23 E
La Gouèra	148	20.48 N	17.08 W
La Goulette	148	36.49 N	10.18 E
Lago Viedma	254	49.48 S	72.07 W
La Granadella	34	41.21 N	0.40 E
La Grand'Combe	62	44.13 N	4.02 E
La Grande	202	45.19 N	118.05 W
La Grande Anse c	241o	16.19 N	61.48 W
La Grande Deux, Réservoir ⊜[1]	176	53.40 N	76.55 W
La Grande Moucherolle ∧	62	45.00 N	5.34 E
La Grande Quatre, Réservoir ⊜[1]	176	54.00 N	73.15 W
La Grange, Austl.	162	18.41 S	121.45 E
LaGrange, Ca., U.S.	226	37.40 N	120.28 W
La Grange, Ga., U.S.	192	33.02 N	85.01 W
La Grange, Il., U.S.	216	41.48 N	87.52 W
Lagrange, In., U.S.	216	41.39 N	85.25 W
La Grange, Ky., U.S.	218	38.24 N	85.22 W
La Grange, Mo., U.S.	219	40.02 N	91.29 W
La Grange, N.C., U.S.	192	35.18 N	77.47 W
Lagrange, Oh., U.S.	214	41.14 N	82.07 W
La Grange, Tx., U.S.	222	29.54 N	96.52 W
Lagrange, Wy., U.S.	198	41.38 N	104.10 W
Lagrange □[6]	216	41.39 N	85.25 W
Lagrange Bay c	162	18.38 S	121.42 E
La Grange Highlands	278	41.50 N	87.51 W
La Grange Lock and Dam ◆[5]	219	39.57 N	90.32 W
La Grange Park	278	41.50 N	87.51 W
Lagrangeville	210	41.39 N	73.46 W
La Granja	286e	33.32 S	70.39 W
La Gran Sabana ≚	246	5.30 N	61.30 W
La Grave	62	45.03 N	6.18 E
La Grita	246	8.08 N	71.59 W
Lagro	216	40.50 N	85.43 W
La Groise	50	50.05 N	3.41 E
La Grue Bayou ≃	194	34.05 N	91.10 W
Lagu	102	26.26 N	101.30 E
La Guadeloupe (Saint-Évariste)	188	45.57 N	70.56 W
La Guaira	246	10.36 N	66.56 W
La Guajira □[5]	246	11.30 N	72.30 W
La Guajira, Península de ›[1]	246	12.00 N	71.40 W
La Guardia, Arg.	252	29.33 S	65.27 W
La Guardia, Bol.	248	17.54 S	63.20 W
La Guardia, Esp.	34	41.54 N	8.53 W
Laguardia, Esp.	34	42.33 N	2.35 W
La Guardia Airport ⊠	210	40.46 N	73.53 W
La Gudiña	34	42.04 N	7.08 W
La Guêpière	261	48.35 N	1.50 E
La Guerche-de-Bretagne	32	47.56 N	1.14 W
La Guerche-sur-l'Aubois	32	46.57 N	2.57 E
Laguiole	32	44.41 N	2.51 E
Laguna, Bra.	252	28.29 S	48.47 W
Laguna, N.M., U.S.	200	35.02 N	107.22 W
Laguna □[4]	116	14.10 N	121.20 E
Laguna ≃, Bra.	250	1.17 S	50.50 W
Laguna ≃, Ca., U.S.	226	38.16 N	121.23 W
Laguna, Ilha da I	250	1.40 S	51.00 W
Laguna Beach	228	33.32 N	117.46 W
Laguna Blanca	240p	20.27 N	76.07 W
Laguna Blanca, Parque Nacional ♠	254	39.00 S	70.18 W
Laguna Carapã	255	22.27 S	55.01 W
Laguna Creek ≃	200	36.54 N	109.45 W
Laguna Dam ◆[6]	200	32.50 N	114.31 W
Laguna de Jaco	232	27.50 N	104.00 W
Laguna Hills	228	33.36 N	117.42 W
Laguna Indian Reservation ◆[4]	200	35.00 N	107.20 W
Laguna Lake ⊜	226	35.16 S	120.42 W
Laguna Larga	252	31.46 S	63.48 W
Laguna Limpia	252	26.29 S	59.41 W
Laguna Niguel	228	33.31 N	117.43 W
Laguna Paiva	252	31.19 S	60.39 W
Laguna Park	222	31.52 N	97.23 W
Lagunas	248	5.14 S	75.38 W
Lagundo	64	46.41 N	11.08 E
Lagunillas, Bol.	248	19.38 S	63.43 W
Lagunillas, Méx.	234	21.34 N	99.35 W
Lagunillas, Ven.	246	8.31 N	71.24 W
Lagunillas → Ciudad Ojeda, Ven.	246	10.12 N	71.19 W
Lagunillás, Laguna ⊜	248	15.44 S	70.43 W
Laguntara c	236	15.12 N	83.30 W
L'agušje	86	54.24 N	77.59 E
Laguyu	104	41.43 N	123.49 E
Laha	89	48.10 N	124.39 E
La Habana (Havana), Cuba	240p	23.08 N	82.22 W
La Habana (Havana), Cuba	286b	23.08 N	82.22 W
La Habana □[4]	240p	22.45 N	82.10 W
La Habana, Bahía de c	286b	23.08 N	82.20 W
La Habana, Universidad de ʊ[2]	286b	23.08 N	82.22 W
La Habra	228	33.55 N	117.56 W
La Habra Heights	280	33.57 N	117.57 W
Lahad Datu	112	5.02 N	118.19 E
Lahad Datu, Telukan c	112	4.50 N	118.30 E
Lahaina	229a	20.52 N	156.40 W
Laham	112	0.22 N	115.24 E
Lahār	124	26.12 N	78.57 E
La Harpe, Il., U.S.	190	40.35 N	90.58 W
La Harpe, Ks., U.S.	198	37.55 N	95.17 W
Lāharpur	124	27.43 N	80.54 E
Lahaska	208	40.21 N	75.02 W
Lahat, Indon.	112	3.48 S	103.32 E
Lahat, Malay.	114	4.33 N	101.02 E
La Hauteville	261	48.42 N	1.37 E
La Havane → La Habana	240p	23.08 N	82.22 W
LaHave ≃	186	44.14 N	64.20 W
La Haye → 's-Gravenhage	52	52.06 N	4.18 E
La Haye-du-Puits	32	49.18 N	1.33 W
La Häy-les-Rosas	261	48.47 N	2.21 E
Lähden	52	52.45 N	7.34 E
Lāhe	110	26.20 N	95.26 E
Laheria Sarai	124	26.07 N	85.54 E
Lahewa	114	1.24 N	97.11 E
Lahfān, Bi'r ╤[4]	132	31.01 N	33.52 E
Lahi, Ava ʯ	174w	21.02 S	175.11 W
La Higuera	252	29.30 S	71.17 W
Lahij	144	13.02 N	44.54 E
Lāhījān	128	37.12 N	50.01 E
Lāhithah	132	32.59 N	36.35 E
Lähn → Wleń	30	51.01 N	15.40 E
Lahn ≃	56	50.18 N	7.37 E
Lahnstein	56	50.19 N	7.36 E
Laholm	26	56.31 N	13.02 E
Laholmsbukten c	26	56.35 N	12.50 E
La Honda	226	37.19 N	122.16 W
La Honda Creek ≃	282	37.18 N	122.16 W
Lahontan Reservoir ⊜[1]	226	39.23 N	119.09 W
Lahontan State Recreation Area ♠	226	39.28 N	119.03 W
Lahor → Lahore, Pāk.	123	31.35 N	74.18 E
Lāhor, Pāk.	123	34.03 N	72.22 E
Lahore	123	31.35 N	74.18 E
La Horqueta	246	3.06 N	72.50 W
La Horqueta, Arroyo ≃	288	34.41 S	58.51 W
La Houssaye-en-Brie	261	48.45 N	2.53 E
Lahr	58	48.20 N	7.52 E
Lahri	120	29.11 N	68.13 E
Lāhrūd	128	38.30 N	47.49 E
Lahṭah, Wādī V	142	29.44 N	32.45 E
Lahti	26	60.58 N	25.40 E
La Huaca	248	4.54 S	80.57 W
La Huacana	234	18.58 N	101.49 W
La Huerta, Méx.	234	19.28 N	104.39 W
La Huerta, N.M., U.S.	196	32.27 N	104.13 W
La Hunière	261	48.36 N	1.52 E
Lahuy Island I	116	13.56 N	123.50 E
Laï	146	9.24 N	16.18 E
Laiagam	164	5.30 S	143.20 E
Lai'an	100	32.27 N	118.25 E
Laibach → Ljubljana	36	46.03 N	14.31 E
Laibin	102	23.42 N	109.22 E
Lai Chau	110	22.02 N	103.10 E
Laichingen	58	48.29 N	9.41 E
Laichow Bay → Laizhou Wan c	98	37.36 N	119.30 E
Laide	46	57.52 N	5.32 W
Laidley	171a	27.38 S	152.24 E
Laidley Creek ≃	171a	27.31 S	152.24 E
Laidon, Loch ⊜	46	56.39 N	4.40 W
Laie	229c	21.39 N	157.55 W
Laifang	100	25.56 N	116.54 E
Laifeng, Zhg.	102	29.31 N	109.15 E
Laifeng, Zhg.	107	30.14 N	105.17 E
Laifengzhen	107	29.26 N	106.13 E
L'Aigle	50	48.45 N	0.38 E
L'Aigle Creek ≃	194	33.12 N	92.08 W
Laignes	50	47.50 N	4.22 E
Laigou	100	33.56 N	117.06 E
Laigueglia	62	43.58 N	8.09 E
Laihia	26	62.58 N	22.01 E
Lai-hka	110	21.16 N	97.40 E
Lailly-en-Val	50	47.46 N	1.41 E
Laïmbélé, Mont ∧	175f	16.20 S	167.31 E
Lainate	266b	45.34 N	9.02 E
Lainbach	61	47.38 N	14.46 E
La Independencia, Bahía de c	248	14.15 S	76.10 W
Laingsburg, S. Afr.	158	33.11 S	20.51 E
Laingsburg, Mi., U.S.	216	42.53 N	84.21 W
Lainioälven ≃	24	67.22 N	23.39 E
Laino Borgo	68	39.57 N	15.59 E
Lainsitz (Lužnice) ≃	61	49.13 N	14.42 E
Lainville	261	49.04 N	1.49 E
Lainz ◆[8]	264b	48.11 N	16.17 E
Lainzer Tiergarten ♠	264b	48.10 N	16.14 E
Lair, Scot., U.K.	46	57.29 N	5.20 W
Lair, Ky., U.S.	218	38.20 N	84.18 W
Laird Hill	222	32.21 N	94.54 W
Lairdsville	210	41.14 N	76.37 W
Lairg	46	58.01 N	4.25 W
Laïri	146	10.49 N	17.06 E
Laïri, Batha de ≃	146	12.28 N	16.45 E
Laïriri, Pic ∧	175f	15.27 S	166.48 E
Lais, Indon.	112	0.47 N	120.27 E
Lais, Indon.	112	3.32 S	102.03 E
Lais, Pil.	116	6.20 N	125.39 E
La Isabela	240p	22.57 N	80.01 W
Laisamis	154	1.36 N	37.48 E
Laiševo	80	55.24 N	49.32 E
Laishan	98	37.24 N	121.23 E
Laishui	105	39.23 N	115.42 E
Laissac	32	44.23 N	2.49 E
Laissey	58	47.18 N	6.14 E
Laisu	107	29.16 N	105.47 E
Laisvall	24	66.05 N	17.10 E
Laitan	107	29.06 N	106.10 E
Laitila	26	60.53 N	21.41 E
Laives (Leifers)	64	46.26 N	11.20 E
Laiwu	98	36.12 N	117.38 E
Laiwui	164	1.22 S	127.40 E
Laixi (Shuiji)	98	36.51 N	120.29 E
Laiya	116	13.40 N	121.24 E
Laiyang	98	36.58 N	120.44 E
Laiyuan, Zhg.	98	39.18 N	114.44 E
Laiyuan, Zhg.	100	25.36 N	117.01 E
Laizhou Wan (Laichow Bay) c	98	37.36 N	119.30 E
Laja ≃, Chile	252	37.16 S	72.43 W
Laja ≃, S.S.S.R.	24	66.20 N	56.16 E
Laja, Laguna de la ⊜	252	37.21 S	71.19 W
Laja, Río de la ≃	234	20.30 N	100.46 W
Laja, Salto del ʟ	252	37.22 S	71.25 W
La Jalca	248	6.29 S	77.43 W
La Jara	200	37.16 N	105.57 W
La Jara ◆[1]	34	39.42 N	4.54 W
La Jara Canyon V	200	36.50 N	107.30 W
La Jara Creek ≃	200	37.22 N	105.46 W
La Jarita	232	28.03 N	103.20 W
La Jarrie	32	46.08 N	1.00 W
Lajas, Méx.	234	23.07 N	105.07 W
Lajas, P.R.	240m	18.03 N	67.04 W
La Javie	62	44.10 N	6.21 E
Laje, Bra.	255	13.10 S	39.25 W
Laje, Bra.	256	21.22 S	44.31 W
Laje, Ilha da I	287a	22.57 S	43.09 W
Laje, Ponta da ›	266c	38.40 N	9.19 W
Laje, Ribeira de ≃	266c	38.41 N	9.19 W
Lajeado	252	29.27 S	51.58 W
Lajeado Velho ◆[8]	287b	23.32 S	46.23 W
Lajedo	250	8.40 S	36.19 W
Lajes, Bra.	250	5.41 S	36.14 W
Lajes, Bra.	252	27.48 S	50.19 W
Lajes, Ribeirão das ≃	256	22.38 S	43.42 W
Lajinha	255	20.09 S	41.37 W
Laji Shan ⋏	102	36.13 N	102.15 E
Lajkovo	265b	55.42 N	37.13 E
La Jolla	228	32.51 N	117.16 W
La Jolla, Point ›	228	32.51 N	117.17 W
Lajord	184	50.14 N	104.09 W
La Jose	214	40.50 N	78.41 W
Lajosmizse	30	47.02 N	19.34 E
La Joya, Méx.	196	26.26 N	101.08 W
La Joya, Méx.	232	32.08 N	114.01 W
La Joya, Perú	248	16.44 S	71.51 W
Lajta (Leitha) ≃	61	47.54 N	17.17 E
Lajtamak	86	58.25 N	67.25 E
Lajturi	84	41.55 N	41.55 E
La Junta, Méx.	232	28.28 N	107.20 W
La Junta, Co., U.S.	198	37.59 N	103.32 W
Lakaband	120	31.00 N	69.30 E
Lakahia, Teluk c	164	4.00 S	134.38 E
Lakamané	150	14.31 N	9.55 W
Lakar Kūh ∧	128	31.02 N	57.06 E
Lakatoro	175f	16.07 S	167.25 E
Lake	194	32.20 N	89.19 W
Lake □[6], Ca., U.S.	226	39.01 N	122.33 W
Lake □[6], Fl., U.S.	220	28.42 N	81.39 W
Lake □[6], Il., U.S.	216	42.22 N	87.50 W
Lake □[6], In., U.S.	216	41.25 N	87.22 W
Lake □[6], Oh., U.S.	214	41.43 N	81.15 W
Lake Accotink Park ♠	284c	38.48 N	77.14 W
Lake Albert	171b	35.10 S	147.23 E
Lake Alfred	220	28.05 N	81.43 W
Lake Alpine	226	38.28 N	120.00 W
Lake Andes	198	43.09 N	98.32 W
Lake Angelus	281	42.42 N	83.19 W
Lake Ariel	210	41.27 N	75.23 W
Lake Arrowhead	228	34.14 N	117.11 W
Lake Arthur, La., U.S.	194	30.04 N	92.40 W
Lake Arthur, N.M., U.S.	196	32.59 N	104.21 W
Lake Barcroft	284c	38.51 N	77.09 W
Lake Bathurst	170	35.01 S	149.36 E
Lake Benton	198	44.15 N	96.17 W
Lake Beseck	207	41.31 N	72.44 W
Lake Bluff	216	42.16 N	87.50 W
Lake Brownwood	196	31.49 N	99.02 W
Lake Buena Vista	220	28.23 N	81.31 W
Lake Butler	192	30.01 N	82.20 W
Lake Cable	214	40.52 N	81.27 W
Lake Camm	162	32.59 S	119.35 E
Lake Cargelligo	166	33.18 S	146.23 E
Lake Carmel	210	41.27 N	73.40 W
Lake Charles	194	30.13 N	93.13 W
Lake Chelan National Recreation Area ♠	224	48.20 N	120.40 W
Lake City, Ar., U.S.	194	35.48 N	90.26 W
Lake City, Co., U.S.	200	38.01 N	107.18 W
Lake City, Fl., U.S.	192	30.11 N	82.38 W
Lake City, Il., U.S.	219	39.45 N	88.43 W
Lake City, Ia., U.S.	198	42.16 N	94.44 W
Lake City, Mi., U.S.	190	44.20 N	85.12 W
Lake City, Mn., U.S.	190	44.26 N	92.16 W
Lake City, Pa., U.S.	214	42.00 N	80.20 W
Lake City, S.C., U.S.	192	33.52 N	79.45 W
Lake City, Tn., U.S.	192	36.13 N	84.09 W
Lake Clarke Shores	220	26.39 N	80.04 W
Lake Clark National Park ♠	180	60.30 N	153.15 W
Lake Coleridge	172	43.22 S	171.32 E
Lake Como, N.Y., U.S.	210	42.41 N	76.18 W
Lake Como, Pa., U.S.	210	41.51 N	75.20 W
Lake Corpus Christi State Park ♠	196	28.05 N	97.52 W
Lake Cowichan	224	48.50 N	124.03 W
Lake Creek ≃	222	30.16 N	95.29 W
Lake Crescent	224	48.06 N	123.50 W
Lake Crystal	190	44.06 N	94.13 W
Lake Dalecarlia	216	41.20 N	87.24 W
Lake Dallas	222	33.07 N	97.02 W
Lake Delta	210	43.17 N	75.28 W
Lake Delton	190	43.36 N	89.47 W
Lakedemonovka	83	47.12 N	38.33 E
Lake Dennison State Park ♠	207	42.38 N	72.05 W
Lake District ◆[1]	44	54.30 N	3.10 W
Lake District National Park ♠	44	54.30 N	3.05 W
Lake Eliza	216	41.26 N	87.10 W
Lake Elsinore	228	33.38 N	117.20 W
Lake Elsinore State Recreation Area ♠	228	33.41 N	117.22 W
Lake Entrance ʯ	170	33.05 S	151.39 E
Lake Errock	224	49.13 N	122.02 W
Lake Eyre National Park ♠	166	28.30 S	137.30 E
Lake Fairfax County Park ♠	284c	38.58 N	77.19 W
Lake Fenton	216	42.52 N	83.43 W
Lakefield, On., Can.	212	44.26 N	78.16 W
Lakefield, S. Afr.	273d	26.11 S	28.18 E
Lakefield, Mn., U.S.	198	43.40 N	95.10 W
Lakefield National Park ♠	164	15.00 S	144.05 E
Lake Forest, Fl., U.S.	192	25.58 N	80.11 W
Lake Forest, Il., U.S.	216	42.12 N	87.53 W
Lake Forest, N.J., U.S.	276	40.58 N	74.36 W
Lake Forest Park	224	47.45 N	122.17 W
Lake Fork	219	39.58 N	89.21 W
Lake Fork ≃, Il., U.S.	219	40.05 N	89.25 W
Lake Fork ≃, Ut,. U.S.	200	40.13 N	110.07 W
Lake Fork, North Fork ≃	219	39.56 N	89.14 W
Lake Fork Creek ≃	222	32.36 N	95.21 W
Lake Fork Reservoir ⊜[1]	222	32.50 N	95.35 W
Lake Geneva	216	42.36 N	88.26 W
Lake George	188	43.25 N	73.42 W
Lake Grace	162	33.06 S	118.28 E
Lake Grinnell	276	41.06 N	74.38 W
Lake Grove	276	40.51 N	73.06 W
Lake Hamilton	220	28.07 N	81.42 W
Lake Harbor	220	26.42 N	80.48 W
Lake Harbour	176	62.51 N	69.53 W
Lake Harmony	210	41.04 N	75.36 W
Lake Havasu City	200	34.29 N	114.19 W
Lake Havasu State Park ♠	200	34.29 N	114.21 W
Lake Helen	220	28.58 N	81.14 W
Lake Hiawatha	210	40.52 N	74.22 W
Lake Hill	210	42.04 N	74.11 W
Lake Hills, In., U.S.	216	41.28 N	87.27 W
Lake Hills, Wa., U.S.	224	47.36 N	122.08 W
Lake Hopatcong	210	40.55 N	74.39 W
Lake Hughes	228	34.40 N	118.26 W
Lake Huntington	210	41.41 N	75.00 W
Lakehurst	208	40.00 N	74.18 W
Lakehurst Naval Air Station ■	208	40.01 N	74.18 W
Lake Illawarra	170	34.33 S	150.52 E
Lake Intervale	276	40.53 N	74.25 W
Lake in the Hills	216	42.10 N	88.19 W
Lake Isabella	204	35.39 N	118.28 W
Lake Jackson	222	29.02 N	95.26 W
Lake Jem	220	28.45 N	81.40 W
Lakekamu ≃	164	8.10 S	146.15 E
Lake Katrine	210	41.59 N	73.59 W
Lake King	162	33.05 S	119.40 E
Lake Lackawanna	210	40.57 N	74.42 W
Lakeland, Fl., U.S.	220	28.03 N	81.57 W
Lakeland, Ga., U.S.	192	31.02 N	83.04 W
Lakeland, Mi., U.S.	216	42.28 N	83.51 W
Lakeland, N.Y., U.S.	210	43.06 N	76.15 W
Lakeland Park	216	42.21 N	88.17 W
Lakeland Village	228	33.39 N	117.22 W
Lake Lenape	210	41.01 N	74.44 W
Lake Linden	190	47.11 N	88.26 W
Lake Lookover	276	41.09 N	74.24 W
Lake Loramie State Park ♠	216	40.23 N	84.20 W
Lake Louise, Ab., Can.	182	51.26 N	116.11 W
Lake Louise, Wa., U.S.	224	47.05 N	122.36 W
Lake Lucerne	214	41.24 N	81.21 W
Lake Luzerne	210	43.18 N	73.50 W
Lake Mackay Reserve ◆[4]	162	22.00 S	129.45 E
Lake Magdalene	220	28.05 N	82.28 W
Lake Malawi National Park ♠	154	14.00 S	34.55 E
Lake Manyara National Park ♠	154	3.30 S	36.25 E
Lake Mary	220	28.45 N	81.19 W
Lakemba	274a	33.55 S	151.05 E
Lakemba Island I	175g	18.13 S	178.47 W
Lakemba Passage ʯ	175g	17.53 S	178.32 W
Lake Mead National Recreation Area ♠	200	36.00 N	114.30 W
Lake Meredith National Recreation Area ♠	196	35.40 N	101.40 W
Lake Mills, Ia., U.S.	190	43.25 N	93.31 W
Lake Mills, Wi., U.S.	216	43.04 N	88.54 W
Lake Milton	214	41.06 N	80.58 W
Lake Minchumina	180	63.53 N	152.19 W
Lake Monroe	220	28.50 N	81.19 W
Lakemont, N.Y., U.S.	210	42.31 N	76.56 W
Lakemont, Pa., U.S.	214	40.28 N	78.23 W
Lakemoor	216	42.20 N	88.12 W
Lakemore	214	41.01 N	81.25 W
Lake Mountain ∧	169	37.31 S	145.54 E
Lake Murray	164	7.00 S	141.29 E
Lake Murray State Park ♠	196	34.01 N	97.00 W
Lake Nakuru National Park ♠	154	0.20 S	36.05 E
Lake Nash	166	21.00 S	137.55 E
Lake Nepessing	216	43.02 N	83.22 W
Lakenheath	42	52.25 N	0.31 E
Lake Norden	198	44.34 N	97.12 W
Lake Normandy Estates	284c	39.03 N	77.11 W
Lake Odessa	216	42.47 N	85.08 W
Lake of the Ozarks State Park ♠	194	38.08 N	92.40 W
Lake of the Woods	216	41.26 N	86.14 W
Lake on the Mountain Provincial Park ♠	212	44.02 N	77.05 W
Lake Orion	216	42.47 N	83.14 W
Lake Orion Heights	216	42.46 N	83.18 W
Lake Oroville State Recreational Area ♠	226	39.32 N	121.27 W
Lake Oswego	224	45.25 N	122.39 W
Lake Ozark	194	38.11 N	92.38 W
Lakepa	174v	18.59 S	169.48 W
Lake Panasoffkee	220	28.46 N	82.07 W
Lake Paringa	172	43.43 S	169.29 E
Lake Park, Fl., U.S.	220	26.48 N	80.04 W
Lake Park, Ia., U.S.	198	43.27 N	95.19 W
Lake Park, Mn., U.S.	198	46.53 N	96.05 W
Lake Pine	208	39.52 N	74.51 W
Lake Placid, Fl., U.S.	220	27.17 N	81.21 W
Lake Placid, N.Y., U.S.	188	44.16 N	73.58 W
Lake Pleasant	188	43.28 N	74.25 W
Lakeport, Ca., U.S.	204	39.02 N	122.54 W
Lakeport, Mi., U.S.	190	43.07 N	82.30 W
Lakeport, N.Y., U.S.	210	43.09 N	75.52 W
Lake Preston	198	44.21 N	97.22 W
Lake Providence	194	32.48 N	91.10 W
Lake Pukaki	172	44.11 S	170.09 E
Lakeridge, Nv., U.S.	226	39.02 N	119.56 W
Lake Ridge, N.J., U.S.	276	40.24 N	74.15 W
Lake Riviera	208	40.03 N	74.10 W
Lake Ronkonkoma	276	40.50 N	73.07 W
Lake Saint Louis	219	38.48 N	90.45 W
Lake Sammamish State Park ♠	224	47.33 N	122.03 W
Lake San Marcos	228	33.09 N	117.12 W
Lake Sawyer	224	47.20 N	122.03 W
Lakes Bay c	208	39.22 N	74.30 W
Lakes District	224	47.10 N	122.31 W
Lakes Entrance	166	37.53 S	147.59 E
Lake Shawnee	276	40.59 N	74.36 W
Lakeshore, Ca., U.S.	226	37.15 N	119.12 W
Lake Shore, Md., U.S.	208	39.06 N	76.29 W
Lake Shore, Mi., U.S.	216	42.38 N	86.14 W
Lakeshore, Ms., U.S.	194	30.14 N	89.26 W
Lake Shore, Wa., U.S.	224	45.42 N	122.42 W
Lakeside, N.S., Can.	186	44.38 N	63.41 W
Lakeside, S. Afr.	273d	26.06 S	28.09 E
Lakeside, Az., U.S.	200	34.09 N	109.58 W
Lakeside, Ca., U.S.	228	32.51 N	116.55 W
Lakeside, Ct., U.S.	207	41.25 N	73.13 W
Lakeside, Ct., U.S.	207	41.40 N	73.14 W
Lakeside, Mi., U.S.	216	41.51 N	86.40 W
Lakeside, Mt., U.S.	202	48.01 N	114.13 W
Lakeside, Oh., U.S.	214	41.32 N	82.44 W
Lakeside, Or., U.S.	202	43.34 N	124.10 W
Lakeside, Va., U.S.	208	37.36 N	77.28 W
Lakeside ◆[9]	281	42.37 N	83.00 W
Lakeside Village	222	32.02 N	97.30 W
Lake Station	216	41.34 N	87.14 W
Lake Stevens	224	48.01 N	122.04 W
Lake Stockholm	276	41.04 N	74.31 W
Lake Success	276	40.46 N	73.43 W
Lake Superior Provincial Park ♠	190	47.32 N	84.50 W
Lake Swannanoa	276	41.01 N	74.31 W
Lake Taghkanic State Park ♠	210	42.06 N	73.43 W
Lake Tahoe Airport ⊠	226	38.54 N	120.00 W
Lake Tahoe-Nevada State Park ♠	226	39.13 N	119.55 W
Lake Tamarack	210	41.06 N	74.32 W
Lake Tekapo	172	44.01 S	170.30 E
Lake Telemark	276	40.57 N	74.30 W

Symbol	English	Deutsch	Español	Français	Português
≃	River	Fluß	Río	Rivière	Rio
≍	Canal	Kanal	Canal	Canal	Canal
ʟ	Waterfall, Rapids	Wasserfall, Stromschnellen	Cascada, Rápidos	Chute d'eau, Rapides	Cascata, Rápidos
ʯ	Strait	Meeresstraße	Estrecho	Détroit	Estreito
c	Bay, Gulf	Bucht, Golf	Bahía, Golfo	Baie, Golfe	Baía, Golfo
⊜	Lake, Lakes	See, Seen	Lago, Lagos	Lac, Lacs	Lago, Lagos
≡	Swamp	Sumpf	Pantano	Marais	Pântano
⊓	Ice Features, Glacier	Eis- und Gletscherformen	Accidentes Glaciales	Formes glaciaires	Acidentes glaciares
╤	Other Hydrographic Features	Andere Hydrographische Objekte	Otros Elementos Hidrográficos	Autres données hydrographiques	Outros acidentes hidrográficos
✢	Submarine Features	Untermeerische Objekte	Accidentes Submarinos	Formes de relief sous-marin	Acidentes submarinos
□	Political Unit	Politische Einheit	Unidad Política	Entité politique	Unidade política
ʊ	Cultural Institution	Kulturelle Institution	Institución Cultural	Institution culturelle	Institução cultural
⊥	Historical Site	Historische Stätte	Sitio Histórico	Site historique	Sitio histórico
♠	Recreational Site	Erholungs- und Ferienort	Sitio de Recreo	Centre de loisirs	Area de Lazer
⊠	Airport	Flughafen	Aeropuerto	Aéroport	Aeroporto
■	Military Installation	Militäranlage	Instalación Militar	Installation militaire	Instalação militar
◆	Miscellaneous	Verschiedenes	Misceláneo	Divers	Diversos

I · 94 **Lake-Lapa**

ENGLISH — Name / Page / Lat.°′ / Long.°′
DEUTSCH — Name / Seite / Breite°′ / Länge°′ E = Ost

Name	Page	Lat.°′	Long.°′
Lake Temescal Regional Park ♠	282	37.51 N	122.14 W
Laketon	216	40.58 N	85.50 W
Laketown	200	41.49 N	111.19 W
Lake Varley	162	32.46 S	119.27 E
Lake View, Ar., U.S.	194	34.24 N	90.50 W
Lakeview, Ca., U.S.	228	33.50 N	117.07 W
Lakeview, Ga., U.S.	192	34.58 N	85.15 W
Lake View, Ia., U.S.	198	42.18 N	95.03 W
Lakeview, Mi., U.S.	190	43.26 N	85.16 W
Lake View, N.Y., U.S.	210	42.42 N	78.56 W
Lakeview, Oh., U.S.	216	40.29 N	83.56 W
Lakeview, Or., U.S.	202	42.11 N	120.20 W
Lake View, S.C., U.S.	192	34.20 N	79.09 W
Lakeview, Tx., U.S.	194	29.55 N	93.54 W
Lakeview, Tx., U.S.	196	34.40 N	100.42 W
Lakeview, Wa., U.S.	224	47.10 N	122.30 W
Lakeview ◆[8]	278	41.57 N	87.39 W
Lakeview Mountain ∧, B.C., Can.	182	49.03 N	120.09 W
Lakeview Mountain ∧, Wa., U.S.	224	46.22 N	121.24 W
Lakeview Park ♠	285	40.12 N	75.32 W
Lake Village, Ar., U.S.	194	33.19 N	91.16 W
Lake Village, In., U.S.	216	41.08 N	87.27 W
Lakeville, Ct., U.S.	207	41.57 N	73.26 W
Lakeville, In., U.S.	216	41.31 N	86.16 W
Lakeville, Mi., U.S.	214	42.49 N	83.09 W
Lakeville, Mn., U.S.	190	44.38 N	93.14 W
Lakeville, N.Y., U.S.	210	42.50 N	77.42 W
Lakeville, Oh., U.S.	214	40.40 N	82.07 W
Lakeville Lake ⊜	214	42.50 N	83.09 W
Lake Wales	220	27.54 N	81.35 W
Lake Whitney State Park ♠	222	31.55 N	97.22 W
Lake Wilson	198	43.59 N	95.57 W
Lake Winola	210	41.30 N	75.50 W
Lakewood, Ca., U.S.	228	33.51 N	118.07 W
Lakewood, Co., U.S.	200	39.42 N	105.04 W
Lakewood, Il., U.S.	216	39.19 N	88.54 W
Lakewood, Mi., U.S.	216	42.18 N	85.31 W
Lakewood, N.J., U.S.	208	40.05 N	74.13 W
Lakewood, N.Y., U.S.	214	42.06 N	79.20 W
Lakewood, Oh., U.S.	214	41.28 N	81.47 W
Lakewood, Pa., U.S.	210	41.51 N	75.22 W
Lakewood, Wa., U.S.	224	48.09 N	122.12 W
Lakewood, Wi., U.S.	190	45.18 N	88.31 W
Lakewood Center ◆[9]	280	33.51 N	118.09 W
Lakewood Park	198	48.04 N	98.56 W
Lakewood Park ♠	279a	41.29 N	81.47 W
Lakewood Shores	216	41.17 N	88.10 W
Lake Worth, Fl., U.S.	220	26.36 N	80.03 W
Lake Worth, Tx., U.S.	222	32.49 N	97.27 W
Lake Zurich	216	42.11 N	88.05 W
Lakhdaria	34	36.34 N	3.35 E
Lākheri	124	25.40 N	76.10 E
Lakhīmpur	124	27.57 N	80.46 E
Lakhipur, India	120	24.48 N	93.01 E
Lakhipur, India	124	26.02 N	90.18 E
Lakhish	132	31.34 N	34.51 E
Lakhish V	132	31.49 N	34.38 E
Lakhnādon	124	22.36 N	79.36 E
Lakhya ≃	126	23.35 N	90.31 E
L'aki	84	40.34 N	47.26 E
Laki ≃	115a	7.30 S	107.25 E
Lakin	198	37.56 N	101.15 W
Lakinsk	80	56.01 N	39.57 E
Lakkadiven → Lakshadweep II	122	10.00 N	73.00 E
Lakki	123	32.36 N	70.55 E
Laknau → Lucknow	124	26.51 N	80.55 E
Lakonikós Kólpos ⊂	38	36.25 N	22.37 E
Lakor, Pulau I	164	8.14 S	128.10 E
Lakota, C. Iv.	150	5.51 N	5.41 W
Lakota, Ia., U.S.	190	43.22 N	94.05 W
Lakota, N.D., U.S.	198	48.02 N	98.20 W
Laksefjorden ⊂[2]	24	70.58 N	27.00 E
Lakselv	24	70.04 N	24.56 E
Lakshadweep □[8]	122	10.00 N	73.00 E
Lakshadweep II	122	10.00 N	73.00 E
Lākshām	124	23.14 N	91.08 E
Lakshamannāth	126	21.51 N	87.13 E
Lakshmanpur	272b	22.38 N	88.16 E
Lakshmeshwar	122	15.08 N	75.28 E
Lakshmi, Char I	126	21.57 N	90.33 E
Lakshmikantapur	126	22.07 N	88.20 E
Lakshmi Narayan Temple †[1]	272a	28.38 N	77.12 E
Lakshmīpur	126	22.57 N	90.50 E
Lakshmisāgar	126	22.55 N	87.01 E
Lala	116	7.59 N	123.46 E
Lalafuta ≃	154	13.57 S	24.41 E
La Laguna → San Cristóbal de la Laguna	148	28.29 N	16.19 W
La Lajilla	232	26.47 N	99.37 W
Lāla Mūsa	123	32.42 N	73.58 E
Lalapansi	154	19.16 S	30.15 E
Lâlapaşa	130	41.50 N	26.44 E
Lalatuncun	104	41.44 N	122.00 E
Lalbenque	32	44.20 N	1.33 E
L'Albufera ⊜	34	39.20 N	0.22 W
Laleham, Austl.	166	23.58 S	148.46 E
Laleham, Eng., U.K.	260	51.25 N	0.30 W
Lāleh Zār, Kūh-e ∧	128	29.24 N	56.45 E
La Leona	196	25.52 N	101.05 W
La Leonesa	252	27.03 S	58.43 W
Lalera	152	0.22 N	11.28 E
Lalevade-d'Ardèche	62	44.39 N	4.19 E
Lālganj	124	25.52 N	85.11 E
Lālgarh	126	22.35 N	87.03 E
Lāliān	123	31.49 N	72.48 E
Lalibela	144	12.02 N	39.02 E
La Libertad, El Sal.	236	13.29 N	89.19 W
La Libertad, Guat.	232	16.47 N	90.07 W
La Libertad, Hond.	236	14.43 N	87.36 W
La Libertad, Nic.	236	12.13 N	85.10 W
La Libertad □[5]	248	8.00 S	78.30 W
La Ligua	252	32.27 S	71.14 W
La Lima, Hond.	236	15.24 N	87.56 W
La Lima, It.	66	44.04 N	10.46 E
La Limpia, Laguna ⊜	258	35.37 S	57.49 W
Lalín	34	42.39 N	8.07 W
Lalin ≃	89	45.29 N	125.26 E
Lalinde	32	44.51 N	0.44 E
Lalindi	115b	10.12 S	120.10 E
Lalindu ≃	112	3.28 S	122.05 E
La Línea	34	36.10 N	5.19 W
L'alino	82	54.29 N	39.06 E
La Lisa ◆[8]	286b	23.04 N	82.26 W
Lalitpur	124	24.41 N	78.25 E
La Llagosta	266d	41.31 N	2.12 E
Lalla Khedidja, Tamgout de ∧	34	36.27 N	4.15 E
Lal Lal Reservoir ⊜[1]	169	37.40 S	144.04 E
Lālmanir Hāt	124	25.54 N	89.27 E
Lālmohan	126	22.13 N	90.42 E
Laloa	112	4.50 S	121.54 E
La Loche	184	56.29 N	109.27 W
La Loche ≃	184	56.09 N	109.08 W
La Loche, Lac ⊜	184	56.25 N	109.30 W
Laloki	164	9.25 S	147.15 E
La Loma	234	22.53 N	105.51 W
La Londe	62	43.08 N	6.14 E
La Lora ⋏[1]	34	42.45 N	4.00 W
Lalor Park	274a	33.45 S	150.56 E
La Loupe	50	48.28 N	1.01 E
Lalouvesc	62	45.07 N	4.32 E
La Louvière	50	50.28 N	4.11 E
L'Alpe-d'Huez	62	45.06 N	6.04 E
Lālpur, Bngl.	126	24.11 N	88.58 E
Lālpur, India	120	22.12 N	69.58 E
Lal'sk	24	60.44 N	47.34 E
Lālsot	124	26.34 N	76.20 E
Lālua	126	21.57 N	90.18 E
La Luz, Méx.	196	25.52 N	97.37 W
La Luz, N.M., U.S.	200	32.58 N	105.56 W
Lam	60	49.12 N	13.03 E
Lama ≃, S.S.S.R.	82	56.29 N	36.10 E
Lama ≃, Zhg.	104	42.11 N	123.29 E
Lama, ozero ⊜	74	69.30 N	90.30 E
L'Amable Lake ⊜	212	45.01 N	77.49 W
La Macarena, Serranía de ⋏	246	2.45 N	73.55 W
La Maddalena	71	41.13 N	9.24 E
Lama dei Peligni	66	42.02 N	14.11 E
La Madeleine	50	50.39 N	3.04 E
Lamadong	98	40.39 N	119.39 E
La Madrague	62	43.14 N	5.22 E
La Madrid, Arg.	252	27.38 S	65.15 W
Lamadrid, Méx.	196	27.05 N	101.50 W
Lamag	112	5.29 N	117.49 E
La Magdalena, Río de ≃	286a	19.21 N	99.11 W
Lamagoumen	105	40.52 N	116.39 E
Lamahuang	104	42.27 N	121.33 E
La Mailleraye-sur-Seine	50	49.29 N	0.46 E
Lamainong	114	3.49 N	96.46 E
La Majada	286c	10.27 N	67.01 W
Lama-Kara	150	9.33 N	1.12 E
La Malbaie	186	47.39 N	70.10 W
La Malinche, Parque Nacional ♠	234	19.15 N	98.05 W
Lamaline	186	46.52 N	55.49 W
La Malmaison ⊥	261	48.52 N	2.10 E
Lamaload Reservoir ⊜[1]	262	53.16 N	2.02 W
Lama Mocogno	64	44.18 N	10.45 E
La Mancha	232	24.52 N	102.47 W
La Mancha ◆[1]	34	38.50 N	3.00 W
La Mancha, Canal de → English Channel ⍖	28	50.20 N	1.00 W
La Manche (English Channel) ⍖	28	50.20 N	1.00 W
Lamandau ≃	112	2.42 S	111.34 E
La Mansión	236	10.06 N	85.22 W
Lamap	175f	16.26 S	167.43 E
Lamar, Co., U.S.	198	38.05 N	102.37 W
Lamar, Mo., U.S.	194	37.29 N	94.16 W
Lamar, Pa., U.S.	210	41.01 N	77.32 W
Lamar, S.C., U.S.	192	34.10 N	80.03 W
Lamar ≃	202	44.56 N	110.24 W
La Mar, Parque ♠	286d	12.04 S	77.02 W
La Marañosa	266a	40.17 N	3.35 W
Lamarche	58	48.04 N	5.47 E
Lamarche-sur-Saône	58	47.16 N	5.23 E
La Mare, Pointe ›	240e	14.47 N	61.13 W
Lamari ≃	164	6.54 S	145.25 E
La Mariposa, Embalse ⊜[1]	286c	10.24 N	66.56 W
La Mariscala	252	34.03 S	54.47 W
La Marmora, Punta ∧	71	39.59 N	9.20 E
La Marolle-en-Sologne	50	47.35 N	1.47 E
La Maroma	196	28.34 N	100.45 W
Lamarque, Arg.	252	39.24 S	65.42 W
La Marque, Tx., U.S.	222	29.22 N	94.58 W
La Marsa	36	36.53 N	10.20 E
La Martre	62	43.46 N	6.36 E
Lamas	248	6.25 S	76.35 W
La Masica	236	15.37 N	87.07 W
Lamastre	62	44.59 N	4.35 E
La Matanza → San Justo	258	34.40 S	58.33 W
Lama Temple †[1]	271a	39.56 N	116.25 E
La Mauricie, Parc National de (La Mauricie National Park) ♠	206	46.50 N	73.00 W
La Maya, Cuba	240p	20.10 N	75.39 W
Lamaya, Zhg.	102	29.50 N	99.53 E
Lamayingzi	104	42.09 N	121.50 E
Lambach	60	48.05 N	13.53 E
Lamballe	32	48.28 N	2.31 W
Lambaréné	152	0.42 S	10.13 E
Lambari	256	21.58 S	45.21 W
Lambari ≃, Bra.	255	19.30 S	45.00 W
Lambari ≃, Bra.	256	21.47 S	45.13 W
Lambasa	175g	16.26 S	179.24 E
Lambayeque	248	6.42 S	79.55 W
Lambayeque □[5]	248	6.20 S	80.00 W
Lambayeque ≃	248	6.43 S	79.54 W
Lambay Island I	48	53.29 N	6.01 W
Lambe	273a	6.42 N	3.21 E
Lambersart	50	50.39 N	3.02 E
Lambert, Ms., U.S.	194	34.12 N	90.17 W
Lambert, Mt., U.S.	198	47.41 N	104.37 W
Lambert, Cape ›, Austl.	162	20.35 S	117.10 E
Lambert, Cape ›, Pap. N. Gui.	164	4.12 S	151.32 E
Lambert Glacier ⊓	9	71.00 S	70.00 E
Lamberton	198	44.13 N	95.15 W
Lambert-Saint Louis International Airport ⊠	219	38.45 N	90.22 W
Lambertsbaai → Lambert's Bay	158	32.05 S	18.17 E
Lambert's Bay	158	32.05 S	18.17 E
Lambertville, Mi., U.S.	216	41.45 N	83.37 W
Lambertville, N.J., U.S.	208	40.21 N	74.56 W
Lambesc	62	43.39 N	5.16 E
Lambeth	214	42.54 N	81.18 W
Lambeth ◆[8]	42	51.30 N	0.07 W
L'ambir'	80	54.17 N	45.07 E
Lambo Katenga	154	5.02 S	28.48 E
Lambomakondro	157b	22.41 S	44.44 E
Lambourn	42	51.31 N	1.31 W
Lambourne ≃	42	51.24 N	1.18 W
Lambourne End	260	51.38 N	0.08 E
Lambrama	248	13.52 S	72.46 W
Lambrate ◆[8]	266b	45.29 N	9.15 E
Lambrecht	56	50.08 N	8.56 E
Lambrechten	60	48.19 N	13.31 E
Lambrechts Drift	158	28.31 S	21.43 E
Lambro ≃	62	45.08 N	9.32 E
Lambro, Parco ♠	266b	45.30 N	9.15 E
Lambs Creek	210	41.51 N	77.06 W
Lambs Terrace	285	39.46 N	75.02 W
Lambton	273d	26.15 S	28.10 E
Lambton □[6]	214	42.45 N	82.15 W
Lambton, Cape ›	176	71.05 N	123.10 W
Lambu	164	3.09 S	151.41 E
Lambunao	116	11.03 N	122.29 E
L'amca	24	64.27 N	37.04 E
Lamdessar	164	7.12 S	131.58 E
Lame, Nig.	150	10.23 N	9.13 E
Lamé, Tchad	146	9.15 N	14.32 E
La Meca → Makkah	144	21.27 N	39.49 E
La Mecque → Makkah	144	21.27 N	39.49 E
Lame Deer	202	45.37 N	106.39 W
La Media Luna, Arrecifes de ✢[2]	236	15.13 N	82.36 W
La Méditerranée → Mediterranean Sea ⊤[2]	10	35.00 N	20.00 E
Lamego	34	41.06 N	7.49 W
La Meije ∧	62	45.00 N	6.18 E
La Membrolle-sur-Choisille	50	47.26 N	0.38 E
La Mendieta	252	24.19 S	64.58 W
L'amen'ga	76	59.51 N	44.31 E
Lamentin	241o	16.16 N	61.38 W
Lamèque	186	47.47 N	64.38 W
Lamèque, Île I	186	47.48 N	64.36 W
La Merced, Arg.	252	28.10 S	65.41 W
La Merced, Arg.	252	24.58 S	65.29 W
La Merced, Perú	248	11.03 S	75.19 W
Lameroo	166	35.20 S	140.31 E
La Mesa, Pan.	236	8.09 N	81.11 W
La Mesa, Ca., U.S.	228	32.46 N	117.01 W
La Mesa, N.M., U.S.	200	32.07 N	106.42 W
Lamesa, Tx., U.S.	196	32.44 N	101.57 W
La Mesa, Cerro ∧	232	26.59 N	113.44 W
La Mesa Dam ◆[6]	269f	14.43 N	121.04 E
La Meta ∧	66	41.41 N	13.56 E
Lamía	38	38.54 N	22.26 E
L'amin ≃	74	61.18 N	71.48 E
Lamine ≃	194	38.59 N	92.51 W
La Minerve	206	46.15 N	74.56 W
Laming ≃	61	47.25 N	15.16 E
Lamington ≃	210	40.38 N	74.41 W
Lamington National Park ♠	166	28.15 S	153.12 E
La Mira	234	18.02 N	102.19 W
La Mirada	228	33.55 N	118.00 W
La Mirada Creek ≃	280	33.53 N	118.01 W
La Misión	204	32.05 N	116.50 W
Lamitan	116	6.39 N	122.08 E
Lamlam, Mount ∧[2]	174p	13.20 N	144.40 E
Lamlash	46	55.32 N	5.08 W
Lamma Island I	271d	22.12 N	114.07 E
Lammefjord ⊂	41	55.48 N	11.43 E
Lammerlaw Top ∧	172	45.40 S	169.38 E
Lammermuir ◆[1]	46	55.50 N	2.25 W
Lammermuir Hills ⋏[2]	46	55.50 N	2.44 W
Lammeulo	114	5.15 N	95.56 E
Lammhulf	26	57.10 N	14.35 E
Lammi	26	61.05 N	25.01 E
Lamming Mills	182	53.22 N	120.18 W
Lamogai	164	5.50 S	149.20 E
La Moille, Il., U.S.	190	41.31 N	89.16 W
Lamoille, Nv., U.S.	204	40.43 N	115.28 W
Lamoille ≃	188	44.35 N	73.10 W
La Moine ≃	194	39.59 N	90.31 W
La Moine, East Fork ≃	194	40.24 N	90.56 W
Lamoka Lake ⊜	210	42.24 N	77.05 W
La Molina	286d	12.05 S	76.57 W
Lamon Bay ⊂	116	14.25 N	122.00 E
La Moncada	234	20.16 N	100.48 W
Lamone ≃	66	44.31 N	12.15 E
Lamongan	115a	7.07 S	112.25 E
Lamongan, Gunung ∧	115a	7.58 S	113.20 E
Lamoni	190	40.37 N	93.56 W
Lamont, Ab., Can.	182	53.46 N	112.48 W
Lamont, Ca., U.S.	228	35.15 N	118.54 W
Lamont, Ia., U.S.	190	42.35 N	91.38 W
Lamont, Mi., U.S.	216	43.01 N	86.09 W
Lamont, Ok., U.S.	196	36.41 N	97.33 W
La Monte	194	38.46 N	93.25 W
La Mora, Monte ∧	236	15.06 N	86.16 W
La Mosquitia □[9]	236	15.00 N	83.45 W
La Mothe, Lac ⊜[1]	186	48.46 N	71.09 W
La Mothe-Achard	32	46.37 N	1.40 W
Lamotrek I[1]	14	7.30 N	146.20 E
La Mott	285	40.04 N	75.08 W
La Motte, Lac ⊜	190	48.24 N	78.03 W
Lamotte-Beuvron	50	47.36 N	2.01 E
La Motte-Chalançon	62	44.29 N	5.23 E
La Motte-du-Caire	62	44.21 N	6.02 E
Lamoura	58	46.24 N	5.58 E
La Moure	198	46.21 N	98.17 W
La Moustique ≃	241o	16.11 N	61.35 W
Lampa	248	15.21 S	70.22 W
Lampang	110	18.18 N	99.31 E
Lampasas	196	31.03 N	98.10 W
Lampasas ≃	196	30.59 N	97.24 W
Lampazos de Naranjo	232	27.01 N	100.31 W
Lampedusa	70a	35.30 N	12.56 E
Lampedusa, Isola di I	70a	35.31 N	12.35 E
Lampertheim	56	49.35 N	8.28 E
Lampeter, Wales, U.K.	42	52.07 N	4.05 W
Lampeter, Pa., U.S.	208	39.58 N	76.14 W
Lamphun	110	18.35 N	99.01 E
Lampinsaari	26	64.25 N	25.09 E
Lampione, Isolotto di I	70a	35.34 N	12.19 E
Lampman	184	49.23 N	102.45 W
Lamprechtshausen	64	47.59 N	12.57 E
Lampung □[4]	112	5.00 S	105.00 E
Lampung, Teluk ⊂	115a	5.40 S	105.20 E
Lamskoje	76	52.57 N	38.02 E
Lamspringe	52	51.58 N	10.00 E
Lamstedt	52	53.38 N	9.05 E
Lāmta	124	22.08 N	80.07 E
Lam Tong Hoi Hap ⍖	271d	22.15 N	114.15 E
Lamu, Kenya	154	2.16 S	40.54 E
Lāmu, Mya.	110	19.14 N	94.10 E
Lamud	248	6.09 S	77.55 W
La Muerte, Cerro ∧	236	9.33 N	83.44 W
Lam Uk Wei	271d	22.26 N	114.22 E
La Mure	62	44.54 N	5.47 E
Lamure-sur-Azergues	58	46.04 N	4.30 E
La Mutua	234	22.23 N	99.18 W
Lan' ≃, S.S.S.R.	76	52.09 N	27.18 E
Lan ≃, Zhg.	104	41.14 N	123.32 E
Lan, Loi ∧	110	19.40 N	97.55 E
Lana	64	46.37 N	11.09 E
Lana, Río de la ≃	234	17.49 N	95.09 W
Lanai I	229a	20.50 N	156.55 W
Lanai City	229a	20.49 N	156.55 W
Lanaihale ∧	229a	20.49 N	156.52 W
Lanaken	56	50.53 N	5.39 E
Lanalhue, Lago ⊜	252	37.55 S	73.18 W
La Nana, Bayou ≃	222	31.27 N	94.43 W
Lanao del Norte □[4]	116	8.10 N	124.00 E
Lanao del Sur □[4]	116	7.50 N	124.25 E
La Napoule	62	43.31 N	6.56 E
Lanarce	62	44.44 N	4.00 E
Lanark, On., Can.	212	45.01 N	76.22 W
Lanark, Scot., U.K.	46	55.41 N	3.46 W
Lanark, Il., U.S.	190	42.06 N	89.50 W
Lanark, Pa., U.S.	208	40.33 N	75.26 W
Lanark □[6]	212	45.05 N	76.20 W
La Nartelle	62	43.19 N	6.39 E
Lanas	112	5.20 N	116.30 E
La Nava de Ricomalillo	34	39.39 N	4.59 W
Lanbi Kyun I	110	10.50 N	98.15 E
Lanboyan Point ›	116	8.18 N	122.56 E
Lancang	102	23.00 N	100.02 E
Lancang → Mekong ≃	12	10.33 N	105.24 E
Lancashire	285	39.49 N	75.29 W
Lancashire □[6]	44	53.45 N	2.40 W
Lancashire Plain ≚	44	53.40 N	2.45 W
Lancaster, On., Can.	206	45.08 N	74.30 W
Lancaster, Eng., U.K.	44	54.03 N	2.48 W
Lancaster, Ca., U.S.	228	34.41 N	118.08 W
Lancaster, Ky., U.S.	192	37.37 N	84.34 W
Lancaster, Ma., U.S.	207	42.27 N	71.40 W
Lancaster, Mn., U.S.	198	48.51 N	96.48 W
Lancaster, Mo., U.S.	194	40.31 N	92.31 W
Lancaster, N.H., U.S.	188	44.29 N	71.34 W
Lancaster, N.Y., U.S.	210	42.54 N	78.40 W
Lancaster, Oh., U.S.	188	39.43 N	82.36 W
Lancaster, Pa., U.S.	208	40.02 N	76.18 W
Lancaster, S.C., U.S.	192	34.43 N	80.46 W
Lancaster, Tx., U.S.	222	32.38 N	96.47 W
Lancaster, Va., U.S.	208	37.46 N	76.28 W
Lancaster, Wi., U.S.	190	42.50 N	90.42 W
Lancaster □[6], Pa., U.S.	208	40.02 N	76.19 W
Lancaster □[6], Va., U.S.	208	37.45 N	76.30 W
Lancaster Canal ≋	262	53.46 N	2.43 W
Lancaster Sound ⍖	176	74.13 N	84.00 W
Lancaster Village	285	39.45 N	75.35 W
Lančchuti	84	42.06 N	42.01 E
Lance Creek	200	43.01 N	104.38 W
Lance Creek ≃	198	43.22 N	104.16 W
Lancefield	169	37.17 S	144.44 E
Lancelin	162	31.02 S	115.20 E
Lancelot, Mount ∧	162	26.13 S	123.12 E
Lancey	62	45.14 N	5.53 E
Lanchang	114	3.30 N	102.11 E
Lanchester	44	54.49 N	1.44 W
Lanchow → Lanzhou	102	36.03 N	103.41 E
Lanciano	66	42.14 N	14.23 E
Lancin, Fr.	62	45.43 N	5.24 E
Lančin, S.S.S.R.	78	48.34 N	24.45 E
Lancing	42	50.50 N	0.19 W
Lanco	254	39.24 S	72.46 W
Lancones	246	4.35 S	80.30 W
Lancun	98	36.24 N	120.10 E
Łańcut	30	50.05 N	22.13 E
Lancy	58	46.11 N	6.07 E
Lândana	152	5.13 S	12.08 E
Landang Gua	116	6.58 N	122.15 E
Landau	56	49.12 N	8.07 E
Landau an der Isar	60	48.40 N	12.43 E
Landay	128	30.31 N	63.47 E
Land Between the Lakes ♠	194	36.55 N	88.05 W
Landeck	58	47.08 N	10.34 E
Landeck in Westpreussen → Lędyczek	30	53.33 N	16.58 E
Landen	56	50.45 N	5.05 E
Landenberg	208	39.47 N	75.46 W
Landenhausen	56	50.36 N	9.28 E
Lander	200	42.49 N	108.43 W
Lander ≃	162	20.25 S	132.00 E
Landerneau	32	48.27 N	4.15 W
Landes □[5]	32	44.20 N	1.00 W
Landes ◆[1]	32	44.15 N	1.00 W
Landesbergen	52	52.33 N	9.07 E
Landeskrone ∧[2]	54	51.08 N	14.56 E
Landess	216	40.37 N	85.34 W
Landete	34	39.54 N	1.22 W
Landham Brook ≃	283	42.22 N	71.25 W
Landhausen	263	51.24 N	7.45 E
Landi	98	36.35 N	119.59 E
Landi Kotal	123	34.06 N	71.09 E
Landina	86	59.12 N	67.02 E
Landing	210	40.54 N	74.40 W
Landing Lake ⊜	184	55.17 N	97.26 W
Landis, Sk., Can.	184	52.12 N	108.28 W
Landis, N.C., U.S.	192	35.32 N	80.36 W
Landisburg	208	40.20 N	77.18 W
Landisville	208	40.06 N	76.25 W
Landivisiau	32	48.31 N	4.04 W
Landkey	42	51.04 N	4.00 W
Landkirchen	54	54.27 N	11.08 E
Lando	192	34.46 N	81.00 W
Land O'Lakes, Fl., U.S.	220	28.11 N	82.34 W
Land O'Lakes, Wi., U.S.	190	46.10 N	89.13 W
Landor	162	25.09 S	116.54 E
Landos	62	44.51 N	3.50 E
Landösjön ⊜	26	63.35 N	14.04 E
Landover Estates	284c	38.56 N	76.54 W
Landover Hills	284c	38.57 N	76.53 W
Landover Mall ◆[9]	284c	38.55 N	76.51 W
Landquart	58	46.58 N	9.33 E
Landquart ≃	58	46.58 N	9.32 E
Landrecies	50	50.08 N	3.42 E
Landres	56	49.19 N	5.48 E
Landreth Draw V	196	31.14 N	102.29 W
Landriano	62	45.19 N	9.15 E
Landri Sales	250	7.16 S	43.55 W
Landro (Höhlenstein)	64	46.39 N	12.14 E
Landrum	192	35.10 N	82.11 W
Landry	62	45.34 N	6.45 E
Landsberg	54	51.31 N	12.10 E
Landsberg am Lech	58	48.05 N	10.55 E
Landsberg an der Warthe → Gorzów Wielkopolski	30	52.44 N	15.15 E
Landsberg in Oberschlesien → Gorzów Śląski	30	51.02 N	18.24 E
Landsberg in Ostpreussen → Górowo Iławeckie	30	54.17 N	20.30 E
Landsborough	166	26.49 S	152.58 E
Landsborough Creek ≃	166	22.30 S	144.33 E
Landsbro	26	57.22 N	14.54 E
Land's End ›, Eng., U.K.	42	50.03 N	5.44 W
Lands End ›, Ca., U.S.	228	33.28 N	118.36 W
Lands End ›, R.I., U.S.	207	41.27 N	71.19 W
Landshut	60	48.33 N	12.09 E
Landskrona	41	55.52 N	12.50 E
Landsman Creek ≃	198	39.35 N	102.19 W
Landsmeer	52	52.26 N	4.52 E
Landštejn	61	49.00 N	15.13 E
Landstuhl	56	49.25 N	7.34 E
Landweg	263	51.29 N	7.37 E
Landwehrbach ≃	263	51.26 N	6.26 E
Land Wursten ◆[1]	52	53.40 N	8.35 E
Lane	219	40.07 N	88.51 W
Lane ≃	50	47.17 N	0.05 E
Lane City	222	29.13 N	96.02 W
Lane Cove	274a	33.49 S	151.10 E
Lane Cove ⊂	274a	33.48 S	151.09 E
Lane Cove River Park ♠	274a	33.47 S	151.09 E
La Negra	252	23.45 S	70.19 W
Lane Mountain ∧	228	35.05 N	116.56 W
Lanersbach	64	47.09 N	11.44 E
Lanesboro, Ma., U.S.	207	42.31 N	73.14 W
Lanesboro, Mn., U.S.	190	43.43 N	91.58 W
Lanesboro, Pa., U.S.	210	41.57 N	75.35 W
Lanester	32	47.46 N	3.21 W
Lanesville, In., U.S.	218	38.14 N	85.59 W
Lanesville, N.Y., U.S.	210	42.08 N	74.16 W
Lanesville, Va., U.S.	208	37.37 N	76.59 W
Lanett	194	32.52 N	85.11 W
La Neuveville	58	47.04 N	7.06 E
Laneville	222	31.58 N	94.49 W
Lanexa	208	37.24 N	76.55 W
Lanezi Lake ⊜	182	53.03 N	120.56 W
Lang	184	49.56 N	104.23 W
La'nga Co ⊜	124	30.42 N	81.16 E
Langadhás	38	40.45 N	23.04 E
Langádhia	38	37.41 N	22.02 E
Langa-Langa	152	3.54 S	15.56 E
Langan Creek ≃	216	40.57 N	87.49 W
Langano, Lake ⊜	144	7.35 N	38.48 E
Langao	102	32.13 N	109.02 E
Langar, Afg.	120	37.02 N	73.47 E
L'angar, S.S.S.R.	85	40.25 N	73.07 E
L'angar, S.S.S.R.	123	37.02 N	72.42 E
Langara	112	4.02 S	123.00 E
Langara Island I	182	54.14 N	133.00 W
Langarūd	128	37.11 N	50.10 E
L'angasovo	80	58.32 N	49.30 E
Langat ≃	114	2.54 N	101.22 E
Langau	61	48.49 N	15.42 E
Langavat, Loch ⊜	46	58.04 N	6.48 W
Långban	40	59.51 N	14.15 E
Langbank	184	50.05 N	102.20 W
Lang Bay	182	49.47 N	124.21 W
Langberg ⋏	158	28.20 S	22.35 E
Langburkersdorf	54	51.02 N	14.14 E
Langda	102	31.12 N	96.59 E
Langdai	102	26.06 N	105.20 E
Langdon	198	48.45 N	98.22 W
Langdondale	214	40.08 N	78.15 W
Langdon Hills	260	51.34 N	0.25 E
Langeac	32	45.06 N	3.30 E
Langeais	50	47.20 N	0.24 E
Langebaan	158	33.06 S	18.02 E
Langeberg ⋏	158	33.55 S	20.30 E
Lange Berge ⋏[2]	56	50.20 N	10.55 E
Langebrück	54	51.07 N	13.50 E
Langeland I	41	55.00 N	10.50 E
Langelandsbælt ⍖	41	54.50 N	10.55 E
Längelmävesi ⊜	26	61.32 N	24.22 E
Langeloth	214	40.21 N	80.24 W
Langelsheim	52	51.56 N	10.19 E
Langemark	50	50.55 N	2.55 E
Langen, B.R.D.	52	53.36 N	8.35 E
Langen, B.R.D.	56	49.59 N	8.41 E
Langenargen	58	47.35 N	9.32 E
Langenau, B.R.D.	58	48.30 N	10.07 E
Langenau, D.D.R.	54	50.50 N	13.18 E
Langenberg, B.R.D.	52	51.46 N	8.19 E
Langenberg, B.R.D.	56	51.21 N	7.09 E
Langenbernsdorf	54	50.45 N	12.19 E
Langenbielau → Bielawa	30	50.41 N	16.38 E
Langenbochum	263	51.37 N	7.07 E
Langenbruck	58	47.21 N	7.46 E
Langenburg, B.R.D.	56	49.15 N	9.50 E
Langenburg, Sk., Can.	184	50.50 N	101.43 W
Langendorf	54	51.11 N	11.58 E
Langendreer ◆[8]	263	51.28 N	7.19 E
Langeneichstädt	54	51.20 N	11.41 E
Langenfeld, B.R.D.	56	51.07 N	6.56 E
Längenfeld, Öst.	64	47.04 N	10.58 E
Langenhagen	52	52.27 N	9.44 E
Langenhessen	54	50.45 N	12.22 E
Langenhorn	41	54.41 N	8.53 E
Langenhorst	263	51.22 N	7.02 E
Langenlois	61	48.28 N	15.40 E
Langennaundorf	54	51.36 N	13.20 E
Langenneufnach	58	48.16 N	10.36 E
Langenselbold	56	50.10 N	9.02 E
Langensteinach	56	49.30 N	10.10 E
Langenthal	58	47.13 N	7.47 E
Langenwang	61	47.34 N	15.37 E
Langenweddingen	54	52.02 N	11.31 E
Langenwetzendorf	54	50.41 N	12.05 E
Langenzenn	56	49.30 N	10.48 E
Langenzersdorf	61	48.18 N	16.22 E
Langeoog	52	53.45 N	7.29 E
Langeoog I	52	53.46 N	7.32 E
Langerfeld ◆[8]	263	51.16 N	7.15 E
Langer See ⊜	264a	52.25 N	13.38 E
Langerwehe	56	50.49 N	6.22 E
Langeskov	41	55.22 N	10.36 E
Langesund	26	59.00 N	9.45 E
Langevåg	26	62.27 N	6.12 E
Langewiesen	54	50.40 N	10.58 E
Langfang → Anci	105	39.31 N	116.41 E
Langfjorden ⊂[2]	26	62.43 N	7.30 E
Langford, B.C., Can.	224	48.27 N	123.30 W
Langford, Eng., U.K.	260	51.45 N	0.40 E
Langford, N.Y., U.S.	210	42.35 N	78.51 W
Langford, S.D., U.S.	198	45.36 N	97.49 W
Langförden	52	52.47 N	8.14 E
Langgam	112	0.15 N	101.43 E
Langgapayung	114	1.43 N	99.59 E
Langgöns	56	50.30 N	8.40 E
Långhalsen ⊜	40	58.56 N	16.41 E
Langham	184	52.22 N	106.57 W
Langhe □[9]	62	44.30 N	8.00 E
Langhirano	64	44.37 N	10.16 E
Langho	262	53.48 N	2.27 W
Langholm	44	55.09 N	3.00 W
Langhorne	208	40.10 N	74.55 W
Langhorne Acres	284c	38.51 N	77.16 W
Langhorne Creek	168b	35.18 S	139.02 E
Langhorne Gardens	285	40.11 N	74.53 W
Langhorne Manor	285	40.10 N	74.55 W
Langhorne Terrace	285	40.10 N	74.57 W
Langji Shan I	100	28.32 N	121.36 E
Langjökull ⊓	24a	64.42 N	20.12 W
Langju	100	27.52 N	116.36 E
Lang Ka, Doi ∧	110	19.00 N	99.24 E
Langkawi, Pulau I	114	6.22 N	99.50 E
Langkesi, Kepulauan II	112	5.18 S	124.20 E
Langklip	158	28.12 S	20.20 E
Langkrans	158	27.47 S	31.03 E
Langlade I	186	46.50 N	56.20 W
Lang Lang ≃	169	38.17 S	145.31 E
Langley, B.C., Can.	224	49.06 N	122.39 W
Langley, Eng., U.K.	260	51.30 N	0.33 W
Langley, Eng., U.K.	260	51.14 N	0.35 E
Langley, Eng., U.K.	262	53.15 N	2.05 W
Langley, Ok., U.S.	196	36.27 N	95.02 W
Langley, S.C., U.S.	192	33.31 N	81.50 W
Langley, Va., U.S.	284c	38.57 N	77.10 W
Langley, Wa., U.S.	224	48.02 N	122.24 W
Langley Air Force Base ■	208	37.05 N	76.21 W
Langley Hill ∧[2]	282	37.20 N	122.14 W
Langley Park	284c	38.59 N	76.58 W
Langleyville	219	39.34 N	89.21 W
Langlo ≃	166	26.26 S	146.05 E
Langlois	202	42.55 N	124.26 W
Langmazong	120	30.52 N	89.58 E
Lang Mo	110	17.14 N	106.27 E
Långnäs	26	60.06 N	20.17 E
Langnau	58	46.57 N	7.47 E
Langogne	62	44.43 N	3.51 E
Langon	32	44.33 N	0.15 W
Langøya I	24	68.44 N	14.50 E
Langping	102	30.38 N	110.21 E
Langport	42	51.02 N	2.50 W
Langqiao	100	30.30 N	118.24 E
Langquaid	60	48.49 N	12.03 E
Langreo → Sama [de Langreo]	34	43.18 N	5.41 W
Langres	58	47.52 N	5.20 E
Langres, Plateau de ⋏[1]	58	47.41 N	5.03 E
Langruth	184	50.24 N	98.38 W
Langruzong	120	31.50 N	91.25 E
Langsa	114	4.28 N	97.58 E
Langsa, Teluk ⊂	114	4.35 N	98.00 E
Langschede	263	51.29 N	7.43 E
Långsele	26	63.11 N	17.04 E
Langshan, Zhg.	102	41.12 N	107.22 E
Langshan, Zhg.	105	40.22 N	115.41 E
Långshyttan	40	60.27 N	16.01 E
Långsjön ⊜	40	59.00 N	17.27 E
Langsnek ⊥	158	27.28 S	29.55 E
Lang Son	110	21.50 N	106.44 E
Langstaff	275b	43.50 N	79.25 W
Langst-Kierst	263	51.18 N	6.43 E
Lang Suan	110	9.57 N	99.04 E
Långsvan ⊜	40	59.43 N	15.49 E
Langtang National Park ♠	124	28.10 N	85.30 E
Langtian	100	25.11 N	113.28 E
Langting	120	25.30 N	93.07 E
Langton	212	42.45 N	80.35 W
Langtoutun	89	46.51 N	121.54 E
Langtuozi	104	41.01 N	121.43 E
Langu	100	27.56 N	118.11 E
Langue	236	13.37 N	87.39 W
Languedoc □[9]	32	44.00 N	4.00 E
L'Anguille ≃	194	34.44 N	90.40 W
Langui y Layo, Laguna de ⊜	248	14.29 S	71.13 W
Langula	54	51.09 N	10.25 E
Langundu, Tanjung ›	115b	8.49 S	118.58 E
Langwarden	52	53.36 N	8.19 E
Langwedel	52	52.59 N	9.12 E
Langweer	52	52.57 N	5.43 E
Langweid	58	48.29 N	10.51 E
Langweiler	56	49.40 N	7.31 E
Langwies	58	46.49 N	9.43 E
Langwo	104	41.13 N	121.44 E
Langwozhuang	105	39.05 N	115.37 E
Langxi	106	31.08 N	119.10 E
Langxi ≃	106	31.10 N	118.59 E
Langzhong	102	31.35 N	105.59 E
Langzishan	104	41.02 N	123.23 E
Lanham	284c	38.58 N	76.51 W
Lanhil Island I	116	6.46 N	122.22 E
Lanibga, Mount ∧	116	10.27 N	123.56 E
Lanigan	184	51.52 N	105.02 W
Lanigan Creek ≃	184	51.23 N	105.13 W
Lanín, Parque Nacional ♠	254	39.36 S	71.24 W
Lanín, Volcán ∧[1]	254	39.38 S	71.30 W
Lanjiang	107	30.24 N	105.11 E
Lankao (Lanfeng)	98	34.50 N	114.49 E
Lanker See ⊜	54	54.12 N	10.17 E
Lankeys Creek	171b	35.49 S	147.39 E
Länkipohja	26	61.44 N	24.48 E
Lanklaar	56	51.01 N	5.44 E
Lank-Latum	263	51.18 N	6.41 E
Lankou	100	23.59 N	115.05 E
Lankoviri	146	9.00 N	11.25 E
Lankwitz ◆[8]	264a	52.26 N	13.21 E
Lanling	89	45.15 N	126.12 E
Lannabruk	40	59.14 N	14.56 E
Lannach	61	46.56 N	15.19 E
Lännaholm	40	59.53 N	17.57 E
Lannaja	78	49.21 N	35.16 E
Lannemezan	32	43.08 N	0.23 E
Lannilis	32	48.34 N	4.31 W
Lannion	32	48.44 N	3.28 W
Lannon	216	43.08 N	88.09 W
L'Annonciation	206	46.25 N	74.52 W
Lanoka Harbor	208	39.52 N	74.10 W
Lanoraie	206	45.58 N	73.13 W
La Noria	258	35.10 S	58.48 W
Lanovcy	78	49.52 N	26.05 E
Lanping	102	26.29 N	99.23 E
Lanqibao	104	40.56 N	122.25 E
Lanqikoucun	104	40.52 N	122.26 E
Lanqipuzi	104	42.12 N	123.15 E
Lanquín	236	15.34 N	89.58 W
Lans, Montagnes de ⋏	62	44.52 N	5.29 E
Lansdale	208	40.14 N	75.17 W
Lansdowne, Austl.	162	17.53 S	126.39 E
Lansdowne, Austl.	274a	33.54 S	150.59 E
Lansdowne, On., Can.	212	44.24 N	76.01 W
Lansdowne, India	124	29.50 N	78.41 E
Lansdowne, Md., U.S.	284b	39.14 N	76.39 W
Lansdowne, Pa., U.S.	285	39.56 N	75.16 W
L'Anse, Mi., U.S.	190	46.45 N	88.27 W
Lanse, Pa., U.S.	214	40.59 N	78.08 W
L'Anse-aux-Meadows National Historic Park ♠	186	51.36 N	55.32 W
L'anse Creuse Bay ⊂	214	42.34 N	82.49 W
L'Anse Indian Reservation ◆[4]	190	46.48 N	88.22 W
Lans-en-Vercors	62	45.07 N	5.35 E
Lansford, N.D., U.S.	198	48.37 N	101.22 W
Lansford, Pa., U.S.	210	40.49 N	75.52 W
Lanshan	102	25.18 N	111.52 E
Lanshantou	98	35.07 N	119.21 E
Lansing, Il., U.S.	216	41.33 N	87.32 W
Lansing, Ia., U.S.	190	43.21 N	91.12 W
Lansing, Ks., U.S.	198	39.14 N	94.54 W
Lansing, Mi., U.S.	216	42.43 N	84.33 W
Lansing, N.Y., U.S.	210	42.32 N	76.30 W
Lansing, Oh., U.S.	214	40.04 N	80.47 W
Lansing ◆[8]	275b	43.45 N	79.25 W
Lansing, Lake ⊜	216	42.46 N	84.25 W
Lansing Municipal Airport ⊠	278	41.32 N	87.32 W
Lanškroun	30	49.55 N	16.37 E
Lanslebourg	62	45.17 N	6.52 E
Lanslevillard	62	45.17 N	6.55 E
Lanstrop ◆[8]	263	51.34 N	7.34 E
Lantana	220	26.35 N	80.03 W
Lantang	100	23.25 N	114.56 E
Lantau Island I	100	22.17 N	113.59 E
Lanta Yai, Ko I	110	7.35 N	99.05 E
Lanterne ≃	58	47.44 N	6.03 E
Lantewa	146	12.16 N	11.44 E
Lantian	102	34.03 N	109.12 E
Lantianba	107	28.52 N	105.26 E
Lantianchang	271a	39.58 N	116.17 E
Lantsch → Laces, It.	64	46.37 N	10.52 E
Lantsch, Schw.	58	46.41 N	9.34 E
Lantschou → Lanzhou	102	36.03 N	103.41 E
Lantzville	224	49.15 N	124.05 W
La Nurra ◆[1]	71	40.45 N	8.15 E
Lanús	258	34.43 S	58.24 W
Lanús □[5]	288	34.42 S	58.28 W
Lanusei	71	39.53 N	9.32 E
Lanuvio	66	41.40 N	12.42 E
Lanuza	116	9.14 N	126.04 E
Lanuza Bay ⊂	116	9.17 N	126.04 E
Lanxi, Zhg.	89	46.15 N	126.14 E
Lanxi, Zhg.	100	29.12 N	119.28 E
Lanxian	102	38.22 N	111.46 E
Lány	54	50.06 N	13.58 E
Lan Yü I	100	22.03 N	121.32 E
Lanzada	64	46.15 N	9.51 E
Lanzarote I	148	29.00 N	13.40 W
Lanzendorf	264b	48.06 N	16.26 E
Lanzhou (Lanchow)	102	36.03 N	103.41 E
Lanzo Torinese	62	45.16 N	7.28 E
Lao → Laos □[1]	110	18.00 N	105.00 E
Lao ≃, It.	68	39.47 N	15.48 E
Lao ≃, Thai	110	19.55 N	99.54 E
Lao ≃, Zhg.	100	29.11 N	116.00 E
Laoag	116	18.12 N	120.36 E
Laoag ≃	116	18.12 N	120.31 E
Laoang	116	12.34 N	125.00 E
Laoang Island I	116	12.35 N	125.01 E
Lao Bao	110	16.37 N	106.36 E
Laobian, Zhg.	104	41.58 N	123.10 E
Laobian, Zhg.	104	40.42 N	122.21 E
La Obra	286e	33.36 S	70.30 W
Lao Cai	110	22.30 N	103.57 E
Laochang, Zhg.	102	24.34 N	104.11 E
Laochang, Zhg.	107	29.30 N	106.36 E
Laocheng	104	42.37 N	124.04 E
Laodafang	104	41.40 N	122.40 E
Laodao ≃	100	28.16 N	112.58 E
Laodaodian	89	51.16 N	126.40 E
Laofengkou	86	46.11 N	83.38 E
Laofu	98	42.13 N	118.17 E
Laogang	106	31.01 N	121.49 E
Laoge	100	32.49 N	119.52 E
Laoguan	100	27.38 N	113.36 E
Laoguanpu	104	40.53 N	120.51 E
Laoha ≃	90	43.24 N	120.39 E
Laohaotuo	104	41.25 N	122.46 E
Laoheba	107	28.51 N	103.49 E
Laoheishan	89	43.45 N	130.52 E
Laoheshangtai	104	40.43 N	120.49 E
Laohokow → Guanghua	102	32.25 N	111.36 E
Laohuk'ou	100	24.53 N	121.03 E
Laohumiao	271a	39.58 N	116.20 E
Laohutuozi	104	42.25 N	122.34 E
Laois □[6]	48	53.00 N	7.24 W
Laojunguan	105	40.22 N	114.47 E
Laojunmiao → Yumen	102	39.56 N	97.51 E
Laoka	89	52.47 N	125.52 E
Laolao, Bahia ⊂	174n	15.08 N	145.46 E
Lao Ling ∧	89	43.27 N	130.11 E
Laolong ≃	106	32.11 N	120.00 E
Laolongtan	107	30.01 N	104.48 E
Laomocun	106	30.51 N	119.11 E
Laon	50	49.34 N	3.40 E
Laona, N.Y., U.S.	214	42.25 N	79.19 W
Laona, Wi., U.S.	190	45.33 N	88.40 W
La Orotava	148	28.23 N	16.31 W
La Oroya	248	11.32 S	75.54 W
Laos (Lao) □[1], Asia	108	18.00 N	105.00 E
Laos (Lao) □[1], Asia	110	18.00 N	105.00 E
Laoshan (Licun)	98	36.10 N	120.25 E
Laoshan Wan ⊂	98	36.24 N	120.45 E
Laosolu	114	3.11 N	98.02 E
Laotto	216	41.17 N	85.12 W
Laou, Oued ≃	34	35.29 N	5.04 W
Laowushi	106	31.43 N	121.00 E
Laoxinkou	100	30.12 N	112.50 E
Laoyemiao	98	41.03 N	119.53 E
Laoyezhuang	106	32.16 N	120.04 E
Laoyingpan	100	26.34 N	115.10 E
Laozha	106	31.35 N	121.07 E
Laozhen	100	31.34 N	118.19 E
Laozhong	98	33.56 N	114.51 E
Laozhuangzi	105	39.44 N	118.05 E
Laozishan	100	33.11 N	118.36 E
Lapa	252	25.45 S	49.42 W
Lapa ◆[8], Bra.	287a	22.55 S	43.11 W
Lapa ◆[8], Bra.	287b	23.32 S	46.42 W
Lapac Island I	116	5.32 N	120.47 E

Symbols in the index entries represent the broad categories identified in the key at the right. Symbols with superior numbers (⋏[1]) identify subcategories (see complete key on page *I · 1*).

Symbole im Register stellen die rechts im Schlüssel erklärten Kategorien dar. Symbole mit hochgestellten Ziffern (⋏[1]) bezeichnen Unterabteilungen einer Kategorie (vgl. vollständiger Schlüssel auf Seite *I · 1*).

Los símbolos incluídos en el texto del índice representan las grandes categorias identificadas con la clave a la derecha. Los símbolos con numeros en su parte superior (⋏[1]) identifican las subcategorías (véase la clave completa en la página *I · 1*).

Les symboles de l'index représentent les catégories indiquées dans la légende à droite. Les symboles suivis d'un indice (⋏[1]) représentent des sous-catégories (voir légende complète à la page *I · 1*).

Os símbolos incluídos no texto do índice representam as grandes categorias identificadas com a chave à direita. Os símbolos com números em sua parte superior (⋏[1]) identificam as subcategorias (veja-se a chave completa à página *I · 1*).

English	Deutsch	Español	Français	Português
∧ Mountain	Berg	Montaña	Montagne	Montanha
⋏ Mountains	Gebirge	Montañas	Montagnes	Montanhas
)(Pass	Paß	Paso	Col	Passo
V Valley, Canyon	Tal, Cañon	Valle, Cañón	Vallée, Canyon	Vale, Canhão
≚ Plain	Ebene	Llano	Plaine	Planície
› Cape	Kap	Cabo	Cap	Cabo
I Island	Insel	Isla	Île	Ilha
II Islands	Inseln	Islas	Îles	Ilhas
⊥ Other Topographic Features	Andere Topographische Objekte	Otros Elementos Topográficos	Autres données topographiques	Outros acidentes topográficos

Lapa-Lawa I · 95

ESPAÑOL — Nombre | Página | Lat.°′ | Long.°′ W = Oeste
FRANÇAIS — Nom | Page | Lat.°′ | Long.°′ W = Ouest
PORTUGUÊS — Nome | Página | Lat.°′ | Long.°′ W = Oeste

Lapai 150 9.06 N 6.45 E
Lapaich, Sgurr na ʌ 46 57.21 N 5.04 W
Lapalisse 32 46.15 N 3.38 E
La Palma, Col. 246 5.22 N 74.24 W
La Palma, El Sal. 236 14.19 N 89.11 W
La Palma, Méx. 234 17.05 N 99.29 W
La Palma, Méx. 234 20.09 N 102.46 W
La Palma, Méx. 234 22.49 N 103.57 W
La Palma, Pan. 246 8.25 N 78.09 W
La Palma, Pan. 246 7.42 N 80.12 W
La Palma, Ca., U.S. 280 33.50 N 118.02 W
La Palma I 148 28.40 N 17.52 W
La Palma ≃ 240p 23.03 N 80.54 W
La Palma de Cervelló 266d 41.25 N 1.58 E
La Palma del Condado 34 37.23 N 6.33 W
La Palmita 196 25.57 N 99.18 W
La Paloma 252 34.40 S 54.10 W
La Palud 62 43.47 N 6.20 E
La Pampa □[4] 252 37.00 S 66.00 W
La Panza Range ⋏ 226 35.18 N 120.18 W
Lapão 250 11.24 S 41.50 W
La Paragua 246 6.50 N 63.20 W
Laparan Island I 116 5.54 N 119.59 E
La Parota, Méx. 234 18.20 N 101.08 W
La Parota, Méx. 234 18.19 N 103.02 W
La Parotita 234 19.07 N 101.15 W
La Paternal ◆[8] 288 34.36 S 58.28 W
La Patrie 206 45.24 N 71.15 W
La Paz, Arg. 252 30.45 S 59.39 W
La Paz, Arg. 252 33.28 S 67.33 W
La Paz, Bol. 248 16.30 S 68.09 W
La Paz, Col. 246 10.23 N 73.10 W
La Paz, Hond. 236 14.16 N 87.40 W
La Paz, Méx. 232 24.10 N 110.18 W
La Paz, Méx. 234 23.41 N 100.43 W
La Paz, Pil. 116 8.19 N 125.43 E
Lapaz, In., U.S. 216 41.28 N 86.18 W
La Paz, Ur. 258 34.21 S 57.18 W
La Paz, Ur. 258 34.46 S 56.15 W
La Paz □[5], Bol. 248 15.30 S 68.00 W
La Paz □[5], Hond. 236 14.15 N 87.50 W
La Paz, Bahía de ⊂ 232 24.09 N 110.25 W
La Paz, Río de ≃ 248 16.27 S 67.19 W
La Paz Centro 236 12.20 N 86.41 W
Lape 115b 8.39 S 117.37 E
La Pedrera 246 1.18 S 69.43 W
Lapeer 216 43.03 N 83.19 W
Lapeer □[6] 216 43.00 N 83.20 W
Lapel 218 40.04 N 85.50 W
Lapela 250 3.44 S 44.45 W
La Penne-sur-Huveaune 62 43.17 N 5.31 E
La Perla, Méx. 196 28.18 N 104.33 W
La Perla, Méx. 232 28.18 N 104.38 W
La Perla, Perú 286d 12.05 S 77.08 W
La Perouse 170 33.59 S 151.14 E
La Perouse, Bahía ⊂ 174z 27.04 S 109.18 W
La Perouse Bay ⊂ 229a 20.35 N 156.25 W
La Perouse Strait ꭒ 89 45.45 N 142.00 E
La Pesca 234 23.46 N 97.47 W
La Pesse 58 46.18 N 5.51 E
La Petite-Pierre 56 48.52 N 7.19 E
Lapford 42 50.55 N 3.47 W
Lapham Hill ʌ[2] 216 43.02 N 88.24 W
L'apičev 80 48.30 N 43.32 E
La Piedad [Cavadas] 234 20.21 N 102.00 W
La Piedra 236 9.29 N 83.40 W
La Pimienta 234 21.28 N 99.01 W
La Pine 202 43.40 N 121.30 W
Lapinin Island I 116 10.06 N 124.34 E
Lapinjärvi (Lappträsk) 26 60.38 N 26.13 E
Lapin lääni □[4] 26 66.00 N 27.00 E
Lapinlahti 26 63.22 N 27.24 E
Lapino 82 54.57 N 37.49 E
La Pintada 236 8.36 N 80.27 W
La Pizzuta ʌ 70 38.00 N 13.16 E
La Place, Il., U.S. 219 39.48 N 88.43 W
La Place, La., U.S. 194 30.03 N 90.28 W
Lap Lae 110 17.39 N 100.02 E
La Plaine 240d 15.20 N 61.15 W
Lapland □[9] 24 68.00 N 25.00 E
Laplandija 24 68.16 N 33.19 E
Laplandskij Zapovednik ◆[4] 24 67.50 N 32.10 E
La Plata, Arg. 258 34.55 S 57.57 W
La Plata, Col. 246 2.23 N 75.53 W
La Plata, Md., U.S. 208 38.31 N 76.58 W
La Plata, Mo., U.S. 194 40.01 N 92.29 W
La Plata □[5] 288 34.55 S 58.04 W
La Plata ≃ 200 36.54 N 108.15 W
La Plata, Isla de I 246 1.16 S 81.06 W
La Plata, Lago ⊜ 254 44.53 S 71.50 W
La Plata, Universidad Nacional de ᵾ[2] 288 35.55 S 57.57 W
La Plata Peak ʌ 200 39.02 N 106.28 W
La Playa ◆[8] 286b 23.06 N 82.27 W
La Plonge Indian Reserve ◆[4] 184 55.15 N 107.36 W
La Plume 210 41.34 N 75.45 W
La Pobla de Segur 34 42.14 N 0.59 E
La Pocatière 186 47.22 N 70.02 W
La Poile 186 47.41 N 58.24 W
La Poile Bay ⊂ 186 47.38 N 58.20 W
Lapominka 24 64.48 N 40.28 E
La Pomme 62 43.25 N 5.35 E
Laponie → Lapland □[9] 24 68.00 N 25.00 E
Laporte, Co., U.S. 200 40.38 N 105.08 W
La Porte, In., U.S. 216 41.36 N 86.43 W
La Porte, Oh., U.S. 279a 41.19 N 82.05 W
Laporte, Pa., U.S. 210 41.25 N 76.30 W
La Porte, Tx., U.S. 222 29.39 N 95.01 W
La Porte □[6] 216 41.36 N 86.43 W
La Porte City 190 42.18 N 92.11 W
La Porteña, Salinas ≋ 252 38.15 S 63.47 W
Laposo, Bulu ʌ 112 4.29 S 119.47 E
La Potherie, Lac ⊜ 176 58.50 N 72.24 W
Lapoutroie 58 48.09 N 7.10 E
La Poveda 266a 40.19 N 3.29 W
Lappago (Lappach) 64 46.55 N 11.48 E
Lappajärvi 26 63.12 N 23.38 E
Lappajärvi ⊜ 26 63.08 N 23.40 E
Lappeenranta 26 61.04 N 28.11 E
Lappfjärd (Lapväärtti) 26 62.15 N 21.32 E
Lappi 26 61.06 N 21.50 E
Lappland → Lapland □[9] 24 68.00 N 25.00 E
Lappträsk → Lapinjärvi 26 60.38 N 26.13 E
La Prairie 206 45.25 N 73.30 W
Laprairie □[6] 206 45.20 N 73.35 W
La Prele Creek ≃ 198 42.50 N 105.30 W
Laprida, Arg. 252 28.23 S 64.33 W
Laprida, Arg. 252 37.33 S 60.49 W
La Pryor 196 28.57 N 99.51 W
Lapšanga 80 57.27 N 45.03 E
Lâpseki 130 40.20 N 26.41 E
Lapta 130 35.20 N 33.10 E
Laptev Sea → Laptevych, more ⊤[2] 74 76.00 N 126.00 E
Laptevych, more (Laptev Sea) ⊤[2] 74 76.00 N 126.00 E
Lapua 26 62.57 N 23.00 E
Lapuanjoki ≃ 26 63.34 N 22.30 E
La Puebla de Cazalla 34 37.14 N 5.19 W
La Puebla de Montalbán 34 39.52 N 4.21 W
La Puente 228 34.01 N 117.56 W
La Puerta 252 28.10 S 65.48 W
Lapu-Lapu (Opon) 116 10.19 N 123.57 E
La Punt 58 46.35 N 9.55 E
La Punta 286d 12.05 S 77.11 W
La Purísima, Chile 286e 33.34 S 70.39 W
La Purísima, Méx. 232 26.10 N 112.04 W
Lăpuș 38 47.30 N 24.01 E
La Push 224 47.54 N 124.38 W
Lapuyan 116 7.36 N 123.12 E
Lapväärtti → Lappfjärd 26 62.15 N 21.32 E
Lapwai 202 46.24 N 116.48 W
Łapy 30 53.00 N 22.53 E
La Quemada ⊥ 234 22.27 N 102.45 W
La Queue-en-Brie 261 48.47 N 2.35 E
La Queue-lès-Yvelines 261 48.48 N 1.46 E
La Quiaca 252 22.06 S 65.37 W
L'Aquila 66 42.22 N 13.22 E
L'Aquila □[4] 66 42.05 N 13.40 E
Lār 128 27.41 N 54.17 E
Lara 169 38.01 S 144.24 E
Lara □[3] 246 10.10 N 69.50 W
Larabanga 150 9.13 N 1.51 W
Laracha 34 43.15 N 8.35 W
Larache 148 35.12 N 6.10 W
Laragne-Montéglin 62 44.19 N 5.49 E
Lārak, Jazīreh-ye I 128 26.52 N 56.22 E
Laramate 248 14.15 S 74.52 W
La Rambla 34 37.36 N 4.44 W
Laramie 200 41.18 N 105.35 W
Laramie ≃ 200 42.12 N 104.32 W
Laramie Mountains ⋏ 200 42.00 N 105.40 W
Laramie Peak ʌ 200 42.17 N 105.27 W
Laranjal 255 21.22 S 42.28 W
Laranjal ≃ 255 23.12 S 53.45 W
Laranjeiras 250 10.48 S 37.10 W
Laranjeiras ◆[8] 287a 22.56 S 43.11 W
Laranjeiras do Sul 252 25.25 S 52.25 W
Larantuka 115b 8.21 S 122.59 E
Laraos 248 12.17 S 75.50 W
Larap 116 14.18 N 122.39 E
Larat 164 7.09 S 131.45 E
Larat, Pulau I 164 7.10 S 131.50 E
Laravale 171a 28.05 S 152.56 E
La Raya, Abra)(248 14.35 S 70.59 W
L'Arbaa Naït Irathen 34 36.38 N 4.12 E
Larb Creek ≃ 202 48.25 N 107.16 W
L'Arbresle 62 45.50 N 4.37 E
Lärbro 26 57.47 N 18.47 E
Larbut, Jazīrat I 140 18.47 N 37.33 E
Larche, Col de (Colle della Maddalena))(62 44.25 N 6.53 E
Larchmont 210 40.55 N 73.45 W
Larchmont Harbor ⊂ 276 40.55 N 73.45 W
Larchwood 198 43.27 N 96.26 W
Lardaro 64 45.58 N 10.39 E
Larde 154 16.28 S 39.43 E
Lardeau 182 50.09 N 116.57 W
Larderello 66 43.14 N 10.53 E
Larder Lake ⊜ 190 48.05 N 79.36 W
Lardier, Cap > 62 43.09 N 6.37 E
L'Ardoise 186 45.37 N 60.45 W
Lardy 261 48.31 N 2.16 E
Lare 154 0.20 N 37.56 E
Laredo, Esp. 34 43.24 N 3.25 W
Laredo, Tx., U.S. 196 27.30 N 99.30 W
Laredo Sound ꭒ 182 52.32 N 128.53 W
La Reforma 232 25.06 N 108.05 W
La Reina 286e 33.27 S 70.33 W
Laren 52 52.15 N 5.14 E
Larena 116 9.15 N 123.35 E
La Réole 32 44.35 N 0.02 W
Lares, Perú 248 13.04 S 72.05 W
Lares, P.R. 240m 18.18 N 66.53 W
Larga 78 48.23 N 26.50 E
Larga, Laguna ⊜, Cuba 286b 23.08 N 82.12 W
Larga, Laguna ⊜, Tx., U.S. 196 27.30 N 97.25 W
Large, Île du I 275a 45.19 N 73.52 W
Largentière 62 44.32 N 4.18 E
L'Argentière-la-Bessée 62 44.47 N 6.33 E
Lar Gerd 120 35.29 N 66.40 E
Largo 220 27.54 N 82.47 W
Largo, Cañon V 200 36.40 N 107.43 W
Largo, Cayo I 240p 21.38 N 81.28 W
Largo Creek ≃ 200 34.29 N 108.51 W
Largoward 46 56.15 N 2.51 W
Largs 46 55.48 N 4.52 W
Largue ≃ 62 43.51 N 5.52 E
Lari, It. 66 43.34 N 10.35 E
Lari, Perú 248 15.37 S 71.46 W
Lariang 112 1.26 S 119.17 E
Lariang ≃ 112 1.25 S 119.17 E
La Ricamarie 62 45.24 N 4.22 E
Larimer 214 40.21 N 79.44 W
Larimore 198 47.54 N 97.37 W
La Rinconada 286d 12.05 S 76.57 W
Larino, It. 66 41.48 N 14.54 E
Larino, S.S.S.R. 83 47.53 N 37.56 E
La Rioja, Arg. 252 29.26 S 66.51 W
La Rioja, Cuba 240p 20.46 N 76.36 W
La Rioja □[4], Arg. 252 30.00 S 67.30 W
La Rioja □[4], Esp. 34 42.15 N 2.30 W
Lárisa 38 39.38 N 22.25 E
Larisa Station ◆[5] 267c 37.58 N 23.42 E
Larjak 74 61.16 N 80.15 E
Larjan 76 59.30 N 33.47 E
Larjegan ≃ 86 60.30 N 77.44 E
Lārkāna 120 27.33 N 68.13 E
Larkhall 46 55.45 N 3.59 W
Lark Harbour 186 49.06 N 58.23 W
Larkhill 42 51.12 N 1.50 W
Larkspur 226 37.56 N 122.30 W
Larksville 210 41.14 N 75.55 W
Larnaca → Lárnax 130 34.55 N 33.38 E
Lárnakos, Kólpos ⊂ 130 34.55 N 33.45 E
Lárnax (Larnaca) 130 34.55 N 33.38 E
Larne 48 54.51 N 5.49 W
Larned 198 38.10 N 99.05 W
Larne Lake ⊜ 44 54.47 N 5.45 W
Laro 146 8.17 N 12.18 E
La Robla 34 42.48 N 5.37 W
La Roca de la Sierra 34 39.07 N 6.41 W
La Roche 58 46.42 N 7.08 E
La Roche-Bernard 32 47.31 N 2.18 W
La Roche-de-Rame 62 44.45 N 6.35 E
La Roche-Derrien 28 48.45 N 3.16 W
La Roche-des-Arnauds 62 44.34 N 5.57 E
La Roche-en-Ardenne 56 50.11 N 5.35 E
La Roche-en-Brenil 50 47.22 N 4.10 E
La Rochefoucauld 32 45.45 N 0.23 E
La Roche-Guyon 50 49.05 N 1.38 E
La Rochelle 32 46.10 N 1.10 W
Laroche-Saint-Cydroine 50 47.58 N 3.31 E
La Roche-sur-Foron 58 46.04 N 6.19 E
La Roche-sur-Yon 32 46.40 N 1.26 W
La Rochette, Fr. 62 45.28 N 6.07 E
La Rochette, Fr. 261 48.30 N 2.40 E
Larochette, Lux. 56 49.47 N 6.15 E
La Roda 34 39.13 N 2.09 W
La Romaine 186 50.13 N 60.40 W
La Romana 238 18.25 N 68.58 W
Larona 112 2.45 S 121.20 E
La Ronge 184 55.06 N 105.17 W
Laroquebrou 32 44.58 N 2.11 E
La Roquebrussanne 62 43.20 N 5.59 E
Larose 194 29.34 N 90.22 W
La Route 261 48.48 N 2.47 E
Larrabee State Park ♠ 224 48.41 N 122.29 W
Larreynaga 236 12.40 N 86.34 W
Larrey Point > 162 19.58 S 119.07 E
Larrimah 164 15.35 S 133.12 E
Larringes 58 46.22 N 6.35 E
Larrison Creek ≃ 222 31.27 N 95.03 W
Larrys Creek ≃ 210 41.13 N 77.13 W
Larrys River 186 45.13 N 61.23 W
Larsen Air Park ⊠ 281 42.11 N 83.33 W
Larsen Bay 180 57.33 N 154.00 W
Larsen Ice Shelf ❄ 9 68.30 S 62.30 W
Larteh Aheneasi 150 5.56 N 0.04 E
La Rubia 252 30.06 S 61.48 W
La Rue, Oh., U.S. 214 40.35 N 83.23 W
Larue, Tx., U.S. 222 32.07 N 95.41 W
La Rumorosa 204 32.34 N 116.06 W
Laruns 32 42.59 N 0.25 W
Larus Lake ⊜ 184 51.17 N 94.40 W
Larvik 26 59.04 N 10.00 E
Larwill 216 41.10 N 85.37 W
Larzac, Causse du ⋏[1] 32 44.00 N 3.15 E
Lasa (Laas) 64 46.37 N 10.42 E
La Sabana 252 27.52 S 59.57 W
Las Adjuntas 286c 10.26 N 67.01 W
La Sagne 58 47.03 N 6.48 E
La Sal 200 38.18 N 109.14 W
La Salada 234 18.01 N 101.58 W
La Salette-Fallavaux 62 44.51 N 5.59 E
La Salle, On., Can. 214 42.14 N 83.06 W
La Salle, P.Q., Can. 206 45.26 N 73.38 W
Lasalle, Fr. 62 44.03 N 3.51 E
La Salle, It. 62 45.45 N 7.04 E
La Salle, Co., U.S. 200 40.20 N 104.42 W
La Salle, Il., U.S. 216 41.20 N 89.06 W
La Salle □[6] 216 41.21 N 88.51 W
La Salle ≃ 184 49.45 N 97.08 W
Lasalle, Parc ♠ 275a 45.26 N 73.40 W
La Salle College ᵾ[2] 285 40.02 N 75.09 W
La Salle Gardens 216 42.39 N 83.21 W
La Sal Mountains ⋏ 200 38.30 N 109.10 W
Lasan 112 1.14 N 115.13 E
Lasanga Island I 164 7.25 S 147.16 E
Las Animas 198 38.04 N 103.13 W
Las Ánimas, Punta > 232 28.50 N 113.15 W
La Santa, Cerro ʌ 240m 18.07 N 66.03 W
Las Arenas 240m 18.02 N 67.09 W
La Sarraz 58 46.40 N 6.31 E
La Sarre 190 48.48 N 79.12 W
La Sarre ≃ 190 48.43 N 79.16 W
Las Arrias 252 30.21 S 63.35 W
La Sauceda 196 28.26 N 100.38 W
La Saulce 62 44.25 N 6.01 E
Las Auras 196 26.25 N 99.20 W
Lasberg 61 48.28 N 14.32 E
Las Blancas 196 25.42 N 97.35 W
Las Bonitas 246 7.52 N 65.40 W
Las Breñas 252 27.05 S 61.05 W
Låsby 41 56.09 N 9.49 E
Las Cabezas de San Juan 34 36.59 N 5.56 W
Las Cabras 252 34.18 S 71.19 W
Lascano 252 33.40 S 54.12 W
Lascar, Volcán ʌ[1] 252 23.23 S 67.45 W
Lascari 70 38.00 N 13.56 E
Las Casas → San Cristóbal de las Casas 234 16.45 N 92.38 W
Las Casitas, Cerro ʌ 232 23.32 N 109.59 W
Las Casuarinas 252 31.48 S 68.19 W
Las Catitas 252 33.18 S 68.02 W
Las Catonas, Arroyo ≃ 288 34.37 S 58.43 W
Lascaux, Grotte de ⊥[5] 32 45.01 N 1.08 E
Las Cejas 252 26.53 S 64.44 W
L'Ascension 206 46.33 N 74.50 W
L'aščevka 78 49.33 N 32.41 E
Las Chacras 258 35.05 S 59.10 W
Las Choapas 234 17.55 N 94.05 W
Las Chorreras 232 28.50 N 105.18 W
Las Cidras 234 19.15 N 101.08 W
La Scie 186 49.57 N 55.36 W
Las Colimas 232 25.21 N 98.40 W
Las Coloradas 254 39.33 S 70.35 W
Las Condes 286e 33.22 S 70.31 W
Lascone, Monte ʌ[2] 267a 41.59 N 12.23 E
Las Cruces, Méx. 234 18.45 N 102.16 W
Las Cruces, N.M., U.S. 200 32.18 N 106.46 W
Las Cruces, Estero de ≃ 286e 33.21 S 70.47 W
Las Cuevas 232 29.38 N 101.19 W
Las Delicias 232 15.58 N 91.50 W
La Selva Beach 226 36.55 N 121.51 W
Lasem 115a 6.42 S 111.26 E
La Serena 252 29.54 S 71.16 W
La Serena ◆[1] 34 38.45 N 5.30 W
Las Escobas 232 30.33 N 115.56 W
La Seyne 32 43.06 N 5.53 E
La Seyne-sur-Mer 62 43.06 N 5.53 E
Las Flores, Arg. 252 36.03 S 59.07 W
Las Flores, Arg. 252 30.19 S 69.12 W
Las Flores, Méx. 234 18.22 N 93.10 W
Las Flores, P.R. 240m 18.03 N 66.22 W
Las Flores, Ven. 286c 10.34 N 66.56 W
Las Flores, Arroyo ≃ 252 35.36 S 59.01 W
Las Flores Canyon V 280 34.03 N 118.38 W
Las Garcitas 252 26.35 S 59.48 W
Las Guayabas 232 24.00 N 97.45 W
Lasham 42 51.11 N 1.03 W
Las Harquetas, Arroyo ≃ 288 34.29 S 58.38 W
Lashburn 184 53.08 N 109.36 W
Lāsh-e Joveyn 128 31.43 N 61.37 E
Las Heras 252 32.51 S 68.49 W
Las Higueras 234 23.41 N 106.06 W
Lashio 110 22.56 N 97.45 E
Lashkar → Gwalior 124 26.13 N 78.10 E
Lashkar Gāh 128 31.35 N 64.21 E
Lasht 123 36.48 N 73.01 E
Lasia, Pulau I 114 2.10 N 96.39 E
La Sierra, Montaña ⋏ 236 14.04 N 87.54 W
Las Iglesias 196 27.35 N 101.21 W
La Sila ⋏ 68 39.15 N 16.30 E
La Siligata 66 43.56 N 12.45 E
La Silla de Caracas ʌ 286c 10.33 N 66.51 W
Łasin 30 53.32 N 19.05 E
Lašino 80 58.16 N 49.59 E
Lāsjerd 128 35.24 N 53.04 E
Las Julianas, Presa ⊜[1] 286a 19.28 N 99.18 W
Las Juntas 236 10.16 N 85.00 W
Łask 30 51.36 N 19.07 E
Łaskarzew 30 51.48 N 21.35 E
L'askel'a 24 61.45 N 30.59 E
Laško 36 46.09 N 15.14 E
L'askoviči 78 52.07 N 28.09 E
Las Lajas, Arg. 252 38.31 S 70.22 W
Las Lajas, Pan. 236 8.15 N 81.52 W
Las Lajitas 252 24.41 S 64.15 W
Las Lomas 246 4.40 S 80.15 W
Las Lomitas 252 24.42 S 60.36 W
Lašma 80 54.56 N 41.09 E
Las Malvinas 252 34.50 S 68.15 W
Lašmanka 80 54.44 N 51.28 E
Las Mareas 240m 17.56 N 66.09 W
Las Margaritas 232 16.19 N 91.59 W
Las Margaritas, Laguna ⊜ 258 35.28 S 57.56 W
Las Marianas 258 35.04 S 59.31 W
Las Marías 240m 18.15 N 67.00 W
Las Marismas ≋ 34 37.00 N 6.15 W
Las Mayas 286c 10.26 N 66.56 W
Las Mercedes 246 9.07 N 66.24 W
Las Mesas 234 17.00 N 99.30 W
Las Minas 286c 10.27 N 66.52 W
Las Minas, Cerro ʌ 236 14.33 N 88.39 W
Las Moras Creek ≃ 196 29.00 N 100.39 W
Las Mulas, Laguna ⊜ 258 35.32 S 57.54 W
Las Navas 116 12.21 N 125.02 E
Las Nieves 232 26.24 N 105.22 W
La Solana 34 38.56 N 3.14 W
Lasolo 112 3.29 S 122.04 E
Lasolo ≃ 112 3.28 S 122.06 E
Las Ortegas, Arroyo ≃ 288 34.45 S 58.32 W
Las Ovejas 252 37.01 S 70.45 W
Las Palmas, Arg. 252 27.04 S 58.42 W
Las Palmas, Arg. 258 34.05 S 59.10 W
Las Palmas, Pan. 236 8.08 N 81.27 W
Las Palmas, P.R. 240m 17.59 N 66.02 W
Las Palmas □[4] 148 28.25 N 14.15 W
Las Palmas de Gran Canaria 148 28.06 N 15.24 W
Las Palomas 200 31.44 N 107.37 W
Las Peñas 234 18.03 N 102.30 W
Las Perdices, Canal de ≍ 286e 33.31 S 70.33 W
La Spezia 62 44.07 N 9.50 E
La Spezia □[4] 62 44.15 N 9.42 E
Las Piedras, Bol. 248 11.06 S 66.10 W
Las Piedras, P.R. 240m 18.11 N 65.52 W
Las Piedras, Ur. 258 34.44 S 56.13 W
Las Piedras, Río de ≃ 248 12.30 S 69.14 W
Las Piñas, Pil. 269f 14.29 N 120.59 E
Las Piñas, P.R. 240m 18.15 N 65.55 W
Las Plumas 254 43.43 S 67.15 W
Lasqueti Island I 182 49.29 N 124.17 W
Las Raices Creek ≃ 196 28.09 N 99.02 W
Las Ramas 246 1.50 S 79.48 W
Las Rejas 286e 33.28 S 70.44 W
Las Rosas, Arg. 252 32.28 S 61.34 W
Las Rosas, Chile 286e 33.35 S 70.37 W
Las Rosas, Méx. 232 16.24 N 92.23 W
Las Rozas de Madrid 266a 40.29 N 3.52 W
Las Salinas de Zipaquirá ᵾ[1] 246 5.04 N 73.56 W
Lassan 54 53.57 N 13.50 E
Lassance 255 17.54 S 44.34 W
Lassater 222 32.49 N 94.30 W
Lassay 32 48.26 N 0.30 W
Lassee 61 48.13 N 16.49 E
Lassellsville 210 43.03 N 74.36 W
Lassen Peak ʌ[1] 204 40.29 N 121.31 W
Lassen Volcanic National Park ♠ 204 40.30 N 121.19 W
Lassigny 50 49.35 N 2.51 E
Lassnitz ≃ 61 46.46 N 15.32 E
Lassnitzhöhe 61 47.05 N 15.35 E
Lasso ʌ[2] 174n 15.02 N 145.38 E
L'Assomption 206 45.50 N 73.25 W
L'Assomption □[6] 206 45.48 N 73.35 W
L'Assomption ≃ 206 45.43 N 73.29 W
Lasswade 46 55.53 N 3.08 W
Lassy 261 49.06 N 2.27 E
Las Tablas 246 7.46 N 80.17 W
Las Taperas 248 17.54 S 60.23 W
Las Tinajas 252 27.27 S 62.55 W
Last Mountain ʌ 184 51.07 N 104.54 W
Last Mountain Lake ⊜ 184 51.05 N 105.10 W
Las Torres 236 13.28 N 85.48 W
Las Tórtolas, Cerro ʌ 252 29.56 S 69.54 W
Las Toscas 252 28.21 S 59.17 W
Lastoursville 152 0.49 S 12.42 E
Lastovo, Otok I 36 42.45 N 16.53 E
Lastovski Kanal ꭒ 36 42.50 N 16.59 E
Lastra a Signa 66 43.46 N 11.06 E
Las Trampas Creek ≃ 282 37.53 N 122.03 W
Las Trampas Peak ʌ 282 37.50 N 122.03 W
Las Trampas Regional Park ♠ 282 37.50 N 122.03 W
Las Trampas Ridge ʌ 282 37.49 N 122.02 W
Las Tres Vírgenes, Volcán ʌ[1] 232 27.27 N 112.34 W
Lästringe 40 58.54 N 17.18 E
Las Truchas 234 17.55 N 102.12 W
Lastrup 52 52.48 N 7.52 E
Las Tunas □[4] 240p 21.00 N 77.00 W
Las Tunas, Arroyo ≃ 288 34.27 S 58.41 W
Las Tunas, Punta > 240m 18.30 N 66.38 W
Las Tunas Beach ♠ 280 34.02 N 118.36 W
Las Tunas Grandes, Laguna ⊜ 252 35.58 S 62.25 W
La Suze 32 47.54 N 0.02 E
Las Varas, Méx. 232 29.29 N 108.01 W
Las Varas, Méx. 234 21.10 N 105.10 W
Las Varillas 252 31.52 S 62.43 W
Las Vegas, Hond. 236 14.49 N 88.06 W
Las Vegas, P.R. 240m 18.11 N 67.02 W
Las Vegas, Nv., U.S. 204 36.10 N 115.08 W
Las Vegas, N.M., U.S. 200 35.36 N 105.13 W
Las Vegas, Ven. 246 9.35 N 68.37 W
Las Vigas 234 19.38 N 97.05 W
Las Vizcachas 286e 33.36 S 70.32 W
La Tabatière 186 50.50 N 58.58 W
Latacunga 246 0.56 S 78.37 W
Latady Island I 9 70.45 S 74.35 W
La Tagua 246 0.03 S 74.40 W
Latakia → Al-Lādhiqīyah 130 35.31 N 35.47 E
Latakia □[9] 130 35.20 N 36.00 E
Latambar 123 33.07 N 70.52 E
Lata Mountain ʌ 174y 14.14 S 169.29 W
La Tapona 234 22.48 N 100.38 W
La Tasajera 236 13.16 N 88.52 W
Låtefossen ⌊ 26 59.57 N 6.37 E
Latehar 124 23.45 N 84.30 E
Lately Common 262 53.29 N 2.30 W
Latera 66 42.38 N 11.50 E
Laterina 66 43.31 N 11.43 E
Laterns 58 47.16 N 9.43 E
Laterrière 186 48.18 N 71.06 W
Laterza 68 40.37 N 16.48 E
La Teste-de-Buch 32 44.38 N 1.09 W
Latexo 222 31.24 N 95.29 W
Latgale □[9] 76 56.20 N 27.10 E
Latham, Austl. 162 29.45 S 116.26 E
Latham, Il., U.S. 219 39.58 N 89.10 W
Latham, N.Y., U.S. 210 42.44 N 73.45 W
Latham, Oh., U.S. 218 39.06 N 83.15 W
Lathan ≃ 50 47.27 N 0.08 E
Lathen 52 52.52 N 7.19 E
Latheron 46 58.17 N 3.23 W
Lāthi 120 21.43 N 71.23 E
Lathrop, Ca., U.S. 226 37.49 N 121.16 W
Lathrop, Mo., U.S. 194 39.32 N 94.19 W
Lathrup Village 281 42.29 N 83.14 W
La Thuile 62 45.43 N 6.57 E
La Tiama 286c 10.26 N 66.46 W
Latian, Mount ʌ 116 6.13 N 125.30 E
Latiano 68 40.33 N 17.43 E
Latimer, Eng., U.K. 260 51.41 N 0.33 W
Latimer, Ia., U.S. 190 42.45 N 93.22 W
Latina 66 41.28 N 12.52 E
Latina □[4] 66 41.27 N 13.06 E
Latino Americana, Universidad Militar ᵾ[2] 286a 19.20 N 99.15 W
Latiri 140 9.10 N 25.43 E
Latisana 64 45.47 N 13.00 E
Latjuga 24 64.16 N 48.46 E
Latnaja 78 51.43 N 38.55 E
La Toma 252 33.03 S 65.37 W
Laton 226 36.26 N 119.41 W
Latonovo 83 47.29 N 38.38 E
Latorica ≃ 30 48.28 N 21.50 E
Latornell ≃ 182 54.58 N 118.00 W
La Torrecilla ʌ 240m 18.12 N 66.20 W
La Tortuga, Isla I 246 10.56 N 65.20 W
Latouche Island I 180 60.00 N 147.55 W
Latouche Treville, Cape > 162 18.27 S 121.49 E
La Tour 62 43.57 N 7.11 E
La Tour-d'Aigues 62 43.44 N 5.33 E
La Tour-d'Auvergne 32 45.32 N 2.41 E
La Tour-de-Peilz 58 46.27 N 6.49 E
La Tour-du-Pin 62 45.34 N 5.27 E
La Tourette Park ♠ 276 40.35 N 74.08 W
Latowicz 30 52.02 N 21.48 E
Lat Phrao, Khlong ≍ 269a 13.48 N 100.35 E
La Tremblade 32 45.46 N 1.08 W
La Trimouille 32 46.28 N 1.02 E
La Trinidad, Arg. 252 27.24 S 65.31 W
La Trinidad, Nic. 236 12.58 N 86.14 W
La Trinidad, Pil. 116 16.28 N 120.35 E
La Trinidad, Ven. 286c 10.27 N 66.52 W
La Trinidad de Orichuna 246 7.07 N 69.45 W
La Trinité 240e 14.44 N 60.58 W
Latrobe, Austl. 166 41.14 S 146.24 E
Latrobe, Pa., U.S. 214 40.19 N 79.22 W
La Trobe ≃ 169 38.10 S 146.32 E
Latrobe University ᵾ[2] 274b 37.43 S 145.03 E
La Tronche 62 45.12 N 5.44 E
Latronico 68 40.05 N 16.01 E
Latta 192 34.20 N 79.25 W
Lattarico 68 39.28 N 16.08 E
Lattasburg 214 40.53 N 82.06 W
Latterbach 58 46.40 N 7.35 E
Lattingtown 276 40.54 N 73.36 W
Latty 216 41.05 N 84.35 W
La Tuilerie 261 48.34 N 2.08 E
La Tuilière 62 44.11 N 5.32 E
Latuna 112 8.23 S 124.06 E
La Tuque 176 47.26 N 72.47 W
Lātūr 122 18.24 N 76.35 E
La Turbie 62 43.45 N 7.24 E
Latvia → Latvijskaja Sovetskaja Socialističeskaja Respublika □[3] 76 57.00 N 25.00 E
Latvijskaja Sovetskaja Socialističeskaja Respublika □[3] 76 57.00 N 25.00 E
Lau, Nig. 146 9.13 N 11.17 E
Lau, Pap. N. Gui. 164 5.50 S 151.20 E
Laubach 56 50.33 N 8.59 E
Lauban → Lubań 30 51.08 N 15.18 E
Lau Basin ✣[1] 14 20.00 S 177.00 W
Laubusch 54 51.28 N 14.10 E
Laubuseschbach 56 50.24 N 8.20 E
Lauca ≃ 248 19.10 S 68.10 W
Laucha 54 51.13 N 11.41 E
Lauchhammer 54 51.30 N 13.47 E
Lauchheim 56 48.52 N 10.14 E
Lauda-Königshofen 56 49.34 N 9.41 E
Lauder 46 55.43 N 2.45 W
Lauderdale 194 32.31 N 88.30 W
Lauderdale V 46 55.43 N 2.42 W
Lauderdale-by-the-Sea 220 26.12 N 80.07 W
Lauderdale Lakes 220 26.09 N 80.12 W
Lauderhill 220 26.08 N 80.12 W
Laudun 62 44.06 N 4.40 E
Lauenbrück 52 53.12 N 9.33 E
Lauenburg, B.R.D. 52 53.22 N 10.33 E
Lauenburg → Lębork, Pol. 30 54.33 N 17.44 E
Lauenförde 52 51.39 N 9.23 E
Lauenstein, B.R.D. 52 52.04 N 9.33 E
Lauenstein, B.R.D. 54 50.31 N 11.20 E
Lauenstein, D.D.R. 54 50.47 N 13.49 E
Lauer ≃ 56 50.18 N 10.10 E
Lauerzer See ⊜ 58 47.02 N 8.36 E
Lauf an der Pegnitz 60 49.30 N 11.17 E
Läufelfingen 58 47.24 N 7.51 E
Laufen, B.R.D. 64 47.57 N 12.56 E
Laufen, Schw. 58 47.25 N 7.30 E
Laufenburg (Baden), B.R.D. 58 47.35 N 8.04 E
Laufenburg (Baden), Schw. 58 47.33 N 8.04 E
Laufersfort, Schloss ⊥ 263 51.25 N 6.37 E
Lauffen am Neckar 56 49.05 N 9.10 E
Laugharne 42 51.47 N 4.28 W
Laughery Creek ≃ 218 39.02 N 84.53 W
Laughlen, Mount ʌ 162 23.23 S 134.23 E
Laughlin Air Force Base ■ 196 29.22 N 100.47 W
Laughlin Peak ʌ 196 36.38 N 104.12 W
Laughlintown 214 40.13 N 79.12 W
Lau Group II 175g 18.20 S 178.30 W
Lauingen 56 48.34 N 10.25 E
Lauis → Lugano 58 46.01 N 8.58 E
Laukaa 26 62.25 N 25.57 E
Laukuva 76 55.37 N 22.14 E
Laul'u 89 45.46 N 135.16 E
Laun 110 10.07 N 98.46 E
Launceston, Austl. 166 41.26 S 147.08 E
Launceston, Eng., U.K. 42 50.38 N 4.21 W
Laundi, Tanjung > 115b 9.28 S 120.12 E
Laune ≃ 48 52.07 N 9.48 W
Launglon 110 13.58 N 98.07 E
Laungowāl 123 30.13 N 75.41 E
La Unión, Chile 254 40.17 S 73.05 W
La Unión, Col. 246 1.36 N 77.09 W
La Unión, El Sal. 236 13.20 N 87.51 W
La Unión, Esp. 34 37.37 N 0.52 W
La Unión, Méx. 234 17.58 N 101.49 W
La Unión, Perú 248 9.46 S 76.48 W
La Unión, Perú 248 5.24 S 80.45 W
La Union, Pil. 116 6.42 N 126.05 E
La Union, N.M., U.S. 200 31.57 N 106.39 W
La Unión, Ven. 246 8.13 N 67.46 W
La Unión, Ven. 286c 10.25 N 66.48 W
La Union □[4] 116 16.35 N 120.25 E
La Unión de Coto 236 8.36 N 83.03 W
Launois-sur-Vence 56 49.39 N 4.32 E
Launsdorf 61 46.46 N 14.27 E
Laupen 58 46.54 N 7.14 E
Laupendahl ◆[8] 263 51.21 N 6.56 E
Laupheim 58 48.14 N 9.52 E
Laur 116 15.35 N 121.11 E
Laura, Austl. 164 15.34 S 144.28 E
Laura, Oh., U.S. 218 39.59 N 84.24 W
La Urbana 246 7.08 N 66.56 W
Laureana di Borrello 68 38.30 N 16.05 E
Laurel, De., U.S. 208 38.33 N 75.34 W
Laurel, Fl., U.S. 220 27.07 N 82.27 W
Laurel, In., U.S. 218 39.30 N 85.11 W
Laurel, Md., U.S. 208 39.05 N 76.50 W
Laurel, Ms., U.S. 194 31.41 N 89.07 W
Laurel, Mt., U.S. 202 45.40 N 108.46 W
Laurel, Ne., U.S. 198 42.25 N 97.05 W
Laurel, Va., U.S. 208 37.38 N 77.30 W
Laurel, Wa., U.S. 224 45.57 N 121.23 W
Laurel ≃ 192 36.57 N 84.18 W
Laurel, Mount ʌ[2] 285 39.56 N 74.53 W
Laurel Bay 192 32.33 N 80.44 W
Laureldale, N.J., U.S. 208 39.29 N 74.41 W
Laureldale, Pa., U.S. 208 40.23 N 75.55 W
Laureles 252 31.22 S 55.51 W
Laureles, Isla de los I 258 33.45 S 59.23 W
Laurel Gardens 279b 40.31 N 80.01 W
Laurel Hill, Austl. 171b 35.37 S 148.05 E
Laurel Hill, N.C., U.S. 192 34.48 N 79.32 W
Laurel Hill ʌ 214 40.15 N 79.05 W
Laurel Hollow 276 40.52 N 73.28 W
Laurel Reservoir ⊜[1] 276 41.10 N 73.33 W
Laurel Ridge State Park ♠ 188 39.58 N 79.23 W
Laurel River Lake ⊜[1] 192 36.55 N 84.15 W
Laurel Run 210 41.13 N 75.51 W
Laurel Run ≃ 208 40.20 N 77.20 W
Laurel Springs 285 39.49 N 75.00 W
Laurelton 210 40.52 N 77.11 W
Laurelville, Oh., U.S. 188 39.28 N 82.44 W
Laurelville, Pa., U.S. 214 40.09 N 79.29 W
Laurenburg 56 50.20 N 7.54 E
Laurence Harbor 276 40.27 N 74.14 W
Laurencekirk 46 56.50 N 2.29 W
Laurens, Ia., U.S. 198 42.50 N 94.51 W
Laurens, N.Y., U.S. 210 42.32 N 75.06 W
Laurens, S.C., U.S. 192 34.29 N 82.00 W
Laurentides 206 45.51 N 73.46 W
Laurentides, Les ⋏[1] 176 48.00 N 71.00 W
Laurentides, Parc Provincial des ♠ 186 47.40 N 71.30 W
Laurenzana 68 40.28 N 15.58 E
Lauria 68 40.02 N 15.50 E
Lau Ridge ✣[3] 14 21.00 S 178.30 W
Laurie Island I 9 60.45 S 44.35 W
Laurie Lake ⊜ 184 56.34 N 101.54 W
Laurier, Mb., Can. 184 50.54 N 99.33 W
Laurier, P.Q., Can. 206 46.32 N 71.38 W
Laurière 32 46.05 N 1.28 E
Laurierville 206 46.18 N 71.39 W
Laurinburg 192 34.46 N 79.27 W
Laurino 68 40.20 N 15.20 E
Laurito 68 40.10 N 15.24 E
Lauritsala 26 61.04 N 28.16 E
Lauritzen Bay ⊂ 9 69.05 S 156.50 E
Laurium 190 47.14 N 88.26 W
Lauriya Nandangarh 124 26.59 N 84.24 E
Lauro, Monte ʌ 70 37.07 N 14.49 E
Lauro Müller 252 28.24 S 49.23 W
Laurys Station 208 40.43 N 75.32 W
Lausanne 58 46.31 N 6.38 E
Lauscha 54 50.28 N 11.10 E
Laut 86 59.18 N 66.02 E
Laut, Pulau I, Indon. 112 3.40 S 116.10 E
Laut, Pulau I, Indon. 112 4.43 N 107.59 E
Laut, Selat ꭒ 112 3.25 S 116.03 E
Lauta 54 51.27 N 14.04 E
Lautaro 252 38.31 S 72.27 W
Lautem 112 8.22 S 126.54 E
Lautenbach 58 47.57 N 7.09 E
Lautenthal 52 51.52 N 10.17 E
Lauter ≃, B.R.D. 56 49.39 N 7.35 E
Lauter ≃, Europe 56 48.58 N 8.11 E
Lauterach 58 47.29 N 9.44 E
Lauterbach, B.R.D. 56 50.38 N 9.24 E
Lauterbach, B.R.D. 58 48.14 N 8.20 E
Lauterbourg 56 48.59 N 8.11 E
Lauterbrunnen 58 46.36 N 7.55 E
Lauterecken 56 49.39 N 7.35 E
Lauterhofen 60 49.22 N 11.37 E
Lauter [Sachsen] 54 50.33 N 12.44 E
Laut Kecil, Kepulauan II 112 4.50 S 115.45 E
Lautoka 175g 17.37 S 177.27 E
Lauttakylä → Huittinen 26 61.11 N 22.42 E
Laut Tawar, Danau ⊜ 114 4.38 N 96.54 E
Lauwe 50 50.48 N 3.11 E
Lauwerszee ⊂ 52 53.20 N 6.12 E
Lauzerte 32 44.15 N 1.08 E
Lauzon 206 46.50 N 71.10 W
Lauzun 32 44.38 N 0.28 E
Lava (Łyna) ≃ 76 54.37 N 21.14 E
Lava, Nosy I 157b 14.33 S 47.36 E
Lava Beds National Monument ♠ 204 41.42 N 121.30 W
Lavaca □[6] 222 29.22 N 96.55 W
Lavaca ≃ 196 28.50 N 96.36 W
Lavaca Bay ⊂ 196 28.35 N 96.35 W
La Vacherie 62 44.53 N 5.11 E
Lavagh More ʌ 48 54.45 N 8.05 W
Lavagna 62 44.18 N 9.20 E
Lavagna ≃ 62 44.21 N 9.20 E
Lava Hot Springs 202 42.37 N 112.00 W
Lavaisse 252 33.49 S 65.25 W
Laval, P.Q., Can. 206 45.35 N 73.45 W
Laval, Fr. 32 48.04 N 0.46 W
Laval-des-Rapides ◆[8] 275a 45.33 N 73.42 W
La Valette → Valletta 36 35.54 N 14.31 E
La Valette-du-Var 62 43.08 N 5.59 E
La Vall d'Uixo 34 39.49 N 0.14 W
Lavalle, Arg. 252 29.01 S 59.11 W
Lavalle, Arg. 252 28.12 S 65.08 W
Lavalleja → Minas 252 34.23 S 55.14 W
Lavallette 208 39.58 N 74.04 W
La Valley 200 37.06 N 105.20 W
Laval-Ouest ◆[8] 275a 45.33 N 73.52 W
Lavaltrie 206 45.53 N 73.17 W
Lavamünd 61 46.39 N 14.56 E
Lāvān, Jazīreh-ye I 128 26.48 N 53.15 E
Lavan, Naḥal V 132 30.57 N 34.21 E
Lavanono 157b 25.24 S 44.55 E
Lavant ≃ 61 46.38 N 14.57 E
Lavapié, Punta > 252 37.09 S 73.35 W
Lávara 38 41.16 N 26.22 E
Lavaraty 157b 23.16 S 46.59 E
Lavardac 32 44.11 N 0.18 E
Lavarone 64 45.56 N 11.15 E
Lavassaare 76 58.31 N 24.22 E
Lava Tudo ≃ 252 28.26 S 50.25 W
Laveaga Peak ʌ 226 36.53 N 121.11 W
La Vecilla de Curueño 34 42.51 N 5.24 W
La Vega ◆[8] 286c 10.28 N 66.57 W
Lavela 24 63.38 N 45.31 E
La Vela, Cabo de > 246 12.15 N 72.11 W
La Vela de Coro 246 11.27 N 69.34 W
Lavelanet 32 42.56 N 1.51 E
Lavelle 208 40.46 N 76.22 W
Lavello 68 41.03 N 15.48 E
Laven 41 56.07 N 9.43 E
La Venada 196 25.50 N 97.30 W
Lavendon 42 52.11 N 0.40 W
Lavenham 42 52.06 N 0.47 E
Laveno 58 45.55 N 8.37 E
Lavenone 64 45.44 N 10.26 E
La Venta ⊥ 234 18.08 N 94.03 W
Laventie 50 50.38 N 2.46 E
La Ventura 232 24.38 N 100.54 W
Laver ≃ 44 54.08 N 1.30 W
Lavéra 62 43.23 N 5.02 E
La Vera ◆[1] 34 40.20 N 5.30 W
La Verde, Arg. 252 27.08 S 59.23 W
La Verde, Arg. 258 34.44 S 59.16 W
Laverdière, Lac ⊜ 206 46.50 N 74.28 W
L'Averdy, Cape > 175e 5.33 S 155.04 E
La Vérendrye, Réserve ♠ 190 47.30 N 77.30 W
La Vergne 194 36.00 N 86.34 W
La Verna ᵾ[1] 66 43.42 N 11.54 E
La Verne, Ca., U.S. 280 34.06 N 117.46 W
Laverne, Ok., U.S. 196 36.42 N 99.53 W
La Vernia 196 29.21 N 98.07 W
Laverock 285 40.05 N 75.11 W
La Verpillière 62 45.38 N 5.09 E
La Verrière 261 48.45 N 1.57 E
Lavers Hill 169 38.40 S 143.24 E
Laverton, Austl. 162 28.38 S 122.25 E
Laverton, Austl. 169 37.52 S 144.45 E
Laverton Royal Australian Air Force Base ■ 169 37.52 S 144.43 E
La Veta 200 37.30 N 105.00 W
Lavezares 116 12.32 N 124.20 E
Lavezzi, Îles II 71 41.20 N 9.15 E
Lavezzola 66 44.34 N 11.52 E
Lavia 26 61.36 N 22.36 E
Laviano 68 40.47 N 15.18 E
Lavic Lake ⊜ 204 34.40 N 116.21 W
La Victoria, Perú 286d 12.04 S 77.02 W
La Victoria, Ven. 246 10.14 N 67.20 W
Lavieille, Lake ⊜ 190 45.51 N 78.14 W
Lavik 26 61.06 N 5.30 E
La Vila Joiosa 34 38.30 N 0.14 W
La Villa 64 46.36 N 11.54 E
La Villa ≃ 236 7.59 N 80.23 W
La Ville-du-Bois 261 48.40 N 2.16 E
La Villeneuve-Saint-Martin 261 49.04 N 1.58 E
Lavillette 186 47.16 N 65.18 W
Lavin 58 46.46 N 10.06 E
La Viña, Arg. 252 25.27 S 65.35 W
Lavina, Mt., U.S. 202 46.17 N 108.56 W
Lavinio Lido di Enea 66 41.30 N 12.05 E
Laviolette, Lac ⊜ 206 46.51 N 73.58 W
La Virginia 246 4.54 N 75.53 W
Lavis 64 46.08 N 11.07 E
La Vista 198 41.11 N 96.01 W
La Volla 204 32.51 N 117.16 W
Lavon 222 33.02 N 96.26 W
Lavonia 192 34.26 N 83.06 W
Lavon Lake ⊜[1] 222 33.05 N 96.28 W
Lavougba 152 5.46 N 23.21 E
La Voulte-sur-Rhône 62 44.48 N 4.47 E
Lavoûte-sur-Loire 62 45.07 N 3.54 E
Lavoutte, Anse ⊂ 241f 14.06 N 60.56 W
Lavradia 266c 38.40 N 9.03 W
Lavras 256 21.14 S 45.00 W
Lavras ≃ 287a 23.00 S 43.33 W
Lavras da Mangabeira 250 6.45 S 38.57 W
Lavras do Sul 252 30.49 S 53.55 W
Lavrentija 180 65.35 N 171.00 W
Lavrentija, zaliv ⊂ 180 65.40 N 171.15 W
Lavrinhas 256 22.35 S 44.54 W
Lávrion 38 37.44 N 24.04 E
Lavumisa 158 27.19 S 31.54 E
Lavushi Manda National Park ♠ 154 12.20 S 30.50 E
Lawa 116 6.12 N 125.41 E

≃ River	Fluß	Río	Rivière	Rio
≍ Canal	Kanal	Canal	Canal	Canal
⌊ Waterfall, Rapids	Wasserfall, Stromschnellen	Cascada, Rápidos	Chute d'eau, Rapides	Cascata, Rápidos
ꭒ Strait	Meeresstraße	Estrecho	Détroit	Estreito
⊂ Bay, Gulf	Bucht, Golf	Bahía, Golfo	Baie, Golfe	Baía, Golfo
⊜ Lake, Lakes	See, Seen	Lago, Lagos	Lac, Lacs	Lago, Lagos
≋ Swamp	Sumpf	Pantano	Marais	Pântano
❄ Ice Features, Glacier	Eis- und Gletscherformen	Accidentes Glaciales	Formes glaciaires	Acidentes glaciares
⊤ Other Hydrographic Features	Andere Hydrographische Objekte	Otros Elementos Hidrográficos	Autres données hydrographiques	Outros acidentes hidrográficos
✣ Submarine Features	Untermeerische Objekte	Accidentes Submarinos	Formes de relief sous-marin	Acidentes submarinos
□ Political Unit	Politische Einheit	Unidad Politica	Entité politique	Unidade política
ᵾ Cultural Institution	Kulturelle Institution	Institución Cultural	Institution culturelle	Instituição cultural
⊥ Historical Site	Historische Stätte	Sitio Histórico	Site historique	Sitio histórico
♠ Recreational Site	Erholungs- und Ferienort	Sitio de Recreo	Centre de loisirs	Area de Lazer
⊠ Airport	Flughafen	Aeropuerto	Aéroport	Aeroporto
■ Military Installation	Militäranlage	Instalación Militar	Installation militaire	Instalação militar
◆ Miscellaneous	Verschiedenes	Misceláneo	Divers	Diversos

Name	Page	Lat.	Long.
Lawai	229b	21.55 N	159.30 W
Lawang	115a	7.49 S	112.42 E
La Wantzenau	58	48.40 N	7.50 E
La Ward	222	28.51 N	96.28 W
Lawas	112	4.51 N	115.24 E
Lawatu	112	2.53 S	120.18 E
Lawdar	144	13.53 N	45.52 E
Lawele	112	5.13 S	122.57 E
Lawers, Ben ▲	46	56.34 N	4.13 W
Laweueng	114	5.31 N	95.52 E
Lawford Lake ☒	184	54.30 N	96.43 W
Lawgi	166	24.34 S	150.39 E
Lawin	114	5.18 N	101.04 E
Lawin, Pulau I	164	1.31 S	128.44 E
Lawit, Gunong ▲	114	5.26 N	102.35 E
Lawksawk	110	21.15 N	96.52 E
Lawler	190	43.04 N	92.09 W
Lawlor, Mount ▲	280	34.16 N	118.06 W
Lawn, Nf., Can.	186	46.57 N	55.32 W
Lawn, Pa., U.S.	208	40.13 N	76.32 W
Lawn, Tx., U.S.	196	32.08 N	99.49 W
Lawn Bay ⊂	186	46.53 N	55.35 W
Lawndale, Ca., U.S.	228	33.53 N	118.21 W
Lawndale, Il., U.S.	219	40.13 N	89.17 W
Lawndale, N.C., U.S.	192	35.24 N	81.33 W
Lawndale ◆⁸, Il., U.S.	278	41.51 N	87.43 W
Lawndale ◆⁸, Pa., U.S.	285	40.03 N	75.05 W
Lawnes Creek ≃	208	37.08 N	76.40 W
Lawn Hill	166	18.35 S	138.35 E
Lawn Hill Creek ≃	166	18.03 S	139.09 E
Lawn Hill National Park ♦	166	18.45 S	138.27 E
Lawnside	285	39.51 N	75.01 W
Lawowa	112	4.26 S	122.56 E
Lawqah	128	29.49 N	42.45 E
Lawra	150	10.39 N	2.52 W
Lawrence, N.Z.	172	45.55 S	169.41 E
Lawrence, In., U.S.	218	39.50 N	86.01 W
Lawrence, Ks., U.S.	198	38.58 N	95.14 W
Lawrence, Ma., U.S.	208	42.43 N	71.09 W
Lawrence, Mi., U.S.	216	42.13 N	86.03 W
Lawrence, Ne., U.S.	198	40.17 N	98.15 W
Lawrence, N.Y., U.S.	276	40.36 N	73.43 W
Lawrence, Pa., U.S.	279b	40.19 N	81.33 W
Lawrence, Tx., U.S.	222	32.45 N	96.21 W
Lawrence □⁶, In., U.S.	218	38.52 N	86.29 W
Lawrence □⁶, Pa., U.S.			
Lawrence, Lake ☒	214	41.00 N	80.20 W
Lawrence Brook ≃	276	40.29 N	74.24 W
Lawrenceburg, In., U.S.	218	39.05 N	84.51 W
Lawrenceburg, Ky., U.S.	218	38.02 N	84.54 W
Lawrenceburg, Tn., U.S.	192	35.14 N	87.20 W
Lawrence Fork ≃	198	41.36 N	103.14 W
Lawrence Institute of Technology ·²	281	42.28 N	83.15 W
Lawrence Marsh ⯑	276	40.36 N	73.42 W
Lawrence Municipal Airport ⯑	283	42.43 N	71.07 W
Lawrence Park	214	42.09 N	80.01 W
Lawrencepur	123	33.50 N	72.30 E
Lawrenceville, Il., U.S.	194	38.43 N	87.40 W
Lawrenceville, N.J., U.S.	208	40.17 N	74.43 W
Lawrenceville, Pa., U.S.	210	42.00 N	77.08 W
Lawrenceville, Va., U.S.	192	36.45 N	77.50 W
Lawrenceville ◆	279b	40.28 N	79.57 W
Lawson, Austl.	170	33.43 S	150.26 E
Lawson, Mo., U.S.	194	39.26 N	94.12 W
Lawson Heights	214	40.18 N	79.23 W
Lawsonia	208	37.58 N	75.50 W
Lawsons Creek ≃	192	32.35 S	149.43 E
Lawtey	192	30.02 N	82.04 W
Lawton, Ky., U.S.	218	38.16 N	83.13 W
Lawton, Mi., U.S.	216	42.10 N	85.50 W
Lawton, N.D., U.S.	198	48.18 N	98.22 W
Lawton, Ok., U.S.	196	34.36 N	98.23 W
Lawton ◆⁸	286b	23.06 N	82.21 W
Lawu, Gunung ▲¹	115a	7.38 S	111.11 E
Lawyer Creek ≃	202	46.14 N	116.01 W
Lawyersville	210	42.42 N	74.30 W
Lawz, Jabal al- ▲	128	28.40 N	35.18 E
Laxá	40	58.09 N	15.36 E
Laxay	46	58.09 N	6.29 W
Laxenburg	264b	48.04 N	16.21 E
Laxenburger Park ♦	264b	48.04 N	16.22 E
Laxey	44	54.14 N	4.23 W
Laxford, Loch ⊂	46	58.23 N	5.06 W
Lax Kw'alaams	182	54.33 N	130.25 W
Laxou	58	48.41 N	6.09 E
Layang Layang	114	1.49 N	103.29 E
Laye ≃	62	43.54 N	5.48 E
La Yesca	234	21.19 N	104.02 W
Layhill	208	39.05 N	77.03 W
Layla	144	22.17 N	46.45 E
Lay Lake ☒¹	194	33.10 N	86.35 W
Layou	241h	13.12 N	61.17 W
Layou ≃	240d	15.23 N	61.26 W
La'youn □⁶	148	27.55 N	12.15 W
Lay-Saint-Christophe	58	48.45 N	6.12 E
Layssan Island I	14	25.50 N	171.50 W
Layton, In., U.S.	210	41.13 N	74.50 W
Layton, Ut., U.S.	200	41.04 N	111.58 W
Laytons Lake ☒	285	39.42 N	75.26 W
Laytonville	204	39.41 N	123.28 W
La Zarca	232	25.50 N	104.44 W
Lazarev	89	52.13 N	141.32 E
Lazarevskoje	80	56.49 N	50.15 E
Lazaro	84	43.55 N	39.20 E
Lazarivo	157b	23.54 S	44.59 E
Lázaro Cárdenas	196	23.23 N	103.10 W
Lázaro Cárdenas, Presa ☒¹	232	25.35 N	105.02 W
Lazdijai	76	54.14 N	23.31 E
Lazha	102	26.26 N	101.50 E
Lazhulong	120	35.08 N	81.33 E
Lazi	116	9.08 N	123.38 E
Lazio □⁴	66	42.00 N	12.30 E
Lazise	64	45.30 N	10.44 E
Lazo	78	50.06 N	32.39 E
Lazorki			
La Zorra, Quebrada ≃	286c	10.36 N	67.03 W
Lazovski zapovednik ♦	89	44.00 N	133.55 E
Lazzaro	68	37.58 N	15.40 E
Lazzate	64	45.40 N	9.05 E
Lea ≃	42	51.30 N	0.01 E
Léach	110	12.21 N	103.46 E
Leach ≃	42	51.41 N	1.39 W
Leach Pond ☒	283	42.04 N	71.09 W
Leachville	194	35.56 N	90.15 W
Leacock	280	40.05 N	76.12 W
Lead	198	44.21 N	103.45 W
Leadbetter Point ⯈	204	46.38 N	124.03 W
Leadburn	46	55.47 N	3.14 W
Leadenham	44	53.04 N	0.33 W
Leaden Roding	260	51.48 N	0.19 E
Leader	184	50.55 N	109.31 W
Leader Water ≃	46	55.36 N	2.41 W
Leadgate	44	54.52 N	1.48 W
Lead Hill ▲²	194	37.06 N	92.38 W
Leadhills	44	55.25 N	3.47 W
Leadon ≃	42	51.53 N	2.16 W
Leadore	202	44.40 N	113.21 W
Leadville	198	39.15 N	106.17 W
Leaf ≃, Ms., U.S.	194	31.00 N	88.45 W
Leaf Lake ☒	184	53.02 N	102.07 W
Leaghur, Lake ☒	166	33.35 S	143.04 E
League ▲	47	54.39 N	8.44 W
League City	222	29.30 N	95.05 W

Name	Page	Lat.	Long.
Leakesville	194	31.09 N	88.33 W
Leakey	196	29.43 N	99.45 W
Leakin Park ♦	284b	39.18 N	76.42 W
Leak Run ≃	279b	40.27 N	79.47 W
Leaksville	192	36.29 N	79.53 W
Lealman	220	27.49 N	82.40 W
Lealui	152	15.10 S	23.02 E
Leamington	214	42.03 N	82.36 W
Leamington Spa → Royal Leamington Spa	42	52.18 N	1.31 W
Le'an	100	27.24 N	115.48 E
Leander	236	15.47 N	87.20 W
Leander Point ⯈	162	29.16 S	114.56 E
Leandro	250	5.59 S	44.55 W
Leandro, Serra do ▲	256	22.55 S	43.55 W
Leandro N. Alem	252	27.36 S	55.19 W
Leane, Lough ☒	48	52.05 N	9.35 W
Leannan ≃	48	55.02 N	7.38 W
Leano, Monte ▲	66	41.20 N	13.13 E
Learmonth	162	22.15 S	114.05 E
Leary	192	31.29 N	84.30 W
Leaside □⁸	275b	43.42 N	79.22 W
Leask	184	53.00 N	106.45 W
Leatherhead	42	51.18 N	0.20 W
Leatherman Peak ▲	202	44.05 N	113.44 W
Leatherwood Creek ≃	218	38.49 N	86.30 W
Lea Town	262	53.46 N	2.48 W
Leavenworth, Ks., U.S.	198	39.18 N	94.55 W
Leavenworth, Wa., U.S.	224	47.35 N	120.39 W
Leavenworth Aerodrome ⯑	260	51.42 N	0.27 W
Leavittsburg	214	41.14 N	80.52 W
Leawood	316	43.09 N	94.31 W
Leba	30	54.47 N	17.33 E
Leba ≃	30	54.47 N	17.33 E
Lebach	56	49.24 N	6.54 E
Lebak	116	6.32 N	124.03 E
Lebam	224	46.33 N	123.32 W
Lébamba	152	2.12 S	11.30 E
Lebanon, Ct., U.S.	207	41.38 N	72.13 W
Lebanon, Il., U.S.	219	38.36 N	89.48 W
Lebanon, In., U.S.	218	40.02 N	86.28 W
Lebanon, Ks., U.S.	198	39.48 N	98.33 W
Lebanon, Ky., U.S.	194	37.34 N	85.15 W
Lebanon, Mo., U.S.	194	37.40 N	92.39 W
Lebanon, N.H., U.S.	188	43.38 N	72.15 W
Lebanon, N.J., U.S.	210	40.38 N	74.50 W
Lebanon, N.Y., U.S.	210	42.47 N	75.39 W
Lebanon, Oh., U.S.	218	39.26 N	84.12 W
Lebanon, Or., U.S.	202	44.32 N	122.54 W
Lebanon, Pa., U.S.	208	40.20 N	76.24 W
Lebanon, S.D., U.S.	198	45.04 N	99.46 W
Lebanon, Tn., U.S.	194	36.12 N	86.17 W
Lebanon, Va., U.S.	192	36.54 N	82.04 W
Lebanon □⁶	208	40.20 N	76.25 W
Lebanon (Al-Lubnān) □¹, Asia	118	34.00 N	36.00 E
Lebanon (Lubnān) □¹, Lebanon Junction	194	37.50 N	85.43 W
Lebanon Mountains → Lubnān, Jabal ▲	132	34.00 N	36.00 E
Lebanon Springs	210	42.29 N	73.23 W
Le Bar-sur-Martin	56	49.07 N	6.09 E
Le Bar-sur-le-Loup	62	43.42 N	6.59 E
Leb'ažje, S.S.S.R.	80	57.25 N	49.32 E
Leb'ažje, S.S.S.R.	86	55.16 N	66.29 E
Leb'ažje, S.S.S.R.	85	51.28 N	77.46 E
Lee Boulevard			
Le Béage	62	44.51 N	4.07 E
Le Beausset	62	43.12 N	5.48 E
Lebec	228	34.50 N	118.51 W
Lebed'an'	76	53.01 N	39.09 E
Lebedevka, S.S.S.R.	80	51.06 N	47.09 E
Lebedevka, S.S.S.R.	86	55.09 N	54.07 E
Lebedin	78	50.36 N	34.30 E
Lebedin, S.S.S.R.	78	51.17 N	37.38 E
Lebedin, S.S.S.R.	78	48.59 N	31.31 E
Lebedino	86	54.39 N	49.50 E
Leben, Oued el V	148	34.37 N	10.01 E
Lebesby	24	70.34 N	26.59 E
Le Bessat	62	45.22 N	4.31 E
Le Bihan Falls ∟	158	29.51 S	28.03 E
Le Biot	62	46.16 N	6.38 E
Le Blanc	114	53.00 N	1.04 E
Le Blanc-Mesnil	261	48.56 N	2.28 E
Le Bleymard	62	44.29 N	3.43 E
Leblon ◆⁸	287a	22.59 S	43.13 W
Lebo, Ks., U.S.	198	38.25 N	95.51 W
Lebo, Zaïre	152	4.25 N	23.25 E
Le Bois-de-Cise	261	48.39 N	1.26 E
Le Bois-Dieu	261	48.39 N	1.43 E
Le Bois-d'Oingt	58	45.55 N	4.35 E
Lebombo Mountains ▲²	156	25.15 S	32.00 E
Lebongtandai	114	2.20 S	101.45 E
Lebon Régis	252	26.56 S	50.42 W
Le Boréon	62	44.07 N	7.17 E
Lebork	30	54.33 N	17.44 E
Le Boulay	58	48.47 N	1.40 E
Le Bourg-d'Oisans	62	45.03 N	6.02 E
Le Bourget	261	48.56 N	2.26 E
Le Bourget-du-Lac	62	45.40 N	5.52 E
Le Brassus	58	46.35 N	6.13 E
Lebrija	34	36.55 N	6.04 W
Le Broc	62	45.54 N	7.07 E
Le Brugeron	62	45.43 N	3.43 E
Łebsko, Jezioro ⊂	30	54.44 N	17.24 E
Lebu	252	37.37 S	73.39 W
Le Bugue	62	44.55 N	0.56 E
Le Buisson de Massoury ♦	261	48.30 N	2.43 E
Lebus	54	52.25 N	14.32 E
Le Caire → Al-Qāhirah	142	30.03 N	31.15 E
Le Camp-du-Castellet	62	43.15 N	5.45 E
Le Cannet	62	43.34 N	7.01 E
Lecanto	220	28.51 N	82.29 W
Le Cap → Cap-Haïtien, Haï.	238	19.45 N	72.12 W
Le Cap → Cape Town, S. Afr.	158	33.55 S	18.22 E
Le Carbet	240e	14.43 N	61.11 W
Le Cateau	50	50.06 N	3.33 E
Le Catelet	58	50.00 N	3.15 E
Lecce	68	40.23 N	18.11 E
Lecce □⁴	68	40.23 N	18.10 E
Lecco	64	45.51 N	9.23 E
Lecco, Lago di ⊂	64	45.51 N	9.23 E
Le Center	190	44.23 N	93.44 W
Lech	32	47.12 N	10.09 E
Le Châble, Fr.	58	48.44 N	10.56 E
Le Châble, Schw.	62	46.05 N	7.12 E
L'Échalp	62	44.45 N	7.00 E
Le Chambon-Feugerolles	62	45.24 N	4.19 E
Le Chambon-sur-Lignon	62	45.03 N	4.18 E
Le Champ-Renault	62	45.48 N	0.53 E
Le Chasseral ▲	58	47.08 N	7.03 E
Le-Châtelard-d'Oléron	32	45.51 N	1.11 W
Le Châtelard	58	45.41 N	6.08 E
Le Châtelet	58	46.39 N	2.17 E
Le Châtelet-en-Brie	58	48.30 N	2.47 E

Name	Page	Lat.	Long.
Leche, Laguna de la ⊂	240p	22.13 N	78.38 W
Le Chêne-Rogneux	261	48.46 N	1.46 E
Le Chesnay	261	48.50 N	2.07 E
Le Chesne	56	49.31 N	4.46 E
Le Cheylard	62	44.54 N	4.25 E
Lechfeld ☰	58	48.10 N	10.50 E
Lechiguanas, Islas de las II	252	33.26 S	59.42 W
Lechiguiri, Cerro ▲	234	16.43 N	95.30 W
Lechlade	42	51.43 N	1.41 W
Lechleiten	58	47.16 N	10.12 E
Lechtal ☰	24	60.49 N	48.28 E
Lechtaler Alpen ▲	64	47.15 N	10.30 E
Lechuga, Arroyo ≃	286b	23.01 N	82.16 W
Lechuguilla, Cerro ▲	234	22.19 N	104.15 W
Lecinone, Monte ▲	267a	41.59 N	12.48 E
Leck	41	54.46 N	8.58 E
Le Claire	190	41.36 N	90.21 W
Lecompte	194	31.05 N	92.24 W
Lecomfield	44	53.52 N	0.27 W
Léconi	152	1.35 S	14.14 E
Lecontes Mills	214	41.05 N	78.17 W
Le Cornate ▲	66	43.10 N	10.57 E
Le Coudray-Montceaux	261	48.34 N	2.31 E
Le Coudray-Saint-Germer	50	49.25 N	1.50 E
Le Creusot	56	46.48 N	4.26 E
Le Croci di Acerno ✕	68	40.45 N	15.02 E
Le Croisic	32	47.18 N	2.31 W
Le Crotoy	50	50.13 N	1.37 E
Łęczna	30	51.19 N	22.52 E
Łęczyca	30	52.04 N	19.13 E
Leda ≃	52	53.12 N	7.26 E
Ledaig	46	56.30 N	5.23 W
Led'anaja, gora ▲	74	61.53 N	171.09 E
Ledang, Gunong ▲	114	2.22 N	102.37 E
Ledava ≃	64	46.29 N	16.35 E
Ledbetter	222	30.09 N	96.48 W
Ledbury	42	52.02 N	2.25 W
Lede	50	50.58 N	3.58 E
Ledenice	61	48.57 N	14.37 E
Lederach	285	40.16 N	75.24 W
Le Deschaux	58	46.55 N	5.33 E
Ledesma	34	41.05 N	6.00 W
Ledgewood	276	40.52 N	74.39 W
Ledi, Ben ▲	46	56.15 N	4.19 W
Le Diamant	240e	14.29 N	61.02 W
Lediba	152	3.03 S	16.32 E
Ledikton	24	71.14 N	50.30 E
Lednice	61	48.48 N	16.48 E
Ledo, India	120	27.18 N	95.44 E
Ledo, Indon.	114	1.02 N	109.36 E
Lêdo, Cabo ⯈	152	9.35 S	13.12 E
Ledong	110	18.45 N	109.09 E
Le Donjon	58	46.21 N	3.48 E
Le Dorat	32	46.13 N	1.05 E
Le Doré, Lac ☒	186	51.17 N	61.23 W
Ledra ≃	64	46.13 N	13.02 E
Ledsham	262	53.16 N	2.58 W
Leduc	182	53.16 N	113.33 W
Ledung	114	2.45 N	99.59 E
Ledyard Bay ⊂	180	69.30 N	164.30 W
Łędyczek	58	53.33 N	16.58 E
Lee, Il., U.S.	216	41.48 N	88.56 W
Lee ≃, Ma., U.S.	207	42.19 N	73.23 W
Lee ≃⁶, Fl., U.S.	220	26.34 N	81.55 W
Lee ≃⁶, Tx., U.S.	216	41.50 N	89.29 W
Lee ≃⁶, Tx., U.S.	222	30.20 N	96.55 W
Lee ≃	48	51.54 N	8.22 W
Lee Boulevard Heights	284c	38.52 N	77.09 W
Lee Center	210	43.18 N	75.31 W
Leechburg	214	40.37 N	79.36 W
Leechburg Airport ⯑	279b	40.37 N	79.34 W
Leech Lake ☒, Sk., Can.	184	51.04 N	102.30 W
Leech Lake ☒, Mn., U.S.	190	47.09 N	94.23 W
Leech Lake Indian Reservation ◆⁴	190	47.30 N	94.27 W
Leechtown	224	48.30 N	123.42 W
Leedey	196	35.52 N	99.21 W
Leeds, Eng., U.K.	44	53.50 N	1.35 W
Leeds, Al., U.S.	194	33.32 N	86.32 W
Leeds, N.Y., U.S.	210	42.15 N	73.54 W
Leeds, N.D., U.S.	198	48.17 N	99.26 W
Leeds and Bradford (Yeadon) Airport ⯑	44	53.52 N	1.38 W
Leeds and Grenville □⁶	212	44.45 N	75.50 W
Leeds and Liverpool Canal ≡	262	53.25 N	2.59 W
Leeds Point	208	39.29 N	74.25 W
Leedstown	42	50.10 N	5.22 W
Leegebruch	54	52.43 N	13.11 E
Leek, Ned.	52	53.09 N	6.24 E
Leek, Eng., U.K.	44	53.06 N	2.01 W
Leelanau, Lake ☒	190	44.55 N	85.43 W
Leelanau Peninsula ⯈¹	190	45.00 N	85.35 W
Leeman	162	29.57 S	114.58 E
Leeming	44	54.17 N	1.32 W
Leenaun	48	53.36 N	9.45 W
Leende	52	51.21 N	5.33 E
Lee-on-the-Solent	42	50.49 N	1.12 W
Lee Park	210	41.14 N	75.55 W
Leeper	214	41.22 N	79.18 W
Leer	52	53.14 N	7.26 E
Leerdam	52	51.54 N	5.05 E
Leerhafe	52	53.32 N	7.47 E
Lees ≃	262	53.32 N	2.04 W
Leesburg, Fl., U.S.	220	28.48 N	81.52 W
Leesburg, Ga., U.S.	192	31.43 N	84.10 W
Leesburg, In., U.S.	218	38.40 N	86.21 W
Leesburg, N.J., U.S.	208	39.15 N	74.59 W
Leesburg, Oh., U.S.	218	39.21 N	83.33 W
Leesburg, Tx., U.S.	222	32.59 N	95.05 W
Leesburg, Va., U.S.	208	39.06 N	77.33 W
Lees Creek ≃	218	39.21 N	83.29 W
Leese	52	52.30 N	9.06 E
Leeshendian	107	28.58 N	106.40 E
Leesi	194	38.55 N	93.25 W
Leeston	172	43.46 S	172.18 E
Leesville, Il., U.S.	216	41.01 N	87.33 W
Leesville, La., U.S.	194	31.08 N	93.16 W
Leesville, Oh., U.S.	214	40.27 N	81.13 W
Leesville, S.C., U.S.	192	33.54 N	81.31 W
Leesville, Tx., U.S.	222	29.24 N	97.45 W
Leesville Lake ☒¹, Oh., U.S.	214	40.30 N	81.10 W
Leesville Lake ☒¹, Va., U.S.	192	37.08 N	79.25 W
Leetonia	214	40.52 N	80.45 W
Leetsdale	214	40.33 N	80.12 W
Leeudoringstad	158	27.15 S	26.10 E
Leeu-Gamka	158	32.47 S	21.59 E
Leeupan ☒	158	26.14 S	28.19 E
Leeuwarden	52	53.12 N	5.46 E
Leeuwin, Cape ⯈	162	34.22 S	115.08 E
Lee Vining	226	37.57 N	119.07 W
Lee Ward Islands II	238	17.00 N	63.00 W
Le Faou	32	48.18 N	4.12 W
Le Fayet	62	45.55 N	6.43 E
Lèfèvre, Pointe ⯈	175f	20.54 S	167.01 E
Leffe	58	45.48 N	9.53 E
Lefferts, Lake ☒	276	40.25 N	74.14 W
Léfini ≃	152	2.57 S	16.12 E
Léfini, Réserve de la ◆⁴	152	2.58 S	15.25 E
Le Fleix	130	35.00 S	21.15 E
La Focette	64	43.55 N	10.13 E
Leforest	50	50.25 N	3.04 E
Lefors	196	35.26 N	100.48 W
Le François	240e	14.37 N	60.54 W
Le Freney-d'Oisans	58	45.02 N	6.07 E

Name	Page	Lat.	Long.
Lefroy, Lake ☒	212	44.16 N	79.34 W
Lefroy, Lake ☒	162	31.15 S	121.40 E
Leftrook Lake ☒	184	56.05 N	98.36 W
Lega Hida	144	7.56 N	41.04 E
Legal	182	53.57 N	113.35 W
Legardes	34	40.19 N	3.45 W
Le Gardeur	206	45.45 N	73.28 W
Legaspi	116	13.08 N	123.44 E
Legau	58	47.51 N	10.07 E
Legden	52	52.02 N	7.07 E
Legendre ≃	206	45.44 N	71.08 W
Legendre Island I	162	20.23 S	116.54 E
Leggett, Ca., U.S.	204	39.51 N	123.42 W
Leggett, Tx., U.S.	222	30.49 N	94.52 W
Leghorn → Livorno	66	43.33 N	10.19 E
Legion Mine	156	21.23 S	28.33 E
Legion of Honor, Palace of the ·²	282	37.47 N	122.30 W
Legionowo	30	52.25 N	20.56 E
Legnago	64	45.11 N	11.18 E
Legnano	62	45.36 N	8.54 E
Legnica (Liegnitz)	30	51.13 N	16.09 E
Legnica □⁴	30	51.25 N	16.10 E
Le Gosier	240e	16.12 N	61.30 W
Le Grand	226	37.13 N	120.14 W
LeGrand, Cape ⯈	162	34.01 S	122.06 E
Le Grand-Lucé	58	47.52 N	0.28 E
Le Grand-Quevilly	50	49.25 N	1.02 E
Le Grand-Serre	62	45.16 N	5.06 E
Le Grand Wintersberg ▲²	56	48.59 N	7.37 E
Le Grau-du-Roi	62	43.32 N	4.08 E
Le Gua	62	45.01 N	5.37 E
La Guelta	34	36.22 N	0.50 E
Leguga	66	3.23 N	25.02 E
Legume	166	28.25 S	152.19 E
Legundi, Pulau I	115a	5.50 S	105.43 E
Leh	123	34.10 N	77.35 E
Le Havre	50	49.30 N	0.08 E
Lehčevo	70	43.32 N	23.32 E
Lehesten	54	50.29 N	11.28 E
Lehi	200	40.23 N	111.51 W
Lehigh, Ia., U.S.	190	42.21 N	94.03 W
Lehigh, Ok., U.S.	196	34.28 N	96.12 W
Lehigh ≃	208	40.36 N	75.29 W
Lehigh ≃	210	40.41 N	75.12 W
Lehigh Acres	220	26.37 N	81.37 W
Lehighton	208	40.50 N	75.42 W
Lehinch	48	52.56 N	9.20 W
Lehliu	54	44.26 N	26.22 E
Lehmi ≃	202	44.38 N	113.32 W
Lehnin	54	52.19 N	12.44 E
Lehnitz See ☒	264a	52.45 N	13.15 E
Leho	140	7.07 N	33.52 E
Le Hohwald	58	48.24 N	7.20 E
Le Houlme	50	49.30 N	1.03 E
Lehr	198	46.17 N	99.21 W
Lehra Gāga	123	29.55 N	75.49 E
Lehrbach	54	50.47 N	9.04 E
Lehrberg	54	49.21 N	10.30 E
Lehre	54	52.19 N	10.40 E
Lehrte	52	52.22 N	9.59 E
Lehsten	54	53.19 N	10.12 E
Lehtimäki	26	62.47 N	23.55 E
Lehtrār Bāla	123	33.42 N	73.26 E
Lehtse	76	59.15 N	25.50 E
Lehua I	229b	22.01 N	160.06 W
Lehututu	156	23.58 S	21.51 E
Leiah	123	30.58 N	70.56 E
Leião	266c	38.44 N	9.18 W
Leibnitz	61	46.47 N	15.32 E
Leibo	102	28.19 N	103.21 E
Leicester, Eng., U.K.	42	52.38 N	1.05 W
Leicester, Ma., U.S.	207	42.14 N	71.54 W
Leicester, N.Y., U.S.	210	42.46 N	77.53 W
Leicestershire □⁶	42	52.40 N	1.10 W
Leichhardt ≃	274a	33.53 S	151.07 E
Leichhardt ≃	166	17.35 S	139.48 E
Leichhardt Falls ∟	166	18.14 S	139.53 E
Leichhardt Range ▲	166	20.40 S	147.25 E
Leichlingen	56	51.06 N	7.01 E
Leiden	52	52.09 N	4.30 E
Leiderdorp	52	52.09 N	4.34 E
Leidschendam	52	52.05 N	4.24 E
Leie (Lys) ≃	50	51.03 N	3.43 E
Leiferde	52	52.26 N	10.26 E
Leigh, N.Z.	172	36.17 S	174.49 E
Leigh, Eng., U.K.	44	53.30 N	2.33 W
Leigh, Eng., U.K.	260	51.12 N	0.13 E
Leigh Canal ≡	263	53.28 N	2.21 W
Leigh Creek	166	30.28 S	138.25 E
Leighlinbridge	48	52.44 N	6.59 W
Leigh-on-Sea	42	51.33 N	0.39 E
Leighton	194	34.42 N	87.31 W
Leighton Buzzard	42	51.55 N	0.40 W
Leikanger	26	61.10 N	6.52 E
Leikhu	110	19.13 N	96.35 E
Leimbach	54	51.36 N	11.28 E
Leimstruth	54	50.58 N	10.01 E
Lein ≃	54	49.54 N	10.00 E
Leinan	184	50.10 N	107.46 W
Leine ≃	52	52.43 N	9.36 E
Leinefelde	54	51.23 N	10.19 E
Leinfelden-Echterdingen	58	48.41 N	9.08 E
Leinster	162	27.51 S	120.36 E
Leinster, Mount ▲	48	52.37 N	6.46 W
Leintwardine	42	52.22 N	2.53 W
Leipalingis	76	54.05 N	23.57 E
Leipo ·²	262	53.32 N	2.04 W
Leipoldtville	158	32.14 S	18.30 E
Leipsic, Oh., U.S.	218	41.06 N	83.59 W
Leipsic ≃	208	39.15 N	75.24 W
Leipzig	54	51.19 N	12.20 E
Leipzig □⁵	54	51.15 N	12.45 E
Leiria	34	39.45 N	8.48 W
Leirvik	26	59.47 N	5.30 E
Leisach	61	46.48 N	12.45 E
Leisi	76	58.34 N	22.38 E
Leisler, Mount ▲	162	23.28 S	129.17 E
Leisnig	54	51.10 N	12.38 E
Leiston	42	52.12 N	1.34 E
Leisure City	220	25.29 N	80.25 W
Leitariegos, Puerto de ✕	34	43.00 N	6.25 W
Leitchfield	194	37.28 N	86.17 W
Leiters Ford	218	41.07 N	86.23 W
Leith	46	55.59 N	3.11 W
Leith, Water of ≃	46	55.59 N	3.11 W
Leitha (Lajta) ≃, Europe	61	47.54 N	17.17 E
Leitha, Öst.	264b	48.06 N	16.33 E
Leithagebirge ▲	61	47.59 N	16.43 E
Leithe ◆⁸	263	51.29 N	7.06 E
Leith Hill ▲²	42	51.11 N	0.23 W
Leitkau	54	52.11 N	11.59 E
Leitchville	166	36.01 S	144.20 E
Leitrim	48	54.00 N	8.04 W
Leitrim □⁶	48	54.08 N	8.00 W
Leiva	122	6.35 N	76.24 E
Leixi	104	27.41 N	114.14 E
Leiyang	100	26.24 N	112.51 E
Lei Yue Mun 凵	271d	22.16 N	114.14 E
Leizhou Bandao ⯈¹	100	21.10 N	110.05 E
Leizhou			

Name	Page	Lat.	Long.
Lekkeroog	158	30.43 S	20.00 E
Lekkerwater	156	23.38 S	17.14 E
Lekma	80	58.18 N	52.04 E
Łęknice	54	51.35 N	14.45 E
Lékoni	152	1.11 S	13.16 E
Lékoumou □⁵	152	3.00 S	13.30 E
Le Kreïder	148	34.06 N	0.02 E
Le Kremlin-Bicêtre	261	48.49 N	2.21 E
Leksand	26	60.44 N	14.59 E
Leksberg	26	59.41 N	13.49 E
Leksozero, ozero ☒	24	63.46 N	30.58 E
Leksvik	26	63.40 N	10.37 E
Lela	152	5.03 S	12.29 E
Le Lac-d'Issarlès	62	44.49 N	4.04 E
Le Lamentin	240e	14.37 N	61.01 W
Leland, Il., U.S.	216	41.37 N	88.48 W
Leland, Ms., U.S.	194	33.24 N	90.53 W
Leland Grove	219	39.47 N	89.41 W
Leland Lake ☒	224	47.53 N	122.53 W
Lelâng ☒	26	59.08 N	12.10 E
Lelant	42	50.11 N	5.26 W
Le Laus	62	44.31 N	6.09 E
Le Lauzet-Ubaye	62	44.26 N	6.26 E
Le Lavandou	62	43.08 N	6.22 E
Lel'čicy	78	51.47 N	28.19 E
Leleiwi Point ⯈	229d	19.44 N	155.00 W
Leleque	254	42.24 S	71.03 W
Leles	115a	7.07 S	107.53 E
Lelewau	112	3.02 S	121.05 E
Lelintah	263	51.08 N	7.40 E
Lelija ▲	70	43.20 N	18.33 E
Leling	98	37.45 N	117.12 E
Lelingluang	164	7.09 S	131.43 E
Lelintah	164	2.03 S	130.16 E
Lengua de Vaca, Punta ⯈	252	30.14 S	71.38 W
Lelystad	52	52.31 N	5.27 E
Lema	150	12.57 N	4.14 E
Le Madonie ▲	68	37.52 N	13.58 E
Lemahabang	115a	6.17 S	107.27 E
Le Maire, Estrecho de 凵	254	54.50 S	65.00 W
Lêman, Lac → Geneva, Lake ☒	58	46.26 N	6.30 E
Lemankoa	175e	5.02 S	154.35 E
Le Mars	190	42.47 N	96.10 W
Le Marin	240e	14.28 N	60.53 W
Le Markstein	58	47.56 N	7.02 E
Le Mars	198	42.47 N	96.09 W
Lema Shilindi	144	4.55 N	42.02 E
Lemay	219	38.32 N	90.17 W
Lemay, Lac ☒	186	50.35 N	68.25 W
Lembach	56	49.00 N	7.48 E
Lembach im Mühlkreis	60	48.29 N	13.53 E
Lemba-Gaba	273b	4.27 S	15.18 E
Lembang	115a	6.49 S	107.36 E
Lembeck	263	51.45 N	7.00 E
Lembeek	50	50.43 N	4.13 E
Lembeni, Pulau I	112	1.26 N	125.13 E
Lemberg, Sk., Can.	184	50.44 N	103.13 W
Lemberg, Fr.	56	49.00 N	7.23 E
Lemberg → L'vov, S.S.S.R.	78	49.50 N	24.00 E
Lemberg ▲	58	48.09 N	8.45 E
Lembruch	52	52.29 N	8.25 E
Lembu, Gunung ▲	148	36.11 N	4.11 E
Lemdiyya	148	36.15 N	2.50 E
Lemdiyya □⁵	148	35.50 N	3.00 E
Leme	255	22.12 S	47.24 W
Leme, Morro do ▲²	287a	22.58 S	43.10 W
Le Mée-sur-Seine	261	48.32 N	2.38 E
Lemei Rock ▲	224	46.01 N	121.41 W
Lemele	52	52.27 N	6.25 E
Le Mêle-sur-Sarthe	58	48.31 N	0.23 E
Lemen	160	1.26 N	32.45 E
Lemeris, Cape ⯈	164	3.15 S	152.03 E
Le Merlerault	58	48.42 N	0.18 E
Lemesós (Limassol)	130	34.40 N	33.02 E
Lemešino ▲	80	51.00 N	49.40 E
Le Mesle	62	45.00 N	4.41 E
Le Mesnil-Amelot	261	49.01 N	2.36 E
Le Mesnil-Aubry	261	49.03 N	2.24 E
Le Mesnil-Saint-Denis	261	48.45 N	1.58 E
Le Mesnil-sur-Oger	56	48.57 N	4.01 E
Lemeson (Limassol)	130	34.40 N	33.02 E
Lemeta	180	64.52 N	147.44 W
Lemförde	52	52.28 N	8.22 E
Lemgo	52	52.02 N	8.54 E
Lemhi ≃	202	45.12 N	113.53 W
Lemhi Pass ✕	202	44.59 N	113.27 W
Lemhi Range ▲	202	44.30 N	113.25 W
Lemieux Islands II	178	64.23 N	64.35 W
Lemin	102	21.11 N	109.42 E
Lemitar	196	34.09 N	106.54 W
Lemmenjoki ≃	24	68.40 N	26.00 E
Lemmenjoen Kansallispuisto ♦	24	68.40 N	26.00 E
Lemmer	52	52.50 N	5.42 E
Lemmon	198	45.56 N	102.09 W
Lemmon, Mount ▲	200	32.26 N	110.47 W
Lemnos → Límnos I	38	39.54 N	25.21 E
Lemoine, Lac ☒	186	48.06 N	77.40 W
Lemon, Lake ☒	218	39.16 N	86.25 W
Lemon Grove	226	32.44 N	117.02 W
Lemont	216	41.40 N	88.00 W
Lemont-Furnace	214	39.53 N	79.41 W
Lemoore	226	36.18 N	119.46 W
Lemoore Naval Air Station ⯑	226	36.15 N	119.57 W
Le Moule	240e	16.20 N	61.21 W
LeMoyne, P.Q., Can.	275a	45.31 N	73.29 W
Lemoyne, Pa., U.S.	208	40.14 N	76.54 W
Lempa ≃	238	13.14 N	88.49 W
Le Mesnil ≃	261	48.58 N	2.10 E
Lempdes	62	45.47 N	3.12 E
Lempira □⁵	236	14.20 N	88.40 W
Lemsid	148	26.33 N	13.51 W
Lemsterland □⁸	52	52.52 N	5.42 E
Lemva ≃	24	66.30 N	61.48 E
Lemvig	26	56.32 N	8.18 E
Lemyethna	110	18.19 N	95.09 E
Lena, Il., U.S.	216	42.23 N	89.49 W
Lena, Wi., U.S.	190	44.57 N	88.02 W
Lena ≃	74	72.25 N	126.40 E
Lenah	162	30.27 S	119.51 E
Lenart	61	46.35 N	15.50 E

Name	Seite	Breite	Länge E = Ost
Lenasia	273d	26.17 S	27.50 E
Lenawee □⁶	216	41.53 N	84.04 W
Lencloître	32	46.49 N	0.20 E
Lençóis	255	12.34 S	41.23 W
Lend	61	47.18 N	13.04 E
Lenda ≃	154	1.20 N	28.01 E
Lenda ≃	61	46.34 N	16.27 E
Lendelede	50	50.53 N	3.14 E
Lendery	24	63.26 N	31.03 E
Lendinara	64	45.05 N	11.36 E
Lendorf	64	46.50 N	13.26 E
Lendringsen	50	49.09 N	0.55 E
Le Neubourg	50	49.09 N	0.55 E
Lengau	58	47.11 N	7.22 E
Lenggong	114	2.17 N	102.49 E
Lengjiagou	104	41.40 N	121.37 E
Lenglingen ☒	26	64.14 N	13.45 E
Lengnau	58	47.11 N	7.22 E
Lengoué ≃	152	0.49 N	15.47 E
Lengshuijiang	100	27.55 N	111.08 E
Lengshuitan	100	26.27 N	111.35 E
Lengeflscheid	263	51.08 N	7.40 E
Lengefeld, D.D.R.	54	50.34 N	12.22 E
Lengenfeld, D.D.R.	56	51.13 N	10.13 E
Lenger	85	42.12 N	69.54 E
Lengerich, B.R.D.	52	52.11 N	7.50 E
Lengerich, B.R.D.	52	52.33 N	7.32 E
Lenggor ≃	114	2.25 N	103.37 E
Lenggries	58	47.41 N	11.34 E
Lenghu	90	38.30 N	93.15 E
Lenglingen	115a	7.32 S	112.04 E
Lengoué ≃	26	64.14 N	13.45 E
Lengnau	58	47.11 N	7.22 E
Lengoué	152	0.49 N	15.43 E
Lengerskeid	263	51.08 N	7.40 E
Lengua National Park ♦	154	16.15 S	34.45 E
Lengzipu	104	41.42 N	122.47 E
Lenham	42	51.14 N	0.43 E
Lenhartsville	208	40.34 N	75.53 W
Lenhovda	26	57.00 N	15.17 E
Lenina, gora ▲²	265b	56.49 N	37.31 E
Lenina, ozero ☒	78	48.33 N	35.12 E
Lenina, pik ▲	85	39.20 N	72.55 E
Leninabad	85	40.17 N	69.37 E
Leninakan	84	40.48 N	43.50 E
Lenin Central Stadium ♦	265b	55.43 N	37.33 E
Leninsk	84	42.07 N	44.29 E
Leningrad, S.S.S.R.	76	59.55 N	30.15 E
Leningrad, S.S.S.R.	265a	59.55 N	30.15 E
Leningrad, Gorod □⁷	265a	59.55 N	30.15 E
Leningrad Airport ⯑	265a	59.48 N	30.16 E
Leningrado → Leningrad	76	59.55 N	30.15 E
Leningradskaja	84	46.19 N	39.24 E
Leningradskij □³	85	69.30 S	159.23 E
Leningradskoje	85	38.06 N	70.01 E
Leningrad State University ·²	265a	59.56 N	30.18 E
Leningrad Station → ✦⁵	265b	55.47 N	37.39 E
Lenino	265b	55.18 N	35.47 E
Leninogorsk, S.S.S.R.	85	50.27 N	83.32 E
Leninogorsk, S.S.S.R.	86	54.36 N	52.30 E
Leninpol'	85	42.29 N	71.55 E
Leninsk, S.S.S.R.	80	48.42 N	45.11 E
Leninsk, S.S.S.R.	85	40.38 N	72.15 E
Leninsk, S.S.S.R.	84	54.55 N	59.54 E
Leninsk ≃	85	46.05 N	63.20 E
Leninskaja Sloboda	80	56.05 N	44.28 E
Leninskij, S.S.S.R.	85	46.31 N	44.28 E
Leninskij, S.S.S.R.	80	56.34 N	45.56 E
Leninskij, S.S.S.R.	80	54.00 N	37.31 E
Leninsk-Kuzneckij	85	54.38 N	86.10 E
Leninskoje, S.S.S.R.	80	58.20 N	47.04 E
Leninskoje, S.S.S.R.	89	48.19 N	133.03 E
Lenin-Stausee → Kujbyševskoje vodochranilišče ☒¹	80	54.30 N	48.30 E
Leninžol	85	40.40 N	71.27 E
Lenk	58	46.28 N	7.27 E
Lenkerville	280	40.30 N	76.58 W
Len'ki	85	52.57 N	80.26 E
Lenkoran'	84	38.45 N	48.50 E
Lennard, Mount ▲²	168a	33.21 S	151.53 E
Lenne ≃	56	51.25 N	7.30 E
Lennebergwiese ♦	56	51.15 N	8.00 E
Lenningen	58	51.11 N	7.16 E
Lennox, S.D., U.S.	198	43.21 N	96.53 W
Lennox, S.D., U.S.	198	40.52 N	94.33 W
Lennox ◆⁸	228	33.56 N	118.21 W
Lennox, Isla I	254	55.18 S	66.50 W
Lennox and Addington □⁶	212	44.30 N	77.00 W
Lennoxtown	44	55.59 N	4.12 W
Lennoxville	206	45.22 N	71.51 W
Leno	64	45.22 N	10.13 E
Lenoir	192	35.54 N	81.32 W
Lenoir City	192	35.47 N	84.15 W
Le Noirmont	58	47.14 N	6.58 E
Lenola	64	41.24 N	13.28 E
Lenora	198	39.37 N	100.00 W
Lenore Lake ☒	184	52.30 N	104.59 W
Le Nouvion-en-Thiérache	50	50.01 N	3.47 E
Lenox, Ga., U.S.	192	31.16 N	83.27 W
Lenox, Ia., U.S.	198	40.53 N	94.33 W
Lenox, Ma., U.S.	207	42.22 N	73.17 W
Lenox, Tn., U.S.	194	36.05 N	89.29 W
Lenox Dale	207	42.21 N	73.15 W
Leno ≃	64	45.53 N	11.00 E
Lens, Fr.	50	50.26 N	2.50 E
Lens, Schw.	62	46.17 N	7.27 E
Lensahn	54	54.13 N	10.53 E
Lenskoje	84	47.02 N	41.21 E
Lenti	61	46.37 N	16.33 E
Lentini	68	37.17 N	15.00 E
Lenting	58	48.49 N	11.28 E
Lentoira	150	10.36 N	5.05 W
Lentvaris	76	54.39 N	25.03 E
Lenzburg	58	47.23 N	8.11 E
Lenzen	273d	26.17 S	27.49 E
Lenzen	54	53.06 N	11.27 E
Lenzerheide (Lai)	58	46.44 N	9.33 E
Lenzinghausen	52	52.07 N	8.27 E
Lenzkirch	58	47.52 N	8.12 E
Léo, Burkina	150	11.06 N	2.06 W
Léo ≃	152	0.28 N	14.30 E
Leoben	61	47.23 N	15.06 E

ESPAÑOL Nombre	Página	Lat.°′	Long.°′ W=Oeste
Leobschütz → Głubczyce	30	50.13 N	17.49 E
Leo Carrillo State Beach ◆	228	34.03 N	118.56 W
Léogane ◆	238	18.31 N	72.38 W
Leogang	64	47.26 N	12.45 E
Leola, Ar., U.S.	194	34.10 N	92.35 W
Leola, Pa., U.S.	208	40.05 N	76.11 W
Leola, S.D., U.S.	198	45.43 N	98.56 W
Leominster, Eng., U.K.	42	52.14 N	2.45 W
Leominster, Ma., U.S.	207	42.31 N	71.45 W
Léon, Esp.	34	42.36 N	5.34 W
Léon, Fr.	32	43.53 N	1.18 W
Leon, Nic.	236	12.26 N	86.53 W
Leon, Pil.	116	10.47 N	122.23 E
Leon, Ia., U.S.	190	40.44 N	93.44 W
Leon, Ks., U.S.	198	37.41 N	96.46 W
Leon, N.Y., U.S.	210	42.18 N	79.01 W
Leon □⁸	236	12.35 N	86.35 W
Leon □⁶	222	31.18 N	95.55 W
Leon □⁹	34	42.00 N	6.00 W
Leon ≃	196	30.59 N	97.24 W
Leon, Montes de ↗	282	37.28 N	122.25 E
Leona	34	42.30 N	6.18 W
Leona	222	31.09 N	95.58 W
Leona ≃	196	28.45 N	99.11 W
Leona, Punta ▶	236	9.41 N	84.41 W
Leonard, Mi., U.S.	214	42.51 N	83.08 W
Leonard, Mo., U.S.	219	39.53 N	92.10 W
Leonard, N.D., U.S.	198	46.39 N	97.14 W
Leonard, Tx., U.S.	196	33.22 N	96.14 W
Leonard ≃	276	40.25 N	74.03 W
Leonardo da Vinci, Aeroporto Intercontinentale ⊠	66	41.48 N	12.13 E
Leonardsburg	214	40.21 N	82.59 W
Leonardsville	210	42.48 N	75.15 W
Leonardtown	208	38.17 N	76.38 W
Leonardville, Namibia	156	23.29 S	18.49 E
Leonardville, Ks., U.S.	198	39.21 N	96.51 W
Leona Vicario	200	32.10 N	115.10 W
Leonberg	56	48.48 N	9.01 E
Leonbronn	56	49.03 N	8.53 E
Leondale	273d	26.18 S	28.12 E
Leondárion	267c	37.59 N	23.51 E
León [de los Aldamas]	234	21.07 N	101.40 W
Leonding	61	48.16 N	14.15 E
Leone, Golfo del → Lion, Golfe du c	174u	14.20 S	170.47 W
Leone, Monte ▲	32	43.00 N	4.00 E
Leones	46	46.15 N	8.06 E
Leonessa	252	32.39 S	62.18 W
Leonforte	66	42.34 N	12.58 E
Leongatha	70	37.38 N	14.23 E
León Guzmán	169	38.29 S	145.57 E
Leonia	196	25.31 N	103.34 W
Leonicha	276	40.51 N	73.59 W
Leonidas	76	59.37 N	38.51 E
Leonidhion	216	42.01 N	85.21 W
Leonidovo	38	37.10 N	22.52 E
Leon Junction	89	49.17 N	142.50 E
Leonova	222	31.20 N	97.36 W
Leonovo	162	28.53 S	121.20 E
Leontjevka	82	55.26 N	38.42 E
Leontjevo	85	57.13 S	65.32 W
Leontville	85	43.03 N	69.50 E
Leopard	56	58.58 N	36.37 E
Leopold	285	40.01 N	75.27 W
Leopold and Astrid Coast ±²	169	38.11 S	144.28 E
Leopoldau ◆⁴	9	67.10 S	84.10 E
Leopold Downs	264b	48.16 N	16.27 E
Leopold II, Lac → Mai-Ndombe, Lac ⊜	162	17.52 S	125.25 E
Leopoldina	152	2.00 S	18.20 E
Leopoldkanaal ≊	256	21.32 S	42.38 W
Leopoldo de Bulhões	50	51.14 N	3.46 E
Leopoldo y Astrid, Costa → Leopold and Astrid Coast ±²	255	15.37 S	48.46 W
Leopoldsburg	9	67.10 S	84.10 E
Leopoldsdorf	56	51.07 N	5.15 E
Leopoldshagen	264b	43.06 N	16.24 E
Leopoldstadt ◆⁸	54	53.46 N	13.53 E
Léopoldville → Kinshasa	264b	48.13 N	16.23 E
Leoti	152	4.18 S	15.18 N
Leoville	198	38.28 N	101.21 W
Leovo	184	53.37 N	107.35 W
Le Pailly	78	46.29 N	28.15 E
Le Palais	58	47.48 N	5.25 E
Lepanto, C.R.	32	47.21 N	3.09 W
Lepanto → Návpaktos, Ellás	236	9.57 N	85.02 W
Lepanto, Ar., U.S.	38	38.23 N	21.50 E
Lepar, Pulau I	194	35.36 N	90.19 W
Le Parcq	112	2.57 S	106.50 E
Le Pâté	58	50.23 N	2.06 E
Lepe	261	48.32 N	2.18 E
Le Péage-de-Roussillon	34	37.15 N	7.12 W
Le Pecq	62	45.24 N	4.48 E
Lepel'	261	48.54 N	2.07 E
Le Pellerin	76	54.53 N	28.42 E
Lepenou	32	47.12 N	1.45 W
Lepanbusu, Keli ↗	115b	8.40 S	121.49 E
Le Perray-en-Yvelines	261		1.51 E
Le Perreux-sur-Marne	261	48.51 N	2.30 E
Lepeški	82	56.05 N	38.07 E
Le Petit-Clamart ◆⁴	261	48.47 N	2.16 E
Le Petit-Couronne	58	49.23 N	1.01 E
Le Petit-Quevilly	58	49.26 N	1.02 E
Lephepe	156	23.20 S	25.50 E
Lépi	152	12.52 S	15.26 E
Le Piastre	58	44.00 N	10.50 E
Lephuhé	254	41.37 S	73.36 W
Le Pin	261	48.55 N	2.38 E
Le Pin-au-Haras	50	48.44 N	0.09 E
L'Épine, Fr.	58	48.54 N	4.28 E
L'Épine, Fr.	261	48.32 N	2.21 E
Leping	100	28.57 N	117.05 E
Lépini, Monti ↗	58	41.33 N	13.00 E
Lépin-le-Lac	62	45.32 N	5.47 E
L'Épiphanie	206	45.51 N	73.30 W
Lepl'avo	78	49.48 N	31.32 E
Le Plessis-aux-Bois	261	49.00 N	2.46 E
Le Plessis-Belleville	58	49.06 N	2.46 E
Le Plessis-Pâté	261	48.37 N	2.20 E
Le Plessis-Trévise	261	48.49 N	2.34 E
Lépo, Lagoa de ⊜	152	17.08 S	19.00 E
Le Poët	58	44.17 N	5.53 E
Le Pont-de-Beauvoisin	58	46.40 N	6.20 E
Le Pont-de-Montvert	62	45.32 N	5.40 E
Le Pontet	62	44.22 N	3.45 E
Lepontine, Alpi ↗	58	48.49 N	1.53 E
Leporano	58	46.25 N	8.40 E
Le Port	157c	40.23 N	17.20 E
Le Portel	50	20.55 S	55.18 W
Le Port-Marly	58	50.42 N	1.34 E
Le Pouzin	261	48.53 N	2.06 E
Lèppävirta	26	62.29 N	27.47 E
Leppin	76	60.45 N	33.25 E
Leppington	274a	33.58 S	150.49 E
Le Pradet	58	39.04 N	174.13 E
Lepreau, Point ▶	186	45.04 N	66.27 W
Le Prêcheur	240e	14.48 N	61.14 W
Le Pré-Saint-Gervais	261		2.25 E
Le Prese	46	46.16 N	10.05 E
Lepsinsk	86	45.32 N	80.37 E
Lepsy, S.S.S.R.	86	46.18 N	78.20 E
Lepsy, S.S.S.R.	86	46.15 N	78.55 E

FRANÇAIS Nom	Page	Lat.°′	Long.°′ W=Ouest
Le Puy	62	45.02 N	3.53 E
Le Quesnoy	50	50.15 N	3.38 E
Léraba ≊	150	9.42 N	4.35 W
Le Raincy	261	48.54 N	2.31 E
Le Rayol-Canadel-sur-Mer	62	43.10 N	6.28 E
La Raysville	210	41.51 N	76.11 W
Lerberget	41	56.11 N	12.33 E
Lercara Friddi	70	37.45 N	13.36 E
Lerche ◆⁸	263	51.37 N	7.43 E
Lerderderg ≊	169	37.42 S	144.30 E
Lerdo → Ciudad Lerdo	196	25.32 N	103.32 W
Lerdo de Tejada	234	18.37 N	95.31 W
Léré, Fr.	50	47.28 N	2.52 E
Léré, Mali	150	15.43 N	4.55 W
Lere, Nig.	150	9.43 N	9.21 E
Léré, Tchad	146	9.39 N	14.13 E
Lereh	164	3.08 S	139.54 E
Lerek ▲	114	3.47 N	102.47 E
Le Reposoir	58	46.00 N	6.33 E
Leri ≊	42	52.32 N	4.02 W
Leribe	158	28.58 S	28.00 E
Lerici	64	44.04 N	9.55 E
Lérida	246	0.10 N	70.42 W
Lérida → Lleida	34	41.37 N	0.37 E
Lerik	84	38.46 N	48.25 E
Lérins, Îles de II	62	43.31 N	7.03 E
Lerma	34	42.02 N	3.45 W
Lerma ≊	234	20.13 N	102.46 W
Lermontova	89	47.10 N	134.20 E
Lermocs	58	47.24 N	10.53 E
Lerno, Monte ▲	71	40.37 N	9.10 E
Le Robert	240e	14.41 N	60.57 W
Léros I, Ellás	38	37.08 N	26.52 E
Léros I, Ellás	267c	37.59 N	23.34 E
Lérouville	56	48.47 N	5.33 E
Leroux Wash V	200	34.54 N	110.12 W
Le Roy, Il., U.S.	216	40.21 N	88.45 W
Leroy, In., U.S.	216	41.22 N	87.16 W
Le Roy, Ks., U.S.	198	38.05 N	95.38 W
Le Roy, Mn., U.S.	190	43.30 N	92.30 W
Le Roy, N.Y., U.S.	210	42.58 N	77.59 W
Le Roy, Pa., U.S.	210	41.41 N	76.43 W
Leroy, Tx., U.S.	222	31.44 N	97.01 W
Lerum	26	57.46 N	12.16 E
Le Russey	58	47.10 N	6.44 E
Léry	206	45.21 N	73.48 W
Lesa	62	45.50 N	8.34 E
Les Abrets	62	45.32 N	5.35 E
Les Abymes	240i	16.16 N	61.31 W
Lesage, Lac ⊜	206	46.19 N	75.03 W
Le Saint-Esprit	240e	14.34 N	60.57 W
Les Aix-d'Angillon	50	47.12 N	2.34 E
Les Allues	62	45.26 N	6.33 E
Les Alluets-le-Roi	261	48.55 N	1.55 E
Les Andelys	58	49.15 N	1.25 E
Les Anses-d'Arlets	240e	14.29 N	61.05 W
Le Sappey-en-Chartreuse	62	45.16 N	5.47 E
Les Arcs	62	43.27 N	6.29 E
Lesatima, Oldoinyo ▲	154	0.19 S	36.37 E
Le Sauze	62	44.22 N	6.41 E
Les Baux-en-Provence	62	43.45 N	4.48 E
Les Bézards	50	47.48 N	2.44 E
Les Bordes	261	48.39 N	1.58 E
Les Borges Blanques	34	41.31 N	0.52 E
Lesbos → Lésvos I	38	39.10 N	26.20 E
Les Bouchoux	62	46.18 N	5.49 E
Les Bréviaires	261	48.42 N	1.49 E
Lesbury	44	55.24 N	1.36 W
L'Escarène	62	43.50 N	7.21 E
Les Cayes	238	18.12 N	73.45 W
Les Chaises	58	44.39 N	4.08 E
Les Chapieux	62	45.42 N	6.44 E
Leschenault, Cape ▶	162	31.18 S	115.27 E
Leschenault Estuary c¹	168a	33.15 S	115.42 E
Leščinovka	78	49.16 N	34.14 E
Les Clayes-sous-Bois	261	48.49 N	1.59 E
Les Contamines-Montjoie	62	45.50 N	6.44 E
Les Diablerets	58	46.21 N	7.10 E
Les Diablerets ▲	58	46.19 N	7.12 E
Lesdidorben	146	8.28 N	29.35 E
Les Echarmeaux	58	46.10 N	4.27 E
Les Échelles	58	45.26 N	5.45 E
Les Écureuils	206	46.39 N	71.43 W
Le Semnoz ▲	62	45.48 N	6.07 E
Les Essarts	58	46.29 N	35.10 E
Les Essarts-le-Roi	261	48.43 N	1.54 E
Les Étangs	56	49.09 N	6.23 E
Les Fonts	266d	41.32 N	2.02 E
Les Fourgs	58	46.50 N	6.25 E
Les Gaillards d'Anjou ◆⁹	275a	45.35 N	73.34 W
Les Gâtines	261	48.48 N	1.58 E
Les Gets	58	46.09 N	6.40 E
Les Granges-le-Roi	261	48.30 N	2.01 E
Les Grésillons	261	48.56 N	2.01 E
Les Halles	62	45.43 N	4.26 E
Leshan	107	29.34 N	103.45 E
Les Haudères	58	46.05 N	7.31 E
Les Hautes-Rivières	56	49.53 N	4.50 E
Les Herbiers	62	46.52 N	1.01 W
Les Houches	62	45.53 N	6.48 E
Lesignano de'Bagni	64	44.39 N	10.18 E
Lésigny	261	48.45 N	2.37 E
Lesima, Monte ▲	62	44.41 N	9.15 E
Lesina	82	56.05 N	38.07 E
Lesina, Lago di ⊜	68	41.53 N	15.21 E
Les Islettes	56	49.06 N	5.00 E
Lesjaskog	26	62.15 N	8.22 E
Lesjöfors	40	59.59 N	14.11 E
Lesken	84	43.16 N	43.48 E
Les'ki	78	49.29 N	32.13 E
Lesko	30	49.28 N	22.21 E
Leskovac	38	42.59 N	21.57 E
Leskov Island I	18	56.40 S	28.10 W
Les Laumes	58	47.32 N	4.27 E
Les Lecques	62	43.11 N	5.40 E
Leslie, S. Afr.	158	26.23 S	28.55 E
Leslie, Scot., U.K.	44	56.12 N	3.13 W
Leslie, Ar., U.S.	194	35.49 N	92.33 W
Leslie, Ga., U.S.	192	31.57 N	84.05 W
Leslie, Mi., U.S.	216	42.27 N	84.25 W
Leslie, W.V., U.S.	188	38.02 N	80.43 W
Les Lilas	261	48.53 N	2.25 E
Les Loges	58	48.34 N	0.46 E
Les Loges-en-Josas	261	48.46 N	2.09 E
Lesmahagow	46	55.39 N	3.55 W
Les Marécottes	58	46.07 N	7.00 E
Les Mées	58	44.02 N	5.59 E
Les Mesnuls	261	48.45 N	1.50 E
Lesmo	266b	45.39 N	9.18 E
Les Molières	261	48.40 N	2.04 E
Les Monges ▲	58	44.23 N	6.22 E
Lesmont	58	48.26 N	4.25 E
Les Mosses	58	46.24 N	7.07 E
Lesmurdie Falls National Park ◆	168a	32.01 S	116.04 E
Les Mureaux	261	48.59 N	1.55 E
Lešna	30	51.20 N	15.16 E
Leśna ≊	30	52.59 N	23.46 E
Lesnaja	76	52.59 N	25.46 E
Les Neyrolles	58	46.13 N	5.40 E
Lešnica	38	44.39 N	19.19 E
Lesnoj, S.S.S.R.	24	54.11 N	22.08 E
Lesnoj, S.S.S.R.	56	58.01 N	57.13 E
Lesnoj ◆⁹	265a	60.10 N	30.19 E
Lesnoje → Konobejevo	82	56.07 N	35.22 E
Lesnoje Mat'unino	80	53.27 N	47.26 E
Lesnoj Gorodok	265b	55.39 N	37.13 E

PORTUGUÊS Nome	Página	Lat.°′	Long.°′ W=Oeste
Lesnoj park ◆	265a	59.59 N	30.21 E
Lesny ◆	60	50.02 N	12.37 E
Lesnyje Pol'any, S.S.S.R.	24	58.58 N	52.26 E
Lesnyje Pol'any, S.S.S.R.	265b	55.57 N	37.53 E
Lesogorsk, S.S.S.R.	80	55.06 N	43.56 E
Lesogorsk, S.S.S.R.	88	56.03 N	99.33 E
Lesogorsk, S.S.S.R.	89	49.27 N	142.08 E
Lesogorskij	24	61.02 N	28.53 E
Lesong, Gunong ▲	114	2.44 N	103.17 E
Lesopil'noje	89	46.44 N	134.20 E
Lesosibirsk	88	58.16 N	92.29 E
Lesotho □¹, Afr.	138	29.30 S	28.30 E
Lesotho □¹, Afr.	158	29.30 S	28.30 E
LesovšČina	78	50.47 N	28.35 E
Lesozavodsk	24	66.44 N	32.49 E
Lesparre-Médoc	32	45.18 N	0.56 W
Les Pavillons-sous-Bois	261	48.55 N	2.30 E
Les Pieux	32	49.31 N	1.48 W
Les Planches-en-Montagne	58	46.40 N	6.01 E
Les Ponts-de-Martel	58	46.54 N	6.41 E
Les Posets ▲	34	42.39 N	0.25 E
Les Praz-de-Chamonix	58	45.56 N	6.52 E
Lesquin	50	50.35 N	3.07 E
Les Riceys	58	47.59 N	4.22 E
Les Roches-l'Evêque	50	47.47 N	0.53 E
Les Rousses	58	46.29 N	6.04 E
Les Ruelles	261	48.40 N	1.37 E
Les Sables-d'Olonne	32	46.30 N	1.47 W
Lessach	64	47.11 N	13.49 E
Les Salles-sur-Verdon	62	43.46 N	6.12 E
Lessay	32	49.13 N	1.32 W
Les Scaffarels	62	43.56 N	6.41 E
Lesse ≊	56	50.14 N	4.54 E
Lessebo	26	56.45 N	15.16 E
Lessen → Lessines	50	50.43 N	3.50 E
Lesser Antilles II	238	15.00 N	61.00 W
Lesser Khingan Range → Xiao Hinggan Ling ↗	89	48.45 N	127.00 E
Lesser Slave ≊	182	55.10 N	114.03 W
Lesser Slave Lake ⊜	182	55.25 N	115.30 W
Lesser Sunda Islands → Tenggara, Nusa II	108	9.00 S	120.00 E
Lessines (Lessen)	50	50.43 N	3.50 E
Lessini, Monti ↗	64	45.41 N	11.13 E
L'Estaque	62	43.22 N	5.20 E
Leste ≈	250	6.20 S	57.46 W
Lester, Pa., U.S.	285	39.52 N	75.17 W
Lester, Wa., U.S.	224	47.12 N	121.29 W
Lester B. Pearson International Airport ⊠	212	43.41 N	79.38 W
Les Tessiers	62	44.24 N	4.16 E
Les Thilliers-en-Vexin	58	49.14 N	1.36 E
Lestijärvi	26	63.32 N	24.39 E
Lestijoki ≊	26	64.04 N	23.38 E
Lestock	182	51.18 N	104.00 W
L'Estréchure	62	44.06 N	3.47 E
Le Sueur	190	44.28 N	93.55 W
Le Sueur ≊	190	44.07 N	94.03 W
Lesueur, Mount ▲²	162	30.10 S	115.11 E
Lešukonskoje	24	64.54 N	45.40 E
Les Ulis	261	48.41 N	2.11 E
Lesung, Tanjung ▶	115a	6.28 S	105.40 E
Lesunovo	80	55.40 N	43.04 E
Les Vans	62	44.24 N	4.08 E
Les Varrières	58	46.54 N	6.33 E
Lésvos I	38	39.10 N	26.20 E
Leszno □⁸	30	51.45 N	16.45 E
Letälven ≊	40	59.05 N	14.20 E
L'Étang-La-Ville	261	48.52 N	2.05 E
Le Teil	58	44.33 N	4.41 E
Le Temple	261	49.00 N	1.58 E
Letenye	30	46.26 N	16.43 E
Le Terfre-Saint-Denis	261	48.56 N	1.36 E
Lethbridge, Austl.	234	33.44 S	150.48 E
Lethbridge, Ab., Can.	182	49.42 N	112.50 W
Lethbridge, Nf., Can.	186	48.21 N	53.52 W
Le Theil-sur-Huisne	58	48.16 N	0.42 E
Lethem	246	3.23 N	59.48 W
Le Thillay	261	49.00 N	2.28 E
Le Thillot	58	47.53 N	6.46 E
Le Thor	58	43.56 N	5.00 E
Le Thoronet	62	43.27 N	6.18 E
Leti, Kepulauan II	164	8.13 S	127.50 E
Leti, Pulau I	112	8.12 S	127.41 E
Leticia	246	4.09 S	69.57 W
Leting	98	39.23 N	118.53 E
Letino	114	41.26 N	14.17 E
Letjiesbos	158	32.34 S	22.16 E
Letka ≊	56	59.36 N	49.22 E
Letlhakane	156	21.27 S	25.02 E
Letlhakeng	156	24.08 S	25.02 E
Letmathe	54	51.22 N	7.37 E
Letn'aja Zolotica	24	64.57 N	36.50 E
Letnerečenskij	24	64.17 N	34.23 E
Le Touquet-Paris-Plage	50	50.31 N	1.35 E
Letovo	265b	55.34 N	37.24 E
Letpadan	110	17.47 N	95.45 E
Le Trait	58	49.28 N	0.49 E
Le Trayas	62	43.29 N	6.56 E
Le Tremblay-sur-Mauldre	261	48.47 N	1.53 E
Le Tréport	58	50.04 N	1.22 E
Letsôk-aw Kyun I	110	11.37 N	98.15 E
Letter ≊	52	52.24 N	9.38 E
Letterfrack	48	53.33 N	10.00 W
Letterkenny	48	54.57 N	7.44 W
Lettermullan	48	53.15 N	9.42 W
Letterston	42	51.56 N	5.00 W
Lettonie → Latvijskaja Sovetskaja Socialisticeskaja Respublika □³	8	57.00 N	25.00 E
Letts	218	39.14 N	85.35 W
Letung	112	2.58 N	105.42 E
Letzlingen	54	52.26 N	11.29 E
Leu	38	44.11 N	24.00 E
Léua	152	11.43 S	20.12 E
Leubnitz ◆⁸	60	50.43 N	12.21 E
Leuca	70	39.48 N	18.21 E
Leucadia ◆	228	33.04 N	117.18 W
Leucate, Étang de c	32	42.51 N	3.00 E
Leuchars	46	56.23 N	2.53 W
Leuchtenberg	60	49.36 N	12.15 E
Leuenberger Forst ◆⁴	261		2.20 E
Leuglay	264a	52.40 N	13.53 E
Leuk	58	46.19 N	7.38 E
Leukerbad	58	46.23 N	7.38 E
Leumeah	274a	34.03 S	150.50 E
Leuna	54	51.19 N	12.01 E
Leupoldsgrün	60	50.17 N	11.47 E
Leura	170	23.48 S	150.20 E
Leura, Mount ▲¹	169	38.15 S	143.09 E

	Página	Lat.°′	Long.°′ W=Oeste
Leuser, Gunung ▲	114	3.45 N	97.11 E
Leušinskij Tuman, ozero ⊜	86	59.42 N	65.35 E
Leutenberg	54	50.34 N	11.28 E
Leutersdorf	54	50.57 N	14.40 E
Leutershausen	56	49.18 N	10.24 E
Leutesdorf	56	50.27 N	7.23 E
Leutkirch	58	47.49 N	10.01 E
Leuven (Louvain)	56	50.53 N	4.42 E
Leuville-sur-Orge	261	48.37 N	2.16 E
Leuwiliang	115a	6.34 S	106.37 E
Leuze, Bel.	50	50.36 N	3.36 E
Leuze, Bel.	56	50.34 N	4.54 E
Levack	188	46.38 N	81.23 W
Levádhia	38	38.25 N	22.54 E
Levaja Mama ≊	88	57.10 N	111.54 E
Le Val-d'Ajol	58	47.55 N	6.29 E
Le Val-d'Albian	261	48.45 N	2.11 E
Levallois-Perret	261	48.54 N	2.18 E
Le Val-Saint-Germain	261	48.34 N	2.08 E
Levan	200	39.33 N	111.51 W
Levanga	26	63.45 N	11.18 E
Levanna, Monte ▲	62	45.24 N	7.12 E
Levant, Île du I	62	43.03 N	6.28 E
Levante, Riviera di ★			
Levanto	62	44.10 N	9.38 E
Levanzo	70	37.59 N	12.20 E
Levanzo, Isola di I	70	38.00 N	12.20 E
Levaši	84	42.27 N	47.20 E
Le Vauclin	240e	14.33 N	60.51 W
Levdym	86	60.29 N	66.19 E
Leveaux Mountain ▲¹	190	47.37 N	90.47 W
Lével	61	47.54 N	17.12 E
Level Green	279b	40.24 N	79.43 W
Levelland	196	33.35 N	102.22 W
Levelock	180	59.07 N	156.52 W
Level Park	216	42.22 N	85.18 W
Leven, Eng., U.K.	44	53.53 N	0.19 W
Leven, Scot., U.K.	46	56.12 N	3.00 W
Leven ≊, Eng., U.K.	44	54.31 N	1.21 W
Leven ≊, Eng., U.K.	44	54.14 N	3.01 W
Leven, Loch ⊜, Scot., U.K.	46	56.12 N	3.22 W
Leven, Loch ⊜, Scot., U.K.	46	56.41 N	5.07 W
Leven Point ▶	158	27.55 S	32.35 E
Levens	62	43.52 N	7.13 E
Levenshulme ◆⁸	262	53.27 N	2.10 W
Levent	130	38.27 N	37.52 E
Leventina, Valle V	58	46.25 N	9.52 E
Leveque, Cape ▶	162	16.24 S	122.56 E
Leverano	68	40.17 N	18.00 E
Leverburgh	46	57.45 N	7.00 W
Leverett Glacier ⊽	9	85.30 S	150.00 W
Leveretts Chapel	222	32.19 N	94.55 W
Levering	190	45.38 N	84.47 W
Leverkusen	56	51.03 N	6.59 E
Lever Park ◆	262	53.37 N	2.34 W
Le Vésinet	261	48.54 N	2.08 E
Le Vigan	62	43.59 N	3.35 E
Levino	76	60.29 N	37.30 E
Lévis	206	46.48 N	71.11 W
Lévis □⁶	206	46.40 N	71.15 W
Levisa Fork ≊	192	38.06 N	82.36 W
Levis-Saint Nom	261	48.43 N	1.58 E
Levittsa I	38	37.00 N	26.28 E
Levittown → Willingboro, N.J., U.S.	208	40.03 N	74.53 W
Levittown, N.Y., U.S.	210	40.43 N	73.30 W
Levittown, Pa., U.S.	208	40.09 N	74.49 W
Levittown Discount World ◆⁹	285	40.09 N	74.49 W
Lévka Óri ▲	38	35.18 N	24.01 E
Levkás	38	38.50 N	20.43 E
Levka, Ostrovul I	38	45.20 N	29.20 E
Levkimmi	38	39.25 N	20.04 E
Levokumskoje	84	44.48 N	44.39 E
Levroux	32	46.59 N	1.37 E
Levski	38	43.22 N	25.08 E
Lev Tolstoj	80	53.13 N	39.27 E
Levúo ≊	76	56.04 N	24.23 E
Levuka	175p	17.41 S	178.50 E
Levy Tuzlov ≊	83	47.35 N	39.23 E
Lewa	110	27.30 N	96.07 E
Lewapaku	115b	9.43 S	119.55 E
Lewbeach	210	41.58 N	74.51 W
Lewe	110	19.38 N	96.07 E
Lewedorp	52	51.30 N	3.45 E
Lewellen	198	41.19 N	102.08 W
Lewes, Eng., U.K.	42	50.52 N	0.01 E
Lewes, De., U.S.	208	38.46 N	75.08 W
Lewin Brzeski	30	50.46 N	17.37 E
Lewis, Ia., U.S.	190	41.18 N	95.04 W
Lewis, Ks., U.S.	198	37.56 N	99.15 W
Lewis, I, Scot., U.K.	46	58.10 N	6.40 W
Lewis ≊, N.Y., U.S.	210	43.47 N	75.29 W
Lewis ≊, Wa., U.S.	224	46.05 N	122.48 W
Lewis, Butt of ▶	46	58.31 N	6.16 W
Lewis, East Fork ≊	224	45.52 N	122.43 W
Lewis, Isle of → Lewis I	46	58.10 N	6.40 W
Lewis, Mount ▲¹	204	40.24 N	116.51 W
Lewis and Clark ≊	224	46.10 N	123.52 W
Lewis and Clark Cavern State Park ◆	202	45.49 N	111.13 W
Lewis and Clark Lake ⊜¹	198	42.50 N	97.45 W
Lewis and Clark Range ↗	202	47.30 N	113.00 W
Lewisberry	208	40.08 N	76.52 W
Lewisburg, Ky., U.S.	192	36.59 N	86.57 W
Lewisburg, Oh., U.S.	218	39.51 N	84.32 W
Lewisburg, Pa., U.S.	208	40.57 N	76.53 W
Lewisburg, Tn., U.S.	194	35.26 N	86.47 W
Lewisburg, W.V., U.S.	188	37.48 N	80.26 W
Lewis Center	214	40.12 N	83.01 W
Lewis Creek ≊, Ca., U.S.	226	35.17 N	120.58 W
Lewis Creek ≊, In., U.S.	218	39.54 N	85.51 W
Lewis Creek Reservoir ⊜¹	222	30.56 N	89.15 W
Lewisham ◆⁸	273d	27.49 S		
Lewisham Location	273d		
Lewis-Lockport Airport ⊠	216	41.36 N	88.05 W
Lewis Pass ⅄	172	42.23 S	172.24 E
Lewisporte	186	49.15 N	55.03 W
Lewis Range ↗, Mt., Austl.	162	20.20 S	128.40 E
Lewis Range ↗, Mt., U.S.	202	48.35 N	113.40 W
Lewis Run	214	41.52 N	78.39 W
Lewis Smith Lake ⊜¹	194	34.05 N	87.07 W
Lewiston, Me., U.S.	188	44.06 N	70.12 W
Lewiston, Mi., U.S.	190	44.53 N	84.18 W

	Página	Lat.°′	Long.°′ W=Oeste
Lewiston, Mn., U.S.	190	43.59 N	91.52 W
Lewiston, N.Y., U.S.	210	43.10 N	79.02 W
Lewiston, Ut., U.S.	200	41.58 N	111.51 W
Lewiston Orchards	202	46.23 N	116.59 W
Lewistown, Il., U.S.	194	40.23 N	90.09 W
Lewistown, Md., U.S.	208	39.32 N	77.24 W
Lewistown, Mt., U.S.	202	47.04 N	109.25 W
Lewistown, Oh., U.S.	216	40.25 N	83.53 W
Lewistown, Pa., U.S.	208	40.35 N	77.34 W
Lewisville, N.B., Can.	186	46.06 N	64.46 W
Lewisville, Ar., U.S.	194	33.21 N	93.34 W
Lewisville, In., U.S.	218	39.48 N	85.21 W
Lewisville, Pa., U.S.	208	39.43 N	75.53 W
Lewisville Dam ◆⁶	222	33.02 N	96.59 W
Lewisville Lake ⊜¹	196	33.08 N	97.00 W
Lewoleba	112	8.23 S	123.24 E
Lewotobi-lakilaki, Ili ▲	115b	8.32 S	122.46 E
Lexa	194	34.35 N	90.44 W
Lexington, Ga., U.S.	192	33.52 N	83.06 W
Lexington, Il., U.S.	216	40.38 N	88.47 W
Lexington, In., U.S.	218	38.39 N	85.37 W
Lexington, Ky., U.S.	218	38.02 N	84.30 W
Lexington, Ma., U.S.	207	42.26 N	71.13 W
Lexington, Mi., U.S.	190	43.16 N	82.31 W
Lexington, Mo., U.S.	194	39.11 N	93.52 W
Lexington, Ne., U.S.	198	40.46 N	99.44 W
Lexington, N.Y., U.S.	210	42.15 N	74.22 W
Lexington, N.C., U.S.	192	35.49 N	80.15 W
Lexington, Ok., U.S.	196	35.00 N	97.20 W
Lexington, Or., U.S.	202	45.26 N	119.41 W
Lexington, S.C., U.S.	192	33.58 N	81.14 W
Lexington, Tn., U.S.	194	35.39 N	88.23 W
Lexington, Tx., U.S.	222	30.25 N	97.01 W
Lexington, Va., U.S.	192	37.47 N	79.26 W
Lexington Park	208	38.16 N	76.27 W
Lexington Reservoir ⊜¹	226	37.12 N	121.59 W
Lexton	169	37.15 S	143.31 E
Leybourne	260	51.18 N	0.25 E
Leyburn	44	54.19 N	1.49 W
Leyden → Leiden	52	52.09 N	4.30 E
Leyland	44	24.48 N	106.34 E
Leymebamba	32	43.42 N	2.42 W
Léyou ≊	152	1.07 S	13.08 E
Leysdown-on-Sea	42	51.24 N	0.55 E
Leysin	58	46.21 N	7.01 E
Leyte I	116	11.23 N	124.49 E
Leyte □⁴	116	10.50 N	124.55 E
Leyte I	116	10.50 N	124.50 E
Leyte Gulf c	116	10.50 N	125.25 E
Leyu	106	31.55 N	120.43 E
Lèz ≊	62	44.13 N	4.43 E
Leža ≊	56	56.46 N	40.53 E
Leža ≊	76	58.54 N	40.45 E
Lezajsk	30	50.16 N	22.24 E
Lezama	246	9.43 N	66.24 W
Lézard, Pointe à ▶	240i	16.08 N	61.47 W
Lézat	240e	14.30 N	5.56 E
Lèze ≊	32	43.30 N	1.22 E
Lezhě	62	41.47 N	19.39 E
Lezhi	107	30.17 N	105.02 E
Lezna	76	55.20 N	30.13 E
Leẑno	56	48.54 N	37.18 E
Lézn'ovo	56	56.46 N	40.53 E
L'gov	78	51.43 N	35.17 E
Lhasa	120	29.40 N	91.09 E
Lhasa ≊	120	29.21 N	90.45 E
Lhaviyani □⁵			
L'Hautil ▲	261	49.00 N	2.01 E
Lhazê	120	29.10 N	87.42 E
L'Hermite, Isla I	254	55.52 S	67.20 W
L'Hilli	34	35.41 N	0.18 W
Lhokkruet	114	4.52 N	95.24 E
Lhokgna	114	5.29 N	95.15 E
Lhokseumawe	114	5.10 N	97.08 E
Lhoksukon	114	5.03 N	97.19 E
L'Hôpital-sous-Rochefort	62	45.54 N	3.56 E
Lhorong	120	30.45 N	96.09 E
L'Hospitalet de Llobregat	34	41.22 N	2.08 E
Lhotse ▲	120	27.57 N	86.56 E
Lhuis	62	45.45 N	5.32 E
Lhuntsi Dzong	120	27.39 N	91.09 E
Lhünzê	120	28.25 N	92.31 E
Li	110	17.48 N	98.57 E
Li ≊ → Thai	110	18.14 N	98.51 E
Li ≊, Zhg.	100	33.11 N	115.07 E
Li ≊, Zhg.	102	24.59 N	112.01 E
Lian ≊, Phil.	116	14.03 N	120.38 E
Lian ≊, Zhg.	102	23.45 N	112.39 E
Liancourt	50	49.20 N	2.28 E
Liane ≊	50	50.43 N	1.36 E
Liang	164	3.30 S	128.19 E
Liangbingtai	100	36.37 N	116.52 E
Liangbingbao	98	34.37 N	105.33 E
Liangcun	98	34.15 N	106.33 E
Liangdang	104	33.57 N	106.18 E
Liangfengwu	102	24.51 N	110.42 E
Lianghu, Zhg.	89	45.09 N	128.45 E
Lianghu, Zhg.	102	24.51 N	110.29 E
Liangheguan	102	32.32 N	109.19 E
Lianghekou, Zhg.	107	28.55 N	106.03 E
Lianghekou, Zhg.	107	30.10 N	108.40 E
Liangjia	98	39.10 N	121.54 E
Liangjiadian	98	39.44 N	122.03 E
Liangjiang	102	23.23 N	108.22 E
Liangjiawazi	98	42.42 N	123.18 E
Liangping	107	30.40 N	107.48 E
Liangshan	100	35.42 N	116.05 E
Liang Shan ▲	107	31.12 N	107.05 E
Liangshui ≊	271a	39.49 N	116.40 E
Liangwu ≊	98	43.33 N	124.40 E
Liangxiang	98	39.43 N	116.08 E
Liangxiangzhen	271a	39.44 N	116.08 E
Liangzhuang	100	34.21 N	117.40 E
Lianhua	102	27.08 N	113.57 E
Lianhua Shan ↗	102	23.05 N	115.31 E
Lianjiang, Zhg.	102	26.12 N	119.31 E

	Página	Lat.°′	Long.°′ W=Oeste
Lianjiang, Zhg.	102	21.38 N	110.15 E
Lianjiechang	107	29.41 N	104.30 E
Liannan (Sanjiang)	102	24.38 N	112.10 E
Lianozovo ◆⁸	265b	55.54 N	37.35 E
Lianping	102	24.22 N	114.31 E
Lianpu	100	26.02 N	118.38 E
Lianshanguan	104	40.58 N	123.46 E
Lianshi	106	30.42 N	120.26 E
Lianshui	100	33.47 N	119.16 E
Liansiji	98	33.58 N	114.24 E
Liantang	106	31.37 N	120.38 E
Lianxian	102	24.48 N	112.25 E
Lianyin	89	53.28 N	123.51 E
Lianyuan (Lantian)	102	27.42 N	111.19 E
Lianyungang (Xinpu), Zhg.	98	34.39 N	119.16 E
Lianyungang, Zhg.	98	34.44 N	119.30 E
Lianyun Shan ↗	100	28.32 N	113.50 E
Lianzhou → Hepu	102	21.39 N	109.11 E
Liao ≈	90	40.50 N	121.48 E
Liaobinta	104	42.08 N	123.04 E
Liaocheng	98	36.30 N	115.59 E
Liaodong Bandao (Liaotung Peninsula) ▶¹	98	40.00 N	122.20 E
Liaodong Wan (Gulf of Liaotung) c	98	40.30 N	121.30 E
Liaohe Kou c¹	104	40.42 N	122.05 E
Liaojiangshi	100	26.05 N	113.17 E
Liaoning □⁴	90	41.00 N	123.00 E
Liaotung, Gulf of → Liaodong Wan c	98	40.30 N	121.30 E
Liaotung Peninsula → Liaodong Bandao ▶¹	98	40.00 N	122.20 E
Liaoyang	104	41.17 N	123.11 E
Liaoyangwopu	89	43.00 N	123.28 E
Liaoyuan	89	42.54 N	125.07 E
Liaozhong	104	41.31 N	122.44 E
Liapádhes	38	39.40 N	19.44 E
Liäqatpur	123	28.56 N	70.57 E
Liard ≊	176	61.52 N	121.18 W
Liäri	120	25.41 N	66.29 E
Liat, Pulau I	112	2.53 S	107.05 E
Liathach ▲	46	57.35 S	5.29 W
Lib I	183	8.19 N	167.25 E
Libagon	116	10.18 N	125.03 E
Liban → Lebanon □¹	128	34.00 N	36.00 E
Libanga	152	0.19 N	18.41 E
Libano	246	4.55 N	75.04 W
Libano → Lebanon □¹	128	34.00 N	36.00 E
Libanon → Lebanon □¹	128	34.00 N	36.00 E
Libau → Liepāja	76	56.31 N	21.01 E
Libby	202	48.23 N	115.33 W
Libby Dam ◆⁶	202	48.24 N	115.20 W
Libčeves	54	50.26 N	13.50 E
Libčice nad Vltavou	54	50.10 N	14.20 E
Libenge	152	3.39 N	18.38 E
Liberal, Ks., U.S.	198	37.02 N	100.55 W
Liberal, Mo., U.S.	194	37.33 N	94.31 W
Liberdade	256	22.01 S	44.19 W
Liberdade ◆⁸	287b	23.35 S	46.37 W
Liberdade, Riozinho da ≊	250	9.40 S	52.17 W
Liberec	30	50.46 N	15.03 E
Liberia	236	10.38 N	85.27 W
Liberia □¹, Afr.	134	6.30 N	9.30 W
Liberia □¹, Afr.	150	6.30 N	9.30 W
Libertad, Arg.	240c	17.02 N	61.47 W
Libertad, Ur.	256	34.42 S	58.41 W
Libertad, Ven.	246	8.20 N	69.37 W
Libertad, Ven.	286c	10.27 N	66.57 W
Libertador General Bernardo O'Higgins □⁴	252	34.30 S	71.00 W
Libertador General San Martín	252	23.48 S	64.48 W
Liberty, Il., U.S.	219	39.53 N	91.06 W
Liberty, In., U.S.	216	39.38 N	84.56 W
Liberty, Ky., U.S.	194	37.19 N	84.56 W
Liberty, Mo., U.S.	194	39.14 N	94.25 W
Liberty, Ms., U.S.	194	31.09 N	90.48 W
Liberty, N.Y., U.S.	210	41.47 N	74.45 W
Liberty, N.C., U.S.	192	35.51 N	79.34 W
Liberty, Pa., U.S.	208	41.33 N	77.06 W
Liberty, S.C., U.S.	192	34.47 N	82.41 W
Liberty, Tx., U.S.	196	30.03 N	94.47 W
Liberty Bell Race Track ◆	285	40.05 N	74.58 W
Liberty Center, In., U.S.	216	40.41 N	85.16 W
Liberty Center, Oh., U.S.	216	41.26 N	84.00 W
Liberty City	222	32.26 N	94.57 W
Liberty Corner	276	40.39 N	74.34 W
Liberty Ditch ≊	226	36.31 N	120.02 W
Liberty Farms	226	38.19 N	121.42 W
Liberty Hill	222	30.40 N	97.55 W
Liberty Lake ⊜¹	208	39.25 N	76.53 W
Liberty Manor	278b	39.21 N	76.47 W
Liberty Mills	216	41.04 N	85.42 W
Liberty Square ◆	282	41.26 N	87.22 W
Libertytown	208	39.29 N	77.14 W
Liberty Tree Mall ◆⁸	277b	42.33 N	70.57 W
Liberty Tunnel ◆⁵	279b	40.01 N	80.01 W
Libertyville	216	42.16 N	87.57 W
Libeznice	54	50.11 N	14.30 E
Libia → Libya □¹	146	27.00 N	17.00 E
Libibi	152	4.31 S	17.44 E
Libishan	106	30.45 N	119.39 E
Libiyah → Libya □¹	146	27.00 N	17.00 E
Libiyah, As-Sahrā' al- (Libyan Desert) ◆²	136	24.00 N	25.00 E
Liblín	54	49.55 N	13.32 E
Libni, Jabal ▲	130	30.44 N	33.37 E
Libobo, Tanjung ▶	164	0.54 S	128.28 E
Libochovice	54	50.24 N	14.03 E
Libode	158	31.33 S	29.02 E
Liboi	154	0.23 N	40.57 E
Libona	116	8.21 N	124.44 E
Libourne	32	44.55 N	0.14 W
Libramont	56	49.55 N	5.23 E
Libreville	152	0.23 N	9.27 E
Librazhd	38	41.11 N	20.19 E
Libro Point ▶	116	11.26 N	119.21 E
Libu	98	37.27 N	113.06 E
Libuican Island I	116	7.58 N	122.55 E
Libula	152	7.23 S	26.37 E
Liburna	64	45.30 N	14.18 E
Libuo	107	25.25 N	107.53 E
Liburnia ◆⁹	64	45.13 N	14.18 E
Libya □¹, Afr.	136	27.00 N	17.00 E
Libya □¹, Afr.	146	27.00 N	17.00 E
Libya (Libyā) □¹, Afr.	146	27.00 N	17.00 E
Libyan Desert → Lībiyah, As-Sahrā' al- ◆²	136	24.00 N	25.00 E

Name	Page	Lat.°′	Long.°′
Libyan Plateau → Aḍ-Ḍiffah ⋏[1]	140	30.30 N	25.30 E
Libye → Libya □[1]	146	27.00 N	17.00 E
Libyen → Libya □[1]	146	27.00 N	17.00 E
Libysche Wüste → Lībīyah, Aṣ-Ṣaḥrā' al- ◆[2]	136	24.00 N	25.00 E
Licantén	252	34.59 S	72.00 W
Licata	70	37.06 N	13.56 E
Licciana Nardi	64	44.16 N	10.02 E
Lice	130	38.28 N	40.39 E
Lich	56	50.33 N	8.50 E
Lichačova, mys >	89	42.44 N	132.51 E
Lichaja ≃	83	48.08 N	40.15 E
Lichang	107	28.53 N	104.26 E
Licheng	102	36.30 N	113.21 E
Lichères-Près-Aigremont	50	47.43 N	3.51 E
Lichfield	42	52.42 N	1.48 W
Lichinga	154	13.18 S	35.14 E
Lichitiseni	38	46.23 N	27.17 E
Lichoborka ≃	265b	55.50 N	37.38 E
Lichoslavl'	76	57.07 N	35.28 E
Lichovka	78	48.41 N	33.55 E
Lichovskoj	83	48.07 N	40.12 E
Lichtaart	56	51.14 N	4.54 E
Lichte	54	50.31 N	11.10 E
Lichtenau	56	48.43 N	8.01 E
Lichtenberg, B.R.D.	54	50.23 N	11.40 E
Lichtenberg, Fr.	56	48.55 N	7.29 E
Lichtenberg ◆[8]	264a	52.31 N	13.29 E
Lichtenburg	158	26.08 S	26.08 E
Lichtendorf	263	51.28 N	7.37 E
Lichtenfels	56	50.09 N	11.04 E
Lichtenplatz ◆[8]	263	51.15 N	7.12 E
Lichtenrade ◆[8]	264a	52.23 N	13.25 E
Lichtensee	54	51.23 N	13.22 E
Lichtensteig	58	47.19 N	9.05 E
Lichtenstein	54	50.45 N	12.37 E
Lichtenstein, Schloss ♁	58	48.24 N	9.15 E
Lichtentanne	54	50.42 N	12.25 E
Lichtenvoorde	52	51.59 N	6.34 E
Lichterfelde ◆[8]	264a	52.26 N	13.19 E
Lichtervelde	50	51.02 N	3.09 E
Lichuan, Zhg.	100	27.18 N	116.53 E
Lichuan, Zhg.	102	30.18 N	108.51 E
Lick Creek ≃, Il., U.S.	219	39.42 N	89.41 W
Lick Creek ≃, In., U.S.	218	38.33 N	86.31 W
Lick Creek ≃, Mo., U.S.	219	39.31 N	91.39 W
Lick Creek ≃, Oh., U.S.	216	41.21 N	84.25 W
Lick Creek ≃, Tn., U.S.	192	36.11 N	83.10 W
Lickershamn	26	57.50 N	18.31 E
Licking	194	37.29 N	91.51 W
Licking □[6]	214	40.10 N	82.30 W
Licking ≃, Ky., U.S.	188	39.06 N	84.30 W
Licking ≃, Oh., U.S.	214	40.03 N	82.20 W
Licking, North Fork ≃, Ky., U.S.	218	38.35 N	84.13 W
Licking, North Fork ≃, Oh., U.S.	214	40.03 N	82.23 W
Licking, South Fork ≃	218	38.41 N	84.20 W
Lickingville	214	41.23 N	79.22 W
Lick Observatory ♁[3]	226	37.22 N	121.37 W
Ličko Polje ≚	36	44.35 N	15.25 E
Lick Run ≃, Pa., U.S.	210	41.12 N	77.32 W
Lick Run ≃, Pa., U.S.	279b	40.17 N	79.57 W
Licodia Eubea	70	37.09 N	14.42 E
Licosa, Punta >	68	40.15 N	14.54 E
Licun	98	38.32 N	117.08 E
Licungo ≃	154	17.40 S	37.15 E
Lid'	76	59.39 N	35.05 E
Lida	76	53.53 N	25.18 E
Lidan ≃	26	58.31 N	13.09 E
Lidao	98	37.15 N	122.32 E
Lidarentuncun	104	41.32 N	123.12 E
Lidcombe	274a	33.52 S	151.03 E
Liddel Water ≃	44	55.04 N	2.57 W
Liddesdale V	44	55.12 N	2.46 W
Liddon Gulf ⊂	176	75.03 N	113.00 W
Liden	26	62.42 N	16.48 E
Lidesi	100	33.33 N	115.53 E
Lidgerwood	198	46.04 N	97.09 W
Lidgetton	158	29.25 S	30.05 E
Lidian	107	28.57 N	103.44 E
Lídice, Bra.	256	22.51 S	44.12 W
Lídice, Pan.	236	8.45 N	79.54 W
Lidice ⊥	54	50.03 N	14.08 E
Lidingö	40	59.22 N	18.08 E
Lidköping	26	58.30 N	13.10 E
Lido	64	45.25 N	12.22 E
Lido, Litorale di ⊥[2]	64	45.23 N	12.21 E
Lido, Porto di ⊂	64	45.26 N	12.25 E
Lido Beach	276	40.35 N	73.38 W
Lido di Camaiore	64	43.54 N	10.13 E
Lido di Castel Fusano ◆[8]	66	41.43 N	12.20 E
Lido di Iesolo	64	45.30 N	12.39 E
Lido di Metaponto	68	40.22 N	16.50 E
Lido di Ostia ◆[8]	66	41.44 N	12.14 E
Lido di Pomposa	66	44.45 N	12.14 E
Lido di Siponto	68	41.37 N	15.55 E
Lido Key I	220	27.19 N	82.35 W
Lidsjön ⊜	40	58.55 N	16.51 E
Lidu	107	30.35 N	106.04 E
Lidzbark	30	53.17 N	19.49 E
Lidzbark Warmiński	30	54.09 N	20.35 E
Liebenau, B.R.D.	52	52.36 N	9.05 E
Liebenau, Öst.	61	48.32 N	14.49 E
Liebenbergsvlei ≃	158	27.20 S	28.31 E
Liebenburg	52	52.01 N	10.26 E
Liebenthal → Lubomierz	30	51.01 N	15.30 E
Liebenwalde	54	52.52 N	13.23 E
Lieberhausen	56	51.03 N	7.40 E
Lieberose	54	51.59 N	14.17 E
Liebertwolkwitz	54	51.17 N	12.28 E
Liebig, Mount ∧	162	23.18 S	131.22 E
Liebstadt	54	50.52 N	13.51 E
Liechtenstein □[1], Europe	22	47.09 N	9.35 E
Liechtenstein □[1], Europe	58	47.09 N	9.35 E
Liechtensteinklamm V	64	47.18 N	13.12 E
Liedberg	263	51.10 N	6.32 E
Liedekerke	50	50.52 N	4.05 E
Liège (Luik)	56	50.38 N	5.34 E
Liège □[4]	56	50.30 N	5.30 E
Liège, Aéroport ⊠	56	50.39 N	5.30 E
Liegnitz → Legnica	30	51.13 N	16.09 E
Lieja → Liège	56	50.38 N	5.34 E
Lieksa	26	63.19 N	30.01 E
Lielais Liepu kalns ∧[2]	76	56.25 N	27.50 E
Lielupe ≃	76	57.01 N	23.56 E
Lielvārde	76	56.43 N	24.51 E
Liemienzhen	107	30.29 N	106.05 E
Lienart	154	3.04 N	25.31 E
Lienchou → Hepu	102	21.39 N	109.11 E
Lienen	52	52.09 N	7.58 E
Lienz	64	46.50 N	12.47 E
Liepāja	76	56.31 N	21.01 E
Liepājas ezers ⊜	76	56.27 N	21.03 E
Liepe	54	53.58 N	13.56 E
Liepna	76	57.25 N	27.25 E
Liepnitzsee ⊜	264a	52.45 N	13.30 E
Lièpvre	58	48.16 N	7.17 E
Lier (Lierre)	50	51.08 N	4.34 E
Lierenfeld ◆[8]	263	51.13 N	6.51 E
Lierna	58	45.57 N	9.18 E
Liernais	50	47.12 N	4.17 E
Lierneux	56	50.18 N	5.48 E
Liershizhai	104	41.49 N	123.43 E
Liesborn	52	51.43 N	8.15 E
Lieser ≃, B.R.D.	56	49.55 N	7.01 E
Lieser ≃, Öst.	64	46.47 N	13.39 E
Lieshout	52	51.32 N	5.35 E
Liesing ◆[8]	264b	48.08 N	16.17 E
Liesing ≃	264b	48.08 N	16.28 E
Liesingbach ≃	61	47.20 N	15.02 E
Liesjärven Kansallispuisto ♦	26	60.40 N	23.54 E
Lieskau	54	51.37 N	13.48 E
Liesse	50	49.37 N	3.48 E
Liessies	50	50.07 N	4.05 E
Liestal	58	47.29 N	7.44 E
Liești	38	45.38 N	27.32 E
Lietzow	54	54.29 N	13.30 E
Lieurey	50	49.14 N	0.29 E
Lieusaint	261	48.38 N	2.33 E
Lieutel ≃	261	48.49 N	1.52 E
Lieutenant Robert J. Palenscar Memorial Airport ⊠	285	39.51 N	75.03 W
Liévin	50	50.25 N	2.46 E
Lièvre, Rivière du ≃	176	45.31 N	75.26 W
Lièvres, Île aux I	186	47.51 N	69.44 W
Liezen	61	47.35 N	14.15 E
Lifanga	152	0.19 N	21.57 E
Liffey ≃	48	53.21 N	6.16 W
Liffol-le-Grand	58	48.19 N	5.35 E
Lifford	48	54.50 N	7.29 W
Liffré	32	48.13 N	1.30 W
Lifjell ∧	26	59.30 N	8.52 E
Lifoku	152	0.04 S	21.18 E
Lifou I	175f	20.53 S	167.13 E
Lifoula	273b	4.06 S	15.25 E
Lifton	42	50.39 N	4.17 W
Liftwood	285	39.47 N	75.31 W
Lifune ≃	152	8.21 S	13.22 E
Ligačovo	265b	55.56 N	37.15 E
Ligang	100	30.04 N	121.52 E
Ligao, Pil.	116	13.14 N	123.32 E
Ligao, Pil.	116	6.17 N	124.09 E
Ligasa	152	0.42 N	23.45 E
Līgatne	76	57.14 N	25.02 E
Ligezhuang, Zhg.	105	39.49 N	115.56 E
Ligezhuang, Zhg.	105	39.42 N	118.12 E
Light ≃	168b	34.35 S	138.22 E
Lightfoot	208	37.20 N	76.45 W
Lighthouse Beach ⊥[2]	273a	6.24 N	3.22 E
Lighthouse Point	220	26.16 N	80.05 W
Lighthouse Point >, On., Can.	214	41.50 N	82.38 W
Lighthouse Point >, Fl., U.S.	192	29.54 N	84.21 W
Lighthouse Point >, Mi., U.S.	190	45.13 N	85.32 W
Lighthouse Reef ✦[2]	232	17.20 N	87.32 W
Lightning Creek ≃, Sk., Can.	184	49.12 N	101.43 W
Lightning Creek ≃, N.A.	224	48.50 N	121.03 W
Lightning Creek ≃, Wy., U.S.	198	43.11 N	104.44 W
Lightning Ridge	166	29.26 S	147.59 E
Lightstreet	210	41.02 N	76.25 W
Lightsville	216	40.18 N	84.42 W
Ligist	61	46.59 N	15.12 E
Lignano Pineta	64	45.40 N	13.07 E
Lignano Sabbiadoro	64	45.42 N	13.09 E
Lignières	32	46.45 N	2.11 E
Lignite	198	48.52 N	102.33 W
Lignon ≃	62	45.44 N	4.08 E
Lignumvitae Key I	220	24.55 N	80.42 W
Ligny-en-Barrois	58	48.41 N	5.20 E
Ligny-en-Cambrésis	50	50.06 N	3.22 E
Ligny-le-Châtel	50	47.54 N	3.45 E
Ligny-le-Ribault	50	47.41 N	1.47 E
Ligonha ≃	154	16.54 S	39.09 E
Ligonier, In., U.S.	216	41.27 N	85.35 W
Ligonier, Pa., U.S.	214	40.14 N	79.14 W
Ligovka	78	49.08 N	36.03 E
Ligovo	76	60.13 N	31.48 E
Ligovo ◆[8]	265a	59.50 N	30.12 E
Ligovskij kanal ≊	265a	59.47 N	30.10 E
Liguantu	105	40.24 N	115.45 E
Ligueil	32	47.03 N	0.49 E
Ligui	232	25.43 N	111.16 W
Ligure, Mar → Ligurian Sea ⫧[2]	36	43.30 N	9.00 E
Liguria □[4]	62	44.30 N	8.50 E
Liguria, Mar de → Ligurian Sea ⫧[2]	36	43.30 N	9.00 E
Ligurian Sea ⫧[2]	36	43.30 N	9.00 E
Ligurisches Meer → Ligurian Sea ⫧[2]	36	43.30 N	9.00 E
Lihir Group II	164	3.05 S	152.40 E
Lihir Island I	164	3.05 S	152.35 E
Lihou Reef and Cays ✦[2]	166	17.25 S	151.40 E
Lihu	100	23.23 N	116.03 E
Lihue	229b	21.58 N	159.22 W
Lihue Airport ⊠	229b	21.59 N	159.21 W
Lihula	76	58.41 N	23.50 E
Liji, Zhg.	100	33.48 N	117.48 E
Liji, Zhg.	100	31.59 N	115.51 E
Lijia, Zhg.	98	37.49 N	118.01 E
Lijia, Zhg.	104	41.43 N	122.20 E
Lijiaba	107	29.37 N	105.33 E
Lijiadian	104	42.07 N	121.14 E
Lijiajie	107	29.49 N	105.30 E
Lijiakou	105	39.12 N	116.29 E
Lijiang	102	26.57 N	100.15 E
Lijiapuzi	104	40.59 N	123.38 E
Lijiaqiao, Zhg.	105	40.03 N	116.40 E
Lijiaqiao, Zhg.	105	39.47 N	117.47 E
Lijiaqiao, Zhg.	106	31.38 N	120.00 E
Lijiatun	104	41.19 N	121.23 E
Lijiatuo	107	29.28 N	106.33 E
Lijiawobao	104	41.00 N	122.26 E
Lijiaxiang	106	30.57 N	119.59 E
Lijiazao	105	39.17 N	118.19 E
Lijin, Zhg.	98	37.29 N	118.16 E
Lijin, Zhg.	104	41.40 N	121.20 E
Lik ≃	110	18.31 N	102.31 E
Likako	152	0.15 N	21.00 E
Likang	100	22.47 N	120.29 E
Likasi (Jadotville)	154	10.59 S	26.44 E
Likati	152	3.21 N	23.53 E
Likati ≃	152	2.53 N	24.03 E
Likely	182	52.37 N	121.34 W
Likėnai	76	56.12 N	24.37 E
Likete	152	0.43 S	21.25 E
Likhu ≃	124	27.15 N	86.12 E
Liki	112	1.36 S	101.11 E
Likimi	152	2.50 N	20.45 E
Likino	82	55.38 N	37.08 E
Likino-Dulevo	82	55.43 N	38.58 E
Liknes	26	58.19 N	6.59 E
Likoma Island I	154	12.05 S	34.45 E
Likou, Zhg.	100	29.53 N	117.28 E
Likou, Zhg.	100	33.51 N	113.20 E
Likou, Zhg.	106	31.24 N	120.37 E
Likouala □[5]	152	2.00 N	17.30 E
Likouala ≃	152	1.13 S	16.48 E
Likouala aux Herbes ≃	152	0.50 S	17.11 E
Likova ≃	265b	55.34 N	37.21 E
Likstammen ⊜	40	58.58 N	17.12 E
Liku	174v	19.02 S	169.47 W
Likupang	112	1.41 N	125.04 E
Likus ≃	236	14.14 N	83.35 W
Likuyu	154	10.20 S	36.14 E
Lilanchengzhen	105	39.12 N	116.43 E
Lilanga	152	0.34 S	23.55 E
Lilasi	124	29.22 N	84.30 E
Lilbert	222	31.44 N	94.54 W
Lilbourn	194	36.35 N	89.36 W
L'Île-Bouchard	32	47.07 N	0.25 E
Lilenga	152	0.54 N	22.06 E
L'Île-Rousse	32	42.38 N	8.56 E
Lili	106	31.00 N	120.42 E
Lilian Point >	174d	0.53 S	169.35 E
Lilienfeld	61	48.03 N	15.36 E
Lilienthal	52	53.08 N	8.55 E
Liling	100	27.40 N	113.30 E
Lilio	116	14.08 N	121.26 E
Liljendal	40	60.08 N	14.04 E
Lilla Bharwana	123	32.34 N	72.45 E
Lilla Edet	26	58.08 N	12.08 E
Lillån	40	59.19 N	15.13 E
Lillby	26	63.28 N	23.00 E
Lille	50	50.38 N	3.04 E
Lillebælt ⋓	41	55.20 N	9.45 E
Lillebonne	50	49.31 N	0.33 E
Lillehammer	26	61.08 N	10.30 E
Lille-Lesquin, Aéroport ⊠	50	50.35 N	3.07 E
Lillerød	41	55.52 N	12.22 E
Lillers	50	50.34 N	2.29 E
Lillesand	26	58.15 N	8.24 E
Lilleshall	42	52.44 N	2.21 W
Lillestrøm	26	59.57 N	11.05 E
Lille Værløse	41	55.47 N	12.23 E
Lillhärdal	26	61.51 N	14.04 E
Lillian	222	32.30 N	97.11 W
Lillington	192	35.23 N	78.48 W
Lillinonah Lake ⊜[1]	207	41.28 N	73.21 W
Lilli Pilli	274a	34.04 S	151.07 E
Lillo	34	39.43 N	3.18 W
Lillooet	182	50.42 N	121.56 W
Lillooet ≃	182	49.45 N	122.08 W
Lillooet Lake ⊜	182	50.13 N	122.29 W
Lilly	214	40.25 N	78.37 W
Lilly Creek ≃	222	32.47 N	94.56 W
Liloan	116	10.09 N	125.07 E
Lilongwe	154	13.59 S	33.44 E
Lilo Viejo	252	26.56 S	62.58 W
Liloy	116	8.08 N	122.40 E
Liluāh	272b	22.35 N	88.23 E
Lily	192	37.01 N	84.04 W
Lily Cache Creek ≃	278	41.41 N	88.07 W
Lilydale, Austl.	166	41.15 S	147.13 E
Lilydale, Austl.	169	37.45 S	145.21 E
Lily Dale, N.Y., U.S.	214	42.21 N	79.19 W
Lilyfield	274a	33.52 S	151.10 E
Lilyvale	273d	26.06 S	28.25 E
Lim ≃, Afr.	152	7.54 N	15.46 E
Lim ≃, Jugo.	38	43.45 N	19.13 E
Lima, Arg.	258	34.03 S	59.12 W
Lima, Para.	252	23.54 S	56.20 W
Lima, Perú	248	12.03 S	77.03 W
Lima, Perú	286d	12.03 S	77.03 W
Lima, Sve.	26	60.56 N	13.26 E
Lima, Il., U.S.	219	40.11 N	91.23 W
Lima, Mt., U.S.	202	44.38 N	112.35 W
Lima, N.Y., U.S.	210	42.54 N	77.36 W
Lima, Oh., U.S.	216	40.44 N	84.06 W
Lima, Pa., U.S.	285	39.55 N	75.26 W
Lima □[5]	248	12.00 S	76.35 W
Lima (Limia) ≃, Europe	34	41.41 N	8.50 W
Lima ≃, It.	64	44.00 N	10.35 E
Lima, Punta >	240m	18.11 N	65.41 W
Lima-Callao, Aeropuerto Internacional ⊠	286d	12.02 S	77.07 W
Lima Center	216	42.47 N	88.49 W
Limache	252	33.01 S	71.16 W
Lima Duarte	256	21.51 S	43.48 W
Lima Duarte, Serra de ⋏[2]	256	21.54 S	43.52 W
Liman, S.S.S.R.	78	49.36 N	36.27 E
Liman, S.S.S.R.	78	45.41 N	29.45 E
Liman, S.S.S.R.	80	45.47 N	47.14 E
Liman, S.S.S.R.	83	49.21 N	38.57 E
Liman, Yis.	132	33.03 N	35.06 E
Liman ≃	115a	6.29 S	105.48 E
Limanowa	30	49.43 N	20.26 E
Limanskoje	78	46.38 N	30.00 E
Lima Nueva	236	15.23 N	87.56 W
Limão ◆[8]	287b	23.30 S	46.40 W
Limapuluh	114	3.10 N	99.26 E
Lima Reservoir ⊜[1]	202	44.38 N	112.17 W
Limarí ≃	252	30.44 S	71.43 W
Limas	112	0.14 N	104.31 E
Limasawa Island I	116	9.56 N	125.05 E
Limassa	152	4.14 N	22.02 E
Limassol → Lemesós	130	34.40 N	33.02 E
Limavady	48	55.03 N	6.57 W
Limaville	214	40.59 N	81.09 W
Limay, Fr.	50	49.00 N	1.44 E
Limay, Pil.	116	14.34 N	120.36 E
Limay ≃	254	38.59 S	68.00 W
Limay Mahuida	252	37.12 S	66.42 W
Limbach-Oberfrohna	54	50.51 N	12.45 E
Limbadi	68	38.33 N	15.58 E
Limbang	112	4.45 N	115.00 E
Limbang ≃	112	4.50 N	115.01 E
Limbani	248	14.08 S	69.42 W
Limbara, Monte ∧	71	40.51 N	9.10 E
Limbaži	76	57.31 N	24.42 E
Līmbdi	120	22.34 N	71.48 E
Limbe	154	15.49 S	35.03 E
Limbiate	62	45.36 N	9.07 E
Limboto	112	0.37 N	122.57 E
Limbourg	56	50.37 N	5.56 E
Limbrick	262	53.38 N	2.36 W
Limbueta	152	12.30 S	18.42 E
Limbunya	164	17.14 S	129.50 E
Limburg □[4], Bel.	56	51.00 N	5.30 E
Limburg □[4], Ned.	52	51.14 N	5.50 E
Limburg an der Lahn	56	50.23 N	8.04 E
Limburgerhof	56	49.25 N	8.24 E
Lim Chu Kang	271c	1.26 N	103.43 E
Limecrest	218	39.54 N	83.48 W
Limefield	262	53.37 N	2.18 W
Limeira	255	22.34 S	47.24 W
Limekiln Canyon V	280	34.18 N	118.33 W
Lime Lake	210	42.26 N	78.29 W
Limen	100	27.07 N	119.19 E
Limena	64	45.29 N	11.50 E
Limentra ≃	64	44.14 N	11.03 E
Limerick, Sk., Can.	184	49.40 N	106.15 W
Limerick, Ire.	48	52.40 N	8.38 W
Limerick, Pa., U.S.	285	40.14 N	75.32 W
Limerick (Luimneach) □[6]	48	52.30 N	8.45 W
Limerick Lake ⊜	212	44.54 N	77.37 W
Limerock	207	41.55 N	71.28 W
Lime Springs	190	43.27 N	92.17 W
Limestone, Austl.	162	21.11 S	119.50 E
Limestone, Fl., U.S.	220	27.21 N	81.53 W
Limestone, Me., U.S.	186	46.54 N	67.49 W
Limestone, N.Y., U.S.	210	42.01 N	78.37 W
Limestone, Pa., U.S.	214	41.08 N	79.20 W
Limestone □[6]	222	31.35 N	96.35 W
Limestone ≃	184	56.31 N	94.07 W
Limestone, Lake ⊜[1]	222	31.25 N	96.20 W
Limestone Bay ⊂	184	53.50 N	98.50 W
Limestone Canyon V	280	33.45 N	117.41 W
Limestone Creek ≃	210	43.06 N	75.58 W
Limestone Lake ⊜, Mb., Can.	184	56.35 N	96.00 W
Limestone Lake ⊜, Sk., Can.	184	54.36 N	103.18 W
Limestone Point >[1]	184	53.50 N	98.50 W
Limestone Point Lake ⊜	184	55.07 N	100.32 W
Lime Street Station ◆[5]	262	53.25 N	2.59 W
Lime Village	180	61.21 N	155.28 W
Limfjorden ⋓	26	56.55 N	9.10 E
Limhamn ◆[8]	41	55.35 N	12.54 E
Limia (Lima) ≃	34	41.41 N	8.50 W
Limina	70	37.56 N	15.17 E
Liminka	26	64.49 N	25.24 E
Liminzhen	98	34.31 N	115.56 E
Limit Brook ≃	283	42.42 N	71.25 W
Limmared	26	57.32 N	13.21 E
Limmaren ⊜	40	59.44 N	18.43 E
Limmen	52	52.34 N	4.41 E
Limmen Bight ⊂[3]	164	14.45 S	135.40 E
Limmen Bight ≃	164	15.07 S	135.44 E
Límnos I	38	39.54 N	25.21 E
Limoeiro	250	7.52 S	35.27 W
Limoeiro do Norte	250	5.08 S	38.05 W
Limoges, On., Can.	212	45.20 N	75.15 W
Limoges, Fr.	32	45.50 N	1.16 E
Limoges-Fourches	261	48.38 N	2.40 E
Limogne	32	44.24 N	1.46 E
Limón, C.R.	236	10.00 N	83.02 W
Limón, Hond.	236	15.52 N	85.33 W
Limon, Co., U.S.	198	39.15 N	103.41 W
Limón □[4]	236	10.00 N	83.15 W
Limonar	240p	22.57 N	81.24 W
Limón de Ramos	232	24.43 N	107.08 W
Limone Piemonte	62	44.12 N	7.34 E
Limone sul Garda	64	45.49 N	10.47 E
Limours	50	48.39 N	2.05 E
Limousin, Plateaux du ⋏[1]	32	45.30 N	1.15 E
Limoux	32	43.04 N	2.14 E
Limpopo ≃	156	25.15 S	33.30 E
Limpsfield	42	51.16 N	0.01 E
Limski kanal ⊂	64	45.07 N	13.38 E
Limu	102	25.02 N	110.51 E
Limuru	154	1.06 S	36.39 E
Linachamari	24	69.40 N	31.20 E
Līnah	128	28.42 N	43.48 E
Lin'an	106	30.14 N	119.43 E
Linanäs	40	59.28 N	18.31 E
Linao Bay ⊂	116	6.45 N	124.00 E
Linapacan Island I	116	11.27 N	119.49 E
Linapacan Strait ⋓	116	11.37 N	119.56 E
Linares, Chile	252	35.51 S	71.36 W
Linares, Col.	246	1.23 N	77.31 W
Linares, Esp.	34	38.05 N	3.38 W
Linares, Méx.	232	24.52 N	99.34 W
Linariá	38	37.24 N	24.57 E
Linaro, Capo >	66	42.02 N	11.50 E
Linas	261	48.38 N	2.16 E
Linas, Monte ∧	71	39.27 N	8.37 E
Linas-Montlhéry, Domaine Militaire de ■	261	48.37 N	2.13 E
Linate, Aeroporto di ⊠	62	45.27 N	9.16 E
Lincai	100	33.50 N	114.56 E
Lincang	102	23.45 N	102.20 E
Lince	286d	12.06 S	77.03 W
Linch	200	43.36 N	106.11 W
Lincheng, Zhg.	98	37.27 N	114.29 E
Lincheng, Zhg.	106	30.55 N	119.47 E
Linch'ing → Linqing	98	36.53 N	115.41 E
Lincoln, Arg.	252	34.52 S	61.32 W
Lincoln, On., Can.	212	43.10 N	79.29 W
Lincoln, N.Z.	172	43.39 S	172.29 E
Lincoln, Eng., U.K.	44	53.14 N	0.33 W
Lincoln, Ar., U.S.	194	35.56 N	94.25 W
Lincoln, Ca., U.S.	226	38.53 N	121.17 W
Lincoln, De., U.S.	208	38.52 N	75.25 W
Lincoln, Il., U.S.	219	40.08 N	89.21 W
Lincoln, In., U.S.	216	40.37 N	86.12 W
Lincoln, Ks., U.S.	198	39.02 N	98.08 W
Lincoln, Me., U.S.	188	45.21 N	68.30 W
Lincoln, Ma., U.S.	207	42.25 N	71.18 W
Lincoln, Mi., U.S.	190	44.41 N	83.24 W
Lincoln, Mo., U.S.	194	38.23 N	93.20 W
Lincoln, Mt., U.S.	202	46.57 N	112.40 W
Lincoln, Ne., U.S.	198	40.48 N	96.40 W
Lincoln, N.H., U.S.	188	44.02 N	71.40 W
Lincoln, Pa., U.S.	208	40.12 N	76.12 W
Lincoln, Pa., U.S.	279b	40.18 N	79.51 W
Lincoln, R.I., U.S.	207	41.54 N	71.25 W
Lincoln, Tx., U.S.	222	30.17 N	96.52 W
Lincoln □[6], Mo., U.S.	219	39.05 N	90.57 W
Lincoln □[6], Or., U.S.	224	44.59 N	123.52 W
Lincoln, Mount ∧	200	39.21 N	106.07 W
Lincoln Acres	228	32.40 N	117.04 W
Lincoln Boyhood National Memorial ⊥	194	38.10 N	86.58 W
Lincoln Cathedral ♁[1]	44	53.14 N	0.33 W
Lincoln Center ♁	276	40.46 N	73.59 W
Lincoln City	224	44.57 N	124.00 W
Lincoln Creek ≃, Ne., U.S.	198	40.54 N	97.06 W
Lincoln Creek ≃, Wa., U.S.	224	46.45 N	123.02 W
Lincolndale	210	41.19 N	73.43 W
Lincoln Estates	278	41.31 N	87.49 W
Lincoln Heights, Oh., U.S.	214	40.47 N	82.30 W
Lincoln Heights, Oh., U.S.	218	39.15 N	84.28 W
Lincoln Heights, Pa., U.S.	279b	40.19 N	79.37 W
Lincoln Home National Historical Site ⊥	219	39.47 N	89.38 W
Lincolnia Heights	284c	38.50 N	77.09 W
Lincoln Memorial ⊥	284c	38.53 N	77.03 W
Lincoln Park, Co., U.S.	200	38.25 N	105.13 W
Lincoln Park, Ga., U.S.	192	32.52 N	84.19 W
Lincoln Park, Mi., U.S.	216	42.15 N	83.10 W
Lincoln Park, N.J., U.S.	276	40.55 N	74.18 W
Lincoln Park, N.Y., U.S.	210	41.57 N	74.00 W
Lincoln Park ♦, Ca., U.S.	282	37.46 N	122.30 W
Lincoln Park ♦, Il., U.S.	278	41.56 N	87.38 W
Lincoln Park Airport ⊠	276	40.57 N	74.19 W
Lincoln Place ◆[8]	279b	40.22 N	79.55 W
Lincoln Sea ⫧[2]	16	83.00 N	56.00 W
Lincolnshire	216	42.11 N	87.54 W
Lincolnshire □[6]	42	52.55 N	0.22 W
Lincoln's New Salem State Park ♦	219	39.58 N	89.52 W
Lincoln Tomb State Memorial ⊥	219	39.50 N	89.39 W
Lincolnton, Ga., U.S.	192	33.47 N	82.28 W
Lincolnton, N.C., U.S.	192	35.28 N	81.15 W
Lincoln Tunnel ◆[5]	276	40.46 N	74.01 W
Lincoln University	208	39.48 N	75.55 W
Lincoln Village, Ca., U.S.	226	38.00 N	121.19 W
Lincoln Village, Oh., U.S.	218	39.57 N	83.03 W
Lincolnville	214	41.47 N	79.51 W
Lincolnwood	278	42.00 N	87.43 W
Lincolnwood Hills	278	41.31 N	87.54 W
Linconia	285	40.08 N	74.59 W
Lincroft	208	40.19 N	74.07 W
Lind	202	46.58 N	118.36 W
Linda, S.S.S.R.	80	56.37 N	44.07 E
Linda, Ca., U.S.	226	39.07 N	121.32 W
Linda-a-Velha	266c	38.43 N	9.14 W
Lindale, Ga., U.S.	192	34.11 N	85.10 W
Lindale, Tx., U.S.	222	32.30 N	95.24 W
Lindau, B.R.D.	41	54.36 N	9.47 E
Lindau, B.R.D.	52	51.39 N	10.07 E
Lindau, B.R.D.	58	47.33 N	9.41 E
Lindau, D.D.R.	54	52.02 N	12.06 E
Lindbergh	219	39.02 N	92.08 W
Lindbergh Field ⊠	228	32.44 N	117.11 W
Lind Coulee V	202	47.00 N	119.10 W
Linde ≃	74	64.57 N	124.36 E
Lindelse	41	54.52 N	10.44 E
Linden, Al., U.S.	194	32.18 N	87.47 W
Linden, Ca., U.S.	226	38.01 N	121.05 W
Linden, In., U.S.	194	40.11 N	86.54 W
Linden, Mi., U.S.	216	42.48 N	83.46 W
Linden, N.J., U.S.	210	40.37 N	74.14 W
Linden, Pa., U.S.	210	41.14 N	77.08 W
Linden, Pa., U.S.	279b	40.14 N	80.08 W
Linden, Tn., U.S.	194	35.37 N	87.50 W
Linden, Tx., U.S.	194	33.00 N	94.21 W
Linden ◆[8]	273d	26.08 S	28.00 E
Linden Airport ⊠	276	40.37 N	74.15 W
Lindenberg, D.D.R.	54	52.36 N	13.31 E
Lindenberg, D.D.R.	54	53.02 N	12.07 E
Lindenberg, D.D.R.	54	52.12 N	14.07 E
Lindenberg im Allgäu	58	47.36 N	9.53 E
Linden-Dahlhausen ◆[8]	263	51.26 N	7.09 E
Lindenfels	56	49.41 N	8.47 E
Lindenhorst ◆[8]	263	51.33 N	7.27 E
Lindenhurst, Il., U.S.	216	42.24 N	88.01 W
Lindenhurst, N.Y., U.S.	210	40.41 N	73.22 W
Lindenhurst, Pa., U.S.	285	40.14 N	74.54 W
Linden Park	216	40.13 N	85.23 W
Lindenthal	54	51.24 N	12.20 E
Lindenwold	208	39.49 N	74.59 W
Lindenwood, Il., U.S.	216	42.03 N	89.02 W
Lindenwood, In., U.S.	218	39.41 N	86.09 W
Linderhausen	263	51.18 N	7.17 E
Linderhof, Schloss ⊥	64	47.34 N	10.57 E
Lindern	52	52.50 N	7.46 E
Linderöd	41	55.56 N	13.49 E
Linderödsåsen ⋏[2]	26	55.53 N	13.56 E
Lindesay, Mount ∧[2]	162	34.49 S	117.18 E
Lindesberg	40	59.35 N	15.15 E
Lindesnäs	40	60.20 N	14.32 E
Lindesnes >	26	58.00 N	7.02 E
Lindfield, Austl.	274a	33.47 S	151.10 E
Lindfield, Eng., U.K.	42	51.01 N	0.05 W
Lindfors	40	59.36 N	13.49 E
Lindholmen	40	59.35 N	18.06 E
Lindhorst	52	52.21 N	9.17 E
Líndhos	38	36.06 N	28.04 E
Líndhos ⊥	38	36.06 N	28.05 E
Lindi	154	10.00 S	39.43 E
Lindi □[4]	154	9.15 S	38.45 E
Lindi ≃	154	0.33 N	25.05 E
Lindian	89	47.11 N	124.52 E
Lindis Pass)(	172	44.36 S	169.40 E
Lindkirchen	60	48.40 N	11.47 E
Lindlar	56	51.01 N	7.23 E
Lindley, S. Afr.	158	28.00 S	27.57 E
Lindley, N.Y., U.S.	210	42.02 N	77.08 W
Lind National Park ♦	166	37.35 S	149.05 E
Lindö	40	58.37 N	16.15 E
Lindóia	256	22.31 S	46.39 W
Lindome	26	57.34 N	12.05 E
Lindon	198	39.44 N	103.24 W
Lindong, Zhg.	100	26.03 N	118.49 E
Lindong, Zhg.	105	39.51 N	117.41 E
Lindow	54	52.58 N	13.00 E
Lind Point >	240m	18.20 N	64.48 W
Lindre, Étang de ⊜[1]	56	48.47 N	6.45 E
Lindsay, On., Can.	212	44.21 N	78.44 W
Lindsay, Ca., U.S.	204	36.12 N	119.05 W
Lindsay, Ne., U.S.	198	41.42 N	97.41 W
Lindsay, Ok., U.S.	196	34.50 N	97.36 W
Lindsborg	198	38.34 N	97.40 W
Lindsey	214	41.25 N	83.13 W
Lindved	41	55.47 N	9.35 E
Lindy Lake	276	41.05 N	74.22 W
Lineboro	208	39.43 N	76.50 W
Line Creek ≃	194	33.34 N	88.42 W
Line Islands II	14	0.05 N	157.00 W
Line Lexington	208	40.17 N	75.16 W
Line Mountain ∧	210	40.45 N	76.37 W
Linesville	214	41.39 N	80.25 W
Lineville, Al., U.S.	194	33.18 N	85.45 W
Lineville, Ia., U.S.	190	40.34 N	93.31 W
Línevo	86	54.05 N	83.24 E
Linfa	287b	23.44 S	46.56 W
Linfen	102	36.05 N	111.32 E
Linfield	208	40.13 N	75.34 W
Linford	260	51.29 N	0.25 E
Ling ≃	46	57.19 N	5.27 W
Ling'an	106	30.36 N	120.30 E
Linganamakki Reservoir ⊜[1]	122	14.04 N	74.54 E
Lingao	102	19.54 N	109.40 E
Lingayen	116	16.01 N	120.14 E
Lingayen Gulf ⊂	116	16.15 N	120.14 E
Lingbi	100	33.33 N	117.33 E
Lingbo	26	61.03 N	16.41 E
Lingchuan, Zhg.	102	25.26 N	110.15 E
Lingchuan, Zhg.	102	35.46 N	113.26 E
Lingda	106	31.12 N	119.18 E
Lingdale	44	54.32 N	0.57 W
Lingdianzhen	106	31.51 N	121.25 E
Lingdou	100	26.22 N	118.56 E
Lingen	52	52.31 N	7.19 E
Lingesestausee ⊜[1]	263	51.06 N	7.32 E
Lingfengwei	100	24.44 N	115.35 E
Lingfield	42	51.11 N	0.01 W
Lingga, Kepulauan II	112	0.05 S	104.35 E
Lingga, Pulau I	112	0.12 S	104.35 E
Lingham Lake ⊜	212	44.46 N	77.25 W
Linghe	98	36.23 N	119.03 E
Linghu	106	30.44 N	120.10 E
Lingig	116	8.02 N	126.24 E
Lingjiachang	107	29.28 N	104.54 E
Lingjiaqiao	106	30.09 N	120.04 E
Lingkar Dzong	124	28.45 N	90.36 E
Lingkou, Zhg.	100	29.16 N	120.38 E
Lingkou, Zhg.	106	31.57 N	119.38 E
Lingle	200	42.08 N	104.20 W
Linglestown	208	40.21 N	76.48 W
Lingling	102	26.13 N	111.37 E
Linglongta	98	40.54 N	119.59 E
Lingma	102	23.22 N	107.53 E
Lingolsheim	58	48.34 N	7.41 E
Lingomo	152	0.38 N	21.59 E
Lingqiu	98	39.24 N	114.13 E
Lingshan, Zhg.	98	36.33 N	120.27 E
Lingshan, Zhg.	102	22.28 N	109.17 E
Lingshanwei	98	35.58 N	120.13 E
Lingshi	102	36.54 N	111.43 E
Lingshou	98	38.18 N	114.24 E
Lingshui	110	18.31 N	110.01 E
Lingtangqiao	100	32.43 N	119.14 E
Linguaglossa	70	37.50 N	15.08 E
Linguère	150	15.24 N	15.07 W
Lingwala	273b	4.22 S	15.17 E
Lingwood	42	52.37 N	1.29 E
Lingwu	102	38.06 N	106.21 E
Lingxian, Zhg.	98	37.21 N	116.34 E
Lingxian, Zhg.	100	26.30 N	113.46 E
Lingxiazhu	100	29.03 N	119.46 E
Lingyuan	98	41.15 N	119.16 E
Lingzhuangzi	105	39.04 N	117.09 E
Lingzinan	105	39.29 N	115.15 E
Linh, Ngoc ∧	110	15.04 N	107.59 E
Linhai	100	28.51 N	121.07 E
Linhares	255	19.25 S	40.04 W
Linh Cam	110	18.31 N	105.34 E
Linhe	102	40.51 N	107.30 E
Linhezhuang	105	40.04 N	117.39 E
Linhigh	284b	39.21 N	76.31 W
Linhó	266c	38.46 N	9.23 W
Linhsia → Linxia	102	35.35 N	103.13 E
Linhuaiguan	100	32.55 N	117.40 E
Linhuanji	100	33.42 N	116.33 E
Lini → Linyi	98	35.04 N	118.22 E
Linjiang, Zhg.	98	41.44 N	126.55 E
Linjiang, Zhg.	100	27.50 N	118.26 E
Linjiang, Zhg.	100	28.04 N	115.21 E
Linjiang, Zhg.	102	33.01 N	105.01 E
Linjiangchang	107	29.14 N	105.58 E
Linjianghu	100	28.41 N	117.54 E
Linjiangsi	107	30.15 N	104.37 E
Linjiatai	104	40.43 N	123.57 E
Linkenheim	56	49.07 N	8.24 E
Linköping	26	58.25 N	15.37 E
Linkou	89	45.15 N	130.16 E
Linksfield ◆[8]	273d	26.10 S	28.06 E
Linksmakalnis	76	54.45 N	23.55 E
Linksness	46	58.56 N	3.19 W
Linkuva	76	56.05 N	23.59 E
Linkwood	208	38.32 N	75.57 W
Linli	102	29.18 N	111.30 E
Linlithgow	46	55.59 N	3.37 W
Linmeyer	273d	26.16 S	28.04 E
Linn, Ks., U.S.	198	39.40 N	97.05 W
Linn, Mo., U.S.	219	38.29 N	91.51 W
Linn ◆[8]	263	51.20 N	6.38 E
Linnancang	105	39.50 N	117.37 E
Linnansaaren Kansallispuisto ♦	26	62.07 N	28.31 E
Linndale	279a	41.27 N	81.46 W
Linne	52	51.10 N	5.57 E
Linnell	226	36.21 N	119.11 W
Linnés Hammarby ⊥	40	59.49 N	17.46 E
Linney Head >	42	51.38 N	5.04 W
Linn Grove	216	40.38 N	85.01 W
Linnhe, Loch ⊂	46	56.39 N	5.21 W
Linnich	56	50.59 N	6.16 E
Linntown	210	40.58 N	76.54 W
Linnville Bayou ≃	222	28.57 N	95.42 W
Linosa	70a	35.51 N	12.52 E
Linosa, Isola di I	70a	35.51 N	12.52 E
Linovica	78	50.28 N	32.22 E
Lin'ovo	80	50.53 N	44.51 E
Linow	54	53.06 N	12.49 E
Linping → Yuhang	106	30.25 N	120.18 E
Linpu	100	30.03 N	120.15 E
Linqi, Zhg.	98	35.48 N	113.53 E
Linqi, Zhg.	100	29.51 N	119.06 E
Linqing	98	36.53 N	115.41 E
Linqu	98	36.32 N	118.31 E
Linquan	100	33.06 N	115.13 E
Linru	100	34.11 N	112.49 E
Linruzhen	100	34.17 N	112.35 E
Lins	255	21.40 S	49.45 W
Linshan	100	30.09 N	120.59 E
Linshanhe	100	30.44 N	114.52 E
Linshengpu	104	41.34 N	123.20 E
Linshui	102	30.21 N	106.59 E
Linslade	42	51.55 N	0.41 W
Linstead	241q	18.08 N	77.02 W
Linta ≃	157b	25.02 S	44.05 E
Lintan	102	34.37 N	103.40 E
Lintao	102	35.27 N	103.46 E
Linté	152	5.24 N	11.42 E
Linth ≃	58	47.07 N	9.07 E
Linthal, Fr.	58	47.56 N	7.08 E
Linthal, Schw.	58	46.55 N	9.00 E
Linthicum Heights	284b	39.12 N	76.39 W
Linthkanal ≊	58	47.13 N	8.57 E
Linthwaite	262	53.37 N	1.51 W
Lintingkou	105	39.39 N	117.30 E
Linton, Austl.	169	37.41 S	143.34 E
Linton, N.Z.	172	40.26 S	175.33 E
Linton, Eng., U.K.	42	52.06 N	0.17 E
Linton, Eng., U.K.	260	51.13 N	0.31 E
Linton, In., U.S.	194	39.02 N	87.09 W
Linton, N.D., U.S.	198	46.16 N	100.13 W
Lintong	102	34.21 N	109.11 E
Linton Park ♦	260	51.13 N	0.31 E
Linum	264a	52.46 N	12.53 E
Linville, Austl.	171a	26.51 S	152.16 E
Linville, N.C., U.S.	192	36.03 N	81.52 W
Linwood, Austl.	168b	34.21 S	138.46 E
Linwood, In., U.S.	218	40.12 N	85.41 W
Linwood, Ma., U.S.	207	42.05 N	71.38 W
Linwood, N.J., U.S.	208	39.20 N	74.34 W
Linwood, Pa., U.S.	285	39.49 N	75.24 W
Linworth	214	40.06 N	83.04 W
Linwu, Zhg.	98	36.14 N	119.17 E
Linwu, Zhg.	102	25.16 N	112.20 E
Linxi, Zhg.	90	43.30 N	118.00 E
Linxi, Zhg.	98	36.52 N	115.32 E
Linxia	102	35.35 N	103.13 E
Linxian, Zhg.	98	36.04 N	113.50 E
Linxian, Zhg.	102	37.58 N	110.59 E
Linxiang	100	29.28 N	113.30 E
Linyanti	156	18.04 S	24.01 E
Linyanti ≃	156	17.58 S	24.16 E
Linyi, Zhg.	98	35.04 N	118.22 E
Linyi, Zhg.	98	37.13 N	116.51 E
Linyi, Zhg.	102	35.15 N	110.59 E
Linying	100	33.50 N	113.57 E
Linyü → Shanhaiguan	98	40.01 N	119.44 E
Linyüan	100	22.30 N	120.23 E
Linz, B.R.D.	56	50.34 N	7.17 E
Linz, Öst.	61	48.18 N	14.18 E
Linze, Zhg.	100	33.03 N	119.38 E
Linze, Zhg.	102	39.19 N	100.17 E
Linzgau ◆[1]	58	47.45 N	9.16 E
Linzhai	100	24.18 N	115.03 E
Linzhang	98	36.21 N	114.36 E
Linzhi	120	29.25 N	94.22 E
Linzikou	100	28.42 N	112.46 E
Linzolo	152	4.25 S	15.07 E
Lioko, Zaïre	152	0.02 N	22.04 E
Lioko, Zaïre	152	1.25 N	23.07 E
Lio Matoh	112	3.10 N	115.14 E
Liomer	50	49.51 N	1.49 E
Lion, Golfe du ⊂	32	43.00 N	4.00 E
Lionel Town	241q	17.48 N	77.14 W
Lioni	68	40.52 N	15.11 E
Lion Rock ∧[2]	271d	22.22 N	114.11 E
Lion Rock Tunnel ◆[5]	271d	22.21 N	114.09 E
Lions Den	154	17.16 S	30.02 E
Lion's Head	212	44.59 N	81.15 W
Lionville	208	40.03 N	75.39 W
Lioppa	112	7.40 S	126.00 E
Liouesso	152	1.02 N	15.43 E
Liozno	76	55.02 N	30.48 E
Lipa	116	13.57 N	121.10 E
Lipan	196	32.31 N	98.03 W
Lipany	30	49.10 N	20.58 E
Lipari	70	38.28 N	14.57 E
Lipari, Isola I	70	38.29 N	14.56 E
Lipatkain	112	0.01 S	101.13 E
Lipayan	104	42.13 N	123.23 E
Lipcy	78	50.13 N	36.25 E
Lipeck	76	52.37 N	39.35 E
Lipeck □[4]	80	52.15 N	40.30 E
Lipeckoje Vtoroje	78	47.46 N	29.41 E
Liperi	26	62.32 N	29.22 E
Lipetsk → Lipeck	76	52.37 N	39.35 E
Lipez, Cerro ∧	248	21.53 S	66.52 W
Liphook	42	51.05 N	0.49 W
Lipiany	30	53.00 N	14.59 E
Lipicy	76	53.22 N	37.17 E
Lipin Bor	76	60.16 N	37.57 E
Liping	102	26.17 N	109.00 E
Lipis ≃	114	4.10 N	102.04 E
Lipiyu	104	41.09 N	123.36 E
Lipka ≃	265b	55.45 N	37.11 E
Lipkany	78	48.16 N	26.48 E
Lipki	76	53.58 N	37.42 E
Lipník nad Bečvou	30	49.31 N	17.35 E
Lipniški	76	54.00 N	25.37 E
Lipno	30	52.51 N	19.10 E
Lipno, údolní nádrž ⊜[1]	60	48.43 N	14.04 E
Lipno nad Vltavou	61	48.38 N	14.14 E
Lipoa Point >	229a	21.02 N	156.38 W
Lipova	38	46.05 N	21.40 E
Lipovaja Dolina	78	50.35 N	33.48 E
Lipovcy	89	44.11 N	131.44 E
Lipovec	78	49.14 N	29.03 E
Lipovka, S.S.S.R.	78	50.52 N	40.02 E
Lipovka, S.S.S.R.	80	52.26 N	46.11 E
Lipovka, S.S.S.R.	80	49.46 N	44.56 E
Lippborg	52	51.40 N	8.02 E
Lippe ≃	52	51.39 N	6.38 E
Lipperode	52	51.41 N	8.22 E
Lippetal	52	51.40 N	8.06 E
Lippoldsberg	52	51.37 N	9.33 E
Lippstadt	52	51.40 N	8.19 E
Lipscomb	196	36.14 N	100.16 W
Lipsko	30	51.09 N	21.39 E
Lipsoí I, Ellás	38	37.20 N	26.45 E
Lipsoí I, Ellás	130	37.20 N	26.45 E
Lipton	184	50.54 N	103.50 W
Liptovská Teplička	30	48.59 N	20.06 E
Liptovský Mikuláš	30	49.06 N	19.37 E
Liptrap, Cape >	166	38.54 S	145.55 E
Lipu	102	24.25 N	110.29 E
Lipu La)(	124	30.21 N	81.05 E
Liqiao	107	29.03 N	104.48 E
Lira, Ug.	154	2.15 N	32.54 E
Lira, Ven.	286c	10.26 N	66.46 W
Liranga	152	0.40 S	17.36 E

Symbols in the index entries represent the broad categories identified in the key at the right. Symbols with superior numbers (⋏[1]) identify subcategories (see complete key on page *I · 1).*

Symbole im Register stellen die rechts im Schlüssel erklärten Kategorien dar. Symbole mit hochgestellten Ziffern (⋏[1]) bezeichnen Unterabteilungen einer Kategorie (vgl. vollständiger Schlüssel auf Seite *I · 1).*

Los símbolos incluídos en el texto del índice representan las grandes categorias identificadas con la clave a la derecha. Los símbolos con numeros en su parte superior (⋏[1]) identifican las subcategorías (véase la clave completa en la página *I · 1).*

Les symboles de l'index représentent les catégories indiquées dans la légende à droite. Les symboles suivis d'un indice (⋏[1]) représentent des sous-catégories (voir légende complète à la page *I · 1).*

Os símbolos incluídos no texto do índice representam as grandes categorias identificadas com a chave à direita. Os símbolos com números em sua parte superior (⋏[1]) identificam as subcategorias (veja-se a chave completa à página *I · 1).*

	English	Deutsch	Español	Français	Português
∧	Mountain	Berg	Montaña	Montagne	Montanha
⋏	Mountains	Gebirge	Montañas	Montagnes	Montanhas
)(	Pass	Paß	Paso	Col	Passo
V	Valley, Canyon	Tal, Cañon	Valle, Cañón	Vallée, Canyon	Vale, Canhão
≚	Plain	Ebene	Llano	Plaine	Planície
>	Cape	Kap	Cabo	Cap	Cabo
I	Island	Insel	Isla	Île	Ilha
II	Islands	Inseln	Islas	Îles	Ilhas
⊥	Other Topographic Features	Andere Topographische Objekte	Otros Elementos Topográficos	Autres données topographiques	Outros acidentes topográficos

Lira-Llan *I* · 99

ESPAÑOL — Nombre | Página | Lat.°′ | Long.°′ W = Oeste
FRANÇAIS — Nom | Page | Lat.°′ | Long.°′ W = Ouest
PORTUGUÊS — Nome | Página | Lat.°′ | Long.°′ W = Oeste

Nombre / Nom / Nome	Página / Page	Lat.°′	Long.°′ W = Oeste / Ouest
Lirangdian	105	39.14 N	116.14 E
Lircay	248	12.56 S	74.43 W
Liren	100	33.55 N	118.47 E
Lirentuncun	104	41.24 N	122.59 E
Liri ≃	66	41.25 N	13.52 E
Liro	175f	16.27 S	168.13 E
Liro ≃	58	46.18 N	9.23 E
Lisa, Punta ›	236	8.00 N	80.22 W
Lisakovsk	86	52.36 N	62.37 E
Lisala	152	2.09 N	21.31 E
Lisavy	82	56.33 N	38.32 E
Lisboa (Lisbon), Port.	34	38.43 N	9.08 W
Lisboa (Lisbon), Port.	266c	38.43 N	9.08 W
Lisboa □[5]	266c	38.48 N	9.16 W
Lisbon → Lisboa, Port.	34	38.43 N	9.08 W
Lisbon, Il., U.S.	216	41.29 N	88.29 W
Lisbon, Md., U.S.	208	39.20 N	77.04 W
Lisbon, N.H., U.S.	188	44.12 N	71.54 W
Lisbon, N.D., U.S.	198	46.26 N	97.40 W
Lisbon, Oh., U.S.	214	40.46 N	80.46 W
Lisbon Falls	188	43.59 N	70.03 W
Lisbonne → Lisboa	34	38.43 N	9.08 W
Lisburn	48	54.31 N	6.03 W
Lisburne, Cape ›	180	68.52 N	166.14 W
Lisburne Peninsula ›[1]	180	68.30 N	165.15 W
Liscannor Bay ⊂	48	52.55 N	9.25 W
Liscarney	48	53.43 N	9.35 W
Liscia ≃	71	41.11 N	9.19 E
Liscia, Lago di ⊜	71	41.00 N	9.16 E
Lisdoonvarna	48	53.01 N	9.15 W
Lisec	78	48.52 N	24.36 E
Liseleje	41	56.01 N	11.59 E
Lishan, Zhg.	100	31.50 N	113.16 E
Lishan, Zhg.	104	41.10 N	123.00 E
Lishangzhuang	105	39.35 N	118.11 E
Lishanke	98	40.41 N	119.53 E
Lishe	100	29.48 N	121.28 E
Lishe ≃	102	24.18 N	101.32 E
Lishi, Zhg.	102	37.32 N	111.09 E
Lishi, Zhg.	106	31.14 N	120.37 E
Lishi, Zhg.	107	29.10 N	105.42 E
Lishizhen, Zhg.	107	29.04 N	106.15 E
Lishizhen, Zhg.	107	29.20 N	105.24 E
Lishu	89	43.21 N	124.37 E
Lishui, Zhg.	100	28.27 N	119.54 E
Lishui, Zhg.	106	31.39 N	119.01 E
Lishuzhen	89	45.05 N	130.41 E
Lisianski Island I	14	26.02 N	174.00 W
Lisica ≃	86	58.34 N	85.11 E
Lisičansk	83	48.55 N	38.26 E
Lisichansk → Lisičansk	83	48.55 N	38.26 E
Lisicy	82	56.47 N	36.21 E
Lisieux, Sk., Can.	184	49.17 N	105.59 W
Lisieux, Fr.	50	49.09 N	0.14 E
Lisij Nos	265a	60.01 N	30.00 E
Líšina	60	49.37 N	13.10 E
Lisitu	154	9.39 S	34.39 E
Lisizhuang	105	38.55 N	115.07 E
Lisja	80	57.15 N	54.22 E
Liska ≃	80	48.32 N	43.08 E
Liskeard	42	50.28 N	4.28 W
Liski → Georgiu-Dež, S.S.S.R.	78	50.59 N	39.30 E
Liski, S.S.S.R.	78	50.56 N	39.29 E
Lískova	60	49.25 N	12.43 E
L'Isle, Schw.	58	46.37 N	6.25 E
Lisle, Il., U.S.	216	41.48 N	88.04 W
Lisle, N.Y., U.S.	210	42.21 N	76.00 W
L'Isle-Adam	50	49.07 N	2.14 E
L'Isle Jourdain	32	46.14 N	0.41 E
L'Isle-sur-la-Sorgue	62	43.55 N	5.03 E
L'Isle-sur-le-Doubs	58	47.27 N	6.35 E
L'Isle-sur-Serein	50	47.35 N	4.00 E
Lisman	194	32.10 N	88.16 W
Lismore, Austl.	166	28.48 S	153.17 E
Lismore, Austl.	169	37.58 S	143.20 E
Lismore, N.S., Can.	186	45.42 N	62.16 W
Lismore, Ire.	48	52.08 N	7.55 W
Lismore Castle ⊥	48	52.08 N	7.52 W
Lismore Island I	46	56.29 N	5.33 W
Lisnaskea	48	54.15 N	7.27 W
Lišn'ovka	78	51.28 N	25.25 E
Lisö ›[1]	40	58.55 N	17.45 E
Lišov	61	49.01 N	14.37 E
Liss	42	51.03 N	0.55 W
Lissabon → Lisboa	34	38.43 N	9.08 W
Lissberg	56	50.22 N	9.05 E
Lisse	52	52.15 N	4.33 E
Lisses	261	48.36 N	2.26 E
Lissewege	50	51.18 N	3.11 E
Lissie	222	29.33 N	96.13 W
Lissingen	56	50.14 N	6.38 E
Lissone	62	45.37 N	9.14 E
Lissy	261	48.38 N	2.42 E
Lista	80	47.44 N	45.54 E
Lista ›[1]	26	58.07 N	6.40 E
Lister ≃	263	51.05 N	7.45 E
Lištica	36	43.23 N	17.36 E
Listowel, On., Can.	212	43.44 N	80.57 W
Listowel, Ire.	48	52.27 N	9.29 W
Listv'anka	88	51.52 N	104.51 E
Listv'anskij	86	54.27 N	83.29 E
Lisui	105	40.05 N	116.44 E
Lit	26	63.19 N	14.49 E
Lita	100	27.22 N	116.34 E
Litang, Malay.	112	5.20 N	118.31 E
Litang, Zhg.	102	23.11 N	109.05 E
Litang, Zhg.	102	30.00 N	100.16 E
Litang ≃	102	28.04 N	101.30 E
Litani (Itany) ≃	250	3.40 N	54.00 W
Līṭānī, Nahr al- ≃	132	33.20 N	35.14 E
Litava ≃	61	49.02 N	16.36 E
Litcham	42	52.44 N	0.47 E
Litchfield, Ct., U.S.	207	41.44 N	73.11 W
Litchfield, Il., U.S.	219	39.10 N	89.39 W
Litchfield, Mi., U.S.	216	42.02 N	84.45 W
Litchfield, Mn., U.S.	190	45.07 N	94.31 W
Litchfield, Ne., U.S.	198	41.09 N	99.09 W
Litchfield, Oh., U.S.	214	41.10 N	82.02 W
Litchfield □[6]	207	41.45 N	73.11 W
Litchfield Park	200	33.29 N	112.21 W
Litchville	198	46.39 N	98.11 W
Literberry	219	39.51 N	90.12 W
Līth, Wādī al- V	144	20.40 N	40.35 E
Litherland	44	53.28 N	2.59 W
Lithgow	170	33.29 S	150.09 E
Lithia	220	27.51 N	82.10 W
Líthinon, Ákra ›	38	34.55 N	24.44 E
Lithonia	192	33.42 N	84.06 W
Lithuania → Litovskaja Sovetskaja Socialističeskaja Respublika □[3]	76	56.00 N	24.00 E
Litian	100	26.58 N	114.10 E
Litija	36	46.03 N	14.50 E
Litin	78	49.20 N	28.05 E
Litipāra	124	24.42 N	87.37 E
Lititz	208	40.09 N	76.18 W
Litke	89	53.57 N	140.15 E
Litókhoron	38	40.06 N	22.30 E
Litoko	154	1.13 S	24.47 E
Litoměřice	54	50.35 N	14.09 E
Litomyšl	30	49.52 N	16.19 E
Litoo	154	9.54 S	38.24 E
Litoral, Cordillera del ⋀	286c	10.33 N	66.52 W
Litouqiao	106	31.15 N	118.54 E
Litovel	30	49.42 N	17.05 E
Litovko	89	49.15 N	135.11 E
Litovskaja Sovetskaja Socialističeskaja Respublika □[3]	76	56.00 N	24.00 E
Litschau	61	48.57 N	15.03 E
Littau	58	47.03 N	8.16 E
Little ≃, Austl.	169	38.01 S	144.35 E
Little ≃, On., Can.	281	42.20 N	82.56 W
Little ≃, U.S.	194	35.32 N	90.25 W
Little ≃, U.S.	194	33.37 N	93.52 W
Little ≃, Al., U.S.	194	31.18 N	87.46 W
Little ≃, Al., U.S.	194	34.16 N	85.40 W
Little ≃, Ct., U.S.	207	41.36 N	72.03 W
Little ≃, Ga., U.S.	192	30.51 N	83.21 W
Little ≃, Ga., U.S.	192	33.14 N	83.24 W
Little ≃, Ga., U.S.	192	33.39 N	82.32 W
Little ≃, In., U.S.	216	40.53 N	85.32 W
Little ≃, Ky., U.S.	194	36.51 N	87.58 W
Little ≃, La., U.S.	194	31.38 N	91.49 W
Little ≃, Ma., U.S.	283	42.37 N	70.42 W
Little ≃, Ma., U.S.	283	42.46 N	70.51 W
Little ≃, N.Y., U.S.	210	43.18 N	75.43 W
Little ≃, N.C., U.S.	192	35.21 N	78.02 W
Little ≃, N.C., U.S.	192	35.15 N	78.42 W
Little ≃, Ok., U.S.	196	35.00 N	96.25 W
Little ≃, S.C., U.S.	192	34.11 N	81.45 W
Little ≃, S.C., U.S.	192	34.10 N	81.11 W
Little ≃, S.C., U.S.	192	33.56 N	82.25 W
Little ≃, Tn., U.S.	192	35.51 N	83.57 W
Little ≃, Tx., U.S.	222	30.51 N	96.41 W
Little ≃, Va., U.S.	192	37.05 N	80.32 W
Little ≃, Va., U.S.	208	37.49 N	77.26 W
Little, Mountain Fork ≃	194	33.57 N	94.34 W
Little Abaco Island I	238	26.53 N	77.43 W
Little Amwell	260	51.47 N	0.02 W
Little Andaman I	110	10.45 N	92.30 E
Little Arkansas ≃	198	37.43 N	97.22 W
Little Auglaize ≃	216	41.07 N	84.25 W
Little Averill Lake ⊜	206	44.57 N	71.44 W
Little Baddow	260	51.44 N	0.35 E
Little Barrier Island I	172	36.12 S	175.05 E
Little Bay	186	47.41 N	58.24 W
Little Bay ⊂	276	40.48 N	73.47 W
Little Bay Islands	186	49.39 N	55.47 W
Little Bear ≃	200	41.42 N	111.57 W
Little Bear Creek ≃	196	37.43 N	101.43 W
Little Bear Creek Reservoir ⊜[1]	194	34.25 N	87.57 W
Little Beaver Creek ≃, U.S.	198	39.49 N	101.03 W
Little Beaver Creek ≃, U.S.	198	46.17 N	103.56 W
Little Beaver Creek ≃, U.S.	214	40.38 N	80.31 W
Little Beaver Creek ≃, Wa., U.S.	224	48.54 N	121.06 W
Little Beaver Creek, Middle Fork ≃	214	40.43 N	80.37 W
Little Beaver Creek, North Fork ≃	214	40.43 N	80.33 W
Little Beaver Creek, West Fork ≃	214	40.43 N	80.37 W
Little Belt → Lillebælt ꭒ	41	55.20 N	9.45 E
Little Belt Mountains ⋀	202	46.45 N	110.35 W
Little Berkhamsted	260	51.45 N	0.08 W
Little Bighorn ≃	202	45.44 N	107.34 W
Little Billabong	171b	35.35 S	147.32 E
Little Bitter Lake → Murrah aṣ-Ṣughrā, Al-Buḥayrah al- ⊜	142	30.13 N	32.33 E
Little Bitterroot ≃	202	47.30 N	114.19 W
Little Black ≃, U.S.	194	36.25 N	90.45 W
Little Black ≃, Ak., U.S.	180	66.26 N	143.49 W
Little Black Bear Indian Reserve ◆[4]	184	51.00 N	103.23 W
Little Blackfoot ≃	202	46.31 N	112.48 W
Little Blue ≃, U.S.	198	39.41 N	96.40 W
Little Blue ≃, In., U.S.	218	39.32 N	85.46 W
Littleborough	44	53.39 N	2.05 W
Little Bow ≃	182	49.53 N	112.29 W
Little Brazos ≃	222	30.38 N	96.31 W
Little Brokenstraw Creek ≃	214	41.50 N	79.23 W
Little Brosna ≃	48	53.10 N	8.05 W
Little Buffalo ≃	176	61.00 N	113.46 W
Little Bullhead	184	51.40 N	96.51 W
Little Burstead	260	51.36 N	0.24 E
Little Calumet ≃	278	41.39 N	87.34 W
Little Catalina	186	48.33 N	53.02 W
Little Cayman I	238	19.41 N	80.03 W
Little Cedar ≃	190	42.57 N	92.31 W
Little Chalfont	260	51.40 N	0.34 W
Little Chartiers Creek ≃	279b	40.17 N	80.08 W
Little Choptank River ⊂	208	38.32 N	76.13 W
Little Churchill ≃	184	57.15 N	95.21 W
Little Chute	190	44.16 N	88.19 W
Little Coco Island I	110	14.00 N	93.13 E
Little Colorado ≃	200	36.11 N	111.48 W
Little Compton	207	41.30 N	71.10 W
Little Cooley	214	41.44 N	79.53 W
Little Cottonwood ≃	198	44.15 N	94.20 W
Little Creek	208	39.10 N	75.26 W
Little Creek ≃	285	39.56 N	74.48 W
Little Creek Naval Amphibious Base ■	208	36.55 N	76.10 W
Little Creek Reservoir ⊜[1]	208	37.20 N	76.50 W
Little Cumbrae Island I	46	55.43 N	4.57 W
Little Current	190	45.58 N	81.56 W
Little Current ≃	176	50.57 N	84.36 W
Little Cypress Bayou ≃	194	32.41 N	94.15 W
Little Cypress Creek ≃	222	32.39 N	94.42 W
Little Darby Creek ≃	218	39.53 N	83.13 W
Little Dart ≃	42	50.54 N	3.51 W
Little Deep Creek ≃	198	48.35 N	100.52 W
Little Deer Creek ≃, In., U.S.	216	40.36 N	86.28 W
Little Deer Creek ≃, Pa., U.S.	279b	40.33 N	79.50 W
Little Deschutes ≃	202	43.51 N	121.27 W
Little Desert ◆[2]	166	36.35 S	141.20 E
Little Desert National Park ♠	166	36.25 S	141.25 E
Little Diomede Island I	180	65.45 N	168.57 W
Little Don ≃	275b	43.42 N	79.20 W
Little Dry Creek ≃, Ca., U.S.	226	39.22 N	121.52 W
Little Dry Creek ≃, Mt., U.S.	202	47.21 N	106.22 W
Little Ease Run ≃	285	39.39 N	75.04 W
Little Eau Pleine ≃	190	44.40 N	89.41 W
Little Egg Harbor ⊂	208	39.35 N	74.18 W
Little Elkhart ≃	216	41.43 N	85.49 W
Little End	260	51.41 N	0.14 E
Little Etobicoke Creek ≃	275b	43.37 N	79.34 W
Little Fabius ≃	219	39.59 N	91.59 W
Little Falls, Mn., U.S.	190	45.58 N	94.21 W
Little Falls, N.J., U.S.	276	40.52 N	74.12 W
Little Falls, N.Y., U.S.	210	43.02 N	74.51 W
Little Falls ≃	208	39.36 N	76.38 W
Little Falls Dam ◆[6]	284c	38.57 N	77.08 W
Little Farms	218	39.57 N	83.10 W
Little Ferry	276	40.51 N	74.02 W
Littlefield	196	33.55 N	102.19 W
Little Flatrock ≃	218	39.26 N	85.33 W
Littlefork	190	48.23 N	93.33 W
Little Fork ≃	190	48.31 N	93.35 W
Little Fort	182	51.25 N	120.12 W
Little Genesee	210	42.02 N	78.13 W
Little Gold ≃	162	18.01 S	126.29 E
Little Gunpowder Falls ≃	208	39.23 N	76.22 W
Littlehampton	42	50.48 N	0.33 W
Little Harbour Deep	186	50.15 N	56.33 W
Little Haw Creek ≃	192	29.23 N	81.24 W
Little Hawk Lake ⊜	212	45.10 N	78.42 W
Little Hoosic ≃	210	42.49 N	73.20 W
Little Hope	214	42.06 N	79.49 W
Little Hulton	262	53.32 N	2.25 W
Little Humboldt ≃	204	41.00 N	117.43 W
Little Humboldt, North Fork ≃	204	41.24 N	117.10 W
Little Humboldt, South Fork ≃	204	41.24 N	117.10 W
Little Hurricane Creek ≃	192	31.23 N	82.19 W
Little Inagua I	238	21.30 N	73.00 W
Little Indian Creek ≃, Il., U.S.	216	41.31 N	88.46 W
Little Indian Creek ≃, In., U.S.	218	38.12 N	86.08 W
Little Island Pond ⊜	283	42.43 N	71.17 W
Littlejohns Creek ≃	226	37.52 N	121.14 W
Little Juniata ≃	214	40.34 N	78.03 W
Little Juniata Creek ≃	208	40.23 N	77.02 W
Little Kanawha ≃	188	39.16 N	81.34 W
Little Kanawha, West Fork ≃	188	38.57 N	81.16 W
Little Karroo (Klein Karroo) ⋀[1]	158	33.45 S	21.30 E
Little Kentucky ≃	218	38.41 N	85.12 W
Little Klickitat ≃	224	45.51 N	121.04 W
Little Koniuji Island I	180	55.01 N	159.26 W
Little Lake ⊜, On., Can.	212	44.26 N	79.40 W
Little Lake ⊜, La., U.S.	194	29.30 N	90.10 W
Little Laramie ≃	200	41.28 N	105.44 W
Little Laver	260	51.46 N	0.14 E
Little Leigh	262	53.17 N	2.35 W
Little Lever	262	53.34 N	2.22 W
Little Limestone Lake ⊜	184	53.46 N	99.18 W
Little London	241q	18.15 N	78.13 W
Little Lost ≃	202	43.46 N	112.58 W
Little Lun ≃	116	6.02 N	125.17 E
Little Mahoning Creek ≃	214	40.49 N	79.00 W
Little Maitland ≃	212	43.52 N	81.18 W
Little Manatee ≃	220	27.42 N	82.28 W
Little Manatee, South Fork ≃	220	27.39 N	82.18 W
Little Manistee ≃	190	44.15 N	86.19 W
Little Manitou Lake ⊜	184	51.45 N	105.30 W
Little Marco Pass ⊂	220	26.01 N	81.46 W
Little Marsh	210	41.53 N	77.24 W
Little Meadows	210	41.59 N	76.08 W
Little Mecatina ≃	176	50.28 N	59.35 W
Little Medicine Bow ≃	200	41.58 N	106.18 W
Little Mexico	196	30.57 N	102.52 W
Little Miami ≃	218	39.05 N	84.26 W
Little Miami, East Fork ≃	218	39.09 N	84.18 W
Little Miami, North Fork ≃	218	39.48 N	83.47 W
Little Miami, Todd Fork ≃	218	39.21 N	84.08 W
Little Miami, Todd Fork, East Fork ≃	218	39.24 N	84.00 W
Littlemill	46	57.32 N	3.49 W
Little Mississippi ≃	212	45.17 N	77.35 W
Little Missouri ≃, U.S.	198	47.30 N	102.25 W
Little Missouri ≃, Ar., U.S.	194	33.49 N	92.54 W
Little Mountain ʌ	208	40.47 N	76.40 W
Little Muddy ≃, Il., U.S.	194	37.50 N	89.11 W
Little Muddy ≃, N.D., U.S.	198	48.12 N	103.36 W
Little Mulberry Creek ≃	194	32.26 N	86.51 W
Little Naches ≃	224	46.58 N	121.08 W
Little Nahant	283	42.25 N	70.56 W
Little Namaqualand □[9]	156	29.00 S	17.00 E
Little Neck	283	42.42 N	70.48 W
Little Neck ◆[8]	276	40.46 N	73.44 W
Little Neck Bay ⊂	276	40.47 N	73.46 W
Little Nemaha ≃	198	40.19 N	95.40 W
Little Neshaminy Creek ≃	285	40.15 N	75.02 W
Little Niangua ≃	194	38.04 N	92.54 W
Little Nicobar I	110	7.20 N	93.40 E
Little Ohoopee ≃	192	32.27 N	82.24 W
Little Osage ≃	194	38.02 N	94.14 W
Little Otter Creek ≃	212	42.44 N	80.51 W
Little Ouse ≃	42	52.30 N	0.22 E
Little Panoche Creek ≃	226	36.50 N	120.42 W
Little Patuxent ≃	284b	39.11 N	76.52 W
Little Paxton	42	52.15 N	0.15 W
Little Peconic Bay ⊂	207	40.59 N	72.24 W
Little Pee Dee ≃	192	33.42 N	79.11 W
Little Pic ≃	190	48.48 N	86.37 W
Little Pine and Lucky Man Indian Reserve ◆[4]	184	52.56 N	109.05 W
Little Pine Creek ≃, Pa., U.S.	210	41.18 N	77.22 W
Little Pine Creek ≃, Pa., U.S.	279b	40.31 N	79.57 W
Little Pine Island I	220	26.36 N	82.05 W
Little Pine Key I	220	24.44 N	81.19 W
Little Pine State Park ♠	210	41.22 N	77.20 W
Little Pipe Creek ≃	208	39.36 N	77.16 W
Little Platte ≃	194	39.24 N	94.41 W
Little Plum Creek ≃	279b	40.30 N	79.51 W
Little Popo Aggie ≃	202	42.54 N	108.35 W
Little Porcupine Creek ≃, Mt., U.S.	202	46.18 N	106.34 W
Little Porcupine Creek ≃, Mt., U.S.	202	48.02 N	106.04 W
Littleport	42	52.28 N	0.19 E
Little Portage Creek ≃	216	42.00 N	85.27 W
Little Powder ≃	198	45.28 N	105.20 W
Little Pucketa Creek ≃	279b	40.33 N	79.45 W
Little Quill Lake ⊜	184	51.55 N	104.05 W
Little Rann of Kachchh ≚	120	23.25 N	71.15 E
Little Red ≃	194	35.11 N	91.27 W
Little Red, Middle Fork ≃	194	35.37 N	92.11 W
Little Red Deer ≃	182	52.04 N	114.09 W
Little Red River Indian Reserve ◆[4]	184	53.30 N	105.58 W
Little Redstone Lake ⊜	212	45.13 N	78.34 W
Little River, Austl.	169	37.58 S	144.30 E
Little River, N.Z.	172	43.46 S	172.47 E
Little River, Ks., U.S.	198	38.23 N	98.00 W
Little River, Tx., U.S.	222	30.59 N	97.22 W
Little Rock, Ar., U.S.	194	34.44 N	92.17 W
Littlerock, Ca., U.S.	228	34.31 N	117.59 W
Little Rock, Il., U.S.	216	41.43 N	88.34 W
Little Rock, Ia., U.S.	198	43.26 N	95.52 W
Littlerock, Wa., U.S.	224	46.54 N	123.01 W
Little Rock ≃	198	43.16 N	96.15 W
Little Rock Air Force Base ■	194	34.55 N	92.10 W
Little Rock Creek ≃	228	34.28 N	118.01 W
Little Rock Wash V	228	34.42 N	118.02 W
Little Rocky Mountains ⋀	202	47.50 N	108.10 W
Little Rouge Creek ≃	212	43.48 N	79.08 W
Little Ruaha ≃	154	7.17 S	35.28 E
Little Sable Point ›	190	43.38 N	86.32 W
Little Sac ≃	194	37.39 N	93.46 W
Little Sachigo Lake ⊜	184	54.09 N	92.11 W
Little Saint Bernard Pass → Petit-Saint-Bernard, Col du)(	62	45.41 N	6.53 E
Little Salkehatchie ≃	192	32.37 N	80.53 W
Little Salmon ≃, Id., U.S.	202	45.25 N	116.19 W
Little Salmon ≃, N.Y., U.S.	212	43.32 N	76.16 W
Little Salmon, North Branch ≃	212	43.24 N	76.09 W
Little Salmon, South Branch ≃	212	43.24 N	76.09 W
Little Salmon Lake ⊜	180	62.12 N	134.45 W
Little Salt Lake ⊜	200	37.55 N	112.53 W
Little Sandy ≃	188	38.35 N	82.51 W
Little Sandy, East Fork ≃	188	38.30 N	82.50 W
Little Sandy Creek ≃	200	42.06 N	109.27 W
Little Sandy Desert ◆[2]	162	24.20 S	120.50 E
Little Saskatchewan ≃	184	49.52 N	100.07 W
Little Scarcies ≃	150	8.51 N	13.09 W
Little Scioto ≃, Oh., U.S.	214	40.31 N	83.12 W
Little Scioto ≃, Oh., U.S.	218	38.46 N	82.53 W
Little Sewickley Creek ≃, Pa., U.S.	279b	40.15 N	79.45 W
Little Sewickley Creek ≃, Pa., U.S.	279b	40.33 N	80.12 W
Little Silver	276	40.20 N	74.02 W
Little Sioux ≃	198	41.49 N	96.04 W
Little Sioux, West Fork ≃	198	42.04 N	96.00 W
Little Sitkin Island I	181a	51.55 N	178.30 E
Little Smoky ≃	182	55.42 N	117.38 W
Little Snake ≃	200	40.27 N	108.26 W
Little Sodus Bay ⊂	210	43.20 N	76.43 W
Little Southwest Miramichi ≃	186	46.57 N	65.50 W
Little Stanney	262	53.15 N	2.53 W
Little Stony Creek ≃	226	39.20 N	122.31 W
Little Stour ≃	42	51.19 N	1.15 E
Littlestown	208	39.44 N	77.05 W
Little Stukeley	42	52.21 N	0.13 W
Little Sugarloaf ʌ[2]	274b	37.41 S	145.19 E
Little Sur ≃	226	36.20 N	121.54 W
Little Sutton	262	53.17 N	2.57 W
Little Swatara Creek ≃	208	40.24 N	76.29 W
Little Tallapoosa ≃	192	33.18 N	85.34 W
Little Tanaga Island I	180	51.48 N	176.10 W
Little Tennessee ≃	192	35.47 N	84.15 W
Little Thurrock	260	51.28 N	0.21 E
Little Timber Creek ≃	285	39.53 N	75.08 W
Little Tinicum Island I	285	39.51 N	75.17 W
Little Tobago I, Br. Vir. Is.	240m	18.26 N	64.51 W
Little Tobago I, Trin.	241r	11.18 N	60.30 W
Little Toby Creek ≃	214	41.22 N	78.49 W
Littleton, Eng., U.K.	260	51.24 N	0.28 W
Littleton, Co., U.S.	200	39.36 N	105.00 W
Littleton, Ma., U.S.	207	42.32 N	71.30 W
Littleton, N.H., U.S.	188	44.18 N	71.46 W
Littleton, N.C., U.S.	192	36.26 N	77.54 W
Littleton, W.V., U.S.	188	39.41 N	80.31 W
Little Traverse Bay ⊂	190	45.24 N	85.03 W
Little Truckee ≃	226	39.25 N	120.05 W
Little Turtle ≃	184	48.46 N	92.36 W
Little Turtle State Recreation Area ♠	216	40.50 N	85.26 W
Little Valley	210	42.15 N	78.48 W
Little Vermilion ≃	216	41.20 N	89.05 W
Little Vermilion Lake ⊜	184	51.16 N	93.50 W
Little Vienna Estates	284c	38.54 N	77.18 W
Little Wabash ≃	194	37.54 N	88.05 W
Little Walsingham	42	52.54 N	0.51 E
Little Waltham	260	51.47 N	0.29 E
Little Warley	260	51.35 N	0.19 E
Little Washita ≃	196	34.58 N	97.51 W
Little White ≃	198	43.44 N	100.40 W
Little White Mountain ʌ	182	49.42 N	119.20 W
Little White Salmon ≃	224	45.43 N	121.38 W
Little Wichita ≃	196	33.54 N	97.59 W
Little Wichita, East Fork ≃	196	33.52 N	98.07 W
Little Wind ≃	202	42.57 N	108.29 W
Little Wind, North Fork ≃	202	43.01 N	108.53 W
Little Wind, South Fork ≃	202	43.01 N	108.53 W
Little Wolf ≃	190	44.23 N	88.48 W
Little Wood ≃	202	42.57 N	114.21 W
Little York, In., U.S.	218	38.42 N	85.54 W
Little York, N.Y., U.S.	210	42.42 N	76.10 W
Little Zab (Zāb-e Kūchek) (Az-Zāb aṣ-Ṣaghīr) ≃	128	35.12 N	43.25 E
Littoral □[4]	152	4.13 N	10.25 E
Litunga	152	13.17 S	16.43 E
Litvínov	54	50.37 N	13.36 E
Litvinovka	83	49.18 N	39.27 E
Litvinovo	76	59.34 N	38.01 E
Litvinskoje	86	50.42 N	72.42 E
Litzmannstadt → Łódź	30	51.46 N	19.30 E
Liu ≃, Zhg.	98	42.45 N	126.04 E
Liu ≃, Zhg.	98	41.48 N	122.43 E
Liu ≃, Zhg.	98	40.38 N	118.09 E
Liu ≃, Zhg.	102	23.52 N	109.45 E
Liu ≃, Zhg.	105	40.38 N	118.09 E
Liu ≃, Zhg.	106	31.31 N	121.18 E
Liuanzhuang	105	39.14 N	117.11 E
Liuba	102	33.32 N	107.07 E
Liubotong	100	31.26 N	116.00 E
Liucao	106	31.07 N	121.41 E
Liuchen	102	23.09 N	110.29 E
Liucheng, Zhg.	100	28.36 N	119.34 E
Liucheng, Zhg.	100	24.03 N	115.08 E
Liucheng, Zhg.	102	24.32 N	109.21 E
Liuchengba	102	27.27 N	102.53 E
Liuch'iu Hsü I	100	22.21 N	120.22 E
Liuchow → Liuzhou	102	24.19 N	109.24 E
Liucun	106	30.44 N	119.23 E
Liucura	252	38.39 S	71.05 W
Liudaogou	98	41.34 N	127.12 E
Liudaohe	105	40.39 N	116.12 E
Liudongqiao	106	31.03 N	119.32 E
Liudu	100	26.44 N	119.33 E
Liuduo	100	34.01 N	120.17 E
Liuduzhuang	105	39.27 N	117.50 E
Liuerbao	104	41.13 N	122.55 E
Liufang	100	27.56 N	116.22 E
Liufangling	100	30.27 N	114.27 E
Liufentzu	269d	24.57 N	121.35 E
Liugezhuang, Zhg.	98	38.33 N	116.30 E
Liugezhuang, Zhg.	105	40.03 N	118.16 E
Liugou	105	40.57 N	118.18 E
Liugu ≃	98	40.22 N	120.26 E
Liuguan	100	29.56 N	113.08 E
Liuguantun	104	41.20 N	121.21 E
Liuhang	106	31.21 N	121.22 E
Liuhe, Zhg.	98	42.15 N	125.43 E
Liuhe, Zhg.	100	33.20 N	112.48 E
Liuhe, Zhg.	100	32.22 N	118.49 E
Liuhe, Zhg.	100	30.46 N	113.12 E
Liuhe, Zhg.	100	30.20 N	115.36 E
Liuhe, Zhg.	105	39.31 N	118.17 E
Liuhe, Zhg.	106	31.30 N	121.15 E
Liuhegou	104	41.56 N	122.44 E
Liuheita	104	42.09 N	123.56 E
Liuhejie	102	24.26 N	101.35 E
Liuhekou	105	40.39 N	118.09 E
Liuheng Dao I	100	29.43 N	122.08 E
Liuhuang	100	23.58 N	116.28 E
Liuhudang	104	42.31 N	122.22 E
Liujia	102	24.54 N	107.49 E
Liujiachang	107	29.46 N	103.49 E
Liujiachuan	105	40.07 N	114.47 E
Liujiadai	106	31.57 N	120.23 E
Liujiadian	89	50.07 N	124.17 E
Liujiadu	106	32.15 N	120.33 E
Liujiafen	105	39.58 N	115.47 E
Liujiagangzi	104	41.28 N	122.33 E
Liujiagou	98	37.47 N	120.53 E
Liujiahe, Zhg.	100	32.06 N	113.21 E
Liujiahe, Zhg.	104	40.40 N	123.58 E
Liujiang	98	40.04 N	119.34 E
Liujiashan	105	40.14 N	114.49 E
Liujiatun, Zhg.	104	41.52 N	122.44 E
Liujiatun, Zhg.	104	41.51 N	122.05 E
Liujiatun, Zhg.	104	42.08 N	122.44 E
Liujiawopeng	104	42.16 N	123.01 E
Liujiazhai	269b	31.21 N	121.27 E
Liujiazhen	106	32.04 N	121.30 E
Liujiazi, Zhg.	98	41.00 N	120.13 E
Liujiazi, Zhg.	104	42.36 N	122.15 E
Liujiazi, Zhg.	104	41.48 N	123.47 E
Liujingcun	105	39.27 N	115.26 E
Liujisu	105	40.01 N	117.13 E
Liukeshu	86	44.59 N	90.12 E
Liuku	102	25.48 N	98.52 E
Liuli	154	11.05 S	34.38 E
Liulicun	271a	39.56 N	116.28 E
Liulidian	106	31.31 N	119.17 E
Liuligou	104	41.24 N	121.29 E
Liulihezhen	105	39.36 N	116.01 E
Liulin	100	31.34 N	113.14 E
Liuliwei	100	24.20 N	114.03 E
Liulongtai	104	41.32 N	120.56 E
Liumachang	107	29.51 N	104.54 E
Liumaogou	89	48.12 N	127.13 E
Liupangtun	104	41.36 N	123.28 E
Liupan Shan ⋀	102	35.40 N	106.40 E
Liuqianhutun	104	42.01 N	123.41 E
Liuqiao	106	32.11 N	120.51 E
Liuquan, Zhg.	98	34.27 N	117.20 E
Liuquan, Zhg.	105	39.22 N	116.18 E
Liurenba	100	29.57 N	114.49 E
Liushi, Zhg.	98	38.33 N	115.44 E
Liushi, Zhg.	100	28.03 N	120.51 E
Liushilipu	100	32.45 N	115.58 E
Liushi Shan ʌ	120	36.15 N	82.05 E
Liushouying	98	39.48 N	119.19 E
Liushudian	98	35.54 N	119.30 E
Liushudixia	104	42.26 N	121.14 E
Liushui	89	44.17 N	124.15 E
Liushuigou	100	31.34 N	112.27 E
Liushuquan	105	39.21 N	118.06 E
Liusiqiao	100	29.47 N	116.21 E
Liusong	105	39.40 N	117.08 E
Liuta	98	35.52 N	115.18 E
Liutai	98	41.20 N	113.43 E
Liutaizi	104	41.46 N	122.39 E
Liutang	102	24.58 N	110.21 E
Liutiaozhaicun	104	41.29 N	123.12 E
Liutuan	98	36.56 N	119.22 E
Liutuhutun	104	40.44 N	120.32 E
Liuwanglou	98	34.48 N	116.28 E
Liuwa Plain ≚	152	14.30 S	22.40 E
Liuwa Plain National Park ♠	152	14.30 S	22.40 E
Liuwei	106	32.16 N	119.28 E
Liuwudian	100	24.36 N	118.13 E
Liuxi ≃	100	23.22 N	112.54 E
Liuxia	106	30.15 N	120.03 E
Liuyang	100	28.09 N	113.38 E
Liuyang ≃	100	28.13 N	112.53 E
Liuyuan	98	36.10 N	114.34 E
Liuyuankou	98	34.54 N	114.20 E
Liuzhai	102	25.15 N	107.20 E
Liuzhou	102	24.19 N	109.24 E
Liuzhuang	100	33.10 N	120.19 E
Livada	38	47.52 N	23.07 E
Livadija	89	42.50 N	132.39 E
Livanátai	38	38.42 N	23.03 E
Līvāni	76	56.22 N	26.11 E
Livanjsko Polje ≚	36	43.55 N	16.45 E
Livanovka	86	52.06 N	61.59 E
Livarot	50	49.01 N	0.09 E
Lively, On., Can.	190	46.26 N	81.09 W
Lively, Va., U.S.	208	37.47 N	76.31 W
Lively Island I	254	52.02 S	58.30 W
Livengood	180	65.32 N	148.33 W
Livenka, S.S.S.R.	78	50.26 N	38.18 E
Livenka, S.S.S.R.	78	50.44 N	40.14 E
Livenza ≃	64	45.35 N	12.51 E
Live Oak, Ca., U.S.	226	39.16 N	121.39 W
Live Oak, Fl., U.S.	192	30.17 N	82.59 W
Live Oak Creek ≃	196	30.39 N	101.42 W
Liverdun	56	48.45 N	6.03 E
Liverdy-en-Brie	261	48.42 N	2.47 E
Livergnano	66	44.19 N	11.21 E
Liveringa	162	18.03 S	124.10 E
Livermore, Ca., U.S.	226	37.40 N	121.46 W
Livermore, Ia., U.S.	190	42.52 N	94.11 W
Livermore, Ky., U.S.	194	37.29 N	87.07 W
Livermore, Mount ʌ	196	30.38 N	104.10 W
Livermore Falls	188	44.28 N	70.11 W
Liverpool, Austl.	170	33.54 S	150.56 E
Liverpool, N.S., Can.	186	44.02 N	64.43 W
Liverpool, Eng., U.K.	44	53.25 N	2.55 W
Liverpool, Eng., U.K.	262	53.25 N	2.55 W
Liverpool, In., U.S.	216	41.34 N	87.18 W
Liverpool, N.Y., U.S.	210	43.06 N	76.13 W
Liverpool, Pa., U.S.	208	40.34 N	76.59 W
Liverpool, Tx., U.S.	222	29.18 N	95.17 W
Liverpool □[8]	262	53.25 N	2.55 W
Liverpool ≃	164	12.02 S	134.13 E
Liverpool (Speke) Airport ⊠	44	53.21 N	2.52 W
Liverpool, Cape ›	176	73.38 N	78.06 W
Liverpool, University of ᵿ[2]	262	53.24 N	2.58 W
Liverpool Bay ⊂, N.T., Can.	180	69.45 N	130.00 W
Liverpool Bay ⊂, N.S., Can.	186	44.02 N	64.41 W
Liverpool Bay ⊂, Eng., U.K.	44	53.30 N	3.16 W
Liverpool Football Ground ♠	262	53.26 N	2.57 W
Liverpool Heights	210	43.07 N	76.13 W
Liverpool Range ⋀	166	31.40 S	150.30 E
Liverpool Street Station ◆[5]	260	51.31 N	0.05 W
Livet-et-Gavet	62	45.06 N	5.56 E
Livigno	64	46.32 N	10.04 E
Livilliers	261	49.06 N	2.06 E
Lívingston, Guat.	236	15.50 N	88.45 W
Livingston, Scot., U.K.	46	55.53 N	3.32 W
Livingston, Al., U.S.	194	32.35 N	88.11 W
Livingston, Ca., U.S.	226	37.23 N	120.43 W
Livingston, Il., U.S.	194	38.58 N	89.45 W
Livingston, Ky., U.S.	192	37.17 N	84.12 W
Livingston, La., U.S.	194	30.30 N	90.44 W
Livingston, Mt., U.S.	202	45.39 N	110.33 W
Livingston, N.J., U.S.	210	40.47 N	74.18 W
Livingston, N.Y., U.S.	210	42.09 N	73.47 W
Livingston, Tn., U.S.	194	36.23 N	85.19 W
Livingston, Tx., U.S.	222	30.42 N	94.55 W
Livingston, Wi., U.S.	190	42.54 N	90.25 W
Livingston □[6], Il., U.S.	216	40.53 N	88.38 W
Livingston □[6], Mi., U.S.	216	42.38 N	83.50 W
Livingston □[6], N.Y., U.S.	210	42.48 N	77.49 W
Livingstone	154	17.50 S	25.53 E
Livingstone, Chutes de (Livingstone Falls) ᒐ	152	4.50 S	14.30 E
Livingstone, Lake ⊜[1]	222	30.50 N	95.30 W
Livingstone Falls → Livingstone, Chutes de ᒐ	152	4.50 S	14.30 E
Livingstone Lake ⊜	212	45.22 N	78.43 W
Livingstonia	154	10.36 S	34.07 E
Livingston Island I	9	62.35 S	60.30 W
Livingston Mall ◆[9]	276	40.47 N	74.21 W
Livingston Manor	210	41.54 N	74.49 W
Livno	36	43.50 N	17.01 E
Livny	76	52.25 N	37.37 E
Livojoki ≃	26	65.24 N	26.48 E
Livonia, In., U.S.	218	38.34 N	86.17 W
Livonia, La., U.S.	194	30.33 N	91.33 W
Livonia, Mi., U.S.	216	42.22 N	83.21 W
Livonia, N.Y., U.S.	210	42.49 N	77.40 W
Livonia Center	210	42.49 N	77.38 W
Livonia Mall ◆[9]	281	42.26 N	83.20 W
Livorno (Leghorn)	66	43.33 N	10.19 E
Livorno □[4]	66	43.14 N	10.35 E
Livorno Ferraris	62	45.17 N	8.05 E
Livourne → Livorno	66	43.33 N	10.19 E
Livramento → Santana do Livramento	252	30.53 S	55.31 W
Livramento do Brumado	255	13.39 S	41.50 W
Livron-sur-Drôme	62	44.46 N	4.51 E
Livry-Gargan	261	48.56 N	2.33 E
Livry-sur-Seine	261	48.31 N	2.41 E
Liwa	112	5.04 S	104.06 E
Liwale	154	9.46 S	37.56 E
Liwale Chini	154	9.41 S	38.01 E
Liwan	154	4.54 N	35.40 E
Liwonde	154	14.52 S	35.28 E
Liwonde National Park ♠	154	14.50 S	35.20 E
Liwung ≃	115a	6.08 S	106.49 E
Lixi, Zhg.	100	27.39 N	116.19 E
Lixi, Zhg.	100	29.15 N	114.46 E
Lixian, Zhg.	98	38.29 N	115.34 E
Lixian, Zhg.	102	34.11 N	105.02 E
Lixian, Zhg.	102	29.30 N	111.37 E
Lixian, Zhg.	105	39.33 N	116.26 E
Lixian → Black ≃	110	21.15 N	105.20 E
Lixin, Zhg.	100	26.52 N	116.42 E
Lixin, Zhg.	100	33.06 N	116.08 E
Lixing	100	33.28 N	115.28 E
Lixingzhuang	105	39.25 N	117.56 E
Lixoúrion	38	38.12 N	20.26 E
Lixus ⊥	34	35.16 N	6.13 W
Liyang, Zhg.	98	37.28 N	113.37 E
Liyang, Zhg.	106	31.26 N	119.29 E
Liyuanbao	100	25.16 N	112.55 E
Liyujiang	100	25.57 N	113.15 E
Lizard	42	49.58 N	5.12 W
Lizarda	250	9.36 S	46.41 W
Lizard Head Peak ʌ	200	42.47 N	109.11 W
Lizard Island I	164	14.40 S	145.28 E
Lizard Point ›	42	49.56 N	5.13 W
Lizard Point Indian Reserve ◆[4]	184	50.40 N	100.57 W
Lize	107	30.08 N	106.11 E
Lizhai	106	31.34 N	121.45 E
Lizhou	102	28.08 N	102.10 E
Lizhu	100	29.56 N	120.30 E
Lizhuang, Zhg.	100	34.24 N	116.30 E
Lizhuang, Zhg.	107	28.47 N	104.46 E
Lizhuangqiao	106	31.48 N	119.37 E
Lizino	83	49.33 N	38.51 E
Lizinovka	78	50.08 N	39.28 E
Liziwei	107	30.19 N	106.39 E
Lizy-sur-Ourcq	50	49.01 N	3.02 E
Lizzana	64	45.51 N	11.03 E
Lizzanello	68	40.18 N	18.13 E
Lizzano	68	40.23 N	17.27 E
Lizzano in Belvedere	64	44.10 N	10.53 E
Ljalovo	82	56.03 N	37.14 E
Ljan	26	59.51 N	10.48 E
Ljubelj (Loiblpass))(	61	46.26 N	14.16 E
Ljubija	36	44.56 N	16.37 E
Ljubimec	38	41.50 N	26.05 E
Ljubinje	38	42.57 N	18.05 E
Ljubljana	36	46.03 N	14.31 E
Ljubovija	38	44.11 N	19.22 E
Ljubuški	36	43.12 N	17.33 E
Ljugarn	26	57.19 N	18.42 E
Ljunga	40	58.31 N	16.21 E
Ljungan ≃	26	62.19 N	17.23 E
Ljungaverk	26	62.29 N	16.03 E
Ljungby	26	56.50 N	13.56 E
Ljungbyhed	41	56.04 N	13.12 E
Ljungbyholm	26	56.38 N	16.10 E
Ljungdalen	26	62.51 N	12.47 E
Ljungsbro	26	58.31 N	15.30 E
Ljungskile	26	58.14 N	11.55 E
Ljusdal	26	61.50 N	16.05 E
Ljusfallshammar	40	58.47 N	15.29 E
Ljusnan ≃	26	61.12 N	17.08 E
Ljusnaren ⊜	40	59.51 N	14.56 E
Ljusne	26	61.13 N	17.08 E
Ljusterö I	40	59.31 N	18.37 E
Ljutomer	61	46.31 N	16.12 E
Llagas Creek ≃	226	36.58 N	121.31 W
Llaima, Volcán ʌ[1]	252	38.43 S	71.43 W
Llallagua	248	18.25 S	66.38 W
Llamara, Salar de ≚	248	21.13 S	69.40 W
Llanaber	42	52.45 N	4.05 W
Llanaelhaearn	42	52.59 N	4.24 W
Llanarth	42	52.12 N	4.18 W
Llanarthney	42	51.52 N	4.09 W
Llanbedrog	42	52.52 N	4.29 W
Llanberis, Pass of V	44	53.06 N	4.04 W
Llanbister	42	52.21 N	3.27 W
Llanboidy	42	51.54 N	4.36 W
Llanbryde	46	57.37 N	3.13 W
Llanbrynmair	42	52.37 N	3.57 W
Llançà	34	42.22 N	3.09 E
Llancanelo, Laguna ⊜	252	35.35 S	69.09 W
Llandaff	42	51.30 N	3.14 W
Llandaff Cathedral ᵿ[1]	42	51.29 N	3.15 W
Llanddewi Brefi	42	52.10 N	3.57 W
Llandeilo	42	51.52 N	3.59 W
Llandilo	274a	33.43 S	150.45 E
Llandinam	42	52.29 N	3.26 W
Llandissilio	42	51.53 N	4.44 W
Llandovery	42	51.59 N	3.48 W
Llandrindod Wells	42	52.15 N	3.23 W
Llandudno	44	53.19 N	3.49 W
Llandybie	42	51.50 N	4.00 W
Llandysul	42	52.02 N	4.19 W
Llanelli	42	51.42 N	4.10 W
Llanelltyd	42	52.45 N	3.54 W
Llanelly	169	36.44 S	143.51 E
Llanenddwyn	42	52.49 N	4.06 W
Llanerchymedd	44	53.20 N	4.22 W
Llanes	34	43.25 N	4.45 W
Llanfaethlu	44	53.21 N	4.32 W
Llanfair-Caereinion	42	52.39 N	3.20 W
Llanfairfechan	44	53.15 N	3.58 W
Llanfairpwllgwyngyll	44	53.13 N	4.12 W
Llanfrynach	42	51.56 N	3.21 W
Llanfyllin	42	52.46 N	3.17 W
Llanfynydd	42	51.56 N	4.06 W
Llanfyrnach	42	51.57 N	4.35 W
Llangadog	42	51.56 N	3.53 W
Llangefni	44	53.16 N	4.18 W
Llangennech	42	51.41 N	4.04 W
Llangollen	42	52.58 N	3.10 W
Llangollen Estates	208	39.39 N	75.37 W
Llangranog	42	52.09 N	4.29 W
Llangurig	42	52.25 N	3.36 W
Llangwyryfon	42	52.19 N	4.03 W
Llangynog	42	52.50 N	3.25 W
Llanharan	42	51.33 N	3.25 W
Llanidloes	42	52.27 N	3.32 W
Llanilar	42	52.21 N	4.01 W
Llanllyfni	44	53.03 N	4.17 W
Llano	196	30.45 N	98.40 W
Llano ≃	196	30.35 N	98.25 W
Llano Colorado	204	31.38 N	115.55 W
Llano Grande	234	20.28 N	105.37 W
Llanon	42	52.17 N	4.10 W
Llanos ≚	246	5.00 N	70.00 W
Llanpumsaint	42	51.56 N	4.18 W
Llanquera	248	18.06 S	67.47 W
Llanquihue	254	41.15 S	73.01 W
Llanquihue, Lago ⊜	254	41.08 S	72.48 W
Llanrhaeadr-ym-Mochnant	42	52.51 N	3.17 W
Llanrhidian	42	51.37 N	4.11 W
Llanrhystud	42	52.18 N	4.09 W
Llanrwst	44	53.08 N	3.48 W
Llansantffraid-ym-Mechain	42	52.47 N	3.08 W

Symbol	English	Deutsch	Español	Français	Português
≃	River	Fluß	Río	Rivière	Rio
≊	Canal	Kanal	Canal	Canal	Canal
ᒐ	Waterfall, Rapids	Wasserfall, Stromschnellen	Cascada, Rápidos	Chute d'eau, Rapides	Cascata, Rápidos
ꭒ	Strait	Meeresstraße	Estrecho	Détroit	Estreito
⊂	Bay, Gulf	Bucht, Golf	Bahía, Golfo	Baie, Golfe	Baía, Golfo
⊜	Lake, Lakes	See, Seen	Lago, Lagos	Lac, Lacs	Lago, Lagos
≡	Swamp	Sumpf	Pantano	Marais	Pântano
⊡	Ice Features, Glacier	Eis- und Gletscherformen	Accidentes Glaciales	Formes glaciaires	Acidentes glaciares
⊤	Other Hydrographic Features	Andere Hydrographische Objekte	Otros Elementos Hidrográficos	Autres données hydrographiques	Outros acidentes hidrográficos
✢	Submarine Features	Untermeerische Objekte	Accidentes Submarinos	Formes de relief sous-marin	Acidentes submarinos
□	Political Unit	Politische Einheit	Unidad Política	Entité politique	Unidade política
ᵿ	Cultural Institution	Kulturelle Institution	Institución Cultural	Institution culturelle	Instituição cultural
⊥	Historical Site	Historische Stätte	Sitio Histórico	Site historique	Sitio histórico
♠	Recreational Site	Erholungs- und Ferienort	Sitio de Recreo	Centre de loisirs	Area de Lazer
⊠	Airport	Flughafen	Aeropuerto	Aéroport	Aeroporto
■	Military Installation	Militäranlage	Instalación Militar	Installation militaire	Instalação militar
◆	Miscellaneous	Verschiedenes	Misceláneo	Divers	Diversos

I · *100* **Llan-Long**

Name	Page	Lat.°′	Long.°′
Llansawel	42	52.01 N	4.00 W
Llanta	252	26.20 S	69.49 W
Llantrisant	42	51.33 N	3.23 W
Llantwit Major	42	51.25 N	3.30 W
Llanuwchllyn	42	52.52 N	3.41 W
Llanwenog	42	52.06 N	4.12 W
Llanwrda	42	51.58 N	3.53 W
Llanwrtyd Wells	42	52.07 N	3.38 W
Llanybydder	42	52.04 N	4.09 W
Llata	248	9.25 S	76.47 W
Llavallol ♦[8]	288	34.48 S	58.28 W
Llay	44	53.06 N	2.59 W
Lleida	34	41.37 N	0.37 E
Llentrisca, Cap ≻	34	38.51 N	1.14 E
Llera	234	23.19 N	99.01 W
Llerena	34	38.14 N	6.01 W
Lleulleu, Lago ⊜	252	38.09 S	73.20 W
Lleyn Peninsula ≻[1]	42	52.54 N	4.30 W
Llica	248	19.52 S	68.16 W
Llico	252	34.46 S	72.05 W
Lliria	34	39.38 N	0.36 W
Llivia	32	42.28 N	1.59 E
Llobregat ≃	34	41.19 N	2.09 E
Llobregat, Delta del ⊻[2]	266d	41.17 N	2.08 E
Llorente	116	11.25 N	125.33 E
Llorente ≃	116	11.25 N	125.33 E
Lloyd	218	38.37 N	82.51 W
Lloyd Harbor	210	40.54 N	73.27 W
Lloyd Harbor ⊂	276	40.55 N	73.27 W
Lloydminster	184	53.17 N	110.00 W
Lloyd Neck ≻[1]	276	40.56 N	73.28 W
Lloyd Point ≻	210	40.57 N	73.29 W
Lloyds ≃	186	48.33 N	57.13 W
Llucena	34	40.08 N	0.17 W
Llucmajor	34	39.29 N	2.54 E
Llullaillaco, Volcán ∧[1]	252	24.43 S	68.33 W
Llusco	248	14.21 S	72.07 W
Lluta ≃	248	18.24 S	70.19 W
Llyswen	42	52.02 N	3.17 W
Lnáře	60	49.28 N	13.47 E
Lo (Panlong) ≃	110	21.18 N	105.25 E
Loa	200	38.24 N	111.38 W
Loa ≃, Chile	244	21.26 S	70.04 W
Loa ≃, Congo	273b	4.20 S	15.11 E
Loami	194	39.40 N	89.51 W
Loanda → Luanda, Ang.	152	8.48 S	13.14 E
Loanda, Bra.	255	22.54 S	53.10 W
Loanda, Gabon	152	0.55 S	9.00 E
Loande ≃	152	8.41 S	17.56 E
Loange (Luangue) ≃	152	4.17 S	20.02 E
Loango Buele	152	5.10 S	12.59 E
Loanhead	46	55.53 N	3.09 W
Loanja ≃	154	17.22 S	24.48 E
Loano	62	44.08 N	8.15 E
Loantaka Brook ≃	276	40.43 N	74.28 W
Lo Aranguiz	286e	33.23 S	70.40 W
Loay	116	9.36 N	124.01 E
Lob' ≃	82	56.29 N	35.51 E
Lobamba	158	26.27 S	31.12 E
Loban	24	65.44 N	45.25 E
Loban' ≃	80	56.58 N	51.12 E
Lobanovo	76	53.04 N	38.14 E
Lobanovskije Vyselki	82	54.18 N	38.58 E
Lo Barnechea	286e	33.21 S	70.31 W
Lobaski	80	54.38 N	45.09 E
Lobatos	234	22.49 N	103.24 W
Lobatse	156	25.11 S	25.40 E
Löbau	54	51.05 N	14.40 E
Lobau ⊻	264b	48.10 N	16.32 E
Lobaye □[5]	152	4.00 N	18.30 E
Lobaye ≃	152	3.41 N	18.35 E
Lobbes	50	50.21 N	4.15 E
Lobbs Run ≃	279b	40.15 N	79.55 W
Lobdell Lake ⊜	216	42.48 N	83.48 W
Löbejün	54	51.38 N	11.53 E
Lobelville	194	35.46 N	87.47 W
Lo Benitez	286e	33.34 S	70.42 W
Lobenstein	54	50.26 N	11.38 E
Lobería	252	38.09 S	58.47 W
Lo Bernales	286e	33.34 S	70.34 W
Löberöd	41	55.47 N	13.30 E
Lobethal	168b	34.54 S	138.52 E
Łobez	30	53.39 N	15.36 E
Lobito	152	12.20 S	13.34 E
Lobitos	246	4.26 S	81.17 W
Lobitos Creek ≃	282	37.22 N	122.24 W
Lobkoviči	76	53.50 N	31.45 E
Lobn'a	82	56.01 N	37.30 E
Löbnitz, D.D.R.	54	54.17 N	12.43 E
Löbnitz, D.D.R.	54	51.35 N	12.28 E
Lobo, Indon.	164	3.45 S	134.05 E
Lobo, Pil.	116	13.39 N	121.13 E
Lobo ≃	150	6.02 N	6.47 W
Loboko	152	0.45 S	16.38 E
Lobos, Arg.	258	35.11 S	59.06 W
Lobos, Méx.	234	20.29 N	105.03 W
Lobos, Cabo ≻	232	29.55 N	112.46 W
Lobos, Cay I	238	22.24 N	77.32 W
Lobos, Estero de ⊂	232	27.22 N	110.33 W
Lobos, Isla de I, Esp.	148	28.45 N	13.49 W
Lobos, Isla de I, Méx.	234	21.27 N	97.13 W
Lobos, Laguna ⊜	258	35.17 S	59.07 W
Lobos, Point ≻	226	37.47 N	122.31 W
Lobos, Puerto de ⊂	234	21.12 N	97.25 W
Lobos, Punta ≻, Chile	248	21.01 S	70.11 W
Lobos, Punta ≻, Ur.	258	34.54 S	56.15 W
Lobos de Afuera, Islas II	248	6.57 S	80.42 W
Lobos de Tierra, Isla I	248	6.27 S	80.52 W
Lo Boza	286e	33.23 S	70.46 W
Lobskoje	24	62.45 N	35.16 E
Lobstädt	54	51.08 N	12.29 E
Löbtau ♦[8]	54	51.03 N	13.42 E
Loburg	54	52.07 N	12.05 E
Lobva	86	59.12 N	60.30 E
Łobżenica	30	53.16 N	17.15 E
Locana	62	45.25 N	7.27 E
Locana, Val di V	62	45.25 N	7.27 E
Locarno	58	46.10 N	8.48 E
Lo Castillo, Aeropuerto ⊠	286e	33.23 S	70.36 W
Locate Triulzi	62	45.21 N	9.13 E
Loccum	52	52.27 N	9.08 E
Loceri	71	39.51 N	9.35 E
Loch	169	38.22 S	145.43 E
Lochaber ♦[1]	46	56.57 N	5.06 W
Lochailort	46	56.53 N	5.40 W
Lochaline	46	56.32 N	5.47 W
Locharbriggs	44	55.06 N	3.35 W
Lochar Water ≃	44	54.59 N	3.27 W
Lochboisdale	46	57.09 N	7.19 W
Lochcarron	46	57.24 N	5.30 W
Lochdon	46	56.26 N	5.41 W
Lochearn	284b	39.21 N	76.43 W
Lochearnhead	46	56.23 N	4.17 W
Lochem	52	52.09 N	6.25 E
Loches	50	47.08 N	1.00 E
Lochgair	46	56.03 N	5.20 W
Loch Garman → Wexford	48	52.20 N	6.27 W
Lochgelly	46	56.08 N	3.19 W
Lochgilphead	46	56.03 N	5.26 W
Lochgoilhead	46	56.10 N	4.54 W
Lochiel	168b	33.56 S	138.10 E
Lochindorb ⊜	46	57.24 N	3.43 W
Lochino	265b	55.42 N	37.19 E
Lochinvar National Park ♠	154	15.55 S	27.15 E
Lochinver	46	58.09 N	5.15 W
Lochmaben	44	55.08 N	3.27 W
Lochmaddy	46	57.36 N	7.11 W
Lochnagar ∧	46	56.57 N	3.16 W
Lochovice	60	49.51 N	13.59 E
Lochranza	46	55.42 N	5.18 W
Loch Raven Dam ♦[6]	284b	39.26 N	76.33 W
Loch Raven Reservoir ⊜[1]	208	39.27 N	76.34 W
Lochristi	50	51.06 N	3.50 E
Lochsa ≃	202	46.08 N	115.36 W
Loch Sheldrake	210	41.46 N	74.39 W
Loch Sport	166	38.03 S	147.36 E
Lochvica	78	50.22 N	33.16 E
Lochwinnoch	46	55.48 N	4.39 W
Lochy, Loch ⊜	46	56.57 N	4.53 W
Lock	166	33.34 S	135.46 E
Lock and Dam No. 20 ♦[6], U.S.	219	40.09 N	91.30 W
Lock and Dam No. 21 ♦[6], U.S.	219	39.54 N	91.26 W
Lock and Dam No. 22 ♦[6], U.S.	219	39.39 N	91.16 W
Lock and Dam No. 24 ♦[6], U.S.	219	39.22 N	90.55 W
Lock and Dam No. 25 ♦[6], U.S.	219	39.01 N	90.41 W
Locke, Ca., U.S.	226	38.15 N	121.31 W
Locke, In., U.S.	216	41.28 N	86.00 W
Locke, N.Y., U.S.	210	42.39 N	76.25 W
Lockeford	226	38.10 N	121.09 W
Lockenhaus	61	47.24 N	16.25 E
Lockeport	186	43.42 N	65.07 W
Lockerbie	44	55.07 N	3.22 W
Lockesburg	194	33.58 N	94.10 W
Lockhart, Austl.	166	35.14 S	146.43 E
Lockhart, Fl., U.S.	220	28.37 N	81.26 W
Lockhart, Tx., U.S.	222	29.53 N	97.40 W
Lockhart River Aboriginal Reserve ♦[4]	164	13.00 S	143.15 E
Lock Haven	210	41.08 N	77.26 W
Lockheed Aircraft Corporation ʋ[3], Ca., U.S.	280	34.12 N	118.22 W
Lockheed Aircraft Corporation ʋ[3], Ca., U.S.	282	37.25 N	122.02 W
Lockington	216	40.12 N	84.13 W
Lock Mountain ∧	214	40.25 N	78.18 W
Lockney	196	34.07 N	101.26 W
Löcknitz	54	53.27 N	14.12 E
Löcknitz ≃, D.D.R.	54	53.07 N	11.16 E
Löcknitz ≃, D.D.R.	264a	52.25 N	13.49 E
Lockport, Mb., Can.	184	50.05 N	96.56 W
Lockport, Il., U.S.	216	41.35 N	88.03 W
Lockport, La., U.S.	194	29.39 N	90.32 W
Lockport, N.Y., U.S.	210	43.10 N	78.41 W
Lockport Lock ♦[5]	278	41.35 N	88.04 W
Locks Heath	42	50.52 N	1.15 W
Locksley Park	210	42.45 N	78.52 W
Lockvattnet ⊜	40	59.03 N	17.05 E
Lockview	279b	40.10 N	79.55 W
Lockwood, Ca., U.S.	226	35.56 N	121.05 W
Lockwood, Mo., U.S.	194	37.23 N	93.57 W
Lockwood Corners	214	41.00 N	81.34 W
Lockyer Creek ≃	171a	27.25 S	152.36 E
Locminé	28	47.53 N	2.50 W
Loc Ninh	110	11.51 N	106.36 E
Loco, Bayou ≃	222	31.28 N	94.44 W
Locon	50	50.34 N	2.40 E
Locorotondo	68	40.45 N	17.20 E
Locri	68	38.14 N	16.16 E
Locri Epizefiri ⊥	68	38.12 N	16.13 E
Locroja	248	12.41 S	74.26 W
Locsin	116	13.09 N	123.43 E
Locumba	248	17.36 S	70.46 W
Locumba ≃	248	17.54 S	70.57 W
Locust	208	40.18 N	73.59 W
Locust Creek ≃	194	39.40 N	93.17 W
Locust Fork ≃	194	33.33 N	87.11 W
Locust Grove, N.Y., U.S.	276	40.48 N	73.30 W
Locust Grove, Ok., U.S.	196	36.12 N	95.10 W
Locust Lake State Park ♠	208	40.46 N	76.08 W
Locust Point ≻	276	40.49 N	73.48 W
Locust Valley	210	40.53 N	73.36 W
Lod (Lydda)	132	31.58 N	34.54 E
Lod, Nemel-Te'Ufa (Ben Gurion Airport) ⊠	132	31.59 N	34.53 E
Loda	216	40.31 N	88.04 W
Lodal Creek ≃	285	40.14 N	75.27 W
Löddeköpinge	41	55.46 N	13.01 E
Loddenhøj ∧[2]	41	56.13 N	9.48 E
Loddon	42	52.32 N	1.29 E
Loddon ≃, Austl.	166	35.32 S	143.52 E
Loddon ≃, Eng., U.K.	42	51.30 N	0.53 W
Lodè	71	40.35 N	9.32 E
Lodejnoje Pole	76	60.44 N	33.30 E
Lodenau	54	51.24 N	14.57 E
Löderburg	54	51.52 N	11.32 E
Lodève	32	43.43 N	3.19 E
Lodge Creek ≃	202	48.35 N	109.10 W
Lodge Grass	202	45.18 N	107.21 W
Lodgepole, Ab., Can.	182	53.06 N	115.19 W
Lodgepole, Ne., U.S.	198	41.08 N	102.38 W
Lodgepole Creek ≃	198	40.57 N	102.22 W
Lodhāsuli	126	22.19 N	87.03 E
Lodhrān	123	29.32 N	71.38 E
Lodi, It.	62	45.19 N	9.30 E
Lodi, Ca., U.S.	226	38.07 N	121.16 W
Lodi, N.J., U.S.	210	40.52 N	74.05 W
Lodi, N.Y., U.S.	210	42.36 N	76.49 W
Lodi, Oh., U.S.	214	41.02 N	82.00 W
Lodi, Wi., U.S.	190	43.18 N	89.31 W
Lodi Park ♠	272a	28.36 N	77.13 E
Lodi Vecchio	62	45.18 N	9.24 E
Lodja	152	3.29 S	23.26 E
Lodosa	34	42.25 N	2.05 W
Lodoyo	115a	8.10 S	112.13 E
Lodrone	64	45.50 N	10.32 E
Lods	58	47.03 N	6.15 E
Lodsch → Łódź	30	51.46 N	19.30 E
Lodwar	154	3.07 N	35.36 E
Łódź	30	51.46 N	19.30 E
Łódź □[4]	30	51.50 N	19.25 E
Loe Āgra	123	34.35 N	71.43 E
Loei	110	17.29 N	101.35 E
Loei ≃	110	17.51 N	101.37 E
Loen	26	61.52 N	6.52 E
Loenen	52	52.07 N	6.01 E
Loengo	154	4.45 S	26.27 E
Loeriesfontein	158	30.56 S	19.26 E
Lo Espejo	286e	33.32 S	70.43 W
Lofa ≃	150	6.36 N	11.08 W
Lofer	64	47.35 N	12.41 E
Löffingen	58	47.53 N	8.20 E
Lofoten II	24	68.30 N	15.00 E
Lofoten Basin ✣[1]	10	70.00 N	4.00 E
Lofthouse	44	53.44 N	1.29 W
Lofthus	26	60.20 N	6.40 E
Loftus, Austl.	274a	34.03 S	151.03 E
Loftus, Eng., U.K.	44	54.33 N	0.53 W
Lofty, Mount ∧, Austl.	168b	34.59 S	138.42 E
Lofty, Mount ∧, Austl.	274b	37.43 S	145.17 E
Log	80	49.29 N	43.52 E
Loga, B.R.D.	52	53.14 N	7.29 E
Loga, Niger	150	13.37 N	3.14 E
Logačovka	80	52.23 N	52.21 E
Logan, Ia., U.S.	198	41.38 N	95.47 W
Logan, Ks., U.S.	198	39.39 N	99.34 W
Logan, N.M., U.S.	196	35.22 N	103.25 W
Logan, Oh., U.S.	188	39.32 N	82.24 W
Logan, Ut., U.S.	200	41.44 N	111.50 W
Logan, W.V., U.S.	188	37.50 N	81.59 W
Logan □[6], Il., U.S.	219	40.09 N	89.22 W
Logan □[6], Oh., U.S.	216	40.22 N	83.46 W
Logan ♦[8]	285	40.02 N	75.09 W
Logan ≃, Austl.	171a	27.43 S	153.18 E
Logan ≃, Ab., Can.	182	55.09 N	111.42 W
Logan ≃, Ut,. U.S.	200	41.44 N	111.57 W
Logan, Mount ∧, Yk., Can.	180	60.34 N	140.24 W
Logan, Mount ∧, Wa., U.S.	224	48.32 N	120.57 W
Logan Creek ≃, Ca., U.S.	226	39.22 N	122.06 W
Logan Creek ≃, Mo., U.S.	194	37.11 N	90.49 W
Logan Creek ≃, Ne., U.S.	198	41.37 N	96.29 W
Logandale	204	36.35 N	114.29 W
Logan International Airport ⊠	283	42.22 N	71.00 W
Logan Lake ⊜	212	44.52 N	78.59 W
Logan Martin Lake ⊜[1]	194	33.40 N	86.15 W
Logan Mountains ⋀	180	61.45 N	128.38 W
Logan Pass)(	202	48.42 N	113.43 W
Logansport, In., U.S.	216	40.45 N	86.21 W
Logansport, La., U.S.	194	31.58 N	93.59 W
Logan Square ♦[8]	278	41.56 N	87.42 W
Loganton	210	41.02 N	77.18 W
Loganville, Ga., U.S.	192	33.50 N	83.54 W
Loganville, Pa., U.S.	208	39.52 N	76.42 W
Logården ⊜	40	60.37 N	16.00 E
Lögdeälven ≃	26	63.33 N	19.25 E
Logduz	76	60.00 N	44.41 E
Loge ≃, Ang.	152	10.12 S	17.00 E
Loge ≃, Ang.	152	7.49 S	13.06 E
Logia	164	2.55 S	151.27 E
Loginovo	82	55.42 N	38.44 E
Logirim	154	4.43 N	33.14 E
Logišin	76	52.20 N	25.59 E
Lognes	261	48.50 N	2.38 E
Lognes-Émerainville, Aérodrome de ⊠	261	48.49 N	2.37 E
Logo	154	5.20 N	30.18 E
Logojsk	76	54.12 N	27.49 E
Logone ≃	146	12.06 N	15.02 E
Logone Birni	146	11.47 N	15.06 E
Logone Gana	146	11.33 N	15.09 E
Logone-Occidental □[5]	146	8.50 N	16.00 E
Logone Occidental ≃	146	9.07 N	16.26 E
Logone-Oriental □[5]	146	8.15 N	16.20 E
Logone Oriental ≃	146	9.07 N	16.26 E
Logoualé	150	7.07 N	7.33 W
Logovskij	80	48.26 N	43.23 E
Log pod Mangartom	64	46.24 N	13.36 E
Logroño	34	42.28 N	2.27 W
Logrosán	34	39.20 N	5.29 W
Løgstør	26	56.58 N	9.15 E
Logtāk Lake ⊜	120	24.33 N	93.50 E
Løgten	41	56.17 N	10.19 E
Logudoro ♦[1]	71	40.35 N	8.40 E
Logue Brook Dam ♦[6]	168a	33.00 S	115.57 E
Løgumgårde	41	55.05 N	8.57 E
Løgumkloster	41	55.03 N	8.57 E
Logumukum	154	0.27 N	36.05 E
Logy Creek ≃	224	46.11 N	120.35 W
Loh I	175f	13.21 S	166.38 E
Lohāgara	126	23.11 N	89.39 E
Lohals	41	55.08 N	10.55 E
Lohārdaga	124	23.26 N	84.41 E
Lohāru	120	28.27 N	75.49 E
Lohatlha	158	28.02 S	23.04 E
Lohausen ♦[8]	263	51.16 N	6.44 E
Lohauserholz ♦[8]	263	51.39 N	7.48 E
Lohberg	263	51.35 N	6.46 E
Löhdorf ♦[8]	263	51.09 N	7.01 E
Lo Hermida	286e	33.29 S	70.33 W
Lohfelden	56	51.16 N	9.32 E
Lohheide ♦[8]	263	51.30 N	6.40 E
Lohiān	123	31.10 N	75.11 E
Lohiniva	24	67.10 N	24.58 E
Lohit ≃	120	27.48 N	95.28 E
Lohja	26	60.15 N	24.05 E
Lohjan harju ∧	26	60.15 N	24.30 E
Lohjanjärvi ⊜	26	60.15 N	23.55 E
Löhlbach	56	51.04 N	8.58 E
Lohmar	56	50.50 N	7.13 E
Lohme, D.D.R.	54	54.35 N	13.37 E
Löhme, D.D.R.	264a	52.37 N	13.40 E
Lohmen, D.D.R.	54	50.59 N	13.59 E
Lohmen, D.D.R.	54	53.41 N	12.05 E
Lohmühle	263	51.31 N	6.40 E
Lohne, B.R.D.	52	52.42 N	8.12 E
Löhne, B.R.D.	52	52.11 N	8.41 E
Löhnen	263	51.36 N	6.39 E
Lohnsburg	60	48.09 N	13.24 E
Loho → Luohe	100	33.35 N	114.01 E
Lohr am Main	56	50.00 N	9.34 E
Lohrville	198	42.16 N	94.32 W
Lohsa	54	51.23 N	14.24 E
Loi ≃	110	21.19 N	100.44 E
Loi, Phou ∧	110	20.16 N	103.12 E
Loiano	66	44.16 N	11.19 E
Loiblpass (Ljubelj))(	61	46.26 N	14.16 E
Loiborsoit	154	3.52 S	36.26 E
Loi-kaw	110	19.41 N	97.13 E
Loile ≃	152	0.52 S	20.12 E
Loimaa	26	60.51 N	23.03 E
Loimijoki ≃	26	61.13 N	22.38 E
Loi Mwe	110	21.11 N	99.46 E
Loing ≃	50	48.23 N	2.48 E
Loing, Canal du ≋	50	48.22 N	2.50 E
Loir ≃	32	47.33 N	0.32 W
Loira → Loire ≃	32	47.16 N	2.11 W
Loire	62	45.33 N	4.48 E
Loire □[5]	32	45.30 N	4.00 E
Loire ≃	32	47.16 N	2.11 W
Loire, Canal latéral à la ≋	50	47.37 N	2.44 E
Loire-Atlantique □[5]	32	47.20 N	1.35 W
Loiret □[5]	50	47.55 N	2.20 E
Loiret ≃	50	47.52 N	1.48 E
Loir-et-Cher □[5]	50	47.30 N	1.30 E
Loïs, Lac ⊜	190	48.34 N	78.44 W
Loisach ≃	64	47.56 N	11.27 E
Loisdale	284c	38.46 N	77.11 W
Loisia	58	46.29 N	5.27 E
Loison ≃	56	49.30 N	5.17 E
Loitz	54	53.58 N	13.07 E
Loíza, Embalse de ⊜[1]	240m	18.17 N	66.00 W
Loíza Aldea	240m	18.26 N	65.53 W
Loja, Ec.	246	4.00 S	79.13 W
Loja, Esp.	34	37.10 N	4.09 W
Loja □[4]	246	4.10 S	79.30 W
Lojang → Luoyang	102	34.41 N	112.28 E
Lojev	78	51.56 N	30.46 E
Lojga	24	61.05 N	44.37 E
Lojno	24	59.44 N	52.39 E
Løjt Kirkeby	41	55.05 N	9.28 E
Loka, Süd.	154	4.16 N	31.01 E
Loka, Zaïre	152	0.20 N	17.57 E
Loka brunn	40	59.36 N	14.28 E
Lokači	78	50.44 N	24.39 E
Lokako	152	2.14 S	21.45 E
Lokalema	152	1.59 N	22.17 E
Lokan ≃	116	5.25 N	117.44 E
Lokandu	154	2.31 S	25.47 E
Lokan tekojärvi ⊜[1]	24	67.55 N	27.40 E
Lokbatan	84	40.20 N	49.43 E
Løken	26	59.48 N	11.29 E
Lokeren	50	51.06 N	4.00 E
Loket	54	50.09 N	12.43 E
Lokichar	154	2.23 N	35.39 E
Lokichokio	154	4.12 N	34.21 E
Lokitaung	154	4.16 N	35.45 E
Lokka	24	67.49 N	27.44 E
Løkken	26	57.22 N	9.43 E
Løkken verk	26	63.08 N	9.42 E
Lokn'a	76	56.50 N	30.09 E
Loknaš ≃	82	56.11 N	36.04 E
Loko	150	8.02 N	7.49 E
Lokofa-Bokolongo	152	0.12 N	19.22 E
Lokoja	150	7.47 N	6.45 E
Lokolama	152	2.34 S	19.53 E
Lokolenge	152	1.11 N	22.40 E
Lokolo ≃	152	0.43 S	19.40 E
Lokomo	152	2.41 N	15.19 E
Lokoro ≃	152	1.43 S	18.23 E
Lokossa	150	6.38 N	1.43 E
Lokosso	150	10.19 N	3.40 W
Lokot', S.S.S.R.	76	52.34 N	34.34 E
Lokot', S.S.S.R.	86	51.11 N	81.11 E
Lokoua ≃	273b	4.06 S	15.16 E
Loksa	76	59.35 N	25.45 E
Loks Land I	176	62.26 N	64.38 W
Loktyši	76	52.50 N	26.43 E
Lokve	64	46.01 N	13.49 E
Loky	157b	12.47 S	49.39 E
Lol	140	6.26 N	29.37 E
Lol ≃	140	9.13 N	28.59 E
Lóla, Ang.	152	14.22 S	13.42 E
Lola, Guinée	150	7.48 N	8.32 W
Lola, Mount ∧	226	39.26 N	120.22 W
Lolengi	152	0.07 N	20.59 E
Loleta	204	40.38 N	124.13 W
Lolingo	152	0.55 N	22.38 E
Loliondo	154	2.03 S	35.37 E
Lolita	222	28.50 N	96.32 W
Lolland I	41	54.46 N	11.30 E
Lollar	56	50.39 N	8.42 E
Lolo, Mt., U.S.	202	46.45 N	114.04 W
Lolo, Zaïre	152	2.13 N	23.00 E
Lolo ≃	152	1.07 S	12.28 E
Lolobau Island I	164	4.55 S	151.10 E
Lolo Creek ≃, Id., U.S.	202	46.26 N	116.10 W
Lolo Creek ≃, Mt., U.S.	202	46.45 N	114.03 W
Lolodorf	152	3.14 N	10.44 E
Lolo Pass)(	202	46.38 N	114.35 W
Lolotique	236	13.33 N	88.21 W
Lolowai	175f	15.18 S	168.00 E
Loltong	175f	15.33 S	168.08 E
Lolvavana, Passage ⩍	175f	15.26 S	168.12 E
Lolwa	154	1.22 N	29.31 E
Lolworth Range ⋀	166	20.20 S	145.15 E
Lom, Blg.	38	43.49 N	23.14 E
Lom, Česko.	54	50.37 N	13.40 E
Lom, Nor.	26	61.50 N	8.33 E
Lom, S.S.S.R.	80	57.54 N	39.12 E
Lom ∧	60	49.54 N	13.12 E
Lom ≃, Afr.	152	5.20 N	13.24 E
Lom ≃, Blg.	38	43.50 N	23.15 E
Loma	144	6.55 N	37.34 E
Loma, Point ≻	228	32.41 N	117.14 W
Loma Blanca, Chile	286e	33.30 S	70.47 W
Loma Blanca, Méx.	200	31.35 N	106.17 W
Loma Bonita	234	18.07 N	95.53 W
Lomakino	85	40.05 N	68.10 E
Lomako ≃	152	0.50 N	20.50 E
Loma Linda, Méx.	286a	19.28 N	99.14 W
Loma Linda, Ca., U.S.	228	34.02 N	117.15 W
Lomaloma	175g	17.17 S	178.59 W
Lomami ≃	138	0.46 N	24.16 E
Loma Mountains ⋀	150	9.10 N	11.07 W
Loma Ridge ∧	280	33.45 N	117.43 W
Lomas	248	15.34 S	74.50 W
Lomas, Bahía ⊂	254	52.35 S	69.05 W
Lomas Alegres	234	17.38 N	92.36 W
Lomas Chapultepec ♦[8]	286a	19.26 N	99.13 W
Lomas del Real	234	22.30 N	97.54 W
Lomas de Monreal	200	31.17 N	110.56 W
Lomas de Zamora	258	34.46 S	58.24 W
Lomas de Zamora □[5]	288	34.45 S	58.24 W
Loma Verde	258	35.16 S	58.24 W
Lomax, Il., U.S.	190	40.41 N	91.04 W
Lomax, Tx., U.S.	222	29.41 N	95.04 W
Łomazy	30	51.55 N	23.10 E
Lomazzo	62	45.42 N	9.02 E
Lomba ≃	152	15.36 S	21.32 E
Lombagin	112	0.55 N	124.04 E
Lombard	216	41.52 N	88.00 W
Lombarda, Serra ⋀[1]	250	2.50 N	51.50 W
Lombardia □[4]	36	45.40 N	9.30 E
Lombardy East	273d	26.07 S	28.08 E
Lombe	152	9.27 S	16.13 E
Lomblen, Pulau I	112	8.25 S	123.30 E
Lombo do Tejo, Mouchão do I	266c	38.52 N	9.00 W
Lombok	115b	8.30 S	116.40 E
Lombok I	115b	8.45 S	116.30 E
Lombok, Selat ⩍	115b	8.30 S	115.50 E
Lombong	114	1.48 N	103.51 E
Lomé	150	6.08 N	1.13 E
Lomela	152	2.18 S	23.17 E
Lomela ≃	152	0.14 S	20.42 E
Lomellina □[9]	62	45.15 N	8.45 E
Lomello	62	45.07 N	8.47 E
Lometa	196	31.13 N	98.23 W
Lomi	24	67.05 N	16.09 E
Lomié	152	3.10 N	13.37 E
Lomira	190	43.35 N	88.26 W
Lo Miranda	252	34.11 S	70.54 W
Lomita	228	33.47 N	118.18 W
Lom Kao	110	16.53 N	101.14 E
Lomma	41	55.41 N	13.05 E
Lommabukten ⊂	41	55.40 N	12.58 E
Lommatzsch	54	51.12 N	13.18 E
Lomme	50	50.39 N	2.59 E
Lomme ≃	56	50.08 N	5.10 E
Lommel	56	51.14 N	5.18 E
Lomnice ≃	60	49.26 N	14.04 E
Lomnice nad Popelkou	30	50.32 N	15.22 E
Lomond	182	50.21 N	112.39 W
Lomond, Loch ⊜, N.S., Can.	186	45.46 N	60.35 W
Lomond, Loch ⊜, On., Can.	190	48.15 N	89.20 W
Lomond, Loch ⊜, Scot., U.K.	46	56.08 N	4.38 W
Lomond, Loch ⊜, Il., U.S.	278	42.17 N	88.01 W
Lomonosov	265a	59.55 N	29.46 E
Lomonosov Moscow State University ʋ[2]	265b	55.43 N	37.32 E
Lomonosovskij	86	52.50 N	66.28 E
Lomovatka	83	48.27 N	38.34 E
Lomovoje	24	64.01 N	40.40 E
Lompobatang, Gunung ∧	112	5.20 S	119.55 E
Lompoc	204	34.38 N	120.27 W
Lom Sak	110	16.47 N	101.15 E
Lomy	88	52.17 N	117.59 E
Łomża	30	53.11 N	22.05 E
łomża □[4]	30	53.00 N	22.15 E
Lonaconing	188	39.33 N	78.58 W
Lonate Pozzolo	62	45.36 N	8.45 E
Lonato	64	45.27 N	10.29 E
Lonāvale	122	18.45 N	73.25 E
Lončakovo	89	47.05 N	134.10 E
Loncoche	254	39.22 S	72.38 W
Loncon ≃	64	45.42 N	12.47 E
Loncopué	252	38.04 S	70.37 W
Londela-Kaye	152	4.51 S	13.24 E
Londerzeel	50	51.00 N	4.18 E
Londinières	50	49.50 N	1.24 E
Londo	154	2.03 N	25.43 E
Londoko	89	49.02 N	131.59 E
London, On., Can.	212	42.59 N	81.14 W
London, Kiribati	174o	1.58 N	157.28 W
London, Eng., U.K.	42	51.30 N	0.10 W
London, Eng., U.K.	260	51.30 N	0.10 W
London, Ar., U.S.	194	35.19 N	93.15 W
London, Ca., U.S.	226	36.30 N	119.25 W
London, Ky., U.S.	192	37.07 N	84.05 W
London, Oh., U.S.	218	39.53 N	83.26 W
London, Tx., U.S.	196	30.41 N	99.35 W
London, Wi., U.S.	216	43.03 N	89.01 W
London (Gatwick) Airport ⊠, Eng., U.K.	42	51.09 N	0.21 W
London (Stansted) Airport ⊠, Eng., U.K.	42	51.40 N	0.15 E
London (Heathrow) Airport ⊠, Eng., U.K.	260	51.27 N	0.28 W
London Bridge Station ♦[5]	260	51.30 N	0.05 W
London Colney	260	51.43 N	0.18 W
Londonderry, N.S., Can.	186	45.29 N	63.36 W
Londonderry (Derry), N. Ire., U.K.	48	54.59 N	7.20 W
Londonderry, N.H., U.S.	207	42.51 N	71.22 W
Londonderry, Oh., U.S.	214	39.16 N	82.47 W
Londonderry, Cape ≻	164	13.45 S	126.55 E
Londonderry, Isla I	254	55.03 S	70.35 W
Londontowne	208	38.59 N	76.32 W
London Zoo ♠	260	51.32 N	0.09 W
Londres, Arg.	252	27.43 S	67.07 W
Londres → London, Eng., U.K.	42	51.30 N	0.10 W
Londrina	255	23.18 S	51.09 W
Lonedell	219	38.18 N	90.50 W
Lone Grove	196	34.10 N	97.15 W
Lonely Lake ⊜	184	51.09 N	99.05 W
Lonelyville	276	40.39 N	73.11 W
Lone Mountain ∧	204	38.02 N	117.29 W
Lone Oak, Ky., U.S.	194	37.02 N	88.39 W
Lone Oak, Tx., U.S.	222	33.01 N	95.57 W
Lone Pine	204	36.36 N	118.03 W
Lone Pine Koala Sanctuary ♠	171a	27.32 S	152.57 E
Lone Rock	190	43.11 N	90.11 W
Lone Star	222	32.56 N	94.43 W
Lone Tree	190	41.29 N	91.25 W
Lone Tree Creek ≃, U.S.	200	40.25 N	104.35 W
Lone Tree Creek ≃, Ca., U.S.	226	37.53 N	121.14 W
Lone Wolf	196	34.59 N	99.14 W
Long	110	18.05 N	99.50 E
Long ≃, Fr.	50	47.41 N	0.28 E
Long ≃, Zhg.	100	23.26 N	114.38 E
Long ≃, Zhg.	102	24.32 N	109.15 E
Long ≃, Zhg.	105	39.23 N	116.49 E
Longa	152	14.42 S	18.32 E
Longa ≃, Ang.	152	10.15 S	13.30 E
Longa ≃, Ang.	152	16.25 N	19.04 E
Longá ≃, Bra.	250	3.09 S	41.56 W
Longa, proliv ⩍	74	70.20 N	178.00 E
Longairo	154	4.30 N	32.17 E
Long Akah	112	3.19 N	114.47 E
Long'an	102	25.03 N	109.00 E
Longana	175f	15.20 S	167.55 E
Long'anqiao	89	47.31 N	124.27 E
Longare	64	45.29 N	11.36 E
Longarone	64	46.16 N	12.18 E
Long Arroyo V	196	33.04 N	104.17 W
Longasy	24	61.58 N	35.09 E
Longaví	252	35.58 S	71.41 W
Longbangun	112	0.36 N	115.11 E
Long Bar Harbor	208	39.27 N	76.15 W
Long Barn	226	38.05 N	120.08 W
Long Bay ⊂, Austl.	274a	33.58 S	151.16 E
Long Bay ⊂, Barb.	241g	13.04 N	59.29 W
Long Bay ⊂, Jam.	241q	17.51 N	77.27 W
Long Bay ⊂, U.S.	192	33.35 N	78.45 W
Long Beach, Ca., U.S.	228	33.46 N	118.11 W
Long Beach, In., U.S.	216	41.44 N	86.51 W
Long Beach, Ms., U.S.	194	30.21 N	89.09 W
Long Beach, N.Y., U.S.	210	40.35 N	73.39 W
Long Beach, Wa., U.S.	224	46.21 N	124.03 W
Long Beach ≛[2]	208	39.39 N	74.11 W
Long Beach Breakwater ♦[5]	280	33.43 N	118.09 W
Long Beach Middle Harbor ⊂	280	33.45 N	118.13 W
Long Beach Municipal Airport ⊠	280	33.49 N	118.09 W
Long Beach Naval Station ■	280	33.45 N	118.14 W
Longbeleh	112	0.16 N	116.11 E
Long Belepai	112	2.45 N	114.04 E
Longbenton	44	55.02 N	1.35 W
Longboat Key	220	27.24 N	82.39 W
Longboat Key I	220	27.23 N	82.39 W
Long Branch, N.J., U.S.	208	40.18 N	73.59 W
Longbranch, Wa., U.S.	224	47.12 N	122.45 W
Long Branch □[8]	275b	43.35 N	79.32 W
Long Branch ≃	219	39.23 N	91.49 W
Long Branch Lake ⊜[1]	194	39.49 N	92.31 W
Longbu	100	25.32 N	115.24 E
Long Buckby	42	52.19 N	1.04 W
Long Cane Creek ≃	192	33.57 N	82.24 W
Long Canyon V	226	38.59 N	120.41 W
Longchamp, Hippodrome de ♠	261	48.51 N	2.14 E
Longchamps, Arg.	258	34.52 S	58.23 W
Longchamps, Bel.	56	50.03 N	5.42 E
Longchang, Zhg.	104	40.53 N	123.08 E
Longchang, Zhg.	107	29.21 N	105.17 E
Longchaumois	58	46.27 N	5.56 E
Longchêne	261	48.38 N	2.00 E
Longchuan, Zhg.	100	24.07 N	115.17 E
Longchuan, Zhg.	102	24.14 N	97.45 E
Longchuan (Shweli) ≃	102	23.56 N	96.17 E
Long Creek, Il., U.S.	219	39.48 N	88.50 W
Long Creek, Or., U.S.	202	44.42 N	119.06 W
Long Creek ≃	184	49.07 N	103.00 W
Long Crendon	42	51.47 N	1.01 W
Longcun	100	23.34 N	115.33 E
Longde	102	35.28 N	106.22 E
Longdendale V	262	53.29 N	1.56 W
Long Ditton	260	51.23 N	0.20 W
Longdongtuo	107	29.59 N	106.21 E
Longdor, gora ∧	88	58.24 N	116.47 E
Longdou	100	27.25 N	117.24 E
Longdu	106	31.51 N	118.56 E
Long Eaton	42	52.54 N	1.15 W
Longeau	58	47.46 N	5.18 E
Long Eddy	210	41.51 N	75.08 W
Longfellow National Historical Site ⊥	283	42.23 N	71.08 W
Longfengchang	107	30.26 N	105.38 E
Longfengkan	104	41.51 N	124.01 E
Longfengyutun	104	40.39 N	122.57 E
Longfield	260	51.24 N	0.18 E
Longford, Austl.	166	38.10 S	147.05 E
Longford, Ire.	48	53.44 N	7.47 W
Longford, Md., U.S.	284b	39.25 N	76.39 W
Longford □[6]	48	53.40 N	7.40 W
Longford Park ♠	262	53.27 N	2.17 W
Longframlington	44	55.18 N	1.47 W
Longgang, Zhg.	100	29.38 N	114.57 E
Longgang, Zhg.	100	33.22 N	120.04 E
Longgang, Zhg.	102	24.41 N	101.09 E
Longgangzi	104	42.09 N	123.26 E
Long Green	208	39.28 N	76.31 W
Long Grove	216	42.11 N	88.00 W
Longguan	105	40.47 N	115.34 E
Longgudu	100	27.45 N	116.14 E
Longguntur	112	0.13 N	112.12 E
Long Harbour	186	47.26 N	53.48 W
Long Harbour ⊂, Nf., Can.	186	47.44 N	55.01 W
Long Harbour ⊂, H.K.	271d	22.27 N	114.20 E
Longhorn Cavern State Park ♠	196	30.20 N	98.30 W
Longhorsley	44	55.15 N	1.46 W
Longhoughton	44	55.26 N	1.36 W
Long Hu ⊜	100	29.58 N	116.10 E
Longhua, Zhg.	98	41.17 N	117.37 E
Longhua, Zhg.	100	23.37 N	114.14 E
Longhua, Zhg.	100	22.42 N	113.59 E
Longhua, Zhg.	106	31.09 N	121.26 E
Longhua Airport ⊠	269b	31.10 N	121.26 E
Longhua Pagoda ʋ[1]	269b	31.11 N	121.26 E
Longhui, Zhg.	100	25.32 N	114.47 E
Longhui (Taohuaping), Zhg.	102	27.00 N	110.59 E
Longhui, Zhg.	107	29.32 N	104.48 E
Longhutang	106	31.52 N	119.59 E
Longi	70	38.01 N	14.45 E
Longido	154	2.44 S	36.41 E
Longiram	112	0.02 S	115.38 E
Long Island I, Antig.	240c	17.08 N	61.45 W
Long Island I, Austl.	166	22.09 S	149.54 E
Long Island I, Ba.	238	23.15 N	75.07 W
Long Island I, Nf., Can.	186	47.35 N	54.05 W
Long Island I, N.T., Can.	176	54.50 N	79.20 W
Long Island I, N.S., Can.	186	44.20 N	66.15 W
Long Island I, Ak., U.S.	182	54.54 N	132.45 W
Long Island I, Ma., U.S.	283	42.19 N	70.58 W
Long Island I, N.Y., U.S.	188	40.50 N	73.00 W
Long Island I, Wa., U.S.	224	46.27 N	123.58 W
Long Island City ♦[8]	276	40.45 N	73.56 W
Long Island MacArthur Airport ⊠	210	40.48 N	73.06 W
Long Island Sound ⩍	188	41.05 N	72.58 W
Long Island University ʋ[2], N.Y., U.S.	276	40.41 N	73.59 W
Long Island University (C.W. Post Center) ʋ[2], N.Y., U.S.	276	40.49 N	73.36 W
Longitudinal, Valle V	252	36.00 S	72.00 W
Long Jetty	170	33.22 S	151.29 E
Longji	107	29.23 N	106.04 E
Longjiadian	104	42.10 N	120.47 E
Longjiang, Zhg.	89	47.19 N	123.12 E
Longjiang, Zhg.	100	22.53 N	113.04 E
Longjiang, Zhg.	100	22.59 N	116.13 E
Longjiang, Zhg.	107	29.48 N	105.03 E
Longjie	107	29.53 N	104.32 E
Longjin	100	28.37 N	116.37 E
Longjing	100	23.53 N	112.52 E
Longjohn Slough ≃	278	41.43 N	87.53 W
Longjumeau	50	48.42 N	2.18 E
Longka	120	33.12 N	79.47 E
Longkamp	56	49.53 N	7.07 E
Longkangji	100	33.09 N	116.54 E
Long Ke	271d	22.23 N	114.22 E
Long Key I, Fl., U.S.	220	24.49 N	80.49 W
Long Key I, Fl., U.S.	220	27.44 N	82.45 W
Long King Creek ≃	222	30.34 N	94.58 W
Longkou, Zhg.	98	37.38 N	120.18 E
Longkou, Zhg.	100	32.56 N	114.57 E
Longkou, Zhg.	100	29.57 N	113.47 E
Longkou, Zhg.	100	26.11 N	115.15 E
Longkouqiao	85	39.40 N	77.09 E
Long Lake, Il., U.S.	216	42.22 N	88.08 W
Long Lake, N.Y., U.S.	188	43.58 N	74.25 W
Long Lake, Tx., U.S.	222	31.39 N	95.47 W
Long Lake ⊜, On., Can.	212	44.41 N	76.45 W
Long Lake ⊜, Mi., U.S.	190	45.12 N	83.30 W
Long Lake ⊜, Mi., U.S.	281	42.37 N	83.44 W
Long Lake ⊜, Mi., U.S.	281	42.36 N	83.28 W
Long Lake ⊜, N.Y., U.S.	188	44.04 N	74.20 W
Long Lake ⊜, N.D., U.S.	198	46.43 N	100.07 W
Long Lake ⊜, Wa., U.S.	224	47.03 N	122.47 W
Long Lake ⊜[1]	202	47.50 N	117.40 W
Long Lake Creek ≃	198	46.40 N	100.13 W
Long Lake Shores	281	42.35 N	83.19 W
Long Lama	112	3.46 N	114.24 E
Longlaville	56	49.32 N	5.47 E
Longleaf	194	31.00 N	92.34 W
Long Leaf Park	192	34.12 N	77.56 W
Longleat ʋ	42	51.12 N	2.17 W
Longlegged Lake ⊜	184	50.46 N	94.08 W
Longli	102	26.26 N	106.58 E
Longlin	102	24.49 N	105.31 E
Longling	102	24.39 N	98.40 E
Longmeadow	207	42.03 N	72.35 W
Long Melford	42	52.05 N	0.43 E
Longmen, Zhg.	89	48.55 N	126.54 E
Longmen, Zhg.	100	29.53 N	119.57 E
Longmen, Zhg.	100	24.56 N	118.04 E
Longmen, Zhg.	100	25.06 N	116.58 E
Longmen, Zhg.	100	23.44 N	114.15 E
Longmen, Zhg.	107	29.27 N	104.59 E
Longmen, Zhg.	107	29.12 N	106.13 E
Longmenchang	107	30.53 N	106.10 E
Longmensuo	98	40.56 N	115.54 E
Longmenzhang	107	28.59 N	106.13 E
Longming	102	22.59 N	107.11 E
Longmire	224	46.45 N	121.49 W
Long Moc	110	18.51 N	105.01 E
Longmont	200	40.10 N	105.06 W
Longmorn	46	57.36 N	3.17 W
Long Mountain ∧	194	36.41 N	92.26 W
Long Mountain ∧[2]	42	52.39 N	3.09 W
Longmu	100	24.16 N	115.28 E
Longnan	100	24.54 N	114.48 E
Longnawan	112	1.54 N	114.53 E
Long Neck ≻[1]	276	41.03 N	73.29 W
Long Neck Point ≻	276	41.02 N	73.29 W
Longniddry	46	55.58 N	2.53 W
Longnüsi	107	30.23 N	106.11 E
Longny-au-Perche	50	48.32 N	0.45 E
Longobucco	68	39.27 N	16.37 E
Longperrier	261	49.03 N	2.40 E
Long Pine	198	42.32 N	99.42 W
Longping	100	29.53 N	115.41 E
Long Plains	168b	34.21 S	138.22 E
Long Point, Austl.	274a	34.01 S	150.54 E
Long Point, Il., U.S.	216	41.00 N	88.54 W
Long Point ≻, Ba.	240b	25.01 N	77.20 W
Long Point ≻, Nf., Can.	186	48.48 N	58.46 W
Long Point ≻, N.S., Can.	186	46.51 N	60.18 W
Long Point ≻, On., Can.	212	44.06 N	76.29 W
Long Point ≻, On., Can.	212	44.32 N	80.18 W
Long Point ≻, Pil.	116	9.39 N	118.20 E
Long Point ≻, Ca., U.S.	280	33.44 N	118.23 W
Long Point ≻, Vir. Is., U.S.	240m	18.18 N	64.53 W
Long Point ≻, Vir. Is., U.S.	241n	17.41 N	64.50 W
Long Point ≻[1], Mb., Can.	184	53.02 N	98.40 W
Long Point ≻[1], On., Can.	214	42.34 N	80.15 W
Long Point Bay ⊂	212	42.40 N	80.14 W
Long Point Creek ≃	216	41.02 N	88.48 W
Long Point Provincial Park ♠	214	42.35 N	80.35 W
Long Pond ⊜, U.S.	283	42.41 N	71.21 W
Long Pond ⊜, Ma., U.S.	207	41.48 N	70.57 W
Long Pond ⊜, Ma., U.S.	207	41.43 N	70.04 W
Longpont, Fr.	50	49.16 N	3.13 E
Longpont, Fr.	261	48.38 N	2.17 E
Longport	208	39.18 N	74.31 W
Long Prairie	198	45.58 N	94.51 W
Long Prairie ≃	198	46.20 N	94.36 W
Longpré-les-Corps-Saints	50	50.01 N	1.59 E
Long Preston	44	54.02 N	2.15 W
Longqiantai	104	41.23 N	120.52 E
Longqu, Zhg.	98	34.16 N	114.49 E
Longqu, Zhg.	98	34.54 N	116.47 E
Longquan	100	28.04 N	119.07 E

Symbols in the index entries represent the broad categories identified in the key at the right. Symbols with superior numbers (⋀[1]) identify subcategories (see complete key on page *I · 1).*

Symbole im Register stellen die rechts im Schlüssel erklärten Kategorien dar. Symbole mit hochgestellten Ziffern (⋀[1]) bezeichnen Unterabteilungen einer Kategorie (vgl. vollständiger Schlüssel auf Seite *I · 1).*

Los símbolos incluídos en el texto del índice representan las grandes categorias identificadas con la clave a la derecha. Los símbolos con numeros en su parte superior (⋀[1]) identifican las subcategorías (véase la clave completa en la página *I · 1).*

Les symboles de l'index représentent les catégories indiquées dans la légende à droite. Les symboles suivis d'un indice (⋀[1]) représentent des sous-catégories (voir légende complète à la page *I · 1).*

Os símbolos incluídos no texto do índice representam as grandes categorias identificadas com a chave à direita. Os símbolos com números em sua parte superior (⋀[1]) identificam as subcategorias (veja-se a chave completa à página *I · 1).*

	English	Deutsch	Español	Français	Português
∧	Mountain	Berg	Montaña	Montagne	Montanha
⋀	Mountains	Gebirge	Montañas	Montagnes	Montanhas
)(	Pass	Paß	Paso	Col	Passo
V	Valley, Canyon	Tal, Cañon	Valle, Cañón	Vallée, Canyon	Vale, Canhão
⊻	Plain	Ebene	Llano	Plaine	Planície
≻	Cape	Kap	Cabo	Cap	Cabo
I	Island	Insel	Isla	Île	Ilha
II	Islands	Inseln	Islas	Îles	Ilhas
≛	Other Topographic Features	Andere Topographische Objekte	Otros Elementos Topográficos	Autres données topographiques	Outros acidentes topográficos

ESPAÑOL

Nombre	Página	Lat.°′	Long.°′ W = Oeste
Longquan ≃	100	28.17 N	119.44 E
Longquanguan	98	38.55 N	113.51 E
Longquan Shan ⋏	107	30.25 N	104.15 E
Longquanyi	107	30.34 N	104.16 E
Longquanzhen	107	30.21 N	104.39 E
Long Range Mountains ⋏	186	49.20 N	57.30 W
Longreach	166	23.26 S	144.15 E
Long Reach c	186	45.26 N	66.09 W
Long Reach ʯ	212	44.07 N	77.04 W
Long Reef ⊹[2]	164	11.11 S	151.40 E
Long Reef Point ›	274a	33.45 S	151.19 E
Longridge	44	53.51 N	2.36 W
Long Run ≃, Il., U.S.	278	41.37 N	88.03 W
Long Run ≃, Pa., U.S.	279b	40.20 N	79.48 W
Long-Sault	206	45.02 N	74.53 W
Long Sault Dam ◆[6]	206	45.00 N	74.45 W
Long Sault Islands II	206	45.00 N	74.55 W
Longsegah	112	2.15 N	116.42 E
Longshan, Zhg.	100	33.36 N	116.18 E
Longshan, Zhg.	102	29.28 N	109.20 E
Longshansuo	100	30.05 N	121.33 E
Longsheng, Zhg.	102	25.48 N	110.00 E
Longsheng, Zhg.	107	30.36 N	105.21 E
Longshizhen, Zhg.	107	30.12 N	106.26 E
Longshizhen, Zhg.	107	29.23 N	105.10 E
Longshu	107	29.33 N	105.45 E
Longs Peak ∧	200	40.15 N	105.37 W
Long Stratton	42	52.29 N	1.14 E
Long Sutton	42	52.47 N	0.08 E
Longtaichang	107	30.04 N	105.34 E
Longtan, Zhg.	100	23.40 N	113.24 E
Longtan, Zhg.	102	28.20 N	108.52 E
Longtan, Zhg.	106	32.11 N	119.04 E
Longtan, Zhg.	106	31.20 N	118.45 E
Longtansi	107	30.42 N	104.10 E
Longtanzhen	107	29.19 N	104.35 E
Long Teru	112	3.52 N	114.15 E
Long Thanh	110	10.47 N	106.57 E
Longtian	100	25.38 N	119.28 E
Longtian'an	106	31.10 N	120.49 E
Long Tom ≃	202	44.23 N	123.15 W
Longton	44	53.43 N	2.47 W
Longton, Ks., U.S.	198	37.22 N	96.04 W
Longtou	98	38.51 N	121.18 E
Longtoupu	100	27.54 N	113.12 E
Longtouwei	100	25.14 N	115.24 E
Longtown	44	55.01 N	2.58 W
Long Truong	269c	10.49 N	106.49 E
Longué	32	47.23 N	0.06 W
Longueau	50	49.52 N	2.21 E
Longuenesse	50	50.44 N	2.14 E
Longuesse	261	49.04 N	1.56 E
Longueuil	206	45.32 N	73.30 W
Longueville, Austl.	274a	33.50 S	151.10 E
Longueville, Fr.	50	48.31 N	3.15 E
Longueville-sur-Scie	50	49.48 N	1.06 E
Longuyon	56	49.26 N	5.36 E
Long Valley	210	40.47 N	74.46 W
Long Valley Creek ≃, Ca., U.S.	226	39.03 N	122.34 W
Long Valley Creek ≃, Nv., U.S.	226	39.31 N	119.39 W
Longvic	58	47.17 N	5.04 E
Longview, Ab., Can.	182	50.32 N	114.14 W
Longview, N.C., U.S.	192	35.43 N	81.23 W
Longview, Tx., U.S.	222	32.30 N	94.44 W
Longview, Wa., U.S.	224	46.08 N	122.56 W
Longview Heights	222	32.30 N	94.41 W
Longvilliers	261	48.35 N	2.00 E
Longvilly	56	50.01 N	5.50 E
Longwai	112	0.42 N	116.39 E
Longwan	105	38.57 N	116.10 E
Longwangmiao, Zhg.	98	36.12 N	115.13 E
Longwangmiao, Zhg.	102	40.36 N	95.52 E
Longwangmiao, Zhg.	104	41.38 N	121.04 E
Longwangmiao, Zhg.	104	42.35 N	123.42 E
Longwarry	169	38.07 S	145.46 E
Longwen	100	24.36 N	116.21 E
Longwo	100	23.28 N	115.17 E
Longwokou	106	32.18 N	119.52 E
Longwood	220	28.42 N	81.20 W
Longwood Gardens ♠	285	39.52 N	75.40 W
Longwood Lake	276	40.59 N	74.52 W
Longwood Park	192	34.55 N	79.42 W
Longworth	182	53.55 N	121.28 W
Longwy	56	49.31 N	5.46 E
Longxi → Zhangzhou, Zhg.	100	24.33 N	117.39 E
Longxi, Zhg.	102	34.56 N	104.47 E
Longxi, Zhg.	107	29.59 N	106.09 E
Longxian, Zhg.	102	34.51 N	106.59 E
Longxian, Zhg.	107	29.09 N	105.50 E
Long Xuyen	110	10.23 N	105.25 E
Longyan	100	25.08 N	117.02 E
Longyao	98	37.23 N	114.41 E
Longyou	100	29.02 N	119.10 E
Longyou ≃	106	32.08 N	120.38 E
Longyuanba	100	24.56 N	114.27 E
Longzhaogou	98	40.49 N	124.36 E
Longzhen	89	48.41 N	126.42 E
Longzhou	102	22.22 N	106.52 E
Loni	272a	28.45 N	77.17 E
Lonigo	64	45.23 N	11.23 E
Löningen	52	52.44 N	7.46 E
Lonja ≃	36	45.27 N	16.41 E
Lonkala	152	4.37 S	23.14 E
Lönnewitz	54	51.34 N	13.11 E
Lonny	56	49.49 N	4.35 E
Lonoke	194	34.47 N	91.53 W
Lönsboda	26	56.24 N	14.19 E
Lønsdal	24	66.44 N	15.28 E
Lonsdale	190	44.28 N	93.25 W
Lonsdale, Point ›	169	38.17 S	144.37 E
Lons-le-Saunier	58	46.40 N	5.33 E
Lonton	110	25.06 N	96.17 E
Lontra ≃	250	6.37 S	48.39 W
Lontra, Ribeirão ≃	255	21.28 S	53.37 W
Lonua ≃	152	1.16 N	22.38 E
Lonzhen	107	30.00 N	103.59 E
Loo	84	43.43 N	39.36 E
Looc	116	12.16 N	121.59 E
Looe	42	50.21 N	4.28 W
Loogootee	194	38.40 N	86.54 W
Looking Glass ≃	216	42.52 N	84.54 W
Lookout	210	41.47 N	75.11 W
Lookout, Cape ›, N.C., U.S.	192	34.35 N	76.32 W
Lookout, Cape ›, Or., U.S.	224	45.20 N	124.00 W
Lookout, Point ›, Austl.	171a	27.26 S	153.33 E
Lookout, Point ›, Md., U.S.	208	38.02 N	76.19 W
Lookout Mountain ∧, U.S.	194	34.25 N	85.40 W
Lookout Mountain ∧, Or., U.S.	202	44.20 N	120.22 W
Lookout Mountain ∧, Or., U.S.	224	45.21 N	121.31 W
Lookout Mountain ∧, Wa., U.S.	224	48.40 N	122.22 W
Lookout Pass)(	202	47.27 N	115.42 W
Lookout Point Lake ⊜[1]	202	43.52 N	122.40 W
Lookout Ridge ⋏	180	69.07 N	158.36 W
Loolmalassin ∧[1]	154	3.03 S	35.49 E
Loomis, Ca., U.S.	226	38.49 N	121.12 W
Loomis, Ne., U.S.	198	40.28 N	99.30 W
Loomis, Wa., U.S.	182	48.49 N	119.37 W
Loon	116	9.48 N	123.47 E
Loon ≃	184	55.50 N	101.59 W
Loon Creek ≃	202	44.49 N	114.49 W
Loongana	162	30.57 S	127.02 E
Loon Lake ⊜, Can.	184	55.51 N	102.00 W
Loon Lake ⊜, Mi., U.S.	281	42.41 N	83.22 W
Loon Lake ⊜[1]	226	39.00 N	120.18 W
Loon op Zand	52	51.38 N	5.04 E
Loop	196	32.55 N	102.25 W
Loop ◆[8]	278	41.53 N	87.38 W

FRANÇAIS

Nom	Page	Lat.°′	Long.°′ W = Ouest
Loop Head ›	48	52.34 N	9.56 W
Lo Ortuzar	286e	33.28 S	70.45 W
Loos	50	50.37 N	3.01 E
Loosdorf	61	48.12 N	15.24 E
Loosduinen ◆[8]	52	52.04 N	4.13 E
Loose, B.R.D.	41	54.31 N	9.53 E
Loose, Eng., U.K.	260	51.14 N	0.31 E
Loose Creek	219	38.30 N	91.57 W
Lop	120	37.02 N	80.15 E
Lop ≃	110	13.18 N	107.37 E
Lopandino	76	52.28 N	34.49 E
Lopanka	80	46.24 N	40.59 E
Lopar'ovo	80	58.20 N	42.41 E
Lopasn'a ≃	82	54.51 N	37.52 E
Lopatiči	76	53.34 N	30.53 E
Lopatin, S.S.S.R.	78	50.13 N	24.50 E
Lopatin, S.S.S.R.	84	43.53 N	47.41 E
Lopatina, gora ∧	89	50.52 N	143.10 E
Lopatino, S.S.S.R.	80	52.37 N	45.47 E
Lopatino, S.S.S.R.	82	54.45 N	37.00 E
Lopatino, S.S.S.R.	89	48.24 N	142.15 E
Lopatinskij	82	55.21 N	38.34 E
Lopatka, mys ›	74	50.52 N	156.40 E
Lopatovo	76	56.08 N	29.12 E
Lop Buri	110	14.48 N	100.37 E
Lopé-Okanda, Réserve de Chasse de ◆[4]	152	0.30 S	11.40 E
Lopévi I	175f	16.30 S	168.21 E
Lopez, Pa., U.S.	210	41.27 N	76.20 W
Lopez, Wa., U.S.	224	48.31 N	122.54 W
López, Arroyo de ≃	258	35.26 S	57.35 W
Lopez, Cap ›	152	0.37 S	8.43 E
Lopez Bay c	116	13.56 N	122.12 E
López Collada	232	31.45 N	113.55 W
Lopez Island I	224	48.30 N	122.54 W
Lopez Lake ⊜[1]	226	35.12 N	120.28 W
Lopik	52	51.58 N	4.56 E
Lop Nor → Lop Nur ⊜	90	40.20 N	90.15 E
Lop Nur (Lop Nor) ⊜	90	40.20 N	90.15 E
Lopori ≃	152	1.14 N	19.49 E
Lopotovo	82	56.04 N	36.49 E
Loppersum	52	53.19 N	6.45 E
Loppi	26	60.43 N	24.27 E
Lo Prado, Embalse ⊜[1]	286e	33.26 S	70.48 W
Lo Prado Arriba	286e	33.26 S	70.45 W
Lopšen'ga	24	64.58 N	37.41 E
L'Opton Ruisseau ≃	261	48.52 N	1.29 E
Lopt'uga	24	63.16 N	47.56 E
Lopuchovka, S.S.S.R.	80	51.59 N	44.42 E
Lopuchovka, S.S.S.R.	80	50.37 N	44.29 E
Łopuszno	30	50.57 N	20.15 E
Lora	123	33.53 N	73.17 E
Lora ≃	246	9.25 N	72.25 W
Lora, Hāmūn-i- ⊜	128	29.20 N	64.50 E
Lora Creek ≃	162	28.10 S	135.22 E
Lora del Río	34	37.39 N	5.32 W
Lorain	214	41.27 N	82.10 W
Lorain □[6]	214	41.22 N	82.06 W
Lorain County Regional Airport ⊠	279a	41.20 N	82.11 W
Loraine, Ca., U.S.	228	35.19 N	118.25 W
Loraine, Il., U.S.	219	40.09 N	91.13 W
Loraine, Tx., U.S.	196	32.24 N	100.42 W
Loralai	120	30.22 N	68.36 E
Loramie, Lake ⊜[1]	216	40.23 N	84.18 W
Loramie Creek ≃	216	40.11 N	84.14 W
Lorca	34	37.40 N	1.42 W
Lorch, B.R.D.	56	48.49 N	9.40 E
Lorch, B.R.D.	56	50.02 N	7.48 E
Lorchhausen	56	50.03 N	7.47 E
Lord Howe Island I	160	31.33 S	159.05 E
Lord Howe Rise ⊹[3]	14	32.00 S	162.00 E
Lord Howe Seamounts ⊹[3]	14	28.00 S	159.00 E
Lord Mayor Bay c	176	69.44 N	92.00 W
Lordsburg	200	32.21 N	108.42 W
Lord's Cricket Ground ♠	260	51.32 N	0.10 W
Lordstown	214	41.09 N	80.53 W
Lords Valley	210	41.23 N	75.04 W
Loreauville	194	30.03 N	91.44 W
Loreley ♠	56	50.08 N	7.44 E
Lorena, Bra.	256	22.44 S	45.08 W
Lorena, Tx., U.S.	222	31.23 N	97.13 W
Lorengau	164	2.00 S	147.15 E
Lorentz ≃	164	5.23 S	138.04 E
Lorentzen	56	48.57 N	7.10 E
Lorenzago di Cadore	64	46.29 N	12.28 E
Lorenzo	196	33.40 N	101.32 W
Lorenzo Geyres (Queguay)	252	32.05 S	57.55 W
Loreo	64	45.04 N	12.11 E
Lorestān □[4]	128	33.30 N	48.30 E
Loreto, Arg.	252	27.46 S	57.17 W
Loreto, Bol.	248	15.13 S	64.40 W
Loreto, Bra.	250	7.05 S	45.09 W
Loreto, Col.	246	3.48 S	70.15 W
Loreto, It.	66	43.26 N	13.36 E
Loreto, Méx.	232	26.01 N	111.21 W
Loreto, Méx.	234	22.16 N	101.58 W
Loreto, Para.	252	23.16 S	57.11 W
Loreto, Pil.	116	10.21 N	125.34 E
Loreto, Pil.	116	8.12 N	125.45 E
Loreto □[5]	246	3.00 S	75.00 W
Loreto Aprutino	66	42.26 N	13.59 E
Lorette, Mb., Can.	184	49.44 N	96.52 W
Lorette, Fr.	62	45.31 N	4.35 E
Loretteville	206	46.51 N	71.21 W
Loretto → Loreto, It.	66	43.26 N	13.36 E
Loretto, Ky., U.S.	194	37.38 N	85.24 W
Loretto, Pa., U.S.	214	40.30 N	78.37 W
Loretto, Tn., U.S.	194	35.04 N	87.26 W
Lorgues	62	43.29 N	6.22 E
Lorian Swamp ≡	154	0.40 N	39.35 E
Lorica	246	9.14 N	75.49 W
Lorida	220	27.26 N	81.15 W
Lorient	32	47.45 N	3.22 W
L'Orignal	206	45.37 N	74.42 W
Lorimer Park ♠	285	40.06 N	75.05 W
Lorimor	194	41.07 N	94.03 W
Loring, Aeródromo de ⊠	266a	40.22 N	3.47 W
Loring Air Force Base ■	186	46.57 N	67.54 W
Lorino	180	65.30 N	171.43 W
Loriol-sur-Drôme	62	44.45 N	4.49 E
Loris	192	34.03 N	78.53 W
Lorman	194	31.49 N	91.03 W
L'Orme	261	48.39 N	1.41 E
Lormes	50	47.17 N	3.49 E
Lorn, Firth of c[1]	46	56.20 N	5.45 W
Lorna Glen	162	26.14 S	121.33 E
Lorne, Austl.	169	38.33 S	143.59 E
Lorne, N.B., Can.	186	47.53 N	66.08 W
Loro Ciuffenna	66	43.35 N	11.38 E
Loronyo	154	4.39 N	32.38 E
Lorquin	58	48.40 N	7.00 E
Lörrach	58	47.37 N	7.40 E
Lorrain, Rivière du ≃	240e	14.50 N	61.03 W
Lorraine □[9]	32	49.00 N	6.00 E
Lorrez-le-Bocage	50	48.14 N	2.54 E
Lorris	50	47.53 N	2.31 E
Lorsch	56	49.39 N	8.34 E
Lorsica	62	44.26 N	9.16 E
Lorup	52	52.55 N	7.38 E
Lorze ≃	58	47.15 N	8.25 E
Los	26	61.44 N	15.10 E
Los, Îles de II	150	9.30 N	13.48 W
Losa, Nuraghe ⊥	71	40.07 N	8.46 E
Losada ≃	246	2.12 N	73.55 W
Los Aguacates	286c	10.35 N	66.48 W
Los Alamitos	280	33.48 N	118.04 W
Los Alamitos Armed Forces Reserve Center ■	280	33.47 N	118.03 W
Los Alamitos Race Course ♠	280	33.48 N	118.03 W

PORTUGUÊS

Nome	Página	Lat.°′	Long.°′ W = Oeste
Los Alamos, Méx.	232	28.40 N	103.30 W
Los Alamos, Ca., U.S.	204	34.44 N	120.16 W
Los Alamos, N.M., U.S.	200	35.53 N	106.19 W
Los Aldamas	232	26.03 N	99.11 W
Los Altos, Méx.	196	26.14 N	98.28 W
Los Altos, Ca., U.S.	226	37.23 N	122.06 W
Los Altos Hills	226	37.22 N	122.08 W
Los Amates, Guat.	236	15.16 N	89.06 W
Los Amates, Méx.	234	18.08 N	102.15 W
Los Andes	252	32.50 S	70.37 W
Los Ángeles, Chile	252	37.28 S	72.21 W
Los Angeles, Ca., U.S.	228	34.03 N	118.14 W
Los Angeles, Ca., U.S.	280	34.03 N	118.14 W
Los Angeles □[6]	228	34.20 N	118.10 W
Los Angeles ≃	228	33.46 N	118.12 W
Los Angeles Aqueduct ≊[1]	204	35.22 N	118.05 W
Los Angeles Coliseum and Sports Arena ♠	280	34.01 N	118.17 W
Los Angeles Convention Center ᵾ	280	34.03 N	118.17 W
Los Angeles County Fairgrounds ♠	280	34.05 N	117.46 W
Los Angeles County Museum of Art ᵾ	280	34.05 N	118.22 W
Los Angeles Harbor c	280	33.42 N	118.16 W
Los Angeles International Airport ⊠	228	33.56 N	118.24 W
Los Antiguos	254	46.33 S	71.37 W
Losantville	218	40.01 N	85.10 W
Losap I[1]	14	6.54 N	152.44 E
Los Arabos	240p	22.44 N	80.43 W
Losarang	115a	6.24 S	108.10 E
Los Arroyos, Laguna de ⊜	248	12.38 S	65.00 W
Los Banos	226	37.03 N	120.50 W
Los Banos Creek ≃	226	37.20 N	120.57 W
Los Banos Creek, North Fork ≃	226	36.57 N	121.07 W
Los Banos Creek, South Fork ≃	226	36.57 N	121.07 W
Los Banos Reservoir ⊜[1]	226	36.59 N	120.57 W
Los Berros	252	31.57 S	68.39 W
Los Blancos	252	23.36 S	62.36 W
Los Burros	232	25.03 N	110.50 W
Los Cardales	258	34.20 S	58.59 W
Los Cerrillos, Arg.	252	31.57 S	65.28 W
Los Cerrillos, Ur.	258	34.37 S	56.22 W
Los Cerrillos, Aeropuerto ⊠	286e	33.30 S	70.43 W
Los Cerritos Center ◆[9]	280	33.52 N	118.05 W
Los Chacos	248	14.33 S	62.11 W
Löschenrod	56	50.30 N	9.41 E
Los Chiles	236	11.02 N	84.43 W
Los Conquistadores	252	30.36 S	58.28 W
Los Coronados, Islas II	204	32.25 N	117.15 W
Los Coyotes Indian Reservation ◆[4]	204	33.20 N	116.35 W
Los Cuatro Álamos	286e	33.32 S	70.44 W
Los Dos Caminos	286c	10.31 N	66.50 W
Los Ebanos, Méx.	232	24.40 N	97.45 W
Los Ebanos, Tx., U.S.	196	26.14 N	98.34 W
Loseley House ⊥	260	51.13 N	0.36 W
Los Esclavos ≃	236	13.50 N	90.20 W
Losevo	78	50.40 N	40.02 E
Los Flamencos, Laguna ⊜	258	35.36 S	58.42 W
Los Frentones	252	26.25 S	61.25 W
Los Fresnos	196	26.04 N	97.29 W
Los Garzas	196	26.23 N	99.46 W
Los Gatos	226	37.13 N	121.58 W
Los Gatos Creek ≃, Ca., U.S.	226	36.13 N	120.08 W
Los Gatos Creek ≃, Ca., U.S.	226	37.20 N	121.54 W
Los Glaciares, Parque Nacional ♠	254	49.52 S	73.05 W
Los Guerras	196	26.25 N	99.05 W
Loshan → Leshan	107	29.34 N	103.45 E
Los Haros	234	22.46 N	102.57 W
Losheim	56	49.30 N	6.44 E
Los Hermanos, Islas II	246	11.45 N	64.25 W
Los Herreras, Méx.	196	25.55 N	99.24 W
Los Herreras, Méx.	232	25.10 N	105.31 W
Losi	273a	6.40 N	3.31 E
Łosice	30	52.14 N	22.43 E
Los Indios, Canal de ʯ	240p	21.56 N	83.16 W
Lošinj, Otok I	36	44.36 N	14.24 E
Losinoborskaja	86	58.27 N	89.28 E
Losino-Petrovskij	82	55.52 N	38.12 E
Losinovka	78	50.51 N	31.54 E
Los Jazmines, Presa ⊜[1]	286a	19.25 N	99.16 W
Los Juríes	252	28.28 S	62.06 W
Loškar'ovka	78	47.57 N	34.12 E
Loskopdam ⊜[1]	156	25.23 S	29.20 E
Loskop Dam Game Reserve ◆[4]	156	25.23 S	29.20 E
Los Lagos	254	39.51 S	72.50 W
Los Lagos □[4]	254	41.45 S	73.00 W
Los Llanos	240m	18.03 N	66.24 W
Los Llanos [de Aridane]	148	28.39 N	17.54 W
Los López	196	26.15 N	99.05 W
Los Lunas	200	34.48 N	106.43 W
Los Mármoles, Parque Nacional ♠	234	20.55 N	99.12 W
Los Médanos, Istmo de ⊥[3]	241s	11.35 N	69.45 W
Los Menucos	254	40.50 S	68.08 W
Los Metates	234	23.46 N	106.02 W
Los Micos, Laguna de c	236	15.45 N	87.36 W
Los'mino	76	55.04 N	34.24 E
Los Mochis	232	25.45 N	108.57 W
Los Molinos	204	40.01 N	122.05 W
Los Muermos	254	41.24 S	73.29 W
Los Naranjos	286c	10.27 N	66.48 W
Los Navalmorales	34	39.43 N	4.38 W
Lošnica	76	54.17 N	28.46 E
Los Nietos	280	33.58 N	118.04 W
Løsning	41	55.48 N	9.42 E
Los Nogales	196	26.16 N	99.43 W
Losolava	175f	14.11 S	167.34 E
Los Olmos Creek ≃, Tx., U.S.	196	27.20 N	97.40 W
Los Olmos Creek ≃, Tx., U.S.	196	26.21 N	98.48 W
Los Osos	226	35.19 N	120.50 W
Los Padillas	200	34.58 N	106.41 W
Los Palacios, Arg.	252	29.22 S	68.11 W
Los Palacios, Cuba	240p	22.35 N	83.15 W
Los Palacios y Villafranca	34	37.10 N	5.56 W
Los Perros, Arroyo ≃	288	34.37 S	58.46 W
Los Pinos ◆[8]	286b	23.04 N	82.23 W
Los Pinos ≃	200	36.56 N	107.36 W
Los Placeres	234	18.13 N	100.54 W
Los Polvorines	288	34.30 S	58.41 W
Los Quillayes	286e	33.34 S	70.37 W
Los Quirquinchos	252	33.22 S	61.43 W
Los Rábanos	240m	18.11 N	66.50 W
Los Ramones	196	25.42 N	99.37 W
Los Remedios ≃	286a	19.31 N	99.05 W
Los Reyes de Salgado	234	19.35 N	102.29 W
Los Reyes la Paz	286a	19.21 N	98.58 W
Los Ríos □[4]	246	1.30 S	79.25 W
Los Rodríguez	232	27.11 N	101.21 W
Los Roques, Islas II	246	11.50 N	66.45 W
Lossa	54	51.13 N	11.25 E
Lossa ≃	54	51.18 N	11.10 E
Los Santos	246	7.56 N	80.25 W
Los Santos □[4]	236	7.55 N	80.25 W
Los Santos de Maimona	34	38.27 N	6.23 W
Los Sauces	252	37.58 S	72.50 W
Lossburg	58	48.25 N	8.27 E
Lössel	263	51.21 N	7.39 E
Losser	52	52.15 N	7.00 E
Los Serranos	228	33.59 N	117.42 W
Lossie ≃	46	57.43 N	3.16 W
Lossiemouth	46	57.43 N	3.18 W
Lössnitz	54	50.37 N	12.43 E
Lost ≃, U.S.	202	41.56 N	121.30 W
Lost ≃, In., U.S.	194	38.33 N	86.49 W
Lost ≃, Mn., U.S.	198	47.51 N	96.02 W
Lost ≃, W.V., U.S.	188	39.05 N	78.36 W
Lostant	216	41.09 N	89.04 W
Los Taques	246	11.50 N	70.16 W
Lost Bridge State Recreation Area ♠	216	40.45 N	85.37 W
Lost Creek ≃, Al., U.S.	194	33.38 N	87.14 W
Lost Creek ≃, Ar., U.S.	194	34.10 N	92.31 W
Lost Creek ≃, Oh., U.S.	218	39.58 N	84.09 W
Lost Creek ≃, Ut,. U.S.	200	41.04 N	111.32 W
Lost Creek ≃, Wy., U.S.	200	42.01 N	108.11 W
Lost Draw V	196	32.58 N	102.02 W
Los Telares	252	28.59 S	63.26 W
Los Teques	246	10.21 N	67.02 W
Los Testigos, Islas II	246	11.22 N	63.06 W
Lost Hills	226	35.36 N	119.41 W
Lostine ≃	202	45.33 N	117.29 W
Lost Lake ⊜, Or., U.S.	224	45.29 N	121.49 W
Lost Lake ⊜, Wa., U.S.	224	47.20 N	121.24 W
Lost Nation	190	41.57 N	90.49 W
Lostock ≃	262	53.40 N	2.48 W
Lostock Gralam	262	53.16 N	2.28 W
Los Trancos Creek ≃	282	37.25 N	122.12 W
Los Trancos Woods	282	37.21 N	122.12 W
Los Tres Palos	232	24.33 N	98.18 W
Lost River Range ⋏	202	44.10 N	113.35 W
Lost Trail Pass)(	202	45.41 N	113.57 W
Lostwithiel	42	50.25 N	4.40 W
Losuia	164	8.32 S	151.04 E
Los Vidrios	232	31.59 N	113.28 W
Los Vilos	252	31.55 S	71.31 W
Los Yébenes	34	39.34 N	3.53 W
Lot □[5]	32	44.35 N	1.40 E
Lot ≃	32	44.18 N	0.20 E
Lota	252	37.05 S	73.10 W
Lotagipi Swamp (Lotikipi Plain) ≡	144	4.36 N	34.55 E
Lotak	112	0.11 S	115.54 E
Lotbinière □[6]	206	46.30 N	71.40 W
Lotela, Lake ⊜	220	27.34 N	81.29 W
Løten	26	60.49 N	11.19 E
Lot-et-Garonne □[5]	32	44.20 N	0.20 E
Lotfābād	128	37.32 N	59.20 E
Lothair, S. Afr.	158	26.26 S	30.27 E
Lothair, Ky., U.S.	192	37.14 N	83.10 W
Lothian □[4]	46	55.55 N	3.05 W
Lothringen → Lorraine □[9]	32	49.00 N	6.00 E
Lotikipi Plain (Lotagipi Swamp) ≡	144	4.36 N	34.55 E
Loto	152	2.49 S	22.29 E
Loto ≃	152	1.55 S	22.09 E
Lotofaga	175a	13.59 S	171.50 W
Lotoi ≃	152	1.35 S	18.30 E
Lotorp	40	58.44 N	15.50 E
Lotošino	76	56.14 N	35.38 E
Lotrului, Munții ⋏	38	45.30 N	23.52 E
Lotsane ≃	156	22.41 S	28.11 E
Lötschberg Tunnel ◆[5]	58	46.25 N	7.45 E
Lötschental V	58	46.25 N	7.50 E
Lotseninsel I	41	54.40 N	10.01 E
Lott	222	31.12 N	97.02 W
Lotta ≃	24	68.36 N	31.06 E
Lottaville	278	41.31 N	87.22 W
Lotte	52	52.17 N	7.55 E
Lottivue	214	42.40 N	82.46 W
Löttringhausen ◆[8]	263	51.27 N	7.27 E
Lottsburg	208	37.57 N	76.31 W
Lotts Creek ≃	192	32.09 N	81.47 W
Lottsford Branch ≃	284c	38.55 N	76.49 W
Lottstetten	58	47.38 N	8.34 E
Lotuke, Jabal ∧	154	4.07 N	33.48 E
Lotung	100	24.41 N	121.46 E
Lötzen → Giżycko	30	54.03 N	21.47 E
Lotzorai	71	39.58 N	9.39 E
Louang Namtha	110	20.57 N	101.25 E
Louangphrabang	110	19.52 N	102.08 E
L'Ouarsenis, Massif de ⋏	34	35.40 N	1.50 E
Loubaresse	62	44.36 N	4.03 E
Loube, Montagne de la ∧	62	43.22 N	5.59 E
Loubetsi	152	3.12 S	12.10 E
Louchi	24	66.04 N	33.00 E
Loučim	60	49.22 N	13.07 E
Loučná ∧	54	50.39 N	13.37 E
Loude	98	35.54 N	117.18 E
Loudéac	32	48.10 N	2.45 W
Louden Cove c	276	41.05 N	73.43 W
Loudes	62	45.05 N	3.45 E
Loudima Poste	152	4.07 S	13.04 E
Loudon	192	35.43 N	84.20 W
Loudonville, N.Y., U.S.	210	42.42 N	73.45 W
Loudonville, Oh., U.S.	214	40.38 N	82.14 W
Loudoun □[6]	208	39.05 N	77.30 W
Loudun	32	47.01 N	0.05 E
Loué	32	48.00 N	0.09 W
Loue ≃	58	47.01 N	5.27 E
Louga	150	15.37 N	16.13 W
Louga □[4]	150	15.25 N	15.30 W
Louge	252	36.57 S	61.40 W
Louge ≃	32	43.27 N	1.20 E
Lougguéré ≃	150	15.35 N	14.47 W
Loughborough	42	52.47 N	1.11 W
Loughborough Lake ⊜	212	44.23 N	76.30 W
Loughermore ∧[2]	48	54.59 N	7.05 W
Loughman	220	28.14 N	81.34 W
Loughor	42	51.40 N	4.04 W
Loughor ≃	42	51.40 N	4.04 W
Loughrea	48	53.12 N	8.34 W
Loughros More Bay c	48	54.47 N	8.35 W
Loughton	260	51.39 N	0.03 E
Louhans	58	46.38 N	5.13 E
Louin	194	32.04 N	89.15 W
Louisa, Ky., U.S.	192	38.06 N	82.36 W
Louisa, Va., U.S.	192	38.01 N	78.00 W
Louisa, Lake ⊜, On., Can.	212	45.28 N	78.30 W
Louisa, Lake ⊜, Fl., U.S.	220	28.29 N	81.44 W
Louisbourg	186	45.55 N	59.58 W
Louis Bull Indian Reserve ◆[4]	182	52.53 N	113.31 W
Louisburg, Ks., U.S.	198	38.37 N	94.40 W
Louisburg, N.C., U.S.	192	36.05 N	78.18 W
Louisburgh	48	53.46 N	9.51 W
Louisdale	186	45.36 N	61.04 W
Louise, Ms., U.S.	194	32.58 N	90.35 W
Louise, Tx., U.S.	222	29.06 N	96.25 W
Louise, Lac ⊜, P.Q., Can.	206	45.43 N	71.25 W
Louise, Lac ⊜, P.Q., Can.	206	45.46 N	74.25 W
Louise, Lake ⊜	180	62.20 N	146.30 W
Louise Island I	182	52.58 N	131.50 W
Louiseville	206	46.15 N	72.57 W
Louis Gentil → Youssoufia	148	32.16 N	8.33 W
Louisiade Archipelago II	160	11.00 S	153.00 E
Louisiana	219	39.26 N	91.03 W
Louisiana □[3], U.S.	178	31.15 N	92.15 W
Louisiana □[3], U.S.	194	31.15 N	92.15 W
Louisiana ᵾ	41	55.58 N	12.33 E
Lou Island I	164	2.25 S	147.20 E
Louis Trichardt	156	23.01 S	29.43 E
Louisvale	158	28.33 S	21.12 E
Louisville, On., Can.	214	42.28 N	82.07 W
Louisville, Al., U.S.	194	31.47 N	85.33 W
Louisville, Ga., U.S.	192	33.00 N	82.24 W
Louisville, Il., U.S.	194	38.46 N	88.30 W
Louisville, Ky., U.S.	218	38.15 N	85.45 W
Louisville, Ms., U.S.	194	33.07 N	89.03 W
Louisville, Ne., U.S.	198	40.59 N	96.09 W
Louisville, Oh., U.S.	214	40.50 N	81.15 W
Louisville Ridge ⊹[3]	14	31.00 S	172.30 W
Louisville Seamount ⊹[3]	14	31.15 S	172.15 W
Louis-XIV, Pointe ›	176	54.37 N	79.45 W
Loujiaying	98	42.04 N	116.04 E
Loukanga	273b	4.20 S	15.09 E
Loukkos, Oued ≃	34	35.12 N	6.09 W
Loukoua ≃	273b	4.09 S	15.08 E
Loulé	34	37.08 N	8.02 W
Loum	152	4.43 N	9.44 E
Loumou	273b	4.08 S	15.09 E
Lount Lake ⊜	184	50.10 N	94.20 W
Louny	54	50.19 N	13.46 E
Loup ≃, Fr.	62	43.38 N	7.09 E
Loup ≃, Ne., U.S.	198	41.24 N	97.19 W
Loup, Gorge du V	56	49.47 N	6.23 E
Loup, Rivière du ≃	206	46.13 N	72.55 W
Loup City	198	41.16 N	98.57 W
Loups Marins, Lacs des ⊜	176	56.30 N	73.45 W
Lourches	50	50.19 N	3.21 E
Lourdes, Nf., Can.	186	48.39 N	59.00 W
Lourdes, Fr.	32	43.06 N	0.03 W
Lourel de Baixo	266c	38.49 N	9.22 W
Lourenço	250	2.30 N	51.40 W
Lourenço Marques → Maputo	156	25.58 S	32.35 E
Lourenço Marques → Maputo □[5]	156	26.00 S	32.25 E
Lourenço Velho	256	22.22 S	45.19 W
Lourenço Velho ≃, Bra.	256	23.26 S	45.35 W
Lourenço Velho ≃, Bra.	256	22.22 S	45.31 W
Loures	34	38.50 N	9.10 W
Loures ≃	266c	38.50 N	9.08 W
Lourinhã	34	39.14 N	9.19 W
Lourmarin	62	43.46 N	5.22 E
Lourosa	34	40.19 N	7.56 W
Loury	50	48.00 N	2.05 E
Lousã, Port.	34	40.07 N	8.15 W
Lousa, Port.	266c	38.53 N	9.12 W
Louse Creek ≃	198	46.22 N	100.57 W
Lou Shan ∧	89	45.15 N	128.58 E
Louta	150	13.30 N	3.10 W
Loutang	106	31.26 N	121.12 E
Loutézou, Île de I	273b	4.22 S	15.10 E
Louth, Austl.	166	30.32 S	145.07 E
Louth, Ire.	44	53.57 N	6.33 W
Louth, Ire.	48	53.37 N	6.53 W
Louth, Eng., U.K.	44	53.22 N	0.01 W
Louth □[6]	48	53.55 N	6.30 W
Louth Bay c	166	34.34 S	136.02 E
Louti, Mayo ≃	146	9.38 N	13.56 E
Loutit Bay c	169	38.33 S	144.00 E
Loutrá Aidhipsoú	38	38.51 N	23.02 E
Loutre ≃	219	38.42 N	91.25 W
Loutre, Bayou de ≃	194	32.41 N	92.08 W
Loutrópirgos	267c	38.02 N	23.28 E
Louvain → Leuven	56	50.53 N	4.42 E
Louveciennes	261	48.52 N	2.07 E
Louveigné	56	50.32 N	5.42 E
Louveira	256	23.04 S	46.58 W
Louviers, Fr.	50	49.13 N	1.10 E
Louviers, Co., U.S.	200	39.28 N	105.00 W
Louvre ᵾ	261	48.52 N	2.20 E
Louvres	50	49.02 N	2.30 E
Louvroil	50	50.16 N	3.58 E
Louwsburg	158	27.37 S	31.07 E
Lou Yaeger, Lake ⊜[1]	219	39.10 N	89.37 W
Lövånger	26	64.22 N	21.18 E
Lovászi	61	46.33 N	16.34 E
Lovat' ≃	76	58.14 N	31.28 E
Lovcy	82	55.00 N	39.15 E
Love	184	53.29 N	104.09 W
Loveč	38	43.08 N	24.43 E
Love Clough	262	53.44 N	2.17 W
Lovedale	279b	40.17 N	79.52 W
Lovejoy	219	38.39 N	90.10 W
Lovelady	222	31.08 N	95.27 W
Loveland, Co., U.S.	200	40.23 N	105.04 W
Loveland, Oh., U.S.	218	39.16 N	84.16 W
Lovell	202	44.50 N	108.23 W
Lovell Island I	283	42.20 N	70.56 W
Lovelock	204	40.10 N	118.28 W
Lovely	192	37.49 N	82.24 W
Love Point ›	208	39.02 N	76.18 W
Lovere	64	45.49 N	10.04 E
Lovering, Lac ⊜	206	45.10 N	72.09 W
Lovero	64	46.14 N	10.14 E
Loves Green	260	51.43 N	0.24 E
Loves Park	216	42.19 N	89.03 W
Loviisa → Lovisa	26	60.27 N	26.14 E
Lovilia	190	41.08 N	92.54 W
Loving, N.M., U.S.	196	32.17 N	104.05 W
Loving, Tx., U.S.	196	33.16 N	98.31 W
Lovingston	192	37.45 N	78.52 W
Lovington, Il., U.S.	219	39.42 N	88.37 W
Lovington, N.M., U.S.	196	32.56 N	103.20 W
Lovisa (Loviisa)	26	60.27 N	26.14 E
Lövő	61	47.30 N	16.47 E
Lovö I	40	59.20 N	17.50 E
Lovoi ≃	154	8.14 S	26.39 E
Lovosice	54	50.31 N	14.03 E
Lovozero, S.S.S.R.	24	65.00 N	29.50 E
Lovozero, S.S.S.R.	24	68.00 N	35.00 E
Lovozero, ozero ⊜	24	67.54 N	35.12 E
Lovrenc	61	46.32 N	15.23 E
Lövstabruk	40	60.24 N	17.53 E
Lövstabukten c	40	60.35 N	17.45 E
Lövstad slott ⊥	40	58.33 N	16.02 E
Lóvua, Ang.	152	7.20 S	20.16 E
Lóvua, Ang.	152	11.36 S	23.53 E
Lovua (Lóvua) ≃	152	6.07 S	20.35 E
Low	188	45.48 N	75.57 W
Low, Cape ›	176	63.07 N	85.18 W
Lowa	154	1.24 S	25.51 E
Lowa ≃	154	1.24 S	25.51 E
Lowāda	126	22.27 N	87.37 E
Lowat → Lovat' ≃	76	58.14 N	31.28 E
Lowber	279b	40.15 N	79.46 W
Lowden	190	41.51 N	90.55 W
Lowder Brook ≃	283	43.14 N	71.11 W
Lowell, Ar., U.S.	194	36.15 N	94.07 W
Lowell, In., U.S.	216	41.17 N	87.25 W
Lowell, Ma., U.S.	207	42.38 N	71.19 W
Lowell, Mi., U.S.	216	42.56 N	85.20 W
Lowell, Or., U.S.	202	43.55 N	122.46 W
Lowell, Lake ⊜[1]	202	43.33 N	116.40 W
Lowell, University of ᵾ[2]	283	42.39 N	71.20 W
Lowell-Dracut State Forest ♠	283	42.40 N	71.22 W
Lowelli	140	5.59 N	33.45 E
Lowellville	214	41.02 N	80.32 W
Löwen → Leuven, Bel.	56	50.53 N	4.42 E
Löwen → Lewin Brzeski, Pol.	30	50.46 N	17.37 E
Löwen ≃	158	26.51 S	18.17 E
Löwenberg	54	52.54 N	13.08 E
Löwenberg → Lwówek Śląski	30	51.07 N	15.35 E
Löwenbruch	264a	52.18 N	13.19 E
Löwenstein	56	49.06 N	9.22 E
Lowe Pond ⊜	283	42.41 N	70.59 W
Lower Aetna Lake ⊜	285	39.51 N	74.48 W
Lower Arrow Lake ⊜	182	49.40 N	118.08 W
Lower Bay c	208	40.33 N	74.02 W
Lower Bear River Reservoir ⊜[1]	226	38.33 N	120.14 W
Lower Bershire Valley	276	40.54 N	74.37 W
Lower Beverley Lake ⊜	212	44.36 N	76.09 W
Lower Broughton ◆[8]	262	53.29 N	2.15 W
Lower Brule Indian Reservation ◆[4]	198	44.05 N	99.44 W
Lower Buckhorn Lake ⊜	212	44.33 N	78.17 W
Lower Burrell	214	40.33 N	79.45 W
Lower California → Baja California ›[1]	232	28.00 N	113.30 W
Lower Chittering	168a	31.34 S	116.06 E
Lower Crystal Springs Reservoir ⊜[1]	226	37.32 N	122.22 W
Lower Darwen	262	53.43 N	2.28 W
Lower Egypt → Mişr Baḩrī □[9]	140	31.00 N	31.00 E
Lower Eltham Park ♠	274b	37.45 S	145.09 E
Lower Elwha Indian Reservation ◆[4]	224	48.09 N	123.33 W
Lower Fort Garry National Historic Park ♠	184	50.07 N	96.55 W
Lower Ganga Canal ≊	124	26.27 N	80.17 E
Lower Gap c	212	44.10 N	76.35 W
Lower Halstow	260	51.22 N	0.40 E
Lower Hay Lake ⊜	212	45.25 N	78.13 W
Lower Higham	260	51.26 N	0.28 E
Lower Huron Metropolitan Park ♠	281	42.12 N	83.25 W
Lower Hutt	172	41.13 S	174.55 E
Lower Kalskag	180	61.31 N	160.22 W
Lower Keechi Creek ≃	222	31.08 N	95.46 W
Lower Klamath Lake ⊜	204	41.55 N	121.42 W
Lower Lake	226	38.55 N	122.36 W
Lower Lake ⊜	204	41.15 N	120.02 W
Lower Loteni	158	29.32 S	29.36 E
Lower Manitou Lake ⊜	184	49.15 N	93.00 W
Lower Matecumbe Key I	220	24.51 N	80.43 W
Lower Montville	276	40.54 N	74.22 W
Lower Mystic Lake ⊜	283	42.26 N	71.09 W
Lower Nazeing	260	51.44 N	0.01 E
Lower Otay Lake ⊜[1]	228	32.37 N	116.55 W
Lower Paia	229a	20.55 N	156.23 W
Lower Paudash Lake ⊜	212	44.58 N	78.01 W
Lower Peirce Reservoir ⊜[1]	271c	1.22 N	103.49 E
Lower Peover	262	53.16 N	2.23 W
Lower Place	262	53.36 N	2.09 W
Lower Plenty	274b	37.44 S	145.06 E
Lower Portland	170	33.27 S	150.53 E
Lower Post	176	59.55 N	128.30 W
Lower Red Lake ⊜	198	48.00 N	94.50 W
Lower River Rouge ≃	281	42.18 N	83.14 W
Lower Rouge Parkway ♠	281	42.18 N	83.20 W
Lower Stoke	260	51.27 N	0.38 E
Lower Trajan's Wall ⊥	38	45.40 N	28.30 E
Lower Ugashik Lake ⊜	180	57.30 N	156.56 W
Lower Van Norman Lake ⊜[1]	280	34.17 N	118.29 W
Lower West Pubnico	186	43.38 N	65.48 W
Lower Whitley	262	53.18 N	2.35 W
Lower Wood's Harbour	186	43.31 N	65.44 W
Lowery, Lake ⊜	220	28.07 N	81.41 W
Lower Zambezi International Game Park ◆[4]	154	15.30 S	29.35 E
Lowestoft	42	52.29 N	1.45 E
Lowgar □[4]	120	33.50 N	69.00 E
Lowick	44	55.38 N	2.00 W
Łowicz	30	52.07 N	19.56 E
Lowman	210	42.02 N	76.44 W
Lowmoor	192	37.47 N	79.53 W
Lowood	171a	27.28 S	152.35 E
Lowrah (Pishīn Lora) ≃	120	29.09 N	64.55 E
Lowries Run ≃	279b	40.30 N	80.05 W
Low Rocky Point ›	166	43.00 S	145.30 E
Lowry Air Force Base ■	198	39.43 N	104.53 W
Lowry City	194	38.08 N	93.43 W
Lowther ≃	44	54.39 N	2.44 W
Lowther Hills ⋏[2]	44	55.19 N	3.38 W
Lowton	262	53.28 N	2.35 W
Lowton Common	262	53.29 N	2.33 W
Lowville, N.Y., U.S.	212	43.47 N	75.29 W
Lowville, Pa., U.S.	214	42.01 N	79.49 W
Loxahatchee	220	26.49 N	80.13 W
Loxley	194	30.37 N	87.45 W
Loxstedt	52	53.28 N	8.38 E
Loxten	52	52.03 N	8.08 E
Loxton, Austl.	166	34.27 S	140.35 E
Loxton, S. Afr.	158	31.30 S	22.22 E
Loyal	190	44.44 N	90.29 W
Loyal, Loch ⊜	46	58.23 N	4.22 W
Loyalhanna	214	40.19 N	79.21 W
Loyalhanna Creek ≃	214	40.28 N	79.27 W
Loyalhanna Lake ⊜[1]	214	40.25 N	79.28 W
Loyalsock Creek ≃	210	41.14 N	76.56 W
Loyalton	204	39.40 N	120.14 W
Loyalty Islands → Loyauté, Îles II	175f	21.00 S	167.00 E
Loyang, Sing.	271c	1.22 N	103.58 E
Loyang → Luoyang, Zhg.	102	34.41 N	112.28 E
Loyauté, Îles (Loyalty Islands) II	175f	21.00 S	167.00 E
Loyne, Loch ⊜	46	57.06 N	5.00 W
Loyola College ᵾ[2]	284b	39.21 N	76.37 W
Loyola University ᵾ[2], Ca., U.S.	280	33.58 N	118.25 W
Loyola University ᵾ[2], Il., U.S.	278	42.00 N	87.39 W
Loyoro	154	3.21 N	34.16 E
Loysburg	214	40.10 N	78.23 W
Loysville	208	40.22 N	77.21 W
Lozano	258	34.51 S	59.03 W
Lozère □[5]	32	44.30 N	3.30 E
Lozère, Mont ∧	62	44.25 N	3.46 E
Loznica	38	44.32 N	19.13 E
Ložnikovo, S.S.S.R.	86	56.54 N	73.56 E
Ložnikovo, S.S.S.R.	88	51.22 N	117.03 E
Lozno-Aleksandrovka	78	49.50 N	38.44 E
Loznoje	80	49.17 N	44.26 E
L'Ozone ◆[8]	273b	4.21 S	15.14 E
Lozovaja, S.S.S.R.	78	48.54 N	36.20 E
Lozovaja, S.S.S.R.	83	49.28 N	37.54 E
Lozovaja, S.S.S.R.	86	53.17 N	77.45 E
Lozovoje, S.S.S.R.	78	49.18 N	27.18 E
Lozovoje, S.S.S.R.	83	49.13 N	37.36 E
Lozovskij	83	48.33 N	38.54 E
Lozoyuela	34	40.55 N	3.37 W
Loz'va ≃	86	59.36 N	62.20 E

≃ River	Fluß	Río	Rivière	Rio
≊ Canal	Kanal	Canal	Canal	Canal
ᒐ Waterfall, Rapids	Wasserfall, Stromschnellen	Cascada, Rápidos	Chute d'eau, Rapides	Cascata, Rápidos
ʯ Strait	Meeresstraße	Estrecho	Détroit	Estreito
c Bay, Gulf	Bucht, Golf	Bahía, Golfo	Baie, Golfe	Baía, Golfo
⊜ Lake, Lakes	See, Seen	Lago, Lagos	Lac, Lacs	Lago, Lagos
≡ Swamp	Sumpf	Pantano	Marais	Pântano
⍓ Ice Features, Glacier	Eis- und Gletscherformen	Accidentes Glaciales	Formes glaciaires	Acidentes glaciares
⍑ Other Hydrographic Features	Andere Hydrographische Objekte	Otros Elementos Hidrográficos	Autres données hydrographiques	Outros acidentes hidrográficos

⊹ Submarine Features	Untermeerische Objekte	Accidentes Submarinos	Formes de relief sous-marin	Acidentes submarinos
□ Political Unit	Politische Einheit	Unidad Politica	Entité politique	Unidade política
ᵾ Cultural Institution	Kulturelle Institution	Institución Cultural	Institution culturelle	Instituição cultural
⊥ Historical Site	Historische Stätte	Sitio Histórico	Site historique	Sitio histórico
♠ Recreational Site	Erholungs- und Ferienort	Sitio de Recreo	Centre de loisirs	Area de Lazer
⊠ Airport	Flughafen	Aeropuerto	Aéroport	Aeroporto
■ Military Installation	Militäranlage	Instalación Militar	Installation militaire	Instalação militar
◆ Miscellaneous	Verschiedenes	Misceláneo	Divers	Diversos

Name / Name	Page / Seite	Lat.°′ / Breite°′	Long.°′ / Länge°′ E = Ost
Lozzo di Cadore	64	46.29 N	12.27 E
Lu	62	45.00 N	8.29 E
Lu ≃	100	27.04 N	115.00 E
Lua ≃	152	2.46 N	18.26 E
Luabo	156	18.30 S	36.10 E
Luabu ≃	152	2.46 S	18.19 E
Luachimo ≃	152	6.33 S	20.59 E
Luaha-sibuha	110	0.31 S	98.28 E
Luala ≃	154	17.57 S	36.30 E
Lualaba ≃	154	0.26 N	25.20 E
Luali	152	5.06 S	12.29 E
Lualoje ≃	152	12.18 S	21.38 E
Luama ≃	154	4.46 S	26.53 E
Luambe National Park ♠	154	12.25 S	32.15 E
Luambimba ≃	152	15.00 S	22.48 E
Luampa	154	15.03 S	24.28 E
Luampa ≃	154	14.33 S	24.10 E
Lu'an	100	31.44 N	116.31 E
Luan ≃	98	39.20 N	119.10 E
Luana ≃	152	7.56 S	21.06 E
Luana Point >	241q	18.02 N	77.52 W
Luan Balu	114	2.38 N	96.13 E
Luancheng, Zhg.	98	37.53 N	114.39 E
Luancheng, Zhg.	102	22.45 N	108.51 E
Luanchuan	102	33.51 N	111.36 E
Luancundo ≃	152	16.25 S	21.27 E
Luanda	152	8.48 S	13.14 E
Luanda □[5]	152	9.00 S	13.15 E
Luando ≃	152	10.19 S	16.40 E
Luando, Réserva do ◆[4]	152	11.10 S	17.30 E
Luang, Khao ∧	110	8.31 N	99.47 E
Luang, Thale c	110	7.30 N	100.15 E
Luang Chiang Dao, Doi ∧	110	19.23 N	98.54 E
Luanginga (Luanguinga) ≃	152	15.11 S	22.56 E
Luang Prabang → Louangphrabang	110	19.52 N	102.08 E
Luang Prabang Range ⋏	110	18.30 N	101.15 E
Luangue	152	7.19 S	19.38 E
Luangue (Loange) ≃	152	4.17 S	20.02 E
Luanguinga (Luanginga) ≃	152	15.11 S	22.56 E
Luangwa (Aruângua) ≃	154	15.36 S	30.25 E
Luanhaizi	120	34.27 N	93.12 E
Luanhe	105	40.57 N	117.44 E
Luannan (Bencheng)	98	39.32 N	118.39 E
Luanping (Anjiangying)	98	40.57 N	117.20 E
Luanshishan	104	42.10 N	123.41 E
Luanshya	154	13.08 S	28.24 E
Luán Toro	252	36.12 S	65.06 W
Luanxian	98	39.45 N	118.44 E
Luanza	154	8.42 S	28.42 E
Luapula □[4]	154	10.55 S	29.00 E
Luapula ≃	154	9.26 S	28.33 E
Luar, Danau ⊜	112	0.55 N	112.15 E
Luarca	34	43.32 N	6.32 W
Luashi	152	10.56 S	23.37 E
Luashi ≃	152	10.41 S	22.55 E
Luassinga ≃	152	15.47 S	18.50 E
Luati	152	14.35 S	21.13 E
Luatira	152	12.52 S	17.14 E
Luau	152	10.42 S	22.12 E
Lua-Vindu ≃	152	3.38 N	19.16 E
Luba	152	3.27 N	8.33 E
Lubaantum ⊥	232	16.17 N	88.58 W
Lubaczów	30	50.10 N	23.07 E
Lubalo	152	9.12 S	19.16 E
Lubalo ≃	152	7.22 S	19.20 E
Lubamiti	152	2.29 S	17.47 E
Lubań, Pol.	30	51.08 N	15.18 E
L'uban', S.S.S.R.	76	59.21 N	31.13 E
L'uban', S.S.S.R.	76	52.37 N	29.08 E
L'uban', S.S.S.R.	76	52.48 N	27.59 E
Lubāna	76	56.54 N	26.43 E
Lubānas ezers ⊜	76	56.46 N	26.53 E
Lubang	116	13.52 N	120.07 E
Lubang Island I	116	13.46 N	120.11 E
Lubang Islands II	116	13.46 N	120.15 E
Lubango	152	14.55 S	13.30 E
Lubanowo	54	53.09 N	14.36 E
Lubansenshi ≃	154	11.21 S	30.35 E
Lub'any	80	56.02 N	51.24 E
Lubao	100	23.22 N	112.55 E
L'ubar	78	49.55 N	27.44 E
Lübars, D.D.R.	54	52.39 N	12.02 E
Lübars, D.D.R.	54	52.10 N	12.09 E
Lübars ◆[8]	264a	52.37 N	13.22 E
Lubartów	30	51.28 N	22.38 E
L'ubašovka	78	47.51 N	30.15 E
Lubawa	30	53.30 N	19.45 E
Lubaynī, Baḥr al- ≋	273c	29.56 N	31.11 E
Lübbecke	52	52.18 N	8.36 E
Lübben	54	51.56 N	13.53 E
Lübbenau	54	51.52 N	13.57 E
Lubber Brook ≃	283	42.33 N	71.09 W
Lubbers Run ≃	276	40.56 N	74.43 W
Lübbesee ⊜	54	53.05 N	13.34 E
Lubbock	196	33.34 N	101.51 W
Lübbow	54	52.54 N	11.10 E
Lubbub Creek ≃	194	33.04 N	88.10 W
L'ubča	76	53.45 N	26.03 E
L'ubeč, S.S.S.R.	78	51.42 N	30.39 E
Lubec, Me., U.S.	188	44.51 N	66.59 W
Lübeck	52	53.52 N	10.40 E
Lübecker Bucht c	54	54.00 N	10.55 E
Lubefu	152	4.43 S	24.25 E
Lubefu ≃	152	4.10 S	23.00 E
Lubelska, Wyżyna ⋏[2]	30	51.00 N	23.00 E
Lubembe (Luembe) ≃	152	6.37 S	21.05 E
Lüben → Lubin	30	51.24 N	16.13 E
Lubenec	54	50.06 N	13.20 E
L'ubercy	82	55.41 N	37.53 E
Lubéron, Montagne du ⋏	62	43.48 N	5.22 E
Lubersac	32	45.27 N	1.24 E
L'ubešov	78	51.46 N	25.31 E
Lübesse	54	53.29 N	11.28 E
Lubi ≃	152	4.58 S	23.26 E
Lubiana → Ljubljana	36	46.03 N	14.31 E
Lubic Island I	116	10.58 N	120.44 E
L'ubickoje	80	51.46 N	49.19 E
Lubień Kujawski	30	52.25 N	19.10 E
Lubilash ≃	152	6.02 S	23.45 E
Lubile	154	2.55 S	26.45 E
L'ubim	80	58.22 N	40.41 E
L'ubimovka, S.S.S.R.	78	51.31 N	35.37 E
L'ubimovka, S.S.S.R.	78	46.47 N	33.34 E
L'ubimovka, S.S.S.R.	86	52.15 N	66.45 E
L'ubimyj	83	47.53 N	39.28 E
Lubin, Pol.	30	51.24 N	16.13 E
Lubin, Pol.	54	53.50 N	14.25 E
L'ubino	86	57.30 N	88.47 E
L'ubinskij	86	55.09 N	72.42 E
Lubishi ≃	152	6.54 S	24.09 E
Lubja ≃	265a	59.58 N	30.30 E
Lublin	30	51.15 N	22.35 E
Lublin □[4]	30	51.30 N	22.30 E
Lubliniec	30	50.40 N	18.41 E
L'ublino ◆[8]	265b	55.41 N	37.44 E
Lubmin	54	54.08 N	13.37 E
Lubnān → Lebanon □[1]	128	34.00 N	36.00 E
Lubnān, Jabal (Lebanon Mountains) ⋏	132	34.00 N	36.00 E
L'ubnica	76	57.58 N	32.42 E
Lubny	78	50.01 N	33.00 E
L'ubochna	76	53.31 N	34.23 E
Lubok China	114	2.27 N	102.04 E
Lubomierz	30	51.01 N	15.30 E
L'uboml'	78	51.14 N	24.01 E
Luboń	30	52.23 N	16.54 E
Lubondai	152	6.34 S	22.39 E
Lubondoi	154	8.02 S	26.31 E
L'ubostan'	78	51.19 N	35.44 E
L'ubotin	78	49.57 N	35.57 E
Lubraniec	30	52.33 N	18.50 E
Lubsko	30	51.46 N	14.59 E
Lubsza ≃	54	51.56 N	14.43 E
Lübtheen	54	53.18 N	11.04 E
Lubu, Indon.	112	0.46 S	122.30 E
Lubu, Zhg.	102	23.09 N	112.13 E
Lubuagan	116	17.21 N	121.10 E
L'ubučany	82	55.15 N	37.33 E
Lubudi, Zaïre	152	6.51 S	21.18 E
Lubudi, Zaïre	154	9.57 S	25.58 E
Lubudi ≃, Zaïre	152	4.03 S	21.23 E
Lubudi ≃, Zaïre	154	9.13 S	25.38 E
Lubue	152	4.09 S	19.52 E
Lubue ≃	152	4.10 S	19.53 E
Lubukambacang	112	0.37 S	101.25 E
Lubukbatang	112	4.03 S	104.12 E
Lubukbertubung	112	0.02 N	102.08 E
Lubuklinggau	112	3.18 S	102.52 E
Lubukpakam	114	3.33 N	98.52 E
Lubukraya, Dolok ∧	114	1.29 N	99.13 E
Lubuksikaping	112	0.08 N	100.10 E
Lubumbaschi → Lubumbashi	154	11.40 S	27.28 E
Lubumbashi (Élisabethville)	154	11.40 S	27.28 E
Lubunda	154	5.10 S	26.40 E
Lubutu	154	0.44 S	26.35 E
Luby	54	50.12 N	12.25 E
L'ubytino	76	58.49 N	33.23 E
Lübz	54	53.27 N	12.01 E
Lučak	85	38.23 N	67.25 E
Lucala	152	9.16 S	15.15 E
Lucala ≃, Ang.	152	6.38 S	12.34 E
Lucala ≃, Ang.	152	9.37 S	14.14 E
Lucan, On., Can.	190	43.11 N	81.24 W
Lucan, Ire.	48	53.22 N	6.27 W
Lucanas	248	14.36 S	74.15 W
Lucania □[9]	68	40.30 N	16.00 E
Lucania, Mount ∧	180	61.01 N	140.28 W
Lucano	152	11.16 S	21.38 E
Lucaogou	102	42.26 N	96.55 E
Lucapa	152	8.36 S	20.54 E
Lucas, Ia., U.S.	190	41.01 N	93.27 W
Lucas, Ks., U.S.	198	39.03 N	98.32 W
Lucas, Oh., U.S.	214	40.45 N	82.30 W
Lucas, Tx., U.S.	222	33.05 N	96.35 W
Lucas □[6]	214	41.39 N	83.32 W
Lucas González	252	32.24 S	59.33 W
Lucas Heights	274a	34.02 S	150.58 E
Lucas Valley	282	38.03 N	122.35 W
Lucasville	218	38.52 N	82.59 W
Lucban	116	14.06 N	121.33 E
Lucca	66	43.50 N	10.29 E
Lucca □[4]	64	44.02 N	10.27 E
Lucca Sicula	70	37.35 N	13.18 E
Lucé	50	48.26 N	1.28 E
Luce, Water of ≃	44	54.52 N	4.48 W
Lucea	241q	18.27 N	78.10 W
Luce Bay c	44	54.47 N	4.50 W
Luce Bayou ≃	222	30.03 N	95.07 W
Lucedale	194	30.55 N	88.35 W
Lucena, Esp.	34	37.24 N	4.29 W
Lucena, Pil.	116	13.56 N	121.37 E
Lucenay-L'Évêque	32	47.05 N	4.15 E
Luc-en-Diois	62	44.37 N	5.27 E
Lučenec	30	48.20 N	19.40 E
Lucens	58	46.42 N	6.50 E
Luceque	152	14.41 S	15.04 E
Lucera	68	41.30 N	15.20 E
Lucéram	62	43.53 N	7.22 E
Lucerne → Luzern, Schw.	58	47.03 N	8.18 E
Lucerne, Ca., U.S.	204	39.05 N	122.47 W
Lucerne, In., U.S.	216	40.52 N	86.24 W
Lucerne, Lake → Vierwaldstätter See ⊜	58	47.00 N	8.28 E
Lucerne Lake ⊜	228	34.31 N	116.57 W
Lucernemines	214	40.33 N	79.09 W
Lucerne Valley	228	34.26 N	116.58 W
Lucero	200	30.49 N	106.30 W
Lucero, Lake ⊜	200	32.42 N	106.25 W
Lučesa ≃	76	55.10 N	30.11 E
Luch	80	57.01 N	42.15 E
Luch ≃	80	56.14 N	42.25 E
Luchang	102	26.23 N	102.18 E
Luchena ≃	34	37.44 N	1.50 W
Lucheng, Zhg.	102	24.21 N	106.00 E
Lücheng, Zhg.	106	31.55 N	119.44 E
Lucheng, Zhg.	106	31.47 N	120.02 E
Luché-Pringé	50	47.42 N	0.05 E
Lucheringo ≃	154	11.43 S	36.17 E
Luchibe ≃	152	12.07 S	21.13 E
Luchico (Lushiko) ≃	152	6.13 S	19.40 E
Luchou	269d	25.05 N	121.28 E
Luchovicy	82	54.59 N	39.03 E
Lüchow, B.R.D.	54	52.58 N	11.10 E
Luchow → Luzhou, Zhg.	107	28.54 N	105.27 E
Lüchtringen	52	51.47 N	9.25 E
Luchuan	102	22.19 N	110.11 E
Luci	100	29.52 N	119.47 E
Lucie ≃	250	3.35 N	57.38 W
Lucikou	100	28.56 N	116.04 E
Lučin	76	53.01 N	30.01 E
Lucinda, Austl.	166	18.32 S	146.20 E
Lucinda, Pa., U.S.	214	41.19 N	79.22 W
Lucindale	166	36.59 S	140.22 E
Lucipara, Kepulauan II	164	5.30 S	127.33 E
Lucira	152	13.51 S	12.31 E
Lucito	66	41.44 N	14.41 E
Luci Yu I	100	25.07 N	119.22 E
Luck, S.S.S.R.	78	50.44 N	25.20 E
Luck, Wi., U.S.	190	45.34 N	92.28 W
Luck, Mount ∧[2]	162	28.47 S	123.33 E
Lucka	54	51.06 N	12.20 E
Luckau	54	51.51 N	13.43 E
Luckeesarai	124	25.11 N	86.05 E
Luckenwalde	54	52.05 N	13.10 E
Luckey	214	41.27 N	83.29 W
Luckhoff	158	29.44 S	24.43 E
Luckiamute ≃	202	44.45 N	123.09 W
Luck Lake ⊜	184	51.05 N	107.07 W
Lucknow, On., Can.	190	43.57 N	81.31 W
Lucknow, India	124	26.51 N	80.55 E
Lucknow, Pa., U.S.	208	40.20 N	76.54 W
Lucknow Branch ≋	124	27.57 N	80.03 E
Lucky Lake	184	51.00 N	107.10 W
Lucky Peak Lake ⊜[1]	202	43.33 N	116.00 W
Luco dei Marsi	66	41.58 N	13.28 E
Lucomagno, Passo del)(	58	46.33 N	8.49 E
Luçon, Fr.	32	46.27 N	1.10 W
Lucon, Pa., U.S.	285	40.14 N	75.25 W
Luconha ≃	152	12.54 S	21.15 E
Lucun, Zhg.	98	36.12 N	118.01 E
Lucun, Zhg.	106	30.49 N	119.26 E
Lucunga ≃	152	6.57 S	12.48 E
Lucungu ≃	152	6.41 S	14.26 E
Lucusse	152	12.32 S	20.48 E
Lucy Creek	166	22.25 S	136.20 E
Lüda → Dalian	98	38.53 N	121.35 E
Luda Kamčija ≃	38	43.03 N	27.29 E
Ludao	89	43.51 N	129.19 E
Ludbreg	36	46.15 N	16.37 E
Luddan	123	29.54 N	72.34 E
Luddenden	262	53.44 N	1.56 W
Luddenham	274a	33.53 S	150.41 E
Luddesdown	260	51.22 N	0.24 E
Lüdenscheid	56	51.13 N	7.38 E
Lüder ≃	56	50.31 N	9.27 E
Lüderitz, D.D.R.	54	52.30 N	11.44 E
Lüderitz, Namibia	156	26.38 S	15.10 E
Lüderitz □[5]	156	26.30 S	15.45 E
Lüdersdorf	54	53.47 N	10.46 E
Ludgershall	42	51.16 N	1.37 W
Ludgo	40	58.55 N	17.08 E
Ludhiāna	123	30.54 N	75.51 E
Ludian	102	27.11 N	103.33 E
Luding	102	29.55 N	102.15 E
Lüdinghausen	52	51.46 N	7.26 E
Ludington	190	43.57 N	86.27 W
Ludingtonville	210	41.29 N	73.39 W
L'udinovo	76	53.52 N	34.27 E
L'udkovo	76	54.36 N	34.43 E
Ludlam Bay c	208	39.10 N	74.42 W
Ludlow, Eng., U.K.	42	52.22 N	2.43 W
Ludlow, Il., U.S.	216	40.23 N	88.08 W
Ludlow, Ky., U.S.	218	39.05 N	84.32 W
Ludlow, Ma., U.S.	207	42.09 N	72.28 W
Ludlow, Pa., U.S.	214	41.43 N	78.56 W
Ludlow, Vt., U.S.	188	43.23 N	72.42 W
Ludlow Falls	218	40.00 N	84.20 W
Ludlowville	210	42.33 N	76.32 W
Ludogorie ◆[1]	38	43.46 N	26.56 E
Ludonghe	102	25.53 N	103.33 E
Ludoni	76	58.12 N	29.21 E
Ludowici	192	31.42 N	81.44 W
Luduș	38	46.29 N	24.05 E
Ludvika	40	60.09 N	15.11 E
Ludwigkanal ≋	60	49.05 N	11.27 E
Ludwigsburg	56	48.53 N	9.11 E
Ludwigsfelde	54	52.17 N	13.16 E
Ludwigsfelder-Heide ◆[3]	264a	52.18 N	13.14 E
Ludwigshafen	56	49.29 N	8.26 E
Ludwigshafen am Bodensee	58	47.49 N	9.03 E
Ludwigslust	54	53.19 N	11.30 E
Ludwigsort → Laduškin	76	54.36 N	20.11 E
Ludwigsstadt	54	50.30 N	11.23 E
Ludwigstein, Burg ⊥	56	51.20 N	9.55 E
Ludza	76	56.33 N	27.43 E
Lue	170	32.39 S	149.51 E
Luebo	152	5.21 S	21.25 E
Lueders	196	32.48 N	99.37 W
Lueg, Pass)(	64	47.34 N	13.12 E
Lueki	154	3.22 S	25.51 E
Luele ≃	152	7.55 S	20.09 E
Luemba	154	3.42 S	28.40 E
Luembe (Lubembe) ≃, Afr.	152	6.37 S	21.05 E
Luembé ≃, Zaïre	154	6.43 S	24.11 E
Luena, Ang.	152	11.47 S	19.52 E
Luena, Zaïre	154	9.27 S	25.47 E
Luena ≃, Ang.	152	12.31 S	22.34 E
Luena ≃, Zam.	152	14.45 S	23.25 E
Luena Flats ≋	152	14.50 S	23.20 E
Luengué ≃	152	16.54 S	21.52 E
Luenha (Ruenya) ≃	154	16.24 S	33.48 E
Lueo ≃	152	9.06 S	23.51 E
Luepa	246	5.43 N	61.31 W
Lueta	152	7.19 S	22.06 E
Lueta ≃	152	7.04 S	21.40 E
Lueyang	102	33.20 N	106.10 E
Lüfangsicun	104	41.25 N	123.22 E
Lufeng, Zhg.	100	22.57 N	115.38 E
Lufeng, Zhg.	102	25.07 N	102.07 E
Lufico	152	6.24 S	13.23 E
Lufira ≃	154	8.16 S	26.27 E
Lufkin	222	31.20 N	94.43 W
Luftekopf ∧[2]	56	50.05 N	7.37 E
Lufubu ≃	154	8.36 S	30.47 E
Lufuidje ≃	152	12.52 S	22.47 E
Lufupa	154	10.37 S	24.56 E
Lufupa ≃	154	14.37 S	26.12 E
Luga	76	58.44 N	29.52 E
Luga ≃	76	59.40 N	28.18 E
Lugagnano Val d'Arda	62	44.49 N	9.50 E
Lugan' ≃	83	48.37 N	39.27 E
Lugančik ≃	83	48.35 N	39.32 E
Lugang, Zhg.	100	31.17 N	118.22 E
Lugang, Zhg.	100	27.23 N	115.36 E
Luganga	154	7.31 S	35.32 E
Lugano	58	46.01 N	8.58 E
Lugano, Lago di ⊜	58	46.00 N	9.00 E
Lugansk → Vorošilovgrad	83	48.34 N	39.20 E
Luganskoje	83	48.26 N	38.15 E
Luganville	175f	15.32 S	167.10 E
Lugards Falls ʟ	154	3.03 S	38.42 E
Lugareño	240p	21.33 N	77.28 W
Lugarno	274a	33.59 S	151.03 E
Lugau	54	50.44 N	12.44 E
Lügde	52	51.57 N	9.15 E
Lugela	154	16.25 S	36.43 E
Lugenda	154	12.30 S	37.43 E
Lugenda ≃	154	11.25 S	38.33 E
Lugg ≃	42	52.02 N	2.38 W
Luggarus → Locarno	58	46.10 N	8.48 E
Luginino	76	57.43 N	35.17 E
Luginy	78	51.04 N	28.24 E
Lugnano in Teverina	66	42.34 N	12.20 E
Lugnaquillia Mountain ∧	48	52.58 N	6.27 W
Lugnås	40	58.39 N	13.42 E
Lugny	58	46.28 N	4.49 E
Lugo, Esp.	34	43.00 N	7.34 W
Lugo, It.	66	44.25 N	11.54 E
Lugoj	38	45.41 N	21.54 E
Lugongshi	106	31.38 N	121.12 E
Lugos → Lugoj	38	45.41 N	21.54 E
Lugouqiao	105	39.51 N	116.13 E
Lugovaja Subbota	86	59.52 N	69.45 E
Lugovoj, S.S.S.R.	85	42.56 N	72.45 E
Lugovoj, S.S.S.R.	86	59.44 N	65.55 E
Lugovoje	85	42.55 N	72.43 E
Lugovskij	88	58.02 N	112.54 E
Lugovskoje	80	50.38 N	46.28 E
Lugu	102	28.21 N	102.09 E
Lugulu ≃	154	2.17 S	26.32 E
Lugunga ∧	154	6.47 S	36.19 E
Luguru	154	2.55 S	33.58 E
Lugus Island I	116	5.41 N	120.50 E
Luhanka	26	61.47 N	25.42 E
Luhe	60	49.35 N	12.09 E
Luhe ≃	52	53.18 N	10.11 E
Lühedian	100	32.33 N	114.28 E
Lühmannsdorf	54	54.00 N	13.38 E
Luhombero ≃	154	8.24 S	37.12 E
Luhsien → Luzhou	107	28.54 N	105.27 E
Luhuo	102	31.26 N	100.48 E
Lui ≃, Ang.	152	8.41 S	17.56 E
Lui ≃, Zam.	152	16.21 S	23.18 E
Lui, Beinn ∧	46	56.24 N	4.49 W
Luia	152	8.26 S	21.45 E
Luia (Ruya) ≃, Afr.	154	16.34 S	33.12 E
Luia ≃, Ang.	152	8.24 S	21.42 E
Lúia ≃, Moç.	154	15.34 S	32.58 E
Luiana	152	17.23 S	23.03 E
Luiana ≃	152	17.27 S	23.14 E
Luichart, Loch ⊜	46	57.37 N	4.46 W
Luido	156	21.31 S	34.41 E
Luie ≃	152	4.33 S	17.41 E
Luik → Liège	56	50.38 N	5.34 E
Luilaka ≃	152	0.52 S	20.12 E
Luilu ≃	152	6.22 S	23.50 E
Luimbale	152	12.15 S	15.19 E
Luimneach → Limerick	48	52.40 N	8.38 W
Luing I	46	56.13 N	5.40 W
Luino	58	46.00 N	8.44 E
Luio ≃	152	13.15 S	21.39 E
Luipaardsvlei	273d	26.16 S	27.42 E
Luiro ≃	24	67.08 N	27.29 E
Luís Alves	252	26.44 S	48.57 W
Luisant	50	48.25 N	1.29 E
Luís Correia	250	2.53 S	41.40 W
Luisen-Berg ∧[2]	264a	52.27 N	13.07 E
Luisenthal	54	50.47 N	10.43 E
Luís Gomes	250	6.25 S	38.23 W
Luis Guillón	288	34.48 S	58.27 W
Luishia	154	11.10 S	27.02 E
Luisiânia	255	21.41 S	50.17 W
Luis Moya, Méx.	234	22.25 N	102.15 W
Luis Moya, Méx.	234	23.05 N	103.56 W
Luis Peña, Cayo de I	240m	18.18 N	65.20 W
Luis Pereira, Arroyo ≃	258	34.33 S	57.02 W
Luita	152	8.04 S	19.25 E
Luitpold Coast ⊥[2]	9	78.30 S	32.00 W
Luiza	152	7.12 S	22.25 E
Luiza ≃	152	7.35 S	22.40 E
Luizavo ≃	152	11.42 S	23.12 E
Luizi	154	6.03 S	27.28 E
Luján, Arg.	252	32.22 S	65.57 W
Luján, Arg.	252	33.03 S	68.52 W
Luján, Arg.	258	34.34 S	59.07 W
Luján ≃	288	34.26 S	58.32 W
Lujia, Zhg.	106	31.15 N	121.37 E
Lujia, Zhg.	106	31.19 N	121.03 E
Lujia, Zhg.	269b	31.22 N	121.18 E
Lujiabang	106	31.20 N	121.01 E
Lujiachang	107	30.14 N	105.34 E
Lujiagangzi	104	42.05 N	122.59 E
Lujiang	100	31.14 N	117.17 E
Lujiao	100	29.10 N	112.52 E
Lujiaoxi	107	28.55 N	105.48 E
Lujiaqiao, Zhg.	106	31.47 N	120.27 E
Lujiaqiao, Zhg.	107	28.50 N	106.21 E
Lujiatun, Zhg.	98	40.14 N	122.11 E
Lujiatun, Zhg.	104	41.58 N	122.38 E
Lujiatun, Zhg.	104	41.10 N	121.56 E
Lujiatun, Zhg.	104	42.18 N	124.15 E
Lujiazhou	100	28.16 N	114.35 E
L'uk	80	56.55 N	52.48 E
Lukachukai Wash V	200	36.39 N	109.36 W
Lukačok	89	53.03 N	132.16 E
Lukala	152	5.31 S	14.32 E
Lukang	100	24.03 N	120.25 E
Lukanga, Zaïre	152	1.00 S	18.08 E
Lukanga, Zaïre	152	1.41 S	18.09 E
Lukanga Swamp ≋	154	14.25 S	27.45 E
Luk'anovo	82	54.52 N	37.25 E
Lukašin	84	40.12 N	44.01 E
Lukaškin Jar	86	60.20 N	78.24 E
Luke, Mount ∧	162	27.13 S	116.48 E
Luke Air Force Base ■	200	33.32 N	112.22 W
Lukenie ≃	152	2.44 S	18.09 E
Lukens, Mount ∧	280	34.16 N	118.14 W
Lukeville	200	31.52 N	112.48 W
Luki	76	53.29 N	26.15 E
Lukino, S.S.S.R.	82	55.26 N	37.04 E
Lukino, S.S.S.R.	82	55.50 N	36.49 E
Lukka	140	14.33 N	23.42 E
Luknovo	80	56.12 N	42.03 E
Lukojanov	80	55.02 N	44.30 E
Lukolela, Zaïre	152	5.23 S	24.32 E
Lukolela, Zaïre	152	1.03 S	17.12 E
Lukong	107	29.31 N	105.39 E
Lukoshi ≃	152	10.05 S	22.59 E
Lukosi	154	18.30 S	26.30 E
Lukoškino	82	55.19 N	37.16 E
Lukou, Zhg.	100	27.14 N	114.04 E
Lukou, Zhg.	106	31.48 N	118.52 E
Lukoupu	100	29.30 N	113.26 E
Lukouyu	100	28.24 N	113.18 E
Lukov	78	51.13 N	24.19 E
Lukovit	38	43.12 N	24.10 E
Lukovskaja	80	50.35 N	41.52 E
Łuków	30	51.56 N	22.23 E
Lükqün	86	42.44 N	89.42 E
Lukuga ≃	154	5.40 S	26.55 E
Lukula	152	5.23 S	12.57 E
Lukula ≃, Afr.	152	5.08 S	12.28 E
Lukula ≃, Zaïre	152	4.13 S	17.58 E
Lukuledi ≃	154	10.05 S	39.42 E
Lukulu	152	14.25 S	23.12 E
Lukulu ≃	154	10.56 S	31.05 E
Lukumburu	154	9.45 S	35.09 E
Lukunga ≃	273b	4.25 S	15.14 E
Lukuni	152	5.52 S	17.11 E
Lukusashi ≃	154	14.38 S	30.00 E
Lukusuzi National Park ♠	154	12.50 S	32.35 E
Lula, It.	71	40.28 N	9.29 E
Lula, Ms., U.S.	194	34.27 N	90.28 W
Lula, Zaïre	152	5.22 S	16.02 E
Luleå	26	65.34 N	22.10 E
Luleälven ≃	24	65.35 N	22.03 E
Lüleburgaz	130	41.24 N	27.21 E
Lules	252	26.56 S	65.21 W
Luliang	102	25.05 N	103.36 E
Lüliang Shan ⋏	102	37.25 N	111.20 E
Luliāni	123	31.15 N	74.25 E
Luliao	269d	25.07 N	121.39 E
Luling	222	29.40 N	97.38 W
Lullingstone Castle ⊥	260	51.21 N	0.12 E
Lulo ≃	152	9.25 S	18.14 E
Lulong	98	39.54 N	118.50 E
Lulonga	152	0.37 N	18.23 E
Lulonga ≃	152	0.43 N	18.23 E
Lulu ≃	152	1.18 N	23.42 E
Lulua ≃	152	5.02 S	21.07 E
Luluabourg → Kananga	152	5.54 S	22.25 E
Lulu Island I, B.C., Can.	224	49.09 N	123.05 W
Lulu Island I, Ak., U.S.	182	55.28 N	133.30 W
Luluo	98	37.06 N	113.58 E
Lulworth, Mount ∧	162	26.53 S	117.42 E
Lumai	152	13.31 S	21.21 E
Lumajang	115a	8.08 S	113.13 E
Lumajangdong Co	120	34.00 N	81.45 E
Lumaku, Gunong ∧	112	4.52 N	115.38 E
Lumaling	120	29.53 N	92.37 E
Lumb	262	53.42 N	1.58 W
Lumbala ≃	152	12.38 S	22.34 E
Lumbala Kaquengue	152	12.39 S	22.34 E
Lumbala N'guimbo	152	14.08 S	21.25 E
Lumbangaraga	114	1.53 N	99.04 E
Lumbanlobu	114	2.31 N	99.08 E
Lumbe ≃	152	16.42 S	23.42 E
Lumber ≃	192	34.12 N	79.10 W
Lumber City	192	31.55 N	82.40 W
Lumberport	188	39.22 N	80.20 W
Lumberton, Ms., U.S.	194	31.00 N	89.27 W
Lumberton, N.J., U.S.	285	39.57 N	74.48 W
Lumberton, N.C., U.S.	192	34.37 N	79.00 W
Lumberton, Tx., U.S.	194	30.16 N	94.10 W
Lumbinī □[8]	124	27.45 N	83.30 E
Lumbis	112	4.18 N	116.15 E
Lumbo	154	15.00 S	40.44 E
Lumbovka	24	67.44 N	40.30 E
Lumbrales	34	40.56 N	6.43 W
Lumbrein	58	46.41 N	9.08 E
Lumbres	50	50.42 N	2.08 E
Lumbwa	154	0.12 S	35.28 E
Lumby	182	50.15 N	118.58 W
Lumding	120	25.45 N	93.10 E
Lumege ≃	152	11.55 S	20.58 E
Lumerau ≃	116	5.21 N	118.53 E
Lumi	164	3.29 S	142.02 E
Lumiei ≃	64	46.24 N	12.51 E
Luminárias	256	21.30 S	44.54 W
Luminosa	256	22.35 S	45.38 W
Lumintao ≃	116	12.43 N	120.55 E
Lummen	56	50.59 N	5.12 E
Lummi Bay c	224	48.46 N	122.41 W
Lummi Indian Reservation ◆[4]	224	48.48 N	122.38 W
Lummi Island	224	48.42 N	122.40 W
Lummi Island I	224	48.42 N	122.40 W
Lumphanan	46	57.07 N	2.41 W
Lumphăt	110	13.30 N	106.59 E
Lumphini Park ♠	269a	13.44 N	100.33 E
Lumpkin	192	32.03 N	84.47 W
Lumpun ≃	80	57.01 N	51.22 E
Lumsån ≃	40	59.59 N	15.26 E
Lumsås	41	55.57 N	11.31 E
Lumsden, Nf., Can.	186	49.19 N	53.37 W
Lumsden, Sk., Can.	184	50.34 N	104.53 W
Lumsden, N.Z.	172	45.44 S	168.27 E
Lumsden, Scot., U.K.	46	57.15 N	2.52 W
Lumsheden	40	60.43 N	16.15 E
Lums Pond State Park ♠	208	39.34 N	75.43 W
Lumu, Indon.	112	2.11 S	119.09 E
Lumu, Zhg.	106	31.22 N	120.37 E
Lumuna	154	3.46 S	26.24 E
Lumuna ≃	152	16.59 S	21.25 E
Lumut, Indon.	114	1.33 N	98.56 E
Lumut, Malay.	114	4.14 N	100.38 E
Lumut, Tanjung >	112	3.50 S	105.57 E
Lumwana	154	11.50 S	25.10 E
Lün, Mong.	88	47.24 N	102.52 E
Lün, Mong.	88	47.52 N	105.15 E
Luna, Pil.	116	16.51 N	120.23 E
Luna, Pil.	116	18.18 N	121.21 E
Luna ≃	246	4.32 S	60.41 W
Lunada Bay c	280	33.46 N	118.25 W
Lunain ≃	50	48.20 N	2.47 E
Lunamatrona	71	39.39 N	8.54 E
Lunan	102	24.49 N	103.16 E
Lunan Bay c	46	56.39 N	2.28 W
Lunano	66	43.44 N	12.26 E
Luna Pier	216	41.48 N	83.26 W
Lūnāvāda	120	23.08 N	73.37 E
Luncarty	46	56.27 N	3.28 W
Lund, B.C., Can.	182	49.58 N	124.44 W
Lund, Sve.	41	55.42 N	13.11 E
Lund, Nv., U.S.	204	38.51 N	115.00 W
Lunda ≃, Ang.	152	6.07 S	13.52 E
L'unda ≃, S.S.S.R.	80	56.32 N	46.03 E
Lundåkrabukten c	41	55.48 N	12.53 E
Lundale	188	37.48 N	81.44 W
Lunda Norte □[5]	152	8.45 S	19.45 E
Lundar	184	50.42 N	98.02 W
Lunda Sul □[5]	152	10.00 S	20.30 E
Lundazi	154	12.19 S	33.13 E
Lundby	41	55.07 N	11.53 E
Lunde	41	55.29 N	10.21 E
Lundeborg	41	55.08 N	10.47 E
Lunden	41	54.20 N	9.01 E
Lunderskov	41	55.29 N	9.18 E
Lundevatn ⊜	26	58.22 N	6.36 E
Lundi ≃	154	21.43 S	32.34 E
Lundsberg	40	59.30 N	14.10 E
Lundsfjärden ⊜	40	59.38 N	14.41 E
Lundy I	42	51.10 N	4.40 W
Lundys Lane	214	41.53 N	80.21 W
Lune ≃	44	54.02 N	2.50 W
Lüneburg	52	53.15 N	10.23 E
Lüneburg □[6]	52	53.15 N	10.00 E
Lüneburger Heide ◆[1]	52	53.10 N	10.20 E
Lunel	62	43.41 N	4.08 E
Lünen	52	51.36 N	7.32 E
Lunenburg, N.S., Can.	186	44.23 N	64.19 W
Lunenburg, Ma., U.S.	207	42.35 N	71.43 W
Lunenburg, Va., U.S.	192	36.57 N	78.15 W
Luneray	50	49.50 N	0.55 E
Lünern	263	51.33 N	7.46 E
Lunéville	56	48.36 N	6.30 E
Lunga I	46	56.13 N	5.42 W
Lunga ≃, Ang.	152	5.59 S	16.20 E
Lunga ≃, Zam.	154	14.34 S	26.25 E
Lungälven ≃	40	59.34 N	14.10 E
Lunga Reservoir ⊜[1]	208	38.32 N	77.28 W
Lungau ◆[1]	64	47.07 N	13.39 E
Lungavilla	62	45.02 N	9.04 E
Lungch'i → Zhangzhou	100	24.33 N	117.39 E
Lunge	152	12.12 S	16.05 E
Lunge'nake	120	31.45 N	85.55 E
Lungern	58	46.47 N	8.10 E
Lunggar	120	31.10 N	84.00 E
Lunghezza ◆[8]	267a	41.55 N	12.35 E
Lungi	150	8.38 N	13.13 W
Lunglei	120	22.53 N	92.44 E
Lungro	68	39.44 N	16.07 E
Lungsang	124	29.51 N	88.41 E
Lungt'an	100	24.52 N	121.12 E
Lungué-Bungo (Lungwebungu) ≃	152	14.19 S	23.14 E
Lunguya	154	3.23 S	32.24 E
Lungwebungu (Lungué-Bungo) ≃	152	14.19 S	23.14 E
Lūni	120	26.00 N	73.00 E
Lūni ≃	120	24.41 N	71.15 E
Luni ⊥	64	44.04 N	10.01 E
Lunia-Bubi	154	7.30 S	24.49 E
Lunigiana ◆[1]	64	44.15 N	9.50 E
Lunin	76	52.18 N	26.38 E
Luninec	76	52.15 N	26.48 E
Lunino, S.S.S.R.	80	53.35 N	45.14 E
Lunino, S.S.S.R.	82	54.09 N	38.29 E
Lunjiao	100	22.53 N	113.13 E
Lūnkaransar	120	28.29 N	73.44 E
Lunnaja, gora ∧	180	68.14 N	174.20 E
Lunndörrsfjällen ∧	26	63.00 N	13.00 E
Lunno	76	53.27 N	24.16 E
Lunongzha	106	31.59 N	120.55 E
Lunsar	150	8.41 N	12.32 W
Lunsemfwa ≃	154	14.54 S	30.12 E
Lunt	262	53.31 N	2.59 W
Lunteren	52	52.05 N	5.37 E
Lunyuk	115b	8.57 S	117.14 E
Lunz am See	61	47.51 N	15.03 E
Lunzenau	54	50.58 N	12.45 E
Lunzhen	98	36.47 N	116.34 E
Luo ≃, Zhg.	102	34.48 N	113.04 E
Luo ≃, Zhg.	102	34.42 N	110.15 E
Luoba, Zhg.	100	24.51 N	114.13 E
Luoba, Zhg.	107	29.08 N	106.11 E
Luobei (Fengxiang)	89	47.34 N	130.50 E
Luobo	102	28.22 N	101.38 E
Luobu	102	24.30 N	109.40 E
Luobumiao	102	40.19 N	107.30 E
Luochanghe	100	31.01 N	117.18 E
Luocheng, Zhg.	102	24.51 N	108.59 E
Luocheng, Zhg.	107	29.23 N	104.01 E
Luochuan	102	35.55 N	109.26 E
Luoci	102	25.19 N	102.18 E
Luodian	106	31.25 N	121.20 E
Luoding	102	22.47 N	111.31 E
Luoduzhen	107	30.22 N	106.35 E
Luofa	105	39.25 N	116.50 E
Luofang, Zhg.	100	28.40 N	115.04 E
Luofang, Zhg.	100	27.52 N	115.06 E
Luofu, Zaïre	154	0.10 S	29.14 E
Luofu, Zhg.	100	24.32 N	115.35 E
Luogang, Zhg.	100	24.25 N	115.38 E
Luogang, Zhg.	100	23.11 N	113.30 E
Luogosanto	71	41.03 N	9.13 E
Luoguhe	89	53.18 N	121.30 E
Luohan Shan ∧	100	25.51 N	119.13 E
Luohe	100	33.35 N	114.01 E
Luoheya	98	35.46 N	118.54 E
Luohua	100	26.35 N	118.43 E
Luoji	100	32.06 N	117.16 E
Luojiachang	107	30.49 N	106.32 E
Luojiang	102	31.21 N	104.28 E
Luojiatang	106	30.18 N	120.13 E
Luojiatun, Zhg.	98	40.11 N	118.34 E
Luojiatun, Zhg.	104	40.55 N	122.04 E
Luojiatun, Zhg.	104	42.06 N	122.44 E
Luojiawei	100	26.55 N	115.02 E
Luoke	100	24.07 N	114.28 E
Luokeng	100	24.32 N	113.23 E
Luokou, Zhg.	100	28.54 N	117.24 E
Luokou, Zhg.	100	25.46 N	115.39 E
Luolong	107	28.49 N	104.46 E
L'Uomo di Cagna ∧	71	41.33 N	9.04 E
Luonan	102	34.05 N	110.04 E
Luoning	102	34.25 N	111.42 E
Luoping	102	24.59 N	104.21 E
Luoqi	102	29.48 N	106.56 E
Luoqiao	100	26.28 N	119.01 E
Luoquanzhen	107	29.50 N	104.31 E
Luoshan, Zhg.	100	32.13 N	114.32 E
Luoshan, Zhg.	100	29.41 N	113.18 E
Luoshan, Zhg.	105	39.55 N	117.33 E
Luoshe, Zhg.	106	30.41 N	120.04 E
Luoshe, Zhg.	106	31.39 N	120.11 E
Luoshuihe	98	39.27 N	114.19 E
Luossa ≃	152	8.24 S	17.03 E
Luotian	100	30.48 N	115.22 E
Luotuodian	100	32.13 N	113.49 E
Luotuoqiao	100	29.56 N	121.32 E
Luotuo Shan ∧	104	42.14 N	121.42 E
Luowenba	102	31.48 N	107.48 E
Luowenyu	105	40.16 N	117.57 E
Luoxi	100	29.05 N	114.58 E
Luoxiao Shan ⋏	100	26.00 N	114.00 E
Luoyang (Loyang), Zhg.	102	34.41 N	112.28 E
Luoyang, Zhg.	106	31.39 N	120.05 E
Luoyuan	100	26.31 N	119.32 E
Luoyuan Wan c	100	26.25 N	119.43 E
Luoyukou	102	38.23 N	110.43 E
Luozhexi	107	29.02 N	103.54 E
Luozi	152	4.57 S	14.08 E
Lupala	156	17.50 S	19.06 E
Lupani	154	18.54 S	27.44 E
Lupao	116	15.53 N	120.54 E
Lupar ≃	112	1.30 N	111.00 E
Łupawa	30	54.26 N	17.24 E
Lupberg	60	49.09 N	11.45 E
Lupembe	154	9.15 S	35.15 E
Lupeni	38	45.22 N	23.13 E
Lupire	152	14.36 S	19.29 E
Lupiro	154	8.23 S	36.40 E
Lupon	116	6.54 N	126.00 E
Lupow → Łupawa	30	54.26 N	17.24 E
Luppa	54	51.20 N	12.57 E
Luputa	152	7.10 S	23.42 E
Luqiao, Zhg.	100	32.34 N	117.14 E
Luqiao, Zhg.	100	28.35 N	121.22 E
Luqu	102	34.41 N	102.22 E
Luque	34	37.33 N	4.16 W
Luquillo	240m	18.22 N	65.43 W
Luquillo, Sierra de ⋏	240m	18.17 N	65.47 W
Lūrah ≃	120	31.33 N	66.33 E
Luray	188	38.39 N	78.27 W
Lure	58	47.41 N	6.30 E
Lure, Montagne de ⋏	62	44.07 N	5.47 E
Lureco ≃	154	12.28 S	37.40 E
Luremo	152	8.31 S	17.50 E
Lurgan	48	54.28 N	6.20 W
Luribay	248	17.06 S	67.39 W
Lurigancho	286d	12.02 S	77.01 W
Lurín	248	12.17 S	76.52 W
Lúrio	154	13.35 S	40.30 E
Lúrio ≃	154	13.35 S	40.32 E
Lurisia	62	44.18 N	7.42 E
Lurnea	274a	33.56 S	150.54 E
Lurö I	26	58.48 N	13.14 E
Lürrip ◆[8]	263	51.12 N	6.28 E
Lusahunga	154	2.52 S	31.15 E
Lusaka, Zaïre	154	7.10 S	29.27 E
Lusaka, Zam.	154	15.25 S	28.17 E
Lusaka □[4]	154	15.25 S	29.00 E
Lusakert	84	40.23 N	44.36 E
Lusambo	152	4.58 S	23.27 E
Lusancay Islands and Reefs II	164	8.25 S	150.20 E
Lusanga	152	4.50 S	18.44 E
Lusangaye	154	4.54 S	26.00 E
Lusangi	154	4.37 S	27.08 E
Luscar	182	53.04 N	117.24 W
Luseke	152	2.51 S	23.08 E
Luseland	184	52.05 N	109.24 W
Lusen ∧	60	48.56 N	13.31 E
Lusenga Plain National Park ♠	154	9.30 S	29.10 E
Lusengo	152	1.46 N	19.29 E
Luserna San Giovanni	62	44.48 N	7.15 E
Lush, Mount ∧	164	17.02 S	127.30 E
Lushan, Zhg.	100	33.45 N	112.53 E
Lushan, Zhg.	102	30.15 N	102.58 E
Lu Shan ∧	100	29.31 N	115.58 E
Lu Shan ⋏	98	36.05 N	118.05 E
Lushanguanliju	100	29.33 N	115.58 E
Lushi	102	34.05 N	111.01 E
Lushiko (Luchico) ≃	152	6.13 S	19.40 E
Lüshikou	100	29.16 N	120.17 E
Lushnje	38	40.56 N	19.42 E
Lushoto	154	4.47 S	38.17 E
Lushui	102	26.00 N	98.51 E
Lüshun (Port Arthur)	98	38.48 N	121.16 E
Lüsi	106	32.03 N	121.36 E
Lusi ≃	115a	7.05 S	110.55 E
Lusiana	64	45.47 N	11.34 E
Lusignan	32	46.26 N	0.07 E
Lusignan, Lac ⊜	206	46.40 N	74.09 W
Lusigny-sur-Barse	50	48.15 N	4.16 E
Lusikisiki	158	31.25 S	29.30 E
L'usino	76	52.38 N	26.31 E
Lusk, Ire.	48	53.32 N	6.10 W
Lusk, Wy., U.S.	200	42.45 N	104.27 W
Lus-la-Croix-Haute	62	44.40 N	5.42 E
Lusongwa	152	12.58 S	24.16 E
Luspebryggan	24	67.01 N	19.51 E
Lussac-les-Châteaux	32	46.24 N	0.44 E
Lussan	62	44.09 N	4.22 E
Luṣṣān, Wādī V	132	30.30 N	34.18 E
Lustenau	58	47.26 N	9.39 E
Luster	26	61.26 N	7.24 E
Lustin	56	50.23 N	4.53 E
Lustrafjorden c[2]	26	61.20 N	7.22 E
Lüstringen	52	52.16 N	8.08 E
Lusutfu (Maputo) (Great Usutu) ≃	158	26.11 S	32.42 E
Luswishi ≃	154	13.55 S	27.24 E
Lūt, Dasht-e ◆[2]	128	32.00 N	58.00 E
Lü-ta → Dalian	98	38.53 N	121.35 E
L'uta ≃	76	58.37 N	28.40 E
Lutago (Luttach)	64	46.57 N	11.55 E
Lutai	100	33.32 N	115.03 E
Lütan, Zhg.	98	34.07 N	114.27 E
Lütan, Zhg.	100	28.57 N	119.46 E
Lutang	100	25.39 N	112.46 E
Lutao	116	10.00 N	124.04 E
Lü Tao I	100	22.40 N	121.29 E
Lutcher	194	30.02 N	90.41 W
Lute	284c	39.04 N	77.03 W
Lutembo	152	13.26 S	21.16 E
Lutembo ≃	152	12.03 S	22.15 E
L'uten'ka	78	50.13 N	34.02 E
Lutesville	194	37.18 N	89.58 W
Lutéte ≃	152	9.21 S	15.14 E
Lutexu ≃	273b	4.24 S	15.12 E
Lütgendortmund ◆[8]	263	51.30 N	7.21 E
Luthe	52	52.26 N	9.28 E
Luther, Mi., U.S.	190	44.02 N	85.40 W
Luther, Ok., U.S.	196	35.39 N	97.11 W
Luther Lake ⊜	212	43.55 N	80.26 W
Luthersburg	214	41.03 N	78.43 W
Lutherville-Timonium	284b	39.25 N	76.37 W
Luthrie	46	56.21 N	3.05 W
Luti	175e	7.14 S	156.59 E
Lutian, Zhg.	100	26.33 N	114.38 E
Lütian, Zhg.	100	23.48 N	113.56 E
Lütjenburg	54	54.17 N	10.35 E
Lütjensee	52	53.39 N	10.22 E
Luton, Eng., U.K.	42	51.53 N	0.25 W
Luton, Eng., U.K.	260	51.22 N	0.32 E
Lutong	112	4.28 N	114.00 E
Lutosn'a ≃	82	56.26 N	36.52 E
Lutou	100	32.16 N	112.53 E
Lutry	58	46.30 N	6.41 E
Lutshi	154	4.09 S	26.30 E
Lutshima ≃	152	5.22 S	18.59 E
Lutsk → Luck	78	50.44 N	25.20 E
Luttach → Lutago	64	46.57 N	11.55 E
Lutter am Barenberge	52	51.59 N	10.16 E
Lutterbach	58	47.46 N	7.17 E
Lutterworth	42	52.28 N	1.10 W
Lüttich → Liège	56	50.38 N	5.34 E
Luttrell	192	36.11 N	83.44 W
Lüttringhausen ◆[8]	263	51.13 N	7.14 E
Lutuai ≃	152	12.33 S	20.16 E

Symbols in the index entries represent the broad categories identified in the key at the right. Symbols with superior numbers (⋏[1]) identify subcategories (see complete key on page I · 1).

Symbole im Register stellen die rechts im Schlüssel erklärten Kategorien dar. Symbole mit hochgestellten Ziffern (⋏[1]) bezeichnen Unterabteilungen einer Kategorie (vgl. vollständiger Schlüssel auf Seite I · 1).

Los símbolos incluídos en el texto del índice representan las grandes categorias identificadas con la clave a la derecha. Los símbolos con numeros en su parte superior (⋏[1]) identifican las subcategorías (véase la clave completa en la página I · 1).

Les symboles de l'index représentent les catégories indiquées dans la légende à droite. Les symboles suivis d'un indice (⋏[1]) représentent des sous-catégories (voir légende complète à la page I · 1).

Os símbolos incluídos no texto do índice representam as grandes categorias identificadas com a chave à direita. Os símbolos com números em sua parte superior (⋏[1]) identificam as subcategorias (veja-se a chave completa à página I · 1).

	English	Deutsch	Español	Français	Português
∧	Mountain	Berg	Montaña	Montagne	Montanha
⋏	Mountains	Gebirge	Montañas	Montagnes	Montanhas
)(	Pass	Paß	Paso	Col	Passo
V	Valley, Canyon	Tal, Cañon	Valle, Cañón	Vallée, Canyon	Vale, Canhão
≡	Plain	Ebene	Llano	Plaine	Planície
>	Cape	Kap	Cabo	Cap	Cabo
I	Island	Insel	Isla	Île	Ilha
II	Islands	Inseln	Islas	Îles	Ilhas
⊥	Other Topographic Features	Andere Topographische Objekte	Otros Elementos Topográficos	Autres données topographiques	Outros acidentes topográficos

≃ River	Fluß	Río	Rivière	Rio
≋ Canal	Kanal	Canal	Canal	Canal
L Waterfall, Rapids	Wasserfall, Stromschnellen	Cascada, Rápidos	Chute d'eau, Rapides	Cascata, Rápidos
⋃ Strait	Meeresstraße	Estrecho	Détroit	Estreito
c Bay, Gulf	Bucht, Golf	Bahía, Golfo	Baie, Golfe	Baía, Golfo
⊜ Lake, Lakes	See, Seen	Lago, Lagos	Lac, Lacs	Lago, Lagos
⊡ Swamp	Sumpf	Pantano	Marais	Pântano
⊞ Ice Features, Glacier	Eis- und Gletscherformen	Accidentes Glaciares	Formes glaciaires	Acidentes glaciares
⊤ Other Hydrographic Features	Andere Hydrographische Objekte	Otros Elementos Hidrográficos	Autres données hydrographiques	Outros acidentes hidrográficos

♦ Submarine Features	Untermeerische Objekte	Accidentes Submarinos	Formes de relief sous-marin	Acidentes submarinos
◻ Political Unit	Politische Einheit	Unidad Política	Entité politique	Unidade política
⊥ Cultural Institution	Kulturelle Institution	Institución Cultural	Institution culturelle	Instituição cultural
⊥ Historical Site	Historische Stätte	Sitio Histórico	Site historique	Sítio histórico
♦ Recreational Site	Erholungs- und Ferienort	Sitio de Recreo	Centre de loisirs	Área de Lazer
⊞ Airport	Flughafen	Aeropuerto	Aéroport	Aeroporto
▪ Military Installation	Militäranlage	Instalación Militar	Installation militaire	Instalação militar
∅ Miscellaneous	Verschiedenes	Misceláneo	Divers	Diversos

McVeytown 214 40.30 N 77.44 W
McVickers Brook ≃ 276 40.45 N 74.38 W
McVille 198 47.45 N 98.10 W
McWilliams 194 31.49 N 87.05 W
Macy 216 40.57 N 86.07 W
Mad ≃, On., Can. 212 44.25 N 79.54 W
Mad ≃, Ca., U.S. 204 40.57 N 124.07 W
Mad ≃, N.Y., U.S. 212 43.20 N 75.44 W
Mad ≃, Oh., U.S. 188 39.46 N 84.11 W
Mad ≃, Vt., U.S. 188 44.18 N 72.41 W
Mada ≃ 150 7.59 N 7.55 E
Ma'dabā 132 31.43 N 35.48 E
Madagascar (Madagasikara) □[1], Afr. 138 19.00 S 46.00 E
Madagascar (Madagasikara) □[1], Afr. 157b 19.00 S 46.00 E
Madagascar Basin ✢[1] 12 27.00 S 53.00 E
Madagascar Plateau ✢[3] 10 30.00 S 45.00 E
Madagasikara → Madagascar □[1] 157b 19.00 S 46.00 E
Madagaskar → Madagascar □[1] 157b 19.00 S 46.00 E
Madagiz 84 40.19 N 46.44 E
Madagoi, Bohol V 144 0.44 N 42.56 E
Madā'in Ṣāliḥ 128 26.48 N 37.53 E
Madajevo 80 54.48 N 44.31 E
Madama 146 21.58 N 13.39 E
Madame, Isle I 186 45.33 N 61.02 W
Madan 38 41.30 N 24.57 E
Madanapalle 122 13.33 N 78.30 E
Madang, Pap. N. Gui. 164 5.15 S 145.50 E
Madang, Zhg. 100 29.58 N 116.40 E
Madang □[5] 164 5.00 S 145.30 E
Madanpur 272b 22.40 N 88.32 E
Madanpur Dabās ◆[8] 272a 28.43 N 77.02 E
Madaoua 150 14.05 N 5.58 E
Mādār Gāng ≃[1] 126 22.12 N 89.04 E
Mādāri Hāt 124 26.42 N 89.17 E
Mādārīpur 124 23.10 N 90.12 E
Madarounfa 150 13.18 N 7.09 E
Mādārpur 272b 22.54 N 88.27 E
Madau Island I 164 8.58 S 152.28 E
Madawaska, On., Can. 212 45.30 N 77.59 W
Madawaska, Me., U.S. 186 47.21 N 68.19 W
Madawaska ≃ 212 45.27 N 76.21 W
Madawaska Highlands ⋀[1] 212 45.15 N 77.35 W
Madawaska Lake ⊜ 212 45.20 N 78.23 W
Madaxmaroodi 144 2.39 N 44.36 E
Madaya, Mya. 110 22.13 N 96.07 E
Maḍāyā, Sūrīy. 132 33.41 N 36.06 E
Madbar 140 6.19 N 30.40 E
Mad Creek ≃ 210 42.55 N 77.59 W
Maddalena, Colle della (Col de Larche))(62 44.25 N 6.53 E
Maddalena, Isola I 71 41.14 N 9.25 E
Maddaloni 68 41.02 N 14.23 E
Maddela 116 16.21 N 121.41 E
Madden, Mount ∧ 162 33.12 S 119.51 E
Maddington 168a 32.03 S 115.59 E
Maddock 198 47.57 N 99.31 W
Maddy, Loch ⊂ 46 57.36 N 7.08 W
Made 52 51.41 N 4.46 E
Madeir 140 7.50 N 29.12 E
Madeira 218 39.11 N 84.21 W
Madeira I 148 32.44 N 17.00 W
Madeira ≃ 242 3.22 S 58.45 W
Madeira, Arquipélago da II 148 32.40 N 16.45 W
Madeira Beach 220 27.48 N 82.48 W
Madeirinha ≃ 248 8.31 S 60.46 W
Madeirinha, Paraná ≃[1] 246 3.25 S 58.51 W
M'adel' 76 54.53 N 26.57 E
Mädelegabel ∧ 58 47.18 N 10.18 E
Madeleine, Îles de la II 186 47.30 N 61.45 W
Madeleine, Pointe › 275a 45.27 N 73.57 W
Madeleine-Centre 186 49.15 N 65.21 W
Madeley, Eng., U.K. 42 52.59 N 2.20 W
Madeley, Eng., U.K. 42 52.39 N 2.28 W
Madelia 190 44.03 N 94.25 W
Madeline Island I 190 46.50 N 90.40 W
Maden, Tür. 130 38.23 N 39.40 E
Maden, Tür. 130 40.11 N 40.25 E
Madenijet 86 47.53 N 78.37 E
Madera, Méx. 232 29.12 N 108.07 W
Madera, Ca., U.S. 226 36.57 N 120.03 W
Madera, Pa., U.S. 214 40.49 N 78.26 W
Madera □[6] 226 37.15 N 119.45 W
Madera Canal ≊ 226 37.05 N 119.59 W
Madera Lake ⊜[1] 226 37.02 N 119.59 W
Madera Peak ∧ 226 37.32 N 119.23 W
Maderas, Islas → Madeira, Arquipélago da II 148 32.40 N 16.45 W
Maderas, Volcán ∧[1] 236 11.27 N 85.31 W
Maderno 64 45.38 N 10.35 E
Madgaon (Margao) 122 15.18 N 73.57 E
Madh ◆[8] 272c 19.08 N 72.47 E
Madhepura 124 25.55 N 86.47 E
Madhkūr, Bi'r ⊤[4] 142 30.42 N 32.32 E
Mādhopur 123 32.22 N 75.36 E
Madhubani 124 26.22 N 86.05 E
Madhudaha 272b 22.31 N 88.25 E
Madhugiri 122 13.40 N 77.12 E
Madhumati ≃[1] 126 22.53 N 89.52 E
Madhupar 126 22.54 N 86.28 E
Madhupur 126 24.16 N 86.39 E
Madhya Bhārat Pathār ◆[1] 124 25.00 N 77.00 E
Madhyamgrām 272b 22.42 N 88.27 E
Madhya Pradesh □[3] 118 23.00 N 79.00 E
Madia 154 7.08 S 26.00 E
Madian 106 32.15 N 119.58 E
Madibi 152 4.18 S 18.24 E
Madibira 154 8.12 S 34.49 E
Madibogo 158 26.25 S 25.10 E
Madida 98 42.57 N 130.48 E
Madidi ≃ 248 12.32 S 66.52 W
Madill 196 34.05 N 96.46 W
Madimba, Ang. 152 6.31 S 14.21 E
Madimba, Zaïre 152 4.58 S 15.08 E
Madina 150 13.24 N 8.51 W
Madina do Boé 150 11.45 N 14.13 W
Madinani 150 9.37 N 6.57 W
Madinat al-Abyār 146 32.11 N 20.36 E
Madīnat ash-Sha'b (Al-Ittiḥad) 144 12.50 N 44.56 E
Madīnat ath Thawrah 130 35.52 N 38.34 E
Madine, Lac de ⊜ 56 48.54 N 5.42 E
Madingo 152 4.07 S 11.22 E
Madingou 152 4.09 S 13.34 E
Madingzi 104 42.08 N 120.52 E
Madi Opei 154 3.37 N 33.05 E
Madirobe 157b 16.04 S 46.15 E
Madirovalo 157b 16.26 S 46.30 E
Madison, Al., U.S. 194 34.41 N 86.44 W
Madison, Ca., U.S. 226 38.41 N 121.58 W
Madison, Ct., U.S. 207 41.16 N 72.35 W
Madison, Fl., U.S. 192 30.28 N 83.24 W
Madison, Ga., U.S. 192 33.35 N 83.28 W
Madison, Il., U.S. 219 38.40 N 90.09 W
Madison, In., U.S. 218 38.44 N 85.22 W
Madison, Ks., U.S. 198 38.08 N 96.08 W
Madison, Me., U.S. 188 44.47 N 69.52 W
Madison, Md., U.S. 208 38.30 N 76.13 W
Madison, Mn., U.S. 198 45.00 N 96.11 W
Madison, Mo., U.S. 219 39.28 N 92.12 W
Madison, Ne., U.S. 198 41.49 N 97.27 W
Madison, N.J., U.S. 210 40.45 N 74.25 W
Madison, N.Y., U.S. 210 42.53 N 75.30 W
Madison, N.C., U.S. 192 36.23 N 79.57 W
Madison, Oh., U.S. 214 41.46 N 81.03 W
Madison, Pa., U.S. 279b 40.15 N 79.41 W
Madison, S.D., U.S. 198 44.00 N 97.06 W
Madison, Va., U.S. 188 38.22 N 78.15 W
Madison, W.V., U.S. 188 38.04 N 81.49 W
Madison, Wi., U.S. 216 43.04 N 89.24 W
Madison □[6], Il., U.S. 219 38.49 N 89.58 W
Madison □[6], In., U.S. 218 40.10 N 85.41 W
Madison □[6], N.Y., U.S. 210 43.05 N 75.42 W
Madison □[6], Oh., U.S. 218 39.53 N 83.27 W
Madison □[6], Tx., U.S. 222 30.58 N 95.55 W
Madison ≃ 202 45.56 N 111.30 W
Madison, West Fork ≃ 202 44.55 N 111.35 W
Madisonburg, Oh., U.S. 214 40.51 N 81.55 W
Madisonburg, Pa., U.S. 210 40.55 N 77.31 W
Madison Heights, Mi., U.S. 216 42.29 N 83.06 W
Madison Heights, Va., U.S. 192 37.25 N 79.07 W
Madison Mills 218 39.40 N 83.20 W
Madison-on-the-Lake 214 41.42 N 81.24 W
Madison Park 276 40.26 N 74.19 W
Madison Range ⋀ 202 45.15 N 111.20 W
Madison Square Garden ♦ 276 40.45 N 74.00 W
Madisonville, Ky., U.S. 194 37.19 N 87.29 W
Madisonville, La., U.S. 194 30.24 N 90.09 W
Madisonville, Tn., U.S. 192 35.31 N 84.21 W
Madisonville, Tx., U.S. 222 30.56 N 95.54 W
Madiun 115a 7.37 S 111.31 E
Madiun ≃ 115a 7.23 S 111.27 E
Madiyi 102 28.14 N 110.30 E
Madjingo 152 1.23 N 14.06 E
Madjoari 150 11.26 N 1.15 E
Madley, Mount ∧ 162 24.31 S 123.58 E
Madoc 212 44.30 N 77.28 W
Mado Gashi 154 0.44 N 39.10 E
Madoi 102 34.53 N 98.24 E
Madol 140 9.02 N 27.46 E
Madon ≃ 58 48.36 N 6.06 E
Madona 76 56.51 N 26.13 E
Madonna (Unserfrau) 64 46.43 N 10.52 E
Madonna della Guardia ⊍[1] 62 44.29 N 8.51 E
Madonna della Quercia ⊍[1] 66 42.25 N 12.06 E
Madonna dell'Olmo 62 44.25 N 7.32 E
Madonna del Sasso ⊍[1] 58 46.11 N 8.33 E
Madonna di Campiglio 64 46.14 N 10.49 E
Madonna di Tirano 64 46.13 N 10.09 E
Madora 76 53.09 N 30.11 E
Madougou 150 14.24 N 3.05 W
Madrakah 144 21.59 N 39.59 E
Madrakah, Ra's al- › 118 19.00 N 57.50 E
Madras, India 122 13.05 N 80.17 E
Madras, Or., U.S. 202 44.38 N 121.07 W
Madras → Tamil Nādu □[3] 122 11.00 N 78.15 E
Madre, Laguna ⊂, Méx. 232 25.00 N 97.40 W
Madre, Laguna ⊂, Tx., U.S. 196 27.00 N 97.35 W
Madre, Sierra ⋀, N.A. 236 15.20 N 92.20 W
Madre, Sierra ⋀, Pil. 116 16.20 N 122.00 E
Madre de Deus de Minas 256 21.29 S 44.20 W
Madre de Dios □[5] 248 12.00 S 70.15 W
Madre de Dios ≃ 248 10.59 S 66.08 W
Madre de Dios, Isla I 254 50.15 S 75.05 W
Madre del Sur, Sierra ⋀ 234 17.00 N 100.00 W
Madre Occidental, Sierra ⋀ 232 25.00 N 105.00 W
Madre Oriental, Sierra ⋀ 232 22.00 N 99.30 W
Madre Vieja ≃ 236 14.01 N 91.26 W
Madrid, Col. 246 4.44 N 74.16 W
Madrid, Esp. 34 40.24 N 3.41 W
Madrid, Esp. 266a 40.24 N 3.41 W
Madrid, Pil. 116 9.15 N 126.00 E
Madrid, Al., U.S. 194 31.02 N 85.23 W
Madrid, Ia., U.S. 190 41.52 N 93.49 W
Madrid, Ne., U.S. 198 40.51 N 101.32 W
Madrid □[4] 34 40.30 N 3.40 W
Madridejos, Esp. 34 39.28 N 3.32 W
Madridejos, Pil. 116 11.18 N 123.44 E
Madrigalejo 34 39.09 N 5.37 W
Madrillon 284c 38.55 N 77.14 W
Madriz □[5] 236 13.30 N 86.30 W
Madroñera 34 39.26 N 5.46 W
Madruga 240p 22.55 N 81.51 W
Madrūsah 146 24.48 N 14.32 E
Madsen 184 50.58 N 93.55 W
Madsūs, Bi'r ⊤[4] 142 29.15 N 32.19 E
Maducang Island I 116 10.42 N 120.15 E
Maduda 152 4.55 S 13.06 E
Maduo 152 1.24 S 20.44 E
Madura, Austl. 162 31.55 S 127.00 E
Madura → Madurai, India 122 9.56 N 78.07 E
Madura I 115a 7.00 S 113.20 E
Madura, Selat ⊔ 115a 7.25 S 113.25 E
Madurai 122 9.56 N 78.07 E
Madurāntakam 122 12.31 N 79.54 E
Madureira, Serra de ⋀ 287a 22.49 S 43.31 W
Madurerira ◆[8] 287a 22.53 S 43.21 W
Maduru ≃ 122 7.52 N 81.31 E
Madwar al-Bighāl ∧[2] 142 29.09 N 29.54 E
Madžalis 84 42.08 N 47.50 E
Mãe, Ilha da I 287a 22.59 S 43.04 W
Maeander Reef ✢[2] 116 8.05 N 119.18 E
Maebaru 92 33.33 N 130.12 E
Maebashi 94 36.23 N 139.04 E
Maeda 270 34.55 N 135.08 E
Mãe dos Homens 256 22.52 S 46.37 W
Maegye-ri 98 34.45 N 126.18 E
Mae Hong Son 110 19.16 N 97.56 E
Mae Klong ≃ 110 13.21 N 100.00 E
Maenclochog 42 51.54 N 4.48 W
Maengsan 98 39.40 N 126.30 E
Maeno ◆[8] 268 35.46 N 139.42 E
Maenza 66 41.31 N 13.11 E
Mae Ramat 110 16.58 N 98.31 E
Mae Rim 110 18.54 N 98.57 E
Maerkansu 85 39.19 N 73.53 E
Ma'erna 102 31.13 N 102.02 E
Maershan ∧ 102 26.18 N 100.20 E
Mae Sariang 110 18.10 N 97.56 E
Maeser 200 40.28 N 109.35 W
Mae Sot 110 16.43 N 98.34 E
Maesteg 42 51.37 N 3.40 W
Maestra, Sierra ⋀ 240p 20.00 N 76.45 W
Maestre de Campo Island I 116 12.56 N 121.42 E
Maestu 34 42.44 N 2.27 W
Mae Tha 110 18.28 N 99.08 E
Maevarano ≃ 157b 14.35 S 47.58 E
Maevatanana 157b 16.56 S 46.49 E
Maéwo I 175f 15.10 S 168.10 E
Ma'fan 146 25.55 N 14.29 E
Mafang 105 40.02 N 117.01 E
Mafangchang 107 29.24 N 106.06 E
Mafangcun 105 40.09 N 116.24 E
Ma Faro ✢[2] 122 5.50 N 73.26 E
Mafeking 184 52.41 N 101.06 W
Mafembage 152 14.32 S 21.42 E
Mafengtun 104 40.49 N 122.54 E
Mafeteng 158 29.51 S 27.15 E
Maffliers 261 49.05 N 2.19 E
Maffra 166 37.58 S 146.59 E
Mafia Channel ⊔ 154 8.10 S 39.40 E
Mafia Island I 154 7.50 S 39.50 E
Mafikeng 156 25.53 S 25.39 E
Mafou ≃ 150 10.32 N 10.08 W
Mafra, Bra. 252 26.07 S 49.49 W
Mafra, Port. 34 38.56 N 9.20 W
Magadan 74 59.34 N 150.48 E
Magadan □[4] 180 66.00 N 178.00 E
Magadi 154 1.54 S 36.17 E
Magadi, Lake ⊜ 154 1.52 S 36.17 E
Magaguadavic Lake ⊜ 186 45.43 N 67.12 W
Magai-butsu ⊍[1] 96 33.05 N 131.45 E
Magalhães Bastos ◆[8] 287a 22.53 S 43.23 W
Magalhães de Almeida 250 3.24 S 42.12 W
Magaliesberg ⋀ 158 25.50 S 27.30 E
Magallanes → Punta Arenas, Chile 254 53.09 S 70.55 W
Magallanes, Pil. 116 12.50 N 123.50 E
Magallanes, Estrecho de (Strait of Magellan) ⊔ 254 54.00 S 71.00 W
Magallanes y Antártica Chilena □[4] 254 53.00 S 72.00 W
Maganga 154 0.51 N 26.22 E
Magangué 246 9.14 N 74.45 W
Magansk 88 55.52 N 93.15 E
Maganuy ≃ 116 6.55 N 124.30 E
Magara, India 126 22.34 N 87.34 E
Mağara, Tür. 130 36.43 N 33.52 E
Magaramkent 84 41.37 N 48.21 E
Magaria 150 13.00 N 8.54 E
Magat ≃ 116 17.02 N 121.49 E
Magazine Mountain ∧ 194 35.10 N 93.38 W
Magazzolo ≃ 70 37.25 N 13.15 E
Magboro 273a 6.43 N 3.24 E
Magburaka 150 8.43 N 11.57 W
Magdagači 89 53.27 N 125.48 E
Magdalena, Arg. 258 35.04 S 57.32 W
Magdalena, Bol. 248 13.20 S 64.08 W
Magdalena, Méx. 234 20.55 N 103.57 W
Magdalena, Perú 248 6.21 S 77.49 W
Magdalena, N.M., U.S. 200 34.07 N 107.14 W
Magdalena □[5] 246 10.00 N 74.00 W
Magdalena ≃, Col. 246 11.06 N 74.51 W
Magdalena ≃, Méx. 232 30.48 N 112.32 W
Magdalena, Bahía ⊂ 232 24.35 N 112.00 W
Magdalena, Isla I 254 44.40 S 73.10 W
Magdalena, Punta › 246 3.56 N 77.21 W
Magdalena Contreras ◆[8] 286a 19.18 N 99.17 W
Magdalena de Kino 232 30.38 N 110.57 W
Magdalena Nueva 286d 12.06 S 77.05 W
Magdalena Peñasco 234 17.14 N 97.34 W
Magdalena Tequisistlán 234 16.22 N 95.15 W
Magdalen Laver 260 51.45 N 0.11 E
Magdalinovka 78 48.55 N 34.54 E
Magdeborn 54 51.14 N 12.26 E
Magdeburg 54 52.07 N 11.38 E
Magdeburg □[5] 54 52.15 N 11.30 E
Magdeburger Börde ≚ 54 52.00 N 11.30 E
Magdeburgo → Magdeburg 54 52.07 N 11.38 E
Magdiwang 116 12.30 N 122.31 E
Magdonskij, porog ⌞ 88 57.45 N 100.55 E
Magé, Bra. 256 22.39 S 43.02 W
Māge, Mya. 110 26.33 N 98.33 E
Magé □[7] 287a 22.41 S 43.07 W
Magé ≃ 256 22.41 S 43.03 W
Magee 194 31.52 N 89.44 W
Magee, Island ›[1] 48 54.49 N 5.42 W
Magelang 115a 7.28 S 110.13 E
Magellan, Strait of → Magallanes, Estrecho de ⊔ 254 54.00 S 71.00 W
Magellan-Strasse → Magallanes, Estrecho de ⊔ 254 54.00 S 71.00 W
Magé-Mirim 287a 22.40 S 43.01 W
Magén 132 31.18 N 34.26 E
Magenta 62 45.28 N 8.53 E
Magenta, Lake ⊜ 162 33.26 S 119.10 E
Magerov 78 50.08 N 23.43 E
Magerøy I 24 71.03 N 25.45 E
Magetan 115a 7.39 S 111.20 E
Magezhuang 105 40.08 N 117.59 E
Maggia 58 46.15 N 8.42 E
Maggia ≃ 58 46.09 N 8.48 E
Maggia, Valle V 58 46.17 N 8.40 E
Maggie Creek ≃ 204 40.43 N 116.05 W
Maggiorasca, Monte ∧ 62 44.33 N 9.29 E
Maggiore ≃, It. 267a 43.43 N 13.06 E
Maggiore ≃, It. 267a 41.54 N 12.16 E
Maggiore, Lago ⊜ 36 46.00 N 8.40 E
Maggiore, Monte ∧ 68 41.14 N 14.12 E
Maghāghah 142 28.39 N 30.50 E
Maghama 150 15.31 N 12.51 W
Maghar 132 32.53 N 35.24 E
Maghdūshah 132 33.31 N 35.23 E
Maghera 48 54.51 N 6.40 W
Magherafelt 48 54.45 N 6.36 W
Maghniyya 148 34.50 N 1.50 W
Magholpur ◆[8] 272a 28.42 N 77.06 E
Maghull 44 53.32 N 2.57 W
Magician Lake ⊜ 216 42.04 N 86.10 W
Magic Mountain ♦ 228 34.26 N 118.36 W
Magic Reservoir ⊜[1] 202 43.17 N 114.23 W
Magill, Lac ⊜ 206 45.35 N 71.17 W
Magill Heights 279b 40.37 N 79.52 W
Magill Lake ⊜ 184 54.45 N 94.58 W
Mágina ∧ 34 37.43 N 3.28 W
Maginu 268 35.35 N 139.36 E
Magione 66 43.08 N 12.12 E
Magisano 68 39.01 N 16.27 E
Magiscatzin 234 22.48 N 98.42 W
Magiss Lake ⊜ 184 52.59 N 91.40 W
Maglaj 38 44.33 N 18.06 E
Magliana ◆[8] 267a 41.50 N 12.25 E
Magliana, Fosso ≃ 267a 41.49 N 12.25 E
Magliano dei Marsi 66 42.05 N 13.22 E
Magliano in Toscana 66 42.36 N 11.17 E
Magliano Sabina 66 42.22 N 12.29 E
Maglie 68 40.07 N 18.19 E
Maglód 264c 47.27 N 19.21 E
M'aglovo 265a 59.53 N 30.41 E
Magnago 266b 45.35 N 8.48 E
Magnanville 261 48.58 N 1.41 E
Magnet 184 51.19 N 99.30 W
Magnetawan ≃ 190 45.46 N 80.37 W
Magnetic Island I 166 19.08 S 146.50 E
Magnetic Springs 214 40.21 N 83.16 W
Magnetischer Nordpol → North Magnetic Pole ◆ 16 77.19 N 101.49 W
Magnetischer Südpol → South Magnetic Pole ◆ 9 65.18 S 139.30 E
Magnières 58 48.27 N 6.34 E
Magnitka 86 55.21 N 59.43 E
Magnitogorsk 86 53.27 N 59.04 E
Magnitostroj 80 51.43 N 53.05 E
Magnolia, Ar., U.S. 194 33.16 N 93.14 W
Magnolia, De., U.S. 208 39.04 N 75.28 W
Magnolia, Ma., U.S. 283 42.35 N 70.43 W
Magnolia, Mn., U.S. 198 43.38 N 96.04 W
Magnolia, Ms., U.S. 194 31.08 N 90.27 W
Magnolia, N.J., U.S. 285 39.51 N 75.02 W
Magnolia, Oh., U.S. 214 40.39 N 81.17 W
Magnolia, Tx., U.S. 222 30.13 N 95.45 W
Magnor 26 59.57 N 12.12 E
Magny-en-Vexin 50 49.09 N 1.47 E
Magny-le-Hongre 261 48.52 N 2.49 E
Magny-les-Hameaux 261 48.44 N 2.04 E
Mago 89 53.15 N 140.13 E
Magog 206 45.16 N 72.09 W
Magog ≃ 206 45.24 N 71.54 W
Magog, Lake ⊜ 206 45.18 N 72.03 W
Magoito 266c 38.52 N 9.26 W
Magome ◆[8] 268 35.35 N 139.43 E
Mago National Park ♦ 144 5.30 N 36.15 E
Magonoy 116 6.54 N 124.33 E
Magoro 154 1.44 N 34.06 E
Magothy Bay ⊂ 208 37.10 N 75.55 W
Magothy River ⊂ 208 39.04 N 76.28 W
Magoúla 267c 38.04 N 23.32 E
Magoye 154 16.00 S 27.37 E
M'agozero 76 60.21 N 34.50 E
Magpie 186 50.19 N 64.30 W
Magpie ≃, On., Can. 190 47.56 N 84.50 W
Magpie ≃, P.Q., Can. 186 50.19 N 64.27 W
Magpie, Lac ⊜ 186 51.00 N 64.41 W
Magpie Ouest ≃ 186 51.02 N 64.42 W
Magra 126 22.59 N 88.22 E
Magra ≃ 64 44.03 N 9.58 E
Magra Hāt 126 22.14 N 88.23 E
Magrath 182 49.25 N 112.52 W
Magrè (Margreid) 64 46.17 N 11.12 E
Magro ≃ 34 39.11 N 0.25 W
Magruder Mountain ∧ 204 37.25 N 117.33 W
Magsaysay (Linugos) 116 9.01 N 125.11 E
Magsingal 116 17.41 N 120.25 E
Magu ≃ 250 2.56 S 41.55 W
Maguan 102 22.59 N 104.19 E
Maguanying 271a 39.52 N 116.17 E
Maguari, Cabo › 250 0.18 S 48.22 W
Magude 156 25.02 S 32.40 E
Magudu 158 27.31 S 31.40 E
Magueyes 196 25.44 N 97.47 W
Maguindanao □[4] 116 6.55 N 124.20 E
Magumeri 146 12.08 N 12.50 E
Māgura 124 23.29 N 89.25 E
Maguru 150 12.28 N 6.35 E
Maguse Lake ⊜ 176 61.40 N 95.10 W
Maguzhan 120 31.15 N 88.00 E
Magway 110 20.09 N 94.55 E
Magway □[8] 110 20.30 N 94.30 E
Magwe 154 4.08 N 32.17 E
Magwood Park ♦ 275b 43.39 N 79.30 W
Magyarország → Hungary □[1] 30 47.00 N 20.00 E
Mahābād 128 36.45 N 45.43 E
Mahābaleshwar 122 17.55 N 73.40 E
Mahabe 157b 17.05 S 45.20 E
Mahābhārat Lek ⋀ 124 27.40 N 84.30 E
Mahabo, Madag. 157b 23.40 S 46.08 E
Mahabo, Madag. 157b 20.23 S 44.40 E
Mahād 122 18.05 N 73.25 E
Mahadday Weyn 144 2.58 N 45.32 E
Mahādebpur 126 23.51 N 89.53 E
Mahādeo Hills ⋀[2] 122 22.22 N 78.34 E
Mahādeo Range ⋀ 122 17.50 N 74.15 E
Mahaffey 214 40.52 N 78.43 W
Mahagi 154 2.18 N 30.59 E
Mahagi Port 154 2.09 N 31.14 E
Mahai 102 38.17 N 94.13 E
Mahaicony Village 246 6.36 N 57.48 W
Mahajamba ≃ 157b 15.33 S 47.08 E
Mahajamba, Helodranon' i ⊂ 157b 15.24 S 47.05 E
Mahājan 123 28.47 N 73.50 E
Mahajanga 157b 15.43 S 46.19 E
Mahajanga □[4] 157b 17.00 S 46.00 E
Mahajilo ≃ 157b 19.42 S 45.22 E
Maḥajjah 132 32.57 N 36.14 E
Mahākālī □[8] 124 29.30 N 80.30 E
Mahākālī (Sārda) ≃ 124 27.21 N 81.23 E
Mahakam ≃ 112 0.35 S 117.17 E
Mahālandi 126 24.04 N 88.07 E
Mahalatswe 156 23.05 S 26.51 E
Mahalla el-Kubra → Al-Maḥallah al-Kubrā 142 30.58 N 31.10 E
Maḥallāt 128 33.55 N 50.27 E
Maḥallat Kayl 142 31.01 N 30.17 E
Maḥallat Marḥūm 142 30.48 N 30.57 E
Maḥallat Minūf 142 30.53 N 30.58 E
Maḥallat Zayyād 142 31.02 N 31.14 E
Maham 124 28.59 N 76.18 E
Mahamba 158 27.07 S 31.10 E
Mahānadi ≃ 118 20.19 N 86.45 E
Mahānadpati 126 23.00 N 88.16 E
Mahānanda ≃ 124 24.29 N 88.18 E
Mahanay Island I 116 10.12 N 124.14 E
Mahanoro 157b 19.54 S 48.48 E
Mahanoy City 208 40.48 N 76.08 W
Mahanoy Creek ≃ 208 40.42 N 76.51 W
Mahantango Creek ≃ 208 40.47 N 76.56 W
Mahantango Mountain ∧ 208 40.40 N 76.45 W
Mahao 89 43.10 N 127.59 E
Mahape 272c 19.07 N 73.01 E
Mahārājganj, India 124 27.09 N 83.34 E
Mahārājganj, India 124 26.07 N 84.29 E
Mahārājpur, India 124 25.01 N 79.44 E
Mahārājpur, India 272a 28.39 N 77.20 E
Mahārāshtra □[3] 122 19.00 N 76.00 E
Maḥārīq, Wādī V 142 27.48 N 31.47 E
Mahārlū, Daryācheh-ye ⊜ 128 29.25 N 52.50 E
Mahāsamund 120 21.06 N 82.06 E
Maha Sarakham 110 16.11 N 103.18 E
Maha Sawat, Khlong ≊ 269a 13.47 N 100.28 E
Mahasoa 157b 22.12 S 46.06 E
Mahasolo 157b 19.07 S 46.22 E
Mahates 246 10.14 N 75.12 W
Mahatsinjo 157b 21.26 S 45.51 E
Maḥaṭṭat al-Ḥafīf 132 32.12 N 37.08 E
Mahaut 240d 15.21 N 61.25 W
Mahavavy ≃, Madag. 157b 15.57 S 45.54 E
Mahavavy ≃, Madag. 157b 13.00 S 48.55 E
Mahaweli ≃ 122 8.27 N 81.13 E
Mahaxai 110 17.25 N 105.12 E
Maḥbas, Wādī al- V 140 15.50 N 29.45 E
Mahbūbābād 122 17.37 N 80.01 E
Mahbūbnagar 122 16.44 N 77.59 E
Mahd adh-Dhahab 128 23.30 N 40.52 E
Mahdāt, Bi'r al- ⊤[4] 142 30.44 N 32.32 E
Mahdia 148 35.30 N 11.04 E
Mahdia □[8] 148 35.18 N 10.45 E
Mahe 122 11.42 N 75.32 E
Mahébourg 157c 20.24 S 57.42 E
Mahé Island I 138 4.40 S 55.28 E
Mahendraganj 124 25.20 N 89.45 E
Mahendragarh 124 28.17 N 76.09 E
Mahendra Giri ∧ 122 18.58 N 84.21 E
Mahendranagar 124 28.52 N 80.17 E
Mahenge, Tan. 154 7.38 S 36.16 E
Mahenge, Tan. 154 8.41 S 36.43 E
Maheno 172 45.10 S 170.50 E
Mahesāna 120 23.36 N 72.24 E
Mahesgādi 272b 22.39 N 88.33 E
Maheshmunda 126 24.13 N 86.24 E
Maheshtala 272b 22.30 N 88.15 E
Maheshwar 120 22.11 N 75.35 E
Mahespur 124 23.21 N 88.55 E
Mahgawān 124 26.29 N 78.37 E
Mahi ≃ 120 22.16 N 72.58 E
Mahia Peninsula ›[1] 172 39.10 S 177.53 E
Mahiāri 272b 22.35 N 88.14 E
Māhikpur 272b 22.32 N 88.14 E
Mahilāra 126 22.56 N 90.16 E
Māhīm ◆[8] 272c 19.03 N 72.49 E
Māhīm ≃ 272c 19.03 N 72.51 E
Māhīm Bay ⊂ 272c 19.02 N 72.50 E
Mahina, Mali 150 13.46 N 10.51 W
Mahina, Poly. fr. 174s 17.31 S 149.30 W
Mahinerangi, Lake ⊜ 172 45.51 S 169.57 E
Mahinog 116 9.09 N 124.47 E
Mahīshādal 126 22.11 N 87.59 E
Mahishdānga 272b 22.54 N 88.11 E
Mahlabatini 158 28.14 S 31.30 E
Mahlangasi 158 27.37 S 31.42 E
Mahlberg 58 48.17 N 7.48 E
Mahlow 54 52.22 N 13.24 E
Mahlsdorf 54 52.47 N 11.13 E
Mahlsdorf-Süd ◆[8] 264a 52.29 N 13.36 E
Maḥmūdābād, India 124 27.18 N 81.07 E
Maḥmūdābād, Īrān 128 36.38 N 52.15 E
Maḥmūd-e Rāqī 120 35.01 N 69.20 E

ENGLISH Name	Page	Lat.°′	Long.°′	DEUTSCH Name	Seite	Breite°′	Länge°′ E = Ost

Maḥmūdīyah, Tur'at al- ≊ 142 31.11 N 29.53 E
Mahmudiye 130 39.30 N 31.00 E
Mahmūdpur, India 272a 28.46 N 77.22 E
Mahmudpur, India 272b 22.41 N 88.09 E
Mahmutbey ◆[8] 267b 41.03 N 28.49 E
Mahmutşevketpaşa 130 41.05 N 29.19 E
Mahmutşevketpaşa ◆[8] 267b 41.09 N 29.11 E
Mahnomen 198 47.18 N 95.58 W
Mahoba 124 25.17 N 79.52 E
Mahogany Mountain ∧ 202 43.14 N 117.16 W
Mahomet 216 40.11 N 88.24 W
Mahone Bay 186 44.27 N 64.23 W
Mahone Bay ⊂ 186 44.30 N 64.15 W
Mahoning □[6] 214 41.06 N 80.39 W
Mahoning ≃ 214 40.58 N 80.23 W
Mahoning, West Branch ≃ 214 41.12 N 80.57 W
Mahoning Creek ≃ 214 40.55 N 79.27 W
Mahoning Creek Lake ⊜[1] 214 40.50 N 79.10 W
Mahony Lake ⊜ 180 65.30 N 125.20 W
Mahood Falls 182 51.50 N 120.39 W
Mahood Lake ⊜ 182 51.55 N 120.24 W
Mahopac 210 41.22 N 73.44 W
Mahopac Falls 210 41.22 N 73.46 W
Mahora 34 39.13 N 1.44 W
Mahoras Brook ≃ 276 40.25 N 74.08 W
Mahrāt, Jabal ⋀[1] 144 17.05 N 51.30 E
Mahrauli ◆[8] 272a 28.31 N 77.11 E
Mahrauni 124 24.35 N 78.43 E
Mähren → Morava □[9] 30 49.20 N 17.00 E
Mahres 148 34.32 N 10.30 E
Mähring 60 49.55 N 12.32 E
Mahuiling 100 29.24 N 115.48 E
Māhul ◆[8] 272c 19.01 N 72.53 E
Mahulia 126 22.39 N 86.24 E
Mahur Island I 164 2.50 S 152.40 E
Mahuta 154 10.52 S 39.27 E
Mahuva 120 21.05 N 71.48 E
Mahwa 124 27.03 N 76.56 E
Mahwah 276 41.06 N 74.09 W
Mahwah ≃ 276 41.06 N 74.10 W
Mai, Île de I 275a 45.36 N 73.50 W
Maia, Am. Sam. 174y 14.13 S 169.28 W
Maia, Port. 34 41.14 N 8.37 W
Mai Aini 144 14.47 N 39.06 E
Maiala National Park ♦ 171a 27.19 S 152.46 E
Maianga 152 14.12 S 21.45 E
Maiano 64 46.11 N 13.04 E
Maiauatá 250 1.51 S 49.02 W
Maicao 246 11.23 N 72.13 W
Maîche 58 47.15 N 6.48 E
Maichen 102 20.29 N 109.59 E
Maici ≃ 248 6.30 S 61.43 W
Maicurú ≃ 250 2.14 S 54.17 W
Maida 68 38.51 N 16.22 E
Maidan ♦ 272b 22.33 N 88.21 E
Maiden 192 35.34 N 81.12 W
Maidenhead 42 51.32 N 0.44 W
Maiden Newton 42 50.46 N 2.35 W
Maidstone, Austl. 274b 37.47 S 144.52 E
Maidstone, On., Can. 214 42.13 N 82.53 W
Maidstone, Sk., Can. 184 53.06 N 109.18 W
Maidstone, Eng., U.K. 42 51.17 N 0.32 E
Maidstone □[8] 260 51.17 N 0.35 E
Maiduguri 146 11.51 N 13.10 E
Maie 154 2.46 N 30.34 E
Maiella, Montagna della ⋀ 66 42.05 N 14.07 E
Maienfeld 58 47.00 N 9.32 E
Maierato 68 38.42 N 16.11 E
Maifeld □[9] 56 50.20 N 7.20 E
Maigatari 150 12.46 N 9.27 E
Maignelay 50 49.33 N 2.31 E
Maigo 116 8.10 N 123.57 E
Mai Gudo ∧ 144 7.29 N 37.12 E
Maihar 124 24.16 N 80.45 E
Maihara 94 35.19 N 136.17 E
Maijoma 196 28.55 N 104.21 W
Maikala Plateau ⋀[1] 124 22.30 N 81.00 E
Maikala Range ⋀ 122 22.30 N 81.30 E
Maikammer 56 49.18 N 9.07 E
Maiko ≃ 154 0.14 N 25.33 E
Maiko, Parc National de la ♦ 154 3.30 N 27.45 E
Maikoor, Pulau I 164 6.15 S 134.15 E
Mailand → Milano 62 45.28 N 9.12 E
Mailāni 124 28.17 N 80.21 E
Maili 229c 21.25 N 158.10 W
Maillane 62 43.50 N 4.47 E
Mailley-et-Chazelot 58 47.32 N 6.03 E
Maillezais 32 46.22 N 0.44 W
Mailly-le-Camp 50 48.40 N 4.13 E
Mailly-le-Château 50 47.36 N 3.38 E
Mailly-Maillet 50 50.04 N 2.36 E
Mailsi 123 29.48 N 72.11 E
Maimbung 116 5.56 N 121.02 E
Mai Mefales 144 14.59 N 38.16 E
Mā'īn 132 31.41 N 35.44 E
Main ≃, B.R.D. 30 50.00 N 8.18 E
Main ≃, N. Ire., U.K. 48 54.43 N 6.18 W
Maināguri 124 26.34 N 88.49 E
Mainart ≃ 255 20.27 S 43.17 W
Mainau 58 47.42 N 9.11 E
Mainburg 60 48.38 N 11.47 E
Main Camp 174o 2.01 N 157.25 W
Main Canal ≊, Ca., U.S. 226 37.25 N 121.05 W
Main Canal ≊, Ca., U.S. 226 37.23 N 120.26 W
Main Canal ≊, Wa., U.S. 224 47.07 N 120.44 W
Main Channel ⊔ 190 45.22 N 81.50 W
Maincourt-sur-Yvette 261 48.43 N 1.58 E
Main Creek ≃ 276 40.34 N 74.11 W
Maincy 261 48.33 N 2.42 E
Mai-Ndombe, Lac ⊜ 152 2.00 S 18.20 E
Main-Donau-Kanal ≊ 60 49.02 N 11.36 E
Main Duck Island I 212 43.56 N 76.37 W
Maine 210 42.11 N 76.03 W
Maine □[9] 32 48.15 N 0.05 W
Maine □[3], U.S. 178 45.15 N 69.15 W
Maine □[3], U.S. 188 45.15 N 69.15 W
Maine ≃ 48 52.09 N 9.45 W
Maine, Gulf of ⊂ 178 43.00 N 68.00 W
Mainebene □[9] 56 50.00 N 8.45 E
Maine-et-Loire □[5] 32 47.25 N 0.30 W
Mainesburg 210 41.47 N 77.07 W
Maïné-Soroa 146 13.12 N 12.02 E
Maineville 218 39.18 N 84.13 W
Mainguerin 261 48.32 N 1.51 E
Mainhardt 56 49.04 N 9.33 E
Mainit 116 9.32 N 125.32 E
Mainit, Lake ⊜ 116 9.26 N 125.32 E
Mainland 285 40.15 N 75.22 W
Mainland I, Scot., U.K. 46 59.00 N 3.15 W
Mainland I, Scot., U.K. 46a 60.16 N 1.16 W
Mainleus 54 50.06 N 11.22 E
Mainoru 164 14.02 S 134.05 E
Mainpuri 124 27.14 N 79.01 E
Main Range National Park ♦ 171a 28.01 S 152.22 E
Maintal 56 50.09 N 8.54 E
Maintenon 50 48.35 N 1.35 E
Maintirano 157b 18.03 S 44.01 E
Main Topsail ∧ 186 49.08 N 56.33 W
Mainvilliers 50 48.27 N 1.28 E
Mainz 56 50.01 N 8.16 E
Maio I 150a 15.15 N 23.10 W
Maiolati Spontini 66 43.28 N 13.06 E
Maiori 68 40.39 N 14.38 E
Maiori, Nuraghe ⊥ 71 40.56 N 9.06 E
Maipa 164 8.21 S 146.33 E
Maipo ≃ 252 33.37 S 71.39 W
Maipo, Volcán ∧[1] 252 34.10 S 69.50 W
Maipú, Arg. 252 32.58 S 68.47 W
Maipú, Arg. 252 36.52 S 57.52 W
Maipú, Chile 252 33.31 S 70.46 W
Maiqihamiao 89 43.22 N 120.46 E
Maiquetía 246 10.36 N 66.57 W
Maiquetía, Aeropuerto ⊠ 286c 10.37 N 66.59 W
Maira ≃ 62 44.49 N 7.38 E
Maira, Valle V 62 44.30 N 7.08 E
Mairābāri 120 26.28 N 92.26 E
Mairi 250 11.43 S 40.08 W
Mairinque 256 23.33 S 47.10 W
Mairiporã 256 23.19 S 46.35 W
Mairiporã □[7] 287b 23.24 S 46.37 W
Mairipotaba 255 17.18 S 49.28 W
Maisach 60 48.13 N 11.16 E
Maisaka 94 34.41 N 137.37 E
Maishi 100 29.11 N 113.58 E
Maišiagala 76 54.52 N 25.04 E
Maiskhāl Island I 120 21.36 N 91.56 E
Maison de Pierre, Lac de la ⊜ 206 46.53 N 74.42 W
Maisonneuve, Parc ♦ 275a 45.33 N 73.34 W
Maisons-Alfort 261 48.48 N 2.26 E
Maisons-Laffitte 50 48.57 N 2.09 E
Maisons-Laffitte, Château de ⊥ 261 48.57 N 2.09 E
Maisse 50 48.24 N 2.23 E
Maissin 56 49.58 N 5.11 E
Maitani 270 34.49 N 135.22 E
Maitengwe 156 20.06 S 27.13 E
Maitengwe ≃ 156 19.59 S 26.26 E
Maithon Reservoir ⊜[1] 126 23.50 N 86.43 E
Maitland, Austl. 168b 34.22 S 137.40 E
Maitland, Austl. 170 32.44 S 151.33 E
Maitland, N.S., Can. 186 45.19 N 63.30 W
Maitland, On., Can. 212 44.38 N 75.37 W
Maitland, Fl., U.S. 220 28.37 N 81.21 W
Maitland ≃ 190 43.45 N 81.43 W
Maitland, Lake ⊜ 162 27.11 S 121.03 E
Maixie 100 27.38 N 115.29 E
Maíz ≃ 236 11.17 N 83.52 W
Maíz, Islas del II 236 12.15 N 83.00 W
Maizefield 158 26.28 S 29.31 E
Maizhokunggar 120 29.50 N 91.45 E
Maizières-lès-Metz 56 49.13 N 6.09 E
Maizières-lès-Vic 58 48.43 N 6.46 E
Maizuru 96 35.28 N 135.24 E
Maja ≃, S.S.S.R. 74 60.24 N 134.30 E
Maja ≃, S.S.S.R. 89 54.31 N 134.41 E
Majābirah, Minqār al- ⊥[4] 142 30.16 N 29.49 E
Majačka ≃ 83 48.44 N 37.33 E
Majačnyj 86 52.41 N 55.44 E
Majadahonda 266a 40.29 N 3.52 W
Majagua 240p 21.55 N 79.00 W
Majagual 246 8.33 N 74.38 W
Majaki, S.S.S.R. 78 46.25 N 30.16 E
Majaki, S.S.S.R. 83 48.57 N 37.37 E
Majakovskij 84 42.06 N 42.48 E
Majalaya 115a 7.03 S 107.45 E
Majalengka 115a 6.50 S 108.13 E
Majana, Ensenada de ⊂ 240p 22.41 N 82.45 W
Majanji 154 0.15 N 33.59 E
Majari ≃ 246 3.29 N 60.58 W
Majayjay 116 14.09 N 121.28 E
Majchura 85 39.02 N 68.35 E
Majdantal 85 43.41 N 68.02 E
Majd el Kurūm 132 32.55 N 35.15 E
Majeigha 140 11.33 N 24.40 E
Majenang 115a 7.18 S 108.45 E
Majene 112 3.33 S 118.57 E
Majenica 216 40.46 N 85.27 W
Majevica ⋀ 38 44.30 N 18.55 E
Maji 144 6.11 N 35.38 E
Majia 100 32.32 N 118.50 E
Majia ≃ 98 38.09 N 117.53 E
Majiacun 106 30.08 N 119.58 E
Majiahe 102 35.20 N 104.46 E
Majian, Zhg. 100 29.19 N 119.36 E
Majian, Zhg. 100 29.43 N 120.00 E
Majiang, Zhg. 102 23.48 N 111.09 E
Majiang, Zhg. 110 26.28 N 107.28 E
Majiangzong 120 30.27 N 90.03 E
Majiaoba 102 32.14 N 104.35 E
Majiaping 102 36.31 N 103.20 E
Majiasi 105 39.03 N 117.05 E
Majiawopu 104 41.46 N 121.06 E
Majiayan 100 27.26 N 112.56 E
Majiazhai 104 42.22 N 124.04 E
Majiazhou 100 26.46 N 114.47 E
Majidun Creek ≃ 273a 6.38 N 3.28 E
Majie, Zhg. 102 23.50 N 105.07 E
Majie, Zhg. 102 25.03 N 103.45 E
Majin 100 29.18 N 118.24 E
Majin ≃ 100 29.00 N 118.21 E
Majinzhuangzi 104 41.55 N 123.53 E
Maji Shan I 106 31.26 N 120.06 E
Majītha 123 31.46 N 74.57 E
Majja 74 61.44 N 130.18 E
Majkain 86 51.27 N 75.52 E
Majkop 84 44.35 N 40.07 E
Majkor 86 59.01 N 55.54 E
Majlibaš 86 45.49 N 62.39 E
Majli-Saj 85 41.17 N 72.29 E
Majlispur 126 24.13 N 90.53 E
Majmak 85 42.40 N 71.15 E
Majna, S.S.S.R. 80 54.07 N 47.37 E
Majna, S.S.S.R. 86 53.00 N 91.28 E
Majnan 272b 22.59 N 88.09 E
Majnic, ozero ⊜ 180 63.15 N 176.40 E
Majno-Gytkino 180 63.36 N 176.30 E
Majŏn-ni, C.M.I.K. 98 39.06 N 127.07 E
Majŏn-ni, Taehan 271b 37.36 N 126.41 E
Major, Puig ∧ 34 39.48 N 2.48 E
Majorca → Mallorca I 34 39.30 N 3.00 E
Major Creek ≃ 169 36.51 S 145.05 E
Major Isidoro 250 9.32 S 37.00 W
Majorque, Île → Mallorca I 34 39.30 N 3.00 E
Majrūr 140 14.01 N 30.27 E
Majrūr, Wādī V 140 15.44 N 26.26 E
Majsk 86 57.49 N 77.16 E
Majskij, S.S.S.R. 83 47.43 N 40.03 E
Majskij, S.S.S.R. 84 43.38 N 44.04 E
Majskij, S.S.S.R. 89 52.18 N 129.38 E
Majskij, S.S.S.R. 89 49.00 N 140.10 E
Majskoje, S.S.S.R. 82 56.08 N 37.55 E
Majskoje, S.S.S.R. 86 50.55 N 78.15 E
Majtan 86 45.46 N 74.20 E
Majtobe 85 43.01 N 70.35 E
Māju 126 22.37 N 88.05 E
Majuba Hill ⊥ 158 27.28 S 29.51 E
Majuqiao 105 39.46 N 116.32 E
Majuro I[1] 14 7.09 N 171.12 E
Majuzigou 104 41.49 N 121.38 E
Maka 150 13.40 N 14.17 W
Makabana 152 2.48 S 12.29 E
Makabe 94 36.16 N 140.06 E
Makadasa ≃ 116 7.22 N 124.36 E
Makaha, Hi., U.S. 229c 21.28 N 158.13 W
Makaha, Zimb. 154 17.17 S 32.37 E
Makaha Point › 229b 22.08 N 159.44 W
Makah Indian Reservation ◆[4] 224 48.20 N 124.41 W
Makahuena Point › 229b 21.52 N 159.27 W
Makak 152 3.33 N 11.02 E
Makala 273b 4.25 S 15.17 E
Makalamabedi 156 20.19 S 23.51 E
Makale 112 3.06 S 119.51 E
Makallé 252 27.13 S 59.17 W
Makālu ∧ 124 27.54 N 87.06 E
Makamba 154 4.08 S 29.49 E
Makanapur 272a 28.38 N 77.21 E
Makanči 86 46.48 N 82.00 E
Makanya 154 4.20 S 37.51 E
Makanza 152 1.36 N 19.07 E
Makaoo Indian Reserve ◆[4] 184 53.40 N 110.02 W
Makapu Point › 174v 18.59 S 169.56 W

Symbols in the index entries represent the broad categories identified in the key at the right. Symbols with superior numbers (⋀[1]) identify subcategories (see complete key on page *I · 1).*

Symbole im Register stellen die rechts im Schlüssel erklärten Kategorien dar. Symbole mit hochgestellten Ziffern (⋀[1]) bezeichnen Unterabteilungen einer Kategorie (vgl. vollständiger Schlüssel auf Seite *I · 1).*

Los símbolos incluídos en el texto del índice representan las grandes categorias identificadas con la clave a la derecha. Los símbolos con numeros en su parte superior (⋀[1]) identifican las subcategorías (véase la clave completa en la página *I · 1).*

Les symboles de l'index représentent les catégories indiquées dans la légende à droite. Les symboles suivis d'un indice (⋀[1]) représentent des sous-catégories (voir légende complète à la page *I · 1).*

Os símbolos incluídos no texto do índice representam as grandes categorias identificadas com a chave à direita. Os símbolos com números em sua parte superior (⋀[1]) identificam as subcategorias (veja-se a chave completa à página *I · 1).*

	English	Deutsch	Español	Français	Português
∧	Mountain	Berg	Montaña	Montagne	Montanha
⋀	Mountains	Gebirge	Montañas	Montagnes	Montanhas
)(	Pass	Paß	Paso	Col	Passo
V	Valley, Canyon	Tal, Cañon	Valle, Cañón	Vallée, Canyon	Vale, Canhão
≚	Plain	Ebene	Llano	Plaine	Planície
›	Cape	Kap	Cabo	Cap	Cabo
I	Island	Insel	Isla	Île	Ilha
II	Islands	Inseln	Islas	Îles	Ilhas
◆	Other Topographic Features	Andere Topographische Objekte	Otros Elementos Topográficos	Autres données topographiques	Outros acidentes topográficos

ESPAÑOL — Nombre | Página | Lat.°′ | Long.°′ W = Oeste
FRANÇAIS — Nom | Page | Lat.°′ | Long.°′ W = Ouest
PORTUGUÊS — Nome | Página | Lat.°′ | Long.°′ W = Oeste

Makapuu Head › 229c 21.19 N 157.39 W
Makarakomburu, Mount ∧ 175e 9.43 S 160.02 E
Makarakskij 86 55.36 N 88.03 E
Makarewa 172 46.20 S 168.21 E
Makari 146 12.35 N 14.28 E
Makar-Ib 24 63.39 N 49.24 E
Makaricha 24 66.15 N 58.20 E
Makarje 80 58.35 N 48.11 E
Makarjev 80 57.52 N 43.48 E
Makarjevo 80 56.06 N 45.06 E
Makarov, S.S.S.R. 78 50.28 N 29.49 E
Makarov, S.S.S.R. 89 48.38 N 142.48 E
Makarovo, S.S.S.R. 80 52.18 N 43.20 E
Makarovo, S.S.S.R. 82 54.22 N 36.40 E
Makarovo, S.S.S.R. 88 57.29 N 107.52 E
Makarska 36 43.18 N 17.02 E
Makasar → Ujungpandang 112 5.07 S 119.24 E
Makasar, Selat (Makassar Strait) ꭒ 112 2.00 S 117.30 E
Makaševka 80 51.30 N 42.36 E
Makassar Strait → Makasar, Selat ꭒ 112 2.00 S 117.30 E
Makasuko 154 6.00 S 34.56 E
Makat 80 47.39 N 53.19 E
Makatea ɪ 14 15.50 S 148.15 W
Makati 269f 14.34 N 121.02 E
Makaw, Mya. 110 26.27 N 96.42 E
Makaw, Zaïre 152 3.29 S 18.19 E
Makawao 229a 20.51 N 156.18 W
Makaweli 229b 21.55 N 159.38 W
Makay, Massif du ⋏ 157b 21.15 S 45.15 E
Makaya 152 3.22 S 18.02 E
Makedonija □[3] 38 41.50 N 22.00 E
Makefu 174v 18.59 S 169.55 W
Makejevka, S.S.S.R. 78 50.40 N 31.50 E
Makejevka, S.S.S.R. 83 48.02 N 37.58 E
Makejevka, S.S.S.R. 83 49.14 N 37.59 E
Makemie Park 208 37.55 N 75.34 W
Makemo ɪ[1] 14 16.35 S 143.40 W
Makena 229a 20.39 N 156.27 W
Makeni 150 8.53 N 12.03 W
Makere 154 4.17 S 30.25 E
Maketu 172 37.46 S 176.27 E
Makeyevka → Makejevka 83 48.02 N 37.58 E
Makgadikgadi ≡ 156 20.45 S 25.30 E
Makgadikgadi Pans Game Reserve ◆[4] 156 20.30 S 24.45 E
Makhachkala → Machačkala 84 42.58 N 47.30 E
Makhad 123 33.08 N 71.44 E
Makhaleng ≃ 158 30.20 S 27.23 E
Mākhālpur 272b 22.56 N 88.10 E
Makham 110 12.40 N 102.12 E
Makhdūmnagar 124 26.28 N 82.46 E
Makhfar al-Quwayrah 132 29.48 N 35.19 E
Makhfar Ramn 132 29.42 N 35.25 E
Makhrūq, Wādī al- V 132 31.30 N 37.10 E
Makhyah, Wādī V 144 17.40 N 49.01 E
Maki, Indon. 164 3.11 S 134.14 E
Maki, Nihon 92 37.45 N 138.53 E
Maki, Nihon 94 37.05 N 138.23 E
Maki, Nihon 270 34.52 N 135.04 E
Makika, Lua ±[6] 229a 20.34 N 156.34 W
Makikihi 172 44.38 S 171.09 E
Makilala 116 6.55 N 125.05 E
Makindu 154 2.17 S 37.49 E
Makino, Nihon 94 35.28 N 136.05 E
M'akino, S.S.S.R. 265b 55.48 N 37.22 E
Makinsk 86 52.37 N 70.26 E
Makio-dam ◆[6] 94 35.50 N 137.36 E
Makioka 94 35.45 N 138.43 E
Makira □[4] 175e 11.00 S 162.30 E
Makira Harbour ⊂ 175e 10.25 S 161.29 E
M'akiševo 76 56.34 N 28.53 E
M'akit 74 61.24 N 152.09 E
Makkah (Mecca) 144 21.27 N 39.49 E
Makkavejevo 88 51.44 N 113.58 E
Makkum 52 53.04 N 5.24 E
Makó, Magy. 30 46.13 N 20.29 E
Mako, Sén. 150 12.52 N 12.21 W
Makoaneng ∧ 158 29.47 S 28.57 E
Makobe Lake ◎ 190 47.27 N 80.25 W
Makoka 154 2.34 S 25.29 E
Makok-ni 271b 37.43 N 126.38 E
Makokou 152 0.34 N 12.52 E
Makoli 154 17.27 S 26.05 E
Makongai Island ɪ 175g 17.27 S 178.58 E
Makongo 154 3.25 N 26.22 E
Makongolosi 154 8.24 S 33.09 E
Makopse 84 43.59 N 39.13 E
Makorako ∧ 172 39.09 S 176.02 E
Makoro 154 3.08 N 29.44 E
Makoshika State Park ♠ 198 47.03 N 104.41 W
Makošino 78 51.27 N 32.18 E
Makotuku 172 40.07 S 176.14 E
Makoua 152 0.01 N 15.39 E
Makov 30 49.23 N 18.30 E
Makovskoje 86 58.12 N 90.52 E
Maków Mazowiecki 30 52.52 N 21.06 E
Maków Podhalański 30 49.44 N 19.41 E
Makrai 124 22.04 N 77.06 E
Makrampur 126 22.44 N 90.14 E
Makrāna 120 27.03 N 74.43 E
Makran Coast ±[2] 128 25.15 N 61.00 E
M'aksa 76 58.54 N 38.12 E
Maksaticha 76 57.48 N 35.53 E
Maksimicha 88 53.15 N 108.43 E
Maksimkin Jar 86 58.42 N 86.48 E
Maksimoviči 78 51.13 N 29.37 E
Maksimovka, S.S.S.R. 80 52.59 N 51.10 E
Maksimovka, S.S.S.R. 83 47.38 N 37.34 E
Maksimovka, S.S.S.R. 89 46.04 N 137.51 E
Maksimovo 82 56.20 N 35.58 E
Maksudangarh 124 24.03 N 77.15 E
Maktar 148 35.51 N 9.12 E
Maktau 154 3.24 S 38.08 E
Mākū, Īrān 128 39.17 N 44.31 E
Maku, Zhg. 105 39.33 N 114.46 E
Makuhari 268 35.39 N 140.03 E
Makuliro 154 9.35 S 37.26 E
Makumbako 154 8.51 S 34.50 E
Makumbi 152 5.51 S 20.41 E
Makung (P'enghu) 100 23.34 N 119.34 E
Makunudu ɪ 122 6.25 N 72.41 E
Makunudu Atoll ɪ[1] 122 6.20 N 72.36 E
Makuragi-san ∧ 96 35.32 N 133.08 E
Makurazaki 92 31.16 N 130.19 E
Makurdi 150 7.45 N 8.32 E
Makushin Volcano ∧[1] 180 53.53 N 166.50 W
Makušino 86 55.13 N 67.13 E
Makuyuni 154 3.33 S 36.06 E
Makwa Lake ◎ 184 54.04 N 109.15 W
Makwassie 158 27.26 S 26.00 E
Makwende-Bayo 154 7.08 S 28.06 E
Makwiro 154 17.58 S 30.28 E
Māl, India 124 26.52 N 88.44 E
Mal, Maur. 150 16.58 N 13.23 W
Mala, Perú 248 12.39 S 76.38 W
Malå, Sve. 26 65.11 N 18.44 E
Mala ≃ 248 12.40 S 76.41 W
Mala, Punta › 246 7.28 N 80.00 W
Malabang 116 7.38 N 124.03 E
Malabar, Austl. 274a 33.58 S 151.15 E
Malabar, Fl., U.S. 220 28.00 N 80.33 W
Malabar Coast ±[2] 122 11.00 N 75.00 E
Malabar Farm State Park ♠ 214 40.38 N 82.25 W
Malabar Hill ∧[2] 272c 18.57 N 72.48 E
Malabar Point › 272c 18.57 N 72.47 E
Malabo 152 3.45 N 8.47 E
Mal Abrigo 258 34.09 S 56.57 W
Malabrigo Point › 116 13.36 N 121.15 E
Malabuyoc 116 9.39 N 123.19 E
Malaca, Estrecho de → Malacca, Strait of ꭒ 110 2.30 N 101.20 E
Malacacheta 255 17.50 S 42.05 W
Malacañang Palace v 269f 14.36 N 120.59 E
Malacca, Strait of ꭒ 110 2.30 N 101.20 E
Malachovka 82 55.39 N 38.00 E
Malachovo, S.S.S.R. 82 54.45 N 37.27 E
Malachovo, S.S.S.R. 82 54.22 N 37.31 E
Malachovskij 80 49.08 N 41.43 E
Malacky 30 48.27 N 17.00 E
Malād ◆[8] 272c 19.11 N 72.51 E
Malad ≃ 200 41.35 N 112.07 W
Malad City 202 42.11 N 112.15 W
Malad Creek ≃ 272c 19.08 N 72.48 E
Malafede ≃ 267a 41.47 N 12.24 E
Málaga, Col. 246 6.42 N 72.44 W
Málaga, Esp. 34 36.43 N 4.25 W
Malaga, Ca., U.S. 226 36.42 N 119.46 W
Malaga, N.J., U.S. 208 39.34 N 75.02 W
Malaga, N.M., U.S. 196 32.13 N 104.04 W
Malagarasi 154 5.06 S 30.50 E
Malagarasi ≃ 154 5.12 S 29.47 E
Malagash 186 45.46 N 63.23 W
Malagasy Republic → Madagascar □[1] 157b 19.00 S 46.00 E
Malago ≃ 116 10.55 N 123.02 E
Malagón 34 39.10 N 3.51 W
Malagón ≃ 34 37.35 N 7.29 W
Malagrotta ◆[8] 66 41.53 N 12.20 E
Mal'agurt 80 57.39 N 52.32 E
Malahat 224 48.32 N 123.34 W
Malahide 48 53.27 N 6.09 W
Malaimbandy 157b 20.20 S 45.36 E
Malaisie → Malaysia □[1] 112 2.30 N 112.30 E
Malaita □[4] 175e 9.00 S 161.00 E
Malaita ɪ 175e 9.00 S 161.00 E
Malaja Beloz'orka 78 47.14 N 34.56 E
Malaja Bessergenovka 83 47.09 N 38.36 E
Malaja Borščovka 82 56.33 N 36.53 E
Malaja Bykovka 80 51.54 N 47.45 E
Malaja Čuja ≃ 88 58.56 N 112.13 E
Malaja Devica 78 50.41 N 32.10 E
Malaja Doroginka 82 54.06 N 38.56 E
Malaja Dubna 82 55.52 N 38.58 E
Malaja Istra ≃ 82 55.54 N 36.50 E
Malaja Ižmora 80 53.32 N 42.48 E
Malaja Janisol' 83 47.22 N 37.20 E
Malaja Jekaterinovka 80 51.26 N 44.17 E
Malaja Kinel' ≃ 80 53.29 N 51.30 E
Malaja Kokšaga ≃ 80 56.09 N 47.53 E
Malaja Konkudera ≃ 88 57.26 N 112.37 E
Malaja Kuril'skaja Gr'ada (Habomai-Shotō) ɪɪ 92a 43.30 N 146.10 E
Malaja Laba ≃ 84 44.16 N 40.53 E
Malaja Neva ≃[1] 265a 59.57 N 30.15 E
Malaja Ochta ◆[8] 265a 59.56 N 30.24 E
Malaja Orlovka 80 47.18 N 41.24 E
Malaja Pera 24 64.11 N 54.47 E
Malaja Serdoba 80 52.28 N 44.56 E
Malaja Sestra ≃ 82 56.17 N 35.57 E
Malaja Tokmačevka 78 47.32 N 35.54 E
Malaja Višera 76 58.51 N 32.14 E
Malaja Viska 78 48.39 N 31.38 E
Malaka → Melaka 114 2.12 N 102.15 E
Malaka, Sempitan ꭒ 114 5.44 N 95.30 E
Malakāl 140 9.31 N 31.39 E
Malākand 123 34.34 N 71.56 E
Mala Kapela ⋏ 36 44.50 N 15.30 E
Malakka, Strasse von → Malacca, Strait of ꭒ 110 2.30 N 101.20 E
Malakoff, Fr. 261 48.49 N 2.19 E
Malakoff, Tx., U.S. 222 32.10 N 96.00 W
Malakpur ◆[8] 272a 28.42 N 77.12 E
Malakula □[8] 175f 16.20 S 167.20 E
Malakula ɪ 175f 16.15 S 167.30 E
Malakwāl 123 32.34 N 73.13 E
Malala 164 5.15 S 147.10 E
Malalag 116 6.36 N 125.24 E
Malalbergo 64 44.43 N 11.32 E
Malamala 112 3.21 S 120.55 E
Mala Mala Game Reserve ◆[4] 156 24.52 S 31.30 E
Malamaui Island ɪ 116 6.44 N 121.58 E
Malambo, Arroyo ≃ 258 33.43 S 58.46 W
Malambunga 116 9.02 N 117.38 E
Malamocco 64 45.22 N 12.20 E
Malampaya Sound ꭒ 116 10.51 N 119.20 E
Malān 110 25.37 N 96.21 E
Malān, Rās › 128 25.18 N 65.11 E
Malanao Island ɪ 116 9.27 N 118.37 E
Malanas ≃ 116 17.41 N 120.43 E
Mālancha 272b 22.55 N 88.26 E
Mālancha ≃[1] 126 21.40 N 89.20 E
Mālandighi 126 23.33 N 87.24 E
Malandji 152 5.56 S 22.18 E
Malang 115a 7.59 S 112.37 E
Malang, Gunung ∧ 115a 7.02 S 107.01 E
Malangali 154 8.34 S 34.51 E
Malangas 116 7.37 N 123.01 E
Malanggwā 124 26.52 N 85.34 E
Malangka, Tanjung › 112 1.20 N 120.48 E
Malan Guan)(105 40.16 N 117.39 E
Malanipa Island ɪ 116 6.53 N 122.16 E
Malanje 152 9.32 S 16.20 E
Malanje □[5] 152 9.30 S 16.30 E
Malanut Bay ⊂ 116 9.16 N 117.59 E
Malanville 150 11.52 N 3.23 E
Malanyu 105 40.11 N 117.42 E
Malanzán 252 30.48 S 66.37 W
Malapane → Ozimek 30 50.41 N 18.13 E
Mała Panew ≃ 30 50.44 N 17.52 E
Malapantao, Mount ∧ 116 9.54 N 122.37 E
Malapardis Brook ≃ 276 40.49 N 74.25 W
Mala Pascua, Cabo › 240m 17.59 N 65.55 W
Mälaren ◎ 40 59.30 N 17.12 E
Malargüe 252 35.28 S 69.35 W
Mälar-See → Mälaren ◎ 40 59.30 N 17.12 E
Malartic 190 48.08 N 78.08 W
Malartic, Lac ◎ 190 48.15 N 78.07 W
Malasia → Malaysia □[1] 112 2.30 N 112.30 E
Malasiqui 116 15.55 N 120.25 E
Malaspina 254 44.56 S 66.54 W
Malaspina Glacier ⊓ 180 59.50 N 140.30 W
Malaspina Strait ꭒ 182 49.44 N 124.20 W
Malassis 261 48.38 N 2.03 E
Malāṭīyah 142 28.42 N 30.51 E
Malatya 130 38.21 N 38.19 E
Malatya □[4] 130 38.30 N 38.10 E
Malau 175f 15.10 S 166.48 E
Malaucène 62 44.10 N 5.08 E
Malaunay 50 49.32 N 1.02 E
Malaut 123 30.13 N 74.29 E
Malavalli 122 12.23 N 77.05 E
Malawali, Pulau ɪ 116 7.03 N 117.18 E
Malawi □[1], Afr. 138 13.30 S 34.00 E
Malawi □[1], Afr. 154 13.30 S 34.00 E
Malawi, Lake → Nyasa, Lake ◎ 154 12.00 S 34.30 E
Malawiya 140 15.16 N 36.12 E
Malaya → Semenanjung Malaysia □[9] 114 4.00 N 102.00 E
Malayagiri ∧ 120 21.23 N 85.16 E
Malayal 116 7.12 N 121.57 E
Malaybalay 116 8.09 N 125.05 E
Malāyer 128 34.17 N 48.50 E
Malay Peninsula ›[1] 110 6.00 N 101.00 E
Malay Reef ✢[2] 166 17.59 S 149.18 E
Malaysia □[1], Asia 108 2.30 N 112.30 E
Malaysia □[1], Asia 112 2.30 N 112.30 E
Malazgirt 130 39.09 N 42.31 E
Malbaie ≃ 186 47.39 N 70.09 W
Malbaie, La ⊂ 186 48.35 N 64.14 W
Malbon 166 21.04 S 140.18 E
Malbooma 162 30.41 S 134.11 E
Malborghetto Valbruna 64 46.30 N 13.26 E
Malbork 30 54.02 N 19.01 E
Malbrán 252 29.21 S 62.27 W
Malbuisson 58 46.48 N 6.18 E
Malbun 58 47.35 N 9.33 E
Malcesine 64 45.46 N 10.48 E
Mal'cevo 265b 55.56 N 37.57 E
Mal'čevskaja 78 49.04 N 40.21 E
Mal'čevsko-Polnenskaja 83 48.58 N 40.12 E
Malchanskij chrebet ⋏ 88 50.45 N 109.30 E
Malchin 54 53.44 N 12.46 E
Malchiner See ◎ 54 53.43 N 12.38 E
Malching 60 48.19 N 13.12 E
Malchow 54 53.28 N 12.25 E
Malchow ◆[8] 264a 52.35 N 13.29 E
Malčin 88 49.44 N 93.18 E
Malcolm 162 28.56 S 121.30 E
Malcolm, Point › 162 33.48 S 123.45 E
Malcolm Island ɪ 182 50.40 N 127.00 W
Malcom 190 41.42 N 92.33 W
Malcompeth → Mahābaleshwar 122 17.55 N 73.40 E
Malcontenta 64 45.25 N 12.13 E
Malczyce 30 51.14 N 16.29 E
Māldah 124 25.02 N 88.09 E
Maldegem 50 51.13 N 3.27 E
Malden, Ma., U.S. 207 42.25 N 71.04 W
Malden, Mo., U.S. 194 36.33 N 89.57 W
Malden ɪ 14 4.03 S 154.59 W
Malden ≃ 283 42.24 N 71.05 W
Malden Bridge 210 42.28 N 73.35 W
Malden on Hudson 210 42.06 N 73.56 W
Maldivas → Maldives □[1] 12 3.15 N 73.00 E
Maldive Islands → Maldives □[1] 12 3.15 N 73.00 E
Mal di Ventre, Isola di ɪ 71 39.59 N 8.18 E
Maldives □[1] 12 3.15 N 73.00 E
Maldon, Austl. 169 37.00 S 144.04 E
Maldon, Eng., U.K. 42 51.45 N 0.40 E
Maldon □[8] 260 51.43 N 0.40 E
Maldonado 252 34.54 S 54.57 W
Maldonado, Punta › 234 16.20 N 98.35 W
Male, It. 64 46.21 N 10.55 E
Male, Mald. 12 4.10 N 73.30 E
Male, Mya. 110 23.02 N 95.58 E
Maléa, Ákra › 38 36.26 N 23.12 E
Malea, Dolok ∧ 114 0.56 N 99.38 E
Malebo, Pool ◎ 152 4.17 S 15.20 E
Malediven → Maldives □[1] 12 3.15 N 73.00 E
Mālegaon 122 20.33 N 74.32 E
Malegno, It. 64 45.56 N 10.14 E
Malegno, It. 64 46.40 N 11.08 E
Malehra 124 24.34 N 79.19 E
Maleit, Lake ◎ 140 7.55 N 28.35 E
Malejevka 78 47.29 N 32.43 E
Malek, S.S.S.R. 85 40.47 N 68.37 E
Malek, Sūd. 140 6.04 N 31.36 E
Malé Karpaty ⋏ 30 48.30 N 17.20 E
Malek Dīn 120 32.25 N 68.04 E
Malek Kandī 128 37.09 N 46.06 E
Malek Sīāh, Kūh-e ∧ 128 29.51 N 60.52 E
Malela, Zaïre 154 2.28 S 26.09 E
Malela, Zaïre 154 4.22 S 26.08 E
Malema 154 14.57 S 37.20 E
Malen'ga 24 63.50 N 36.25 E
Malengoya 154 3.32 N 25.25 E
Malente 54 54.10 N 10.33 E
Maleo 62 45.10 N 9.46 E
Māler Kotla 124 30.31 N 75.53 E
Malesco 58 46.08 N 8.30 E
Malesherbes 50 48.18 N 2.25 E
Malestroit 32 47.49 N 2.23 W
Maleta 88 50.50 N 108.25 E
Maletto 70 37.49 N 14.52 E
Malfa 70 38.35 N 14.50 E
Malgas 158 34.18 S 20.35 E
Malgersdorf 60 48.32 N 12.45 E
Malgobek 84 43.32 N 44.34 E
Malgomaj ◎ 26 64.47 N 16.12 E
Malha Wells 140 15.08 N 26.12 E
Malheur ≃ 202 44.03 N 116.59 W
Malheur, North Fork ≃ 202 43.45 N 118.04 W
Malheur, South Fork ≃ 202 43.33 N 118.10 W
Malheureux, Cap › 157c 19.59 S 57.36 E
Malheur Lake ◎ 202 43.20 N 118.45 W
Mali, Guinée 150 12.05 N 12.18 W
Mali, Zaïre 154 2.48 S 26.08 E
Mali □[1], Afr. 134 17.00 N 4.00 W
Mali □[1], Afr. 150 17.00 N 4.00 W
Mali ≃ 102 25.43 N 97.29 E
Maliangping 102 31.29 N 111.20 E
Malianjingzi 102 41.32 N 95.23 E
Malibamatšo ≃ 158 29.20 S 29.28 E
Malibu 228 34.02 N 118.42 W
Malibu Lake ◎[1] 228 34.07 N 118.45 W
Malien ≃ 269d 25.11 N 121.41 E
Malienkang 269d 25.10 N 121.39 E
Maligay Bay ⊂ 116 7.30 N 123.14 E
Malighati 126 22.33 N 87.40 E
Maligne ≃ 182 52.56 N 118.02 W
Maligne Lake ◎ 182 52.40 N 117.31 W
Malīhābād 124 26.55 N 80.43 E
Māliḥah, Wādī V 142 29.21 N 32.35 E
Malik 112 0.34 S 123.14 E
Malik, Wādī al- V 140 18.02 N 30.58 E
Mali Kyun ɪ 110 13.06 N 98.16 E
Malili 112 2.38 S 121.06 E
Målilla 26 57.23 N 15.48 E
Malimba, Monts ⋏ 154 7.32 S 29.30 E
Malim Nawar 114 4.21 N 101.07 E
Malimono 116 9.34 N 125.25 E
Malin, Ire. 48 55.18 N 7.15 W
Malin, S.S.S.R. 78 50.46 N 29.15 E
Malin, Or., U.S. 202 42.00 N 121.24 W
Malinalco ⊥ 234 18.57 N 99.30 W
Malinaltepec 234 17.03 N 98.40 W
Malinau 112 3.35 N 116.38 E
Malin Beg 48 54.40 N 8.48 W
Malindang, Mount ∧ 116 8.13 N 123.38 E
Malindi 154 3.13 S 40.07 E
Malindi Marine National Park ♠ 154 3.15 S 40.10 E
Malines → Mechelen 50 51.02 N 4.28 E
Malinga 152 2.25 S 12.14 E
Malingping 115a 6.46 S 106.01 E
Malingsbosjön ◎ 40 59.55 N 15.27 E
Malin Head › 48 55.23 N 7.24 W
Malinki 82 54.05 N 38.59 E
Malinniki 82 56.17 N 38.24 E
Malino, Indon. 112 5.15 S 119.51 E
Malino, S.S.S.R. 82 55.06 N 38.11 E
Malino, S.S.S.R. 265b 55.58 N 37.13 E
Malino, Bukit ∧ 112 0.45 N 120.47 E
Malinoa ɪ 174w 21.02 S 175.08 W
Malinovka, S.S.S.R. 78 49.47 N 36.43 E
Malinovka, S.S.S.R. 80 51.47 N 43.26 E
Malinovka, S.S.S.R. 86 53.24 N 87.17 E
Malinta 216 41.19 N 84.02 W
Malinyi 154 8.56 S 36.08 E
Malipara 272b 22.57 N 88.14 E
Mali Rajinac ∧ 36 44.48 N 15.02 E
Malita 116 6.25 N 125.36 E
Malitbog 116 10.10 N 125.00 E
Maliuchang 107 29.05 N 104.07 E
Maliuping 107 29.55 N 106.23 E
Ma Liu Shui 271d 22.25 N 114.12 E
Malivo 82 55.07 N 39.02 E
Maliwun 110 10.14 N 98.37 E
Malizhen 102 23.10 N 104.35 E
Maljamar 196 32.51 N 103.46 W
Malka, S.S.S.R. 74 53.20 N 157.30 E
Malka, S.S.S.R. 84 43.47 N 43.21 E
Malka ≃ 84 43.44 N 44.15 E
Malkāpur 120 20.53 N 76.12 E
Malkara 130 40.53 N 26.54 E
Malkerns 158 26.32 S 31.11 E
Malko Târnovo 38 41.59 N 27.32 E
Mallāḥ 132 32.30 N 36.51 E
Mallaig, Ab., Can. 182 54.13 N 111.22 W
Mallaig, Scot., U.K. 46 57.00 N 5.50 W
Mallala 168b 34.26 S 138.30 E
Mallaoua 150 13.02 N 9.36 E
Mallapunyah 164 16.59 S 135.49 E
Mallaranny 48 53.54 N 9.49 W
Mallard Reservoir ◎[1] 282 38.01 N 122.03 W
Mallawī 142 27.44 N 30.50 E
Mallee Cliffs National Park ♠ 166 34.15 S 142.40 E
Mallemort 62 43.44 N 5.11 E
Mallersdorf 60 48.47 N 12.16 E
Mallery Lake ◎ 176 63.55 N 98.25 W
Malles Venosta (Mals) 64 46.41 N 10.32 E
Mallet 252 25.55 S 50.50 W
Mallig 116 17.08 N 121.41 E
Malligasta 252 29.11 S 67.26 W
Mallina 162 20.53 S 118.02 E
Malling 41 56.02 N 10.10 E
Mallnitz 64 46.59 N 13.10 E
Mallorca ɪ 34 39.30 N 3.00 E
Mallorytown 212 44.29 N 75.53 W
Mallow 48 52.08 N 8.39 W
Mallwitz → Małowice 30 51.34 N 15.27 E
Mallwood 216 42.51 N 89.02 W
Malm 26 64.04 N 11.13 E
Malmbäck 26 57.35 N 14.28 E
Malmberget 24 67.10 N 20.40 E
Malmédy 56 50.25 N 6.02 E
Malmesbury, S. Afr. 158 33.28 S 18.44 E
Malmesbury, Eng., U.K. 42 51.36 N 2.06 W
Malmesbury, Vale of V 42 51.22 N 2.10 W
Malmköping 40 59.08 N 16.44 E
Malmlången ◎ 40 59.27 N 14.42 E
Malmö 41 55.36 N 13.00 E
Malmöhus Län □[6] 26 55.45 N 13.30 E
Malmsbury 169 37.12 S 144.23 E
Malmsbury Reservoir ◎[1] 169 37.13 S 144.22 E
Malmslätt 26 58.25 N 15.30 E
Malmstrom Air Force Base ■ 202 47.30 N 111.10 W
Malmyž 80 56.31 N 50.41 E
Malna 116 8.08 N 124.27 E
Malnate 62 45.48 N 8.53 E
Malnoue 261 48.50 N 2.36 E
Malo 64 45.39 N 11.24 E
Malo ɪ 175f 15.40 S 167.11 E
Malo, Arroyo ≃ 258 33.43 S 58.52 W
Maloarchangel'sk 76 52.24 N 36.30 E
Maloarchangel'skoje 88 50.24 N 108.50 E
Maloba 154 6.18 S 27.39 E
Malodel'skaja 80 50.11 N 43.53 E
Maloduša 78 52.09 N 30.14 E
Maloelap ɪ[1] 14 8.45 N 171.03 E
Malo-Iljinovka ◆[8] 83 48.38 N 37.59 E
Maloja 58 46.24 N 9.41 E
Malojapass)(58 46.24 N 9.41 E
Malojaroslavec 82 55.01 N 36.28 E
Malojaz 86 55.13 N 58.09 E
Maloje Goloustnoje 88 52.18 N 105.18 E
Malojekaterinovka 78 47.39 N 35.16 E
Maloje Kozino 80 56.26 N 43.41 E
Maloje Polesje ◆[1] 78 50.10 N 25.00 E
Maloje-Ščerbedino, S.S.S.R. 80 51.59 N 42.50 E
Maloje Ščerbedino, S.S.S.R. 80 47.56 N 44.41 E
Maloje Skuratovo 76 53.33 N 37.00 E
Malokirsanovka 83 47.28 N 38.31 E
Malokrasnojarka 86 56.28 N 76.01 E
Malo-les-Bains 50 51.03 N 2.24 E
Malolo 154 7.18 S 36.35 E
Malolos, Guam 174p 13.18 N 144.46 E
Malolos, Pil. 116 14.51 N 120.49 E
Malom 164 3.10 S 151.50 E
Maloma 158 27.00 S 31.40 E
Malombe, Lake ◎ 154 14.38 S 35.12 E
Malomichajlovka 78 48.06 N 36.23 E
Malonabatovskij 80 48.57 N 43.40 E
Malone, Fl., U.S. 192 30.57 N 85.09 W
Malone, N.Y., U.S. 188 44.50 N 74.17 W
Malone, Tx., U.S. 222 31.55 N 96.54 W
Malone, Wa., U.S. 224 46.58 N 123.20 W
Malonga 152 10.24 S 23.10 E
Malonno 64 46.07 N 10.18 E
Malonty 61 48.41 N 14.35 E
Małopolska ◆[1] 30 50.10 N 21.30 E
Malor'azancevo 83 48.53 N 38.23 E
Malorita 78 51.47 N 24.05 E
Malorossijskij 86 53.12 N 62.30 E
Malošujka 24 63.45 N 37.22 E
Malott 182 48.16 N 119.42 W
Måløv 41 55.45 N 12.20 E
Małowice 30 51.34 N 15.27 E
Måløy 26 61.56 N 5.07 E
Malozemel'skaja Tundra ◆[1] 24 67.50 N 51.00 E
Malpaisillo 236 12.35 N 86.41 W
Malpartida de Plasencia 34 39.59 N 6.02 W
Malpas, Austl. 166 34.43 S 140.37 E
Malpas, Eng., U.K. 44 53.01 N 2.46 W
Malpaso 234 22.37 N 102.46 W
Malpe 122 13.21 N 74.43 E
Malpelo, Isla de ɪ 242 3.59 N 81.35 W
Malpensa, Aeroporto della ⊠ 62 45.38 N 8.44 E
Malpeque Bay ⊂ 186 46.30 N 63.47 W
Malprabha ≃ 122 16.12 N 76.03 E
Mālpura 120 26.17 N 75.23 E
Mals → Malles Venosta 64 46.41 N 10.32 E
Målsåker slott ⊥ 40 59.23 N 17.18 E
Malsch 56 48.53 N 8.19 E
Malše (Maltsch) ≃ 61 48.58 N 14.28 E
Målselva ≃ 24 69.14 N 18.30 E
Malta, Bra. 250 6.54 S 37.31 W
Malta, Öst. 64 46.57 N 13.30 E
Malta, S.S.S.R. 76 56.21 N 27.10 E
Malta, Il., U.S. 216 41.56 N 88.52 W
Malta, Mt., U.S. 202 48.21 N 107.52 W
Malta, Oh., U.S. 188 39.38 N 81.51 W
Malta □[1], Europe 22 35.50 N 14.35 E
Malta □[1], Europe 36 35.50 N 14.35 E
Malta ɪ 36 35.53 N 14.27 E
Malta ≃ 76 56.44 N 26.53 E
Malta Channel ꭒ 36 36.20 N 15.00 E
Maltahöhe 156 24.50 S 17.00 E
Maltahöhe □[5] 156 25.00 S 16.30 E
Malta-Tal V 64 47.03 N 13.24 E
Maltby 44 53.26 N 1.11 W
Malte → Malta □[1] 36 35.50 N 14.35 E
Malte Brun ∧ 172 43.34 S 170.18 E
Maltepe ◆[8] 267b 40.55 N 29.08 E
Malton 44 54.08 N 0.48 W
Malton ◆[8] 275b 43.42 N 79.38 W
Maltrata 234 18.48 N 97.16 W
Maltsch → Malczyce 30 51.14 N 16.29 E
Maltsch (Malše) ≃ 61 48.58 N 14.28 E
Malugou 89 43.39 N 128.27 E
Maluku □[4] 164 5.00 S 130.00 E
Maluku (Moluccas) ɪɪ 108 2.00 S 128.00 E
Maluku, Laut (Molucca Sea) ⊤[2] 108 0.00 125.00 E
Maluku-Maes 152 4.06 S 15.31 E
Ma'lūlā 130 33.50 N 36.33 E
Ma'lūlā, Jabal ∧ 132 33.54 N 36.36 E
Malu Mare 38 44.15 N 23.51 E
Malumfashi 150 11.47 N 7.37 E
Malunda 112 3.00 S 118.50 E
Malung 26 60.40 N 13.44 E
Maluso 116 6.33 N 121.53 E
Malūṭ 140 10.26 N 32.12 E
Maluti 126 24.09 N 87.41 E
Maluwe 150 8.40 N 2.17 W
Maluzhen 106 31.20 N 121.16 E
Malvaglia 58 46.25 N 8.59 E
Malvaglio 266b 45.31 N 8.47 E
Malvagna 70 37.55 N 15.04 E
Mālvan 122 16.04 N 73.28 E
Malveira 266c 38.45 N 9.27 W
Malvern, Austl. 274b 37.52 S 145.02 E
Malvern, Ar., U.S. 194 34.21 N 92.48 W
Malvern, Ia., U.S. 198 41.00 N 95.35 W
Malvern, Oh., U.S. 214 40.41 N 81.10 W
Malvern, Pa., U.S. 285 40.02 N 75.31 W
Malvern ◆[8] 273d 26.12 S 28.06 E
Malverne 276 40.40 N 73.40 W
Malvern Hills ⋏[2] 42 52.05 N 2.21 W
Malvérnia 156 22.06 S 31.42 E
Malvern Link 42 52.08 N 2.18 W
Malvinas 252 29.37 S 58.59 W
Malvito 68 39.36 N 16.03 E
Malwal 140 9.19 N 31.35 E
Mālwa Plateau ⋏[1] 124 23.50 N 77.30 E
Malybaj 85 43.30 N 78.25 E
Malý Dunaj ≃ 30 47.45 N 18.09 E
Malyi Nesvetaj ≃ 83 47.32 N 39.49 E
Malyj, ostrov ɪ 76 60.02 N 28.02 E
Malyj An'uj ≃ 74 68.30 N 160.49 E
Malyj Čeremšan ≃ 80 54.18 N 50.01 E
Malyj Chamar-Daban, chrebet ⋏ 88 51.00 N 105.00 E
Malyj Civil' ≃ 80 55.54 N 47.28 E
Malyje Alabuchi 80 51.33 N 42.10 E
Malyje Čany, ozero ◎ 86 54.33 N 78.02 E
Malyje Gorod'atiči 76 52.33 N 28.20 E
Malyje Jagury 80 45.26 N 43.01 E
Malyje Kamkaly 86 44.44 N 71.31 E
Malyje Karmakuly 72 72.23 N 52.44 E
Malyje Porogi 265a 59.47 N 30.42 E
Malyj Irgiz ≃ 80 52.12 N 47.58 E
Malyj Jenisej (Ka-Chem) ≃ 88 51.43 N 94.26 E
Malyj Jugan ≃ 86 60.40 N 73.54 E
Malyj Kavkaz ⋏ 84 41.00 N 44.35 E
Malyj Kundyš ≃ 80 56.22 N 47.53 E
Malyj Šantar, ostrov ɪ 89 54.30 N 137.36 E
Malyj Sarybulak 86 52.10 N 72.35 E
Malyj Tajmyr, ostrov ɪ 74 78.08 N 107.12 E
Malyj T'uters, ostrov ɪ 76 59.49 N 26.56 E
Malyj Uran ≃ 80 52.30 N 53.01 E
Malyj Uzen' ≃ 80 48.50 N 49.39 E
Malyj Zelenčuk ≃ 84 44.24 N 41.56 E
Malyn' 82 54.36 N 38.40 E
Malyševo 76 57.50 N 35.36 E
Malzéville 58 48.43 N 6.12 E
Mama 88 58.18 N 112.54 E
Mama ≃ 88 58.18 N 112.55 E
Ma Ma Creek ≃ 171a 27.35 S 152.13 E
Mamadyš 80 55.44 N 51.25 E
Mamagota 175e 6.46 S 155.24 E
Mamahuolang 104 42.24 N 124.12 E
Mamajiecun 104 41.26 N 122.51 E
Mamakan 88 57.48 N 114.01 E
Mamaku 172 38.06 S 176.05 E
Mamakwash Lake ◎ 184 51.38 N 92.56 W
Mamala Bay ⊂ 229a 21.18 N 157.57 W
Mamalu Bay ⊂ 229a 20.37 N 156.09 W
Mamanguape 250 6.50 S 35.07 W
Mama'o, Hakau ✢[2] 174w 21.00 S 175.12 W
Mamara 248 14.14 S 72.35 W
Mamaroneck 210 40.56 N 73.43 W
Mamaroneck ≃ 276 40.57 N 73.44 W
Mamaroneck Harbor ⊂ 276 40.56 N 73.43 W
Mamasa 112 2.56 S 119.22 E
Mamasa ≃ 112 3.30 S 119.42 E
Mamba 94 36.07 N 138.55 E
Mambaí 255 14.28 S 46.07 W
Mambajao 116 9.15 N 124.43 E
Mambajao, Mount ∧ 116 9.10 N 124.44 E
Mambali 154 4.33 S 32.41 E
Mambalot 116 8.51 N 117.55 E
Mambare ≃ 164 8.20 S 147.55 E
Mambasa 154 1.21 N 29.03 E
Mamberamo ≃ 164 1.26 S 137.53 E
Mambéré ≃ 152 3.31 N 16.03 E
Mambili ≃ 152 0.07 N 16.08 E
Mambrui 154 3.07 S 40.09 E
Mambucaba 256 23.01 S 44.31 W
Mambucaba ≃ 256 23.02 S 44.32 W
Mamburao 116 13.14 N 120.35 E
Mambusao ≃ 116 11.24 N 122.41 E
Mamdūḥ, Rujm ∧ 132 32.14 N 36.15 E
Mamedkala 84 42.10 N 48.06 E
Mamehaktebo 112 0.08 N 115.32 E
Mamelodi 158 25.45 S 28.18 E
Ma-Me-O Beach 182 52.58 N 113.59 W
Mamera 286c 10.27 N 66.59 W
Mamera, Quebrada ≃ 286c 10.27 N 66.59 W
Mamers 50 48.21 N 0.23 E
Mamfe 152 5.46 N 9.17 E
Mamiá ≃ 250 1.55 S 55.07 W
Mamiá, Lago ◎ 246 4.15 S 63.03 W
Mamiao 98 35.04 N 116.10 E
Mamie 192 36.07 N 75.50 W
Mamiña 248 20.05 S 69.14 W
Maminigui 150 7.24 N 5.50 W
Mamirolle 58 47.12 N 6.10 E
Mamisonskij, pereval)(84 42.43 N 43.48 E
Maml'utka 86 54.57 N 68.35 E
Mammendorf 60 48.12 N 11.09 E
Mammola 68 38.22 N 16.15 E
Mammoth, Az., U.S. 200 32.43 N 110.38 W
Mammoth, W.V., U.S. 188 38.15 N 81.22 W
Mammoth Cave National Park ♠ 194 37.08 N 86.13 W
Mammoth Lakes 204 37.38 N 118.58 W
Mammoth Pool Reservoir ◎[1] 226 37.20 N 119.20 W
Mammoth Spring 194 36.29 N 91.32 W
Mamoiada 71 40.13 N 9.17 E
Mamonovo, S.S.S.R. 76 54.28 N 19.57 E
Mamonovo, S.S.S.R. 265b 55.36 N 37.49 E
Mamonovo, S.S.S.R. 265b 55.41 N 37.19 E
Mamont 279b 40.29 N 79.36 W
Mamontovo, S.S.S.R. 86 52.43 N 81.37 E
Mamontovo, S.S.S.R. 86 51.45 N 81.25 E
Mamoré ≃ 248 10.23 S 65.23 W
Mamori, Lago ◎ 246 3.38 S 60.07 W
Mamoriá ≃ 248 7.30 S 66.21 W
Mamoritanas ≃ 246 1.39 S 67.22 W
Mamou, Guinée 150 10.23 N 12.05 W
Mamou, La., U.S. 194 30.38 N 92.25 W
Mamoutzou 157a 12.47 S 45.14 E
Mampikony 157b 16.06 S 47.38 E
Mampong 150 7.04 N 1.24 W
Mamraš 84 41.44 N 48.19 E
Mamre 158 33.30 S 18.29 E
Mamry, Jezioro ◎ 30 54.08 N 21.42 E
Mamuchi 98 35.41 N 118.17 E
Mamué 152 13.35 S 13.13 E
Mamuil Malal, Paso)(254 39.35 S 71.28 W
Mamuju 112 2.41 S 118.54 E
Mamulique 196 26.08 N 100.20 W
Ma'mūn 140 12.15 N 22.41 E
Mamuno 156 22.16 S 20.01 E
Mamuru ≃ 250 2.42 S 56.44 W
Mamykovo 80 54.38 N 50.37 E
Mamyl' 24 61.57 N 56.41 E
Man, C. Iv. 150 7.24 N 7.33 W
Man, India 120 33.51 N 78.32 E
Man, W.V., U.S. 192 37.44 N 81.52 W
Man (Île de) → Isle of Man □[2] 44 54.15 N 4.30 W
Man, Isle of → Isle of Man □[2] 44 54.15 N 4.30 W
Mana 229b 22.02 N 159.46 W
Mana ≃, Guy. fr. 250 5.44 N 53.54 W
Mana ≃, S.S.S.R. 86 55.57 N 92.28 E
Manabí □[4] 246 0.40 S 80.05 W
Manabique, Punta de › 236 15.56 N 88.37 W
Manacá ≃ 246 2.52 S 61.50 W
Manacacías ≃ 246 4.23 N 72.04 W
Manacapuru 246 3.18 S 60.37 W
Manacle Point › 42 50.03 N 5.03 W
Manacor 34 39.34 N 3.12 E
Manado 112 1.29 N 124.51 E
Managua 236 12.09 N 86.17 W
Managua □[5] 236 12.00 N 86.25 W
Managua, Aeropuerto ⊠ 286b 23.00 N 82.17 W
Managua, Lago de ◎ 236 12.20 N 86.20 W
Manahawkin 208 39.41 N 74.15 W
Manahawkin Bay ⊂ 208 39.40 N 74.12 W
Manaia 172 39.33 S 174.08 E
Manā'if, Bi'r al- ⊤[4] 142 30.31 N 32.12 E
Manajenki 76 53.42 N 36.27 E
Manakalampona ∧ 157b 15.23 S 48.50 E
Manakara 157b 22.08 S 48.01 E
Manakau 172 40.43 S 175.13 E
Manakau ∧ 172 42.14 S 173.37 E
Manākhah 144 15.07 N 43.44 E
Manalapan Brook ≃ 276 40.24 N 74.23 W
Manāli 123 32.15 N 77.10 E
Manama → Al-Manāmah 128 26.13 N 50.35 E
Manambaho ≃ 157b 17.41 S 44.04 E
Manambato, Madag. 157b 13.14 S 49.54 E
Manambato, Madag. 157b 13.43 S 49.07 E
Manambolo ≃ 157b 19.18 S 44.24 E
Manambolosy 157b 16.02 S 49.40 E
Manam Island ɪ 164 4.05 S 145.05 E
Mánamo, Caño ≃[1] 246 9.55 N 62.16 W
Manamoc Island ɪ 116 11.19 N 120.41 E
Manana Island ɪ 229c 21.20 N 157.40 W
Mananantanana ≃ 157b 21.25 S 45.33 E
Mananao 116 13.30 N 120.34 E
Mananara 157b 16.10 S 49.46 E
Mananara ≃ 157b 23.21 S 47.42 E
Manandaza 157b 19.19 S 45.23 E
Mananjary 157b 21.13 S 48.20 E
Manankoro 150 10.28 N 7.27 W
Manantenina 157b 24.17 S 47.19 E
Manantiales Behr 254 45.41 S 67.31 W
Manaoag 116 16.03 N 120.29 E
Manáos → Manaus 246 3.08 S 60.01 W
Manapatrana 157b 21.40 S 47.35 E
Manapiare ≃ 246 5.04 N 66.30 W
Manapire ≃ 246 7.42 N 66.07 W
Manapla 116 10.58 N 123.07 E
Mana Point › 229b 22.03 N 159.47 W
Mana Pools National Park ♠ 154 16.00 S 28.35 E
Manapouri 172 45.34 S 167.36 E
Manapouri, Lake ◎ 172 45.30 S 167.30 E
Manappārai 122 10.36 N 78.25 E
Manaquiri, Lago ◎ 246 3.29 S 60.31 W
Manār ≃ 122 18.39 N 77.44 E
Manaravolo 157b 23.59 S 45.39 E
Manas, Som. 144 2.57 N 43.28 E
Manas, Zhg. 86 44.18 N 86.13 E
Manās ≃, Asia 120 26.13 N 90.38 E
Manas ≃, Zhg. 86 45.38 N 85.12 E
Manas, gora ∧ 85 42.18 N 71.01 E
Manas Hu ◎ 86 45.45 N 85.55 E
Manāslu ∧ 124 28.33 N 84.33 E
Manasota Key ɪ 220 26.58 N 82.23 W
Manasquan 208 40.07 N 74.02 W
Manasquan ≃ 208 40.06 N 74.02 W
Manassa 200 37.10 N 105.56 W
Manassas 208 38.45 N 77.28 W
Manassas National Battlefield Park ♠ 208 38.50 N 77.32 W
Manassas Park 208 38.46 N 77.27 W
Manastash Creek ≃ 224 46.59 N 120.35 W
Manastash Creek, North Fork ≃ 224 46.57 N 120.44 W
Manastash Creek, South Fork ≃ 224 46.57 N 120.44 W
Manastash Ridge ∧ 224 46.55 N 120.30 W
Manatang 112 8.26 S 124.28 E
Manatawny 208 40.17 N 75.41 W
Manatawny Creek ≃ 208 40.14 N 75.39 W
Manatee □[6] 220 27.26 N 82.25 W
Manatee ≃ 220 27.32 N 82.38 W
Manatee, Lake ◎[1] 220 27.29 N 82.20 W
Manatí, Col. 246 10.27 N 74.58 W
Manatí, Cuba 240p 21.19 N 76.56 W
Manatí, P.R. 240m 18.26 N 66.29 W
Manatí ≃ 240p 21.40 N 79.50 W
Manatí, Bahía de ⊂ 240p 21.24 N 76.48 W
Manatuto 112 8.30 S 126.01 E
Manaul 116 12.27 N 121.25 E
Manaung 110 18.51 N 93.44 E
Manaus 246 3.08 S 60.01 W
Manavgat 130 36.47 N 31.26 E
Manawa 190 44.27 N 88.55 W
Mānāwāla 123 31.35 N 73.41 E
Manawan Lake ◎ 184 55.24 N 103.14 W
Manāwar 120 22.14 N 75.05 E
Manawatu ≃ 172 40.28 S 175.13 E
Manawoka, Pulau ɪ 164 4.05 S 131.20 E
Manay 116 7.13 N 126.32 E
Manayunk ◆[8] 285 40.01 N 75.13 W
Manazuru 94 35.09 N 139.08 E
Manazuru-misaki › 94 35.08 N 139.10 E
Manban 102 23.04 N 103.11 E
Mānbāzār 126 23.04 N 86.39 E
Manbian 102 24.19 N 100.32 E
Manbij 130 36.31 N 37.57 E
Manby 44 53.22 N 0.06 E
Mancelona 190 44.54 N 85.03 W
Mancenillier, Anse du ⊂ 241o 16.15 N 61.15 W
Mancha Blanca 254 40.47 S 65.27 W
Mancha Real 34 37.47 N 3.37 W
Manchaug 207 42.05 N 71.44 W
Manche □[5] 32 49.00 N 1.10 W
Mancheng 105 38.56 N 115.20 E
Mancherāl 122 18.52 N 79.26 E
Manchester, Eng., U.K. 44 53.28 N 2.15 W
Manchester, Eng., U.K. 262 53.28 N 2.15 W
Manchester, Ct., U.S. 207 41.46 N 72.31 W
Manchester, Ga., U.S. 192 32.51 N 84.37 W
Manchester, Il., U.S. 219 39.33 N 90.20 W
Manchester, Ia., U.S. 190 42.29 N 91.27 W
Manchester, Ky., U.S. 192 37.09 N 83.45 W
Manchester, Md., U.S. 208 39.39 N 76.53 W
Manchester, Ma., U.S. 207 42.34 N 70.46 W
Manchester, Mi., U.S. 216 42.09 N 84.02 W
Manchester, N.H., U.S. 188 42.59 N 71.27 W
Manchester, N.Y., U.S. 210 42.58 N 77.13 W
Manchester, Oh., U.S. 218 38.41 N 83.36 W
Manchester, Pa., U.S. 208 40.03 N 76.43 W
Manchester, Tn., U.S. 194 35.28 N 86.05 W
Manchester, Vt., U.S. 210 43.09 N 73.04 W
Manchester, Wa., U.S. 224 47.33 N 122.33 W
Manchester □[8] 262 53.27 N 2.13 W
Manchester Airport ⊠ 44 53.21 N 2.15 W
Manchester Bridge 210 41.41 N 73.52 W
Manchester City Football Ground ♠ 262 53.27 N 2.14 W
Manchester Docks ◆[5] 262 53.28 N 2.17 W
Manchester Race Course ♠ 262 53.30 N 2.16 W
Manchester Ship Canal ≊ 262 53.19 N 2.57 W

≃ River	Fluß	Río	Rivière	Rio
≊ Canal	Kanal	Canal	Canal	Canal
⌞ Waterfall, Rapids	Wasserfall, Stromschnellen	Cascada, Rápidos	Chute d'eau, Rapides	Cascata, Rápidos
ꭒ Strait	Meeresstraße	Estrecho	Détroit	Estreito
⊂ Bay, Gulf	Bucht, Golf	Bahía, Golfo	Baie, Golfe	Baía, Golfo
◎ Lake, Lakes	See, Seen	Lago, Lagos	Lac, Lacs	Lago, Lagos
≡ Swamp	Sumpf	Pantano	Marais	Pântano
⊓ Ice Features, Glacier	Eis- und Gletscherformen	Accidentes Glaciales	Formes glaciaires	Acidentes glaciares
⊤ Other Hydrographic Features	Andere Hydrographische Objekte	Otros Elementos Hidrográficos	Autres données hydrographiques	Outros acidentes hidrográficos

✢ Submarine Features	Untermeerische Objekte	Accidentes Submarinos	Formes de relief sous-marin	Acidentes submarinos
□ Political Unit	Politische Einheit	Unidad Politica	Entité politique	Unidade política
v Cultural Institution	Kulturelle Institution	Institución Cultural	Institution culturelle	Institução cultural
⊥ Historical Site	Historische Stätte	Sitio Histórico	Site historique	Sitio histórico
♠ Recreational Site	Erholungs- und Ferienort	Sitio de Recreo	Centre de loisirs	Area de Lazer
⊠ Airport	Flughafen	Aeropuerto	Aéroport	Aeroporto
■ Military Installation	Militäranlage	Instalación Militar	Installation militaire	Instalação militar
◆ Miscellaneous	Verschiedenes	Misceláneo	Divers	Diversos

Name	Page	Lat.°′	Long.°′
Manchester United Football Ground ♠	262	53.28 N	2.18 W
Manching	60	48.43 N	11.30 E
Manchioneal	241q	18.02 N	76.17 W
Manchouli → Manzhouli	88	49.35 N	117.22 E
Manchuria □⁹	90	47.00 N	125.00 E
Manciano	66	42.35 N	11.31 E
Mancieulles	56	49.17 N	5.53 E
Máncora	246	4.06 S	81.05 W
Mancos	200	37.20 N	108.17 W
Mancos ≃	200	36.59 N	108.59 W
Mand	128	26.07 N	62.03 E
Mānd ≃, India	120	21.42 N	83.15 E
Mand ≃, Īrān	128	28.11 N	51.17 E
Manda, India	126	22.06 N	86.14 E
Manda, Tan.	154	7.58 S	32.26 E
Manda, Tan.	154	8.30 S	32.44 E
Manda, Tan.	154	10.28 S	34.35 E
Manda, Tchad	146	9.12 N	18.10 E
Manda, Jabal ∧	140	8.39 N	24.27 E
Mandabe, Madag.	157b	21.03 S	44.55 E
Mandabe, Madag.	157b	20.55 S	45.49 E
Mandach	102	44.28 N	108.11 E
Mandaguaçu	255	23.20 S	52.05 W
Mandaguari	255	23.32 S	51.42 W
Mandai Orchard Gardens ♠	271c	1.24 N	103.47 E
Manda Island I	154	2.15 S	40.57 E
Mandal	26	58.02 N	7.27 E
Mandal, Jibāl ∧²	140	12.09 N	29.31 E
Mandala, Puncak ∧	164	4.44 S	140.20 E
Mandalay	110	22.00 N	96.05 E
Mandalay □⁵	110	21.00 N	96.00 E
Mandale	216	41.01 N	84.20 W
Mandale Station ◆⁵	272c	19.03 N	72.56 E
Mandalgov'	102	45.45 N	106.12 E
Mandalī	128	33.45 N	45.32 E
Mandalkia	272b	22.43 N	88.08 E
Mandal-Ovoo	102	44.35 N	104.05 E
Mandalselva ≃	26	58.02 N	7.28 E
Mandaluyong	269f	14.35 N	121.02 E
Mandan	198	46.49 N	100.53 W
Mandanici	70	38.00 N	15.19 E
Mandāoli ◆⁸	272a	28.38 N	77.18 E
Mandaon	116	12.14 N	123.17 E
Mandapur	126	23.00 N	88.29 E
Mandar, Teluk ⊂	112	3.40 S	119.15 E
Mandara Mountains (Monts Mandara) ⋏	146	10.45 N	13.40 E
Mandas	71	39.38 N	9.07 E
Mandatoriccio	68	39.28 N	16.50 E
Mandau ≃	114	0.48 N	101.47 E
Mandaue	116	10.20 N	123.56 E
Mandāwar	124	29.30 N	78.08 E
Mandeb, Bab el ⊔	144	12.40 N	43.20 E
Mandehu	104	42.07 N	121.33 E
Mandel	128	33.17 N	61.52 E
Mandélia	146	11.43 N	15.15 E
Mandelieu	62	43.33 N	6.56 E
Mandello del Lario	58	45.54 N	9.19 E
Mandera	154	3.56 N	41.52 E
Manderfeld	56	50.20 N	6.20 E
Manderscheid	56	50.05 N	6.49 E
Manderson	202	44.16 N	107.57 W
Mandeure	58	47.27 N	6.48 E
Mandeville, P.Q., Can.	206	46.22 N	73.22 W
Mandeville, Jam.	241q	18.02 N	77.30 W
Mandeville, N.Z.	172	46.00 S	168.49 E
Mandeville, La., U.S.	194	30.21 N	90.03 W
Mandi	123	31.43 N	76.55 E
Mandiana	150	10.38 N	8.41 W
Mandiangin	112	2.01 S	102.58 E
Mandi Angin, Gunong ∧	114	4.42 N	102.52 E
Mandi Bahāuddīn	123	32.35 N	73.30 E
Mandi Būrewāla	123	30.09 N	72.41 E
Mandi Dabwāli	123	29.58 N	74.42 E
Mandié	154	16.30 S	33.30 E
Mandimba	154	14.21 S	35.39 E
Mandinga	246	9.27 N	79.04 W
Mandini	158	29.09 S	31.25 E
Mandioli, Pulau I	108	0.44 S	127.14 E
Mandioré, Lagoa ⊜	248	18.08 S	57.33 W
Mandira ⊜¹	124	22.20 N	84.35 E
Mandiri ≃	115a	7.02 S	106.32 E
Mandi Sādiqganj	123	30.10 N	73.44 E
Mandjafa	146	11.11 N	15.25 E
Mandjé, Lac ⊜	152	2.50 S	10.22 E
Mandji	152	1.36 S	10.26 E
Mandla	124	22.36 N	80.23 E
Mandora	162	19.44 S	120.51 E
Mandoto	157b	19.34 S	46.17 E
Mandoul ≃	146	8.56 N	17.58 E
Mandouri	150	10.51 N	0.49 E
Mándra, Ellás	267c	38.04 N	23.30 E
Māndrā, India	272b	22.55 N	88.07 E
Mandra, Pāk.	123	33.22 N	73.14 E
Mandrare ≃	157b	25.10 S	46.27 E
Mandres-les-Roses	261	48.42 N	2.33 E
Mandriola ◆⁸	267a	41.45 N	12.30 E
Mandriole	64	44.33 N	12.14 E
Mandrioli, Passo dei)(	64	43.48 N	11.55 E
Mandritsara	157b	15.50 S	48.49 E
Mandronarivo	157b	21.07 S	45.38 E
Mandsaur	120	24.04 N	75.04 E
Māndu	122	22.22 N	75.23 E
Mandu, Ribeirão do ≃	256	22.14 S	45.55 W
Manduba, Ponta ›	256	24.05 S	46.18 W
Manduhu	104	41.36 N	122.38 E
Mandun	102	22.17 N	100.05 E
Mandurah	168a	32.32 S	115.43 E
Manduri	255	23.01 S	49.19 W
Manduria	68	40.24 N	17.38 E
Māndvi, India	120	21.15 N	73.18 E
Māndvi, India	120	22.50 N	69.22 E
Mandvi ◆⁸	272c	18.57 N	72.50 E
Mandya	122	12.33 N	76.54 E
Mané	150	12.59 N	1.21 W
Måne ≃	26	59.00 N	9.40 E
Manea	42	52.30 N	0.11 E
Manebach	54	50.41 N	10.51 E
Manek Urai	114	5.23 N	102.14 E
Manendragarh	124	23.13 N	82.13 E
Manera	157b	22.55 S	44.20 E
Manerbio	64	45.21 N	10.08 E
Manětín	60	49.59 N	13.14 E
Manevīči	78	51.17 N	25.33 E
Manfalūṭ	142	27.19 N	30.58 E
Manfredonia	68	41.38 N	15.55 E
Manfredonia, Golfo di ⊂	68	41.35 N	16.05 E
Manga, Bra.	255	14.46 S	43.56 W
Manga, Burkina	150	11.40 N	1.04 W
Manga, Ur.	258	34.49 S	56.06 W
Manga ◆¹	146	15.00 N	14.00 E
Mangabeiras, Chapada das ⋏²	250	10.00 S	46.30 W
Mangagoy	116	8.11 N	126.21 E
Mangahao ≃	172	40.23 S	175.50 E
Mangai	164	2.45 S	151.05 E
Mangaia I	14	21.55 S	157.55 W
Mangakino	172	38.22 S	175.47 E
Mangala	152	1.02 N	23.50 E
Mangalagiri	122	16.26 N	80.33 E
Mangaldai	120	26.26 N	92.02 E
Mangaldan	116	16.04 N	120.24 E
Mangalia	38	43.50 N	28.35 E
Mangalkot	126	23.33 N	87.54 E
Mangalmé	146	12.21 N	19.37 E
Mangalore	122	12.52 N	74.53 E
Mangalpaita	126	23.19 N	89.11 E
Mangalvedha	122	17.31 N	75.28 E
Mangamahu	172	39.49 S	175.22 E
Manganji	268	35.40 N	139.26 E
Mangaoka	157b	12.19 S	49.07 E
Mangapehi	172	38.31 S	175.18 E
Mangaratiba	256	22.57 S	44.02 W
Mangart, Monte (Mangrt) ∧	64	46.25 N	13.40 E
Mangatarem	116	15.47 N	120.17 E
Mangawān	124	24.41 N	81.33 E
Mangaweka	172	39.48 S	175.47 E
Mangaweka ∧	172	39.49 S	176.05 E
Mangcao Point ›	116	11.02 N	123.54 E
Mangchang	102	25.08 N	107.31 E
Mangde ≃	124	27.35 N	90.28 E
Mange, S.L.	150	8.55 N	12.51 W
Mange, Zaïre	152	0.54 N	20.30 E
Mange, Zhg.	120	32.25 N	83.35 E
Mangeigne	146	10.31 N	21.19 E
Mangerton Mountain ∧	48	51.57 N	9.29 W
Mangfall ≃	64	47.51 N	12.08 E
Manggar	112	2.53 S	108.16 E
Manggeng	114	3.36 N	96.55 E
Manggonggri	164	3.30 S	133.19 E
Mangguar, Tanjung ›	164	2.53 S	134.51 E
Mangham	194	32.18 N	91.46 W
Mangichu ≃	126	23.24 N	90.48 E
Mangindrano	157b	14.17 S	48.58 E
Mangin Range ⋏	110	24.20 N	95.42 E
Mangkalihat, Tanjung ›	112	1.02 N	118.59 E
Mangkutana	112	2.24 S	120.48 E
Manglares, Cabo ›	246	1.36 N	79.02 W
Mangla Reservoir ⊜¹	123	33.10 N	73.40 E
Manglaur	124	29.48 N	77.52 E
Manglisi	84	41.43 N	44.24 E
Mangnai	120	37.40 N	91.50 E
Mangniu ≃, Zhg.	104	41.45 N	120.53 E
Mangniu ≃, Zhg.	105	39.04 N	116.26 E
Mangnuiyingzi	104	41.37 N	120.43 E
Mango	220	28.00 N	82.19 W
Mangochi	154	14.28 S	35.16 E
Mango Island I	175g	17.27 S	179.09 W
Mangoky ≃, Madag.	157b	21.29 S	43.41 E
Mangoky ≃, Madag.	157b	23.27 S	45.13 E
Mangole, Pulau I	112	1.53 S	125.50 E
Mangombe	154	1.25 S	26.54 E
Mangone	68	39.12 N	16.20 E
Mangonia Park	220	26.46 N	80.05 W
Mangonui	172	34.59 S	173.32 E
Mangoplah	171b	35.23 S	147.15 E
Mangoro ≃	157b	20.00 S	48.45 E
Mangotsfield	42	51.28 N	2.28 W
Mangoupa	140	5.53 N	24.40 E
Mangrol	120	21.07 N	70.07 E
Mangrove Cay I	238	24.10 N	77.45 W
Mangrove Creek ≃	170	33.28 S	151.10 E
Mangrove Creek Dam ◆⁶	170	33.13 S	151.07 E
Mangrove Mountain	170	33.19 S	151.14 E
Mangrove Point ›	220	26.56 N	82.08 W
Mangrt (Monte Mangart) ∧	64	46.25 N	13.40 E
Mangrullo, Cuchilla ⋏²	258	34.34 S	56.42 W
Mangrūl Pīr	122	20.19 N	77.21 E
Mångsälven ≃	40	59.59 N	14.36 E
Mangsang	112	2.10 S	104.00 E
Mangu ≃	273b	4.24 S	15.24 E
Mangualde	34	40.36 N	7.46 W
Mangueira, Lagoa ⊂	252	33.06 S	52.48 W
Mangueirinha	252	25.57 S	52.09 W
Manguéni, Plateau du ⋏¹	146	22.35 N	12.40 E
Mangues ≃	250	10.21 S	48.27 W
Mangui	89	52.03 N	122.13 E
Manguinho, Aeroporto de ⊠	287a	22.52 S	43.15 W
Manguito	240p	22.35 N	80.55 W
Mangulile	236	15.03 N	86.49 W
Mangum	196	34.52 N	99.30 W
Mangungu	152	5.13 S	19.35 E
Mangut, S.S.S.R.	86	55.47 N	70.46 E
Mangut, S.S.S.R.	88	49.46 N	112.38 E
Mangya	90	37.40 N	90.50 E
Man'gyŏng	98	35.52 N	126.48 E
Mangyšlak □⁴	86	44.00 N	54.30 E
Manhan ≃	207	42.17 N	72.38 W
Manhartsberg ∧	61	48.32 N	15.44 E
Manhasset	276	40.47 N	73.42 W
Manhasset Bay ⊂	276	40.50 N	73.43 W
Manhasset Hills	276	40.46 N	73.41 W
Manhasset Neck ›¹	276	40.50 N	73.42 W
Manhattan, Il., U.S.	216	41.25 N	87.59 W
Manhattan, Ks., U.S.	198	39.11 N	96.34 W
Manhattan, Mt., U.S.	202	45.51 N	111.19 W
Manhattan □⁸	276	40.46 N	73.55 W
Manhattan Beach	228	33.53 N	118.24 W
Manhattan Beach State Park ♠	280	33.54 N	118.25 W
Manhattan Bridge ◆⁵	276	40.42 N	73.59 W
Manhattan College ☩²	276	40.53 N	73.54 W
Manheim	208	40.09 N	76.23 W
Manhiça	156	25.24 S	32.48 E
Mān Hpāng	110	22.41 N	98.36 E
Manhuaçu	255	20.15 S	42.02 W
Manhuaçu ≃	255	19.30 S	41.06 W
Manhumirim	255	20.22 S	41.57 W
Maní, P.R.	240m	18.15 N	67.10 W
Mani, Zaïre	154	6.27 S	25.20 E
Mānī', Jabal al- ∧	132	33.19 N	36.17 E
Mania ≃	157b	19.42 S	45.22 E
Maniago	64	46.10 N	12.43 E
Maniamba	154	12.43 S	35.00 E
Manianga	273b	4.10 S	15.19 E
Manica □⁵	156	19.00 S	33.15 E
Manicahan	116	7.01 N	122.12 E
Manicaland □⁴	154	19.30 S	32.15 E
Manicani Island I	116	10.59 N	125.38 E
Manicaragua	240p	22.09 N	79.58 W
Maniçauá-Miçu ≃	250	10.58 S	53.20 W
Manic Deux, Réservoir ⊜¹	186	49.25 N	68.25 W
Manicoré	248	5.49 S	61.17 W
Manicoré ≃	248	5.51 S	61.19 W
Manicouagan ≃	186	49.11 N	68.13 W
Manicouagan, Réservoir ⊜¹	186	51.30 N	68.19 W
Manic Trois, Réservoir ⊜¹	186	50.00 N	68.40 W
Manifold ≃	44	53.03 N	1.47 W
Maniganggo	102	32.01 N	99.11 E
Manignan	150	10.00 N	7.50 W
Manigotagan	184	51.06 N	96.18 W
Manigotagan ≃	184	51.07 N	96.20 W
Manihāri	124	25.21 N	87.38 E
Manihiki I¹	14	10.24 S	161.01 W
Manika, Plateau de la ⋏¹	154	10.00 S	26.00 E
Manikanāli	126	23.19 N	87.03 E
Mānikganj	124	23.52 N	90.00 E
Mānikpur	124	25.04 N	81.07 E
Manila, Pil.	116	14.35 N	121.00 E
Manila, Pil.	269f	14.35 N	121.00 E
Manila, Ar., U.S.	194	35.52 N	90.10 W
Manila, Ut,. U.S.	200	40.59 N	109.43 W
Manila Bay ⊂	116	14.30 N	120.45 E
Manila Cathedral ☩¹	269f	14.35 N	120.59 E
Manila International Airport ⊠	269f	14.31 N	121.01 E
Manilla, Austl.	166	30.45 S	150.43 E
Manilla, In., U.S.	218	39.34 N	85.37 W
Manilla, Ia., U.S.	198	41.53 N	95.13 W
Manille → Manila	116	14.35 N	121.00 E
Manily	74	62.29 N	165.36 E
Mani Majra	123	30.43 N	76.50 E
Manimbaya, Tanjung ›	112	0.01 N	119.36 E
Manimpé	150	14.09 N	5.31 W
Maningory ≃	157b	17.13 S	49.28 E
Maningrida	164	12.03 S	134.13 E
Maninjau, Danau ⊜	112	0.20 S	100.11 E
Manino	76	53.58 N	34.20 E
Manipa, Pulau I	164	3.17 S	127.35 E
Manipa, Selat ⊔	164	3.20 S	127.23 E
Manipur □³	120	25.00 N	94.00 E
Manipur ≃	110	22.52 N	94.05 E
Manique de Baixo	266c	38.44 N	9.22 W
Maniquin Island I	116	11.36 N	121.45 E
Manirāmpur	126	23.01 N	89.14 E
Manisa	130	38.36 N	27.26 E
Manisa □⁴	130	38.50 N	28.10 E
Manistee	190	44.14 N	86.19 W
Manistee ≃	190	44.15 N	86.21 W
Manistique	190	45.57 N	86.14 W
Manistique ≃	190	45.57 N	86.15 W
Manistique, West Branch ≃	190	46.02 N	86.09 W
Manistique Lake ⊜	190	46.15 N	85.45 W
Manito	194	40.25 N	89.46 W
Manitoba □⁴, Can.	176	54.00 N	97.00 W
Manitoba □⁴, Can.	184	54.00 N	97.00 W
Manitoba, Lake ⊜	184	51.00 N	98.45 W
Manitou	184	49.15 N	98.31 W
Manitou ≃, On., Can.	184	48.58 N	93.20 W
Manitou ≃, P.Q., Can.	186	50.18 N	65.15 W
Manitou, Lac ⊜, P.Q., Can.	186	50.29 N	63.54 W
Manitou, Lac ⊜, P.Q., Can.	186	50.54 N	65.18 W
Manitou, Lac ⊜, P.Q., Can.	206	46.03 N	74.23 W
Manitou, Lake ⊜, On., Can.	190	45.48 N	82.00 W
Manitou, Lake ⊜, In., U.S.	216	41.03 N	86.11 W
Manitou Beach, Sk., Can.	184	51.43 N	105.26 W
Manitou Beach, Mi., U.S.	216	41.58 N	84.19 W
Manitou Lake ⊜, On., Can.	190	46.01 N	79.00 W
Manitou Lake ⊜, Sk., Can.	184	52.45 N	109.45 W
Manitoulin Island I	190	45.50 N	82.20 W
Manitou Springs	200	38.51 N	104.55 W
Manitouwabing Lake ⊜	212	45.29 N	79.54 W
Manitowaning	190	45.45 N	81.49 W
Manitowik Lake ⊜	190	48.10 N	84.24 W
Manitowish Waters	190	46.09 N	89.53 W
Manitowoc	190	44.05 N	87.39 W
Manitowoc ≃	190	44.05 N	87.39 W
Maniwaki	188	46.23 N	75.58 W
Ma'nīyā	142	30.50 N	30.39 E
Manizales	246	5.05 N	75.32 W
Manja, Madag.	157b	21.26 S	44.20 E
Manjā, Urd.	132	31.45 N	35.51 E
Manjacaze	156	24.44 S	33.53 E
Manjakandriana	157b	18.55 S	47.47 E
Manjeri	122	11.07 N	76.07 E
Manjiang	98	41.57 N	127.36 E
Manjimup	162	34.14 S	116.09 E
Manjing	107	29.55 N	104.07 E
Mānjra ≃	122	18.49 N	77.52 E
Manjuyod	116	9.41 N	123.09 E
Mank	61	48.06 N	15.20 E
Mankanaj	86	48.58 N	60.58 E
Månkarbo	40	60.14 N	17.28 E
Mān Kāt	110	22.05 N	98.01 E
Mankato, Ks., U.S.	198	39.47 N	98.12 W
Mankato, Mn., U.S.	190	44.09 N	93.59 W
Mankayane	158	26.42 S	31.00 E
Mankent	85	42.25 N	69.50 E
Mankera	123	31.23 N	71.26 E
Mankim	152	5.01 N	12.00 E
Mankinholes	262	53.42 N	2.03 W
Mankono	150	8.04 N	6.12 W
Mankota	184	49.25 N	107.04 W
Man'kovka, S.S.S.R.	78	48.58 N	30.20 E
Man'kovka, S.S.S.R.	83	49.34 N	38.27 E
Man'kovo	83	49.24 N	40.17 E
Man'kovo-Ber'ozovskaja	80	48.47 N	41.33 E
Mankoya	154	14.47 S	24.48 E
Mānkundu	272b	22.50 N	88.22 E
Mānkur, India	126	22.30 N	87.54 E
Mānkur, India	126	23.20 N	87.33 E
Manlaj	102	44.07 N	106.50 E
Manley	262	53.14 N	2.45 W
Manley Hot Springs	180	65.00 N	150.37 W
Manleys Corner	283	42.03 N	71.04 W
Manlius	210	43.00 N	75.58 W
Manlleu	34	42.00 N	2.17 E
Manly, Austl.	170	33.48 S	151.17 E
Manly, Austl.	171a	27.28 S	153.15 E
Manly, Ia., U.S.	190	43.17 N	93.12 W
Manly Warringah War Memorial Park ♠	274a	33.46 S	151.15 E
Manmād	122	20.15 N	74.27 E
Mann ≃	164	12.20 S	134.07 E
Mann, Mount ∧	162	25.59 S	129.42 E
Manna, Indon.	112	4.27 S	102.55 E
Mān Na, Mya.	110	23.27 N	97.14 E
Mannahill	166	32.26 S	139.59 E
Mannar	122	8.59 N	79.54 E
Mannar, Gulf of ⊂	122	8.30 N	79.00 E
Mannārgudi	122	10.40 N	79.26 E
Mannar Island I	122	9.03 N	79.50 E
Mann Creek ≃	281	42.32 N	83.44 W
Männedorf	58	47.15 N	8.42 E
Mannersdorf am Leithagebirge	61	47.58 N	16.36 E
Mannersdorf an der Rabnitz	61	47.25 N	16.31 E
Mannford	196	36.09 N	96.23 W
Mannheim	56	49.29 N	8.29 E
Manni	120	34.48 N	87.15 E
Manning, Ia., U.S.	198	41.54 N	95.03 W
Manning, N.D., U.S.	198	47.13 N	102.46 W
Manning, S.C., U.S.	192	33.41 N	80.12 W
Manning, Cape ›	174o	2.02 N	157.26 W
Manning Provincial Park ♠	224	49.07 N	120.54 W
Manning Strait ⊔	175e	7.24 S	158.00 E
Mannington	188	39.31 N	80.20 W
Manningtree	42	51.57 N	1.04 E
Mannō	96	34.11 N	133.51 E
Mann Ranges ⋏	162	26.00 S	129.30 E
Mannsville	212	43.42 N	76.03 W
Mannswörth ◆⁸	264b	48.09 N	16.31 E
Mannu	71	39.18 N	8.58 E
Mannu ≃	71	40.50 N	8.23 E
Mannu, Capo ›	71	40.47 N	8.09 E
Mannu, Monte ∧	71	40.23 N	8.25 E
Mannum	166	34.55 S	139.18 E
Mannus	171b	35.48 S	147.57 E
Mannus Creek ≃	171b	35.58 S	148.03 E
Mannville	182	53.20 N	111.10 W
Mano	150	8.02 N	12.06 W
Mano ≃	150	6.56 N	11.31 W
Manoa	248	9.40 S	65.27 W
Manohardi	126	24.08 N	90.43 E
Manoharpur, India	124	22.23 N	85.12 E
Manoharpur, India	126	21.59 N	87.18 E
Manokin ≃	208	38.05 N	75.55 W
Manokotak	180	58.40 N	159.09 W
Manokwari	164	0.52 S	134.05 E
Manolo Fortich (Maluko)	116	8.25 N	124.58 E
Manoma ≃	89	49.18 N	136.37 E
Manombo	157b	22.57 S	43.28 E
Manomet	207	41.55 N	70.34 W
Manomet Hill ∧²	207	41.55 N	70.36 W
Manong	114	4.36 N	100.53 E
Manonga ≃	154	4.08 S	34.12 E
Manono	154	7.18 S	27.25 E
Manono I	175a	13.50 S	172.05 W
Manoora	168b	34.00 S	138.49 E
Manoppello	66	42.15 N	14.03 E
Manor, Sk., Can.	184	49.36 N	102.05 W
Manor, Pa., U.S.	214	40.20 N	79.40 W
Manor, Tx., U.S.	222	30.20 N	97.33 W
Manorbier	42	51.39 N	4.48 W
Manorhamilton	48	54.18 N	8.10 W
Manorhaven	276	40.50 N	73.42 W
Manor Hill	214	40.38 N	77.55 W
Manori ◆⁸	272c	19.12 N	72.47 E
Manori Creek ⊂	272c	19.12 N	72.48 E
Manorina National Park ♠	171a	27.23 S	152.47 E
Manori Point ›	272c	19.11 N	72.47 E
Manoron	110	11.38 N	99.04 E
Manorville	214	40.47 N	79.31 W
Manosque	62	43.50 N	5.47 E
Manotick	212	45.13 N	75.41 W
Manouane ≃	186	49.30 N	71.11 W
Manouane, Lac ⊜	186	50.41 N	70.45 W
Manouanis ≃	186	50.28 N	70.08 W
Manouanis, Lac ⊜	186	50.51 N	70.20 W
Manown	279b	40.13 N	79.54 W
Manpaka	273b	4.18 S	15.12 E
Manpitou	100	22.17 N	112.52 E
Manp'o	98	41.10 N	126.17 E
Mānpur, India	122	20.22 N	80.43 E
Mānpur, India	124	23.46 N	81.08 E
Manqabād	142	27.12 N	31.07 E
Manqaṭīn	142	28.20 N	30.40 E
Manquehue, Cerro ∧	286e	33.21 S	70.36 W
Manra I¹	14	4.27 S	171.15 W
Manresa	34	41.44 N	1.50 E
Manresa Island I	276	41.04 N	73.25 W
Mānsa, India	120	23.26 N	72.40 E
Mānsa, India	123	29.59 N	75.23 E
Mansa (Fort Rosebery), Zam.	154	11.12 S	28.53 E
Mansabá	150	12.18 N	15.15 W
Mansafīs	142	28.00 N	30.49 E
Mansalay	116	12.31 N	121.26 E
Mansara	150	13.20 N	4.39 W
Manse ≃	50	47.08 N	0.25 E
Manseau	206	46.22 N	72.00 W
Mānsehra	123	34.20 N	73.12 E
Mansein	110	25.12 N	95.58 E
Mansel Island I	176	62.00 N	79.50 W
Mansfeld	54	51.35 N	11.27 E
Mansfield, Austl.	169	37.03 S	146.05 E
Mansfield, Eng., U.K.	44	53.09 N	1.11 W
Mansfield, Ar., U.S.	194	35.04 N	94.13 W
Mansfield, Ga., U.S.	192	33.31 N	83.44 W
Mansfield, Il., U.S.	216	40.12 N	88.30 W
Mansfield, La., U.S.	194	32.02 N	93.42 W
Mansfield, Ma., U.S.	207	42.02 N	71.13 W
Mansfield, Mo., U.S.	194	37.06 N	92.34 W
Mansfield, N.J., U.S.	285	40.05 N	74.43 W
Mansfield, Oh., U.S.	214	40.45 N	82.30 W
Mansfield, Pa., U.S.	210	41.48 N	77.04 W
Mansfield, Tx., U.S.	222	32.33 N	97.08 W
Mansfield, Mount ∧	188	44.33 N	72.49 W
Mansfield Center	207	41.45 N	72.11 W
Mansfield Hollow Lake ⊜¹	207	41.45 N	72.11 W
Mansfield Hollow State Park ♠	207	41.46 N	72.10 W
Mansfield Municipal Airport ⊠	283	42.00 N	71.12 W
Mansfield Woodhouse	44	53.11 N	1.12 W
Man Shan I	106	31.14 N	120.17 E
Mansieville Location	273d	26.05 S	27.45 E
Mānsinhapur	272b	22.39 N	88.09 E
Manskoje belogorje ⋏	88	54.35 N	94.00 E
Mansle	32	45.53 N	0.11 E
Manso ≃, Bra.	248	14.42 S	56.16 W
Manso ≃, Bra.	255	13.18 S	46.51 W
Mansôa	150	12.10 N	14.36 W
Manson, Ia., U.S.	198	42.32 N	94.32 W
Manson, Wa., U.S.	182	47.53 N	120.09 W
Manson ≃	182	55.42 N	123.47 W
Manson Creek	182	55.41 N	124.29 W
Mansonville	206	45.03 N	72.23 W
Mansourah	34	36.04 N	4.28 E
Mansura → Al-Manṣūrah, Miṣr	142	31.03 N	31.23 E
Mansura, La., U.S.	194	31.03 N	92.02 W
Manṣūrīyah, Tur'at al- ≋	142	31.03 N	31.24 E
Mansurovo	82	55.52 N	36.36 E
Manta, Ec.	246	0.57 S	80.44 W
Manta, It.	62	44.37 N	7.29 E
Manta, Bahía de ⊂	246	0.54 S	80.42 W
Mantabuan Island I	116	5.02 N	120.13 E
Mantagao ≃	184	51.50 N	97.48 W
Mantalingajan, Mount ∧	116	8.48 N	117.40 E
Mantalingajan Range ⋏	116	8.46 N	117.40 E
Mantanani Besar, Pulau I	112	6.45 N	116.17 E
Mantangule Island I	116	8.10 N	117.10 E
Mantantale	152	2.10 S	20.06 E
Mantare	154	2.43 S	33.13 E
Mantaro ≃	248	12.15 S	73.58 W
Manteca	226	37.47 N	121.12 W
Mantecal	246	7.33 N	69.09 W
Mantel	60	49.39 N	12.03 E
Manteno	216	41.15 N	87.49 W
Manteo	192	35.54 N	75.40 W
Mantes-Chérence, Aérodrome de ⊠	261	49.05 N	1.41 E
Mantes-la-Jolie	50	48.59 N	1.43 E
Mantes-la-Ville	261	48.58 N	1.42 E
Manteswar	126	23.26 N	88.06 E
Manteuil-le-Haudouin	50	49.08 N	2.48 E
Manthelan	50	47.08 N	0.47 E
Manti	200	39.16 N	111.38 W
Manticao	116	8.24 N	124.17 E
Mantilla ◆⁸	286b	23.04 N	82.20 W
Mantin	114	2.49 N	101.54 E
Mantiqueira, Serra da ⋏	256	22.00 S	44.45 W
Mantok	112	1.09 S	123.14 E
Manton	190	44.24 N	85.23 W
Mantorville	190	44.04 N	92.45 W
Mantos Blancos	252	23.25 S	70.05 W
Mantou	104	42.27 N	122.26 E
Mantova	64	45.09 N	10.48 E
Mantova □⁴	64	45.10 N	10.47 E
Māntri	126	21.39 N	86.49 E
Mänttä	26	62.02 N	24.38 E
Mantua, Cuba	240p	22.17 N	84.17 W
Mantua → Mantova, It.	64	45.09 N	10.48 E
Mantua, N.J., U.S.	208	39.47 N	75.10 W
Mantua, Oh., U.S.	214	41.17 N	81.13 W
Mantua, Va., U.S.	284c	38.51 N	77.15 W
Mantua ≃	240p	22.12 N	84.25 W
Mantua Creek ≃	285	39.51 N	75.14 W
Mantua Creek, Chestnut Branch ≃	285	39.47 N	75.10 W
Mantua Creek, Porch Branch ≃	285	39.46 N	75.07 W
Mantua Hills	284c	38.51 N	77.16 W
Mantua Terrace	285	39.48 N	75.10 W
Manturovo, S.S.S.R.	78	51.28 N	37.07 E
Manturovo, S.S.S.R.	80	58.20 N	44.46 E
Mäntyharju	26	61.25 N	26.53 E
Mäntyluoto	26	61.35 N	21.29 E
Manu	248	12.15 S	70.50 W
Manú ≃	248	12.16 S	70.51 W
Manuae I¹, Cook Is.	14	19.21 S	158.56 W
Manuae I¹, Poly. fr.	14	16.30 S	154.40 W
Manua Islands II	174y	14.13 S	169.35 W
Manuel	234	22.44 N	98.19 W
Manuel Alves ≃	250	11.19 S	48.28 W
Manuel Alves Grande ≃	250	7.27 S	47.35 W
Manuel Benavides	232	29.05 N	103.55 W
Manuel Derqui	252	27.50 S	58.48 W
Manuel Duarte	256	22.06 S	43.34 W
Manuel M. Diéguez	234	19.34 N	102.55 W
Manuel Ribas	252	24.31 S	51.39 W
Manuel Rodríguez, Isla I	254	52.35 S	73.50 W
Manuel Urbano	248	8.53 S	69.18 W
Manués-Açu ≃	250	3.22 S	57.44 W
Manuguru	122	17.59 N	80.43 E
Manuhangi I¹	14	19.12 S	141.16 W
Manuherikia ≃	172	45.16 S	169.24 E
Manui, Pulau I	112	3.35 S	123.08 E
Manuilovskaja	76	60.29 N	40.40 E
Manu Island I	164	1.17 S	143.35 E
Manūjān	128	27.24 N	57.32 E
Manuk ≃	115a	6.14 S	108.13 E
Manuk, Pulau I	164	5.33 S	130.18 E
Manukan	116	8.31 N	123.06 E
Manukau	172	37.02 S	174.54 E
Manukau Harbour ⊂	172	37.01 S	174.44 E
Manulla ≃	48	53.57 N	9.12 W
Manulu Lagoon ⊂	174o	1.56 N	157.20 W
Manumuskin ≃	208	39.18 N	75.00 W
Manundi, Tanjung ›	164	0.38 S	135.22 E
Manunui	172	38.53 S	175.20 E
Manuoha ∧	172	38.39 S	177.07 E
Manupari ≃	248	11.50 S	67.16 W
Manurimi ≃	248	11.42 S	67.16 W
Manuripe (Manuripi) ≃	248	11.06 S	67.36 W
Manursing Island I	276	40.58 N	73.40 W
Manursing Island Park ♠	276	40.58 N	73.40 W
Manus □⁵	164	2.00 S	147.00 E
Mānushmuria	126	22.22 N	86.47 E
Manus Island I	164	2.05 S	147.00 E
Manutahi	172	39.40 S	174.24 E
Manutuke	172	38.41 S	177.55 E
Manvel, N.D., U.S.	198	48.04 N	97.10 W
Manvel, Tx., U.S.	222	29.28 N	95.22 W
Manville, N.J., U.S.	210	40.32 N	74.35 W
Manville, R.I., U.S.	207	41.58 N	71.28 W
Mānwat	122	19.18 N	76.30 E
Many	194	31.34 N	93.29 W
Manyal Shīḥah	273c	29.57 N	31.14 E
Manyana	156	23.23 S	21.44 E
Manyani	154	3.05 S	38.30 E
Manyara, Lake ⊜	154	3.35 S	35.50 E
Manyas	130	40.02 N	27.58 E
Manyberries	184	49.24 N	110.42 W
Manyč ≃	72	47.15 N	40.00 E
Manyč-Gudilo, ozero ⊜	80	46.24 N	42.38 E
Manyeleti Game Reserve ◆⁴	156	25.42 S	31.30 E
Many Island Lake ⊜	184	50.08 N	110.03 W
Manyoni	154	5.45 S	34.50 E
Many Peaks	166	24.33 S	151.23 E
Manytsch → Manyč ≃	72	47.15 N	40.00 E
Manz'a	86	58.29 N	96.15 E
Mānzai	120	30.07 N	68.52 E
Manzanares	34	39.00 N	3.22 W
Manzanares ≃	34	40.19 N	3.32 W
Manzanares, Canal del ≋	266a	40.23 N	3.41 W
Manzanillo, Cuba	240p	20.21 N	77.07 W
Manzanillo, Méx.	234	19.03 N	104.20 W
Manzanillo, Bahía ⊂	234	19.04 N	104.22 W
Manzanillo, Punta ›, Pan.	236	9.38 N	79.32 W
Manzanillo, Punta ›, Ven.	241s	11.32 N	69.17 W
Manzanillo Bay ⊂	238	19.45 N	71.46 W
Manzanita, Or., U.S.	224	45.43 N	123.56 W
Manzanita, Wa., U.S.	224	47.42 N	122.33 W
Manzano, It.	64	45.59 N	13.23 E
Manzano, N.M., U.S.	200	34.38 N	106.20 W
Manzanola	198	38.06 N	103.51 W
Manzano Peak ∧	200	34.35 N	106.26 W
Manželija	78	49.19 N	33.38 E
Manzhouli	88	49.35 N	117.22 E
Manziana	66	42.08 N	12.08 E
Manzil	128	29.15 N	63.05 E
Manzilah, Birkat al- ⊜	142	31.08 N	31.56 E
Manzilah, Buḥayrat al- ⊜	142	31.15 N	32.00 E
Manzini	158	26.30 S	31.25 E
Manzone	258	34.29 S	58.52 W
Manzurka	88	53.30 N	106.04 E
Maó, Esp.	34	39.53 N	4.15 E
Mao, Rep. Dom.	238	19.34 N	71.05 W
Mao, Tchad	146	14.07 N	15.19 E
Maoba	102	30.02 N	108.59 E
Maocifan	100	31.40 N	112.53 E
Maocun	98	34.25 N	117.16 E
Maodianzi, Zhg.	107	29.45 N	104.55 E
Maodianzi, Zhg.	107	30.42 N	104.25 E
Mao'ertuo	107	29.19 N	106.24 E
Maojiagou	104	40.58 N	120.51 E
Maojiaji	100	31.32 N	114.16 E
Maojiakou	100	29.53 N	112.58 E
Maojiaping	105	40.34 N	114.43 E
Maojiapuzi	104	41.10 N	123.32 E
Maojiatun	104	41.05 N	121.58 E
Maojiazao	98	39.53 N	113.26 E
Maoke, Pegunungan ⋏	164	4.00 S	138.00 E
Maolin, Zhg.	89	43.58 N	123.24 E
Maolin, Zhg.	100	30.32 N	118.14 E
Maomao Shan ∧	102	37.12 N	103.10 E
Maoming	102	21.39 N	110.54 E
Maomu	102	40.18 N	99.28 E
Ma On Shan ∧	271d	22.25 N	114.15 E
Ma On Shan Tsuen	271d	22.24 N	114.14 E
Maoping	102	30.23 N	110.33 E
Maopora, Pulau I	112	7.35 S	127.35 E
Maoshan	105	40.17 N	117.26 E
Mao Shan ⋏	106	31.43 N	119.17 E
Maoshi	100	26.57 N	113.05 E
Maospati	115a	7.36 S	111.26 E
Maouri, Dallol V	150	12.05 N	3.32 E
Maowen	102	31.30 N	103.39 E
Maoxing	89	45.32 N	124.33 E
Mao Yü I	100	23.19 N	119.19 E
Maozhou	105	38.51 N	116.06 E
Mapaga	112	0.06 S	119.48 E
Mapam Yumco ⊜	120	30.42 N	81.27 E
Mapan	112	2.21 S	111.10 E
Mapanda	152	9.32 S	24.16 E
Mapane	112	1.24 S	120.40 E
Mapanza	154	16.15 S	26.55 E
Mapaoni ≃	250	1.55 N	54.13 W
Mapari ≃	250	0.45 N	53.07 W
Mapastepec	234	15.26 N	92.54 W
Mapaville	219	38.14 N	90.29 W
Mapi	164	7.07 S	139.23 E
Mapi ≃	164	7.00 S	139.16 E
Mapia, Kepulauan II	108	0.50 N	134.20 E
Mapida	112	0.33 S	119.46 E
Mapimí	232	25.49 N	103.51 W
Mapimí, Bolsón de ◆²	232	27.30 N	103.30 W
Mapimí, Bufa de ∧	196	25.47 N	103.48 W
Maping, Zhg.	100	24.16 N	117.54 E
Maping, Zhg.	100	31.36 N	113.32 E
Mapinga	154	6.36 S	39.04 E
Mapinhane	156	22.19 S	35.03 E
Mapire	246	7.45 N	64.42 W
Mapiri	248	15.15 S	68.10 W
Mapiri ≃	248	9.52 S	66.21 W
Mapixari, Ilha I	246	2.10 S	65.08 W
Maple ◆⁸	275b	43.51 N	79.31 W
Maple ≃, U.S.	198	45.47 N	98.33 W
Maple ≃, Ia., U.S.	198	42.00 N	95.59 W
Maple ≃, Mi., U.S.	190	42.59 N	84.57 W
Maple ≃, Mn., U.S.	190	44.05 N	94.00 W
Maple ≃, N.D., U.S.	198	46.56 N	96.55 W
Maple Airfield ⊠	275b	43.51 N	79.32 W
Maple Bay	224	48.49 N	123.36 W
Maple Bluff	216	43.07 N	89.22 W
Maple Creek	184	49.55 N	109.27 W
Maple Creek ≃	198	41.33 N	96.27 W
Maplecrest	210	42.17 N	74.11 W
Maple Cross	260	51.37 N	0.30 W
Mapledale	214	41.23 N	79.51 W
Maple Falls	224	48.55 N	122.04 W
Maple Glen	285	40.11 N	75.11 W
Maple Grove, On., Can.	212	43.55 N	78.44 W
Maple Grove, P.Q., Can.	206	45.19 N	73.50 W
Maple Heights	214	41.24 N	81.33 W
Maple Lake	190	45.13 N	94.00 W
Maple Lake ⊜	212	45.06 N	78.40 W
Maple Lane	216	41.45 N	86.14 W
Maple Leaf Gardens ♠	275b	43.40 N	79.23 W
Maple Meadow Brook ≃	283	42.33 N	71.09 W
Maple Mount	194	37.42 N	87.26 W
Maple Park	216	41.55 N	88.36 W
Maples	216	41.01 N	84.58 W
Maple Shade	285	39.57 N	74.59 W
Maple Springs	214	42.12 N	79.25 W
Maplesville	194	32.47 N	86.52 W
Mapleton, S. Afr.	158	26.20 S	28.14 E
Mapleton, Ia., U.S.	198	42.09 N	95.47 W
Mapleton, Mn., U.S.	190	43.55 N	93.57 W
Mapleton, Or., U.S.	202	44.01 N	123.51 W
Mapleton, Ut,. U.S.	200	40.07 N	111.34 W
Mapleton Depot	214	40.24 N	77.57 W
Maple Valley	224	47.25 N	122.03 W
Mapleville	207	41.56 N	71.38 W
Maplewood, Mo., U.S.	219	38.36 N	90.19 W
Maplewood, N.J., U.S.	276	40.43 N	74.14 W
Maplewood, Oh., U.S.	216	40.23 N	84.02 W
Maplewood, Wa., U.S.	224	47.30 N	122.07 W
Maplewood Terrace	279b	40.17 N	79.32 W
Mapocho ≃	286e	33.25 S	70.47 W
Mapocho, Estación ◆⁵	286e	33.26 S	70.40 W
Mapoi	154	5.28 N	27.40 E
Mapoon Aboriginal Reserve ◆⁴	164	11.40 S	142.25 E
Mappsville	208	37.51 N	75.34 W
Maprik	164	3.40 S	143.05 E
Mapuera ≃	250	1.05 S	57.02 W
Mapujiang	105	40.24 N	114.56 E
Mapulanguene	156	24.29 S	32.06 E
Mapulau ≃	246	1.23 N	63.24 W
Mapumulo	158	29.11 S	31.02 E
Maputa	158	26.59 S	32.46 E
Maputo	156	25.58 S	32.35 E
Maputo □⁵	156	26.00 S	32.25 E
Maputo (Great Usutu) (Lusutfu) ≃	158	26.11 S	32.42 E
Maputo, Baia de ⊂	158	25.48 S	32.51 E
Maqên Gangri ∧	102	34.55 N	99.18 E
Maqiangou	105	39.30 N	115.02 E
Maqiao, Zhg.	100	29.48 N	114.22 E
Maqiao, Zhg.	106	30.28 N	120.42 E
Maqna	128	28.24 N	34.45 E
Maqṭeïr ⊤⁴	148	22.10 N	10.50 W
Maquan ≃	124	29.35 N	84.10 E
Maqueda	34	40.04 N	4.22 W
Maqueda Bay ⊂	116	11.44 N	124.58 E
Maqueda Channel ⊔	116	13.42 N	124.01 E
Maquela do Zombo	152	6.03 S	15.07 E
Maquereau, Pointe au ›	186	48.12 N	64.47 W
Maquiling, Mount ∧	116	14.08 N	121.12 E
Maquinchao	254	41.15 S	68.44 W
Maquinchao ≃	254	41.13 S	69.25 W
Maquoketa	190	42.04 N	90.39 W
Maquoketa ≃	190	42.11 N	90.19 W
Maquoketa, North Fork ≃	190	42.05 N	90.40 W
Mar, Serra do ±⁴	252	26.00 S	48.00 W
Mara, India	120	28.11 N	94.06 E
Mara, Perú	248	14.06 S	72.07 W
Mara, Zhg.	120	28.11 N	94.08 E
Mara □⁴	154	1.45 S	34.30 E
Mara ≃, Afr.	154	1.31 S	33.56 E
Mara ≃, S.S.S.R.	88	58.06 N	104.06 E
Maraã, Bra.	246	1.50 S	65.22 W
Maraa, Poly. fr.	174s	17.46 S	149.34 W
Marabá	250	5.21 S	49.07 W
Marabahan	112	3.00 S	114.45 E
Marabut	116	11.07 N	125.13 E
Maracá ≃	250	0.26 S	51.26 W
Maracá, Ilha de I, Bra.	246	3.25 N	61.40 W
Maracá, Ilha de I, Bra.	250	2.05 N	50.25 W
Maracaçumé ≃	250	1.23 S	45.42 W
Maracaí	255	22.36 S	50.39 W
Maracaibo	246	10.40 N	71.37 W
Maracaibo, Lago de ⊜	246	9.50 N	71.30 W
Maracaju	255	21.38 S	55.09 W
Maracaju, Serra de ⋏²	255	20.45 S	55.00 W
Maracalagonis	71	39.17 N	9.13 E
Maracanã	250	0.46 S	47.27 W
Maracanã ◆⁸	287a	22.54 S	43.14 W
Maracanã ≃	248	8.22 S	59.41 W
Maracanã, Estádio Municipal ♠	287a	22.55 S	43.14 W
Maracanaú	250	3.52 S	38.38 W
Maracás	255	13.26 S	40.27 W
Maracay	246	10.15 N	67.36 W
Maracossic Creek ≃	208	37.53 N	77.11 W
Marādah	146	29.14 N	19.13 E
Maradi	150	13.29 N	7.06 E
Maradi □⁵	150	14.00 N	7.00 E
Maradi, Goulbin ≃	150	13.38 N	6.20 E
Marāghah, Sabkhat al- ⊜	130	35.39 N	37.39 E
Marāgheh	128	37.23 N	46.13 E
Maragiu, Capo ›	71	40.20 N	8.23 E
Maragogi	250	9.01 S	35.13 W
Maragogipe	255	12.46 S	38.55 W
Marahoué, Parc National de la ♠	150	7.00 N	6.00 W
Mārahra	124	27.44 N	78.35 E
Marahuaca, Cerro ∧	246	3.34 N	65.27 W
Maraial	250	8.47 S	35.50 W
Maraiche Lake ⊜	184	54.28 N	102.01 W
Marainviller	58	48.35 N	6.36 E
Maraisburg → Roodepoort-Maraisburg	273d	26.11 S	27.56 E
Marais des Cygnes ≃	194	38.02 N	94.14 W
Marais Temps Clair ⊜	219	38.54 N	90.24 W
Marajó, Baía de ⊂	250	1.00 S	48.30 W
Marajó, Ilha de I	250	1.00 S	49.30 W
Marakabei	158	29.32 S	28.09 E
Ma'rakah	132	33.16 N	35.18 E
Mārākand	84	38.52 N	45.14 E
Marakwini	164	3.42 S	141.31 E
Maralal	154	1.06 N	36.42 E
Maralaleng	156	25.47 S	22.45 E
Maralal Game Sanctuary ◆⁴	154	1.09 N	36.38 E
Maraldy	86	52.26 N	77.45 E
Marali	152	6.01 N	18.24 E
Maralik	84	40.35 N	43.52 E
Maralinga	162	30.10 S	131.35 E
Maralinga Lands ◆⁴	162	29.15 S	130.50 E
Maram	120	25.25 N	94.06 E
Maramag	116	7.46 N	125.00 E
Maramasike I	175e	9.32 S	161.27 E
Marambaia ≃	256	21.44 S	46.25 W
Marambaia, Ilha da I	256	23.04 S	43.58 W
Marambaia, Pico da ∧	256	23.04 S	43.59 W
Marambio ☩³	9	64.14 S	56.43 W
Marampa	150	8.41 N	12.28 W
Maramsilli Reservoir ⊜¹	122	20.32 N	81.41 E
Maramureș □⁶	38	47.40 N	24.00 E
Maran	114	3.35 N	102.46 E
Mārān, Koh-i- ∧	120	29.26 N	66.48 E
Marana, Mali	150	14.38 N	11.55 W
Marana, Az., U.S.	200	32.26 N	111.13 W
Maranalgo	162	29.23 S	117.48 E
Maranboy	164	14.30 S	132.45 E
Maranchón	34	41.03 N	2.12 W
Marand	128	38.26 N	45.46 E
Maranello	64	44.32 N	10.52 E
Marang, Malay.	114	5.12 N	103.13 E
Marang, Mya.	110	10.27 N	98.47 E
Marangá ≃	287a	22.51 S	43.23 W

Symbols in the index entries represent the broad categories identified in the key at the right. Symbols with superior numbers (⋏¹) identify subcategories (see complete key on page *I · 1*).

Symbole im Register stellen die rechts im Schlüssel erklärten Kategorien dar. Symbole mit hochgestellten Ziffern (⋏¹) bezeichnen Unterabteilungen einer Kategorie (vgl. vollständiger Schlüssel auf Seite *I · 1*).

Los símbolos incluídos en el texto del índice representan las grandes categorías identificadas con la clave a la derecha. Los símbolos con numeros en su parte superior (⋏¹) identifican las subcategorías (véase la clave completa en la página *I · 1*).

Les symboles de l'index représentent les catégories indiquées dans la légende à droite. Les symboles suivis d'un indice (⋏¹) représentent des sous-catégories (voir légende complète à la page *I · 1*).

Os símbolos incluídos no texto do índice representam as grandes categorias identificadas com a chave à direita. Os símbolos com números em sua parte superior (⋏¹) identificam as subcategorias (veja-se a chave completa à página *I · 1*).

	English	Deutsch	Español	Français	Português
∧	Mountain	Berg	Montaña	Montagne	Montanha
⋏	Mountains	Gebirge	Montañas	Montagnes	Montanhas
)(	Pass	Paß	Paso	Col	Passo
V	Valley, Canyon	Tal, Cañon	Valle, Cañón	Vallée, Canyon	Vale, Canhão
≚	Plain	Ebene	Llano	Plaine	Planície
›	Cape	Kap	Cabo	Cap	Cabo
I	Island	Insel	Isla	Île	Ilha
II	Islands	Inseln	Islas	Îles	Ilhas
±	Other Topographic Features	Andere Topographische Objekte	Otros Elementos Topográficos	Autres données topographiques	Outros acidentes topográficos

ESPAÑOL			FRANÇAIS			PORTUGUÊS		
Nombre	Página	Lat.°' / Long.°' W=Oeste	Nom	Page	Lat.°' / Long.°' W=Ouest	Nome	Página	Lat.°' / Long.°' W=Oeste

Column 1 (ESPAÑOL)

Nombre	Página	Lat.	Long.
Marangani	248	14.22 S	71.10 W
Marangas	116	8.40 N	117.38 E
Marange-Zondrange	56	49.07 N	6.32 E
Maranguape	250	3.53 S	38.40 W
Maranhão ◻³	250	5.00 S	45.00 W
Maranhão	255	14.34 S	49.02 W
Maranhão, Cachoeira ㄴ	250	4.49 S	56.18 W
Marano	266b	45.38 N	8.38 E
Marano, Laguna di ◠	64	45.44 N	13.10 E
Marano sul Panaro	64	44.27 N	10.58 E
Marano Vicentino	64	45.41 N	11.25 E
Marans	32	46.19 N	1.00 W
Maraoli ⬥⁸	250	0.42 S	47.42 W
Marapanim			
Marapendi, Lagoa de ◠	287a	23.01 S	43.24 W
Marapicu	250	0.37 N	55.58 W
Marapicu, Morro do ∧	256	22.48 S	43.35 W
	287a	22.50 S	43.36 W
Mararoa ≃	172	45.34 S	167.36 E
Mararui	154	1.56 S	41.18 E
Marasa	248	13.20 S	72.09 W
Maraş → Kahramanmaraş	130	37.36 N	36.55 E
Marasany	80	57.21 N	54.25 E
Marasende, Pulau ı	112	5.08 S	118.09 E
Márășești	38	45.52 N	27.14 E
Maratasã ≃	250	4.14 S	42.15 W
Maratea	68	39.59 N	15.45 E
Marathon, Austl.	166	20.49 S	143.34 E
Marathon, On., Can.	190	48.43 N	86.23 W
Marathón, Ellás	38	38.10 N	23.58 E
Marathon, Fl., U.S.	220	24.42 N	81.05 W
Marathon, N.Y., U.S.	210	42.26 N	76.01 W
Marathon, Tx., U.S.	196	30.12 N	103.15 W
Marathon, Wi., U.S.	190	44.55 N	89.50 W
Maratua, Pulau ı	112	2.15 N	118.36 E
Marau, Bra.	252	28.27 S	52.12 W
Maraú, Bra.	255	14.06 S	39.00 W
Maraúiá ≃	246	0.23 S	65.13 W
Marausa	70	37.56 N	12.30 E
Maravari	175e	7.51 S	156.42 E
Maravatío de Ocampo	234	19.54 N	100.27 W
Maravilha, Bra.	250	9.14 S	37.21 W
Maravilha, Bra.	252	26.47 S	53.09 W
Maravillas	252	27.22 N	104.29 W
Maravillas Creek ≃	196	29.34 N	102.47 W
Mara Vista	207	41.33 N	70.34 W
Mara'y Lake ◠	120	29.04 N	69.18 E
Maravovo	175e	9.17 S	159.38 E
Marāwah	146	32.29 N	21.25 E
Marawi, Pil.	116	8.01 N	124.18 E
Marwi, Süd.	140	18.29 N	31.49 E
Marawwah ı	128	24.18 N	53.18 E
Maraye-en-Othe	50	48.10 N	3.51 E
Marayes	252	31.29 S	67.20 W
Marayong	274a	33.45 S	150.54 E
Marazion	84	40.33 N	48.56 E
Marbach, B.R.D.	42	50.08 N	5.28 W
Marbach, D.D.R.	56	50.37 N	9.43 E
Marbach, Schw.	58	46.52 N	7.55 E
Marbach am Neckar	48	48.56 N	9.14 E
Marbache	56	48.48 N	6.05 E
Marbais	50	50.63 N	4.31 E
Marbeck	52	51.49 N	6.52 E
Marbella	34	36.31 N	4.53 W
Marble, Mn., U.S.	190	47.19 N	93.17 W
Marble, N.C., U.S.	192	35.10 N	83.55 W
Marble, Pa., U.S.	214	41.20 N	79.25 W
Marble Bar	162	21.11 S	119.44 E
Marble Canyon V	200	36.30 N	111.50 W
Marble Falls	196	30.34 N	98.16 W
Marble Hall	156	24.57 S	29.13 E
Marblehead, Il., U.S.	219	38.50 N	91.22 W
Marblehead, Ma., U.S.	207	42.30 N	70.51 W
Marblehead Neck >¹	214	41.32 N	82.44 W
Marble Hill	283	42.29 N	70.51 W
Marble Hill	194	37.18 N	89.58 W
Marble Lake ◠	216	41.54 N	84.54 W
Marblemount	224	48.31 N	121.26 W
Marble Rock	190	42.57 N	92.52 W
Marbleton	226	45.37 N	71.35 W
Marburg, Austl.	171a	27.34 S	152.35 E
Marburg, B.R.D.	56	50.49 N	8.46 E
Marburg, S. Afr.	158	30.44 S	30.26 E
Marburg an der Drau → Maribor	208	39.48 N	76.53 W
Marbury	36	46.33 N	15.39 E
Marc ⬥	218	38.34 N	77.09 W
Marca, Ponta da ▸	152	16.31 S	11.42 E
Maracaconga	248	13.59 S	71.34 W
Marcala	234	37.41 N	17.32 E
Marcali	236	14.07 N	88.00 W
Marcalo con Casone	266b	46.35 N	17.25 E
Marcaria	186	45.29 N	8.62 E
Marceau, Lac ◠	186	51.25 N	66.41 W
Marcedusa	68	39.02 N	16.50 E
Marcelin	184	52.55 N	106.47 W
Marceline	219	39.42 N	92.56 W
Marcelino Ramos	252	27.28 S	51.54 W
Marcella	276	40.59 N	74.28 W
Marcellus, Mi., U.S.	216	42.01 N	85.48 W
Marcellus, N.Y., U.S.	210	42.59 N	76.20 W
Marcellus Falls	210	43.00 N	76.24 W
Marcevo	82	47.15 N	38.53 E
March	42	52.33 N	0.06 E
March (Morava) ≃	30	48.10 N	16.59 E
Marcha	74	60.37 N	123.18 E
Marchand	184	49.27 N	96.24 W
March Air Force Base ⬥	228	33.54 N	117.15 W
Marchais	261	48.31 N	2.03 E
Marchal	152	15.34 S	14.58 E
Marchamat	85	40.30 N	72.19 E
Marchand	214	40.55 N	79.02 W
Marchaux	58	47.19 N	6.08 E
Marche ◻⁴	68	43.30 N	13.15 E
Marche-en-Famenne	56	50.12 N	5.20 E
Marchegg	161	43.17 N	16.55 E
Marche-les-Dames	56	50.30 N	4.58 E
Marchemoret	261	49.02 N	2.41 E
Marchena	34	37.20 N	5.24 W
Marchena, Isla ı	246a	0.21 N	90.29 W
Marchenoir	50	47.49 N	1.24 E
Marchesato ◻¹	68	39.07 N	16.58 E
Marchfeld ◻¹	30	48.18 N	16.31 E
Marchienne-au-Pont	50	50.24 N	4.23 E
Marchinbar Island ı	166	11.15 S	136.45 E
Marching	60	48.49 N	11.43 E
Mar Chiquita, Laguna ◠	252	37.37 S	57.24 W
Mar Chiquita, Laguna ◠	250	30.42 S	62.36 W
Marchtrenk	61	48.11 N	14.07 E
Marciana	66	42.47 N	10.10 E
Marciana Marina	66	42.48 N	10.12 E
Marcianise	68	41.02 N	14.17 E
Marcichina Buda	78	51.58 N	34.03 E
Marciginsky	32	46.17 N	4.02 E
Marcillac-Vallon	52	44.29 N	2.28 E
Marcilloles	62	45.20 N	5.11 E
Marcilly	261	49.02 N	2.53 E
Marcilly-la-Campagne	50	48.50 N	1.13 E
Marcilly-sur-Eure	50	48.49 N	1.21 E
Marck	50	50.57 N	1.57 E

Column 2 (FRANÇAIS)

Nom	Page	Lat.	Long.
Marckolsheim	58	48.10 N	7.33 E
Marco, Bra.	250	3.05 S	40.09 W
Marco, It.	64	45.51 N	11.01 E
Marco, Fl., U.S.	220	25.58 N	81.43 W
Marcoing	50	50.07 N	3.11 E
Marco Island ı	220	25.55 N	81.45 W
Marcola	202	44.10 N	122.51 W
Marcolino, Igarapé ≃	250	11.03 S	58.35 W
Marcona	248	15.03 S	75.01 W
Marco Polo, Aeroporto ⬥	64	45.30 N	12.21 E
Marco Polo Bridge ⬥⁵	271a	39.52 N	116.12 E
Marcos Juárez	252	32.42 S	62.06 W
Marcos Paz	258	34.46 S	58.50 W
Marcos Paz ◻⁵	258	34.48 S	58.49 W
Marcotte, Lac ◠	206	46.47 N	73.12 W
Marcoussis	261	48.39 N	2.14 E
Marcq	261	48.52 N	1.49 E
Marco-en-Barœul	50	50.40 N	3.05 E
Marčugi	82	55.21 N	38.33 E
Marcus	198	42.49 N	95.48 W
Marcus Baker, Mount ∧	180	61.26 N	147.45 W
Marcus Hook	208	39.49 N	75.25 W
Marcus Hook Creek ≃	285	39.49 N	75.25 W
Marcus Island → Minami-Tori-shima ı	14	24.18 N	153.58 E
Marcy, Mount ∧	188	44.07 N	73.56 W
Marda	162	30.13 S	119.17 E
Mardakert	84	40.12 N	46.48 E
Mardān	123	34.12 N	72.02 E
Mardarovka	78	47.37 N	29.44 E
Mar de Cães, Vala de ≃	266c	38.51 N	8.59 W
Mar de Espanha	256	21.52 S	43.00 W
Mardela Springs	208	38.27 N	75.45 W
Mar del Plata	252	38.00 S	57.33 W
Marden	42	51.10 N	0.29 E
Mardin	162	21.11 S	115.57 E
Mardin ◻⁴	130	37.18 N	40.44 E
Mardin ◻⁴	128	37.25 N	41.00 E
Mar Dyke ≃	260	51.29 N	0.14 E
Maré ı	175f	21.30 S	168.00 E
Mare à Brăilei, Insula ı	38	45.00 N	28.00 E
Marecchia ≃	66	44.04 N	12.34 E
Marechal Cândido Rondon	252	24.34 S	54.04 W
Marechal Deodoro	250	9.43 S	35.54 W
Marene, Loch ◠	46	57.42 N	5.30 W
Mareeba	166	17.00 S	145.26 E
Mareetsane	158	26.09 S	25.25 E
Mareil-en-France	261	49.04 N	2.26 E
Mareil-le-Guyon	261	48.47 N	1.51 E
Mareil-Marly	261	48.53 N	2.05 E
Mare Island Naval Shipyard ⬥	282	38.06 N	122.17 W
Mare Island Strait ᴗ	282	38.06 N	122.17 W
Mareje, Gunung ∧	115b	8.46 S	116.08 E
Marek	112	4.48 S	120.21 E
Maremma ◻¹	66	42.30 N	11.30 E
Marene	62	44.39 N	7.44 E
Marengo, Il., U.S.	216	42.14 N	88.36 W
Marengo, In., U.S.	218	38.22 N	86.20 W
Marengo, Ia., U.S.	190	41.47 N	92.04 W
Marengo, Mi., U.S.	216	42.17 N	84.54 W
Marengo, Oh., U.S.	214	40.24 N	82.49 W
Marengo ⬥¹	62	44.55 N	8.40 E
Marengo Cave ⬥⁵	218	38.23 N	86.21 W
Marennes	52	45.49 N	1.06 W
Marenisco	192	46.22 N	89.41 W
Marenne	42	45.50 N	1.06 W
Marennes	157b	21.23 S	44.52 E
Maresias	256	23.48 S	45.34 W
Marettimo	70	37.58 N	12.04 E
Marettimo, Isola ı	70	37.58 N	12.03 E
Mareuil-en-Brie	50	48.53 N	3.45 E
Mareuil-lès-Meaux	261	48.56 N	2.52 E
Mareuil-sur-Aÿ	50	49.03 N	4.02 E
Mareuil-sur-Belle	32	45.28 N	0.28 E
Marevo	76	57.19 N	32.05 E
Marey-sur-Tille	58	47.35 N	5.03 E
Marfa	196	30.18 N	104.01 W
Marfinka	83	46.38 N	38.32 E
Marfino	83	46.05 N	48.44 E
Mar Forest ⬥⁴	46	57.00 N	3.35 W
Margai Caka ◠	120	35.00 N	87.00 E
Margam, Īrān	120	34.12 N	72.02 E
Margam, Wales, U.K.	42	51.34 N	3.44 W
Marganec	78	47.38 N	34.40 E
Margao → Madgaon	122	15.18 N	73.57 E
Margaree	186	46.26 N	61.05 W
Margaree Harbour	186	46.26 N	61.07 W
Margaret ⬥¹	166	18.10 S	125.37 E
Margaret, Mount ∧	162	18.18 N	122.08 W
Margaret Bay	182	51.20 N	127.29 W
Margaret Creek ≃	166	29.26 S	137.07 E
Margarethenhöhe ⬥⁸	263	51.26 N	6.58 E
Margaret River, Austl.	162	33.57 S	115.04 E
Margaret River, Austl.	162	18.38 S	126.52 E
Margaret Roding	260	51.47 N	0.19 E
Margaretting	260	51.41 N	0.25 E
Margaretville	208	36.32 N	77.21 W
Margareville	210	42.08 N	74.38 W
Margarita, Bahía ◠	287a	22.59 S	43.06 W
Margarita, Isla ı	246	9.05 N	64.00 W
Margarita, Isla de ı	246	11.00 N	64.00 W
Margarita Belén	252	27.16 S	58.58 W
Margarita Peak ∧	228	33.26 N	117.23 W
Margaritovka	83	46.55 N	38.52 E
Margate, S. Afr.	158	30.55 S	30.15 E
Margate, Eng., U.K.	42	51.24 N	1.24 E
Margate, Fl., U.S.	220	26.14 N	80.12 W
Margate City	208	39.19 N	74.30 W
Margecany	30	48.54 N	21.01 E
Margelan → Margilan	85	40.28 N	71.44 E
Margerice, Monts de ∧	32	45.09 N	5.03 E
Margès	62	45.09 N	5.03 E
Margherita	120	27.17 N	95.41 E
Margherita → Jamaame	144	0.04 N	42.45 E
Margherita di Savoia	61	41.23 N	16.09 E
Margherita Peak ∧	154	0.22 N	29.51 E
Margi	128	34.58 N	66.31 E
Margilan	85	40.28 N	71.44 E
Margit ≃	70	37.16 N	14.58 E
Margit Hid ⬥¹	264c	47.31 N	19.02 E
Margit-sziget ı	264c	47.32 N	19.03 E
Margny-lès-Compiègne	50	49.26 N	2.49 E
Margonin	30	52.59 N	17.05 E
Margosatubig	116	7.34 N	123.10 E
Margow, Dasht-e ⬟²	128	30.45 N	63.10 E
Margreid			
→ Magrè			
Marguareis, Pic ∧	62	44.08 N	7.41 E
Marguerite	182	52.29 N	122.25 W
→ Margherita Peak	154	0.22 N	29.51 E
Marguerite Bay ◠	5	68.30 S	68.30 W
Marguerittes	62	43.51 N	4.27 E
Margyang	124	29.57 N	90.09 E
Mari	248	9.10 S	141.40 E
Maria	186	48.11 N	65.59 W
Maria, Îles ıı	13	21.48 S	154.41 W

Column 3 (PORTUGUÊS)

Nome	Página	Lat.	Long.
Mariabrunn ⬥⁸	264b	48.12 N	16.14 E
María Cleofas, Isla ı	234	21.16 N	106.14 W
María da Fé	256	22.18 S	45.23 W
María Elena	252	22.21 S	69.40 W
María Enzersdorf	61	48.06 N	16.17 E
María Gail	64	46.36 N	13.52 E
Mariager	26	56.39 N	10.00 E
Mariāhu	124	25.37 N	82.37 E
María Ignacia (Vela)	252	37.24 S	59.30 W
María Island ı, Austl.	164	14.52 S	135.40 E
María Island ı, Austl.	166	42.39 S	148.04 E
María Island National Park ⬥	166	42.39 S	148.06 E
Mariakani	154	3.52 S	39.28 E
María Laach v¹	56	50.24 N	7.14 E
María la Baja	246	9.59 N	75.17 W
María Lanzendorf	264b	48.06 N	16.25 E
María Luggau	64	46.42 N	12.45 E
María Madre, Isla ı	234	21.35 N	106.33 W
María Magdalena, Isla ı	234	21.25 N	106.24 W
Marian, Lake ◠	220	27.52 N	81.06 W
Mariana	255	20.23 S	43.25 W
Mariana Basin ⬥¹	14	17.30 N	145.00 E
Mariana Islands ıı	108	16.00 N	145.30 E
Mariana Ridge ⬥³	14	17.00 N	146.00 E
Mariana Trench ⬥¹	14	15.00 N	147.30 E
Mariāni	120	26.40 N	94.20 E
Marian Lake ◠	176	63.00 N	116.10 W
Marianna, Ar., U.S.	194	34.46 N	90.45 W
Marianna, Fl., U.S.	192	30.46 N	85.13 W
Mariannelund	26	57.37 N	15.34 E
Mariannhill	158	29.52 S	30.50 E
Mariano Acosta	258	34.43 S	58.48 W
Mariano Comense	62	45.42 N	9.11 E
Mariano del Friuli	64	45.55 N	13.27 E
Mariano I. Loza	252	29.22 S	58.12 W
Mariano J. Haedo	258	34.38 S	58.36 W
Mariano Moreno, Arg.	252	38.44 S	70.01 W
Mariano Moreno → Moreno, Arg.	258	34.39 S	58.48 W
Marianópoli	70	37.36 N	13.55 E
Marianópolis	250	4.47 S	44.38 W
Mariánské Lázně	60	49.59 N	12.43 E
María Paula	287a	22.54 S	43.02 W
Mariar	164	2.48 S	132.50 E
Mariarano	157b	15.29 S	46.42 E
Marias, Dry Fork ≃	202	47.56 N	110.30 W
Marías, Islas ıı	234	21.25 N	106.28 W
Marias Pass ㅅ	202	48.19 N	113.21 W
Marias Stein	216	40.24 N	84.28 W
María Teresa	252	34.01 S	61.54 W
Maria-Theresiopel → Subotica	38	46.06 N	19.39 E
Mariato, Punta ▸	246	7.13 N	80.53 W
Maria van Diemen, Cape ▸	172	34.28 S	172.39 E
Mariaville	210	42.49 N	74.08 W
Mariazell	61	47.47 N	15.19 E
Ma'rib	144	15.30 N	45.20 E
Maribios, Cordillera de los ∧	236	12.35 N	86.50 W
Maribo	41	54.46 N	11.31 E
Maribojoc Bay ◠	116	9.42 N	123.50 E
Maribor	61	46.33 N	15.39 E
Maribyrnong	274b	37.46 S	144.54 E
Marica, Blg.	38	42.02 N	25.50 E
Marica, Bra.	256	22.55 S	42.49 W
Marica, S.S.S.R.	78	51.45 N	35.16 E
Maricá ◠¹	287a	22.57 S	42.59 W
Maricá, Lagoa de ◠	256	22.56 S	42.50 W
Maricaban Island ı	116	13.39 N	120.53 E
Maricha Bil ◠	272b	22.55 N	88.31 E
Marico ≃	156	24.12 S	26.52 E
Maricopa, Az., U.S.	200	33.03 N	112.02 W
Maricopa, Ca., U.S.	204	35.03 N	119.24 W
Maricopa Indian Reservation ⬥⁴	200	33.02 N	112.05 W
Maricunga, Salar de ⬟	252	26.55 S	69.05 W
Maridagao ≃	116	7.13 N	124.41 E
Maridī	148	4.55 N	29.28 E
Maridī ≃	148	6.05 N	29.24 E
Marié ≃	246	0.27 S	66.26 W
Marie Byrd Land ⬥¹	5	80.00 S	120.00 W
Marie Curtis Park ⬥	275b	43.35 N	79.33 W
Mariefred	40	59.16 N	17.14 E
Marie-Galante ı	241o	15.56 N	61.16 W
Mariehamn	26	60.06 N	19.57 E
Mariehamn	40	60.06 N	19.57 E
Mariel	240p	22.59 N	82.45 W
Mariembourg	50	50.06 N	4.31 E
Marie-Lefranc, Lac ◠	206	46.08 N	75.00 W
Marienbad	50	50.06 N	4.31 E
→ Mariánské Lázně	60	49.59 N	12.43 E
Marienbaum	52	51.41 N	6.22 E
Marienberg, B.R.D.	56	50.39 N	7.57 E
Marienberg, D.D.R.	54	50.39 N	13.10 E
Marienberg, Pap. N. Gui.		3.55 S	144.15 E
Marien-Berg ∧²	264a	52.22 N	13.32 E
Marienborn	54	52.12 N	11.08 E
Marienburg → Malbork	30	54.02 N	19.01 E
Mariendorf ⬥⁸	264a	52.26 N	13.23 E
Marienfelde ⬥⁸	264a	52.25 N	13.22 E
Marienhafe	54	53.31 N	7.16 E
Marienhede	54	51.05 N	7.32 E
Mariental, B.R.D.	54	52.16 N	10.56 E
Mariental, Namibia	156	24.36 S	17.59 E
Mariental ⬥⁸	156	25.00 S	19.00 E
Marienville	214	41.28 N	79.07 W
Maries ◻⁶	219	38.15 N	91.56 W
Maries ≃	219	38.30 N	91.54 W
Mariestad	40	58.43 N	13.51 E
Marietta, Ga., U.S.	192	33.57 N	84.33 W
Marietta, In., U.S.	218	39.24 N	85.53 W
Marietta, Oh., U.S.	188	39.24 N	81.27 W
Marietta, Ok., U.S.	196	33.56 N	97.07 W
Marietta, Pa., U.S.	208	40.03 N	76.33 W
Marietta, Tx., U.S.	196	33.10 N	94.33 W
Marietta, Wa., U.S.	224	48.47 N	122.34 W
Marieville	206	45.26 N	73.10 W
Mariga ≃	150	9.40 N	5.55 E
Marignane	62	43.25 N	5.13 E
Marigot	46	46.06 N	6.31 W
Marigny-le-Châtel	50	48.25 N	3.44 E
Marigny-L'Église	58	47.18 N	4.05 E
Marigot, Dom.	240d	15.32 N	61.18 W
Marigot, Guad.	238	14.00 N	60.58 W
Marī Jijis ⬥³	261	30.04 N	31.14 E
Marī 'Uyūn	132	33.22 N	35.35 E
Marijampolė	86	54.33 N	23.21 E
Marija, Som.	144	1.43 N	44.52 E
Märjäk, Urd.	132	31.59 N	35.59 E
Marka ≃	144	1.43 N	44.53 E
Mark Azres	279b	40.21 N	79.42 W
Markakol', ozero ◠	102	48.46 N	85.48 E
Markala	150	13.41 N	6.05 W
Markapur	122	15.44 N	79.17 E
Markaryd	26	56.26 N	13.36 E
Markdale	212	44.19 N	80.39 W
Marken ı	56	52.26 N	5.07 E
Markelo	52	52.14 N	6.30 E
Markerwaard ⬥	56	52.33 N	5.15 E

Column 4 (ESPAÑOL)

Nombre	Página	Lat.	Long.
Markermeer ◠	52	52.33 N	5.15 E
Markesan	190	43.42 N	88.59 W
Märket ı	40	60.18 N	19.08 E
Market Bosworth	42	52.37 N	1.24 W
Market Deeping	42	52.41 N	0.19 W
Market Drayton	42	52.54 N	2.29 W
Market Harborough	42	52.29 N	0.55 W
Markethill	48	54.18 N	6.31 W
Market Lavington	42	51.18 N	1.59 W
Market Rasen	44	53.24 N	0.21 W
Market Weighton	44	53.52 N	0.40 W
Markfield	42	52.40 N	1.17 W
Markgröningen	56	48.54 N	9.05 E
Markham, On., Can.	212	43.52 N	79.16 W
Markham, Tx., U.S.	222	28.57 N	96.04 W
Markham ≃	164	6.35 S	146.25 E
Markham, Mount ∧	9	82.51 S	161.21 E
Markham Bay ◠	176	63.30 N	71.48 W
Markit	85	38.55 N	77.38 E
Markkleeberg	54	51.17 N	12.23 E
Markland Dam ⬥⁶	218	38.47 N	84.58 W
Markle, In., U.S.	216	40.50 N	85.20 W
Markle, Pa., U.S.	279b	40.30 N	79.39 W
Markleeville	226	38.41 N	119.46 W
Markleville	218	39.58 N	85.36 W
Markley Canyon V	282	38.00 N	121.50 W
Marklissa → Leśna	30	51.02 N	15.16 E
Marknesse	52	52.43 N	5.52 E
Markneukirchen	54	50.18 N	12.19 E
Markoldendorf	54	51.48 N	9.46 E
Márkópoulon	267c	37.54 N	23.54 E
Markounda	152	7.37 N	16.59 E
Markovka	83	49.31 N	39.34 E
Markovo, S.S.S.R.	74	64.40 N	170.25 E
Markovo, S.S.S.R.	82	57.01 N	40.30 E
Markovo, S.S.S.R.	83	55.52 N	39.17 E
Markovy	85	57.20 N	107.04 E
Markoya	150	14.39 N	0.02 E
Markranstädt	54	51.18 N	12.13 E
Marks, S. Afr.	80	51.42 N	46.46 E
Marks, Ms., U.S.	194	34.15 N	90.16 W
Marks Tey	42	51.52 N	0.47 E
Marksuhl	56	50.53 N	10.11 E
Marksville	194	31.07 N	92.03 W
Markt Bibart	56	49.39 N	10.26 E
Markt Rettenbach	60	48.00 N	10.26 E
Marktschellenberg	64	47.42 N	13.02 E
Markt Schwaben	60	48.11 N	11.51 E
Mark Twain Lake ±⁵	219	39.29 N	91.21 W
Mark Twain Lake ◠¹	219	39.30 N	91.45 W
Mark Twain State Park ⬥	219	39.30 N	91.48 W
Markuleby	78	47.52 N	28.14 E
Markundi	140	11.33 N	23.49 E
Markvue Manor	279b	40.00 N	79.46 W
Marl	52	51.38 N	7.05 E
Marlasi	164	5.30 S	134.38 E
Marlboro, Ab., Can.	182	53.33 N	116.45 W
Marlboro, N.J., U.S.	208	40.18 N	74.14 W
Marlboro, N.Y., U.S.	214	41.36 N	73.58 W
Marlboro, Oh., U.S.	214	40.53 N	81.12 W
Marlboro, Va., U.S.	208	39.06 N	76.55 W
Marlborough, Austl.	166	22.49 S	149.53 E
Marlborough, Guy.	246	7.29 N	58.38 W
Marlborough, Ct., U.S.	207	41.37 N	72.27 W
Marlborough Downs ⬟¹	42	51.30 N	1.45 W
Marldon	50	50.28 N	3.36 W
Marle	50	49.44 N	3.46 E
Marlehlen	58	48.37 N	7.30 E
Marlenheim	58	48.37 N	7.30 E
Marles-les-Mines	261	48.31 N	2.31 E
Marlette	190	43.19 N	83.04 W
Marley, Il., U.S.	278	41.33 N	87.53 W
Marley, N.J., U.S.	208	39.09 N	76.35 W
Marley Neck ▸¹	284b	39.12 N	76.33 W
Marlieux	62	46.02 N	5.05 E
Marlin	196	31.18 N	96.53 W
Mar-Lou-Ehmühle, Flughafen ⬥	263	51.35 N	7.10 E
Marlow, D.D.R.	54	54.09 N	12.34 E
Marlow, Eng., U.K.	42	51.35 N	0.48 W
Marlow, Ok., U.S.	196	34.39 N	97.57 W
Marlton	208	39.53 N	74.55 W
Marly	58	50.20 N	3.32 E
Marly, Forêt de ⬥⁴	261	48.50 N	2.03 E
Marly-la-Ville	261	49.02 N	2.31 E
Marly-le-Roi	261	48.52 N	2.05 E
Marma, Sve.	40	60.53 N	17.25 E
Marmagne	58	46.50 N	4.21 E
Marmande	32	44.30 N	0.10 E
Marmara Adası ı	130	40.38 N	27.37 E
Marmara Denizi (Sea of Marmara) ⬟²	130	40.40 N	28.15 E
Marmara Ereğlisi	130	40.58 N	27.57 E
Marmara Gölü ◠	130	38.37 N	28.02 E
Marmaris	130	36.51 N	28.16 E
Marmarth	198	46.18 N	103.54 W
Marmelos, Rio dos ≃	248	6.06 S	61.46 W
Marmet	214	38.14 N	81.34 W
Marmion Lake ◠¹	204	48.55 N	91.30 W
Marmirolo	66	45.13 N	10.43 E
Marmolada ∧	64	46.26 N	11.51 E
Marmora	212	44.29 N	77.41 W
Marmore ≃	68	42.33 N	12.43 E
Marmore, Cascata ⚡	66	42.33 N	12.43 E
Marmot Island ı	181	58.13 N	151.51 W
Marnay	58	47.17 N	5.46 E
Marne	50	49.00 N	4.10 E
Marne ◻⁵	50	48.55 N	4.10 E
Marne, B.R.D.	54	53.57 N	9.00 E
Marne, Mn., U.S.	190	45.18 N	95.56 W
Marne ≃	50	48.49 N	2.24 E
Marne à la Saône, Canal de la ☰	50	48.00 N	5.15 E
Marne au Rhin, Canal de la ☰	58	48.44 N	4.36 E

Column 5 (FRANÇAIS)

Nom	Page	Lat.	Long.
Maroala	157b	15.23 S	47.59 E
Maroantsetra	157b	15.26 S	49.44 E
Marobi Raghza	120	32.36 N	69.52 E
Maroc → Morocco ◻¹	148	32.00 N	5.00 W
Maroelaboom	156	19.15 S	18.53 E
Marofandilia	157b	20.07 S	44.34 E
Maroglio ⬥	70	37.03 N	14.15 E
Marokko → Morocco ◻¹	148	32.00 N	5.00 W
Marol ⬥⁸	272c	19.07 N	72.53 E
Marolambo	157b	20.02 S	48.07 E
Maroldsweisach	56	50.12 N	10.39 E
Marolles-en-Brie	261	48.44 N	2.33 E
Marolles-en-Hurepoix	261	48.34 N	2.18 E
Marolles-les-Braults	50	48.15 N	0.19 E
Maromandia	157b	14.13 S	48.08 E
Maromme	50	49.28 N	1.02 E
Maromokotro ∧	157b	14.01 S	48.59 E
Maromdera	154	18.11 S	31.36 E
Marone	64	45.44 N	10.05 E
Marong	171a	36.45 S	144.07 E
Maronghi Creek ≃	171a	26.58 S	152.22 E
Maroni (Marowijne) ≃	250	5.45 N	53.58 W
Maroon	171a	28.10 S	152.44 E
Maroon, Mount ∧	171a	28.13 S	152.44 E
Maroondah Aqueduct ☰¹	274b	37.42 S	145.01 E
Maros	112	5.00 S	119.34 E
Maros (Mureș) ≃	38	46.15 N	20.13 E
Maroseranana	157b	18.32 S	48.51 E
Marostica	64	45.45 N	11.39 E
Marosvásárhely → Tîrgu Mureș	38	46.33 N	24.33 E
Marotandrano	157b	16.10 S	48.50 E
Marotiri, Îles ıı	14	27.55 S	143.26 W
Marotta	66	43.46 N	13.08 E
Maroua	146	10.36 N	14.20 E
Maroubra	274a	33.57 S	151.16 E
Marouini ≃	250	3.18 N	54.04 W
Marovato, Madag.	157b	13.59 S	48.36 E
Marovato, Madag.	157b	15.48 S	48.05 E
Marovato, Madag.	157b	16.28 S	48.25 E
Marovoay	157b	16.06 S	46.39 E
Marovoay Nord	157b	16.57 S	44.34 E
Marowijne ≃	250	4.15 N	54.35 W
Marowijne (Maroni) ◻	250	5.45 N	53.58 W
Marpent	50	50.18 N	4.05 E
Marple	44	53.24 N	2.03 W
Marquand	224	45.04 N	122.41 W
Marquard	194	37.25 N	90.10 W
Marquard	158	28.54 S	27.28 E
Marquardt	54	52.27 N	12.57 E
Marquartstein	64	47.45 N	12.28 E
Marquesas Islands → Marquises, Îles ıı	6	9.00 S	139.30 W
Marquesas Keys ıı	220	24.34 N	82.08 W
Marquette, Ks., U.S.	198	38.33 N	97.50 W
Marquette, Mi., U.S.	190	46.32 N	87.23 W
Marquez, Mi., U.S.	190	46.32 N	87.23 W
Márquez, Perú	286d	11.57 S	77.08 W
Márquez, Tx., U.S.	222	31.14 N	96.15 W
Marquion	50	50.13 N	3.05 E
Marquise	241k	12.06 N	61.37 W
Marquis, Cape ▸	241f	14.03 N	60.54 W
Marquise	50	50.49 N	1.42 E
Marquises, Îles (Marquesas Islands) ıı	6	9.00 S	139.30 W
Marrabel	168b	34.08 S	138.53 E
Marra Creek ≃	166	30.05 S	147.05 E
Marradi	66	44.04 N	11.37 E
Marradong	168a	32.52 S	116.27 E
Marrah, Jabal ∧	140	13.04 N	24.21 E
Marra Hills ⬟²	261	27.33 E
Marrakech → Marrakech ◻⁴	148	31.38 N	8.00 W
Marrakech ◻⁴	148	31.30 N	8.05 W
Marramarra National Park ⬥	170	33.32 S	151.04 E
Marrawah	166	40.56 S	144.41 E
Marrero	194	29.39 S	138.04 E
Marrickville	274a	33.55 S	151.09 E
Marroú	156	18.20 S	35.56 E
Marrowstone Island ı	224	48.04 N	122.41 W
Marrubiu	71	39.45 N	8.38 E
Marruecos → Morocco ◻¹	148	32.00 N	5.00 W
Marrupa	154	13.08 S	37.30 E
Marsa	214	40.41 N	80.00 W
Marsā al-Burayqah	146	30.25 N	19.34 E
Marsabit	154	2.20 N	38.00 E
Marsabit National Park ⬥	154	2.20 N	38.00 E
Marsac-en-Livradois	62	45.23 N	3.44 E
Marsa Fatma → Ahmad Hashibb	144	30.25 N	31.15 E
Marsal	56	48.49 N	6.36 E
Marsā Matrūh	140	31.21 N	27.14 E
Marsā Matrūh ◻⁶	140	30.30 N	27.00 E
Marsala	70	37.48 N	12.26 E
Marsannay-la-Côte	58	47.16 N	4.59 E
Marsanne	62	44.39 N	4.52 E
Marsassum	150	12.50 N	16.00 W
Marsberg	54	51.27 N	8.51 E
Marsciano	66	42.54 N	12.20 E
Marsden, Austl.	166	33.45 S	147.32 E
Marsden, Eng., U.K.	44	53.36 N	1.56 W
Marsden, Point ▸	168b	35.33 S	137.56 E
Marsden ⬥⁸	275b	43.46 N	79.22 W
Marseille	62	43.18 N	5.24 E
Marseille-Marignane, Aéroport de ⬥	62	43.27 N	5.13 E
Marseilles, Il., U.S.	216	41.19 N	88.42 W
Marseilles, Oh., U.S.	214	40.43 N	83.23 W
Marsella → Marseille	62	43.18 N	5.24 E
Marsfjället ∧	24	65.05 N	15.28 E
Marseilles → Marseille	274a	33.47 S	151.07 E
Marshall, Liber.	150	6.08 N	10.23 W
Marshall, Ar., U.S.	194	35.54 N	92.37 W
Marshall, Il., U.S.	216	39.23 N	87.41 W
Marshall, Mi., U.S.	216	42.16 N	84.57 W
Marshall, Mn., U.S.	198	44.27 N	95.47 W
Marshall, Mo., U.S.	219	39.07 N	93.11 W
Marshall, N.C., U.S.	192	35.47 N	82.41 W
Marshall, Tx., U.S.	196	32.32 N	94.22 W
Marshall ≃	166	22.59 S	136.59 E
Marshall Bennett Islands ıı	162	32.50 S	151.50 E
Marshallberg	192	34.43 N	76.30 W
Marshall Gold Discovery State Historical Park ⬥	226	38.48 N	120.53 W
Marshall Hall	218	38.41 N	77.06 W
Marshall Islands ◻¹	10	9.00 N	168.00 E
Marshall Islands ıı	10	9.00 N	168.00 E
Marshallton, De., U.S.	208	39.43 N	75.39 W
Marshallton, Pa., U.S.	208	40.02 N	76.33 W
Marshallton, Pa., U.S.	214	40.12 N	78.19 W
Marshallville, Oh., U.S.	214	40.54 N	81.44 W
Marshbrook	279b	40.19 N	79.37 W
Marshfield, Austl.	32	48.49 N	2.24 E

Column 6 (PORTUGUÊS)

Nome	Página	Lat.	Long.
Marina	226	36.41 N	121.48 W
Marina ⬥⁸	282	37.47 N	122.27 W
Marina del Rey	282	33.50 N	118.25 W
Marina del Rey ◠	280	33.58 N	118.27 W
Marina di Andora	62	43.57 N	8.08 E
Marina di Campo	66	42.44 N	10.14 E
Marina di Carrara	66	44.02 N	10.02 E
Marina di Caronia	66	43.18 N	10.29 E
Marina di Cecina	66		
Marina di Gioiosa Ionica	68	38.18 N	16.20 E
Marina di Grosseto	66	42.43 N	10.59 E
Marina di Massa	66	44.00 N	10.06 E
Marina di Minturno	68	41.16 N	13.45 E
Marina di Orosei	71	40.22 N	9.43 E
Marina di Palma ⬥⁸	70	37.11 N	13.43 E
Marina di Pietrasanta	64	43.56 N	10.12 E
Marina di Pisa	66	43.40 N	10.16 E
Marina di Ragusa	70	36.47 N	14.33 E
Marina di Ravenna	68	44.29 N	12.17 E
Marina Fall ㄴ	246	5.22 N	59.29 W
Marine City	282	37.52 N	122.21 W
Marinduque ı	116	13.25 N	121.55 E
Marinduque Island ı	116	13.24 N	121.58 E
Marine City	216	42.43 N	82.30 W
Marine Ehrenmal ⬥	54	54.23 N	10.15 E
Marineland of the Pacific ⬥³	228	33.44 N	118.24 W
Marinella	70	37.35 N	12.50 E
Marine Museum v	280	33.43 N	118.17 W
Marine Park ⬥	283	42.20 N	71.01 W
Marine Parkway Bridge ⬥⁵	276	40.34 N	73.53 W
Mariners Museum ⬥	208	37.03 N	76.30 W
Marines	50	49.09 N	1.59 E
Marinette	190	45.06 N	87.37 W
Marine World/Africa USA ⬥	282	37.32 N	122.16 W
Maringá	252	23.25 S	51.55 W
Maringa ≃	152	1.14 N	19.48 E
Maringouin	194	30.29 N	91.31 W
Maringué	154	17.55 S	34.24 E
Marinha Grande	34	39.45 N	8.56 W
Marin Mall ⬥	282	37.56 N	122.31 W
Marino, It.	66	41.46 N	12.39 E
Marino, Vanuatu	175f	15.00 S	168.09 E
Marinovka, S.S.S.R.	80	48.41 N	43.49 E
Marinovka, S.S.S.R.	83	47.54 N	38.51 E
Marin Peninsula ▸¹	282	37.51 N	122.31 W
Marinskij Posad	80	56.07 N	47.43 E
Marinwood	282	38.02 N	122.32 W
Mario, Monte ∧²	267a	41.55 N	12.27 E
Marion, Austl.	168b	35.01 S	138.34 E
Marion, Al., U.S.	194	32.37 N	87.19 W
Marion, Ar., U.S.	194	35.12 N	90.11 W
Marion, Ct., U.S.	207	41.35 N	72.54 W
Marion, Il., U.S.	194	37.43 N	88.55 W
Marion, Ia., U.S.	216	40.33 N	85.39 W
Marion, Ia., U.S.	190	42.02 N	91.35 W
Marion, Ky., U.S.	194	37.19 N	88.04 W
Marion, La., U.S.	194	32.54 N	92.14 W
Marion, Ma., U.S.	207	41.42 N	70.45 W
Marion, N.Y., U.S.	210	43.08 N	77.11 W
Marion, N.C., U.S.	192	35.41 N	82.00 W
Marion, N.D., U.S.	198	46.36 N	98.19 W
Marion, Oh., U.S.	214	40.35 N	83.07 W
Marion, S.C., U.S.	192	34.10 N	79.24 W
Marion, S.D., U.S.	198	43.25 N	97.15 W
Marion, Va., U.S.	192	36.50 N	81.30 W
Marion, Wi., U.S.	190	44.40 N	88.53 W
Marion ◻⁶, Fl., U.S.	220	29.00 N	82.03 W
Marion ◻⁶, Il., U.S.	219	38.38 N	88.57 W
Marion ◻⁶, In., U.S.	218	39.46 N	86.09 W
Marion ◻⁶, Ks., U.S.	219	38.38 N	91.37 W
Marion ◻⁶, Oh., U.S.	214	40.35 N	83.08 W
Marion ◻⁶, Or., U.S.	224	45.06 N	122.47 W
Marion, Lake ◠	192	33.30 N	80.25 W
Marion Bay ◠	166	42.48 S	147.55 E
Marion Center	214	40.46 N	79.03 W
Marion Downs	166	23.22 S	139.39 E
Marion Heights	210	40.48 N	76.28 W
Marion Hill	279b	40.41 N	80.16 W
Marion Junction	194	32.26 N	87.14 W
Marion Lake ◠	224	44.34 N	121.46 W
Marion Reef ⬥²	166	19.10 S	152.17 E
Marion Station	208	38.02 N	75.45 W
Marióplis	252	26.20 S	52.33 W
Mariópolis	252	26.20 S	52.33 W
Maripa	246	7.26 N	65.09 W
Maripá de Minas	256	21.48 S	42.56 W
Maripasoula	250	3.40 N	54.02 W
Mariposa	226	37.29 N	119.57 W
Mariposa ◻⁶	226	37.14 N	120.03 W
Mariposa Creek ≃	226	37.12 N	120.46 W
Mariposa Slough ≃	282	37.54 N	122.07 W
Mariquita, Cerro ∧	234	23.15 N	98.22 W
Marisa	112	0.28 N	121.56 E
Marisa ◻⁶	112	0.28 N	121.56 E
Mariscal Estigarribia	252	22.02 S	60.38 W
Marisco, Ponta do ▸	287a	23.01 S	43.17 W
Mariscos	236	15.21 N	89.31 W
Marissa	219	38.15 N	89.45 W
Maritime Alps (Alpes Maritimes) (Alpi Marittime) ∧	62	44.15 N	7.10 E
Maritime, Alpes → Maritime Alps ∧	62	44.15 N	7.10 E
Maritsa → Marica	38	42.02 N	25.50 E
Mari-Turek	80	56.47 N	49.36 E
Maritzburg → Pietermaritzburg	158	29.37 S	30.16 E
Mariupol' (Ždanov)	83	47.06 N	37.33 E
Mariusa, Caño ≃¹	241r	9.66 N	61.26 W
Mariusa, Isla ı	241r	9.35 N	61.13 W
Marīvān	128	35.31 N	46.10 E
Marivelles	116	14.26 N	120.29 E
Marjanovka, S.S.S.R.	82	54.58 N	72.38 E
Marjanovka, S.S.S.R.	83	48.31 N	39.58 E
Marjina Gorka	76	53.30 N	28.09 E
Marjuni	85	43.31 N	54.67 E
Mark ≃, Austl.	168b	34.53 S	139.18 E
Mark ≃, Eur.	32	48.49 N	2.24 E

ENGLISH

Name	Page	Lat.°′	Long.°′

DEUTSCH

Name	Seite	Breite°′	Länge°′ E = Ost

Marsh Creek ≃, Ca., U.S. · 282 · 37.53 N 121.49 W
Marsh Creek ≃, Mi., U.S. · 281 · 42.06 N 83.13 W
Marsh Creek ≃, Pa., U.S. · 214 · 41.03 N 77.36 W
Marsh Creek ≃, Pa., U.S. · 285 · 40.03 N 75.43 W
Marsh Creek ≃, Wi., U.S. · 216 · 42.13 N 89.04 W
Marsh Creek Lake ⊜¹ · 208 · 40.04 N 75.44 W
Marshes Creek ≃ · 276 · 40.36 N 74.13 W
Marshfield, Eng., U.K. · 42 · 51.28 N 2.19 W
Marshfield, Ma., U.S. · 207 · 42.05 N 70.42 W
Marshfield, Mo., U.S. · 194 · 37.20 N 92.54 W
Marshfield, Wi., U.S. · 190 · 44.40 N 90.10 W
Marshfield Airport ≈ · 283 · 42.06 N 70.40 W
Marshfield Center · 283 · 42.07 N 70.43 W
Marshfield Hills · 207 · 42.08 N 70.44 W
Marsh Harbour · 238 · 26.33 N 77.03 W
Mars Hill · 210 · 41.29 N 78.58 W
Mars Hill, In., U.S. · 218 · 39.43 N 86.09 W
Mars Hill, Me., U.S. · 186 · 46.30 N 67.52 W
Mars Hill, N.C., U.S. · 192 · 35.49 N 82.32 W
Marsh Island · 194 · 29.35 N 91.53 W
Marsh Lake ⊜ · 180 · 60.25 N 134.18 W
Marsh Peak ∧ · 200 · 40.43 N 109.50 W
Marshside · 262 · 53.40 N 2.58 W
Marshville · 192 · 34.59 N 80.22 W
Marshyhope Creek ≃ · 208 · 38.32 N 75.45 W
Marsica ⬩¹ · 66 · 41.50 N 13.45 E
Marsico Nuovo · 68 · 40.25 N 15.44 E
Marsico Vetere · 68 · 40.23 N 15.49 E
Marsillargues · 62 · 43.40 N 4.11 E
Marsimang, Tanjung ⟩ · 164 · 3.27 S 130.49 E
Marsing · 202 · 43.32 N 116.48 W
Marske-by-the-Sea · 44 · 54.36 N 1.01 W
Mars-la-Tour · 56 · 49.06 S 5.54 E
Marson · 56 · 48.55 N 4.32 E
Marssum · 52 · 53.12 N 5.42 E
Märsta · 40 · 59.37 N 17.51 E
Marstal · 41 · 54.51 N 10.31 E
Marsteller · 214 · 40.39 N 78.48 W
Märstetten · 58 · 47.36 N 9.04 E
Marston · 262 · 53.16 N 1.17 W
Marston Moor ⬩ · 44 · 53.57 N 1.17 W
Marston Moor Battlesite ⬩ · 44 · 53.57 N 1.17 W
Marstons Mills · 207 · 41.39 N 70.25 W
Marstrand · 26 · 57.53 N 11.35 E
Marsyangdĭ ≃ · 124 · 28.05 N 84.28 E
Mart · 222 · 31.32 N 96.50 W
Marta · 66 · 42.32 N 11.55 E
Marta ≃ · 66 · 42.14 N 11.42 E
Martaban · 110 · 16.32 N 97.37 E
Martaban, Gulf of c · 110 · 16.30 N 97.00 E
Martap · 152 · 6.54 N 13.03 E
Martapura, Indon. · 112 · 3.25 S 114.51 E
Martapura, Indon. · 112 · 4.19 S 104.22 E
Marte · 146 · 12.22 N 13.51 E
Marteg ≃ · 42 · 52.20 N 3.33 W
Martel, Fr. · 34 · 44.56 N 1.37 E
Martel, Oh., U.S. · 214 · 40.40 N 82.55 W
Martelange · 56 · 49.50 N 5.44 E
Martell · 226 · 38.22 N 120.48 W
Martello · 64 · 46.34 N 10.47 E
Martello, Val V · 64 · 46.31 N 10.45 E
Martemjanovskij · 86 · 55.54 N 80.22 E
Marten ⬩⁸ · 263 · 51.31 N 7.23 E
Marten Lake ⊜ · 190 · 46.42 N 79.41 W
Marten Mountain ∧ · 182 · 55.28 N 114.43 W
Marte R. Gomez, Presa ⊜¹ · 196 · 26.10 N 99.00 W
Martha · 52 · 52.52 N 9.04 E
Marthaguy Creek ≃ · 166 · 30.16 S 147.35 E
Martha Lake · 224 · 47.51 N 122.20 W
Marthall · 262 · 53.17 N 2.18 W
Martham · 42 · 52.42 N 1.38 E
Marthasville · 219 · 38.37 N 91.03 W
Martha's Vineyard I · 207 · 41.25 N 70.40 W
Marti, Cuba · 240p · 21.09 N 77.27 W
Marti, Cuba · 240p · 22.57 N 80.55 W
Marti, Pico ∧ · 240p · 20.01 N 76.35 W
Martignacco · 64 · 46.05 N 13.08 E
Martignat · 58 · 46.08 N 5.36 E
Martigny · 58 · 48.06 N 7.04 E
Martigny-les-Bains · 58 · 48.06 N 5.49 E
Martigues · 62 · 43.24 N 5.03 E
Martil · 34 · 35.37 N 5.17 W
Martim Francisco · 256 · 22.31 S 46.57 W
Martin, Česko. · 30 · 49.05 N 18.55 E
Martin, Ky., U.S. · 192 · 37.34 N 82.45 W
Martin, Mi., U.S. · 216 · 42.32 N 85.38 W
Martin, N.D., U.S. · 198 · 47.49 N 100.06 W
Martin, Oh., U.S. · 214 · 41.33 N 83.20 W
Martin, S.D., U.S. · 198 · 43.10 N 101.43 W
Martin, Tn., U.S. · 194 · 36.20 N 88.51 W
Martin ⬩⁶ · 220 · 27.00 N 80.31 W
Martin ≃ · 34 · 41.18 N 0.19 W
Martín, Arroyo ≃ · 288 · 34.51 S 58.04 W
Martin, Isle I · 46 · 57.55 N 5.14 W
Martina · 68 · 46.53 N 10.28 E
Martina Franca · 68 · 40.42 N 17.21 E
Martinborough · 172 · 41.13 S 175.28 E
Martin Chico, Punta ⟩ · 288 · 34.10 S 58.13 W
Martindale · 196 · 29.50 N 97.51 W
Martindale Creek ≃, Austl. · 170 · 32.32 S 150.42 E
Martindale Creek ≃, In., U.S. · 218 · 39.48 N 86.09 W
Martindale Pond · 284a · 43.11 N 79.16 W
Martin-Église · 50 · 49.54 N 1.09 E
Martinengo · 62 · 45.34 N 9.46 E
Martineşti · 38 · 45.30 N 27.18 E
Martínez, Ca., U.S. · 226 · 38.01 N 122.07 W
Martínez, Ga., U.S. · 192 · 33.31 N 82.04 W
Martínez ⬩⁸ · 34 · 34.29 S 58.30 W
Martínez de la Torre · 234 · 20.04 N 97.03 W
Martín García, Isla I · 286 · 34.13 S 58.15 W
Martinho Campos · 255 · 19.20 S 45.13 W
Martinica → Martinique □² · 240e · 14.40 N 61.00 W
Martini Creek ≃ · 282 · 37.33 N 122.31 W
Martinique □², N.A. · 240e · 14.40 N 61.00 W
Martinique □², N.A. · 240e · 14.40 N 61.00 W
Martin Lake ⊜¹, Tx., U.S. · 194 · 32.50 N 94.35 W
Martin Marietta Corporation ⬩³ · 284b · 39.20 N 76.26 W
Martinniemi · 26 · 65.13 N 25.18 E
Martinópole · 250 · 3.13 S 40.41 W
Martin Peninsula ⟩¹ · 74 · 74.25 S 114.10 W
Martín Pérez · 285b · 23.07 N 82.20 W
Martin Point ⟩ · 180 · 70.08 N 143.16 W
Martin Run ≃ · 279a · 41.01 N 79.55 W
Martins · 250 · 6.05 S 37.55 W
Martinsberg · 68 · 48.23 N 15.10 E
Martins Brook ≃ · 283 · 42.34 N 71.06 W
Martinsburg, Mo., U.S. · 219 · 39.06 N 91.38 W
Martinsburg, N.Y., U.S. · 212 · 43.44 N 75.28 W
Martinsburg, Pa., U.S. · 214 · 40.18 N 78.20 W
Martinsburg, W.V., U.S. · 188 · 39.27 N 77.57 W
Martins Creek · 285 · 40.46 N 75.11 W
Martins Creek ≃ · 208 · 41.37 N 75.46 W
Martinscroft · 262 · 53.24 N 2.31 W
Martins Ferry · 214 · 40.05 N 80.43 W
Martins Mills · 222 · 32.05 N 95.40 W
Martins Pond ⊜ · 283 · 42.36 N 71.08 W
Martinstal · 58 · 49.48 N 7.32 E
Martinsthal · 56 · 50.04 N 8.17 E
Martinsville, Austl. · 170 · 33.03 S 151.25 E
Martinsville, Il., U.S. · 194 · 39.20 N 87.52 W
Martinsville, In., U.S. · 218 · 39.25 N 86.25 W
Martinsville, N.J., U.S. · 276 · 40.36 N 74.34 W
Martinsville, Oh., U.S. · 218 · 39.19 N 83.48 W
Martinsville, Va., U.S. · 192 · 36.41 N 79.52 W
Martinton · 216 · 40.55 N 87.44 W
Martintown · 206 · 45.09 N 74.42 W
Martin Van Buren National Historic Site ⬩ · 210 · 42.22 N 73.43 W
Martin Vaz, Ilhas II · 244 · 20.30 S 28.51 W
Martis · 71 · 56.34 N 31.55 E
Martisovo · 76 · 56.34 N 31.55 E
Martock · 42 · 50.59 N 2.46 W
Martofte · 41 · 55.33 N 10.40 E
Marton, N.Z. · 172 · 40.05 S 175.23 E
Marton, Eng., U.K. · 262 · 53.12 N 2.13 W
Martorell · 34 · 41.28 N 1.56 E
Martorelles de Baix · 266d · 41.32 N 2.14 E
Martos · 34 · 37.43 N 3.58 W
Martovaja · 78 · 49.57 N 36.57 E
Martre, Lac la ⊜ · 176 · 63.15 N 117.55 W
Martti · 24 · 67.28 N 28.28 E
Martūbah · 146 · 32.35 N 22.46 E
Martuk · 86 · 50.46 N 56.31 E
Martuni, S.S.S.R. · 84 · 39.55 N 47.06 E
Martuni, S.S.S.R. · 84 · 40.08 N 45.19 E
Martvila · 210 · 43.17 N 76.38 W
Martynoviči · 78 · 51.17 N 29.37 E
Martynovka · 78 · 49.38 N 31.18 E
Martynovo · 80 · 50.43 N 50.23 E
Maru · 150 · 12.22 N 6.22 E
Marudi · 112 · 4.11 N 114.19 E
Marudu, Telukan c · 112 · 6.45 N 116.55 E
Marugame · 96 · 34.17 N 133.47 E
Maruggio · 68 · 40.19 N 17.34 E
Maruia · 172 · 42.11 S 172.13 E
Maruia ≃ · 172 · 41.47 S 172.12 E
Maruim · 250 · 10.45 S 37.05 W
Maruko ≃ · 96 · 36.19 N 138.16 E
Marula · 154 · 20.26 S 28.06 E
Marulan · 170 · 34.43 S 150.00 E
Marulan South · 170 · 34.46 S 150.02 E
Marum · 52 · 53.08 N 6.16 E
Marum, Mont ∧ · 175f · 16.15 S 168.07 E
Maruoka · 96 · 36.09 N 136.16 E
Marúp · 41 · 55.11 N 8.32 E
Marungu · 154 · 3.44 S 30.48 E
Marungu ⬩¹ · 154 · 7.42 S 30.00 E
Maruoka · 96 · 36.09 N 136.16 E

ESPAÑOL

Nombre	Página	Lat.°′	Long.°′ W = Oeste
Matutum, Mount ∧	116	6.22 N	125.05 E
Matuzaka → Matsusaka	94	34.34 N	136.32 E
Matvejevka	80	53.32 N	53.29 E
Matvejev Kurgan	83	47.35 N	38.52 E
Matvejevo, S.S.S.R.	76	58.38 N	43.30 E
Matvejevo, S.S.S.R.	86	57.47 N	57.51 E
Mátyásföld ◆[8]	264c	47.31 N	19.13 E
Matyra ≃	76	52.38 N	39.38 E
Matyševo	80	50.49 N	44.12 E
Mau	124	25.17 N	81.23 E
Maú (Ireng) ≃	246	3.33 N	59.51 W
Mauá, Bra.	256	23.40 S	46.27 W
Maúa, Moç.	154	13.51 S	37.10 E
Mauá □[7]	287b	23.40 S	46.27 W
Mau Aimma	124	25.42 N	81.55 E
Mauban	116	14.12 N	121.44 E
Maubara	112	8.37 S	125.12 E
Maubeuge	50	50.17 N	3.58 E
Mauchamps	261	48.32 N	2.12 E
Mauchline	46	55.31 N	4.24 W
Maud, Scot., U.K.	46	57.31 N	2.06 W
Maud, Mo., U.S.	219	39.37 N	92.15 W
Maud, Oh., U.S.	218	39.21 N	84.23 W
Maud, Ok., U.S.	196	35.08 N	96.46 W
Maud, Tx., U.S.	194	33.20 N	94.21 W
Maud, Point ≻	162	23.06 S	113.45 E
Maudaha	124	25.41 N	80.07 E
Maude	166	34.28 S	144.18 E
Maudétour-en-Vexin	261	49.06 N	1.47 E
Mau-é-ele	156	24.21 S	34.07 E
Mauensee	58	47.10 N	8.04 E
Mauer ◆[8]	264b	48.09 N	16.16 E
Mauerbach	264b	48.15 N	16.10 E
Mauerbach ≃	264b	48.12 N	16.14 E
Mauerkirchen	60	48.11 N	13.08 E
Maués	250	3.24 S	57.42 W
Maués-Açu ≃	246	3.22 S	57.44 W
Maug ≃	116	8.20 N	125.53 E
Mauganj	124	24.41 N	81.53 E
Mauga Silisili ∧	175a	13.35 S	172.27 W
Maughold	44	54.18 N	4.17 W
Maug Islands II	108	20.01 N	145.13 E
Mauguio	62	43.37 N	4.01 E
Mauguio, Étang de ⊂	62	43.35 N	4.02 E
Maui □[6]	229a	20.53 N	156.30 W
Maui I	229a	20.45 N	156.15 W
Mauk	115a	6.04 S	106.30 E
Mauke I	14	20.09 S	157.23 W
Maulbach	56	50.43 N	9.04 E
Maulbronn	56	49.00 N	8.49 E
Maulde	50	50.30 N	3.26 E
Mauldin	192	34.46 N	82.18 W
Mauldre ≃	261	48.58 N	1.49 E
Maule	50	48.55 N	1.51 E
Maule □[4]	252	35.30 S	71.30 W
Maule ≃	252	35.19 S	72.25 W
Maule, Laguna del ⊜	252	36.04 S	70.30 W
Mauléon	32	46.56 N	0.45 W
Mauléon-Licharre	32	43.14 N	0.53 W
Maulette	261	48.48 N	1.37 E
Maullín	254	41.38 S	73.37 W
Maulvi Bāzār	120	24.29 N	91.47 E
Maumaupaki ∧	172	36.58 S	175.35 E
Maumee	214	41.33 N	83.39 W
Maumee ≃	216	41.42 N	83.28 W
Maumee Bay ⊂	214	41.43 N	83.26 W
Maumelle, Lake ⊜[1]	194	34.55 N	92.40 W
Maumere	115b	8.37 S	122.14 E
Maun	156	20.00 S	23.25 E
Maunabo	240m	18.01 N	65.54 W
Mauna Kea ∧[1]	229d	19.50 N	155.28 W
Maunaloa	229a	21.08 N	157.13 W
Mauna Loa ∧[1]	229d	19.29 N	155.36 W
Maunalua Bay ⊂	229c	21.17 N	157.44 W
Maunath Bhanjan	124	25.57 N	83.33 E
Maunatlala	156	22.32 S	27.28 E
Maunesha ≃	216	43.13 N	88.57 W
Maungahaumi ∧	172	38.18 S	177.40 E
Maunga Roa ∧	174k	21.13 S	159.48 W
Maungatapere	172	35.45 S	174.12 E
Maungaturoto	172	36.06 S	174.22 E
Maungdaw	110	20.50 N	92.21 E
Maungmagan	110	14.09 N	98.06 E
Maungu	154	3.33 S	38.45 E
Maunoir, Lac ⊜	180	67.30 N	125.00 W
Maupihaa I[1]	14	16.50 S	153.55 W
Maupin	224	45.10 N	121.04 W
Maur	123	30.05 N	75.15 E
Mau Rānīpur	124	25.15 N	79.08 E
Maurecourt	261	49.00 N	2.04 E
Maure-de-Bretagne	32	47.54 N	1.59 W
Mauregard	261	49.02 N	2.35 E
Maurepas	261	48.45 N	1.55 E
Maurepas, Lake ⊜	194	30.15 N	90.30 W
Maures ⋏	62	43.16 N	6.23 E
Mauretanien → Mauritania □[1]	134	20.00 N	12.00 W
Mauri ≃	248	17.18 S	68.41 W
Mauria, Passo della)(	64	46.27 N	12.31 E
Mauriac	32	45.13 N	2.20 E
Maurice (Île) → Mauritius □[1]	157c	20.17 S	57.33 E
Maurice ≃	208	39.13 N	75.02 W
Maurice, Lake ⊜	162	29.28 S	130.58 E
Maurice K. Goddard State Park ♠	214	41.23 N	81.10 W
Mauricetown	208	39.17 N	74.58 W
Mauriceville	172	40.47 S	175.42 E
Mauricio → Mauritius □[1]	157c	20.17 S	57.33 E
Maurienne ∨	62	45.13 N	6.30 E
Mauritania (Mauritanie) □[1]	134	20.00 N	12.00 W
Mauritanie → Mauritania □[1]	134	20.00 N	12.00 W
Mauriti	250	7.23 S	38.46 W
Mauritius □[1], Afr.	138	20.17 S	57.33 E
Mauritius □[1], Afr.	157c	20.17 S	57.33 E
Mauritius I	157c	20.17 S	57.33 E
Mauron	32	48.05 N	2.18 W
Maurs	32	44.43 N	2.11 E
Maurui	154	5.07 S	38.23 E
Maury ≃	192	37.37 N	79.27 W
Maury Channel ⊔	176	75.44 N	94.40 W
Maury Island ≻[1]	224	47.20 N	122.24 W
Maussane	62	43.43 N	4.48 E
Mauston	190	43.47 N	90.04 W
Mautala	126	22.25 N	89.05 E
Mautau, Pointe ≻	174x	9.42 S	138.58 W
Mautern an der Donau	61	48.24 N	15.35 E
Mauterndorf	64	47.08 N	13.40 E
Mautern in Steiermark	61	47.24 N	14.50 E
Mauth	60	48.53 N	13.35 E
Mauthausen	61	48.14 N	14.32 E
Mauthen	64	46.40 N	13.00 E
Mauvais Coulee ∨	198	48.21 N	99.06 W
Mauvaise Terre Creek ≃	219	39.43 N	90.38 W
Mauvaise Terre Lake ⊜[1]	219	39.42 N	90.12 W
Mauvezin	32	43.44 N	0.55 E
Mava	164	6.50 S	141.25 E
Mavá ≃	246	0.44 N	69.30 W
Mavaca ≃	246	2.31 N	65.11 W
Mavanza	156	22.43 S	35.08 E
Māvelikara	122	9.16 N	76.33 E
Maverick	200	33.43 N	109.32 W
Mavinga	152	15.50 S	20.21 E
Mavita	156	19.33 S	33.10 E
Mavonde	156	18.32 S	33.02 E
Mavuradona Mountains ⋏	154	16.30 S	31.20 E
Mawa	154	2.43 N	26.42 E
Mawai	114	1.52 N	103.57 E
Ma Wan I	271d	22.21 N	114.03 E
Mawāna	124	29.06 N	77.55 E
Mawangkanli Shan ∧	120	34.19 N	80.03 E
Mawangtang	106	30.42 N	120.42 E
Mawasangka	112	5.17 S	122.18 E
Mawchi	110	18.49 N	97.09 E

FRANÇAIS

Nom	Page	Lat.°′	Long.°′ W = Ouest
Maw-daung Pass)(	110	11.47 N	99.39 E
Mawdesley	262	53.38 N	2.46 W
Mawdesley Lake ⊜	184	54.01 N	100.39 W
Mawgan	42	50.06 N	5.06 W
Mawi	272a	28.39 N	77.25 E
Mawiwi	154	3.06 N	27.40 E
Māwiyah	144	13.35 N	44.21 E
Mawjib, Wādī al- ∨	132	31.28 N	35.34 E
Mawkhi	110	16.17 N	98.53 E
Mawlaik	110	23.38 N	94.24 E
Mawlamyaing → Mawlamyine	110	16.30 N	97.38 E
Mawlamyine (Moulmein)	110	16.30 N	97.38 E
Mawr, Wādī ∨	144	15.41 N	42.42 E
Mawshij	144	13.43 N	43.17 E
Mawson ⊌[3]	9	67.40 S	63.43 E
Mawson Escarpment ⫠[4]	9	73.05 S	68.10 E
Mawson Peninsula ≻[1]	9	68.35 S	154.11 E
Maw Taung ∧	110	11.39 N	99.35 E
Mawuba	102	29.50 N	108.11 E
Max	198	47.49 N	101.17 W
Maxaranguape	250	5.31 S	35.16 W
Maxatawny	208	40.33 N	75.41 W
Maxcanú	232	20.35 N	89.59 W
Maxéville	58	48.43 N	6.10 E
Maxglan, Flughafen ⊠	64	47.48 N	13.02 E
Maxhütte Haidhof	60	49.12 N	12.05 E
Maxiang	100	24.41 N	118.15 E
Maximo	214	40.53 N	81.11 W
Maximo Paz	258	34.56 S	58.37 W
Maxinkuckee, Lake ⊜	216	41.12 N	86.24 W
Maxixe	156	23.51 S	35.21 E
Maxon Creek ≃	196	29.53 N	102.24 W
Maxton	192	34.44 N	79.20 W
Maxville	206	45.17 N	74.51 W
Maxwell, Ca., U.S.	226	39.16 N	122.11 W
Maxwell, In., U.S.	218	39.51 N	85.46 W
Maxwell, Ia., U.S.	190	41.53 N	93.23 W
Maxwell, Ne., U.S.	198	41.04 N	100.31 W
Maxwell, N.M., U.S.	196	36.32 N	104.32 W
Maxwell, Tx., U.S.	222	29.53 N	97.48 W
Maxwell Air Force Base ■	194	32.23 N	86.21 W
Maxwell Bay ⊂	176	74.35 N	89.00 W
May	196	31.59 N	98.55 W
May ≃, Austl.	162	17.07 S	123.50 E
May ≃, Ab., Can.	182	55.43 N	111.22 W
May ≃, Pap. N. Gui.	164	4.35 S	141.35 E
May, Cape ≻[1]	208	38.58 N	74.55 W
May, Isle of I	46	56.11 N	2.34 W
May, Mount ∧	182	54.02 N	119.58 W
Maya, Pulau I	112	1.10 S	109.35 E
May Aché	146	12.00 N	15.44 E
Mayaguana I	238	22.23 N	72.57 W
Mayaguana Passage ⊔	238	22.32 N	73.15 W
Mayagüez	240m	18.12 N	67.09 W
Mayagüez, Aeropuerto ⊠	240m	18.15 N	67.09 W
Mayagüez, Bahía de ⊂	240m	18.12 N	67.10 W
Mayahi	150	13.58 N	7.40 E
Mayajigua	240p	22.14 N	79.04 W
Mayaka	152	5.17 N	16.52 E
Mayala	273b	4.21 S	15.09 E
Mayales, Punta ≻	236	11.52 N	85.26 W
Mayama	152	3.51 S	14.54 E
Mayamba	152	4.46 S	16.52 E
Mayāmey	128	36.24 N	55.42 E
Maya Mountains ⋏	232	16.40 N	88.50 W
Mayang	102	27.41 N	109.35 E
Mayang-do I	98	40.00 N	128.12 E
Mayantoc	116	15.37 N	120.23 E
Mayao	106	30.50 N	120.23 E
Mayapan ⊥	232	20.38 N	89.27 W
Māyāpur	272b	22.27 N	88.08 E
Mayarí	240p	20.40 N	75.41 W
Mayarí Arriba	240p	20.25 N	75.32 W
Mayaro Bay ⊂	241r	10.15 N	60.58 W
Maya-san ∧	96	34.44 N	135.12 E
Maybee	216	42.00 N	83.30 W
Maybeury	192	37.22 N	81.22 W
Maybole	44	55.21 N	4.41 W
Maybrook	210	41.29 N	74.13 W
Maychew	144	13.02 N	39.34 E
Maydelle	222	31.48 N	95.18 W
Maydena	166	42.55 S	146.30 E
Maydh	144	11.00 N	47.07 E
Maydī	144	16.20 N	42.46 E
Maydolong	116	11.30 N	125.30 E
Maydūm	142	29.22 N	31.10 E
Mayen	56	50.19 N	7.13 E
Mayence → Mainz	56	50.01 N	8.16 E
Mayenne	32	48.18 N	0.37 W
Mayenne □[5]	32	48.05 N	0.40 W
Mayenne ≃	32	47.30 N	0.33 W
Mayer	200	34.23 N	112.14 W
Mayerling	61	48.03 N	16.06 E
Mayersville	194	32.54 N	91.03 W
Mayerthorpe	182	53.57 N	115.08 W
Mayet	50	47.46 N	0.17 E
Mayfair ◆[8], S. Afr.	273d	26.12 S	28.01 E
Mayfair ◆[8], Pa., U.S.	285	40.02 N	75.03 W
Mayfield, N.Z.	172	43.49 S	171.25 E
Mayfield, Eng., U.K.	42	51.01 N	0.15 E
Mayfield, Eng., U.K.	44	53.01 N	1.45 W
Mayfield, Scot., U.K.	46	55.52 N	3.02 W
Mayfield, In., U.S.	218	40.11 N	85.21 W
Mayfield, Ky., U.S.	194	36.44 N	88.38 W
Mayfield, N.Y., U.S.	210	43.06 N	74.15 W
Mayfield, Oh., U.S.	279a	41.33 N	81.26 W
Mayfield, Pa., U.S.	210	41.32 N	75.32 W
Mayfield, Ut,. U.S.	200	39.06 N	111.42 W
Mayfield Creek ≃	194	36.57 N	89.05 W
Mayfield Dam ◆[6]	224	46.30 N	122.35 W
Mayfield Heights	214	41.31 N	81.27 W
Mayfield Lake ⊜[1]	224	46.31 N	122.32 W
Mayflower	194	34.57 N	92.25 W
Mayford	260	51.18 N	0.34 W
May Inlet ⊂	176	76.15 N	100.45 W
Māyir, Sūrīy.	130	36.23 N	37.02 E
Māyir, Sūrīy.	130	36.28 N	37.11 E
May Jirgui	150	13.44 N	8.08 E
Maykop → Majkop	84	44.35 N	40.07 E
Mayland	42	51.39 N	0.47 E
Maymont	184	52.33 N	107.40 W
Maymūn, Wādī ∨	146	30.10 N	10.27 E
Maymyo	110	22.02 N	96.28 E
Mayna	126	22.14 N	87.47 E
Maynāmati	124	23.29 N	91.07 E
Maynard, Ia., U.S.	190	42.46 N	91.52 W
Maynard, Ma., U.S.	207	42.26 N	71.27 W
Maynard, Oh., U.S.	214	40.07 N	80.53 W
Maynardville	192	36.15 N	83.47 W
Mayne	224	48.51 N	123.18 W
Mayne ≃	166	23.34 S	141.18 E
Mayne Island I	224	48.51 N	123.17 W
Maynooth	48	53.23 N	6.35 W
Mayo, Yk., Can.	180	63.35 N	135.54 W
Mayo, Fl., U.S.	192	30.03 N	83.10 W
Mayo, Md., U.S.	208	38.53 N	76.30 W
Mayo □[6]	48	53.54 N	9.15 W
Mayo ≃, Arg.	254	45.46 S	69.43 W
Mayo ≃, Col.	246	1.40 N	77.21 W
Mayo ≃, Méx.	232	26.45 N	109.47 W
Mayo ≃, Perú	248	6.37 S	76.16 W
Mayoba	154	17.13 S	26.16 E
Mayo Bay ⊂	116	6.56 N	126.22 E
Mayodan	192	36.24 N	79.58 W
Mayo Faran	146	8.57 N	12.04 E
Mayo-Kébbi □[5]	146	10.00 N	15.30 E
Mayoko, Congo	152	2.18 S	12.49 E
Mayoko, Zaïre	152	1.05 S	23.49 E
Mayola ≃	44	54.45 N	6.31 W
Mayo Lake ⊜	180	63.46 N	135.10 W
Mayo Ndaga	146	6.54 N	11.25 E
Mayon Volcano ∧[1]	116	13.15 N	123.41 E
Mayor Buratovich	252	39.15 S	62.37 W

PORTUGUÊS

Nome	Página	Lat.°′	Long.°′ W = Oeste
Mayo Reservoir ⊜[1]	192	36.00 N	78.53 W
Mayor Island I	172	37.18 S	176.16 E
Mayor Pablo Lagerenza	248	19.58 S	60.45 W
Mayotte □[2], Afr.	138	12.50 S	45.10 E
Mayotte □[2], Afr.	157a	12.50 S	45.10 E
Mayoyao	116	16.59 N	121.14 E
Maypearl	222	32.19 N	97.01 W
May Pen	241q	17.58 N	77.14 W
Mayport Naval Station ■	192	30.22 N	81.24 W
Mayraira Point ≻	116	18.39 N	120.51 E
Mayrán, Desierto de ◆[2]	196	25.45 N	102.45 W
Mayres	62	44.40 N	4.07 E
Mayrhofen	64	47.10 N	11.52 E
Mays	218	39.45 N	85.26 W
Maysah, Tall al- ∧	132	31.08 N	35.40 E
Maysān □[4]	128	32.00 N	47.00 E
Maysfield	222	30.54 N	96.51 W
Mays Landing	208	39.27 N	74.43 W
Mays Lick	218	38.31 N	83.50 W
Maysville, Ky., U.S.	218	38.38 N	83.44 W
Maysville, Mo., U.S.	194	39.53 N	94.21 W
Maysville, N.C., U.S.	192	34.54 N	77.13 W
Maysville, Ok., U.S.	196	34.49 N	97.24 W
Maythalūn	132	32.21 N	35.16 E
Maytiguid Island I	116	11.03 N	119.36 E
Maytown	208	40.04 N	76.35 W
Mayu	100	27.48 N	120.26 E
Mayumba	152	3.25 S	10.39 E
Mayung	114	0.49 N	103.03 E
Māyūram	122	11.06 N	79.40 E
Mayville, Mi., U.S.	190	43.20 N	83.21 W
Mayville, N.Y., U.S.	214	42.15 N	79.30 W
Mayville, N.D., U.S.	198	47.29 N	97.19 W
Mayville, Wi., U.S.	190	43.29 N	88.32 W
Maywood, Ca., U.S.	280	33.59 N	118.11 W
Maywood, Il., U.S.	216	41.52 N	87.50 W
Maywood, Mo., U.S.	219	39.57 N	91.36 W
Maywood, Ne., U.S.	198	40.39 N	100.37 W
Maywood, N.J., U.S.	276	40.54 N	74.03 W
Maywood, N.Y., U.S.	210	42.42 N	73.52 W
Maywood Race Track ♠	278	41.44 N	87.50 W
Mayyit, Al-Baḥr al- → Dead Sea ⊜	132	31.30 N	35.30 E
Maza, Arg.	252	36.50 S	63.19 W
Maza, S.S.S.R.	80	57.14 N	44.13 E
Mazabuka	154	15.51 S	27.46 E
Mazagan → El-Jadida	148	33.16 N	8.30 W
Mazagão	250	0.07 S	51.17 W
Mazagaon ◆[8]	272c	18.57 N	72.50 E
Mazagão Velho	250	0.13 S	51.25 W
Maʿzah, Jabal ∧	130	35.51 N	40.38 E
Mazamet	32	43.30 N	2.24 E
Mazamitla	234	19.55 N	103.02 W
Mazamitote, Arroyo de ≃	232	24.51 N	103.12 W
Mazán ≃	246	3.28 S	73.11 W
Māzandarān □[4]	128	36.30 N	53.30 E
Mazanovo	89	51.40 N	128.52 E
Mazār, Jabal ∧	132	33.34 N	36.03 E
Mazar, Oued ∨	148	31.50 N	1.36 E
Mazara, Val di ◆[1]	70	37.50 N	13.00 E
Mazara del Vallo	70	37.39 N	12.35 E
Mazār-e Sharīf	120	36.42 N	67.06 E
Mazargues	62	43.15 N	5.24 E
Mazaro ≃	70	37.39 N	12.35 E
Mazarredo	254	47.05 S	66.42 W
Mazarrón	34	37.36 N	1.19 W
Mazarrón, Golfo de ⊂	34	37.30 N	1.18 W
Mazarsu	85	41.56 N	72.40 E
Mazaruni ≃	246	6.25 N	58.38 W
Mazaruni-Potaro □[5]	246	6.00 N	60.00 W
Mazatenango	236	14.32 N	91.30 W
Mazatlán	234	23.13 N	106.25 W
Mazatlán de Flores	234	18.02 N	96.54 W
Mazatzal Mountains ⋏	200	34.00 N	111.55 W
Mazatzal Peak ∧	200	34.03 N	111.28 W
Maze	94	35.52 N	137.10 E
Maze ≃	94	35.40 N	137.10 E
Mažeikiai	76	56.19 N	22.20 E
Mazenod	184	49.53 N	106.14 W
Mazeppa, Mn., U.S.	190	44.16 N	92.32 W
Mazeppa, Pa., U.S.	210	40.59 N	76.59 W
Mazha	100	23.27 N	114.00 E
Māzhān, Īrān	128	32.35 N	59.01 E
Mazhan, Zhg.	98	36.04 N	118.45 E
Mazhangfang, Zhg.	104	42.23 N	122.26 E
Mazhangfang, Zhg.	104	40.44 N	120.53 E
Mazhuang, Zhg.	98	37.47 N	115.17 E
Mazhuang, Zhg.	100	32.54 N	114.03 E
Mazhuang, Zhg.	105	39.11 N	116.15 E
Maẓhūr, Khubb al- ⫠[8]	128	27.45 N	43.55 E
Mazıdağı	130	37.30 N	40.30 E
Mazigou	105	40.28 N	114.48 E
Mazilovo ◆[8]	265b	55.44 N	37.26 E
Mazīnān	128	36.18 N	56.46 E
Mazinaw Lake ⊜	212	44.55 N	77.12 W
Mazirbe	76	57.41 N	22.21 E
Mazoco	154	11.40 S	35.48 E
Mazoe ≃	154	16.32 S	33.25 E
Mazomanie	190	43.10 N	89.47 W
Mazomba ≃	256	22.53 S	43.45 W
Mazon	216	41.14 N	88.25 W
Mazon ≃	216	41.21 N	88.25 W
Mazon, East Fork ≃	216	41.11 N	88.18 W
Mazon, West Fork ≃	216	41.15 N	88.21 W
Mazong Shan ∧	102	41.28 N	97.10 E
Mazong Shan ⋏	102	41.30 N	97.30 E
Mazorra ◆[8]	286b	23.01 N	82.24 W
Mazou ≃	50	47.15 N	2.59 E
Mazraʿat-Bayt Jinn	132	33.19 N	35.55 E
Mazsalaca	76	57.52 N	25.03 E
Mazul'skij	86	56.16 N	90.28 E
Mazunga	154	21.45 S	29.52 E
Mazury ◆[1]	30	53.45 N	21.00 E
Mazzarino	70	37.18 N	14.13 E
Mazzarrà Sant'andrea	70	38.05 N	15.08 E
Mazzin	64	46.27 N	11.42 E
Mba	175g	17.33 S	177.41 E
Mbabala Island I	154	11.18 S	29.44 E
Mbabane	158	26.18 S	31.06 E
Mbabo, Tchabal ∧	152	7.16 N	12.09 E
Mbacké	150	14.48 N	15.55 W
Mbaéré ≃	152	3.47 N	17.31 E
Mbage	140	5.30 N	25.13 E
M'bahiakro	150	7.27 N	4.20 W
Mbaïki	152	3.53 N	18.00 E
Mbakaou, Barrage de ◆[5]	152	6.15 N	12.46 E
Mbala, Centraf.	152	7.48 N	20.51 E
Mbala (Abercorn), Zam.	154	8.50 S	31.22 E
Mbalam	152	2.13 N	13.49 E
Mbale	154	1.05 N	34.10 E
Mbali	152	2.50 S	16.12 E
Mbali ≃	152	4.26 N	18.20 E
Mbalizi	154	8.56 S	33.22 E
Mbalmayo	152	3.31 N	11.30 E
Mbalouro ≃	273b	4.09 S	15.21 E
Mbalourou	273b	4.09 S	15.21 E
Mbam ≃	152	4.24 N	11.17 E
Mbamba Bay	154	11.17 S	34.46 E
Mbamou, Île I	152	4.13 S	15.25 E
Mbamou, Pointe ≻	273b	4.16 S	15.19 E
Mbandaka (Coquilhatville)	152	0.04 N	18.16 E
Mbanga	152	4.30 N	9.34 E
Mbanika Island I	175e	9.05 S	159.12 E
M'banza Congo	152	6.16 S	14.15 E
Mbanza-Ngungu	152	5.15 S	14.52 E
Mbarangandu ≃	154	8.57 S	37.24 E
Mbarara	154	0.37 S	30.39 E
Mbari ≃	152	4.34 N	22.43 E
Mbarizunga Game Reserve ◆[4]	154	4.45 N	28.06 E
Mbashe ≃	158	32.15 S	28.53 E

Mbassay	146	7.39 N	15.40 E
Mbate	154	8.52 S	39.10 E
M'batto	150	6.28 N	4.22 W
Mbava Island I	175e	7.49 S	156.33 E
Mbé, Cam.	152	7.43 N	13.30 E
Mbé, Congo	152	3.18 S	15.54 E
Mbé ≃	152	0.27 N	9.41 E
Mbemba	154	10.03 S	38.36 E
Mbengga I	175g	18.23 S	178.08 E
M'bengué	150	10.00 N	5.54 W
Mbéré	146	10.49 N	15.44 E
Mbéré ≃	152	7.45 N	15.36 E
Mberengwa	154	20.30 S	29.53 E
Mbereshi Mission	154	9.45 S	28.46 E
Mberubu	150	6.10 N	7.38 E
Mbeya	154	8.54 S	33.27 E
Mbeya □[4]	154	8.00 S	33.30 E
Mbi ≃	152	4.26 N	18.16 E
Mbia	140	6.15 N	29.19 E
M'bigou	152	1.53 S	11.56 E
Mbinda	152	2.00 S	12.55 E
Mbindawina	152	15.57 S	23.18 E
Mbinga	154	10.56 S	35.01 E
Mbini	152	1.35 N	9.37 E
Mbini ≃	152	1.35 N	9.37 E
Mbirira	154	4.21 S	30.10 E
Mbirizi	154	0.23 S	31.27 E
Mbogo	154	7.26 S	33.26 E
Mboie	152	6.56 S	21.54 E
Mbola	175e	9.37 S	160.39 E
Mboli	152	4.08 N	23.09 E
Mbomou □[5]	152	5.00 N	23.30 E
Mbomou (Bomu) ≃	136	4.08 N	22.26 E
Mbonge	152	4.33 N	9.05 E
Mboro, Sén.	150	15.09 N	16.54 W
Mboro, Sūd.	140	6.18 N	28.45 E
Mborokua I	175e	9.00 S	158.40 E
Mborong	115b	8.49 S	120.37 E
Mboté	152	3.56 S	12.43 E
Mbotou ≃	152	6.49 N	24.14 E
Mbouda	152	5.38 N	10.15 E
Mboula	152	4.27 N	16.29 E
Mbour	150	14.24 N	16.58 W
Mbout	150	16.02 N	12.35 W
Mbrès	152	6.40 N	19.48 E
M'Bridge ≃	152	7.14 S	12.52 E
Mbua	175g	16.48 S	178.37 E
Mbua Bay ⊂	175g	16.49 S	178.35 E
Mbuji-Mayi (Bakwanga)	152	6.09 S	23.38 E
Mbulu	154	3.51 S	35.32 E
Mbulula	154	5.26 S	27.26 E
Mbuluzane ≃	158	26.08 S	31.52 E
Mbuluzi ≃	158	26.08 S	31.52 E
Mbuma	154	3.32 N	24.50 E
Mburucuyá	252	28.03 S	58.14 W
Mbutha	175g	16.39 S	179.50 E
Mbwemkuru ≃	154	9.29 S	39.39 E
M'Chedallah	34	36.21 N	4.16 E
M'Clintock Channel ⊔	176	72.00 N	102.00 W
M'Clure Strait ⊔	176	74.30 N	116.00 W
Mdandu	154	9.09 S	34.42 E
Mdantsana	158	32.56 S	27.42 E
M'Daourouch	36	36.05 N	7.49 E
Meacham	184	52.08 N	105.45 W
Mead	198	41.14 N	96.30 W
Mead, Lake ⊜[1]	200	36.05 N	114.25 W
Meade, Ks., U.S.	198	37.17 N	100.20 W
Meade, Mi., U.S.	214	42.43 N	82.52 W
Meade ≃	180	70.50 N	156.25 W
Meaden Peak ∧	200	40.46 N	107.03 W
Meade Peak ∧	202	42.30 N	111.15 W
Meadie, Loch ⊜	46	58.20 N	4.33 W
Meadow, Tx., U.S.	196	33.20 N	102.12 W
Meadow, Ut,. U.S.	200	38.53 N	112.24 W
Meadowbank Park ♠	274a	33.49 S	151.06 E
Meadowbrook, Il., U.S.	219	38.54 N	90.01 W
Meadowbrook, In., U.S.	216	41.03 N	85.03 W
Meadow Brook ≃, Ma., U.S.	283	42.03 N	70.58 W
Meadow Brook ≃, Pa., U.S.	285	40.07 N	75.04 W
Meadow Creek ≃	202	46.03 N	115.18 W
Meadowdale	278	41.32 N	87.21 W
Meadow Flat	170	33.26 S	149.56 E
Meadow Island I	276	40.36 N	73.33 W
Meadow Lake	184	54.08 N	108.26 W
Meadow Lake ⊜, Sk., Can.	184	54.07 N	108.20 W
Meadow Lake ⊜, N.Y., U.S.	276	40.44 N	73.50 W
Meadow Lake Provincial Park ♠	184	54.28 N	109.10 W
Meadow Lands	214	40.13 N	80.13 W
Meadowlands Sports Complex ♠	276	40.49 N	74.05 W
Meadowlark Airport ⊠	280	33.43 N	118.02 W
Meadowood, De., U.S.	285	39.43 N	75.47 W
Meadowood, Md., U.S.	284c	39.04 N	77.00 W
Meadows	168b	35.11 S	138.46 E
Meadows, Island of I	276	40.34 N	74.12 W
Meadows Field ⊠	226	35.26 N	119.03 W
Meadowvale ◆[8]	275b	43.37 N	79.43 W
Meadow Valley Wash ∨	204	36.39 N	114.35 W
Meadowview	192	36.46 N	81.52 W
Meadow Vista	226	39.06 N	121.01 W
Meads Creek ≃	210	42.10 N	77.07 W
Meadville, Ms., U.S.	194	31.28 N	90.53 W
Meadville, Mo., U.S.	194	39.47 N	93.18 W
Meadville, Pa., U.S.	214	41.38 N	80.09 W
Meaford	212	44.36 N	80.35 W
Meaghers Grant	186	44.55 N	63.15 W
Me-akan-dake ∧	92a	43.23 N	144.01 E
Mealasta Isle I	46	58.05 N	7.08 W
Mealhada	34	40.22 N	8.27 W
Méan	56	50.22 N	5.20 E
Meana	128	36.55 N	60.30 E
Meana Sardo	71	39.57 N	9.04 E
Meandarra	166	27.20 S	149.53 E
Meander Creek Reservoir ⊜[1]	214	41.09 N	80.47 W
Meander River	176	59.02 N	117.42 W
Mearim ≃	250	3.04 S	44.35 W
Measham	42	52.43 N	1.29 W
Meath □[6]	48	53.35 N	6.40 W
Meath □[9]	48	53.40 N	7.00 W
Meaux	50	48.57 N	2.52 E
Meaux-Esbly, Aérodrome de ⊠	261	48.55 N	2.50 E
Mebane	192	36.05 N	79.16 W
Mebisere	273a	6.42 N	3.31 E
Mebtoûh, Oued el ≃	34	35.16 N	0.32 W
Meča ≃	82	54.50 N	39.10 E
Meca, La → Makkah	144	21.27 N	39.49 E
Mecanhelas	154	15.12 S	35.54 E
Mecatán	234	21.32 N	105.08 W
Mecatlán	234	20.13 N	97.41 W
Mecaya ≃	246	0.29 N	75.11 W
Mecca → Makkah	144	21.27 N	39.49 E
Mečebilovo	78	49.04 N	36.41 E
Mečetinskaja	78	46.46 N	40.27 E
Mečetka	78	50.54 N	40.05 E
Mechanic Falls	188	44.06 N	70.23 W
Mechanicsburg, Il., U.S.	219	39.48 N	89.24 W
Mechanicsburg, In., U.S.	218	40.09 N	86.28 W
Mechanicsburg, Oh., U.S.	218	40.04 N	83.33 W
Mechanicsburg, Pa., U.S.	208	40.12 N	77.00 W
Mechanicstown, N.Y., U.S.	210	41.27 N	74.24 W
Mechanicstown, Oh., U.S.	214	40.37 N	80.57 W

Mechanicsville, Ia., U.S.	190	41.54 N	91.15 W
Mechanicsville, Md., U.S.	208	38.26 N	76.44 W
Mechanicsville, Va., U.S.	192	37.36 N	77.22 W
Mechanicville	210	42.54 N	73.41 W
Mechara	144	8.32 N	40.22 E
Mechelen (Malines)	50	51.02 N	4.28 E
Mechel'ta	84	42.48 N	46.30 E
Mechernich	56	50.35 N	6.38 E
Mechī □[8]	124	27.15 N	87.45 E
Mechī ≃	124	26.14 N	87.58 E
Mechita	252	35.04 S	60.24 W
Mechlin → Mechelen	50	51.02 N	4.28 E
Mechonskoje	86	56.09 N	64.34 E
Mechra Safsaf	34	34.52 N	2.36 W
Mechren'ga	24	61.46 N	40.57 E
Mechrenga ≃	24	63.15 N	41.20 E
Mechriyya	148	33.35 N	0.18 W
Mechroha	36	36.21 N	7.51 E
Mecidiye, Tür.	130	38.53 N	27.42 E
Mecidiye, Tür.	130	40.38 N	26.32 E
Mečigmen	180	65.28 N	172.05 W
Mečigmeskij zaliv ⊂	180	65.25 N	172.00 W
Meçitözü	130	40.31 N	35.19 E
Meckelfeld	52	53.25 N	10.01 E
Meckenbeuren	58	47.42 N	9.34 E
Meckenheim	56	50.37 N	7.07 E
Meckering	162	31.38 S	117.01 E
Meckesheim	56	49.19 N	8.49 E
Meckinghoven	263	51.37 N	7.19 E
Mecklenburg, D.D.R.	54	53.47 N	11.28 E
Mecklenburg, N.Y., U.S.	210	42.27 N	76.43 W
Mecklenburg □[9]	54	53.30 N	13.00 E
Mecklenburger Bucht ⊂	54	54.20 N	11.40 E
Mecklenburgische Seenplatte ◆[1]	54	53.30 N	12.00 E
Meclov	60	49.31 N	12.52 E
Meco	210	43.03 N	74.23 W
Mecoacán	234	18.23 N	93.07 W
Mecoacán, Laguna ⊂	234	18.22 N	93.09 W
Meconta	154	14.49 S	39.50 E
Mecox Bay ⊂	207	40.54 N	72.20 W
Mecque, La → Makkah	144	21.27 N	39.49 E
Mecsek ⋏	30	46.15 N	18.05 E
Mecubúri	154	14.39 S	38.54 E
Mecubúri ≃	154	14.10 S	40.31 E
Mecúfi	154	13.17 S	40.30 E
Mecula	154	12.04 S	37.40 E
Meda, It.	62	45.40 N	9.09 E
Meda, Port.	34	40.58 N	7.16 W
Medak	122	18.02 N	78.16 E
Medākul	126	23.03 N	90.11 E
Médan, Fr.	261	48.57 N	2.00 E
Medan, Indon.	114	3.35 N	98.40 E
Medang	114	2.06 N	101.38 E
Medang, Pulau I	115b	8.09 S	117.23 E
Medang, Tanjung ≻	114	2.08 N	101.39 E
Médanos	252	38.50 S	62.41 W
Medanosa, Punta ≻	254	48.06 S	65.55 W
Medaryville	216	41.04 N	86.53 W
Mede	62	45.06 N	8.44 E
Medebach	56	51.12 N	8.42 E
Medeiros Neto	255	17.20 S	40.14 W
Medel, Val ∨	58	46.37 N	8.50 E
Medellín, Col.	246	6.15 N	75.35 W
Medellin, Pil.	116	11.08 N	123.58 E
Medelpad □[9]	26	62.40 N	16.15 E
Medemblik	52	52.46 N	5.06 E
Měděnec	54	50.25 N	13.05 E
Medenica	78	49.26 N	23.45 E
Médenine	148	33.21 N	10.30 E
Médenine □[8]	148	32.00 N	10.00 E
Mederdra	150	16.55 N	15.39 W
Medesano	64	44.45 N	10.08 E
Medevi	40	58.40 N	14.57 E
Medfield	207	42.11 N	71.18 W
Medford, Ma., U.S.	207	42.25 N	71.06 W
Medford, N.J., U.S.	208	39.54 N	74.49 W
Medford, N.Y., U.S.	210	40.49 N	73.00 W
Medford, Ok., U.S.	196	36.48 N	97.44 W
Medford, Or., U.S.	202	42.19 N	122.52 W
Medford, Wi., U.S.	190	45.08 N	90.20 W
Medford Farms	285	39.52 N	74.45 W
Medford Lakes	285	39.51 N	74.48 W
Medfra	180	63.06 N	154.44 W
Medgidia	38	44.15 N	28.16 E
Medgyes → Mediaș	38	46.10 N	24.21 E
Medi	154	5.04 N	30.44 E
Media	208	39.55 N	75.23 W
Mediapolis	190	41.00 N	91.09 W
Mediaș	38	46.10 N	24.21 E
Medical Lake	202	47.34 N	117.40 W
Medicina	66	44.28 N	11.38 E
Medicine Bow	200	41.53 N	106.12 W
Medicine Bow ≃	200	42.00 N	106.40 W
Medicine Bow Mountains ⋏	200	41.10 N	106.10 W
Medicine Bow Peak ∧	200	41.21 N	106.19 W
Medicine Creek ≃, Mo., U.S.	194	39.43 N	93.24 W
Medicine Creek ≃, Ne., U.S.	198	40.17 N	100.10 W
Medicine Creek ≃, S.D., U.S.	198	44.06 N	99.42 W
Medicine Hat	184	50.03 N	110.40 W
Medicine Knoll Creek ≃	198	44.19 N	100.05 W
Medicine Lake	198	48.30 N	104.30 W
Medicine Lake ⊜	198	48.28 N	104.24 W
Medicine Lodge	198	37.16 N	98.34 W
Medicine Lodge ≃	196	36.49 N	98.20 W
Medicine Rocks State Park ♠	198	46.01 N	104.35 W
Medina → Al-Madīnah, Ar. Su.	128	24.28 N	39.36 E
Medina, Bra.	255	16.15 S	41.29 W
Medina, Pil.	116	8.55 N	125.01 E
Medina, N.Y., U.S.	210	43.13 N	78.23 W
Medina, N.D., U.S.	198	46.53 N	99.17 W
Medina, Oh., U.S.	214	41.08 N	81.51 W
Medina, Tx., U.S.	196	29.48 N	99.15 W
Medina, Wa., U.S.	224	47.37 N	122.13 W
Medina □[6]	214	41.08 N	81.52 W
Medina ≃	196	29.12 N	98.20 W
Medinaceli	34	41.10 N	2.26 W
Medina del Campo	34	41.18 N	4.55 W
Medina de Ríoseco	34	41.53 N	5.02 W
Médina Gonasse	150	13.08 N	13.45 W
Medinah	278	41.59 N	88.01 W
Medina Lake ⊜[1]	196	29.35 N	98.58 W
Médina Sabak	150	13.36 N	15.35 W
Medina-Sidonia	34	36.27 N	5.55 W
Medinat al-Faiyum → Al-Fayyūm	142	29.19 N	30.50 E
Medininkai	76	54.32 N	25.40 E
Medinīpur	126	22.26 N	87.20 E
Medino	164	9.40 S	149.40 E
Medio, Arroyo del ≃	258	33.49 S	57.43 W
Medio Creek ≃	196	28.19 N	97.19 W
Mediterranean Sea ⊤[2]	10	35.00 N	20.00 E
Mediterraneo, Mare → Mediterranean Sea ⊤[2]	10	35.00 N	20.00 E
Medjana	34	36.08 N	4.41 E
Medje	154	2.25 N	27.18 E
Medjerda, Monts de la ⋏	36	36.35 N	8.15 E
Medkovec	38	43.37 N	23.10 E
Mednogorsk	86	51.24 N	57.37 E
Mednoje	76	56.56 N	35.29 E
Mednyj, ostrov I	74	54.45 N	167.35 E
Médoc ◆[1]	32	45.20 N	1.00 W
Mêdog	120	29.20 N	95.15 E

Medolla	64	44.51 N	11.04 E
Medora, Il., U.S.	219	39.11 N	90.09 W
Medora, In., U.S.	218	38.49 N	86.10 W
Medora, N.D., U.S.	198	46.54 N	103.31 W
Médouneu	152	0.57 N	10.47 E
Medow	54	53.50 N	13.32 E
Medstead, Sk., Can.	184	53.19 N	108.02 W
Medstead, Eng., U.K.	42	51.08 N	1.04 W
Medua	126	22.38 N	90.44 E
Meductic	186	46.00 N	67.29 W
Medulla	220	27.58 N	81.58 W
Međumurje ◆[1]	61	46.25 N	16.30 E
Meduna ≃	64	45.49 N	12.34 E
Medveđa	38	42.50 N	21.35 E
Medvedevo, S.S.S.R.	76	60.02 N	43.01 E
Medvedevo, S.S.S.R.	80	56.37 N	47.47 E
Medvedevo, S.S.S.R.	86	60.37 N	77.21 E
Medvedevskoje	76	58.58 N	35.58 E
Medvedica ≃, S.S.S.R.	76	57.05 N	37.32 E
Medvedica ≃, S.S.S.R.	80	49.35 N	42.41 E
Medvedickij	80	50.47 N	44.43 E
Medvědí hora ∧	60	48.59 N	13.25 E
Medvedkovo ◆[8]	265b	55.53 N	37.38 E
Medvedok	80	57.23 N	50.05 E
Medvedovskaja	78	45.27 N	39.01 E
Medvenka, S.S.S.R.	78	51.26 N	36.07 E
Medvenka, S.S.S.R.	82	54.15 N	37.42 E
Medvežij, ostrov I	89	54.41 N	136.18 E
Medvežinka	83	48.10 N	39.31 E
Medvežje, ozero ⊜	86	55.07 N	68.00 E
Medvežjegorsk	24	62.55 N	34.23 E
Medvežji ostrova II	74	70.52 N	161.26 E
Medvežji ozera ⊜	265b	55.52 N	38.00 E
Medvežji Oz'ora	265b	55.52 N	37.59 E
Medvežskaja	24	64.57 N	57.34 E
Medviagalis ∧[2]	76	55.38 N	22.45 E
Medvin	78	49.23 N	30.47 E
Medv'onka ≃	265b	55.44 N	37.12 E
Medway, Ma., U.S.	207	42.08 N	71.23 W
Medway, Oh., U.S.	218	39.53 N	83.59 W
Medway □[8]	260	51.24 N	0.31 E
Medway ≃, N.S., Can.	186	44.08 N	64.36 W
Medway ≃, Eng., U.K.	42	51.27 N	0.44 E
Medyn'	82	54.58 N	35.52 E
Medynka ≃	82	54.44 N	36.02 E
Medynskij Zavorot, mys ≻	24	68.58 N	59.17 E
Medžibož	78	49.26 N	27.25 E
Medzilaborce	30	49.16 N	21.55 E
Meeberrie	162	26.58 S	115.58 E
Meekatharra	162	26.36 S	118.29 E
Meeker, Co., U.S.	200	40.02 N	107.54 W
Meeker, Oh., U.S.	214	40.39 N	83.18 W
Meeks Bay	226	39.02 N	120.08 W
Meelpaeg Lake ⊜[1]	186	48.16 N	56.35 W
Meenaar	168a	31.38 S	116.53 E
Meentheena	162	21.17 S	120.28 E
Meer	52	51.27 N	4.44 E
Meeralpen → Maritime Alps ⋏	62	44.15 N	7.10 E
Meerane	54	50.51 N	12.28 E
Meerbeck	263	51.28 N	6.39 E
Meerbeke	50	50.50 N	4.02 E
Meerbusch	56	51.15 N	6.41 E
Meerhout	56	51.08 N	5.05 E
Meerhusener Moor ◆[3]	52	53.35 N	7.30 E
Meerkerk	52	51.45 N	5.00 E
Meerle	52	51.28 N	4.48 E
Meersburg	58	47.41 N	9.16 E
Meerssen	56	50.53 N	5.45 E
Meerut	124	28.59 N	77.42 E
Meese ≃	42	52.40 N	2.39 W
Meeteetse	202	44.09 N	108.52 W
Mega, Indon.	164	0.41 S	131.53 E
Mega, Ityo.	144	4.07 N	38.16 E
Mega, Pulau I	112	4.00 S	101.02 E
Megalo	144	6.55 N	41.48 E
Megálon Khoríon	38	36.27 N	27.21 E
Megalópolis	38	37.24 N	22.08 E
Meganom, mys ≻	78	44.48 N	35.05 E
Mégantic □[6]	206	46.10 N	71.30 W
Mégantic, Lac ⊜	188	45.32 N	70.53 W
Mégantic, Mont ∧	206	45.28 N	71.09 W
Mégara	38	38.01 N	23.21 E
Megargel	196	33.27 N	98.56 W
Mégaron, Kólpos ⊂	267c	37.56 N	23.20 E
Megaruma ≃	154	13.28 S	40.32 E
Megasini ∧	126	21.38 N	86.21 E
Meget	88	52.24 N	104.03 E
Megève	62	45.52 N	6.37 E
Mégevette	58	46.12 N	6.30 E
Megezez ∧	144	9.17 N	39.32 E
Megget Reservoir ⊜[1]	46	55.29 N	3.17 W
Meghālaya □[3]	120	25.30 N	91.15 E
Meghna ≃	120	22.50 N	90.50 E
Megi-jima I	96	34.24 N	134.03 E
Mégiscane ≃	190	48.29 N	77.08 W
Mégiscane, Lac ⊜	190	48.35 N	75.55 W
Meglino, ozero ⊜	76	58.25 N	35.07 E
Megra, S.S.S.R.	24	66.09 N	41.37 E
Megra, S.S.S.R.	76	60.10 N	37.13 E
Megri	84	38.56 N	46.16 E
Meguro ◆[8]	268	35.38 N	139.42 E
Meguro ≃	268	35.37 N	139.45 E
Mehadia	38	44.55 N	22.22 E
Méhaigne ≃	56	50.32 N	5.13 E
Mehaïguene, Oued ∨	148	32.15 N	2.59 E
Mehakit	112	2.51 S	115.57 E
Mehar	120	27.11 N	67.49 E
Meharry, Mount ∧	162	22.59 S	118.35 E
Mehdia	148	35.26 N	1.40 E
Mehede	40	60.27 N	17.24 E
Mehedinți □[6]	38	44.30 N	22.50 E
Meheisa	140	19.37 N	32.57 E
Mehekar	122	20.09 N	76.34 E
Mehendiganj	126	22.49 N	90.32 E
Meherpur	124	23.46 N	88.38 E
Meherrin ≃	192	36.26 N	76.57 W
Mehetia I	14	17.52 S	148.03 W
Mehidpur	120	23.49 N	75.40 E
Mehikoorma	76	58.14 N	27.28 E
Mehlsack → Pieniężno	30	54.15 N	20.08 E
Mehlteuer	54	50.32 N	12.02 E
Mehlville	219	38.30 N	90.19 W
Mehnagar	124	25.53 N	83.07 E
Mehndāwal	124	26.59 N	83.07 E
Mehoopany	210	41.34 N	76.04 W
Mehoopany Creek ≃	210	41.34 N	76.03 W
Mehpālpur ◆[8]	272a	28.33 N	77.08 E
Mehr	52	51.43 N	6.29 E
Mehrābād	128	36.53 N	47.55 E
Mehrābād ◆[8]	267d	35.40 N	51.20 E
Mehram Nagar ◆[8]	272a	28.34 N	77.07 E
Mehrān	128	33.07 N	46.10 E
Mehrān ≃	128	26.52 N	55.24 E
Mehring	56	49.48 N	6.49 E
Mehrīz	128	31.35 N	54.28 E
Mehrow	264a	52.34 N	13.37 E
Mehrum	263	51.35 N	6.37 E
Mè-hsa-tè	110	19.33 N	97.38 E
Mehtarlām	120	34.39 N	70.10 E
Mehun-sur-Yèvre	50	47.09 N	2.13 E
Mei ≃, Zhg.	100	24.24 N	116.34 E
Mei ≃, Zhg.	100	26.00 N	115.23 E
Mei ≃, Zhg.	105	39.21 N	117.50 E
Meia Meia	154	5.49 S	35.48 E
Meia Ponte ≃	255	18.32 S	49.36 W
Meichang	105	39.22 N	117.10 E
Meichuan	100	30.10 N	115.36 E
Meicun, Zhg.	100	25.30 N	116.56 E
Meicun, Zhg.	106	30.22 N	119.01 E
Meicun, Zhg.	106	31.33 N	120.24 E
Meicun, Zhg.	106	30.40 N	119.04 E
Meide	263	51.11 N	6.55 E
Meiderich ◆[8]	263	51.28 N	6.46 E
Meidling ◆[8]	264b	48.11 N	16.20 E
Méier ◆[8]	287a	22.54 S	43.16 W

≃ River	Fluß	Río	Rivière	Rio
≡ Canal	Kanal	Canal	Canal	Canal
⌊ Waterfall, Rapids	Wasserfall, Stromschnellen	Cascada, Rápidos	Chute d'eau, Rapides	Cascata, Rápidos
⊔ Strait	Meeresstraße	Estrecho	Détroit	Estreito
⊂ Bay, Gulf	Bucht, Golf	Bahía, Golfo	Baie, Golfe	Baía, Golfo
⊜ Lake, Lakes	See, Seen	Lago, Lagos	Lac, Lacs	Lago, Lagos
≋ Swamp	Sumpf	Pantano	Marais	Pântano
⊓ Ice Features, Glacier	Eis- und Gletscherformen	Accidentes Glaciales	Formes glaciaires	Acidentes glaciares
⊤ Other Hydrographic Features	Andere Hydrographische Objekte	Otros Elementos Hidrográficos	Autres données hydrographiques	Outros acidentes hidrográficos

◆ Submarine Features	Untermeerische Objekte	Accidentes Submarinos	Formes de relief sous-marin	Acidentes submarinos
□ Political Unit	Politische Einheit	Unidad Politica	Entité politique	Unidade política
⊌ Cultural Institution	Kulturelle Institution	Institución Cultural	Institution culturelle	Instituição cultural
⊥ Historical Site	Historische Stätte	Sitio Histórico	Site historique	Sitio histórico
♠ Recreational Site	Erholungs- und Ferienort	Sitio de Recreo	Centre de loisirs	Area de Lazer
⊠ Airport	Flughafen	Aeropuerto	Aéroport	Aeroporto
■ Military Installation	Militäranlage	Instalación Militar	Installation militaire	Instalação militar
◆ Miscellaneous	Verschiedenes	Misceláneo	Divers	Diversos

Name	Page	Lat.°′	Long.°′
Meierij ✧[1]	**52**	51.35 N	5.40 E
Meierkaisong	**120**	30.54 N	84.31 E
Meiersberg	**263**	51.17 N	6.57 E
Meig ≃	**46**	57.34 N	4.41 W
Meiganga	**152**	6.31 N	14.11 E
Meigle	**46**	56.35 N	3.09 W
Meigs	**192**	31.04 N	84.05 W
Meigs Field ⊠	**278**	41.51 N	87.36 W
Meihsien → Meixian	**100**	24.21 N	116.08 E
Meihua	**100**	26.02 N	119.40 E
Meihuajie	**100**	25.14 N	113.05 E
Meijel	**52**	51.21 N	5.53 E
Meijino-Mori-Minō-kokutei-kōen ♦	**94**	34.51 N	135.29 E
Meiji Shrine ʊ[1]	**268**	35.41 N	139.42 E
Meikeng	**100**	23.59 N	114.05 E
Meikle Millyea ʌ	**44**	55.07 N	4.19 W
Meikle Says Law ʌ	**46**	55.55 N	2.40 W
Meiktila	**110**	20.52 N	95.52 E
Meila	**54**	51.09 N	13.13 E
Meilen	**58**	47.16 N	8.38 E
Meili	**106**	31.42 N	120.53 E
Meilie	**100**	26.18 N	117.38 E
Meilin, Zhg.	**100**	23.18 N	115.58 E
Meilin, Zhg.	**106**	30.35 N	119.04 E
Meillerie	**58**	46.24 N	6.43 E
Meilong	**100**	22.56 N	115.17 E
Meilunyingzi	**104**	42.18 N	122.10 E
Meina	**62**	45.47 N	8.32 E
Meine	**52**	52.23 N	10.32 E
Meiners Oaks	**228**	34.26 N	119.17 W
Meinerzhagen	**56**	51.06 N	7.38 E
Meiningen	**54**	50.34 N	10.25 E
Meinung	**100**	22.54 N	120.32 E
Meio, Ilha do I	**287a**	23.02 S	43.17 W
Meio, Rio do ≃	**255**	17.47 S	39.47 W
Meiringen	**58**	46.43 N	8.12 E
Meisburg	**56**	50.06 N	6.41 E
Meisenheim	**56**	49.42 N	7.40 E
Meishan, Zhg.	**106**	31.06 N	119.43 E
Meishan, Zhg.	**107**	30.02 N	103.49 E
Meissen	**54**	51.10 N	13.28 E
Meissendorf	**52**	52.43 N	9.50 E
Meiss Lake ⊜	**204**	41.52 N	122.04 W
Meissner ʌ	**56**	51.12 N	9.50 E
Meitan	**102**	27.46 N	107.35 E
Meitian	**100**	25.21 N	112.47 E
Meitingen	**56**	48.32 N	10.50 E
Meiwa	**94**	34.33 N	136.39 E
Meixi	**106**	30.48 N	119.45 E
Meixian, Zhg.	**100**	24.21 N	116.08 E
Meixian, Zhg.	**100**	28.52 N	113.38 E
Meiyao	**89**	49.37 N	124.30 E
Meiyino	**140**	6.12 N	34.40 E
Meizhai	**102**	25.30 N	108.50 E
Meizhou	**100**	23.50 N	117.20 E
Meizhou Dao I	**100**	25.06 N	119.07 E
Meizhou Wan c	**100**	25.06 N	119.00 E
Meizhu	**106**	31.16 N	119.13 E
Mejeckyn, ostrov I	**180**	65.26 N	178.00 W
Mejerda, Oued (Oued Medjerda) ≃	**36**	37.07 N	10.13 E
Mejez el Bab	**148**	36.39 N	9.37 E
Mejia	**126**	23.34 N	87.06 E
Mejicanos	**236**	13.43 N	89.12 W
Mejillones	**252**	23.06 S	70.27 W
Mejillones, Península ≻[1]	**252**	23.17 S	70.34 W
Mejillones del Sur, Bahía de c	**252**	23.03 S	70.27 W
Mejnypil'gyno	**74**	62.32 N	177.02 E
Mejorada del Campo	**266a**	40.24 N	3.29 W
Meka	**162**	27.26 S	116.48 E
Mekada, Garaet el ≋	**36**	36.48 N	8.00 E
Mékambo	**152**	1.01 N	13.56 E
Mekele	**144**	13.33 N	39.30 E
Mekerra, Oued ≃	**34**	35.00 N	0.45 W
Mekhé	**150**	15.07 N	16.38 W
Mekhliganj	**124**	26.21 N	88.55 E
Mekhtar	**120**	30.28 N	69.22 E
Mékinac ≃	**206**	46.51 N	72.46 W
Mekka → Makkah	**144**	21.27 N	39.49 E
Meknès	**148**	33.53 N	5.37 W
Meknès □[4]	**148**	33.50 N	5.30 W
Mekong ≃	**12**	10.33 N	105.24 E
Mekongga, Gunung ʌ	**112**	3.38 S	121.15 E
Mekongga, Pegunungan ⩓	**112**	3.35 S	121.15 E
Mékôngk → Mekong ≃	**12**	10.33 N	105.24 E
Mekoryuk	**180**	60.23 N	166.12 W
Mékrou ≃	**150**	12.24 N	2.49 E
Mel	**64**	46.04 N	12.05 E
Melado ≃	**252**	35.43 S	71.05 W
Melah, Oued el V, Alg.	**148**	28.21 N	6.00 E
Melah, Oued el V, Tun.	**148**	34.03 N	8.06 E
Melah, Sebkhet el ⊜	**148**	29.05 N	1.10 W
Melaka	**114**	2.12 N	102.15 E
Melaka □[3]	**114**	2.15 N	102.15 E
Melalap	**112**	5.14 N	116.00 E
Melandro ≃	**68**	40.37 N	15.27 E
Melanesia II	**14**	13.00 S	164.00 E
Melanesian Basin ✦[1]	**14**	0.05 N	160.35 E
Melappālaiyam	**122**	8.42 N	77.43 E
Melara	**64**	45.03 N	11.11 E
Melaune	**54**	51.11 N	14.44 E
Melawi ≃	**112**	0.05 N	111.29 E
Melayu ≃	**271c**	1.27 N	103.42 E
Melbern	**216**	41.28 N	84.39 W
Melbost	**46**	58.15 N	6.22 W
Melbourn	**42**	52.05 N	0.01 E
Melbourne, Austl.	**169**	37.49 S	144.58 E
Melbourne, Austl.	**274b**	37.49 S	144.58 E
Melbourne, On., Can.	**214**	42.49 N	81.33 W
Melbourne, Eng., U.K.	**42**	52.49 N	1.25 W
Melbourne, Ar., U.S.	**194**	36.03 N	91.54 W
Melbourne, Fl., U.S.	**220**	28.04 N	80.36 W
Melbourne, Ia., U.S.	**190**	41.56 N	93.06 W
Melbourne, University of ʊ[2]	**274b**	37.48 S	144.58 E
Melbourne Beach	**220**	28.04 N	80.33 W
Melbourne Island I	**176**	68.30 N	104.45 W
Melbourne Regional Airport ⊠	**220**	28.06 N	80.38 W
Mel'cany	**80**	54.28 N	44.43 E
Melcher	**190**	41.13 N	93.14 W
Melchor, Isla I	**254**	45.08 S	73.57 W
Melchor Ocampo	**196**	26.03 N	99.33 W
Melchor Romero ✧[8]	**258**	34.56 S	58.03 W
Melchtal	**58**	46.50 N	8.17 E
Melcroft	**214**	40.03 N	79.24 W
Melderskin ʌ	**26**	60.01 N	6.05 E
Meldola	**66**	44.07 N	12.05 E
Meldorf	**30**	54.05 N	9.05 E
Meldrum Bay	**190**	45.56 N	83.07 W
Meldrum Creek	**182**	52.07 N	122.20 W
Mélé, Centraf.	**146**	9.46 N	21.33 E
Mele, India	**272b**	22.49 N	88.09 E
Mele, It.	**62**	44.27 N	8.45 E
Mélé, Baie c	**175f**	17.43 S	168.15 E
Mele, Capo ≻	**62**	43.57 N	8.10 E
Melechovo	**80**	56.17 N	41.17 E
Meleck	**86**	57.25 N	90.12 E
Meleden	**144**	10.25 N	49.51 E
Melegnano	**62**	45.21 N	9.19 E
Meleješt'	**78**	46.59 N	29.33 E
Melekeok	**175b**	7.29 N	134.38 E
Melekess → Dimitrovgrad	**80**	54.14 N	49.39 E
Melela ≃	**154**	17.04 S	38.36 E
Melena del Sur	**240p**	22.47 N	82.09 W
Melendiz Dağı ʌ	**130**	38.07 N	34.25 E
Melendugno	**68**	40.16 N	18.20 E
Melenki	**80**	55.20 N	41.38 E
Meleškoviči	**78**	51.56 N	28.59 E
Meleuz	**86**	52.58 N	55.55 E
Mélèzes, Rivière aux ≃	**176**	57.40 N	69.29 W
Melfa	**208**	37.39 N	75.45 W
Melfa ≃	**66**	41.30 N	13.35 E
Melfi, It.	**68**	41.00 N	15.39 E
Melfi, Tchad	**146**	11.04 N	17.56 E
Melfort, Sk., Can.	**184**	52.52 N	104.36 W
Melfort, Zimb.	**154**	17.59 S	31.19 E
Melfort, Loch c	**46**	56.15 N	5.31 W
Melgaço, Bra.	**250**	1.47 S	50.44 W
Melgaço, Port.	**34**	42.07 N	8.16 W
Melgar	**246**	4.12 N	74.39 W
Melghir, Chott ⊜	**148**	34.20 N	6.20 E
Mel'guny	**80**	52.09 N	40.52 E
Melhus	**26**	63.17 N	10.16 E
Meli ≃	**150**	8.16 N	10.42 W
Meliane, Oued ≃	**36**	36.46 N	10.18 E
Meliau	**112**	0.08 S	110.18 E
Meliau, Gunong ʌ	**116**	5.50 N	117.14 E
Melibocus ʌ	**56**	49.42 N	8.40 E
Melichovo, S.S.S.R.	**78**	50.42 N	36.48 E
Melichovo, S.S.S.R.	**82**	55.07 N	37.39 E
Melicuccà	**68**	38.18 N	15.53 E
Melide, Esp.	**34**	42.55 N	8.00 W
Melide, Schw.	**58**	45.57 N	8.57 E
Meligalás	**38**	37.13 N	21.59 E
Melilla	**34**	35.19 N	2.58 W
Melilli	**70**	37.11 N	15.07 E
Melimoyu, Cerro ʌ	**254**	44.05 S	72.52 W
Melincué	**252**	33.39 S	61.27 W
Melipilla	**252**	33.42 S	71.13 W
Mélisey	**58**	47.45 N	6.35 E
Melissa	**68**	39.18 N	17.01 E
Melissano	**68**	39.58 N	18.07 E
Melíssia	**267c**	38.03 N	23.50 E
Melita	**184**	49.16 N	101.00 W
Melito di Porto Salvo	**68**	37.55 N	15.47 E
Melitopol'	**78**	46.50 N	35.22 E
Melívoia	**38**	39.45 N	22.48 E
Melk	**61**	48.14 N	15.20 E
Melk ≃	**61**	48.14 N	15.19 E
Melk ʊ[1]	**61**	48.14 N	15.20 E
Melka Teka	**144**	6.05 N	43.08 E
Melkbosstrand	**158**	33.43 S	18.27 E
Melksham	**42**	51.23 N	2.09 W
Mella ≃	**64**	45.13 N	10.13 E
Mellansel	**26**	63.26 N	18.19 E
Mellau	**58**	47.21 N	9.53 E
Melle, B.R.D.	**52**	52.12 N	8.20 E
Melle, Fr.	**32**	46.13 N	0.09 W
Melleck	**64**	47.40 N	12.45 E
Mellègue, Oued ≃	**36**	36.32 N	8.51 E
Mellen	**190**	46.19 N	90.39 W
Mellendorf	**52**	52.33 N	9.43 E
Mellenville	**210**	42.15 N	73.40 W
Mellerud	**26**	58.42 N	12.28 E
Mellette	**198**	45.09 N	98.29 W
Mellier ≃	**56**	49.43 N	5.32 E
Melling	**262**	53.30 N	2.56 W
Mellingen	**54**	50.56 N	11.23 E
Mellish Reef I[1]	**160**	17.25 S	155.50 E
Mellish Rise ✦[3]	**14**	17.00 S	156.00 E
Mellit	**140**	14.08 N	25.33 E
Mellone, Monte ʌ	**267a**	41.50 N	12.43 E
Mellong Range ⩓	**170**	33.06 S	150.43 E
Mellon Udrigle	**46**	57.55 N	5.39 W
Mellor	**262**	53.46 N	2.32 W
Mellor Brook	**262**	53.47 N	2.33 W
Mellor Glacier ᴨ	**9**	73.30 S	66.30 E
Mellösa	**40**	59.06 N	16.33 E
Mellrichstadt	**56**	50.26 N	10.18 E
Mellum I	**52**	53.40 N	8.10 E
Melmerby	**44**	54.44 N	2.35 W
Melmore	**214**	41.02 N	83.07 W
Melmoth	**158**	28.38 S	31.24 E
Mel'nica-Podol'skaja	**78**	48.37 N	26.10 E
Mělník	**54**	50.20 N	14.29 E
Mel'nikovo, S.S.S.R.	**26**	61.05 N	29.22 E
Mel'nikovo, S.S.S.R.	**85**	40.19 N	70.19 E
Mel'nikovo, S.S.S.R.	**86**	56.34 N	84.05 E
Melo	**252**	32.22 S	54.11 W
Melo ≃	**248**	21.27 S	57.52 W
Melo, Ilha de I	**150**	11.02 N	15.13 W
Melocheville	**206**	45.19 N	73.56 W
Meloco	**154**	13.25 S	39.08 E
Melolo	**115b**	9.53 S	120.40 E
Melolo ≃	**115b**	9.52 S	120.41 E
Melong	**152**	5.07 N	9.57 E
Melos → Mílos I	**38**	36.41 N	24.15 E
Melovaja ≃	**83**	49.23 N	40.16 E
Melovatka	**83**	49.21 N	38.11 E
Melovoje	**83**	49.22 N	40.06 E
Melovoj Syrt ʌ	**80**	52.15 N	52.35 E
Melozitna ≃	**180**	64.46 N	155.29 W
Melrose, Austl.	**162**	27.56 S	121.19 E
Melrose, Austl.	**166**	32.42 S	146.58 E
Melrose, Scot., U.K.	**46**	55.36 N	2.44 W
Melrose, Ma., U.S.	**207**	42.27 N	71.04 W
Melrose, Mn., U.S.	**198**	45.40 N	94.48 W
Melrose, N.M., U.S.	**196**	34.25 N	103.37 W
Melrose, N.Y., U.S.	**210**	42.50 N	73.37 W
Melrose, Oh., U.S.	**216**	41.05 N	84.25 W
Melrose, Wi., U.S.	**190**	44.07 N	90.59 W
Melrose ✧[8]	**276**	40.49 N	73.55 W
Melrose Abbey ʊ[1]	**46**	55.37 N	2.45 W
Melrose Park, Fl., U.S.	**220**	26.06 N	80.12 W
Melrose Park, Il., U.S.	**216**	41.54 N	87.51 W
Melrose Park, N.Y., U.S.	**212**	42.54 N	76.32 W
Melrose Park, Pa., U.S.	**285**	40.04 N	75.08 W
Mels	**58**	47.03 N	9.25 E
Melstone	**202**	46.35 N	107.52 W
Melsungen	**56**	51.08 N	9.32 E
Meltaus	**24**	66.54 N	25.22 E
Meltham, Eng., U.K.	**44**	53.35 N	1.51 W
Meltham, Eng., U.K.	**262**	53.36 N	1.51 W
Melton, Austl.	**168b**	34.05 S	137.59 E
Melton, Austl.	**169**	37.41 S	144.35 E
Melton Constable	**42**	52.53 N	1.01 E
Melton Hill Lake ⊜[1]	**192**	36.00 N	84.15 W
Melton Mowbray	**42**	52.46 N	0.53 W
Melton Reservoir ⊜[1]	**169**	37.43 S	144.32 E
Melúa	**246**	3.55 N	72.50 W
Meluan	**112**	1.52 N	111.56 E
Meluco	**154**	12.36 S	39.38 E
Melúli ≃	**154**	16.28 S	39.44 E
Melun, Fr.	**50**	48.32 N	2.40 E
Melun, Mya.	**110**	20.14 N	93.24 E
Melunga	**152**	17.16 S	16.24 E
Melūr	**122**	10.03 N	78.20 E
Melvaig	**46**	57.48 N	5.49 W
Melvern	**198**	38.30 N	95.38 W
Melvern Lake ⊜[1]	**198**	38.30 N	95.50 W
Melvich	**46**	58.33 N	3.55 W
Melville, Austl.	**168a**	32.03 S	115.49 E
Melville, Sk., Can.	**184**	50.55 N	102.48 W
Melville, La., U.S.	**194**	30.41 N	91.44 W
Melville, N.Y., U.S.	**276**	40.47 N	73.24 W
Melville ✧[8]	**273d**	26.11 S	28.00 E
Melville, Cape ≻, Austl.	**164**	14.11 S	144.30 E
Melville, Cape ≻, Pil.	**116**	7.49 N	117.01 E
Melville, Détroit de → Viscount Melville Sound ʯ	**176**	74.10 N	108.00 W
Melville, Lake ⊜	**176**	53.45 N	59.30 W
Melville Bugt c	**16**	75.30 N	63.00 W
Melville Hall Airport ⊠	**240d**	15.33 N	61.18 W
Melville Hills ⩓[2]	**180**	69.15 N	124.00 W
Melville Island I, Austl.	**164**	11.40 S	131.00 E
Melville Island I, N.T., Can.	**16**	75.15 N	110.00 W
Melville Island Aboriginal Reserve ✧[4]	**164**	11.40 S	131.00 E
Melville Peninsula ≻[1]	**176**	68.00 N	84.00 W
Melville Sound ʯ, N.T., Can.	**176**	68.05 N	107.30 W
Melville Sound ʯ, On., Can.	**212**	44.57 N	81.05 W
Melvin, Il., U.S.	**216**	40.34 N	88.15 W
Melvin, Ky., U.S.	**192**	37.21 N	82.41 W
Melvin, Tx., U.S.	**196**	31.13 N	99.35 W
Melvin, Lough ⊜	**48**	54.26 N	8.10 W
Melvindale	**214**	42.16 N	83.10 W
Melvin Lake ⊜	**184**	57.08 N	100.15 W
Melyana	**148**	36.15 N	2.15 E
Mélykút	**30**	46.13 N	19.24 E
Melzo	**62**	45.30 N	9.25 E
Memala	**112**	1.44 S	112.36 E
Mêmar Co ⊜	**120**	34.15 N	82.20 E
Memāri	**126**	23.12 N	88.07 E
Memba	**154**	14.11 S	40.30 E
Membalong	**112**	3.09 S	107.38 E
Memboro	**115b**	9.22 S	119.32 E
Membre	**56**	49.52 N	4.54 E
Même ≃	**50**	48.11 N	0.39 E
Memel → Klaipėda, S.S.S.R.	**76**	55.43 N	21.07 E
Memel, S. Afr.	**158**	27.43 S	29.30 E
Memel → Nemunas ≃	**76**	55.18 N	21.23 E
Mēmele ≃	**76**	56.24 N	24.10 E
Memewin, Lac ⊜	**190**	46.29 N	78.42 W
Memmert I	**52**	53.39 N	6.53 E
Memmingen	**58**	47.59 N	10.11 E
Memo ≃	**246**	9.16 N	66.40 W
Memori, Tanjung ≻	**164**	0.52 S	134.08 E
Memorial Bridge ✧[5]	**269a**	13.44 N	100.30 E
Memorial Stadium ♦	**284b**	39.20 N	76.36 W
Mémót	**110**	11.49 N	106.11 E
Mempawah	**112**	0.22 N	108.58 E
Memphis, Fl., U.S.	**220**	27.32 N	82.33 W
Memphis, In., U.S.	**218**	38.29 N	85.45 W
Memphis, Mi., U.S.	**214**	42.54 N	82.46 W
Memphis, Mo., U.S.	**194**	40.27 N	92.10 W
Memphis, Tn., U.S.	**194**	35.08 N	90.02 W
Memphis, Tx., U.S.	**196**	34.43 N	100.32 W
Memphis → Mīt Ruhaynah ⊥	**142**	29.51 N	31.15 E
Memphis Naval Air Station ■	**194**	35.21 N	89.52 W
Memphremagog, Lake ⊜	**206**	45.05 N	72.15 W
Memsie	**46**	57.39 N	2.02 W
Mena, Ityo.	**144**	6.25 N	39.51 E
Mena, S.S.S.R.	**78**	51.31 N	32.13 E
Mena, Ar., U.S.	**194**	34.35 N	94.14 W
Menado → Manado	**112**	1.29 N	124.51 E
Menaggio	**58**	46.01 N	9.14 E
Menahga	**198**	46.45 N	95.06 W
Menai	**274a**	34.01 S	151.01 E
Menai Bridge	**44**	53.14 N	4.10 W
Menai Strait ʯ	**44**	53.12 N	4.12 W
Ménaka	**150**	15.55 N	2.24 E
Menaldum	**52**	53.12 N	5.39 E
Menan	**202**	43.43 N	111.59 W
Menands	**210**	42.41 N	73.43 W
Menangina	**162**	29.50 S	121.54 E
Menantico Creek ≃	**208**	39.20 N	75.00 W
Menarandra ≃	**157b**	25.17 S	44.30 E
Menard	**196**	30.55 N	99.47 W
Menard □[6]	**219**	40.01 N	89.51 W
Menard Creek ≃	**222**	30.29 N	94.50 W
Menars	**50**	47.38 N	1.24 E
Menasha	**190**	44.12 N	88.26 W
Menate	**112**	0.14 S	113.02 E
Menawashei	**140**	12.40 N	24.59 E
Menchang	**105**	38.54 N	117.01 E
Menčikury	**78**	47.04 N	34.48 E
Mencué	**254**	40.25 S	69.38 W
Mend	**89**	43.40 N	123.08 E
Mendanau, Pulau I	**112**	2.51 S	107.26 E
Mendarik, Pulau I	**112**	1.18 N	107.02 E
Mendatai	**102**	38.51 N	94.39 E
Mendatica	**62**	44.05 N	7.49 E
Mendawai	**112**	2.59 S	113.16 E
Mendawai ≃	**112**	3.17 S	113.21 E
Mendaya	**115a**	8.23 S	114.42 E
Mende	**32**	44.30 N	3.30 E
Mendebo ⩓	**144**	6.50 N	39.40 E
Mendel' ≃	**86**	58.13 N	90.08 E
Mendelejevsk	**80**	55.54 N	52.20 E
Menden	**56**	51.26 N	7.47 E
Menden ✧[8]	**263**	51.24 N	6.54 E
Mendenhall, Ms., U.S.	**194**	31.57 N	89.52 W
Mendenhall, Pa., U.S.	**285**	39.51 N	75.38 W
Mendenhall, Cape ≻	**180**	59.51 N	166.15 W
Mendes	**256**	22.32 S	43.44 W
Méndez	**246**	2.43 S	78.19 W
Mendez-Nuñez	**116**	14.08 N	120.54 E
Mendham	**210**	40.46 N	74.36 W
Mendi, Ityo.	**144**	9.50 N	35.06 E
Mendi, Pap. N. Gui.	**164**	6.10 S	143.40 E
Mendig	**56**	50.21 N	7.15 E
Mendip Hills ⩓[2]	**42**	51.15 N	2.40 W
Mendlesham	**42**	52.16 N	1.05 E
Mendocino	**204**	39.18 N	123.47 W
Mendocino, Cape ≻	**204**	40.25 N	124.25 W
Mendocino Fracture Zone ✦	**16**	40.00 N	145.00 W
Mendola ≃	**70**	37.44 N	13.32 E
Mendon, Il., U.S.	**219**	40.05 N	91.17 W
Mendon, Ma., U.S.	**207**	42.06 N	71.33 W
Mendon, Mi., U.S.	**216**	42.00 N	85.27 W
Mendon, N.Y., U.S.	**210**	43.00 N	77.34 W
Mendon, Oh., U.S.	**216**	40.40 N	84.31 W
Mendon, Pa., U.S.	**279b**	40.11 N	79.41 W
Mendota, Ca., U.S.	**226**	36.45 N	120.22 W
Mendota, Il., U.S.	**216**	41.32 N	89.07 W
Mendota, Lake ⊜	**216**	43.05 N	89.25 W
Mendoza, Arg.	**252**	32.53 S	68.49 W
Mendoza, Perú	**248**	6.20 S	77.24 W
Mendoza, Perú	**286d**	12.06 S	76.59 W
Mendoza, Ur.	**258**	34.17 S	56.13 W
Mendoza □[4]	**252**	34.30 S	68.30 W
Mendoza ≃	**252**	32.21 S	68.18 W
Mendoza, Arroyo de ≃	**258**	34.21 S	56.18 W
Mendrisio	**58**	45.52 N	8.59 E
Mend'ukino	**82**	54.47 N	38.51 E
Mendung	**112**	0.31 N	103.13 E
Ménéac	**32**	48.09 N	2.28 W
Mene de Mauroa	**246**	10.43 N	71.01 W
Mene Grande	**246**	9.49 N	70.56 W
Menemen	**130**	38.36 N	27.04 E
Menen	**50**	50.48 N	3.07 E
Meneng Point ≻	**174b**	0.32 S	166.57 E
Menes	**115a**	6.23 S	105.55 E
Menfi	**70**	37.36 N	12.58 E
Mengalum, Pulau I	**112**	6.16 N	115.12 E
Mengban	**102**	23.08 N	100.19 E
Mengbang	**102**	21.28 N	101.19 E
Mengcheng	**100**	33.17 N	116.33 E
Mengchi ≃	**107**	29.47 N	104.56 E
Mengcun	**98**	38.06 N	117.05 E
Mengdapu	**104**	41.35 N	123.12 E
Mengede ✧[8]	**263**	51.34 N	7.23 E
Mengeh Jek	**120**	37.02 N	66.07 E
Mengen, B.R.D.	**58**	48.03 N	9.20 E
Mengen, Tür.	**130**	40.56 N	32.04 E
Mengeringhausen	**56**	51.22 N	8.59 E
Mengersgereuth-Hämmern	**54**	50.24 N	11.07 E
Menges Mills	**208**	39.52 N	76.54 W
Menggala	**112**	4.28 S	105.17 E
Menggu	**102**	26.34 N	102.57 E
Menggubao	**104**	42.27 N	122.23 E
Menggudai	**102**	38.10 N	108.15 E
Menghai	**102**	22.00 N	100.26 E
Menghe	**106**	32.03 N	119.47 E
Menghun	**102**	21.44 N	100.23 E
Mengjiacun	**106**	31.33 N	118.46 E
Mengjiagang	**89**	46.22 N	130.40 E
Mengjiatai	**104**	42.06 N	123.21 E
Mengjiawan	**102**	38.35 N	109.25 E
Mengjiawopeng	**104**	41.22 N	121.51 E
Mengjiayuanjia	**105**	40.52 N	118.08 E
Mengjiazhai	**269b**	31.18 N	121.19 E
Mengka	**102**	25.10 N	98.01 E
Mengkibol	**114**	1.58 N	103.20 E
Mengkuang	**114**	3.11 N	102.24 E
Menglian	**102**	22.20 N	99.38 E
Menglinghausen ✧[8]	**263**	51.28 N	7.25 E
Mengluchang	**107**	29.19 N	103.35 E
Mengmucun	**106**	31.59 N	119.01 E
Mengong	**152**	2.56 N	11.25 E
Mengqigou	**104**	42.00 N	121.08 E
Mengshan	**102**	24.07 N	110.33 E
Meng Shan ⩓, Zhg.	**98**	35.44 N	117.45 E
Meng Shan ⩓, Zhg.	**104**	41.50 N	121.10 E
Mengtong	**107**	30.44 N	105.53 E
Mengulek, gora ʌ	**86**	50.58 N	89.30 E
Mengwang	**102**	22.26 N	100.34 E
Mengyin	**98**	35.45 N	117.57 E
Mengzhe	**102**	22.02 N	100.16 E
Mengzhi	**102**	24.10 N	99.46 E
Mengzi	**102**	23.22 N	103.20 E
Menihek Lakes ⊜	**176**	54.00 N	66.35 W
Ménil-la-Tour	**56**	48.46 N	5.52 E
Menindee	**166**	32.24 S	142.26 E
Menindee Lake ⊜	**166**	32.21 S	142.20 E
Meningie	**166**	35.42 S	139.20 E
Menjiaqiangzi	**104**	42.29 N	119.21 E
Menkoutang	**106**	31.01 N	119.27 E
Menlo	**224**	46.37 N	123.38 W
Menlo Park	**226**	37.27 N	122.10 W
Menlo Park Mall ✧[9]	**276**	40.32 N	74.20 W
Menlo Park Terrace	**276**	40.32 N	74.20 W
Mennecy	**261**	48.34 N	2.26 E
Mennetou-sur-Cher	**50**	47.16 N	1.53 E
Mennighüffen	**52**	52.13 N	8.43 E
Menno	**198**	43.14 N	97.34 W
Meno, Indon.	**164**	3.52 S	135.31 E
Meno, Ok., U.S.	**196**	36.23 N	98.10 W
Menominee	**190**	45.06 N	87.36 W
Menominee ≃	**190**	45.05 N	87.36 W
Menominee Indian Reservation ✧[4]	**190**	45.00 N	88.45 W
Menomonee ≃	**216**	43.02 N	87.54 W
Menomonee Falls	**216**	43.10 N	88.07 W
Menomonie	**190**	44.52 N	91.55 W
Menongue	**152**	14.36 S	17.48 E
Menor, Mar c	**34**	37.43 N	0.48 W
Menorca I	**34**	40.00 N	4.00 E
Mens	**62**	44.49 N	5.45 E
Menslage	**52**	52.41 N	7.49 E
Menston	**44**	53.53 N	1.44 W
Menstrup	**41**	55.13 N	11.36 E
Mentana	**66**	42.02 N	12.38 E
Mentasta Lake	**180**	62.55 N	143.45 W
Mentasta Mountains ⩓	**180**	62.40 N	143.07 W
Mentawai, Kepulauan II	**108**	2.00 S	99.30 E
Mentawai, Selat ʯ	**108**	1.45 S	100.00 E
Mentekab	**114**	3.29 N	102.21 E
Menteke, peski ✧[2]	**80**	47.20 N	50.40 E
Menteng ✧[8]	**269e**	6.12 S	106.50 E
Menteroda	**54**	51.18 N	10.33 E
Menthon-Saint-Bernard	**62**	45.51 N	6.12 E
Menton	**62**	43.47 N	7.30 E
Mentone, Austl.	**274b**	37.59 S	145.05 E
Mentone → Menton, Fr.	**62**	43.47 N	7.30 E
Mentone, Ca., U.S.	**228**	34.05 N	117.08 W
Mentone, In., U.S.	**216**	41.10 N	86.02 W
Mentone, Tx., U.S.	**196**	31.42 N	103.36 W
Mentor, Ky., U.S.	**218**	38.53 N	84.14 W
Mentor, Oh., U.S.	**214**	41.39 N	81.20 W
Mentor-on-the-Lake	**214**	41.42 N	81.21 W
Mentougou	**105**	39.56 N	116.03 E
Mentzdam ⊜[1]	**158**	33.10 S	25.09 E
Menucourt	**261**	49.02 N	1.59 E
Menuma	**94**	36.13 N	139.23 E
Men'uša	**76**	58.23 N	30.42 E
Menyamya	**164**	7.10 S	146.00 E
Menyapa, Gunung ʌ	**112**	1.05 N	116.05 E
Menyuan	**102**	37.27 N	101.48 E
Menza ≃	**88**	50.14 N	108.38 E
Menzel Bourguiba	**148**	37.10 N	9.48 E
Menzel Bou Zelfa	**36**	36.41 N	10.36 E
Menzel Djemil	**36**	37.14 N	9.55 E
Menzelen	**52**	51.37 N	6.32 E
Menzelerheide	**263**	51.37 N	6.31 E
Menzelinsk	**80**	55.43 N	53.08 E
Menzel Temime	**148**	36.47 N	10.59 E
Menzenschwand	**58**	47.49 N	8.04 E
Menzies	**162**	29.41 S	121.02 E
Menzies, Mount ʌ	**9**	73.30 S	61.50 E
Menziken	**58**	47.14 N	8.12 E
Meobbaai c	**156**	24.25 S	14.34 E
Meola Āgri	**272a**	28.42 N	77.23 E
Meolo	**64**	45.37 N	12.27 E
Meon ≃	**42**	50.48 N	1.15 W
Meopham	**260**	51.22 N	0.22 E
Meopham Station	**260**	51.23 N	0.21 E
Meoqui	**232**	28.17 N	105.29 W
Meota	**184**	53.02 N	108.27 W
Méouge ≃	**62**	44.16 N	5.50 E
Méounes-lès-Montrieux	**62**	43.17 N	5.58 E
Mepal	**42**	52.24 N	0.07 E
Mepisckaro, gora ʌ	**84**	41.50 N	42.40 E
Meppel	**52**	52.42 N	6.11 E
Meppen	**52**	52.41 N	7.17 E
Meqerghane, Sebkha ≚	**148**	26.19 N	1.20 E
Meqruur	**174q**	9.31 N	138.09 E
Mequinenza, Embalse de ⊜[1]	**34**	41.20 N	0.05 E
Mequon	**216**	43.13 N	87.59 W
Mer	**50**	47.42 N	1.30 E
Mera ≃	**58**	46.11 N	9.25 E
Merah	**112**	0.50 N	116.48 E
Merai	**164**	4.50 S	152.20 E
Meråker	**26**	63.26 N	11.45 E
Merakurak	**115a**	6.53 S	111.59 E
Meramangye, Lake ⊜	**162**	28.25 S	132.13 E
Merambéllou, Kólpos c	**38**	35.14 N	25.47 E
Meramec ≃	**194**	38.23 N	90.21 W
Meramec Caverns ⩡[5]	**219**	38.15 N	91.06 W
Meramec State Park ♦	**219**	38.14 N	91.05 W
Meran → Merano, It.	**64**	46.40 N	11.09 E
Meran, Nig.	**273a**	6.38 N	3.16 E
Meranggau	**112**	0.12 S	110.17 E
Merangin ≃	**112**	2.09 S	102.47 E
Merano (Meran)	**64**	46.40 N	11.09 E
Merapi, Gunung ʌ	**115a**	8.03 S	114.15 E
Merapoh	**114**	4.41 N	101.59 E
Merasheen	**186**	47.25 N	54.21 W
Merasheen Island I	**186**	47.30 N	54.15 W
Merate	**62**	45.42 N	9.25 E
Meratus, Pegunungan ⩓	**112**	2.45 S	115.40 E
Merauke	**164**	8.28 S	140.20 E
Merauke ≃	**164**	8.30 S	140.24 E
Merbabu, Gunung ʌ	**115a**	7.27 S	110.26 E
Merbau, Indon.	**114**	1.07 N	102.33 E
Merbau, Indon.	**114**	2.16 N	99.50 E
Merbein	**166**	34.11 S	142.04 E
Merca → Marka	**144**	1.43 N	44.53 E
Mercaderes	**246**	1.47 N	77.10 W
Mercantour, Parc National du ♦	**62**	44.10 N	7.00 E
Mercāra	**122**	12.25 N	75.44 E
Mercatale	**66**	43.15 N	12.08 E
Mercato San Severino	**68**	40.47 N	14.46 E
Mercato Saraceno	**66**	43.57 N	12.12 E
Merced	**226**	37.18 N	120.28 W
Merced □[6]	**226**	37.15 N	120.40 W
Merced ≃	**226**	37.21 N	120.58 W
Merced, Lake ⊜	**282**	37.43 N	122.29 W
Merced, North Fork ≃	**226**	37.37 N	120.03 W
Merced, South Fork ≃	**226**	37.39 N	119.53 W
Merced Airport ⊠	**226**	37.17 N	120.31 W
Mercedario, Cerro ʌ	**252**	31.59 S	70.07 W
Mercedes, Arg.	**252**	29.12 S	58.05 W
Mercedes, Arg.	**252**	33.40 S	65.28 W
Mercedes, Arg.	**258**	34.39 S	59.27 W
Mercedes, Pil.	**116**	14.07 N	123.01 E
Mercedes, Tx., U.S.	**196**	26.08 N	97.54 W
Mercedes, Ur.	**252**	33.16 S	58.01 W
Mercedita, Aeropuerto ⊠	**240m**	18.01 N	66.34 W
Mercer, N.Z.	**172**	37.16 S	175.03 E
Mercer, Mo., U.S.	**194**	40.30 N	93.31 W
Mercer, Oh., U.S.	**216**	40.40 N	84.35 W
Mercer, Pa., U.S.	**214**	41.13 N	80.14 W
Mercer, Wi., U.S.	**190**	46.09 N	90.03 W
Mercer □[6], N.J., U.S.	**208**	40.13 N	74.45 W
Mercer □[6], Oh., U.S.	**216**	40.33 N	84.34 W
Mercer □[6], Pa., U.S.	**214**	41.14 N	80.15 W
Mercer Island	**224**	47.35 N	122.15 W
Mercersburg	**188**	39.49 N	77.54 W
Mercerville	**208**	40.14 N	74.41 W
Mercês, Bra.	**256**	21.12 S	43.21 W
Mercês, Port.	**266c**	38.47 N	9.19 W
Merchants Bay c	**176**	67.10 N	62.50 W
Merchants Millpond ⊜	**208**	36.26 N	76.41 W
Merchantville	**285**	39.56 N	75.04 W
Merchong ≃	**114**	3.03 N	103.27 E
Merchtem	**50**	50.58 N	4.14 E
Mercier (Saint-Philomène)	**275a**	45.19 N	73.45 W
Mercier, Pont ✧[5]	**275a**	45.25 N	73.39 W
Mercoal	**182**	53.10 N	117.05 W
Mercogliano	**68**	40.55 N	14.44 E
Mercury	**204**	36.40 N	115.59 W
Mercury Islands II	**172**	36.35 S	175.55 E
Mercy, Cape ≻	**176**	64.53 N	63.32 W
Mercy Bay c	**176**	74.05 N	119.00 W
Mercy-le-Bas	**56**	49.23 N	5.45 E
Merdeka Bridge ✧[5]	**271c**	1.18 N	103.53 E
Méré, Fr.	**261**	48.47 N	1.49 E
Mere, Eng., U.K.	**42**	51.06 N	2.16 W
Mere, Eng., U.K.	**262**	53.20 N	2.25 W
Mere Brow	**262**	53.40 N	2.53 W
Mereckij	**85**	43.48 N	74.42 E
Mereclough	**262**	53.46 N	2.11 W
Meredale	**273d**	26.17 S	27.59 E
Meredith, Austl.	**169**	37.51 S	144.04 E
Meredith, N.H., U.S.	**188**	43.39 N	71.30 W
Meredith, Cape ≻	**254**	52.15 S	60.39 W
Meredith, Lake ⊜[1]	**196**	35.36 N	101.42 W
Meredosia	**219**	39.50 N	90.34 W
Meredosia Lake ⊜	**219**	39.52 N	90.33 W
Mereeg	**144**	3.46 N	47.18 E
Merefa	**78**	49.49 N	36.03 E
Méré Lava I	**175f**	14.25 S	168.03 E
Merelbeke	**50**	51.00 N	3.45 E
Merenkurkku (Norra Kvarken) ʯ	**26**	63.36 N	20.43 E
Mereny	**78**	46.58 N	29.04 E
Merevari ≃	**246**	4.28 N	63.57 W
Méréville	**50**	48.19 N	2.05 E
Merewa	**144**	7.40 N	37.00 E
Merewether	**170**	32.57 S	151.46 E
Mereworth	**260**	51.15 N	0.23 E
Mergenevo	**80**	49.56 N	51.17 E
Mergozzo	**58**	45.58 N	8.26 E
Mergui (Myeik)	**110**	12.26 N	98.36 E
Mergui Archipelago II	**110**	12.00 N	98.00 E
Merḩavya	**132**	32.36 N	35.19 E
Meria	**272b**	22.59 N	88.20 E
Meribah	**166**	34.42 S	140.51 E
Méribel	**62**	45.25 N	6.34 E
Meriç	**130**	41.11 N	26.25 E
Meriç (Marica) (Évros) ≃	**38**	40.52 N	26.12 E
Méricourt	**50**	50.24 N	2.52 E
Mérida, Esp.	**34**	38.55 N	6.20 W
Mérida, Méx.	**200**	32.39 N	114.58 W
Mérida, Méx.	**232**	20.58 N	89.37 W
Merida, Pil.	**116**	10.55 N	124.32 E
Mérida, Ven.	**246**	8.36 N	71.08 W
Mérida □[3]	**246**	8.30 N	71.10 W
Mérida, Cordillera de ⩓	**246**	8.40 N	71.00 W
Meridale	**210**	42.22 N	74.57 W
Meriden, Eng., U.K.	**42**	52.26 N	1.37 W
Meriden, Ct., U.S.	**207**	41.32 N	72.48 W
Meriden, N.J., U.S.	**276**	40.57 N	74.28 W
Meridian, Ca., U.S.	**226**	39.09 N	121.55 W
Meridian, Ga., U.S.	**192**	31.27 N	81.22 W
Meridian, Id., U.S.	**202**	43.36 N	116.23 W
Meridian, Ms., U.S.	**194**	32.21 N	88.42 W
Meridian, N.Y., U.S.	**210**	43.09 N	76.32 W
Meridian, Pa., U.S.	**214**	40.51 N	79.58 W
Meridian, Tx., U.S.	**222**	31.55 N	97.39 W
Meridian Hills	**218**	39.53 N	86.09 W
Meridian Naval Air Station ■	**194**	32.33 N	88.34 W
Meridianville	**194**	34.51 N	86.34 W
Mériel	**261**	49.05 N	2.12 E
Mérignac	**32**	44.50 N	0.42 W
Merigold	**194**	33.50 N	90.43 W
Merikarvia	**26**	61.51 N	21.30 E
Merille, Laga ≃	**154**	1.25 N	38.26 E
Merimbula	**166**	36.53 S	149.54 E
Merín, Laguna (Lagoa Mirim) c	**252**	32.45 S	52.50 W
Merinda	**166**	20.01 S	148.10 E
Mering	**60**	48.16 N	10.59 E
Meringa	**146**	10.44 N	12.09 E
Merin Gubai	**144**	1.26 N	44.20 E
Meringur	**166**	34.24 S	141.16 E
Merino	**198**	40.28 N	103.21 W
Merinos	**252**	32.24 S	56.54 W
Merion Station	**285**	39.59 N	75.15 W
Merir I	**108**	4.19 N	132.19 E
Merishausen	**58**	47.45 N	8.37 E
Merit	**222**	33.13 N	96.17 W
Meriti ≃	**287a**	22.48 S	43.20 W
Merivale Gardens	**212**	45.19 N	75.44 W
Meriwether Farms	**285**	39.58 N	75.34 W
Merizo	**174p**	13.16 N	144.40 E
Merke	**85**	42.52 N	73.11 E
Merkel	**196**	32.28 N	100.00 W
Merkem	**50**	50.57 N	2.51 E
Merkendorf	**56**	49.12 N	10.42 E
Merkinė	**76**	54.10 N	24.10 E
Merklin	**60**	49.34 N	13.07 E
Merklingen	**58**	48.30 N	9.44 E
Merkourovoúni ʌ	**267c**	37.54 N	23.48 E
Merksem	**50**	51.15 N	4.27 E
Merksplas	**56**	51.22 N	4.52 E
Merkulovíči	**76**	52.58 N	30.36 E
Merkys ≃	**76**	54.10 N	24.11 E
Merlara	**64**	45.10 N	11.26 E
Merlejevo	**82**	55.05 N	37.13 E
Merlimau, Pulau I	**271c**	1.17 N	103.42 E
Merlimont-Plage	**50**	50.28 N	1.35 E
Merlin, On., Can.	**214**	42.14 N	82.14 W
Merlin, Or., U.S.	**202**	42.31 N	123.25 W
Merlin Seamount ✦[3]	**14**	9.05 S	150.44 W
Merlo, Arg.	**252**	32.21 S	65.02 W
Merlo, Arg.	**258**	34.40 S	58.45 W
Merlo □[5]	**288**	34.40 S	58.45 W
Merlo, Aeródromo ⊠	**288**	34.41 S	58.45 W
Merlynston	**274b**	37.43 S	144.58 E
Mermaid Beach	**171a**	28.03 S	153.27 E
Mern	**41**	55.03 N	12.04 E
Merna	**198**	41.29 N	99.45 W
Mernye	**30**	46.30 N	17.50 E
Meroe ⊥	**140**	16.56 N	33.43 E
Meron	**132**	32.59 N	35.26 E
Meron, Hare ʌ	**132**	32.58 N	35.25 E
Meros, Ponta dos ≻	**256**	23.13 S	44.21 W
Merotai Besar	**112**	4.26 N	117.46 E
Merouana	**34**	35.38 N	5.55 E
Merouane, Chott ⊜	**148**	34.00 N	6.02 E
Mer'oža	**76**	59.02 N	36.23 E
Merredin	**162**	31.29 S	118.16 E

ENGLISH | **DEUTSCH**

Name	Seite	Breite°′	Länge°′ E = Ost
Merrick	**276**	40.39 N	73.33 W
Merrick ʌ	**44**	55.08 N	4.29 W
Merrick Bay c	**276**	40.38 N	73.33 W
Merrickville	**212**	44.55 N	75.50 W
Merri Creek ≃	**169**	37.48 S	145.01 E
Merriewold Lake	**210**	41.22 N	74.12 W
Merrifield	**284c**	38.52 N	77.13 W
Merrill, Ia., U.S.	**198**	42.43 N	96.14 W
Merrill, Mi., U.S.	**190**	43.24 N	84.19 W
Merrill, Or., U.S.	**202**	42.01 N	121.35 W
Merrill, Wi., U.S.	**190**	45.10 N	89.41 W
Merrillan	**190**	44.27 N	90.50 W
Merrill C. Meigs Field ⊠	**278**	41.52 N	87.37 W
Merrill Lake ⊜	**212**	44.55 N	77.24 W
Merrillville	**216**	41.28 N	87.19 W
Merrimac	**207**	42.49 N	71.00 W
Merrimack ≃	**188**	42.49 N	70.49 W
Merrimack College ʊ[2]	**283**	42.40 N	71.08 W
Merrimac Terrace	**283**	42.49 N	71.00 W
Merriman, S. Afr.	**158**	31.13 S	23.38 E
Merriman, Ne., U.S.	**198**	42.55 N	101.42 W
Merrionette Park	**278**	41.41 N	87.42 W
Merriott	**42**	50.54 N	2.48 W
Merritt, B.C., Can.	**182**	50.07 N	120.47 W
Merritt, Wa., U.S.	**224**	47.47 N	120.51 W
Merritt, Lake ⊜[1]	**282**	37.48 N	122.16 W
Merritt Island	**220**	28.21 N	80.42 W
Merritt Island I	**220**	28.33 N	80.40 W
Merritt Reservoir ⊜[1]	**198**	42.35 N	100.55 W
Merriwa	**166**	32.08 S	150.21 E
Mer Rouge	**194**	32.46 N	91.47 W
Merrow	**207**	41.49 N	72.18 W
Merrygoen	**166**	31.50 S	149.14 E
Merrylands	**274a**	33.50 S	150.59 E
Merrymount Park ♦	**283**	42.16 N	71.01 W
Merryville	**194**	30.45 N	93.32 W
Mersa Fatma	**144**	14.55 N	40.20 E
Mersa Matruh → Marsā Maṭrūḥ	**140**	31.21 N	27.14 E
Mersch	**56**	49.46 N	6.06 E
Merscheid ✧[8]	**263**	51.10 N	7.01 E
Merse V	**46**	55.39 N	2.15 W
Merse ≃	**66**	43.05 N	11.22 E
Mersea Island I	**42**	51.47 N	0.55 E
Merseburg	**54**	51.21 N	11.59 E
Mersey ≃, Austl.	**166**	41.10 S	146.22 E
Mersey ≃, N.S., Can.	**186**	44.02 N	64.43 W
Mersey ≃, Eng., U.K.	**44**	53.25 N	3.00 W
Merseyside □[6]	**44**	53.25 N	2.50 W
Mersey Tunnel ✧[5]	**262**	53.24 N	3.00 W
Mersin → İçel	**130**	36.48 N	34.38 E
Mersing	**114**	2.26 N	103.50 E
Mers-les-Bains	**50**	50.04 N	1.23 E
Mērsrags	**76**	57.21 N	23.07 E
Mersthaw	**260**	51.16 N	0.09 W
Merta	**120**	26.39 N	74.02 E
Merta Road	**120**	26.43 N	73.55 E
Merthyr Tydfil	**42**	51.46 N	3.23 W
Merti	**154**	1.04 N	38.40 E
Mertingen	**56**	48.39 N	10.47 E
Mértola	**34**	37.38 N	7.40 W
Merton, Austl.	**169**	36.59 S	145.42 E
Merton, Wi., U.S.	**216**	43.08 N	88.18 W
Merton ✧[8]	**42**	51.25 N	0.12 W
Mertz Glacier Tongue ᴨ	**9**	67.40 S	144.45 E
Mertzon	**196**	31.16 N	100.49 W
Mertztown	**208**	40.30 N	75.40 W
Méru, Fr.	**50**	49.14 N	2.08 E
Meru, Kenya	**154**	0.03 N	37.39 E
Meru, Mount ʌ	**154**	3.14 S	36.45 E
Meru National Park ♦	**154**	0.10 N	38.15 E
Meruoca	**250**	3.28 S	40.28 W
Merv → Mary	**128**	37.36 N	61.50 E
Mervans	**58**	46.48 N	5.11 E
Merville	**50**	50.38 N	2.38 E
Mervin	**184**	53.20 N	108.53 W
Merwede	**158**	31.38 S	23.48 E
Merweville	**158**	32.40 S	21.31 E
Merwin, Lake ⊜[1]	**224**	45.59 N	122.26 W
Merxleben	**54**	51.07 N	10.40 E
Mery	**82**	55.49 N	36.36 E
Méry-la-Bataille	**50**	49.33 N	2.38 E
Méry-sur-Oise	**261**	49.04 N	2.11 E
Méry-sur-Seine	**50**	48.30 N	3.53 E
Merzdorf	**54**	51.23 N	14.32 E
Merzhausen	**58**	47.58 N	7.49 E
Merzifon	**130**	40.53 N	35.29 E
Merzig	**56**	49.27 N	6.36 E
Mesa, Moç.	**154**	13.00 S	39.33 E
Mesa, S. Afr.	**158**	26.29 S	26.59 E
Mesa, T.T.P.I.	**175c**	7.21 N	151.51 E
Mesa, Az., U.S.	**200**	33.25 N	111.49 W
Mesa ≃	**34**	41.15 N	1.48 W
Mesa, Cerro ʌ	**254**	48.46 S	71.29 W
Mesabi Range ⩓[2]	**190**	47.30 N	92.50 W
Mesachie Lake	**224**	48.49 N	124.07 W
Mesa del Nayar	**234**	22.16 N	104.35 W
Mesa de Santa Rita	**234**	23.04 N	105.31 W
Mesagne	**68**	40.33 N	17.49 E
Mes'agutovo	**86**	55.35 N	58.20 E
Mesaména	**152**	3.44 N	12.50 E
Mesa Mountain ʌ	**200**	37.55 N	106.38 W
Mesarás, Kólpos c	**38**	34.58 N	24.36 E
Mesa Verde National Park ♦	**200**	37.13 N	108.30 W
Mescalero	**200**	33.09 N	105.46 W
Mescalero Apache Indian Reservation ✧[4]	**200**	33.12 N	105.40 W
Meščerino, S.S.S.R.	**76**	53.37 N	37.23 E
Meščerino, S.S.S.R.	**82**	55.11 N	38.21 E
Meščerskij	**265b**	55.40 N	37.25 E
Meščerskoje	**82**	55.17 N	37.38 E
Meschede	**56**	51.20 N	8.17 E
Meschetskij chrebet ⩓	**84**	41.48 N	42.30 E
Mescit Tepe ʌ	**130**	40.22 N	41.11 E
Meščovsk	**76**	54.19 N	35.17 E
Meščura	**24**	63.20 N	50.52 E
Mese	**58**	46.17 N	9.21 E
Mèsè Atet	**110**	18.38 N	97.39 E
Mesen-Bucht → Mezenskaja guba c	**24**	66.40 N	43.45 E
Meseritz → Międzyrzecz	**30**	52.28 N	15.35 E
Mesero	**266b**	45.30 N	8.51 E
Mesewa → Mitsiwa	**144**	15.38 N	39.28 E
Mesfinto	**144**	13.20 N	37.19 E
Mesgarābād	**267d**	35.37 N	51.31 E
Mesgouez, Lac ⊜	**176**	51.24 N	75.05 W
Meshed → Mashhad	**128**	36.18 N	59.36 E
Meshgīn Shahr	**128**	38.24 N	47.40 E
Meshomasic Mountain ʌ	**207**	41.38 N	72.32 W
Meshoppen	**210**	41.34 N	76.03 W
Meshoppen Creek ≃	**210**	41.37 N	76.03 W
Mesick	**190**	44.24 N	85.42 W
Mesier, Canal ʯ	**254**	48.20 S	74.33 W
Mesilinka ≃	**182**	56.09 N	124.28 W
Mesilla	**200**	32.16 N	106.48 W
Mesillas, Méx.	**234**	23.14 N	106.03 W
Mesillas, Méx.	**234**	23.33 N	103.35 W
Mesima ≃	**68**	38.30 N	16.15 E
Meskiana	**148**	35.39 N	7.41 E
Meskiana, Oued ≃	**36**	35.49 N	7.53 E
Meskine	**146**	11.25 N	15.21 E
Meškuičiai	**76**	56.05 N	23.28 E
Meskum	**114**	1.34 N	102.01 E
Meslay-du-Maine	**32**	47.57 N	0.33 W
Meslay-le-Grenet	**50**	48.22 N	1.23 E
Mesnil-Val-Plage	**50**	50.03 N	1.20 E
Mesocco	**58**	46.23 N	9.14 E
Mesola	**66**	44.55 N	12.14 E
Mesolcina, Valle V	**58**	46.20 N	9.10 E
Mesolóngion	**38**	38.21 N	21.17 E
Mesomikenda Lake ⊜	**190**	47.40 N	81.53 W

Symbols in the index entries represent the broad categories identified in the key at the right. Symbols with superior numbers (⩓[1]) identify subcategories (see complete key on page *I · 1).*

Symbole im Register stellen die rechts im Schlüssel erklärten Kategorien dar. Symbole mit hochgestellten Ziffern (⩓[1]) bezeichnen Unterabteilungen einer Kategorie (vgl. vollständiger Schlüssel auf Seite *I · 1).*

Los símbolos incluídos en el texto del índice representan las grandes categorias identificadas con la clave a la derecha. Los símbolos con numeros en su parte superior (⩓[1]) identifican las subcategorías (véase la clave completa en la página *I · 1).*

Les symboles de l'index représentent les catégories indiquées dans la légende à droite. Les symboles suivis d'un indice (⩓[1]) représentent des sous-catégories (voir légende complète à la page *I · 1).*

Os símbolos incluídos no texto do índice representam as grandes categorias identificadas com a chave à direita. Os símbolos com números em sua parte superior (⩓[1]) identificam as subcategorias (veja-se a chave completa à página *I · 1).*

	English	Deutsch	Español	Français	Português
ʌ	Mountain	Berg	Montaña	Montagne	Montanha
⩓	Mountains	Gebirge	Montañas	Montagnes	Montanhas
)(	Pass	Paß	Paso	Col	Passo
V	Valley, Canyon	Tal, Cañon	Valle, Cañón	Vallée, Canyon	Vale, Canhão
≚	Plain	Ebene	Llano	Plaine	Planície
≻	Cape	Kap	Cabo	Cap	Cabo
I	Island	Insel	Isla	Île	Ilha
II	Islands	Inseln	Islas	Îles	Ilhas
⩡	Other Topographic Features	Andere Topographische Objekte	Otros Elementos Topográficos	Autres données topographiques	Outros acidentes topográficos

ESPAÑOL

Nombre	Página	Lat.°′	Long.°′ W = Oeste
Mesopotamia	214	41.27 N	80.57 W
Mesopotamia □[9]	128	34.00 N	44.00 E
Mesoraca	68	39.05 N	16.48 E
Mesóyia □[9]	267c	37.56 N	23.53 E
Mespelbrunn ⊥	56	49.54 N	9.19 E
Mesquita, Bra.	255	19.13 S	42.35 W
Mesquita, Bra.	256	22.48 S	43.26 W
Mesquite, Nv., U.S.	204	36.48 N	114.03 W
Mesquite, Tx., U.S.	222	32.46 N	96.35 W
Messach Mellet ⋏[2]	146	24.30 N	11.35 E
Messalo ≃	154	11.40 S	40.26 E
Messaoud, Oued ∨	148	27.28 N	0.21 W
Messdorf	54	52.43 N	11.33 E
Messina, It.	70	38.11 N	15.33 E
Messina, S. Afr.	156	22.23 S	30.00 E
Messina □[4]	70	38.03 N	14.52 E
Messina, Stretto di ⊔	70	38.15 N	15.35 E
Messinge ≃	154	11.34 S	35.25 E
Messingham	44	53.32 N	0.39 W
Messíni	38	37.04 N	22.00 E
Messíni ⊥	38	37.11 N	21.57 E
Messiniakós Kólpos ⊂	38	36.58 N	22.00 E
Messix Peak ∧	202	41.29 N	112.31 W
Messkirch	58	47.59 N	9.07 E
Messojacha ≃	74	67.52 N	77.27 E
Messondo	152	3.43 N	10.28 E
Messtetten	58	48.11 N	8.58 E
Messy	261	48.58 N	2.42 E
Mestá	38	38.15 N	25.55 E
Mesta (Néstos) ≃	38	40.41 N	24.44 E
Mestasa	148	35.07 N	4.25 W
Městečko	60	50.03 N	13.52 E
Mestghanem	148	35.51 N	0.07 E
Mestghanem □[5]	148	36.00 N	0.30 E
Mestia	84	43.03 N	42.43 E
Mestlin	54	53.35 N	11.56 E
Město Touškov	60	49.46 N	13.15 E
Mestre	64	45.29 N	12.15 E
Mestrino	64	45.26 N	11.45 E
Mesudiye	130	40.28 N	37.46 E
Mesuji ≃	112	4.08 S	105.52 E
Mesum	52	52.13 N	7.29 E
Meszah Peak ∧	180	58.28 N	131.26 W
Meta, It.	68	40.39 N	14.24 E
Meta, Mo., U.S.	219	38.18 N	92.09 W
Meta □[5]	246	3.30 N	73.00 W
Meta ≃	246	6.12 N	67.28 W
Métabief	58	46.47 N	6.21 E
Metagācha	272b	22.38 N	88.31 E
Metahara	144	8.54 N	39.55 E
Meta Incognita Peninsula ›[1]	176	62.45 N	68.30 W
Metairie	194	29.59 N	90.09 W
Metaline Falls	202	48.51 N	117.22 W
Metallifere, Colline ⋏	66	43.15 N	11.00 E
Metallostroj	265a	59.47 N	30.33 E
Metamora, Il., U.S.	190	40.47 N	89.21 W
Metamora, In., U.S.	218	39.26 N	85.08 W
Metamora, Mi., U.S.	216	42.56 N	83.17 W
Metamora, Oh., U.S.	216	41.42 N	83.54 W
Metán	252	25.29 S	64.57 W
Metangula	154	12.43 S	34.49 E
Metapán	236	14.20 N	89.27 W
Metapontum ⊥	68	40.23 N	16.50 E
Metarica	154	14.20 S	36.48 E
Metaurilia	66	43.49 N	13.03 E
Metauro ≃	66	43.50 N	13.03 E
Metcalfe	212	45.14 N	75.28 W
Metchosin	224	48.22 N	123.33 W
Metechi	84	41.55 N	44.21 E
Metedeconk, South Branch ≃	208	40.04 N	74.09 W
Meteghan	186	44.11 N	66.10 W
Metelen	52	52.08 N	7.12 E
Metema	144	12.57 N	36.12 E
Metéora ⊍[1]	38	39.46 N	21.36 E
Meteor Crater ⏏[6]	200	35.02 N	111.02 W
Meteor Seamount ✣[3]	8	48.00 S	8.30 E
Metepec, Méx.	234	19.15 N	99.36 W
Metepec, Méx.	234	18.56 N	98.28 W
Metharaw	110	16.12 N	98.08 E
Metheringham	44	53.08 N	0.24 W
Methil	46	56.10 N	3.01 W
Methler	263	51.35 N	7.37 E
Methlick	46	57.25 N	2.14 W
Methóni	38	36.50 N	21.43 E
Methow	182	48.07 N	120.00 W
Methow ≃	202	48.03 N	119.53 W
Methuen	207	42.43 N	71.11 W
Methven	172	43.38 S	171.39 E
Methwold	42	52.31 N	0.33 E
Methyen	46	56.25 N	3.34 W
Metiskow	184	52.24 N	110.38 W
Metković	36	43.03 N	17.39 E
Metlakatla, B.C., Can.	182	54.20 N	130.27 W
Metlakatla, Ak., U.S.	182	55.08 N	131.35 W
Metlaoui	148	34.20 N	8.24 E
Metlatonoc	234	17.11 N	98.20 W
Metlika	36	45.39 N	15.19 E
Metlili, Oued ∨	148	31.54 N	4.53 E
Metlili ech Chaâmba	148	32.18 N	3.40 E
Metnitz	61	46.59 N	14.13 E
Meto, Bayou ≃	194	34.05 N	91.26 W
Metolius ≃	202	44.36 N	121.17 W
Metompkin Bay ⊂	208	37.43 N	75.35 W
Metompkin Inlet ⊂	208	37.41 N	75.35 W
Metro	115a	5.05 S	105.20 E
Metropolis	194	37.09 N	88.43 W
Metropolitan	190	46.00 N	87.53 W
Metropolitana □[4]	252	33.30 S	70.30 W
Metropolitan Beach ♠	281	42.35 N	82.48 W
Metropolitan Museum of Art ⊍	276	40.47 N	73.58 W
Metropolitan Oakland International Airport ⊠	226	37.43 N	122.13 W
Metschow	54	53.49 N	12.58 E
Metsematluku	156	24.01 S	24.40 E
Metsera	154	2.35 S	26.07 E
Métsovon	38	39.46 N	21.11 E
Mettawa	278	42.14 N	87.56 W
Metten	60	48.52 N	12.55 E
Mettendorf	56	49.57 N	6.19 E
Metter	192	32.23 N	82.03 W
Mettet	56	50.19 N	4.40 E
Mettetal Airport ⊠	281	42.21 N	83.27 W
Mettingen	52	52.18 N	7.46 E
Mettlach	56	49.30 N	6.36 E
Mettmach	60	48.10 N	13.21 E
Mettmann	56	51.15 N	6.58 E
Mettray	50	47.27 N	0.39 E
Mettuppālaiyam	122	11.18 N	76.57 E
Mettūr	122	11.48 N	77.48 E
Metu	144	8.20 N	35.36 E
Metuchen	210	40.32 N	74.21 W
Metuge	154	12.58 S	40.20 E
Metulla	132	33.16 N	35.35 E
Metundo, Ilha I	154	11.10 S	40.41 E
Metz	56	49.08 N	6.10 E
Metzervisse	56	49.19 N	6.17 E
Metzger	224	45.26 N	122.45 W
Metzingen	56	48.32 N	9.17 E
Metzkausen	263	51.16 N	6.57 E
Metztitlán	234	20.36 N	98.45 W
Metztitlán, Laguna ⊜	234	20.40 N	98.50 W
Meu ≃	32	48.02 N	1.47 W
Meudon	261	48.48 N	2.14 E
Meudon, Bois de ♠	261	48.47 N	2.12 E
Meul ≃	158	27.56 S	28.50 E
Meulaboh	114	4.09 N	96.08 E
Meulan	50	49.01 N	1.54 E
Meulebeke	50	50.57 N	3.17 E
Meung-sur-Loire	50	47.50 N	1.42 E
Meureubo ≃	114	4.09 N	96.09 E
Meureudu	114	5.16 N	96.16 E
Meursault	58	46.59 N	4.46 E
Meurthe ≃	32	48.47 N	6.09 E
Meurthe-et-Moselle □[5]	32	48.35 N	6.10 E
Meuse	58	47.59 N	5.33 E

FRANÇAIS

Nom	Page	Lat.°′	Long.°′ W = Ouest
Meuse □[5]	56	49.00 N	5.30 E
Meuse (Maas) ≃	30	51.49 N	5.01 E
Meuselwitz	54	51.02 N	12.17 E
Meuvette ≃	50	48.45 N	1.08 E
Meux Creek ≃	212	44.07 N	81.02 W
Mevagissey	42	50.16 N	4.48 W
Mevang	152	0.07 N	11.05 E
Mewāt Plain ≚	124	27.40 N	77.15 E
Mexborough	44	53.30 N	1.17 W
Mexcala	234	17.56 N	99.37 W
Mexia	222	31.40 N	96.28 W
Mexia Lake ⊜[1]	222	31.39 N	96.36 W
Mexiana, Ilha I	250	0.02 S	49.35 W
Mexicali	232	32.40 N	115.29 W
Mexican Hat	200	37.09 N	109.52 W
Mexico, In., U.S.	216	40.49 N	86.06 W
Mexico, Me., U.S.	188	44.33 N	70.32 W
Mexico, Mo., U.S.	219	39.10 N	91.52 W
Mexico, N.Y., U.S.	212	43.27 N	76.13 W
Mexico, Pa., U.S.	208	40.32 N	77.21 W
México □[3]	234	19.20 N	99.45 W
Mexico (México) □[1], N.A.	230	23.00 N	102.00 W
Mexico (México) □[1], N.A.	232	23.00 N	102.00 W
México, Golfo de → Mexico, Gulf of ⊂	230	25.00 N	90.00 W
Mexico, Gulf of ⊂	230	25.00 N	90.00 W
Mexico Basin ✣[1]	16	25.00 N	92.00 W
Mexico Bay ⊂	212	43.31 N	76.17 W
Mexico Beach	192	29.58 N	85.24 W
Mexico City → Ciudad de México	234	19.24 N	99.09 W
Mexiko → Ciudad de México	234	19.24 N	99.09 W
Mexiko → Mexico □[1]	232	23.00 N	102.00 W
Mexiko, Golf von → Mexico, Gulf of ⊂	230	25.00 N	90.00 W
Meximieux	58	45.54 N	5.12 E
Mexique → Mexico □[1]	230	23.00 N	102.00 W
Mexique, Golfe du → Mexico, Gulf of ⊂	230	25.00 N	90.00 W
Mexticacán	234	21.13 N	102.43 W
Mey, Castle of ⊥	46	58.38 N	3.14 W
Meyanodas	164	7.38 S	131.38 E
Meycauayan	116	14.44 N	120.58 E
Meydan	130	38.21 N	41.47 E
Meydancık	130	41.25 N	42.14 E
Meydān-e Gel ≚	128	29.04 N	54.50 E
Meydān Khvolah	120	33.36 N	69.51 E
Meyenburg	54	53.18 N	12.14 E
Meyers Chuck	182	55.44 N	132.15 W
Meyersdale	188	39.48 N	79.01 W
Meyers Lake	214	40.52 N	81.24 W
Meyersville	222	28.55 N	97.21 W
Meyerton	158	26.33 S	28.01 E
Meyísti I	130	36.08 N	29.34 E
Meymac	32	45.32 N	2.09 E
Meymaneh	120	35.55 N	64.47 E
Meymeh	128	33.27 N	51.10 E
Meymeh ≃	128	32.05 N	47.16 E
Meynypilgino	180	62.32 N	177.02 E
Meyo Centre	152	2.33 N	11.02 E
Meyrargues	62	43.38 N	5.32 E
Meyrin	58	46.14 N	6.05 E
Meyronne	184	49.39 N	106.50 W
Meyrueis	32	44.10 N	3.26 E
Meyungs	175b	7.20 N	134.27 E
Meža ≃	61	46.35 N	15.02 E
Meẓada, Ḥorvot (Masada) ⊥	132	31.19 N	35.21 E
Mezapa	236	15.33 N	87.23 W
Mezdra	38	43.09 N	23.42 E
Meždurečensk	86	53.42 N	88.03 E
Meždurečenskij	86	59.36 N	65.53 E
Mèze	32	43.25 N	3.36 E
Mézel	62	43.59 N	6.12 E
Mezen'	24	65.50 N	44.13 E
Mezen' ≃	24	66.11 N	43.59 E
Mézenc, Mont ∧	62	44.55 N	4.11 E
Mezenskaja guba ⊂	24	66.40 N	43.45 E
Meževaja	78	48.16 N	36.44 E
Mežgorje	78	48.32 N	23.30 E
Meziadin Lake ⊜	182	56.04 N	129.18 W
Mežica	61	46.31 N	14.52 E
Mézières-en-Brenne	32	46.49 N	1.13 E
Mézières-sur-Seine	261	48.58 N	1.48 E
Mézilhac	62	44.48 N	4.21 E
Mézin	32	44.03 N	0.16 E
Mezinovskij	76	55.30 N	40.21 E
Mežirič	78	50.43 N	34.29 E
Mezőberény	30	46.50 N	21.02 E
Mezőcsát	30	47.49 N	20.55 E
Mezőkovácsháza	30	46.25 N	20.55 E
Mezőkövesd	30	47.50 N	20.34 E
Mezőtúr	30	47.00 N	20.38 E
Mežoz'ornyj	86	54.09 N	59.23 E
Mezquital	234	23.29 N	104.23 W
Mezquital ≃	232	22.35 N	104.54 W
Mezquital del Oro	234	21.10 N	103.23 W
Mezquitic	234	22.23 N	103.41 W
Mezraa	130	41.12 N	35.08 E
Mézy	261	49.00 N	1.53 E
Mezzana	64	46.19 N	10.48 E
Mezzano	64	46.09 N	11.48 E
Mezzenile	62	45.17 N	7.23 E
Mezzocorona	64	46.13 N	11.07 E
Mezzoiuso	70	37.52 N	13.28 E
Mezzola, Lago di ⊜	58	46.12 N	9.26 E
Mezzoldo	58	46.01 N	9.40 E
Mezzolombardo	64	46.13 N	11.05 E
Mezzomerico	266b	45.37 N	8.36 E
Mfangano Island I	154	0.28 S	34.01 E
Mfolozi ≃	158	28.25 S	32.26 E
Mfou	152	3.43 N	11.38 E
Mfuwe	154	13.04 S	31.46 E
Mgači	89	51.05 N	142.17 E
Mgeni ≃	158	29.48 S	31.02 E
Mgeta	154	8.19 S	36.08 E
Mglin	76	53.04 N	32.51 E
M'goun, Irhil ∧	148	31.31 N	6.25 W
M'hai, B'nom ∧	110	11.21 N	107.50 E
Mhasvād	122	17.38 N	74.47 E
Mhlatuze ≃	158	28.47 S	32.06 E
Mhlume	158	26.02 S	31.50 E
Mholach, Beinn ∧[2]	46	56.45 N	4.18 W
Mhòr, Beinn ∧	46	57.17 N	7.19 W
Mhòr, Loch ⊜	46	57.14 N	4.26 W
Mhow	120	22.33 N	75.46 E
Mi ≃, Zhg.	98	37.12 N	119.10 E
Mi ≃, Zhg.	100	27.09 N	112.51 E
Mia, Oued ∨	148	30.47 N	4.54 E
Miacatlán	234	18.46 N	99.22 W
Mia-dong ✦[8]	271b	37.37 N	127.01 E
Miagao	116	10.39 N	122.14 E
Miahuatlán de Porfirio Díaz	234	16.20 N	96.36 W
Miajadas	34	39.09 N	5.54 W
Miaméré	146	8.52 N	19.50 E
Miami, Mb., Can.	184	49.21 N	98.11 W
Miami, Az., U.S.	200	33.23 N	110.52 W
Miami, Fl., U.S.	220	25.46 N	80.11 W
Miami, In., U.S.	216	40.36 N	86.06 W
Miami, Ok., U.S.	196	36.52 N	94.52 W
Miami, Tx., U.S.	196	35.42 N	100.38 W
Miami □[6], In., U.S.	216	40.45 N	86.04 W
Miami □[6], Oh., U.S.	218	40.02 N	84.13 W
Miami ≃	224	45.33 N	123.53 W
Miami Beach, On., Can.	212	44.13 N	79.29 W
Miami Beach, Fl., U.S.	220	25.47 N	80.07 W
Miami Canal ⌸	220	25.47 N	80.15 W
Miami Creek ≃	226	37.21 N	119.44 W
Miami International Airport ⊠	220	25.48 N	80.17 W

PORTUGUÊS

Nome	Página	Lat.°′	Long.°′ W = Oeste
Miami Lakes	220	25.53 N	80.18 W
Miamisburg	218	39.38 N	84.17 W
Miamisburg Mound State Memorial ⊥	218	39.38 N	84.17 W
Miami Shores	220	25.51 N	80.11 W
Miami Springs	220	25.49 N	80.17 W
Miami State Recreation Area ♠	216	40.40 N	85.55 W
Miamiville	218	39.13 N	84.18 W
Miān Channūn	123	30.27 N	72.22 E
Mianchi	102	34.48 N	111.49 E
Mīāndoāb	128	36.58 N	46.06 E
Miandrivazo	157b	19.31 S	45.28 E
Mianduhe	89	49.05 N	121.06 E
Miane	64	45.57 N	12.06 E
Mīāneh	128	37.26 N	47.42 E
Miang, Phu ∧	110	17.42 N	101.01 E
Miangas, Pulau I	108	5.35 N	126.35 E
Mianhu	100	23.28 N	116.09 E
Mianhuadi	104	41.15 N	120.49 E
Miāni	123	32.32 N	73.04 E
Miāni Hōr ⊂	120	25.34 N	66.19 E
Mianning	102	28.39 N	102.09 E
Mianus ≃	207	41.03 N	73.35 W
Mianus, East Branch ≃	276	41.06 N	73.35 W
Mianus Reservoir ⊜[1]	276	41.08 N	73.37 W
Miānwāli	123	32.35 N	71.33 E
Mianxian	102	33.09 N	106.48 E
Mianyang, Zhg.	100	30.23 N	113.25 E
Mianyang, Zhg.	102	31.30 N	104.49 E
Mianzhu	102	31.20 N	104.09 E
Miao Dao I	98	37.56 N	120.45 E
Miaodao Qundao II	98	38.10 N	120.40 E
Miao'ergou	86	45.32 N	83.52 E
Miaofengshan	105	40.04 N	116.13 E
Miaogou	104	41.12 N	120.40 E
Miaojiagou	104	42.16 N	123.22 E
Miaojiatun	104	40.54 N	120.55 E
Miaokou	98	35.48 N	114.09 E
Miaoli	100	24.34 N	120.49 E
Miao Ling ⋏	102	26.15 N	107.26 E
Miaopu	106	31.00 N	118.44 E
Miaoqian	100	30.33 N	117.44 E
Miaotou	106	30.58 N	120.33 E
Miaowan	100	33.07 N	114.41 E
Miaoyang	98	40.49 N	124.24 E
Miaozhen	106	31.43 N	121.21 E
Miaozigou	107	30.17 N	104.35 E
Miarayon	116	8.04 N	124.50 E
Miarinarivo, Madag.	157b	16.38 S	48.15 E
Miarinarivo, Madag.	157b	18.57 S	46.55 E
Miarinavaratra	157b	20.13 S	47.31 E
Miasa	94	36.34 N	137.53 E
Miass	86	54.59 N	60.06 E
Miass ≃	86	56.06 N	64.30 E
Miasteczko Krajeńskie	30	53.06 N	17.01 E
Miastko	30	54.01 N	17.00 E
Miboro-dam ✦[6]	94	36.08 N	136.55 E
Mibu	94	36.25 N	139.48 E
Mibu ≃	94	35.49 N	137.57 E
Mica	156	24.10 S	30.48 E
Mica Mountain ∧	200	32.13 N	110.33 W
Micang Shan ⋏	102	32.45 N	107.20 E
Micanopy	192	29.30 N	82.16 W
Micaúne	156	18.18 S	36.35 E
Mičavičevnik	24	64.14 N	57.58 E
Miccosukee, Lake ⊜[1]	192	30.34 N	83.58 W
Miccosukee Indian Reservation ✦[4]	220	26.10 N	80.50 W
Micha Cchakaja	84	42.17 N	42.04 E
Michael, Mount ∧	164	6.25 S	145.20 E
Michael J. Kirwan Reservoir ⊜[1]	214	41.10 N	81.10 W
Michajlo-Koc'ubinskoje	78	51.27 N	31.04 E
Michajlov	82	54.14 N	39.02 E
Michajlovka, S.S.S.R.	78	49.53 N	39.38 E
Michajlovka, S.S.S.R.	78	49.19 N	36.28 E
Michajlovka, S.S.S.R.	78	47.16 N	35.14 E
Michajlovka, S.S.S.R.	80	47.38 N	46.54 E
Michajlovka, S.S.S.R.	80	50.05 N	43.15 E
Michajlovka, S.S.S.R.	83	48.30 N	38.54 E
Michajlovka, S.S.S.R.	83	48.09 N	37.22 E
Michajlovka, S.S.S.R.	83	48.44 N	37.16 E
Michajlovka, S.S.S.R.	85	43.06 N	71.36 E
Michajlovka, S.S.S.R.	85	42.50 N	75.42 E
Michajlovka, S.S.S.R.	85	42.37 N	78.20 E
Michajlovka, S.S.S.R.	86	51.49 N	79.45 E
Michajlovka, S.S.S.R.	86	56.26 N	78.53 E
Michajlovka, S.S.S.R.	86	53.51 N	76.32 E
Michajlovka, S.S.S.R.	88	50.26 N	104.10 E
Michajlovka, S.S.S.R.	88	55.30 N	114.09 E
Michajlovka, S.S.S.R.	88	51.07 N	119.20 E
Michajlovka, S.S.S.R.	88	52.57 N	103.18 E
Michajlovka, S.S.S.R.	89	49.13 N	129.56 E
Michajlovka, S.S.S.R.	89	43.56 N	132.00 E
Michajlovka, S.S.S.R.	265a	60.04 N	30.14 E
Michajlovka, S.S.S.R.	265a	59.43 N	30.01 E
Michajlovo	80	56.56 N	45.04 E
Michajlovo-Aleksandrovskij	83	49.13 N	40.15 E
Michajlovskaja	80	50.58 N	41.52 E
Michajlovskaja Celina, zapovednik ♠	78	50.45 N	34.10 E
Michajlovskij, S.S.S.R.	76	60.05 N	43.29 E
Michajlovskij, S.S.S.R.	86	51.41 N	79.47 E
Michajlovskij, S.S.S.R.	86	50.17 N	55.23 E
Michajlovskoje, S.S.S.R.	76	58.23 N	37.40 E
Michajlovskoje, S.S.S.R.	80	56.11 N	45.47 E
Michajlovskoje, S.S.S.R.	82	55.50 N	36.20 E
Michajlovskoje, S.S.S.R.	265b	55.35 N	37.35 E
Michalevo	82	55.27 N	38.26 E
Michali	82	55.17 N	39.05 E
Michalkovo	82	54.11 N	37.33 E
Michalovce	30	48.45 N	21.55 E
Michalovy Hory	60	49.55 N	12.47 E
Michanoviči	76	53.45 N	27.40 E
Michaud, Point ›	186	45.34 N	60.40 W
Micheal Peak ∧	182	53.35 N	126.26 W
Michejevo	88	57.10 N	104.53 E
Michel	182	49.43 N	114.49 W
Michelago	171b	35.43 S	149.10 E
Michelau	56	50.10 N	11.06 E
Micheldever	42	51.09 N	1.15 W
Micheldorf in Oberösterreich	61	47.52 N	14.08 E
Michelsneukirchen	60	49.08 N	12.33 E
Michelson, Mount ∧	180	69.19 N	144.17 W
Michel'sonovskij	265b	55.42 N	37.54 E
Michelstadt	56	49.41 N	9.00 E
Michendorf	54	52.18 N	13.01 E
Miches	238	18.59 N	69.03 W
Micheta	84	41.52 N	44.44 E
Michiana	216	41.46 N	86.48 W
Michiana Regional Airport ⊠	216	41.42 N	86.19 W
Michigamme ≃	190	46.04 N	88.13 W
Michigan	198	48.01 N	98.07 W
Michigan □[3], U.S.	178	44.00 N	85.00 W
Michigan □[3], U.S.	190	44.00 N	85.00 W
Michigan ≃	200	40.52 N	106.20 W
Michigan, Lake ⊜	190	44.00 N	87.00 W
Michigan, University of ⊍[2]	281	42.17 N	83.44 W
Michigan Center	216	42.13 N	84.19 W
Michigan City	216	41.42 N	86.53 W
Michigan International Speedway ♠	216	42.03 N	84.15 W
Michigan Stadium ♠	281	42.16 N	83.45 W
Michigan State Fair Grounds ♠	281	42.27 N	83.07 W
Michigantown	216	40.19 N	86.23 W
Michika	146	10.38 N	13.24 E
Michillinda	280	34.07 N	118.05 W
Michipicoten Bay ⊂	190	47.55 N	84.56 W
Michipicoten Island I	190	47.45 N	85.45 W
Michnevo	82	55.07 N	37.58 E
Michninskaja	24	60.26 N	46.14 E
Michoacán	204	32.28 N	115.20 W
Michoacán □[3]	234	19.10 N	101.50 W
Michoacanejo	234	21.33 N	102.36 W
Michów	30	51.32 N	22.19 E
Michurinsk → Mičurinsk	80	52.54 N	40.30 E
Mickle Fell ∧	44	54.37 N	2.18 W
Mickleham	260	51.16 N	0.19 W
Mickleover	42	52.24 N	1.34 W
Mickleton	285	39.47 N	75.14 W
Mickle Trafford	262	53.13 N	2.50 W
Mickleyville	218	39.45 N	86.16 W
Mico ≃	236	12.11 N	84.16 W
Mico, Montañas del ⋏	236	15.30 N	88.55 W
Miconge	152	4.26 S	12.51 E
Micoud	241f	13.50 N	60.54 W
Micronesia II	14	11.00 N	159.00 E
Micronesia, Federated States of □[1]	14	5.00 N	152.00 E
Mičurin	38	42.10 N	27.51 E
Mičurinsk	80	52.54 N	40.30 E
Midai, Pulau I	112	3.00 N	107.47 E
Midale	184	49.22 N	103.27 W
Midar	148	34.58 N	3.30 W
Mid-Atlantic Ridge ✣[3]	8	0.00	20.00 W
Midbar Yehuda → Wilderness of Judæa ✦[2]	132	31.30 N	35.18 E
Middalya	162	23.55 S	114.45 E
Middelburg, Ned.	52	51.30 N	3.37 E
Middelburg, S. Afr.	158	25.47 S	29.28 E
Middelburg, S. Afr.	158	31.30 S	25.00 E
Middelfart	41	55.30 N	9.45 E
Middelharnis	52	51.45 N	4.11 E
Middelkerke	50	51.11 N	2.49 E
Middelkerke, Vliegveld ⊠	50	51.12 N	2.52 E
Middelpos	158	31.55 S	20.13 E
Middelstum	52	53.20 N	6.38 E
Middelwater	156	23.17 S	30.16 E
Middelwit	156	24.58 S	27.00 E
Middenbeemster	52	52.33 N	4.55 E
Middenin	158	27.43 S	28.02 E
Middenmeer	52	52.47 N	5.00 E
Middle ≃, B.C., Can.	182	54.50 N	125.08 W
Middle ≃, Ca., U.S.	226	38.03 N	121.31 W
Middle ≃, Ia., U.S.	194	41.29 N	93.24 W
Middle ≃, Mn., U.S.	198	48.22 N	97.04 W
Middle ≃, Mo., U.S.	219	38.39 N	91.53 W
Middle Alkali Lake ⊜	204	41.28 N	120.04 W
Middle America Trench ✣[1]	16	15.00 N	95.00 W
Middle Andaman I	110	12.30 N	92.50 E
Middle Barton	42	51.56 N	1.22 W
Middle Bass	214	41.41 N	82.50 W
Middle Bass Island I	214	41.41 N	82.49 W
Middle-Bay	186	51.28 N	57.30 W
Middle Bay ⊂	276	40.37 N	73.36 W
Middleboro	207	41.53 N	70.54 W
Middle Bosque ≃	222	31.31 N	97.16 W
Middlebourne	188	39.29 N	80.54 W
Middlebranch	214	40.54 N	81.20 W
Middle Breakwater ✦[5]	280	33.43 N	118.13 W
Middlebro	184	49.01 N	95.21 W
Middle Brook	186	48.45 N	54.13 W
Middle Brook ≃, N.J., U.S.	276	40.39 N	74.41 W
Middle Brook ≃, N.J., U.S.	276	40.33 N	74.33 W
Middle Brook, East Branch ≃	276	40.35 N	74.33 W
Middle Brook, West Branch ≃	276	40.35 N	74.33 W
Middleburg, Md., U.S.	208	39.35 N	77.12 W
Middleburg, N.Y., U.S.	210	42.36 N	74.20 W
Middleburg, Oh., U.S.	216	40.17 N	83.34 W
Middleburg, Pa., U.S.	208	40.47 N	77.02 W
Middleburg Heights	214	41.22 N	81.48 W
Middlebury, Ct., U.S.	207	41.31 N	73.07 W
Middlebury, In., U.S.	216	41.40 N	85.42 W
Middlebury, Vt., U.S.	188	44.00 N	73.10 W
Middlebush	276	40.29 N	74.32 W
Middle Caicos I	238	21.47 N	71.43 W
Middle Cape ›	220	25.09 N	81.09 W
Middle Castor ≃	212	45.16 N	75.24 W
Middle Channel ≃[1], N.T., Can.	180	69.21 N	135.33 W
Middle Channel ≃[1], Mi., U.S.	281	42.33 N	82.42 W
Middle Concho ≃	196	31.27 N	100.25 W
Middle Creek ≃, U.S.	208	39.41 N	76.18 W
Middle Creek ≃, Pa., U.S.	210	40.46 N	76.52 W
Middle Creek ≃, Pa., U.S.	210	41.28 N	75.11 W
Middle Fabius ≃	194	39.58 N	91.35 W
Middle Falls	210	43.07 N	73.32 W
Middlefield, Ct., U.S.	207	41.31 N	72.42 W
Middlefield, N.Y., U.S.	210	42.41 N	74.50 W
Middlefield, Oh., U.S.	214	41.27 N	81.04 W
Middle Fork Reservoir ⊜[1]	218	39.51 N	84.51 W
Middle Ground I	272c	18.55 N	72.51 E
Middle Ground ✣[2]	174g	28.15 N	177.25 W
Middle Grove, Mo., U.S.	219	39.24 N	92.16 W
Middle Grove, N.Y., U.S.	210	43.05 N	73.55 W
Middle Haddam	207	41.33 N	72.33 W
Middleham	44	54.17 N	1.49 W
Middle Harbour ⊂	274a	33.48 S	151.14 E
Middle Head ›	274a	33.50 S	151.16 E
Middle Hope	210	41.34 N	74.01 W
Middle Island	210	40.53 N	72.56 W
Middle Island I	162	34.07 S	123.12 E
Middle Level Main Drain ⌸	42	52.43 N	0.22 E
Middle Loup ≃	198	41.17 N	98.23 W
Middle Maitland ≃	212	43.53 N	81.19 W
Middlemarch	172	45.31 S	170.07 E
Middlemount	166	22.49 S	148.40 E
Middle Musquodoboit	186	45.03 N	63.09 W
Middle Nodaway ≃	194	40.54 N	95.00 W
Middle Pease ≃	196	34.15 N	100.07 W
Middle Point	216	40.51 N	84.27 W
Middleport, N.Y., U.S.	210	43.12 N	78.28 W
Middleport, Oh., U.S.	188	39.00 N	82.02 W
Middleport, Pa., U.S.	208	40.44 N	76.05 W
Middle Raccoon ≃	198	41.34 N	94.12 W
Middle Reservoir ⊜[1]	283	42.27 N	71.07 W
Middle River	208	39.20 N	76.26 W
Middle River ⊂	208	39.19 N	76.25 W
Middle River Neck ›[1]	284b	39.22 N	76.23 W
Middle River Rouge ≃	281	42.20 N	83.15 W
Middle Rouge Parkway ♠	281	42.21 N	83.21 W
Middle Run ≃	285	39.41 N	75.43 W
Middlesboro	192	36.36 N	83.43 W
Middlesbrough	44	54.35 N	1.14 W
Middlesex, Belize	232	17.02 N	88.31 W
Middlesex, N.J., U.S.	276	40.34 N	74.29 W
Middlesex, N.Y., U.S.	210	42.42 N	77.16 W
Middlesex, N.C., U.S.	192	35.47 N	78.12 W
Middlesex □[6], On., Can.	212	43.00 N	81.08 W
Middlesex □[6], Ct., U.S.	207	41.33 N	72.39 W
Middlesex □[6], Ma., U.S.	207	42.30 N	71.25 W
Middlesex □[6], N.J., U.S.	208	40.29 N	74.27 W
Middlesex □[6], Va., U.S.	208	37.40 N	76.35 W
Middlesex Fells Reservation ♠	283	42.27 N	71.07 W
Middlesex Reservoir ⊜[1]	276	40.37 N	74.19 W
Middle Stewiacke	186	45.13 N	63.08 W
Middle Swan	168a	31.52 S	116.00 E
Middle Thames ≃	212	42.59 N	80.58 W
Middleton, Austl.	166	22.22 S	141.32 E
Middleton, N.S., Can.	186	44.57 N	65.04 W
Middleton, Eng., U.K.	42	52.43 N	0.28 E
Middleton, Eng., U.K.	44	53.33 N	2.13 W
Middleton, Ma., U.S.	207	42.35 N	71.01 W
Middleton, Mi., U.S.	190	43.11 N	84.42 W
Middleton, Tn., U.S.	194	35.03 N	88.53 W
Middleton, Wi., U.S.	216	43.05 N	89.30 W
Middleton-in-Teesdale	44	54.38 N	2.04 W
Middleton Island I	180	59.25 N	146.25 W
Middleton-on-the-Wolds	44	53.56 N	0.33 W
Middleton Pond ⊜	283	42.36 N	71.02 W
Middleton Reef I[1]	160	29.28 S	159.06 E
Middleton Saint George	44	54.30 N	1.28 W
Middletown, N. Ire., U.K.	48	54.18 N	6.50 W
Middletown, Ca., U.S.	226	38.45 N	122.36 W
Middletown, Ct., U.S.	207	41.33 N	72.39 W
Middletown, De., U.S.	208	39.26 N	75.43 W
Middletown, Il., U.S.	219	40.11 N	89.35 W
Middletown, In., U.S.	218	40.03 N	85.32 W
Middletown, Ky., U.S.	218	38.14 N	85.32 W
Middletown, Md., U.S.	208	39.26 N	77.32 W
Middletown, Mo., U.S.	219	39.07 N	91.24 W
Middletown, N.J., U.S.	208	40.23 N	74.07 W
Middletown, N.Y., U.S.	210	41.26 N	74.25 W
Middletown, Oh., U.S.	218	39.30 N	84.23 W
Middletown, Pa., U.S.	208	40.11 N	76.43 W
Middletown, R.I., U.S.	207	41.32 N	71.17 W
Middletown, Va., U.S.	188	39.01 N	78.16 W
Middletown Park	218	40.09 N	85.26 W
Middle Tuolumne ≃	226	37.50 N	120.01 W
Middleville, Mi., U.S.	216	42.42 N	85.27 W
Middleville, N.Y., U.S.	210	43.08 N	74.58 W
Middleville, N.Y., U.S.	276	43.08 N	74.58 W
Middlewich	44	53.11 N	2.27 W
Middle Yegua Creek ≃	222	30.19 N	96.47 W
Middle Yuba ≃	226	39.22 N	121.12 W
Midelt	148	32.41 N	4.43 W
Midfield	222	28.56 N	96.13 W
Midge Hall	262	53.42 N	2.45 W
Midgic	186	45.59 N	64.18 W
Mid Glamorgan □[6]	42	51.40 N	3.30 W
Midgley	262	53.44 N	1.58 W
Midhurst, On., Can.	212	44.27 N	79.44 W
Midhurst, Eng., U.K.	42	50.59 N	0.45 W
Midi, Aiguille du ∧	62	45.52 N	6.53 E
Midi, Canal du ⌸	32	43.26 N	1.58 E
Midi de Bigorre, Pic du ∧	32	42.56 N	0.08 E
Mid Illovo	158	29.59 S	30.25 E
Mid-Indian Basin ✣[1]	12	10.00 S	80.00 E
Mid-Indian Ridge ✣[3]	6	30.00 S	75.00 E
Midland, Austl.	168a	31.53 S	116.00 E
Midland, On., Can.	212	44.45 N	79.53 W
Midland, Ca., U.S.	204	33.52 N	114.48 W
Midland, Mi., U.S.	190	43.36 N	84.14 W
Midland, N.C., U.S.	192	35.13 N	80.30 W
Midland, Oh., U.S.	218	39.18 N	83.54 W
Midland, Pa., U.S.	214	40.37 N	80.26 W
Midland, Pa., U.S.	214	40.37 N	80.26 W
Midland, S.D., U.S.	198	44.04 N	101.09 W
Midland, Tx., U.S.	196	31.59 N	102.04 W
Midland, Wa., U.S.	224	47.10 N	122.24 W
Midland Bay ⊂	212	44.47 N	79.52 W
Midland Beach ✦[8]	276	40.34 N	74.05 W
Midland City	219	40.09 N	89.08 W
Midland Park, Mi., U.S.	216	42.23 N	85.22 W
Midland Park, N.J., U.S.	276	40.59 N	74.08 W
Midland Park Lake ⊜	212	44.44 N	79.53 W
Midlands □[4]	154	19.00 S	29.45 E
Midleton	48	51.55 N	8.10 W
Midlothian, Il., U.S.	216	41.37 N	87.43 W
Midlothian, Tx., U.S.	222	32.28 N	96.59 W
Midlothian Creek ≃	278	41.39 N	87.40 W
Midlum	52	53.43 N	8.37 E
Midnapore	182	50.55 N	114.05 W
Midnapore Canal ⌸	126	22.25 N	87.53 E
Midnapore Plain ≚	126	22.00 N	87.45 E
Mid-Ohio Sports Car Course ♠	214	40.40 N	82.38 W
Midongy Nord	157b	20.45 S	46.13 E
Midongy Sud	157b	23.35 S	47.01 E
Midori	96	34.43 N	132.37 E
Midori ✦[8]	268	35.32 N	139.34 E
Midori ≃	92	32.42 N	130.37 E
Midou ≃	32	43.54 N	0.30 W
Mid-Pacific Mountains ✣[3]	14	20.00 N	170.00 E
Midpines	226	37.32 N	119.55 W
Midreshet Ben Gurion	132	30.21 N	34.46 E
Midsayap	116	7.12 N	124.32 E
Midshipman Point ›	282	38.07 N	122.27 W
Midsland	52	53.22 N	5.16 E
Midsomer Norton	42	51.18 N	2.28 W
Midu	102	25.22 N	100.31 E
Midvale, De., U.S.	285	39.39 N	75.37 W
Midvale, Id., U.S.	202	44.28 N	116.44 W
Midvale, Oh., U.S.	214	40.26 N	81.22 W
Midville	192	32.49 N	82.14 W
Midway, B.C., Can.	182	49.01 N	118.47 W
Midway, B.C., Can.	202	49.01 N	118.46 W
Midway, Al., U.S.	194	32.04 N	85.31 W
Midway, In., U.S.	216	41.37 N	85.55 W
Midway, Ky., U.S.	218	38.09 N	84.41 W
Midway, Pa., U.S.	279b	40.22 N	80.17 W
Midway, Tx., U.S.	222	31.02 N	95.45 W
Midway, Ut,. U.S.	200	40.30 N	111.28 W
Midway City	280	33.45 N	118.00 W
Midway Islands □[2], Oc.	6	28.13 N	177.22 W
Midway Islands □[2], Oc.	174g	28.13 N	177.22 W
Midway Mall ✦[9]	279a	41.24 N	82.07 W
Midway Naval Station ■	174g	28.13 N	177.26 W
Midway Park	192	34.43 N	77.21 W
Midwest	200	43.24 N	106.16 W
Midwest City	196	35.26 N	97.23 W
Midwolda	52	53.12 N	7.00 E
Midyan ✦[1]	128	27.40 N	35.35 E
Midyat	130	37.25 N	41.23 E
Midyobe	152	1.21 N	10.18 E
Midžor (Midžur) ∧	38	43.23 N	22.42 E
Mie	96	32.58 N	131.35 E
Mie □[5]	92	34.30 N	136.30 E
Miechów	30	50.23 N	20.01 E
Miedwie, Jezioro ⊜	54	53.17 N	14.52 E
Międzybórz	30	51.24 N	17.40 E
Międzychód	30	52.36 N	15.55 E
Międzylesie	30	50.10 N	16.40 E
Międzyrzec Podlaski	30	52.00 N	22.47 E
Międzyrzecz	30	52.28 N	15.35 E
Międzyzdroje	30	53.55 N	14.28 E
Miehuapu	105	39.11 N	117.44 E
Miejska Górka	30	51.40 N	16.58 E
Miélan	32	43.26 N	0.19 E
Mielec	30	50.18 N	21.25 E
Mielno	30	54.16 N	16.01 E
Mien ⊜	26	56.25 N	14.51 E
Mienga	152	17.17 S	19.48 E
Mienhua Yü I	100	25.29 N	122.06 E
Mient'ienhuo Shan ∧	269d	25.11 N	121.30 E
Miercurea-Ciuc	38	46.22 N	25.48 E
Mieres	34	43.15 N	5.46 W
Mierlo	52	51.27 N	5.37 E
Mieroszów	30	50.41 N	16.10 E
Miersdorf	264a	52.20 N	13.37 E
Miersig	38	46.53 N	21.51 E
Mier y Noriega	234	23.25 N	100.07 W
Miesaituo	120	35.52 N	93.40 E
Miesbach	64	47.47 N	11.50 E
Miesenbach	61	47.22 N	15.46 E
Mieso	144	9.15 N	40.48 E
Mieste	54	52.28 N	11.11 E
Miesterhorst	54	52.27 N	11.09 E
Mieszkowice	30	52.46 N	14.30 E
Mifflin, Oh., U.S.	214	40.47 N	82.22 W
Mifflin, Pa., U.S.	208	40.34 N	77.24 W
Mifflin □[6]	210	40.40 N	77.33 W
Mifflinburg	210	40.55 N	77.02 W
Mifflintown	208	40.34 N	77.23 W
Mifflinville	210	41.01 N	76.18 W
Miftāḥ, Wādī ∨	142	30.15 N	31.46 E
Migdal	132	32.50 N	35.30 E
Migdal Ha'Emeq	132	32.41 N	35.15 E
Migdol	158	26.54 S	25.27 E
Migennes	50	47.58 N	3.31 E
Migliarino	66	44.46 N	11.56 E
Migliaro	64	44.48 N	11.58 E
Miglionico	68	40.34 N	16.30 E
Mignano Monte Lungo	68	41.23 N	13.58 E
Mignone ≃	66	42.11 N	11.44 E
Mignoviči	76	54.16 N	31.34 E
Mignovillard	58	46.48 N	6.08 E
Migori ≃	154	0.59 S	34.15 E
Miguel Alemán, Presa ⊜[1]	234	18.13 N	96.32 W
Miguel Alves	250	4.10 S	42.54 W
Miguel Auza	232	24.18 N	103.25 W
Miguel Calmon	250	11.26 S	40.36 W
Miguel Couto	287a	22.43 S	43.27 W
Miguel de la Borda	236	9.09 N	80.19 W
Migueles, Arroyo de los ≃	266a	40.20 N	3.32 W
Miguelete	258	34.01 S	57.39 W
Miguelete, Arroyo ≃	258	34.14 S	57.54 W
Miguel Hidalgo □[7]	286a	19.26 N	99.11 W
Miguel Hidalgo, Presa ⊜[1]	232	26.30 N	108.35 W
Miguelópolis	255	20.12 S	48.03 W
Miguel Pereira	256	22.27 S	43.22 W
Miguel Riglos	252	36.51 S	63.42 W
Migulinskaja	80	49.42 N	41.16 E
Migvie	46	57.08 N	2.56 W
Migyaunglaung	110	14.40 N	98.09 E
Mihăeşti	38	45.07 N	25.00 E
Mihai Viteazu	38	44.39 N	28.41 E
Mihajlovgrad	38	43.25 N	23.13 E
Mihalgazi	130	40.02 N	30.34 E
Mihalıççık	130	39.52 N	31.30 E
Mihama, Nihon	94	34.46 N	136.54 E
Mihama, Nihon	94	35.36 N	135.56 E
Mihama, Nihon	96	33.54 N	135.08 E
Mihara, Nihon	96	34.24 N	133.05 E
Mihara, Nihon	96	34.17 N	134.46 E
Mihara, Nihon	96	34.32 N	135.34 E
Mihara-yama ∧	94	34.43 N	139.23 E
Mihla	54	51.04 N	10.20 E
Miho	94	36.00 N	140.18 E
Mihonoseki	96	35.34 N	133.19 E
Miho-wan ⊂	96	35.30 N	133.23 E
Mihuangzhuang	105	39.07 N	116.12 E
Mijaly	86	48.57 N	53.42 E
Mijares ≃	34	39.55 N	0.01 W
Mijdaḥah	144	14.00 N	48.26 E
Mijdrecht	52	52.13 N	4.52 E
Mijiang	98	43.01 N	130.08 E
Mijoux	58	46.22 N	6.00 E
Mikabo-yama ∧	94	36.09 N	138.55 E
Mikame	96	33.25 N	132.27 E
Mikamo, Nihon	96	34.05 N	133.57 E
Mikamo, Nihon	96	35.09 N	133.37 E
Mikasa	92a	43.14 N	141.53 E
Mikaševiči	78	52.13 N	27.28 E
Mikata	94	35.33 N	135.55 E
Mikata-ko ⊜	94	35.34 N	135.53 E
Mikatou	273b	4.16 S	15.08 E
Mikawa, Nihon	94	36.29 N	136.29 E
Mikawa, Nihon	96	33.37 N	132.58 E
Mikawa-wan ⊂	94	34.43 N	137.10 E
Mikawa-wan-kokutei-kōen ♠	94	34.42 N	137.10 E
Mikazuki	96	34.58 N	134.27 E
Mikese	154	6.46 S	37.54 E
Mikhaylov, Cape ›	9	66.51 S	118.33 E
Mikhrot Shelomo Hamelekh (Timna') (King Solomon's Mines) ⊥	132	29.45 N	34.56 E
Miki, Nihon	96	34.17 N	134.05 E
Miki, Nihon	96	34.48 N	134.59 E
Mikínai ⊥	38	37.44 N	22.45 E
Mikindani	154	10.17 S	40.07 E
Mikinduri	154	0.07 N	37.50 E
Mikkabi	94	34.48 N	137.33 E
Mikkaichi	270	34.26 N	135.35 E
Mikkeli	26	61.41 N	27.15 E
Mikkelin lääni □[4]	26	62.00 N	27.30 E
Mikkwa ≃	176	58.25 N	114.45 W
Mikołajki	30	53.49 N	21.36 E
Mikołów	30	50.11 N	18.55 E
Mikomeseng	152	2.08 N	10.37 E
Mikomoto-jima I	94	34.34 N	138.56 E
Míkonos	38	37.26 N	25.20 E
Míkonos I	38	37.29 N	25.25 E
Mikope	152	5.03 S	20.48 E
Mikre	38	43.02 N	24.31 E
Mikrí Préspa, Límni ⊜	38	40.46 N	21.04 E
Miksimil	126	22.52 N	89.23 E
Mikšino	76	57.15 N	35.43 E
Mikstat	30	51.32 N	17.59 E
Mikulášovice	54	50.58 N	14.20 E
Mikulincy	78	49.24 N	25.38 E
Mikulino	76	55.02 N	31.07 E
Mikulkin, mys ›	24	67.48 N	46.40 E
Mikulov	61	48.49 N	16.39 E
Mikumi	154	7.24 S	36.59 E
Mikumi National Park ♠	154	7.12 S	37.05 E
Mikun'	24	62.21 N	50.06 E
Mikuni	94	36.13 N	136.09 E
Mikuni-sammyaku ⋏	94	36.50 N	138.40 E
Mikuni-tōge)(	94	36.46 N	138.50 E
Mikuni-yama ∧	94	35.59 N	138.43 E
Mikura-jima I	92	33.52 N	139.36 E
Mila	34	36.27 N	6.16 E
Milaca	190	45.45 N	93.39 W
Miladummadulu Atoll I[1]	122	6.15 N	73.15 E
Milagre	256	21.18 S	47.00 W
Milagres	250	7.17 S	38.57 W
Milagro	246	2.07 S	79.36 W
Milagros	116	12.13 N	123.30 E
Milam □[6]	222	30.47 N	96.57 W
Milan → Milano, It.	62	45.28 N	9.12 E
Milan, Ga., U.S.	192	32.01 N	83.03 W
Milan, In., U.S.	218	39.07 N	85.07 W
Milan, Mi., U.S.	216	42.05 N	83.40 W
Milan, Mn., U.S.	198	45.06 N	95.54 W
Milan, Mo., U.S.	194	40.12 N	93.07 W
Milan, N.M., U.S.	200	35.10 N	107.53 W
Milan, Oh., U.S.	214	41.17 N	82.36 W
Milan, Pa., U.S.	210	41.54 N	76.32 W
Milan, Tn., U.S.	194	35.55 N	88.45 W
Milando	152	8.45 S	17.36 E
Milan Federal Correctional Institution ⊍	281	42.06 N	83.40 W

≃ River	Fluß	Río	Rivière	Rio
⌸ Canal	Kanal	Canal	Canal	Canal
ʟ Waterfall, Rapids	Wasserfall, Stromschnellen	Cascada, Rápidos	Chute d'eau, Rapides	Cascata, Rápidos
⊔ Strait	Meeresstraße	Estrecho	Détroit	Estreito
⊂ Bay, Gulf	Bucht, Golf	Bahía, Golfo	Baie, Golfe	Baía, Golfo
⊜ Lake, Lakes	See, Seen	Lago, Lagos	Lac, Lacs	Lago, Lagos
≡ Swamp	Sumpf	Pantano	Marais	Pântano
⊓ Ice Features, Glacier	Eis- und Gletscherformen	Accidentes Glaciales	Formes glaciaires	Acidentes glaciares
⫪ Other Hydrographic Features	Andere Hydrographische Objekte	Otros Elementos Hidrográficos	Autres données hydrographiques	Outros acidentes hidrográficos

✣ Submarine Features	Untermeerische Objekte	Accidentes Submarinos	Formes de relief sous-marin	Acidentes submarinos
□ Political Unit	Politische Einheit	Unidad Politica	Entité politique	Unidade política
⊍ Cultural Institution	Kulturelle Institution	Institución Cultural	Institution culturelle	Institução cultural
⊥ Historical Site	Historische Stätte	Sitio Histórico	Site historique	Sitio histórico
♠ Recreational Site	Erholungs- und Ferienort	Sitio de Recreo	Centre de loisirs	Area de Lazer
⊠ Airport	Flughafen	Aeropuerto	Aéroport	Aeroporto
■ Military Installation	Militäranlage	Instalación Militar	Installation militaire	Instalação militar
✦ Miscellaneous	Verschiedenes	Misceláneo	Divers	Diversos

ENGLISH — Name | Page | Lat.°′ | Long.°′
DEUTSCH — Name | Seite | Breite°′ | Länge°′ E = Ost

Milang 168b 35.25 S 138.58 E
Milano (Milan), It. 62 45.28 N 9.12 E
Milano (Milan), It. 266b 45.28 N 9.12 E
Milano, Tx., U.S. 222 30.43 N 96.52 W
Milano □[4] 62 45.30 N 9.30 E
Milanoa 157b 13.35 S 49.47 E
Milano Marittima 66 44.16 N 12.21 E
Milanville 210 41.40 N 75.04 W
Milâs 130 37.19 N 27.47 E
Milaševiči 78 51.39 N 27.56 E
Mil'atino, S.S.S.R. 76 54.29 N 34.18 E
Mil'atino, S.S.S.R. 82 55.41 N 35.48 E
Milazzo 70 38.13 N 15.14 E
Milazzo, Capo di ≻ 70 38.16 N 15.14 E
Milazzo, Golfo di c 70 38.15 N 15.20 E
Milbank 198 45.13 N 96.38 W
Milbanke Sound ⊔ 182 52.18 N 128.33 W
Milborne Port 42 50.58 N 2.27 W
Milbuk 116 6.10 N 124.16 E
Milburn 196 34.14 N 96.32 W
Milburn Creek ≃ 276 40.38 N 73.36 W
Milden 184 51.30 N 107.31 W
Mildenau 54 50.35 N 13.04 E
Mildenhall 42 52.21 N 0.30 E
Milders 64 47.06 N 11.16 E
Mildmay 212 44.03 N 81.07 W
Mildred, Il., U.S. 219 39.46 N 89.38 W
Mildred, Pa., U.S. 210 41.28 N 76.22 W
Mildura 166 34.12 S 142.09 E
Mile 102 24.26 N 103.26 E
Miléai 38 39.20 N 23.09 E
Milena 70 37.28 N 13.44 E
Milendella 168b 34.49 S 139.12 E
Milepa 154 11.43 S 36.20 E
Miles, Austl. 166 26.40 S 150.11 E
Miles, Tx., U.S. 196 31.35 N 100.10 W
Miles ≃ 283 42.40 N 70.51 W
Milesburg 214 40.56 N 77.47 W
Miles City 202 46.24 N 105.50 W
Miles Creek c 208 38.46 N 76.12 W
Miles Creek ≃ 226 37.12 N 120.21 W
Mile Seven Hundred Thirty Three 180 60.03 N 131.07 W
Milešovka ∧ 54 50.33 N 13.56 E
Milestone 184 50.00 N 104.30 W
Milesville 279b 40.12 N 79.52 W
Milet (Miletus) ⊥ 130 37.28 N 27.15 E
Mileto 68 38.36 N 16.04 E
Miletto, Monte ∧ 68 41.27 N 14.22 E
Miletus → Milet ⊥ 130 37.28 N 27.15 E
Mileura 162 26.23 S 117.20 E
Milevsko 30 49.27 N 14.22 E
Milford, Eng., U.K. 42 51.11 N 1.38 W
Milford, Ct., U.S. 207 41.13 N 73.04 W
Milford, De., U.S. 208 38.54 N 75.25 W
Milford, Il., U.S. 216 40.37 N 87.41 W
Milford, In., U.S. 216 41.24 N 85.50 W
Milford, Ia., U.S. 198 43.19 N 95.08 W
Milford, Ky., U.S. 218 38.34 N 84.09 W
Milford, Me., U.S. 188 44.56 N 68.38 W
Milford, Md., U.S. 284b 39.21 N 76.44 W
Milford, Ma., U.S. 207 42.08 N 71.31 W
Milford, Mi., U.S. 216 42.35 N 83.35 W
Milford, N.H., U.S. 207 42.50 N 71.38 W
Milford, N.J., U.S. 210 40.34 N 75.05 W
Milford, N.Y., U.S. 210 42.35 N 74.56 W
Milford, Oh., U.S. 218 39.10 N 84.17 W
Milford, Pa., U.S. 210 41.19 N 74.48 W
Milford, Tx., U.S. 222 32.07 N 96.57 W
Milford, Ut,. U.S. 200 38.23 N 113.00 W
Milford, Va., U.S. 208 38.01 N 77.22 W
Milford Brook ≃ 276 40.19 N 74.17 W
Milford Center 218 40.10 N 83.26 W
Milford Cross Roads 285 39.43 N 75.44 W
Milford Haven 42 51.40 N 5.02 W
Milford Haven c 42 51.42 N 5.03 W
Milford Lake ⊜[1] 198 39.15 N 97.00 W
Milford on Sea 42 50.44 N 1.36 W
Milford Ridge 284b 39.21 N 76.45 W
Milford Sound 172 44.40 S 167.54 E
Milford Sound ⊔ 172 44.35 S 167.47 E
Milford Station 186 45.03 N 63.26 W
Milgis ≃ 154 1.48 N 38.06 E
Milgoo ∧ 162 28.51 S 118.07 E
Mil'guvejem ≃ 180 68.22 N 171.30 E
Milḥ, Baḥr al- ⊜ 128 32.40 N 43.35 E
Milḥat Ashqar ⊜ 128 35.18 N 41.55 E
Milḥat Ashqar ≋ 130 35.18 N 41.55 E
Milhaud 62 43.47 N 4.18 E
Mili I[1] 14 6.08 N 171.55 E
Milian ≃ 112 5.13 N 117.25 E
Milibangalala, Ponta ≻ 158 26.26 S 32.56 E
Milicia ≃ 70 38.04 N 13.33 E
Milicz 30 51.32 N 17.17 E
Milieu, Rivière du ≃ 206 46.47 N 73.56 W
Milīj 142 30.36 N 31.03 E
Milim 164 5.10 S 152.00 E
Milín 60 49.39 N 14.02 E
Miling 162 30.30 S 116.21 E
Milis 71 40.03 N 8.38 E
Militello in Val di Catania 70 37.16 N 14.48 E
Militello Rosmarino 70 38.03 N 14.41 E
Militsch → Milicz 30 51.32 N 17.17 E
Milk ≃ 202 48.05 N 106.15 W
Milk Creek ≃, Co., U.S. 200 40.24 N 107.45 W
Milk Creek ≃, Or., U.S. 224 45.15 N 122.41 W
Milk Hill ∧[2] 42 51.23 N 1.51 W
Mil'kovo 74 54.43 N 158.37 E
Milk River 182 49.09 N 112.05 W
Milk River Ridge Reservoir ⊜[1] 182 49.22 N 112.35 W
Mill 52 51.41 N 5.47 E
Mill ≃, Ct., U.S. 276 41.08 N 73.16 W
Mill ≃, Ma., U.S. 207 42.18 N 72.37 W
Mill ≃, Ma., U.S. 283 42.44 N 70.52 W
Mill ≃, Ma., U.S. 283 42.38 N 70.41 W
Mill ≃, Ma., U.S. 283 42.12 N 70.57 W
Mill ≃, Ma., U.S. 283 42.08 N 71.21 W
Mill ≃, N.Y., U.S. 276 40.38 N 73.39 W
Millard 198 41.13 N 96.07 W
Millau 32 44.06 N 3.05 E
Mill Bay 224 48.39 N 123.34 W
Millboro 192 37.59 N 79.36 W
Millbourne 285 39.58 N 75.15 W
Millbrae 226 37.35 N 122.23 W
Millbrook, On., Can. 212 44.09 N 78.27 W
Millbrook, Eng., U.K. 42 50.20 N 4.13 W
Millbrook, Ma., U.S. 283 42.03 N 70.41 W
Millbrook, N.J., U.S. 276 40.52 N 74.33 W
Millbrook, N.Y., U.S. 210 41.47 N 73.41 W
Mill Brook ≃, Ma., U.S. 283 42.31 N 71.18 W
Mill Brook ≃, N.J., U.S. 276 40.53 N 74.32 W
Mill Brook ≃, N.J., U.S. 276 40.25 N 74.06 W
Mill Brook ≃, N.J., U.S. 276 40.29 N 74.23 W
Millburn 276 40.44 N 74.18 W
Millbury, Ma., U.S. 207 42.11 N 71.45 W
Millbury, Oh., U.S. 214 41.33 N 83.25 W
Mill City 202 44.45 N 122.29 W
Mill Creek, Pa., U.S. 214 40.26 N 77.56 W
Millcreek, Ut,. U.S. 200 40.27 N 111.54 W
Mill Creek, W.V., U.S. 188 38.43 N 79.58 W
Mill Creek ≃, Austl. 274a 33.59 S 151.01 E
Mill Creek ≃, Ca., U.S. 226 36.49 N 119.21 W
Mill Creek ≃, Ca., U.S. 228 34.05 N 117.06 W
Mill Creek ≃, De., U.S. 285 39.42 N 75.39 W
Mill Creek ≃, Il., U.S. 219 39.50 N 91.24 W
Mill Creek ≃, In., U.S. 194 39.30 N 86.57 W
Mill Creek ≃, In., U.S. 216 41.01 N 86.36 W
Mill Creek ≃, Ia., U.S. 198 42.47 N 95.31 W
Mill Creek ≃, Ks., U.S. 198 39.55 N 96.56 W
Mill Creek ≃, Ky., U.S. 218 38.28 N 84.20 W
Mill Creek ≃, N.J., U.S. 276 40.48 N 74.03 W
Mill Creek ≃, N.J., U.S. 285 40.02 N 74.55 W
Mill Creek ≃, N.Y., U.S. 212 43.57 N 76.08 W
Mill Creek ≃, Oh., U.S. 214 41.06 N 80.40 W
Mill Creek ≃, Oh., U.S. 214 40.14 N 83.09 W
Mill Creek ≃, Oh., U.S. 218 39.06 N 84.32 W
Mill Creek ≃, Oh., U.S. 279a 41.25 N 81.38 W
Mill Creek ≃, Or., U.S. 224 45.36 N 121.11 W
Mill Creek ≃, Pa., U.S. 208 40.00 N 76.18 W
Mill Creek ≃, Pa., U.S. 210 41.53 N 77.08 W
Mill Creek ≃, Pa., U.S. 214 41.09 N 79.03 W
Mill Creek ≃, Pa., U.S. 285 40.03 N 75.16 W
Mill Creek ≃, Pa., U.S. 285 40.08 N 74.52 W
Mill Creek ≃, Tx., U.S. 222 29.50 N 96.07 W
Mill Creek ≃, Tx., U.S. 222 32.46 N 95.46 W
Mill Creek ≃, Tx., U.S. 222 30.08 N 95.37 W
Mill Creek ≃, Va., U.S. 208 38.09 N 77.10 W
Mill Creek, North Fork ≃ 224 45.33 N 121.18 W
Mill Creek, South Fork ≃ 224 45.36 N 121.12 W
Millcreek Township 214 42.05 N 80.10 W
Milldale 207 41.33 N 72.53 W
Milledgeville, Ga., U.S. 192 33.04 N 83.13 W
Milledgeville, Il., U.S. 190 41.57 N 89.46 W
Milledgeville, Oh., U.S. 218 39.36 N 83.35 W
Mille Îles, Rivière des ≃ 206 45.42 N 73.32 W
Mille Lacs, Lac des ⊜ 190 48.50 N 90.30 W
Mille Lacs Kathio State Park ♠ 190 46.08 N 93.43 W
Mille Lacs Lake ⊜ 190 46.15 N 93.40 W
Millemont 261 48.49 N 1.45 E
Millen 192 32.48 N 81.56 W
Millendon 168a 31.48 S 116.02 E
Miller, Mo., U.S. 194 37.13 N 93.50 W
Miller, S.D., U.S. 198 44.31 N 98.59 W
Miller □[6] 219 38.15 N 92.15 W
Miller, Mount ∧ 180 60.25 N 142.23 W
Miller City 216 41.06 N 84.08 W
Miller Creek ≃ 282 38.02 N 122.30 W
Miller House 180 65.32 N 145.11 W
Miller Mountain ∧ 204 38.03 N 118.12 W
Millerovo, S.S.S.R. 78 48.55 N 40.25 E
Millerovo, S.S.S.R. 83 47.49 N 39.15 E
Miller Peak ∧ 200 31.23 N 110.17 W
Miller Place 210 40.58 N 73.00 W
Millers ≃ 207 42.35 N 72.30 W
Millersburg, In., U.S. 216 41.31 N 85.41 W
Millersburg, In., U.S. 218 41.31 N 85.41 W
Millersburg, Ky., U.S. 218 38.18 N 84.08 W
Millersburg, Mi., U.S. 190 45.20 N 84.03 W
Millersburg, Oh., U.S. 214 40.33 N 81.55 W
Millersburg, Pa., U.S. 208 40.32 N 76.57 W
Millers Creek ≃ 196 33.27 N 99.14 W
Miller Seamount ✢[3] 16 53.30 N 144.20 W
Millers Falls 207 42.34 N 72.29 W
Millers Ferry 194 32.05 N 87.22 W
Millers Flat 172 45.40 S 169.25 E
Millers Island 284b 39.14 N 76.24 W
Millers Pond ⊜ 276 40.51 N 73.12 W
Millersport 188 39.54 N 82.32 W
Millers Run ≃ 279b 40.22 N 80.07 W
Millerstown 210 40.32 N 77.09 W
Millersville, Il., U.S. 219 39.25 N 89.07 W
Millersville, Oh., U.S. 214 41.18 N 83.16 W
Millersville, Pa., U.S. 208 39.59 N 76.21 W
Millerton, N.Y., U.S. 210 41.57 N 73.30 W
Millerton, Pa., U.S. 210 41.59 N 76.56 W
Millerton Lake ⊜[1] 226 37.01 N 119.41 W
Millerton Lake State Recreation Area ♠ 226 37.02 N 119.37 W
Millertown 186 48.49 N 56.33 W
Millertown Junction 186 49.01 N 56.21 W
Millesimo 62 44.22 N 8.12 E
Millet 182 53.06 N 113.28 W
Millett, Mi., U.S. 216 42.42 N 84.38 W
Millett, Tx., U.S. 196 28.35 N 99.12 W
Milleur Point ≻ 44 55.01 N 5.06 W
Millevaches, Plateau de ⩘[1] 32 45.30 N 2.10 E
Millford 48 55.07 N 7.43 W
Mill Green 260 51.41 N 0.22 E
Mill Grove 216 40.25 N 85.17 W
Mill Hall 210 41.06 N 77.29 W
Millheim 210 40.53 N 77.28 W
Mill Hill ◆[8] 260 51.37 N 0.13 W
Mill Hill ∧[2] 262 53.25 N 1.54 W
Millhousen 218 39.13 N 85.26 W
Millican 222 30.28 N 96.12 W
Millicent 166 37.36 S 140.22 E
Milligan, Fl., U.S. 194 30.45 N 86.38 W
Milligan, Ne., U.S. 198 40.30 N 97.23 W
Milligan Gulch V 200 33.37 N 107.02 W
Milligantown 279b 40.33 N 79.41 W
Milliken 275b 43.49 N 79.18 W
Millingen aan de Rijn 52 51.52 N 6.02 E
Millington, Il., U.S. 216 41.34 N 88.36 W
Millington, Md., U.S. 208 39.15 N 75.50 W
Millington, Mi., U.S. 190 43.16 N 83.31 W
Millington, N.J., U.S. 210 40.40 N 74.31 W
Millington, Tn., U.S. 194 35.20 N 89.53 W
Millinocket 188 45.39 N 68.42 W
Millionnyj 89 54.30 N 126.19 E
Millis 207 42.10 N 71.21 W
Mill Island I, Ant. 9 65.30 S 100.40 E
Mill Island I, N.T., Can. 176 64.00 N 78.00 W
Millisle 48 54.36 N 5.32 W
Mill Lake ⊜ 212 45.22 N 80.00 W
Millmerran 166 27.52 S 151.16 E
Millmont 210 40.53 N 77.08 W
Mill Neck 276 40.52 N 73.34 W
Mill Neck ≻[1] 276 40.53 N 73.33 W
Mill Neck Creek c 276 40.54 N 73.33 W
Millom 44 54.13 N 3.18 W
Mill Pond ⊜ 276 40.53 N 73.22 W
Millport, Scot., U.K. 46 55.46 N 4.55 W
Millport, Al., U.S. 194 33.33 N 88.04 W
Millport, N.Y., U.S. 210 42.16 N 76.50 W
Millport, Pa., U.S. 214 41.55 N 78.07 W
Millrift 210 41.25 N 74.45 W
Mill River 207 42.06 N 73.16 W
Mill Run Acres 284c 38.58 N 77.17 W
Millry 194 31.38 N 88.18 W
Mills, Pa., U.S. 214 41.57 N 77.41 W
Mills, Wy., U.S. 202 42.50 N 106.21 W
Mills, Lake ⊜[1] 224 47.59 N 123.36 W
Millsboro 208 38.35 N 75.17 W
Mills Creek ≃, Austl. 166 22.23 S 143.05 E
Mills Creek ≃, Ca., U.S. 282 37.27 N 122.25 W
Mills Lake ⊜ 176 61.30 N 118.10 W
Mills Mansion State Historic Site ⊥ 210 41.52 N 73.57 W
Millstadt 219 38.27 N 90.05 W
Millstatt 64 46.48 N 13.35 E
Millstätter See ⊜ 64 46.47 N 13.35 E
Millstone 276 40.29 N 74.35 W
Millstone ≃ 276 40.33 N 74.34 W
Millstream, Austl. 162 21.35 S 117.04 E
Millstream, B.C., Can. 224 48.30 N 123.31 W
Millstream Chichester National Park ♠ 162 21.25 S 117.20 E
Millstreet 48 52.03 N 9.04 W
Milltown, Scot., U.K. 46 57.14 N 2.52 W
Milltown, In., U.S. 218 38.20 N 86.16 W
Milltown, Mt., U.S. 202 46.52 N 113.52 W
Milltown, N.J., U.S. 208 40.27 N 74.26 W
Milltown, Wi., U.S. 190 45.31 N 92.30 W
Milltown Malbay 48 52.50 N 9.23 W
Millvale 279b 40.28 N 79.58 W
Mill Valley 226 37.54 N 122.32 W
Mill Village 214 41.53 N 79.58 W
Millville, Ma., U.S. 207 42.01 N 71.34 W
Millville, N.J., U.S. 208 39.24 N 75.02 W
Millville, Oh., U.S. 218 39.24 N 84.40 W
Millville, Pa., U.S. 210 41.07 N 76.31 W
Millville Lake 283 42.48 N 71.13 W
Millville Lake ⊜ 283 42.48 N 71.13 W
Millwood, Md., U.S. 284c 38.53 N 76.53 W
Millwood, N.Y., U.S. 210 41.11 N 73.48 W
Millwood, Va., U.S. 188 39.04 N 78.02 W
Millwood Lake ⊜[1] 194 33.45 N 94.00 W
Milly-la-Forêt 50 48.24 N 2.28 E
Milly-Lamartine 58 46.21 N 4.42 E
Milmay 208 39.26 N 74.51 W
Milmersdorf 54 53.06 N 13.38 E
Milmine 219 39.54 N 88.39 W
Milmont Park 285 39.53 N 75.20 W
Milne Bay □[5] 164 10.00 S 152.30 E
Milne Bay c 164 10.22 S 150.30 E
Milner 224 49.20 N 122.42 W
Milnesville 210 40.59 N 75.59 W
Milngavie 46 55.57 N 4.20 W
Milnor 198 46.15 N 97.27 W
Milnrow 44 53.37 N 2.06 W
Milnthorpe 44 54.14 N 2.46 W
Milo, Ab., Can. 182 50.34 N 112.53 W
Milo, Ia., U.S. 190 41.17 N 93.26 W
Milo, Me., U.S. 188 45.15 N 68.59 W
Milo ≃ 150 11.04 N 9.14 W
Milon-la-Chapelle 261 48.44 N 2.03 E
Mílos 38 36.45 N 24.27 E
Mílos I 38 36.41 N 24.15 E
Miloslaviči 76 53.41 N 32.15 E
Miloslavskoje 76 53.34 N 39.24 E
Miłosław 30 52.13 N 17.29 E
Milow, D.D.R. 54 53.11 N 11.32 E
Milow, D.D.R. 54 52.31 N 12.18 E
Milpa Alta □[7] 286a 19.11 N 99.02 W
Milpa Alta ◆[8] 286a 19.11 N 99.01 W
Milparinka 166 29.44 S 141.53 E
Milpitas 226 37.25 N 121.54 W
Milpitas Wash V 204 33.18 N 114.44 W
Milroy, In., U.S. 218 39.29 N 85.28 W
Milroy, Pa., U.S. 208 40.42 N 77.35 W
Milseburg ∧ 56 50.32 N 9.53 E
Mil'skaja ravnina ≚ 84 40.00 N 48.00 E
Milspe 263 51.18 N 7.21 E
Miltach 60 49.09 N 12.46 E
Miltenberg 56 49.42 N 9.15 E
Miltitz 54 51.19 N 12.16 E
Milton, Austl. 170 35.19 S 150.26 E
Milton, On., Can. 212 43.31 N 79.53 W
Milton, N.Z. 172 46.07 S 169.58 E
Milton, Eng., U.K. 42 52.14 N 0.09 W
Milton, De., U.S. 208 38.46 N 75.18 W
Milton, Fl., U.S. 194 30.37 N 87.02 W
Milton, Il., U.S. 219 39.34 N 90.39 W
Milton, In., U.S. 218 38.58 N 85.01 W
Milton, In., U.S. 218 39.47 N 85.09 W
Milton, Ia., U.S. 190 40.40 N 92.09 W
Milton, Ky., U.S. 218 38.43 N 85.22 W
Milton, Ma., U.S. 207 42.15 N 71.05 W
Milton, N.J., U.S. 276 41.02 N 74.32 W
Milton, N.Y., U.S. 210 41.39 N 73.57 W
Milton, N.D., U.S. 198 48.37 N 98.02 W
Milton, Pa., U.S. 210 41.00 N 76.50 W
Milton, Vt., U.S. 188 44.38 N 73.06 W
Milton, Wa., U.S. 224 47.14 N 122.18 W
Milton, W.V., U.S. 188 38.26 N 82.07 W
Milton, Wi., U.S. 216 42.46 N 88.56 W
Milton, Lake ⊜ 214 41.06 N 80.58 W
Milton Abbot 42 50.35 N 4.15 W
Milton-Freewater 202 45.55 N 118.23 W
Milton Harbor c 276 40.57 N 73.42 W
Milton Keynes 42 52.02 N 0.42 W
Milton Point ≻ 276 40.57 N 73.42 W
Miltonvale 198 39.20 N 97.26 W
Miltou 146 10.14 N 17.26 E
Miltzow 54 54.12 N 13.13 E
Milumba 154 7.06 S 31.04 E
Miluo 100 28.50 N 113.04 E
Miluo ≃ 100 28.50 N 113.06 E
Mil'utinskaja 80 48.38 N 41.40 E
Mil'utkej, gora ∧ 180 65.42 N 178.03 W
Milverton, On., Can. 212 43.34 N 80.55 W
Milverton, Eng., U.K. 42 51.02 N 3.16 W
Milwaukee 216 43.02 N 87.54 W
Milwaukee □[6] 216 43.02 N 87.58 W
Milwaukee ≃ 190 43.02 N 87.54 W
Milwaukee Bay c 216 43.02 N 87.53 W
Milwaukie 224 45.26 N 122.38 W
Mim 150 6.54 N 2.34 W
Mima 96 33.17 N 132.36 E
Mimasaka 96 35.00 N 134.10 E
Mimbres ≃ 200 32.13 N 107.28 W
Mimbres Mountains ⩘ 200 32.45 N 107.45 W
Mimi ≃ 92 32.20 N 131.37 E
Mimico ◆[8] 275b 43.37 N 79.30 W
Mimico Creek ≃ 275b 43.37 N 79.29 W
Mimizan 32 44.12 N 1.14 W
Mimmaya 92 41.12 N 140.26 E
Mimoň 54 50.40 N 14.44 E
Mimongo 152 1.11 S 11.36 E
Mimoso, Bra. 248 16.17 S 55.48 W
Mimoso, Bra. 255 15.10 S 48.05 W
Mimoso do Sul 255 21.04 S 41.22 W
Mims 220 28.39 N 80.50 W
Mimuro-yama ∧ 96 35.14 N 134.28 E
Min ≃, Zhg. 100 26.05 N 119.32 E
Min ≃, Zhg. 102 28.46 N 104.38 E
Mina, Méx. 196 26.01 N 100.32 W
Mina, Nv., U.S. 204 38.23 N 118.06 W
Mina ≃ 112 10.09 S 124.12 E
Mîna, Oued ≃ 34 35.47 N 0.30 E
Mīnā' al-Aḥmadī 128 29.04 N 48.08 E
Mīnāb 128 27.09 N 57.05 E
Mīnāb ≃ 128 27.01 N 56.53 E
Minabe 96 33.46 N 135.19 E
Minabegawa 96 33.47 N 135.20 E
Mina el Limón 236 12.45 N 86.44 W
Minago ≃ 184 54.34 N 98.08 W
Minahasa ≻[1] 112 1.00 N 124.35 E
Minäj ≃[1] 126 22.31 N 89.22 E
Minakami 94 36.46 N 138.58 E
Minakuchi 94 34.58 N 136.10 E
Minam ≃ 202 45.37 N 117.43 W
Minamata 92 32.13 N 130.24 E
Minami 94 35.39 N 136.57 E
Minami ◆[8], Nihon 268 35.24 N 139.36 E
Minami ◆[8], Nihon 270 34.40 N 135.31 E
Minami ◆[8], Nihon 270 34.58 N 135.45 E
Minami ≃ 94 35.30 N 135.49 E
Minamiaiki 94 36.02 N 138.33 E
Minami-Alps-kokuritsu-kōen ♠ 94 35.40 N 138.13 E
Minamiashigara 94 35.19 N 139.07 E
Minami-Bōsō-kokutei-kōen ♠ 94 35.10 N 140.05 E
Minamichita 94 34.44 N 136.52 E
Minami-Daitō-jima I 90 25.50 N 131.15 E
Minami-Iō-jima I 14 24.14 N 141.28 E
Minamiizu 94 34.39 N 138.50 E
Minamimaki 94 36.00 N 138.30 E
Minaminasu 94 36.39 N 140.06 E
Minamisenju ◆[8] 268 35.44 N 139.48 E
Minamishinano 94 35.19 N 137.56 E
Minami-Tori-shima (Marcus Island) I 14 24.18 N 153.58 E
Minano 94 36.04 N 139.06 E
Mina Pirquitas 252 22.41 S 66.31 W
Minard, S. Afr. 158 31.17 S 27.35 E
Minard, Scot., U.K. 46 56.07 N 5.15 W
Minas, Cuba 240p 21.29 N 77.37 W
Minas, Indon. 114 0.50 N 101.29 E
Minas, Ur. 252 34.23 S 55.14 W
Minas, Sierra de las ⩘ 236 15.10 N 89.40 W
Minas Basin c 186 45.20 N 64.00 W
Minas Channel ⊔ 186 45.15 N 64.45 W
Minas de Barroterán 232 27.40 N 101.20 W
Minas de Corrales 252 31.35 S 55.28 W
Minas de Matahambre 240p 22.35 N 83.57 W
Minas de Oro 236 14.46 N 87.20 W
Minas de Ríotinto 34 37.42 N 6.35 W
Minas Gerais □[3] 255 18.00 S 44.00 W
Minas Novas 255 17.15 S 42.36 W
Mînăstirea 38 44.13 N 26.54 E
Minatare 198 41.48 N 103.30 W
Minatitlán 234 17.59 N 94.31 W
Minato 268 35.13 N 139.52 E
Minato ◆[8], Nihon 268 35.39 N 139.45 E
Minato ◆[8], Nihon 270 34.39 N 135.26 E
Minato ≃ 268 35.13 N 139.52 E
Minbāl 142 28.24 N 30.41 E
Minbu 110 20.11 N 94.52 E
Minbulak 85 41.30 N 75.53 E
Minbya 110 20.22 N 93.15 E
Minbyin 110 19.17 N 93.32 E
Minchināhād 123 30.10 N 73.34 E
Minchinhampton 42 51.42 N 2.10 W
Minchinmávida, Volcán ∧[1] 254 42.49 S 72.28 W
Minchumina, Lake ⊜ 180 63.52 N 152.15 W
Mincio ≃ 64 45.04 N 10.59 E
Minco 196 35.18 N 97.56 W
Minčol ∧ 30 49.15 N 20.59 E
Mind'ak 86 54.02 N 58.48 E
Mindanao I 116 8.00 N 125.00 E
Mindanao ≃ 116 7.07 N 124.24 E
Mindego Creek ≃ 282 37.18 N 122.15 W
Mindego Hill ∧[2] 282 37.18 N 122.13 W
Mindel ≃ 58 48.31 N 10.23 E
Mindelheim 58 48.03 N 10.29 E
Mindelo 150a 16.53 N 25.00 W
Mindemoya 190 45.44 N 82.10 W
Minden, B.R.D. 52 52.17 N 8.55 E
Minden, On., Can. 212 44.55 N 78.43 W
Minden, La., U.S. 194 32.36 N 93.17 W
Minden, Ne., U.S. 198 40.29 N 98.56 W
Minden, Nv., U.S. 226 38.57 N 119.45 W
Minden, W.V., U.S. 188 37.58 N 81.07 W
Minden City 190 43.40 N 82.46 W
Mindenmines 194 37.28 N 94.35 W
Minderoo 162 22.00 S 115.02 E
Mindif 146 10.24 N 14.26 E
Mindiptana 164 5.45 S 140.42 E
Mindon 110 19.21 N 94.44 E
Mindoro I 116 12.50 N 121.05 E
Mindoro Occidental □[4] 116 13.00 N 121.00 E
Mindoro Oriental □[4] 116 13.00 N 121.20 E
Mindoro Strait ⊔ 116 12.20 N 120.40 E
Mindouli 152 4.17 S 14.21 E
Mindourou, Cam. 152 4.06 N 14.34 E
Mindourou, Cam. 152 3.25 N 13.32 E
Minduri 256 21.41 S 44.37 W
Mindživan 84 39.03 N 46.42 E
Mine, Ityo. 144 8.20 N 40.09 E
Mine, Nihon 96 33.17 N 130.26 E
Mine, Nihon 96 34.10 N 131.13 E
Minear Lake ⊜ 278 42.17 N 87.57 W
Minebank Run ≃ 284b 39.25 N 76.32 W
Mine Brook ≃, Ma., U.S. 283 42.08 N 71.26 W
Mine Brook ≃, Ma., U.S. 283 42.09 N 71.15 W
Mine Brook ≃, N.J., U.S. 276 40.41 N 74.38 W
Mine Centre 190 48.45 N 92.37 W
Minehead 42 51.13 N 3.29 W
Mine Hill 210 40.52 N 74.35 W
Mineiros 255 17.34 S 52.34 W
Mineo 70 37.16 N 14.42 E
Mineola, N.Y., U.S. 210 40.44 N 73.38 W
Mineola, Tx., U.S. 222 32.39 N 95.29 W
Miner ≃ 180 66.30 N 138.25 W
Mineral 224 46.43 N 122.10 W
Mineral City 214 40.36 N 81.21 W
Mineral Creek ≃ 224 46.45 N 122.08 W
Mineral del Monte 234 20.08 N 98.40 W
Mineral del Oro 234 19.48 N 100.08 W
Mineral'nyje Vody 84 44.12 N 43.08 E
Mineral Point, Pa., U.S. 214 40.23 N 78.50 W
Mineral Point, Wi., U.S. 190 42.51 N 90.10 W
Mineral Ridge 214 41.08 N 80.46 W
Mineral Springs, Ar., U.S. 194 33.52 N 93.54 W
Mineral Springs, Pa., U.S. 214 41.00 N 78.22 W
Mineral Wells 196 32.48 N 98.06 W
Minerbe 64 45.14 N 11.20 E
Minerbio 64 44.37 N 11.29 E
Minersville, Pa., U.S. 208 40.41 N 76.16 W
Minersville, Ut,. U.S. 200 38.12 N 112.55 W
Mine Run ≃ 285 40.15 N 75.28 W
Minerva, Ky., U.S. 218 38.42 N 83.55 W
Minerva, Oh., U.S. 214 40.43 N 81.06 W
Minerva, Tx., U.S. 222 30.46 N 96.59 W
Minerva Park 214 40.04 N 83.00 W
Minervino Murge 68 41.05 N 16.05 E
Minesing Swamp ≋ 212 44.23 N 79.51 W
Minetto 210 43.23 N 76.28 W
Mineville 188 44.05 N 73.31 W
Mineyama 96 35.37 N 135.04 E
Minfeng 120 37.05 N 82.40 E
Minga 154 11.08 S 27.57 E
Mingala 152 5.06 N 21.49 E
Mingan 186 50.18 N 64.02 W
Mingan ≃ 186 50.18 N 63.59 W
Mingan, Îles de II 186 50.12 N 63.35 W
Mingan Archipelago National Park ♠ 186 50.12 N 63.35 W
Mingan Mountains ⩘ 116 15.29 N 121.24 E
Mingāora 123 34.47 N 72.22 E
Mingardo ≃ 68 40.02 N 15.18 E
Mingary 166 32.08 S 140.44 E
Mingcheng 89 43.11 N 125.59 E
Mingečaur 84 40.45 N 47.03 E
Mingečaurskoje vodochranilišče ⊜[1] 84 40.50 N 46.50 E
Mingela 166 19.53 S 146.38 E
Mingenew 162 29.11 S 115.26 E
Mingera Creek ≃ 166 20.38 S 138.10 E
Minggang 100 32.29 N 114.03 E
Minggao 100 34.20 N 112.15 E
Minghuang 106 31.41 N 119.56 E
Mingin 110 22.52 N 94.39 E
Mingjuesi 106 31.34 N 118.53 E
Minglanilla 34 39.32 N 1.36 W
Ming Ming 164 5.30 S 146.10 E
Mingo, Congo 152 1.55 S 14.59 E
Mingo, Oh., U.S. 216 40.13 N 83.38 W
Mingo Creek ≃, Pa., U.S. 279b 40.13 N 79.57 W
Mingo Creek ≃, Pa., U.S. 285 40.10 N 75.32 W
Mingo Junction 214 40.19 N 80.36 W
Mingorría 34 40.45 N 4.40 W
Mingoville 214 40.56 N 77.39 W
Mingoyo 154 10.06 S 39.38 E
Mingrel'skaja 78 45.01 N 38.20 E
Mingshantou 100 29.18 N 112.33 E
Mingshui, Zhg. 89 47.10 N 125.55 E
Mingshui, Zhg. 102 42.06 N 96.04 E
Mingulay I 46 56.49 N 7.38 W
Mingwan 106 31.04 N 120.17 E
Mingxi 100 26.24 N 117.13 E
Mingyuegou 89 43.07 N 128.54 E
Mingyuelu 85 39.34 N 75.26 E
Minhang 106 31.01 N 121.24 E
Minhla, Mya. 110 19.58 N 95.03 E
Minhla, Mya. 110 17.59 N 95.43 E
Minho □[9] 34 41.40 N 8.30 W
Minho (Miño) ≃ 34 41.52 N 8.51 W
Minhou 100 26.12 N 119.06 E
Minianko 150 9.58 N 8.22 W
Minićevo 38 43.41 N 22.18 E
Minicoy Island I 122 8.17 N 73.02 E
Minier 194 40.26 N 89.18 W
Minigwal, Lake ⊜ 162 29.35 S 123.12 E
Minija ≃ 76 55.21 N 21.17 E
Minilya 162 23.51 S 113.58 E
Minilya ≃ 162 23.56 S 113.51 E
Minimarg 123 34.47 N 75.05 E
Minīn 132 33.39 N 36.18 E
Miniota 184 50.08 N 101.00 W
Minisinakwa Lake ⊜ 190 47.40 N 81.43 W
Ministikwan Lake ⊜ 184 54.01 N 109.39 W
Ministro Ramos Mexía 254 40.30 S 67.17 W
Ministro Rivadavia 288 34.51 S 58.22 W
Minitonas 184 52.07 N 101.00 W
Minj 164 5.54 S 144.39 E
Minjar 86 55.04 N 57.33 E
Minjary, Mount ∧ 171b 35.14 S 148.08 E
Minjiadianzi 104 41.35 N 121.41 E
Minjiaji 100 31.08 N 115.01 E
Minkamman 140 6.03 N 31.32 E
Min'kovo 76 59.42 N 43.28 E
Min-Kuš 85 41.41 N 74.28 E
Minlaton 168b 34.46 S 137.36 E
Minle, Zhg. 100 22.59 N 112.58 E
Minle, Zhg. 102 38.27 N 100.56 E
Minna 150 9.37 N 6.33 E
Minna Bluff ≻[1] 9 78.32 S 166.30 E
Minna-shima I, Nihon 174m 26.39 N 127.49 E
Minna-shima I, Nihon 175d 24.45 N 124.42 E
Minneapolis, Ks., U.S. 198 39.07 N 97.42 W
Minneapolis, Mn., U.S. 190 44.58 N 93.15 W
Minnechaduza Creek ≃ 198 42.54 N 100.29 W
Minnedosa 184 50.14 N 99.51 W
Minnehaha 224 45.39 N 122.37 W
Minnehaha, Lake ⊜ 220 28.31 N 81.46 W
Minneola, Fl., U.S. 220 28.35 N 81.45 W
Minneola, Ks., U.S. 198 37.26 N 100.00 W
Minneola, Lake ⊜ 220 28.34 N 81.46 W
Minneosa Creek ≃ 196 35.31 N 102.48 W
Minneota 198 44.34 N 95.59 W
Minnertsga 52 53.15 N 5.35 E
Minnesota □[3] 178 46.00 N 94.15 W
Minnesota ≃ 178 44.54 N 93.10 W
Minnesota Lake 190 43.50 N 93.49 W
Minnewanka, Lake ⊜ 182 51.15 N 115.20 W
Minnewaukan 198 48.04 N 99.15 W
Minnie Creek 162 24.02 S 115.42 E
Minnigaff 44 54.58 N 4.30 W
Minnipa 162 32.51 S 135.09 E
Minnitaki Lake ⊜ 184 49.58 N 92.00 W
Minnoch, Water of ≃ 44 55.02 N 4.33 W
Mino, Nihon 94 35.32 N 136.55 E
Minō, Nihon 96 34.50 N 135.28 E
Miño (Minho) ≃, Europe 34 41.52 N 8.51 W
Minō ≃, Nihon 270 34.47 N 134.57 E
Minoa 210 43.04 N 76.00 W
Minobu 94 35.22 N 138.26 E
Minobu-san ∧ 94 35.24 N 138.25 E
Minobu-sanchi ⩘ 94 35.14 N 138.20 E
Minocqua 190 45.52 N 89.42 W
Minokamo 94 35.26 N 137.01 E
Mino-Mikawa-kōgen ⩘[1] 94 35.11 N 137.23 E
Minong 190 46.05 N 91.49 W
Minonk 216 40.54 N 89.02 W
Minooka 216 41.27 N 88.16 W
Minorca → Menorca I 34 40.00 N 4.00 E
Minori 94 36.14 N 140.21 E
Minorsville 218 38.20 N 84.42 W
Minoshō 270 34.39 N 135.49 E
Minot, Ma., U.S. 283 42.14 N 70.45 W
Minot, N.D., U.S. 198 48.13 N 101.17 W
Minot Air Force Base ■ 198 48.26 N 101.21 W
Minowa 94 35.55 N 137.59 E
Minqiao 100 32.53 N 119.13 E
Minqin 102 38.42 N 103.11 E
Minqing 100 26.12 N 118.51 E
Minquadale 285 39.42 N 75.34 W
Minquan 98 34.41 N 115.11 E
Minquiers, Plateau des II 32 48.57 N 2.09 W
Minsen 52 53.42 N 7.58 E
Min Shan ⩘ 102 33.35 N 103.00 E
Minshāt adh-Dhahab 142 28.00 N 30.42 E
Minshat al-Amir Muhammad 'Ali 142 29.10 N 30.38 E
Minshāt al-Bakkārī 273c 30.01 N 31.08 E
Minshāt al-Ikhwah 142 30.56 N 31.21 E
Minshāt al-Mughālaqah 142 27.44 N 30.47 E
Minshāt Būlīn 142 31.11 N 30.10 E
Minshāt Sulṭān 142 30.32 N 30.55 E
Minsk 76 53.54 N 27.34 E
Minsk □[4] 24 54.30 N 28.00 E
Minskaja vozvyšennost' ⩘[1] 76 54.00 N 27.10 E
Mińsk Mazowiecki 30 52.11 N 21.34 E
Minster, Eng., U.K. 42 51.20 N 1.19 E
Minster, Eng., U.K. 42 51.26 N 0.49 E
Minster, Oh., U.S. 216 40.24 N 84.23 W
Minsterley 42 52.39 N 2.55 W
Minta 152 4.35 N 12.48 E
Mintaka Pass)(123 37.00 N 74.50 E
Mintard 263 51.22 N 6.54 E
Mintaro 168b 33.55 S 138.43 E
Mint Canyon 228 34.26 N 118.25 W
Mintlaw 46 57.31 N 2.00 W
Minto, Austl. 274a 34.01 S 150.51 E
Minto, Mb., Can. 184 49.25 N 100.01 W
Minto, N.B., Can. 186 46.05 N 66.05 W
Minto, Yk., Can. 180 62.34 N 136.51 W
Minto, Ak., U.S. 180 65.09 N 149.21 W
Minto, N.D., U.S. 198 48.17 N 97.22 W
Minto, Lac ⊜ 176 57.13 N 75.00 W
Minto Inlet c 176 71.20 N 117.00 W
Mintom II 152 2.42 N 13.17 E
Minton 184 49.10 N 104.35 W
Mintoum 152 0.27 N 12.16 E
Minturn 200 39.35 N 106.25 W
Minturnae ⊥ 68 41.14 N 13.45 E
Minturno 66 41.15 N 13.45 E
Minūf 142 30.28 N 30.56 E
Minulovo 265a 60.03 N 30.45 E
Minumadai-yōsui ≍ 268 35.50 N 139.42 E
Minur'uk 85 40.56 N 73.22 E
Minusinsk 86 53.43 N 91.42 E
Minutang 120 28.13 N 96.32 E
Minute Man National Historical Park ♠ 207 42.27 N 71.17 W
Minvoul 152 2.09 N 12.08 E
Minwakh 144 16.50 N 48.05 E
Minxian 102 34.26 N 104.02 E
Minya → Al-Minyā 142 28.06 N 30.45 E
Minyā al-Qamḥ 142 30.31 N 31.21 E
Minya Konka → Gongga Shan ∧ 102 29.35 N 101.51 E
Minyat an-Naṣr 142 31.07 N 31.39 E
Minyat as-Sīrij ◆[8] 273c 30.05 N 31.15 E
Minyat Sandūb 142 31.00 N 31.23 E
Miržir 78 46.40 N 28.19 E
Mirzow 54 53.23 N 12.30 E
Mio 190 44.39 N 84.07 W
Mioglia 62 44.29 N 8.25 E
Mionica 38 44.15 N 20.05 E
Miory 76 55.37 N 27.38 E
Mipi 120 28.57 N 95.48 E
Miquan 86 44.06 N 87.35 E
Miquelon I 186 47.03 N 56.20 W
Miquihuana 234 23.34 N 99.47 W
Miquon 285 40.04 N 75.16 W
Mīr, Miṣr 142 27.27 N 30.44 E
Mir, Niger 146 14.05 N 11.59 E
Mir, S.S.S.R. 76 53.27 N 26.28 E
Mira 34 40.26 N 8.44 W
Mira ≃, N.S., Can. 186 46.03 N 60.00 W
Mira ≃, Col. 246 1.36 N 79.01 W
Mira ≃, Port. 34 37.43 N 8.47 W
Mīrābād 128 30.25 N 61.50 E
Mira Bay c 186 46.02 N 59.56 W
Mirabeau 62 43.42 N 5.39 E
Mirabel 206 45.39 N 74.05 W
Mirabel, Aéroport International de ⊠ 206 45.41 N 74.02 W
Mirabella Eclano 68 41.02 N 14.59 E
Mirabella Imbaccari 70 37.19 N 14.27 E
Mirabello, Ippodromo ♠ 266b 45.36 N 9.17 E
Mirabello Monferrato 62 45.02 N 8.31 E
Miracema do Norte 250 9.33 S 48.24 W
Mirada Hills → La Mirada 228 33.54 N 118.01 W
Mirador 250 6.22 S 44.22 W
Mirador, Cerro ∧ 286d 11.57 S 77.02 W
Miradouro 255 20.53 S 42.21 W
Miraflores, Arg. 252 28.36 S 65.55 W
Miraflores, Col. 246 5.12 N 73.12 W
Miraflores, Col. 246 1.25 N 72.13 W
Miraflores, Perú 286d 12.07 S 77.02 W
Miraflores, Palacio ⊍ 286c 10.31 N 66.55 W
Miraflores Locks ◆[5] 236 9.00 N 79.36 W
Mīrah, Wādī al- V 128 32.26 N 41.42 E
Miraí 256 21.12 S 42.37 W
Miraj 122 16.50 N 74.38 E
Miraki 85 39.02 N 67.10 E
Miraleste 228 33.46 N 118.19 W
Mira Loma 228 34.01 N 117.31 W
Miramar, Arg. 252 38.16 S 57.51 W
Miramar, Arg. 252 30.54 S 62.40 W
Miramar, C.R. 236 10.06 N 84.44 W
Miramar, Fr. 62 43.30 N 6.57 E
Miramar, Moç. 156 23.50 S 35.34 E
Miramar, Fl., U.S. 220 25.59 N 80.13 W
Miramar ◆[8] 286b 23.07 N 82.25 W
Miramar, Laguna ⊜ 236 16.23 N 91.16 W
Miramare 66 44.02 N 12.38 E
Miramare, Aeroporto di ⊠ 66 44.02 N 12.35 E
Miramare, Castello di ⊥ 64 45.42 N 13.43 E
Miramar Naval Air Station ■ 228 32.52 N 117.07 W
Miramas 62 43.35 N 5.00 E
Mirambeau 32 45.23 N 0.34 W
Miramichi Bay c 186 47.08 N 65.08 W
Mira Monte 228 36.42 N 119.03 W
Mīram Shāh 120 33.01 N 70.04 E
Mīrān 123 31.24 N 70.43 E
Miranda, Austl. 274a 34.02 S 151.06 E
Miranda, Bra. 248 20.14 S 56.22 W
Miranda, Col. 246 3.15 N 76.14 W
Miranda, Ca., U.S. 204 40.14 N 123.49 W
Miranda □[3] 246 10.15 N 66.25 W
Miranda ≃ 248 19.25 S 57.20 W
Miranda de Ebro 34 42.41 N 2.57 W
Miranda do Douro 34 41.30 N 6.16 W
Mirande 32 43.31 N 0.25 E
Mirandela 34 41.29 N 7.11 W
Mirando City 196 27.26 N 99.00 W
Mirandola 64 44.53 N 11.04 E
Mirano 64 45.30 N 12.07 E
Mirantão 256 22.15 S 44.30 W
Mirante do Paranapanema 255 22.17 S 51.54 W
Mirapuxi ≃ 255 13.06 S 51.10 W
Mirasaka 96 34.46 N 132.58 E
Mira Taglio 64 45.26 N 12.08 E
Miravalles, Volcán ∧[1] 236 10.45 N 85.10 W
Miravete, Puerto de)(34 39.43 N 5.43 W
Mīr Bacheh Kowt 120 34.45 N 69.08 E
Mir-Bašir 84 40.20 N 46.55 E
Mirbāṭ 118 17.00 N 54.45 E
Mirboo North 169 38.24 S 146.10 E
Mirebeau-sur-Bèze 58 47.24 N 5.19 E
Mirecourt 58 48.18 N 6.08 E
Miren 64 45.54 N 13.37 E
Mirfield 44 53.40 N 1.41 W
Mirgorod 78 49.58 N 33.36 E
Mirgorodka 80 50.58 N 53.33 E
Miri 112 4.23 N 113.59 E
Miriam Vale 166 24.20 S 151.34 E
Mirim, Lagoa (Laguna Merín) c 252 32.45 S 52.50 W
Mirimichi, Lake ⊜ 283 42.02 N 71.18 W
Mírina 38 39.52 N 25.04 E
Miriñay ≃ 252 30.10 S 57.39 W
Mirinzal 250 2.01 S 44.43 W
Miriti 248 6.15 S 59.00 W
Miritiparaná ≃ 246 1.11 S 70.02 W
Miriyama 164 3.57 S 141.45 E
Mīrjāveh 128 29.01 N 61.28 E
Mirke ◆[8] 263 51.16 N 7.09 E
Mirna ≃ 64 45.19 N 13.36 E
Mirnock ∧ 64 46.46 N 13.43 E
Mirnoje Ozero 86 57.44 N 78.45 E
Mirnyj, S.S.S.R. 74 62.33 N 113.53 E
Mirnyj, S.S.S.R. 78 50.57 N 28.34 E
Mirnyj, S.S.S.R. 80 53.30 N 50.18 E
Mirnyy ⊍[3] 9 66.33 S 93.00 E
Mirond Lake ⊜ 184 55.06 N 102.47 W
Mironeasa 38 46.58 N 27.25 E
Mironovka 78 49.39 N 30.59 E
Mironovo 88 58.19 N 109.38 E
Mironovskij 83 48.29 N 38.17 E
Miropol' 78 50.07 N 27.41 E
Miropolje 78 51.02 N 35.16 E
Miroslav 61 48.57 N 16.18 E
Mirosławiec 30 53.21 N 16.05 E
Mirošov 60 49.41 N 13.40 E
Mirovice 60 49.31 N 14.02 E
Mirovoje 78 47.45 N 34.45 E
Mirovskoje 78 48.05 N 33.23 E
Mirow 54 53.16 N 12.49 E
Mīrpur, Bngl. 126 23.47 N 90.21 E
Mīrpur, Bngl. 126 23.56 N 88.59 E
Mīrpur, Pāk. 123 33.11 N 73.47 E
Mīrpur Batoro 120 24.44 N 68.16 E
Mīrpur Bībīwāri 120 28.32 N 67.44 E
Mīrpur Khās 120 25.32 N 69.00 E
Mīrpur Sakro 120 24.33 N 67.37 E
Mirria 150 13.43 N 9.07 E
Mirror 182 52.28 N 113.07 W
Mirror Lake ⊜, Ma., U.S. 283 42.05 N 71.20 W
Mirror Lake ⊜, N.J., U.S. 276 40.29 N 74.22 W
Mirtağ 130 38.23 N 41.56 E
Mirto 70 38.05 N 14.45 E
Mirtóön Pélagos ⊤[2] 38 36.51 N 23.18 E
Miryang 98 35.31 N 128.44 E
Miry Run ≃ 285 40.15 N 74.49 W
Mirza-Aki 85 40.45 N 73.25 E
Mirzaani 84 41.23 N 46.09 E
Mirzāganj 126 22.21 N 90.14 E
Mīrzākalu 126 22.29 N 90.48 E
Mirzāpur, Bngl. 126 24.06 N 90.06 E
Mirzāpur, India 124 25.09 N 82.35 E
Mirzāpur, India 272b 22.50 N 88.24 E
Mis 64 46.12 N 11.57 E
Misa ≃ 66 43.43 N 13.14 E
Misāḥah, Bi'r ⊤[4] 140 22.12 N 27.57 E
Misailovo 265b 55.34 N 37.49 E
Misaka 94 35.38 N 138.40 E
Misaka-tōge)(96 33.42 N 132.52 E
Misaki → Miura, Nihon 94 35.08 N 139.37 E
Misaki, Nihon 94 35.18 N 140.22 E

Symbols in the index entries represent the broad categories identified in the key at the right. Symbols with superior numbers (⩘[1]) identify subcategories (see complete key on page *I · 1).*

Symbole im Register stellen die rechts im Schlüssel erklärten Kategorien dar. Symbole mit hochgestellten Ziffern (⩘[1]) bezeichnen Unterabteilungen einer Kategorie (vgl. vollständiger Schlüssel auf Seite *I · 1).*

Los símbolos incluídos en el texto del índice representan las grandes categorias identificadas con la clave a la derecha. Los símbolos con numeros en su parte superior (⩘[1]) identifican las subcategorías (véase la clave completa en la página *I · 1).*

Les symboles de l'index représentent les catégories indiquées dans la légende à droite. Les symboles suivis d'un indice (⩘[1]) représentent des sous-catégories (voir légende complète à la page *I · 1).*

Os símbolos incluídos no texto do índice representam as grandes categorias identificadas com a chave à direita. Os símbolos com números em sua parte superior (⩘[1]) identificam as subcategorias (veja-se a chave completa à página *I · 1).*

∧	Mountain	Berg	Montaña	Montagne	Montanha
⩘	Mountains	Gebirge	Montañas	Montagnes	Montanhas
)(	Pass	Paß	Paso	Col	Passo
V	Valley, Canyon	Tal, Cañon	Valle, Cañón	Vallée, Canyon	Vale, Canhão
≚	Plain	Ebene	Llano	Plaine	Planície
≻	Cape	Kap	Cabo	Cap	Cabo
I	Island	Insel	Isla	Île	Ilha
II	Islands	Inseln	Islas	Îles	Ilhas
⊥	Other Topographic Features	Andere Topographische Objekte	Otros Elementos Topográficos	Autres données topographiques	Outros acidentes topográficos

ESPAÑOL — Nombre · Página · Lat.°′ · Long.°′ W = Oeste
FRANÇAIS — Nom · Page · Lat.°′ · Long.°′ W = Ouest
PORTUGUÊS — Nome · Página · Lat.°′ · Long.°′ W = Oeste

Nombre	Página	Lat.°′	Long.°′ W = Oeste
Misaki, Nihon	96	33.23 N	132.07 E
Misaki, Nihon	96	34.19 N	135.09 E
Misakubo	94	35.09 N	137.52 E
Misallah, Ra's ›	142	29.50 N	32.36 E
Misamis Occidental □[4]	116	8.20 N	123.42 E
Misamis Oriental □[4]	116	8.45 N	125.00 E
Misano Adriatico	66	43.57 N	12.39 E
Misantla	234	19.56 N	96.50 W
Misasa	96	35.24 N	133.54 E
Misasagi → Fujiidera	96	34.34 N	135.36 E
Misato, Nihon	94	36.23 N	138.57 E
Misato, Nihon	94	34.43 N	136.24 E
Misato, Nihon	94	36.15 N	137.54 E
Misato, Nihon	96	34.09 N	135.22 E
Misato, Nihon	268	35.50 N	139.53 E
Misawa	92	40.41 N	141.24 E
Misbourne ≃	260	51.34 N	0.29 W
Misburg	52	52.23 N	9.51 E
Miscou Centre	186	47.57 N	64.34 W
Miscou Island I	186	47.57 N	64.33 W
Miscou Point ›	186	48.03 N	64.32 W
Miševka	88	52.51 N	103.09 E
Misema ≃	190	47.54 N	79.53 W
Mi-sen ʌ	96	34.16 N	132.19 E
Misenheimer	192	35.29 N	80.17 W
Miseno	68	40.47 N	14.05 E
Misericórdia, Serra da ʌ	287a	22.51 S	43.17 W
Misery, Mount ʌ	169	37.24 S	143.36 E
Misgār	123	36.47 N	74.47 E
Mish'āb, Ra's al- ›	128	28.12 N	48.39 E
Mishan	89	45.33 N	131.52 E
Mishansha ≃	248	11.13 S	72.59 W
Mishawaka	216	41.39 N	86.09 W
Mishawum Lake ⊜	283	42.30 N	71.08 W
Mishbiḥ, Jabal ʌ	140	22.38 N	34.44 E
Misheguk Mountain ʌ	180	68.15 N	161.03 W
Mishe-Mokwa, Lake ⊜	285	39.52 N	74.48 W
Mishibishu Lake ⊜	190	48.05 N	85.25 W
Mishicot	190	44.14 N	87.38 W
Mishima, Nihon	94	35.07 N	138.55 E
Mishima → Settsu, Nihon	96	34.46 N	135.33 E
Mi-shima I	96	34.46 N	131.09 E
Mishmar HaNegev	132	31.21 N	34.43 E
Mishmi Hills ⋏[2]	120	29.00 N	96.00 E
Mishō	96	32.57 N	132.34 E
Mishqal, Jabal al- ʌ	132	31.53 N	36.08 E
Mišicha	88	51.38 N	105.35 E
Misikan	120	35.45 N	89.25 E
Misilmeri	70	38.02 N	13.27 E
Misima Island I	164	10.40 S	152.45 E
Misinto	266b	45.40 N	9.05 E
Misiones □[4]	252	27.00 S	55.00 W
Misiones □[5]	252	27.00 S	57.00 W
Misión San Francisco de Laishí	252	26.14 S	58.38 W
Misirevo	82	56.16 N	36.45 E
Miskī	140	14.51 N	24.13 E
Miski, Enneri V	146	20.00 N	17.55 E
Miškino, S.S.S.R.	86	55.20 N	63.55 E
Miškino, S.S.S.R.	265a	59.42 N	30.45 E
Miskito Channel ʊ	236	14.20 N	83.08 W
Miskitos, Cayos II	236	14.23 N	82.46 W
Miskitos Reef ✢[2]	236	14.28 N	82.42 W
Miskolc	30	48.06 N	20.47 E
Misli	130	38.10 N	34.52 E
Mislinja	61	46.28 N	15.14 E
Mislinja ≃	61	46.35 N	15.02 E
Mislippi	146	10.00 N	15.37 E
Mislivna ʌ	61	48.40 N	14.44 E
Mismār	140	18.13 N	35.38 E
Mismār, Jabal ʌ	140	18.06 N	35.42 E
Mišn'ovo	76	53.58 N	36.21 E
Misoke	154	1.06 S	28.38 E
Misool, Pulau I	164	1.52 S	130.10 E
Mispillion ≃	208	38.57 N	75.20 W
Misquamaebin Lake ⊜	184	53.30 N	91.05 W
Misquamicut	207	41.20 N	71.49 W
Miṣr → Egypt □[1]	140	27.00 N	30.00 E
Miṣr al-Jadīdah (Heliopolis) ◆[8]	273c	30.06 N	31.20 E
Miṣr al-Qadīmah (Old Cairo) ◆[8]	273c	30.00 N	31.14 E
Misrātah	146	32.23 N	15.06 E
Miṣr Baḥrī □[9]	140	31.00 N	31.00 E
Misrikh	124	27.27 N	80.31 E
Missanello	68	40.17 N	16.10 E
Missão Santa Cruz	152	16.14 S	21.57 E
Missão Velha	250	7.15 S	39.08 W
Misserghin	34	35.37 N	0.45 W
Missinaibi ≃	176	50.44 N	81.29 W
Missinaibi Lake ⊜	190	48.23 N	83.40 W
Missinaibi Lake Provincial Park ♦	190	48.25 N	83.35 W
Mission, S.D., U.S.	198	43.18 N	100.39 W
Mission, Tx., U.S.	196	26.12 N	98.19 W
Mission ◆[8]	282	37.45 N	122.25 W
Mission Bay c	228	32.47 N	117.15 W
Mission Beach	166	17.52 S	146.06 E
Mission City	224	49.08 N	122.18 W
Mission Creek ≃	282	37.32 N	121.55 W
Mission Hills ◆[8]	280	34.16 N	118.27 W
Mission Mountain ʌ[2]	194	36.02 N	94.35 W
Mission Peak ʌ	282	37.31 N	121.53 W
Mission Range ⋏	202	47.30 N	113.55 W
Mission Texas State Historic Park ♦	222	31.33 N	95.15 W
Mission Valley	222	28.54 N	97.12 W
Mission Viejo	228	33.36 N	117.40 W
Missisquoi □[6]	206	45.10 N	72.55 W
Missisquoi ≃	206	45.00 N	73.08 W
Missisquoi Bay c	206	45.05 N	73.10 W
Missisquoi-Nord ≃	206	45.02 N	72.26 W
Mississagagon Lake ⊜	212	44.52 N	77.05 W
Mississagi ≃	190	46.10 N	83.01 W
Mississagi Provincial Park ♦	190	46.35 N	82.45 W
Mississagua ≃	212	44.34 N	78.20 W
Mississagua Lake ⊜	212	44.42 N	78.19 W
Mississauga	212	43.35 N	79.39 W
Mississinewa ≃	216	40.46 N	86.02 W
Mississinewa Lake ⊜[1]	216	40.42 N	85.52 W
Mississippi □[3], U.S.	178	32.50 N	89.30 W
Mississippi □[3], U.S.	194	32.50 N	89.30 W
Mississippi ≃, On., Can.	212	45.26 N	76.16 W
Mississippi ≃, U.S.	178	29.00 N	89.15 W
Mississippi Bay c	162	34.00 S	122.17 E
Mississippi Delta ⁝[2]	194	29.10 N	89.15 W
Mississippi Lake ⊜	212	45.05 N	76.12 W
Mississippi Sound ʊ	194	30.15 N	88.40 W
Mississippi State	194	33.26 N	88.47 W
Missolonghi → Mesolóngion	38	38.21 N	21.17 E
Missoula	202	46.52 N	113.59 W
Missouri □[3], U.S.	178	38.30 N	93.30 W
Missouri □[3], U.S.	194	38.30 N	93.30 W
Missouri ≃	178	38.50 N	90.08 W
Missouri, Coteau du ⋏[2]	198	46.00 N	99.30 W
Missouri Buttes ʌ	198	44.37 N	104.47 W
Missouri City	222	29.37 N	95.32 W
Missouri Creek ≃	219	40.07 N	90.43 W
Missouri Valley	198	41.33 N	95.53 W
Mistake, Mount ʌ	171a	27.52 S	152.20 E
Mistake Creek	164	17.06 S	129.04 E
Mistake Creek ≃	166	21.38 S	146.50 E
Mistake Mountains ⋏	171a	27.52 S	152.22 E
Mistaken Point ›	186	46.38 N	53.10 W
Mistanipisipou ≃	186	51.32 N	61.50 W
Mistassibi ≃	176	48.53 N	72.13 W
Mistassibi Nord-Est ≃	186	49.50 N	71.56 W
Mistassini	176	50.25 N	73.52 W
Mistassini, Lac ⊜	176	51.00 N	73.37 W
Mistatim	184	52.52 N	103.22 W
Mistawasis Indian Reserve ◆[4]	184	53.06 N	106.48 W
Mistelbach, B.R.D.	60	49.55 N	11.31 E
Mistelbach, Öst.	61	48.34 N	16.35 E
Mistelgau	60	49.55 N	11.28 E
Misteln ⊜	40	59.07 N	16.57 E
Misterbianco	70	37.31 N	15.00 E
Misterei	140	13.07 N	22.09 E
Misteriosa Bank ✢[2]	238	18.50 N	83.50 W
Misterton, Eng., U.K.	42	50.52 N	2.47 W
Misterton, Eng., U.K.	44	53.27 N	0.51 W
Misti, Volcán ʌ[1]	248	16.18 S	71.24 W
Mistikokan ≃	184	57.01 N	91.27 W
Mistley	42	51.56 N	1.05 E
Mistrás ⊥	38	37.04 N	22.21 E
Mistretta	70	37.56 N	14.22 E
Misugi	94	34.33 N	136.16 E
Misumi, Nihon	92	32.37 N	130.27 E
Misumi, Nihon	96	34.22 N	131.15 E
Misumi, Nihon	96	34.46 N	131.58 E
Misumi ≃	96	34.47 N	131.56 E
Misurina	64	46.35 N	12.15 E
Mišurin Rog	78	48.50 N	33.58 E
Mišutino, S.S.S.R.	76	59.31 N	36.01 E
Mišutino, S.S.S.R.	82	56.23 N	38.06 E
Mita, Punta ›	234	20.47 N	105.33 W
Mīt Abū Ghālib	142	31.17 N	31.40 E
Mita Hills Dam ◆[6]	154	14.15 S	29.06 E
Mit'ajevo, S.S.S.R.	82	55.16 N	36.32 E
Mit'ajevo, S.S.S.R.	86	60.17 N	61.06 E
Mitaka	94	35.40 N	139.33 E
Mitake, Nihon	94	35.51 N	137.37 E
Mitake, Nihon	94	35.25 N	137.08 E
Mit'akinka ≃	83	48.35 N	39.50 E
Mit'akino	82	54.24 N	38.50 E
Mit'akinskaja	83	48.36 N	39.47 E
Mīt al-'Āmil	142	30.54 N	31.21 E
Mitatib	140	16.03 N	36.11 E
Mitau → Jelgava	76	56.39 N	23.42 E
Mīt Badr Ḥalāwah	142	30.51 N	31.14 E
Mīt Bashshār	142	30.31 N	31.24 E
Mitcham, Austl.	168b	34.59 S	138.36 E
Mitcham, Austl.	274b	37.49 S	145.12 E
Mitcham ◆[8]	260	51.24 N	0.10 W
Mitcheldean	42	51.53 N	2.30 W
Mitchell, Austl.	166	26.29 S	147.58 E
Mitchell, On., Can.	212	43.28 N	81.12 W
Mitchell, Il., U.S.	219	38.46 N	90.06 W
Mitchell, In., U.S.	218	38.43 N	86.28 W
Mitchell, Ne., U.S.	198	41.56 N	103.48 W
Mitchell, Or., U.S.	202	44.34 N	120.09 W
Mitchell, S.D., U.S.	198	43.42 N	98.01 W
Mitchell ≃, Austl.	164	15.12 S	141.35 E
Mitchell ≃, Austl.	164	14.28 S	125.43 E
Mitchell ≃, Austl.	166	37.53 S	147.41 E
Mitchell, Lake ⊜[1]	194	32.50 N	86.30 W
Mitchell, Mount ʌ	192	35.46 N	82.16 W
Mitchell and Alice Rivers National Park ♦	164	15.30 S	142.05 E
Mitchell Bay c	214	42.28 N	82.26 W
Mitchell Corners	212	43.57 N	78.48 W
Mitchell Field ⊠	278	41.55 N	88.15 W
Mitchell Lake ⊜, B.C., Can.	182	52.53 N	120.36 W
Mitchell Lake ⊜, On., Can.	212	44.34 N	78.58 W
Mitchell Point ›	214	42.26 N	82.26 W
Mitchellville	190	41.40 N	93.21 W
Mitchelstown	48	52.16 N	8.16 W
Mīt Fāris	142	31.02 N	31.36 E
Mīt Ghamr	142	30.43 N	31.16 E
Mīt Ḥalfah	273c	30.10 N	31.14 E
Mīt Ḥamal	142	30.26 N	31.32 E
Mithapur	120	22.25 N	69.00 E
Mitha Tiwāna	123	32.15 N	72.07 E
Mithi	120	24.44 N	69.48 E
Míthimna	38	39.22 N	26.10 E
Mitiaro I	14	19.49 S	157.43 W
Mitidja, Plaine de la ⁝	34	36.45 N	3.00 E
Mitilíni	38	39.06 N	26.32 E
Mitino	265b	55.51 N	37.21 E
Mitis, Lac ⊜	186	48.17 N	67.45 W
Mitishto ≃	184	54.50 N	98.58 W
Mitiškovo	76	54.40 N	33.31 E
Mitiwanga	214	41.22 N	82.27 W
Mitkof Island I	180	56.45 N	132.50 W
Mitla ⊥	234	16.55 N	96.17 W
Mitla, Laguna c	234	17.03 N	100.25 W
Mitla, Mamarr (Mitla Pass))(	142	30.00 N	32.53 E
Mitla Pass → Mitla, Mamarr)(	142	30.00 N	32.53 E
Mito, Nihon	94	34.49 N	137.19 E
Mito, Nihon	94	36.22 N	140.28 E
Mito, Nihon	96	34.40 N	131.59 E
Mitō, Nihon	96	34.13 N	131.21 E
Mito, Nihon	268	35.10 N	139.37 E
Mitomi	94	35.47 N	138.44 E
Mitoya	96	35.17 N	132.52 E
Mitra, Monte ʌ	152	1.23 N	9.57 E
Mitra do Bispo ʌ	256	22.10 S	44.34 W
Mitre ʌ	172	40.48 S	175.27 E
Mitre, Península ›[1]	254	54.48 S	65.40 W
Mitre Peak ʌ	172	44.38 S	167.50 E
Mitrofania Island I	180	55.51 N	158.49 W
Mitrofanovka	78	49.58 N	39.42 E
Mitrofanovo	24	63.13 N	56.00 E
Mīt Ruhaynah	273c	29.51 N	31.15 E
Mīt Ruhaynah (Memphis) ⊥	142	29.51 N	31.15 E
Mitry-le-Neuf	261	48.57 N	2.36 E
Mitry-Mory	261	48.59 N	2.37 E
Mitsamiouli	157a	11.23 S	43.18 E
Mitsinjo	157b	16.01 S	45.52 E
Mitsio, Nosy I	157b	12.54 S	48.36 E
Mitsiwa (Massawa)	144	15.38 N	39.28 E
Mitsiwa Channel ʊ	144	15.30 N	40.00 E
Mitsu, Nihon	96	34.47 N	134.33 E
Mitsu, Nihon	96	34.48 N	133.56 E
Mitsubori	268	35.56 N	139.56 E
Mitsue	94	34.29 N	136.10 E
Mitsugi	96	34.30 N	133.09 E
Mitsuike Park ♦	268	35.31 N	139.39 E
Mitsukaidō	94	36.01 N	139.59 E
Mitsuke	92	37.32 N	138.56 E
Mitsumarenge-dake ʌ	94	36.23 N	137.35 E
Mitsushima	92	34.16 N	129.19 E
Mitsuzaku	268	35.25 N	140.00 E
Mitsuzawa Park Race Track ♦	268	35.27 N	139.36 E
Mitta, Oued el V	148	34.20 N	6.44 E
Mittagong	170	34.27 S	150.27 E
Mittagskogel (Kepa) ʌ	61	46.31 N	13.57 E
Mittainville	261	48.40 N	1.39 E
Mitta Mitta ≃	171b	36.12 S	147.11 E
Mitte ◆[8]	264a	52.31 N	13.24 E
Mittelberg, B.R.D.	58	47.38 N	10.25 E
Mittelberg, Öst.	58	47.20 N	10.10 E
Mitteldorf → Międzychód	30	52.36 N	15.55 E
Mittelfischach	56	49.02 N	9.52 E
Mittelfranken □[5]	56	49.20 N	10.40 E
Mittellandkanal ≍	30	52.16 N	11.41 E
Mittelmeer → Mediterranean Sea ⍑[2]	10	35.00 N	20.00 E
Mittelsaida	54	50.46 N	13.18 E
Mittelstetten	60	48.15 N	11.06 E
Mittenwald	64	47.27 N	11.15 E
Mittenwalde, D.D.R.	54	53.11 N	13.39 E
Mittenwalde, D.D.R.	54	52.16 N	13.32 E
Mitterndorf	64	47.33 N	13.55 E
Mittersill	64	47.16 N	12.29 E
Mitterskirchen	60	48.21 N	12.44 E
Mitterteich	60	49.57 N	12.15 E
Mittewald an der Drau	64	46.46 N	12.36 E
Mittwalde → Międzylesie	30	50.10 N	16.40 E
Mittweida	54	50.59 N	12.59 E
Mitú	246	1.08 N	70.03 W
Mitumba, Monts ⋏	154	6.00 S	29.00 E
Mituo	107	28.53 N	105.37 E
Mitwaba	154	8.38 S	27.20 E
Mitwitz	56	50.15 N	11.12 E
Mityana	154	0.24 N	32.03 E
Mīt Yazīd	142	30.30 N	31.20 E
Mitzic	152	0.47 N	11.34 E
Miura	94	35.08 N	139.37 E
Miura-chosuichi ⊜[1]	94	35.49 N	137.23 E
Miura-dam ◆[6]	94	35.49 N	137.24 E
Miura-hantō ›[1]	94	35.15 N	139.39 E
Mius	80	51.26 N	47.56 E
Mius ≃	83	47.18 N	38.49 E
Miusinsk	83	48.05 N	38.53 E
Miusskij liman c[1]	83	47.15 N	38.40 E
Miwa, Nihon	94	35.11 N	136.47 E
Miwa, Nihon	94	36.39 N	140.18 E
Miwa, Nihon	96	34.39 N	132.51 E
Miwa, Nihon	96	35.12 N	135.14 E
Miwa, Nihon	96	34.13 N	132.06 E
Miwa, Nihon	270	34.31 N	135.51 E
Mi-Wuk Village	226	38.05 N	120.13 W
Mixcoac ◆[8]	286a	19.23 N	99.12 W
Mixcoac, Presa de ⊜[1]	286a	19.22 N	99.14 W
Mixco Viejo ⊥	236	14.52 N	90.40 W
Mixian	100	34.31 N	113.22 E
Mixin	107	30.23 N	105.46 E
Mixquiahuala	234	20.14 N	99.13 W
Mixtán	234	17.55 N	95.51 W
Mixteco ≃	234	18.11 N	98.30 W
Mixtlán	234	20.26 N	104.25 W
Miya	94	36.05 N	137.15 E
Miya ≃, Nihon	94	34.32 N	136.44 E
Miya ≃, Nihon	94	36.28 N	137.15 E
Miyagawa, Nihon	94	36.19 N	137.09 E
Miyagawa, Nihon	94	34.22 N	136.21 E
Miyagi □[5]	92	38.22 N	140.52 E
Miyagi-jima I	174m	26.21 N	127.57 E
Miyāh, Wādī al- V	140	25.00 N	33.23 E
Miyahara	268	35.56 N	139.37 E
Miyajima	96	34.18 N	132.19 E
Miyake	270	34.35 N	135.47 E
Miyake-jima I	92	34.05 N	139.32 E
Miyako	92	39.38 N	141.57 E
Miyakojima ◆[8]	270	34.43 N	135.33 E
Miyako-jima I	175d	24.47 N	125.20 E
Miyakonojō	92	31.44 N	131.04 E
Miyako-rettō II	175d	24.24 N	125.00 E
Miyama, Nihon	92	34.06 N	136.14 E
Miyama, Nihon	94	36.00 N	136.22 E
Miyama, Nihon	94	35.33 N	136.45 E
Miyama, Nihon	96	35.16 N	135.33 E
Miyama, Nihon	96	33.59 N	135.22 E
Miyāni	120	21.51 N	69.23 E
Miyanojō	92	31.54 N	130.27 E
Miyanoura-dake ʌ	93b	30.20 N	130.31 E
Miyara	175d	24.20 N	124.14 E
Miyata	96	33.44 N	130.40 E
Miyazaki, Nihon	92	31.54 N	131.26 E
Miyazaki, Nihon	94	35.56 N	136.05 E
Miyazakino-hana ›	96	34.04 N	135.05 E
Miyazu	96	35.32 N	135.11 E
Miyi	102	27.00 N	102.08 E
Miyoshi, Nihon	96	33.57 N	133.03 E
Miyoshi, Nihon	96	34.48 N	132.51 E
Miyoshi, Nihon	96	34.02 N	133.52 E
Miyoshi, Nihon	268	35.50 N	139.31 E
Miyota	94	36.18 N	138.30 E
Miyun	105	40.22 N	116.50 E
Miyun Shuiku ⊜[1]	105	40.30 N	116.58 E
Mizan Teferi	144	6.53 N	35.28 E
Mizdah	146	31.26 N	12.59 E
Mize	194	31.52 N	89.33 W
Mizen Head ›, Ire.	48	52.51 N	6.01 W
Mizen Head ›, Ire.	48	51.27 N	9.49 W
Miževiči	76	52.59 N	25.05 E
Mizhi	102	37.49 N	110.02 E
Mizil	38	45.00 N	26.26 E
Mizoč	78	50.24 N	26.09 E
Mizoguchi	96	35.21 N	133.26 E
Mizonokuchi	268	35.36 N	139.37 E
Mizonuma	268	35.48 N	139.36 E
Mizoram □[3]	120	23.30 N	93.00 E
Mizpah	208	39.29 N	74.50 W
Mizpah Creek ≃	198	46.16 N	105.17 W
Miẓpé Ramon	132	30.36 N	34.48 E
Mizque	248	17.56 S	65.19 W
Mizque ≃	248	18.39 S	64.20 W
Mizue ◆[8]	268	35.41 N	139.54 E
Mizuho, Nihon	94	35.46 N	139.21 E
Mizuho, Nihon	96	35.10 N	135.22 E
Mizuho, Nihon	96	34.51 N	132.31 E
Mizukaidō → Mitsukaidō	94	36.01 N	139.59 E
Mizuko	268	35.50 N	139.34 E
Mizumaki	96	33.51 N	130.42 E
Mizunami	94	35.22 N	137.15 E
Mizunoko-jima I	96	33.02 N	132.11 E
Mizusawa	92	39.08 N	141.08 E
Mizushima-nada c	96	34.25 N	133.40 E
Mizutori	270	34.47 N	135.45 E
Mizuwake-tōge)(	96	33.15 N	131.17 E
Mjälgen	40	60.33 N	15.07 E
Mjällom	26	62.59 N	18.26 E
Mjangad	86	48.15 N	91.57 E
Mjanyana	158	31.50 S	28.10 E
Mjölby	26	58.19 N	15.08 E
Mjøndalen	26	59.45 N	10.01 E
Mjörn ⊜	26	57.54 N	12.25 E
Mjøsa ⊜	26	60.40 N	11.00 E
Mkalama	154	4.07 S	34.38 E
Mkata	154	5.47 S	38.17 E
Mkhondvo ≃	158	26.39 S	31.25 E
Mkokotoni	154	5.52 S	39.15 E
Mkomazi ≃	158	30.12 S	30.50 E
Mkomazi Game Reserve ◆[4]	154	4.10 S	38.10 E
Mkulwe	154	8.35 S	32.19 E
Mkumvura ≃	154	15.55 S	31.07 E
Mkunumbi	154	2.18 S	40.42 E
Mkushi	154	13.40 S	29.20 E
Mkushi ≃	154	14.40 S	29.07 E
Mkushi River	154	13.32 S	29.45 E
Mkuze	158	27.37 S	32.02 E
Mkuze ≃	158	27.53 S	32.29 E
Mkuzi Game Reserve ◆[4]	158	27.40 S	32.15 E
Mkwaja	154	5.47 S	38.51 E
Mkwaya	154	10.06 S	39.40 E
Mladá Boleslav	54	50.23 N	14.59 E
Mladenovac	38	44.26 N	20.42 E
Mladotice	60	49.58 N	13.18 E
Mlala Hills ⋏[2]	154	6.47 S	31.45 E
M'Lang	116	6.55 N	124.53 E
M'Lang ≃	116	6.52 N	124.45 E
Mlanje Peak → Sapitwa ʌ	154	15.57 S	35.36 E
Mlava ≃	38	44.45 N	21.13 E
Mława	30	53.06 N	20.23 E
Mlawula	158	26.11 S	32.01 E
Mliba	158	26.14 S	31.36 E
Mlinov	78	50.31 N	25.37 E
Mljet, Otok I	36	42.45 N	17.30 E
Mljet Nacionalni Park ♦	36	42.47 N	17.25 E
Mljetski Kanal ʊ	36	42.48 N	17.35 E
Mmabatho	138	25.51 S	25.38 E
Mmadinare	156	21.57 S	27.52 E
Mnazi	154	8.54 S	39.06 E
Mnevniki ◆[8]	265b	55.45 N	37.28 E
Mnichov	60	50.03 N	12.49 E
Mníšek pod Brdy	30	49.52 N	14.16 E
Mo	24	66.15 N	14.08 E
Mo ≃	150	8.45 N	0.11 E
Moa ≃, Afr.	150	6.59 N	11.36 W
Moa ≃, Bra.	248	7.39 S	72.41 W
Moa, Pulau I	164	8.10 S	127.56 E
Moab	200	38.34 N	109.32 W
Moabi	152	2.15 S	11.00 E
Moaco ≃	248	7.41 S	68.18 W
Moa Island I	164	10.12 S	142.16 E
Moala Island I	175g	18.36 S	179.53 E
Moalboal	116	9.56 N	123.23 E
Moama	333	36.07 S	144.47 E
Moamba	156	25.35 S	32.13 E
Moana	168b	35.13 S	138.29 E
Moanda	152	1.34 S	13.11 E
Moanza	152	5.25 S	17.30 E
Moar Lake ⊜	184	52.00 N	95.09 W
Moate	48	53.24 N	7.58 W
Moatize	154	16.08 S	33.45 E
Moawhango	172	39.35 S	175.52 E
Moba, Nig.	273a	6.27 N	3.28 E
Moba, Zaïre	154	7.03 S	29.47 E
Mobara	94	35.25 N	140.18 E
Mobārakpur	126	22.58 N	89.10 E
Mobaye	152	4.19 N	21.11 E
Mobayi-Mbongo	152	4.18 N	21.11 E
Mobberley	262	53.19 N	2.20 W
Mobeetie	196	35.31 N	100.26 W
Mobeka	152	1.53 N	19.46 E
Mobenzélé	152	0.54 N	17.51 E
Moberly	194	39.25 N	92.26 W
Moberly ≃	182	56.12 N	120.55 W
Moberly Lake	182	55.48 N	121.45 W
Moberly Lake ⊜	182	55.49 N	121.45 W
Mobile, Al., U.S.	194	30.41 N	88.02 W
Mobile, Az., U.S.	200	33.03 N	112.16 W
Mobile ≃	194	30.29 N	88.01 W
Mobile Bay c	194	30.25 N	88.00 W
Mobjack	208	37.23 N	76.21 W
Mobjack Bay c	208	37.19 N	76.21 W
Mobridge	198	45.32 N	100.25 W
Moca, P.R.	240m	18.24 N	67.07 W
Moca, Rep. Dom.	238	19.24 N	70.31 W
Moča ≃	82	55.25 N	37.28 E
Mocajuba	250	2.35 S	49.30 W
Mocal ≃	236	14.00 N	88.33 W
Močalejevka	80	53.38 N	51.46 E
Močališče	80	56.21 N	48.23 E
Moçambique	154	15.03 S	40.45 E
Moçambique → Mozambique □[1]	138	18.15 S	35.00 E
Mocanaqua	210	41.08 N	76.08 W
Mocanguê Grande, Ilha I	287a	22.52 S	43.08 W
Mocassins, Lac des ⊜	206	46.35 N	74.25 W
Mo Cay	110	10.08 N	106.20 E
Moccasin, Ca., U.S.	226	37.49 N	120.18 W
Moccasin, Il., U.S.	219	39.09 N	88.45 W
Moc Chau	110	20.51 N	104.37 E
Moccoidumis	144	1.36 N	44.26 E
Mocha → Al-Makhā'	144	13.19 N	43.15 E
Mocha, Isla I	252	38.22 S	73.56 W
Moche ≃	248	8.10 S	79.03 W
Mocheng	106	31.35 N	120.43 E
Mochh	123	32.45 N	71.31 E
Mochigase	96	35.20 N	134.12 E
Mochitlán	234	17.30 N	99.18 W
Mochizuki	94	36.16 N	138.22 E
Mocho, Arroyo ≃	226	37.41 N	121.55 W
Mochov	54	50.08 N	14.50 E
Mochtín	60	49.22 N	13.21 E
Mochudi	156	24.28 S	26.05 E
Močily	82	54.20 N	38.41 E
Mocímboa da Praia	154	11.20 S	40.21 E
Mocímboa do Rovuma	154	11.20 S	39.18 E
Möckeln ⊜, Sve.	26	56.40 N	14.10 E
Möckeln ⊜, Sve.	40	59.18 N	14.30 E
Möckern	54	52.08 N	11.57 E
Mockfjärd	40	60.30 N	14.58 E
Mockhorn Island I	208	37.13 N	75.53 W
Möckmühl	56	49.19 N	9.22 E
Mockrehna	54	51.30 N	12.49 E
Mocksville	192	35.53 N	80.33 W
Moclips	224	47.14 N	124.12 W
Mocó ≃	246	1.49 S	66.48 W
Môco, Serra do ʌ	152	12.28 S	15.10 E
Mocoa	246	1.09 N	76.37 W
Mococa	256	21.28 S	47.01 W
Mocoduene	156	23.40 S	35.10 E
Mocomoco	248	15.22 S	68.59 W
Mocoretá	252	30.38 S	57.58 W
Mocorito	232	25.29 N	107.55 W
Moctezuma, Méx.	232	29.48 N	109.42 W
Moctezuma, Méx.	234	22.45 N	101.05 W
Moctezuma ≃, Méx.	232	29.09 N	109.40 W
Moctezuma ≃, Méx.	234	21.59 N	98.34 W
Mocuba	154	16.50 S	36.59 E
Močurica ≃	38	42.31 N	26.32 E
Modane	62	45.12 N	6.40 E
Modāsa	120	23.28 N	73.18 E
Modau ≃	56	49.49 N	8.28 E
Modbury	42	50.21 N	3.53 W
Modder ≃	158	29.02 S	24.37 E
Modderbee	273d	26.10 S	28.24 E
Modder East	273d	26.11 S	28.26 E
Modderfontein	273d	26.06 S	28.09 E
Modderfontein ≃	273d	26.13 S	28.10 E
Modderrivier	158	29.02 S	24.38 E
Model City	284a	43.11 N	78.59 W
Modena, It.	64	44.40 N	10.55 E
Modena, N.Y., U.S.	210	41.40 N	74.07 W
Modena □[4]	64	44.30 N	10.54 E
Moder ≃	56	48.49 N	8.06 E
Möderbrugg	61	47.17 N	14.29 E
Modern Art, Museum of ᴗ	276	40.46 N	73.58 W
Modeste, Mount ʌ	224	48.37 N	124.06 W
Modesto, Ca., U.S.	226	37.38 N	120.59 W
Modesto, Il., U.S.	219	39.29 N	89.59 W
Modesto City-County Airport ⊠	226	37.39 N	120.57 W
Modesto Main Canal ≍	226	37.39 N	120.27 W
Modesto Reservoir ⊜[1]	226	37.26 N	121.58 W
Modica	70	36.52 N	14.46 E
Modigliana	66	44.09 N	11.47 E
Modinagar	124	28.51 N	77.37 E
Modione ≃	70	37.34 N	12.49 E
Modjamboli	152	2.28 N	22.06 E
Modjeska	280	33.43 N	117.37 W
Mödling	264b	48.05 N	16.17 E
Mödling ≃	264b	48.04 N	16.22 E
Modoc	218	40.02 N	85.07 W
Modon ≃	50	47.16 N	1.27 E
Modowi	164	4.05 S	134.39 E
Modra, Česko.	30	48.21 N	17.17 E
Modra, Tchad	146	20.43 N	17.42 E
Modra špilja ⍊[5]	36	43.00 N	16.02 E
Mödrath	56	50.53 N	6.43 E
Modriča	38	44.57 N	18.18 E
Modřice	61	49.07 N	16.37 E
Mo Duc	110	14.57 N	108.53 E
Modugno	68	41.05 N	16.47 E
Moe	169	38.10 S	146.15 E
Moe ≃, Austl.	169	38.08 S	146.17 E
Moe ≃, P.Q., Can.	206	45.19 N	71.49 W
Moecherville	216	41.44 N	88.17 W
Moeda	255	20.20 S	44.03 W
Moehau ʌ	172	36.35 S	175.24 E
Moel Fferna ʌ	42	52.57 N	3.18 W
Moelv	26	60.56 N	10.42 E
Moema	255	19.50 S	45.24 W
Moen	50	50.46 N	3.24 E
Moen I	175c	7.26 N	151.52 E
Moena	64	46.22 N	11.39 E
Moengo	250	5.37 N	54.24 W
Moen-jo-Daro ⊥	120	27.18 N	68.15 E
Moenkopi	200	36.06 N	111.13 W
Moenkopi Wash V	200	35.54 N	111.26 W
Moeraki Point ›	172	45.22 S	170.52 E
Moerbeke, Bel.	50	50.45 N	3.55 E
Moerbeke, Bel.	50	51.10 N	3.56 E
Moerdijk	52	51.43 N	4.38 E
Moerewa	172	35.23 S	174.02 E
Moergestel	52	51.33 N	5.11 E
Moero, Lago → Mweru, Lake ⊜	154	9.00 S	28.45 E
Moers	56	51.27 N	6.37 E
Moersbach ≃	263	51.33 N	6.36 E
Moesa ≃	58	46.13 N	9.03 E
Moffat	44	55.20 N	3.27 W
Moffat Peak ʌ	172	45.02 S	168.07 E
Moffatt	222	31.12 N	97.28 W
Moffatt, Lac ⊜	206	45.34 N	71.19 W
Moffat Water ≃	44	55.18 N	3.25 W
Moffet Point ›	180	55.26 N	162.32 W
Moffett Field Naval Air Station ■	226	37.24 N	122.03 W
Moffit	198	46.40 N	100.17 W
Mofoluku	273a	6.33 N	3.20 E
Moga	123	30.48 N	75.10 E
Mogadiscio → Muqdisho	144	2.04 N	45.22 E
Mogadishu → Muqdisho	144	2.04 N	45.22 E
Mogador → Essaouira	148	31.30 N	9.47 W
Mogadore	214	41.02 N	81.23 W
Mogadore Reservoir ⊜[1]	214	41.04 N	81.21 W
Mogadouro	34	41.20 N	6.39 W
Mogalakwena ≃	156	23.00 S	28.40 E
Mogalo	152	3.10 N	19.04 E
Mogami ≃	92	38.55 N	139.48 E
Mogan Shan ʌ	106	30.36 N	119.52 E
Mogapinyana	156	22.19 S	27.27 E
Mogaung	110	25.18 N	96.56 E
Mogdy	89	50.35 N	133.51 E
Mogees	285	40.06 N	75.19 W
Møgeltønder	41	54.56 N	8.49 E
Mogenstrup	41	55.11 N	11.53 E
Mogent ≃	266d	41.33 N	2.15 E
Moggio Udinese	64	46.25 N	13.12 E
Mogi, Serra do ⋏	287b	23.47 S	46.20 W
Mogi das Cruzes	256	23.31 S	46.11 W
Mogielnica	30	51.42 N	20.43 E
Mogi-Guaçu	256	22.22 S	46.57 W
Mogila-Bel'mak, gora ʌ[2]	78	47.20 N	36.35 E
Mogila-Mečetnaja, gora ʌ[2]	83	48.16 N	38.53 E
Mogilev → Mogil'ov	76	53.54 N	30.21 E
Mogilno	30	52.40 N	17.58 E
Mogil'ov, S.S.S.R.	76	53.54 N	30.21 E
Mogil'ov, S.S.S.R.	78	48.52 N	34.29 E
Mogil'ov-Podol'skij	78	48.27 N	27.48 E
Mogi-Mirim	256	22.26 S	46.57 W
Mogincual	154	15.35 S	40.25 E
Moglal, Wādī V	140	19.18 N	34.29 E
Moglia	64	44.56 N	10.55 E
Mogliano Veneto	64	45.33 N	12.14 E
Mogoča	88	53.44 N	119.44 E
Mogoča ≃	76	58.00 N	36.26 E
Mogočin	86	57.43 N	83.34 E
Mogod	88	48.24 N	103.00 E
Mogogh	140	8.26 N	31.19 E
Mogojto	88	54.25 N	110.27 E
Mogojtuj	88	51.17 N	114.55 E
Mogok	110	22.55 N	96.30 E
Mogollon Mountains ⋏	200	33.25 N	108.40 W
Mogollon Rim ⍊[4]	200	34.25 N	110.50 W
Mogor	120	32.52 N	67.47 E
Mogorella	71	39.52 N	8.51 E
Mogoro	71	39.41 N	8.47 E
Mogotes	246	6.30 N	72.58 W
Mogotón, Pico ʌ	236	13.45 N	86.23 W
Mograt Island I	140	19.30 N	33.15 E
Mogroum	146	11.06 N	15.25 E
Moguer	34	37.16 N	6.50 W
Mogyoród	264c	47.36 N	19.15 E
Mogyoródi-patak ≃	264c	47.36 N	19.05 E
Mogzon	88	51.45 N	111.58 E
Mohács	30	45.59 N	18.42 E
Mohaka	172	39.07 S	177.11 E
Mohaka ≃	172	39.07 S	177.12 E
Mohall	198	48.45 N	101.30 W
Moḥammadābād	128	30.53 N	61.28 E
Mohammedia (Fedala)	148	33.44 N	7.24 W
Mohana	124	25.54 N	77.45 E
Mohangi	154	0.03 N	29.05 E
Mohania	124	25.11 N	83.37 E
Mohanpur, Bngl.	126	23.24 N	90.36 E
Mohanpur, India	126	21.51 N	87.26 E
Mohanpur, India	272a	28.44 N	77.10 E
Mohave, Lake ⊜[1]	204	35.25 N	114.38 W
Mohawk, Mi., U.S.	190	47.18 N	88.21 W
Mohawk, N.Y., U.S.	210	43.00 N	75.00 W
Mohawk ≃	210	42.47 N	73.42 W
Mohawk, East Branch ≃	212	43.22 N	75.28 W
Mohawk, Lake ⊜	276	41.02 N	74.41 W
Mohawk Dam ◆[6]	214	40.20 N	82.05 W
Mohawk Mountain ʌ	207	41.49 N	73.17 W
Mohawk Point ›	212	42.51 N	79.29 W
Mohe	89	53.29 N	122.19 E
Moheda	26	57.00 N	14.34 E
Mohegan	207	41.28 N	72.06 W
Mohegan Lake	210	41.19 N	73.51 W
Mohelnice	30	49.46 N	16.55 E
Moher, Cliffs of ⍊[4]	48	52.57 N	9.26 W
Mohican ≃	214	40.22 N	82.09 W
Mohican, Black Fork ≃	214	40.35 N	82.17 W
Mohican, Cape ›	180	60.12 N	167.28 W
Mohican, Clear Fork ≃	214	40.35 N	82.12 W
Mohican, Jerome Fork ≃	214	40.45 N	82.23 W
Mohican, Lake Fork ≃	214	40.27 N	82.12 W
Mohican, Muddy Fork ≃	214	40.45 N	82.08 W
Mohican State Park ♦	214	40.37 N	82.16 W
Mohicanville Dam ◆[6]	214	40.44 N	82.09 W
Mohili ◆[8]	272c	19.06 N	72.53 E
Mohill	48	53.54 N	7.52 W
Mohinora, Cerro ʌ	232	26.06 N	107.04 W
Mohlakeng	273d	26.13 S	27.42 E
Möhlau	54	51.44 N	12.21 E
Möhlin	58	47.34 N	7.51 E
Möhne ≃	52	51.27 N	7.57 E
Möhnestausee ⊜[1]	52	51.29 N	8.08 E
Mohns Ridge ✢[3]	16	72.30 N	5.00 E
Mohnton	208	40.17 N	75.59 W
Mohnyin	110	24.47 N	96.22 E
Moho ≃	236	16.04 N	88.52 W
Mohokare (Caledon) ≃	158	30.31 S	26.05 E
Moholm	40	58.37 N	14.02 E
Mohon	56	49.45 N	4.44 E
Mohorn	54	51.00 N	13.28 E
Mohoro	154	8.08 S	39.10 E
Möhringen	58	47.57 N	8.46 E
Mohrsville	208	40.28 N	75.59 W
Mohrungen → Morąg	30	53.56 N	19.56 E
Moi	26	58.28 N	6.32 E
Moiano, It.	68	41.05 N	14.32 E
Moiano, It.	68	40.39 N	14.28 E
Moindou	175f	21.42 S	165.41 E
Moinești	38	46.28 N	26.29 E
Moingbi	140	5.46 N	28.49 E
Moinhos	256	22.43 S	46.20 W
Moinkum	85	43.48 N	73.41 E
Mointy	86	47.13 N	73.21 E
Moio Alcantara	70	37.54 N	15.03 E
Moiporá	255	16.34 S	50.42 W
Moira	48	54.30 N	6.17 W
Moira ≃	212	44.09 N	77.23 W
Moiraba	250	2.27 S	49.25 W
Moira Lake ⊜	212	44.29 N	77.27 W
Moirans	62	45.20 N	5.34 E
Moirans-en-Montagne	58	46.26 N	5.44 E
Mõisaküla	76	58.06 N	25.11 E
Moisdon	32	47.37 N	1.22 W
Moisejeviči	76	53.13 N	28.17 E
Moisejevka, S.S.S.R.	83	49.14 N	39.51 E
Moisejevka, S.S.S.R.	86	58.05 N	76.16 E
Moisejevo Alabuška	76	51.54 N	42.06 E
Moisenay	261	48.34 N	2.44 E
Moisés Ville	252	30.43 S	61.29 W
Moisie	186	50.11 N	66.05 W
Moisie ≃	176	50.11 N	66.05 W
Moisie, Baie de c	186	50.16 N	65.56 W
Moisling ◆[8]	52	53.50 N	10.38 E
Moison Creek ≃	281	42.18 N	82.40 W
Moissac	32	44.06 N	1.05 E
Moïssala	146	8.21 N	17.46 E
Moisselles	261	49.03 N	2.20 E
Moisson	261	49.05 N	1.40 E
Moisson, Forêt de ♦	261	49.03 N	1.39 E
Moissy-Cramayel	261	48.38 N	2.36 E
Moita	34	38.39 N	8.59 W
Moitaco	246	8.01 N	64.21 W
Moivre ≃	56	48.52 N	4.28 E
Mojácar	34	37.08 N	1.51 W
Mojana, Caño ≃[1]	246	9.02 N	74.46 W
Mojave	228	35.03 N	118.10 W
Mojave ≃	204	35.06 N	116.04 W
Mojave Desert ◆[2]	204	35.00 N	117.00 W
Mojave River Forks Reservoir ⊜[1]	228	34.20 N	117.15 W
Moji	85	38.59 N	74.24 E
Mojiang	102	23.28 N	101.39 E
Moji-Guaçu ≃	255	20.53 S	48.10 W
Mojjero ≃	74	68.44 N	103.42 E
Mojnalyk	88	51.18 N	95.33 E
Mojo	144	8.36 N	39.07 E
Mojoagung	115a	7.34 S	112.21 E
Mojokerto	115a	7.28 S	112.26 E
Mojosari	115a	7.31 S	112.33 E
Mojstrana	64	46.27 N	13.56 E
Moju	250	1.53 S	48.46 W
Moju ≃	250	1.40 S	48.25 W
Mōka	94	36.26 N	140.01 E
Mokai	172	38.32 S	175.54 E
Mokāma	124	25.24 N	85.55 E
Mokambo	154	12.25 S	28.21 E
Mokane	219	38.40 N	91.52 W
Mokapu Peninsula ›[1]	229c	21.27 N	157.45 W
Mokaria	152	2.00 N	23.20 E
Mokarta, Castello di ⊥	70	37.48 N	12.45 E
Mokau	172	38.41 S	174.37 E
Mokau ≃	172	38.42 S	174.37 E
Moke	102	30.14 N	100.01 E
Mokelumne ≃	226	38.13 N	121.28 W
Mokelumne, Middle Fork ≃	226	38.22 N	120.37 W
Mokelumne, North Fork ≃	226	38.22 N	120.37 W
Mokelumne, South Fork ≃	226	38.23 N	120.35 W
Mokelumne Aqueduct ≍[1]	226	37.54 N	122.07 W
Mokelumne Hill	226	38.18 N	120.42 W
Mokena	216	41.31 N	87.53 W
Mokhotlong	158	29.22 S	29.02 E
Mokil I[1]	14	6.40 N	159.47 E
Mokimbo	154	6.20 S	28.42 E
Mokino	80	57.27 N	49.11 E
Moklakan	88	54.56 N	118.56 E
Möklinta	40	60.05 N	16.32 E
Moknine	148	35.38 N	10.54 E
Mokochu, Khao ʌ	110	15.56 N	99.06 E
Mokohinau Islands II	172	35.55 S	175.07 E
Mokokchūng	120	26.20 N	94.32 E
Mokolo, Cam.	146	10.45 N	13.48 E
Mokolo, Zaïre	152	1.57 N	18.05 E
Mokolo ≃	156	23.14 S	27.43 E
Mokombe	152	0.14 S	23.48 E
Mokoreta ≃	172	46.21 S	168.51 E
Mokou	273b	4.13 S	15.13 E
Mokpalin	110	17.26 N	96.53 E
Mokp'o	98	34.48 N	126.22 E
Mokraja Jel'muta	80	46.51 N	41.41 E
Mokraja Ol'chovka	80	50.28 N	44.59 E
Mokraja Sura ≃	78	48.19 N	35.09 E
Mokraja Volnovacha ≃	83	47.30 N	37.15 E
Mokrany	78	51.50 N	24.14 E
Mokrisset	34	34.59 N	5.20 W
Mokro-Jelančik	83	47.42 N	38.31 E
Mokrous	80	51.14 N	47.37 E
Mokrousovo	86	55.48 N	66.45 E
Mokrušinskoje	86	57.31 N	93.11 E
Mokryje Jaly ≃	78	48.05 N	36.44 E
Mokryj Gašun	80	46.53 N	42.45 E
Mokryj Jelančik ≃	83	47.08 N	38.20 E
Mokryj Kor	82	54.34 N	37.58 E
Mokša ≃	80	54.44 N	41.53 E
Mokšan	80	53.26 N	44.37 E
Moku	154	2.57 N	29.22 E
Mokuleia	229c	21.35 N	158.09 W
Mokumbusu	152	1.44 N	21.04 E
Mokvin	78	50.57 N	26.48 E
Mokwa	150	9.20 N	5.02 E
Mol	56	51.11 N	5.06 E
Mola di Bari	68	41.04 N	17.05 E
Molale	144	10.08 N	39.42 E
Molalla	224	45.08 N	122.34 W
Molalla ≃	224	45.18 N	122.43 W
Molalla, North Fork ≃	224	45.05 N	122.29 W
Molanda	152	2.28 N	20.48 E
Molanosa	184	54.30 N	105.33 W
Moláoi	38	36.48 N	22.52 E
Molara, Isola I	71	40.52 N	9.43 E
Molaretto	62	45.10 N	7.00 E
Molat, Otok I	36	44.15 N	14.49 E
Molbergen	52	52.51 N	7.55 E
Molčanovka	83	46.52 N	38.37 E
Molčanovo	86	57.35 N	83.48 E
Mold	44	53.10 N	3.08 W
Moldary	86	50.47 N	78.29 E
Moldau → Vltava ≃	30	50.21 N	14.30 E
Moldavia → Moldavskaja Sovetskaja Socialističeskaja Respublika □[3]	78	47.00 N	29.00 E
Moldavia □[9]	38	47.00 N	27.15 E
Moldavskaja Sovetskaja Socialističeskaja Respublika □[3]	78	47.00 N	29.00 E
Molde	26	62.44 N	7.11 E
Moldotau, chrebet ⋏	85	41.35 N	74.40 E
Moldova ≃	38	46.54 N	26.58 E
Moldova Nouă	38	44.44 N	21.40 E
Moldoveanu, Vîrful ʌ	38	45.36 N	24.44 E
Môle ≃, Fr.	62	43.15 N	6.32 E
Mole ≃, Eng., U.K.	42	50.57 N	3.54 W
Mole ≃, Eng., U.K.	42	51.24 N	0.21 W
Môle, Cap du ›	238	19.50 N	73.25 W
Mole Creek	166	41.33 S	146.24 E
Moledet	132	32.35 N	35.26 E
Molega Lake ⊜	186	44.22 N	64.53 W
Mole Game Reserve ◆[4]	150	9.30 N	2.00 W
Molegbe	152	4.14 N	20.53 E
Molenbeek-St.-Jean	50	50.51 N	4.19 E
Molepolole	156	24.25 S	25.30 E
Moléson ʌ	58	46.33 N	7.01 E
Molėtai	76	55.14 N	25.25 E
Mole Valley □[8]	260	51.16 N	0.18 W
Molfetta	68	41.12 N	16.36 E
Molibagu	112	0.23 N	123.59 E
Molières-sur-Cèze	62	44.15 N	4.09 E
Molimiao	89	43.34 N	121.54 E
Molina	252	35.07 S	71.17 W
Molina de Aragón	34	40.51 N	1.53 W
Molina de Segura	34	38.03 N	1.12 W
Molina di Ledro	64	45.56 N	10.46 E
Molinara	68	41.18 N	14.54 E
Moline, Il., U.S.	190	41.30 N	90.30 W
Moline, Ks., U.S.	198	37.21 N	96.18 W
Moline, Mi., U.S.	216	42.44 N	85.39 W

Symbol	English	Deutsch	Español	Français	Português
≃	River	Fluß	Río	Rivière	Rio
≍	Canal	Kanal	Canal	Canal	Canal
ʟ	Waterfall, Rapids	Wasserfall, Stromschnellen	Cascada, Rápidos	Chute d'eau, Rapides	Cascata, Rápidos
ʊ	Strait	Meeresstraße	Estrecho	Détroit	Estreito
c	Bay, Gulf	Bucht, Golf	Bahía, Golfo	Baie, Golfe	Baía, Golfo
⊜	Lake, Lakes	See, Seen	Lago, Lagos	Lac, Lacs	Lago, Lagos
⁝	Swamp	Sumpf	Pantano	Marais	Pântano
⊓	Ice Features, Glacier	Eis- und Gletscherformen	Accidentes Glaciales	Formes glaciaires	Acidentes glaciares
⍑	Other Hydrographic Features	Andere Hydrographische Objekte	Otros Elementos Hidrográficos	Autres données hydrographiques	Outros acidentes hidrográficos
✢	Submarine Features	Untermeerische Objekte	Accidentes Submarinos	Formes de relief sous-marin	Acidentes submarinos
□	Political Unit	Politische Einheit	Unidad Politica	Entité politique	Unidade política
ᴗ	Cultural Institution	Kulturelle Institution	Institución Cultural	Institution culturelle	Instituição cultural
⊥	Historical Site	Historische Stätte	Sitio Histórico	Site historique	Sitio histórico
♦	Recreational Site	Erholungs- und Ferienort	Sitio de Recreo	Centre de loisirs	Area de Lazer
⊠	Airport	Flughafen	Aeropuerto	Aéroport	Aeroporto
■	Military Installation	Militäranlage	Instalación Militar	Installation militaire	Instalação militar
◆	Miscellaneous	Verschiedenes	Misceláneo	Divers	Diversos

ENGLISH / DEUTSCH

Name	Page	Lat.°′	Long.°′
Molinella	64	44.37 N	11.40 E
Molinges	58	46.21 N	5.46 E
Molingguan	106	31.50 N	118.50 E
Molini di Tures (Mühlen)	64	46.54 N	11.56 E
Moliniere Point ≻	241k	12.05 N	61.45 W
Molino	194	30.43 N	87.18 W
Molino de Rosas ♦[8]	286a	19.22 N	99.13 W
Molinos	252	25.25 S	66.19 W
Molins de Rei	34	41.25 N	2.01 E
Moliro	154	8.13 S	30.34 E
Molise □[4]	66	41.35 N	14.30 E
Moliterno	68	40.14 N	50.52 E
Mölkau	54	51.20 N	12.26 E
Molkom	40	59.36 N	13.43 E
Möll ≃	64	46.50 N	13.26 E
Mollahasan	130	39.22 N	42.37 E
Mollāhāt	126	22.56 N	89.48 E
Mollakendi	130	38.36 N	39.20 E
Mollaro	64	46.16 N	11.05 E
Möllbrücke	64	46.50 N	13.22 E
Mölle	41	56.17 N	12.29 E
Möllen	263	51.35 N	6.42 E
Möllenbeck, D.D.R.	54	53.17 N	11.44 E
Möllenbeck, D.D.R.	54	53.23 N	13.20 E
Mollendo	248	17.02 S	72.01 W
Möllensee ⊜	264a	52.26 N	13.51 E
Mollepata	248	13.31 S	72.32 W
Moller, Port ⊂	180	55.51 N	160.25 W
Möllersdorf	264b	48.02 N	16.18 E
Mollet del Vallès	266d	41.33 N	2.13 E
Mollia	62	45.49 N	8.02 E
Molliens-Vidame	50	49.53 N	2.01 E
Mollington	262	53.13 N	2.55 W
Mollis	58	47.05 N	9.04 E
Mölln, B.R.D.	54	53.37 N	10.41 E
Molln, Öst.	61	47.53 N	14.15 E
Mollösund	26	58.04 N	11.28 E
Mollusk	208	37.43 N	76.32 W
Molly Ann Brook ≃	276	40.55 N	74.11 W
Mölnbo	40	59.03 N	17.25 E
Mölndal	26	57.39 N	12.01 E
Mölnlycke	26	57.39 N	12.09 E
Mölntorp	40	59.33 N	16.15 E
Molocaboc Island I	116	10.58 N	123.34 E
Moločansk	78	47.12 N	35.36 E
Molochio	68	38.18 N	16.02 E
Moločnaja ≃	78	46.42 N	35.20 E
Moločnoje	76	59.17 N	39.41 E
Moločnoje, ozero ⊜	78	46.30 N	35.20 E
Molócuè ≃	154	17.03 S	38.52 E
Molodečno	76	54.19 N	26.49 E
Molodežnaja ♉[3]	9	67.35 S	46.35 E
Molodi	82	55.17 N	37.31 E
Molodo	150	14.14 N	6.02 W
Molodogvardejsk	83	48.20 N	39.40 E
Molodoj Tud	76	56.26 N	33.36 E
Molod'ožnyj	89	50.23 N	136.48 E
Mologa ≃	76	58.50 N	37.11 E
Molokai I	229a	21.07 N	157.00 W
Molokai Fracture Zone ✢	14	23.00 N	148.00 W
Molokai Fracture Zone ✢	16	23.00 N	130.00 W
Molokča ≃	82	56.15 N	38.45 E
Molokini I	229a	20.38 N	156.30 W
Molokovo, S.S.S.R.	76	58.10 N	36.45 E
Molokovo, S.S.S.R.	82	55.34 N	37.52 E
Moloma ≃	24	58.20 N	48.28 E
Molong	166	33.06 S	148.52 E
Molonglo ≃	171b	35.15 S	148.58 E
Molopo ≃	156	28.30 S	20.13 E
Molotkoviči	78	52.07 N	25.56 E
Molotov → Perm'	86	58.00 N	56.15 E
Molotovsk → Severodvinsk	24	64.34 N	39.50 E
Molou	146	13.42 N	21.44 E
Moloundou	152	2.03 N	15.10 E
Molowaie	152	5.47 S	23.20 E
Moloy	58	47.32 N	4.55 E
Molsheim	58	48.32 N	7.29 E
Molson Lake ⊜	184	54.12 N	96.45 W
Molteno	158	31.22 S	26.22 E
Moltrasio	58	45.52 N	9.05 E
Molu, Pulau I	164	6.45 S	131.33 E
Moluca, Mar de la → Maluku, Laut ⊽[2]	108	0.00	125.00 E
Molucas, Islas → Maluku II	108	2.00 S	128.00 E
Moluccas → Maluku II	108	2.00 S	128.00 E
Molucca Sea → Maluku, Laut ⊽[2]	108	0.00	125.00 E
Molukken → Maluku II	108	2.00 S	128.00 E
Molumbo	154	15.27 S	30.15 E
Molundo	116	7.56 N	124.23 E
Moluques → Maluku II	108	2.00 S	128.00 E
Molveno, Lago di ⊜	64	46.08 N	10.57 E
Molvoticy	76	57.25 N	32.20 E
Molžaninovo	82	55.56 N	37.22 E
Moma, Moç.	154	16.44 S	39.14 E
Moma, Zaïre	152	1.36 S	23.57 E
Moma ≃	74	66.26 N	143.06 E
Momanga	156	18.12 S	21.42 E
Momats ≃	164	5.20 S	137.47 E
Momax	234	21.56 N	103.19 W
Momba ≃	154	8.28 S	32.40 E
Mombaça	250	5.45 S	39.38 W
Mombachito, Cerro ∧	236	12.24 N	85.34 W
Mombacho, Volcán ∧[1]	236	11.50 N	85.58 W
Mombango	152	1.45 N	24.26 E
Mombaruzzo	62	44.46 N	8.27 E
Mombasa	154	4.03 S	39.40 E
Mombetsu	92a	44.21 N	143.22 E
Mombo	154	4.53 S	38.17 E
Mombongo	152	1.39 N	23.09 E
Momboyo ≃	152	0.16 S	19.00 E
Mombuey	34	42.02 N	6.20 W
Mombum	164	8.23 S	138.51 E
Momčilgrad	38	41.32 N	25.25 E
Momence	216	41.10 N	87.39 W
Momfafa, Tanjung ≻	164	0.18 S	131.20 E
Momi	175g	17.55 S	177.17 E
Momignies	50	50.02 N	4.10 E
Mommark	41	54.55 N	10.03 E
Mommenheim	56	48.45 N	7.39 E
Momo	152	1.52 N	11.48 E
Momotombo, Volcán ∧[1]	236	12.26 N	86.33 W
Momozaka	270	34.51 N	135.02 E
Mompog Island I	116	13.31 N	122.11 E
Mompog Pass ꭒ	116	13.34 N	122.13 E
Mompono	152	0.04 N	21.48 E
Mompós	246	9.14 N	74.26 W
Momskij chrebet ⩕	74	66.00 N	146.00 E
Mon	110	18.31 N	96.38 E
Mon □[8]	110	17.30 N	97.00 E
Møn I	41	55.00 N	12.20 E
Mon ≃	110	20.20 N	94.54 E
Mona	200	39.48 N	111.51 W
Mona, Canal de la ꭒ	238	18.30 N	67.45 W
Mona, Isla de I	238	18.05 N	67.54 W
Mona, Punta ≻	236	9.38 N	82.37 W
Monaca	214	40.41 N	80.16 W
Monach, Sound of ꭒ	46	57.34 N	7.35 W
Monach Islands II	46	57.31 N	7.40 W
Monachovo	83	48.09 N	38.07 E
Monaci, Fiume dei ≃	70	37.24 N	14.48 E
Monaco	62	43.42 N	7.23 E
Monaco □[1], Europe	22	43.45 N	7.25 E
Monaco □[1], Europe	62	43.45 N	7.25 E
Monadhliath Mountains ⩕	46	57.10 N	4.00 W
Monadnock Mountain ∧	207	42.52 N	72.07 W
Monagas □[3]	246	9.20 N	63.00 W
Monaghan	48	54.15 N	6.58 W
Monaghan □[6]	48	54.10 N	7.00 W
Monagrillo	236	7.59 N	80.26 W
Monahans	196	31.35 N	102.53 W
Monahans Draw V	196	31.55 N	101.46 W
Monahans Sandhills State Park ♠	196	31.38 N	102.50 W
Monakino	89	43.24 N	133.29 E
Mona Lake ⊜	216	43.11 N	86.17 W
Monamolin	48	52.33 N	6.20 W
Monango	198	46.10 N	98.35 W
Monapo	154	14.57 S	40.17 E
Monapo ≃	154	15.07 S	40.33 E
Mona Quimbundo	152	9.55 S	19.58 E
Monar, Loch ⊜	46	57.25 N	5.06 W
Monarch	192	34.43 N	81.35 W
Monarch Mountain ∧	182	51.54 N	125.53 W
Monarch Pass)(	200	38.30 N	106.19 W
Monaro Range ⩕	171b	36.22 S	149.03 E
Monarto South	168b	35.08 S	139.08 E
Monaš	80	46.58 N	50.36 E
Monashee Mountains ⩕	182	50.30 N	118.30 W
Monashee Provincial Park ♠	182	50.28 N	118.11 W
Monash University ♉[2]	274b	37.55 S	145.08 E
Monasterace	68	38.27 N	16.33 E
Monasterevin	48	53.07 N	7.02 W
Monasterolo di Savigliano	62	44.40 N	7.37 E
Monastir, It.	71	39.23 N	9.02 E
Monastir → Bitola, Jugo.	38	41.01 N	21.20 E
Monastir, Tun.	148	35.47 N	10.50 E
Monastir □[8]	148	35.15 N	10.45 E
Monastyrišče	78	49.00 N	29.49 E
Monastyriska	78	49.06 N	25.11 E
Monastyrščina	76	54.21 N	31.50 E
Monatélé	152	4.16 N	11.12 E
Mona Vale	170	33.41 S	151.18 E
Monbulk	274b	37.52 S	145.25 E
Monbulk Creek ≃	274b	37.54 S	145.15 E
Moncada	116	15.44 N	120.34 E
Moncalieri	62	45.00 N	7.41 E
Moncalvo	62	45.03 N	8.16 E
Monção, Bra.	250	3.30 S	45.15 W
Moncão, Port.	34	42.05 N	8.29 W
Monceau-sur-Sambre	50	50.25 N	4.22 E
Mončegorsk	24	67.54 N	32.58 E
Mönchdorf	61	48.21 N	14.48 E
Mönchengladbach	56	51.12 N	6.28 E
Mönchengladbach, Flughafen ⊠	263	51.14 N	6.29 E
Mönchhof	61	47.52 N	16.56 E
Monchique	34	37.19 N	8.33 W
Mönchweiler	58	48.06 N	8.25 E
Moncks Corner	192	33.11 N	80.00 W
Monclova	232	26.54 N	101.25 W
Moncontour	32	48.21 N	2.39 W
Moncoutant	32	46.43 N	0.35 W
Moncton	186	46.06 N	64.47 W
Mondaí	252	27.05 S	53.25 W
Mondaino	66	43.51 N	12.41 E
Mondavio	66	43.40 N	12.58 E
Monday ≃	252	25.33 S	54.41 W
Mondego ≃	34	40.09 N	8.52 W
Mondego, Cabo ≻	34	40.11 N	8.55 W
Mondello	70	38.13 N	13.20 E
Mondeodo	112	3.33 S	122.12 E
Mondeor	273d	26.17 S	28.00 E
Mondimbi	152	1.43 N	22.58 E
Mondo, Tan.	154	4.59 S	35.54 E
Mondo, Tchad	146	13.47 N	15.32 E
Mondolè, Monte ∧	62	44.13 N	7.46 E
Mondolfo	66	43.45 N	13.06 E
Mondombe	152	0.53 S	22.45 E
Mondoñedo	34	43.26 N	7.22 W
Mondorf-les-Bains	56	49.31 N	6.16 E
Mondoro	150	14.40 N	1.57 W
Mondoubleau	50	47.59 N	0.54 E
Mondovi	190	44.34 N	91.40 W
Mondragon, Fr.	62	44.14 N	4.43 E
Mondragon, Pil.	116	12.31 N	124.45 E
Mondragone	68	41.07 N	13.53 E
Mondrain Island I	162	34.08 S	122.15 E
Mondsee	64	47.52 N	13.21 E
Mondsee ⊜	64	47.49 N	13.23 E
Monds Island I	285	39.50 N	75.19 W
Mondy	88	51.40 N	100.59 E
Monee	216	41.25 N	87.45 W
Moneglia	62	44.14 N	9.30 E
Monemvasía	38	36.41 N	23.03 E
Monero	200	36.54 N	106.52 W
Moneron, ostrov I	89	46.17 N	141.15 E
Monesiglio	62	44.28 N	8.07 E
Monessen	214	40.08 N	79.53 W
Monesterio	34	38.05 N	6.16 W
Monestier-de-Clermont	62	44.54 N	5.38 E
Monetnyj	86	57.03 N	60.53 E
Monett	194	36.55 N	93.55 W
Monette	194	35.53 N	90.20 W
Money Creek ≃	216	40.40 N	88.58 W
Moneygall	48	52.53 N	7.57 W
Moneymore	48	54.42 N	6.40 W
Monfalcone	64	45.49 N	13.32 E
Monferrato □[9]	62	44.55 N	8.05 E
Monflanquin	32	44.32 N	0.46 E
Monforte	34	39.03 N	7.26 W
Monforte de Lemos	34	42.31 N	7.30 W
Monforte San Giorgio	70	38.09 N	15.23 E
Monfort Heights	218	39.12 N	84.37 W
Monga	152	4.12 N	22.49 E
Mongaguá	256	24.06 S	46.37 W
Mongai-Musenge	152	4.04 S	19.34 E
Mongala ≃	152	1.53 N	19.46 E
Mongalla	154	5.12 N	31.46 E
Mongalla Game Reserve ♦[4]	154	5.12 N	31.33 E
Mongandjo	152	1.21 N	24.20 E
Mongarlowe ≃	170	35.15 S	149.52 E
Mongat	266d	41.28 N	2.17 E
Mongaup ≃	210	41.25 N	74.45 W
Mongaup Valley	210	41.40 N	74.47 W
Mongbwalu	154	1.57 N	30.02 E
Mongbyŏn-ni	271b	37.40 N	126.44 E
Mong Cai	110	21.32 N	107.58 E
Monge ∧	266c	38.46 N	9.26 W
Monger, Îles II	186	51.05 N	58.45 W
Mongeri	150	8.19 N	11.44 W
Mongers Lake ⊜	162	29.15 S	117.05 E
Monggon Qulu	89	48.35 N	119.49 E
Monggŭmp'o	98	38.09 N	124.47 E
Möng Hai	110	20.46 N	99.49 E
Möng Hawm	110	23.51 N	98.20 E
Monghidoro	66	44.13 N	11.19 E
Möng Hpāyak	110	20.53 N	99.54 E
Möng Hsat	110	20.32 N	99.15 E
Monghyr → Munger	124	25.23 N	86.28 E
Mongi ≃	164	6.35 S	147.35 E
Mongiana	68	38.31 N	16.19 E
Mongibello → Etna, Monte ∧[1]	70	37.46 N	15.00 E
Mongiuffi	70	37.55 N	15.17 E
Möng Küng	110	21.36 N	97.32 E
Möng Ma	110	21.37 N	99.54 E
Möng Mit	110	23.07 N	96.41 E
Möng Nai	110	20.31 N	97.52 E
Möng Nawng	110	21.39 N	98.08 E
Mongo, Tchad	146	12.11 N	18.42 E
Mongo, In., U.S.	216	41.41 N	85.17 W
Mongo ≃	150	9.34 N	12.11 W
Mongoj	88	53.57 N	113.50 E
Mongol Altajn nuruu ⩕	90	46.30 N	93.00 E
Mongol Ard Uls → Mongolia □[1]	90	46.00 N	105.00 E
Mongolei → Mongolia □[1]	90	46.00 N	105.00 E
Mongol els ♦[2]	88	47.45 N	94.30 E
Mongolia (Mongol Ard Uls) □[1]	90	46.00 N	105.00 E
Mongolie → Mongolia □[1]	90	46.00 N	105.00 E
Mongomo	152	1.38 N	11.19 E
Möngön Mor't	88	48.11 N	108.29 E
Mongororo	146	12.01 N	22.28 E
Mongoumba	152	3.38 N	18.36 E
Möng Pai	110	19.44 N	97.05 E
Möng Pan	110	20.19 N	98.22 E
Möng Pawn	110	20.49 N	97.28 E
Möng Ping	110	22.22 N	99.02 E
Mongpong ≃	116	12.44 N	120.48 E
Mongrando	62	45.31 N	8.00 E
Mongrove, Punta ≻	234	17.56 N	102.11 W
Möng Si	110	23.40 N	98.23 E
Mong Tung Hang	271d	22.20 N	114.02 E
Mongu	152	15.15 S	23.09 E
Môngua	152	16.43 S	15.23 E
Monguelfo (Welsberg)	64	46.45 N	12.06 E
Monguno	146	12.40 N	13.38 E
Möng Yai	110	22.25 N	98.02 E
Möng Yawng	110	21.11 N	100.22 E
Monheim, B.R.D.	56	48.50 N	10.51 E
Monheim, B.R.D.	56	51.05 N	6.52 E
Moniaive	44	55.12 N	3.55 W
Mönichkirchen	61	47.31 N	16.02 E
Monico	190	45.34 N	89.09 W
Monida Pass)(	202	44.33 N	112.18 W
Mon Idée	50	49.53 N	4.23 E
Monie	152	4.00 S	17.22 E
Monie Bay ⊂	208	38.13 N	75.51 W
Monie Creek ≃	208	38.14 N	75.50 W
Monifieth	46	56.29 N	2.49 W
Monimail	46	56.18 N	3.08 W
Moninger	214	40.14 N	80.13 W
Monino	82	55.50 N	38.11 E
Moniquirá	246	5.52 N	73.36 W
Mõniste	76	57.35 N	26.33 E
Monistrol-d'Allier	62	44.57 N	3.38 E
Monistrol-sur-Loire	62	45.17 N	4.10 E
Monitor Range ⩕	204	38.45 N	116.30 W
Monitor Valley V	204	39.00 N	116.40 W
Monívea	48	53.23 N	8.43 W
Monjolo	256	22.49 S	42.57 W
Monk, Pointe ≻	275a	45.29 N	73.57 W
Monkayo	116	7.50 N	126.03 E
Mönkebude	54	53.46 N	13.57 E
Monken Hadley ♦[8]	260	51.40 N	0.11 W
Monkey Bay	154	14.05 S	34.55 E
Monkey Point ≻	236	11.36 N	83.39 W
Monkey River	236	16.22 N	88.29 W
Mońki	30	53.24 N	22.49 E
Monkira	166	24.49 S	140.34 E
Monkoto	152	1.38 S	20.39 E
Monks Heath	262	53.16 N	2.14 W
Monkton	212	43.35 N	81.05 W
Monmouth, Wales, U.K.	42	51.50 N	2.43 W
Monmouth, Il., U.S.	190	40.54 N	90.38 W
Monmouth, In., U.S.	216	40.52 N	84.57 W
Monmouth, Or., U.S.	202	44.50 N	123.13 W
Monmouth □[6]	208	40.16 N	74.17 W
Monmouth Beach	276	40.19 N	73.58 W
Monmouth Hills	276	40.24 N	74.00 W
Monmouth Junction	208	40.22 N	74.32 W
Monmouth Mountain ∧	182	51.00 N	123.47 W
Monnickendam	52	52.27 N	5.02 E
Monnow ≃	42	51.48 N	2.42 W
Mono □[5]	150	6.45 N	1.50 E
Mono □[6]	226	38.18 N	119.22 W
Mono ≃	150	6.17 N	1.51 E
Mono, Caño ≃	246	4.25 N	67.47 W
Monobe	96	33.42 N	133.53 E
Monobe ≃	96	33.32 N	133.41 E
Monocacy ≃	208	39.13 N	77.27 W
Monocacy Station	208	40.16 N	75.46 W
Monogarovo	82	54.42 N	38.45 E
Mono Island I	175e	7.21 S	155.34 E
Mono Lake ⊜	204	38.00 N	119.00 W
Monolith	228	35.07 N	118.22 W
Monomoy Island I	207	41.35 N	69.59 W
Monomoy Point ≻	207	41.33 N	70.02 W
Monon	216	40.52 N	86.52 W
Monona, Ia., U.S.	190	43.03 N	91.23 W
Monona, Wi., U.S.	216	43.03 N	89.20 W
Monona, Lake ⊜	216	43.03 N	89.22 W
Monongahela	214	40.12 N	79.55 W
Monongahela ≃	188	40.27 N	80.00 W
Monongahela Brook ≃	285	39.47 N	75.09 W
Monopoli	68	40.57 N	17.19 E
Monor	30	47.21 N	19.27 E
Mono Road Station	275b	43.51 N	79.51 W
Monos ⊥	232	18.27 N	89.02 W
Monòver	34	38.26 N	0.50 W
Monowai, Lake ⊜	172	45.52 S	167.27 E
Monponsett	207	42.01 N	70.50 W
Monponsett Pond ⊜	283	42.01 N	70.51 W
Monreal	34	42.42 N	1.30 W
Monreal del Campo	34	40.47 N	1.21 W
Monreale	70	38.05 N	13.17 E
Monreale, Castello di ⊥	71	39.38 N	8.49 E
Monroe, Ct., U.S.	207	41.19 N	73.12 W
Monroe, Fl., U.S.	220	25.52 N	81.06 W
Monroe, Ga., U.S.	192	33.47 N	83.42 W
Monroe, In., U.S.	216	40.44 N	84.56 W
Monroe, Ia., U.S.	190	41.31 N	93.06 W
Monroe, La., U.S.	194	32.30 N	92.07 W
Monroe, Mi., U.S.	214	41.54 N	83.23 W
Monroe, Ne., U.S.	198	41.28 N	97.35 W
Monroe, N.J., U.S.	276	41.06 N	74.38 W
Monroe, N.Y., U.S.	210	41.19 N	74.11 W
Monroe, N.C., U.S.	192	34.59 N	80.32 W
Monroe, Oh., U.S.	218	39.26 N	84.21 W
Monroe, Or., U.S.	202	44.18 N	123.17 W
Monroe, Ut,. U.S.	200	38.37 N	112.07 W
Monroe, Va., U.S.	192	37.30 N	79.07 W
Monroe, Wa., U.S.	224	47.51 N	121.58 W
Monroe, Wi., U.S.	190	42.36 N	89.38 W
Monroe □[6], Fl., U.S.	220	25.10 N	81.10 W
Monroe □[6], Il., U.S.	219	38.20 N	90.09 W
Monroe □[6], In., U.S.	218	39.10 N	86.26 W
Monroe □[6], Mi., U.S.	216	41.55 N	83.26 W
Monroe □[6], Mo., U.S.	219	39.30 N	92.00 W
Monroe □[6], N.Y., U.S.	210	43.10 N	77.36 W
Monroe □[6], Pa., U.S.	210	40.59 N	75.12 W
Monroe, Lake ⊜	220	28.52 N	81.16 W
Monroe Bridge	207	42.43 N	72.56 W
Monroe Center, Ct., U.S.	207	41.20 N	73.12 W
Monroe Center, Il., U.S.	216	42.06 N	89.00 W
Monroe City, In., U.S.	194	38.36 N	87.21 W
Monroe City, Mo., U.S.	219	39.39 N	91.44 W
Monroe City, Tx., U.S.	222	29.47 N	94.35 W
Monroe Lake ⊜[1]	218	39.05 N	86.25 W
Monroe Manor	216	41.36 N	86.40 W
Monroeton	210	41.43 N	76.30 W
Monroeville, Al., U.S.	194	31.31 N	87.19 W
Monroeville, In., U.S.	216	40.58 N	84.52 W
Monroeville, N.J., U.S.	208	39.37 N	75.09 W
Monroeville, Oh., U.S.	214	41.14 N	82.41 W
Monroeville, Pa., U.S.	214	40.26 N	79.47 W
Monroeville Mall ♦[9]	279b	40.26 N	79.48 W
Monrovia, Liber.	150	6.18 N	10.47 W
Monrovia, Ca., U.S.	228	34.08 N	117.59 W
Monrovia, In., U.S.	218	39.34 N	86.28 W
Monrovia Mountain Park ♠	280	34.10 N	118.10 W
Monrovia Peak ∧	280	34.13 N	117.58 W
Mons (Bergen), Bel.	50	50.27 N	3.56 E
Mons, Fr.	62	43.41 N	6.43 E
Monsarás, Ponta do ≻	255	19.35 S	39.45 W
Monschau	56	50.33 N	6.14 E
Monse	112	4.07 S	123.15 E
Monsefú	248	6.52 S	79.52 W
Monselice	64	45.14 N	11.45 E
Monsenhor Hipólito	250	6.59 S	41.07 W
Monsenhor Paulo	256	21.46 S	45.33 W
Monsenhor Tabosa	250	4.47 S	40.04 W
Monserrato	71	39.15 N	9.08 E
Monsey	210	41.06 N	74.04 W
Monsheim, B.R.D.	56	49.38 N	8.12 E
Mönsheim, B.R.D.	56	48.52 N	8.52 E
Møns Klint ⊥[4]	41	54.58 N	12.33 E
Monsols	58	46.13 N	4.31 E
Monson, Me., U.S.	188	45.17 N	69.30 W
Monson, Ma., U.S.	207	42.06 N	72.19 W
Monster	52	52.02 N	4.10 E
Mönsterås	26	57.02 N	16.26 E
Monsummano Terme	66	43.52 N	10.49 E
Montà	62	44.48 N	7.57 E
Montabaur	56	50.26 N	7.50 E
Montabaur □[5]	56	50.30 N	7.40 E
Montafon V	58	47.02 N	9.57 E
Montagano	66	41.39 N	14.40 E
Montagnana	64	45.14 N	11.28 E
Montagnareale	70	38.07 N	14.57 E
Montagne d'Ambre, Parque National de la ♠	157b	12.40 S	49.05 E
Montagnola ⩕	66	43.17 N	11.11 E
Montagrier	32	45.16 N	0.29 E
Montagu	158	33.45 S	20.08 E
Montague, P.E., Can.	186	46.10 N	62.39 W
Montague, Ca., U.S.	204	41.43 N	122.31 W
Montague, Ma., U.S.	207	42.32 N	72.32 W
Montague, Mi., U.S.	190	43.25 N	86.21 W
Montague, Tx., U.S.	196	33.40 N	97.43 W
Montague, Isla I	232	31.45 N	114.48 W
Montague City	207	42.35 N	72.35 W
Montague Island I	180	60.00 N	147.30 W
Montague Peak ∧	180	60.15 N	147.01 W
Montagu Island I	18	58.25 S	26.20 W
Montaigle, Château de ⊥	56	50.18 N	4.49 E
Montaigu	32	46.59 N	1.19 W
Montaigut-en-Combraille	32	46.11 N	2.48 E
Montainville	261	48.53 N	1.52 E
Montaione	66	43.33 N	10.55 E
Montaj-Taš	85	42.06 N	68.58 E
Montalba	222	31.53 N	95.38 W
Montalbán	34	40.50 N	0.48 W
Montalbancito	286c	10.28 N	66.59 W
Montalbano Elicona	70	38.02 N	15.01 E
Montalbano Ionico	68	40.17 N	16.34 E
Montalcino	66	43.03 N	11.29 E
Montaldo di Cosola	62	44.40 N	9.11 E
Montale	66	43.56 N	11.01 E
Montalegre	34	41.49 N	7.48 W
Montalet-le-Bois	261	49.03 N	1.50 E
Montalieu-Vercieu	62	45.49 N	5.24 E
Montallegro	70	37.23 N	13.21 E
Mont Alto	208	39.50 N	77.33 W
Montalto ∧	68	38.10 N	15.55 E
Montalto delle Marche	66	42.59 N	13.36 E
Montalto di Castro	66	42.21 N	11.37 E
Montalto Ligure	62	43.56 N	7.51 E
Montalto Uffugo	68	39.25 N	16.10 E
Montalvin Manor	226	37.59 N	122.21 W
Montalvo	228	34.15 N	119.12 W
Montana, Schw.	58	46.18 N	7.29 E
Montana, Ak., U.S.	180	62.05 N	150.04 W
Montana □[3], U.S.	178	47.00 N	110.00 W
Montana □[3], U.S.	202	47.00 N	110.00 W
Montana de Oro State Park ♠	226	35.15 N	120.50 W
Montana Indian Reserve ♦[4]	182	52.43 N	113.25 W
Montanaro	62	45.14 N	7.51 E
Montánchez	34	39.13 N	6.09 W
Montandon	210	40.58 N	76.51 W
Montano Antilia	68	40.10 N	15.22 E
Montara	226	37.33 N	122.31 W
Montara Beach ♠	282	37.33 N	122.31 W
Montara Mountain ⩕	282	37.32 N	122.27 W
Montargil	34	39.05 N	8.10 W
Montargis	50	48.00 N	2.45 E
Montataire	50	49.16 N	2.26 E
Montauban	32	44.01 N	1.21 E
Montauban, Lac ⊜	206	46.52 N	72.10 W
Montauban-les-Mines	206	46.50 N	72.20 W
Montauk	207	41.02 N	71.57 W
Montauk, Lake ⊜	207	41.04 N	71.55 W
Montauk Point ≻	207	41.04 N	71.52 W
Montauroux	62	43.37 N	6.46 E
Monta Vista	226	37.19 N	122.03 W
Montazzoli	66	41.57 N	14.26 E
Montbard	50	47.37 N	4.20 E
Montbarrey	58	47.01 N	5.39 E
Montbazon	50	47.17 N	0.43 E
Montbéliard	58	47.31 N	6.48 E
Mont Belvieu	222	29.50 N	94.53 W
Montbenoît	58	46.59 N	6.28 E
Montblanc	34	41.22 N	1.10 E
Mont Blanc, Tunnel du ♦[5]	58	45.50 N	6.53 E
Mont-Bonvillers	56	49.20 N	5.51 E
Montbovon	58	46.29 N	7.03 E
Montbozon	58	47.28 N	6.16 E
Montbrison	62	45.36 N	4.03 E
Montbron	32	45.40 N	0.30 E
Montbronn	56	48.59 N	7.19 E
Montcada i Reixas	266d	41.29 N	2.11 E
Montcalm □[6]	206	46.20 N	74.20 W
Montceau-les-Mines	58	46.40 N	4.22 E
Montcenis	58	46.47 N	4.23 E
Mont Cenis, Col du)(	62	45.15 N	6.54 E
Mont Cenis, Lac du ⊜	62	45.14 N	6.55 E
Montcevelles, Lac ⊜	186	51.07 N	60.38 W
Montchanin, Fr.	58	46.45 N	4.27 E
Montchanin, De., U.S.	285	39.47 N	75.35 W
Montchauvet	261	48.54 N	1.38 E
Montclair, Ca., U.S.	228	34.06 N	117.41 W
Montclair, N.J., U.S.	210	40.49 N	74.12 W
Montclair State College ♉[2]	276	40.51 N	74.12 W
Mont Clare	285	40.08 N	75.30 W
Montcornet	50	49.41 N	4.01 E
Montdale	210	41.32 N	75.37 W
Mont-de-Marsan	32	43.53 N	0.30 W
Montdidier	50	49.39 N	2.34 E
Mont-Dore	175f	22.16 S	166.34 E
Monte, Castel del ⊥	68	41.05 N	16.16 E
Monte, Laguna del ⊜, Arg.	252	37.00 S	62.28 W
Monte, Laguna del ⊜, Arg.	258	35.28 S	58.49 W
Montea ∧	68	39.40 N	15.57 E
Monte Adone, Galleria di ♦[5]	64	44.21 N	11.25 E
Monteagle	194	35.15 N	85.50 W
Monteagudo	248	19.49 S	63.59 W
Monte Albán ⊥	234	17.02 N	96.45 W
Monte Alegre, Bra.	250	2.01 S	54.04 W
Monte Alegre, Bra.	250	6.04 S	35.20 W
Monte Alegre de Goiás	255	13.14 S	47.10 W
Monte Alegre de Minas	255	18.52 S	48.52 W
Monte Alegre de Sergipe	250	10.02 S	37.33 W
Monte Alegre do Piauí	250	9.46 S	45.18 W
Monte Alegre do Sul	256	22.40 S	46.41 W
Monte Azul	255	15.09 S	42.53 W
Monte Azul Paulista	255	20.55 S	48.38 W
Montebello, P.Q., Can.	206	45.39 N	74.56 W
Montebello, It.	62	45.00 N	9.06 E
Montebello, P.R.	240m	18.22 N	66.31 W
Montebello, Ca., U.S.	228	34.00 N	118.06 W
Montebello Iónico	68	37.59 N	15.45 E
Monte Bello Islands II	162	20.25 S	115.32 E
Montebello Vicentino	64	45.27 N	11.23 E
Montebelluna	64	45.47 N	12.03 E
Monte Belo	256	21.20 S	46.23 W
Montebruno	62	44.31 N	9.15 E
Monte Buey	252	32.55 S	62.27 W
Montecalvo Irpino	68	41.11 N	15.02 E
Monte Campatri	267a	41.48 N	12.44 E
Montecarlo	252	26.34 S	54.47 W
Monte Carlo ♦[8]	62	43.44 N	7.25 E
Montecarotto	66	43.31 N	13.04 E
Monte Caseros	252	30.15 S	57.39 W
Montecassiano	66	43.21 N	13.26 E
Montecassino, Abbazia di ♉[1]	66	41.29 N	13.48 E
Montecastrilli	66	42.39 N	12.29 E
Montecatini-Terme	66	43.53 N	10.46 E
Monte Cavallo	66	42.59 N	13.00 E
Montecchio	66	43.51 N	12.46 E
Montecchio Emilia	64	44.42 N	10.27 E
Montecchio Maggiore	64	45.30 N	11.24 E
Montecelio	66	42.01 N	12.44 E
Montechiaro d'Asti	62	45.01 N	8.07 E
Montechiarugolo	64	44.42 N	10.25 E
Monte Chingolo ♦[8]	288	34.45 S	58.20 W
Monteciccardo	66	43.49 N	12.48 E
Montecilfone	66	41.54 N	14.50 E
Montecillos, Cordillera de ⩕	236	14.25 N	87.51 W
Montecito	204	34.26 N	119.37 W
Monte Comán	252	34.36 S	67.54 W
Montecorice	68	40.14 N	14.59 E
Montecorvino Pugliano	68	40.41 N	14.57 E
Montecorvino Rovella	68	40.42 N	14.59 E
Montecosaro	66	43.19 N	13.37 E
Monte Creek	182	50.39 N	119.57 W
Montecreto	64	44.14 N	10.41 E
Montecristi	246	1.03 S	80.40 W
Monte Cristo	248	14.43 S	61.14 W
Monte Cristo, Cerro ∧	236	14.25 N	89.21 W
Montecristo, Isola di I	36	42.20 N	10.19 E
Montecuccolo ♉[1]	64	44.19 N	10.50 E
Montedinove	66	42.58 N	13.35 E
Monte di Procida	68	40.48 N	14.03 E
Monte do Carmo	250	10.45 S	48.07 W
Montedoro	70	37.27 N	13.49 E
Monte Escobedo	234	22.18 N	103.35 W
Monte Estoril	266c	38.42 N	9.24 W
Montefalcione	68	40.58 N	14.53 E
Montefalco	66	42.54 N	12.39 E
Montefalcone di Val Fortore	68	41.20 N	15.00 E
Montefano	66	43.25 N	13.26 E
Montefeltro ♦[1]	66	43.50 N	12.15 E
Montefiascone	66	42.32 N	12.02 E
Montefiorino	64	44.22 N	10.37 E
Monteforte d'Alpone	64	45.25 N	11.17 E
Monteforte Irpino	68	40.54 N	14.42 E
Montefrío	34	37.19 N	4.01 W
Montegallo	66	42.50 N	13.19 E
Montegiordano	68	40.02 N	16.32 E
Montegiorgio	66	43.08 N	13.32 E
Monte Giovi, Passo di (Jaufen Pass))(	64	46.50 N	11.19 E
Montego Bay	241q	18.28 N	77.55 W
Montegranaro	66	43.14 N	13.38 E
Monte Grande	252	30.06 S	70.31 W
Monte Grande, Aeródromo ⊠	288	34.48 S	58.28 W
Monte Grimano	66	43.52 N	12.29 E
Montegrotto Terme	64	45.19 N	11.46 E
Montegut	194	29.28 N	90.33 W
Monteiasi	68	40.30 N	17.23 E
Monteiro	250	7.53 S	37.07 W
Monteiro Lobato	256	22.58 S	45.50 W
Monteith, Mount ∧	182	55.45 N	122.30 W
Montejicar	34	37.34 N	3.30 W
Montejinni	164	16.40 S	131.45 E
Montelavar	266c	38.51 N	9.20 W
Monteleone di Puglia	68	41.10 N	15.15 E
Monteleone di Spoleto	66	42.39 N	12.58 E
Monteleone Rocco Doria	71	40.29 N	8.34 E
Monteleone Sabino	66	42.14 N	12.51 E
Montelepre	70	38.05 N	13.10 E
Montelíbano	246	8.05 N	75.29 W
Montélimar	62	44.34 N	4.45 E
Montelindo ≃	252	23.56 S	57.12 W
Montella	68	40.51 N	15.01 E
Montellano	34	37.00 N	5.34 W
Montello, Nv., U.S.	204	41.15 N	114.11 W
Montello, Wi., U.S.	190	43.47 N	89.19 W
Monteluco ♉[1]	66	42.43 N	12.45 E
Montelungo	64	44.24 N	9.54 E
Montelupo Fiorentino	66	43.44 N	11.01 E
Montemaggiore Belsito	70	37.51 N	13.46 E
Montemagno	62	44.59 N	8.20 E
Monte Maíz	252	33.12 S	62.36 W
Montemarano	68	40.55 N	15.00 E
Montemarciano	66	43.38 N	13.19 E
Montemayor, Meseta de ⩕[1]	254	44.20 S	66.10 W
Montemesola	68	40.34 N	17.20 E
Montemiletto	68	41.01 N	14.54 E
Montemilone	68	41.02 N	15.38 E
Montemor	266c	38.49 N	9.12 W
Montemor ∧	266c	38.49 N	9.12 W
Montemorelos	232	25.12 N	99.49 W
Montemor-o-Novo	34	38.39 N	8.13 W
Montemor-o-Vehlo	34	40.10 N	8.41 W
Montemuro ∧	34	40.58 N	7.56 W
Montemurro	68	40.18 N	15.59 E
Montendre	32	45.17 N	0.24 W
Montenegro	252	29.42 S	51.28 W
Montenegro → Crna Gora □[3]	38	42.30 N	19.18 E
Montenero	66	43.30 N	10.21 E
Montenero ∧	68	39.13 N	16.35 E
Montenero di Bisaccia	66	41.57 N	14.47 E
Monteodorisio	66	42.05 N	14.39 E
Monte Oliveto Maggiore, Abbazia del ♉[1]	66	43.12 N	11.32 E
Monte Pascoal, Parque Nacional de ♠	255	16.54 S	39.24 W
Monte Patria	252	30.42 S	70.58 W
Montepescali	66	42.53 N	11.05 E
Monte Porzio Catone	267a	41.49 N	12.43 E
Monteprandone	66	42.55 N	13.50 E
Montepuez	154	13.07 S	39.00 E
Montepuez ≃	154	12.32 S	40.27 E
Montepulciano	66	43.05 N	11.47 E
Monte Quemado	252	25.48 S	62.52 W
Monterado	112	0.45 N	109.08 E
Monterchi	66	43.29 N	12.07 E
Montereale	66	42.31 N	13.15 E
Montereale Valcellina	64	46.10 N	12.39 E
Montereau	50	47.51 N	2.34 E
Montereau-Faut-Yonne	50	48.23 N	2.57 E
Montereau-sur-le-Jard	261	48.35 N	2.40 E
Monterey, Ca., U.S.	226	36.36 N	121.53 W
Monterey, In., U.S.	216	41.09 N	86.28 W
Monterey, Ky., U.S.	218	38.25 N	84.52 W
Monterey, Ma., U.S.	207	42.10 N	73.12 W
Monterey, N.Y., U.S.	210	42.18 N	77.03 W
Monterey, Tn., U.S.	194	36.08 N	85.16 W
Monterey, Va., U.S.	188	38.24 N	79.34 W
Monterey □[6]	226	36.40 N	121.38 W
Monterey Bay ⊂	226	36.45 N	121.55 W
Monterey Park	228	34.03 N	118.07 W
Monterey Peninsula Airport ⊠	226	36.35 N	121.51 W
Montería	246	8.46 N	75.53 W
Monteriggioni	66	43.23 N	11.13 E
Montero	248	17.20 S	63.15 W
Monte Romano	66	42.16 N	11.54 E
Monteroni d'Arbia	66	43.14 N	11.25 E

Name	Seite	Breite°′	Länge°′ E = Ost
Monteroni di Lecce	68	40.19 N	18.06 E
Monteros	252	27.10 S	65.30 W
Monterosso al Mare	62	44.09 N	9.39 E
Monterosso Almo	70	37.05 N	14.46 E
Monterosso Calabro	68	38.43 N	16.17 E
Monterotondo	66	42.03 N	12.37 E
Monterotondo Marittimo	66	43.09 N	10.51 E
Monterrey, Méx.	232	25.40 N	100.19 W
Monterrey, Méx.	234	16.05 N	93.23 W
Monterrico, Hipódromo de ♠	286d	12.06 S	76.59 W
Monterubbiano	66	43.05 N	13.43 E
Montes Altos	250	5.50 S	47.04 W
Monte San Biagio	66	41.21 N	13.21 E
Monte San Giovanni Campano	66	41.38 N	13.31 E
Montesano, It.	36	40.16 N	15.43 E
Montesano, Wa., U.S.	224	46.58 N	123.36 W
Montesano sulla Marcellana	68	40.16 N	15.42 E
Monte San Savino	66	43.20 N	11.43 E
Monte Santa Maria Tiberina	66	43.26 N	12.09 E
Monte Sant'Angelo	68	41.42 N	15.57 E
Monte Santo, Bra.	250	10.26 S	39.20 W
Monte Santo, Bra.	250	9.54 S	49.03 W
Monte Santo de Minas	256	21.12 S	46.59 W
Monte Santu, Capo di ≻	71	40.05 N	9.44 E
Montesarchio	68	41.04 N	14.38 E
Montescaglioso	68	40.33 N	16.40 E
Montes Claros	255	16.43 S	43.52 W
Montescudaio	66	43.18 N	10.40 E
Montese	64	44.16 N	10.56 E
Monte Sereno	226	37.15 N	122.01 W
Monte Sião	256	22.26 S	46.34 W
Montesilvano Marina	66	42.31 N	14.09 E
Montespaccato ♦[8]	267a	41.54 N	12.23 E
Montespertoli	66	43.38 N	11.04 E
Montespluga	58	46.30 N	9.21 E
Montets, Col des)(	58	46.00 N	6.55 E
Monteux	62	44.02 N	5.00 E
Montevago	70	37.42 N	12.58 E
Montevallo	194	33.06 N	86.51 W
Montevarchi	66	43.31 N	11.34 E
Monteverde	68	41.00 N	15.32 E
Monte Verde ≃	256	21.55 S	43.33 W
Monteverde Nuovo ♦[8]	267a	41.51 N	12.27 E
Montevergine, Santuario di ♉[1]	68	40.55 N	14.45 E
Montevideo, Mn., U.S.	198	44.56 N	95.43 W
Montevideo, Ur.	258	34.53 S	56.11 W
Montevideo □[5]	258	34.50 S	56.12 W
Monte Vista	200	37.34 N	106.08 W
Montévrain	261	48.53 N	2.45 E
Montezemolo	62	44.22 N	8.08 E
Montezuma, Ca., U.S.	282	38.05 N	121.53 W
Montezuma, Ga., U.S.	192	32.18 N	84.01 W
Montezuma, In., U.S.	194	39.47 N	87.22 W
Montezuma, Ia., U.S.	190	41.35 N	92.31 W
Montezuma, Ks., U.S.	198	37.35 N	100.26 W
Montezuma, N.Y., U.S.	210	43.00 N	76.42 W
Montezuma, Oh., U.S.	216	40.29 N	84.33 W
Montezuma Castle National Monument ♠	200	34.38 N	110.49 W
Montezuma Creek ≃	200	37.17 N	109.20 W
Montezuma Hills ⩕[2]	282	38.07 N	121.51 W
Montezuma Slough ≃	226	38.04 N	121.52 W
Montfaucon, Fr.	56	49.17 N	5.08 E
Montfaucon, Fr.	62	45.10 N	4.18 E
Montfaucon, Schw.	58	47.17 N	7.03 E
Montfermeil	261	48.54 N	2.34 E
Montfleur	58	46.19 N	5.26 E
Montfort, Fr.	32	48.08 N	1.58 W
Montfort, Wi., U.S.	190	42.58 N	90.25 W
Montfort-l'Amaury	50	48.47 N	1.49 E
Montfort-le-Rotrou	50	48.03 N	0.25 E
Montfort-sur-Risle	50	49.18 N	0.40 E
Montfrin	62	43.53 N	4.36 E
Montgé	261	49.02 N	2.45 E
Montgenèvre	62	44.56 N	6.43 E
Montgenèvre, Col de)(	62	44.56 N	6.44 E
Montgeron	261	48.42 N	2.27 E
Montgeroult	261	49.05 N	2.00 E
Montgesoye	58	47.05 N	6.12 E
Montgomery → Sāhīwāl	123	30.40 N	73.06 E
Montgomery, Wales, U.K.	42	52.33 N	3.03 W
Montgomery, Al., U.S.	194	32.23 N	86.18 W
Montgomery, Il., U.S.	216	41.43 N	88.20 W
Montgomery, La., U.S.	194	31.40 N	92.53 W
Montgomery, Mi., U.S.	216	41.46 N	84.48 W
Montgomery, Mn., U.S.	190	44.26 N	93.34 W
Montgomery, N.Y., U.S.	210	41.31 N	74.14 W
Montgomery, Oh., U.S.	218	39.13 N	84.21 W
Montgomery, Pa., U.S.	210	41.10 N	76.52 W
Montgomery, Tx., U.S.	222	30.23 N	95.42 W
Montgomery, W.V., U.S.	188	38.11 N	81.19 W
Montgomery □[6], Il., U.S.	219	39.09 N	89.29 W
Montgomery □[6], Md., U.S.	208	39.05 N	77.09 W
Montgomery □[6], Mo., U.S.	219	38.57 N	91.27 W
Montgomery □[6], N.Y., U.S.	210	42.57 N	74.22 W
Montgomery □[6], Oh., U.S.	218	39.45 N	84.15 W
Montgomery □[6], Pa., U.S.	208	40.07 N	75.21 W
Montgomery □[6], Tx., U.S.	222	30.18 N	95.30 W
Montgomery City	219	38.58 N	91.30 W
Montgomery Dam ♦[6]	214	40.39 N	80.24 W
Montgomery Knolls	284b	39.14 N	76.48 W
Montgomery Mall ♦[9]	284c	39.01 N	77.09 W
Montgomery Square	284c	39.04 N	77.09 W
Montgomeryville	285	40.15 N	75.15 W
Montgomeryville Airport ⊠	285	40.15 N	75.14 W
Montguyon	32	45.13 N	0.11 W
Monthermé	56	49.53 N	4.44 E
Monthey	58	46.15 N	6.57 E
Monthois	56	49.19 N	4.43 E
Monthureux-sur-Saône	58	48.02 N	5.58 E
Monthyon	261	49.00 N	2.50 E
Monti	71	40.49 N	9.19 E
Monticelli d'Ongina	64	45.05 N	9.56 E
Monticello, Ar., U.S.	194	33.37 N	91.47 W
Monticello, Fl., U.S.	192	30.32 N	83.52 W
Monticello, Ga., U.S.	192	33.18 N	83.41 W
Monticello, Il., U.S.	194	40.01 N	88.34 W
Monticello, In., U.S.	216	40.44 N	86.45 W
Monticello, Ia., U.S.	190	42.14 N	91.11 W
Monticello, Ky., U.S.	194	36.49 N	84.50 W
Monticello, Mn., U.S.	190	45.18 N	93.47 W
Monticello, Ms., U.S.	194	31.33 N	90.06 W
Monticello, Mo., U.S.	219	40.07 N	91.42 W

Symbols in the index entries represent the broad categories identified in the key at the right. Symbols with superior numbers (⩕[1]) identify subcategories (see complete key on page *I · 1)*.

Symbole im Register stellen die rechts im Schlüssel erklärten Kategorien dar. Symbole mit hochgestellten Ziffern (⩕[1]) bezeichnen Unterabteilungen einer Kategorie (vgl. vollständiger Schlüssel auf Seite *I · 1)*.

Los símbolos incluídos en el texto del índice representan las grandes categorias identificadas con la clave a la derecha. Los símbolos con numeros en su parte superior (⩕[1]) identifican las subcategorías (véase la clave completa en la página *I · 1)*.

Les symboles de l'index représentent les catégories indiquées dans la légende à droite. Les symboles suivis d'un indice (⩕[1]) représentent des sous-catégories (voir légende complète à la page *I · 1)*.

Os símbolos incluídos no texto do índice representam as grandes categorias identificadas com a chave à direita. Os símbolos com números em sua parte superior (⩕[1]) identificam as subcategorias (veja-se a chave completa à página *I · 1)*.

∧ Mountain	Berg	Montaña	Montagne	Montanha
⩕ Mountains	Gebirge	Montañas	Montagnes	Montanhas
)(Pass	Paß	Paso	Col	Passo
V Valley, Canyon	Tal, Cañon	Valle, Cañón	Vallée, Canyon	Vale, Canhão
≃ Plain	Ebene	Llano	Plaine	Planície
≻ Cape	Kap	Cabo	Cap	Cabo
I Island	Insel	Isla	Île	Ilha
II Islands	Inseln	Islas	Îles	Ilhas
⊥ Other Topographic Features	Andere Topographische Objekte	Otros Elementos Topográficos	Autres données topographiques	Outros acidentes topográficos

Mont-Mort I · 115

ESPAÑOL — Nombre | Página | Lat.°′ | Long.°′ W = Oeste
FRANÇAIS — Nom | Page | Lat.°′ | Long.°′ W = Ouest
PORTUGUÊS — Nome | Página | Lat.°′ | Long.°′ W = Oeste

Nombre / Nom / Nome	Página / Page	Lat.°′	Long.°′
Monticello, N.Y., U.S.	210	41.39 N	74.41 W
Monticello, Ut,. U.S.	200	37.52 N	109.20 W
Monticello, Wi., U.S.	190	42.44 N	89.35 W
Monticello ⊥	188	38.00 N	78.30 W
Monticello Conte Otto	64	45.35 N	11.35 E
Monticello Dam ◆[6]	226	38.30 N	122.07 W
Monticello Woods	284c	38.47 N	77.10 W
Montichiari	64	45.25 N	10.23 E
Monticiano	66	43.08 N	11.11 E
Montiel, Campo de ≚	34	38.46 N	2.44 W
Montier-en-Der	58	48.29 N	4.46 E
Montieri	66	43.08 N	11.01 E
Montieri, Poggio di ∧	66	43.08 N	11.00 E
Montiers-sur-Saulx	58	48.32 N	5.16 E
Montignac	32	45.04 N	1.10 E
Montigny	58	48.31 N	6.48 E
Montigny-Devant-Sassey	56	49.26 N	5.09 E
Montigny-le-Bretonneux	261	48.46 N	2.02 E
Montigny-le-Roi	58	48.00 N	5.30 E
Montigny-lès-Cormeilles	261	48.59 N	2.12 E
Montigny-lès-Metz	56	49.06 N	6.09 E
Montigny-sur-Aube	58	47.57 N	4.46 E
Montijo, Esp.	34	38.55 N	6.37 W
Montijo, Pan.	236	7.59 N	81.03 W
Montijo, Port.	34	38.42 N	8.58 W
Montijo, Aeroporto ⊠	266c	38.42 N	9.02 W
Montijo, Golfo de ⊂	246	7.40 N	81.07 W
Montilla	34	37.35 N	4.38 W
Montividiu	255	17.24 S	51.14 W
Montivilliers	50	49.33 N	0.12 E
Montjay-la-Tour	261	48.55 N	2.40 E
Montjoie, Lac ⊜, P.Q., Can.	206	46.17 N	75.08 W
Montjoie, Lac ⊜, P.Q., Can.	206	45.25 N	72.06 W
Mont-Joli	186	48.35 N	68.11 W
Montjovet	62	45.43 N	7.40 E
Montjuich, Estadio de ♦	266d	41.22 N	2.09 E
Montjuich, Faro de ◆[5]	266d	41.21 N	2.11 E
Montjuich, Parque de ♦	266d	41.21 N	2.09 E
Mont-Laurier	176	46.33 N	75.30 W
Montlebon	58	47.02 N	6.37 E
Montlhéry	50	48.38 N	2.16 E
Montlhéry, Tour de ⊛	261	48.38 N	2.16 E
Montlhéry, Tour de ♦	261	48.38 N	2.16 E
Montlignon	261	49.01 N	2.17 E
Montlouet	261	48.31 N	1.43 E
Mont-Louis	32	42.31 N	2.07 E
Montlouis-sur-Loire	50	47.23 N	0.50 E
Montluçon	32	46.21 N	2.36 E
Montluel	62	45.51 N	5.03 E
Montmagny, P.Q., Can.	186	46.59 N	70.33 W
Montmagny, Fr.	261	48.58 N	2.21 E
Montmajour, Abbaye de ⊛[1]	62	43.43 N	4.40 E
Montmartre ◆[8]	261	48.53 N	2.21 E
Montmédy	56	49.31 N	5.22 E
Montmélian	62	45.30 N	6.04 E
Montmeló	266d	41.33 N	2.15 E
Montmerle-sur-Saône	58	46.05 N	4.46 E
Montmin	62	45.48 N	6.16 E
Montmirail, Fr.	50	48.06 N	0.48 E
Montmirail, Fr.	50	48.52 N	3.32 E
Montmirey-le-Château	58	47.13 N	5.32 E
Montmoreau-Saint-Cybard	32	45.24 N	0.08 E
Montmorenci	216	40.28 N	87.02 W
Montmorency	274b	37.43 S	145.07 E
Montmorency → Beauport	186	46.52 N	71.11 W
Montmorency	261	49.00 N	2.20 E
Montmorency ≃	186	46.53 N	71.07 W
Montmorency, Forêt de ♦	261	49.02 N	2.16 E
Montmorillon	32	46.26 N	0.52 E
Montmort	50	48.55 N	3.49 E
Monto	166	24.52 S	151.07 E
Montodine	62	45.17 N	9.42 E
Montoggio	62	44.31 N	9.03 E
Montoire-sur-le-Loir	50	47.45 N	0.52 E
Montone	66	43.22 N	12.20 E
Montone ≃, It.	64	44.24 N	12.14 E
Montone ≃, It.	66	43.22 N	12.20 E
Montopoli in Val d'Arno	66	43.40 N	10.45 E
Mont Orford, Parc du ♦	206	45.22 N	72.05 W
Montorio al Vomano	66	42.35 N	13.38 E
Montorio nei Frentani	66	41.46 N	14.55 E
Montoro	34	38.01 N	4.23 W
Mont'Orso, Galleria di ◆[5]	66	41.20 N	13.15 E
Montour □[6]	210	40.58 N	76.37 W
Montour Falls	210	42.20 N	76.50 W
Montour Run ≃, Pa., U.S.	279b	40.31 N	80.08 W
Montour Run ≃, Pa., U.S.	279b	40.36 N	79.57 W
Montoursville	210	41.15 N	76.55 W
Mont Park	274b	37.43 S	145.04 E
Montparnasse, Gare ◆[5]	261	48.51 N	2.19 E
Mont Peko, Parc National du ♦	150	7.00 N	7.15 W
Montpelier, Jam.	241q	18.22 N	77.56 W
Montpelier, Id., U.S.	202	42.19 N	111.17 W
Montpelier, In., U.S.	216	40.33 N	85.16 W
Montpelier, Md., U.S.	284c	39.04 N	76.51 W
Montpelier, Ms., U.S.	194	33.43 N	88.56 W
Montpelier, Oh., U.S.	216	41.35 N	84.36 W
Montpelier, Vt., U.S.	188	44.15 N	72.34 W
Montpellier	62	43.36 N	3.53 E
Montpellier-Fréjorgues, Aéroport de ⊠	62	43.33 N	4.00 E
Montpezat-sous-Bauzon	62	44.43 N	4.12 E
Mont-Pichet	261	48.53 N	2.54 E
Montpon-Ménesterol	32	45.00 N	0.10 E
Montpont-en-Bresse	58	46.33 N	5.09 E
Montréal, P.Q., Can.	206	45.31 N	73.34 W
Montréal, P.Q., Can.	275a	45.31 N	73.34 W
Montréal, Fr.	50	47.32 N	4.02 E
Montreal, Wi., U.S.	190	46.25 N	90.14 W
Montreal ≃, On., Can.	190	47.14 N	84.39 W
Montreal ≃, On., Can.	190	47.08 N	79.27 W
Montreal ≃, Sk., Can.	184	55.06 N	105.19 W
Montreal ≃, U.S.	190	46.44 N	90.25 W
Montréal, Base des Forces Canadiennes ■	275a	45.31 N	73.25 W
Montréal, Île de I	206	45.30 N	73.40 W
Montréal, Université de ⊛[2]	275a	45.30 N	73.37 W
Montréal-Est	206	45.38 N	73.31 W
Montreal International Airport ⊠	206	45.28 N	73.45 W
Montreal Lake	184	54.03 N	105.46 W
Montreal Lake ⊜	184	54.20 N	105.40 W
Montreal Lake Indian Reserve ◆[4]	184	54.00 N	105.45 W
Montréal-Nord	206	45.36 N	73.38 W
Montréal-Quest	275a	45.27 N	73.39 W
Montreal Water Works Aqueduct ≍[1]	275a	45.26 N	73.36 W
Montrésor	50	47.09 N	1.12 E
Montresta	71	40.22 N	8.30 E
Montret	58	46.41 N	5.07 E
Montreuil	261	48.52 N	2.26 E
Montreuil-Bellay	32	47.08 N	0.09 W
Montreuil-sous-Bois	50	48.52 N	2.26 E
Montreuil-sur-Mer	50	50.28 N	1.46 E
Montreux	58	46.26 N	6.55 E
Montrevel-en-Bresse	58	46.20 N	5.08 E
Montrichard	50	47.21 N	1.11 E
Montriond	58	46.12 N	6.41 E
Mont-Rolland	206	45.57 N	74.07 W
Montrond-les-Bains	62	45.38 N	4.14 E
Montrose, Austl.	274b	37.49 S	145.21 E
Montrose, Scot., U.K.	46	56.43 N	2.29 W
Montrose, Ca., U.S.	228	34.12 N	118.13 W
Montrose, Co., U.S.	200	38.28 N	107.52 W
Montrose, Ia., U.S.	190	40.31 N	91.24 W
Montrose, Mi., U.S.	190	43.10 N	83.53 W
Montrose, N.Y., U.S.	210	41.15 N	73.56 W
Montrose, Oh., U.S.	214	41.08 N	81.37 W
Montrose, Pa., U.S.	210	41.50 N	75.52 W
Montrose, S.D., U.S.	198	43.41 N	97.11 W
Montrose Harbor ⊂	278	41.58 N	87.38 W
Montrose Hill	279b	40.30 N	79.51 W
Montross	208	38.05 N	76.49 W
Montrouge	261	48.49 N	2.19 E
Mont-Royal	206	45.31 N	73.39 W
Mont Royal, Parc ♦	275a	45.31 N	73.35 W
Mont Royal Tunnel ◆[5]	275a	45.31 N	73.38 W
Montry	261	48.53 N	2.50 E
Monts	50	47.17 N	0.37 E
Monts, Pointe des ›	186	49.20 N	67.23 W
Mont-Saint-Aignan	50	49.28 N	1.05 E
Mont-Sainte-Anne, Parc du ♦	186	47.08 N	70.55 W
Mont-Saint-Hilaire	206	45.34 N	73.11 W
Mont-Saint-Martin	56	49.32 N	5.47 E
Mont-Saint-Michel → Le Mont-Saint-Michel ⊛[1]	32	48.38 N	1.32 W
Mont-Saint-Vincent	58	46.38 N	4.29 E
Montsauche	50	47.13 N	4.01 E
Montsec	56	48.53 N	5.43 E
Montserrat □[2], N.A.	230	16.45 N	62.12 W
Montserrat □[2], N.A.	238	16.45 N	62.12 W
Montserrat, Monasterio de ⊛[1]	34	41.36 N	1.49 E
Montsoult	261	49.04 N	2.19 E
Montsûrs	28	48.08 N	0.33 W
Mont-sur-Vaudrey	58	46.58 N	5.36 E
Mont-Tremblant, Parc provincial du ♦	206	46.42 N	74.20 W
Montuenga	34	41.03 N	4.37 W
Montvale, N.J., U.S.	276	41.02 N	74.01 W
Montvale, Va., U.S.	192	37.23 N	79.43 W
Montverde	220	28.36 N	81.41 W
Montville, Ct., U.S.	207	41.27 N	72.08 W
Montville, N.J., U.S.	276	40.54 N	74.23 W
Montville, Oh., U.S.	214	41.36 N	81.03 W
Montville Airpark ⊠	276	40.56 N	74.20 W
Monument, S. Afr.	273d	26.06 S	27.43 E
Monument, Or., U.S.	202	44.49 N	119.25 W
Monument, Pa., U.S.	214	41.07 N	77.42 W
Monument Beach	207	41.43 N	70.36 W
Monument Draw V, U.S.	196	32.27 N	102.20 W
Monument Draw V, Tx., U.S.	196	30.51 N	102.33 W
Monument Hill State Historic Site ⊥	222	29.53 N	96.54 W
Monumento	256	22.44 S	43.51 W
Monument Peak ∧, Co., U.S.	200	39.43 N	107.55 W
Monument Peak ∧, Id., U.S.	202	42.07 N	114.14 W
Monument Valley V	200	37.05 N	110.20 W
Monundilla, Mount ∧	170	32.45 S	150.29 E
Monveda	152	2.57 N	21.27 E
Monymusk	46	57.13 N	2.31 W
Monyo	110	17.59 N	95.30 E
Monywa	110	22.05 N	95.08 E
Monza	62	45.35 N	9.16 E
Monze	154	16.16 S	27.28 E
Monzen	92	37.17 N	136.46 E
Monzie	46	56.24 N	3.48 W
Monzón, Esp.	34	41.55 N	0.12 E
Monzón, Perú	248	9.10 S	76.23 W
Moóca ◆[8]	287b	23.33 S	46.35 W
Moóca, Ribeirão da ≃	287b	23.36 S	46.35 W
Moodie Island I	176	64.37 N	65.30 W
Moodus	207	41.30 N	72.27 W
Moodus Reservoir ⊜[1]	207	41.30 N	72.24 W
Moody	222	31.18 N	97.21 W
Moody Air Force Base ■	192	30.59 N	83.11 W
Moody Wood Dale Airport ⊠	278	41.59 N	87.58 W
Mooers	206	44.58 N	73.35 W
Mooi ≃, S. Afr.	158	28.45 S	30.34 E
Mooi ≃, S. Afr.	158	26.53 S	26.56 E
Mooirivier	158	29.13 S	29.50 E
Mook	52	51.45 N	5.54 E
Mookane	156	24.59 S	24.33 E
Mooketsi	156	23.35 S	30.05 E
Moolawatana	166	29.55 S	139.43 E
Moolman	158	27.10 S	30.53 E
Mooloogool	162	26.06 S	119.05 E
Moon	214	40.31 N	80.14 W
Moon ≃	212	45.08 N	79.59 W
Moon, Mountains of the → Ruwenzori Range ⋀	154	0.23 N	29.54 E
Moonachie	276	40.50 N	74.02 W
Moonachie Creek ≃	276	40.48 N	74.03 W
Moonah Creek ≃	166	22.03 S	138.33 E
Moon Crest	279b	40.32 N	80.11 W
Moondarra Reservoir ⊜[1]	169	38.04 S	146.22 E
Moonee Valley Racecourse ♦	274b	37.46 S	144.56 E
Moonie	166	27.43 S	150.22 E
Moonie ≃	166	29.19 S	148.43 E
Moon Island I, On., Can.	212	45.09 N	80.01 W
Moon Island I, Ma., U.S.	283	42.18 N	71.00 W
Moon Run	214	40.27 N	80.06 W
Moonta	168b	34.04 S	137.35 E
Moor, Kepulauan II	164	2.57 S	135.45 E
Moora	162	30.39 S	116.00 E
Moorabbin	169	37.56 S	145.02 E
Moorabbin Airport ⊠	274b	37.59 S	145.09 E
Mooraberree	166	25.14 S	140.59 E
Moorabool ≃	169	38.09 S	144.19 E
Moorarie	162	25.56 S	117.35 E
Moorburg	52	53.17 N	7.53 E
Moorcroft	198	44.15 N	104.56 W
Moordorf	52	53.28 N	7.23 E
Moordrecht	52	51.59 N	4.40 E
Moore, Austl.	171a	26.53 S	152.18 E
Moore, Eng., U.K.	262	53.21 N	2.38 W
Moore, Id., U.S.	202	43.44 N	113.21 W
Moore, Mt., U.S.	202	46.58 N	109.41 W
Moore, Ok., U.S.	196	35.20 N	97.29 W
Moore, Tx., U.S.	196	29.03 N	99.01 W
Moore ≃	162	31.22 S	115.29 E
Moore, Lake ⊜	162	29.50 S	117.35 E
Moorea I	174s	17.32 S	149.50 W
Moorebank	274a	33.56 S	150.56 E
Moore Creek ≃	212	45.29 N	77.58 W
Moorefield, Ky., U.S.	218	38.16 N	83.55 W
Moorefield, Oh., U.S.	214	40.12 N	81.10 W
Moorefield, W.V., U.S.	188	39.03 N	78.58 W
Moore Haven	220	26.49 N	81.05 W
Moore Haven Lock ◆[5]	220	26.51 N	81.05 W
Moore Lake ⊜, On., Can.	212	45.26 N	78.01 W
Moore Lake ⊜, On., Can.	212	44.48 N	78.48 W
Moore Lake ⊜, Mi., U.S.	281	42.37 N	83.36 W
Mooreland, In., U.S.	218	39.59 N	85.15 W
Mooreland, Ok., U.S.	196	36.26 N	99.12 W
Moore Point ›	275b	43.48 N	79.03 W
Moore Reservoir ⊜[1]	188	44.25 N	71.50 W
Mooresburg	210	40.59 N	76.43 W
Moores Creek National Battlefield ♦	192	34.24 N	78.08 W
Moores Hill	218	39.06 N	85.05 W
Moore Station	222	32.11 N	95.35 W
Moorestown	208	39.58 N	74.56 W
Moorestown Mall ◆[9]	285	39.56 N	74.58 W
Mooresville, In., U.S.	218	39.36 N	86.22 W
Mooresville, N.C., U.S.	192	35.35 N	80.48 W
Mooreville	281	42.06 N	83.44 W
Moorfoot Hills ⋀[2]	46	55.45 N	3.02 W
Moorhead, Mn., U.S.	198	46.52 N	96.46 W
Moorhead, Ms., U.S.	194	33.27 N	90.30 W
Mooring	222	30.41 N	96.33 W
Mooringsport	194	32.41 N	93.57 W
Moormerland	52	53.20 N	7.27 E
Moornanyah Lake ⊜	166	33.02 S	143.58 E
Moorooka	171a	27.32 S	153.02 E
Mooroolbark	274b	37.47 S	145.19 E
Moorpark	228	34.17 N	118.53 W
Moorreesburg	158	33.08 S	18.40 E
Moorrege	52	53.40 N	9.39 E
Moorriem	52	53.15 N	8.19 E
Moorsel	50	50.57 N	4.06 E
Moorside	262	53.34 N	2.04 W
Moorslede	50	50.53 N	3.04 E
Moos → Moso, It.	64	46.41 N	12.23 E
Moos → Moso in Passiria, It.	64	46.50 N	11.10 E
Moosach ◆[8]	60	48.11 N	11.31 E
Moosbrunn	264b	48.01 N	16.28 E
Moosburg, B.R.D.	30	48.29 N	11.57 E
Moosburg, Öst.	61	46.39 N	14.10 E
Moosburg an der Isar	60	48.29 N	11.57 E
Moose ≃, Me., U.S.	188	45.40 N	69.42 W
Moose ≃, N.Y., U.S.	212	43.37 N	75.22 W
Moose Creek	206	45.15 N	74.58 W
Moose Creek ≃	206	45.23 N	75.04 W
Moosehead Lake ⊜	188	45.40 N	69.40 W
Mooseheart	216	41.49 N	88.20 W
Moose Heights	182	53.05 N	122.30 W
Moose Hill ∧[2]	283	42.07 N	71.13 W
Moose Island I	184	51.42 N	97.10 W
Moose Jaw	184	50.23 N	105.32 W
Moose Jaw ≃	184	50.34 N	105.17 W
Moose Lake, Mb., Can.	184	53.43 N	100.20 W
Moose Lake, Mn., U.S.	190	46.27 N	92.45 W
Moose Lake ⊜, Ab., Can.	182	54.15 N	110.55 W
Moose Lake ⊜, Mb., Can.	184	53.55 N	99.45 W
Moose Lake ⊜, On., Can.	212	45.09 N	78.28 W
Mooselookmeguntic Lake ⊜	188	44.53 N	70.48 W
Moose Mountain ∧	184	49.45 N	102.37 W
Moose Mountain Creek ≃	184	49.12 N	102.10 W
Moose Mountain Provincial Park ♦	184	49.48 N	102.25 W
Moose Pass	180	60.29 N	149.22 W
Moosomin	184	50.07 N	101.40 W
Moosomin Indian Reserve ◆[4]	184	53.06 N	108.14 W
Moosonee	176	51.17 N	80.39 W
Moosup	207	41.42 N	71.52 W
Mooti	144	0.35 N	41.56 E
Moots Creek ≃	216	40.32 N	86.47 W
Mootwingee National Park ♦	166	31.07 S	142.23 E
Mopane	156	22.37 S	29.52 E
Mopeia Velha	156	17.59 S	35.44 E
Mopipi	156	21.07 S	24.55 E
Mopo	100	33.07 N	113.02 E
Moppo → Mokp'o	98	34.48 N	126.22 E
Mopti	150	14.30 N	4.12 W
Mopti □[4]	150	14.40 N	4.15 W
Moqokorei	144	4.04 N	46.08 E
Moquegua	248	17.12 S	70.56 W
Moquegua □[5]	248	16.50 S	70.55 W
Mór	30	47.23 N	18.12 E
Mor ≃	126	24.01 N	88.03 E
Mòr, Glen V	46	57.10 N	4.40 W
Mor, Sgurr ∧	46	57.42 N	5.03 W
Mora, Cam.	146	11.03 N	14.09 E
Mora, Esp.	34	39.41 N	3.46 W
Mora, India	272c	18.54 N	72.56 E
Mora, Port.	34	38.56 N	8.10 W
Mora, Sve.	26	61.00 N	14.33 E
Mora, Mn., U.S.	190	45.52 N	93.17 W
Mora, N.M., U.S.	200	35.58 N	105.19 W
Mora ≃	196	35.44 N	104.23 W
Mora, Arroyo de la ≃	196	34.05 N	104.18 W
Moraby	40	60.23 N	15.35 E
Morača, Manastir ⊛[1]	38	42.44 N	19.20 E
Morada	226	38.01 N	121.15 W
Morādābād	124	28.50 N	78.47 E
Morada Nova	250	5.07 S	38.23 W
Morada Nova de Minas	255	18.37 S	45.22 W
Mora de Rubielos	34	40.15 N	0.45 W
Morado Primero, Cerro ∧	252	22.49 S	65.26 W
Moraduccio	66	44.10 N	11.29 E
Morafenobe	157b	17.49 S	44.55 E
Morąg	30	53.56 N	19.56 E
Moraga	226	37.50 N	122.08 W
Mórahalom	30	46.13 N	19.54 E
Moraine	218	39.42 N	84.13 W
Moraine Hills State Park ♦	216	42.18 N	88.15 W
Moraine State Park ♦	214	40.56 N	80.07 W
Morainvilliers	261	48.56 N	1.56 E
Morākhi ≃	126	24.01 N	88.10 E
Morākhi Reservoir ⊜[1]	126	24.10 N	87.15 E
Mor'akovskij Zaton	86	56.45 N	84.41 E
Moral de Calatrava	34	38.50 N	3.35 W
Moraleda, Canal de ‖	254	44.30 S	73.30 W
Morales, Guat.	236	15.29 N	88.49 W
Morales, Perú	248	6.28 S	76.28 W
Morales, Arroyo ≃	258	34.48 S	58.36 W
Morales, Laguna de ⊂	234	23.35 N	97.47 W
Moramanga	157b	18.56 S	48.12 E
Moran, Ks., U.S.	198	37.54 N	95.10 W
Moran, Mi., U.S.	190	45.59 N	84.49 W
Moran, Tx., U.S.	196	32.33 N	99.10 W
Moran ≃	164	15.16 S	125.33 E
Moranbah	166	22.00 S	148.02 E
Morangis	261	48.42 N	2.20 E
Morangup Hill ∧[2]	168a	31.41 S	116.19 E
Morann	214	40.48 N	78.21 W
Morano Calabro	68	39.50 N	16.08 E
Morano sul Po	62	45.10 N	8.22 E
Moran State Park ♦	224	48.41 N	122.52 W
Morant Bay	241q	17.53 N	76.25 W
Morant Cays II	238	17.24 N	75.59 W
Morant Point ›	241q	17.55 N	76.10 W
Morar, Loch ⊜	46	56.57 N	5.43 W
Mörarp	41	56.04 N	12.52 E
Morasverdes	34	40.36 N	6.16 W
Morat, Lac de (Murtensee) ⊜	58	46.55 N	7.05 E
Moratalla	34	38.12 N	1.53 W
Morattico	208	37.47 N	76.37 W
Moratuwa	122	6.46 N	79.53 E
Morava □[9]	30	49.30 N	17.00 E
Morava (March) ≃	30	48.10 N	16.59 E
Morāveh Tappeh	128	37.55 N	55.57 E
Moravia, C.R.	236	9.51 N	83.26 W
Moravia, Ia., U.S.	190	40.53 N	92.48 W
Moravia, N.Y., U.S.	210	42.42 N	76.25 W
Moravia → Morava □[9]	30	49.20 N	17.00 E
Moravian Indian Reserve ◆[4]	214	42.34 N	81.53 W
Moravská Dyje ≃	61	48.51 N	15.30 E
Moravská Ostrava → Ostrava	30	49.50 N	18.17 E
Moravská Třebová	30	49.45 N	16.40 E
Moravské Budějovice	61	49.03 N	15.49 E
Moravský Krumlov	61	49.03 N	16.19 E
Morawa	162	29.13 S	116.00 E
Morawhanna	246	8.16 N	59.45 W
Moraya	248	21.45 S	65.32 W
Morayfield	171a	27.07 S	152.57 E
Moray Firth ⊂[1]	46	57.50 N	3.30 W
Morazán, Guat.	236	14.56 N	90.09 W
Morazán, Hond.	236	15.17 N	87.34 W
Morbach	56	49.48 N	7.07 E
Morbegno	36	46.08 N	9.34 E
Morbi	120	22.49 N	70.50 E
Morbihan □[5]	32	47.55 N	2.50 W
Mörbisch am See	61	47.45 N	16.40 E
Morbras ≃	261	48.47 N	2.29 E
Mörbylånga	26	56.31 N	16.23 E
Morcenx	32	44.02 N	0.55 W
Morciano di Romagna	66	43.55 N	12.38 E
Morcone	68	41.20 N	14.40 E
Morcote	58	45.56 N	8.55 E
Morcy	80	51.18 N	47.51 E
Morden	184	49.11 N	98.05 W
Morden ◆[8]	260	51.24 N	0.12 W
Mordialloc	169	38.00 S	145.05 E
Mordino	24	61.21 N	51.52 E
Mordoğan	130	38.30 N	26.37 E
Mordovo, S.S.S.R.	80	51.07 N	45.48 E
Mordovo, S.S.S.R.	80	52.05 N	40.46 E
Mordovo-Adel'akovo	80	53.47 N	51.36 E
Mordovskaja Avtonomnaja Sovetskaja Socialističeskaja Respublika □[3]	80	54.30 N	44.00 E
Mordovskij Buguruslan	80	53.48 N	52.31 E
Mordovskij Zapovednik ◆[4]	80	54.48 N	43.20 E
Mordves	82	54.34 N	38.13 E
Mordy	30	52.13 N	22.31 E
More, Ben ∧, Scot., U.K.	46	56.21 N	4.35 W
More, Ben ∧, Scot., U.K.	46	56.25 N	6.01 W
More, Loch ⊜	46	58.17 N	4.52 W
More Assynt, Ben ∧	46	58.08 N	4.53 W
Moreau ≃, Mo., U.S.	219	38.33 N	92.06 W
Moreau ≃, S.D., U.S.	198	45.18 N	100.43 W
Moreau, North Fork ≃	198	45.09 N	102.50 W
Moreau, South Fork ≃	198	45.09 N	102.50 W
Moreau Peak ∧	198	45.21 N	103.43 W
Moreauville	194	31.02 N	91.58 W
Morec	80	51.03 N	44.03 E
Morecambe	44	54.04 N	2.53 W
Morecambe Bay ⊂	44	54.07 N	3.00 W
Moree, Austl.	166	29.28 S	149.51 E
Morée, Fr.	50	47.54 N	1.14 E
Morehead, Pap. N. Gui.	164	8.40 S	141.35 E
Morehead, Ky., U.S.	218	38.11 N	83.25 W
Morehead ≃	164	9.00 S	141.25 E
Morehead City	192	34.43 N	76.43 W
Morehouse	194	36.50 N	89.41 W
Moreira César	256	22.55 S	45.22 W
Moreland, Austl.	274b	37.45 S	144.58 E
Moreland, Ga., U.S.	192	33.17 N	84.46 W
Moreland, Ky., U.S.	194	37.30 N	84.48 W
Moreland Hills	279a	41.27 N	81.29 W
Morelia	234	19.42 N	101.07 W
Morell	186	46.25 N	62.42 W
Morella, Austl.	166	22.59 S	143.52 E
Morella, Esp.	34	40.37 N	0.06 W
Morello ≃	70	37.29 N	14.08 E
Morelos, Méx.	196	28.25 N	100.53 W
Morelos, Méx.	232	26.42 N	107.40 W
Morelos, Méx.	234	22.53 N	102.37 W
Morelos □[3]	234	18.45 N	99.00 W
Morelos ◆[8]	286a	19.27 N	99.07 W
Moremi Wildlife Reserve ◆[4]	156	19.10 S	23.15 E
Morena	124	26.30 N	78.09 E
Morena, Sierra ∧	282	37.25 N	122.18 W
Morena, Sierra ⋀	34	38.00 N	5.00 W
Morenci, Az., U.S.	200	33.04 N	109.21 W
Morenci, Mi., U.S.	216	41.43 N	84.13 W
Moreni	38	45.00 N	25.39 E
Moreno, Arg.	258	34.39 S	58.48 W
Moreno, Ca., U.S.	228	33.55 N	117.09 W
Moreno □[5]	288	34.36 S	58.48 W
Moreno ≃	234	18.32 N	96.01 W
Moreno, Bahía ⊂	252	23.35 S	70.30 W
Møre og Romsdal □[6]	26	62.40 N	7.50 E
Mores	71	40.33 N	8.50 E
Moresby Island I, B.C., Can.	182	52.50 N	131.55 W
Moresby Island I, B.C., Can.	224	48.40 N	123.20 W
Mores Island I	238	26.18 N	77.33 W
Moresnet	56	50.43 N	5.59 E
Morestel	62	45.40 N	5.28 E
Moreton, Austl.	164	12.28 S	142.38 E
Moreton, Eng., U.K.	44	53.24 N	3.07 W
Moreton, Eng., U.K.	260	51.44 N	0.14 E
Moreton, Cape ›	171a	27.02 S	153.28 E
Moreton Bay ⊂	171a	27.20 S	153.15 E
Moretonhampstead	42	50.40 N	3.45 W
Moreton-in-Marsh	42	51.59 N	1.42 W
Moreton Island I	171a	27.10 S	153.25 E
Moreton Island National Park ♦	171a	27.09 S	153.25 E
Moret-sur-Loing	50	48.22 N	2.49 E
Moretta	62	44.46 N	7.32 E
Moreuil	50	49.46 N	2.29 E
Morey Park	210	42.33 N	73.43 W
Morey Peak ∧	204	38.37 N	116.17 W
Morez	58	46.31 N	6.02 E
Morfa Nefyn	42	52.56 N	4.33 W
Mörfelden-Walldorf	56	49.58 N	8.34 E
Morga	80	54.26 N	46.29 E
Morgan, Austl.	166	34.02 S	139.40 E
Morgan, Ga., U.S.	192	31.32 N	84.35 W
Morgan, Ky., U.S.	218	38.36 N	84.23 W
Morgan, Mn., U.S.	198	44.25 N	94.55 W
Morgan, Pa., U.S.	279b	40.22 N	80.08 W
Morgan, Tx., U.S.	222	32.01 N	97.37 W
Morgan, Ut,. U.S.	200	41.02 N	111.40 W
Morgan □[6], Il., U.S.	219	39.44 N	90.14 W
Morgan □[6], In., U.S.	218	39.30 N	86.25 W
Morgan, Mount ∧	171b	35.44 S	148.47 E
Morgan City, Al., U.S.	194	34.28 N	86.34 W
Morgan City, La., U.S.	194	29.41 N	91.12 W
Morgan Creek ≃	196	32.19 N	100.55 W
Morganfield	194	37.41 N	87.55 W
Morgan Hill	226	37.07 N	121.39 W
Morganito	246	5.04 N	67.44 W
Morgan Park ◆[8]	278	41.42 N	87.40 W
Morgan's Bay	158	32.43 S	28.20 E
Morgan's Point	222	29.41 N	94.59 W
Morgans Point ›	212	42.52 N	79.21 W
Morgan State College ⊛[2]	284b	39.21 N	76.35 W
Morgantina ⊥	70	37.25 N	14.29 E
Morganton	192	35.44 N	81.41 W
Morgantown, In., U.S.	218	39.22 N	86.15 W
Morgantown, Ky., U.S.	194	37.13 N	86.41 W
Morgantown, Md., U.S.	208	38.21 N	76.58 W
Morgantown, Ms., U.S.	194	31.18 N	89.54 W
Morgantown, Ms., U.S.	194	31.34 N	91.20 W
Morgantown, Oh., U.S.	218	39.08 N	83.13 W
Morgantown, Pa., U.S.	208	40.09 N	75.54 W
Morgantown, W.V., U.S.	188	39.37 N	79.57 W
Morganville	208	40.23 N	74.15 W
Morgan Whyalla Pipeline ≍[1]	168b	33.48 S	138.56 E
Morganza	194	30.44 N	91.35 W
Morgårdshammar	40	60.09 N	15.23 E
Morgauši	80	55.58 N	46.47 E
Morgenzon	158	26.45 S	29.36 E
Morges	58	46.31 N	6.30 E
Morgex	62	45.45 N	7.02 E
Morghāb (Murgab) ≃	128	38.18 N	61.12 E
Morghar	126	23.40 N	89.37 E
Morghūm, Kūh-e ∧	128	33.06 N	57.30 E
Morgongåva	40	59.56 N	16.57 E
Morgongiori	71	39.45 N	8.46 E
Morguilla, Punta ›	252	37.46 S	73.40 W
Morhange	56	48.55 N	6.38 E
Mori, It.	64	45.51 N	10.59 E
Mori, Nihon	92a	42.06 N	140.35 E
Mori, Nihon	94	34.50 N	137.56 E
Mori, Nihon	270	34.32 N	135.00 E
Mori ≃	164	10.00 S	148.30 E
Moriah	241r	11.15 N	60.43 W
Moriah, Mount ∧	204	39.17 N	114.12 W
Morialta Conservation Park ♦	168b	34.55 S	138.40 E
Moriarty	200	34.59 N	106.02 W
Moriarty, Mount ∧	224	49.08 N	124.26 W
Morib	114	2.45 N	101.26 E
Moribaya	150	9.53 N	9.33 W
Morice ≃	182	54.24 N	126.45 W
Morice Lake ⊜	182	54.00 N	127.37 W
Morichal Largo ≃	246	9.27 N	62.25 W
Moricsala ♦	76	57.17 N	22.11 E
Morie, Loch ⊜	46	57.44 N	4.28 W
Morienval	50	49.18 N	2.56 E
Morigerati	68	40.08 N	15.33 E
Moriguchi	96	34.44 N	135.34 E
Morija	158	29.34 S	27.31 E
Moriki	150	12.52 N	6.30 E
Morin Dawa	89	48.28 N	124.27 E
Moringen	52	51.42 N	9.52 E
Morino, It.	66	41.53 N	13.25 E
Morino, S.S.S.R.	76	57.54 N	30.22 E
Morinville	182	53.48 N	113.39 W
Morioka	92	39.42 N	141.09 E
Morīri, Tso ⊜	120	32.54 N	78.20 E
Morisset	170	33.06 S	151.29 E
Moriston ≃	46	57.12 N	4.36 W
Moritzburg ⊥	54	51.09 N	13.40 E
Morivione ◆[8]	266b	45.26 N	9.12 E
Moriya	94	35.56 N	140.00 E
Moriyama	94	35.04 N	135.59 E
Moriyama-chūtonchi, Rikujō-jieitai- ■	94	35.12 N	136.57 E
Moriyoshi-zan ∧	92	39.58 N	140.33 E
Morki	80	56.25 N	49.01 E
Morkill ≃	182	53.42 N	120.30 W
Morkiny Gory	76	57.33 N	36.18 E
Mörkö I	40	58.59 N	17.40 E
Morkoka ≃	74	65.10 N	115.52 E
Mørkøv	41	55.40 N	11.32 E
Morlaix	32	48.35 N	3.50 W
Morlanwelz	50	50.27 N	4.14 E
Morles	56	50.38 N	9.51 E
Morley, Eng., U.K.	44	53.46 N	1.36 W
Morley, Mi., U.S.	190	43.29 N	85.26 W
Morley, N.Y., U.S.	212	44.40 N	75.12 W
Morley Green	262	53.20 N	2.16 W
Mörlunda	26	57.19 N	15.51 E
Mormal'	76	52.45 N	29.53 E
Mormanno	68	39.53 N	16.00 E
Mormant	50	48.36 N	2.53 E
Mormoiron	62	44.04 N	5.11 E
Mormon Bar	226	37.28 N	119.57 W
Mormon Lake ⊜	200	34.57 N	111.27 W
Mormon Peak ∧	204	36.57 N	114.30 W
Mormon Reservoir ⊜[1]	202	43.16 N	114.49 W
Mormon Slough ≃	226	37.57 N	121.18 W
Mormon Station Historical State Monument ♦	226	39.00 N	119.50 W
Mormugao	122	15.24 N	73.48 E
Morna	272a	28.35 N	77.22 E
Mornant	62	45.37 N	4.40 E
Mornas	62	44.12 N	4.44 E
Morne, Pointe ›	241o	16.20 N	61.18 W
Morne-à-l'Eau	241o	16.21 N	61.31 W
Morne-Rouge	240e	14.46 N	61.08 W
Morney	166	25.22 S	141.28 E
Morningdale	207	42.18 N	71.45 W
Morningside	284c	38.50 N	76.53 W
Morningside Park ♦	275b	43.47 N	79.12 W
Morningstar ≃	48	52.27 N	8.41 W
Morning Sun	190	41.05 N	91.15 W
Mornington	169	38.13 S	145.03 E
Mornington, Isla I	254	49.45 S	75.23 W
Mornington Island I	164	16.33 S	139.24 E
Mornington Island Aboriginal Land Trust ◆[4]	164	16.20 S	139.20 E
Mornington Peninsula ›[1]	169	38.20 S	145.05 E
Morno	150	8.41 N	1.31 W
Mornou, Hadjer ∧	146	17.12 N	23.08 E
Moro, Indon.	114	0.46 N	103.43 E
Moro, Or., U.S.	224	45.29 N	120.43 W
Moro ≃	150	7.25 N	11.03 W
Morobe	164	7.45 S	147.35 E
Morobe □[5]	164	7.00 S	146.30 E
Moroč'	76	52.34 N	27.36 E
Moroč' ≃	76	52.35 N	27.35 E
Morocco	216	40.56 N	87.27 W
Morocco (Al-Magreb) □[1], Afr.	134	32.00 N	5.00 W
Morocco (Al-Magreb) □[1], Afr.	148	32.00 N	5.00 W
Morococala	248	18.10 S	66.44 W
Morococha	248	11.37 S	76.09 W
Moro Creek ≃	194	33.18 N	92.22 W
Morogoro	154	6.49 S	37.40 E
Morogoro □[4]	154	8.00 S	37.15 E
Moro Gulf ⊂	116	6.51 N	123.00 E
Moroka	273d	26.16 S	27.52 E
Morokweng	158	26.12 S	23.45 E
Moroleón	234	20.08 N	101.12 W
Morombe	157b	21.45 S	43.22 E
Morón, Arg.	258	34.39 S	58.37 W
Morón, Cuba	240p	22.06 N	78.38 W
Mörön, Mong.	88	48.15 N	100.23 E
Mörön, Mong.	88	49.38 N	100.10 E
Mörön, Mong.	88	47.24 N	110.16 E
Morón, Ven.	246	10.29 N	68.11 W
Morón □[5]	288	34.37 S	58.37 W
Mörön ≃	88	47.14 N	110.37 E
Morón, Aeródromo ⊠	288	34.41 S	58.38 W
Morón, Arroyo ≃	288	34.33 S	58.37 W
Morona ≃	246	4.45 S	77.04 W
Morona-Santiago □[4]	246	2.30 S	78.00 W
Morondava	157b	20.17 S	44.17 E
Morón de Almazán	34	41.25 N	2.25 W
Morón de la Frontera	34	37.08 N	5.27 W
Morones, Sierra ⋀	234	21.45 N	103.10 W
Morong	116	14.41 N	120.16 E
Morongo Indian Reservation ◆[4]	204	33.59 N	116.50 W
Moroni, Comores	157a	11.41 S	43.16 E
Moroni, Ut,. U.S.	200	39.31 N	111.35 W
Moron Us ≃, Zhg.	90	34.42 N	94.50 E
Moron Us ≃, Zhg.	120	34.40 N	95.00 E
Moros ≃	34	41.03 N	4.15 W
Morošečnoje	74	56.24 N	156.12 E
Morotai I	108	2.20 N	128.25 E
Moroto	154	2.32 N	34.39 E
Moroto ∧	154	2.32 N	34.46 E
Morouba	152	6.11 N	20.13 E
Morovis	240m	18.20 N	66.24 W
Morovsk	78	51.06 N	30.50 E
Morowali	112	1.52 S	121.30 E
Moroyama	94	35.56 N	139.19 E
Morozkovo	86	59.29 N	61.01 E
Morozovka, S.S.S.R.	78	50.09 N	39.38 E
Morozovka, S.S.S.R.	83	49.28 N	39.54 E
Morozovsk	80	48.22 N	41.50 E
Morozovskaja	24	61.10 N	50.18 E
Morpeth, On., Can.	214	42.23 N	81.51 W
Morpeth, Eng., U.K.	44	55.10 N	1.41 W
Morphett Vale	168b	35.07 S	138.31 E
Morra, Monte ∧	267a	42.02 N	12.50 E
Morral	214	40.41 N	83.12 W
Morral, Arroyo del ≃	266d	41.29 N	2.03 E
Morrelganj	126	22.28 N	89.51 E
Morretes	252	25.28 S	48.49 W
Morrice	216	42.50 N	84.11 W
Morrill	198	41.57 N	103.55 W
Morrilton	194	35.09 N	92.44 W
Morrin	182	51.40 N	112.47 W
Morrinhos, Bra.	250	3.14 S	40.07 W
Morrinhos, Bra.	255	17.44 S	49.07 W
Morrinsville	172	37.39 S	175.32 E
Morris, Mb., Can.	184	49.21 N	97.22 W
Morris, Ct., U.S.	207	41.41 N	73.11 W
Morris, Il., U.S.	216	41.21 N	88.25 W
Morris, In., U.S.	218	39.16 N	85.10 W
Morris, Mn., U.S.	198	45.35 N	95.54 W
Morris, N.Y., U.S.	210	42.32 N	75.14 W
Morris, Ok., U.S.	196	35.36 N	95.51 W
Morris, Pa., U.S.	210	41.36 N	77.18 W
Morris □[6], N.J., U.S.	210	40.48 N	74.29 W
Morris □[6], Tx., U.S.	222	33.05 N	94.45 W
Morris ≃	184	49.21 N	97.22 W
Morris, Mount ∧	162	26.09 S	131.04 E
Morrisburg	212	44.54 N	75.11 W
Morrisdale	214	40.56 N	78.13 W
Morris Dam ◆[6]	280	34.11 N	117.53 W
Morris Jesup, Kap ›	16	83.38 N	33.52 W
Morris Lake ⊜	276	41.03 N	74.37 W
Morrison, Arg.	252	32.36 S	62.50 W
Morrison, Il., U.S.	190	41.48 N	89.57 W
Morrison, Mo., U.S.	219	38.40 N	91.38 W
Morrison, Point ›	168b	35.44 S	137.47 E
Morrison Creek ≃	275b	43.28 N	79.39 W
Morrison Lake ⊜, On., Can.	212	44.52 N	79.28 W
Morrison Lake ⊜, Mi., U.S.	216	42.53 N	85.13 W
Morrisonville	219	39.25 N	89.27 W
Morris Park ♦	285	39.59 N	75.15 W
Morris Plains	210	40.49 N	74.28 W
Morris Reservoir ⊜[1]	228	34.12 N	117.52 W
Morris Run	210	41.40 N	77.01 W
Morristown, Az., U.S.	200	33.51 N	112.37 W
Morristown, Il., U.S.	216	42.10 N	89.03 W
Morristown, In., U.S.	218	39.40 N	85.41 W
Morristown, Mn., U.S.	190	44.14 N	93.26 W
Morristown, N.J., U.S.	210	40.47 N	74.28 W
Morristown, N.Y., U.S.	212	44.35 N	75.38 W
Morristown, Oh., U.S.	214	40.04 N	81.05 W
Morristown, S.D., U.S.	198	45.56 N	101.43 W
Morristown, Tn., U.S.	192	36.12 N	83.17 W
Morristown Airport ⊠	276	40.48 N	74.25 W
Morristown National Historical Park ♦	210	40.46 N	74.32 W
Morrisville, N.Y., U.S.	210	42.53 N	75.38 W
Morrisville, Pa., U.S.	208	40.12 N	74.47 W
Morrisville, Vt., U.S.	188	44.33 N	72.35 W
Morro	246	2.39 S	80.19 W
Morro, Castillo del (Morro Castle) ⊥	286b	23.09 N	82.21 W
Morro, Punta ›	252	27.07 S	70.57 W
Morro, Punta del ›	234	19.51 N	96.27 W
Morro Agudo	287a	22.45 S	43.29 W
Morro Bay	226	35.21 N	120.50 W
Morro Bay ⊂	226	35.20 N	120.51 W
Morro Bay State Park ♦	226	35.20 N	120.52 W
Morro Creek ≃	226	35.23 N	120.52 W
Morro de Mazatán	234	16.07 N	95.27 W
Morro do Chapéu	250	11.33 S	41.09 W
Morro do Pilar	255	19.12 S	43.23 W
Morro d'Oro	66	42.39 N	13.54 E
Morrone del Sannio	66	41.43 N	14.47 E
Morropón	248	5.15 S	80.00 W
Morros	250	2.52 S	44.03 W
Morrosquillo, Golfo de ⊂	246	9.35 N	75.40 W
Morrow, La., U.S.	194	30.49 N	92.04 W
Morrow, Oh., U.S.	218	39.21 N	84.07 W
Morrow □[6]	214	40.33 N	82.50 W
Morrow Island I	282	38.07 N	122.05 W
Morrow Mountain State Park ♦	192	35.23 N	80.05 W
Morrow Point Reservoir ⊜[1]	200	38.25 N	107.30 W
Mörrum	26	56.11 N	14.45 E
Morrumbala	154	17.22 S	35.36 E
Morrumbene	156	23.39 S	35.20 E
Mörrumsån ≃	26	56.09 N	14.44 E
Mors I	26	56.50 N	8.45 E
Morsains	50	48.48 N	3.32 E
Morsang-sur-Orge	261	48.40 N	2.21 E
Moršansk	80	53.26 N	41.49 E
Morsbach	56	50.52 N	7.43 E
Mörsch	56	48.58 N	8.17 E
Morschwiller-le-Bas	58	47.45 N	7.16 E
Morščichino	265b	55.56 N	37.20 E
Morse, Sk., Can.	184	50.25 N	107.03 W
Morse, La., U.S.	194	30.07 N	92.29 W
Morse, Tx., U.S.	196	36.04 N	101.29 W
Morse Mill	219	38.17 N	90.40 W
Mörsenbroich ◆[8]	263	51.15 N	6.48 E
Morse Reservoir ⊜[1]	218	40.06 N	86.02 W
Morses Pond ⊜	283	42.18 N	71.19 W
Morsi	120	21.21 N	78.00 E
Morskaja Masel'ga	24	63.06 N	34.54 E
Morskoj Bir'učok, ostrov I	84	44.42 N	47.02 E
Morson	184	49.03 N	94.18 W
Morsott	36	35.40 N	8.01 E
Morstein	285	40.01 N	75.35 W
Mort	272a	28.43 N	77.25 E
Morta	272a	28.44 N	77.27 E
Mortagne	32	48.31 N	0.33 E
Mortagne ≃	58	48.33 N	6.27 E
Mortagne-au-Perche	50	48.31 N	0.33 E
Mortagne-sur-Sèvre	32	47.00 N	0.57 W
Mortain	32	48.39 N	0.56 W
Mortana	162	33.02 S	134.07 E
Mortara	62	45.15 N	8.44 E
Morteau	58	47.04 N	6.37 E
Mortefontaine	50	49.07 N	2.36 E
Mortegliano	64	45.57 N	13.10 E
Morte Point ›	42	51.11 N	4.13 W
Morteratsch, Piz ∧	58	46.22 N	9.51 E
Morteros	252	30.42 S	62.00 W
Mortes, Rio das ≃, Bra.	255	11.45 S	50.44 W
Mortes, Rio das ≃, Bra.	256	21.18 S	43.58 W
Mortesoro	140	10.12 N	34.09 E
Mort-Homme, Forêt du ◆[3]	56	49.15 N	5.15 E
Mortimer	42	51.22 N	1.04 W
Mortlach	184	50.28 N	106.03 W
Mortlake, Austl.	166	38.05 S	142.48 E
Mortlake, Austl.	274a	33.51 S	151.07 E
Mortlake ◆[8]	260	51.28 N	0.16 W
Mortlock ≃	168a	31.42 S	116.55 E
Mortlock North ≃	168a	31.38 S	116.42 E
Mortola Inferiore	62	43.47 N	7.33 E
Morton, Il., U.S.	190	40.36 N	89.27 W
Morton, Mn., U.S.	198	44.33 N	94.59 W

Symbol	English	Deutsch	Español	Français	Português
≃	River	Fluß	Río	Rivière	Rio
≍	Canal	Kanal	Canal	Canal	Canal
⌊	Waterfall, Rapids	Wasserfall, Stromschnellen	Cascada, Rápidos	Chute d'eau, Rapides	Cascata, Rápidos
‖	Strait	Meeresstraße	Estrecho	Détroit	Estreito
⊂	Bay, Gulf	Bucht, Golf	Bahía, Golfo	Baie, Golfe	Baía, Golfo
⊜	Lake, Lakes	See, Seen	Lago, Lagos	Lac, Lacs	Lago, Lagos
⊞	Swamp	Sumpf	Pantano	Marais	Pântano
✱	Ice Features, Glacier	Eis- und Gletscherformen	Accidentes Glaciales	Formes glaciaires	Acidentes glaciares
⊤	Other Hydrographic Features	Andere Hydrographische Objekte	Otros Elementos Hidrográficos	Autres données hydrographiques	Outros acidentes hidrográficos
✣	Submarine Features	Untermeerische Objekte	Accidentes Submarinos	Formes de relief sous-marin	Acidentes submarinos
□	Political Unit	Politische Einheit	Unidad Política	Entité politique	Unidade política
⊛	Cultural Institution	Kulturelle Institution	Institución Cultural	Institution culturelle	Instituição cultural
⊥	Historical Site	Historische Stätte	Sitio Histórico	Site historique	Sitio histórico
♦	Recreational Site	Erholungs- und Ferienort	Sitio de Recreo	Centre de loisirs	Area de Lazer
⊠	Airport	Flughafen	Aeropuerto	Aéroport	Aeroporto
■	Military Installation	Militäranlage	Instalación Militar	Installation militaire	Instalação militar
◆	Miscellaneous	Verschiedenes	Misceláneo	Divers	Diversos

ENGLISH: Name | Page | Lat. °′ | Long. °′
DEUTSCH: Name | Seite | Breite °′ | Länge °′ E = Ost

Morton, Ms., U.S. 194 32.21 N 89.39 W
Morton, N.Y., U.S. 210 43.20 N 78.00 W
Morton, Pa., U.S. 285 39.55 N 75.20 W
Morton, Tx., U.S. 196 33.43 N 102.45 W
Morton, Wa., U.S. 224 46.33 N 122.16 W
Morton, Mount ∧ [2] 274b 37.56 S 145.20 E
Morton Arboretum ✈ [4] 278 41.49 N 88.04 W
Morton Craig Range ⩕ 162 28.12 S 124.41 E
Morton Grove 216 42.02 N 87.46 W
Morton National Park ♦ 170 35.00 S 150.10 E
Mortons Gap 194 37.14 N 87.28 W
Mortorio, Isola I 71 41.05 N 9.36 E
Mortornès del Vallès 266d 41.33 N 2.16 E
Mortrée 50 48.38 N 0.05 E
Mörtschach 64 46.55 N 12.55 E
Mortsel 50 51.10 N 4.28 E
M'ortvyj Donec ≃ 83 47.15 N 39.14 E
Morty 80 55.49 N 51.44 E
Morua 175f 16.54 S 168.32 E
Morumbi ✈ [8] 287b 23.36 S 46.42 E
Morumbi, Estádio do ♦ 287b 23.37 S 46.43 W
Morungaba 256 22.52 S 46.48 W
Morungole ∧ 154 3.49 N 34.02 E
Moruya 166 35.55 S 150.05 E
Morvan ⩕ 32 47.05 N 4.00 E
Morven, Austl. 166 26.25 S 147.07 E
Morven, N.Z. 172 44.50 S 171.07 E
Morven, Ga., U.S. 192 30.56 N 83.29 W
Morven, N.C., U.S. 192 34.51 N 80.00 W
Morven ∧, Scot., U.K. 46 58.14 N 3.42 W
Morven ∧, Scot., U.K. 46 57.07 N 3.02 W
Morwell 169 38.14 S 146.24 E
Morwell ≃ 169 38.10 S 146.23 E
Morwenstow 42 50.54 N 4.33 W
Moryń 30 52.49 N 14.13 E
Morženga 76 59.37 N 40.12 E
Morzhovoi 180 54.55 N 163.18 W
Morzine 58 46.11 N 6.43 E
Moržovec, ostrov I 24 66.44 N 42.35 E
Moša ≃, S.S.S.R. 24 62.25 N 39.46 E
M'oša ≃, S.S.S.R. 80 55.25 N 49.22 E
Mosal'sk 76 54.29 N 34.59 E
Mosambik → Mozambique □ [1] 138 18.15 S 35.00 E
Mošanicy 82 54.56 N 38.23 E
Mosås 40 59.12 N 15.08 E
Mosbach 56 49.21 N 9.08 E
Mosborough 44 53.19 N 1.22 W
Mosby 26 58.14 N 7.54 E
Mosby Woods 284c 38.52 N 77.18 W
Moscavide 266c 38.47 N 9.06 W
Mosciano Sant'Angelo 66 42.45 N 13.53 E
Moščnyj, ostrov I 76 60.01 N 27.50 E
Moscos Islands II 110 14.00 N 97.45 E
Moscou → Moskva 82 55.45 N 37.35 E
Moscow → Moskva, S.S.S.R. 82 55.45 N 37.35 E
Moscow, Id., U.S. 202 46.43 N 116.59 W
Moscow, In., U.S. 218 39.29 N 85.34 W
Moscow, Oh., U.S. 218 38.51 N 84.13 W
Moscow, Pa., U.S. 210 41.20 N 75.31 W
Moscow, Tx., U.S. 222 30.55 N 94.50 W
Moscow → Moskva ≃ 76 55.05 N 38.50 E
Moscow Air Terminal ✈ 265b 55.48 N 37.32 E
Moscow Circus ♦ 265b 55.43 N 37.33 E
Moscow Mills 219 38.56 N 90.55 W
Moscow Station ✈ [5] 265a 59.56 N 30.22 E
Moscow Zoo ♦ 265b 55.46 N 37.34 E
Moscú → Moskva 82 55.45 N 37.35 E
Moscufo 66 42.25 N 14.03 E
Mosel 54 50.47 N 12.28 E
Mosel (Moselle) ≃ 32 50.22 N 7.36 E
Moselebe ≃ 156 25.03 S 23.13 E
Moselle, Ms., U.S. 194 31.30 N 89.16 W
Moselle, Mo., U.S. 219 38.23 N 90.54 W
Moselle □ [5] 56 49.00 N 6.30 E
Moselle (Mosel) ≃ 32 50.22 N 7.36 E
Moselotte ≃ 58 48.01 N 6.38 E
Mosenskoje 76 58.31 N 34.35 E
Mosermandl ∧ 64 47.12 N 13.24 E
Mosers River 186 44.59 N 62.15 W
Moses Lake 202 47.07 N 119.16 W
Moses Lake ⊜ [1] 202 47.10 N 119.20 W
Moses Point 180 64.42 N 162.03 W
Moses Power Plant ✈ [5] 284a 43.09 N 79.02 W
Mosetse 156 20.37 S 26.32 E
Mosgiel 172 45.53 S 170.21 E
Moshannon 214 41.02 N 78.00 W
Moshannon Creek ≃ 214 41.04 N 78.06 W
Moshanpu 100 29.34 N 112.41 E
Moshaweng ≃ 158 26.35 S 22.50 E
Mosheim, Tn., U.S. 192 36.11 N 82.57 W
Mosheim, Tx., U.S. 222 31.38 N 97.36 W
Moshi 154 3.21 S 37.20 E
Moshi ≃ 150 9.18 N 4.38 E
Moshiyu 104 41.15 N 124.05 E
Mosier 224 45.41 N 121.23 W
Mosier Hill ∧ [2] 214 40.06 N 80.24 W
Mosina 30 52.16 N 16.51 E
Mosinee 190 44.47 N 89.42 W
Mosjøen 24 65.50 N 13.10 E
Moskal'onki 86 54.59 N 71.54 E
Moskal'vo 89 53.35 N 142.30 E
Moskau → Moskva 82 55.45 N 37.35 E
Moskenesøya I 24 67.59 N 13.00 E
Moskháton 267c 37.57 N 23.41 E
Moškino 80 57.45 N 45.20 E
Moskito-Golf → Mosquitos, Golfo de los ⊂ 236 9.00 N 81.15 W
Moškovo 86 55.18 N 83.37 E
Moskovskaja Slav'anka 265a 59.45 N 30.30 E
Moskovskaja vozvyšennost' ⩕ [1] 76 56.15 N 37.30 E
Moskovskij park Pobedy ♦ 265a 59.52 N 30.20 E
Moskva (Moscow), S.S.S.R. 82 55.45 N 37.35 E
Moskva (Moscow), S.S.S.R. 265b 55.45 N 37.35 E
Moskva □ [4] 82 55.45 N 37.30 E
Moskva ≃ 76 55.05 N 38.50 E
Moskva, Gorod □ [7] 265b 55.45 N 37.35 E
Moskva, pik ∧ 85 38.57 N 71.49 E
Moskvy, kanal imeni ≅ 82 56.43 N 37.08 E
Mosman 170 33.49 S 151.14 E
Mosman Park 168a 32.01 S 115.46 E
Mošny 78 49.32 N 31.44 E
Moso (Moos) 64 46.41 N 12.23 E
Moso in Passiria (Moos) 64 46.50 N 11.10 E
Mošok 80 55.48 N 41.17 E
Mosolovo 80 54.17 N 40.32 E
Mosomane 156 24.04 S 26.15 E
Mosoni-Duna ≃ 61 47.54 N 17.17 E
Mosonmagyaróvár 30 47.51 N 17.17 E
Mosonszolnok 61 47.51 N 17.11 E
Mosopa 156 24.50 S 25.31 E
Mospino 83 47.53 N 38.03 E
Mosqueiro 250 1.10 S 48.28 W
Mosquera 246 2.30 N 78.29 W
Mosquero 196 35.46 N 103.57 W
Mosquic, Lac ⊜ 206 46.39 N 74.28 W
Mosquito, Punta > 246 9.07 N 77.53 W
Mosquito, Riacho ≃ 252 22.02 S 57.57 W
Mosquito Brook ≃ 283 42.40 N 71.02 W
Mosquito Creek ≃, Ia., U.S. 198 41.11 N 95.50 W
Mosquito Creek ≃, Oh., U.S. 214 41.10 N 80.45 W
Mosquito Creek ≃, Pa., U.S. 214 41.07 N 78.07 W
Mosquito Creek Lake ⊜ [1] 214 41.22 N 80.45 W
Mosquito Creek State Park ♦ 214 41.22 N 80.45 W
Mosquito Indian Reserve ✈ [4] 184 52.30 N 108.15 W
Mosquito Lagoon ⊂ 220 28.45 N 80.45 W
Mosquitos, Costa de □ [9] 236 13.00 N 83.45 W
Mosquitos, Golfo de los ⊂ 236 9.00 N 81.15 W
Moss 26 59.26 N 10.42 E
Mossaka 152 1.13 S 16.48 E
Mossâmedes 255 16.07 S 50.11 W
Mossbank, Sk., Can. 184 49.55 N 105.59 W
Moss Bank, Eng., U.K. 262 53.29 N 2.44 W
Mossbank, Scot., U.K. 46a 60.27 N 1.12 W
Moss Bank Park ♦ 262 53.36 N 2.28 W
Moss Beach 282 37.32 N 122.31 W
Mossburn 172 45.40 S 168.15 E
Mosselbaai (Mossel Bay) 158 34.11 S 22.08 E
Mosselbaai ⊂ 158 34.06 S 22.20 E
Mossendjo 152 2.57 S 12.44 E
Mosses, Col des)(58 46.24 N 7.06 E
Mossgiel 166 33.15 S 144.34 E
Moss Hill 222 30.15 N 94.45 W
Mossig ≃ 58 48.33 N 7.30 E
Mössingen 58 48.24 N 9.03 E
Moss Landing 226 36.48 N 121.47 W
Mossleigh 182 50.43 N 113.20 W
Mossley 262 53.32 N 2.02 W
Mossley Hill ✈ [8] 262 53.23 N 2.55 W
Mossman 164 16.28 S 145.22 E
Mossmans Brook ≃ 276 41.03 N 74.27 W
Moss Moor ✈ [3] 262 53.37 N 2.00 W
Moss Mountain ∧ 194 34.50 N 92.40 W
Mossø ⊜ 41 56.02 N 9.48 E
Mosson ≃ 62 43.33 N 3.54 E
Mossoró 250 5.11 S 37.20 W
Mosso Santa Maria 62 45.38 N 8.08 E
Moss Point 194 30.24 N 88.32 W
Moss Point > 279a 41.37 N 81.32 W
Moss Side 262 53.46 N 2.57 W
Mossuril 154 14.58 S 40.42 E
Moss Vale 170 34.33 S 150.22 E
Mossy ≃, Mb., Can. 184 51.39 N 99.55 W
Mossy ≃, Sk., Can. 184 54.05 N 103.00 W
Mossyrock 224 46.31 N 122.29 W
Mossyrock Dam ✈ [6] 224 46.32 N 122.25 W
Most 54 50.32 N 13.39 E
Mosta 80 56.32 N 42.10 E
Mostar 36 43.20 N 17.49 E
Mostardas 252 31.06 S 50.57 W
Møsting, Kap > 176 64.00 N 41.00 W
Mostiska 78 49.48 N 23.09 E
Mostiștea ≃ 38 44.15 N 27.10 E
Mostizzolo 64 46.24 N 11.01 E
Mostki 83 49.19 N 38.30 E
Most na Soči 64 46.09 N 13.44 E
Mostok 76 53.59 N 30.28 E
Móstoles 266a 40.19 N 3.51 W
Mostoos Hills ⩕ [2] 184 55.00 N 109.15 W
Mostovaja 76 56.13 N 33.08 E
Mostovka 86 58.10 N 65.31 E
Mostovoje 78 47.24 N 30.59 E
Mostovskoj 84 44.25 N 40.48 E
Mostovskoje 86 55.46 N 66.22 E
Mostrim (Edgeworthstown) 48 53.42 N 7.36 W
Mostva ≃ 78 52.00 N 27.33 E
Mosty 76 53.25 N 24.32 E
Mostyn, Malay. 112 4.40 N 118.11 E
Mostyn, Wales, U.K. 44 53.19 N 3.16 W
Mosul → Al-Mawșil 128 36.20 N 43.08 E
Møsvatnet ⊜ 26 59.52 N 8.05 E
Mota 144 11.02 N 37.52 E
Mota I 175f 13.49 S 167.42 E
Motaba ≃ 152 2.03 N 18.03 E
Mota del Cuervo 34 39.30 N 2.52 W
Mota del Marqués 34 41.38 N 5.10 W
Motagua ≃ 236 15.44 N 88.14 W
Motala 26 58.33 N 15.03 E
Motala ström ≃ 40 58.38 N 16.10 E
Mota Lava I 175f 13.40 S 167.40 E
Motane I 174x 9.59 S 138.49 W
Motatán 246 9.24 N 70.36 W
Motaze 156 24.48 S 32.52 E
Motegi 94 36.32 N 140.11 E
Mote Park ♦ 260 51.17 N 0.34 E
Moteve, Cap > 174x 9.58 S 139.02 W
Moth 124 25.43 N 78.57 E
Mother Brook ≅ 283 42.15 N 71.10 W
Motherwell 46 55.48 N 4.00 W
Motihāri 124 26.39 N 84.55 E
Motilla del Palancar 34 39.34 N 1.53 W
Motiong 116 11.47 N 125.00 E
Motiti Island I 172 37.38 S 176.26 E
Motjärnshyttan 40 59.56 N 13.58 E
Motloutse 156 21.28 S 27.24 E
Motloutse ≃ 156 22.15 S 29.00 E
Moto-ara ≃ 94 35.53 N 139.50 E
Motobu 174m 26.39 N 127.54 E
Motol' 76 52.19 N 25.36 E
Motola, Monte ∧ 68 40.22 N 15.26 E
Motopu 174x 9.55 S 139.03 W
Motor Island I 284a 42.58 N 78.56 W
Motorki 80 56.53 N 51.29 E
Motorovo 86 56.31 N 71.10 E
Motosu 94 35.29 N 136.40 E
Motosu-ko ⊜ 94 35.28 N 138.35 E
Motou 106 32.18 N 120.34 E
Motovilovo 80 55.36 N 43.51 E
Motovun 64 45.20 N 13.50 E
Motoyama 96 33.45 N 133.35 E
Moto-yama ∧ [2] 174f 24.48 N 141.20 E
Motozintla de Mendoza 232 15.22 N 92.14 W
Motril 34 36.45 N 3.31 W
Motrone 64 43.54 N 10.12 E
Motru 38 44.50 N 23.00 E
Mott 198 46.22 N 102.19 W
Motta 64 45.36 N 11.29 E
Motta Camastra 70 37.54 N 15.10 E
Motta d'Affermo 70 37.59 N 14.18 E
Motta di Livenza 64 45.47 N 12.36 E
Mottafollone 68 39.39 N 16.04 E
Motta Montecorvino 68 41.30 N 15.07 E
Motta San Giovanni 70 38.00 N 15.41 E
Motta Sant'Anastasia 70 37.31 N 14.58 E
Motta Visconti 62 45.17 N 8.59 E
Möttingen 56 48.48 N 10.35 E
Mottingham ✈ [8] 260 51.26 N 0.03 E
Mottisfont 42 51.02 N 1.32 W
Mottola 68 40.38 N 17.03 E
Mottram in Longdendale 262 53.27 N 2.01 W
Motts Creek ≃ 276 40.38 N 73.45 W
Mottville, Mi., U.S. 216 41.48 N 85.45 W
Mottville, N.Y., U.S. 210 42.59 N 76.27 W
Motu ≃ 172 37.51 S 177.35 E
Motueka 172 41.07 S 173.00 E
Motueka ≃ 172 41.05 S 173.01 E
Motul [de Felipe Carrillo Puerto] 232 21.06 N 89.17 W
Motu One I [1] 14 15.48 S 154.33 W
Motupe 248 6.09 S 79.44 W
Motupena Point > 175e 6.32 S 155.09 E
Motutapu I 174k 21.14 S 159.43 W
Motygino 86 58.11 N 94.40 E
Motyklejka 74 59.26 N 148.38 E
Motyžin 78 50.23 N 29.55 E
Motyzlej 80 54.54 N 42.54 E
Mou 175f 21.05 S 165.26 E
Mouanko 152 3.39 N 9.49 E
Mouans-Sartoux 62 43.37 N 6.58 E
Mouaskar 148 35.45 N 0.01 E
Mouaskar □ [5] 148 35.10 N 0.00
Mouchard 58 46.58 N 5.48 E
Mouchoir Bank ✈ [2] 238 20.57 N 70.42 W
Mouchoir Passage)(238 21.10 N 71.00 W
Moúdhros 38 39.52 N 25.16 E
Mouding 102 25.24 N 101.35 E
Moudjéria 150 17.53 N 12.20 W
Moudon 58 46.40 N 6.48 E
Moudongouma ≃ 152 1.36 N 17.24 E
Mouila 152 1.52 S 11.01 E
Mouit 150 16.35 N 13.05 W
Mouka 152 7.16 N 21.52 E
Moukden → Shenyang 104 41.48 N 123.27 E
Moulamein 166 35.05 S 144.02 E
Moulay-bou-Selham 34 34.53 N 6.15 W
Moulay-Idriss 148 34.02 N 5.27 W
Mouldsworth 262 53.14 N 2.44 W
Moule à Chique, Cap > 241f 13.43 N 60.57 W
Moulhoulé 144 12.36 N 43.12 E
Moulin, Île du I 275a 45.41 N 73.32 W
Moulin-des-Ponts 58 46.20 N 5.19 E
Moulineaux 50 49.21 N 0.58 E
Moulinet 62 43.57 N 7.25 E
Moulins 32 46.34 N 3.20 E
Moulins-la-Marche 50 48.39 N 0.29 E
Moulmein → Mawlamyine 110 16.30 N 97.38 E
Moulmeingyun 110 16.23 N 95.16 E
Moulouya, Oued ≃ 148 35.05 N 2.25 W
Moulton, Eng., U.K. 262 53.13 N 2.31 W
Moulton, Al., U.S. 194 34.28 N 87.17 W
Moulton, Ia., U.S. 190 40.41 N 92.40 W
Moulton, Tx., U.S. 222 29.34 N 97.09 W
Moultrie 192 31.10 N 83.47 W
Moultrie □ [6] 219 39.36 N 88.37 W
Moultrie, Lake ⊜ [1] 192 33.20 N 80.05 W
Mouly 175f 20.42 S 166.25 E
Mound 222 31.21 N 97.38 W
Mound Bayou 194 33.52 N 90.43 W
Mound City, Il., U.S. 194 37.05 N 89.09 W
Mound City, Ks., U.S. 198 38.08 N 94.48 W
Mound City, Mo., U.S. 194 40.07 N 95.13 W
Mound City, S.D., U.S. 198 45.43 N 100.04 W
Mound City Group National Monument ♦ 218 39.23 N 83.00 W
Mound Lake ⊜ 219 40.05 N 90.17 W
Moundou 146 8.34 N 16.05 E
Moundridge 198 38.12 N 97.31 W
Mounds, Il., U.S. 194 37.06 N 89.11 W
Mounds, Ok., U.S. 196 35.52 N 96.03 W
Mounds State Park ♦ 218 40.07 N 85.37 W
Mounds State Recreation Area ♦ 218 39.30 N 84.59 W
Moundsville 188 39.55 N 80.44 W
Moundville 194 32.59 N 87.37 W
Moungali ✈ [8] 273b 4.15 S 15.17 E
Moung Roessei 110 12.46 N 103.27 E
Mounianzé ≃ 152 0.32 N 12.52 E
Mounier, Mont ∧ 62 44.09 N 6.58 E
Mounlapamôk 110 14.20 N 105.52 E
Mount Aetna 208 40.25 N 76.18 W
Mountain 190 45.11 N 88.28 W
Mountain □ [4] 116 17.20 N 121.10 E
Mountain ≃ 180 65.41 N 128.50 W
Mountainair 200 34.31 N 106.14 W
Mountainaire 200 35.05 N 111.39 W
Mountain Ash 42 51.42 N 3.24 W
Mountain Brook 194 33.30 N 86.45 W
Mountain Chute Dam ✈ [6] 212 45.11 N 76.54 W
Mountain City, Ga., U.S. 192 34.55 N 83.23 W
Mountain City, Nv., U.S. 204 41.50 N 115.57 W
Mountain City, Tn., U.S. 192 36.28 N 81.48 W
Mountain Creek 194 32.43 N 86.29 W
Mountain Creek ≃, Pa., U.S. 208 40.09 N 77.11 W
Mountain Creek ≃, Tx., U.S. 222 32.42 N 96.58 W
Mountain Creek Lake ⊜ [1] 222 32.43 N 96.58 W
Mountain Dale 210 41.41 N 74.31 W
Mountain Grove 194 37.07 N 92.15 W
Mountain Home, Ar., U.S. 194 36.20 N 92.23 W
Mountain Home, Id., U.S. 202 43.07 N 115.41 W
Mountainhome, Pa., U.S. 210 41.11 N 75.17 W
Mountain Home Air Force Base ■ 202 43.03 N 115.52 W
Mountain Iron 190 47.31 N 92.37 W
Mountain Lake, Fl., U.S. 220 27.57 N 81.36 W
Mountain Lake, Mn., U.S. 198 43.56 N 94.55 W
Mountain Lake ⊜, On., Can. 212 44.42 N 81.03 W
Mountain Lake ⊜, On., Can. 212 44.59 N 78.43 W
Mountain Lake ⊜, N.J., U.S. 276 40.53 N 74.27 W
Mountain Lakes 210 40.53 N 74.26 W
Mountain Lodge 210 41.23 N 74.09 W
Mountain Nile (Bahr al-Jabal) ≃ 136 9.30 N 30.30 E
Mountain Park 182 52.55 N 117.14 W
Mountain Pine 194 34.34 N 93.10 W
Mountain Point 182 55.18 N 131.32 W
Mountain Ranch 226 38.14 N 120.33 W
Mountainside 208 40.40 N 74.21 W
Mountain Spring Lakes 276 41.02 N 74.23 W
Mountain Valley Lake ⊜ 279b 40.18 N 79.35 W
Mountain View, Ar., U.S. 194 35.52 N 92.07 W
Mountain View, Ca., U.S. 226 37.23 N 122.04 W
Mountain View, Mo., U.S. 194 36.59 N 91.42 W
Mountain View, Ok., U.S. 196 35.05 N 98.44 W
Mountain View, Wy., U.S. 200 41.16 N 110.20 W
Mountain View, Wy., U.S. 200 42.51 N 106.23 W
Mountain View Acres 228 34.31 N 117.24 W
Mountain Village 180 62.05 N 163.44 W
Mountain Zebra National Park ♦ 158 32.16 S 25.29 E
Mount Airy, Md., U.S. 208 39.22 N 77.09 W
Mount Airy, N.C., U.S. 192 36.29 N 80.36 W
Mount Airy ✈ [8] 285 40.04 N 75.12 W
Mount Albert 212 44.08 N 79.19 W
Mount Alford 171a 28.04 S 152.36 E
Mount Alida 158 29.09 S 30.18 E
Mount Alverno 285 39.53 N 75.25 W
Mount Angel 224 45.04 N 122.47 W
Mount Ann Park ♦ 283 42.37 N 70.44 W
Mount Arlington 210 40.55 N 74.38 W
Mount Assiniboine Provincial Park ♦ 182 50.54 N 115.40 W
Mount Auburn 219 39.46 N 89.16 W
Mount Augustus 162 24.19 S 116.54 E
Mount Ayliff 158 30.54 S 29.20 E
Mount Ayr, In., U.S. 216 40.57 N 87.18 W
Mount Ayr, Ia., U.S. 198 40.42 N 94.14 W
Mount Baldy 280 34.14 N 117.40 W
Mount Barker, Austl. 162 34.38 S 117.40 E
Mount Barker, Austl. 168b 35.04 S 138.52 E
Mount Bellew Bridge 48 53.28 N 8.29 W
Mount Berry 194 34.17 N 85.11 W
Mount Bethel 210 40.54 N 75.07 W
Mount Blanchard 216 40.53 N 83.33 W
Mount Bold Reservoir ⊜ [1] 168b 35.07 S 138.42 E
Mount Brydges 214 42.54 N 81.29 W
Mount Buffalo National Park ♦ 166 36.45 S 146.45 E
Mount Buller 169 37.10 S 146.27 E
Mount Calm 222 31.45 N 96.53 W
Mount Carleton Provincial Park ♦ 186 47.23 N 66.50 W
Mount Carmel, Nf., Can. 186 47.09 N 53.29 W
Mount Carmel, Il., U.S. 194 38.24 N 87.45 W
Mount Carmel, Ky., U.S. 218 38.29 N 83.38 W
Mount Carmel, Oh., U.S. 218 39.06 N 84.18 W
Mount Carmel, Pa., U.S. 208 40.47 N 76.24 W
Mount Carmel Heights 218 39.07 N 84.18 W
Mount Carroll 190 42.05 N 89.58 W
Mount Cavenagh 162 25.58 S 133.15 E
Mount Charles 275b 43.41 N 79.40 W
Mount Clare 188 39.13 N 80.21 W
Mount Clemens 214 42.35 N 82.52 W
Mount Colah 274a 33.41 S 151.07 E
Mount Compass 168b 35.22 S 138.37 E
Mount Cook 172 43.44 S 170.06 E
Mount Cook National Park ♦ 172 43.35 S 170.15 E
Mount Coot-tha Park ♦ 171a 27.28 S 152.56 E
Mount Cory 216 40.56 N 83.50 W
Mount Crawford 168b 34.40 S 138.57 E
Mount Crosby 171a 27.32 S 152.48 E
Mount Currie Indian Reserve ✈ [4] 182 50.19 N 122.42 W
Mount Dandenong 274b 37.50 S 145.22 E
Mount Dennis ✈ [8] 275b 43.42 N 79.30 W
Mount Desert Island I 188 44.20 N 68.20 W
Mount Diablo Creek ≃ 282 38.02 N 122.02 W
Mount Diablo State Park ♦ 226 37.51 N 121.55 W
Mount Dora 220 28.48 N 81.38 W
Mount Doreen 162 22.03 S 131.18 E
Mount Druitt 274a 33.46 S 150.49 E
Mount Eaton 214 40.42 N 81.42 W
Mount Eba 166 30.12 S 135.40 E
Mount Eden 226 37.38 N 122.06 W
Mount Edgecumbe 180 57.03 N 135.21 W
Mount Edwards 171a 28.01 S 152.31 E
Mount Elgon National Park ♦ 154 1.07 N 34.44 E
Mount Elizabeth 164 16.15 S 126.12 E
Mount Emu Creek ≃ 169 38.18 S 142.55 E
Mount Enterprise 222 31.55 N 94.41 W
Mount Ephraim 285 39.52 N 75.05 W
Mount Evelyn 274b 37.47 S 145.23 E
Mount Fern 276 40.52 N 74.34 W
Mount Field National Park ♦ 166 42.40 S 146.35 E
Mount Fletcher 158 30.40 S 28.30 E
Mount Forest 212 43.59 N 80.44 W
Mount Freedom 210 40.49 N 74.34 W
Mount Frere 158 31.00 S 28.58 E
Mount Gambier 166 37.50 S 140.46 E
Mount Garnet 166 17.41 S 145.07 E
Mount Gay 188 37.51 N 82.00 W
Mount Gilead, N.C., U.S. 192 35.12 N 80.00 W
Mount Gilead, Oh., U.S. 214 40.32 N 82.49 W
Mount Glorious National Park ♦ 171a 27.19 S 152.47 E
Mount Gravatt 171a 27.33 S 153.06 E
Mount Greenwood ✈ [8] 278 41.42 N 87.43 W
Mount Gunson 162 31.27 S 137.11 E
Mount Hagen 164 5.50 S 144.15 E
Mount Hawke 42 50.17 N 5.12 W
Mount Hawthorn 168a 31.55 S 115.50 E
Mount Healthy 218 39.14 N 84.32 W
Mount Hebron 284b 39.18 N 76.50 W
Mount Helena 168a 31.53 S 116.13 E
Mount Hermon, Ca., U.S. 226 37.03 N 122.04 W
Mount Hermon, Ma., U.S. 207 42.40 N 72.29 W
Mount Holly, N.J., U.S. 208 39.59 N 74.47 W
Mount Holly, N.C., U.S. 192 35.17 N 81.00 W
Mount Holly Springs 208 40.07 N 77.11 W
Mount Hope, Austl. 166 34.07 S 135.23 E
Mount Hope, On., Can. 212 43.09 N 79.55 W
Mount Hope, Ks., U.S. 198 37.52 N 97.39 W
Mount Hope, N.J., U.S. 276 40.56 N 74.33 W
Mount Hope, Oh., U.S. 214 40.38 N 81.47 W
Mount Hope, W.V., U.S. 188 37.53 N 81.09 W
Mount Hope Lake ⊜ 276 40.56 N 74.32 W
Mount Horeb 190 43.00 N 89.44 W
Mount Houston 222 29.54 N 95.18 W
Mount Howitt 166 26.31 S 142.16 E
Mount Hunter Rivulet ≃ 274a 34.02 S 150.42 E
Mount Ida 194 34.33 N 93.38 W
Mount Isa 166 20.44 S 139.30 E
Mount Jackson, Pa., U.S. 214 40.58 N 80.26 W
Mount Jackson, Va., U.S. 188 38.44 N 78.38 W
Mount Jewett 214 41.43 N 78.38 W
Mount Juliet 194 36.12 N 86.31 W
Mount Kaputar National Park ♦ 166 30.16 S 150.10 E
Mount Kenya National Park ♦ 154 0.09 S 37.19 E
Mount Kisco 210 41.12 N 73.43 W
Mount Kokeby 168a 32.13 S 116.58 E
Mountlake Terrace 224 47.47 N 122.18 W
Mount Laurel 285 39.56 N 74.54 W
Mount Lebanon 214 40.21 N 80.02 W
Mount Liberty 214 40.21 N 82.38 W
Mount Lofty Ranges ⩕ 168b 34.45 S 139.00 E
Mount Magnet 162 28.04 S 117.49 E
Mount Manara 166 32.29 S 143.56 E
Mount Margaret, Austl. 162 28.47 S 122.11 E
Mount Margaret, Austl. 166 26.54 S 143.21 E
Mount Marion 210 42.02 N 73.59 W
Mount Martha 169 38.17 S 145.01 E
Mount Maunganui 172 37.37 S 176.11 E
Mount McKinley National Park → Denali National Park ♦ 180 63.15 N 150.30 W
Mount Mee 171a 27.04 S 152.46 E
Mountmellick 48 53.07 N 7.20 W
Mount Misery Point > 276 40.58 N 73.05 W
Mount Mistake National Park ♦ 171a 27.53 S 152.20 E
Mount Molloy 164 16.41 S 145.20 E
Mount Monger 162 30.59 S 121.53 E
Mount Moorosi 158 30.16 S 27.53 E
Mount Morgan 166 23.39 S 150.23 E
Mount Morris, Il., U.S. 190 42.03 N 89.25 W
Mount Morris, Mi., U.S. 190 43.07 N 83.41 W
Mount Morris, N.Y., U.S. 210 42.43 N 77.52 W
Mount Morris Dam ✈ [6] 210 42.44 N 77.53 W
Mount Mulligan 166 16.51 S 144.52 E
Mount Nebo 279b 40.33 N 80.06 W
Mountnessing 260 51.39 N 0.21 E
Mount Olive, Il., U.S. 219 39.04 N 89.43 W
Mount Olive, Ms., U.S. 194 31.45 N 89.39 W
Mount Olive, N.C., U.S. 192 35.11 N 78.04 W
Mount Oliver 279b 40.28 N 79.59 W
Mount Olivet 218 38.31 N 84.02 W
Mount Orab 218 39.01 N 83.55 W
Mount Penn 208 40.20 N 75.54 W
Mount Perry 166 25.11 S 151.39 E
Mount Pleasant, Austl. 168b 34.47 S 139.02 E
Mount Pleasant, On., Can. 212 43.05 N 80.19 W
Mount Pleasant, In., U.S. 218 38.07 N 86.31 W
Mount Pleasant, Ia., U.S. 190 40.57 N 91.33 W
Mount Pleasant, Mi., U.S. 190 43.35 N 84.46 W
Mount Pleasant, N.C., U.S. 192 35.23 N 80.26 W
Mount Pleasant, Oh., U.S. 214 40.11 N 80.48 W
Mount Pleasant, Pa., U.S. 214 40.08 N 79.32 W
Mount Pleasant, S.C., U.S. 192 32.47 N 79.51 W
Mount Pleasant, Tn., U.S. 194 35.32 N 87.12 W
Mount Pleasant, Tx., U.S. 222 33.09 N 94.58 W
Mount Pleasant, Ut., U.S. 200 39.32 N 111.27 W
Mount Pleasant Mills 208 40.43 N 77.01 W
Mount Pleasant Park ♦ 284b 39.22 N 76.35 W
Mount Pocono 210 41.07 N 75.21 W
Mount Pritchard 274a 33.54 S 150.54 E
Mount Prospect, S. Afr. 158 27.29 S 29.53 E
Mount Prospect, Il., U.S. 216 42.03 N 87.56 W
Mount Pulaski 219 40.00 N 89.16 W
Mount Rainier 284c 38.56 N 76.57 W
Mount Rainier National Park ♦ 224 46.52 N 121.43 W
Mountrath 48 53.00 N 7.27 W
Mount Repose 218 39.10 N 84.14 W
Mount Revelstoke National Park ♦ 182 51.06 N 118.00 W
Mount Riddock 162 23.03 S 134.40 E
Mount Robson Provincial Park ♦ 182 52.58 N 118.50 W
Mount Rogers National Recreation Area ♦ 192 36.42 N 81.30 W
Mount Roskill 172 36.55 S 174.45 E
Mount Royal 285 39.49 N 75.13 W
Mount Rushmore National Memorial ⊥ 198 43.50 N 103.24 W
Mount Saint Helens National Volcanic Monument ♦ 224 46.12 N 122.11 W
Mount Sandiman 162 24.24 S 115.23 E
Mount Sarah 162 26.57 S 135.22 E
Mount Savage 188 39.41 N 78.52 W
Mount's Bay ⊂ 42 50.03 N 5.25 W
Mount Selinda 154 20.25 S 32.43 E
Mount Selman 222 32.04 N 95.17 W
Mount Seymour Provincial Park ♦ 182 49.23 N 122.57 W
Mount Shasta 204 41.18 N 122.18 W
Mount Sinai 276 40.57 N 73.02 W
Mount Sinai Harbor ⊂ 276 40.57 N 73.02 W
Mount Sinai Ridge ∧ 218 39.04 N 84.58 W
Mount Somers 172 43.43 S 171.24 E
Mountsorrel 42 52.44 N 1.07 W
Mount Spokane State Park ♦ 202 47.58 N 117.13 W
Mount Sterling, Il., U.S. 219 39.59 N 90.45 W
Mount Sterling, Ky., U.S. 192 38.03 N 83.56 W
Mount Sterling, Mo., U.S. 219 38.28 N 91.38 W
Mount Sterling, Oh., U.S. 218 39.43 N 83.15 W
Mount Stewart, P.E., Can. 186 46.22 N 62.52 W
Mount Stewart, S. Afr. 158 33.10 S 24.26 E
Mount Stromlo Observatory ⊍ [3] 171b 35.20 S 149.00 E
Mount Summit 218 40.00 N 85.23 W
Mount Surprise 166 18.09 S 144.19 E
Mount Sylvia 171a 27.44 S 152.14 E
Mount Tamalpais State Park ♦ 226 37.54 N 122.34 W
Mount Torrens 168b 34.52 S 138.57 E
Mount Tremper 210 42.03 N 74.17 W
Mount Uniacke 186 44.54 N 63.50 W
Mount Union 214 40.23 N 77.52 W
Mount Upton 210 42.25 N 75.23 W
Mount Vernon, Austl. 162 24.13 S 118.14 E
Mount Vernon, Al., U.S. 194 31.05 N 88.00 W
Mount Vernon, Ga., U.S. 192 32.10 N 82.35 W
Mount Vernon, Il., U.S. 219 38.19 N 88.54 W
Mount Vernon, In., U.S. 194 37.55 N 87.53 W
Mount Vernon, Ia., U.S. 190 41.55 N 91.25 W
Mount Vernon, Ky., U.S. 192 37.21 N 84.20 W
Mount Vernon, Md., U.S. 208 38.14 N 75.49 W
Mount Vernon, Mo., U.S. 194 37.06 N 93.49 W
Mount Vernon, N.Y., U.S. 210 42.45 N 78.53 W
Mount Vernon, N.Y., U.S. 210 40.54 N 73.50 W
Mount Vernon, Oh., U.S. 214 40.23 N 82.29 W
Mount Vernon, Or., U.S. 202 44.25 N 119.06 W
Mount Vernon, Pa., U.S. 279b 40.17 N 79.48 W
Mount Vernon, S.D., U.S. 198 43.42 N 98.15 W
Mount Vernon, Tx., U.S. 222 33.11 N 95.13 W
Mount Vernon, Wa., U.S. 224 48.25 N 122.19 W
Mount Vernon ⊥ 208 38.47 N 77.06 W
Mount Victoria 170 33.35 S 150.15 E
Mount Victory 216 40.32 N 83.31 W
Mount View 207 41.38 N 71.24 W
Mountville 208 40.02 N 76.26 W
Mount Vision 210 42.35 N 75.04 W
Mount Washington 284b 39.23 N 76.41 W
Mount Washington ✈ [8] 284b 39.22 N 76.40 W
Mount Waverley 274b 37.53 S 145.08 E
Mount Wedge, Austl. 162 22.45 S 132.09 E
Mount Wedge, Austl. 162 33.29 S 135.10 E
Mount Wellington 172 36.54 S 174.51 E
Mount Wilhelm National Park ♦ 164 5.45 S 145.05 E
Mount William National Park ♦ 166 40.56 S 148.15 E
Mount Willoughby 162 27.58 S 134.08 E
Mount Wilson Observatory ⊍ [3] 228 34.14 N 118.03 W
Mount Wolf 208 40.03 N 76.42 W
Mount Zion 219 39.46 N 88.53 W
Mounyaz 146 10.41 N 21.18 E
Moura, Austl. 166 24.35 S 149.58 E
Moura, Bra. 246 1.27 S 61.38 W
Moura, Port. 34 38.08 N 7.27 W
Moura, Tchad 146 13.47 N 21.13 E
Mouraya 146 11.27 N 20.59 E
Mourdi, Dépression du ± [7] 146 18.10 N 23.00 E
Mourdiah 150 14.28 N 7.28 W
Mouriès 62 43.41 N 4.52 E
Mourindi 152 2.32 S 10.48 E
Mourmelon-le-Grand 50 49.08 N 4.22 E
Mourne ≃ 48 54.49 N 7.28 W
Mourne Beg ≃ 48 54.41 N 7.39 W
Mourne Mountains ⩕ 48 54.10 N 6.04 W
Mousa I 46a 60.00 N 1.11 W
Mouscron 50 50.44 N 3.13 E
Mousgougou 146 10.47 N 16.09 E
Moussa Ali ∧ 144 12.28 N 42.24 E
Mousseaux-sur-Seine 261 49.03 N 1.39 E
Moussey 58 48.40 N 6.47 E
Moussoro 146 13.39 N 16.29 E
Moussy-le-Neuf 261 49.04 N 2.36 E
Moussy-le-Vieux 261 49.03 N 2.38 E
Moustiers-Sainte-Marie 62 43.51 N 6.13 E
Mouthe 58 46.43 N 6.12 E
Mouthier-Haute-Pierre 58 47.02 N 6.16 E
Moutier 58 47.17 N 7.23 E
Moûtiers 62 45.29 N 6.32 E
Moutiers-au-Perche 50 48.29 N 0.51 E
Moutnice 61 49.02 N 16.46 E
Moutohora 172 38.17 S 177.32 E
Moutomoukadi 152 4.41 S 13.15 E
Moutong 112 0.28 N 121.13 E
Mouy 50 49.19 N 2.19 E
Mouydir ⩕ 148 24.45 N 4.05 E
Mouyondzi 152 3.58 S 13.57 E
Mouzákion 38 39.26 N 21.40 E
Mouzarak 146 13.11 N 15.58 E
Mouzon 56 49.36 N 5.05 E
Mouzon ≃ 58 48.21 N 5.41 E
Móvano 232 26.42 N 103.39 W
Moville, Ire. 48 55.11 N 7.03 W
Moville, Ia., U.S. 198 42.29 N 96.04 W
Mowang 100 30.31 N 113.34 E
Moweaqua 219 39.37 N 89.01 W
Mowein 140 7.36 N 28.11 E
Mowry Slough ≃ 282 37.29 N 122.03 W
Mowrystown 218 39.02 N 83.44 W
Mowu 100 26.50 N 117.42 E
Moxhe 56 50.38 N 5.05 E
Moxi 107 30.18 N 105.41 E
Moxico □ [5] 152 13.00 S 20.30 E
Moxotó ≃ 250 9.19 S 38.14 W
Moy 48 54.27 N 6.42 W
Moy ≃ 48 54.12 N 9.08 W
Moy, Cnoc ∧ [2] 46 55.22 N 5.46 W
Moya, Comores 157a 12.18 S 44.27 E
Moya, Perú 248 12.24 S 75.10 W
Moyagee 162 27.45 S 117.54 E
Moyahua 234 21.16 N 103.10 W
Moyale, Ityo. 144 3.30 N 39.07 E
Moyale, Kenya 154 3.32 N 39.03 E
Moyamba 150 8.10 N 12.26 W
Moycullen 48 53.21 N 9.09 W
Moydans 62 44.24 N 5.30 E
Moÿ-de-l'Aisne 50 49.45 N 3.22 E
Moye Dao I 98 36.55 N 122.32 E
Moyen Atlas ⩕ 148 33.30 N 5.00 W
Moyen-Chari □ [5] 146 9.00 N 18.00 E
Moyenmoutier 58 48.23 N 6.55 E
Moyenne-Sido 146 8.13 N 18.43 E
Moyenneville 50 50.04 N 1.45 E
Moyen-Ogooué □ [4] 152 0.30 S 10.30 E
Moyenvic 56 48.47 N 6.33 E
Moyeuvre-Grande 56 49.15 N 6.02 E
Moyie 182 49.17 N 115.50 W
Moyie ≃ 202 48.42 N 116.11 W
Moyie Springs 202 48.43 N 116.11 W
Moylan 285 39.54 N 75.23 W
Moyle ≃ 48 52.24 N 7.39 W
Moyo 154 3.39 N 31.43 E
Moyo ≃ 115b 8.26 S 117.28 E
Moyo, Pulau I 115b 8.15 S 117.34 E
Moyobamba 248 6.03 S 76.58 W
Moyock 208 36.31 N 76.10 W
Moyogalpa 236 11.32 N 85.42 W
Moyowosi ≃ 154 4.50 S 31.24 E
Moyu 120 37.17 N 79.44 E
Moyuta, Volcán ∧ [1] 236 14.02 N 90.06 W
M'oža ≃, S.S.S.R. 76 55.27 N 30.43 E
M'oža ≃, S.S.S.R. 80 58.23 N 44.54 E
Možajevka 83 48.44 N 39.45 E
Možajsk 82 55.30 N 36.01 E
Možajskij 265a 59.43 N 30.07 E
Možajskoje vodochranilišče ⊜ [1] 82 55.35 N 35.50 E
Mozambique → Moçambique 154 15.03 S 40.42 E
Mozambique (Moçambique) □ [1] 138 18.15 S 35.00 E
Mozambique Channel)(138 19.00 S 41.00 E
Mozambique Plateau ✈ [3] 10 32.00 S 35.00 E
Mozarlândia 255 14.47 S 50.35 W
Možarovka 86 51.09 N 59.05 E
Možarov Majdan 80 55.37 N 45.53 E
Možary 80 53.53 N 41.02 E
Mozdok 84 43.44 N 44.38 E
Možga 80 56.23 N 52.17 E
Mozhabong Lake ⊜ 190 46.57 N 82.05 W
Mozia ⊥ 70 37.52 N 12.28 E
Mozichang 107 29.20 N 103.53 E
Mozolevo 76 59.19 N 33.51 E
Mozu 270 34.34 N 135.29 E
Mozuli 76 56.36 N 28.11 E
Mozyr' 78 52.03 N 29.14 E
Mozzanica 62 45.29 N 9.41 E
Mozzano 66 42.50 N 13.31 E
Mozzate 266b 45.41 N 8.57 E
Mpaka 158 26.26 S 31.47 E
Mpala 154 6.45 S 29.31 E
Mpama ≃ 152 0.57 S 15.39 E
Mpanda 154 6.22 S 31.02 E
Mpé 152 2.54 S 14.43 E
Mpese 152 5.14 S 15.33 E
Mpessoba 150 12.40 N 5.43 W
Mphoengs 154 21.10 S 27.51 E
Mpigi 154 0.13 N 32.42 E
Mpika 154 11.54 S 31.26 E
Mpila ✈ [8] 273b 4.14 S 15.18 E
Mpoka 152 1.26 S 17.02 E
Mpoko ≃ 152 4.19 N 18.33 E
Mporokoso 154 9.23 S 30.05 E
Mpouya 152 2.37 S 16.13 E
Mpraeso 150 6.35 N 0.44 W
Mpui 154 8.21 S 31.50 E
Mpulungu 154 8.46 S 31.07 E
Mpwapwa 154 6.21 S 36.29 E
Mqanduli 158 31.48 S 28.46 E
Mrągowo 30 53.52 N 21.19 E
Mrakovo 86 52.43 N 56.38 E
M'Ramani 157a 12.21 S 44.32 E
Mranggen 115a 7.01 S 110.31 E
Mras-Su ≃ 86 53.45 N 87.49 E
Mrhila, Jebel ∧ 36 35.25 N 9.14 E
Mrijo 154 5.10 S 36.15 E
Mrkonjić Grad 36 44.25 N 17.05 E
Mrkopalj 36 45.19 N 14.51 E
Mrocza 30 53.14 N 17.36 E
Msagali 154 6.21 S 36.18 E
M'Saken 148 35.44 N 10.35 E
Msata 154 6.20 S 38.23 E
Mšec 54 50.10 N 13.54 E
Mšeno 54 50.27 N 14.38 E
M'Sila 148 35.46 N 4.31 E
M'sila □ [5] 148 35.00 N 4.20 E

Symbols in the index entries represent the broad categories identified in the key at the right. Symbols with superior numbers (⩕ [1]) identify subcategories (see complete key on page I · 1).

Symbole im Register stellen die rechts im Schlüssel erklärten Kategorien dar. Symbole mit hochgestellten Ziffern (⩕ [1]) bezeichnen Unterabteilungen einer Kategorie (vgl. vollständiger Schlüssel auf Seite I · 1).

Los símbolos incluidos en el texto del índice representan las grandes categorías identificadas con la clave a la derecha. Los símbolos con números en su parte superior (⩕ [1]) identifican las subcategorías (véase la clave completa en la página I · 1).

Les symboles de l'index représentent les catégories indiquées dans la légende à droite. Les symboles suivis d'un indice (⩕ [1]) représentent des sous-catégories (voir légende complète à la page I · 1).

Os símbolos incluídos no texto do índice representam as grandes categorias identificadas com a chave à direita. Os símbolos com números em sua parte superior (⩕ [1]) identificam as subcategorias (veja-se a chave completa à página I · 1).

∧	Mountain	Berg	Montaña	Montagne	Montanha
⩕	Mountains	Gebirge	Montañas	Montagnes	Montanhas
)(	Pass	Paß	Paso	Col	Passo
∨	Valley, Canyon	Tal, Cañon	Valle, Cañón	Vallée, Canyon	Vale, Canhão
≐	Plain	Ebene	Llano	Plaine	Planície
>	Cape	Kap	Cabo	Cap	Cabo
I	Island	Insel	Isla	Île	Ilha
II	Islands	Inseln	Islas	Îles	Ilhas
±	Other Topographic Features	Andere Topographische Objekte	Otros Elementos Topográficos	Autres données topographiques	Outros acidentes topográficos

ESPAÑOL Nombre	Página	Lat.°'	Long.°' W=Oeste
M'Sila, Oued ⩲	34	35.46 N	4.34 E
Mšinskaja	76	59.01 N	29.57 E
Msoro	154	13.36 S	31.55 E
Msta	76	57.55 N	34.29 E
Msta ⩲	76	58.25 N	31.20 E
Mstera	80	56.23 N	41.56 E
Mstislavl'	76	54.02 N	31.42 E
Mstíž	76	54.34 N	28.10 E
Mszana Dolna	30	49.42 N	20.05 E
Mszczonów	30	51.58 N	20.31 E
Mtakataka	154	14.12 S	34.32 E
Mtakuja	154	7.22 S	30.37 E
Mtama	154	10.18 S	39.22 E
Mtamvuna ⩲	158	31.06 S	30.12 E
Mtarazi National Park	154	18.36 S	32.50 E
Mtata	158	31.58 S	29.10 E
Mtelo ⋀	154	1.39 N	35.23 E
Mtilikwe ⩲	154	21.09 S	31.30 E
Mtito Andei	154	2.41 S	38.10 E
Mtowabaga	154	2.30 S	35.53 E
Mtsensk → Mcensk	76	53.17 N	36.35 E
Mtubatuba	158	28.30 S	32.08 E
Mtunzini	158	28.57 S	31.46 E
Mtwara	154	10.16 S	40.11 E
Mtwara □⁴	154	11.00 S	39.00 E
Mtyangimbori	154	10.16 S	35.31 E
Mu ⩲, Mya.	110	21.56 N	95.38 E
Mu ⩲, Nihon	92a	42.33 N	141.56 E
Mu, Cerro ⋀	246	9.29 N	73.07 W
Mu'a	174w	21.11 S	175.07 W
Muacandala	102	10.02 S	19.40 E
Mualama	154	16.53 S	38.17 E
Mualang	112	0.42 N	111.18 E
Mu 'Allaqah, Lubnān	132	33.50 N	35.54 E
Mu 'Allaqah, Süd.	140	13.28 N	23.57 E
Muan	98	34.58 N	126.26 E
Muaná	250	1.32 S	49.13 W
Muang	152	5.56 S	12.21 E
Muangai	152	12.32 S	19.51 E
Muang Bèng	110	20.22 N	101.44 E
Muang Hay	110	21.03 N	101.49 E
Muang Hinboun	110	17.35 N	104.36 E
Muang Hôngsa	110	19.43 N	101.20 E
Muang Houn	110	20.09 N	101.27 E
Muang Hounxianghoung	110	21.37 N	102.18 E
Muang Huang	110	18.63 N	103.42 E
Muang Khammouan	110	17.24 N	104.48 E
Muang Khao	110	19.47 N	103.29 E
Muang Khi	110	18.27 N	101.46 E
Muang Khòng	110	14.07 N	105.51 E
Muang Khôngxédôn	110	15.34 N	105.49 E
Muang La	110	20.52 N	102.07 E
Muang Liap	110	18.29 N	101.40 E
Muang Long	110	20.57 N	100.48 E
Muang Meung	110	20.43 N	100.28 E
Muang Ngoy, Lao	102	20.43 N	102.41 E
Muang Ngoy, Lao	110	20.43 N	102.41 E
Muang Nong	110	16.22 N	106.30 E
Muang Ou Nua	110	22.18 N	101.48 E
Muang Ou Tai	110	22.07 N	101.48 E
Muang Pakbèng	110	19.54 N	101.08 E
Muang Pak-Lay	110	18.12 N	101.25 E
Muang Paktha	110	20.06 N	100.36 E
Muang Pakxan	110	18.22 N	103.39 E
Muang Peun	110	20.13 N	103.52 E
Muang Phalan	110	16.39 N	105.34 E
Muang Phiang	110	19.06 N	101.32 E
Muang Phônthong	110	16.35 N	105.39 E
Muang Phoun	110	19.07 N	102.43 E
Muang Sam Sip	110	15.31 N	104.44 E
Muang Sing	110	21.11 N	101.09 E
Muang Soum	110	18.45 N	102.36 E
Muang Souvannakhili	110	15.23 N	105.49 E
Souy	110	19.33 N	102.52 E
Muang Sung	110	20.19 N	102.27 E
Muang Thadua	110	19.26 N	101.50 E
Muang Thatèng	110	15.26 N	106.23 E
Muang Thathôm	110	19.06 N	103.20 E
Muang Va	110	21.53 N	102.19 E
Muang Vangviang	110	18.56 N	102.27 E
Muang Vapi	110	15.40 N	105.55 E
Muang Xaignabouri	110	19.15 N	101.45 E
Muang Xamtong	110	19.51 N	103.51 E
Muang Xay	110	20.42 N	101.59 E
Muang Xépôn	110	16.41 N	106.14 E
Muang Xon	110	20.27 N	103.19 E
Muang Yo	110	21.31 N	101.51 E
Muang Yong	110	19.49 N	102.50 E
Muanza	156	18.59 S	34.48 E
Muar (Bandar Maharani)	114	2.02 N	102.34 E
Muar ⩲	114	2.03 N	102.35 E
Muara	112	5.02 S	115.02 E
Muaraaman	112	3.07 S	102.12 E
Muaraancalung	112	0.27 N	116.41 E
Muarabeliti	112	3.15 S	103.02 E
Muarabengin	112	0.58 S	115.19 E
Muarabinuangeun	115a	6.50 S	105.53 E
Muarabulian	112	1.43 S	103.15 E
Muarabungo	112	1.28 S	102.07 E
Muaradua	112	4.32 S	104.05 E
Muaraenim	112	3.39 S	103.48 E
Muaragusung	112	1.37 N	117.17 E
Muarajuloi	112	0.12 S	114.03 E
Muarakaman	112	0.12 S	116.45 E
Muarakelingi	112	3.05 S	103.14 E
Muarakumpe	112	1.24 S	104.00 E
Muaralabuh	112	1.29 S	101.03 E
Muaralakitan	112	2.51 S	103.19 E
Muaralaksan	112	1.48 N	117.12 E
Muaralembu	112	0.24 S	101.21 E
Muaramawai	112	0.37 N	116.49 E
Muarapangean	112	0.38 N	116.41 E
Muarapantai	112	0.01 N	116.58 E
Muarapayang	112	1.32 S	115.48 E
Muararupit	112	2.44 S	102.54 E
Muarasabak	112	1.08 S	103.51 E
Muarasiberut	108	1.36 S	99.11 E
Muarasipongi	112	0.44 N	100.05 E
Muaratebo	112	1.17 N	99.21 E
Muarateladang	112	1.30 S	102.26 E
Muaratembesi	112	1.42 S	103.07 E
Muaratewe	112	0.57 S	114.53 E
Muaratuhup	112	0.34 S	114.50 E
Muarawahau	112	1.02 N	116.39 E
Muarawahau	112	1.04 N	116.92 E
Mu'āri, Rās ›	120	24.49 N	66.40 E
Muasdale	46	55.36 N	5.41 W
Muá Ximica	152	9.50 S	18.41 E
Mubārakpur	120	26.06 N	83.18 E
Mubārakpur Dabās □⁸	272a	28.43 N	77.03 E
Mubayyad ⊤⁴	142	30.55 N	32.48 E
Mubende	154	0.35 N	31.23 E
Mubi	146	10.18 N	13.20 E
Mubur, Pulau I	112	3.20 N	106.12 E
Mucaitá ⩲	250	6.59 S	42.40 W
Mucajai ⩲	248	2.25 N	60.52 W
Mucambo	250	3.54 S	40.44 W
Mucári	152	9.30 S	16.06 E
Muccan	162	20.38 S	120.04 E
Muccia	66	43.03 N	13.02 E
Mucha	56	50.54 N	7.25 E
Muchangpu	269d	24.59 N	121.34 E
Muchanovo	100	31.55 N	120.36 E
Muchavec ⩲	82	56.31 N	38.20 E
Much Dewchurch	42	51.59 N	2.46 W
Muchea	168a	31.35 S	115.59 E
Mücheln	54	51.18 N	11.48 E
Mücheln	54	48.10 N	135.13 E
Muchengzhen	107	29.47 N	120.29 E
Much Hoole	262	51.39 N	2.48 W
Muchinga Escarpment ⩲⁴	154	14.45 S	29.30 E
Muchinga Mountains	154	12.20 S	31.00 E
Muchino, S.S.S.R.	80	58.11 N	51.02 E
Muchino, S.S.S.R.	89	52.16 N	127.14 E

FRANÇAIS Nom	Page	Lat.°'	Long.°' W=Ouest
Muchor-Konduj	88	52.25 N	113.16 E
Muchorŝibir'	88	51.03 N	107.50 E
Muchrani	84	41.56 N	44.35 E
Muchtadir	84	41.41 N	48.46 E
Muchtolovo	80	55.27 N	43.13 E
Muchuan	107	28.55 N	103.58 E
Much Wenlock	42	52.36 N	2.34 W
Mucifal	266c	38.48 N	9.26 W
Mučikan	88	53.02 N	120.27 E
Mück I	46	56.50 N	6.15 W
Mücka	54	51.18 N	14.40 E
Muckadilla	166	26.35 S	148.23 E
Muckalee Creek ⩲	192	31.38 N	84.09 W
Muckamore	48	54.41 N	6.10 W
Mučkapskij	80	51.52 N	42.28 E
Muckle Roe I	46a	60.22 N	1.27 W
Muckleshoot Indian Reservation ⩲⁴	224	47.16 N	122.09 W
Muckno Lough ⊜	48	54.07 N	6.42 W
Mucojo	154	12.04 S	40.28 E
Mucoma	152	15.18 S	13.39 E
Muconda	152	10.34 S	21.17 E
Mucope, Ang.	152	8.42 S	21.43 E
Mucope, Ang.	152	16.24 S	14.53 E
Mucrone, Monte ⋀	62	45.36 N	7.56 E
Mucubela	154	16.55 S	37.52 E
Mucuchies	246	8.45 N	70.55 W
M'uc'ucl'u	84	40.28 N	47.55 E
Mucucuaú ⩲	246	0.37 S	61.24 W
Mucuim ⩲	248	6.33 S	64.18 W
Mucuio	152	16.47 S	14.51 E
Mucum	252	29.10 S	51.53 W
Mucumbura	154	16.09 S	31.31 E
Mucun	100	26.44 N	114.00 E
Mucupia	108	18.01 S	36.48 E
Mucupina, Monte ⋀	236	15.08 N	86.38 W
Mucuri	255	18.05 S	39.34 W
Mucuri ⩲	255	18.05 S	39.34 W
Mucusso	152	18.01 S	21.25 E
Mud ⩲, Ky., U.S.	194	37.13 N	86.54 W
Mud ⩲, W.V., U.S.	188	38.25 N	82.17 W
Mudan ⩲	89	46.22 N	129.33 E
Mudanjiang	89	44.35 N	129.36 E
Mudanjiang ⩲	89	46.22 N	129.33 E
Mudau	58	49.32 N	9.11 E
Mudayŝiŝât, Jabal ⋀	132	31.39 N	36.14 E
Mud Creek ⩲, N.A.	206	45.01 N	72.34 W
Mud Creek ⩲, U.S.	198	43.17 N	96.15 W
Mud Creek ⩲, Il., U.S.	219	38.21 N	89.48 W
Mud Creek ⩲, In., U.S.	216	41.06 N	86.21 W
Mud Creek ⩲, Ne., U.S.	216	40.26 N	85.55 W
Mud Creek ⩲, N.Y., U.S.	198	41.01 N	96.44 W
Mud Creek ⩲, N.Y., U.S.	210	43.05 N	78.43 W
Mud Creek ⩲, N.Y., U.S.	210	42.17 N	77.13 W
Mud Creek ⩲, Ok., U.S.	196	33.55 N	97.28 W
Mud Creek ⩲, S.D., U.S.	198	45.11 N	98.24 W
Mud Creek ⩲, Tx., U.S.	196	32.19 N	95.30 W
Muddus Nationalpark	24	67.00 N	20.16 E
Muddy ⩲, Nv., U.S.	200	36.27 N	114.22 W
Muddy ⩲, Wa., U.S.	224	46.04 N	122.01 W
Muddy Boggy Creek ⩲	196	34.03 N	95.47 W
Muddy Branch ⩲	284c	39.03 N	77.18 W
Muddy Brook ⩲	276	41.07 N	73.20 W
Muddy Creek ⩲, U.S.	276	41.27 N	75.39 W
Muddy Creek ⩲, Mo., U.S.	194	38.51 N	93.03 W
Muddy Creek ⩲, Mt., U.S.	202	47.56 N	111.46 W
Muddy Creek ⩲, Oh., U.S.	214	40.21 N	83.03 W
Muddy Creek ⩲, Pa., U.S.	208	39.47 N	76.18 W
Muddy Creek ⩲, Ut., U.S.	200	38.24 N	110.42 W
Muddy Creek ⩲, Wy., U.S.	198	42.35 N	104.57 W
Muddy Creek ⩲, Wy., U.S.	200	41.59 N	106.08 W
Muddy Creek ⩲, Wy., U.S.	200	41.32 N	110.13 W
Muddy Creek ⩲, Wy., U.S.	200	41.07 N	107.42 W
Muddy Fork ⩲	202	43.17 N	104.14 W
Muddy Gut ⩲	284b	39.17 N	76.26 W
Muddy Peak ⋀	200	36.18 N	114.42 W
Müden, B.R.D.	52	52.52 N	10.07 E
Müden, B.R.D.	54	52.31 N	10.22 E
Mudgee	166	32.36 S	149.35 E
Mudgeeraba	171a	28.04 S	153.22 E
Mudhol	122	16.21 N	75.17 E
Mud Island I	171a	27.20 S	153.15 E
Mud Islands II	169	38.17 S	144.45 E
Mudjatik ⩲	184	56.02 N	107.36 W
Mud Lake ⊜, Id., U.S.	202	43.53 N	112.24 W
Mud Lake ⊜, Nv., U.S.	200		
Mud Lake ⊜, N.Y., U.S.	204	37.52 N	117.04 W
Mud Lake Reservoir ⊜	198		
Mudon	110	16.15 N	97.44 E
Mudongzhen	102	29.35 N	106.51 E
Mudug □⁴	144	6.15 N	48.00 E
Mudug □⁴	144	11.16 N	47.30 E
Mud'u'ur'um ⩲	85	40.49 N	76.38 E
Mud'ug ⩲	85	40.49 N	76.38 E
Muduru	154	11.39 S	39.33 E
Muelle de los Bueyes	236	12.04 N	84.32 W
Mueller, Mount ⋀²	166	19.54 S	127.51 E
Muenster	196	33.39 N	97.23 W
Mu'er ⩲	107	29.48 N	106.37 E
Muerte, Valle de la → Death Valley ⩲	204	36.30 N	117.00 W
Muerto, Mar c	234	16.10 N	94.10 W
Muerto, Mar c	234	16.10 N	94.10 W
Mufufuma	152	9.04 S	17.06 E
Mufu Shan ⋀	100	29.02 N	113.54 E
Mufu Shan ⋀	100	29.00 N	114.00 E
Mufulira	154	12.33 S	28.14 E
Mugang	100	29.44 N	115.14 E
Mugançskaja ravnina ≃	84	39.40 N	48.15 E
Mugazine	158	26.07 S	32.30 E
Mugeba	154	35.31 N	136.51 E
Mugello V	66	43.55 N	11.30 E
Muger ⩲	144	9.54 N	37.57 E
Müggelberge ⋀²	264a	52.25 N	13.39 E
Müggelheim □⁸	264a	52.25 N	13.40 E
Muggia	64	45.36 N	13.46 E
Mughal Sarāī	126b	25.18 N	83.07 E
Mugi, Nihon	90	33.45 N	135.28 E
Mugi, Nihon	90	33.40 N	134.25 E
Mugia, Ría de ⊜	110	17.40 N	105.47 E
Muginsa	152	8.20 S	13.37 E

PORTUGUÊS Nome	Página	Lat.°'	Long.°' W=Oeste
Muğla	130	37.12 N	28.22 E
Muğla □⁴	130	37.10 N	28.30 E
Mugodžarskaja	86	48.36 N	58.27 E
Mugodžary, gory ⋀²	86	49.00 N	58.40 E
Mugombazi	154	5.50 S	30.14 E
Mugo-ri	98	38.58 N	126.31 E
Mugrejevskij	80	56.36 N	42.21 E
Mugron	32	43.45 N	0.45 W
Mugu Karnāli ⩲	124	29.38 N	81.52 E
Mugur-Aksy	86	50.21 N	90.30 E
Muhaïdi	124	30.34 N	38.20 E
Muhammdi	124	27.57 N	80.13 E
Muhammad, Ra's ›	140	27.44 N	34.15 E
Muhammadābād	124	26.02 N	83.23 E
Muhammadpur	124	23.24 N	89.36 E
Muhammad Qawl	140	20.54 N	37.05 E
Muhayshī, Birkat ⊜	142	30.43 N	31.56 E
Muheza	154	5.10 S	38.47 E
Muhīt, Masrif al-	273c	30.07 N	31.06 E
Mühlau	56	50.54 N	12.45 E
Mühlbach am Hochkönig	64	47.22 N	13.08 E
Mühlbach-sur-Munster	58	48.02 N	7.05 E
Mühlberg	54	51.26 N	13.13 E
Mühldorf	61	48.22 N	15.21 E
Mühldorf am Inn	60	48.15 N	12.32 E
Mühlen → Molini di Tures	64	46.54 N	11.56 E
Mühlenbeck	54	52.40 N	13.22 E
Mühlenbecker See ⊜	264a	52.41 N	13.24 E
Mühlenberg	210	41.14 N	76.09 W
Mühlen-Berg ⋀²	264a	52.23 N	13.15 E
Mühlen Eichsen	54	53.45 N	11.15 E
Mühlenfliess ⩲	264a	52.26 N	13.41 E
Mühlenrahmede	263	51.16 N	7.40 E
Mühlhausen, B.R.D.	263	51.33 N	7.44 E
Mühlhausen, D.D.R.	54	51.12 N	10.27 E
Mühlhausen im Täle	58	48.34 N	9.39 E
Mühlheim an der Donau	58	48.01 N	8.53 E
Mühlig-Hofmann Mountains ⋀	9	72.00 S	5.20 E
Mühlleiten	264b	48.10 N	16.32 E
Mühltroff	54	50.32 N	11.55 E
Mühlviertel ➜¹	30	48.25 N	14.10 E
Muhola	26	63.20 N	25.05 E
Muhoro	154	1.01 S	34.07 E
Muhos	26	64.48 N	25.59 E
Muhradah	130	35.15 N	36.35 E
Muhu I	76	58.38 N	23.15 E
Muhula	154	13.53 S	39.30 E
Muhulu	154	1.03 S	27.17 E
Muhutwe	154	1.33 S	31.42 E
Muhu vāin ⊔	76	58.45 N	23.20 E
Muhwesi ⩲	154	11.16 S	37.58 E
Muick, Loch ⊜	46	56.55 N	3.10 W
Muiden	52	52.19 N	5.04 E
Muiderslot ⌂¹	52	52.20 N	5.10 E
Muides-sur-Loire	50	47.40 N	1.31 E
Mué	152	14.25 S	20.36 E
Mui Hopohoponga Point ›	174w	21.09 S	175.02 W
Muikaichi	96	37.04 N	131.56 E
Muikamachi	94	37.04 N	138.53 E
Muine Bheag	48	52.41 N	6.58 W
Muir, Nv., U.S.	204	42.59 N	84.46 W
Muir, Pa., U.S.	208	40.36 N	76.31 W
Muir, Mount ⋀	180	61.06 N	148.24 W
Muir Beach	282	37.52 N	122.35 W
Muirdrum	46	56.31 N	2.42 W
Muirkirk, Scot., U.K.	46	55.31 N	4.04 W
Muirkirk, Md., U.S.	284c	39.04 N	76.53 W
Muir of Ord	46	57.31 N	4.27 W
Muiron Islands II	162	21.35 S	114.22 W
Muir Seamount ⊔³	16	33.41 N	62.30 W
Muir Woods	282	46.16 N	3.45 W
Muir Woods National Monument ✦	282	37.53 N	122.34 W
Muiskraal	158	33.56 S	21.13 E
Muisne	246	0.36 N	80.02 W
Muite	154	14.02 S	39.00 E
Mui Wo	271d	22.16 N	113.59 E
Muizen	50	51.01 N	4.31 E
Muja ⩲	88	56.24 N	115.39 E
Muja, S.S.S.R.	88	56.24 N	115.39 E
Muja ⩲	272a	28.34 N	77.13 E
Mujähidpur ➜⁸	272a	28.34 N	77.13 E
Mujezerskij	76	63.58 N	32.03 E
Mujiapucun	104	41.06 N	122.48 E
Mujisyu	105	24.04 N	116.55 E
Mujimbeji Mission	154	12.11 S	24.57 E
Mujnak	86	43.48 N	59.02 E
Mujo	98	36.02 N	127.40 E
Mujugin, peski ⩲²	86	48.27 N	22.45 E
Mukačevo	78	48.27 N	22.45 E
Mukah	112	2.54 N	112.06 E
Mukaishima	96	34.20 N	133.10 E
Mukalla → Al-Mukallā	144	14.32 N	49.08 E
Mukandwara	122	24.49 N	75.59 E
Mukawa	152	35.47 N	138.23 E
Mukáwir ⌂¹	132	31.34 N	35.38 E
Mukáwir ⊥	132	31.34 N	35.38 E
Mukawwar I	140	20.48 N	37.13 E
Mukdahan	110	16.32 N	104.43 E
Mukden → Shenyang	104	41.48 N	123.27 E
Muke Arba	144	8.57 N	42.09 E
Mukeru	154	6.49 S	28.03 E
Mukharram al-Fawqānī	130	34.49 N	37.04 E
Mukhmās	132	31.53 N	35.17 E
Mukho	98	37.33 N	129.06 E
Mukilteo	224	47.56 N	122.18 W
Mukinbudin	162	30.54 S	118.13 E
Mukinge Hill	154	13.29 S	25.52 E
Mukō	96	34.56 N	135.42 E
Muko ⩲	154	34.41 N	135.23 E
Mukomuko	112	2.35 S	101.07 E
Mukomwenze	154	6.52 S	27.16 E
Mukoshima-rettō II	95	27.37 N	142.10 E
Mukry	128	37.36 N	65.44 E
Muksu ⩲	85	39.15 N	71.23 E
Mukš ūdpur	126	23.18 N	89.51 E
Muktāgācha	124	24.46 N	90.14 E
Mukutawa ⩲	184	53.10 N	97.24 W
Mukwela	154	17.02 S	26.39 E
Mukwonago	216	42.51 N	88.19 W
Mül	22	56.20 N	9.51 E
Mula, Esp.	34	38.03 N	1.30 W
Mula, Zhg.	102	29.40 N	100.39 E
Mūla ⩲, India	122	19.32 N	74.50 E
Mūla ⩲, Pāk.	120	27.57 N	67.36 E
Muladu I	122	7.01 N	72.59 E
Mulaly	85	45.27 N	78.19 E
Mulanay	109	13.31 N	122.24 E
Mulanda	152	14.41 S	21.48 E
Mulanje, Malawi	154	16.02 S	35.31 E
Mulanje, Moç.	154	15.57 S	35.33 E
Mulargia, Lago ⊜	71	39.37 N	9.14 E
Mulas, Punta de ›	240p	21.01 N	75.35 W
Mulatos	232	28.39 N	108.51 W
Mulatupo	246	8.20 S	77.48 E

... (continued columns, right side)			
Mulayit Taung ⋀	110	16.11 N	98.32 E
Mulazzo	64	44.19 N	9.53 E
Mulbāgal	122	13.10 N	78.24 E
Mulben	46	57.31 N	3.06 W
Mulberry, Ar., U.S.	194	35.30 N	94.03 W
Mulberry, Fl., U.S.	220	27.53 N	81.58 W
Mulberry, In., U.S.	216	40.20 N	86.39 W
Mulberry, Oh., U.S.	218	39.11 N	84.14 W
Mulberry ⩲	194	35.28 N	94.03 W
Mulberry Creek ⩲, Al., U.S.	194	32.27 N	86.52 W
Mulberry Creek ⩲, Tx., U.S.	196	34.37 N	100.55 W
Mulberry Fork ⩲	194	33.33 N	87.11 W
Mulberry Grove	219	38.55 N	89.16 W
Mulberry Mountain ⋀	194	35.42 N	92.56 W
Mulchatna ⩲	180	59.39 N	157.08 W
Mulchén	252	37.43 S	72.14 W
Mulda, D.D.R.	54	50.48 N	13.25 E
Mul'da, S.S.S.R.	24	67.28 N	63.34 E
Mulde ⩲	54	51.52 N	12.15 E
Muldenstein	54	51.40 N	12.19 E
Muldersdrif se Loop ⩲	273d	26.06 S	27.51 E
Muldoon	200	30.41 S	22.13 E
Muldraugh	194	37.56 N	85.59 W
Muldrow	194	35.24 N	94.35 W
Mule, Lac la ⊜	186	51.33 N	65.35 W
Mulegé	232	26.53 N	112.01 W
Mulei	86	43.49 N	90.11 E
Mules (Mauls)	64	46.51 N	11.24 E
Mules, Pulau I	115b	8.54 S	120.17 E
Muleshoe	196	34.13 N	102.43 W
Mulga Downs	162	22.08 S	118.26 E
Mulgathing	162	30.15 S	134.00 E
Mulgathing Rocks ⋀	162	30.14 S	133.58 E
Mulgoa	170	33.50 S	150.40 E
Mulgoa Creek ⩲	274a	33.46 S	150.39 E
Mulgowie	171a	27.43 S	152.22 E
Mulgrave, Austl.	166	25.36 S	151.18 E
Mulgrave, N.S., Can.	186	45.37 N	61.23 W
Mulgrave Hills ⋀²	180	67.12 N	163.04 W
Mulgul	162	24.49 S	118.26 E
Mulhacén ⋀	34	37.03 N	3.19 W
Mulhall	196	36.03 N	97.24 W
Mülhausen → Mulhouse	58	47.45 N	7.20 E
Mülheim an der Ruhr	58	49.54 N	7.01 E
Mülheim-Kärlich	56	51.24 N	6.54 E
Mülheim (Mülhausen)	58	47.45 N	7.20 E
Muli	102	27.50 N	101.15 E
Muling, Zhg.	89	44.56 N	130.31 E
Muling, Zhg.	89	44.31 N	130.13 E
Muling ⩲	89	45.53 N	133.30 E
Mulini, Capo ›	70	37.34 N	15.10 E
Mulinu'u, Cape ›	175a	13.26 S	172.43 W
Mulita	116	7.18 N	124.52 E
Mülkeær ⩲	48	52.59 N	8.33 W
Mülki	122	13.06 N	74.48 E
Mull, Island of I	46	56.27 N	6.00 W
Mull, Sound of ⊔	46	56.32 N	5.50 W
Mullagh	48	53.49 N	6.57 W
Mullaghareirk Mountains ⋀	48	52.20 N	9.10 W
Mullaghcleevaun ⋀	48	53.06 N	6.24 W
Mullaghmore ›	48	54.52 N	6.51 W
Mullaloo Point ›	168a	31.48 S	115.44 W
Mullan	202	47.28 N	115.48 W
Mullen	198	42.02 N	101.02 W
Müllenbach	56	50.19 N	6.55 E
Mullengudgery	166	31.41 S	147.26 E
Mullens	192	37.34 N	81.22 W
Muller, Pegunungan ⋀²	112	0.40 N	113.50 E
Muller Creek ⩲	162	22.29 S	134.30 E
Muller Range ⋀	164	5.35 S	142.15 E
Mullerup	22	55.34 N	11.13 E
Mullet Key I	220	27.37 N	82.44 W
Mullet Peninsula ›¹	48	54.15 N	10.03 W
Mullet Lake ⊜	190	45.30 N	84.30 W
Mullewa	162	28.33 S	115.31 E
Mull Head ›, Scot., U.K.	46	59.23 N	2.54 W
Mull Head ›, Scot., U.K.	46	58.58 N	2.43 W
Müllheim	58	47.48 N	7.38 E
Mullhyttan	40	59.09 N	14.41 E
Mullica ⩲	208	39.33 N	74.25 W
Mullica, Alquatka Branch ⩲	285	39.47 N	74.48 W
Mullica, Sleeper Branch ⩲	285	39.44 N	74.40 W
Mullica Hill	208	39.44 N	75.13 W
Mulligan ⩲	166	25.00 S	138.30 E
Mulliken	216	42.45 N	84.53 W
Mullinahone	48	52.30 N	7.30 W
Mullinavat	48	52.21 N	7.10 W
Mullingar	48	53.31 N	7.20 W
Mullins	192	34.12 N	79.15 W
Mullinville	198	37.35 N	99.28 W
Mullion	42	50.01 N	5.15 W
Mulloon Creek ⩲	171b	35.12 S	149.38 E
Mullovka	80	54.13 N	49.25 E
Mullrose	54	52.14 N	14.25 E
Mullsjö	40	57.55 N	13.53 E
Mullumbimby	166	28.33 S	153.30 E
Mulm Mullum Creek ⩲	274b	37.46 S	145.10 E
Mulobezi	154	16.48 S	25.09 E
Mulonda Funda	154	11.06 S	25.28 E
Mulondo	152	15.39 S	15.14 E
Mulonga Plain ⩲	154	16.11 S	22.59 E
Mulonga ⩲	154	14.40 S	28.50 E
Mulonge Lake ⊜	122	10.30 N	73.30 E
Multai	122	21.46 N	78.15 E
Multān	123	30.11 N	71.29 E
Multé	232	17.41 N	91.24 W
Multen	40	59.09 N	14.37 E
Multia	26	62.25 N	24.47 E
Multnomah □⁶	224	45.31 N	122.22 W
Multnomah Channel ⩲	224	45.51 N	122.52 W
Multnomah Falls ⩲	224	45.34 N	122.06 W
Mulu, Gunong ⋀	112	4.04 N	114.56 E
Mulumbe, Monts ⋀	154	8.56 S	27.15 E
Mulungu	250	10.02 S	37.18 W
Mulungushi	154	14.28 S	28.50 E
Mulungushi Dam ⊤⁶	154	14.16 S	28.45 E
Mulvane	198	37.28 N	97.14 W
Mulwad	140	18.45 N	30.34 E
Mulyah Mountain ⋀	152	30.37 S	144.31 E
Mumbai → Bombay	122	18.58 N	72.50 E
Mumbeji	154	12.33 S	23.08 E
Mumbles Head ›	42	51.34 N	3.58 W
Mumbondo	152	10.09 S	14.15 E
Mumbwa	154	14.59 S	27.04 E
Mumcular	130	37.06 N	27.40 E
Mumeng	164	7.04 S	146.35 E
Mumra	84	45.45 N	47.41 E
Muna ⩲	72	37.43 N	3.30 W
Muna ⩲	88	67.52 N	123.06 E
Muna ⩲	232	20.29 N	89.43 W
Muna, Méx.	232	20.29 N	89.43 W
Muna, Pulau I	112	5.00 S	122.30 E
Muna, Selat ⊔	112	5.15 S	122.10 E
Munā al-Amīr	142	29.54 N	31.15 E
Munābāo	120	25.45 N	70.17 E
Munak	86	46.47 N	54.31 E
Munakata	90	33.50 N	130.35 E
Munam-ni	98	38.41 N	126.54 E
Munam-san ⋀	98	40.26 N	127.22 E
Munbong-ni	271b	37.43 N	126.49 E
Muncar	115a	8.26 S	114.20 E
Münchberg	54	50.11 N	11.47 E
Müncheberg	54	52.30 N	14.08 E
München	264a	52.30 N	13.40 E
München	60	48.08 N	11.34 E
Münchenbernsdorf	54	50.49 N	11.56 E
München-Gladbach → Mönchengladbach	56	51.12 N	6.28 E
Münchhausen	56	51.00 N	8.43 E
Münchweiler an der Rodalb	58	49.11 N	7.37 E
Muncie	216	40.11 N	85.23 W
Muncoon	130	52.28 N	31.41 E
Muncy	210	41.12 N	76.47 W
Muncy Creek ⩲	210	41.13 N	76.48 W
Muncy Valley	210	41.21 N	76.35 W
Mundare	182	53.36 N	112.20 W
Mundelein	216	42.15 N	88.00 W
Münder	56	52.11 N	9.39 E
Munderfing	60	48.05 N	13.11 E
Munderkingen	58	48.14 N	9.38 E
Mundersheim	58	49.49 N	8.07 E
Mundo ⩲	34	38.19 N	1.40 W
Mundolsheim	58	48.39 N	7.42 E
Mundo Nuevo	255	11.52 S	63.28 W
Mundra	120	22.51 N	69.44 E
Mundrabilla	162	31.52 S	127.51 E
Mundubbera	166	25.36 S	151.18 E
Mundybaš	86	53.14 N	87.19 E
Mundytau, gora ⋀	85	38.00 N	68.27 E
Munene	154	20.38 S	30.03 E
Munenga	152	10.02 S	14.41 E
Munera	34	39.02 N	2.28 W
Munford	194	35.26 N	89.48 W
Munfordville	194	37.16 N	85.53 W
Mungana	166	17.09 S	144.24 E
Mungaoli	122	24.24 N	78.07 E
Mungari	154	17.12 S	33.31 E
Munger	124	25.23 N	86.28 E
Mungeranie	166	28.00 S	138.39 E
Mungindi	166	28.58 S	148.59 E
Mungkan → Kabalega Falls	154		
Mungo National Park	166	33.44 S	143.02 E
Mungra Badshāhpur	124	25.40 N	82.11 E
Mungun-Tajga, gora ⋀	86		
Mun'gyŏng	98	36.44 N	128.07 E
Munhall	214	40.23 N	79.54 W
Munhamade	154	16.37 S	36.58 E
Munhango	152	12.12 S	18.42 E
Munhango ⩲	152	11.20 S	19.50 E
Munhoz	255	22.37 S	46.22 W
Munhyŏ-ri	98	38.10 N	127.19 E
Munich → München	60	48.08 N	11.34 E
Muniesa	34	41.02 N	0.48 W
Munika ⩲	272a	28.34 N	77.10 E
Munising	190	46.24 N	86.38 W
Munith	216	42.23 N	84.15 W
Muñiz	258	34.33 S	58.42 W
Muniz Freire	255	20.28 S	41.25 W
Munkács → Mukačevo	78	48.27 N	22.45 E
Munkebjerg	41	55.51 N	9.37 E
Munkebo	22	55.27 N	10.34 E
Munkedal	40	58.29 N	11.40 E
Munkerud	40	59.50 N	13.31 E
Munkfors	40	59.50 N	13.32 E
Munksund	26	65.17 N	21.29 E
Munktorp	40	59.31 N	16.23 E
Munku-Sardyk, gora ⋀	88	51.45 N	100.32 E
Munlochy	46	57.32 N	4.15 W
Munnerstadt	56	50.15 N	10.11 E
Munnsville	210	42.58 N	75.35 W
Muñoz	116	15.43 N	120.54 E
Muñoz ⩲	240p	21.22 N	78.32 W
Muñozero	80	67.05 N	34.12 E
Muñoz Gamero, Península ›¹	254	52.30 S	73.10 W
Munro ➜	258	34.32 S	58.31 W
Munroe Falls	214	41.08 N	81.26 W
Munsan	274b	37.51 N	126.48 E
Munsang	98	37.51 N	126.48 E
Munsar	124	24.18 N	88.26 E
Munsey Park	284a	40.47 N	73.40 W
Munshiganj	124	23.33 N	90.32 E
Munsing	26	46.24 N	86.38 W
Münsingen, B.R.D.	58	48.25 N	9.30 E
Münsingen, Schw.	61	46.53 N	7.34 E
Munsö I	40	59.19 N	17.39 E
Munson, Ab., Can.	182	51.34 N	112.45 W
Munson, Pa., U.S.	214	40.57 N	78.10 W
Munster, Fr.	58	48.02 N	7.08 E
Münster, B.R.D.	56	51.57 N	7.37 E
Münster, B.R.D.	58	49.54 N	8.52 E
Münster, Schw.	61	46.29 N	8.16 E
Munster, In., U.S.	216	41.33 N	87.30 W
Münster ➜⁹	56	52.00 N	7.40 E
Münsterkirchen ➜	60	48.20 N	13.25 E
Münsterland ➜¹	56	51.57 N	7.35 E
Münstermaifeld	56	50.14 N	7.22 E
Münster ➜ (Münster-Zwiesel)	58	48.33 N	9.14 E
Munte	115b	0.25 S	119.46 E
Muntele Mare, Vîrful ⋀	68	46.29 N	23.14 E
Muong Het	110	20.49 N	104.01 E
Muong Hinh	110	19.49 N	105.03 E
Muong Khoua	110	21.05 N	102.31 E
Muong Saiapoun	110	18.24 N	101.31 E
Muong Te	110	22.28 N	102.37 E
Muonio	24	67.57 N	23.42 E
Muoro	36	40.20 N	9.20 E
Muotathal	58	46.59 N	8.46 E
Mupa	152	16.59 S	15.44 E
Mupa, Parque Nacional da ➜⁴	152	16.00 S	15.35 E
Muping	98	37.24 N	121.35 E
Mupini	158	17.50 S	19.40 E
Mup'ungjang	98	35.58 N	127.49 E
Muqaddam, Wādī ⩲	140	18.04 N	31.30 E
Muqatta'	140	14.40 N	35.51 E
Muqaybirah, Bi'r al-	142	30.53 N	32.50 E
Muqayshit I	128	24.10 N	53.45 E
Muqdisho (Mogadishu)	144	2.04 N	45.22 E
Muqi	98	41.46 N	124.28 E
Muqsam, Jabal ⋀	140	13.38 N	27.42 E
Muquequete	152	14.50 S	14.16 E
Muqui	255	20.57 S	41.20 W
Mura (Mur) ⩲	30	46.18 N	16.53 E
Mura (Mur) ⩲	Europe		
Mura ⩲, S.S.S.R.	88	58.27 N	98.34 E
Muradiye, Tür.	84	38.59 N	43.46 E
Muradiye, Tür.	130	38.39 N	27.21 E
Murafa ⩲	78	48.13 N	28.14 E
Murāgācha	126	23.32 N	88.24 E
Muraglione, Passo del ✕	66	43.56 N	11.39 E
Murai Reservoir ⊜¹	271c	1.24 N	103.41 E
Murajá	250	0.47 S	47.57 W
Murakami	92	38.14 N	139.29 E
Murallón, Cerro ⋀	254	49.48 S	73.25 W
Murambi	154	1.46 S	30.23 E
Muramvya	154	3.16 S	29.37 E
Muran	90	33.40 N	20.02 E
Murana	164	3.33 S	133.49 E
Murano, Isola di I	64	45.28 N	12.21 E
Muránska planina ⋀²	78	48.44 N	20.02 E
Muranskij porog ⌇	88	58.02 N	112.16 E
Muraoka	96	35.28 N	134.35 E
Murashi	80	59.24 N	48.55 E
Muraški	265b	59.24 N	37.45 E
Murat	32	45.07 N	2.52 E
Murat ⩲	84	38.39 N	39.50 E
Murat Dağı ⋀	130	38.55 N	29.43 E
Muratkovo	86	58.26 N	62.23 E
Murati	110	14.30 N	27.30 E
Muratovo	83	48.48 N	38.45 E
Muratpur	272b	28.50 N	88.27 E
Murauaeá ⩲	246	0.09 N	60.40 W
Muravera	71	39.25 N	9.34 E
Muravjovka	89	49.50 N	127.44 E
Muravyovo	56	56.14 N	14.14 E
Murayama	92	38.29 N	140.22 E
Murayama-chosuichi ⊜¹	268	35.45 N	139.25 E
Muraysah, Ra's al- ›	144	31.55 N	25.02 E
Murça	34	41.24 N	7.27 W
Murcanyo	144	11.44 N	50.27 E
Mürchin	54	53.54 N	13.44 E
Murchison, Austl.	166	36.37 S	145.14 E
Murchison, N.Z.	172	41.48 S	172.20 E
Murchison, Tx., U.S.	222	32.17 N	95.45 W
Murchison ⩲	162	27.42 S	114.09 E
Murchison, Mount ⋀, Austl.	162	26.46 S	116.25 E
Murchison, Mount ⋀, N.Z.	172	43.01 S	171.22 E
Murchison Falls → Kabalega Falls	154		
Murchison Range ✕	162	20.11 S	134.26 E
Murcia, Esp.	34	37.59 N	1.07 W
Murcia, Pil.	116	10.36 N	123.02 E
Murcia ➜⁴, Esp.	34	38.00 N	1.10 W
Murciélago	236	10.55 N	85.44 W
Murciélagos, Islas II	236	10.51 N	85.57 W
Murciélagos Bay c	116	8.39 N	123.33 E
Murdeduke, Lake ⊜	169	38.11 S	143.53 E
Mure ⩲	84	44.51 N	2.39 E
Mureaux, Aérodrome des ➜	261	49.00 N	1.57 E
Mureck	60	46.42 N	15.46 E
Mureş (Maros) ⩲	78	46.15 N	20.13 E
Mureş ➜⁴	32	46.35 N	24.40 E
Muret	32	43.28 N	1.21 E
Murfreesboro, Ar., U.S.	194	34.04 N	93.41 W
Murfreesboro, N.C., U.S.	192	36.26 N	77.05 W
Murfreesboro, Tn., U.S.	194	35.50 N	86.23 W
Murg	58	47.33 N	8.01 E
Murg ⩲	58	48.55 N	8.10 E
Murgab ⩲ → Murgab (Morghāb)	128	38.18 N	61.12 E
Murgab (Morghāb) ⩲, Asia	128	38.18 N	61.12 E
Murgab, S.S.S.R.	128	38.10 N	74.00 E
Murgenella	164	11.33 S	132.55 E
Murgeni	68	46.12 N	28.02 E
Murgenthal	61	47.16 N	7.50 E
Murgha Kibzai	120	30.44 N	69.25 E
Murghab, Daryā-ye ⩲	120	36.50 N	64.51 E
Muri, Cook Is.	174k	21.14 S	159.43 W
Muri, Ngr.	146	9.11 N	10.53 E
Muri, Schw.	61	47.16 N	8.20 E
Muri, Schw.	61	46.56 N	7.29 E
Muria ⩲	248	4.15 S	55.13 E
Muriaé	255	21.08 S	42.22 W
Muriaé ⩲	255	21.08 S	41.08 W
Murias de Paredes	34	42.51 N	6.11 W
Muribeca	255	10.26 S	36.59 W
Muribeca dos Guararapes	250	8.10 S	35.01 W
Muriege	152	9.19 S	21.17 E
Murilo I¹	176	8.40 N	152.15 E
Mürîtz ⊜	54	53.25 N	12.43 E
Muriwai	173	38.46 S	177.55 E
Murkong Selek	124	27.54 N	95.16 E
Murliganj	124	25.54 N	86.59 E
Murmansk	76	68.58 N	33.05 E
Murmansk Rise ➜³	12	75.00 N	37.00 E
Murmansk ➜⁴ (Oblast)			
Murmerwoude	52	53.16 N	6.00 E

(key to symbols)

Symbol	English	Deutsch	Español	Français	Português
⩲	River	Fluß	Río	Rivière	Rio
	Canal	Kanal	Canal	Canal	Canal
⌇	Waterfall, Rapics	Wasserfall, Stromschnellen	Cascada, Rápidos	Chute d'eau, Rapides	Cascata, Rápidos
⊔	Strait	Meeresstraße	Estrecho	Détroit	Estreito
c	Bay, Gulf	Bucht, Golf	Bahía, Golfo	Baie, Golfe	Baía, Golfo
⊜	Lake, Lakes	See, Seen	Lago, Lagos	Lac, Lacs	Lago, Lagos
	Swamp	Sumpf	Pantano	Marais	Pântano
	Ice Features, Glacier	Eis- und Gletscherformen	Accidentes Glaciares	Formes glaciaires	Acidentes glaciares
⊤	Other Hydrographic Features	Andere Hydrographische Objekte	Otros Elementos Hidrográficos	Autres données hydrographiques	Outros acidentes hidrográficos
✦	Submarine Features	Untermeerische Objekte	Accidentes Submarinos	Formes de relief sous-marin	Acidentes submarinos
□	Political Unit	Politische Einheit	Unidad Política	Entité politique	Unidade política
⌂	Cultural Institution	Kulturelle Institution	Institución Cultural	Institution culturelle	Instituição cultural
	Historical Site	Historische Stätte	Sitio Histórico	Site historique	Sítio Histórico
■	Recreational Site	Erholungs- und Ferienort	Sitio de Recreo	Centre de loisirs	Area de Lazer
	Airport	Flughafen	Aeropuerto	Aéroport	Aeroporto
	Military Installation	Militäranlage	Instalación Militar	Installation militaire	Instalação militar
	Miscellaneous	Verschiedenes	Misceláneo	Divers	Diversos

Name	Page	Lat.°/	Long.°/
Murmino	80	54.36 N	40.03 E
Murnau	64	47.40 N	11.12 E
Murnei	140	12.57 N	22.52 E
Murō	94	34.34 N	136.02 E
Murō-Akame-Aoyama-kokutei-kōen ♦	94	34.30 N	136.10 E
Muro Lucano	68	40.45 N	15.29 E
Murom	80	55.34 N	42.02 E
Muromcevo	86	56.23 N	75.14 E
Muroran	92a	42.18 N	140.59 E
Muros	34	42.47 N	9.02 W
Muros y Noya, Ría de c ¹	34	42.45 N	9.00 W
Muroto	96	33.18 N	134.09 E
Muroto-Anan-kaigan-kokutei-kōen ♦	96	33.41 N	134.32 E
Muroto-zaki ‣	96	33.15 N	134.11 E
Murovanyje Kurilovcy	78	48.43 N	27.31 E
Murowana Goślina	30	52.35 N	17.01 E
Murphy, Id., U.S.	202	43.13 N	116.33 W
Murphy, Mo., U.S.	219	38.29 N	90.29 W
Murphy, N.C., U.S.	192	35.05 N	84.02 W
Murphy Lake	182	52.03 N	121.14 W
Murphys	226	38.08 N	120.27 W
Murphysboro	194	37.45 N	89.20 W
Murphy Slough ≃	226	36.28 N	120.00 W
Murr ≃	48	48.57 N	9.16 E
Murr, Wādī ⩔	142	28.27 N	32.18 E
Murrah, Qārat al- ∧²	142	30.00 N	32.41 E
Murrah al-Kubrā, Al-Buhayrah al- (Great Bitter Lake)	142	30.20 N	32.23 E
Murrah as-Sughrā, Al-Buhayrah al- (Little Bitter Lake)	142	30.13 N	32.33 E
Murra Murra	166	28.16 S	146.48 E
Murrāt, Ābār ⩔	140	21.03 N	32.55 E
Murray, la., U.S.	196	41.02 N	93.56 W
Murray, Ky., U.S.	194	36.36 N	88.18 W
Murray, Ut., U.S.	200	40.40 N	111.53 W
Murray, Austl.	166	35.22 S	139.22 E
Murray ≃, Austl.	168a	32.35 S	115.46 E
Murray ≃, B.C., Can.	182	55.40 N	121.10 W
Murray, Lake ⊜	164	7.00 S	141.30 E
Murray, Lake ⊜ ¹	192	34.04 N	81.23 W
Murray, Mount ∧, Yk., Can.	180	60.54 N	128.49 W
Murray, Mount ∧, Pap. N. Gui.	164	6.46 S	144.01 E
Murray Bay	186	47.39 N	70.10 W
— La Malbaie	186	47.39 N	70.10 W
Murray Bridge	168b	35.07 S	139.17 E
Murray Canal ≃	212	44.04 N	77.35 W
Murray City	188	39.30 N	82.09 W
Murray Downs	162	21.04 S	134.40 E
Murray Fracture Zone ⧫	16	34.00 N	135.00 W
Murray Harbour	186	46.00 N	62.31 W
Murray Head ‣	186	46.00 N	62.28 W
Murray Maxwell Bay c	176	70.00 N	80.00 W
Murray Mouth ≃¹	168b	35.34 S	138.54 E
Murray River	186	46.01 N	62.37 W
Murraysville, B.C., Can.	224	49.10 N	122.36 W
Murraysville, Il., U.S.	194	39.35 N	90.15 W
Murrébué	154	13.02 S	40.30 E
Murree	123	33.54 N	73.24 E
Murren	58	46.34 N	7.54 E
Murrhardt	56	48.59 N	9.34 E
Murrī	246	6.33 N	76.52 W
Murrieta	228	33.33 N	117.12 W
Murro di Porca, Capo ‣	70	37.00 N	15.20 E
Murrumbidgee ≃	166	34.43 S	143.12 E
Murrumburrah	166	34.33 S	148.21 E
Murrupula	154	15.27 S	38.47 E
Murry Hill	279b	40.17 N	80.09 W
Murrysville	226	40.29 N	79.41 W
Mursal	130	39.11 N	37.59 E
Mursala, Pulau I	114	1.38 N	98.32 E
Murshidābād	126	24.11 N	88.16 E
Mürşitpınar	130	36.54 N	38.19 E
Murski, porog ⟱	86	46.40 N	116.10 E
Mursko središće	61	46.31 N	16.27 E
Murtajipar	122	20.44 N	77.23 E
Murtal	266c	38.42 N	9.22 W
Murten	58	46.56 N	7.08 E
Murtensee ⊜	—		
— Morat, Lac de ⊜	58	46.55 N	7.05 E
Murter, Otok I	36	43.48 N	15.37 E
Murtle Lake ⊜	182	52.08 N	119.38 W
Murtoa	166	36.37 S	142.28 E
Murton	44	54.49 N	1.24 W
Murtosa	34	40.44 N	8.38 W
Muru ≃	140	6.36 N	29.15 E
Muru ≃	248	8.09 S	70.45 W
Muru, Capu di ‣	36	41.44 N	8.40 E
Murud	122	18.19 N	72.58 E
Murud, Gunong ∧	112	3.52 N	115.30 E
Murung ≃	112	0.58 S	114.35 E
Murupara	172	38.28 S	176.42 E
Mururoa I ¹	6	21.52 S	138.55 W
Murutinga	246	3.26 S	59.12 W
Murvaul, Lake ⊜	222	32.03 N	94.12 W
Murval Creek ≃	194	32.05 N	94.12 W
Murwāra	124	23.51 N	80.24 E
Murwillumbah	166	28.19 S	153.24 E
Mürz ≃	61	47.24 N	15.17 E
Mürzsteg	61	47.40 N	15.29 E
Mürzzuschlag	61	47.36 N	15.41 E
Muş	130	38.44 N	41.30 E
Muş ⊡⁴	128	39.00 N	42.00 E
Musa	204	2.40 N	19.18 E
Musa ≃, Pap. N. Gui.	164	9.25 S	148.50 E
Mūša ≃, S.S.S.R.	76	56.24 N	23.43 E
Mūsá, Jabal (Mount Sinai)	140	28.32 N	33.59 E
Mūsá, 'Uyūn (Springs of Moses) ⧫	142	29.52 N	32.39 E
Musabeyli	130	39.51 N	34.37 E
Musadi	152	2.34 S	22.47 E
Musaid	146	31.35 N	25.03 E
Mūsá Khel	123	32.54 N	71.14 E
Mūsá Khel Bāzār	120	30.52 N	69.49 E
Musala ∧	38	42.11 N	23.34 E
Musan	98	42.14 N	129.13 E
Musandam Peninsula ‣¹	142	26.18 N	56.24 E
Musao	154	7.43 S	26.17 E
Mūsá Qal'eh	128	32.22 N	64.46 E
Mūsá Qal'eh ≃	128	32.05 N	64.51 E
Musar	272b	22.54 N	88.14 E
Musashi	154	3.21 S	31.33 E
Musashi — Iruma, Nihon	96	35.50 N	139.24 E
Musashi, Nihon	96	33.30 N	131.43 E
Musashimurayama	96	35.45 N	139.23 E
Musashino	96	35.42 N	139.34 E
Musashino-daichi ⌒¹	268	35.45 N	139.28 E
Musau	58	47.32 N	10.40 E
Musay'īd	142	24.59 N	51.32 E
Musaymīr	142	13.27 N	44.37 E
Mūsāzai	120	30.23 N	66.32 E
Muscat — Masqaṭ	128	23.37 N	58.35 E
Muscat and Oman — Oman ⊡¹	128		
Muscatatuck ≃	218	38.46 N	86.10 W
Muscatatuck, Grassy Fork ≃	218	38.45 N	85.07 W
Muscatatuck, Vernon Fork ≃	218	38.45 N	85.07 W
Muscatine	190	41.25 N	91.03 W
Müsch	52	50.19 N	6.52 E
Mus-Chaja, gora ∧	74	62.35 N	140.50 E

Name	Page	Lat.°/	Long.°/
Muschu Island I	164	3.25 S	143.35 E
Muschwitz	54	51.11 N	12.07 E
Muscle Shoals	194	34.44 N	87.40 W
Musclow, Mount ∧	182	53.17 N	127.09 W
Musclow Lake ⊜	184	51.25 N	94.56 W
Muscoda	190	43.11 N	90.26 W
Musconetcong ≃	210	40.36 N	75.11 W
Musconetcong, Lake ⊜	276	40.54 N	74.42 W
Muscongus Bay c	188	43.55 N	69.20 W
Muscote Bay c	212	44.06 N	77.18 W
Muscowpetung Indian Reserve ◆⁴	184	50.45 N	104.15 W
Muscoy	228	34.09 N	117.20 W
Muse	214	40.17 N	80.12 W
Musengezi ≃	154	15.43 S	31.14 E
Museo Nacional de Antropología ⧫	286a	19.25 N	99.11 W
Museum, Bergbau ∨	263	51.29 N	7.13 E
Musgrave, Austl.	166	14.47 S	143.30 E
Musgrave, B.C., Can.	224	48.45 N	123.32 W
Musgrave, Mount ∧	172	43.48 S	170.43 E
Musgrave Ranges ⩙	162	26.10 S	131.50 E
Musgravetown	186	48.24 N	53.53 W
Mūshā	142	27.08 N	31.18 E
Mushābāni	126	22.31 N	86.27 E
Mushenge	152	4.32 S	21.21 E
Mushie	152	3.01 S	16.54 E
Mushima	154	14.13 S	25.05 E
Mushin	150	6.32 N	3.22 E
Mushi ≃, India	122	16.41 N	79.40 E
Musi ≃, Indon.	112	2.20 S	104.56 E
Musicians Seamounts ⦁³	6	31.00 N	162.00 W
Muskauer Heide ⇻	54	51.25 N	14.40 E
Muskeg ≃	182	54.01 N	119.03 W
Muskeget Channel ⥹	207	41.25 N	70.20 W
Muskeget Island I	207	41.20 N	70.18 W
Muskeg Lake Indian Reserve ◆⁴	184	52.58 N	106.57 W
Muskego	216	42.53 N	88.08 W
Muskego Lake ⊜	216	42.53 N	88.07 W
Muskegon	216	43.13 N	86.14 W
Muskegon ≃	216	43.14 N	86.20 W
Muskegon ≃⁶	216	43.12 N	86.08 W
Muskegon ≃⁷	216	43.14 N	86.20 W
Muskegon County Airport ⩥	216	43.10 N	86.14 W
Muskegon Heights	216	43.12 N	86.14 W
Muskegon Lake ⊜	216	43.14 N	86.16 W
Muskegon State Park ◆	216	43.14 N	86.20 W
Mušketova, gora ∧	88	53.35 N	113.32 E
Muskingum ≃	214	40.06 N	81.51 W
Muskingum ≃	188	39.27 N	81.30 W
Muskingum Brook ≃	285	39.48 N	74.44 W
Muskira	124	25.40 N	79.48 E
Muskö I	40	59.00 N	18.06 E
Muskoday Indian Reserve ◆⁴	184	53.05 N	105.30 W
Muskogee	196	35.44 N	95.22 W
Muskoka ≃⁶	212	45.05 N	79.03 W
Muskoka, Lake ⊜	212	45.00 N	79.25 W
Muskoka, North Branch ≃	212	45.02 N	79.19 W
Muskoka, South Branch ≃	212	45.02 N	79.19 W
Muskosh Channel ⥹	212	44.55 N	79.53 W
Muskowekwan Indian Reserve ◆⁴	184	51.19 N	104.06 W
Muskrat Creek ≃	202	43.09 N	108.11 W
Muskrat Dam Lake ⊜	184	53.25 N	91.40 W
Muskrat Lake ⊜	184	55.40 N	76.55 W
Muskwa ≃	176	58.45 N	122.35 W
Muskwa Lake ⊜	182	56.09 N	114.38 W
Muslimbāgh	120	30.49 N	67.45 E
Musl'umovo	80	55.18 N	53.12 E
Musmus	132	32.32 N	35.09 E
Musocco ≃	266b	45.30 N	9.08 E
Musofu Mission	154	13.31 S	29.02 E
Musoma	154	1.30 S	33.48 E
Musone ≃, lt.	64	45.50 N	11.55 E
Musone ≃, lt.	66	43.28 N	13.38 E
Musoshi	154	11.54 S	27.46 E
Musquanousse, Lac ⊜	186	50.22 N	61.05 W
Musquapsink Brook ≃	276	40.59 N	74.01 W
Musquaro, Lac ⊜	186	50.38 N	61.05 W
Musquash ≃	212	44.57 N	79.52 W
Musquash Brook ≃	283	42.42 N	71.26 W
Musquashcut Pond ⊜	283	42.13 N	70.46 W
Musquodoboit Harbour	186	44.47 N	63.09 W
Musseau Island I	164	1.30 S	149.40 E
Musselburgh	46	55.57 N	3.04 W
Musselkanaal	52	52.56 N	7.00 E
Musselshell ≃	202	47.21 N	107.58 W
Mussende	152	10.32 S	16.05 E
Mussidan	32	45.02 N	0.22 E
Mussoorie	124	30.27 N	78.05 E
Mussuco	152	17.08 S	19.05 E
Mussuma	152	12.01 S	28.44 E
Mussy-sur-Seine	58	47.58 N	4.30 E
Mustafakemalpaşa	130	40.02 N	28.24 E
Mustafa Kemal Paşa ≃	130	40.07 N	28.33 E
Mustafino	80	55.01 N	53.38 E
Mustahil	144	5.12 N	44.17 E
Müstair	58	46.37 N	10.27 E
Mustajevo	80	51.48 N	53.25 E
Mustajõe	76	57.59 N	26.58 E
Mustang	196	35.22 N	97.43 W
Mustang Draw ⩔	196	32.23 N	101.36 W
Mustang Island I	196	28.00 N	96.55 W
Mustāfā	126	30.37 N	31.09 E
Musters, Lago ⊜	254	45.27 S	69.13 W
Mustinka ≃	198	45.45 N	96.38 W
Mustjala	76	58.28 N	22.14 E
Mustla	76	58.14 N	25.52 E
Musturud	273c	30.08 N	31.17 E
Mustvee	76	58.51 N	26.56 E
Mutalau	174r	18.56 S	169.50 W
Mutambara	154	19.36 S	32.33 E
Mutanchiang — Mudanjiang	89	44.35 N	129.36 E
Mutanda, Moç.	156	21.02 S	33.31 E
Mutanda, Zaïre	152	5.17 S	16.34 E
Mutanda Mission	154	12.24 S	26.16 E
Mutankiang — Mudanjiang	89	44.35 N	129.36 E
Mutararé, Jabal al- ∧²	142	31.04 N	36.06 E
Mutare	154	18.58 S	32.40 E
Mutis ∧	110	9.33 S	124.14 E
Mutis (Rezovska) ≃	108	41.59 N	28.01 E
Mutoko	154	17.24 S	32.13 E
Mutombo-Mukulu	152	7.58 S	24.00 E
Mutoraj	74	61.20 N	100.30 E
Mutouchengzi	98	44.15 N	89.01 E
Mutouhao	107	28.49 N	105.04 E
Mutsamudu	152	12.09 S	44.25 E
Mutsamba ≃	152	13.09 S	34.27 E

Name	Page	Lat.°/	Long.°/
Mutsu	92	41.17 N	141.10 E
Mutsuai	268	35.08 N	139.38 E
Mutsumi	96	34.26 N	131.34 E
Mutsuura ≃	268	35.19 N	139.37 E
Mutsu-wan c	92	41.05 N	140.55 E
Muttaburra	166	22.36 S	144.33 E
Mutte Kopf ∧	58	47.16 N	10.39 E
Muttenz	58	47.32 N	7.39 E
Muttra	124	27.30 N	77.41 E
— Mathura	124	27.30 N	77.41 E
Mutton Island I	48	52.49 N	9.32 W
Muttonbird Islands II	172	47.15 S	167.24 E
Muttontown	276	40.49 N	73.33 W
Mutual, Oh., U.S.	218	40.05 N	83.38 W
Mutual, Pa., U.S.	279b	40.14 N	79.30 W
Mutūbis	142	31.18 N	30.31 E
Mutuca, Ribeirão da ≃	256	21.36 S	45.39 W
Mutucu, Lago ⊜	250	1.21 N	50.24 W
Mutuípe	255	13.15 S	39.31 W
Mutum	255	19.49 S	41.26 W
Mutum ≃	246	4.25 S	68.03 W
Mutum Biyu	146	8.38 N	10.46 E
Mutumbo	152	13.14 S	17.17 E
Mutunópolis	255	13.40 S	49.15 W
Muturi ≃	164	2.06 S	133.43 E
Muturi ≃	164	2.13 S	133.40 E
Mututi, Ilha I	250	0.45 S	51.00 W
Mutzig	58	48.32 N	7.28 E
Mutzschen	54	51.16 N	12.53 E
Mu Us Shamo ⇻²	102	38.45 N	109.10 E
Muvattupula	122	9.58 N	76.35 E
Muvukoni	154	0.24 S	38.14 E
Muwaqqar	132	31.49 N	36.06 E
Muwopu	104	41.03 N	121.12 E
Muxaluando	152	8.07 S	14.17 E
Muxihe	100	31.03 N	115.21 E
Muxima	152	9.31 S	13.56 E
Muyaga	154	3.14 S	30.33 E
Muyang	100	27.06 N	119.34 E
Muying ≃	100	27.00 N	119.41 E
Muyinga	154	2.51 S	30.20 E
Muymanu ≃	248	11.27 S	69.03 W
Muy Muy	236	12.46 N	85.38 W
Muyua Island I	164	9.02 S	152.50 E
Muyuka	152	4.17 N	9.25 E
Muyumba	154	7.15 S	26.59 E
Mužač°	82	54.22 N	36.21 E
Muzaffarābād	123	34.22 N	73.28 E
Muzaffargarh	123	30.04 N	71.12 E
Muzaffarnagar	124	29.28 N	77.41 E
Muzaffarpur	124	26.07 N	85.24 E
Muzambinho	256	21.22 S	46.32 W
Muzambo ≃	256	21.15 S	46.26 W
Muzambo ≃	256	21.17 S	46.16 W
Muzat ≃	90	41.15 N	83.27 E
Muzayrīb	132	32.42 N	36.01 E
Muzbek, gora ∧	85	40.23 N	69.33 E
Muzdar ⁻¹	86	50.15 N	70.50 E
Muzeze ≃	152	15.03 S	17.43 E
Muži	74	65.22 N	64.40 E
Mužiči	86	43.03 N	44.59 E
Mužiksu ≃	86	47.42 N	84.58 E
Muzkol, chrebet ⩙	85	38.25 N	73.30 E
Muzoka	154	16.41 S	27.19 E
Muzon, Cape ‣	182	54.41 N	132.44 W
Muztag ∧, Zhg.	120	36.03 N	80.07 E
Muztag ∧, Zhg.	120	36.25 N	87.25 E
Muztagata ∧	85	38.17 N	75.11 E
Muztor	85	41.26 N	76.12 E
Muzzana del Turgnano	64	45.49 N	13.08 E
Mvam ≃	152	0.13 S	9.39 E
Mvangan	152	2.38 N	11.44 E
Mvela	152	3.37 N	15.16 E
Mvolo	140	6.03 N	29.56 E
Mvomero	154	6.20 S	37.25 E
Mvoti ≃	158	29.24 S	31.22 E
Mvoung ≃	152	0.04 N	12.18 E
Mvouti	152	4.15 S	12.29 E
Mvuma	154	19.19 S	30.35 E
Mwadi-Kalumba	152	7.53 S	18.46 E
Mwadui	154	3.33 S	33.36 E
Mwali (Mohéli) I	157a	12.15 S	43.45 E
Mwami	154	16.40 S	29.46 E
Mwanamugimbe	152	15.31 S	23.30 E
Mwango	152	6.51 S	24.13 E
Mwanza, Malawi	154	15.37 S	34.31 E
Mwanza, Tan.	154	2.31 S	32.54 E
Mwanza, Zaïre	152	7.54 S	26.45 E
Mwanza, Zam.	152	17.02 S	24.27 E
Mwanza ⊡⁴	154	2.35 S	32.51 E
Mwanza Gulf c	154	2.35 S	33.11 E
Mwaya, Tan.	154	8.55 S	36.50 E
Mwaya, Tan.	154	9.33 S	33.57 E
Mweelrea ∧	48	53.38 N	9.50 W
Mwehu	154	5.44 S	26.40 E
Mweka	152	4.51 S	21.34 E
Mwemena	154	10.19 S	27.28 E
Mwenda	154	12.01 S	28.44 E
Mwendjila	152	7.12 S	18.51 E
Mwene-Ditu	152	7.03 S	23.27 E
Mwenezi	154	21.22 S	30.45 E
Mwenga	154	3.02 S	28.26 E
Mwepo	154	11.56 S	26.11 E
Mweresandu	154	9.59 S	30.23 E
Mwereni	154	4.20 S	39.08 E
Mweru, Lake ⊜	154	9.00 S	28.45 E
Mweru Mantipa — National Park ♦	154	8.45 S	29.30 E
Mweru Wantipa, Lake ⊜	154	8.45 S	29.10 E
Mwimbi	154	8.39 S	31.40 E
Mwinilunga	154	11.44 S	24.26 E
Mwitikira	154	6.31 S	35.39 E
Mwomboshi ≃	154	12.52 S	29.10 E
Myadaung	116	23.08 N	96.02 E
My Tho	110	10.21 N	106.21 E
Mytholm	262	53.44 N	2.01 W
Mytholmroyd	262	53.44 N	1.59 W
Mytilene — Mitilíni	38	39.06 N	26.32 E
Mytíshchi	82	55.55 N	37.46 E
— Mytíšči	82	55.55 N	37.46 E
Mýtna	76	54.54 N	34.01 E
Mýto	54	49.47 N	13.44 E
Myton	200	40.11 N	110.03 W
Myvatn ⊜	24a	65.37 N	16.58 W
Myzovo	78	51.22 N	24.31 E
M'zab, Oued ⩔	148	32.19 N	5.24 E
Mže ≃	60	49.46 N	13.24 E
Mzenga	154	6.56 S	38.43 E
Mziha	154	5.55 S	37.47 E
Mzimba	154	11.52 S	33.34 E
Mzimkulu ≃	158	30.44 S	30.28 E
Mzimvubu ≃	158	31.38 S	29.32 E
Mzintlava ≃	158	31.12 S	29.18 E
Mzuzu	154	11.27 S	33.55 E
Mzymta ≃	84	43.27 N	39.56 E

N

Name	Page	Lat.°/	Long.°/
Na I (Tengtiao) ≃	110	6.52 S	158.22 E
Naab ≃	60	49.01 N	12.02 E
Naach, Jbel ∧	34	34.53 N	3.22 W
Naachtpunkt Brook ≃	276	40.54 N	74.15 W
Naaldwijk	52	52.00 N	4.12 E
Naalehu	229d	19.03 N	155.35 W
Na'ama, Sebkhet en ≃	148	35.42 N	1.19 W
Naaman Creek, South Branch ≃	285	39.48 N	75.27 W
Naamans Garden	285	39.49 N	75.31 W
Naantali	26	60.27 N	22.02 E
Naarden	52	52.17 N	5.09 E
Naarn ≃	61	48.14 N	14.49 E
Naas	48	53.13 N	6.39 W
Naas ≃	171b	35.48 S	149.08 E
Naast, Bel.	50	50.36 N	4.08 E
Naast, Scot., U.K.	46	57.47 N	5.39 W
Na'ayur, Hasy ⩔	148	30.05 N	35.00 E
Nabā, Jabal an- (Mount Nebo) ∧	132	31.46 N	35.44 E
Nababeep	158	29.36 S	17.46 E
Nābabū ≃	272b	22.42 N	88.12 E
Nabaganga ≃	272a	23.04 N	89.34 E
Nabagram	272b	24.06 N	88.06 E
Nabalat Al-Hajanah	132	33.17 N	36.36 E
Nabari	94	34.37 N	136.05 E
Nabas	116	11.50 N	122.05 E
Nabawa	166	28.31 S	114.47 E
Nabberu, Lake ⊜	162	25.36 S	120.30 E
Nabburg	60	49.27 N	12.11 E
Nabeina	174t	1.26 N	173.05 E
Naberera	154	4.12 S	36.56 E
Naberežnyje Čelny	80	55.42 N	52.19 E
Nabesna	180	62.22 N	143.00 W
Nabesna ≃	180	63.27 N	141.00 W
Nabeul	146	36.27 N	10.44 E
Nābha	124	30.22 N	76.09 E
Nabīb ∧⁸	38	40.35 N	20.05 E
Nabi Hārūn, Jabal an- ∧	132	30.20 N	35.26 E
Nabigou	146	9.31 N	1.12 E
Nabil' ≃	74	51.40 N	143.32 E
Nabīl Shu'ayb, Jabal an- ∧	144	15.17 N	43.59 E
Nabisipi ≃	186	50.14 N	62.13 W

Name	Page	Lat.°/	Long.°/
Myllendonk, Schloss ⧫	263	51.13 N	6.29 E
Myllykoski	26	60.47 N	26.48 E
Myllymäki	26	62.32 N	24.17 E
Mylor	168b	35.03 S	138.45 E
Mymensingh	124	24.45 N	90.24 E
Mynämäki	26	60.40 N	22.00 E
Mynaral	85	45.25 N	73.41 E
Mynbulak, gora ∧	85	41.43 N	69.49 E
Mynfontein	158	30.55 S	23.57 E
Mynydd Bach ∧²	36	13.24 N	123.22 E
Mynydd Eppynt ∧	42	52.05 N	3.30 W
Mynydd Hiraethog ⌒	44	53.05 N	3.33 W
Mynydd Pencarreg ∧	—		
Mynydd Preseli ⩙	42	52.04 N	4.04 W
Mynydd Y Fân	42	51.58 N	4.42 W
Myōga	94	35.51 N	137.02 E
Myōgi	94	36.17 N	138.49 E
Myōgi-Arafune-Saku-kōgen-kokutei-kōen ♦	94	36.12 N	138.10 E
Myōgi-san ∧	94	36.17 N	138.44 E
Myō-gyi	110	21.27 N	96.22 E
Myōhaung	110	20.36 N	93.10 E
Myohyang-san ∧	98	40.02 N	126.17 E
Myohyang-sanmaek ⩙	—		
Myojin-dake ∧	268	40.30 N	127.00 E
Myōken-san ∧	96	34.57 N	135.36 E
Myōken-san ∧	96	33.34 N	133.04 E
Myōken-san ∧	95	35.24 N	134.39 E
Myōken-zan ∧	270	34.56 N	135.28 E
Myōken-zan ∧²	268	34.30 N	134.57 E
Myōkō	94	36.56 N	138.13 E
Myōkō-kōgen	94	36.54 N	138.11 E
Myōnmong-ni ⩔⁸	271b	37.35 N	127.05 E
Myponga	168b	35.24 S	138.28 E
Myponga Reservoir ⊜¹	168b	35.24 S	138.26 E
Myra ≃	130	36.15 N	29.54 E
Myrdalsjökull 囗	24a	63.40 N	19.06 W
Myriam	182	53.40 N	111.14 W
Myroodah	162	18.08 S	124.16 E
Myrskylä (Mörskom)	26	60.40 N	25.51 E
Myrtle Beach	192	33.41 N	78.53 W
Myrtle Beach Air Force Base ⧫	192	33.41 N	78.56 W
Myrtle Beach State Park ◆	192	33.37 N	78.58 W
Myrtle Creek	202	43.01 N	123.17 W
Myrtle Grove	190	30.25 N	87.18 W
Myrtle Point	222	43.03 N	124.08 W
Myrtle Springs	222	32.37 N	95.56 W
Myrtletowne	204	40.47 N	124.04 W
Myrtleville	170	34.29 S	149.49 E
Myšega	82	54.31 N	37.02 E
Mysen	26	59.33 N	11.20 E
Mysia ⁻⁹	130	39.40 N	27.51 E
Mysingen ⥹	40	59.00 N	18.15 E
Myski	86	53.42 N	87.48 E
Myškino	82	57.47 N	38.27 E
Myšľa ≃	54	52.40 N	14.29 E
Myślenice	30	49.51 N	19.56 E
Myślibórz	30	52.55 N	14.52 E
Mysłowice	30	50.15 N	19.07 E
Mysore	122	12.18 N	76.39 E
Mys Šmidta	180	68.56 N	179.26 W
Mysovka	76	55.11 N	21.17 E
Mys Seaport ⧫	267	41.22 N	71.58 W
Mys Vchodnoj	74	73.53 N	86.43 E
Mysy	74	60.34 N	53.57 E
Mys Želanija	72	76.56 N	68.35 E
Myszków	30	50.36 N	19.20 E
Myt	80	56.48 N	42.21 E
Mzymta ≃	84	43.27 N	39.56 E

Name	Seite	Breite°/	Länge°/
Nabiswera	154	1.28 N	32.16 E
Nabī Yūnus, Ra's an- ‣	132	33.39 N	35.24 E
Nabnasset	207	42.36 N	71.25 W
Nabnasset Pond ⊜	283	42.37 N	71.26 W
Nabogame	232	26.14 N	106.57 W
Naboomspruit	156	24.32 S	28.36 E
Nabordo	150	10.10 N	9.20 E
Nabou	150	11.27 N	2.43 W
Nabq	140	28.04 N	34.25 E
Nabula	120	31.55 N	80.10 E
Nabulus	132	32.13 N	35.16 E
Nabunturan	116	7.35 N	125.58 E
Nacajuca	234	18.08 N	93.01 W
Nacala	154	14.34 S	40.41 E
Nacala-Velha	154	14.32 S	40.37 E
Nacaome	236	13.31 N	87.30 W
Nacastillo	234	19.35 N	104.55 W
Nacchie	144	7.23 N	40.10 E
Naceredine	34	36.08 N	3.26 E
Náchabinka ⌓	265b	55.51 N	37.22 E
Náchabino	82	55.51 N	37.11 E
Naches	224	46.43 N	120.41 W
Naches ≃	202	46.38 N	120.31 W
Náchičevan'	84	39.13 N	45.24 E
Náchičevanskaja Avtonomnaja Sovetskaja Socialističeskaja Respublika ⊡³	84	39.20 N	45.30 E
Nachi-katsuura	92	33.30 N	135.55 E
Nāchinda	126	21.53 N	87.46 E
Nachingwea	154	10.23 S	38.46 E
Náchna	120	27.30 N	71.43 E
Náchod	30	50.25 N	16.10 E
Nachodka — Karabachskaja Avtonomnaja Oblast' ⊡³	84	40.00 N	46.40 E
Nagomyj, S.S.S.R.	74	55.58 N	124.57 E
Nagomyj, S.S.S.R.	265a	59.43 N	30.16 E
Nagorsk	80	59.18 N	50.48 E
Nagorskoje	82	56.54 N	38.06 E
Nago-wan c	174m	26.34 N	127.57 E
Nagoya	94	35.10 N	136.55 E
Nagoya-kūkō ⩥	94	35.15 N	136.55 E
Nāgpur	120	21.09 N	79.06 E
Nagqu	120	31.34 N	92.00 E
Nagqu ≃	123	34.23 N	77.21 E
Nāgrākāta	124	26.54 N	88.55 E
Nagrota	123	32.03 N	76.05 E
Nagu I	26	60.10 N	21.48 E
Nagua	238	19.23 N	69.50 W
Naguabo	240m	18.13 N	65.44 W
Nácori Chico	232	29.39 N	109.01 W
Nacozari [de García]	232	30.24 N	109.39 W
Nacunday	252	26.01 S	54.46 W
Nada ⊡	108	19.31 N	109.34 E
Nada ⌂	270	34.44 N	135.14 E
Nadābhānga ≃	272b	22.24 N	88.14 E
Nadachi	94	37.09 N	138.06 E
Nadaleen Mountain ∧	180	64.15 N	133.04 W
Nadasaki	96	34.32 N	133.52 E
Nadasd	61	46.58 N	16.37 E
Nadbai	124	27.14 N	77.12 E
Nadder ≃	42	51.03 N	1.52 W
Nadela	34	42.58 N	7.30 W
Nadelkap	—		
— Agulhas, Cape ‣	158	34.52 S	20.00 E
Naden Harbour c	182	54.00 N	132.35 W
Nadi	89	48.38 N	133.11 E
Nadi ≃	140	18.40 N	33.42 E
Nādiād	124	22.42 N	72.52 E
Nādīr, Mişr	132	30.33 N	30.51 E
Nādir, Vir. Is., U.S.	240m	18.19 N	64.53 W
Nādlac	38	46.10 N	20.45 E
Nador	148	35.12 N	2.55 W
Nadoua ⊡⁴	148	35.09 N	3.04 W
Nadporožje	76	60.28 N	34.17 E
Nadrin	50	50.10 N	5.41 E
Nadterečnaja	84	43.37 N	45.22 E
Nadvoicy	24	63.52 N	34.15 E
Nadvornaja	78	48.38 N	24.34 E
Nadym	72	65.35 N	72.42 E
Nadym ≃	74	66.12 N	72.00 E
Nadyrovo	80	54.53 N	52.28 E
Naeba-san ∧	94	36.51 N	138.41 E
Nae-dong	98	37.16 N	126.27 E
Naejang-san Kukrip Kongwön ♦	98	35.28 N	126.52 E
Naenwa	120	25.46 N	75.51 E
Nærbø	26	58.40 N	5.39 E
Nærsby	41	55.18 N	10.22 E
Næstved	41	55.14 N	11.46 E
Nafada	146	11.08 N	11.20 E
Nafels	58	47.06 N	9.04 E
Nafarros	266c	38.49 N	9.25 W
Nahma	190	45.50 N	86.39 W
Nahmer ≃	263	51.20 N	7.35 E
Nahmer ⌂	263	51.21 N	7.36 E
Nahodi, Cap ‣	175f	14.39 S	166.37 E
Nahr Ouassel, Oued ≃	148	35.42 N	2.33 E

Name	Seite	Breite°/	Länge°/
Nagatino ⌓⁸	265b	55.41 N	37.41 E
Nagato, Nihon	94	36.15 N	138.16 E
Nagato, Nihon	96	34.21 N	131.10 E
Nagatsuda ⌓⁸	268	35.32 N	139.30 E
Nagaur	120	27.12 N	73.44 E
Nāgāvali ≃	122	18.13 N	83.56 E
Nagawicka Lake ⊜	216	43.05 N	88.23 W
Nagawa	94	36.05 N	137.41 E
Nagcarlan	116	14.08 N	121.25 E
Nagele	52	52.37 N	5.44 E
Nāgercoil	122	8.10 N	77.26 E
Nagi	96	35.07 N	134.11 E
Nagiba	116	13.41 N	120.53 E
Nagibino	86	55.46 N	72.43 E
Nagichot	154	4.16 N	33.34 E
Nagina	124	29.27 N	78.27 E
Nāgirāt	126	23.38 N	89.18 E
Nagi-san ∧	96	35.10 N	134.11 E
Nagiso	94	35.35 N	137.37 E
Nagla	272a	28.31 N	77.27 E
Naglarby	40	60.25 N	15.34 E
Nagles Mountains ⩙	48	52.05 N	8.30 W
Nago	174m	26.35 N	127.59 E
Nāgod	124	24.34 N	80.36 E
Nagog Pond ⊜	283	42.31 N	71.26 W
Nagoya ⌂	94	35.10 N	136.55 E
Nagold ≃	56	48.33 N	8.43 E
Nagold ⌓	56	48.52 N	8.42 E
Nagol'naja ≃	83	47.57 N	38.58 E
Nagol'no-Tarasovka	83	48.00 N	39.29 E
Nagorje	76	56.55 N	38.16 E
Nagornoje	78	45.26 N	28.27 E
Nagqu	120	31.34 N	92.00 E
Nagqu ≃	123	34.23 N	77.21 E
Nagra, Az., U.S.	200	31.20 N	109.56 W
Nacogdoches	222	31.36 N	94.39 W
Nacogdoches, Lake ⊜	222	31.37 N	94.50 W
Náca	232	29.30 N	109.01 W
Naco, Méx.	232	31.20 N	109.56 W
Naco, Az., U.S.	200	31.20 N	109.56 W
Nagumbaya Point ‣	116	13.34 N	124.21 E
Naguri	268	35.53 N	139.11 E
Nagyatád	38	46.14 N	17.22 E
Nagybajom	38	46.23 N	17.31 E
Nagybánya — Baia Mare	38	47.40 N	23.35 E
Nagyberki	61	47.36 N	16.42 E
Nagyecsed	38	47.52 N	22.24 E
Nagykálló	78	47.53 N	21.51 E
Nagykanizsa	36	46.27 N	17.00 E
Nagykáta	38	47.25 N	19.45 E
Nagy-Kevély ∧²	264c	47.37 N	18.59 E
Nagykőrös	30	47.02 N	19.47 E
Nagy-Milic ∧	64	47.22 N	18.04 E
Nagytarcsa	264c	47.32 N	19.17 E
Nagytétény ⩔⁸	264c	47.24 N	18.59 E
Nagyvárad — Oradea	38	47.03 N	21.57 E
Naha	174m	26.13 N	127.40 E
Naha Airfield ⧫	174m	26.13 N	127.40 E
Nahanbuan	116	0.49 N	114.05 E
Nahma ⌂	180	61.40 N	126.00 W
Nahaha ⌓⁸	207	42.25 N	70.55 W
Nahant	207	42.25 N	70.55 W
Nahant Bay c	207	42.27 N	70.56 W
Nahant Beach ∧²	283	42.26 N	70.58 W
Nahari	96	33.25 N	134.01 E
Nahariyya	132	33.01 N	35.06 E
Naharpur ⌓	272a	28.42 N	77.07 E
Nāhāvand	128	34.12 N	48.22 E
Nahbollenbach	56	49.45 N	7.21 E
Nahe ≃	56	49.58 N	7.57 E
Nahma	190	45.50 N	86.39 W
Nahodi, Cap ‣	175f	14.39 S	166.37 E

Name	Seite	Breite°/	Länge°/
Nagaragawa ≃	94	35.01 N	136.43 E
Nagara-gawa ≃	94	35.01 N	136.43 E
Nāgārjuna Sāgar ⊜¹	122	16.35 N	79.21 E
Nāgārjuna Sāgar ⊜¹	122	16.35 N	79.21 E
Nagasaki	96	32.48 N	129.56 E
Nagasaki ⊡⁴	96	33.00 N	129.30 E
Nagasaki Kūkō ⩥	96	32.55 N	129.55 E
Nagashima ∧	96	34.12 N	131.21 E
Naga-shima I, Nihon	96	33.35 N	136.42 E
Naga-shima I, Nihon	96	34.14 N	134.15 E
Nagashima	94	35.05 N	136.43 E
Nagasu	96	32.56 N	130.27 E
Nagato ⊡	96	34.22 N	131.12 E
Nahuala, Laguna c	234	16.46 N	99.44 W
Nahuala	236	14.51 N	91.19 W
Nahuatate ≃	234	19.42 N	100.48 W
Nahuel Huapi	254	41.03 S	71.09 W
Nahuel Huapi, Lago ⊜	254	41.03 S	71.09 W
Nahuel Huapi, Parque Nacional ♦	254	41.00 S	71.48 W
Nahuel Niyeu	254	40.30 S	66.33 W
Nahuizalco	236	13.46 N	89.45 W
Nahunta	192	31.12 N	81.58 W
Nahyā	273c	30.04 N	31.07 E
Naia	66	44.06 N	12.22 E
Naiba ≃	116	12.04 N	124.10 E
Naic	116	14.19 N	120.46 E
Naica	232	27.52 N	105.30 W
Naiguatá	242	10.37 N	66.44 W
Naiguatá, Pico ∧	286c	10.32 N	66.46 W
Naihāti	272b	22.49 N	88.25 E
Naij, India	120	22.28 N	71.24 E
Naij Gol ≃, Zhg.	90	36.00 N	94.49 E
Naiji Gol ≃	90	36.02 N	95.50 E
Naijin	124	23.20 N	80.10 E
Naikoon Provincial Park ◆	182	53.50 N	131.50 W
Nailsea	50	51.26 N	2.46 W
Nain, Nf., Can.	176	56.32 N	61.41 W
Nā'īn, Īrān	128	32.52 N	53.05 E
Nainpur	124	22.26 N	80.07 E
Nairai I	174g	17.49 S	179.24 E
Nairn, Nf., Can.	175g	17.49 S	179.24 E
Nairn, Scot., U.K.	46	57.35 N	3.53 W
Nairn, La., U.S.	194	29.23 N	89.34 W
Nairn ≃	46	57.36 N	3.55 W
Nairobi	154	1.17 S	36.49 E
Nairobi Airport ⩥	276	41.08 N	74.21 W
Nairobi National Park ♦	154	1.24 S	36.50 E
Naissaar I	76	59.33 N	24.32 E
Naissus Island I	175f	13.57 S	166.58 E
Naivasha	154	0.43 S	36.26 E
Naivasha, Lake ⊜	154	0.46 S	36.22 E
Naivos	114	2.30 S	96.10 E
Najac	32	44.13 N	1.58 E
Najafābād	128	32.37 N	51.21 E
Najd ⌂¹	128	25.00 N	44.30 E
N'aizichen	89	43.41 N	127.29 E

ESPAÑOL — Nombre | Página | Lat.°′ | Long.°′ W = Oeste

FRANÇAIS — Nom | Page | Lat.°′ | Long.°′ W = Ouest

PORTUGUÊS — Nome | Página | Lat.°′ | Long.°′ W = Oeste

Nombre / Nom / Nome	Página / Page	Lat.°′	Long.°′
Najac	32	44.13 N	1.59 E
Najafābād	128	32.37 N	51.21 E
Najafgarh ◆[8]	272a	28.37 N	76.59 E
Najafgarh Drain ≍	272a	28.43 N	77.14 E
Najasa ≃	240p	20.42 N	77.55 W
Najd □[8]	144	21.00 N	46.00 E
Najd □[9]	118	25.00 N	44.30 E
Nájera	34	42.25 N	2.44 W
Najhā	132	33.23 N	36.22 E
Naj' Ḥammādī	140	26.03 N	32.15 E
Najībābād	124	29.38 N	78.20 E
Najin	98	42.15 N	130.18 E
Najinkouzi	89	50.23 N	126.57 E
Najio	270	34.50 N	135.18 E
Najstenjarvi	24	62.16 N	32.38 E
Naju	98	35.03 N	126.43 E
Najza, gora ∧	86	49.24 N	70.42 E
Naka, Nihon	94	36.27 N	140.30 E
Naka, Nihon	96	35.02 N	134.55 E
Naka, Nihon	268	35.49 N	140.03 E
Naka, Nihon	270	34.50 N	135.56 E
Naka, Nihon	270	34.50 N	135.48 E
Naka, Nihon	270	34.42 N	135.45 E
Naka ◆[8]	268	35.27 N	139.39 E
Naka ≃, Nihon	94	36.20 N	140.36 E
Naka ≃, Nihon	96	33.56 N	134.42 E
Naka ≃, Nihon	268	35.39 N	139.51 E
Nakadōri-shima I	92	32.57 N	129.04 E
Nakagami	268	35.49 N	139.21 E
Nakagawa	94	35.38 N	137.56 E
Nakagawa ◆[8]	268	35.33 N	139.35 E
Nakagō	94	36.58 N	138.14 E
Nakagusuku	174m	26.15 N	127.49 E
Nakagusuku-wan ⊂	174m	26.14 N	127.53 E
Nakagyō ◆[8]	270	35.01 N	135.45 E
Nakaheji	96	33.47 N	135.31 E
Nakai	94	35.20 N	139.14 E
Nakaizu	94	34.57 N	139.00 E
Nakajima, Nihon	94	37.07 N	136.51 E
Nakajima, Nihon	96	33.58 N	132.07 E
Nakajima, Nihon	268	35.26 N	139.56 E
Nakajima, Nihon	268	35.18 N	139.58 E
Naka-jima I	96	33.58 N	132.37 E
Nakajō, Nihon	92	38.03 N	139.24 E
Nakajō, Nihon	94	36.36 N	138.02 E
Nakakawane	94	35.03 N	138.05 E
Nāka Khārari	120	25.15 N	66.44 E
Nakalele Point ›	229a	21.02 N	156.35 W
Nākālia	126	24.02 N	89.40 E
Nakama, Nihon	96	33.50 N	130.43 E
Nakama, Nihon	174m	26.16 N	127.44 E
Nakaminato	94	36.21 N	140.36 E
Nakamura	96	32.59 N	132.56 E
Nakanai Mountains ⋏	164	5.35 S	151.10 E
Nakano, Nihon	94	36.45 N	138.22 E
Nakano, Nihon	268	35.20 N	139.54 E
Nakano, Nihon	270	34.58 N	135.58 E
Nakano ◆[8]	268	35.42 N	139.42 E
Nakanobu ◆[8]	268	35.36 N	139.43 E
Nakanojō	94	36.35 N	138.51 E
Nakano-shima I	93b	29.49 N	129.52 E
Nakanoshima-suidō I	93b	29.44 N	129.49 E
Nakanougan-jima I	175d	24.11 N	123.33 E
Nakaosu	174m	26.37 N	128.02 E
Nakaōzō ◆[8]	270	34.51 N	135.11 E
Nakape	140	5.47 N	28.37 E
Nakashibetsu	92a	43.33 N	144.59 E
Nākāsipāra	126	23.35 N	88.21 E
Nakasongola	154	1.19 N	32.28 E
Nakatō	268	35.45 N	139.24 E
Nakatomi, Nihon	94	35.28 N	138.26 E
Nakatomi, Nihon	268	35.49 N	139.30 E
Nakatosa	96	33.20 N	133.14 E
Nakatsu, Nihon	96	33.34 N	131.13 E
Nakatsu, Nihon	96	33.57 N	135.18 E
Nakatsu, Nihon	268	35.30 N	139.20 E
Nakatsu ≃	94	37.00 N	138.39 E
Nakatsue	96	33.08 N	130.56 E
Nakatsugawa	94	35.29 N	137.30 E
Nakatsumine-yama ∧	96	33.58 N	134.31 E
Nakauchigami	270	34.56 N	135.10 E
Naka-umi ⊂	96	35.28 N	133.12 E
Nakayama, Nihon	96	33.38 N	132.42 E
Nakayama, Nihon	96	35.31 N	133.35 E
Nakayama ◆[8]	268	35.31 N	139.33 E
Nakayama ≃	96	33.55 N	133.08 E
Nakazato, Nihon	94	36.05 N	138.50 E
Nakazato, Nihon	94	37.03 N	138.42 E
Nakazuma	268	35.58 N	139.35 E
Nakéty	175f	21.33 S	166.03 E
Nakfa	144	16.43 N	38.32 E
Nakhola	120	26.07 N	92.11 E
Nakhon Nayok	110	14.12 N	101.13 E
Nakhon Pathom	110	13.49 N	100.03 E
Nakhon Phanom	110	17.24 N	104.47 E
Nakhon Ratchasima	110	14.58 N	102.07 E
Nakhon Sawan	110	15.41 N	100.07 E
Nakhon Si Thammarat	110	8.26 N	99.58 E
Nakhon Thai	110	17.07 N	100.50 E
Nakhtarana	120	23.20 N	69.15 E
Nakina	176	50.10 N	86.42 W
Nakkaş ≃	267b	41.00 N	28.45 E
Nakło nad Notecią	30	53.08 N	17.35 E
Naknek	180	58.44 N	157.02 W
Naknek Lake ⊜	180	58.40 N	156.15 W
Nako	150	10.38 N	3.04 W
Nakodar	123	31.07 N	75.29 E
Nakonde	154	9.20 S	32.42 E
Nakoso-no-seki-ato ⊥	94	36.53 N	140.46 E
Nakou	100	27.09 N	117.38 E
Nakskov	41	54.50 N	11.09 E
Nakskov Fjord ⊂	41	54.50 N	11.02 E
Näkten ⊜	26	62.52 N	14.38 E
Naktong-gang ≃	98	35.07 N	128.57 E
Nakūr	124	29.55 N	77.18 E
Nakuru	154	0.17 S	36.04 E
Nakuru, Lake ⊜	154	0.22 S	36.05 E
Nakusp	182	50.15 N	117.48 W
Nāl ≃	120	26.02 N	65.19 E
Nālāgarh	123	31.03 N	76.43 E
Nalajch	88	47.45 N	107.16 E
Nālanda	124	25.07 N	85.25 E
Nalao	102	24.22 N	105.23 E
Nalázi	156	24.03 S	33.20 E
Nalbāri	120	26.25 N	91.26 E
Nalcayec, Isla I	254	46.06 S	73.49 W
Nalchik → Nal'čik	84	43.29 N	43.37 E
Nālchiti	124	22.38 N	90.17 E
Nal'čik	84	43.29 N	43.37 E
Naldānga	126	23.26 N	89.11 E
Nāldera	123	31.11 N	77.11 E
Näldsjön ⊜	26	63.23 N	14.17 E
Nałęczów	30	51.18 N	22.11 E
Nalgonda	122	17.03 N	79.16 E
Nalgora	126	22.52 N	90.39 E
Nalhāti	126	24.18 N	87.49 E
Naliagrām	126	23.36 N	89.37 E
Naliang	102	21.43 N	107.51 E
Nālikul	272b	22.49 N	88.11 E
Nalinnes	50	50.19 N	4.26 E
Nalisan	104	42.06 N	122.12 E
Nallamalla Hills ⋏	122	15.30 N	78.45 E
Nalles (Nals)	64	46.32 N	11.12 E
Nallıhan	130	40.11 N	31.21 E
Na Logu	64	46.23 N	13.45 E
Nalolo	152	15.35 S	23.07 E
Nalón ≃	34	43.32 N	6.04 W
Nalong	102	23.35 N	106.05 E
Nalusa	152	14.55 S	22.13 E
Nālūt	146	31.52 N	10.59 E
Nalžovské Hory	60	49.20 N	13.33 E
Nam ≃	110	21.33 N	98.38 E
Namaacha	156	25.58 S	32.01 E
Namachire	152	11.26 S	22.43 E
Namacunde	152	17.18 S	15.50 E
Namacurra	154	17.29 S	37.01 E
Namadgi National Park ♠	171b	35.09 S	148.57 E
Namak, Daryācheh-ye ⊜	128	34.30 N	51.50 E
Namak, Kavīr-e ◆[2]	128	34.45 N	57.45 E
Namakan Lake ⊜	190	48.27 N	92.35 W
Nāmakkal	122	11.14 N	78.10 E
Namaksār, Kowl-e ⊜	128	34.00 N	64.30 E
Namakula	174v	18.57 S	169.54 W
Namaland □[5]	156	25.50 S	18.00 E
Namamugi ◆[8]	268	35.29 N	139.41 E
Namanga	154	2.33 S	36.46 E
Namangan	85	41.00 N	71.40 E
Namanyere	154	7.31 S	31.03 E
Namapa	154	13.43 S	39.50 E
Namarodu, Cape ›	164	3.38 S	152.30 E
Namarrói	154	15.58 S	36.55 E
Namasagali	154	1.01 N	32.57 E
Namatanai	164	3.40 S	152.25 E
Nambe Indian Reservation ◆[4]	200	35.52 N	105.57 W
Namber	164	1.04 S	134.49 E
Nambi	162	28.54 S	121.41 E
Nambour	166	26.38 S	152.58 E
Nambouwalu	175g	16.59 S	178.42 E
Nambuangongo	152	8.01 S	14.12 E
Nambucca Heads	166	30.39 S	153.00 E
Nam Can	110	8.46 N	104.59 E
Namcha Barwa → Namjagbarwa Feng ∧	102	29.38 N	95.04 E
Namch'ang	98	35.26 N	129.16 E
Nam Co ⊜	120	30.42 N	90.30 E
Namdae-ch'ŏn ≃	98	40.26 N	128.57 E
Namdanak	85	41.11 N	69.42 E
Nam Dinh	110	20.25 N	106.10 E
Nämdö I	40	59.12 N	18.41 E
Nämdöfjärden ⊔	40	59.12 N	18.34 E
Nam Du, Quan Dao II	110	9.42 N	104.22 E
Namegawa	94	36.04 N	139.22 E
Nameh	112	2.34 N	116.21 E
Nameigos Lake ⊜	190	48.46 N	84.43 W
Namekagon ≃	190	46.05 N	92.06 W
Namen → Namur	56	50.28 N	4.52 E
Namerikawa	94	36.46 N	137.20 E
Náměšť	61	49.12 N	16.10 E
Námestovo	30	49.25 N	19.30 E
Nametil	154	15.43 S	39.21 E
Namew Lake ⊜	184	54.13 N	101.56 W
Nam-gang ≃	98	39.03 N	125.52 E
Namhae	98	34.50 N	127.54 E
Namhae-do I	98	34.48 N	127.57 E
Namhan-gang ≃	98	37.31 N	127.18 E
Namhkam	110	23.50 N	97.41 E
Namho-ri	98	38.07 N	125.10 E
Namhsan	110	22.58 N	97.10 E
Namiai	94	35.22 N	137.41 E
Namib Desert ◆[2]	156	23.00 S	15.00 E
Namibe	152	15.10 S	12.09 E
Namibe □[5]	152	15.20 S	12.30 E
Namibia (South West Africa) □[2], Afr.	138	22.00 S	17.00 E
Namibia (South West Africa) □[2], Afr.	156	22.00 S	17.00 E
Namibie → Namibia (South West Africa) □[2]	156	22.00 S	17.00 E
Namib-Naukluft Park ♠	156	23.30 S	15.30 E
Namie	92	37.29 N	141.00 E
Namies	158	29.18 S	19.13 E
Namīn	128	38.25 N	48.30 E
Naminga	88	56.33 N	118.41 E
Namjagbarwa Feng ∧	102	29.38 N	95.04 E
Nāmja La)(	124	29.27 N	82.34 E
Namji-ri	98	35.23 N	128.29 E
Nāmkhāna	126	21.46 N	88.14 E
Nam Kwo Chau I	271d	22.15 N	114.21 E
Namlan	110	22.15 N	97.24 E
Nāmlāng ≃	124	29.28 N	82.50 E
Namlea	164	3.18 S	127.06 E
Namling	120	29.41 N	89.04 E
Namlos	58	47.21 N	10.40 E
Nam Ngum Reservoir ⊜[1]	110	18.30 N	102.40 E
Namnoi, Khao ∧	110	10.36 N	98.38 E
Namo	112	1.24 S	119.57 E
Namoi ≃	166	30.00 S	148.07 E
Namoluk I[1]	14	5.55 N	153.08 E
Namonuito I[1]	14	8.46 N	150.02 E
Namorik I[1]	14	5.36 N	168.07 E
Namoruputh	154	4.34 N	35.57 E
Namounou	150	11.52 N	1.42 E
Namous, Oued en V	148	31.00 N	0.15 W
Namoya	154	4.01 S	27.34 E
Nampa, Ab., Can.	182	56.02 N	117.08 W
Nampa, Id., U.S.	202	43.32 N	116.33 W
Nampala	150	15.17 N	5.33 W
Nam Pat	110	17.43 N	100.41 E
Nampawng	110	22.45 N	97.52 E
Nam Phan □[9]	110	11.00 N	107.00 E
Nam Phong	110	16.42 N	102.52 E
Nampicuan	116	15.44 N	120.38 E
Namp'o	98	38.45 N	125.23 E
Nampont-Saint-Martin	50	50.21 N	1.45 E
Namp'ot'ae-san ∧	98	41.44 N	128.24 E
Nampuecha	154	13.59 S	40.18 E
Nampula	154	15.07 S	39.15 E
Nampula □[5]	154	15.00 S	39.00 E
Namsang	110	20.53 N	97.43 E
Namsan Park ♠	271b	37.34 N	126.59 E
Namsanyŏng-ni	98	38.59 N	127.26 E
Namsen ≃	24	64.27 N	11.28 E
Namsi	98	39.54 N	124.36 E
Namslau → Namysłów	30	51.05 N	17.42 E
Namsos	24	64.29 N	11.30 E
Nam Tok	110	14.14 N	99.04 E
Namtu	110	23.05 N	97.24 E
Namu	182	51.49 N	127.52 W
Namu I[1]	14	8.00 N	168.10 E
Namuka-I-Lau I	175g	18.51 S	178.38 W
Namúli, Serra ⋏	154	15.15 S	37.08 E
Namur, Bel.	56	50.28 N	4.52 E
Namur, P.Q., Can.	206	45.54 N	74.56 W
Namur □[4]	56	50.20 N	4.50 E
Namuruputh	154	4.34 N	35.57 E
Namutoni	156	18.49 S	16.55 E
Namwala	154	15.45 S	26.26 E
Namwera	154	14.22 S	35.30 E
Namwŏn	98	35.25 N	127.21 E
Namyang, C.M.I.K.	98	42.57 N	129.53 E
Namyang, Taehan	98	37.14 N	126.44 E
Namyit Island I	108	10.11 N	114.22 E
Namysłów	30	51.05 N	17.42 E
Nan	110	18.47 N	100.47 E
Nan ≃, Thai	110	15.42 N	100.09 E
Nan ≃, Zhg.	100	28.15 N	120.43 E
Nana ≃	152	5.00 N	15.50 E
Nana Barya ≃	146	7.59 N	17.43 E
Nana Barya, Réserve de Faune de la ◆[4]	146	7.30 N	17.30 E
Nanacamilpa	234	19.29 N	98.33 W
Nanaimo	224	49.10 N	123.56 W
Nanaimo ≃	224	49.08 N	123.54 W
Nanaimo Lakes ⊜	224	49.07 N	124.11 W
Nānakheri ◆[8]	272a	28.31 N	76.59 E
Nana Kru	150	4.50 N	8.44 W
Nanakuli	229c	21.23 N	158.09 W
Nanam	98	41.43 N	129.41 E
Nana-Mambéré □[5]	152	5.30 N	15.30 E
Nan'an	100	24.58 N	118.23 E
Nan'anba	107	28.46 N	104.38 E
Nanango	166	26.40 S	152.00 E
Nanantun	110	24.45 N	95.41 E
Nanao, Nihon	94	37.03 N	136.58 E
Nanao, T'aiwan	100	24.28 N	121.48 E
Nan'ao, Zhg.	100	23.27 N	117.02 E
Nan'ao Dao I	100	23.26 N	117.03 E
Nanao-wan ⊂	94	37.06 N	137.00 E
Nanas Channel ⊔	271c	1.25 N	103.58 E
Nanatsu-jima II	92	37.36 N	136.53 E
Nanatsuka	94	36.44 N	136.41 E
Nanay ≃	246	3.42 S	73.16 W
Nanba	102	32.20 N	104.58 E
Nanbaita	105	38.58 N	115.39 E
Nanbaixia	98	35.45 N	117.23 E
Nanbaozhen	106	31.32 N	121.37 E
Nanbu, Nihon	94	35.17 N	138.27 E
Nanbu, Zhg.	102	31.23 N	106.02 E
Nancaicun	105	39.28 N	117.01 E
Nancefield	273d	26.17 S	27.53 E
Nancha	89	47.08 N	129.19 E
Nanchang, Zhg.	100	28.41 N	115.53 E
Nanchang (Liantang), Zhg.	100	28.34 N	115.56 E
Nancheng, Zhg.	100	25.39 N	118.26 E
Nancheng, Zhg.	100	27.35 N	116.40 E
Nancheng → Hanzhong, Zhg.	102	33.08 N	107.02 E
Nanching → Nanjing	106	32.03 N	118.47 E
Nanchital	234	18.04 N	94.24 W
Nanchong	107	30.48 N	106.04 E
Nanchuan	102	29.08 N	107.07 E
Nanchuang	100	24.36 N	120.59 E
Nanch'ung → Nanchong	107	30.48 N	106.04 E
Nancowry Island I	110	7.59 N	93.32 E
Nancroix	62	45.32 N	6.46 E
Nancun, Zhg.	98	36.32 N	120.06 E
Nancun, Zhg.	98	39.46 N	114.07 E
Nancy	58	48.41 N	6.12 E
Nanda Devi ∧	124	30.23 N	79.59 E
Nāndāha	272b	22.50 N	88.17 E
Nandaime	236	11.46 N	86.03 W
Nanda Kot ∧	124	30.17 N	80.05 E
Nandan	96	34.15 N	134.43 E
Nandarivatu	175g	17.34 S	177.58 E
Nandashan	100	29.01 N	112.43 E
Nānded	122	19.09 N	77.20 E
Nāndgaon, India	122	20.19 N	74.39 E
Nāndgaon, India	272c	18.58 N	73.08 E
Nandi	175g	17.48 S	177.25 E
Nandi Bay ⊂	175g	17.44 S	177.25 E
Nandi Drug ∧	122	13.25 N	77.42 E
Nandigrām	126	22.01 N	87.58 E
Nandikotkūr	122	15.52 N	78.16 E
Nanding ≃, Asia	102	23.25 N	98.41 E
Nanding ≃, Asia	110	23.25 N	98.41 E
Nandlstadt	60	48.32 N	11.48 E
Nandom	150	10.51 N	2.45 W
N'andoma	24	61.40 N	40.12 E
Nandu	106	31.27 N	119.19 E
Nandu ≃	110	20.04 N	110.22 E
Nanduluohe	105	40.11 N	117.13 E
Nāndūra	122	20.50 N	76.27 E
Nandurbār	122	21.22 N	74.15 E
Nanduri	175g	16.27 S	179.09 E
Nandy	261	48.35 N	2.34 E
Nandyāl	122	15.29 N	78.29 E
Nanfangquan	106	31.26 N	120.16 E
Nanfen	104	41.06 N	123.44 E
Nanfeng, Zhg.	100	27.15 N	116.32 E
Nanfeng, Zhg.	100	29.16 N	116.32 E
Nangabadau	112	1.02 N	111.54 E
Nangade	154	11.05 S	39.36 E
Nanga Eboko	152	4.41 N	12.22 E
Nangahale	115b	8.34 S	122.32 E
Nangakelawit	112	0.23 N	112.26 E
Nāngal	123	31.24 N	76.14 E
Nangalangki	112	1.15 S	111.40 E
Nangalao Island I	116	11.27 N	120.11 E
Nangal Dewat ◆[8]	272a	28.33 N	77.06 E
Nangamau	112	0.06 S	111.55 E
Nangamesi, Teluk ⊂	115b	9.37 S	120.20 E
Nangamuntatai	112	0.22 S	112.23 E
Nangang	100	31.22 N	116.59 E
Nan Gang ⊂	100	23.30 N	117.00 E
Nan'gangwa	105	39.46 N	116.09 E
Nangaobat	112	0.57 N	113.13 E
Nangaocun	105	39.25 N	115.58 E
Nanga Parbat ∧	123	35.15 N	74.36 E
Nangapinoh	112	0.20 S	111.44 E
Nangaraun	112	0.38 N	113.11 E
Nangarhār □[4]	120	34.15 N	70.30 E
Nangatayap	112	1.32 S	110.34 E
Nangezhuang	105	39.31 N	116.23 E
Nanggala Hill ∧	175e	8.16 S	157.43 E
Nanggulan	115a	7.46 S	110.12 E
Nangi	272b	22.31 N	88.13 E
Nangin	110	10.31 N	98.31 E
Nangis	50	48.33 N	3.00 E
Nangka ≃	269f	14.41 N	121.06 E
Nanglal ≃	126	24.20 N	90.04 E
Nangloi ◆[8], India	272a	28.41 N	77.05 E
Nāngloi ◆[8], India	272a	28.40 N	77.02 E
Nangloi Jat ◆[8]	272a	28.41 N	77.04 E
Nangnim	98	40.58 N	127.08 E
Nangnim-sanmaek ⋏	98	40.00 N	127.00 E
Nangō, Nihon	92	31.32 N	131.23 E
Nangō, Nihon	94	37.13 N	139.33 E
Nangola	150	12.40 N	6.36 W
Nangoma	152	15.30 S	23.08 E
Nangong	98	37.24 N	115.22 E
Nangou	89	43.17 N	128.37 E
Nangō-yama-tunnel ◆[6]	94	35.12 N	139.10 E
Nangqên	102	32.22 N	96.21 E
Nang Rong	110	14.38 N	102.48 E
Nanguan	102	37.00 N	112.31 E
Nangweshi	152	16.26 S	23.17 E
Nanhai → Foshan	100	23.03 N	113.09 E
Nanhai → South China Sea ⊤[2]	108	10.00 N	113.00 E
Nanhe	98	37.01 N	114.41 E
Nanhedian	100	33.23 N	112.25 E
Nanhekan	107	30.24 N	103.27 E
Nanhezhao	105	39.05 N	115.56 E
Nanhsi	100	23.11 N	120.29 E
Nanhu	102	39.57 N	94.13 E
Nanhua	102	25.14 N	101.13 E
Nanhualou	104	42.30 N	123.53 E
Nanhuang	98	36.58 N	121.47 E
Nanhui	106	31.03 N	121.45 E
Nan Hulsan Hu ⊜	102	36.39 N	96.20 E
Nanhuta Shan ∧	100	24.22 N	121.26 E
Nanhutou	89	43.44 N	128.55 E
Nanika Lake ⊜	182	53.45 N	127.40 W
Naniwa ◆[8]	270	34.39 N	135.30 E
Nanjangūd	122	12.06 N	76.42 E
Nanjemoy	208	38.27 N	77.13 W
Nanjemoy Creek ⊂	208	38.25 N	77.07 W
Nanji I	100	27.28 N	121.04 E
Nanjiang, Zhg.	100	32.44 N	120.52 E
Nanjiang, Zhg.	102	32.33 N	107.30 E
Nanjiangqiao	100	28.58 N	113.44 E
Nanjie	107	29.11 N	105.00 E
Nanjing, Zhg.	100	24.41 N	114.25 E
Nanjing, Zhg.	100	24.32 N	117.22 E
Nanjing (Nanking), Zhg.	106	32.03 N	118.47 E
Nanjing, Zhg.	107	28.49 N	105.12 E
Nanjinyi	107	30.02 N	104.42 E
Nanjirinji	154	9.39 S	39.04 E
Nanjō	94	35.50 N	136.13 E
Nanjuma ≃	105	39.24 N	115.43 E
Nankan	96	33.03 N	130.32 E
Nankāna Sāhib	123	31.27 N	73.42 E
Nankang	100	25.42 N	114.44 E
Nankang ◆[8]	269d	25.03 N	121.36 E
Nankin	214	40.55 N	82.17 W
Nanking → Nanjing	106	32.03 N	118.47 E
Nanko-kōen ♠	94	37.05 N	140.14 E
Nankoku	96	33.39 N	133.44 E
Nankou	100	26.38 N	117.24 E
Nankouzhen	105	40.14 N	116.07 E
Nanku	106	31.06 N	120.37 E
Nankye	110	14.20 N	98.11 E
Nanle	98	36.04 N	115.10 E
Nanling, Zhg.	100	23.21 N	115.25 E
Nanling, Zhg.	100	30.56 N	118.20 E
Nanling, Zhg.	104	41.37 N	120.56 E
Nan Ling ⋏	90	25.00 N	112.00 E
Nanlinqiao	100	29.35 N	114.19 E
Nanliu ≃	102	21.38 N	109.00 E
Nanliucun	105	40.10 N	116.04 E
Nanlongba	102	28.02 N	107.31 E
Nanlou Shan ∧	89	43.27 N	126.42 E
Nanma	102	24.17 N	101.03 E
Nanmatang	106	32.18 N	120.38 E
Nanmeng	105	39.11 N	116.22 E
Nanmoku	94	36.10 N	138.44 E
Nannerch	262	53.13 N	3.15 W
Nannine	162	26.53 S	118.20 E
Nanning	102	22.48 N	108.20 E
Nanniwan	102	36.29 N	109.40 E
Nannō	94	35.13 N	136.36 E
Nannup	162	33.59 S	115.45 E
Nanny ≃	48	53.40 N	6.14 W
Na Noi	110	18.19 N	100.43 E
Nānole ◆[8]	272c	19.01 N	72.55 E
Nanoose Bay	224	49.16 N	124.12 W
Nanoose Harbour ⊂	224	49.20 N	124.10 W
Nanoshi	272c	18.56 N	73.05 E
Nanowin ≃	184	53.13 N	97.13 W
Nanpan ≃, Zhg.	102	25.07 N	106.00 E
Nanpan ≃, Zhg.	102	24.34 N	103.04 E
Nānpāra	124	27.52 N	81.30 E
Nanpengchang	107	29.21 N	106.38 E
Nanpi	98	38.02 N	116.42 E
Nanpiao	104	41.12 N	120.39 E
Nanping, Zhg.	89	43.24 N	129.05 E
Nanping, Zhg.	98	42.16 N	129.09 E
Nanping, Zhg.	100	26.38 N	118.10 E
Nanping, Zhg.	102	21.50 N	107.28 E
Nanping, Zhg.	102	33.07 N	104.20 E
Nanpingji	100	33.30 N	116.51 E
Nanpu	105	39.16 N	118.12 E
Nanpu ≃	100	27.02 N	118.18 E
Nanqingtuo	105	39.37 N	117.53 E
Nanqu	104	40.44 N	122.08 E
Nanquan	98	36.24 N	120.17 E
Nanri Dao I	100	25.13 N	119.30 E
Nansa ≃	34	43.22 N	4.29 W
Nansei	92	34.22 N	136.41 E
Nansei-shotō (Ryukyu Islands) II	90	26.30 N	128.00 E
Nansemond □[6]	208	36.43 N	76.40 W
Nansen, Lago ⊜	254	47.57 S	72.21 W
Nan Sha I	106	31.36 N	121.22 E
Nanshahe	98	35.03 N	117.12 E
Nanshan, Zhg.	100	26.38 N	118.20 E
Nanshan, Zhg.	105	39.21 N	115.34 E
Nanshan → Qilian Shan ⋏	102	39.06 N	98.40 E
Nanshanba	100	25.34 N	116.32 E
Nanshanchengzi	98	42.09 N	125.19 E
Nanshan Island I	108	10.45 N	115.49 E
Nanshankou	102	43.09 N	93.41 E
Nanshanlingcun	105	39.09 N	117.26 E
Nanshuang Dao I	100	26.35 N	120.08 E
Nanshui	100	22.02 N	113.16 E
Nansifa	105	39.27 N	116.27 E
Nansio	154	2.08 S	33.03 E
Nans-les-Pins	62	43.22 N	5.47 E
Nansunzhai	269b	31.21 N	121.27 E
Nant	32	44.01 N	3.18 E
Nant ≃	50	47.30 N	1.14 E
Nantai	104	40.55 N	122.47 E
Nantais, Lac ⊜	176	60.59 N	74.00 W
Nantai-san ∧	94	36.43 N	140.26 E
Nantai-zan ∧	94	36.46 N	139.29 E
Nantang	100	26.08 N	115.12 E
Nantangdun	106	31.15 N	120.56 E
Nantangmei	105	38.51 N	114.56 E
Nantasket Beach	283	42.16 N	70.52 W
Nantawarra	168b	34.00 S	138.14 E
Nant Bran ≃	42	51.57 N	3.28 W
Nanterre	50	48.53 N	2.12 E
Nantes	32	47.13 N	1.33 W
Nanteuil-le-Haudouin	50	49.08 N	2.48 E
Nanteuil-lès-Meaux	261	48.56 N	2.54 E
Nantian, Zhg.	100	27.57 N	119.56 E
Nantian, Zhg.	100	29.08 N	121.56 E
Nantianmen	104	40.56 N	123.04 E
Nanticoke, On., Can.	212	42.54 N	80.11 E
Nanticoke, Md., U.S.	208	38.16 N	75.54 W
Nanticoke, Pa., U.S.	210	41.12 N	76.00 W
Nanticoke ≃	208	38.16 N	75.56 W
Nanticoke Creek ≃, On., Can.	212	42.48 N	80.04 W
Nanticoke Creek ≃, N.Y., U.S.	210	42.05 N	76.05 W
Nantmeal Village	285	40.08 N	75.42 W
Nanto	92	34.20 N	136.31 E
Nanton	182	50.21 N	113.46 W
Nantong	106	32.02 N	120.53 E
Nant'ou, T'aiwan	100	23.55 N	120.41 E
Nantou, Zhg.	100	22.33 N	113.55 E
Nantouillet	261	49.00 N	2.42 E
Nantschang → Nanchang	100	28.41 N	115.53 E
Nantua	58	46.09 N	5.37 E
Nantuantingzhuang	105	40.17 N	118.17 E
Nantucket	207	41.17 N	70.06 W
Nantucket □[6]	207	41.17 N	70.06 W
Nantucket Island I	207	41.16 N	70.03 W
Nantucket Sound ⊔	207	41.30 N	70.15 W
Nantuego	154	11.21 S	38.24 E
Nantulo	154	12.17 S	39.03 E
Nantung → Nantong	106	32.02 N	120.53 E
Nantwich	44	53.04 N	2.32 W
Nanty Glo	214	40.28 N	78.50 W
Nant-y-Moch Reservoir ⊜[1]	42	52.27 N	3.50 W
Nanu	164	8.50 S	142.40 E
Nanuet	210	41.05 N	74.00 W
Nanuet Mall ◆[9]	276	41.06 N	74.01 W
Nanuku Passage ⊔	175g	16.45 S	179.15 W
Nanumanga I	14	6.18 S	176.20 E
Nanumea I[1]	14	5.39 S	176.08 E
Nanuque	255	17.50 S	40.21 W
Nānūr	126	23.42 N	87.52 E
Nanusa, Kepulauan II	108	4.42 N	127.06 E
Nanushuk ≃	180	69.18 N	151.00 W
Nanwan	100	32.09 N	113.57 E
Nan Wan ⊂	100	21.55 N	120.47 E
Nanwengkouzi	89	51.10 N	125.25 E
Nanwenquan	107	29.26 N	106.35 E
Nanxi, Zhg.	100	31.31 N	115.38 E
Nanxi, Zhg.	100	26.24 N	118.24 E
Nanxi, Zhg.	107	28.51 N	104.58 E
Nanxian	102	29.20 N	112.19 E
Nanxiang	106	31.17 N	121.18 E
Nanxikou	107	30.43 N	106.07 E
Nanxin, Zhg.	98	35.33 N	117.12 E
Nanxin, Zhg.	105	39.11 N	115.38 E
Nanxing Hu ⊜	106	31.08 N	120.48 E
Nanxinzhuang	98	36.39 N	115.15 E
Nanxiong	100	25.10 N	114.20 E
Nanxun	106	30.53 N	120.26 E
Nanya	100	26.52 N	118.19 E
Nanyandang Shan ∧	100	27.36 N	120.04 E
Nanyang, Zhg.	100	27.24 N	119.39 E
Nanyang, Zhg.	100	33.25 N	120.13 E
Nanyang, Zhg.	100	33.00 N	112.32 E
Nanyangcun	106	31.53 N	121.43 E
Nanyanggangzi	89	48.43 N	125.27 E
Nanyang Hu ⊜	98	35.12 N	116.41 E
Nanyang Shan ∧	106	31.20 N	120.28 E
Nanyang Technological Institute ᵾ[2]	271c	1.21 N	103.41 E
Nanyi Hu ⊜	106	31.07 N	118.57 E
Nan-yō	92	38.03 N	140.10 E
Nanyu	100	25.59 N	119.14 E
Nanyuan	105	39.48 N	116.23 E
Nanyuan Airport ⊠	271a	39.47 N	116.23 E
Nanyue	100	27.13 N	112.43 E
Nanyuki	154	0.01 N	37.04 E
Nanyulin	105	40.09 N	115.23 E
Nanzamu	98	41.56 N	124.23 E
Nanzha	106	31.51 N	120.15 E
Nanzhai	106	31.34 N	120.02 E
Nanzhang, Zhg.	102	31.50 N	111.41 E
Nanzhang, Zhg.	105	39.03 N	115.46 E
Nanzhao	100	33.30 N	112.27 E
Nanzhaoji	100	32.38 N	115.58 E
Nanzhen	100	26.59 N	119.57 E
Nanzhenjie	106	31.48 N	119.17 E
Nanzhila	154	16.05 S	26.07 E
Nanzhuang, Zhg.	105	40.22 N	116.21 E
Nanzhuang, Zhg.	105	40.43 N	114.58 E
Nao	152	4.35 N	15.09 E
Naoābād	272b	22.28 N	88.27 E
Naoāpāra	126	22.45 N	89.39 E
Naococane, Lac ⊜	176	52.52 N	70.40 W
Naoetsu	94	37.11 N	138.15 E
Naogaon	124	24.47 N	88.56 E
Naoiri	96	33.04 N	131.23 E
Naokot	120	24.51 N	69.27 E
Naoli ≃	89	47.20 N	134.10 E
Naolinco de Victoria	234	19.39 N	96.51 W
Não-me-Toque	252	28.28 S	52.49 W
Naong, Bukit ∧	112	2.40 N	112.45 E
Nāopāra	126	24.09 N	88.54 E
Naopukuria	272b	22.55 N	88.16 E
Naosap Lake ⊜	184	54.51 N	101.24 W
Naoshima	96	34.27 N	133.59 E
Naours	50	50.02 N	2.17 E
Náousa	38	40.37 N	22.05 E
Naozhou Dao I	102	20.57 N	110.34 E
Napa	226	38.17 N	122.17 W
Napa □[6]	226	38.18 N	122.17 W
Napa ≃	226	38.07 N	122.18 W
Napacao Point ›	116	9.43 N	124.31 E
Napajedla	30	49.10 N	17.31 E
Napakiak	180	60.42 N	161.57 W
Napaku	112	2.32 N	115.58 E
Na Pali Coast State Park ♠	229b	22.09 N	159.41 W
Napalkovo	74	70.03 N	73.47 E
Napamute	180	61.33 N	158.42 W
Napanee	212	44.15 N	76.57 W
Napanee ≃	212	44.12 N	77.02 W
Napanoch	210	41.44 N	74.22 W
Napareuli	84	42.03 N	45.31 E
Napas	86	59.53 N	81.58 E
Napaskiak	180	60.42 N	161.45 W
Napa Valley V	226	38.18 N	122.18 W
Napavine	224	46.34 N	122.54 W
Napayauan Island I	116	12.22 N	123.14 E
Napè	110	18.18 N	105.06 E
Napenay	252	26.44 S	60.37 W
Naperville	216	41.47 N	88.08 W
Napetipi ≃	186	51.21 N	58.08 W
Napf ∧	58	47.00 N	7.56 E
Napido	164	0.41 S	135.23 E
Napiéolédougou	150	9.18 N	5.35 W
Napier, N.Z.	172	39.29 S	176.55 E
Napier, S. Afr.	158	34.29 S	19.53 E
Napier, Mount ∧[2]	162	17.32 S	129.10 E
Napier Mountains ⋏	9	66.30 S	53.40 E
Napierville	206	45.11 N	73.25 W
Napierville □[6]	206	45.10 N	73.35 W
Napinka	184	49.17 N	100.50 W
Naplate	216	41.20 N	88.54 W
Naples → Napoli, It.	68	40.51 N	14.17 E
Naples, Fl., U.S.	220	26.08 N	81.47 W
Naples, Id., U.S.	202	48.34 N	116.23 W
Naples, Il., U.S.	219	39.45 N	90.36 W
Naples, N.Y., U.S.	210	42.36 N	77.24 W
Naples, Tx., U.S.	222	33.12 N	94.40 W
Naples Park	220	26.16 N	81.48 W
Napo	102	23.16 N	105.54 E
Napo □[4]	246	0.20 S	76.50 W
Napo ≃	246	3.20 S	72.40 W
Napola	70	37.59 N	12.38 E
Napoleon, In., U.S.	218	39.12 N	85.19 W
Napoleon, Ky., U.S.	218	38.46 N	84.47 W
Napoleon, Mi., U.S.	216	42.10 N	84.15 W
Napoleon, N.D., U.S.	198	46.30 N	99.46 W
Napoleon, Oh., U.S.	216	41.23 N	84.07 W
Napoleonville	194	29.56 N	91.01 W
Nápoles → Napoli	68	40.51 N	14.17 E
Napoli (Naples)	68	40.51 N	14.17 E
Napoli □[4]	68	40.53 N	14.25 E
Napoli, Golfo di ⊂	68	40.43 N	14.10 E
Napopo	154	4.12 N	28.02 E
Nappamerry	166	27.36 S	141.07 E
Nappanee	216	41.26 N	86.00 W
Nappan Island I	212	44.23 N	77.49 W
Napton on the Hill	42	52.15 N	1.24 W
Napu	115b	9.24 S	119.56 E
Napudalutai Shan ∧	89	51.06 N	122.13 E
Naqādah	140	25.54 N	32.43 E
Naqadeh	128	36.57 N	45.23 E
Naqb, Ra's an- ∧	132	29.50 N	35.40 E
Nar ≃	42	52.45 N	0.24 E
Nara, Mali	150	15.10 N	7.17 W
Nara, Nihon	96	34.41 N	135.50 E
Nara □[5]	96	34.30 N	135.50 E
Nāra ≃, Pāk.	120	24.07 N	69.07 E
Nara ≃, S.S.S.R.	82	54.53 N	37.26 E
Nara-bonchi ≚[1]	270	34.38 N	135.50 E
Naracoorte	166	36.58 S	140.44 E
Naradhan	166	33.37 S	146.19 E
Narai ≃	94	36.20 N	137.55 E
Narāil	126	23.10 N	89.30 E
Naraina ◆[8]	272a	28.37 N	77.08 E
Naraini	124	25.11 N	80.29 E
Narainpur	126	24.03 N	86.36 E
Narakawa	94	35.59 N	137.50 E
Naramata	182	49.36 N	119.35 W
Naran	88	48.34 N	98.17 E
Naran Bulag	86	49.22 N	92.33 E
Nārang	123	31.54 N	74.31 E
Narangba	171a	27.12 S	152.58 E
Naranja	220	25.31 N	80.25 W
Naranjal, Ec.	246	2.42 S	79.37 W
Naranjal, Perú	286d	11.58 S	77.06 W
Naranjal, Ven.	286c	10.28 N	67.02 W
Naranjito, Hond.	236	14.57 N	88.41 W
Naranjito, P.R.	240m	18.18 N	66.15 W
Naranjo	236	10.06 N	84.22 W
Naranjo ≃	236	14.30 N	92.11 W
Naranjo, Río del ≃	234	18.54 N	103.37 W
Naranjo Islands II	116	12.23 N	124.03 E
Naranjos	234	21.21 N	97.41 W
Narao	92	32.50 N	129.04 E
Nara Park ♠	270	34.41 N	135.52 E
Narasannapeta	122	18.25 N	84.03 E
Narasapur	122	16.27 N	81.40 E
Narasaraopet	122	16.15 N	80.04 E
Narashino	94	35.41 N	140.02 E
Narasun	88	50.06 N	112.58 E
Narat	86	43.28 N	83.44 E
Narathiwat	110	6.26 N	101.50 E
Nara Visa	196	35.36 N	103.05 W
Nara Women's University ᵾ[2]	270	34.42 N	135.49 E
Nārāyanganj	124	23.37 N	90.30 E
Nārāyaṇī □[8]	124	27.15 N	85.00 E
Nārāyaṇi ≃	124	25.39 N	85.13 E
Nārāyanpāra	272b	22.54 N	88.19 E
Nārāyanpet	122	16.44 N	77.30 E
Nārāyanpur	272b	22.29 N	88.34 E
Narazeni	84	42.27 N	41.57 E
Narberth, Wales, U.K.	42	51.48 N	4.45 W
Narberth, Pa., U.S.	285	40.00 N	75.15 W
Narbonne	32	43.11 N	3.00 E
Narcao	71	39.10 N	8.40 E
Narcea ≃	34	43.28 N	6.06 W
Narcondam Island I	110	13.20 N	94.16 E
Narcosli Creek ≃	182	52.49 N	122.28 W
Nardò	68	40.11 N	18.02 E
Nare ≃	246	6.12 N	74.35 W
Narellan	170	34.02 S	150.44 E
Narembeen	162	32.04 S	118.24 E
Narenbulake	89	49.52 N	120.23 E
Narendranagar	124	30.10 N	78.18 E
Nares Strait ⊔	16	80.30 N	68.00 W
Naretha	162	31.00 S	124.50 E
Narew ≃	30	52.26 N	20.42 E
Nargund	122	15.43 N	75.23 E
Narhan	272c	19.08 N	73.07 E
Nāri ≃	120	28.35 N	67.50 E
Naria	124	23.18 N	90.25 E
Nariai	270	34.53 N	135.38 E
Nariel	171b	36.26 S	147.50 E
Narijn ≃	88	50.20 N	93.24 E
Narijnteel	102	45.57 N	101.29 E
Nārikelbāria	126	23.17 N	89.21 E
Nariman	85	40.34 N	72.48 E
Narimanabad	84	38.53 N	48.52 E
Narimba, Her Majesty's Air Station (Royal Australian Navy Airfield) ■	274a	33.43 S	150.53 E
Narin ≃	120	36.54 N	92.51 E
Narince	130	37.52 N	38.46 E
Narinda, Baie de ⊂	157b	14.55 S	47.30 E
Nariño □[5]	246	1.30 N	78.00 W
Narita	94	35.47 N	140.19 E
Nariwa	96	34.47 N	133.33 E
Nariwa ≃	96	34.46 N	133.36 E
Narizón, Punta ›	232	27.52 N	110.54 W
Nar'jan-Mar	24	67.39 N	53.00 E
Nārkanda	123	31.16 N	77.27 E
Narkatiāganj	124	27.06 N	84.28 E
Närke □[9]	40	59.06 N	15.03 E
Närkes Marieberg	40	59.12 N	15.10 E
Narlı	130	37.27 N	37.09 E
Narma	80	54.46 N	42.01 E
Narmada ≃	120	21.38 N	72.36 E
Narmada Valley V	124	22.30 N	77.00 E
Narmak ◆[8]	267d	35.43 N	51.29 E
Narman	130	40.21 N	41.52 E
Narmušad'	80	54.40 N	41.07 E
Nar-Nar-Goon	169	38.05 S	145.34 E
Nārnaul	124	28.03 N	76.07 E
Narni	66	42.31 N	12.31 E
Naro	70	37.18 N	13.47 E
Naro ≃	70	37.14 N	13.37 E
Naroč' ≃	76	54.26 N	26.39 E
Naroč', ozero ⊜	76	54.52 N	26.45 E
Narodiči	78	51.13 N	29.03 E
Narodnaja, gora ∧	24	65.04 N	60.09 E
Naro-Fominsk	82	55.23 N	36.43 E
Naro Island I	116	11.53 N	123.40 E
Narok	154	1.05 S	35.52 E
Narol	30	50.22 N	23.21 E
Narón	34	43.32 N	8.10 W
Narooma	166	36.14 S	150.03 E
Naro-Osakovo	82	55.33 N	36.33 E
Narovčat	80	53.52 N	43.41 E
Narovl'a	78	51.48 N	29.29 E
Nārowāl	123	32.06 N	74.53 E
Närpes (Närpiö)	26	62.28 N	21.20 E
Närpiö → Närpes	26	62.28 N	21.20 E
Narrabeen	170	33.43 S	151.18 E
Narrabeen Lagoon ⊂	274a	33.43 S	151.17 E
Narrabri	166	30.19 S	149.47 E
Narragansett	207	41.25 N	71.27 W
Narragansett Bay ⊂	207	41.40 N	71.20 W
Narran ≃	166	29.45 S	147.20 E
Narra Narra ∧	171b	35.50 S	147.27 E
Narrandera	166	34.45 S	146.33 E
Narraway ≃	182	54.48 N	119.56 W
Narraweena	274a	33.45 S	151.16 E
Narre Warren	274b	38.02 S	145.19 E
Narre Warren North	274b	37.59 S	145.19 E
Narrogin	162	32.56 S	117.10 E
Narromine	166	32.14 S	148.15 E
Narrows, Md., U.S.	208	38.58 N	76.15 W
Narrows, Va., U.S.	192	37.19 N	80.48 W
Narrowsburg	210	41.36 N	75.03 W
Närsen ⊜	40	60.17 N	14.23 E
Narsimhapur	124	22.57 N	79.12 E
Narsinghdi	124	23.55 N	90.43 E
Narsinghgarh	124	23.42 N	77.06 E
Narsīpatnam	122	17.40 N	82.37 E
Narskije Prudy, ozero ⊜[1]	82	55.32 N	36.36 E
Narssaq	176	60.54 N	46.00 W
Nartkala	84	43.33 N	43.50 E
Nartuby ≃	62	43.28 N	6.34 E
Naru	92	32.49 N	128.56 E
Narubis, Namibia	158	26.55 S	18.35 E
Narubis, Namibia	158	27.10 S	19.05 E
Naruko	92	38.44 N	140.43 E
Naruksovo	80	54.37 N	44.33 E
Naruo	270	34.43 N	135.23 E
Narusawa	94	35.29 N	138.41 E
Narutō, Nihon	94	35.36 N	140.25 E
Naruto, Nihon	96	34.11 N	134.37 E
Naruto-kaikyō ⊔	96	34.14 N	134.39 E
Narva, S.S.S.R.	76	59.23 N	28.12 E
Narva, S.S.S.R.	86	55.25 N	93.39 E
Narva ≃	76	59.27 N	28.02 E
Narvacan	116	17.25 N	120.28 E
Narva-Jõesuu	76	59.27 N	28.03 E
Narvan	85	40.15 N	67.12 E
Narvik	24	68.26 N	17.25 E
Narvskij zaliv (Narva laht) ⊂	76	59.30 N	27.40 E
Narvskoje vodochranilišče ⊜[1]	76	59.18 N	28.14 E
Narwāna	124	29.37 N	76.07 E
Narwietooma	162	23.15 S	132.35 E
Narym	86	58.58 N	81.30 E
Naryn, S.S.S.R.	85	41.26 N	75.59 E
Naryn, S.S.S.R.	88	50.13 N	96.27 E
Naryn □[4]	85	41.30 N	75.30 E
Naryn ≃	85	40.54 N	71.45 E
Narynkol	72	42.43 N	80.12 E
Naryntau, gory ⋏	85	41.25 N	76.50 E
Naryškino	76	52.58 N	35.44 E
Naryū-zaki ›	96	35.36 N	135.28 E
Narzole	62	44.35 N	7.52 E
Nås, Sve.	40	60.27 N	14.29 E
Näs, Sve.	40	58.41 N	15.50 E
Nasadkino	82	56.29 N	37.21 E
Näsåker	26	63.26 N	16.54 E
Na San, Thai	110	8.48 N	99.22 E
Na San, Viet.	110	21.12 N	104.02 E
Nasarawa	150	8.30 N	7.40 E
Năsăud	38	47.17 N	24.24 E
Nasawa	175f	15.13 S	168.09 E
NASA Wallops Station ᵾ[3]	208	37.52 N	75.28 W
Nasbinals	32	44.40 N	3.03 E
Naschel	252	32.55 S	65.23 W
Nase → Naze	93b	28.23 N	129.30 E
Naseby, N.Z.	172	45.02 S	170.09 E
Naseby, Eng., U.K.	42	52.25 N	0.58 W
Naselle	224	46.21 N	123.48 W
Naselle ≃	224	46.25 N	123.55 W
Nash	194	33.27 N	94.08 W
Nashawena Island I	207	41.26 N	70.53 W
Nāshik	122	19.59 N	73.48 E
Nashoba Brook ≃	283	42.28 N	71.24 W
Nashport	214	40.04 N	82.09 W
Nashū', Wādī an- V	146	26.25 N	14.15 E
Nashua, Ia., U.S.	190	42.57 N	92.32 W
Nashua, Mt., U.S.	202	48.07 N	106.21 W
Nashua, N.H., U.S.	207	42.45 N	71.28 W
Nashua ≃	207	42.46 N	71.27 W
Nashuixi	102	30.09 N	108.40 E
Näshultasjön ⊜	40	59.14 N	16.21 E
Nashville, On., Can.	275b	43.50 N	79.40 W

≃ River	Fluß	Río	Rivière	Rio
≍ Canal	Kanal	Canal	Canal	Canal
⌞ Waterfall, Rapids	Wasserfall, Stromschnellen	Cascada, Rápidos	Chute d'eau, Rapides	Cascata, Rápidos
⊔ Strait	Meeresstraße	Estrecho	Détroit	Estreito
⊂ Bay, Gulf	Bucht, Golf	Bahía, Golfo	Baie, Golfe	Baía, Golfo
⊜ Lake, Lakes	See, Seen	Lago, Lagos	Lac, Lacs	Lago, Lagos
⩸ Swamp	Sumpf	Pantano	Marais	Pântano
⍓ Ice Features, Glacier	Eis- und Gletscherformen	Accidentes Glaciales	Formes glaciaires	Acidentes glaciares
⊤ Other Hydrographic Features	Andere Hydrographische Objekte	Otros Elementos Hidrográficos	Autres données hydrographiques	Outros acidentes hidrográficos

✦ Submarine Features	Untermeerische Objekte	Accidentes Submarinos	Formes de relief sous-marin	Acidentes submarinos
□ Political Unit	Politische Einheit	Unidad Politica	Entité politique	Unidade política
ᵾ Cultural Institution	Kulturelle Institution	Institución Cultural	Institution culturelle	Instituição cultural
⊥ Historical Site	Historische Stätte	Sitio Histórico	Site historique	Sitio histórico
♠ Recreational Site	Erholungs- und Ferienort	Sitio de Recreo	Centre de loisirs	Area de Lazer
⊠ Airport	Flughafen	Aeropuerto	Aéroport	Aeroporto
■ Military Installation	Militäranlage	Instalación Militar	Installation militaire	Instalação militar
◆ Miscellaneous	Verschiedenes	Misceláneo	Divers	Diversos

ENGLISH / DEUTSCH

Name	Page	Lat.°′	Long.°′
Nashville, Ar., U.S.	194	33.56 N	93.50 W
Nashville, Ga., U.S.	192	31.12 N	83.15 W
Nashville, Il., U.S.	219	38.20 N	89.22 W
Nashville, In., U.S.	218	39.12 N	86.15 W
Nashville, Mi., U.S.	216	42.36 N	85.05 W
Nashville, N.C., U.S.	192	35.58 N	77.57 W
Nashville, Oh., U.S.	214	40.36 N	82.07 W
Nashville, Tn., U.S.	194	36.09 N	86.47 W
Nashwaak ≃	186	45.57 N	66.37 W
Nashwaaksis	186	45.59 N	66.39 W
Nashwah	142	30.30 N	31.29 E
Nashwauk	190	47.22 N	93.10 W
Nasia	150	10.09 N	0.48 W
Naṣīb	132	32.33 N	36.11 E
Našice	38	45.29 N	18.06 E
Nasielsk	30	52.36 N	20.48 E
Näsijärvi ⊜	26	61.37 N	23.42 E
Nāṣir	140	8.36 N	33.04 E
Nāṣir, Buḥayrat (Lake Nasser) ⊜[1]	140	22.40 N	32.00 E
Nasīrābād, India	120	26.18 N	74.44 E
Nasīrābād, Pāk.	120	28.23 N	68.24 E
Naskaftym	80	52.57 N	45.38 E
Naskaupi ≃	176	53.45 N	60.50 W
Näsnaren ⊜	40	58.51 N	16.18 E
Naso	70	38.07 N	14.47 E
Nasondoye	154	10.22 S	25.06 E
Naso Point ›	116	10.25 N	121.57 E
Nasorolevu ∧	175g	16.38 S	178.42 E
Nasosnyj	84	40.37 N	49.34 E
Naṣr	142	30.36 N	30.23 E
Naṣrābād	128	34.08 N	51.26 E
Naṣrānī, Jabal an- ∧	130	34.06 N	37.24 E
Nasriddinbek	85	40.41 N	71.55 E
Nāsriganj	124	25.03 N	84.20 E
Nass ≃	182	55.00 N	129.50 W
Nassau, Ba.	240b	25.05 N	77.21 W
Nassau, B.R.D.	56	50.19 N	7.47 E
Nassau, D.D.R.	54	50.46 N	13.32 E
Nassau, N.Y., U.S.	210	42.30 N	73.36 W
Nassau □[6]	210	40.45 N	73.38 W
Nassau, Bahía c	254	55.25 S	67.40 W
Nassau Bay	222	29.32 N	95.05 W
Nassau Coliseum ♦	276	40.43 N	73.36 W
Nassau International Airport ⊠	240b	25.02 N	77.28 W
Nassau Island I	14	11.33 S	165.25 W
Nassau Shores	276	40.39 N	73.26 W
Nassawadox	208	37.28 N	75.51 W
Nassawango Creek ≃	208	38.10 N	75.25 W
Nassenfels	60	48.48 N	11.16 E
Nassenheide	54	52.49 N	13.12 E
Nasser, Lake → Nāṣir, Buḥayrat ⊜[1]	140	22.40 N	32.00 E
Nassereith	58	47.19 N	10.50 E
Nassian	150	8.27 N	3.29 W
Nässjö	26	57.39 N	14.41 E
Nastapoca ≃	176	56.55 N	76.33 W
Nastapoka Islands II	176	57.00 N	76.50 W
Nastasjino	82	54.28 N	38.16 E
Nastaška	78	49.39 N	30.19 E
Nastätten	56	50.12 N	7.51 E
Nastauli	272a	28.43 N	77.22 E
Nastf, Bi'r ▼[4]	142	30.18 N	30.28 E
Nasu	94	37.01 N	140.07 E
Nasu-dake ∧, Nihon	92	37.07 N	139.58 E
Nasu-dake ∧, Nihon	94	37.09 N	139.58 E
Nasugbu	116	14.05 N	120.38 E
Nasukoin Mountain ∧	202	48.48 N	114.35 W
Nasva	76	56.35 N	30.10 E
Nat ≃	190	48.48 N	82.07 W
Nata, Bots.	156	20.12 S	26.12 E
Natá, Pan.	236	8.20 N	80.31 W
Nata ≃	156	20.14 S	26.10 E
Natagaima	246	3.37 N	75.06 W
Nātāgarh	272b	22.42 N	88.25 E
Natal, Bra.	250	5.47 S	35.13 W
Natal, B.C., Can.	182	49.44 N	114.50 W
Natal, Indon.	110	0.33 N	99.07 E
Natal □[4]	158	28.40 S	30.40 E
Natal Basin ✢[1]	10	30.00 S	40.00 E
Natalia	196	29.11 N	98.51 W
Nataljevka	83	47.10 N	38.29 E
Nataljin Jar	80	51.46 N	50.35 E
Nataljino	80	52.56 N	49.02 E
Natalkuz Lake ⊜	182	53.26 N	125.20 W
Natalspruit ≃	273d	26.19 S	28.10 E
Natanes Plateau ⋀[1]	200	33.35 N	110.15 W
Natash, Wādī V	140	24.25 N	33.26 E
Natashō	96	35.24 N	135.38 E
Natashquan	186	50.12 N	61.49 W
Natashquan ≃	176	50.06 N	61.49 W
Natashquan, Pointe de ›	186	50.06 N	61.44 W
Natashquan Est ≃	186	51.20 N	61.40 W
Natchez	194	31.33 N	91.24 W
Natchez Trace Parkway ♦	194	32.00 N	91.00 W
Natchitoches	194	31.45 N	93.05 W
Natco Lake ⊜	276	40.26 N	74.09 W
Natércia	256	22.07 S	45.30 W
Naters	58	46.20 N	7.59 E
Natewa Bay c	175g	16.35 S	179.40 E
Na Thawi	110	6.45 N	100.42 E
Nāthdwāra	120	24.56 N	73.49 E
Nathia Gali	123	34.04 N	73.24 E
Nathkaw	102	26.53 N	96.13 E
Nathula I	175g	16.53 S	177.25 E
Natick	207	42.17 N	71.21 W
Natick Laboratories ■	283	42.17 N	71.22 W
Natimuk	166	36.45 S	141.57 E
Nation ≃	182	55.28 N	123.35 W
National Agricultural Research Center ʋ[3]	284c	39.02 N	76.52 W
National Airport ⊠	281	42.19 N	83.25 W
National Arboretum ♦	284c	38.54 N	76.58 W
National Assembly ʋ	269a	13.46 N	100.31 E
National Baseball Hall of Fame and Museum ʋ	210	42.42 N	74.57 W
National City	228	32.40 N	117.05 W
National Gallery ʋ	260	51.31 N	0.08 W
National Institute of Health ʋ	284c	39.00 N	77.06 W
National Maritime Museum ʋ	260	51.29 N	0.00
National Park	285	39.51 N	75.10 W
National Taiwan Normal University ʋ[2]	269d	25.02 N	121.31 E
National Taiwan University ʋ[2]	269d	25.01 N	121.32 E
National Zoological Park ♦	284c	38.56 N	77.03 W
Natipi, Lac ⊜	186	51.27 N	71.23 W
Natisone ≃	64	45.57 N	13.22 E
Natitingou	150	10.19 N	1.22 E
Native Bay c	176	63.52 N	82.30 W
Natividade	250	11.43 S	47.47 W
Natividade da Serra	256	23.24 S	45.26 W
Natívitas ◂[8]	286a	19.14 N	99.05 W
Nativity, Church of the ʋ[1]	132	31.43 N	35.12 E
Natkyizin	110	14.55 N	97.57 E
Natl	132	31.39 N	35.52 E
Natoma	198	39.11 N	99.01 W
Natong	102	23.01 N	107.50 E
Nator	124	24.25 N	88.59 E
Natori	92	38.08 N	140.55 E
Natorp	263	51.30 N	7.38 E
Natron, Lake ⊜	154	2.25 S	36.00 E
Natrona Heights	214	40.37 N	79.43 W
Naṭrūn, Wādī an- ±[7]	142	30.25 N	30.13 E
Natsui ≃	94	37.03 N	140.59 E
Nattai ≃	170	34.05 S	150.25 E
Nattai River	170	34.04 S	150.27 E
Nattam	122	10.14 N	78.14 E
Nåttarö I	40	58.52 N	18.07 E
Nattaset ∧	24	68.12 N	27.20 E
Nattaung ∧	110	18.48 N	97.02 E
Natters	64	47.14 N	11.22 E
Nattwerder	264a	52.26 N	12.56 E
Natuchajevskaja	78	44.54 N	37.34 E
Nātudaha	126	23.39 N	88.41 E
Natukanaoka Pan ≚	156	18.40 S	15.45 E
Natuna Besar I	112	4.00 N	108.15 E
Natuna Besar, Kepulauan II	112	4.40 N	108.00 E
Natuna Selatan, Kepulauan II	112	2.45 N	109.00 E
Natural Bridge	212	44.04 N	75.29 W
Natural Bridge ♦	192	37.38 N	79.33 W
Natural Bridges National Monument ♦	200	37.30 N	110.08 W
Natural Bridge State Resort Park ♦	192	37.47 N	83.42 W
Naturaliste, Cape ›	162	33.32 S	115.01 E
Naturaliste Channel ⊔	162	25.25 S	113.00 E
Naturita	200	38.13 N	108.34 W
Naturita Creek ≃	200	38.13 N	108.32 W
Naturno (Naturns)	64	46.39 N	11.00 E
Natzungen	52	51.36 N	9.14 E
Nau	85	40.09 N	69.22 E
Nau, Cap de la ›	34	38.44 N	0.14 E
Naucalpan → Ciudad de Naucalpan de Juárez	286a	19.28 N	99.14 W
Naucalpan □[7]	286a	19.26 N	99.17 W
Naucelle	32	44.12 N	2.20 E
Naučnyj	78	44.44 N	34.01 E
Naude	272c	19.03 N	73.06 E
Nauders	58	46.53 N	10.30 E
Nauen	54	52.36 N	12.52 E
Nauener Luch ≡	264a	52.37 N	12.55 E
Nauener Stadtforst ♦	264a	52.38 N	12.58 E
Naugachhia	124	25.24 N	87.06 E
Naugatuck	207	41.30 N	73.05 W
Naugatuck ≃	207	41.19 N	73.05 W
Naughton	190	46.24 N	81.12 W
Naugol'noje	82	56.22 N	38.11 E
Naui	140	18.28 N	30.43 E
Naujamiestis	76	55.41 N	24.04 E
Naujan	116	13.20 N	121.18 E
Naujan, Lake ⊜	116	13.10 N	121.21 E
Naujoji Akmenė	76	56.19 N	22.55 E
Naukan	180	66.01 N	169.43 W
Naulavaara ∧[2]	26	63.53 N	28.13 E
Naulila	152	17.12 S	14.42 E
Naumburg, B.R.D.	56	51.15 N	9.10 E
Naumburg, D.D.R.	54	51.09 N	11.48 E
Naumburg am Queiss → Nowogrodziec	30	51.12 N	15.25 E
Naumovščina	76	58.23 N	28.20 E
Naunak	86	59.00 N	80.13 E
Naundorf	54	50.56 N	13.25 E
Naunglon	110	16.48 N	97.45 E
Naungpale	110	19.33 N	97.08 E
Naunhof	54	51.16 N	12.35 E
Naupada ◂[8]	272c	19.04 N	72.50 E
Ñaupe	248	5.36 S	79.54 W
Nā'ūr	132	31.53 N	35.50 E
Nauraushaun Brook ≃	276	41.03 N	73.59 W
Nauroth	56	50.42 N	7.52 E
Nauroz Kalāt	128	28.47 N	65.38 E
Naurskaja	84	43.38 N	45.19 E
Nauru □[1], Oc.	14	0.32 S	166.55 E
Nauru □[1], Oc.	174b	0.32 S	166.55 E
Naurzumskij zapovednik ♦	86	52.30 N	64.20 E
Naushahro Fīroz	120	26.50 N	68.07 E
Naushon Island I	207	41.29 N	70.45 W
Nauški	88	50.28 N	106.07 E
Nausori	175g	18.02 S	178.32 E
Naussac, Barrage de ◂[6]	62	44.46 N	3.49 E
Naustdal	26	61.31 N	5.43 E
Nauta	246	4.32 S	73.33 W
Nautanwa	124	27.26 N	83.25 E
Nautilus Park	207	41.22 N	72.05 W
Nautla	234	20.13 N	96.47 W
Nautla ≃	234	20.15 N	96.47 W
Nauvoo	190	40.33 N	91.23 W
Nava	232	28.25 N	100.46 W
Nava, Arroyo de la ≃	266a	40.31 N	3.46 W
Nava, Colle di)(	62	44.05 N	7.53 E
Nava del Rey	34	41.20 N	5.05 W
Navadwip	126	23.25 N	88.22 E
Navahermosa	34	39.38 N	4.28 W
Navajo	200	35.55 N	109.01 W
Navajo ≃	200	37.01 N	107.10 W
Navajo Creek ≃	200	36.59 N	111.24 W
Navajo Hopi Joint Use Area ◂[4]	200	36.15 N	110.30 W
Navajo Indian Reservation ◂[4]	200	36.25 N	110.00 W
Navajo Mountain ∧	200	37.02 N	110.52 W
Navajo National Monument ♦	200	36.40 N	110.33 W
Navajo Reservoir ⊜[1]	200	36.55 N	107.30 W
Naval	116	11.34 N	124.23 E
Navalmoral de la Mata	34	39.54 N	5.32 W
Naval Ordnance Test Station ■	228	35.32 N	117.05 W
Navalvillar de Pela	34	39.06 N	5.28 W
Navan	48	53.39 N	6.41 W
Navāpur	122	21.09 N	73.48 E
Navarin, mys ›	180	62.16 N	179.10 E
Navarino → Pílos	38	36.55 N	21.43 E
Navarino, Isla I	254	55.05 S	67.40 W
Navarra □[4]	34	42.40 N	1.30 W
Navarre, Austl.	169	36.54 S	143.07 E
Navarre, Oh., U.S.	214	40.43 N	81.31 W
Navarro	258	35.01 S	59.16 W
Navarro □[6]	222	32.05 N	96.30 W
Navarro ≃	204	39.11 N	123.45 W
Navarro, Cañada ≃	258	35.00 S	59.18 W
Navarro, Laguna ⊜	258	35.01 S	59.18 W
Navarro Mills Lake ⊜[1]	222	31.56 N	96.45 W
Navašino	80	55.32 N	42.12 E
Navasota	222	30.23 N	96.05 W
Navasota ≃	222	30.20 N	96.09 W
Navassa	192	34.15 N	78.00 W
Navassa Island I	238	18.24 N	75.01 W
Nave	64	45.35 N	10.17 E
Nävekvarn	40	58.38 N	16.49 E
Navenne	58	47.36 N	6.10 E
Naver ≃	46	58.32 N	4.15 W
Naver, Loch ⊜	46	58.17 N	4.23 W
Navesink	276	40.23 N	74.02 W
Navesink River c	276	40.23 N	73.58 W
Navesnoje	76	52.17 N	37.57 E
Nâves-Parmelan	58	45.56 N	6.11 E
Navesti ≃	76	58.30 N	24.54 E
Navestock	260	51.39 N	0.13 E
Navestock Side	260	51.39 N	0.16 E
Navia, Arg.	252	34.47 S	66.35 W
Navia, Esp.	34	43.32 N	6.43 W
Navia ≃	34	43.33 N	6.44 W
Navidad, Chile	252	33.57 S	71.50 W
Navidad, Méx.	234	20.35 N	104.42 W
Navidad ≃	196	28.41 N	96.35 W
Navidad, Bahía c	234	19.12 N	104.43 W
Navidad Bank ✢[3]	238	20.00 N	68.50 W
Navio, Riacho do ≃	250	8.39 S	38.36 W
Naviraí	255	23.08 S	54.13 W
Navis	64	47.07 N	11.32 E
Naviti I	175g	17.07 S	177.15 E
Navl'a	76	52.51 N	34.30 E
Navl'a ≃	76	52.42 N	34.01 E
Năvodari	38	44.19 N	28.36 E
Navoi	72	40.15 N	65.15 E
Navojoa	232	27.06 N	109.26 W
Navolato	232	24.47 N	107.42 W
Navoloki	80	57.28 N	41.59 E
Navotas	269f	14.39 N	120.57 E
Návpaktos	38	38.23 N	21.50 E
Návplion	38	37.34 N	22.48 E
Navrongo	150	10.54 N	1.06 W
Navsāri	120	20.51 N	72.55 E
Navua	175g	18.14 S	178.10 E
Navy Island I	284a	43.04 N	79.01 W
Navy Pier ◂[5]	278	41.53 N	87.36 W
Navy Yard City	224	47.32 N	122.41 W
Nawa, Nihon	96	35.30 N	133.30 E
Nawa → Naha, Nihon	174m	26.13 N	127.40 E
Nawá, Sūrīy.	132	32.53 N	36.03 E
Nawābganj, Bngl.	124	24.36 N	88.17 E
Nawābganj, Bngl.	126	23.40 N	90.10 E
Nawābganj, India	124	28.33 N	79.38 E
Nawābganj, India	124	26.52 N	82.08 E
Nawābganj, India	124	26.56 N	81.13 E
Nawābshāh	120	26.15 N	68.25 E
Nawāda	124	24.53 N	85.32 E
Nāwah	120	32.19 N	67.53 E
Nawa Kot	120	28.20 N	71.22 E
Nawalapitiya	122	7.03 N	80.32 E
Nawalgarh	120	27.51 N	75.16 E
Nawān Kot	123	31.06 N	71.32 E
Nawanshahr	123	31.07 N	76.08 E
Nawāpāra, Bngl.	126	23.02 N	89.23 E
Nawāpāra, India	122	20.58 N	81.51 E
Nawapārā, India	126	23.29 N	88.15 E
Nawasā al-Ghayṭ	142	30.58 N	31.19 E
Nawāshahr	123	34.10 N	73.16 E
Nawāṣīf, Ḥarrat ±[9]	144	21.20 N	42.10 E
Nawāy	142	27.47 N	30.46 E
Nawiliwili Bay c	229b	21.57 N	159.21 W
Nawinda Kuta	152	16.25 S	24.28 E
Nawŏn-ni	98	36.25 N	126.40 E
Naxera	208	37.20 N	76.27 W
Naxi	107	28.47 N	105.22 E
Náxos	38	37.06 N	25.23 E
Náxos I	38	37.02 N	25.35 E
Naxos ⊥	70	37.49 N	15.17 E
Nayābās	272a	28.35 N	77.19 E
Nayāgaon	126	23.32 N	90.46 E
Nayāgarh	120	20.08 N	85.06 E
Nayāgrām	126	22.02 N	87.11 E
Nayak	120	34.44 N	66.57 E
Nayāpāra	126	21.35 N	87.01 E
Nayarit	204	32.20 N	115.19 W
Nayarit □[3]	234	22.00 N	105.00 W
Nayau Island I	175g	17.58 S	179.03 W
Nāy Band, Īrān	128	32.20 N	57.34 E
Nāy Band, Īrān	128	27.23 N	52.38 E
Nāy Band, Kūh-e ∧	128	32.26 N	57.22 E
Nayland	42	51.59 N	0.52 E
Naylor	194	36.34 N	90.36 W
Nayong	102	26.50 N	105.13 E
Nayoro	92a	44.21 N	142.28 E
Nazālī Ṭāhā'	142	28.11 N	30.42 E
Nazaré, Bra.	250	6.23 S	47.40 W
Nazaré, Bra.	255	13.02 S	39.00 W
Nazaré, Port.	34	39.36 N	9.04 W
Nazaré da Mata	250	7.44 S	35.14 W
Nazaré do Piauí	250	6.59 S	42.40 W
Nazareno	256	21.13 S	44.37 W
Nazaré Paulista	256	23.11 S	46.24 W
Nazareth, Bel.	50	50.58 N	3.36 E
Nazareth, Pa., U.S.	208	40.44 N	75.18 W
Nazareth, Vanuatu	175f	15.21 S	167.50 E
Nazareth, Vanuatu	175f	15.29 S	168.10 E
Nazareth → Naẓerat, Yis.	132	32.42 N	35.18 E
Nazareth Bank ✢[4]	12	14.30 S	60.45 E
Nazário	255	16.36 S	49.54 W
Nazarjevo, S.S.S.R.	82	55.22 N	36.24 E
Nazarjevo, S.S.S.R.	265b	55.59 N	37.16 E
Nazarovo	86	56.01 N	90.26 E
Nazarovskij	78	49.33 N	40.56 E
Nazas	232	25.14 N	104.08 W
Nazas ≃	232	25.35 N	105.00 W
Nazca	248	14.50 S	74.57 W
Nazca Ridge ✢[3]	18	22.00 S	82.00 W
Naze	93b	28.23 N	129.30 E
Nazeing	260	51.44 N	0.03 E
N'azepetrovsk	86	56.03 N	59.36 E
Naẓerat (Nazareth)	132	32.42 N	35.18 E
Naẓerat 'Illit	132	32.42 N	35.19 E
Nazija	76	59.50 N	31.35 E
Nazik Gölü ⊜	130	38.50 N	42.16 E
Nazilli	130	37.55 N	28.21 E
Nazimicha	265b	55.59 N	38.08 E
Nazımiye	130	39.11 N	39.50 E
Nazimovo	86	59.30 N	90.58 E
Nazina	86	60.07 N	78.52 E
Nāzira	120	26.55 N	94.44 E
Nāzir Hāt	120	22.38 N	91.47 E
Nāzirpur	126	22.43 N	89.58 E
Nazko ≃	182	53.07 N	123.34 W
Nazlat al-'Amūdayn	142	28.14 N	30.42 E
Nazlat al-Badramān	142	27.40 N	30.44 E
Nazlat as-Sammān	273c	29.59 N	31.08 E
Nazlat Khalīfah	273c	30.01 N	31.10 E
Nazlat Quftan Bāshā	142	28.57 N	30.49 E
Nazlat Thābit	142	28.25 N	30.47 E
Nazran'	84	43.13 N	44.46 E
Nazret	144	8.33 N	39.16 E
Nazyvajevsk	86	55.34 N	71.21 E
N. B. C. Studios ʋ[3]	280	34.09 N	118.20 W
Nchanga	154	12.30 S	27.53 E
Nchelenge	154	9.20 S	28.50 E
Ncue	152	2.01 N	10.28 E
Ndabala	154	13.28 S	29.50 E
Ndala	154	4.46 S	33.16 E
N'dalatando	152	9.18 S	14.54 E
Ndali	150	9.51 N	2.43 E
Ndanda	152	5.12 N	22.21 E
Ndande	150	15.16 N	16.30 W
Ndarassa	152	6.49 N	22.15 E
Ndélé	146	8.24 N	20.39 E
Ndélélé	152	4.02 N	14.56 E
Ndemba	152	0.11 N	14.19 E
Ndendé	152	2.23 S	11.23 E
Ndikiniméki	152	4.46 N	10.50 E
Ndindi	152	3.46 S	11.09 E
N'Djamena	146	12.07 N	15.03 E
Ndji ≃	152	6.47 N	22.14 E
Ndjili ◂[8]	273b	4.20 S	15.22 E
Ndjili ≃	273b	4.19 S	15.24 E
Ndjili, Grande Île de la I	273b	4.19 S	15.24 E
Ndjim ≃	152	4.38 N	11.24 E
Ndjo	152	1.15 S	14.30 E
Ndjolé	152	0.11 S	10.45 E
Ndogo, Lagune c	152	2.35 S	10.00 E
Ndola	154	12.58 S	28.38 E
Ndolo ◂[8]	273b	4.19 S	15.19 E
Ndona	115b	8.46 S	121.45 E
Ndongo	152	2.19 S	13.38 E
Ndouba	152	0.11 S	14.09 E
Ndougou	152	1.39 S	9.40 E
Ndu	152	4.41 N	22.49 E
Nduguti	154	4.18 S	34.42 E
Nduindui	175f	15.24 S	167.46 E
Ndumbwe	154	10.14 S	39.58 E
Ndumu Game Reserve ◂[4]	158	26.53 S	32.15 E
Nduye	154	1.50 N	29.01 E
Ne	268	35.47 N	140.03 E
Nea ≃	26	63.13 N	11.02 E
Neabul Creek ≃	166	27.45 S	147.32 E
Néa Erithraía	267c	38.05 N	23.49 E
Néa Filadhélfia	267c	38.02 N	23.44 E
Neagari	94	36.27 N	136.27 E
Neagh, Lough ⊜	48	54.38 N	6.24 W
Neah Bay	224	48.22 N	124.37 W
Néa Ionía	267c	38.02 N	23.45 E
Neajlov ≃	38	44.11 N	26.12 E
Néa Khalkidhón	267c	38.02 N	23.43 E
Neale, Lake ⊜	162	24.22 S	130.00 E
Neales ≃	162	28.08 S	136.47 E
Neales Flat	168b	34.15 S	139.10 E
Néa Liósia	267c	38.02 N	23.42 E
Neamț □[6]	38	47.00 N	26.30 E
Neandertal, Naturschutzgebiet ♦	263	51.15 N	7.00 E
Néa Páfos (Paphos)	130	34.45 N	32.25 E
Neapel → Napoli	68	40.51 N	14.17 E
Néa Pendéli	267c	38.04 N	23.52 E
Néa Péramos	267c	38.00 N	23.26 E
Neápolis, Ellás	38	36.30 N	23.04 E
Neápolis, Ellás	38	35.15 N	25.37 E
Neapolis, Oh., U.S.	216	41.29 N	83.52 W
Néa Psará	38	38.23 N	23.48 E
Near Islands II	181a	52.40 N	173.30 E
Near North Side ◂[8]	278	41.54 N	87.38 W
Néa Smírni	267c	37.57 N	23.43 E
Neasons Hill	214	41.37 N	80.08 W
Neatahwanta, Lake ⊜	210	43.18 N	76.27 W
Neath	42	51.40 N	3.48 W
Neath ≃	42	51.37 N	3.50 W
Neauphle-le-Château	50	48.49 N	1.54 E
Neauphle-le-Vieux	261	48.49 N	1.52 E
Neavitt	208	38.43 N	76.16 W
Neba	94	35.15 N	137.35 E
Nebaj	236	15.24 N	91.08 W
Nebbou	150	11.18 N	1.53 W
Nebelhorn ∧	58	47.25 N	10.20 E
Nebesnaja, gora ∧	86	43.19 N	80.44 E
Nebeur	36	36.17 N	8.47 E
Nebine Creek ≃	166	29.07 S	146.56 E
Nebit-Dag	128	39.30 N	54.22 E
Neblina, Pico da ∧	246	0.48 N	66.02 W
Nebo	194	39.27 N	90.47 W
Nebo, Mount ∧, Ut,. U.S.	200	39.49 N	111.46 W
Nebo, Mount → Nabā, Jabal an- ∧, Urd.	132	31.46 N	35.45 E
Nebolči	76	59.08 N	33.18 E
Nebra	54	51.17 N	11.34 E
Nebraska	218	39.04 N	85.28 W
Nebraska □[3], U.S.	178	41.30 N	100.00 W
Nebraska □[3], U.S.	198	41.30 N	100.00 W
Nebraska City	198	40.40 N	95.51 W
Nebrodi ⋀	70	37.54 N	14.35 E
Nebyloje	80	56.22 N	39.59 E
Nečajannoje	78	46.57 N	31.33 E
Nečajevka	80	53.17 N	44.27 E
Nečajevo	82	54.42 N	37.23 E
Necaxa ≃	234	20.16 N	97.27 W
Necedah	190	44.01 N	90.04 W
Nechajevskij	80	50.25 N	41.44 E
Nechako ≃	182	53.56 N	122.42 W
Nechako Plateau ⋀[1]	182	54.00 N	124.30 W
Nechako Range ⋀	182	53.20 N	124.30 W
Nechako Reservoir ⊜[1]	182	53.25 N	125.10 W
Neche	198	48.59 N	97.33 W
Neches	222	31.52 N	95.30 W
Neches ≃	194	29.55 N	93.52 W
Nechí	246	8.07 N	74.46 W
Nechí ≃	246	8.08 N	74.46 W
Nechisar National Park ♦	144	6.00 N	37.50 E
Nechmeya	36	36.36 N	7.31 E
Nechranická Přehradová Nádrž ⊜[1]	54	50.20 N	13.20 E
Nechvorošča	78	49.09 N	34.44 E
Neckar ≃	30	49.31 N	8.26 E
Neckarbischofsheim	56	49.17 N	8.57 E
Neckarelz	56	49.20 N	9.06 E
Neckargemünd	56	49.23 N	8.47 E
Neckarsteinach	56	49.25 N	8.53 E
Neckarsulm	56	49.12 N	9.13 E
Neckartailfingen	56	48.36 N	9.16 E
Neckartenzlingen	56	48.35 N	9.14 E
Neck Creek ≃	276	40.36 N	74.12 W
Necker	284b	39.23 N	76.29 W
Necker Island I, Br. Vir. Is.	240m	18.33 N	64.21 W
Necker Island I, Hi., U.S.	14	23.35 N	164.42 W
Necker Ridge ✢[3]	14	22.00 N	167.15 W
Necochea	252	38.33 S	58.45 W
Necrópolis ◂	266a	40.25 N	3.38 W
Nedalssjön ⊜	26	62.56 N	12.11 E
Nedančiči	78	51.30 N	30.37 E
Ned Brown Preserve ♦	278	42.02 N	88.01 W
Nedel'noje	82	54.50 N	36.39 E
Nederland	194	29.58 N	93.59 W
Nederland → Netherlands □[1]	30	52.15 N	5.30 E
Nederlandse Antillen → Netherlands Antilles □[2]	241s	12.15 N	69.00 W
Neder-Rijn ≃[1]	52	51.58 N	5.20 E
Nederweert	52	51.17 N	5.45 E
Nederzwalm-Hermelgem	50	50.53 N	3.41 E
Nedlands	168a	31.59 S	115.49 E
Nedlitz	54	52.04 N	12.14 E
Nedlitz ◂[8]	264a	52.26 N	13.03 E
Nêdong	120	29.14 N	91.46 E
Nedre Soppero	24	68.01 N	21.44 E
Nedre Vättern ⊜	40	59.49 N	15.40 E
Nedrigajlov	78	50.50 N	33.53 E
Nédroma	148	35.01 N	1.45 W
Nedrow	210	42.58 N	76.08 W
Nedstrand	26	59.21 N	5.51 E
Neebish Island I	190	46.16 N	84.09 W
Neede	52	52.08 N	6.36 E
Needham, In., U.S.	218	39.32 N	85.58 W
Needham, Ma., U.S.	207	42.17 N	71.14 W
Needham Market	42	52.09 N	1.03 E
Needhams Point ›	241g	13.05 N	59.36 W
Needle Mountain ∧	202	44.05 N	109.37 W
Needles	204	34.50 N	114.36 W
Needling Hill ∧[2]	168a	31.53 S	116.56 E
Needville	222	29.23 N	95.50 W
Neelyton	214	40.10 N	77.50 W
Ñeembucú □[5]	252	27.00 S	58.00 W
Neenah	190	44.11 N	88.27 W
Neepawa	184	50.13 N	99.29 W
Neerabup National Park ♦	168a	31.41 S	115.43 E
Neerim South	169	38.01 S	145.58 E
Neermoor	52	53.18 N	7.26 E
Neeroeteren	56	51.05 N	5.42 E
Neerpelt	56	51.13 N	5.25 E
Neersen	263	51.15 N	6.29 E
Nee Soon	271c	1.24 N	103.49 E
Neetze	52	53.15 N	10.39 E
Neetze ≃	54	53.20 N	10.28 E
Nefedjevo, S.S.S.R.	82	54.39 N	37.56 E
Nefedjevo, S.S.S.R.	265b	55.54 N	37.10 E
Neffs	208	40.42 N	75.37 W
Neffsville	208	40.06 N	76.18 W
Nef'odovo	86	58.48 N	72.34 E
Nefta	148	33.52 N	7.33 E
Nefteabad	85	40.12 N	70.34 E
Neftečala	84	39.23 N	49.16 E
Neftegorsk	84	44.22 N	39.42 E
Neftekamsk	80	56.06 N	54.17 E
Neftekumsk	84	44.45 N	44.48 E
Nefyn	42	52.57 N	4.31 W
Nefza	36	36.58 N	9.05 E
Negage	152	7.45 S	15.16 E
Négala	150	12.52 N	8.27 W
Negapatam → Nāgappattinam	122	10.46 N	79.50 E
Negara, Indon.	112	2.37 S	115.06 E
Negara, Indon.	115a	8.22 S	114.37 E
Negara ≃	112	3.00 S	114.45 E
Negast	54	54.15 N	13.01 E
Negaunee	190	46.29 N	87.36 W
Negba	132	31.40 N	34.41 E
Negele	144	5.20 N	39.36 E
Negenborn	52	51.53 N	9.34 E
Negeribatin	112	4.35 S	104.32 E
Negeri Sembilan □[3]	114	2.45 N	102.10 E
Negev Desert → HaNegev ◂[1]	132	30.30 N	34.55 E
Negishi	268	35.51 N	139.23 E
Negley	214	40.47 N	80.32 W
Negola	152	14.10 S	14.30 E
Negomano	154	11.27 S	38.31 E
Negombo	122	7.13 N	79.50 E
Negonego I[1]	14	18.47 S	141.48 W
Negoreloje	76	53.36 N	27.04 E
Negotin	38	44.14 N	22.32 E
Negra, Laguna ⊜	252	34.03 S	53.40 W
Negra, Ponta ›	256	22.58 S	42.42 W
Negra, Punta ›, Belize	232	16.17 N	88.34 W
Negra, Punta ›, Perú	248	6.06 S	81.09 W
Negra, Serra ∧, Bra.	250	6.30 S	46.15 W
Negra, Serra ∧, Bra.	256	21.58 S	43.54 W
Negrais	266c	38.53 N	9.17 W
Negras, Lomas ∧[2]	286d	11.55 S	77.06 W
Negreira	34	42.54 N	8.44 W
Nègres, Pointe des ›	240e	14.36 N	61.06 W
Negrești	38	46.50 N	27.27 E
Negrești-Oaș	38	47.52 N	23.25 E
Negrine	148	34.30 N	7.30 E
Negritos	246	4.38 S	81.19 W
Negro ≃, Arg.	254	41.02 S	62.47 W
Negro ≃, Bol.	248	14.11 S	63.07 W
Negro ≃, Bol.	248	9.49 S	65.42 W
Negro ≃, Bra.	248	5.15 S	70.53 W
Negro ≃, Bra.	248	19.13 S	57.17 W
Negro ≃, Bra.	250	9.15 S	47.34 W
Negro ≃, Bra.	252	26.01 S	50.30 W
Negro ≃, Col.	246	5.44 N	74.39 W
Negro ≃, N.A.	236	13.02 N	87.17 W
Negro ≃, Para.	252	24.23 S	57.11 W
Negro ≃, S.A.	246	3.08 S	59.55 W
Negro ≃, S.A.	252	33.24 S	58.22 W
Negro ≃, Ven.	246	9.36 N	72.15 W
Negro, Baia del c	144	7.55 N	49.55 E
Negro, Cerro ∧, Arg.	254	46.55 S	70.12 W
Negro, Cerro ∧, Arg.	254	44.09 S	69.30 W
Negro, Mar → Black Sea ▼[2]	22	43.00 N	35.00 E
Negros I	116	10.00 N	123.00 E
Negros Occidental □[4]	116	10.20 N	123.00 E
Negros Oriental □[4]	116	9.40 N	123.00 E
Negru-Vodă	38	43.50 N	28.12 E
Neguac	186	47.15 N	65.05 W
Nehalem	224	45.43 N	123.53 W
Nehalem ≃	224	45.40 N	123.56 W
Nehawka	198	40.49 N	95.59 W
Nehbandān	128	31.32 N	60.02 E
Neheim-Hüsten	56	51.27 N	7.57 E
Nehonsey Brook ≃	285	39.49 N	75.18 W
Néhoué, Baie de c	175f	20.21 S	164.09 E
Nehru Planetarium ʋ	272c	18.59 N	72.49 E
Neiba	238	18.28 N	71.25 W
Neiba, Bahía de c	238	18.15 N	71.02 W
Neichiang → Neijiang	107	29.35 N	105.03 E
Neidenburg → Nidzica	30	53.22 N	20.26 E
Neidpath	184	50.13 N	107.15 W
Neige, Crêt de la ∧	58	46.16 N	5.56 E
Neiges, Piton des ∧	157c	21.05 S	55.29 E
Neihart	202	46.56 N	110.44 W
Neihe ≃	100	22.54 N	115.38 E
Neihu	269d	25.05 N	121.34 E
Neihuang	98	35.59 N	114.55 E
Neijiang	107	29.35 N	105.03 E
Neikiang → Neijiang	107	29.35 N	105.03 E
Neilburg	184	52.50 N	109.38 W
Neillsville	190	44.33 N	90.35 W
Neilston	46	55.47 N	4.27 W
Neimen	263	51.29 N	7.48 E
Nei Monggol Zizhiqu (Inner Mongolia) □[4]	90	43.00 N	115.00 E
Nein	132	32.38 N	35.21 E
Neindorf	54	52.20 N	10.50 E
Neinstedt	54	51.45 N	11.05 E
Neiqiu	98	37.17 N	114.31 E
Neira	246	5.10 N	75.32 W
Neirone	62	44.27 N	9.11 E
Neishuishan	269d	25.09 N	121.43 E
Neisse (Nysa Łużycka) (Nisa) ≃	30	52.04 N	14.46 E
Neiva	246	2.56 N	75.18 W
Neiwufuquan	105	40.11 N	117.39 E
Neixiang	102	33.12 N	111.57 E
Neizeng Shan ∧	100	24.02 N	117.32 E
Neja, S.S.S.R.	80	58.24 N	46.31 E
Neja, S.S.S.R.	80	58.18 N	43.54 E
Neja ≃	80	57.48 N	43.42 E
Nejapa de Madero	234	16.37 N	95.59 W
Nejd — Najd □[9]	118	25.00 N	44.30 E
Nejdek	54	50.17 N	12.42 E
Nejo	144	9.30 N	35.30 E
Nejva ≃	86	57.54 N	62.18 E
Nejvo-Šajtanskij	86	57.44 N	61.15 E
Nekalagba	154	2.50 N	28.01 E
Nekemte	144	9.02 N	36.31 E
Nekhab ⊥	140	25.10 N	32.48 E
Nekl'udovo	80	56.24 N	43.59 E
Nekoosa	190	44.18 N	89.54 W
Nekor, Oued ≃	34	35.14 N	3.45 W
Neko-zaki ›	96	35.40 N	134.46 E
Nekrasino	82	56.18 N	36.33 E
Nekrasovka	265b	55.41 N	37.56 E
Nekrasovo, S.S.S.R.	80	51.10 N	45.18 E
Nekrasovo, S.S.S.R.	82	54.30 N	38.57 E
Nekrasovskoje	80	57.41 N	40.22 E
Nekselø I	41	55.47 N	11.18 E
Neksø	26	55.04 N	15.09 E
Nela Park ♦	279a	41.33 N	81.33 W
Nel'aty	88	56.29 N	115.41 E
Nelichu ∧	140	6.08 N	34.25 E
Nelidovo	76	56.13 N	32.46 E
Neligh	198	42.07 N	98.01 W
Nel'kan	74	57.40 N	136.13 E
Nellie	214	40.20 N	82.04 W
Nellikuppam	122	11.46 N	79.41 E
Nellingen	56	48.33 N	9.47 E
Nellis Air Force Base ■	204	36.14 N	115.02 W
Nelliston	210	42.56 N	74.37 W
Nellis Weapons Range ■	204	37.15 N	116.20 W
Nellore	122	14.26 N	79.58 E
Nel'ma	89	47.39 N	139.09 E
Nelson, B.C., Can.	182	49.29 N	117.17 W
Nelson, N.Z.	172	41.17 S	173.17 E
Nelson, Eng., U.K.	44	53.51 N	2.13 W
Nelson, Ne., U.S.	198	40.12 N	98.04 W
Nelson, Pa., U.S.	210	41.59 N	77.14 W
Nelson ≃	184	57.04 N	92.30 W
Nelson, Cape ›, Austl.	166	38.26 S	141.33 E
Nelson, Cape ›, Pap. N. Gui.	164	9.00 S	149.15 E
Nelson, Estrecho ⊔	254	51.37 S	75.00 W
Nelson Creek ≃	222	30.56 N	95.31 W
Nelson House	184	55.47 N	98.51 W
Nelson Island I	180	60.35 N	164.45 W
Nelson-Kennedy Ledges State Park ♦	214	41.18 N	81.04 W
Nelson Lake ⊜	184	55.44 N	100.00 W
Nelson Lakes National Park ♦	172	41.50 S	172.40 E
Nelson Reservoir ⊜[1]	202	48.30 N	107.34 W
Nelsons Dockyard ⊥	240c	17.00 N	61.46 W
Nelsonville, N.Y., U.S.	210	41.25 N	73.57 W
Nelsonville, Oh., U.S.	188	39.27 N	82.14 W
Nelspoort	158	32.07 S	23.00 E
Nelspoortjie	158	29.58 S	22.25 E
Nelspruit	156	25.30 S	30.58 E
Néma, Maur.	150	16.37 N	7.15 W
Nema, S.S.S.R.	80	57.31 N	50.31 E
Néma, Dahr ±[4]	150	16.40 N	7.13 W
Nemadji ≃	190	46.41 N	92.02 W
Nemah	224	46.31 N	123.51 W
Nemaha	198	40.20 N	95.40 W
Neman	76	55.02 N	22.02 E
Neman (Nemunas) ≃	76	55.18 N	21.23 E
Nematābād ◂[8]	267d	35.38 N	51.21 E
Nembe	150	4.35 N	6.26 E
Nembrala	112	10.53 S	122.50 E
Nembro	62	45.45 N	9.45 E
Nemčinovka	265b	55.43 N	37.23 E
Nemda ≃, S.S.S.R.	80	57.35 N	48.56 E
Nemda ≃, S.S.S.R.	80	57.21 N	43.08 E
Nemegosenda ≃	190	48.31 N	82.53 W
Nemegt uul ⋀	102	43.40 N	101.10 E
Nemeiben Lake ⊜	184	55.20 N	105.20 W
Nemenčinė	76	54.51 N	25.29 E
Nementcha, Monts de ⋀	148	34.52 N	7.05 E
Nemeriči	76	53.51 N	33.59 E
Nemi	66	41.43 N	12.43 E
Nemi, Lago di ⊜	267a	41.43 N	12.42 E
Nemira Mare, Vîrful ∧	38	46.15 N	26.19 E
Nemirov, S.S.S.R.	78	50.07 N	23.25 E
Nemirov, S.S.S.R.	78	48.58 N	28.50 E
Nemirovo	82	55.54 N	36.12 E
Nemo	222	32.16 N	97.39 W
Nemoli	68	40.04 N	15.48 E
Nemor ≃	89	48.23 N	124.32 E
Nemours	50	48.16 N	2.42 E
Nemoviči	78	51.16 N	26.38 E
Nemrut Gölü ⊜	130	38.37 N	42.12 E
Nemuna, Bjeshkët e ⋀	38	42.27 N	19.47 E
Nemunas (Neman) ≃	76	55.18 N	21.23 E
Nemuro	92a	43.20 N	145.35 E
Nemuro-hantō ›[1]	92a	43.21 N	145.42 E
Nemuro Strait ⊔	92a	44.00 N	145.20 E
Nemzeti Museum ʋ	264c	47.29 N	19.05 E
Nen ≃	89	45.25 N	124.40 E
Nena Creek ≃	224	45.07 N	121.07 W
Nenagh	48	52.52 N	8.12 W
Nenagh ≃	48	52.56 N	8.17 W
Nenana	180	64.34 N	149.07 W
Nenana ≃	180	64.30 N	149.00 W
Nenaševo	82	54.34 N	37.28 E
Nenasi	114	3.08 N	103.27 E
Nendaz	58	46.11 N	7.18 E
Nendeln	58	47.12 N	9.32 E
Nendo I	14	10.45 S	165.54 E
Nene ≃	42	52.48 N	0.13 E
Neneckij Nacional'nyj Okrug □[8]	24	67.30 N	54.00 E
Nenggiri ≃	114	4.53 N	101.48 E
Nengjia	104	41.38 N	120.46 E
Nengo ≃	152	14.27 S	22.09 E
Nenneper ≃	263	51.32 N	6.26 E
Neno	154	15.24 S	34.39 E
Nentón ≃	236	15.48 N	91.52 W
Nenzing	58	47.11 N	9.42 E
Neo	94	35.38 N	136.37 E
Neo ≃	94	35.24 N	136.34 E
Neodesha	198	37.25 N	95.40 W
Neoga	194	39.19 N	88.27 W
Neola, Ia., U.S.	198	41.26 N	95.36 W
Neola, Ut,. U.S.	200	40.26 N	110.01 W
Neoneli	71	40.04 N	8.57 E
Néon Fáliron	267c	37.57 N	23.40 E
Néon Karlovásion	38	37.48 N	26.44 E
Néon Psikhikón	267c	38.00 N	23.47 E
Neopit	190	44.58 N	88.49 W
Neópolis	250	10.18 S	36.35 W
Neoshera	123	33.09 N	74.14 E
Neosho	194	36.52 N	94.22 W
Neosho ≃	194	35.48 N	95.18 W
Neotsu	224	45.00 N	123.58 W
Nepa ≃	88	59.16 N	108.16 E
Nepal (Nepāl) □[1], Asia	118	28.00 N	84.00 E
Nepal (Nepāl) □[1], Asia	124	28.00 N	84.00 E
Nepālgañj	124	28.03 N	81.37 E
Nepa Nagar	120	21.28 N	76.23 E
Nepaug Reservoir ⊜[1]	207	41.48 N	72.57 W
Nepean	212	45.18 N	75.47 W
Nepean ≃	170	33.27 S	150.53 E
Nepean, Point ›	169	38.18 S	144.39 E
Nepean Bay c	168b	35.42 S	137.44 E
Nepean Island I	174c	29.04 S	167.58 E
Nepean Reservoir ⊜[1]	170	34.22 S	150.35 E
Nepecino	82	55.12 N	38.37 E
Nepeña	248	9.10 S	78.23 W
Nepewassi Lake ⊜	190	46.20 N	80.40 W
Nephi	200	39.42 N	111.50 W
Nephin ∧	48	54.01 N	9.22 W
Nephin Beg Range ⋀	48	54.00 N	9.35 W
Nepi	66	42.14 N	12.21 E
Nepisiguit ≃	186	47.37 N	65.38 W
Nepisiguit Bay c	186	47.46 N	65.32 W
Népliget ♦	264c	47.29 N	19.07 E
Nepoko ≃	154	1.40 N	27.01 E
Nepomuceno	256	21.14 S	45.15 W
Nepomuk	60	49.29 N	13.36 E
Neponset ≃	283	42.17 N	71.02 W
Neponset Reservoir ⊜[1]	283	42.05 N	71.15 W
Neponset River Reservation ♦	283	42.13 N	71.08 W
Neppermin	54	53.56 N	14.02 E
Nepr'adva ≃	76	53.40 N	38.39 E
Nép-sziget I	264c	47.34 N	19.05 E
Neptune, N.J., U.S.	208	40.12 N	74.02 W
Neptune, Oh., U.S.	216	40.36 N	84.30 W
Neptune Beach	192	30.18 N	81.23 W
Neptune City	208	40.12 N	74.02 W
Neqarot, Naḥal V	132	30.40 N	35.15 E
Nera ≃, Europe	38	44.49 N	21.22 E
Nera ≃, It.	66	42.26 N	12.24 E
Nérac	32	44.08 N	0.20 E
Nerákion	267c	38.01 N	23.27 E
Nerang	171a	28.00 S	153.20 E
Nerang ≃	171a	28.03 S	153.17 E
Neratovice	54	50.14 N	14.31 E
Nerča ≃	88	51.56 N	116.40 E
Nerchau	54	51.16 N	12.47 E
Nerčinsk	88	51.58 N	116.35 E
Nerčinskij Zavod	88	51.19 N	119.36 E
Nère ≃	50	47.34 N	2.18 E
Nerechta	80	57.28 N	40.34 E
Nerenstetten	56	48.31 N	10.06 E
Neresheim	56	48.45 N	10.15 E
Nereta	76	56.13 N	25.18 E
Nereto	66	42.49 N	13.49 E
Neretva ≃	36	43.01 N	17.27 E
Nerevoznoje	80	56.53 N	53.54 E
Nerima ◂[8]	268	35.44 N	139.39 E
Neringa	76	55.18 N	21.01 E
Neris ≃	76	54.54 N	23.53 E
Nerito	66	42.32 N	13.28 E
Nerja	34	36.44 N	3.52 W
Nerka, Lake ⊜	180	59.30 N	158.45 W
Nerl', S.S.S.R.	76	57.03 N	37.59 E
Nerl', S.S.S.R.	80	56.40 N	40.24 E
Nerl' ≃, S.S.S.R.	76	57.07 N	37.39 E
Nerl' ≃, S.S.S.R.	80	56.11 N	40.34 E
Nero, ozero ⊜	80	57.07 N	39.27 E
Neroj	88	54.28 N	97.49 E
Néronde	62	45.50 N	4.14 E
Nérondes	32	47.00 N	2.49 E
Nerópolis	255	16.25 S	49.14 W
Nerriga	170	35.07 S	150.05 E
Nerrima	162	18.24 S	124.29 E
Nerrimunga Creek ≃	170	34.57 S	150.04 E
Nersingen	58	48.25 N	10.07 E
Nerskaja ≃	82	55.23 N	38.35 E
Nerul	272c	19.02 N	73.01 E
Nerus ≃	114	5.20 N	103.05 E
Nerussa ≃	76	52.33 N	33.47 E
Nerva	34	37.42 N	6.32 W

Symbols in the index entries represent the broad categories identified in the key at the right. Symbols with superior numbers (⋀[1]) identify subcategories (see complete key on page *I · 1).*

Symbole im Register stellen die rechts im Schlüssel erklärten Kategorien dar. Symbole mit hochgestellten Ziffern (⋀[1]) bezeichnen Unterabteilungen einer Kategorie (vgl. vollständiger Schlüssel auf Seite *I · 1).*

Los símbolos incluídos en el texto del índice representan las grandes categorias identificadas con la clave a la derecha. Los símbolos con numeros en su parte superior (⋀[1]) identifican las subcategorías (véase la clave completa en la página *I · 1).*

Les symboles de l'index représentent les catégories indiquées dans la légende à droite. Les symboles suivis d'un indice (⋀[1]) représentent des sous-catégories (voir légende complète à la page *I · 1).*

Os símbolos incluídos no texto do índice representam as grandes categorias identificadas com a chave à direita. Os símbolos com números em sua parte superior (⋀[1]) identificam as subcategorias (veja-se a chave completa à página *I · 1).*

∧ Mountain	Berg	Montaña	Montagne	Montanha
⋀ Mountains	Gebirge	Montañas	Montagnes	Montanhas
)(Pass	Paß	Paso	Col	Passo
V Valley, Canyon	Tal, Cañon	Valle, Cañon	Vallée, Canyon	Vale, Canhão
≚ Plain	Ebene	Llano	Plaine	Planície
› Cape	Kap	Cabo	Cap	Cabo
I Island	Insel	Isla	Île	Ilha
II Islands	Inseln	Islas	Îles	Ilhas
± Other Topographic Features	Andere Topographische Objekte	Otros Elementos Topográficos	Autres données topographiques	Outros acidentes topográficos

ESPAÑOL

Nombre	Página	Lat.°′	Long.°′ W = Oeste
Nervi	62	44.23 N	9.02 E
Nervia ≃	62	43.47 N	7.38 E
Nerviano	266b	45.33 N	8.58 E
Nerville-la-Forêt	261	49.05 N	2.17 E
Nes, Ned.	52	53.26 N	5.45 E
Nes, Ned.	52	53.04 N	5.51 E
Nes, Nor.	26	60.34 N	9.59 E
Nes', S.S.S.R.	24	66.37 N	44.36 E
Nes, Har ∧	132	30.22 N	34.37 E
Nesbyen	26	60.34 N	9.09 E
Neščerdo, ozero ⊜	76	55.54 N	29.04 E
Neščeretovo	83	49.24 N	38.48 E
Nesco	208	39.38 N	74.41 W
Nescochague Creek ≃	285	39.39 N	74.41 W
Nescochague Creek, Great Swamp Branch ≃	285	39.41 N	74.43 W
Nesconset	276	40.51 N	73.09 W
Nescopeck	210	41.03 N	76.13 W
Nescopeck Creek ≃	210	41.03 N	76.14 W
Nescopeck Mountain ∧	210	41.03 N	76.05 W
Nesebâr	38	42.39 N	27.44 E
Neshaminy Creek ≃	208	40.04 N	74.55 W
Neshaminy Hills	285	40.10 N	74.57 W
Neshaminy Mall ◆[9]	285	40.08 N	74.57 W
Neshaminy State Park ♦	285	40.05 N	74.55 W
Neshaminy Woods	285	40.10 N	74.57 W
Neshannock Creek ≃	214	40.59 N	80.21 W
Nesher	132	32.46 N	35.03 E
Nesjøen ⊜[1]	26	63.02 N	12.01 E
Neškan	180	67.03 N	173.01 W
Neskaupstaður	24a	65.10 N	13.43 W
Neskowin	224	45.06 N	123.58 W
Neskynpil'gyn, laguna ⊂	180	66.57 N	172.45 W
Nesle	50	49.46 N	2.55 E
Nesna	24	66.12 N	13.02 E
Nespelem	182	48.10 N	118.58 W
Nesque ≃	62	43.59 N	4.59 E
Nesquehoning	210	40.51 N	75.48 W
Ness	262	53.17 N	3.03 W
Ness, Loch ⊜	46	57.15 N	4.30 W
Ness City	198	38.27 N	99.54 W
Nesse ≃	54	50.59 N	10.32 E
Nesselrode, Mount ∧	180	58.58 N	134.18 W
Nesselwang	58	47.37 N	10.30 E
Nesselwängle	58	47.29 N	10.37 E
Nesslau	58	47.13 N	9.13 E
Nessmersiel	52	53.40 N	7.21 E
Nesso	58	45.55 N	9.08 E
Neštěmice	54	50.40 N	14.07 E
Nesterkovo	76	59.10 N	30.33 E
Nesterov, S.S.S.R.	76	54.38 N	22.34 E
Nesterov, S.S.S.R.	78	50.04 N	23.58 E
Nesterovka	80	52.26 N	53.42 E
Nesterovo, S.S.S.R.	80	54.31 N	41.49 E
Nesterovo, S.S.S.R.	82	56.45 N	36.30 E
Nesterovo, S.S.S.R.	88	52.22 N	107.53 E
Nestiary	80	56.34 N	45.21 E
Nestoita	78	47.47 N	29.21 E
Neston	44	53.18 N	3.04 W
Nestore ≃	66	43.21 N	12.15 E
Néstos (Mesta) ≃	38	40.41 N	24.44 E
Nesttun	26	60.19 N	5.20 E
Nestucca ≃	224	45.12 N	123.57 W
Nesvetaj	83	47.27 N	39.40 E
Nesviž	76	53.13 N	26.40 E
Nes Ẕiyyona	132	31.55 N	34.48 E
Netanya	132	32.20 N	34.51 E
Netarhāt	124	23.29 N	84.16 E
Netarts	224	45.26 N	123.56 W
Netarts Bay ⊂	224	45.24 N	123.56 W
Netcong	210	40.53 N	74.42 W
Nethan ≃	46	55.42 N	3.52 W
Nether Alderley	262	53.17 N	2.14 W
Netherdale	166	21.08 S	148.32 E
Netherlands (Nederland) □[1], Europe	22	52.15 N	5.30 E
Netherlands (Nederland) □[1], Europe	30	52.15 N	5.30 E
Netherlands Antilles (Nederlandse Antillen) □[2], N.A.	230	12.15 N	68.45 W
Netherlands Antilles (Nederlandse Antillen) □[2], N.A.	241s	12.15 N	68.45 W
Netherton	262	53.30 N	2.58 W
Nethy Bridge	46	57.16 N	3.38 W
Netia	154	14.48 S	39.59 E
Netley Marsh	42	50.53 N	1.21 W
Neto ≃	68	39.13 N	17.08 E
Netolice	61	49.03 N	14.12 E
Netphen	56	50.55 N	8.06 E
Netra	56	51.06 N	10.05 E
Netrakona	124	24.53 N	90.43 E
Netstal	58	47.03 N	9.03 E
Nettancourt	56	48.52 N	4.57 E
Nette	52	52.02 N	10.05 E
Nette ◆[8]	263	51.33 N	7.25 E
Nettelstedt	52	52.18 N	8.41 E
Nettetal	56	51.18 N	6.16 E
Nettilling Fiord ⊂[2]	176	66.02 N	68.12 W
Nettilling Lake ⊜	176	66.30 N	70.40 W
Nett Lake ⊜	190	48.10 N	93.10 W
Nett Lake Indian Reservation ◆[4]	190	48.06 N	93.10 W
Nettlebed	42	51.35 N	1.00 W
Nettle Creek ≃	218	40.03 N	83.48 W
Nettleden	260	51.47 N	0.32 W
Nettleham	44	53.16 N	0.29 W
Nettlestead	260	51.15 N	0.25 E
Nettlestead Green	260	51.14 N	0.25 E
Nettleton	194	34.05 N	88.37 W
Nettuno	66	41.27 N	12.39 E
Nettuno, Grotta di ⊥[5]	71	40.34 N	8.09 E
Netze → Noteć ≃	30	52.44 N	15.26 E
Netzschkau	54	50.36 N	12.14 E
Neualbenreuth	60	49.59 N	12.27 E
Neu-Anspach	56	50.17 N	8.29 E
Neuastenberg	56	51.10 N	8.29 E
Neubeckum	52	51.48 N	8.01 E
Neu Bentschen → Zbąszynek	30	52.15 N	15.50 E
Neubrandenburg	54	53.33 N	13.15 E
Neubrandenburg □[5]	54	53.30 N	13.15 E
Neubraunschweig → New Brunswick □[4]	186	46.30 N	66.15 W
Neubritannien → New Britain I	164	6.00 S	150.00 E
Neu Büddenstedt	54	52.10 N	10.31 E
Neubukow	54	54.02 N	11.40 E
Neuburg am Inn	60	48.30 N	13.27 E
Neuburg an der Donau	60	48.44 N	11.11 E
Neuchâtel	58	46.59 N	6.56 E
Neuchâtel □[3]	58	47.00 N	6.55 E
Neuchâtel, Lac de ⊜	58	46.52 N	6.50 E
Neudamm → Dębno	30	52.45 N	14.40 E
Neu-Delhi → New Delhi	124	28.36 N	77.12 E
Neudenau	56	49.17 N	9.16 E
Neudietendorf	54	50.55 N	10.55 E
Neudorf, Sk., Can.	184	50.44 N	102.59 W
Neudorf, D.D.R.	54	50.29 N	12.58 E
Neudorf ◆[8]	263	51.25 N	6.47 E
Neudörfl	61	47.48 N	16.17 E
Neue Hebriden → Vanuatu □[1]	175f	16.00 S	167.00 E
Neuemühle	264a	52.18 N	13.39 E
Neuenburg, B.R.D.	52	53.23 N	7.57 E
Neuenbürg, B.R.D.	56	48.50 N	8.35 E
Neuenburg, B.R.D.	58	47.49 N	7.35 E

FRANÇAIS

Nom	Page	Lat.°′	Long.°′ W = Ouest
Neuenburg → Neuchâtel, Schw.	58	46.59 N	6.56 E
Neuendettelsau	56	49.17 N	10.47 E
Neuendorf	54	54.31 N	13.05 E
Neuendorfer See ⊜	54	52.07 N	13.55 E
Neuenegg	58	46.54 N	7.18 E
Neuenhagen bei Berlin	54	52.32 N	13.41 E
Neuenhaus	52	52.30 N	6.59 E
Neuenhof ◆[8]	263	51.10 N	7.13 E
Neuenhoven	263	51.08 N	6.31 E
Neue Niers ≃	263	51.16 N	6.26 E
Neuenkamp ◆[8]	263	51.26 N	6.44 E
Neuenkirchen, B.R.D.	52	52.30 N	8.04 E
Neuenkirchen, B.R.D.	52	51.50 N	8.26 E
Neuenkirchen, B.R.D.	52	53.14 N	8.31 E
Neuenkirchen, B.R.D.	52	53.02 N	9.42 E
Neuenkirchen, B.R.D.	52	52.14 N	7.22 E
Neuenkirchen, B.R.D.	52	53.46 N	8.53 E
Neuenkirchen, D.D.R.	54	54.32 N	13.20 E
Neuenrade	56	51.17 N	7.47 E
Neuensalz	54	50.30 N	12.13 E
Neuenstadt am Kocher	56	49.14 N	9.20 E
Neuenwalde	52	53.40 N	8.40 E
Neuerburg	56	50.00 N	6.17 E
Neu-Erlaa ◆[8]	264b	48.08 N	16.19 E
Neues Palais ⊥	264a	52.24 N	13.01 E
Neu Fahrland	264a	52.26 N	13.03 E
Neufahrn bei Freising	60	48.19 N	11.40 E
Neufahrn in Niederbayern	60	48.44 N	12.11 E
Neuf-Brisach	58	48.01 N	7.32 E
Neufchâteau, Bel.	56	49.50 N	5.26 E
Neufchâteau, Fr.	58	48.21 N	5.42 E
Neufchâtel-en-Bray	50	49.44 N	1.27 E
Neufchâtel-sur-Aisne	50	49.26 N	4.02 E
Neufelden	61	48.29 N	14.00 E
Neuffen	56	48.33 N	9.22 E
Neuffossé, Canal de ≅	50	50.45 N	2.15 E
Neufmanil	56	49.49 N	4.48 E
Neuf-Marché	50	49.25 N	1.43 E
Neufmontiers-lès-Meaux	261	48.58 N	2.50 E
Neufundland → Newfoundland □[4]	176	52.00 N	56.00 W
Neufvilles	50	50.34 N	4.00 E
Neugersdorf	54	50.59 N	14.36 E
Neuglobsow	54	53.09 N	13.02 E
Neugraben-Fischbek ◆[8]	52	53.28 N	9.52 E
Neuguinea → New Guinea I	164	5.00 S	140.00 E
Neuharlingersiel	52	53.42 N	7.42 E
Neu-Hartmannsdorf	264a	52.22 N	13.51 E
Neuhaus, B.R.D.	58	47.48 N	8.34 E
Neuhaus, D.D.R.	54	50.30 N	11.08 E
Neuhaus, D.D.R.	54	53.17 N	10.55 E
Neuhaus, Öst.	61	47.47 N	15.11 E
Neuhaus an der Oste	52	53.48 N	9.02 E
Neuhausen, B.R.D.	58	47.58 N	8.55 E
Neuhausen, D.D.R.	54	50.41 N	13.28 E
Neuhausen, Schw.	58	47.41 N	8.37 E
Neuhaus im Solling	52	51.45 N	9.31 E
Neuhaus-Schierschnitz	54	50.19 N	11.14 E
Neuheum	114	5.34 N	95.32 E
Neuhof	56	50.27 N	9.40 E
Neuhof an der Zenn	56	49.27 N	10.38 E
Neuhofen	56	49.25 N	8.26 E
Neuhofen an der Krems	61	48.08 N	14.14 E
Neuillé-Pont-Pierre	50	47.33 N	0.33 E
Neuilly-en-Thelle	50	49.13 N	2.17 E
Neuilly-L'Évêque	58	47.55 N	5.26 E
Neuilly-Saint-Front	50	49.10 N	3.16 E
Neuilly-sur-Marne	261	48.51 N	2.32 E
Neuilly-sur-Seine	50	48.53 N	2.16 E
Neuirland → New Ireland I	164	3.20 S	152.00 E
Neu-Isenburg	56	50.03 N	8.41 E
Neukagran ◆[8]	264b	48.14 N	16.27 E
Neu-Kaledonien → New Caledonia □[2]	175f	21.30 S	165.30 E
Neukalen	54	53.49 N	12.47 E
Neu Kaliss	54	53.10 N	11.17 E
Neukieritzsch	54	51.10 N	12.25 E
Neukirch, B.R.D.	58	47.39 N	9.41 E
Neukirch, D.D.R.	54	51.17 N	13.58 E
Neukirch, D.D.R.	54	51.05 N	14.20 E
Neukirchen, B.R.D.	41	54.52 N	8.44 E
Neukirchen, B.R.D.	54	54.19 N	11.01 E
Neukirchen, B.R.D.	56	50.46 N	9.41 E
Neukirchen, B.R.D.	56	49.29 N	6.50 E
Neukirchen, B.R.D.	60	49.05 N	11.45 E
Neukirchen, B.R.D.	263	51.07 N	6.41 E
Neukirchen, D.D.R.	54	50.46 N	12.52 E
Neukirchen, D.D.R.	54	51.05 N	12.32 E
Neukirchen, D.D.R.	54	50.47 N	12.22 E
Neukirchen, Öst.	64	47.15 N	12.17 E
Neukirchen am Walde	60	48.24 N	13.46 E
Neukirchen bei Sulzbach-Rosenberg	60	49.32 N	11.38 E
Neukirchen-Vluyn	56	51.27 N	6.33 E
Neukloster	54	53.52 N	11.41 E
Neukölln ◆[8]	264a	52.29 N	13.27 E
Neulangerwisch	264a	52.19 N	13.04 E
Neulengbach	61	48.12 N	15.55 E
Neulienken	54	53.27 N	14.22 E
Neu Lübbenau	54	52.04 N	13.53 E
Neulussheim	56	49.17 N	8.31 E
Neumagen	56	49.51 N	6.53 E
Neuman Creek ≃	284a	42.42 N	78.48 W
Neumark	54	50.39 N	12.21 E
Neumark ◆[1]	54	52.40 N	14.50 E
Neumarkt → Środa Śląska	30	51.10 N	16.36 E
Neumarkt → Tîrgu Mureș, Rom.	38	46.33 N	24.33 E
Neumarkt → Tîrgu-Secuiesc, Rom.	38	46.00 N	26.08 E
Neumarkt am Wallersee	64	47.57 N	13.14 E
Neumarkt im Hausruckkreis	60	48.16 N	13.45 E
Neumarkt in der Oberpfalz	60	49.16 N	11.28 E
Neumarkt in Steiermark	61	47.04 N	14.25 E
Neumarkt-Sankt Veit	60	48.22 N	12.30 E
Neumittelwalde → Międzybórz	30	51.24 N	17.40 E
Neumünster	30	54.04 N	9.59 E
Neun ≃	110	19.42 N	104.03 E
Neunburg vorm Wald	60	49.21 N	12.24 E
Neundorf	54	51.49 N	11.34 E
Neung-sur-Beuvron	50	47.32 N	1.48 E
Neunkirchen, B.R.D.	56	50.48 N	8.00 E
Neunkirchen, B.R.D.	56	50.32 N	8.06 E
Neunkirchen, B.R.D.	56	49.20 N	7.10 E
Neunkirchen, Öst.	61	47.43 N	16.05 E
Neunkirchen am Brand	60	49.37 N	11.08 E
Neunkirchen am Potzberg	56	49.30 N	7.29 E
Neunkirchen-Seelscheid	56	50.51 N	7.20 E
Neuötting	60	48.14 N	12.42 E
Neupetershain	54	51.36 N	14.09 E
Neuquén	252	38.57 S	68.04 W
Neuquén □[4]	254	39.00 S	70.00 W
Neuquén ≃	252	38.59 S	68.00 W

PORTUGUÊS

Nome	Página	Lat.°′	Long.°′ W = Oeste
Neurara	252	24.10 S	68.29 W
Neuravensburg	58	47.38 N	9.46 E
Neureisenberg	264b	48.01 N	16.30 E
Neurode → Nowa Ruda	30	50.35 N	16.31 E
Neuruppin	54	52.55 N	12.48 E
Neusalz → Nowa Sól	30	51.48 N	15.44 E
Neusalza-Spremberg	54	51.02 N	14.32 E
Neu Sankt Johann	58	47.14 N	9.12 E
Neusatz → Novi Sad	38	45.15 N	19.50 E
Neuschottland → Nova Scotia □[4]	186	45.00 N	63.00 W
Neuschwanstein, Schloss ⊍	64	47.35 N	10.44 E
Neuse ≃	192	35.06 N	76.30 W
Neuseddin	264a	52.18 N	12.59 E
Neuseeland → New Zealand □[1]	172	41.00 S	174.00 E
Neusibirische Inseln → Novosibirskije ostrova II	74	75.00 N	142.00 E
Neusiedl am See	61	47.57 N	16.51 E
Neusiedler See (Fertő) ⊜	61	47.50 N	16.45 E
Neusohl → Banská Bystrica	30	48.44 N	19.07 E
Neusorg	60	49.56 N	11.58 E
Neuss	56	51.12 N	6.41 E
Neusserweyhe	263	51.13 N	6.39 E
Neustadt, B.R.D.	56	50.37 N	7.26 E
Neustadt, B.R.D.	56	50.51 N	9.07 E
Neustadt, On., Can.	212	44.05 N	81.00 W
Neustadt, D.D.R.	54	52.52 N	12.25 E
Neustadt, D.D.R.	54	51.01 N	14.13 E
Neustadt, D.D.R.	54	50.44 N	11.44 E
Neustadt ◆[8]	52	53.04 N	8.47 E
Neustadt am Rübenberge	52	52.30 N	9.28 E
Neustadt an der Aisch	56	49.34 N	10.37 E
Neustadt an der Donau	60	48.48 N	11.46 E
Neustadt an der Waldnaab	60	49.44 N	12.11 E
Neustadt an der Weinstrasse	56	49.21 N	8.08 E
Neustadt bei Coburg	56	50.19 N	11.07 E
Neustädtel → Nowe Miasteczko	30	51.42 N	15.45 E
Neustädter Bucht ⊂	54	54.02 N	10.50 E
Neustadt-Glewe	54	53.25 N	11.36 E
Neustadt in Holstein	54	54.06 N	10.48 E
Neustadt in Oberschlesien → Prudnik	30	50.19 N	17.34 E
Neustettin → Szczecinek	30	53.43 N	16.42 E
Neustift am Walde ◆[8]	264b	48.15 N	16.18 E
Neustift im Stubaital	64	47.07 N	11.19 E
Neustrelitz	54	53.21 N	13.04 E
Neuteich → Nowy Staw	30	54.09 N	19.00 E
Neu Töplitz	264a	52.27 N	12.54 E
Neutral Hills ⋏[2]	184	52.10 N	110.50 W
Neutral Zone □[2]	128	29.10 N	45.30 E
Neutraubling	60	48.59 N	12.12 E
Neutrebbin	54	52.40 N	14.13 E
Neu-Ulm	58	48.23 N	10.01 E
Neuve-Chapelle	50	50.35 N	2.47 E
Neuves-Maisons	58	48.37 N	6.06 E
Neuvic	32	45.23 N	2.16 E
Neuville-aux-Bois	50	48.04 N	2.03 E
Neuville-de-Poitou	32	46.41 N	0.15 E
Neuville-en-Condroz	56	50.32 N	5.27 E
Neuville-lès-Dieppe	50	49.55 N	1.06 E
Neuville-sur-Oise	261	49.01 N	2.04 E
Neuville-sur-Saône	62	45.52 N	4.51 E
Neuvy-le-Roi	50	47.36 N	0.36 E
Neuvy-sur-Barangeon	50	47.19 N	2.15 E
Neuvy-sur-Loire	50	47.31 N	2.53 E
Neuwaldegg ◆[8]	264b	48.14 N	16.17 E
Neuwarp → Nowe Warpno	30	53.44 N	14.16 E
Neuwedell → Drawno	30	53.13 N	15.45 E
Neuwerk ◆[8]	263	51.13 N	6.28 E
Neuwerk I	52	53.55 N	8.30 E
Neuwied	56	50.25 N	7.27 E
Neuwiller-lès-Saverne	56	48.49 N	7.24 E
Neu Wulmstorf	52	53.28 N	9.48 E
Neuzelle	54	52.05 N	14.38 E
Neu Zittau	54	52.23 N	13.44 E
Neva ≃	265a	59.57 N	30.20 E
Névache	62	45.01 N	6.37 E
Nevada, Ia., U.S.	190	42.01 N	93.27 W
Nevada, Mo., U.S.	194	37.50 N	94.21 W
Nevada, Oh., U.S.	214	40.49 N	83.07 W
Nevada, Tx., U.S.	222	33.02 N	96.22 W
Nevada □[6]	226	39.16 N	121.01 W
Nevada □[3], U.S.	178	39.00 N	117.00 W
Nevada □[3], U.S.	204	39.00 N	117.00 W
Nevada, Sierra ⋏, Esp.	34	37.05 N	3.10 W
Nevada, Sierra ⋏, Ca., U.S.	204	38.00 N	119.15 W
Nevada City	226	39.15 N	121.00 W
Nevada Creek ≃	202	46.54 N	113.02 W
Nevado, Cerro ∧	246	3.59 N	74.04 W
Nevado de Toluca, Parque Nacional ♦	234	19.10 N	99.50 W
Neval'cevo	86	58.38 N	81.53 E
Nevali	272c	19.01 N	73.07 E
Nevanka	88	56.30 N	98.54 E
Neve, Serra da ⋏	152	13.52 S	13.26 E
Nevel'	76	56.02 N	29.55 E
Nevel'sk	89	46.40 N	141.53 E
Nevel'skogo, proliv ⌁	89	52.05 N	141.35 E
Nevendon	260	51.36 N	0.30 E
Never	89	53.58 N	124.05 E
Neverkino	80	52.47 N	46.44 E
Neverovo	80	55.07 N	44.24 E
Nevers	32	47.00 N	3.09 E
Neversink ≃	210	41.21 N	74.42 W
Neversink Reservoir ⊜[1]	210	41.48 N	74.42 W
Nevertire	166	31.52 S	147.39 E
Neves	256	22.51 S	43.06 W
Nevesinje	38	43.15 N	18.07 E
Nevėžis ≃	76	54.56 N	23.46 E
Nevežkino	80	53.07 N	43.19 E
Neviano	68	40.06 N	18.06 E
Neviano degli Arduini	64	44.35 N	10.19 E
Neviges	56	51.19 N	7.05 E
Neville Island	279b	40.31 N	80.08 W
Neville Island I	279b	40.31 N	80.08 W
Nevinnomyssk	84	44.38 N	41.56 E
Nevis I	238	17.10 N	62.34 W
Nevis ≃	46	56.50 N	5.00 W
Nevis, Ben ∧	46	56.48 N	5.01 W
Nevis, Loch ⊂	46	57.01 N	5.43 W
Nevjansk	86	57.32 N	60.13 E
Nevlunghamn	26	58.58 N	9.52 E
Nevon	88	58.07 N	102.49 E
Nevşehir	130	38.38 N	34.43 E
Nevşehir □[4]	130	38.50 N	34.40 E
Nevskoje	76	58.08 N	30.26 E
New ≃, Belize	232	18.22 N	88.24 W
New ≃, Guy.	246	3.23 N	57.36 W
New ≃, N.A.	204	33.08 N	115.44 W
New ≃, Eng., U.K.	260	51.40 N	0.01 W
New ≃, U.S.	192	38.10 N	81.12 W
New ≃, Az., U.S.	200	33.31 N	112.18 W
New ≃, Fl., U.S.	192	29.50 N	84.40 W
New ≃, Fl., U.S.	192	29.55 N	82.25 W
New ≃, N.C., U.S.	192	34.32 N	77.20 W
New ≃, S.C., U.S.	192	32.09 N	80.50 W

Nome	Página	Lat.°′	Long.°′ W = Oeste
New ≃, Tn., U.S.	192	36.25 N	84.38 W
New, North Fork ≃	192	36.33 N	81.21 W
Newabāgam	272b	22.48 N	88.24 E
New Abbey	44	54.59 N	3.38 W
New Addington ◆[8]	260	51.21 N	0.01 W
Newala	154	10.56 S	39.18 E
New Albany, In., U.S.	218	38.17 N	85.49 W
New Albany, Ms., U.S.	194	34.29 N	89.00 W
New Albany, Oh., U.S.	214	40.05 N	82.49 W
New Albany, Pa., U.S.	210	41.36 N	76.27 W
New Albin	190	43.29 N	91.17 W
New Alexandria, Oh., U.S.	214	40.17 N	80.40 W
New Alexandria, Pa., U.S.	214	40.24 N	79.25 W
New Alexandria, Va., U.S.	284c	38.47 N	77.03 W
New Alfa	140	15.10 N	35.40 E
New Almaden	226	37.11 N	121.49 W
New Alresford	42	51.06 N	1.10 W
New Amsterdam	246	6.15 N	57.31 W
New Angledool	166	29.07 S	147.57 E
Newark, Ar., U.S.	194	35.42 N	91.26 W
Newark, Ca., U.S.	226	37.31 N	122.02 W
Newark, De., U.S.	208	39.41 N	75.45 W
Newark, Il., U.S.	216	41.32 N	88.35 W
Newark, Md., U.S.	208	38.15 N	75.17 W
Newark, Mo., U.S.	219	39.59 N	91.59 W
Newark, N.J., U.S.	210	40.44 N	74.10 W
Newark, N.Y., U.S.	210	43.02 N	77.05 W
Newark, Oh., U.S.	214	40.04 N	82.24 W
Newark, Tx., U.S.	222	33.00 N	97.29 W
Newark Bay ⊂, U.S.	276	40.39 N	74.09 W
Newark Bay ⊂, N.J., U.S.	276	40.40 N	74.08 W
Newark Bay Bridge ◆[5]	276	40.42 N	74.07 W
Newark International Airport ⊠	210	40.42 N	74.10 W
Newark Lake ⊜	204	39.41 N	115.44 W
Newark-on-Trent	42	53.05 N	0.49 W
Newark Slough ≃	282	37.31 N	122.05 W
Newark Valley	210	42.13 N	76.11 W
New Athens, Il., U.S.	219	38.19 N	89.52 W
New Athens, Oh., U.S.	214	40.11 N	80.59 W
New Augusta	194	31.12 N	89.02 W
Newaukum, North Fork ≃	224	46.36 N	122.51 W
Newaukum, South Fork ≃	224	46.36 N	122.51 W
Newaygo	190	43.25 N	85.48 W
New Baden, Il., U.S.	219	38.32 N	89.42 W
New Baden, Tx., U.S.	222	31.03 N	96.26 W
New Baltimore, Mi., U.S.	214	42.40 N	82.44 W
New Baltimore, N.Y., U.S.	210	42.26 N	73.47 W
New Bavaria	216	41.12 N	84.10 W
New Bedford, Ma., U.S.	207	41.38 N	70.56 W
New Bedford, Pa., U.S.	214	41.06 N	80.30 W
New Bedford ≃	42	52.35 N	0.20 E
Newberg	224	45.18 N	122.58 W
New Berlin, Il., U.S.	219	39.43 N	89.54 W
New Berlin, N.Y., U.S.	210	42.37 N	75.19 W
New Berlin, Pa., U.S.	210	40.53 N	76.59 W
New Berlin, Wi., U.S.	216	42.58 N	88.06 W
New Berlinville	208	40.20 N	75.38 W
Newbern, Al., U.S.	194	32.35 N	87.31 W
Newbern, Il., U.S.	219	39.01 N	90.20 W
New Bern, N.C., U.S.	192	35.06 N	77.02 W
Newbern, Tn., U.S.	194	36.06 N	89.15 W
Newberry, Fl., U.S.	192	29.38 N	82.36 W
Newberry, Mi., U.S.	190	46.21 N	85.30 W
Newberry, S.C., U.S.	192	34.16 N	81.37 W
New Bethlehem	214	41.00 N	79.19 W
Newbiggin-by-the-Sea	44	55.11 N	1.30 W
New Bloomfield, Mo., U.S.	219	38.43 N	92.05 W
New Bloomfield, Pa., U.S.	208	40.25 N	77.11 W
New Bloomington	214	40.35 N	83.19 W
Newbold Island I	285	40.08 N	74.45 W
Newboro	212	44.39 N	76.19 W
Newboro Lake ⊜	212	44.38 N	76.20 W
Newborough, Austl.	169	38.11 S	146.17 E
Newborough, Wales, U.K.	44	53.09 N	4.22 W
New Boston, Il., U.S.	190	41.10 N	90.59 W
New Boston, Mi., U.S.	216	42.09 N	83.24 W
New Boston, Oh., U.S.	218	38.45 N	82.56 W
New Boston, Tx., U.S.	194	33.27 N	94.24 W
New Braintree	207	42.19 N	72.07 W
New Braunfels	196	29.42 N	98.07 W
New Bremen	216	40.26 N	84.22 W
Newbridge → Droichead Nua	48	53.11 N	6.48 W
Newbridge on Wye	42	52.13 N	3.27 W
New Brighton, N.Z.	172	43.31 S	172.44 E
New Brighton, Eng., U.K.	262	53.26 N	3.03 W
New Brighton, Pa., U.S.	214	40.43 N	80.18 W
New Brighton ◆[8]	276	40.38 N	74.06 W
New Britain, Ct., U.S.	207	41.39 N	72.46 W
New Britain, Pa., U.S.	208	40.18 N	75.11 W
New Britain I	164	6.00 S	150.00 E
New Britain Trench ⊹[1]	14	6.00 S	153.00 E
New Brockton	194	31.23 N	85.55 W
Newbrook	182	54.19 N	112.57 W
New Brooklyn County Park ♦	285	39.43 N	74.57 W
New Brunswick, In., U.S.	218	39.57 N	86.31 W
New Brunswick, N.J., U.S.	208	40.29 N	74.27 W
New Brunswick □[4], Can.	176	46.30 N	66.15 W
New Brunswick □[4], Can.	186	46.30 N	66.15 W
New Buffalo, Mi., U.S.	216	41.47 N	86.44 W
New Buffalo, Pa., U.S.	208	40.27 N	76.58 W
New Buildings	48	54.57 N	7.21 W
New Bullards Bar Lake ⊜[1]	226	39.25 N	121.08 W
Newburg, Mo., U.S.	194	37.54 N	91.54 W
Newburg, Pa., U.S.	208	40.08 N	77.32 W
Newburg, Pa., U.S.	214	40.31 N	78.25 W
Newburgh, On., Can.	212	44.19 N	76.52 W
Newburgh, Eng., U.K.	262	53.35 N	2.47 W
Newburgh, Scot., U.K.	46	57.18 N	2.00 W
Newburgh, Scot., U.K.	46	56.20 N	3.15 W
Newburgh, In., U.S.	194	37.56 N	87.24 W
Newburgh, N.Y., U.S.	210	41.30 N	74.00 W
Newburgh Heights	279a	41.27 N	81.39 W
Newburn	44	54.59 N	1.43 W
Newbury, On., Can.	214	42.41 N	81.48 W
Newbury, Eng., U.K.	42	51.25 N	1.20 W
Newbury, Ma., U.S.	207	42.49 N	70.53 W
Newbury Old Town	207	42.46 N	70.51 W
Newbury Park	228	34.11 N	118.53 W
Newburyport	207	42.48 N	70.52 W
Newby	44	54.20 N	0.28 W

Nome	Página	Lat.°′	Long.°′ W = Oeste
Newby Bridge	44	54.16 N	2.58 W
New Caledonia (Nouvelle-Calédonie) □[2], Oc.	14	21.30 S	165.30 E
New Caledonia (Nouvelle-Calédonie) □[2], Oc.	175f	21.30 S	165.30 E
New Caledonia Basin ⊹[1]	14	30.00 S	165.00 E
New Canaan	207	41.08 N	73.29 W
New Canada ◆[8]	273d	26.13 S	27.57 E
New Caney	222	30.09 N	95.13 W
New Canton	219	39.38 N	91.06 W
New-Carlisle, P.Q., Can.	186	48.01 N	65.20 W
New Carlisle, In., U.S.	216	41.42 N	86.30 W
New Carlisle, Oh., U.S.	218	39.56 N	84.01 W
New Carrollton	284c	38.58 N	76.52 W
New Cassel	276	40.45 N	73.34 W
Newcastle, Austl.	170	32.56 S	151.46 E
Newcastle, N.B., Can.	186	47.00 N	65.34 W
Newcastle, On., Can.	212	43.55 N	78.35 W
Newcastle, Ire.	48	52.16 N	7.48 W
Newcastle, S. Afr.	158	27.49 S	29.55 E
Newcastle, Eng., U.K.	42	52.26 N	3.06 W
Newcastle, N. Ire., U.K.	48	54.12 N	5.54 W
Newcastle, Ca., U.S.	226	38.53 N	121.08 W
New Castle, Co., U.S.	200	39.34 N	107.32 W
New Castle, De., U.S.	208	39.39 N	75.34 W
New Castle, In., U.S.	218	39.55 N	85.22 W
New Castle, Ky., U.S.	218	38.26 N	85.10 W
Newcastle, Ne., U.S.	198	42.33 N	96.42 W
Newcastle, Oh., U.S.	214	40.20 N	82.10 W
Newcastle, Ok., U.S.	196	35.15 N	97.36 W
New Castle, Pa., U.S.	214	41.00 N	80.20 W
Newcastle, Tx., U.S.	196	33.11 N	98.44 W
New Castle, Va., U.S.	192	37.30 N	80.06 W
Newcastle, Wy., U.S.	198	43.51 N	104.12 W
New Castle □[6]	208	39.44 N	75.33 W
Newcastle (Ouston) Airport ⊠	44	55.01 N	1.53 W
Newcastle Bay ⊂	164	10.50 S	142.37 E
Newcastle Bight ⊂[3]	170	32.51 S	151.54 E
Newcastle Creek ≃	164	17.20 S	133.23 E
Newcastle Emlyn	42	52.02 N	4.28 W
Newcastle Mine	182	51.28 N	112.46 W
Newcastleton	44	55.11 N	2.49 W
Newcastle-under-Lyme	44	53.00 N	2.14 W
Newcastle upon Tyne	44	54.59 N	1.35 W
Newcastle Waters	162	17.24 S	133.24 E
Newcastle West	48	52.27 N	9.03 W
New Centerville	285	40.04 N	75.26 W
Newcestown	48	51.47 N	8.51 W
New Chicago	216	41.34 N	87.16 W
Newchurch, Wales, U.K.	42	52.09 N	3.08 W
New Church, Va., U.S.	208	37.59 N	75.32 W
New City	210	41.08 N	73.59 W
Newclare ◆[8]	273d	26.11 S	27.58 E
New Columbia	210	41.02 N	76.52 W
New Columbus	210	41.10 N	76.18 W
Newcomerstown	214	40.16 N	81.36 W
New Concord	188	39.59 N	81.44 W
New Corydon	216	40.34 N	84.51 W
New Croton Aqueduct ≅[1]	276	41.11 N	73.49 W
New Croton Reservoir ⊜[1]	210	41.14 N	73.46 W
New Cumberland, Pa., U.S.	208	40.13 N	76.53 W
New Cumberland, W.V., U.S.	214	40.29 N	80.36 W
New Cumberland Dam ◆[6]	214	40.32 N	80.37 W
New Cumnock	44	55.24 N	4.12 W
New Dayton	182	49.25 N	112.23 W
New Deer	46	57.30 N	2.12 W
Newdegate	162	33.06 S	119.01 E
New Delhi, India	124	28.36 N	77.12 E
New Delhi, India	272a	28.36 N	77.12 E
New Delhi Railroad Station ◆[5]	272a	28.39 N	77.13 E
New Denver	182	49.59 N	117.22 W
New Derry	214	40.21 N	79.19 W
New Dundee	212	43.21 N	80.31 W
New Eagle	214	40.12 N	79.56 W
New Edinburg	194	33.45 N	92.14 W
New Effington	198	45.51 N	96.55 W
New Egypt	208	40.04 N	74.31 W
Newell, Ia., U.S.	198	42.36 N	95.00 W
Newell, S.D., U.S.	198	44.42 N	103.25 W
Newell, W.V., U.S.	214	40.37 N	80.36 W
Newell, Lake ⊜, Austl.	162	24.50 S	126.10 E
Newell, Lake ⊜, Ab., Can.	182	50.25 N	111.56 W
New Ellenton	192	33.25 N	81.41 W
Newellton	194	32.04 N	91.14 W
New Eltham ◆[8]	260	51.26 N	0.04 E
New England	198	46.32 N	102.52 W
New England National Park ♦	166	30.30 S	152.15 E
New England Range ⋏	166	30.00 S	151.50 E
Newenham, Cape ≻	180	58.37 N	162.12 W
Newent	42	51.56 N	2.24 W
New Enterprise	214	40.10 N	78.25 W
New Ermelo	158	26.32 S	30.02 E
New Falconwood	284a	42.59 N	78.58 W
Newfane, N.Y., U.S.	210	43.17 N	78.42 W
Newfane, Vt., U.S.	188	42.59 N	72.39 W
New Ferry	262	53.22 N	2.59 W
Newfield, N.J., U.S.	208	39.32 N	75.01 W
Newfield, N.Y., U.S.	210	42.22 N	76.35 W
Newfield Pond ⊜	283	42.38 N	71.22 W
New Florence, Mo., U.S.	219	38.54 N	91.26 W
New Florence, Pa., U.S.	214	40.22 N	79.04 W
New Forest ◆[3]	42	50.53 N	1.35 W
New Fork ≃	200	42.33 N	109.58 W
Newfound Gap)(	192	35.37 N	83.25 W
Newfoundland, N.J., U.S.	276	40.44 N	74.29 W
Newfoundland, Pa., U.S.	210	41.19 N	75.19 W
Newfoundland □[4]	176	52.00 N	56.00 W
Newfoundland I	186	48.30 N	56.00 W
Newfoundland Basin ⊹[1]	8	45.00 N	40.00 W
Newfoundland Ridge ⊹[3]	8	40.30 N	48.00 W
New Franklin	194	39.01 N	92.44 W
New Freedom	208	39.44 N	76.42 W
New Galilee	214	40.50 N	80.24 W
New Galloway	44	55.05 N	4.10 W
New Garden	285	39.49 N	75.45 W
Newgate	182	49.00 N	115.10 W
Newgate Street	260	51.44 N	0.07 W
New Georgia I	175e	8.15 S	157.30 E
New Georgia Group II	175e	8.30 S	157.20 E
New Georgia Sound ⌁	175e	8.00 S	158.10 E
New Germantown	208	40.18 N	77.34 W
New Germany	186	44.33 N	64.43 W
New Glarus	190	42.48 N	89.38 W
New Glasgow	186	45.35 N	62.39 W
New Gretna	208	39.35 N	74.27 W

Nome	Página	Lat.°′	Long.°′ W = Oeste
New Guinea I	164	5.00 S	140.00 E
Newgulf	222	29.16 N	95.54 W
Newhalem	224	48.40 N	121.14 W
Newhalen	180	59.43 N	154.54 W
Newhall, Eng., U.K.	42	52.48 N	1.34 W
Newhall, Ca., U.S.	228	34.23 N	118.31 W
Newham ◆[8]	42	51.32 N	0.03 E
New Hamburg, On., Can.	212	43.23 N	80.42 W
New Hamburg, N.Y., U.S.	210	41.35 N	73.57 W
New Hampshire	216	40.33 N	83.57 W
New Hampshire □[3], U.S.	178	43.35 N	71.40 W
New Hampshire □[3], U.S.	188	43.35 N	71.40 W
New Hampton, Ia., U.S.	190	43.03 N	92.19 W
New Hampton, N.Y., U.S.	210	41.25 N	74.24 W
New Hanover, S. Afr.	158	29.28 S	30.28 E
New Hanover, Il., U.S.	219	38.23 N	90.13 W
New Hanover I	164	2.30 S	150.15 E
New Harmony	194	38.07 N	87.56 W
New Hartford, Ct., U.S.	207	41.52 N	72.58 W
New Hartford, Ia., U.S.	190	42.34 N	92.37 W
New Hartford, Mo., U.S.	219	39.12 N	91.16 W
New Hartford, N.Y., U.S.	210	43.04 N	75.18 W
Newhaven, Eng., U.K.	42	50.47 N	0.03 E
New Haven, Ct., U.S.	207	41.18 N	72.56 W
New Haven, Il., U.S.	194	37.54 N	88.07 W
New Haven, In., U.S.	216	41.04 N	85.00 W
New Haven, Ky., U.S.	194	37.39 N	85.35 W
New Haven, Mi., U.S.	214	42.43 N	82.48 W
New Haven, Mo., U.S.	219	38.36 N	91.13 W
New Haven, N.Y., U.S.	212	43.29 N	76.19 W
New Haven, Oh., U.S.	214	41.02 N	82.41 W
New Haven, W.V., U.S.	188	38.59 N	81.58 W
New Haven □[6]	207	41.18 N	72.56 W
New Hazelton	182	55.15 N	127.35 W
New Hebrides → Vanuatu □[1]	175f	16.00 S	167.00 E
New Hebrides II	175f	16.00 S	167.00 E
New Hebrides Trench ⊹[1]	14	22.30 S	170.00 E
Newhebron	194	31.44 N	89.58 W
New Hempstead	276	41.08 N	74.03 W
New Hey	262	53.36 N	2.06 W
New Hogan Lake ⊜[1]	226	38.09 N	120.48 W
New Holland, Eng., U.K.	44	53.42 N	0.22 W
New Holland, Il., U.S.	219	40.11 N	89.36 W
New Holland, Oh., U.S.	218	39.33 N	83.15 W
New Holland, Pa., U.S.	208	40.06 N	76.05 W
New Holstein	190	43.57 N	88.05 W
New Hope, Al., U.S.	194	34.32 N	86.23 W
New Hope, Pa., U.S.	208	40.21 N	74.57 W
New Hudson	281	42.30 N	83.36 W
New Hyde Park	276	40.44 N	73.41 W
New Hythe	260	51.19 N	0.27 E
New Iberia	194	30.00 N	91.49 W
Newick	42	50.58 N	0.01 E
Newington, On., Can.	206	45.07 N	75.01 W
Newington, Eng., U.K.	42	51.05 N	1.08 E
Newington, Eng., U.K.	260	51.21 N	0.40 E
Newington, Ct., U.S.	207	41.42 N	72.43 W
Newinn	48	52.26 N	7.53 W
New Ipswich	207	42.44 N	71.51 W
New Ireland □[5]	164	3.00 S	151.30 E
New Ireland I	164	3.20 S	152.00 E
New Island I	126	21.31 N	88.12 E
New Jersey □[3], U.S.	178	40.15 N	74.30 W
New Jersey □[3], U.S.	188	40.15 N	74.30 W
New Jersey Institute of Technology ⊍[2]	276	40.45 N	74.11 W
New Johnsonville	194	36.01 N	87.58 W
New Kensington	214	40.34 N	79.45 W
New Kent	208	37.31 N	76.58 W
New Kent □[6]	208	37.30 N	77.00 W
New Kingstown	208	40.13 N	77.07 W
Newkirk	196	36.52 N	97.03 W
Newkirk Estates	285	39.42 N	75.36 W
New Knoxville	216	40.29 N	84.18 W
New Kowloon (Xinjiulong)	271d	22.20 N	114.10 E
New Lagos ◆[8]	273a	6.30 N	3.22 E
New Lake ⊜	192	35.38 N	76.20 W
Newland	192	36.05 N	81.55 W
Newland Head ≻	168b	35.39 S	138.31 E
Newland Range ⋏	162	27.53 S	123.58 E
Newlands	166	21.11 S	147.54 E
Newlands ◆[8]	273d	26.11 S	27.58 E
New Lane	262	53.37 N	2.52 W
New Lebanon, N.Y., U.S.	210	42.27 N	73.23 W
New Lebanon, Oh., U.S.	218	39.45 N	84.23 W
New Lebanon, Pa., U.S.	214	41.25 N	80.04 W
New Lebanon Center	210	42.28 N	73.25 W
New Leipzig	198	46.22 N	101.56 W
New Lenox	216	41.30 N	87.57 W
New Lexington	188	39.42 N	82.12 W
New Liberty	218	38.36 N	84.54 W
New Lisbon	190	43.52 N	90.09 W
New Liskeard	190	47.30 N	79.40 W
Newllano	194	31.06 N	93.16 W
New London, Ct., U.S.	207	41.21 N	72.07 W
New London, Ia., U.S.	190	40.55 N	91.23 W
New London, Mn., U.S.	198	45.18 N	94.56 W
New London, Mo., U.S.	219	39.35 N	91.24 W
New London, N.H., U.S.	188	43.24 N	71.59 W
New London, Oh., U.S.	214	41.05 N	82.24 W
New London, Pa., U.S.	208	39.47 N	75.52 W
New London, Tx., U.S.	222	32.15 N	94.56 W
New London, Wi., U.S.	190	44.23 N	88.44 W
New London □[6]	207	41.21 N	72.07 W
New London Submarine Base ■	207	41.24 N	72.05 W
New Longton	262	53.44 N	2.45 W
Newlonsburg	279b	40.25 N	79.40 W
New Lyme	214	41.36 N	80.47 W
Newlyn, Austl.	169	37.25 S	143.59 E
Newlyn, Eng., U.K.	42	50.06 N	5.33 W
Newlyn East	42	50.22 N	5.03 W
Newmachar	46	57.16 N	2.11 W
New Machavie	158	26.48 S	26.57 E
New Madison	218	39.58 N	84.42 W
New Madrid	194	36.35 N	89.31 W
Newmains	44	55.47 N	3.53 W
Newman, Austl.	162	23.20 S	119.46 E
Newman, Ca., U.S.	226	37.18 N	121.01 W
Newman, Il., U.S.	194	39.47 N	87.59 W
Newman, Mount ∧	162	23.16 S	119.33 E
New Manchester	214	40.31 N	80.34 W
Newman Grove	198	41.45 N	97.46 W

Symbol	English	Deutsch	Español	Français	Português
≃	River	Fluß	Río	Rivière	Rio
≅	Canal	Kanal	Canal	Canal	Canal
⌞	Waterfall, Rapids	Wasserfall, Stromschnellen	Cascada, Rápidos	Chute d'eau, Rapides	Cascata, Rápidos
⌁	Strait	Meeresstraße	Estrecho	Détroit	Estreito
⊂	Bay, Gulf	Bucht, Golf	Bahía, Golfo	Baie, Golfe	Baía, Golfo
⊜	Lake, Lakes	See, Seen	Lago, Lagos	Lac, Lacs	Lago, Lagos
⁝	Swamp	Sumpf	Pantano	Marais	Pântano
⌂	Ice Features, Glacier	Eis- und Gletscherformen	Accidentes Glaciales	Formes glaciaires	Acidentes glaciares
⫧	Other Hydrographic Features	Andere Hydrographische Objekte	Otros Elementos Hidrográficos	Autres données hydrographiques	Outros acidentes hidrográficos
⊹	Submarine Features	Untermeerische Objekte	Accidentes Submarinos	Formes de relief sous-marin	Acidentes submarinos
□	Political Unit	Politische Einheit	Unidad Politica	Entité politique	Unidade política
⊍	Cultural Institution	Kulturelle Institution	Institución Cultural	Institution culturelle	Instituição cultural
⊥	Historical Site	Historische Stätte	Sitio Histórico	Site historique	Sitio histórico
♦	Recreational Site	Erholungs- und Ferienort	Sitio de Recreo	Centre de loisirs	Area de Lazer
⊠	Airport	Flughafen	Aeropuerto	Aéroport	Aeroporto
■	Military Installation	Militäranlage	Instalación Militar	Installation militaire	Instalação militar
◆	Miscellaneous	Verschiedenes	Misceláneo	Divers	Diversos

Name	Page	Lat.°′	Long.°′
Newmanstown	208	40.20 N	76.12 W
Newmansville	219	40.00 N	90.01 W
New Marion	218	39.00 N	85.22 W
Newmarket, Austl.	171a	27.25 S	153.01 E
Newmarket, On., Can.	212	44.03 N	79.28 W
Newmarket, Ire.	48	52.13 N	9.00 W
Newmarket, S. Afr.	273d	26.17 S	28.08 E
Newmarket, Eng., U.K.	42	52.15 N	0.25 E
New Market, Al., U.S.	194	34.54 N	86.25 W
New Market, Ia., U.S.	198	40.43 N	94.53 W
New Market, Md., U.S.	208	39.22 N	77.16 W
Newmarket, N.H., U.S.	188	43.04 N	70.56 W
New Market, N.J., U.S.	276	40.34 N	74.27 W
New Market, Va., U.S.	188	38.39 N	78.40 W
Newmarket on Fergus	48	52.45 N	8.53 W
Newmarket Race Course ♦	273d	26.17 S	28.08 E
New Marske	44	54.34 N	1.02 W
New Martinsville	188	39.38 N	80.51 W
New Meadows	202	44.58 N	116.16 W
New Melle	219	38.42 N	90.52 W
New Melones Lake ⊜[1]	226	38.00 N	120.32 W
New Memphis	219	38.29 N	89.41 W
New Mexico □[3]	178	34.30 N	106.00 W
New Miami	218	39.26 N	84.32 W
New Middletown	214	40.58 N	80.34 W
New Milford, Ct., U.S.	207	41.34 N	73.24 W
New Milford, Il., U.S.	216	42.11 N	89.04 W
New Milford, N.J., U.S.	276	40.56 N	74.01 W
New Milford, Pa., U.S.	210	41.52 N	75.43 W
New Millpond ⊜	276	40.50 N	73.13 W
New Millport	214	40.54 N	78.32 W
New Mills	44	53.23 N	2.00 W
Newmilns	46	55.37 N	4.20 W
New Milton	42	50.44 N	1.40 W
New Minden	219	38.26 N	89.22 W
New Munster	216	42.34 N	88.13 W
Newnan	192	33.22 N	84.47 W
Newnans Lake ⊜	192	29.39 N	82.13 W
Newnham	42	51.49 N	2.27 W
New Norcia	162	30.58 S	116.13 E
New Norfolk	166	42.47 S	147.03 E
New Norway	182	52.53 N	112.58 W
New Orleans	194	29.57 N	90.04 W
New Orleans Naval Air Station ■	194	29.51 N	90.01 W
New Oxford	208	39.51 N	77.03 W
New Palestine	218	39.43 N	85.53 W
New Paltz	210	41.44 N	74.05 W
New Paris, In., U.S.	216	41.30 N	85.49 W
New Paris, Oh., U.S.	218	39.51 N	84.47 W
New Paris, Pa., U.S.	214	40.06 N	78.39 W
New Philadelphia, Oh., U.S.	214	40.30 N	81.27 W
New Philadelphia, Pa., U.S.	208	40.43 N	76.06 W
New Pine Creek	202	41.59 N	120.17 W
New Pitsligo	46	57.35 N	2.11 W
New Pittsburg	214	40.50 N	82.06 W
New Plymouth, N.Z.	172	39.04 S	174.05 E
New Plymouth, Id., U.S.	202	43.58 N	116.49 W
New Point	218	39.18 N	85.19 W
New Point Comfort ›	208	37.18 N	76.17 W
Newport, Austl.	274a	33.40 S	151.19 E
Newport, Austl.	274b	37.51 S	144.53 E
Newport, P.Q., Can.	186	48.16 N	64.45 W
Newport, Ire.	48	52.42 N	8.24 W
Newport, Ire.	48	53.53 N	9.34 W
New Port, Ned. Ant.	241s	12.03 N	68.49 W
Newport, Eng., U.K.	42	51.59 N	0.15 E
Newport, Eng., U.K.	42	50.42 N	1.18 W
Newport, Eng., U.K.	42	52.47 N	2.22 W
Newport, Wales, U.K.	42	51.35 N	3.00 W
Newport, Wales, U.K.	42	52.01 N	4.51 W
Newport, Ar., U.S.	194	35.36 N	91.16 W
Newport, De., U.S.	208	39.42 N	75.36 W
Newport, In., U.S.	194	39.53 N	87.24 W
Newport, Ky., U.S.	218	39.05 N	84.29 W
Newport, Me., U.S.	188	44.50 N	69.16 W
Newport, Md., U.S.	208	38.25 N	76.54 W
Newport, Mi., U.S.	216	42.00 N	83.18 W
Newport, N.H., U.S.	188	43.21 N	72.10 W
Newport, N.J., U.S.	208	39.17 N	75.10 W
Newport, N.Y., U.S.	210	43.11 N	75.00 W
Newport, N.C., U.S.	192	34.47 N	76.51 W
Newport, Oh., U.S.	216	39.23 N	81.13 W
Newport, Or., U.S.	202	44.38 N	124.03 W
Newport, Pa., U.S.	208	40.28 N	77.07 W
Newport, R.I., U.S.	207	41.29 N	71.18 W
Newport, Tn., U.S.	192	35.58 N	83.11 W
Newport, Vt., U.S.	206	44.56 N	72.12 W
Newport, Wa., U.S.	202	48.11 N	117.02 W
Newport □[6]	207	41.35 N	71.15 W
Newport Bay c	208	38.14 N	75.13 W
Newport Beach	228	33.37 N	117.55 W
Newport Center	206	44.57 N	72.18 W
Newport Hills	224	47.32 N	122.10 W
Newport News	208	36.58 N	76.25 W
Newport-on-Tay	46	56.26 N	2.55 W
Newport Pagnell	42	52.05 N	0.44 W
New Port Richey	220	28.14 N	82.43 W
Newportville	285	40.09 N	74.53 W
Newportville Terrace	285	40.07 N	74.54 W
New Prague	190	44.32 N	93.34 W
New Preston	207	41.40 N	73.21 W
New Providence, N.J., U.S.	210	40.41 N	74.24 W
New Providence, Pa., U.S.	208	39.56 N	76.12 W
New Providence, Tn., U.S.	194	36.32 N	87.23 W
New Providence I	240b	25.02 N	77.24 W
Newquay, Eng., U.K.	42	50.25 N	5.05 W
New Quay, Wales, U.K.	42	52.13 N	4.22 W
New Redruth	273d	26.16 S	28.07 E
New Richland	190	43.53 N	93.29 W
New-Richmond, P.Q., Can.	186	48.10 N	65.52 W
New Richmond, Oh., U.S.	218	38.56 N	84.16 W
New Richmond, Wi., U.S.	190	45.07 N	92.32 W
New Riegel	214	41.03 N	83.19 W
New Rim Ditch ≅	228	35.08 N	118.58 W
New Ringgold	208	40.41 N	76.00 W
New Road	186	44.45 N	63.28 W
New Roads	194	30.42 N	91.26 W
New Rochelle	210	40.54 N	73.46 W
New Rockford	198	47.40 N	99.08 W
New Romney	42	50.59 N	0.57 E
New Ross, N.S., Can.	186	44.44 N	64.27 W
New Ross, Ire.	48	52.24 N	6.56 W
New Rossington	44	53.29 N	1.04 W
Newry, N. Ire., U.K.	48	54.11 N	6.20 W
Newry, Pa., U.S.	214	40.24 N	78.26 W
Newry, S.C., U.S.	192	34.43 N	82.54 W
New Salem, In., U.S.	218	39.32 N	85.22 W
New Salem, N.D., U.S.	198	46.50 N	101.24 W
New Salisbury	218	38.19 N	86.06 W
New Sarum → Salisbury	42	51.05 N	1.48 W
New Schwabenland ◆[1]	9	72.30 S	1.00 E
New Scone	46	56.25 N	3.24 W
Newsham Park ♦	262	53.25 N	2.56 W
New Sharon	190	41.28 N	92.39 W
New Sheffield	214	40.36 N	80.17 W
New Shrewsbury	276	40.19 N	74.04 W
New Siberian Islands → Novosibirskoje ostrova II	74	75.00 N	142.00 E
New Smyrna Beach	220	29.01 N	80.55 W
Newsome	222	32.59 N	95.08 W
Newsoms	208	36.37 N	77.07 W
New South Wales □[3]	166	33.00 S	146.00 E
New South Wales, University of ᵾ[2]	274a	33.55 S	151.14 E
New South Wales Lawn Tennis Association Courts ♦	274a	33.53 S	151.14 E
New Springfield	214	40.55 N	80.36 W
New Square	276	41.08 N	74.02 W
New Stanton	214	40.13 N	79.37 W
Newstead	169	37.07 S	144.04 E
New Stuyahok	180	59.29 N	157.20 W
New Suffolk	207	41.00 N	72.28 W
New Summerfield	222	31.59 N	95.06 W
New Tazewell	192	36.27 N	83.33 W
New Terrell City Lake ⊜[1]	222	32.44 N	96.14 W
New Territories □[8]	271d	22.24 N	114.10 E
New Thunderchild Indian Reserve ◆[4]	184	53.30 N	108.50 W
Newtok	180	60.56 N	164.38 W
Newton, Eng., U.K.	44	53.57 N	2.27 W
Newton, Eng., U.K.	262	53.16 N	2.43 W
Newton, Ga., U.S.	192	31.18 N	84.20 W
Newton, Il., U.S.	194	38.59 N	88.09 W
Newton, Ia., U.S.	190	41.41 N	93.02 W
Newton, Ks., U.S.	198	38.02 N	97.20 W
Newton, Ma., U.S.	207	42.20 N	71.12 W
Newton, Ms., U.S.	194	32.19 N	89.09 W
Newton, N.J., U.S.	210	41.03 N	74.45 W
Newton, N.C., U.S.	192	35.40 N	81.13 W
Newton, Tx., U.S.	194	30.50 N	93.45 W
Newton □[6]	216	40.46 N	87.27 W
Newton Abbot	42	50.32 N	3.36 W
Newton Arlosh	44	54.53 N	3.15 W
Newton Aycliffe	44	54.36 N	1.32 W
Newton Brook ◆[8]	275b	43.48 N	79.24 W
Newton Center	283	42.20 N	71.12 W
Newton Falls, N.Y., U.S.	188	44.12 N	74.59 W
Newton Falls, Oh., U.S.	214	41.11 N	80.58 W
Newton Ferrers	42	50.18 N	4.02 W
Newton Flotman	42	52.32 N	1.16 E
Newton Hamilton	214	40.24 N	77.51 W
Newton Highlands	283	42.19 N	71.13 W
Newton-le-Willows	44	53.28 N	2.37 W
Newton Longville	42	51.58 N	0.46 W
Newton Lower Falls	283	42.19 N	71.23 W
Newtonmore	46	57.04 N	4.08 W
Newton Stewart	44	54.57 N	4.29 W
Newtonsville	218	39.11 N	84.05 W
Newton Upper Falls	283	42.19 N	71.13 W
Newtonville, On., Can.	212	43.56 N	78.30 W
Newtonville, Ma., U.S.	283	42.21 N	71.13 W
Newtonville, N.J., U.S.	208	39.33 N	74.51 W
New Toronto ◆[8]	275b	43.36 N	79.30 W
Newtown, Austl.	169	38.09 S	144.20 E
Newtown, Nf., Can.	186	49.12 N	53.31 W
Newtown, Eng., U.K.	262	53.21 N	2.00 W
Newtown, Wales, U.K.	42	52.32 N	3.19 W
Newtown, Ct., U.S.	207	41.24 N	73.18 W
Newtown, In., U.S.	216	40.12 N	87.08 W
Newtown, Ky., U.S.	218	38.13 N	84.57 W
New Town, N.D., U.S.	198	47.58 N	102.29 W
Newtown, Pa., U.S.	208	40.14 N	74.56 W
Newtown ◆[8]	274a	33.54 S	151.11 E
Newtownabbey	48	54.42 N	5.54 W
Newtownards	48	54.36 N	5.41 W
Newtownbutler	48	54.12 N	7.23 W
Newtown Creek ≏, N.Y., U.S.	276	40.44 N	73.58 W
Newtown Creek ≏, Pa., U.S.	285	40.13 N	74.56 W
Newtown Crommelin	48	54.59 N	6.13 W
Newtown Forbes	48	53.46 N	7.50 W
Newtownhamilton	48	54.12 N	6.35 W
Newtown Mount Kennedy	48	53.05 N	6.07 W
Newtown Saint Boswells	46	55.34 N	2.40 W
Newtown Square	208	39.59 N	75.24 W
Newtownstewart	48	54.43 N	7.24 W
New Tredegar	42	51.43 N	3.14 W
New Tripoli	208	40.41 N	75.45 W
New Troy	216	41.53 N	86.33 W
New Truxton	219	38.58 N	91.15 W
New Ulm, Mn., U.S.	190	44.18 N	94.27 W
New Ulm, Tx., U.S.	222	29.53 N	96.29 W
New Uosenow	54	53.47 N	13.46 E
New Utrecht ◆[8]	276	40.36 N	73.59 W
New Vernon	276	40.45 N	74.30 W
New Vienna	218	39.19 N	83.41 W
Newville, In., U.S.	216	41.21 N	84.51 W
Newville, Pa., U.S.	208	40.10 N	77.23 W
New Vineyard	188	44.48 N	70.07 W
New Waltham	44	53.32 N	0.04 W
New Washington, Pil.	116	11.39 N	122.26 E
New Washington, In., U.S.	218	38.33 N	85.32 W
New Washington, Oh., U.S.	214	40.57 N	82.51 W
New Waterford, N.S., Can.	186	46.15 N	60.05 W
New Waterford, Oh., U.S.	214	40.50 N	80.36 W
New Waverly, In., U.S.	216	40.46 N	86.12 W
New Waverly, Tx., U.S.	222	30.32 N	95.29 W
New Westminster	224	49.12 N	122.55 W
New Whiteland	218	39.33 N	86.05 W
New Wilmington	214	41.07 N	80.19 W
New Windsor → Windsor, Eng., U.K.	42	51.29 N	0.38 W
New Windsor, Md., U.S.	208	39.32 N	77.06 W
New Windsor, N.Y., U.S.	210	41.30 N	74.01 W
New Woodbine Racetrack ♦	275b	43.43 N	79.36 W
New Woodstock	210	42.50 N	75.51 W
New World Island I	186	49.35 N	54.40 W
New Year Creek ≏	222	30.08 N	96.12 W
New York, N.Y., U.S.	210	40.43 N	74.01 W
New York, N.Y., U.S.	276	40.43 N	74.01 W
New York □[6]	276	40.47 N	73.58 W
New York □[3], U.S.	178	43.00 N	75.00 W
New York □[3], U.S.	188	43.00 N	75.00 W
New York, City College of ᵾ[2]	276	40.49 N	73.57 W
New York, Polytechnic Institute of ᵾ[2]	276	40.42 N	73.59 W
New York, State University of (Stony Brook) ᵾ[2], N.Y., U.S.	276	40.55 N	73.08 W
New York, State University of (Buffalo) ᵾ[2], N.Y., U.S.	284a	42.57 N	78.49 W
New York, State University of, College at Buffalo ᵾ[2]	284a	42.56 N	78.53 W
New York at Buffalo, State University of ᵾ[2]	284a	42.56 N	78.49 W
New York Mills, Mn., U.S.	198	46.31 N	95.22 W
New York Mills, N.Y., U.S.	210	43.06 N	75.18 W
New York State Barge Canal ≅	210	43.05 N	78.43 W
New York Stock Exchange ᵾ	276	40.42 N	74.01 W
New Zealand □[1]	172	41.00 S	174.00 E
New Zealand Plateau ✢[3]	9	51.00 S	170.00 E
Nexapa ≏	234	18.07 N	98.46 W
Nexon	32	45.41 N	1.11 E
Nexpa ≏	234	18.05 N	102.46 W
Ney	216	41.23 N	84.32 W
Neyagawa	96	34.46 N	135.38 E
Neye	263	51.07 N	7.22 E
Neyestausee ⊜[1]	263	51.08 N	7.24 E
Ney Lake ⊜	184	54.38 N	92.25 W
Neyland	42	51.43 N	4.57 W
Neylandville	222	33.12 N	96.00 W
Neyrīz	128	29.12 N	54.19 E
Neyshābūr	128	36.12 N	58.50 E
Neyyāttinkara	122	8.24 N	77.05 E
Nezahualcóyotl, Presa ⊜[1]	234	17.10 N	93.40 W
Nezamajevskaja	78	46.09 N	40.16 E
Nezameno-toko ♦	94	35.46 N	137.42 E
Nežárka ≏	61	49.11 N	14.41 E
Nezavertajlovka	78	46.37 N	29.56 E
Nežin	78	51.03 N	31.54 E
Nezlobnaja	84	44.08 N	43.23 E
Neznanka ≏	265b	55.34 N	37.21 E
Neznanovo	80	54.02 N	40.06 E
Nezperce	202	46.14 N	116.14 W
Nez Perce Indian Reservation ◆[4]	202	46.20 N	116.30 W
Nez Perce National Historical Park ♦	202	45.50 N	116.15 W
Nezpique, Bayou ≏	194	30.12 N	92.35 W
Nezvěstice	60	49.39 N	13.32 E
Ngabang	112	0.23 N	109.57 E
Ngabé	152	3.12 S	16.11 E
Ngabordamlu, Tanjung ›	164	6.56 S	134.11 E
Ngadda ≏	146	12.40 N	13.50 E
Ngadirojo	115a	8.13 S	111.19 E
Ngadza	152	5.10 N	20.12 E
Ngahere	172	42.24 S	171.27 E
Ngala	146	12.20 N	14.10 E
Ngale	152	2.56 N	21.20 E
Ngali	152	2.27 S	19.20 E
Ngaliema, Baie de c	273b	4.19 S	15.16 E
Ngalipaeng	112	3.24 N	125.37 E
Ngaloa Harbour c	175g	19.06 S	178.11 E
Ngamaba	273b	4.14 S	15.16 E
Ngamba ◆[8]	273b	4.15 S	15.18 E
Ngambé	152	4.14 N	10.37 E
Ngamdu	146	11.48 N	12.18 E
Ngami, Lake ⊜	156	20.37 S	22.40 E
Ngamiland □[5]	156	19.09 S	22.47 E
Ngamo	154	19.08 S	27.32 E
Ngamouéri	273b	4.14 S	15.14 E
Ngamring	124	29.14 N	87.10 E
Nganda ∧	154	10.25 S	33.50 E
Ngangala	154	4.42 N	31.55 E
Ngangla Ringco ⊜	120	31.40 N	83.00 E
Nganglong Kangri ∧	120	32.45 N	81.12 E
Nganglong Kangri ⋏	120	32.00 N	83.00 E
Ngangzê Co ⊜	120	31.05 N	86.55 E
Nganjuk	115a	7.36 S	111.55 E
Ngao	110	18.46 N	99.59 E
Ngaoui, Mont ∧	152	6.40 N	14.57 E
Ngaoundéré	152	7.19 N	13.35 E
Ngapali	110	18.26 N	94.19 E
Ngapara	172	44.57 S	170.45 E
Ngape	110	20.04 N	94.38 E
Ngaputaw	110	16.32 N	94.42 E
Ngara	154	2.28 S	30.39 E
Ngaramasch	175b	6.54 N	134.08 E
Ngarimbi	154	8.28 S	38.36 E
Ngaruawahia	172	37.40 S	175.09 E
Ngaruroro ≏	172	39.34 S	176.56 E
Ngasamo	154	2.33 S	33.53 E
Ngat ≏	110	19.09 N	99.01 E
Ngatangiia	174k	21.14 S	159.43 W
Ngatangiia Harbour c	174k	21.14 S	159.45 W
Ngatea	172	37.17 S	175.30 E
Ngathainggyaung	110	17.24 N	95.05 E
Ngatik I[1]	14	5.51 N	157.16 E
Ngau I	175g	18.02 S	179.18 E
Ngauruhoe, Mount ∧	172	39.09 S	175.38 E
Ngau Tau Kok → Kwun Tong	271d	22.19 N	114.12 E
Ngawen	115a	7.00 S	111.18 E
Ngawi	115a	7.24 S	111.26 E
Ngay Nua	110	21.50 N	101.54 E
Ngebel	115a	7.46 S	111.37 E
Ngele	152	0.29 S	20.25 E
Ngemelis Islands II	175b	7.07 N	134.15 E
Ngerengere	154	6.45 S	38.07 E
Ngerkeel	175b	7.25 N	134.30 E
Ngermechau	175b	7.35 N	134.39 E
Ngeruktabel I	175b	7.15 N	134.24 E
Ngetbong	175b	7.37 N	134.35 E
Ngetera	146	12.31 N	12.38 E
Nggamea Island I	175g	16.46 S	179.46 W
Nggatokae Island I	175e	8.46 S	158.11 E
Nggela Pile I	175e	9.05 S	160.15 E
Nggela Sule I	175e	9.05 S	160.15 E
Nggelelevu I	175g	16.05 S	179.09 W
Nggwavuma ≏	158	26.58 S	32.17 E
Nghia Dan	110	19.18 N	105.26 E
Nghia Hanh	110	15.03 N	108.47 E
Nghia Lo	110	21.36 N	104.31 E
Ngiap ≏	110	18.24 N	103.36 E
Ngidinga	152	5.37 S	15.17 E
Ngimbang	115a	7.17 S	112.12 E
Ng'iro ∧	154	2.08 N	36.51 E
Ngiro, Ewaso ≏, Kenya	154	2.04 S	36.07 E
Ng'iro, Ewaso ≏, Kenya	154	0.28 N	39.55 E
Ngo	152	2.29 S	15.45 E
Ngoangoa ≏	140	5.48 N	25.09 E
Ngoboli	154	4.57 N	32.37 E
Ngoko ≏, Afr.	152	1.40 N	16.03 E
Ngoko ≏, Congo	152	0.25 S	15.29 E
Ngol-Kedju Hill ∧[2]	152	6.20 N	9.45 E
Ngolo	146	9.56 N	22.16 E
Ngom ≏	102	31.11 N	97.15 E
Ngomahuru	154	20.26 S	30.43 E
Ngomba	154	8.23 S	32.53 E
Ngomba ∧	154	5.43 S	35.52 E
Ngombe, Zaïre	152	6.35 S	20.42 E
Ngombe, Zaïre	273b	4.24 S	15.11 E
Ngome	158	27.46 S	31.28 E
Ngomedzap	152	3.15 N	11.12 E
Ngomeni, Ras ›	154	2.59 S	40.14 E
Ngong	154	1.22 S	36.39 E
Ngongotaha	172	38.05 S	176.12 E
Ngono ≏	154	1.08 S	31.35 E
Ngonye Falls L	152	16.40 S	23.35 E
Ngop	140	6.16 N	30.12 E
Ngora	154	1.27 N	33.46 E
Ngorengore	154	1.02 S	35.30 E
Ngoring Hu ⊜	102	34.50 N	97.35 E
Ngoro	115a	7.41 S	112.16 E
Ngorongoro Crater ≗[6]	154	3.10 S	35.35 E
Ngote	154	2.14 N	30.48 E
Ngoto	152	4.00 N	17.21 E
Ngotwane ≏	156	23.35 S	26.58 E
Ngoulémakong	152	3.07 N	11.25 E
Ngouma	150	15.38 N	3.22 W
Ngounié □[4]	152	1.30 S	11.00 E
Ngounié ≏	152	0.37 S	10.18 E
Ngouri	146	13.38 N	15.22 E
Ngouroundou	152	6.27 N	22.37 E
Ngourti	146	15.19 N	13.12 E
Ngoywa	154	5.56 S	32.48 E
Ngozi	154	2.54 S	29.50 E
Ngqeleni	158	31.40 S	29.02 E
Ngudiabaka ≏	273b	4.25 S	15.11 E
Nguélémendouka	152	4.23 N	12.55 E
Ngugha ≏	156	19.21 S	23.15 E
Nguigmi	146	14.15 N	13.07 E
Nguila	152	4.43 N	11.41 E
Nguiu	164	11.45 S	130.38 E
Ngulu I[1]	108	8.27 N	137.29 E
Ngum ≏	110	18.09 N	103.06 E
Nguna, Île I	175f	17.26 S	168.21 E
Ngunga	154	3.41 S	33.34 E
Ngunju, Tanjung ›	115b	10.19 S	120.28 E
Ngunut	115a	8.06 S	112.01 E
Ngurore	146	9.18 N	12.14 E
Nguru	146	12.52 N	10.27 E
Ngwempisi ≏	158	26.42 S	31.26 E
Ngweni	158	27.56 S	32.15 E
Ngwenya ∧	158	26.11 S	31.02 E
Ngwerere	154	15.18 S	28.20 E
Ngweze ≏	154	17.40 S	25.07 E
Nha Be	269c	10.42 N	106.44 E
Nhabe ≏, Bots.	156	20.22 S	22.58 E
Nha Be ≏, Viet.	269c	10.39 N	106.44 E
Nhacoongo	156	24.18 S	35.14 E
Nhamacolomo	156	18.05 S	34.26 E
Nhamundá	250	2.14 S	56.43 W
Nhamundá ≏	246	2.12 S	56.41 W
Nha Nam	110	21.27 N	106.06 E
Nhandeara	255	20.40 S	50.02 W
Nhareia	152	11.25 S	17.03 E
Nha Trang	110	12.15 N	109.11 E
Nhecolândia	248	19.16 S	57.04 W
Nhia ≏	152	10.15 S	14.12 E
Nhill	166	36.20 S	141.39 E
Nhlangano	158	27.06 S	31.12 E
Nhlazatshe	158	28.10 S	31.14 E
Nhoma ≏	156	18.52 S	20.53 E
Nhon Trach	269c	10.43 N	106.51 E
Nhulunbuy	164	12.11 S	136.47 E
Nhundo	152	14.25 S	21.23 E
Nhunguaçu	256	22.21 S	42.53 W
Niabembe	154	2.14 S	27.44 E
Niafounké	150	15.56 N	4.00 W
Niagara	190	45.46 N	87.59 W
Niagara □[6], On., Can.	212	43.05 N	79.20 W
Niagara □[6], N.Y., U.S.	210	43.10 N	78.42 W
Niagara ≏	212	43.15 N	79.04 W
Niagara County Historical Center ᵾ	284a	43.10 N	78.43 W
Niagara Falls, On., Can.	212	43.06 N	79.04 W
Niagara Falls, On., Can.	284a	43.06 N	79.04 W
Niagara Falls, N.Y., U.S.	210	43.05 N	79.03 W
Niagara Falls, N.Y., U.S.	284a	43.05 N	79.03 W
Niagara Falls L	212	43.05 N	79.04 W
Niagara Falls Airport ⊠	284a	43.02 N	79.08 W
Niagara Falls International Airport ⊠	284a	43.06 N	78.56 W
Niagara-on-the-Lake	212	43.15 N	79.04 W
Niagara University ᵾ[2]	284a	43.08 N	79.02 W
Niagassola	150	12.19 N	9.07 W
Niah	112	3.52 N	113.44 E
Niakaramandougou	150	8.40 N	5.17 W
Niamey	150	13.31 N	2.07 E
Niamey □[5]	150	14.00 N	2.00 E
Niamtougou	150	9.46 N	1.06 E
Nianbadu	100	28.17 N	118.28 E
Niandan ≏	150	10.30 N	10.26 W
Niandan Koro	150	11.05 N	9.15 W
Nianforando	150	9.32 N	10.31 W
Niangara	154	3.42 N	27.52 E
Niangay, Lac ⊜	150	15.50 N	3.00 W
Niangmake	102	30.14 N	99.40 E
Niangnianggong	104	41.00 N	121.13 E
Niangniangmiao	98	42.34 N	118.05 E
Niangniangwa	105	40.33 N	117.30 E
Niangoloko	150	10.17 N	4.55 W
Niangua ≏	194	37.58 N	92.48 W
Niangzizhuang	105	40.02 N	118.05 E
Nia-Nia	154	1.24 N	27.36 E
Nianpan	104	41.48 N	124.02 E
Niantic, Ct., U.S.	207	41.19 N	72.11 W
Niantic, Il., U.S.	219	39.51 N	89.10 W
Nianyugou	104	42.00 N	123.59 E
Nianyushan	100	29.11 N	117.04 E
Nianzhuang	98	34.19 N	117.47 E
Nianzigang	100	31.03 N	114.18 E
Nianzishan	89	47.32 N	122.52 E
Niapu	154	2.25 N	26.28 E
Niari □[5]	152	3.15 S	12.30 E
Niari ≏	152	3.56 S	12.12 E
Niaro	140	10.38 N	31.31 E
Nias, Pulau I	114	1.05 N	97.35 E
Niassa □[5]	154	13.30 S	36.00 E
Nibbiano	62	44.54 N	9.19 E
Nibe	26	56.59 N	9.38 E
Nibong Tebal	114	5.10 N	100.29 E
Nibra	272b	22.36 N	88.16 E
Nīca	76	56.19 N	21.04 E
Nica ≏	86	57.29 N	64.33 E
Nicaragua □[1], N.A.	230	13.00 N	85.00 W
Nicaragua □[1], N.A.	236	13.00 N	85.00 W
Nicaragua, Lago de ⊜	236	11.30 N	85.30 W
Nicaro	240p	20.42 N	75.33 W
Nicastro	68	38.59 N	16.20 E
Ničatka, ozero ⊜	88	57.45 N	117.30 E
Nice	62	43.42 N	7.15 E
Nice-Côte d'Azur, Aéroport de ⊠	62	43.40 N	7.14 E
Niceville	194	30.31 N	86.28 W
Nichelino	62	44.59 N	7.38 E
Nicheng	106	30.55 N	121.49 E
Nichihara	96	34.33 N	131.50 E
Nichinan, Nihon	92	31.36 N	131.23 E
Nichinan, Nihon	96	35.09 N	133.16 E
Nicholas □[6]	218	38.20 N	84.02 W
Nicholas Channel ⋓	238	23.25 N	80.05 W
Nicholasville	192	37.52 N	84.34 W
Nicholls	192	31.31 N	82.38 W
Nichols, Ca., U.S.	282	38.02 N	121.59 W
Nichols, Fl., U.S.	220	27.54 N	82.02 W
Nichols, N.Y., U.S.	210	42.01 N	76.22 W
Nichols Brook ≏	283	42.37 N	70.59 W
Nicholson, Austl.	162	18.02 S	128.54 E
Nicholson, Ky., U.S.	218	38.54 N	84.33 W
Nicholson, Ms., U.S.	194	30.28 N	89.41 W
Nicholson, Pa., U.S.	210	41.37 N	75.46 W
Nicholson ≏, Austl.	162	17.34 S	128.38 E
Nicholson ≏, Austl.	166	17.31 S	139.36 E
Nicholson Island I	212	43.56 N	77.31 W
Nicholson Range ⋏	162	27.15 S	116.45 E
Nicholson River Aboriginal Reserve ◆[4]	162	18.00 S	137.30 E
Nichols Run ≏	284b	39.03 N	77.18 W
Nickerie □[5]	250	4.00 N	57.30 W
Nickerie ≏	250	5.59 N	57.00 W
Nickerson	198	38.08 N	98.05 W
Nickol Bay c	162	20.39 S	116.52 E
Nicktown	214	40.37 N	78.48 W
Nicobar Islands II	110	8.00 N	93.30 E
Nicola	182	50.10 N	120.40 W
Nicola ≏	182	50.25 N	121.18 W
Nicolae Bălcescu	38	47.34 N	26.52 E
Nicolai Mountain ∧	224	46.05 N	123.28 W
Nicola Lake ⊜	182	50.10 N	120.25 W
Nicola Mameet Indian Reserve ◆[4]	182	50.11 N	120.49 W
Nicolás Bravo	234	18.21 N	93.10 W
Nicolás Pérez, Sierra de ⋏	234	22.27 N	99.08 W
Nicolás Romero □[7]	286a	19.37 N	99.17 W
Nicolaus	226	38.54 N	121.35 W
Nicolet	206	46.13 N	72.37 W
Nicolet □[6]	206	46.15 N	72.20 W
Nicolet ≏	206	46.14 N	72.39 W
Nicolet, Lac ⊜	206	45.50 N	71.33 W
Nicolet, Lake ⊜	190	46.20 N	84.15 W
Nicolet Centre ≏	206	45.46 N	71.50 W
Nicolet Sud-Ouest ≏	206	46.13 N	72.36 W
Nicoll Bay c	276	40.43 N	73.07 W
Nicollet	190	44.16 N	94.11 W
Nicoll Point ›	276	40.42 N	73.09 W
Nicolls Town	238	25.08 N	78.00 W
Nicolosi	70	37.37 N	15.01 E
Nicosia, It.	70	37.45 N	14.24 E
Nicosia (Levkosía), Kípros	130	35.10 N	33.22 E
Nicosia (Lefkoşa), Kıbrıs	130	35.10 N	33.22 E
Nicotera	68	38.34 N	15.57 E
Nicoya	236	10.09 N	85.27 W
Nicoya, Golfo de c	236	9.47 N	84.48 W
Nicoya, Península de ›[1]	236	10.00 N	85.25 W
Nictheroy → Niterói	256	22.53 S	43.07 W
Nida ≏	30	50.18 N	20.52 E
Nidadavole	122	16.55 N	81.40 E
Nidau	58	47.07 N	7.14 E
Nidd ≏	44	54.01 N	1.12 W
Nidda	56	50.24 N	9.00 E
Nidda ≏	56	50.06 N	8.34 E
Nidder ≏	56	50.12 N	8.47 E
Nidderau	56	50.14 N	8.52 E
Nide	102	31.51 N	96.19 E
Nideggen	56	50.47 N	6.29 E
Nidelva ≏	26	58.24 N	8.48 E
Nidwalden □[3]	58	46.55 N	8.28 E
Nidž	84	40.56 N	47.41 E
Nidzica	30	53.22 N	20.26 E
Niebüll	41	54.48 N	8.50 E
Nied ≏	56	49.23 N	6.40 E
Nied Allemande ≏	56	49.10 N	6.26 E
Nieddu, Monte ∧	71	40.45 N	9.34 E
Niederanven	56	49.39 N	6.16 E
Niederau	54	51.10 N	13.32 E
Niederaula	56	50.48 N	9.36 E
Niederbayern □[5]	60	48.45 N	12.45 E
Niederbipp	58	47.16 N	7.39 E
Niederbobritzsch	54	50.54 N	13.26 E
Niederbonsfeld	263	51.23 N	7.08 E
Niederbronn-Les-Bains	56	48.57 N	7.38 E
Niederdonk	263	51.14 N	6.41 E
Niederelfringhausen	263	51.21 N	7.10 E
Niedere Tauern ⋏	30	47.18 N	14.00 E
Niederfinow	54	52.50 N	13.55 E
Niederfrohna	54	50.53 N	12.43 E
Niederhaverbeck	52	53.09 N	9.54 E
Niederheimbach	56	50.02 N	7.48 E
Niederhone	56	51.13 N	10.06 E
Niederkassel	56	50.49 N	7.02 E
Nieder-Kassel ◆[8]	263	51.14 N	6.45 E
Niederkrüchten	56	51.12 N	6.13 E
Niederlande → Netherlands □[1]	30	52.15 N	5.30 E
Niederländische Antillen → Netherlands Antilles □[2]	241s	12.15 N	69.00 W
Niederlausitz □[9]	54	51.40 N	14.15 E
Niederlehme	54	52.19 N	13.39 E
Niedermarsberg	56	51.28 N	8.50 E
Niedermarschacht	52	53.25 N	10.21 E
Nieder-Mörlen	56	50.23 N	8.43 E
Niederndodeleben	54	52.08 N	11.30 E
Nieder-Neuendorf	264a	52.37 N	13.12 E
Niedernhall	56	49.17 N	9.36 E
Niedernwöhren	52	52.21 N	9.08 E
Niederoderwitz	54	50.57 N	14.44 E
Nieder-Ohmen	56	50.38 N	9.02 E
Nieder-Olm	56	49.55 N	8.11 E
Niederorschel	54	51.22 N	10.25 E
Niederösterreich □[3]	61	48.20 N	15.50 E
Niedersachsen □[3]	30	52.40 N	9.00 E
Niedersachswerfen	54	51.33 N	10.46 E
Niederschöneweide ◆[8]	264a	52.27 N	13.31 E
Niederschönhausen ◆[8]	54	52.35 N	13.23 E
Niedersee → Ruciane-Nida	30	53.39 N	21.35 E
Niedersonthofen	58	47.38 N	10.13 E
Niederstetten	56	49.24 N	9.55 E
Niederstotzingen	56	48.32 N	10.14 E
Niedersulz	61	48.29 N	16.40 E
Niederurnen	58	47.07 N	9.03 E
Niederwald	58	46.26 N	8.12 E
Niederwalgern	56	50.44 N	8.41 E
Niederweningen	58	47.30 N	8.23 E
Niederwiesa	54	50.51 N	13.01 E
Niederwürschnitz	54	50.43 N	12.45 E
Nied Française ≏	56	49.10 N	6.26 E
Niedu	100	25.28 N	114.08 E
Niefang	152	1.50 N	10.14 E
Nieheim	52	51.48 N	9.06 E
Niekerkshoop	158	29.19 S	22.51 E
Niel	50	51.07 N	4.20 E
Niellé	150	10.12 N	5.38 W
Niellim	146	9.42 N	17.49 E
Niem	152	6.12 N	15.14 E
Niemba	154	5.57 S	28.26 E
Niemegk	54	52.04 N	12.41 E
Niemeyer ◆[8]	287a	23.00 S	43.15 W
Niemodlin	30	50.39 N	17.37 E
Niena	150	11.26 N	6.21 W
Nienberge	52	52.00 N	7.34 E
Nienborg-Wigbold	52	52.08 N	7.06 E
Nienburg, B.R.D.	52	52.38 N	9.13 E
Nienburg, D.D.R.	54	51.50 N	11.46 E
Niendorf	54	53.59 N	10.50 E
Nienhagen, B.R.D.	52	52.33 N	10.05 E
Nienhagen, D.D.R.	54	51.57 N	11.09 E
Niénokoué, Mont ∧[2]	150	5.26 N	7.10 W
Niepkuhlen ≏	263	51.29 N	6.31 E
Niepołomice	30	50.03 N	20.13 E
Nieppe	50	50.42 N	2.50 E
Nier ≏	48	52.17 N	7.48 W
Niéré	146	14.30 N	21.09 E
Niéré, Hadjer ∧	146	14.21 N	21.40 E
Niéri Ko ≏	150	13.21 N	13.23 W
Niers ≏	52	51.43 N	5.57 E
Nierst	263	51.19 N	6.43 E
Nierstein	56	49.52 N	8.20 E
Niesen ∧	58	46.39 N	7.39 E
Niesky	54	51.17 N	14.49 E
Nieszawa	30	52.50 N	18.55 E
Nieto, Cañada de ≏	258	34.00 S	58.15 W
Nieu Bethesda	158	31.51 S	24.34 E
Nieuw-Amsterdam, Ned	52	52.44 N	6.51 E
Nieuw Amsterdam, Sur.	250	5.53 N	55.05 W
Nieuw-Buinen	52	52.57 N	6.55 E
Nieuwefontein	158	28.01 S	19.06 E
Nieuwegein	52	52.03 N	5.05 E
Nieuwe-Niedorp	52	52.45 N	4.54 E
Nieuwe-Pekela	52	53.04 N	6.58 E
Nieuweschans	52	53.11 N	7.12 E
Nieuwkoop	52	52.08 N	4.47 E
Nieuw Nickerie	250	5.57 N	56.59 W
Nieuwolda	52	53.14 N	6.59 E
Nieuwoudtville	158	31.23 S	19.07 E
Nieuwpoort	50	51.08 N	2.45 E
Nieuwpoort-Bad	50	51.09 N	2.42 E
Nieuw-Schoonebeek	52	52.38 N	6.59 E
Nieuw-Vennep	52	52.16 N	4.38 E
Nieuw-Weerdinge	52	52.52 N	6.59 E
Nieva ≏	246	4.35 S	77.53 W

Name	Seite	Breite°′	Länge°′ E = Ost
Nievenheim	56	51.07 N	6.46 E
Nievería	286d	11.59 S	76.55 W
Nieves	234	24.00 N	103.01 W
Nièvre □[5]	32	47.05 N	3.30 E
Nièvre ≏	50	47.10 N	3.13 E
Niga	150	13.38 N	5.27 W
Nigan	126	23.30 N	87.59 E
Niğde	130	37.59 N	34.42 E
Niğde □[4]	130	38.15 N	34.15 E
Nigei Island I	182	50.55 N	127.50 W
Nigel	158	26.30 S	28.28 E
Niger □[3]	150	10.00 N	6.00 E
Niger □[1]	134	16.00 N	8.00 E
Niger ≏	150	5.33 N	6.33 E
Niger Delta ≚[2]	150	4.50 N	6.00 E
Nigeria □[1]	134	10.00 N	8.00 E
Nigerian Museum ᵾ	273a	6.20 N	3.24 E
Nigg	46	57.43 N	4.00 W
Nighāsan	124	28.14 N	80.52 E
Nightcaps	172	45.58 S	168.02 E
Nighthawk	182	48.58 N	119.38 W
Night Hawk Lake ⊜	190	48.28 N	81.00 W
Nightingale Island I	10	37.24 S	12.28 W
Nightmute	180	60.29 N	164.43 W
Nigríta	38	40.55 N	23.30 E
Nihe	104	41.27 N	121.13 E
Nihing (Nahang) ≏	128	26.00 N	62.44 E
Nihoa I	14	23.06 N	161.58 W
Nihommatsu	92	37.35 N	140.26 E
Nihon → Japan □[1]	92	36.00 N	138.00 E
Nihonbashi ◆[8]	268	35.41 N	139.47 E
Nihon-kai → Japan, Sea of ≑[2]	90	40.00 N	135.00 E
Nihon University ᵾ[2]	268	35.42 N	139.45 E
Nihtaur	124	29.20 N	78.23 E
Nihuil, Embalse del ⊜[1]	252	35.05 S	68.45 W
Niida ≏	96	33.11 N	132.58 E
Niigata	92	37.55 N	139.03 E
Niigata □[5]	94	37.08 N	138.30 E
Niihama	96	33.58 N	133.16 E
Niihari	94	36.07 N	140.09 E
Niiharu	94	36.41 N	138.55 E
Niihau I	229b	21.55 N	160.10 W
Nii-jima I	92	34.22 N	139.16 E
Niimi	96	34.59 N	133.28 E
Niinisalo	26	61.50 N	22.29 E
Niitsu	92	37.48 N	139.07 E
Niiza	94	35.48 N	139.34 E
Níjar	34	36.58 N	2.12 W
Nijiaqiao	269b	31.14 N	121.21 E
Nijil	132	30.31 N	35.33 E
Nijkerk	52	52.13 N	5.30 E
Nijlen	56	51.10 N	4.39 E
Nijmegen	52	51.50 N	5.50 E
Nijo Castle ⊥	270	35.01 N	135.45 E
Nijvel → Nivelles	50	50.36 N	4.20 E
Nijverdal	52	52.22 N	6.27 E
Níkaia	267c	37.58 N	23.39 E
Nikel'	24	69.24 N	30.12 E
Nikel'tau	86	50.23 N	58.13 E
Nikiforovo	265b	55.50 N	38.05 E
Nikiniki	112	9.49 S	124.28 E
Nikip Lake ⊜	184	52.53 N	91.53 W
Nikitovka, S.S.S.R.	78	50.23 N	38.25 E
Nikitovka, S.S.S.R.	83	48.21 N	38.02 E
Nikitsch	61	47.32 N	16.40 E
Nikitskoje, S.S.S.R.	82	55.18 N	38.28 E
Nikitskoje, S.S.S.R.	82	55.13 N	35.46 E
Nikki	150	9.56 N	3.12 E
Nikkō	94	36.45 N	139.37 E
Nikkō-kokuritsu-kōen ♦	94	36.49 N	139.33 E
Niklā al-'Inab	142	30.55 N	30.46 E
Niklasdorf	61	47.24 N	15.10 E
Nikobaren → Nicobar Islands II	110	8.00 N	93.30 E
Nikolai	180	62.58 N	154.09 W
Nikolaiken → Mikołajki	30	53.49 N	21.36 E
Nikolajev, S.S.S.R.	78	46.58 N	32.00 E
Nikolajev, S.S.S.R.	78	49.32 N	23.58 E
Nikolajevka, S.S.S.R.	78	51.04 N	34.02 E
Nikolajevka, S.S.S.R.	78	47.38 N	33.12 E
Nikolajevka, S.S.S.R.	78	47.06 N	34.14 E
Nikolajevka, S.S.S.R.	78	44.58 N	33.37 E
Nikolajevka, S.S.S.R.	78	46.23 N	29.24 E
Nikolajevka, S.S.S.R.	78	47.33 N	30.25 E
Nikolajevka, S.S.S.R.	80	46.21 N	47.44 E
Nikolajevka, S.S.S.R.	80	52.28 N	49.14 E
Nikolajevka, S.S.S.R.	80	52.11 N	48.04 E
Nikolajevka, S.S.S.R.	80	53.08 N	47.12 E
Nikolajevka, S.S.S.R.	83	47.18 N	38.50 E
Nikolajevka, S.S.S.R.	83	48.51 N	37.46 E
Nikolajevka, S.S.S.R.	83	48.46 N	38.20 E
Nikolajevka, S.S.S.R.	83	47.39 N	37.41 E
Nikolajevka, S.S.S.R.	86	56.29 N	95.06 E
Nikolajevka, S.S.S.R.	86	54.57 N	75.44 E
Nikolajevka, S.S.S.R.	86	49.10 N	81.59 E
Nikolajevka, S.S.S.R.	88	55.46 N	98.10 E
Nikolajevka, S.S.S.R.	89	48.34 N	134.47 E
Nikolajevo	76	58.16 N	29.29 E
Nikolajevo-Kozlovskij	83	47.13 N	38.21 E
Nikolajevsk	80	50.01 N	45.28 E
Nikolajevskaja	80	47.37 N	41.29 E
Nikolajevsk-Na-Amure	89	53.08 N	140.44 E
Nikolajevskoje, S.S.S.R.	78	45.08 N	39.36 E
Nikolajevskoje, S.S.S.R.	88	51.04 N	111.48 E
Nikolajevskoje, S.S.S.R.	88	52.21 N	117.00 E
Nikolassee ◆[8]	264a	52.26 N	13.12 E
Nikolayev → Nikolajev	78	46.58 N	32.00 E
Nikolo-Berezovec	76	58.38 N	42.17 E
Nikolo-Ber'ozovka	80	56.08 N	54.09 E
Nikolo-Chovanskoje	265b	55.36 N	37.27 E
Nikologory	80	56.09 N	41.59 E
Nikolo-Kropotki	82	56.44 N	37.55 E
Nikolo-L'vovsk	89	43.54 N	131.23 E
Nikolo-Makarovo	80	57.38 N	43.34 E
Nikolsdorf	64	46.47 N	12.55 E
Nikol'sk, S.S.S.R.	24	59.30 N	45.27 E
Nikol'sk, S.S.S.R.	80	53.45 N	46.05 E
Nikolski	180	52.56 N	168.52 W
Nikol'skij, S.S.S.R.	24	60.55 N	34.00 E
Nikol'skij, S.S.S.R.	86	56.18 N	68.58 E
Nikol'skij, S.S.S.R.	86	47.55 N	67.28 E
Nikol'skij Toržok	76	59.53 N	38.46 E
Nikol'skoje, S.S.S.R.	74	55.12 N	166.00 E
Nikol'skoje, S.S.S.R.	76	52.39 N	36.04 E
Nikol'skoje, S.S.S.R.	76	55.26 N	35.04 E
Nikol'skoje, S.S.S.R.	76	59.23 N	44.36 E
Nikol'skoje, S.S.S.R.	76	59.30 N	42.32 E
Nikol'skoje, S.S.S.R.	78	50.35 N	41.10 E
Nikol'skoje, S.S.S.R.	80	47.46 N	46.24 E
Nikol'skoje, S.S.S.R.	80	52.37 N	43.49 E
Nikol'skoje, S.S.S.R.	82	56.09 N	36.43 E
Nikol'skoje, S.S.S.R.	82	54.27 N	36.24 E
Nikol'skoje, S.S.S.R.	82	54.18 N	35.53 E
Nikol'skoje, S.S.S.R.	82	55.15 N	36.04 E
Nikol'skoje, S.S.S.R.	82	55.53 N	36.26 E
Nikol'skoje, S.S.S.R.	82	54.30 N	36.50 E
Nikol'skoje, S.S.S.R.	82	55.37 N	36.41 E
Nikol'skoje, S.S.S.R.	82	54.51 N	35.53 E
Nikol'skoje, S.S.S.R.	82	54.03 N	37.10 E
Nikol'skoje, S.S.S.R.	83	47.46 N	37.18 E
Nikol'skoje, S.S.S.R.	86	52.02 N	55.43 E
Nikol'skoje, S.S.S.R.	86	57.12 N	84.21 E
Nikol'skoje, S.S.S.R.	265a	59.41 N	30.47 E
Nikol'skoje, S.S.S.R.	265b	55.46 N	37.54 E
Nikol'skoje-na-Čeremšane	80	54.03 N	49.14 E
Nikol'skoje-na-Dnepre	78	48.12 N	35.12 E
Nikol'skoje-Ur'upino	265b	55.48 N	37.13 E

Symbols in the index entries represent the broad categories identified in the key at the right. Symbols with superior numbers (⋏[1]) identify subcategories (see complete key on page *I · 1).*

Symbole im Register stellen die rechts im Schlüssel erklärten Kategorien dar. Symbole mit hochgestellten Ziffern (⋏[1]) bezeichnen Unterabteilungen einer Kategorie (vgl. vollständiger Schlüssel auf Seite *I · 1).*

Los símbolos incluídos en el texto del índice representan las grandes categorias identificadas con la clave a la derecha. Los símbolos con numeros en su parte superior (⋏[1]) identifican las subcategorías (véase la clave completa en la página *I · 1).*

Les symboles de l'index représentent les catégories indiquées dans la légende à droite. Les symboles suivis d'un indice (⋏[1]) représentent des sous-catégories (voir légende complète à la page *I · 1).*

Os símbolos incluídos no texto do índice representam as grandes categorias identificadas com a chave à direita. Os símbolos com números em sua parte superior (⋏[1]) identificam as subcategorias (veja-se a chave completa à página *I · 1).*

∧ Mountain	Berg	Montaña	Montagne	Montanha
⋏ Mountains	Gebirge	Montañas	Montagnes	Montanhas
)(Pass	Paß	Paso	Col	Passo
V Valley, Canyon	Tal, Cañon	Valle, Cañón	Vallée, Canyon	Vale, Canhão
≚ Plain	Ebene	Llano	Plaine	Planície
› Cape	Kap	Cabo	Cap	Cabo
I Island	Insel	Isla	Île	Ilha
II Islands	Inseln	Islas	Îles	Ilhas
≗ Other Topographic Features	Andere Topographische Objekte	Otros Elementos Topográficos	Autres données topographiques	Outros acidentes topográficos

Niko-Nori I · 123

ESPAÑOL: Nombre · Página · Lat.°′ · Long.°′ W = Oeste
FRANÇAIS: Nom · Page · Lat.°′ · Long.°′ W = Ouest
PORTUGUÊS: Nome · Página · Lat.°′ · Long.°′ W = Oeste

Nikonga ≃ 154 4.40 S 31.28 E
Nikonorovka 83 49.07 N 39.59 E
Nikonova Gora 76 60.22 N 36.07 E
Nikonovskoje 82 55.17 N 38.10 E
Nikopol, Blg. 38 43.42 N 24.54 E
Nikopol', S.S.S.R. 78 47.35 N 34.25 E
Niksar 130 40.36 N 36.58 E
Nīkshahr 128 26.13 N 60.12 E
Nikšić 38 42.46 N 18.56 E
Nikulino, S.S.S.R. 76 55.16 N 33.46 E
Nikulino, S.S.S.R. 80 58.05 N 44.14 E
Nikulino, S.S.S.R. 82 56.48 N 35.50 E
Nikulino ◆[8] 265b 55.40 N 37.28 E
Nikulkino 82 56.07 N 38.38 E
Nikul'skoje 82 55.10 N 38.41 E
Nikumaroro I[1] 14 4.40 S 174.32 W
Nikunau I 14 1.23 S 176.26 E
Nil
→ Nile ≃ 140 30.10 N 31.06 E
Nīl, Nahr an-
→ Nile ≃ 140 30.10 N 31.06 E
Nila, Pulau I 164 6.44 S 129.31 E
Nilakka ⊜ 26 63.07 N 26.33 E
Niland 204 33.14 N 115.31 W
Nil Blanc
→ White Nile ≃ 140 15.38 N 32.31 E
Nile □[5] 154 3.00 N 31.30 E
Nile (Nahr an-Nīl) ≃ 140 30.10 N 31.06 E
Niles, Il., U.S. 216 42.01 N 87.48 W
Niles, Mi., U.S. 216 41.49 N 86.15 W
Niles, Oh., U.S. 214 41.10 N 80.45 W
Niles Pond ⊜ 283 42.35 N 70.40 W
Nilgani 272b 22.46 N 88.26 E
Nilgaut, Lac ⊜ 190 46.36 N 77.15 W
Nilgiri 126 21.28 N 86.46 E
Nilka 86 43.47 N 82.20 E
Nilkitkwa ≃ 182 55.27 N 126.43 W
Nillahcootie, Lake ⊜[1] 169 36.54 S 146.00 E
Nilo
→ Nile ≃ 140 30.10 N 31.06 E
Nilo Azul
→ Blue Nile ≃ 140 15.38 N 32.31 E
Nilo Blanco
→ White Nile ≃ 140 15.38 N 32.31 E
Nilo Peçanha 255 13.37 S 39.06 W
Nilópolis 256 22.49 S 43.25 W
Nilópolis □[7] 287a 22.49 S 43.26 W
Nilphāmāri 124 25.56 N 88.51 E
Nilsiä 26 63.12 N 28.05 E
Niltepec 234 16.34 N 94.37 W
Nilüfer ≃ 130 40.18 N 28.27 E
Nilwāl ◆[8] 272a 28.40 N 76.59 E
Nilwood 219 39.24 N 89.49 W
Nima 96 35.09 N 132.24 E
Nīmach 120 24.28 N 74.52 E
Niman ≃ 89 51.24 N 132.45 E
Nimančik 89 52.09 N 133.47 E
Nimba, Mount ∧ 150 7.37 N 8.25 W
Nimbāhera 120 24.37 N 74.41 E
Nimba Range ∧ 150 7.30 N 8.30 W
Nimboran,
Pegunungan ∧ 164 2.45 S 140.20 E
Nimelen ≃ 89 52.27 N 136.32 E
Nîmes 62 43.50 N 4.21 E
Nimis 64 46.12 N 13.16 E
Nimishillen Creek ≃ 214 40.38 N 81.22 W
Nimisila 214 40.56 N 81.34 W
Nimisila Reservoir ⊜[1] 214 40.57 N 81.31 W
Nīm Ka Thāna 120 27.44 N 75.48 E
Nimmitabel 156 36.31 S 149.16 E
Nimmonsburg 210 42.09 N 75.55 W
Nimpkish Lake ⊜ 182 50.25 N 126.59 W
Nimrod Glacier ⊟ 9 82.27 S 161.00 E
Nimrod Lake ⊜[1] 194 34.55 N 93.20 W
Nimrūz □[4] 128 30.30 N 62.00 E
Nims ≃ 56 49.51 N 6.28 E
Nimta 272b 22.40 N 88.25 E
Nimule 154 3.36 N 32.03 E
Nimule National Park
♦ 154 3.50 N 31.35 E
Nimy 50 50.28 N 3.57 E
Nīnah, Wādī V 146 30.02 N 15.22 E
Nīnawá □[4] 128 36.10 N 42.35 E
Nīnawá (Nineveh) ⊥ 128 36.25 N 43.10 E
Nin Bay c 116 12.13 N 123.15 E
Ninda 152 14.47 S 21.24 E
Nindigully 166 28.21 S 148.49 E
Nindiri 236 12.00 N 86.08 W
Nine Ashes 260 51.42 N 0.18 E
Nine Degree Channel
ʊ 122 9.00 N 73.00 E
Ninemile Creek ≃,
N.Y., U.S. 210 43.24 N 76.38 W
Ninemile Creek ≃,
N.Y., U.S. 210 43.11 N 75.20 W
Ninemile Creek ≃,
N.Y., U.S. 210 43.06 N 76.14 W
Nine Mile Creek ≃,
Ut., U.S. 200 39.50 N 109.53 W
Ninemile Island I 279b 40.29 N 79.52 W
Nine Mile Lake ⊜ 212 44.57 N 79.34 W
Nine Mile Point > 212 44.09 N 76.34 W
Ninepin Group II 271d 22.16 N 114.21 E
Nineteen Hundred
Five Memorial
Cemetery ◆ 265a 59.51 N 30.27 E
Ninette 184 49.24 N 99.38 W
Ninetyeast Ridge ⊸[3] 6 4.00 S 90.00 E
Ninety Mile Beach
⊥[2], Austl. 166 38.13 S 147.23 E
Ninety Mile Beach
⊥[2], N.Z. 172 34.48 S 173.00 E
Ninety Six 192 34.10 N 82.01 W
Nineveh, In., U.S. 218 39.22 N 86.05 W
Nineveh, N.Y., U.S. 210 42.12 N 75.36 W
Nineveh
→ Nīnawá ⊥ 128 36.25 N 43.10 E
Ninfa ⊥ 66 41.36 N 12.58 E
Ninfas, Punta > 254 42.56 S 64.20 W
Ninfield 42 50.53 N 0.25 E
Ninga 184 49.13 N 99.51 W
Ningaloo 162 22.42 S 113.40 E
Ning'an 89 44.22 N 129.25 E
Ningbo 100 29.52 N 121.31 E
Ningcheng (Tianyi) 98 41.33 N 119.20 E
Ningde 100 26.43 N 119.33 E
Ningdu 100 26.31 N 115.58 E
Ningerum 164 5.41 S 141.08 E
Ninggang 100 26.50 N 114.02 E
Ningguo 100 30.38 N 118.58 E
Ninghai 100 29.17 N 121.25 E
Ninghe (Lutai) 98 39.20 N 117.48 E
Ninghepu 100 40.43 N 116.07 E
Ninghua 100 26.15 N 116.38 E
Ningi 150 11.04 N 9.32 E
Ningjin, Zhg. 98 37.37 N 114.55 E
Ningjin, Zhg. 98 37.39 N 116.48 E
Ningjing Shan ∧ 102 29.45 N 98.45 E
Ningling 98 34.27 N 115.21 E
Ningming 102 22.07 N 107.05 E
Ningnan 102 27.11 N 102.36 E
Ningpo
→ Ningbo 100 29.52 N 121.31 E
Ningqiang 102 32.44 N 106.19 E
Ningshan 102 33.04 N 108.39 E
Ningsia
→ Yinchuan 98 38.30 N 106.18 E
Ningsia Hui
Autonomous
Region
→ Ningxia Huizu
Zizhiqu □[4] 102 37.00 N 106.00 E
Ningwu 102 39.01 N 112.21 E
Ningxi 100 28.35 N 121.00 E
Ningxia Huizu Zizhicu
(Ningsia Hui) □[4] 102 37.00 N 106.00 E
Ningxian 102 35.31 N 108.01 E
Ningxiang 100 28.15 N 112.33 E
Ningyang 98 35.47 N 116.47 E
Ningyō-tōge)(96 35.19 N 133.56 E
Ningyuan 102 25.37 N 111.46 E
Ningyuanbao 102 38.38 N 102.30 E
Ningyuanpu 105 40.44 N 114.54 E
Ninh Binh 110 20.15 N 105.59 E
Ninh Hoa 110 12.29 N 109.08 E
Ninhue 252 36.24 S 72.24 W
Ninigo Group II 164 1.15 S 144.15 E
Ninilchik 180 60.03 N 151.41 W
Ninnescah ≃ 198 37.20 N 97.10 W
Ninnescah, North
Fork ≃ 198 37.34 N 97.42 W
Ninnescah, South
Fork ≃ 198 37.34 N 97.42 W
Ninnis Glacier
Tongue ⊟ 9 68.12 S 147.12 E
Ninohe 92 40.16 N 141.18 E
Ninomiya, Nihon 94 35.18 N 139.16 E
Ninomiya, Nihon 94 36.22 N 139.58 E
Ninove 50 50.50 N 4.01 E
Niny 84 44.29 N 43.57 E
Nio 96 34.12 N 133.39 E
Nioaque 248 21.08 S 55.48 W
Nioaque ≃ 248 20.46 S 56.04 W
Niobe 214 42.01 N 79.27 W
Niobrara 198 42.45 N 98.01 W
Niobrara ≃ 198 42.45 N 98.00 W
Nioka 154 2.10 N 30.39 E
Nioki 152 2.43 S 17.41 E
Niokolo Koba 150 13.04 N 12.43 W
Niokolo Koba, Parc
National du ♦ 150 13.00 N 13.00 W
Niono 150 14.15 N 6.00 W
Nionsamoridougou 150 8.43 N 8.50 W
Nioro du Rip 150 13.45 N 15.48 W
Nioro du Sahel 150 15.15 N 9.35 W
Niort 32 46.19 N 0.27 W
Niota 192 35.30 N 84.32 W
Nioût ⊤[4] 150 16.03 N 6.52 W
Nipa 166 24.47 S 150.01 E
Nipāni 122 16.24 N 74.23 E
Nipawin 184 53.22 N 104.00 W
Nipawin Provincial
Park ♦ 184 54.00 N 104.40 W
Nipe, Bahía de c 240p 20.47 N 75.42 W
Nipe, Sierra de ∧ 240p 20.28 N 75.49 W
Nipekamew ≃ 184 54.59 N 104.52 W
Nipekamew Lake ⊜ 184 54.24 N 104.58 W
Nipepe 154 14.01 S 37.55 E
Nipigon 190 49.01 N 88.16 W
Nipigon, Lake ⊜ 176 49.50 N 88.30 W
Nipigon Bay c 190 48.53 N 87.50 W
Nipin ≃ 184 55.45 N 109.02 W
Nipisi Lake ⊜ 182 55.47 N 114.57 W
Nipissing □[6] 212 45.30 N 78.50 W
Nipissing, Lake ⊜ 190 46.17 N 80.00 W
Nipissis, Lac ⊜ 186 51.02 N 66.10 W
Nipissis ≃ 186 50.52 N 65.50 W
Nipomo 204 35.02 N 120.28 W
Nippenicket, Lake ⊜ 283 41.58 N 71.03 W
Nippers Harbour 186 49.48 N 55.52 W
Nippersink Creek ≃ 216 42.23 N 88.22 W
Niqiu 100 33.25 N 115.38 E
Niquelândia 255 14.27 S 48.27 W
Niquero 240p 20.03 N 77.35 W
Niquivil 252 30.25 S 68.42 W
Nīr 128 38.02 N 47.59 E
Nīr, Jabal an- ∧[2] 128 24.10 N 43.20 E
Nīra ≃ 122 17.59 N 75.07 E
Nīr'am 132 31.31 N 34.35 E
Nirasaki 94 35.42 N 138.27 E
Nirayama 94 35.03 N 138.57 E
Nirgua 246 10.09 N 68.34 W
Nirim 132 31.20 N 34.24 E
Nirmal 122 19.06 N 78.21 E
Nirmāli 124 26.19 N 86.35 E
Nirsa 126 23.47 N 86.43 E
Niš 38 43.19 N 21.54 E
Nisa 34 39.31 N 7.39 W
Nisa (Neisse) (Nysa
Łużycka) ≃ 30 52.04 N 14.46 E
Nisāb, Ar. Su. 128 29.11 N 44.43 E
Niṣāb, J.Y.D.S. 144 14.31 N 46.30 E
Nišava ≃ 38 43.22 N 21.46 E
Nisbet 210 41.13 N 77.07 W
Niscemi 70 37.09 N 14.23 E
Nischintapur 272b 22.26 N 88.22 E
Nisf Thānī Bashbīsh 142 31.07 N 31.11 E
Nish
→ Niš 38 43.19 N 21.54 E
Nishan 120 33.35 N 85.30 E
Nishi ◆[8], Nihon 268 35.27 N 139.38 E
Nishi ◆[8], Nihon 270 34.41 N 135.30 E
Nishiarai ◆[8] 268 35.47 N 139.47 E
Nishiazai 94 35.31 N 136.10 E
Nishibetsuin 270 34.58 N 135.31 E
Nishi-Chūgoku-
sanchi-kokutei-
kōen ♦ 96 34.40 N 132.10 E
Nishigō 94 37.09 N 140.10 E
Nishihiyayama 96 33.53 N 133.49 E
Nishiizu 94 34.46 N 138.47 E
Nishi-jima I 96 34.39 N 134.29 E
Nishikata 94 36.28 N 139.45 E
Nishikatsura 94 35.31 N 138.51 E
Nishiki 96 34.16 N 131.57 E
Nishiki ≃ 96 34.09 N 132.15 E
Nishikiori 270 34.29 N 135.34 E
Nishikyō ◆[8] 270 34.59 N 135.40 E
Nishimori ◆[8] 270 34.35 N 135.01 E
Nishinari ◆[8] 270 34.38 N 135.28 E
Nishinasuno 94 36.53 N 139.59 E
Nishinomiya 270 34.43 N 135.20 E
Nishinoomote 93b 30.44 N 131.00 E
Nishio 94 34.52 N 137.03 E
Nishitoda ◆[8] 270 34.33 N 135.00 E
Nishitosa 96 33.09 N 132.47 E
Nishiwaki 96 34.59 N 134.58 E
Nishiyodogawa ◆[8] 270 34.42 N 135.27 E
Nishinomiya
→ Nishinomiya 96 34.43 N 135.20 E
Nisiros I 38 36.35 N 27.10 E
Niska Lake ⊜ 184 55.35 N 108.38 W
Niskayuna 210 42.46 N 73.50 W
Nisko 30 50.31 N 22.09 E
Nisling ≃ 180 62.27 N 139.30 W
Nismes 56 50.05 N 4.33 E
Nispen 52 51.29 N 4.28 E
Nisporeny 78 47.06 N 28.11 E
Nisqually ≃ 224 47.06 N 122.42 W
Nisqually Indian
Reservation ◆[4] 224 47.02 N 122.42 W
Nisqually Reach c 224 47.07 N 122.45 W
Nissan ≃ 26 56.40 N 12.51 E
Nissedal 26 59.10 N 8.30 E
Nissequogue 276 40.54 N 73.12 W
Nissequogue ≃ 276 40.54 N 73.13 W
Nissequogue,
Northeast Branch
≃ 276 40.50 N 73.13 W
Nissequogue River
State Park ♦ 276 40.51 N 73.13 W
Nisser ⊜ 26 59.10 N 8.30 E
Nisshin 94 35.08 N 137.02 E
Nissoria 70 37.39 N 14.27 E
Nissum Bredning c 26 56.38 N 8.22 E
Nissum Fjord c[2] 26 56.21 N 8.14 E
Nisswa 190 46.31 N 94.17 W
Nistelrode 52 51.43 N 5.33 E
Nister ≃ 56 50.47 N 7.43 E
Nisutlin ≃ 180 60.10 N 132.30 W
Nita, Indon. 115b 8.40 S 122.11 E
Nita, Nihon 96 35.12 N 133.01 E
Nitalas 272c 19.06 N 73.08 E
Nitaure 76 57.10 N 25.10 E
Niterói 256 22.53 S 43.07 W
Niterói □[7] 287a 22.53 S 43.04 W
Nith ≃, On., Can. 212 43.12 N 80.22 W
Nith ≃, Scot., U.K. 44 55.00 N 3.35 W
Nithāri 272a 28.35 N 77.20 E
Nithāri ◆[8] 272a 28.42 N 77.03 E
Nithi River 182 54.01 N 125.01 W
Nithsdale V 44 55.14 N 3.46 W
Nitibe 112 9.19 S 124.12 E
Nitinat 224 48.55 N 124.29 W
Nitinat ≃ 224 48.49 N 124.37 W
Nitinat Lake ⊜ 182 48.45 N 124.45 W
Niton 42 50.35 N 1.16 W
Nitra 30 48.20 N 18.05 E
Nitra ≃ 30 47.46 N 18.10 E
Nitro 188 38.24 N 81.50 W
Nitry 50 47.40 N 3.53 E
Nitse Óros (Nidže) ∧ 38 40.58 N 21.49 E
Nitta 94 36.17 N 139.18 E
Nittälven ≃ 40 59.51 N 14.50 E
Nittany Mountain ∧ 210 41.00 N 77.25 W
Nittedal 26 60.04 N 10.53 E
Nittenau 60 49.12 N 12.16 E
Nittendorf 60 49.02 N 11.58 E
Niu Aunfo Point > 174w 21.04 S 175.20 W
Niubaotun 105 39.46 N 116.41 E
Niubu 100 31.02 N 117.39 E
Niuchuntuncun 104 41.28 N 122.58 E
Niuduoguang 100 24.51 N 115.44 E
Niue □[2], Oc. 14 19.02 S 169.52 W
Niue □[2], Oc. 174v 19.02 S 169.52 W
Niu'erhe 89 51.30 N 121.49 E
Niufentai 89 47.05 N 120.02 E
Niufozhen 107 29.23 N 105.02 E
Niuhang 100 28.44 N 115.51 E
Niuhuaxi 107 29.29 N 103.48 E
Niujie 102 27.47 N 104.56 E
Niujingjie 110 25.46 N 100.33 E
Niuke 120 30.41 N 82.01 E
Niulakita I 14 10.45 S 179.30 E
Niulan ≃ 102 27.28 N 103.10 E
Niulanshan 105 40.13 N 116.39 E
Niumaowu 98 40.58 N 124.59 E
Niupeng 106 31.32 N 121.50 E
Niupichang 107 30.35 N 103.40 E
Niushitun 98 35.18 N 114.24 E
Niut, Gunung ∧ 112 1.00 N 109.55 E
Niutan 107 29.05 N 105.21 E
Niutao I 14 6.06 S 177.17 E
Niuti 100 32.58 N 113.35 E
Niutian 100 27.17 N 115.46 E
Niutoushan 89 45.09 N 126.45 E
Niutou Shan I 100 29.07 N 121.56 E
Niutuo 105 39.15 N 116.20 E
Niutuoshan 106 31.04 N 119.37 E
Niuxichang 107 28.47 N 104.51 E
Niuxintai 104 41.21 N 123.53 E
Niuxintun 104 41.56 N 121.21 E
Niuyuanzi 105 40.20 N 117.47 E
Niuzhuang, Zhg. 98 37.21 N 118.29 E
Niuzhuang, Zhg. 104 40.58 N 122.32 E
Nivå 41 55.56 N 12.31 E
Nivala 26 63.55 N 24.58 E
Nive ≃, Austl. 166 26.02 S 146.25 E
Nive ≃, Fr. 32 43.30 N 1.29 W
Nivelles (Nijvel) 50 50.36 N 4.20 E
Nivernais □[9] 32 47.00 N 3.30 E
Nivernais, Canal du ≍ 50 47.40 N 3.40 E
Niverville, Mb., Can. 184 49.37 N 97.01 W
Niverville, N.Y., U.S. 210 42.26 N 73.40 W
Nivillers 50 49.28 N 2.10 E
Nivnoje 76 53.11 N 32.35 E
Nivskij 24 67.16 N 32.23 E
Niwāno 128 26.22 N 62.43 E
Nixa 194 37.02 N 93.17 W
Nixi 102 27.58 N 99.27 E
Nixis 107 30.08 N 106.19 E
Nixizhen 107 29.02 N 104.16 E
Nixon, Nv., U.S. 204 39.49 N 119.21 W
Nixon, Pa., U.S. 214 40.45 N 79.56 W
Nixon, Tx., U.S. 222 29.16 N 97.45 W
Niyodo 96 33.32 N 133.08 E
Niyodo ≃ 96 33.27 N 133.29 E
Niyor 114 2.05 N 103.17 E
Niyu Shan I 100 27.51 N 121.03 E
Niža 80 56.53 N 44.27 E
Niža 24 66.20 N 43.16 E
Nizāmābād 122 18.40 N 78.07 E
Nizamghāt 120 28.16 N 95.42 E
Nizām Sāgar ⊜[1] 122 18.10 N 77.55 E
Nižankoviči 78 49.40 N 22.47 E
Nizgān ≃ 128 33.13 N 63.40 E
Nizhnij Tagil
→ Nižnij Tagil 86 57.55 N 59.57 E
Nizhny Novgorod
→ Gor'kij 80 56.20 N 44.00 E
Nižin 76 52.38 N 28.10 E
Nizino 265a 59.50 N 29.53 E
Nizip 130 37.01 N 37.46 E
Nízke Tatry ∧ 30 48.54 N 19.40 E
Nízke Tatry, národní
park ♦ 30 47.48 N 19.35 E
Nižn'aja 80 56.34 N 49.07 E
Nižn'aja Čvorovaja 86 59.11 N 77.31 E
Nižnaja Dobrinka 80 50.18 N 45.42 E
Nižn'aja Duvanka 83 49.35 N 38.10 E
Nižn'aja-Gerasimovka 83 48.46 N 39.44 E
Nižn'aja Grajvoronka 78 51.47 N 37.46 E
Nižn'aja Irga 86 56.51 N 57.26 E
Nižn'aja Ivanovka ◆[8] 83 48.09 N 38.46 E
Nižn'aja Karelina 88 57.55 N 107.44 E
Nižn'aja Keul'skaja,
šivera ⌞ 88 58.25 N 102.46 E
Nižn'aja Krynka 83 48.07 N 38.11 E
Nižnaja Matrenka 80 52.16 N 40.06 E
Nižn'aja-Ol'chovaja 83 48.44 N 39.35 E
Nižn'aja Omka 86 55.26 N 74.55 E
Nižn'aja Omra 24 62.46 N 55.46 E
Nižn'aja Ošma 80 55.44 N 51.18 E
Nižn'aja Peša 24 66.48 N 47.38 E
Nižn'aja Pojma 88 56.11 N 97.13 E
Nižn'aja Pokrovka 80 51.40 N 50.07 E
Nižn'aja Šachtama 88 51.24 N 117.40 E
Nižn'aja Salda 86 58.05 N 60.43 E
Nižn'aja Syzran' 80 53.04 N 48.34 E
Nižn'aja Tavda 86 57.40 N 66.12 E
Nižn'aja Tunguska ≃ 74 65.48 N 88.04 E
Nižn'aja Tura 86 58.37 N 59.49 E
Nižn'aja Vol'dža 86 58.19 N 79.20 E
Nižn'aja Zaimka 88 56.09 N 98.14 E
Nižneangarsk 88 55.47 N 109.33 E
Nižnebakanskij 78 44.52 N 37.52 E
Nižne-Baranikovka 83 49.05 N 39.51 E
Nižnečujskij 83 43.12 N 74.21 E
Nižnedevick 78 51.33 N 38.20 E
Nižne-Gnilovskoj ◆[8] 83 47.11 N 39.36 E
Nižnegnutov 80 48.02 N 42.22 E
Nižnegorskij 78 45.27 N 34.44 E
Nižneilimsk 88 57.11 N 103.16 E
Nižneje 83 48.46 N 38.37 E
Nižneje Al'kejevo 80 54.46 N 50.03 E
Nižneje Gir'unino 88 51.12 N 116.58 E
Nižneje Kučukovo 80 56.13 N 52.57 E
Nižneje Kujto, ozero
⊜ 24 64.58 N 31.38 E
Nižneje M'ačkovo 82 55.33 N 37.59 E
Nižneje Pešelevo 80 53.38 N 42.31 E
Nižnejepravalje ≃ 83 48.17 N 39.57 E
Nižneje Romanovo 86 59.47 N 69.35 E
Nižneje Sančelejevo 80 53.40 N 49.27 E
Nižnekamsk 80 55.38 N 51.58 E
Nižnekamskoje
vodochranilišče ⊜[1] 24 55.50 N 53.00 E
Nižnekundr'učen-
Skaja 80 47.45 N 40.57 E
Nižnelemskij 24 64.01 N 56.16 E
Nižne-Mit'akin Pervyj 83 48.41 N 40.02 E
Nižneozërnoje 80 51.37 N 53.56 E
Nižne-Podpol'nyj 83 47.12 N 40.01 E
Nižne-Pokrovka 83 49.13 N 38.32 E
Nižnetambovskoje 89 50.54 N 138.13 E
Nižne-T'oploje 83 48.48 N 39.23 E
Nižnetroickij 80 54.20 N 53.41 E
Nižneudinsk 88 54.54 N 99.03 E
Nižnevartovsk 74 60.56 N 76.31 E
Nižnij Baskunčak 80 48.13 N 46.50 E
Nižnij Casučej 88 50.31 N 115.08 E
Nižnij Čir 80 48.22 N 43.03 E
Nižnij Čulym 86 54.37 N 78.56 E
Nižnij Černi 80 47.41 N 43.26 E
Nižnije Čeršely 80 54.40 N 52.08 E
Nižnije Ostrovcy 82 55.35 N 38.01 E
Nižnije Sergi 86 56.40 N 59.18 E
Nižnije Serogozy 78 46.50 N 34.23 E
Nižnije Timers'any 80 54.34 N 47.45 E
Nižnije V'azovyje 80 55.49 N 48.32 E
Nižnij Ingaš 88 56.12 N 96.31 E
Nižnij Kisl'aj 78 50.50 N 40.11 E
Nižnij Kuranach 74 58.49 N 125.32 E
Nižnij Lomov 80 53.32 N 43.41 E
Nižnij Mamon 78 50.11 N 40.30 E
Nižnij Odes 24 63.40 N 54.52 E
Nižnij Ol'šan 78 50.45 N 38.55 E
Nižnij P'andž 120 37.08 N 68.32 E
Nižnij Paramonov 80 47.57 N 41.55 E
Nižnij Rogačik 78 47.21 N 34.02 E
Nižnij Šerebr'akov 80 48.07 N 41.02 E
Nižnij Škaft 80 53.36 N 45.40 E
Nižnij Stan 88 52.18 N 115.44 E
Nižnij Tagil 86 57.55 N 59.57 E
Nižnij Takanyš 80 55.57 N 51.04 E
Nižnij Ufalej 86 55.55 N 59.59 E
Nižnij V'aloz'orskij 24 66.44 N 35.10 E
Nižnyj Nagol'čik 83 48.01 N 39.04 E
Nizwā 128 22.56 N 57.32 E
Nizy 78 50.47 N 34.46 E
Nizy-le-Comte 50 49.34 N 4.03 E
Nizza Monferrato 62 44.46 N 8.21 E
Nizzana 132 30.53 N 34.27 E
Nizzana, Naḥal V 132 30.57 N 34.23 E
Nizzanim 132 31.43 N 34.38 E
Njassa-See
→ Nyasa, Lake ⊜ 154 12.00 S 34.30 E
Njazidja (Grande
Comore) I 157a 11.35 S 43.20 E
Njinjo 154 8.48 S 38.54 E
Njoko ≃ 152 17.10 S 24.05 E
Njombe 154 9.20 S 34.46 E
Njombe ≃ 154 6.56 S 35.06 E
Njupeskär ⌞ 26 61.38 N 12.41 E
Njurunda 26 62.16 N 17.22 E
Nkambe 152 6.38 N 10.40 E
Nkandla 158 28.37 S 31.05 E
Nkawkaw 150 6.33 N 0.47 W
Nkayi 154 19.00 S 28.54 E
Nkhata Bay 154 11.33 S 34.18 E
Nkhotakota 154 12.57 S 34.17 E
Nkolabona 152 1.14 N 11.43 E
Nkomi, Lagune c 152 1.35 S 9.17 E
Nkongsamba 152 4.57 N 9.56 E
Nkonkwena 154 6.20 S 34.58 E
Nkoso 152 2.42 S 22.39 E
Nkoto 152 1.56 S 19.41 E
Nkunga 152 4.41 S 18.34 E
Nkurenkuru 158 17.38 S 18.35 E
Nkwalini 158 28.45 S 31.33 E
Nmai ≃ 102 25.42 N 97.30 E
Nnewi 150 6.00 N 6.59 E
Nō 94 37.06 N 137.59 E
Noābād 272b 22.34 N 88.31 E
Noailles 50 49.20 N 2.12 E
Noākhāli 124 22.49 N 91.06 E
Noak Hill ◆[8] 260 51.37 N 0.14 E
Noale 64 45.32 N 12.04 E
Noāmundi 124 22.09 N 85.32 E
Noank 207 41.19 N 71.59 W
Noarlunga 168b 35.11 S 138.30 E
Noasca 62 45.27 N 7.19 E
Noatak 180 67.34 N 162.59 W
Noatak ≃ 180 67.00 N 162.30 W
Nobby 171a 27.51 S 151.54 E
Nobel 212 45.25 N 80.06 W
Nobeoka 92 32.35 N 131.40 E
Nobidome 268 35.48 N 139.35 E
Nobidome-yōsui ≍[1] 268 35.44 N 139.27 E
Nōbi-heiya ≃ 94 35.15 N 136.45 E
Nobili 150 11.33 N 1.12 W
Noblefield 54 50.58 N 12.29 E
Noble, Il., U.S. 194 38.41 N 88.13 W
Noble, Ok., U.S. 196 35.08 N 97.23 W
Noble □[6] 216 41.24 N 85.25 W
Noble Park 274b 37.58 S 145.10 E
Noblestown 279b 40.24 N 80.12 W
Noblesville 218 40.02 N 86.00 W
Nobleton, On., Can. 212 43.54 N 79.40 W
Nobleton, Fl., U.S. 220 28.38 N 82.15 W
Noboribetsu 92a 42.27 N 141.11 E
Noborito 268 35.37 N 139.34 E
Nobres 248 14.44 S 56.20 W
Nobsa 246 5.46 N 72.57 W
Nocatee 220 27.09 N 81.52 W
Noccundra 166 27.50 S 142.36 E
Nocé 50 48.22 N 0.42 E
Noce ≃ 64 46.09 N 11.04 E
Nocera Inferiore 68 40.44 N 14.38 E
Nocera Superiore 68 40.44 N 14.40 E
Nocera Tirinese 68 39.02 N 16.09 E
Nocera Umbra 66 43.07 N 12.47 E
Noceto 64 44.48 N 10.11 E
Nochistlán 234 21.22 N 102.51 W
Nochten 54 51.26 N 14.36 E
Noci 68 40.48 N 17.08 E
Nociglia 68 40.02 N 18.20 E
Nockamixon Lake ⊜[1] 208 40.28 N 75.14 W
Nockamixon State
Park ♦ 208 40.27 N 75.16 W
Nockatunga 166 27.43 S 142.43 E
Nocona 196 33.47 N 97.43 W
Nocupétaro 234 18.48 N 101.04 W
Noda 94 35.56 N 139.52 E
Nodagawa 96 35.31 N 135.06 E
Nodaway ≃ 194 39.54 N 94.58 W
Nodera 270 34.45 N 134.56 E
Nods 58 47.06 N 6.20 E
Noé, Ouadi V 146 15.39 N 21.19 E
Noel 194 36.32 N 94.29 W
Noenieput 158 27.29 S 20.06 E
Noepoli 68 40.05 N 16.20 E
Noer 41 54.27 N 10.00 E
Noetinger 252 32.22 S 62.19 W
Nœux-les-Mines 50 50.29 N 2.40 E
Nofels 58 47.15 N 9.34 E
Nogah 132 31.37 N 34.42 E
Nogajskaja step' ≃ 84 44.17 N 46.05 E
Nogales, Chile 252 32.44 S 71.15 W
Nogales, Méx. 232 31.20 N 110.56 W
Nogales, Méx. 234 18.49 N 97.10 W
Nogales, Az., U.S. 200 31.20 N 110.56 W
Nogami 94 36.07 N 139.07 E
Nogamigin 98 39.30 N 125.23 E
Nogara 64 45.11 N 11.04 E
Nogara, Ityo. 144 13.53 N 36.32 E
Nogaro 32 43.46 N 0.02 W
Nōgata 96 33.44 N 130.44 E
Nogent-en-Bassigny 58 48.02 N 5.21 E
Nogent-le-Roi 50 48.39 N 1.32 E
Nogent-le-Rotrou 50 48.19 N 0.50 E
Nogent-sur-Marne 261 48.50 N 2.29 E
Nogent-sur-Oise 50 49.16 N 2.28 E
Nogent-sur-Seine 50 48.29 N 3.30 E
Nogent-sur-Vernisson 50 47.51 N 2.45 E
Nogi 94 36.14 N 139.44 E
Noginsk 82 55.51 N 38.27 E
Nogisaki 268 35.57 N 139.58 E
Nogliki 89 51.48 N 143.10 E
Nogmung 102 27.30 N 97.49 E
Nogoa ≃ 166 23.33 S 148.32 E
Nogohaku-san ∧ 94 35.46 N 136.31 E
Nogoon Nuur 86 49.30 N 90.17 E
Nogoyá 252 32.24 S 59.48 W
Nógrád □[6] 30 48.00 N 19.35 E
Noguera Pallaresa ≃ 34 42.15 N 0.54 E
Noguera Ribagorzana
≃ 34 41.40 N 0.43 E
Nohain ≃ 50 47.24 N 2.55 E
Nohar 123 29.11 N 74.46 E
Noheji 92 40.52 N 141.08 E
Nohili Point > 229b 22.04 N 159.47 W
Nohjhīl 124 27.51 N 77.39 E
Nohta 124 23.40 N 79.34 E
Nohwa-do I 98 34.12 N 126.35 E
Noicattaro 68 41.02 N 16.59 E
Noichi 96 33.33 N 133.42 E
Noir, Causse ∧[1] 32 44.10 N 3.15 E
Noir, Isla I 254 54.29 S 73.02 W
Noire ≃, P.Q., Can. 190 45.54 N 76.57 W
Noire ≃, P.Q., Can. 206 45.33 N 72.58 W
Noire ≃, P.Q., Can. 206 46.39 N 72.08 W
Noire, Mer du
→ Black Sea ⊤[2] 22 43.00 N 35.00 E
Noire, Montagne ∧ 206 46.14 N 74.18 W
Noire, Montagne ∧ 32 43.28 N 2.18 E
Noirétable 62 45.49 N 3.46 E
Noirmoutier 32 47.00 N 2.14 W
Noirmoutier, Île de I 32 47.00 N 2.15 W
Noiseau 261 48.47 N 2.33 E
Noisiel 261 48.51 N 2.37 E
Noisy ≃ 212 44.19 N 80.08 W
Noisy-le-Grand 261 48.51 N 2.33 E
Noisy-le-Roi 261 48.51 N 2.04 E
Noisy-le-Sec 261 48.53 N 2.28 E
Nojember'an 84 41.12 N 45.01 E
Nojima-zaki > 94 34.56 N 139.53 E
Nojiri-ko ⊜ 94 36.49 N 138.13 E
Nojon 102 43.10 N 102.07 E
Nojon uul ∧ 102 43.10 N 101.30 E
Nokami 96 34.15 N 135.20 E
Nokaneng 156 19.40 S 22.16 E
Nōke 270 34.26 N 135.29 E
Nokha Mandi 120 27.35 N 73.29 E
Nokia 26 61.28 N 23.30 E
Nokilalaki, Bulu ∧ 112 1.13 S 120.08 E
Nok Kundi 128 28.46 N 62.46 E
Nokogiri-yama ∧[2] 268 35.09 N 139.51 E
Nokomis, Sk., Can. 184 51.30 N 105.00 W
Nokomis, Fl., U.S. 220 27.07 N 82.26 W
Nokomis, Il., U.S. 219 39.18 N 89.17 W
Nokomis Lake ⊜ 184 56.58 N 103.02 W
Nokou 146 14.35 N 14.47 E
Nokpan-ni ◆[8] 271b 37.36 N 126.56 E
Nokrek ∧ 124 25.27 N 90.20 E
Nokuku 175f 14.53 S 166.35 E
Nola, Centraf. 152 3.32 N 16.04 E
Nola, It. 68 40.55 N 14.33 E
Nolan 222 32.07 N 97.26 W
Nolan Creek ≃ 222 31.02 N 97.26 W
Nolanville 222 31.05 N 97.36 W
Nolay 58 46.57 N 4.38 E
Nole 62 45.15 N 7.35 E
Noli 62 44.12 N 8.26 E
Noli, Capo di > 62 44.12 N 8.25 E
Nolichucky ≃ 192 36.07 N 83.14 W
Nolin ≃ 194 37.13 N 86.15 W
Nolin Lake ⊜[1] 194 37.20 N 86.10 W
Nolinsk 80 57.33 N 49.57 E
Nomad 164 6.18 S 142.14 E
Nomahegan Brook ≃ 276 40.41 N 74.18 W
Nomans Land I 207 41.15 N 70.49 W
Nombre de Dios,
Méx. 232 28.41 N 106.05 W
Nombre de Dios,
Méx. 234 23.51 N 104.14 W
Nombre de Dios,
Pan. 236 9.35 N 79.28 W
Nombre de Dios,
Cordillera ∧ 236 15.35 N 86.55 W
Nome 180 64.30 N 165.24 W
Noměny 58 48.54 N 6.14 E
Nomexy 58 48.18 N 6.23 E
Nomgon, Mong. 102 45.26 N 105.08 E
Nomgon, Mong. 102 42.50 N 105.07 E
Nomgon uul ∧ 102 42.20 N 105.16 E
Nomingue, Petit lac ⊜ 206 46.21 N 75.00 W
Nomini Bay c 208 38.09 N 76.43 W
Nominingue 206 46.24 N 75.02 W
Nominingue, Lac ⊜ 206 46.26 N 74.59 W
Nomoi Islands II 14 5.27 N 153.40 E
Nomoneas II 175c 7.24 N 151.53 E
Nomozaki 92 32.35 N 129.45 E
Nomtsas 156 24.22 S 16.47 E
Nomura 96 33.22 N 132.38 E
Nona, Lake ⊜ 220 28.24 N 81.15 W
Nonacho Lake ⊜ 176 61.42 N 109.40 W
Nonancourt 50 48.46 N 1.12 E
Nonant-le-Pin 50 48.42 N 0.13 E
Nonantola 64 44.41 N 11.02 E
Nonburg 24 65.34 N 50.32 E
Nonceveux 56 50.28 N 5.44 E
Nondalton 180 60.00 N 154.49 W
Nondwa 154 6.26 S 35.20 E
Nondweni 158 28.11 S 30.49 E
None 62 44.56 N 7.32 E
Nonette ≃ 50 49.12 N 2.24 E
None-yama ∧ 96 33.29 N 134.10 E
Nong'an 89 44.25 N 125.10 E
Nong Bua Lamphu 110 17.11 N 102.25 E
Nong Han 110 17.21 N 103.07 E
Nong Hèt 110 19.29 N 103.59 E
Nong Khai 110 17.52 N 102.44 E
Nongoma 158 27.58 S 31.35 E
Nongpoh 120 25.54 N 91.53 E
Nongstoin 120 25.31 N 91.16 E
Nonnenhorn 58 47.34 N 9.36 E
Nonnevitz 54 54.39 N 13.17 E
Nonning 166 32.30 S 136.30 E
Nonnweiler 56 49.36 N 6.58 E
Nono 144 8.32 N 37.26 E
Nonoai 252 27.21 S 52.47 W
Nonoava 232 27.28 N 106.44 W
Nonoc Island I 116 9.51 N 125.37 E
Nono de Julho, Túnel
◆[5] 287b 23.34 S 46.39 W
Nonogasta 252 29.18 S 67.30 W
Nonoichi 94 36.32 N 136.37 E
Nonouti I[1] 14 0.40 S 174.21 E
Nonsan 98 36.12 N 127.05 E
Nonsuch Bay c 240c 17.03 N 61.42 W
Non Sung 110 15.11 N 102.16 E
Nonthaburi 110 13.50 N 100.29 E
Nonthaburi □[4] 269a 13.52 N 100.27 E
Nontron 32 45.32 N 0.40 E
Nonvianuk Lake ⊜ 180 59.00 N 155.15 W
Noojee 169 37.55 S 146.00 E
Nookawarra 162 26.19 S 116.52 E
Nooksack 224 48.55 N 122.19 W
Nooksack ≃ 224 48.46 N 122.35 W
Nooksack, Middle
Fork ≃ 224 48.50 N 122.08 W
Nooksack, North
Fork ≃ 224 48.50 N 122.11 W
Nooksack, South
Fork ≃ 224 48.50 N 122.11 W
Noonamah 164 12.38 S 131.04 E
Noonan 198 48.53 N 103.00 W
Noon Hill ∧[2] 283 42.09 N 71.19 W
Noonkanbah 162 18.30 S 124.50 E
Noorat 169 38.12 S 142.56 E
Noord-Beveland I 52 51.35 N 3.45 E
Noord-Brabant □[4] 52 51.30 N 5.00 E
Noord-Holland □[4] 52 52.40 N 4.50 E
Noordhorn 52 53.16 N 6.24 E
Noordoewer 156 28.45 S 17.37 E
Noordoost Polder ◆[1] 52 52.42 N 5.45 E
Noordpunt > 241s 12.23 N 69.10 W
Noord-Scharwoude 52 52.43 N 4.47 E
Noordwijk aan Zee 52 52.14 N 4.26 E
Noordwijk-Binnen 52 52.13 N 4.27 E
Noordwijkerhout 52 52.15 N 4.30 E
Noordwolde 52 52.54 N 6.09 E
Noormarkku 26 61.35 N 21.52 E
Noorvik 180 66.50 N 161.12 W
Noosaville 166 26.24 S 153.04 E
Nootka Island I 182 49.32 N 126.42 W
Nootka Sound ʊ 182 49.32 N 126.38 W
Nopaltepec 234 18.17 N 95.59 W
No Point, Point > 276 41.09 N 73.08 W
Nóqui 152 5.51 S 13.25 E
Nora, Sve. 40 59.31 N 15.02 E
Nora, In., U.S. 218 39.55 N 86.08 W
Nora ≃ 89 52.26 N 129.58 E
Nora ⊥ 71 39.00 N 9.01 E
Nor Ačin 84 40.19 N 44.35 E
Norah Head > 170 33.17 S 151.35 E
Nora Islands II 144 16.02 N 40.03 E
Norala 116 6.28 N 124.38 E
Noralee 182 53.59 N 126.26 W
Noranda 190 48.15 N 79.02 W
Noraskög ∧ 40 59.39 N 14.50 E
Nora Springs 190 43.08 N 93.00 W
Norberg 40 60.04 N 15.56 E
Norberto de la
Riestra 252 35.16 S 59.46 W
Norborne 194 39.18 N 93.40 W
Norcan Lake ⊜ 212 45.10 N 76.53 W
Norcatur 198 39.50 N 100.11 W
Norchia ⊥ 66 42.20 N 11.57 E
Norcia 66 42.48 N 13.05 E
Norco 228 33.56 N 117.33 W
Norcott, Mount ∧ 162 32.07 S 121.59 E
Norcross 192 33.56 N 84.12 W
Nord □[4] 146 9.00 N 13.30 E
Nord □[5] 50 50.20 N 3.40 E
Nord, Canal du ≍ 50 50.16 N 3.05 E
Nord, Cap
→ Nordkapp > 24 71.11 N 25.48 E
Nord, Gare ◆[5] 261 48.53 N 2.21 E
Nord, Grand lac du ⊜ 186 50.54 N 67.06 W
Nord, Petit lac du ⊜ 186 50.50 N 67.10 W
Nord, Rivière du ≃ 206 45.31 N 74.20 W
Nordamerika
→ North America
⊥[1] 16 45.00 N 100.00 W
Nordanholen 40 60.30 N 14.57 E
Nordausques 50 50.49 N 2.05 E
Nordaustlandet I 12 79.48 N 22.24 E
Nordbögge 263 51.37 N 7.44 E
Nordborg 41 55.03 N 9.45 E
Nordby 41 55.58 N 10.34 E
Nord Dakota
→ North Dakota
□[3] 198 47.30 N 100.15 W
Norddeich 52 53.37 N 7.09 E
Nordegg 182 52.28 N 116.04 W
Nordegg ≃ 182 52.53 N 115.18 W
Norden, B.R.D. 52 53.36 N 7.12 E
Norden, Eng., U.K. 262 53.38 N 2.13 W
Norden, Ca., U.S. 226 39.20 N 120.22 W
Nordendorf 56 48.36 N 10.50 E
Nordenham 52 53.29 N 8.28 E
Nordenšel'da,
archipelag II 74 76.45 N 96.00 E
Nordenskiold ≃ 180 62.05 N 136.18 W
Norderney 52 53.42 N 7.08 E
Norderney I 52 53.42 N 7.10 E
Norderstapel 41 54.21 N 9.14 E
Norderstedt 52 53.43 N 10.00 E
Nordfjord c[2] 26 61.54 N 5.12 E
Nordfjordeid 26 61.54 N 6.00 E
Nordfold 24 67.46 N 15.12 E
Nordfriesische Inseln
→ North Frisian
Islands II 24 54.50 N 8.12 E
Nordfriesland ◆[1] 41 54.40 N 9.10 E
Nordgermersleben 54 52.13 N 11.20 E
Nordhalben 54 50.22 N 11.30 E
Nordhausen 54 51.30 N 10.47 E
Nordheim 222 28.55 N 97.36 W
Nordheim von der
Rhön 56 50.28 N 10.11 E
Nordhelle ∧[2] 263 51.09 N 7.46 E
Nordhorn 52 52.27 N 7.05 E
Nordic Park 278 41.57 N 88.02 W
Nordingrå 26 62.56 N 18.16 E
Nordirland
→ Northern Ireland
□[8] 48 54.40 N 6.45 W
Nordiyya 132 32.19 N 34.54 E
Nordkanal ≍ 263 51.10 N 6.42 E
Nordkapp > 24 71.11 N 25.48 E
Nordkinnhalvøya >[1] 24 70.55 N 27.45 E
Nordkirchen 52 51.44 N 7.31 E
Nordkjosbotn 24 69.13 N 19.30 E
Nord-Korea
→ Korea, North □[1] 98 40.00 N 127.00 E
Nordland 224 48.03 N 122.41 W
Nordland □[6] 24 67.00 N 14.40 E
Nördliche Dwina
→ Severnaja Dvina
≃ 24 64.32 N 40.30 E
Nördliches Eismeer
→ Arctic Ocean
⊤[1] 16 85.00 N 170.00 E
Nördlingen 56 48.51 N 10.30 E
Nordmaling 26 63.34 N 19.30 E
Nordmark 40 59.50 N 14.06 E
Nordmarka ◆[1] 26 60.00 N 10.25 E
Nordostrundingen > 16 81.36 N 12.09 W
Nord-Ostsee-Kanal ≍ 30 53.53 N 9.08 E
Nord-Ouest □[4] 152 6.30 N 10.30 E
Nordpfälzer Bergland
∧ 56 49.40 N 7.40 E
Nordradde ≃ 52 52.43 N 7.17 E
Nordreisa 24 69.46 N 21.03 E
Nordre Strømfjord c[2] 176 67.50 N 52.00 W
Nordrhein-Westfalen
□[3] 30 51.30 N 7.30 E
Nordsee
→ North Sea ⊤[2] 22 55.20 N 3.00 E
Nordstemmen 52 52.09 N 9.46 E
Nordstrand I 41 54.30 N 8.53 E
Nordstrandischmoor I 41 54.33 N 8.48 E
Nord-Trøndelag □[6] 24 64.25 N 12.00 E
Nordvik 74 74.02 N 111.32 E
Nordwalde 52 52.05 N 7.28 E
Nordwest-Kap
→ North West
Cape > 162 21.45 S 114.10 E
Nore 26 60.10 N 9.01 E
Nore ≃ 48 52.25 N 6.58 W
Norenberg
→ Nürnberg 60 49.27 N 11.04 E
Norenberg
→ Ińsko 30 53.27 N 15.33 E
Norf 263 51.09 N 6.43 E
Norf ≃ 263 51.11 N 6.44 E
Norfolk, Ct., U.S. 207 41.59 N 73.12 W
Norfolk, Ma., U.S. 283 42.07 N 71.19 W
Norfolk, Ne., U.S. 198 42.02 N 97.25 W
Norfolk, Va., U.S. 208 36.50 N 76.17 W
Norfolk □[6], Eng., U.K. 42 52.35 N 1.00 E
Norfolk □[6], Ma., U.S. 207 42.10 N 71.15 W
Norfolk Broads ◆[1] 42 52.40 N 1.30 E
Norfolk-Insel
→ Norfolk Island
□[2] 174c 29.02 S 167.57 E
Norfolk International
Airport ✈ 208 36.54 N 76.12 W
Norfolk Island □[2], Oc. 14 29.02 S 167.57 E
Norfolk Island □[2], Oc. 174c 29.02 S 167.57 E
Norfolk Island
Aerodome ✈ 174c 29.03 S 167.56 E
Norfolk Naval
Shipyard ■ 208 36.49 N 76.18 W
Norfolk Naval Station
■ 208 36.57 N 76.18 W
Norfolk Ridge ⊸[3] 14 29.00 S 168.00 E
Norfork Lake ⊜[1] 194 36.25 N 92.10 W
Norg 52 53.04 N 6.27 E
Norge 208 37.22 N 76.46 W
Norge
→ Norway □[1] 24 62.00 N 10.00 E
Norham 44 55.43 N 2.10 W
Norheimsund 26 60.22 N 6.08 E
Norikura-dake ∧ 94 36.06 N 137.33 E

Symbol	English	Deutsch	Español	Français	Português
≃	River	Fluß	Río	Rivière	Rio
≍	Canal	Kanal	Canal	Canal	Canal
⌞	Waterfall, Rapids	Wasserfall, Stromschnellen	Cascada, Rápidos	Chute d'eau, Rapides	Cascata, Rápidos
ʊ	Strait	Meeresstraße	Estrecho	Détroit	Estreito
c	Bay, Gulf	Bucht, Golf	Bahía, Golfo	Baie, Golfe	Baía, Golfo
⊜	Lake, Lakes	See, Seen	Lago, Lagos	Lac, Lacs	Lago, Lagos
≡	Swamp	Sumpf	Pantano	Marais	Pântano
⊟	Ice Features, Glacier	Eis- und Gletscherformen	Accidentes Glaciales	Formes glaciaires	Acidentes glaciares
⊤	Other Hydrographic Features	Andere Hydrographische Objekte	Otros Elementos Hidrográficos	Autres données hydrographiques	Outros acidentes hidrográficos
⊸	Submarine Features	Untermeerische Objekte	Accidentes Submarinos	Formes de relief sous-marin	Acidentes submarinos
□	Political Unit	Politische Einheit	Unidad Política	Entité politique	Unidade política
⊙	Cultural Institution	Kulturelle Institution	Institución Cultural	Institution culturelle	Instituição cultural
⊥	Historical Site	Historische Stätte	Sitio Histórico	Site historique	Sitio histórico
♦	Recreational Site	Erholungs- und Ferienort	Sitio de Recreo	Centre de loisirs	Area de Lazer
✈	Airport	Flughafen	Aeropuerto	Aéroport	Aeroporto
■	Military Installation	Militäranlage	Instalación Militar	Installation militaire	Instalação militar
◆	Miscellaneous	Verschiedenes	Misceláneo	Divers	Diversos

I · 124 Nori-Norw

ENGLISH: Name Page Lat.°′ Long.°′
DEUTSCH: Name Seite Breite°′ Länge°′ E = Ost

Noril'sk 74 69.20 N 88.06 E
Noring, Gunong ∧ 114 5.24 N 101.44 E
Norland, On., Can. 212 44.43 N 78.49 W
Norland, Fl., U.S. 220 25.57 N 80.12 W
Norlane 169 38.06 S 144.21 E
Norley 262 53.15 N 2.39 W
Norlina 192 36.26 N 78.11 W
Norma, It. 66 41.35 N 12.58 E
Norma, N.J., U.S. 208 39.29 N 75.05 W
Normal, Al., U.S. 194 34.47 N 86.34 W
Normal, Il., U.S. 216 40.30 N 88.59 W
Norman, Ar., U.S. 194 34.27 N 93.40 W
Norman, In., U.S. 218 38.57 N 86.16 W
Norman, Ok., U.S. 196 35.13 N 97.26 W
Norman ≃ 166 17.28 S 140.49 E
Norman, Lake ◎[1] 192 35.35 N 80.55 W
Normanby, Austl. 171a 27.28 S 153.01 E
Normanby, N.Z. 172 39.32 S 174.17 E
Normanby ≃ 164 14.25 S 144.08 E
Normanby Island I 164 10.05 S 151.05 E
Norman Creek c 284b 39.18 N 76.25 W
Normandie □[9] 32 49.00 N 0.05 W
Normandie, Collines de ⋏[2] 32 48.40 N 0.30 W
Normandien 158 27.57 S 29.47 E
Normandy → Normandie □[9] 32 49.00 N 0.05 W
Normandy Heights 284b 39.17 N 76.48 W
Normandy Park 224 47.27 N 122.21 W
Normangee 222 31.02 N 96.07 W
Normanhurst 274a 33.43 S 151.06 E
Normanhurst, Mount ∧ 162 25.04 S 122.32 E
Norman Island I 240m 18.20 N 64.37 W
Normannische Inseln → Channel Islands II 28 49.20 N 2.20 W
Norman Park 192 31.16 N 83.41 W
Normans Kill ≃ 210 42.36 N 73.44 W
Normanton, Austl. 166 17.40 S 141.05 E
Normanton, Eng., U.K. 44 53.41 N 1.27 W
Normanville 168b 35.27 S 138.19 E
Norman Wells 180 65.17 N 126.51 W
Nor Marsh ≡ 260 51.24 N 0.38 E
Nornalup 162 35.00 S 116.49 E
Norogachic 232 27.15 N 107.07 W
Noroton ≃ 276 41.03 N 73.31 W
Noroton Point ➤ 276 41.03 N 73.26 W
Norovlin 88 48.40 N 112.00 E
Noroy-le-Bourg 58 47.37 N 6.18 E
Norphlet 194 33.18 N 92.39 W
Norquay 184 51.53 N 102.05 W
Ñorquinco 254 41.51 S 70.54 W
Norra Barken ◎ 40 60.07 N 15.31 E
Norra Björkfjärden c 40 59.27 N 17.28 E
Norrahammar 26 57.42 N 14.06 E
Norra Hörken ◎ 40 60.04 N 14.53 E
Norra Kvarken (Merenkurkku) ɥ 26 63.36 N 20.43 E
Norra Kvills Nationalpark ♦ 26 57.44 N 15.37 E
Norrälgen ◎ 40 59.50 N 14.34 E
Norra Rörum 41 56.01 N 13.30 E
Norra Storfjället ∧ 24 65.52 N 15.18 E
Norra Yngern ◎ 40 59.09 N 17.22 E
Norrboda 40 60.28 N 18.25 E
Norrbotten □[9] 26 66.45 N 23.00 E
Norrbottens Län □[6] 24 66.00 N 20.00 E
Nørre Åby 41 55.27 N 9.54 E
Nørre Alslev 41 54.54 N 11.54 E
Nørre Broby 41 55.15 N 10.14 E
Nørre Nærå 41 55.34 N 10.17 E
Norrent-Fontes 50 50.35 N 2.24 E
Nørre Snede 41 55.58 N 9.25 E
Nørresundby 26 57.04 N 9.55 E
Nørre Vejrup 41 55.31 N 8.47 E
Norrfjärden 26 65.25 N 21.27 E
Norridge 216 41.57 N 87.49 W
Norridgewock 188 44.42 N 69.47 W
Norris 192 36.11 N 84.04 W
Norris, Lake ◎ 220 28.57 N 81.32 W
Norris Arm 186 49.05 N 55.15 W
Norris Bridge ◆[5] 208 37.37 N 76.26 W
Norris City 194 37.58 N 88.19 W
Norris Dam State Park ♦ 192 36.14 N 84.07 W
Norrish Creek ≃ 224 49.10 N 122.08 W
Norris Lake ◎[1] 192 36.20 N 83.55 W
Norris Point 186 49.31 N 57.53 W
Norristown 208 40.07 N 75.20 W
Norrköping 40 58.36 N 16.11 E
Norroway Brook ≃ 283 42.11 N 71.03 W
Norrskedika 40 60.17 N 18.17 E
Norrsundet 26 60.56 N 17.08 E
Norrtälje 40 59.46 N 18.42 E
Norrtäljeviken c 40 59.47 N 18.53 E
Norseman 162 32.12 S 121.46 E
Norsewood 172 40.04 S 176.13 E
Norsjå ◎ 26 59.18 N 9.20 E
Norsjö 26 64.55 N 19.29 E
Norsk 89 52.20 N 129.55 E
Norsminde 41 56.01 N 10.16 E
Norsup 175f 16.05 S 167.23 E
Norte, Cabo ➤, Bra. 250 1.40 N 49.55 W
Norte, Cabo ➤, Chile 174z 27.03 S 109.24 W
Norte, Cabo → Nordkapp ➤ 24 71.11 N 25.48 E
Norte, Canal do ɥ 250 0.30 N 50.30 W
Norte, Cayo I 240m 18.20 N 65.15 W
Norte, Estación del ◆[5], Esp. 266a 40.25 N 3.43 W
Norte, Estación del ◆[5], Esp. 266d 41.24 N 2.02 E
Norte, Mar del → North Sea ⊤[2] 22 55.20 N 3.00 E
Norte, Punta ➤, Arg. 252 36.17 S 56.47 W
Norte, Punta ➤, Arg. 254 42.04 S 63.45 W
Norte, Serra do ⋏[1] 248 11.20 S 59.00 W
Norte de Santander □[5] 246 8.00 N 73.00 W
Nortelândia 248 14.25 S 56.48 W
Nörten-Hardenberg 52 51.38 N 9.56 E
North, S.C., U.S. 192 33.36 N 81.06 W
North, Va., U.S. 208 37.26 N 76.24 W
North ≃, Nf., Can. 176 57.30 N 62.05 W
North ≃, On., Can. 212 44.44 N 79.39 W
North ≃, Al., U.S. 194 33.15 N 87.30 W
North ≃, Ia., U.S. 194 41.31 N 93.27 W
North ≃, Ma., U.S. 283 42.10 N 70.43 W
North ≃, Mo., U.S. 219 39.52 N 91.27 W
North ≃, Wa., U.S. 224 46.45 N 123.53 W
North, Cape ➤ 186 47.02 N 60.25 W
North Abington 207 42.07 N 70.57 W
North Adams, Ma., U.S. 207 42.42 N 73.06 W
North Adams, Mi., U.S. 216 41.58 N 84.32 W
North Albany 202 44.39 N 123.06 W
Northallerton 44 54.20 N 1.26 W
Northam, Austl. 168a 31.39 S 116.40 E
Northam, S. Afr. 156 25.03 S 27.11 E
Northam, Eng., U.K. 42 51.02 N 4.12 W
North America ⋏[1] 4 45.00 N 100.00 W
North America ⋏[1] 16 45.00 N 100.00 W
North American Basin ✣[1] 8 30.00 N 60.00 W
North Amherst 207 42.24 N 72.31 W
North Amityville 276 40.41 N 73.25 W
Northampton, Austl. 162 28.21 S 114.37 E
Northampton, Eng., U.K. 42 52.14 N 0.54 W
Northampton, Md., U.S. 284c 38.52 N 76.49 W
Northampton, Ma., U.S. 207 42.19 N 72.38 W
Northampton, N.Y., U.S. 207 40.54 N 72.40 W
Northampton, Pa., U.S. 208 40.41 N 75.29 W
Northampton □[6], N.C., U.S. 208 36.28 N 77.21 W
Northampton □[6], Pa., U.S. 210 40.45 N 75.18 W
Northampton □[6], Va., U.S. 208 37.20 N 75.50 W
Northamptonshire □[6] 42 52.20 N 0.50 W
North Andaman I 110 13.15 N 92.55 E
North Andover 207 42.41 N 71.08 W
North Andrews Gardens 220 26.12 N 80.07 W
North Anna ≃ 192 37.48 N 77.25 W
North Anson 188 44.51 N 69.54 W
North Apollo 214 40.35 N 79.33 W
North Arlington 276 40.47 N 74.08 W
North Arm ≃[1] 224 49.12 N 123.10 W
North Asheboro 192 35.44 N 79.49 W
North Atlanta 192 33.51 N 84.20 W
North Attleboro 207 41.59 N 71.20 W
North Attleboro National Fish Hatchery ♦ 283 42.00 N 71.17 W
North Auburn 274a 33.50 S 151.02 E
North Augusta 192 33.30 N 81.57 W
North Aulatsivik Island I 176 59.50 N 64.00 W
North Aurora 216 41.48 N 88.19 W
North Australian Basin ✣[1] 14 14.30 S 116.30 E
Northaw 260 51.42 N 0.09 W
North Babylon 276 40.42 N 73.19 W
North Balabac Strait ɥ 116 8.10 N 117.04 E
North Baltimore 216 41.10 N 83.40 W
North Balwyn 274b 37.48 S 145.05 E
North Bannister 168a 32.35 S 116.26 E
North Bārākpur 126 22.46 N 88.22 E
North Bass Island I 214 41.43 N 82.49 W
North Battleford 184 52.47 N 108.17 W
North Bay, On., Can. 190 46.19 N 79.28 W
North Bay, N.Y., U.S. 210 43.14 N 75.45 W
North Bay, Wi., U.S. 216 42.46 N 87.47 W
North Bay c, On., Can. 212 44.53 N 79.48 W
North Bay c, Wa., U.S. 224 46.59 N 124.04 W
North Bay Village 220 25.51 N 80.08 W
North Beach 168a 31.52 S 115.45 E
North Beach ◆[8] 282 37.48 N 122.25 W
North Beach Peninsula ➤[1] 224 46.30 N 124.02 W
North Belle Vernon 214 40.08 N 79.52 W
North Bellmore 276 40.41 N 73.32 W
North Bend, B.C., Can. 182 49.53 N 121.27 W
North Bend, Ne., U.S. 198 41.27 N 96.46 W
North Bend, Oh., U.S. 218 39.09 N 84.44 W
North Bend, Or., U.S. 202 43.24 N 124.13 W
North Bend, Pa., U.S. 214 41.21 N 77.42 W
North Bend, Wa., U.S. 224 47.29 N 121.47 W
North Benfleet 260 51.35 N 0.32 E
North Bengal Plains ≚, Asia 124 26.20 N 88.30 E
North Bengal Plains ≚, Asia 124 26.15 N 88.35 E
North Bennington 210 42.55 N 73.14 W
North Bergen 276 40.47 N 74.02 W
North Berwick, Scot., U.K. 46 56.04 N 2.44 W
North Berwick, Me., U.S. 188 43.18 N 70.44 W
North Bethlehem 210 42.40 N 73.50 W
North Bihar Plains ≚ 124 26.20 N 86.00 E
North Billerica 207 42.35 N 71.17 W
North Bloomfield 214 41.27 N 80.52 W
North Boggy Creek ≃ 196 34.23 N 96.04 W
North Bonneville 224 45.38 N 121.58 W
Northborough 207 42.19 N 71.38 W
North Bosque ≃ 196 31.40 N 97.24 W
North Boston 210 42.41 N 78.47 W
North Bourke 166 30.03 S 145.57 E
North Box Hill 274b 37.48 S 145.07 E
North Braddock 279b 40.23 N 79.50 W
North Branch, Mi., U.S. 190 43.13 N 83.11 W
North Branch, Mn., U.S. 190 45.30 N 92.58 W
North Branch, N.J., U.S. 210 40.36 N 74.41 W
North Branch Canal ≅ 224 47.12 N 120.40 W
North Branford 207 41.19 N 72.46 W
North Breakers ✣[2] 174g 28.14 N 177.25 W
Northbridge, Austl. 274a 33.49 S 151.13 E
Northbridge, Ma., U.S. 207 42.09 N 71.39 W
North Bristol 214 41.24 N 80.52 W
Northbrook, On., Can. 212 44.44 N 77.10 W
Northbrook, Il., U.S. 216 42.07 N 87.49 W
Northbrook, Pa., U.S. 285 39.55 N 75.41 W
North Brookfield, Ma., U.S. 207 42.16 N 72.05 W
North Brookfield, N.Y., U.S. 210 42.51 N 75.24 W
North Brunswick 208 40.28 N 74.28 W
North Buganda □[5] 154 1.00 N 32.15 E
North Caicos I 238 21.56 N 71.59 W
North Caldwell 276 40.51 N 74.16 W
North Canadian ≃ 196 35.17 N 95.31 W
North Canton, Ct., U.S. 207 41.53 N 72.53 W
North Canton, Ga., U.S. 192 34.14 N 84.29 W
North Canton, Oh., U.S. 214 40.52 N 81.24 W
North Cape 216 42.47 N 88.05 W
North Cape ➤, P.E., Can. 186 47.05 N 64.00 W
North Cape ➤, N.Z. 172 34.25 S 173.02 E
North Cape → Nordkapp ➤, Nor. 24 71.11 N 25.48 E
North Cape ➤, Pap. N. Gui. 164 2.32 S 150.49 E
North Cape ➤, Mi., U.S. 216 41.44 N 83.25 W
North Cape May 208 38.58 N 74.57 W
North Captiva Island I 220 26.35 N 82.13 W
North Caribou Lake ◎ 176 52.50 N 90.40 W
North Carolina □[3], U.S. 178 35.30 N 80.00 W
North Carolina □[3], U.S. 192 35.30 N 80.00 W
North Carver 207 41.55 N 70.48 W
North Cascades National Park ♦ 224 48.30 N 121.00 W
North Castor ≃ 212 45.16 N 75.24 W
North Catasauqua 208 40.40 N 75.29 W
North Chagrin Reservation ♦ 279a 41.34 N 81.26 W
North Channel ɥ, On., Can. 190 46.02 N 82.50 W
North Channel ɥ, On., Can. 212 44.10 N 76.45 W
North Channel ɥ, U.K. 44 55.10 N 5.40 W
North Channel ɥ, N.Y., U.S. 276 40.36 N 73.53 W
North Channel ≃[1] 281 42.38 N 82.40 W
North Charleroi 214 40.09 N 79.54 W
North Charleston 192 32.53 N 79.58 W
North Chatham 210 42.29 N 73.38 W
North Chelmsford 207 42.38 N 71.23 W
North Chicago 216 42.19 N 87.50 W
North Chili 210 43.06 N 77.45 W
Northchurch 260 51.46 N 0.36 W
North City 224 47.45 N 122.18 W
North Cleveland 222 30.21 N 95.06 W
Northcliff ◆[8] 273d 26.09 S 27.58 E
Northcliffe 162 34.36 S 116.07 E
North Clymer 214 42.04 N 79.34 W
North Cohasset 283 42.15 N 70.50 W
North Cohocton 210 42.34 N 77.28 W
North College Hill 218 39.13 N 84.33 W
North Collins 210 42.35 N 78.56 W
North Commerce Lake ◎ 281 42.35 N 83.30 W
North Concho ≃ 196 31.27 N 100.25 W
North Conway 188 44.03 N 71.07 W
North Cotabato □[4] 116 7.15 N 124.50 E
Northcote 274b 37.46 S 145.00 E
North Cray ◆[8] 260 51.26 N 0.08 E
North Creek 188 43.41 N 73.59 W
North Creek ≃ 278 41.33 N 87.37 W
Northcrest 222 31.38 N 97.06 W
North Crossett 194 33.09 N 91.56 W
North Crosswicks 285 40.10 N 74.39 W
North Croton Creek ≃ 196 33.24 N 100.00 W
North Dakota □[3], U.S. 178 47.30 N 100.15 W
North Dakota □[3], U.S. 198 47.30 N 100.15 W
North Dandalup 168a 32.31 S 115.58 E
North Dandalup ≃ 168a 32.36 S 115.53 E
North Dartmouth 207 41.38 N 70.58 W
North Dighton 207 41.51 N 71.07 W
North Dorset Downs ⋏[1] 42 50.47 N 2.30 W
North Downs ⋏[1] 42 51.20 N 0.10 E
North Dum Dum 126 22.38 N 88.23 E
North Eagle Butte 198 45.02 N 101.15 W
North East, Md., U.S. 208 39.36 N 75.56 W
North East, Pa., U.S. 214 42.12 N 79.50 W
North-East □[5] 156 21.00 S 27.30 E
Northeast Cape 180 63.18 N 168.42 W
Northeast Cape ➤ 180 63.17 N 168.45 W
Northeast Cape Fear ≃ 192 34.11 N 77.57 W
Northeast Creek ≃ 284b 39.18 N 76.29 W
North Eastern □[4] 154 1.00 N 40.15 E
Northeastern University ᵿ[2] 283 42.20 N 71.05 W
North Eastham 207 41.51 N 69.59 W
Northeast Henrietta 210 43.04 N 77.36 W
Northeast Islands II 175c 7.36 N 151.57 E
North Easton 207 42.04 N 71.06 W
Northeast Pass ɥ 175c 7.30 N 151.59 E
Northeast Point ➤, Ba. 238 22.43 N 73.50 W
Northeast Point ➤, Ba. 238 21.20 N 73.01 W
North East Point ➤, Kiribati 174o 1.57 N 157.16 W
Northeast Point ➤, St. Vin. 241h 13.03 N 61.13 W
Northeast Providence Channel ɥ 238 25.40 N 77.09 W
North Edwards 228 35.01 N 117.44 W
North Egremont 207 42.11 N 73.26 W
Northeim 52 51.42 N 10.00 E
North Elkhorn Creek ≃ 218 38.13 N 84.48 W
North Elm Creek ≃ 222 30.53 N 97.00 W
North English 190 41.30 N 92.04 W
Northern □[4], Ghana 150 9.30 N 1.00 W
Northern □[4], Malawi 154 11.00 S 34.00 E
Northern □[4], S.L. 150 9.15 N 11.45 W
Northern □[4], Zam. 154 11.00 S 31.00 E
Northern □[5], Pap. N. Gui. 164 9.00 S 148.30 E
Northern □[5], Ug. 154 2.50 N 32.45 E
Northern Aire Estates 278 42.08 N 88.02 W
Northern Arm 186 49.10 N 55.23 W
Northern Cheyenne Indian Reservation ◆[4] 202 45.31 N 106.45 W
Northern Circārs ⋏[2] 122 18.00 N 83.15 E
Northern Cook Islands II 14 10.00 S 161.00 W
Northern Division □[5] 175g 16.30 S 179.30 E
Northern Dvina → Severnaja Dvina ≃ 24 64.32 N 40.30 E
Northern Indian Lake ◎ 176 57.20 N 97.20 W
Northern Ireland □[8] 48 54.40 N 6.45 W
Northern Light Lake ◎ 190 48.15 N 90.38 W
Northern Mariana Islands □[2] 14 16.00 N 149.00 E
Northern Samar □[4] 116 12.30 N 124.30 E
Northern Territory □[8] 160 20.00 S 134.00 E
North Esk ≃, Scot., U.K. 46 56.44 N 2.28 W
North Esk ≃, Scot., U.K. 46 55.54 N 3.04 W
North Essendon 274b 37.45 S 144.54 E
North Evans 210 42.42 N 78.56 W
Northey Island I 260 51.44 N 0.43 E
North Fabius ≃ 194 39.54 N 91.30 W
North Fairfield 214 41.06 N 82.36 W
North Fair Oaks 282 37.28 N 122.12 W
North Falmouth 207 41.38 N 70.37 W
North Ferriby 44 53.43 N 0.30 W
Northfield, B.C., Can. 224 49.11 N 123.59 W
Northfield, Ct., U.S. 207 41.41 N 73.06 W
Northfield, Il., U.S. 278 42.05 N 87.46 W
Northfield, Ma., U.S. 207 42.41 N 72.27 W
Northfield, Mn., U.S. 190 44.27 N 93.09 W
Northfield, N.J., U.S. 208 39.22 N 74.33 W
Northfield, Oh., U.S. 214 41.20 N 81.32 W
Northfield, Vt., U.S. 188 44.09 N 72.39 W
Northfield Airport ⊠ 279a 41.17 N 81.31 W
Northfield Center 279a 41.19 N 81.32 W
Northfield Park Race Track ♦ 279a 41.21 N 81.31 W
Northfield Village 279a 41.21 N 81.31 W
Northfield Woods 278 42.05 N 87.52 W
North Fiji Basin ✣[1] 14 16.00 S 174.00 E
North Fillmore 228 34.24 N 118.56 W
North Fitzroy 274b 37.47 S 144.59 E
Northfleet 42 51.27 N 0.21 E
North Flinders Range ⋏ 166 31.00 S 139.00 E
North Fond du Lac 190 43.48 N 88.29 W
Northford 207 41.23 N 72.47 W
North Foreland ➤ 42 51.23 N 1.27 E
North Fork 226 37.13 N 119.30 W
North Fork ≃ 194 36.13 N 92.17 W
North Fork Lake ◎[1] 226 38.56 N 121.00 W
North Fork Reservoir ◎[1] 224 45.13 N 122.15 W
North Fork Village 218 39.21 N 83.02 W
North Fort Myers 220 26.40 N 81.52 W
North Freedom 190 43.27 N 89.52 W
North Frisian Islands II 24 54.50 N 8.12 E
Northgate 216 43.01 N 85.36 W
Northgate ◆[9] 282 38.00 N 122.33 W
North Georgetown 214 40.51 N 80.59 W
North Glanford 212 43.11 N 79.54 W
North Glen Ellyn 278 41.54 N 88.04 W
Northglenn 200 39.53 N 104.59 W
North Gower 212 45.08 N 75.43 W
North Grafton 207 42.14 N 71.42 W
North Granby 207 41.59 N 72.49 W
North Grand Island Bridge ◆[5] 284a 43.04 N 78.59 W
North Great River 276 40.44 N 73.10 W
North Greece 212 43.15 N 77.44 W
North Grosvenordale 207 41.59 N 71.53 W
North Grove 216 40.37 N 85.58 W
North Gulfport 194 30.24 N 89.06 W
North Hadley 207 42.23 N 72.36 W
North Haledon 276 40.57 N 74.11 W
North Hampton 218 39.59 N 83.56 W
North Hanover 283 42.08 N 70.52 W
North Harbor c 269f 14.36 N 120.57 E
North Harbour c 274a 33.49 S 151.17 E
North Haven 207 41.23 N 72.51 W
North Head ➤, Austl. 274a 33.49 S 151.18 E
North Head ➤, N.Z. 172 36.25 S 174.03 E
North Henderson 192 36.21 N 78.22 W
North Henik Lake ◎ 176 61.45 N 97.40 W
North Hero 188 44.49 N 73.17 W
North Highlands 226 38.41 N 121.22 W
North Hill 42 50.34 N 4.25 W
North Hills, De., U.S. 285 39.46 N 75.30 W
North Hills, Il., U.S. 278 42.18 N 88.01 W
North Hills, N.Y., U.S. 276 40.47 N 73.41 W
North Hinksey 42 51.45 N 1.16 W
North Hogan Creek ≃ 218 39.03 N 84.54 W
North Hollywood ◆[8] 280 34.10 N 118.23 W
North Holmwood 260 51.13 N 0.20 W
North Honcut Creek ≃ 226 39.19 N 121.36 W
North Hoosick 210 42.56 N 73.21 W
North Hornell 210 42.21 N 77.40 W
North Horr 154 3.19 N 37.04 E
North Houston 222 29.54 N 95.31 W
Northiam 42 50.59 N 0.36 E
North Industry 214 40.44 N 81.22 W
North Irwin 279b 40.20 N 79.43 W
North Island I, India 122 10.08 N 72.20 E
North Island I, Kenya 154 4.04 N 36.03 E
North Island I, N.Z. 172 39.00 S 176.00 E
North Island Naval Air Station ■ 228 32.42 N 117.12 W
North Islet I 116 8.56 N 120.02 E
North Jackson 214 41.06 N 80.52 W
North Java 210 42.41 N 78.20 W
North Judson 216 41.12 N 86.46 W
North Kenai 180 60.44 N 151.19 W
North Kingstown 207 41.38 N 71.25 W
North Kingsville 214 41.54 N 80.42 W
North Knife Lake ◎ 176 58.05 N 97.05 W
North Knob ∧ 210 41.43 N 75.33 W
North Korea → Korea, North □[1] 98 40.00 N 127.00 E
North La Junta 198 37.59 N 103.31 W
Northlake, Il., U.S. 278 41.50 N 87.58 W
North Lake, Wi., U.S. 216 43.09 N 88.22 W
North Lake ◎, N.Y., U.S. 276 41.09 N 73.41 W
North Lake ◎, Tx., U.S. 222 32.57 N 96.58 W
North Lakhimpur 120 27.14 N 94.07 E
Northland ◆[9] 281 42.27 N 83.13 W
North Landing ≃ 208 36.31 N 76.01 W
North Laramie ≃ 198 42.08 N 104.56 W
North Las Vegas 204 36.11 N 115.07 W
North La Veta Pass)(200 37.37 N 105.11 W
North Lawrence 214 40.51 N 81.38 W
Northleach 42 51.51 N 1.50 W
North Lewisburg 216 40.13 N 83.33 W
North Liberty 216 41.32 N 86.25 W
North Lima 214 40.56 N 80.39 W
North Lindenhurst 276 40.42 N 73.22 W
North Line Island I 276 40.38 N 73.29 W
Northline Terrace 222 29.55 N 95.25 W
North Little Rock 194 34.46 N 92.16 W
North Llano ≃ 196 30.30 N 99.46 W
North Logan 202 41.46 N 111.48 W
North Loma Linda 228 34.02 N 117.05 W
North Loon Mountain ∧ 202 45.07 N 115.52 W
North Loup 198 41.29 N 98.46 W
North Loup ≃ 198 41.17 N 98.23 W
North Luangwa National Park ♦ 154 11.50 S 32.15 E
North Luconia Shoals ✣[2] 108 5.40 N 112.35 E
North Macmillan ≃ 180 63.03 N 133.18 W
North Madison 214 41.48 N 81.03 W
North Magnetic Pole ◆ 16 77.19 N 101.49 W
North Malosmadulu Atoll I[1] 122 5.35 N 72.55 E
North Mamm Peak ∧ 200 39.23 N 107.52 W
North Manchester 216 41.00 N 85.46 W
North Manitou Island I 190 45.06 N 86.01 W
North Mankato 190 44.10 N 94.02 W
North Manly 274a 33.46 S 151.16 E
North Maroota 170 33.29 S 150.56 E
North Marshfield 283 42.08 N 70.46 W
North Marysville 224 48.07 N 122.09 W
North Massapequa 276 40.42 N 73.27 W
Northmead, Austl. 274a 33.47 S 151.00 E
Northmead, S. Afr. 273d 26.10 S 28.20 E
North Merrick 276 40.41 N 73.33 W
North Miami 220 25.53 N 80.11 W
North Miami Beach 220 25.55 N 80.09 W
North Middleboro 207 41.56 N 70.58 W
North Milk ≃ 202 49.08 N 112.23 W
North Mokelumne ≃ 226 38.08 N 121.35 W
North Moose Lake ◎ 184 54.08 N 100.13 W
North Moreau Creek ≃ 194 38.30 N 92.18 W
North Muskegon 216 43.15 N 86.16 W
North Myrtle Beach 192 33.49 N 78.40 W
North Nahanni ≃ 180 62.05 N 124.30 W
North Naples 220 26.13 N 81.47 W
North Narrabeen 274a 33.42 S 151.18 E
North Nemah ≃ 224 46.30 N 123.53 W
North New Hyde Park 276 40.44 N 73.41 W
North New River Canal ≅ 220 26.05 N 80.12 W
North Newton 198 38.04 N 97.21 W
North Niles 216 41.52 N 86.15 W
North Norwich 210 42.37 N 75.31 W
North Oaks 222 30.22 N 97.41 W
North Ockendon ◆[8] 260 51.32 N 0.18 E
North Ogden 200 41.18 N 111.57 W
North Olmsted 214 41.24 N 81.55 W
Northolt Aerodrome ⊠ 260 51.33 N 0.23 W
Northome 190 47.52 N 94.16 W
Northop 262 53.12 N 3.08 W
North Ore Creek ≃ 281 42.43 N 83.47 W
North Orwell 210 41.55 N 76.19 W
Northowram 262 53.44 N 1.50 W
North Oxford 207 42.09 N 71.52 W
North Palisade ∧ 204 37.06 N 118.31 W
North Palm Beach 220 26.49 N 80.04 W
North Para ≃ 168b 34.36 S 138.45 E
North Park ◆[8] 278 41.59 N 87.43 W
North Park ♦ 279b 40.36 N 80.00 W
North Park Lake ◎ 279b 40.36 N 80.00 W
North Parramatta 274a 33.48 S 151.00 E
North Pass ɥ 175c 7.41 N 151.48 E
North Patchogue 276 40.47 N 73.00 W
North Peak ∧, Ak., U.S. 180 62.34 N 162.23 W
North Peak ∧, Ca., U.S. 282 37.33 N 122.28 W
North Pease ≃ 196 34.15 N 100.07 W
North Pelham, N.H., U.S. 283 42.46 N 71.21 W
North Pelham, N.Y., U.S. 276 40.55 N 73.48 W
North Pembroke 207 42.05 N 70.47 W
North Pender Island I 224 48.49 N 123.17 W
North Perry 214 41.47 N 81.07 W
North Petherton 42 51.06 N 3.01 W
North Philadelphia ◆[8] 285 39.58 N 75.09 W
North Philadelphia Airport ⊠ 285 40.05 N 75.01 W
North Pine ≃ 171a 27.17 S 153.01 E
North Pine Grove 214 41.11 N 79.13 W
North Piney Creek ≃ 200 42.31 N 110.05 W
North Pitcher 210 42.37 N 75.49 W
North Plainfield 210 40.37 N 74.25 W
North Plains 224 45.35 N 122.59 W
North Plains ≚ 200 34.40 N 108.15 W
North Platte 198 41.07 N 100.45 W
North Platte ≃ 178 41.07 N 100.42 W
North Pleasureville 218 38.22 N 85.07 W
North Plympton 283 41.59 N 70.48 W
North Point, H.K. 271d 22.17 N 114.12 E
Northpoint, Pa., U.S. 214 40.54 N 79.08 W
North Point ➤, Barb. 241g 13.20 N 59.36 W
North Point ➤, Md., U.S. 284b 39.12 N 76.27 W
North Point ➤, Mi., U.S. 190 45.02 N 83.16 W
North Pole 180 64.45 N 147.21 W
North Pole ◆ 16 90.00 N 0.00
Northport, Al., U.S. 194 33.13 N 87.34 W
North Port, Fl., U.S. 220 27.03 N 82.15 W
Northport, Mi., U.S. 190 45.07 N 85.37 W
Northport, N.Y., U.S. 210 40.53 N 73.20 W
Northport, Wa., U.S. 202 48.54 N 117.46 W
North Portal 184 49.00 N 102.33 W
Northport Bay c 276 40.55 N 73.23 W
Northport Harbor c 276 40.53 N 73.22 W
North Powder 202 45.01 N 117.55 W
North Pownal 207 42.47 N 73.15 W
North Prairie 216 42.56 N 88.24 W
North Providence 207 41.50 N 71.25 W
North Puyallup 224 47.12 N 122.17 W
North Queensferry 46 56.01 N 3.25 W
North Quincy 219 39.58 N 91.24 W
North Raccoon ≃ 198 41.50 N 94.08 W
North Raisin ≃ 206 45.09 N 74.43 W
North Ram ≃ 182 52.16 N 115.38 W
North Randall 279a 41.27 N 81.32 W
North Reading 207 42.34 N 71.04 W
North Reservoir ◎[1] 283 42.28 N 71.07 W
North Richland Hills 222 32.50 N 97.13 W
North Richmond 282 37.57 N 122.22 W
Northridge, Oh., U.S. 218 39.59 N 83.46 W
Northridge, Oh., U.S. 218 39.48 N 84.11 W
Northridge ◆[8] 280 34.14 N 118.33 W
Northridge Fashion Center ◆[9] 280 34.13 N 118.33 W
North Ridge Village 218 39.57 N 86.09 W
North Ridgeville 214 41.23 N 82.01 W
North Rim 200 36.12 N 112.03 W
North River c 208 37.25 N 76.25 W
North Riverside 278 41.50 N 87.49 W
North Riverside Park Mall ◆[9] 278 41.51 N 87.49 W
North Robinson 214 40.48 N 82.51 W
North Rocks 274a 33.46 S 151.02 E
North Ronaldsay I 46 59.22 N 2.26 W
North Ronaldsay Firth ɥ 46 59.20 N 2.25 W
North Rose 210 43.11 N 76.53 W
North Royalton 214 41.18 N 81.43 W
North Rustico 186 46.27 N 63.19 W
North Ryde 274a 33.48 S 151.07 E
North Salem 214 40.09 N 81.33 W
North Salt Lake 200 40.50 N 111.54 W
North San Juan 226 39.22 N 121.06 W
North Santiam ≃ 202 44.41 N 123.00 W
North Saskatchewan ≃ 176 53.15 N 105.05 W
North Saugeen ≃ 212 44.19 N 81.17 W
North Scituate, Ma., U.S. 207 42.13 N 70.47 W
North Scituate, R.I., U.S. 207 41.49 N 71.35 W
North Sea ⊤[2] 22 56.00 N 3.00 E
North Seaton Colliery 44 55.11 N 1.32 W
North Sentinel Island I 110 11.33 N 92.15 E
North Shafter 226 35.31 N 119.18 W
North Shields 44 55.01 N 1.27 W
Norths Highland ⋏[1] 9 66.40 S 126.00 E
North Shoal Lake ◎ 184 50.29 N 97.40 W
North Shore 216 42.16 N 88.23 W
Northshore ◆[9] 283 42.32 N 70.57 W
North Shore Channel ≅ 278 42.05 N 87.41 W
North Shores 216 41.50 N 83.25 W
North Shoshone Peak ∧ 204 39.09 N 117.29 W
North Siberian Lowland → Severo-Sibirskaja nizmennost' ≚ 74 73.00 N 100.00 E
Northside 174h 2.47 S 171.43 W
North Singa 126 23.16 N 89.30 E
North Sioux City 198 42.31 N 96.28 W
North Skunk ≃ 190 41.15 N 92.02 W
North Somercotes 44 53.28 N 0.08 E
North Sound ɥ, Antig. 240c 17.07 N 61.45 W
North Sound ɥ, Ire. 48 53.11 N 9.43 W
North Sound ɥ, Scot., U.K. 46 59.18 N 2.46 W
North Spicer Island I 176 68.30 N 78.55 W
North Spirit Lake ◎ 184 52.30 N 92.53 W
North Spot I 236 16.15 N 88.11 W
North Springfield, Pa., U.S. 214 41.59 N 80.26 W
North Springfield, Va., U.S. 284c 38.48 N 77.12 W
North Stamford Reservoir ◎[1] 276 41.08 N 73.32 W
North Star, De., U.S. 285 39.46 N 75.43 W
North Star, Oh., U.S. 216 40.19 N 84.34 W
North Sterling Reservoir ◎[1] 198 40.47 N 103.17 W
North Stradbroke Island I 171a 27.35 S 153.28 E
North Sudbury 283 42.24 N 71.24 W
North Sulphur ≃ 196 33.23 N 95.18 W
North Sunday Creek ≃ 202 46.27 N 105.54 W
North Sunderland 44 55.34 N 1.39 W
North Swansea 207 41.46 N 71.15 W
North Sydenham ≃ 214 42.35 N 82.23 W
North Sydney, Austl. 274a 33.50 S 151.13 E
North Sydney, N.S., Can. 186 46.13 N 60.15 W
North Syracuse 210 43.08 N 76.07 W
North Tamborine 171a 27.56 S 153.11 E
North Taranaki Bight c[3] 172 38.42 S 174.15 E
North Tarrytown 276 41.05 N 73.51 W
North Tawton 42 50.48 N 3.53 W
North Tea Lake ◎ 190 45.56 N 79.03 W
North Terre Haute 194 39.31 N 87.21 W
North Tewksbury 283 42.38 N 71.14 W
North Thames ≃ 212 42.59 N 81.16 W
North Thompson ≃ 182 50.41 N 120.21 W
North Thoresby 44 53.28 N 0.03 W
North Tidworth 42 51.16 N 1.40 W
North Toe ≃ 192 36.00 N 82.16 W
North Tolsta 46 58.20 N 6.13 W
North Tonawanda 210 43.02 N 78.51 W
North Towanda 210 41.47 N 76.28 W
North Troy 206 44.59 N 72.24 W
North Truro 207 42.02 N 70.05 W
North Tule Draw V 196 34.30 N 101.36 W
North Tunica 194 34.42 N 90.23 W
North Turlock 226 37.31 N 120.51 W
North Turramurra 274a 33.43 S 150.09 E
North Twin Lake ◎ 186 49.16 N 55.56 W
North Tyne ≃ 44 54.59 N 2.08 W
North Ubian Island I 116 6.09 N 120.27 E
North Uist I 46 57.36 N 7.18 W
Northumberland 210 40.53 N 76.47 W
Northumberland □[6], On., Can. 212 44.10 N 78.00 W
Northumberland □[6], Eng., U.K. 44 55.15 N 2.05 W
Northumberland □[6], Pa., U.S. 210 40.49 N 76.39 W
Northumberland □[6], Va., U.S. 208 37.50 N 76.25 W
Northumberland Isles II 166 21.40 S 150.00 E
Northumberland National Park ♦ 44 55.15 N 2.20 W
Northumberland Strait ɥ 186 46.00 N 63.30 W
North Umpqua ≃ 202 43.16 N 123.27 W
North Uxbridge 207 42.05 N 71.38 W
Northvale 276 41.00 N 73.56 W
North Valley Hills ⋏[2] 285 40.02 N 75.40 W
North Valley Stream 276 40.41 N 73.42 W
North Vancouver 224 49.19 N 123.04 W
North Vandergrift 279b 40.36 N 79.34 W
North Vernon 218 39.00 N 85.37 W
North Versailles 279b 40.22 N 79.48 W
North Vietnam → Vietnam □[1] 108 16.00 N 108.00 E
Northville, Mi., U.S. 216 42.25 N 83.29 W
Northville, N.Y., U.S. 210 43.13 N 74.10 W
Northville Downs ♦ 281 42.26 N 83.29 W
Northvue 214 40.54 N 79.56 W
North Wabasca Lake ◎ 182 56.00 N 113.55 W
North Wales 208 40.12 N 75.16 W
Northwall 46 59.16 N 2.17 W
North Walsham 42 52.50 N 1.24 E
North Wantagh 276 40.41 N 73.30 W
North Warren 214 41.52 N 79.09 W
North Washington, Pa., U.S. 214 41.03 N 79.49 W
North Washington, Pa., U.S. 279b 40.32 N 79.36 W
North Watuppa Pond ◎ 207 41.42 N 71.06 W
Northway 180 62.58 N 141.56 W
North Weald Bassett 42 51.43 N 0.10 E
North Webster 216 41.19 N 85.41 W
North Weissport 210 40.50 N 75.41 W
North West □[5] 246 7.45 N 59.30 W
Northwest ≃ 208 36.31 N 76.05 W
North West Cape ➤, Austl. 162 21.45 S 114.10 E
Northwest Cape ➤, Ak., U.S. 180 63.46 N 171.45 W
Northwest Cape ➤, Fl., U.S. 220 25.13 N 81.11 W
North Westchester 207 41.34 N 72.24 W
North Western 210 43.20 N 75.22 W
North-Western □[4] 154 13.00 S 25.00 E
Northwestern University ᵿ[2], Il., U.S. 278 42.04 N 87.40 W
Northwestern University (Chicago Campus) ᵿ[2], Il., U.S. 278 41.54 N 87.37 W
Northwest Frontier □[4] 120 34.30 N 72.00 E
Northwest Gander ≃ 186 48.50 N 55.00 W
Northwest Harbor c 284b 39.16 N 76.35 W
Northwest Head ➤ 116 10.08 N 118.45 E
Northwest Miramichi ≃ 186 46.58 N 65.35 W
Northwest Pacific Basin ✣[1] 6 40.00 N 155.00 E
North West Point ➤ 174o 2.02 N 157.29 W
Northwest Providence Channel ɥ 238 26.10 N 78.20 W
North West River 176 53.32 N 60.08 W
Northwest Territories □[4] 176 70.00 N 100.00 W
North Weymouth 283 42.15 N 70.57 W
Northwich 44 53.16 N 2.32 W
North Wichita ≃ 196 33.43 N 99.29 W
North Wilbraham 207 42.09 N 72.25 W
North Wildwood 208 39.00 N 74.47 W
North Wilkesboro 192 36.09 N 81.08 W
North Willow Creek ≃ 202 46.51 N 107.54 W
North Wilmington 283 42.34 N 71.09 W
North Windham, Ct., U.S. 207 41.44 N 72.09 W
North Windham, Me., U.S. 188 43.50 N 70.26 W
Northwold 42 52.33 N 0.35 E
Northwood, Eng., U.K. 42 50.44 N 1.19 W
Northwood, Ia., U.S. 190 43.26 N 93.13 W
Northwood, Mi., U.S. 216 42.19 N 85.38 W
Northwood, N.D., U.S. 198 47.44 N 97.33 W
Northwood, Oh., U.S. 214 41.36 N 83.28 W
Northwood ◆[8] 260 51.37 N 0.25 W
North Woodslee 281 42.13 N 82.43 W
Northwood Village 284c 39.02 N 77.01 W
North Yamhill ≃ 224 45.13 N 123.08 W
North Yelta 168b 34.03 S 137.37 E
North York 212 43.46 N 79.25 W
North York Moors ⋏[2] 44 54.24 N 0.53 W
North York Moors National Park ♦ 44 54.23 N 0.50 W
North Yorkshire □[6] 44 54.15 N 1.30 W
North Yuba ≃ 226 39.22 N 121.08 W
North Zulch 222 30.55 N 96.07 W
Norton, N.B., Can. 186 45.38 N 65.42 W
Norton, Eng., U.K. 44 54.09 N 0.47 W
Norton, Eng., U.K. 262 53.20 N 2.40 W
Norton, Ks., U.S. 198 39.50 N 99.53 W
Norton, Ma., U.S. 207 41.58 N 71.11 W
Norton, Oh., U.S. 214 41.01 N 81.39 W
Norton, Vt., U.S. 206 45.00 N 71.47 W
Norton, Va., U.S. 192 36.56 N 82.37 W
Norton, Zimb. 154 17.53 S 30.42 E
Norton Air Force Base ■ 228 34.06 N 117.14 W
Norton Basin c 276 40.36 N 73.47 W
Norton Bay c 180 64.45 N 161.15 W
Norton Creek ≃ 281 42.34 N 83.34 W
Norton Fitzwarren 42 51.02 N 3.09 W
Norton Grove 207 42.00 N 71.12 W
Norton Heath 260 51.43 N 0.19 E
Norton Hill 210 42.25 N 74.04 W
Norton Pond ◎ 206 44.56 N 71.51 W
Norton Reservoir ◎[1] 283 41.59 N 71.12 W
Norton Shores 216 43.10 N 86.15 W
Norton Sound ɥ 180 63.50 N 164.00 W
Nortonville, On., Can. 275b 43.43 N 79.44 W
Nortonville, Ks., U.S. 198 39.25 N 95.20 W
Nortorf, B.R.D. 30 54.10 N 9.50 E
Nortorf, B.R.D. 52 53.55 N 9.16 E
Nort-sur-Erdre 32 47.26 N 1.30 W
Noruega → Norway □[1] 24 62.00 N 10.00 E
Noruega, Mar de → Norwegian Sea ⊤[2] 10 70.00 N 2.00 E
Norumbega Reservoir ◎[1] 283 42.20 N 71.18 W
Nørup 41 55.43 N 9.19 E
Norval 212 43.39 N 79.51 W
Norvalspont 158 30.38 S 25.27 E
Norvège → Norway □[1] 24 62.00 N 10.00 E
Norvegia, Cape ➤ 9 71.25 S 12.18 W
Norvell 216 42.10 N 84.11 W
Norvelt 214 40.12 N 79.32 W
Norvin Green State Forest ♦ 276 41.03 N 74.20 W
Norwalk, Ca., U.S. 228 33.54 N 118.04 W
Norwalk, Ct., U.S. 207 41.07 N 73.24 W
Norwalk, Ia., U.S. 190 41.28 N 93.40 W
Norwalk, Oh., U.S. 214 41.14 N 82.36 W
Norwalk ≃ 207 41.06 N 73.25 W
Norwalk Harbor c 276 41.06 N 73.24 W
Norwalk Islands II 276 41.04 N 73.23 W
Norway, In., U.S. 216 40.47 N 86.46 W
Norway, Ia., U.S. 190 41.54 N 91.55 W
Norway, Me., U.S. 188 44.12 N 70.32 W
Norway, Mi., U.S. 190 45.47 N 87.54 W

Symbols in the index entries represent the broad categories identified in the key at the right. Symbols with superior numbers (⋏[1]) identify subcategories (see complete key on page I · 1).

Symbole im Register stellen die rechts im Schlüssel erklärten Kategorien dar. Symbole mit hochgestellten Ziffern (⋏[1]) bezeichnen Unterabteilungen einer Kategorie (vgl. vollständiger Schlüssel auf Seite I · 1).

Los símbolos incluidos en el texto del índice representan las grandes categorías identificadas con la clave a la derecha. Los símbolos con numeros en su parte superior (⋏[1]) identifican las subcategorías (véase la clave completa en la página I · 1).

Les symboles de l'index représentent les catégories indiquées dans la légende à droite. Les symboles suivis d'un indice (⋏[1]) représentent des sous-catégories (voir légende complète à la page I · 1).

Os símbolos incluídos no texto do índice representam as grandes categorias identificadas com a chave à direita. Os símbolos com números em sua parte superior (⋏[1]) identificam as subcategorias (veja-se a chave completa à página I · 1).

∧ Mountain	Berg	Montaña	Montagne	Montanha
⋏ Mountains	Gebirge	Montañas	Montagnes	Montanhas
)(Pass	Paß	Paso	Col	Passo
V Valley, Canyon	Tal, Cañon	Valle, Cañón	Vallée, Canyon	Vale, Canhão
≚ Plain	Ebene	Llano	Plaine	Planície
➤ Cape	Kap	Cabo	Cap	Cabo
I Island	Insel	Isla	Île	Ilha
II Islands	Inseln	Islas	Îles	Ilhas
⋏ Other Topographic Features	Andere Topographische Objekte	Otros Elementos Topográficos	Autres données topographiques	Outros acidentes topográficos

ESPAÑOL

Nombre	Página	Lat.° ′	Long.° ′ W = Oeste
Norway (Norge) □¹, Europe	22	62.00 N	10.00 E
Norway (Norge) □¹, Europe	24	62.00 N	10.00 E
Norway Bay c	176	71.08 N	104.35 W
Norway House	184	53.59 N	97.50 W
Norway Lake ◎	184	45.20 N	76.43 W
Norwegen → Norway □¹	24	62.00 N	10.00 E
Norwegian Basin ←¹	10	68.00 N	2.00 W
Norwegian Sea ▽²	10	70.00 N	2.00 E
Norwegian Trench ←¹	10	59.00 N	4.30 E
Norwell	283	42.09 N	70.47 W
Norwich, On., Car.	212	42.59 N	80.36 W
Norwich, Eng., U.K.	42	52.38 N	1.18 E
Norwich, Ct., U.S.	207	41.32 N	72.05 W
Norwich, Ks., U.S.	198	37.27 N	97.50 W
Norwich, N.Y., U.S.	210	42.31 N	75.31 W
Norwich Airport ⊠	42	52.31 N	1.15 E
Norwin Heights	279b	40.20 N	79.44 W
Norwood, On., Can.	212	44.23 N	77.59 W
Norwood, Co., U.S.	208	38.07 N	108.17 W
Norwood, Ma., U.S.	207	42.11 N	71.12 W
Norwood, Mn., U.S.	190	44.46 N	93.55 W
Norwood, N.J., U.S.	276	40.59 N	73.57 W
Norwood, N.Y., U.S.	188	44.45 N	74.59 W
Norwood, N.C., U.S.	192	35.13 N	80.07 W
Norwood, Oh., U.S.	218	39.10 N	84.27 W
Norwood, Pa., U.S.	285	39.53 N	75.17 W
Norwood ←⁸	273d	26.10 S	28.04 E
Norwood Memorial Airport ⊠	283	42.11 N	71.10 W
Norwood Park ←⁸	273	41.59 N	87.48 W
Norwood Pond ◎	283	42.35 N	70.52 W
Norwoodville	190	41.39 N	93.33 W
Noryang	98	34.56 N	127.52 E
Nosaka	94	35.39 N	140.34 E
Nosapu-misaki ►	92a	43.23 N	145.49 E
Nosate	266b	45.33 N	8.43 E
Nosbonsing, Lake ◎	190	46.12 N	79.13 W
Nose	96	34.58 N	135.24 E
Nose ←⁸	270	34.49 N	135.09 E
Nose Creek ≃	182	40.12 N	140.02 E
Noshiro	92	40.12 N	140.02 E
Noska ≃	86	58.53 N	68.40 E
Nosop (Nossob) ≃	156	26.55 S	20.37 E
Nosova	86	59.30 N	63.13 E
Nosovaja, S.S.S.R.	24	68.15 N	54.35 E
Nosovaja, S.S.S.R.	80	57.15 N	45.35 E
Nosovka	78	50.55 N	31.35 E
Nosovo, S.S.S.R.	78	57.07 N	27.50 E
Nosovo, S.S.S.R.	83	47.16 N	38.40 E
Nosovščina	24	62.56 N	37.03 E
Nosratābād	128	29.54 N	59.59 E
Noss, Isle of ►	46a	60.09 N	1.01 W
Nossa Senhora da Aparecida	283	22.02 S	42.48 W
Nossa Senhora das Dores	250	10.29 S	37.13 W
Nossa Senhora do Amparo	256	22.22 S	44.05 W
Nossa Senhora do Livramento	248	15.48 S	56.22 W
Nossa Senhora do Ó ←⁸	237b	23.30 S	46.41 W
Nossebro	26	58.11 N	12.43 E
Nossen	54	51.03 N	13.17 E
Nossentiner Heide ←³	54	53.35 N	12.25 E
Noss Head ►	46	58.28 N	3.04 W
Nossob	156	22.18 S	17.10 E
Nossob (Nosop) ≃	156	26.55 S	20.37 E
Nossombougou	150	13.06 N	7.56 W
Nošul'	24	60.09 N	49.28 E
Nosy Varika	157b	20.35 S	48.32 E
Notasulga	194	32.33 N	85.40 W
Notch Cliff	284b	39.27 N	76.31 W
Notch Hill	182	50.52 N	119.26 W
Notch Peak ∧	200	39.08 N	113.24 W
Noteć ≃	52	52.44 N	15.26 E
Notengo, Laguna de c	234	16.12 N	98.07 W
Notigi Lake ◎	184	55.57 N	99.18 W
Notikewin ≃	176	57.15 N	117.05 W
Noto, It.	70	36.53 N	15.04 E
Noto, Nihon	92	37.18 N	137.09 E
Noto, Golfo di c	70	36.51 N	15.12 E
Noto, Val di ←¹	70	37.05 N	14.35 E
Noto Antica ↓¹	70	36.56 N	15.02 E
Notodden	26	59.34 N	9.17 E
Notogawa	94	35.10 N	136.10 E
Noto-hantō ►¹	92	37.20 N	137.00 E
Noto-hantō-kokutei-kōen ←	94	37.10 N	136.50 E
Noto-jima I	94	37.08 N	137.00 E
Noto-jima I	94	37.07 N	137.00 E
Nōtori-dake ∧	94	35.37 N	138.15 E
Notoro-ko ◎	92a	44.05 N	144.10 E
Notozero, ozero ◎	24	66.28 N	32.05 E
Notre-Dame	186	46.19 N	64.43 W
Notre-Dame, Bois ←⁸	261	48.51 N	2.21 E
Notre-Dame, Monts ⊀	186	48.10 N	68.00 W
Notre-Dame, Ruisseau ≃	275a	45.41 N	73.26 W
Notre Dame Bay c	188	49.45 N	55.15 W
Notre-Dame-de-Bellecombe	62	45.48 N	6.31 E
Notre-Dame-de-Lorette ↓¹	50	50.25 N	2.42 E
Notre-Dame-de-Lourdes	184	49.32 N	98.33 W
Notre-Dame-de-Pierreville	206	46.06 N	72.53 W
Notre-Dame-des-Victoires ↓¹	275a	45.35 N	73.34 W
Notre-Dame-du-Haut ↓¹	58	47.43 N	6.37 E
Notre-Dame-du-Laus	188	46.05 N	75.37 W
Notre-Dame-du-Nord	190	47.36 N	79.30 W
Notrees	196	31.55 N	102.45 W
Notreure ≃	50	47.41 N	2.36 E
Notsu	96	33.02 N	131.42 E
Notsuharu	96	33.09 N	131.32 E
Nottawa	216	45.11 N	85.27 W
Nottawa Creek ≃	216	42.01 N	85.24 W
Nottawasaga ≃	212	44.32 N	80.01 W
Nottawasaga Bay c	212	44.35 N	80.15 W
Nottaway ≃	176	51.22 N	79.55 W
Nottingham, Eng., U.K.	42	52.58 N	1.10 W
Nottingham, Pa., U.S.	208	39.45 N	76.01 W
Nottingham, Pa., U.S.	285	40.07 N	74.58 W
Nottingham Island I	176	63.20 N	77.55 W
Nottingham Park	278	41.46 N	87.42 W
Nottingham Road	158	29.22 S	30.00 E
Nottinghamshire □⁶	42	53.00 N	1.00 W
Notting Hill	274b	37.54 S	145.08 E
Nottleben	54	50.58 N	10.50 E
Nottoway ≃	192	36.33 N	76.55 W
Nottoway ≃	192	36.33 N	76.55 W
Nottuln	52	51.55 N	7.22 E
Notukeu Creek ≃	184	50.15 N	106.30 W
Nouâdhibou	150	20.54 N	17.04 W
Nouâdhibou, Râs ►	148	20.46 N	17.03 W
Nouakchott	150	18.06 N	15.57 W
Nouâmghâr	150	19.22 N	16.31 W
Nouan-le-Fuzelier	50	47.32 N	2.02 E
Nouans-les-Fontaines	50	47.08 N	1.18 E
Nouméa	175f	22.16 S	166.27 E
Noun ≃	152	4.55 N	11.06 E
Nouna	150	12.44 N	3.52 W
Nounsley	260	51.46 N	0.36 E
Noupoort	158	31.10 S	24.57 E
Nous ≃	158	28.44 S	19.52 E
Nouveau Brunswick → New Brunswick □⁴	186	46.30 N	66.15 W

FRANÇAIS

Nom	Page	Lat.° ′	Long.° ′ W = Ouest
Nouveau Mexique → New Mexico □³	178	34.30 N	106.00 W
Nouveau-Québec, Cratère du ⊾⁶	176	61.17 N	73.40 W
Nouvelle	186	48.08 N	66.19 W
Nouvelle □	186	48.07 N	66.18 W
Nouvelle-Calédonie → New Caledonia ←¹	175f	21.30 S	165.30 E
Nouvelle-Calédonie (New Caledonia) □²	175f	21.30 S	165.30 E
Nouvelle Écosse → Nova Scotia □⁴	186	45.00 N	63.00 W
Nouvelle-France, Cap de ►	176	62.27 N	73.42 W
Nouvelle Galles du Sud → New South Wales □³	166	33.00 S	146.00 E
Nouvelle-Orléans → New Orleans	194	29.58 N	90.07 W
Nouvelles-Hébrides → Vanuatu □¹	175f	16.00 S	167.00 E
Nouvelle Zélande → New Zealand □¹	172	41.00 S	174.00 E
Nouvelle Zemble → Novaja Zeml'a II	72	74.00 N	57.00 E
Nouvion-en-Ponthieu	50	50.12 N	1.47 E
Nouvion-sur-Meuse	50	49.42 N	4.48 E
Nouzonville	50	49.49 N	4.45 E
Nova, Mägy.	61	46.41 N	16.41 E
Nova, Oh., U.S.	214	41.02 N	82.18 W
Nova, Ilha I	250	0.20 N	49.40 W
Nova América	255	15.01 S	49.56 W
Nova Andradina	255	22.10 S	53.15 W
Nova Aurora	255	18.04 S	48.16 W
Novabad, S.S.S.R.	85	38.37 N	68.45 E
Novabad, S.S.S.R.	85	39.01 N	70.09 E
Nova Baña	30	48.26 N	18.39 E
Nová Bystřice	61	49.01 N	15.06 E
Nova Cachoeirinha ←⁸	287b	23.28 S	46.40 W
Nova Caipemba	152	7.26 S	14.38 E
Novacella v¹	66	46.44 N	11.39 E
Nova Cintra	255	22.13 S	46.46 W
Nova Era	255	19.45 S	43.03 W
Nova Esperança	255	23.08 S	52.13 W
Nova Fátima	255	23.29 S	50.33 W
Novafeltria	66	43.53 N	12.17 E
Nova Friburgo	256	22.16 S	42.32 W
Nova Gôa → Panaji	122	15.29 N	73.50 E
Nova Gorica	64	45.57 N	13.39 E
Nova Gradiška	36	45.16 N	17.23 E
Nova Granada	255	20.29 S	49.19 W
Nova Iguaçu	256	22.45 S	43.27 W
Nova Iguaçu □⁷	287a	22.45 S	43.29 W
Novaja, S.S.S.R.	82	55.13 N	38.54 E
Novaja, S.S.S.R.	265b	55.48 N	38.03 E
Novaja ←⁸	265a	60.02 N	30.28 E
Novaja Astrachan'	83	49.07 N	38.36 E
Novaja Belaja	78	49.46 N	39.11 E
Novaja Belokorovići	78	51.07 N	28.02 E
Novaja Binaradka	80	53.48 N	49.56 E
Novaja Borovaja	78	50.42 N	28.39 E
Novaja Čigla	78	51.13 N	40.28 E
Novaja Derevn'a, S.S.S.R.	82	54.01 N	38.53 E
Novaja Derevn'a, S.S.S.R.	—	57.15 N	103.08 E
Novaja Ivanovka	78	45.55 N	29.05 E
Novaja Janisol'	83	47.17 N	37.16 E
Novaja Kachovka	78	46.45 N	33.23 E
Novaja Kalitva	78	50.06 N	40.01 E
Novaja Kazanka	80	48.57 N	49.36 E
Novaja Kazmaska	80	56.49 N	53.31 E
Novaja Kriuša	78	50.16 N	41.16 E
Novaja Ladoga	76	60.05 N	32.16 E
Novaja Majačka	78	46.36 N	33.14 E
Novaja Maluksa	76	59.39 N	31.21 E
Novaja Malykla	80	54.13 N	49.57 E
Novaja Mojgora	82	54.27 N	38.32 E
Novaja Odessa	78	47.19 N	31.47 E
Novaja Porubežka	80	51.45 N	49.40 E
Novaja Praga	78	48.33 N	32.54 E
Novaja Ropša	265a	59.45 N	29.53 E
Novaja Sibir', ostrov I	74	75.00 N	149.00 E
Novaja Sloboda	78	51.23 N	34.08 E
Novaja Slobodka	78	54.56 N	36.47 E
Novaja Sol'ba	88	54.07 N	103.33 E
Novaja Uda	88	54.11 N	103.01 E
Novaja Ušica	78	48.49 N	27.16 E
Novaja Usman'	78	51.37 N	39.24 E
Novaja Vodolaga	78	49.43 N	35.52 E
Novaja Zburjevka	78	46.28 N	32.24 E
Novaja Zeml'a II	72	74.00 N	57.00 E
Nováky	30	48.43 N	18.34 E
Nova Lamego	150	12.19 N	14.11 W
Novale (Rauth)	64	46.24 N	11.30 E
Novalesa	62	45.11 N	7.01 E
Novaliches Reservoir ◎¹	269f	14.43 N	121.05 E
Nova Lima	255	19.59 S	43.51 W
Nova Lisboa → Huambo	152	12.44 S	15.47 E
Nova Lusitânia	156	19.54 S	34.35 E
Nova Mambone	156	20.59 S	35.01 E
Nova Milanese	266b	45.35 N	9.12 E
Nova Nabúri	156	16.46 S	38.57 E
Nova Olinda	250	7.06 S	39.40 W
Nova Olinda, Riacho ≃	250	8.05 S	42.34 W
Nova Olinda do Norte	246	3.45 S	59.03 W
Nova Paka	30	50.29 N	15.31 E
Nova Ponente (Deutschnofen)	64	46.25 N	11.25 E
Nova Ponte	255	19.08 S	47.41 W
Nova Prata	252	28.47 S	51.36 W
Novara	62	45.27 N	79.15 W
Novara □	62	45.28 N	8.40 E
Novara di Sicilia	70	38.01 N	15.08 E
Nova Resende	255	21.08 S	46.25 W
Nová Role	54	50.15 N	12.47 E
Nova Roma	250	13.51 S	46.57 W
Nova Russas	250	4.42 S	40.34 W
Nova Scotia □⁴, Can.	176	45.00 N	63.00 W
Nova Scotia □⁴, Can.	188	45.00 N	63.00 W
Nova Siri	68	40.09 N	16.32 E
Nova Sofala	156	20.09 S	34.42 E
Nova Soure	250	11.14 S	38.29 W
Novate Mezzola	58	46.15 N	9.27 E
Novate Milanese	266b	45.32 N	9.08 E
Nova Timboteua	250	1.12 S	47.24 W
Novato	226	38.06 N	122.34 W
Novato Creek ≃	282	38.06 N	122.29 W
Nova Vandúzi	156	18.57 S	33.16 E
Nova Varoš	38	43.28 N	19.48 E
Nova Venécia	255	18.43 S	40.24 W
Nova Veneza	255	28.39 S	49.30 W
Nova Vida, Cachoeira ⌇	—	—	—
Nova Zagora	38	42.29 N	26.01 E
Nové Hrady	61	48.47 N	14.47 E
Novellara	64	44.51 N	10.44 E
Novelty	219	40.00 N	92.12 W
Nové Mesto nad Váhom	30	48.46 N	17.49 E
Nové Město na Moravě	30	49.34 N	16.04 E
Nové Mlýny, údolní nádrž ◎¹	61	48.54 N	16.34 E
Nové di Piave	64	45.40 N	12.31 E

PORTUGUÊS

Nome	Página	Lat.° ′	Long.° ′ W = Oeste
Noves	62	43.52 N	4.54 E
Nové Sedlo	54	50.10 N	12.42 E
Nové Strašecí	54	50.07 N	13.53 E
Nové Údol	60	48.48 N	13.48 E
Nové Zámky	30	47.59 N	18.11 E
Novgorod	76	58.31 N	31.17 E
Novgorodka	78	48.21 N	32.39 E
Novgorod-Severskij	78	51.59 N	33.16 E
Novgorodskoje	83	48.20 N	37.50 E
Novi	216	42.28 N	83.28 W
Novi Bečej	38	45.36 N	20.08 E
Novi Beograd	38	44.49 N	20.27 E
Novice	196	31.59 N	99.37 W
Novičícha	80	52.13 N	81.24 E
Novi di Modena	64	44.54 N	10.54 E
Novigrad, Jugo.	36	45.19 N	13.34 E
Novigrad, Jugo.	36	44.11 N	15.33 E
Novikovo, S.S.S.R.	86	58.15 N	80.39 E
Novikovo, S.S.S.R.	89	46.23 N	143.20 E
Novi Ligure	62	44.46 N	8.47 E
Novilla	56	50.40 N	5.23 E
Novi Lyon Drain ≃	281	42.30 N	83.38 W
Novinger	194	40.13 N	92.42 W
Novinka	76	59.49 N	33.20 E
Novion-Porcien	50	49.36 N	4.25 E
Novi Pazar, Blg.	38	43.21 N	27.12 E
Novi Pazar, Jugo.	38	43.08 N	20.31 E
Novi Sad	38	45.15 N	19.50 E
Novi Vinodolski	36	45.08 N	14.48 E
Novka	76	55.27 N	30.24 E
Novki	80	56.22 N	41.06 E
Novl'anka	80	55.48 N	41.44 E
Novlenskoje	76	59.37 N	39.20 E
Nôvo ≃, Bra.	248	4.55 S	70.33 W
Nôvo ≃, Bra.	250	4.30 S	53.50 W
Nôvo ≃, Bra.	250	6.22 S	55.42 W
Nôvo ≃, Bra.	256	21.23 S	42.44 W
Novo, Lago ⊚	250	1.30 N	50.40 W
Novoachtyrka	83	48.55 N	38.49 E
Nôvo Acôrdo	255	13.10 S	46.48 W
Novoajdar	83	48.57 N	39.00 E
Novoaleksandrovka, S.S.S.R.	80	51.56 N	52.26 E
Novoaleksandrovka, S.S.S.R.	83	48.17 N	39.37 E
Novoaleksandrovka, S.S.S.R.	83	49.08 N	39.17 E
Novoaleksandrovo, S.S.S.R.	85	51.47 N	68.49 E
Novoaleksandrovsk	80	45.29 N	41.16 E
Novoaleksejevka, S.S.S.R.	78	46.06 N	32.30 E
Novoaleksejevka, S.S.S.R.	86	52.56 N	64.41 E
Novoaleksejevka, S.S.S.R.	86	52.47 N	74.54 E
Novoaltajsk	86	53.24 N	83.58 E
Novoannenskij	80	50.32 N	42.41 E
Novoarchangel'sk	78	48.39 N	30.50 E
Novoarchangel'skoje	265b	55.55 N	37.33 E
Novo Aripuanã	246	5.08 S	60.22 W
Novoasbest	86	57.44 N	60.45 E
Novoazovsk	83	47.08 N	38.05 E
Novobachmutovka	83	48.15 N	37.48 E
Novobatajsk	83	46.54 N	39.47 E
Novobelaja	78	49.49 N	39.18 E
Novobessergenovka	83	47.11 N	38.51 E
Novobogatinskoje	80	47.22 N	51.11 E
Novobogdanovka	78	47.06 N	35.29 E
Novobogorodskoje	83	53.11 N	53.56 E
Novoborovaja	78	50.16 N	41.16 E
Novo Brasil	255	16.11 S	50.38 W
Novobratcevskij	265b	55.51 N	37.23 E
Novoburejskij	89	49.49 N	129.54 E
Novočeboksarsk	80	56.08 N	47.30 E
Novo Čeremšansk	80	54.13 N	49.57 E
Novočerkassk	83	47.25 N	40.06 E
Novočernorečenskij	88	56.16 N	91.06 E
Novocharitonovo	265b	55.35 N	38.30 E
Novocherkassk → Novočerkassk	83	47.25 N	40.06 E
Novochop'orsk	78	51.07 N	41.37 E
Novochop'orskij	78	51.23 N	41.33 E
Novochovrino ←⁸	265b	55.52 N	37.30 E
Novocimľ'anskaja	80	47.59 N	42.17 E
Nôvo Cruzeiro	255	17.29 S	41.53 W
Novodanilovka	78	46.38 N	35.00 E
Novoderev'ankov-skaja	78	46.19 N	38.45 E
Novodevičje	80	53.37 N	48.52 E
Novodolinskij	86	49.44 N	72.45 E
Novodoroninskoje	88	51.08 N	112.08 E
Novodubovoje	78	52.19 N	39.13 E
Novodugino	76	55.36 N	34.18 E
Novoderelijevskaja	78	45.46 N	38.41 E
Novoekonomičeskoje	83	48.18 N	37.15 E
Novofetinino	76	56.14 N	39.17 E
Novogaritovo	82	52.47 N	40.07 E
Novogigrejevo ←⁸	265b	55.48 N	37.48 E
Novograd-Volynskij	78	50.36 N	27.36 E
Novogrigorjevka	78	46.24 N	34.59 E
Novogrigorjevskaja	83	49.26 N	43.37 E
Novogrodovka	83	48.11 N	37.20 E
Novogromenskij	84	43.15 N	46.15 E
Novogruzok	83	53.36 N	25.50 E
Novogupalovka	78	48.02 N	35.29 E
Novo Hamburgo	252	29.41 S	51.08 W
Novo Horizonte	255	21.28 S	49.13 W
Novoignatjevka	83	47.38 N	37.41 E
Novoilijnsk	88	51.42 N	108.41 E
Novoilljinskij	87	57.54 N	55.30 E
Novoivanovka, S.S.S.R.	78	49.44 N	39.36 E
Novoivanovka, S.S.S.R.	83	47.41 N	38.23 E
Novoivanovka, S.S.S.R.	83	45.08 N	71.26 E
Novoizborsk	265b	55.43 N	37.22 E
Novojampol'	89	52.55 N	127.38 E
Novoje ≃	265a	59.54 N	30.34 E
Novoje Pavlino	82	54.23 N	38.46 E
Novoje Zarečje	77	55.55 N	37.00 E
Novokačalinsk	89	45.06 N	132.01 E
Novokašali	84	40.20 N	49.54 E
Novokašali	84	39.50 N	46.27 E
Novokuznetsk → Novokuzneck	86	53.45 N	87.06 E
Novolakskoje	84	43.07 N	46.29 E
Novolazarevskaja v³	9	70.45 S	11.50 E
Novoleušcovskaja	78	46.19 N	39.36 E
Novoli	68	40.23 N	18.03 E
Novolimarevka	83	49.17 N	39.36 E
Novol'vovsk	82	53.55 N	38.47 E
Novomalorossijskaja	83	45.38 N	39.53 E
Novomansurkino	80	53.52 N	51.52 E
Novomargaritovka	83	46.54 N	38.50 E
Novomarkivka	83	49.42 N	39.06 E
Novomarkovka	86	51.44 N	72.17 E
Novomel'nikov	84	43.56 N	45.09 E
Novomelovatka	78	50.27 N	40.46 E
Novomelovoje	78	51.23 N	38.13 E
Novo Mesto	36	45.48 N	15.10 E
Novomichajlovka, S.S.S.R.	78	47.19 N	36.04 E
Novomichajlovka, S.S.S.R.	86	55.13 N	81.57 E
Novomichajlovskoje	84	44.15 N	38.51 E
Novominskaja	78	46.19 N	38.57 E
Novomirgorod	78	48.47 N	31.39 E
Novomoskovsk, S.S.S.R.	82	54.05 N	38.13 E
Novomoskovsk, S.S.S.R.	78	48.38 N	35.14 E
Novonikolajevka, S.S.S.R.	80	52.20 N	70.28 E
Novonikolajevka, S.S.S.R.	80	50.58 N	42.22 E
Novonikolajevka, S.S.S.R.	83	48.17 N	39.37 E
Novonikolajevka, S.S.S.R.	83	49.08 N	39.17 E
Novonikolajevskij	80	50.58 N	42.22 E
Novonikolajevsk → Novosibirsk	86	55.02 N	82.55 E
Novonikol'skoje	82	53.08 N	41.05 E
Novonikol'skoje	80	59.25 N	33.13 E
Novooleksandrovka	78	47.59 N	35.55 E
Novooleksijivka → Novoaleksejevka, S.S.S.R.	78	46.06 N	32.30 E
Novoomskij	86	54.54 N	73.30 E
Novoorsk	80	51.23 N	58.58 E
Novoorskij	80	51.23 N	58.58 E
Novopavlovka	83	43.58 N	43.38 E
Novopavlovskoje	88	50.56 N	111.35 E
Novopetrovo	82	57.11 N	69.10 E
Novopokrovka, S.S.S.R.	78	55.59 N	36.28 E
Novopokrovka, S.S.S.R.	82	57.19 N	41.54 E
Novopodrezkovo	82	55.57 N	37.21 E
Novopokrovka, S.S.S.R.	78	48.03 N	34.37 E
Novopokrovka, S.S.S.R.	85	42.52 N	74.45 E
Novopokrovka, S.S.S.R.	88	50.41 N	80.28 E
Novopokrovskoje	80	45.52 N	134.28 E
Novopolock	76	55.31 N	28.38 E
Novopskov	83	49.33 N	39.05 E
Novorahačinsk	84	43.18 N	42.39 E
Novor'ažsk	82	53.44 N	40.07 E
Novorepnoje	80	51.06 N	48.24 E
Novorossijsk	83	44.45 N	37.45 E
Novorossijskoje	86	53.40 N	59.08 E
Novorossijsk → Novorossijsk	83	44.45 N	37.45 E
Novorossošč	83	49.32 N	39.15 E
Novorudnyj	80	51.30 N	58.10 E
Novorybnaja	74	72.50 N	105.50 E
Novorybnoje	74	72.50 N	105.50 E
Novošachtinsk	83	47.47 N	39.56 E
Novosanžary	83	49.21 N	34.19 E
Novoščerbinovskaja	86	46.28 N	38.38 E
Novosel'e	76	58.10 N	29.10 E
Novoselenginsk	88	51.06 N	106.37 E
Novoselica	88	48.14 N	26.17 E
Novoselickoje	84	44.45 N	43.26 E
Novoselki	76	55.48 N	25.03 E
Novoselki, S.S.S.R.	265b	55.08 N	37.33 E
Novoselki, S.S.S.R.	82	55.08 N	37.33 E
Novosel'nyj	86	54.00 N	58.51 E
Novoselovka Pervaja	82	55.10 N	40.06 E
Novosel'skoje	84	45.20 N	28.33 E
Novosel'skoje	78	45.20 N	28.43 E
Novosergejevka	80	52.06 N	53.39 E
Novosergijevka → Novošachtinsk	83	47.47 N	39.56 E
Novoselavino	82	55.00 N	51.15 E
Novošešminsk	80	55.04 N	51.15 E
Novosibirsk	86	55.02 N	82.55 E
Novosibirskije ostrova II	74	75.00 N	142.00 E
Novosibirskoje vodochranilišče ◎¹	86	54.35 N	82.35 E
Novosil'	82	52.58 N	37.03 E
Novosil'skij	86	56.10 N	62.36 E
Novosil' skol'niki	76	56.21 N	30.10 E
Novosokol'niki	76	56.21 N	30.10 E
Novospasskoje	80	53.08 N	47.45 E
Novostrojevka	84	45.29 N	47.55 E
Novotitarovskaja	83	45.14 N	38.58 E
Novotroickoje, S.S.S.R.	83	46.21 N	34.21 E
Novotroickoje, S.S.S.R.	84	45.08 N	44.07 E
Novotroickoje, S.S.S.R.	86	56.11 N	78.41 E
Novotroick → Novotroick	86	—	—
Novotul'skij	82	54.10 N	37.43 E
Novoukrainka	78	48.19 N	31.32 E
Novoul'janovsk	80	54.08 N	48.24 E
Novoural'sk	86	51.15 N	57.16 E
Novouzensk	80	50.28 N	48.08 E
Novovaršavka	86	54.11 N	74.42 E
Novovasiljevka, S.S.S.R.	78	46.51 N	36.46 E
Novovelička	265d	25.06 N	121.44 E
Novovolynsk	78	50.50 N	24.05 E
Novovoroncovka	78	47.29 N	33.54 E
Novovoronežskij	78	51.16 N	39.11 E
Novozagorje	82	55.39 N	38.38 E
Novozavidovskij	76	56.33 N	36.26 E
Novozilovskaja	24	64.50 N	51.20 E
Novozizevka	80	50.48 N	49.08 E
Novozybkov	76	52.32 N	31.56 E
Novoselskij	—	—	—
Novský Bohumín	30	49.56 N	18.20 E
Nový Bor	54	50.45 N	14.33 E
Nový Bydžov	30	50.14 N	15.30 E
Novyj	86	55.39 N	86.39 E
Novyj Afon	84	43.06 N	40.48 E
Novyj Bor	24	66.43 N	52.16 E
Novyj Bug	78	47.41 N	32.30 E
Novyj Bujan	80	53.41 N	50.04 E
Novyj Bykov	78	50.36 N	31.39 E
Novyj Donbass ←⁸	83	48.08 N	38.46 E
Novyj Dvor	76	52.50 N	24.21 E
Novyje Aljhesi	80	54.49 N	47.02 E
Novyje Aneny	78	46.52 N	29.14 E
Novyje Basy	78	50.53 N	34.51 E
Novyje Burasy	80	52.04 N	46.06 E
Novyje Denisoviči	76	54.12 N	29.13 E
Novyje Gorki	80	56.42 N	41.06 E
Novyje Maty	80	55.15 N	54.04 E
Novyje Salty	80	56.04 N	53.26 E
Novyje Senžary	78	49.21 N	34.19 E
Novyje Z'atcy	80	57.27 N	52.36 E
Nový Jičín	30	49.36 N	18.00 E
Novyj Jaryčev	78	49.55 N	24.18 E
Novyj Jegorlyk	80	46.24 N	41.54 E
Novyj Karačaj	84	43.49 N	41.58 E
Novyj Kiner	80	56.24 N	49.44 E
Novyj Multan	80	57.09 N	52.19 E
Novyj Nekouz	76	57.54 N	38.04 E
Novyj Oskol	78	50.46 N	37.53 E
Novyj Pogost	76	55.30 N	27.49 E
Novyj Port	74	67.40 N	72.52 E
Novyj Put'	85	43.29 N	73.52 E
Novyj Ropsk	78	52.18 N	32.19 E
Novyj Stan	82	56.18 N	37.00 E
Novyj Svet	83	47.48 N	38.00 E
Novyj Tap	86	57.04 N	67.49 E
Novyj Terek ≃	84	43.37 N	47.25 E
Novyj Tevriz	86	58.02 N	75.08 E
Novyj Uzen	72	43.18 N	52.48 E
Novyj Vas'ugan	86	58.34 N	76.29 E
Novyj Torjal	80	57.00 N	48.44 E
Nowa Dęba	30	50.26 N	21.46 E
Nowaja Semlja → Novaja Zeml'a II	72	74.00 N	57.00 E
Nowa Ruda	30	50.35 N	16.31 E
Nowa Sól (Neusalz)	30	51.48 N	15.44 E
Nowata	196	36.42 N	95.38 W
Nowater Creek ≃	202	43.57 N	108.00 W
Nowbaran	128	35.08 N	48.42 E
Nowe	30	53.40 N	18.43 E
Nowe Miasto Lubawskie	30	53.27 N	19.35 E
Nowe Miasto nad Pilicą	30	51.38 N	20.35 E
Nowe Warpno	52	53.44 N	14.16 E
Nowfel low Shātow	128	34.23 N	50.32 E
Nowgong	124	25.04 N	79.27 E
Nowingi	166	34.36 S	142.14 E
Nowitna ≃	180	64.55 N	154.17 W
Nowodniki	82	54.59 N	—
Nowogard	52	53.40 N	15.08 E
Nowogrodziec	30	51.12 N	15.25 E
Nowra	170	34.53 S	150.36 E
Nowrangapur	122	19.14 N	82.33 E
Nowshak ∧	84	36.26 N	71.50 E
Nowshera	123	34.01 N	71.59 E
Nowy Dwór Gdański	30	54.13 N	19.06 E
Nowy Dwór Mazowiecki	30	52.26 N	20.43 E
Nowy Sącz	30	49.38 N	20.42 E
Nowy Sącz □⁴	30	49.30 N	20.15 E
Nowy Staw	30	54.09 N	19.02 E
Nowy Targ	30	49.29 N	20.02 E
Nowy Tomyśl	30	52.19 N	16.08 E
Now Zād	120	32.24 N	64.28 E
Noxapater	194	32.59 N	89.03 W
Noxe ≃	54	48.33 N	3.35 E
Noxen	210	41.25 N	76.04 W
Noxon	202	48.00 N	115.47 W
Noxon Reservoir ◎¹	202	47.54 N	115.44 W
Noxubee ≃	194	32.50 N	88.10 W
Noy ≃	110	17.05 N	105.02 E
Noya ≃	152	0.58 N	9.48 E
Noyant	50	47.31 N	0.08 E
Noyelles-sur-Mer	50	50.11 N	1.43 E
Noyers, Ruisseau des ≃	275a	45.21 N	73.22 W
Noyes Island I	182	55.30 N	133.40 W
Noyon	50	49.35 N	3.00 E
Nozay-Jurt	84	43.18 N	45.48 E
Nozay, Fr.	50	47.34 N	1.38 W
Nozay, Fr.	261	48.41 N	2.14 E
Nozeroy	58	46.47 N	6.02 E
Nozori-dam ◎⁶	94	36.43 N	138.39 E
Nozori-ko ◎	94	36.42 N	138.39 E
Nqamakwe	158	32.12 S	27.56 E
Nqutu	158	28.13 S	30.40 E
N'Riquinha	156	16.10 S	21.45 E
N'Rougas ≃	158	29.07 S	21.09 E
Nsa, Oued en ≃	148	32.28 N	5.24 E
Nsaba	152	5.39 N	0.45 W
Nsah	152	0.32 S	14.38 E
Nsanje	156	16.55 S	35.12 E
Nsawam	152	5.50 N	0.20 W
Nsefu Game Reserve ⁴	156	13.07 S	32.10 E
Nsele ≃	154	4.14 S	15.33 E
Nsiza	158	20.03 S	29.22 E
Nsoko	158	27.03 S	31.53 E
Nsukka	152	6.52 N	7.24 E
Nsuta	152	5.17 N	1.58 W
Ntakat, chrebet ∧	84	41.40 N	46.52 E
Ntambanana	158	28.39 S	31.39 E
Ntandembele	154	2.11 S	18.08 E
Nteko	152	14.55 S	34.00 E
Ntem ≃	150	2.10 N	9.45 E
Ntibane	158	31.22 S	28.37 E
N'Tsaoueni	157a	11.27 S	43.16 E
Ntui	152	4.27 N	11.38 E
Ntungamo	154	0.53 S	30.16 E
Ntusi	154	0.03 N	31.13 E
Ntwetwe Pan ≃	156	20.30 S	25.20 E
Nuala	154	13.27 S	28.16 E
Nuanchang	104	41.02 N	120.41 E
Nuanetsi ≃	156	22.40 S	31.50 E
Nuangola	210	41.09 N	75.58 W
Nuanli	102	23.26 N	100.51 E
Nuannan	269d	25.06 N	121.44 E
Nuanshui	100	28.53 N	117.51 E
Nuanzhouying	100	25.22 N	117.22 E
Nuasjärvi ◎	26	64.10 N	28.05 E
Nuatabu	174t	1.33 N	172.59 E
Nuatja	150	6.57 N	1.10 E
Nu'aymah	132	32.38 N	36.10 E
Nūbah, Jibāl an- ∧	142	30.29 N	31.33 E
Nūbah, Jibāl an- ∧	140	11.00 N	30.45 E
Nubian Desert ←²	140	20.30 N	33.00 E
Ñuble ≃	252	36.39 S	72.27 W
Nubra ≃	123	34.39 N	77.36 E
Nucet	38	46.28 N	22.35 E
Nucetto	62	44.21 N	8.04 E
Nucha → Šeki	84	41.12 N	47.12 E
Nuchatlitz Inlet c	182	49.45 N	126.55 W
N'uchča	24	63.27 N	46.28 E
Nuch'on-ni	98	38.14 N	126.16 E
Nucla	200	38.16 N	108.32 W
Núcleo Colonial São Bento	287a	22.43 S	43.18 W
N'učpas	24	60.51 N	51.18 E
Nucuray ≃	246	5.02 S	75.34 W
Nuda, Monte la ∧	64	44.17 N	10.15 E
Nudaybah	142	30.59 N	30.22 E
Nudol' ≃	82	56.07 N	36.42 E
Nudol'-Šarino	82	56.06 N	36.31 E
Nudow	264a	52.20 N	13.10 E
Nueces ≃	196	27.50 N	97.30 W
Nueces Plains ≃	196	28.30 N	99.15 W
Nueltin Lake ◎	176	60.20 N	99.50 W
Nuenen	52	51.29 N	5.33 E
Nu'erhe ≃	104	40.57 N	121.19 E
Nuestra Señora de las Lajas v¹	246	0.49 N	77.36 W
Nuestra Señora de Talavera	252	25.26 S	63.48 W
Nueva, Isla I	252	55.13 S	66.30 W
Nueva Antioquia	246	6.05 N	69.26 W
Nueva Asunción □⁴	248	21.00 S	61.00 W
Nueva Atzacoalco ←⁸	286a	19.29 N	99.05 W
Nueva Brunswick → New Brunswick	—	—	—
Nueva Caledonia → New Caledonia □²	175f	21.30 S	165.30 E
Nueva California	252	32.45 S	68.20 W
Nueva Casas Grandes	232	30.25 N	107.55 W
Nueva Chicago ←⁸	288	34.40 S	58.30 W
Nueva Ciudad Guerrero	232	26.35 N	99.15 W
Nueva Concepción	236	14.08 N	89.18 W
Nueva Cuadrilla	234	18.04 N	101.33 W
Nueva Ecija □⁴	116	15.35 N	121.00 E
Nueva Escocia → Nova Scotia □³	188	45.00 N	63.00 W
Nueva Esparta □³	246	11.00 N	64.00 W
Nueva Francia	252	28.11 S	64.12 W
Nueva Galia	252	35.07 S	65.15 W
Nueva Germania	252	23.54 S	56.45 W
Nueva Gerona	240p	21.53 N	82.48 W
Nueva Guinea I → New Guinea I	164	5.00 S	140.00 E
Nueva Helvecia	258	34.19 S	57.13 W
Nueva Imperial	252	38.44 S	72.57 W
Nueva Italia de Ruiz	234	19.01 N	102.06 W
Nueva Lubecka	254	44.32 S	70.24 W
Nueva Ocotepeque	236	14.24 N	89.13 W
Nueva Palmira	258	33.53 S	58.25 W
Nueva Paz	240p	22.46 N	81.45 W
Nueva Pompeya ←⁸	288	34.39 S	58.25 W
Nueva Rosita	232	27.57 N	101.13 W
Nueva San Salvador	236	13.41 N	89.17 W
Nueva Segovia □³	236	13.40 N	86.10 W
Nueva Siberia, Islas → Novosibirskije ostrova II	74	75.00 N	142.00 E
Nueva Vizcaya □⁴	116	16.25 N	121.10 E
Nueva Zelandia → New Zealand □¹	172	41.00 S	174.00 E
Nueva Zembla, Isla → Novaja Zeml'a II	72	74.00 N	57.00 E
Nueve, Canal Numero ≃	252	36.11 S	57.18 W
Nueve de Julio	252	35.27 S	60.52 W
Nuevitas	240p	21.33 N	77.16 W
Nuevitas, Bahía de c	240p	21.30 N	77.12 W
Nuevo, Golfo c	254	42.42 S	64.36 W
Nuevo Berlín	258	32.59 S	58.03 W
Nuevo Camarón	232	27.05 N	99.55 W
Nuevo Chagres	240r	9.14 N	80.05 W
Nuevo Laredo	232	27.30 N	99.31 W
Nuevo León □³	232	25.40 N	100.00 W
Nuevo México	234	17.31 N	95.02 W
Nuevo Necaxa	234	20.13 N	98.00 W
Nuevo Poblado el Oro	196	26.50 N	101.19 W
Nuevo Primero de Mayo	196	26.01 N	98.02 W
Nuevo Progreso	232	18.38 N	92.18 W
Nuevo Rocafuerte	246	0.56 S	75.24 W
Nuevo Saucillo	196	27.20 N	104.54 W
Nufcor	273d	26.37 S	27.44 E
Nugaal ≃	148	8.30 N	49.00 E
Nugaaled, Dooxo ∨	144	8.35 N	48.30 E
Nugget Point ►	172	46.27 S	169.49 E
Nugssuaq ►¹	176	70.25 N	52.30 W
Nguang ≃	152	6.30 N	7.28 E
Nguru Islands II	3	13.20 S	154.45 E
Nuhaka	172	39.03 S	177.45 E
Nuhak'iyah ▽⁴	132	31.27 N	35.49 E
Nuhūd, Jabal an- ∧	140	14.50 N	29.53 E
Nui I	174i	7.15 S	177.10 E
Nuia	76	58.02 N	25.32 E
Nuich'ang	102	24.14 N	99.00 E
Nuits-Saint-Georges	58	47.08 N	4.57 E
Nuits-sur-Armançon	58	47.44 N	4.12 E
Nújar	76	60.50 N	31.10 E
Nujiang → Saluen ≃	102	24.11 S	97.38 E
Nūjūm, Ḥāssī an- ◎¹	148	26.07 N	1.52 E
N'uk, ozero ◎	24	64.27 N	31.45 E
Nukalaelae ↓¹	174i	9.23 S	179.52 E
Nukha → Šeki	84	41.12 N	47.12 E
Nukey Bluff ∧⁴	166	32.33 S	135.40 E
Nuku I	174w	21.08 S	175.12 W
Nuku'alofa	174w	21.08 S	175.12 W
Nukufetau ↓¹	174i	8.00 S	178.22 E
Nukuhiva I	164	8.55 S	140.05 W
Nukulaelae ↓¹	174i	9.23 S	179.52 E
Nukumanu Islands II	166	4.35 S	159.35 E
Nukunonu I	3	9.10 S	171.50 W
Nukunuku	174w	21.08 S	175.18 W

Legend (symbols)

≃ River	Fluß	Río	Rio
⋍ Canal	Kanal	Canal	Canal
∟ Waterfall, Rapids	Wasserfall, Stromschnellen	Cascada, Rápidos	Cascata, Rápidos
) (Strait	Meeresstraße	Estrecho	Chute d'eau, Rapides; Détroit
c Bay, Gulf	Bucht, Golf	Baie, Golfe	Baía, Golfo
◎ Lake, Lakes	See, Seen	Lac, Lacs	Lago, Lagos
≈ Swamp	Sumpf	Pântano	Marais
⊠ Ice Features, Glacier	Eis- und Gletscherformen	Accidentes Glaciales	Formes glaciaires
▽ Other Hydrographic Features	Andere Hydrographische Objekte	Otros Elementos Hidrográficos	Autres données hydrographiques
← Submarine Features	Untermeerische Objekte	Accidentes Submarinos	Formes de relief sous-marin
↨ Political Unit	Politische Einheit	Unidad Política	Entité politique
v Cultural Institution	Kulturelle Institution	Institución Cultural	Institution culturelle
↓ Historical Site	Historische Stätte	Sitio Histórico	Site historique
≋ Recreational Site	Erholungs- und Ferienort	Sitio de Recreo	Centre de loisirs
⊞ Airport	Flughafen	Aeropuerto	Aéroport
■ Military Installation	Militäranlage	Instalación Militar	Installation militaire
⋈ Miscellaneous	Verschiedenes	Misceláneo	Divers

Rio	Accidentes Submarinos	Formes de relief sous-marin
Canal	Unidad Política	Entité politique
Cascata, Rápidos	Institución Cultural	Institution culturelle
Estreito	Sitio Histórico	Site historique
Baia, Golfo	Sitio de Recreo	Centre de loisirs
Lago, Lagos	Aeropuerto	Aéroport
Pântano	Instalación Militar	Installation militaire
Acidentes glaciares	Misceláneo	Divers
Outros acidentes hidrográficos		
Acidentes Submarinos	Formes de relief sous-marin	Acidentes submarinos
Unidade política	Entité politique	Unidade política
Instituição Cultural	Institution culturelle	Instituição cultural
Sítio Histórico	Site historique	Sítio histórico
Área de Lazer	Centre de loisirs	Area de Lazer
Aeroporto	Aéroport	Aeroporto
Instalação Militar	Installation militaire	Instalação militar
Diversos	Divers	Diversos

Nukuoro I[1] 14 3.51 N 154.58 E
Nukus 72 42.50 N 59.29 E
Nul 175f 16.49 S 168.24 E
Nulato 180 64.43 N 158.06 W
Nullagine 162 21.53 S 120.06 E
Nullagine ≃ 162 20.43 S 120.33 E
Nullarbor 162 31.26 S 130.55 E
Nullarbor National Park ◆ 162 31.30 S 130.30 E
Nullarbor Plain ≍ 162 31.00 S 129.00 E
Nulltown 218 39.35 N 85.10 W
Nul'vand 85 38.16 N 70.32 E
Nulvi 71 40.47 N 8.45 E
Num, Mios I 164 1.30 S 135.13 E
Numabin Bay c 184 56.30 N 103.08 W
Numakuma 96 34.23 N 133.20 E
Numan 146 9.28 N 12.02 E
Numana 66 43.31 N 13.37 E
Numancia 116 9.52 N 125.58 E
Numancia ⊥ 34 41.48 N 2.25 W
Numansdorp 52 51.44 N 4.26 E
Numara I 122 6.26 N 73.03 E
Numarán 234 20.15 N 101.56 W
Numata, Nihon 92a 43.48 N 141.57 E
Numata, Nihon 94 36.38 N 139.03 E
Numata, Nihon 96 34.27 N 132.24 E
Numatinna ≃ 140 7.14 N 27.37 E
Numazu 94 35.06 N 138.52 E
Numbargulme, Mount ∧ 164 14.56 S 145.03 E
Number 5 Mine 214 41.08 N 80.11 W
Numedal V 26 60.06 N 9.06 E
Numeralla 171b 36.11 S 149.20 E
Numeralla ≃ 171b 36.06 S 149.11 E
Numfoor, Pulau I 164 1.03 S 134.54 E
Numidia 210 40.53 N 76.24 W
Numila 229b 21.54 N 159.33 W
Nu Mine 214 40.48 N 79.18 W
Numto 74 63.40 N 71.20 E
Numurkah 166 36.06 S 145.26 E
Nun ≃[1] 150 4.20 N 6.00 E
Nun'amo 180 65.37 N 170.40 W
Nunapitchuk 180 60.54 N 162.29 W
Nunawading 169 37.49 S 145.10 E
Nünchritz 54 51.18 N 13.23 E
Nunda 210 42.34 N 77.56 W
Nundah 171a 27.24 S 153.04 E
Nundu 154 3.49 S 29.05 E
Nuneaton 42 52.32 N 1.28 W
Núñez ◆[8] 288 34.33 S 58.27 W
Nunez ≃ 150 10.36 N 14.40 W
Núñez, Isla I 254 53.31 S 73.48 W
Nungarin 162 31.11 S 118.06 E
Nungesser Lake ⊜ 184 51.28 N 93.35 W
Nungwe 154 2.46 S 32.01 E
Nunica 216 43.04 N 86.04 W
Nunivak Island I 180 60.00 N 166.30 W
Nunjiang 89 49.10 N 125.11 E
Nunjikompita 162 32.16 S 134.19 E
Nunkini 232 20.20 N 90.11 W
Nunkun ∧ 123 33.59 N 76.01 E
Nunligran 180 64.48 N 175.24 W
Nunnelly 194 35.51 N 87.28 W
Ñuñoa 286e 33.28 S 70.36 W
Nunshan 89 48.59 N 125.14 E
Nunspeet 52 52.23 N 5.46 E
Nuomin ≃ 89 48.06 N 124.26 E
Nuomin Dashan ∧ 89 50.15 N 122.46 E
Nuon ≃ 150 6.30 N 8.36 W
Nuoro 71 40.19 N 9.20 E
Nuoro □[4] 71 40.10 N 9.20 E
Nuqruș, Jabal ∧ 140 24.49 N 34.36 E
Nuquí 246 5.42 N 77.17 W
Nura 86 48.53 N 62.20 E
Nura ≃ 86 50.30 N 69.59 E
Nurallao 71 39.47 N 9.05 E
Nuraminis 71 39.26 N 9.01 E
Nuratau, chrebet ∧ 85 40.20 N 67.15 E
Nuraxi, Nuraghe su ⊥ 71 39.42 N 9.00 E
N'urba 74 63.17 N 118.20 E
Nürburg 56 50.21 N 6.57 E
Nürburgring ◆ 56 50.21 N 6.58 E
Nur Dağları ∧ 130 36.45 N 36.20 E
Nure ≃ 62 45.03 N 9.49 E
Nurek 85 38.23 N 69.19 E
Nurekskoje vodochranilišče ⊜[1] 85 38.30 N 69.30 E
Nuremberg → Nürnberg, B.R.D. 60 49.27 N 11.04 E
Nuremberg, Pa., U.S. 210 40.56 N 76.10 W
Nürenbei 107 30.11 N 106.04 E
Nūrestān □[9] 123 35.30 N 70.45 E
Nurettin 130 39.14 N 42.25 E
Nurhak 130 37.58 N 37.25 E
Nuri 232 28.02 N 109.22 W
Nuria, Monte ∧ 66 42.21 N 13.05 E
Nuriootpa 168b 34.29 S 139.00 E
Nurlat 80 54.26 N 50.46 E
Nurlaty 80 55.37 N 48.18 E
Nurmahal 123 31.06 N 75.36 E
Nurmes 26 63.33 N 29.07 E
Nurmijärvi 26 60.28 N 24.48 E
Nurnagar 126 22.20 N 89.03 E
Nürnberg 60 49.27 N 11.04 E
Nürnberg, Flughafen ≋ 60 49.30 N 11.06 E
Nūrpur, India 123 31.10 N 76.29 E
Nūrpur, India 123 32.18 N 75.54 E
Nurpur, India 126 22.13 N 88.05 E
Nurpur, Pāk. 123 31.53 N 71.54 E
Nurrari Lakes ⊜ 162 29.01 S 130.05 E
Nurri 71 39.43 N 9.14 E
Nurri, Mount ∧[2] 166 31.42 S 146.02 E
Nursery 222 28.56 N 97.06 W
Nürtingen 56 48.38 N 9.20 E
Nus 62 45.45 N 7.28 E
Nūsah 144 14.00 N 46.43 E
Nusa Tenggara Barat □[4] 115b 8.50 S 117.30 E
Nusa Tenggara Timur □[4] 112 9.30 S 122.00 E
Nusaybin 130 37.03 N 41.13 E
Nusayrīyah, Jabal an- ∧ 130 35.30 N 36.12 E
Nusco 68 40.53 N 15.05 E
Nushagak ≃ 180 59.00 N 158.30 W
Nushagak Bay c 180 58.40 N 158.40 W
Nushagak Peninsula › 180 58.30 N 159.00 W
Nu Shan ∧ 102 27.00 N 99.00 E
Nüshan Hu ⊜ 100 32.57 N 118.03 E
Nu-shima I 96 34.10 N 134.50 E
Nushki 120 29.33 N 66.01 E
Nusplingen 58 48.08 N 8.53 E
Nušpoly 82 56.39 N 37.44 E
Nussdorf ◆[8] 264b 48.15 N 16.22 E
Nussdorf am Attersee 64 47.53 N 13.31 E
Nuta ≃ 96 34.23 N 133.04 E
Nutauge, laguna c 180 67.55 N 176.45 W
Nutepel'men, S.S.S.R. 180 67.26 N 174.56 W
Nutepelmen, S.S.S.R. 180 65.31 N 178.30 W
Nutfield 260 51.14 N 0.07 W
Nuth 56 50.55 N 5.54 E
Nuthe ≃, D.D.R. 54 51.58 N 11.53 E
Nuthe ≃, D.D.R. 54 52.23 N 13.04 E
Nut Lake Indian Reserve ◆[4] 184 52.20 N 103.30 W
Nutley 210 40.49 N 74.09 W
Nutrioso 200 33.57 N 109.12 W
Nut Swamp Brook ≃ 276 40.21 N 74.06 W
Nuttby Mountain ∧[2] 186 45.33 N 63.13 W
Nutter Fort 188 39.15 N 80.19 W
Nutting Lake 207 42.32 N 71.16 W
Nutting Lake ⊜ 283 42.32 N 71.16 W
Nutwood 219 39.05 N 90.39 W
Nutwood Downs 164 15.49 S 134.10 E
Nutzotin Mountains ∧ 180 62.10 N 141.40 W
Nu'ūmīyah, Wādī an- V 142 29.31 N 31.17 E
Nuupere, Pointe › 174s 17.36 S 149.47 W
Nu'uuli 174u 14.18 S 170.42 W
N'uvčim 24 61.22 N 50.42 E
Nuwākot 124 28.08 N 83.53 E
Nuwaybiʻ al-Muzayyinah 140 28.58 N 34.39 E
Nuwerus 158 31.08 S 18.24 E
Nuweveldberge ∧ 158 32.13 S 22.10 E
Nuxis 71 39.09 N 8.44 E
Nuyakuk Lake ⊜ 180 60.00 N 158.40 W
Nuyts, Point › 162 35.04 S 116.37 E
Nuyts Archipelago II 162 32.35 S 133.17 E
Nüzvīd 122 16.47 N 80.51 E
N'Vinda 152 13.04 S 18.57 E
Nwa 152 6.30 N 11.00 E
Nxainxai 156 19.50 S 21.13 E
Nxai Pan National Park ◆ 156 19.45 S 24.50 E
Nxaunxau 156 18.19 S 21.04 E
Nyaake 150 4.52 N 7.37 W
Nyabéssan 152 2.24 N 10.24 E
Nyabing 162 33.32 S 118.09 E
Nyac 180 61.01 N 159.57 W
Nyack 210 41.05 N 73.55 W
Nyack Beach State Park ◆ 276 41.07 N 73.55 W
Nyadiri ≃ 154 16.44 S 32.33 E
Nyahanga 154 2.23 S 33.33 E
Nyahua 154 5.24 S 33.19 E
Nyahururu Falls 154 0.02 N 36.22 E
Nyah West 166 35.11 S 143.22 E
Nyainqêntanglha Feng ∧ 124 30.22 N 90.35 E
Nyainqêntanglha Shan ∧ 120 30.00 N 90.00 E
Nyainrong 120 32.09 N 92.11 E
Nyakabindi 154 2.38 S 33.59 E
Nyakakiri 154 2.15 S 31.28 E
Nyakanazi 154 3.00 S 31.15 E
Nyakrom 150 5.37 N 0.48 W
Nyakulenga 152 13.03 S 23.29 E
Nyala 140 12.03 N 24.53 E
Nyalam 120 28.11 N 85.58 E
Nyalas 114 2.26 N 102.28 E
Nyamandhlovu 154 19.50 S 28.16 E
Nyamina 150 13.19 N 6.59 W
Nyamlell 140 9.07 N 26.58 E
Nyamougo 154 1.29 S 34.33 E
Nyamtumbo 154 10.29 S 36.02 E
Nyamwage 154 8.08 S 39.00 E
Nyandekwa 154 3.55 S 32.30 E
Nyanding, Khawr V 140 8.40 N 32.41 E
Nyang ≃ 124 29.25 N 94.22 E
Nyanga □[4] 152 3.00 S 11.00 E
Nyanga ≃ 152 2.58 S 10.15 E
Nyanga, Lake ⊜ 162 29.57 S 126.10 E
Nyangana 156 18.00 S 20.41 E
Nyangui ∧ 154 17.53 S 32.44 E
Nyangui Mission 154 14.23 S 31.48 E
Nyanza □[4] 154 0.30 S 34.30 E
Nyanza-Lac 154 4.21 S 29.36 E
Nyasa, Lake (Lake Malawi) ⊜ 154 12.00 S 34.30 E
Nyaunglebin 110 17.57 N 96.44 E
Nyavikungu 154 11.26 S 25.54 E
Nyazura 154 18.43 S 32.10 E
Nyazvidzi ≃ 154 20.00 S 32.17 E
Nybergsund 26 61.15 N 12.19 E
Nyborg 41 55.19 N 10.48 E
Nybro 26 56.45 N 15.54 E
Nyda 74 66.36 N 72.54 E
Nydmo 124 29.25 N 90.08 E
Nyengo Swamp ≋ 152 14.51 S 22.07 E
Nyeri 154 0.25 S 36.57 E
Nyerol 140 8.41 N 32.02 E
Nyfer ≃ 42 52.02 N 4.50 W
Nygčigen, mys › 180 65.05 N 172.06 W
Nyhammar 40 60.17 N 14.58 E
Nyhyttan 40 59.31 N 14.48 E
Nyiel 140 6.06 N 31.13 E
Nyika National Park ◆ 154 10.48 S 33.48 E
Nyika Plateau ∧[1] 154 10.40 S 33.50 E
Nyimba 154 14.35 S 30.52 E
Nyingchi 120 29.32 N 94.25 E
Nyíradony 30 47.41 N 21.55 E
Nyírbátor 30 47.50 N 22.08 E
Nyíregyháza 30 47.59 N 21.43 E
Nykøbing, Dan. 26 56.48 N 8.52 E
Nykøbing, Dan. 41 54.46 N 11.53 E
Nykøbing, Dan. 41 55.55 N 11.41 E
Nyköping 40 58.45 N 17.00 E
Nykroppa 40 59.38 N 14.18 E
Nykvarn 40 59.11 N 17.26 E
Nyland 26 63.00 N 17.46 E
Nyland Acres 228 34.14 N 119.09 W
Nylga, S.S.S.R. 80 56.46 N 52.22 E
Nylga, S.S.S.R. 89 51.38 N 127.35 E
Nylstroom 156 24.42 S 28.20 E
Nymagee 166 32.04 S 146.20 E
Nymboida ≃ 166 29.39 S 152.30 E
Nymburk 30 50.11 N 15.03 E
Nymphenburg ◆[8] 60 48.09 N 11.30 E
Nynäshamn 40 58.54 N 17.57 E
Nyngan 166 31.34 S 147.11 E
Nyoma 120 33.11 N 78.38 E
Nyon 58 46.23 N 6.14 E
Nyong ≃ 152 3.17 N 9.54 E
Nyons 62 44.22 N 5.08 E
Nyord I 41 55.03 N 12.13 E
Nyou 150 12.46 N 1.56 W
Nyřany 60 49.43 N 13.12 E
Nyrov 24 60.42 N 56.40 E
Nyrsko 60 49.18 N 13.09 E
Nyš 89 51.31 N 142.46 E
Nysa, Pol. 30 50.29 N 17.20 E
Nyša, S.S.S.R. 80 56.23 N 51.51 E
Nysa Kłodzka ≃ 30 50.49 N 17.50 E
Nysa Łużycka (Neisse) (Nisa) ≃ 30 52.04 N 14.46 E
Nyslott → Savonlinna 26 61.52 N 28.53 E
Nysø 41 55.08 N 12.02 E
Nyssa 202 43.52 N 116.59 W
Nysted 41 54.40 N 11.45 E
Nytva 86 57.56 N 55.20 E
Nyūdō-zaki › 92 40.00 N 139.42 E
Nyugati Pályaudvar ◆[5] 264c 47.31 N 19.04 E
Nyūkawa 94 36.10 N 137.19 E
Nyumba ya Mungu Dam ◆[6] 154 3.51 S 37.28 E
Nyungwe 154 10.16 S 34.07 E
Nyunzu 154 5.57 S 28.01 E
Nyuri 120 27.42 N 92.13 E
Nyūzen 94 36.57 N 137.30 E
Nyvång 41 56.08 N 12.54 E
Nyvrovo 89 54.19 N 142.36 E
Nzaba 273b 4.06 S 15.16 E
Nzébéla 150 8.05 N 9.06 W
Nzega 154 4.13 S 33.11 E
Nzéla 152 1.25 S 12.39 E
Nzérékoré 150 7.45 N 8.49 W
N'zeto 152 7.14 S 12.52 E
Nzheleledam ⊜[1] 156 22.44 S 30.06 E
Nzi ≃ 150 5.57 N 4.50 W
Nzima 154 3.03 S 32.48 E
Nziro 152 3.17 N 24.06 E
Nzo ≃ 150 6.16 N 7.03 W
Nzoia ≃ 154 0.04 N 33.57 E
Nzubuka 154 4.45 S 32.50 E
Nzwani (Anjouan) I 157a 12.15 S 44.25 E

O

Oa, Mull of › 46 55.35 N 6.20 W
Oacoma 198 43.47 N 99.23 W
Oadby 42 52.36 N 1.04 W
Oad Street 260 51.20 N 0.41 E
Oahe, Lake ⊜[1] 198 45.30 N 100.25 W
Oahe Dam ◆[6] 198 44.27 N 100.23 W
Oahu I 229c 21.30 N 158.00 W
Oak ≃ 184 49.51 N 100.28 W
O-Akan-dake ∧ 92a 43.27 N 144.10 E
Oakbank, Austl. 162 33.03 S 140.35 E
Oakbank, Austl. 168b 34.59 S 138.51 E
Oak Bay 224 48.27 N 123.18 W
Oak Beach 276 40.38 N 73.17 W
Oak Bluffs 207 41.27 N 70.33 W
Oakboro 192 35.13 N 80.19 W
Oak Brook 278 41.49 N 87.55 W
Oakbrook Center ◆[9] 278 41.52 N 87.57 W
Oakbrook Terrace 278 41.52 N 87.58 W
Oakburn 184 50.35 N 100.32 W
Oak City, N.C., U.S. 192 35.57 N 77.18 W
Oak City, Ut., U.S. 200 39.22 N 112.20 W
Oak Creek, Co., U.S. 200 40.16 N 106.57 W
Oak Creek, Wi., U.S. 216 42.53 N 87.55 W
Oak Creek ≃, U.S. 198 45.39 N 100.31 W
Oak Creek ≃, Az., U.S. 200 34.41 N 111.56 W
Oak Creek ≃, Co., U.S. 200 40.25 N 106.50 W
Oak Creek ≃, Ks., U.S. 198 39.29 N 98.28 W
Oak Creek ≃, N.D., U.S. 198 48.38 N 100.24 W
Oak Creek ≃, Tx., U.S. 196 31.48 N 100.13 W
Oakdale, Ca., U.S. 226 37.46 N 120.50 W
Oakdale, Ct., U.S. 207 41.27 N 72.09 W
Oakdale, Il., U.S. 219 38.16 N 89.30 W
Oakdale, La., U.S. 194 30.48 N 92.39 W
Oakdale, Ma., U.S. 207 42.23 N 71.47 W
Oakdale, Ne., U.S. 198 42.04 N 97.58 W
Oakdale, N.J., U.S. 285 39.59 N 74.49 W
Oakdale, N.Y., U.S. 210 40.44 N 73.08 W
Oakdale, Pa., U.S. 214 40.23 N 80.11 W
Oakdale, Tn., U.S. 192 35.59 N 84.33 W
Oakdale Woods 278 41.56 N 87.58 W
Oakengates 42 52.42 N 2.28 W
Oakes 198 46.08 N 98.05 W
Oakesdale 202 47.07 N 117.14 W
Oakey 171a 27.26 S 151.43 E
Oakeys Brook ≃ 276 40.25 N 74.30 W
Oakfield, Me., U.S. 188 46.05 N 68.09 W
Oakfield, N.Y., U.S. 210 43.03 N 78.16 W
Oakfield, Wi., U.S. 190 43.41 N 88.32 W
Oakford, Il., U.S. 219 40.06 N 89.58 W
Oakford, In., U.S. 216 40.25 N 86.06 W
Oakford, Pa., U.S. 208 40.09 N 74.58 W
Oak Forest 216 41.36 N 87.44 W
Oakgrove, Eng., U.K. 262 53.13 N 2.07 W
Oak Grove, La., U.S. 194 32.51 N 91.23 W
Oak Grove, Or., U.S. 224 45.25 N 122.38 W
Oak Hall 208 37.56 N 75.33 W
Oakham 42 52.40 N 0.43 W
Oak Harbor, Oh., U.S. 214 41.30 N 83.09 W
Oak Harbor, Wa., U.S. 224 48.17 N 122.38 W
Oak Hill, De., U.S. 285 39.44 N 75.36 W
Oak Hill, Fl., U.S. 220 28.51 N 80.51 W
Oak Hill, Mi., U.S. 190 44.13 N 86.18 W
Oak Hill, N.Y., U.S. 210 42.25 N 74.09 W
Oak Hill, Oh., U.S. 188 38.54 N 82.34 W
Oak Hill, W.V., U.S. 188 37.58 N 81.08 W
Oakhurst, Ca., U.S. 226 37.19 N 119.40 W
Oakhurst, N.J., U.S. 208 40.16 N 74.01 W
Oakhurst, Tx., U.S. 222 30.44 N 95.19 W
Oak Island I, N.S., Can. 186 44.31 N 64.18 W
Oak Island I, N.Y., U.S. 276 40.39 N 73.18 W
Oak Knolls 204 34.51 N 120.27 W
Oak Lake 184 49.47 N 100.38 W
Oak Lake ⊜, Mb., Can. 184 49.40 N 100.45 W
Oak Lake ⊜, On., Can. 184 50.26 N 93.50 W
Oak Lake ⊜, On., Can. 212 44.36 N 77.55 W
Oakland, On., Can. 214 42.09 N 82.36 W
Oakland, Ca., U.S. 226 37.48 N 122.16 W
Oakland, Ca., U.S. 282 37.48 N 122.16 W
Oakland, Fl., U.S. 220 28.33 N 81.38 W
Oakland, Il., U.S. 194 39.39 N 88.01 W
Oakland, Ia., U.S. 198 41.18 N 95.23 W
Oakland, Me., U.S. 188 44.32 N 69.43 W
Oakland, Md., U.S. 188 39.24 N 79.24 W
Oakland, Md., U.S. 284c 38.51 N 76.55 W
Oakland, Ms., U.S. 194 34.03 N 89.54 W
Oakland, Ne., U.S. 198 41.50 N 96.28 W
Oakland, N.J., U.S. 210 41.00 N 74.15 W
Oakland, Or., U.S. 202 43.25 N 123.17 W
Oakland, Pa., U.S. 210 41.57 N 75.36 W
Oakland, Pa., U.S. 214 40.59 N 80.22 W
Oakland, Tx., U.S. 222 29.36 N 96.50 W
Oakland □[6] 216 42.40 N 83.23 W
Oakland ◆[8] 279b 40.26 N 79.58 W
Oakland-Alameda County Coliseum ◆ 282 37.45 N 122.12 W
Oakland Army Base ■ 282 37.49 N 122.19 W
Oakland Beach 214 41.37 N 80.18 W
Oakland City 194 38.20 N 87.20 W
Oakland Gardens ◆[8] 276 40.45 N 73.45 W
Oakland Mall ◆[9] 281 42.32 N 83.07 W
Oakland Park 220 26.10 N 80.07 W
Oakland-Pontiac Airport ⊠ 281 42.40 N 83.24 W
Oaklands 168b 35.00 S 137.41 E
Oaklands ◆[8] 273d 26.09 S 28.04 E
Oakland Southwest Airport ⊠ 281 42.30 N 83.37 W
Oakland University v[2] 281 42.41 N 83.13 W
Oak Lane Manor 285 39.47 N 75.32 W
Oak Lawn, Il., U.S. 216 41.43 N 87.45 W
Oaklawn, Ks., U.S. 198 37.36 N 97.17 W
Oaklawn, Md., U.S. 284c 38.47 N 76.57 W
Oakleigh 169 37.54 S 145.06 E
Oakleigh South 274b 37.56 S 145.05 E
Oakley, Eng., U.K. 42 51.15 N 1.11 W
Oakley, Scot., U.K. 46 56.04 N 3.33 W
Oakley, Ca., U.S. 226 37.58 N 121.43 W
Oakley, Id., U.S. 202 42.14 N 113.52 W
Oakley, Il., U.S. 219 39.53 N 88.48 W
Oakley, Ks., U.S. 198 39.08 N 100.51 W
Oakley Park 216 42.36 N 83.30 W
Oaklyn 285 39.54 N 75.05 W
Oakman 194 33.42 N 87.23 W
Oakmont 214 40.31 N 79.50 W
Oak Mountain State Park ◆ 194 33.22 N 86.41 W
Oakmulgee Creek ≃ 194 32.28 N 87.09 W
Oak Neck › 276 40.54 N 73.34 W
Oak Neck Point › 276 40.55 N 73.34 W
Oakohay Creek ≃ 194 31.44 N 89.25 W
Oak Orchard Creek ≃ 210 43.22 N 78.12 W
Oak Orchard Swamp ≋ 210 43.07 N 78.18 W
Oakover ≃ 162 20.43 S 120.33 E
Oak Park, Austl. 274b 37.43 S 144.55 E
Oak Park, Ca., U.S. 228 34.11 N 118.45 W
Oak Park, Il., U.S. 216 41.53 N 87.47 W
Oak Park, Mi., U.S. 216 42.27 N 83.10 W
Oak Park, Pa., U.S. 285 40.15 N 75.18 W
Oak Point 184 50.30 N 98.00 W
Oakridge, Ca., U.S. 226 38.03 N 121.20 W
Oak Ridge, N.J., U.S. 210 41.03 N 74.29 W
Oakridge, Or., U.S. 202 43.44 N 122.27 W
Oak Ridge, Pa., U.S. 214 41.00 N 79.18 W
Oak Ridge, Tn., U.S. 192 36.00 N 84.16 W
Oak Ridge Lake 276 41.00 N 74.32 W
Oak Ridge National Laboratory v[3] 192 36.00 N 84.15 W
Oak Ridge Reservoir ⊜[1] 276 41.03 N 74.30 W
Oaks 285 40.08 N 75.27 W
Oaks Corners 210 42.56 N 77.01 W
Oak Shades 276 40.26 N 74.13 W
Oakton 284c 38.52 N 77.18 W
Oaktown 194 38.52 N 87.26 W
Oakura 172 39.07 S 173.57 E
Oak Valley, N.J., U.S. 208 39.48 N 75.09 W
Oak Valley, Va., U.S. 284c 38.54 N 77.18 W
Oak View, Ca., U.S. 228 34.24 N 119.18 W
Oak View, Md., U.S. 284c 39.01 N 76.59 W
Oakview, N.J., U.S. 285 39.51 N 75.09 W
Oakview Beach 212 44.29 N 80.03 W
Oakville, Mb., Can. 184 49.56 N 97.58 W
Oakville, On., Can. 212 43.27 N 79.41 W
Oakville, Ct., U.S. 207 41.35 N 73.05 W
Oakville, Il., U.S. 218 40.05 N 85.23 W
Oakville, Mo., U.S. 219 38.28 N 90.18 W
Oakville, Wa., U.S. 224 46.50 N 123.13 W
Oakwood, On., Can. 212 44.20 N 78.53 W
Oakwood, N.J., U.S. 285 39.52 N 74.50 W
Oakwood, Oh., U.S. 214 41.23 N 81.29 W
Oakwood, Oh., U.S. 216 41.05 N 84.22 W
Oakwood, Oh., U.S. 218 39.44 N 84.10 W
Oakwood, Tx., U.S. 222 31.35 N 95.50 W
Oakwood Beach 208 39.33 N 75.31 W
Oakwood Park ◆ 279a 41.26 N 82.06 W
Oamaru 172 45.06 S 170.58 E
Ōamishirasato 94 35.31 N 140.19 E
Ōana 268 35.45 N 140.04 E
Oancea 38 45.55 N 28.06 E
Ōarai 94 36.18 N 140.34 E
Oaro 172 42.31 S 173.30 E
Ōasa 96 34.46 N 132.28 E
Oat Creek ≃ 226 38.50 N 121.56 W
Oates Coast ⊥[2] 9 70.00 S 160.00 E
Oatka Creek ≃ 210 43.01 N 77.44 W
Oatlands 166 42.18 S 147.21 E
Oatley 274a 33.59 S 151.05 E
Oatley Park ◆ 274a 33.59 S 151.04 E
Oatman 200 35.01 N 114.22 W
Oaxaca □[3] 234 17.00 N 96.30 W
Oaxaca [de Juárez] 234 17.03 N 96.43 W
Ob' ≃ 72 66.45 N 69.30 E
Oba 190 48.55 N 84.17 W
Oba ≃ 152 2.00 S 16.10 E
Obabika Lake ⊜ 190 47.05 N 80.17 W
Obala 152 4.10 N 11.32 E
Oba Lake ⊜ 190 48.38 N 84.18 W
Obama, Nihon 92 32.43 N 130.13 E
Obama, Nihon 94 35.30 N 135.45 E
Obama-wan c 94 35.30 N 135.42 E
Oban, Austl. 166 21.14 S 139.03 E
Oban, Nig. 150 5.17 N 8.35 E
Oban, Scot., U.K. 46 56.25 N 5.29 W
Obanazawa 92 38.36 N 140.24 E
Obando 269f 14.43 N 120.56 E
Oban Hills ∧[2] 150 5.35 N 8.35 E
Obara 94 35.15 N 137.18 E
Obasa 94 34.30 N 136.40 E
Obata 94 34.33 N 136.38 E
Ob' Bay c 9 70.35 S 163.22 E
Obbo 144 3.36 N 38.54 E
Obbola 26 63.42 N 20.19 E
Občuga 76 54.30 N 29.22 E
Obdach 61 47.04 N 14.41 E
Obed 182 53.33 N 117.12 W
Obed ≃ 192 36.04 N 84.39 W
Obeliai 76 55.56 N 25.48 E
Obelisk ∧ 172 45.20 S 169.12 E
Oberá 252 27.29 S 55.08 W
Oberägeri 58 47.08 N 8.37 E
Oberalpass x 58 46.39 N 8.40 E
Oberalpstock ∧ 58 46.44 N 8.46 E
Oberammergau 64 47.35 N 11.04 E
Oberau 64 47.33 N 11.08 E
Oberaudorf 64 47.39 N 12.10 E
Oberbauer 263 51.17 N 7.26 E
Oberbayern □[5] 60 48.00 N 11.45 E
Oberbieber 56 50.28 N 7.29 E
Oberbonsfeld 263 51.22 N 7.08 E
Oberbrügge 263 51.11 N 7.34 E
Obercunnersdorf 54 51.02 N 14.40 E
Oberdiessbach 58 46.51 N 7.38 E
Oberdolling 60 48.50 N 11.35 E
Oberdorla 54 51.10 N 10.25 E
Oberdrauburg 64 46.45 N 12.58 E
Oberelfringhausen 263 51.20 N 7.11 E
Ober Engadin V 58 46.37 N 9.58 E
Oberengstringen 58 47.25 N 8.28 E
Oberer See → Superior, Lake ⊜ 190 48.00 N 88.00 W
Oberfranken □[5] 60 49.50 N 11.20 E
Obergeis 56 50.54 N 9.35 E
Oberglogau → Głogówek 30 50.22 N 17.51 E
Ober-Grafendorf 61 48.09 N 15.33 E
Obergum 52 53.20 N 6.31 E
Obergünzburg 58 47.51 N 10.25 E
Obergurgl 64 46.52 N 11.01 E
Obergurig 54 51.07 N 14.24 E
Oberhaan 263 51.13 N 7.02 E
Oberhaching 60 48.02 N 11.37 E
Oberharmersbach 58 48.22 N 8.07 E
Oberhaslach 58 48.33 N 7.20 E
Oberhausen 56 51.28 N 6.50 E
Oberhof 54 50.41 N 10.44 E
Oberhofen 58 46.44 N 7.40 E
Oberinntal V 64 47.13 N 10.45 E
Oberjettingen 58 48.34 N 8.46 E
Oberjoch 58 47.31 N 10.23 E
Ober-Kassel ◆[8] 263 51.14 N 6.46 E
Oberkirch 58 48.31 N 8.05 E
Ober-Kirchbach 264b 48.17 N 16.12 E
Oberkirchen 56 51.09 N 8.22 E
Oberkochen 58 48.47 N 10.06 E
Oberkotzau 54 50.16 N 11.56 E
Oberlaa ◆[8] 264b 48.08 N 16.24 E
Oberlaapark ◆ 264b 48.08 N 16.25 E
Oberlausitz □[9] 54 51.15 N 14.30 E
Oberlin, Ks., U.S. 198 39.49 N 100.31 W
Oberlin, La., U.S. 194 30.37 N 92.45 W
Oberlin, Oh., U.S. 214 41.17 N 82.13 W
Oberlin, Pa., U.S. 208 40.14 N 76.49 W
Oberloisdorf 61 47.27 N 16.30 E
Oberlungwitz 54 50.47 N 12.44 E
Obermarchtal 58 48.14 N 9.34 E
Obermeiser 56 51.26 N 9.19 E
Obermieming 64 47.18 N 10.59 E
Obermodern 58 48.51 N 7.32 E
Obermoschel 56 49.44 N 7.46 E
Obermünstertal 58 47.52 N 7.49 E
Obernai 58 48.28 N 7.29 E
Obernbeck 52 52.12 N 8.41 E
Obernberg am Inn 60 48.19 N 13.20 E
Obernburg am Main 56 49.50 N 9.08 E
Oberndorf 52 53.45 N 9.08 E
Oberndorf am Neckar 58 48.18 N 8.34 E
Oberndorf bei Salzburg 64 47.57 N 12.56 E
Oberndorf in Tirol 64 47.30 N 12.23 E
Oberne 171b 35.24 S 147.50 E
Oberne Hill ∧[2] 171b 35.22 S 147.44 E
Obernhausen 56 50.29 N 9.56 E
Obernkirchen 52 52.16 N 9.07 E
Obernzell 60 48.34 N 13.39 E
Oberoderwitz 54 50.58 N 14.42 E
Oberon 170 33.43 S 149.52 E
Oberösterreich □[3] 30 48.15 N 14.00 E
Oberpfalz □[5] 60 49.30 N 12.10 E
Oberpleis 56 50.43 N 7.16 E
Oberpullendorf 61 47.31 N 16.31 E
Ober-Ramstadt 56 49.49 N 8.44 E
Oberried 58 46.44 N 7.58 E
Oberriet 58 47.19 N 9.33 E
Oberrimsingen 58 47.59 N 7.40 E
Oberröblingen 54 51.26 N 11.18 E
Ober Sankt Veit ◆[8] 264b 48.11 N 16.16 E
Oberscheidental 56 49.30 N 9.09 E
Oberscheinfeld 56 49.42 N 10.26 E

ENGLISH Name	Page	Lat.°′	Long.°′

Oberscheld 56 50.44 N 8.20 E
Oberschleissheim 60 48.15 N 11.34 E
Oberschöneweide ◆[8] 264a 52.28 N 13.31 E
Oberseebach 56 48.58 N 7.59 E
Obersickte 54 52.13 N 10.38 E
Oberspier 54 51.19 N 10.51 E
Oberstadtfeld 56 50.10 N 6.46 E
Oberstaufen 58 47.33 N 10.01 E
Oberstdorf 58 47.24 N 10.16 E
Obersteinbach 56 49.02 N 7.41 E
Oberstreu 56 50.24 N 10.17 E
Obersuhl 56 50.56 N 10.02 E
Obersulm 56 49.08 N 9.27 E
Obertheres 56 50.01 N 10.26 E
Obertilliach 64 46.42 N 12.37 E
Obertin 78 48.42 N 25.11 E
Obertraubling 60 48.58 N 12.10 E
Obertraun 64 47.33 N 13.41 E
Obertrum 64 47.56 N 13.05 E
Obertrumer See ⊜ 60 47.58 N 13.06 E
Obertürken 60 48.19 N 12.50 E
Oberueckersee ⊜ 54 53.12 N 13.52 E
Oberursel 56 50.11 N 8.35 E
Oberuzwil 58 47.26 N 9.08 E
Obervellach 64 46.56 N 13.12 E
Oberviechtach 60 49.28 N 12.25 E
Obervolta → Burkina Faso □[1] 150 13.00 N 1.30 W
Oberwald 58 46.32 N 8.21 E
Oberwart 61 47.17 N 16.13 E
Oberweissbach 54 50.35 N 11.08 E
Oberwengern 263 51.23 N 7.22 E
Oberwesel 56 50.06 N 7.43 E
Oberwiesenthal 54 50.25 N 12.59 E
Oberwolfach 58 48.19 N 8.12 E
Oberwölz Stadt 61 47.13 N 14.17 E
Oberzeiring 61 47.15 N 14.29 E
Obetz 218 39.52 N 82.57 W
Obey, East Fork ≃ 192 36.27 N 85.07 W
Obey, West Fork ≃ 192 36.27 N 85.09 W
Obgruiten 263 51.13 N 7.01 E
Obhausen 54 51.23 N 11.39 E
Obi 150 8.22 N 8.46 E
Obi, Kepulauan II 164 1.30 S 127.45 E
Obi, Selat ꞩ 164 0.52 S 127.33 E
Obi, Pulau I 164 1.30 S 127.45 E
Obiaruku 150 5.51 N 6.09 E
Obichingou ≃ 85 38.53 N 70.01 E
Obichody 78 51.02 N 28.59 E
Óbidos 250 1.55 S 55.31 W
Obi-Garm 85 38.43 N 69.42 E
Obihiro 92a 42.55 N 143.12 E
Obikanda 85 39.10 N 67.10 E
Obilatu, Pulau I 108 1.25 S 127.20 E
Obil'noje 80 47.31 N 44.25 E
Obing 60 48.00 N 12.24 E
Obion 194 36.15 N 89.11 W
Obion ≃ 194 35.55 N 89.39 W
Obion, Middle Fork ≃ 194 36.13 N 88.56 W
Obion, Rutherford Fork ≃ 194 36.17 N 89.01 W
Obion, South Fork ≃ 194 36.17 N 89.03 W
Obion Creek ≃ 194 36.35 N 89.11 W
Obiou, Grande Tête de l' ∧ 62 44.46 N 5.50 E
Obira 92a 44.00 N 141.35 E
Obitočnaja kosa ›[2] 78 46.33 N 36.13 E
Obitočnyj zaliv c 78 46.35 N 36.00 E
Obitsu ≃ 94 35.24 N 139.54 E
Objačevo 24 60.20 N 49.34 E
Oblačnaja, gora ∧ 89 43.45 N 134.10 E
Öblarn 61 47.27 N 13.59 E
Oblastnaja 80 56.59 N 52.37 E
Oblivskaja 80 48.32 N 42.30 E
Oblong 194 39.00 N 87.54 W
Oblučje 89 49.03 N 131.04 E
Obninsk 82 55.05 N 36.37 E
Obnora ≃ 76 58.14 N 40.58 E
Obnova 38 43.26 N 24.59 E
Obo 154 5.24 N 26.30 E
Obobogorap 158 27.18 S 20.04 E
Obock 144 11.59 N 43.16 E
Obojan' 78 51.13 N 36.16 E
Ō-boke ◆ 96 33.55 N 133.46 E
Obokote 154 0.52 S 26.19 E
Obol' 76 55.22 N 29.17 E
Obol' ≃ 76 55.24 N 29.02 E
Oboldino 265b 55.53 N 37.56 E
Obolon' 78 49.36 N 32.52 E
Oborniki 30 52.39 N 16.51 E
Obot 144 4.30 N 37.20 E
Obouya 152 0.56 S 15.43 E
Oboz'orskij 24 63.28 N 40.18 E
Obra ≃ 30 52.36 N 15.28 E
Obrazcovo-Travino 80 45.58 N 48.02 E
Obree, Mount ∧ 164 9.30 S 148.05 E
Obrenovac 38 44.39 N 20.12 E
O'Brien 202 42.04 N 123.42 W
O'Brien Coulee V 202 48.38 N 110.22 W
Obrighoven-Lackhausen 52 51.40 N 6.38 E
Obrovac 36 44.12 N 15.41 E
Obrovo 76 52.30 N 25.34 E
Obručeva, gora ∧ 88 53.36 N 113.52 E
Obručevka 85 42.30 N 69.05 E
Obruk 130 38.10 N 33.12 E
Obryta 54 53.13 N 14.59 E
Obryvistoje 89 48.46 N 144.40 E
Obša ≃ 76 55.55 N 32.32 E
Obšarovka 80 53.07 N 48.52 E
Obščij Syrt ∧ 80 52.00 N 51.30 E
Observation Peak ∧ 204 40.46 N 120.10 W
Observatoire, Caye de l' I 160 21.25 S 158.50 E
Observatory Inlet c 182 55.10 N 129.54 W
Obskaja guba c 72 69.00 N 73.00 E
Obsteig 64 47.18 N 10.56 E
Obtovo 78 51.37 N 33.13 E
Ob' Trench ◆[1] 14 33.00 S 98.00 E
Ōbu 94 35.00 N 136.58 E
Obu ◆[8] 270 34.44 N 135.09 E
Obuasi 150 6.14 N 1.39 W
Obubra 150 6.05 N 8.21 E
Obuchov 78 50.08 N 30.37 E
Obuchova 76 56.06 N 32.22 E
Obuchoviči 78 51.00 N 29.46 E
Obuchovka 86 46.13 N 81.05 E
Obuchovo, S.S.S.R. 82 55.50 N 38.16 E
Obuchovo, S.S.S.R. 82 56.09 N 36.55 E
Óbuda ◆[8] 264c 47.33 N 19.02 E
Óbudai-sziget I 264c 47.33 N 19.04 E
Obudu 150 6.40 N 9.09 E
Obuse 94 36.42 N 138.19 E
Obushkong Lake ⊜ 190 47.42 N 80.48 W
Obuškovo 82 55.47 N 37.02 E
Obu-tōge x 270 34.44 N 135.10 E
Obva ≃ 86 58.32 N 55.18 E
Obvinsk 86 58.29 N 54.51 E
Obwalden □[3] 58 46.50 N 8.14 E
Obžericha 80 57.11 N 42.58 E
Očakov 78 46.37 N 31.33 E
Očakovo ◆[8] 265b 55.41 N 37.27 E
Ocala 192 29.11 N 82.08 W
Ocallí 248 6.09 S 78.18 W
Očamčira 84 42.44 N 41.28 E
Ocamo ≃ 246 2.48 N 65.14 W
Ocampo, Méx. 232 28.11 N 108.23 W
Ocampo, Méx. 232 27.20 N 102.21 W
Ocampo, Méx. 234 21.39 N 101.30 W
Ocaña, Col. 246 8.15 N 73.20 W
Ocaña, Esp. 34 39.56 N 3.31 W
Ocate Creek ≃ 196 36.17 N 104.30 W
Occaquan ≃ 208 38.40 N 77.14 W
Occaquan Reservoir ⊜[1] 208 38.43 N 77.22 W
Očchamuri 84 41.52 N 41.50 E
Occhieppo Inferiore 62 45.33 N 8.01 E
Occhiobello 64 44.55 N 11.35 E
Occidental, Cordillera ∧, Col. 246 5.00 N 76.00 W

DEUTSCH Name	Seite	Breite°′	Länge°′ E = Ost

Occidental, Cordillera ∧, Perú 248 10.00 S 77.00 W
Occidental College v[2] 280 34.08 N 118.13 W
Occidental de Zapata, Ciénaga ≋ 240p 22.25 N 81.20 W
Occimiano 62 45.03 N 8.30 E
Occoquan 208 38.41 N 77.15 W
Occoquan Bay c 208 38.37 N 77.13 W
Ocean □[6] 208 39.58 N 74.12 W
Oceana 192 37.41 N 81.37 W
Oceana Naval Air Station ■ 208 36.50 N 76.02 W
Ocean Bay Park 276 40.39 N 73.08 W
Ocean Beach 276 40.38 N 73.18 W
Ocean Bluff 207 42.05 N 70.39 W
Ocean Breeze Park 220 27.15 N 80.14 W
Ocean Cape › 180 59.30 N 139.45 W
Ocean City, Md., U.S. 208 38.20 N 75.05 W
Ocean City, N.J., U.S. 208 39.16 N 74.34 W
Ocean City, Wa., U.S. 224 47.04 N 124.09 W
Ocean Falls 182 52.21 N 127.40 W
Ocean Gate 208 39.55 N 74.08 W
Ocean Grove, Austl. 169 38.16 S 144.32 E
Ocean Grove, Ma., U.S. 207 41.43 N 71.12 W
Ocean Heights 207 41.24 N 70.33 W
Ocean Island → Banaba I 174d 0.52 S 169.35 E
Ocean Lake ⊜[1] 202 43.11 N 108.36 W
Oceano 204 35.06 N 120.37 W
Ocean Park, B.C., Can. 224 49.02 N 122.53 W
Ocean Park, Wa., U.S. 224 46.29 N 124.02 W
Ocean Park ◆ 271d 22.15 N 114.09 E
Ocean Port 276 40.19 N 74.00 W
Ocean Shores 224 47.01 N 124.09 W
Oceanside, Ca., U.S. 228 33.11 N 117.22 W
Oceanside, N.Y., U.S. 210 40.38 N 73.38 W
Ocean Springs 194 30.24 N 88.49 W
Ocean View, De., U.S. 208 38.32 N 75.05 W
Ocean View, N.J., U.S. 208 39.10 N 74.44 W
Oceanville 208 39.28 N 74.27 W
Oceola 214 40.51 N 83.06 W
Očer 80 57.53 N 54.42 E
Očeretino 83 48.14 N 37.36 E
O. C. Fisher Lake ⊜[1] 196 31.30 N 100.30 W
Ocha 89 53.34 N 142.56 E
Ochagavía, Canal de ≍ 286e 33.30 S 70.49 W
Ochanomizu Women's University v[2] 268 35.43 N 139.44 E
Ochansk 86 57.43 N 55.23 E
Ochapowace Indian Reserve ◆[4] 184 50.30 N 102.24 W
Ocheyedan 198 43.24 N 95.32 W
Ocheyedan ≃ 198 43.08 N 95.09 W
Ōchi, Nihon 96 35.04 N 132.36 E
Ochi, Nihon 96 33.32 N 133.15 E
Ōchi, Nihon 96 34.16 N 134.18 E
Ochiai 96 35.01 N 133.45 E
Ochiai ◆[8] 268 35.43 N 139.42 E
O'Chiese Indian Reserve ◆[4] 182 52.50 N 115.28 W
Ochil Hills ∧[2] 46 56.14 N 3.40 W
Ochiltree 44 55.28 N 4.23 W
Ōchise ≃ 94 35.03 N 137.46 E
Ochlocknee 192 30.58 N 84.03 W
Ochlockonee ≃ 192 29.58 N 84.21 W
Ochoco Creek ≃ 202 44.19 N 120.53 W
Ochoco Mountains ∧ 202 44.30 N 120.35 W
Ochopee 220 25.54 N 81.18 W
Ocho Rios 241q 18.25 N 77.07 W
Ochota ≃ 74 59.20 N 143.04 E
Ochotsk 74 59.23 N 143.18 E
Ochotskisches Meer → Okhotsk, Sea of ▼[2] 74 53.00 N 150.00 E
Ochotskoje more → Okhotsk, Sea of ▼[2] 74 53.00 N 150.00 E
Ochre River 184 51.03 N 99.47 W
Ochsenfurt 56 49.40 N 10.03 E
Ochsenhausen 58 48.04 N 9.56 E
Ochsenwerder ◆[8] 52 53.28 N 10.05 E
Ochta ≃ 265a 59.57 N 30.24 E
Ochtrup 52 52.13 N 7.11 E
Ochvat 76 56.46 N 32.27 E
Oci ≃ 152 15.14 S 15.16 E
Ocilla 192 31.35 N 83.15 W
Ock ≃ 42 51.39 N 1.17 W
Ockelbo 26 60.53 N 16.43 E
Öckerö 26 57.43 N 11.39 E
Ockham 260 51.18 N 0.27 W
Ockholm 41 54.40 N 8.49 E
Ockies 158 31.31 S 21.41 E
Ocklawaha, Lake ⊜[1] 192 29.30 N 81.50 W
Ocmulgee ≃ 192 31.58 N 82.32 W
Ocmulgee National Monument ◆ 192 32.43 N 83.38 W
Ocna Mureș 38 46.23 N 23.51 E
Ocoa, Bahía de c 238 18.22 N 70.39 W
Ocoee 220 28.34 N 81.32 W
Ocoee (Toccoa) ≃ 192 35.12 N 84.40 W
Ocoña 248 16.26 S 73.07 W
Ocoña ≃ 248 16.28 S 73.07 W
Oconee 219 39.17 N 89.07 W
Oconee ≃ 192 31.58 N 82.32 W
Oconee, Lake ⊜[1] 192 33.30 N 83.15 W
Ocongate 248 13.38 S 71.24 W
O'Connell 170 33.32 S 149.44 E
Oconomowoc 216 43.06 N 88.29 W
Oconomowoc ≃ 216 43.07 N 88.37 W
Oconomowoc Lake 216 42.37 N 88.28 W
Oconomowoc Lake ⊜ 216 43.06 N 88.27 W
Oconto 190 44.53 N 87.51 W
Oconto ≃ 190 44.53 N 87.50 W
Oconto, North Branch ≃ 190 45.00 N 88.23 W
Oconto Falls 190 44.52 N 88.08 W
Ocós 236 14.31 N 92.11 W
Ocotal 236 13.38 N 86.29 W
Ocotepec 234 17.13 N 93.09 W
Ocotepeque □[5] 236 14.30 N 89.00 W
Ocotlán 234 20.21 N 102.46 W
Ocotlán de Morelos 234 16.48 N 96.40 W
Ocoyoacac 234 19.16 N 99.26 W
Ocozingo 232 16.54 N 92.07 W
Ocozocoautla [de Espinosa] 234 16.46 N 93.22 W
Ocracoke 192 35.06 N 75.58 W
Ocracoke Island I 192 35.09 N 75.53 W
Ocre, Monte ∧ 66 42.15 N 13.26 E
Ocros 248 10.24 S 77.24 W
Octoraro Creek ≃ 208 39.39 N 76.09 W
Octoraro Creek, East Branch ≃ 208 39.49 N 76.02 W
Octoraro Creek, West Branch ≃ 208 39.49 N 76.05 W
Octoraro Lake ⊜[1] 208 39.48 N 76.02 W
Ocú 236 7.57 N 80.47 W
Ocuilán de Arteaga 234 18.58 N 99.25 W
Ocumare del Tuy 246 10.07 N 66.46 W
Ocurí 248 18.50 S 65.50 W
Ocussi 112 9.12 S 124.21 E
Oda, Ghana 150 5.55 N 0.59 W
Oda, Nihon 96 33.34 N 132.48 E
Ōda, Nihon 96 35.11 N 132.30 E
Oda ≃ 96 34.37 N 133.44 E
Oda, Jabal ∧ 140 20.21 N 36.39 E
Ŏdaejin 98 41.34 N 129.40 E
Odae-san Kukrip Kongwŏn ◆ 98 37.46 N 128.37 E
Ōdai 94 34.24 N 136.25 E
Ōdaigahara-zan ∧ 92 34.11 N 136.05 E

Symbols in the index entries represent the broad categories identified in the key at the right. Symbols with superior numbers (∧[1]) identify subcategories (see complete key on page *I · 1).*

Symbole im Register stellen die rechts im Schlüssel erklärten Kategorien dar. Symbole mit hochgestellten Ziffern (∧[1]) bezeichnen Unterabteilungen einer Kategorie (vgl. vollständiger Schlüssel auf Seite *I · 1).*

Los símbolos incluídos en el texto del índice representan las grandes categorias identificadas con la clave a la derecha. Los símbolos con numeros en su parte superior (∧[1]) identifican las subcategorías (véase la clave completa en la página *I · 1).*

Les symboles de l'index représentent les catégories indiquées dans la légende à droite. Les symboles suivis d'un indice (∧[1]) représentent des sous-catégories (voir légende complète à la page *I · 1).*

Os símbolos incluídos no texto do índice representam as grandes categorias identificadas com a chave à direita. Os símbolos com números em sua parte superior (∧[1]) identificam as subcategorias (veja-se a chave completa à página *I · 1).*

∧ Mountain	Berg	Montaña	Montagne	Montanha
∧ Mountains	Gebirge	Montañas	Montagnes	Montanhas
x Pass	Paß	Paso	Col	Passo
V Valley, Canyon	Tal, Cañon	Valle, Cañón	Vallée, Canyon	Vale, Canhão
≍ Plain	Ebene	Llano	Plaine	Planície
› Cape	Kap	Cabo	Cap	Cabo
I Island	Insel	Isla	Île	Ilha
II Islands	Inseln	Islas	Îles	Ilhas
⊥ Other Topographic Features	Andere Topographische Objekte	Otros Elementos Topográficos	Autres données topographiques	Outros acidentes topográficos

ESPAÑOL Nombre	Página	Lat.°′	Long.°′ W = Oeste

FRANÇAIS Nom	Page	Lat.°′	Long.°′ W = Ouest

PORTUGUÊS Nome	Página	Lat.°′	Long.°′ W = Oeste

Odaka 92 37.34 N 141.00 E
Ödåkra 41 56.06 N 12.44 E
Odanakumadona 156 20.53 S 24.45 E
Ōdate 92 40.16 N 140.34 E
Odawara 94 35.15 N 139.10 E
Odayeri ◆[8] 267b 41.14 N 28.51 E
Odda 26 60.04 N 6.33 E
Odden 41 55.58 N 11.22 E
Odder 41 55.58 N 10.10 E
Oddville 218 38.27 N 84.15 W
Odebolt 198 42.18 N 95.15 W
Ödeby 40 59.24 N 15.25 E
Odei ≃ 184 56.06 N 96.55 W
Odeleite, Ribeira de ≃ 34 37.21 N 7.27 W
Odell, Il., U.S. 216 41.00 N 88.31 W
Odell, Ne., U.S. 198 40.03 N 96.48 W
Odell, Or., U.S. 224 45.37 N 121.32 W
Odell, Tx., U.S. 196 34.21 N 99.25 W
Odell Lake ⊜ 202 43.34 N 122.00 W
Odelzhausen 60 48.19 N 11.12 E
Odem 196 27.57 N 97.34 W
Odemira 34 37.36 N 8.38 W
Ödemiş 130 38.13 N 27.59 E
Ödenburg → Sopron 61 47.41 N 16.36 E
Odendaalsrus 158 27.48 S 26.45 E
Odenkirchen ◆[8] 263 51.08 N 6.27 E
Odensbacken 40 59.10 N 15.32 E
Odense 41 55.24 N 10.23 E
Odense Å ≃ 41 55.26 N 10.26 E
Odense Fjord c 41 55.30 N 10.34 E
Odenthal 56 51.02 N 7.07 E
Odenton 208 39.05 N 76.42 W
Odenwald ʎ 56 49.40 N 9.00 E
Oder ≃, B.R.D. 52 51.40 N 10.06 E
Oder (Odra) ≃, Europe 30 53.32 N 14.38 E
Oderberg 54 52.52 N 14.02 E
Oderbruch ◆[1] 54 52.40 N 14.15 E
Oderen 58 47.55 N 6.59 E
Oderhaff (Zalew Szczeciński) c 54 53.46 N 14.14 E
Oder-Havel-Kanal ≊ 54 52.52 N 14.02 E
Oder-Spree-Kanal ≊ 54 52.23 N 13.41 E
Odertalsperre ◆[6] 54 51.38 N 10.30 E
Oderzo 64 45.47 N 12.29 E
Odesa → Odessa 78 46.28 N 30.44 E
Ödeshög 26 58.14 N 14.39 E
Odessa, On., Can. 212 44.17 N 76.43 W
Odessa, S.S.S.R. 78 46.28 N 30.44 E
Odessa, De., U.S. 208 39.27 N 75.39 W
Odessa, Fl., U.S. 220 28.11 N 82.35 W
Odessa, Mo., U.S. 194 38.59 N 93.57 W
Odessa, N.Y., U.S. 210 42.20 N 76.47 W
Odessa, Tx., U.S. 196 31.50 N 102.22 W
Odessa, Wa., U.S. 202 47.20 N 118.41 W
Odessa □[4] 38 47.30 N 30.00 E
Odessa Lake ⊜ 212 44.19 N 76.41 W
Odesskoje 86 54.13 N 72.58 E
Odiakwe 156 20.01 S 25.17 E
Odib, Wādī V 140 22.38 N 36.06 E
Odiel ≃ 34 37.10 N 6.54 W
Odienné 150 9.30 N 7.34 W
Odiham 42 51.15 N 0.57 W
Odin 219 38.37 N 89.03 W
Odin, Mount ∧ 182 50.33 N 118.08 W
Odincovo, S.S.S.R. 82 55.41 N 37.17 E
Odincovo, S.S.S.R. 82 54.40 N 38.00 E
Odiongan 116 12.24 N 121.59 E
Odiongan Bay c 116 12.25 N 121.58 E
Odivelas 266c 38.47 N 9.11 W
Odobeşti 38 45.45 N 27.04 E
Odojev 76 53.56 N 36.41 E
Odolanów 30 51.35 N 17.39 E
Ōdomari-chosuichi ⊜ 96 34.43 N 132.18 E
Odon 194 38.50 N 86.59 W
Ŏdŏngk 110 11.48 N 104.45 E
O'Donnell 196 32.57 N 101.49 W
O'Donnell ≃ 162 18.22 S 126.36 E
Odoorn 52 52.51 N 6.51 E
Odorheiu Secuiesc 38 46.18 N 25.18 E
Odra (Oder) ≃ 30 53.32 N 14.38 E
Odra Port 54 53.52 N 14.14 E
Odrinhas 266c 38.53 N 9.22 W
Odrzywół 30 51.32 N 20.33 E
Ødsted 41 55.39 N 9.25 E
Odum 192 31.39 N 82.01 W
Odžaci 38 45.30 N 19.16 E
Odzala, Parc National d' ♠ 152 1.00 S 15.00 E
Odzi 154 18.58 S 32.23 E
Odzi ≃ 154 19.45 S 32.24 E
Odziba 152 3.35 S 15.31 E
Ōe 96 35.23 N 135.09 E
Oebisfelde 54 52.25 N 10.59 E
Oedelem 50 51.10 N 3.20 E
Oederan 54 50.52 N 13.09 E
Oeding 52 51.56 N 6.49 E
Oedt 56 51.19 N 6.22 E
Oegstgeest 52 52.10 N 4.29 E
Oeiras, Bra. 250 7.01 S 42.08 W
Oeiras, Port. 266c 38.41 N 9.21 W
Oeiras do Pará 250 1.58 S 49.51 W
Oelde 52 51.49 N 8.08 E
Oelemari ≃ 250 3.13 N 54.09 W
Oella 284b 39.16 N 76.47 W
Oels → Oleśnica 30 51.13 N 17.23 E
Oelsig 54 51.41 N 13.22 E
Oelsnitz, D.D.R. 54 50.24 N 12.10 E
Oelsnitz, D.D.R. 54 50.43 N 12.41 E
Oelwein 190 42.40 N 91.54 W
Oenpelli 164 12.20 S 133.04 E
Oensingen 58 47.17 N 7.44 E
Oepping 60 48.36 N 13.56 E
Oeraro-do I 98 34.27 N 127.30 E
Oer-Erkenschwick 52 51.39 N 7.15 E
Oerlinghausen 52 51.57 N 8.39 E
Oermten 263 51.29 N 6.27 E
Oesede 52 52.12 N 8.04 E
Oespel ◆[8] 263 51.30 N 7.23 E
Oeste, Canal del ≊ 266a 40.32 N 3.42 W
Oeste, Parque del ♠ 266a 40.26 N 3.44 W
Oesterdam ◆[5] 52 51.29 N 4.15 E
Oestrich 263 51.22 N 7.38 E
Oestrich ◆[8] 263 51.34 N 7.22 E
Oestrum ◆[8] 263 51.25 N 6.40 E
Ōetaka-yama ∧ 96 35.04 N 132.26 E
Oettingen in Bayern 56 48.57 N 10.36 E
Oetz 58 47.12 N 10.54 E
Oeuf ≃ 50 48.11 N 2.21 E
Oeventrop 56 51.23 N 8.08 E
Oeversee 41 54.42 N 9.26 E
Ōe-yama ∧ 96 35.27 N 135.07 E
Oeyŏn-do I 98 36.14 N 126.05 E
Of 130 40.57 N 40.18 E
O'Fallon, Il., U.S. 219 38.35 N 89.54 W
O'Fallon, Mo., U.S. 219 38.48 N 90.41 W
O'Fallon Creek ≃ 198 46.50 N 105.09 W
Ofanto ≃ 68 41.22 N 16.13 E
Ofaqim 132 31.17 N 34.37 E
Ofenpass → Fuorn, Pass dal)(58 46.37 N 10.15 E
Offa 150 8.09 N 4.44 E
Offaly □[6] 48 53.20 N 7.30 W
Offanengo 62 45.22 N 9.44 E
Offemont 58 47.40 N 6.53 E
Offenbach 56 50.08 N 8.47 E
Offenburg 58 48.28 N 7.57 E
Offendorf 58 48.43 N 7.55 E
Offerdal 26 63.28 N 14.00 E
Offham 260 51.17 N 0.23 E
Officer 274b 38.04 S 145.25 E
Officer Creek ≃ 162 27.45 S 132.24 E
Offida 66 42.56 N 13.41 E
Offingen 58 48.29 N 10.21 E
Offranville 50 49.52 N 1.03 E
Offutt Air Force Base ■ 198 41.08 N 95.56 W
Oficina Alianza 248 20.46 S 69.42 W
Oficina Chile 252 25.09 S 69.54 W
Oficina Pedro de Valdivia 252 22.36 S 69.40 W
Oficina Victoria 248 20.44 S 69.42 W
Ofin 273a 6.33 N 3.30 E
Öflingen 58 47.35 N 7.55 E
Ofotfjorden c[2] 24 68.23 N 16.10 E
Oftringen 58 47.19 N 7.56 E
Ofu 174y 14.10 S 169.42 W
Ofu I 174y 14.11 S 169.42 W
Ōfukuroshinden 268 35.53 N 139.27 E
Ōfuna 268 35.21 N 139.32 E
Ōfunato 92 39.04 N 141.43 E
Oga 92 39.53 N 139.51 E
Ogaden ◆[1] 144 8.00 N 44.00 E
Oga-hantō ›[1] 92 39.55 N 139.50 E
Ōgaki, Nihon 94 35.21 N 136.37 E
Ōgaki, Nihon 96 34.06 N 132.30 E
Ogallala 198 41.07 N 101.43 W
Ogan ≃ 112 3.01 S 104.44 E
Ogano 94 36.01 N 139.00 E
Ogasa 94 34.41 N 138.06 E
Ogasawara-guntō (Bonin Islands) II 14 27.00 N 142.10 E
Ōgata, Nihon 94 37.13 N 138.20 E
Ōgata, Nihon 96 33.01 N 133.01 E
Ogata, Nihon 96 32.58 N 131.29 E
Ōga-tō ∧ 94 36.13 N 138.06 E
Ogatsu 92 38.31 N 141.28 E
Ogawa, Nihon 92 32.35 N 130.43 E
Ogawa, Nihon 94 36.03 N 139.16 E
Ogawa, Nihon 94 36.10 N 140.21 E
Ogawa, Nihon 94 36.45 N 140.08 E
Ogawa, Nihon 94 36.37 N 137.58 E
Ogawa, Nihon 268 35.44 N 139.28 E
Ogawara-ko ⊜ 92 40.47 N 141.20 E
Ogbomosho 150 8.08 N 4.15 E
Ogden, Ia., U.S. 190 42.02 N 94.01 W
Ogden, Ks., U.S. 198 39.06 N 96.42 W
Ogden, Pa., U.S. 208 39.49 N 75.27 W
Ogden, Ut., U.S. 200 41.13 N 111.58 W
Ogden, Mount ∧ 180 58.26 N 133.23 W
Ogden Dunes 216 41.38 N 87.12 W
Ogden Island I 212 44.52 N 75.12 W
Ogden Reservoir ⊜[1] 262 53.42 N 2.22 W
Ogdensburg, N.J., U.S. 210 41.04 N 74.35 W
Ogdensburg, N.Y., U.S. 212 44.41 N 75.29 W
Ogeechee ≃ 192 31.51 N 81.06 W
Ōge-jima I 96 34.12 N 134.38 E
Ogema 184 49.35 N 104.55 W
Oggersheim 56 49.29 N 8.22 E
Oghi Fort 123 34.31 N 73.01 E
Ogibalovo 76 60.34 N 39.40 E
Ogidaki Mountain ∧[2] 190 46.58 N 83.58 W
Ogies 158 26.02 S 29.04 E
Ogi-jima I 96 34.26 N 134.04 E
Ogijo 273a 6.42 N 3.31 E
Ogilvie, Austl. 162 28.09 S 114.38 E
Ogilvie, Mn., U.S. 190 45.49 N 93.25 W
Ogilvie ≃ 180 65.52 N 137.16 W
Ogilvie Mountains ʎ 180 65.00 N 139.30 W
Ogilville 218 39.08 N 86.01 W
Ōgimi 174m 26.42 N 128.07 E
Ōgino-sen ∧ 96 35.26 N 134.26 E
Ogle □[6] 216 42.01 N 89.20 W
Oglesby, Il., U.S. 216 41.17 N 89.03 W
Oglesby, Tx., U.S. 222 31.25 N 97.31 W
Oglethorpe 192 32.17 N 84.03 W
Ogliastra ◆[1] 71 39.56 N 9.37 E
Ogliastro Cilento 68 40.21 N 15.03 E
Oglio ≃ 64 45.02 N 10.39 E
Ogmore 166 22.37 S 149.40 E
Ogmore ≃ 42 51.28 N 3.38 W
Ogmore Vale 42 51.38 N 3.31 W
Ogni 86 51.54 N 83.31 E
Ognica 54 53.07 N 14.27 E
Ognon ≃ 58 47.20 N 5.29 E
Ogn'ov Jar 86 58.23 N 76.29 E
Ogn'ovka 86 49.36 N 83.25 E
Ōgo 94 36.25 N 139.10 E
Ōgo ◆[8] 270 34.49 N 135.06 E
Ōgo ≃ 270 34.47 N 135.04 E
Ogoamas, Bulu ∧ 112 0.40 N 120.12 E
Ogōchi-dam ◆[6] 94 35.47 N 139.04 E
Ogodža 89 52.44 N 132.31 E
Ogoja 150 6.40 N 8.48 E
Ogoki ≃ 176 51.38 N 85.57 W
Ogol, Khaṭṭ el V 150 20.01 N 15.29 W
Ogooué ≃ 152 0.49 S 9.00 E
Ogooué-Ivindo □[4] 152 1.00 N 13.00 E
Ogooué-Lolo □[4] 152 1.00 S 12.30 E
Ogooué-Maritime □[4] 152 2.00 S 9.30 E
Ogōri, Nihon 96 34.06 N 131.24 E
Ogōri, Nihon 96 33.22 N 130.32 E
Ogorodnoje 78 45.53 N 28.50 E
Ogose 94 35.58 N 139.18 E
Ogosta ≃ 38 43.45 N 23.51 E
Ogou ≃ 150 7.50 N 1.19 E
Ogoyo 273a 6.26 N 3.29 E
Ogr 140 12.02 N 27.06 E
Ogre 76 56.51 N 24.36 E
Ogre ≃ 76 56.48 N 24.36 E
Ogrodzieniec 30 50.27 N 19.31 E
Ogrosen 54 51.42 N 14.02 E
Ōguchi 94 35.20 N 136.55 E
Ŏgu-dong 98 38.57 N 126.56 E
Ogudu 273a 6.34 N 3.24 E
Ogulin 36 45.16 N 15.14 E
Ogun □[3] 150 6.45 N 3.25 E
Ogun ≃ 150 6.36 N 3.27 E
Ogun Forest Reserve ♠ 273a 6.37 N 3.26 E
Oguni, Nihon 92 38.04 N 139.45 E
Oguni, Nihon 96 33.07 N 131.04 E
Ogunlogun 273a 6.41 N 3.28 E
Ogunquit 188 43.14 N 70.35 W
Ogura-san ∧ 94 36.02 N 138.37 E
Ogurčinskij, ostrov I 128 38.55 N 53.02 E
Oguta 150 5.44 N 6.44 E
Oğuz, Tür. 130 37.49 N 41.22 E
Oğuz, Tür. 130 39.32 N 38.51 E
Oğuzeli 130 36.59 N 37.30 E
Ogwashi-Uku 150 6.10 N 6.31 E
Ohakune 172 39.25 S 175.24 E
Ohanapecosh ≃ 224 46.38 N 121.37 W
Ohanet 148 28.45 N 8.55 E
Ohār 124 27.21 N 84.37 E
Ōhara, Nihon 94 35.15 N 140.23 E
Ōhara, Nihon 96 35.07 N 134.20 E
Ōharano ◆[8] 270 34.58 N 135.40 E
Ōhara-tunnel ◆[5] 94 35.12 N 137.50 E
Ōhata 92 41.24 N 141.10 E
Ōhatake 268 35.57 N 139.46 E
Ohau, Lake ⊜ 172 44.15 S 169.51 E
Ohaupo 172 37.55 S 175.19 E
Ohey 56 50.26 N 5.08 E
O'Higgins, Cabo › 174z 27.05 S 109.15 W
O'Higgins, Cerro ∧ 254 48.48 S 73.11 W
O'Higgins, Lago (Lago San Martín) ⊜ 254 49.00 S 72.40 W
Ohingaiti 172 39.52 S 175.43 E
Ohio 190 41.34 N 89.28 W
Ohio □[6], In., U.S. 218 38.57 N 84.51 W
Ohio □[6], W.V., U.S. 214 40.09 N 80.35 W
Ohio □[3], U.S. 178 40.15 N 82.45 W
Ohio □[3], U.S. 188 40.15 N 82.45 W
Ohio ≃ 178 36.59 N 89.08 W
Ohio Brush Creek ≃ 218 38.41 N 83.27 W
Ohio Brush Creek, Baker Fork ≃ 218 39.02 N 83.26 W
Ohio Brush Creek, Little West Fork ≃ 218 38.58 N 83.34 W
Ohio Brush Creek, West Fork ≃ 218 38.56 N 83.28 W
Ohio Canal ≊ 279a 41.26 N 81.40 W
Ohio Caverns ⊥[5] 216 40.14 N 83.43 W
Ohio City 216 40.46 N 84.36 W
Ohio Peak ∧ 200 38.49 N 107.07 W
Ohiopyle State Park ♠ 188 39.50 N 79.31 W
Ohioville, N.Y., U.S. 210 41.45 N 74.03 W
Ohioville, Pa., U.S. 214 40.40 N 80.29 W
Ōhira 94 36.20 N 139.42 E
Ōhira-yama ∧ 96 34.20 N 133.57 E
Ōhito 94 35.01 N 138.56 E
Ohlau → Oława 30 50.57 N 17.17 E
Ohligs ◆[8] 263 51.09 N 7.00 E
Ohlman 219 39.21 N 89.13 W
Ohlsdorf 64 47.57 N 13.47 E
Ohm ≃ 56 50.51 N 8.48 E
Ōho 94 36.08 N 140.06 E
Ohoitom 164 5.56 S 132.41 E
'Ohonua 174w 21.20 S 174.57 W
Ohoopee ≃ 192 31.54 N 82.07 W
Ōhori 268 35.20 N 139.52 E
Ohorn 54 51.10 N 14.02 E
Ohra Stausee ⊜[1] 54 50.46 N 10.42 E
Ohrdruf 54 50.50 N 10.44 E
Ohře (Eger) ≃, Europe 54 50.32 N 14.08 E
Ohre ≃, Europe 54 52.18 N 11.47 E
Ohrid 38 41.07 N 20.47 E
Ohrid, Lake ⊜ 38 41.02 N 20.43 E
Ohrigstad 156 24.49 S 30.33 E
Öhringen 56 49.12 N 9.29 E
Ohrnberg 56 49.15 N 9.27 E
Ohuira, Bahía de c 232 25.38 N 108.58 W
Ohura 172 38.50 S 174.59 E
Ōi, Nihon 96 35.28 N 135.37 E
Ōi, Nihon 268 35.51 N 139.30 E
Oi ◆[8] 268 35.35 N 139.45 E
Ōi ≃, Nihon 94 34.46 N 138.18 E
Ōi ≃, Nihon 96 35.01 N 135.39 E
Oiapoque 250 3.50 N 51.50 W
Oiapoque (Oyapock) ≃ 250 4.08 N 51.40 W
Oies, Île aux I 186 47.07 N 70.30 W
Ōigawa 94 34.48 N 138.17 E
Oignies 50 50.28 N 2.59 E
Oil Center 196 32.29 N 103.15 W
Oil City, La., U.S. 194 32.44 N 93.58 W
Oil City, Pa., U.S. 214 41.26 N 79.42 W
Oil Creek ≃ 214 41.26 N 79.42 W
Oil Creek State Park ♠ 214 41.33 N 79.40 W
Oildale 226 35.25 N 119.01 W
Oilmont 182 48.44 N 111.50 W
Oil Springs 214 42.47 N 82.07 W
Oilton, Ok., U.S. 196 36.05 N 96.35 W
Oilton, Tx., U.S. 196 27.33 N 98.59 W
Oil Trough 194 35.37 N 91.27 W
Oinville-sur-Montcient 261 49.02 N 1.51 E
Oir, Beinn an ∧ 46 55.54 N 6.00 W
Oirschot 52 51.30 N 5.18 E
Oise □[5] 50 49.30 N 2.30 E
Oise ≃ 50 49.00 N 2.04 E
Oise à l'Aisne, Canal de l' ≊ 50 49.36 N 3.11 E
Oisemont 50 49.57 N 1.46 E
Ōiso, Nihon 94 35.18 N 139.19 E
Ōiso, Nihon 270 34.33 N 135.01 E
Oissel 50 49.20 N 1.06 E
Oissery 261 49.04 N 2.49 E
Oisterwijk 52 51.35 N 5.12 E
Oistins 241g 13.04 N 59.32 W
Oistins Bay c 241g 13.03 N 59.33 W
Ōita 96 33.14 N 131.36 E
Ōita □[5] 96 33.15 N 131.30 E
Ōita ≃ 96 33.15 N 131.37 E
Oiticica 250 5.03 S 41.05 W
Oituz, Pasul)(38 46.03 N 26.23 E
Ōiwa 270 34.53 N 135.33 E
Oiyung 124 29.39 N 89.46 E
Ōizumi, Nihon 94 36.15 N 139.25 E
Ōizumi, Nihon 94 35.52 N 138.23 E
Oizuruga-dake ∧ 94 36.18 N 136.47 E
Öja I 40 58.45 N 17.52 E
Oja ≃ 86 53.26 N 91.55 E
Ojai 228 34.26 N 119.14 W
Öjaren ⊜ 40 60.43 N 16.50 E
Ojat' ≃ 76 60.31 N 33.00 E
Ojcowski Park Narodowy ♠ 30 50.15 N 19.50 E
Öje 26 60.49 N 13.51 E
Ojgon nuur ⊜ 88 49.10 N 96.36 E
Ojgor 86 49.10 N 89.17 E
Ōji 96 34.35 N 135.42 E
Ōjima 94 36.15 N 139.20 E
Ojinaga 232 29.34 N 104.25 W
Ojitlán 234 18.04 N 96.23 W
Ojiya 92 37.18 N 138.48 E
Ojm'akon 74 63.28 N 142.49 E
Ojocaliente 234 22.34 N 102.15 W
Ojo de Agua de Alférez 234 22.51 N 99.42 W
Ojo de la Casa 200 31.23 N 106.32 W
Ojo de Liebre, Laguna c 232 27.45 N 114.15 W
Ojok 88 52.35 N 104.27 E
Ojos del Salado, Nevado ∧ 252 27.06 S 68.32 W
Ojota 273a 6.35 N 3.23 E
Ojtal, S.S.S.R. 85 42.55 N 73.17 E
Ojtal, S.S.S.R. 85 40.24 N 74.06 E
Oju 150 6.53 N 8.26 E
Ojuelos de Jalisco 234 21.52 N 101.35 W
Ojus 220 25.57 N 80.09 W
Oka 150 7.29 N 5.49 E
Oka ≃, S.S.S.R. 80 56.20 N 43.59 E
Oka ≃, S.S.S.R. 88 55.15 N 102.10 E
Okaba 164 8.06 S 139.42 E
Okabe, Nihon 94 36.12 N 139.15 E
Okabe, Nihon 94 34.55 N 138.17 E
Okagaki 96 33.50 N 130.38 E
Okahandja 156 21.59 S 16.58 E
Okahandja □[5] 156 21.30 S 17.00 E
Okahukura 172 38.47 S 175.13 E
Okahumpka 220 28.45 N 81.54 W
Okaihau 172 35.19 S 173.47 E
Okalataka 152 0.20 S 14.59 E
Okaloacoochee Slough ≃ 220 26.16 N 81.17 W
Okamoto 270 34.59 N 135.58 E
Okamoto ◆[8] 270 34.44 N 135.16 E
Okanagan (Okanogan) ≃ 182 48.06 N 119.43 W
Okanagan Centre 182 50.03 N 119.27 W
Okanagan Falls 182 49.21 N 119.34 W
Okanagan Indian Reserve ◆[4] 182 50.21 N 119.17 W
Okanagan Lake ⊜ 182 50.00 N 119.28 W
Okanagan Landing 182 50.14 N 119.22 W
Okanagan Mountain Provincial Park ♠ 182 49.45 N 119.40 W
Okanagan Range (Okanogan Range) ʎ 182 49.00 N 120.00 W
Okanogan 202 48.21 N 119.34 W
Okanogan □[6] 224 48.39 N 120.41 W
Okanogan (Okanagan) ≃ 182 48.06 N 119.43 W
Okanogan Range (Okanagan Range) ʎ 182 49.00 N 120.00 W
Okapilco Creek ≃ 192 30.45 N 83.30 W
Okaputa 156 20.09 S 16.56 E
Okāra 123 30.49 N 73.27 E
Okarche 196 35.44 N 97.58 W
Okarito 172 43.14 S 170.11 E
Okasaki 270 34.46 N 135.52 E
Okatibbee Reservoir ⊜[1] 194 32.30 N 88.47 W
Okato 172 39.12 S 173.53 E
Okauchee 216 43.06 N 88.26 W
Okauchee Lake ⊜ 216 43.07 N 88.26 W
Okaukuejo 156 19.10 S 15.54 E
Okavango (Cubango) ≃ 138 18.50 S 22.25 E
Okavango Delta ⊻[2] 156 18.45 S 22.45 E
Ōkawa, Nihon 92 33.12 N 130.23 E
Ōkawa, Nihon 94 35.05 N 138.15 E
Ōkawa, Nihon 96 33.47 N 133.26 E
Ōkawachi 96 35.04 N 134.45 E
Ōkawado 268 35.56 N 139.50 E
Okawville 219 38.26 N 89.33 W
Okaya 94 36.03 N 138.03 E
Okayama 96 34.39 N 133.55 E
Okayama □[5] 96 35.00 N 134.00 E
Okazaki 94 34.57 N 137.10 E
Okch'ŏn 98 36.20 N 127.34 E
Oke-Aro 273a 6.41 N 3.19 E
Okeechobee 220 27.14 N 80.49 W
Okeechobee □[6] 220 27.25 N 80.52 W
Okeechobee, Lake ⊜ 220 26.55 N 80.45 W
O'Keefe Centre ʊ 275b 43.37 N 79.22 W
Okeene 196 36.06 N 98.19 W
Okefenokee Swamp ≡ 192 30.42 N 82.20 W
Okegawa 94 36.00 N 139.35 E
Okehampton 42 50.44 N 4.00 W
Okeigbo 150 7.09 N 4.43 E
Okemah 196 35.25 N 96.18 W
Okement ≃ 42 50.50 N 4.01 W
Okemos 216 42.43 N 84.25 W
Okene 150 7.33 N 6.15 E
Oke-Ode 150 8.33 N 5.02 E
Oke Ogbe 273a 6.24 N 3.23 E
Oker 52 51.54 N 10.29 E
Oker ≃ 54 52.30 N 10.22 E
Okere ≃ 154 2.07 N 33.55 E
Okhaldungga 124 27.19 N 86.30 E
Okhla ◆[8] 272a 28.34 N 77.18 E
Okhotsk, Sea of (Ochotskoje more) ⫪[2] 74 53.00 N 150.00 E
Okhotsk Basin ✣[1] 12 53.00 N 148.00 E
Okiep 156 29.39 S 17.53 E
Okinawa 174m 26.20 N 127.50 E
Okinawa □[5] 93b 26.31 N 127.59 E
Okinawa-jima I 174m 26.30 N 128.00 E
Okinawa-shotō II 93b 26.40 N 128.00 E
Okino-Daitō-jima I 90 24.28 N 131.11 E
Okino-Erabu-shima I 93b 27.22 N 128.35 E
Okino-Kl'uči 88 50.36 N 107.06 E
Okino-shima I, Nihon 94 35.12 N 136.04 E
Okino-shima I, Nihon 96 34.07 N 135.06 E
Okino-Tori-shima (Parece Vela) I 90 20.25 N 136.00 E
Oki-shotō II 92 36.15 N 133.15 E
Okitipupa 150 6.29 N 4.46 E
Okitsu-zaki › 96 33.09 N 133.14 E
Okkang-ni 98 40.18 N 124.42 E
Okkerbil' ≃ 265a 59.56 N 30.26 E
Okladnevo 76 58.36 N 33.39 E
Oklahoma, Pa., U.S. 214 41.07 N 78.44 W
Oklahoma, Pa., U.S. 279b 40.35 N 79.35 W
Oklahoma □[3], U.S. 178 35.30 N 98.00 W
Oklahoma □[3], U.S. 196 35.30 N 98.00 W
Oklahoma City 196 35.28 N 97.30 W
Oklawaha 220 29.02 N 81.55 W
Oklawaha ≃, Fl., U.S. 192 29.28 N 81.41 W
Oklawaha ≃, Fl., U.S. 220 29.03 N 81.52 W
Oklee 198 47.50 N 95.51 W
Okmulgee 196 35.37 N 95.57 W
Oknica 78 48.24 N 27.29 E
Okno 78 48.34 N 25.58 E
Oko, Wādī V 140 21.15 N 35.56 E
Okobojo Creek ≃ 198 44.38 N 100.28 W
Okok ≃ 154 2.06 N 33.53 E
Okoka 152 2.57 S 23.27 E
Okola 152 4.01 N 11.23 E
Okollo 154 2.40 N 31.08 E
Okolo 152 3.46 S 23.55 E
Okolona, Ar., U.S. 194 33.59 N 93.20 W
Okolona, Ky., U.S. 194 38.08 N 85.41 W
Okolona, Ms., U.S. 194 34.00 N 88.45 W
Okombahe 156 21.23 S 15.22 E
Okondja 152 0.41 S 13.47 E
Okonek 30 53.33 N 16.50 E
Okonešnikovo 86 54.50 N 75.05 E
Okotoks 182 50.44 N 113.59 W
Okoyo 152 1.28 S 15.04 E
Okpara ≃ 150 7.40 N 2.35 E
Okrika 150 4.47 N 7.04 E
Oksbøl 26 55.38 N 8.17 E
Okskij Zapovednik ◆[4] 80 54.45 N 40.45 E
Oksko-Donskaja ravnina ⊻ 80 53.00 N 40.30 E
Oksovskij 24 62.37 N 39.55 E
Oksskolten ∧ 24 65.59 N 14.15 E
Oksu ≃, S.S.S.R. 85 40.12 N 69.16 E
Oksu ≃, S.S.S.R. 85 38.09 N 73.57 E
Okt'abr', S.S.S.R. 76 57.50 N 37.26 E
Okt'abr', S.S.S.R. 85 43.41 N 77.12 E
Okt'abr', S.S.S.R. 86 45.45 N 61.34 E
Okt'abr'sk, S.S.S.R. 80 53.11 N 48.40 E
Okt'abr'sk, S.S.S.R. 86 49.28 N 57.25 E
Okt'abr'skij, S.S.S.R. 24 61.04 N 43.08 E
Okt'abr'skij, S.S.S.R. 24 59.29 N 48.50 E
Okt'abr'skij, S.S.S.R. 76 53.47 N 39.29 E
Okt'abr'skij, S.S.S.R. 76 52.38 N 28.53 E
Okt'abr'skij, S.S.S.R. 78 44.56 N 39.00 E
Okt'abr'skij, S.S.S.R. 78 50.26 N 36.22 E
Okt'abr'skij, S.S.S.R. 80 56.35 N 53.58 E
Okt'abr'skij, S.S.S.R. 80 54.28 N 53.28 E
Okt'abr'skij, S.S.S.R. 80 47.58 N 43.38 E
Okt'abr'skij, S.S.S.R. 80 56.17 N 44.12 E
Okt'abr'skij, S.S.S.R. 80 57.08 N 40.20 E
Okt'abr'skij, S.S.S.R. 80 58.19 N 44.19 E
Okt'abr'skij, S.S.S.R. 82 54.14 N 38.54 E
Okt'abr'skij, S.S.S.R. 82 55.37 N 37.58 E
Okt'abr'skij, S.S.S.R. 83 47.28 N 40.04 E
Okt'abr'skij, S.S.S.R. 85 38.33 N 68.22 E
Okt'abr'skij, S.S.S.R. 86 56.31 N 57.12 E
Okt'abr'skij, S.S.S.R. 86 52.35 N 62.40 E
Okt'abr'skij, S.S.S.R. 86 49.38 N 83.35 E
Okt'abr'skij, S.S.S.R. 88 50.04 N 118.04 E
Okt'abr'skij, S.S.S.R. 88 56.05 N 99.26 E
Okt'abr'skij, S.S.S.R. 89 53.01 N 128.37 E
Okt'abr'skij, S.S.S.R. 89 49.02 N 140.11 E
Okt'abr'skoje, S.S.S.R. 74 62.28 N 66.03 E
Okt'abr'skoje, S.S.S.R. 76 52.18 N 39.44 E
Okt'abr'skoje, S.S.S.R. 78 48.38 N 33.04 E
Okt'abr'skoje, S.S.S.R. 78 45.18 N 34.09 E
Okt'abr'skoje, S.S.S.R. 80 52.54 N 46.30 E
Okt'abr'skoje, S.S.S.R. 80 45.37 N 42.49 E
Okt'abr'skoje, S.S.S.R. 83 48.28 N 37.22 E
Okt'abr'skoje, S.S.S.R. 86 52.20 N 55.30 E
Okt'abr'skoje, S.S.S.R. 86 54.26 N 62.44 E
Okt'abr'skoje, S.S.S.R. 86 52.07 N 65.40 E
Okt'abr'skoj Revol'ucii, ostrov I 74 79.30 N 97.00 E
Ok Tedi 164 5.44 S 141.09 E
Oktember'an 84 40.09 N 44.02 E
Oktong-ni 98 38.27 N 127.07 E
Oktwin 110 18.49 N 96.26 E
Oktyabr'skiy → Okt'abr'skij 80 54.28 N 53.28 E
Oku, Nihon 96 34.40 N 134.05 E
Oku, Nihon 174m 26.50 N 128.17 E
Ōkubo, Nihon 268 35.21 N 139.56 E
Ōkubo, Nihon 270 34.41 N 134.57 E
Ōkubo ◆[8] 268 35.24 N 139.35 E
Okučani 36 45.16 N 17.12 E
Ōkuchi, Nihon 92 32.04 N 130.37 E
Ōkuchi, Nihon 94 36.17 N 136.39 E
Okuku ≃ 172 43.16 S 172.28 E
Okulovka 76 58.26 N 33.18 E
Okuma Bay c 9 77.48 S 158.35 W
Okumi 84 42.43 N 41.45 E
Okundi 150 6.22 N 8.44 E
Okun'ov Nos 24 66.15 N 52.28 E
Ōkura-yama ∧ 96 35.08 N 133.22 E
Okusawa ◆[8] 268 35.36 N 139.40 E
Okushiri 92a 42.10 N 139.31 E
Okushiri-tō I 92a 42.10 N 139.27 E
Ōkusu-yama ∧[2] 268 35.15 N 139.38 E
Okuta 150 9.14 N 3.15 E
Okutadami Dam ◆[6] 94 37.09 N 139.15 E
Okutama 94 35.47 N 139.02 E
Okutama-ko ⊜ 94 35.47 N 139.02 E
Okutsu 96 35.14 N 133.56 E
Ōkuwa 94 35.41 N 137.40 E
Okwa (Chapman's) ≃ 156 22.30 S 23.00 E
Okwoga 150 7.01 N 7.50 E
Olá, Pan. 236 8.25 N 80.39 W
Ola, S.S.S.R. 74 59.35 N 151.17 E
Ola, Ar., U.S. 194 35.01 N 93.13 W
Ola ≃ 76 52.41 N 29.39 E
Ólafsfjörður 24a 66.06 N 18.38 W
Olambwe Valley Game Reserve ◆[4] 154 0.37 S 34.15 E
Olancha 204 36.16 N 118.00 W
Olancha Peak ∧ 204 36.16 N 118.07 W
Olanchito 236 15.30 N 86.35 W
Olancho □[5] 236 14.45 N 86.00 W
Öland I 26 56.45 N 16.38 E
Olandsån ≃ 40 60.20 N 18.14 E
Olango Island I 116 10.16 N 124.03 E
Olanta 192 33.56 N 79.55 W
Olar 192 33.10 N 81.11 W
Olarevo 76 59.22 N 40.04 E
Olaria, Bra. 256 21.52 S 43.56 W
Olaria, Bra. 287a 22.41 S 43.08 W
Olaria ◆[8] 287a 22.52 S 43.15 W
Olary 166 32.17 S 140.19 E
Olascoaga 252 35.12 S 60.36 W
Olasore 273a 6.40 N 3.17 E
Olathe, Co., U.S. 200 38.36 N 107.58 W
Olathe, Ks., U.S. 198 38.52 N 94.49 W
Olavarría 252 36.54 S 60.17 W
Olavinlinna ⊥ 26 61.52 N 29.00 E
Oława 30 50.57 N 17.17 E
Olbernhau 54 50.39 N 13.20 E
Olbersdorf 54 50.52 N 14.46 E
Olbersleben 54 51.09 N 11.20 E
Olbia 71 40.55 N 9.31 E
Olbia, Golfo di c 71 40.55 N 9.39 E
Ølby Lyng 41 55.29 N 12.09 E
Olca, Volcán ∧[1] 248 20.57 S 68.30 W
Ol'chi 80 53.53 N 41.28 E
Olching 60 48.12 N 11.20 E
Ol'chon, ostrov I 88 53.09 N 107.24 E
Ol'chovaja ≃, S.S.S.R. 80 48.47 N 40.51 E
Ol'chovaja ≃, S.S.S.R. 83 48.35 N 39.17 E
Ol'chovatka, S.S.S.R. 78 50.18 N 39.17 E
Ol'chovatka, S.S.S.R. 83 48.15 N 38.25 E
Ol'chovčik ◆[8] 83 48.04 N 38.31 E
Ol'chovka, S.S.S.R. 80 49.52 N 44.34 E
Ol'chovka, S.S.S.R. 86 56.22 N 63.46 E
Ol'chovoje 83 48.40 N 39.34 E
Olcott 210 43.20 N 78.42 W
Old ≃, Ca., U.S. 226 38.04 N 121.35 W
Old ≃, Tx., U.S. 222 30.25 N 96.19 W
Old Bahama Channel ⊔ 238 22.30 N 78.50 W
Old Bedford ≃ 42 52.35 N 0.20 E
Old Bennington 210 42.52 N 73.12 W
Old Bethpage 276 40.45 N 73.27 W
Old Bethpage Village ⊥ 276 40.47 N 73.28 W
Old Bight 238 24.15 N 75.21 W
Old Brazoria 222 29.04 N 95.34 W
Old Bridge 276 40.24 N 74.21 W
Old Brookville 276 40.49 N 73.36 W
Oldbury 42 52.30 N 2.00 W
Old Cairo → Mişr al-Qadīmah ◆[8] 273c 30.00 N 31.14 E
Oldcastle 48 53.46 N 7.10 W
Old Colwyn 44 53.18 N 3.43 W
Old Cork 166 22.56 S 141.52 E
Old Creek Estates 284c 38.50 N 77.16 W
Old Crow 180 67.35 N 139.50 W
Old Crow ≃ 180 67.35 N 139.50 W
Oldeani 154 3.21 S 35.33 E
Oldebroek 52 52.26 N 5.54 E
Old Economy ⊥ 279b 40.36 N 80.14 W
Olden, Nor. 26 61.50 N 6.49 E
Olden, Tx., U.S. 196 32.25 N 98.45 W
Oldenbrok 52 53.17 N 8.23 E
Oldenburg, B.R.D. 52 53.08 N 8.13 E
Oldenburg, In., U.S. 218 39.20 N 85.12 W
Oldenburg □[9] 52 53.00 N 8.00 E
Oldenburg in Holstein 54 54.17 N 10.52 E
Oldendorf 52 53.35 N 9.14 E
Oldenstadt 52 52.58 N 10.35 E
Oldenswort 41 54.22 N 8.56 E
Oldenzaal 52 52.19 N 6.56 E
Oldersum 52 53.20 N 7.20 E
Old Faithful Geyser ⫪[4] 202 44.30 N 110.45 W
Old Farm 284c 39.03 N 77.09 W
Old Field 276 40.57 N 73.08 W
Old Field Point › 276 40.58 N 73.07 W
Old Forge, N.Y., U.S. 188 43.42 N 74.58 W
Old Forge, Pa., U.S. 210 41.22 N 75.44 W
Old Forge Village 276 40.49 N 74.29 W
Old Fort 214 41.15 N 83.09 W
Old Fort Erie ⊥ 284a 42.53 N 78.56 W
Old Fort Henry ⊥ 212 44.14 N 76.28 W
Old Fort Mountain ∧ 182 55.05 N 126.30 W
Old Fort Niagara ⊥ 284a 43.16 N 79.03 W
Old Fort Parker State Historic Site ⊥ 222 31.34 N 96.34 W
Old Fort Point › 240b 25.03 N 77.29 W
Old Greenwich 276 41.02 N 73.34 W
Oldham, Eng., U.K. 44 53.33 N 2.07 W
Oldham, S.D., U.S. 198 44.13 N 97.18 W
Oldham □[6] 218 38.23 N 85.27 W
Oldham □[8] 262 53.34 N 2.03 W
Oldham Pines 283 42.05 N 70.50 W
Oldham Pond ⊜ 283 42.03 N 70.51 W
Oldham Village 207 42.04 N 70.49 W
Old Harbor 180 57.12 N 153.19 W
Old Harbour 241q 17.56 N 77.07 W
Old Hickory Lake ⊜[1] 194 36.18 N 86.30 W
Old Howe ≃ 44 53.57 N 0.21 W
Oldisleben 54 51.18 N 11.10 E
Old Lyme 207 41.18 N 72.19 W
Old Malden ◆[8] 260 51.23 N 0.15 W
Oldman ≃ 182 49.56 N 111.42 W
Old Man House ⊥ 224 47.43 N 122.34 W
Old Man Mountain ∧ 186 49.08 N 57.43 W
Old Manor 276 40.24 N 74.11 W
Oldmans Creek ≃ 208 39.47 N 75.27 W
Oldmeldrum 46 57.20 N 2.20 W
Old Mkushi 154 14.22 S 29.22 E
Old Monroe 219 38.55 N 90.44 W
Old Mystic 207 41.23 N 71.57 W
Old Nene ≃ 42 52.40 N 0.10 E
Old North Bridge ⊥ 283 42.28 N 71.21 W
Old North Church ʊ[1] 283 42.22 N 71.03 W
Old Ocean 222 29.05 N 95.45 W
Ol Doinyo Sapuk National Park ♠ 154 1.09 S 37.12 E
Ol'doj ≃ 89 53.33 N 123.21 E
Old Orchard ◆[9] 278 42.04 N 87.45 W
Old Orchard Beach 188 43.31 N 70.22 W
Old Perlican 186 48.05 N 53.01 W
Old Place Creek ≃ 276 40.38 N 74.12 W
Old Point Comfort › 208 37.00 N 76.19 W
Old Rhodes Key I 220 25.22 N 80.14 W
Old Ripley 219 38.54 N 89.34 W
Old Road 240c 17.01 N 61.50 W
Old Road Bay c 284b 39.12 N 76.27 W
Old Road Bluff › 240c 16.59 N 61.50 W
Old Round Rock 222 30.31 N 97.42 W
Olds 182 51.47 N 114.06 W
Old Saybrook 207 41.17 N 72.22 W
Oldsmar 220 28.02 N 82.39 W
Old Speck Mountain ∧ 188 44.34 N 70.57 W
Old Sturbridge Village ⊥ 207 42.07 N 72.07 W
Old Swamp ≃ 283 42.11 N 70.57 W
Old Swedes Church ʊ[1] 285 39.44 N 75.32 W
Old Tampa Bay c 220 27.56 N 82.35 W
Old Tappan 276 41.00 N 73.59 W
Old Tate 156 21.22 S 27.46 E
Old Town 188 44.56 N 68.38 W
Old Trafford Cricket Ground ♠ 262 53.28 N 2.17 W
Old Trap 192 36.15 N 76.02 W
Olduvai Gorge V 154 2.58 S 35.22 E
Old Westbury 276 40.47 N 73.37 W
Old Westbury Gardens ♠ 276 40.46 N 73.36 W
Oldwick 210 40.40 N 74.44 W
Old Windsor 260 51.28 N 0.35 W
Old Wives Lake ⊜ 184 50.06 N 106.00 W
Old Woman Creek ≃ 198 43.19 N 104.21 W
Öldzijt, Mong. 88 48.07 N 102.34 E
Öldzijt, Mong. 102 45.18 N 106.12 E
Old Zoinsville 208 40.29 N 75.31 W
Olean 210 42.04 N 78.25 W
Olean Creek ≃ 210 42.04 N 78.25 W
O'Leary 186 46.42 N 64.13 W
Olecko 30 54.03 N 22.30 E
Olegário Maciel 256 22.19 S 45.35 W
Oleggio 62 45.36 N 8.38 E
Olekma → Ol'okma ≃ 74 60.22 N 120.42 E
Olema 24 64.30 N 46.08 E
Olen, Bel. 56 51.09 N 4.51 E
Ølen, Nor. 26 59.36 N 5.48 E
Ölen ⊜ 40 59.13 N 14.31 E
Olenegorsk 24 68.09 N 33.15 E
Olenevka 78 45.23 N 32.32 E
Olenica 24 66.29 N 35.20 E
Olenij, ostrov I 74 72.25 N 77.45 E
Olenino 76 56.12 N 33.29 E
Olenja Rečka 86 52.48 N 93.14 E
Olen'kovo 82 54.34 N 38.06 E
Olen'ok 74 68.33 N 112.18 E
Olen'ok ≃ 74 73.00 N 119.55 E
Olen'okskij zaliv c 74 73.20 N 121.00 E
Olentangy ≃ 214 39.58 N 83.06 W
Olenty 80 50.02 N 52.07 E
Olenty ≃ 80 49.50 N 52.03 E
Oleopolis 214 41.27 N 79.37 W
Oléron, Île d' I 32 45.56 N 1.15 W
Olesko 78 49.58 N 24.53 E
Olešná 60 49.46 N 13.48 E
Oleśnica 30 51.13 N 17.23 E
Olesno 30 50.53 N 18.25 E
Olevano Romano 66 41.52 N 13.02 E
Olevano sul Tusciano 68 40.40 N 15.01 E
Olevsk 78 51.13 N 27.39 E
Oley 208 40.23 N 75.47 W
Olfen 52 51.42 N 7.23 E
Ol'ga, S.S.S.R. 89 43.45 N 135.18 E
Olga, Wa., U.S. 224 48.37 N 122.50 W
Olga, Mount ∧, Austl. 162 25.19 S 130.46 E
Olga, Mount ∧, Vt., U.S. 207 42.51 N 72.48 W
Olgiata 267a 42.02 N 12.22 E
Olgiate Comasco 62 45.48 N 8.58 E
Olgiate Olona 62 45.38 N 8.53 E
Ölgij, Mong. 86 48.56 N 89.57 E
Ölgij, Mong. 86 48.59 N 92.01 E
Olginate 62 45.48 N 9.24 E
Ol'ginka, S.S.S.R. 78 44.14 N 38.53 E
Ol'ginka, S.S.S.R. 83 47.42 N 37.31 E
Ol'gino 89 52.53 N 125.47 E
Ol'gino ◆[8] 265a 60.00 N 30.09 E
Ol'ginskaja, S.S.S.R. 78 45.57 N 38.34 E
Ol'ginskaja, S.S.S.R. 83 47.11 N 39.56 E
Ølgod 26 55.49 N 8.37 E
Ol'gopol' 78 48.12 N 29.29 E
Ol'govo 82 56.16 N 37.21 E
Olhão 34 37.02 N 7.50 W
Ôlho d'Água das Cunhãs 250 4.43 S 44.34 W
Ôlho-d'Água das Flores 250 9.33 S 37.17 W
Oli ≃ 150 9.45 N 4.38 E
Olib, Otok I 36 44.22 N 14.48 E
Oliden 258 35.11 S 57.57 W
Oliena 71 40.16 N 9.24 E
Olifants (Rio dos Elefantes) ≃, Afr. 156 24.10 S 32.40 E
Olifants ≃, Namibia 156 25.30 S 19.30 E
Olifants ≃, S. Afr. 158 29.39 S 21.10 E
Olifants ≃, S. Afr. 158 33.41 S 21.42 E
Olifants ≃, S. Afr. 158 31.42 S 18.12 E
Olifantshoek 158 27.57 S 22.42 E
Olifantsrivierberge ʎ 158 32.40 S 19.00 E
Oliki 265a 59.46 N 29.55 E
Olimarao I[1] 108 7.41 N 145.52 E
Olimbía ⊥ 38 37.38 N 21.41 E
Ólimbos 38 35.44 N 27.11 E
Ólimbos ∧, Ellás 38 40.05 N 22.21 E
Ólimbos ∧, Kípros 130 34.56 N 32.52 E
Olímpia 255 20.44 S 48.54 W
Olímpico, Estadio ♠ 286a 19.20 N 99.12 W
Olímpio Noronha 256 22.04 S 45.16 W
Olimpo → Ólimbos ∧ 38 40.05 N 22.21 E
Olin 190 41.59 N 91.08 W
Olinalá 234 17.50 N 98.51 W
Olinda, Austl. 170 32.50 S 150.08 E
Olinda, Austl. 274b 37.51 S 145.22 E
Olinda, Bra. 250 8.01 S 34.51 W
Olinda, Bra. 256 22.49 S 43.25 W
Olinda, Mount ∧ 274b 37.52 S 145.21 E
Olinda Creek ≃ 274b 37.41 S 145.21 E
Olindina 250 11.22 S 38.21 W
Olinsk 88 52.24 N 116.13 E
Olio 166 21.54 S 143.13 E
Olišovka 78 51.13 N 31.18 E
Olite 34 42.29 N 1.39 W
Oliva, Arg. 252 32.03 S 63.34 W
Oliva, Esp. 34 38.55 N 0.07 W
Oliva de la Frontera 34 38.16 N 6.55 W
Olivais ◆[8] 266c 38.46 N 9.06 E
Olival Basto 266c 38.47 N 9.10 W
Olivare, Cerro de ∧ 252 30.18 S 69.55 W
Olive Branch 194 34.57 N 89.49 W
Olivebridge 210 41.55 N 74.13 W
Olive Hill 218 38.18 N 83.10 W
Olivehurst 226 39.05 N 121.33 W
Oliveira 255 20.41 S 44.49 W
Oliveira dos Brejinhos 255 12.19 S 42.54 W
Oliveira Fortes 256 21.20 S 43.27 W
Olivelifuri I 122 5.17 N 73.35 E
Olive Mount ◆[8] 262 53.24 N 2.55 W
Olivença 154 11.47 S 35.13 E
Olivenza 34 38.41 N 7.06 W
Oliver 182 49.11 N 119.33 W
Olivera 258 34.38 S 59.15 W
Oliver Creek ≃ 222 33.06 N 97.17 W
Oliver Ditch ≊ 216 41.00 N 87.10 W
Oliverea 210 42.04 N 74.28 W
Oliver Estates 284c 38.59 N 77.18 W
Oliveri 70 38.07 N 15.03 E
Oliver Lake ⊜ 184 56.56 N 103.22 W

≃ River	Fluß	Río	Rivière	Rio
≊ Canal	Kanal	Canal	Canal	Canal
⌞ Waterfall, Rapids	Wasserfall, Stromschnellen	Cascada, Rápidos	Chute d'eau, Rapides	Cascata, Rápidos
⊔ Strait	Meeresstraße	Estrecho	Détroit	Estreito
c Bay, Gulf	Bucht, Golf	Bahía, Golfo	Baie, Golfe	Baía, Golfo
⊜ Lake, Lakes	See, Seen	Lago, Lagos	Lac, Lacs	Lago, Lagos
≡ Swamp	Sumpf	Pantano	Marais	Pântano
⍓ Ice Features, Glacier	Eis- und Gletscherformen	Accidentes Glaciales	Formes glaciaires	Acidentes glaciares
⫪ Other Hydrographic Features	Andere Hydrographische Objekte	Otros Elementos Hidrográficos	Autres données hydrographiques	Outros acidentes hidrográficos
✣ Submarine Features	Untermeerische Objekte	Accidentes Submarinos	Formes de relief sous-marin	Acidentes submarinos
□ Political Unit	Politische Einheit	Unidad Politica	Entité politique	Unidade política
ʊ Cultural Institution	Kulturelle Institution	Institución Cultural	Institution culturelle	Instituição cultural
⊥ Historical Site	Historische Stätte	Sitio Histórico	Site historique	Sitio histórico
♠ Recreational Site	Erholungs- und Ferienort	Sitio de Recreo	Centre de loisirs	Area de Lazer
⊠ Airport	Flughafen	Aeropuerto	Aéroport	Aeroporto
■ Military Installation	Militäranlage	Instalación Militar	Installation militaire	Instalação militar
◆ Miscellaneous	Verschiedenes	Misceláneo	Divers	Diversos

Column 1

Oliver Springs 192 36.02 N 84.20 W
Olivet, Fr. 50 47.52 N 1.54 E
Olivet, Mi., U.S. 216 42.26 N 84.55 W
Olivet, S.D., U.S. 198 43.14 N 97.40 W
Oliveto Citra 68 40.41 N 15.14 E
Oliveto Lucano 68 40.32 N 16.11 E
Olivia 198 44.46 N 94.59 W
Olivine Range ⋌ 172 44.48 S 168.30 E
Olivo 116 10.52 N 123.53 E
Olivo ⋍ 70 37.22 N 14.15 E
Olivone 58 46.32 N 8.57 E
Olivos ⋍⁸ 258 34.32 S 58.29 W
Öljaren ⊜ 40 59.08 N 16.02 E
Olji Moron ⋍ 88 44.16 N 121.42 E
Olla 194 31.54 N 92.14 W
Ollagüe 248 21.14 S 68.16 W
Ollagüe, Volcán ⋀¹ 248 21.18 S 68.12 W
Ollainville 261 48.35 N 2.13 E
Ollantaytambo 248 13.16 S 72.16 W
Ollatrim ⋍ 48 52.52 N 8.13 W
Ollei 175b 7.43 N 134.37 E
Ollerton 262 53.17 N 2.20 W
Ollerup 41 55.04 N 10.30 E
Olliergues 62 45.40 N 3.38 E
Ollioules 62 43.08 N 5.51 E
Ollomont 62 45.50 N 7.22 E
Ollon 58 46.18 N 7.00 E
Olloua 152 0.56 S 14.34 E
Olmedillo de Roa 34 41.47 N 3.56 W
Olmedo, Esp. 34 41.23 N 4.41 W
Olmedo, It. 71 40.39 N 8.23 E
Olmo al Brembo 58 45.58 N 9.39 E
Olmos 248 5.59 S 79.46 W
Olmsted 214 41.24 N 81.44 W
Olmsted Falls 279a 41.22 N 81.54 W
Olmütz
  → Olomouc 30 49.36 N 17.16 E
Olney, Eng., U.K. 42 52.09 N 0.42 W
Olney, Il., U.S. 194 38.44 N 88.05 W
Olney, Md., U.S. 208 39.09 N 77.04 W
Olney, Mt., U.S. 182 48.32 N 114.34 W
Olney, Tx., U.S. 196 33.22 N 98.45 W
Olney ⋍⁸ 285 40.02 N 75.08 W
Oločí 89 51.21 N 119.55 E
Olofström 26 56.16 N 14.30 E
Oloj ⋍ 74 66.29 N 159.29 E
Ol'okma ⋍ 74 60.22 N 120.42 E
Ol'okminsk 74 60.24 N 120.24 E
Ol'okminskij Stanovik ⋀ 88 54.30 N 120.00 E
Olokui ⋀ 229a 21.08 N 156.51 W
Olomane ⋍ 186 50.14 N 60.37 W
Olombo 152 1.18 S 15.53 E
Olomega, Laguna de ⊜ 236 13.19 N 88.04 W
Olomouc 30 49.36 N 17.16 E
Olona ⋍ 62 45.06 N 9.21 E
Olonec 24 61.00 N 32.57 E
Olongapo 116 14.50 N 120.16 E
Olonki 88 52.54 N 103.45 E
Olorgasailie National Monument ⋆ 154 1.40 S 36.22 E
Oloron, Gave d' ⋍ 32 43.33 N 1.05 W
Oloron-Sainte-Marie 32 43.12 N 0.36 W
Olosega 174y 14.11 S 169.39 W
Olosega I 174y 14.11 S 169.39 W
Olot 34 42.11 N 2.29 E
Olov'annaja, S.S.S.R. 88 50.56 N 115.35 E
Olov'annaja, S.S.S.R. 180 66.10 N 178.59 W
Olovi 50 50.11 N 12.33 E
Olpe, B.R.D. 56 51.02 N 7.51 E
Olpe, Ks., U.S. 198 38.15 N 96.10 W
Olperer ⋀ 64 47.03 N 11.39 E
Ol'ša 76 54.51 N 31.52 E
Olsabach ⋍ 61 46.56 N 14.25 E
Øm Kloster ⋆ 56 56.03 N 9.45 E
Ommanney, Cape ⋗ 180 56.10 N 134.39 W
Ommanney Bay c 176 70.00 N 101.11 W
Omme ⋍ 41 55.53 N 8.40 E
Ommen 52 52.32 N 6.25 E
Ömnödelger 88 47.52 N 109.55 E
Ömnögov' ⋍ 88 49.06 N 91.43 E
Ömnögov' ⋍⁴ 102 43.00 N 104.00 E
Ome I 94 55.09 N 11.10 E
om ⋍ 144 43.10 N 35.59 E
Omoa, Bahía de c 236 15.45 N 88.00 W
Omogo 96 33.41 N 133.02 E
Omoi ⋗ 94 36.09 N 139.41 E
Omoko 150 5.20 N 6.39 E
Omole 273a 6.38 N 3.22 E
Omolon ⋍ 74 71.10 N 132.08 E
Omolon ⋍ 74 68.42 N 158.36 E
Omo National Park ⋆ 144 6.00 N 35.45 E
Omont 56 49.46 N 4.44 E
Omo Ranch 226 38.35 N 120.35 W
Omori ⋗⁸ 268 36.34 N 136.44 E
Omotego ⋍ 94 37.03 N 140.18 E
Omoy 152 1.21 S 13.09 E
Omrel'kaj 180 68.24 N 170.30 E
Omro 190 44.02 N 88.44 W
Omsino 80 58.36 N 50.28 E
Omsk 74 55.00 N 73.24 E
Omsukčan 74 62.32 N 155.48 E
O-mu, Mya. 110 22.58 N 99.18 E
Ōmu, Nihon 92a 44.34 N 142.58 E
Omu-Aran 150 8.09 N 5.07 E
Ōmuta 150 33.02 N 130.27 E
Omulew ⋍ 30 53.05 N 21.32 E
Ōmura 92 32.54 N 129.57 E
Ōmura-wan c 92 32.57 N 129.52 E
Ōmuro 268 35.54 N 139.58 E
Omuta 96 33.02 N 130.27 E
Omutinskij 82 56.31 N 67.41 E
Ōmuta 96 33.02 N 130.27 E
Ōmyōnbo 98 41.16 N 127.36 E
On 110 21.40 N 106.35 E
Ona, Nor. 26 62.52 N 6.34 E
Ona, Fl., U.S. 220 27.26 N 81.55 W
Ona ⋍, S.S.S.R. 86 52.34 N 89.50 E
Ona
  → Bir'usa ⋍, S.S.S.R. 88 57.43 N 95.24 E
Onagadokondo 156 3.52 S 24.10 E
Onaga 198 39.29 N 96.10 W
Onagawa 94 38.26 N 141.27 E
Onaha 94 36.57 N 140.54 E
Onalaska, Tx., U.S. 222 30.48 N 95.07 W
Onalaska, Wa., U.S. 224 46.34 N 122.43 W
Onamia 190 46.04 N 93.40 W
Onancock 208 37.42 N 75.44 W
Onaping, Lac ⊜ 190 46.57 N 81.18 W
Onaping Lake ⊜ 190 47.00 N 81.30 W
Onarga 216 40.42 N 88.00 W
Onawa 198 42.02 N 96.05 W
Oncativo 252 31.55 S 63.40 W
Once ⋆⁸ 281 34.36 S 58.24 W
Once, Canal Numero Dos ⋈ 252 22.57 N 105.15 E
Onda, Esp. 34 39.58 N 0.15 W
Onda, India 126 23.08 N 87.12 E
Ondas, Rio das ⋍ 255 12.08 S 45.00 W
Ondava ⋍ 30 48.27 N 21.48 E
Ondawa 96 37.43 N 139.52 E
Ondčen-dong 102 40.31 N 129.07 E
Ondo, India 126 23.08 N 87.12 E

Column 2

Omaha, Ne., U.S. 198 41.15 N 95.56 W
Omaha, Tx., U.S. 222 33.11 N 94.45 W
Omaha Indian Reservation ⋆⁴ 198 42.08 N 96.22 W
Omak 202 48.24 N 119.31 W
Omakau 172 45.05 S 169.36 E
Omak Lake ⊜ 202 48.16 N 119.23 W
Ōmama 84 42.23 N 45.38 E
Ōmama 94 36.26 N 139.17 E
Oman ('Umān) □¹ 118 22.00 N 58.00 E
Oman, Gulf of c 118 24.30 N 58.30 E
Omapere, Lake ⊜ 172 35.21 S 173.47 E
Omar 192 37.45 N 81.59 W
Omarama 172 44.29 S 169.58 E
Omaruru 156 21.28 S 15.56 E
Omaruru □⁵ 156 21.00 N 15.00 E
Omaruru ⋍ 156 22.07 S 14.15 E
Omas 248 12.31 S 76.17 W
Omatako ⋀ 156 21.07 S 16.43 E
Omatako ⋍ 156 17.59 S 20.30 E
Omate 248 16.41 S 70.59 W
Ōma-zaki ⋗ 92 41.32 N 140.55 E
Ombai, Selat ⋃ 112 8.30 S 125.00 E
Ombella-Mpoko □⁵ 152 5.00 N 18.00 E
Omberg ⋀² 26 58.20 N 14.39 E
Ombersley 42 52.17 N 2.13 W
Ombō 156 13.43 S 13.53 E
Ombrone ⋍ 66 42.39 N 11.00 E
Omčerli Baraji ⊟¹ 130 41.00 N 29.20 E
Omerville 206 45.17 N 72.07 W
Ometepe, Isla de I 236 11.30 N 85.35 W
Ometepec 234 16.41 N 98.25 W
Ometepec ⋍ 234 16.30 N 98.45 W
Om Hajer 144 14.24 N 36.46 E
Ōmi, Nihon 94 36.27 N 138.03 E
Ōmi, Nihon 94 37.01 N 137.48 E
Ōmi, Nihon 94 35.31 N 136.24 E
Ōmigawa 94 35.51 N 140.37 E
Ōmi-hachiman 94 35.08 N 136.06 E
Ōmin-ni ⋍⁸ 271b 37.27 N 127.01 E
Ōmino 94 34.32 N 135.03 E
Omišalj 36 45.13 N 14.34 E
Ōmi-shima I, Nihon 96 34.15 N 133.00 E
Ōmi-shima I, Nihon 96 34.15 N 131.13 E
Omitara 156 22.18 S 18.01 E
Omitlán ⋍ 234 17.06 N 99.34 W
Ōmiya, Nihon 94 36.33 N 140.25 E
Ōmiya, Nihon 94 35.54 N 139.38 E
Ōmiya, Nihon 94 35.35 N 135.06 E
Ōmiya-ōiči ⋍¹ 268 35.54 N 139.38 E
Ōmiya Park Race Track ⋆ 268 35.55 N 139.38 E
Ømmosse 56 49.46 N 4.44 E
Omnina 110 24.30 N 91.30 E
Onance ⋍ 54 52.09 N 11.34 E
Onega 24 63.55 N 38.05 E
Onega ⋍ 24 63.58 N 37.55 E
Onega, Lake
  → Onežskoje ozero ⊜ 24 61.30 N 35.45 E
Oneco, Ct., U.S. 207 41.41 N 71.48 W
Oneco, Fl., U.S. 220 27.26 N 82.32 W
Oneida, Ky., U.S. 192 37.16 N 83.38 W
Oneida, N.Y., U.S. 210 43.05 N 75.39 W
Oneida, Oh., U.S. 218 39.28 N 84.23 W
Oneida, Pa., U.S. 210 40.54 N 76.08 W
Oneida, Tn., U.S. 192 36.29 N 84.30 W
Oneida ⋍ 210 43.10 N 75.20 W
Oneida ⋍ 210 43.12 N 76.17 W
Oneida Castle 210 43.05 N 75.40 W
Oneida County Airport ⋆ 210 43.09 N 75.23 W
Oneida Creek ⋍ 210 43.10 N 75.44 W
Oneida Indian Reservation ⋆⁴ 190 44.30 N 88.10 W
Oneida Indian Reserve ⋆⁴ 214 42.49 N 81.24 W
Oneida Lake ⊜ 210 43.13 N 76.00 W
O'Neil Forebay ⊟¹ 226 37.05 N 121.03 W
O'Neill 198 42.27 N 98.38 W
Onekama 190 44.21 N 86.12 W
Onekotan, ostrov I 74 49.25 N 154.45 E
Onema 152 4.33 S 24.31 E
Onemen, zaliv c 180 64.45 N 176.35 E
Oneonta, Al., U.S. 192 33.56 N 86.28 W
Oneonta, N.Y., U.S. 210 42.27 N 75.03 W
One Tree Hill 168b 34.43 S 138.46 E
One Tree Hill ⋀² 174 37.52 S 145.19 E
One Tree Hill Lookout ⋆ 169 36.48 S 144.18 E
Onevai I 174w 21.05 S 175.07 W
Onex 58 46.10 N 6.06 E
Onežskaja guba c 24 64.20 N 36.30 E
Onežskij poluostrov ⋗¹ 24 64.35 N 38.00 E
Onežskoje ozero (Lake Onega) ⊜ 24 61.30 N 35.45 E
Ongandjera 156 17.40 S 15.04 E
Ongandjera ⊿ 152 4.33 S 24.31 E
Ongangana 172 39.55 S 176.25 E
Ong Con, Cu Lao I 269c 10.45 N 106.50 E
Ongea Levu I 175g 19.08 S 178.24 W
Ongeluks ⋍ 158 32.24 S 19.46 E
Ongerup 158 33.58 S 118.29 E
Ongjin 102 38.00 N 125.25 E
Ongjin 102 44.30 N 103.40 E
Ongka 98 37.57 N 125.21 E
Ongoka 154 1.23 S 26.02 E
Ongon 122 15.31 N 80.04 E
Ongud ⊿ 102 42.51 N 113.09 E
Oni 86 42.34 N 43.27 E
Onich 46 56.42 N 5.13 W
Onida 198 44.42 N 100.03 W
Onifai 71 40.24 N 9.39 E
Oniferi 71 40.16 N 9.10 E
Oniojaô-yama ⋀ 94 33.00 N 132.41 E
Onilahy ⋍ 157b 23.34 S 43.45 E
Onin, Jazirah ⋗¹ 164 2.50 S 132.05 E
Onion Creek ⋍ 222 30.12 N 97.35 W
Onion Peak ⋀ 224 45.49 N 123.53 W
Onishi 94 36.09 N 139.04 E
Onistagane, Lac ⊜ 186 50.42 N 71.19 W
Onitsha 150 6.09 N 6.47 E
Onji 270 34.37 N 135.38 E
Onjuku 94 35.11 N 140.22 E
Onkaparinga ⋍ 168b 35.10 N 138.28 E
Onkivesi ⊜ 26 63.18 N 27.18 E
Onko 152 4.07 S 19.59 E
Onna 208 38.36 N 120.35 W
Onna 174m 26.30 N 127.51 E
Onnaing 56 50.23 N 3.36 E
Onny ⋍ 42 55.55 N 9.17 E
Ōno, Nihon 94 35.59 N 136.29 E
Ōno, Nihon 94 35.38 N 136.37 E
Ōno, Nihon 94 35.02 N 131.30 E
Ōno, Nihon 94 34.18 N 132.17 E
Ōno, Nihon 94 34.51 N 134.56 E
Ōno, Nihon 94 34.57 N 135.14 E
Ōno, Pa., U.S. 208 40.24 N 76.32 W
Ōno I 175g 18.54 S 178.29 E
Onocoy 248 13.15 N 131.43 E
Onoda 96 34.00 N 131.11 E
Onogami ⋍ 94 36.33 N 138.56 E
Ono-i-Lau I 175g 20.39 S 178.42 W
Onojō 96 33.32 N 130.28 E
Onolimbu 114 1.03 N 97.53 E
Onomichi 96 34.25 N 133.12 E
Onon ⋍ 88 51.42 N 115.50 E
Ononda ⊿ 88 50.05 N 110.07 E
Onondaga, Mi., U.S. 216 42.26 N 84.33 W
Onondaga, N.Y., U.S. 210 43.00 N 76.11 W
Onondaga Creek ⋍ 210 43.04 N 76.11 W
Onondaga Indian Reservation ⋆⁴ 210 42.55 N 76.06 W
Onota 94 50.11 N 142.40 E
Onotoa ⋓ 162 1.52 S 175.34 E
Onotoa I¹ 14 1.52 S 175.34 E
Onsan 98 35.26 N 129.22 E
Ons, Isla de I 34 42.23 N 8.56 W
Ons 94 55.51 N 10.35 E
Onseepkans 158 28.46 S 19.14 E
Onset 196 33.33 N 134.29 E
Onslow 162 21.39 S 115.06 E
Onslow Bay c 192 34.20 N 77.20 W
Onslow Village 216 38.35 N 120.35 W
Onstwedde 52 53.02 N 7.02 E
Ontake-san ⋀ 94 35.53 N 137.29 E
Ontario, Ca., U.S. 226 34.03 N 117.39 W
Ontario, N.Y., U.S. 210 43.13 N 77.17 W
Ontario, Oh., U.S. 214 40.45 N 82.36 W
Ontario, Or., U.S. 202 44.01 N 116.57 W
Ontario □¹ 176 51.00 N 85.00 W
Ontario, Lake ⊜ 176 43.40 N 78.00 W
Ontario Agricultural Museum ⋆ 275c 43.30 N 79.56 W
Ontario Center 210 43.14 N 77.17 W
Ontario International Airport ⋆ 226 34.04 N 117.36 W
Ontario Place ⋆ 275b 43.38 N 79.25 W

Column 3

Ondo, Nihon 96 34.11 N 132.32 E
Ondo □³ 150 7.00 N 5.15 E
Ondo-ōhashi ⋍⁵ 96 34.12 N 132.33 E
Ōndörchaan 88 47.19 N 110.39 E
Ōndörchangaj 88 47.19 N 100.50 E
Ōndör-Önc 102 45.51 N 103.11 E
Öndöršireet 88 47.27 N 104.50 E
Ōndör-Uulaan 88 48.00 N 100.30 E
Ondozero, ozero ⊜ 24 63.48 N 33.20 E
O'Neals 226 37.08 N 119.42 W
One Arrow Indian Reserve ⋆⁴ 184 52.48 N 106.03 W
Oneco, Ct., U.S. 207 41.41 N 71.48 W
Oneco, Fl., U.S. 220 27.26 N 82.32 W
Onega 24 63.55 N 38.05 E
Onega ⋍ 24 63.58 N 37.55 E
Onega, Lake
  → Onežskoje ozero ⊜ 24 61.30 N 35.45 E
Onward 216 40.42 N 86.12 W
Onyang, Taehan 98 36.46 N 126.59 E
Onyang, Taehan 98 36.47 N 127.00 E
Onzain 50 47.30 N 1.11 E
Oolitic 216 38.54 N 86.31 W
Oologah 196 36.26 N 95.42 W
Oologah Lake ⊟¹ 196 36.33 N 95.36 W
Oona River ⋍ 184 53.57 N 130.18 W
Ooratippra 162 22.00 S 136.00 E
Ooratippra ⋍ 162 21.55 S 136.05 E
Oorlogskloof ⋍ 158 31.52 S 19.01 E
Oos ⋍ 56 48.47 N 8.11 E
Oos-Londen
  → East London 158 33.00 S 27.55 E
Oostburg, Ned. 52 51.20 N 3.30 E
Oostburg, Wi., U.S. 190 43.37 N 87.47 W
Oost-Cappel 50 50.55 N 2.36 E
Oostduinkerke 50 51.07 N 2.41 E
Oostelijk Flevoland ⋍ 52 52.30 N 5.45 E
Oostende (Ostende) 50 51.13 N 2.55 E
Oosterbeek 52 52.00 N 5.50 E
Oosterend 52 53.05 N 4.52 E
Oosterhout 52 51.38 N 4.51 E
Oosterschelde c 52 51.30 N 4.00 E
Oosterscheldedam ⋆⁶ 52 51.38 N 3.42 E
Oosterwolde 52 52.59 N 6.17 E
Oosterzele 52 50.57 N 3.48 E
Oosthuizen 52 52.34 N 4.59 E
Oostkamp 50 51.09 N 3.14 E
Oostmahorn 52 53.24 N 6.09 E
Oostmalle 52 51.18 N 4.44 E
Oost-Souburg 52 51.27 N 3.35 E
Oost-Vlaanderen □⁴ 50 51.00 N 3.45 E
Oost-Vleteren 50 50.56 N 2.44 E
Oost-Vlieland 52 53.17 N 5.04 E
Oostmarsum 52 52.19 N 6.54 E
Oostvoorne 52 51.55 N 4.06 E
Oostzaan 52 52.26 N 4.52 E
Ootacamund 124 11.24 N 76.44 E
Ootmarsum 52 52.24 N 6.54 E
Ootsa Lake 182 53.47 N 126.03 W
Ootsa Lake ⊜ 156 29.02 S 25.45 E
Ootsi 156 25.02 S 25.45 E
Ootsi 174x 18.02 S 178.59 E
Ootha, Mont ⋀ 154 4.23 N 31.58 E
Opaka 38 43.27 N 26.10 E
Opala 152 0.40 S 24.21 E
Opalaca, Cordillera ⋌ 236 14.30 N 88.20 W
Opal Cliffs 226 36.57 N 121.57 W
Opala, Côte d' ⋍² 247 50.40 N 1.35 E
Opaľnaja 214 40.31 N 82.13 W
Opaličha 265b 55.49 N 37.15 E
Opa-Locka 220 25.54 N 80.15 W
Opari 154 3.52 N 32.03 E
Oparino 24 59.52 N 48.17 E
Opasatica, Lac ⊜ 190 48.04 N 79.19 W
Opasatika Lake ⊜ 184 53.16 N 93.34 W
Opasatika Lake ⊜ 184 53.16 N 93.34 W
Opasquia ⋍ 184 53.16 N 93.35 W
Opasquia Lake ⊜ 184 53.18 N 93.34 W
Opatija 36 45.21 N 14.19 E
Opatów 30 50.49 N 21.26 E
Opava ⋍ 30 50.49 N 17.54 E
Opeepeeskij Posad 76 58.16 N 34.07 E
Opeepeeway Lake ⊜ 185c 51.23 N 20.17 E
Opeinu ⋍ 273a 6.42 N 3.18 E
Opelika 192 32.38 N 85.22 W
Opelousas 194 30.32 N 92.04 W
Open Bay c 164 4.50 S 151.20 E
Open Door 258 35.30 S 59.05 W
Opeongo 190 45.30 N 77.57 W
Opeongo Lake ⊜ 190 45.42 N 78.23 W
Opfikon 58 47.26 N 8.35 E
Ophain-Bois-Seigneur-Isaac 50 50.40 N 4.21 E
Ophasselt 50 50.49 N 3.53 E
Opheim 202 48.51 N 106.24 W
Opherdicke 263 51.29 N 7.38 E
Opheusden 52 51.56 N 5.38 E
Ophir, Ak., U.S. 180 63.08 N 156.31 W
Ophir, Or., U.S. 202 42.33 N 124.22 W
Ophthalmia Range ⋌ 162 23.15 S 119.30 E
Opi 66 41.47 N 13.50 E
Opiango 196 52.15 N 78.02 W
Opinaca ⋍ 186 52.15 N 78.02 W
Opinaca, Réservoir ⊟¹ 186 52.39 N 76.20 W
Opinicon Lake ⊜ 212 44.33 N 76.20 W
Opiscotéo, Lac ⊜ 176 53.10 N 68.10 W
Opladen 54 51.04 N 7.00 E
Opmeer 52 52.42 N 4.57 E
Opobo 150 4.30 N 7.27 E
Opobo Town 150 4.34 N 7.27 E
Opočno 30 50.16 N 16.13 E
Opočka 76 56.43 N 28.38 E
Opoczno 30 51.23 N 20.17 E
Opol 116 8.31 N 124.34 E
Opole (Oppeln) 30 50.41 N 17.55 E
Opole □⁴ 30 50.30 N 17.45 E
Opole Lubelskie 30 51.09 N 21.58 E
Opon
  → Lapu-Lapu 116 10.19 N 123.57 E
Opononi 172 35.31 S 173.23 E
Opotiki 172 38.00 S 177.17 E
Opp 194 31.16 N 86.15 W
Oppach 54 51.03 N 14.30 E
Oppeln
  → Opole 30 50.41 N 17.55 E
Oppenau 54 48.38 N 8.10 E
Oppenheim, B.R.D. 54 49.51 N 8.21 E
Oppenheim Park ⋆ 284a 43.06 N 78.54 W
Oppido Lucano 68 40.47 N 16.00 E
Oppido Mamertina 68 38.16 N 15.59 E
Oppio 66 44.10 N 10.51 E
Oppland □⁴ 26 61.10 N 9.40 E

Ontario Science Centre ⋆ 275b 43.43 N 79.21 W
Ontelaunee, Lake ⊟¹ 208 40.27 N 75.55 W
Ontinyent
  (Onteniente) 34 38.49 N 0.37 W
Ontojärvi ⊜ 26 64.08 N 29.09 E
Ontonagon 190 46.52 N 89.18 W
Ontonagon ⋍ 190 46.52 N 89.20 W
Ontonagon, East Branch ⋍ 190 46.42 N 89.11 W
Ontonagon, Middle Branch ⋍ 190 46.42 N 89.11 W
Ontonagon, West Branch ⋍ 190 46.42 N 89.14 W
Ontong Java I¹ 175c 5.20 S 159.30 E
Onuma ⊜ 94 41.59 N 140.41 E
Ōnuma 268 35.32 N 139.25 E
Onverwacht 250 5.36 N 55.12 W
Onward 216 40.42 N 86.12 W
Onyang, Taehan 98 36.46 N 126.59 E
Onyang, Taehan 98 36.47 N 127.00 E
Onzain 50 47.30 N 1.11 E
Onzo 152 8.12 S 13.16 E
Oodagooma 162 16.46 S 123.59 E
Oodnadatta 162 27.33 S 135.28 E
Ood Weyne 144 9.25 N 45.04 E
Ooka 96 36.30 N 137.59 E
Ooldea 162 30.27 S 131.50 E
Oolitic 216 38.54 N 86.31 W
Oologah 196 36.26 N 95.42 W
Oologah Lake ⊟¹ 196 36.33 N 95.36 W
Oona River ⋍ 184 53.57 N 130.18 W
Ooratippra 162 22.00 S 136.00 E
Ooratippra ⋍ 162 21.55 S 136.05 E
Oorlogskloof ⋍ 158 31.52 S 19.01 E
Oos ⋍ 56 48.47 N 8.11 E

(Weiteres folgt analog; siehe Spalte 3)

Opsaheden 40 60.28 N 13.59 E
Optic Lake ⊜ 184 54.46 N 101.13 W
Optima Lake ⊟¹ 196 36.40 N 101.10 W
Opua 172 35.19 S 174.07 E
Opunake 172 39.27 S 173.51 E
Opunohu, Baie d' c 174a 17.30 S 149.51 W
Opuwo 152 18.03 S 13.45 E
Opwijk 50 50.58 N 4.11 E
Oquawka 190 40.55 N 90.56 W
Oquendo, Perú 286d 11.58 S 77.08 W
Oquendo, Pil. 222 22.50 N 96.58 W
O'Quinn 222 29.40 N 96.48 W
Or ⋍ 86 51.12 N 58.30 E
Cr ⋍ 58 47.10 N 4.50 E
Cr, Côte d' ⋀ 58 47.10 N 4.50 E
Cr, Étang d' ⊟ 261 48.38 N 1.51 E
Ora, Libiyā 146 28.33 N 19.24 E
Ōra, Nihon 268 35.32 N 139.25 E
Ora (Auer), It. 64 46.21 N 11.18 E
Ōra ⋍, Nihon 174m 26.33 N 128.02 E
Ōra Banda 162 30.22 S 121.04 E
Oracle 200 32.36 N 110.46 W
Oradea 38 47.03 N 21.57 E
Oradell 276 40.57 N 74.02 W
Oradell Reservoir ⊟¹ 276 40.58 N 74.01 W
Ōʻæfajökull ▨ 24a 64.03 N 16.38 W
Oʻahovica 38 45.31 N 17.53 E
O-ai 124 20.59 S 79.28 E
Oʻaibi Wash ⋁ 200 35.26 N 110.49 W
Oʻraison 62 43.55 N 5.55 E
Oran
  → Wahran 148 35.43 N 0.43 W
Oran 194 37.05 N 89.39 W
Oran, Sebkha d' ⊜ 34 35.32 N 0.48 W
Orange, Austl. 166 33.17 S 149.06 E
Orange, Fr. 62 44.08 N 4.48 E
Orange, Ca., U.S. 228 33.47 N 117.51 W
Orange, Ct., U.S. 207 41.16 N 73.01 W
Orange, Ma., U.S. 207 42.35 N 72.19 W
Orange, N.J., U.S. 276 40.46 N 74.13 W
Orange, Oh., U.S. 279a 41.26 N 81.29 W
Orange, Tx., U.S. 194 30.05 N 93.44 W
Orange, Va., U.S. 188 38.14 N 78.06 W
Orange ⋍⁶, Ca., U.S. 228 33.43 N 117.54 W
Orange ⋍⁶, Fl., U.S. 220 28.32 N 81.16 W
Orange ⋍⁶, In., U.S. 218 38.30 N 86.28 W
Orange ⋍⁷, N.Y., U.S. 210 41.24 N 74.20 W
Orange (Oranje) ⋍ 156 28.41 S 16.28 E
Orange, Cabo ⋗ 250 4.24 N 51.33 W
Orange Bowl ⋆ 220 25.46 N 80.14 W
Orangeburg, Ky., U.S. 218 38.35 N 83.39 W
Orangeburg, N.Y., U.S. 210 41.03 N 73.57 W
Orangeburg, S.C., U.S. 192 33.29 N 80.51 W
Orange City, Fl., U.S. 220 28.56 N 81.18 W
Orange City, Ia., U.S. 198 43.00 N 96.03 W
Orange County Airport ⋆ 228 33.40 N 117.51 W
Orange Cove 226 36.37 N 119.19 W
Orange Free State
  (Oranje-Vrystaat) 158 28.30 S 27.00 E
Orange Grove 196 27.57 N 97.56 W
Orange Grove ⋍⁸ 273d 26.10 S 28.05 E
Orange Lake, Fl., U.S. 220 29.25 N 82.13 W
Orange Lake, N.Y., U.S. 210 41.33 N 74.06 W
Orange Lake ⊜ 192 29.29 N 82.10 W
Orangemouth 156 28.38 S 16.24 E
  → Oranjemund 156 28.38 S 16.24 E
Orange Park 190 30.09 N 81.42 W
Orange Park Acres 280 33.48 N 117.47 W
Orange Reservoir ⊟¹ 276 33.48 N 117.54 W
Orangevale 226 38.40 N 121.13 W
Orangeville, Oh., U.S. 214 41.17 N 80.33 W
Orangeville, Pa., U.S. 210 41.05 N 76.24 W
Orangeville, Ut., U.S. 200 39.13 N 111.03 W
Orange Walk 232 18.06 N 88.33 W
Orani 116 14.48 N 120.32 E
Oranje
  → Orange ⋍ 156 28.38 S 16.24 E
Oranjefontein 156 23.25 S 27.41 E
Oranje Gebergte ⋌ 250 3.00 N 55.05 W
Oranjemund 156 28.38 S 16.24 E
Oranjerivier 156 29.40 S 24.13 E
Oranjestad 241s 12.33 N 70.06 W
Oranjeville 158 27.00 S 28.15 E
Oranjewoud 52 53.00 N 5.58 E
Oranmore 48 53.16 N 8.54 W
Ōranʻn-ni 66 41.34 N 126.29 E
Oranželand 172 45.50 N 47.36 E
Or 'Aqiva 132 32.30 N 34.55 E
Orarak 154 6.15 N 32.23 E
Oras 116 12.08 N 125.26 E
Ōren 130 37.02 N 27.57 E
Orás Bay c 116 12.08 N 125.28 E
Orāşṭie 38 45.50 N 23.12 E
Oraşul Stalin
  → Braşov 38 45.39 N 25.37 E
Oratório, Ribeirão do ⋍ 287b 23.37 S 46.32 W
Oravais (Oravainen) 26 63.18 N 22.21 E
Oravița 38 45.01 N 21.41 E
Orba ⋍ 62 44.53 N 8.37 E
Orba Co ⊜ 120 35.03 N 83.12 E
Orbassano 64 45.01 N 7.32 E
Orbe 58 46.43 N 6.31 E
Orbe ⋍ 58 46.47 N 6.39 E
Orbe-en-Auge 58 46.44 N 6.40 E
Orbetello 66 42.27 N 11.13 E
Orbetello, Laguna di c 66 42.26 N 11.10 E
Orbey 56 48.08 N 7.10 E
Orbigny 50 47.14 N 1.14 E
Orbisnia 214 40.15 N 77.54 W
Orbost 166 37.42 S 148.27 E
Orbøy ⋍⁸ 41 56.10 N 10.25 E
Orcas Island I 224 48.39 N 122.59 W
Orcera 34 38.19 N 2.39 W
Orchamps 58 47.08 N 5.34 E
Orchard, Ne., U.S. 198 42.20 N 98.14 W
Orchard, Tx., U.S. 222 29.36 N 95.59 W
Orchard City 200 38.49 N 107.58 W
Orchard Hills, Austl. 274a 33.47 S 150.43 E
Orchard Hills ⋍⁸ 279b 40.30 N 79.32 W
Orchard Homes 202 46.51 N 114.02 W
Orchard Island ⋆ 184 56.24 N 102.39 W
Orchard Lake 281 42.35 N 83.21 W
Orchard Lake Village 216 42.35 N 83.22 W
Orchard Mesa 200 39.03 N 108.33 W
Orchard Park 210 42.46 N 78.44 W

Opsaheden 40 60.28 N 13.59 E
Orchard Park Airport ⋆ 284a 42.48 N 78.45 W
Orchard Peak ⋀ 226 35.44 N 120.08 W
Orchards 224 45.40 N 122.33 W
Orchard Valley 200 41.05 N 104.48 W
Orchard View 285 40.04 N 74.53 W
Orchha 124 25.21 N 78.38 E
Orchies 50 50.28 N 3.14 E
Orchila, Isla I 246 11.48 N 66.09 W
Orchon 88 49.09 N 105.21 E
Orchon ⋍ 88 50.21 N 106.05 E
Orchon Tuul 88 48.58 N 104.59 E
Orcia ⋍ 66 42.58 N 11.21 E
Orcières 62 44.41 N 6.20 E
Orčik ⋍ 78 49.10 N 35.04 E
Orco ⋍ 62 45.10 N 7.52 E
Orcotuna 248 11.58 S 75.20 W
Ord 198 41.36 N 98.55 W
Ord ⋍ 160 15.30 S 128.21 E
Ord, Mount ⋀ 162 17.20 S 125.34 E
Orda 86 51.10 N 7.52 E
Ordenes 34 43.04 N 8.24 W
Orderville 200 37.16 N 112.38 W
Ordesa, Parque Nacional de ⋆ 34 42.39 N 0.02 E
Ord Mountain ⋀ 204 34.40 N 116.49 W
Ord Mountains ⋌ 228 34.42 N 117.10 W
Ordoqui 252 35.54 S 61.10 W
Ord River 162 17.23 S 128.51 E
Ordu 130 41.00 N 37.53 E
Ordu □⁴ 130 40.45 N 37.30 E
Ordubad 84 38.56 N 46.02 E
Ordway 198 38.13 N 103.45 W
Ordynskoje 86 54.22 N 81.56 E
Ordžonikidze
  → Jenakijevo, S.S.S.R. 83 48.14 N 38.13 E
Ordžonikidze
  → Ordžonikidze, S.S.S.R. 84 43.03 N 44.40 E
Ordžonikidze, S.S.S.R. 84 43.03 N 44.40 E
Ordžonikidze, S.S.S.R. 78 47.40 N 34.04 E
Ordžonikidze, S.S.S.R. 78 44.57 N 35.22 E
Ordžonikidze, S.S.S.R. 84 40.53 N 47.23 E
Ordžonikidze, S.S.S.R. 84 43.03 N 44.40 E
Ordžonikidze, S.S.S.R. 84 42.01 N 43.12 E
Ordžonikidze 86 52.28 N 61.46 E
Ordžonikidzeabad 85 38.34 N 69.01 E
Ordžonikidzevskaja 84 43.18 N 45.03 E
Ordžonikidzevskij, S.S.S.R. 84 43.51 N 41.54 E
Ordžonikidzevskij, S.S.S.R. 86 54.46 N 88.59 E
Ore ⋍ 150 6.44 N 4.52 E
Öreälven ⋍ 26 63.32 N 19.44 E
Oreana 226 36.37 N 119.19 W
Örebro 26 59.17 N 15.13 E
Örebro Län □⁶ 40 59.30 N 15.00 E
Orechov 78 47.34 N 35.47 E
Orechovka, S.S.S.R. 80 52.56 N 48.14 E
Orechovka, S.S.S.R. 83 48.17 N 39.13 E
Orechovsk 80 55.28 N 41.58 E
Orechovo-Zujevo 82 55.49 N 38.59 E
Orechovo ⋍⁸ 78 54.41 N 30.30 E
Orechowo ⋍⁸ 78 48.01 N 38.42 E
Ore City 222 32.48 N 94.43 W
Oredež 76 58.49 N 30.13 E
Oredež ⋍ 76 58.49 N 30.00 E
Orefield 208 40.38 N 75.35 W
Oregon, Il., U.S. 190 42.00 N 89.19 W
Oregon, Mo., U.S. 198 39.59 N 95.08 W
Oregon, Wi., U.S. 216 42.55 N 89.23 W
Oregon □³, U.S. 178 44.00 N 121.00 W
Oregon □³, U.S. 202 44.00 N 121.00 W
Oregon Caves National Monument ⋆ 202 42.06 N 123.24 W
Oregon City 224 45.21 N 122.36 W
Oregon Creek ⋍ 226 39.23 N 121.05 W
Oregon Dunes National Recreation Area ⋆ 202 43.45 N 124.12 W
Oregon House 226 39.21 N 121.17 W
Öregrund 40 60.20 N 18.26 E
Öregrundsgrepen c 40 60.18 N 18.30 E
Orehoved 41 54.57 N 11.52 E
Orekhovo-Zuyevo
  → Orechovo-Zujevo 82 55.49 N 38.59 E
Orel
  → Or'ol 76 52.59 N 36.05 E
Orel', ozero ⊜ 89 52.10 N 139.42 E
Oreland 285 40.07 N 75.10 W
Orellana 246 6.54 S 75.04 W
Orellana, Embalse de ⊟¹ 34 39.00 N 5.25 W
Ören 200 40.17 N 111.41 W
Ören 130 37.02 N 27.57 E
Orenburg 86 51.54 N 55.06 E
Orenburg □⁴ 86 51.30 N 55.00 E
Orenčik 78 53.00 N 27.23 E
Oreng, Indon. 114 4.03 N 97.28 E
Oreng, Indon. 114 4.03 N 97.28 E
Orense, Arg. 252 38.40 S 59.47 W
Orense, Esp. 34 42.20 N 7.51 W
Orense □⁴ 34 42.20 N 7.51 W
Örepuki 172 46.17 S 167.44 E
Orešak 38 42.42 N 24.32 E
Orešje ⋍⁸ 76 53.43 N 36.21 E
Orestes 216 40.16 N 85.43 W
Orestiás 38 41.30 N 26.31 E
Orestimba Creek ⋍ 226 37.25 N 121.00 W
Øresund ⋃
  → The Sound ⋃ 41 55.50 N 12.40 E
Oreti ⋍ 172 46.28 S 168.17 E
Orewa 172 36.34 S 174.42 E
Oreye 50 50.44 N 5.22 E
Orfanoú, Kólpos c 38 40.40 N 23.50 E
Orford, Eng., U.K. 42 52.06 N 1.31 E
Orford, Eng., U.K. 262 45.19 N 72.15 W
Orford Ness ⋗ 42 52.05 N 1.35 E
Orfordville 190 42.37 N 89.15 W
Organ Needle ⋀ 200 32.21 N 106.33 W
Organ Pipe Cactus National Monument ⋆ 200 32.00 N 112.55 W
Órgãos, Serra dos ⋌ 256 22.30 S 42.45 W
Orge ⋍ 261 48.31 N 2.24 E
Orgelet 58 46.31 N 5.37 E
Orgères-en-Beauce 50 48.09 N 1.42 E
Orgeval 261 48.55 N 1.58 E
Orgiano 64 45.20 N 11.28 E
Orgiva 34 36.54 N 3.25 W
Orgnac-l'Aven ⋆ 62 44.19 N 4.27 E
Orgon 62 43.47 N 5.03 E
Orgosolo 72 40.12 N 9.21 E
Orgūn 121 32.57 N 69.11 E
Orhaneli 130 39.54 N 28.59 E
Orhangazi 130 40.30 N 29.18 E
Orhaniye 130 40.30 N 27.38 E
Orhei 78 47.23 N 28.49 E
Oria, Esp. 34 37.31 N 2.17 W
Oria, Zaïre 154 3.17 N 30.41 E
Orica 236 14.41 N 86.58 W
Oriçanga, Rio de ⋍ 256 22.18 S 47.03 W
Orichuna ⋍ 246 7.36 N 68.44 W
Oriči 80 58.24 N 49.05 E

ESPAÑOL — Nombre / Página / Lat.°′ / Long.°′ W = Oeste
FRANÇAIS — Nom / Page / Lat.°′ / Long.°′ W = Ouest
PORTUGUÊS — Nome / Página / Lat.°′ / Long.°′ W = Oeste

	English	Deutsch	Español	Français	Português
≃	River	Fluß	Río	Rivière	Rio
≡	Canal	Kanal	Canal	Canal	Canal
⌊	Waterfall, Rapids	Wasserfall, Stromschnellen	Cascada, Rápidos	Chute d'eau, Rapides	Cascata, Rápidos
⊔	Strait	Meeresstraße	Estrecho	Détroit	Estreito
ᑕ	Bay, Gulf	Bucht, Golf	Bahía, Golfo	Baie, Golfe	Baía, Golfo
◎	Lake, Lakes	See, Seen	Lago, Lagos	Lac, Lacs	Lago, Lagos
≡	Swamp	Sumpf	Pantano	Marais	Pântano
⁂	Ice Features, Glacier	Eis- und Gletscherformen	Accidentes Glaciales	Formes glaciaires	Acidentes glaciares
✧	Other Hydrographic Features	Andere Hydrographische Objekte	Otros Elementos Hidrográficos	Autres données hydrographiques	Outros acidentes hidrográficos

	English	Deutsch	Español	Français	Português
✧	Submarine Features	Untermeerische Objekte	Accidentes Submarinos	Formes de relief sous-marin	Acidentes submarinos
□	Political Unit	Politische Einheit	Unidad Política	Entité politique	Unidade política
∪	Cultural Institution	Kulturelle Institution	Institución Cultural	Institution culturelle	Instituição cultural
⊥	Historical Site	Historische Stätte	Sitio Histórico	Site historique	Sitio histórico
♦	Recreational Site	Erholungs- und Ferienort	Sitio de Recreo	Centre de loisirs	Area de Lazer
⊠	Airport	Flughafen	Aeropuerto	Aéroport	Aeroporto
■	Military Installation	Militäranlage	Instalación Militar	Installation militaire	Instalação militar
✦	Miscellaneous	Verschiedenes	Misceláneo	Divers	Diversos

Otter Creek ≃, In., U.S. 218 38.58 N 85.37 W
Otter Creek ≃, Ia., U.S. 190 41.20 N 93.30 W
Otter Creek ≃, Mo., U.S. 219 39.31 N 91.51 W
Otter Creek ≃, Mt., U.S. 202 45.36 N 106.17 W
Otter Creek ≃, N.Y., U.S. 212 43.43 N 75.23 W
Otter Creek ≃, Ut,. U.S. 200 38.10 N 112.02 W
Otter Creek ≃, Vt., U.S. 188 44.13 N 73.17 W
Otter Creek Reservoir ⊜[1] 200 38.12 N 111.59 W
Otterhöfen 56 48.33 N 8.12 E
Otter-Lake, P.Q., Can. 188 45.51 N 76.26 W
Otter Lake, Mi., U.S. 190 43.13 N 83.28 W
Otter Lake ⊜, On., Can. 212 44.47 N 76.07 W
Otter Lake ⊜, On., Can. 212 45.17 N 79.56 W
Otter Lake ⊜, Sk., Can. 184 55.35 N 104.39 W
Otter Lake ⊜[1] 219 39.26 N 89.54 W
Otterlo 52 52.06 N 5.45 E
Otterndorf 52 53.48 N 8.53 E
Otterøya I 26 62.42 N 6.48 E
Otter River 207 42.35 N 72.03 W
Ottersberg 52 53.06 N 9.08 E
Ottershaw 260 51.22 N 0.32 W
Ottersleben ◆[8] 54 52.05 N 11.34 E
Otter Tail ≃ 198 46.16 N 96.36 W
Otter Tail Lake ⊜ 198 46.23 N 95.40 W
Otterup 41 55.31 N 10.24 E
Otterville, On., Can. 212 42.55 N 80.36 W
Otterville, Il., U.S. 219 39.03 N 90.24 W
Otterville, Mo., U.S. 194 38.41 N 93.00 W
Ottery ≃ 42 50.39 N 4.20 W
Ottery Saint Mary 42 50.45 N 3.17 W
Ottignies 56 50.40 N 4.34 E
Ottine 222 29.36 N 97.35 W
Ottleben 54 52.05 N 11.07 E
Ottmachau → Otmuchów 30 50.28 N 17.10 E
Ottmarsbocholt 52 51.49 N 7.32 E
Ottnang 60 48.06 N 13.40 E
Ottnaren ⊜ 40 60.29 N 16.37 E
Otto, N.Y., U.S. 210 42.21 N 78.50 W
Otto, Tx., U.S. 222 31.27 N 96.49 W
Ottobeuren 58 47.56 N 10.18 E
Ottobeuren, Klosterkirche ✝[1] 58 47.56 N 10.18 E
Ottobiano 62 45.09 N 8.50 E
Ottobrunn 60 48.04 N 11.40 E
Ottone 62 44.37 N 9.20 E
Ottoschwanden 58 48.12 N 7.52 E
Ottosdal 158 26.58 S 26.00 E
Ottoshoop 156 25.45 S 25.59 E
Ottoville 216 40.55 N 84.20 W
Ottuk, S.S.S.R. 85 42.18 N 76.18 E
Ottuk, S.S.S.R. 85 41.38 N 75.51 E
Ottumwa 190 41.00 N 92.22 W
Ottweiler 56 49.24 N 7.09 E
Otty Lake ⊜ 212 44.50 N 76.13 W
Otu 150 8.14 N 3.24 E
Otu → Ōtsu 96 35.00 N 135.52 E
Otukpa 150 7.09 N 7.41 E
Otumpa 252 27.19 S 62.13 W
Otun 273a 6.42 N 3.22 E
Otuquis, Bañados de ≣ 248 19.20 S 58.30 W
Oturkpo 150 7.14 N 8.08 E
Otuzco 248 7.54 S 78.35 W
Otway, Bahía ⊌ 254 53.20 S 74.00 W
Otway, Cape > 166 38.52 S 143.31 E
Otway, Seno c 254 53.05 S 71.30 W
Otway Range ⋏ 169 38.30 S 143.50 E
Otwock 30 52.07 N 21.16 E
Otyn'a 78 48.44 N 24.51 E
Ötztal V 64 47.05 N 10.55 E
Ötztaler Ache ≃ 64 47.14 N 10.50 E
Ötztaler Alpen (Alpi Venoste) ⋏ 64 46.45 N 10.55 E
Ou ≃, Lao 110 20.04 N 102.13 E
Ou ≃, Zhg. 100 28.01 N 120.44 E
Ou ≃, Zhg. 100 26.02 N 113.09 E
Oua ≃ 152 0.43 N 12.55 E
Ouachita ≃ 194 31.38 N 91.49 W
Ouachita, Lake ⊜[1] 194 34.40 N 93.25 W
Ouachita Mountains ⋏ 194 34.40 N 94.25 W
Ouaco 175f 20.50 S 164.29 E
Ouadâne 148 20.56 N 11.37 W
Ouadda 152 8.04 N 22.24 E
Ouaddaï □[5] 146 13.00 N 21.00 E
Ouadey, Ouadi el V 146 13.34 N 18.03 E
Ouagadougou 150 12.22 N 1.31 W
Ouahigouya 150 13.35 N 2.25 W
Ouahran → Wahran 148 35.43 N 0.43 W
Ouaka □[5] 152 6.00 N 21.00 E
Ouaka ≃ 152 4.59 N 19.56 E
Oualâta 150 17.18 N 7.02 W
Ouâlata, Dahr ⊥[4] 150 17.48 N 7.24 W
Oualé ≃ 150 10.52 N 0.51 E
Oualidia 148 32.44 N 9.08 W
Ouallam 150 14.19 N 2.05 E
Ouallene 148 24.37 N 1.14 E
Oualto 150 9.01 N 10.06 W
Ouanary 250 4.13 N 51.40 W
Ouanda Djallé 146 8.54 N 22.48 E
Ouandago 146 7.10 N 18.42 E
Ouandja ≃ 146 9.35 N 21.43 E
Ouandja-Vakaga, Réserve de la ◆[4] 146 9.00 N 21.30 E
Ouango 152 4.19 N 22.33 E
Ouangolodougou 150 9.58 N 5.09 W
Ouaninou 150 8.11 N 7.51 W
Ouanne ≃ 50 47.57 N 2.47 E
Ouan Taredert 148 27.33 N 9.32 E
Ouaquaga 210 42.08 N 75.39 W
Ouara ≃ 154 5.05 N 24.26 E
Ouarâne ◆[1] 134 21.00 N 10.30 W
Ouararda, Passe de)(148 21.01 N 13.03 W
Ouareau ≃ 206 45.56 N 73.25 W
Ouareau, Lac ⊜[1] 206 46.17 N 74.09 W
Ouargaye 150 11.32 N 0.01 E
Ouarkoye 150 12.05 N 3.40 W
Ouarkziz, Jbel ⋏ 148 28.50 N 9.00 W
Ouarsenis, Djebel ∧ 34 35.53 N 1.38 E
Ouarville 50 48.21 N 1.46 E
Ouarzazate 148 30.57 N 6.50 W
Ouarzazate □[4] 148 30.55 N 6.45 W
Ouassoulou ≃ 150 11.35 N 8.11 W
Ouatcha 150 13.22 N 9.18 E
Oubangui (Ubangi) ≃ 152 0.30 S 17.42 E
Ouche ≃ 58 47.06 N 5.16 E
Oucques 50 47.49 N 1.18 E
Ōuda 94 34.28 N 135.56 E
Oudaze Lake ⊜ 212 45.27 N 79.11 W
Oud-Beijerland 52 51.49 N 4.25 E
Ouddorp 52 51.18 N 3.56 E
Oude IJssel (Issel) ≃ 52 52.00 N 6.10 E
Oudenaarde 50 50.51 N 3.36 E
Oudenbosch 52 51.35 N 4.31 E
Oudenburg 50 50.46 N 3.53 E
Oude-Pekela 52 53.04 N 6.58 E
Oude Rijn ≃ 52 52.05 N 4.20 E
Oudeschild 52 53.02 N 4.50 E
Oude-Tonge 52 51.41 N 4.12 E
Oudewater 52 52.02 N 4.52 E
Oud-Gastel 52 51.35 N 4.27 E
Oudjda → Oujda 148 34.41 N 1.45 W
Oud-Loosdrecht 52 52.13 N 5.04 E
Oudtshoorn 158 33.35 S 22.14 E
Oudyoumoudi 150 14.04 N 0.28 W
Oued Athmenia 34 36.15 N 6.17 E
Oued Cheham 36 36.23 N 7.46 E
Oued edh Dheheb, Khlij c 148 23.45 N 15.47 W
Oued Fodda 34 36.11 N 1.32 E
Oued Meliz 36 36.27 N 8.34 E
Oued Rhiou 34 35.58 N 0.55 E
Oued Tlelat 34 35.34 N 0.27 W
Oued Zarga 36 36.40 N 9.25 E
Oued-Zem 148 32.55 N 6.33 W
Ouellé 150 7.18 N 4.01 W
Ouémé □[5] 150 7.00 N 2.35 E
Ouémé ≃ 150 6.29 N 2.32 E
Ouen, Île I 175f 22.26 S 166.49 E
Ouenkoro 150 13.23 N 3.50 W
Ouenza, Djebel ∧ 36 35.57 N 8.05 E
Ouenzé ◆[8] 273b 4.14 S 15.17 E
Ouessa 150 11.03 N 2.47 W
Ouessant, Île d' (Ushant) I 32 48.28 N 5.05 W
Ouesso 152 1.37 N 16.04 E
Ouest □[4] 152 5.23 N 10.45 E
Ouest, Pointe de l' > 186 49.52 N 64.31 W
Ouest, Rivière de l' ≃ 206 45.39 N 74.21 W
Ouezzane 148 34.52 N 5.35 W
Ouffet 56 50.26 N 5.28 E
Ouganda → Uganda □[1] 154 1.00 N 32.00 E
Ougarou 150 12.09 N 0.56 E
Oughter, Lough ⊜ 48 54.00 N 7.30 W
Oughterard 48 53.25 N 9.17 W
Oughtibridge 44 53.26 N 1.33 W
Ouham □[5] 152 7.00 N 18.00 E
Ouham ≃ 136 9.18 N 18.14 E
Ouham-Pendé □[5] 152 7.00 N 16.00 E
Ouidah 150 6.22 N 2.05 E
Ouidi 146 14.07 N 12.58 E
Ouimet Canyon V 190 48.47 N 88.40 W
Oujda 148 34.41 N 1.45 W
Oujda □[4] 148 34.05 N 2.10 W
Oulad Naïl, Monts des ⋏ 148 34.33 N 3.28 E
Oulainen 26 64.16 N 24.48 E
Oulangan Kansallispuisto ♠ 24 66.12 N 29.30 E
Oulchy-le-Château 50 49.12 N 3.21 E
Oule ≃ 62 44.25 N 5.21 E
Ouled Agla 34 35.58 N 4.45 E
Ouleout Creek ≃ 210 42.20 N 75.18 W
Oulins 50 48.52 N 1.28 E
Oullins 62 45.43 N 4.48 E
Oulou, Bahr ≃ 146 9.48 N 21.32 E
Oulton Broad 42 52.31 N 1.42 E
Oulu 26 65.01 N 25.28 E
Oulujärvi ⊜ 26 64.20 N 27.15 E
Oulujoki ≃ 26 65.01 N 25.25 E
Oulun lääni □[4] 24 65.00 N 27.00 E
Oulx 62 45.02 N 6.50 E
Oumba 152 4.55 N 19.04 E
Oum-Chalouba 146 15.48 N 20.46 E
Oumé 150 6.23 N 5.25 W
Oum El Bouagui 148 35.53 N 7.07 E
Oum El Bouagui □[5] 148 35.50 N 7.15 E
Oum er Rbia, Oued ≃ 148 33.19 N 8.21 W
Oum-Hadjer 146 13.18 N 19.41 E
Oum Hadjer, Ouadi V 146 16.38 N 20.14 E
Oumiao 102 31.55 N 112.09 E
Oumm ed Droûs Guebli, Sebkhet ⊜ 148 24.03 N 11.45 W
Oumm ed Droûs Telli, Sebkhet ⊜ 148 24.20 N 11.30 W
Ounâne, Bîr ⊤[4] 148 21.28 N 3.56 W
Ounara 148 31.33 N 9.28 W
Ounasjoki ≃ 24 66.30 N 25.45 E
Oundle 42 52.29 N 0.29 W
Ounianga Kébir 146 19.04 N 20.29 E
Ouolossébougou 150 12.00 N 7.55 W
Our ≃ 56 49.53 N 6.18 E
Ouragahio 150 6.19 N 5.56 W
Ōura-wan c 174m 26.32 N 128.04 E
Ouray 200 38.01 N 107.40 W
Ouray, Mount ∧ 200 38.25 N 106.14 W
Ource ≃ 58 48.06 N 4.23 E
Ourcq ≃ 50 49.01 N 3.01 E
Ourcq, Canal de l' ≋ 50 48.51 N 2.22 E
Ourém 250 1.33 S 47.06 W
Ouri 146 21.34 N 19.13 E
Ouri, Tarso ∧ 146 21.25 N 18.56 E
Ouricuri 250 7.53 S 40.05 W
Ourimbah 170 33.22 S 151.23 E
Ourinhos 255 22.59 S 49.52 W
Ourique 34 37.39 N 8.13 W
Ournie 171b 35.56 S 147.51 E
Ouro, Paraná do ≃ 248 8.29 S 70.30 W
Ouro, Ponta do > 158 26.51 S 32.54 E
Ouro, Rio d' ≃ 287a 22.42 S 43.35 W
Ouro Branco 250 6.42 S 36.57 W
Ouro Fino 256 22.17 S 46.22 W
Ouro Prêto 255 20.23 S 43.30 W
Ouro Prêto ≃ 248 11.02 S 65.13 W
Ouroufa, Vallée d' V 150 14.42 N 7.00 E
Ours, Grand Lac de l' → Great Bear Lake ⊜ 176 66.00 N 120.00 W
Oursi 150 14.41 N 0.27 W
Ourthe ≃ 56 50.38 N 5.35 E
Ourthe Occidentale ≃ 56 50.08 N 5.41 E
Ourthe Orientale ≃ 56 50.08 N 5.41 E
Ourville-en-Caux 50 49.44 N 0.36 E
Ōu-sammyaku ⋏ 92 38.45 N 140.50 E
Ouse ≃, On., Can. 212 44.17 N 78.03 W
Ouse ≃, Eng., U.K. 42 50.47 N 0.03 E
Ouse ≃, Eng., U.K. 44 53.42 N 0.41 W
Oust ≃ 32 47.39 N 2.06 W
Outaouais, Rivière des → Ottawa ≃ 176 45.20 N 73.58 W
Outardes, Baie aux c 186 49.02 N 68.30 W
Outardes, Rivière aux ≃ 176 49.04 N 68.28 W
Outardes Est, Rivière aux ≃ 206 45.06 N 74.04 W
Outardes Quatre, Réservoir ⊜[1] 186 49.50 N 68.58 W
Outardes Trois, Barrage ◆[6] 186 49.34 N 68.48 W
Outarville 50 48.13 N 2.01 E
Outcalt 276 40.23 N 74.24 W
Outeniekwaberge ⋏ 158 33.53 S 22.35 E
Outerbridge Crossing ◆[5] 276 40.31 N 74.15 W
Outer Harbour 168b 34.47 S 138.30 E
Outer Hebrides II 46 57.45 N 7.00 W
Outer Island I 190 47.03 N 90.30 W
Outer Santa Barbara Passage ⊌ 228 33.10 N 118.30 W
Outer Sister Island I 166 39.39 S 148.00 E
Outjo 156 20.08 S 16.08 E
Outjo □[5] 156 19.30 S 15.30 E
Outlane 262 53.39 N 1.53 W
Outlet Bay c 208 37.22 N 75.49 W
Outlook, Sk., Can. 184 51.30 N 107.03 W
Outlook, Mt., U.S. 198 48.53 N 104.46 W
Outokumpu 26 62.44 N 29.01 E
Outpost Mountain ∧ 180 69.08 N 151.12 W
Outreau 50 50.42 N 1.35 E
Outremont 206 45.31 N 73.38 W
Outside Canal ≋ 226 37.13 N 121.02 W
Out Skerries II 46a 60.25 N 0.42 W
Outwell 42 52.37 N 0.14 E
Ouvéa I 175f 20.30 S 166.35 E
Ouvéa, Lagon d' c 175f 20.33 S 166.27 E
Ouvèze ≃ 62 43.59 N 4.51 E
Ouvidor 255 18.14 S 47.50 W
Ouye, Forêt de l' ♠ 261 48.32 N 2.00 E
Ouyen 166 35.04 S 142.20 E
Ouzinkie 180 57.55 N 152.30 W
Ouzouer-le-Marché 50 47.55 N 1.32 E
Ouzouer-sur-Loire 50 47.46 N 2.29 E
Ouzzal, Oued i-n- V 148 21.35 N 2.00 E
Ovabağ 130 37.43 N 39.59 E
Ovacık, Tür. 130 39.22 N 39.13 E
Ovacık, Tür. 130 41.05 N 32.55 E
Ovada 62 44.38 N 8.38 E
Ovakent 130 38.06 N 28.02 E
Oval 210 41.09 N 77.11 W
Ovalau I 175g 17.40 S 178.48 E
Ovalle 252 30.36 S 71.12 W
Ovamboland □[9] 156 17.45 S 16.30 E
Ovana, Cerro ∧ 246 4.38 N 66.57 W
Ovar 34 40.52 N 8.38 W
Ovaro 64 46.29 N 12.52 E
Ovčinino 82 56.02 N 39.03 E
Ovcyno 265a 59.48 N 30.37 E
Övedskloster 41 55.41 N 13.38 E
Ovejas 246 9.32 N 75.14 W
Ovelgönne 52 53.20 N 8.25 E
Ovenden 262 53.44 N 1.53 W
Oveng 152 2.25 N 12.16 E
Overath 56 50.55 N 7.14 E
Overberge 263 51.37 N 7.41 E
Overbrook 198 38.46 N 95.33 W
Overbrook ◆[8], Pa., U.S. 279b 40.24 N 79.59 W
Overbrook ◆[8], Pa., U.S. 285 39.58 N 75.16 W
Overdinkel 52 52.14 N 7.01 E
Overflakkee I 52 51.45 N 4.10 E
Overflowing ≃ 184 53.10 N 101.05 W
Overhalla 24 64.30 N 11.57 E
Overijse 56 50.46 N 4.32 E
Overijssel □[4] 52 52.25 N 6.30 E
Over Jerstal 41 55.12 N 9.18 E
Överkalix 24 66.21 N 22.56 E
Overland 219 38.42 N 90.21 W
Overland Park 198 38.58 N 94.40 W
Overlea 208 39.22 N 76.31 W
Overloon 52 51.35 N 5.57 E
Övermark (Ylimarkku) 26 62.38 N 21.30 E
Overpeck Creek ≃ 276 40.51 N 74.02 W
Overpelt 56 51.13 N 5.25 E
Overseal 42 52.44 N 1.34 W
Overstrand 42 52.56 N 1.20 E
Overton, Eng., U.K. 42 51.15 N 1.15 W
Overton, Ne., U.S. 198 40.44 N 99.32 W
Overton, Nv., U.S. 204 36.32 N 114.26 W
Overton, Tx., U.S. 222 32.16 N 94.58 W
Overton Arm c 204 36.20 N 114.25 W
Övertorneå 24 66.23 N 23.40 E
Överum 26 57.59 N 16.19 E
Over Wallop 42 51.09 N 1.35 W
Ovett 194 31.29 N 89.01 W
Ovid, Mi., U.S. 216 43.00 N 84.22 W
Ovid, N.Y., U.S. 210 42.40 N 76.49 W
Ovidiopol' 78 46.17 N 30.27 E
Oviedo, Esp. 34 43.22 N 5.50 W
Oviedo, Fl., U.S. 220 28.40 N 81.13 W
Oviglio 62 44.52 N 8.29 E
Oviken 26 62.59 N 14.24 E
Oviksfjällen ⋏ 26 63.02 N 13.51 E
Ovilla 222 32.32 N 96.53 W
Ovindoli 66 42.08 N 13.31 E
Ovinišče 76 58.22 N 37.02 E
Ovino 76 59.41 N 33.11 E
Oviši 76 57.34 N 21.45 E
Övörchangaj □[4] 102 46.00 N 102.30 E
Øvre Anarjokka Nasjonalpark ♠ 24 69.00 N 25.00 E
Øvre Årdal 26 61.19 N 7.48 E
Øvre Dividal Nasjonalpark ♠ 24 68.39 N 19.45 E
Øvre Pasvik Nasjonalpark ♠ 24 69.06 N 28.55 E
Øvre Rendal 26 61.53 N 11.05 E
Övre Vättern ⊜ 40 59.52 N 15.40 E
Ovruč 78 51.21 N 28.49 E
Ovs'anikovo 76 60.09 N 45.16 E
Ovs'anka, S.S.S.R. 86 55.57 N 92.33 E
Ovs'anka, S.S.S.R. 89 53.35 N 126.57 E
Ovs'annikovo 82 56.54 N 37.33 E
Ovstug 76 53.24 N 33.52 E
Ōwada 268 35.49 N 139.33 E
Owaka 172 46.27 S 169.40 E
Owambo □[5] 156 18.00 S 16.00 E
Owambo ≃ 156 18.45 S 17.03 E
Owando 152 0.29 S 15.55 E
Owaneco 219 39.29 N 89.12 W
Owariashi 94 35.12 N 137.02 E
Owasco 210 42.51 N 76.28 W
Owasco Inlet ≃ 210 42.45 N 76.28 W
Owasco Lake ⊜ 210 42.52 N 76.32 W
Owasco Outlet ≃ 210 43.04 N 76.39 W
Owase 92 34.04 N 136.12 E
Owasso 196 36.16 N 95.51 W
Owatonna 190 44.05 N 93.13 W
Owbeh 128 34.22 N 63.10 E
Owe 272c 19.04 N 73.04 E
Owego 210 42.06 N 76.15 W
Owego Creek, East Branch ≃ 210 42.10 N 76.15 W
Owego Creek, West Branch ≃ 210 42.10 N 76.15 W
Owel, Lough ⊜ 48 53.34 N 7.25 W
Owen, Austl. 168b 34.16 S 138.33 E
Owen, B.R.D. 56 48.35 N 9.27 E
Owen, In., U.S. 218 38.27 N 85.34 W
Owen, Wi., U.S. 190 44.57 N 90.33 W
Owen □[6] 218 38.33 N 84.49 W
Owen, Mount ∧ 172 41.33 S 172.32 E
Owenboy ≃ 48 51.48 N 8.18 W
Owendo 152 0.17 N 9.30 E
Owenea ≃ 48 54.47 N 8.26 W
Owen Falls Dam ◆[6] 154 0.27 N 33.11 E
Owen Fracture Zone ✣ 12 12.00 N 58.00 E
Owenkillew ≃ 48 54.44 N 7.18 W
Owenmore ≃ 48 54.07 N 9.50 W
Owen River 172 41.39 S 172.27 E
Owens ≃ 204 36.31 N 117.57 W
Owensboro 194 37.46 N 87.06 W
Owens Creek ≃, Ca., U.S. 226 37.13 N 120.42 W
Owens Creek ≃, Md., U.S. 208 39.33 N 77.20 W
Owens Lake ⊜ 204 36.25 N 117.56 W
Owen Sound 212 44.34 N 80.56 W
Owen Sound c 212 44.40 N 80.55 W
Owen Stanley Range ⋏ 164 9.20 S 147.55 E
Owensville, In., U.S. 194 38.16 N 87.41 W
Owensville, Mo., U.S. 219 38.20 N 91.30 W
Owensville, Oh., U.S. 218 39.07 N 84.08 W
Owenton, Ky., U.S. 218 38.32 N 84.50 W
Owenton, Va., U.S. 208 37.53 N 77.06 W
Owentown 222 32.26 N 95.12 W
Owerri 150 5.29 N 7.02 E
Owhango 172 39.00 S 175.23 E
Owikeno Lake ⊜ 182 51.41 N 127.00 W
Owings 208 38.43 N 76.36 W
Owings Mills 284b 39.25 N 76.46 W
Owingsville 188 38.08 N 83.45 W
Owl ≃, Ab., Can. 182 54.54 N 111.57 W
Owl ≃, Mb., Can. 176 57.51 N 92.44 W
Owl Creek ≃, U.S. 198 44.41 N 103.29 W
Owl Creek ≃, Mt., U.S. 202 45.18 N 107.21 W
Owl Creek ≃, Wy., U.S. 202 43.41 N 108.11 W
Owl Creek, South Fork ≃ 202 43.43 N 108.32 W
Owl Creek Mountains ⋏ 202 43.30 N 108.35 W
Owo 150 7.15 N 5.37 E
Oworonsoki 273a 6.33 N 3.24 E
Owosso 216 42.59 N 84.10 W
Owuru ≃ 273a 6.39 N 3.27 E
Owyhee 204 41.56 N 116.05 W
Owyhee ≃ 202 43.46 N 117.02 W
Owyhee, Lake ⊜[1] 202 43.28 N 117.20 W
Owyhee, South Fork ≃ 202 42.26 N 116.53 W
Oxapampa 248 10.34 S 75.24 W
Öxarfjörður c 24a 66.15 N 16.45 W
Oxbow, Sk., Can. 184 49.14 N 102.11 W
Oxbow, Mi., U.S. 281 42.38 N 83.28 W
Oxbow, N.Y., U.S. 212 44.17 N 75.37 W
Oxbow Lake ⊜ 281 42.38 N 83.28 W
Ox Creek ≃ 198 48.37 N 100.17 W
Oxelösund 40 58.40 N 17.06 E
Oxford, N.S., Can. 186 45.44 N 63.52 W
Oxford, N.Z. 172 43.18 S 172.11 E
Oxford, Eng., U.K. 42 51.46 N 1.15 W
Oxford, Al., U.S. 194 33.36 N 85.50 W
Oxford, Ct., U.S. 207 41.26 N 73.07 W
Oxford, Fl., U.S. 220 28.55 N 82.02 W
Oxford, In., U.S. 216 40.31 N 87.14 W
Oxford, Ia., U.S. 190 41.43 N 91.47 W
Oxford, Ks., U.S. 198 37.16 N 97.10 W
Oxford, Ky., U.S. 218 38.16 N 84.30 W
Oxford, Me., U.S. 188 44.07 N 70.29 W
Oxford, Md., U.S. 208 38.41 N 76.10 W
Oxford, Ma., U.S. 207 42.07 N 71.51 W
Oxford, Mi., U.S. 216 42.49 N 83.15 W
Oxford, Ms., U.S. 194 34.21 N 89.31 W
Oxford, Ne., U.S. 198 40.15 N 99.38 W
Oxford, N.J., U.S. 210 40.48 N 74.59 W
Oxford, N.Y., U.S. 210 42.26 N 75.35 W
Oxford, N.C., U.S. 192 36.18 N 78.35 W
Oxford, Oh., U.S. 218 39.30 N 84.44 W
Oxford, Pa., U.S. 208 39.47 N 75.58 W
Oxford, Wi., U.S. 190 43.46 N 89.34 W
Oxford □[6] 212 43.08 N 80.50 W
Oxford Falls 274a 33.44 S 151.15 E
Oxford House 184 54.56 N 95.16 W
Oxford House Indian Reserve ◆[4] 184 54.54 N 95.15 W
Oxford Junction 190 41.59 N 90.57 W
Oxford Lake ⊜ 184 54.51 N 95.37 W
Oxford Peak ∧ 202 42.16 N 112.06 W
Oxfordshire □[6] 42 51.50 N 1.15 W
Oxford Valley Mall ◆[9] 285 40.11 N 74.53 W
Oxhey 260 51.39 N 0.23 W
Oxie 41 55.33 N 13.04 E
Oxley 166 34.12 S 144.06 E
Oxley Creek ≃ 171a 27.32 S 153.00 E
Oxnard 228 34.11 N 119.10 W
Oxnard Beach 228 34.09 N 119.13 W
Oxon Hill 284c 38.48 N 76.59 W
Oxon Run ≃ 284b 38.49 N 77.00 W
Ox Pasture Brook ≃ 283 42.45 N 70.54 W
Oxshott 260 51.20 N 0.21 W
Oxted 42 51.16 N 0.01 W
Oxtongue ≃ 212 45.19 N 79.01 W
Oxtongue Lake ⊜ 212 45.22 N 78.55 W
Oxus → Amu Darya ≃ 72 43.40 N 59.01 E
Oy 58 47.38 N 10.28 E
Oya, Malay. 112 2.52 N 111.53 E
Ōya, Nihon 96 35.20 N 134.40 E
Oya ≃ 112 2.52 N 111.52 E
Oyabe 94 36.40 N 136.52 E
Oyabe ≃ 94 36.48 N 137.04 E
Ōya-ji ✝[1] 94 36.38 N 139.48 E
Ōyake-yama ∧[2] 270 34.48 N 135.51 E
Oyalı 130 37.14 N 41.45 E
Oyama, B.C., Can. 182 50.07 N 119.22 W
Oyama, Nihon 94 35.21 N 139.00 E
Oyama, Nihon 94 36.18 N 139.48 E
Ōyama, Nihon 94 36.36 N 137.18 E
Oyama, Nihon 268 35.36 N 139.22 E
Ōyamada 94 34.46 N 136.13 E
Ōyamazaki 270 34.54 N 135.42 E
Oyameles 234 19.43 N 97.32 W
Oyan 152 0.02 N 10.17 E
Ōyano 92 32.35 N 130.26 E
Oyapock (Oiapoque) ≃ 250 4.08 N 51.40 W
Oyashirazu ♠ 94 36.59 N 137.40 E
Oybin 54 50.50 N 14.44 E
Oye-et-Pallet 58 46.51 N 6.20 E
Oyem 152 1.37 N 11.35 E
Oyen 184 51.22 N 110.28 W
Øyeren ⊜ 26 59.48 N 11.14 E
Oykel ≃ 46 57.56 N 4.25 W
Oykel Bridge 46 57.58 N 4.43 W
Oymyakon → Ojm'akon 74 63.28 N 142.49 E
Oyo, Congo 152 0.01 N 15.54 E
Oyo, Nig. 150 7.51 N 3.56 E
Oyo □[3] 150 8.00 N 3.50 E
Oyo ≃ 115a 7.57 S 110.22 E
Ōyodo 96 34.23 N 135.48 E
Oyodo ◆[8] 270 34.43 N 135.30 E
Ōyodo ≃ 92 31.53 N 131.28 E
Oyón 248 10.39 S 76.47 W
Oyonnax 58 46.15 N 5.40 E
Ōyorogi-san ∧ 96 35.05 N 132.51 E
Oyotún 248 6.51 S 79.19 W
Oyster 208 37.17 N 75.55 W
Oyster Bay 210 40.51 N 73.31 W
Oyster Bay c 276 40.55 N 73.30 W
Oyster Bay Cove 276 40.52 N 73.31 W
Oyster Bay Harbor c 276 40.53 N 73.32 W
Oyster Creek 222 29.00 N 95.20 W
Oyster Creek ≃ 222 28.59 N 95.18 W
Oyster Point ∧ 282 37.50 N 121.52 W
Oyster Point > 168b 34.55 S 137.48 E
Oyster Rock I[2] 272c 18.54 N 72.50 E
Oysterville 224 46.33 N 124.02 W
Øystese 26 60.23 N 6.13 E
Oyten 52 53.04 N 9.01 E
Ozaki 268 35.59 N 139.51 E
Ozamiz 116 8.08 N 123.50 E
Ozanne ≃ 50 48.11 N 1.22 E
Ozariči 76 52.28 N 29.16 E
Ozark, Al., U.S. 194 31.27 N 85.38 W
Ozark, Ar., U.S. 194 35.29 N 93.49 W
Ozark, Mo., U.S. 194 37.01 N 93.12 W
Ozark National Scenic Riverways ♠ 194 37.10 N 91.10 W
Ozark Plateau ⋏[1] 194 37.00 N 93.00 W
Ozark Reservoir ⊜[1] 194 35.35 N 94.00 W
Ozarks, Lake of the ⊜[1] 194 38.10 N 92.50 W
Ozaukee □[6] 216 44.14 N 88.00 W
Ozbourn Seamount ✣[3] 14 26.00 S 174.50 W
Ózd 30 48.14 N 20.18 E
Ozd'atiči 76 54.06 N 28.50 E
Oze ≃ 96 34.12 N 132.14 E
Ozeblin ∧ 36 44.35 N 15.53 E
Ozek 86 46.35 N 60.41 E
Ozereckoje 82 56.04 N 37.23 E
Ožerelje 82 54.48 N 38.17 E
Ožerelki 82 55.51 N 38.52 E
Ozerišče 76 54.48 N 33.13 E
Ozerki, S.S.S.R. 80 51.13 N 53.56 E
Ozerki, S.S.S.R. 80 51.32 N 45.16 E
Ozerki, S.S.S.R. 80 52.01 N 45.29 E
Ozerki, S.S.S.R. 86 53.38 N 83.44 E
Ozerki, S.S.S.R. 265a 59.54 N 30.44 E
Ozerna ≃ 82 55.44 N 36.08 E
Ozerninskoje vodochranilišče ⊜[1] 82 55.45 N 36.15 E
Ozernoje 78 50.11 N 28.42 E
Ozernovskij 74 51.30 N 156.31 E
Ozernyj 180 66.24 N 179.06 W
Ozero 80 56.58 N 44.43 E
Ozery 82 54.51 N 38.34 E
Ozette Lake ⊜ 224 48.06 N 124.38 W
Ozgoryš 85 41.15 N 74.45 E
Ozieri 71 40.35 N 9.00 E
Ozimek 30 50.41 N 18.13 E
Ozinki 80 51.12 N 49.45 E
Ožogino, ozero ⊜ 74 69.16 N 146.36 E
Ozoir-la-Ferrière 261 48.46 N 2.40 E
Ozona, Fl., U.S. 220 28.04 N 82.46 W

ENGLISH				DEUTSCH			
Name	Page	Lat.°′	Long.°′	Name	Seite	Breite°′	Länge°′ E = Ost

Ozona, Tx., U.S. 196 30.42 N 101.12 W
Ozone Park ◆[8] 276 40.40 N 73.51 W
Ozorków 30 51.58 N 19.19 E
Oz'ornaja, S.S.S.R. 86 51.08 N 60.50 E
Oz'ornaja, S.S.S.R. 86 53.25 N 63.15 E
Oz'ornoje, S.S.S.R. 80 51.41 N 44.55 E
Oz'ornoje, S.S.S.R. 80 51.46 N 51.28 E
Oz'ornoje, S.S.S.R. 86 56.48 N 71.15 E
Oz'ornyj 80 57.10 N 40.59 E
Oz'orsk, S.S.S.R. 76 54.25 N 22.01 E
Oz'orsk, S.S.S.R. 78 51.43 N 26.24 E
Oz'orskij 89 46.36 N 143.08 E
Oz'ory 76 53.43 N 24.11 E
Ozouer-le-Voulgis 261 48.40 N 2.47 E
Özpınar 130 37.57 N 42.16 E
Ōzu, Nihon 92 32.52 N 130.52 E
Ōzu, Nihon 96 33.30 N 132.33 E
Ozubulu 150 5.57 N 6.51 E
Ozuluama 234 21.40 N 97.51 W
Ozumba de Alzate 234 19.03 N 98.48 W

P

Pâ 150 11.33 N 3.15 W
Paagoumène 175f 20.29 S 164.11 E
Paal 56 51.02 N 5.11 E
Paama □[8] 175f 16.28 S 168.18 E
Paama I 175f 16.28 S 168.14 E
Paar ≃ 60 48.45 N 11.33 E
Paardekraal Monument ⊥ 273d 26.06 S 27.47 E
Paaren 264a 52.39 N 12.59 E
Paarl 158 33.45 S 18.56 E
Paasbach ≃ 263 51.25 N 7.11 E
Paauilo 229d 53.23 N 1.28 W
Pabarabuk 164 6.05 S 144.05 E
Pabbay I, Scot., U.K. 46 56.51 N 7.35 W
Pabbay I, Scot., U.K. 46 57.46 N 7.15 W
Pabbi 123 34.01 N 71.47 E
Pabbiring, Kepulauan II 112 4.55 S 119.25 E
Pabean 112 6.50 S 115.19 E
Pabellón, Ensenada del c 232 24.27 N 107.36 W
Pabellón, Punta > 254 43.14 S 74.23 W
Pabellon de Arteaga 234 22.10 N 102.21 W
Pabianice 30 51.40 N 19.22 E
Pabillonis 71 39.35 N 8.43 E
Pablo 202 47.36 N 114.07 W
Pābna 124 24.00 N 89.15 E
Pabo 154 3.00 N 32.09 E
Pabradė 76 54.59 N 25.44 E
Paca 115b 8.29 S 120.11 E
Pacaás Novos ≃ 248 10.51 S 65.20 W
Pacaás Novos, Serra dos ⋏ 248 10.45 S 64.15 W
Pacaembu 255 21.34 S 51.17 W
Pacaembú, Estádio do ♠ 287b 23.33 S 46.39 W
Pacahuaras ≃ 248 10.04 S 65.46 W
Pacajá ≃ 250 1.56 S 50.50 W
Pacajus 250 4.10 S 38.28 W
Pacaltsdorp 158 34.00 S 22.28 E
Pacaraima, Sierra de → Pakaraima Mountains ⋏ 246 5.30 N 60.40 W
Pacarán 248 12.52 S 76.03 W
Pacaraos 248 11.11 S 76.44 W
Pacasmayo 248 7.24 S 79.34 W
Pacatuba 250 3.58 S 38.37 W
Paccha ≃ 248 9.05 S 76.54 W
Pace, Fl., U.S. 194 30.35 N 87.09 W
Pace, Ms., U.S. 194 33.47 N 90.51 W
Paceco 70 37.59 N 12.33 E
Pačelma, S.S.S.R. 80 53.15 N 43.21 E
Pačelma, S.S.S.R. 80 53.20 N 43.20 E
Pacet 115a 6.45 S 107.03 E
Pachača 74 60.34 N 169.03 E
Pachacamac 248 12.14 S 76.53 W
Pachacamac ⊥ 248 12.14 S 76.52 W
Pachamba 126 24.12 N 86.16 E
Pachaug Pond ⊜ 207 41.34 N 71.54 W
Pacheco 226 37.59 N 122.04 W
Pacheco Creek ≃ 226 36.58 N 121.28 W
Pacheco Pass)(226 37.03 N 121.13 W
Pachecos 256 22.48 S 42.50 W
Pāchh Elāsin 126 24.08 N 89.54 E
Pachino 70 36.43 N 15.05 E
Pachitea ≃ 248 8.46 S 74.32 W
Pachiza 248 7.16 S 76.46 W
Pachkoli ◆[8] 272c 19.08 N 72.54 E
Pachmarhi 124 22.28 N 78.26 E
Pacho 246 5.08 N 74.10 W
Pachomovo 82 54.38 N 37.33 E
Pachor 124 23.42 N 76.44 E
Pāchora 122 20.40 N 75.21 E
Pachotnyj Ugol 80 52.58 N 41.56 E
Pachra ≃ 82 55.32 N 37.59 E
Pachtaabad 85 38.28 N 68.10 E
Pachuca [de Soto] 234 20.07 N 98.44 W
Paciência ◆[8] 256 22.55 S 43.38 W
Pacific, B.C., Can. 182 54.46 N 128.17 W
Pacific, Mo., U.S. 219 38.28 N 90.44 W
Pacific, Wa., U.S. 224 47.15 N 122.14 W
Pacific □[6] 224 46.30 N 123.39 W
Pacifica 226 37.37 N 122.29 W
Pacific-Antarctic Ridge ✣[3] 6 62.00 S 157.00 W
Pacific Beach 224 47.12 N 124.12 W
Pacific City 224 45.12 N 123.57 W
Pacific Creek ≃ 200 42.08 N 109.24 W
Pacific Gardens 226 37.58 N 121.20 W
Pacific Grove 226 36.38 N 121.56 W
Pacific Islands, Trust Territory of the □[2] 14 5.00 N 137.00 E
Pacific Missile Test Center ■ 228 34.07 N 119.07 W
Pacífico, Océano → Pacific Ocean ⊤[1] 6 10.00 S 150.00 W
Pacific Ocean ⊤[1] 4 10.00 S 150.00 W
Pacific Ocean ⊤[1] 6 10.00 S 150.00 W
Pacifico Mountain ∧ 228 34.23 N 118.02 W
Pacific Palisades ◆[8] 280 34.03 N 118.32 W
Pacific Ranges ⋏ 182 50.45 N 125.30 W
Pacific Rim National Park ♠ 182 48.45 N 125.40 W
Pacifique, Océan → Pacific Ocean ⊤[1] 6 10.00 S 150.00 W
Pacijan Island I 116 10.39 N 124.20 E
Pacinan, Tanjung > 115a 7.36 S 114.02 E
Paciran 115a 6.52 S 112.20 E
Pacitan 115a 8.12 S 111.07 E
Pack 61 46.58 N 14.59 E
Packanack Lake ⊜ 276 40.56 N 74.15 W
Packard Mountain ∧[2] 207 42.28 N 72.21 W
Páckevei-Duna ≃[1] 264c 47.19 N 19.02 E
Pack Monadnock Mountain ∧ 207 42.52 N 71.52 W
Packsattel)(61 46.58 N 14.58 E
Packwood 224 46.36 N 121.40 W
Packwood Lake ⊜ 224 46.35 N 121.34 W
Paclłón 248 10.18 S 77.07 W
Pacock Brook ≃ 276 41.05 N 74.31 W
Paço de Arcos 266c 38.42 N 9.17 W
Paço do Lumiar 250 2.31 S 44.07 W
Pacoima ◆[8] 280 34.16 N 118.26 W
Pacolet ≃ 192 34.50 N 81.27 W
Pacolet Mills 192 34.55 N 81.44 W
Pácora, Col. 246 5.31 N 75.27 W
Pacora, Pan. 246 9.05 N 79.17 W
Pacoti 250 4.13 S 38.56 W
Pacov 30 49.28 N 15.00 E
Pacquet 186 49.59 N 55.53 W
Pacuare ≃ 236 10.14 N 83.17 W
Pacuí ≃ 255 16.46 S 45.01 W
Pacuneiro ≃ 255 13.02 S 53.25 W
Pacy-sur-Eure 50 49.01 N 1.23 E
Paczkow 30 50.27 N 17.00 E
Padada 116 6.42 N 125.22 E
Padada ≃ 116 6.42 N 125.23 E
Padaido, Kepulauan II 164 1.15 S 136.30 E
Padam 123 33.28 N 76.53 E
Padamarang, Pulau I 112 4.07 S 121.24 E
Padamo ≃ 246 2.54 N 65.17 W
Padampur 120 20.59 N 83.04 E
Padang, Indon. 112 1.39 S 108.55 E
Padang, Indon. 112 2.59 N 105.40 E
Padang, Indon. 112 6.11 S 120.26 E
Padang, Indon. 112 0.57 S 100.21 E
Padang, Pulau I 114 1.10 N 102.20 E
Padang Besar 114 6.40 N 100.19 E
Padangbetuah 112 3.39 S 102.13 E
Padang Endau 114 2.40 N 103.37 E
Padangpanjang 112 0.27 S 100.25 E
Padangsidempuan 114 1.22 N 99.16 E
Padangtiji 114 5.22 N 95.50 E
Padangtikar, Pulau I 112 0.50 S 109.30 E
Padang Tungku 114 4.14 N 101.59 E
Padany 24 63.17 N 33.22 E
Padas 115a 7.25 S 111.32 E
Padas ≃ 112 5.14 N 115.34 E
Padasjoki 26 61.21 N 25.17 E
Padauiri ≃ 246 0.15 S 64.05 W
Padborg 41 54.49 N 9.22 E
Padcaya 248 21.52 S 64.48 W
Paddington ◆[8] 260 51.31 N 0.10 W
Paddington Station ◆[5] 260 51.31 N 0.11 W
Paddle ≃ 182 54.05 N 114.15 W
Paddle Prairie 176 57.57 N 117.29 W
Paddock Lake 216 42.34 N 88.06 W
Paddock Wood 42 51.11 N 0.23 E
Padea 38 44.01 N 23.52 E
Padea-besar I 112 3.30 S 123.05 E
Padeghar 272c 18.58 N 73.03 E
Paden City 188 39.36 N 80.56 W
Paderborn 52 51.43 N 8.45 E
Paderno Dugnano 266b 45.34 N 9.10 E
Paderno Ponchielli 64 45.14 N 9.55 E
Padghe 272c 19.03 N 73.07 E
Padibe 154 3.28 N 32.50 E
Padiham 44 53.49 N 2.19 W
Padilla 248 19.19 S 64.20 W
Padilla Bay c 224 48.35 N 122.32 W
Padjelanta Nationalpark ♠ 24 67.28 N 16.41 E
Padle 272c 19.09 N 73.03 E
Padloping Island I 176 67.07 N 62.35 W
Padma → Ganges ≃ 124 23.22 N 90.32 E
Padola 64 46.36 N 12.28 E
Padoue → Padova 64 45.25 N 11.53 E
Padova 64 45.25 N 11.53 E
Padova □[4] 64 45.21 N 11.49 E
Padovka 80 52.28 N 49.31 E
Pādra 120 22.14 N 73.05 E
Padrão, Ponta do > 152 6.03 S 12.18 E
Padrauna 124 26.55 N 83.59 E
Padre Bernardo 255 15.21 S 48.30 W
Padre Brito 256 21.18 S 43.59 W
Padre Burgos 116 10.02 N 125.01 E
Padre Island I 196 27.00 N 97.15 W
Padre Island National Seashore ♠ 196 27.00 N 97.25 W
Padre Miguel ◆[8] 287a 22.53 S 43.26 W
Padre Paraíso 255 17.06 S 41.31 W
Padria 71 40.24 N 8.38 E
Padrón 34 42.44 N 8.40 W
Padrone, Cape > 158 33.46 S 26.30 E
Padrt' 60 49.40 N 13.46 E
Padstow, Austl. 274a 33.57 S 151.02 E
Padstow, Eng., U.K. 42 50.33 N 4.56 W
Padua → Padova 64 45.25 N 11.53 E
Paduari ≃ 246 2.08 S 61.15 W
Paducah, Ky., U.S. 194 37.05 N 88.36 W
Paducah, Tx., U.S. 196 34.00 N 100.18 W
Padula 68 40.20 N 15.39 E
Paduli 68 41.10 N 14.53 E
Padunskaja 86 55.02 N 85.02 E
Paea 174s 17.41 S 149.35 W
Paedun 98 35.03 N 128.21 E
Paekakariki 172 40.59 S 174.57 E
Paektu-san ∧ 98 42.00 N 128.03 E
Paengaroa 172 37.49 S 176.25 E
Paengnyŏng-do I 98 37.57 N 124.40 E
Paerdegat Basin c 276 40.37 N 73.54 W
Paeroa 172 37.23 S 175.40 E
Paesana 62 44.41 N 7.16 E
Paese 64 45.40 N 12.10 E
Paestum ⊥ 68 40.25 N 15.00 E
Paete 116 14.23 N 121.29 E
Páez ≃ 246 2.28 N 75.34 W
Pafúri 156 22.27 S 31.21 E
Pag 36 44.27 N 15.04 E
Pag, Otok I 36 44.30 N 15.00 E
Paga 150 10.58 N 1.06 W
Pagadenbaru 115a 6.28 S 107.48 E
Pagadian 116 7.49 N 123.25 E
Pagadian Bay c 116 7.48 N 123.31 E
Pagai Selatan, Pulau I 112 3.00 S 100.20 E
Pagai Utara, Pulau I 112 2.42 S 100.07 E
Pagalungan 116 7.04 N 124.41 E
Pagan 110 21.10 N 94.51 E
Pagan I 108 18.07 N 145.46 E
Pagancillo 252 29.34 S 68.03 W
Paganella ∧ 64 46.08 N 11.02 E
Pagani 68 40.45 N 14.37 E
Paganica 66 42.21 N 13.28 E
Paganico 66 42.56 N 11.16 E
Pagaralam 112 4.01 S 103.16 E
Pagasitikós Kólpos c 38 39.15 N 22.51 E
Pagatan 112 3.36 S 115.56 E
Pagato ≃ 184 55.49 N 102.05 W
Pagato Lake ⊜ 184 56.08 N 102.30 W
Pagbilao 116 13.58 N 121.41 E
Pagbilao Grande Island I 116 13.55 N 121.46 E
Pagdanan Bay c 116 10.31 N 119.15 E
Page, Az., U.S. 200 36.54 N 111.28 W
Page, N.D., U.S. 198 47.09 N 97.34 W
Page Field ⊠ 220 26.35 N 81.52 W
Pagėgiai 76 55.09 N 21.54 E
Pageland 192 34.46 N 80.23 W
Page Manor 218 39.45 N 84.06 W
Pager ≃ 154 3.09 N 32.30 E
Pagerdewa 112 3.46 S 105.18 E
Paget, Mount ∧ 244 54.26 S 36.33 W
Paghmān 120 34.36 N 68.57 E
Paglia ≃ 66 42.42 N 12.11 E
Pagliara 70 37.59 N 15.22 E
Paglieta 66 42.10 N 14.30 E
Pagliete, Bonifica delle ◆[1] 267a 41.53 N 12.12 E
Pagny-sur-Moselle 56 48.59 N 6.01 E
Pago Bay c 174p 13.25 N 144.48 E
Pagoda Peak ∧ 200 40.10 N 107.20 W
Pagoda Point > 110 15.57 N 94.15 E
Pagon, Bukit ∧ 112 4.18 N 115.19 E
Pago Pago 174u 14.16 S 170.42 W
Pago Pago Harbor c 174u 14.17 S 170.40 W
Pago Pago International Airport ⊠ 174u 14.20 S 170.43 W
Pagosa Springs 200 37.16 N 107.00 W
Pagote 272c 18.54 N 72.59 E
Pagouda 150 9.45 N 1.19 E
Pagri 124 27.44 N 89.09 E
Pagsangahan 116 13.13 N 122.33 E
Pagsanjan 116 14.15 N 121.25 E
Pagua Bay c 240d 15.32 N 61.17 W
Paguate 200 35.08 N 107.22 W
Pagudpud 116 18.34 N 120.47 E
Pagueras, Torrente de ≃ 266d 41.28 N 1.58 E

Symbols in the index entries represent the broad categories identified in the key at the right. Symbols with superior numbers (⋏[1]) identify subcategories (see complete key on page *I · 1).*

Symbole im Register stellen die rechts im Schlüssel erklärten Kategorien dar. Symbole mit hochgestellten Ziffern (⋏[1]) bezeichnen Unterabteilungen einer Kategorie (vgl. vollständiger Schlüssel auf Seite *I · 1).*

Los símbolos incluidos en el texto del índice representan las grandes categorias identificadas con la clave a la derecha. Los símbolos con numeros en su parte superior (⋏[1]) identifican las subcategorías (véase la clave completa en la página *I · 1).*

Les symboles de l'index représentent les catégories indiquées dans la légende à droite. Les symboles suivis d'un indice (⋏[1]) représentent des sous-catégories (voir légende complète à la page *I · 1).*

Os símbolos incluídos no texto do índice representam as grandes categorias identificadas com a chave à direita. Os símbolos com números em sua parte superior (⋏[1]) identificam as subcategorias (veja-se a chave completa à página *I · 1).*

∧ Mountain	Berg	Montaña	Montagne	Montanha
⋏ Mountains	Gebirge	Montañas	Montagnes	Montanhas
)(Pass	Paß	Paso	Col	Passo
V Valley, Canyon	Tal, Cañon	Valle, Cañón	Vallée, Canyon	Vale, Canhão
≍ Plain	Ebene	Llano	Plaine	Planície
> Cape	Kap	Cabo	Cap	Cabo
I Island	Insel	Isla	Île	Ilha
II Islands	Inseln	Islas	Îles	Ilhas
⊥ Other Topographic Features	Andere Topographische Objekte	Otros Elementos Topográficos	Autres données topographiques	Outros acidentes topográficos

ESPAÑOL

Nombre	Página	Lat.°′	Long.°′ W = Oeste
Paguyaman ≏	112	0.31 N	122.38 E
Pagwi	164	4.03 S	143.02 E
Pah	84	39.08 N	39.40 E
Pahādi ◆[8]	272c	19.10 N	72.51 E
Pahala	229d	19.12 N	155.28 W
Pahalgam	123	34.02 N	75.20 E
Pahang □[3]	114	3.30 N	102.45 E
Pahang ≏	114	3.32 N	103.28 E
Páhara, Laguna ᑕ	236	14.18 N	83.15 W
Pahāsu	124	28.11 N	78.03 E
Pahau Point ›	229b	21.49 N	160.15 W
Pahi	114	5.28 N	102.13 E
Pahia Point ›	172	46.19 S	167.41 E
Pahiatua	172	40.27 S	175.50 E
Pahlād Garhi	272a	28.40 N	77.21 E
Pahlavī → Bandar-e Anzalī	128	37.28 N	49.27 E
Pahlevī → Bandar-e Anzalī	128	37.28 N	49.27 E
Pahoa	229d	19.29 N	154.57 W
Pahokee	220	26.49 N	80.39 W
Pahrump	204	36.12 N	115.58 W
Pahsimeroi ≏	202	44.41 N	114.03 W
Pahuatlán de Valle	234	20.17 N	98.09 W
Pahvant Range ʎ	200	38.45 N	112.15 W
Pai	110	19.19 N	98.27 E
Pai ≏	110	19.09 N	97.33 E
Pai, Ilha do I	287a	22.59 S	43.05 W
Paia	229a	20.54 N	156.22 W
Paianía	267c	37.57 N	23.51 E
Paicines	226	36.44 N	121.17 W
Paico	248	14.02 S	73.39 W
Paide	76	58.54 N	25.33 E
Paidorzu, Monte ∧	71	40.30 N	9.05 E
Paifangchang	107	30.31 N	106.38 E
Paige	222	30.13 N	97.07 W
Paignton	42	50.26 N	3.34 W
Paiguano	252	30.01 S	70.32 W
Paihia	172	35.17 S	174.05 E
Paiho	100	23.21 N	120.25 E
Paiján	248	7.44 S	79.19 W
Päijänne ⊜	26	61.35 N	25.30 E
Pāikgācha	126	22.35 N	89.20 E
Paikü Co ⊜	124	28.48 N	85.36 E
Pail	123	32.38 N	72.27 E
Paila ≏	248	16.02 S	64.12 W
Paila, Sierra la ʎ	196	25.50 N	101.30 W
Pailin	110	12.51 N	102.36 E
Pailitas	246	8.58 N	73.38 W
Paillaco	254	40.04 S	72.53 W
Pailolo Channel ʉ	229a	21.05 N	156.42 W
Pailoutou	106	30.56 N	121.16 E
Pailoutun	104	40.44 N	122.49 E
Paimboeuf	32	47.17 N	2.02 W
Paimio	26	60.27 N	22.42 E
Paimpol	32	48.46 N	3.03 W
Painan	112	1.21 S	100.34 E
Paincourt	214	42.23 N	82.17 W
Painesdale	190	47.02 N	88.40 W
Painesville	214	41.43 N	81.14 W
Pains	255	20.22 S	45.40 W
Painscastle	42	52.07 N	3.12 W
Painshawfield	44	54.56 N	1.54 W
Painswick	42	51.48 N	2.11 W
Paint ≏	190	45.58 N	88.15 W
Paint Creek ≏, Mi., U.S.	281	42.06 N	83.36 W
Paint Creek ≏, Oh., U.S.	218	39.18 N	82.56 W
Paint Creek ≏, Pa., U.S.	214	41.10 N	79.28 W
Paint Creek ≏, Tx., U.S.	196	30.18 N	99.54 W
Paint Creek, East Fork ≏	218	39.32 N	83.25 W
Paint Creek, North Fork ≏	218	39.18 N	83.02 W
Paint Creek Lake ⊜[1]	218	39.15 N	83.22 W
Painted Desert ◆[2]	200	36.00 N	111.20 W
Painted Post	210	42.09 N	77.05 W
Painted Rock Reservoir ⊜[1]	200	33.00 N	112.50 W
Painten	60	49.00 N	11.49 E
Painter	208	37.35 N	75.47 W
Painter Creek ≏	218	40.05 N	84.21 W
Paintertown	279b	40.21 N	79.42 W
Paint Lake ⊜	184	55.28 N	97.57 W
Paint Rock	196	31.30 N	99.55 W
Paint Rock ≏	194	34.28 N	86.28 W
Paintsville	192	37.48 N	82.48 W
Paiol da Vargem	256	22.41 S	46.26 W
Paiolinho	256	21.52 S	45.54 W
Paisco	64	46.04 N	10.17 E
Paisha	100	23.40 N	119.35 E
Paisley, Austl.	274b	37.51 S	144.51 E
Paisley, On., Can.	212	44.18 N	81.16 W
Paisley, Scot., U.K.	46	55.50 N	4.26 W
Paisley, Fl., U.S.	220	28.59 N	81.32 W
Paisley, Or., U.S.	202	42.41 N	120.32 W
Païta, N. Cal.	175f	22.08 S	166.22 E
Paita, Perú	248	5.06 S	81.07 W
Paita, Bahía de ᑕ	248	5.04 S	81.05 W
Paitan	100	23.31 N	113.46 E
Paitan ≏	116	6.30 N	117.30 E
Paitan, Teluk ᑕ	116	6.45 N	117.20 E
Paiton	115a	7.43 S	113.30 E
Paiva	256	21.18 S	43.25 W
Paiva ≏	34	41.04 N	8.16 W
Paizhou	100	30.13 N	113.56 E
Paj	24	61:13 N	34.24 E
Pajacuarán	234	20.07 N	102.34 W
Pajala	24	67.11 N	23.22 E
Paján	246	1.34 S	80.25 W
Pajapan	234	18.15 N	94.42 W
Pajares, Puerto de)(	34	43.00 N	5.46 W
Pajaro	226	36.54 N	121.39 W
Pajaro ≏	226	36.51 N	121.48 W
Pajaros Point ›	240m	18.31 N	64.18 W
Paj-Choj ʎ[2]	72	69.00 N	63.00 E
Pajdugina ≏	86	58.50 N	81.47 E
Pajęczno	30	51.09 N	19.00 E
Pajeú ≏	250	8.55 S	38.42 W
Pajiangkou	100	23.46 N	113.14 E
Pajjer, gora ∧	24	66.42 N	64.25 E
Pajtug	85	40.53 N	72.15 E
Pak ≏	110	21.05 N	102.31 E
Páka, Magy.	61	46.36 N	16.39 E
Paka, Malay.	114	4.39 N	103.26 E
Paka ≏	114	4.40 N	103.27 E
Pākāla	122	13.28 N	79.07 E
Pakaraima Mountains ʎ	246	5.30 N	60.40 W
Pākaur	124	24.38 N	87.51 E
Pak Ban	110	21.14 N	102.28 E
Pakch'ŏn	98	39.45 N	125.35 E
Pak Chong	110	14.42 N	101.25 E
Pakeng	140	6.55 N	30.40 E
Pakenham, Austl.	169	38.04 S	145.29 E
Pakenham, On., Can.	212	45.20 N	76.17 W
Pākhāl ⊜[1]	122	17.57 N	79.59 E
Pákhi	267c	37.59 N	23.22 E
Pákhi I	267c	37.58 N	23.22 E
Pákhna	130	34.46 N	32.48 E
Pakhoi → Beihai	102	21.29 N	109.05 E
Pakin I[1]	14	7.04 N	157.48 E
Pakipaki	172	39.41 S	176.48 E
Pakistan (Pākistān) □[1], Asia	118	30.00 N	70.00 E
Pakistan (Pākistān) □[1], Asia	120	30.00 N	70.00 E
Pakistan, East → Bangladesh □[1]	120	24.00 N	90.00 E
Pak Kong	271d	22.23 N	114.15 E
Pak Kret	269a	13.55 N	100.30 E
Pak Kwo Chau I	271d	22.16 N	114.20 E
Paklenica Nacionalni Park ♠	36	44.21 N	15.23 E
Pakokku	110	21.20 N	95.05 E
Pakość	30	52.49 N	18.05 E

FRANÇAIS

Nom	Page	Lat.°′	Long.°′ W = Ouest
Pakouabo	150	7.10 N	5.48 W
Pakowki Lake ⊜	184	49.22 N	110.57 W
Pākpattan	123	30.21 N	73.24 E
Pak Phanang	110	8.21 N	100.12 E
Pak Phayun	110	7.21 N	100.19 E
Pak Phraek	110	8.13 N	100.12 E
Pakrac	36	45.26 N	17.12 E
Pākrāganj	126	24.00 N	90.41 E
Pakruojis	76	55.58 N	23.52 E
Paks	30	46.39 N	18.53 E
Pak Sane → Muang Pakxan	110	18.22 N	103.39 E
Pāksey	126	24.05 N	89.03 E
Pak Thong Chai	110	14.43 N	102.01 E
Paktīā □[4]	120	33.30 N	69.30 E
Paktīkā □[4]	120	32.30 N	68.45 E
Pākundia	126	24.20 N	90.42 E
P'akupur ≏	74	65.00 N	77.48 E
Pakwach	154	2.28 N	31.30 E
Pakwash Lake ⊜	184	50.45 N	93.30 W
Pakxé	110	15.07 N	105.47 E
Pala, Mya.	110	12.51 N	98.40 E
Pala, Tchad	146	9.22 N	14.54 E
Pala, Ca., U.S.	228	33.22 N	117.05 W
Palaau State Park ♠	229a	21.11 N	157.00 W
Palabek	154	3.26 N	32.34 E
Palacios	196	28.42 N	96.13 W
Palacios ≏	248	16.36 S	64.18 W
Paladru	62	45.28 N	5.33 E
Palagano	64	44.20 N	10.39 E
Palagianello	68	40.37 N	16.58 E
Palagiano	68	40.35 N	17.02 E
Palagonia	70	37.19 N	14.45 E
Palagruža, Otoci II	36	42.24 N	16.15 E
Palai	122	9.44 N	76.41 E
Palai, Punta ∧	71	40.20 N	8.55 E
Palaia	66	43.36 N	10.46 E
Palaiá Epídhavros	38	37.38 N	23.09 E
Palaiá Psará	38	38.46 N	25.36 E
Palaikhóri	130	34.55 N	33.05 E
Pala Indian Reservation ◆[4]	228	33.21 N	117.04 W
Palaiokhóra	38	35.14 N	23.41 E
Palaión Fáliron	267c	37.55 N	23.41 E
Palaiseau	50	48.43 N	2.15 E
Pālakodu	122	16.32 N	81.44 E
Pālam ◆[8]	272a	28.35 N	77.05 E
Palam Airport ⊠	123	28.35 N	77.07 E
Palamás	38	39.28 N	22.05 E
Palamós	34	41.51 N	3.08 E
Pālampur	123	32.07 N	76.32 E
Palamuse	76	58.41 N	26.35 E
Palamut	130	38.59 N	27.41 E
Palana	74	59.07 N	159.58 E
Palanan, Mount ∧	116	17.03 N	122.15 E
Palanan Bay ᑕ	116	17.09 N	122.27 E
Palanan Point ›	116	17.09 N	122.30 E
Palanas	116	12.09 N	123.55 E
Palandöken Dağları ʎ	130	39.47 N	41.15 E
Pālang	126	23.13 N	90.21 E
Pālang ≏[1]	126	23.15 N	90.21 E
Palanga	76	55.55 N	21.03 E
Palanganene	152	6.26 S	18.50 E
Palangkaraya	112	2.16 S	113.56 E
Palani	122	10.28 N	77.32 E
Pālanpur	120	24.10 N	72.26 E
Palanquinos	34	42.27 N	5.31 W
Palanzano	64	44.26 N	10.11 E
Palaoa Point ›	229a	20.44 N	156.58 W
Palapag	116	12.33 N	125.07 E
Palapye	156	22.37 S	27.06 E
Pālār ≏	122	12.28 N	80.10 E
Palasan Island I	116	14.52 N	122.03 E
Palas de Rei	34	42.52 N	7.52 W
Palāshdānga	126	23.24 N	87.22 E
Palāspol	126	22.43 N	89.05 E
Palasthali	126	23.51 N	87.03 E
Palata	66	41.53 N	14.47 E
Palatcy	86	49.09 N	83.43 E
Palatine	216	42.06 N	88.02 W
Palatine Bridge	210	42.55 N	74.35 W
Palatka, S.S.S.R.	74	60.06 N	150.54 E
Palatka, Fl., U.S.	192	29.38 N	81.38 W
Palau, It.	71	41.11 N	9.23 E
Palau, Méx.	196	27.54 N	101.26 W
Palau (Belau) □[2], Oc.	14	5.00 N	137.00 E
Palau (Belau) □[2], Oc.	175b	7.30 N	134.30 E
Palauig	116	15.26 N	119.54 E
Palaui Island I	116	18.33 N	122.08 E
Palau Islands II	175b	7.30 N	134.30 E
Palauk	110	13.16 N	98.38 E
Pal'avaam ≏	180	68.50 N	170.45 E
Pal'avaamskij chrebet ʎ	180	68.20 N	177.00 E
Palavas-les-Flots	62	43.32 N	3.56 E
Palaw	110	12.58 N	98.39 E
Palawai Basin ⊻[1]	229a	20.47 N	156.55 W
Palawan □[4]	116	10.00 N	118.50 E
Palawan I	116	9.30 N	118.30 E
Palawan Passage ʉ	116	10.00 N	118.00 E
Palayan	116	15.33 N	121.06 E
Pālayankottai	122	8.43 N	77.44 E
Palazzo Adriano	70	37.41 N	13.23 E
Palazzolo Acreide	70	37.04 N	14.54 E
Palazzolo dello Stella	64	45.48 N	13.05 E
Palazzolo sull'Oglio	62	45.36 N	9.53 E
Palazzolo Vercellese	62	45.11 N	8.14 E
Palazzo San Gervasio	68	40.56 N	16.00 E
Palazzuolo sul Senio	66	44.07 N	11.33 E
P'albong-san ∧	98	40.16 N	127.57 E
Palca, Bol.	248	16.34 S	67.59 W
Palca, Perú	248	11.21 S	75.31 W
Palcamayo	248	11.18 S	75.46 W
Pal'co	76	53.17 N	34.56 E
Paldi	224	48.48 N	123.51 W
Paldiski	76	59.20 N	24.06 E
Pāldor ∧	124	28.16 N	85.11 E
Palech	80	56.48 N	41.51 E
Palel	120	24.27 N	94.02 E
Paleleh	112	1.04 N	121.57 E
Palembang	112	2.55 S	104.45 E
Palena	66	41.59 N	14.08 E
Palena ≏	254	43.50 S	72.59 W
Palena, Lago (Lago General Vintter) ⊜	254	43.55 S	71.40 W
Palencia	34	42.01 N	4.32 W
Palen Lake ⊜	204	33.46 N	115.12 W
Palenque	232	17.31 N	91.58 W
Palenque ⊥	232	17.30 N	92.00 W
Palenque, Punta ›	238	18.14 N	70.09 W
Palenville	210	42.10 N	74.01 W
Paleparto, Monte ∧	68	39.28 N	16.34 E
Palermo, Col.	246	2.54 N	75.26 W
Palermo, It.	70	38.07 N	13.21 E
Palermo, Ca., U.S.	226	39.26 N	121.33 W
Palermo, Ur.	252	33.48 S	55.59 W
Palermo □[4]	70	37.49 N	13.35 E
Palermo ◆[8]	288	34.35 S	58.25 W
Palermo, Golfo di ᑕ	70	38.08 N	13.26 E
Palese, Aeroporto di ⊠	68	41.10 N	16.47 E
Palestina, Bra.	255	20.23 S	49.25 W
Palestina, Méx.	196	29.10 N	100.55 W
Palestine, Ar., U.S.	194	34.58 N	90.54 W
Palestine, Il., U.S.	194	39.00 N	87.36 W
Palestine, Oh., U.S.	218	40.03 N	84.45 W
Palestine, Tx., U.S.	222	31.45 N	95.37 W
Palestine □[9]	132	32.00 N	35.15 E
Palestine, Lake ⊜[1]	222	32.06 N	95.27 W
Palestrina	66	41.50 N	12.53 E
Paletwa	110	21.18 N	92.51 E
Palézieux	58	46.33 N	6.50 E
Palfau	61	47.42 N	14.48 E
Pālghāt	122	10.47 N	76.39 E
Palgrave, Mount ∧	162	23.22 S	115.58 E
Palgrave Point ›	156	20.45 S	13.20 E
Palhais	266c	38.37 N	9.03 W
Palhano	250	4.44 S	37.57 W
Palhano ≏	250	4.33 S	37.42 W

PORTUGUÊS

Nome	Página	Lat.°′	Long.°′ W = Oeste
Pāli, India	120	25.46 N	73.20 E
Pali, India	124	25.51 N	76.33 E
Paliano	66	41.48 N	13.03 E
Palikea ∧	229c	21.26 N	158.06 W
Palima	112	4.20 S	120.22 E
Palimanan	115a	6.42 S	108.26 E
Palimbang	116	6.12 N	124.12 E
Palimé	150	6.54 N	0.38 E
Palín	236	14.24 N	90.42 W
Palinges	32	46.33 N	4.13 E
Palinuro	68	40.02 N	15.17 E
Palinuro, Capo ›	68	40.02 N	15.16 E
Palisade, Co., U.S.	200	39.06 N	108.21 W
Palisade, Ne., U.S.	198	40.20 N	101.06 W
Palisades, Id., U.S.	202	43.21 N	111.13 W
Palisades, N.Y., U.S.	276	41.01 N	73.55 W
Palisades Amusement Park ♠	276	40.50 N	73.59 W
Palisades Interstate Park ♠	210	40.56 N	73.55 W
Palisades Park, Mi., U.S.	216	42.18 N	86.19 W
Palisades Park, N.J., U.S.	276	40.50 N	73.59 W
Palisades Reservoir ⊜[1]	202	43.15 N	111.05 W
Paliseul	56	49.54 N	5.08 E
Pālitāna	120	21.31 N	71.50 E
Palivere	76	58.59 N	23.52 E
Palizada	232	18.15 N	92.05 W
Palizzi	68	37.58 N	15.59 E
Paljakka ∧[2]	26	64.41 N	28.08 E
Pälkäne	26	61.20 N	24.16 E
Palk Bay ᑕ	122	9.30 N	79.15 E
Palkino, S.S.S.R.	76	57.32 N	28.01 E
Palkino, S.S.S.R.	80	58.15 N	42.56 E
Pālkonda	122	18.36 N	83.45 E
Pālkonda Range ʎ	122	14.05 N	79.05 E
Palk Strait ʉ	122	10.00 N	79.45 E
Palla Bianca (Weisskugel) ∧	64	46.48 N	10.44 E
Pallagorio	68	39.18 N	16.54 E
Pallamana	168b	35.02 S	139.12 E
Pallasca	248	8.15 S	78.01 W
Pallas Grean	48	52.33 N	8.22 W
Pallaskenry	48	52.39 N	8.52 W
Pallas-Ounastunturin Kansallispuisto ♠	24	68.06 N	24.00 E
Pallasovka	80	50.03 N	46.53 E
Pallastunturi ∧	24	68.06 N	24.00 E
Pallejà	266d	41.25 N	2.00 E
Pallës, Bishti i ›	38	41.24 N	19.24 E
Palling	182	54.21 N	125.55 W
Pallíni	267c	38.00 N	23.53 E
Pallinup ≏	162	34.29 S	118.54 E
Pallisa	154	1.10 N	33.42 E
Palliser, Cape ›	172	41.37 S	175.17 E
Palliser Bay ᑕ	172	41.25 S	175.05 E
Pallu	123	28.56 N	74.13 E
Palluau	32	46.48 N	1.37 W
Palma, Bra.	255	21.22 S	42.19 W
Palma, Moç.	154	10.46 S	40.29 E
P'al'ma, S.S.S.R.	24	62.26 N	35.53 E
Palma ≏	255	12.33 S	47.52 W
Palma, Badia de ᑕ	34	39.27 N	2.35 E
Palmácia	250	4.08 S	38.50 W
Palma del Río	34	37.42 N	5.17 W
Palma [de Mallorca]	34	39.34 N	2.39 E
Palma di Montechiaro	70	37.11 N	13.46 E
Palmaḥim	132	31.56 N	34.42 E
Palma Pegada	234	22.42 N	101.48 W
Palmar ≏	246	10.10 N	71.50 W
Palmar Camp	232	16.26 N	88.53 W
Palmar de Cariaco	286c	10.34 N	66.55 W
Palmar de Sepúlveda	232	25.43 N	107.55 W
Palmar de Varela	246	10.45 N	74.45 W
Palmarejo	240m	18.03 N	67.05 W
Palmares, Bra.	250	8.41 S	35.36 W
Palmares, C.R.	236	10.03 N	84.26 W
Palmares, C.R.	236	9.21 N	83.40 W
Palmares do Sul	252	30.16 S	50.31 W
Palmaria, Isola I	62	44.02 N	9.51 E
Palmarito	246	7.37 N	70.10 W
Palmarito [Tochapan]	234	18.54 N	97.37 W
Palmarola, Isola I	66	40.56 N	12.51 E
Palmar Sur	236	8.58 N	83.29 W
Palmas	252	26.30 S	52.00 W
Palmas, Canal de las ≊	288	34.36 S	58.18 W
Palmas, Golfo di ᑕ	71	39.02 N	8.31 E
Palmas, Ilha das I, Bra.	287a	23.02 S	43.12 W
Palmas, Ilha das I, Bra.	287a	23.04 S	43.31 W
Palmas Bellas	236	9.14 N	80.05 W
Palmas de Monte Alto	255	14.16 S	43.10 W
Palma Sola	220	27.31 N	82.38 W
Palma Soriano	240p	20.13 N	76.00 W
Palm Bay	220	28.02 N	80.35 W
Palm Beach, Austl.	170	33.36 S	151.19 E
Palm Beach, Austl.	171a	28.08 S	153.28 E
Palm Beach, Fl., U.S.	220	26.42 N	80.02 W
Palm Beach □[6]	220	26.38 N	80.27 W
Palm Beach Gardens	220	26.49 N	80.06 W
Palm Beach International Airport ⊠	220	26.41 N	80.05 W
Palm City	220	27.09 N	80.16 W
Palmdale, Ca., U.S.	228	34.34 N	118.06 W
Palmdale, Fl., U.S.	220	26.56 N	81.18 W
Palmdale, Pa., U.S.	208	40.18 N	76.37 W
Palmdale, Lake ⊜[1]	228	34.33 N	118.07 W
Palm Desert	204	33.43 N	116.23 W
Palmeira, Bra.	252	25.25 S	50.00 W
Palmeira, C.V.	150a	16.46 N	22.59 W
Palmeira das Missões	252	27.55 S	53.17 W
Palmeira d'Oeste	255	20.23 S	50.47 W
Palmeira dos Indios	250	9.25 S	36.37 W
Palmeirais	250	5.58 S	43.04 W
Palmeiral	256	21.38 S	46.31 W
Palmeirante	250	7.49 S	48.09 W
Palmeiras	255	12.31 S	41.34 W
Palmeiras ≏, Bra.	250	12.22 S	47.08 W
Palmeiras ≏, Bra.	255	15.25 S	51.10 W
Palmeirina	250	8.56 S	36.17 W
Palmeirinhas, Ponta das ›	152	9.05 S	13.00 E
Palmela ≏	256	21.38 S	45.23 W
Palmelo	255	17.20 S	48.27 W
Palmer, Austl.	168b	34.51 S	139.10 E
Palmer, P.R.	240m	18.22 N	65.46 W
Palmer, Ak., U.S.	180	61.36 N	149.07 W
Palmer, Il., U.S.	219	39.27 N	89.24 W
Palmer, Ma., U.S.	207	42.09 N	72.19 W
Palmer, Ms., U.S.	194	31.16 N	89.15 W
Palmer, Ne., U.S.	198	41.13 N	98.15 W
Palmer, Tn., U.S.	194	35.21 N	85.34 W
Palmer, Tx., U.S.	222	32.26 N	96.40 W
Palmer ≏, Austl.	162	24.46 S	133.25 E
Palmer ≏, Austl.	164	15.34 S	142.26 E
Palmer ≏, P.Q., Can.	206	46.19 N	71.27 W
Palmer ʊ[3]	9	64.46 S	64.03 W
Palmerah ◆[8]	269e	6.12 S	106.47 E
Palmer Heights	208	40.42 N	75.16 W
Palmer Lake	200	38.52 N	104.48 W
Palmer Land ◆[1]	9	71.30 S	65.00 W
Palmer Mill Brook ≏	283	41.58 N	70.52 W
Palmer Park	284c	38.55 N	76.52 W
Palmer Park ♠	281	42.26 N	83.07 W
Palmerston, On., Can.	212	43.50 N	80.51 W
Palmerston, N.Z.	172	45.29 S	170.43 E
Palmerston I[1]	14	18.04 S	163.10 W
Palmerston, Cape ›	166	21.32 S	149.29 E
Palmerston Lake ⊜	212	45.01 N	76.50 W
Palmerston North	172	40.21 S	175.37 E
Palmerton	210	40.48 N	75.36 W
Palmerville	164	15.59 S	144.05 E
Palmetto, Fl., U.S.	220	27.31 N	82.34 W
Palmetto, Ga., U.S.	192	33.31 N	84.40 W
Palmetto, La., U.S.	194	30.43 N	91.54 W
Palmford	158	27.11 S	29.42 E
Palm Harbor	220	28.04 N	82.45 W
Palmi	68	38.21 N	15.51 E
Palminópolis	255	16.47 S	50.08 W
Palmira, Arg.	252	33.03 S	68.34 W
Palmira, Col.	246	3.32 N	76.16 W
Palmira, Cuba	240p	22.14 N	80.23 W
Palmira, Ec.	246	2.05 S	78.43 W
Palmira, Méx.	196	28.58 N	100.47 W
Palmitas	252	33.31 S	57.49 W
Palmitos	252	27.05 S	53.08 W
Palmnicken → Jantarnyj	76	54.52 N	19.57 E
Palmoli	66	41.56 N	14.32 E
Palm River	220	27.56 N	82.23 W
Palms ◆[8]	280	34.02 N	118.25 W
Palm Shores	220	28.11 N	80.35 W
Palm Springs, Ca., U.S.	204	33.49 N	116.32 W
Palm Springs, Fl., U.S.	220	26.39 N	80.06 W
Palmyra → Tudmur, Sūrīy.	130	34.33 N	38.17 E
Palmyra, Il., U.S.	219	39.26 N	89.59 W
Palmyra, In., U.S.	218	38.24 N	86.06 W
Palmyra, Mi., U.S.	216	41.52 N	83.56 W
Palmyra, Mo., U.S.	219	39.47 N	91.31 W
Palmyra, N.J., U.S.	208	40.00 N	75.01 W
Palmyra, N.Y., U.S.	210	43.03 N	77.14 W
Palmyra, Oh., U.S.	214	41.07 N	81.02 W
Palmyra, Pa., U.S.	208	40.18 N	76.35 W
Palmyra, Va., U.S.	192	37.51 N	78.15 W
Palmyra, Wi., U.S.	216	42.52 N	88.35 W
Palmyra ⊥	130	34.33 N	38.17 E
Palmyra Atoll I[1]	14	5.52 N	162.06 W
Palo, It.	66	41.56 N	12.06 E
Palo, Pil.	116	11.10 N	124.59 E
Palo Alto, Méx.	196	26.32 N	99.45 W
Palo Alto, Ca., U.S.	226	37.26 N	122.08 W
Palo Alto, Pa., U.S.	208	40.41 N	76.11 W
Palo Alto Airport ⊠	282	37.28 N	122.07 W
Palo Blanco, Méx.	196	26.45 N	101.32 W
Palo Blanco, P.R.	240m	18.26 N	66.39 W
Palo Blanco Creek ≏	196	27.10 N	97.52 W
Paločka	86	58.25 N	84.32 E
Palo del Colle	68	41.03 N	16.42 E
Palo Duro Canyon State Park ♠	196	34.55 N	101.42 W
Palo Duro Creek ≏, U.S.	196	36.39 N	100.58 W
Palo Duro Creek ≏, Tx., U.S.	196	35.00 N	101.55 W
Paloe, Pulau I	115b	8.20 S	121.43 E
Paloemeu ≏	250	3.21 N	55.26 W
Palo Flechado Pass)(	200	36.25 N	105.20 W
Paloh, Indon.	112	1.43 N	109.18 E
Paloh, Malay.	112	2.25 N	111.15 E
Paloh, Malay.	114	2.11 N	103.12 E
Paloich, Sūd.	140	6.45 N	30.08 E
Paloich, Sūd.	140	10.28 N	32.32 E
Palojoensuu	24	68.17 N	23.05 E
Paloma Creek ≏	226	36.15 N	121.26 W
Palomares	286d	12.00 S	77.01 W
Palomares Creek ≏	282	37.42 N	122.02 W
Palomar Mountain ∧	204	33.22 N	116.50 W
Palomar Mountain State Park ♠	228	33.19 N	116.53 W
Palomar Park	282	37.29 N	122.16 W
Palomas, Méx.	196	28.43 N	103.45 W
Palomas, Méx.	232	31.44 N	107.37 W
Palomas, Mesa de ∧	232	28.46 N	103.41 W
Palombara Sabina	66	42.04 N	12.46 E
Palominos, Isla I	240m	18.21 N	65.34 W
Palomonte	68	40.40 N	15.17 E
Palompon	116	11.03 N	124.23 E
Palo Negro	246	10.11 N	67.33 W
Palo Pinto	196	32.46 N	98.18 W
Palo Pinto Reservoir ⊜[1]	196	32.38 N	98.18 W
Palopo	112	3.00 S	120.12 E
Palora ≏	246	1.51 S	77.49 W
Palos	240p	22.48 N	81.44 W
Palos → Palos de la Frontera	34	37.14 N	6.53 W
Palos, Cabo de ›	34	37.38 N	0.41 W
Palo Santo	252	25.34 S	59.21 W
Palos de la Frontera	34	37.14 N	6.53 W
Palo Seco	240m	18.28 N	66.09 W
Palos Gardens	278	41.40 N	87.48 W
Palos Heights	216	41.40 N	87.47 W
Palos Hills	278	41.41 N	87.49 W
Palos Hills ♠	278	41.42 N	87.53 W
Palos Park	278	41.40 N	87.49 W
Palos Verdes Estates	228	33.48 N	118.23 W
Palos Verdes Hills ʎ[2]	280	33.46 N	118.21 W
Palos Verdes Point ›	228	33.47 N	118.26 W
Palotai-sziget I	264c	47.35 N	19.05 E
Paloúkia	267c	37.58 N	23.31 E
Palouse	202	46.54 N	117.04 W
Palouse ≏	202	46.35 N	118.13 W
Palouse, South Fork ≏	202	46.53 N	117.22 W
Palo Verde	204	33.25 N	114.43 W
P'alovskoje vodochranilišče ⊜[1]	82	56.03 N	37.40 E
Palpa	248	14.32 S	75.11 W
Palpalá	252	24.15 S	65.12 W
Pålsboda	40	59.04 N	15.20 E
Pālsit	126	23.12 N	88.03 E
Paltamo	26	64.25 N	27.50 E
Paltenbach ≏	61	47.34 N	14.20 E
Palu, Indon.	112	0.53 S	119.53 E
Palu, Tür.	130	38.42 N	39.57 E
Palu ≏	112	0.52 S	119.51 E
Palu, Teluk ᑕ	112	0.40 S	119.45 E
Paluan	116	13.25 N	120.28 E
Paluan Bay ᑕ	116	13.23 N	120.25 E
Palù del Fersina	64	46.08 N	11.21 E
Paludi	68	39.32 N	16.41 E
Paluga	24	65.16 N	45.11 E
Paluke	150	5.02 N	8.06 W
Paluška ∧	61	48.45 N	14.24 E
Paluxy ≏	196	32.15 N	97.43 W
Paluzza	64	46.32 N	13.01 E
Palvantaš	85	40.34 N	72.12 E
Palvār, Kūh-e ∧	128	30.04 N	57.28 E
Palvart	128	38.11 N	64.34 E
Palwal	124	28.09 N	77.20 E
Pal-Waukee Airport ⊠	278	42.07 N	87.54 W
Pam	175f	20.16 S	164.19 E
Pama	150	11.15 N	0.42 E
Pama ≏	152	4.23 N	18.27 E
Pamaluan	112	1.04 S	116.39 E
Pamanukan	115a	6.16 S	107.49 E
Pamarayan	115a	6.16 S	106.17 E
Pam'ati 13 Borcov	86	56.13 N	92.20 E
Pam'atnaja	86	56.01 N	65.42 E
Pam'at' Parižskoj Kommuny	80	56.06 N	44.31 E
Pāmban Channel ʉ	122	9.17 N	79.10 E
Pāmban Island I	122	9.15 N	79.20 E
Pambeguwa	150	10.40 N	8.19 E
Pambuhan	116	13.59 N	123.05 E
Pambuhan ≏	116	12.34 N	124.55 E
Pambujan	116	12.34 N	124.56 E
Pamekasan	115a	7.10 S	113.28 E
Pamel	50	50.50 N	4.04 E
Pamenang	112	2.07 S	102.31 E
Pameungpeuk	115a	7.38 S	107.43 E
Pamiers	32	43.07 N	1.36 E
Pamir ʎ	118	38.00 N	73.00 E
Pamlico ≏	192	35.20 N	76.30 W
Pamlico Sound ʉ	192	35.20 N	75.55 W
Pamotan	115a	6.46 S	111.29 E
Pampa	196	35.32 N	100.57 W
Pampā ≏	255	17.43 S	40.36 W
Pampa ◆[1]	252	35.00 S	63.00 W
Pampa Almirón	252	26.42 S	59.08 W
Pampacolca	248	15.43 S	72.33 W
Pampa del Castillo	254	45.48 S	68.05 W
Pampa del Chañar	252	30.11 S	68.43 W
Pampa del Indio	252	26.02 S	59.55 W
Pampa del Infierno	252	26.31 S	61.10 W
Pampa de los Guanacos	252	26.14 S	61.51 W
Pampa Grande	248	18.05 S	64.06 W
Pampana ≏	150	8.24 N	12.00 W
Pampanga □[4]	116	15.05 N	120.40 E
Pampanga ≏	116	14.47 N	120.39 E
Pampanua	112	4.14 S	120.08 E
Pamparato	62	44.17 N	7.55 E
Pampas	248	12.24 S	74.54 W
Pampas ≏	248	13.23 S	73.15 W
Pampeluna → Pamplona	34	42.49 N	1.38 W
Pamphylia □[9]	130	37.00 N	31.00 E
Pamplico	192	33.59 N	79.34 W
Pamplona, Col.	246	7.23 N	72.39 W
Pamplona, Esp.	34	42.49 N	1.38 W
Pampoenpoort	158	31.03 S	22.40 E
Pampow	54	53.32 N	14.15 E
Pāmpur	123	34.01 N	74.56 E
Pamukkale (Hierapolis) ⊥	130	37.58 N	29.19 E
Pamukova	130	40.31 N	30.09 E
Pamunkey ≏	208	37.32 N	76.48 W
Pana	219	39.23 N	89.04 W
Panabá	232	21.17 N	88.16 W
Panabo	116	7.19 N	125.42 E
Panaca	204	37.47 N	114.23 W
Panacachi	248	18.23 S	66.21 W
Panacan	116	9.16 N	118.25 E
Panacea	192	30.02 N	84.23 W
Panache, Lake ⊜	190	46.15 N	81.20 W
Panadura	122	6.43 N	79.54 E
Panaeati Island I	164	10.40 S	152.20 E
Panāgar	124	23.18 N	79.59 E
Panagjurište	38	42.30 N	24.11 E
Panagtaran Point ›	116	9.41 N	118.45 E
Panahan	112	1.44 S	111.49 E
Panaitan, Pulau I	115a	6.36 S	105.12 E
Panaitan, Selat ʉ	115a	6.40 S	105.16 E
Panaji (Panjim)	122	15.29 N	73.50 E
Pānākua	272b	22.23 N	88.21 E
Panamá, Bra.	255	18.11 S	49.21 W
Panamá, Pan.	236	8.58 N	79.32 W
Panama, Il., U.S.	219	39.02 N	89.32 W
Panama, N.Y., U.S.	214	42.04 N	79.29 W
Panama, Ok., U.S.	194	35.10 N	94.40 W
Panamá □[4]	236	8.48 N	79.55 W
Panama (Panamá) □[1], N.A.	230	9.00 N	80.00 W
Panama (Panamá) □[1], N.A.	246	9.00 N	80.00 W
Panamá, Bahía de ᑕ	246	8.50 N	79.20 W
Panamá, Golfo de ᑕ	246	8.00 N	79.30 W
Panamá, Istmo de ⫠[3]	246	9.00 N	80.00 W
Panama Basin ✣[1]	18	5.00 N	83.30 W
Panama Canal ≊	236	9.20 N	79.55 W
Panama City	194	30.09 N	85.39 W
Panamá La Vieja ⊥	236	9.00 N	79.29 W
Panambi	252	28.18 S	53.30 W
Panamint Range ʎ	204	36.30 N	117.20 W
Panamint Valley V	204	36.15 N	117.20 W
Pan'an	100	29.06 N	120.27 E
Panao, Perú	248	9.49 S	76.00 W
Pan'ao, Zhg.	107	30.09 N	103.37 E
Panaon Island I	116	10.03 N	125.13 E
Panarea, Isola I	70	38.38 N	15.04 E
Panaro ≏	64	44.55 N	11.25 E
Panarukan	115a	7.42 S	113.56 E
Panasoffkee, Lake ⊜	220	28.47 N	82.08 W
Panatinane Island I	164	11.15 S	153.10 E
Panay I	116	11.15 N	122.30 E
Panay ≏	116	11.35 N	122.43 E
Panay Gulf ᑕ	116	10.15 N	122.15 E
Panayía	38	39.56 N	25.20 E
Panay Island I	116	13.58 N	124.20 E
Pancalieri	62	44.50 N	7.35 E
Pancas	266c	38.48 N	8.55 W
Pančevo, Jugo.	38	44.52 N	20.39 E
Pančevo, S.S.S.R.	78	48.44 N	31.51 E
Panchagarh	124	26.20 N	88.34 E
Pānchāl	126	23.15 N	87.18 E
Pānchet Hill ∧[2]	126	23.37 N	86.47 E
Pānchet Reservoir ⊜[1]	126	23.40 N	86.45 E
Pānchghara	272b	22.44 N	88.16 E
Panchgram	126	24.12 N	88.01 E
Panch'iao	269d	25.01 N	121.27 E
Panchla	126	22.32 N	88.09 E
Panchor	114	2.10 N	102.43 E
Pancho Simón, Arroyo ≏	286b	23.03 N	82.21 W
Pānchur	272b	22.32 N	88.16 E
Pānchuria	272b	22.33 N	88.29 E
Panciu	38	45.55 N	27.05 E
Panda	156	24.02 S	34.45 E
Pandakan	115a	7.39 S	112.41 E
Pandamatenga	156	18.35 S	25.42 E
Pandan, Malay.	112	3.09 N	113.22 E
Pandan, Pil.	116	11.43 N	122.06 E
Pandan, Pil.	116	14.03 N	124.10 E
Pandan, Selat ʉ	271c	1.15 N	103.44 E
Pandanan Island I	116	8.17 N	117.13 E
Pandan Bay ᑕ	116	11.43 N	122.04 E
Pandan Reservoir ⊜[1]	271c	1.19 N	103.44 E
Pandaria	124	22.14 N	81.25 E
Pandarochan Bay ᑕ	116	12.12 N	121.10 E
Pandasan	112	6.28 N	116.32 E
Pan de Azúcar	252	34.48 S	55.14 W
Pan de Azucar Island I	116	11.17 N	123.10 E
Pandegelang	115a	6.18 S	106.06 E
Pandělys	76	56.01 N	25.13 E
Pāndharkawada	122	20.01 N	78.32 E
Pandharpur	122	17.40 N	75.20 E
Pāndhurna	122	21.36 N	78.31 E
Pandian	98	36.38 N	116.27 E
Pandino	62	45.24 N	9.33 E
Pando	252	34.43 S	55.57 W
Pando □[5]	248	11.20 S	67.40 W
Pando, Cerro ∧	236	8.55 N	82.43 W
Pandora	216	40.56 N	83.57 W
Pandu	152	5.01 N	19.16 E
Pandua, India	124	25.08 N	88.10 E
Pāndua, India	126	23.05 N	88.17 E
P'andž (Panj) ≏	120	37.06 N	68.20 E
Panebianco ≏	70	37.24 N	15.04 E
Panelas	250	8.40 S	36.01 W
Paneveggio	64	46.18 N	11.44 E
Panevėžys	76	55.44 N	24.21 E
Panfang	100	27.54 N	115.57 E
Panfilov	86	44.10 N	80.01 E
Panfilovo	80	50.26 N	42.55 E
Pāng ≏	110	20.58 N	98.30 E
Panga	154	1.51 N	26.25 E
Pangala	152	3.19 S	14.34 E
Pangalanes, Canal des ≊	157b	22.40 S	47.50 E
Pangandaran	115a	7.41 S	108.39 E
Pangani	154	5.26 S	38.58 E
Pangani ≏	154	5.26 S	38.58 E
Panganiran	116	13.02 N	123.26 E
Pangantocan	116	7.50 N	124.49 E
Panganuran	116	7.24 N	122.03 E
Pangasinan □[4]	116	16.00 N	120.20 E
Pangbourne	42	51.29 N	1.05 W
Pangburn	194	35.25 N	91.50 W
Pange	56	49.05 N	6.22 E
Pangfou → Bengbu	100	32.58 N	117.24 E
Pangga, Tanjung ›	115b	8.55 S	116.02 E
Panggezhuang, Zhg.	105	39.38 N	116.19 E
Panggezhuang, Zhg.	105	39.16 N	115.49 E
Panghkam	110	23.53 N	97.37 E
Pangi	154	3.11 S	26.38 E
Pangian	112	1.06 S	119.24 E
Pangjiabu	105	40.36 N	115.27 E
Pangkah	115a	6.58 S	109.10 E
Pangkajene	112	4.50 S	119.32 E
Pangkalanbrandan	114	4.01 N	98.17 E
Pangkalanbuun	112	2.41 S	111.37 E
Pangkalansusu	114	4.06 N	98.14 E
Pangkalaseang, Tanjung ›	112	0.42 S	123.26 E
Pangkalpinang	112	2.08 S	106.08 E
Pangkatan	114	2.09 N	100.00 E
Pangke	114	1.01 N	103.10 E
Pangkor, Pulau I	114	4.13 N	100.33 E
Panglao	116	9.35 N	123.45 E
Panglao Island I	116	9.35 N	123.48 E
Pangman	184	49.39 N	104.38 W
Pangnirtung	176	66.08 N	65.44 W
Pango Aluquém	152	8.43 S	14.27 E
Pangŏjin	98	35.29 N	129.26 E
Pangong Tso ⊜	120	33.45 N	78.43 E
Pangp'u → Bengbu	100	32.58 N	117.24 E
Pāngsa	126	23.47 N	89.25 E
Pangtara	110	20.57 N	96.40 E
Pangubatan	116	6.57 N	125.47 E
Panguil Bay ᑕ	116	8.01 N	123.43 E
Panguipulli	254	39.38 S	72.20 W
Panguipulli, Lago ⊜	254	39.43 S	72.13 W
Panguiranan	116	12.04 N	123.19 E
Panguitch	200	37.49 N	112.26 W
Pangururan	114	2.37 N	98.42 E
Pangutaran	116	6.18 N	120.35 E
Pangutaran Group II	116	6.15 N	120.30 E
Pangutaran Island I	116	6.18 N	120.34 E
Pangutaran Passage ʉ	116	6.13 N	120.30 E
Pangzidian	107	30.38 N	105.04 E
Panhandle	196	35.20 N	101.22 W
Paniai, Danau ⊜	164	3.50 S	136.15 E
Pania-Mutombo	152	5.11 S	23.51 E
Paniau ∧	229b	21.57 N	160.05 W
Panié, Mont ∧	175f	20.36 S	164.46 E
Pānihāti	126	22.42 N	88.22 E
Panika	80	50.59 N	50.11 E
Panindícuaro	234	19.59 N	101.46 W
Panino, S.S.S.R.	76	56.25 N	34.34 E
Panino, S.S.S.R.	78	51.38 N	40.08 E
Panino-Nesterovo	82	55.23 N	38.11 E
Panīpāt	124	29.23 N	76.58 E
Paniqui	116	15.40 N	120.35 E
Panissières	62	45.47 N	4.20 E
Panitan	116	11.28 N	122.46 E
Panitian	116	9.05 N	118.05 E
Panj (P'andž) ≏	120	37.06 N	68.20 E
Panjāb	120	34.22 N	67.01 E
Panjang	115a	5.28 S	105.18 E
Panjang, Pulau I	112	2.44 N	108.55 E
Panjang, Selat ʉ	114	0.40 N	102.30 E
Panje	272c	18.54 N	72.57 E
Panjgūr	128	26.58 N	64.06 E
Panji	114	2.34 N	97.50 E
Panjiapie	100	32.54 N	120.42 E
Panjiatun	104	41.04 N	121.38 E
Panjim → Panaji	122	15.29 N	73.50 E
Pānjkora ≏	123	34.39 N	71.44 E
Panjnad ≏	123	28.57 N	70.30 E
Panjpāi	120	29.55 N	66.30 E
Panjshār ≏	120	34.38 N	69.42 E
Pankakoski	26	63.19 N	30.09 E
Panke ≏	264a	52.32 N	13.22 E
Panker	54	54.20 N	10.34 E
Pānkhāli	126	22.37 N	89.31 E
Pankof, Cape ›	180	54.40 N	163.04 W
Pankow ◆[8]	54	52.34 N	13.25 E
Pankratovo	76	59.10 N	43.30 E
Pankshin	150	9.20 N	9.24 E
Panlong, Zhg.	100	25.52 N	114.52 E
Panlong, Zhg.	106	31.58 N	121.35 E
Panlong, Zhg.	106	31.11 N	121.16 E
Panlong (Lo) ≏	110	21.18 N	105.25 E
Panlongzhen	107	29.31 N	105.17 E
P'anmunjŏm	98	37.57 N	126.40 E
Panna	124	24.43 N	80.12 E
Pannawonica	162	21.44 S	116.22 E
Panni	68	41.13 N	15.16 E
Panningen	52	51.20 N	5.59 E
Pannonhalma ʊ[1]	30	47.28 N	17.50 E
Panoche Creek ≏	226	36.44 N	120.31 W
Panola	194	31.58 N	86.23 W
Panola □[6]	222	32.07 N	94.30 W
Páno Lévkara	130	34.52 N	33.18 E
Panopah	112	1.56 S	111.11 E
Páno Panayiá	130	34.55 N	32.38 E
Páno Plátres	130	34.53 N	32.52 E
Panora	198	41.41 N	94.21 W
Panorama	255	21.21 S	51.51 W
Pánormos	38	37.38 N	25.02 E
Panovo, S.S.S.R.	24	59.48 N	46.27 E
Panovo, S.S.S.R.	88	58.58 N	101.58 E
P'anp'yŏng-ni	98	40.28 N	125.49 E
Panruti	122	11.46 N	79.33 E
Pansfelde	54	51.39 N	11.16 E
Panshan	104	41.12 N	122.04 E
Panshanger Aerodrome ⊠	260	51.48 N	0.08 W
Pansik, Rápido ʟ	236	14.30 N	85.15 W
Pansionat	265b	55.59 N	37.41 E
Pānskura	126	22.25 N	87.42 E
Pantabañgan	116	15.50 N	121.09 E
Pantajevka	78	48.41 N	32.53 E
Pantalica, Necropoli di ⊥	70	37.08 N	15.01 E
Pantanaw	110	16.59 N	95.28 E
Pântano	256	22.23 S	46.01 W
Pântano, Ribeirão do ≏	256	22.15 S	45.59 W
Pantar, Pulau I	112	8.25 S	124.07 E
Pantelejmonovka	83	48.12 N	37.59 E
Pantelleria	70	36.50 N	11.57 E
Pantelleria, Isola di I	70	36.47 N	12.00 E
Panteón Nacional ⊥	286c	10.31 N	66.55 W
Pantepec ≏	234	20.56 N	97.44 W
Pantha	110	23.49 N	94.33 E
Pantheon ⊥	267a	41.55 N	12.29 E
Panther Creek ≏, Id., U.S.	202	45.19 N	114.24 W
Panther Creek ≏, Ky., U.S.	194	37.45 N	87.19 W
Panther Creek, South Fork ≏	194	37.42 N	87.05 W
Panther Lake	210	43.19 N	75.54 W
Pantin	50	48.54 N	2.24 E
Pantitlán ◆[8]	286a	19.25 N	99.05 W
Panto, Tanjung ›	115a	6.51 S	105.54 E
Panton, Mount ∧[2]	162	17.21 S	129.13 E
Pantonlabu	114	5.08 N	97.28 E
Pantry Brook ≏	283	42.24 N	71.22 W
Panu	152	3.48 S	19.07 E
Pánuco	234	22.03 N	98.10 W
Pánuco ≏	234	22.16 N	97.47 W
Panuke Lake ⊜	186	44.48 N	64.07 W
Panukulan	116	14.56 N	121.49 E
Pānuria	126	23.49 N	86.58 E
Pan'utino	78	48.56 N	36.17 E
Panvel	122	18.59 N	73.06 E
Panvel ≏	272c	19.01 N	73.04 W
Panvel Creek ≏	272c	18.59 N	73.00 E
Panwāri	124	25.27 N	79.29 E
Panxi	106	30.35 N	119.20 E
Panxian	102	25.50 N	104.36 E
Panxidu	98	35.39 N	115.52 E
Panyabungan	114	0.51 N	99.33 E
Panyam	150	9.25 N	9.13 E
Panyang	140	10.04 N	29.58 E
Panyčevo	86	57.05 N	81.49 E
Panyu	100	22.57 N	113.20 E
Panzerstausee ⊜[1]	263	51.11 N	7.16 E

Symbol	English	Deutsch	Español	Français	Português
≏	River	Fluß	Río	Rivière	Rio
≊	Canal	Kanal	Canal	Canal	Canal
ʟ	Waterfall, Rapids	Wasserfall, Stromschnellen	Cascada, Rápidos	Chute d'eau, Rapides	Cascata, Rápidos
ʉ	Strait	Meeresstraße	Estrecho	Détroit	Estreito
ᑕ	Bay, Gulf	Bucht, Golf	Bahía, Golfo	Baie, Golfe	Baía, Golfo
⊜	Lake, Lakes	See, Seen	Lago, Lagos	Lac, Lacs	Lago, Lagos
≣	Swamp	Sumpf	Pantano	Marais	Pântano
⊓	Ice Features, Glacier	Eis- und Gletscherformen	Accidentes Glaciales	Formes glaciaires	Acidentes glaciares
⍑	Other Hydrographic Features	Andere Hydrographische Objekte	Otros Elementos Hidrográficos	Autres données hydrographiques	Outros acidentes hidrográficos
✣	Submarine Features	Untermeerische Objekte	Accidentes Submarinos	Formes de relief sous-marin	Acidentes submarinos
□	Political Unit	Politische Einheit	Unidad Politica	Entité politique	Unidade política
ʊ	Cultural Institution	Kulturelle Institution	Institución Cultural	Institution culturelle	Instituição cultural
⊥	Historical Site	Historische Stätte	Sitio Histórico	Site historique	Sitio histórico
♠	Recreational Site	Erholungs- und Ferienort	Sitio de Recreo	Centre de loisirs	Area de Lazer
⊠	Airport	Flughafen	Aeropuerto	Aéroport	Aeroporto
▪	Military Installation	Militäranlage	Instalación Militar	Installation militaire	Instalação militar
◆	Miscellaneous	Verschiedenes	Misceláneo	Divers	Diversos

Name	Page	Lat.°′	Long.°′
Panzhuang	105	39.20 N	117.28 E
Panzi	152	7.13 S	17.58 E
Panzós	236	15.24 N	89.40 W
Pao ≏, Thai	110	16.13 N	103.43 E
Pao ≏, Ven.	246	8.33 N	68.01 W
Pao ≏, Ven.	246	8.06 N	64.17 W
Paochi → Baoji	102	34.23 N	107.09 E
Pão de Açúcar	250	9.45 S	37.26 W
Pão de Açúcar (Sugar Loaf) ∧	287a	22.57 S	43.09 W
Paoki → Baoji	102	34.23 N	107.09 E
Paola, It.	68	39.22 N	16.03 E
Paola, Ks., U.S.	198	38.34 N	94.52 W
Paoli, In., U.S.	218	38.33 N	86.28 W
Paoli, Pa., U.S.	208	40.02 N	75.28 W
Paoli, Wi., U.S.	216	42.56 N	89.32 W
Paonia	200	38.52 N	107.35 W
Pāonta Sāhib	124	30.27 N	77.37 E
Paopao	174s	17.31 S	149.49 W
Paoshenmiao	98	41.12 N	118.17 E
Paotai Yingzi	98	41.48 N	115.12 E
Paoting → Baoding	105	38.52 N	115.29 E
Paotow → Baotou	102	40.40 N	109.59 E
Paoua	152	7.15 N	16.26 E
Paoying → Baoying	100	33.16 N	119.20 E
P'aozero, ozero ⊜	24	66.05 N	30.58 E
Paozi	104	42.13 N	122.19 E
Pap	85	40.53 N	71.07 E
Pápa	30	47.19 N	17.28 E
Papa, Sound of ʯ	46a	60.18 N	1.41 W
Papagaio	250	6.01 S	45.21 W
Papagaio ≏	246	1.53 S	62.35 W
Papagayo ≏	234	16.46 N	99.43 W
Papagayo, Golfo de c	236	10.42 N	85.50 W
Papago Indian Reservation ◆[4]	200	32.20 N	112.00 W
Papaikou	229d	19.47 N	155.05 W
Papakating Creek ≏	276	41.11 N	74.38 W
Papakura	172	37.04 S	174.57 E
Papalia	112	5.58 S	124.01 E
Papaloapan ≏	234	18.42 N	95.38 W
Papanoa	234	17.21 N	101.02 W
Papantla [de Olarte]	234	20.27 N	97.19 W
Papar, Indon.	115a	7.41 S	112.04 E
Papar, Malay.	112	5.44 N	115.56 E
Papara, Poly. fr.	174s	17.44 S	149.21 W
Papara, Sol.Is.	175e	7.02 S	156.48 E
Paparoa	172	36.06 S	174.14 E
Paparoa National Park ♠	172	42.05 S	171.25 E
Paparoa Range ⋏	172	42.00 S	171.35 E
Papasidero	68	39.52 N	15.54 E
Papa Stour I	46a	60.20 N	1.42 W
Papatoetoe	172	36.58 S	174.52 E
Papawai Point ≻	229a	20.47 N	156.33 W
Papa Westray I	46	59.21 N	2.54 W
Papayacu, Lago ⊜	248	5.03 S	76.25 W
Papeari	174s	17.45 S	149.21 W
Papeete	174s	17.32 S	149.34 W
Papelón	286c	10.27 N	66.47 W
Papenburg	52	53.05 N	7.23 E
Papendrecht	52	51.50 N	4.40 E
Papenoo	174s	17.30 S	149.25 W
Papenoo ≏	174s	17.30 S	149.25 W
Papetoai	174s	17.29 S	149.52 W
Papey I	24a	64.37 N	14.11 W
Paphlagonia □[9]	130	41.10 N	32.45 E
Paphos → Néa Páfos	130	34.45 N	32.25 E
Papigochic ≏	232	29.09 N	109.40 W
Papilė	76	56.09 N	22.48 E
Papillion	198	41.09 N	96.02 W
Papineau	216	40.58 N	87.43 W
Papineau □[6]	206	45.50 N	75.00 W
Papineau, Lac ⊜	206	45.48 N	74.46 W
Papineau Creek ≏	212	45.13 N	77.43 W
Papineau-Labelle, Réserve ♠	188	45.55 N	75.20 W
Papineau Lake ⊜	212	45.20 N	77.50 W
Papineauville	206	45.37 N	75.01 W
Paposo	252	25.01 S	70.28 W
Papouasie Nouvelle-Guinée → Papua New Guinea □[1]	164	6.00 S	150.00 E
Papozze	64	44.59 N	12.02 E
Pappenheim, B.R.D.	56	48.56 N	10.58 E
Pappenheim, D.D.R.	54	50.47 N	10.27 E
Paps of Jura ∧	46	55.55 N	6.00 W
Papua, Gulf of c	164	8.30 S	145.00 E
Papua Neuguinea → Papua New Guinea □[1]	164	6.00 S	150.00 E
Papua New Guinea □[1]	164	6.00 S	147.00 E
Papuasia Nueva Guinea → Papua New Guinea □[1]	164	6.00 S	150.00 E
Papudo	252	32.31 S	71.27 W
Papulovo	24	60.34 N	48.00 E
Papun	110	18.04 N	97.27 E
Papunava ≏	246	2.09 N	70.32 W
Papunya	162	23.16 S	131.54 E
Papurí ≏	246	0.36 N	69.11 W
Paquequer ≏	256	22.12 S	42.54 W
Paquequer, Serra do ⋏	256	22.12 S	42.48 W
Paquequer Pequeno	256	22.20 S	43.02 W
Paquera	236	9.50 N	84.56 W
Paquetá, Ilha de I	287a	22.46 S	43.06 W
Paquica, Cabo ≻	252	21.54 S	70.12 W
Par	42	50.21 N	4.43 W
Pará → Belém	250	1.27 S	48.29 W
Pará □[3]	250	4.00 S	53.00 W
Para □[5]	250	5.30 N	55.15 W
Pará ≏, Bra.	250	1.30 S	48.55 W
Pará ≏, Bra.	255	19.13 S	45.07 W
Para ≏, S.S.S.R.	80	54.23 N	40.52 E
Pará, Ilha do I	250	0.18 S	51.15 W
Para, Pulau I	112	3.05 N	125.30 E
Parabel'	86	58.43 N	81.31 E
Parabel' ≏	86	58.44 N	81.35 E
Parabiago	62	45.33 N	8.57 E
Parabita	68	40.03 N	18.08 E
Paraburdoo	162	23.14 S	117.48 E
Paracale	116	14.17 N	122.48 E
Paracambi	256	22.37 S	43.43 W
Paracari ≏	250	4.36 S	57.47 W
Paracas, Bahía de c	248	13.50 S	76.17 W
Paracas, Península ≻[1]	248	13.48 S	76.24 W
Paracatu	255	17.13 S	46.52 W
Paracatu ≏, Bra.	255	16.30 S	45.04 W
Paracatu ≏, Bra.	255	16.35 S	45.06 W
Paracel Islands → Xisha Qundao II	108	16.30 N	112.15 E
Parachilna	166	31.08 S	138.23 E
Pārachinār	120	33.54 N	70.06 E
Paracho [de Verduzco]	234	19.39 N	102.04 W
Parachute	200	39.27 N	108.03 W
Paraćin	38	43.52 N	21.24 E
Parácuaro	234	20.09 N	100.46 W
Paracuellos de Jarama	266a	40.30 N	3.32 W
Paracuru	250	3.24 S	39.04 W
Parád	30	47.55 N	20.02 E
Parada, Punta ≻	248	15.22 S	75.12 W
Paradas	34	37.18 N	5.30 W
Paradino	76	53.59 N	31.51 E
Paradise, Ca., U.S.	204	39.44 N	121.38 W
Paradise, Mt., U.S.	202	47.23 N	114.48 W
Paradise, Nv., U.S.	204	36.09 N	115.10 W
Paradise, Pa., U.S.	208	40.01 N	76.08 W
Paradise, Tx., U.S.	222	33.09 N	97.41 W
Paradise Hill, Sk., Can.	184	53.32 N	109.28 W
Paradise Hill, Ak., U.S.	180	62.25 N	160.03 W
Paradise Island I	240b	25.05 N	77.19 W
Paradise Mountain ∧	171a	27.45 S	152.02 E
Paradise Valley, Az., U.S.	200	33.31 N	111.56 W
Paradise Valley, Nv., U.S.	204	41.29 N	117.32 W
Parado	115b	8.45 S	118.36 E
Parado ≏	250	10.17 S	55.39 W
Pāradwīp	120	20.16 N	86.37 E
Parafield	168b	34.47 S	138.38 E
Parafijevka	78	50.53 N	32.38 E
Paragačaj	84	39.07 N	45.56 E
Paragon	218	39.23 N	86.33 W
Paragonah	200	37.53 N	112.46 W
Paragould	194	36.03 N	90.30 W
Paraguá ≏, Bol.	248	13.34 S	61.53 W
Paragua ≏, Ven.	246	6.55 N	62.55 W
Paraguaçu	256	21.33 S	45.44 W
Paraguaçu ≏	255	12.45 S	38.54 W
Paraguaçu Paulista	255	22.25 S	50.34 W
Paraguaipoa	246	11.21 N	71.57 W
Paraguaná, Península de ≻[1]	246	11.55 N	70.00 W
Paraguarí	252	25.38 S	57.09 W
Paraguarí □[5]	252	26.00 S	57.10 W
Paraguay □[1], S.A.	244	23.00 S	58.00 W
Paraguay □[1], S.A.	252	23.00 S	58.00 W
Paraguay (Paraguai) ≏	18	27.18 S	58.38 W
Parahyba → João Pessoa	250	7.07 S	34.52 W
Paraí, Represa ⊜[1]	256	23.20 S	45.35 W
Paraíba □[3]	250	7.15 S	36.30 W
Paraíba do Sul	256	22.09 S	43.17 W
Paraíba do Sul ≏	255	21.37 S	41.03 W
Paraibano	250	6.30 S	44.01 W
Paraibuna	256	23.23 S	45.39 W
Paraibuna ≏, Bra.	256	22.06 S	43.08 W
Paraibuna ≏, Bra.	256	23.22 S	45.40 W
Paraibuna, Represa do ⊜[1]	256	23.25 S	45.30 W
Paraíso, Bra.	255	19.03 S	52.59 W
Paraíso, Bra.	256	22.19 S	45.42 W
Paraíso, C.R.	236	9.50 N	83.51 W
Paraíso, Méx.	234	18.24 N	93.14 W
Paraiso, Pan.	236	9.02 N	79.38 W
Paraíso do Norte	255	23.13 S	52.38 W
Paraíso Garcia	256	21.32 S	43.53 W
Paraíso Novillero	234	18.16 N	95.59 W
Paraisópolis	256	22.33 S	45.47 W
Paraitinga ≏, Bra.	256	23.34 S	46.02 W
Paraitinga ≏, Bra.	256	23.22 S	45.40 W
Parakan	115a	7.17 S	110.06 E
Parakou	150	9.21 N	2.37 E
Paralía Aspropírgos	267c	38.02 N	23.35 E
Paralímni	130	35.02 N	33.59 E
Parama Island I	164	9.00 S	143.25 E
Paramakkudi	122	9.33 N	78.36 E
Paramaribo	250	5.50 N	55.10 W
Parambu	250	6.13 S	40.43 W
Paramillo, Nudo de ∧	246	7.04 N	75.55 W
Paramirim	255	13.26 S	42.15 W
Paramirim ≏	250	11.34 S	43.18 W
Paramithiá	38	39.28 N	20.30 E
Paramonga	248	10.40 S	77.50 W
Paramoti	250	4.06 S	39.15 W
Paramount	228	33.53 N	118.09 W
Paramus	210	40.56 N	74.04 W
Paramušir, ostrov I	74	50.25 N	155.50 E
Paramus Park ◆[9]	276	40.57 N	74.04 W
Paran, Naḥal (Wādī al-Jirāfī) ∨	132	30.24 N	35.10 E
Paraná, Arg.	252	31.44 S	60.32 W
Paranã, Bra.	255	12.33 S	47.52 W
Paraná □[3]	252	24.00 S	51.00 W
Paranã ≏, Bra.	255	12.30 S	48.14 W
Paraná ≏, S.A.	18	33.43 S	59.15 W
Paranabi	256	23.54 S	45.14 W
Paraná Bravo ≏[1]	258	33.53 S	58.27 W
Paranacito ≏	258	33.44 S	58.33 W
Paraná de las Palmas ≏[1]	258	34.18 S	58.33 W
Paranaguá	252	25.31 S	48.30 W
Paranaguá, Baía c	252	25.29 S	48.33 W
Paraná Guazú ≏[1]	258	34.00 S	58.25 W
Paranaíba	255	19.40 S	51.11 W
Paranaíba ≏	255	20.07 S	51.05 W
Paraná Ibicuy ≏[1]	258	33.48 S	59.10 W
Paranaidji	250	6.33 S	47.27 W
Paranaíta ≏	250	9.28 S	56.43 W
Paranam	250	5.37 N	55.06 W
Paraná Miní ≏[1]	258	34.13 S	58.25 W
Paranapanema ≏	255	22.40 S	53.09 W
Paranapiacaba	256	23.47 S	46.19 W
Paranapiacaba, Serra do ⋏	252	24.20 S	49.00 W
Parañaque	269f	14.30 N	120.59 E
Paranavaí	255	23.04 S	52.28 W
Parang, Pil.	116	7.23 N	124.16 E
Parang, Pil.	116	5.55 N	120.54 E
Parang, Pulau I	115a	5.45 S	110.14 E
Paran'ga	80	56.43 N	49.24 E
Paranhos	255	23.55 S	55.25 W
Paranjang	98	37.08 N	126.55 E
Párao de Masa, Puerto de)(	34	42.38 N	3.46 W
Paraopeba	255	19.18 S	44.25 W
Parapara	246	9.44 N	67.18 W
Paraparaumu	172	40.55 S	175.01 E
Paraparaumu Beach	172	40.54 S	174.59 E
Parapayè	58	45.55 N	7.32 E
Parapetí ≏	248	18.58 S	62.21 W
Parara	112	2.37 S	120.07 E
Parás, Méx.	196	26.30 N	99.31 W
Paras, Perú	248	13.30 S	74.35 W
Parasan	116	8.05 N	123.33 E
Parāsī	124	27.32 N	83.40 E
Parāsia	124	22.12 N	78.46 E
Parasida	126	23.46 N	87.20 E
Parasnāth	124	23.59 N	86.02 E
Paratei	256	23.14 S	46.00 W
Parateí ≏	256	23.12 S	46.00 W
Parati	256	23.13 S	44.43 W
Paratico	64	45.39 N	9.57 E
Parati-Mirim	256	23.14 S	44.38 W
Paratinga	255	12.42 S	43.10 W
Paratoo	166	32.42 S	139.22 E
Parauapebas ≏	250	5.35 S	49.41 W
Parauari ≏	250	4.36 S	57.47 W
Paraúna	255	17.02 S	50.26 W
Paravani, ozero ⊜	84	41.26 N	43.48 E
Para Wirra Recreation Park ♠	168b	34.43 S	138.50 E
Paray-le-Monial	32	46.27 N	4.07 E
Parbakalan	114	2.38 N	98.27 E
Pārbati ≏	124	25.51 N	76.36 E
Pārbatipur	124	25.39 N	88.55 E
Parbhani	122	19.16 N	76.47 E
Parbig	86	57.14 N	81.24 E
Parbig ≏	86	57.37 N	82.18 E
Parbold	262	53.36 N	2.46 W
Parburuan	114	1.52 N	99.55 E
Parchen	54	52.21 N	12.05 E
Parchim	54	53.25 N	11.51 E
Parchment	216	42.19 N	85.34 W
Parchomenko	83	48.34 N	39.43 E
Parchomovka	78	50.08 N	35.01 E
Parchwitz → Prochowice	30	51.17 N	16.22 E
Parcines (Partschins)	64	46.41 N	11.04 E
Parczew	30	51.39 N	22.54 E
Pardee Reservoir ⊜[1]	226	38.16 N	120.51 W
Pardeeville	190	43.32 N	89.18 W
Pardes Hanna-Karkur	132	32.28 N	34.58 E
Pārdi	122	20.31 N	72.57 E
Parding	120	32.52 N	88.39 E
Pardo ≏, Bra.	250	5.21 S	52.53 W
Pardo ≏, Bra.	252	29.59 S	52.23 W
Pardo ≏, Bra.	255	15.48 S	44.48 W
Pardo ≏, Bra.	255	21.46 S	52.09 W
Pardo ≏, Bra.	255	20.10 S	48.38 W
Pardo ≏, Bra.	255	22.55 S	49.58 W
Pardo ≏, Bra.	255	15.39 S	38.57 W
Pardo ≏, Bra.	256	23.32 S	45.30 W
Pardo ≏, Bra.	256	21.25 S	42.39 W
Pardomuan	114	2.06 N	98.20 E
Pardubice	30	50.02 N	15.47 E
Pare	115a	7.46 S	112.11 E
Parece Vela → Okino-Tori-shima I	90	20.25 N	136.00 E
Parecis	248	14.09 S	56.56 W
Parecis ≏	248	12.56 S	56.43 W
Parecis, Chapada dos ⋏	248	13.00 S	60.00 W
Parede	266c	38.41 N	9.21 W
Paredes de Nava	34	42.09 N	4.41 W
Paredes do Sapucaí	256	21.48 S	45.43 W
Paredón	232	25.56 N	100.58 W
Parelhas	250	6.41 S	36.39 W
Parelheiros ◆[8]	256	23.51 S	46.44 W
Pareloup, Lac de ⊜	32	44.15 N	2.45 E
Paremata	172	41.07 S	174.52 E
Parempei I	174r	7.01 N	158.15 E
Paren'	74	62.28 N	163.05 E
Paren' ≏	74	62.25 N	163.10 E
Parengarenga Harbour c	172	34.31 S	172.57 E
Parent	176	47.55 N	74.37 W
Parent, Lac ⊜	190	48.38 N	77.03 W
Parentis-en-Born	32	44.21 N	1.05 W
Pareora	172	44.30 S	171.12 E
Parepare	112	4.01 S	119.38 E
Parera	252	35.08 S	64.32 W
Parets del Vallès	266d	41.34 N	2.14 E
Parey	54	52.22 N	11.59 E
Parfenjevo, S.S.S.R.	24	61.21 N	42.43 E
Parfenjevo, S.S.S.R.	80	58.29 N	43.25 E
Parfentevo	82	55.06 N	38.49 E
Parfino	76	57.58 N	31.41 E
Parforce-Heide ◆[3]	264a	52.22 N	13.10 E
Párga	38	39.17 N	20.23 E
Pārgaon	272c	18.59 N	73.05 E
Pargarutan	114	1.28 N	99.20 E
Pargas (Parainen)	26	60.18 N	22.18 E
Pargey Creek ≏	285	39.49 N	75.18 W
Pargny-sur-Saulx	56	48.46 N	4.50 E
Pargolovo	76	60.04 N	30.18 E
Parham	240c	17.05 N	61.46 W
Parhebangan	114	2.15 N	98.45 E
Pari ◆[8]	287b	23.32 S	46.37 W
Paria ≏	200	36.52 N	111.36 W
Paria, Gulf of c	246	10.20 N	62.00 W
Paria, Península de ≻[1]	241r	10.40 N	62.10 W
Pariaguán	246	8.51 N	64.43 W
Pariaman	112	0.38 S	100.08 E
Pariamanu ≏	248	12.26 S	69.16 W
Paricá, Lago ⊜	246	1.53 S	65.45 W
Pariči	76	52.48 N	29.25 E
Paricutín ∧[1]	234	19.28 N	102.15 W
Parida, Isla I	236	8.07 N	82.20 W
Pariette Draw ∨	200	40.02 N	109.45 W
Parigi, Indon.	112	0.48 S	120.10 E
Parigi, Indon.	115a	6.12 S	106.22 E
Parigné-L'Évêque	50	47.56 N	0.22 E
Parika	246	6.52 N	58.25 W
Parikkala	26	61.33 N	29.30 E
Parima ≏	246	3.34 N	63.47 W
Parima, Sierra ⋏	246	2.30 N	64.00 W
Pariñas, Punta ≻	246	4.40 S	81.20 W
Parîngu Mare, Vîrful ∧	38	45.22 N	23.33 E
Parintins	250	2.36 S	56.44 W
Paripiranga	250	10.41 S	37.52 W
Pariquera-Açu	252	24.43 S	47.53 W
Paris, On., Can.	212	43.12 N	80.23 W
Paris, Fr.	50	48.52 N	2.20 E
Paris, Fr.	261	48.52 N	2.20 E
Paris, Ar., U.S.	194	35.17 N	93.43 W
Paris, Id., U.S.	202	42.13 N	111.24 W
Paris, Il., U.S.	194	39.36 N	87.41 W
Paris, Ky., U.S.	218	38.12 N	84.15 W
Paris, Me., U.S.	188	44.15 N	70.30 W
Paris, Mo., U.S.	219	39.28 N	92.00 W
Paris, Oh., U.S.	214	40.48 N	81.10 W
Paris, Pa., U.S.	214	40.24 N	80.31 W
Paris, Tn., U.S.	194	36.18 N	88.19 W
Paris, Tx., U.S.	196	33.39 N	95.33 W
Paris □[5]	261	48.52 N	2.20 E
Paris, Port de c	261	48.57 N	2.17 E
Parish	210	43.24 N	76.07 W
Parisien de Pantin, Cimetière ◆	261	48.54 N	2.23 E
Parisienne, Ile I	190	46.41 N	84.44 W
Paris-le-Bourget, Aéroport de ⊠	50	49.00 N	2.25 E
Parismina	236	10.12 N	83.38 W
Parismina ≏	236	10.19 N	83.21 W
Paris-Orly, Aéroport de ⊠	50	48.43 N	2.22 E
Paris-Plage, Aéroport ⊠	50	50.31 N	1.38 E
Parit	112	3.10 S	104.38 E
Parita, Bahía de c	236	8.08 N	80.24 W
Parit Bunga	114	2.04 N	102.33 E
Parit Buntar	114	5.07 N	100.30 E
Pariti	112	10.01 S	123.43 E
Parit Jawa	114	1.57 N	102.39 E
Parižskaja Kommuna ◆[8]	83	48.26 N	38.49 E
Park ≏	198	48.28 N	97.09 W
Park, North Branch ≏	198	48.26 N	97.27 W
Park, South Branch ≏	198	48.26 N	97.27 W
Parka	154	4.31 N	27.20 E
Parkano	26	62.01 N	23.01 E
Parkany	78	46.49 N	29.31 E
Parkchester	285	40.00 N	75.35 W
Park City, Il., U.S.	216	42.21 N	87.53 W
Park City, Ks., U.S.	198	37.48 N	97.19 W
Park City, Mt., U.S.	202	45.37 N	108.55 W
Park City, Ut,. U.S.	200	40.38 N	111.29 W
Park Creek ≏	285	40.13 N	75.08 W
Parkdale, P.E., Can.	186	46.15 N	63.07 W
Parkdale, Mo., U.S.	219	38.29 N	90.32 W
Parkdale, Or., U.S.	224	45.31 N	121.35 W
Parkdene	273d	26.14 S	28.16 E
Parkent	85	41.18 N	69.40 E
Parker, Az., U.S.	200	34.09 N	114.17 W
Parker, Co., U.S.	198	39.31 N	104.45 W
Parker, Fl., U.S.	194	30.07 N	85.36 W
Parker, Pa., U.S.	214	41.05 N	79.41 W
Parker, S.D., U.S.	198	43.23 N	97.08 W
Parker □[6]	222	32.48 N	97.42 W
Parker ≏	207	42.45 N	70.49 W
Parker, Cape ≻	176	75.04 N	79.40 W
Parker, Lake ⊜	220	28.04 N	81.56 W
Parker City	218	40.11 N	85.12 W
Parker Dam	204	34.17 N	114.08 W
Parker Dam ◆[6]	200	34.18 N	114.10 W
Parker Ford	285	40.12 N	75.35 W
Parker Peak ∧	198	43.24 N	103.41 W
Parker Range	162	31.38 S	119.35 E
Parker River National Wildlife Refuge ◆[4]	283	42.45 N	70.48 W
Parkersburg, Il., U.S.	194	38.36 N	88.03 W
Parkersburg, Ia., U.S.	190	42.34 N	92.47 W
Parkersburg, W.V., U.S.	188	39.16 N	81.33 W
Parkers Creek ≏	285	40.00 N	74.53 W
Parkers Prairie	198	46.09 N	95.19 W
Parkerville	168a	31.53 S	116.09 E
Parker Volcano ∧[1]	116	6.07 N	124.54 E
Parkes	166	33.08 S	148.11 E
Parkesburg	208	39.57 N	75.55 W
Park Falls	190	45.56 N	90.26 W
Park Forest	216	41.28 N	87.38 W
Parkgate, Eng., U.K.	262	53.18 N	3.05 W
Parkgate, Eng., U.K.	262	53.16 N	2.20 W
Park Hall	208	38.13 N	76.25 W
Parkhill, On., Can.	190	43.09 N	81.41 W
Parkhill, Pa., U.S.	214	40.22 N	78.52 W
Parkhill Gardens	273d	26.14 S	28.11 E
Parkin	194	35.15 N	90.34 W
Park Lake	216	42.48 N	84.27 W
Parkland, Pa., U.S.	285	40.09 N	74.56 W
Parkland, Wa., U.S.	224	47.09 N	122.25 W
Parklawn	284c	38.50 N	77.09 W
Park Layne	218	39.53 N	84.03 W
Parklea	274a	33.44 S	150.57 E
Parkman	214	41.22 N	81.03 W
Park Meadows	279b	40.18 N	79.44 W
Parkmore	44	55.02 N	6.06 W
Park Orchards	274b	37.46 S	145.13 E
Park Plateau ⋏[1]	198	37.15 N	104.45 W
Park Range ⋏	200	40.40 N	106.40 W
Park Rapids	198	46.55 N	95.03 W
Park Ridge, Il., U.S.	216	42.00 N	87.50 W
Park Ridge, N.J., U.S.	276	41.02 N	74.02 W
Park Ridge Farms	285	40.10 N	74.42 W
Park River	198	48.23 N	97.44 W
Parkrose	224	45.33 N	122.33 W
Park Rynie	158	30.25 S	30.35 E
Parks	180	57.38 N	154.00 W
Parks Creek ≏	212	44.17 N	77.21 W
Park Shore Resort	216	41.55 N	85.59 W
Parkside, Md., U.S.	284c	39.02 N	77.06 W
Parkside, Pa., U.S.	285	39.52 N	75.23 W
Parksley	208	37.46 N	75.39 W
Park Station ◆[5]	273d	26.12 S	28.03 E
Parkstein	60	49.44 N	12.04 E
Parkstetten	60	48.55 N	12.36 E
Parkston	198	43.23 N	97.59 W
Parksville, B.C., Can.	182	49.19 N	124.19 W
Parksville, N.Y., U.S.	210	41.51 N	74.45 W
Parktown ◆[8]	273d	26.11 S	28.03 E
Parktown North ◆[8]	273d	26.09 S	28.02 E
Parkview	279b	40.30 N	79.56 W
Parkville, Md., U.S.	208	39.22 N	76.32 W
Parkville, Mo., U.S.	194	39.11 N	94.40 W
Parkwater	202	47.40 N	117.19 W
Parkway, Ca., U.S.	226	38.29 N	121.27 W
Parkway, Mo., U.S.	219	38.20 N	90.57 W
Parkwood	284c	39.01 N	77.05 W
Parla	34	40.14 N	3.46 W
Parlākimidi	122	18.47 N	84.06 E
Parle, Lac qui ⊜	198	45.07 N	96.00 W
Parli	122	18.51 N	76.32 E
Parliament, Houses of ♦	260	51.30 N	0.07 W
Parlier	226	36.36 N	119.31 W
Parma, It.	64	44.48 N	10.20 E
Parma, Id., U.S.	202	43.47 N	116.56 W
Parma, Mi., U.S.	216	42.15 N	84.35 W
Parma, Mo., U.S.	194	36.36 N	89.48 W
Parma, Oh., U.S.	214	41.24 N	81.43 W
Parma □[4]	64	44.40 N	10.10 E
Parma ≏	64	44.56 N	10.26 E
Parma Heights	214	41.23 N	81.45 W
Parmain	261	49.07 N	2.12 E
Parmatown Mall ◆[9]	279a	41.23 N	81.44 W
Parnaguá	250	10.13 S	44.38 W
Parnahyba → Parnaíba	250	2.54 S	41.47 W
Parnaíba	250	2.54 S	41.47 W
Parnaíba ≏	250	3.00 S	41.50 W
Parnaibinha ≏	250	9.17 S	45.55 W
Parnamirim, Bra.	250	8.05 S	39.34 W
Parnamirim, Bra.	250	5.55 S	35.15 W
Parnarama	250	5.41 S	43.06 W
Parnassós ∧	38	38.32 N	22.35 E
Parnassus	172	42.43 S	173.18 E
Parndorf	61	47.59 N	16.51 E
Parnell	216	40.14 N	88.42 W
Párnis ∧	38	38.11 N	23.42 E
Párnis Óros ⋏	267c	38.07 N	23.41 E
Parnon ⋏	38	37.18 N	22.35 E
Pärnu	76	58.24 N	24.32 E
Pärnu ≏	76	58.23 N	24.29 E
Pärnu-Jaagupi	76	58.37 N	24.30 E
Pärnu laht c	76	58.15 N	24.25 E
Paro	124	27.26 N	89.25 E
Pārola	120	20.53 N	75.07 E
Paromaj	89	52.50 N	143.02 E
Paroo	162	26.16 S	119.46 E
Paroo ≏	166	31.28 S	143.32 E
Parorā	272b	22.48 N	88.09 E
Páros	38	37.04 N	25.08 E
Páros I	38	37.08 N	25.12 E
Parow	158	33.53 S	18.37 E
Parowan	200	37.50 N	112.49 W
Parpaillon ⋏	62	44.30 N	6.40 E
Parpan	58	46.46 N	9.33 E
Parr	216	41.02 N	87.13 W
Parral, Chile	252	36.09 S	71.50 W
Parral → Hidalgo del Parral, Méx.	232	26.56 N	105.40 W
Parral, Oh., U.S.	214	40.33 N	81.30 W
Parramatta	170	33.49 S	151.00 E
Parramatta ≏	274a	33.51 S	151.14 E
Parramatta Park ♠	274a	33.49 S	151.00 E
Parramore Island I	208	37.32 N	75.38 W
Parras de la Fuente	232	25.25 N	102.11 W
Parrett ≏	42	51.13 N	3.01 W
Parrish, Al., U.S.	194	33.43 N	87.17 W
Parrish, Fl., U.S.	220	27.35 N	82.25 W
Parris Island Marine Corps Recruit Depot ■	192	32.21 N	80.41 W
Parrita	236	9.30 N	84.19 W
Parrsboro	186	45.24 N	64.20 W
Parry, Cape ≻	176	70.08 N	124.24 W
Parry, Mount ∧	182	52.53 N	128.45 W
Parry Bay c	176	68.07 N	82.00 W
Parry Channel ʯ	16	74.20 N	98.00 W
Parry Island I	212	45.18 N	80.10 W
Parry Island Indian Reserve ◆[4]	212	45.18 N	80.10 W
Parry Peninsula ≻[1]	180	69.45 N	124.30 W
Parry Sound	212	45.21 N	80.02 W
Parry Sound □[6]	212	45.25 N	79.55 W
Parry Sound ʯ	212	45.21 N	80.06 W
Parryville	208	40.49 N	75.40 W
Parsberg	60	49.09 N	11.43 E
Parsdorf	60	48.09 N	11.47 E
Parseier Spitze ∧	58	47.10 N	10.28 E
Parsęta ≏	30	54.12 N	15.33 E
Parshād	120	24.11 N	73.42 E
Parshall	198	47.57 N	102.08 W
Parshallville	281	42.41 N	83.46 W
Paršino	88	59.10 N	111.48 E
Parsippany	210	40.51 N	74.25 W
Parsippany, Lake ⊜	276	40.51 N	74.26 W
Parsnāth ∧	124	23.53 N	86.08 E
Parsnip ≏	182	55.10 N	123.00 W
Parsoburan	114	2.19 N	99.20 E
Parsonage Island I	276	40.37 N	73.37 W
Parsons, Ks., U.S.	198	37.20 N	95.15 W
Parsons, Tn., U.S.	194	35.38 N	88.07 W
Parsons, W.V., U.S.	188	39.05 N	79.40 W
Parsons, Mount ∧[2]	164	13.33 S	135.09 E
Parson's Pond	186	50.02 N	57.43 W
Parsons Pond ⊜	186	50.00 N	57.35 W
Parsons Range ⋏	164	13.30 S	135.15 E
Parsteiner See ⊜	54	52.55 N	13.59 E
Pärsti	76	58.25 N	25.32 E
Partābpur	124	23.29 N	83.13 E
Partanna	70	37.43 N	12.53 E
Partāppur	126	21.48 N	86.44 E
Partenen	58	46.58 N	10.03 E
Parthala	272a	28.36 N	77.24 E
Parthe ≏	54	51.22 N	12.21 E
Parthenay	32	46.39 N	0.15 W
Partington	262	53.25 N	2.26 W
Partinico	70	38.03 N	13.07 E
Partizansk	89	43.08 N	133.09 E
Partizánske	30	48.39 N	18.23 E
Partizanskoje	86	55.30 N	94.24 E
Parton	44	54.34 N	3.35 W
Partridge, Point ≻	224	48.13 N	122.46 W
Partridge Creek ≏	212	44.44 N	77.13 W
Partridge Crop Lake ⊜	184	55.38 N	97.27 W
Partridge Point ≻	186	50.09 N	56.10 W
Partry	48	53.41 N	9.19 W
Partschins → Parcines	64	46.41 N	11.04 E
Paru ≏, Bra.	250	1.33 S	52.38 W
Parú ≏, Ven.	246	4.20 N	66.27 W
Parubcan	116	13.43 N	123.45 E
Parucito ≏	246	5.18 N	65.59 W
Paru de Este ≏	250	1.10 N	54.40 W
Paru de Oeste ≏	250	1.30 S	56.00 W
Parung	115a	6.25 S	106.42 E
Pårup, Dan.	41	55.24 N	10.20 E
Pårup, Dan.	41	56.08 N	9.21 E
Parūr	122	10.09 N	76.14 E
Paruro	248	13.46 S	71.51 W
Parutino	78	46.43 N	31.53 E
Parvān □[4]	120	35.15 N	69.30 E
Pārvatīpuram	122	18.47 N	83.26 E
Parvin State Park ♠	208	39.30 N	75.09 W
Pârvomaj	38	42.06 N	25.13 E
Paryang	120	30.11 N	83.09 E
Påryd	26	56.34 N	15.55 E
Parys	158	27.04 S	27.16 E
Paša ≏	76	60.29 N	32.55 E
Paşabahçe ◆[8]	267b	41.06 N	29.05 E
Pasacao	116	13.31 N	123.03 E
Pasaco	236	13.59 N	90.12 W
Pasadena, Nf., Can.	186	49.01 N	57.36 W
Pasadena, Ca., U.S.	228	34.08 N	118.08 W
Pasadena, Md., U.S.	208	39.06 N	76.34 W
Pasadena, Tx., U.S.	222	29.41 N	95.12 W
Pasado, Cabo ≻	246	0.22 S	80.30 W
Pasaje	246	3.20 S	79.49 W
Pasaje ≏	252	25.35 S	63.57 W
Pasaje Talavera ≏[1]	258	33.53 S	58.55 W
Pa Sak ≏	110	14.21 N	100.35 E
Paşaköy	130	35.09 N	33.36 E
Pasaleng Bay c	116	18.36 N	120.56 E
Paşalimanı Adası I	130	40.28 N	27.37 E
Pasān	124	22.51 N	82.12 E
Pasanauri	84	42.21 N	44.41 E
Pasangkayu	112	1.10 S	119.20 E
Pasarbantal	112	2.45 S	101.20 E
Pasarseluma	112	4.09 S	102.32 E
Pasar Senen Station ◆[5]	269e	6.10 S	106.50 E
Pasarsorkam	114	1.53 N	98.34 E
Pasarwajo	112	5.29 S	122.50 E
Pasatiempo	226	37.02 N	122.02 W
Pasaunda	272a	28.42 N	77.21 E
Pasawng	110	18.52 N	97.18 E
Pasay	269f	14.33 N	121.00 E
Pasayten ≏	224	49.08 N	120.35 W
Pasayten, Middle Fork ≏	224	48.53 N	120.37 W
Pasayten, West Fork ≏	224	48.53 N	120.37 W
Pascack Brook ≏	276	40.59 N	73.59 W
Pascagama, Lac ⊜	190	48.34 N	75.36 W
Pascagoula	194	30.21 N	88.33 W
Pascagoula ≏	194	30.21 N	88.34 W
Pascalis, Lac ⊜	190	48.16 N	77.24 W
Paşcani	38	47.15 N	26.44 E
Pasching	61	48.15 N	14.12 E
Pasco	202	46.13 N	119.05 W
Pasco □[5]	248	10.30 S	75.15 W
Pasco □[6]	220	28.20 N	82.27 W
Pascoag	207	41.57 N	71.42 W
Pascoe Vale	274b	37.44 S	144.56 E
Pascua ≏	254	48.13 S	73.22 W
Pascua, Isla de (Easter Island) (Rapa Nui) I	174z	27.07 S	109.22 W
Pascuales, Boca ≏[1]	234	18.52 N	103.58 W
Pas-de-Calais □[5]	50	50.30 N	2.20 E
Pas-en-Artois	50	50.09 N	2.30 E
Pasewalk	54	53.30 N	14.00 E
Pashmāl	123	35.26 N	72.36 E
Pasian di Prato	64	46.03 N	13.11 E
Pasiano di Pordenone	64	45.51 N	12.37 E
Pasig	116	14.33 N	121.05 E
Pasig ≏	269f	14.36 N	120.58 E
Pāsighāt	120	28.04 N	95.20 E
Pašija	86	58.26 N	58.16 E
P'asina ≏	74	73.50 N	87.10 E
Pasinler (Hasankale)	130	39.59 N	41.41 E
Pašino	86	55.11 N	83.00 E
P'asino, ozero ⊜	74	69.45 N	87.45 E
P'asinskij zaliv c	74	74.00 N	86.00 E
Pasion, Rió de la ≏	232	16.28 N	90.33 W
Pasirganting	112	2.02 S	100.53 E
Pasir Gudang	271c	1.27 N	103.53 E
Pasirian	115a	8.13 S	113.06 E
Pasir Mas	114	6.02 N	102.08 E
Pasir Panjang	271c	1.17 N	103.47 E
Pasirpengarayan	114	0.51 N	100.16 E
Pasir Puteh, Malay.	114	5.50 N	102.24 E
Pasir Puteh, Malay.	271c	1.26 N	103.56 E
Påskallavik	26	57.10 N	16.27 E
Paskeville	168b	34.02 S	137.54 E
Paškovo, S.S.S.R.	80	53.39 N	42.25 E
Paškovo, S.S.S.R.	89	48.54 N	130.42 E
Paškovskij	78	45.02 N	39.06 E
Pasłęk	30	54.05 N	19.39 E
Pasłęka ≏	30	54.26 N	19.45 E
Pasley, Cape ≻	162	33.57 S	123.31 E
Pasley Bay c	176	70.40 N	96.27 W
Pašman, Otok I	36	43.58 N	15.21 E
Pasmore ≏	166	31.07 S	139.48 E
Pašn'a	24	63.21 N	56.28 E
Pasni	128	25.16 N	63.28 E
Paso de Indios	254	43.52 S	69.06 W
Paso del Cerro	252	31.29 S	55.50 W
Paso del Macho	234	18.58 N	96.43 W
Paso de los Libres	252	29.43 S	57.05 W
Paso de los Toros	252	32.49 S	56.31 W
Paso del Rey	288	34.39 S	58.46 W
Paso del Toro	234	19.02 N	96.07 W
Paso de Ovejas	234	19.17 N	96.26 W
Paso de Patria	252	27.13 S	58.35 W
Paso de San Antonio	196	29.05 N	103.55 W
Paso Hondo	232	15.49 N	92.02 W
Paso Limay	254	40.33 S	70.26 W
Pasorapa	248	18.16 S	64.37 W
Paso Real de Sarabia	234	17.03 N	95.01 W
Paso Robles	226	35.37 N	120.41 W
Paso Seco	240m	17.59 N	66.23 W
Pašozero	76	60.02 N	34.37 E
Pasqua Indian Reserve ◆[4]	184	50.45 N	104.02 W
Pasque Island I	207	41.27 N	70.50 W
Pasquia Hills ⋏[2]	184	53.13 N	102.37 W
Pasquotank □[6]	208	36.26 N	76.26 W
Pasquotank ≏	192	36.10 N	76.03 W
Pasrūr	123	32.16 N	74.40 E
Passa-Cinco, Corredeira ∟	256	21.19 S	43.08 W
Passadumkeag	188	45.11 N	68.37 W
Passadumkeag Mountain ∧[2]	188	45.10 N	68.20 W
Passage East	48	52.13 N	6.59 W
Passagem Franca	250	6.10 S	43.47 W
Passage Point ≻	176	73.29 N	115.17 W
Passage West	48	51.52 N	8.20 W
Passaic	210	40.51 N	74.07 W
Passaic □[6]	210	40.55 N	74.10 W
Passaic ≏	276	40.43 N	74.07 W
Passamaquoddy Bay c	186	45.06 N	66.59 W
Passa Quatro	256	22.23 S	44.58 W
Passa Três	256	22.42 S	44.00 W
Passau	60	48.35 N	13.28 E
Passa Vinte	256	22.13 S	44.15 W
Pass Creek ≏	198	43.45 N	101.28 W
Passero, Capo ≻	70	36.40 N	15.09 E
Passignano sul Trasimeno	66	43.11 N	12.08 E
Passirio (Passer) ≏	64	46.41 N	11.10 E
Pass Island	186	47.29 N	56.11 W
Pašskij Perevoz	76	60.24 N	32.59 E
Passo Corese	66	42.09 N	12.39 E
Passo de Camaragibe	250	9.14 S	35.29 W
Passo Fundo	252	28.15 S	52.24 W
Passo Fundo ≏	252	27.16 S	52.42 W
Passopisciaro	70	37.52 N	15.02 E
Passos	255	20.43 S	46.37 W
Passow	54	53.08 N	14.06 E
Passy	58	45.55 N	6.41 E
Passy ◆[8]	261	48.52 N	2.17 E
Pastaza □[4]	246	1.45 S	76.50 W
Pastaza ≏	246	4.50 S	76.25 W
Pastecho ≏	182	56.07 N	114.15 W
Pasteur, Lac ⊜	186	50.13 N	66.58 W
Pastillo	240m	17.59 N	66.29 W
Pasto	246	1.13 N	77.17 W
Pastol Bay c	180	63.07 N	163.15 W
Pastora Peak ∧	200	36.47 N	109.10 W
Pastoría, Laguna de c	234	15.59 N	97.40 W
Pastoria Creek ≏	228	35.01 N	118.51 W
Pastos Bons	250	6.36 S	44.05 W
Pastrana	34	40.25 N	2.55 W
Pastrengo	64	45.29 N	10.48 E
Pašukovo	82	55.55 N	38.16 E
Pasuquin	116	18.20 N	120.37 E
Pasuruan	115a	7.38 S	112.54 E
Pasvalys	76	56.04 N	24.24 E
Pásztó	30	47.55 N	19.42 E
Pata	116	5.51 N	121.10 E
Patacamaya	248	17.14 S	67.55 W
Pātāchārkuchi	120	26.31 N	91.16 E
Patagonia	200	31.32 N	110.45 W
Patagonia ◆[1]	254	44.00 S	68.00 W
Pataha Creek ≏	202	46.31 N	117.59 W
Pata Island I	116	5.49 N	121.10 E
Patamban	234	19.48 N	102.18 W
Pātan, India	120	23.50 N	72.07 E
Pātan, India	124	23.18 N	79.42 E
Patapsco	208	39.32 N	76.53 W
Patapsco ≏	208	39.09 N	76.27 W
Patapsco, Cooks Branch ≏	284b	39.27 N	76.53 W
Patapsco, Davis Branch ≏	284b	39.19 N	76.51 W
Patapsco, North Branch ≏	208	39.21 N	76.53 W
Patapsco, Rockburn Branch ≏	284b	39.14 N	76.43 W
Patapsco, Soapstone Branch ≏	284b	39.13 N	76.43 W
Patapsco, South Branch ≏	208	39.21 N	76.53 W
Patapsco River Neck ≻[1]	284b	39.14 N	76.27 W
Patapsco Valley State Park ♠	208	39.20 N	76.55 W
Patargān, Daqq-e ≡	128	33.30 N	60.40 E
Pataudi	124	28.19 N	76.47 E
Pataula Creek ≏	192	31.46 N	85.02 W
Patay	50	48.03 N	1.42 E
Pataz	248	7.44 S	77.37 W
Patchewollock	166	35.23 S	142.11 E
Patchogue	210	40.45 N	73.00 W
Patchogue Bay c	276	40.44 N	73.01 W
Patchway	42	51.32 N	2.34 W
Pat Cleburne, Lake ⊜[1]	222	32.25 N	97.30 W
Pate	154	2.08 S	41.00 E
Patea	172	39.45 S	174.28 E
Patea ≏	172	39.46 S	174.29 E
Patearoa	172	45.16 S	170.03 E
Pategi	150	8.44 N	5.44 E
Pate Island I	154	2.07 S	41.03 E
Pateley Bridge	44	54.05 N	1.45 W
Patel Nagar ◆[8]	272a	28.39 N	77.10 E
Patensie	158	33.46 S	24.49 E
Patéras Óros ∧	267c	38.07 N	23.25 E
Patergassen	64	46.49 N	13.52 E
Paterna	34	39.30 N	0.26 W
Paternion	64	46.43 N	13.38 E
Paternò	70	37.34 N	14.54 E
Pateros, Pil.	269f	14.33 N	121.04 E
Pateros, Wa., U.S.	202	48.03 N	119.54 W
Patersdorf	60	49.01 N	12.59 E
Paterson, Austl.	170	32.36 S	151.37 E
Paterson, S. Afr.	158	33.26 S	25.58 E
Paterson, N.J., U.S.	210	40.55 N	74.10 W
Paterson ≏	170	32.43 S	151.39 E
Paterson, Cape ≻	169	38.40 S	145.36 E
Paterson Inlet c	172	46.55 S	168.03 E
Paterswolde	52	53.08 N	6.35 E
Pātghāti	126	22.53 N	89.55 E
Pathalgaon	124	22.34 N	83.28 E
Pathānkot	123	32.17 N	75.39 E
Pathānkot Airport ⊠	123	32.15 N	75.37 E
Pātharghāra	272b	22.34 N	88.35 E
Patharia	124	23.54 N	79.12 E
Pathein (Bassein)	110	16.47 N	94.44 E
Pathfinder Reservoir ⊜[1]	200	42.30 N	106.50 W
Pathfinder Seamount ✦[3]	16	50.55 N	143.15 W
Pathiong	140	6.46 N	30.54 E
Pathiu	110	10.42 N	99.19 E
Path of Condie	46	56.15 N	3.30 W
Pāthrāil	126	24.12 N	89.56 E
Pathro ≏	126	24.12 N	86.48 E
Pathum Thani	110	14.01 N	100.32 E
Pati, Indon.	112	0.33 S	111.19 E
Pati, Indon.	115a	6.45 S	111.01 E
Pati ≏	246	3.41 S	67.37 W
Patía	246	2.04 N	77.04 W
Patía ≏	246	2.13 N	78.40 W
Patiāla	123	30.19 N	76.24 E
Patiāla ∧	123	32.32 N	72.11 E
P'atichatki	78	48.24 N	33.42 E
Pati do Alferes	256	22.25 S	43.25 W
P'atigorsk	84	44.03 N	43.04 E
Pātihāl	272b	22.39 N	88.08 E
Patikul	116	6.04 N	121.06 E
Patillas	240m	18.00 N	66.01 W
P'atimar	80	49.31 N	50.32 E
Patinti, Selat ʯ	164	0.30 S	127.45 E
Patipāda	272c	19.04 N	73.05 E
Pati Point ≻	174p	13.36 N	144.57 E
Pātiram	124	25.19 N	88.45 E
Patire, Convento del ♦[1]	68	39.34 N	16.35 E
Pătîrlagele	38	45.19 N	26.22 E
Pativilca	248	10.42 S	77.47 W
Pativilca ≏	248	10.44 S	77.48 W
Pātkai Range ⋏	120	27.00 N	96.00 E
Pat Mayse Reservoir ⊜[1]	196	33.40 N	95.35 W
Pátmos I	38	37.20 N	26.33 E
Patna, India	124	25.36 N	85.07 E
Patna, India	126	21.56 N	87.52 E
Pātna, India	272b	22.59 N	88.18 E
Patna, Scot., U.K.	44	55.21 N	4.30 W
Patnāgarh	122	20.43 N	83.09 E
Patnanongan Island I	116	14.48 N	122.11 E
P'atnica, S.S.S.R.	82	54.46 N	38.09 E
P'atnica, S.S.S.R.	82	56.05 N	36.48 E
P'atnickoje, S.S.S.R.	78	50.25 N	37.51 E
P'atnickoje, S.S.S.R.	82	54.20 N	35.53 E
Pātnoli	272c	18.57 N	73.05 E
Patnoñgon	116	10.55 N	122.00 E
Patnos	84	39.14 N	42.52 E
Pato Branco	252	26.13 S	52.40 W
Patoka	219	38.45 N	89.05 W

Symbols in the index entries represent the broad categories identified in the key at the right. Symbols with superior numbers (⋏[1]) identify subcategories (see complete key on page I · 1).

Symbole im Register stellen die rechts im Schlüssel erklärten Kategorien dar. Symbole mit hochgestellten Ziffern (⋏[1]) bezeichnen Unterabteilungen einer Kategorie (vgl. vollständiger Schlüssel auf Seite I · 1).

Los símbolos incluídos en el texto del índice representan las grandes categorias identificadas con la clave a la derecha. Los símbolos con numeros en su parte superior (⋏[1]) identifican las subcategorías (véase la clave completa en la página I · 1).

Les symboles de l'index représentent les catégories indiquées dans la légende à droite. Les symboles suivis d'un indice (⋏[1]) représentent des sous-catégories (voir légende complète à la page I · 1).

Os símbolos incluídos no texto do índice representam as grandes categorias identificadas com a chave à direita. Os símbolos com números em sua parte superior (⋏[1]) identificam as subcategorias (veja-se a chave completa à página I · 1).

	English	Deutsch	Español	Français	Português
∧	Mountain	Berg	Montaña	Montagne	Montanha
⋏	Mountains	Gebirge	Montañas	Montagnes	Montanhas
)(	Pass	Paß	Paso	Col	Passo
∨	Valley, Canyon	Tal, Cañon	Valle, Cañón	Vallée, Canyon	Vale, Canhão
≚	Plain	Ebene	Llano	Plaine	Planície
≻	Cape	Kap	Cabo	Cap	Cabo
I	Island	Insel	Isla	Île	Ilha
II	Islands	Inseln	Islas	Îles	Ilhas
⊥	Other Topographic Features	Andere Topographische Objekte	Otros Elementos Topográficos	Autres données topographiques	Outros acidentes topográficos

ESPAÑOL — Nombre | Página | Lat.°′ | Long.°′ W = Oeste

Patoka ≃ 194 38.25 N 87.44 W
Patoka Lake ⊜[1] 194 38.20 N 86.40 W
Patokino 82 56.27 N 39.06 E
Patomskoje nagorje ⋏[1] 88 59.00 N 115.00 E
Paton, Île I 275a 45.31 N 73.45 W
Patonga 154 2.46 N 33.18 E
Patos 250 7.01 S 37.16 W
Patos, Cachoeira dos ⌞ 248 9.20 S 60.15 W
Patos, Lagoa dos C 252 31.06 S 51.15 W
Patos, Río de los ≃ 252 31.18 S 69.25 W
Patos, Rio dos ≃, Bra. 248 13.33 S 56.29 W
Patos, Rio dos ≃, Bra. 255 14.59 S 48.46 W
Patos de Minas 255 18.35 S 46.32 W
Patos Island I 224 48.47 N 122.56 W
P'atovskij 82 54.41 N 36.04 E
Patquía 252 30.03 S 66.53 W
Pátrai 38 38.15 N 21.44 E
Patraïkós Kólpos C 38 38.14 N 21.15 E
Patras → Pátrai 38 38.15 N 21.44 E
Pātrasāer 124 23.13 N 87.31 E
Patricio Lynch, Isla I 254 48.37 S 75.26 W
Patrick Air Force Base ■ 220 28.15 N 80.36 W
Patrick Henry International Airport ⊠ 208 37.08 N 76.30 W
Patrick Point › 214 42.35 N 81.28 W
Patrington 44 53.41 N 0.02 W
Patriot 218 38.50 N 84.49 W
Patrocínio 255 18.57 S 46.59 W
Patrocínio Paulista 255 20.38 S 47.17 W
Patsaliga Creek ≃ 194 31.22 N 86.31 W
Patscherkofel ∧ 64 47.13 N 11.28 E
Pattada 71 40.35 N 9.06 E
Pattani 110 6.52 N 101.16 E
Pattani ≃ 110 6.53 N 101.16 E
Patten 188 45.59 N 68.26 W
Pattenburg 210 40.38 N 75.01 W
Pattensen 52 52.15 N 9.46 E
Pattenville 283 42.35 N 71.14 W
Patterdale 44 54.32 N 2.56 W
Patterson, Ca., U.S. 226 37.28 N 121.07 W
Patterson, Ga., U.S. 192 31.23 N 82.08 W
Patterson, Il., U.S. 219 39.29 N 90.29 W
Patterson, La., U.S. 194 29.41 N 91.18 W
Patterson, N.Y., U.S. 210 41.30 N 73.36 W
Patterson, Oh., U.S. 216 40.47 N 83.32 W
Patterson ≃ 274b 38.05 S 145.07 E
Patterson, Mount ∧ 180 64.04 N 134.39 W
Patterson Creek ≃ 188 39.34 N 78.44 W
Patterson Gardens 216 41.56 N 83.25 W
Patterson Heights 214 40.45 N 80.19 W
Patterson Island I 190 48.39 N 87.00 W
Patterson Park ♠ 284b 39.17 N 76.35 W
Pattersonville 210 42.53 N 74.05 W
Patti, India 123 31.17 N 74.51 E
Patti, India 124 25.55 N 82.12 E
Patti, It. 70 38.08 N 14.58 E
Patti, Golfo di C 36 38.12 N 15.05 E
Pattison, Ms., U.S. 194 31.53 N 90.53 W
Pattison, Tx., U.S. 222 29.49 N 95.60 W
Pattoki 123 31.01 N 73.51 E
Patton 214 40.37 N 78.39 W
Patton, Cape › 169 38.42 S 143.50 E
Patton Park ♠ 281 42.19 N 83.10 W
Pattonsburg 194 40.02 N 94.08 W
Patton Seamounts ✢[3] 16 54.20 N 149.30 W
Pattscheid ◆[8] 263 51.05 N 7.03 E
Pattukkottai 122 10.26 N 79.19 E
Pattullo, Mount ∧ 180 56.14 N 129.39 W
Patu 250 6.06 S 37.38 W
Pātua 126 22.06 N 90.23 E
Patuākhāli 124 22.21 N 90.21 E
Patuca ≃ 236 15.50 N 84.17 W
Patuca, Punta › 236 15.51 N 84.18 W
Patuha, Gunung ∧ 115a 7.10 S 107.23 E
Pātul 272b 22.45 N 88.10 E
Patul ∧ 246 2.40 S 79.03 W
Pātuli 126 23.33 N 88.15 E
Patulul 236 14.25 N 91.10 W
Patumahoe 172 37.11 S 174.50 E
Pātūr 122 20.27 N 76.56 E
Patusi 164 2.10 S 147.10 E
Patutu ∧ 172 39.15 S 175.51 E
Patuxent ≃ 208 38.18 N 76.25 W
Patuxent, Western Branch ≃ 208 38.47 N 76.43 W
Patuxent River Naval Air Test Center ■ 208 38.17 N 76.25 W
Patuxent Wildlife Research Center ᴗ[3] 284c 39.03 N 76.48 W
Patvinsuon kansallispuisto ♠ 24 63.10 N 30.55 E
Patwāri 272a 28.35 N 77.27 E
Pátzcuaro 234 19.31 N 101.36 W
Pátzcuaro, Lago de ⊜ 234 19.35 N 101.35 W
Patzicía 236 14.38 N 90.56 W
Patzig 54 54.28 N 13.24 E
Patzún 236 14.41 N 91.01 W
Pau 32 43.18 N 0.22 W
Pau, Gave de ≃ 32 43.33 N 1.12 W
Pau Brasil 255 15.27 S 39.39 W
Paucarbamba 248 12.25 S 74.36 W
Paucarpata 248 16.26 S 71.30 W
Paucartambo 248 13.18 S 71.40 W
Pau d'Arco 250 7.30 S 49.22 W
Paudash Lake ⊜ 212 44.58 N 78.04 W
Pau dos Ferros 250 6.07 S 38.10 W
Pauh 112 2.08 S 102.48 E
Pauhunri ∧ 124 27.58 N 88.50 E
Pauini 248 7.40 S 66.58 W
Pauini ≃, Bra. 246 1.42 S 62.50 W
Pauini ≃, Bra. 248 7.47 S 67.05 W
Pauk 110 21.27 N 94.27 E
Pauksa Taung ∧ 110 19.55 N 94.18 E
Paul 202 42.36 N 113.46 W
Paul, Lac à ⊜ 186 49.52 N 70.46 W
Paula Lima 256 21.35 S 43.29 W
Paularo 64 46.32 N 13.07 E
Paulaya ≃ 236 15.51 N 85.06 W
Paulding, Ms., U.S. 194 32.01 N 89.02 W
Paulding, Oh., U.S. 216 41.08 N 84.34 W
Paulding □[6] 216 41.08 N 84.35 W
Paulding Bay C 9 66.35 S 123.00 E
Paulhan 32 43.32 N 3.27 E
Paulicéia 255 21.17 S 51.51 W
Paulilatino 71 40.05 N 8.46 E
Paulina Peak ∧ 202 43.41 N 121.15 W
Pauline, Mount ∧ 182 53.33 N 119.54 W
Paulinenaue 54 52.40 N 12.43 E
Paulínia 256 22.45 S 47.10 W
Paulino Neves 250 2.43 S 42.33 W
Paulins Kill 210 41.03 N 74.49 W
Paulins Kill ≃ 210 40.55 N 75.05 W
Paulinzella ⊥ 54 50.42 N 11.06 E
Paulis → Isiro 154 2.47 N 27.37 E
Paulista 250 7.57 S 34.53 W
Paulistana 250 8.09 S 41.09 W
Paulistas 255 18.25 S 42.52 W
Paullina 198 42.58 N 95.41 W
Paull Lake ⊜ 184 56.08 N 104.50 W
Paullo 62 45.25 N 9.24 E
Paulo Afonso 250 9.21 S 38.14 W
Paulo Afonso, Parque Nacional de ♠ 250 9.20 S 38.12 W
Paulo de Faria 255 20.02 S 49.24 W
Paulo e Virginia, Gruta ⊥[5] 287a 22.57 S 43.18 W
Pauloff Harbor (Pavlof Harbor) 180 54.27 N 162.42 W

FRANÇAIS — Nom | Page | Lat.°′ | Long.°′ W = Ouest

Paulpietersburg 158 27.30 S 30.51 E
Paul Roux 158 28.18 S 27.59 E
Paul-Sauvé, Parc ♠ 275a 45.28 N 74.02 W
Paulsboro 208 39.49 N 75.14 W
Pauls Cross Roads 208 37.52 N 76.53 W
Paul Seamount ✢[3] 14 23.26 N 172.36 W
Paulstown → Whitehall 48 52.41 N 7.01 W
Pauls Valley 196 34.44 N 97.13 W
Paulton, Eng., U.K. 42 51.18 N 2.30 W
Paulton, Pa., U.S. 279b 40.34 N 79.34 W
Pauma Indian Reservation ◆[4] 228 33.22 N 116.58 W
Pāunān 272b 22.57 N 88.17 E
Paung 110 16.37 N 97.28 E
Paungbyin 110 24.16 N 94.49 E
Paungde 110 18.29 N 95.30 E
Paunggyi 110 17.19 N 96.11 E
Paup 164 3.15 S 142.35 E
Paupack 210 41.24 N 75.14 W
Pauri 124 30.09 N 78.47 E
Pausa, D.D.R. 54 50.35 N 12.00 E
Pausa, Perú 248 15.16 S 73.20 W
Pausania 36 40.55 N 9.06 E
Pausin 264a 52.38 N 13.03 E
Paute 246 2.47 S 78.50 W
Paute ≃ 246 2.46 S 78.16 W
Pauto ≃ 246 5.09 N 70.55 W
Pautou → Baotou 102 40.40 N 109.59 E
Pauwalu Point › 229a 20.52 N 156.08 W
Pauwela 229a 20.56 N 156.19 W
Pauwela Point › 229a 20.57 N 156.19 W
Pavai ◆[8] 272c 19.07 N 72.55 E
Pavai Lake ⊜ 272c 19.07 N 72.55 E
Pavda 86 59.15 N 59.30 E
Pāveh 128 35.03 N 46.22 E
Pavel'cevo 82 56.15 N 36.26 E
Pavelec 76 53.50 N 39.16 E
Pavelec Station ◆[5] 265b 55.44 N 37.38 E
Pavia 62 45.10 N 9.10 E
Pavia □[4] 62 45.07 N 9.08 E
Pavia, Naviglio di ≍ 266b 45.27 N 9.11 E
Pavia di Udine 64 45.59 N 13.17 E
Pavilion, B.C., Can. 182 50.52 N 121.50 W
Pavilion, N.Y., U.S. 210 42.52 N 78.01 W
Pavilion Key I 220 25.42 N 81.22 W
Pavillion 200 43.14 N 108.41 W
Pavilly 50 49.34 N 0.58 E
Pāvilosta 76 56.53 N 21.14 E
Pavino 24 59.07 N 46.07 E
Pavione, Monte ∧ 64 46.07 N 11.50 E
Pavlice 61 48.59 N 15.53 E
Pavlikeni 38 43.14 N 25.18 E
Pavliščevo, S.S.S.R. 82 55.11 N 35.59 E
Pavliščevo, S.S.S.R. 82 55.34 N 35.59 E
Pavlodar 86 52.18 N 76.57 E
Pavlof Bay C 180 55.30 N 161.32 W
Pavlof Volcano ∧[1] 180 55.24 N 161.52 W
Pavlograd 78 48.32 N 35.53 E
Pavlogradka 86 54.12 N 73.33 E
Pavlopol' 83 47.16 N 37.47 E
Pavlovka, S.S.S.R. 78 47.45 N 37.14 E
Pavlovka, S.S.S.R. 80 52.41 N 47.09 E
Pavlovka, S.S.S.R. 83 48.08 N 39.33 E
Pavlovka, S.S.S.R. 83 49.36 N 38.42 E
Pavlovka, S.S.S.R. 86 51.55 N 54.47 E
Pavlovka, S.S.S.R. 86 55.25 N 56.33 E
Pavlovo, S.S.S.R. 76 60.05 N 45.17 E
Pavlovo, S.S.S.R. 80 55.58 N 43.04 E
Pavlovo, S.S.S.R. 265a 59.56 N 30.40 E
Pavlovo, S.S.S.R. 265a 59.49 N 30.54 E
Pavlovsk, S.S.S.R. 76 59.41 N 30.27 E
Pavlovsk, S.S.S.R. 78 50.27 N 40.08 E
Pavlovsk, S.S.S.R. 86 53.20 N 82.59 E
Pavlovskaja 78 46.08 N 39.48 E
Pavlovskaja Sloboda 82 55.49 N 37.05 E
Pavlovskij, S.S.S.R. 80 57.50 N 54.51 E
Pavlovskij, S.S.S.R. 86 52.32 N 63.06 E
Pavlovskij Posad 82 55.47 N 38.40 E
Pavlyš 78 48.55 N 33.21 E
Pavne 272c 19.05 N 73.01 E
Pavo 192 31.02 N 84.04 W
Pavón, Arg. 258 34.23 S 59.03 W
Pavón, Col. 246 3.37 N 72.15 W
Pavón, Arroyo ≃ 258 34.30 S 57.05 W
Pavona 267a 41.43 N 12.37 E
Pavonia 214 40.49 N 82.26 W
Pavšino 265b 55.49 N 37.21 E
Pavšozero 76 60.38 N 35.34 E
Pavullo nel Frignano 64 44.20 N 10.50 E
Pavuna, Arroio ≃ 287a 22.58 S 43.23 W
Pavuvu Island I 175e 9.03 S 159.06 E
Pavy 76 58.03 N 29.30 E
Pawai, Pulau I 271c 1.12 N 103.43 E
Pawan ≃ 112 1.51 S 109.57 E
Pawāyān 124 28.04 N 80.06 E
Pawcatuck 207 41.22 N 71.50 W
Paw Creek 192 35.16 N 80.56 W
Päwesin 54 52.31 N 12.42 E
Pawhuska 196 36.40 N 96.20 W
Pawling 210 41.33 N 73.36 W
Pawn ≃ 110 18.53 N 97.19 E
Pawnee, Il., U.S. 219 39.35 N 89.34 W
Pawnee, Ok., U.S. 196 36.20 N 96.48 W
Pawnee ≃ 198 38.10 N 99.06 W
Pawnee City 198 40.06 N 96.09 W
Pawnee Creek ≃ 198 40.34 N 103.14 W
Pawnee Rock 198 38.15 N 98.58 W
Pawni 122 20.47 N 79.38 E
Pawota 110 17.46 N 97.17 E
Paw Paw, Il., U.S. 216 41.41 N 88.59 W
Paw Paw, Mi., U.S. 216 42.13 N 85.53 W
Paw Paw, W.V., U.S. 188 39.31 N 78.27 W
Paw Paw ≃ 216 42.07 N 86.29 W
Paw Paw Creek ≃ 216 40.52 N 85.58 W
Paw Paw Lake 216 42.12 N 86.15 W
Paw Paw Lake ⊜ 216 42.12 N 86.16 W
Pawtucket 207 41.52 N 71.22 W
Pawtucket Falls ⌞ 207 42.39 N 71.20 W
Paxoí I 38 39.12 N 20.12 E
Paxson 180 63.02 N 145.30 W
Paxton, Austl. 170 32.54 S 151.16 E
Paxton, Il., U.S. 216 40.27 N 88.05 W
Paxton, Ma., U.S. 207 42.18 N 71.55 W
Paxton, Ne., U.S. 198 41.07 N 101.21 W
Paxtonia 208 40.19 N 76.48 W
Paxtonville 208 40.46 N 77.05 W
Paya 236 15.37 N 85.17 W
Paya Besar 114 3.47 N 103.16 E
Payadapu 114 3.05 N 97.23 E
Payāgpur 124 27.25 N 81.48 E
Payagyi 110 17.29 N 96.32 E
Payakumbuh 112 0.14 S 100.38 E
Paya Lebar 271c 1.22 N 103.53 E
Paya Lebar Airport ⊠ 271c 1.21 N 103.54 E
Payamlı 130 37.01 N 38.35 E
Payangan 115b 8.26 S 115.15 E
Payas, Cerro ∧ 236 15.50 N 85.00 W
Payerne 58 46.49 N 6.56 E
Payeti 115b 9.41 S 120.20 E
Payette 202 44.04 N 116.55 W
Payette ≃ 202 44.05 N 116.57 W
Payette, Middle Fork ≃ 202 44.05 N 116.07 W
Payette, North Fork ≃ 202 44.05 N 116.07 W
Payette, South Fork ≃ 202 44.06 N 116.00 W
Payette Lake ⊜[1] 202 44.57 N 116.05 W
Paylampur 272b 22.47 N 88.16 E
Payne 216 41.04 N 84.43 W
Payne ≃ 206 45.14 N 75.08 W
Payne, Lac ⊜ 176 59.25 N 74.00 W
Payne Bay C 176 60.00 N 70.00 W
Payneham 168b 34.53 S 138.38 E
Paynes Creek ≃ 204 40.16 N 122.11 W
Paynes Find 162 29.15 S 117.41 E
Paynesville, S. Afr. 273d 26.14 S 28.28 E
Paynesville, Mn., U.S. 198 45.22 N 94.42 W

PORTUGUÊS — Nome | Página | Lat.°′ | Long.°′ W = Oeste

Paynesville, Mo., U.S. 219 39.16 N 90.54 W
Paynetown State Recreation Area ♠ 218 39.05 N 86.27 W
Paynton 184 53.01 N 108.56 W
Paysandú 252 32.19 S 58.05 W
Pays-Bas → Netherlands □[1] 30 52.15 N 5.30 E
Payson, Az., U.S. 200 34.13 N 111.19 W
Payson, Il., U.S. 219 39.49 N 91.14 W
Payson, Ut,. U.S. 200 40.02 N 111.43 W
Payún, Cerro ∧ 252 36.30 S 69.18 W
Paz ≃ 236 13.45 N 90.08 W
Paz, Cañada de la ≃ 288 34.53 S 58.38 W
Paz, Ribeirão da ≃ 250 9.14 S 52.01 W
Pazar, Tür. 130 40.17 N 36.18 E
Pazar, Tür. 130 41.11 N 40.53 E
Pazarbaşi › 130 41.10 N 30.11 E
Pazarcık 130 37.31 N 37.19 E
Pazardžik 38 42.12 N 24.20 E
Pazarköy, Tür. 130 39.51 N 27.24 E
Pazarköy, Tür. 130 40.55 N 32.11 E
Pazarören 130 38.41 N 36.11 E
Pazaryeri, Tür. 130 38.05 N 28.14 E
Pazaryeri, Tür. 130 40.00 N 29.54 E
Paz de Ariporo 246 5.53 N 71.54 W
Paz de Río 246 5.59 N 72.47 W
Pazifischer Ozean → Pacific Ocean ∓[1] 6 10.00 S 150.00 W
P'ažijeva Sel'ga 24 61.29 N 34.29 E
Pazin 36 45.14 N 13.56 E
Pazña 248 18.36 S 66.55 W
Paznaun V 58 47.03 N 10.20 E
Pčevža 76 59.23 N 32.20 E
Pčevža ≃ 76 59.21 N 31.54 E
Pchery 54 50.10 N 14.08 E
Pe 110 13.28 N 98.31 E
Pea 174w 21.10 S 175.14 W
Pea ≃ 194 31.01 N 85.51 W
Peabody, Ks., U.S. 198 38.10 N 97.06 W
Peabody, Ma., U.S. 207 42.31 N 70.55 W
Peace ≃, Can. 176 59.00 N 111.25 W
Peace ≃, Fl., U.S. 220 26.55 N 82.05 W
Peace Arch ⊥ 224 49.00 N 122.45 W
Peace Bridge ◆[5] 284a 42.54 N 78.55 W
Peace Canyon Dam ◆[6] 182 55.59 N 121.59 W
Peace Dale 207 41.27 N 71.29 W
Peacehaven 42 50.47 N 0.01 E
Peace River 182 56.14 N 117.17 W
Peach Creek 188 37.52 N 81.59 W
Peach Creek ≃, Tx., U.S. 222 30.07 N 95.10 W
Peach Creek ≃, Tx., U.S. 222 29.24 N 97.19 W
Peach Creek, Sandy Fork ≃ 222 29.34 N 97.19 W
Peachdale 158 26.30 S 24.42 E
Peachland 182 49.46 N 119.44 W
Peach Orchard 192 33.28 N 82.04 W
Peach Springs 200 35.31 N 113.25 W
Peacock Hills ⋏[2] 176 66.05 N 110.45 W
Peacock Point ›, On., Can. 212 42.47 N 79.59 W
Peacock Point ›, Wake I. 174a 19.16 N 166.37 E
Peacock Sound ∪ 9 72.55 S 100.00 W
Pea Hill Branch ≃ 284c 38.45 N 76.57 W
Peak Charles National Park ♠ 162 32.55 S 121.06 E
Peak Crossing 171a 27.47 S 152.44 E
Peak Dale 262 53.17 N 1.52 W
Peak District National Park ♠ 44 53.17 N 1.45 W
Peak Downs 166 22.12 S 148.10 E
Peake Creek ≃ 162 28.05 S 136.07 E
Peaked Mountain ∧ 186 46.34 N 68.49 W
Peak Forest 262 53.19 N 1.50 W
Peak Forest Canal ≍ 262 53.29 N 2.06 W
Peak Hill, Austl. 162 25.38 S 118.43 E
Peak Hill, Austl. 166 32.44 S 148.12 E
Peakhurst 274a 33.58 S 151.04 E
Peakview 171b 36.04 S 149.24 E
Peäldoajvi ∧ 24 69.11 N 26.36 E
Peale, Mount ∧ 200 38.26 N 109.14 W
Peale Island I 174a 19.19 N 166.35 E
Peapack Brook ≃ 276 40.41 N 74.39 W
Pearblossom 228 34.30 N 117.55 W
Pearce 200 31.54 N 109.49 W
Pearce, Royal Australian Air Force Station ■ 168a 31.41 S 116.01 E
Pearce Point › 164 14.25 S 129.21 E
Peard Bay C 180 70.51 N 159.10 W
Pea Ridge ∧ 218 38.25 N 83.36 W
Pea Ridge National Military Park ♠ 194 36.29 N 94.06 W
Pearisburg 192 37.19 N 80.44 W
Pearl, Il., U.S. 194 39.28 N 90.38 W
Pearl, Ms., U.S. 194 32.16 N 90.07 W
Pearl ≃ 194 30.11 N 89.32 W
Pearl, Lake ⊜ 283 42.04 N 71.21 W
Pearland 222 29.33 N 95.17 W
Pearl and Hermes Atoll I[1] 14 27.55 N 175.45 W
Pearl Bank ✢[4] 116 5.49 N 119.42 E
Pearl Beach 214 42.37 N 82.35 W
Pearl City 229c 21.23 N 157.58 W
Pearl Creek ≃ 198 44.15 N 98.08 W
Pearl Harbor C 229c 21.22 N 157.58 W
Pearl Harbor Naval Station ■ 229c 21.21 N 157.57 W
Pearl Peak ∧ 204 40.14 N 115.32 W
Pearl River, La., U.S. 194 30.22 N 89.44 W
Pearl River, N.Y., U.S. 210 41.03 N 74.01 W
Pearls Airport ⊠ 241k 12.09 N 61.37 W
Pearns Point › 240c 17.05 N 61.54 W
Pearsall 196 28.53 N 99.05 W
Pearse Island I 182 54.51 N 130.21 W
Pearsoll Peak ∧ 202 42.18 N 123.50 W
Pearson 192 31.17 N 82.51 W
Pearson Lake ⊜ 184 56.15 N 97.15 W
Pearston 158 32.35 S 25.08 E
Peary Land ◆[1] 16 83.00 N 35.00 W
Pease ≃ 196 34.12 N 99.07 W
Pease Air Force Base ■ 188 43.06 N 70.49 W
Peasedown Saint John 42 51.19 N 2.27 W
Peaster 222 32.52 N 97.52 W
Peat Inn 46 56.17 N 2.53 W
Pebane 154 17.10 S 38.08 E
Pebas 246 3.20 S 71.49 W
Pebble Beach 226 36.34 N 121.57 W
Pebble Island I 254 51.18 S 59.35 W
Peć 38 42.40 N 20.19 E
Pecan Bayou ≃ 196 31.28 N 98.43 W
Pecangakan 115a 6.41 S 110.42 E
Pecan Gap 196 33.26 N 95.51 W
Peçanha 255 18.33 S 42.34 W
Peças, Ilha das I 252 25.26 S 48.19 W
Pecatonica 190 42.18 N 89.21 W
Pecatonica ≃ 190 42.27 N 89.05 W
Pecatu 115b 8.50 S 115.07 E
Peccioli 66 43.33 N 10.43 E
Pécel 264c 47.29 N 19.21 E
Pečenegi 78 49.52 N 36.55 E
Peçenek 130 40.25 N 32.19 E
Pečenežin 78 48.32 N 24.54 E
Pečenga 24 69.33 N 31.07 E
Pečerniki 82 54.39 N 39.14 E
Pečernikovskije Vyselki 82 54.10 N 39.10 E
Pechanga Indian Reservation ◆[4] 228 33.27 N 117.04 W
Peche Island I 281 42.21 N 82.56 W
Pechincha ◆[8] 287a 22.56 S 43.21 W
Pechora → Pečora ≃ 24 68.13 N 54.15 E

Pechorka ≃ 265b 55.35 N 38.03 E
Pechra-Jakovlevskaja 265b 55.48 N 37.58 E
Pechra-Pokrovskoje 265b 55.50 N 37.57 E
Pechu 84 43.24 N 40.49 E
Peči 80 54.48 N 44.19 E
Pecica 38 46.10 N 21.05 E
Pečicy 82 55.36 N 38.27 E
Pecixe, Ilha de I 150 11.50 N 16.05 W
Peck 190 43.15 N 82.49 W
Peck Bay C 208 39.16 N 74.37 W
Peck-Berge ⋏[2] 264a 52.36 N 13.34 E
Peckeloh 52 52.01 N 8.07 E
Peckelsheim 52 51.36 N 9.07 E
Pecket Well 262 53.46 N 2.00 W
Peck Lake ⊜ 210 43.07 N 74.25 W
Peckman ≃ 276 40.53 N 74.13 W
Peconic ≃ 207 40.55 N 72.37 W
Pečora, S.S.S.R. 24 65.10 N 57.11 E
Pečora, S.S.S.R. 78 48.52 N 28.42 E
Pečora ≃ 24 68.13 N 54.15 E
Pecora, Capo › 71 39.27 N 8.23 E
Pecoraro, Monte ∧ 68 38.32 N 16.20 E
Pečoro-Ilyčskij Zapovednik ◆[4] 24 62.20 N 59.00 E
Pečorskaja guba C 24 68.40 N 54.45 E
Pečorskoje more ∓[2] 24 70.00 N 54.00 E
Pečory 76 57.49 N 27.36 E
Pecos, N.M., U.S. 200 35.34 N 105.40 W
Pecos, Tx., U.S. 196 31.25 N 103.29 W
Pecos ≃ 178 29.42 N 101.22 W
Pecos National Monument ♠ 200 35.26 N 105.56 W
Pecos Plains ≌ 196 33.20 N 104.30 W
Pecq 50 50.41 N 3.20 E
Pecquencourt 50 50.23 N 3.13 E
Pecqueuse 261 48.39 N 2.03 E
Pécs 30 46.05 N 18.13 E
Pedana 122 16.16 N 81.10 E
Pedas 114 2.37 N 102.04 E
Pedasí 246 7.32 N 80.02 W
Pedaso 66 43.06 N 13.50 E
Peddāpuram 122 17.05 N 82.08 E
Pedder, Lake ⊜[1] 166 42.54 S 146.12 E
Peddie 158 33.12 S 27.07 E
Peddocks Island I 283 42.17 N 70.56 W
Pededze ≃ 76 56.56 N 26.54 E
Pedernales, Arg. 252 35.15 S 59.39 W
Pedernales, Méx. 234 19.08 N 101.28 W
Pedernales, Rep. Dom. 238 18.02 N 71.45 W
Pedernales, Ven. 246 9.58 N 62.16 W
Pedernales ≃ 196 30.26 N 98.04 W
Pedernales, Salar de ≌ 252 26.15 S 69.10 W
Pedernales Falls State Park ♠ 196 30.20 N 98.14 W
Pederobba 64 45.53 N 11.58 E
Pedersborg 41 55.27 N 11.34 E
Pederstrup 41 54.54 N 11.16 E
Pedesina 58 46.05 N 9.33 E
Pedhoulás 130 34.58 N 32.50 E
Pedja ≃ 76 58.25 N 26.11 E
Pedley 228 33.59 N 117.28 W
Pé do Morro 256 22.20 S 44.57 W
Pedra 250 8.30 S 36.57 W
Pedra Azul 255 16.01 S 41.16 W
Pedra Bela 256 22.47 S 46.27 W
Pedra Branca 250 5.27 S 39.43 W
Pedra Branca ∧ 256 22.56 S 43.28 W
Pedra Branca, Serra da ∧ 287a 22.56 S 43.29 W
Pedra da Gávea ∧ 287a 23.00 S 43.17 W
Pedra de Guaratiba ◆[8] 256 23.00 S 43.39 W
Pedra do Sino ∧ 256 22.30 S 43.03 W
Pedra Grande, Recifes da ✢[2] 255 17.45 S 38.58 W
Pedra Lume 150a 16.46 N 22.54 W
Pedralva 256 22.14 S 45.28 W
Pedras 250 2.48 S 57.16 W
Pedras, Rio das ≃, Bra. 255 12.13 S 45.15 W
Pedras, Rio das ≃, Bra. 287a 22.51 S 43.01 W
Pedras de Fogo 250 7.23 S 35.07 W
Pedra Selada 256 22.21 S 44.26 W
Pedras Negras 248 12.51 S 62.54 W
Pedras Salgadas 34 41.32 N 7.36 W
Pedraza 246 10.11 N 74.55 W
Pedregal, Pan. 236 8.22 N 82.26 W
Pedregal, Ven. 246 11.01 N 70.08 W
Pedregulho 255 20.16 S 47.29 W
Pedreira 256 22.43 S 46.55 W
Pedreira ≃ 250 0.12 N 50.47 W
Pedreiras 250 4.34 S 44.39 W
Pedreros 286d 12.01 S 76.57 W
Pedriceña 232 25.06 N 103.47 W
Pedricktown 208 39.46 N 75.24 W
Pedrinhas 250 11.12 S 37.41 W
Pedro, Point › 122 9.50 N 80.14 E
Pedro Afonso 250 8.59 S 48.11 W
Pedro Avelino 250 5.31 S 36.23 W
Pedro Bay 180 59.47 N 154.07 W
Pedro Betancourt 240p 22.44 N 81.17 W
Pedro Cays II 238 17.00 N 77.50 W
Pedro do Rio 256 22.20 S 43.09 W
Pedrógão Grande 34 39.55 N 8.09 W
Pedro Gomes 255 18.04 S 54.32 W
Pedro González, Isla I 246 8.24 N 79.06 W
Pedro II 250 4.25 S 41.28 W
Pedro II, Ilha I 246 1.10 N 66.40 W
Pedro Juan Caballero 252 22.34 S 55.37 W
Pedro Leopoldo 255 19.38 S 44.03 W
Pedro Luro 252 39.29 S 62.41 W
Pedro Muñoz 34 39.24 N 2.58 W
Pedro Osório 252 31.51 S 52.45 W
Pedro R. Fernández 252 28.45 S 58.39 W
Pedro Teixeira 256 21.43 S 43.44 W
Pedro Velho 250 6.26 S 35.14 W
Peebinga 166 34.56 S 140.55 E
Peebles, Scot., U.K. 46 55.39 N 3.12 W
Peebles, Oh., U.S. 218 38.56 N 83.24 W
Peedamullah 162 21.50 S 115.38 E
Pee Dee ≃ 192 34.43 N 79.52 W
Peekaboo Mountain ∧[2] 188 45.45 N 67.53 W
Peekskill 210 41.17 N 73.55 W
Peel, Austl. 170 33.19 S 149.38 E
Peel, I. of Man 44 54.13 N 4.40 W
Peel □[6] 212 43.45 N 79.47 W
Peel ≃ 180 67.37 N 134.40 W
Peel Channel ≃[1] 180 68.13 N 135.00 W
Peel Fell ∧ 44 55.17 N 2.35 W
Peel Inlet C 168a 32.35 S 115.44 E
Peel Island I 171a 27.30 S 153.22 E
Pe Ell 224 46.34 N 123.17 W
Peel Point › 176 73.22 N 114.35 W
Peel Sound ∪ 176 73.15 N 96.30 W
Peene ≃ 54 54.09 N 13.46 E
Peenemünde 54 54.08 N 13.46 E
Peepeekisis Indian Reserve ◆[4] 184 50.52 N 103.24 W
Peer 56 51.08 N 5.28 E
Peerless 202 48.46 N 105.49 W
Peers 182 53.40 N 116.00 W
Peesane 184 52.52 N 103.36 W
Peetz 198 40.57 N 103.06 W
Peetzsee ⊜ 264a 52.26 N 13.50 E
Pefferlaw 212 44.19 N 79.12 W
Pefferlaw Brook ≃ 212 44.15 N 79.13 W
Pegasus, Port C 172 47.12 S 167.41 E
Pegasus Bay C 172 43.20 S 173.00 E
Pegau 54 51.10 N 12.14 E
Pegli 62 44.26 N 8.48 E
Peglia, Monte ∧ 66 42.49 N 12.13 E
Pegnitz 60 49.45 N 11.33 E
Pegnitz ≃ 60 49.29 N 11.00 E
Pego 34 38.51 N 0.07 W
Pegolotte 64 45.12 N 12.02 E

Pegswood 44 55.11 N 1.38 W
Pegtymel' ≃ 180 69.25 N 174.35 E
Pegtymel'skij chrebet ⋏ 180 68.30 N 177.00 E
Pegu → Bago 110 17.20 N 96.29 E
Pegu ≃ 110 16.47 N 96.13 E
Pegueros 234 20.57 N 102.40 W
Peguis Indian Reserve ◆[4] 184 51.20 N 97.35 W
Pegu Yoma ⋏ 110 19.00 N 95.50 E
Pegwell Bay C 42 51.18 N 1.26 E
Pegyš 24 63.26 N 50.30 E
Pehčevo 38 41.46 N 22.54 E
Pehladpur ◆[8] 272a 28.35 N 77.06 E
Pehlivanköy 130 41.21 N 26.55 E
Pehowa 124 29.59 N 76.35 E
Pehuajó 252 35.48 S 61.53 W
Pehula 26 61.17 N 22.42 E
Peian → Bei'an 89 48.16 N 126.36 E
Peiching → Beijing 105 39.55 N 116.25 E
Peigan Indian Reserve ◆[4] 182 49.35 N 113.40 W
Peihai → Beihai 102 21.29 N 109.05 E
Peij 52 51.06 N 5.53 E
Peijiatun 98 39.19 N 121.41 E
Peikang 100 23.34 N 120.18 E
Peikang ≃ 100 23.31 N 120.08 E
Peikant'ang Tao I 100 26.13 N 119.59 E
Peilstein im Mühlviertel 60 48.37 N 13.53 E
Peinan 100 22.47 N 121.07 E
Peinan ≃ 100 22.46 N 121.10 E
Peine 52 52.19 N 10.13 E
Peine, Pointe à › 240d 15.23 N 61.15 W
Peinnechaung I 110 19.59 N 93.04 E
Peio 64 46.22 N 10.40 E
Peip'ing → Beijing 105 39.55 N 116.25 E
Peipsi järv → Čudskoje ozero ⊜ 76 58.45 N 27.25 E
Peipus, Lake → Čudskoje ozero ⊜ 76 58.45 N 27.25 E
Peïra-Cava 62 43.56 N 7.22 E
Peirce, Cape › 180 58.35 N 161.47 W
Peisey-Nancroix 62 45.33 N 6.45 E
Peiskretscham → Pyskowice 30 50.24 N 18.38 E
Peissenberg 64 47.48 N 11.04 E
Peissenberg ∧, B.R.D. 60 47.48 N 11.01 E
Peissenberg ∧, B.R.D. 64 47.48 N 11.01 E
Peiting 58 47.47 N 10.55 E
Peit'ou ◆[8] 269d 25.08 N 121.30 E
Peitz 54 51.51 N 14.24 E
Peixe 255 12.03 S 48.32 W
Peixe, Rio do ≃, Bra. 255 14.06 S 50.51 W
Peixe, Rio do ≃, Bra. 255 21.31 S 51.58 W
Peixe, Rio do ≃, Bra. 256 23.24 S 45.28 W
Peixe, Rio do ≃, Bra. 256 23.12 S 46.06 W
Peixe, Rio do ≃, Bra. 256 21.55 S 43.21 W
Peixe, Rio do ≃, Bra. 256 21.38 S 45.11 W
Peixe, Rio do ≃, Bra. 256 22.23 S 46.51 W
Peixe-Boi 250 1.12 S 47.18 W
Peixes, Rio dos ≃ 250 10.42 S 57.56 W
Peixian, Zhg. 98 34.44 N 116.59 E
Peixian (Yunhe), Zhg. 98 34.21 N 117.59 E
Peixoto de Azevedo ≃ 250 10.06 S 55.31 W
Peiziyan 98 35.07 N 115.01 E
Pejantan, Pulau I 112 0.07 N 107.14 E
Pejelagartero 234 18.04 N 93.45 W
Pek ≃ 38 44.46 N 21.33 E
Pekalongan 115a 6.53 S 109.40 E
Pekan 114 3.30 N 103.25 E
Pekanbaru 112 0.32 N 101.27 E
Pekanheran 112 0.21 S 102.26 E
Pekin, Il., U.S. 190 40.34 N 89.38 W
Pekin, In., U.S. 218 38.29 N 86.01 W
Pekin, N.Y., U.S. 284a 43.10 N 78.53 W
Pekin, Oh., U.S. 214 40.43 N 81.07 W
Pékin → Beijing, Zhg. 105 39.55 N 116.25 E
Peking → Beijing 105 39.55 N 116.25 E
Peking National Library ᴗ 271a 39.56 N 116.22 E
Peking Railway Station ◆[5] 271a 39.54 N 116.26 E
Peking University ᴗ[2] 271a 39.59 N 116.18 E
Peking Zoo ♠ 271a 39.56 N 116.19 E
Peklino 76 53.33 N 33.32 E
Pekša ≃ 80 55.53 N 39.40 E
Pektubajevo 80 57.02 N 48.23 E
Pekul'nej, chrebet ⋏ 180 66.00 N 175.00 E
Pekul'nejskoje, ozero ⊜ 180 62.40 N 177.00 E
Péla 150 7.37 N 9.07 W
Pelabuhandagang 112 1.08 S 103.05 E
Pelabuhan Kelang 114 3.00 N 101.24 E
Pelabuhanratu 115a 6.59 S 106.33 E
Pelabuhanratu, Teluk C 115a 7.03 S 106.27 E
Pel'a-Chovanskaja 80 54.36 N 44.56 E
Pelado, Cerro ∧ 286a 19.09 N 99.13 W
Pelagejevka 83 48.06 N 38.36 E
Pelagie, Isole II 70a 35.40 N 12.40 E
Pelago 66 43.46 N 11.30 E
Pelahatchie 194 32.18 N 89.47 W
Pelaihari 112 3.48 S 114.45 E
Pelalawan 112 0.27 N 102.05 E
Pelat, Mont ∧ 62 44.16 N 6.42 E
Pelawan 114 2.47 N 102.55 E
Pełczyce 30 53.03 N 15.18 E
Pélé, Mont ∧ 152 3.15 S 11.14 E
Peleaga, Vîrful ∧ 38 45.22 N 22.54 E
Pelechuco 248 14.48 S 69.04 W
Peleduj 74 59.36 N 112.45 E
Pelée, Montagne ∧ 240e 14.48 N 61.10 W
Pelee, Point › 214 41.54 N 82.30 W
Pelee Island I 214 41.46 N 82.39 W
Pelee Passage ∪ 214 41.52 N 82.37 W
Pelekech ∧ 154 3.48 N 35.04 E
Peleliu I 175b 7.01 N 134.15 E
Peleng, Pulau I 112 1.20 S 123.10 E
Peleng, Selat ∪ 112 1.10 S 122.45 E
Pelenija 78 47.53 N 27.50 E
Pelf, Monte ∧ 64 46.14 N 12.12 E
Pelham, On., Can. 212 43.02 N 79.17 W
Pelham, Al., U.S. 194 33.17 N 86.48 W
Pelham, Ga., U.S. 192 31.07 N 84.09 W
Pelham, Ma., U.S. 207 42.23 N 72.24 W
Pelham, N.H., U.S. 207 42.44 N 71.19 W
Pelham, N.Y., U.S. 276 40.54 N 73.48 W
Pelham Bay C 276 40.52 N 73.47 W
Pelham Bay Park ♠ 276 40.52 N 73.49 W
Pelham Manor 276 40.53 N 73.48 W
Pelhřimov 30 49.26 N 15.13 E
Pelican 180 57.57 N 136.14 W
Pelican ≃ 198 46.17 N 96.08 W
Pelican, Punta › 200 31.19 N 113.43 W
Pelican Bay C 184 52.45 N 100.20 W
Pelican Island I, Mo., U.S. 219 38.52 N 90.18 W
Pelican Island I, Tx., U.S. 222 29.20 N 94.48 W
Pelican Lagoon C 168b 35.50 S 137.47 E
Pelican Lake 190 45.30 N 89.10 W
Pelican Lake ⊜, Ab., Can. 182 55.47 N 113.15 W
Pelican Lake ⊜, Mb., Can. 184 53.50 N 96.08 W
Pelican Lake ⊜, Mb., Can. 184 52.30 N 100.20 W

Pelican Lake ⊜, Mb., Can. 184 49.20 N 99.35 W
Pelican Lake ⊜, Sk., Can. 184 55.08 N 103.00 W
Pelican Lake ⊜, Sk., Can. 184 50.32 N 106.00 W
Pelican Lake ⊜, Mn., U.S. 190 48.05 N 92.54 W
Pelican Lake ⊜, S.D., U.S. 198 44.52 N 97.11 W
Pelican Mountain ∧ 182 55.35 N 113.40 W
Pelican Narrows 184 55.10 N 102.56 W
Pelican Point › 168b 34.48 S 138.29 E
Pelican Rapids, Mb., Can. 184 52.45 N 100.42 W
Pelican Rapids, Mn., U.S. 198 46.34 N 96.04 W
Pelileo 246 1.19 S 78.32 W
Pelister ∧ 38 41.00 N 21.12 E
Pelješac, Poluotok ›[1] 36 42.58 N 17.20 E
Pelkosenniemi 24 67.07 N 27.30 E
Pelkum, B.R.D. 52 51.39 N 7.46 E
Pelkum, B.R.D. 263 51.40 N 7.24 E
Pella, S. Afr. 158 29.01 S 19.06 E
Pella, Ia., U.S. 190 41.24 N 92.54 W
Pélla ⊥ 38 40.45 N 22.33 E
Pellaro 68 38.01 N 15.39 E
Pell City 194 33.35 N 86.17 W
Pellechia, Monte ∧ 66 42.07 N 12.52 E
Pellegrini 252 36.16 S 63.09 W
Pellegrini, Lago ⊜ 252 38.40 S 68.00 W
Pellegrino, Cozzo ∧ 68 39.45 N 16.03 E
Pellegrino, Monte ∧ 70 38.10 N 13.21 E
Pellegrino Parmense 64 44.44 N 9.55 E
Pellendorf 264b 48.06 N 16.27 E
Peller, Monte ∧ 64 46.18 N 10.57 E
Pellestrina, Litorale di ⊥[2] 64 45.16 N 12.18 E
Pelletier Lake ⊜ 184 56.30 N 97.00 W
Pellice ≃ 62 44.50 N 7.38 E
Pellingen 56 49.40 N 6.40 E
Pell Lake 216 42.32 N 88.21 W
Pello 24 66.47 N 24.00 E
Pellston 190 45.33 N 84.47 W
Pellworm I 30 54.31 N 8.38 E
Pelly 184 51.52 N 101.55 W
Pelly ≃ 180 62.47 N 137.19 W
Pelly Bay C 176 68.53 N 89.51 W
Pelly Crossing 180 62.50 N 136.35 W
Pelly Lake ⊜ 176 65.59 N 101.12 W
Pelly Mountains ⋏ 180 62.00 N 133.00 W
Peloncillo Mountains ⋏ 200 32.15 N 109.00 W
Pelón de Ñado, Cerro ∧ 234 20.05 N 99.55 W
Pelopónnisos ›[1] 38 37.30 N 22.00 E
Peloritani, Monti ⋏ 70 38.03 N 15.20 E
Pelotas 252 31.46 S 52.20 W
Pelotas ≃ 252 27.28 S 51.55 W
Pelplin 30 53.56 N 18.42 E
Pelque ≃ 254 51.03 S 70.58 W
Pelsin 54 53.48 N 13.40 E
Pelusium Bay → Ṭīnah, Khalīj aṭ- C 140 31.08 N 32.40 E
Pel'ušn'a 76 58.56 N 32.52 E
Pélussin 62 45.25 N 4.41 E
Pelvo d'Elva ∧ 62 44.33 N 9.15 E
Pelym 86 59.38 N 63.05 E
Pemadumcook Lake ⊜ 188 45.40 N 68.55 W
Pemalang 115a 6.54 S 109.22 E
Pemalang, Ujung › 115a 6.47 S 109.29 E
Pemali ≃ 115a 6.47 S 109.01 E
Pemangkat 112 1.10 N 108.58 E
Pematang 112 0.12 S 102.04 E
Pematangsiantar 114 2.57 N 99.03 E
Pematangtanahjawa 114 2.53 N 99.12 E
Pemba, Moç. 154 12.58 S 40.30 E
Pemba, Zam. 154 16.31 S 27.22 E
Pemba I 154 5.10 S 39.48 E
Pemba Channel ∪ 154 5.10 S 39.20 E
Pembarisan, Pegunungan ⋏ 115a 7.13 S 108.45 E
Pemberton, Austl. 162 34.28 S 116.01 E
Pemberton, B.C., Can. 182 50.20 N 122.48 W
Pemberton, Eng., U.K. 262 53.32 N 2.41 W
Pemberton, N.J., U.S. 208 39.58 N 74.41 W
Pemberton, Oh., U.S. 216 40.18 N 84.02 W
Pemberton Airport ⊠ 285 39.59 N 74.41 W
Pemberton Heights 285 39.58 N 74.41 W
Pemberville 214 41.24 N 83.27 W
Pembina 198 48.57 N 97.14 W
Pembina ≃, Ab., Can. 182 54.45 N 114.15 W
Pembina ≃, N.A. 184 48.57 N 97.14 W
Pembina Hills ⋏[2] 198 49.10 N 98.25 W
Pembine 190 45.38 N 87.59 W
Pembrey 42 51.42 N 4.16 W
Pembroke, On., Can. 190 45.49 N 77.07 W
Pembroke, Wales, U.K. 42 51.41 N 4.55 W
Pembroke, Ga., U.S. 192 32.08 N 81.37 W
Pembroke, Ky., U.S. 194 36.46 N 87.21 W
Pembroke, Me., U.S. 188 44.57 N 67.09 W
Pembroke, N.Y., U.S. 210 43.00 N 78.27 W
Pembroke, N.C., U.S. 192 34.40 N 79.11 W
Pembroke, Va., U.S. 192 37.19 N 80.38 W
Pembroke, Cape › 176 62.56 N 81.55 W
Pembroke Castle ⊥ 42 51.41 N 4.56 W
Pembroke Dock 42 51.42 N 4.56 W
Pembroke Pines 220 26.00 N 80.13 W
Pembrokeshire Coast National Park ♠ 42 51.47 N 5.06 W
Pembuang 112 2.34 S 112.19 E
Pembuang ≃ 112 3.24 S 112.33 E
Pembury 42 51.09 N 0.20 E
Pemfling 60 49.16 N 12.37 E
Pemichigamau Lake ⊜ 184 56.16 N 99.33 W
Pemigewasset ≃ 188 43.26 N 71.40 W
Pemmican Portage 184 53.56 N 102.17 W
Pemuco 252 36.58 S 72.06 W
Pemynoos Indian Reserve ◆[4] 182 50.29 N 121.15 W
Pemzašen 84 40.35 N 43.57 E
Pena, Parque de ♠ 266c 38.47 N 9.23 W
Peña Blanca 236 8.27 N 81.40 W
Peña Blanca, Macizos de ∧ 236 13.15 N 85.41 W
Peñafiel, Esp. 34 41.36 N 4.07 W
Penafiel, Port. 34 41.12 N 8.17 W
Pen'agino 265b 55.50 N 37.21 E
Peña Gorda, Cerro ∧ 234 20.44 N 104.50 W
Peña Grande ◆[8] 266a 40.29 N 3.44 W
Pen'akša 80 56.22 N 44.56 E
Peñalara ∧ 34 40.51 N 3.57 W
Peñalolén 286e 33.29 S 70.32 W
Pena-Lunanga 154 4.16 S 28.10 E
Penalva 250 3.18 S 45.10 W
Penambulai, Pulau I 164 6.24 S 134.48 E
Peña Negra, Punta › 246 4.17 S 81.15 W
Peña Nevada, Cerro ∧ 234 23.46 N 99.52 W
Penang → George Town 114 5.25 N 100.20 E
Penanjung, Teluk C 115a 7.45 S 108.37 E
Penápolis 255 21.24 S 50.04 W
Peñaranda de Bracamonte 34 40.54 N 5.12 W
Pen Argyl 210 40.52 N 75.15 W
Penaron 114 4.38 N 97.40 E
Peñarroya-Pueblonuevo 34 38.18 N 5.16 W
Penarth 42 51.27 N 3.11 W
Peñas, Cabo de › 34 43.39 N 5.51 W
Penas, Golfo de C 254 47.22 S 74.50 W

Symbol	English	Deutsch	Español	Français	Português
≃	River	Fluß	Río	Rivière	Rio
≍	Canal	Kanal	Canal	Canal	Canal
⌞	Waterfall, Rapids	Wasserfall, Stromschnellen	Cascada, Rápidos	Chute d'eau, Rapides	Cascata, Rápidos
∪	Strait	Meeresstraße	Estrecho	Détroit	Estreito
C	Bay, Gulf	Bucht, Golf	Bahía, Golfo	Baie, Golfe	Baía, Golfo
⊜	Lake, Lakes	See, Seen	Lago, Lagos	Lac, Lacs	Lago, Lagos
≌	Swamp	Sumpf	Pantano	Marais	Pântano
⊓	Ice Features, Glacier	Eis- und Gletscherformen	Accidentes Glaciales	Formes glaciaires	Acidentes glaciares
∓	Other Hydrographic Features	Andere Hydrographische Objekte	Otros Elementos Hidrográficos	Autres données hydrographiques	Outros acidentes hidrográficos
✢	Submarine Features	Untermeerische Objekte	Accidentes Submarinos	Formes de relief sous-marin	Acidentes submarinos
□	Political Unit	Politische Einheit	Unidad Politica	Entité politique	Unidade política
ᴗ	Cultural Institution	Kulturelle Institution	Institución Cultural	Institution culturelle	Institução cultural
⊥	Historical Site	Historische Stätte	Sitio Histórico	Site historique	Sitio histórico
♠	Recreational Site	Erholungs- und Ferienort	Sitio de Recreo	Centre de loisirs	Area de Lazer
⊠	Airport	Flughafen	Aeropuerto	Aéroport	Aeroporto
■	Military Installation	Militäranlage	Instalación Militar	Installation militaire	Instalação militar
◆	Miscellaneous	Verschiedenes	Misceláneo	Divers	Diversos

Column 1

Penasco, Rio 200 36.10 N 105.41 W
Peñasco, Rio 196 32.45 N 104.19 W
Penataquit Creek ≃ 276 40.43 N 73.14 W
Penbrook 208 40.16 N 76.50 W
Pencader 42 52.01 N 4.16 W
Pencahue 252 35.24 S 71.49 W
Pence 190 46.25 N 90.16 W
Pen Centre ↗9 284a 43.08 N 79.14 W
Penchard 261 48.59 N 2.52 E
Penck Trough ∨ 9 73.00 S 2.45 W
Pencoed 42 51.32 N 3.30 W
Pendang, Indon. 112 1.28 S 114.51 E
Pendang, Malay. 114 6.00 N 100.28 E
Pendé ≃ 146 7.55 N 16.36 E
Pendédi 267c 38.03 N 23.52 E
Pendelikón Óros ▲ 267c 38.06 N 23.54 E
Pendembu, S.L. 150 8.06 N 10.42 W
Pendembu, S.L. 150 9.06 N 12.12 W
Pendências 250 5.15 S 36.43 W
Pendeng 114 4.46 N 97.36 E
Pender 198 42.06 N 96.42 W
Pender Bay ⊂ 116 16.45 S 122.42 E
Pendhar 272c 19.04 N 73.06 E
Pendik 267b 40.53 N 29.13 E
Pendjari ≃ 150 10.54 N 0.51 E
Pendjari, Parc
  National de la ◆ 150 11.20 N 1.15 E
Pendlebury 262 53.31 N 2.20 W
Pendle Hill 274a 33.48 S 150.57 E
Pendle Hill ▲² 44 53.52 N 2.17 W
Pendleton, In., U.S. 218 39.59 N 85.44 W
Pendleton, N.Y., U.S. 284a 43.06 N 78.44 W
Pendleton, Or., U.S. 202 45.40 N 118.47 W
Pendleton, S.C., U.S. 192 34.39 N 82.47 W
Pendleton ⊡⁶ 218 38.42 N 84.22 W
Pendolo 112 2.05 S 120.42 E
Pendopo 112 3.17 S 103.52 E
Pend Oreille ≃ 202 49.04 N 117.37 W
Pend Oreille, Lake ⊕ 202 48.10 N 116.11 W
Pend Oreille, Mount ▲ 202 48.25 N 116.10 W
Pendotiba ≃ 287a 22.53 S 43.02 W
Pendžikent 85 39.29 N 67.35 E
Penebel 115b 8.25 S 115.09 E
Penedo 250 10.17 S 36.36 W
Penedono 34 40.59 N 7.24 W
Penela 34 40.02 N 8.23 W
Penelope 222 31.52 N 96.56 W
Penetang Harbour ⊂ 212 44.47 N 79.57 W
Penetanguishene 212 44.47 N 79.55 W
Penfield, Il., U.S. 216 40.18 N 87.57 W
Penfield, N.Y., U.S. 210 43.07 N 77.28 W
Penfield, Oh., U.S. 214 41.10 N 82.08 W
Penfield, Pa., U.S. 214 41.13 N 78.34 W
Pengango ≃ 122 19.53 N 79.09 E
Pengastulan 115b 8.11 S 114.55 E
Peng Chau I 271d 22.17 N 114.02 E
P'engchia Yü I 100 25.38 N 122.04 E
Penge, S. Afr. 156 24.22 S 30.13 E
Penge, Zaïre 154 5.31 S 24.37 E
Penge ↗8 ≃ 260 51.25 N 0.04 W
Penggong 106 30.27 N 119.57 E
Penggongmiao 100 26.07 N 113.34 E
Penghu 100 25.24 N 118.11 E
P'enghu Ch'üntao
  (Pescadores) II 100 23.30 N 119.30 E
P'enghu Shuitao ∐ 100 23.30 N 119.50 E
Pengiki, Pulau I 112 0.15 N 108.03 E
Pengjiachang 107 30.36 N 103.53 E
Pengjialouzi 104 41.56 N 123.40 E
Pengjiawan 102 32.16 N 114.04 E
Pengjiawu 105 39.41 N 117.10 E
Pengkalan Baharu 114 4.28 N 100.38 E
Pengkou 106 25.32 N 116.42 E
Penglai (Dengzhou) 98 37.48 N 120.42 E
Penglaizhen 105 30.36 N 105.14 E
Penglang 106 31.23 N 121.05 E
Pengnan 107 30.25 N 105.53 E
Pengpu,
  → Bengbu 100 32.58 N 117.24 E
Pengshan 100 30.13 N 103.52 E
Pengshi 100 30.28 N 113.10 E
Pengshui 102 29.18 N 108.09 E
Penguin 166 41.07 S 146.04 E
Pengwaluote Shan ▲ 120 33.30 N 86.35 E
Pengxi 102 30.49 N 105.41 E
Pengxian 102 31.00 N 103.50 E
Pengze 100 29.53 N 116.33 E
Pengzhai 100 24.49 N 106.33 E
Pengzhuangzi 105 40.06 N 114.51 E
Penha 256 26.46 S 48.39 W
Penha ↗2 287a 22.49 S 43.17 W
Penha, Ribeirão da ≃ 256 22.24 S 46.50 W
Penha de França ≃ 287b 23.32 S 46.36 W
Penha Longa, Bra. 256 22.04 S 43.05 W
Penhalonga, Zimb. 154 18.54 S 32.40 E
Penhold, Canadian
  Forces Base ◆ 182 52.12 N 113.53 W
Penhook Creek ≃ 276 40.45 N 74.05 W
Penhsi,
  → Benxi 104 41.18 N 123.45 E
Peniche 34 39.21 N 9.23 W
Penicuik 46 55.50 N 3.14 W
Penida, Nusa I 115b 8.44 S 115.32 E
Peniq 54 56.56 N 12.41 E
Peningo Neck ↗1 276 40.57 N 73.41 W
Peninjai 112 1.26 S 101.50 E
Peninsula Lake ⊕ 212 45.20 N 79.05 W
Peninsula State Park
  ◆ 190 45.09 N 87.14 W
Penistone 44 53.32 N 1.37 W
Penitas 196 26.17 N 98.27 W
Penitencia Creek ≃ 282 37.27 N 121.55 W
Penitente, Serra do ∧ 250 8.45 S 46.20 W
Penjamillo [de
  Degollado] 234 20.06 N 101.54 W
Pénjamo 234 20.26 N 101.44 W
Penketh 262 53.23 N 2.40 W
Penki,
  → Benxi 104 41.18 N 123.45 E
Penkino 42 54.50 N 38.53 E
Penkridge 42 52.44 N 2.07 W
Penkun 42 53.17 N 14.14 E
Pen Lake ⊕ 212 45.28 N 78.23 W
Penllyn 285 40.10 N 75.15 W
Penmaenmawr 44 53.16 N 3.54 W
Penmarc'h, Pointe de ≻ 32 47.48 N 4.22 W
Penn 279b 40.20 N 79.38 W
Penna, Punta della ≻ 66 42.10 N 14.43 E
Pennabilli 66 43.49 N 12.16 E
Penn Acres 285 39.40 N 75.34 W
Pennant Hills 274a 33.44 S 151.04 E
Pennant Hills Park ◆ 274a 33.45 S 151.04 E
Pennant Point ↗1 186 44.26 N 63.39 W
Pennant Station 184 50.33 N 108.12 W
Pennask Lake ⊕ 182 50.00 N 120.05 W
Pennask Mountain ▲ 182 49.53 N 120.07 W
Penn Creek ≃ 283 42.44 N 70.59 W
Penn Cove ⊂ 284 48.14 N 122.41 W
Penn Cove Park 285 40.09 N 74.55 W
Penndel 66 42.37 N 13.55 E
Penne, Punta ≻ 208 40.41 N 17.56 E
Penne-d'Agenais 32 44.23 N 0.49 E
Pennedepie 50 49.25 N 0.11 E
Pennel Creek ≃ 198 46.34 N 104.52 W
Penneru ≃ 122 14.35 N 80.10 E
Pennes (Pens) 64 46.47 N 11.25 E
Pennes, Val di ✓ 64 46.47 N 11.25 E
Penneshaw 168b 35.44 S 137.56 E
Penn Hills Center ↗9 279b 40.28 N 79.50 W
Pennines ▲ 44 54.10 N 2.05 W
Pennines, Alpes ▲ 58 46.05 N 7.50 E
Penningby 40 59.41 N 18.40 E
Penningby slott ⊥ 40 59.41 N 18.40 E

Column 2

Pennington, N.J.,
  U.S. 208 40.19 N 74.47 W
Pennington, Tx., U.S. 222 31.11 N 95.14 W
Pennington ≃¹ 150 4.45 N 5.35 E
Pennington Gap 192 36.45 N 83.01 W
Pennino, Monte ▲ 66 43.06 N 12.53 E
Penn Run 214 40.37 N 79.01 W
Pennsauken 208 39.58 N 75.04 W
Pennsauken Creek ≃ 285 39.59 N 75.03 W
Pennsauken Creek,
  North Branch ≃ 285 39.58 N 75.01 W
Pennsauken Creek,
  South Branch ≃ 285 39.58 N 75.01 W
Penns Brook ≃ 276 40.43 N 74.32 W
Pennsburg 208 40.23 N 75.29 W
Pennsbury Heights 285 40.12 N 74.49 W
Pennsbury Manor ⊥ 285 40.08 N 74.46 W
Penn's Cave ±5 210 40.53 N 77.36 W
Penns Creek 210 40.52 N 77.04 W
Penns Creek ≃ 210 40.51 N 76.51 W
Pennsdale 210 41.15 N 76.48 W
Penns Grove 208 39.43 N 75.28 W
Pennside 208 40.20 N 75.53 W
Penns Neck 276 40.20 N 74.38 W
Pennsuco 220 25.53 N 80.22 W
Pennsville 208 39.39 N 75.31 W
Penns Woods 279b 40.21 N 79.46 W
Pennsylvania □³, U.S. 178 40.45 N 77.30 W
Pennsylvania □³, U.S. 188 40.45 N 77.30 W
Pennsylvania,
  University of ↗2 285 39.57 N 75.12 W
Pennsylvania Canal ∐ 285 40.13 N 74.47 W
Pennsylvania Station
  ↗ 276 40.45 N 74.00 W
Penn Valley, Ca.,
  U.S. 226 39.12 N 121.11 W
Penn Valley, Pa.,
  U.S. 285 40.01 N 75.16 W
Penn Valley Terrace 285 40.11 N 74.47 W
Pennville 216 40.29 N 85.08 W
Penn Wynne 285 39.59 N 75.16 W
Penny 182 53.50 N 121.17 W
Penn Yan 210 42.39 N 77.03 W
Pennycutaway ≃ 184 56.43 N 92.44 W
Penny Hill 285 39.46 N 75.33 W
Penny Ice Cap ⊓ 176 67.10 N 66.00 W
Pennypack Creek ≃ 285 40.02 N 75.00 W
Pennypack Park ◆ 285 40.04 N 75.03 W
Penny Strait ∐ 176 76.30 N 97.00 W
Peno 76 56.55 N 32.45 E
Penobscot 184 44.07 N 75.54 W
Penobscot ≃ 188 44.30 N 68.50 W
Penobscot, East
  Branch ≃ 186 45.35 N 68.32 W
Penobscot, West
  Branch ≃ 188 45.35 N 68.32 W
Penobscot Bay ⊂ 188 44.15 N 68.49 W
Peno Creek ≃ 219 39.32 N 91.16 W
Penola 168 36.58 S 140.50 E
Peñoles, Cerro ▲ 286a 19.19 N 99.00 W
Peñón, Cerro ▲ 286a 19.19 N 99.00 W
Peñón Blanco 232 24.47 N 104.02 W
Peñón del Rosario,
  Cerro ▲ 234 19.40 N 98.11 W
Penong 162 31.55 S 133.01 E
Penonomé 236 8.31 N 80.22 W
Penrhyn I¹ 14 9.00 S 158.00 W
Penrhyn Bay 44 53.19 N 3.45 W
Penrhyndeudraeth 42 52.56 N 4.04 W
Penrith, Austl. 164 33.45 S 150.42 E
Penrith, Eng., U.K. 44 54.40 N 2.44 W
Penryn, Eng., U.K. 42 50.09 N 5.06 W
Penryn, Ca., U.S. 226 38.51 N 121.10 W
Penryn, Pa., U.S. 208 40.12 N 76.22 W
Pens
  → Pennes 64 46.47 N 11.25 E
Pensacola 194 30.25 N 87.13 W
Pensacola Bay ⊂ 194 30.25 N 87.06 W
Pensacola Mountains ∧ 9 83.45 S 55.00 W
Pensacola Naval Air
  Station ◆ 194 30.21 N 87.19 W
Pensacola Seamount ↗3 14 18.17 N 157.20 W
Pensaukee ≃ 190 44.49 N 87.55 W
Pensby 262 53.20 N 3.06 W
Pense 184 50.25 N 105.00 W
Penshaw 44 54.53 N 1.29 W
Pensiangan 112 4.33 N 116.19 E
Pensilva 42 50.30 N 4.25 W
Pensilvania 246 5.31 N 75.05 W
Pentagna 256 22.09 S 43.45 W
Pentagon ↯ 284c 38.52 N 77.03 W
Pentagon Mountain ▲ 202 47.56 N 113.07 W
Pentecost ↗8 156 15.45 S 168.12 E
Pentecoste 250 3.48 S 39.16 W
Pentecôte I 175f 15.42 S 168.10 E
Pentecôte ≃ 186 49.47 N 67.10 W
Pentecôte, Lac ⊕ 186 49.53 N 67.20 W
Penticton 182 49.30 N 119.35 W
Penticton Indian
  Reserve ◆ 182 49.30 N 119.40 W
Pentin Point ↗ 42 50.36 N 4.55 W
Pentland 166 20.32 S 145.24 E
Pentland Firth ∐ 46 58.44 N 3.07 W
Pentland Hills ▲² 44 55.48 N 3.25 W
Pentraeth 44 53.17 N 4.12 W
Pentre Halkyn 262 53.12 N 3.11 W
Pentucket, Lake ⊕ 283 42.47 N 71.05 W
Pentucket Pond ⊕ 283 42.44 N 71.00 W
Pentwater 190 43.46 N 86.25 W
Penuba 112 0.20 S 104.28 E
Peñuelas 240m 18.03 N 66.43 W
Penugonda 122 14.05 N 77.35 E
Penunjok, Tanjong ≻ 114 4.22 N 103.29 E
Pênwégon 110 18.13 N 96.34 E
Penwell 196 31.44 N 102.35 W
Penyagolosa ▲ 34 40.13 N 0.21 W
Penyal d'Ifac ≻ 34 38.38 N 0.05 E
Penyengat 114 0.54 N 104.28 E
Pen-y-Ghent ▲ 44 54.09 N 2.14 W
Penygroes, Wales,
  U.K. 42 51.49 N 4.02 W
Penygroes, Wales,
  U.K. 44 53.04 N 4.17 W
Penyu, Kepulauan II 115a 5.30 N 125.47 E
Penyu, Teluk ⊂ 115a 7.45 S 109.15 E
Penza 80 53.13 N 45.00 E
Penza □⁴ 76 53.30 N 43.00 E
Penzance 42 50.07 N 5.33 W
Penzberg 64 47.45 N 11.23 E
Penzig,
  → Pieńsk 30 51.15 N 15.03 E
Penžina ≃ 74 62.28 N 165.18 E
Penzing ↗8 264b 48.12 N 16.18 E
Penzino 80 52.07 N 50.27 E
Penžinskaja guba ⊂ 74 61.00 N 162.00 E
Penžinskij chrebet ✗ 74 62.50 N 167.00 E
Penzlin 42 53.30 N 13.05 E
Péone 52 44.07 N 6.59 E
Peonias, Quebrada ≃ 286c 10.32 N 67.01 W
Peoples Creek ≃ 198 48.24 N 108.19 W
Peoples Ditch ∐ 226 36.15 N 119.41 W
Peoria, Az., U.S. 200 33.34 N 112.14 W
Peoria, Il., U.S. 216 40.41 N 89.35 W
Peoria, Oh., U.S. 216 40.49 N 83.27 W
Peoria Heights 216 40.45 N 89.36 W
Peotillas 234 22.30 N 100.37 W
Peotone 216 41.19 N 87.47 W
Peover Eye ≃ 262 53.15 N 2.31 W
Peover Heath 262 53.15 N 2.24 W
Pepa 154 7.42 S 29.47 E

Column 3

Pepin 190 44.26 N 92.08 W
Pepin, Lake ⊕ 190 44.30 N 92.15 W
Pepinster 56 50.34 N 5.49 E
Péplos 62 40.58 N 26.16 E
Pepperdine University
  ↗2 280 33.58 N 118.18 W
Pepperell 207 42.40 N 71.35 W
Pepper Park State
  Recreation Area ◆ 220 27.30 N 80.18 W
Pepper Pike 279a 41.28 N 81.27 W
Peqi'in Ḥadasha 132 32.59 N 35.20 E
Peqin 38 41.03 N 19.45 E
Pequannock 210 40.57 N 74.17 W
Pequannock ≃ 276 40.58 N 74.17 W
Pequannut Brook ≃ 283 42.01 N 71.08 W
Pequea Creek ≃ 208 40.03 N 76.22 W
Pequena ≃ 287a 22.55 S 43.25 W
Pequeri 256 21.50 S 43.06 W
Pequeri ≃ 248 17.39 S 55.09 W
Pequest ≃ 210 40.50 N 75.05 W
Pequez 208 39.53 N 76.22 W
Pequizeiro 250 8.32 S 48.58 W
Pequop Mountains ∧ 204 40.45 N 114.40 W
Pequot Lakes 190 46.36 N 94.18 W
Perabumulih 112 3.27 S 104.15 E
Perak □³ 114 5.00 N 101.00 E
Perak ≃ 114 3.58 N 100.53 E
Perak, Kuala ⊂ 114 4.00 N 100.47 E
Peralba, Monte ▲ 64 46.37 N 12.43 E
Perales de Alfambra 34 40.38 N 1.00 W
Perales del Rio 266a 40.19 N 3.38 W
Peralillo 252 34.29 S 71.29 W
Peralta 200 34.50 N 106.41 W
Pérama 267c 37.58 N 23.34 E
Perambalur 122 11.14 N 78.53 E
Peráméri
  (Bottenviken) ⊂ 26 65.00 N 23.00 E
Perani, Ákra ≻ 267c 37.54 N 23.31 E
Peraralo di Cadore 64 46.24 N 12.21 E
Peräseinäjoki 26 62.34 N 23.04 E
Percé 186 48.31 N 64.13 W
Percée, Pointe ▲ 52 45.54 N 6.33 E
Perch ≃ 212 44.00 N 76.05 W
Perchas 240m 18.19 N 66.59 W
Perchau 61 47.06 N 14.27 E
Perchauer Sattel ✗ 61 47.07 N 14.27 E
Perche, Collines du
  ↗2 50 48.25 N 0.40 E
Perche Creek ≃ 194 38.49 N 92.24 W
Perche, Lac ⊕ 212 44.07 N 75.54 W
Perchtoldsdorf 264b 48.07 N 16.17 E
Perchuškovo 265b 55.41 N 37.10 E
Percival Lakes ⊕ 162 21.25 S 125.00 E
Percy Creek ≃ 212 44.15 N 77.49 W
Percy Isles II 166 21.39 S 150.16 E
Percy Lake ⊕ 212 45.13 N 78.22 W
Percy Reach ⊕ 212 44.15 N 77.45 W
Perdagangan-tomuon 114 3.09 N 99.20 E
Perdasdefogu 79 39.41 N 9.26 E
Perdeberg 158 28.59 S 25.05 E
Perdekop 158 27.13 S 29.38 E
Perdices, Arroyo de
  las ≃ 288 34.41 S 58.22 W
Perdido 250 9.13 S 47.59 W
Perdido ≃ 194 31.00 N 87.37 W
Perdido ≃, Bra. 248 22.10 S 57.33 W
Perdido ≃, U.S. 194 30.29 N 87.26 W
Perdido, Arroyo ≃ 254 42.55 S 67.00 W
Perdido, Arroyo del
  ≃² 258 33.37 S 57.23 W
Perdido, Cuchilla del
  ≃² 258 33.43 S 57.17 W
Perdido, Monte ▲ 34 42.40 N 0.05 E
Perdido Bay ⊂ 194 30.21 N 87.27 W
Perdifumo 68 40.16 N 15.01 E
Perdix 208 40.22 N 76.57 W
Perdizes 250 19.21 S 47.17 W
Perdreauville 261 48.58 N 1.38 E
Perdu, Lac ⊕ 186 50.44 N 70.14 W
Perdue 184 52.04 N 107.32 W
Perebrody 78 51.43 N 27.20 E
Perečin 78 48.44 N 22.26 E
Peredel 76 55.12 N 35.41 E
Peredel cy 82 55.36 N 37.21 E
Peredelkino 265b 55.39 N 37.21 E
Peregino 76 53.36 N 31.21 E
Pereginskoje 78 48.49 N 24.12 E
Peregonovka 78 48.32 N 30.31 E
Pereira 246 4.49 N 75.43 W
Pereira, Cachoeira ∟ 250 4.25 S 56.17 W
Pereira Barreto 250 20.38 S 51.07 W
Pereiras 256 22.42 S 46.24 W
Pereiro 250 6.03 S 38.28 W
Perejaslav-
  Chmel'nickij 78 50.06 N 31.30 E
Perejaslavskaja 78 47.58 N 135.06 E
Perejaslavskaja ≃ 83 45.11 N 39.02 E
Perejezdnoje 83 48.47 N 38.04 E
Perejž'na ▲ 78 47.46 N 48.12 E
Perekopnoje 80 51.13 N 48.04 E
Perekopovka 78 50.57 N 33.53 E
Perekopskaja 80 49.21 N 43.20 E
Père-Lachaise,
  Cimetière du ◆ 261 48.51 N 2.25 E
Perelazovskij 80 49.09 N 42.33 E
Perelazy 78 51.02 N 31.28 E
Perelesinskij 78 51.44 N 40.07 E
Perel'ub 80 51.52 N 50.22 E
Pere Marquette, Big
  South Branch ≃ 190 43.56 N 86.10 W
Pere Marquette State
  Park ◆ 219 39.00 N 90.30 W
Perem'otnoje 80 51.11 N 50.49 E
Peremyšl' 82 54.16 N 36.10 E
Peremyšl'any 78 49.40 N 24.33 E
Perené ≃ 248 11.09 S 74.18 W
Perenjori 162 29.26 S 116.17 E
Perepravka ≃ 78 46.29 S 138.17 E
Pererov 78 49.01 N 35.22 E
Pereščepno 78 50.32 N 45.06 E
Pereslavl'-Zalesskij 80 56.44 N 38.51 E
Peresypkino Pervoje 80 52.54 N 42.55 E
Peretrusovo 83 56.51 N 36.53 E
Pereval'sk 83 48.26 N 38.50 E
Perevoz, S.S.S.R. 82 56.51 N 44.32 E
Perevoz, S.S.S.R. 88 59.03 N 116.57 E
Perevoz, S.S.S.R. 265a 59.43 N 30.47 E
Pereyra, Arroyo ≃ 288 34.47 S 58.00 W
Pereyra, Punta ≻ 258 34.14 S 58.04 W
Pérez 252 33.00 S 60.46 W
Perfugas 71 40.50 N 8.53 E
Pergamino 252 33.53 S 60.34 W
Pergamum I 130 39.10 N 27.13 E
Pergau ≃ 114 5.23 N 102.02 E
Pergine Valdarno 66 43.34 N 11.41 E
Pergine Valsugana 64 46.04 N 11.14 E
Pergusa, Lago di ⊕ 70 37.31 N 14.18 E
Perho 26 63.13 N 24.25 E
Peri 130 38.50 N 39.35 E
Peribán de Ramos 234 19.31 N 102.25 W
Péribonca, Lac ⊕ 186 50.04 N 71.15 W
Perico, Arg. 252 24.23 S 65.06 W
Perico, Cuba 240p 22.46 N 81.01 W
Pericumã ≃ 250 2.17 S 44.42 W
Perigi 112 4.33 S 104.25 E
Perigirafa 112 0.16 S 103.30 E
Périgord ∧³ 32 45.20 N 1.00 E
Perigoso, Canal ∐ 250 0.54 N 49.40 W
Périgueux 32 45.11 N 0.43 E
Perija, Sierra de ✗ 246 10.00 N 73.00 W

Column 4

Perim
  → Barīm I 144 12.39 N 43.25 E
Perisque, Golfe
  → Persian Gulf ⊂ 128 27.00 N 51.00 E
Peri-Mirim 250 2.38 S 44.54 W
Persischer Golf
  → Persian Gulf ⊂ 128 27.00 N 51.00 E
Perinaldo 62 43.52 N 7.40 E
Peringat 114 6.02 N 102.17 E
Periprava 38 45.24 N 29.32 E
Perisher Valley ◆ 171b 36.23 S 145.24 E
Péristérion 267c 38.01 N 23.42 E
Perito 68 40.18 N 15.09 E
Perito Moreno 254 46.36 S 70.56 W
Peritoró 250 4.20 S 44.18 W
Perivale ↗8 260 51.32 N 0.19 W
Periyakulam 122 10.07 N 77.33 E
Periyār ≃ 122 10.11 N 76.13 E
Perkasie 208 40.22 N 75.17 W
Perkins 198 35.58 N 97.02 W
Perkins Observatory
  ↗3 214 40.14 N 83.02 W
Perkinston 194 30.46 N 89.08 W
Perkinsville, In., U.S. 218 40.09 N 85.52 W
Perkinsville ≃ 214 42.32 N 77.38 W
Perkiomen Creek ≃ 208 40.07 N 75.28 W
Perkiomen Creek,
  East Branch ≃ 208 40.15 N 75.27 W
Perkiomen Junction
  Pawling 285 40.21 N 75.25 W
Perkiomen Valley 285 40.21 N 75.25 W
Perl 56 49.28 N 6.36 E
Perlas, Archipiélago
  de las II 236 8.25 N 79.00 W
Perlas, Laguna de ⊂ 236 12.30 N 83.40 W
Perlas, Punta ≻ 236 12.23 N 83.30 W
Perleberg 54 53.04 N 11.51 E
Perlez 38 45.12 N 20.24 E
Perlis □³ 114 6.30 N 100.15 E
Perl'ovka 78 51.51 N 38.51 E
Perm' 80 58.00 N 56.15 E
Perm' □⁴ 80 57.30 N 54.30 E
Permanente Creek ≃ 282 37.25 N 122.05 W
Permas 24 59.00 N 56.00 E
Permisi 80 54.06 N 45.48 E
Permskaja Oblast' □⁴ 24 59.00 N 56.00 E
Pernambuco
  → Recife 250 8.03 S 34.54 W
Pernambuco □³ 250 8.00 S 37.00 W
Pernate 266b 45.27 N 8.41 E
Pernatty Lagoon ⊕ 166 31.31 S 137.14 E
Pernay 50 47.27 N 0.30 E
Pernegg an der Mur 61 47.22 N 15.21 E
Pernes-les-Fontaines 52 44.00 N 5.03 E
Pernik 38 42.36 N 23.02 E
Perniö 26 60.12 N 23.08 E
Pernió 54 47.54 N 15.58 E
Pernovo 82 55.58 N 39.10 E
Pero 266b 45.35 N 9.05 E
Peroba, Ribeirão do
  ≃ 287b 23.27 S 46.22 W
Pérols, Étang de ⊕ 62 43.33 N 3.56 E
Peron, Cape ≻ 168a 32.17 S 115.41 E
Péronnes 56 50.26 N 4.08 E
Péronnes ≃ 50 50.06 N 2.56 E
Peron Peninsula ↗1 162 25.55 S 113.30 E
Pero Pinheiro 266c 38.51 N 9.20 W
Perosa Argentina 66 44.58 N 7.10 E
Perote 234 19.34 N 97.14 W
Perotó 248 14.50 S 64.31 W
Pérou
  → Peru □¹ 244 10.00 S 76.00 W
Pérouges 58 45.54 N 5.11 E
Peroulaz 62 45.42 N 7.19 E
Perovo ↗8 265b 55.44 N 37.46 E
Perpendicular, Point ≻ 170 35.06 S 150.48 E
Perpignan 32 42.41 N 2.53 E
Perranporth 42 50.20 N 5.09 W
Perrault Falls 184 50.19 N 93.11 W
Perray ≃ 261 48.31 N 1.42 E
Perrero 66 44.56 N 7.05 E
Perrier 50 45.31 N 3.05 E
Perrignier 58 46.18 N 6.27 E
Perrine 220 25.36 N 80.21 W
Perrineville 276 40.13 N 74.26 W
Perris, Lake ⊕¹ 228 33.46 N 117.13 W
Perro, Laguna del ⊕ 200 34.40 N 105.57 W
Perro, Punta del ≻ 34 36.45 N 6.25 W
Perros, Bahía de los
  ⊂ 240p 22.25 N 78.30 W
Perros-Guirec 32 48.49 N 3.27 W
Perry, Fl., U.S. 192 30.07 N 83.34 W
Perry, Ga., U.S. 192 32.27 N 83.43 W
Perry, Ia., U.S. 190 41.50 N 94.06 W
Perry, Ks., U.S. 198 39.04 N 95.23 W
Perry, Me., U.S. 186 44.58 N 67.04 W
Perry, Mi., U.S. 216 42.49 N 84.13 W
Perry, Mo., U.S. 219 39.26 N 91.40 W
Perry, N.Y., U.S. 210 42.43 N 78.00 W
Perry, Oh., U.S. 214 41.46 N 81.09 W
Perry, Ok., U.S. 196 36.17 N 97.17 W
Perry, Tx., U.S. 222 31.14 N 96.55 W
Perry, Ut., U.S. 204 41.27 N 112.02 W
Perry □⁶ 214 40.22 N 77.35 W
Perrydale 226 44.59 N 123.15 W
Perry Hall 208 39.24 N 76.28 W
Perry Heights 214 40.47 N 81.28 W
Perry-Jōriku-kinenhi ⊥ 198 39.20 N 95.30 W
Perry Lake ⊕¹ 198 39.07 N 95.30 W
Perryman 208 39.27 N 76.12 W
Perrymont 279b 40.21 N 43.37 W
Perrysburg 214 41.33 N 83.38 W
Perrysville 279a 40.32 N 80.01 W
Perryton 196 36.24 N 100.48 W
Perryville, Ak., U.S. 180 55.54 N 159.10 W
Perryville, Ar., U.S. 196 35.00 N 92.48 W
Perryville, In., U.S. 194 37.39 N 84.57 W
Perryville, Md., U.S. 208 39.33 N 76.04 W
Perryville, Mo., U.S. 194 37.43 N 89.51 W
Perryville, N.Y., U.S. 210 43.04 N 75.53 W
Perșani, Munții ✗ 38 45.43 N 25.25 E
Persan 261 49.09 N 2.16 E
Persberg 40 59.45 N 14.15 E
Perschling ≃ 264a 48.20 N 15.53 E
Persembe 130 41.04 N 37.46 E
Persépolis
  → Takht-e Jamshīd 128 29.57 N 52.52 E
Perseverance, Mount
  ▲ 171a 27.25 S 152.10 E
Perseverancia 248 14.44 S 62.48 W
Pershagen 40 59.10 N 17.39 E
Pershing 42 39.49 N 84.53 W
Pershore 42 52.07 N 2.05 W
Pershtejn 198 59.30 N 15.00 E
Persia 198 41.34 N 95.34 W

Column 5 (Deutsch)

Persimmon Creek ≃ 194 31.31 N 86.50 W
Peščanokopskoje 80 46.12 N 41.04 E
Pescantina 64 45.29 N 10.51 E
Peščanyj 83 47.02 N 37.28 E
Peščanye, ostrova II 83 46.52 N 38.17 E
Pescara 66 42.28 N 14.13 E
Pescara ≃ 66 42.28 N 14.13 E
Pescasseroli 66 41.48 N 13.47 E
Pesch 263 51.11 N 6.32 E
Pesch, Schloss ⊥ 263 51.18 N 6.39 E
Peschiera del Garda 66 45.26 N 10.42 E
Peschio, Monte ▲ 287a 41.43 N 12.46 E
Pescia 66 43.54 N 10.41 E
Pescina 66 42.02 N 13.39 E
Pescocostanzo 66 41.53 N 14.04 E
Pescolanciano 66 41.41 N 14.20 E
Pescopagano 68 40.50 N 15.24 E
Pescocchiano 68 42.12 N 13.09 E
Pesco Sannita 68 41.14 N 14.49 E
Pesé 236 7.54 N 80.37 W
Pesek, Pulau I 271c 1.17 N 103.41 E
Peseux 58 46.59 N 6.53 E
Peshastin 224 47.34 N 120.36 W
Peshastin Creek ≃ 224 47.28 N 120.36 W
Peshawar 123 34.01 N 71.33 E
Peshtän Jän 128 33.25 N 61.28 E
Peshkopi 38 41.41 N 20.26 E
Peshtigo 190 45.03 N 87.44 W
Peshtigo ≃ 190 44.58 N 87.40 W
Pesio ≃ 62 44.28 N 7.53 E
Peski ≃ 82 56.01 N 38.48 E
Peski, S.S.S.R. 76 53.21 N 24.38 E
Peski, S.S.S.R. 78 50.23 N 33.27 E
Peski, S.S.S.R. 80 51.16 N 42.27 E
Peski, S.S.S.R. 85 55.13 N 38.46 E
Peski, S.S.S.R. 82 56.08 N 37.04 E
Peski, S.S.S.R. 83 49.29 N 38.59 E
Peski, S.S.S.R. 83 49.17 N 37.36 E
Peski-Radʹkovskije 83 49.17 N 37.36 E
Peskovatskoje 80 50.43 N 43.53 E
Peskovka, S.S.S.R. 78 50.42 N 29.38 E
Peskovka, S.S.S.R. 86 59.04 N 52.22 E
Peškovo 83 47.02 N 39.24 E
Peškovo Grecovo 82 47.04 N 39.24 E
Peškovskoje 86 53.45 N 62.23 E
Pesmes 58 47.17 N 5.34 E
Pesnica 61 46.36 N 15.41 E
Pesnica ≃ 61 46.24 N 16.05 E
Pešnoj, poluostrov ↗2 80 46.52 N 51.42 E
Pesočenskij 82 54.10 N 36.06 E
Pesočin 78 49.59 N 36.06 E
Pesočnoje 80 54.07 N 40.50 E
Pesočnoje, S.S.S.R. 82 53.20 N 27.06 E
Pesočnoje, S.S.S.R. 82 58.01 N 39.10 E
Pesočnyj 76 60.07 N 30.08 E
Peso da Régua 34 41.10 N 7.47 W
Pespire 236 13.35 S 87.22 W
Pesqueira 250 8.22 S 36.42 W
Pesqueira Maja 196 25.54 N 100.03 W
Pesquería 196 25.54 N 99.11 W
Pessac 32 44.48 N 0.38 W
Pessin 54 52.38 N 12.40 E
Pessinetto 62 45.17 N 7.24 E
Pest □⁴ 30 47.30 N 19.20 E
Pest'aki 82 56.43 N 42.40 E
Peštera 38 42.02 N 24.18 E
Pesterzsébet ↗8 264c 47.26 N 19.07 E
Pesthidegkút ↗8 264c 47.34 N 18.58 E
Pestime ↗4 264c 47.24 N 19.12 E
Pestlörinc ↗8 264c 47.26 N 19.12 E
Pestovo, S.S.S.R. 76 58.36 N 35.48 E
Pestovo, S.S.S.R. 82 48.37 N 38.35 E
Pestovskoje
  vodochranilišče ⊕¹ 82 56.06 N 37.40 E
Pestravka 80 52.24 N 49.58 E
Pestrecy 85 55.46 N 49.39 E
Pestrikovo 82 53.54 N 25.23 E
Pestújhely ↗4 264c 47.32 N 19.07 E
Petacalco, Bahía de
  ⊂ 234 17.57 N 102.05 W
Petaḥ Tiqwa 132 32.05 N 34.53 E
Petäjävesi 26 62.15 N 25.12 E
Petal 194 31.20 N 89.15 W
Petalcingo 234 17.19 N 92.27 W
Petaling Jaya 114 3.05 N 101.39 E
Petalión, Kólpos ⊂ 38 37.59 N 24.02 E
Petaluma 226 38.06 N 122.30 W
Petaluma ≃ 282 38.04 N 122.30 W
Pétange 56 49.34 N 5.52 E
Petare 246 10.29 N 66.49 W
Petatlán 234 17.31 N 101.16 W
Petauke 154 14.15 S 31.20 E
Petawawa 212 45.54 N 77.17 W
Petawawa ≃ 190 45.55 N 77.15 W
Pété 146 10.58 N 14.30 W
Petegem 56 50.58 N 3.32 E
Petén Itzá, Lago ⊕ 236 16.59 N 89.50 W
Petenwell Lake ⊕¹ 232 16.59 N 89.50 W
Peter and Paul
  Fortress ⊥ 265a 59.57 N 30.19 E
Peterboro 210 42.58 S 75.41 W
Peterborough, Austl. 166 32.58 S 138.50 E
Peterborough, On.,
  Can. 212 44.18 N 78.19 W
Peterborough, Eng.,
  U.K. 42 52.35 N 0.15 W
Peterborough, N.H.,
  U.S. 188 42.52 N 71.57 W
Petercider □⁶ 210 42.50 N 103.20 W
Peterhead 46 57.30 N 1.49 W
Peter Hill ▲ 46 57.00 N 2.41 W
Peter I Island I 9 68.47 S 90.35 W
Peter Island I, N.T.,
  Can. 240m 18.22 N 64.35 W
Peter Lake ⊕, Sk.,
  Can. 184 57.15 N 103.53 W
Peterlee 44 54.46 N 1.19 W
Peter Lougheed
  Provincial Park ◆ 182 50.45 N 115.15 W
Peterman 194 31.35 N 87.15 W
Petermann Ranges ✗ 162 25.00 S 129.46 E
Petermann Reserve
  ◆⁴ 162 25.00 S 130.15 E
Peter Pond Lake ⊕ 184 55.55 N 108.44 W
Peter Pond Lake
  Indian Reserve ◆ 184 55.55 N 109.00 W
Petersberg 54 50.33 N 9.43 E
Peters Brook ≃ 276 40.33 N 74.37 W
Petersburg, Ak., U.S. 180 56.49 N 132.57 W
Petersburg, Il., U.S. 216 39.59 N 89.50 W
Petersburg, In., U.S. 194 38.29 N 87.16 W
Petersburg, Mi., U.S. 214 41.54 N 83.42 W
Petersburg, N.D.,
  U.S. 198 48.01 N 98.00 W
Petersburg, N.J.,
  U.S. 208 39.15 N 74.43 W
Petersburg, Oh., U.S. 210 40.54 N 80.32 W
Petersburg, Pa., U.S. 208 40.34 N 78.03 W
Petersburg, Va., U.S. 192 37.13 N 77.24 W
Petersburg, W.V.,
  U.S. 188 38.59 N 79.07 W
Petersburg National
  Battlefield ◆ 208 37.14 N 77.22 W
Peters Canyon ≃ 280 33.47 N 117.45 W
Peters Creek ≃, Ca.,
  U.S. 282 37.07 N 122.13 W
Peters Creek ≃, Pa.,
  U.S. 279b 40.18 N 79.52 W

	English	Deutsch	Español	Français	Português
▲	Mountain	Berg	Montaña	Montagne	Montanha
∧	Mountains	Gebirge	Montañas	Montagnes	Montanhas
∨	Valley, Canyon	Tal, Cañon	Valle, Cañón	Vallée, Canyon	Vale, Canhão
≃	Plain	Ebene	Llano	Plaine	Planície
≻	Cape	Kap	Cabo	Cap	Cabo
I	Island	Insel	Isla	Île	Ilha
II	Islands	Inseln	Islas	Îles	Ilhas
±	Other Topographic Features	Andere Topographische Objekte	Otros Elementos Topográficos	Autres données topographiques	Outros acidentes topográficos

ESPAÑOL

Nombre	Página	Lat.°′	Long.°′ W = Oeste
Petershagen, B.R.D.	52	52.23 N	8.58 E
Petershagen, D.D.R.	54	52.24 N	14.20 E
Petershagen bei Berlin	54	52.31 N	13.46 E
Petersham, Austl.	274a	33.54 S	151.09 E
Petersham, Ma., U.S.	207	42.29 N	72.11 W
Peters Hill ∧ [2]	163b	34.11 S	138.50 E
Peterson	198	42.55 N	95.20 W
Peterson Air Force Base ■	198	38.49 N	104.42 W
Peters Pond ⊜	283	42.43 N	71.16 W
Peterswald Hill ∧ [2]	162	26.43 S	123.39 E
Peter the Great Bay → Petra Velikogo, zaliv ⊂	89	42.40 N	132.00 E
Peter the Great Monument ⊥	265a	59.56 N	30.18 E
Pétervására	30	48.01 N	20.06 E
Petilia Policastro	68	39.07 N	16.47 E
Pétionville	238	18.31 N	72.17 W
Petit	273d	26.06 S	28.22 E
Petit Bois Island I	194	30.12 N	88.26 W
Petit-Bourg	241o	16.12 N	61.36 W
Petit-Canal	241o	16.23 N	61.29 W
Petitcodiac	186	45.56 N	65.10 W
Petitcodiac ≃	186	45.50 N	64.33 W
Petit Cul-de-Sac Marin ⊂	241o	16.12 N	61.33 W
Petite Nation, Rivière de la ≃	206	45.35 N	75.06 W
Petite Rivière du Chêne ≃	206	46.34 N	72.02 W
Petite Rivière Noire, Piton de la ∧	157c	20.24 S	57.24 E
Petite Rivière Rouge ≃	206	45.45 N	75.00 W
Petite Sauldre ≃	50	47.27 N	2.05 E
Petite Terre, Îles de la II	241o	16.10 N	61.07 W
Petit Forte	186	47.24 N	54.40 W
Petit-Fort-Philippe	50	51.00 N	2.07 E
Petit-Goâve	238	18.26 N	72.52 W
Petit Jean ≃	194	35.10 N	92.56 W
Petit Jean State Park ♦	194	35.06 N	92.57 W
Petit Loango	152	2.16 S	9.35 E
Petit Loango, Parc National du ♦	152	2.15 S	9.36 E
Petit Mécatina, Île du I	186	50.33 N	59.20 W
Petit Morin ≃	50	48.56 N	3.07 E
Petitot ≃	176	60.14 N	123.29 W
Petit Rhône ≃	62	43.27 N	4.24 E
Petit-Saint-Bernard, Col du)(	62	45.41 N	6.53 E
Petitsikapau Lake ⊜	176	54.45 N	66.25 W
Petkeljärven Kansallispuisto ♦	24	62.35 N	31.12 E
Petkus	54	51.59 N	13.21 E
Petlād	120	22.28 N	72.48 E
Petlalcingo	234	18.05 N	97.54 W
Peto	232	20.08 N	88.55 W
Petoh	114	2.53 N	103.15 E
Petone	172	41.13 S	174.52 E
Petorca	252	32.15 S	70.56 W
Petoskey	190	45.22 N	84.57 W
Petownikip Lake ⊜	184	52.56 N	92.02 W
Petra → Baṭrā ⊥	132	30.20 N	35.26 E
Petralia Soprana	70	37.47 N	14.06 E
Petralia Sottana	70	37.48 N	14.05 E
Petras, Mount ∧	9	75.52 S	128.38 W
Petra Velikogo, zaliv (Peter the Great Bay) ⊂	89	42.40 N	132.00 E
Petre, Point ›	212	43.50 N	77.09 W
Petrecovo	24	61.18 N	57.07 E
Petrella, Monte ∧	66	41.18 N	13.40 E
Petrella Salto	66	42.18 N	13.04 E
Petrella Tifernina	66	41.41 N	14.42 E
Petrič	38	41.24 N	23.13 E
Petrie	171a	27.16 S	152.59 E
Petrified Forest National Park ♦	200	34.55 N	109.49 W
Petrikov	78	52.08 N	28.30 E
Petrikovka	78	48.43 N	34.37 E
Petrila	38	45.27 N	23.25 E
Petrinja	36	45.26 N	16.17 E
Petriščevo, S.S.S.R.	82	54.37 N	36.57 E
Petriščevo, S.S.S.R.	82	55.30 N	36.18 E
Petrítis, Ákra ›	267c	37.56 N	23.24 E
Petrodvorec	76	59.53 N	29.54 E
Petroglyphs Provincial Park ♦	212	44.33 N	77.53 W
Petrograd → Leningrad	76	59.55 N	30.15 E
Petrogrado-Doneckoje ◆ [8]	83	48.42 N	38.41 E
Petrohué	254	41.08 S	72.25 W
Petrokrepost'	76	59.57 N	31.02 E
Petrolândia	250	9.05 S	38.18 W
Petrólea	246	8.30 N	72.35 W
Petroleum	216	40.36 N	85.09 W
Petrolia, On., Can.	214	42.52 N	82.09 W
Petrolia, Pa., U.S.	214	41.01 N	79.43 W
Petrolia, Tx., U.S.	196	34.01 N	98.14 W
Petrolina	250	9.24 S	40.30 W
Petrolina de Goiás	255	16.06 S	49.20 W
Petronà	68	39.03 N	16.45 E
Petrona, Punta ›	240m	17.56 N	66.23 W
Petronila Creek ≃	196	27.32 N	97.32 W
Petropavlovka, S.S.S.R.	78	50.06 N	40.54 E
Petropavlovka, S.S.S.R.	78	48.27 N	36.26 E
Petropavlovka, S.S.S.R.	83	49.43 N	37.42 E
Petropavlovka, S.S.S.R.	88	50.38 N	105.19 E
Petropavlovsk, S.S.S.R.	86	56.20 N	57.09 E
Petropavlovsk, S.S.S.R.	86	54.54 N	69.06 E
Petropavlovsk-Kamčatskij	74	53.01 N	158.39 E
Petropavlovskoje, S.S.S.R.	86	52.04 N	84.08 E
Petropavlovskoje, S.S.S.R.	88	58.13 N	108.59 E
Petrópolis	256	22.31 S	43.10 W
Petros	192	36.05 N	84.26 W
Petroșani	38	45.25 N	23.22 E
Petrosino	70	37.43 N	12.29 E
Petro-Slav'anka	265a	59.48 N	30.31 E
Petroso, Monte ∧	66	41.44 N	13.55 E
Petroúpolis	267c	38.03 N	23.41 E
Petrovac	38	44.22 N	21.27 E
Petrovgrad → Zrenjanin	38	45.23 N	20.24 E
Petrovka, S.S.S.R.	78	46.54 N	30.44 E
Petrovka, S.S.S.R.	80	53.13 N	51.58 E
Petrovka, S.S.S.R.	83	48.53 N	39.52 E
Petrovka, S.S.S.R.	83	48.48 N	39.16 E
Petrovo, S.S.S.R.	76	58.22 N	35.09 E
Petrovo, S.S.S.R.	78	48.20 N	33.16 E
Petrovo, S.S.S.R.	82	55.00 N	38.08 E
Petrovo, S.S.S.R.	88	54.30 N	105.15 E
Petrovo-Dal'neje	265b	55.45 N	37.11 E
Petrovo-Krasnoselje ◆ [8]	83	48.18 N	38.52 E
Petrovsk	80	52.19 N	45.23 E
Petrovskaja	78	45.25 N	37.57 E
Petrovskij, S.S.S.R.	80	56.39 N	40.19 E
Petrovskij, S.S.S.R.	80	50.45 N	41.59 E
Petrovskij, S.S.S.R.	82	54.29 N	36.59 E
Petrovskoje, S.S.S.R.	78	49.10 N	36.54 E
Petrovskoje, S.S.S.R.	80	52.39 N	40.15 E
Petrovskoje, S.S.S.R.	80	57.01 N	39.16 E
Petrovskoje, S.S.S.R.	82	55.27 N	38.21 E
Petrovskoje, S.S.S.R.	82	55.32 N	36.59 E

FRANÇAIS

Nom	Page	Lat.°′	Long.°′ W = Ouest
Petrovskoje, S.S.S.R.	83	48.18 N	38.52 E
Petrovskoje, S.S.S.R.	265b	55.36 N	37.53 E
Petrovsko-Razumovskoje ◆ [8]	265b	55.50 N	37.34 E
Petrovsk-Zabajkal'skij	88	51.17 N	108.50 E
Petrov Val	80	50.09 N	45.12 E
Petrozavodsk	24	61.47 N	34.20 E
Petrozsény → Petroșani	38	45.25 N	23.22 E
Petrun'	24	66.28 N	60.43 E
Petrusburg	158	29.08 S	25.27 E
Petrušino	265a	59.48 N	30.50 E
Petrus Steyn	158	27.38 S	28.08 E
Petrusville	158	30.05 S	24.41 E
Petschora → Pečora ≃	24	68.13 N	54.15 E
Petten	52	52.45 N	4.39 E
Pettenbach	61	47.57 N	14.01 E
Petteril ≃	44	54.54 N	2.55 W
Petticoat Creek ≃	275b	43.48 N	79.06 W
Pettigoe	48	54.33 N	7.50 W
Pettinascura, Monte ∧	68	39.22 N	16.37 E
Pettineo	70	37.58 N	14.17 E
Pettisville	216	41.31 N	84.13 W
Pettnau	64	47.18 N	11.08 E
Pettneu am Arlberg	58	47.09 N	10.20 E
Pettus	196	28.37 N	97.48 W
Petty Harbour	186	47.28 N	52.43 W
Petty Island I	285	39.58 N	75.07 W
Petua	272b	22.25 N	88.27 E
Petuchovo	86	55.06 N	67.58 E
Petuški	80	55.55 N	39.28 E
Petworth	42	50.59 N	0.38 W
Petzow	264a	52.21 N	12.56 E
Peudada	114	5.12 N	96.35 E
Peuerbach	60	48.21 N	13.56 E
Peuetsagoe, Gunung ∧	114	4.55 N	96.20 E
Peureulak	114	4.48 N	97.53 E
Peureulak ≃	114	4.54 N	97.53 E
Peureulak, Ujung ›	114	4.54 N	97.54 E
Peusangan ≃	114	5.16 N	96.51 E
Peusangan, Ujung ›	114	5.16 N	96.50 E
Pevek	74	69.42 N	170.17 E
Pevely	219	38.17 N	90.23 W
Pevensey	42	50.49 N	0.20 E
Pevensey Levels ⩨	42	50.50 N	0.20 E
Peveragno	62	44.20 N	7.37 E
Pewamo	216	43.00 N	84.50 W
Pewaukee	216	43.04 N	88.15 W
Pewaukee Lake ⊜	216	43.04 N	88.19 W
Pewee Valley	218	38.18 N	85.29 W
Pews Creek ≃	276	40.27 N	74.06 W
Pewsey	42	51.21 N	1.46 W
Pewsey, Vale of V	42	51.20 N	1.48 W
Péyia	130	34.53 N	32.23 E
Peykjahlid	24a	65.40 N	16.50 W
Peyrolles-en-Provence	62	43.39 N	5.35 E
Peyruis	62	44.02 N	5.56 E
Peza ≃	24	65.36 N	44.35 E
Pezas	86	54.39 N	87.46 E
Pezawa Taung ∧	110	19.33 N	94.31 E
Pézenas	32	43.27 N	3.25 E
Peženga	76	59.10 N	44.16 E
Pezinok	30	48.18 N	17.17 E
Pezu	123	32.19 N	70.44 E
Pezzana	62	45.16 N	8.29 E
Pfäfers	58	46.59 N	9.30 E
Pfaffenhausen	58	48.07 N	10.27 E
Pfaffenhofen an der Ilm	60	48.31 N	11.30 E
Pfaffenhoffen	56	48.51 N	7.37 E
Pfaffenöden ∧ [2]	264b	48.04 N	16.33 E
Pfäffikersee ⊜	58	47.21 N	8.48 E
Pfäffikon	58	47.22 N	8.47 E
Pfaffnau	58	47.14 N	7.54 E
Pfaffstätten	264b	48.01 N	16.16 E
Pfalz □ [5]	56	49.20 N	8.00 E
Pfalzdorf	52	51.42 N	6.11 E
Pfalzel	56	49.47 N	6.41 E
Pfänder ∧	58	47.30 N	9.47 E
Pfarrkirchen	60	48.27 N	12.56 E
Pfarrweisach	56	50.09 N	10.44 E
Pfastatt	58	47.47 N	7.18 E
Pfatter	60	48.58 N	12.23 E
Pfaueninsel, Schloss ⊥	264a	52.26 N	13.07 E
Pfeddersheim	56	49.38 N	8.16 E
Pfeffenhausen	60	48.40 N	11.58 E
Pfeiffer-Big Sur State Park ♦	226	36.15 N	121.47 W
Pferderennbahn ♦	263	51.31 N	7.32 E
Pflugerville	222	30.26 N	97.37 W
Pförten → Brody	30	51.45 N	14.45 E
Pforzen	58	47.55 N	10.37 E
Pforzheim	56	48.54 N	8.42 E
Pfreimd ≃	60	49.29 N	12.11 E
Pfrimm ≃	56	49.39 N	8.22 E
Pfronten	58	47.34 N	10.33 E
Pfuhl	58	48.24 N	10.02 E
Pfullendorf	58	47.55 N	9.15 E
Pfullingen	58	48.28 N	9.13 E
Pfunds	58	46.58 N	10.33 E
Pfungstadt	56	49.48 N	8.36 E
Pfyn	58	47.36 N	8.57 E
Pha-an	110	16.53 N	97.38 E
Phachi ≃	110	13.56 N	99.24 E
Phaéton, Port ⊂	174s	17.44 S	149.21 W
Phagwāra	123	31.14 N	75.46 E
Phala	156	23.45 S	26.57 E
Phalaborwa	156	23.55 S	31.13 E
Phalanx	214	41.15 N	80.58 W
Phalempin	50	50.31 N	3.01 E
Phālia	123	32.26 N	73.35 E
Phalodi	120	27.08 N	72.22 E
Phalsbourg	56	48.46 N	7.16 E
Phalta	126	22.17 N	88.07 E
Phaltan	122	17.59 N	74.26 E
Phalti	272b	22.46 N	88.34 E
Phan	110	19.28 N	99.43 E
Phanat Nikhom	110	13.27 N	101.11 E
Phangan, Ko I	110	9.45 N	100.04 E
Phang Hoei, Khao ∧	110	15.15 N	101.23 E
Phangnga	110	8.28 N	98.32 E
Phaniang ≃	110	16.49 N	102.24 E
Phanom Dongrak, Thiu Khao ⋏	110	14.25 N	103.30 E
Phanom Thuan	110	14.07 N	99.42 E
Phan Rang	110	11.34 N	108.59 E
Phan Thiet	110	10.56 N	108.06 E
Phan Thong	110	13.28 N	101.06 E
Phantom Lake	216	42.52 N	88.21 W
Pharenda	124	27.06 N	83.17 E
Phariāro	120	27.12 N	68.59 E
Pharr	196	26.11 N	98.11 W
Phasi Charoen	269a	13.43 N	100.26 E
Phasi Charoen, Khlong ≅	269a	13.44 N	100.30 E
Phat Diem	110	20.06 N	106.06 E
Phato	110	9.48 N	98.48 E
Phatthalung	110	7.37 N	100.05 E
Phayao	110	19.10 N	99.55 E
Pheasant Creek ≃	184	50.35 N	103.28 W
Pheba	194	33.35 N	88.56 W
Phelan	228	34.25 N	117.34 W
Phelps, N.Y., U.S.	210	42.57 N	77.03 W
Phelps, Tx., U.S.	222	30.42 N	95.27 W
Phelps, Wi., U.S.	190	46.03 N	89.05 W
Phelps Lake ⊜	192	35.46 N	76.27 W
Phenix City	192	32.28 N	85.00 W
Phepane ≃	156	25.50 S	22.45 E
Phet Buri ≃	110	13.13 N	99.59 E
Phetchabun	110	16.25 N	101.08 E
Phetchabun, Thiu Khao ⋏	110	16.20 N	100.55 E
Phetchaburi	110	13.06 N	99.57 E
Phibun Mangsahan	110	15.14 N	105.14 E

PORTUGUÊS

Nome	Página	Lat.°′	Long.°′ W = Oeste
Phichai	110	17.17 N	100.05 E
Phichit	110	16.26 N	100.22 E
Philadelphia, S. Afr.	158	33.40 S	18.36 E
Philadelphia, Il., U.S.	219	39.58 N	90.07 W
Philadelphia, Ms., U.S.	194	32.46 N	89.07 W
Philadelphia, Mo., U.S.	219	39.50 N	91.44 W
Philadelphia, N.Y., U.S.	212	44.09 N	75.42 W
Philadelphia, Pa., U.S.	208	39.57 N	75.09 W
Philadelphia, Pa., U.S.	285	39.57 N	75.09 W
Philadelphia, Tn., U.S.	192	35.40 N	84.24 W
Philadelphia □ [6]	285	39.57 N	75.07 W
Philadelphia International Airport ⊠	208	39.53 N	75.14 W
Philadelphia Museum of Art ❦	285	39.58 N	75.11 W
Philadelphia Naval Shipyard ■	285	39.53 N	75.11 W
Philae ⊥	140	24.01 N	32.53 E
Phil Campbell	194	34.21 N	87.42 W
Philip	198	44.02 N	101.39 W
Philipp	194	33.45 N	90.12 W
Philippeville → Skikda, Alg.	148	36.50 N	6.58 E
Philippeville, Bel.	50	50.12 N	4.32 E
Philippi	188	39.09 N	80.02 W
Philippi, Lake ⊜	166	24.22 S	139.00 E
Philippi Glacier ⊓	9	66.45 S	88.20 E
Philippine Basin ✦ [1]	14	17.00 N	132.00 E
Philippine International Convention Center ♦	269f	14.32 N	120.59 E
Philippinen → Philippines □ [1]	116	13.00 N	122.00 E
Philippines (Pilipinas) □ [1], Asia	108	13.00 N	122.00 E
Philippines (Pilipinas) □ [1], Asia	116	13.00 N	122.00 E
Philippines, University of the ❦ [2]	269f	14.39 N	121.04 E
Philippine Sea ⊤ [2]	14	20.00 N	135.00 E
Philippine Trench ✦ [1]	14	9.00 N	127.00 E
Philippolis	158	30.19 S	25.13 E
Philippopolis → Plovdiv	38	42.09 N	24.45 E
Philippsreut	60	48.52 N	13.41 E
Philippsthal	264a	52.20 N	13.09 E
Philipsburg, P.Q., Can.	206	45.02 N	73.05 W
Philipsburg, Ned. Ant.	238	17.59 N	63.10 W
Philipsburg, Mt., U.S.	202	46.19 N	113.17 W
Philipsburg, Pa., U.S.	214	40.53 N	78.13 W
Philipsburg Manor ⊥	276	41.05 N	73.52 W
Philipse Manor Hall State Historic Site ⊥	276	40.56 N	73.54 W
Philip Smith Mountains ⋏	180	68.30 N	148.00 W
Philipstown	158	30.26 S	24.29 E
Phillaur	123	31.01 N	75.47 E
Phillip Island I	169	38.29 S	145.14 E
Phillips, Me., U.S.	188	44.49 N	70.20 W
Phillips, Tx., U.S.	196	35.41 N	101.21 W
Phillips, Wi., U.S.	190	45.41 N	90.24 W
Phillipsburg, Ga., U.S.	192	31.34 N	83.31 W
Phillipsburg, Ks., U.S.	198	39.45 N	99.19 W
Phillipsburg, N.J., U.S.	210	40.41 N	75.11 W
Philmont	210	42.14 N	73.39 W
Philo, Il., U.S.	194	40.01 N	88.09 W
Philo, Oh., U.S.	188	39.51 N	81.54 W
Philomath	202	44.32 N	123.21 W
Philpots Island I	176	74.48 N	80.00 W
Phimai	110	15.13 N	102.30 E
Phinga	272b	22.41 N	88.25 E
Phitsanulok	110	16.50 N	100.15 E
Phnom Penh → Phnum Pénh	110	11.33 N	104.55 E
Phnum Pénh	110	11.33 N	104.55 E
Phnum Tbêng Méanchey	110	13.49 N	104.58 E
Pho ≃	124	27.41 N	89.53 E
Phoenicia	210	42.05 N	74.18 W
Phoenix, Az., U.S.	200	33.26 N	112.04 W
Phoenix, Il., U.S.	278	41.36 N	87.38 W
Phoenix, Md., U.S.	208	39.30 N	76.36 W
Phoenix, N.Y., U.S.	210	43.13 N	76.18 W
Phoenix Islands II	14	4.00 S	172.00 W
Phoenix Lake ⊜ [1]	282	37.57 N	122.35 W
Phoenix Park ♦	281	42.24 N	83.27 W
Phoenixville	208	40.07 N	75.30 W
Phon	110	15.49 N	102.36 E
Phong ≃	110	16.23 N	102.56 E
Phôngsali	110	21.41 N	102.06 E
Phong Tho	110	22.32 N	103.21 E
Phon Phisai	110	18.01 N	103.05 E
Phosphate Hill	166	21.52 S	139.51 E
Phrae	110	18.09 N	100.08 E
Phra Khanong ◆ [8]	269a	13.42 N	100.35 E
Phra Nakhon → Krung Thep	110	13.45 N	100.31 E
Phra Nakhon Si Ayutthaya	110	14.21 N	100.33 E
Phran Kratai	110	16.40 N	99.36 E
Phrao	110	19.22 N	99.13 E
Phra Pradaeng	269a	13.40 N	100.32 E
Phra Rop, Khao ∧	110	13.11 N	99.31 E
Phrom Phiram	110	17.02 N	100.12 E
Phrygia □ [9]	130	39.00 N	30.00 E
Phsar Réam	110	10.30 N	103.37 E
Phu Cat	110	14.01 N	109.03 E
Phu Huu, Viet.	110	18.58 N	105.31 E
Phu Huu, Viet.	269c	10.43 N	106.47 E
Phuket	110	7.53 N	98.24 E
Phuket, Ko I	110	8.00 N	98.22 E
Phularwān	123	32.22 N	73.00 E
Phulbari	126	21.52 N	88.08 E
Phulbāria	126	23.22 N	89.50 E
Phuljhuri	126	22.12 N	90.04 E
Phulkusma	126	22.43 N	86.52 E
Phu Loc	110	16.16 N	107.53 E
Phūlpur	124	25.33 N	82.06 E
Phulra	123	34.20 N	73.03 E
Phultala	126	22.59 N	89.28 E
Phu Ly	110	20.32 N	105.56 E
Phum Duang ≃	110	9.10 N	99.20 E
Phumĭ Bâ Khăm	110	13.51 N	107.22 E
Phumĭ Banam	110	11.19 N	105.18 E
Phumĭ Béng	110	13.05 N	104.18 E
Phumĭ Châmbák	110	11.14 N	104.49 E
Phumĭ Chângho Ândêng	110	12.39 N	104.35 E
Phumĭ Chhuk	110	10.50 N	104.28 E
Phumĭ Chruŏy Slêng	110	13.14 N	105.57 E
Phumĭ Dăk Dăm	110	12.20 N	107.21 E
Phumĭ Kâmpóng Srâlau	110	14.05 N	105.46 E
Phumĭ Kâmpóng Trâbâk	110	13.06 N	105.14 E
Phumĭ Kântuŏt Sâmraông	110	14.12 N	104.37 E
Phumĭ Kaôh Kért	110	13.47 N	104.32 E
Phumĭ Kaôh Kŏng	110	11.26 N	103.11 E
Phumĭ Khpôb	110	11.02 N	105.12 E
Phumĭ Krêk	110	11.46 N	105.56 E
Phumĭ Lvéa Kraôm	110	13.21 N	102.54 E
Phumĭ Moŭng	110	13.45 N	103.33 E
Phumĭ Narŭng	110	13.53 N	105.34 E
Phumĭ Phnum Srâlau	110	11.03 N	103.42 E
Phumĭ Prêk Kák	110	12.15 N	105.32 E
Phumĭ Prêk Sândêk	110	11.51 N	105.22 E
Phumĭ Prey Toch	110	12.54 N	103.23 E
Phumĭ Puŏk Chăs	110	13.26 N	103.44 E
Phumĭ Rôluŏs Chăs	110	13.19 N	104.00 E
Phumĭ Sâmraông	110	14.11 N	103.31 E
Phumĭ Spœ Tbong	110	12.20 N	105.19 E
Phumĭ Srê Kôkir	110	13.08 N	106.04 E
Phumĭ Srê Rônéam	110	12.16 N	106.25 E
Phumĭ Tbêng	110	13.35 N	104.55 E
Phumĭ Thalabârĭvăt	110	13.33 N	105.57 E
Phumĭ Thmâ Pôk	110	13.57 N	103.04 E
Phumĭ Tnaôt	110	12.56 N	104.34 E
Phumĭ Tœk Choŭ	110	13.36 N	103.24 E
Phu My	110	14.10 N	109.03 E
Phung Hiep	110	9.49 N	105.50 E
Phuntsholing	124	26.53 N	89.23 E
Phuoc Binh	110	11.50 N	106.58 E
Phuoc Khanh	269c	10.40 N	106.48 E
Phuoc Long	110	9.26 N	105.28 E
Phuoc Long Xa	269c	10.49 N	106.46 E
Phuoc Luong	269c	10.45 N	106.48 E
Phu Quoc	110	10.13 N	103.58 E
Phu Quoc, Dao I	110	10.12 N	104.00 E
Phurphura	272b	22.44 N	88.08 E
Phu Tho	110	21.24 N	105.13 E
Phu Tho Hoa	269c	10.46 N	106.38 E
Phu Tho Race Track ♦	269c	10.46 N	106.40 E
Phutthaisong	110	15.32 N	103.01 E
Phu Vang	110	16.31 N	107.37 E
Phu Yen	110	21.16 N	104.39 E
Pi ≃	100	32.26 N	116.34 E
Pia	154	4.00 N	26.17 E
Piaanu Pass ⊔	175c	7.20 N	151.26 E
Piabas	250	1.12 S	46.54 W
Piabetá	256	22.37 S	43.10 W
Piacá	250	7.42 S	47.18 W
Piaçabuçu	250	10.24 S	36.25 W
Piacatu	255	21.38 S	50.30 W
Piacatuba	256	21.29 S	42.47 W
Piacenza	62	45.01 N	9.40 E
Piacenza □ [4]	62	44.53 N	9.35 E
Piacouadie, Lac ⊜	186	51.16 N	70.54 W
Piadena	64	45.08 N	10.22 E
Piaggine	68	40.21 N	15.23 E
Piako ≃	172	37.12 S	175.30 E
Pialba	166	25.17 S	152.51 E
Piāli ≃	272b	22.23 N	88.35 E
Piana	36	42.14 N	8.38 E
Piana, Isola I	71	40.58 N	8.13 E
Piana Crixia	62	44.29 N	8.18 E
Piana degli Albanesi	70	38.00 N	13.17 E
Piana degli Albanesi, Lago di ⊜	70	37.58 N	13.18 E
Piana Mwanga	154	7.40 S	28.10 E
Piancastagnaio	66	42.51 N	11.41 E
Piancó	250	7.12 S	37.57 W
Pian Creek ≃	166	30.02 S	148.12 E
Pian di Sco	66	43.38 N	11.33 E
Pianella	66	42.24 N	14.02 E
Pianello Val Tidone	62	44.57 N	9.24 E
Pianezza	62	45.06 N	7.33 E
Pianguan	102	39.24 N	111.30 E
Pianjiaojie	102	26.01 N	100.32 E
Piankatank ≃	208	37.32 N	76.18 W
Pianling	104	41.24 N	123.58 E
Piano	64	45.46 N	11.08 E
Piano d'Arta	64	46.29 N	13.01 E
Piano del Voglio	66	44.10 N	11.13 E
Pianoro	64	44.22 N	11.20 E
Pianosa, Isola I, It.	36	42.35 N	10.04 E
Pianosa, Isola I, It.	66	42.13 N	15.45 E
Pianosinatico	66	44.07 N	10.44 E
Pianottoli-Caldarello, Fr.	71	41.29 N	9.03 E
Pianottoli-Caldarello, Fr.	71	41.29 N	9.03 E
Pians	58	47.08 N	10.30 E
Piapot	184	49.59 N	109.07 W
Piapot Indian Reserve ◆ [4]	184	50.45 N	104.26 W
Piares, Punta ›	234	16.49 N	99.55 W
Piasa	219	39.07 N	90.07 W
Piasa Creek ≃	219	38.56 N	90.17 W
Piaseczno	30	52.05 N	21.01 E
Piashti, Lac ⊜	186	50.29 N	62.52 W
Piaski	30	51.08 N	22.51 E
Piat	116	17.48 N	121.29 E
Piatã	255	13.09 S	41.48 W
Piatra-Neamț	38	46.56 N	26.22 E
Piatra Olt	38	44.24 N	24.16 E
Piatt □ [6]	219	40.00 N	88.35 W
Piau	256	21.31 S	43.19 W
Piauí □ [3]	250	7.00 S	43.00 W
Piauí ≃, Bra.	250	6.38 S	42.42 W
Piauí ≃, Bra.	255	16.41 S	41.53 W
Piaus, Rio dos ≃	255	12.27 S	49.32 W
Piave ≃	64	45.32 N	12.44 E
Piawaning	162	30.51 S	116.22 E
Piaxtla ≃	232	23.42 N	106.49 W
Piazza Armerina	70	37.23 N	14.22 E
Piazzola sul Brenta	64	45.32 N	11.47 E
Piberegg	61	47.05 N	15.05 E
Pibor ≃	140	8.26 N	33.13 E
Pibor Post	140	6.48 N	33.08 E
Pibroch	182	54.16 N	113.52 W
Pic ≃	190	48.36 N	86.18 W
Pica	248	20.30 S	69.21 W
Picacho	200	32.42 N	111.29 W
Picacho, Cerro del ∧	286a	19.35 N	99.06 W
Pičajevo	80	53.15 N	42.12 E
Picanoc ≃	190	46.05 N	76.03 W
Picardie □ [9]	50	49.45 N	2.50 E
Picatinny Arsenal ■	276	40.57 N	74.33 W
Picatinny Lake ⊜	276	40.57 N	74.33 W
Picayune	194	30.31 N	89.40 W
Piccadilly	186	48.34 N	58.55 W
Piccadilly Station ◆ [5]	262	53.28 N	2.14 W
Piccione	66	43.11 N	12.31 E
Piccolo, Mar (Taranto) ⊤ [2]	68	40.29 N	17.16 E
Piccotts End	260	51.46 N	0.28 W
Pic de Tio ∧	150	8.52 N	8.54 W
Piceance Creek ≃	200	40.05 N	108.14 W
Picentini, Monti ∧	68	40.45 N	15.00 E
Picerno	68	40.38 N	15.38 E
Pičeury	80	54.19 N	45.50 E
Pīch ≃	123	34.52 N	71.09 E
Pichana ≃	246	3.31 S	71.43 W
Pichanal	252	23.19 S	64.13 W
Picháṭaro	234	19.30 N	101.46 W
Picheng	106	32.07 N	119.42 E
Picher	196	36.59 N	94.49 W
Pichhor	124	25.58 N	78.24 E
Pichilemu	252	34.23 S	72.00 W
Pichileufú, Arroyo ≃	254	40.35 S	70.39 W
Pichimá	246	4.24 N	77.21 W
Pichi-Mahuída	252	38.50 S	64.57 W
Pichinango, Arroyo ≃	258	34.10 S	57.15 W
Pichincha □ [4]	246	0.10 S	78.40 W
Pichis ≃	248	9.59 S	74.59 W
Pichl bei Wels	60	48.11 N	13.54 E
Pichor	124	25.11 N	78.11 E
Pichtovka	86	56.00 N	82.42 E
Pichucalco	234	17.31 N	93.09 W
Pichucalco ≃	234	17.57 N	92.55 W
Picinguaba	256	23.22 S	44.50 W
Picinisco	66	41.39 N	13.52 E
Pic Island I	190	48.43 N	86.38 W
Pickardville	182	54.03 N	113.53 W
Pickaway □ [6]	218	39.36 N	82.57 W
Pickens, Ms., U.S.	194	32.53 N	89.58 W
Pickens, S.C., U.S.	192	34.53 N	82.42 W
Pickens, W.V., U.S.	188	38.39 N	80.12 W
Pickensville	194	33.14 N	88.16 W
Pickerel ≃	190	45.55 N	80.50 W
Pickerel Lake ⊜	184	52.36 N	99.30 W
Pickering, On., Can.	212	43.52 N	79.02 W
Pickering, Eng., U.K.	44	54.14 N	0.46 W
Pickering, Vale of V	44	54.12 N	0.45 W
Pickering Beach	212	43.50 N	78.59 W
Pickering Brook	168a	32.03 S	116.08 E
Pickering Creek ≃	285	40.08 N	75.30 W
Pickering Creek Reservoir ⊜ [1]	285	40.07 N	75.30 W
Pickett, Lake ⊜	220	28.36 N	81.07 W
Pickford	190	46.09 N	84.21 W
Pičkir'ajevo	80	54.12 N	42.27 E
Pickle Crow	176	51.30 N	90.04 W
Pickmere	262	53.17 N	2.28 W
Pick Mere ⊜	262	53.17 N	2.29 W
Pickstown	198	43.04 N	98.31 W
Pickton	222	33.02 N	95.24 W
Pickwick Lake ⊜ [1]	194	34.55 N	88.10 W
Pickwick Landing Dam ◆ [6]	194	35.00 N	88.21 W
Picnic Point ›	274b	37.57 S	145.00 E
Pico	66	41.27 N	13.34 E
Pico ∧	150a	14.56 N	24.21 W
Pico I	148a	38.28 N	28.20 W
Pico, Ponta do ∧	148a	38.28 N	28.25 W
Pico de Orizaba, Parque Nacional ♦	234	19.05 N	97.16 W
Pico de Oro	234	18.01 N	93.37 W
Pico de Tancítaro, Parque Nacional ♦	234	19.27 N	102.22 W
Pico Rivera	228	33.58 N	118.05 W
Picos	250	7.05 S	41.28 W
Picos, Riacho dos ≃	255	12.46 S	41.47 W
Picota	248	6.55 S	76.20 W
Pico Truncado	254	46.48 S	67.58 W
Picquigny	50	49.57 N	2.09 E
Picton, Austl.	170	34.11 S	150.36 E
Picton, On., Can.	212	44.00 N	77.08 W
Picton, N.Z.	172	41.18 S	174.01 E
Picton, Eng., U.K.	262	53.14 N	2.51 W
Picton, Isla I	254	55.02 S	66.57 W
Picton Bay ⊂	212	44.03 N	77.08 W
Picton Junction	168a	33.21 S	115.41 E
Pictou	186	45.41 N	62.43 W
Pictou Island I	186	45.50 N	62.34 W
Picture Butte	182	49.53 N	112.47 W
Pictured Rocks National Lakeshore ♦	190	46.35 N	86.20 W
Picture Rocks	210	41.17 N	76.43 W
Picúa, Punta ›	240m	18.25 N	65.46 W
Picuí	250	6.31 S	36.21 W
Picunda	84	43.12 N	40.21 E
Picún Leufú	254	39.31 S	69.15 W
Picún Leufú, Arroyo ≃	254	39.31 S	69.08 W
Picuris Indian Reservation ◆ [4]	200	36.12 N	105.42 W
Pidálion, Akrotírion ›	130	34.56 N	34.05 E
Pidarak	128	25.51 N	63.14 E
Piddle ≃	42	50.42 N	2.04 W
Piddletrenthide	42	50.48 N	2.25 W
Pide Adası I	267b	40.53 N	29.04 E
Pidie, Ujung ›	114	5.30 N	95.53 E
Piding	64	47.46 N	12.55 E
Pidurutalagala ∧	122	7.00 N	80.46 E
Piedade	287a	22.41 S	43.05 W
Piedade ◆ [8]	287a	22.53 S	43.19 W
Piedade do Baruel	287b	23.37 S	46.18 W
Piedade do Rio Grande	256	21.28 S	44.12 W
Piedecuesta	246	6.59 N	73.03 W
Piedicavallo	62	45.42 N	7.57 E
Piedicroce	32	42.23 N	9.23 E
Piediluco	66	42.32 N	12.45 E
Piedimonte Etneo	70	37.48 N	15.12 E
Piedimonte Matese	68	41.21 N	14.22 E
Piedimonte San Germano	66	41.30 N	13.45 E
Piedimulera	58	46.01 N	8.16 E
Piè di Ripa	66	43.15 N	13.29 E
Piedmont, Al., U.S.	194	33.55 N	85.36 W
Piedmont, Ca., U.S.	226	37.49 N	122.13 W
Piedmont, Mo., U.S.	194	37.09 N	90.41 W
Piedmont, Oh., U.S.	214	40.11 N	81.12 W
Piedmont, S.C., U.S.	192	34.54 N	82.21 W
Piedmont Lake ⊜ [1]	214	40.08 N	81.11 W
Piedra	226	36.48 N	119.22 W
Piedra ≃	200	37.01 N	107.24 W
Piedra, Cerro ∧	252	37.41 S	73.07 W
Piedra Azul, Quebrada ≃	286c	10.36 N	66.57 W
Piedra Blanca	232	29.05 N	102.19 W
Piedrabuena	34	39.02 N	4.10 W
Piedra del Águila	254	40.03 S	70.05 W
Piedrafita, Puerto de)(	34	42.40 N	7.01 W
Piedrahita	34	40.28 N	5.19 W
Piedra Roja	236	8.38 N	81.48 W
Piedras, Arroyo de las ≃	288	34.43 S	58.19 W
Piedras, Punta ›, Arg.	258	35.25 S	57.08 W
Piedras, Punta ›, Ur.	258	33.59 S	58.17 W
Piedras, Punta ›, Ven.	246	10.40 N	61.40 W
Piedras, Punta de ›	234	20.50 N	97.14 W
Piedras Blancas	252	31.11 S	59.56 W
Piedras Blancas, Point ›	226	35.40 N	121.17 W
Piedras Coloradas	252	32.23 S	57.36 W
Piedras de Tunja ♦	246	4.49 N	74.20 W
Piedras Negras, Guat.	232	17.11 N	91.15 W
Piedras Negras, Méx.	232	28.42 N	100.31 W
Piedras Negras ⊥	232	17.12 N	91.15 W
Piedra Sola	252	32.04 S	56.21 W
Piegaro	66	42.58 N	12.05 E
Pie Island I	190	48.15 N	89.05 W
Pieksämäki	26	62.18 N	27.08 E
Piéla	150	12.42 N	0.08 W
Pielach ≃	61	48.15 N	15.22 E
Pielavesi	26	63.14 N	26.45 E
Pielavesi ⊜	26	63.18 N	26.35 E
Pielinen ⊜	26	63.15 N	29.40 E
Pieljekaise Nationalpark ♦	24	66.18 N	16.58 E
Piemonte □ [4]	62	45.00 N	8.00 E
Pienaarsrivier	156	25.15 S	28.18 E
Piendamó	246	2.38 N	76.30 W
Pieniężno	30	54.15 N	20.08 E
Pieniński Park Narodowy ♦	30	49.25 N	20.25 E
Pieni-Salpausselkä ∧	26	61.08 N	27.20 E
Piennes	56	49.19 N	5.47 E
Pieńsk	30	51.15 N	15.03 E
Pienza	66	43.04 N	11.41 E
Pierce, Co., U.S.	200	40.38 N	104.45 W
Pierce, Fl., U.S.	220	27.50 N	81.58 W
Pierce, Id., U.S.	202	46.29 N	115.47 W
Pierce, Ne., U.S.	198	42.11 N	97.31 W
Pierce, Tx., U.S.	222	29.14 N	96.12 W
Pierce □ [6]	224	47.04 N	122.07 W
Pierce, Lake ⊜	220	27.58 N	81.31 W
Pierce City	194	36.56 N	94.00 W
Pierce Lake ⊜, Can.	184	54.10 N	92.56 W
Pierce Lake ⊜, Sk., Can.	184	54.30 N	109.42 W
Pierceton	216	41.12 N	85.42 W
Piermont	210	41.03 N	73.55 W
Pierowall	46	59.20 N	2.59 W
Pierpont, Oh., U.S.	214	41.45 N	80.34 W
Pierpont, S.D., U.S.	198	45.29 N	97.49 W
Pierre	198	44.22 N	100.21 W
Pierre, Bayou ≃, La., U.S.	194	31.51 N	93.06 W
Pierre, Bayou ≃, Ms., U.S.	194	31.55 N	91.11 W
Pierre-Buffière	32	45.42 N	1.21 E
Pierreclos	58	46.20 N	4.41 E
Pierre-de-Bresse	58	46.53 N	5.15 E
Pierrefeu-du-Var	62	43.13 N	6.08 E
Pierrefitte-sur-Aire	56	48.54 N	5.20 E
Pierrefitte-sur-Sauldre	50	47.30 N	2.09 E
Pierrefitte-sur-Seine	261	48.58 N	2.22 E
Pierrefonds, P.Q., Can.	206	45.29 N	73.52 W
Pierrefonds, Fr.	50	49.21 N	2.59 E
Pierrefontaine-les-Varans	58	47.13 N	6.33 E
Pierrelatte	62	44.23 N	4.42 E
Pierrelaye	261	49.01 N	2.09 E
Pierre Part	194	29.57 N	91.12 W
Pierre Pertuis, Col de)(	58	47.12 N	7.11 E
Pierrepont Manor	212	43.44 N	76.04 W
Pierre-sur-Haut ∧	62	45.39 N	3.49 E
Pierreville, P.Q., Can.	206	46.04 N	72.49 W
Pierreville, Trin.	241r	10.18 N	61.01 W
Pierron	219	38.47 N	89.36 W
Pierron, Lac ⊜	206	46.53 N	74.20 W
Pierry	50	49.01 N	3.56 E
Pierson	192	29.14 N	81.27 W
Piersonville	285	40.10 N	74.42 W
Pierz	190	45.58 N	94.06 W
Piesendorf	64	47.17 N	12.43 E
Pieštʼany	30	48.36 N	17.50 E
Piesting ≃	61	48.02 N	16.30 E
Pietarsaari → Jakobstad	26	63.40 N	22.42 E
Pieterburen	52	53.24 N	6.27 E
Pieterlen	58	47.11 N	7.20 E
Pietermaritzburg	158	29.37 S	30.16 E
Pietersburg	156	23.54 S	29.25 E
Pietrabbondante	66	41.45 N	14.23 E
Pietracamela	66	42.31 N	13.33 E
Pietracatella	66	41.35 N	14.52 E
Pietra del Pertusillo, Lago di ⊜	68	40.17 N	15.58 E
Pietragalla	68	40.45 N	15.53 E
Pietra Ligure	62	44.09 N	8.17 E
Pietralunga	66	43.26 N	12.26 E
Pietramala	66	44.10 N	11.20 E
Pietramelara	68	41.16 N	14.11 E
Pietramontecorvino	68	41.32 N	15.07 E
Pietrapaola	68	39.29 N	16.49 E
Pietrapertosa	68	40.31 N	16.04 E
Pietraperzia	70	37.25 N	14.08 E
Pietrasanta	64	43.57 N	10.14 E
Pietrelcina	68	41.12 N	14.51 E
Piet Retief	158	27.01 S	30.50 E
Pietrosu, Vîrful ∧, Rom.	38	47.36 N	24.38 E
Pietrosu, Vîrful ∧, Rom.	38	47.08 N	25.11 E
Pieve	64	45.46 N	10.45 E
Pieve d'Alpago	64	46.10 N	12.21 E
Pieve del Cairo	62	45.03 N	8.48 E
Pieve di Cadore	64	46.26 N	12.22 E
Pieve di Cento	64	44.43 N	11.18 E
Pieve di Soligo	64	45.53 N	12.10 E
Pieve di Teco	62	44.03 N	7.56 E
Pieve Fosciana	64	44.08 N	10.25 E
Pievepelago	64	44.12 N	10.37 E
Pieve Porto Morone	62	45.07 N	9.26 E
Pieve Santo Stefano	66	43.40 N	12.02 E
Piffard	210	42.50 N	77.51 W
Pigari	80	51.24 N	49.42 E
Pigeon, Mi., U.S.	190	43.49 N	83.16 W
Pigeon, Pa., U.S.	214	41.32 N	79.03 W
Pigeon ≃, Mb., Can.	184	52.15 N	97.00 W
Pigeon ≃, On., Can.	212	44.22 N	78.31 W
Pigeon ≃, N.A.	190	48.00 N	89.34 W
Pigeon ≃, U.S.	192	36.00 N	83.11 W
Pigeon ≃, U.S.	216	41.46 N	85.47 W
Pigeon ≃, Mi., U.S.	190	43.56 N	83.17 W
Pigeon ≃, Mi., U.S.	190	45.27 N	84.33 W
Pigeon ≃, Mi., U.S.	216	42.54 N	86.11 W
Pigeon Bay ⊂	214	42.01 N	82.40 W
Pigeon Cove	207	42.40 N	70.38 W
Pigeon Creek ≃, Al., U.S.	194	31.20 N	86.42 W
Pigeon Creek ≃, In., U.S.	194	37.59 N	87.35 W
Pigeon Creek ≃, In., U.S.	216	41.41 N	85.17 W
Pigeon Creek ≃, Pa., U.S.	279b	40.12 N	79.55 W
Pigeon Creek ≃, Pa., U.S.	285	40.12 N	75.35 W
Pigeon Forge	192	35.47 N	83.33 W
Pigeon Lake ⊜, Ab., Can.	182	53.00 N	114.00 W
Pigeon Lake ⊜, On., Can.	212	44.30 N	78.30 W
Pigeon Run ≃	285	40.06 N	75.35 W
Pigeon Swamp ⩨	276	40.23 N	74.29 W
Pigezhuang	105	39.39 N	116.15 E
Pigg ≃	192	37.00 N	79.29 W
Piggott	194	36.22 N	90.11 W
Piggs Peak	158	25.38 S	31.15 E
Pigkawagan	116	7.12 N	124.32 E
Piglio	66	41.49 N	13.08 E
Pigna	62	43.56 N	7.40 E
Pignans	62	43.18 N	6.13 E
Pignataro Maggiore	68	41.11 N	14.10 E
Pignola	68	40.34 N	15.47 E
Pigs, Bay of → Cochinos, Bahía de ⊂	240p	22.07 N	81.10 W
Pigüé	252	37.37 S	62.25 W
Pigŭm-do I	98	34.45 N	125.55 E
Pihama	172	39.30 S	173.56 E
Piha Passage ⊔	174w	21.07 S	175.05 W
Pihāri	124	27.38 N	80.12 E
Pihlajavesi ⊜	26	61.45 N	28.50 E
Pihlava	26	61.33 N	21.36 E
Pihtipudas	26	63.23 N	25.34 E
Pihuamo	234	19.15 N	103.23 W
P'ihyŏn	98	40.01 N	124.37 E
Piikkiö	26	60.26 N	22.31 E
Piippola	26	64.10 N	25.58 E
Pijijiapan	234	15.42 N	93.14 W
Pijnacker	52	52.02 N	4.27 E
Pijol, Pico ∧	236	15.06 N	87.35 W
Pikal'ovo	76	59.31 N	34.06 E
Pikangikum	184	51.49 N	94.00 W
Pikangikum Lake ⊜	184	51.48 N	94.00 W
Pike	210	42.33 N	78.09 W
Pike □ [6], Il., U.S.	219	39.36 N	90.48 W
Pike □ [6], Mo., U.S.	219	39.21 N	91.10 W
Pike □ [6], Oh., U.S.	218	39.05 N	83.06 W
Pike □ [6], Pa., U.S.	210	41.19 N	74.48 W
Pike ≃, N.A.	206	45.04 N	73.06 W
Pike ≃, Wi., U.S.	190	45.26 N	87.52 W
Pike, North Branch ≃	190	45.30 N	88.01 W
Pike, South Branch ≃	190	45.30 N	88.01 W
Pike Creek ≃, On., Can.	281	42.19 N	82.51 W
Pike Creek ≃, De., U.S.	285	39.42 N	75.42 W
Pike Lake ⊜	212	44.46 N	76.21 W
Pikelot I	14	8.05 N	147.38 E
Pike Lowe ∧ [2]	262	53.42 N	2.34 W
Pike Run ≃	276	40.25 N	74.38 W
Pikes Peak	218	39.08 N	86.09 W
Pikes Peak ∧	200	38.51 N	105.03 W
Pikes Rocks ∧ [2]	214	41.56 N	79.24 W
Pikesville	208	39.22 N	76.43 W
Piketberg	158	32.54 S	18.46 E
Piketon	218	39.04 N	83.00 W
Piketown	208	40.23 N	76.45 W
Pikeville, Ky., U.S.	192	37.28 N	82.31 W
Pikeville, Tn., U.S.	194	35.36 N	85.11 W
Pikkola	265a	59.42 N	30.08 E
Pikou	98	39.24 N	122.20 E
Pikounda	152	0.33 N	16.42 E
Pikwitonei	184	55.35 N	97.09 W
Pila, Arg.	252	36.01 S	58.08 W
Pila, It.	62	45.41 N	7.18 E
Piła (Schneidemühl), Pol.	30	53.10 N	16.44 E
Piła □ [4]	30	53.15 N	16.30 E
Pilanesberg ∧	156	25.14 S	27.04 E

Symbol	English	Deutsch	Español	Français	Português
≃	River	Fluß	Río	Rivière	Rio
≅	Canal	Kanal	Canal	Canal	Canal
⌊	Waterfall, Rapids	Wasserfall, Stromschnellen	Cascada, Rápidos	Chute d'eau, Rapides	Cascata, Rápidos
⊔	Strait	Meeresstraße	Estrecho	Détroit	Estreito
⊂	Bay, Gulf	Bucht, Golf	Bahía, Golfo	Baie, Golfe	Baía, Golfo
⊜	Lake, Lakes	See, Seen	Lago, Lagos	Lac, Lacs	Lago, Lagos
⩨	Swamp	Sumpf	Pantano	Marais	Pântano
⊓	Ice Features, Glacier	Eis- und Gletscherformen	Accidentes Glaciales	Formes glaciaires	Acidentes glaciares
⊤	Other Hydrographic Features	Andere Hydrographische Objekte	Otros Elementos Hidrográficos	Autres données hydrographiques	Outros acidentes hidrográficos
✦	Submarine Features	Untermeerische Objekte	Accidentes Submarinos	Formes de relief sous-marin	Acidentes submarinos
□	Political Unit	Politische Einheit	Unidad Politica	Entité politique	Unidade política
❦	Cultural Institution	Kulturelle Institution	Institución Cultural	Institution culturelle	Instituição cultural
⊥	Historical Site	Historische Stätte	Sitio Histórico	Site historique	Sitio histórico
♦	Recreational Site	Erholungs- und Ferienort	Sitio de Recreo	Centre de loisirs	Area de Lazer
⊠	Airport	Flughafen	Aeropuerto	Aéroport	Aeroporto
■	Military Installation	Militäranlage	Instalación Militar	Installation militaire	Instalação militar
◆	Miscellaneous	Verschiedenes	Misceláneo	Divers	Diversos

ENGLISH — Name / Page / Lat.°′ / Long.°′
DEUTSCH — Name / Seite / Breite°′ / Länge°′ E = Ost

Pilanesberg Game Reserve ◆[4] 156 25.15 S 27.05 E
Pilão Arcado 250 10.09 S 42.26 W
Pilar, Arg. 252 31.41 S 63.54 W
Pilar, Arg. 252 31.27 S 61.15 W
Pilar, Arg. 258 34.27 S 58.54 W
Pilar, Bra. 250 9.36 S 35.56 W
Pilar, Bra. 287a 22.42 S 43.19 W
Pilar, Para. 252 26.52 S 58.23 W
Pilar, Pil. 116 11.29 N 123.00 E
Pilar, Pil. 116 9.52 N 126.06 E
Pilar □[5] 288 34.28 S 58.52 W
Pilar Bay ⊂ 116 11.34 N 123.00 E
Pilarcitos Creek ≃ 282 37.28 N 122.27 W
Pilarcitos Lake ⊜ 282 37.33 N 122.25 W
Pilar de Goiás 255 14.41 S 49.27 W
Pilar do Sul 255 23.49 S 47.42 W
Pilares 196 30.24 N 104.52 W
Pilas Group II 116 6.45 N 121.35 E
Pilas Island I 116 6.38 N 121.37 E
Pilatus ∧ 58 46.59 N 8.15 E
Pilawa 30 51.58 N 21.31 E
Pilaya ≃ 248 20.55 S 64.04 W
Pilcher Park ♦ 278 41.32 N 88.01 W
Pilchuck ≃ 224 47.55 N 122.02 W
Pilchuck Creek ≃ 224 48.12 N 122.13 W
Pilcomayo ≃ 18 25.21 S 57.42 W
Pilcomayo, Brazo Norte ≃ 252 24.56 S 58.16 W
Pilcomayo, Brazo Sur ≃ 252 24.56 S 58.16 W
Pil'dozero 24 65.43 N 33.28 E
Piles Creek ≃ 276 40.37 N 74.12 W
Pilga 162 21.29 S 119.25 E
Pilger 198 42.00 N 97.03 W
Pilgrim Gardens 285 39.57 N 75.19 W
Pilgrim Memorial Monument ⊥ 207 42.04 N 70.12 W
Pilgrims Hatch 260 51.38 N 0.17 E
Pilgrim's Rest 156 24.55 S 30.44 E
Pil'gyn 180 69.18 N 179.08 E
Pili 116 13.33 N 123.16 E
Pīlībhīt 124 28.38 N 79.48 E
Pilica ≃ 30 51.52 N 21.17 E
Pilipinas → Philippines □[1] 116 13.00 N 122.00 E
Pilis ⩘ 264c 47.37 N 18.59 E
Pilisborosjenő 264c 47.36 N 19.00 E
Pilkhua 124 28.43 N 77.39 E
Píllaro 246 1.10 S 78.32 W
Pillar Point ≻ 282 37.30 N 122.30 W
Pillar Point ≻[1] 212 43.59 N 76.09 W
Pillau → Baltijsk 76 54.39 N 19.55 E
Pilley's Island 186 49.31 N 55.44 W
Pilliga 166 30.21 S 148.54 E
Pillings Pond ⊜ 283 42.32 N 71.02 W
Pillnitz ◆[8] 54 51.00 N 13.52 E
Pillon, Col du)(58 46.22 N 7.13 E
Pillow 208 40.38 N 76.48 W
Pillsbury Sound ʊ 240m 18.20 N 64.49 W
Pil'na 80 55.33 N 45.55 E
Pilón ≃ 232 25.22 N 99.32 W
Pílos 38 36.55 N 21.43 E
Pilot ∧ 166 36.45 S 148.13 E
Pilot Butte 184 50.28 N 104.25 W
Pilot Grove 194 38.52 N 92.54 W
Pilot Hill 226 38.50 N 121.02 W
Pilot Knob 194 37.37 N 90.38 W
Pilot Knob ∧, Ar., U.S. 194 35.42 N 93.57 W
Pilot Knob ∧, Id., U.S. 202 45.54 N 115.42 W
Pilot Mound 184 49.16 N 98.55 W
Pilot Mountain 192 36.23 N 80.28 W
Pilot Peak ∧, Nv., U.S. 204 38.21 N 117.58 W
Pilot Peak ∧, Nv., U.S. 204 41.02 N 114.06 W
Pilot Peak ∧, Wy., U.S. 202 44.58 N 109.53 W
Pilot Point, Ak., U.S. 180 57.34 N 157.35 W
Pilot Point, Tx., U.S. 196 33.23 N 96.57 W
Pilot Rock 202 45.29 N 118.49 W
Pilot Rock ∧ 200 35.09 N 109.53 W
Pilot Station 180 61.56 N 162.54 W
Pilottown 194 29.10 N 89.15 W
Pilpah Range ⩘ 166 20.23 S 138.34 E
Pilsen → Plzeň 60 49.45 N 13.23 E
Pilsensee ⊜ 60 48.01 N 11.11 E
Pilsum 52 53.29 N 7.04 E
Piltene 76 57.13 N 21.40 E
Pilu ≃ 110 19.33 N 97.24 E
Piluchang 107 29.13 N 105.37 E
Pil'ugino 80 53.25 N 52.26 E
Pilusi 106 32.05 N 120.05 E
Pilzno 30 49.59 N 21.17 E
Pim ≃ 74 61.18 N 71.57 E
Pima 200 32.53 N 109.49 W
Pimah 110 15.36 N 107.25 E
Pimba 166 31.15 S 136.47 E
Pimelles 50 47.50 N 4.10 E
Pimenteira, Vereda ≃ 250 10.04 S 42.25 W
Pimenteiras 250 6.14 S 41.25 W
Pimentel, Bra. 250 3.43 S 45.30 W
Pimentel, Perú 248 6.50 S 79.57 W
Pimlico Race Course ♦ 284b 39.21 N 76.40 W
Pimmit Hills 284c 38.54 N 77.12 W
Pimmit Run ≃ 284c 38.55 N 77.07 W
Pimu-Lendo 152 1.46 N 20.54 E
Pimville ◆[8] 273d 26.16 S 27.54 E
Pina, Cuba 240p 22.01 N 78.43 W
Pina, Esp. 34 41.29 N 0.32 W
Pina ≃ 78 52.10 N 26.14 E
Pinacanauan ≃ 116 17.37 N 121.44 E
Pinamalayan 116 13.02 N 121.29 E
Pinang → George Town 114 5.25 N 100.20 E
Pinang □[3] 114 5.20 N 100.20 E
Pinang, Pulau I 114 5.23 N 100.15 E
Pinangah 112 5.12 N 116.50 E
Pınarbaşı, Tür. 130 41.36 N 33.07 E
Pınarbaşı, Tür. 130 38.44 N 36.24 E
Pinar del Río 240p 22.25 N 83.42 W
Pinar del Río □[4] 240p 22.30 N 83.45 W
Pinardville 188 42.59 N 71.30 W
Pınarhisar 130 41.37 N 27.30 E
Pınarlar 130 38.53 N 39.29 E
Pinas, Arg. 252 31.09 S 65.29 W
Piñas, Ec. 246 3.42 S 79.42 W
Piñas, Cerro ∧ 236 15.25 N 85.47 W
Pinatubo, Mount ∧ 116 15.08 N 120.21 E
Pinazo, Arroyo ≃ 288 34.24 S 58.48 W
Pinchbeck 42 52.48 N 0.09 W
Pincher Creek 182 49.29 N 113.57 W
Pinchi Lake ⊜ 182 54.35 N 124.20 W
Pinckney 216 42.27 N 83.56 W
Pinckney State Recreation Area ♦ 216 42.25 N 84.04 W
Pinckneyville 194 38.04 N 89.22 W
Pinconning 190 43.51 N 83.57 W
Pincourt 206 45.23 N 74.00 W
Pinčuga 86 58.23 N 96.59 E
Pińczów 30 50.32 N 20.35 E
Pindaíba, Ribeirão ≃ 255 14.18 S 51.45 W
Pindale 110 21.11 N 95.51 E
Pindamonhangaba 256 22.55 S 45.28 W
Pindar 162 28.29 S 115.48 E
Pindaré ≃ 250 3.17 S 44.47 W
Pindaré-Mirim 250 3.37 S 45.21 W
Pind Dādan Khān 123 32.35 N 73.03 E
Pinde → Píndhos Óros ⩘ 38 39.49 N 21.14 E
Pinder Point ≻ 192 26.28 N 78.39 W
Píndhos Óros ⩘ 38 39.49 N 21.14 E
Pindi Bhattiān 123 31.54 N 73.16 E
Pindiga 146 9.59 N 10.54 E
Pindi Gheb 123 33.14 N 72.16 E
Pindo → Píndhos Óros ⩘ 38 39.49 N 21.14 E
Pindobaçu 250 10.44 S 40.21 W
Pindorama de Goiás 250 10.55 S 47.40 W
Pindoyacu ≃ 246 2.07 S 76.03 W
Pinduši 24 62.56 N 34.35 E
Pindus Mountains → Píndhos Óros ⩘ 38 39.49 N 21.14 E
Pindwāra 120 24.48 N 73.04 E
Pine ≃, B.C., Can. 182 56.08 N 120.41 W
Pine ≃, Mb., Can. 184 52.00 N 100.09 W
Pine ≃, On., Can. 212 44.20 N 79.52 W
Pine ≃, Mi., U.S. 190 44.15 N 85.55 W
Pine ≃, Mi., U.S. 190 43.35 N 84.08 W
Pine ≃, Mi., U.S. 190 44.26 N 83.21 W
Pine ≃, Mi., U.S. 190 46.03 N 84.40 W
Pine ≃, Mi., U.S. 214 42.49 N 82.29 W
Pine ≃, Wi., U.S. 190 44.08 N 88.54 W
Pine ≃, Wi., U.S. 190 45.50 N 88.08 W
Pine ≃, Wi., U.S. 190 43.12 N 90.18 W
Pine Apple 194 31.52 N 86.59 W
Pine Banks Park ♦ 283 42.26 N 71.04 W
Pine Barrens ◆[1] 208 39.48 N 74.35 W
Pine Beach 206 45.32 N 73.57 W
Pine Bluff 194 34.13 N 92.00 W
Pine Bluffs 198 41.10 N 104.04 W
Pine Brook 276 40.52 N 74.20 W
Pine Brook ≃, U.S. 276 41.04 N 74.05 W
Pine Brook ≃, Ma., U.S. 283 42.00 N 70.47 W
Pine Brook ≃, N.J., U.S. 276 40.19 N 74.20 W
Pine Bush 210 41.36 N 74.17 W
Pine Castle 220 28.28 N 81.22 W
Pine City, Mn., U.S. 190 45.49 N 92.58 W
Pine City, N.Y., U.S. 210 42.02 N 76.52 W
Pinecliff Lake ⊜ 276 41.08 N 74.23 W
Pinecraft 220 27.19 N 82.30 W
Pine Creek 164 13.49 S 131.49 E
Pine Creek ≃, Ab., Can. 182 54.56 N 112.31 W
Pine Creek ≃, Ca., U.S. 204 40.40 N 120.46 W
Pine Creek ≃, Ca., U.S. 282 37.58 N 122.02 W
Pine Creek ≃, Nv., U.S. 204 40.36 N 116.10 W
Pine Creek ≃, Pa., U.S. 210 41.10 N 77.16 W
Pine Creek ≃, Pa., U.S. 279b 40.30 N 79.57 W
Pine Creek ≃, Pa., U.S. 285 40.05 N 75.37 W
Pine Creek, West Branch ≃ 210 41.43 N 77.38 W
Pine Creek Indian Reserve ◆[4] 184 52.03 N 100.14 W
Pine Creek Lake ⊜[1] 196 34.05 N 95.05 W
Pine Creek Point ≻ 276 41.07 N 73.16 W
Pine Crest, Fl., U.S. 220 28.01 N 82.32 W
Pinecrest, Va., U.S. 208 38.50 N 77.09 W
Pinecrest Lake ⊜ 226 38.12 N 119.58 W
Pine Crest Point ≻ 284a 42.52 N 79.11 W
Pinedale, Ca., U.S. 226 36.50 N 119.48 W
Pinedale, Wy., U.S. 200 42.52 N 109.51 W
Pine Falls 184 50.35 N 96.15 W
Pine Flat Lake ⊜[1] 226 36.52 N 119.18 W
Pinega 24 64.42 N 43.19 E
Pinega ≃ 24 64.08 N 41.54 E
Pine Glen 212 45.19 N 75.43 W
Pine Grove, On., Can. 275b 43.48 N 79.35 W
Pine Grove, Ca., U.S. 226 38.25 N 120.39 W
Pine Grove, Fl., U.S. 220 28.16 N 81.11 W
Pine Grove, N.J., U.S. 285 39.53 N 74.52 W
Pine Grove, Pa., U.S. 208 40.32 N 76.23 W
Pine Grove, W.V., U.S. 188 39.33 N 80.40 W
Pine Grove Mills 214 40.44 N 77.53 W
Pine Hill, Austl. 166 23.39 S 146.58 E
Pine Hill, Al., U.S. 194 31.58 N 87.35 W
Pine Hill, N.J., U.S. 208 39.47 N 74.59 W
Pine Hill, N.Y., U.S. 210 42.08 N 74.29 W
Pinehill, Tx., U.S. 222 32.06 N 94.36 W
Pine Hills 220 28.33 N 81.27 W
Pinehouse Lake 184 55.31 N 106.36 W
Pinehouse Lake ⊜ 184 55.32 N 106.35 W
Pinehurst, Ga., U.S. 192 32.11 N 83.45 W
Pinehurst, Id., U.S. 202 45.15 N 116.20 W
Pinehurst, Ma., U.S. 207 42.31 N 71.13 W
Pinehurst, N.Y., U.S. 284a 42.44 N 78.57 W
Pinehurst, N.C., U.S. 192 35.11 N 79.28 W
Pinehurst, Tx., U.S. 222 30.10 N 95.41 W
Pinehurst Lake ⊜ 182 54.39 N 111.25 W
Pine Island, Mn., U.S. 190 44.12 N 92.38 W
Pine Island, N.Y., U.S. 210 41.17 N 74.27 W
Pine Island I 220 26.35 N 82.06 W
Pine Island Bay ⊂ 9 74.50 S 102.05 W
Pine Island Bayou ≃ 194 30.10 N 94.07 W
Pine Island Creek ≃ 283 42.47 N 70.48 W
Pine Island Dam ◆[6] 214 40.08 N 80.43 W
Pine Island Sound ʊ 220 26.33 N 82.10 W
Pine Lake, In., U.S. 216 41.38 N 86.45 W
Pine Lake, Ma., U.S. 283 42.23 N 71.27 W
Pine Lake ⊜, On., Can. 212 44.57 N 79.27 W
Pine Lake ⊜, Mi., U.S. 281 42.35 N 83.20 W
Pine Lake ⊜, N.Y., U.S. 210 43.12 N 74.31 W
Pineland 194 31.14 N 93.58 W
Pine Lawn 219 38.41 N 90.16 W
Pinellas □[6] 220 27.53 N 82.43 W
Pinellas, Point ≻ 220 27.42 N 82.38 W
Pinellas Park 220 27.50 N 82.41 W
Pine Marsh ≋ 276 40.37 N 73.34 W
Pine Meadow Lake ⊜ 276 41.11 N 74.07 W
Pine Mountain ∧, U.S. 192 36.55 N 83.20 W
Pine Mountain ∧, Ca., U.S. 226 35.41 N 121.05 W
Pine Mountain ∧, Ca., U.S. 280 34.13 N 117.54 W
Pine Mountain ∧, Ct., U.S. 207 41.58 N 72.56 W
Pine Mountain ∧, Ga., U.S. 192 32.51 N 84.47 W
Pine Mountain ∧, Or., U.S. 202 43.47 N 120.54 W
Pine Mountain ∧, Wy., U.S. 200 41.02 N 109.01 W
Pine Nut Mountains ⩘ 226 39.00 N 119.25 W
Pine Orchard Meadows 284b 39.17 N 76.52 W
Pine Pass)(182 55.22 N 122.40 W
Pine Plains 210 41.59 N 73.40 W
Pine Point, Austl. 168b 34.34 S 137.52 E
Pine Point, N.T., Can. 176 61.01 N 114.15 W
Pine Point Park ♦ 275b 43.43 N 79.33 W
Pine Portage Dam ◆[6] 176 49.18 N 88.19 W
Pine Prairie 194 30.47 N 92.25 W
Piner 218 38.50 N 84.32 W
Pine Rest 283 42.23 N 71.26 W
Pine Ridge, Pa., U.S. 285 39.55 N 75.22 W
Pine Ridge, S.D., U.S. 198 43.01 N 102.33 W
Pine Ridge, Va., U.S. 284c 38.52 N 77.14 W
Pine Ridge ∧ 198 42.40 N 103.00 W
Pine Ridge Estates 276 41.02 N 73.41 W
Pine Ridge Indian Reservation ◆[4] 198 43.25 N 102.21 W
Pine River, Mb., Can. 184 51.47 N 100.32 W
Pine River, Mn., U.S. 190 46.43 N 94.24 W
Piñero 258 34.32 S 58.45 W
Pinerolo 62 44.53 N 7.21 E
Piñeros, Isla I 240m 18.15 N 65.35 W
Pinerovka 80 51.34 N 43.04 E
Pine Run ≃ 279b 40.37 N 79.35 W
Pines ≃ 283 42.27 N 70.58 W
Pines, Isle of → Juventud, Isla de la I 240p 21.40 N 82.50 W
Pines, Lake o' the ⊜[1] 222 32.46 N 94.35 W
Pines, Point of ≻ 283 42.26 N 70.58 W
Pine Shores 220 27.17 N 82.32 W
Pines Lake ⊜ 276 41.00 N 74.16 W
Pines Run ≃ 285 39.50 N 75.05 W
Pine Swamp Knob ∧ 188 39.33 N 79.31 W
Pineto 66 42.36 N 14.04 E
Pinetop 200 34.07 N 109.56 W
Pinetops 192 35.47 N 77.38 W
Pinetown 158 29.52 S 30.46 E
Pine Tree Hill ∧ 114 3.43 N 101.42 E
Pine Valley, Md., U.S. 284b 39.26 N 76.39 W
Pine Valley, N.Y., U.S. 210 42.14 N 76.51 W
Pine Valley V 204 38.25 N 113.40 W
Pine Village 216 40.27 N 87.15 W
Pineville, Ky., U.S. 192 36.45 N 83.41 W
Pineville, La., U.S. 194 31.19 N 92.26 W
Pineville, Mo., U.S. 194 36.35 N 94.23 W
Pineville, N.C., U.S. 192 35.04 N 80.53 W
Pineville, Pa., U.S. 208 40.18 N 75.00 W
Pineville, W.V., U.S. 192 37.34 N 81.32 W
Pinewood, Fl., U.S. 220 25.53 N 80.14 W
Pinewood, S.C., U.S. 192 33.44 N 80.27 W
Piney 50 48.22 N 4.20 E
Piney ≃ 194 35.49 N 87.33 W
Piney Branch ≃ 284c 38.56 N 77.18 W
Piney Creek ≃, Tx., U.S. 222 31.03 N 94.34 W
Piney Creek ≃, Wy., U.S. 202 44.34 N 106.32 W
Piney Fork 214 40.15 N 80.50 W
Piney Point 222 29.46 N 95.31 W
Piney Point ≻ 208 38.08 N 76.32 W
Piney Run ≃ 284c 38.58 N 77.17 W
Piney Woods 194 32.03 N 89.59 W
Pinfold 262 53.36 N 2.55 W
Ping ≃, Thai 110 15.42 N 100.09 E
Ping ≃, Zhg. 100 25.59 N 115.07 E
Pinga 154 1.01 S 28.42 E
Ping'an, Zhg. 89 45.20 N 123.42 E
Ping'an, Zhg. 104 41.11 N 123.26 E
Ping'an, Zhg. 107 30.36 N 104.42 E
Ping'anbu 98 41.45 N 116.13 E
Ping'ancheng 105 40.03 N 117.48 E
Ping'andi 104 42.34 N 121.52 E
Pingaring 162 32.45 S 118.37 E
Pingba, Zhg. 100 31.19 N 113.18 E
Pingba, Zhg. 102 26.22 N 106.09 E
Pingchang 102 31.35 N 107.03 E
Pingchao 106 32.07 N 120.45 E
Pingding 98 37.48 N 113.37 E
Pingdingpu 104 42.22 N 123.55 E
Pingdingshan, Zhg. 98 41.26 N 124.45 E
Pingdingshan, Zhg. 100 33.45 N 113.17 E
Pingding Shan ∧ 89 46.38 N 128.27 E
Pingdu 98 36.47 N 119.54 E
Pingelap I[1] 14 6.13 N 160.42 E
Pingelly 162 32.32 S 117.05 E
Pingfang, Zhg. 100 30.07 N 113.48 E
Pingfang, Zhg. 104 41.17 N 120.40 E
Pingfang, Zhg. 104 41.28 N 120.48 E
Pingfang, Zhg. 104 42.14 N 120.38 E
Pingfang, Zhg. 104 42.27 N 120.38 E
Pingfang, Zhg. 271a 39.56 N 116.33 E
Pingfangdu 104 41.45 N 121.12 E
Pingfangzi 104 41.31 N 121.21 E
Pinggau 61 47.27 N 16.04 E
Pinggu 105 40.09 N 117.07 E
Pingguo 102 23.19 N 107.39 E
Pinghai, Zhg. 100 25.14 N 119.15 E
Pinghai, Zhg. 100 22.39 N 114.53 E
Pinghe, Zhg. 100 24.25 N 117.22 E
Pinghe, Zhg. 102 22.51 N 102.30 E
Pinghe ≃ 100 24.25 N 116.36 E
P'inghsiang → Pingxiang 102 22.09 N 106.43 E
Pinghu, Zhg. 100 26.46 N 118.48 E
Pinghu, Zhg. 100 30.56 N 115.22 E
Pinghu, Zhg. 100 22.42 N 114.08 E
Pinghu, Zhg. 106 30.42 N 121.01 E
Pingjiang 100 28.44 N 113.34 E
Pingjing 105 39.20 N 116.06 E
Pinglan 100 22.22 N 113.27 E
Pingle, Zhg. 102 24.37 N 110.40 E
Pingle, Zhg. 102 24.31 N 106.59 E
Pingli 102 32.19 N 109.21 E
Pingliang 102 35.32 N 106.41 E
Pinglidian 98 37.17 N 119.59 E
Pingling 100 23.39 N 114.23 E
Pinglucheng 102 39.50 N 112.19 E
Pingluo 102 38.57 N 106.35 E
Pingluopu 104 41.56 N 123.20 E
Pingnan, Zhg. 100 26.56 N 119.02 E
Pingnan, Zhg. 102 23.30 N 110.30 E
Pingqiao 100 33.24 N 119.13 E
Pingquan 98 40.59 N 118.34 E
Pingrup 162 33.32 S 118.31 E
Ping Shan, H.K. 271d 22.27 N 114.00 E
Pingshan, Zhg. 100 25.36 N 117.52 E
Pingshan, Zhg. 100 23.26 N 113.15 E
Pingshan, Zhg. 100 22.43 N 114.22 E
Pingshan, Zhg. 102 38.15 N 114.10 E
Pingshang 98 35.11 N 119.07 E
Pingshi, Zhg. 100 32.32 N 113.03 E
Pingshi, Zhg. 100 25.20 N 113.02 E
Pingshui 100 29.53 N 120.38 E
Pingtaizi 105 40.44 N 116.25 E
Pingtan, Zhg. 100 25.31 N 119.47 E
Pingtan, Zhg. 100 23.04 N 114.38 E
Pingtan, Zhg. 107 29.50 N 105.56 E
Pingtan, Zhg. 107 29.38 N 105.16 E
Pingtan Dao I 100 25.33 N 119.48 E
Pingtang 102 25.50 N 107.19 E
Pingtian 100 25.19 N 113.31 E
P'ingtung 100 22.40 N 120.29 E
Pingües, Cayos II 240p 20.47 N 78.15 W
Pingüicas, Cerro ∧ 234 21.10 N 99.42 W
Pingwang 106 30.59 N 120.38 E
Pingwu 102 32.29 N 104.37 E
Pingxiang, Zhg. 100 27.38 N 113.50 E
Pingxiang, Zhg. 102 22.09 N 106.43 E
Pingyang, Zhg. 89 48.13 N 124.23 E
Pingyang, Zhg. 100 27.41 N 120.33 E
Pingyao, Zhg. 102 37.16 N 112.09 E
Pingyao, Zhg. 106 30.24 N 119.58 E
Pingyi 98 35.34 N 117.37 E
Pingyin 98 36.19 N 116.22 E
Pingyu 100 32.57 N 114.41 E
Pingyuan, Zhg. 98 37.11 N 116.25 E
Pingyuan, Zhg. 100 24.36 N 115.54 E
Pingzhai 102 24.07 N 104.22 E
Pingzhuang 98 42.03 N 119.22 E
Pinhal 256 22.12 S 46.45 W
Pinhal, Ribeirão do ≃ 256 22.42 S 46.42 W
Pinhal Novo 34 38.38 N 8.55 W
Pinhalzinho 256 22.46 S 46.36 W
Pinhão 250 10.34 S 37.44 W
Pinheiral 256 22.31 S 43.59 W
Pinheirinhos 256 22.26 S 44.59 W
Pinheiro 250 2.31 S 45.05 W
Pinheiro de Loures 266c 38.50 N 9.12 W
Pinheiro Machado 252 31.34 S 53.23 W
Pinheiros 256 22.32 S 44.54 W
Pinheiros ≃ 287b 23.32 S 46.44 W
Pinhel 34 40.46 N 7.04 W
Pinhoe 42 50.44 N 3.27 W
Pinhuã ≃ 248 6.21 S 65.00 W
Pini, Pulau I 110 0.08 N 98.40 E
Pinillos 246 8.55 N 74.28 W
Piniós ≃ 38 39.54 N 22.45 E
Pinitos, Sierra de ⩘ 200 31.08 N 110.50 W
Pinjar, Lake ⊜ 168a 31.38 S 115.49 E
Pinjarra 168a 32.37 S 115.53 E
Pinjor Garden ♦ 123 30.47 N 76.47 E
Pinka ≃ 61 47.00 N 16.35 E
Pinkafeld 61 47.22 N 16.07 E
Pinkiang → Harbin 89 45.45 N 126.41 E
Pinlaung 110 20.08 N 96.47 E
Pinlebu 110 24.05 N 95.21 E
Pinn ≃ 260 51.31 N 0.29 W
Pinnacle ∧, N.Z. 172 41.49 S 173.17 E
Pinnacle ∧, N.Y., U.S. 188 43.13 N 74.23 W
Pinnacle ∧, Va., U.S. 188 39.08 N 78.26 W
Pinnacle Buttes ∧ 202 43.44 N 109.57 W
Pinnacle Island I 180 60.12 N 172.46 W
Pinnacle Peak ∧ 224 46.45 N 121.43 W
Pinnacles National Monument ♦ 226 36.28 N 121.19 W
Pinnaroo 166 35.16 S 140.55 E
Pinneberg 52 53.40 N 9.47 E
Pinner ◆[8] 260 51.36 N 0.23 W
Pino, Sierra del ⩘ 196 28.15 N 103.03 W
Pin Oak Creek ≃ 222 31.57 N 96.28 W
Pinocchio 66 43.35 N 13.30 E
Pinochle Peak ∧ 224 45.43 N 123.36 W
Pinole 226 38.00 N 122.17 W
Pinole Creek ≃ 282 38.01 N 122.18 W
Pinole Point ≻ 282 38.01 N 122.22 W
Pinole Ridge ∧ 282 37.59 N 122.15 W
Pinos 234 22.18 N 101.34 W
Pinos, Mount ∧ 228 34.50 N 119.09 W
Pinos, Point ≻ 226 36.38 N 121.56 W
Pinos-Puente 34 37.15 N 3.45 W
Pinotepa de Don Luis 234 16.25 N 97.55 W
Pinotepa Nacional 234 16.19 N 98.01 W
Pinrang 112 3.48 S 119.38 E
Pins, Île de → Juventud, Isla de la I 240p 21.40 N 82.50 W
Pins, Île des I 175f 22.37 S 167.30 E
Pins, Pointe aux ≻ 214 42.15 N 81.51 W
Pins, Rivière des ≃ 206 46.01 N 72.03 W
Pinsk 78 52.07 N 26.04 E
Pinson 194 33.41 N 86.41 W
Pinsot 62 45.21 N 6.06 E
Pinta, Isla I 246a 0.35 N 90.44 W
Pintada Arroyo V 196 34.53 N 104.39 W
Pintado 258 33.50 S 56.18 W
Pintado ≃ 255 13.33 S 50.16 W
Pintado, Arroyo de ≃ 258 34.08 S 56.14 W
Pintado, Cuchilla del ⩘[2] 258 34.12 S 56.25 W
Pintados 248 20.37 S 69.38 W
Pintados, Salar de ≚ 248 20.30 S 69.42 W
Pintasan 112 5.26 N 117.43 E
Pinteus 266c 38.52 N 9.09 W
Pintlala Creek ≃ 194 32.21 N 86.30 W
Pinto 252 29.09 S 62.39 W
Pinto Butte ∧ 184 49.22 N 107.25 W
Pinto Creek ≃, Ab., Can. 182 53.51 N 117.35 W
Pinto Creek ≃, Sk., Can. 184 49.40 N 106.42 W
Pintos, Arroyo de ≃ 258 33.55 S 56.51 W
Pintos Negreiros 256 22.18 S 45.13 W
Pintoyacu ≃ 246 3.35 S 73.55 W
Pinturas ≃ 254 46.35 S 70.18 W
Pintuyan 116 9.57 N 125.15 E
Pin'ug 24 60.15 N 47.48 E
Pinukpuk 116 17.35 N 121.22 E
Pinwherry 44 55.09 N 4.50 W
Pinxton 42 53.06 N 1.19 W
Pinzano al Tagliamento 64 46.11 N 12.57 E
Pinzgau V 64 47.15 N 12.40 E
Pinzón, Isla I 246a 0.36 S 90.40 W
Piobbico 66 43.35 N 12.31 E
Pioche 204 37.55 N 114.27 W
Pio IX 250 6.50 S 40.37 W
Piolenc 62 44.11 N 4.46 E
Piombino 66 42.55 N 10.32 E
Piombino, Canale di ʊ 66 42.53 N 10.30 E
Pioneer, Austl. 162 31.48 S 121.43 E
Pioneer, Ca., U.S. 226 38.25 N 120.33 W
Pioneer, Oh., U.S. 216 41.40 N 84.33 W
Pioneer Mine 182 50.46 N 122.46 W
Pioneer Mountains ⩘ 202 45.40 N 113.00 W
Pioneer Park ♦ 273d 26.14 S 28.04 E
Pioner, ostrov I 74 79.50 N 92.30 E
Pionerskij 76 54.57 N 20.20 E
Pionierbivak 164 2.16 S 138.02 E
Pionki 30 51.30 N 21.27 E
Pio Pico State Historical Monument ♦ 280 33.59 N 118.04 W
Piopio 172 38.28 S 175.01 E
Pioppo 70 38.03 N 13.14 E
Piora, Mount ∧ 164 6.45 S 146.00 E
Pioraco 66 43.11 N 12.59 E
Piorini ≃ 246 3.23 S 63.30 W
Piorini, Lago ⊜ 246 3.34 S 63.15 W
Piotrków Trybunalski 30 51.25 N 19.42 E
Piotrków Trybunalski □[4] 30 51.30 N 19.45 E
Piotta 58 46.31 N 8.40 E
Pio V. Corpus (Limbujan) 116 11.53 N 124.03 E
Piove di Sacco 64 45.18 N 12.02 E
Piovene-Rocchette 64 45.45 N 11.25 E
Pio XII 250 3.53 S 45.17 W
Pipa 107 29.07 N 105.05 E
Pipalkoti 124 30.26 N 79.27 E
Pipanaco, Salar de ≚ 252 28.07 S 66.25 W
Pīpār 120 26.23 N 73.32 E
Piparia 124 22.45 N 78.21 E
Pīpar Road 120 26.27 N 73.27 E
Pipas 152 14.56 S 12.12 E
Pipe Creek ≃, In., U.S. 194 40.08 N 85.52 W
Pipe Creek ≃, In., U.S. 216 40.45 N 86.13 W
Pipe Creek ≃, In., U.S. 218 39.26 N 85.06 W
Piper City 216 40.45 N 88.11 W
Pipe Spring National Monument ♦ 200 36.43 N 112.33 W
Pipestem Creek ≃ 198 46.54 N 98.43 W
Pipestem State Park ♦ 192 37.32 N 81.00 W
Pipestone 198 44.00 N 96.19 W
Pipestone ≃ 176 52.53 N 89.23 W
Pipestone Creek ≃, Can. 184 49.42 N 100.45 W
Pipestone Creek ≃, Mi., U.S. 216 42.04 N 86.24 W
Pipestone National Monument ♦ 198 44.00 N 96.18 W
Pipi ≃ 146 7.27 N 22.48 E
Pipinas 258 35.32 S 57.20 W
Piping Brook ≃ 276 41.08 N 73.37 W
Pipiriki 172 39.29 S 175.03 E
Piplān 123 32.17 N 71.21 E
Piplūn 126 23.21 N 88.07 E
Pipmuacan, Réservoir ⊜[1] 186 49.35 N 70.30 W
Pipri 124 23.58 N 82.40 E
Pipriac 28 47.49 N 1.57 W
Piqiang 85 40.20 N 77.38 E
Piqiao 106 31.34 N 119.27 E
Piqua 218 40.08 N 84.14 W
Piquet Carneiro 250 5.48 S 39.25 W
Piquete 256 22.36 S 45.11 W
Piquete, Ribeirão ≃ 256 22.36 S 45.01 W
Piquiri ≃ 252 24.03 S 54.14 W
Pira 150 8.30 N 1.44 E
Piracaia 256 23.03 S 46.21 W
Piracanjuba 255 17.18 S 49.01 W
Piracanjuba ≃, Bra. 255 18.14 S 48.48 W
Piracanjuba ≃, Bra. 255 17.18 S 48.13 W
Piracão ≃ 287a 23.02 S 43.36 W
Piracicaba 255 22.43 S 47.38 W
Piracicaba ≃ 255 22.36 S 48.19 W
Piracuruca 250 3.56 S 41.42 W
Pirae 174s 17.32 S 149.33 W
Piraeus → Piraiévs 38 37.57 N 23.38 E
Pirahmet 130 38.11 N 39.51 E
Piraí 256 22.38 S 43.54 W
Piraí ≃ 256 22.28 S 43.50 W
Piraí do Sul 252 24.31 S 49.56 W
Piraiévs (Piraeus) 38 37.57 N 23.38 E
Piraino 70 38.10 N 14.52 E
Piraju 255 23.12 S 49.23 W
Pirajuba 255 19.54 S 48.42 W
Pirajucara, Ribeirão ≃ 287b 23.34 S 46.43 W
Pirajuí 255 21.59 S 49.29 W
Pirakata 126 22.34 N 87.11 E
Piramida, gora ∧ 88 54.15 N 95.45 E
Piramidal'nyj, pik ∧ 85 39.34 N 69.57 E
Pirámide de Cuicuilco ⊥ 286a 19.18 N 99.11 W
Pirámide de Santa Cecilia ⊥ 286a 19.35 N 99.11 W
Pirámide de Tenayuca ⊥ 286a 19.32 N 99.11 W
Pirámide Xochicalco ⊥ 234 18.48 N 99.19 W
Piram Island I 120 21.36 N 72.41 E
Piran 36 45.32 N 13.34 E
Piraña, Arroyo ≃ 288 34.24 S 58.30 W
Pirané 252 25.43 S 59.06 W
Piranga 255 20.41 S 43.18 W
Pirangaí 256 22.34 S 44.37 W
Piranguinho 256 22.24 S 45.32 W
Piranha ≃ 250 5.56 S 48.15 W
Piranhas, Bra. 250 9.27 S 37.46 W
Piranhas, Bra. 255 16.31 S 51.51 W
Piranhas ≃, Bra. 250 5.15 S 36.45 W
Piranhas ≃, Bra. 250 8.40 S 49.28 W
Piranji ≃ 250 4.23 S 37.48 W
Pīrān Shahr 128 36.41 N 45.08 E
Pirapemas 250 3.43 S 44.14 W
Pirapetinga 256 21.54 S 43.40 W
Pirapetinga ≃ 256 21.37 S 42.32 W
Pirapetinga, Ribeirão ≃ 256 21.49 S 43.36 W
Pirapó ≃ 255 22.30 S 52.01 W
Pirapora 255 17.21 S 44.56 W
Pirapora do Bom Jesus 256 23.24 S 47.00 W
Pirapora do Bom Jesus □[7] 287b 23.24 S 46.56 W
Piraputanga 255 20.26 S 55.32 W
Piraquara 252 25.26 S 49.04 W
Piraquê ≃ 287a 23.01 S 43.37 W
Pirarajá 252 33.44 S 54.45 W
Piraras, Cachoeira de ㄴ 255 14.02 S 53.25 W
Pirassununga 255 21.59 S 47.25 W
Pirata, Monte ∧[2] 240m 18.06 N 65.33 W
Pirate Creek ≃ 282 37.33 N 121.52 W
Pir'atin 78 50.15 N 32.30 E
Piratinga ≃ 255 15.41 S 46.07 W
Piratini 252 31.27 S 53.06 W
Piratini ≃ 252 28.06 S 55.27 W
Piratininga 287a 22.57 S 43.04 W
Piratininga, Lagoa de ⊂ 256 22.57 S 43.05 W
Piratuba 252 27.27 S 51.48 W
Piratuba, Lago ⊂ 250 1.37 N 50.10 W
Piratucu ≃ 250 1.59 S 56.58 W
Piraúba 256 21.17 S 43.02 W
Piraube, Lac ⊜ 186 50.33 N 71.42 W
Piray ≃ 248 16.32 S 63.45 W
Piraziz 130 40.58 N 38.08 E
Pirbright 260 51.18 N 0.39 W
Pirdop 38 42.42 N 24.11 E
Pirenópolis 255 15.51 S 48.57 W
Pires, Ribeirão ≃ 287b 23.43 S 46.25 W
Pires do Rio 255 17.18 S 48.17 W
Pírgos 38 37.41 N 21.28 E
Piriá 250 1.40 S 50.02 W
Piriápolis 252 34.54 S 55.17 W
Piribebuy 252 25.29 S 57.03 W
Pirin ⩘ 38 41.40 N 23.30 E
Pirinççi ◆[8] 267b 41.10 N 28.50 E
Pirineos → Pyrenees ⩘ 34 42.40 N 1.00 E
Piripiri 250 4.16 S 41.47 W
Piritiba 250 11.44 S 40.34 W
Píritu, Ven. 246 11.22 N 69.08 W
Píritu, Ven. 246 9.23 N 69.12 W
Pirituba ◆[8] 287b 23.29 S 46.43 W
Pirk 54 50.25 N 12.04 E
Pīr Mahal 123 30.46 N 72.26 E
Pirmasens 56 49.12 N 7.36 E
Pirna 54 50.58 N 13.56 E
Piroči 82 55.04 N 38.57 E
Pirogovka 78 51.54 N 33.18 E
Pirogovskij 265b 55.59 N 37.44 E
Pirogovskoje vodochranilišče ⊜[1] 82 55.58 N 37.40 E
Pirojpur 126 22.34 N 89.59 E
Pirón ≃ 34 41.23 N 4.31 W
Pirongia 172 38.00 S 175.12 E
Pirot 38 43.09 N 22.35 E
Pirovano 252 36.30 S 61.34 W
Pirovskoje 86 57.37 N 92.16 E
Pīr Panjāl Range ⩘ 123 33.37 N 74.32 E
Pirpirituba 250 6.46 S 35.30 W
Pirreşit Tepe ∧ 84 38.56 N 43.55 E
Pirrís ≃ 236 9.29 N 84.19 W
Pirsagat 84 39.54 N 49.24 E
Pirsagat ≃ 84 39.53 N 49.19 E
Pirtleville 200 31.22 N 109.34 W
Piru, Indon. 164 3.04 S 128.12 E
Piru, Ca., U.S. 228 34.25 N 118.48 W
Piru, Lake ⊜[1] 228 34.30 N 118.45 W
Piru, Teluk ⊂ 164 3.10 S 128.08 E
Piru Creek ≃ 228 34.23 N 118.47 W
Pisa 66 43.43 N 10.23 E
Pisa □[4] 66 43.25 N 10.43 E
Pisa ∧[2] 26 63.13 N 28.18 E
Pisa ≃ 30 53.15 N 21.52 E
Pisa, Certosa di ᵥ[1] 66 43.45 N 10.31 E
Pisa, Mount ∧ 172 44.52 S 169.11 E
Pisac ⊥ 248 13.25 S 71.53 W
Pisagua 248 19.36 S 70.13 W
Pisam-bong ∧ 98 40.41 N 126.34 E
Pisang, Pulau I 164 1.23 S 128.55 E
Pisarevka 78 49.53 N 40.12 E
Pisarve 272c 19.06 N 73.05 E
Pisau, Tanjong ≻ 116 6.04 N 118.03 E
Piščalje 80 58.14 N 48.42 E
Piscasaw Creek ≃ 216 42.16 N 88.49 W
Piscataway 210 40.29 N 74.23 W
Piscataway Creek ≃, Md., U.S. 208 38.42 N 77.02 W
Piscataway Creek ≃, Va., U.S. 208 37.54 N 76.50 W
Pişchia 38 45.55 N 21.20 E
Pisciotta 68 40.06 N 15.14 E
Pisco 248 13.42 S 76.13 W
Pisco ≃ 248 13.42 S 76.15 W
Pişcolt 38 47.35 N 22.18 E
Piscovo 80 57.11 N 40.32 E
Piseco Lake ⊜ 210 43.23 N 74.36 W
Písek 30 49.19 N 14.10 E
Pisgah, Md., U.S. 208 38.32 N 77.08 W
Pisgah, Oh., U.S. 218 39.19 N 84.22 W
Pisgah Forest 192 35.15 N 82.42 W
Pishan 120 37.37 N 78.18 E
Pishīn 120 30.35 N 67.00 E
Pishīn Lora (Lowrah) ≃ 120 29.09 N 64.55 E
Pisidia □[9] 130 37.30 N 31.00 E
Pisinemo 200 32.02 N 112.18 W
Pising 112 5.05 S 121.54 E
Pis'mennoje 78 48.13 N 35.48 E
Pismo Beach 226 35.08 N 120.38 W
Pišnur 80 57.47 N 47.58 E
Piso, Lake ⊜ 150 6.48 N 11.17 W
Pisogne 64 45.48 N 10.06 E
Pisqui ≃ 248 7.45 S 75.01 W
Pissila 150 13.10 N 0.49 W
Pissos 32 44.19 N 0.47 W
Pistakee Highlands 216 42.25 N 88.11 W
Pistakee Lake ⊜ 216 42.23 N 88.12 W
Pisticci 68 40.23 N 16.34 E
Pistoia 66 43.55 N 10.54 E
Pistoia □[4] 64 43.58 N 10.50 E
Pistolet Bay ⊂ 186 51.32 N 55.50 W
Pistuk Peak ∧ 180 59.43 N 159.42 W
Pisuerga ≃ 34 41.33 N 4.52 W
Pisz 30 53.38 N 21.49 E
Pit ≃ 204 40.45 N 122.22 W
Pit, North Fork ≃ 204 41.28 N 120.33 W
Pit, South Fork ≃ 204 41.28 N 120.33 W
Pita 150 11.05 N 12.24 W
Pital 246 2.16 N 75.49 W
Pitalito 246 1.51 N 76.02 W
Pitampura Kālan ◆[8] 272a 28.42 N 77.08 E
Pitanga 252 24.46 S 51.44 W
Pitangueiras 255 21.02 S 48.13 W
Pitangueiras, Ribeirão das ≃ 256 21.27 S 44.27 W
Pitangui 255 19.40 S 44.54 W
Pitcairn 279b 40.24 N 79.46 W
Pitcairn □[2], Oc. 6 25.04 S 130.05 W
Pitcairn □[2], Oc. 174e 25.04 S 130.05 W
Pitcher 210 42.35 N 75.52 W
Pitch Place 260 51.16 N 0.36 W
Piteå 26 65.20 N 21.30 E
Piteälven ≃ 24 65.14 N 21.32 E
Piteglio 66 44.01 N 10.46 E
Pitelino 80 54.34 N 41.49 E
Piterka 80 50.42 N 47.27 E
Pitești 38 44.52 N 24.52 E
Pithapuram 122 17.07 N 82.16 E
Pithara 162 30.24 S 116.40 E
Pithiviers 50 48.10 N 2.15 E
Pithorāgarh 124 29.35 N 80.13 E
Piti, Lagoa ⊜ 158 26.34 S 32.53 E
Pitigliano 66 42.38 N 11.40 E
Pitillal del Norte 234 20.40 N 105.01 W
Pitim 80 53.12 N 42.21 E
Pitiquito 232 30.42 N 112.02 W
Pitjantjatjara Lands ◆[4] 162 27.00 S 130.30 E
Pitk'aranta 24 61.34 N 31.27 E
Pitkas Point 180 62.02 N 163.17 W
Pitlochry 46 56.43 N 3.45 W
Pitman 208 39.43 N 75.07 W
Pitman Airport ⊠ 285 39.45 N 75.08 W
Pitmedden 46 57.20 N 2.11 W
Pitner Ditch ≍ 216 41.14 N 86.53 W
Pitogo 116 10.08 N 124.33 E
Pitomača 36 45.57 N 17.14 E
Pitou, Zhg. 100 25.01 N 114.35 E
Pitou, Zhg. 100 23.34 N 116.05 E
Pitou, Zhg. 100 24.26 N 114.22 E
Pitrufquén 254 38.59 S 72.39 W
Pitschen → Byczyna 30 51.07 N 18.11 E
Pitsea 260 51.34 N 0.31 E
Pitseng 158 28.58 S 28.16 E
Pitsford Reservoir ⊜[1] 42 52.20 N 0.52 W
Pitt ≃ 224 49.12 N 122.47 W
Pitt, Mount ∧ 174c 29.01 S 167.56 E
Pittem 50 51.00 N 3.16 E
Pitten ≃ 61 47.44 N 16.14 E
Pittenweem 46 56.12 N 2.44 W
Pitti Island I 122 10.50 N 72.38 E
Pitt Island I 182 53.35 N 129.45 W
Pitt Lake ⊜ 182 49.25 N 122.32 W
Pittsboro, In., U.S. 218 39.51 N 86.28 W
Pittsboro, Ms., U.S. 194 33.56 N 89.20 W
Pittsboro, N.C., U.S. 192 35.43 N 79.10 W
Pittsburg, Ca., U.S. 226 38.01 N 121.53 W
Pittsburg, In., U.S. 216 40.37 N 86.42 W
Pittsburg, Ks., U.S. 198 37.24 N 94.42 W
Pittsburg, N.H., U.S. 206 45.03 N 71.23 W
Pittsburg, Tx., U.S. 222 32.59 N 94.57 W
Pittsburgh, Pa., U.S. 214 40.26 N 79.59 W
Pittsburgh, Pa., U.S. 279b 40.26 N 79.59 W
Pittsburgh, University of ᵥ[2] 279b 40.27 N 79.58 W
Pittsburgh-Monroeville Airport ⊠ 279b 40.27 N 79.46 W
Pittsfield, Il., U.S. 219 39.36 N 90.48 W
Pittsfield, Me., U.S. 188 44.46 N 69.23 W
Pittsfield, Ma., U.S. 207 42.27 N 73.14 W
Pittsfield, N.H., U.S. 188 43.18 N 71.19 W
Pittsfield, Pa., U.S. 214 41.50 N 79.23 W
Pittsford, Mi., U.S. 216 41.52 N 84.28 W
Pittsford, N.Y., U.S. 210 43.05 N 77.31 W
Pitt Stadium ♦ 279b 40.27 N 79.58 W
Pittston 210 41.19 N 75.47 W
Pittsview 194 32.11 N 85.09 W
Pittsville 208 38.23 N 75.24 W
Pittsworth 166 27.43 S 151.38 E
Pitt Water ⊂ 170 33.37 S 151.18 E
Pituil 252 28.34 S 67.27 W
Pitumarca 248 13.59 S 71.25 W
Pituri Creek ≃ 166 22.58 S 138.50 E
Pitzbach ≃ 64 47.13 N 10.46 E
Pitztal V 58 47.07 N 10.47 E
Pium 250 10.27 S 49.11 W
Pium ≃ 250 10.12 S 49.57 W
Piura 248 5.12 S 80.38 W
Piura □[5] 248 5.10 S 80.00 W
Piura ≃ 248 5.32 S 80.53 W
Piute Peak ∧ 204 35.27 N 118.24 W
Piute Reservoir ⊜[1] 200 38.17 N 112.12 W
Piva ≃ 38 43.21 N 18.51 E
Pivan' 89 50.29 N 137.06 E
Piverone 62 45.27 N 8.00 E
Pivijay 246 10.28 N 74.37 W
Piwniczna 30 49.27 N 20.42 E
Pixian 102 30.49 N 103.49 E
Pixley 226 35.58 N 119.17 W
Pižanka 80 57.28 N 48.33 E
Pižma 80 57.52 N 47.06 E
Pižma ≃ 80 57.37 N 48.58 E
Pizzighettone 62 45.11 N 9.47 E
Pizzillo, Monte ∧ 70 37.48 N 15.01 E
Pizzo 68 38.44 N 16.10 E
Pizzoferrato 66 41.55 N 14.14 E
Pizzoli 66 42.26 N 13.18 E
Pizzone 66 41.40 N 14.02 E
Pjalka 24 66.43 N 40.59 E
Pjana ≃ 80 55.40 N 45.57 E
Pjöngjang → P'yŏngyang 98 39.01 N 125.45 E
P. K. le Rouxdam ⊜[1] 158 30.12 S 24.54 E
Placanica 68 38.25 N 16.27 E
Place Bonaventure ◆[9] 275a 45.30 N 73.34 W
Placentia, Nf., Can. 186 47.14 N 53.58 W
Placentia, Ca., U.S. 228 33.52 N 117.52 W
Placentia Bay ⊂ 186 47.15 N 54.30 W
Placer, Pil. 116 9.39 N 125.36 E
Placer, Pil. 116 11.52 N 123.55 E
Placer □[6] 226 38.54 N 121.04 W
Placeres de Picacho 234 23.11 N 105.42 W
Placerville 226 38.43 N 120.47 W
Placetas 240p 22.19 N 79.40 W
Place Versailles ◆[9] 275a 45.35 N 73.32 W
Plachino 76 54.28 N 39.20 E
Plachtejevka 78 46.07 N 29.43 E
Placid, Lake ⊜ 220 27.14 N 81.22 W
Placida 220 26.49 N 82.15 W
Plácido de Castro 248 10.20 S 67.11 W
Plácido Rosas 252 32.45 S 53.44 W
Plačkovica ⩘ 38 41.45 N 22.35 E
Plaffeien 58 46.44 N 7.17 E
Plages, Lac des ⊜ 206 45.59 N 74.54 W
Plage-Sainte-Cécile 50 50.34 N 1.35 E
Plailly 261 49.06 N 2.35 E
Plai Mat ≃ 110 15.22 N 102.45 E
Plain 224 47.46 N 120.39 W
Plain City, Oh., U.S. 214 40.06 N 83.16 W
Plain City, Ut,. U.S. 200 41.17 N 112.05 W
Plain Dealing 194 32.54 N 93.41 W

Symbols in the index entries represent the broad categories identified in the key at the right. Symbols with superior numbers (⩘[1]) identify subcategories (see complete key on page *I · 1).*

Symbole im Register stellen die rechts im Schlüssel erklärten Kategorien dar. Symbole mit hochgestellten Ziffern (⩘[1]) bezeichnen Unterabteilungen einer Kategorie (vgl. vollständiger Schlüssel auf Seite *I · 1).*

Los símbolos incluídos en el texto del índice representan las grandes categorias identificadas con la clave a la derecha. Los símbolos con numeros en su parte superior (⩘[1]) identifican las subcategorías (véase la clave completa en la página *I · 1).*

Les symboles de l'index représentent les catégories indiquées dans la légende à droite. Les symboles suivis d'un indice (⩘[1]) représentent des sous-catégories (voir légende complète à la page *I · 1).*

Os símbolos incluídos no texto do índice representam as grandes categorias identificadas com a chave à direita. Os símbolos com números em sua parte superior (⩘[1]) identificam as subcategorias (veja-se a chave completa à página *I · 1).*

English	Deutsch	Español	Français	Português
∧ Mountain	Berg	Montaña	Montagne	Montanha
⩘ Mountains	Gebirge	Montañas	Montagnes	Montanhas
)(Pass	Paß	Paso	Col	Passo
V Valley, Canyon	Tal, Cañon	Valle, Cañón	Vallée, Canyon	Vale, Canhão
≚ Plain	Ebene	Llano	Plaine	Planície
≻ Cape	Kap	Cabo	Cap	Cabo
I Island	Insel	Isla	Île	Ilha
II Islands	Inseln	Islas	Îles	Ilhas
⊥ Other Topographic Features	Andere Topographische Objekte	Otros Elementos Topográficos	Autres données topographiques	Outros acidentes topográficos

Nombre / Nom / Nome — Página/Page — Lat.°' — Long.°' W = Oeste / W = Ouest

Name	Página	Lat.°'	Long.°'
Plaines, Île aux I	275a	45.21 N	73.50 W
Plainfield, Ct., U.S.	207	41.40 N	71.54 W
Plainfield, Il., U.S.	216	41.37 N	88.12 W
Plainfield, In., U.S.	218	39.42 N	86.23 W
Plainfield, Ma., U.S.	207	42.30 N	72.55 W
Plainfield, N.J., U.S.	210	40.37 N	74.26 W
Plainfield, Oh., U.S.	214	40.13 N	81.43 W
Plainfield, Pa., U.S.	208	40.12 N	77.17 W
Plainfield, Wi., U.S.	190	44.12 N	89.29 W
Plainfield Heights	216	43.01 N	85.37 W
Plains, Ga., U.S.	192	32.02 N	84.23 W
Plains, Ks., U.S.	198	37.15 N	100.35 W
Plains, Mt., U.S.	202	47.27 N	114.52 W
Plains, Tx., U.S.	196	33.11 N	102.50 W
Plainsboro	208	40.20 N	74.36 W
Plainview, Ca., U.S.	226	36.08 N	119.08 W
Plainview, Il., U.S.	219	39.10 N	89.59 W
Plainview, Mn., U.S.	190	44.09 N	92.10 W
Plainview, Ne., U.S.	198	42.20 N	97.47 W
Plainview, N.Y., U.S.	210	40.46 N	73.28 W
Plainview, Tx., U.S.	196	34.11 N	101.42 W
Plainville, Ct., U.S.	207	41.40 N	72.51 W
Plainville, Il., U.S.	219	39.47 N	91.11 W
Plainville, In., U.S.	194	38.48 N	87.09 W
Plainville, Ks., U.S.	198	39.14 N	99.17 W
Plainville, Ma., U.S.	207	42.00 N	71.20 W
Plainville, N.Y., U.S.	210	43.10 N	76.27 W
Plainwell	216	42.26 N	85.38 W
Plaisance, Baie de c	186	47.18 N	61.53 W
Plaisir	281	48.49 N	1.57 E
Plaistow	207	42.50 N	71.05 W
Plaksino	76	56.11 N	30.42 E
Plamondon	182	54.51 N	112.19 W
Plampang	115b	8.48 S	117.48 E
Planá	60	49.52 N	12.44 E
Plana, Illa I	34	38.10 N	0.28 W
Planada	226	37.18 N	120.19 W
Planalto, Bra.	252	27.20 S	53.03 W
Planalto, Bra.	255	14.39 S	40.29 W
Planches	56	48.42 N	0.22 E
Plandome	276	40.48 N	73.42 W
Plandome Heights	276	40.48 N	73.42 W
Plandome Manor	276	40.49 N	73.42 W
Plan-d'Orgon	62	43.48 N	5.00 E
Plane ≃	54	52.23 N	12.30 E
Planegg	60	48.06 N	11.25 E
Planerskoje	78	44.57 N	35.14 E
Planeta Rica	248	8.25 N	75.36 W
Plangeross	58	46.59 N	10.52 E
Plankenfels	60	49.59 N	11.20 E
Plankinton	198	43.42 N	98.29 W
Plano, Il., U.S.	216	41.39 N	88.32 W
Plano, Tx., U.S.	222	33.01 N	96.41 W
Plano ≃	64	41.28 N	10.48 E
Planta de Evaporación v³	286a	19.35 N	99.00 W
Plantagenet	206	45.32 N	75.00 W
Plantation, Fl., U.S.	220	26.07 N	80.14 W
Plantation, Fl., U.S.	220	24.59 N	80.33 W
Plantation Key I	220	24.58 N	80.33 W
Plant City	220	28.01 N	82.06 W
Plantersville, Al., U.S.	194	32.39 N	86.55 W
Plantersville, Ms., U.S.		34.12 N	88.39 W
Plantersville, Tx., U.S.	222	30.20 N	95.52 W
Planting Fields Arboretum State Park ♦	276	40.52 N	73.33 W
Plantsite	200	33.03 N	109.19 W
Plantsville	207	41.35 N	72.53 W
Plaquemine	194	30.17 N	91.14 W
Plaridel, Pil.	116	10.12 N	124.46 E
Plaridel, Pil.	116	8.37 N	123.43 E
Plasencia	34	40.02 N	6.05 W
Plaški	36	45.05 N	15.22 E
Plassenburg ⊥	60	50.06 N	11.28 E
Plassey	126	23.47 N	88.15 E
Plaster Rock	186	46.54 N	67.24 W
Plastovo	82	54.17 N	37.03 E
Plastun	89	44.45 N	136.19 E
Plastunovskaja	78	45.18 N	39.16 E
Plasy	60	49.56 N	13.24 E
Plata, Río de la c¹	258	35.00 S	57.00 W
Plata, Río de la ≃	240m	18.29 N	66.15 W
Platani ≃	70	37.24 N	13.16 E
Platania ≃	68	39.00 N	16.19 E
Plátanos	288	34.47 S	58.11 W
Plátanos, Arroyo c	288	34.45 S	58.08 W
Plate, Île I	275a	45.22 N	73.48 W
Plateau ᵤ³	150	8.45 N	10.59 E
Plateau Creek ≃	200	39.11 N	108.18 W
Plateaux ᵤ⁵	152	2.15 S	15.30 E
Plathe → Płoty	30	53.49 N	15.16 E
Plati	68	38.13 N	16.03 E
Platinum	180	59.01 N	161.49 W
Platnirovskaja	78	45.23 N	39.23 E
Plato	246	9.47 N	74.47 W
Platono-Petrovka	83	46.59 N	39.28 E
Platonovka	80	52.43 N	41.57 E
Platón Sánchez	236	21.17 N	98.22 W
Platovo	83	48.05 N	39.53 E
Platt	158	27.08 S	29.29 E
Platta ≃	260	51.17 N	0.20 E
Platte	58	46.40 N	8.51 E
Platte ≃	198	43.23 N	98.50 W
Platte, Il., U.S.	194	39.16 N	94.50 W
Platte, Mn., U.S.	190	45.47 N	94.17 W
Platte ≃, Ne., U.S.	198	41.04 N	95.53 W
Platte ≃, Wi., U.S.	190	42.40 N	90.40 W
Platte Center	198	41.32 N	97.29 W
Platte City	194	39.22 N	94.46 W
Platte Creek ≃	198	43.19 N	99.00 W
Platte Island I	138	5.52 S	55.23 E
Plattekill	210	41.37 N	74.05 W
Platteville, Co., U.S.	200	40.12 N	104.49 W
Platteville, Wi., U.S.	190	42.44 N	90.28 W
Platt Hall ∴	262	53.27 N	2.13 W
Plattling	60	48.47 N	12.53 E
Plattsburg	194	39.33 N	94.26 W
Plattsburgh	188	44.41 N	73.27 W
Plattsburgh Air Force Base ■	188	44.40 N	73.28 W
Plattsmouth	198	41.00 N	95.52 W
Plattsville	212	43.18 N	80.37 W
Platveld	156	19.58 S	17.07 E
Plau	54	53.27 N	12.16 E
Plaue, D.D.R.	54	50.47 N	12.25 E
Plaue, D.D.R.	54	50.47 N	10.54 E
Plauen	54	50.30 N	12.08 E
Plauer See ∅	54	53.30 N	12.20 E
Plav	38	42.36 N	19.56 E
Plave	64	46.02 N	13.36 E
Plavinas	76	56.37 N	25.43 E
Plavsk	76	53.43 N	37.18 E
Plaxtol	260	51.15 N	0.18 E
Playa Azul	234	17.59 N	102.24 W
Playa Baracoa	286b	23.03 N	82.34 W
Playa Bonita	236	9.39 N	84.27 W
Playa de Fajardo	240m	18.20 N	65.38 W
Playa de Guayanés	240m	18.01 N	65.46 W
Playa de Guayanilla	240m	18.01 N	66.46 W
Playa del Carmen	238	20.36 N	87.06 W
Playa del Rey ⊶	228	33.58 N	118.26 W
Playa de Naguabo	240m	18.12 N	65.43 W
Playa de Ponce	240m	18.00 N	66.37 W
Playa Noriega, Laguna ∅	232	29.10 N	111.50 W
Playas Lake ∅	200	31.50 N	108.34 W
Playa Vicente	234	17.50 N	95.49 W
Playa Vicente ≃	234	18.00 N	95.42 W
Play Cu	110	13.59 N	108.00 E
Playford	162	19.03 S	135.35 E
Playgreen Lake ∅	184	54.00 N	98.10 W
Playland ⛱	276	40.58 N	73.41 W
Playon Grande	246	9.21 N	78.20 W

Nom	Page	Lat.°'	Long.°'
Plaza	198	48.01 N	101.57 W
Plaza at Mid Island ♦⁹	276	40.46 N	73.32 W
Plaza Caisan	236	8.42 N	82.45 W
Plaza de Mayo ♦	288	34.36 S	58.23 W
Plaza de Toros ⊡	266a	40.26 N	3.39 W
Plaza de Toros Monumental ♦	266d	41.23 N	2.09 W
Plaza de Toros Las Arenas ♦	266d	41.24 N	2.11 E
Plaza Huincul	252	38.55 S	69.09 W
Plaza Park	285	40.04 N	74.53 W
Plazas de Soberanía en el Norte de Africa ◻²	34	35.53 N	5.19 W
Pleasant	275b	43.41 N	79.49 W
Pleasant, Lake ∅¹	200	33.53 N	112.16 W
Pleasant, Mount ∧¹	192	37.44 N	79.10 W
Pleasant, Mount ∧²	186	45.26 N	66.49 W
Pleasant Bay	186	46.49 N	60.48 W
Pleasantdale, Sk., Can.	184	52.35 N	104.30 W
Pleasantdale, N.Y., U.S.	210	42.47 N	73.40 W
Pleasant Gap	208	40.52 N	77.44 W
Pleasant Garden	192	35.57 N	79.45 W
Pleasant Grove, Ca., U.S.	226	38.49 N	121.29 W
Pleasant Grove, Ut., U.S.	200	40.21 N	111.44 W
Pleasant Grove Creek ≃	226	38.48 N	121.32 W
Pleasant Hill, Ca., U.S.	226	37.56 N	122.03 W
Pleasant Hill, Il., U.S.	219	39.26 N	90.52 W
Pleasant Hill, La., U.S.	194	31.49 N	93.31 W
Pleasant Hill, Mo., U.S.	194	38.47 N	94.16 W
Pleasant Hill, N.C., U.S.	208	36.32 N	77.32 W
Pleasant Hill, Oh., U.S.	218	40.03 N	84.20 W
Pleasant Hill Lake ∅¹	214	40.38 N	82.21 W
Pleasant Hills	214	40.20 N	79.57 W
Pleasant Lake, In., U.S.	216	41.34 N	85.00 W
Pleasant Lake, Mi., U.S.	216	42.23 N	84.22 W
Pleasant Lake ∅	216	42.13 N	83.56 W
Pleasant Mills	216	40.47 N	84.51 W
Pleasant Mount	218	41.44 N	75.26 W
Pleasanton, Ca., U.S.	226	37.39 N	121.52 W
Pleasanton, Ks., U.S.	198	38.10 N	94.42 W
Pleasanton, Tx., U.S.	196	28.58 N	98.28 W
Pleasanton Ridge ∧	282	37.40 N	121.55 W
Pleasant Plains, Il., U.S.	219	39.52 N	89.55 W
Pleasant Plains, N.J., U.S.	208	40.00 N	74.13 W
Pleasant Point	172	44.16 S	171.08 E
Pleasant Prairie	216	42.33 N	87.57 W
Pleasant Ridge	281	42.31 N	83.10 W
Pleasant Unity	214	40.15 N	79.28 W
Pleasant Valley, N.Y., U.S.	210	41.44 N	73.49 W
Pleasant Valley, Oh., U.S.	218	39.22 N	83.03 W
Pleasant Valley, Pa., U.S.	279b	40.31 N	75.18 W
Pleasantville, Ia., U.S.	190	41.23 N	93.16 W
Pleasantville, Md., U.S.	284b	39.11 N	76.38 W
Pleasantville, N.J., U.S.	208	39.23 N	74.31 W
Pleasantville, N.Y., U.S.	210	41.07 N	73.47 W
Pleasantville, Pa., U.S.	214	41.35 N	79.34 W
Pleasington	262	53.44 N	2.34 W
Pleasure Beach	207	41.18 N	72.08 W
Pleasure Ridge Park	218	38.09 N	85.51 W
Pleasureville	218	38.33 N	85.04 W
Plechanovo	32	45.08 N	2.14 E
Plechanovo	82	54.14 N	37.33 E
Plechovo	76	52.39 N	39.50 E
Plechovo	78	51.07 N	35.18 E
Plechý (Plöckenstein) ∧	60	48.46 N	13.51 E
Pledger	222	29.11 N	95.55 W
Pleebo	150	4.35 N	7.40 W
Pleinfeld	56	49.06 N	10.59 E
Peissa	54	50.50 N	12.46 E
Peisse ≃	54	51.20 N	12.22 E
Pléneuf	56	48.36 N	2.33 W
Plenty	188	51.47 N	108.36 W
Plenty ≃, Austl.	162	23.25 S	136.31 E
Plenty ≃, Austl.	162	37.45 S	145.07 E
Plenty, Bay of c	172	37.40 S	177.00 E
Plentywood	198	48.46 N	104.33 W
Plered	115a	6.38 S	107.23 E
Pleščejevo, ozero ∅	76	56.46 N	38.47 E
Pleščenicy	76	54.25 N	27.50 E
Pleseck	74	62.43 N	40.20 E
Pleška	82	54.23 N	37.09 E
Plesna ≃	54	50.07 N	12.28 E
Pless, B.R.D.	58	48.05 N	10.08 E
Pless → Pszczyna, Pol.	30	49.59 N	18.57 E
Plessa	54	51.28 N	13.37 E
Plessisville	206	46.14 N	71.47 W
Pleszew	30	51.54 N	17.48 E
Pletenevka	82	54.31 N	36.06 E
Pleternica	36	45.17 N	17.48 E
Plétipi, Lac ∅	178	51.44 N	70.08 W
Plet'onyj Tašlyk ≃	78	48.12 N	31.40 E
Plettenberg	56	51.13 N	7.52 E
Plettenbergbaai	158	34.04 S	23.22 E
Pleurs	50	48.41 N	3.52 E
Pleven	38	43.25 N	24.37 E
Plevna, Mo., U.S.	219	39.58 N	92.05 W
Plevna, Mt., U.S.	198	46.25 N	104.31 W
Pleyben	32	48.14 N	3.58 W
Pleystein	60	49.39 N	12.25 E
Pliening	60	48.12 N	11.48 E
Pliezhausen	56	48.33 N	9.12 E
Plimmerton	172	41.05 S	174.52 E
Plimoth Plantation ∴	207	41.57 N	70.38 W
Plintovka	265a	60.01 N	30.46 E
Pliski	78	51.07 N	32.24 E
Plisskov	78	49.23 N	29.18 E
Pliszka ≃	54	52.14 N	14.42 E
Plitvička Jezera Nacionalni Park ♦	36	44.53 N	15.38 E
Plješevica ∧	36	44.45 N	15.45 E
Ploaghe	71	40.40 N	8.45 E
Pločê	36	43.03 N	17.26 E
Plochingen	56	48.42 N	9.25 E
Plock	30	52.33 N	19.42 E
Plöckenpass ⛰	64	46.36 N	12.58 E
Plöckenstein (Plechý) ∧	60	48.46 N	13.51 E
Pločno ∧	36	43.23 N	17.57 E
Ploegsteert	50	50.43 N	2.53 E
Plœrdorodnoje	78	50.43 N	35.33 E
Plœsti → Ploiești	38	44.56 N	26.02 E
Ploegsteert-Saint-Germain	28	47.59 N	4.16 W
Plomàrin	38	38.58 N	26.22 E
Plomb du Cantal ∧	32	45.03 N	2.46 E
Plombières-les-Bains	32	47.58 N	6.27 E
Plombières-lès-Dijon	32	47.20 N	4.58 E
Plomer	258	34.48 S	59.02 W

Nome	Página	Lat.°'	Long.°'
Plomer, Point ⊳	166	31.19 S	152.58 E
Plön	54	54.09 N	10.25 E
Plonge, Lac la ∅	184	55.08 N	107.25 W
Płońsk	30	52.38 N	20.23 E
Pl'os	80	57.27 N	41.31 E
Plose, Cima delle ∧	64	46.42 N	11.44 E
Ploskij	78	46.17 N	40.15 E
Ploskoje	76	52.45 N	38.21 E
Ploskoš	76	56.46 N	31.16 E
Pl'oso	76	59.47 N	35.43 E
Plotbišče	80	56.50 N	50.35 E
Plotina	83	48.33 N	40.05 E
Plotnica	78	52.03 N	26.39 E
Plottier	252	38.58 S	68.14 W
Ploty	30	53.49 N	15.16 E
Plötz	54	51.38 N	11.56 E
Plouay	32	47.55 N	3.20 W
Ploučnice ≃	54	50.47 N	14.13 E
Ploudalmézeau	32	48.32 N	4.39 W
Plouguenast	32	48.17 N	2.43 W
Plouha	32	48.41 N	2.56 W
Plovdiv	38	42.09 N	24.45 E
Plover ≃	190	44.29 N	89.15 W
Plover Islands II	180	71.15 N	155.30 W
Pluckemin	276	40.39 N	74.39 W
Plum, Pa., U.S.	214	40.31 N	79.45 W
Plum, Pa., U.S.	214	43.35 N	79.51 W
Plum, Tx., U.S.	222	29.56 N	96.58 W
Plum Hidalgo	234	15.55 N	96.25 W
Plumas	184	50.25 N	99.02 W
Plumbridge	54	54.46 N	7.15 W
Plum Brook ≃	281	42.34 N	82.58 W
Plum Creek ≃, Il., U.S.	278	41.33 N	87.29 W
Plum Creek ≃, Ne., U.S.	198	41.52 N	96.44 W
Plum Creek ≃, Oh., U.S.	279a	41.18 N	82.09 W
Plum Creek ≃, S.D., U.S.	279b	40.31 N	79.51 W
Plum Creek ≃, Tx., U.S.	198	44.13 N	100.43 W
Plum Creek, Clear Fork ≃	196	29.38 N	97.36 W
Plumerville	222	29.45 N	97.37 W
Plum Grove	278	35.09 N	92.38 W
Plum Grove Estates	278	42.04 N	88.02 W
Plum Island	283	42.04 N	70.59 W
Plum Island I, Ma., U.S.	207	42.45 N	70.48 W
Plum Island I, N.Y., U.S.	207	41.11 N	72.12 W
Plum Island Airport ⊠	283	42.48 N	70.50 W
Plum Island Sound ⨆	283	42.45 N	70.48 W
Plum Island State Park ♦	283	42.42 N	70.47 W
Plumley	262	53.17 N	2.25 W
Plummer	202	47.20 N	116.53 W
Plummers Landing	218	38.19 N	83.33 W
Plumper Sound ⨆	287	48.47 N	123.13 W
Plum Point ⊳	276	40.50 N	40.43 W
Plumpton	274a	33.45 S	150.50 E
Plumridge Lakes ∅	162	29.55 S	125.25 E
Plum Run ≃	279b	40.15 N	80.13 W
Plumsteadville	208	40.23 N	75.09 W
Plumtree	154	20.30 S	27.50 E
Plumville	214	40.48 N	79.11 W
Plumwood	218	40.01 N	83.23 W
Plungé	76	55.55 N	21.51 E
Pl'uskovo	76	52.46 N	33.49 E
Pl'ussa ≃	76	58.26 N	29.21 E
Pl'ussa ≃	76	59.19 N	28.11 E
Pluviger	32	47.46 N	3.01 E
Plym ≃	52	50.12 N	4.07 W
Plymouth, Monts.	238	16.42 N	62.13 W
Plymouth, Trin.	241f	11.13 N	60.47 W
Plymouth, Eng., U.K.	42	50.23 N	4.10 W
Plymouth, Ct., U.S.	226	38.29 N	120.51 W
Plymouth, Ct., U.S.	207	41.40 N	73.03 W
Plymouth, Il., U.S.	194	40.17 N	90.55 W
Plymouth, In., U.S.	216	41.00 N	86.18 W
Plymouth, Ma., U.S.	207	41.57 N	70.40 W
Plymouth, N.H., U.S.	188	43.45 N	71.41 W
Plymouth, N.C., U.S.	208	35.52 N	76.44 W
Plymouth, N.Y., U.S.	210	42.38 N	75.37 W
Plymouth, Oh., U.S.	214	41.00 N	82.40 W
Plymouth, Pa., U.S.	210	41.14 N	75.56 W
Plymouth, Wi., U.S.	216	43.44 N	87.58 W
Plymouth ◻⁶	238	16.42 N	62.13 W
Plymouth Airport ⊠	283	42.12 N	70.43 W
Plymouth Bay c	207	41.58 N	70.37 W
Plymouth Harbor c	283	41.58 N	70.39 W
Plymouth Meeting	285	40.06 N	75.16 W
Plymouth Meeting Mall ♦⁹	285	40.06 N	75.17 W
Plymouth Rock ∴	207	41.57 N	70.39 W
Plymouth Valley	285	40.07 N	75.23 W
Plympton, Eng., U.K.	52	50.23 N	4.03 W
Plympton, Ma., U.S.	207	41.57 N	70.48 W
Plymptonville	214	41.03 N	78.28 W
Plymstock	42	50.21 N	4.04 W
Plymwan ≃	42	52.29 N	3.47 W
Plzeň	60	49.45 N	13.23 E
Pniewy	30	52.31 N	16.15 E
Pô	150	11.10 N	1.09 W
Pô ≃, It.	30	44.57 N	12.04 E
Pô ≃, Zhg.	100	28.57 N	116.39 E
Pô, Foci del ≃¹	64	44.52 N	12.30 E
Pô, Parc National de ♦	150	11.30 N	1.15 W
Poá	256	23.32 S	46.20 W
Poana ≃	287b	32.35 S	46.45 W
Poarta Orientală, Pasul ⛰	38	45.06 N	22.18 E
Poás, Volcán ∧¹	236	10.11 N	84.13 W
Pobé, Bénin	150	6.58 N	2.41 E
Pobé, Burkina	150	11.53 N	1.45 W
Pobeda, gora ∧	74	65.12 N	146.12 E
Pobeda Ice Island I	9	64.30 S	97.00 E
Pobedino	74	49.51 N	142.49 E
Pobedy, pik ∧	94	42.02 N	80.05 E
Pobershau	54	50.38 N	13.13 E
Poběžovice	60	49.31 N	12.48 E
Poblado Cerro Gordo	240m	18.29 N	66.20 W
Poblado Jacaguas	240m	18.03 N	66.32 W
Poblado Mediania Alta	240m	18.25 N	65.50 W
Poblado Sábalos	240m	18.11 N	67.09 W
Poblado Santana	240m	18.10 N	67.10 W
Poblet	34	41.23 N	1.05 E
Pochahontas, Ar., U.S.	194	36.15 N	90.58 W
Pocahontas, Il., U.S.	219	38.49 N	89.32 W
Pocahontas, Ia., U.S.	190	42.44 N	94.40 W
Pocahontas State Park ♦	208	37.23 N	77.34 W
Pocatalico ≃	192	38.31 N	81.49 W
Pocatello	202	42.52 N	112.26 W
Počep	76	52.56 N	33.31 E
Počinkovskij	82	53.17 N	34.20 E
Poçe-sur-Cisse	32	47.34 N	0.58 E
Pocé-sur-Cisse	50	47.34 N	0.58 E
Pochinok	76	54.17 N	32.27 E
Pochotitla	234	15.44 N	96.38 W
Pochvistnevo	80	53.38 N	52.08 E
Pocinhos do Rio Verde	256	21.56 S	46.25 W
Počinki	80	54.42 N	44.51 E
Počinnaja Sopka ∧¹	88	58.25 N	34.22 E
Počinok	76	54.25 N	32.27 E

Nome	Página	Lat.°'	Long.°'
Pocitos, Salar ≃	252	24.30 S	67.03 W
Pockau	54	50.43 N	13.27 E
Pocking	60	48.24 N	13.19 E
Pocklington	44	53.56 N	0.46 W
Pocoata	248	18.41 S	66.11 W
Poçoça Cruz, Açude ◎¹	250	8.30 S	37.35 W
Poço do Bispo ◻⁸	266c	38.44 N	9.06 W
Poções	255	14.31 S	40.21 W
Poço Fundo	256	21.48 S	45.58 W
Poço Fundo, Cachoeira do ⌐	256	22.10 S	44.13 W
Pocol	64	46.31 N	12.07 E
Pocola	194	35.13 N	94.28 W
Pocomoke ≃	208	37.58 N	75.39 W
Pocomoke City	208	38.04 N	75.34 W
Pocomoke Sound ⨆	208	37.52 N	75.49 W
Pocona	248	17.39 S	65.24 W
Poconé	248	16.15 S	56.37 W
Pocono International Raceway ♦	210	41.03 N	75.31 W
Pocono Lake	210	41.06 N	75.31 W
Pocono Manor	210	41.06 N	75.22 W
Pocono Mountains ∧²	210	41.10 N	75.20 W
Pocono Pines	210	41.05 N	75.29 W
Pocono Summit	210	41.07 N	75.25 W
Pocopson	285	39.54 N	75.37 W
Pocopson Creek ≃	285	39.54 N	75.37 W
Poço Redondo	250	9.49 S	37.41 W
Poços de Caldas	256	21.48 S	46.34 W
Poço Verde	250	10.42 S	38.11 W
Pocrane	255	19.37 S	41.37 W
Pocrí	236	8.16 N	80.33 W
Podbel'skaja	88	53.37 N	51.50 E
Podberezje, S.S.S.R.	76	56.31 N	30.38 E
Podberezje, S.S.S.R.	82	56.46 N	37.10 E
Podbořany	54	50.11 N	13.25 E
Podborovje	82	54.11 N	35.56 E
Podbuž	78	49.22 N	23.15 E
Podbužje	82	53.30 N	34.56 E
Podčaše	82	63.57 N	37.34 E
Podčečje	82	54.19 N	38.34 E
Podčinnyj	80	50.52 N	45.13 E
Poddebice	30	51.53 N	18.58 E
Poddemjur	82	64.05 N	53.26 E
Poddolgoje	76	53.12 N	38.04 E
Poddorje	76	57.28 N	31.07 E
Poddubrady	60	50.08 N	15.07 E
Podejuch → Podjuchy ◻⁸	54	53.20 N	14.36 E
Po delle Donzella ≃	64	44.48 N	12.25 E
Po delle Tolle ≃	64	44.50 N	12.28 E
Podensac	32	44.39 N	0.22 W
Podenzano	64	44.55 N	9.41 E
Podersdorf am See	61	47.51 N	16.50 E
Podgajcy	78	49.19 N	25.08 E
Podgorenskij	80	50.24 N	39.39 E
Podgorica → Titograd	38	42.26 N	19.14 E
Podgornaja	80	50.28 N	41.10 E
Podgornoje, S.S.S.R.	78	51.43 N	39.07 E
Podgornoje, S.S.S.R.	80	50.27 N	39.37 E
Podgornoje, S.S.S.R.	88	56.33 N	43.07 E
Podgornoje, S.S.S.R.	92	42.55 N	72.25 E
Podgornoje, S.S.S.R.	88	57.47 N	82.36 E
Podgorodnaja	78	48.07 N	30.15 E
Podgorodnoje	78	48.38 N	35.08 E
Podhůři	60	48.28 N	13.40 E
Podi	112	1.08 S	121.16 E
Po di Goro ≃	64	44.48 N	12.27 E
Po di Volano ≃	64	44.49 N	12.15 E
Podjom-Michajlovka	80	52.49 N	50.32 E
Podjuchy ◻⁸	54	53.20 N	14.36 E
Podkamen'	82	51.41 N	35.29 E
Podkamennaja Tunguska ≃	74	61.36 N	90.09 E
Podkamennaja Tunguska ≃	74	61.36 N	90.18 E
Podkumok ≃	84	44.14 N	43.36 E
Podlasie ⁺¹	30	52.30 N	23.00 E
Podlesnoje	80	51.50 N	47.03 E
Podlopatki	88	50.55 N	107.05 E
Podmoklovo	82	56.23 N	37.24 E
Podolsk	76	55.26 N	37.33 E
Podol'skaja vozvyšennost' ∧¹	78	49.00 N	27.00 E
Podor, Maur.	150	16.40 N	15.00 W
Podor, Sén.	150	16.40 N	14.57 W
Podora	24	62.22 N	54.19 E
Podosinovec	24	60.17 N	47.04 E
Podozorskij	74	60.12 N	42.20 E
Poporožje	24	60.53 N	34.03 E
Podravina ⁺¹	38	45.40 N	17.40 E
Podravska Slatina	36	45.42 N	17.42 E
Podrečča	24	59.22 N	51.28 E
Podstepnyj	80	51.05 N	51.28 E
Podsvilje	76	55.09 N	27.58 E
Podt'osovo	88	58.36 N	92.06 E
Pod'uga	24	61.06 N	40.53 E
Podujevo	38	42.55 N	21.11 E
Poduškino	265b	55.43 N	37.17 E
Podu Turcului	38	46.11 N	27.26 E
Podvoločisk	78	49.33 N	26.09 E
Podymachino	88	57.04 N	106.11 E
Podvotje	76	52.03 N	34.08 E
Poe	216	40.56 N	85.05 W
Poel I	54	54.00 N	11.26 E
Poeldijk	52	52.00 N	4.17 E
Poeleela, Lagoa ⨆	156	24.38 S	35.00 E
Poekapelle	50	50.55 N	2.57 E
Poestenkill	210	42.41 N	73.34 W
Poestenkill ≃	210	42.43 N	73.42 W
Poetto	71	39.12 N	9.10 E
Pofadder	158	46.57 N	81.50 W...
Pogamasing Lake ∅	190	46.57 N	81.50 W
Pogan, Zhg.	100	28.18 N	116.46 E
Pogan, Zhg.	100	27.40 N	116.46 E
Pogānis ≃	38	45.41 N	21.22 E
Pogar	76	52.33 N	33.16 E
Poge, Cape ⊳	207	41.25 N	70.27 W
Poggendorf	54	54.06 N	13.07 E
Poggibonsi	66	43.28 N	11.09 E
Poggio	64	44.28 N	11.00 E
Poggio Bustone	66	42.33 N	12.54 E
Poggio Imperiale	66	41.49 N	15.22 E
Poggiomarino	68	40.48 N	14.33 E
Poggio Mirteto	66	42.16 N	12.41 E
Poggio Moiano	66	42.15 N	12.54 E
Poggioreale	70	37.47 N	13.01 E
Poggio Renatico	64	44.46 N	11.29 E
Poggio Rusco	64	44.58 N	11.07 E
Poggio Sannita	66	41.49 N	14.24 E
Pogoanele	38	44.55 N	27.00 E
Pogorelje	82	56.24 N	34.56 E
Pogoreloje Gorodišče	152	6.46 S	17.12 E
Pogost, S.S.S.R.	76	52.51 N	39.11 E
Pogost, S.S.S.R.	82	52.51 N	37.16 E
Po Grande ≃	64	44.57 N	12.04 E
Pogradec	38	40.54 N	20.39 E
Pogranicnyj, S.S.S.R.	84	50.22 N	48.57 E
Pogranicnyj, S.S.S.R.	89	44.24 N	131.24 E
Pogrebišče	78	49.29 N	29.16 E

Nome	Página	Lat.°'	Long.°'
Pogromni Volcano ∧¹	180	54.33 N	164.45 W
Pogromnoje	80	52.35 N	52.32 E
Pogruznaja	80	54.14 N	50.29 E
Poh	112	0.46 S	122.49 E
P'ohang	98	36.03 N	129.20 E
Pohatcong Creek ≃	210	40.37 N	75.11 W
Pohénégamook	186	47.31 N	69.16 W
Pohick Creek ≃	256	38.44 N	77.14 W
Pohick Creek, Rabbit Branch ≃	284c	38.48 N	77.17 W
Pohick Creek, Sideburn Branch ≃	284c	38.48 N	77.17 W
Pohjanmaa ⁺¹	26	64.00 N	25.00 E
Pohjois-Karjalan lääni ◻⁴	24	63.00 N	30.00 E
Pöhl, Talsperre ◎⁶	54	50.33 N	12.12 E
Pöhla	54	50.31 N	12.49 E
Pöhlde	52	51.37 N	10.18 E
Pohl-Göns	56	50.28 N	8.39 E
Pohlheim	56	50.34 N	8.45 E
Pohnpei I	174r	6.55 N	158.15 E
Pohorelice	61	48.59 N	16.32 E
Pohorje ∧	36	46.30 N	15.20 E
Pohri	124	25.32 N	77.21 E
Pohsien → Boxian	100	33.53 N	115.45 E
Pohue Bay c	229d	19.00 N	155.48 W
Poiana Mare	38	43.55 N	23.04 E
Poiana Ruscă, Munţii ∧	38	45.41 N	22.30 E
Poide	76	58.31 N	23.03 E
Poigny-la-Forêt	261	48.41 N	1.45 E
Poim	80	53.01 N	43.11 E
Poinsett, Cape ⊳	9	65.42 S	113.18 E
Poinsett, Lake ∅, Fl., S.D., U.S.	220	28.20 N	80.50 W
Poinsett, Lake ∅, S.D., U.S.	198	44.34 N	97.05 W
Point	222	32.56 N	95.52 W
Point Arena	204	38.54 N	123.41 W
Point au Fer Island I	194	29.15 N	91.15 W
Point Baker	180	56.21 N	133.37 W
Point Comfort	222	28.40 N	96.33 W
Point Cook	274b	37.56 S	144.45 E
Point Cook Royal Australian Air Force Station ■	169	37.56 S	144.45 E
Point-du-Chêne	186	46.15 N	64.30 W
Pointe-aux-Peaux Farms	216	41.57 N	83.16 W
Pointe-aux-Trembles	275a	45.39 N	73.30 W
Pointe-Calumet	275a	45.30 N	73.58 W
Pointe-Claire	275a	45.26 N	73.50 W
Pointe-des-Cascades	275a	45.20 N	73.58 W
Pointe-des-Galets → Le Port	157c	20.55 S	55.18 E
Pointe-du-Moulin	275a	45.38 N	74.45 W
Pointe-Noire, Congo	152	4.48 S	11.51 E
Pointe-Noire, Guad.	241o	16.14 N	61.47 W
Point Enterprise	222	31.40 N	96.26 W
Pointers	208	39.35 N	75.26 W
Point Fortin	241f	10.11 N	61.41 W
Point Hope	180	68.21 N	166.41 W
Point Imperial ∧²	200	36.16 N	111.58 W
Point Independence	207	41.44 N	70.39 W
Point Lake ∅	176	65.15 N	113.04 W
Point Leamington	186	49.20 N	55.24 W
Point Lookout, Md., U.S.	208	38.02 N	76.19 W
Point Lookout, N.Y., U.S.	276	40.35 N	73.35 W
Point Marion	188	39.44 N	79.53 W
Point McLeay	168b	35.32 S	139.06 E
Point Nepean National Park ■	169	38.16 N	77.32 W
Point of Rocks	208	39.16 N	77.32 W
Point of Woods	276	40.45 N	73.04 W
Point Pass	168b	34.05 S	139.03 E
Point Pelee National Park ■	214	41.57 N	82.31 W
Point Peninsula ⊳¹	212	44.01 N	76.15 W
Point Pleasant, Md., U.S.			
Point Pleasant, N.J., U.S.	284b	39.11 N	76.35 W
Point Pleasant, Oh., U.S.	218	40.04 N	74.04 W
Point Pleasant, Pa., U.S.	208	40.25 N	75.04 W
Point Pleasant, W.V., U.S.	188	38.50 N	82.08 W
Point Pleasant Beach	208	40.05 N	74.02 W
Point Reyes National Seashore ■	226	38.00 N	122.58 W
Point Roberts	287	48.59 N	123.05 W
Point Samson	166	20.36 S	117.12 E
Point Sapin	186	46.58 N	64.50 W
Point View Reservoir ◎¹	276	40.57 N	74.15 W
Point Whitehead	180	65.28 N	145.57 W
Poirino	64	44.55 N	7.51 E
Poisevo	82	56.44 N	53.00 E
Poison Creek ≃	202	43.15 N	108.09 W
Poison Spider Creek ≃	200	42.46 N	106.31 W
Poisson Blanc, Réservoir du ◎¹	210	46.00 N	75.44 W
Poissonnier Point ⊳¹	162	19.57 S	119.11 E
Poissons	50	48.26 N	5.13 E
Poissy	50	48.56 N	2.03 E
Poitiers	32	46.35 N	0.20 E
Poitou ⁺⁹	32	46.20 N	0.20 E
Poix-Terron	50	49.47 N	4.39 E
Pojarkovo	89	49.38 N	128.38 E
Pojma ≃	88	56.54 N	97.48 W...
Pojo	248	17.48 S	64.49 W
Pojoaque Valley	200	35.59 N	106.00 W
Pojuca	255	12.21 S	38.20 W
Pokagon State Park ■	216	41.43 N	85.01 W
Pokaran	124	26.55 N	71.55 E
Pokataroo	166	29.35 S	148.42 E
Pokatello, S.S.S.R.	74	61.29 N	129.00 E
Pokatello, S.S.S.R.	88	56.39 N	99.35 E
Pokka	22	68.10 N	25.48 E
Poko, Süd.	154	5.38 S	31.47 E
Poko, Zaïre	154	3.09 N	26.53 E
Pokoinoje	84	44.48 N	44.16 E
Pokosnoje	88	56.27 N	100.13 E
Pokrov	80	55.55 N	39.09 E
Pokrova, S.S.S.R.	78	50.47 N	35.50 E
Pokrovka, S.S.S.R.	80	53.47 N	53.11 E
Pokrovka, S.S.S.R.	92	42.55 N	78.18 E

Nome	Página	Lat.°'	Long.°'
Pokrovskij	78	46.32 N	31.38 E
Pokrovskoje, S.S.S.R.	76	52.38 N	36.51 E
Pokrovskoje, S.S.S.R.	78	49.44 N	38.13 E
Pokrovskoje, S.S.S.R.	78	47.59 N	36.14 E
Pokrovskoje, S.S.S.R.	80	54.04 N	43.37 E
Pokrovskoje, S.S.S.R.	80	53.54 N	40.26 E
Pokrovskoje, S.S.S.R.	82	56.25 N	37.03 E
Pokrovskoje, S.S.S.R.	83	55.53 N	36.54 E
Pokrovskoje, S.S.S.R.	83	47.25 N	38.54 E
Pokrovskoje, S.S.S.R.	83	48.37 N	38.09 E
Pokrovskoje, S.S.S.R.	86	57.14 N	66.48 E
Pokrovskoje ♦⁸	265a	59.44 N	30.46 E
Pokrovsko-Strešnevo ♦⁸	265b	55.37 N	37.37 E
Pokrovsk-Ural'skij	86	60.10 N	59.49 E
Pokur	74	61.02 N	75.26 E
Pola → Pula, Jugo.	64	44.52 N	13.50 E
Pola, Pil.	116	13.09 N	121.26 E
Pola ≃, S.S.S.R.	76	57.56 N	31.50 E
Pola ≃, S.S.S.R.	76	58.04 N	31.37 E
Pola Bay c	116	13.10 N	121.28 E
Polacca	200	35.50 N	110.22 W
Polacca Wash ∨	200	35.22 N	110.50 W
Pola de Laviana	34	43.15 N	5.34 W
Pola de Lena	34	43.10 N	5.49 W
Pola de Siero	34	43.23 N	5.40 W
Polän	128	25.35 N	61.12 E
Polanco	252	33.54 S	55.09 W
Poland, Kiribati	174o	1.59 N	157.32 W
Poland, N.Y., U.S.	210	43.13 N	75.03 W
Poland, Oh., U.S.	214	41.01 N	80.37 W
Poland (Polska) ◻¹ Europe	22	52.00 N	19.00 E
Poland (Polska) ◻¹ Europe	30	52.00 N	19.00 E
Polangui	116	13.17 N	123.29 E
Polapara ≃	115b	9.43 S	119.06 E
Pol'arnik	180	67.03 N	178.53 W
Pol'arnyj, S.S.S.R.	24	69.12 N	33.22 E
Pol'arnyj, S.S.S.R.	74	69.10 N	178.48 E
Pol'arnyj Ural ∧	24	66.55 N	64.30 E
Polar Record Glacier ⧫	9	69.43 S	75.30 E
Polatli	100	39.36 N	32.09 E
Polba	272b	22.57 N	88.18 E
Polbeth	46	55.52 N	3.33 W
Polch	56	50.18 N	7.18 E
Polcirkeln	20	66.34 N	21.05 E
Polcura	252	37.17 S	71.43 W
Połczyn Zdrój	30	53.46 N	16.06 E
Polden Hills ∧²	42	51.08 N	2.50 W
Poldnevica	80	58.37 N	46.38 E
Pol'dorak	85	39.25 N	69.56 E
Poleang	112	4.45 S	121.31 E
Polebridge	182	48.45 N	114.17 W
Polecat Creek ≃	196	36.00 N	95.57 W
Polednik ∧	60	49.04 N	13.24 E
Polee, Pulau I	164	2.12 S	130.15 E
Polegate	42	50.49 N	0.15 E
Pole-e Khomrī	120	35.56 N	68.43 E
Pole Moor	262	53.39 N	1.54 W
Polen → Poland ◻¹	30	52.00 N	19.00 E
Polenebówký ♦⁸	267b	41.07 N	29.12 E
Pole-e Safid	128	36.06 N	53.01 E
Polesden Lacey ⊥	260	51.15 N	0.22 W
Polesella	64	44.58 N	11.45 E
Polesine ⁺¹	64	45.00 N	11.45 E
Polesine Parmense	64	45.01 N	10.04 E
Polesje	76	53.05 N	31.17 E
Polesje ≃	72	52.00 N	27.00 E
Polesk	76	54.52 N	21.05 E
Polessk [Labiau]	30	54.52 N	21.06 E
Polesworth	42	52.37 N	1.36 W
Polevaja	78	50.31 N	36.30 E
Polevoj'sk	86	56.26 N	60.11 E
Polewali	112	3.25 S	119.20 E
Połgár	128	34.28 N	45.52 E
Polgár	30	47.52 N	21.08 E
Polgolla	132	7.19 N	80.38 E
Poli, Cam.	148	8.29 N	13.15 E
Poli, Zhg.	98	35.57 N	119.47 E...
Poli, Zhg.	68	38.45 N	16.19 E
Poliaigos I	68	36.46 N	24.38 E
Policastro, Golfo di c	68	40.00 N	15.30 E
Policastro Bussentino	68	40.05 N	15.32 E
Police	54	53.34 N	14.33 E
Poličná	61	49.28 N	17.58 E
Policoro	68	40.13 N	16.41 E
Poligny	58	46.50 N	5.43 E
Polihale State Park ■	229b	22.05 N	159.45 W
Polikastron	38	41.01 N	22.34 E
Polikhnitos	38	39.05 N	26.11 E
Polillo	116	14.43 N	121.56 E
Polillo Island I	116	14.43 N	121.57 E
Polillo Islands II	116	14.50 N	122.05 E
Polillo Strait ⨆	116	14.44 N	121.51 E
Polinésia Francesa → French Polynesia ◻²	14	15.00 S	140.00 W
Polinyà	266d	41.33 N	2.10 E
Polinyà de Vallès	266d	41.33 N	2.10 E
Polis	130	35.02 N	32.25 E
Polist' ≃	76	58.06 N	31.31 E
Polistovo ∧¹	76	57.00 N	31.00 E
Politécnico Nacional, Ciudad ◻⁸	286a	19.30 N	99.08 W
Politotdel'skoe	84	47.33 N	39.05 E
Politz → Police	30	53.35 N	14.33 E
Polivanovo ♦⁸	265b	55.36 N	37.23 E
Poliyiros	38	40.23 N	23.27 E
Polk, Ne., U.S.	198	41.04 N	97.47 W
Polk, Pa., U.S.	214	41.22 N	79.56 W
Polk, Oh., U.S.	214	40.57 N	82.13 W
Polkan-gora ∧	88	56.58 N	92.58 E
Polk City, Fl., U.S.	220	28.11 N	81.49 W
Polk City, Ia., U.S.	190	41.46 N	93.43 W
Polk City, Ia., U.S.	220	28.01 N	81.49 W
Polkowice [Heerwegen]	54	51.30 N	16.04 E
Polla	68	40.31 N	15.29 E
Pollachi	132	10.40 N	77.01 E
Pollard	194	31.01 N	87.12 W
Pollença	34	39.53 N	3.01 E
Pollica	68	40.11 N	15.05 E
Pollino, Monte ∧	68	39.55 N	16.11 E
Pollnow → Polanów	30	54.07 N	16.39 W...
Pollock, La., U.S.	194	31.31 N	92.24 W
Pollock, S.D., U.S.	198	45.54 N	100.17 W
Pollock Pines	226	38.46 N	120.34 W

| — Glossary of map symbols — |
| ≃ River / Fluß / Río / Rivière / Rio |
| ⌐ Canal / Kanal / Canal / Canal / Canal |
| ⌐ Waterfall, Rapids / Wasserfall, Stromschnellen / Cascada, Rápidos / Chute d'eau, Rapides / Cascata, Rápidos |
| c Bay, Gulf / Bucht, Golf / Bahía, Golfo / Baie, Golfe / Baía, Golfo |
| ∅ Lake, Lakes / See, Seen / Lago, Lagos / Lac, Lacs / Lago, Lagos |
| ≃ Swamp / Sumpf / Pantano / Marais / Pântano |
| ⊡ Ice Features, Glacier / Eis- und Gletscherformen / Accidentes Glaciares / Formes glaciaires / Acidentes glaciares |
| ⊤ Other Hydrographic Features / Andere Hydrographische Objekte / Otros Elementos Hidrográficos / Autres données hydrographiques / Outros acidentes hidrográficos |
| ⊷ Submarine Features / Untermeerische Objekte / Accidentes Submarinos / Formes de relief sous-marin / Acidentes submarinos |
| ◻ Political Unit / Politische Einheit / Unidad Política / Entité politique / Unidade política |
| ∴ Historical Site / Historische Stätte / Sitio Histórico / Site historique / Sítio histórico |
| ⛱ Recreational Site / Erholungs- und Ferienort / Sitio de Recreo / Site de loisirs / Area de Lazer |
| ⊠ Airport / Flughafen / Aeropuerto / Aéroport / Aeroporto |
| ■ Military Installation / Militäranlage / Instalación Militar / Installation militaire / Instalação militar |
| ♦ Miscellaneous / Verschiedenes / Misceláneo / Divers / Diversos |

ENGLISH | DEUTSCH

Name	Page	Lat.°′	Long.°′
Pollock Run ≃	279b	40.14 N	79.47 W
Pollok	222	31.27 N	94.52 W
Pollutri	66	42.08 N	14.35 E
Pollux ∧	172	44.14 S	168.53 E
Polmak	24	70.04 N	28.00 E
Polmont	46	55.59 N	3.42 W
Polná	30	49.29 N	15.43 E
Polnaja ≃	83	48.54 N	39.50 E
Pol'noje-Jaltunovo	80	53.59 N	41.52 E
Polnovo-Seliger	76	57.32 N	32.55 E
Polo, Il., U.S.	190	41.59 N	89.34 W
Polo, Mo., U.S.	194	39.33 N	94.02 W
Polochic ≃	236	15.28 N	89.22 W
Polock, S.S.S.R.	76	55.31 N	28.46 E
Polock, S.S.S.R.	86	52.46 N	59.42 E
Pologi	78	47.29 N	36.15 E
Pologne → Poland □[1]	30	52.00 N	19.00 E
Pologoje Zajmišče	80	48.29 N	45.57 E
Pologrudovo	86	57.07 N	74.13 E
Polom, S.S.S.R.	24	59.13 N	50.50 E
Polom, S.S.S.R.	80	57.47 N	53.29 E
Polo Magnético del Sur → South Magnetic Pole ◆	9	65.18 S	139.30 E
Pölömäki ∧[2]	26	63.21 N	27.03 E
Polomet' ≃	76	57.41 N	32.12 E
Polomolo	116	6.14 N	125.03 E
Polonia → Poland □[1]	30	52.00 N	19.00 E
Polonio, Cabo ≻	252	34.24 S	53.46 W
Polonnaruwa	122	7.56 N	81.00 E
Polonnaruwa ⊥	122	7.56 N	81.00 E
Polonnoje	78	50.07 N	27.30 E
Pološkovo	82	54.08 N	35.53 E
Polo Sur → South Pole ◆	9	90.00 S	0.00
Polotn'anyj	82	54.45 N	36.00 E
Polotsk → Polock	76	55.31 N	28.46 E
Polovinkino	83	49.14 N	38.55 E
Polovinnoje, S.S.S.R.	86	54.43 N	63.50 E
Polovinnoje, S.S.S.R.	86	53.46 N	79.15 E
Polovo	76	57.03 N	32.27 E
Polperro	42	50.19 N	4.31 W
Polruan	42	50.19 N	4.36 W
Pöls	61	47.11 N	14.45 E
Pölsbach ≃	61	47.11 N	14.45 E
Polska → Poland □[1]	30	52.00 N	19.00 E
Polski Trâmbeš	38	43.22 N	25.38 E
Polson	202	47.41 N	114.09 W
Polster ∧	61	47.32 N	14.58 E
Polsum	52	51.37 N	7.03 E
Poltava	78	49.35 N	34.34 E
Poltavka	86	54.22 N	71.45 E
Poltevy Pen'ki	80	54.35 N	42.06 E
Poltimore	188	45.47 N	75.43 W
Põltsamaa	76	58.38 N	25.58 E
Põltsamaa ≃	76	58.27 N	26.09 E
Poludino	86	54.51 N	69.55 E
Poluj ≃	74	66.31 N	66.33 E
Polunočnoje	72	60.52 N	60.25 E
Polur	122	12.30 N	79.08 E
Polur'adinki	82	54.51 N	38.41 E
Poluškino	265b	55.41 N	38.05 E
Pol'ustrovo ◆[8]	265a	59.58 N	30.25 E
Põlva	76	58.03 N	27.03 E
Polvaredas	258	35.35 S	59.30 W
Polverigi	66	43.31 N	13.23 E
Polvijärvi	26	62.51 N	29.22 E
Polvoranca	266a	40.19 N	3.48 W
Polynesia II	14	4.00 S	156.00 W
Polynesian Cultural Center ʊ	229c	21.39 N	157.55 W
Polynésie française → French Polynesia □[2]	14	15.00 S	140.00 W
Polynnoje	80	46.51 N	46.56 E
Polysajevo	86	54.35 N	86.14 E
Pölzig	54	50.57 N	12.11 E
Poma, Lago ⊜[1]	70	37.55 N	13.06 E
Pomabamba	248	8.50 S	77.28 W
Pomacanchi	248	14.02 S	71.34 W
Pomahaka ≃	172	46.09 S	169.34 E
Pomarance	66	43.18 N	10.52 E
Pomarico	68	40.31 N	16.33 E
Pomarkku	26	61.42 N	22.00 E
Pomaro	234	18.20 N	103.18 W
Pomata	248	16.16 S	69.18 W
Pomáz	264c	47.39 N	19.02 E
Pomba ≃	256	21.24 S	42.32 W
Pombais, Ribeira de ≃	266c	38.48 N	9.07 W
Pombal, Bra.	250	6.46 S	37.47 W
Pombal, Port.	34	39.55 N	8.38 W
Pombas, Rio das ≃	248	6.27 S	60.18 W
Pombia	266b	45.39 N	8.38 E
Pomellen	54	53.20 N	14.23 E
Pomene	156	22.53 S	35.33 E
Pomerania □[9]	30	54.00 N	16.00 E
Pomeranian Bay ⊂	54	54.00 N	14.15 E
Pomerene	200	31.59 N	110.17 W
Pomerode	252	26.45 S	49.11 W
Pomeroon ≃	246	7.37 N	58.45 W
Pomeroy, S. Afr.	158	28.33 S	30.26 E
Pomeroy, N. Ire., U.K.	48	54.36 N	6.55 W
Pomeroy, Ia., U.S.	198	42.33 N	94.41 W
Pomeroy, Oh., U.S.	188	39.01 N	82.02 W
Pomeroy, Pa., U.S.	208	39.58 N	75.53 W
Pomeroy, Wa., U.S.	202	46.28 N	117.36 W
Pomezia	66	41.40 N	12.30 E
Pomfret, S. Afr.	156	25.50 S	23.32 E
Pomfret, Ct., U.S.	207	41.53 N	71.57 W
Pomfret, Md., U.S.	208	38.34 N	77.01 W
Pomi	38	47.42 N	23.19 E
Pomigliano	66	40.54 N	14.23 E
Pominovo	82	55.26 N	39.11 E
Pomio	164	5.30 S	151.30 E
Pommard	58	47.01 N	4.47 E
Pomme de Terre ≃, Mn., U.S.	198	45.10 N	96.05 W
Pomme de Terre ≃, Mo., U.S.	194	38.11 N	93.24 W
Pomme de Terre Lake ⊜[1]	194	37.51 N	93.19 W
Pommera	50	50.10 N	2.26 E
Pommern → Pomerania □[9]	30	54.00 N	16.00 E
Pommersche Bucht → Pomeranian Bay ⊂	54	54.00 N	14.15 E
Pommersfelden	56	49.46 N	10.49 E
Pomona, Namibia	156	27.09 S	15.18 E
Pomona, Ca., U.S.	228	34.03 N	117.45 W
Pomona, Ks., U.S.	198	38.36 N	95.27 W
Pomona, N.J., U.S.	208	39.28 N	74.34 W
Pomona, N.Y., U.S.	276	41.10 N	74.02 W
Pomona College ʊ[2]	280	34.06 N	117.44 W
Pomona Estates	273d	26.06 S	28.15 E
Pomona Lake ⊜[1]	198	38.40 N	95.35 W
Pomona Park	192	29.30 N	81.35 W
Pomongo	152	5.00 S	19.08 E
Pomor'any	78	49.38 N	24.56 E
Pomorie	38	42.33 N	27.39 E
Pomorskij proliv ⊔	24	68.30 N	50.00 E
Pomorze → Pomerania □[9]	30	54.00 N	16.00 E
Pomošnaja	78	48.14 N	31.26 E
Pomozdino	24	62.12 N	54.06 E
Pompano Beach	220	26.14 N	80.07 W
Pompano Beach Highlands	220	26.16 N	80.06 W
Pompei	68	40.45 N	14.30 E
Pompei ⊥	68	40.45 N	14.30 E
Pompéia	255	22.08 S	50.10 W
Pompejevka	89	48.23 N	130.46 E
Pompeston Creek ≃	285	40.01 N	75.01 W
Pompéu	255	19.12 S	44.59 W
Pompey, Fr.	56	48.46 N	6.07 E
Pompey, N.Y., U.S.	210	42.54 N	76.01 W
Pomponio Creek ≃	282	37.18 N	122.25 W
Pomponio State Beach ♠	282	37.17 N	122.24 W
Pomponne	261	48.53 N	2.41 E
Pompon-yama ∧	270	34.56 N	135.37 E
Pomposa	66	44.49 N	12.11 E
Pomposa, Abbazia di ʊ[1]	64	44.49 N	12.11 E
Pompton ≃	276	40.54 N	74.16 W
Pompton Lakes	210	41.00 N	74.17 W
Pompton Lakes ⊜	276	41.00 N	74.17 W
Pompton Plains	276	40.58 N	74.18 W
Pomquet	186	45.38 N	61.51 W
Pomssen	54	51.14 N	12.37 E
Ponape → Pohnpei I	174r	6.55 N	158.15 E
Ponask Lake ⊜	184	54.00 N	92.41 W
Ponass Lakes ⊜	184	52.18 N	103.58 W
Ponazyrevo	80	58.21 N	46.19 E
Ponca	198	42.33 N	96.42 W
Ponca City	196	36.42 N	97.05 W
Ponca Creek ≃	198	42.48 N	98.05 W
Ponce	240m	18.01 N	66.37 W
Ponce de Leon	194	30.43 N	85.56 W
Ponce de Leon Bay ⊂	220	25.21 N	81.07 W
Ponce de Leon Inlet ⊂	192	29.04 N	80.55 W
Poncé-sur-le-Loir	50	47.46 N	0.40 E
Poncha Pass)(	200	38.25 N	106.05 W
Ponchatoula	194	30.26 N	90.26 W
Poncin	58	46.05 N	5.24 E
Poncitlán	234	20.22 N	102.55 W
Pond ≃	194	37.32 N	87.21 W
Pond Brook ≃, N.J., U.S.	276	41.02 N	74.15 W
Pond Brook ≃, Oh., U.S.	279a	41.17 N	81.24 W
Pondcreek	196	36.40 N	97.48 W
Pond Creek ≃, U.S.	196	36.40 N	97.33 W
Pond Creek ≃, Tx., U.S.	222	31.02 N	96.46 W
Pond Eddy	210	41.27 N	74.49 W
Ponder	222	33.11 N	97.17 W
Pondera Coulee V	202	48.16 N	111.03 W
Ponders End ◆[8]	260	51.39 N	0.03 W
Pondicherry	122	11.56 N	79.53 E
Pondicherry □[8]	122	11.56 N	79.50 E
Pond Inlet	176	72.41 N	78.00 W
Pond Inlet ⊂	176	72.46 N	77.00 W
Pondok Tanjong	114	5.00 N	100.44 E
Pondoland □[9]	158	31.10 S	29.30 E
Pondosa	204	41.12 N	121.41 W
Pond Run ≃	285	40.13 N	74.44 W
Poneas Island I	116	9.55 N	125.57 E
Ponente, Capo ≻	70a	35.31 N	12.31 E
Ponente, Riviera di ⏊[2]	62	44.10 N	8.20 E
Ponérihouen	175f	21.05 S	165.24 E
Poneto	216	40.39 N	85.13 W
Ponežukaj	78	44.53 N	39.22 E
Ponferrada	34	42.33 N	6.35 W
Pong	110	19.10 N	100.17 E
Pongani	164	9.05 S	148.35 E
Pongara, Pointe ≻	152	0.21 N	9.21 E
Pongaroa	172	40.33 S	176.11 E
Pongau V	64	47.21 N	13.14 E
Pong Dam ◆[6]	123	31.59 N	75.57 E
Ponghyŏn	98	37.49 N	125.36 E
Pongo ≃	140	8.42 N	27.40 E
Pongolo ≃	158	26.57 S	32.17 E
Pon'goma	24	65.21 N	34.25 E
Pong Tamale	150	9.41 N	0.49 W
Ponhook Lake ⊜	186	44.19 N	64.53 W
Poni ≃	208	38.07 N	77.26 W
Poniatowa	30	51.11 N	22.05 E
Poniec	30	51.47 N	16.50 E
Ponil Creek ≃	196	36.29 N	104.48 W
Poninka	78	50.12 N	27.32 E
Ponino	80	58.16 N	52.49 E
Pönitz, B.R.D.	54	54.03 N	10.40 E
Ponitz, D.D.R.	54	50.51 N	12.25 E
Ponizovje	76	55.17 N	31.04 E
Ponkapog Pond ⊜	283	42.12 N	71.06 W
Pônley	110	12.26 N	104.27 E
Ponnaiyār ≃	122	11.46 N	79.47 E
Ponnāni	122	10.46 N	75.54 E
Ponnūru Nidubrolu	122	16.04 N	80.34 E
Pono	164	6.22 S	134.36 E
Ponoj	24	67.05 N	41.07 E
Ponoj ≃	24	66.59 N	41.17 E
Ponoka	182	52.42 N	113.35 W
Ponomar'ovka, S.S.S.R.	80	53.19 N	54.08 E
Ponomar'ovka, S.S.S.R.	86	56.08 N	82.23 E
Ponornica	78	51.43 N	32.49 E
Ponorogo	115a	7.52 S	111.27 E
Ponpāj	272b	22.56 N	88.15 E
Pons	32	45.35 N	0.33 W
Ponsacco	66	43.37 N	10.38 E
Ponson Island I	116	10.46 N	124.32 E
Ponsul ≃	34	39.40 N	7.31 W
Pont	62	45.34 N	7.07 E
Pont-à-Celles	50	50.30 N	4.21 E
Ponta Delgada	148a	37.44 N	25.40 W
Ponta Delgada □[5]	148a	37.40 N	25.30 W
Ponta de Pedras	250	1.23 S	48.52 W
Ponta Grossa	252	25.05 S	50.09 W
Pontal ≃	250	9.08 S	40.12 W
Pontalete	256	21.27 S	45.40 W
Pontalina	255	17.31 S	49.27 W
Pontallier-sur-Saône	58	47.18 N	5.25 E
Pont-à-Marcq	50	50.31 N	3.07 E
Pont-à-Mousson	56	48.54 N	6.04 E
Pontão	34	39.55 N	8.22 W
Ponta Porã	255	22.32 S	55.43 W
Pontardawe	42	51.44 N	3.51 W
Pontardulais	42	51.43 N	4.03 W
Pontarlier	58	46.54 N	6.22 E
Pontas de Pedra	250	7.38 S	34.48 W
Pontassieve	66	43.46 N	11.26 E
Pontaubert	50	47.29 N	3.52 E
Pont-Audemer	50	49.21 N	0.31 E
Pontault-Combault	261	48.47 N	2.36 E
Pontaumur	32	45.52 N	2.40 E
Pont-Aven	32	47.51 N	3.45 W
Pontbriand	206	46.09 N	71.15 W
Pont Canavese	62	45.25 N	7.36 E
Pontcarré	261	48.48 N	2.42 E
Pontcharra	62	45.26 N	6.01 E
Pontchartrain	261	48.48 N	1.54 E
Pontchartrain, Lake ⊜	194	30.10 N	90.10 W
Pontchâteau	32	47.26 N	2.05 W
Pont-Croix	32	48.02 N	4.29 W
Pont-d'Ain	58	46.03 N	5.20 E
Pont d'Arc ♠	62	44.23 N	4.26 E
Pont-de-Bonne	56	50.27 N	5.17 E
Pont-de-Chéruy	62	45.45 N	5.11 E
Pont-de-l'Arche	50	49.18 N	1.10 E
Pont-de-Pany	58	47.18 N	4.49 E
Pont-de-Poitte	58	46.35 N	5.41 E
Pont-de-Roide	58	47.23 N	6.46 E
Pont-de-Ruan	50	47.15 N	0.35 E
Pont-de-Salars	32	44.17 N	2.44 E
Pont-de-Vaux	58	46.26 N	4.56 E
Pont-de-Veyle	58	46.16 N	4.53 E
Ponte a Elsa	66	43.41 N	10.54 E
Ponte Alta	256	22.26 S	47.06 W
Ponte Alta do Bom Jesus	255	12.06 S	46.29 W
Ponte Alta do Norte	250	10.45 S	47.34 W
Ponte a Moriano	66	43.54 N	10.31 E
Ponteareas	34	42.11 N	8.30 W
Pontebba	64	46.30 N	13.18 E
Ponte Branca	255	16.27 S	52.40 W
Ponte Caffaro	64	45.50 N	10.32 E
Pontecagnano	68	40.39 N	14.52 E
Ponte Caldelas	34	42.23 N	8.30 W
Pontecchio Marconi	64	44.25 N	11.15 E
Pontecchio Polesine	64	45.01 N	11.49 E
Pontecorvo	66	41.27 N	13.40 E
Pontecurone	62	44.57 N	8.56 E
Ponte da Barca	34	41.48 N	8.25 W
Ponte d'Arbia	66	43.10 N	11.28 E
Ponte delle Arche	64	46.02 N	10.52 E
Ponte dell'Olio	62	44.52 N	9.39 E
Pontedera	66	43.40 N	10.38 E
Ponte de Sor	34	39.15 N	8.01 W
Pontedeume	34	43.24 N	8.10 W
Ponte di Barbarano	64	45.23 N	11.34 E
Ponte di Legno	64	46.16 N	10.31 E
Ponte di Nava	62	44.08 N	7.53 E
Ponte di Piave	64	45.43 N	12.28 E
Ponte do Lima	34	41.46 N	8.35 W
Ponte do Púngoè	156	19.30 S	34.32 E
Pontefract	44	53.42 N	1.18 W
Ponte Galeria ◆[8]	267a	41.49 N	12.21 E
Ponte Gardena (Waidbruck)	64	46.36 N	11.32 E
Ponte Ghiereto	66	43.59 N	11.15 E
Pontegrande	58	45.59 N	8.09 E
Ponte in Valtellina	64	46.12 N	9.59 E
Ponteix	184	49.45 N	107.29 W
Pontelagoscuro	64	44.53 N	11.36 E
Ponteland	44	55.03 N	1.44 W
Pontelandolfo	68	41.17 N	14.41 E
Pontelongo	64	45.15 N	12.02 E
Ponte nell'Alpi	64	46.11 N	12.16 E
Ponte Nova	255	20.24 S	42.54 W
Pont-en-Royans	62	45.04 N	5.21 E
Ponte Nuovo	66	43.01 N	12.28 E
Pontenure	62	44.59 N	9.47 E
Pontepetri	66	44.02 N	10.53 E
Pontericcioli	66	43.26 N	12.38 E
Ponte Rocchetta	64	46.14 N	11.04 E
Ponterwyd	42	52.25 N	3.50 W
Pontes	256	22.26 S	46.28 W
Ponte San Giovanni	66	43.05 N	12.26 E
Ponte San Pietro	62	45.42 N	9.35 E
Pontesbury	42	52.39 N	2.54 W
Ponte Selva	64	45.52 N	9.54 E
Ponte Serrada	252	26.52 S	51.58 W
Pontestura	62	45.08 N	8.20 E
Ponte Tresa	58	45.58 N	8.52 E
Pontevedra, Arg.	258	34.45 S	58.42 W
Pontevedra, Esp.	34	42.26 N	8.38 W
Pontevedra, Pil.	116	10.22 N	122.52 E
Pontevedra, Ría de ⊂[1]	34	42.22 N	8.45 W
Ponte Vedra Beach	192	30.14 N	81.23 W
Pont-Évêque	62	45.32 N	4.55 E
Pontevico	64	45.16 N	10.05 E
Pontfaverger-Moronvilliers	50	49.18 N	4.19 E
Pontgibaud	32	45.50 N	2.52 E
Ponthévrard	261	48.33 N	1.55 E
Ponthierry	261	48.32 N	2.33 E
Ponthierville → Ubundu	154	0.21 S	25.29 E
Pontiac, Il., U.S.	216	40.52 N	88.37 W
Pontiac, Mi., U.S.	216	42.38 N	83.17 W
Pontiac □[6]	212	46.30 N	77.00 W
Pontiac Lake	281	42.40 N	83.28 W
Pontiac Lake ⊜	281	42.40 N	83.28 W
Pontiac Lake State Recreation Area ♠	216	42.41 N	83.28 W
Pontiac Mall ◆[9]	281	42.39 N	83.20 W
Pontiac State Recreation Area ♠	281	42.41 N	83.28 W
Pontianak	112	0.02 S	109.20 E
Pontian Kechil	114	1.29 N	103.23 E
Pontida	62	45.43 N	9.30 E
Pontigny	50	47.55 N	3.43 E
Pontinha ◆[8]	266c	38.46 N	9.11 W
Pontinia	66	41.24 N	13.02 E
Pontivy	32	48.04 N	2.59 W
Pont-l'Abbé	32	47.52 N	4.13 W
Pont-lès-Moulins	58	47.19 N	6.22 E
Pont-L'Évêque	50	49.18 N	0.11 E
Pontlevoy	50	47.23 N	1.15 E
Pontoise	50	49.03 N	2.06 E
Pontoise-Cormeilles-en-Vexin, Aérodrome ⊠	261	49.06 N	2.02 E
Ponton Creek ≃	162	31.10 S	124.25 E
Pontonnyj	265a	59.47 N	30.38 E
Pontoon Beach	219	38.43 N	90.04 W
Pontorson	32	48.33 N	1.31 W
Pontotoc, Ms., U.S.	194	34.14 N	88.59 W
Pontotoc, Tx., U.S.	196	30.54 N	98.59 W
Pontremoli	62	44.22 N	9.53 E
Pont-Remy	50	50.03 N	1.55 E
Pontresina	58	46.28 N	9.53 E
Pontrhydfendigaid	42	52.17 N	3.51 W
Pont-Rouge	206	46.45 N	71.42 W
Pont-Royal	62	43.43 N	5.11 E
Ponts	34	41.55 N	1.12 E
Pont-Sainte-Marie	50	48.19 N	4.06 E
Pont-Sainte-Maxence	50	49.18 N	2.36 E
Pont-Saint-Esprit	62	44.15 N	4.39 E
Pont-Saint-Martin	62	45.36 N	7.48 E
Pont-Scorff	28	47.50 N	3.24 W
Ponts Quentin, Ruisseau des ≃	261	48.44 N	1.48 E
Pont-sur-Yonne	50	48.17 N	3.12 E
Pontuda, Ilha I	287a	23.02 S	43.18 W
Pontus □[9]	130	40.15 N	38.00 E
Pontvallain	50	47.45 N	0.12 E
Pont-Viau ◆[8]	275a	45.34 N	73.41 W
Pontyberem	42	51.17 N	4.09 W
Pontycymer	42	51.37 N	3.34 W
Pontypool	42	51.43 N	3.02 W
Pontypridd	42	51.37 N	3.22 W
Pony	202	45.39 N	111.53 W
Ponyri	76	52.19 N	36.20 E
Ponza	66	40.54 N	12.58 E
Ponza, Isola di I	66	40.55 N	12.57 E
Ponziane, Isole II	66	40.55 N	12.57 E
Ponzone	62	44.35 N	8.27 E
Poochera	162	32.43 S	134.51 E
Pool □[5]	152	3.30 S	15.00 E
Poole	42	50.43 N	1.59 W
Poole, Mount ∧	166	29.37 S	141.46 E
Poole Bay ⊂	42	50.42 N	1.52 W
Pooler	192	32.06 N	81.14 W
Poole's Cavern ⏊[5]	262	53.14 N	1.56 W
Pooles Island I	208	39.17 N	76.16 W
Poolesville	208	39.08 N	77.25 W
Poolewe	46	57.45 N	5.37 W
Pooley Island I	182	52.44 N	128.16 W
Pool's Cove	186	47.41 N	55.26 W
Poolville	222	32.58 N	97.52 W
Poona → Pune	122	18.32 N	73.52 E
Pooncarie	166	33.23 S	142.34 E
Poondinna, Mount ∧	162	27.20 S	129.59 E
Poopó	248	18.23 S	66.59 W
Poopó, Lago ⊜	248	18.45 S	67.07 W
Pooraka	168b	34.50 S	138.37 E
Poor Knights Islands II	172	35.30 S	174.45 E
Poor Man Indian Reserve ◆[4]	184	51.30 N	104.23 W
Poor Meadow Brook ≃	283	42.01 N	70.55 W
Poortjie	158	30.13 S	22.44 E
Poowong	169	38.21 S	145.46 E
Popa, Isla I	236	9.11 N	82.07 W
Popasnaja	83	48.37 N	38.20 E
Popasnoje	78	48.48 N	35.31 E
Popayán	246	2.27 N	76.36 W
Pope	194	34.12 N	89.56 W
Pope Creek ≃	226	38.37 N	122.17 W
Popel'n'a	78	49.57 N	29.27 E
Popel'nastoje	78	48.39 N	33.43 E
Poperečnoje	88	52.23 N	110.42 E
Poperinge	50	50.51 N	2.43 E
Popești	38	47.14 N	22.25 E
Popești-Leordeni	38	44.23 N	26.10 E
Pope Valley	226	38.37 N	122.26 W
Popham Bay ⊂	176	64.10 N	65.10 W
Popigaj	74	71.55 N	110.47 E
Popigaj ≃	74	72.54 N	106.36 E
Popiltah Lake ⊜	166	33.10 S	141.43 E
Popinci	38	42.25 N	24.17 E
Popki	80	50.11 N	44.30 E
Popkum	224	49.12 N	121.44 W
Poplar, Ca., U.S.	226	36.03 N	119.08 W
Poplar, Mt., U.S.	198	48.06 N	105.11 W
Poplar, Wi., U.S.	190	46.35 N	91.47 W
Poplar ◆[8]	260	51.31 N	0.01 W
Poplar ≃, Can.	184	53.00 N	97.24 W
Poplar ≃, N.A.	198	48.05 N	105.11 W
Poplar ≃, Mn., U.S.	198	47.51 N	96.04 W
Poplar, West Fork ≃	198	48.31 N	105.22 W
Poplar Bluff	194	36.45 N	90.23 W
Poplar Grove	216	42.22 N	88.49 W
Poplar Heights	284c	38.53 N	77.12 W
Poplar Hill	184	52.05 N	94.18 W
Poplar Mountain ∧	194	36.43 N	85.03 W
Poplar Point	184	50.04 N	97.57 W
Poplar Ridge	210	42.44 N	76.37 W
Poplar Springs	208	39.21 N	77.06 W
Poplarville	194	30.50 N	89.32 W
Poplevinskij	76	53.41 N	39.33 E
Popocatépetl, Volcán ∧[1]	234	19.02 N	98.38 W
Popof Island I	180	55.17 N	160.25 W
Popoh	115a	8.15 S	111.48 E
Popokabaka	152	5.42 S	16.35 E
Popoli	66	42.10 N	13.50 E
Popondetta	164	8.46 S	148.14 E
Popova	89	42.58 N	131.42 E
Popovka, S.S.S.R.	76	60.08 N	39.21 E
Popovka, S.S.S.R.	80	49.14 N	41.12 E
Popovkino	82	56.07 N	36.01 E
Popovo	38	43.21 N	26.13 E
Poppberg ∧	60	49.25 N	11.35 E
Poppel	56	51.27 N	5.02 E
Poppenbüttel ◆[8]	52	53.39 N	10.04 E
Poppenhausen	56	50.06 N	10.08 E
Poppi	66	43.43 N	11.46 E
Popple ≃	190	45.50 N	88.21 W
Poprad	30	49.03 N	20.18 E
Poprad ≃	30	49.38 N	20.42 E
Popricani	38	47.18 N	27.31 E
Pŏpsŏng	98	35.22 N	126.27 E
Pŏptong	98	38.59 N	127.05 E
Poptún	236	16.21 N	89.26 W
Populonia	66	42.59 N	10.29 E
Poputnaja	84	44.31 N	41.27 E
Poquessing Creek ≃	285	40.03 N	74.58 W
Poquetanuck	207	41.29 N	72.02 W
Poquonock	207	41.54 N	72.40 W
Poquonock Bridge	207	41.20 N	72.01 W
Poquoson	208	37.07 N	76.21 W
Poquoson ≃	208	37.10 N	76.24 W
Poquott	276	40.57 N	73.05 W
Porādaha	126	23.51 N	89.01 E
Porādiha	126	21.33 N	86.26 E
Porāli Nai ≃	120	25.58 N	66.26 E
Poranga	250	4.44 S	40.55 W
Porangahau	172	40.18 S	176.37 E
Porangatu	255	13.26 S	49.10 W
Porbandar	120	21.38 N	69.36 E
Porce ≃	246	7.28 N	74.53 W
Porchaman	128	33.08 N	63.51 E
Porcher Island I	182	53.57 N	130.30 W
Porcheville	261	48.58 N	1.47 E
Porchov	76	57.46 N	29.34 E
Porcia	64	45.57 N	12.36 E
Porciúncula	255	20.58 S	42.02 W
Porco	248	19.50 S	65.59 W
Porcos, Rio dos ≃	255	12.42 S	45.07 W
Porcuna	34	37.52 N	4.11 W
Porcupine ≃	180	66.35 N	145.15 W
Porcupine Brook ≃	283	42.46 N	71.13 W
Porcupine Creek ≃	202	48.07 N	106.20 W
Porcupine Creek, Middle Fork ≃	202	48.31 N	106.30 W
Porcupine Creek, West Fork ≃	202	48.31 N	106.30 W
Porcupine Dome ∧	180	65.31 N	145.31 W
Porcupine Hills ⋏[2]	184	52.30 N	101.45 W
Porcupine Mountains State Park ♠	190	46.47 N	89.50 W
Pordenone	64	45.57 N	12.39 E
Pordenone □[4]	64	46.00 N	12.45 E
Pordim	38	43.23 N	24.51 E
Poreč	36	45.13 N	13.37 E
Porecatu	255	22.43 S	51.24 W
Porečje, S.S.S.R.	76	55.43 N	35.33 E
Porečje, S.S.S.R.	76	56.06 N	30.29 E
Porečje, S.S.S.R.	76	53.55 N	24.07 E
Porečje-Rybnoje	80	57.06 N	39.23 E
Poreckoje	80	55.12 N	46.20 E
Porez	80	57.40 N	51.10 E
Pori	26	61.29 N	21.47 E
Poricy Brook ≃	276	40.21 N	74.05 W
Poringland	42	52.33 N	1.21 E
Porirua	172	41.08 S	174.51 E
Porjaguba	24	66.47 N	33.45 E
Porkkala	26	59.59 N	24.26 E
Porlamar	246	10.57 N	63.51 W
Porlezza	58	46.03 N	9.07 E
Porlock	42	51.14 N	3.36 W
Porma ≃	34	42.29 N	5.28 W
Pornassio	62	44.04 N	7.52 E
Pörnbach	60	48.37 N	11.28 E
Pornic	32	47.07 N	2.06 W
Poro ∧	154	1.14 N	36.37 E
Porog, S.S.S.R.	24	63.50 N	38.29 E
Porog, S.S.S.R.	76	59.16 N	33.24 E
Porogi	265a	59.46 N	30.47 E
Poro Island I	116	10.40 N	124.27 E
Porokylä	26	63.33 N	29.06 E
Poroma	248	18.29 S	65.30 W
Poronaj ≃	89	49.14 N	143.06 E
Poronajsk	89	49.14 N	143.04 E
Porong	115a	7.32 S	112.41 E
Porong ≃	115a	7.32 S	112.51 E
Poropotank ≃	208	37.27 N	76.42 W
Poroškovo	78	48.41 N	22.45 E
Porosozero	24	62.43 N	32.42 E
Poroto Mountains ⋏	154	9.00 S	33.45 E
Porozovo	76	52.56 N	24.22 E
Porožskij	88	56.04 N	101.46 E
Porpoise Bay ⊂	9	66.30 S	128.30 E
Porpoise Channel ⊔	276	40.55 N	73.09 W
Porquerolles	62	43.00 N	6.12 E
Porquerolles, Île de I	62	43.00 N	6.13 E
Porrentruy	58	47.25 N	7.05 E
Porretta Terme	64	44.09 N	10.59 E
Porsangen ⊂[2]	24	70.58 N	27.00 E
Porsangerhalvøya ≻[1]	24	70.50 N	25.00 E
Porsea	114	2.27 N	99.09 E
Porsgrunn	26	59.09 N	9.40 E
Porsuk ≃	130	39.42 N	31.59 E
Port → Le Port	157c	20.55 S	55.18 E
Portachuelo	248	17.21 S	63.24 W
Portacloy	48	54.19 N	9.48 W
Port Adelaide	168b	34.51 S	138.30 E
Portadown	48	54.26 N	6.27 W
Portaferry	48	54.23 N	5.33 W
Portage, In., U.S.	216	41.34 N	87.10 W
Portage, Mi., U.S.	216	42.12 N	85.34 W
Portage, Oh., U.S.	216	41.20 N	83.39 W
Portage, Pa., U.S.	214	40.23 N	78.40 W
Portage, Ut,. U.S.	200	41.58 N	112.14 W
Portage, Wi., U.S.	190	43.32 N	89.27 W
Portage □[6]	214	41.09 N	81.15 W
Portage ≃, Mi., U.S.	216	41.57 N	85.38 W
Portage ≃, Oh., U.S.	214	41.31 N	83.05 W
Portage, East Branch ≃	216	41.17 N	83.31 W
Portage, Middle Branch ≃	216	41.22 N	83.28 W
Portage, North Branch ≃	216	41.25 N	83.27 W
Portage, South Branch ≃	216	41.22 N	83.30 W
Portage Bay ⊂	184	51.33 N	98.50 W
Portage Des Sioux	219	38.55 N	90.20 W
Portage Lake ⊜, Mi., U.S.	190	47.04 N	88.30 W
Portage Lake ⊜, Mi., U.S.	216	42.25 N	83.54 W
Portage Lake ⊜, Mi., U.S.	216	42.03 N	85.31 W
Portage Lakes	214	40.59 N	81.32 W
Portage Lakes ⊜	214	40.59 N	81.32 W
Portage Lakes State Park ♠	214	40.57 N	81.32 W
Portage-la-Prairie	184	49.59 N	98.18 W
Portage Park ◆[8]	278	41.57 N	87.46 W
Portageville, Mo., U.S.	194	36.25 N	89.41 W
Portageville, N.Y., U.S.	210	42.34 N	78.02 W
Portal, Ga., U.S.	192	32.32 N	81.55 W
Portal, N.D., U.S.	198	48.59 N	102.32 W
Port Alberni	224	49.14 N	124.48 W
Portal del Infierno ∟	236	14.22 N	85.38 W
Portalegre, Bra.	250	6.02 S	38.00 W
Portalegre, Port.	34	39.17 N	7.26 W
Portales	196	34.11 N	103.20 W
Port Alexander	180	56.15 N	134.39 W
Port Alfred (Kowie)	158	33.36 S	26.55 E
Port Alice	182	50.23 N	127.27 W
Port Allegany	214	41.48 N	78.16 W
Port Allen	194	30.27 N	91.12 W
Port Alma, Austl.	166	23.35 S	150.51 E
Port Alma, On., Can.	214	42.11 N	82.15 W
Port Alsworth	180	60.12 N	154.20 W
Port Angeles	224	48.07 N	123.25 W
Port Angeles Harbor ⊂	224	48.07 N	123.24 W
Port Anson	186	49.32 N	55.50 W
Port Antonio	241q	18.11 N	76.28 W
Port Aransas	196	27.50 N	97.04 W
Portarlington, Austl.	169	38.07 S	144.39 E
Portarlington, Ire.	48	53.10 N	7.11 W
Port Arthur, Austl.	166	43.09 S	147.51 E
Port Arthur → Thunder Bay, On., Can.	190	48.23 N	89.15 W
Port Arthur, Tx., U.S.	194	29.53 N	93.55 W
Port Arthur → Lüshun, Zhg.	98	38.48 N	121.16 E
Port Ashton	180	60.04 N	148.01 W
Port Askaig	46	55.51 N	6.07 W
Port Augusta	166	32.30 S	137.46 E
Port au Port	186	48.33 N	58.44 W
Port au Port Bay ⊂	186	48.40 N	58.45 W
Port au Port Peninsula ≻[1]	186	48.35 N	59.00 W
Port-au-Prince	238	18.32 N	72.20 W
Port-au-Prince, Baie de ⊂	238	18.40 N	72.30 W
Port Austin	190	44.02 N	82.59 W
Port-aux-Basques → Channel-Port-aux-Basques	186	47.34 N	59.09 W
Portavogie	48	54.27 N	5.27 W
Porta Westfalica	52	52.14 N	8.55 E
Porta Westfalica ♠	52	52.14 N	8.55 E
Port Bannatyne	46	55.52 N	5.05 W
Port Barre	194	30.33 N	91.57 W
Port Bell	154	0.17 N	32.39 E
Port-Bergé	157b	15.33 S	47.40 E
Port Blair	110	11.40 N	92.45 E
Port Blakely	224	47.37 N	122.28 W
Port Blandford	186	48.21 N	54.10 W
Port Bolivar	222	29.23 N	94.46 W
Port Borden	186	46.15 N	63.42 W
Port-Bouët	150	5.15 N	3.58 W
Port Broughton	166	33.36 S	137.56 E
Port Burwell	212	42.39 N	80.49 W
Port Byron, Il., U.S.	190	41.36 N	90.20 W
Port Byron, N.Y., U.S.	210	43.02 N	76.37 W
Port Campbell	169	38.37 S	143.00 E
Port Campbell National Park ♠	169	38.38 S	142.55 E
Port Canning	126	22.18 N	88.40 E
Port Carbon	208	40.42 N	76.10 W
Port Carling	212	45.07 N	79.35 W
Port-Cartier	186	50.01 N	66.52 W
Port-Cartier Sept-Îles, Réserve ♠	186	50.35 N	67.10 W
Port Chalmers	172	45.49 S	170.37 E
Port Charlotte	220	26.58 N	82.05 W
Port Chester	210	41.00 N	73.39 W
Port Chester Harbor ⊂	276	40.59 N	73.40 W
Port Chicago	226	38.03 N	122.01 W
Port Clements	182	53.42 N	132.11 W
Port Clinton, Austl.	168b	34.14 S	138.01 E
Port Clinton, Oh., U.S.	214	41.30 N	82.56 W
Port Clinton, Pa., U.S.	208	40.35 N	76.02 W
Port Clyde	188	43.55 N	69.15 W
Port Colborne	212	42.53 N	79.14 W
Port Colden	210	40.45 N	74.57 W
Port Columbus International Airport ⊠	218	40.00 N	82.53 W
Port Coquitlam	224	49.16 N	122.46 W
Port Costa	226	38.03 N	122.11 W
Port Crane	210	42.10 N	75.50 W
Port Credit	212	43.33 N	79.35 W
Port-Cros	62	43.00 N	6.23 E
Port-Cros, Île de I	62	43.00 N	6.24 E
Port-Cros, Parc National de ♠	62	43.01 N	6.24 E
Port-Daniel, Réserve ♠	186	48.18 N	64.55 W
Port-de-Bouc	62	43.24 N	4.59 E
Port-de-Paix	238	19.57 N	72.50 W
Port Deposit	208	39.36 N	76.06 W
Port Dickinson	210	42.08 N	75.53 W
Port Dickson	114	2.31 N	101.48 E
Porte Crayon, Mount ∧	188	38.56 N	79.27 W
Port Edward, B.C., Can.	182	54.14 N	130.18 W
Port Edward, S. Afr.	158	31.02 S	30.13 E
Port Edward → Weihai, Zhg.	98	37.28 N	122.07 E
Port Edwards	190	44.21 N	89.51 W
Portegolpe	236	10.20 N	85.46 W
Porteiras	250	7.31 S	39.07 W
Porteirinha	255	15.44 S	43.02 W
Portel, Bra.	250	1.57 S	50.49 W
Portel, Port.	34	38.18 N	7.42 W
Portela ≃	287a	23.00 S	43.27 W
Portela, Aeroporto da ⊠	266c	38.46 N	9.08 W
Port Elgin, N.B., Can.	186	46.03 N	64.05 W
Port Elgin, On., Can.	190	44.26 N	81.24 W
Port Elizabeth, St. Vin.	241h	13.03 N	61.13 W
Port Elizabeth, S. Afr.	158	33.58 S	25.40 E
Port Elizabeth, N.J., U.S.	208	39.18 N	74.58 W
Port Ellen	46	55.39 N	6.12 W
Port Elliot	168b	35.32 S	138.41 E
Porteña	252	31.01 S	62.04 W
Port-en-Bessin	32	49.21 N	0.45 W
Porter, In., U.S.	216	41.36 N	87.04 W
Porter, Ok., U.S.	196	35.52 N	95.31 W
Porter, Tx., U.S.	222	30.06 N	95.14 W
Porter, Wa., U.S.	224	46.56 N	123.18 W
Porter □[6]	216	41.28 N	87.04 W
Port'Ercole	66	42.23 N	11.12 E
Porter Corners	210	43.09 N	73.53 W
Porter Creek ≃	279a	41.41 N	81.56 W
Port Erin	44	54.06 N	4.44 W
Porter Lake ⊜	184	56.21 N	107.20 W
Porter Springs	222	31.16 N	95.36 W
Porters Retreat	170	34.00 S	149.48 E
Porters Run ≃	279b	40.27 N	79.33 W
Portersville	214	40.56 N	80.09 W
Porterville, S. Afr.	158	33.00 S	19.00 E
Porterville, Ca., U.S.	204	36.03 N	119.00 W
Porterville, Ms., U.S.	194	32.41 N	88.28 W
Portes-lés-Valence	62	44.52 N	4.53 E
Port Essington	182	54.09 N	129.57 W
Portete, Bahía de ⊂	246	12.13 N	71.55 W
Port-Étienne → Nouâdhibou	148	20.54 N	17.04 W
Port Ewen	210	41.54 N	73.58 W
Port-Eynon	42	51.33 N	4.13 W
Port-Eynon Point ≻	42	51.32 N	4.12 W
Portezuelo	234	20.25 N	102.31 W
Port Fairy	166	38.23 S	142.14 E
Port Fitzroy	172	36.10 S	175.21 E
Port Gamble	224	47.51 N	122.34 W
Port Gamble Indian Reservation ◆[4]	224	47.53 N	122.34 W
Port Gentil	152	0.43 S	8.47 E
Port Germein	166	33.01 S	138.00 E
Port Gibson, Ms., U.S.	194	31.57 N	90.59 W
Port Gibson, N.Y., U.S.	210	43.02 N	77.09 W
Port Glasgow	46	55.57 N	4.41 W
Portglenone	48	54.52 N	6.29 W
Port Graham	180	59.21 N	151.50 W
Port Greville	186	45.24 N	64.33 W
Porth	42	51.38 N	3.25 W
Port Hacking	274a	34.04 S	151.08 E
Port Hacking Point ≻	170	34.05 S	151.10 E
Port Hammond	224	49.13 N	122.39 W
Port Harcourt	150	4.43 N	7.05 E
Port Hardy	182	50.43 N	127.29 W
Port Hawkesbury	186	45.37 N	61.21 W
Porthcawl	42	51.29 N	3.43 W
Port Hedland	162	20.19 S	118.34 E
Port Heiden	180	56.55 N	158.41 W
Port Henry	188	44.02 N	73.27 W
Port Hill	186	46.35 N	63.53 W
Porthleven	42	50.05 N	5.19 W
Porthmadog	42	52.55 N	4.08 W
Porth Neigwl ⊂	42	52.48 N	4.34 W
Port Hood	186	46.01 N	61.32 W
Port Hope, On., Can.	212	43.57 N	78.18 W
Port Hope, Mi., U.S.	190	43.56 N	82.42 W
Port Hueneme	228	34.08 N	119.11 W
Port Hughes	168b	34.04 S	137.32 E
Port Huron	214	42.58 N	82.25 W
Portici	68	40.49 N	14.20 E
Portico di Romagna	66	44.01 N	11.47 E
Portigliola	68	38.14 N	16.13 E
Port-Iljič	84	38.53 N	48.48 E
Portillo	240p	19.55 N	77.11 W
Portimão	34	37.08 N	8.32 W
Portinho, Rio do ≃	287a	23.03 S	43.35 W
Port Isaac	42	50.35 N	4.49 W
Port Isabel	196	26.04 N	97.12 W
Portishead	42	51.30 N	2.46 W
Port Jefferson, N.Y., U.S.	210	40.56 N	73.03 W
Port Jefferson, Oh., U.S.	216	40.19 N	84.05 W
Port Jefferson Harbor ⊂	276	40.58 N	73.05 W
Port Jefferson Station	210	40.55 N	73.02 W
Port Jervis	210	41.22 N	74.41 W
Port Julia	168b	34.40 S	137.52 E
Port-Katon	83	46.52 N	38.46 E
Port Kembla	170	34.29 S	150.54 E
Port Kennedy	285	40.06 N	75.25 W
Port Kenny	162	33.10 S	134.42 E
Portknockie	46	57.41 N	2.51 W
Port Láirge → Waterford	48	52.15 N	7.06 W
Port Lambton	214	42.39 N	82.30 W
Portland, Austl.	166	38.21 S	141.36 E
Portland, Austl.	170	33.22 S	150.00 E
Portland, N.Z.	172	35.48 S	174.19 E
Portland, Ar., U.S.	194	33.14 N	91.30 W
Portland, Ct., U.S.	207	41.34 N	72.38 W
Portland, In., U.S.	216	40.26 N	84.58 W
Portland, Me., U.S.	188	43.39 N	70.15 W
Portland, Mi., U.S.	216	42.52 N	84.54 W
Portland, Mo., U.S.	219	38.42 N	91.43 W
Portland, N.Y., U.S.	214	42.22 N	79.28 W
Portland, N.D., U.S.	198	47.29 N	97.22 W
Portland, Or., U.S.	224	45.31 N	122.40 W
Portland, Pa., U.S.	210	40.55 N	75.06 W
Portland, Tn., U.S.	194	36.34 N	86.30 W
Portland, Tx., U.S.	196	27.52 N	97.19 W
Portland, Wi., U.S.	216	43.12 N	88.58 W
Portland, Bill of ≻	42	50.31 N	2.27 W
Portland, Cape ≻	166	40.45 S	147.57 E
Portland, Isle of I	42	50.33 N	2.27 W
Portland Bay ⊂	166	38.19 S	141.47 E
Portland Bight ⊂[3]	241q	17.53 N	77.08 W
Portland Canal ⊂	182	55.10 N	130.08 W
Portland Creek Pond ⊜	186	50.12 N	57.34 W
Portland Inlet ⊂	182	54.50 N	130.15 W
Portland International Airport ⊠	224	45.35 N	122.36 W
Portland Island I	172	39.17 S	177.52 E
Portland Mills	214	41.23 N	78.50 W
Portland Point ≻	241q	17.42 N	77.11 W
Portlandville	210	42.32 N	74.58 W
Port Laoise (Maryborough)	48	53.02 N	7.17 W
Port Lavaca	196	28.36 N	96.37 W
Portlaw	48	52.17 N	7.19 W
Port-Lesney	58	47.00 N	5.49 E
Portlethen	46	57.03 N	2.06 W
Port Leyden	212	43.35 N	75.21 W
Port Lincoln	166	34.44 S	135.52 E
Port Lions	180	57.52 N	152.53 W
Portlock Reefs ✣[2]	164	9.30 S	144.45 E
Port Logan	44	54.43 N	4.56 W
Port Loko	150	8.46 N	12.47 W
Port-Louis, Fr.	32	47.43 N	3.21 W
Port-Louis, Guad.	241o	16.25 N	61.32 W
Port Louis, Maus.	157c	20.10 S	57.30 E
Port Ludlow	224	47.55 N	122.40 W
Port-Lyautey → Kenitra	148	34.16 N	6.40 W
Port MacDonnell	166	38.03 S	140.42 E
Port Macquarie	166	31.26 S	152.55 E
Port Madison Indian Reservation ◆[4]	224	47.45 N	122.35 W
Portmahomack	46	57.49 N	3.50 W
Port Maitland, N.S., Can.	186	43.59 N	66.09 W
Port Maitland, On., Can.	214	42.52 N	79.34 W
Port Maria	241q	18.22 N	76.54 W
Portmarnock	48	53.25 N	6.08 W
Port Matilda	214	40.48 N	78.03 W
Port Mayaca	220	27.08 N	80.12 W
Port McNeill	182	50.35 N	127.06 W
Port McNicoll	212	44.45 N	79.49 W
Port Melbourne	274b	37.51 S	144.56 E
Port Mellon	182	49.32 N	123.29 W
Port-Menier	186	49.48 N	64.20 W
Port Moller	180	55.59 N	160.34 W
Port Monmouth	276	40.25 N	74.05 W
Port Moody	224	49.17 N	122.51 W
Port Morant	241q	17.54 N	76.19 W
Portmore	241q	17.58 N	76.53 W
Port Moresby	164	9.30 S	147.10 E
Port Moresby □[5]	164	9.30 S	147.10 E
Port Morien	186	46.08 N	59.52 W
Port Morris	276	40.54 N	74.41 W
Port Mouton	186	43.56 N	64.51 W
Port Murray	210	40.47 N	74.54 W
Portnaguran	46	58.17 N	6.13 W
Portnahaven	46	55.41 N	6.31 W

DEUTSCH: Name | Seite | Breite°′ | Länge°′ E = Ost

Symbols in the index entries represent the broad categories identified in the key at the right. Symbols with superior numbers (⋏[1]) identify subcategories (see complete key on page *I · 1).*

Symbole im Register stellen die rechts im Schlüssel erklärten Kategorien dar. Symbole mit hochgestellten Ziffern (⋏[1]) bezeichnen Unterabteilungen einer Kategorie (vgl. vollständiger Schlüssel auf Seite *I · 1).*

Los símbolos incluídos en el texto del índice representan las grandes categorias identificadas con la clave a la derecha. Los símbolos con numeros en su parte superior (⋏[1]) identifican las subcategorías (véase la clave completa en la página *I · 1).*

Les symboles de l'index représentent les catégories indiquées dans la légende à droite. Les symboles suivis d'un indice (⋏[1]) représentent des sous-catégories (voir légende complète à la page *I · 1).*

Os símbolos incluídos no texto do índice representam as grandes categorias identificadas com a chave à direita. Os símbolos com números em sua parte superior (⋏[1]) identificam as subcategorias (veja-se a chave completa à página *I · 1).*

English	Deutsch	Español	Français	Português
∧ Mountain	Berg	Montaña	Montagne	Montanha
⋏ Mountains	Gebirge	Montañas	Montagnes	Montanhas
)(Pass	Paß	Paso	Col	Passo
V Valley, Canyon	Tal, Cañon	Valle, Cañón	Vallée, Canyon	Vale, Canhão
⌣ Plain	Ebene	Llano	Plaine	Planície
≻ Cape	Kap	Cabo	Cap	Cabo
I Island	Insel	Isla	Île	Ilha
II Islands	Inseln	Islas	Îles	Ilhas
⏊ Other Topographic Features	Andere Topographische Objekte	Otros Elementos Topográficos	Autres données topographiques	Outros acidentes topográficos

Port-Pres *I* · *139*

ESPAÑOL

Nombre	Página	Lat.°′	Long.°′ W = Oeste
Port Neches	194	29.59 N	93.57 W
Port Neill	166	34.07 S	136.20 E
Port Nelson	184	57.03 N	92.36 W
Portneuf	206	46.42 N	71.53 W
Portneuf □[6]	206	46.45 N	72.00 W
Portneuf ≃, P.Q., Can.	186	48.38 N	69.05 W
Portneuf ≃, P.Q., Can.	206	46.42 N	71.53 W
Portneuf ≃, Id., U.S.	202	42.58 N	112.35 W
Portneuf, Lac ⊜	186	49.08 N	70.18 W
Portneuf-Station	206	46.43 N	71.54 W
Portneuf-sur-Mer	186	48.37 N	69.06 W
Port Neville	182	50.29 N	126.05 W
Port Noarlunga	168b	35.09 S	138.28 E
Port Nolloth	156	29.17 S	16.51 E
Port Norris	208	39.14 N	75.02 W
Porto, Bra.	250	3.54 S	42.42 W
Porto, Port.	34	41.11 N	8.36 W
Porto, Bonifica di ◆[1]	267a	41.48 N	12.16 E
Porto Acre	248	9.34 S	67.31 W
Porto Alegre, Bra.	252	30.04 S	51.11 W
Porto Alegre, S. Tom./P.	152	0.02 N	6.32 E
Porto Amazonas	252	25.33 S	49.53 W
Porto Amboim	152	10.44 S	13.44 E
Porto Azzurro	66	42.46 N	10.24 E
Portobello	46	55.58 N	3.07 W
Porto Belo, Bra.	252	27.10 S	48.33 W
Portobelo, Pan.	236	9.33 N	79.39 W
Porto Calvo	250	9.04 S	35.24 W
Porto Ceresio	58	45.54 N	8.55 E
Port O'Connor	196	28.27 N	96.24 W
Porto das Caixas	256	22.42 S	42.53 W
Porto d'Ascoli	66	42.55 N	13.53 E
Porto das Flôres	256	22.05 S	43.34 W
Porto das Gabarras	250	3.07 S	44.34 W
Pôrto de Mós	34	39.36 N	8.39 W
Porto de Moz	250	1.45 S	52.14 W
Porto de Pedras	250	9.10 S	35.17 W
Porto di Potenza Picena	66	43.21 N	13.42 E
Porto di Traiano, Necropoli del ⊥	267a	41.46 N	12.16 E
Porto Empedocle	70	37.17 N	13.32 E
Porto Esperança	248	19.37 S	57.27 W
Porto Esperidião	248	15.51 S	58.28 W
Porto Farina	36	37.10 N	10.12 E
Porto Feliz	255	23.13 S	47.32 W
Portoferraio	66	42.49 N	10.19 E
Porto Ferreira	255	21.51 S	47.28 W
Portofino	62	44.18 N	9.12 E
Port of Ness	46	58.29 N	6.13 W
Porto Franco	250	6.20 S	47.24 W
Port of Spain	241r	10.39 N	61.31 W
Porto Garibaldi	66	44.41 N	12.14 E
Porto Grande	250	0.42 N	51.24 W
Portogruaro	64	45.47 N	12.50 E
Porto Inglês	150a	15.08 N	23.13 W
Portola	204	39.48 N	120.28 W
Portola State Park ♦	226	37.15 N	122.13 W
Portola Valley	226	37.23 N	122.13 W
Porto Lucena	252	27.51 S	55.01 W
Pörtom (Pirttikylä)	26	62.42 N	21.37 E
Portomaggiore	64	44.42 N	11.48 E
Porto Maurizio	62	43.52 N	8.01 E
Porto Mendes	252	24.30 S	54.20 W
Porto Murtinho	248	21.42 S	57.52 W
Porto Nacional	250	10.42 S	48.25 W
Porto-Novo, Bénin	150	6.29 N	2.37 E
Porto Novo, India	122	11.29 N	79.46 E
Porto Novo Creek c	273a	6.26 N	3.20 E
Portopalo, It.	70	36.41 N	15.08 E
Porto Palo, It.	70	37.34 N	12.54 E
Port Orange	192	29.06 N	80.59 W
Port Orchard	224	47.32 N	122.38 W
Porto Real	256	22.25 S	44.20 W
Porto Real do Colégio	250	10.11 S	36.49 W
Porto Recanati	66	43.26 N	13.40 E
Port Orford	202	42.44 N	124.29 W
Porto Rico	152	6.08 S	12.30 E
Porto Rico → Puerto Rico □[2]	240m	18.15 N	66.30 W
Portorož	64	45.31 N	13.36 E
Porto Salvo	256c	38.43 N	9.18 W
Porto San Giorgio	66	43.11 N	13.48 E
Porto Santana	250	0.03 S	51.11 W
Porto Sant'Elpidio	66	43.15 N	13.45 E
Porto Santo I	148	33.04 N	16.20 W
Porto Santo Stefano	66	42.26 N	11.07 E
Porto São José	255	22.43 S	53.10 W
Portoscuso	71	39.12 N	8.23 E
Porto Seguro, Bra.	255	16.26 S	39.05 W
Porto-Séguro, Togo	150	6.12 N	1.29 E
Porto Torres	71	40.50 N	8.24 E
Porto União	252	26.15 S	51.05 W
Porto Válter	248	8.15 S	72.45 W
Porto Valtravaglia	58	45.58 N	8.41 E
Porto-Vecchio	36	41.35 N	9.16 E
Porto Velho	248	8.46 S	63.54 W
Porto Velho do Cunha	256	21.50 S	42.32 W
Portovenere	62	44.03 N	9.51 E
Portoviejo	246	1.03 S	80.27 W
Portpatrick, Scot., U.K.	44	54.51 N	5.07 W
Port Patrick, Vanuatu	175f	20.08 S	169.47 E
Port Penn	208	39.31 N	75.34 W
Port Perry	212	44.06 N	78.57 W
Port Phillip Bay c	169	38.07 S	144.48 E
Port Pirie	166	33.11 S	138.01 E
Port Providence	285	40.08 N	75.30 W
Portraine	48	53.30 N	6.07 W
Port Reading	276	40.33 N	74.15 W
Portree	46	57.24 N	6.12 W
Port Renfrew	224	48.33 N	124.25 W
Port Republic	208	39.31 N	74.29 W
Port Rexton	186	48.23 N	53.20 W
Port Richey	220	28.16 N	82.43 W
Port Richmond	208	37.33 N	76.49 W
Port Robinson	284a	43.02 N	79.13 W
Port Rowan	214	42.37 N	80.28 W
Port Royal, Jam.	241q	17.56 N	76.51 W
Port Royal, Ky., U.S.	218	38.33 N	85.04 W
Port Royal, Pa., U.S.	208	40.32 N	77.23 W
Port Royal, S.C., U.S.	192	32.22 N	80.41 W
Port Royal, Va., U.S.	208	38.10 N	77.11 W
Port-Royal-des-Champs, Abbaye de ♁[1]	261	48.45 N	2.01 E
Port Royal National Historic Park ♦	186	44.44 N	65.40 W
Portrush	48	55.12 N	6.40 W
Port Said → Būr Sa'īd	142	31.16 N	32.18 E
Port-Sainte-Marie	32	44.15 N	0.24 E
Port Saint Joe	192	29.49 N	85.18 W
Port Saint Johns	158	31.38 S	29.33 E
Port-Saint-Louis	62	43.23 N	4.48 E
Port Saint Lucie	220	27.20 N	80.20 W
Port Saint Mary	44	54.05 N	4.43 W
Port-Saint-Servan	186	51.19 N	58.02 W
Port Salerno	220	27.08 N	80.12 W
Portsalon	48	55.13 N	7.37 W
Port Sanilac	190	43.25 N	82.32 W
Port Saunders	186	50.39 N	57.18 W
Pörtschach	61	46.37 N	14.08 E
Portsea	169	38.19 S	144.43 E
Port Seton	46	55.58 N	2.57 W
Port Shepstone	158	30.46 S	30.22 E
Portslade	42	50.50 N	0.11 W
Portsmouth, Dom.	240d	15.35 N	61.28 W
Portsmouth, Eng., U.K.	42	50.48 N	1.05 W
Portsmouth, N.H., U.S.	188	43.04 N	70.45 W
Portsmouth, Oh., U.S.	218	38.43 N	82.59 W

FRANÇAIS

Nom	Page	Lat.°′	Long.°′ W = Ouest
Portsmouth, R.I., U.S.	207	41.36 N	71.15 W
Portsmouth, Va., U.S.	208	36.50 N	76.17 W
Portsmouth Naval Shipyard ■	188	43.05 N	70.45 W
Portsoy	46	57.41 N	2.41 W
Port Stanley, On., Can.	214	42.40 N	81.13 W
Port Stanley → Stanley, Falk. Is.	254	51.42 S	57.51 W
Portstewart	48	55.11 N	6.43 W
Port Sudan → Būr Sūdān	140	19.37 N	37.14 E
Port Sulphur	194	29.28 N	89.41 W
Port Sunlight	262	53.21 N	2.59 W
Port-sur-Saône	58	47.41 N	6.03 E
Port Talbot	42	51.36 N	3.47 W
Port Taufiq → Būr Tawfīq	128	29.57 N	32.34 E
Porttipahdan tekojärvi ⊜[1]	24	68.08 N	26.40 E
Port Tobacco River c	208	38.27 N	77.02 W
Port Townsend	224	48.07 N	122.45 W
Port Trevorton	208	40.42 N	76.52 W
Portugal □[1], Europe	22	39.30 N	8.00 W
Portugal □[1], Europe	34	39.30 N	8.00 W
Portugal, Cachoeira L	248	9.55 S	64.16 W
Portugal Cove South	186	46.42 N	53.15 W
Portugalete	34	43.19 N	3.01 W
Portuguesa □[3]	246	9.10 N	69.15 W
Portuguesa ≃	246	7.57 N	67.32 W
Portuguese Guinea → Guinea-Bissau □[1]	150	12.00 N	15.00 W
Portumna	48	53.06 N	8.13 W
Port Union, Nf., Can.	186	48.30 N	53.05 W
Port Union, On., Can.	275b	43.47 N	79.08 W
Port-Vendres	32	42.31 N	3.07 E
Port Victoria → Victoria	138	4.38 S	55.27 E
Port Vila	175f	17.44 S	168.19 E
Portville	210	42.02 N	78.20 W
Port Vincent	168b	34.47 S	137.51 E
Port-Vladimir	24	69.25 N	33.06 E
Port Vue	279b	40.20 N	79.52 W
Port Waikato	172	37.23 S	174.44 E
Port Wakefield, Austl.	168b	34.11 S	138.09 E
Port Wakefield, Ak., U.S.	180	58.03 N	153.03 W
Port Washington, B.C., Can.	224	48.49 N	123.19 W
Port Washington, N.Y., U.S.	210	40.49 N	73.41 W
Port Washington, Oh., U.S.	214	40.27 N	81.37 W
Port Washington, Wi., U.S.	190	43.23 N	87.52 W
Port Weld	114	4.50 N	100.38 E
Port Welshpool	169	38.42 S	146.28 E
Port Wentworth	192	32.08 N	81.09 W
Port William, Scot., U.K.	44	54.46 N	4.35 W
Port William, Oh., U.S.	218	39.33 N	83.47 W
Port Wing	190	46.46 N	91.23 W
Porum	196	35.21 N	95.15 W
Porus	241q	18.02 N	77.25 W
Porvenir	254	53.18 S	70.22 W
Porvoo (Borgå)	26	60.24 N	25.40 E
Porvoonjoki ≃	26	60.23 N	25.40 E
Porz	56	50.53 N	7.03 E
Porzdni	80	57.00 N	42.33 E
Porzuna	34	39.09 N	4.09 W
Posada	71	40.38 N	9.43 E
Posada ≃	71	40.39 N	9.45 E
Posadas, Arg.	252	27.23 S	55.53 W
Posadas, Esp.	34	37.48 N	5.06 W
Posavina V	36	45.10 N	17.20 E
Poščharv	85	38.24 N	71.10 E
Poschiavino ≃	58	46.12 N	10.10 E
Poschiavo	58	46.18 N	10.04 E
Pošechonje-Volodarsk	76	58.30 N	39.07 E
Posen → Poznań, Pol.	30	52.25 N	16.55 E
Posen, Il., U.S.	278	41.37 N	87.40 W
Posen, Mi., U.S.	190	45.15 N	83.41 W
Poseritz	54	54.18 N	13.16 E
Posesión, Bahía c	254	52.17 S	69.14 W
Posevnaja	86	54.18 N	83.20 E
Poshan → Boshan	98	36.29 N	117.50 E
Poshiwu	106	30.22 N	119.36 E
Posieux	58	46.46 N	7.06 E
Posina	64	45.47 N	11.15 E
Pösing	60	49.14 N	12.33 E
Posio	26	66.06 N	28.09 E
Positano	68	40.38 N	14.29 E
Posjet	89	42.39 N	130.50 E
Poso	112	1.23 S	120.44 E
Poso, Danau ⊜	112	1.52 S	120.35 E
Poso, Teluk c	112	1.15 S	120.55 E
Poso Creek ≃	226	35.41 N	119.22 W
Posof	130	41.31 N	42.42 E
Pos'olki	80	53.08 N	46.29 E
Pos'olok	265a	59.43 N	30.12 E
Posŏng	98	34.47 N	127.04 E
Posooy, Mount ∧	116	17.21 N	120.48 E
Pospelicha	86	51.57 N	81.46 E
Possagno	64	45.51 N	11.51 E
Posse	255	14.05 S	46.22 W
Posse dos Coutinhos	256	22.49 S	42.45 W
Possel	152	5.01 N	19.15 E
Possendorf	54	50.57 N	13.42 E
Posses	256	21.43 S	46.08 W
Possession Islands II	9	71.27 S	171.08 E
Possession Sound Ʉ	224	48.00 N	122.20 W
Possidhonia ⊥	38	37.40 N	24.00 E
Pössneck	54	50.42 N	11.37 E
Possruck (Kozjak) ⋏	61	46.37 N	15.28 E
Possum Kingdom Lake ⊜[1]	196	32.55 N	98.28 W
Post	196	33.11 N	101.22 W
Posta	66	42.31 N	13.06 E
Postal (Burgstall)	64	46.36 N	11.11 E
Postau	60	48.39 N	12.20 E
Postavy	76	55.07 N	26.50 E
Postbauer	60	49.19 N	11.21 E
Post Creek ≃	210	42.09 N	77.02 W
Poste-de-la-Baleine	176	55.17 N	77.45 W
Postelle	192	35.02 N	84.22 W
Poste Ramartina	157b	19.38 S	45.58 E
Posterholt	52	51.07 N	6.03 E
Post Falls	202	47.43 N	116.57 W
Postiglione	68	40.33 N	15.13 E
Postmasburg	158	28.18 S	23.05 E
Pôsto do Registro	256	22.23 S	42.35 W
Postojna	36	45.47 N	14.13 E
Postojnska jama ⏏[7]	36	45.47 N	14.12 E
Postoloprty	54	50.20 N	13.40 E
P'ostraja Dresva	74	61.34 N	156.41 E
Postrevalle	248	18.29 S	63.51 W
Postsee ⊜	54	54.13 N	10.13 E
Poststadion ♦	264a	52.32 N	13.21 E
Postville	190	43.05 N	91.34 W
Pota	115b	8.20 S	120.46 E
Potaizi	104	41.34 N	121.08 E
Potake Pond ⊜	276	41.08 N	74.13 W
Pótam	232	27.36 N	110.23 W
Potanino	76	60.16 N	32.47 E
Potaro ≃	246	5.22 N	58.54 W
Potaro Landing	246	5.23 N	59.08 W
Potato Creek ≃, Ga., U.S.	192	32.47 N	84.21 W
Potato Creek ≃, Pa., U.S.	214	41.53 N	78.23 W
Potawatomie Woods ♦	278	42.08 N	87.53 W

PORTUGUÊS

Nome	Página	Lat.°′	Long.°′ W = Oeste
Potchefstroom	158	26.46 S	27.01 E
Poté	255	17.49 S	41.49 W
Poteau	194	35.03 N	94.37 W
Poteau ≃	194	35.23 N	94.26 W
Poteet	196	29.02 N	98.34 W
Potengi	250	7.06 S	40.00 W
Potengi ≃	250	5.47 S	35.16 W
Pötenitz	54	53.57 N	10.58 E
Pötenitzer Wiek c	54	53.55 N	10.55 E
Potenza	68	40.38 N	15.49 E
Potenza □[4]	68	40.30 N	15.50 E
Potenza ≃	66	43.25 N	13.40 E
Potenza Picena	66	43.22 N	13.37 E
Poteriteri, Lake ⊜	172	46.06 S	167.08 E
Potes	34	43.09 N	4.37 W
Potfontein	158	30.12 S	24.08 E
Potgietersrus	156	24.15 S	28.55 E
Poth	196	29.04 N	98.05 W
Potholes Reservoir ⊜[1]	202	47.01 N	119.19 W
Poti	84	42.09 N	41.40 E
Poti ≃	250	5.02 S	42.50 W
Potic Creek ≃	210	42.16 N	73.55 W
Potijevka	78	50.37 N	28.58 E
Potiraguá	255	15.36 S	39.53 W
Potirendaba	255	21.08 S	49.08 W
Potiskum	146	11.43 N	11.05 E
Potlatch	202	46.55 N	116.53 W
Potlatch ≃	202	46.28 N	116.46 W
Po Toi Island I	271d	22.10 N	114.15 E
Po Toi Island Group II	271d	22.11 N	114.16 E
Potol Point >	116	11.56 N	121.57 E
Potomac, Il., U.S.	216	40.18 N	87.48 W
Potomac, Md., U.S.	284c	39.01 N	77.12 W
Potomac ≃	188	38.00 N	76.18 W
Potomac, South Branch ≃	188	39.31 N	78.35 W
Potomac, South Branch, North Fork ≃	188	38.59 N	79.11 W
Potomac, South Branch, South Fork ≃	188	39.04 N	78.59 W
Potomac Creek ≃	208	38.21 N	77.18 W
Potomac Creek, Long Branch ≃	208	38.23 N	77.29 W
Potomac Heights	208	38.36 N	77.08 W
Poto-Poto ◆[8]	273b	4.15 S	15.18 E
Potosí, Bol.	248	19.35 S	65.45 W
Potosi, Mo., U.S.	194	37.56 N	90.47 W
Potosí □[5]	248	20.40 S	67.00 W
Potosí, Bahía c	234	17.34 N	101.30 W
Potosí, Cerro ∧	232	24.52 N	100.13 W
Pototan	116	10.55 N	122.40 E
Potrerillos, Chile	252	26.26 S	69.29 W
Potrerillos, Hond.	236	15.11 N	87.58 W
Potrerillos Arriba	236	8.41 N	82.30 W
Potrero ◆[8]	282	37.48 N	122.24 W
Potrero de Gallegos	234	22.38 N	103.41 W
Potrero del Llano	196	29.12 N	104.28 W
Potrero Grande, C.R.	236	9.00 N	83.11 W
Potrero Grande, Méx.	232	24.59 N	106.26 W
Potsdam, D.D.R.	54	52.24 N	13.04 E
Potsdam, N.Y., U.S.	188	44.40 N	74.58 W
Potsdam, Oh., U.S.	218	39.58 N	84.25 W
Potsdam □[5]	54	52.30 N	12.45 E
Potsdam, Staatsforst ♦	264a	52.26 N	13.04 E
Potshausen	52	53.11 N	7.37 E
Pott, Île I	175f	19.35 S	163.36 E
Pottawatomie Creek ≃	198	38.29 N	94.55 W
Pottawatomi Indian Reservation ◆[4]	198	39.20 N	95.50 W
Pottendorf	61	47.55 N	16.23 E
Potten End	260	51.46 N	0.31 W
Pottenhofen	61	48.46 N	16.33 E
Pottenstein	60	49.46 N	11.25 E
Potter	198	41.13 N	103.18 W
Potter □[6]	214	41.47 N	78.01 W
Potter Hollow	210	42.25 N	74.13 W
Potter Lake	216	42.50 N	88.21 W
Potter Point >	274a	34.03 S	151.13 E
Potters Bar	42	51.42 N	0.11 W
Potters Mills	208	40.48 N	77.32 W
Potter Street	260	51.46 N	0.08 E
Pottersville	276	40.42 N	74.43 W
Potterville	216	42.38 N	84.45 W
Pöttmes	60	48.35 N	11.06 E
Potton	42	52.08 N	0.14 W
Potts Camp	194	34.38 N	89.18 W
Potts Creek ≃	192	37.45 N	80.00 W
Potts Grove	210	41.00 N	76.48 W
Potts Hill Reservoirs ⊜[1]	274a	33.54 S	151.02 E
Pott Shrigley	262	53.19 N	2.05 W
Pottstown	208	40.14 N	75.39 W
Pottstown Landing	285	40.14 N	75.40 W
Pottstown Limerick Airport ⊠	285	40.14 N	75.34 W
Pottstown Municipal Airport ⊠	285	40.16 N	75.40 W
Pottsville	208	40.41 N	76.11 W
Potwin	198	37.56 N	97.01 W
Pötzleinsdorf ◆[8]	264b	48.15 N	16.19 E
Pötzleinsdorfer Park ♦	264b	48.14 N	16.18 E
P'otzu	100	23.28 N	120.14 E
Pouancé	32	47.44 N	1.11 W
Pouce-Coupe	182	55.43 N	120.08 W
Pouce Coupé ≃	182	56.08 N	119.52 W
Pouch	54	51.37 N	12.24 E
Pouch Cove	186	47.46 N	52.46 W
Pouembout	175f	21.08 S	164.53 E
Poughkeepsie	210	41.42 N	73.55 W
Poughquag	210	41.37 N	73.41 W
Pouilly-en-Auxois	58	47.16 N	4.33 E
Pouilly-sur-Loire	50	47.17 N	2.57 E
Pouilly-sur-Meuse	56	49.32 N	5.07 E
Poulain, Étang ⊜	261	48.43 N	1.44 E
Poulan	192	31.30 N	83.47 W
Poulaphouca Reservoir ⊜[1]	48	53.08 N	6.31 W
Poulin-de-Courval, Lac ⊜	186	48.52 N	70.27 W
Poulsbo	224	47.44 N	122.38 W
Poulter, Lac ⊜	190	47.07 N	76.45 W
Poultney	188	43.31 N	73.14 W
Poulton-le-Fylde	44	53.51 N	2.59 W
Poum	175f	20.14 S	164.02 E
Poŭn	98	36.29 N	127.43 E
Pound	192	37.07 N	82.36 W
Poundmaker Indian Reserve ◆[4]	184	52.51 N	109.00 W
Poundstock	42	50.46 N	4.33 W
Pouoanuu, Mont ∧	174x	9.49 S	139.07 W
Pourri, Mont ∧	62	45.32 N	6.52 E
Pouru-Saint-Rémy	56	49.41 N	5.05 E
Pourville-sur-Mer	50	49.55 N	1.02 E
Pouso Alegre	256	22.13 S	45.56 W
Pouso Alto	256	22.11 S	44.58 W
Pouso Redondo	252	27.15 S	49.57 W
Pouso Sêco	256	22.41 S	44.10 W
Pouss	146	10.51 N	15.03 E
Poutasi	175a	14.01 S	171.41 W
Poŭthĭsăt	110	12.32 N	103.55 E
Poŭthĭsăt ≃	110	12.41 N	104.09 E
Pouxeux	58	48.06 N	6.34 E
Pouzauges	32	46.47 N	0.50 W
Považská Bystrica	30	49.08 N	18.27 E
Povenec	24	62.51 N	34.45 E
Poverello, Monte ∧	70	38.05 N	15.22 E
Poverennyj	80	46.45 N	43.12 E
Poverty Bay c	172	38.42 S	177.58 E
Povetkino	82	54.20 N	38.23 E
Poviglio	64	44.51 N	10.32 E
Povljen ⋏	38	43.55 N	19.30 E
Póvoa, Mouchão da I	266c	38.51 N	9.03 W
Povoação	148a	37.45 N	25.15 W

Póvoa de Santa Iria	266c	38.52 N	9.04 W
Póvoa de Santo Adrião	266c	38.48 N	9.10 W
Póvoa de Varzim	34	41.23 N	8.46 W
Povorino	80	51.12 N	42.14 E
Povorotnyj, mys >	89	42.42 N	133.04 E
Povorsk	78	51.16 N	25.07 E
Povrly	54	50.40 N	14.10 E
Povungnituk	176	60.02 N	77.10 W
Povungnituk, Rivière de ≃	176	60.03 N	77.15 W
Powassan	190	46.05 N	79.22 W
Poway	228	32.57 N	117.02 W
Powder ≃, U.S.	178	46.44 N	105.26 W
Powder ≃, Or., U.S.	202	44.45 N	117.03 W
Powder, Dry Fork ≃	200	43.47 N	106.15 W
Powder, Middle Fork ≃	200	43.42 N	106.33 W
Powder, North Fork ≃	202	43.42 N	106.33 W
Powder, Red Fork ≃	202	43.39 N	106.47 W
Powder, South Fork ≃	202	43.40 N	106.30 W
Powder Horn Lake ⊜	278	41.38 N	87.32 W
Powderly, Ky., U.S.	194	37.09 N	87.10 W
Powderly, Tx., U.S.	196	33.49 N	95.31 W
Powdermaker Ditch ≅	279a	41.30 N	82.02 W
Powder Mill Village	284c	39.03 N	76.57 W
Powder River Pass)(	202	44.09 N	107.04 W
Powell, Oh., U.S.	214	40.09 N	83.05 W
Powell, Pa., U.S.	210	41.42 N	76.31 W
Powell, Tx., U.S.	222	32.07 N	96.20 W
Powell, Wy., U.S.	202	44.45 N	108.45 W
Powell ≃	192	36.29 N	83.42 W
Powell, Lake ⊜[1]	200	37.25 N	110.45 W
Powell, Mount ∧	200	39.46 N	106.20 W
Powell Creek ≃, Austl.	166	25.02 S	143.40 E
Powell Creek ≃, Oh., U.S.	216	41.17 N	84.21 W
Powellhurst	224	45.30 N	122.32 W
Powell Lake ⊜	182	50.11 N	124.24 W
Powell River	182	49.52 N	124.33 W
Powells Valley	208	40.26 N	76.56 W
Powellton	188	38.05 N	81.19 W
Powellville	208	38.19 N	75.22 W
Powers, Mi., U.S.	190	45.41 N	87.31 W
Powers, Or., U.S.	202	42.53 N	124.04 W
Powers Lake, N.D., U.S.	198	48.33 N	102.38 W
Powers Lake, Wi., U.S.	216	42.33 N	88.17 W
Powers Lookout ♦	169	36.50 S	146.22 E
Powhatan, La., U.S.	194	31.52 N	93.12 W
Powhatan, Va., U.S.	192	37.32 N	77.55 W
Powhatan Mill	284b	39.20 N	76.43 W
Powhatan Point	188	39.51 N	80.48 W
Powis, Vale of V	42	52.38 N	3.08 W
Powissett Brook ≃	283	42.16 N	71.14 W
Powlett ≃	169	38.35 S	145.32 E
Pownal	210	42.45 N	73.14 W
Powys □[6]	42	52.17 N	3.20 W
Poxoréu	255	15.50 S	54.23 W
Poya	175f	21.19 S	165.07 E
Poyang Hu ⊜	100	29.00 N	116.25 E
Poyan Reservoir ⊜[1]	271c	1.23 N	103.40 E
Poyen	194	34.19 N	92.38 W
Poygan, Lake ⊜	190	44.09 N	88.50 W
Poyle	260	51.28 N	0.31 W
Poynette	190	43.23 N	89.24 W
Poynor	222	32.04 N	95.36 W
Poynton	44	53.21 N	2.07 W
Poyntz Pass	48	54.18 N	6.23 W
Poyraz ◆[8]	267b	41.12 N	29.07 E
Poyraz Burnu >	267b	41.12 N	29.08 E
Poysdorf	61	48.40 N	16.38 E
Poza Grande	232	25.50 N	112.05 W
Pozantı	130	37.25 N	34.52 E
Požarevac	38	44.37 N	21.11 E
Poza Rica de Hidalgo	234	20.33 N	97.27 W
Požarskoje	89	46.16 N	134.04 E
Pozdejevka	89	50.36 N	128.56 E
Požega	38	43.50 N	20.02 E
Poznań	30	52.25 N	16.55 E
Poznań □[4]	30	52.20 N	16.55 E
Pozo Alcón	34	37.42 N	2.56 W
Pozo Almonte	248	20.16 S	69.48 W
Pozoblanco	34	38.22 N	4.51 W
Pozo-Cañada	34	38.48 N	1.45 W
Pozo Colorado	252	23.28 S	58.51 W
Pozo del Molle	252	32.02 S	62.55 W
Pozo del Tigre	252	24.54 S	60.19 W
Pozo Hondo	252	27.10 S	64.30 W
Pozos	234	21.14 N	100.29 W
Pozos, Arroyo de los ≃	288	34.57 S	58.45 W
Pozos, Punta >	254	47.57 S	65.47 W
Pozsony → Bratislava	30	48.09 N	17.07 E
Pozuelo de Alarcón, Esp.	34	40.26 N	3.49 W
Pozuelo de Alarcón, Esp.	266a	40.26 N	3.49 W
Pozuelos	246	10.11 N	64.39 W
Pozuelos, Laguna de ⊜	252	22.22 S	66.01 W
Pozuzo	248	10.04 S	75.32 W
Pozuzo ≃	248	9.52 S	75.12 W
Požva	86	59.05 N	56.05 E
Pozzallo	70	36.43 N	14.51 E
Pozzillo, Lago di ⊜	70	37.40 N	14.35 E
Pozzolo Formigaro	62	44.48 N	8.47 E
Pozzomaggiore	71	40.24 N	8.39 E
Pozzuoli	68	40.49 N	14.07 E
Pozzuolo del Friuli	64	45.59 N	13.12 E
Pra ≃, Ghana	150	5.01 N	1.37 W
Pra ≃, S.S.S.R.	80	54.45 N	41.01 E
Prabuty	30	53.46 N	19.10 E
Pracai ≃	250	2.26 S	51.19 W
Praça Sêca ◆[8]	287a	22.54 S	43.21 W
Prachatice	30	49.01 N	14.00 E
Prachin Buri	110	14.03 N	101.22 E
Prachuap Khiri Khan	110	11.49 N	99.48 E
Prackenbach	60	49.06 N	12.50 E
Pracupi ≃	250	2.06 S	51.30 W
Pradelles	62	44.46 N	3.53 E
Pradera	246	3.25 N	76.15 W
Prades	32	42.37 N	2.26 E
Pradleves	62	44.25 N	7.17 E
Prado	255	17.21 S	39.13 W
Prado, Museo del ♁	266a	40.25 N	3.41 W
Prado Dam ◆[6]	280	33.54 N	117.39 W
Prado Flood Control Basin ⩸[1]	280	33.54 N	117.38 W
Prados	255	21.03 S	44.05 W
Pr'adovka	78	48.55 N	34.41 E
Prads	62	44.13 N	6.27 E
Præstø	41	55.07 N	12.03 E
Prag → Praha	54	50.05 N	14.26 E
Praga → Praha	54	50.05 N	14.26 E
Pragelato	62	45.01 N	6.57 E
Pragersko	61	46.23 N	15.40 E
Praglia, Monastero di ♁[1]	64	45.23 N	11.45 E
Prägraten	64	47.01 N	12.23 E
Prague → Praha, Česko.	54	50.05 N	14.26 E
Prague, Ne., U.S.	198	41.18 N	96.48 W
Prague, Ok., U.S.	196	35.29 N	96.41 W
Praha (Prague)	54	50.05 N	14.26 E
Praha ∧	60	49.40 N	13.49 E
Prahova □[6]	38	45.00 N	26.00 E
Prahova ≃	38	44.43 N	26.27 E
Prahran	274b	37.51 S	144.59 E
Praia	150a	14.55 N	23.31 W
Praia a Mare	68	39.54 N	15.47 E
Praia da Cruz Quebrada	266c	38.42 N	9.14 W
Praia das Maçãs	266c	38.50 N	9.28 W
Praia da Vitória	148a	38.44 N	27.04 W
Praia de Araçatiba	256	23.06 S	44.15 W
Praia Funda, Ponta da >	287a	23.05 S	43.33 W
Praia Grande, Bra.	252	29.12 S	49.57 W
Praia Grande, Bra.	256	24.01 S	46.25 W
Praiano	68	40.37 N	14.32 E
Praikalogu	115b	9.45 S	119.25 E
Prainha, Bra.	248	7.16 S	60.23 W
Prainha, Bra.	250	1.48 S	53.29 W
Prairie	166	20.52 S	144.36 E
Prairie ≃, Mi., U.S.	216	41.55 N	85.38 W
Prairie ≃, Mn., U.S.	190	47.18 N	93.29 W
Prairie ≃, Wi., U.S.	190	45.10 N	89.42 W
Prairie City, Il., U.S.	190	40.37 N	90.28 W
Prairie City, Ia., U.S.	190	41.35 N	93.14 W
Prairie City, Or., U.S.	202	44.27 N	118.42 W
Prairie Creek ≃, Fl., U.S.	220	26.59 N	81.56 W
Prairie Creek ≃, Il., U.S.	216	41.21 N	88.12 W
Prairie Creek ≃, Il., U.S.	216	40.55 N	87.49 W
Prairie Creek ≃, Il., U.S.	278	41.36 N	87.40 W
Prairie Creek ≃, Mi., U.S.	216	42.59 N	85.01 W
Prairie Creek ≃, Ne., U.S.	198	41.22 N	97.32 W
Prairie Creek Reservoir ⊜[1]	218	40.08 N	85.17 W
Prairie Dog Creek ≃	198	40.00 N	99.23 W
Prairie du Chien	190	43.03 N	91.08 W
Prairie du Sac	190	43.17 N	89.43 W
Prairie Elk Creek ≃	198	48.00 N	105.51 W
Prairie Grove	194	35.58 N	94.19 W
Prairie Hill	222	31.39 N	96.47 W
Prairie Lea	222	29.44 N	97.45 W
Prairie River	184	52.52 N	103.00 W
Prairies, Coteau des ⋏[2]	198	44.30 N	96.45 W
Prairies, Lake of the ⊜[1]	184	51.05 N	101.25 W
Prairies, Rivière des ≃	275a	45.42 N	73.29 W
Prairie View, Il., U.S.	278	42.12 N	87.57 W
Prairie View, Tx., U.S.	222	30.05 N	95.59 W
Prairie Village	198	38.59 N	94.38 W
Prajekan	115a	7.47 S	113.59 E
Prakhon Chai	110	14.37 N	103.05 E
Pralboino	64	45.16 N	10.13 E
Prali	62	44.54 N	7.03 E
Pralls Island I	276	40.37 N	74.12 W
Pralognan-la-Vanoise	62	45.23 N	6.43 E
Pram	60	48.14 N	13.37 E
Pram ≃	60	48.28 N	13.26 E
Pramaggiore, Monte ∧	64	46.22 N	12.33 E
Prambachkirchen	60	48.19 N	13.55 E
Prambanan	115a	7.45 S	110.30 E
Pr'amicyno	78	51.39 N	35.56 E
Pramort	54	54.26 N	12.55 E
Prampram	150	5.42 N	0.07 E
Pran Buri	110	12.23 N	99.55 E
Pran Buri ≃	110	12.24 N	100.00 E
Prang	150	7.59 N	0.53 W
Prangli I	76	59.38 N	25.02 E
Prānhita ≃	122	18.49 N	79.55 E
Pranzo	64	45.55 N	10.48 E
Prapa, Khlong ≅	269a	13.46 N	100.32 E
Prapat	114	2.40 N	98.56 E
Praraye	58	45.55 N	7.32 E
Prärien → Great Plains ⩸	16	42.00 N	100.00 W
Praskoveja	84	44.43 N	44.12 E
Praskovejevka	83	48.40 N	38.00 E
Praslin, Lac ⊜	186	50.03 N	69.48 W
Praslin, Port c	241f	13.53 N	60.54 W
Praslin Island I	138	4.19 S	55.44 E
Prasonísi, Ákra >	38	35.42 N	27.46 E
Praszka	30	51.04 N	18.26 E
Prat, Isla I	254	48.15 S	75.00 W
Prata, Bra.	250	7.41 S	37.06 W
Prata, Bra.	255	19.18 S	48.55 W
Prata, Bra.	287a	22.45 S	43.25 W
Prata, Rio da ≃, Bra.	255	17.28 S	46.35 W
Prata, Rio da ≃, Bra.	255	18.49 S	49.54 W
Prata, Rio da ≃, Bra.	255	18.50 S	52.11 W
Prata, Rio da ≃, Bra.	287a	22.56 S	43.34 W
Pratāpgarh, India	120	24.02 N	74.47 E
Pratāpgarh, India	124	25.54 N	81.58 E
Pratāpnagar	126	22.23 N	89.13 E
Pratápolis	255	20.45 S	46.52 W
Pratas Island → Tungsha Tao I	90	20.42 N	116.43 E
Pratau	54	51.50 N	12.38 E
Pratella	68	41.24 N	14.11 E
Prater ♦	264b	48.12 N	16.25 E
Prathet Thai → Thailand □[1]	110	15.00 N	100.00 E
Pratinha	255	19.46 S	46.24 W
Prato	66	43.53 N	11.06 E
Prato allo Stelvio	64	46.37 N	10.35 E
Pratola Peligna	66	42.06 N	13.52 E
Pratola Serra	68	40.59 N	14.51 E
Pratolino	66	43.52 N	11.18 E
Pratomagno ⋏	66	43.39 N	11.39 E
Pratt	198	37.38 N	98.44 W
Pratteln	58	47.31 N	7.42 E
Prättigau V	58	46.55 N	9.45 E
Pratt's Bottom ◆[8]	260	51.20 N	0.07 E
Prattsburg	210	42.31 N	77.17 W
Prattsville	210	42.18 N	74.26 W
Prattville	194	32.27 N	86.27 W
Pratudão ≃	255	13.56 S	44.55 W
Prauthoy	58	47.40 N	5.17 E
Pravaja Mama ≃	88	57.10 N	111.54 E
Pravda	89	47.00 N	142.01 E
Pravdinsk, S.S.S.R.	76	54.27 N	21.01 E
Pravdinsk, S.S.S.R.	80	56.32 N	43.34 E
Pravdinskij	82	56.04 N	37.51 E
Pravia	34	43.29 N	6.07 W
Prawet Buri Rom, Khlong ≅	269a	13.42 N	100.35 E
Prawle Point >	42	50.13 N	3.42 W
Praya	115b	8.42 S	116.17 E
Pr'aža	24	61.42 N	33.35 E
Praz-sur-Arly	62	45.50 N	6.34 E
Prazzo	62	44.29 N	7.03 E
Preakness Brook ≃	276	40.54 N	74.15 W
Preakness Mountain ∧	276	40.58 N	74.13 W
Preakness Valley Park ♦	276	40.55 N	74.14 W
Preble, In., U.S.	216	40.50 N	85.01 W
Preble, N.Y., U.S.	210	42.44 N	76.09 W
Preble □[6]	218	39.45 N	84.38 W
Preci	66	42.53 N	13.02 E
Prečistoje, S.S.S.R.	76	55.41 N	34.56 E
Prečistoje, S.S.S.R.	76	55.31 N	32.22 E
Prečistoje, S.S.S.R.	80	58.27 N	40.19 E
Précy-sous-Thil	50	47.23 N	4.19 E
Précy-sur-Marne	261	48.56 N	2.47 E
Précy-sur-Oise	50	49.12 N	2.22 E
Preda	58	46.36 N	9.46 E
Predappio	66	44.06 N	11.58 E
Predazzo	64	46.19 N	11.36 E
Predeal	38	45.30 N	25.35 E
Prédecelle ≃	261	48.35 N	2.07 E
Predești	38	44.21 N	23.36 E
Predgornoje	86	47.10 N	81.02 E
Predigtstuhl ∧	61	48.48 N	15.22 E
Předin	61	49.12 N	15.40 E
Predivinsk	86	57.04 N	93.27 E
Predlitz	64	47.04 N	13.55 E
Predmostnoje	78	45.57 N	34.37 E
Predoi (Prettau)	64	47.02 N	12.06 E
Predore	64	45.40 N	10.01 E
Preeceville	184	51.58 N	102.40 W
Pré-en-Pail	32	48.27 N	0.12 W
Preesall	44	53.55 N	2.58 W
Preetz	54	54.14 N	10.16 E
Pregarten	61	48.21 N	14.32 E
Pregel → Pregol'a ≃	76	54.41 N	20.22 E
Pregnana	266b	45.31 N	9.00 E
Pregol'a ≃	76	54.41 N	20.22 E
Pregonero	246	8.01 N	71.46 W
Pregos	256	21.46 S	42.54 W
Pregradnaja	84	43.58 N	41.12 E
Pregradnoje	80	45.49 N	41.45 E
Preguiças ≃	250	2.34 S	42.44 W
Preila	76	55.22 N	21.04 E
Preiļi	76	56.18 N	26.43 E
Preissac, Lac ⊜	190	48.20 N	78.20 W
Prekestolen ♦	26	59.00 N	6.01 E
Preko	36	44.05 N	15.11 E
Prekomurje ◆[1]	61	46.40 N	16.10 E
Prěk Poŭthĭ	110	11.51 N	105.07 E
Prelate	184	50.51 N	109.23 W
Přelouč	30	50.02 N	15.34 E
Premana	58	46.03 N	9.25 E
Prembun	115a	7.43 S	109.48 E
Prémery	50	47.10 N	3.20 E
Premià de Dalt	266d	41.31 N	2.21 E
Premià de Mar	266d	41.29 N	2.21 E
Premnitz	54	52.32 N	12.19 E
Prémont, P.Q., Can.	206	46.22 N	73.03 W
Premont, Tx., U.S.	196	27.21 N	98.07 W
Prémontré	50	49.33 N	3.24 E
Premosello	58	46.00 N	8.20 E
Premuda, Otok I	36	44.20 N	14.37 E
Prenestini, Monti ⋏	66	41.50 N	12.55 E
Prenjas	38	41.04 N	20.32 E
Prentice	190	45.32 N	90.17 W
Prentiss	194	31.35 N	89.52 W
Prenton	262	53.22 N	3.03 W
Prenzlau	54	53.19 N	13.52 E
Prenzlauer Berg ◆[8]	264a	52.32 N	13.26 E
Preobraženije	89	42.57 N	133.55 E
Preobražennoje	83	49.32 N	38.10 E
Preobraženovka	89	48.04 N	131.55 E
Preparis Island I	110	14.52 N	93.41 E
Preparis North Channel Ʉ	110	15.27 N	94.05 E
Preparis South Channel Ʉ	110	14.40 N	94.00 E
Přerov	30	49.27 N	17.27 E
Prerow	54	54.26 N	12.35 E
Pré-Saint-Didier	62	45.46 N	6.59 E
Presanella, Cima ∧	64	46.13 N	10.40 E
Prescot	44	53.26 N	2.48 W
Prescott, On., Can.	212	44.43 N	75.31 W
Prescott, Az., U.S.	200	34.32 N	112.28 W
Prescott, Ar., U.S.	194	33.48 N	93.22 W
Prescott, Or., U.S.	224	46.02 N	122.53 W
Prescott, Wi., U.S.	190	44.44 N	92.48 W
Prescott and Russell □[6]	206	45.25 N	75.00 W
Prescott Island I	176	73.01 N	96.50 W
Preševo	38	42.18 N	21.39 E
Presho	198	43.54 N	100.03 W
Presicce	68	39.54 N	18.16 E
Presidencia de la Plaza	252	27.01 S	59.51 W
Presidencia Roca	252	26.08 S	59.36 W
Presidencia Roque Sáenz Peña	252	26.47 S	60.27 W
Presidente Costa e Silva, Ponte ◆[5]	287a	22.53 S	43.10 W
Presidente Derqui	258	34.29 S	58.51 W
Presidente Dutra	250	5.15 S	44.30 W
Presidente Epitácio	255	21.46 S	52.06 W
Presidente Getúlio	252	27.03 S	49.37 W
Presidente Hayes □[5]	252	24.00 S	59.00 W
Presidente Nicolás Avellaneda, Parque ♦	288	34.39 S	58.29 W
Presidente Olegário	255	18.25 S	46.25 W
Presidente Prudente	255	22.07 S	51.22 W
Presidente Ríos, Lago ⊜	254	46.28 S	74.25 W
Presidente Roosevelt, Estação ◆[5]	287b	23.33 S	46.36 W
Presidente Venceslau	255	21.52 S	51.50 W
Presidential Heights	279b	40.34 N	80.03 W
President Roxas	116	11.26 N	122.56 E
Presidio	196	29.33 N	104.22 W
Presidio, Río del ≃	234	23.06 N	106.17 W
Presidio of San Francisco ■	226	37.48 N	122.28 W
Presles	56	50.23 N	4.35 E
Presles-en-Brie	261	48.43 N	2.45 E
Presnogor'kovka	86	54.30 N	65.45 E
Presnovka	86	54.40 N	67.09 E
Presolana, Passo della)(	64	45.55 N	10.06 E
Prešov	30	49.00 N	21.15 E
Prespa, Lake ⊜	38	40.55 N	21.00 E
Prespansko Jezero → Prespa, Lake ⊜	38	40.55 N	21.00 E
Presque Isle	186	46.40 N	68.00 W
Presque Isle >[1]	214	42.09 N	80.06 W
Presque Isle ≃	190	46.43 N	89.59 W
Presque Isle State Park ♦	214	42.09 N	80.06 W
Presqu'ile Bay c	212	44.01 N	77.43 W
Presqu'ile Peninsula >[1]	212	44.00 N	77.41 W
Presqu'ile Provincial Park ♦	212	44.00 N	77.42 W
Pressana	64	45.17 N	11.24 E
Pressath	60	49.46 N	11.56 E
Pressbaum	61	48.11 N	16.05 E
Pressburg → Bratislava	30	48.09 N	17.07 E
Pressel	54	51.34 N	12.41 E
Prestatyn	44	53.20 N	3.24 W
Prestbury	262	53.17 N	2.09 W
Prestea	150	5.27 N	2.08 W
Presteigne	42	52.17 N	3.00 W
Přeštice	60	49.34 N	13.20 E
Presto, Bol.	248	18.55 S	64.56 W
Presto, Pa., U.S.	279b	40.23 N	80.07 W
Preston, Austl.	169	37.45 S	145.01 E
Preston, Cuba	240p	20.46 N	75.39 W
Preston, Eng., U.K.	42	50.39 N	2.25 W
Preston, Eng., U.K.	44	53.46 N	2.42 W
Preston, Eng., U.K.	44	53.46 N	0.12 W
Preston, Ga., U.S.	192	32.03 N	84.32 W
Preston, Id., U.S.	202	42.05 N	111.52 W
Preston, Ia., U.S.	190	42.03 N	90.24 W
Preston, Ks., U.S.	198	37.45 N	98.33 W
Preston, Md., U.S.	208	38.42 N	75.54 W
Preston, Mn., U.S.	190	43.40 N	92.04 W
Preston, Wa., U.S.	224	47.31 N	121.55 W
Preston □[8]	262	53.48 N	2.42 W
Preston ≃, Austl.	168a	33.20 S	115.40 E
Preston ≃, P.Q., Can.	206	46.05 N	75.04 W
Preston, Cape >	162	20.51 S	116.12 E
Preston, Lac ⊜	206	46.05 N	75.04 W
Preston, Lake ⊜, Austl.	168a	32.59 S	115.42 E
Preston, Lake ⊜, Fl., U.S.	220	28.18 N	81.08 W
Preston Airport ⊠	276	40.22 N	74.15 W
Preston Brook	262	53.19 N	2.39 W
Preston Brook Canal Tunnel ◆[5]	262	53.19 N	2.38 W
Preston Heights	216	41.28 N	88.08 W
Preston Hollow	210	42.27 N	74.13 W
Preston North End Football Ground ♦	262	53.47 N	2.42 W
Prestonpans	46	55.57 N	3.00 W
Preston Peak ∧	204	41.50 N	123.37 W

≃	River	Fluß	Río	Rivière	Rio
≅	Canal	Kanal	Canal	Canal	Canal
L	Waterfall, Rapids	Wasserfall, Stromschnellen	Cascada, Rápidos	Chute d'eau, Rapides	Cascata, Rápidos
Ʉ	Strait	Meeresstraße	Estrecho	Détroit	Estreito
c	Bay, Gulf	Bucht, Golf	Bahía, Golfo	Baie, Golfe	Baía, Golfo
⊜	Lake, Lakes	See, Seen	Lago, Lagos	Lac, Lacs	Lago, Lagos
⩸	Swamp	Sumpf	Pantano	Marais	Pântano
⍓	Ice Features, Glacier	Eis- und Gletscherformen	Accidentes Glaciales	Formes glaciaires	Acidentes glaciares
⏏	Other Hydrographic Features	Andere Hydrographische Objekte	Otros Elementos Hidrográficos	Autres données hydrographiques	Outros acidentes hidrográficos

✣	Submarine Features	Untermeerische Objekte	Accidentes Submarinos	Formes de relief sous-marin	Acidentes submarinos
□	Political Unit	Politische Einheit	Unidad Politica	Entité politique	Unidade política
♁	Cultural Institution	Kulturelle Institution	Institución Cultural	Institution culturelle	Instituição cultural
⊥	Historical Site	Historische Stätte	Sitio Histórico	Site historique	Sítio histórico
♦	Recreational Site	Erholungs- und Ferienort	Sitio de Recreo	Centre de loisirs	Área de Lazer
⊠	Airport	Flughafen	Aeropuerto	Aéroport	Aeroporto
■	Military Installation	Militäranlage	Instalación Militar	Installation militaire	Instalação militar
◆	Miscellaneous	Verschiedenes	Misceláneo	Divers	Diversos

ENGLISH Name	Page	Lat.°′	Long.°′
DEUTSCH Name	Seite	Breite°′	Länge°′ E = Ost

Prestonsburg 192 37.39 N 82.46 W
Prestrud Inlet ⊂ 9 78.18 S 156.00 W
Preststranda 26 59.06 N 9.04 E
Prestville 182 55.44 N 118.37 W
Prestwich 44 53.32 N 2.17 W
Prestwick 46 55.29 N 4.37 W
Prestwick Airport ⊠ 46 55.30 N 4.36 W
Prêto ≃, Bra. 246 1.41 S 63.48 W
Prêto ≃, Bra. 248 8.03 S 62.54 W
Prêto ≃, Bra. 250 11.21 S 43.52 W
Prêto ≃, Bra. 250 3.32 S 43.46 W
Prêto ≃, Bra. 255 13.37 S 48.06 W
Prêto ≃, Bra. 255 17.00 S 46.12 W
Prêto ≃, Bra. 255 18.25 S 39.47 W
Prêto ≃, Bra. 255 18.44 S 50.23 W
Prêto ≃, Bra. 255 19.22 S 41.56 W
Prêto ≃, Bra. 255 20.08 S 49.38 W
Preto ≃, Bra. 256 22.14 S 43.07 W
Preto ≃, Bra. 256 22.01 S 43.20 W
Prêto, Igarapé ≃ 246 4.10 S 68.57 W
Prêto do Igapó-Açu ≃ 246 4.26 S 59.48 W
Pretoria 158 25.45 S 28.10 E
Pretoriusvlei 158 28.30 S 22.59 E
Prettau → Predoi 64 47.02 N 12.06 E
Prettin 54 51.39 N 12.55 E
Prettyboy Reservoir ⊜[1] 208 39.38 N 76.45 W
Pretty Prairie 198 37.46 N 98.01 W
Pretzfeld 60 49.45 N 11.11 E
Pretzier 54 52.49 N 11.15 E
Pretzsch 54 51.42 N 12.48 E
Preussisch Eylau → Bagrationovsk 76 54.23 N 20.39 E
Preussisch Friedland → Debrzno 30 53.33 N 17.14 E
Preussisch Holland → Pasłęk 30 54.05 N 19.39 E
Preussisch Königsdorf → Olesno 30 50.53 N 18.25 E
Preussisch-Oldendorf 52 52.18 N 8.30 E
Preussisch-Ströhen 52 52.29 N 8.40 E
Prevalje 61 46.32 N 14.55 E
Préveza 38 38.57 N 20.44 E
Prévost 206 45.52 N 74.05 W
Prevost Island I 224 48.50 N 123.22 W
Prey Lvéa 110 11.10 N 104.57 E
Prey Nób 110 10.38 N 103.47 E
Prey Vêng 110 11.29 N 105.19 E
Prezza, Monte ∧ 66 42.02 N 13.49 E
Priaral'skije Karakumy ◆[2] 86 47.00 N 63.30 E
Priargunsk 88 50.27 N 119.00 E
Priay 58 46.00 N 5.17 E
Priazovskaja vozvyšennost' ⋏[1] 83 47.30 N 37.30 E
Priazovskoje 78 46.43 N 35.38 E
Pribilof Islands II 180 57.00 N 170.00 W
Priboj 38 43.35 N 19.31 E
Příbram 30 49.42 N 14.01 E
Pribylovo 76 60.26 N 28.40 E
Priccio, Cozzo ∧ 70 37.01 N 14.46 E
Price, Austl. 168b 34.17 S 138.00 E
Price, Tx., U.S. 222 32.08 N 94.57 W
Price, Ut,. U.S. 200 39.35 N 110.48 W
Price ≃ 200 39.10 N 110.06 W
Price, Cape › 110 13.34 N 93.03 E
Price Bend ⊂ 276 40.55 N 73.24 W
Price Island I 182 52.23 N 128.36 W
Prichard 194 30.44 N 88.04 W
Prickly Point › 241k 11.59 N 61.45 W
Pričornomorskaja nizmennost' ≚ 78 47.00 N 33.00 E
Priddy 196 31.40 N 98.31 W
Pridneprovskaja nizmennost' ≚ 78 50.00 N 32.00 E
Pridneprovskaja vozvyšennost' ⋏[1] 78 49.00 N 32.00 E
Priego 34 40.27 N 2.18 W
Priego de Córdoba 34 37.26 N 4.11 W
Priekule, S.S.S.R. 76 56.26 N 21.35 E
Priekule, S.S.S.R. 76 55.33 N 21.19 E
Prienai 76 54.38 N 23.57 E
Prien am Chiemsee 64 47.51 N 12.20 E
Prieros 54 52.13 N 13.46 E
Prieska 158 29.40 S 22.42 E
Priest ≃ 202 48.11 N 116.53 W
Priestewitz 54 51.15 N 13.30 E
Priest Island I 46 57.58 N 5.30 W
Priest Lake ⊜ 202 48.34 N 116.52 W
Priestley, Mount ∧ 182 55.13 N 128.53 W
Priest Rapids Lake ⊜[1] 202 46.45 N 119.55 W
Priest River 202 48.10 N 116.54 W
Prieta, Loma ∧ 226 37.07 N 121.51 W
Prieta, Peña ∧ 34 43.01 N 4.44 W
Prieto ≃ 240m 18.15 N 66.54 W
Prieto Diaz 116 13.02 N 124.12 E
Prievidza 30 48.47 N 18.37 E
Prignitz ◆[1] 54 53.05 N 12.15 E
Priirtyšskaja ravnina ≚ 86 52.30 N 76.15 E
Priiskovyj, S.S.S.R. 86 54.39 N 88.42 E
Priiskovyj, S.S.S.R. 88 51.57 N 116.39 E
Prijedor 36 44.59 N 16.43 E
Prijepolje 38 43.23 N 19.39 E
Prijutnoje 80 46.06 N 43.31 E
Prijutovo 80 53.54 N 53.56 E
Prikaspijskaja nizmennost' ≚ 80 48.00 N 52.00 E
Prikolotnoje 78 50.09 N 37.21 E
Prikro 150 7.39 N 3.59 W
Prilep 38 41.20 N 21.33 E
Prilepy 82 54.03 N 37.42 E
Prilly 58 46.32 N 6.36 E
Priluki, S.S.S.R. 76 59.16 N 39.53 E
Priluki, S.S.S.R. 78 50.36 N 32.24 E
Priluki, S.S.S.R. 82 54.51 N 37.53 E
Prima Porta ◆[8] 267a 42.00 N 12.29 E
Primavera 250 0.56 S 47.06 W
Přimda 60 49.41 N 12.41 E
Primeira Cruz 250 2.30 S 43.26 W
Primeiro de Maio 255 22.48 S 51.01 W
Primera 196 26.14 N 97.43 W
Primero ≃ 252 31.00 S 63.12 W
Primero de Mayo 196 27.12 N 101.15 W
Primghar 198 43.05 N 95.37 W
Primkenau → Przemków 30 51.32 N 15.48 E
Primolano 64 45.58 N 11.42 E
Primorje [Warnicken] 76 54.57 N 20.02 E
Primorka 83 47.16 N 39.03 E
Primorsk, S.S.S.R. 76 60.22 N 28.36 E
Primorsk, S.S.S.R. 76 54.44 N 20.01 E
Primorsk, S.S.S.R. 78 46.44 N 36.20 E
Primorsk, S.S.S.R. 80 49.16 N 45.03 E
Primorsk, S.S.S.R. 84 40.13 N 49.33 E
Primorskij, S.S.S.R. 78 45.07 N 35.29 E
Primorskij, S.S.S.R. 89 43.07 N 131.38 E
Primorskij chrebet ⋏ 88 52.30 N 106.00 E
Primorskij Kraj □[4] 89 45.25 N 135.25 E
Primorsko 38 42.16 N 27.46 E
Primorsko-Achtarsk 78 46.03 N 38.11 E
Primorskoje 83 47.11 N 37.42 E
Primos 285 39.55 N 75.18 W
Primrose, S. Afr. 273d 26.12 S 28.10 E
Primrose, Pa., U.S. 210 40.42 N 76.17 W
Primrose, Pa., U.S. 279b 40.21 N 80.16 W
Primrose Brook ≃ 276 40.43 N 74.31 W
Primrose Lake ⊜ 184 54.55 N 109.45 W
Prims ≃ 56 49.20 N 6.44 E
Primstal 56 49.32 N 6.58 E
Prince, Lake ⊜[1] 208 36.48 N 76.38 W
Prince Albert, On., Can. 212 44.05 N 78.58 W
Prince Albert, Sk., Can. 184 53.12 N 105.46 W
Prince Albert, S. Afr. 158 33.13 S 22.02 E
Prince Albert Mountains ⋏ 9 76.00 S 161.30 E
Prince Albert National Park ♦ 184 54.00 N 106.25 W
Prince Albert Road 158 33.01 S 21.40 E
Prince Albert Sound ʯ 176 70.25 N 115.00 W
Prince Alexander Mountains ⋏ 164 3.30 S 142.50 E
Prince Alfred Hamlet 158 33.18 S 19.20 E
Prince Charles Island I 176 67.50 N 76.00 W
Prince Charles Mountains ⋏ 9 72.00 S 67.00 E
Prince-de-Galles, Île du → Prince of Wales Island I, Austl. 164 10.40 S 142.10 E
Prince-de-Galles, Île du → Prince of Wales Island I, N.T., Can. 176 72.40 N 99.00 W
Prince Edward □[6] 212 44.00 N 77.15 W
Prince Edward Bay ⊂ 212 43.57 N 76.57 W
Prince Edward Island □[4], Can. 176 46.20 N 63.20 W
Prince Edward Island □[4], Can. 186 46.20 N 63.20 W
Prince Edward Island National Park ♦ 186 46.31 N 63.26 W
Prince Edward Islands II 6 46.35 S 37.56 E
Prince Edward Park ♦ 274a 34.02 S 151.03 E
Prince Edward Point › 212 43.56 N 76.52 W
Prince Frederick 208 38.32 N 76.35 W
Prince Gallitzin State Park ♦ 214 40.40 N 78.32 W
Prince George, B.C., Can. 182 53.55 N 122.45 W
Prince George, Va., U.S. 208 37.13 N 77.17 W
Prince George □[6] 208 37.13 N 77.10 W
Prince Georges □[6] 208 38.49 N 76.45 W
Prince Georges Plaza ◆[9] 284c 38.58 N 76.57 W
Prince Leopold Island I 176 74.02 N 89.55 W
Prince of Wales, Cape › 180 65.40 N 168.05 W
Prince of Wales Island I, Austl. 164 10.40 S 142.10 E
Prince of Wales Island I, N.T., Can. 176 72.40 N 99.00 W
Prince of Wales Island I, Ak., U.S. 180 55.47 N 132.50 W
Prince of Wales Strait ʯ 176 73.00 N 117.00 W
Prince Olav Coast ⊥[2] 9 68.30 S 42.30 E
Prince Patrick Island I 16 76.45 N 119.30 W
Prince Regent ≃ 164 15.28 S 125.05 E
Prince Regent Inlet ⊂ 176 73.00 N 90.30 W
Prince Regent Nature Reserve ♦ 164 15.30 S 125.30 E
Prince Rupert 182 54.19 N 130.19 W
Prince Rupert Bay ⊂ 240d 15.34 N 61.29 W
Prince Rupert Bluff Point › 240d 15.35 N 61.29 W
Princesa, Puerto ⊂ 116 9.45 N 118.43 E
Princesa Astrid, Costa → Princess Astrid Coast ⊥[2] 9 70.45 S 12.30 E
Princesa Carlota, Bahía → Princess Charlotte Bay ⊂ 164 14.25 S 144.00 E
Princesa Isabel 250 7.44 S 38.00 W
Princesa Marta, Costa → Princess Martha Coast ⊥[2] 9 72.00 S 7.30 W
Princesa Ragnhild, Costa → Princess Ragnhild Coast ⊥[2] 9 70.15 S 27.30 E
Princes Bay ⊂ 276 40.31 N 74.12 W
Princes Risborough 42 51.44 N 0.51 W
Princess Anne 208 38.12 N 75.41 W
Princess Astrid Coast ⊥[2] 9 70.45 S 12.30 E
Princess Charlotte Bay ⊂ 164 14.25 S 144.00 E
Princess Martha Coast ⊥[2] 9 72.00 S 7.30 W
Princess Ragnhild Coast ⊥[2] 9 70.15 S 27.30 E
Princess Ranges ⋏ 162 26.08 S 121.55 E
Princess Royal Channel ʯ 182 53.10 N 128.37 W
Princess Royal Island I 182 52.57 N 128.49 W
Princes Town 241r 10.16 N 61.23 W
Princeton, B.C., Can. 182 49.27 N 120.31 W
Princeton, Nf., Can. 186 48.25 N 53.36 W
Princeton, On., Can. 212 43.10 N 80.32 W
Princeton, Ca., U.S. 226 39.24 N 122.00 W
Princeton, Fl., U.S. 220 25.32 N 80.24 W
Princeton, Il., U.S. 190 41.22 N 89.27 W
Princeton, In., U.S. 194 38.21 N 87.34 W
Princeton, Ky., U.S. 194 37.06 N 87.52 W
Princeton, Me., U.S. 188 45.13 N 67.34 W
Princeton, Mi., U.S. 190 46.17 N 87.28 W
Princeton, Mn., U.S. 190 45.34 N 93.34 W
Princeton, Mo., U.S. 194 40.24 N 93.34 W
Princeton, N.J., U.S. 208 40.20 N 74.39 W
Princeton, N.C., U.S. 192 35.27 N 78.09 W
Princeton, Tx., U.S. 222 33.11 N 96.30 W
Princeton, W.V., U.S. 192 37.21 N 81.06 W
Princeton, Wi., U.S. 190 43.51 N 89.07 W
Princeton Airfield ⊠ 276 40.24 N 74.39 W
Princeton Battlefield Park ⊥ 276 40.20 N 74.41 W
Princeton Junction 208 40.19 N 74.37 W
Princeton Township 276 40.22 N 74.40 W
Princeton University ᵾ[2] 276 40.21 N 74.39 W
Princetown 42 50.33 N 4.00 W
Princeville, P.Q., Can. 206 46.10 N 71.53 W
Princeville, Il., U.S. 190 40.56 N 89.45 W
Princeville, N.C., U.S. 192 35.53 N 77.31 W
Prince William □[6] 208 38.42 N 77.27 W
Prince William Forest Park ♦ 208 38.36 N 77.23 W
Prince William Sound ʯ 180 60.40 N 147.00 W
Príncipe I 152 1.37 N 7.25 E
Príncipe Alberto, Montes → Prince Albert Mountains ⋏ 9 76.00 S 161.30 E
Príncipe Carlos, Montes → Prince Charles Mountains ⋏ 9 72.00 S 67.00 E
Principe Channel ʯ 182 53.28 N 130.00 W
Príncipe da Beira 248 12.25 S 64.25 W
Príncipe de Gales, Isla → Prince of Wales Island I, Austl. 164 10.40 S 142.10 E
Príncipe de Gales, Isla → Prince of Wales Island I, N.T., Can. 176 72.40 N 99.00 W
Príncipe Eduardo, Isla → Prince Edward Island □[4] 186 46.20 N 63.20 W
Príncipe Olav, Costa → Prince Olav Coast ⊥[2] 9 68.30 S 42.30 E
Príncipe Patricio, Isla → Prince Patrick Island I 16 76.45 N 119.30 W
Prineville 202 44.18 N 120.51 W
Prineville Reservoir ⊜[1] 202 44.08 N 120.42 W
Prineville Southeast 202 44.17 N 120.53 W
Pringgabaja 115b 8.34 S 116.37 E
Pringsewu 112 5.24 S 104.55 E
Pringy 261 48.31 N 2.34 E
Prinsenbeek 52 51.36 N 4.42 E
Prinses Margrietkanaal ≡ 52 53.10 N 5.55 E
Prinshof 158 32.06 S 20.53 E
Prinzapolka 236 13.24 N 83.34 W
Prinzapolka ≃ 236 13.24 N 83.34 W
Prinzessin Astrid-Küste → Princess Astrid Coast ⊥[2] 9 70.45 S 12.30 E
Prinzessin Charlotte Bucht → Princess Charlotte Bay ⊂ 164 14.25 S 144.00 E
Prinzessin Martha-Küste → Princess Martha Coast ⊥[2] 9 72.00 S 7.30 W
Prinzessin Ragnhild-Küste → Princess Ragnhild Coast ⊥[2] 9 70.15 S 27.30 E
Priobskoje plato ⋏[1] 86 52.40 N 83.00 E
Prioksko-Terrasnyj Zapovednik ◆[4] 82 54.51 N 37.36 E
Priolo Gargallo 70 37.09 N 15.11 E
Prior, Cabo › 34 43.34 N 8.19 W
Priort 264a 52.31 N 12.58 E
Priozernyj 80 47.23 N 45.14 E
Prioz'ornyj 86 47.50 N 84.13 E
Prioz'orsk 24 61.02 N 30.04 E
Prip'at' ≃ 78 51.21 N 30.09 E
Pripet → Prip'at' ≃ 78 51.21 N 30.09 E
Pripet Marshes → Polesje ◆[1] 72 52.00 N 27.00 E
Pripol'arnyj Ural ⋏ 24 65.00 N 60.00 E
Priputni 78 50.57 N 32.14 E
Prirečje 88 55.07 N 101.03 E
Prirečnyj 80 51.03 N 52.26 E
Přísečnice 54 50.27 N 13.06 E
Priselje 76 55.09 N 32.49 E
Prišib, S.S.S.R. 78 47.16 N 35.21 E
Prišib, S.S.S.R. 84 39.08 N 48.36 E
Prislon 82 56.48 N 37.16 E
Pristan'-Prževal'sk 85 42.34 N 78.18 E
Pristen', S.S.S.R. 78 51.15 N 36.41 E
Pristen', S.S.S.R. 83 49.36 N 37.38 E
Priština 38 42.39 N 21.10 E
Pritchett 198 37.22 N 102.51 W
Přitluky 61 48.51 N 16.46 E
Pritzerbe 54 52.30 N 12.27 E
Pritzier 54 53.22 N 11.04 E
Pritzwalk 54 53.09 N 12.10 E
Priural'nyj 80 51.29 N 53.06 E
Privas 62 44.44 N 4.36 E
Priverno 66 41.28 N 13.11 E
Privetnoje 78 44.50 N 34.41 E
Privodino 24 61.05 N 46.28 E
Privokzal'nyj, S.S.S.R. 82 55.59 N 35.56 E
Privokzal'nyj, S.S.S.R. 86 58.53 N 60.43 E
Privolje, S.S.S.R. 83 49.01 N 38.18 E
Privolje, S.S.S.R. 83 48.52 N 37.16 E
Privol'naja 78 46.09 N 38.42 E
Privol'n'anskij ◆[8] 83 48.41 N 38.28 E
Privol'noje, S.S.S.R. 78 47.29 N 32.17 E
Privol'noje, S.S.S.R. 80 50.57 N 46.06 E
Privolžje 80 52.52 N 48.37 E
Privolžsk 80 57.23 N 41.17 E
Privolžskaja vozvyšennost' ⋏[1] 80 52.00 N 46.00 E
Privolžskij, S.S.S.R. 80 46.24 N 48.00 E
Privolžskij, S.S.S.R. 80 51.24 N 46.02 E
Privolžskoje 80 51.06 N 45.57 E
Prizren 38 42.12 N 20.44 E
Prizzi 70 37.43 N 13.26 E
Prizzi, Lago di ⊜ 70 37.44 N 13.25 E
Prnjavor 36 44.52 N 17.40 E
Pro 286d 11.57 S 77.05 W
Probolinggo 115a 7.45 S 113.13 E
Proboštov 54 50.39 N 13.50 E
Probstzella 54 50.32 N 11.22 E
Probus 42 50.17 N 4.57 W
Procchio 66 42.47 N 10.15 E
Prochladnoje 86 48.30 N 82.41 E
Prochladnyj 84 43.46 N 44.00 E
Prochorkino 86 59.34 N 79.26 E
Prochorovka 82 54.07 N 38.11 E
Prochowice 30 51.17 N 16.22 E
Procida 68 40.46 N 14.02 E
Procida, Isola di I 68 40.45 N 14.01 E
Procter 182 49.37 N 116.57 W
Proctor, Mn., U.S. 190 46.44 N 92.13 W
Proctor, Vt., U.S. 188 43.39 N 73.02 W
Proctor Brook ≃ 283 42.32 N 70.54 W
Proctor Lake ⊜ 228 35.07 N 118.21 W
Proctor Lake ⊜[1] 196 32.02 N 98.32 W
Proddatūr 122 14.44 N 78.33 E
Proença-a-Nova 34 39.45 N 7.55 W
Profen 54 51.07 N 12.13 E
Pro Football Hall of Fame ᵾ 214 40.49 N 81.25 W
Prognoj 83 48.45 N 39.51 E
Progreso, Méx. 196 27.28 N 100.59 W
Progreso, Méx. 232 21.17 N 89.40 W
Progreso, Ur. 258 34.40 S 56.13 W
Progreso Industrial 234 19.38 N 99.21 W
Progress, S.S.S.R. 89 49.42 N 129.39 E
Progress, Or., U.S. 224 45.28 N 122.47 W
Progress, Pa., U.S. 208 40.08 N 76.34 W
Project City 204 40.41 N 122.21 W
Prokopjeva 88 58.03 N 100.39 E
Prokopjevsk 86 53.53 N 86.45 E
Prokopyevsk → Prokopjevsk 86 53.53 N 86.45 E
Prokuplje 38 43.14 N 21.36 E
Prokuševo 76 59.55 N 34.56 E
Prokutkino 86 56.19 N 69.46 E
Proletarij 76 58.26 N 31.44 E
Proletarsk, S.S.S.R. 78 48.56 N 38.23 E
Proletarsk, S.S.S.R. 80 46.42 N 41.44 E
Proletarsk, S.S.S.R. 85 40.10 N 69.30 E
Proletarsk ◆[8] 83 48.56 N 38.23 E
Proletarskij, S.S.S.R. 78 50.47 N 35.47 E
Proletarskij, S.S.S.R. 82 55.01 N 37.23 E
Proletarskij ◆[8] 83 48.08 N 39.18 E
Prolysovo 76 52.54 N 34.09 E
Prome (Pyè) 110 18.49 N 95.13 E
Promised Land State Park ♦ 210 41.18 N 75.11 W
Promissão 255 21.32 S 49.52 W
Promitorio 267a 42.03 N 12.39 E
Promontogno 58 46.21 N 9.34 E
Prompton 210 41.35 N 75.19 W
Prompton Lake ⊜[1] 210 41.36 N 75.20 W
Prompton Lake State Park ♦ 210 41.37 N 75.22 W
Promyšlennaja 86 54.55 N 85.40 E
Promyšlennovskij 86 55.29 N 86.12 E
Promyšlennyj 24 67.35 N 63.55 E
Promyslovka 80 45.44 N 47.10 E
Pron'a ≃, S.S.S.R. 76 53.25 N 31.01 E
Pron'a ≃, S.S.S.R. 80 54.21 N 40.24 E
Pron'a Gorodišče 82 54.15 N 38.43 E
Pronin 80 49.12 N 42.11 E
Pronsfeld 56 50.10 N 6.20 E
Pronsk 76 54.07 N 39.37 E
Prony, Baie du ⊂ 175f 22.22 S 166.53 E
Prophet ≃ 176 58.45 N 122.45 W
Prophetstown 190 41.40 N 89.56 W
Propriá 250 10.13 S 36.51 W
Propriano 36 41.40 N 8.55 E
Prorer Wiek ⊂ 54 54.27 N 13.38 E
Prorva 86 46.03 N 53.15 E
Proryvnoje 86 54.23 N 64.26 E
Pros'anaja 78 48.07 N 36.23 E
Pros'anov 78 49.42 N 35.47 E
Prösen 54 51.25 N 13.30 E
Proserpine 166 20.24 S 148.34 E
Prosigk 54 51.42 N 12.03 E
Proskurov → Chmel'nickij 78 49.25 N 27.00 E
Prosna ≃ 30 52.10 N 17.39 E
Prosnica 80 58.26 N 50.15 E
Prosotsáni 38 41.10 N 23.59 E
Prospect, Austl. 168b 34.54 S 138.35 E
Prospect, Austl. 274a 33.48 S 150.56 E
Prospect, Ct., U.S. 207 41.30 N 72.58 W
Prospect, N.Y., U.S. 210 43.18 N 75.09 W
Prospect, Oh., U.S. 214 40.27 N 83.11 W
Prospect, Pa., U.S. 214 40.54 N 80.03 W
Prospect Bay ⊂ 208 38.56 N 76.14 W
Prospect Creek ≃ 274a 33.55 S 150.59 E
Prospect Heights 278 42.05 N 87.56 W
Prospect Hill 168b 35.13 S 138.44 E
Prospect Hill ∧[2], Ma., U.S. 207 41.21 N 70.45 W
Prospect Hill ∧[2], Ma., U.S. 283 42.23 N 71.15 W
Prospect Hill Park ♦ 283 42.23 N 71.15 W
Prospect Meadows 278 42.05 N 87.57 W
Prospect Park, N.J., U.S. 276 40.56 N 74.10 W
Prospect Park, Pa., U.S. 214 41.31 N 78.13 W
Prospect Park, Pa., U.S. 285 39.53 N 75.18 W
Prospect Park ♦ 276 40.40 N 73.58 W
Prospect Park Lake ⊜ 276 40.39 N 73.57 W
Prospect Plains 276 40.19 N 74.28 W
Prospect Point 276 40.58 N 74.38 W
Prospect Point › 276 40.52 N 73.43 W
Prospect Reservoir ⊜[1] 274a 33.49 S 150.54 E
Prospectville 285 40.13 N 75.11 W
Prosper 222 33.14 N 96.48 W
Prosperi Airport ⊠ 278 41.33 N 87.47 W
Prosperidad 116 8.34 N 125.52 E
Prosser 202 46.12 N 119.46 W
Prosser Creek Reservoir ⊜[1] 226 39.22 N 120.08 W
Prostějov 30 49.29 N 17.07 E
Prostken → Prostki 30 53.43 N 22.26 E
Prostki 30 53.43 N 22.26 E
Proston 166 26.10 S 151.36 E
Proszowice 30 50.12 N 20.18 E
Protasovo, S.S.S.R. 82 54.48 N 38.35 E
Protasovo, S.S.S.R. 82 54.11 N 37.00 E
Protasovo, S.S.S.R. 82 56.08 N 37.36 E
Protasy 76 52.47 N 29.05 E
Protea 273d 26.17 S 27.51 E
Protection 198 37.12 N 99.29 W
Protection Island I 224 48.07 N 122.55 W
Protem 158 34.16 S 20.05 E
Protestantes 256 22.44 S 46.18 W
Protivín 61 49.12 N 14.13 E
Protoka ≃ 78 45.43 N 37.46 E
Protva 82 55.01 N 36.41 E
Protva ≃ 82 54.51 N 37.16 E
Protville 36 36.54 N 10.01 E
Prötzel 54 52.38 N 13.59 E
Proud Lake State Recreation Area ♦ 281 42.34 N 83.33 W
Proulxville 206 46.40 N 72.30 W
Provadija 38 43.11 N 27.26 E
Provencal 194 31.39 N 93.12 W
Provence □[9] 62 44.00 N 6.00 E
Provence, Alpes de ⋏ 62 43.40 N 6.00 E
Provenchères-sur-Fave 58 48.19 N 7.05 E
Providence, Ky., U.S. 194 37.23 N 87.45 W
Providence, R.I., U.S. 207 41.49 N 71.24 W
Providence, Ut,. U.S. 200 41.42 N 111.48 W
Providence □[6] 207 41.52 N 71.36 W
Providence ≃ 207 41.43 N 71.21 W
Providence Forge 208 37.26 N 77.02 W
Providence Island I 138 9.14 S 51.02 E
Providência, Bra. 256 21.40 S 42.35 W
Providencia, Chile 286e 33.26 S 70.37 W
Providencia, Méx. 196 27.06 N 103.32 W
Providencia, Isla de I 236 13.21 N 81.22 W
Providenciales I 238 21.47 N 72.17 W
Providenija 180 64.23 N 173.18 W
Providenija, buchta ⊂ 180 64.30 N 173.20 W
Provincetown 207 42.03 N 70.10 W
Provincia, Cerro de la ∧ 286e 33.25 S 70.26 W
Provins 50 48.33 N 3.18 E
Provo 200 40.14 N 111.39 W
Provo ≃ 200 40.14 N 111.44 W
Provost 184 52.21 N 110.16 W
Provost, Lac ⊜ 206 46.22 N 74.00 W
Prozor 36 43.49 N 17.37 E
Pru ≃ 150 7.58 N 0.53 W
Prud'anka 78 50.14 N 36.09 E
Prudence Island I 207 41.37 N 71.19 W
Prudentópolis 252 25.12 S 50.57 W
Prudentov 80 49.39 N 46.19 E
Prudhoe 44 54.58 N 1.51 W
Prudhoe Bay ⊂ 180 70.20 N 148.20 W
Prudhoe Island I 166 21.19 S 149.40 E
Prudišči 82 54.24 N 38.26 E
Prudki 82 54.46 N 36.29 E
Prudnik 30 50.19 N 17.34 E
Prudy 76 53.47 N 26.32 E
Pruggern 64 47.25 N 13.52 E
Prüm 56 50.12 N 6.25 E
Prüm ≃ 56 49.49 N 6.28 E
Pruna, Punta sa ∧ 71 40.11 N 9.26 E
Prunay-le-Temple 261 48.52 N 1.40 E
Prunay-sous-Ablis 261 48.32 N 1.48 E
Prunedale 226 36.47 N 121.40 W
Prunéřov 54 50.25 N 13.16 E
Prunières 62 44.33 N 6.20 E
Prunn, Schloss ⊥ 60 48.57 N 11.44 E
Pruszków 30 52.11 N 20.48 E
Prut ≃ 78 45.30 N 28.12 E
Pruth → Prut ≃ 78 45.30 N 28.12 E
Prutting 64 47.53 N 12.11 E
Prutz 58 47.05 N 10.40 E
Pružany 76 52.33 N 24.28 E
Prydz Bay ⊂ 9 69.00 S 76.00 E
Pryor 196 36.19 N 95.19 W
Pryor Creek ≃ 202 45.54 N 108.19 W
Pryor Mountain ∧[2] 222 31.43 N 95.12 W
Prysor ≃ 42 52.56 N 4.00 W
Przasnysz 30 53.01 N 20.55 E
Przedbórz 30 51.06 N 19.53 E
Przemków 30 51.32 N 15.48 E
Przemocze 54 53.27 N 14.55 E
Przemyśl 30 49.47 N 22.47 E
Przemyśl □[4] 30 50.00 N 22.40 E
Prževal'sk 85 42.29 N 78.24 E
Prževal'sk □[4] 85 42.00 N 77.45 E
Przeworsk 30 50.05 N 22.29 E
Przewóz 54 51.29 N 14.59 E
Przybiernów 54 53.46 N 14.46 E
Przysucha 30 51.22 N 20.38 E
Pšagar 85 39.58 N 68.08 E
Psakhná 38 38.35 N 23.38 E
Psará I 38 38.35 N 25.37 E
Psárion 38 37.20 N 21.51 E
Psebaj 84 44.07 N 40.47 E
Pšecha ≃ 78 44.47 N 39.48 E
Psekups ≃ 78 45.00 N 39.09 E
Pselec 78 51.17 N 36.32 E
Psikhikón 267c 38.01 N 23.46 E
Pšiš ≃ 78 45.01 N 39.18 E
Pšiš, gora ∧ 84 43.24 N 41.12 E
Psittália I 267c 37.56 N 23.35 E
Pskem 85 41.56 N 70.22 E
Pskem ≃ 85 41.38 N 70.01 E
Pskent 85 40.54 N 69.20 E
Pskov 76 57.50 N 28.20 E
Pskovskoje ozero ⊜ 76 58.00 N 28.00 E
Pskowsee → Pskovskoje ozero ⊜ 76 58.00 N 28.00 E
Ps'ol ≃ 78 49.02 N 33.33 E
Pšov 54 50.10 N 13.29 E
Pszczyna 30 49.59 N 18.57 E
Ptarmigan, Cape › 176 71.04 N 118.07 W
Ptič' 78 52.09 N 28.52 E
Ptič' ≃ 76 52.09 N 28.52 E
Ptolemaís 38 40.31 N 21.41 E
Ptolemais ⊥ 146 32.43 N 20.57 E
Ptuj 61 46.25 N 15.52 E
Pu ≃, Zhg. 104 41.21 N 122.47 E
Pu ≃, Zhg. 107 30.25 N 103.49 E
Puah, Pulau I 112 0.30 S 122.34 E
Puakonikai 174d 0.52 S 169.36 E
Puamau, Baie ⊂ 174x 9.46 S 138.52 W
Puán, Arg. 252 37.33 S 62.43 W
Puan, Taehan 98 35.45 N 126.44 E
Pubāil 126 23.56 N 90.29 E
Pubnico 186 43.42 N 65.47 W
Pucallpa 248 8.23 S 74.32 W
Pucará 248 18.43 S 64.11 W
Pucarani 248 16.23 S 68.30 W
Puccia, Serra di ∧ 70 37.44 N 13.56 E
Puce 214 42.18 N 82.47 W
Puces ≃ 281 42.18 N 82.47 W
Pučevejem ≃ 180 68.48 N 170.30 E
Pučež 80 56.59 N 43.11 E
Puchberg am Schneeberg 61 47.47 N 15.54 E
Pucheng, Zhg. 100 27.55 N 118.31 E
Pucheng, Zhg. 102 34.59 N 109.29 E
Pucheta 252 29.54 S 57.34 W
Puchheim 60 48.09 N 11.20 E
Púchov 30 49.08 N 18.20 E
Puchoviči 76 53.32 N 28.15 E
Pucioasa 38 45.04 N 25.26 E
Pucio Point › 116 11.46 N 121.51 E
Pučišća 36 43.21 N 16.44 E
Puck 30 54.44 N 18.27 E
Puckapunyal 169 37.01 S 145.03 E
Pucketa Creek ≃ 279b 40.33 N 79.45 W
Pudahuel, Aeropuerto de ⊠ 286e 33.23 S 70.49 W
Pudding ≃ 224 45.18 N 122.43 W
Puddingstone Reservoir ⊜[1] 280 34.05 N 117.48 W
Puddington 262 53.15 N 3.00 W
Puddletown 42 50.45 N 2.21 W
Pūdeh Tal ≃ 128 31.03 N 62.15 E
Pudem 80 58.18 N 52.10 E
Pudi 102 27.58 N 99.05 E
Pudimoe 158 27.26 S 24.44 E
Puding 102 26.21 N 105.40 E
Pudino 86 57.34 N 79.24 E
Pudops Dam ◆[6] 186 48.09 N 56.50 W
Pudož 24 61.48 N 36.32 E
Pudsey 44 53.48 N 1.40 W
Pudu ≃ 102 26.19 N 102.45 E
Puduhe 102 25.39 N 102.39 E
Pudukkottai 122 10.23 N 78.49 E
Puebla □[3] 234 18.50 N 98.00 W
Puebla de Alcocer 34 38.59 N 5.15 W
Puebla de Don Fadrique 34 37.58 N 2.26 W
Puebla de Don Rodrigo 34 39.05 N 4.37 W
Puebla de Sanabria 34 42.03 N 6.38 W
Puebla de Trives 34 42.20 N 7.15 W
Puebla [de Zaragoza] 234 19.03 N 98.12 W
Pueblito de Ponce 240m 18.26 N 66.58 W
Pueblo 198 38.15 N 104.36 W
Pueblo Ledesma 252 23.50 S 64.46 W
Pueblo Libertador 252 30.13 S 59.23 W
Pueblo Libre 286d 12.05 S 77.04 W
Pueblo Mountain ∧ 202 42.06 N 118.39 W
Pueblonuevo, Col. 246 8.31 N 75.15 W
Pueblo Nuevo, Méx. 234 20.31 N 101.22 W
Pueblo Nuevo, Nic. 236 13.23 N 86.29 W
Pueblo Nuevo, P.R. 240m 18.28 N 66.51 W
Pueblo Nuevo, Ur. 258 34.26 S 56.29 W
Pueblo Nuevo, Ven. 246 11.58 N 69.55 W
Pueblo Nuevo ◆[8] 266a 40.26 N 3.39 W
Pueblo of Acoma 200 35.03 N 107.35 W
Pueblo Reservoir ⊜[1] 198 38.15 N 104.45 W
Puebloviejo, Ec. 246 1.34 S 79.30 W
Pueblo Viejo, Méx. 234 17.33 N 100.05 W
Pueblo Viejo, Méx. 234 17.24 N 93.47 W
Pueblo Viejo, Laguna de ⊂ 234 22.10 N 97.53 W
Puelches 252 38.09 S 65.55 W
Puente Alto 252 33.37 S 70.35 W
Puente de Arganda 266a 40.19 N 3.31 W
Puente de Camotlán 234 21.32 N 104.12 W
Puente de Ixtla 234 18.37 N 99.20 W
Puente-Genil 34 37.23 N 4.47 W
Puente Hills ⋏[2] 280 34.00 N 117.55 W
Puente Hills Mall ◆[9] 280 33.59 N 117.56 W
Puente la Reina 34 42.40 N 1.49 W
Puente Negro 196 27.55 N 101.01 W
Puente Nuevo, Embalse de ⊜[1] 34 38.00 N 5.00 W
Pueo Point › 229b 21.54 N 160.04 W
Pu'er 102 23.07 N 101.00 E
Puerca, Punta › 240m 18.14 N 65.36 W
Puerco ≃ 200 34.53 N 110.07 W
Puerco, Rio ≃ 200 34.22 N 106.50 W
Fu'erdu 102 28.08 N 104.24 E
Puerto Acosta 248 15.32 S 69.15 W
Puerto Adela 252 24.33 S 54.22 W
Puerto Aisén 254 45.24 S 72.42 W
Puerto Alegre 248 13.53 S 61.36 W
Puerto Alfonso 246 2.11 S 71.01 W
Puerto Ángel 234 15.40 N 96.29 W
Puerto Armuelles 236 8.17 N 82.52 W
Puerto Asís 246 0.30 N 76.31 W
Puerto Ayacucho 246 5.40 N 67.35 W
Puerto Bahía Negra 248 20.15 S 58.12 W
Puerto Baquerizo Moreno 246a 0.54 S 89.36 W
Puerto Barrios 236 15.43 N 88.36 W
Puerto Belgrano 252 38.54 S 62.06 W
Puerto Bermejo 252 26.56 S 58.30 W
Puerto Bermúdez 248 10.20 S 74.54 W
Puerto Berrío 246 6.29 N 74.24 W
Puerto Bolívar 246 3.16 S 79.59 W
Puerto Boyacá 246 5.45 N 74.39 W
Puerto Busch 248 20.02 S 57.55 W
Puerto Cabello 246 10.28 N 68.01 W
Puerto Cabezas 236 14.02 N 83.23 W
Puerto Carreño 246 6.12 N 67.22 W
Puerto Casado 252 22.20 S 57.55 W
Puerto Castilla 236 16.01 N 86.01 W
Puerto Chicama 248 7.42 S 79.27 W
Puerto Colombia 246 10.59 N 74.58 W
Puerto Constanza 258 33.50 S 59.03 W
Puerto Cortés, C.R. 236 8.58 N 83.32 W
Puerto Cortés, Hond. 236 15.48 N 87.56 W
Puerto Cumarebo 246 11.29 N 69.21 W
Puerto de Lajas, Cerro ∧ 232 28.59 N 107.02 W
Puerto Delicia 252 26.12 S 54.35 W
Puerto Delón 236 14.22 N 85.53 W
Puerto de los Ángeles y Barranca de los Negros, Parques Nacionales de ♦ 234 23.40 N 105.18 W
Puerto del Rosario 148 28.30 N 13.52 W
Puerto de San José 236 13.55 N 90.49 W
Puerto de San Juan de Dios 234 22.19 N 99.33 W
Puerto Deseado 254 47.45 S 65.54 W
Puerto El Triunfo 236 13.17 N 88.33 W
Puerto Escondido 234 15.50 N 97.10 W
Puerto Espãna → Port of Spain 241r 10.39 N 61.31 W
Puerto Esperanza 252 26.01 S 54.39 W
Puerto Felipe, Bahía → Port Phillip Bay ⊂ 169 38.07 S 144.48 E
Puerto Fonciere 252 22.29 S 57.48 W
Puerto Francisco de Orellana 246 0.28 S 76.58 W
Puerto Guaraní 248 21.18 S 57.55 W
Puerto Heath 248 12.30 S 68.40 W
Puerto Iguazú 252 25.34 S 54.34 W
Puerto Ingeniero Ibáñez 254 46.18 S 71.56 W
Puerto Inírida 246 3.53 N 67.52 W
Puerto Jiménez 236 8.33 N 83.19 W
Puerto Juárez 232 21.11 N 86.49 W
Puerto la Cruz 246 10.13 N 64.38 W
Puerto la Plata, Zona Nacional □[5] 288 34.52 S 57.52 W
Puerto Leda 248 20.41 S 58.02 W
Puerto Leguízamo 246 0.12 S 74.46 W
Puerto Lempira 236 15.13 N 83.47 W
Puerto Libertad, Arg. 252 25.55 S 54.36 W
Puerto Libertad, Méx. 232 29.55 N 112.43 W
Puerto Limón, Col. 246 3.23 N 73.30 W
Puerto Limón → Limón, C.R. 236 10.00 N 83.02 W
Puertollano 34 38.41 N 4.07 W
Puerto Lobos 254 42.00 S 65.06 W
Puerto López 246 4.05 N 72.58 W
Puerto Madero 236 14.44 N 92.25 W
Puerto Madryn 254 42.46 S 65.03 W
Puerto Maldonado 248 12.36 S 69.11 W
Puerto Manatí 240p 21.22 N 76.50 W
Puerto Mihanovich 248 20.52 S 57.59 W
Puerto Montt 254 41.28 S 72.57 W
Puerto Morazán 236 12.51 N 87.11 W
Puerto Morelos 232 20.50 N 86.52 W
Puerto Morrito 236 11.37 N 85.05 W
Puerto Nariño 246 4.56 N 67.48 W
Puerto Natales 254 51.44 S 72.31 W
Puerto Nuevo, Punta › 240m 18.30 N 66.24 W
Puerto Octay 254 40.58 S 72.54 W
Puerto Ordaz → Ciudad Guayana 246 8.22 N 62.40 W
Puerto Padre 240p 21.12 N 76.36 W
Puerto Páez 246 6.13 N 67.28 W
Puerto Palmer, Pico ∧ 196 27.08 N 101.47 W
Puerto Peñasco 232 31.20 N 113.33 W
Puerto Pilón 236 9.22 N 79.48 W
Puerto Pinasco 252 22.43 S 57.50 W
Puerto Pirámides 254 42.34 S 64.17 W
Puerto Piray 252 26.28 S 54.42 W
Puerto Píritu 246 10.04 N 65.03 W
Puerto Portillo 248 9.46 S 72.45 W
Puerto Potrero 236 10.28 N 85.47 W
Puerto Presidente Stroessner 252 25.30 S 54.36 W
Puerto Princesa, Pil. 116 9.44 N 118.44 E
Puerto Princesa, Pil. 116 10.06 N 125.29 E
Puerto Real, Esp. 34 36.32 N 6.11 W
Puerto Real, P.R. 240m 18.05 N 67.11 W
Puerto Reyes 246 0.59 S 73.17 W
Puerto Rico, Arg. 252 26.48 S 55.02 W
Puerto Rico, Bol. 248 11.05 S 67.38 W
Puerto Rico, Col. 246 1.54 N 75.10 W
Puerto Rico □[2], N.A. 230 18.15 N 66.30 W
Puerto Rico □[2], N.A. 240m 18.15 N 66.30 W
Puerto Rico, International Airport Of ⊠ 240m 18.27 N 66.00 W
Puerto Rico Trench ✦[1] 16 20.00 N 66.00 W
Puerto Rondón 246 6.17 N 71.06 W
Puerto Saavedra 252 38.47 S 73.24 W
Puerto Salgar 246 5.28 N 74.39 W
Puerto Sandino 236 12.12 N 86.46 W
Puerto Santa Cruz 254 50.01 S 68.31 W
Puerto Sastre 252 22.06 S 57.59 W
Puerto Siles 248 12.48 S 65.05 W
Puerto Suárez 248 18.57 S 57.51 W
Puerto Supe 248 10.49 S 77.45 W
Puerto Tejada 246 3.14 N 76.24 W
Puerto Toledo 246 0.59 S 74.09 W
Puerto Umbría 246 0.52 N 76.33 W
Puerto Vallarta 234 20.37 N 105.15 W
Puerto Varas 254 41.19 S 72.59 W
Puerto Victoria, Arg. 252 26.20 S 54.39 W
Puerto Victoria, Perú 248 9.54 S 74.58 W
Puerto Viejo, C.R. 236 9.39 N 82.45 W
Puerto Viejo, C.R. 236 10.26 N 83.59 W
Puerto Villamizar 246 8.19 N 72.26 W
Puerto Villaroel 248 16.50 S 64.47 W
Puerto Visser 254 45.24 S 67.08 W
Puerto Wilches 246 7.21 N 73.54 W
Puerto Ybapobó 252 23.42 S 57.12 W
Pueyrredón, Lago (Lago Cochrane) ⊜ 254 47.20 S 72.00 W
Puffendorf 56 50.56 N 6.13 E
Puffing Billy Railroad Station ◆[5] 274b 37.55 S 145.21 E
Pugačov 80 52.01 N 48.50 E
Pugač'ovo 80 56.35 N 53.02 E
Puge, Tan. 154 4.45 S 33.07 E
Puge, Zhg. 102 27.28 N 102.31 E
Puget, Cape › 180 59.52 N 148.26 W
Puget Island I 224 46.10 N 123.23 W
Puget Sound ʯ 224 47.50 N 122.30 W
Puget Sound Naval Shipyard ■ 224 47.33 N 122.38 W
Puget-sur-Argens 62 43.27 N 6.41 E
Puget-Théniers 62 43.57 N 6.54 E
Puget-Ville 62 43.17 N 6.08 E
Pugh Mountain ∧ 224 48.08 N 121.22 W
Pughtown 285 40.10 N 75.40 W
Puglia □[4] 68 41.15 N 16.15 E
Pugong-ni 271b 37.43 N 126.58 E
Pugŏ-ri 98 42.01 N 129.59 E
Pugwash 186 45.51 N 63.40 W
Puhe 104 41.57 N 123.36 E
Puhi 229b 21.58 N 159.23 W
Puhja 76 58.20 N 26.19 E
Puhos 26 62.05 N 29.54 E
Puhosjärvi ⊜ 26 65.19 N 27.55 E
Puica 248 15.04 S 72.42 W
Puiești 38 46.25 N 27.33 E
Puigcerdá 34 42.26 N 1.56 E
Puigmal ∧ 34 42.23 N 2.07 E
Puimoisson 62 43.52 N 6.08 E
Puinahua, Canal de ≃[1] 248 5.20 S 74.13 W
Puinān 272b 22.56 N 88.13 E
Puir 89 53.10 N 141.25 E
Puisaye, Collines de la ⋏[2] 50 47.40 N 3.15 E
Puiseaux 50 48.12 N 2.28 E
Puiseaux ≃ 50 48.00 N 2.44 E
Puiseux-en-France 261 49.04 N 2.29 E
Puiseux-Pontoise 261 49.03 N 2.01 E
Puisieux 50 50.07 N 2.42 E
Puits ≃ 50 48.31 N 4.15 E
Pujada Bay ⊂ 116 6.51 N 126.14 E
Pujehun 150 7.21 N 11.42 W
Puji, Zhg. 100 27.59 N 113.25 E
Puji, Zhg. 100 29.58 N 112.32 E
Pujiang, Zhg. 100 29.28 N 119.53 E
Pujiang, Zhg. 107 30.12 N 103.30 E
Pujilí 246 0.57 S 78.41 W
Pujon 115a 7.50 S 112.28 E
Pujun 112 1.20 S 114.20 E
Pujut 114 1.25 N 100.39 E
Pujut, Tanjung › 115a 5.52 S 106.02 E
Pukaki, Lake ⊜ 172 44.07 S 170.10 E
Pukalani 229a 20.50 N 156.20 W
Pukaskwa ≃ 190 48.00 N 85.53 W

Symbols in the index entries represent the broad categories identified in the key at the right. Symbols with superior numbers (⋏[1]) identify subcategories (see complete key on page *I · 1).*

Symbole im Register stellen die rechts im Schlüssel erklärten Kategorien dar. Symbole mit hochgestellten Ziffern (⋏[1]) bezeichnen Unterabteilungen einer Kategorie (vgl. vollständiger Schlüssel auf Seite *I · 1).*

Los símbolos incluídos en el texto del índice representan las grandes categorias identificadas con la clave a la derecha. Los símbolos con numeros en su parte superior (⋏[1]) identifican las subcategorías (véase la clave completa en la página *I · 1).*

Les symboles de l'index représentent les catégories indiquées dans la légende à droite. Les symboles suivis d'un indice (⋏[1]) représentent des sous-catégories (voir légende complète à la page *I · 1).*

Os símbolos incluídos no texto do índice representam as grandes categorias identificadas com a chave à direita. Os símbolos com números em sua parte superior (⋏[1]) identificam as subcategorias (veja-se a chave completa à página *I · 1).*

∧	Mountain	Berg	Montaña	Montagne	Montanha
⋏	Mountains	Gebirge	Montañas	Montagnes	Montanhas
)(	Pass	Paß	Paso	Col	Passo
∨	Valley, Canyon	Tal, Cañon	Valle, Cañón	Vallée, Canyon	Vale, Canhão
≚	Plain	Ebene	Llano	Plaine	Planície
›	Cape	Kap	Cabo	Cap	Cabo
I	Island	Insel	Isla	Île	Ilha
II	Islands	Inseln	Islas	Îles	Ilhas
⊥	Other Topographic Features	Andere Topographische Objekte	Otros Elementos Topográficos	Autres données topographiques	Outros acidentes topográficos

ESPAÑOL — Nombre | Página | Lat.°′ | Long.°′ W = Oeste
FRANÇAIS — Nom | Page | Lat.°′ | Long.°′ W = Ouest
PORTUGUÊS — Nome | Página | Lat.°′ | Long.°′ W = Oeste

Pukaskwa National
  Park ♠ 190 48.20 N 85.50 W
Pukch'ang 98 39.36 N 126.17 E
Pukchin 98 40.10 N 125.43 E
Pukch'ŏn 98 36.13 N 126.45 E
Pukch'ŏng 98 40.15 N 128.20 E
Pukë 38 42.03 N 19.54 E
Pukeashun Mountain
  ∧ 182 51.12 N 119.14 W
Pukekohe 172 37.12 S 174.55 E
Puketeraki Range ⩘ 172 42.58 S 172.12 E
Puketoi Range ⩘ 172 40.30 S 176.05 E
Pukeuri Junction 172 45.02 S 171.02 E
Pukhan-gang ≃ 98 37.31 N 127.18 E
Pūkhan-san ∧ 271b 37.41 N 127.00 E
Pukhrāyān 124 26.14 N 79.51 E
Pukoo 229d 21.04 N 156.48 W
Pukou, Zhg. 100 26.16 N 119.35 E
Pukou, Zhg. 106 32.07 N 118.43 E
Puksoozero 24 62.38 N 40.36 E
Puksubaek-san ∧ 98 40.42 N 127.44 E
Puktae-ch'ŏn ≃ 98 40.28 N 129.00 E
Pula, It. 71 39.01 N 9.00 E
Pula, Jugo. 64 44.52 N 13.50 E
Pulacayo 248 20.25 S 66.41 W
Pulandian Wan c 98 39.18 N 121.35 E
Pulanduta Point > 116 11.54 N 123.10 E
Pulangi ≃ 116 7.18 N 124.50 E
Pulangpisau 112 2.46 S 114.14 E
Pulap I[1] 14 7.35 N 149.24 E
Púlar, Cerro ∧ 252 24.11 S 68.04 W
Pulaski, In., U.S. 216 40.59 N 86.40 W
Pulaski, Mi., U.S. 216 42.07 N 84.40 W
Pulaski, N.Y., U.S. 212 43.34 N 76.07 W
Pulaski, Oh., U.S. 216 41.30 N 84.26 W
Pulaski, Pa., U.S. 214 41.07 N 80.26 W
Pulaski, Tn., U.S. 194 35.11 N 87.01 W
Pulaski, Va., U.S. 192 37.02 N 80.46 W
Pulaski, Wi., U.S. 190 44.40 N 88.14 W
Pulaski □[6] 216 41.03 N 86.36 W
Pulau ≃ 164 5.50 S 138.15 E
Pulaukida 112 2.44 S 102.34 E
Pulaukijang 112 0.42 S 103.12 E
Pulaumerak, Indon. 115a 5.56 S 106.00 E
Pulaumerak, Indon. 115a 5.56 S 106.00 E
Pulauraja 114 2.42 N 99.37 E
Puławy 30 51.25 N 21.57 E
Pulborough 42 50.58 N 0.30 W
Pul'chakim 85 38.10 N 67.21 E
Pulehu Gulch V 229a 20.50 N 156.28 W
Pulfero 64 46.11 N 13.29 E
Pulga 123 31.59 N 77.26 E
Pulgaon 122 20.44 N 78.20 E
Pulham Market 42 52.26 N 1.14 E
Pulheim 56 51.00 N 6.47 E
Puli 100 23.58 N 120.57 E
Pulicat 122 13.25 N 80.19 E
Pulicat Lake c 122 13.40 N 80.10 E
Pulichatum 128 35.57 N 61.07 E
Puliciano 66 43.23 N 11.51 E
Puliyangudi 122 9.10 N 77.25 E
Pulj
  → Pula 64 44.52 N 13.50 E
Pulkau 61 48.42 N 15.51 E
Pulkau ≃ 61 48.43 N 16.21 E
Pulkkila 26 64.16 N 25.52 E
Pulkovo ⬥[8] 265a 59.46 N 30.20 E
Pullman, Mi., U.S. 216 42.29 N 86.05 W
Pullman, Wa., U.S. 202 46.43 N 117.10 W
Pullman ⬥[8] 278 41.43 N 87.36 W
Pullo 248 15.14 S 73.50 W
Pully 58 46.31 N 6.39 E
Pul'mo 78 51.31 N 23.47 E
Pulo ⊥ 68 41.12 N 16.34 E
Pulo Anna I 108 4.40 N 131.58 E
Pulog, Mount ∧ 116 16.36 N 120.54 E
Pulogadung ⬥[8] 269e 6.11 S 106.54 E
Pulon'ga 24 66.17 N 40.02 E
Púlpito do Sul 152 15.46 S 12.00 E
Pulsano 68 40.23 N 17.22 E
Pulsen 54 51.23 N 13.26 E
Pulsnitz 54 51.11 N 14.01 E
Pulsnitz ≃ 54 51.27 N 13.30 E
Pulteney 210 42.31 N 77.10 W
Pulteneyville 210 43.17 N 77.11 W
Pułtusk 30 52.43 N 21.05 E
Pulü, Zhg. 107 29.50 N 106.11 E
Pulu, Zhg. 120 36.11 N 81.30 E
Pulupandan 116 10.31 N 122.48 E
Pulur 130 40.10 N 39.53 E
Pulusuk I 14 6.42 N 149.19 E
Pulversheim 58 47.51 N 7.18 E
Puma Yumco ◎ 124 28.35 N 90.20 E
Pumbi 152 3.26 N 22.11 E
Pumei 102 23.28 N 105.15 E
Pumphrey 284b 39.13 N 76.38 W
Pumpkin Buttes ∧ 200 43.44 N 105.54 W
Pumpkin Center 228 35.18 N 119.05 W
Pumpkin Creek ≃,
  Mt., U.S. 198 46.15 N 105.45 W
Pumpkin Creek ≃,
  Ne., U.S. 198 41.38 N 103.01 W
Pumsaint 42 52.03 N 3.58 W
Pumsi 80 57.12 N 51.39 E
Puna 248 19.46 S 65.28 W
Puná, Isla I 246 2.50 S 80.08 W
Punaauia 174s 17.38 S 149.36 W
Punaauia, Pointe de > 174s 17.38 S 149.36 W
Punakha 124 27.37 N 89.52 E
Punaluu 229c 21.35 N 157.53 W
Punan, Indon. 112 1.20 N 115.34 E
Punan, Indon. 112 3.24 N 116.16 E
Punan, Zhg. 100 24.39 N 117.41 E
Punata 248 17.32 S 65.50 W
Pūnch 123 33.46 N 74.06 E
Pūnch ≃ 123 33.12 N 73.40 E
Puncha 126 23.10 N 86.39 E
Punchaw 182 53.28 N 123.13 W
Punchbowl 274a 33.56 S 151.03 E
Pundaguitan 116 6.22 N 126.10 E
Punda Maria 156 22.40 S 31.05 E
Pünderich 56 50.02 N 7.08 E
Pūndri 124 29.45 N 76.33 E
Punduga 76 60.08 N 40.12 E
Pune (Poona) 122 18.32 N 73.52 E
P'ungam-ni 98 37.43 N 128.11 E
Pungan 85 40.45 N 70.49 E
Punganūru 122 13.22 N 78.35 E
Pungeşti 38 46.42 N 27.20 E
Punggol 271c 1.25 N 103.55 E
Punggol ≃ 271c 1.25 N 103.54 E
Pungki 114 4.17 N 96.13 E
Pungo ≃ 192 35.23 N 76.33 W
Pungo Andongo 152 9.40 S 15.35 E
Púngoè ≃ 154 19.50 S 34.48 E
P'ungsan, C.M.I.K. 98 38.28 N 125.01 E
P'ungsan, C.M.I.K. 98 40.47 N 128.10 E
P'ungsong-ni 98 39.56 N 127.11 E
Punia 154 1.28 S 26.27 E
Punilla, Sierra de la ⩘ 252 28.55 S 69.00 W
Puning 100 23.18 N 116.12 E
Punitaqui 252 30.50 S 71.16 W
Punjab □[3] 123 31.00 N 75.30 E
Punjab □[4] 120 31.00 N 72.00 E
Punkaharju ♠ 26 61.47 N 29.20 E
Punkalaidun 26 61.07 N 23.06 E
Punnichy 184 51.23 N 104.18 W
Puno 248 15.50 S 70.02 W
Puno □[5] 248 15.00 S 70.00 W
Punta, Castillo de la
  ⊥ 286b 23.09 N 82.21 W
Punta, Cerro de ∧ 240m 18.10 N 66.36 W
Punta Alegre 240p 22.23 N 78.49 W
Punta Alta 254 38.53 S 62.05 W
Punta Arenas 254 53.09 S 70.55 W
Punta Banda, Cabo > 232 31.45 N 116.45 W
Punta Brava ⬥[8] 286b 23.01 N 82.30 W
Punta Cardón 246 11.38 N 70.14 W

Punta de Agua Creek
  (Tramperos Creek)
  ≃ 196 35.32 N 102.27 W
Punta de Bombón 248 17.11 S 71.48 W
Punta de Díaz 252 28.03 S 70.37 W
Punta del Cobre 252 27.30 S 70.16 W
Punta del Este 252 34.58 S 54.57 W
Punta Delgada 254 42.46 S 63.38 W
Punta de los Llanos 252 30.09 S 66.33 W
Punta de Mata 246 9.43 N 63.38 W
Punta Flecha 116 7.23 N 123.25 E
Punta Gorda, Belize 232 16.07 N 88.48 W
Punta Gorda, Fl.,
  U.S. 220 26.55 N 82.02 W
Punta Gorda ≃ 236 11.30 N 83.47 W
Punta Gorda, Bahía
  de c 236 11.15 N 83.45 W
Punta Indio, Canal ≅ 258 34.36 S 58.16 W
Punta Moreno 248 7.36 S 78.54 W
Punta Negra, Salar
  de ≚ 252 24.35 S 69.00 W
Punta Piedras 246 10.54 N 64.06 W
Punta Porá 252 25.13 S 58.31 W
Punta Prieta 232 28.58 N 114.17 W
Punta Raisi,
  Aeroporto di ⊠ 70 38.11 N 13.06 E
Puntarenas 236 9.58 N 84.50 W
Puntarenas □[4] 236 9.00 N 83.15 W
Punta Santiago 240m 18.10 N 65.45 W
Puntas del Sauce 258 33.51 S 57.01 W
Punto Fijo 246 11.42 N 70.13 W
Puntzi Lake ◎ 182 52.12 N 124.02 W
Punung 115a 8.08 S 111.01 E
Punxsutawney 214 40.56 N 78.58 W
Puolanka 26 64.52 N 27.40 E
Puolo Point > 229b 21.54 N 159.36 W
Puper 164 0.10 S 131.18 E
Pup'yŏng 271b 37.30 N 126.43 E
Puqi, Zhg. 100 28.11 N 121.01 E
Puqi, Zhg. 100 29.43 N 113.53 E
Puqian, Zhg. 100 23.34 N 114.38 E
Puqian, Zhg. 102 20.03 N 110.36 E
Puquio 248 14.42 S 74.08 W
Pur ≃ 74 67.31 N 77.55 E
Purabiya Plain ≚ 124 25.50 N 82.30 E
Puracé, Volcán ∧[1] 246 2.21 N 76.23 W
Purandarpur 126 23.51 N 87.36 E
Pūranpur 124 28.31 N 80.09 E
Purari ≃ 164 7.25 S 145.05 E
Purba 114 2.54 N 98.42 E
Purbashthāli 126 23.28 N 88.21 E
Purbeck, Isle of I 42 50.38 N 2.00 W
Purbolinggo 115a 7.24 S 109.22 E
Purcell 196 35.00 N 97.21 W
Purcell Mountains ⩘ 182 50.00 N 116.30 W
Purcellville 188 39.08 N 77.42 W
Purchase 276 41.02 N 73.43 W
Purchena 34 37.21 N 2.22 W
Purdon 222 31.57 N 96.37 W
Purdoški 80 54.40 N 43.32 E
Purdy 194 36.49 N 93.55 W
Purech 80 56.39 N 43.05 E
Pureora ∧ 172 38.33 S 175.38 E
Purépero 234 19.55 N 102.01 W
Purfleet 42 51.29 N 0.15 E
Purga 171a 27.43 S 152.44 E
Purga Creek ≃ 171a 27.42 S 152.45 E
Purgatoire ≃ 198 38.04 N 103.10 W
Purgatory Brook ≃ 283 42.11 N 71.11 W
Purgg 61 47.32 N 14.04 E
Purgstall an der
  Erlauf 61 48.03 N 15.08 E
Puri 120 19.48 N 85.51 E
Purial, Sierra del ⩘ 240p 20.12 N 74.42 W
Purificación, Col. 246 3.51 N 74.55 W
Purificación, Méx. 234 19.43 N 104.38 W
Purificación ≃, Méx. 232 23.58 N 98.42 W
Purificación ≃, Méx. 234 19.18 N 104.54 W
Purikari neem > 76 59.40 N 25.43 E
Purísima, Méx. 196 29.09 N 100.46 W
Purísima, Méx. 232 25.25 N 105.26 W
Purísima, Sierra de la
  ⩘ 196 26.30 N 101.44 W
Purisima Creek ≃ 282 37.24 N 122.26 W
Purísima de Bustos 234 21.02 N 101.52 W
Purkersdorf 264b 48.12 N 16.11 E
Purleigh 260 51.41 N 0.40 E
Purley 222 33.05 N 95.16 W
Purley ⬥[8] 260 51.20 N 0.07 W
Purling 210 42.17 N 74.00 W
Purmerend 52 52.31 N 4.57 E
Pūrna ≃, India 122 19.07 N 77.02 E
Pūrna ≃, India 122 21.05 N 76.00 E
Pūrnia 124 25.47 N 87.31 E
Puronga 76 60.09 N 40.54 E
Purranque 254 40.55 S 73.10 W
Purrorumba Hill ∧ 171b 35.10 S 149.23 E
Purros 156 18.38 S 12.59 E
Purrumbete, Lake ◎ 169 38.17 S 143.14 E
Pursat
  → Poŭthĭsăt 110 12.32 N 103.55 E
Purton 42 51.36 N 1.52 W
Puruándiro 234 20.05 N 101.30 W
Puruarán 234 19.06 N 101.32 W
Puruchuca 286d 12.04 S 76.57 W
Puruê ≃ 246 1.40 S 68.08 W
Purukcahu 112 0.35 S 114.35 E
Puruliya 126 23.20 N 86.22 E
Puruni ≃ 246 6.00 N 59.12 W
Purus (Purús) ≃ 242 3.42 S 61.28 W
Puruvesi ◎ 26 61.50 N 29.27 E
Purvis 194 31.08 N 89.24 W
Purwakarta 115a 6.34 S 107.26 E
Purwantoro 115a 7.51 S 111.15 E
Purwareja 115a 7.28 S 109.25 E
Purwodadi, Indon. 115a 7.49 S 110.00 E
Purwodadi, Indon. 115a 7.05 S 110.54 E
Purwokerto 115a 7.25 S 109.14 E
Purworejo 115a 7.43 S 110.01 E
Pusa 112 1.36 N 111.17 E
Pusad 122 19.54 N 77.35 E
Pusan 98 35.06 N 129.03 E
Pusan □[4] 98 35.10 N 129.05 E
Pūsa Road 124 25.59 N 85.41 E
Pusat Gayo,
  Pegunungan ⩘ 114 4.15 N 97.05 E
Puščino 82 54.50 N 37.36 E
Pusgo Point > 116 13.31 N 122.38 E
Pushang 98 36.08 N 119.42 E
Pushkar 120 26.30 N 74.33 E
Pushkin
  → Puškin 76 59.43 N 30.25 E
Pushkin Airport ⊠ 265a 59.41 N 30.21 E
Pushkin Drama
  Theatre ⊍ 265a 59.56 N 30.21 E
Pushthrough 186 47.39 N 56.10 W
Puškar'ovka 78 48.40 N 34.16 E
Puskiakiwenin Indian
  Reserve ⬥[4] 184 53.57 N 110.26 W
Puškin 76 59.43 N 30.25 E
Puškino, S.S.S.R. 80 51.14 N 46.59 E
Puškino, S.S.S.R. 82 56.36 N 35.46 E
Puškino, S.S.S.R. 82 56.01 N 37.51 E
Puškino, S.S.S.R. 84 39.27 N 48.33 E
Puškinskij 265a 59.43 N 30.18 E
Puškinskije Gory 76 57.01 N 28.54 E
Puskwaskau ≃ 182 55.29 N 118.10 W
Puslinch Lake ◎ 212 43.25 N 80.16 W
Pusŏng-ni 98 40.19 N 127.19 E
Püspökladány 30 47.19 N 21.07 E
Pussay 50 48.21 N 2.00 E
Püssi 76 59.24 N 27.01 E
Puster-Tal V 64 46.45 N 12.20 E
Pustin' 76 59.54 N 35.32 E
Pustomyty 78 49.42 N 23.56 E
Pustoš' 76 60.07 N 42.45 E
Pustoška 76 56.20 N 29.22 E
Pustozersk 24 67.33 N 52.27 E
Pusur ≃[1] 126 21.45 N 89.30 E
Puszczykowo 30 52.17 N 16.52 E

Putaendo 252 32.38 S 70.44 W
Putah Creek ≃ 226 38.33 N 121.42 W
Putai 100 23.23 N 120.09 E
Putang ≃ 269e 6.13 S 106.54 E
Putangqiao 106 31.34 N 118.59 E
Putao 102 27.21 N 97.24 E
Putaruru 172 38.03 S 175.47 E
Put'atin 89 42.52 N 132.25 E
Put'atino 80 54.10 N 41.07 E
Putbus 54 54.21 N 13.28 E
Puteaux 261 48.53 N 2.14 E
Puteran, Pulau I 115a 7.05 S 114.00 E
Putfontein
  Landbouhoewes 273d 26.08 S 28.24 E
Putgarten 54 54.40 N 13.25 E
Puth Kalān ⬥[8] 272a 28.43 N 77.05 E
Putian, Zhg. 100 29.16 N 114.58 E
Putian, Zhg. 100 25.26 N 119.01 E
Putifigari 71 40.34 N 8.27 E
Putignano 68 40.51 N 17.07 E
Putila 78 48.01 N 25.03 E
Putilkovo 265b 55.52 N 37.23 E
Putina 248 14.55 S 69.52 W
Put-in-Bay 214 41.39 N 82.49 W
Putincevo 86 49.50 N 84.22 E
Puting, Tanjung > 112 3.31 S 111.46 E
Putivl' 78 51.21 N 33.52 E
Putla de Guerrero 234 17.02 N 97.56 W
Putlitz 54 53.15 N 12.02 E
Putnam, Ct., U.S. 207 41.54 N 71.54 W
Putnam, Tx., U.S. 196 32.22 N 99.12 W
Putnam □[6], N.Y.,
  U.S. 210 41.26 N 73.41 W
Putnam □[6], Oh., U.S. 216 41.01 N 84.03 W
Putnam Lake 210 41.28 N 73.35 W
Putnam Lake ◎ 276 41.05 N 73.38 W
Putnam Valley 210 41.20 N 73.52 W
Putnamville Reservoir
  ◎[1] 283 42.36 N 70.57 W
Putney, Ga., U.S. 192 31.29 N 84.07 W
Putney, Vt., U.S. 188 42.58 N 72.31 W
Putney ⬥[8] 260 51.28 N 0.13 W
Putney Island I 126 21.42 N 89.20 E
Puto 175e 5.41 S 154.43 E
Putorana, plato ⩘[1] 74 69.00 N 95.00 E
Putorino 172 39.08 S 177.00 E
Putre 248 18.12 S 69.35 W
Putri Narrows ʯ 271c 1.27 N 103.42 E
Putsonderwater 158 29.09 S 21.51 E
Pütt 263 51.11 N 6.59 E
Puttalam 122 8.02 N 79.49 E
Puttalam Lagoon c 122 8.07 N 79.47 E
Putte, Bel. 56 51.04 N 4.38 E
Putte, Ned. 52 51.22 N 4.23 E
Puttelange-lès-
  Farschviller 56 49.03 N 6.56 E
Putten 52 52.15 N 5.36 E
Putten I 52 51.50 N 4.15 E
Puttgarden 41 54.30 N 11.13 E
Püttlingen 56 49.17 N 6.53 E
Puttūr 122 13.27 N 79.33 E
Putty 170 32.57 S 150.40 E
Putty Creek ≃ 170 33.05 S 150.37 E
Putú 252 35.13 S 72.17 W
Putumayo □[8] 246 0.30 N 76.00 W
Putumayo (Içá) ≃ 246 3.07 S 67.58 W
Putuo 100 29.58 N 122.17 E
Putu Range ⩘ 150 5.30 N 8.10 W
Pütürge 130 38.12 N 38.53 E
Putussibau 112 0.50 N 112.56 E
Putzkau 54 51.06 N 14.13 E
Putzu Idu 71 40.02 N 8.25 E
Pu'uhonua o
  Honaunau National
  Historical Park ♠ 229d 19.25 N 155.54 W
Puu Kaaumakua ∧ 229c 21.30 N 157.54 W
Puu Keahiakahoe ∧ 229c 21.23 N 157.49 W
Puukohola National
  Historic Site ⊥ 229d 20.00 N 155.46 W
Puukolii 229a 20.56 N 156.40 W
Puu Kukui ∧ 229a 20.52 N 156.35 W
Puula ◎ 26 61.50 N 26.42 E
Puumala 26 61.32 N 28.11 E
Puunene 229a 20.51 N 156.27 W
Pu'upu'a 175a 13.34 S 172.09 W
Puurmani 76 58.34 N 26.17 E
Puurs 50 51.05 N 4.17 E
Puuwai 229b 21.54 N 160.12 W
Puxcatán ≃ 234 17.37 N 92.34 W
Puxi 100 25.10 N 119.08 E
Puxian 102 36.30 N 111.02 E
Puxico 194 36.56 N 90.09 W
Puxingchang 107 30.41 N 105.06 E
Puxmetacán ≃ 234 17.22 N 95.36 W
Puyallup 224 47.11 N 122.17 W
Puyallup ≃ 224 47.15 N 122.24 W
Puyang 98 35.42 N 114.59 E
Puyang ≃ 100 30.05 N 120.11 E
Puyango (Tumbes) ≃ 246 3.30 S 80.27 W
Puy-de-Dôme □[5] 32 45.45 N 3.05 E
Puyehue 254 40.40 S 72.37 W
Puyehue, Volcán ∧[1] 254 40.35 S 72.08 W
Puylaurens 32 43.34 N 2.01 E
Puy-l'Évêque 32 44.30 N 1.08 E
Puyloubier 62 43.31 N 5.41 E
Puymorens, Col de)(32 42.30 N 1.50 E
Puyo, Ec. 246 1.28 S 77.59 W
Puyŏ, Taehan 98 36.18 N 126.54 E
Puysegur Point > 172 46.09 S 166.36 E
Puyuan 106 30.41 N 120.38 E
Puyuguapi, Canal ʯ 254 44.45 S 72.48 W
Puyun-dong 98 41.55 N 129.30 E
Pūzak, Hāmūn-e ◎ 128 31.30 N 61.45 E
Puzhen 106 32.09 N 118.41 E
Puzzle Creek ≃ 162 17.58 S 135.41 E
Puzzle Lake ◎, On.,
  Can. 212 44.36 N 76.58 W
Puzzle Lake ◎, Fl.,
  U.S. 220 28.41 N 81.02 W
Pwalagu 150 10.35 N 0.50 W
Pwani □[4] 154 7.00 S 39.00 E
Pweto 154 8.28 S 28.54 E
Pwinbyu 110 20.22 N 94.40 E
Pwllheli 42 52.53 N 4.25 W
Pyalo 110 19.09 N 95.11 E
Pyalong 169 37.07 S 144.54 E
Pyamalaw ≃[1] 110 15.49 N 94.42 E
Pyapon 110 16.17 N 95.41 E
Pyatigorsk
  → P'atigorsk 84 44.03 N 43.04 E
Pyawbwe 110 20.35 N 96.04 E
Pyaye 110 19.15 N 95.06 E
Pyčas 80 56.29 N 52.28 E
Pye Islands II 180 59.22 N 150.25 W
Pygmalion Point > 110 6.45 N 93.49 E
Pyhäjärvi ◎, Suomi 26 61.00 N 22.18 E
Pyhäjärvi ◎, Suomi 26 61.53 N 30.00 E
Pyhäjärvi ◎, Suomi 26 62.46 N 25.30 E
Pyhäjärvi ◎, Suomi 26 61.28 N 23.35 E
Pyhäjärvi ◎, Suomi 26 63.35 N 25.57 E
Pyhäjoki 26 64.28 N 24.14 E
Pyhäjoki ≃ 26 64.28 N 24.13 E
Pyhämaa I 26 60.57 N 21.20 E
Pyhän-Häkin
  kansallispuisto ♠ 26 62.52 N 25.30 E
Pyhäsalmi 26 63.41 N 25.59 E
Pyhäselkä 26 62.26 N 29.58 E
Pyhäselkä ◎ 26 62.26 N 29.58 E
Pyhätunturi ∧ 24 67.01 N 27.09 E
Pyhätunturin
  Kansallispuisto ♠ 24 67.01 N 27.10 E
Pyhra 61 48.10 N 15.41 E
Pyhtää (Pyttis) 26 60.29 N 26.32 E
Pyinbongyi 110 17.34 N 96.34 E
Pyingaing 110 23.09 N 94.51 E
Pyinkayaing 110 15.58 N 94.24 E
Pyinmana 110 19.44 N 96.13 E
Pyle 42 51.32 N 3.42 W
Pylos
  → Pílos 38 36.55 N 21.43 E

Pymatuning Creek ≃ 214 41.18 N 80.27 W
Pymatuning
  Reservoir ◎[1] 214 41.37 N 80.30 W
Pymatuning State
  Park ♠, Oh., U.S. 214 41.38 N 80.33 W
Pymatuning State
  Park ♠, Pa., U.S. 214 41.30 N 80.27 W
Pymble 274a 33.45 S 151.09 E
Pyngopil'gyn, laguna
  c 180 67.24 N 175.10 W
Pyŏktong 98 40.35 N 125.20 E
Pyŏlch'ang-ni 98 39.17 N 126.26 E
P'yŏngan Namdo □[4] 98 39.20 N 126.00 E
P'yŏngan Pukdo □[4] 98 40.10 N 125.20 E
P'yŏngch'ang 98 37.23 N 128.22 E
P'yŏngdong-ni 98 37.10 N 128.02 E
P'yŏnggang 98 38.26 N 127.16 E
P'yonghae 98 36.46 N 129.28 E
P'yŏngsan 98 38.19 N 126.23 E
P'yŏngt'aek 98 37.00 N 127.05 E
P'yŏngyang 98 39.01 N 125.45 E
P'yŏngyang □[4] 98 39.05 N 125.50 E
Pyŏrha-ri 98 40.48 N 126.32 E
Pyote 196 31.32 N 103.08 W
Pyramid Head > 228 32.49 N 118.21 W
Pyramid Lake ◎ 204 40.00 N 119.35 W
Pyramid Lake ◎[1] 228 34.39 N 118.47 W
Pyramid Lake Indian
  Reservation ⬥[4] 204 40.20 N 119.35 W
Pyramid Peak ∧, Ca.,
  U.S. 226 38.50 N 120.19 W
Pyramid Peak ∧,
  Wa., U.S. 224 47.07 N 121.24 W
Pyramid Peak ∧,
  Wy., U.S. 200 43.27 N 110.28 W
Pyramid Point > 174h 2.52 S 171.37 W
Pyramids of Giza
  → Jīzah, Ahrāmāt
  al- ⊥ 142 29.59 N 31.08 E
Pyrenäen
  → Pyrenees ⩘ 34 42.40 N 1.00 E
Pyrenees ⩘ 34 42.40 N 1.00 E
Pyrénées-Atlantiques
  □[5] 32 43.15 N 0.50 W
Pyrénées Occident,
  Parc National des ♠ 32 42.48 N 0.08 W
Pyrénées-Orientales
  □[5] 32 42.30 N 2.20 E
Pyre Peak ∧ 180 52.20 N 172.31 W
Pyrford 260 51.19 N 0.30 W
Pyrgi ⊥ 66 42.01 N 11.58 E
Pyrgos
  → Pírgos 38 37.41 N 21.28 E
Pyritz
  → Pyrzyce 30 53.10 N 14.55 E
Pyrkanajjan, gora ∧ 180 69.14 N 175.50 E
Pyrkino 80 53.29 N 45.07 E
Pyrmont 216 40.28 N 86.41 W
Pyrzyce 30 53.10 N 14.55 E
Pyšma 86 56.56 N 63.13 E
Pyšma ≃ 86 57.08 N 66.18 E
Pytalovo 76 57.04 N 27.56 E
Pythonga, Lac ◎ 190 46.23 N 76.25 W
Pyu 110 18.29 N 96.26 E
Pyuntaza 110 17.52 N 96.44 E
Pyūthān 124 28.06 N 82.54 E
Pyvèsa ≃ 76 56.06 N 24.27 E
Pyzdry 30 52.11 N 17.41 E

Q

Qabāṭīyah 132 32.25 N 35.17 E
Qabbāsīn 130 36.25 N 37.34 E
Qabb Ilyās 132 33.48 N 35.49 E
Qabr Hūd 144 16.08 N 49.37 E
Qacentina
  (Constantine) 148 36.22 N 6.37 E
Qacentina □[5] 148 36.20 N 6.40 E
Qaddīs Anṭūn, Dayr
  al- (Monastery of
  Saint Anthony) ⊍[1] 142 28.55 N 32.21 E
Qaddīs Būlus, Dayr
  al- (Monastery of
  Saint Paul) ⊍[1] 142 28.52 N 32.33 E
Qāderābād 128 30.17 N 53.16 E
Qādiān 123 31.49 N 75.23 E
Qā'emshahr 128 36.28 N 52.53 E
Qā'en 128 33.44 N 59.11 E
Qāfilah 142 31.04 N 30.16 E
Qagan 88 49.14 N 118.08 E
Qagan Nur ◎, Zhg. 98 41.23 N 113.55 E
Qagan Nur ◎, Zhg. 102 43.37 N 114.40 E
Qahā 142 30.17 N 31.12 E
Qahar Youyi Zhongqi 102 41.09 N 112.38 E
Qahbûna 142 30.48 N 31.54 E
Qaidam ≃ 102 36.39 N 96.20 E
Qaidam Pendi ≚[1] 120 37.00 N 95.00 E
Qakar 120 36.32 N 80.43 E
Qala' an-Naḥl 140 13.38 N 34.57 E
Qalabshū 142 31.26 N 31.19 E
Qalamshāh 142 29.10 N 30.50 E
Qalandīyah 132 31.50 N 35.14 E
Qalandūl 142 27.49 N 30.50 E
Qalāt 120 32.07 N 66.54 E
Qal'At ash-Shaqīf
  (Beaufort Castle) ⊥ 132 33.19 N 35.32 E
Qal'at Bīshah 144 20.01 N 42.36 E
Qal'at Ṣāliḥ 128 31.31 N 47.16 E
Qal'at Sukkar 128 31.51 N 46.05 E
Qal'eh Shahr 120 35.33 N 65.34 E
Qal'eh-ye Deh-e
  Bārez 128 27.26 N 57.12 E
Qal'eh-ye Now, Afg. 120 35.27 N 67.08 E
Qal'eh-ye Now, Afg. 128 34.59 N 63.08 E
Qal'eh-ye Panjeh 123 37.00 N 72.36 E
Qal'eh-ye Sarkārī 120 35.54 N 67.17 E
Qallābāt, Sūd. 140 12.43 N 23.26 E
Qallābāt, Sūd. 140 12.58 N 36.09 E
Qallīn 142 31.03 N 30.51 E
Qalqīlīya 132 32.11 N 34.58 E
Qalyūb 142 30.11 N 31.12 E
Qamar, Ghubbat al-
  c 118 16.00 N 52.30 E
Qamata 158 32.00 S 27.21 E
Qamdo 102 31.11 N 97.15 E
Qamīnis 146 31.39 N 20.03 E
Qamr-ud-dīn Kārez 120 31.39 N 68.25 E
Qamṣar 128 33.45 N 51.26 E
Qanā, Ar. Su. 128 27.47 N 41.25 E
Qānā, Lubnān 132 33.13 N 35.18 E
Qanāyah 132 33.01 N 36.11 E
Qandahār 120 31.32 N 65.30 E
Qandahār □[4] 120 31.00 N 65.45 E
Qandala 144 11.28 N 49.52 E
Qanṭarah, Jabal ∧[2] 142 30.09 N 30.15 E
Qantur 140 9.45 N 25.52 E
Qārah, Ar. Su. 128 29.52 N 40.15 E
Qārah, Sūrīy. 130 34.09 N 36.44 E
Qarah Bāgh 128 34.56 N 61.46 E
Qarak 85 38.23 N 76.58 E
Qarāvol 120 37.14 N 68.46 E
Qardho 144 9.30 N 49.05 E
Qareh ≃ 128 34.52 N 51.25 E
Qareh Sū ≃ 128 39.27 N 47.23 E
Qareh Ẕīā' od Dīn 84 38.54 N 45.02 E
Qarqan ≃ 90 39.25 N 88.20 E
Qarqīn 120 37.25 N 66.03 E
Qarṭabā 130 34.06 N 35.51 E
Qārūn, Birkat (Lake
  Moeris) ◎ 142 29.28 N 30.40 E
Qaryat al-Qaddāḥīyah 146 31.22 N 15.14 E
Qaryat al-Zuwaytīnah 146 30.58 N 20.07 E
Qaṣa-e Qand 128 26.12 N 60.45 E
Qāsh, Nahr al- (Gash)
  ≃ 140 16.48 N 35.51 E
Qashqeh, Kūh-e ∧ 128 28.23 N 55.18 E
Qāsim 132 32.59 N 36.05 E
Qāsimwāla 123 30.09 N 73.50 E

Qaṣr ad-Dayr, Jabal
  ∧ 132 30.48 N 35.34 E
Qaṣr al-Azraq ⊥ 132 31.53 N 36.49 E
Qasr al-Dubārā
  (Garden City) ⬥[8] 273c 30.02 N 31.14 E
Qaṣr al-Farāfirah 140 27.03 N 27.58 E
Qaṣr al-Jibālī 142 29.20 N 30.38 E
Qaṣr al-Kharānah ⊥ 132 31.44 N 36.28 E
Qaṣr al-Mushāsh ⊥ 132 31.49 N 36.19 E
Qaṣr al-Mushattā ⊥ 132 31.44 N 36.01 E
Qaṣr al Qarābūllī 146 32.45 N 13.43 E
Qaṣr 'Amrah ⊥ 132 31.48 N 36.35 E
Qaṣr aṭ-Ṭūbah ⊥ 132 31.20 N 36.34 E
Qaṣr Baghdād 142 30.44 N 30.53 E
Qaṣr Bū-Hādī 146 31.03 N 16.40 E
Qaṣr Ḍab'ah ⊥ 132 31.36 N 36.03 E
Qaṣr-e Fīrūzeh 267d 35.40 N 51.32 E
Qasr el-Boukhari 148 35.51 N 2.52 E
Qaṣr-e Shīrīn 128 34.31 N 45.35 E
Qaṣr Qārūn 142 29.25 N 30.25 E
Qa'ṭabah 144 13.51 N 44.42 E
Qaṭanā 132 33.26 N 36.05 E
Qatar (Qaṭar) □[1],
  Asia 118 25.00 N 51.10 E
Qatar (Qaṭar) □[1],
  Asia 128 25.00 N 51.10 E
Qaṭia, Bi'r ⍑[4] 142 30.58 N 32.45 E
Qaṭmah 130 36.36 N 36.57 E
Qaṭrānī, Jabal ∧[2] 142 29.41 N 30.35 E
Qattāntyah, Ghurd al-
  ⊻[8] 142 29.50 N 30.17 E
Qattara Depression
  → Qaṭṭārah,
  Munkhafaḍ al- ⊻[7] 140 30.00 N 27.30 E
Qaṭṭārah, Munkhafaḍ
  al- (Qattara
  Depression) ⊻[7] 140 30.00 N 27.30 E
Qaṭṭīnah, Buḥayrat
  ◎[1] 130 34.39 N 36.34 E
Qawz Rajab 140 16.04 N 35.34 E
Qāy 142 29.09 N 30.57 E
Qayṭah 132 33.04 N 36.08 E
Qāzigund 123 33.38 N 75.09 E
Qazvīn 128 36.16 N 50.00 E
Qeh 102 42.18 N 100.59 E
Qena
  → Qinā 140 26.10 N 32.43 E
Qeqertaq I 176 71.55 N 55.30 W
Qesari, Ḥorbat
  (Cæsarea) ⊥ 132 32.30 N 34.53 E
Qeshm 128 26.58 N 56.16 E
Qeshm, Jazīreh-ye I 128 26.45 N 55.45 E
Qetura 132 29.58 N 35.03 E
Qeydār 128 36.07 N 48.35 E
Qeyṣār 120 35.41 N 64.17 E
Qezel Owzan ≃ 128 36.45 N 49.22 E
Qezel Qeshlāq 84 39.08 N 45.21 E
Qi ≃, Zhg. 98 35.30 N 114.17 E
Qi ≃, Zhg. 100 30.09 N 115.20 E
Qi ≃, Zhg. 107 30.38 N 105.26 E
Qi ≃, Zhg. 107 29.15 N 106.24 E
Qiakemake 85 40.05 N 75.24 E
Qian ≃ 102 23.25 N 110.10 E
Qian'an, Zhg. 89 45.00 N 124.01 E
Qian'an, Zhg. 98 39.59 N 118.40 E
Qiancaijiatun 104 41.14 N 121.38 E
Qiandiwu 105 39.16 N 116.38 E
Qiandong 100 23.41 N 116.55 E
Qiandun 106 31.16 N 121.00 E
Qianertaizi 104 42.04 N 122.42 E
Qianfang 100 28.32 N 116.13 E
Qian Gorlos 89 45.08 N 124.47 E
Qiangzilu 105 40.26 N 117.13 E
Qianhonghepu 104 41.23 N 123.07 E
Qianhuang 106 31.36 N 119.58 E
Qianji 100 33.55 N 118.56 E
Qianjiadian 89 43.42 N 122.35 E
Qianjiang, Zhg. 100 30.25 N 112.51 E
Qianjiang, Zhg. 102 23.37 N 109.00 E
Qianjian'gangzi 104 41.34 N 122.26 E
Qianjiangtai 104 41.46 N 122.03 E
Qianjiaqiao 106 30.53 N 121.31 E
Qianjiaying 105 39.35 N 118.21 E
Qianjiazhuang 106 32.16 N 120.17 E
Qianjing 106 31.33 N 121.15 E
Qianjinmiao 100 25.09 N 118.20 E
Qiankeng 106 30.43 N 119.47 E
Qiankoutou 105 39.42 N 117.01 E
Qianlijiazhuang 105 39.25 N 118.17 E
Qianluanshanzi 104 42.17 N 122.27 E
Qianmajiagushanzi 104 42.23 N 123.33 E
Qianmintun 104 41.49 N 123.15 E
Qianning 102 30.30 N 101.31 E
Qianpai 102 22.22 N 111.11 E
Qianqi 100 27.20 N 120.20 E
Qianqianjianglugou 104 41.59 N 120.58 E
Qiansandaoliangzi 104 42.06 N 120.44 E
Qianshahezi 104 41.46 N 123.01 E
Qianshan, Zhg. 100 30.38 N 116.33 E
Qianshan, Zhg. 100 22.16 N 113.33 E
Qianshan, Zhg. 106 31.06 N 120.24 E
Qian Shan ⩘ 104 40.52 N 123.25 E
Qianshuangshanzi 104 41.22 N 121.13 E
Qiansuo 100 28.44 N 121.27 E
Qiantang ≃ 106 30.23 N 120.33 E
Qiantangzhen 107 30.12 N 106.18 E
Qianwei, Zhg. 98 40.12 N 120.06 E
Qianwei, Zhg. 107 29.12 N 103.57 E
Qianxi, Zhg. 102 26.57 N 106.00 E
Qianxi, Zhg. 105 40.09 N 118.19 E
Qianxiatazi 104 42.23 N 123.53 E
Qianyamen 104 42.04 N 121.26 E
Qianyang 102 27.11 N 110.04 E
Qianyaopu 104 42.02 N 123.37 E
Qi'anzhen 106 32.11 N 121.03 E
Qianzhou 106 31.42 N 120.13 E
Qiaodun 100 27.29 N 120.18 E
Qiaoershan ⩘ 102 31.48 N 99.10 E
Qiaogou 100 32.26 N 115.45 E
Qiaohengjin 102 29.30 N 99.50 E
Qiaojia 102 26.57 N 102.52 E
Qiaojiang 269b 31.15 N 121.19 E
Qiaokou 100 25.55 N 113.10 E
Qiaolima 120 34.35 N 81.00 E
Qiaolin 100 31.57 N 118.32 E
Qiaomu 98 39.34 N 114.27 E
Qiaopurikebazha 85 38.48 N 76.19 E
Qiaoqi 106 31.49 N 120.18 E
Qiaoshe 100 28.48 N 115.58 E
Qiaosi 106 30.21 N 120.18 E
Qiaotou, Zhg. 100 33.05 N 112.46 E
Qiaotou, Zhg. 102 28.17 N 99.22 E
Qiaotou, Zhg. 104 41.13 N 123.44 E
Qiaotou, Zhg. 106 32.11 N 119.14 E
Qiaotou, Zhg. 107 29.18 N 104.39 E
Qiaotoucun 106 30.36 N 119.08 E
Qiaotouji 100 31.45 N 117.34 E
Qiaotoupu 106 30.33 N 118.50 E
Qiaotouyi 100 28.24 N 112.58 E
Qiaotouzhen 106 30.49 N 119.13 E
Qiaowan 102 40.36 N 96.55 E
Qiaowei 102 22.51 N 109.50 E
Qiaoxia 106 31.09 N 119.35 E
Qiaoxiajie 100 28.10 N 120.34 E
Qiaozhen 106 31.39 N 121.24 E
Qibao 106 31.09 N 121.20 E
Qibyā 132 31.59 N 35.01 E
Qichun 100 30.17 N 115.26 E
Qiddīsah Kātrīnā,
  Dayr al-
  (Monastery of
  Saint Catherine) ⊍[1] 140 28.29 N 34.01 E
Qidong, Zhg. 102 26.44 N 112.04 E
Qidong, Zhg. 106 31.49 N 121.40 E
Qidu 100 30.16 N 117.46 E
Qiemo 120 38.08 N 85.32 E
Qiesanglinzi 104 41.42 N 123.30 E
Qieshikou 271a 39.59 N 116.24 E
Qiezixi 107 29.25 N 106.30 E
Qifosi 107 29.27 N 105.58 E

Qifṭ (Coptos) 140 26.00 N 32.49 E
Qigong 102 28.38 N 100.38 E
Qigongtai 104 41.50 N 123.08 E
Qihe (Yancheng) 98 36.48 N 116.44 E
Qiji 98 37.16 N 115.21 E
Qijiadian 89 46.48 N 125.36 E
Qijian 107 30.14 N 106.09 E
Qijiang 107 29.02 N 106.39 E
Qijiapuzi 104 40.54 N 122.31 E
Qijiawan 100 30.53 N 114.13 E
Qijiawopeng 104 41.02 N 121.26 E
Qijiazi 104 41.54 N 122.58 E
Qika 89 50.35 N 119.16 E
Qikou 98 38.35 N 117.31 E
Qila Abdullāh 120 30.43 N 66.38 E
Qila Dīdār Singh 123 32.08 N 74.01 E
Qilaguganni Shan ∧ 124 28.46 N 87.38 E
Qila Lādgasht 128 27.54 N 62.57 E
Qila Saifullāh 120 30.43 N 68.21 E
Qila Sobha Singh 123 32.14 N 74.46 E
Qilian 102 38.05 N 100.12 E
Qilian Shan ∧ 102 39.12 N 98.35 E
Qilian Shan ⩘ 102 39.06 N 98.40 E
Qili Hai ≋ 105 39.19 N 117.33 E
Qilihe, Zhg. 104 41.21 N 121.16 E
Qilihe, Zhg. 104 41.30 N 121.15 E
Qilihezi 104 40.56 N 121.02 E
Qiling 100 24.05 N 115.27 E
Qilingzicun 104 41.05 N 123.06 E
Qilinmen 106 32.04 N 118.55 E
Qilinzhen 106 31.56 N 121.21 E
Qiliping 100 31.27 N 114.39 E
Qiliqiao 106 31.35 N 120.48 E
Qilizhen, Zhg. 102 35.43 N 108.59 E
Qilizhen, Zhg. 106 32.19 N 121.05 E
Qilṭ, 'Ayn al- ⍑[4] 132 31.50 N 35.23 E
Qimafang 98 40.08 N 114.31 E
Qiman al-'Arūs 142 29.18 N 31.10 E
Qimen, Zhg. 100 29.52 N 117.42 E
Qimen, Zhg. 100 25.18 N 113.15 E
Qimoudi 105 39.35 N 115.32 E
Qimu Jiao > 98 37.46 N 120.12 E
Qin ≃, Zhg. 100 23.58 N 115.47 E
Qin ≃, Zhg. 100 26.16 N 115.52 E
Qin ≃, Zhg. 102 35.01 N 113.25 E
Qinā 140 26.10 N 32.43 E
Qinā, Wādī V, Miṣr 140 26.12 N 32.44 E
Qinā, Wādī V, Miṣr 142 29.39 N 31.53 E
Qincaigou 104 40.38 N 120.37 E
Qing ≃, Zhg. 98 42.26 N 123.50 E
Qing ≃, Zhg. 102 30.22 N 111.20 E
Qing'an 89 46.52 N 127.30 E
Qingbaikou 105 40.01 N 115.50 E
Qingcaoge 100 30.50 N 116.46 E
Qingcheng 98 37.12 N 117.40 E
Qingchengzi 104 40.44 N 123.36 E
Qingchuan 102 32.36 N 105.09 E
Qingcungang 106 30.56 N 121.34 E
Qingdao (Tsingtao) 98 36.06 N 120.19 E
Qingdian 105 39.51 N 117.22 E
Qingduizi, Zhg. 98 39.50 N 123.18 E
Qingduizi, Zhg. 104 41.28 N 121.53 E
Qingfeng 98 35.54 N 115.07 E
Qingfengtuo 98 40.59 N 116.04 E
Qingfu 102 28.29 N 104.35 E
Qinggang 89 46.43 N 126.07 E
Qingguang 105 39.11 N 117.02 E
Qingguji 98 34.45 N 115.47 E
Qinghai (Tsinghai) □[4] 90 36.00 N 96.00 E
Qinghai Hu ◎ 102 36.50 N 100.20 E
Qinghai Nanshan ⩘ 102 37.06 N 99.05 E
Qinghe, Zhg. 86 46.36 N 90.39 E
Qinghe, Zhg. 98 40.02 N 122.35 E
Qinghe, Zhg. 104 42.32 N 124.09 E
Qinghe, Zhg. 105 40.01 N 116.20 E
Qinghecheng 104 41.28 N 124.15 E
Qinghechengzi 104 41.44 N 121.25 E
Qinghemen 104 41.45 N 121.25 E
Qinghezhen 98 37.16 N 117.39 E
Qinghu 100 28.40 N 118.34 E
Qinghua 100 29.24 N 117.46 E
Qinghuayuan 105 40.00 N 116.19 E
Qinghuazhen 100 32.55 N 112.19 E
Qingjian 102 37.10 N 110.00 E
Qingjiang, Zhg. 100 28.16 N 121.06 E
Qingjiang, Zhg. 100 33.35 N 119.02 E
Qingjiang, Zhg. 100 28.05 N 115.29 E
Qingjiang, Zhg. 107 29.17 N 105.34 E
Qingjujie 107 30.42 N 106.07 E
Qinglian 100 24.27 N 112.45 E
Qingliu 100 26.12 N 116.52 E
Qingliuzhen 107 29.56 N 105.19 E
Qinglong, Zhg. 98 40.24 N 118.54 E
Qinglong, Zhg. 100 25.28 N 114.28 E
Qinglong, Zhg. 102 25.50 N 105.10 E
Qinglong ≃, Zhg. 98 39.51 N 118.51 E
Qinglong ≃, Zhg. 105 39.35 N 117.46 E
Qinglongchang, Zhg. 107 28.50 N 106.31 E
Qinglongchang, Zhg. 107 29.51 N 105.40 E
Qinglongchang, Zhg. 107 30.20 N 103.51 E
Qinglonggang 106 31.51 N 121.15 E
Qinglongguan 107 30.25 N 104.48 E
Qinglongji 98 34.05 N 116.37 E
Qinglongwan ≃ 105 39.19 N 117.32 E
Qingmuguan 107 29.41 N 106.18 E
Qingningsi 106 31.16 N 121.33 E
Qingping, Zhg. 98 36.47 N 116.06 E
Qingping, Zhg. 107 30.14 N 106.12 E
Qingping, Zhg. 107 29.00 N 106.21 E
Qingpu 106 31.09 N 121.06 E
Qingshan, Zhg. 100 31.33 N 116.22 E
Qingshan, Zhg. 100 30.38 N 114.23 E
Qingshan, Zhg. 106 30.43 N 120.03 E
Qingshan, Zhg. 106 30.15 N 119.52 E
Qingshan, Zhg. 106 30.36 N 119.41 E
Qingshanpu 100 29.27 N 114.01 E
Qingshen 107 29.50 N 103.50 E
Qingshui, Zhg. 102 34.42 N 106.21 E
Qingshui, Zhg. 102 39.23 N 99.09 E
Qingshui, Zhg. 107 30.10 N 104.03 E
Qingshui ≃, Zhg. 102 37.30 N 105.30 E
Qingshui ≃, Zhg. 102 27.08 N 109.36 E
Qingshuihe 86 44.12 N 80.45 E
Qingshuijian 105 39.59 N 115.58 E
Qingshuilang Shan ⩘ 102 26.15 N 99.35 E
Qingshuixi 102 29.09 N 103.55 E
Qingtan 100 31.48 N 112.48 E
Qingtang, Zhg. 100 26.28 N 115.48 E
Qingtang, Zhg. 100 24.14 N 113.51 E
Qingtian 100 28.10 N 120.17 E
Qingtong 107 29.28 N 103.27 E
Qingtongxia 102 37.53 N 105.54 E
Qingtuosi 98 35.29 N 118.20 E
Qingtuozi, Zhg. 104 41.05 N 121.28 E
Qingtuozi, Zhg. 105 39.08 N 117.45 E
Qingxi, Zhg. 89 49.19 N 127.10 E
Qingxi, Zhg. 100 31.40 N 118.00 E
Qingxi, Zhg. 107 30.40 N 106.14 E
Qingxian 98 38.34 N 116.46 E
Qingxizhen 107 29.09 N 103.55 E
Qingyang, Zhg. 89 45.20 N 128.47 E
Qingyang, Zhg. 100 30.38 N 117.48 E
Qingyang, Zhg. 102 36.06 N 107.47 E
Qingyangzhen 106 31.46 N 120.15 E
Qingyi ≃ 107 29.34 N 103.42 E
Qingyuan, Zhg. 98 42.13 N 124.56 E
Qingyuan, Zhg. 100 27.38 N 119.04 E
Qingyuan, Zhg. 100 23.42 N 113.02 E
Qingyuan
  → Baoding, Zhg. 105 38.52 N 115.29 E
Qingyun (Xiejiaji) 98 37.52 N 117.21 E
Qingyunbao 104 42.34 N 123.50 E
Qingyundian 105 39.38 N 116.29 E
Qing Zang Gaoyuan
  ⩘[1] 12 33.00 N 92.00 E
Qingzhen, Zhg. 102 26.29 N 106.22 E
Qingzhen, Zhg. 106 30.45 N 120.30 E
Qingzhou 100 23.39 N 116.57 E
Qinhuai ≃ 106 32.01 N 118.50 E

Symbol	English	Deutsch	Español	Français	Português
≃	River	Fluß	Río	Rivière	Rio
≅	Canal	Kanal	Canal	Canal	Canal
ᒪ	Waterfall, Rapids	Wasserfall, Stromschnellen	Cascada, Rápidos	Chute d'eau, Rapides	Cascata, Rápidos
ʯ	Strait	Meeresstraße	Estrecho	Détroit	Estreito
c	Bay, Gulf	Bucht, Golf	Bahía, Golfo	Baie, Golfe	Baía, Golfo
◎	Lake, Lakes	See, Seen	Lago, Lagos	Lac, Lacs	Lago, Lagos
≋	Swamp	Sumpf	Pantano	Marais	Pântano
⊞	Ice Features, Glacier	Eis- und Gletscherformen	Accidentes Glaciales	Formes glaciaires	Acidentes glaciares
⍑	Other Hydrographic Features	Andere Hydrographische Objekte	Otros Elementos Hidrográficos	Autres données hydrographiques	Outros acidentes hidrográficos
✣	Submarine Features	Untermeerische Objekte	Accidentes Submarinos	Formes de relief sous-marin	Acidentes submarinos
□	Political Unit	Politische Einheit	Unidad Politica	Entité politique	Unidade política
⊍	Cultural Institution	Kulturelle Institution	Institución Cultural	Institution culturelle	Instituição cultural
⊥	Historical Site	Historische Stätte	Sitio Histórico	Site historique	Sitio histórico
♠	Recreational Site	Erholungs- und Ferienort	Sitio de Recreo	Centre de loisirs	Area de Lazer
⊠	Airport	Flughafen	Aeropuerto	Aéroport	Aeroporto
■	Military Installation	Militäranlage	Instalación Militar	Installation militaire	Instalação militar
⬥	Miscellaneous	Verschiedenes	Misceláneo	Divers	Diversos

ENGLISH — Name | Page | Lat.°′ | Long.°′

DEUTSCH — Name | Seite | Breite°′ | Länge°′ E = Ost

Qinhuangdao (Chinwangtao)	98	39.56 N	119.36 E
Qinjia	89	46.47 N	127.00 E
Qinlan	100	32.37 N	119.08 E
Qin Ling (Tsinlingshan) ⋏	102	34.00 N	108.00 E
Qinnan	100	33.16 N	119.55 E
Qinshui	102	35.41 N	112.11 E
Qintong	100	32.39 N	120.08 E
Qinxian	102	36.48 N	112.41 E
Qinyang	102	35.06 N	112.57 E
Qinyuan	102	36.30 N	112.15 E
Qinzhou	102	21.59 N	108.36 E
Qionghai (Jiaji)	110	19.20 N	110.30 E
Qionglai	107	30.25 N	103.27 E
Qionglaishan ⋏	102	31.21 N	102.50 E
Qionglong Shan ∧	106	31.15 N	120.25 E
Qiongzhong, Zhg.	90	19.02 N	109.49 E
Qiongzhong, Zhg.	110	19.04 N	109.48 E
Qiongzhou Haixia ⋓	102	20.10 N	110.15 E
Qipandi	105	39.46 N	115.12 E
Qipanshan	98	42.05 N	117.30 E
Qiqian	89	52.12 N	120.49 E
Qiqihar (Tsitsihar)	89	47.19 N	123.55 E
Qira	120	37.00 N	80.47 E
Qirʿawn, Buḥayrat al- ⊜[1]	132	33.34 N	35.42 E
Qiryat	132	32.49 N	35.06 E
Qiryat ʿAnavim	132	31.48 N	35.07 E
Qiryat Ata	132	32.48 N	35.06 E
Qiryat Bialik	132	32.50 N	35.05 E
Qiryat Gat	132	31.36 N	34.46 E
Qiryat Ḥayyim	132	32.49 N	35.04 E
Qiryat Mal'akhi	132	31.44 N	34.44 E
Qiryat Motzkin	132	32.50 N	35.04 E
Qiryat Ono	132	32.04 N	34.51 E
Qiryat Shemona	132	33.13 N	35.34 E
Qiryat Tivʿon	132	32.43 N	35.08 E
Qiryat Yam	132	32.51 N	35.04 E
Qirzah, Wādī V	146	30.56 N	14.31 E
Qiseqi Shan ∧	89	48.37 N	122.32 E
Qishn	144	15.26 N	51.40 E
Qishon ≃	132	32.49 N	35.02 E
Qishrān I	144	20.14 N	40.05 E
Qishudang	107	29.13 N	104.39 E
Qishuyan	106	31.44 N	120.04 E
Qiṣrāyā	130	34.53 N	36.26 E
Qitai	86	44.01 N	89.28 E
Qitaihe	89	45.48 N	130.53 E
Qitaizi	104	41.33 N	122.11 E
Qitamu	89	44.22 N	126.20 E
Qitangzhen	107	29.47 N	106.16 E
Qiting	100	31.02 N	114.44 E
Qitingqiao	106	31.26 N	119.52 E
Qitou	100	24.54 N	117.29 E
Qiubei	102	24.07 N	104.12 E
Qiuchang	107	28.59 N	104.42 E
Qiuji	100	33.51 N	118.01 E
Qiujia	106	31.49 N	121.51 E
Qiujiatun	104	41.20 N	121.00 E
Qiujin	100	29.10 N	115.42 E
Qiuxi ≃	107	29.58 N	104.40 E
Qiuxizhen	107	29.56 N	104.41 E
Qiweigang	106	32.01 N	119.59 E
Qixia	98	37.17 N	120.48 E
Qixian (Zhaoge), Zhg.	98	35.38 N	114.11 E
Qixian, Zhg.	100	34.33 N	114.47 E
Qixianji	100	33.28 N	117.01 E
Qixiashan	106	32.10 N	118.57 E
Qi Xia Si ʊ[1]	106	32.12 N	118.58 E
Qixingqiao	106	30.49 N	120.51 E
Qiyahe	89	53.02 N	120.33 E
Qiyang	102	26.29 N	111.43 E
Qiyi	100	32.30 N	112.54 E
Qiying	102	36.38 N	106.25 E
Qizhou	100	30.04 N	115.20 E
Qizil Jilga	120	35.21 N	78.52 E
Qizil Langar	120	35.13 N	77.59 E
Qnadsa	148	31.48 N	2.26 W
Qogir Feng (K2) ∧	123	35.53 N	76.30 E
Qolhak ◆[8]	267d	35.47 N	51.26 E
Qom	128	34.39 N	50.54 E
Qom ≃	128	34.48 N	51.02 E
Qomolangma Feng → Everest, Mount ∧	124	27.59 N	86.56 E
Qomsheh	128	32.01 N	51.52 E
Qondūz ≃	120	37.00 N	68.16 E
Qorveh	128	35.10 N	47.48 E
Qoṭbābād	128	28.42 N	53.34 E
Qoṭūr	128	38.28 N	44.25 E
Qu ≃, Zhg.	100	29.12 N	119.27 E
Qu ≃, Zhg.	102	30.01 N	106.24 E
Quabbin Reservoir ⊜[1]	207	42.22 N	72.18 W
Quaddick Reservoir ⊜[1]	207	41.57 N	71.49 W
Quadra Island I	182	50.08 N	125.16 W
Quadraro ◆[8]	267a	41.51 N	12.33 E
Quadrath-Ichendorf	56	50.56 N	6.41 E
Quadros, Lagoa dos c	252	29.42 S	50.05 W
Quāidābād	123	32.20 N	71.52 E
Quail Lake ⊜[1]	228	34.47 N	118.45 W
Quail Valley	228	33.43 N	117.15 W
Quairading	162	32.01 S	117.25 E
Quakake	210	40.51 N	76.02 W
Quakenbrück	52	52.40 N	7.57 E
Quaker Hill, Ct., U.S.	207	41.22 N	72.06 W
Quaker Hill, N.Y., U.S.	210	41.35 N	73.33 W
Quakers Hill	170	33.43 S	150.53 E
Quakers Knob ∧[2]	214	40.21 N	80.24 W
Quaker Street	210	42.44 N	74.11 W
Quakertown, N.J., U.S.	210	40.33 N	74.56 W
Quakertown, Pa., U.S.	208	40.26 N	75.20 W
Qualicum Beach	182	49.21 N	124.27 W
Quambatook	166	35.51 S	143.31 E
Quanah	196	34.17 N	99.44 W
Quanbao Shan ∧	102	34.09 N	111.29 E
Quanery, Anse c	240d	15.26 N	61.15 W
Quangang	100	28.10 N	115.34 E
Quang Ngai	110	15.07 N	108.48 E
Quang Trach	110	17.45 N	106.27 E
Quanjiang	100	27.43 N	113.59 E
Quanjiao	100	32.06 N	118.16 E
Quan Long → Ca Mau	110	9.11 N	105.08 E
Quanmian	104	42.02 N	122.13 E
Quannan	100	24.44 N	114.31 E
Quannapowitt, Lake ⊜	283	42.31 N	71.05 W
Quanshang	100	26.25 N	116.55 E
Quanshengpu	104	41.59 N	123.22 E
Quanshui	104	41.18 N	124.11 E
Quanshuitou	105	40.24 N	116.39 E
Quantico, Md., U.S.	208	38.22 N	75.44 W
Quantico, Va., U.S.	208	38.31 N	77.17 W
Quantico Marine Corps Air Station ■	208	38.31 N	77.19 W
Quantock Hills ⋏[2]	42	51.07 N	3.10 W
Quantou	89	42.52 N	124.07 E
Quanxishi	100	26.51 N	112.45 E
Quanyanhezi	104	40.52 N	123.26 E
Quanzhou (Chuanchou)	100	24.54 N	118.35 E
Quanzhou Gang c	100	24.52 N	118.37 E
Qu'Appelle	184	50.33 N	103.52 W
Qu'Appelle ≃	184	50.25 N	101.20 W
Qu'Appelle Dam ◆[6]	184	51.00 N	106.25 W
Quaraí	252	30.23 S	56.27 W
Quaraí (Guareim) ≃	252	30.12 S	57.36 W
Quaregnon	50	50.26 N	3.51 E
Quarles, Pegunungan ⋏	112	2.55 S	119.30 E
Quarrata	66	43.51 N	10.58 E
Quarré-les-Tombes	50	47.22 N	3.59 E
Quarry	222	30.18 N	96.30 W
Quarry Heights	276	41.04 N	73.45 W
Quarryville, Ct., U.S.	207	41.51 N	72.25 W
Quarryville, Pa., U.S.	208	39.53 N	76.09 W
Quartu Sant'Elena	71	39.14 N	9.11 E
Quartz Hill	228	34.39 N	118.13 W
Quartz Lake ⊜	176	70.55 N	80.33 W
Quartz Mountain ∧	202	43.10 N	122.40 W
Quartzsite	200	33.39 N	114.13 W
Quatá	255	22.16 S	50.42 W
Quatis	256	22.25 S	44.16 W
Quatre, Isle I	241h	12.57 N	61.15 W
Quatsino Sound ⋓	182	50.25 N	127.55 W
Qubei	124	28.18 N	86.53 E
Qūchān	128	37.06 N	58.30 E
Quchijie	102	28.03 N	111.53 E
Qudaym	130	35.03 N	38.25 E
Qudi	98	37.06 N	117.15 E
Qudsia Gardens ♦	272a	28.40 N	77.13 E
Quê ≃	152	14.45 S	14.45 E
Queanbeyan	171b	35.21 S	149.14 E
Queanbeyan ≃	171b	35.20 S	149.14 E
Québec	206	46.49 N	71.14 W
Québec □[6]	206	46.50 N	71.20 W
Québec □[4]	176	52.00 N	72.00 W
Quebec Airport ⊠	206	46.47 N	71.23 W
Quebec House ⊥	260	51.14 N	0.05 E
Quebeck	194	35.49 N	85.34 W
Quebra-Anzol ≃	255	19.09 S	47.38 W
Quebra-Cangalha, Serra do ⋏	256	22.55 S	45.10 W
Quebracho	252	31.57 S	57.53 W
Quebrada Seca	240m	18.14 N	65.40 W
Quebradillas	240m	18.29 N	66.56 W
Quebrangulo	250	9.20 S	36.29 W
Quecholac	234	18.57 N	97.40 W
Quechultenango	234	17.25 N	99.13 W
Quecreek	214	40.06 N	79.05 W
Quedal, Cabo ›	254	40.59 S	73.59 W
Quedas	156	19.30 S	33.29 E
Quedlinburg	54	51.48 N	11.09 E
Queen	214	40.16 N	78.31 W
Queen Alexandra Range ⋏	9	84.00 S	168.00 E
Queen Alia International Airport ⊠	132	31.44 N	35.59 E
Queen Anne	208	38.55 N	75.57 W
Queen Anne Creek ≃	285	40.08 N	74.53 W
Queen Annes □[6]	208	39.03 N	76.04 W
Queen Bess, Mount ∧	182	51.16 N	124.34 W
Queenborough	42	51.26 N	0.45 E
Queen Charlotte	182	53.16 N	132.05 W
Queen Charlotte Bay c	254	51.50 S	60.40 W
Queen Charlotte Islands II	182	53.00 N	132.00 W
Queen Charlotte Mountains ⋏	182	53.00 N	132.00 W
Queen Charlotte Sound ⋓	182	51.30 N	129.30 W
Queen Charlotte Strait ⋓	182	50.50 N	127.25 W
Queen City, Mo., U.S.	194	40.24 N	92.34 W
Queen City, Tx., U.S.	194	33.08 N	94.09 W
Queen Elizabeth II Reservoir ⊜[1]	260	51.23 N	0.24 W
Queen Elizabeth Islands II	16	78.00 N	95.00 W
Queen Fabiola Mountains ⋏	9	71.30 S	35.40 E
Queen Mary ◆	280	33.45 N	118.12 W
Queen Mary Coast •[2]	9	67.00 S	96.00 E
Queen Mary Reservoir ⊜[1]	260	51.25 N	0.28 W
Queen Maud Gulf c	176	68.25 N	102.30 W
Queen Maud Land ◆[1]	9	72.30 S	12.00 E
Queen Maud Mountains ⋏	9	86.00 S	160.00 W
Queens □[6]	210	40.34 N	73.52 W
Queensbury	44	53.46 N	1.50 W
Queens Channel ⋓, Austl.	164	14.46 S	129.24 E
Queens Channel ⋓, N.T., Can.	176	76.11 N	96.00 W
Queenscliff	169	38.16 S	144.40 E
Queensferry, Scot., U.K.	46	55.59 N	3.25 W
Queensferry, Wales, U.K.	44	53.12 N	3.01 W
Queensland □[3]	160	22.00 S	145.00 E
Queensland Plateau ✦[3]	14	17.00 S	150.00 E
Queens Park ♦, Austl.	274a	33.54 S	151.16 E
Queens Park ♦, On., Can.	275b	43.40 N	79.24 W
Queens Park ♦, Eng., U.K.	262	53.30 N	2.13 W
Queens Park ♦, Eng., U.K.	262	53.35 N	2.27 W
Queen's Park ♦, Eng., U.K.	262	53.44 N	2.28 W
Queensport	186	45.20 N	61.16 W
Queens Sound ⋓	182	51.55 N	128.11 W
Queenston	284a	43.10 N	79.03 W
Queenston Chippawa Power Canal ≊	284a	43.08 N	79.03 W
Queenstown, Austl.	166	42.05 S	145.33 E
Queenstown, Guy.	246	7.12 N	58.29 W
Queenstown → Cobh, Ire.	48	51.51 N	8.17 W
Queenstown, N.Z.	172	45.02 S	168.40 E
Queenstown, S. Afr.	158	31.52 S	26.52 E
Queenstown, Md., U.S.	208	38.59 N	76.09 W
Queensville	212	44.08 N	79.28 W
Queen Victoria Park ♦	284a	43.05 N	79.05 W
Que'er'ao I	100	28.48 N	121.51 E
Queerhe	104	40.57 N	121.35 E
Queets	224	47.32 N	124.19 W
Queets ≃	224	47.33 N	124.21 W
Queguay Grande ≃	252	32.09 S	58.09 W
Queich ≃	56	49.14 N	8.23 E
Queige	62	45.43 N	6.28 E
Queimada, Ilha I	250	0.10 S	50.50 W
Queimada Nova	250	8.35 S	41.25 W
Queimadas	250	10.58 S	39.38 W
Queimados	256	22.42 S	43.34 W
Quela	152	9.16 S	17.02 E
Quelimane	156	17.53 S	36.51 E
Quelizhen	106	30.54 N	121.26 E
Quelle	52	52.00 N	8.29 E
Quellendorf	54	51.45 N	12.07 E
Quellón	254	43.07 S	73.37 W
Quelo	152	6.27 S	12.48 E
Quelpart Island → Cheju-do I	90	33.20 N	126.30 E
Queluz → Conselheiro Lafaiete, Bra.	255	20.40 S	43.48 W
Queluz, Bra.	256	22.32 S	44.46 W
Queluz, Port.	266c	38.45 N	9.15 W
Quemado, N.M., U.S.	200	34.20 N	108.29 W
Quemado, Tx., U.S.	196	28.56 N	100.38 W
Quemado, Punta del ›	240p	20.13 N	74.08 W
Quemado de Güines	240p	22.48 N	80.15 W
Quemahoning Reservoir ⊜[1]	214	40.09 N	78.57 W
Quembo ≃	152	14.57 S	20.22 E
Quemchi	254	42.09 S	73.29 W
Quemoy → Chinmen Tao I	100	24.27 N	118.23 E
Quemú Quemú	252	36.03 S	63.33 W
Quend	50	50.19 N	1.38 E
Quend Plage	50	50.19 N	1.33 E
Queñi, Nevado de ∧	254	40.14 S	71.49 W
Quenouilles, Lac aux ⊜	206	46.10 N	74.23 W
Quentin	208	40.17 N	76.26 W
Quepos	236	9.27 N	84.09 W
Quepos, Punta ›	236	9.23 N	84.10 W
Quequén	252	38.32 S	58.42 W
Quequén Salado ≃	254	38.56 S	60.31 W
Querary ≃	246	1.04 N	69.51 W
Quercianella	66	43.27 N	10.22 E
Quercy □[9]	32	44.30 N	1.25 E
Querecotillo	248	4.50 S	80.40 W
Querenburg ◆[8]	263	51.27 N	7.16 E
Querência do Norte	255	23.00 S	53.28 W
Querenhorst	54	52.20 N	10.57 E
Querétaro	234	20.36 N	100.23 W
Querétaro □[3]	234	21.00 N	99.55 W
Querfurt	54	51.23 N	11.36 E
Quero	64	45.55 N	11.56 E
Querobabi	232	30.03 N	111.01 W
Querobamba	248	13.52 S	73.50 W
Quesada, C.R.	236	10.19 N	84.26 W
Quesada, Esp.	34	37.51 N	3.04 W
Queset Brook ≃	283	42.02 N	71.04 W
Queshan	100	32.48 N	114.01 E
Quesnel	182	52.59 N	122.30 W
Quesnel ≃	182	53.00 N	122.30 W
Quesnel Lake ⊜	182	52.32 N	121.05 W
Quesnoy	50	50.43 N	3.00 E
Que Son	110	15.40 N	108.14 E
Questa	200	36.42 N	105.35 W
Questembert	32	47.40 N	2.27 W
Quetena	248	22.10 S	67.25 W
Quetico Lake ⊜	190	48.34 N	91.52 W
Quetico Provincial Park ♦	190	48.30 N	91.30 W
Quetta	120	30.12 N	67.00 E
Quettehou	32	49.36 N	1.18 W
Quetzala ≃	234	16.35 N	98.30 W
Quevedo	246	1.02 S	79.29 W
Quevedo ≃	246	1.02 S	79.28 W
Quezaltenango	236	14.50 N	91.31 W
Quezaltenango □[5]	236	14.45 N	91.40 W
Quezaltepeque, El Sal.	236	13.50 N	89.17 W
Quezaltepeque, Guat.	236	14.38 N	89.27 W
Quezon, Pil.	116	14.01 N	122.11 E
Quezon, Pil.	116	15.34 N	120.49 E
Quezon □[4]	116	13.58 N	122.02 E
Quezon City	116	14.38 N	121.03 E
Quezon Memorial ⊥	269f	14.39 N	121.03 E
Qufu	98	35.36 N	117.02 E
Qugou, Zhg.	102	36.10 N	100.56 E
Qugou, Zhg.	105	39.17 N	116.15 E
Quiabaya	248	15.37 S	68.46 W
Quibala	152	10.46 S	14.59 E
Quibaxi	152	8.29 S	14.36 E
Quibdó	246	5.42 N	76.40 W
Quiberon	32	47.29 N	3.07 W
Quiberville	50	49.54 N	0.55 E
Quíbor	246	9.56 N	69.37 W
Quibray Bay c	274a	34.01 S	151.11 E
Quibú ≃	286b	23.05 N	82.27 W
Quiçama, Parque Nacional de ♦	152	9.45 S	13.30 E
Qui Chau	110	19.33 N	105.06 E
Quiches	248	8.25 S	77.27 W
Quickborn	52	53.44 N	9.53 E
Quiculungo	152	8.31 S	15.19 E
Quidapil Point ›	116	6.49 N	123.57 E
Quidnessett	207	41.37 N	71.27 W
Quidnick	207	41.41 N	71.32 W
Quien Sabe Creek ≃	226	36.43 N	121.09 W
Quiévrain	50	50.24 N	3.41 E
Quiévy	50	50.10 N	3.25 E
Quiindy	252	25.58 S	57.16 W
Quilá	232	24.23 N	107.13 W
Quilalí	236	13.34 N	86.02 W
Quilates, Cap ›	34	35.20 N	3.45 W
Quilcene	224	47.49 N	122.52 W
Quilenda	152	10.33 S	14.22 E
Quilengues	152	14.05 S	14.04 E
Quileute Indian Reservation ◆[4]	224	47.55 N	124.38 W
Quilicura	286e	33.22 S	70.45 W
Quilicura, Canal de ≊	286e	33.22 S	70.47 W
Quilimarí	252	32.07 S	71.30 W
Quilino	252	30.12 S	64.29 W
Quillabamba	248	12.49 S	72.43 W
Quillacas	248	19.14 S	66.58 W
Quillacollo	248	17.26 S	66.17 W
Quillagua	248	21.39 S	69.33 W
Quillan	32	42.52 N	2.11 E
Quillebeuf-sur-Seine	50	49.29 N	0.31 E
Quill Lake	184	52.05 N	104.15 W
Quillota	252	32.53 S	71.16 W
Quilmes	258	34.44 S	58.16 W
Quilmes □[5]	288	34.44 S	58.16 W
Quilmes, Aeródromo ⊠	288	34.42 S	58.15 W
Quilombo ≃	256	23.52 S	46.21 W
Quilon	122	8.53 N	76.36 E
Quilotosa Wash V	200	32.56 N	112.46 W
Quilpie	166	26.37 S	144.15 E
Quilpué	252	33.03 S	71.27 W
Quilty	48	52.47 N	9.26 W
Quimarí, Alto de ∧	246	8.07 N	76.23 W
Quimbango	152	11.01 S	17.26 E
Quimbaya	246	4.38 N	75.47 W
Quimbele	152	6.28 S	16.13 E
Quimbo	152	13.59 S	16.05 E
Quimbonge	152	8.36 S	18.30 E
Quimbumbe	152	7.50 S	14.03 E
Quimby	198	42.37 N	95.38 W
Quime	248	17.02 S	67.15 W
Quimichis	234	22.21 N	105.32 W
Quimilí	252	27.38 S	62.25 W
Quimper	32	48.00 N	4.06 W
Quimperlé	32	47.52 N	3.33 W
Quimpitirique	248	12.15 S	73.52 W
Quinalasag Island I	116	13.56 N	123.38 E
Quinault	224	47.28 N	123.50 W
Quinault ≃	224	47.23 N	124.18 W
Quinault, North Fork ≃	224	47.32 N	123.40 W
Quinault Indian Reservation ◆[4]	224	47.24 N	124.10 W
Quinault Lake ⊜	224	47.28 N	123.52 W
Quinby Inlet c	208	37.28 N	75.40 W
Quincampoix	50	49.32 N	1.11 E
Quincemil	248	13.16 S	70.38 W
Quinches	248	12.13 S	76.05 W
Quincy, Ca., U.S.	204	39.56 N	120.56 W
Quincy, Fl., U.S.	192	30.35 N	84.35 W
Quincy, Il., U.S.	219	39.56 N	91.24 W
Quincy, Ky., U.S.	218	38.37 N	83.07 W
Quincy, Ma., U.S.	207	42.15 N	71.00 W
Quincy, Mi., U.S.	216	41.56 N	84.53 W
Quincy, Oh., U.S.	216	40.17 N	83.58 W
Quincy, Or., U.S.	224	46.08 N	123.09 W
Quincy, Pa., U.S.	208	39.48 N	77.35 W
Quincy, Wa., U.S.	202	47.14 N	119.51 W
Quincy Bay c	283	42.17 N	70.58 W
Quincy-sous-Sénart	261	48.40 N	2.33 E
Quincy-Voisins	261	48.54 N	2.53 E
Quindanning	168a	33.03 S	116.34 E
Quindío □[5]	246	4.30 N	75.40 W
Quinebaug	207	42.01 N	71.57 W
Quinebaug ≃	207	41.33 N	72.03 W
Quines	252	32.13 S	65.48 W
Quinga	154	15.49 S	40.15 E
Quingey	58	47.06 N	5.53 E
Quingyi ≃	100	31.12 N	118.29 E
Quinhagak	180	59.45 N	161.43 W
Qui Nhon	110	13.46 N	109.14 E
Quiniluban Islands II	116	11.27 N	120.48 E
Quinjenje	152	12.49 S	14.55 E
Quinlan	222	32.55 N	96.08 W
Quinn ≃	204	40.52 N	119.03 W
Quiñones, Arroyo de los ≃	266a	40.33 N	3.34 W
Quinson	62	43.42 N	6.02 E
Quinta da Boa Vista ♦	287a	22.54 S	43.15 W
Quintanar de la Orden	34	39.34 N	3.03 W
Quintana Roo □[3]	232	19.40 N	88.30 W
Quinta Normal	286e	33.27 S	70.42 W
Quinta Normal de Agricultura ʊ[2]	286e	33.27 S	70.42 W
Quinte, Bay of c	212	44.07 N	77.15 W
Quinter	198	39.04 N	100.13 W
Quintero	252	32.47 S	71.32 W
Quintette Mountain ∧	182	54.52 N	120.53 W
Quintin	32	48.24 N	2.55 W
Quintino Sella, Canale ≊	266b	45.29 N	8.38 E
Quinto	34	41.25 N	0.29 W
Quinto ≃	252	34.14 S	64.10 W
Quinto Creek ≃	226	37.11 N	121.02 W
Quinto de Noviembre, Presa ◆[6]	236	13.59 N	88.44 W
Quinton, Sk., Can.	184	51.23 N	104.24 W
Quinton, N.J., U.S.	208	39.32 N	75.24 W
Quinton, Ok., U.S.	196	35.07 N	95.22 W
Quinto Romano ◆[8]	266b	45.29 N	9.05 E
Quinzano d'Oglio	64	45.19 N	10.00 E
Quinzáu	152	6.51 S	12.46 E
Quinze, Lac des ⊜	190	47.35 N	79.05 W
Quionga	154	10.37 S	40.30 E
Quiotepec ≃	234	17.35 N	97.00 W
Quiotepec ⊥	234	17.54 N	96.58 W
Quipapá	250	8.50 S	36.02 W
Quipar ≃	34	38.14 N	1.36 W
Quipeio	152	12.26 S	15.30 E
Quipemba	152	7.12 S	15.06 E
Quipit ≃	116	8.04 N	122.29 E
Quipungo	152	14.51 S	14.30 E
Quirauk Mountain ∧	208	39.42 N	77.31 W
Quiriguá ⊥	236	15.17 N	89.04 W
Quirihue	252	36.17 S	72.32 W
Quirima	152	10.48 S	18.09 E
Quirimba, Ilha I	154	12.20 S	40.36 E
Quirimbo	152	10.36 S	14.12 E
Quirindi	166	31.31 S	150.41 E
Quirino □[4]	116	16.25 N	121.35 E
Quirinópolis	255	18.32 S	50.30 W
Quiriquire	246	9.59 N	63.13 W
Quiriri ≃	152	15.13 S	18.47 E
Quiririm	256	23.02 S	45.38 W
Quirke Lake ⊜	190	46.28 N	82.33 W
Quiroga, Esp.	34	42.29 N	7.16 W
Quiroga, Méx.	234	19.40 N	101.32 W
Quirós	252	28.47 S	65.07 W
Quiros, Cap ›	175f	14.55 S	167.01 E
Quirpon Island I	186	51.35 N	55.25 W
Quirra, Salto di ◆[1]	71	39.35 N	9.33 E
Quiruvilca	248	8.00 S	78.19 W
Quissac	62	43.55 N	4.00 E
Quissanga	154	12.25 S	40.29 E
Quissico	156	24.42 S	34.44 E
Quissongo	152	10.01 S	15.07 E
Quistello	64	45.00 N	10.59 E
Quitapa	152	10.23 S	18.14 E
Quitaque	196	34.22 N	101.04 W
Quita Sueño Bank ✦[4]	236	14.20 N	81.15 W
Quitaúna	287b	23.31 S	46.47 W
Quiterajo	154	11.48 S	40.25 E
Quitéria ≃	255	20.16 S	51.08 W
Quitilipi	252	26.52 S	60.13 W
Quitman, Ga., U.S.	192	30.47 N	83.33 W
Quitman, Ms., U.S.	194	32.02 N	88.43 W
Quitman, Tx., U.S.	222	32.47 N	95.27 W
Quitman, Lake ⊜[1]	222	32.52 N	95.27 W
Quito	246	0.13 S	78.30 W
Quitzdorf, Speicherbecken ⊜[1]	54	51.17 N	14.45 E
Quivilla	248	9.32 S	76.41 W
Quixadá	250	4.58 S	39.01 W
Quixeramobim	250	5.12 S	39.17 W
Quixeré	250	5.05 S	37.59 W
Quixico	152	7.59 S	14.25 E
Quixinge	152	9.52 S	14.23 E
Quixito ≃	246	4.29 S	70.18 W
Quizenga	152	9.21 S	15.28 E
Qujiadian	89	43.13 N	123.53 E
Qujiang, Zhg.	100	24.41 N	113.35 E
Qujiang, Zhg.	100	24.48 N	113.17 E
Qujiang, Zhg.	100	28.15 N	115.45 E
Qujing	102	25.32 N	103.41 E
Qujiu	102	22.28 N	107.40 E
Qukou	105	39.46 N	117.07 E
Qulayʿah, Ra's al- ›	128	28.53 N	48.18 E
Qulin	194	36.35 N	90.14 W
Qulubbā	142	27.45 N	30.50 E
Qulūd, Jabal ∧[2]	140	11.41 N	29.31 E
Qulūṣanā	142	28.21 N	30.44 E
Qulzum, Baḥr al- c	142	29.55 N	32.31 E
Qumar ≃, Zhg.	90	34.42 N	94.50 E
Qumar ≃, Zhg.	120	34.39 N	95.00 E
Qumarlêb	102	34.35 N	95.27 E
Qumbu	158	31.10 S	28.48 E
Qumrān, Khirbat ⊥	132	31.44 N	35.27 E
Qunayfidhah, Nafūd •[8]	128	24.45 N	45.30 E
Qunbush Al-Ḥamrā'	142	29.00 N	30.59 E
Qungtag	120	29.59 N	87.33 E
Qunshen'guan	105	39.49 N	117.59 E
Quobba, Point ›	162	24.23 S	113.24 E
Quoich ≃	176	64.00 N	93.30 W
Quoich, Loch ⊜	46	57.04 N	5.17 W
Quoile ≃	48	54.21 N	5.42 W
Quoin Point ›	158	34.46 S	19.37 E
Quonochontaug	207	41.21 N	71.43 W
Quorn	166	32.21 S	138.03 E
Quorndon	42	52.45 N	1.09 W
Quoxo ≃	156	22.16 S	24.02 E
Qurayyah, Wādī V	132	30.26 N	34.01 E
Qurayyāt	128	23.17 N	58.55 E
Qurdūd	140	10.17 N	29.56 E
Qurrāṣah	140	14.38 N	32.12 E
Qurūn Ḥarḥash ∧[2]	142	28.09 N	31.42 E
Qūṣ	140	25.55 N	32.45 E
Quṣayr ad-Daffah ⊥	146	30.20 N	23.57 E
Qūshchī	128	37.59 N	45.03 E
Qushui	107	30.41 N	106.02 E
Qutang	100	32.30 N	120.21 E
Qutbapur ◆[8]	272a	28.35 N	77.01 E
Qutb Minar ʊ[1]	272a	28.32 N	77.11 E
Qutdligssat	176	70.04 N	53.01 W
Quthing	158	30.30 S	27.36 E
Quṭūr	142	30.59 N	30.57 E
Quwaysinā	142	30.34 N	31.09 E
Quxi, Zhg.	100	28.00 N	120.31 E
Quxi, Zhg.	100	23.36 N	116.26 E
Quxia	106	32.06 N	120.09 E
Quxian, Zhg.	100	28.58 N	118.52 E
Quxian, Zhg.	102	30.51 N	106.59 E
Quxingji	98	34.52 N	114.39 E
Quxiong	102	31.09 N	96.00 E
Qüxü	120	29.22 N	90.43 E
Quyang	98	38.34 N	114.42 E
Qūyjāq-e-Bālā	84	39.16 N	47.07 E
Quyon	188	45.31 N	76.14 W
Quyquyó	252	26.14 S	57.01 W
Quzaymah, Jabal ∧	132	30.34 N	36.21 E
Quzhou	98	36.46 N	114.57 E
Quzong	102	30.08 N	96.00 E

R

Råå	41	56.00 N	12.44 E
Raab → Győr, Magy.	30	47.42 N	17.38 E
Raab, Öst.	60	48.21 N	13.39 E
Raab (Rába) ≃	30	47.42 N	17.38 E
Raabs an der Thaya	61	48.51 N	15.30 E
Raadt ◆[8]	263	51.24 N	6.56 E
Raahe	26	64.41 N	24.29 E
Rääkkylä	26	62.19 N	29.37 E
Raalte	52	52.24 N	6.16 E
Raamsdonksveer	52	51.42 N	4.56 E
Raʿananna	132	32.11 N	34.53 E
Raas, Pulau I	115a	7.09 S	114.32 E
Raasay I	46	57.23 N	6.04 W
Raasay, Sound of ⋓	46	57.27 N	6.06 W
Raasdorf	264b	48.15 N	16.34 E
Raasiku	76	59.22 N	25.11 E
Rab	36	44.46 N	14.46 E
Rab, Otok I	36	44.47 N	14.45 E
Raba	115b	8.27 S	118.46 E
Rába (Raab) ≃, Europe	30	47.42 N	17.38 E
Raba ≃, Pol.	30	50.09 N	20.30 E
Rabaable	144	8.17 N	48.18 E
Rabaçal ≃	34	41.30 N	7.12 W
Rábade	34	43.07 N	7.37 W
Rábahidvég	61	47.04 N	16.45 E
Rabai	154	3.58 S	39.37 E
Rabak	140	13.09 N	32.44 E
Rabal	164	6.22 S	134.52 E
Rabaraba	164	10.00 S	149.50 E
Rabat, Magreb	148	34.02 N	6.51 W
Rabat, Malta	36	35.52 N	14.25 E
Rabat (Victoria), Malta	36	36.02 N	14.14 E
Rabat □[4]	148	33.57 N	6.50 W
Rabaul	164	4.12 S	152.12 E
Rabbit ≃	216	42.38 N	86.06 W
Rabbit, Lac ⊜	190	47.30 N	78.22 W
Rabbit Creek ≃, S.D., U.S.	198	45.13 N	102.10 W
Rabbit Creek ≃, Tx., U.S.	222	32.26 N	94.47 W
Rabbit Ears Pass)(	200	40.23 N	106.37 W
Rabbit Lake ⊜, On., Can.	190	47.00 N	79.37 W
Rabbit Lake ⊜, Ca., U.S.	228	34.27 N	117.01 W
Rabbs Creek ≃	222	29.59 N	96.55 W
Rábca ≃	61	47.43 N	17.17 E
R'abcevo	76	54.39 N	32.19 E
Rabeira, Ponta da ›	287a	22.49 S	43.10 W
Rabenau	54	50.57 N	13.38 E
Rabette, Ruisseau la ≃	261	48.35 N	2.00 E
Rābiʿ, Ash-Shallāl ar- (Fourth Cataract) ⌊	140	18.47 N	32.03 E
Rābigh	128	22.48 N	39.01 E
Rabinal	236	15.06 N	90.27 W
Rabiusa ≃	58	46.48 N	9.20 E
Rabka	30	49.36 N	19.56 E
Rabkavi Banhatti	122	16.28 N	75.06 E
Rabnābād Channel ⋓	126	21.50 N	90.19 E
Rabnābād Islands II	126	21.58 N	90.24 E
Rabočeostrovsk	24	64.59 N	34.48 E
Rabočij	86	59.07 N	79.00 E
Rabong, Gunong ∧	114	4.48 N	102.07 E
Rabotki	80	56.03 N	44.38 E
R abovskij	80	50.01 N	41.53 E
Rabun Bald ∧	192	34.58 N	83.18 W
Rabwāh	123	31.44 N	72.50 E
Raby	262	53.19 N	3.02 W
Rabyānah ⊤[4]	146	24.15 N	22.00 E
Rabyānah, Ṣaḥrā' ◆[2]	146	24.30 N	21.00 E
Racale	68	39.57 N	18.06 E
Racalmuto	70	37.24 N	13.44 E
Răcari	38	44.38 N	25.45 E
Racconigi	62	44.46 N	7.46 E
Raccoon ≃	194	41.35 N	93.37 W
Raccoon Creek ≃, N.J., U.S.	208	39.48 N	75.23 W
Raccoon Creek ≃, Oh., U.S.	188	38.43 N	82.11 W
Raccoon Creek ≃, Oh., U.S.	214	40.02 N	82.24 W
Raccoon Creek ≃, Pa., U.S.	214	40.38 N	80.22 W
Raccoon Creek ≃, Pa., U.S.	285	39.48 N	75.23 W
Raccoon Creek ≃, Va., U.S.	208	36.48 N	77.10 W
Raccoon Creek, South Branch ≃	285	39.44 N	75.15 W
Raccoon Creek State Park ♦	214	40.30 N	80.27 W
Raccoon Island I	285	39.49 N	75.22 W
Raccuia	70	38.03 N	14.54 E
Race, Cape ›	186	46.40 N	53.10 W
Raceland	194	29.43 N	90.35 W
Race Point ›	207	42.04 N	70.14 W
Racette, Lac ⊜	206	46.34 N	74.03 W
Racette, Ruisseau ≃	206	46.36 N	74.04 W
Raceview	273d	26.17 S	28.08 E
Rach'a	76	60.05 N	30.49 E
Rach Gia	110	10.01 N	105.05 E
Rach Gia, Vinh c	110	10.00 N	105.00 E
Rachmanovka, S.S.S.R.	78	47.48 N	33.13 E
Rachmanovka, S.S.S.R.	80	51.57 N	49.29 E
Rachmanovo	82	55.44 N	38.37 E
Rachny Lesovyje	78	48.47 N	28.29 E
Rachov	78	48.03 N	24.12 E
Raciąż	30	52.47 N	20.06 E
Racibórz (Ratibor)	30	50.06 N	18.13 E
Racine, Pa., U.S.	214	40.49 N	80.20 W
Racine, Wi., U.S.	216	42.43 N	87.46 W
Racine □[6]	216	42.45 N	88.05 W
Racines	64	46.52 N	11.18 E
Račinskij chrebet ⋏	84	42.30 N	43.30 E
Rackerby	226	39.26 N	121.20 W
Ráckeve	30	47.10 N	18.56 E
Rackwick	46	58.52 N	3.23 W
R'ad	76	57.56 N	35.04 E
Råda	40	60.00 N	13.36 E
Radama, Nosy II	157b	14.00 S	47.47 E
Radama, Presqu'île ›	157b	14.16 S	47.53 E
Rådasjön ⊜	40	59.58 N	13.38 E
Radaur	124	30.02 N	77.09 E
Rădăuţi	38	47.51 N	25.55 E
Radbuza ≃	60	49.46 N	13.24 E
Radčenskoje	78	49.48 N	40.32 E
Radcliff	194	37.50 N	85.56 W
Radcliffe	44	53.34 N	2.20 W
Radcliffe on Trent	42	52.57 N	1.03 W
Radda in Chianti	66	43.29 N	11.22 E
Raddusa	70	37.28 N	14.32 E
Råde	26	59.21 N	10.51 E
Radebaugh	279b	40.19 N	79.35 W
Radeberg	54	51.07 N	13.55 E
Radebeul	54	51.06 N	13.40 E
Radeburg	54	51.13 N	13.43 E
Radeče	36	46.04 N	15.11 E
Radechov	78	50.18 N	24.37 E
Radegast	54	51.39 N	12.05 E
Radenci	61	46.38 N	16.03 E
Radenthein	64	46.48 N	13.43 E
Radevormwald	56	51.12 N	7.21 E
Radford	192	37.07 N	80.34 W
Rādhānagar, India	126	23.09 N	87.19 E
Rādhānagar, India	272b	22.27 N	88.28 E
Rādhanpur	120	23.50 N	71.36 E
Radici, Foce delle)(	64	44.12 N	10.31 E
Radicofani	66	42.54 N	11.46 E
Radicondoli	66	43.16 N	11.02 E
Rădineşti	38	44.48 N	23.46 E
Radiščevo	80	52.51 N	47.53 E
Radisson	184	52.27 N	107.23 W
Radiumbad Brambach	54	50.13 N	12.19 E
Radium Hot Springs	182	50.38 N	116.03 W
Radix, Point ›	241r	10.20 N	60.59 W
Rad'kovka	78	51.06 N	36.58 E
Radlett	42	51.42 N	0.20 W
Radlett Aerodrome ⊠	260	51.43 N	0.19 W
Radley Run ≃	285	39.54 N	75.37 W
Radlje ob Dravi	61	46.37 N	15.13 E
Rådmansö ›[1]	40	59.45 N	18.55 E
Radnevo	38	42.18 N	25.56 E
Radnice	60	49.51 N	13.37 E
Radnor, Oh., U.S.	214	40.23 N	83.09 W
Radnor, Pa., U.S.	285	40.02 N	75.21 W
Radnor Forest ∧	42	52.18 N	3.10 W
Radnor Mere ⊜	262	53.17 N	2.14 W
Radofinnikovo	76	59.09 N	30.55 E
Radogošča	76	59.47 N	34.51 E
Radoj'a	78	47.44 N	28.09 E
Radolfzell	58	47.44 N	8.58 E
Radom, Pol.	30	51.25 N	21.10 E
Radom, Il., U.S.	219	38.17 N	89.12 W
Radom □[4]	30	51.25 N	21.15 E
Radomicko	54	52.10 N	14.58 E
Radomir	38	42.33 N	22.58 E
Radomka	78	51.56 N	32.32 E
Radomka ≃	30	51.43 N	21.26 E
Radomsko	30	51.05 N	19.25 E
Radomyšl'	78	50.30 N	29.14 E
Radomyśl Wielki	30	50.12 N	21.16 E
Radošice	60	49.33 N	13.39 E
Radoškoviči	76	54.09 N	27.14 E
Radotin	30	50.00 N	14.22 E
Radovicy	80	55.06 N	39.32 E
Radoviš	38	41.38 N	22.28 E
Radovljica	36	46.21 N	14.11 E
Radstadt	64	47.23 N	13.27 E
Radstädter Tauern)(	64	47.15 N	13.24 E
Radstock	42	51.18 N	2.28 W
Radstock, Cape ›	162	33.12 S	134.20 E
Raduha ∧	61	46.25 N	14.45 E
Radul'	78	51.49 N	30.42 E
Radun'	76	54.03 N	25.00 E
Radušnoje	78	47.49 N	33.29 E
Radutino	76	52.39 N	33.57 E
Radvaniči	78	52.02 N	24.02 E
Radviliškis	76	55.50 N	23.31 E
Radville	184	49.27 N	104.17 W
Radway	182	54.04 N	112.57 W
Radykovskoje	80	45.56 N	41.57 E
Radymno	30	49.57 N	22.48 E
Radyr	42	51.31 N	3.15 W
Radziejów	30	52.38 N	18.32 E
Radzyń Chełmiński	30	53.24 N	18.56 E
Radzyń Podlaski	30	51.48 N	22.38 E
Rae	176	62.50 N	116.03 W
Rae ≃	176	67.55 N	115.30 W
Rāe Bareli	124	26.13 N	81.14 E
Raeford	192	34.58 N	79.13 W
Rae Isthmus •[3]	176	66.55 N	86.10 W
Rāenda	126	22.18 N	89.51 E
Raeren	56	50.41 N	6.07 E
Raesfeld	52	51.46 N	6.50 E
Raeside, Lake ⊜	162	29.30 S	122.00 E
Rae Strait ⋓	176	68.45 N	95.00 W
Raetihi	172	39.26 S	175.17 E
Rafael, Cachoeira do ⌊	248	10.25 S	63.15 W
Rafaela	252	31.16 S	61.29 W
Rafael Calzada	258	34.48 S	58.22 W
Rafael Castillo	288	34.43 S	58.37 W
Rafael Perazza	258	34.32 S	56.47 W
Rafaḥ	132	31.18 N	34.15 E
Rafaï	152	4.58 N	23.56 E
Rafalovka	78	51.22 N	25.52 E
Raffadali	70	37.24 N	13.32 E
Raffelberg, Rennbahn ♦	263	51.26 N	6.50 E
Raffili Mission	140	6.53 N	27.58 E
Rafḥā'	128	29.42 N	43.30 E
Rafinesque, Mount ∧[2]	210	42.47 N	73.37 W
Rafsanjān	128	30.24 N	56.01 E
Raft ≃	202	42.37 N	113.15 W
Raft River Mountains ⋏	200	41.55 N	113.25 W
Rafz	58	47.37 N	8.32 E
Raga	140	8.28 N	25.41 E
Ragada	64	46.10 N	10.38 E
Ragang, Mount ∧	116	7.43 N	124.32 E
Ragay	116	13.49 N	122.47 E
Ragay Gulf c	116	13.30 N	122.45 E
Rågeleje	41	56.06 N	12.10 E
Rägelin	54	53.01 N	12.38 E
Ragewitz	54	51.14 N	12.51 E
Ragged, Mount ∧	162	33.27 S	123.25 E
Ragged Island I	238	22.12 N	75.44 W
Ragged Island Range II	238	22.40 N	75.54 W
Ragged Lake ⊜	212	45.28 N	78.38 W
Ragged Top Mountain ∧	200	41.27 N	105.20 W
Raghabpur	272b	22.25 N	88.21 E
Rāghogarh	124	24.27 N	77.12 E
Raghumāthbāri	126	22.22 N	87.47 E
Raghunāthpur, Bngl.	126	23.12 N	89.31 E
Raghunāthpur, India	126	23.33 N	86.40 E
Raglan, Austl.	170	33.26 S	149.36 E
Raglan, N.Z.	172	37.48 S	174.53 E
Raglan, Wales, U.K.	42	51.47 N	2.51 W
Ragland	194	33.44 N	86.09 W
Ragnitz	61	46.50 N	15.35 E
Rago Nasjonalpark ♦	24	67.26 N	16.00 E
Ragow	264a	52.17 N	13.33 E
Ragozino	86	59.15 N	77.52 E
Rågsveden	40	60.29 N	14.05 E
Raguda, Ghubbet c	144	10.45 N	46.34 E
Raguhn	54	51.42 N	12.17 E
Raguli	80	45.38 N	43.42 E
Ragusa, It.	70	36.55 N	14.44 E
Ragusa → Dubrovnik, Jugo.	38	42.38 N	18.07 E
Ragusa □[4]	70	36.55 N	14.36 E
Raguva	76	55.34 N	24.36 E
Raha	112	4.51 S	122.43 E
Rahad, Nahr ar- (Rahad) ≃	140	14.28 N	33.31 E
Rahad al-Bardī	140	11.18 N	23.53 E
Rahad Game Reserve ◆[4]	140	13.06 N	35.05 E
Rahaṭ, Ḥarrat •[9]	144	22.20 N	40.05 E
Rahatgaon	124	22.15 N	77.14 E
Rāhatgarh	124	23.47 N	78.22 E
Raḥbah	130	34.30 N	36.09 E
Rahden	52	52.26 N	8.36 E
Rahimatpur	122	17.36 N	74.12 E
Rahīm Ki Bāzār	120	24.19 N	69.09 E
Rahīmyār Khān	120	28.25 N	70.18 E
Rahlstedt ◆[8]	52	53.36 N	10.09 E
Rahm	263	51.26 N	6.26 E
Rahm ◆[8], B.R.D.	263	51.32 N	7.23 E
Rahm ◆[8], B.R.D.	263	51.21 N	6.47 E
Rahmer See ⊜	264a	52.45 N	13.25 E
Rahns	285	40.12 N	75.27 W
Rahnsdorf ◆[8]	264a	52.26 N	13.42 E
Rāhon	123	31.03 N	76.07 E
Rahotu	172	39.20 S	173.48 E
Rahouia	34	35.32 N	1.01 E
Rāhwāli	123	32.15 N	74.10 E
Rahway	210	40.36 N	74.16 W
Rahway ≃	276	40.35 N	74.12 W
Rahway, East Branch ≃	276	40.42 N	74.18 W
Rahway, Robinsons Branch ≃	276	40.37 N	74.17 W
Rahway, South Branch ≃	276	40.36 N	74.17 W
Rahway, West Branch ≃	276	40.42 N	74.18 W
Rahway River Parkway ♦	276	40.41 N	74.19 W
Raiano	66	42.06 N	13.49 E
Raiatea I	14	16.50 S	151.25 W
Rāichūr	122	16.12 N	77.22 E
Raidak ≃	124	26.22 N	89.45 E
Rāidighi	126	22.00 N	88.26 E
Raiding	61	47.34 N	16.32 E
Raiford	192	30.03 N	82.14 W

Symbols in the index entries represent the broad categories identified in the key at the right. Symbols with superior numbers (⋏[1]) identify subcategories (see complete key on page *I · 1*).

Symbole im Register stellen die rechts im Schlüssel erklärten Kategorien dar. Symbole mit hochgestellten Ziffern (⋏[1]) bezeichnen Unterabteilungen einer Kategorie (vgl. vollständiger Schlüssel auf Seite *I · 1*).

Los símbolos incluídos en el texto del índice representan las grandes categorias identificadas con la clave a la derecha. Los símbolos con numeros en su parte superior (⋏[1]) identifican las subcategorías (véase la clave completa en la página *I · 1*).

Les symboles de l'index représentent les catégories indiquées dans la légende à droite. Les symboles suivis d'un indice (⋏[1]) représentent des sous-catégories (voir légende complète à la page *I · 1*).

Os símbolos incluídos no texto do índice representam as grandes categorias identificadas com a chave à direita. Os símbolos com números em sua parte superior (⋏[1]) identificam as subcategorias (veja-se a chave completa à página *I · 1*).

∧ Mountain	Berg	Montaña	Montagne	Montanha
⋏ Mountains	Gebirge	Montañas	Montagnes	Montanhas
)(Pass	Paß	Paso	Col	Passo
V Valley, Canyon	Tal Cañon	Valle, Cañón	Vallée, Canyon	Vale, Canhão
≚ Plain	Ebene	Llano	Plaine	Planície
› Cape	Kap	Cabo	Cap	Cabo
I Island	Insel	Isla	Île	Ilha
II Islands	Inseln	Islas	Îles	Ilhas
• Other Topographic Features	Andere Topographische Objekte	Otros Elementos Topográficos	Autres données topographiques	Outros acidentes topográficos

ESPAÑOL: Nombre · Página · Lat.°′ · Long.°′ W = Oeste
FRANÇAIS: Nom · Page · Lat.°′ · Long.°′ W = Ouest
PORTUGUÊS: Nome · Página · Lat.°′ · Long.°′ W = Oeste

Raiganj	124	25.37 N	88.07 E
Raigarh	122	21.54 N	83.24 E
Raijua, Pulau I	112	10.37 S	121.36 E
Rāikot	123	30.39 N	75.36 E
Railroad	208	39.46 N	76.42 W
Railroad Canyon Reservoir ⊜[1]	228	33.42 N	117.16 W
Railroad Creek ≃	224	48.12 N	120.36 W
Rail Road Flat	226	38.20 N	120.30 W
Railroad Valley V	204	38.25 N	115.40 W
Railton	166	41.21 S	146.25 E
Raimangal ≃	126	21.47 N	89.08 E
Rain	56	48.41 N	10.55 E
Rainbach im Innkreis	60	48.27 N	13.32 E
Rainbow	228	33.24 N	117.10 W
Rainbow Bridge ✦[5]	284a	43.05 N	79.04 W
Rainbow Bridge National Monument ♠	200	37.06 N	110.57 W
Rainbow City	236	9.21 N	79.53 W
Rainbow Falls ∟	182	52.23 N	119.59 W
Rainbow Lakes	276	40.52 N	74.28 W
Rainbow Park ♠	278	41.46 N	87.33 W
Rainbow Shores	212	43.37 N	76.12 W
Rainelle	188	37.58 N	80.46 W
Rainford	44	53.30 N	2.48 W
Rainham	42	51.23 N	0.36 E
Rainham ✦[8]	260	51.31 N	0.12 E
Rainhill	262	53.26 N	2.46 W
Rainhill Stoops	262	53.24 N	2.45 W
Rainier, Or., U.S.	224	46.05 N	122.56 W
Rainier, Wa., U.S.	224	46.53 N	122.41 W
Rainier, Mount ∧	224	46.52 N	121.46 W
Rainow	262	53.17 N	2.04 W
Rains → Riva di Tures	64	46.57 N	12.04 E
Rains ▫[6]	222	32.50 N	95.47 W
Rainsboro	218	39.13 N	83.25 W
Rainsford Island I	283	42.18 N	70.57 W
Rainworth	44	53.07 N	1.08 W
Rainy ≃, N.A.	184	48.50 N	94.41 W
Rainy ≃, Mi., U.S.	190	45.27 N	84.13 W
Rainy Lake ⊜, On., Can.	212	45.32 N	79.30 W
Rainy Lake ⊜, N.A.	184	48.42 N	93.10 W
Rainy Pass)(	224	48.32 N	120.39 W
Rainy River	190	48.43 N	94.34 W
Rāipur, Bngl.	126	23.03 N	90.46 E
Raipur, India	122	21.14 N	81.38 E
Raipur, India	124	30.19 N	78.06 E
Raipur, India	126	22.48 N	86.57 E
Raipur, India	272a	28.32 N	77.20 E
Raipur, India	272b	22.24 N	88.09 E
Rāipura	126	23.59 N	90.53 E
Raipur Uplands ⋀[1]	122	21.00 N	82.20 E
Rairākhol	120	21.04 N	84.21 E
Ra'īs	128	23.34 N	38.36 E
Raisdorf	54	54.17 N	10.16 E
Raisen	124	23.20 N	77.48 E
Ráisi, Punta ≻	70	38.11 N	13.06 E
Raisin	226	36.36 N	119.54 W
Raisin ≃, On., Can.	206	45.08 N	74.29 W
Raisin ≃, Mi., U.S.	216	41.53 N	83.20 W
Rāisinghnagar	123	29.32 N	73.27 E
Raismes	50	50.23 N	3.29 E
Raita	126	24.07 N	88.57 E
Raitenbuch	60	49.01 N	11.08 E
Raiti	236	14.35 N	85.02 W
Raivavae I	14	23.52 S	147.40 W
Rāiwind	123	31.15 N	74.13 E
Raizeux	261	48.37 N	1.41 E
Raja, Gili I	115a	7.14 S	113.47 E
Raja, Ujung ≻	114	3.45 N	96.33 E
Rājābāri	126	23.23 N	90.28 E
Rajabasa	112	5.25 S	104.24 E
Rājābhāt Khāwa	124	26.37 N	89.32 E
Rājābhita	126	23.52 N	86.20 E
Rājahmundry	122	16.59 N	81.47 E
Rajāj	140	10.55 N	24.43 E
Rāja Jang	123	31.13 N	74.16 E
Raja-Jooseppi	24	68.28 N	28.21 E
Rājākhera	124	26.55 N	78.11 E
Rājaldesar	120	28.02 N	74.28 E
Raj-Aleksandrovka	83	48.48 N	37.51 E
Rājāluka	126	22.09 N	86.38 E
Rajamäki	26	60.32 N	24.45 E
Rājampet	122	14.11 N	79.10 E
Rajang ≃	112	2.04 N	111.12 E
Rājanpur	120	29.06 N	70.19 E
Rājapālaiyam	122	9.27 N	77.34 E
Rājāpur, Bngl.	126	22.34 N	90.09 E
Rājāpur, India	122	16.40 N	73.31 E
Rājāpur, India	124	25.23 N	81.09 E
Rājāpur, India	272b	22.39 N	88.11 E
Rājapur Canal ≊	272b	22.30 N	88.07 E
Rājasthān ▫[3]	120	27.00 N	74.00 E
Rājauri	123	33.23 N	74.18 E
Rājbāri, Bngl.	124	23.46 N	89.39 E
Rājbāri, India	126	22.25 N	88.48 E
Raj Bhavan ʊ	272b	22.34 N	88.21 E
Rājbirāj	124	26.32 N	86.44 E
Rajčichinsk	89	49.46 N	129.25 E
Rājendrapur	126	24.06 N	90.27 E
Rajevskij	86	54.04 N	54.56 E
Rāj Gangpur	124	22.11 N	84.36 E
Rājganj ≃[1]	126	22.21 N	90.16 E
Rājgarh, India	123	28.38 N	75.23 E
Rājgarh, India	124	23.56 N	76.58 E
Rājgarh, India	124	27.14 N	76.38 E
Rajghat ʊ[1]	272a	28.39 N	77.15 E
Rājgīr	124	25.02 N	85.25 E
Rajgorod	80	48.26 N	44.55 E
Rajgorodka, S.S.S.R.	83	49.22 N	37.57 E
Rajgorodka, S.S.S.R.	83	48.50 N	39.04 E
Rajgorodok, S.S.S.R.	80	48.48 N	52.53 E
Rajgorodok, S.S.S.R.	83	48.54 N	37.43 E
Rajgród	30	53.44 N	22.42 E
Rājhāt	272b	22.56 N	88.21 E
Rajhrad	61	49.05 N	16.37 E
Rājibpur	272b	22.49 N	88.34 E
Rajik	112	2.36 S	105.56 E
Rajka	61	48.02 N	17.11 E
Rājkot	120	22.18 N	70.47 E
Rajkuzi	265a	59.47 N	29.57 E
Rājmahāl	124	25.03 N	87.50 E
Rājmahāl Hills ⋀[2]	124	24.40 N	87.25 E
Rājnagar	126	23.57 N	87.19 E
Rāj Nāndgaon	120	21.06 N	81.02 E
Rajokri ✦[8]	272a	28.31 N	77.07 E
Rājpipla	120	21.47 N	73.34 E
Rājpur, India	120	21.56 N	75.08 E
Rājpur, India	126	22.25 N	88.25 E
Rājpur, India	272a	28.44 N	77.22 E
Rājpur ✦[8]	272a	28.41 N	77.12 E
Rājpura	124	30.29 N	76.36 E
Rājshāhi	124	24.22 N	88.36 E
Rājshāhi ▫[5]	124	25.15 N	89.15 E
Rajskoje	83	48.34 N	37.25 E
Rājula	122	21.03 N	71.26 E
Raka	124	29.26 N	85.50 E
Raka ≃	124	29.24 N	87.58 E
Rakaia	172	43.45 S	172.01 E
Rakaia ≃	172	43.56 S	172.13 E
Rakamaz	30	48.08 N	21.30 E
Rakaposhi ∧	123	36.10 N	74.30 E
Rakata, Pulau I	115a	6.10 S	105.26 E
Rakha La)(	124	27.53 N	87.34 E
Rakhawt, Wādī V	144	17.40 N	51.40 E
Rakhine ▫[8]	110	19.00 N	94.15 E
Rakhneh	128	31.39 N	59.13 E
Rakhni	120	30.03 N	69.55 E
Rakhshān ≃	128	27.10 N	63.25 E
Rākīn	132	31.14 N	35.42 E
Rakitnoje, S.S.S.R.	78	50.51 N	35.50 E
Rakitnoje, S.S.S.R.	78	49.42 N	30.27 E
Rakitnoje, S.S.S.R.	78	51.17 N	27.14 E
Rakitnoje, S.S.S.R.	89	45.36 N	134.17 E
Rakke	76	58.59 N	26.15 E
Rakkestad	26	59.26 N	11.21 E
Rakoniewice	30	52.10 N	16.16 E
Rakops	156	21.00 S	24.32 E
Rákoscsaba ✦[8]	264c	47.29 N	19.17 E
Rákoshegy ✦[8]	264c	47.28 N	19.14 E
Rákoskeresztúr ✦[8]	264c	47.29 N	19.15 E
Rákoskert ✦[8]	264c	47.28 N	19.19 E
Rákosliget ✦[8]	264c	47.30 N	19.16 E
Rákospalota ✦[8]	264c	47.34 N	19.08 E
Rákos-patak ≃	264c	47.33 N	19.04 E
Rákosszentmihály ✦[8]	264c	47.32 N	19.11 E
Rakovnická plošina ⋀[1]	54	50.08 N	13.47 E
Rakovník	54	50.05 N	13.43 E
Rakovski	38	42.18 N	24.58 E
Rakša	80	53.33 N	41.37 E
Raksakiny	86	60.37 N	73.52 E
Rakuša	80	47.03 N	52.47 E
Råkvåg	26	63.46 N	10.05 E
Rakvere	76	59.22 N	26.20 E
Rakwa	164	2.42 S	134.30 E
Raleigh, Nf., Can.	186	51.34 N	55.44 W
Raleigh, Ms., U.S.	194	32.02 N	89.31 W
Raleigh, N.C., U.S.	192	35.46 N	78.38 W
Raleigh Hills	224	45.29 N	122.45 W
Ralik Chain II	14	8.00 N	167.00 E
Ralls	196	33.40 N	101.23 W
Ralls ▫[6]	219	39.34 N	91.30 W
Ralsko ∧	54	50.42 N	14.47 E
Ralston, Ne., U.S.	198	41.12 N	96.02 W
Ralston, Pa., U.S.	210	41.31 N	76.57 W
Ram ≃	182	52.23 N	115.25 W
Rama, Nic.	236	12.09 N	84.15 W
Rama, Yis.	132	32.56 N	35.22 E
Rama ≃	236	12.08 N	84.13 W
Ramacca	70	37.23 N	14.42 E
Rāmachandrapuram	122	16.51 N	82.01 E
Ramādah	144	13.38 N	43.56 E
Ramah	200	35.07 N	108.29 W
Ramah Indian Reservation ✦[4]	200	34.50 N	108.25 W
Rama Indian Reserve ✦[4]	212	44.41 N	79.15 W
Ramales de la Victoria	34	43.15 N	3.27 W
Ramalho, Serra do ⋀	255	13.45 S	44.00 W
Rām Allāh	132	31.54 N	35.12 E
Rāman	123	29.58 N	74.58 E
Rāmanagaram	122	12.43 N	77.18 E
Rāmanāthapuram	122	9.23 N	78.50 E
Ramānāthpur	272b	22.41 N	88.14 E
Ramanbāti	272b	22.47 N	88.08 E
Rāmānuj Ganj	124	23.48 N	83.42 E
Ramapo	276	41.08 N	74.10 W
Ramapo ≃	276	40.58 N	74.17 W
Ramapo Lake ⊜	276	41.02 N	74.16 W
Ramapo Mountains ⋀	276	41.08 N	74.12 W
Ramapo Valley Airport ⊠	276	41.06 N	74.02 W
Ramas, Cape ≻	122	15.07 N	73.55 E
Ramasaig	46	57.24 N	6.44 W
Ramasucha	76	52.46 N	33.33 E
Ramat Gan	132	32.05 N	34.49 E
Ramat HaSharon	132	32.09 N	34.50 E
Ramat HaShofét	132	32.37 N	35.06 E
Ramathlabama	156	25.40 S	25.35 E
Ramatuelle	62	43.13 N	6.37 E
Rama VI Bridge ✦[5]	269a	13.48 N	100.31 E
Rāmban	123	33.15 N	75.15 E
Rambervillers	58	48.21 N	6.38 E
Rambi I	175g	16.30 S	179.59 E
Rambipuji	115a	8.13 S	113.36 E
Rambleton Acres	208	39.39 N	75.38 W
Ramblewood	285	39.55 N	74.56 W
Rambouillet	50	48.39 N	1.50 E
Rambouillet, Château de ⊥	261	48.39 N	1.49 E
Rambouillet, Forêt de ♠	261	48.40 N	1.50 E
Rambutyo Island I	164	2.20 S	147.50 E
Rām Dās	123	31.58 N	74.54 E
Rāmdia	126	23.42 N	89.32 E
Rāmdurg	122	15.57 N	75.18 E
Ramea	186	47.31 N	57.23 W
Ramea Islands II	186	47.31 N	57.21 W
Rāmechhāp	124	27.20 N	86.05 E
Rame Head ≻, Transkei	158	31.48 S	29.22 E
Rame Head ≻, Eng., U.K.	42	50.19 N	4.13 W
Rämen ⊜	40	60.18 N	15.10 E
Ramenje, S.S.S.R.	76	60.17 N	43.46 E
Ramenje, S.S.S.R.	82	56.34 N	37.13 E
Ramenka ✦[8]	265b	55.41 N	37.30 E
Ramenskoje	82	55.34 N	38.14 E
Ramer	194	32.03 N	86.13 W
Ramerupt	50	48.31 N	4.18 E
Rameški	76	57.21 N	36.03 E
Rāmeswaram	122	9.17 N	79.18 E
Ramey	214	40.48 N	78.24 W
Ramey Air Force Base ■	240m	18.30 N	67.08 W
Rāmganj	126	23.06 N	90.51 E
Rāmgarh, Bngl.	120	22.59 N	91.44 E
Rāmgarh, India	120	27.15 N	75.11 E
Rāmgarh, India	120	27.22 N	70.30 E
Rāmgarh, India	124	23.38 N	85.31 E
Rāmgarh, India	124	24.34 N	87.15 E
Rāmgarh, India	126	22.42 N	87.04 E
Rāmgarh Hills ⋀[2]	124	22.50 N	83.10 E
Ram Head ≻	240m	18.18 N	64.42 W
Rāmhormoz	128	31.16 N	49.36 E
Ramingining	164	12.19 S	135.03 E
Ramingstein	64	47.04 N	13.50 E
Ramírez, Méx.	196	27.20 N	100.58 W
Ramírez, Méx.	196	25.57 N	97.46 W
Ramiriquí	246	5.24 N	73.20 W
Ramis ≃	144	7.59 N	41.34 E
Rāmjībanpur	126	22.50 N	87.37 E
Rāmkānāli	126	23.35 N	86.45 E
Raml, Qārat ar- ∧[2]	142	30.02 N	30.39 E
Ramla	132	31.55 N	34.52 E
Ramlu ∧	144	13.24 N	41.51 E
Ramm, Jabal ∧	132	29.35 N	35.24 E
Rämmen	40	60.07 N	14.08 E
Rāmnagar, India	123	32.49 N	75.19 E
Rāmnagar, India	124	25.17 N	83.02 E
Rāmnagar, India	124	29.24 N	79.07 E
Rāmnagar, India	126	21.41 N	87.33 E
Rāmnagar, India	272b	22.23 N	88.19 E
Ramnäs	40	59.46 N	16.12 E
Ramo	144	6.42 N	41.23 E
Ramon'	78	51.54 N	39.20 E
Ramon, Har ∧	132	30.30 N	34.38 E
Ramon, Makhtésh ⍛[7]	132	30.36 N	34.49 E
Ramon, Naḥal V	132	30.36 N	34.55 E
Ramona, Ca., U.S.	228	33.02 N	116.52 W
Ramona, Ok., U.S.	196	36.31 N	95.55 W
Ramona, S.D., U.S.	198	44.07 N	97.12 W
Ramor, Lough ⊜	48	53.49 N	7.05 W
Ramos	234	22.50 N	101.55 W
Ramos ✦[8]	287a	22.51 S	43.15 W
Ramos ≃[1]	150	5.08 N	5.22 E
Ramos Arizpe	232	25.33 N	100.58 W
Ramosch	58	46.50 N	10.22 E
Ramos Island I	116	8.06 N	117.02 E
Ramos Mejía	258	34.38 S	58.34 W
Ramot	132	32.46 N	35.40 E
Ramotswa	156	24.56 S	25.50 E
Rāmpāl	126	22.34 N	89.39 E
Rampart	180	65.30 N	150.11 W
Ramparts ≃	180	66.11 N	129.03 W
Rampillon	50	48.33 N	3.04 E
Rampside	44	54.05 N	3.10 W
Rāmpur, India	120	31.27 N	77.38 E
Rāmpur, India	123	29.49 N	77.27 E
Rāmpur, India	124	28.49 N	79.02 E
Rāmpura	120	24.28 N	75.26 E
Rāmpura Phūl	123	30.17 N	75.14 E
Rampur Boalia → Rājshāhi	124	24.22 N	88.36 E
Rāmpur Hāt	126	24.10 N	87.47 E
Ramrath	263	51.06 N	6.41 E
Ramree Island I	110	19.06 N	93.48 E
Rāmsāgar	126	23.05 N	87.17 E
Ramsau	64	47.36 N	12.54 E
Ramsay Range ⋀	162	18.31 S	127.03 E
Ramsbeck	56	51.18 N	8.24 E
Ramsberg	40	59.46 N	15.17 E
Ramsbottom	44	53.40 N	2.19 W
Ramsden Bellhouse	260	51.37 N	0.29 E
Ramsden Heath	260	51.38 N	0.28 E
Ramsdorf	52	51.54 N	6.55 E
Ramsele	26	63.33 N	16.29 E
Ramsenthal	60	50.01 N	11.35 E
Ramseur	192	35.44 N	79.39 W
Ramsey, I. of Man	44	54.20 N	4.21 W
Ramsey, Eng., U.K.	42	51.56 N	1.14 E
Ramsey, Eng., U.K.	42	52.27 N	0.07 W
Ramsey, Il., U.S.	219	39.08 N	89.06 W
Ramsey, N.J., U.S.	210	41.03 N	74.08 W
Ramsey Bay ⊂	44	54.20 N	4.20 W
Ramsey Brook ≃	276	41.02 N	74.08 W
Ramsey Creek ≃	219	39.03 N	89.04 W
Ramsey Island I	42	51.52 N	5.10 W
Ramsey Lake ⊜	190	47.15 N	82.16 W
Ramsey Lake State Park ♠	219	39.10 N	89.08 W
Ramsgate, Austl.	274a	33.59 S	151.08 E
Ramsgate, S. Afr.	158	30.55 S	30.20 E
Ramsgate, Eng., U.K.	42	51.20 N	1.25 E
Rāmshai	124	26.44 N	88.51 E
Rāmshīr	128	30.54 N	49.24 E
Ramshorn Peak ∧	202	45.09 N	111.06 W
Rämshyttan	40	60.18 N	15.13 E
Ramsjö	26	62.11 N	15.39 E
Ramsloh	52	53.06 N	7.40 E
Ramstein	56	49.27 N	7.33 E
Rāmtek	120	21.24 N	79.20 E
Rāmu, Bngl.	120	21.25 N	92.07 E
Ramu, Kenya	154	3.56 N	41.13 E
Ramu ≃	164	5.00 S	144.40 E
Ramuševo	76	57.50 N	31.37 E
Ramvik	26	62.49 N	17.51 E
Ramville, Îlet I	240e	14.42 N	60.53 W
Ramygala	76	55.31 N	24.18 E
Ramzaj	80	53.18 N	44.44 E
Rānāghāt	126	23.11 N	88.35 E
Rana Kao, Volcán ∧[1]	174z	27.11 S	109.27 W
Ranalt	64	47.02 N	11.13 E
Rāna Pratāp Sāgar ⊜[1]	120	24.50 N	75.35 E
Rånäs	40	59.48 N	18.17 E
Ranau	112	5.58 N	116.41 E
Ranau, Danau ⊜	112	4.50 S	103.55 E
Ranbīrsinghpura	123	32.38 N	74.44 E
Ranburne	194	33.31 N	85.20 W
Ranburn Woods	278	41.33 N	87.22 W
Rancabali	115a	7.08 S	107.21 E
Rancagua	252	34.10 S	70.45 W
Rancah	115a	7.12 S	108.30 E
Rance ≃	32	48.31 N	1.59 W
Rancevo, S.S.S.R.	76	56.40 N	33.02 E
Rancevo, S.S.S.R.	76	56.56 N	34.03 E
Rancharia	255	22.15 S	50.55 W
Rancheria	180	60.05 N	130.40 W
Ranchería ≃	246	11.34 N	72.54 W
Rancheria Rock ∧	202	44.53 N	120.08 W
Ranches of Taos	200	36.22 N	105.37 W
Ranchester	202	44.54 N	107.09 W
Rānchi	124	23.21 N	85.20 E
Ranchillos	252	26.57 S	65.03 W
Rānchi Plateau ⋀[1]	124	23.20 N	84.50 E
Ranch Lake ⊜	184	52.30 N	104.46 W
Rancho Colorado, Presa de ⊜[1]	286a	19.29 N	99.17 W
Rancho Cordova	226	38.35 N	121.18 W
Rancho Del Mar	226	38.10 N	122.15 W
Rancho Nuevo, Méx.	196	26.22 N	99.54 W
Rancho Nuevo, Méx.	234	23.12 N	97.48 W
Rancho Palos Verdes	228	33.45 N	118.24 W
Rancho Rinconado	226	37.18 N	122.01 W
Rancho Santa Fe	228	33.01 N	117.12 W
Rancho Veloz	240p	22.53 N	80.23 W
Ranchuelo	240p	22.23 N	80.09 W
Ranco, Lago ⊜	254	40.14 S	72.24 W
Rancocas	208	40.00 N	74.52 W
Rancocas Creek ≃	285	40.02 N	74.59 W
Rancocas Creek, North Branch ≃	208	40.00 N	74.52 W
Rancocas Creek, South Branch ≃	208	40.00 N	74.52 W
Rancocas Creek, Southwest Branch ≃	285	39.57 N	74.48 W
Rancocas Heights	285	39.59 N	74.51 W
Rancocas State Park ♠	285	40.00 N	74.50 W
Rancocas Woods	285	39.59 N	74.51 W
Rancul	252	35.03 S	64.42 W
Rand	166	35.36 S	146.35 E
Rand (Germiston) Airport ⊠	273d	26.15 S	28.09 E
Randa	58	46.07 N	7.47 E
Randall Lake ⊜	216	41.57 N	85.02 W
Randall Park Mall ✦[9]	279a	41.26 N	81.32 W
Randalls Island I	276	40.48 N	73.55 W
Randallstown	284b	39.22 N	76.48 W
Randalstown	48	54.45 N	6.19 W
Randan	32	46.01 N	3.21 E
Rāndaveswar	126	23.43 N	87.17 E
Randazzo	70	37.53 N	14.57 E
Randbøl	41	55.42 N	9.16 E
Randburg	273d	26.06 S	27.59 E
Randers	26	56.28 N	10.03 E
Randfontein	158	26.11 S	27.42 E
Randfontein ▫[5]	273d	26.13 S	27.40 E
Randgate	273d	26.11 S	27.41 E
Randhurst ✦[9]	278	42.05 N	87.56 W
Randle	224	46.32 N	121.57 W
Randleman	192	35.49 N	79.48 W
Randlett	196	34.10 N	98.27 W
Randolph, Az., U.S.	200	32.55 N	111.30 W
Randolph, Me., U.S.	188	44.13 N	69.46 W
Randolph, Ma., U.S.	207	42.09 N	71.02 W
Randolph, Ne., U.S.	198	42.22 N	97.21 W
Randolph, N.Y., U.S.	210	42.09 N	78.58 W
Randolph, Oh., U.S.	214	41.01 N	81.14 W
Randolph, Ut,. U.S.	200	41.39 N	111.10 W
Randolph, Vt., U.S.	188	43.55 N	72.39 W
Randolph, Wi., U.S.	190	43.32 N	89.00 W
Randolph ▫[6], In., U.S.	218	40.10 N	85.00 W
Randolph ▫[6], Mo., U.S.	219	39.22 N	92.20 W
Randolph Air Force Base ■	196	29.32 N	98.16 W
Randolph Hills	284c	39.03 N	77.05 W
Randolph Village	284c	38.53 N	76.52 W
Random Island I	186	48.08 N	53.45 W
Random Lake	190	43.33 N	87.57 W
Randow ≃	54	53.41 N	14.04 E
Randowaya	164	1.52 S	136.31 E
Randowbruch ≣	54	53.15 N	14.10 E
Randsburg	228	35.22 N	117.39 W
Randse Afrikaanse Universiteit ʊ[2]	273d	26.11 S	27.50 E
Randsfjorden ⊜	26	60.25 N	10.24 E
Rand Stadium ♠	273d	26.14 S	28.03 E
Randublatung	115a	7.12 S	111.23 E
Randudongkal	115a	7.06 S	109.19 E
Randwick	170	33.55 S	151.15 E
Randwick Racecourse ♠	274a	33.54 S	151.14 E
Råneå	26	65.52 N	22.18 E
Ranelagh	258	34.48 S	58.12 W
Rāner	123	28.53 N	73.17 E
Ranérou	150	15.18 N	13.58 W
Rāneswar	126	24.02 N	87.25 E
Raneue	114	5.03 N	95.20 E
Ranford	168a	32.48 S	116.31 E
Ranfurly, N.Z.	172	45.08 S	170.06 E
Ranfurly, Scot., U.K.	46	55.52 N	4.33 W
Rangae	114	6.17 N	101.44 E
Rāngāmāti	120	22.38 N	92.12 E
Rangantemiang	112	0.35 S	113.19 E
Rangas, Tanjung ≻	112	2.38 S	118.49 E
Rangasa, Tanjung ≻	112	3.33 S	118.56 E
Rangaunu Bay ⊂	172	34.50 S	173.15 E
Range Creek ≃	200	39.18 N	110.04 W
Range Indian Reserve ✦[4]	182	49.09 N	119.50 W
Rangeley	188	44.57 N	70.38 W
Rangely	200	40.05 N	108.48 W
Ranger	196	32.28 N	98.40 W
Ranger Lake ⊜	190	46.54 N	83.35 W
Rangersdorf	64	46.51 N	12.58 E
Ranghe	100	33.43 N	112.51 E
Rangia	120	26.28 N	91.38 E
Rangiora	172	43.18 S	172.36 E
Rangitaiki ≃	172	37.54 S	176.53 E
Rangitata ≃	172	44.12 S	171.30 E
Rangitikei ≃	172	40.18 S	175.14 E
Rangitukia	172	37.46 S	178.27 E
Rangkasbitung	115a	6.21 S	106.15 E
Rangkul'	85	38.29 N	74.22 E
Rangoon → Yangon	110	16.47 N	96.10 E
Rangoon ≃	110	16.29 N	96.21 E
Rangpo	124	27.11 N	88.32 E
Rangpur, Bngl.	124	25.45 N	89.15 E
Rangpur, Pāk.	123	30.31 N	71.34 E
Rangpuri ⊥	272a	28.33 N	77.08 E
Rangsang, Pulau I	114	1.00 N	102.55 E
Rangsdorf	54	52.17 N	13.25 E
Rangsdorfer See ⊜	264a	52.17 N	13.24 E
Ranguana Cay I	236	16.20 N	88.09 W
Ranguana Entrance ʯ	236	16.19 N	88.09 W
Rangun → Yangon	110	16.47 N	96.10 E
Ranholas	266c	38.47 N	9.22 W
Rānībāndh	126	22.52 N	86.47 E
Rānībennur	122	14.37 N	75.37 E
Rānīganj	126	23.37 N	87.08 E
Rānikhet	124	29.39 N	79.25 E
Ranino	80	52.58 N	40.15 E
Ranis	54	50.39 N	11.34 E
Rānīwāra	120	24.45 N	72.13 E
Rāniyah	128	36.15 N	44.53 E
Rankamhaeng National Park ♠	110	17.10 N	99.58 E
Ranken ≃	166	20.31 S	137.36 E
Ranken Store	166	19.35 S	136.55 E
Rankin, Il., U.S.	216	40.27 N	87.53 W
Rankin, Mi., U.S.	216	42.55 N	83.46 W
Rankin, Pa., U.S.	279b	40.24 N	79.52 W
Rankin, Tx., U.S.	196	31.13 N	101.56 W
Rankin Inlet	176	62.45 N	92.10 W
Rankins Springs	166	33.50 S	146.16 E
Rankūs	132	33.45 N	36.23 E
Rankweil	58	47.17 N	9.39 E
Ranlo	192	35.17 N	81.07 W
Ranneje	80	51.29 N	52.37 E
Rannersdorf	264b	48.08 N	16.28 E
Rannoch, Loch ⊜	46	56.41 N	4.20 W
Rannoch Moor ✦[3]	46	56.38 N	4.40 W
Rann of Kutch → Kutch, Rann of ✦[1]	120	24.05 N	70.10 E
Ranobe ≃	157b	17.10 S	44.08 E
Ranohira	157b	22.29 S	45.24 E
Ranomafana, Madag.	157b	18.57 S	48.50 E
Ranomafana, Madag.	157b	24.36 S	46.58 E
Ranomena	157b	23.25 S	47.17 E
Ranong	110	9.58 N	98.38 E
Ranongga Island I	175e	8.05 S	156.34 E
Ranopiso	157b	25.03 S	46.40 E
Ranot	110	7.46 N	100.19 E
Ranotsara Nord	157b	22.48 S	46.36 E
Rānsai	272c	18.53 N	73.05 E
Ransäter	40	59.46 N	13.26 E
Ransiki	164	1.30 S	134.10 E
Ransom, Il., U.S.	216	41.09 N	88.39 W
Ransom, Ks., U.S.	198	38.38 N	99.56 W
Ransom, Pa., U.S.	210	41.24 N	75.50 W
Ransom Creek ≃	284a	43.04 N	78.45 W
Ransomville	210	43.14 N	78.54 W
Ranson	188	39.17 N	77.51 W
Ransta	40	59.48 N	16.38 E
Ranstadt	56	50.21 N	8.59 E
Rantabe	157b	15.42 S	49.39 E
Rantasalmi	26	62.04 N	28.18 E
Rantau, Indon.	112	2.56 S	115.09 E
Rantau, Malay.	114	2.35 N	101.58 E
Rantaukampar	114	1.24 N	100.59 E
Rantaupanjang, Indon.	112	1.51 S	102.19 E
Rantaupanjang, Indon.	112	1.16 S	101.49 E
Rantaupanjang, Indon.	114	0.58 N	99.13 E
Rantauprapat	114	2.06 N	99.50 E
Rantekombola, Bulu ∧	112	3.21 S	120.01 E
Ranten	61	47.09 N	14.05 E
Rantepao	112	2.59 S	119.54 E
Rantigny	50	49.20 N	2.26 E
Rantoul	216	40.09 N	88.20 W
Rantsila	26	64.31 N	25.39 E
Rantzau	54	54.15 N	10.30 E
Ranua	26	65.55 N	26.32 E
Rānvād	272c	18.53 N	72.55 E
Ranwanalenaus	156	19.35 S	22.47 E
Råö	26	57.24 N	11.56 E
Rao'er	100	28.48 N	117.40 E
Raohe	89	46.47 N	134.00 E
Raon-L'Étape	58	48.24 N	6.51 E
Raon-sur-Plaine	58	48.31 N	7.06 E
Raoping	100	23.43 N	117.01 E
Raoui, 'Erg er ✦[2]	148	29.17 N	2.20 W
Raoul	192	34.27 N	83.36 W
Raoul Island I	14	29.16 S	177.54 W
Raoyang	98	38.16 N	115.44 E
Raoyang ≃	104	41.50 N	122.35 E
Raoyanghe	104	41.46 N	122.26 E
Rapa I	14	27.36 S	144.20 W
Rapa, Ponta do ≻	252	27.22 S	48.26 W
Rapallo	62	44.21 N	9.14 E
Rapang	112	3.50 S	119.48 E
Rāpar	120	23.34 N	70.38 E
Raparo, Monte ∧	68	40.12 N	15.59 E
Rapatovo	80	55.04 N	54.37 E
Rāpch ≃	128	25.28 N	59.21 E
Rapel ≃	252	33.55 S	71.51 W
Rapel, Embalse ⊜[1]	252	34.12 S	71.30 W
Rapelli	252	26.24 S	64.29 W
Raphoe	48	54.52 N	7.36 W
Rapid ≃, Mi., U.S.	190	45.55 N	86.58 W
Rapid ≃, Mn., U.S.	198	48.42 N	94.26 W
Rapid ≃, Wa., U.S.	224	47.48 N	121.18 W
Rapidan ≃	188	38.22 N	77.37 W
Rapid Bay	168b	35.32 S	138.12 E
Rapid City, Mb., Can.	184	50.08 N	100.02 W
Rapid City, Mi., U.S.	190	44.50 N	85.16 W
Rapid City, S.D., U.S.	198	44.04 N	103.13 W
Rapid Creek ≃	198	43.54 N	102.37 W
Rapide Taureau, Barrage du ✦[6]	206	46.52 N	73.39 W
Rapid River	190	45.55 N	86.58 W
Räpina	76	58.06 N	27.27 E
Rapkan	85	40.22 N	70.40 E
Rapla	76	59.01 N	24.47 E
Rapness	46	59.14 N	2.51 W
Rapolano Terme	66	43.17 N	11.36 E
Rapolla	68	40.58 N	15.41 E
Rapone	68	40.51 N	15.30 E
Raposo ∧[2]	266c	38.40 N	9.11 W
Rappahannock ≃	208	37.34 N	76.18 W
Rappbodestausee ⊜[1]	54	51.09 N	10.58 E
Rappenlochschlucht ∟	58	47.23 N	9.47 E
Rappottenstein	61	48.31 N	15.05 E
Rāptī ▫[8]	124	28.15 N	82.30 E
Rāpti (Raptī) ≃, Asia	124	26.18 N	83.41 E
Rāptī ≃, Nepāl	124	27.33 N	84.07 E
Rápulo ≃	248	13.43 S	65.32 W
Rapu-Rapu	116	13.11 N	124.08 E
Rapu Rapu Island I	116	13.12 N	124.09 E
Raqabah, Khashm ar- ∧[2]	142	28.18 N	31.43 E
Raquette ≃	206	45.00 N	74.42 W
Raraka I[1]	14	16.10 S	144.54 W
Rara National Park ♠	124	29.35 N	82.05 E
Rārh Plains ≚	126	23.13 N	87.20 E
Rāribahāl	126	24.05 N	87.21 E
Raritan	210	40.34 N	74.38 W
Raritan ≃	208	40.29 N	74.17 W
Raritan, North Branch ≃	210	40.33 N	74.41 W
Raritan, South Branch ≃	210	40.33 N	74.41 W
Raritan Bay ⊂	208	40.28 N	74.12 W
Raroïa I	14	16.01 S	142.27 W
Raron	58	46.19 N	7.48 E
Rarotonga I	174k	21.14 S	159.46 W
Rarotonga International Airport ⊠	174k	21.12 S	159.49 W
Rarz	85	39.23 N	68.44 E
Rasa, Ilha I	287a	23.04 S	43.09 W
Rasa, Punta ≻	254	40.51 S	62.19 W
Rašaant	88	49.07 N	101.25 E
Rasa da Guaratiba, Ilha I	256	23.05 S	43.34 W
Rasa Island I	116	9.14 N	118.27 E
Ra's al-'Ayn	130	36.51 N	40.04 E
Ra's al-Barr	142	31.31 N	31.50 E
Ra's al-Khalīj	142	31.15 N	31.39 E
Ra's al-Khaymah	128	25.47 N	55.57 E
Ra's al-Unūf	146	30.31 N	18.34 E
Ra's al-Ushsh ✦[8]	142	31.08 N	32.18 E
Ra's an-Naqb, Miṣr	132	29.36 N	34.51 E
Ra's an-Naqb, Urd.	132	30.00 N	35.29 E
Rasawi	164	2.04 S	134.01 E
Ra's Ba'labakk	130	34.15 N	36.25 E
Rasbo	40	59.57 N	17.53 E
Raschau	54	50.32 N	12.50 E
Ras Dashen Terara ∧	144	13.16 N	38.24 E
Rasdorf	56	50.43 N	9.53 E
Raseborg	26	59.59 N	23.39 E
Raseiniai	76	55.24 N	23.07 E
Râs el Aïoun	36	35.30 N	8.18 E
Ras el Ma, Alg.	148	34.31 N	0.46 W
Râs el Mâ, Mali	150	16.37 N	4.28 W
Ras el Oued	34	35.57 N	5.03 E
Rasen-Antholz → Anterselva di Sopra	64	46.52 N	12.08 E
Raševka	78	50.14 N	33.54 E
Rashād	140	11.51 N	31.04 E
Rāshayyā	132	33.30 N	35.51 E
Rashīd (Rosetta)	142	31.24 N	30.25 E
Rashīd, Far' (Rosetta Branch) ≃	142	31.30 N	30.21 E
Rashīd, Maṣabb (Rosetta Mouth) ≃[1]	142	31.30 N	30.20 E
Rashīd Qal'eh	120	31.31 N	67.31 E
Rashin → Najin	98	42.15 N	130.18 E
Rasht	128	37.16 N	49.36 E
Rashtrapati Bhawan ʊ	272a	28.37 N	77.12 E
Rasina ≃	38	43.37 N	21.22 E
Rāsipuram	122	11.28 N	78.10 E
Rasi Salai	110	15.20 N	104.09 E
Rāsk	128	26.13 N	61.25 E
Raška	38	43.17 N	20.37 E
Rask Mølle	41	55.52 N	9.37 E
Rās Koh ∧	128	28.50 N	65.12 E
Raškov	78	47.57 N	28.50 E
Raskunda	126	22.48 N	87.26 E
Rasm al-Arwām, Sabkhat ⊜	130	35.53 N	37.40 E
R'asna	76	54.01 N	31.12 E
R'asnopol'	78	47.04 N	31.12 E
Raso, Cabo ≻	266c	38.43 N	9.29 W
Raso, Ilhéu I	150a	16.37 N	24.36 W
Rasocolmo, Capo ≻	70	38.18 N	15.31 E
Rason Lake ⊜	162	28.46 S	124.20 E
Raspberry Peak ∧	194	34.23 N	94.01 W
Raspopinskaja	80	49.24 N	42.52 E
Rasra	124	25.51 N	83.51 E
Rass Jebel	36	37.13 N	10.09 E
Rasskazovka	265b	55.38 N	37.20 E
Rasskazovo	80	52.40 N	41.53 E
Rasšua, ostrov I	74	47.45 N	153.01 E
Rassudovo	82	55.29 N	36.54 E
Rassvet, S.S.S.R.	84	43.58 N	46.44 E
Rassvet, S.S.S.R.	84	43.58 N	46.44 E
Rassvet, S.S.S.R.	86	57.02 N	91.34 E
Rassvet, S.S.S.R.	88	57.02 N	91.34 E
Rassypnaja	80	51.35 N	53.37 E
Rassypnoje	83	48.08 N	38.34 E
Rast	38	43.53 N	23.17 E
Rastälven ≃	40	59.37 N	14.56 E
Ra's Tannūrah	128	26.42 N	50.06 E
Rastatt	56	48.51 N	8.12 E
Rastavica ≃	78	49.44 N	30.01 E
Rastede	52	53.15 N	8.11 E
Rastegai'sa ∧	24	70.00 N	26.18 E
Rastenberg	54	51.10 N	11.25 E
Rastenburg → Kętrzyn	30	54.06 N	21.23 E
Rastorf	54	54.16 N	10.19 E
Rastorgujevo	82	55.33 N	37.41 E
Rastovcy	82	56.39 N	37.35 E
Rastunovo	82	55.16 N	37.50 E
Rasu, Monte ∧	71	40.25 N	9.00 E
Rasūl	123	32.42 N	73.34 E
Rasūlnagar	123	32.20 N	73.47 E
Rasulpur	272a	28.37 N	77.22 E
Rasulpur ✦[8]	272a	28.42 N	77.01 E
Rasun di sopra	64	46.48 N	12.03 E
Rasun di sotto	64	46.47 N	12.02 E
Rasura	58	46.06 N	9.33 E
Råsvalen ⊜	40	59.40 N	15.10 E
Răsvani	38	44.25 N	26.53 E
Rat ≃, Mb., Can.	184	55.41 N	99.04 W
Rat ≃, Mb., Can.	184	49.35 N	97.08 W
Ratahan	112	1.04 N	124.48 E
Ratak Chain II	14	9.00 N	171.00 E
Ratangarh	120	28.05 N	74.36 E
Ratanpur, India	126	23.07 N	87.04 E
Ratanpur, India	272b	22.50 N	88.14 E
Rätansbyn	26	62.29 N	14.32 E
Rat Burana	269a	13.41 N	100.30 E
Ratčino, S.S.S.R.	80	53.02 N	39.55 E
Ratčino, S.S.S.R.	82	55.16 N	38.39 E
Ratcliff	222	31.24 N	95.08 W
Rateče	64	46.30 N	13.43 E
Ratekau	54	53.57 N	10.44 E
Rāth	124	25.35 N	79.34 E
Rath ✦[8]	263	51.17 N	6.49 E
Rathangan	48	53.12 N	6.59 W
Rathbone	210	42.08 N	77.19 W
Rathbun Lake ⊜	212	44.47 N	78.12 W
Rathbun Lake ⊜[1]	190	40.54 N	93.05 W
Rathcoole	48	53.16 N	6.28 W
Rathcormack	48	52.05 N	8.17 W
Rathdowney, Austl.	171a	28.12 S	152.52 E
Rathdowney, Ire.	48	52.50 N	7.34 W
Rathdrum, Ire.	48	52.56 N	6.13 W
Rathdrum, Id., U.S.	202	47.48 N	116.53 W
Rathebur	54	53.44 N	13.46 E
Ratheim	52	51.04 N	6.10 E
Rathen	46	57.38 N	2.02 W
Rathenow	54	52.36 N	12.20 E
Rathfriland	48	54.14 N	6.10 W
Rathkeale	48	52.32 N	8.56 W
Rathlin Island I	48	55.18 N	6.13 W
Rathlin Sound ʯ	48	55.15 N	6.15 W
Ráth Luirc (Charleville)	48	52.21 N	8.41 W
Rathmecke	263	51.15 N	7.38 E
Rathmelton	48	55.02 N	7.38 W
Rathmore	48	52.03 N	9.13 W
Rathmullan	48	55.06 N	7.33 W
Rathnew	48	53.00 N	6.05 W
Ratho	46	55.55 N	3.22 W
Rathowen	48	53.40 N	7.31 W
Rathstock	54	52.31 N	14.32 E
Rathwell	184	49.40 N	98.32 W
Ratibor → Racibórz	30	50.06 N	18.13 E
Raticosa, Passo della)(	66	44.10 N	11.20 E
Rätikon ⋀	58	47.03 N	9.40 E
Ratingen	56	51.18 N	6.51 E
Ratisbon → Regensburg	60	49.01 N	12.06 E
Rätische Alpen → Rhaetian Alps ⋀	58	46.30 N	10.00 E
Rat Island I	181a	51.55 N	178.20 E
Rat Islands II	181a	51.40 N	178.30 E
Rat'kovo	82	56.01 N	38.38 E
Rat Lake ⊜	184	56.10 N	99.40 W
Ratlām	120	23.19 N	75.04 E
Ratmanova, ostrov I	180	65.46 N	169.02 W
Ratnāgiri	122	16.59 N	73.18 E
Ratnapura	122	6.41 N	80.24 E
Ratno	78	51.40 N	24.31 E
Ratodero	120	27.48 N	68.18 E
Ratomka	76	53.56 N	27.21 E
Raton	196	36.54 N	104.26 W
Raton Pass)(	196	36.59 N	104.29 W
Ratqah, Wādī ar- V	130	34.25 N	40.55 E
Ratt ≃	224	47.27 N	124.21 W
Rattanaburi	110	15.19 N	103.51 E
Rattaphum	110	7.08 N	100.16 E
Ratten	61	47.29 N	15.43 E
Rattlesnake	202	46.56 N	113.59 W
Rattlesnake Creek ≃, Ks., U.S.	198	38.13 N	98.22 W
Rattlesnake Creek ≃, Oh., U.S.	218	39.16 N	83.23 W
Rattlesnake Creek ≃, Or., U.S.	202	42.44 N	117.47 W
Rattlesnake Creek ≃, Wa., U.S.	224	45.48 N	121.29 W
Rattlesnake Creek ≃, Wa., U.S.	224	46.45 N	120.55 W
Rattlesnake Mountain ∧	207	41.42 N	72.50 W
Rattlesnake Peak ∧	280	34.16 N	117.47 W
Rattling Brook	186	49.38 N	56.10 W
Rattling Run ≃	279b	40.33 N	79.32 W
Rattray	46	56.35 N	3.19 W
Rattray Head ≻	46	57.37 N	1.49 W
Rattu	123	35.08 N	74.48 E
Rättvik	26	60.53 N	15.06 E
Ratz, Mount ∧	180	57.23 N	132.19 W
Ratzebuhr → Okonek	30	53.33 N	16.50 E
Ratzeburg	54	53.42 N	10.46 E
Ratzeburger See ⊜	54	53.45 N	10.47 E
Rätzlingen	54	52.23 N	11.08 E
Rau	112	0.34 N	100.01 E
Raub, Malay.	114	3.48 N	101.52 E
Raub, In., U.S.	216	40.44 N	87.29 W
Raubsville	208	40.38 N	75.12 W
Rauch	252	36.46 S	59.06 W
Raucheck ∧	64	47.30 N	13.14 E
Rauchenwarth	264b	48.05 N	16.32 E
Rauchtown	210	41.07 N	77.14 W
Raucourt-et-Flaba	56	49.36 N	4.57 E
Rauen	54	52.20 N	14.01 E
Rauenstein	54	50.24 N	11.03 E
Raufarhöfn	24a	66.30 N	15.57 W
Raufoss	26	60.43 N	10.37 E
Rauhe Ebrach ≃	56	49.50 N	10.56 E
Raukumara Range ⋀	172	37.47 S	178.02 E
Raul Soares	255	20.05 S	42.22 W
Rauma	26	61.08 N	21.30 E
Rauma ≃	26	62.33 N	7.43 E
Raumünzach	56	48.38 N	8.21 E
Rauna	76	57.20 N	25.43 E
Raunds	42	52.21 N	0.33 W
Raung, Gunung ∧	115a	8.08 S	114.03 E
Raunheim	56	50.01 N	8.28 E
Raupal'an	180	65.28 N	171.59 W
Raurimu	172	39.07 S	175.24 E
Rauris	64	47.13 N	13.00 E
Raurkela	124	22.13 N	84.53 E
Rauschenberg	56	50.53 N	8.55 E
Rausu	92a	44.01 N	145.12 E
Rautalampi	26	62.38 N	26.50 E
Rāutara	272b	22.51 N	88.28 E
Rautavaara	26	63.29 N	28.18 E
Ravahere I[1]	14	18.14 S	142.09 W
Ravalgaon	122	20.38 N	74.25 E
Ravanica, Manastir ʊ[1]	38	43.58 N	21.26 E
Ravānsar	128	34.43 N	46.40 E
Ravanusa	70	37.16 N	13.58 E
Rāvar	128	31.15 N	56.53 E
Ravarano	64	44.35 N	10.04 E
Ravarino	64	44.44 N	11.06 E
Rava-Russkaja	78	50.14 N	23.37 E
Ravascletto	64	46.32 N	12.57 E
Ravat	85	39.54 N	70.12 E
Ravello	68	40.39 N	14.37 E
Ravelo	248	18.48 S	65.32 W
Raven	192	37.05 N	81.51 W
Ravena	210	42.28 N	73.49 W
Ravenglass	44	54.21 N	3.24 W
Raven Lake ⊜	212	45.13 N	78.51 W
Ravenna, It.	66	44.25 N	12.12 E
Ravenna, Ky., U.S.	192	37.41 N	83.57 W
Ravenna, Mi., U.S.	216	43.11 N	85.56 W
Ravenna, Ne., U.S.	198	41.01 N	98.54 W
Ravenna, Oh., U.S.	214	41.09 N	81.14 W
Ravenna ▫[4]	66	44.25 N	11.59 E
Ravensbourne	171a	27.22 S	152.10 E
Ravensbourne National Park ♠	171a	27.21 S	152.15 E
Ravensburg	58	47.47 N	9.37 E
Ravenscrag	184	49.30 N	109.05 W
Ravensdale	224	47.21 N	121.58 W
Ravenshoe	166	17.37 S	145.29 E
Ravensthorpe, Austl.	162	33.35 S	120.02 E
Ravensthorpe, Eng., U.K.	44	53.42 N	1.35 W
Ravenswood, S. Afr.	273d	26.11 S	28.15 E
Ravenswood, Mi., U.S.	216	42.45 N	84.36 W
Ravenswood, W.V., U.S.	188	38.56 N	81.45 W
Ravenswood Park ♠	283	42.36 N	70.42 W
Ravenswood Point ≻	282	37.30 N	122.08 W
Ravensworth	284c	38.48 N	77.13 W
Rāver	120	21.15 N	76.02 E
Ravernet ≃	48	54.30 N	6.04 W
Rāvi ≃	123	30.35 N	71.49 E
Ravières	50	47.45 N	4.17 E
Ravine	208	40.34 N	76.24 W
Ravine Lake ⊜[1]	276	40.43 N	74.38 W
Ravinia Park ♠	278	42.09 N	87.46 W
Ravna Gora	36	45.23 N	14.57 E
Ravne	61	46.33 N	14.58 E
Ravnina	128	37.57 N	62.40 E
Ravsted	41	55.01 N	9.08 E
Rāwah	128	34.28 N	41.55 E
Rawaki I[1]	14	3.43 S	170.43 W
Rāwala Kot	123	33.52 N	73.46 E
Rāwalpindi	123	33.36 N	73.04 E
Rawa Mazowiecka	30	51.46 N	20.16 E
Rāwāndūz	128	36.37 N	44.31 E

≃ River	Fluß	Río	Rivière	Rio
≊ Canal	Kanal	Canal	Canal	Canal
∟ Waterfall, Rapids	Wasserfall, Stromschnellen	Cascada, Rápidos	Chute d'eau, Rapides	Cascata, Rápidos
ʯ Strait	Meeresstraße	Estrecho	Détroit	Estreito
⊂ Bay, Gulf	Bucht, Golf	Bahía, Golfo	Baie, Golfe	Baía, Golfo
⊜ Lake, Lakes	See, Seen	Lago, Lagos	Lac, Lacs	Lago, Lagos
≣ Swamp	Sumpf	Pantano	Marais	Pântano
⍓ Ice Features, Glacier	Eis- und Gletscherformen	Accidentes Glaciales	Formes glaciaires	Acidentes glaciares
⍑ Other Hydrographic Features	Andere Hydrographische Objekte	Otros Elementos Hidrográficos	Autres données hydrographiques	Outros acidentes hidrográficos

✤ Submarine Features	Untermeerische Objekte	Accidentes Submarinos	Formes de relief sous-marin	Acidentes submarinos
▫ Political Unit	Politische Einheit	Unidad Politica	Entité politique	Unidade política
ʊ Cultural Institution	Kulturelle Institution	Institución Cultural	Institution culturelle	Institução cultural
⊥ Historical Site	Historische Stätte	Sitio Histórico	Site historique	Sitio histórico
♠ Recreational Site	Erholungs- und Ferienort	Sitio de Recreo	Centre de loisirs	Area de Lazer
⊠ Airport	Flughafen	Aeropuerto	Aéroport	Aeroporto
■ Military Installation	Militäranlage	Instalación Militar	Installation militaire	Instalação militar
✦ Miscellaneous	Verschiedenes	Misceláneo	Divers	Diversos

ENGLISH				DEUTSCH			
Name	Page	Lat.°/′	Long.°/′	Name	Seite	Breite°/′	Länge°/′ E = Ost

The following is a multi-column gazetteer index. Entries are listed in reading order.

Left page columns (Name, Page, Lat, Long):

- Rawang 114 3.19 N 101.35 E
- Rawas ≃ 112 2.42 S 103.24 E
- Rāwatsar 123 29.17 N 74.23 E
- Rawāwis, Wādī ∨ 146 30.26 N 15.24 E
- Rawdah 130 35.15 N 41.05 E
- Rawdah, Wādī ar- ∨ 130 34.22 N 37.21 E
- Rawd al-Faraj ⬩ ⁸ 273c 30.05 N 31.14 E
- Rawdaw, Jazīrat ar- I 273c 30.01 N 31.13 E
- Rawson 206 46.03 N 73.43 W
- Rawene 172 35.24 S 173.30 E
- Rawhah 144 19.28 N 41.48 E
- Rawhide Creek ≃ 198 42.06 N 104.20 W
- Rawhide Lake ⊚ 190 46.39 N 82.37 W
- Rawhide Mountain ∧ 204 38.17 N 116.25 W
- Rawi 112 2.07 S 113.56 E
- Rawi, Ko I 114 6.33 N 99.14 E
- Rawicz 30 51.37 N 16.52 E
- Rawlina 162 31.01 S 125.20 E
- Rawlins 200 41.47 N 107.14 W
- Rawlinson, Mount ∧ 162 25.58 S 127.28 E
- Rawlinson Range ∧ 162 24.31 S 127.30 E
- Rawmarsh 44 53.27 N 1.21 W
- Rawreth 260 51.37 N 0.35 E
- Rawson, Arg. 252 34.36 S 60.04 W
- Rawson, Arg. 254 43.18 S 65.06 W
- Rawson, Oh., U.S. 216 40.57 N 83.47 W
- Rawsonville 158 33.41 S 19.20 E
- Rawtenstall 44 53.42 N 2.18 W
- Rawu 102 29.30 N 96.45 E
- Rax ∧ 61 47.42 N 15.43 E
- Raxăul 124 26.59 N 84.51 E
- Ray, Il., U.S. 219 40.12 N 90.29 W
- Ray, In., U.S. 211 41.45 N 84.53 W
- Ray, N.D., U.S. 198 48.20 N 103.09 W
- Ray ≃ 42 51.48 N 1.05 W
- Ray, Cape ⊁ 186 47.40 N 59.18 W
- Raya 112 1.05 N 118.32 E
- Raya, Bukit ∧ 112 0.40 S 112.41 E
- Raya, Gunong ∧ 114 6.22 N 99.49 E
- Raya, Pulau I 114 4.52 N 95.22 E
- Rayachoti 122 14.03 N 78.45 E
- Rayadurg 122 14.42 N 76.52 E
- Rāyagarha 122 19.10 N 83.25 E
- Rayburn 222 30.35 N 94.56 W
- Rāyen, B.R.D. 263 51.28 N 6.32 E
- Rāyen, Īrān 128 29.34 N 57.26 E
- Ray Hubbard, Lake ⊚ ¹ 222 32.53 N 96.35 W
- Rāyikhah I 128 26.21 N 36.21 E
- Rayland 214 40.11 N 80.41 W
- Rayleigh 42 51.36 N 0.36 E
- Raymond, Ab., Can. 182 49.27 N 112.39 W
- Raymond, Ca., U.S. 226 37.13 N 119.54 W
- Raymond, Il., U.S. 219 39.19 N 89.34 W
- Raymond, Mn., U.S. 198 45.00 N 95.14 W
- Raymond, Ms., U.S. 194 32.15 N 90.25 W
- Raymond, Oh., U.S. 216 40.20 N 83.28 W
- Raymond, Wa., U.S. 224 46.41 N 123.43 W
- Raymond Terrace 170 32.46 S 151.44 E
- Raymondville 196 26.29 N 97.47 W
- Raymore 184 51.25 N 104.31 W
- Ray Mountains ∧ 180 65.45 N 151.30 W
- Rāyna 126 23.05 N 87.54 E
- Rayne 194 30.14 N 92.16 W
- Rayner Glacier ⊠ 9 67.40 S 48.30 E
- Raynham Dog Track 207 41.56 N 71.04 W
- ⁺ 283 41.59 N 71.04 W
- Rayón, Méx. 232 29.43 N 110.35 W
- Rayón, Méx. 234 17.12 N 93.40 W
- Rayón, Méx. 234 21.51 N 99.40 W
- Rayón, Parque Nacional ♦ 234 19.54 N 100.10 W
- Rayones 232 25.01 N 100.05 W
- Rayong 110 12.40 N 101.17 E
- Rāypur 272b 22.25 N 88.31 E
- Rayrah ∨ 140 15.21 N 34.41 E
- Rayse Creek ≃ 219 38.13 N 88.51 W
- Raystown Lake ⊚ ¹ 214 40.20 N 78.05 W
- Rayton 158 25.45 S 28.32 E
- Raytown 194 39.00 N 94.27 W
- Rayville 194 32.28 N 91.45 W
- Raywood 222 30.02 N 94.40 W
- Raz, Pointe du ⊁ 32 48.02 N 4.43 W
- Raza, Punta ⊁ 234 21.02 N 105.20 W
- Razan, Īrān 128 35.23 N 49.02 E
- R'azan', S.S.S.R. 80 54.38 N 39.44 E
- R'azan', S.S.S.R. 82 54.15 N 39.00 E
- R'azancevo 82 56.42 N 39.12 E
- R'azancevo 38 43.40 N 21.33 E
- R'azanovo 38 43.40 N 21.33 E
- Razbegaj 265a 59.47 N 29.56 E
- Razboeni 38 47.05 N 26.32 E
- Razdan 84 40.30 N 44.46 E
- Razdan ≃ 84 39.58 N 44.27 E
- Razdel'naja 78 46.51 N 30.05 E
- Razdol'e 86 58.25 N 94.38 E
- Razdol'noje 88 52.27 N 103.13 E
- Razdol'noje, S.S.S.R. 78 45.47 N 33.29 E
- Razdol'noje, S.S.S.R. 88 47.37 N 38.01 E
- Razdol'noje, S.S.S.R. 89 43.30 N 131.52 E
- Razdol'nyj 86 46.38 N 42.57 E
- Razdorskaja 78 47.33 N 40.38 E
- Razdory, S.S.S.R. 78 43.07 N 44.50 E
- Razdory, S.S.S.R. 265b 55.45 N 37.18 E
- Ra'ženoje 86 57.31 N 38.52 E
- Raževo 86 56.09 N 68.25 E
- Razgrad 38 43.32 N 26.31 E
- Razlog 38 41.54 N 23.28 E
- Razmachnino 80 54.17 N 115.28 E
- Razmitlevo 285a 59.54 N 30.41 E
- Raznočinovka 80 46.37 N 47.57 E
- Raznomojka 86 52.29 N 55.52 E
- Razorback Mountain ∧ 182 51.35 N 124.42 W
- R'ažsk 80 53.43 N 40.04 E
- Razvil'noje 80 46.14 N 41.18 E
- Razzoli, Isola I 71 41.18 N 9.21 E
- Ré, Île de I 32 46.12 S 1.25 W
- Rea ≃ 42 52.18 N 2.32 W
- Read 282 53.49 N 2.21 W
- Reading, Eng., U.K. 42 51.28 N 0.59 W
- Reading, Il., U.S. 216 41.05 N 88.51 W
- Reading, Ks., U.S. 198 38.31 N 95.57 W
- Reading, Ma., U.S. 207 42.31 N 71.05 W
- Reading, Mi., U.S. 216 41.50 N 84.44 W
- Reading, Oh., U.S. 218 39.13 N 84.27 W
- Reading, Pa., U.S. 208 40.20 N 75.55 W
- Reading Center 210 42.26 N 76.56 W
- Reading Station ⁺ 285 39.57 N 75.10 W
- Readington 210 40.34 N 74.44 W
- Readlyn 219 42.42 N 92.13 W
- Readsboro 207 42.46 N 72.56 W
- Readstown 219 43.25 N 90.45 W
- Reagan 222 31.13 N 96.47 W
- Real 116 14.40 N 121.36 E
- Real, Cordillera ∧ 250 11.27 S 37.22 W
- Real, Estero ≃ 236 12.56 N 87.23 W
- Real del Castillo 232 31.58 N 116.19 W
- Real del Padre 252 34.50 S 67.46 W
- Real de San Carlos 258 34.26 S 57.53 W
- Realengo ⁸ 273a 22.53 S 43.22 W
- Real Felipe, Castillo ⅄ 286d 12.04 S 77.09 W
- Realicó 252 35.02 S 64.15 W
- Realitos 196 27.27 N 98.32 W
- Realmonte 70 37.18 N 13.28 E
- Reamstown 208 40.12 N 76.07 W
- Reana del Roiale 64 46.12 N 13.13 E
- Reardan 202 47.40 N 117.52 W
- Reatini, Monti ∧ 66 42.28 N 13.01 E
- Réau 261 48.37 N 2.38 E
- Reay 44 58.33 N 3.47 W
- Reay Forest ♦ 46 58.22 N 4.58 W
- Rebecca, Lake ⊚ 162 29.53 S 122.10 E
- Rebecq-Rognon 50 50.39 N 4.08 E
- Rebeida, Wādī ∨ 140 20.45 N 34.06 E
- Rebel Hill 285 40.04 N 75.20 W
- Rebersburg 210 40.57 N 77.27 W

Second column (Rebi...):

- Rebi 164 6.23 S 134.06 E
- Rebiana Sand Sea → Rabyānah, Sahrā ⬩ ² 146 24.20 N 20.37 E
- Rebild Bakker ♦ 26 56.50 N 9.51 E
- Reboly 24 63.50 N 30.47 E
- Rebouças 252 25.36 S 50.42 W
- Rebricha 86 53.05 N 82.20 E
- Rebun-tō I 92a 45.23 N 141.02 E
- Recale 252 36.39 S 61.05 W
- Recanati 66 43.24 N 13.32 E
- Rečane 76 56.25 N 31.39 E
- Recco 62 44.22 N 9.09 E
- Recey-sur-Ource 58 47.47 N 4.52 E
- Rechitsa 76 52.22 N 30.25 E
- Rechberghausen 56 48.44 N 9.38 E
- Recherche, Archipelago of the II 162 34.05 S 122.45 E
- Recherche, Cape ⊁ 175e 10.11 S 161.19 E
- Réchicourt-le-Château 58 48.40 N 6.51 E
- Rechlin 54 53.20 N 12.43 E
- Rechna Doāb ⁺ ¹ 123 31.35 N 73.30 E
- Rechnitz 61 47.18 N 16.27 E
- Rečica, S.S.S.R. 76 52.22 N 30.25 E
- Rečica, S.S.S.R. 78 51.52 N 26.48 E
- Recife 250 8.03 S 34.54 W
- Recife, Kaap ⊁ 158 34.02 S 25.44 E
- Recinto 252 36.48 S 71.44 W
- Recke 52 52.20 N 7.43 E
- Rečki 78 51.07 N 34.30 E
- Recklinghausen 52 51.36 N 7.13 E
- Reconquista 252 29.09 S 59.39 W
- Reconquista ≃ 252 29.09 S 59.39 W
- Recovery Glacier ⊠ 9 81.10 S 28.00 W
- Recreio, Bra. 248 8.11 S 58.14 W
- Recreio, Bra. 255 21.32 S 42.28 W
- Recreo 252 29.16 S 65.04 W
- Rector 194 36.16 N 90.17 W
- Rectorville 218 38.34 N 83.39 W
- Recuay 248 9.43 S 77.28 W
- Recz 30 53.16 N 15.33 E
- Red (Hong) (Yuan) ≃, Asia 110 20.17 N 106.34 E
- Red ≃, N.A. 178 32.00 N 96.48 W
- Red ≃, U.S. 178 31.00 N 91.40 W
- Red ≃, U.S. 194 36.32 N 87.22 W
- Red ≃, U.S. 192 37.51 N 84.05 W
- Red ≃, N.M., U.S. 200 36.39 N 105.42 W
- Red ≃, Wi., U.S. 190 44.49 N 88.38 W
- Red ≃, Elm Fork ≃ 196 34.53 N 99.19 W
- Red, North Fork ≃ 196 34.24 N 99.14 W
- Red, Prairie Dog Town Fork ≃ 196 34.35 N 99.58 W
- Red, Salt Fork ≃ 196 34.27 N 99.22 W
- Red, South Fork ≃ 196 36.41 N 86.56 W
- Red, West Fork ≃ 194 36.32 N 87.21 W
- Reda 50 54.37 N 18.21 E
- Redang, Pulau I 114 5.47 N 103.00 E
- Redange 56 49.46 N 5.54 E
- Redcar 44 54.37 N 1.04 W
- Red Dial 42 54.48 N 3.10 W
- Redditch 42 52.19 N 1.56 W
- Rede 46 55.12 N 34.41 E
- Redefin 54 53.21 N 11.11 E
- Redenhuys 158 30.30 S 18.33 E
- Redenção da Serra 256 23.16 S 45.33 W
- Redesdale ∨ 44 55.17 N 2.16 W
- Redes Mere ⊚ 262 53.16 N 2.14 W
- Redeye ≃ 198 46.26 N 94.49 W
- Redfield, Ia., U.S. 198 41.35 N 94.11 W
- Redfield, N.Y., U.S. 210 43.37 N 75.51 W
- Redfield, S.D., U.S. 198 44.52 N 98.31 W
- Redfish Lake ⊚ 184 44.07 N 114.56 W
- Redford 207 44.29 N 104.10 W
- Redford Township 216 42.25 N 83.18 W
- Red Fox Forest 204 38.49 N 77.15 W
- Redhead 241r 10.47 N 60.57 W
- Red Hill, Austl. 162 21.59 S 116.03 E
- Red Hill, Eng., U.K. 42 51.14 N 0.11 W
- Red Hill, Ca., U.S. 208 33.45 N 117.48 W
- Red Hill, Pa., U.S. 208 40.23 N 75.29 W
- Red Hill Aerodrome ⊞ 261 48.46 N 16.58 E
- Red Hill Branch ≃ 284b 39.14 N 76.51 W
- Red Hook 210 41.59 N 73.52 W
- Redhouse Creek ≃ 284b 39.18 N 76.45 W
- Rédics 61 46.36 N 16.30 E
- Red Indian Lake ⊚ 186 48.40 N 56.50 W
- Redinger Lake ⊚ ¹ 226 37.07 N 119.25 W
- Red Island I 76 58.05 N 31.33 E
- Redja ≃ 76 58.05 N 31.33 E
- Redkino 82 56.38 N 36.17 E

Third column (Red Lake...):

- Red Lake, On., Can. 184 51.03 N 93.49 W
- Redlake, Mn., U.S. 198 47.53 N 95.01 W
- Red Lake ≃, On., Can. 184 51.01 N 95.05 W
- Red Lake ⊚, Az., U.S. 200 35.40 N 114.04 W
- Red Lake ⊚, S.D., U.S. 198 43.44 N 99.13 W
- Red Lake ⊚ 222 31.40 N 95.58 W
- Red Lake ≃ 198 47.55 N 97.01 W
- Red Lake Falls 198 47.52 N 96.16 W
- Red Lake Indian Reservation ⬩ ⁴ 198 48.05 N 95.05 W
- Red Lake Road 184 49.58 N 93.22 W
- Redland, Scot., U.K. 46 59.05 N 3.05 W
- Redland, Tx., U.S. 222 31.25 N 94.43 W
- Redland Bay 171a 27.37 S 153.18 E
- Redlands, S. Afr. 158 29.52 S 22.57 E
- Redlands, Ca., U.S. 228 34.01 N 117.12 W
- Red Level 194 31.24 N 86.36 W
- Red Lick 194 31.47 N 90.58 W
- Redlin 54 53.22 N 12.01 E
- Red Lion, Pa., U.S. 208 39.54 N 76.36 W
- Red Lion, Pa., U.S. 285 39.53 N 75.41 W
- Red Lion Airport ⊞ 285 39.54 N 74.45 W
- Red Lodge 200 45.11 N 109.14 W
- Red Mill 206 46.25 N 72.28 W
- Redmond, Or., U.S. 224 44.16 N 121.10 W
- Redmond, Wa., U.S. 224 47.40 N 122.07 W
- Red Mountain ∧, Ca., U.S. 204 41.35 N 123.06 W
- Red Mountain ∧, Ca., U.S. 228 35.21 N 117.36 W
- Red Mountain ∧, Mt., U.S. 202 47.07 N 112.44 W
- Red Mountain Pass ⋋ 200 37.54 N 107.43 W
- Rednitz ≃ 56 49.28 N 10.59 E
- Red Oak, Ia., U.S. 198 41.00 N 95.13 W
- Red Oak, Ok., U.S. 196 34.57 N 95.04 W
- Red Oak, Tx., U.S. 222 32.31 N 96.48 W
- Red Oak Creek ≃ 222 32.28 N 96.30 W
- Red Oaks Mill 210 41.40 N 73.52 W
- Redon 32 47.39 N 2.05 W
- Redonda I 238 16.55 N 62.19 W
- Redonda, Isla I 256 23.04 S 43.12 W
- Redonda Islands II 182 50.13 N 124.48 W
- Redondela 34 42.17 N 8.36 W
- Redondo, Port. 34 38.39 N 7.33 W
- Redondo, Mount ∧ 224 47.20 N 122.19 W
- Redondo, Mount ∧ 116 10.21 N 125.38 E
- Redondo Beach 228 33.50 N 118.23 W
- Redondo Beach State Park ♦ 280 33.50 N 118.24 W
- Redoubt, Mount ∧ 224 48.57 N 121.18 W
- Redoubt Volcano ∧¹ 180 60.29 N 152.45 W
- Red Pass 182 52.59 N 118.59 W
- Red Pheasant Indian Reserve ⬩ ⁴ 184 52.30 N 108.07 W
- Red Pine Lake ⊚ 212 45.12 N 78.42 W
- Red Point ⊁ 170 34.29 S 150.55 E
- Red Rock, B.C., Can. 182 53.39 N 122.41 W
- Red Rock, On., Can. 190 48.58 N 88.15 W
- Red Rock, Tx., U.S. 222 29.58 N 97.27 W
- Red Rock ≃ 282 37.56 N 122.26 W
- Red Rock ∧ 202 44.59 N 112.52 W
- Red Rock, Lake ⊚¹ 198 41.30 N 93.02 W
- Red Rock Canyon State Park ♦ 228 35.23 N 118.00 W
- Red Rocks Point ⊁ 162 32.13 S 127.32 E
- Red Root Creek ≃ 276 40.30 N 74.19 W
- Red Run ≃, Md., U.S. 284b 39.24 N 76.47 W
- Red Run ≃, Mi., U.S. 281 42.34 N 82.58 W
- Redruth 42 50.13 N 5.14 W
- Red Sea ≃ ² 136 20.00 N 38.00 E
- Red Springs 192 34.48 N 79.11 W
- Redstone 182 52.08 N 123.42 W
- Redstone ≃, N.T., Can. 180 64.17 N 124.33 W
- Redstone ≃, On., Can. 212 45.12 N 78.32 W
- Redstone Arsenal ♦ 194 34.38 N 86.38 W
- Redstone Creek ≃ 198 44.04 N 98.05 W
- Redstone Lake ⊚ 212 45.11 N 78.32 W
- Red Sucker Lake ⊚ 184 54.09 N 93.40 W
- Reduction 279b 40.11 N 79.46 W
- Redut 80 47.22 N 51.53 E
- Redvers 184 49.33 N 101.39 W
- Redwater 182 53.57 N 113.06 W
- Redwater ≃ 198 48.03 N 105.13 W
- Red Wharf Bay ⊂ 262 53.18 N 4.10 W
- Redwillow ≃ 182 55.04 N 119.21 W
- Red Willow Creek ≃ 198 40.13 N 100.00 W
- Red Wing 198 44.33 N 92.32 W
- Redwood ≃ 212 44.44 N 95.05 W
- Redwood City 226 37.29 N 122.14 W
- Redwood Creek ≃, Ca., U.S. 204 41.18 N 124.05 W
- Redwood Creek ≃, Ca., U.S. 226 38.18 N 122.18 W
- Redwood Creek ≃, Ca., U.S. 282 37.31 N 122.12 W
- Redwood Estates 282 37.10 N 121.59 W
- Redwood Falls 198 44.32 N 95.07 W
- Redwood National Park ♦ 204 41.30 N 124.05 W
- Redwood Point ⊁ 282 37.31 N 122.12 W
- Redwood Regional Park ♦ 282 37.48 N 122.10 W
- Redwood Terrace 204 37.19 N 122.18 W
- Redwood Valley 226 39.15 N 123.12 W
- Ree, Lough ⊚ 48 53.35 N 8.00 W
- Reed City 216 43.52 N 85.30 W
- Reeder 198 46.06 N 102.56 W
- Reed Lake ⊚, Mb., Can. 184 54.37 N 100.30 W
- Reed Lake ⊚, Sk., Can. 184 50.24 N 107.05 W
- Reedley 226 36.35 N 119.26 W
- Reedsburg, Oh., U.S. 216 40.49 N 82.07 W
- Reedsburg, Wi., U.S. 198 43.31 N 90.00 W
- Reeds Peak ∧ 200 33.10 N 107.35 W
- Reedsport 224 43.42 N 124.05 W
- Reedsville, Pa., U.S. 208 40.39 N 77.35 W
- Reedsville, Wi., U.S. 190 44.09 N 87.57 W
- Reedville 208 37.50 N 76.16 W
- Reedy Creek ≃ 208 28.04 N 81.21 W
- Reedy Creek Swamp ≃ 220 28.17 N 81.31 W
- Reedy Lake ⊚ 162 27.44 N 81.22 W
- Reefton 172 42.07 S 171.52 E
- Reefoot Lake ⊚ 194 36.25 N 89.22 W
- Reepham 42 52.46 N 1.07 E
- Reerse ⁺¹ 54 55.31 N 11.06 E
- Rees 52 51.45 N 6.23 E
- Reese 216 43.27 N 83.42 W
- Reese ≃ 204 40.39 N 116.54 W
- Reese Air Force Base ♦ 196 33.36 N 102.02 W
- Reeseville 190 43.18 N 88.50 W
- Reetz 54 52.21 N 12.32 E
- Reetz in der Neumark → Recz 30 53.16 N 15.33 E
- Reeuwijk 50 52.03 N 4.42 E
- Refahiye 130 39.54 N 38.46 E
- Reforma de Pineda 234 16.24 N 94.28 W

Fourth column (Refton...):

- Refton 208 39.57 N 76.14 W
- Refuge Cove 182 50.07 N 124.50 W
- Refugio 196 28.18 N 97.16 W
- Refugio, Isla I 254 43.58 S 73.12 W
- Refugio Creek ≃ 282 38.01 N 122.17 W
- Rega ≃ 30 54.10 N 15.18 E
- Regalia 34 35.38 N 5.46 W
- Regalbuto 70 37.39 N 14.38 E
- Regau 64 47.59 N 13.41 E
- Regen 64 48.59 N 13.07 E
- Regen ≃ 60 49.01 N 12.06 E
- Regência 255 19.36 S 39.49 W
- Regency Estates 284c 39.05 N 76.41 W
- Regensburg 60 49.01 N 12.06 E
- Regensburg ⁺ 60 49.01 N 12.06 E
- Regenstauf 60 49.08 N 12.08 E
- Regent, Austl. 274b 37.44 S 145.00 E
- Regent, N.D., U.S. 198 46.25 N 102.33 W
- Regents Park 274a 33.53 S 151.02 E
- Regents Park ⬩ ⁸ 273d 26.15 S 28.04 E
- Regent's Park ♦ 260 51.32 N 0.09 W
- Regentville 233 33.47 S 150.40 E
- Reggâne 148 26.42 N 0.16 E
- Regge ≃ 52 52.31 N 6.22 E
- Reggio di Calabria 68 38.06 N 15.39 E
- Reggio di Calabria ⬩ ⁸ 68 38.10 N 16.00 E
- Reggiolo 64 44.55 N 10.48 E
- Reggio nell'Emilia 64 44.43 N 10.36 E
- Reggio nell'Emilia ⬩ ⁸ 64 44.37 N 10.37 E
- Reghaïen ⁻ 40 58.54 N 15.46 E
- Reghin 38 46.47 N 24.42 E
- Regina, Sk., Can. 184 50.25 N 104.39 W
- Regina, Guy. fr. 250 4.19 N 52.08 W
- Regina, S. Afr. 158 27.02 S 26.30 E
- Regina Beach 184 50.47 N 105.00 W
- Regina Elena, Canale ≃ 266b 45.11 N 8.39 E
- Regis-Breitingen 54 51.05 N 12.26 E
- Registro 252 24.30 S 47.50 W
- Registro do Araguaia 255 15.44 S 51.50 W
- Regiwar 120 25.57 N 65.44 E
- Regla ⬩ ⁸ 286b 23.08 N 82.20 W
- Regla 240p 23.08 N 82.20 W
- Regnitz ≃ 56 49.54 N 10.49 E
- Rego Park ⬩ ⁸ 276 40.44 N 73.52 W
- Regozero 24 65.28 N 31.10 E
- Regstrup 26 55.40 N 11.37 E
- Reguengos de Monsaraz 34 38.25 N 7.32 W
- Reh 263 51.22 N 7.33 E
- Rehau 54 50.15 N 12.02 E
- Rehbach ≃ 56 49.27 N 8.27 E
- Rehberg 54 52.43 N 12.10 E
- Rehberge, Volkspark ♦ 264a 52.35 N 13.11 E
- Rehburg 52 52.28 N 9.13 E
- Rehden 52 52.37 N 8.29 E
- Rehe ≃ 56 50.38 N 8.07 E
- Rehefeld-Zaunhaus 54 50.45 N 13.32 E
- Rehetobel 56 47.24 N 9.28 E
- Rehfelde 54 52.30 N 13.54 E
- Rehli 124 23.38 N 79.05 E
- Rehme 52 52.12 N 8.49 E
- Rehna 54 53.47 N 11.03 E
- Rehoboth, Namibia 156 17.53 S 15.04 E
- Rehoboth, Namibia 156 23.35 S 17.04 E
- Rehoboth Bay ⊂ 208 38.40 N 75.06 W
- Rehoboth Beach 208 38.43 N 75.04 W
- Rehoboth Seamount ⬩³ 16 37.30 N 59.50 W
- Rehon 56 49.30 N 5.45 E
- Rehti 124 22.44 N 77.26 E
- Reiche Ebrach ≃ 56 49.49 N 10.58 E
- Reiche Liesing ≃ 264b 48.08 N 16.16 E
- Reichelsheim 56 49.43 N 8.50 E
- Reichenau, B.R.D. 58 47.41 N 9.03 E
- Reichenau → Bogatynia, Pol. 30 50.53 N 15.00 E
- Reichenau, Schw. 56 46.49 N 9.24 E
- Reichenau an der Rax 61 47.42 N 15.50 E
- Reichenbach, D.D.R. 54 51.08 N 14.48 E
- Reichenbach, D.D.R. 54 50.37 N 12.18 E
- Reichenbach → Dzierżoniów, Pol. 30 50.44 N 16.39 E
- Reichenbach, Schw. 56 46.37 N 7.42 E
- Reichenberg → Liberec 30 50.46 N 15.03 E
- Reichenhofen 58 47.50 N 10.05 E
- Reichensachsen 52 51.09 N 9.59 E
- Reichen Spitze ∧ 64 47.09 N 12.07 E
- Reichertshausen 60 48.28 N 11.31 E
- Reichertsheim 60 48.12 N 12.17 E
- Reichraming 61 47.42 N 14.20 E
- Reichsbrücke ⁵ 264b 48.14 N 16.25 E
- Reichshoffen 56 48.56 N 7.40 E
- Reid 162 30.49 S 128.26 E
- Reid, Mount ∧, Austl. 162 17.58 S 130.38 E
- Reid, Mount ∧, Ak., U.S. 182 55.42 N 131.15 W
- Reidsville, Ga., U.S. 192 32.05 N 82.07 W
- Reidsville, N.C., U.S. 192 36.21 N 79.39 W
- Reiffton 208 40.19 N 75.53 W
- Reigate 42 51.14 N 0.13 W
- Reigate and Banstead ⬩ ⁸ 260 51.17 N 0.12 W
- Reignac-sur-Indre 58 47.13 N 0.55 E
- Reignier 58 46.08 N 6.16 E
- Reigoldswil 56 47.24 N 7.41 E
- Reihoku 91 32.31 N 130.02 E
- Reillanne 58 43.53 N 5.40 E
- Reims 50 49.15 N 4.02 E
- Reims, Montagne de ♦² 50 49.08 N 4.10 E
- Reina, Cerro ∧ 286e 33.24 N 70.44 W
- Reina Adelaida, Archipiélago II 254 52.10 S 74.25 W
- Reina Alejandra → Queen Alexandra Range ∧ 9 84.00 S 168.00 E
- Reina Carlota, Estrecho de la → Queen Charlotte Sound ≃ 182 51.30 N 129.30 W
- Reinach, Schw. 56 47.30 N 7.35 E
- Reinach, Schw. 56 47.15 N 8.11 E
- Reina Fabiola → Queen Fabiola Mountains ∧ 9 71.30 S 35.40 E
- Reina Maria, Costa de la → Queen Mary Coast ⊁ 9 67.00 S 96.00 E
- Reina Maud, Tierras de la → Queen Maud Land ⁺ 9 73.00 S 12.00 E
- Reina Maud, Tierras de la → Queen Maud Mountains ∧ 9 86.00 S 160.00 W
- Reinach, Schw. 128 25.57 N 95.53 E
- Reinbek 190 42.19 N 92.35 W
- Reinbeck 190 42.19 N 92.35 W
- Reinberg 54 54.09 N 13.15 E
- Reinach 9 71.30 S 35.40 E
- Reindeer Island I 184 52.30 N 98.10 W
- Reindeer Lake ⊚ 176 57.15 N 102.40 W
- Reindeer Station 176 68.42 N 134.06 W
- Reine 22 67.56 N 13.06 E
- Reinen 22 67.56 N 13.06 E
- Reinga, Cape ⊁ 172 34.25 S 172.41 E
- Reinhardswald ♦² 52 51.30 N 9.30 E

Right page columns (DEUTSCH — Name, Seite, Breite, Länge):

- Reinhardtsdorf 54 50.53 N 14.11 E
- Reinheim 56 49.49 N 8.50 E
- Reinickendorf ⬩ ⁸ 264a 52.35 N 13.21 E
- Reinosa 34 43.00 N 4.08 W
- Reino Unido → United Kingdom ⁺¹ 30 54.00 N 2.00 W
- Reinsdorf, D.D.R. 54 50.42 N 12.33 E
- Reinsdorf, D.D.R. 54 51.54 N 12.37 E
- Reinshagen ⁺ 263 51.10 N 7.09 E
- Reinstorf 52 53.16 N 10.30 E
- Reis 130 38.16 N 31.35 E
- Reisach 64 46.39 N 13.09 E
- Reisaelva ≃ 24 69.48 N 21.00 E
- Reischach 60 48.17 N 12.44 E
- Reisdorf 56 49.52 N 6.16 E
- Reisdorf, Camp ⁺ 273b 4.21 S 15.15 E
- Reisholz ⬩ ⁸ 263 51.11 N 6.52 E
- Reisjärvi 26 63.37 N 24.54 E
- Reisterstown 208 39.28 N 76.49 W
- Reisterstown Road ⁺⁹ 284b 39.02 N 76.42 W
- Reitano 70 37.58 N 14.20 E
- Reitdiep ≃ 52 53.20 N 6.18 E
- Reith bei Seefeld 64 47.18 N 11.12 E
- Reit im Winkl 64 47.40 N 12.28 E
- Reitz 158 27.53 S 28.31 E
- Reitzenhain 54 50.33 N 13.13 E
- Reivilo 158 27.36 S 24.08 E
- Rejinagar 126 23.53 N 88.15 E
- Rejmyra 40 58.50 N 15.55 E
- Rejowiec Fabryczny 30 51.08 N 23.13 E
- Rejšteyn 60 49.09 N 13.31 E
- Rekarne ≃ 40 59.26 N 16.20 E
- Rekarne ≃ 40 59.17 N 16.25 E
- Rekata 118 7.50 N 159.30 E
- Rekovac 38 43.51 N 21.06 E
- Reliance, N.T., Can. 176 62.42 N 109.08 W
- Reliance, Wy., U.S. 200 41.40 N 109.11 W
- Relief Reservoir ⊚¹ 226 38.16 N 119.44 W
- Religione, Punta ⊁ 70 36.42 N 14.46 E
- Feliz Creek ≃ 226 36.19 N 121.18 W
- Fellingen 52 53.59 N 9.51 E
- Fellinghausen ⬩ ⁸ 263 51.25 N 7.04 E
- Felócavi, Seno ⊂ 254 41.40 S 72.35 W
- Femada 148 32.19 N 10.24 E
- Femagen 56 50.34 N 7.13 E
- Fémalard 50 48.26 N 0.42 E
- Femansão 250 4.25 S 49.34 W
- Femanso 250 9.41 S 42.04 W
- Femarde ≃ 162 48.35 S 2.15 E
- Femarkable, Mount ∧ 162 32.48 S 138.10 E
- Fembau 114 2.35 N 102.06 E
- Fembia 114 2.20 N 102.13 E
- Femchi 34 35.04 N 1.26 W
- Femedios, Col. 246 7.02 N 74.41 W
- Femedios, Cuba 240p 22.29 N 79.33 W
- Femedios, Pan. 236 8.14 N 81.51 W
- Femedios, Punta ⊁ 236 13.31 N 89.49 W
- Femedios, Santuario de los ⁺¹ 286a 19.28 N 99.15 W
- Femedello di Escalada ⬩ ⁸ 258 34.43 S 58.23 W
- Femels ≃ 52 52.44 E
- Femenncy 82 54.36 N 36.36 E
- Femer 190 47.03 N 93.54 W
- Femeshk 128 26.56 N 58.49 E
- Femhoogte 158 29.53 S 23.09 E
- Femich Airport ⊞ 279b 50.00 N 5.39 E
- Fémigny, Lac ⊚ 190 47.51 N 79.12 W
- Fémilly 50 49.01 N 6.24 E
- Fémindell 214 41.20 N 81.23 W
- Femington, In., U.S. 216 40.45 N 87.09 W
- Femington, Va., U.S. 208 38.32 N 77.48 W
- Fémire 250 4.53 N 52.17 W
- Fémiremont 56 48.01 N 6.35 E
- Fémo ⬩ ⁸ 273a 6.42 N 3.29 E
- Femolá, Estany del ⊂ 266d 41.17 N 2.04 E
- Femollon 58 44.28 N 6.10 E
- Femoray 58 46.46 N 4.34 E
- Femoulins 50 48.53 N 4.34 E
- Femovka ⁻ ⁸ 52 52.59 N 38.43 E
- Fempang, Pulau I 114 0.51 N 104.10 E
- Femptendorf 54 51.08 N 11.39 E
- Femscheid 56 48.52 N 9.16 E
- Femscheid 52 51.11 N 7.11 E
- Femscheider-Stausee ⊚¹ 263 51.10 N 7.14 E
- Femsen, Ia., U.S. 198 42.48 N 95.58 W
- Femsen, N.Y., U.S. 210 43.19 N 75.11 W
- Femsfeld 52 52.43 N 8.32 E
- Femstein 126 28.42 N 80.19 E
- Femuna 126 21.33 N 86.54 E
- Femus 190 43.36 N 85.09 W
- Femuzat 64 44.24 N 5.12 E
- Fena 26 61.08 N 11.22 E
- Fenaix 50 50.45 N 3.36 E
- Fenälla Khurd 123 26.08 N 80.19 E
- Fena Point ⊁ 118 16.10 N 119.45 E
- Fenard Islands II 164 10.50 S 150.05 E
- Fenata 182 30.50 S 118.06 W
- Fenca 286e 33.24 S 70.44 W
- Fenchen 56 48.35 N 8.01 E
- Fencontre East 186 47.38 N 55.12 W
- Fencun 107 31.15 N 106.48 E
- Fenda, Ityo. 76 36.19 N 113.52 E
- Fenda, S.S.S.R. 76 57.09 N 22.52 E
- Fende 158 33.59 S 18.11 E
- Fendina, Valle ∨ 58 46.08 N 6.16 E
- Fenland Island I 9 67.00 S 68.00 W
- Fendova Island I 175e 8.32 S 157.20 E
- Fendsburg 54 54.18 N 9.40 E
- Fenesse 52 51.39 N 9.17 E
- Fenews 186 46.56 N 52.56 W
- Fenews, On., Can. 212 44.56 N 78.33 W
- Fenfrew, Scot., U.K. 46 55.53 N 4.24 W
- Fenfrew, Pa., U.S. 214 41.00 N 79.59 W
- Fengam 42 51.39 N 3.15 W
- Feng gang 107 32.32 N 112.08 E
- Fengasdegnklok 115a 6.09 S 107.17 E
- Fengat 112 2.07 S 102.43 E
- Fengel 115a 7.04 S 112.02 E
- Fengo 252 34.25 S 70.52 W
- Fengoldsweil 56 47.24 N 7.41 E
- Fengzhuang 105 39.45 N 118.10 E
- Feni 130 37.45 N 28.17 E
- Fenish Point ⊁ 48 54.19 N 8.28 W
- Fenishaw 44 53.18 N 1.21 W
- Fenishaw 106 24.51 N 115.54 E
- Fenk ⁻ 258 24.39 S 53.29 W
- Fenkum 52 51.58 N 5.45 E
- Fenmark 156 17.48 S 16.58 E
- Fenmin 105 34.11 N 140.45 E
- Fenmin 30 51.42 N 3.42 W
- Fenland Sound ⋋ 182 51.30 N 129.30 W
- Fennebont, Scot., Loch ⊂ 46 58.03 N 7.06 E
- Fennes, Lac du → Reindeer Lake ⊚ 176 57.15 N 102.40 W
- Renne, Rivière le ≃ 206 45.41 N 72.39 W
- Rennell I 160 11.40 S 160.10 E
- Rennell, Isla I 254 52.05 S 74.00 W
- Rennell Sound ⋋ 182 53.25 N 132.40 W
- Renner 222 32.59 N 96.47 W
- Rennerdale 279b 40.24 N 80.08 W
- Rennerod 56 50.36 N 8.04 E
- Renner Springs 162 18.20 S 133.48 E
- Rennertshofen 60 48.45 N 11.02 E
- Rennes 32 48.05 N 1.41 W
- Rennick Bay ⊂ 9 70.18 S 161.45 E
- Rennick Glacier ⊠ 9 70.30 S 161.45 E
- Rennie 184 49.51 N 95.33 W
- Rennie's Mill 271d 22.18 N 114.15 E
- Renningen 56 48.46 N 8.56 E
- Renr'tier-See → Reindeer Lake ⊚ 176 57.15 N 102.40 W
- Renrweg 64 47.01 N 13.37 E
- Renc, Nv., U.S. 226 39.31 N 119.48 W
- Renc, Pa., U.S. 214 41.25 N 79.45 W
- Renc, Tx., U.S. 222 32.56 N 97.05 W
- Renc Beach 214 44.30 N 83.15 W
- Renc Hill ∧ 200 42.35 N 106.03 W
- Renc International Airport ⊞ 226 39.30 N 119.46 W
- Rencster ≃ 158 31.37 S 20.37 E
- Rencus 186 46.49 N 65.48 W
- Rencus ≃ 186 46.50 N 65.50 W
- Rencvo 214 41.19 N 77.45 W
- Rendiao 100 33.27 N 117.16 E
- Rendiu 98 33.42 N 116.05 E
- Rens 41 54.54 N 9.06 E
- Renshan 100 22.50 N 114.48 E
- Renshou, Zhg. 100 29.59 N 117.51 E
- Renshou, Zhg. 107 30.00 N 104.08 E
- Rensión 24 68.05 N 19.49 E
- Rensselaer, In., U.S. 216 40.56 N 87.09 W
- Rensselaer, Mo., U.S. 219 39.40 N 91.33 W
- Rensselaer, N.Y., U.S. 210 42.38 N 73.44 W
- Rensselaer ≃ 210 42.38 N 73.44 W
- Rensselaer Falls 212 44.35 N 75.19 W
- Rensselaerville 210 42.30 N 74.08 W
- Rentería 34 43.19 N 1.54 W
- Rentford ⁺ ⁸ 263 51.35 N 6.57 E
- Rentien 107 27.28 N 122.12 E
- Rentsu 107 29.14 N 106.23 E
- Rentweinsdorf 56 50.04 N 10.47 E
- Renu ⁺ 114 3.05 N 97.55 E
- Renville 198 44.47 N 95.12 W
- Renwez 50 49.50 N 4.36 E
- Renwick, N.Z. 172 41.30 S 173.50 E
- Renwick, Ia., U.S. 190 42.49 N 93.58 W
- Renyichang 107 29.29 N 105.28 E
- Renziehausen Park ⬩ ⁸ 279b 40.21 N 79.50 W
- Réo, Burkina 150 12.19 N 2.28 W
- Reola 115b 8.19 S 120.30 E
- Reotipur 126 25.33 N 83.46 E
- Repartición 286d 12.00 S 74.02 E
- Repartimento 250 6.06 S 50.40 W
- Repaupo 285 39.48 N 75.18 W
- Repbäcken 40 60.31 N 15.20 E
- Répce ≃ 30 47.41 N 17.03 E
- Repentigny 206 45.44 N 73.28 W
- Repetek 84 38.34 N 63.11 E
- Repino 76 60.10 N 29.52 E
- Repki 30 52.22 N 22.23 E
- Repolka 76 59.16 N 29.34 E
- Repoo 172 60.40 N 69.50 E
- Reposaari 26 61.37 N 21.27 E
- Reppen 56 52.22 N 10.40 E
- → Rzepin 30 52.21 N 14.50 E
- Repton 42 52.50 N 1.33 W
- Republic, Ks., U.S. 198 39.55 N 97.49 W
- Republic, Mi., U.S. 190 46.25 N 87.59 W
- Republic, Oh., U.S. 214 41.07 N 83.00 W
- Republic, Wa., U.S. 202 48.38 N 118.44 W
- República Centroafricana → Central African Republic ⁺¹ 136 7.00 N 21.00 E
- Republican ≃ 198 39.03 N 96.48 W
- Republican, North Fork ≃ 198 40.01 N 101.59 W
- Republican, South Fork ≃ 198 40.03 N 101.31 W
- Republic Observatory ♦³ 273d 26.11 S 28.05 E
- Republic Steel Corporation ⁺ 279a 41.28 N 81.40 W
- République Centrafricaine → Central African Republic ⁺¹ 136 7.00 N 21.00 E
- Repuebio de Oriente 286a 19.25 N 99.33 W
- Repulse Bay 176 66.32 N 86.15 W
- Repulse Bay ⊂ 160 20.36 S 148.43 E
- Repvåg ² 24 70.45 N 25.41 E
- Requena, Esp. 34 39.29 N 1.06 W
- Requena, Perú 248 4.58 S 73.50 W
- Requista 32 44.02 N 2.32 E
- Rère ≃ 58 47.21 N 1.50 E
- Reriutaba 250 4.10 S 40.35 W
- Resadiye 130 40.24 N 37.21 E
- Reşadiye Yarımadası ⊁¹ 130 36.40 N 27.45 E
- Resaca 192 34.35 N 84.56 W
- Resanovci 66 44.28 N 16.15 E
- Resava ≃ 38 44.01 N 21.19 E
- Reschenpass (Passo di Resia) ⋋ 64 46.50 N 10.30 E
- Reschenscheideck ≃ 64 46.51 N 10.33 E
- Rescue 226 38.43 N 120.59 W
- Research 274b 37.42 S 145.11 E
- Resen 38 41.05 N 21.01 E
- Reseda 280 34.12 N 118.32 W
- Reserva 252 24.39 S 50.51 W
- Reserva ⬩ ⁸ 252 22.28 S 44.27 W
- Reserve 194 30.03 N 90.33 W
- Reserve, N.M., U.S. 200 33.42 N 108.45 W
- Reservoir 274b 37.43 S 145.00 E
- Reservoir Pond ⊚ 283 42.10 N 71.07 W
- Resetilovka 78 49.34 N 34.03 E
- Rešetnikovo 82 56.27 N 36.34 E
- Rešetylivka 78 49.34 N 34.03 E
- Reshui 99 24.00 N 101.00 E
- Reşiţa 38 45.17 N 21.53 E
- Resko 30 53.47 N 15.25 E
- Resolis 46 57.41 N 4.10 W
- Resolute 176 74.41 N 94.54 W
- Resolution Island I, N.T., Can. 176 61.30 N 65.00 W
- Resolution Island I, N.Z. 172 45.40 S 166.40 E
- Resolven 42 51.42 N 3.42 W

Legend / Symbol key (bottom of page):

Symbols in the index entries represent the broad categories identified in the key at the right. Symbols with superior numbers (⬩¹) identify subcategories (see complete key on page I · 1).

Symbole im Register stellen die rechts im Schlüssel erklärten Kategorien dar. Symbole mit hochgestellten Ziffern (⬩¹) bezeichnen Unterteilungen einer Kategorie (vgl. vollständigen Schlüssel auf Seite I · 1).

Los símbolos incluidos en el texto del índice representan las grandes categorías identificadas con la clave a la derecha. Los símbolos con números en su parte superior (⬩¹) identifican las subcategorías (véase la clave completa en la página I · 1).

Les symboles de l'index représentent les catégories indiquées dans la légende à droite. Les symboles suivis d'un indice (⬩¹) représentent des sous-catégories (voir légende complète à la page I · 1).

Os símbolos incluídos no texto do índice representam as grandes categorias identificadas com a clave à direita. Os símbolos com números em sua parte superior (⬩¹) identificam as subcategorias (veja-se a chave completa à página I · 1).

	English	Deutsch	Español	Français	Português
∧	Mountain	Berg	Montaña	Montagne	Montanha
∧	Mountains	Gebirge	Montañas	Montagnes	Montanhas
⋋	Pass	Paß	Paso	Col	Passo
∨	Valley, Canyon	Tal, Cañon	Valle, Cañón	Vallée, Canyon	Vale, Canhão
⁺	Plain	Ebene	Llano	Plaine	Planície
⊁	Cape	Kap	Cabo	Cap	Cabo
I	Island	Insel	Isla	Île	Ilha
II	Islands	Inseln	Islas	Îles	Ilhas
⁺	Other Topographic Features	Andere Topographische Objekte	Otros Elementos Topográficos	Autres données topographiques	Outros acidentes topográficos

ESPAÑOL Nombre	Página	Lat.°′	Long.°′ W = Oeste
FRANÇAIS Nom	Page	Lat.°′	Long.°′ W = Ouest
PORTUGUÊS Nome	Página	Lat.°′	Long.°′ W = Oeste

Resse ◆[8] 263 51.34 N 7.07 E
Resseta ≃ 76 53.49 N 35.15 E
Ressons-sur-Matz 50 49.33 N 2.45 E
Resta ≃ 76 53.36 N 30.56 E
Resthaven 216 41.16 N 88.09 W
Restigouche (Ristigouche) ≃ 186 48.04 N 66.20 W
Restinga 34 35.42 N 5.23 W
Restinga Sêca 252 29.49 S 53.23 W
Reston, Mb., Can. 184 49.35 N 101.02 W
Reston, Scot., U.K. 46 55.51 N 2.11 W
Reston, Va., U.S. 208 38.58 N 77.20 W
Restoule Lake ⊜ 190 46.03 N 79.47 W
Restrepo, Col. 246 4.15 N 73.33 W
Restrepo, Col. 246 3.48 N 76.31 W
Resurrección 234 19.06 N 98.07 W
Resuttano 70 37.41 N 14.02 E
Retalhuleu 236 14.32 N 91.41 W
Retalhuleu □[5] 236 14.20 N 91.50 W
Retamosa 252 33.35 S 54.44 W
Retem, Oued er V 148 33.30 N 5.45 E
Řetenice 54 50.38 N 13.46 E
Retezat, Parcul Național ♠ 38 45.20 N 22.50 E
Retezatului, Munții ⩚ 38 45.25 N 23.00 E
Rethel 50 49.31 N 4.22 E
Rethem 52 52.45 N 9.23 E
Réthimnon 38 35.22 N 24.29 E
Retiche, Alpi → Rhaetian Alps ⩚ 58 46.30 N 10.00 E
Retie 56 51.16 N 5.04 E
Retiers 28 47.55 N 1.23 W
Retiro, Estacion ◆[5] 288 34.36 S 58.22 W
Retiro, Parque del ♦ 266a 40.25 N 3.41 W
Retournac 62 45.12 N 4.02 E
Retreat 222 32.03 N 96.29 W
Retreat ≃ 170 34.07 S 149.38 E
Retsof 210 42.50 N 77.53 W
Rettenberg 58 47.35 N 10.17 E
Rettendon 260 51.39 N 0.33 E
Rettendon Place 260 51.38 N 0.34 E
Rettichovka 89 44.10 N 132.47 E
Rettin 54 54.06 N 10.53 E
Return Creek ≃ 226 37.56 N 119.28 W
Retz 61 48.45 N 15.57 E
Retzow 54 52.37 N 12.41 E
Reuden 54 52.04 N 12.18 E
Reungeut 114 4.34 N 96.22 E
Reunion (Réunion) □[2], Afr. 138 21.06 S 55.36 E
Reunion (Réunion) □[2], Afr. 157c 21.06 S 55.36 E
Réunion I 157c 21.06 S 55.36 E
Reus 34 41.09 N 1.07 E
Reuschenberg 263 51.10 N 6.42 E
Reusel 52 51.21 N 5.22 E
Reusrath 263 51.06 N 6.57 E
Reuss ≃ 58 47.28 N 8.14 E
Reut ≃ 78 47.15 N 29.09 E
Reuterstadt Stavenhagen 54 53.42 N 12.53 E
Reutlingen 58 48.29 N 9.11 E
Reutov 82 55.46 N 37.52 E
Reutte 58 47.29 N 10.43 E
Reuver 52 51.17 N 6.05 E
Revadim 132 31.46 N 34.48 E
Rev'akino 82 54.22 N 37.40 E
Reval → Tallinn 76 59.25 N 24.45 E
Revda, S.S.S.R. 24 67.58 N 34.32 E
Revda, S.S.S.R. 86 56.48 N 59.57 E
Réveillon, Ruisseau le ≃ 261 48.42 N 2.30 E
Revel 62 45.11 N 5.52 E
Revelganj 124 25.47 N 84.40 E
Revelstoke 182 50.59 N 118.12 W
Reventazón 248 6.10 S 80.58 W
Reventazón ≃ 236 10.17 N 83.24 W
Revere, It. 64 45.03 N 11.08 E
Revere, Ma., U.S. 207 42.24 N 71.00 W
Revere, Pa., U.S. 208 40.31 N 75.10 W
Revere Beach ♠[2] 283 42.25 N 70.59 W
Revermont ⩚[2] 58 46.27 N 5.25 E
Revesby 274a 33.57 S 151.01 E
Revest-du-Bion 62 44.05 N 5.33 E
Revia 154 13.23 S 36.31 E
Reviga 38 44.42 N 27.06 E
Revigny-sur-Ornain 56 48.50 N 4.59 E
Revilla del Campo 34 42.13 N 3.32 W
Revillagigedo, Islas II 232 19.00 N 111.30 W
Revillagigedo Channel ꓵ 182 55.10 N 131.13 W
Revillagigedo Island I 182 55.35 N 131.23 W
Revillo 198 45.01 N 96.34 W
Revin 56 49.56 N 4.38 E
Revloc 214 40.29 N 78.45 W
Řevničov 54 50.08 N 13.45 E
Revò 64 46.23 N 11.03 E
Revol'ucii, pik ∧ 85 38.31 N 72.21 E
Revolution, Museum of the v 265b 55.46 N 37.36 E
Revsundssjön ⊜ 26 62.49 N 15.17 E
Revúboè ≃ 154 16.13 S 33.37 E
Revuè ≃ 156 19.45 S 34.00 E
Rew 214 41.54 N 78.32 W
Rewa 124 24.32 N 81.18 E
Rewa ≃ 246 3.53 N 58.45 W
Rewāri 124 28.11 N 76.37 E
Rewataya, Take ◆[2] 112 6.05 S 118.55 E
Rex, Mount ∧ 9 74.57 S 76.00 W
Rexburg 202 43.49 N 111.47 W
Rexdale ◆[8] 275b 43.43 N 79.35 W
Rexford, Ks., U.S. 198 39.28 N 100.44 W
Rexford, Mt., U.S. 202 48.52 N 115.13 W
Rexhame 283 42.06 N 70.40 W
Rexton 186 45.39 N 64.52 W
Rexville, In., U.S. 218 41.31 N 87.21 W
Rexville, N.Y., U.S. 210 42.05 N 77.40 W
Rey, Arroyo del ≃ 288 34.46 S 58.27 W
Rey, Embalse del ⊜[1] 266a 40.18 N 3.32 W
Rey, Estrecho del → King Sound ꓵ 162 17.00 S 123.30 E
Rey, Isla del I 246 8.22 N 78.55 W
Rey, Laguna del ⊜ 196 27.01 N 103.26 W
Rey Bouba 146 8.40 N 14.11 E
Reyes 248 14.19 S 67.23 W
Reyes, Point > 204 38.00 N 123.01 W
Reyes Peak ∧ 228 34.38 N 119.17 W
Reyhanlı 130 36.18 N 36.32 E
Rey Jorge, Estrecho → King George Sound ꓵ 162 35.03 S 117.57 E
Rey Jorge, Isla → King George Island I 9 62.00 S 58.15 W
Reykjanes >[1] 24a 63.49 N 22.43 W
Reykjanes Ridge ✢[3] 10 62.00 N 27.00 W
Reykjavík 24a 64.09 N 21.51 W
Reynella 168b 35.06 S 138.32 E
Reyno 194 36.21 N 90.45 W
Reynolds, Ga., U.S. 192 32.33 N 84.05 W
Reynolds, In., U.S. 216 40.44 N 86.52 W
Reynolds, N.D., U.S. 198 47.57 N 97.45 W
Reynolds Channel ꓵ 276 40.36 N 73.40 W
Reynolds Creek ≃, Austl. 171a 27.56 S 152.36 E
Reynolds Creek ≃, On., Can. 212 43.00 N 80.58 W
Reynoldsville 214 41.05 N 78.53 W
Reynosa 232 26.07 N 98.18 W
Reyssouze ≃ 58 46.27 N 4.54 E
Režė ≃ 86 57.23 N 61.24 E
Rež ≃ 86 57.54 N 62.18 E
Reza, gora (Küh-e Rizeh) ∧ 128 37.47 N 58.05 E
Rezé 32 47.12 N 1.34 W
Rēzekne 76 56.30 N 27.19 E
Rēzekne ≃ 76 56.46 N 26.58 E
Rezeny 78 46.46 N 28.54 E
Rezina 78 47.44 N 28.58 E
Rezino 86 55.51 N 75.18 E
Rēznas ezers ⊜ 76 56.20 N 27.27 E
Rezovo 38 41.59 N 28.02 E
Rezovska (Mutlu) ≃ 130 41.59 N 28.01 E
Rezvānshahr 128 37.33 N 49.09 E
Rezzato 64 45.31 N 10.19 E
Rezzoaglio 62 44.32 N 9.23 E
Rezzonico 58 46.04 N 9.16 E
Rhade 52 53.19 N 9.07 E
Rhadeswood Reservoir ⊜[1] 262 53.29 N 1.56 W
Rhaetian Alps (Rätische Alpen) (Alpi Retiche) ⩚ 58 46.30 N 10.00 E
Rhallamane, Sebkha de ⩩ 148 23.41 N 9.50 W
Rhame 198 46.13 N 103.39 W
Rharbi, Île I 148 34.39 N 11.03 E
Rharbi, Zahrez ⊜ 148 34.50 N 2.50 E
Rhauderfehn 52 53.08 N 7.35 E
Rhaunen 56 49.52 N 7.20 E
Rhayader 42 52.18 N 3.30 W
Rhea Creek ≃ 202 45.30 N 119.46 W
Rheda-Wiedenbrück 52 51.50 N 8.18 E
Rhede, B.R.D. 52 51.50 N 6.11 E
Rhede, B.R.D. 52 53.03 N 7.16 E
Rheden 52 52.01 N 6.02 E
Rheems 208 40.08 N 76.34 W
Rheem Valley 226 37.52 N 122.07 W
Rheidol ≃ 42 52.25 N 4.05 W
Rheims → Reims 50 49.15 N 4.02 E
Rhein, Sk., Can. 184 51.22 N 102.10 W
Rhein → Ryn, Pol. 30 53.56 N 21.33 E
Rhein → Rhine ≃ 30 51.52 N 6.02 E
Rheinau 56 48.41 N 7.56 E
Rheinbach 56 50.37 N 6.57 E
Rheinberg 52 51.33 N 6.35 E
Rheinböllen 56 49.59 N 7.40 E
Rheinbrohl 56 50.30 N 7.19 E
Rheinbrücke ◆[5] 263 51.12 N 6.44 E
Rheindürkheim 56 49.42 N 8.21 E
Rheine 52 52.17 N 7.26 E
Rheineck 58 47.28 N 9.35 E
Rheinen 263 51.27 N 7.38 E
Rheinfall ↳ 58 47.41 N 8.38 E
Rheinfelden, B.R.D. 58 47.33 N 7.47 E
Rheinfelden, Schw. 58 47.33 N 7.48 E
Rheinhausen 56 51.24 N 6.44 E
Rhein-Herne-Kanal ≋ 263 51.27 N 6.47 E
Rheinhessen □[5] 56 49.40 N 8.40 E
Rheinkamp 52 51.30 N 6.37 E
Rheinland-Pfalz □[3] 56 50.00 N 7.00 E
Rheinsberg 54 53.06 N 12.53 E
Rheinstadion ♠ 263 51.16 N 6.44 E
Rheinstein, Burg ⊥ 56 50.00 N 7.50 E
Rheinwald V 58 46.32 N 9.17 E
Rheinwaldhorn ∧ 58 46.30 N 9.02 E
Rheris, Oued V 148 30.39 N 4.26 W
Rhêmes-Notre-Dame 62 45.34 N 7.07 E
Rhenen 52 51.57 N 5.34 E
Rhens 56 50.17 N 7.37 E
Rheurdt 263 51.27 N 6.28 E
Rheydt 56 51.10 N 6.25 E
Rheydt, Schloss ⊥ 263 51.11 N 6.28 E
Rhin ≃, D.D.R. 54 52.59 N 12.55 E
Rhin → Rhine ≃, Europe 30 51.52 N 6.02 E
Rhinau 58 48.19 N 7.42 E
Rhine 192 31.59 N 83.12 W
Rhine (Rhein) (Rhin) ≃ 30 51.52 N 6.02 E
Rhinebeck 210 41.55 N 73.54 W
Rhinecliff 210 41.55 N 73.57 W
Rhineland 219 38.43 N 91.31 W
Rhinelander 190 45.38 N 89.24 W
Rhin Kanal ≋ 54 52.47 N 12.24 E
Rhinluch ⩩ 54 52.50 N 12.50 E
Rhinns of Kells ⩚ 44 55.07 N 4.22 W
Rhinns Point > 46 55.40 N 6.30 W
Rhino Camp 154 2.58 N 31.24 E
Rhinow 54 52.45 N 12.20 E
Rhiou, Oued ≃ 34 36.00 N 0.55 E
Rhir, Cap > 148 30.38 N 9.55 W
Rhis, Oued ≃ 34 35.14 N 3.57 W
Rhiw ≃ 42 52.36 N 3.11 W
Rho 62 45.32 N 9.02 E
Rhode Island □[3], U.S. 178 41.40 N 71.30 W
Rhode Island □[3], U.S. 207 41.40 N 71.30 W
Rhode Island I 207 41.33 N 71.15 W
Rhode Island Sound ꓵ 207 41.25 N 71.15 W
Rhoden 52 51.28 N 9.00 E
Rhodes, Austl. 274a 33.50 S 151.05 E
Rhodes → Ródhos, Ellás 38 36.26 N 28.13 E
Rhodes, S. Afr. 158 30.47 S 27.59 E
Rhodes, Eng., U.K. 262 53.33 N 2.14 W
Rhodes → Ródhos I 38 36.10 N 28.00 E
Rhodesia → Zimbabwe □[1] 154 20.00 S 30.00 E
Rhodes Inyanga National Park ♠ 154 18.12 S 32.45 E
Rhodes Matopos National Park ♠ 154 20.33 S 28.20 E
Rhodes Park ♠ 273d 26.12 S 28.06 E
Rhodes Peak ∧ 202 46.41 N 114.47 W
Rhodes' Tomb ⊥ 154 20.30 S 28.30 E
Rhododendron 224 45.20 N 121.55 W
Rhododendron State Park ♠ 207 42.47 N 72.12 W
Rhodon 261 48.43 N 2.04 E
Rhodon, Ruisseau le ≃ 261 48.42 N 2.04 E
Rhodope Mountains ⩚ 38 41.30 N 24.30 E
Rhodt 56 49.16 N 8.07 E
Rhome 222 33.03 N 97.28 W
Rhondda 42 51.40 N 3.27 W
Rhône □[5] 62 45.55 N 4.40 E
Rhône ≃ 32 43.20 N 4.50 E
Rhône à Sète, Canal du ≋ 62 43.25 N 3.42 E
Rhône au Rhin, Canal du ≋ 58 47.06 N 5.19 E
Rhoose 42 51.24 N 3.20 W
Rhosesmor 262 53.12 N 3.10 W
Rhosllanerchrugog 44 53.00 N 3.03 W
Rhosneigr 44 53.14 N 4.31 W
Rhos-on-Sea 44 53.19 N 3.45 W
Rhossili 42 51.34 N 4.17 W
Rhourde-El-Baguel 148 31.24 N 6.57 E
Rhuddlan 44 53.18 N 3.27 W
Rhue ≃ 32 45.23 N 2.29 E
Rhum I 46 57.00 N 6.20 W
Rhum, Sound of ꓵ 46 56.56 N 6.14 W
Rhyl 44 53.19 N 3.29 W
Rhymney 42 51.46 N 3.18 W
Rhymney ≃ 42 51.28 N 3.10 W
Rhynie 46 57.20 N 2.50 W
Riaba 152 3.23 N 8.46 E
Riace 68 38.25 N 16.29 E
Riachão 250 7.22 S 46.37 W
Riachão do Dantas 250 11.04 S 37.44 W
Riachão do Jacuípe 250 11.48 S 39.21 W
Riacho de Santana 250 13.37 S 42.57 W
Riacho Grande 256 23.48 S 46.35 W
Riachos, Islas de los II 254 40.10 S 62.08 W
Riachuelo, Bra. 250 10.44 S 37.11 W
Riachuelo, Chile 254 40.49 S 73.21 W
Riachuelo, Ur. 258 34.26 S 57.44 W
Riachuelo, Arroyo ≃ 258 34.27 S 57.44 W
Rialma 255 15.18 S 49.34 W
Rialto, Bra. 256 22.35 S 44.16 W
Rialto, Ca., U.S. 228 34.06 N 117.22 W
Riamkanan, Waduk ⊜[1] 112 3.30 S 115.05 E
Rianápolis 255 15.29 S 49.28 W
Riang 120 27.32 N 92.56 E
Riangnom 140 9.55 N 30.01 E
Riano 34 42.58 N 5.01 W
Rians 62 43.37 N 5.45 E
Riánsares ≃ 34 39.32 N 3.18 W
Riāsi 123 33.05 N 74.50 E
Riau □[4] 112 1.00 N 102.00 E
Riau, Kepulauan II 112 1.00 N 104.30 E
Riaz 58 46.38 N 7.04 E
Riaza 34 41.17 N 3.28 W
Riaza ≃ 34 41.42 N 3.55 W
Ribadavia 34 42.17 N 8.08 W
Ribadeo 34 43.32 N 7.02 W
Ribadesella 34 43.28 N 5.04 W
Ribamar 250 2.33 S 44.03 W
Ribas de Jarama 266a 40.23 N 3.31 W
Ribas do Rio Pardo 255 20.27 S 53.46 W
Ribauè 154 14.57 S 38.17 E
Ribble ≃ 44 53.44 N 2.50 W
Ribbleton 262 53.46 N 2.40 W
Ribble Valley □[8] 262 53.48 N 2.31 W
Ribbon Fall ↳ 226 37.44 N 119.39 W
Ribchester 262 53.49 N 2.32 W
Ribe 41 55.21 N 8.46 E
Ribe □[6] 41 55.35 N 8.50 E
Ribe Å ≃ 41 55.21 N 8.40 E
Ribeauvillé 58 48.12 N 7.19 E
Ribécourt 50 49.31 N 2.55 E
Ribeira 252 24.40 S 49.01 W
Ribeira de Iguape ≃ 252 24.40 S 47.24 W
Ribeira do Amparo 250 11.03 S 38.26 W
Ribeira do Pombal 250 10.50 S 38.32 W
Ribeira Grande, C.V. 150a 17.11 N 25.04 W
Ribeira Grande, Port. 148a 37.49 N 25.31 W
Ribeirão, Bra. 250 8.31 S 35.23 W
Ribeirão, Bra. 256 23.17 S 45.36 W
Ribeirão, Bra. 287b 23.35 S 46.55 W
Ribeirão das Lajes, Represa do ⊜[1] 256 22.45 S 43.55 W
Ribeirão de São Joaquim 256 22.17 S 44.11 W
Ribeirão do Pinhal 255 23.24 S 50.18 W
Ribeirão do Pote 256 23.36 S 45.50 W
Ribeirão Fundo 256 22.40 S 46.15 W
Ribeirão Grande 256 22.48 S 45.27 W
Ribeirão Pires 256 23.43 S 46.25 W
Ribeirão Prêto 255 21.10 S 47.48 W
Ribeirão Vermelho 255 21.11 S 45.03 W
Ribeirãozinho 255 16.27 S 52.35 W
Ribeiro Gonçalves 250 7.32 S 45.14 W
Ribeiro Junqueira 256 21.28 S 42.31 W
Ribeiros 256 21.59 S 45.35 W
Ribemont 50 49.48 N 3.28 E
Ribera 70 37.30 N 13.16 E
Ribérac 32 45.15 N 0.20 E
Riberalta 248 10.59 S 66.06 W
Riberão Pires □[7] 287b 23.43 S 46.21 W
Ribiers 62 44.14 N 5.52 E
Rib Lake 190 45.19 N 90.12 W
Ribnica, Jugo. 36 45.44 N 14.44 E
Ribnica, Jugo. 61 46.32 N 15.16 E
Ribnitz-Damgarten 54 54.15 N 12.28 E
Ribstone Creek ≃ 184 52.51 N 110.05 W
Ricadi 68 38.37 N 15.52 E
Ricarda, Estany de la c 266d 41.18 N 2.07 E
Ricardo Flores Magón 232 29.58 N 106.58 W
Ricaurte 246 1.13 N 77.59 W
Riccall 44 53.50 N 1.04 W
Riccarton 172 43.32 S 172.36 E
Riccia 66 41.29 N 14.50 E
Riccione 66 43.59 N 12.39 E
Rice 222 32.15 N 96.30 W
Rice Creek ≃ 216 42.16 N 84.57 W
Rice Lake 190 45.30 N 91.44 W
Rice Lake ⊜, On., Can. 190 47.42 N 82.08 W
Rice Lake ⊜, On., Can. 212 44.08 N 78.13 W
Rice Lake Indian Reserve ◆[4] 212 44.10 N 78.12 W
Riceville, Ia., U.S. 190 43.22 N 92.33 W
Riceville, Pa., U.S. 214 41.47 N 79.48 W
Riceville, Tn., U.S. 192 35.23 N 84.41 W
Rich, Cape > 212 44.43 N 80.38 W
Richan 184 49.59 N 92.49 W
Richard B. Russell Lake ⊜[1] 192 34.05 N 82.39 W
Richard Collinson Inlet c 176 72.45 N 113.45 W
Richards 222 30.32 N 95.51 W
Richard's Bay 158 28.47 S 32.06 E
Richard's Bay c 158 28.50 S 32.02 E
Richards-Gebaur Air Force Base ■ 194 38.51 N 94.33 W
Richard's Harbour 186 47.37 N 56.24 W
Richards Island I 180 69.20 N 134.30 W
Richardson 222 32.56 N 96.43 W
Richardson ≃ 176 58.30 N 111.30 W
Richardson, Mount ∧ 162 28.49 S 119.59 E
Richardson Bay c 282 37.52 N 122.29 W
Richardson Mountains ⩚, Can. 180 67.15 N 136.30 W
Richardson Mountains ⩚, N.Z. 172 44.45 S 168.31 E
Richardson Park 285 39.44 N 75.35 W
Richardsville 214 41.14 N 79.01 W
Richard-Toll 150 16.28 N 15.41 W
Richardton 198 46.53 N 102.18 W
Rîchât, Guelb er ∧[2] 148 21.07 N 11.24 W
Richboro 208 40.13 N 75.01 W
Richburg 210 42.05 N 78.09 W
Riche, Pointe > 186 50.42 N 57.25 W
Richebourg 261 48.49 N 1.38 E
Richelieu, P.Q., Can. 206 45.27 N 73.15 W
Richelieu, Fr. 32 47.01 N 0.19 E
Richelieu □[6] 206 45.55 N 73.00 W
Richelieu ≃ 206 46.03 N 73.07 W
Richer 184 49.39 N 96.28 W
Richey 198 47.38 N 105.04 W
Richfield, Id., U.S. 202 43.02 N 114.09 W
Richfield, Mn., U.S. 190 44.53 N 93.16 W
Richfield, Oh., U.S. 214 41.14 N 81.39 W
Richfield, Pa., U.S. 208 40.41 N 77.07 W
Richfield, Ut,. U.S. 200 38.46 N 112.05 W
Richfield Springs 210 42.51 N 74.59 W
Richford, N.Y., U.S. 210 42.21 N 76.12 W
Richford, Vt., U.S. 206 44.59 N 72.40 W
Rich Fountain 219 38.24 N 91.53 W
Richgrove 226 35.48 N 119.07 W
Richhill, N. Ire., U.K. 48 54.23 N 6.33 W
Rich Hill, Mo., U.S. 194 38.05 N 94.12 W
Richibucto 186 46.41 N 64.52 W
Richisau 58 47.02 N 8.54 E
Richland, Ga., U.S. 192 32.05 N 84.40 W
Richland, Mi., U.S. 216 42.22 N 85.27 W
Richland, Mo., U.S. 194 37.51 N 92.24 W
Richland, N.J., U.S. 208 39.29 N 74.52 W
Richland, N.Y., U.S. 212 43.34 N 76.03 W
Richland, Pa., U.S. 208 40.21 N 76.16 W
Richland, Tx., U.S. 222 31.56 N 96.26 W
Richland, Tx., U.S. 222 32.57 N 95.49 W
Richland, Wa., U.S. 202 46.17 N 119.17 W
Richland □[6] 214 40.46 N 82.31 W
Richland Center 190 43.20 N 90.23 W
Richland Creek ≃, Il., U.S. 219 38.14 N 89.54 W
Richland Creek ≃, Tn., U.S. 194 35.02 N 86.55 W
Richland Creek ≃, Tx., U.S. 222 31.58 N 96.03 W
Richlands, N.C., U.S. 192 34.53 N 77.32 W
Richlands, Va., U.S. 192 37.05 N 81.47 W
Richland Springs 196 31.16 N 98.57 W
Richmond, Austl. 166 20.44 S 143.08 E
Richmond, Austl. 170 33.36 S 150.46 E
Richmond, Austl. 274b 37.49 S 145.00 E
Richmond, B.C., Can. 224 49.09 N 123.06 W
Richmond, On., Can. 212 45.11 N 75.50 W
Richmond, P.Q., Can. 206 45.40 N 72.09 W
Richmond, N.Z. 172 41.20 S 173.11 E
Richmond, S. Afr. 158 31.23 S 23.56 E
Richmond, S. Afr. 158 29.54 S 30.08 E
Richmond, Eng., U.K. 44 54.24 N 1.44 W
Richmond, Ca., U.S. 226 37.56 N 122.20 W
Richmond, Il., U.S. 216 42.28 N 88.18 W
Richmond, In., U.S. 218 39.49 N 84.53 W
Richmond, Ks., U.S. 198 38.24 N 95.15 W
Richmond, Ky., U.S. 192 37.44 N 84.17 W
Richmond, Me., U.S. 188 44.05 N 69.47 W
Richmond, Ma., U.S. 207 42.22 N 73.22 W
Richmond, Mi., U.S. 214 42.48 N 82.45 W
Richmond, Mn., U.S. 190 45.27 N 94.31 W
Richmond, Mo., U.S. 194 39.16 N 93.58 W
Richmond, Oh., U.S. 214 40.26 N 80.46 W
Richmond, Tx., U.S. 222 29.34 N 95.45 W
Richmond, Ut,. U.S. 200 41.55 N 111.48 W
Richmond, Vt., U.S. 188 44.24 N 72.59 W
Richmond, Va., U.S. 208 37.33 N 77.27 W
Richmond □[6], P.Q., Can. 206 45.40 N 72.00 W
Richmond □[6], N.Y., U.S. 210 40.38 N 74.05 W
Richmond □[6], Va., U.S. 208 37.32 N 77.28 W
Richmond ◆[8], Eng., U.K. 42 51.28 N 0.18 W
Richmond ◆[8], Ca., U.S. 282 37.46 N 122.29 W
Richmond ◆[8], Pa., U.S. 285 39.59 N 75.06 W
Richmond, Mount ∧ 172 41.29 S 173.24 E
Richmond, Point > 282 37.55 N 122.23 W
Richmond Beach 224 47.46 N 122.23 W
Richmond Creek ≃ 276 40.34 N 74.11 W
Richmond Heights, Fl., U.S. 220 25.37 N 80.22 W
Richmond Heights, Mo., U.S. 219 38.37 N 90.19 W
Richmond Heights, Oh., U.S. 214 41.33 N 81.30 W
Richmond Highlands 224 47.45 N 122.20 W
Richmond Hill, On., Can. 212 43.52 N 79.27 W
Richmond Hill, Ga., U.S. 192 31.56 N 81.18 W
Richmond Hill ◆[8] 276 40.42 N 73.49 W
Richmond International Airport ⊠ 208 37.30 N 77.19 W
Richmond Mall ◆[9] 279a 41.32 N 81.30 W
Richmond National Battlefield Park ♠ 208 37.25 N 77.23 W
Richmond Park ♠ 260 51.26 N 0.16 W
Richmond Peak ∧ 241h 13.17 N 61.13 W
Richmond Range ⩚ 172 41.27 S 173.30 E
Richmond Royal Australian Air Force Base ■ 170 33.37 S 150.48 E
Richmond-San Rafael Bridge ◆[5] 282 37.56 N 122.27 W
Richmondtown Restoration ⊥ 276 40.34 N 74.09 W
Richmond Valley ◆[8] 276 40.31 N 74.13 W
Richmondville 210 42.38 N 74.33 W
Richrath 263 51.08 N 6.56 E
Rich Square 192 36.16 N 77.17 W
Rich Stadium ♠ 284a 42.57 N 78.47 W
Richtenberg 54 54.12 N 12.53 E
Richterswil 58 47.13 N 8.42 E
Richton 194 31.20 N 88.56 W
Richton Park 216 41.29 N 87.42 W
Richvale, On., Can. 212 43.51 N 79.26 W
Richvale, Ca., U.S. 226 39.30 N 121.45 W
Richview 219 38.23 N 89.11 W
Richville, N.Y., U.S. 212 44.25 N 75.23 E
Richville, Oh., U.S. 214 40.45 N 81.27 W
Richwood, N.J., U.S. 285 39.43 N 75.10 W
Richwood, Oh., U.S. 214 40.25 N 83.17 W
Richwood, W.V., U.S. 188 38.13 N 80.32 W
Richwood Village 222 29.04 N 95.25 W
Ricinskij zapovednik ♠ 84 43.25 N 40.30 E
Rickenbacker Air Force Base ■ 218 39.48 N 82.56 W
Rickenpass)(58 47.14 N 9.02 E
Ricken Tunnel ◆[5] 58 47.12 N 9.05 E
Ricketts Glen State Park ♠ 210 41.20 N 76.18 W
Ricketts Point > 274b 38.00 S 145.02 E
Rickleån ≃ 26 64.05 N 20.56 E
Rickling 54 54.01 N 10.13 E
Rickmansworth 42 51.39 N 0.29 W
Rico 200 37.41 N 108.01 W
Ricoa ≃ 241s 11.30 N 69.12 W
Ricobayo, Embalse de ⊜[1] 34 41.30 N 5.55 W
Ricupe 152 14.37 S 21.25 E
Ridā' 144 14.38 N 44.54 E
Ridanna (Ridnaun) 64 46.55 N 11.15 E
Riddarhyttan 40 59.48 N 15.33 E
Ridderkerk 52 51.52 N 4.36 E
Riddes 58 46.10 N 7.13 E
Riddle 202 42.57 N 123.21 W
Riddle Mountain ∧ 202 43.07 N 118.30 W
Riddlesburg 214 40.10 N 78.15 W
Riddlewood 285 39.54 N 75.26 W
Riddon, Loch c 46 55.58 N 5.12 W
Rideau ≃ 212 45.27 N 75.42 W
Ridge, Eng., U.K. 260 51.41 N 0.15 W
Ridge, N.Y., U.S. 207 40.54 N 72.53 W
Ridge, Tx., U.S. 222 31.09 N 96.19 W
Ridge Acres 276 40.41 N 74.32 W
Ridgecrest, Ca., U.S. 204 35.37 N 117.40 W
Ridgecrest, Wa., U.S. 224 47.45 N 122.21 W
Ridgedale 184 53.04 N 104.09 W
Ridge Farm 194 39.53 N 87.39 W
Ridgefield, Ct., U.S. 207 41.16 N 73.29 W
Ridgefield, Il., U.S. 216 42.16 N 88.22 W
Ridgefield, N.J., U.S. 210 40.50 N 74.00 W
Ridgefield, Wa., U.S. 224 45.48 N 122.44 W
Ridgefield Park 276 40.51 N 74.01 W
Ridgeland, Ms., U.S. 194 32.25 N 90.07 W
Ridgeland, S.C., U.S. 192 32.28 N 80.58 W
Ridgely, Md., U.S. 208 38.56 N 75.53 W
Ridgely, Tn., U.S. 194 36.15 N 89.29 W
Ridge Manor 220 28.31 N 82.10 W
Ridgemont 210 43.13 N 77.43 W
Ridgetown 214 42.26 N 81.54 W
Ridgeville, Mb., Can. 184 49.04 N 97.01 W
Ridgeville, In., U.S. 216 40.17 N 85.01 W
Ridgeville, S.C., U.S. 192 33.05 N 80.18 W
Ridgeville Corners 216 41.26 N 84.15 W
Ridgeway, On., Can. 284a 42.53 N 79.03 W
Ridgeway, Mi., U.S. 216 41.59 N 83.51 W
Ridgeway, Mo., U.S. 194 40.22 N 93.56 W
Ridgeway, N.J., U.S. 208 40.01 N 74.17 W
Ridgeway, Oh., U.S. 216 40.30 N 83.34 W
Ridgeway, Tx., U.S. 222 33.11 N 95.46 W
Ridgeway, Wi., U.S. 190 43.00 N 89.59 W
Ridgeway Ditch ≋ 279a 41.25 N 82.05 W
Ridgewood 210 40.58 N 74.07 W
Ridgewood ◆[8] 276 40.42 N 73.53 W
Ridgewood Farm 285 39.57 N 75.34 W
Ridgewood Reservoir ⊜[1] 276 40.41 N 73.53 W
Ridgway, Co., U.S. 200 38.09 N 107.46 W
Ridgway, Il., U.S. 194 37.47 N 88.15 W
Ridgway, Pa., U.S. 214 41.25 N 78.43 W
Riding Mountain ∧ 184 50.37 N 99.37 W
Riding Mountain National Park ♠ 184 50.55 N 100.25 W
Riḍīwajār 124 27.57 N 83.26 E
Ridley Creek ≃ 285 39.51 N 75.21 W
Ridley Creek State Park ♠ 285 39.57 N 75.27 W
Ridley Park 285 39.52 N 75.19 W
Ridnaun → Ridanna 64 46.55 N 11.15 E
Riebeek-Kasteel 158 33.23 S 18.53 E
Riebeek-Oos 158 33.10 S 26.10 E
Riebeek-Wes 158 33.21 S 18.52 E
Riecawr, Loch ⊜ 44 55.13 N 4.27 W
Riedau 60 48.18 N 13.38 E
Riedelbach 56 50.18 N 8.23 E
Rieden 60 49.19 N 11.57 E
Riedenburg 60 48.58 N 11.41 E
Rieder 54 51.44 N 11.10 E
Riederalp 58 46.23 N 8.01 E
Riedern 56 49.40 N 9.23 E
Ried im Innkreis 60 48.13 N 13.30 E
Ried im Oberinntal 58 47.03 N 10.39 E
Riedisheim 58 47.45 N 7.22 E
Riedlingen 58 48.09 N 9.28 E
Riedstadt 56 49.50 N 8.30 E
Riegel 58 48.09 N 7.45 E
Riegelsville, N.J., U.S. 210 40.49 N 74.52 W
Riegelsville, Pa., U.S. 208 40.36 N 75.12 W
Riegelwood 192 34.20 N 78.15 W
Riegersburg 61 47.00 N 15.56 E
Riegersburg, Schloss ⊥ 61 47.01 N 15.56 E
Riegersdorf 64 46.33 N 13.47 E
Riehen 58 47.35 N 7.39 E
Rieka → Rijeka 36 45.20 N 14.27 E
Rielasingen 58 47.44 N 8.50 E
Riemke ◆[8] 263 51.30 N 7.13 E
Riemst 56 50.48 N 5.36 E
Rieneck 56 50.05 N 9.38 E
Rienza (Rienz) ≃ 64 46.43 N 11.39 E
Rienzi 194 34.45 N 88.31 W
Riesa 54 51.18 N 13.17 E
Riesco, Isla I 254 53.00 S 72.30 W
Rieseby 41 54.32 N 9.48 E
Riesel 222 31.28 N 96.56 W
Riesenbeck 52 52.16 N 7.37 E
Riesenburg → Prabuty 30 53.46 N 19.10 E
Riese Pio X 64 45.44 N 11.55 E
Riesi 70 37.17 N 14.05 E
Riestedt 54 51.29 N 11.21 E
Riet ≃, S. Afr. 158 29.00 S 23.54 E
Riet ≃, S. Afr. 158 31.20 S 20.17 E
Rietavas 76 55.44 N 21.56 E
Rietberg 52 51.47 N 8.25 E
Rietbron 158 32.54 S 23.10 E
Rietfontein 156 21.58 S 20.58 E
Riethuiskraal 158 34.20 S 21.22 E
Rieti 66 42.24 N 12.51 E
Rieti □[4] 66 42.18 N 12.52 E
Rietschen 54 51.23 N 14.47 E
Rietspruit ≃, S. Afr. 273d 26.19 S 28.18 E
Rietspruit ≃, S. Afr. 273d 26.06 S 27.39 E
Rietvlei 158 30.29 S 29.51 E
Rietzer See ⊜ 54 52.22 N 12.39 E
Rievaulx Abbey v[1] 44 54.16 N 1.07 W
Riez 62 43.49 N 6.06 E
Riezlern 58 47.21 N 10.11 E
Rif ⩚ 148 35.00 N 4.00 W
Riffe Lake ⊜[1] 224 46.30 N 122.20 W
Rifflart 273b 4.25 S 15.21 E
Rifiano (Riffian) 64 46.42 N 11.11 E
Rifle 200 39.32 N 107.46 W
Rifle ≃ 190 44.00 N 83.49 W
Rifstangi > 24a 66.35 N 16.10 W
Rifton 210 41.50 N 74.03 W
Rift Valley □[4] 154 0.30 N 36.00 E
Rift Valley V 10 3.00 S 29.00 E
Rift Valley Lakes National Park ♠ 144 7.30 N 38.30 E
Rīga, S.S.S.R. 76 56.57 N 24.06 E
Riga, S.S.S.R. 88 56.36 N 106.17 E
Riga, Mi., U.S. 216 41.49 N 83.50 W
Riga, Gulf of → Rižskij zaliv c 76 57.30 N 23.35 E
Riga, Mount ∧ 162 21.59 S 116.25 E
Rigacikun 150 10.40 N 7.28 E
Rigaih 114 4.40 N 95.34 E
Rīgān 128 28.37 N 58.58 E
Rīgas Jūras līcis → Rižskij zaliv c 76 57.30 N 23.35 E
Rīga Station ◆[5] 265b 55.48 N 37.38 E
Rigaud 206 45.29 N 74.18 W
Rigaud ≃ 206 45.29 N 74.18 W
Rigby 202 43.40 N 111.54 W
Rīgestān ◆[1] 128 31.00 N 65.00 E
Riggins 202 45.25 N 116.18 W
Riggisberg 58 46.48 N 7.29 E
Riggston 219 39.42 N 90.25 W
Righedo, Passo del)(64 44.27 N 9.55 E
Rigi ∧ 58 47.05 N 8.30 E
Rignano Flaminio 66 42.12 N 12.29 E
Rignano Garganico 68 41.40 N 15.35 E
Rignano sull'Arno 66 43.43 N 11.27 E
Rigney 58 47.23 N 6.11 E
Rigney Bluff 210 43.19 N 77.38 W
Rigny-Ussé 50 47.15 N 0.18 E
Rigo 164 9.47 S 147.34 E
Rigolet 176 54.20 N 58.35 W
Rig-Rig 146 14.16 N 14.21 E
Rigside 46 55.36 N 3.47 W
Riguldi 76 59.08 N 23.33 E
Rīḥ, Jazīrat ar- I 140 18.10 N 38.27 E
Riḥāb 132 32.19 N 36.06 E
Rihand ≃ 124 24.33 N 82.59 E
Rihand Dam ◆[6] 124 24.05 N 82.45 E
Riihimäki 26 60.45 N 24.46 E
Riiser-Larsen Peninsula >[1] 9 68.55 S 34.00 E
Rijau 150 11.07 N 5.14 E
Riječki Zaljev c 36 45.15 N 14.25 E
Rijeka 36 45.20 N 14.27 E
Rijen 52 51.35 N 4.55 E
Rijkevorsel 56 51.21 N 4.46 E
Rijksdorp 52 52.09 N 4.25 E
Rijn → Rhine ≃ 30 51.52 N 6.02 E
Rijnsburg 52 52.12 N 4.27 E
Rijssel → Lille 50 50.38 N 3.04 E
Rijssen 52 52.18 N 6.30 E
Rijswijk 52 52.04 N 4.20 E
Rike 144 10.42 N 39.55 E
Rikers Island I 276 40.47 N 73.53 W
Rikers Island Channel ꓵ 276 40.47 N 73.52 W
Rikkavesi ⊜ 26 62.50 N 28.44 E
Riksgränsen 24 68.24 N 18.12 E
Rikuchū-kaigan-kokuritsu-kōen ♠ 92 39.25 N 141.57 E
Rikuzen-takata 92 39.01 N 141.38 E
Rila ⩚ 38 42.08 N 23.33 E
Riley 198 39.17 N 96.49 W
Riley, Mount ∧ 200 31.55 N 107.07 W
Riley, Point > 168b 33.53 S 137.36 E
Riley Creek ≃ 216 41.02 N 84.00 W
Riley Lake ⊜ 212 44.50 N 79.11 W
Rileys Range ⩚ 170 34.21 S 150.10 E
Rilievo 70 37.55 N 12.33 E
Rillieux 62 45.49 N 4.54 E
Rillington 44 54.09 N 0.42 W
Rillito 200 32.24 N 111.09 W
Rillton 214 40.17 N 79.44 W
Rilly-la-Montagne 50 49.10 N 4.03 E
Rilski manastir v[1] 38 42.08 N 23.20 E
Rima ≃ 150 13.04 N 5.10 E
Rímac 286d 12.03 S 77.03 W
Rímac ≃ 248 12.02 S 77.09 W
Rímachi, Lago ⊜ 246 4.25 S 76.43 W
Rimāḥ, Jabal ar- ∧ 132 32.19 N 36.52 E
Rima San Giuseppe 62 45.52 N 8.00 E
Rimatara I 14 22.38 S 152.51 W
Rimavská Sobota 30 48.23 N 20.02 E
Rimbey 182 52.38 N 114.14 W
Rimbo 40 59.45 N 18.22 E
Rimé, Ouadi V 146 14.02 N 18.03 E
Rimersburg 214 41.02 N 79.30 W
Rimforsa 26 58.08 N 15.40 E
Rimi 150 12.58 N 7.43 E
Rimini 66 44.04 N 12.34 E
Rîmna ≃ 38 45.39 N 27.19 E
Rîmnicu Sărat 38 45.23 N 27.03 E
Rîmnicu Vîlcea 38 45.06 N 24.22 E
Rimo Glacier ⊼ 123 35.25 N 77.30 E
Rimogne 56 49.50 N 4.33 E
Rimouski 186 48.26 N 68.33 W
Rimouski ≃ 186 48.27 N 68.32 W
Rimouski, Réserve ♠ 186 48.03 N 68.15 W
Rimpar 56 49.51 N 9.57 E
Rimrock Lake ⊜[1] 224 46.38 N 121.12 W
Rimsko-Korsakovka 80 51.34 N 48.31 E
Rín → Rhine ≃ 30 51.52 N 6.02 E
Rinbung 124 29.21 N 89.57 E
Rinca 115b 8.37 S 119.48 E
Rinca, Pulau I 115b 8.41 S 119.42 E
Rinchnach 60 48.57 N 13.12 E
Rinčin Lchumbe 88 51.07 N 99.40 E
Rincón, C.R. 236 8.42 N 83.29 W
Rincon, Ned. Ant. 241s 12.15 N 68.20 W
Rincón, P.R. 240m 18.20 N 67.15 W
Rincon, Ga., U.S. 192 32.17 N 81.14 W
Rincon, N.M., U.S. 200 32.40 N 107.03 W
Rincón, Bahía de c 240m 17.58 N 66.20 W
Rinconada 252 22.26 S 66.10 W
Rinconada, Hipódromo de la ♠ 286c 10.26 N 66.56 W
Rincón del Bonete, Lago Artificial ⊜[1] 252 32.45 S 56.00 W
Rincón del Ocote, Cerro ∧ 236 13.36 N 87.10 W
Rincón de Romos 234 22.14 N 102.18 W
Rincón de Tamayo 234 20.25 N 100.45 W
Rincon Indian Reservation ◆[4] 228 33.15 N 116.57 W
Rincon Valley 226 38.28 N 122.39 W
Rindal 26 63.03 N 9.13 E
Rindown Castle ⊥ 48 53.32 N 7.59 W
Rīngas 120 27.21 N 75.34 E
Ringdove 175f 16.38 S 168.09 E
Ringe 41 55.14 N 10.29 E
Ringebu 26 61.31 N 10.10 E
Ringenwalde 54 53.03 N 13.42 E
Ringertown 279b 40.25 N 79.36 W
Ringford 44 54.54 N 4.03 W
Ringgau ◆[1] 56 51.04 N 10.04 E
Ringgit, Gunung ∧ 115a 7.43 S 113.50 E
Ringgold, Ga., U.S. 192 34.54 N 85.06 W
Ringgold, La., U.S. 194 32.19 N 93.16 W
Ringgold, Pa., U.S. 214 41.00 N 79.10 W
Ringgold Isles II 175g 16.15 S 179.25 W
Ringim 150 12.08 N 9.10 E
Ringkøbing 26 56.05 N 8.15 E
Ringkøbing □[6] 41 56.10 N 8.50 E
Ringkøbing Fjord c[2] 26 56.00 N 8.15 E
Ringlet 114 4.25 N 101.23 E
Ringling 196 34.10 N 97.35 W
Ringling Museums v 220 27.23 N 82.34 W
Ringmer 42 50.53 N 0.04 E
Ringoes 208 40.26 N 74.52 W
Rings Island 283 42.49 N 70.52 W
Ringsted, Dan. 41 55.27 N 11.49 E
Ringsted, Ia., U.S. 198 43.17 N 94.30 W
Ringtown 210 40.51 N 76.14 W
Ringvassøy I 24 69.55 N 19.15 E
Ringville 48 52.02 N 7.34 W
Ringwood, Austl. 169 37.49 S 145.14 E
Ringwood, Eng., U.K. 42 50.51 N 1.47 W
Ringwood, N.J., U.S. 210 41.06 N 74.14 W
Ringwood Manor ⊥ 276 41.08 N 74.15 W
Ringwood North 274b 37.48 S 145.14 E
Ringwood State Park ♠ 210 41.08 N 74.16 W
Riñihue 254 39.49 S 72.27 W
Riñihue, Lago ⊜ 254 39.50 S 72.18 W
Rinjani, Gunung ∧ 115b 8.24 S 116.28 E
Rinkenæs 41 54.54 N 9.34 E
Rinkerode 52 51.50 N 7.41 E
Rinnes, Ben ∧ 46 57.23 N 3.15 W
Rinnthal 56 49.13 N 7.55 E
Rinsumageest 52 53.18 N 5.57 E
Rinteln 52 52.11 N 9.04 E
Rinxent 50 50.48 N 1.44 E
Rio, Fl., U.S. 220 27.13 N 80.14 W
Rio, Wi., U.S. 190 43.26 N 89.14 W
Rio Azul 252 25.43 S 50.47 W
Río Balsas 234 17.59 N 99.47 W
Riobamba 246 1.40 S 78.38 W
Río Blanco, Chile 252 32.55 S 70.19 W
Río Blanco (Tenango de Rio Blanco), Méx. 234 18.50 N 97.09 W
Rio Bonito 256 22.43 S 42.37 W
Rio Bonito ◆[8] 287b 23.43 S 46.41 W
Rio Branco, Bra. 248 9.58 S 67.48 W
Río Branco, Ur. 252 32.34 S 53.25 W
Río Bravo, Méx. 196 28.17 N 100.55 W
Río Bravo, Méx. 232 25.59 N 98.06 W
Rio Brilhante 255 21.48 S 54.33 W
Río Bueno 254 40.19 S 72.58 W
Río Caribe 246 10.42 N 63.07 W
Rio Casca 255 20.13 S 42.39 W
Río Cauto 240p 20.33 N 76.55 W
Río Ceballos 252 31.10 S 64.20 W
Río Chico, Arg. 254 41.43 S 70.30 W
Río Chico, Ven. 246 10.18 N 65.59 W
Rio Claro, Bra. 255 22.24 S 47.33 W
Rio Claro, Bra. 256 22.43 S 44.09 W
Rio Claro, Trin. 241r 10.18 N 61.11 W
Rio Claro, Represa do ⊜[1] 256 23.39 S 45.54 W
Río Colorado 252 39.01 S 64.05 W
Rio Comprido ◆[8] 287a 22.55 S 43.12 W
Río Cuarto 252 33.08 S 64.21 W
Rio da Conceição 250 11.24 S 46.54 W
Rio das Antas 252 26.55 S 51.04 W
Rio das Flores 256 22.10 S 43.35 W
Rio das Pedras 156 23.12 S 35.23 E
Rio de Contas 255 13.36 S 41.48 W
Rio de Janeiro, Bra. 256 22.54 S 43.14 W
Rio de Janeiro, Bra. 287a 22.54 S 43.14 W
Rio de Janeiro □[3] 255 22.00 S 42.30 W
Rio de Janeiro □[7] 287a 22.55 S 43.30 W
Río de Jesús 236 7.59 N 81.10 W
Río de las Playas 234 17.51 N 94.02 W
Rio Dell 204 40.29 N 124.06 W
Rio de Mouro 266c 38.46 N 9.20 W
Río de Oro 246 8.17 N 73.23 W
Rio d'Oeste 252 27.12 S 49.48 W
Rio do Ouro 256 22.51 S 42.59 W
Rio do Prado 255 16.35 S 40.34 W
Rio do Sul 252 27.13 S 49.39 W
Rio d'Ouro 287a 22.39 S 43.32 W
Rio Espera 255 20.51 S 43.29 W
Rio Fortuna 252 28.06 S 49.07 W
Río Gallegos 254 51.38 S 69.13 W
Río Grande, Arg. 254 53.47 S 67.42 W
Rio Grande, Bra. 252 32.02 S 52.05 W
Río Grande, Méx. 234 15.59 N 97.27 W
Río Grande, Méx. 234 23.50 N 103.02 W
Río Grande, Pan. 236 8.37 N 81.17 W
Río Grande, P.R. 240m 18.23 N 65.50 W
Rio Grande, N.J., U.S. 208 39.00 N 74.52 W
Río Grande, Ven. 286c 10.35 N 66.57 W
Rio Grande → Grande, Rio ≃ 178 25.57 N 97.09 W
Rio Grande, Barragem do ◆[6] 287b 23.42 S 46.40 W
Rio Grande, Ponte do ◆[5] 287b 23.46 S 46.31 W

Symbol	English	Deutsch	Español	Français	Português
≃	River	Fluß	Río	Rivière	Rio
≋	Canal	Kanal	Canal	Canal	Canal
↳	Waterfall, Rapids	Wasserfall, Stromschnellen	Cascada, Rápidos	Chute d'eau, Rapides	Cascata, Rápidos
ꓵ	Strait	Meeresstraße	Estrecho	Détroit	Estreito
c	Bay, Gulf	Bucht, Golf	Bahía, Golfo	Baie, Golfe	Baía, Golfo
⊜	Lake, Lakes	See, Seen	Lago, Lagos	Lac, Lacs	Lago, Lagos
⩩	Swamp	Sumpf	Pantano	Marais	Pântano
⊼	Ice Features, Glacier	Eis- und Gletscherformen	Accidentes Glaciales	Formes glaciaires	Acidentes glaciares
⍑	Other Hydrographic Features	Andere Hydrographische Objekte	Otros Elementos Hidrográficos	Autres données hydrographiques	Outros acidentes hidrográficos
✢	Submarine Features	Untermeerische Objekte	Accidentes Submarinos	Formes de relief sous-marin	Acidentes submarinos
□	Political Unit	Politische Einheit	Unidad Politica	Entité politique	Unidade política
v	Cultural Institution	Kulturelle Institution	Institución Cultural	Institution culturelle	Instituição cultural
⊥	Historical Site	Historische Stätte	Sitio Histórico	Site historique	Sitio histórico
♠	Recreational Site	Erholungs- und Ferienort	Sitio de Recreo	Centre de loisirs	Area de Lazer
⊠	Airport	Flughafen	Aeropuerto	Aéroport	Aeroporto
■	Military Installation	Militäranlage	Instalación Militar	Installation militaire	Instalação militar
◆	Miscellaneous	Verschiedenes	Misceláneo	Divers	Diversos

ENGLISH — Name | Page | Lat.°′ | Long.°′
DEUTSCH — Name | Seite | Breite°′ | Länge°′ E = Ost

Name	Page	Lat.°′	Long.°′
Rio Grande, Reservatório do ⊜[1]	256	23.47 S	46.37 W
Rio Grande City	196	26.22 N	98.49 W
Rio Grande da Serra	287b	23.44 S	46.24 W
Rio Grande da Serra □[7]	287b	23.45 S	46.23 W
Rio Grande do Norte □[3]	250	5.45 S	36.00 W
Rio Grande do Sul → Rio Grande	252	32.02 S	52.05 W
Rio Grande do Sul □[3]	252	30.00 S	54.00 W
Riograndina	256	22.11 S	42.30 W
Ríohacha	246	11.33 N	72.55 W
Río Hato	236	8.23 N	80.10 W
Río Hondo, Méx.	286a	19.25 N	99.16 W
Rio Hondo, Tx., U.S.	196	26.14 N	97.34 W
Rioja	248	6.05 S	77.09 W
Río Jueyes	240m	18.01 N	66.20 W
Riola	64	44.16 N	11.04 E
Río Lagartos	232	21.36 N	88.10 W
Riolândia	255	19.59 S	49.40 W
Rio Largo	250	9.29 S	35.51 W
Riola Sardo	71	39.59 N	8.32 E
Rio Linda	226	38.41 N	121.26 W
Riolo Terme	66	44.16 N	11.43 E
Río Luján	258	34.17 S	58.54 W
Riom	32	45.54 N	3.07 E
Riomaggiore	62	44.06 N	9.44 E
Rio Marina	66	42.49 N	10.25 E
Río Mayo	254	45.41 S	70.16 W
Río Mulatos	248	19.42 S	66.47 W
Río Muni □[4]	152	1.30 N	10.30 E
Riondel	182	49.46 N	116.52 W
Rio Negrinho	252	26.15 S	49.31 W
Rio Negro, Bra.	252	26.06 S	49.48 W
Rio Negro, Bra.	255	19.27 S	54.58 W
Río Negro, Chile	254	40.47 S	73.14 W
Ríonegro, Col.	246	6.09 N	75.22 W
Rionegro, Col.	246	7.16 N	73.09 W
Río Negro □[4]	254	40.00 S	67.00 W
Rio Negro, Pantanal do ≋	248	19.00 S	56.00 W
Rionero in Vulture	68	40.56 N	15.41 E
Rionero Sannitico	66	41.42 N	14.08 E
Rioni ≃	84	42.08 N	41.39 E
Rio Novo	256	21.29 S	43.08 W
Rio Novo do Sul	255	20.52 S	40.56 W
Riópar	34	38.30 N	2.27 W
Rio Pardo	252	29.59 S	52.22 W
Rio Pardo de Minas	255	15.37 S	42.33 W
Rio Pequeno, Reservatório do ⊜[1]	287b	23.46 S	46.30 W
Río Pico	254	44.13 S	71.21 W
Río Piedras, Arg.	252	25.18 S	64.54 W
Río Piedras, P.R.	240m	18.24 N	66.03 W
Río Pilcomayo, Parque Nacional ♠	252	25.10 S	58.00 W
Rio Piracicaba	255	19.55 S	43.11 W
Rio Pomba	256	21.17 S	43.11 W
Rio Prêto → São José do Rio Prêto, Bra.	256	22.10 S	42.57 W
Rio Prêto, Bra.	256	22.06 S	43.50 W
Rio Prêto, Bra.	256	22.48 S	45.46 W
Rio Rancho	200	35.14 N	106.38 W
Rio Real	250	11.28 S	37.56 W
Rio Saliceto	64	44.49 N	10.49 E
Río San Juan □[5]	236	11.10 N	84.30 W
Rio Sêco	256	22.46 S	42.40 W
Río Segundo	252	31.40 S	63.55 W
Rio Sorocaba, Represa do ⊜[1]	256	23.37 S	47.16 W
Río Sucio, Col.	246	5.25 N	75.42 W
Ríosucio, Col.	246	7.27 N	77.07 W
Río Tercero	252	32.11 S	64.06 W
Rio Tinto	250	6.48 S	35.05 W
Riotord	62	45.14 N	4.24 E
Rio Tuba	116	8.30 N	117.25 E
Riou, Île de I	62	43.11 N	5.24 E
Rioveggio	64	44.17 N	11.14 E
Rio Verde, Bra.	255	17.43 S	50.56 W
Ríoverde, Méx.	234	21.56 N	99.59 W
Rio Verde de Mato Grosso	255	18.56 S	54.52 W
Rio Vermelho	255	18.18 S	43.00 W
Rio Vista, Ca., U.S.	226	38.09 N	121.41 W
Rio Vista, Tx., U.S.	222	32.14 N	97.23 W
Rioz	58	47.25 N	6.04 E
Riozinho ≃, Bra.	246	2.55 S	67.07 W
Riozinho ≃, Bra.	250	8.25 S	45.43 W
Riozinho ≃, Bra.	250	10.22 S	49.50 W
Riozinho ≃, Bra.	250	7.06 S	51.40 W
Říp ∧	54	50.24 N	14.18 E
Ripacandida	68	40.55 N	15.43 E
Ripalti, Punta dei ›	66	42.42 N	10.25 E
Ripatransone	66	43.00 N	13.46 E
Ripley, Eng., U.K.	42	53.03 N	1.24 W
Ripley, Eng., U.K.	260	51.18 N	0.29 W
Ripley, Il., U.S.	219	40.01 N	90.38 W
Ripley, In., U.S.	216	41.06 N	86.39 W
Ripley, Ms., U.S.	194	34.43 N	88.57 W
Ripley, N.Y., U.S.	214	42.16 N	79.42 W
Ripley, Oh., U.S.	218	38.44 N	83.50 W
Ripley, Tn., U.S.	194	35.44 N	89.31 W
Ripley, W.V., U.S.	188	38.49 N	81.42 W
Ripley □[6]	218	39.04 N	85.15 W
Ripoll	34	42.12 N	2.12 E
Ripoll ≃	266d	41.29 N	2.12 E
Ripollet	266d	41.30 N	2.10 E
Ripon, P.Q., Can.	206	45.47 N	75.06 W
Ripon, Eng., U.K.	44	54.08 N	1.31 W
Ripon, Ca., U.S.	226	37.44 N	121.07 W
Ripon, Wi., U.S.	190	43.50 N	88.50 W
Riposto	70	37.44 N	15.12 E
Rippling Ridge	284b	39.11 N	76.37 W
Ripponden	44	53.41 N	1.57 W
Rippowam ≃	276	41.03 N	73.33 W
Riquewihr	58	48.10 N	7.18 E
Ririba, Laga ≃	154	3.34 N	37.15 E
Ririe	202	43.37 N	111.46 W
Risālpur Cantonment	123	34.04 N	72.00 E
Risaralda □[5]	246	5.00 N	76.00 W
Risasi	154	0.25 S	25.44 E
Risbäck	26	64.42 N	15.32 E
Risca	42	51.37 N	3.07 W
Rischenau	52	51.53 N	9.17 E
Riscle	32	43.40 N	0.05 W
Rishā', Wādī ar- V	128	25.33 N	44.05 E
Rīshahr	128	28.55 N	50.50 E
Rishīkesh	124	30.07 N	78.19 E
Rishiri-Rebun-Sarobetsu-kokuritsu-kōen ♠	92a	45.10 N	141.35 E
Rishiri-suidō ᴚ	92a	45.10 N	141.25 E
Rishiri-tō I	92a	45.11 N	141.15 E
Rishiri-zan ∧	92a	45.11 N	141.15 E
Rishmayyā	132	33.44 N	35.36 E
Rishon LeẔiyyon	132	31.58 N	34.48 E
Rishpon	132	32.12 N	34.49 E
Rishra	272b	22.43 N	88.21 E
Rishrāsh, Wādī V	142	29.29 N	31.16 E
Rishton	262	53.46 N	2.25 W
Rishworth	262	53.40 N	1.57 W
Rishworth Moor ◆[3]	262	53.39 N	2.01 W
Risinge	40	58.42 N	15.51 E
Rising Star	196	32.05 N	98.57 W
Rising Sun, In., U.S.	218	38.56 N	84.51 W
Rising Sun, Md., U.S.	208	39.41 N	76.03 W
Risingsun, Oh., U.S.	214	41.16 N	83.25 W
Risle ≃	50	49.26 N	0.23 E
Risnjak ∧	36	45.26 N	14.37 E
Rîşnov	38	45.36 N	25.28 E
Risø	41	55.42 N	12.06 E
Rison, Ar., U.S.	194	33.57 N	92.11 W
Rison, Md., U.S.	208	38.32 N	77.10 W
Risør	26	58.43 N	9.14 E
Ris-Orangis	50	48.39 N	2.25 E
Riss ≃	58	48.17 N	9.49 E
Rissani	148	31.23 N	4.09 W
Risskov ◆[8]	41	56.11 N	10.14 E
Risstissen	58	48.16 N	9.49 E
Risti	76	58.59 N	24.03 E
Ristigouche (Restigouche) ≃	186	48.04 N	66.20 W
Ristiina	26	61.30 N	27.16 E
Ristijärvi	26	64.44 N	28.24 E
Ristinge	41	54.50 N	10.38 E
Ristna	76	58.56 N	22.05 E
Risum-Lindholm	41	54.45 N	8.53 E
Rita Blanca Creek ≃	196	35.40 N	102.29 W
Ritchie, S. Afr.	158	29.02 S	24.38 E
Ritchie, Md., U.S.	284c	38.52 N	76.52 W
Ritchie Branch ≃	284c	38.53 N	76.52 W
Rithāla ◆[8]	272a	28.43 N	77.06 E
Ritidian Point ›	174p	13.39 N	144.51 E
Ritscher Upland ∧∧[1]	9	73.20 S	9.30 W
Ritsumeikan University ʋ[2]	270	35.01 N	135.46 E
Ritsurin-kōen ♠	96	34.21 N	134.02 E
Ritta Island I	220	26.44 N	80.48 W
Ritter, Mount ∧	226	37.42 N	119.12 W
Ritterhude	52	53.11 N	8.45 E
Rittersgrün	54	50.29 N	12.47 E
Rittman	214	40.58 N	81.46 W
Rittō	94	35.01 N	136.00 E
Ritzleben	54	52.50 N	11.21 E
Ritzville	202	47.07 N	118.22 W
Riu	120	28.19 N	95.03 E
Riva	208	38.57 N	76.35 W
Rivadavia, Arg.	252	35.28 S	62.57 W
Rivadavia, Arg.	252	24.11 S	62.53 W
Rivadavia, Arg.	252	33.11 S	68.28 W
Rivadavia, Arg.	252	31.33 S	68.37 W
Rivadavia, Chile	252	29.58 S	70.34 W
Riva del Garda	64	45.53 N	10.50 E
Riva del Sole	66	42.46 N	10.52 E
Riva di Tures (Rain)	64	46.57 N	12.04 E
Rivanazzano	62	44.56 N	9.01 E
Rivanna ≃	192	37.45 N	78.10 W
Rivare	216	40.49 N	84.50 W
Rivarolo Canavese	62	45.19 N	7.43 E
Rivarolo Mantovano	64	45.04 N	10.26 E
Rivas	236	11.26 N	85.50 W
Rivas □[5]	236	11.25 N	85.50 W
Rivasdale	273d	26.17 S	27.56 E
Rīvash	128	35.26 N	58.26 E
Rivas-Vaciamadrid	266a	40.20 N	3.31 W
Riva Trigoso	62	44.16 N	9.26 E
Rive, Île de la I	273b	4.21 S	15.26 E
Rive d'Arcano	64	46.08 N	13.02 E
Rive-de-Gier	62	45.32 N	4.37 E
Rivello	68	40.04 N	15.45 E
Rivera, Arg.	252	37.12 S	63.14 W
Rivera, Col.	246	2.47 N	75.15 W
Rivera, Ur.	252	30.54 S	55.31 W
Riverbank	226	37.44 N	120.56 W
River Cess	150	5.28 N	9.32 W
Riverdale, Ca., U.S.	226	36.25 N	119.51 W
Riverdale, Il., U.S.	278	41.38 N	87.37 W
Riverdale, Md., U.S.	284c	38.57 N	76.55 W
Riverdale, N.J., U.S.	276	40.59 N	74.18 W
Riverdale, N.D., U.S.	198	47.29 N	101.22 W
Riverdale, Or., U.S.	224	45.27 N	122.41 W
Riverdale ◆[8]	276	40.54 N	73.54 W
Riverdale Heights	284c	38.58 N	76.55 W
Riverdale Park ♠	275b	43.40 N	79.21 W
River Drive Park	212	44.08 N	79.31 W
River Edge, N.J., U.S.	276	40.55 N	74.02 W
River Edge, Oh., U.S.	279a	41.25 N	81.51 W
River Falls, Al., U.S.	194	31.21 N	86.32 W
River Falls, Wi., U.S.	190	44.51 N	92.37 W
River Forest	278	41.53 N	87.48 W
Rivergaro	62	44.55 N	9.36 E
River Grove	278	41.55 N	87.50 W
Riverhaven	216	41.05 N	85.02 W
Riverhead, Eng., U.K.	260	51.17 N	0.10 E
Riverhead, N.Y., U.S.	207	40.55 N	72.39 W
River Hébert	186	45.42 N	64.23 W
River Hill	279b	40.12 N	79.54 W
River Hills	216	43.10 N	87.55 W
Riverhurst	184	50.53 N	106.52 W
Riverina ◆[1]	166	35.30 S	145.30 E
River John	186	45.45 N	63.03 W
River Jordan	224	48.25 N	124.03 W
Riverlea	214	40.05 N	83.02 W
River Lea Navigation ≊	260	51.32 N	0.02 W
River Meadow Brook ≃	283	42.38 N	71.17 W
Rivermont	192	35.13 N	77.38 W
Rivero, Isla I	254	45.37 S	74.20 W
River Oaks	284c	38.57 N	77.11 W
River of Ponds	186	50.32 N	57.24 W
River Pines, Ca., U.S.	226	38.33 N	120.45 W
River Pines, Ma., U.S.	207	42.33 N	71.17 W
River Plaza	208	40.21 N	74.05 W
River Ridge Estates	284c	38.47 N	77.00 W
River Road	202	44.03 N	123.05 W
River Rouge	216	42.16 N	83.08 W
River Rouge Park ♠	281	42.22 N	83.15 W
Rivers	184	50.02 N	100.12 W
Rivers □[3]	150	4.30 N	6.30 E
Rivers, Lake of the ⊜	184	49.45 N	105.45 W
Riversdale, N.Z.	172	45.54 S	168.45 E
Riversdale, S. Afr.	158	34.07 S	21.15 E
Riverside, Ca., U.S.	228	33.57 N	117.23 W
Riverside, Ct., U.S.	276	41.02 N	73.35 W
Riverside, Il., U.S.	278	41.50 N	87.49 W
Riverside, Ia., U.S.	190	41.28 N	91.34 W
Riverside, Mi., U.S.	216	42.11 N	86.23 W
Riverside, Mi., U.S.	216	42.17 N	84.29 W
Riverside, N.J., U.S.	208	40.01 N	74.57 W
Riverside, N.Y., U.S.	210	42.08 N	77.01 W
Riverside, N.Y., U.S.	210	42.55 N	73.40 W
Riverside, Pa., U.S.	210	40.57 N	76.38 W
Riverside, Tx., U.S.	222	30.57 N	95.24 W
Riverside, Wa., U.S.	182	48.30 N	119.30 W
Riverside □[6]	228	33.45 N	117.10 W
Riverside ◆[8]	281	42.20 N	82.57 W
Riverside International Raceway ♠	228	33.57 N	117.17 W
Riverside Manors	284a	43.11 N	79.03 W
Riverside Park ♠, Mi., U.S.	281	42.22 N	83.26 W
Riverside Park ♠, N.Y., U.S.	284a	42.57 N	78.54 W
Rivers Inlet	182	51.41 N	127.15 W
Rivers Inlet ⊂	182	51.39 N	127.30 W
Riversleigh	166	19.02 S	138.44 E
Riverstone	170	33.40 S	150.52 E
Riverton, Austl.	168b	34.09 S	138.45 E
Riverton, Mb., Can.	184	50.59 N	96.59 W
Riverton, N.Z.	172	46.21 S	168.01 E
Riverton, Il., U.S.	219	39.51 N	89.33 W
Riverton, Ne., U.S.	198	40.05 N	98.45 W
Riverton, N.J., U.S.	208	40.00 N	75.00 W
Riverton, Ut,. U.S.	200	40.31 N	111.56 W
Riverton, Va., U.S.	188	38.56 N	78.11 W
Riverton, Wy., U.S.	200	43.01 N	108.22 W
Riverton Heights	224	47.28 N	122.18 W
River Vale	276	40.59 N	74.00 W
Riverview, S. Afr.	158	28.27 S	32.10 E
River View, Al., U.S.	194	32.47 N	85.08 W
Riverview, Fl., U.S.	220	27.51 N	82.19 W
Riverview, Ks., U.S.	198	37.47 N	97.22 W
Riverview, Mi., U.S.	216	42.10 N	83.10 W
Riverview Park ♠	279b	40.29 N	80.01 W
Riverwood, Austl.	274a	33.57 S	151.03 E
Riverwood, In., U.S.	218	40.06 N	85.58 W
Riverwoods	278	42.10 N	87.54 W
Rives, Fr.	62	45.21 N	5.30 E
Rives, Tn., U.S.	194	36.21 N	89.02 W
Rivesaltes	32	42.46 N	2.52 E
Rives Junction	216	42.23 N	84.27 W
Rive Sud, Canal de la ≊	275a	45.25 N	73.41 W
Rivesville	188	39.31 N	80.07 W
Riviera, Az., U.S.	204	35.04 N	114.35 W
Riviera, Tx., U.S.	196	27.18 N	97.49 W
Riviera V	58	46.15 N	8.58 E
Riviera Beach, Fl., U.S.	220	26.46 N	80.03 W
Riviera Beach, Md., U.S.	208	39.10 N	76.30 W
Rivière-à-Claude	186	49.13 N	65.54 W
Rivière à Goyaves, Pointe de la ›	241o	16.11 N	61.35 W
Rivière-au-Tonnerre	186	50.16 N	64.47 W
Rivière-Bleue	186	47.26 N	69.03 W
Rivière-Bois-Clair	206	46.34 N	71.50 W
Rivière-de-la-Chaloupe	186	49.08 N	62.32 W
Rivière-des-Prairies ◆[8]	275a	45.39 N	73.33 W
Rivière-du-Loup	186	47.50 N	69.32 W
Rivière du Rempart	157c	20.06 S	57.41 E
Rivière-Matane	186	48.39 N	67.20 W
Rivière-Mékinac	206	46.47 N	72.48 W
Rivière-Pentecôte	186	49.47 N	67.10 W
Rivière-Pilote	240e	14.29 N	60.54 W
Rivière-Salée	240e	14.32 N	60.59 W
Rivière-Verte	186	47.19 N	68.09 W
Riviersonderend	158	34.09 S	19.55 E
Rivignano	64	45.52 N	13.03 E
Rivington	262	53.37 N	2.34 W
Rivington Reservoirs ⊜[1]	262	53.37 N	2.34 W
Rivisondoli	66	41.52 N	14.04 E
Rivoli	62	45.04 N	7.31 E
Rivoli Bay ⊂	166	37.32 S	140.04 E
Rivolta d'Adda	62	45.28 N	9.31 E
Rivoltella	64	45.27 N	10.33 E
Riwaka	172	41.05 S	173.00 E
Rixford	214	41.55 N	78.30 W
Rixheim	58	47.46 N	7.24 E
Riyadh → Ar-Riyāḍ	128	24.38 N	46.43 E
Rīyāq	132	33.51 N	36.00 E
Rizal, Pil.	116	15.43 N	121.06 E
Rizal → Pasay, Pil.	269f	14.33 N	121.00 E
Rizal □[4]	116	14.35 N	121.10 E
Rizal Memorial Stadium ♠	269f	14.34 N	120.59 E
Rize	130	41.02 N	40.31 E
Rize □[4]	130	40.55 N	40.55 E
Rīzeh, Kūh-e (gora Reza) ∧	128	37.47 N	58.05 E
Rizhao	98	35.27 N	119.29 E
Rižskij zaliv (Rīgas Jūras līcis) (Gulf of Riga) ⊂	76	57.30 N	23.35 E
Rizziconi	68	38.25 N	15.57 E
Rizzuto, Capo ›	68	38.54 N	17.06 E
Rjukan	26	59.52 N	8.34 E
Rkîz, Lac ⊜	150	16.50 N	15.19 W
Rô	175f	21.22 S	167.50 E
Roa, Esp.	34	41.42 N	3.55 W
Roa, Nor.	26	60.17 N	10.37 E
Roa, Zaïre	154	3.49 N	24.56 E
Roachdale	194	39.50 N	86.48 W
Roade	42	52.09 N	0.53 W
Roadhead	44	55.04 N	2.46 W
Roadknight, Point ›	169	38.26 S	144.11 E
Roadside	158	27.31 S	28.52 E
Road Town	240m	18.27 N	64.37 W
Roag, East Loch ⊂	46	58.14 N	6.48 W
Roag, West Loch ⊂	46	58.13 N	6.53 W
Roaming Rock, Lake ⊜[1]	214	41.38 N	80.49 W
Roaming Shores	214	41.39 N	80.49 W
Roana	64	45.52 N	11.28 E
Roan Cliffs ⍊[4]	200	39.20 N	109.40 W
Roan Creek ≃	200	39.20 N	108.13 W
Roan Fell ∧	44	55.13 N	2.52 W
Roan Mountain	192	36.11 N	82.04 W
Roann	216	40.54 N	85.55 W
Roanne	32	46.02 N	4.04 E
Roanoke, Al., U.S.	194	33.09 N	85.22 W
Roanoke, Il., U.S.	190	40.47 N	89.11 W
Roanoke, In., U.S.	216	40.57 N	85.22 W
Roanoke, Tx., U.S.	222	33.01 N	97.14 W
Roanoke, Va., U.S.	192	37.16 N	79.56 W
Roanoke (Staunton) ≃	192	35.56 N	76.43 W
Roanoke Island I	192	35.53 N	75.39 W
Roanoke Rapids	192	36.27 N	77.39 W
Roanoke Rapids Dam ◆[6]	192	36.24 N	77.40 W
Roan Plateau ∧∧[1]	200	39.30 N	109.40 W
Roans Prairie	222	30.35 N	95.57 W
Roaring ≃	224	45.13 N	122.12 W
Roaring Branch	210	41.34 N	76.57 W
Roaring Brook ≃	212	43.44 N	75.24 W
Roaring Fork ≃	200	39.33 N	107.20 W
Roaring River Slough ≃	282	38.05 N	121.55 W
Roaring Run ≃	279b	40.33 N	79.32 W
Roaring Spring	214	40.20 N	78.23 W
Roaring Springs	196	33.54 N	100.52 W
Roaringwater Bay ⊂	48	51.25 N	9.35 W
Roatán	236	16.18 N	86.35 W
Roatán, Isla de I	236	16.23 N	86.30 W
Robâa Oued Yahia	36	36.05 N	9.35 E
Robāṭ Karīm	128	35.28 N	51.05 E
Robbeneiland I	158	33.49 S	18.22 E
Robbers Cave State Park ♠	196	35.01 N	95.27 W
Robbins, Ca., U.S.	226	38.53 N	121.42 W
Robbins, Il., U.S.	216	41.38 N	87.42 W
Robbins, N.C., U.S.	192	35.26 N	79.35 W
Robbins, Tn., U.S.	192	36.21 N	84.35 W
Robbins Airport ⊠	283	42.34 N	70.58 W
Robbins Ditch ≊	216	41.21 N	86.43 W
Robbins Island I	166	40.41 S	144.57 E
Robbins Pond ⊜	283	42.00 N	70.55 W
Robbins Rest	276	40.39 N	73.10 W
Robbinsville, N.J., U.S.	208	40.13 N	74.37 W
Robbinsville, N.C., U.S.	192	35.19 N	83.48 W
Robbio	62	45.17 N	8.35 E
Robe, Austl.	166	37.11 S	139.45 E
Robe, Ityo.	144	7.52 N	39.38 E
Robe ≃, Austl.	162	21.19 S	115.40 E
Robe ≃, Ire.	48	53.37 N	9.16 W
Robe, Mount ∧[2]	166	31.40 S	141.20 E
Robecchetto con Induno	266b	45.32 N	8.46 E
Robecco d'Oglio	64	45.15 N	10.04 E
Robecco sul Naviglio	266b	45.26 N	8.53 E
Röbel	54	53.23 N	12.35 E
Robeline	194	31.41 N	93.18 W
Röberget ∧[2]	40	59.45 N	14.54 E
Robersonville	192	35.49 N	77.15 W
Robert, Havre du ⊂	240e	14.40 N	60.55 W
Roberta	192	32.43 N	84.00 W
Roberta Mills	192	35.22 N	80.38 W
Robert E. Lee Memorial Park ♠	284b	39.23 N	76.39 W
Robert E. Lee's Birthplace ⊥	208	38.10 N	76.49 W
Robert-Espagne	56	48.45 N	5.02 E
Robert F. Kennedy Memorial Stadium ♠	284c	38.53 N	76.58 W
Robert H. Treman State Park ♠	210	42.24 N	76.35 W
Robert Lee	196	31.54 N	100.29 W
Robert Louis Stevenson Memorial State Park ♠	226	38.40 N	122.36 W
Robert Louis Stevenson's Tomb ⊥	175a	13.50 S	171.44 W
Robert Morse College ʋ[2]	279b	40.31 N	80.12 W
Robert Moses State Park ♠	210	40.37 N	73.16 W
Robert Mueller Municipal Airport ⊠	222	30.18 N	97.42 W
Roberto Payró	258	35.10 S	57.39 W
Robert Point ›	168a	32.31 S	115.42 E
Roberts, Id., U.S.	202	43.43 N	112.07 W
Roberts, Il., U.S.	216	40.37 N	88.11 W
Roberts, Mt., U.S.	202	45.21 N	109.10 W
Roberts, Mount ∧	171a	28.13 S	152.28 E
Roberts, Point ›	224	49.00 N	123.06 W
Robert's Arm	186	49.29 N	55.49 W
Robertsbridge	42	50.59 N	0.29 E
Roberts Canyon V	280	34.11 N	117.54 W
Roberts Creek Mountain ∧	204	39.52 N	116.18 W
Robertsdale, Al., U.S.	194	30.33 N	87.42 W
Robertsdale, Pa., U.S.	214	40.11 N	78.06 W
Robertsfield	150	6.15 N	10.24 W
Robertsfors	26	64.11 N	20.51 E
Robertsganj	124	24.42 N	83.04 E
Robertsham ◆[8]	273d	26.15 S	28.00 E
Robertsholm	40	60.35 N	76.16 E
Robert S. Kerr Lake ⊜[1]	194	35.25 N	95.00 W
Roberts Mountain ∧	180	60.03 N	166.16 W
Robertson, Austl.	170	34.35 S	150.35 E
Robertson, S. Afr.	158	33.46 S	19.50 E
Robertson □[6], Ky., U.S.	218	38.32 N	84.04 W
Robertson □[6], Tx., U.S.	222	31.00 N	96.30 W
Robertson, Lac ⊜	186	51.00 N	59.10 W
Robertson Bay ⊂	9	71.25 S	170.00 E
Robertson Range ∧∧	162	23.10 S	121.00 E
Robertsonville	206	46.09 N	71.13 W
Roberts Park	278	41.44 N	87.49 W
Roberts Peak ∧	182	52.57 N	120.32 W
Robertsport	150	6.45 N	11.22 W
Robertstown, Austl.	168b	34.00 S	139.05 E
Robertstown, Ire.	48	53.15 N	6.59 W
Robertsville	214	40.46 N	81.11 W
Robertville	56	50.27 N	6.07 E
Roberval	176	48.31 N	72.13 W
Robin Hood's Bay	44	54.25 N	0.33 W
Robins Air Force Base ■	192	32.38 N	83.35 W
Robins Island I	207	40.58 N	72.28 W
Robinson, Il., U.S.	194	39.00 N	87.44 W
Robinson, Tx., U.S.	222	31.28 N	97.06 W
Robinson ≃	164	16.03 S	137.16 E
Robinson, Lake ⊜[1]	192	34.26 N	80.10 W
Robinson Brook ≃	283	43.02 N	71.13 W
Robinson Creek ≃	226	38.16 N	119.15 W
Róbinson Crusoe, Isla (Isla Más a Tierra) I	244	33.38 S	78.52 W
Robinson Gorge National Park ♠	166	25.15 S	149.10 E
Robinson Lake ⊜	222	29.35 N	94.36 W
Robinson Lake Aerodrome ⊠	273d	26.08 S	27.42 E
Robinson Pond ⊜	283	42.48 N	71.23 W
Robinson Range ∧∧	162	25.45 S	119.00 E
Robinson Run ≃	279b	40.23 N	80.06 W
Robinson Run, North Branch ≃	279b	40.23 N	80.11 W
Robinsons	186	48.15 N	58.48 W
Robinvale	166	34.36 S	142.46 E
Robleda	34	40.23 N	6.36 W
Robledo	34	38.46 N	2.26 W
Roblin	184	51.14 N	101.21 W
Röblingen	54	51.28 N	11.40 E
Roboré	248	18.20 S	59.45 W
Röbrinken	40	58.36 N	15.53 E
Rob Roy Island I	175e	7.25 S	157.35 E
Robson, Mount ∧	182	53.07 N	119.09 W
Robstown	196	27.47 N	97.40 W
Roby, Eng., U.K.	262	53.25 N	2.51 W
Roby, Il., U.S.	219	39.44 N	89.24 W
Roby, Tx., U.S.	196	32.44 N	100.22 W
Roby Mill	262	53.34 N	2.44 W
Roca, Cabo da ›	34	38.47 N	9.30 W
Roçado	250	6.40 S	44.19 W
Rocafuerte	246	0.55 S	80.28 W
Roça Grande	256	21.36 S	42.58 W
Rocanville	184	50.24 N	101.43 W
Roca Partida, Isla I	232	19.01 N	112.02 W
Roca Partida, Punta ›	234	18.42 N	95.10 W
Rocas, Atol das I[1]	250	3.52 S	33.59 W
Roccabernarda	68	39.08 N	16.52 E
Roccacasale	66	42.07 N	13.53 E
Roccadaspide	68	40.26 N	15.12 E
Rocca di Cambio	66	42.14 N	13.29 E
Rocca di Mezzo	66	42.12 N	13.31 E
Rocca di Neto	68	39.11 N	17.00 E
Rocca di Papa	66	41.46 N	12.42 E
Roccafluvione	66	42.51 N	13.29 E
Roccagloriosa	68	40.06 N	15.26 E
Roccalbegna	66	42.47 N	11.30 E
Roccalumera	70	37.58 N	15.24 E
Rocca Massima	66	41.41 N	12.55 E
Roccamena	70	37.50 N	13.09 E
Roccamonfina	68	41.17 N	13.59 E
Roccanova	68	40.13 N	16.12 E
Roccapalumba	70	37.48 N	13.39 E
Rocca Pia	66	41.56 N	13.59 E
Rocca Pietore	64	46.26 N	11.59 E
Roccaprebalza	64	44.31 N	9.57 E
Rocca Priora	267a	41.48 N	12.45 E
Roccaraso	66	41.51 N	14.05 E
Rocca San Casciano	66	44.03 N	11.50 E
Rocca Santa Maria	66	42.41 N	13.30 E
Roccasecca	66	41.33 N	13.40 E
Roccasecca dei Volsci	66	41.29 N	13.13 E
Roccastrada	66	43.00 N	11.10 E
Roccavione	62	44.19 N	7.29 E
Roccavivara	66	41.50 N	14.36 E
Roccelito, Monte ∧	70	37.50 N	13.47 E
Roccella Ionica	68	38.19 N	16.24 E
Roccella Valdemone	70	37.56 N	15.00 E
Rocchetta Sant'Antonio	68	41.06 N	15.27 E
Rocciamelone ∧	62	45.12 N	7.05 E
Ročegda	24	62.42 N	43.23 E
Roch ≃	44	53.34 N	2.18 W
Rocha, Bra.	256	21.28 S	45.49 W
Rocha, Ur.	252	34.29 S	54.20 W
Rocha Miranda ◆[8]	287a	22.52 S	43.22 W
Rocha Sobrinho	287a	22.47 S	43.25 W
Rochdale, Eng., U.K.	44	53.38 N	2.09 W
Rochdale, Ma., U.S.	207	42.11 N	71.54 W
Rochdale, N.Y., U.S.	210	41.43 N	73.50 W
Rochdale □[8]	262	53.37 N	2.08 W
Rochdale Canal ≊	262	53.43 N	1.54 W
Roche	42	50.24 N	4.48 W
Rochebrune, Pic de ∧	62	44.49 N	6.51 E
Rochechouart	32	45.50 N	0.50 E
Rochedinho	255	20.14 S	54.33 W
Rochedo	255	19.57 S	54.52 W
Rochedo de Minas	256	21.38 S	43.01 W
Rochefort, Bel.	56	50.10 N	5.13 E
Rochefort, Fr.	32	45.57 N	0.58 W
Rochefort-en-Yvelines	50	48.35 N	1.59 E
Rochefort-Montagne	32	45.41 N	2.48 E
Rochefort-sur-Nenon	58	47.07 N	5.34 E
Roche Harbor	224	48.36 N	123.08 W
Rochehaut	56	49.51 N	5.00 E
Roche-la-Molière	62	45.26 N	4.19 E
Roche-lez-Beaupré	58	47.17 N	6.07 E
Rochelle, Ga., U.S.	192	31.57 N	83.27 W
Rochelle, Il., U.S.	216	41.55 N	89.04 W
Rochelle, Tx., U.S.	196	31.13 N	99.13 W
Rochelle Park	276	40.54 N	74.04 W
Rochemaure	62	44.35 N	4.42 E
Roche-Percée	184	49.03 N	102.45 W
Rochepot, Château de la ⊥	58	46.57 N	4.40 E
Rocher Fendu, Rapides du ↳	275a	45.19 N	73.57 W
Rochester, Austl.	166	36.22 S	144.42 E
Rochester, Eng., U.K.	42	51.24 N	0.30 E
Rochester, Eng., U.K.	44	55.16 N	2.16 W
Rochester, Il., U.S.	219	39.45 N	89.32 W
Rochester, In., U.S.	216	41.03 N	86.12 W
Rochester, Ma., U.S.	207	41.43 N	70.49 W
Rochester, Mi., U.S.	214	42.40 N	83.08 W
Rochester, Mn., U.S.	190	44.01 N	92.28 W
Rochester, N.H., U.S.	188	43.18 N	70.58 W
Rochester, N.Y., U.S.	210	43.09 N	77.36 W
Rochester, Oh., U.S.	214	41.07 N	82.18 W
Rochester, Pa., U.S.	214	40.42 N	80.17 W
Rochester, Tx., U.S.	196	33.19 N	99.51 W
Rochester, Wa., U.S.	224	46.49 N	123.05 W
Rochester, Wi., U.S.	216	42.44 N	88.13 W
Rochester City Airport ⊠	260	51.21 N	0.30 E
Rochester Hills	214	42.40 N	83.09 W
Rochester Mills	214	40.49 N	78.59 W
Rochester-Monroe County Airport ⊠	210	43.07 N	77.40 W
Rochester-Utica State Recreation Area ♠	214	42.39 N	83.04 W
Rochetaillée	62	45.25 N	4.27 E
Rocheuses → Rocky Mountains ∧∧	16	48.00 N	116.00 W
Rochford	42	51.36 N	0.43 E
Rochford □[8]	260	51.36 N	0.39 E
Rochfortbridge	48	53.23 N	7.17 W
Rochlitz	54	51.03 N	12.47 E
Rochon, Lac ⊜	206	46.43 N	75.14 W
Rock	190	46.04 N	87.09 W
Rock □[6]	216	42.41 N	89.05 W
Rock ≃, U.S.	190	41.29 N	90.37 W
Rock ≃, U.S.	198	43.05 N	96.27 W
Rockall I	22	57.35 N	13.48 W
Rockall Rise ✦[3]	10	59.00 N	14.00 W
Rockanje	52	51.53 N	4.05 E
Rockaway, N.J., U.S.	210	40.54 N	74.30 W
Rockaway, Or., U.S.	224	45.36 N	123.56 W
Rockaway ≃	210	40.51 N	74.21 W
Rockaway Inlet ⊂	276	40.34 N	73.55 W
Rockaway Neck	276	40.51 N	74.21 W
Rockaway Park ◆[8]	276	40.35 N	73.50 W
Rockaway Point ◆[8]	276	40.33 N	73.55 W
Rockaway Point ›	276	40.33 N	73.56 W
Rockaways' Playland ♠	276	40.35 N	73.49 W
Rockbank	274b	37.43 S	144.39 E
Rock Bay	182	50.20 N	125.29 W
Rockbridge	219	39.16 N	90.12 W
Rock Bridge State Park ♠	219	38.53 N	92.19 W
Rock Brook ≃	276	40.25 N	74.40 W
Rock Candy Mountain ∧	224	47.01 N	123.07 W
Rockcastle ≃	192	36.58 N	84.21 W
Rock City Falls	210	43.04 N	73.55 W
Rockcliffe Park	212	45.27 N	75.41 W
Rockcorry	48	54.07 N	7.01 W
Rock Creek, B.C., Can.	182	49.06 N	118.58 W
Rock Creek, Oh., U.S.	214	41.39 N	80.51 W
Rock Creek ≃, N.A.	202	48.25 N	107.05 W
Rock Creek ≃, U.S.	208	39.43 N	77.13 W
Rock Creek ≃, U.S.	284c	38.54 N	77.04 W
Rock Creek ≃, Ca., U.S.	226	37.55 N	120.58 W
Rock Creek ≃, Co., U.S.	198	40.20 N	102.31 W
Rock Creek ≃, Il., U.S.	216	41.12 N	87.59 W
Rock Creek ≃, In., U.S.	216	40.49 N	85.23 W
Rock Creek ≃, In., U.S.	216	40.42 N	86.35 W
Rock Creek ≃, Mt., U.S.	202	45.31 N	108.49 W
Rock Creek ≃, Mt., U.S.	202	46.43 N	113.40 W
Rock Creek ≃, Nv., U.S.	204	40.39 N	116.54 W
Rock Creek ≃, Or., U.S.	202	45.34 N	120.25 W
Rock Creek ≃, Or., U.S.	202	42.39 N	119.08 W
Rock Creek ≃, Or., U.S.	224	45.51 N	123.12 W
Rock Creek ≃, S.D., U.S.	198	43.44 N	97.58 W
Rock Creek ≃, Ut,. U.S.	200	40.17 N	110.30 W
Rock Creek ≃, Wa., U.S.	202	46.55 N	117.56 W
Rock Creek ≃, Wa., U.S.	202	45.42 N	120.29 W
Rock Creek ≃, Wy., U.S.	200	41.54 N	106.08 W
Rock Creek Butte ∧	202	44.49 N	118.07 W
Rock Creek Hills	284c	39.01 N	77.04 W
Rock Creek Park ♠	284c	38.58 N	77.03 W
Rock Cut State Park ♠	216	42.20 N	89.00 W
Rockdale, Austl.	170	33.57 S	151.08 E
Rockdale, Il., U.S.	216	41.30 N	88.06 W
Rockdale, Md., U.S.	284b	39.21 N	76.45 W
Rockdale, Pa., U.S.	285	39.53 N	75.26 W
Rockdale, Tx., U.S.	222	30.39 N	97.00 W
Rockdale, W.V., U.S.	214	40.18 N	80.35 W
Rockefeller Center ʋ	276	40.45 N	74.00 W
Rockefeller Park ♠	279a	41.32 N	81.38 W
Rockefeller Plateau ∧∧[1]	9	80.00 S	135.00 W
Rockenhausen	56	49.38 N	7.49 E
Rockensüss	56	51.03 N	9.50 E
Rockfall	207	41.31 N	72.41 W
Rock Falls	190	41.46 N	89.41 W
Rock Ferry	262	53.22 N	3.00 W
Rockfield	216	40.38 N	86.34 W
Rock Flat	171b	36.21 S	149.12 E
Rock Flat Creek ≃	171b	36.07 S	149.12 E
Rockford, Al., U.S.	194	32.53 N	86.13 W
Rockford, Il., U.S.	216	42.16 N	89.05 W
Rockford, In., U.S.	218	38.59 N	85.54 W
Rockford, Ia., U.S.	190	43.03 N	92.56 W
Rockford, Mi., U.S.	190	43.07 N	85.33 W
Rockford, Oh., U.S.	216	40.41 N	84.38 W
Rockford, Tn., U.S.	192	35.49 N	83.56 W
Rock Forest	206	45.20 N	71.59 W
Rockglen, Sk., Can.	184	49.10 N	105.57 W
Rock Glen, N.Y., U.S.	210	42.41 N	78.07 W
Rock Hall	208	39.08 N	76.14 W
Rockhammar	40	59.32 N	15.26 E
Rockhampton	166	23.23 S	150.31 E
Rockhampton Downs	162	18.57 S	135.01 E
Rock Hill, N.Y., U.S.	210	41.38 N	74.36 W
Rock Hill, S.C., U.S.	192	34.55 N	81.01 W
Rockhill Furnace	214	40.15 N	77.54 W
Rockingham, Austl.	168a	32.17 S	115.44 E
Rockingham, N.C., U.S.	192	34.56 N	79.46 W
Rockingham □[6]	207	42.50 N	71.15 W
Rockingham Bay ⊂	166	18.10 S	146.05 E
Rockingham Forest ◆[3]	42	52.30 N	0.37 W
Rockingham State Historic Site ⊥	276	40.24 N	74.37 W
Rock Island, P.Q., Can.	206	45.01 N	72.06 W
Rock Island, Il., U.S.	190	41.30 N	90.34 W
Rock Island, Tx., U.S.	222	29.32 N	96.35 W
Rocklake	198	48.47 N	99.15 W
Rock Lake ⊜, Mb., Can.	184	49.11 N	99.12 W
Rock Lake ⊜, On., Can.	212	45.30 N	78.23 W
Rock Lake ⊜, Il., U.S.	278	41.40 N	88.03 W
Rock Lake ⊜, N.D., U.S.	198	48.50 N	99.10 W
Rock Lake ⊜, Wi., U.S.	216	43.04 N	88.56 W
Rockland, On., Can.	188	45.33 N	75.17 W
Rockland, De., U.S.	285	39.47 N	75.34 W
Rockland, Id., U.S.	202	42.34 N	112.52 W
Rockland, Me., U.S.	188	44.06 N	69.06 W
Rockland, Ma., U.S.	207	42.07 N	70.55 W
Rockland, Mi., U.S.	190	46.44 N	89.10 W
Rockland, N.Y., U.S.	210	41.58 N	74.54 W
Rockland □[6]	210	41.09 N	73.59 W
Rockland Lake	276	41.09 N	73.55 W
Rockland Lake ⊜	276	41.08 N	73.55 W
Rockland Lake State Park ♠	276	41.08 N	73.55 W
Rocklands Reservoir ⊜[1]	166	37.15 S	142.00 E
Rockledge, Fl., U.S.	220	28.21 N	80.43 W
Rockledge, Pa., U.S.	285	40.03 N	75.05 W
Rockleigh	276	41.00 N	73.55 W
Rocklin	226	38.47 N	121.14 W
Rockmart	192	34.00 N	85.02 W
Rock Meadow Brook ≃	283	42.16 N	71.13 W
Rock of Cashel ⊥	48	52.31 N	7.53 W
Rock Point	208	38.16 N	76.50 W
Rock Point Provincial Park ♠	212	42.51 N	79.33 W
Rock Pond ⊜	283	42.44 N	71.00 W
Rockport, Il., U.S.	219	39.32 N	91.00 W
Rockport, Ky., U.S.	194	37.20 N	86.59 W
Rockport, Me., U.S.	188	44.11 N	69.04 W
Rockport, Ma., U.S.	207	42.39 N	70.37 W
Rock Port, Mo., U.S.	194	40.24 N	95.30 W
Rockport, Tx., U.S.	196	28.01 N	97.03 W
Rock Rapids	198	43.25 N	96.10 W
Rock River	200	41.44 N	105.58 W
Rock Run	208	39.59 N	75.50 W
Rock Run ≃	284c	38.58 N	77.11 W
Rock Sound	238	24.54 N	76.12 W
Rocksprings, Tx., U.S.	196	30.00 N	100.12 W
Rock Springs, Wy., U.S.	200	41.35 N	109.12 W
Rockstone	246	5.59 N	58.33 W
Rock Stream	210	42.28 N	76.56 W
Rockton, Il., U.S.	216	42.27 N	89.04 W
Rockton, Pa., U.S.	214	41.05 N	78.39 W
Rock Valley	198	43.12 N	96.17 W
Rockville, N.Z.	172	40.44 S	172.38 E
Rockville, Ct., U.S.	207	41.52 N	72.27 W
Rockville, In., U.S.	194	39.45 N	87.13 W
Rockville, Md., U.S.	208	39.05 N	77.09 W
Rockville, Ma., U.S.	283	42.08 N	71.21 W
Rockville, Pa., U.S.	208	40.20 N	76.54 W
Rockville, R.I., U.S.	207	41.27 N	71.30 W
Rockville Centre	210	40.39 N	73.38 W
Rockwall	222	32.55 N	96.27 W
Rockwall □[6]	222	32.55 N	96.23 W
Rockwell, Ia., U.S.	190	42.59 N	93.11 W
Rockwell, N.C., U.S.	192	35.33 N	80.24 W
Rockwell, Lake ⊜	214	41.12 N	81.19 W
Rockwell City	198	42.23 N	94.38 W
Rockwell International Corporation ʋ[3]	280	33.52 N	117.51 W
Rockwood, On., Can.	212	43.37 N	80.08 W
Rockwood, Me., U.S.	188	45.41 N	69.44 W
Rockwood, Mi., U.S.	216	42.04 N	83.14 W
Rockwood, Or., U.S.	224	45.31 N	122.28 W
Rockwood, Pa., U.S.	188	39.54 N	79.09 W
Rockwood, Tn., U.S.	192	35.51 N	84.41 W
Rockwood Lake ⊜	276	41.06 N	73.38 W
Rockwood Lake Brook ≃	276	41.03 N	73.36 W
Rocky	196	35.09 N	99.03 W
Rocky ≃, Ab., Can.	182	53.08 N	117.59 W
Rocky ≃, Mi., U.S.	216	41.57 N	85.39 W
Rocky ≃, N.C., U.S.	192	35.37 N	79.09 W
Rocky ≃, Oh., U.S.	214	41.30 N	81.49 W
Rocky, East Branch ≃	279a	41.24 N	81.53 W
Rocky, West Branch ≃	214	41.24 N	81.53 W
Rocky Arroyo V	196	32.32 N	104.21 W
Rocky Boy's Indian Reservation ◆[4]	202	48.18 N	109.45 W
Rocky Branch ≃	284c	38.53 N	77.19 W
Rocky Cape National Park ♠	166	40.56 S	145.35 E
Rocky Comfort Creek ≃	192	32.59 N	82.25 W
Rocky Coulee V	202	47.10 N	119.16 W
Rocky Creek ≃	192	35.53 N	80.47 W
Rockyford, Ab., Can.	182	51.13 N	113.08 W
Rocky Ford, Co., U.S.	198	38.06 N	103.43 W
Rocky Ford Creek ≃	216	41.19 N	83.37 W
Rocky Fork Lake ⊜	218	39.11 N	83.28 W
Rocky Fork State Park ♠	218	39.11 N	83.30 W
Rocky Gorge Reservoir ⊜[1]	208	39.07 N	77.54 W
Rocky Grove	214	41.25 N	79.49 W
Rocky Gully	162	34.30 S	116.48 E
Rocky Harbour	186	49.36 N	57.55 W
Rocky Harbour ⊂	271d	22.20 N	114.19 E
Rocky Hill, Ct., U.S.	207	41.40 N	72.39 W
Rocky Hill, N.J., U.S.	276	40.24 N	74.38 W
Rocky Island Lake ⊜[1]	190	46.56 N	83.04 W
Rocky Lake ⊜	184	54.08 N	101.30 W
Rocky Mount, N.C., U.S.	192	35.57 N	77.48 W
Rocky Mount, Va., U.S.	192	36.59 N	79.53 W
Rocky Mountain ∧	202	47.49 N	112.49 W
Rocky Mountain House	182	52.22 N	114.55 W
Rocky Mountain National Park ♠	200	40.19 N	105.42 W
Rocky Mountains ∧∧	16	48.00 N	116.00 W
Rocky Point, N.Y., U.S.	207	40.57 N	72.56 W
Rocky Point, Wa., U.S.	224	47.35 N	122.41 W
Rocky Point ›, Ba.	192	26.00 N	77.25 W
Rocky Point ›, Ire.	48	54.42 N	8.48 W
Rocky Point ›, Namibia	156	19.03 S	12.30 E
Rocky Point ›, Norf. I.	174c	29.03 S	167.55 E
Rocky Point ›, Ak., U.S.	180	64.25 N	163.10 W
Rocky Point ›, Ma., U.S.	207	41.57 N	70.35 W
Rocky Point ›, N.Y., U.S.	276	40.55 N	73.32 W
Rocky Ridge	214	41.32 N	83.13 W
Rocky Ridge ∧	282	37.48 N	122.03 W
Rocky River	214	41.28 N	81.50 W
Rocky River Reservation ♠	279a	41.27 N	81.50 W
Rocky Run ≃, N.D., U.S.	198	47.38 N	99.02 W
Rocky Run ≃, Pa., U.S.	285	39.54 N	75.28 W
Rocky Run ≃, Va., U.S.	284c	38.58 N	77.15 W
Rocky Saugeen ≃	212	44.13 N	80.53 W
Rocky Top ∧	202	44.47 N	122.17 W
Roclenge-sur-Geer	56	50.45 N	5.36 E
Rocosas, Montañas → Rocky Mountains ∧∧	16	48.00 N	116.00 W
Rocquencourt	261	48.50 N	2.07 E
Rocroi	50	49.55 N	4.31 E

Symbols in the index entries represent the broad categories identified in the key at the right. Symbols with superior numbers (∧∧[1]) identify subcategories (see complete key on page *I · 1)*.

Symbole im Register stellen die rechts im Schlüssel erklärten Kategorien dar. Symbole mit hochgestellten Ziffern (∧∧[1]) bezeichnen Unterabteilungen einer Kategorie (vgl. vollständiger Schlüssel auf Seite *I · 1)*.

Los símbolos incluidos en el texto del índice representan las grandes categorias identificadas con la clave a la derecha. Los símbolos con numeros en su parte superior (∧∧[1]) identifican las subcategorías (véase la clave completa en la página *I · 1)*.

Les symboles de l'index représentent les catégories indiquées dans la légende à droite. Les symboles suivis d'un indice (∧∧[1]) représentent des sous-catégories (voir légende complète à la page *I · 1)*.

Os símbolos incluídos no texto do índice representam as grandes categorias identificadas com a chave à direita. Os símbolos com números em sua parte superior (∧∧[1]) identificam as subcategorias (veja-se a chave completa à página *I · 1)*.

∧ Mountain	Berg	Montaña	Montagne	Montanha
∧∧ Mountains	Gebirge	Montañas	Montagnes	Montanhas
)(Pass	Paß	Paso	Col	Passo
V Valley, Canyon	Tal, Cañon	Valle, Cañón	Vallée, Canyon	Vale, Canhão
≚ Plain	Ebene	Llano	Plaine	Planície
› Cape	Kap	Cabo	Cap	Cabo
I Island	Insel	Isla	Île	Ilha
II Islands	Inseln	Islas	Îles	Ilhas
⍊ Other Topographic Features	Andere Topographische Objekte	Otros Elementos Topográficos	Autres données topographiques	Outros acidentes topográficos

ESPAÑOL

Nombre	Página	Lat.°′	Long.°′ W = Oeste
Roda	192	36.58 N	82.49 W
Roda ≃	54	50.52 N	11.44 E
Rodach	56	50.20 N	10.46 E
Rodach ≃	56	50.08 N	10.52 E
Rodakovo	83	48.33 N	39.02 E
Rodalben	56	49.14 N	7.38 E
Rodalquilar	34	37.40 N	2.08 W
Rodas	240p	22.20 N	80.33 W
Rodas, Isla de → Ródhos I	38	36.10 N	28.00 E
Rodaun ◆[8]	264b	48.08 N	16.16 E
Rødberg	26	60.16 N	8.58 E
Rødby	41	54.42 N	11.24 E
Rødbyhavn	41	54.39 N	11.21 E
Roddickton	186	50.52 N	56.08 W
Rødding	41	55.23 N	9.06 E
Rodeio	252	26.57 S	49.23 W
Rodeiro	256	21.12 S	42.52 W
Rødekro	41	55.04 N	9.21 E
Rodel	46	57.41 N	7.05 W
Roden	52	53.07 N	6.26 E
Roden ≃	42	52.43 N	2.36 W
Rodenberg	52	52.18 N	9.21 E
Rodenkirchen, B.R.D.	52	53.24 N	8.26 E
Rodenkirchen, B.R.D.	56	50.54 N	6.59 E
Rödental	54	50.17 N	11.01 E
Rodeo, Arg.	252	30.12 S	69.06 W
Rodeo, Méx.	232	25.11 N	104.34 W
Rodeo, Ca., U.S.	226	38.01 N	122.15 W
Rodeo, N.M., U.S.	200	31.50 N	109.01 W
Rodeo Lagoon c	282	37.50 N	122.31 W
Röderau	54	51.19 N	13.19 E
Roderick ≃	162	26.57 S	116.13 E
Roderick Island I	182	52.40 N	128.22 W
Rödermark	56	49.59 N	8.50 E
Rodewisch	54	50.32 N	12.24 E
Rodez	32	44.21 N	2.35 E
Rodgau	56	50.02 N	8.54 E
Rodheim-Bieber	56	50.37 N	8.35 E
Rodhópis, Orosirá → Rhodope Mountains ⋏	38	41.30 N	24.30 E
Ródhos (Rhodes)	38	36.26 N	28.13 E
Ródhos (Rhodes) I	38	36.10 N	28.00 E
Rodi Garganico	68	41.55 N	15.53 E
Roding	60	49.12 N	12.32 E
Roding ≃	42	51.31 N	0.06 E
Rodinka	80	57.24 N	43.34 E
Rodino, S.S.S.R.	76	58.57 N	44.59 E
Rodino, S.S.S.R.	86	52.30 N	80.15 E
Rodionovo-Nesvetajskaja	83	47.36 N	39.42 E
Rodman	180	57.28 N	135.21 W
Rodman Naval Station ■	236	8.56 N	79.36 W
Rodn'a	76	56.22 N	34.55 E
Rodnei, Munții ⋏	38	47.35 N	24.40 E
Rodney, On., Can.	214	42.34 N	81.41 W
Rodney, Ms., U.S.	194	31.51 N	91.11 W
Rodney, Cape ›, N.Z.	172	36.17 S	174.49 E
Rodney, Cape ›, Ak., U.S.	180	64.39 N	166.24 W
Rodney Village	208	39.07 N	75.31 W
Rodničok	80	51.26 N	42.54 E
Rodniki, S.S.S.R.	80	57.06 N	41.44 E
Rodniki, S.S.S.R.	265b	55.39 N	38.04 E
Rodnikovskij	86	50.39 N	57.12 E
Rodolfo, Lago → Rudolf, Lake ⊜	144	3.30 N	36.05 E
Rodolfo Iselín	252	34.39 S	68.01 W
Rodonit, Kep i ›	38	41.35 N	19.27 E
Rodostov	78	51.58 N	24.57 E
Rødovre	41	55.41 N	12.29 E
Rodrigo de Freitas, Lagoa c	287a	22.58 S	43.13 W
Rodrigues I	12	19.42 S	63.25 E
Rodriguez, Méx.	196	27.10 N	100.01 W
Rodriguez, Ur.	258	34.23 S	56.33 W
Rodriguez, Arroyo ≃	288	34.52 S	58.02 W
Roduco	208	36.27 N	76.48 W
Rødven	26	62.38 N	7.33 E
Rødvig	41	55.15 N	12.23 E
Roe ≃	48	55.07 N	6.59 W
Roebling	208	40.06 N	74.47 W
Roebourne	162	20.47 S	117.09 E
Roebuck Bay c	162	18.04 S	122.17 E
Roehampton ◆[8]	260	51.27 N	0.14 W
Roe Island I	282	38.04 N	122.02 W
Roeland Park	198	39.02 N	94.37 W
Roelands	168a	33.18 S	115.50 E
Roeliff Jansen Kill ≃	210	42.11 N	73.52 W
Roelofarendsveen	52	52.12 N	4.38 E
Roelofskamp	158	26.10 S	24.24 E
Roen, Monte ∧	64	46.22 N	11.11 E
Roer (Rur) ≃	56	51.12 N	5.59 E
Roermond	52	51.12 N	6.00 E
Roesbrugge-Haringe	50	50.55 N	2.37 E
Roeselare (Roulers)	50	50.57 N	3.08 E
Roesinger, Lake ⊜	224	47.58 N	121.55 W
Roessleville	210	42.41 N	73.48 W
Roes Welcome Sound ʉ	176	64.00 N	88.00 W
Roetgen	56	50.39 N	6.12 E
Rœulx	50	50.30 N	4.06 E
Roff	196	34.37 N	96.50 W
Röfors	40	58.57 N	14.37 E
Rofrano	68	40.12 N	15.25 E
Rogačevo	82	56.26 N	37.10 E
Rogačov	76	53.05 N	30.03 E
Rogačovka	78	51.30 N	39.34 E
Rogagua, Laguna ⊜	248	13.43 S	66.54 W
Rogaguado, Laguna ⊜	248	12.52 S	65.43 W
Rogaland □[6]	26	59.00 N	6.15 E
Rogalik	83	48.56 N	40.03 E
Rogan'	78	49.54 N	36.29 E
Rogans Hill	274a	33.44 S	151.01 E
Rogan's Seat ∧	44	54.25 N	2.07 W
Rogart	46	58.00 N	4.08 W
Rogäsen	54	52.19 N	12.20 E
Rogaška Slatina	36	46.14 N	15.38 E
Rogatica	38	43.48 N	19.00 E
Rogatin	78	49.25 N	24.37 E
Rogätz	54	52.19 N	11.46 E
Rogen ⊜	26	62.19 N	12.23 E
Roger, Lac ⊜	190	47.50 N	78.51 W
Roger Island I	283	42.43 N	70.50 W
Rogers, Ar., U.S.	194	36.19 N	94.07 W
Rogers, Ct., U.S.	207	41.50 N	71.54 W
Rogers, Oh., U.S.	214	40.48 N	80.38 W
Rogers, Tx., U.S.	222	30.55 N	97.13 W
Rogers, Mount ∧	192	36.39 N	81.33 W
Rogers City	190	45.25 N	83.49 W
Rogers Lake ⊜	228	34.52 N	117.51 W
Rogers Park ◆[8]	278	42.01 N	87.40 W
Rogers Pass)(	182	51.17 N	117.31 W
Rogersville, N.B., Can.	186	46.44 N	65.26 W
Rogersville, Al., U.S.	194	34.49 N	87.17 W
Rogersville, Tn., U.S.	192	36.24 N	83.00 W
Roggeveldberge ⋏	158	32.17 S	20.08 E
Roggewein, Cabo ›	174z	27.07 S	109.15 W
Roggiano Gravina	68	39.37 N	16.09 E
Roghudi	68	38.03 N	15.55 E
Rogliano, Fr.	62	42.57 N	9.25 E
Rogliano, It.	68	39.11 N	16.20 E
Rognac	62	43.29 N	5.14 E
Rognedino	76	53.48 N	33.33 E
Rögnitz ≃	54	53.19 N	10.57 E
Rognon ≃	58	48.23 N	5.10 E
Rogny	50	47.45 N	2.53 E
Rogojampi	115a	8.19 S	114.17 E
Rogovatoje	78	51.14 N	38.22 E
Rogovo	82	55.13 N	37.05 E
Rogovskaja	78	45.44 N	38.44 E
Rogovskoje	80	58.33 N	50.43 E
Rogožkino	83	47.10 N	39.21 E
Rogoźno	30	52.46 N	17.00 E
Rogozov	78	50.14 N	31.03 E
Rogue ≃, Mi., U.S.	190	43.04 N	85.35 W

FRANÇAIS

Nom	Page	Lat.°′	Long.°′ W = Ouest
Rogue ≃, Or., U.S.	202	42.26 N	124.25 W
Rogue River	202	42.26 N	123.10 W
Rohdenhaus	263	51.18 N	7.01 E
Rohilkhand Plains ⩸	124	28.20 N	79.30 E
Rohinjan	272c	19.06 N	73.04 E
Rohitpur	126	23.42 N	90.19 E
Rohl ≃	140	6.22 N	29.46 E
Röhlinghausen ◆[8]	263	51.36 N	7.14 E
Rohnert Park	226	38.20 N	122.42 W
Rohr	60	48.46 N	11.58 E
Rohrbach in Oberösterreich	60	48.34 N	13.59 E
Rohrbach-lès-Bitche	56	49.03 N	7.16 E
Rohrbeck	264a	52.32 N	13.02 E
Rohrberg	54	52.42 N	11.02 E
Röhrenfurth	56	51.09 N	9.32 E
Rohri	120	27.41 N	68.54 E
Röhrsdorf	54	50.51 N	12.50 E
Rohtak	123	28.54 N	76.34 E
Roi, Île du → King Island I	166	39.50 S	144.00 E
Roia (Roya) ≃	62	43.48 N	7.35 E
Roi Et	110	16.03 N	103.40 E
Roi Georges, Îles du II	14	14.32 S	145.08 W
Roi Léopold, Monts du → King Leopold Ranges ⋏	160	17.30 S	125.45 E
Roine ⊜	26	61.24 N	24.06 E
Roinville	261	48.32 N	2.03 E
Roisel	50	49.57 N	3.06 E
Roissy	261	48.47 N	2.39 E
Roissy-en-France	261	49.00 N	2.31 E
Roitzsch	54	51.34 N	12.16 E
Roja, S.S.S.R.	76	57.30 N	22.49 E
Roja, S.S.S.R.	83	47.59 N	37.20 E
Rojas	252	34.12 S	60.44 W
Rojl'anka	78	46.17 N	29.46 E
Rojo → Red ≃	178	31.00 N	91.40 W
Rojo, Cabo ›, Méx.	234	21.33 N	97.20 W
Rojo, Cabo ›, P.R.	240m	17.56 N	67.11 W
Rojo, Mar → Red Sea ⊤[2]	136	20.00 N	38.00 E
Rokan	112	0.34 N	100.25 E
Rokan ≃	114	2.00 N	100.52 E
Rokan-kanan ≃	114	1.23 N	100.56 E
Rokan-kiri ≃	114	1.23 N	100.56 E
Röke	41	56.14 N	13.30 E
Rokeby National Park ♠	164	13.40 S	142.55 E
Rokel ≃	150	8.33 N	12.48 W
Rokewood	169	37.54 S	143.43 E
Rokewood Junction	169	37.51 S	143.41 E
Rokhah	120	35.16 N	69.28 E
Rokiškis	76	55.58 N	25.35 E
Rokkō-san ∧	96	34.46 N	135.16 E
Rokkō-sanchi ⋏	270	34.45 N	135.13 E
Roklum	54	52.04 N	10.44 E
Rokuan Kansallispuisto ♠	26	64.32 N	26.33 E
Rokugō	94	35.29 N	138.27 E
Rokugō ◆[8]	268	35.33 N	139.43 E
Rokusei	94	36.58 N	136.52 E
Rokycany	60	49.45 N	13.36 E
Rokytná ≃	61	49.05 N	16.22 E
Rolampont	58	47.57 N	5.16 E
Roland, Mb., Can.	184	49.25 N	97.55 W
Roland, Ar., U.S.	194	34.54 N	92.29 W
Roland, Ia., U.S.	190	42.09 N	93.30 W
Roland, Lake ⊜[1]	284b	39.23 N	76.38 W
Roland C. Nickerson State Park ♠	207	41.46 N	70.03 W
Rolândia	255	23.18 S	51.22 W
Roland Park ◆[8]	284b	39.22 N	76.39 W
Roland Run ≃	284b	39.23 N	76.39 W
Rolava ≃	54	50.15 N	12.51 E
Røldal	26	59.49 N	6.48 E
Roldán	252	32.54 S	60.54 W
Roldanillo	246	4.24 N	76.09 W
Rolde	52	52.58 N	6.38 E
Roldskov ◆[3]	26	56.48 N	9.50 E
Rolette	198	48.39 N	99.50 W
Roleystone	168a	32.08 S	116.04 E
Rolfe	198	42.48 N	94.31 W
Roll, Az., U.S.	200	32.45 N	113.59 W
Roll, In., U.S.	216	40.33 N	85.23 W
Rolla, B.C., Can.	182	55.54 N	120.09 W
Rolla, Ks., U.S.	198	37.07 N	101.07 W
Rolla, Mo., U.S.	194	37.57 N	91.46 W
Rolla, N.D., U.S.	198	48.51 N	99.37 W
Rolle	58	46.28 N	6.20 E
Rolle, Passo di)(	64	46.18 N	11.47 E
Rolleboise	261	49.01 N	1.36 E
Rolleston, Austl.	166	24.28 S	148.37 E
Rolleston, N.Z.	172	43.35 S	172.23 E
Rolling Acres	284b	39.17 N	76.52 W
Rollingbay	224	47.39 N	122.30 W
Rolling Fork	194	32.54 N	90.52 W
Rolling Fork ≃	194	37.55 N	85.50 W
Rolling Hills	280	33.46 N	118.21 W
Rolling Hills Estates	280	33.47 N	118.21 W
Rolling Meadows	216	42.05 N	88.00 W
Rolling Prairie	216	41.40 N	86.37 W
Rolling River Indian Reserve ◆[4]	184	50.27 N	100.00 W
Rollingstone	166	19.03 S	146.24 E
Rollingwood	226	37.57 N	122.20 W
Rollins	182	47.54 N	114.11 W
Rollins Reservoir ⊜[1]	226	39.08 N	120.57 W
Rolvsøya I	24	71.00 N	24.00 E
Rom → Roma	66	41.54 N	12.29 E
Roma, Austl.	166	26.35 S	148.47 E
Roma (Rome), It.	66	41.54 N	12.29 E
Roma (Rome), It.	267a	41.54 N	12.29 E
Roma, Leso.	158	29.27 S	27.45 E
Roma, Tx., U.S.	196	26.25 N	99.01 W
Roma □[4]	66	41.58 N	12.40 E
Romagna □[9]	64	44.30 N	12.15 E
Romagnano Sesia	62	45.38 N	8.23 E
Romagne-sous-Montfaucon	56	49.20 N	5.05 E
Romain, Cape ›	192	33.00 N	79.22 W
Romaine ≃	176	50.18 N	63.47 W
Romainmôtier	58	46.42 N	6.29 E
Romainville	261	48.53 N	2.26 E
Romakloster	26	57.31 N	18.27 E
Roman, Blg.	38	43.09 N	23.55 E
Roman, Rom.	38	46.55 N	26.56 E
Roman ≃	42	51.51 N	0.57 E
Romanche ≃	62	45.05 N	5.43 E
Romanche Gap ✣[1]	10	0.10 S	18.15 W
Romang, Pulau I	164	7.35 S	127.26 E
Romang, Selat ʉ	164	7.30 S	127.00 E
Romania (România) □[1], Europe	22	46.00 N	25.30 E
Romania (România) □[1], Europe	38	46.00 N	25.30 E
Roman-Koš, gora ∧	78	44.37 N	34.15 E
Romankovcy	78	48.29 N	27.13 E
Roman Nose Mountain ∧	202	43.55 N	123.44 W
Romano, Cape ›	220	25.50 N	81.41 W
Romano, Cayo I	240p	22.04 N	77.50 W
Romano Banco	266b	45.25 N	9.06 E
Romano di Lombardia	62	45.31 N	9.45 E
Romanova	88	57.04 N	103.24 E
Romanovka, S.S.S.R.	80	51.24 N	47.23 E
Romanovka, S.S.S.R.	80	49.47 N	45.05 E
Romanovka, S.S.S.R.	80	51.45 N	42.45 E
Romanovka, S.S.S.R.	86	54.38 N	76.03 E
Romanovka, S.S.S.R.	88	53.14 N	112.46 E
Romanovka, S.S.S.R.	265a	60.03 N	30.42 E
Romanovo, S.S.S.R.	82	56.39 N	39.14 E
Romanovo, S.S.S.R.	86	53.58 N	80.30 E
Romanovo, S.S.S.R.	86	52.37 N	81.14 E
Romanovo, S.S.S.R.	86	59.09 N	61.30 E

PORTUGUÊS

Nome	Página	Lat.°′	Long.°′ W = Oeste
Romans d'Isonzo	64	45.53 N	13.26 E
Romanshorn	58	47.34 N	9.22 E
Romans-sur-Isère	62	45.03 N	5.03 E
Romansville	285	39.57 N	75.45 W
Romanzof Mountains ⋏	180	69.00 N	144.00 W
Romaški	80	50.13 N	46.41 E
Romaškino	80	52.29 N	51.48 E
Romaškovo	265b	55.44 N	37.20 E
Romayor	222	30.27 N	94.50 W
Rombari	154	4.33 N	31.02 E
Romblon	116	12.35 N	122.15 E
Romblon □[4]	116	12.30 N	122.10 E
Romblon Island I	116	12.33 N	122.17 E
Romblon Passage ʉ	116	12.27 N	122.12 E
Rombo, Ilhéus do II	150a	14.58 N	24.40 W
Rome → Roma, It.	66	41.54 N	12.29 E
Rome, Ga., U.S.	192	34.15 N	85.09 W
Rome, Il., U.S.	190	40.53 N	89.30 W
Rome, Ms., U.S.	194	33.57 N	90.28 W
Rome, N.Y., U.S.	210	43.12 N	75.27 W
Rome, Oh., U.S.	214	41.36 N	80.52 W
Rome, Pa., U.S.	210	41.51 N	76.21 W
Rome, Wi., U.S.	216	42.58 N	88.38 W
Rome City	216	41.29 N	85.22 W
Romeleåsen ⋏[2]	41	55.34 N	13.33 E
Romenay	58	46.30 N	5.04 E
Romeno	64	46.24 N	11.07 E
Romentino	62	45.28 N	8.42 E
Romeo	214	42.48 N	83.00 W
Romeoville	216	41.38 N	88.05 W
Römerberg	56	49.17 N	8.24 E
Romero, Isla I	258	33.48 S	59.20 W
Rometan	128	39.56 N	64.23 E
Rometta	70	38.10 N	15.25 E
Romfartuna	40	59.44 N	16.35 E
Romford ◆[8]	260	51.35 N	0.11 E
Römhild	54	50.24 N	10.32 E
Romiley	262	53.25 N	2.05 W
Romilly, Mount ∧[2]	162	20.27 S	126.34 E
Romilly-sur-Seine	50	48.31 N	3.43 E
Romit	85	38.44 N	69.17 E
Romit, zapovednik ♠	85	38.52 N	69.20 E
Romita	234	20.52 N	101.31 W
Romitorio	267a	42.01 N	12.39 E
Rommani	148	34.34 N	6.37 W
Romme	40	60.26 N	15.30 E
Rommerskirchen	56	51.02 N	6.40 E
Romney, In., U.S.	216	40.14 N	86.54 W
Romney, W.V., U.S.	188	39.20 N	78.45 W
Romney Marsh ≡	42	51.03 N	0.55 E
Romny, S.S.S.R.	78	50.45 N	33.30 E
Romny, S.S.S.R.	89	50.44 N	129.15 E
Rømø I	26	55.08 N	8.31 E
Romodan	78	49.59 N	33.19 E
Romodanovo	80	54.26 N	45.20 E
Romoland	228	33.45 N	117.10 W
Romont	58	46.42 N	6.55 E
Romorantin-Lanthenay	50	47.22 N	1.45 E
Rompin, Malay.	114	2.42 N	102.31 E
Rompin, Malay.	114	2.48 N	103.29 E
Rompin ≃	114	2.49 N	103.29 E
Romrod	56	50.43 N	9.13 E
Romsdalen ∨	26	62.15 N	8.05 E
Romsdalsfjorden c[2]	26	62.39 N	7.15 E
Romsey, Austl.	169	37.21 S	144.45 E
Romsey, Eng., U.K.	42	50.59 N	1.30 W
Romsø I	41	55.31 N	10.48 E
Romulus, Mi., U.S.	216	42.13 N	83.23 W
Romulus, N.Y., U.S.	210	42.45 N	76.50 W
Røn, Nor.	26	61.03 N	9.03 E
Ron, Viet.	110	17.53 N	106.27 E
Ron, Mui ›	110	18.07 N	106.27 E
Rona, Schw.	58	46.34 N	9.38 E
Rona, Zaïre	154	2.14 N	30.52 E
Rona I, Scot., U.K.	46	59.07 N	5.49 W
Rona I, Scot., U.K.	46	57.34 N	5.59 W
Ronald	224	47.14 N	121.01 W
Ronan	202	47.31 N	114.06 W
Ronas Hill ∧[2]	46a	60.31 N	1.28 W
Ronas Voe c	46a	60.32 N	1.29 W
Ronay I	46	57.29 N	7.11 W
Roncade	64	45.38 N	12.22 E
Roncador, Serra do ⋏[1]	242	12.00 S	52.00 W
Roncador Bank ✣[4]	236	13.32 N	80.03 W
Roncador Reef ✣[2]	175e	6.13 S	159.22 E
Roncegno	64	46.03 N	11.25 E
Roncesvalles	34	43.01 N	1.19 W
Ronceverte	192	37.44 N	80.27 W
Ronchamp	58	47.42 N	6.39 E
Ronchi dei Legionari	64	45.50 N	13.30 E
Ronchin	50	50.36 N	3.06 E
Ronchis	64	45.49 N	13.00 E
Ronciglione	66	42.17 N	12.13 E
Ronco	58	46.08 N	8.44 E
Ronco Canavese	62	45.30 N	7.32 E
Roncofreddo	66	44.02 N	12.20 E
Roncone	64	45.59 N	10.40 E
Ronco Scrivia	62	44.37 N	8.59 E
Roncq	50	50.45 N	3.07 E
Rond, Sommet ∧	206	45.05 N	72.33 W
Ronda	34	36.44 N	5.10 W
Ronda, Serranía de ⋏	34	36.44 N	5.03 W
Rondane ∧	26	61.55 N	9.45 E
Rondane Nasjonal Park ♠	26	61.50 N	9.50 E
Rønde	41	56.18 N	10.29 E
Rondeau Harbour c	214	42.18 N	81.53 W
Rondeau Provincial Park ♠	214	42.16 N	81.51 W
Rondebult	273d	26.18 S	28.14 E
Ronde Island I	241k	12.18 N	61.35 W
Rondissone	62	45.15 N	7.58 E
Rondon	255	23.23 S	52.48 W
Rondônia	248	10.52 S	61.57 W
Rondônia □[3]	248	11.00 S	63.00 W
Rondonópolis	255	16.28 S	54.38 W
Rondout	278	42.17 N	87.53 W
Rondout Creek ≃	210	41.55 N	73.53 W
Rondout Reservoir ⊜[1]	210	41.50 N	74.29 W
Rone ≃	50	50.46 N	3.27 E
Ronehamn	26	57.10 N	18.29 E
Rong ≃	102	24.32 N	109.15 E
Ronga	80	56.43 N	48.32 E
Rongai	154	0.10 S	35.51 E
Rong'an	102	25.10 N	109.20 E
Rongbaca	102	31.48 N	99.40 E
Rongchang	107	29.24 N	105.36 E
Rongcheng, Zhg.	98	37.08 N	122.23 E
Rongcheng, Zhg.	105	39.03 N	115.52 E
Rongding	107	28.57 N	103.40 E
Ronge, Lac la ⊜	184	55.10 N	105.00 W
Rongelap I[1]	14	11.20 N	166.50 E
Rongjiang	102	25.52 N	108.37 E
Rongkop	115a	8.10 S	110.45 E
Rongola	158	27.22 S	31.37 E
Rongotea	172	40.18 S	175.25 E
Rõngu	76	58.09 N	26.15 E
Rongui, Ilha I	154	10.50 S	40.40 E
Rongwanshi	100	28.10 N	112.57 E
Rongxian, Zhg.	102	22.50 N	110.38 E
Rongxian, Zhg.	107	29.28 N	104.25 E
Ronkiti Harbor c	174r	6.48 N	158.10 E
Ronkonkoma	276	40.48 N	73.06 W
Ronkonkoma, Lake ⊜	276	40.50 N	73.07 W
Rønne	26	55.06 N	14.42 E
Rönne ≃	41	56.16 N	12.50 E
Ronneburg	54	50.51 N	12.10 E
Ronneby	26	56.12 N	15.18 E
Ronne Entrance c	9	72.30 S	74.00 W
Ronne Ice Shelf ⍓	9	78.30 S	61.00 W
Ronnenberg	52	52.20 N	9.40 E
Rönneshytta	40	58.56 N	15.02 E
Rönninge	40	59.12 N	17.44 E
Ronroni	175e	9.37 S	159.58 E
Rönsahl	263	51.07 N	7.30 E

Ronsdorf ◆[8]	263	51.14 N	7.12 E
Ronse (Renaix-Gleiche)	50	50.45 N	3.36 E
Röntgenmuseum ℧	263	51.12 N	7.16 E
Ronuro ≃	255	11.56 S	53.33 W
Roodepoort □[5]	273d	26.10 S	27.52 E
Roodepoort-Maraisburg	158	26.11 S	27.54 E
Roodeschool	52	53.25 N	6.45 E
Roodhouse	219	39.29 N	90.22 W
Roof Butte ∧	200	36.28 N	109.05 W
Rooiberge ∧	158	28.27 S	28.26 E
Rooiboklaagte ≃	156	20.50 S	21.00 E
Rooidam	158	28.07 S	21.15 E
Rooilyf	158	28.49 S	21.57 E
Rooiwal	158	27.18 S	27.32 E
Rooks Creek ≃	216	40.57 N	88.44 W
Rookwood Cemetery ◆	274a	33.53 S	151.04 E
Roon, Pulau I	164	2.23 S	134.33 E
Rooniu, Mont ∧	174s	17.49 S	149.12 W
Roordahuizum	52	53.06 N	5.46 E
Roorkee	124	29.52 N	77.53 E
Roosboom	158	28.36 S	29.44 E
Roosendaal	52	51.32 N	4.28 E
Roosevelt, Az., U.S.	200	33.40 N	111.08 W
Roosevelt, Mn., U.S.	198	48.48 N	95.05 W
Roosevelt, N.J., U.S.	208	40.13 N	74.28 W
Roosevelt, N.Y., U.S.	276	40.40 N	73.35 W
Roosevelt, Ok., U.S.	196	34.50 N	99.01 W
Roosevelt, Ut,. U.S.	200	40.17 N	109.59 W
Roosevelt ≃	248	7.35 S	60.20 W
Roosevelt Beach	210	43.19 N	78.52 W
Roosevelt Campobello International Park ♠	186	44.52 N	66.58 W
Roosevelt Field ◆[9]	276	40.45 N	73.37 W
Roosevelt Island I	9	79.30 S	162.00 W
Roosevelt Park	216	43.11 N	86.15 W
Roosevelt Park ♠	276	40.33 N	74.21 W
Roosevelt Raceway ♠	276	40.44 N	73.36 W
Roosevelt Roads Naval Station ■	240m	18.15 N	65.38 W
Roosevelt Terrace	226	38.08 N	122.16 W
Root	58	47.07 N	8.23 E
Root ≃, N.T., Can.	180	62.50 N	123.40 W
Root ≃, Mn., U.S.	190	43.46 N	91.15 W
Root ≃, Wi., U.S.	216	42.44 N	87.47 W
Root, North Branch ≃	190	43.49 N	92.10 W
Root, South Branch ≃	190	43.44 N	91.58 W
Root Lake ⊜	184	54.04 N	101.24 W
Rootstown	214	41.05 N	81.14 W
Rooty Hill	170	33.46 S	150.50 E
Ropang	115b	8.52 S	117.29 E
Ropaži	76	57.08 N	24.30 E
Ropča	24	63.02 N	52.16 E
Ropczyce	30	50.03 N	21.37 E
Roper	192	35.52 N	76.36 W
Roper ≃	164	14.43 S	135.27 E
Roper Bar	164	14.44 S	134.44 E
Roper Valley	164	14.56 S	134.00 E
Ropes Creek ≃	274a	33.43 S	150.47 E
Ropesville	196	33.26 N	102.09 W
Roppe	58	47.40 N	6.55 E
Ropša	265a	59.44 N	29.52 E
Roque	250	3.01 S	45.23 W
Roquebillière	62	44.01 N	7.18 E
Roquebrune-Cap-Martin	62	43.46 N	7.28 E
Roquebrune-sur-Argens	62	43.26 N	6.38 E
Roquefavour, Aqueduc de ⊼[1]	62	43.31 N	5.19 E
Roquefort	32	44.02 N	0.19 W
Roquemaure	62	44.03 N	4.47 E
Roque Pérez	258	35.25 S	59.20 W
Roquestéron	62	43.52 N	7.00 E
Roquevaire	62	43.21 N	5.36 E
Rora Head ›	46	58.52 N	3.25 W
Roraima □[8]	246	1.00 N	61.00 W
Roraima, Mount ∧	246	5.12 N	60.44 W
Rörbäcksnäs	26	61.08 N	12.49 E
Roreto Chisone	62	44.59 N	7.06 E
Rorey Lake ⊜	180	66.55 N	128.25 W
Rorke Lake ⊜	184	54.33 N	92.30 W
Rorke's Drift ⊥	158	28.20 S	30.32 E
Rorketon	184	51.26 N	99.32 W
Røros	26	62.35 N	11.20 E
Rorschach	58	47.29 N	9.30 E
Rørvig	41	55.57 N	11.46 E
Rørvik	24	64.51 N	11.14 E
Ros' ≃	78	49.39 N	31.35 E
Rosà, It.	64	45.43 N	11.45 E
Rosa, Zam.	154	9.38 S	31.21 E
Rosa, Cap ›	36	36.58 N	8.14 E
Rosa, Lake ⊜	238	21.00 N	73.30 W
Rosa, Monte ∧	58	45.55 N	7.53 E
Rosairinho	266c	38.40 N	9.01 W
Rošal'	80	55.40 N	39.51 E
Rosales, Méx.	232	28.12 N	105.33 W
Rosales, Pil.	116	15.54 N	120.38 E
Rosalia	202	47.14 N	117.22 W
Rosalie, Lake ⊜	220	27.58 N	81.28 W
Rosalind Bank ✣[4]	238	16.30 N	80.30 W
Rosamond, Ca., U.S.	228	34.51 N	118.09 W
Rosamond, Il., U.S.	219	39.23 N	89.10 W
Rosamond Lake ⊜	228	34.50 N	118.04 W
Rosamorada	234	22.08 N	105.12 W
Rosana	255	22.33 S	53.00 W
Rosander, Mount ∧	224	48.46 N	124.42 W
Rosanky	222	29.56 N	97.18 W
Rosanna	274b	37.45 S	145.04 E
Rosans	62	44.23 N	5.28 E
Rosario, Arg.	252	32.57 S	60.40 W
Rosário, Bra.	250	2.57 S	44.14 W
Rosario, Méx.	232	30.01 N	115.40 W
Rosario, Méx.	234	23.00 N	105.52 W
Rosario, Para.	252	24.27 S	57.03 W
Rosario, Pil.	116	13.51 N	121.12 E
Rosario, Pil.	116	16.14 N	120.29 E
Rosario, Ur.	258	34.19 S	57.21 W
Rosario, Ven.	246	10.19 N	72.19 W
Rosario ≃, Arg.	252	24.50 S	65.43 W
Rosario ≃, Ur.	258	34.26 S	57.21 W
Rosario, Bahía del c	232	29.52 N	115.45 W
Rosario, Cayo del I	240p	21.38 N	81.53 W
Rosario, Islas del II	246	10.10 N	75.46 W
Rosario, Laguna ⊜	234	17.52 N	93.48 W
Rosario Bank ✣[2]	238	18.30 N	84.05 W
Rosario de la Frontera	252	25.48 S	64.58 W
Rosario de Lerma	252	24.59 S	65.35 W
Rosario del Tala	252	32.18 S	59.09 W
Rosário de Minas	256	21.43 S	43.38 W
Rosário do Sul	252	30.15 S	54.55 W
Rosário Oeste	248	14.50 S	56.25 W
Rosario Strait ʉ	224	48.30 N	122.45 W
Rosarito, Méx.	204	32.20 N	117.02 W
Rosarito, Méx.	232	26.27 N	111.38 W
Rosarito, Méx.	232	28.38 N	114.04 W
Rosarito, Embalse de ⊜[1]	34	40.05 N	5.15 W
Rosarno	68	38.29 N	15.59 E
Rosas	196	26.09 N	103.27 W
Rosazza	62	45.41 N	7.58 E
Rošča	82	54.47 N	36.51 E
Roščino	76	60.15 N	29.37 E
Rosciolo	66	42.07 N	13.20 E
Roscoe, Il., U.S.	216	42.25 N	89.01 W
Roscoe, N.Y., U.S.	210	41.55 N	74.54 W
Roscoe, Pa., U.S.	214	40.04 N	79.51 W
Roscoe, S.D., U.S.	198	45.26 N	99.20 W
Roscoe, Tx., U.S.	196	32.26 N	100.32 W
Roscoe ≃	180	69.40 N	120.57 W
Roscoe Glacier ⍓	9	66.30 S	95.20 E
Roscoe Village ⊥	214	40.18 N	81.54 W
Roscoff	32	48.44 N	3.59 E
Roscommon, Ire.	48	53.38 N	8.11 W

Roscommon, Mi., U.S.	190	44.29 N	84.35 W
Roscommon □[6]	48	53.45 N	8.15 W
Roscrea	48	52.57 N	7.47 W
Rosdorf	52	51.30 N	9.53 E
Rose, It.	68	39.24 N	16.17 E
Rose, N.Y., U.S.	210	43.09 N	76.53 W
Rose, Monte ∧	70	37.39 N	13.25 E
Rose, Mount ∧	226	39.21 N	119.55 W
Rose, Pointe de la ›	240e	14.40 N	60.53 W
Roseau, Dom.	240d	15.18 N	61.24 W
Roseau, Mn., U.S.	198	48.50 N	95.45 W
Roseau ≃, Dom.	240d	15.18 N	61.24 W
Roseau ≃, N.A.	198	49.08 N	97.15 W
Roseau ≃, St. Luc.	241f	13.58 N	61.02 W
Rosebank ◆[8]	273d	26.09 S	28.02 E
Rosebank Station	275b	43.47 N	79.07 W
Roseberry Lakes ⊜	184	52.40 N	92.30 W
Roseberth	166	25.47 S	139.37 E
Rosebery	166	41.46 S	145.32 E
Rosebery ◆[8]	274a	33.55 S	151.12 E
Rose-Blanche	186	47.37 N	58.41 W
Roseboom	210	42.45 N	74.47 W
Roseboro	192	34.57 N	78.30 W
Rose Bowl ♠	280	34.10 N	118.09 W
Rosebud, Austl.	169	38.21 S	144.54 E
Rosebud, Mo., U.S.	219	38.23 N	91.24 W
Rosebud, Mt., U.S.	202	46.16 N	106.26 W
Rose Bud, Pa., U.S.	214	40.45 N	78.33 W
Rosebud, S.D., U.S.	198	43.13 N	100.51 W
Rosebud, Tx., U.S.	222	31.04 N	96.58 W
Rosebud ≃	182	51.25 N	112.37 W
Rosebud Creek ≃	202	46.16 N	106.28 W
Rosebud Indian Reservation ◆[4]	198	43.25 N	100.28 W
Roseburg	202	43.13 N	123.20 W
Rosebush	190	43.41 N	84.46 W
Rose City	190	44.25 N	84.07 W
Rose Creek ≃, U.S.	198	40.04 N	97.07 W
Rose Creek ≃, Ca., U.S.	226	38.07 N	120.24 W
Rosecroft Raceway ♠	284c	38.48 N	76.58 W
Rosedale, Austl.	166	24.38 S	151.55 E
Rosedale, Ab., Can.	182	51.25 N	112.38 W
Rosedale, B.C., Can.	224	49.11 N	121.48 W
Rosedale, In., U.S.	194	39.37 N	87.17 W
Rosedale, La., U.S.	194	30.27 N	91.27 W
Rosedale, Md., U.S.	284b	39.19 N	76.30 W
Rosedale, Ms., U.S.	194	33.51 N	91.01 W
Rosedale ◆[8], On., Can.	275b	43.41 N	79.22 W
Rosedale ◆[8], N.Y., U.S.	276	40.39 N	73.45 W
Rosedale Estates	284c	38.47 N	76.58 W
Rosedale Hills	218	39.42 N	86.07 W
Rosedene	158	32.01 S	22.07 E
Rose Hall	246	6.16 N	57.21 W
Rosehearty	46	57.42 N	2.07 W
Rose-Hill, Maus.	157c	20.14 S	57.27 E
Rose Hill, N.C., U.S.	192	34.49 N	78.01 W
Rose Hill, Va., U.S.	192	36.40 N	83.22 W
Rose Hill, Wa., U.S.	224	47.42 N	122.10 W
Rosehill Cemetery ◆	278	41.59 N	87.41 W
Rosehill Racecourse ♠	274a	33.49 S	151.02 E
Rose Hills Memorial Park ◆	280	34.01 N	118.02 W
Roseira	256	22.54 S	45.18 W
Roseiras	256	22.49 S	46.17 W
Rose Island I, Am. Sam.	14	14.32 S	168.08 W
Rose Island I, Ba.	192	25.06 N	77.14 W
Rose Lake	182	54.24 N	126.02 W
Roseland, Ca., U.S.	226	38.30 N	122.55 W
Roseland, In., U.S.	216	41.42 N	86.15 W
Roseland, La., U.S.	194	30.45 N	90.30 W
Roseland, N.J., U.S.	276	40.49 N	74.17 W
Roseland, Oh., U.S.	214	40.47 N	82.32 W
Roseland ◆[8]	278	41.42 N	87.38 W
Roselawn	216	41.09 N	87.19 W
Roselle, Il., U.S.	216	41.59 N	88.04 W
Roselle, N.J., U.S.	276	40.39 N	74.15 W
Roselle Field ⊠	278	41.59 N	88.06 W
Rosellen	263	51.08 N	6.43 E
Roselle Park	276	40.39 N	74.15 W
Rosellerheide	263	51.07 N	6.44 E
Rose Lodge	224	45.01 N	123.52 W
Rosemary	182	50.46 N	112.05 W
Rosemary Brook ≃	283	42.19 N	71.15 W
Rosemead	280	34.04 N	118.04 W
Rosemère	206	45.38 N	73.48 W
Rosemont, Ca., U.S.	226	38.34 N	121.20 W
Rosemont, Il., U.S.	278	41.59 N	87.52 W
Rosemont, Ky., U.S.	218	38.01 N	84.32 W
Rosemont, Oh., U.S.	214	41.03 N	80.53 W
Rosemont, Pa., U.S.	285	40.01 N	75.19 W
Rosemont Horizon ♠	278	42.00 N	87.53 W
Rosenberg → Susz, Pol.	30	53.44 N	19.20 E
Rosenberg, Tx., U.S.	222	29.33 N	95.48 W
Rosendaël	50	51.02 N	2.24 E
Rosendal, Nor.	26	59.59 N	6.01 E
Rosendal, S. Afr.	158	28.30 S	27.55 E
Rosendale	210	41.51 N	74.05 W
Roseneath	273d	26.17 S	28.11 E
Rosenfeld	58	48.17 N	8.43 E
Rosengarten	52	53.23 N	9.54 E
Rosenhayn	208	39.28 N	75.07 W
Rosenheim	64	47.51 N	12.07 E
Rosenhügel ◆[8]	263	51.10 N	7.12 E
Rosenthal, B.R.D.	56	50.58 N	8.52 E
Rosenthal, D.D.R.	54	50.51 N	14.04 E
Rosenthal ◆[8]	264a	52.36 N	13.23 E
Rose Peak ∧	200	33.26 N	109.22 W
Rosepine	194	30.55 N	93.17 W
Rose Point ›	182	54.13 N	131.35 W
Rosersberg	40	59.35 N	17.53 E
Rosersberg ⊥	40	59.34 N	17.50 E
Roses, Golf de c	34	42.10 N	3.15 E
Roseto	210	40.52 N	75.12 W
Roseto Capo Spulico	68	39.59 N	16.36 E
Roseto degli Abruzzi	66	42.41 N	14.01 E
Roseto Valfortore	68	41.22 N	15.06 E
Rosetown	184	51.33 N	108.00 W
Rose Tree	285	39.56 N	75.23 W
Rose Tree Park ♠	285	39.56 N	75.24 W
Rosetta → Rashīd	142	31.24 N	30.25 E
Rosetta Branch → Rashīd, Far' ≃	142	31.30 N	30.21 E
Rosetta Mouth → Rashīd, Maṣabb ≃[1]	142	31.30 N	30.20 E
Rosettenville ◆[8]	273d	26.15 S	28.03 E
Rosevale	171a	27.51 S	152.29 E
Rose Valley, Sk., Can.	184	52.18 N	103.50 W
Rose Valley, Pa., U.S.	285	39.53 N	75.23 W
Rose Valley, Pa., U.S.	285	40.10 N	75.13 W
Rose Valley, Wa., U.S.	224	46.06 N	122.50 W
Roseville, Austl.	274a	33.47 S	151.11 E
Roseville, Ca., U.S.	226	38.45 N	121.17 W
Roseville, Il., U.S.	190	40.43 N	90.39 W
Roseville, Mi., U.S.	214	42.29 N	82.56 W
Roseville, Mn., U.S.	190	45.00 N	93.09 W
Roseville, Oh., U.S.	188	39.48 N	82.04 W
Roseville, Pa., U.S.	210	41.51 N	76.57 W
Roseville Park	285	39.42 N	75.43 W
Rosewood, Austl.	171a	27.39 S	152.35 E
Rosewood, Austl.	171b	35.41 S	147.52 E
Rosewood, Oh., U.S.	216	40.13 N	83.58 W
Rosewood Heights	219	38.53 N	90.05 W
Roseworthy	168b	34.32 S	138.44 E
Roshanara Gardens ♠	272a	28.40 N	77.12 E
Rosharon	222	29.21 N	95.28 W
Rosheim	58	48.30 N	7.28 E
Rosherville Dam ⊜[1]	273d	26.14 S	28.07 E

Rosh Ha'Ayin	132	32.06 N	34.57 E
Rosholt, S.D., U.S.	198	45.52 N	96.43 W
Rosholt, Wi., U.S.	190	44.37 N	89.18 W
Rosh Pinna	132	32.58 N	35.32 E
Rosica ≃	38	43.15 N	25.42 E
Rosice	30	49.11 N	16.23 E
Rosiclare	194	37.25 N	88.20 W
Rosières-aux-Salines	58	48.36 N	6.20 E
Rosières-en-Santerre	50	49.49 N	2.43 E
Rosiers, Rivière des ≃	206	45.59 N	72.07 W
Rosignano Marittimo	66	43.24 N	10.28 E
Rosignano Solvay	66	43.23 N	10.26 E
Rosignol	246	6.17 N	57.32 W
Roșiori de Vede	38	44.07 N	25.00 E
Rosita	236	13.53 N	84.24 W
Rositz	54	51.01 N	12.22 E
Roskilde	41	55.39 N	12.05 E
Roskilde □[6]	41	55.30 N	12.05 E
Roskilde Fjord c	41	55.56 N	12.00 E
Roskow	54	52.28 N	12.42 E
Roslagen □[9]	40	59.30 N	18.40 E
Roslags-Bro	40	59.50 N	18.44 E
Rosl'akovo	24	69.03 N	33.09 E
Rosl'atino	76	59.46 N	44.15 E
Roslavl'	76	53.57 N	32.52 E
Roslev	26	56.42 N	8.59 E
Roslindale ◆[8]	283	42.18 N	71.07 W
Roslyn, N.Y., U.S.	276	40.48 N	73.39 W
Roslyn, Pa., U.S.	208	40.07 N	75.08 W
Roslyn, Pa., U.S.	285	39.57 N	75.36 W
Roslyn, Wa., U.S.	224	47.13 N	120.59 W
Roslyn Estates	276	40.47 N	73.40 W
Roslyn Harbor	276	40.49 N	73.38 W
Roslyn Heights	276	40.47 N	73.38 W
Rosmalen	52	51.43 N	5.22 E
Rosman	192	35.08 N	82.49 W
Rosmead	158	31.29 S	25.08 E
Ros Mhic Thriúin → New Ross	48	52.24 N	6.56 W
Røsnæs ›[1]	41	55.44 N	10.59 E
Rosne, Ruisseau le ≃	261	48.58 N	2.25 E
Rosneath	46	56.01 N	4.49 W
Rosny-sous-Bois	261	48.53 N	2.29 E
Rosny-sur-Seine	50	49.00 N	1.38 E
Rosolina	64	45.05 N	12.15 E
Rosolini	70	36.49 N	14.57 E
Rošore	85	38.20 N	72.19 E
Rosporden	32	47.58 N	3.50 W
Rösrath	56	50.54 N	7.11 E
Ross, Austl.	166	42.02 S	147.29 E
Ross, N.Z.	172	42.54 S	170.49 E
Ross', S.S.S.R.	76	53.17 N	24.24 E
Ross, Ca., U.S.	226	37.55 N	122.32 W
Ross, In., U.S.	278	41.32 N	87.23 W
Ross, Oh., U.S.	218	39.19 N	84.39 W
Ross □[6]	218	39.20 N	83.06 W
Ross ≃	180	61.59 N	132.26 W
Ross, Cape ›	116	10.56 N	119.13 E
Ross, Mount ∧	172	41.28 S	175.21 E
Ross, Point ›	174c	29.04 S	167.56 E
Ross, Pointe ›	275a	45.21 N	73.48 W
Rossa	58	46.22 N	9.08 E
Rossach	56	50.09 N	10.56 E
Rossano	68	39.35 N	16.39 E
Rossasna	76	54.39 N	30.53 E
Rossau	54	52.47 N	11.38 E
Rossbach	54	51.15 N	11.53 E
Ross Behy	48	52.02 N	9.58 W
Ross-Béthio	150	16.16 N	16.08 W
Rossburg	216	40.17 N	84.38 W
Rossburn	184	50.40 N	100.52 W
Ross Carbery	48	51.35 N	9.01 W
Rosscott Manor	285	39.39 N	75.44 W
Ross Dam ◆[6]	224	48.44 N	121.04 W
Rossdorf	56	49.51 N	8.45 E
Rosseau	212	45.16 N	79.39 W
Rosseau, Lake ⊜	212	45.10 N	79.35 W
Rossel, Cap ›	175f	20.23 S	166.36 E
Rossell y Rius	252	33.11 S	55.42 W
Rossen ⊜	40	60.19 N	16.26 E
Rossendale □[8]	262	53.43 N	2.14 W
Rosser	222	32.28 N	96.27 W
Rosses Bay c	48	55.10 N	8.27 W
Rosses Point	48	54.18 N	8.33 W
Rossford	214	41.37 N	83.33 W
Ross Fork Creek ≃	202	47.05 N	109.43 W
Rosshaupten	58	47.39 N	10.43 E
Rosshyttan	40	60.04 N	16.21 E
Ross Ice Shelf ⍓	9	81.30 S	175.00 W
Rossiglione	62	44.34 N	8.40 E
Rossignol, Lake ⊜	186	44.10 N	65.10 W
Rossijskaja Sovetskaja Federativnaja Socialističeskaja Respublika (Russian Soviet Federative Socialist Republic) □[3]	72	60.00 N	80.00 E
Rössing	156	22.31 S	14.52 E
Rossio, Estação do ◆[5]	266c	38.43 N	9.09 W
Ross Island I, Ant.	9	77.30 S	168.00 E
Ross Island I, Mb., Can.	184	54.14 N	97.45 W
Rossiter	214	40.53 N	78.55 W
Rossitten → Rybačij	76	55.09 N	20.51 E
Rossla	54	51.28 N	11.04 E
Ross Lake ⊜[1]	224	48.53 N	121.04 W
Ross Lake National Recreation Area ♠	224	48.45 N	121.00 W
Rossland	182	49.05 N	117.48 W
Rosslare	48	52.17 N	6.23 W
Rosslare Harbour	48	52.15 N	6.22 W
Rosslau	54	51.53 N	12.14 E
Rosslea	48	54.14 N	7.11 W
Rossleben	54	51.17 N	11.25 E
Rosslyn Farms	279b	40.26 N	80.05 W
Rossmoor	280	33.47 N	118.05 W
Rossmore	274a	33.57 S	150.46 E
Rossmoyne	208	40.13 N	76.57 W
Rosso	150	16.30 N	15.49 W
Rossön	26	63.55 N	16.21 E
Ross-on-Wye	42	51.55 N	2.35 W
Rossony	76	55.53 N	28.49 E
Rossoš', S.S.S.R.	78	51.08 N	38.29 E
Rossoš', S.S.S.R.	78	50.12 N	39.34 E
Rossouw	158	31.09 S	27.18 E
Ross R. Barnett Reservoir ⊜[1]	194	32.30 N	90.00 W
Ross River	180	61.59 N	132.27 W
Ross-Schelfeis → Ross Ice Shelf ⍓	9	81.30 S	175.00 W
Ross Sea ⊤[2]	9	76.00 S	175.00 W
Rosstal	56	49.25 N	10.52 E
Rosston	218	40.03 N	86.17 W
Rossu, Capu ›	36	42.14 N	8.33 E
Røssvatnet ⊜	24	65.45 N	14.00 E
Rossville, Ga., U.S.	192	34.58 N	85.17 W
Rossville, Il., U.S.	216	40.22 N	87.40 W
Rossville, In., U.S.	216	40.25 N	86.35 W
Rossville, Ks., U.S.	198	39.08 N	95.57 W
Rossville, Md., U.S.	284b	39.20 N	76.29 W
Rosswein	54	51.03 N	13.10 E
Røst II	24	67.28 N	11.59 E
Rostāq	120	37.07 N	69.49 E
Röstånga	41	56.00 N	13.17 E
Rosthern	184	52.40 N	106.17 W
Rostherne	262	53.21 N	2.23 W
Rostherne Mere ⊜	262	53.21 N	2.23 W
Roštkala	120	37.16 N	71.49 E
Rostock	54	54.05 N	12.07 E
Rostock □[5]	54	54.15 N	12.30 E
Rostov	80	57.11 N	39.25 E
Rostov □[4]	83	47.30 N	39.30 E
Rostov-na-Donu	83	47.14 N	39.42 E

≃ River	Fluß	Río	Rivière	Rio	✣ Submarine Features	Untermeerische Objekte	Accidentes Submarinos	Formes de relief sous-marin	Acidentes submarinos
⊼ Canal	Kanal	Canal	Canal	Canal	□ Political Unit	Politische Einheit	Unidad Política	Entité politique	Unidade política
⌊ Waterfall, Rapids	Wasserfall, Stromschnellen	Cascada, Rápidos	Chute d'eau, Rapides	Cascata, Rápidos	℧ Cultural Institution	Kulturelle Institution	Institución Cultural	Institution culturelle	Instituição cultural
ʉ Strait	Meeresstraße	Estrecho	Détroit	Estreito	⊥ Historical Site	Historische Stätte	Sitio Histórico	Site historique	Sitio histórico
c Bay, Gulf	Bucht, Golf	Bahía, Golfo	Baie, Golfe	Baía, Golfo	♠ Recreational Site	Erholungs- und Ferienort	Sitio de Recreo	Centre de loisirs	Area de Lazer
⊜ Lake, Lakes	See, Seen	Lago, Lagos	Lac, Lacs	Lago, Lagos	⊠ Airport	Flughafen	Aeropuerto	Aéroport	Aeroporto
≡ Swamp	Sumpf	Pantano	Marais	Pântano	■ Military Installation	Militäranlage	Instalación Militar	Installation militaire	Instalação militar
⍓ Ice Features, Glacier	Eis- und Gletscherformen	Accidentes Glaciales	Formes glaciaires	Acidentes glaciares	◆ Miscellaneous	Verschiedenes	Misceláneo	Divers	Diversos
⊤ Other Hydrographic Features	Andere Hydrographische Objekte	Otros Elementos Hidrográficos	Autres données hydrographiques	Outros acidentes hidrográficos					

ENGLISH — Name · Page · Lat.°′ · Long.°′
DEUTSCH — Name · Seite · Breite°′ · Länge°′ E = Ost

Rostrataville **158** 26.49 S 25.39 E
Rostraver Airport ⊠ **279b** 40.13 N 79.50 W
Rostrevor **48** 54.06 N 6.12 W
Rosvinskoje **24** 66.32 N 52.26 E
Roswell, Ga., U.S. **192** 34.01 N 84.21 W
Roswell, N.M., U.S. **196** 33.23 N 104.31 W
Roswell, Oh., U.S. **214** 40.28 N 81.21 W
Rosyth **46** 56.03 N 3.26 W
Rot ≃ **58** 48.19 N 9.54 E
Rota **34** 36.37 N 6.21 W
Rota I **108** 14.10 N 145.12 E
Rot am See **56** 49.15 N 10.01 E
Rotan **196** 32.51 N 100.27 W
Rotanda **156** 19.33 S 32.50 E
Rotary Island I **285** 40.14 N 74.49 W
Rotbach ≃ **263** 51.34 N 6.41 E
Rotberg **264a** 52.21 N 13.31 E
Rote-Erde, Stadion ♠ **263** 51.30 N 7.27 E
Rotenburg **52** 53.06 N 9.24 E
Rotenburg an der Fulda **56** 51.00 N 9.45 E
Roter Main ≃ **54** 50.04 N 11.24 E
Rotes Meer → Red Sea ▾[2] **136** 20.00 N 38.00 E
Roth, B.R.D. **56** 50.46 N 7.42 E
Roth, B.R.D. **60** 49.15 N 11.06 E
Roth ≃ **58** 48.27 N 10.10 E
Rötha **54** 51.12 N 12.25 E
Rothaargebirge ⁎ **56** 51.05 N 8.15 E
Rothbury **44** 55.19 N 1.55 W
Rothbury Forest ◆[3] **44** 55.18 N 1.54 W
Rothemühl **54** 53.36 N 13.49 E
Röthenbach, B.R.D. **58** 47.37 N 9.59 E
Röthenbach, Schw. **58** 46.51 N 7.45 E
Röthenbach an der Pegnitz **60** 49.29 N 11.15 E
Rothenburg **54** 51.20 N 14.58 E
Rothenburg an der Oder → Czerwieńsk **30** 52.01 N 15.25 E
Rothenburg ob der Tauber **56** 49.23 N 10.10 E
Rothenkirchen **54** 50.33 N 12.30 E
Rothenschirmbach **54** 51.27 N 11.33 E
Rothenstein ∧[2] **263** 51.07 N 7.41 E
Rother ≃ **42** 50.57 N 0.32 W
Rothera ᴕ[3] **9** 67.34 S 68.08 W
Rotherham, N.Z. **172** 42.42 S 172.57 E
Rotherham, Eng., U.K. **44** 53.26 N 1.20 W
Rothes **46** 57.31 N 3.13 W
Rothesay, N.B., Can. **186** 45.23 N 66.00 W
Rothesay, Scot., U.K. **46** 55.51 N 5.03 W
Roth-Neusiedl ◆[8] **264b** 48.08 N 16.23 E
Rothrist **58** 47.19 N 7.53 E
Rothsay, Austl. **162** 29.17 S 116.53 E
Rothsay, Mn., U.S. **198** 46.28 N 96.16 W
Rothschild **190** 44.53 N 89.37 W
Rothsville **208** 40.09 N 76.15 W
Rothwell, N.B., Can. **186** 46.04 N 66.04 W
Rothwell, Eng., U.K. **42** 52.25 N 0.48 W
Rothwell, Eng., U.K. **44** 53.46 N 1.29 W
Roti, Pulau I **112** 10.45 S 123.10 E
Roti, Selat ⋈ **112** 10.25 S 123.25 E
Roto **166** 33.03 S 145.28 E
Rotoiti, Lake ⊜, N.Z. **172** 41.50 S 172.50 E
Rotoiti, Lake ⊜, N.Z. **172** 38.02 S 176.25 E
Rotomanu **172** 42.39 S 171.32 E
Rotonda **68** 39.57 N 16.02 E
Rotondella **68** 40.10 N 16.32 E
Rotondo, Monte ∧ **36** 42.13 N 9.03 E
Rotoroa, Lake ⊜ **172** 41.52 S 172.38 E
Rotorua **172** 38.09 S 176.15 E
Rotorua, Lake ⊜ **172** 38.05 S 176.16 E
Rotowaro **172** 37.36 S 175.05 E
Rott **64** 47.54 N 10.59 E
Rott ≃ **60** 48.27 N 13.26 E
Rottach-Egern **64** 47.41 N 11.46 E
Rott am Inn **64** 47.59 N 12.07 E
Rotten ≃ **58** 46.17 N 7.33 E
Röttenbach **60** 49.09 N 11.02 E
Rottenbach-Tremersdorf **56** 50.21 N 10.56 E
Rottenbuch **64** 47.44 N 10.58 E
Rottenburg am Neckar **58** 48.28 N 8.56 E
Rottenburg an der Laaber **60** 48.42 N 12.02 E
Rottenmann **61** 47.31 N 14.22 E
Rotterdam, Ned. **52** 51.55 N 4.28 E
Rotterdam, N.Y., U.S. **210** 42.48 N 73.59 W
Rotterdam, Luchthaven ⊠ **52** 51.58 N 4.30 E
Rotterdam Junction **210** 42.52 N 74.03 W
Rotthalmünster **60** 48.21 N 13.12 E
Rotthausen ◆[8] **263** 51.30 N 7.05 E
Rottingdean **42** 50.48 N 0.04 W
Röttingen **56** 49.30 N 9.58 E
Rottleberode **54** 51.31 N 10.57 E
Rottnest Island I **168a** 32.00 S 115.30 E
Rottofreno **62** 45.03 N 9.34 E
Rottum **263** 51.36 N 7.42 E
Rottumeroog I **52** 53.30 N 6.30 E
Rottumerplaat I **52** 53.32 N 6.30 E
Rottweil **58** 48.10 N 8.37 E
Rotuma I **14** 12.30 S 177.05 E
Rotwand ∧ **64** 47.39 N 11.56 E
Rötz **60** 49.21 N 12.32 E
Roubaix **50** 50.42 N 3.10 E
Roubideau Creek ≃ **200** 38.44 N 108.10 W
Roubidoux Creek ≃ **194** 37.51 N 92.13 W
Roubion ≃ **62** 44.31 N 4.42 E
Rouceux **58** 48.22 N 5.41 E
Roudnice [nad Labem] **54** 50.22 N 14.16 E
Rouen **50** 49.26 N 1.05 E
Rougé **32** 47.47 N 1.27 W
Rouge ≃, On., Can. **212** 43.48 N 79.07 W
Rouge ≃, P.Q., Can. **206** 45.39 N 74.42 W
Rouge ≃, P.Q., Can. **206** 45.33 N 74.20 W
Rouge → Red ≃, U.S. **178** 31.00 N 91.40 W
Rouge, Bell Branch ≃ **281** 42.23 N 83.16 W
Rouge, Lac ⊜ **206** 46.56 N 74.38 W
Rouge, Mer → Red Sea ▾[2] **136** 20.00 N 38.00 E
Rouge, River ≃ **281** 42.17 N 83.06 W
Rougeau, Forêt de ♠ **261** 48.35 N 2.30 E
Rougemont, Fr. **58** 47.29 N 6.21 E
Rougemont, Schw. **58** 46.29 N 7.12 E
Rougemont-le-Château **58** 47.44 N 6.58 E
Rough ≃ **194** 37.29 N 87.08 W
Rough And Ready **226** 39.14 N 121.08 W
Rough River Lake ⊜[1] **194** 37.40 N 86.25 W
Rouiba **34** 36.44 N 3.17 E
Rouillac **32** 45.47 N 0.04 W
Rouillon **261** 48.33 N 2.00 E
Roujol, Pointe de > **241o** 16.12 N 61.35 W
Roulans **58** 47.19 N 6.14 E
Rouleau **184** 50.11 N 104.55 W
Roulers → Roeselare **50** 50.57 N 3.08 E
Roulette **214** 41.46 N 78.09 W
Roumanie → Romania ▫[1] **38** 46.00 N 25.30 E
Round, Point > **240d** 15.33 N 61.29 W
Round Harbour **186** 49.51 N 55.40 W
Roundhead **216** 40.34 N 83.50 W
Round Hill Head > **166** 24.10 S 151.53 E
Round Hill Regional Park ♠ **279b** 40.15 N 79.51 W
Round Knowe ∧[2] **48** 55.08 N 6.55 W
Round Lake, Il., U.S. **278** 42.21 N 88.05 W
Round Lake, Mn., U.S. **198** 43.32 N 95.28 W
Round Lake, N.Y., U.S. **210** 42.56 N 73.47 W
Round Lake ⊜, Nf., Can. **186** 51.08 N 56.33 W
Round Lake ⊜, On., Can. **190** 45.38 N 77.32 W
Round Lake ⊜, On., Can. **212** 44.30 N 77.52 W
Round Lake ⊜, On., Can. **212** 45.28 N 79.24 W
Round Lake ⊜, Sk., Can. **184** 50.33 N 102.23 W
Round Lake ⊜, Il., U.S. **278** 42.22 N 88.05 W
Round Lake ⊜, Mi., U.S. **216** 41.58 N 84.17 W
Round Lake Beach **216** 42.22 N 88.05 W
Round Lake Park **216** 42.21 N 88.04 W
Round Mound ∧[2] **198** 38.55 N 99.39 W
Round Mountain **204** 38.42 N 117.04 W
Round Mountain ∧, Austl. **166** 30.27 S 152.14 E
Round Mountain ∧, Austl. **171b** 36.15 S 148.34 E
Round Pond ⊜, Nf., Can. **186** 48.10 N 56.00 W
Round Pond ⊜, Ma., U.S. **283** 42.36 N 70.49 W
Round Rock **222** 30.30 N 97.40 W
Roundstone **48** 53.23 N 9.53 W
Round Top **210** 42.16 N 74.02 W
Round Top ∧[2] **208** 40.30 N 76.42 W
Round Top Regional Park ♠ **282** 37.51 N 122.12 W
Roundup **202** 46.26 N 108.32 W
Round Valley Indian Reservation ◆[4] **204** 39.50 N 123.20 W
Round Valley Reservoir ⊜[1] **210** 40.36 N 74.50 W
Roundwood **48** 53.04 N 6.13 W
Roura **250** 4.44 N 52.20 W
Rourkela → Raurkela **124** 22.13 N 84.53 E
Rousay I **46** 59.10 N 3.02 W
Rouse Hill **274a** 33.41 S 150.56 E
Rouses Point **206** 45.00 N 73.22 W
Rouseville **214** 41.28 N 79.41 W
Rousies **50** 50.16 N 4.00 E
Rousseau, Lake ⊜[1] **220** 29.02 N 82.32 W
Rousset, Col de)(**62** 44.50 N 5.24 E
Roussigny **261** 48.39 N 2.06 E
Roussillon, Fr. **62** 43.54 N 5.17 E
Roussillon, Fr. **62** 45.22 N 4.49 E
Roussillon ▫[9] **32** 42.30 N 2.30 E
Roussy-le-Village **56** 49.27 N 6.10 E
Routhierville **186** 48.11 N 67.09 W
Routot **50** 49.23 N 0.44 E
Rouveen **52** 52.36 N 6.11 E
Rouvignies **50** 50.20 N 3.26 E
Rouville ▫[6] **206** 45.23 N 73.04 W
Rouvray **50** 47.25 N 4.06 E
Rouvray, Lac ⊜ **186** 49.18 N 70.49 W
Rouxville **158** 30.29 S 26.46 E
Rouyn **190** 48.15 N 79.01 W
Rouzerville **208** 39.44 N 77.32 W
Rovaniemi **24** 66.34 N 25.48 E
Rovasenda **62** 45.32 N 8.19 E
Rovato **64** 45.34 N 10.00 E
Rovbickskaja **76** 52.40 N 24.05 E
Rove, Tunnel du ◆[5] **62** 43.22 N 5.17 E
Rovegno **62** 44.35 N 9.17 E
Rovellasca **62** 45.40 N 9.03 E
Rovello Porro **62** 45.39 N 9.02 E
Roven'ki, S.S.S.R. **78** 49.56 N 38.54 E
Roven'ki, S.S.S.R. **83** 48.05 N 39.21 E
Rovenskaja Sloboda **78** 52.13 N 30.19 E
Roverbella **64** 45.16 N 10.46 E
Rovere **66** 42.10 N 13.31 E
Roverè della Luna **64** 46.15 N 11.10 E
Roveredo **58** 46.14 N 9.08 E
Rovereto **64** 45.53 N 11.02 E
Roverè Veronese **64** 45.36 N 11.03 E
Rövershagen **54** 54.10 N 12.15 E
Roversi **252** 27.35 S 61.57 W
Roverud **26** 60.15 N 12.03 E
Roviano **66** 42.01 N 13.00 E
Rovigo **64** 45.04 N 11.47 E
Rovigo ▫[4] **64** 45.02 N 11.50 E
Rovinj **36** 45.05 N 13.38 E
Rovira **246** 4.14 N 75.14 W
Rovno **78** 50.37 N 26.15 E
Rovnoje, S.S.S.R. **78** 48.15 N 31.45 E
Rovnoje, S.S.S.R. **80** 50.47 N 46.05 E
Rovnoje, S.S.S.R. **85** 42.53 N 73.32 E
Rovubu (Ruvubu) ≃ **154** 2.23 S 30.47 E
Rovuma (Ruvuma) ≃ **154** 10.29 S 40.28 E
Rów **54** 52.58 N 14.45 E
Rowan ▫[6] **218** 38.17 N 83.26 W
Rowan Lake ⊜ **184** 49.18 N 93.32 W
Rowanty Creek ≃ **208** 36.58 N 77.21 W
Rowena, Austl. **166** 29.49 S 148.54 E
Rowena, Tx., U.S. **196** 31.39 N 100.03 W
Rowe Park ♠ **273a** 6.30 N 3.23 E
Rowhill **273d** 26.14 S 28.26 E
Rowland, N.C., U.S. **192** 34.32 N 79.17 W
Rowland, Pa., U.S. **210** 41.28 N 75.03 W
Rowland Flat **168b** 34.35 S 138.56 E
Rowland Heights **280** 33.58 N 117.54 W
Rowlands Gill **44** 54.54 N 1.45 W
Rowlesburg **188** 39.20 N 79.40 W
Rowlett **222** 32.54 N 96.33 W
Rowlett, Isla I **254** 44.48 S 74.25 W
Rowlett Creek ≃ **222** 32.49 N 96.31 W
Rowley **207** 42.43 N 70.52 W
Rowley ≃, N.T., Can. **176** 70.16 N 77.45 W
Rowley ≃, Ma., U.S. **283** 42.43 N 70.49 W
Rowley Island I **176** 69.08 N 78.50 W
Rowley Regis **42** 52.29 N 2.03 W
Rowley Shoals ✢[2] **162** 17.30 S 119.00 E
Rowntree Mill Park ♠ **275b** 43.45 N 79.35 W
Rowsburg **214** 40.52 N 82.10 W
Rowville **274b** 37.56 S 145.14 E
Roxa, Ilha I **150** 11.15 N 15.40 W
Roxana **219** 38.50 N 90.04 W
Roxas, Pil. **108** 11.35 N 122.45 E
Roxas, Pil. **116** 17.08 N 121.36 E
Roxas, Pil. **116** 12.35 N 121.31 E
Roxas, Pil. **116** 10.20 N 119.21 E
Roxas (Capiz), Pil. **116** 11.35 N 122.45 E
Roxboro, P.Q., Can. **275a** 45.31 N 73.48 W
Roxboro, N.C., U.S. **192** 36.23 N 78.58 W
Roxborough **241r** 11.15 N 60.35 W
Roxborough ◆[8] **285** 40.02 N 75.13 W
Roxburgh, N.Z. **172** 45.32 S 169.19 E
Roxburgh, Scot., U.K. **46** 55.34 N 2.30 W
Roxbury, Ct., U.S. **207** 41.33 N 73.18 W
Roxbury, N.Y., U.S. **210** 42.17 N 74.33 W
Roxbury, Pa., U.S. **214** 40.07 N 77.40 W
Roxbury, Va., U.S. **208** 37.28 N 77.09 W
Roxbury ◆[8], Ma., U.S. **283** 42.20 N 71.06 W
Roxbury ◆[8], N.Y., U.S. **276** 40.34 N 73.54 W
Roxby Downs **162** 30.43 S 136.46 E
Roxel **52** 51.57 N 7.32 E
Roxen ⊜ **26** 58.30 N 15.41 E
Roxie **194** 31.30 N 91.04 W
Roxo, Cap > **150** 12.20 N 16.43 W
Roxton **196** 33.33 N 95.44 W
Roxton Pond (Sainte-Pudentienne) **206** 45.29 N 72.40 W
Roxwell **260** 51.45 N 0.23 E
Roy, N.M., U.S. **196** 35.56 N 104.11 W
Roy, Ut,. U.S. **200** 41.09 N 112.01 W
Roy, Wa., U.S. **224** 47.00 N 122.32 W
Roya (Roia) ≃ **62** 43.48 N 7.35 E
Royal **198** 43.03 N 95.17 W
Royal Albert Hall ᴕ **260** 51.30 N 0.11 W
Royal Australian Naval College ᴕ[2] **170** 35.07 S 150.42 E
Royal Bangkok Sports Club ♠ **269a** 13.44 N 100.33 E
Royal Botanic Gardens ♠, Austl. **274a** 33.52 S 151.13 E
Royal Botanic Gardens ♠, Austl. **274b** 37.50 S 144.59 E
Royal Canal ≊ **48** 53.21 N 6.15 W
Royal Center **216** 40.51 N 86.29 W
Royal Chitwan National Park ♠ **124** 27.30 N 84.30 E
Royal City **202** 46.54 N 119.38 W
Royale, Isle I **190** 48.00 N 89.00 W
Royal Festival Hall ᴕ **260** 51.30 N 0.07 W
Royal Gorge V **200** 38.17 N 105.45 W
Royal Island I **192** 25.31 N 76.51 W
Royalla **171b** 35.31 S 149.09 E
Royal Leamington Spa **42** 52.18 N 1.31 W
Royal Natal National Park ♠ **158** 28.45 S 28.57 E
Royal National Park ♠ **170** 34.10 S 151.05 E
Royal Naval College ▪ **260** 51.29 N 0.01 W
Royal Oak, B.C., Can. **224** 48.30 N 123.23 W
Royal Oak, Md., U.S. **208** 38.44 N 76.10 W
Royal Oak, Mi., U.S. **216** 42.29 N 83.08 W
Royal Oak Township **281** 42.27 N 83.10 W
Royal Ontario Museum ᴕ **275b** 43.40 N 79.24 W
Royal Opera House ᴕ **260** 51.30 N 0.08 W
Royal Palms State Beach ♠ **280** 33.44 N 118.19 W
Royal Park ♠ **274b** 37.47 S 144.57 E
Royal Roads ⊂ **224** 48.26 N 123.26 W
Royalton, In., U.S. **218** 39.56 N 86.21 W
Royalton, Mn., U.S. **190** 45.49 N 94.17 W
Royalton, Pa., U.S. **208** 40.11 N 76.44 W
Royal Tunbridge Wells **42** 51.08 N 0.16 E
Royal Turf Club ♠ **269a** 13.46 N 100.32 E
Royan **32** 45.37 N 1.01 W
Royaume-Uni → United Kingdom ▫[1] **28** 54.00 N 2.00 W
Roybon **62** 45.15 N 5.15 E
Royce Brook ≃ **276** 40.32 N 70.35 W
Roydon, Eng., U.K. **42** 52.50 N 0.32 E
Roydon, Eng., U.K. **42** 51.46 N 0.03 E
Roye **50** 49.42 N 2.48 E
Royersford **208** 40.11 N 75.32 W
Royerton **216** 40.15 N 85.21 W
Roy Hill **162** 22.38 S 119.57 E
Royse City **222** 32.58 N 96.19 W
Royston, Eng., U.K. **42** 52.03 N 0.01 W
Royston, Eng., U.K. **44** 53.37 N 1.27 W
Royston, Ga., U.S. **192** 34.17 N 83.06 W
Royton **44** 53.34 N 2.08 W
Rožaj **38** 42.50 N 20.10 E
Różan **30** 52.53 N 21.25 E
Rozay-en-Brie **50** 48.41 N 2.58 E
Roždestvenka, S.S.S.R. **86** 55.21 N 77.29 E
Roždestvenka, S.S.S.R. **86** 55.42 N 70.00 E
Roždestvenka, S.S.S.R. **86** 50.52 N 71.22 E
Roždestveno, S.S.S.R. **76** 57.44 N 37.57 E
Roždestveno, S.S.S.R. **80** 53.15 N 50.04 E
Roždestveno, S.S.S.R. **82** 56.51 N 36.33 E
Roždestveno, S.S.S.R. **82** 55.57 N 36.23 E
Roždestvenskaja Chava **78** 51.38 N 39.40 E
Roždestvenskoje, S.S.S.R. **80** 58.09 N 45.35 E
Roždestvenskoje, S.S.S.R. **80** 52.47 N 42.10 E
Roždestvenskoje, S.S.S.R. **80** 51.14 N 42.10 E
Roždestvo **76** 57.36 N 33.48 E
Rozel **43b** 49.14 N 2.03 W
Rozelle **274a** 33.52 S 151.10 E
Roželov **60** 49.33 N 13.48 E
Rozewie, Przylądek > **30** 54.51 N 18.21 E
Rozhnof, Cape > **180** 55.58 N 160.58 W
Rožišče **78** 50.54 N 25.15 E
Rožki **80** 56.41 N 50.31 E
Rožkov **80** 51.39 N 52.19 E
Rožmberk ⊜ **61** 49.04 N 14.47 E
Rožmberk nad Vltavou **61** 48.39 N 14.22 E
Rožmitál pod Třemšínem **60** 49.36 N 13.52 E
Rožn'atov **78** 48.56 N 24.09 E
Rožňava **30** 48.40 N 20.32 E
Roznov **38** 46.50 N 26.31 E
Rožnov pod Radhoštěm **30** 49.28 N 18.10 E
Rożnów **30** 49.46 N 20.42 E
Rozovka **78** 47.23 N 37.04 E
Rozoy-sur-Serre **50** 49.43 N 4.08 E
Roztoczański Park Narodowy ♠ **78** 50.35 N 23.03 E
Roztocze ⁎[2] **30** 50.30 N 23.20 E
Roztoky **54** 50.09 N 14.22 E
Rozzano **62** 45.20 N 9.06 E
Rrëshen **38** 41.47 N 19.54 E
Rrogozhinë **38** 41.05 N 19.40 E
Rtiščevo **80** 52.16 N 43.47 E
Ru ≃ **100** 32.43 N 115.01 E
Ru, Tanjong > **114** 2.50 N 101.17 E
Ruabon **42** 52.59 N 3.02 W
Ruacaná **152** 17.25 S 14.12 E
Ruacana Falls L **152** 17.22 S 14.12 E
Ruaha National Park ♠ **154** 7.30 S 34.40 E
Ruahine Range ⁎ **172** 40.00 S 176.06 E
Ruahmi, Ra's > **142** 28.44 N 32.50 E
Ruanda **154** 10.33 S 34.57 E
Ruanda → Rwanda ▫[1] **154** 2.00 S 30.00 E
Ruango **164** 5.35 S 150.10 E
Ruapehu, Mount ∧ **172** 39.17 S 175.34 E
Ruapuke Island I **172** 46.47 S 168.30 E
Ruatahuna **172** 38.33 S 176.57 E
Ruatapu **172** 42.48 S 170.53 E
Ruathair, Lochan ⊜ **46** 58.18 N 3.56 W
Ruatoria **172** 37.53 S 178.20 E
Ruawai **172** 36.08 S 174.02 E
Rub' al Khali → Ar-Rub' al-Khālī ◆[2] **118** 20.00 N 51.00 E
Rubanovka **78** 47.00 N 34.10 E
Rubbestadneset **26** 59.49 N 5.17 E
Rubcovsk **86** 51.33 N 81.10 E
Rubcy **83** 49.12 N 37.33 E
Rubeho Mountains ⁎ **154** 6.55 S 36.30 E
Rubel' **78** 51.58 N 27.04 E
Rübeland **54** 51.45 N 10.50 E
Rubelles **261** 48.34 N 2.41 E
Rubery **42** 52.24 N 2.00 W
Rubeshibe **92a** 43.47 N 143.38 E
Rubežka **80** 51.26 N 51.59 E
Rubežnoje **83** 49.01 N 38.23 E
Rubí, Esp. **266d** 41.29 N 2.02 E
Rubi, Zaïre **154** 2.49 N 25.14 E
Rubí ≃, Esp. **266d** 41.26 N 2.00 E
Rubi ≃, Zaïre **152** 2.48 N 23.54 E
Rubiana **62** 45.08 N 7.23 E
Rubiataba **255** 15.08 S 49.48 W
Rubicon ≃ **226** 39.00 N 120.44 W
Rubicone ≃ **66** 44.08 N 12.28 E
Rubidoux **228** 33.59 N 117.24 W
Rubiera **64** 44.39 N 10.45 E
Rubim **255** 16.23 S 40.32 W
Rubinéia **255** 20.11 S 50.58 W
Rubino **150** 6.04 N 4.18 W
Rubio **246** 7.43 N 72.22 W
Rubio Woods ♠ **278** 41.38 N 87.46 W
Rubl'ovka **78** 49.15 N 33.19 E
Rubl'ovo **82** 55.47 N 37.21 E
Ruboani **140** 8.06 N 30.45 E
Rubona **154** 0.33 N 30.10 E
Rubondo Island I **154** 2.20 S 31.52 E
Rubondo Island National Park ♠ **154** 2.20 S 31.52 E
Rubtsovsk → Rubcovsk **86** 51.33 N 81.10 E
Ruby, Ak., U.S. **180** 64.44 N 155.30 W
Ruby, N.Y., U.S. **210** 42.01 N 74.01 W
Ruby ≃ **202** 45.34 N 112.21 W
Ruby Creek ≃ **224** 48.43 N 120.59 W
Ruby Dome ∧ **204** 40.37 N 115.28 W
Ruby Lake ≡ **204** 40.10 N 115.30 W
Ruby Mountains ⁎ **204** 40.25 N 115.35 W
Ruby Valley V **204** 40.30 N 115.15 W
Rucava **76** 56.09 N 21.10 E
Ruchan' **76** 53.33 N 32.48 E
Ruche **261** 49.02 N 2.27 E
Rucheng **100** 25.34 N 113.41 E
Ruciane-Nida **30** 53.39 N 21.35 E
Ručji ◆[8] **265a** 60.01 N 30.24 E
Ručjuvom **24** 66.42 N 61.08 E
Rucphen **52** 51.32 N 4.34 E
Ruda **64** 45.50 N 13.24 E
Rudall **166** 33.41 S 136.16 E
Rudall ≃ **162** 22.16 S 122.47 E
Rudall River National Park ♠ **162** 22.25 S 122.40 E
Ruda Śląska **30** 50.18 N 18.51 E
Rudauli **124** 26.45 N 81.45 E
Ruḍaymat al-Liwā' **132** 33.01 N 36.35 E
Rūdbār, Afg. **128** 30.09 N 62.36 E
Rūdbār, Īrān **128** 36.48 N 49.24 E
Rudbøl **41** 54.54 N 8.45 E
Ruddervoorde **50** 51.06 N 3.12 E
Ruddiman Terrace **216** 43.12 N 86.17 W
Rudelsburg ⊥ **54** 51.07 N 11.43 E
Ruden I **54** 54.12 N 13.46 E
Rudensk **76** 53.36 N 27.52 E
Rüdersdorf, D.D.R. **54** 52.29 N 13.47 E
Rudersdorf, Öst. **61** 47.03 N 16.07 E
Rüdersdorf, Forst ◆[3] **264a** 52.26 N 13.50 E
Rüdesheim am Rhein **56** 49.59 N 7.56 E
Rudeville **276** 41.09 N 74.33 W
Rudewa **154** 10.06 S 34.39 E
Rudge Ramos **287b** 23.41 S 46.34 W
Rūdiškės **76** 54.31 N 24.50 E
Rudki **78** 49.39 N 23.29 E
Rudkino **78** 51.27 N 39.01 E
Rudkøbing **41** 54.56 N 10.43 E
Rudn'a, S.S.S.R. **76** 54.57 N 31.06 E
Rudn'a, S.S.S.R. **80** 50.48 N 44.33 E
Rudnaja Pristan' **89** 44.22 N 135.48 E
Rudnevka ≃ **265b** 55.43 N 37.56 E
Rudnevo **82** 54.44 N 38.09 E
Rudnica **78** 48.15 N 28.55 E
Rudničnyj, S.S.S.R. **24** 59.38 N 52.27 E
Rudničnyj, S.S.S.R. **86** 56.08 N 86.12 E
Rudničnyj, S.S.S.R. **86** 59.42 N 60.18 E
Rudničnyj, S.S.S.R. **86** 44.40 N 78.55 E
Rudnik **30** 50.28 N 22.15 E
Rüdnitz **54** 52.43 N 13.37 E
Rudnyj, S.S.S.R. **86** 52.57 N 63.07 E
Rudnyj, S.S.S.R. **89** 44.21 N 134.58 E
Rudo **38** 43.37 N 19.22 E
Rudolf, Lake (Lake Turkana) ⊜ **144** 3.30 N 36.00 E
Rudolfov **61** 48.59 N 14.34 E
Rudolph **216** 41.17 N 83.40 W
Rudolstadt **54** 50.43 N 11.20 E
Rudong, Zhg. **102** 21.39 N 111.23 E
Rudong, Zhg. **106** 32.19 N 121.12 E
Rudovka, S.S.S.R. **80** 53.07 N 42.23 E
Rudovka, S.S.S.R. **83** 49.24 N 38.27 E
Rudow ◆[8] **264a** 52.25 N 13.30 E
Rudrón ≃ **34** 42.47 N 3.45 W
Rūdsar **128** 37.08 N 50.18 E
Ruds Vedby **41** 55.33 N 11.23 E
Rudyard, Mi., U.S. **190** 46.13 N 84.36 W
Rudyard, Mt., U.S. **202** 48.33 N 110.33 W
Rudyerd Bay ⊂ **182** 55.35 N 130.44 W
Rue, Fr. **50** 50.16 N 1.40 E
Rue, Schw. **58** 46.37 N 6.50 E
Ruecas ≃ **34** 39.00 N 5.55 W
Rueil-Malmaison **261** 48.53 N 2.11 E
Ruen ∧ **38** 42.10 N 22.31 E
Ruenya (Luenha) ≃ **154** 16.24 S 33.48 E
Rufā'ah **140** 14.46 N 33.22 E
Ruffano **68** 39.59 N 18.15 E
Ruffec **32** 46.01 N 0.12 E
Ruffieu **58** 46.00 N 5.40 E
Ruffieux **62** 45.51 N 5.50 E
Ruffin **192** 33.00 N 80.48 W
Ruffle Bar I **276** 40.36 N 46.51 W
Rufford **262** 53.38 N 2.49 W
Rufford Old Hall ⊥ **262** 53.38 N 2.49 W
Ruffs Dale **279b** 40.10 N 79.37 W
Rufidschi → Rufiji ≃ **154** 8.00 S 39.20 E
Rufiji ≃ **154** 8.00 S 39.20 E
Rufina **66** 43.49 N 11.29 E
Rufino **252** 34.16 S 62.42 W
Rufisque **150** 14.43 N 17.17 W
Rufunsa **154** 15.05 S 29.40 E
Rufus **224** 45.41 N 120.44 W
Rufus, Mount ∧ **168b** 34.20 S 139.07 E
Rugāji **76** 57.00 N 27.08 E
Rugao **100** 32.25 N 120.36 E
Rugby, Eng., U.K. **42** 52.23 N 1.15 W
Rugby, N.D., U.S. **198** 48.22 N 99.59 W
Rugeley **42** 52.46 N 1.55 W
Rügen I **54** 54.25 N 13.24 E
Rügenwalde → Darłowo **30** 54.26 N 16.23 E
Rüggeberg **263** 51.16 N 7.22 E
Rugged Mountain ∧ **182** 50.02 N 126.41 W
Ruggles Beach **214** 41.22 N 82.29 W
Rugles **50** 48.49 N 0.42 E
Rugufu ≃ **154** 5.10 S 30.14 E
Ruguj **76** 59.28 N 32.50 E
Ruḥama **132** 31.30 N 34.42 E
Ruhea **124** 26.10 N 88.25 E
Ruhengeri **154** 1.30 S 29.38 E
Ruhla **54** 50.53 N 10.22 E
Ruhland **54** 51.27 N 13.52 E
Ruhlsdorf **264a** 52.23 N 13.16 E
Ruhmannsfelden **60** 48.59 N 12.59 E
Ruhner Berge ⁎[2] **54** 53.17 N 11.55 E
Ruhnu saar I **76** 57.48 N 23.15 E
Ruhpolding **64** 47.45 N 12.38 E
Ruhr ≃ **52** 51.27 N 6.44 E
Ruhrort ◆[8] **263** 51.26 N 6.45 E
Ruhr-Universität ᴕ[2] **263** 51.27 N 7.16 E
Ruhstorf an der Rott **60** 48.26 N 13.20 E
Ruhudji ≃ **154** 8.52 S 36.01 E
Ruhuhu ≃ **154** 10.31 S 34.34 E
Ruhunu National Park ♠ **122** 6.30 N 81.30 E
Rui'an **100** 27.49 N 120.38 E
Ruichang **100** 29.41 N 115.40 E
Ruicheng **102** 34.45 N 110.45 E
Ruidoso **200** 33.19 N 105.40 W
Ruidoso, Rio ≃ **200** 33.23 N 105.16 W
Ruidoso Downs **200** 33.19 N 105.36 W
Ruifeng Sha I **106** 31.25 N 121.36 E
Ruihong **100** 28.45 N 116.23 E
Ruijin **100** 25.50 N 116.00 E
Ruinen **52** 52.46 N 6.22 E
Ruiselede **50** 51.03 N 3.24 E
Ruislip ◆[8] **260** 51.34 N 0.25 W
Ruivo, Pico ∧ **148** 32.45 N 16.56 W
Ruiz **234** 21.57 N 105.09 W
Ruiz de Montoya **252** 26.59 S 55.03 W
Rūjiena **76** 57.54 N 25.21 E
Rujm ar-Rashīd, Jabal ∧ **132** 31.53 N 36.18 E
Rujm aṣ-Ṣakhrī **132** 31.02 N 35.43 E
Rukan-shō ✢[2] **174m** 26.06 N 127.32 E
Rukatunturi ∧[2] **26** 66.09 N 29.10 E
Ruki ≃ **152** 0.05 N 18.17 E
Rukni **126** 23.33 N 86.33 E
Rukungiri **154** 0.48 S 29.55 E
Rukwa ▫[4] **154** 7.00 S 31.30 E
Rukwa, Lake ⊜ **154** 8.00 S 32.25 E
Rule **196** 33.11 N 99.53 W
Rule Creek ≃ **198** 38.02 N 103.02 W
Ruleville **194** 33.43 N 90.33 W
Rulle **52** 52.20 N 8.04 E
Rully **58** 46.52 N 4.45 E
Rulo **198** 40.03 N 95.25 W
Rülzheim **56** 49.09 N 8.16 E
Rum **61** 47.08 N 16.51 E
Rum ≃ **190** 45.11 N 93.23 W
Ruma **38** 45.00 N 19.49 E
Rumaat **164** 5.49 S 132.48 E
Rumāh **128** 25.34 N 47.09 E
Rumahtinggih **164** 6.23 S 140.17 E
Rum'ancevo, S.S.S.R. **82** 55.38 N 37.26 E
Rum'ancevo, S.S.S.R. **82** 55.58 N 36.32 E
Rum'ancevo ◆[8] **83** 48.21 N 38.06 E
Rumänien → Romania ▫[1] **38** 46.00 N 25.30 E
Rumaysh **132** 33.05 N 35.22 E
Rumbek **140** 6.48 N 29.41 E
Rumbeke **50** 50.56 N 3.10 E
Rumberpon, Pulau I **164** 1.50 S 134.15 E
Rumbling Bridge **46** 56.10 N 3.35 W
Rumburk **54** 50.57 N 14.32 E
Rum Cay I **238** 23.40 N 74.53 W
Rumelange **56** 49.28 N 6.02 E
Rumelifeneri ◆[8] **267b** 41.14 N 29.06 E
Rumelihisarı ◆[8] **267b** 41.05 N 29.03 E
Rumelihisarı ⊥ **267b** 41.05 N 29.02 E
Rumelikavağı ◆[8] **267b** 41.11 N 29.04 E
Rumford **188** 44.33 N 70.33 W
Rumford ≃ **283** 41.58 N 71.11 W
Rumia **30** 54.35 N 18.25 E
Rumigny **50** 49.48 N 4.16 E
Rumilly **62** 45.52 N 5.57 E
R'uminskoje **82** 56.31 N 38.47 E
Rum Jungle **164** 13.01 S 131.00 E
R'umki **265a** 59.47 N 30.02 E
Rümlang **58** 47.27 N 8.32 E
Rummah, Wādī ar- V **128** 26.12 N 44.04 E
Rummānah **142** 31.01 N 32.40 E
Rummānah, Bi'r ar- ▾[4] **142** 31.00 N 32.40 E
Rummel **214** 40.13 N 78.48 W
Rummelsburg → Miastko **30** 54.01 N 17.00 E
Rummelsburg ◆[8] **264a** 52.30 N 13.29 E
Rummenohl ◆[8] **263** 51.17 N 7.32 E
Rumney **42** 51.31 N 3.07 W
Rumoi **92a** 43.56 N 141.39 E
Rumont **56** 48.50 N 5.17 E
Rumphi **154** 11.01 S 33.52 E
Rump Mountain ∧ **188** 45.12 N 71.04 W
Rumson **208** 40.22 N 73.59 W
Rumst **50** 51.05 N 4.25 E
Rumula **164** 16.35 S 145.20 E
Rumung I **174q** 9.37 N 138.10 E
Rumuruti **154** 0.16 N 36.32 E
Runan **100** 33.01 N 114.22 E
Runanga **172** 42.24 S 171.16 E
Runaway, Cape > **172** 37.32 S 177.59 E
Runazi **154** 2.47 S 31.28 E
Runcorn ◆[8] **44** 53.20 N 2.44 W
Rundeng **114** 2.39 N 97.52 E
Rundēni **76** 56.16 N 27.50 E
Rundu **156** 17.52 S 19.43 E
Rundvik **26** 63.32 N 19.26 E
Runere **154** 3.06 S 33.16 E
Rŭng, Kaôh I **110** 10.44 N 103.14 E
Rungāni **120** 26.38 N 65.43 E
Runge **222** 28.52 N 97.42 W
Rungis **261** 48.45 N 2.21 E
Rungis-Halles, Marché de ᴕ **261** 48.46 N 2.21 E
Rungsted **41** 55.53 N 12.33 E
Rungus Point > **116** 13.43 N 123.58 E
Rungwa, Tan. **154** 7.21 S 31.40 E
Rungwa, Tan. **154** 6.57 S 33.31 E
Rungwa ≃ **154** 7.36 S 31.50 E
Rungwa Game Reserve ◆[4] **154** 7.00 S 34.10 E
Rungwe **154** 9.10 S 33.36 E
Runhällen **40** 60.02 N 16.49 E
Runheji **100** 32.30 N 116.05 E
Runkel **56** 50.24 N 8.10 E
Runmarö I **40** 59.17 N 18.46 E
Runn ⊜ **40** 60.33 N 15.40 E
Runnemede **285** 39.51 N 75.04 W
Running Springs **228** 34.12 N 117.07 W
Running Water Draw V **196** 33.58 N 101.30 W
Runnymede ▫[8] **260** 51.24 N 0.32 W
Runnymede ⊥ **260** 51.26 N 0.34 W
Rünthe **263** 51.39 N 7.39 E
Runwell **260** 51.37 N 0.32 E
Ruo ≃, Afr. **154** 16.33 S 35.09 E
Ruo ≃, Zhg. **102** 41.00 N 100.10 E
Ruo'ergai **102** 33.16 N 102.55 E
Ruoheng **100** 28.24 N 121.31 E
Ruokolahti **26** 61.17 N 28.50 E
Ruoms **62** 44.27 N 4.21 E
Ruoqiang **90** 38.30 N 88.05 E
Ruoti **68** 40.43 N 15.41 E
Ruovesi **26** 61.59 N 24.05 E
Ruoxi **100** 29.18 N 115.20 E
Rupanco **254** 40.46 S 72.42 W
Rupanco, Lago ⊜ **254** 40.49 S 72.28 W
Rupari **168b** 35.37 S 139.09 E
Rupat, Pulau I **114** 1.50 N 101.35 E
Rupat, Selat ⋈ **114** 1.50 N 101.25 E
Rupdia **126** 23.08 N 89.18 E
Rupea **38** 46.02 N 25.13 E
Rupert, Id., U.S. **202** 42.37 N 113.40 W
Rupert, Vt., U.S. **210** 43.15 N 73.13 W
Rupert, W.V., U.S. **188** 37.57 N 80.41 W
Rupert, Rivière de ≃ **176** 51.29 N 78.45 W
Rupert Creek ≃ **166** 20.53 S 142.23 E
Rupganj **126** 23.48 N 90.31 E
Rūpnagar **123** 30.59 N 76.31 E
Rūpnārāyan ≃ **126** 22.13 N 88.03 E
Ruponda **154** 10.15 S 38.42 E
Ruppertenrod **56** 50.37 N 9.05 E
Ruppiner See ⊜ **54** 52.48 N 12.50 E
Rupprechtseck ∧ **61** 47.14 N 14.00 E
Rupt de Mad ≃ **56** 49.01 N 6.02 E
Rupt-sur-Moselle **58** 47.56 N 6.40 E
Rupununi ▫[5] **246** 3.00 N 59.00 W
Rupununi ≃ **246** 4.03 N 58.34 W
Ruqqād, Wādī ar- V **132** 32.44 N 35.46 E
Rur (Roer) ≃ **56** 51.12 N 5.59 E
Rural Hall **192** 36.14 N 80.17 W
Rural Retreat **192** 36.53 N 81.16 W
Rural Ridge **279b** 40.35 N 79.50 W
Rural Valley **214** 40.48 N 79.18 W
Rurberg **56** 50.37 N 6.22 E
Ruri-kei ♠ **96** 35.03 N 135.26 E
Rurrenabaque **248** 14.28 S 67.34 W
Rurstausee ⊜[1] **56** 50.36 N 6.22 E
Rurutu I **14** 22.26 S 151.20 W
Rusambo **154** 16.35 S 32.12 E
Rušan **120** 37.58 N 71.30 E
Rusanov **78** 50.29 N 31.09 E
Rusanovka **78** 50.32 N 33.44 E
Rusape **154** 18.32 S 32.07 E
Rusavkina-Popovščina **265b** 55.42 N 38.04 E
Ruṣayriṣ, Khazzān ar- ⊜[1] **140** 11.40 N 34.20 E
Ruschuk → Ruse **38** 43.50 N 25.57 E
Ruscom ≃ **214** 42.18 N 82.38 W
Ruscom Station **214** 42.13 N 82.39 W
Ruse, Blg. **38** 43.50 N 25.57 E
Ruše, Jugo. **61** 46.32 N 15.31 E
Rusera **124** 25.45 N 86.02 E
Rush, Ire. **48** 53.32 N 6.06 W
Rush, N.Y., U.S. **210** 42.59 N 77.39 W
Rush, Pa., U.S. **210** 41.47 N 76.03 W
Rush ▫[6] **218** 39.37 N 85.27 W
Rush ≃, N.D., U.S. **198** 47.00 N 96.54 W
Rush ≃, Wi., U.S. **190** 44.34 N 92.19 W
Rushan (Xiacun) **98** 36.54 N 121.29 E
Rush Center **198** 38.27 N 99.18 W
Rush City **190** 45.41 N 92.57 W
Rush Creek ≃, Co., U.S. **198** 38.22 N 102.32 W
Rush Creek ≃, Ne., U.S. **198** 41.27 N 102.32 W
Rush Creek ≃, N.Y., U.S. **284a** 42.00 N 78.52 W
Rush Creek ≃, Oh., U.S. **188** 39.38 N 82.33 W
Rush Creek ≃, Oh., U.S. **214** 40.34 N 83.20 W
Rush Creek ≃, Ok., U.S. **196** 34.42 N 97.10 W
Rushden **42** 52.17 N 0.36 W
Rushford, Mn., U.S. **190** 43.48 N 91.45 W
Rushford, N.Y., U.S. **210** 42.23 N 78.15 W
Rush Hill **219** 39.13 N 91.43 W
Rush Lake ⊜, On., Can. **190** 47.48 N 82.12 W
Rush Lake ⊜, Wi., U.S. **190** 43.56 N 88.49 W
Rushland **285** 40.15 N 75.02 W
Rushmore **198** 43.37 N 95.48 W
Rusholme ◆[8] **262** 53.27 N 2.12 W
Rush Springs **196** 34.46 N 97.57 W
Rushsylvania **216** 40.27 N 83.40 W
Rushville, Il., U.S. **219** 40.07 N 90.33 W
Rushville, In., U.S. **218** 39.36 N 85.26 W
Rushville, Ne., U.S. **198** 42.43 N 102.27 W
Rushville, N.Y., U.S. **210** 42.45 N 77.13 W
Rusinga Island I **154** 0.24 S 34.10 E
Rusizi (Ruzizi) ≃ **154** 3.16 S 29.14 E
Rusk **222** 31.47 N 95.09 W
Rusk ▫[6] **222** 32.10 N 94.50 W
Rusken ⊜ **26** 57.17 N 14.20 E
Ruskin, B.C., Can. **224** 49.12 N 122.28 W
Ruskin, Fl., U.S. **220** 27.43 N 82.26 W
Ruskington **44** 53.02 N 0.23 W
Rusnė **76** 55.18 N 21.22 E
Rušonu ezers ⊜ **76** 56.11 N 27.02 E
Rusovce **61** 48.04 N 17.10 E
Russa **272b** 22.29 N 88.21 E
Russas **250** 4.56 S 37.58 W
Russbach ≃ **264b** 48.17 N 16.35 E
Russee **41** 54.18 N 10.04 E
Russell, Mb., Can. **184** 50.47 N 101.15 W
Russell, On., Can. **212** 45.15 N 75.22 W
Russell, N.Z. **172** 35.16 S 174.07 E
Russell, Ia., U.S. **190** 40.58 N 93.11 W
Russell, Ks., U.S. **198** 38.53 N 98.51 W
Russell, Ky., U.S. **188** 38.31 N 82.41 W
Russell, Ma., U.S. **207** 42.11 N 72.51 W
Russell, Mn., U.S. **198** 44.19 N 95.57 W
Russell, Pa., U.S. **214** 41.56 N 79.08 W
Russell, Cape > **176** 75.15 N 117.35 W
Russell, Mount ∧ **180** 62.48 N 151.52 W
Russell Cave National Monument ♠ **194** 34.54 N 85.48 W
Russell Creek ≃ **194** 37.14 N 85.30 W
Russell Gardens **276** 40.47 N 73.43 W
Russell Island I **176** 73.55 N 98.25 W
Russell Islands II **175e** 9.04 S 159.12 E
Russellkonda **120** 19.56 N 84.35 E
Russell Lake ⊜ **184** 56.15 N 101.30 W
Russell Range ⁎ **162** 33.24 S 123.28 E
Russells Point **216** 40.28 N 83.54 W
Russell Springs **194** 37.03 N 85.05 W
Russellton **214** 40.37 N 79.50 W
Russellville, Al., U.S. **194** 34.30 N 87.43 W
Russellville, Ar., U.S. **194** 35.16 N 93.08 W
Russellville, Ky., U.S. **194** 36.50 N 86.53 W
Russellville, Mo., U.S. **194** 38.30 N 92.26 W
Russellville, Oh., U.S. **218** 38.51 N 83.47 W
Russellville, Or., U.S. **224** 45.31 N 122.33 W
Rüsselsheim **56** 50.00 N 8.25 E
Russi **66** 44.22 N 12.02 E
Russia **216** 40.14 N 84.24 W
Russian ≃ **204** 38.27 N 123.08 W
Russian Mission **180** 61.47 N 161.19 W
Russian Soviet Federative Socialist Republic → Rossijskaja Sovetskaja Federativnaja Socialističeskaja Respublika ▫[3] **72** 60.00 N 80.00 E
Russiaville **216** 40.25 N 86.16 W
Russka **76** 58.59 N 28.30 E
Russkaja ᴕ[3] **9** 74.46 S 136.52 W
Russkaja Bujlovka **78** 50.22 N 40.03 E
Russkaja Gavan' **74** 76.10 N 62.35 E
Russkaja Pol'ana **86** 53.47 N 73.53 E
Russkaja Ṭalovka **80** 49.59 N 49.05 E
Russkaja Žuravka **80** 50.21 N 40.33 E
Russkij **89** 43.03 N 131.50 E
Russkij, ostrov I **74** 77.00 N 96.00 E
Russkij Aktaš **80** 55.02 N 52.07 E
Russkij Brod **76** 52.36 N 37.22 E
Russkij Kameškir **80** 52.52 N 46.06 E
Russkij Turek **80** 57.03 N 50.13 E
Russkij Vožoj **80** 56.57 N 53.22 E
Russkij Zavorot, mys > **24** 68.58 N 54.34 E
Russkoje **83** 47.45 N 38.56 E
Russkoje-Dobrino **80** 54.22 N 52.28 E
Russko-Vysockoje **265a** 59.42 N 29.56 E
Rust, B.R.D. **58** 48.16 N 7.43 E
Rust, Öst. **61** 47.48 N 16.41 E
Rustajskij **80** 56.31 N 44.49 E
Rustam **123** 34.21 N 72.17 E
Rustavi **84** 41.33 N 45.02 E
Rustburg **192** 37.16 N 79.06 W
Rustenburg **158** 25.37 S 27.08 E
Rustfontein **158** 30.28 S 29.17 E
Rustic Canyon V **280** 34.04 N 118.31 W
Rustig **158** 27.22 S 27.09 E
Rustington **42** 50.48 N 0.31 W
Ruston, La., U.S. **194** 32.31 N 92.38 W
Ruston, Wa., U.S. **224** 47.17 N 122.30 W
Rusville **273d** 26.10 S 28.18 E
Rutana **154** 3.55 S 30.00 E
Rutčenkovo **83** 47.57 N 37.44 E
Rute **34** 37.19 N 4.22 W
Rütenbrock **52** 52.50 N 7.10 E
Ruteng **115b** 8.36 S 120.27 E
Rutenga **154** 21.08 S 30.45 E
Rutersville **222** 29.57 N 96.48 W
Rutgers University ᴕ[2], N.J., U.S. **276** 40.30 N 74.27 W
Rutgers University (Newark) ᴕ[2], N.J., U.S. **276** 40.44 N 74.10 W
Rutgers University (Camden) ᴕ[2], N.J., U.S. **285** 39.56 N 75.07 W
Ruth, Ms., U.S. **194** 31.22 N 90.18 W
Ruth, Nv., U.S. **204** 39.16 N 114.59 W
Rüthen **52** 51.29 N 8.25 E
Rutherford, Ca., U.S. **226** 38.28 N 122.25 W
Rutherford, N.J., U.S. **210** 40.49 N 74.06 W
Rutherford, Tn., U.S. **194** 36.07 N 88.59 W
Rutherfordton **192** 35.22 N 81.57 W
Rutherglen, Scot., U.K. **46** 55.50 N 4.12 W
Ruther Glen, Va., U.S. **208** 37.56 N 77.27 W
Ruthin **44** 53.07 N 3.18 W
Ruthton **198** 44.10 N 96.06 W
Ruthven, On., Can. **214** 42.03 N 82.40 W

Symbols in the index entries represent the broad categories identified in the key at the right. Symbols with superior numbers (⁎[1]) identify subcategories (see complete key on page *I · 1)*.

Symbole im Register stellen die rechts im Schlüssel erklärten Kategorien dar. Symbole mit hochgestellten Ziffern (⁎[1]) bezeichnen Unterabteilungen einer Kategorie (vgl. vollständiger Schlüssel auf Seite *I · 1)*.

Los símbolos incluídos en el texto del índice representan las grandes categorias identificadas con la clave a la derecha. Los símbolos con numeros en su parte superior (⁎[1]) identifican las subcategorías (véase la clave completa en la página *I · 1)*.

Les symboles de l'index représentent les catégories indiquées dans la légende à droite. Les symboles suivis d'un indice (⁎[1]) représentent des sous-catégories (voir légende complète à la page *I · 1)*.

Os símbolos incluídos no texto do índice representam as grandes categorias identificadas com a chave à direita. Os símbolos com números em sua parte superior (⁎[1]) identificam as subcategorias (veja-se a chave completa à página *I · 1)*.

	English	Deutsch	Español	Français	Português
∧	Mountain	Berg	Montaña	Montagne	Montanha
⁎	Mountains	Gebirge	Montañas	Montagnes	Montanhas
)(	Pass	Paß	Paso	Col	Passo
V	Valley, Canyon	Tal, Cañon	Valle, Cañón	Vallée, Canyon	Vale, Canhão
≚	Plain	Ebene	Llano	Plaine	Planície
>	Cape	Kap	Cabo	Cap	Cabo
I	Island	Insel	Isla	Île	Ilha
II	Islands	Inseln	Islas	Îles	Ilhas
⩲	Other Topographic Features	Andere Topographische Objekte	Otros Elementos Topográficos	Autres données topographiques	Outros acidentes topográficos

ESPAÑOL Nombre	Página	Lat.°'	Long.°' W = Oeste
Ruthven, Ia., U.S.	198	43.07 N	94.53 W
Rūti	58	47.16 N	8.51 E
Rutigliano	68	41.01 N	17.00 E
Rutino	68	40.18 N	15.04 E
Rutka ≃	80	56.22 N	46.38 E
Rutland, B.C., Can.	182	49.53 N	119.24 W
Rutland, Fl., U.S.	220	28.51 N	82.13 W
Rutland, II., U.S.	216	40.59 N	89.03 W
Rutland, Ma., U.S.	207	42.21 N	71.56 W
Rutland, N.D., U.S.	198	46.03 N	97.30 W
Rutland, Vt., U.S.	188	43.36 N	72.58 W
Rutland ◻ [6]	210	43.21 N	71.59 W
Rutland Island I	110	11.25 N	92.40 E
Rutland State Park ♦	207	42.23 N	72.01 W
Rutledge ≃	42	52.39 N	0.38 W
Rutledge, Ga., U.S.	192	33.37 N	83.36 W
Rutledge, Pa., U.S.	285	39.54 N	75.20 W
Rutledge, Tn., U.S.	192	36.16 N	83.30 W
Rutog	120	33.28 N	79.40 E
Rutshuru	154	1.11 S	29.27 E
Rüttenscheid •◻ [8]	263	51.27 N	6.59 E
Rutter	190	46.06 N	80.40 W
Rutul	84	41.33 N	47.25 E
Ruukki	26	64.40 N	25.06 E
Ruurlo	52	52.05 N	6.26 E
Ruvo del Monte	68	40.51 N	15.32 E
Ruvo di Puglia	68	41.07 N	16.29 E
Ruvu	154	6.48 S	38.39 E
Ruvu ≃	154	6.23 S	38.52 E
Ruvubu (Rovubu) ≃	154	3.23 S	30.47 E
Ruvuma ◻ [4]	154	11.00 S	36.00 E
Ruvuma (Rovuma) ≃	154	10.29 S	40.28 E
Ruwayān, Wādī ar- ≃ [7]	142	29.07 N	30.10 E
Ruwaybah ≃ [4]	140	15.39 N	28.45 E
Ruwayfi, Jabal ar- ∧	132	31.12 N	36.00 E
Ruwenzori National Park ♦	154	0.15 S	30.00 E
Ruwenzori Range ∧	154	0.23 N	29.54 E
Ruwer ≃	56	49.47 N	6.43 E
Ruwer ≃	56	49.47 N	6.42 E
Ruya (Luia) ≃	154	16.34 S	33.12 E
Ruya	100	34.10 N	112.26 E
Ruy Barbosa	255	12.18 S	40.27 W
Ruyigi	154	3.29 S	30.15 E
Ruyton-Eleven-Towns	42	52.48 N	2.54 W
Ruza	80	55.42 N	36.12 E
Ruza ≃	80	55.38 N	36.17 E
Ruzajevka, S.S.S.R.	80	54.04 N	44.57 E
Ruzajevka, S.S.S.R.	86	52.49 N	66.57 E
Ružany	76	52.52 N	24.53 E
Ružičnaja	78	49.24 N	26.58 E
Ružín	78	49.43 N	29.14 E
Ruzizi (Rusizi) ≃	154	3.16 S	29.14 E
Ružomberok	30	49.06 N	19.18 E
Ruzskoje vodochranilišče ◻ [1]	80	55.47 N	36.00 E
Ruzyně ◻ [8]	54	50.06 N	14.17 E
Ruzzah, Jabal ∧ [2]	142	30.01 N	30.26 E
Rwamagana	154	1.57 S	30.34 E
Rwanda ◻ [1], Afr.	138	2.00 S	30.00 E
Rwanda ◻ [1], Afr.	154	2.00 S	30.00 E
Rwashamaire	154	0.49 S	30.08 E
Ry	41	56.05 N	9.46 E
Ryal Fold	262	53.41 N	2.30 W
Ryan	196	34.01 N	97.57 W
Ryan, Loch ⊂	44	54.58 N	5.02 W
Ryan Peak ∧	202	43.54 N	114.25 W
Ryans Creek ≃	169	36.43 S	146.12 E
Ryarsh	260	51.19 N	0.24 E
Ryazan' → R'azan'	80	54.38 N	39.44 E
Rybačij	76	55.09 N	20.51 E
Rybačij, poluostrov ≻ [1]	24	69.42 N	32.36 E
Rybačje, S.S.S.R.	85	42.26 N	76.12 E
Rybačje, S.S.S.R.	86	46.27 N	81.32 E
Rybackaja •◻ [8]	265a	60.00 N	30.30 E
Rybackoje •◻ [8]	265a	59.50 N	30.30 E
Rybakovka	78	46.37 N	31.20 E
Rybinsk (Andropov)	76	58.03 N	38.52 E
Rybinskoje Stausee → Rybinskoje vodochranilišče ◻ [1]	76	58.30 N	38.25 E
Rybinskije Budy	78	51.13 N	35.57 E
Rybinskoje	86	55.47 N	94.47 E
Rybinskoje vodochranilišče ◻ [1]	76	58.30 N	38.25 E
Rybkino	80	54.15 N	43.46 E
Rybnaja Sloboda	80	55.29 N	50.09 E
Rybnica	78	47.45 N	29.01 E
Rybnik	30	50.06 N	18.32 E
Rybnoje, S.S.S.R.	80	54.44 N	39.30 E
Rybnoje, S.S.S.R.	86	58.08 N	94.30 E
Rybnovsk	89	53.12 N	141.50 E
Ryburn ≃	262	53.43 N	1.54 W
Rybuška	80	51.17 N	45.26 E
Rychnov nad Kněžnou	30	50.10 N	16.17 E
Rychwał	30	52.05 N	18.09 E
Ryčkovo	86	58.09 N	61.43 E
Rycroft	182	55.45 N	118.43 W
Ryd	26	56.28 N	14.41 E
Rydaholm	26	56.59 N	14.16 E
Rydal, Austl.	170	33.29 S	150.02 E
Rydal, Pa., U.S.	285	40.06 N	75.06 W
Rydalmere	274a	33.49 S	151.02 E
Rydoo	40	59.28 N	18.11 E
Ryde, Austl.	170	33.49 S	151.06 E
Ryde, Eng., U.K.	42	50.44 N	1.10 W
Ryder	198	47.55 N	101.40 W
Ryder's Hill ∧ [2]	30	50.31 N	3.53 W
Ryderwood	224	46.22 N	123.02 W
Rydsgård	41	55.28 N	13.35 E
Rydzyna	30	51.48 N	16.40 E
Rye, Austl.	169	38.23 S	144.49 E
Rye, Eng., U.K.	42	50.57 N	0.44 E
Rye, N.Y., U.S.	210	40.58 N	73.41 W
Rye, Tx., U.S.	222	30.27 N	94.49 W
Rye ≃	44	54.10 N	0.45 W
Ryegate	202	46.17 N	109.15 W
Rye Hills-Rye Brook	285	41.02 N	73.41 W
Rye Lake @	276	41.04 N	73.43 W
Ryeosu → Yŏsu	98	34.46 N	127.44 E
Rye Patch Reservoir @	204	40.38 N	118.18 W
Ryer Island I	282	38.05 N	121.47 W
Ryes	32	49.19 N	0.37 W
Ryfoss	26	61.09 N	8.49 E
Ryfylke •◻ [9]	26	59.30 N	5.60 E
Rygge	26	59.23 N	10.43 E
Rygnestad	26	59.13 N	7.29 E
Ryhope	44	54.52 N	1.21 W
Rykaartspos	158	26.32 S	26.39 E
Ryker Lake @	276	41.03 N	74.33 W
Rykerts	182	49.00 N	116.35 W
Ryki	30	51.39 N	21.56 E
Rykonec	76	59.33 N	36.34 E
Ryley	182	53.17 N	112.26 W
Rylovici	76	52.31 N	32.04 E
Ryl'sk	78	51.34 N	34.43 E
Rylstone	170	32.48 S	149.58 E
Rymanów	30	49.34 N	21.53 E
Rymařov	30	49.56 N	17.16 E
Ryn	30	53.56 N	21.33 E
Rynfield	273d	26.09 S	28.22 E
Rynok	80	48.49 N	44.40 E
Ryn-Peski ◾²	80	48.24 N	49.00 E
Ryō	94	34.44 N	135.59 E
Ryōhaku-sanchi ∧	94	36.09 N	136.45 E
Ryojun → Lüshun	100	38.48 N	121.16 E
Ryōkami	94	36.00 N	138.58 E
Ryōke	268	35.58 N	139.33 E
Ryōnan	94	34.15 N	133.55 E
Ryōtsu	92	38.05 N	138.26 E
Rypin	30	53.05 N	19.25 E
Ryškany	78	47.58 N	27.32 E

FRANÇAIS Nom	Page	Lat.°'	Long.°' W = Ouest
Ryslinge	41	55.15 N	10.33 E
Rysy ∧	30	49.12 N	20.04 E
Ryton ∨	44	54.59 N	1.46 W
Ryton ≃	44	53.25 N	1.00 W
Ryton-on-Dunsmore	42	52.22 N	1.26 W
Ryūga-do ◻ [5]	96	33.39 N	133.45 E
Ryūgasaki	92	35.54 N	140.11 E
Ryūjin	96	33.53 N	135.29 E
Ryukyu Islands → Nansei-shotō II	90	26.30 N	128.00 E
Ryukyu Trench ◻ [1]	12	24.45 N	128.00 E
Ryūmon-dake ∧	270	34.26 N	135.53 E
Ryūō, Nihon	94	35.39 N	138.30 E
Ryūō, Nihon	94	35.04 N	136.07 E
Ryūsen	270	34.28 N	135.37 E
Ryūyō	94	34.40 N	137.48 E
Ržaksa	80	52.09 N	42.02 E
Ržanica	78	53.26 N	33.55 E
Ržava	78	51.14 N	36.43 E
Rzepin	30	52.22 N	14.50 E
Rzeszów	30	50.03 N	22.00 E
Rzeszów ◻ [4]	30	50.00 N	22.00 E
Ržev	76	56.16 N	34.20 E
Ržiščev	78	49.58 N	31.03 E
Ržovka •◻ [8]	265a	59.58 N	30.30 E

S

Nom	Page	Lat.°'	Long.°' W = Ouest
Sa	110	18.34 N	100.45 E
Sa ≃	105	40.22 N	117.58 E
Saa	152	4.22 N	11.27 E
Sa'ad	132	31.28 N	34.32 E
Sa'ādatābād	128	30.06 N	53.08 E
Sääksjärvi @	26	61.24 N	22.24 E
Saal ≃	54	54.19 N	12.29 E
Saalach ≃	64	47.51 N	13.00 E
Saal an der Donau	60	48.54 N	11.56 E
Saal an der Saale	56	50.19 N	10.21 E
Saalbach ≃	64	47.23 N	12.38 E
Saalburg	56	50.30 N	11.43 E
Saaldorf	54	51.57 N	11.55 E
Saaler Bodden ⊂	54	54.20 N	12.28 E
Saales	58	48.21 N	7.07 E
Saaletalsperre ◻ [6]	54	50.30 N	11.35 E
Saalfeld	54	50.39 N	11.22 E
Saalfelden	64	47.25 N	12.51 E
Saamar	88	52.08 N	106.10 E
Saanen, ∼, Fr.	50	49.54 N	0.56 E
Saane ≃, Schw.	58	46.59 N	7.16 E
Saanen	58	46.29 N	7.16 E
Saanenmöser	58	46.31 N	7.18 E
Saanich Inlet ⊂	224	48.38 N	123.30 W
Saar → Saarland ◻ [3]	56	49.20 N	7.00 E
Saar (Sarre) ≃	56	49.42 N	6.34 E
Saarbrücken	56	49.14 N	6.59 E
Saarburg	56	49.36 N	6.33 E
Saäre	78	57.56 N	22.02 E
Saarelouis → Saarlouis	56	49.21 N	6.45 E
Saaremaa I	76	58.25 N	22.5 J E
Saarijärvi	26	62.43 N	25.16 E
Saaristomeren kansallispuisto ♦	26	59.50 N	21.50 E
Saarland ◻ [3]	56	49.20 N	7.00 E
Saarlautern → Saarlouis	56	49.20 N	6.45 E
Saarlouis	56	49.20 N	6.45 E
Saarmund	264a	52.19 N	13.07 E
Saarn •◻ [8]	263	51.24 N	6.53 E
Saarnberg •◻ [8]	263	51.25 N	6.53 E
Saas Almagell	58	46.07 N	7.58 E
Saas Fee	58	46.07 N	7.55 E
Saas Grund	58	46.08 N	7.56 E
Saastal ∨	58	46.10 N	7.56 E
Saatly	84	39.56 N	48.23 E
Saavedra	252	37.45 S	62.22 W
Saavedra •◻ [8]	288	34.33 S	58.28 W
Saba ◻	96	34.02 N	131.30 E
Saba ≃, Nihon	96	59.08 N	29.00 E
Sabā', Wādī al- ∨	128	28.35 N	36.35 E
Saba Bank ◾²	238	17.30 N	63.30 W
Šabac	34	44.45 N	19.42 E
Sabadell	34	41.33 N	2.06 E
Sab'ah	142	30.15 N	32.33 E
Sabah ◻ [3]	112	5.20 N	117.10 E
Sabajevo	80	53.59 N	45.43 E
Sabak Bernam	112	3.46 N	100.59 E
Sabal	112	0.59 S	123.14 E
Sabalán ∧	128	38.15 N	47.48 E
Sabalana, Kepulauan II	112	6.45 S	118.50 E
Sabalgarh	124	26.15 N	77.24 E
Sabaluka Game Reserve ♦	140	16.18 N	32.40 E
Sabana, Archipiélago de II	240m	18.20 N	65.44 W
Sabana-Camagüey, Archipiélago de II	240p	23.00 N	80.00 W
Sabana de la Mar	238	19.04 N	69.23 W
Sabana de Mendoza	246	09.26 N	70.46 W
Sabanagrande, Hond.	236	13.48 N	87.15 W
Sabana Grande, P.R.	240m	18.05 N	66.58 W
Sabanalamar, Ensenada ⊂	240p	21.36 N	84.44 W
Sabanalarga	244	10.38 N	74.55 W
Sabana Llana	240m	18.02 N	66.15 W
Sabancuy	232	18.58 N	91.11 W
Sabaneta, Rep. Dom.	238	19.30 N	71.21 W
Sabaneta, Ven.	246	8.46 N	69.56 W
Sabaneta, Puntan ≻	174n	15.17 N	145.49 E
Sabang, India	126	22.11 N	87.36 E
Sabang (Dampelas), Indon.	112	0.11 N	119.51 E
Sabang, Indon.	114	5.55 N	95.19 E
Sabinilla	232	25.08 N	101.44 W
Sabanözü	130	40.29 N	33.18 E
Sabará	255	19.54 S	43.48 W
Šabašovo	76	56.02 N	35.29 E
Sabattis	276	44.09 N	74.40 W
Sabaudia	66	41.18 N	13.02 E
Sabaudia, Lago di ⊂	66	41.16 N	13.02 E
Sabaúna	256	23.29 S	46.05 W
Saba Wanak	144	10.33 N	44.08 E
Sabaya	248	19.01 S	68.23 W
Sabdjah, Jabal ∧	84	35.51 N	41.41 E
Sabenba	84	42.14 N	43.48 E
Sabetha	48	45.00 N	10.39 E
Sabé	272c	19.11 N	73.02 E
Šabel'kovka	83	48.51 N	37.29 E
Šabel'sk	80	46.33 N	38.42 E
Sāberī, Hāmūn-e @	128	31.30 N	61.20 E
Sabha, S.S.S.R.	80	57.15 N	51.04 E
Sabhā, Lībiyā	148	27.03 N	14.26 E
Sabhā, Urd.	132	32.20 N	36.30 E
Šabino	80	58.10 N	49.30 E
Sabina ◻ [9]	36	42.15 N	12.42 E

PORTUGUÊS Nome	Página	Lat.°'	Long.°' W = Oeste
Sabinal	196	29.19 N	99.27 W
Sabinal ≃	196	29.06 N	99.27 W
Sabinal, Península de ≻ [1]	240p	21.40 N	77.18 W
Sabiñánigo	34	42.31 N	0.22 W
Sabinas	232	27.51 N	101.07 W
Sabinas ≃, Méx.	232	26.51 N	99.34 W
Sabinas ≃, Méx.	232	27.37 N	100.42 W
Sabinas, Méx.	232	22.59 N	98.58 W
Sabinas Hidalgo	232	26.30 N	100.10 W
Sabine ≃	178	30.00 N	93.45 W
Sabine, Mount ∧, Ant.	9	71.55 S	169.33 E
Sabine, Mount ∧, Austl.	169	38.38 S	143.44 E
Sabine, South Fork ≃	222	32.52 N	96.10 W
Sabine Bay ⊂	176	75.35 N	109.30 W
Sabine Lake ⊂	194	29.50 N	93.50 W
Sabine Pass ⊂	194	29.44 N	93.52 W
Sabine Peninsula ≻ [1]	176	76.20 N	109.30 W
Sabini, Monti ∧	66	42.13 N	12.50 E
Sabinópolis	255	18.40 S	43.06 W
Sabinov	30	49.06 N	21.06 E
Sabinsville	210	41.52 N	77.31 W
Săcueni	38	47.21 N	22.06 E
Sacul	222	31.50 N	94.56 W
Sacupana	246	8.35 N	61.39 W
Sacuriuiná ≃	248	12.52 S	57.22 W
Sada, Esp.	34	43.21 N	8.15 W
Sada, Nihon	96	35.15 N	132.43 E
Sadaba	34	42.17 N	1.16 W
Sadābād, India	124	27.27 N	78.03 E
Sa'dābād, Īrān	128	34.51 N	50.36 E
Sa'dābād, Īrān	128	29.23 N	51.07 E
Sadad	130	34.18 N	36.56 E
Sadaik Taung ∧	110	15.00 N	98.12 E
Sadali	71	39.49 N	9.16 E
Sada-misaki ≻	96	33.20 N	132.01 E
Sada-misaki-hantō ≻ [1]	96	33.26 N	132.13 E
Sadamitsu	96	34.02 N	134.04 E
Sadane ≃	115a	6.01 S	106.37 E
Sadang ≃	112	3.43 S	119.27 E
Sadanga	116	17.09 N	121.02 E
Sadani	154	6.03 S	38.47 E
Sadao	110	6.38 N	100.26 E
Sadarpur, Bngl.	126	23.28 N	90.02 E
Sadarpur, India	272a	28.33 N	77.21 E
Sadčikovka	86	53.01 N	63.27 E
Saddakh	132	31.42 N	35.09 E
Sadda	120	33.42 N	70.20 E
Saddle ∧	276	40.52 N	74.07 W
Saddleback ∧	44	54.38 N	3.03 W
Saddleback, Mount ∧	168a	32.58 S	116.28 E
Saddle Brook	276	40.54 N	74.06 W
Saddleback Keys II	220	24.37 N	81.37 W
Saddle Lake Indian Reserve ♦	182	54.00 N	111.40 W
Saddle Mountain ∧, Co., U.S.	200	38.50 N	105.28 W
Saddle Mountain ∧, Or., U.S.	224	45.58 N	123.41 W
Saddle Mountains ∧	202	46.50 N	119.55 W
Saddle Mountain State Park ♦	224	45.58 N	123.41 W
Saddle Peak ∧, India	110	13.09 N	93.01 E
Saddle Peak ∧, India	110	13.09 N	93.01 E
Saddle River ≃	276	40.54 N	74.05 W
Saddle Rock	276	40.48 N	73.45 W
Saddleworth, Austl.	168b	34.05 S	138.47 E
Saddleworth, Eng., U.K.	262	53.33 N	1.59 W
Saddleworth Moor ≃ [3]	262	53.33 N	1.59 W
Sa Dec	110	10.18 N	105.46 E
Sadelkow ≃	54	53.34 N	13.26 E
Sādhāura	124	30.23 N	77.13 E
Sādhuhāti	126	23.34 N	89.01 E
Sadieville	218	38.23 N	84.32 W
Sadilovo	80	59.28 N	70.08 E
Sadiya	120	27.50 N	95.40 E
Sa'dīyah, Wādī ∨	144	20.36 N	39.38 E
Sa'dīyat, Ra's as-	132	33.41 N	35.25 E
Sadler Lake @	184	55.17 N	103.45 W
Sado I	92	38.00 N	138.25 E
Sado-kaikyō ⋈	92	37.50 N	138.40 E
Sadovoje, S.S.S.R.	80	42.45 N	44.40 E
Sadovoje, S.S.S.R.	80	47.56 N	44.30 E
Sadovoje Pervoje	78	51.33 N	40.29 E
Sadowara	96	32.03 N	131.26 E
Sădri	124	25.11 N	73.26 E
Sadrinsk	86	56.05 N	63.38 E
Sadsburyville	208	39.59 N	75.53 W
Sădulpur	124	28.27 N	75.41 E
Sädvaluspen ≃	24	66.24 N	16.12 E
Saeby, Dan.	41	55.33 N	11.19 E
Saeby, Dan.	26	57.20 N	10.32 E
Saegertown	214	41.43 N	80.09 W
Sae Islands II	164	4.05 S	145.15 E
Saeki → Saiki, Nihon	96	32.57 N	131.54 E
Saeki, Nihon	96	34.22 N	132.11 E
Saeki, Nihon	96	34.31 N	134.06 E
Saengjil-to I	98	34.19 N	126.59 E
Saensuk	110	13.18 N	100.55 E
Saergorod	84	38.29 N	47.57 E
Saerslev, Dan.	41	55.31 N	10.11 E
Saerslev, Dan.	41	55.34 N	9.44 E
Safā, Tulūl as- ◻ [1]	132	33.02 N	37.12 E
Safad → Zefat	132	32.58 N	35.30 E
Safājah, Jazīrat I	140	26.45 N	33.59 E
Safakulevo	86	54.59 N	62.33 E
Safānīkovo	130	39.43 N	30.20 E
Safdar Jang Airport ⫟	272a	28.37 N	77.13 E
Safdar Jang's Tomb ⫟	272a	28.35 N	77.13 E
Safed Koh Range ∧	123	33.56 N	70.25 E
Safe Harbor Dam •◻ [6]	208	39.56 N	76.28 W
Safety Bay	168a	32.18 S	115.43 E
Safety Harbor	220	28.00 N	82.41 W
Safford	196	32.50 N	109.42 W
Saffron Walden	42	52.01 N	0.15 E
Safi	148	32.20 N	9.17 W
Safia	132	36.40 N	38.14 E
Safīd ≃	128	37.24 N	49.58 E
Safīd Kūh, Selseleh-ye ∧	123	34.30 N	63.30 E
Safienthal ∨	58	46.35 N	9.18 E
Safioune, Sebkhet ⊂	148	32.16 N	5.27 W
Safītā	130	34.49 N	36.07 E
Safonovo, S.S.S.R.	24	65.40 N	47.37 E
Safonovo, S.S.S.R.	76	55.06 N	33.15 E
Safonovo, S.S.S.R.	76	55.02 N	33.15 E
Safotu	181a	13.27 S	172.24 W
Safranbolu	130	41.15 N	32.41 E
Saft al-'Inab	142	30.05 N	31.25 E
Saft al-Khammār	142	28.02 N	30.44 E
Saft al-Laban	273d	30.01 N	31.08 E
Saft al-Mulūk	142	28.08 N	30.51 E
Saft Rāshin	142	29.00 N	31.12 E
Saft Turāb	142	28.55 N	30.49 E
Safwān	128	30.07 N	47.43 E
Saga ◻ [42]	92	33.15 N	130.18 E
Saga, Nihon	96	33.05 N	133.06 E
Saga, S.S.S.R.	86	50.23 N	64.15 E

Nome	Página	Lat.°'	Long.°' W = Oeste
Sacramento ◻ [6]	226	38.35 N	121.30 W
Sacramento ≃, Ca., U.S.	226	38.32 N	121.56 W
Sacramento ≃, N.M., U.S.	200	32.16 N	105.31 W
Sacramento, Pampa del ≃	248	8.00 S	75.50 W
Sacramento Metropolitan Airport ⫟	226	38.42 N	121.37 W
Sacramento Mountains ∧	200	32.45 N	105.30 W
Sacramento River Deep Water Ship Channel ⫝	226	38.15 N	121.40 W
Sacramento South	226	38.32 N	121.26 W
Sacramento Valley ∨	200	39.15 N	122.00 W
Sacramento Wash ∨	200	34.43 N	114.28 W
Sacre ≃	248	12.56 S	58.18 W
Sacré-Coeur ⫟	261	48.53 N	2.21 E
Sacred Heart	198	44.47 N	95.21 W
Sacriston	44	54.49 N	1.37 W
Sacro, Monte ∧	68	40.13 N	15.20 E
Sacro Monte ⫟ [1]	62	45.49 N	8.15 E
Sacrow ◻ [8]	264a	52.26 N	13.06 E
Sacrower See ⊂	264a	52.27 N	13.06 E
Sacul	222	31.50 N	94.56 W
Saga, S.S.S.R.	86	49.25 N	55.17 E
Saga, Zhg.	120	29.30 N	85.22 E
Saga ◻ [5]	96	33.21 N	130.28 E
Sagae	92	38.22 N	140.17 E
Sagaing	110	21.52 N	95.59 E
Sagaing ◻ [3]	110	24.00 N	95.00 E
Sagak, Cape ≻	180	52.48 N	169.08 W
Sagalaherang	115a	6.40 S	107.39 E
Sagalakasa	80	46.54 N	50.43 E
Sagami ≃	94	35.19 N	139.22 E
Sagamihara	94	35.34 N	139.23 E
Sagamihara-daichi ≃ [1]	268	35.27 N	139.27 E
Sagamiko	94	35.37 N	139.12 E
Sagami-ko @	94	35.35 N	139.16 E
Sagami-nada ⊂	94	35.00 N	139.30 E
Sagami-wan ⊂	94	35.15 N	139.25 E
Sagamore, Ma., U.S.	207	41.46 N	70.31 W
Sagamore, Pa., U.S.	214	40.46 N	79.13 W
Sagamore Beach	207	41.47 N	70.31 W
Sagamore Hill National Historic Site ⫟	276	40.53 N	73.30 W
Sagamore Hills	279a	41.20 N	81.26 W
Saganaga Lake @	190	48.14 N	90.52 W
Saganoseki	96	33.15 N	131.53 E
Saganthit Kyun I	110	11.56 N	98.29 E
Ságany, ozero @	78	45.43 N	29.53 E
Sagaon	272c	19.12 N	73.06 E
Sāgar, India	124	14.10 N	75.02 E
Sāgar, India	124	23.50 N	78.43 E
Sagara	94	34.41 N	138.12 E
Sagaranten	115a	7.13 S	106.52 E
Sagard	54	54.31 N	13.33 E
Sāgar Island I	126	21.43 N	88.06 E
Sagarmatha → Everest, Mount ∧	124	27.59 N	86.56 E
Sagarmatha National Park ♦	124	27.50 N	86.45 E
Ságar Plateau ≃ [1]	124	23.30 N	78.30 E
Sāgavanirktok ≃	180	70.20 N	148.00 W
Sagay	116	10.57 N	123.25 E
Sage, Mount ∧	240m	18.25 N	64.39 W
Sage Creek ≃, N.A.	202	48.58 N	110.06 W
Sage Creek ≃, U.S.	202	44.50 N	108.26 W
Sage Creek ≃, Mt., U.S.	202	47.16 N	109.43 W
Sage Creek ≃, Mt., U.S.	202	48.20 N	110.03 W
Sagemace Bay ⊂	184	51.49 N	100.03 W
Sagerton	196	33.05 N	99.58 W
Saggaubach ≃	64	46.43 N	15.24 E
Sag Harbor	207	40.59 N	72.17 W
Saghbīn	132	33.37 N	35.42 E
Saghīr, Al-Bahr as- ≃	142	31.09 N	31.56 E
Sagil	86	50.18 N	91.40 E
Saginaw, Mi., U.S.	190	43.25 N	83.56 W
Saginaw, Tx., U.S.	222	32.52 N	97.22 W
Saginaw Bay ⊂	190	43.50 N	83.40 W
Sagiz, S.S.S.R.	86	47.31 N	53.16 E
Sagiz, S.S.S.R.	86	48.12 N	54.56 E
Sagiz ≃	86	48.05 N	53.20 E
Sağkaya	130	37.11 N	35.41 E
Sagleipie	150	7.10 N	8.52 W
Saglek Bay ⊂	176	58.35 N	63.00 W
Sagleik Fiord ⊂	176	58.30 N	63.00 W
Saglouc → Salluit	176	62.14 N	75.38 W
Saguache Creek ≃	200	37.52 N	106.51 W
Sagua de Tánamo	240p	20.35 N	75.14 W
Sagua la Chica ≃	240p	22.40 N	80.01 W
Sagua la Grande	240p	22.49 N	80.05 W
Sagua la Grande ≃	240p	22.56 N	80.01 W
Saguaro National Monument ♦	200	32.12 N	110.38 W
Saguenay ≃	176	48.08 N	69.44 W
Sagunto	272p	39.41 N	0.16 W
Saguna	148	39.41 N	0.16 W
Sagunovka	78	50.39 N	39.15 E
Sagunto	34	39.41 N	0.16 W
Sagwon	180	69.23 N	148.42 W
Sah	150	4.40 N	10.52 E
Sahagún, Col.	246	8.57 N	75.27 W
Sahagún, Esp.	34	42.22 N	5.02 W
Sahah al-Jawlān ≃	132	35.31 N	33.05 E
Sahala	26	62.52 N	24.11 E
Sahalin, ostrov I	89	51.00 N	143.00 E
Sahalinskij zaliv ⊂	89	53.45 N	141.30 E
Sahand ∧	84	37.44 N	46.27 E
Sahara ≃ [2]	138	24.30 N	13.00 W
Sahara Occidental → Western Sahara ◻ [1]	148	24.30 N	13.00 W
Sahara Occidentale → Western Sahara ◻ [1]	148	24.30 N	13.00 W
Saharsa	124	25.53 N	86.36 E
Sahasinaka	157b	21.49 S	47.49 E
Sahasrail	126	23.19 N	89.43 E
Sahaspur	124	29.07 N	78.37 E
Sahat, Canal de ⫝	190	46.26 N	63.28 W
Sahaturn ⫟	34	22.04 N	114.10 E
Sahel, Oued ≃	72	36.28 N	5.04 E
Sahiwal •◻ [8]	272a	28.45 N	77.05 E
Sāhibganj	124	25.15 N	87.39 E
Sāhib Nangli	272a	28.45 N	77.09 E
Sahibiti ◻	132	40.01 N	26.60 E
Sāhibzāda •◻ [8]	272a	28.45 N	77.05 E
Sāhil ≃	144	10.00 N	45.00 E
Sāhīwal, Pāk.	123	30.40 N	73.06 E
Sāhīwal, Pāk.	120	30.40 N	73.06 E
Sahlenburg	54	53.52 N	8.37 E
Sahneh	128	34.29 N	47.41 E
Sahrā', Bi'r ≃ [4]	140	24.34 N	25.43 E
Sahrajat al-Kubrā wa Kafr Jirjis Yūsuf	142	30.38 N	31.17 E
Sahuaripa	232	29.03 N	109.14 W
Sahuayo	232	20.04 N	102.43 W
Sahul Shelf ◾⁴	164	12.30 S	125.00 E
Sahwaj	142	30.07 N	31.45 E
Šahy	30	48.05 N	18.57 E
Sai ≃, India	124	25.39 N	82.47 E
Sai ≃, Nihon	94	36.38 N	138.10 E
Sai Buri	110	6.43 N	101.37 E
Šaʿib, Wādī aš- ≃	132	31.51 N	35.41 E

Nome	Página	Lat.°'	Long.°' W = Oeste
Saidaiji	96	34.39 N	134.02 E
Saïda	148	35.04 N	2.15 W
Sa'idīyeh	128	36.26 N	48.48 E
Saïdo	152	11.17 S	23.07 E
Saidor	164	5.35 S	146.30 E
Saidpur, Bngl.	124	25.47 N	88.54 E
Saidpur, India	124	25.33 N	83.11 E
Saidu	123	34.45 N	72.21 E
Saigawa	96	33.39 N	130.57 E
Saignelégier	58	47.15 N	7.00 E
Saignon	62	43.52 N	5.26 E
Saigō	96	36.12 N	133.20 E
Saigon → Thanh Pho Ho Chi Minh	269c	10.45 N	106.40 E
Sai Gon ≃	269c	10.45 N	106.45 E
Saihaku	96	35.20 N	133.20 E
Saihan Toroi	102	41.41 N	100.26 E
Saijō, Nihon	96	34.56 N	133.07 E
Saijō, Nihon	96	33.55 N	133.11 E
Saijō	96	34.48 N	132.51 E
Saikai-kokuritsu-kōen ♦	92	33.12 N	129.22 E
Sai Keng	271d	22.26 N	114.16 E
Sai-kawa ≃	96	32.57 N	131.54 E
Saiki-wan ⊂	96	33.00 N	131.58 E
Sainjang	98	39.15 N	125.51 E
Sainō-ha'iji ⫟	96	35.29 N	133.39 E
Sains-du-Nord	50	50.06 N	4.00 E
Sains-en-Gohelle	50	50.27 N	2.41 E
Sains-Richaumont	50	49.49 N	3.42 E
Saint Ab's Head ≻	46	55.54 N	2.09 W
Sainte-Adèle	206	45.57 N	74.07 W
Saint-Adresse	50	49.30 N	0.05 E
Saint-Adrien	206	45.49 N	71.43 W
Saint-Affrique	62	43.57 N	2.53 E
Saint-Agapit	206	46.34 N	71.27 W
Saint Agatha	212	43.26 N	80.36 W
Sainte-Agathe, Mb., Can.	184	49.34 N	97.10 W
Sainte-Agathe, Fr.	62	45.49 N	3.37 E
Sainte-Agathe [-de-Lotbinière]	206	46.23 N	71.24 W
Sainte-Agathe-des-Monts	206	46.03 N	74.17 W
Sainte-Agnès, Fr.	62	43.48 N	7.28 E
Saint Agnes, Eng., U.K.	42	50.18 S	5.13 W
Saint Agnes I	42a	49.54 N	6.20 W
Saint-Agrève	62	45.01 N	4.24 E
Saint-Aignan	50	47.16 N	1.23 E
Saint-Aimé (Massueville)	206	45.55 N	72.56 W
Saint Albans, Austl.	169	37.44 S	144.48 E
Saint Albans, Nf., Can.	176	47.52 N	55.51 W
Saint Alban's, Nf., Can.	176	47.52 N	55.51 W
Saint Albans, Mo., U.S.	42	51.46 N	0.21 W
Saint Albans, Vt., U.S.	188	38.23 N	81.50 W
Saint Albans, W.V., U.S.	188	44.49 N	73.05 W
Saint Albans ◻ [8]	260	40.42 N	73.46 W
Saint Albans, Cape ≻	168b	35.49 S	138.07 E
Saint Alban's Head ≻	42	50.34 N	2.04 W
Saint-Albert, Ab., Can.	182	53.38 N	113.38 W
Saint-Albert, P.Q., Can.	206	46.00 N	72.05 W
Saint Aldhelm's Head	42	50.34 N	2.04 W
Saint-Alexandre-de-Kamouraska	206	47.41 N	69.38 W
Saint-Amable	275a	45.39 N	73.18 W
Saint-Amand-en-Puisaye	50	47.31 N	3.04 E
Saint-Amand-les-Eaux	50	50.27 N	3.26 E
Saint-Amand-Longpré	50	47.41 N	1.01 E
Saint-Amant-Roche-Savine	62	45.39 N	3.38 E
Sainte-Amélie	184	50.59 N	99.21 W
Sainte-Amour	50	46.26 N	5.21 E
Saint-André, Cap ≻	157b	16.11 S	44.27 E
Saint-André, Réunion	275a	20.57 S	55.39 E
Saint-André-Avellin	206	45.43 N	75.03 W
Saint-André-de-l'Eure	50	48.54 N	1.17 E
Saint-André-de-Valborgne	62	44.09 N	3.41 E
St.-André-Est	206	45.34 N	74.20 W
Saint-André-les-Alpes	62	43.58 N	6.30 E
Saillans	62	44.42 N	5.11 E
Saint André, Mount ∧	241d	13.11 N	61.13 W
Saint Andrew Lakes @	212	44.36 N	76.40 W
Saint Andrews, N.B., Can.	176	45.05 N	67.03 W
Saint Andrews, Scot., U.K.	46	56.20 N	2.48 W
Saint Andrews, S.C., U.S.	192	36.04 N	79.59 W
Saint Andrews Bay ⊂	192	30.00 N	85.45 W
Saint Andrew's Cathedral ⫟ [1]	271c	1.18 N	103.51 E
Sainte-Anne, Guad.	241b	16.14 N	61.23 W
Sainte-Anne, Mart.	240e	14.26 N	60.53 W
Sainte-Anne, Il., U.S.	216	41.01 N	87.42 W
Sainte Anne, Lac @	182	53.42 N	114.27 W
Sainte-Anne ≃	273b	4.18 S	15.19 E
Sainte-Anne, Lac @ Ab., Can.	182	53.43 N	114.27 W
Sainte-Anne, Lac @ P.Q., Can.	186	50.05 N	67.50 W
Sainte-Anne-de-Beaupré	206	47.02 N	70.56 W
Sainte-Anne-de-Bellevue	275a	45.24 N	73.57 W
Sainte-Anne-de-la-Pérade	206	46.35 N	72.12 W

Symbols legend:

≃ River	Fluß	Río	Rivière	Rio	⫝ Submarine Features	Untermeerische Objekte
⫝ Canal	Kanal	Canal	Canal	Canal	◻ Political Unit	Politische Einheit
⌐ Waterfall, Rapids	Wasserfall, Stromschnellen	Cascada, Rápidos	Chute d'eau, Rapides	Cascata, Rápidos	⫟ Cultural Institution	Kulturelle Institution
⋈ Strait	Meeresstraße	Estrecho	Détroit	Estreito	⫟ Historical Site	Historische Stätte
⊂ Bay, Gulf	Bucht, Golf	Bahía, Golfo	Baie, Golfe	Baía, Golfo	♦ Recreational Site	Erholungs- und Ferienort
@ Lake, Lakes	See, Seen	Lago, Lagos	Lac, Lacs	Lago, Lagos	⫟ Airport	Flughafen
⋈ Swamp	Sumpf	Pantano	Marais	Pântano	⫟ Military Installation	Militäranlage
▨ Ice Features, Glacier	Eis- und Gletscherformen	Accidentes Glaciales	Formes glaciaires	Acidentes glaciares	◦ Miscellaneous	Verschiedenes
⫟ Other Hydrographic Features	Andere Hydrographische Objekte	Otros Elementos Hidrográficos	Autres données hydrographiques	Outros acidentes hidrográficos		

Accidentes Submarinos	Formes de relief sous-marin	Acidentes submarinos	
Unidad Política	Entité politique	Unidade política	
Institución Cultural	Institution culturelle	Instituição cultural	
Sitio Histórico	Site historique	Sitio histórico	
Sitio de Recreo	Centre de loisirs	Area de Lazer	
Aeropuerto	Aéroport	Aeroporto	
Instalación Militar	Installation militaire	Instalação militar	
Misceláneo	Divers	Diversos	

Name	Page	Lat.°′	Long.°′
Sainte-Anne-de-Madawaska	186	47.15 N	68.02 W
Sainte-Anne-des-Chênes	184	49.40 N	96.40 W
Sainte-Anne-des-Monts	186	49.08 N	66.30 W
Sainte-Anne-des-Plaines	206	46.46 N	73.48 W
Saint Anne of the Congo ᵿ1	273b	4.16 S	15.17 E
Saint Anne's	44	53.45 N	3.02 W
Saint Ann's Bay	241q	18.26 N	77.08 W
Saint Anns Bay c	186	46.20 N	60.30 W
Saint Ann's Head ›	42	51.41 N	5.10 W
Saint-Anselme	186	46.37 N	70.58 W
Saint Ansgar	190	43.22 N	92.55 W
Saint-Anthème	58	45.31 N	3.55 E
Saint Anthony, N.B., Can.	186	46.22 N	64.45 W
Saint Anthony, Nf., Can.	186	51.22 N	55.35 W
Saint Anthony, Id., U.S.	202	43.57 N	111.40 W
Saint-Antoine, P.Q., Can.	206	45.46 N	73.59 W
Saint-Antoine, Fr.	62	45.10 N	5.13 E
Saint-Antonin	32	44.09 N	1.45 E
Saint-Apollinaire (Francoeur)	206	46.37 N	71.31 W
Saint Arnaud, Austl.	166	36.37 S	143.15 E
Saint Arnaud, N.Z.	172	41.48 S	172.50 E
Saint-Arnoult, Forêt de ♦	261	48.35 N	1.55 E
Saint-Arnoult-en-Yvelines	50	48.34 N	1.56 E
Saint Arvans	42	51.40 N	2.41 W
Saint Asaph	44	53.16 N	3.26 W
Saint-Astier	32	45.09 N	0.32 E
Saint Athan	42	51.24 N	3.25 W
Saint-Auban	62	43.51 N	6.44 E
Saint-Aubert, Mont ∧2	50	50.39 N	3.24 E
Saint Aubert Island I	219	38.40 N	91.52 W
Saint-Aubin, Fr.	50	49.53 N	0.53 E
Saint-Aubin, Fr.	58	47.02 N	5.20 E
Saint Aubin, Jersey	43b	49.11 N	2.10 W
Saint-Aubin, Schw.	58	46.54 N	6.47 E
Saint-Aubin-d'Aubigné	32	48.15 N	1.36 W
Saint-Aubin-lès-Elbeuf	50	49.18 N	1.01 E
Saint-Aubin-sur-Aire	58	48.42 N	5.27 E
Saint Augustin	157b	23.33 S	43.46 E
Saint-Augustin ≃	176	51.14 N	58.41 W
Saint-Augustin-Deux-Montagnes	275a	45.38 N	73.59 W
Saint Augustine	192	29.53 N	81.18 W
Saint-Augustin Nord-Ouest ≃	186	51.16 N	58.42 W
Saint-Augustin-Saguenay	186	51.14 N	58.39 W
Saint-Aulaye	32	45.12 N	0.08 E
Saint Austell	42	50.20 N	4.48 W
Saint-Avertin	50	47.22 N	0.44 E
Saint-Avold	56	49.06 N	6.42 E
Saint-Ay	50	47.51 N	1.45 E
Saint-Aygulf	62	43.23 N	6.44 E
Saint Barbe	186	51.12 N	56.46 W
Saint Barnabas Chapel ᵿ1	174c	29.02 S	167.55 E
Saint-Barthélemy I	238	17.54 N	62.50 W
Saint-Basile	186	47.21 N	68.14 W
Saint-Basile-de-Portneuf	206	46.45 N	71.49 W
Saint-Basile-le-Grand	206	45.32 N	73.17 W
Saint Bathans, Mount ∧	172	44.44 S	169.46 E
Sainte-Baume, Chaîne de la ⩘	62	43.20 N	5.45 E
Saint-Béat	32	42.55 N	0.42 E
Saint Bees	44	54.30 N	3.37 W
Saint Bees Head ›	44	54.32 N	3.38 W
Saint Benedict	214	40.38 N	78.44 W
Saint-Benoît, Fr.	261	48.40 N	1.55 E
Saint-Benoît, Réu.	157c	21.02 S	55.43 E
Saint-Benoît-du-Sault	32	46.27 N	1.23 E
Saint-Benoît-en-Woëvre	56	48.59 N	5.47 E
Saint Bernard	218	39.10 N	84.29 W
Saint-Bernard, Île I	275a	45.23 N	73.45 W
Saint-Bernard-de-Dorchester	206	46.30 N	71.08 W
Saint-Béron	62	45.30 N	5.43 E
Saint-Blaise, P.Q., Can.	206	45.13 N	73.17 W
Saint-Blaise, Schw.	58	47.01 N	6.59 E
Saint-Blaise-la-Roche	58	48.24 N	7.10 E
Saint Blaize, Cape ›	158	34.11 S	22.10 E
Saint Blazey	42	50.22 N	4.43 W
Saint-Blin	58	48.16 N	5.25 E
Saint Bonaventure, P.Q., Can.	206	45.58 N	72.41 W
Saint Bonaventure, N.Y., U.S.	210	42.05 N	78.28 W
Saint-Boniface-de-Shawinigan	206	46.30 N	72.49 W
Saint-Bonnet	62	44.41 N	6.05 E
Saint-Bonnet-de-Joux	58	46.29 N	4.27 E
Saint-Bonnet-le-Château	62	45.25 N	4.04 E
Saint-Bonnet-le-Froid	62	45.09 N	4.27 E
Saint Boswells	46	55.34 N	2.39 W
Saint Brendan's	186	48.52 N	53.40 W
Saint-Brice-sous-Forêt	261	49.00 N	2.21 E
Saint Bride, Mount ∧	182	51.30 N	115.57 W
Saint Bride's	186	46.55 N	54.10 W
Saint Brides Bay c	42	51.48 N	5.15 W
Saint Bride's Major	42	51.28 N	3.38 W
Saint-Brieuc	32	48.31 N	2.47 W
Saint-Brieux	184	52.38 N	104.52 W
Saint-Broing-Les-Moines, Fr.	58	47.41 N	4.50 E
Saint-Broing-les-Moines, Fr.	58	48.32 N	6.36 E
Saint-Bruno	206	45.32 N	73.21 W
Saint-Bruno, Mont ∧2	275a	45.33 N	73.19 W
Saint-Calais	50	47.55 N	0.45 E
Saint-Calixte-de-Kilkenny	206	45.57 N	73.51 W
Saint-Cannat	62	43.37 N	5.18 E
Saint-Casimir	206	46.40 N	72.08 W
Saint-Cassien, Lac de ⊜1	62	43.35 N	6.48 E
Saint Catharines	212	43.10 N	79.15 W
Saint Catharines Airport ⊠	284a	43.11 N	79.10 W
Saint Catherine	220	28.37 N	82.08 W
Saint Catherine, Monastery of → Qiddīsah Kātrīnā, Dayr al- ᵿ1	140	28.29 N	34.01 E
Saint Catherine, Mount ∧	241k	12.10 N	61.40 W
Sainte-Catherine-de-Fierbois	50	47.09 N	0.39 E
Saint Catherines Island I	192	31.38 N	81.10 W
Saint Catherine's Point ›	42	50.34 N	1.15 W
Saint-Célestin (Annaville)	206	46.13 N	72.26 W
Saint-Céré	32	44.52 N	1.53 E
Saint-Cergue	58	46.27 N	6.09 E
Saint-Césaire	206	45.25 N	73.00 W
Saint-Cézaire-sur-Siagne	62	43.39 N	6.48 E
Saint-Chamas	62	43.33 N	5.02 E
Saint-Chamond	62	45.28 N	4.30 E
Saint-Chaptes	62	43.58 N	4.17 E
Saint Charles, Ar., U.S.	194	34.22 N	91.08 W
Saint Charles, Id., U.S.	202	42.06 N	111.23 W
Saint Charles, Il., U.S.	216	41.54 N	88.18 W
Saint Charles, Md., U.S.	208	38.36 N	76.56 W
Saint Charles, Mi., U.S.	190	43.17 N	84.08 W
Saint Charles, Mn., U.S.	190	43.58 N	92.03 W
Saint Charles, Mo., U.S.	219	38.47 N	90.28 W
Saint Charles □6	219	38.47 N	90.43 W
Saint-Charles ≃	275a	45.40 N	73.27 W
Saint-Charles, Lac ⊜	206	46.55 N	71.23 W
Saint-Charles-de-Drummond	206	45.54 N	72.28 W
Saint Charles Mesa	198	38.15 N	104.32 W
Saint-Charles-sur-Richelieu	206	45.41 N	73.11 W
Saint-Chef	62	45.38 N	5.22 E
Saint-Chély-d'Apcher	32	44.48 N	3.17 E
Saint-Chéron	261	48.33 N	2.07 E
Saint-Christophe-en-Bazelle	50	47.11 N	1.43 E
Saint-Christophe-Nevis → Saint Christopher-Nevis □1	238	17.20 N	62.45 W
Saint Christopher (Saint Kitts) I	238	17.20 N	62.45 W
Saint Christopher-Nevis □1, N.A.	230	17.20 N	62.45 W
Saint Christopher-Nevis □1, N.A.	238	17.20 N	62.45 W
Saint-Chrysostome	206	45.06 N	73.46 W
Saint-Ciers-sur-Gironde	32	45.18 N	0.37 W
Saint Clair, Mi., U.S.	214	42.48 N	82.29 W
Saint Clair, Mo., U.S.	219	38.20 N	90.58 W
Saint Clair, Pa., U.S.	208	40.43 N	76.11 W
Saint Clair, Pa., U.S.	279b	40.16 N	79.33 W
Saint Clair □6, Il., U.S.	219	38.31 N	90.00 W
Saint Clair □6, Mi., U.S.	214	42.50 N	82.42 W
Saint Clair ≃	214	42.37 N	82.31 W
Saint Clair, Lake ⊜	214	42.25 N	82.41 W
Saint Clair Beach	214	42.19 N	82.51 W
Saint Clair Flats	214	42.32 N	82.37 W
Saint Clair Flats ≃	281	42.35 N	82.36 W
Saint Clair Flats Canal ≅	214	42.20 N	82.58 W
Saint Clair Flats State Wildlife Area ♦4	281	42.36 N	82.40 W
Saint Clair Haven	214	42.34 N	82.47 W
Saint Clair Shores	214	42.29 N	82.53 W
Saint-Clair-sur-Epte	50	49.12 N	1.41 E
Saint Clairsville, Oh., U.S.	214	40.04 N	80.54 W
Saint Clairsville, Pa., U.S.	214	40.09 N	78.31 W
Saint Clair Tunnel ♦5	214	42.57 N	82.25 W
Saint-Claud	32	45.53 N	0.23 E
Saint-Claude, Mb., Can.	184	49.40 N	98.22 W
Saint-Claude, Fr.	58	46.23 N	5.52 E
Saint-Claude, Guad.	241o	16.02 N	61.42 W
Saint-Claude, Ruisseau ≃	275a	45.25 N	73.28 W
Saint Clears	42	51.50 N	4.30 W
Saint Clements	212	43.31 N	80.39 W
Saint Clements Bay c	208	38.17 N	76.42 W
Sainte-Clothilde	206	45.59 N	72.14 W
Sainte-Clotilde-de-Châteauguay	206	45.10 N	73.41 W
Saint-Cloud, Fr.	50	48.50 N	2.11 E
Saint Cloud, Fl., U.S.	220	28.14 N	81.16 W
Saint Cloud, Mn., U.S.	190	45.33 N	94.09 W
Saint-Cloud, Parc de ♦	261	48.50 N	2.13 E
Saint-Colomban-des-Villards	62	45.18 N	6.14 E
Saint-Colombe	58	47.52 N	4.32 E
Saint Columb Major	42	50.26 N	5.03 W
Saint Combs	46	57.39 N	1.54 W
Saint-Constant	206	45.22 N	73.37 W
Saint-Cosme-en-Vairais	50	48.16 N	0.28 E
Sainte-Croix, P.Q., Can.	206	46.38 N	71.44 W
Sainte-Croix, Schw.	58	46.49 N	6.31 E
Saint Croix I	241n	17.45 N	64.45 W
Saint Croix ≃, N.A.	186	45.10 N	67.10 W
Saint Croix ≃, U.S.	190	44.45 N	92.49 W
Sainte-Croix-aux-Mines	58	48.16 N	7.13 E
Saint Croix Falls	190	45.24 N	92.38 W
Saint Croix Island I	158	33.48 S	25.45 E
Saint Croix Island National Monument ♦	188	45.08 N	67.08 W
Saint Croix National Scenic Riverway ♦	190	46.00 N	92.25 W
Saint Croix State Park ♦	190	46.00 N	92.40 W
Sainte-Croix-Vallée-Française	62	44.11 N	3.44 E
Saint-Cuthbert	206	46.09 N	73.14 W
Saint-Cyprien	32	44.52 N	1.02 E
Saint-Cyrille-de-Wendover	206	45.56 N	72.26 W
Saint-Cyr-L'École	50	48.48 N	2.04 E
Saint-Cyr-l'École, Aérodrome de ⊠	261	48.49 N	2.04 E
Saint Cyr Range ⩘	180	61.10 N	131.10 W
Sainte-Cyr-sous-Dourdan	261	48.34 N	2.02 E
Saint-Cyr-sur-Loire	50	47.24 N	0.40 E
Saint-Cyr-sur-Mer	62	43.11 N	5.43 E
Saint-Dalmas-de-Tende	62	44.03 N	7.35 E
Saint-Damien-de-Brandon	206	46.20 N	73.29 W
Saint David, Az., U.S.	200	31.54 N	110.12 W
Saint David, Il., U.S.	190	40.29 N	90.02 W
Saint David's, Nf., Can.	186	48.12 N	58.52 W
Saint Davids, On., Can.	284a	43.10 N	79.06 W
Saint David's, Wales, U.K.	42	51.54 N	5.16 W
Saint Davids, Pa., U.S.	285	40.02 N	75.22 W
Saint David's Cathedral ᵿ1	42	51.54 N	5.16 W
Saint David's Head ›	42	51.55 N	5.19 W
Saint David's Island I	240a	32.22 N	64.39 W
Saint Day	42	50.14 N	5.11 W
Saint-Denis, Fr.	50	48.56 N	2.22 E
Saint-Denis, Réu.	157c	20.52 S	55.28 E
Saint-Denis, Basilique ᵿ1	261	48.56 N	2.22 E
Saint-Denis-de-l'Hôtel	50	47.52 N	2.07 E
Saint-Denis-en-Bugey	58	45.57 N	5.20 E
Saint-Denis-Rivière-Richelieu	206	45.47 N	73.09 W
Saint Dennis	42	50.23 N	4.53 W
Saint-Didier-en-Velay	62	45.18 N	4.17 E
Saint-Didier-les-Bains	62	44.00 N	5.07 E
Saint-Dié	58	48.17 N	6.57 E
Saint-Disdier	62	44.44 N	5.54 E
Saint-Dizier	58	48.38 N	4.57 E
Saint Dogmaels	42	52.05 N	4.40 W
Saint-Donat-de-Montcalm	206	46.19 N	74.13 W
Saint-Donat-sur-l'Herbasse	62	45.07 N	5.00 E
Sainte-Dorothée ♦8	275a	45.32 N	73.49 W
Saint-Dyé-sur-Loire	50	47.39 N	1.29 E
Saint-Édouard-de-Maskinongé	206	46.20 N	73.09 W
Saint Edward	198	41.34 N	97.52 W
Saint-Égrève	62	45.14 N	5.41 E
Saint Eleanor's	186	46.25 N	63.49 W
Saint Elias, Cape ›	180	59.52 N	144.30 W
Saint Elias, Mount ∧	180	60.18 N	140.55 W
Saint Elias Mountains ⩘	180	60.30 N	139.30 W
Saint-Élie	250	4.50 N	53.17 W
Saint Elmo	219	39.01 N	88.50 W
Saint-Éloi	186	48.02 N	69.14 W
Saint-Émile-de-Montcalm	206	46.06 N	74.00 W
Saint-Émile-de-Québec	206	46.52 N	71.20 W
Saint-Émile-de-Suffolk	206	45.56 N	74.55 W
Sainte-Enimie	32	44.22 N	3.26 E
Saint-Épain	50	47.08 N	0.32 E
Saint-Esprit ≃	206	45.52 N	73.27 W
Saint-Étienne	62	45.26 N	4.24 E
Saint-Étienne-de-Lugdarès	62	44.39 N	3.57 E
Saint-Étienne-de-Saint-Geoirs	62	45.20 N	5.21 E
Saint-Étienne-des-Grès	206	46.26 N	72.46 W
Saint-Étienne-de-Tinée	62	44.15 N	6.55 E
Saint-Étienne-du-Rouvray	50	49.23 N	1.06 E
Saint-Étienne-en-Dévoluy	62	44.42 N	5.56 E
Saint-Étienne-le-Laus	62	44.30 N	6.10 E
Saint-Étienne-les-Orgues	62	44.03 N	5.47 E
Saint-Étienne-lès-Remiremont	58	48.02 N	6.37 E
Saint-Eugène	206	45.30 N	74.28 W
Saint-Eustache	206	45.34 N	73.54 W
Saint-Evroult-Notre-Dame-du-Bois	50	48.48 N	0.28 E
Saint-Fabien	186	48.18 N	68.52 W
Saint Faith's	158	30.30 S	30.12 E
Saint-Fargeau	50	47.38 N	3.04 E
Saint-Fargeau-Ponthierry	261	48.33 N	2.32 E
Saint-Félicien, P.Q., Can.	176	48.39 N	72.26 W
Saint-Félicien, Fr.	62	45.05 N	4.38 E
Sainte-Félicité	186	48.54 N	67.20 W
Saint-Félix	62	45.48 N	5.58 E
Saint-Félix-de-Kingsey	206	45.48 N	72.12 W
Saint-Félix-de-Valois	206	46.10 N	73.26 W
Saint-Ferdinand (Bernierville)	206	46.06 N	71.34 W
Saintfield	48	54.28 N	5.50 W
Saint Fillans	46	56.23 N	4.07 W
Saint-Firmin	62	44.47 N	6.02 E
Saint-Firmin-sur-Loire	50	47.37 N	2.44 E
Saint-Flavien	206	46.31 N	71.36 W
Saint-Florent	36	42.41 N	9.18 E
Saint-Florentin	50	48.00 N	3.44 E
Saint-Florent-sur-Cher	32	46.59 N	2.15 E
Saint-Floris, Parc National ♦	146	9.40 N	21.35 E
Saint-Flour	32	45.02 N	3.05 E
Saint-Fons	62	45.42 N	4.52 E
Saint-Fortunat	206	45.58 N	71.36 W
Sainte-Foy	206	46.47 N	71.17 W
Sainte-Foy-la-Grande	32	44.50 N	0.13 E
Sainte-Foy-l'Argentière	62	45.42 N	4.28 E
Sainte-Foy-lès-Lyon	62	45.44 N	4.48 E
Sainte-Foy-Tarentaise	62	45.35 N	6.53 E
Saint Francis, Ks., U.S.	198	39.46 N	101.47 W
Saint Francis, S.D., U.S.	198	43.08 N	100.54 W
Saint Francis, Wi., U.S.	216	42.58 N	87.52 W
Saint Francis ≃, N.A.	186	47.10 N	68.57 W
Saint Francis ≃, U.S.	194	34.38 N	90.35 W
Saint Francis, Cape ›, Nf., Can.	186	47.50 N	52.47 W
Saint Francis, Cape ›, S. Afr.	158	34.14 S	24.49 E
Saint Francis, Lake ⊜	206	45.08 N	74.25 W
Saint Francis Bay c	158	34.35 S	25.10 E
Saint Francisville	194	30.46 N	91.22 W
Saint-François	241o	16.15 N	61.17 W
Saint-François ≃	206	46.07 N	72.55 W
Saint-François, Lac ⊜	206	45.55 N	71.10 W
Saint-François de Boundji	152	1.03 S	15.22 E
Saint-François-de-Laval ♦8	275a	45.40 N	73.34 W
Saint-François-du-Lac	206	46.04 N	72.50 W
Saint Francois Mountains ⩘2	194	37.30 N	90.35 W
Saint-François-sur-Bugeon	62	45.24 N	6.21 E
Saint-Front	62	44.59 N	4.08 E
Saint-Gabriel	206	46.17 N	73.23 W
Saint-Gabriel-de-Gaspé	186	48.31 N	64.32 W
Saint-Gabriel-de-Rimouski	186	48.25 N	68.10 W
Saint-Gall → Sankt Gallen	58	47.25 N	9.23 E
Saint-Galmier	62	45.35 N	4.19 E
Sainte-Gauburge-Sainte-Colombe	50	48.42 N	0.26 E
Saint-Gaudens	32	43.07 N	0.44 E
Saint-Gaudens National Historic Site ⊥	188	43.29 N	72.19 W
Saint-Gaultier	32	46.38 N	1.25 E
Saint-Gély-du-Fesc	62	43.42 N	3.48 E
Saint-Genest-Lerpt	62	45.27 N	4.20 E
Saint-Genest-Malifaux	62	45.20 N	4.25 E
Sainte-Geneviève, P.Q., Can.	275a	45.29 N	73.52 W
Sainte Genevieve, Mo., U.S.	194	37.59 N	90.03 W
Sainte-Geneviève-de-Batiscan	206	46.32 N	72.20 W
Sainte-Geneviève-des-Bois	50	48.38 N	2.20 E
Saint-Genis-de-Saintonge	32	45.29 N	0.34 W
Saint-Genis-Laval	62	45.41 N	4.48 E
Saint-Genis-Pouilly	58	46.15 N	6.01 E
Saint-Genix-sur-Guiers	62	45.36 N	5.38 E
Saint-Geoire-en-Valdaine	62	45.27 N	5.38 E
Saint George, Austl.	166	28.02 S	148.35 E
Saint George, Ber.	240a	32.22 N	64.40 W
Saint George, N.B., Can.	186	45.08 N	66.49 W
Saint George, On., Can.	212	43.15 N	80.15 W
Saint George, Pa., U.S.	214	41.15 N	79.47 W
Saint George, S.C., U.S.	192	33.11 N	80.34 W
Saint George, Ut,. U.S.	200	37.06 N	113.34 W
Saint George ♦8	276	40.39 N	74.05 W
Saint George, Cape ›, Nf., Can.	186	48.28 N	59.15 W
Saint George, Cape ›, Pap. N. Gui.	164	4.52 S	152.52 E
Saint George, Cape ›, Fl., U.S.	192	29.35 N	85.04 W
Saint George, Point ›	204	41.47 N	124.15 W
Saint George Island, Ak., U.S.	180	56.36 N	169.32 W
Saint George Island, Md., U.S.	208	38.07 N	76.29 W
Saint George Island I, Ak., U.S.	180	56.35 N	169.35 W
Saint George Island I, Fl., U.S.	192	29.39 N	84.55 W
Saint George's, Nf., Can.	186	48.26 N	58.29 W
Saint-Georges, P.Q., Can.	188	46.07 N	70.40 W
Saint-Georges, P.Q., Can.	206	46.37 N	72.40 W
Saint-Georges, Fr.	58	48.40 N	6.56 E
Saint George's, Gren.	241k	12.03 N	61.45 W
Saint-Georges, Guy. fr.	250	3.54 N	51.48 W
Saint Georges, De., U.S.	208	39.33 N	75.39 W
Saint Georges Basin c	170	35.07 S	150.36 E
Saint George's Bay c, Nf., Can.	186	48.20 N	59.00 W
Saint Georges Bay c, N.S., Can.	186	45.50 N	61.45 W
Saint George's Channel ʊ, Europe	28	52.00 N	6.00 W
Saint George's Channel ʊ, Pap. N. Gui.	164	4.30 S	152.30 E
Saint-Georges-de-Reneins	58	46.04 N	4.43 E
Saint-Georges-de-Windsor	206	45.42 N	71.50 W
Saint-Georges-en-Couzan	62	45.42 N	3.56 E
Saint Georges Head ›	170	35.12 S	150.42 E
Saint George's Island I	240a	32.22 N	64.40 W
Saint George Sound ʊ	192	29.47 N	84.42 W
Saint-Gérard, Bel.	56	50.21 N	4.45 E
Saint-Gérard, P.Q., Can.	206	45.46 N	71.25 W
Saint-Germain	32	48.54 N	2.05 E
Saint-Germain ≃	206	45.55 N	72.30 W
Saint-Germain, Forêt de ♦	261	48.55 N	2.05 E
Saint-Germain-de-Calberte	62	44.13 N	3.48 E
Saint-Germain-de-Grantham	206	45.50 N	72.34 W
Saint-Germain-de-Joux	58	46.11 N	5.44 E
Saint-Germain-des-Champs	50	47.25 N	3.55 E
Saint-Germain-du-Bois	58	46.45 N	5.15 E
Saint-Germain-du-Plain	58	46.42 N	4.58 E
Saint-Germain-en-Laye	50	48.54 N	2.05 E
Saint-Germain-en-Laye, Château de ⊥	261	48.54 N	2.06 E
Saint-Germain-Laval	62	45.50 N	4.01 E
Saint-Germain-Laxis	261	48.35 N	2.43 E
Saint-Germain-Lembron	32	45.28 N	3.14 E
Saint-Germain-lès-Arlay	58	46.46 N	5.34 E
Saint-Germain-lès-Corbeil	261	48.37 N	2.29 E
Saint-Germain-l'Herm	32	45.28 N	3.33 E
Saint-Germain-sur-Morin	261	48.53 N	2.51 E
Saint Germans	42	50.24 N	4.18 W
Saint-Germer-de-Fly	50	49.27 N	1.47 E
Saint-Gervais-d'Auvergne	32	46.02 N	2.49 E
Saint-Gervais-les-Bains	62	45.54 N	6.43 E
Saint-Gervasy	62	43.53 N	4.29 E
Saint-Géry	62	44.29 N	1.35 E
Saint-Gilles, Bel.	50	50.49 N	4.20 E
Saint-Gilles, P.Q., Can.	206	46.31 N	71.22 W
Saint-Gilles, Fr.	62	43.41 N	4.26 E
Saint-Gilles-Croix-de-Vie	32	46.42 N	1.57 W
Saint-Gingolph	58	46.24 N	6.52 E
Saint-Girons	32	42.59 N	1.09 E
Saint-Gobain	50	49.36 N	3.23 E
Saint Gotthard Pass → San Gottardo, Passo del ✕	58	46.33 N	8.34 E
Saint Govan's Head ›	42	51.36 N	4.55 W
Saint-Gratien	261	48.58 N	2.17 E
Saint-Grégoire (Larochelle)	206	46.16 N	72.30 W
Saint Gregory, Mount ∧	186	49.19 N	58.13 W
Saint-Guénolé	32	47.49 N	4.20 W
Saint-Guillaume-d'Upton	206	45.53 N	72.46 W
Saint-Héand	62	45.31 N	4.22 E
Saint Helena	226	38.30 N	122.28 W
Saint Helena □2	10	15.57 S	5.42 W
Saint Helena, Mount ∧	226	38.40 N	122.38 W
Saint Helena Sound ʊ	192	32.27 N	80.25 W
Sainte-Hélène, Île I	275a	45.31 N	73.32 W
Sainte-Hélène-de-Bagot	206	45.44 N	72.44 W
Saint Helens, Austl.	166	41.20 S	148.15 E
Saint Helens, Eng., U.K.	42	50.42 N	1.06 W
Saint Helens, Eng., U.K.	44	53.28 N	2.44 W
Saint Helens, Or., U.S.	224	45.51 N	122.48 W
Saint Helens □8	262	53.28 N	2.45 W
Saint Helens, Mount ∧1	224	46.12 N	122.11 W
Saint Helens Canal ≅	262	53.27 N	2.42 W
Saint Helier	43b	49.11 N	2.06 W
Saint Henry	216	40.25 N	84.38 W
Sainte-Hermine	32	46.33 N	1.04 W
Saint-Hilaire-du-Harcouët	32	48.35 N	1.06 W
Saint-Hilarion	261	48.37 N	1.44 E
Saint-Hippolyte, Fr.	58	47.19 N	6.49 E
Saint-Hippolyte, Fr.	62	43.38 N	4.45 E
Saint-Hippolyte-de-Kilkenny	206	45.56 N	74.01 W
Saint-Hippolyte-du-Fort	62	43.58 N	3.51 E
Saint-Honorat, Mont ∧	62	44.05 N	6.46 E
Saint-Hubert, Bel.	56	50.01 N	5.23 E
Saint-Hubert, P.Q., Can.	206	45.30 N	73.25 W
Saint-Hubert, Étang de ⊜	261	48.43 N	1.51 E
Saint-Hubert-le-Roi	261	48.43 N	1.52 E
Saint-Hugues	206	45.48 N	72.52 W
Saint-Hyacinthe	206	45.37 N	72.57 W
Saint-Hyacinthe □6	206	45.40 N	73.05 W
Saint-Ignace, N.B., Can.	186	46.42 N	65.05 W
Saint Ignace, Mi., U.S.	190	45.52 N	84.43 W
Saint Ignace Island I	190	48.48 N	87.55 W
Saint Ignatius, Guy.	246	3.20 N	59.47 W
Saint Ignatius, Mt., U.S.	202	47.19 N	114.05 W
Saint-Imier	58	47.09 N	7.00 E
Saint-Imier, Vallon de V	58	47.10 N	7.00 E
Saint-Isidore	186	47.33 N	65.03 W
Saint-Isidore-d'Auckland	206	45.16 N	71.31 W
Saint-Isidore-de-Laprairie	275a	45.18 N	73.41 W
Saint Ives, Austl.	274a	33.44 S	151.10 E
Saint Ives, Eng., U.K.	32	50.12 N	5.29 W
Saint Ives, Eng., U.K.	42	52.20 N	0.05 W
Saint Ives Bay c	42	50.14 N	5.28 W
Saint Jacob	219	38.43 N	89.46 W
Saint Jacobs	212	43.32 N	80.33 W
Saint-Jacques	206	45.57 N	73.34 W
Saint-Jacques ≃	275a	45.26 N	73.29 W
Saint James, Il., U.S.	219	38.57 N	88.51 W
Saint James, Mi., U.S.	190	45.45 N	85.30 W
Saint James, Mn., U.S.	198	43.58 N	94.37 W
Saint James, Mo., U.S.	194	37.59 N	91.36 W
Saint James, N.Y., U.S.	210	40.52 N	73.09 W
Saint James, Cape ›	182	51.56 N	131.01 W
Saint James City	220	26.29 N	82.04 W
Saint James Islands II	240m	18.19 N	64.50 W
Saint James Palace ᵿ	260	51.30 N	0.08 W
Saint-Janvier	275a	45.43 N	73.56 W
Saint-Jean □6	206	45.15 N	73.20 W
Saint-Jean ≃, P.Q., Can.	186	48.46 N	64.26 W
Saint-Jean ≃, P.Q., Can.	186	50.17 N	64.20 W
Saint-Jean, Île I	275a	45.41 N	73.39 W
Saint-Jean, Lac ⊜	176	48.35 N	72.05 W
Saint-Jean, Rapides de ⊔	275a	45.19 N	73.15 W
Saint-Jean Airport ⊠	275a	45.18 N	73.17 W
Saint-Jean-aux-Bois	50	49.21 N	2.55 E
Saint-Jean-Baptiste	184	49.16 N	97.21 W
Saint-Jean-Baptiste-de-Rouville	206	45.31 N	73.07 W
Saint-Jean-Cap-Ferrat	62	43.41 N	7.20 E
Saint-Jean-d'Angély	32	45.57 N	0.31 W
Saint-Jean-d'Assé	50	48.09 N	0.07 E
Saint-Jean-de-Bournay	62	45.29 N	5.08 E
Saint-Jean-de-Braye	50	47.54 N	1.58 E
Saint-Jean-de-la-Ruelle	50	47.55 N	1.52 E
Saint-Jean-de-Losne	58	47.06 N	5.15 E
Saint-Jean-de-Luz	32	43.23 N	1.40 W
Saint-Jean-de-Maurienne	62	45.17 N	6.21 E
Saint-Jean-de-Monts	32	46.48 N	2.03 W
Saint-Jean-des-Piles	206	46.41 N	72.45 W
Saint-Jean-du-Gard	62	44.06 N	3.53 E
Saint-Jean-en-Royans	62	45.01 N	5.18 E
Saint-Jean-Pied-de-Port	32	43.10 N	1.14 W
Saint-Jean-Port-Joli	186	47.13 N	70.16 W
Saint-Jean-Soleymieux	62	45.30 N	4.02 E
Saint-Jean-sur-Richelieu	206	45.19 N	73.16 W
Saint-Jeoire	58	46.09 N	6.28 E
Saint-Jérôme	206	45.47 N	74.00 W
Saint Jo	196	33.41 N	97.31 W
Saint Joachim	214	42.16 N	82.38 W
Saint Joe	216	41.18 N	84.54 W
Saint Joe ≃	202	47.21 N	116.42 W
Saint John, N.B., Can.	186	45.16 N	66.03 W
Saint John, Jersey	43b	49.15 N	2.08 W
Saint John, In., U.S.	216	41.27 N	87.28 W
Saint John, Ks., U.S.	198	38.00 N	98.45 W
Saint John, N.D., U.S.	198	48.56 N	99.42 W
Saint John, Wa., U.S.	202	47.05 N	117.34 W
Saint John I	240m	18.20 N	64.45 W
Saint John ≃, Liber.	150	6.40 N	9.10 W
Saint John ≃, N.A.	186	45.15 N	66.04 W
Saint John, Cape ›	186	50.00 N	55.32 W
Saint John, Lake ⊜, Nf., Can.	186	48.23 N	54.41 W
Saint John, Lake ⊜, On., Can.	212	44.41 N	79.20 W
Saint John Bay c	186	50.54 N	57.08 W
Saint John Island I	186	50.49 N	57.14 W
Saint Johns, Antig.	240c	17.06 N	61.51 W
Saint John's, Nf., Can.	186	47.34 N	52.43 W
Saint Johns → Saint-Jean-sur-Richelieu	206	45.19 N	73.16 W
Saint John's, I. of Man	44	54.13 N	4.38 W
Saint Johns, Az., U.S.	200	34.30 N	109.21 W
Saint Johns, Mi., U.S.	216	43.00 N	84.33 W
Saint Johns, Mo., U.S.	219	38.42 N	90.20 W
Saint Johns, Oh., U.S.	216	40.33 N	84.05 W
Saint Johns ≃, Ca., U.S.	226	36.25 N	119.25 W
Saint Johns ≃, Fl., U.S.	192	30.24 N	81.24 W
Saint Johnsburg	210	43.05 N	78.53 W
Saint Johnsbury	188	44.25 N	72.00 W
Saint Johns Creek ≃	219	38.34 N	91.01 W
Saint John's Jerusalem ⊥	260	51.25 N	0.14 E
Saint Johns Marsh ≃	220	27.45 N	80.40 W
Saint John's Point ›	48	54.13 N	5.40 W
Saint John's University ᵿ2	276	40.43 N	73.48 W
Saint Johnsville	210	42.59 N	74.41 W
Saint Joseph, N.B., Can.	186	45.59 N	64.34 W
Saint Joseph, Dom.	240d	15.26 N	61.26 W
Saint Joseph, Mart.	240e	14.40 N	61.03 W
Saint Joseph, N. Cal.	175f	20.27 S	166.36 E
Saint-Joseph, Réu.	157c	21.22 S	55.36 E
Saint Joseph, Il., U.S.	194	40.06 N	88.02 W
Saint Joseph, La., U.S.	194	31.55 N	91.14 W
Saint Joseph, Mi., U.S.	216	42.05 N	86.29 W
Saint Joseph, Mn., U.S.	190	45.33 N	94.19 W
Saint Joseph, Mo., U.S.	194	39.46 N	94.50 W
Saint Joseph, Tn., U.S.	194	35.02 N	87.30 W
Saint Joseph □6, In., U.S.	216	41.41 N	86.15 W
Saint Joseph □6, Mi., U.S.	216	41.55 N	85.31 W
Saint Joseph ≃, U.S.	216	41.05 N	85.08 W
Saint Joseph ≃, U.S.	216	42.06 N	86.29 W
Saint Joseph, East Branch ≃	216	41.39 N	84.34 W
Saint-Joseph, Lac ⊜	206	46.54 N	71.38 W
Saint Joseph, Lake ⊜	176	51.05 N	90.35 W
Saint Joseph, West Branch ≃	216	41.39 N	84.34 W
Saint Joseph Bay c	192	29.47 N	85.21 W
Saint Joseph Channel ʊ	190	46.19 N	84.04 W
Saint-Joseph-d'Alma → Alma	186	48.33 N	71.39 W
Saint-Joseph-de-Beauce	186	46.18 N	70.53 W
Saint-Joseph-de-Mékinac	206	46.55 N	72.42 W
Saint-Joseph-de-Sorel	206	46.02 N	73.07 W
Saint-Joseph-du-Lac	275a	45.32 N	74.00 W
Saint Joseph Island I	190	46.13 N	83.57 W
Saint Joseph's University ᵿ2	285	40.00 N	75.14 W
Saint-Jouin-Bruneval	50	49.39 N	0.10 E
Saint-Jovite	206	46.07 N	74.36 W
Sainte-Julie	206	45.35 N	73.19 W
Saint-Julien	58	46.23 N	5.27 E
Saint-Julien-Chapteuil	62	45.02 N	4.04 E
Saint-Julien-du-Sault	50	48.02 N	3.18 E
Saint-Julien-du-Verdon	62	43.55 N	6.32 E
Saint-Julien-en-Beauchêne	62	44.37 N	5.42 E
Saint-Julien-en-Born	32	44.04 N	1.14 W
Saint-Julien-en-Genevois	58	46.08 N	6.05 E
Saint-Julien-en-Jarez	62	45.28 N	4.31 E
Saint-Julien-les-Villas	50	48.16 N	4.06 E
Saint-Julien-Molin-Molette	62	45.19 N	4.37 E
Sainte-Julienne	206	45.58 N	73.43 W
Saint-Junien	32	45.53 N	0.54 E
Saint Just, P.R.	240m	18.23 N	66.00 W
Saint Just, Eng., U.K.	42	50.07 N	5.42 W
Saint-Just-en-Chaussée	50	49.30 N	2.26 E
Saint-Just-en-Chevalet	32	45.55 N	3.50 E
Saint-Justin	206	46.15 N	73.05 W
Saint-Just-Malmont	62	45.20 N	4.19 E
Saint-Just-sur-Loire	62	45.29 N	4.16 E
Saint Keverne	42	50.03 N	5.06 W
Saint Kilda, Austl.	168b	34.44 S	138.32 E
Saint Kilda, Austl.	169	37.52 S	144.59 E
Saint Kilda, N.Z.	172	45.54 S	170.30 E
Saint Kilda I	28	57.49 N	8.36 W
Saint Kitts	168b	34.21 S	139.04 E
Saint Kitts → Saint Christopher I	238	17.20 N	62.45 W
Saint-Lambert, P.Q., Can.	206	45.30 N	73.30 W
Saint-Lambert, Fr.	261	48.44 N	2.01 E
Saint Landry	194	30.50 N	92.15 W
Saint-Laurent, Mb., Can.	184	50.24 N	97.56 W
Saint-Laurent, P.Q., Can.	206	45.30 N	73.40 W
Saint-Laurent, Fr.	58	48.09 N	6.27 E
Saint-Laurent → Saint Lawrence ≃	176	49.30 N	67.00 W
Saint-Laurent-Blangy	50	50.18 N	2.48 E
Saint-Laurent-de-Chamousset	62	45.44 N	4.28 E
Saint-Laurent-du-Maroni	250	5.30 N	54.02 W
Saint-Laurent du Maroni □8	250	4.00 N	53.30 W
Saint-Laurent-du-Pont	62	45.23 N	5.44 E
Saint-Laurent-du-Var	62	43.40 N	7.11 E
Saint-Laurent-en-Caux	50	49.45 N	0.53 E
Saint-Laurent-en-Grandvaux	58	46.35 N	5.57 E
Saint-Laurent-et-Benon	32	45.09 N	0.49 W
Saint-Laurent-les-Bains	62	44.37 N	3.58 E
Saint-Laurent-sur-Saône	58	46.18 N	4.50 E
Saint Lawrence, Austl.	166	22.21 S	149.31 E
Saint Lawrence, Nf., Can.	186	46.55 N	55.24 W
Saint Lawrence □6	212	44.30 N	75.27 W
Saint Lawrence ≃	176	49.30 N	67.00 W
Saint Lawrence, Cape ›	186	47.03 N	60.37 W
Saint Lawrence, Gulf of c	186	48.00 N	62.00 W
Saint Lawrence, Lake ⊜	206	44.56 N	75.04 W
Saint Lawrence Island I	180	63.30 N	170.30 W
Saint Lawrence Islands National Park ♦	212	44.18 N	76.08 W
Saint Lawrence Seaway ≅	275a	45.43 N	73.25 W
Saint-Lazare	184	50.26 N	101.16 W
Saint-Lazare, Gare ♦5	261	48.53 N	2.20 E
Saint-Léandre	186	48.44 N	67.36 W
Saint-Léger-en-Yvelines	261	48.43 N	1.46 E
Saint-Léger-sur-Dheune	58	46.51 N	4.38 E
Saint Leo	220	28.20 N	82.15 W
Saint Leon	218	39.17 N	84.57 W
Saint-Léonard, N.B., Can.	186	47.10 N	67.56 W
Saint-Léonard, P.Q., Can.	206	45.35 N	73.35 W
Saint Leonard, Md., U.S.	208	38.28 N	76.30 W
Saint-Léonard-d'Aston	206	46.06 N	72.22 W
Saint-Léonard-de-Noblat	32	45.50 N	1.29 E
Saint Leonards, Eng., U.K.	42	50.51 N	0.34 E
Saint Leonards, Eng., U.K.	42	50.49 N	1.51 W
Saint-Leu-d'Esserent	50	49.13 N	2.25 E
Saint-Leu-la-Forêt	50	49.01 N	2.15 E
Saint-Liboire	206	45.39 N	72.46 W
Saint-Lô	32	49.07 N	1.05 W
Saint-Louis, Sk., Can.	184	52.56 N	105.49 W
Saint-Louis, Fr.	58	47.35 N	7.34 E
Saint-Louis, Guad.	241o	15.57 N	61.19 W
Saint-Louis, Réu.	157c	21.16 S	55.25 E
Saint-Louis, Sén.	150	16.02 N	16.30 W
Saint Louis, Mi., U.S.	190	43.24 N	84.36 W
Saint Louis, Mo., U.S.	219	38.37 N	90.11 W
Saint Louis, Tx., U.S.	222	32.18 N	95.20 W
Saint-Louis □4	150	16.00 N	14.30 W
Saint Louis □6	219	38.39 N	90.25 W
Saint-Louis ≃, P.Q., Can.	275a	45.19 N	73.53 W
Saint Louis ≃, U.S.	190	46.45 N	92.06 W
Saint-Louis, Baie de c	241o	15.57 N	61.20 W
Saint-Louis, Lac ⊜	206	45.24 N	73.48 W
Saint-Louis, Pointe ›	275a	45.19 N	73.53 W
Saint Louis Crossing	218	39.19 N	85.51 W
Saint-Louis-de-Champlain	206	46.25 N	72.36 W
Saint-Louis-de-Kent	186	46.44 N	64.58 W
Saint Louis Park	190	44.56 N	93.20 W
Saint Louisville	214	40.10 N	82.25 W
Saint-Loup-sur-Aujon	58	47.53 N	5.05 E
Saint-Loup-sur-Semouse	58	47.53 N	6.16 E
Saint-Luc, P.Q., Can.	206	45.22 N	73.18 W
Saint-Luc, Schw.	58	46.13 N	7.36 E
Sainte-Luce	240e	14.28 N	60.56 W
Saint Lucia □1, N.A.	230	13.53 N	60.58 W
Saint Lucia □1, N.A.	241f	13.53 N	60.58 W
Saint Lucia, Cape ›	158	28.25 S	32.25 E

Symbols in the index entries represent the broad categories identified in the key at the right. Symbols with superior numbers (⩘1) identify subcategories (see complete key on page *I · 1).*

Symbole im Register stellen die rechts im Schlüssel erklärten Kategorien dar. Symbole mit hochgestellten Ziffern (⩘1) bezeichnen Unterabteilungen einer Kategorie (vgl. vollständiger Schlüssel auf Seite *I · 1).*

Los símbolos incluidos en el texto del índice representan las grandes categorías identificadas con la clave a la derecha. Los símbolos con numeros en su parte superior (⩘1) identifican las subcategorías (véase la clave completa en la página *I · 1).*

Les symboles de l'index représentent les catégories indiquées dans la légende à droite. Les symboles suivis d'un indice (⩘1) représentent des sous-catégories (voir légende complète à la page *I · 1).*

Os símbolos incluídos no texto do índice representam as grandes categorias identificadas com a chave à direita. Os símbolos com números em sua parte superior (⩘1) identificam as subcategorias (veja-se a chave completa à página *I · 1).*

ENGLISH	DEUTSCH			
∧ Mountain	Berg	Montaña	Montagne	Montanha
⩘ Mountains	Gebirge	Montañas	Montagnes	Montanhas
✕ Pass	Paß	Paso	Col	Passo
V Valley, Canyon	Tal, Cañon	Valle, Cañón	Vallée, Canyon	Vale, Canhão
⩦ Plain	Ebene	Llano	Plaine	Planície
› Cape	Kap	Cabo	Cap	Cabo
I Island	Insel	Isla	Île	Ilha
II Islands	Inseln	Islas	Îles	Ilhas
⊥ Other Topographic Features	Andere Topographische Objekte	Otros Elementos Topográficos	Autres données topographiques	Outros acidentes topográficos

ESPAÑOL

Nombre	Página	Lat.°′	Long.°′ W = Oeste
Saint Lucia, Lake ⬚	158	28.05 S	32.26 E
Saint Lucia Channel ṵ	238	14.09 N	60.57 W
Saint Lucia Estuary	158	28.22 S	32.25 E
Saint Lucia Game Reserve ⬧4	158	28.10 S	32.28 E
Sainte-Lucie, Fr.	36	41.42 N	9.22 E
Saint Lucie, Fl., U.S.	220	27.29 N	80.20 W
Saint Lucie ⬚6	220	27.23 N	80.26 W
Saint Lucie Canal ᴸ	220	27.10 N	80.15 W
Saint Lucie Inlet ᴄ	220	27.10 N	80.10 W
Saint Lucie Lock ⬥5	220	27.07 N	80.17 W
Saint-Lucien	261	48.39 N	1.38 E
Saint-Lupicin	58	46.24 N	5.47 E
Sainte-Magnance	50	47.27 N	4.04 E
Saint Magnus Bay c	46a	60.24 N	1.34 W
Saint Magnus Cathedral ⬧1	46	58.58 N	2.57 W
Saint-Malo, P.Q., Can.	206	45.12 N	71.30 W
Saint-Malo, Fr.	32	48.39 N	2.01 W
Saint-Malo, Golfe de c	32	48.45 N	2.00 W
Saint-Mamert-du-Gard	62	43.53 N	4.12 E
Saint-Mammès	50	48.23 N	2.49 E
Saint-Mandé	261	48.50 N	2.25 E
Saint-Mandrier-sur-Mer	62	43.04 N	5.56 E
Saint-Marc	238	19.07 N	72.42 W
Saint-Marc, Canal de ṵ	238	18.50 N	72.45 W
Saint-Marc-des-Carrières	206	46.41 N	72.03 W
Saint-Marcel	58	46.47 N	4.54 E
Saint-Marcellin	62	45.09 N	5.19 E
Saint-Marcelline-de-Kildare	206	46.07 N	73.36 W
Saint-Marc-sur-Richelieu	275a	45.41 N	73.12 W
Saint-Mard	261	49.02 N	2.42 E
Saint Margaret Bay c	186	51.01 N	56.58 W
Saint Margaret's at Cliffe	42	51.09 N	1.24 E
Saint Margarets Bay c	186	44.35 N	64.00 W
Saint Margaret's Hope	46	58.49 N	2.57 W
Sainte-Marguerite, Fr.	176	50.09 N	66.36 W
Sainte-Marguerite, Baie c	206	50.06 N	66.36 W
Sainte-Marguerite-sur-Mer	50	49.55 N	0.57 E
Sainte-Marie	240e	14.47 N	61.00 W
Sainte-Marie, Cap ⧽	157b	25.36 S	45.08 E
Sainte-Marie-aux-Mines (Markirch)	58	48.15 N	7.11 E
Saint Maries	202	47.18 N	116.33 W
Saint Maries ≃	202	47.19 N	116.33 W
Saint-Marin → San Marino ⬚	66	43.56 N	12.25 E
Saint Marks, S. Afr.	158	32.01 S	27.22 E
Saint Marks, Fl., U.S.	192	30.09 N	84.12 W
Saint Marks ≃	192	30.08 N	84.12 W
Sainte-Marthe-de-Gaspé	186	49.12 N	66.10 W
Sainte-Marthe-sur-le-Lac	275a	45.32 N	73.56 W
Saint-Martin (Sint Maarten) I	238	18.04 N	63.04 W
Saint-Martin, Cap ⧽	240e	14.52 N	61.13 W
Saint-Martin, Lake ⬚	184	51.37 N	98.29 W
Saint-Martin-Boulogne	50	50.43 N	1.38 E
Saint-Martin-d'Ardèche	62	44.18 N	4.35 E
Saint-Martin-d'Auxigny	50	47.12 N	2.25 E
Saint-Martin-de-Belleville	62	45.23 N	6.30 E
Saint-Martin-de-Bossenay	50	48.26 N	3.41 E
Saint-Martin-de-Bréthencourt	261	48.31 N	1.56 E
Saint-Martin-de-Crau	62	43.38 N	4.49 E
Saint-Martin-de-Londres	62	43.47 N	3.44 E
Saint-Martin-de-Nigelles	261	48.37 N	1.37 E
Saint-Martin-d'Entraunes	62	44.08 N	6.46 E
Saint-Martin-des-Champs	261	48.53 N	1.43 E
Saint-Martin-de-Valamas	62	44.56 N	4.22 E
Saint-Martin-d'Hères	62	45.10 N	5.46 E
Saint-Martin-du-Puy	50	47.20 N	3.52 E
Saint-Martin-du-Tertre	261	49.06 N	2.21 E
Saint-Martin-du-Var	62	43.49 N	7.12 E
Sainte-Martine	206	45.15 N	73.48 W
Saint-Martin-en-Bresse	58	46.49 N	5.04 E
Saint-Martin-la-Garenne	261	49.02 N	1.41 E
Saint-Martin-la-Plaine	62	45.32 N	4.36 E
Saint Martins, N.B., Can.	186	45.21 N	65.32 W
Saint Martin's, Eng., U.K.	42a	52.55 N	2.59 W
Saint Martin's I	42a	49.58 N	6.20 W
Saint Martins Keys II	220	28.47 N	82.44 W
Saint-Martin-Vésubie	62	44.04 N	7.15 E
Saint Martinville	194	30.07 N	91.49 W
Saint Mary	194	37.52 N	89.58 W
Saint Mary ≃, B.C., Can.	182	49.37 N	115.38 W
Saint Mary ≃, N.A.	182	49.37 N	112.52 W
Saint Mary, Cape ⧽	150	13.28 N	16.40 W
Saint Mary, Mount ⩓	164	8.10 S	147.00 E
Saint Mary Bourne	42	51.16 N	1.24 W
Saint Mary Cray ⬥8	260	51.23 N	0.07 E
Saint Mary Lake ⬚	202	48.40 N	113.30 W
Saint Marylebone ⬥	260	51.31 N	0.10 W
Saint Mary of the Lake Seminary ⬧2	278	42.17 N	88.00 W
Saint Mary Peak ⩓	166	31.30 S	138.33 E
Saint Mary Reservoir ⬚1	182	49.19 N	113.12 W
Saint Marys, Austl.	166	41.35 S	148.10 E
Saint Marys, Austl.	170	33.47 S	150.47 E
Saint Mary's, Nf., Can.	186	46.55 N	53.34 W
Saint Mary's, On., Can.	212	43.16 N	81.08 W
Saint Marys, Ak., U.S.	180	62.04 N	163.10 W
Saint Marys, Ga., U.S.	192	30.43 N	81.32 W
Saint Marys, Ks., U.S.	198	39.11 N	96.04 W
Saint Marys, Oh., U.S.	198	40.32 N	84.23 W
Saint Marys, Pa., U.S.	214	41.26 N	78.33 W
Saint Marys, W.V., U.S.	188	39.23 N	81.12 W
Saint Mary's I	42a	49.55 N	6.18 W
Saint Marys ≃, N.S., Can.	186	45.02 N	61.54 W
Saint Marys ≃, N.A.	192	30.44 N	81.33 W
Saint Marys ≃, U.S.	192	30.43 N	81.27 W
Saint Marys ≃, U.S.	216	41.05 N	85.08 W
Saint Mary's, Cape ⧽, Nf., Can.	186	46.49 N	54.12 W
Saint Marys, Cape ⧽, N.S., Can.	186	44.05 N	66.13 W

FRANÇAIS

Nom	Page	Lat.°′	Long.°′ W = Ouest
Saint Marys, North Prong ≃	192	30.22 N	82.06 W
Saint Marys, South Prong ≃	192	30.22 N	82.06 W
Saint Mary's Bay	42	51.00 N	0.58 E
Saint Mary's Bay c, Nf., Can.	186	46.50 N	53.47 W
Saint Marys Bay c, N.S., Can.	186	44.25 N	66.10 W
Saint Marys City	208	38.11 N	76.26 W
Saint Mary's Hoo	260	51.28 N	0.36 E
Saint Marys Lake ⬚	278	42.17 N	87.59 W
Saint Mary's Marshes ⩵	260	51.28 N	0.35 E
Saint-Mathieu	32	45.42 N	0.46 E
Saint-Mathieu, Pointe de ⧽	32	48.20 N	4.46 W
Saint-Mathieu-de-Laprairie	275a	45.19 N	73.31 W
Saint Matthew Island	180	60.30 N	172.45 W
Saint Matthews, Ky., U.S.	218	38.15 N	85.39 W
Saint Matthews, S.C., U.S.	192	33.39 N	80.46 W
Saint Matthias Group II	164	1.30 S	149.40 E
Saint-Maur-des-Fossés	50	48.48 N	2.30 E
Sainte-Maure-de-Touraine	32	47.07 N	0.37 E
Saint-Maurice, Fr.	261	48.49 N	2.25 E
Saint-Maurice, Schw.	58	46.13 N	7.00 E
Saint-Maurice ≃6	206	46.35 N	73.00 W
Saint-Maurice ≃	176	46.21 N	72.31 W
Saint-Maurice, Parc de ⬤	206	46.52 N	73.10 W
Saint-Maurice-en-Montagne	58	46.34 N	5.50 E
Saint-Maurice-Montcouronne	261	48.35 N	2.07 E
Saint Mawes	42	50.09 N	5.01 W
Saint Mawgan	42	50.28 N	4.58 W
Saint-Max	58	48.42 N	6.13 E
Sainte-Maxime	62	43.18 N	6.38 E
Saint-Maximin-la-Sainte-Baume	62	43.27 N	5.52 E
Saint-Méen-le-Grand	32	48.11 N	2.12 W
Saint Meinrad	194	38.10 N	86.48 W
Sainte-Menehould	56	49.05 N	4.54 E
Saint-Menges	56	49.44 N	4.56 E
Sainte-Mère-Église	32	49.25 N	1.19 W
Saint Merryn	42	50.31 N	4.58 W
Saint-Méry	261	48.35 N	2.50 E
Sainte-Mesme	261	48.32 N	1.58 E
Saint-Mesmes	261	48.59 N	2.42 E
Saint Michael, Ak., U.S.	180	63.29 N	162.02 W
Saint Michael, Pa., U.S.	214	40.20 N	78.46 W
Saint Michaels	208	38.47 N	76.13 W
Saint-Michel, Fr.	62	49.55 N	4.08 E
Saint-Michel, Fr.	62	43.13 N	6.28 E
Saint-Michel ⬥8	275a	45.35 N	73.35 W
Saint-Michel-de-Napierville	206	45.14 N	73.34 W
Saint-Michel-des-Saints	206	46.41 N	73.55 W
Saint-Michel-sur-Meurthe	58	48.19 N	6.54 E
Saint-Michel-sur-Orge	261	48.38 N	2.18 E
Saint-Mihiel	58	48.54 N	5.33 E
Saint Monance	46	56.12 N	2.46 W
Sainte-Monique-des-Deux-Montagnes	275a	45.46 N	74.00 W
Sainte-Montaine	50	47.29 N	2.19 E
Saint-Moritz → Sankt Moritz	58	46.30 N	9.50 E
Saint-Narcisse	206	46.34 N	72.28 W
Saint-Nazaire	32	47.17 N	2.12 W
Saint-Nazaire-les-Royans	62	45.04 N	5.15 E
Saint-Nazaire-le-Désert	62	44.34 N	5.17 E
Saint Nazianz	190	44.00 N	87.55 W
Saint Neots	42	52.14 N	0.17 W
Saint-Nicéphore	206	45.50 N	72.25 W
Saint-Nicolas → Sint-Niklaas, Bel.	50	51.10 N	4.08 E
Saint-Nicolas, Bel.	50	50.38 N	5.32 E
Saint-Nicolas, P.Q., Can.	206	46.42 N	71.24 W
Saint-Nicolas-aux-Bois	50	49.36 N	3.25 E
Saint-Nicolas-d'Aliermont	50	49.53 N	1.13 E
Saint-Nizier-du-Moucherotte	62	45.10 N	5.38 E
Saint-Nom-la-Bretèche	261	48.51 N	2.01 E
Saint Nora Lake ⬚	212	45.08 N	78.49 W
Saint-Norbert-d'Arthabaska	206	46.07 N	71.50 W
Sainte-Odile ⬥1	58	48.26 N	7.24 E
Saint-Omer	50	50.45 N	2.15 E
Saintonge ⬚9	32	45.30 N	0.30 W
Saint-Ouen, Fr.	50	50.02 N	2.03 E
Saint-Ouen, Fr.	261	48.54 N	2.20 E
Saint-Ouen-l'Aumône	50	49.03 N	2.06 E
Saint-Pacôme	186	47.24 N	69.57 W
Saint-Pamphile	186	46.58 N	69.47 W
Saint-Pancras ⬥8	260	51.32 N	0.07 W
Saint Pancras Station ⬥	260	51.32 N	0.08 W
Saint Paris	218	40.07 N	83.57 W
Saint-Pascal	186	47.32 N	69.49 W
Saint-Paterne	50	48.24 N	0.07 E
Saint-Pathus	261	49.04 N	2.48 E
Saint-Patrice, Lac ⬚	190	46.22 N	77.20 W
Saint Paul, Ab., Can.	182	53.59 N	111.17 W
Saint-Paul, Fr.	62	43.42 N	7.07 E
Saint-Paul, Réu.	157c	21.00 S	55.16 E
Saint Paul, In., U.S.	218	39.26 N	85.28 W
Saint Paul, Ks., U.S.	198	37.31 N	95.10 W
Saint Paul, Mn., U.S.	190	44.57 N	93.05 W
Saint Paul, Ne., U.S.	198	41.13 N	98.27 W
Saint Paul, Or., U.S.	224	45.13 N	122.58 W
Saint Paul, Va., U.S.	192	36.54 N	82.18 W
Saint-Paul ≃, Liber.	150	6.23 N	10.48 W
Saint-Paul, Cape ⧽	150	5.49 N	0.57 E
Saint-Paul, Île I	6	38.43 S	77.29 E
Saint-Paul, Lac ⬚	206	46.18 N	72.29 W
Saint-Paul-du-Var	62	43.42 N	7.07 E
Saint-Paul-et-Valmalle	62	43.38 N	3.40 E
Saint-Paulien	62	45.08 N	3.49 E
Saint Paul Island I	180	57.07 N	170.17 W
Saint Paul Island I, N.S., Can.	186	47.15 N	60.10 W
Saint Paul Island I, Ak., U.S.	180	57.10 N	170.15 W
Saint-Paul-Trois-Châteaux	62	44.21 N	4.46 E
Saint-Péravy-la-Colombe	50	48.00 N	1.42 E
Saint-Péray	62	44.57 N	4.50 E
Saint-Père	50	47.28 N	3.46 E
Saint Peter, II., U.S.	219	38.52 N	88.51 W

PORTUGUÊS

Nome	Página	Lat.°′	Long.°′ W = Oeste
Saint Peter, Mn., U.S.	190	44.19 N	93.57 W
Saint Peter, Lake ⬚	212	45.18 N	78.02 W
Saint Peter Island I	162	32.17 S	133.35 E
Saint Peter Port	43b	49.27 N	2.32 W
Saint Peters, N.S., Can.	186	45.40 N	60.52 W
Saint Peters, Mo., U.S.	219	38.48 N	90.37 W
Saint Peters, Pa., U.S.	285	40.11 N	75.44 W
Saint Peters Bay	186	46.25 N	62.35 W
Saint Petersburg → Leningrad, S.S.S.R.	76	59.55 N	30.15 E
Saint Petersburg, Fl., U.S.	220	27.46 N	82.40 W
Saint Petersburg, Pa., U.S.	214	41.10 N	79.37 W
Saint Petersburg Beach	220	27.43 N	82.44 W
Saint Peter's College ⊥	276	40.44 N	74.05 W
Saint-Philippe-d'Argenteuil	206	45.37 N	74.25 W
Saint-Philippe-de-Laprairie	275a	45.21 N	73.28 W
Saint-Pie	206	45.30 N	72.54 W
Saint-Pierre, P.Q., Can.	275a	45.27 N	73.39 W
Saint-Pierre, Fr.	62	45.40 N	3.45 E
Saint-Pierre, It.	62	45.42 N	7.14 E
Saint-Pierre, Mart.	240e	14.45 N	61.11 W
Saint-Pierre, Réu.	157c	21.19 S	55.29 E
Saint-Pierre, St. P./M.	186	46.47 N	56.11 W
Saint-Pierre I	186	46.47 N	56.11 W
Saint-Pierre ≃	275a	45.23 N	73.34 W
Saint-Pierre, Lac ⬚, P.Q., Can.	186	50.08 N	68.26 W
Saint-Pierre, Lac ⬚, P.Q., Can.	186	46.12 N	72.52 W
Saint-Pierre, Rade de c3	240e	14.44 N	61.11 W
Saint Pierre and Miquelon (Saint-Pierre-et-Miquelon) □2, N.A.	176	46.55 N	56.20 W
Saint Pierre and Miquelon (Saint-Pierre-et-Miquelon) □2, N.A.	186	46.55 N	56.20 W
Saint-Pierre-d'Albigny	62	45.34 N	6.09 E
Saint-Pierre-de-Bœuf	62	45.22 N	4.45 E
Saint-Pierre-de-Broughton	206	46.15 N	71.12 W
Saint-Pierre-de-Chartreuse	62	45.20 N	5.49 E
Saint-Pierre-des-Corps	50	47.23 N	0.44 E
Saint-Pierre-de-Vauquière	62	43.52 N	4.13 E
Saint-Pierre-du-Vauvray	50	49.14 N	1.13 E
Saint-Pierre-Église	32	49.40 N	1.24 W
Saint-Pierre-en-Port	50	49.48 N	0.29 E
Saint-Pierre-et-Miquelon → Saint Pierre and Miquelon □2	186	46.55 N	56.20 W
Saint Pierre Island I	138	9.19 S	50.43 E
Saint-Pierre-Jolys	184	49.26 N	96.59 W
Saint-Pierre-le-Moûtier	32	46.48 N	3.07 E
Saint-Pierre-lès-Elbeuf	50	49.16 N	1.03 E
Saint-Pierre-sur-Dives	28	49.01 N	0.02 W
Saint-Pierreville	62	44.49 N	4.29 E
Saint-Point, Lac de ⬚	58	46.49 N	6.19 E
Saint-Pol-de-Léon	32	48.41 N	3.59 W
Saint-Pol-sur-Mer	50	51.02 N	2.21 E
Saint-Pol-sur-Ternoise	50	50.23 N	2.20 E
Saint-Polycarpe	206	45.18 N	74.18 W
Saint-Pons	32	43.29 N	2.46 E
Saint-Pourçain-sur-Sioule	32	46.19 N	3.17 E
Saint-Prex	58	46.29 N	6.28 E
Saint-Priest	62	45.42 N	4.57 E
Saint-Priest-en-Jarez	261	45.28 N	4.22 E
Saint-Prix	261	49.01 N	2.16 E
Saint-Prosper-de-Dorchester	188	46.13 N	70.29 W
Saint-Quentin, N.B., Can.	186	47.30 N	67.23 W
Saint-Quentin, Fr.	50	49.51 N	3.17 E
Saint-Quentin, Canal de ᴸ	50	49.36 N	3.11 E
Saint-Quentin, Étang de ⬚	261	48.47 N	2.01 E
Saint-Rambert-d'Albon	62	45.17 N	4.49 E
Saint-Rambert-en-Bugey	62	45.57 N	5.26 E
Saint-Rambert-sur-Loire	62	45.30 N	4.15 E
Saint-Raphaël	62	43.25 N	6.46 E
Saint-Raymond	206	46.54 N	71.50 W
Saint-Rédempter-de-Lévis	206	46.42 N	71.17 W
Saint Regis ≃	207	44.40 N	74.40 W
Saint-Régis ≃, P.Q., Can.	275a	45.00 N	74.34 W
Saint Regis ≃, N.A.	188	45.00 N	74.39 W
Saint Regis ≃, Mt., U.S.	202	47.18 N	115.05 W
Saint Regis, West Branch ≃	207	44.46 N	74.46 W
Saint Regis Falls	188	44.40 N	74.32 W
Saint Regis Indian Reservation ⬧4	207	44.58 N	74.39 W
Saint-Rémi	206	45.16 N	73.37 W
Saint-Rémi-d'Amherst	206	46.01 N	74.46 W
Saint-Rémy, Fr.	58	46.46 N	4.50 E
Saint-Rémy, N.Y., U.S.	210	41.54 N	74.01 W
Saint-Rémy-de-Provence	62	43.47 N	4.50 E
Saint-Rémy-lès-Chevreuse	261	48.42 N	2.05 E
Saint-Rémy-l'Honoré	261	48.45 N	1.53 E
Saint-Rémy-sur-Avre	50	48.46 N	1.15 E
Saint-Renan	32	48.26 N	4.37 W
Saint-Révérien	50	47.13 N	3.30 E
Saint-Rhémy	62	45.50 N	7.11 E
Saint-Riquier	50	50.08 N	1.57 E
Saint Robert	194	37.50 N	92.09 W
Saint-Roch-de-l'Achigan	206	45.51 N	73.36 W
Saint-Romain-de-Colbosc	50	49.32 N	0.22 E
Saint-Romain-le-Puy	62	45.33 N	4.08 E
Saint-Romans	62	45.07 N	5.19 E
Sainte-Rosalie	206	46.45 N	72.16 W
Sainte-Rose	240a	16.20 N	61.42 W
Sainte-Rose-du-Lac	184	51.03 N	99.32 W
Saintry-sur-Seine	261	48.38 N	2.28 E
Saintes, Bel.	50	50.42 N	4.10 E
Saintes, Fr.	32	45.45 N	0.38 W
Saintes, Îles des II	240a	15.52 N	61.37 W
Saint-Saëns	50	49.41 N	1.17 E
Saint Sampson	43b	49.29 N	2.31 W
Saint-Saturnin-d'Apt	62	43.51 N	5.23 E
Saint-Sauveur, Fr.	50	48.58 N	3.46 E
Saint-Sauveur, Fr.	58	47.37 N	3.13 E
Saint-Sauveur, Fr.	58	47.48 N	6.23 E

Saint-Sauveur-des-Monts	206	45.52 N	74.10 W
Saint-Sauveur-sur-Tinée	62	44.05 N	7.06 E
Saint-Savin	32	46.34 N	0.52 E
Sainte-Savine	50	48.18 N	4.03 E
Saint-Savinien	32	45.53 N	0.41 W
Saint Saviour	43b	49.11 N	2.06 W
Saint Sebastian Bay c	158	34.25 S	21.00 E
Saint-Sébastien	206	45.07 N	73.09 W
Saint-Sébastien, Cap ⧽	157b	12.26 S	48.44 E
Saint-Seine-l'Abbaye	58	47.26 N	4.47 E
Saint Séverin	56	50.32 N	5.25 E
Saint Shotts	186	46.38 N	53.35 W
Sainte-Sigolène	62	45.14 N	4.15 E
Saint-Siméon	186	47.50 N	69.53 W
Saint-Simon	50	49.45 N	3.10 E
Saint Simons Island	192	31.09 N	81.22 W
Saint Simons Island I	192	31.14 N	81.21 W
Saint-Sixte	206	45.39 N	74.05 W
Saintes-Maries, Golfe des c	62	43.25 N	4.31 E
Saintes-Maries-de-la-Mer	62	43.27 N	4.26 E
Sainte-Sophie-de-Mégantic	206	46.09 N	71.42 W
Saint-Soupplets	261	49.02 N	2.48 E
Saint Stanislas Bay c	174o	1.53 N	157.30 W
Saint-Stanislas-de-Kosta	206	45.11 N	74.08 W
Saint Stephen, N.B., Can.	186	45.12 N	67.17 W
Saint Stephen, S.C., U.S.	192	33.24 N	79.55 W
Saint-Sulpice-de-Favières	261	48.33 N	2.11 E
Saint-Sulpice-les-Feuilles	32	46.19 N	1.22 E
Sainte-Suzanne	58	47.30 N	6.46 E
Saint-Sylvestre	206	46.22 N	71.14 W
Saint-Symphorien, Fr.	32	44.26 N	0.30 W
Saint-Symphorien, Fr.	261	48.31 N	1.46 E
Saint-Symphorien-d'Ozon	62	45.38 N	4.52 E
Saint-Symphorien-sur-Coise	62	45.38 N	4.27 E
Sainte-Thècle	206	46.49 N	72.31 W
Saint-Théodore-d'Acton	206	45.41 N	72.35 W
Sainte-Thérèse	206	45.22 N	73.51 W
Sainte-Thérèse, Île I, P.Q., Can.	275a	45.41 N	73.28 W
Sainte-Thérèse, Île I, P.Q., Can.	275a	45.22 N	73.15 W
Saint-Thibault-des-Vignes	261	48.52 N	2.41 E
Saint Thomas, On., Can.	212	42.47 N	81.12 W
Saint Thomas, Mo., U.S.	219	38.22 N	92.13 W
Saint Thomas, N.D., U.S.	198	48.37 N	97.26 W
Saint Thomas → Charlotte Amalie, Vir. Is., U.S.	240m	18.21 N	64.56 W
Saint Thomas I	240m	18.21 N	64.55 W
Saint-Timothée	206	45.18 N	74.02 W
Saint-Tite	206	46.44 N	72.34 W
Saint-Tite-des-Caps	186	47.08 N	70.47 W
Saint-Trivier-de-Courtes	58	46.28 N	5.05 E
Saint-Trivier-sur-Moignans	58	46.04 N	4.54 E
Saint-Tropez	62	43.16 N	6.38 E
Saint Tudy	42	50.33 N	4.43 W
Sainte-Tulle	62	43.47 N	5.46 E
Saint-Ubald	206	46.45 N	72.16 W
Saint-Urbain-de-Charlevoix	186	47.34 N	70.32 W
Saint-Ursanne	58	47.22 N	7.10 E
Saint-Uze	62	45.11 N	4.52 E
Saint-Valérien	58	48.11 N	3.06 E
Saint-Valéry-en-Caux	50	49.52 N	0.44 E
Saint-Valéry-sur-Somme	50	50.11 N	1.38 E
Saint-Vallier, Fr.	58	46.38 N	4.22 E
Saint-Vallier, Fr.	62	45.10 N	4.49 E
Saint-Vallier-de-Thiey	62	43.42 N	6.51 E
Saint-Varent	32	46.53 N	0.14 W
Saint-Venant	50	50.37 N	2.33 E
Saint-Vérax	62	44.42 N	6.52 E
Sainte-Victoire, Montagne ⩓	62	43.32 N	5.39 E
Saint-Victoret	62	43.25 N	5.14 E
Saint Vincent	198	43.58 N	97.13 W
Saint Vincent I	241h	13.15 N	61.12 W
Saint Vincent, Baie de c	175f	22.00 S	166.05 E
Saint Vincent, Cap ⧽	157b	21.57 S	43.16 E
Saint Vincent, Cape ⧽	192	29.38 N	85.02 W
Saint Vincent, Cape → São Vicente, Cabo de ⧽	34	37.01 N	9.00 W
Saint Vincent, Gulf c	168b	35.00 S	138.05 E
Saint Vincent and the Grenadines □1, N.A.	230	13.15 N	61.12 W
Saint Vincent and the Grenadines □1, N.A.	241h	13.15 N	61.12 W
Saint-Vincent-de-Paul	275a	45.37 N	73.39 W
Saint-Vincent-de-Tyrosse	32	43.40 N	1.18 W
Saint Vincent Island I	192	29.40 N	85.08 W
Saint Vincent's	58	47.11 N	5.49 E
Saint-Vith	56	50.17 N	6.08 E
Saint-Vivien-de-Médoc	32	45.26 N	1.02 W
Saint Walburg	184	53.39 N	109.12 W
Saint-Wandrille-Rançon	50	49.32 N	0.46 E
Saint-Wenceslas	206	46.18 N	72.23 W
Saint Williams	212	42.40 N	80.25 W
Saint-Witz	261	49.05 N	2.34 E
Saint-Yrieix-la-Perche	32	45.31 N	1.12 E
Saint-Yvon	186	49.10 N	64.48 W
Saint-Zacharie	62	43.23 N	5.43 E
Saint-Zénon	206	46.33 N	73.49 W
Sainthya	126	23.57 N	87.40 E
Saipan I	174n	15.12 N	145.45 E
Saipan Channel ṵ	174n	15.15 N	145.41 E
Saipan International Airport ⬥	174n	15.07 N	145.43 E
Saiqi	258	27.00 N	119.43 E
Sairecábur, Cerro ⩓	248	22.43 S	67.54 W
Saishu-to → Cheju-do I	96	33.20 N	126.30 E
Saita	96	34.08 N	133.49 E
Saitama □5	94	36.00 N	139.30 E
Saitama University ⊥2	268	35.52 N	139.36 E
Saito	94	32.06 N	131.24 E
Saïwa Swamp National Park ⬤	154	1.06 N	35.12 E
Saiydiābād ⬥8	272a	28.40 N	77.05 E
Sai Yok	110	14.09 N	98.52 E
Sajak	164	0.53 S	132.41 E
Sajama, Nevado ⩓	248	18.06 S	68.54 W

Sajan → Sayan Mountains ⩓	88	52.45 N	96.00 E
Sajanogorsk	86	53.08 N	91.29 E
Sajano-Šušenskoje vodochranilišče ⬚1	88	52.20 N	92.25 E
Sajantuj	88	51.44 N	107.30 E
Sajasan	84	43.03 N	46.17 E
Sajat	88	38.47 N	63.53 E
Sajchan	88	48.40 N	102.39 E
Sajchandulaan	102	44.40 N	109.01 E
Sajchan-Ovoo	102	45.27 N	103.54 E
Sajchin	80	48.50 N	46.47 E
Sajen	115a	7.40 S	112.31 E
Sajgino	80	57.46 N	46.51 E
Sajlli I	144	16.52 N	41.50 E
Sajma' ⬚	120	37.27 N	74.44 E
Sajnšand	102	44.52 N	110.09 E
Sajó ≃	30	47.56 N	21.08 E
Sajószentpéter	30	48.13 N	20.44 E
Sajram	85	42.18 N	69.45 E
Sajukino	80	52.47 N	41.59 E
Sâjûr (Bağırsak) ≃	130	36.40 N	38.05 E
Sak ≃	158	30.02 S	20.40 E
Saka, Kenya	154	0.09 S	39.20 E
Saka, Nihon	96	34.20 N	132.31 E
Sakado	94	35.57 N	139.24 E
Sakae, Nihon	94	35.50 N	140.15 E
Sakae, Nihon	94	36.58 N	138.35 E
Sa Kaeo	110	13.49 N	102.04 E
Sakahogi	94	35.26 N	136.59 E
Sakai, Nihon	94	36.16 N	139.15 E
Sakai, Nihon	94	36.10 N	136.14 E
Sakai, Nihon	94	36.06 N	139.48 E
Sakai, Nihon	96	34.35 N	135.28 E
Sakai, Nihon	268	35.25 N	139.22 E
Sakaide	94	35.18 N	139.29 E
Sakaide	94	34.19 N	133.52 E
Sakaigawa	94	35.35 N	138.37 E
Sakaiminato	96	35.33 N	133.15 E
Sakākah	128	29.59 N	40.06 E
Sakakawea, Lake ⬚1	198	47.50 N	102.20 W
Sakaki	94	36.28 N	138.11 E
Sakakita	94	36.25 N	138.01 E
Sakala, Pulau I	112	6.54 S	116.15 E
Sakami ≃	176	53.40 N	76.40 W
Sakami, Lac ⬚	176	53.15 N	76.45 W
Sakania	154	12.45 S	28.34 E
Sakar ⩓	38	41.59 N	26.16 E
Sakaraha	157b	22.55 S	44.32 E
Sakar-Čaga	128	37.38 N	61.40 E
Sakar Island I	164	5.25 S	148.05 E
Sakarya □4	130	40.45 N	30.35 E
Sakarya ≃	130	41.07 N	30.39 E
Sakashita	94	35.34 N	137.32 E
Sakassou	150	7.27 N	5.18 W
Sakata	92	38.55 N	139.50 E
Sakawa	94	35.36 N	136.25 E
Sakawa ≃	94	35.15 N	139.11 E
Sakchu	100	40.23 N	125.05 E
Sakesar	123	32.33 N	71.56 E
Sakété	150	6.43 N	2.40 E
Sakhā ≃	142	31.05 N	30.57 E
Sakhalin → Sachalin, ostrov I	89	51.00 N	143.00 E
Sakhi Sarwar	120	29.59 N	70.18 E
Sakhnin	132	32.52 N	35.17 E
Sakhrīyät, Jabal as- ⩓	132	31.01 N	36.21 E
Sakht Sar	128	36.53 N	50.41 E
Säki ⬥8	272c	19.06 N	72.53 E
Sakiai	48	54.57 N	23.03 E
Sakib	132	32.17 N	35.49 E
Sakijang Bendera, Pulau I	271c	1.13 N	103.51 E
Sakijang Pelepah, Pulau I	271c	1.13 N	103.51 E
Sakishima-shotō II	175d	24.46 N	124.00 E
Sakito	94	33.02 N	129.32 E
Sakkara	142	29.51 N	31.13 E
Sakkara → Saqqārāh	142	29.51 N	31.13 E
Sakmara	78	51.46 N	55.01 E
Sakmara ≃	82	54.55 N	56.05 E
Sakoku	270	34.55 N	138.30 E
Sakon Nakhon	110	17.10 N	104.09 E
Sakonnet	207	41.28 N	71.12 W
Sakonnet Point ⧽	207	41.27 N	71.12 W
Sakoyra	150	14.17 N	1.24 E
Sakra, Pulau I	271c	1.16 N	103.42 E
Sakrand	120	26.08 N	68.16 E
Sakrivier	158	30.54 S	20.28 E
Sakrow-Paretzer Kanal ᴸ	264a	52.28 N	12.55 E
Saks	194	33.42 N	85.52 W
Saksagan' ≃2	78	47.53 N	33.18 E
Saksauldala ⬥2	86	54.48 N	73.00 E
Saksköbing	22	54.48 N	11.39 E
Sakti	124	22.02 N	82.58 E
Saku, Nihon	94	36.19 N	138.30 E
Saku, Nihon	94	35.18 N	138.30 E
Sakubva	154	34.52 S	32.10 E
Sakugi	94	34.50 N	132.43 E
Sakura	94	35.43 N	140.14 E
Sakurai	96	34.31 N	135.51 E
Sakurai ≃	96	35.30 N	135.53 E
Sakura-dam ⬚6	94	35.43 N	140.14 E
Sakura-ko ⬚1	94	35.08 N	137.47 E
Sakura-shima I	94	34.43 N	137.23 E
Sakura-tōge ᕽ	270	34.36 N	135.53 E
Sakuto	94	35.01 N	134.11 E
Sakwaso Lake ⬚	184	53.01 N	91.55 W
Sakyiä	158	33.03 S	25.40 E
Sakyō ⬥5	270	35.00 N	135.48 E
Sal ≃	80	47.31 N	40.45 E
Sal, Cay I	238	23.42 N	80.24 W
Sal, Ilha do I	150a	16.45 N	22.55 W
Sal, Ponta do ⧽	266c	38.41 N	9.22 W
Sal, Punta ⧽	238	15.53 N	87.37 W
Sal'a, Č.	30	48.09 N	17.52 E
Sal'a, S.S.S.R.	88	57.15 N	88.43 E
Sala, Sve.	22	59.55 N	16.36 E
Sala Baganza	36	44.43 N	10.14 E
Salabangka, Kepulauan II	112	3.02 S	122.25 E
Salaberry-de-Valleyfield	206	45.15 N	74.08 W
Salaca ≃	76	57.45 N	24.21 E
Salacgrīva	76	57.45 N	24.21 E
Sala Consilina	36	40.24 N	15.36 E
Salada, Laguna ⬚, Arg.	252	30.58 S	59.24 W
Salada, Laguna ⬚, Méx.	232	32.20 N	115.40 W
Saladas	252	28.15 S	58.38 W
Saladillo ≃, Arg.	252	26.50 S	60.30 W
Saladillo, Arroyo ≃	258	35.33 S	59.01 W

Salado, Arroyo ≃, Arg.	254	41.37 S	65.02 W
Salado, Arroyo ≃, Arg.	254	40.35 S	66.33 W
Salado, Arroyo ≃, Méx.	232	24.25 N	111.34 W
Salado, Rio ≃	200	34.16 N	106.52 W
Salado Creek ≃, Tx., U.S.	196	29.14 N	98.25 W
Salado Creek ≃, Tx., U.S.	222	30.59 N	97.25 W
Salaga	150	8.33 N	0.31 W
Salagle	144	1.50 N	42.17 E
Sālah	132	32.38 N	36.46 E
Salāh ad-Dīn □4	128	34.15 N	43.55 E
Salahin	144	2.57 N	46.26 E
Salā'ilua	175a	13.41 S	172.34 W
Salak ⩓	86	54.15 N	85.47 E
Salak ⩓	114	2.34 N	98.20 E
Salak, Gunung ⩓	115a	6.42 S	106.44 E
Salakas	76	55.35 N	26.08 E
Salal	115a	7.35 S	110.08 E
Salal	146	14.51 N	17.13 E
Salala, Chile	252	30.41 S	71.32 W
Salala, Liber.	150	6.40 N	10.05 W
Salālah, Süd.	144	21.19 N	36.13 E
Salālah, 'Umān	118	17.00 N	54.06 E
Salamá, Guat.	236	15.06 N	90.16 W
Salamá, Hond.	236	14.50 N	86.36 W
Salamajärven kansallispuisto ⬤	26	63.20 N	24.40 E
Salaman	115a	7.35 S	110.08 E
Salamanca, Chile	252	31.47 S	70.58 W
Salamanca, Esp.	34	40.58 N	5.39 W
Salamanca, Méx.	234	20.34 N	101.12 W
Salamanca, Perú	248	15.31 S	72.50 W
Salamanca, Perú	286d	12.05 S	77.00 W
Salamanca, N.Y., U.S.	210	42.09 N	78.42 W
Salamanga	158	26.28 S	32.39 E
Salamat □5	146	11.00 N	20.30 E
Salamat, Bahr ≃	146	9.27 N	18.06 E
Salämbek	120	28.18 N	65.09 E
Salamina	246	5.25 N	75.29 W
Salamínos, Órmos c	267c	37.56 N	23.27 E
Salamis	38	37.59 N	23.28 E
Salamis I	38	37.54 N	23.26 E
Salamíyah	130	35.01 N	37.03 E
Salamīyah	120	31.47 N	66.45 E
Salamonia	216	40.23 N	84.52 W
Salamonie ≃	216	40.46 N	85.37 W
Salamonie Lake ⬚1	216	40.45 N	85.39 W
Salamún	142	30.31 N	31.11 E
Salandra	36	40.31 N	16.19 E
Sālang, Tünel-e ⬥	120	35.19 N	69.02 E
Salani	175a	14.00 S	171.33 W
Salantai	76	56.04 N	21.32 E
Salaparuta	36	37.47 N	13.00 E
Salas	34	43.25 N	6.16 W
Salaspils	76	56.51 N	24.21 E
Salat ≃	32	43.10 N	0.58 E
Salataš	115a	7.53 S	110.30 E
Salau	80	55.59 N	52.53 E
Salavat	86	53.21 N	55.55 E
Salavaux	58	46.56 N	7.02 E
Salavina	248	28.14 S	78.58 W
Salawa	252	28.48 S	63.25 W
Salawati I	164	1.07 S	130.52 E
Salawe	154	3.19 S	32.52 E
Salay	114	8.52 N	124.47 E
Salazie	157c	21.02 S	55.32 E
Sala y Gómez, Isla I	18	26.28 S	105.28 W
Sala y Gomez Ridge ⬥3	18	25.00 S	98.00 W
Salazgar	38	42.12 N	22.01 E
Salba	88	53.14 N	92.36 E
Salbani	126	22.38 N	87.20 E
Salbohed	22	59.55 N	16.21 E
Salbojšon ⬥	40	59.50 N	14.54 E
Sabris	50	47.26 N	2.03 E
Šalbudag, gora ⩓	84	41.19 N	47.48 E
Salcajá	236	14.53 N	91.27 W
Salcantay, Nevado ⩓	248	13.20 S	72.33 W
Salcedo, Pil.	116	11.09 N	125.01 E
Salcedo, Rep. Dom.	238	19.23 N	70.25 W
Salcha ≃	180	64.29 N	147.00 W
Salching	264a	48.49 N	12.34 E
Šalčininkai	76	54.18 N	25.23 E
Salcombe	42	50.13 N	3.47 W
Salda ⬚	130	37.33 N	29.42 E
Saldaña	34	42.31 N	4.44 W
Saldaña ≃	246	4.01 N	74.52 W
Saldana	158	33.00 S	17.56 E
Saldanha	158	33.00 S	17.56 E
Saldanhabaai c	158	33.06 S	17.10 E
Saldedž	76	57.46 N	24.48 E
Saldungaray	252	38.12 S	61.47 W
Saldus	76	56.40 N	22.30 E
Sale, Austl.	166	38.06 S	147.04 E
Salé, Magreb	148	34.03 N	6.51 W
Sale, Eng., U.K.	44	53.26 N	2.19 W
Sale Creek	194	35.22 N	85.06 W
Salé, Rivière à ≃	240o	16.17 N	61.33 W
Saleh, Teluk c	115b	8.34 S	117.57 E
Salekhard → Salechard	62	66.33 N	66.40 E
Salem, B.R.D.	264c	47.46 N	9.16 E
Salem, On., Can.	212	43.42 N	80.27 W
Salem, India	111	11.39 N	78.10 E
Salem, S. Afr.	158	33.29 S	26.29 E
Salem, Il., U.S.	190	38.37 N	88.56 W
Salem, In., U.S.	218	38.36 N	86.06 W
Salem, Ma., U.S.	210	42.31 N	70.53 W
Salem, Mo., U.S.	194	37.39 N	91.32 W
Salem, N.J., U.S.	208	39.34 N	75.28 W
Salem, N.Y., U.S.	210	43.10 N	73.20 W
Salem, Oh., U.S.	214	40.54 N	80.51 W
Salem, Or., U.S.	224	44.56 N	123.02 W
Salem, S.D., U.S.	198	43.43 N	97.23 W
Salem, Ut., U.S.	200	40.03 N	111.40 W
Salem, Va., U.S.	192	37.17 N	80.03 W
Salem, W.V., U.S.	188	39.16 N	80.33 W
Salem, Wi., U.S.	278	42.33 N	88.06 W
Salem □4	111	11.30 N	78.15 E
Salem Airfield ⬥	281	42.31 N	70.51 W
Sale Marasino	36	45.42 N	10.06 E
Salem Canal ᴸ	285	39.41 N	75.31 W
Salem Depot	281	42.47 N	71.12 W
Salem Harbor c	281	42.30 N	70.53 W
Salem Heights	283	44.54 N	123.02 W
Salémi	36	37.49 N	12.48 E
Salem Maritime National Historic Site ⬧	281	42.31 N	70.53 W
Salem State College ⊥	281	42.30 N	70.54 W
Sālem Upland ⩓1	194	37.25 N	91.30 W
Salen, Sve.	40	61.10 N	13.16 E
Salen, Scot., U.K.	46	56.31 N	5.57 W
Salen, Scot., U.K.	46	56.43 N	5.47 W

Symbol	English	Deutsch	Español	Français	Português
≃	River	Fluß	Río	Rivière	Rio
ᴸ	Canal	Kanal	Canal	Canal	Canal
⇟	Waterfall, Rapids	Wasserfall, Stromschnellen	Cascada, Rápidos	Chute d'eau, Rapides	Cascata, Rápidos
ṵ	Strait	Meeresstraße	Estrecho	Détroit	Estreito
c	Bay, Gulf	Bucht, Golf	Bahía, Golfo	Baie, Golfe	Baía, Golfo
⬚	Lakes	See, Seen	Lago, Lagos	Lac, Lacs	Lago, Lagos
⩵	Swamp	Sumpf	Pantano	Marais	Pântano
⛰	Ice Features, Glacier	Eis- und Gletscherformen	Accidentes Glaciares	Formes glaciaires	Acidentes glaciares
⛆	Other Hydrographic Features	Andere Hydrographische Objekte	Otros Elementos Hidrográficos	Autres données hydrographiques	Outros acidentes hidrográficos
⬥	Submarine Features	Untermeerische Objekte	Accidentes Submarinos	Formes de relief sous-marin	Acidentes submarinos
□	Political Unit	Politische Einheit	Unidad Política	Entité politique	Unidade política
⊥	Cultural Institution	Kulturelle Institution	Institución Cultural	Institution culturelle	Instituição cultural
⬧	Historical Site	Historische Stätte	Sitio Histórico	Site historique	Sitio histórico
⬤	Recreational Site	Erholungs- und Ferienort	Sitio de Recreo	Centre de loisirs	Area de Lazer
⬥	Airport	Flughafen	Aeropuerto	Aéroport	Aeroporto
⬥	Military Installation	Militäranlage	Instalación Militar	Installation militaire	Instalação militar
⬥	Miscellaneous	Verschiedenes	Misceláneo	Divers	Diversos

I · 152 Sale-Sanb

Salentina, Penisola >[1] 68 40.25 N 18.00 E
Salentine, Murge ✦[1] 68 40.02 N 18.13 E
Salento 68 40.15 N 15.11 E
Salernes 62 43.33 N 6.14 E
Salerno 68 40.41 N 14.47 E
Salerno □[4] 68 40.27 N 15.16 E
Salerno, Golfo di c 68 40.32 N 14.42 E
Salers 32 45.08 N 2.30 E
Salesbury 262 53.47 N 2.30 W
Salesópolis 256 23.32 S 45.51 W
Salève, Mont ∧ 58 46.07 N 6.10 E
Salford 44 53.28 N 2.18 W
Salford □[8] 262 53.28 N 2.23 W
Salfords 260 51.12 N 0.10 W
Šalgačova 24 62.19 N 39.35 E
Salgado 250 11.02 S 37.28 W
Salgan 80 55.14 N 45.30 E
Salgar 246 5.58 N 75.59 W
Šalgija 86 47.35 N 70.36 E
Salgir ≃ 78 45.38 N 35.01 E
Salgótarján 30 48.07 N 19.48 E
Salgueiro 250 8.04 S 39.06 W
Salher ∧ 122 20.43 N 73.56 E
Sali, Alg. 148 26.58 N 0.01 W
Sali, Jugo. 36 43.56 N 15.10 E
Šali, S.S.S.R. 80 55.41 N 49.40 E
Šali, S.S.S.R. 84 43.08 N 45.54 E
Salí ≃ 252 27.33 S 64.57 W
Salice Salentino 68 40.23 N 17.58 E
Salice Terme 62 44.55 N 9.01 E
Salici, Monte ∧ 70 37.44 N 14.38 E
Salida, Ca., U.S. 226 37.42 N 121.05 W
Salida, Co., U.S. 200 38.32 N 105.59 W
Salies-de-Béarn 32 43.29 N 0.55 W
Salīf 144 15.18 N 42.40 E
Salignac-Eyvignes 32 44.59 N 1.19 E
Salihli 130 38.29 N 28.09 E
Šālikha 126 23.18 N 89.22 E
Šalikovo 82 55.30 N 36.13 E
Salim 140 12.52 N 28.40 E
Salima 154 13.47 S 34.26 E
Salīmah, Wāḥat ⊽[4] 140 21.22 N 29.19 E
Salimani 157a 11.47 S 43.17 E
Salimbatu 112 2.57 N 117.21 E
Salimgarh Fort ⊥ 272a 28.40 N 77.14 E
Salimi 152 9.24 S 23.35 E
Salin 110 20.35 N 94.39 E
Salina, Ks., U.S. 198 38.50 N 97.36 W
Salina, Ok., U.S. 196 36.17 N 95.09 W
Salina, Pa., U.S. 214 40.31 N 79.30 W
Salina, Ut,. U.S. 200 38.57 N 111.51 W
Salina, Canale di ≍ 70 38.32 N 14.54 E
Salina, Isola I 70 38.34 N 14.50 E
Salina Cruz 234 16.10 N 95.12 W
Salina Point > 238 22.13 N 74.18 W
Salinas, Bra. 255 16.10 S 42.17 W
Salinas, Ec. 246 2.13 S 80.58 W
Salinas, P.R. 240m 17.59 N 66.18 W
Salinas, Ca., U.S. 226 36.40 N 121.39 W
Salinas ≃, Bra. 255 16.37 S 42.18 W
Salinas ≃, N.A. 236 16.28 N 90.33 W
Salinas ≃, Ca., U.S. 226 36.45 N 121.48 W
Salinas, Pampa de las ≐ 252 31.58 S 66.42 W
Salinas, Ponta das > 152 12.50 S 12.56 E
Salinas, Sierra de ⋏ 226 36.18 N 121.20 W
Salinas de Garci Mendoza 248 19.38 S 67.43 W
Salinas de Hidalgo 234 22.38 N 101.43 W
Salinas del Rey 196 27.38 N 102.24 W
Salinas Municipal Airport ⊠ 226 36.40 N 121.40 W
Salinas National Monument ♦ 200 34.05 N 106.14 W
Salinas Valley V 226 36.15 N 121.15 W
Salinas Victoria 196 25.53 N 100.19 W
Salin-de-Giraud 62 43.25 N 4.44 E
Salindres 62 44.10 N 4.10 E
Saline, La., U.S. 194 32.09 N 92.58 W
Saline, Mi., U.S. 216 42.10 N 83.46 W
Saline ≃, Ar., U.S. 194 33.10 N 92.08 W
Saline ≃, Ar., U.S. 194 33.44 N 93.58 W
Saline ≃, Il., U.S. 194 37.35 N 88.08 W
Saline ≃, Ks., U.S. 198 38.51 N 97.30 W
Saline ≃, Mi., U.S. 216 41.59 N 83.37 W
Saline, North Fork ≃ 194 37.44 N 88.19 W
Saline Bayou ≃ 194 31.45 N 92.58 W
Saline di Volterra 66 43.22 N 10.49 E
Saline Lake ◎[1] 194 31.55 N 92.55 W
Salines, Point > 241k 12.00 N 61.48 W
Salines, Pointe des > 240e 14.24 N 60.53 W
Salineville 214 40.37 N 80.51 W
Salingyi 110 21.58 N 95.03 E
Salinópolis 250 0.37 S 47.20 W
Šalinskoje 86 55.43 N 93.46 E
Salins-les-Bains 58 46.57 N 5.53 E
Salins-les-Thermes 62 45.28 N 6.32 E
Salipolo 112 3.45 S 119.29 E
Salisbury, Austl. 168b 34.46 S 138.38 E
Salisbury, Dom. 240d 15.26 N 61.27 W
Salisbury, Eng., U.K. 42 51.05 N 1.48 W
Salisbury, Ct., U.S. 207 41.59 N 73.25 W
Salisbury, Md., U.S. 208 38.21 N 75.35 W
Salisbury, Ma., U.S. 207 42.50 N 70.51 W
Salisbury, Mo., U.S. 194 39.25 N 92.48 W
Salisbury, N.C., U.S. 192 35.40 N 80.28 W
Salisbury, Pa., U.S. 188 39.45 N 79.04 W
Salisbury → Harare 154 17.50 S 31.03 E
Salisbury Cathedral ⊍[1] 42 51.05 N 1.48 W
Salisbury Center 210 43.09 N 74.47 W
Salisbury Hall ⊥ 260 51.43 N 0.16 W
Salisbury Island I, Austl. 162 34.21 S 123.32 E
Salisbury Island I, N.T., Can. 176 63.30 N 77.00 W
Salisbury Mills 210 41.26 N 74.08 W
Salisbury Plain ≐ 42 51.12 N 1.55 W
Salisbury Plain ≐ 283 42.02 N 70.58 W
Salish Mountains ⋏ 202 48.15 N 114.45 W
Salito ≃ 70 37.29 N 13.46 E
Salitpa 194 31.37 N 88.01 W
Salitre ≃ 250 9.29 S 40.39 W
Salix 214 40.18 N 78.46 W
Šaljany 84 39.34 N 48.58 E
Šalkar, S.S.S.R. 80 48.03 N 48.56 E
Šalkar, S.S.S.R. 80 50.32 N 51.51 E
Šalkar, ozero ◎ 80 50.33 N 51.40 E
Šalkar-Jega-Kara, ozero ◎ 86 50.45 N 60.54 E
Salkehatchie ≃ 192 32.37 N 80.53 W
Şalkhad 132 32.29 N 36.43 E
Salkhia 272b 22.35 N 88.21 E
Salkum 224 46.31 N 122.37 W
Salla 24 66.50 N 28.40 E
Salladasburg 210 41.17 N 77.14 W
Sallagriffon 62 43.53 N 6.54 E
Sallanches 58 45.56 N 6.38 E
Salland ✦[1] 52 52.20 N 6.20 E
Salles-Curan 32 44.11 N 2.47 E
Salles-sous-Bois 62 44.27 N 4.56 E
Sallgast 54 51.35 N 13.51 E
Salling ✦[1] 26 56.40 N 9.00 E
Salliqueló 252 36.45 S 62.56 W
Sallisaw 196 35.27 N 94.47 W
Sallisaw Creek ≃ 194 35.23 N 94.52 W
Salluit 176 62.14 N 75.38 W
Sallūm 140 19.23 N 37.06 E
Sallūm, Khalīj as- c 146 31.41 N 25.21 E
Salluyo, Nevado ∧ 248 14.38 S 69.14 W
Salm ≃, Bel. 56 50.22 N 5.52 E
Salm ≃, B.R.D. 56 49.51 N 6.51 E
Salmās 128 38.11 N 44.47 E
Salmchâteau 56 50.16 N 5.54 E
Salme 76 58.10 N 22.15 E
Salmi 24 61.22 N 31.53 E
Salmo 182 49.12 N 117.17 W
Salmon 202 45.10 N 113.53 W
Salmon ≃, B.C., Can. 182 54.05 N 122.34 W
Salmon ≃, N.B., Can. 186 46.06 N 65.56 W
Salmon ≃, On., Can. 212 44.11 N 77.15 W
Salmon ≃, N.A. 188 45.02 N 74.31 W
Salmon ≃, Ct., U.S. 207 41.29 N 72.29 W
Salmon ≃, Id., U.S. 202 45.51 N 116.46 W
Salmon ≃, N.Y., U.S. 212 43.35 N 76.12 W
Salmon ≃, Or., U.S. 224 45.22 N 122.02 W
Salmon ≃, Or., U.S. 224 45.03 N 124.00 W
Salmon, East Fork ≃ 202 44.16 N 114.19 W
Salmon, Middle Fork ≃ 202 45.18 N 114.36 W
Salmon, North Branch ≃ 212 43.32 N 75.48 W
Salmon, South Fork ≃ 202 45.23 N 115.31 W
Salmon Arm 182 50.42 N 119.16 W
Salmon-Bay 186 51.26 N 57.36 W
Salmon Creek ≃, N.Y., U.S. 210 43.16 N 77.02 W
Salmon Creek ≃, N.Y., U.S. 210 43.19 N 77.43 W
Salmon Creek ≃, Wa., U.S. 224 45.44 N 122.45 W
Salmon Creek ≃, Wa., U.S. 224 46.26 N 122.52 W
Salmon Falls Creek ≃ 202 42.43 N 114.51 W
Salmon Falls Creek Reservoir ◎[1] 202 42.08 N 114.45 W
Salmon Gums 162 32.59 S 121.38 E
Salmon Lake ◎ 212 44.49 N 78.28 W
Salmon Mountain ∧ 188 45.14 N 71.08 W
Salmon Mountains ⋏ 204 41.00 N 123.00 W
Salmon Peak ∧ 196 29.28 N 100.10 W
Salmon Point > 212 43.52 N 77.14 W
Salmon River Mountains ⋏ 202 44.45 N 115.30 W
Salmon River Reservoir ◎[1] 212 43.32 N 75.52 W
Salmon Valley 182 54.05 N 122.41 W
Salmyš ≃ 86 52.01 N 55.21 E
Sal'nica 78 49.44 N 28.02 E
Salo, Centraf. 152 3.12 N 16.07 E
Salò, It. 64 45.36 N 10.31 E
Salo, Suomi 26 60.23 N 23.08 E
Salobel'ak 80 57.07 N 48.05 E
Salobra ≃ 248 20.12 S 56.29 W
Salomatino 80 50.01 N 44.50 E
Salome 200 33.46 N 113.36 W
Salomon, Cap > 240e 14.30 N 61.06 W
Salomon, Îles → Solomon Islands □[1] 175e 8.00 S 159.00 E
Salomón, Islas → Solomon Islands □[1] 175e 8.00 S 159.00 E
Salomone, Monte ∧ 267a 41.47 N 12.44 E
Salomon-Inseln → Solomon Islands □[1] 175e 8.00 S 159.00 E
Salon ≃ 58 47.32 N 5.41 E
Salona 210 41.05 N 77.28 W
Salon-de-Provence 62 43.38 N 5.06 E
Salonga ≃ 152 0.10 S 19.50 E
Salonga, Parc National de la ♦ 152 1.45 S 21.20 E
Salonika → Thessaloníki 38 40.38 N 22.56 E
Salonta 38 46.48 N 21.40 E
Salor ≃, Esp. 34 39.42 N 6.28 W
Salor ≃, Esp. 34 39.39 N 7.03 W
Salorno (Salurn) 64 46.14 N 11.13 E
Saloslovo 265b 55.42 N 37.09 E
Saloum ≃ 150 13.50 N 16.45 W
Šalovka ≃ 265b 55.47 N 38.12 E
Salpausselkä ∧ 26 61.00 N 26.30 E
Şalpazarı 130 40.59 N 39.10 E
Şalqīn 130 36.08 N 36.27 E
Sal Rei 150a 16.11 N 22.55 W
Salsacate 252 31.19 S 65.05 W
Salsette Island I 272c 19.10 N 72.53 E
Salsilgo, Qawz ⊥[8] 140 10.49 N 22.54 E
Salsipuedes, Canal de ʮ 232 28.37 N 113.00 W
Salsipuedes, Punta >, C.R. 236 8.28 N 83.37 W
Salsipuedes, Punta >, Méx. 232 32.05 N 116.53 W
Sal'sk 80 46.28 N 41.33 E
Šal'skij 24 61.48 N 35.58 E
Sal'sko-Manyčskaja gr'ada ∧ 80 46.40 N 42.30 E
Salso ≃ 70 37.06 N 13.57 E
Salsomaggiore Terme 64 44.49 N 9.59 E
Salt ≃, U.S. 202 43.08 N 111.02 W
Salt ≃, Az., U.S. 200 33.23 N 112.18 W
Salt ≃, Ky., U.S. 194 38.00 N 85.57 W
Salt ≃, Mi., U.S. 281 42.39 N 82.47 W
Salt ≃, Mo., U.S. 219 39.28 N 91.04 W
Salt, Elk Fork ≃ 219 39.28 N 91.53 W
Salt, Middle Fork ≃ 219 39.28 N 91.49 W
Salt, North Fork ≃ 219 39.30 N 91.47 W
Salt, South Fork ≃ 219 39.28 N 91.49 W
Salta 252 24.47 S 65.25 W
Salta □[4] 252 25.00 S 64.30 W
Saltaim, ozero ◎ 86 56.10 N 71.45 E
Saltair 224 48.57 N 123.46 W
Saltaire 276 40.39 N 73.12 W
Saltanovka 76 52.47 N 34.17 E
Saltara 66 43.45 N 12.54 E
Salt Ash, Austl. 170 32.47 S 151.55 E
Saltash, Eng., U.K. 42 50.24 N 4.12 W
Saltbæk Vig c 41 55.43 N 11.12 E
Salt Basin ◎ 196 31.50 N 105.00 W
Saltburn-by-the-Sea 44 54.35 N 0.58 W
Salt Cay I 240b 25.06 N 77.18 W
Saltcoats, Sk., Can. 184 51.03 N 102.12 W
Saltcoats, Scot., U.K. 46 55.38 N 4.47 W
Salt Creek ≃, On., Can. 275b 43.48 N 79.42 W
Salt Creek ≃, Ca., U.S. 204 36.15 N 116.49 W
Salt Creek ≃, Il., U.S. 194 40.08 N 89.50 W
Salt Creek ≃, Il., U.S. 278 41.49 N 87.50 W
Salt Creek ≃, In., U.S. 216 41.37 N 87.09 W
Salt Creek ≃, In., U.S. 218 39.27 N 85.09 W
Salt Creek ≃, In., U.S. 218 38.50 N 86.32 W
Salt Creek ≃, Ks., U.S. 198 39.06 N 97.44 W
Salt Creek ≃, N.M., U.S. 196 33.35 N 104.23 W
Salt Creek ≃, Ok., U.S. 196 36.32 N 96.43 W
Salt Creek ≃, Or., U.S. 202 43.43 N 122.26 W
Salt Creek ≃, Or., U.S. 224 45.09 N 123.13 W
Salt Creek ≃, Wy., U.S. 202 43.41 N 106.20 W
Salt Creek, Middle Fork ≃ 218 39.04 N 86.15 W
Salt Creek, North Fork ≃, Il., U.S. 216 40.13 N 88.50 W
Salt Creek, North Fork ≃, In., U.S. 218 39.08 N 86.21 W
Salt Creek, West Branch ≃ 278 42.02 N 88.01 W
Salt Creek South Fork ≃ 218 39.02 N 86.16 W
Salt Draw V 196 31.19 N 103.28 W
Saltee Islands II 48 52.07 N 6.36 W
Salten 41 56.05 N 9.35 E
Saltfleet 44 53.25 N 0.11 E
Saltford 42 51.24 N 2.27 W
Salt Fork Lake ◎[1] 214 41.07 N 81.30 W
Salt Fork State Park ♦ 214 40.06 N 81.29 W
Saltholm I 41 55.38 N 12.46 E
Saltillo, Méx. 232 25.25 N 101.00 W
Saltillo, Ms., U.S. 194 34.22 N 88.40 W
Saltillo, Pa., U.S. 214 40.13 N 78.01 W
Saltillo, Tn., U.S. 194 35.22 N 88.12 W
Saltillo, Tx., U.S. 222 33.11 N 95.20 W
Salt Island I 240m 18.23 N 64.31 W
Salt Lake 158 29.16 S 24.00 E
Salt Lake ◎ 196 34.05 N 103.05 W
Salt Lake City 200 40.45 N 111.53 W
Salto, Arg. 252 34.17 S 60.15 W
Salto, Bra. 255 23.12 S 47.17 W
Salto, Ur. 252 31.23 S 57.58 W
Salto ≃ 66 42.23 N 12.54 E
Salto, Lago del ◎ 66 42.15 N 13.02 E
Salto da Divisa 255 16.00 S 39.57 W
Salto de las Rosas 252 34.43 S 68.14 W
Salto del Fraile > 286d 12.11 S 77.03 W
Salto Grande 255 22.54 S 49.59 W
Salton City 204 33.19 N 115.59 W
Salton Sea ◎ 204 33.19 N 115.50 W
Salton Sea State Recreation Area ♦ 204 33.29 N 115.53 W
Saltonstall, Lake ◎ 283 42.47 N 71.04 W
Sāltora 126 23.32 N 86.56 E
Saltoro Range ⋏ 123 35.17 N 77.03 E
Saltos del Guaira 252 24.03 S 54.17 W
Salt Pan Creek ≃ 274a 33.59 S 151.02 E
Saltpeter Creek c 284b 39.20 N 76.22 W
Salt Point 210 41.44 N 73.42 W
Saltpond 150 5.12 N 1.04 W
Salt Range ⋏ 123 32.40 N 72.35 E
Salt River Indian Reservation ✦[4] 200 33.31 N 111.48 W
Saltsburg 214 40.29 N 79.27 W
Saltsjöbaden 40 59.17 N 18.18 E
Salt Slough ≃ 226 37.18 N 120.54 W
Saltspring Island I 224 48.47 N 123.30 W
Salt Springs Reservoir ◎[1] 226 38.30 N 120.11 W
Saltville 192 36.52 N 81.45 W
Salt Wells Creek ≃ 200 41.39 N 108.59 W
Saltykovka, S.S.S.R. 80 52.07 N 44.05 E
Saltykovka, S.S.S.R. 265b 55.46 N 37.55 E
Saluda, S.C., U.S. 192 34.00 N 81.46 W
Saluda, Va., U.S. 208 37.36 N 76.35 W
Saluda ≃ 192 34.00 N 81.04 W
Saludecio 66 43.52 N 12.40 E
Saluën → Salween ≃ 12 16.31 N 97.37 E
Salue Timpaus, Selat ʮ 112 1.55 S 124.00 E
Salug 116 8.07 N 122.47 E
Saluggia 62 45.14 N 8.00 E
Sālūmbar 120 24.08 N 74.03 E
Salunga 208 40.06 N 76.26 W
Saluping Island I 116 6.20 N 122.02 E
Salūq 'Atīq 130 36.36 N 39.07 E
Sālūr 122 18.32 N 83.13 E
Salurn → Salorno 64 46.14 N 11.13 E
Salussola 62 45.27 N 8.07 E
Salutáris 256 22.10 S 43.17 W
Saluzzo 62 44.39 N 7.29 E
Salvación, Bahía c 254 50.55 S 75.05 W
Salvado, Mount ∧ 162 25.15 S 121.01 E
Salvador, Bra. 255 12.59 S 38.31 W
Salvador, Pil. 116 7.54 N 123.50 E
Salvador, Ca., U.S. 226 38.20 N 122.18 W
Salvador, El → El Salvador □[1] 236 13.50 N 88.55 W
Salvador, Lake ◎ 194 29.45 N 90.15 W
Salvador Island I 116 15.31 N 119.55 E
Salvador María 258 35.18 S 59.10 W
Salvador Mazza 252 22.04 S 63.43 W
Salvage 186 48.41 N 53.38 W
Salvail ≃ 206 45.49 N 72.58 W
Salvaleón de Higüey 238 18.37 N 68.42 W
Salvaterra 250 0.46 S 48.31 W
Salvaterra de Magos 34 39.01 N 8.48 W
Salvatierra 234 20.13 N 100.53 W
Salve 68 39.51 N 18.17 E
Salviac 32 44.41 N 1.16 E
Salwā, Dawḥat c 128 25.30 N 50.40 E
Salwā Baḥrī 140 24.44 N 32.56 E
Salween ≃ 12 16.31 N 97.37 E
Salyān 124 28.22 N 82.10 E
Salyer 204 40.53 N 123.35 W
Salyersville 192 37.45 N 83.04 W
Šalygino 78 51.34 N 34.07 E
Salza ≃, D.D.R. 54 51.23 N 11.50 E
Salza ≃, Öst. 61 47.40 N 14.43 E
Salzach ≃ 30 48.12 N 12.56 E
Salza Irpina 68 40.55 N 14.53 E
Salzbergen 52 52.19 N 7.20 E
Salzböde ≃ 56 50.40 N 8.42 E
Salzbrunn 156 24.23 S 18.00 E
Salzburg 64 47.48 N 13.02 E
Salzburg □[3] 64 47.25 N 13.15 E
Salzgitter 54 52.10 N 10.25 E
Salzgitter-Bad ✦[8] 52 52.04 N 10.23 E
Salzgitter-Barum ✦[8] 52 52.07 N 10.25 E
Salzgitter-Immendorf ✦[8] 52 52.09 N 10.26 E
Salzgitter-Lebenstedt ✦[8] 52 52.09 N 10.20 E
Salzgitter-Thiede ✦[8] 52 52.11 N 10.29 E
Salzgitter-Watenstedt ✦[8] 52 52.06 N 10.22 E
Salzhaff c 54 54.06 N 11.36 E
Salzhausen 52 53.13 N 10.09 E
Salzhemmendorf 52 52.04 N 9.35 E
Salzkammergut ✦[1] 64 47.45 N 13.30 E
Salzkotten 52 51.40 N 8.36 E
Salzmünde 54 51.31 N 11.49 E
Salzwedel 54 52.51 N 11.09 E
Sam, Gabon 152 0.58 N 11.16 E
Sām, India 120 26.50 N 70.31 E
Samā 132 32.28 N 36.14 E
Sama ≃ 248 18.10 S 70.40 W
Sam A. Baker State Park ♦ 194 37.16 N 90.34 W
Samacá 246 5.29 N 73.29 W
Samacimbo 152 13.33 S 16.59 E
Sama [de Langreo] 34 43.18 N 5.41 W
Samādūn 142 30.20 N 30.57 E
Samagaltaj 88 50.36 N 95.03 E
Samah 146 28.12 N 19.09 E
Samāika ✦[8] 272a 28.32 N 77.05 E
Samaipata 248 18.09 S 63.52 W
Samal (Peñaplata) 116 7.05 N 125.42 E
Samalá ≃ 236 14.11 N 91.47 W
Samalanga 114 5.13 N 96.22 E
Samalayuca 200 31.21 N 106.28 W
Šamaldy-Saj 85 41.12 N 72.11 E
Samales Group II 116 6.00 N 121.45 E
Samalga Pass ʮ 180 52.48 N 169.25 W
Samal Island I 116 7.03 N 125.44 E
Sāmalkot 122 17.03 N 82.11 E
Samālūt 142 28.18 N 30.42 E
Samambaia ≃ 255 22.45 S 53.21 W
Samāna 124 30.09 N 76.12 E
Samaná, Bahía de c 238 19.10 N 69.25 W
Samaná, Cabo > 238 19.18 N 69.09 W
Samana Cay I 238 23.06 N 73.42 W
Samandağı 130 36.07 N 35.56 E
Samandıra 130 40.59 N 29.13 E
Samandıra ≃ 267b 40.59 N 29.15 E
Samangān 120 36.16 N 68.01 E
Samangān □[4] 120 36.15 N 67.40 E
Samangwa 152 4.24 S 24.10 E
Samani 92a 42.07 N 142.56 E
Samaniego 246 1.20 N 77.35 W
Samanlı Dağları ⋏ 130 40.36 N 29.30 E
Samannūd 142 30.58 N 31.15 E
Samar 132 29.49 N 35.01 E
Samar □[4] 116 11.50 N 125.00 E
Samar I 116 12.00 N 125.00 E
Samara → Kujbyšev 80 53.12 N 50.09 E
Samara ≃, S.S.S.R. 78 48.27 N 35.07 E
Samara ≃, S.S.S.R. 80 53.10 N 50.04 E
Samarai 164 10.37 S 150.40 E
Samarate 62 45.38 N 8.47 E
Samarga 89 47.17 N 138.48 E
Samarga ≃ 89 47.15 N 138.46 E
Samaria, Id., U.S. 202 42.07 N 112.20 W
Samaria, Mi., U.S. 216 41.48 N 83.35 W
Samaria (As-Sāmirah) □[9] 132 32.15 N 35.10 E
Samaria, Mount ∧ 169 36.52 S 146.03 E
Samaria Gorge → Farángi Samariás V 38 35.18 N 24.00 E
Samariapo 246 5.15 N 67.48 W
Samarinda 112 0.30 S 117.09 E
Samarka 89 44.44 N 134.13 E
Samarkand 85 39.40 N 66.48 E
Samarkand □[4] 85 40.00 N 67.00 E
Sāmarrā' 128 34.12 N 43.52 E
Samar Sea ⊽[2] 116 12.15 N 124.15 E
Samarskoje, S.S.S.R. 83 46.56 N 39.41 E
Samarskoje, S.S.S.R. 86 49.00 N 83.23 E
Şamarskoje, S.S.S.R. 86 52.02 N 58.10 E
Šamary 86 57.21 N 58.14 E
Samasata 123 29.21 N 71.33 E
Samassi 71 39.29 N 8.54 E
Samastīpur 124 25.51 N 85.47 E
Samatya ✦[8] 267b 41.00 N 28.56 E
Samawāri 120 28.34 N 66.46 E
Samba, Centraf. 152 6.49 N 21.12 E
Samba, India 123 32.34 N 75.07 E
Samba, Zaïre 152 0.14 N 21.19 E
Samba, Zaïre 154 4.38 S 26.22 E
Samba Caju 152 8.46 S 15.24 E
Sambaetiba 256 22.41 S 42.48 W
Sambaíba 250 7.08 S 45.21 W
Sambalpur 120 21.27 N 83.58 E
Sambar, Tanjung > 112 2.59 S 110.19 E
Sambas 112 1.20 N 109.15 E
Sambava 157b 14.16 S 50.10 E
Sambawizi 154 18.21 S 26.16 E
Şambayat 130 37.41 N 38.03 E
Šambāza 120 31.49 N 69.20 E
Sambek, S.S.S.R. 83 47.45 N 39.48 E
Sambek, S.S.S.R. 83 47.20 N 39.01 E
Sambek ≃ 83 47.16 N 39.01 E
Sambesi → Zambezi ≃ 138 18.55 S 36.04 E
Sambhal 124 28.35 N 78.33 E
Sāmbhar 120 26.55 N 75.12 E
Sāmbhar Lake ◎ 120 26.58 N 75.05 E
Sambia → Zambia □[1] 154 14.30 S 27.30 E
Sambiase 68 38.58 N 16.17 E
Sambit, Pulau I 112 1.46 N 119.03 E
Sambito ≃ 250 5.40 S 42.10 W
Sambo 152 12.57 S 16.05 E
Samboan 116 9.32 N 123.18 E
Samboja 112 1.02 S 117.02 E
Sambolabbo 152 7.05 N 11.59 E
Sâmbor, Kam. 110 12.46 N 105.58 E
Sambor, S.S.S.R. 78 49.32 N 23.11 E
Samborombón ≃ 252 35.43 S 57.20 W
Samborombón, Bahía c 252 36.00 S 57.12 W
Samborondón 246 1.57 S 79.44 W
Sambre ≃ 32 50.28 N 4.52 E
Sambre à l'Oise, Canal de la ≍ 50 49.39 N 3.20 E
Sambreville 56 50.26 N 4.37 E
Sambriāl 123 32.28 N 74.21 E
Sambú ≃ 246 8.05 N 78.18 W
Sambuca di Sicilia 70 37.39 N 13.07 E
Sambuca Pistoiese 66 44.06 N 11.00 E
Sambughetti, Monte ∧ 70 37.50 N 14.22 E
Sambungo 152 8.39 S 20.43 E
Sambusu 156 17.50 S 19.20 E
Samch'ŏk 98 37.27 N 129.10 E
Sam Chom, Khao ∧ 110 8.07 N 99.26 E
Şamch'ŏnp'o 98 34.57 N 128.03 E
Šamchor 84 40.50 N 46.02 E
Samdžir, gora ∧ 88 52.32 N 93.53 E
Same 154 4.04 S 37.44 E
Same ≃ 94 36.54 N 140.49 E
Samedan 58 46.33 N 9.52 E
Samegawa 94 37.02 N 140.31 E
Sāmen 128 34.12 N 48.42 E
Samene, Oued V 148 26.49 N 7.08 E
Samer 50 50.38 N 1.45 E
Sameru Dando ∧ 124 27.02 N 90.20 E
Samet' 80 57.49 N 40.44 E
Samford 171a 27.23 S 152.53 E
Samfya 154 11.21 S 29.32 E
Samga 98 35.25 N 128.05 E
Samho 98 39.56 N 127.53 E
Saminka ≃ 265b 55.45 N 37.17 E
Samiria ≃ 246 4.42 S 74.13 W
Samish 224 48.35 N 122.33 W
Samish ≃ 224 48.38 N 122.29 W
Samish Bay c 224 48.36 N 122.28 W
Samish Lake ◎ 224 48.39 N 122.24 W
Samj 132 32.27 N 36.30 E
Samka 110 20.09 N 96.57 E
Samlesbury 262 53.46 N 2.38 W
Samlesbury Aerodrome ⊠ 262 53.47 N 2.34 W
Samlesbury Bottoms 262 53.45 N 2.34 W
Samlesbury Higher Hall ⊥ 262 53.46 N 2.34 W
Şamlı 130 39.48 N 27.51 E
Sammamish, Lake ◎ 224 47.36 N 122.06 W
Sammichele di Bari 68 40.53 N 16.57 E
Samnangjin 98 35.23 N 128.50 E
Samnaun 58 46.56 N 10.22 E
Samnaungruppe ⋏ 58 47.00 N 10.25 E
Sam Ngao 110 17.15 N 99.01 E
Samnū 146 27.17 N 14.53 E
Samnye 98 35.55 N 127.05 E
Samo 164 3.58 S 152.51 E
Samoa → American Samoa □[2] 175a 14.20 S 170.00 W
Samoa americane → American Samoa □[2] 175a 14.20 S 170.00 W
Samoa Basin ✦[1] 14 16.00 S 166.00 W
Samoa i Sisifo → Western Samoa □[1] 175a 13.55 S 172.00 W
Samoa Islands II 175a 14.00 S 171.00 W
Samo Alto 252 30.25 S 70.58 W
Samoa Occidental → Western Samoa □[1] 175a 13.55 S 172.00 W
Samoa Occidentales → Western Samoa □[1] 175a 13.55 S 172.00 W
Samobor 36 45.48 N 15.43 E
Samoded 24 63.38 N 40.29 E
Samoëns 58 46.05 N 6.44 E
Samofalovka 80 48.57 N 44.13 E
Samoggia ≃ 64 44.41 N 11.15 E
Samojlovka 80 51.12 N 43.43 E
Samokov 38 42.20 N 23.33 E
Samolaco 58 46.15 N 9.21 E
Samora ≃ 266c 38.50 N 8.57 W
Sámos 38 37.45 N 27.00 E
Sámos I 38 37.48 N 26.44 E
Samosdelka 80 46.02 N 47.53 E
Samoset 220 27.28 N 82.32 W
Samosir, Pulau I 114 2.35 N 98.50 E
Samotevići 76 53.13 N 31.50 E
Samothrace → Samothráki I 38 40.30 N 25.32 E
Samothráki 38 40.28 N 25.31 E
Samothráki I 38 40.30 N 25.32 E

ENGLISH

Name Page Lat.°′ Long.°′
Şamouco 266c 38.43 N 9.00 W
Šamovo 76 54.12 N 31.22 E
Samovol'no-Ivanovka 80 52.33 N 50.53 E
S amozero 24 61.54 N 33.18 E
Sampacho 252 33.23 S 64.43 W
Sampaga 112 2.19 S 119.07 E
Sampaio Correia 256 22.52 S 42.36 W
Sampalan 115b 8.41 S 115.34 E
Sampanahan 112 2.38 S 116.11 E
Sampang 115a 7.12 S 113.14 E
Sampara ≃ 112 3.49 S 122.28 E
Sampawams Creek ≃ 276 40.41 N 73.19 W
Sam Pervyj 86 45.28 N 56.06 E
Sampéyre 62 44.34 N 7.11 E
Sampford Peverell 42 50.56 N 3.22 W
Sampieri 70 36.43 N 14.44 E
Sampit 112 2.32 S 112.57 E
Sampit ≃ 112 2.44 S 112.54 E
Sampit, Teluk c 112 3.05 S 113.03 E
Sampolawa 112 5.36 S 122.43 E
Sampson 279b 40.10 N 79.53 W
Sampson State Park ♦ 210 42.44 N 76.55 W
Sampués 246 9.11 N 75.23 W
Sampur 80 52.19 N 41.37 E
Sampwe 154 9.20 S 27.26 E
Šamrajevka 78 49.46 N 29.49 E
Samrāla 123 30.51 N 76.11 E
Sam Rayburn Reservoir ◎[1] 194 31.27 N 94.37 W
Samre 144 13.07 N 39.10 E
Samreboi 150 5.36 N 2.34 W
Samro, ozero ◎ 76 58.57 N 28.49 E
Samrong, Khlong ≍ 269a 13.39 N 100.34 E
Sams ≃ 224 47.38 N 124.01 W
Samsang 120 30.31 N 82.37 E
Samsat 130 37.30 N 38.31 E
Samsø I 41 55.52 N 10.37 E
Samsø Bælt ʮ 41 55.48 N 10.47 E
Samson, Al., U.S. 194 31.06 N 86.02 W
Sam Son, Viet. 110 19.44 N 105.54 E
Samson I 42a 49.56 N 6.22 W
Samson Indian Reserve ✦[4] 182 52.48 N 113.10 W
Samsonovka 85 42.44 N 70.32 E
Samsonvale, Lake ◎[1] 171a 27.15 S 152.55 E
Samsonville 210 41.53 N 74.18 W
Sams Point ∧ 210 41.40 N 74.22 W
Samsu 98 41.19 N 127.59 E
Samsun 130 41.17 N 36.20 E
Samsun □[4] 130 41.15 N 36.00 E
Samsun Körfezi c 130 41.18 N 36.21 E
Samtens 54 54.21 N 13.17 E
Samthar 124 25.51 N 78.55 E
Samtown 194 31.16 N 92.26 W
Samtredia 84 42.10 N 42.20 E
Samu 112 2.01 S 115.57 E
Samūdragarh 126 23.21 N 88.20 E
Samuel, Mount ∧ 162 19.41 S 134.09 E
Samuel P. Taylor State Park ♦ 226 38.01 N 122.44 W
Samugheo 71 39.57 N 8.56 E
Samuhú 252 27.31 S 60.24 W
Samui, Ko I 110 9.30 N 100.00 E
Samukawa 94 35.22 N 139.23 E
Samundri 123 31.04 N 72.58 E
Samur ≃ 84 41.53 N 48.32 E
Samur-Apšeronskij kanal ≍ 84 41.38 N 48.25 E
Samus' 86 56.46 N 84.44 E
Samusele 152 10.06 S 24.05 E
Samut Prakan 110 13.36 N 100.36 E
Samut Prakan □[4] 269a 13.35 N 100.35 E
Samut Sakhon 110 13.32 N 100.17 E
Samut Songkhram 110 13.24 N 100.00 E
Samuyi Shankou)(124 29.55 N 84.46 E
S'amža 76 60.01 N 41.02 E
San 150 13.18 N 4.54 W
San (Xan) ≃, Asia 110 13.32 N 105.58 E
San ≃, Europe 30 50.44 N 21.50 E
San ≃, Zhg. 100 33.02 N 119.21 E
Saña, Perú 248 6.55 S 79.35 W
Şan'ā', Yaman 144 15.23 N 44.12 E
Sana ≃, Jugo. 36 45.03 N 16.23 E
Šan'a ≃, S.S.S.R. 82 54.41 N 35.55 E
Sanaag □[4] 144 10.30 N 47.45 E
Sanaba 150 12.25 N 3.49 W
Sanaba ≃ 150 15.06 N 10.55 W
Şanabū 142 27.30 N 30.47 E
Sanada 94 36.27 N 138.20 E
Sanaduva 252 27.57 S 51.48 W
Sanae ⊍[3] 9 70.30 S 2.30 W
Sanafā 142 30.47 N 31.21 E
Şanāfīr I 128 27.55 N 34.40 E
Sanaga ≃ 152 3.35 N 9.38 E
Sanage-yama ∧ 94 35.12 N 137.10 E
Sanagōchi 96 33.59 N 134.28 E
San Agustín, Arg. 252 31.59 S 64.23 W
San Agustín, Arg. 252 38.01 S 58.21 W
San Agustín, Col. 246 1.53 N 76.16 W
San Agustín, Méx. 200 31.31 N 106.15 W
San Agustín, Perú 286d 12.02 S 77.07 W
San Agustin, Pil. 116 12.25 N 120.59 E
San Agustin, Pil. 116 16.30 N 121.45 E
San Agustin, Cape > 116 6.16 N 126.11 E
San Agustin, Plains of ≐ 200 33.50 N 108.00 W
San Agustín Atenango 234 17.38 N 97.59 W
San Agustín de Valle Fértil 252 30.38 S 67.27 W
San Agustín Loxicha 234 16.01 N 96.38 W
San Agustín Oapan 234 17.58 N 99.27 W
San Agustín Tlaxiaca 234 20.07 N 98.53 W
Sanak Islands II 180 54.25 N 162.35 W
San Alberto 196 27.30 N 101.20 W
San Alejo 236 13.26 N 87.58 W
Şān al-Ḥajar, Birkat ◎ 142 31.03 N 31.54 E
Şān al-Ḥajar al-Qiblīyah 142 30.58 N 31.52 E
Sanalona, Presa ◎[1] 232 24.53 N 107.00 W
San Ambrosio, Isla I 244 26.21 S 79.52 W
Sanam Chai, Khlong ≍ 269a 13.38 N 100.27 E
Sanana 112 2.04 S 125.58 E
Sanana, Pulau I 112 2.12 S 125.55 E
Sānand 120 22.59 N 72.23 E
Sanandaj 128 35.19 N 47.00 E
Sanandita 248 21.40 S 63.35 W
San Andreas 226 38.11 N 120.40 W
San Andreas Lake ◎ 282 37.36 N 122.26 W
San Andreas Rift Zone V 282 37.25 N 122.15 W
San Andrés, Col. 236 12.35 N 81.42 W
San Andrés, Col. 246 6.49 N 72.52 W
San Andrés, Méx. 232 27.14 N 114.14 W
San Andrés, Pan. 236 8.36 N 82.44 W
San Andrés, Cerro ∧ 234 19.48 N 100.36 W
San Andrés, Isla de I 236 12.32 N 81.42 W
San Andrés, Laguna de c 234 22.40 N 97.52 W
San Andrés Cohamiata 234 22.12 N 104.03 W
San Andrés de Giles 258 34.27 S 59.27 W
San Andres Mountains ⋏ 200 32.55 N 106.45 W
San Andres Point > 116 13.34 N 121.52 E
San Andrés Sajcabajá 236 15.13 N 90.55 W
San Andrés Totoltepec ✦[8] 286a 19.15 N 99.10 W
San Andrés Tuxtla 234 18.27 N 95.13 W
San Andrés y Providencia □[8] 238 12.30 N 81.45 W
San Angel → Villa Obregón ✦[8] 286a 19.21 N 99.12 W
San Angelo 196 31.27 N 100.26 W
San Anselmo 226 37.58 N 122.33 W

DEUTSCH

Name Seite Breite°′ Länge°′ E = Ost
San Antero 246 9.23 N 75.46 W
San Antonio, Arg. 252 28.56 S 65.06 W
San Antonio, Arg. 252 24.22 S 65.20 W
San Antonio, Belize 236 16.15 N 89.02 W
San Antonio, Chile 252 33.35 S 71.38 W
San Antonio, Chile 252 27.53 S 70.03 W
San Antonio, Col. 246 3.55 N 75.28 W
San Antonio, C.R. 236 10.12 N 85.26 W
San Antonio, Perú 248 6.22 S 76.21 W
San Antonio, Pil. 116 12.25 N 124.17 E
San Antonio, Pil. 116 14.57 N 120.05 E
San Antonio, P.R. 240m 18.30 N 67.07 W
San Antonio, T.T.P.I. 174n 15.08 N 145.43 E
San Antonio, Fl., U.S. 220 28.20 N 82.16 W
San Antonio, N.M., U.S. 200 35.06 N 106.22 W
San Antonio, Tx., U.S. 196 29.25 N 98.29 W
San Antonio, Ur. 252 31.22 S 57.48 W
San Antonio, Ur. 258 34.27 S 56.05 W
San Antonio □[7] 286b 22.55 N 82.29 W
San Antonio ≃, Méx. 196 29.13 N 103.47 W
San Antonio ≃, Méx. 232 31.00 N 116.15 W
San Antonio ≃, Méx. 234 18.14 N 101.52 W
San Antonio ≃, Ca., U.S. 226 35.52 N 120.48 W
San Antonio ≃, Tx., U.S. 196 28.30 N 96.50 W
San Antonio ≃[1] 288 34.24 S 58.31 W
San Antonio, Cabo >, Arg. 252 36.40 S 56.42 W
San Antonio, Cabo >, Cuba 240p 21.52 N 84.57 W
San Antonio, Lake ◎[1] 226 35.55 N 121.00 W
San Antonio, Mount ∧ 228 34.17 N 117.39 W
San Antonio, Punta >, Méx. 232 29.46 N 115.42 W
San Antonio, Punta >, Méx. 232 26.31 N 111.28 W
San Antonio, Rio ≃ 200 37.11 N 105.55 W
San Antonio Bay c, Pil. 116 8.38 N 117 35 E
San Antonio Bay c, Tx., U.S. 196 28.20 N 96.45 W
San Antonio Canyon V 280 34.12 N 117.40 W
San Antonio Creek ≃ 226 38.09 N 122.33 W
San Antonio Dam ✦[6] 280 34.09 N 117.41 W
San Antonio de Areco 258 34.15 S 59.28 W
San Antonio de Bravo 232 30.10 N 104.42 W
San Antonio de Galipán 286c 10.33 N 66.53 W
San Antonio de las Alazanas 232 25.16 N 100.36 W
San Antonio del Golfo 246 10.27 N 63.50 W
San Antonio de los Baños 240p 22.53 N 82.30 W
San Antonio de los Cobres 252 24.11 S 66.21 W
San Antonio del Táchira 246 7.50 N 72.27 W
San Antonio de Padua, Arg. 258 34.40 S 58.42 W
San Antônio de Pádua, Bra. 255 21.32 S 42.11 W
San Antonio de Padua, Méx. 234 22.35 N 104.30 W
San Antonio de Padua, Mission ⊍[1] 226 36.01 N 121.15 W
San Antonio de Tamanaco 246 9.41 N 66.03 W
San Antonio Eloxochitlán 234 18.11 N 96.52 W
San Antonio Heights 228 34.10 N 117.40 W
San Antonio Mountain ∧ 200 36.52 N 106.02 W
San Antonio Nogalar 234 23.04 N 98.22 W
San Antonio Oeste 254 40.44 S 64.56 W
San Antonio Reservoir ◎[1] 226 37.35 N 121.50 W
San Antonio Suchitepéquez 236 14.32 N 91.25 W
San Antonio Tecómitl ✦[8] 286a 19.13 N 98.59 W
San Antonio Ticino 266b 45.35 N 8.46 E
San Antonio Zomeyucan 286a 19.27 N 99.16 W
San Ardo 226 36.01 N 120.54 W
Sanaroa Island I 164 9.35 S 151.00 E
Sanary-sur-Mer 62 43.07 N 5.48 E
Sanatoga 285 40.15 N 75.36 W
Sanatoga Creek ≃ 285 40.14 N 75.36 W
Sanatorium 194 31.53 N 89.46 W
San Augustine 194 31.31 N 94.06 W
San Augustin Pass)(200 32.26 N 106.34 W
Sanaur 124 30.18 N 76.27 E
Sanāw 144 17.50 N 51.00 E
Sanāwad 120 22.11 N 76.04 E
Sanāwān 123 30.19 N 70.59 E
Sanbao, Zhg. 102 43.00 N 93.19 E
Sanbao, Zhg. 105 40.20 N 116.02 E
Sanbaoyingzi 104 41.34 N 120.56 E
San Bartolomé Ayautla 234 18.02 N 96.40 W
San Bartolomeo in Galdo 68 41.24 N 15.01 E
San Bartolo Morelos 234 19.41 N 99.29 W
San Basilio 71 39.32 N 9.11 E
San Benedetto, Alpe di ⋏ 66 43.53 N 11.43 E
San Benedetto del Tronto 66 42.57 N 13.53 E
San Benedetto in Alpe 66 43.59 N 11.41 E
San Benedetto Po 64 45.02 N 10.55 E
San Benedicto, Isla I 232 19.18 N 110.49 W
San Benigno Canavese 62 45.13 N 7.46 E
San Benito, Bol. 248 17.31 S 65.55 W
San Benito, Guat. 232 16.55 N 89.54 W
San Benito, Perú 248 7.26 S 78.56 W
San Benito, Tx., U.S. 196 26.07 N 97.37 W
San Benito □[6] 226 36.51 N 121.24 W
San Benito ≃ 226 36.53 N 121.34 W
San Benito Mountain ∧ 226 36.22 N 120.38 W
San Bernard ≃ 222 28.52 N 95.27 W
San Bernardino, Schw. 58 46.28 N 9.12 E
San Bernardino, Ca., U.S. 228 34.07 N 117.18 W
San Bernardino □[6] 228 34.40 N 117.17 W
San Bernardino, Passo del)(58 46.30 N 9.11 E
San Bernardino Mountains ⋏ 204 34.10 N 116.45 W
San Bernardino National Forest ♦ 280 34.12 N 117.38 W
San Bernardino Strait ʮ 116 12.32 N 124.10 E
San Bernardo, Arg. 252 27.17 S 60.42 W
San Bernardo, Chile 252 33.36 S 70.43 W
San Bernardo, Méx. 232 25.59 N 105.33 W
San Bernardo, Canal ≍ 286e 33.36 S 70.41 W
San Bernardo, Isla I 236 11.32 N 85.06 W
San Bernardo, Islas de II 246 9.45 N 75.50 W
San Bernardo del Viento 246 9.21 N 75.57 W
Sanbe-yama ∧ 96 35.08 N 132.37 E
San Biagio 66 44.35 N 11.52 E
San Biagio di Callalta 64 45.41 N 12.22 E
San Biagio Platani 70 37.31 N 13.32 E

Symbols in the index entries represent the broad categories identified in the key at the right. Symbols with superior numbers (⋏[1]) identify subcategories (see complete key on page I · 1).

Symbole im Register stellen die rechts im Schlüssel erklärten Kategorien dar. Symbole mit hochgestellten Ziffern (⋏[1]) bezeichnen Unterabteilungen einer Kategorie (vgl. vollständiger Schlüssel auf Seite I · 1).

Los símbolos incluidos en el texto del índice representan las grandes categorías identificadas con la clave a la derecha. Los símbolos con numeros en su parte superior (⋏[1]) identifican las subcategorías (véase la clave completa en la página I · 1).

Les symboles de l'index représentent les catégories indiquées dans la légende à droite. Les symboles suivis d'un indice (⋏[1]) représentent des sous-catégories (voir légende complète à la page I · 1).

Os símbolos incluídos no texto do índice representam as grandes categorias identificadas com a chave à direita. Os símbolos com números em sua parte superior (⋏[1]) identificam as subcategorias (veja-se a chave completa à página I · 1).

∧ Mountain	Berg	Montaña	Montagne	Montanha
⋏ Mountains	Gebirge	Montañas	Montagnes	Montanhas
)(Pass	Paß	Paso	Col	Passo
V Valley, Canyon	Tal, Cañon	Valle, Cañón	Vallée, Canyon	Vale, Canhão
≐ Plain	Ebene	Llano	Plaine	Planície
> Cape	Kap	Cabo	Cap	Cabo
I Island	Insel	Isla	Île	Ilha
II Islands	Inseln	Islas	Îles	Ilhas
⊥ Other Topographic Features	Andere Topographische Objekte	Otros Elementos Topográficos	Autres données topographiques	Outros acidentes topográficos

ESPAÑOL — Nombre · Página · Lat.°' · Long.°' W = Oeste
FRANÇAIS — Nom · Page · Lat.°' · Long.°' W = Ouest
PORTUGUÊS — Nome · Página · Lat.°' · Long.°' W = Oeste

San Biagio Saracinisco 66 41.37 N 13.55 E
San Blas, Méx. 232 26.05 N 108.46 W
San Blas, Méx. 234 21.31 N 105.16 W
San Blas, Cape ➤ 192 29.40 N 85.22 W
San Blas, Cordillera de ⋏ 246 9.18 N 79.00 W
San Blas, Golfo de ⊂ 246 9.30 N 79.00 W
San Blas Atempa 234 16.16 N 95.10 W
San Blas de los Sauces 252 28.24 S 67.05 W
San Bonifacio 64 45.24 N 11.16 E
San Borja 248 14.49 S 66.51 W
Sanborn, Ia., U.S. 198 43.10 N 95.39 W
Sanborn, Mn., U.S. 198 44.12 N 95.07 W
Sanborn, N.Y., U.S. 210 43.08 N 78.53 W
Sanborn, N.D., U.S. 198 46.56 N 98.13 W
San Bovio 266b 45.28 N 9.19 E
San Bruno 226 37.37 N 122.24 W
San Bruno, Point ➤ 282 37.39 N 122.22 W
San Bruno Mountain ⋏ 282 37.42 N 122.25 W
Sanbu 94 35.39 N 140.23 E
San Buena Ventura, Bol. 248 14.28 S 67.35 W
San Buenaventura, Méx. 232 27.05 N 101.32 W
San Buenaventura → Ventura, Ca., U.S. 228 34.17 N 119.18 W
San Buono 66 41.59 N 14.34 E
San Calogero 68 38.34 N 16.01 E
San Calogero, Monte ⋏ 70 37.57 N 13.44 E
San Candido (Innichen) 64 46.44 N 12.17 E
Sancang 100 32.45 N 120.43 E
San Carlo 58 46.25 N 8.32 E
San Carlos, Arg. 252 25.56 S 65.56 W
San Carlos, Arg. 252 27.45 S 55.54 W
San Carlos, Arg. 252 33.46 S 69.02 W
San Carlos, Chile 252 36.25 S 71.58 W
San Carlos, Chile 286e 33.36 S 70.35 W
San Carlos, Méx. 232 29.01 N 100.51 W
San Carlos, Méx. 232 24.35 N 98.56 W
San Carlos, Nic. 236 11.07 N 84.47 W
San Carlos, Pan. 236 8.29 N 79.57 W
San Carlos, Para. 252 22.16 S 57.18 W
San Carlos, Pil. 116 10.30 N 123.25 E
San Carlos, Pil. 116 15.55 N 120.20 E
San Carlos, Az., U.S. 200 33.20 N 110.27 W
San Carlos, Ca., U.S. 226 37.29 N 122.15 W
San Carlos, Ur. 252 34.48 S 54.55 W
San Carlos, Ven. 246 9.40 N 68.36 W
San Carlos ≃, C.R. 236 10.47 N 84.12 W
San Carlos ≃, Az., U.S. 200 33.16 N 110.27 W
San Carlos ≃, Ven. 246 9.07 N 68.25 W
San Carlos, Canal ≅ 286e 33.25 S 70.38 W
San Carlos, Riacho ≃ 252 22.51 S 57.51 W
San Carlos Airport ⊠ 282 37.31 N 122.15 W
San Carlos Bay ⊂ 220 26.28 N 82.03 W
San Carlos Borromeo, Mission ✝1 226 36.34 N 121.55 W
San Carlos Centro 252 31.44 S 61.06 W
San Carlos de Bariloche 254 41.09 S 71.18 W
San Carlos de Bolívar 252 36.15 S 61.06 W
San Carlos de Chena 286e 33.35 S 70.44 W
San Carlos de Guaroa 246 3.44 N 73.14 W
San Carlos del Zulia 246 9.01 N 71.55 W
San Carlos de Río Negro 246 1.55 N 67.04 W
San Carlos Indian Reservation ◆4 200 33.23 N 110.09 W
San Carlos Reservoir ⊜1 200 33.13 N 110.24 W
San Carpoforo Creek ≃ 226 35.47 N 121.19 W
San Casciano dei Bagni 66 42.52 N 11.53 E
San Casciano in Val di Pesa 66 43.39 N 11.11 E
San Cataldo, It. 68 40.23 N 18.17 E
San Cataldo, It. 70 37.29 N 13.59 E
San Cayetano 252 38.20 S 59.37 W
Sancergues 50 47.09 N 2.55 E
Sancerre 50 47.20 N 2.51 E
Sancerrois, Collines du ⋏2 50 47.25 N 2.45 E
San Cesario di Lecce 68 40.18 N 18.10 E
San Cesario sul Panaro 64 44.34 N 11.02 E
Sancey-le-Grand 58 47.18 N 6.35 E
Sancha, Zhg. 105 40.27 N 116.26 E
Sancha, Zhg. 106 31.52 N 119.06 E
Sancha ≃ 102 26.55 N 106.06 E
Sanchaba 107 30.19 N 104.14 E
Sanchahe 89 44.59 N 126.04 E
Sanchakou 105 39.47 N 117.19 E
Sanchang 106 31.54 N 121.15 E
Sanchazi 104 41.07 N 124.15 E
Sanchazicun 104 42.03 N 123.59 E
Sanchenglong 89 44.02 N 120.58 E
Sánchez 238 19.14 N 69.36 W
Sanchez Creek ≃ 222 32.36 N 97.50 W
Sánchez Magallanes 234 18.14 N 93.52 W
Sanchi 124 23.29 N 77.44 E
Sanchih 100 25.16 N 121.30 E
San Chirico Raparo 68 40.11 N 16.05 E
Sanch'ŏng 98 35.26 N 127.54 E
Sanchung 269d 25.04 N 121.30 E
Sanch'ungch'iao 269d 25.12 N 121.35 E
San Cipirello 70 37.58 N 13.10 E
San Cipriano Picentino 68 40.43 N 14.52 E
San Ciro de Acosta 234 21.38 N 99.49 W
San Clemente, Esp. 34 39.24 N 2.26 W
San Clemente, Ca., U.S. 228 33.25 N 117.36 W
San Clemente, Arroyo de ≃ 266d 41.20 N 2.00 E
San Clemente a Casauria ✝1 66 42.14 N 13.55 E
San Clemente Island I 228 32.54 N 118.29 W
Sancoins 32 46.50 N 2.55 E
San Colombano al Lambro 62 45.11 N 9.29 E
San Cono 70 37.17 N 14.22 E
Sanco Point ➤ 116 8.15 N 126.27 E
San Cosme 252 27.22 S 58.31 W
San Cosme Xalostoc 234 19.24 N 98.03 W
San Cosmo Albanese 68 39.35 N 16.25 E
San Costantino Albanese 68 40.02 N 16.18 E
San Cristóbal, Arg. 252 30.19 S 61.14 W
San Cristóbal, Cuba 240p 22.43 N 83.03 W
San Cristóbal, Ven. 246 7.46 N 72.14 W
San Cristobal I 175e 10.36 S 161.45 E
San Cristóbal ≃ 234 18.02 N 96.12 W
San Cristóbal, Bahía de ⊂ 232 27.23 N 114.38 W
San Cristóbal, Cerro ⋏, Chile 286e 33.25 S 70.39 W
San Cristóbal, Cerro ⋏, Perú 286d 12.02 S 77.01 W
San Cristóbal, Isla I 246a 0.50 S 89.26 W
San Cristóbal, Nevis → Saint Christopher-Nevis □1 238 17.20 N 62.45 W
San Cristóbal, Volcán ⋏1 236 12.42 N 87.01 W
San Cristóbal de la Barranca 234 21.03 N 103.26 W
San Cristóbal de la Laguna 148 28.29 N 16.19 W
San Cristóbal de las Casas 234 16.45 N 92.38 W
San Cristóbal Totonicapán 236 14.55 N 91.26 W
San Cristobal Trench ✦1 14 11.15 S 162.45 E
San Cristóbal Verapaz 236 15.23 N 90.24 W
San Cristobal Wash V 200 32.47 N 113.44 W
San Croce, Monte ⋏ 66 41.17 N 13.58 E
Sancti-Spíritus 240p 21.56 N 79.27 W
Sancti-Spíritus □4 240p 22.00 N 79.20 W
San Cugat, Riera de ≃ 266d 41.29 N 2.11 E
Sančursk 80 56.57 N 47.15 E
Sancy, Puy de ⋏ 32 45.32 N 2.49 E
Sand, B.R.D. 56 48.32 N 7.55 E
Sand, Nor. 26 59.29 N 6.15 E
Sand ≃, Ab., Can. 184 54.22 N 111.05 W
Sand ≃, S. Afr. 156 22.25 S 30.05 E
Sand ≃, S. Afr. 158 28.05 S 26.25 E
Sanda, Nihon 96 34.53 N 135.14 E
Sanda, Nihon 268 35.28 N 139.21 E
Sandafā al-Fa'r 142 28.32 N 30.40 E
Sandai 112 1.15 S 110.31 E
Sanda Island I 44 55.18 N 5.34 W
Sandakan 112 5.50 N 118.07 E
Sandakan, Pelabuhan ⊂ 116 5.45 N 118.05 E
Sandal, Baie du ⊂ 175f 20.50 S 167.05 E
San Damián 248 12.02 S 76.24 W
San Damiano d'Asti 62 44.50 N 8.04 E
San Damiano Macra 62 44.29 N 7.16 E
Sândân 110 12.42 N 106.01 E
Sandan, Chāh ▾4 128 28.59 N 63.27 E
Sandane 26 61.46 N 6.13 E
San Daniele del Friuli 64 46.09 N 13.00 E
Sandan-kyō ♦ 96 34.38 N 132.13 E
Sandanski 38 41.34 N 23.17 E
Sandaogang 89 46.08 N 130.05 E
Sandaogou, Zhg. 104 41.39 N 121.45 E
Sandaogou, Zhg. 105 39.33 N 115.27 E
Sandaohe 86 44.21 N 85.37 E
Sandaoliangzi 104 41.20 N 122.07 E
Sandaolingzi 104 40.58 N 124.08 E
Sandaozhen 89 47.25 N 126.25 E
Sandaré 150 14.42 N 10.18 W
Sandared 26 57.43 N 12.47 E
Sandarne 26 61.16 N 17.10 E
Sand Arroyo V 196 37.29 N 101.29 W
Sandata 80 46.16 N 41.46 E
Sandau 54 52.47 N 12.02 E
Sanday I 46 59.15 N 2.35 W
Sanday Sound ⊂ 46 59.11 N 2.31 W
Sandbach 44 53.09 N 2.22 W
Sandbank 46 55.59 N 4.58 W
Sandbanks Provincial Park ♦ 212 43.55 N 77.17 W
Sandbochum ◆8 263 51.40 N 7.41 E
Sand City 226 36.37 N 121.51 W
Sand Coulee 202 47.23 N 111.10 W
Sand Coulee Creek ≃ 202 47.27 N 111.18 W
Sand Creek ≃, U.S. 200 41.13 N 105.43 W
Sand Creek ≃, In., U.S. 218 39.03 N 85.51 W
Sand Creek ≃, Ks., U.S. 198 37.26 N 98.12 W
Sand Creek ≃, Mn., U.S. 190 45.56 N 92.39 W
Sand Creek ≃, Mt., U.S. 202 47.18 N 106.45 W
Sand Creek ≃, S.D., U.S. 198 44.02 N 98.05 W
Sand Creek ≃, Wy., U.S. 200 43.27 N 105.26 W
Sand Creek ≃, Wy., U.S. 200 41.02 N 107.52 W
Sand Creek ≃, Wy., U.S. 202 44.16 N 107.55 W
Sand Cut 220 26.56 N 80.35 W
Sande, B.R.D. 52 51.45 N 8.39 E
Sande, B.R.D. 52 53.30 N 8.01 E
Sandefjord 26 59.08 N 10.14 E
San Demetrio Corone 68 39.34 N 16.22 E
San Demetrio ne'Vestini 66 42.17 N 13.34 E
Sanders, Az., U.S. 200 35.12 N 109.19 W
Sanders, Ky., U.S. 218 38.39 N 84.56 W
Sandersdorf, B.R.D. 60 48.54 N 11.37 E
Sandersdorf, D.D.R. 54 51.37 N 12.15 E
Sandersleben 54 51.40 N 11.34 E
Sanderson 196 30.08 N 102.23 W
Sanderstead ◆8 260 51.20 N 0.05 W
Sanderston 168b 34.46 S 139.13 E
Sandersville, Ga., U.S. 192 32.58 N 82.48 W
Sandersville, Ms., U.S. 194 31.47 N 89.01 W
Sandeshkhali 126 22.22 N 88.53 E
Sandesneben 52 53.41 N 10.30 E
Sandfly Lake ⊜ 184 55.45 N 106.05 W
Sand Fork 188 38.54 N 80.45 W
Sandgate, Austl. 171a 27.20 S 153.05 E
Sandgate, Eng., U.K. 42 51.05 N 1.08 E
Sandhammaren ➤ 26 55.23 N 14.12 E
Sandhamn 40 59.17 N 18.55 E
Sandhead 44 54.48 N 4.58 W
Sandheuwel 158 31.46 S 20.48 E
Sandhill, On., Can. 275b 43.50 N 79.49 W
Sand Hill, Ma., U.S. 207 42.13 N 70.44 W
Sand Hill ⋏2 210 42.31 N 77.37 W
Sand Hill ≃ 198 47.36 N 96.52 W
Sand Hills ⋏2 198 42.00 N 101.00 W
Sandhorst 52 53.29 N 7.29 E
Sandhurst 42 51.19 N 0.48 W
Sāndi 124 27.18 N 79.57 E
Sandia 248 14.17 S 69.26 W
Sandia Crest ⋏ 200 35.13 N 106.27 W
Sandia Indian Reservation ◆4 200 35.15 N 106.30 W
San Diego, Ca., U.S. 228 32.42 N 117.09 W
San Diego, Tx., U.S. 196 27.45 N 98.14 W
San Diego □6 228 33.00 N 117.05 W
San Diego ≃, Cuba 240p 22.20 N 83.16 W
San Diego ≃, Ca., U.S. 204 32.46 N 117.13 W
San Diego, Cabo ➤ 254 54.38 S 65.07 W
San Diego Aqueduct ≅1 228 32.55 N 116.55 W
San Diego Bay ⊂ 228 32.37 N 117.07 W
San Diego Creek ≃ 196 27.47 N 98.03 W
San Diego de Alcala, Mission ✝1 228 32.48 N 117.06 W
San Diego de la Unión 234 21.28 N 100.52 W
San Diego Naval Training Center ■ 228 32.44 N 117.13 W
San Dieguito ≃ 228 32.58 N 117.16 W
Sandies Creek ≃ 222 29.06 N 97.20 W
Sandıklı 130 38.28 N 30.17 E
Sandila 124 27.05 N 80.31 E
Sandilands 168b 34.31 S 137.46 E
Sandilands Village 240b 25.02 N 77.18 W
San Dimas 228 34.06 N 117.48 W
San Dimas Canyon V 280 34.10 N 117.46 W
San Dimas Reservoir ⊜1 280 34.09 N 117.43 W
San Dionisio, Nic. 236 12.45 N 85.51 W
San Dionisio, Pil. 116 11.16 N 123.06 E
Sand Island I, Mid. Is. 174g 28.12 N 177.23 W
Sand Island I, Hi., U.S. 229c 21.18 N 157.53 W
Sand Islet I 174g 28.16 N 177.23 W
Sandiway 262 53.14 N 2.36 W
Sand Key I 220 27.53 N 82.51 W
Sandkrug 54 52.53 N 13.52 E
Sandl 61 48.33 N 14.38 E
Sand Lake 210 42.38 N 73.32 W
Sand Lake ⊜, On., Can. 184 50.05 N 94.39 W
Sand Lake ⊜, On., Can. 212 44.56 N 77.02 W
Sand Lake ⊜, On., Can. 212 44.34 N 76.15 W
Sandling ⋏ 64 47.39 N 13.43 E
Sandnes 26 58.51 N 5.44 E
Sandness 46a 60.17 N 1.38 W
Sandoa 152 9.41 S 22.52 E
Sandogora 80 58.12 N 40.59 E
Sandomierz 30 50.41 N 21.45 E
San Domingo Creek ≃ 226 38.07 N 120.40 W
San Domino, Isola I 66 42.07 N 15.29 E
Sandon 260 51.43 N 0.32 E
Sandoná 246 1.17 N 77.28 W
San Donaci 68 40.27 N 17.55 E
San Donà di Piave 64 45.38 N 12.34 E
San Donato di Lecce 68 40.15 N 18.10 E
San Donato di Ninea 68 39.42 N 16.03 E
San Donato Milanese 62 45.24 N 9.16 E
San Donato Val di Comino 66 41.42 N 13.49 E
Sandongo 152 15.30 S 21.28 E
San Dorligo della Valle 64 45.36 N 13.51 E
Sandouping 102 30.48 N 110.49 E
Sandoval 219 38.36 N 89.06 W
Sandovalina 255 22.27 S 51.44 W
Sandover ≃ 162 21.43 S 136.32 E
Sandovo 76 58.28 N 36.25 E
Sandoway 110 18.28 N 94.22 E
Sandown 42 50.39 N 1.09 W
Sandown Park Racecourse ♦, Austl. 274b 37.57 S 145.10 E
Sandown Park Race Course ♦, Eng., U.K. 260 51.22 N 0.22 W
Sand Point, Ak., U.S. 180 55.20 N 160.30 W
Sandpoint, Id., U.S. 202 48.16 N 116.33 W
Sandrancourt 261 49.02 N 1.39 E
Sandray I 46 56.53 N 7.30 W
Sandridge, Eng., U.K. 260 51.47 N 0.18 W
Sand Ridge, N.Y., U.S. 210 43.15 N 76.14 W
Sandrigo 64 45.39 N 11.36 E
Sandringham, Austl. 166 24.05 S 139.04 E
Sandringham, Austl. 169 37.57 S 145.00 E
Sandringham, Eng., U.K. 42 52.50 N 0.30 E
Sandringham ◆8 273d 26.09 S 28.07 E
Sandringham House ⊥ 42 52.50 N 0.30 E
Sand River Valley 158 28.28 S 29.33 E
Sandrovka 78 48.57 N 35.46 E
Sands Key I 220 25.30 N 80.11 W
Sandslån 26 63.01 N 17.47 E
Sandspit 182 53.14 N 131.50 W
Sands Point 276 40.51 N 73.43 W
Sands Point ➤ 276 40.52 N 73.44 W
Sand Springs, Ok., U.S. 196 36.08 N 96.06 W
Sand Springs, Tx., U.S. 196 32.15 N 101.22 W
Sandspruit 158 27.18 S 29.48 E
Sandspruit ≃ 273d 26.07 S 28.04 E
Sandstedt 52 53.21 N 8.31 E
Sandston 208 37.31 N 77.18 W
Sandstone, Austl. 162 27.59 S 119.17 E
Sandstone, Mn., U.S. 190 46.07 N 92.52 W
Sandstone Creek ≃ 216 42.23 N 84.33 W
Sandu, Zhg. 100 26.02 N 113.16 E
Sandu, Zhg. 100 29.46 N 120.12 E
Sandu, Zhg. 102 29.12 N 114.40 E
Sandu, Zhg. 102 25.59 N 107.52 E
Sanduan 104 41.10 N 121.27 E
Sandu Ao ⊂ 100 26.35 N 119.50 E
Sandugan Point ➤ 116 9.18 N 123.36 E
Sandumba 152 13.45 S 17.29 E
Sandun, Zhg. 106 31.52 N 121.50 E
Sandun, Zhg. 106 30.19 N 120.05 E
Sanduo 100 32.49 N 119.42 E
Sandusky, In., U.S. 218 39.25 N 85.29 W
Sandusky, Mi., U.S. 190 43.25 N 82.49 W
Sandusky, N.Y., U.S. 210 42.30 N 78.23 W
Sandusky, Oh., U.S. 214 41.26 N 82.42 W
Sandusky □6 214 41.21 N 83.07 W
Sandusky ≃ 214 41.27 N 83.00 W
Sandusky Bay ⊂ 214 41.27 N 82.52 W
Sand uul ⋏ 102 43.27 N 104.04 E
Sandvig 26 55.17 N 14.47 E
Sandvika 26 59.54 N 10.31 E
Sandviken 40 60.37 N 16.46 E
Sandweiler 56 49.37 N 6.13 E
Sandwich, Eng., U.K. 42 51.17 N 1.20 E
Sandwich, Il., U.S. 216 41.38 N 88.37 W
Sandwich, Ma., U.S. 207 41.45 N 70.29 W
Sandwich Bay ⊂, Nf., Can. 176 53.35 N 57.15 W
Sandwich Bay ⊂, Namibia 156 23.22 S 14.30 E
Sandwich del Sur, Islas → South Sandwich Islands II 18 57.45 S 26.30 W
Sandwick, B.C., Can. 182 49.42 N 124.59 W
Sandwick, Scot., U.K. 46a 60.00 N 1.15 W
Sand Wick ⊂ 46a 60.42 N 0.52 W
Sandwīp 124 22.29 N 91.26 E
Sandwīp Channel ʊ 124 22.30 N 91.35 E
Sandwīp Island I 124 22.30 N 91.25 E
Sandy, Eng., U.K. 42 52.08 N 0.18 W
Sandy, Or., U.S. 224 45.23 N 122.15 W
Sandy, Pa., U.S. 214 41.07 N 78.47 W
Sandy, Ut,. U.S. 200 40.35 N 111.53 W
Sandy ≃, Me., U.S. 188 44.45 N 69.52 W
Sandy ≃, Or., U.S. 224 45.34 N 122.24 W
Sandy ≃, Va., U.S. 192 36.35 N 79.25 W
Sandy Bay ⊂, Nic. 236 14.28 N 83.16 W
Sandy Bay ⊂, Ma., U.S. 283 42.40 N 70.37 W
Sandy Bay Indian Reserve ◆4 184 50.33 N 98.40 W
Sandy Bay Mountain ⋏ 188 45.47 N 70.25 W
Sandy Beach 210 43.04 N 78.55 W
Sandy Branch ≃ 284c 39.03 N 77.16 W
Sandy Cape ➤, Austl. 166 41.25 S 144.45 E
Sandy Cape ➤, Austl. 166 24.42 S 153.17 E
Sandy Creek 212 43.38 N 76.05 W
Sandy Creek ≃, Austl. 166 32.10 S 144.39 E
Sandy Creek ≃, U.S. 196 34.25 N 99.35 W
Sandy Creek ≃, U.S. 196 36.50 N 98.10 W
Sandy Creek ≃, Il., U.S. 219 39.34 N 90.35 W
Sandy Creek ≃, N.Y., U.S. 212 43.44 N 76.15 W
Sandy Creek ≃, N.Y., U.S. 212 43.20 N 77.55 W
Sandy Creek ≃, N.C., U.S. 192 36.08 N 78.02 W
Sandy Creek ≃, Oh., U.S. 214 40.38 N 81.26 W
Sandy Creek ≃, Pa., U.S. 214 41.18 N 79.51 W
Sandy Creek ≃, Tx., U.S. 196 30.34 N 98.26 W
Sandy Creek ≃, Tx., U.S. 222 29.02 N 96.33 W
Sandy Creek, East Branch ≃ 210 43.17 N 78.03 W
Sandy Creek, North Branch ≃ 212 43.51 N 75.58 W
Sandy Creek, West Branch ≃ 210 43.17 N 78.03 W
Sandy Desert ◆2 128 28.40 N 62.30 E
Sandy Hook, Ct., U.S. 207 41.25 N 73.16 W
Sandy Hook, Ky., U.S. 192 38.05 N 83.07 W
Sandy Hook, Ms., U.S. 194 31.02 N 89.48 W
Sandy Hook ➤2 208 40.27 N 74.00 W
Sandy Hook Bay ⊂ 276 40.26 N 74.03 W
Sandykači 128 36.33 N 62.34 E
Sandy Key I 220 25.02 N 81.01 W
Sandy Lake 214 41.20 N 80.04 W
Sandy Lake ⊜, Nf., Can. 186 49.16 N 57.00 W
Sandy Lake ⊜, On., Can. 184 53.02 N 93.00 W
Sandy Lake ⊜, On., Can. 212 44.33 N 78.24 W
Sandy Lick Creek ≃ 214 41.09 N 79.05 W
Sandy Point 238 17.22 N 62.50 W
Sandy Point ➤, Austl. 168b 34.16 S 138.09 E
Sandy Point ➤, Trin. 241r 11.09 N 60.50 W
Sandy Point ➤, R.I., U.S. 207 41.14 N 71.35 W
Sandy Pond ⊜ 283 42.26 N 71.19 W
Sandy Ridge 214 40.49 N 78.14 W
Sandy Springs 192 33.55 N 84.22 W
Sandyville, Md., U.S. 208 39.31 N 76.55 W
Sandyville, Oh., U.S. 214 40.38 N 81.23 W
Sandžak ◆1 38 43.10 N 19.30 E
San Eladio 258 34.46 S 59.11 W
San Elizario 200 31.35 N 106.16 W
San Emigdio Creek ≃ 228 35.02 N 119.11 W
San Emilio 116 17.14 N 120.37 E
Sanen ≃ 115a 8.23 S 113.37 E
San Enrique 252 35.47 S 60.22 W
San Estanislao, Col. 246 10.24 N 75.09 W
San Estanislao, Para. 252 24.39 S 56.26 W
San Esteban 236 15.17 N 85.52 W
San Esteban, Bahía ⊂ 232 25.38 N 109.14 W
San Esteban, Isla I 232 28.42 N 112.36 W
San Esteban de Gormaz 34 41.35 N 3.12 W
San Fele 68 40.49 N 15.32 E
San Felice (Sankt Felix) 64 46.30 N 11.08 E
San Felice Circeo 66 41.14 N 13.05 E
San Felice sul Panaro 64 44.50 N 11.08 E
San Felipe, Chile 252 32.45 S 70.44 W
San Felipe, Col. 246 1.55 N 67.06 W
San Felipe, Méx. 232 31.00 N 114.52 W
San Felipe, Méx. 234 21.29 N 101.13 W
San Felipe, Pil. 116 15.04 N 120.04 E
San Felipe, Tx., U.S. 222 29.48 N 96.06 W
San Felipe, Ven. 246 10.20 N 68.44 W
San Felipe, Castillo de ⊥ 236 15.39 N 89.01 W
San Felipe, Cayos de II 240p 21.58 N 83.30 W
San Felipe Aztatán 234 22.23 N 105.24 W
San Felipe Creek ≃ 204 33.09 N 115.46 W
San Felipe de Puerto Plata 238 19.48 N 70.41 W
San Felipe de Vichayal 248 4.52 S 81.05 W
San Felipe Indian Reservation ◆4 200 35.26 N 106.26 W
San Felipe Nuevo Mercurio 232 24.22 N 102.06 W
San Felipe Pueblo 200 35.27 N 106.28 W
San Félix ≃ 236 8.10 N 81.51 W
San Félix, Isla I 244 26.17 S 80.05 W
San Ferdinando di Puglia 68 41.18 N 16.04 E
San Fermin 196 26.20 N 104.49 W
San Fermín, Punta ➤ 232 30.25 N 114.40 W
San Fernando, Arg. 258 34.26 S 58.34 W
San Fernando, Chile 252 34.35 S 71.00 W
San Fernando, Esp. 34 36.28 N 6.12 W
San Fernando, Méx. 196 28.32 N 100.54 W
San Fernando, Méx. 200 31.16 N 110.36 W
San Fernando, Méx. 232 24.50 N 98.10 W
San Fernando, Méx. 234 16.52 N 93.13 W
San Fernando, Pil. 116 16.37 N 120.19 E
San Fernando, Pil. 116 12.30 N 123.46 E
San Fernando, Pil. 116 15.01 N 120.41 E
San Fernando, Trin. 241r 10.17 N 61.28 W
San Fernando, Ca., U.S. 228 34.16 N 118.26 W
San Fernando □5 288 34.28 S 58.34 W
San Fernando ≃ 232 24.55 N 97.40 W
San Fernando, Aeródromo ⊠ 288 34.27 S 58.35 W
San Fernando Airport ⊠ 280 34.17 N 118.25 W
San Fernando Creek ≃ 196 27.28 N 97.46 W
San Fernando de Apure 246 7.54 N 67.28 W
San Fernando de Atabapo 246 4.03 N 67.42 W
San Fernando de Henares 266a 40.26 N 3.32 W
San Fernando del Valle de Catamarca 252 28.28 S 65.47 W
San Fernando Mission ✝1 280 34.16 N 118.28 W
San Fernando Point ➤ 116 16.38 N 120.17 E
San Fernando Valley V 280 34.13 N 118.27 W
San Fili 68 39.20 N 16.09 E
San Filippo del Mela 70 38.10 N 15.17 E
Sånfjället ⋏ 26 62.17 N 13.32 E
Sånfjällets Nationalpark ♦ 26 62.20 N 13.40 E
San Floriano 64 46.02 N 12.18 E
Sanford, Co., U.S. 200 37.15 N 105.54 W
Sanford, Fl., U.S. 220 28.48 N 81.16 W
Sanford, Me., U.S. 188 43.26 N 70.46 W
Sanford, Mi., U.S. 190 43.40 N 84.22 W
Sanford, N.C., U.S. 192 35.28 N 79.10 W
Sanford, Tx., U.S. 196 35.42 N 101.32 W
Sanford ≃ 162 27.22 S 115.53 E
Sanford, Mount ⋏ 180 62.13 N 144.09 W
San Francesco, Convento ✝1, It. 66 42.28 N 12.45 E
San Francesco, Convento ✝1, It. 267a 42.03 N 12.46 E
San Francisco, Arg. 252 31.26 S 62.05 W
San Francisco, Col. 246 1.11 N 76.53 W
San Francisco, C.R. 236 9.49 N 85.15 W
San Francisco, Pan. 236 8.15 N 80.58 W
San Francisco, Pil. 116 8.30 N 125.56 E
San Francisco, Pil. 116 10.04 N 125.09 E
San Francisco, Ca., U.S. 226 37.46 N 122.25 W
San Francisco, Ca., U.S. 282 37.46 N 122.25 W
San Francisco □6 282 37.45 N 122.22 W
San Francisco ≃, Arg. 252 23.16 S 64.03 W
San Francisco → São Francisco ≃, Bra. 242 10.30 S 36.24 W
San Francisco ≃, U.S. 200 32.59 N 109.22 W
San Francisco, Arroyo ≃ 288 34.43 S 58.19 W
San Francisco, La Cadena ⋏ 240m 18.19 N 67.10 W
San Francisco, Paso de)(252 26.53 S 68.19 W
San Francisco, University of ✝2 282 37.46 N 122.26 W
San Francisco Bay ⊂ 226 37.43 N 122.17 W
San Francisco Creek ≃ 196 29.53 N 102.19 W
San Francisco Culhuacán ◆8 286a 19.20 N 99.08 W
San Francisco de Arriba 232 26.15 N 102.50 W
San Francisco de Borja 232 27.53 N 106.41 W
San Francisco de Horizonte 196 25.56 N 103.26 W
San Francisco de la Paz 236 14.55 N 86.14 W
San Francisco del Carnicero 236 12.30 N 86.18 W
San Francisco del Chañar 252 29.47 S 63.56 W
San Francisco del Mar 234 16.14 N 94.39 W
San Francisco del Monte de Oro 252 32.36 S 66.08 W
San Francisco del Oro 232 26.52 N 105.51 W
San Francisco del Rincón 234 21.01 N 101.51 W
San Francisco de Macorís 238 19.18 N 70.15 W
San Francisco de Mostazal 252 33.59 S 70.43 W
San Francisco el Grande, Iglesia de ✝1 266a 40.25 N 3.43 W
San Francisco Gotera 236 13.42 N 88.06 W
San Francisco International Airport ⊠ 226 37.37 N 122.23 W
San Francisco Ixhuatán 234 16.22 N 94.29 W
San Francisco Maritime State Historical Park ♦ 282 37.48 N 122.27 W
San Francisco-Oakland Bay Bridge ◆5 282 37.48 N 122.22 W
San Francisco State Fish and Game Refuge ◆4 282 37.35 N 122.25 W
San Francisco State University ✝2 282 37.43 N 122.28 W
San Francisco Tlalcilalcalpa 234 19.18 N 99.46 W
San Francisco Zoological Gardens ♦ 282 37.44 N 122.30 W
San Francisquito Creek ≃ 282 37.28 N 122.07 W
San Franco, Cerro ⋏ 236 15.25 N 87.18 W
San Fratello 70 38.01 N 14.36 E
San Fratello ≃ 70 38.02 N 14.34 E
Sanga, Ang. 152 11.07 S 15.22 E
Sanga, Burkina 150 11.10 N 0.10 E
Sanga, Mali 150 14.28 N 3.19 W
Sanga, Zaïre 154 7.02 S 28.21 E
San Gabriel, Ec. 246 0.36 N 77.49 W
San Gabriel, Ca., U.S. 228 34.05 N 118.06 W
San Gabriel ≃, Ca., U.S. 280 33.45 N 118.07 W
San Gabriel ≃, Tx., U.S. 222 30.46 N 97.01 W
San Gabriel, Isla I 258 34.28 S 57.54 W
San Gabriel, North Fork ≃, Ca., U.S. 280 34.15 N 117.52 W
San Gabriel, North Fork ≃, Tx., U.S. 196 30.38 N 97.41 W
San Gabriel, South Fork ≃ 196 30.38 N 97.41 W
San Gabriel Arcangel, Mission ✝1 280 34.06 N 118.06 W
San Gabriel Chilac 234 18.19 N 97.21 W
San Gabriel Dam ◆6 280 34.13 N 117.52 W
San Gabriel Mountains ⋏ 228 34.20 N 118.00 W
San Gabriel Peak ⋏ 280 34.15 N 118.06 W
San Gabriel Reservoir ⊜1 228 34.13 N 117.51 W
Sangačal, mys ➤ 84 40.07 N 49.30 E
San Galgano, Abbazia di ✝1 66 43.10 N 11.10 E
San Gallán, Isla I 248 13.51 S 76.28 W
Sangaly 24 61.08 N 43.19 E
Sangamankanda Point ➤ 122 7.01 N 81.52 E
Sangamner 122 19.34 N 74.13 E
Sangamon □6 219 39.47 N 89.40 W
Sangamon ≃ 194 40.07 N 90.20 W
Sangamon, South Fork ≃ 219 39.48 N 89.32 W
Sanga Puitã 255 22.40 S 55.36 W
Sangar 74 63.55 N 127.31 E
Sangar Sarāy 120 34.24 N 70.38 E
Sangasanga-dalam 112 0.40 S 117.14 E
Sanga Sanga Island I 116 5.04 N 119.47 E
Sangat 123 30.05 N 74.50 E
Sangatte 50 50.56 N 1.45 E
San Gavino Monreale 71 39.33 N 8.47 E
Sangay, Volcán ⋏1 246 2.00 S 78.20 W
Sang Bast 128 35.59 N 59.46 E
Sangbé 152 6.03 N 12.28 E
Sangchris Lake ⊜1 219 39.35 N 89.30 W
Sangchris Lake State Park ♦ 219 39.38 N 89.28 W
Sangchungshih 100 25.04 N 121.29 E
Sangeang, Pulau I 115b 8.12 S 119.04 E
Sang-e Māsheh 120 33.08 N 67.27 E
San Gemini 66 42.37 N 12.33 E
San Genesio Atesino 64 46.32 N 11.20 E
Sangenjaya ◆8 268 35.38 N 139.40 E
Sanger, Ca., U.S. 226 36.42 N 119.33 W
Sanger, Tx., U.S. 196 33.21 N 97.10 W
Sangerhausen 54 51.28 N 11.17 E
San Germán, Cuba 240p 20.36 N 76.08 W
San Germán, P.R. 240m 18.05 N 67.03 W
San Germano Vercellese 62 45.21 N 8.15 E
San Geronimo 226 38.01 N 122.39 W
San Gerónimo, Arroyo ≃ 258 33.57 S 56.05 W
Sangerville 188 45.09 N 69.21 W
Sanggan ≃ 90 40.21 N 115.21 E
Sanggar, Teluk ⊂ 115b 8.20 S 118.18 E
Sanggau 112 0.08 N 110.36 E
Sangge-ri ◆8 271b 37.41 N 127.05 E
Sanggin Dalai 102 38.11 N 105.17 E
Sanggona 112 3.52 S 121.46 E
Sangha □5, Centraf. 152 3.35 N 16.20 E
Sangha □5, Congo 152 1.00 N 15.30 E
Sangha ≃ 152 1.13 S 16.49 E
Sanghar 120 26.02 N 68.57 E
San Giacomo (Sankt Jakob in Pfitsch) 64 46.57 N 11.36 E
San Giacomo Filippo 58 46.20 N 9.21 E
Sangihe, Kepulauan II 112 3.00 N 125.30 E
Sangihe, Pulau I 112 3.35 N 125.32 E
Sangijn dalaj nuur ⊜ 88 49.17 N 99.00 E
San Gil 246 6.33 N 73.08 W
Sangilen, chrebet ⋏ 88 50.18 N 96.30 E
San Gimignano 66 43.28 N 11.02 E
San Ginesio 66 43.06 N 13.19 E
San Gion 58 46.38 N 8.50 E
San Giorgio 68 40.51 N 14.23 E
San Giorgio Canavese 62 45.20 N 7.48 E
San Giorgio della Richinvelda 64 46.03 N 12.52 E
San Giorgio del Sannio 68 41.04 N 14.51 E
San Giorgio di Lomellina 62 45.10 N 8.47 E
San Giorgio di Nogaro 64 45.50 N 13.13 E
San Giorgio di Piano 64 44.39 N 11.22 E
San Giorgio Ionico 68 40.27 N 17.23 E
San Giorgio la Molara 68 41.16 N 14.55 E
San Giorgio Lucano 68 40.07 N 16.23 E
San Giorgio Monferrato 62 45.07 N 8.23 E
San Giorgio Morgeto 68 38.23 N 16.06 E
San Giorgio Piacentino 62 44.57 N 9.44 E
San Giorgio su Legnano 266b 45.34 N 8.55 E
San Giovanni (Sankt Johann) 64 46.38 N 11.44 E
San Giovanni al Timavo (Sankt Johann in Ahrn) 64 46.58 N 11.57 E
San Giovanni a Piro 68 40.03 N 15.27 E
San Giovanni-Bianco 58 45.52 N 9.39 E
San Giovanni d'Asso 66 43.09 N 11.35 E
San Giovanni Gemini 70 37.38 N 13.39 E
San Giovanni Ilarione 64 45.30 N 11.15 E
San Giovanni in Croce 64 45.05 N 10.22 E
San Giovanni in Fiore 68 39.15 N 16.42 E
San Giovanni in Laterano ✝1 267a 41.53 N 12.30 E
San Giovanni in Persiceto 64 44.38 N 11.11 E
San Giovanni la Punta 70 37.35 N 15.07 E
San Giovanni Lupatoto 64 45.23 N 11.03 E
San Giovanni Rotondo 68 41.42 N 15.44 E
San Giovanni Suergiu 71 39.07 N 8.31 E
San Giovanni Valdarno 66 43.34 N 11.32 E
San Giuliano, Lago di ⊜ 68 40.37 N 16.30 E
San Giuliano Milanese 266b 45.24 N 9.17 E
San Giuliano Terme 66 43.46 N 10.26 E
San Giuseppe, It. 62 44.22 N 8.18 E
San Giuseppe, It. 70 37.58 N 13.11 E
San Giuseppe Vesuviano 68 40.50 N 14.30 E
San Giustino 66 43.33 N 12.10 E
San Giusto, Aeroporto di ⊠ 66 43.11 N 10.21 E
San Giusto Canavese 62 45.19 N 7.49 E
Sangju 98 36.26 N 128.09 E
Sangkapura 115a 5.52 S 112.40 E
Sângkê ≃ 110 13.13 N 103.41 E
Sangkhai 110 14.39 N 103.52 E
Sangkulirang 112 0.59 N 117.58 E
Sāngla 123 31.43 N 73.23 E
Sangley Point ➤ 269f 14.30 N 120.55 E
Sāngli 122 16.52 N 74.34 E
Sanglin 100 27.54 N 114.46 E
Sangluoshu 98 37.31 N 117.43 E
Sangmélima 152 2.56 N 11.59 E
Sangngagqoiling 120 28.33 N 93.00 E
Sangnyŏng-ni 98 38.14 N 126.54 E
Sango 270 34.36 N 135.42 E
San Godenzo 66 43.55 N 11.37 E
Sāngole 122 17.26 N 75.12 E
Sangolquí 246 0.19 S 78.27 W
San Gorgonio Mountain ⋏ 204 34.06 N 116.50 W
San Gottardo, Passo del)(58 46.33 N 8.34 E
Sangou 98 41.02 N 118.11 E
Sangre de Cristo Mountains ⋏ 200 37.30 N 105.15 W
San Gregorio, Arg. 252 34.19 S 62.02 W
San Gregorio, It. 66 42.19 N 13.29 E
San Gregorio, Ca., U.S. 226 37.19 N 122.23 W
San Gregorio, Ur. 252 32.37 S 55.40 W
San Gregorio, Ur. 258 33.57 S 56.45 W
San Gregorio, Arroyo ≃ 258 33.59 S 56.50 W
San Gregorio Atlapulco ◆8 286a 19.15 N 99.03 W
San Gregorio Creek ≃ 282 37.19 N 122.25 W
San Gregorio Magno 68 40.39 N 15.24 E
San Gregorio State Beach ♦ 282 37.19 N 122.24 W
Sangre Grande 241r 10.35 N 61.07 W
Sangro ≃ 66 42.14 N 14.32 E
Sangrūr 123 30.14 N 75.50 E
Sangsang 120 29.25 N 86.40 E
Sangshuyuan 86 42.23 N 88.30 E
Sangsues, Lac aux ⊜ 190 46.29 N 77.57 W
Sangtuda 85 38.04 N 69.04 E
Sanguandian 100 31.19 N 118.05 E
Sanguang 106 31.47 N 121.16 E
Sanguanmiao 100 32.25 N 114.04 E
Sanguanyingzi 104 41.39 N 120.44 E
Sangudo 182 53.53 N 114.54 W
Sangue, Rio do ≃ 248 11.01 S 58.39 W
Sangüesa 34 42.35 N 1.17 W
Sanguinetto 64 45.11 N 11.09 E
Sanguliu 104 40.45 N 124.14 E
Sângurli 272c 18.56 N 73.07 E
Sangutane ≃ 156 24.07 S 33.47 E
Sangvor, S.S.S.R. 85 38.47 N 71.12 E
Sangvor, S.S.S.R. 85 38.53 N 71.06 E
Sangwa 154 5.30 S 26.00 E
Sangya 120 30.52 N 91.40 E
Sangyuanbao 105 40.15 N 115.32 E
Sangyuanbu 106 31.37 N 118.53 E
Sangyuanzhen 107 30.30 N 103.26 E
Sangzhi 102 29.18 N 110.02 E
Sangzidian 98 36.46 N 116.55 E
Sanharó 250 8.21 S 36.34 W
Sanhe, Zhg. 100 24.24 N 116.34 E
Sanhe, Zhg. 105 39.59 N 117.04 E
Sanhechang, Zhg. 102 31.22 N 106.48 E
Sanhechang, Zhg. 107 30.04 N 105.01 E
Sanhecun 98 42.28 N 129.39 E
Sanheji 100 32.42 N 117.55 E
Sanhekou 106 31.50 N 120.08 E
Sanhetun 104 42.38 N 123.38 E
Sanhezhan 89 52.34 N 126.02 E
Sanhezhen 100 31.30 N 117.14 E
Sanhezhuang 105 40.04 N 116.18 E
San Hipólito, Punta ➤ 232 26.59 N 113.59 W
Sanhsient'ai I 100 23.08 N 121.25 E
Sanhsing 100 24.40 N 121.39 E
Sanhu 100 27.55 N 115.24 E
Sanhui, Zhg. 107 30.06 N 106.36 E
Sanhui, Zhg. 107 29.57 N 105.53 E
Sanhūr 142 29.25 N 30.46 E
Sanhūr al-Madīnah 142 31.07 N 30.44 E
Sani 100 24.25 N 120.46 E
Sanibel 220 26.26 N 82.01 W
Sanibel Island I 220 26.27 N 82.06 W
Sānī Bherī ≃ 124 28.42 N 82.16 E
San Ignacio, Arg. 252 27.16 S 55.32 W
San Ignacio, Bol. 248 14.53 S 65.36 W
San Ignacio, Bol. 248 16.23 S 60.59 W
San Ignacio, C.R. 236 9.48 N 84.09 W
San Ignacio, Hond. 236 14.38 N 87.02 W
San Ignacio, Méx. 232 27.27 N 112.51 W
San Ignacio, Méx. 234 23.55 N 106.25 W
San Ignacio, Méx. 234 23.12 N 100.12 W
San Ignacio, Para. 252 26.52 S 57.03 W
San Ignacio, Isla de I 232 25.25 N 108.54 W
San Ignacio, Laguna ⊜ 232 26.54 N 113.13 W
San Ildefonso, Cape ➤ 116 16.02 N 121.59 E
San Ildefonso, Cerro ⋏ 236 15.31 N 88.17 W
San Ildefonso Indian Reservation ◆4 200 35.53 N 106.08 W

Symbol	English	Deutsch	Español	Français	Português
≃	River	Fluß	Río	Rivière	Rio
≅	Canal	Kanal	Canal	Canal	Canal
⌊	Waterfall, Rapids	Wasserfall, Stromschnellen	Cascada, Rápidos	Chute d'eau, Rapides	Cascata, Rápidos
ʊ	Strait	Meeresstraße	Estrecho	Détroit	Estreito
⊂	Bay, Gulf	Bucht, Golf	Bahía, Golfo	Baie, Golfe	Baía, Golfo
⊜	Lake, Lakes	See, Seen	Lago, Lagos	Lac, Lacs	Lago, Lagos
⊞	Swamp	Sumpf	Pantano	Marais	Pântano
⊓	Ice Features, Glacier	Eis- und Gletscherformen	Accidentes Glaciales	Formes glaciaires	Acidentes glaciares
▾	Other Hydrographic Features	Andere Hydrographische Objekte	Otros Elementos Hidrográficos	Autres données hydrographiques	Outros acidentes hidrográficos
✦	Submarine Features	Untermeerische Objekte	Accidentes Submarinos	Formes de relief sous-marin	Acidentes submarinos
□	Political Unit	Politische Einheit	Unidad Política	Entité politique	Unidade política
✝	Cultural Institution	Kulturelle Institution	Institución Cultural	Institution culturelle	Instituição cultural
⊥	Historical Site	Historische Stätte	Sitio Histórico	Site historique	Sítio histórico
♦	Recreational Site	Erholungs- und Ferienort	Sitio de Recreo	Centre de loisirs	Área de Lazer
⊠	Airport	Flughafen	Aeropuerto	Aéroport	Aeroporto
■	Military Installation	Militäranlage	Instalación Militar	Installation militaire	Instalação militar
◆	Miscellaneous	Verschiedenes	Misceláneo	Divers	Diversos

San Ildefonso o La Granja 34 40.54 N 4.00 W
San Ildefonso Peninsula ≻[1] 116 16.10 N 122.05 E
San'in-kaigan-kokuritsu-kōen ♠ 96 35.38 N 134.38 E
Sanino 265a 59.50 N 29.54 E
Sani Pass)(158 29.34 S 29.19 E
San Isidro, Arg. 252 28.27 S 65.44 W
San Isidro, Arg. 258 34.27 S 58.30 W
San Isidro, C.R. 236 9.22 N 83.42 W
San Isidro, Méx. 200 31.31 N 106.18 W
San Isidro, Méx. 234 21.55 N 100.15 W
San Isidro, Nic. 236 12.56 N 86.12 W
San Isidro, Perú 286d 12.07 S 77.03 W
San Isidro, Pil. 116 11.24 N 124.21 E
San Isidro, Tx., U.S. 196 26.42 N 98.27 W
San Isidro □[5] 288 34.29 S 58.33 W
San Isidro el Real, Catedral de ●[1] 266a 40.25 N 3.42 W
Sanitaria Springs 210 42.09 N 75.46 W
Sanitatas 156 18.11 S 12.47 E
Sanitz 54 54.04 N 12.22 E
San Jacinto, Col. 246 9.50 N 75.08 W
San Jacinto, Méx. 196 25.29 N 103.44 W
San Jacinto, Pil. 116 12.34 N 123.44 E
San Jacinto, Ca., U.S. 228 33.47 N 116.57 W
San Jacinto □[6] 222 30.35 N 95.10 W
San Jacinto ≏, Ca., U.S. 228 33.43 N 117.16 W
San Jacinto ≏, Tx., U.S. 222 29.46 N 95.05 W
San Jacinto, East Fork ≏ 222 30.05 N 95.09 W
San Jacinto, West Fork ≏ 222 30.02 N 95.15 W
San Jacinto Monument ⊥ 222 29.45 N 95.01 W
San Jacinto Peak ∧ 204 33.49 N 116.41 W
San Jacinto Valley V 228 33.50 N 117.05 W
Sanjahā 142 30.50 N 31.38 E
San Javier, Arg. 252 27.53 S 55.08 W
San Javier, Arg. 252 30.35 S 59.57 W
San Javier, Bol. 248 16.20 S 62.38 W
San Javier, Bol. 248 14.34 S 64.42 W
San Javier, Méx. 196 26.16 N 99.27 W
San Javier, Ur. 252 32.41 S 58.08 W
San Javier ≏ 252 31.30 S 60.20 W
San Javier de Loncomilla 252 35.35 S 71.45 W
Sanjāwi 120 30.17 N 68.21 E
Sanje 154 0.46 S 31.30 E
San Jerónimo 236 15.03 N 90.12 W
San Jerónimo de Juárez 234 17.08 N 100.28 W
San Jerónimo Norte 252 31.33 S 61.05 W
Sanjiadian, Zhg. 105 40.09 N 116.36 E
Sanjiadian, Zhg. 105 39.58 N 116.06 E
Sanjiadian, Zhg. 105 39.22 N 115.58 E
Sanjiang, Zhg. 102 25.42 N 109.23 E
Sanjiang, Zhg. 107 29.33 N 104.03 E
Sanjiangzhen 107 30.31 N 103.48 E
Sanjiaocheng 102 36.47 N 104.40 E
Sanjiaopao 104 41.22 N 122.17 E
Sanjiaoshancun 104 40.42 N 122.49 E
Sanjiazhen 107 30.17 N 105.32 E
Sanjiazi, Zhg. 104 40.54 N 121.59 E
Sanjiazi, Zhg. 104 42.02 N 122.20 E
Sanjiazi, Zhg. 104 42.33 N 121.38 E
Sanjiazi, Zhg. 104 41.53 N 121.42 E
Sanjiazi, Zhg. 104 40.42 N 123.16 E
Sanjiaziyingzi 104 41.52 N 120.49 E
Sanjie, Zhg. 100 32.35 N 118.08 E
Sanjie, Zhg. 102 25.01 N 101.02 E
Sanjō 92 37.37 N 138.57 E
San Joaquín, Bol. 248 13.04 S 64.49 W
San Joaquín, Para. 252 24.57 S 56.07 W
San Joaquin, Pil. 116 10.35 N 122.08 E
San Joaquin, Ca., U.S. 226 36.36 N 120.11 W
San Joaquin □[6] 226 37.57 N 121.17 W
San Joaquín ≏, Bol. 248 13.08 S 63.41 W
San Joaquin ≏, Ca., U.S. 226 38.03 N 121.50 W
San Joaquin, Middle Fork ≏ 226 37.32 N 119.11 W
San Joaquin, North Fork ≏ 226 37.32 N 119.11 W
San Joaquin, South Fork ≏ 226 37.26 N 119.14 W
San Joaquin Valley V 204 36.50 N 120.10 W
San Jon 196 35.06 N 103.19 W
San Jorge, Arg. 252 31.54 S 61.52 W
San Jorge, El Sal. 236 13.25 N 88.21 W
San Jorge, Nic. 236 11.27 N 85.48 W
San Jorge ≏ 246 9.07 N 74.44 W
San Jorge, Bahía de c 232 31.12 N 113.15 W
San Jorge, Cabo ≻ 254 45.47 S 67.21 W
San Jorge, Canal de → Saint George's Channel ⲓ 28 52.00 N 6.00 W
San Jorge, Golfo c 254 46.00 S 67.00 W
San Jorge Island I 175e 8.27 S 159.35 E
San José, Arg. 252 27.46 S 55.47 W
San José, Bol. 248 14.13 S 68.05 W
San José, C.R. 236 9.56 N 84.05 W
San José, Ec. 246 1.42 S 79.01 W
San José, Hond. 236 14.54 N 88.44 W
San José, Méx. 196 28.16 N 100.15 W
San José, Méx. 232 27.32 N 110.09 W
San José, Para. 252 25.33 S 56.45 W
San Jose, Pil. 116 10.45 N 121.56 E
San Jose, Pil. 116 15.48 N 121.00 E
San Jose, Pil. 116 12.27 N 121.03 E
San Jose, T.T.P.I. 174n 15.09 N 145.43 E
San Jose, Ca., U.S. 226 37.20 N 121.53 W
San Jose, Ca., U.S. 282 37.20 N 121.53 W
San Jose, Il., U.S. 194 40.18 N 89.36 W
San Jose, N.M., U.S. 200 35.23 N 105.28 W
San José, Ven. 286c 10.34 N 66.57 W
San José □[4] 236 9.40 N 84.00 W
San José □[5] 258 34.15 S 56.45 W
San José □[7] 286b 22.57 N 82.14 W
San Jose ≏, B.C., Can. 182 52.14 N 122.15 W
San José ≏, Ur. 258 34.38 S 56.29 W
San Jose, Arroyo ≏ 282 38.03 N 122.30 W
San José, Golfo c 254 42.20 S 64.18 W
San José, Isla I, Méx. 232 25.00 N 110.38 W
San José, Isla I, Pan. 246 8.15 N 79.07 W
San José, Laguna c 240m 18.25 N 66.01 W
San Jose, Mission ●[1] 282 37.32 N 121.55 W
San Jose, Rio ≏ 200 34.52 N 107.01 W
San José Ayuquila 234 17.58 N 97.57 W
San Jose Creek ≏ 280 34.01 N 118.03 W
San José de Achuapa 236 13.03 N 86.35 W
San José de Aura 196 27.34 N 101.23 W
San Jose de Buan 116 12.02 N 125.01 E
San José de Chiquitos 248 17.51 S 60.47 W
San José de Feliciano 252 30.23 S 58.45 W
San José de Galipán 286c 10.35 N 66.54 W
San José de Galipán, Quebrada ≏ 286c 10.37 N 66.54 W
San José de Gauribe 246 9.52 N 65.48 W
San José de Gracia 234 20.40 N 102.35 W
San José de Guanipa 246 8.54 N 64.09 W
San José de Jáchal 252 30.14 S 68.45 W
San José de la Esquina 252 33.06 S 61.42 W
San José de la Parilla 234 23.44 N 104.07 W
San José de la Popa 196 26.10 N 100.47 W
San José de las Flores 234 17.20 N 95.24 W
San José de las Lajas 240p 22.58 N 82.09 W
San José del Cabo 232 23.03 N 109.41 W
San José del Guaviare 246 2.35 N 72.38 W
San José de Llanetes 234 22.55 N 103.16 W
San José de los Molinos 248 13.57 S 75.41 W
San José de Lourdes 234 23.18 N 103.01 W
San José de Mayo 258 34.20 S 56.42 W
San José de Ocoa 238 18.33 N 70.30 W
San José de Ocuné 246 4.15 N 70.20 W
San José de Raíces 232 24.35 N 100.14 W
San José de Sisa 248 6.37 S 76.39 W
San José de Tiznados 246 9.23 N 67.33 W
San Jose Hills ∧[2] 280 34.04 N 117.49 W
San Jose Island I 196 28.10 N 96.45 W
San José Iturbide 234 21.00 N 100.23 W
San Jose Municipal Airport ≋ 226 37.22 N 121.56 W
San Jose State University ●[2] 282 37.20 N 121.53 W
San Juan, Arg. 252 31.32 S 68.31 W
San Juan, Guat. 236 15.52 N 88.53 W
San Juan, Méx. 196 29.34 N 104.36 W
San Juan, Méx. 232 27.47 N 103.57 W
San Juan, Perú 248 15.21 S 75.10 W
San Juan, Pil. 116 13.50 N 121.24 E
San Juan, Pil. 116 16.40 N 120.20 E
San Juan, Pil. 116 8.25 N 126.20 E
San Juan, P.R. 240m 18.28 N 66.07 W
San Juan □[4] 252 31.00 S 69.00 W
San Juan □[6] 224 48.34 N 122.59 W
San Juan ≏, Arg. 252 32.17 S 67.22 W
San Juan ≏, B.C., Can. 224 48.34 N 124.24 W
San Juan ≏, Col. 246 4.03 N 77.27 W
San Juan ≏, Méx. 232 26.22 N 98.51 W
San Juan ≏, N.A. 236 10.56 N 83.42 W
San Juan ≏, Perú 248 13.27 S 76.11 W
San Juan ≏, Pil. 269f 14.35 N 121.01 E
San Juan ≏, S.A. 246 1.11 N 78.33 W
San Juan ≏, U.S. 200 37.18 N 110.28 W
San Juan ≏, Ur. 258 34.17 S 57.58 W
San Juan ≏, Ven. 246 10.14 N 62.38 W
San Juan, Bahía de c 240m 18.27 N 66.07 W
San Juan, Cabezas de ≻ 240m 18.23 N 65.37 W
San Juan, Cabo ≻, Arg. 254 54.44 S 63.44 W
San Juan, Cabo ≻, Gui. Ecu. 152 1.08 N 9.23 E
San Juan, Embalse de ⊜[1] 34 40.30 N 4.15 W
San Juan, Pasaje de ⲓ 240m 18.24 N 65.37 W
San Juan, Pico ∧ 240p 21.59 N 80.09 W
San Juan, Port c 224 48.34 N 124.27 W
San Juan, Punta ≻ 174z 27.03 S 109.22 W
San Juan Basin ≐[1] 200 36.15 N 108.20 W
San Juan Bautista, Méx. 196 26.58 N 101.24 W
San Juan Bautista, Para. 252 26.38 S 57.10 W
San Juan Bautista, Ca., U.S. 226 36.51 N 121.32 W
San Juan Bautista Cuicatlán 234 17.48 N 96.58 W
San Juan Bautista State Historical Park ♦ 226 36.51 N 121.31 W
San Juan Capistrano 228 33.30 N 117.39 W
San Juan Capistrano Mission ●[1] 228 33.31 N 117.40 W
San Juan Colorado 234 16.32 N 97.55 W
San Juan Cotzal 236 15.26 N 91.01 W
San Juan Creek ≏, Ca., U.S. 226 35.40 N 120.22 W
San Juan Creek ≏, Ca., U.S. 228 33.28 N 117.41 W
San Juan de Abajo 234 20.48 N 105.13 W
San Juan de Aragón, Bosque ♦ 286a 19.28 N 99.04 W
San Juan de Aragón, Zoológico de ♦ 286a 19.28 N 99.05 W
San Juan de Colón 246 8.02 N 72.16 W
San Juan de Dios 286c 10.35 N 66.55 W
San Juan de Guadalupe 232 24.38 N 102.44 W
San Juan [de la Maguana] 238 18.48 N 71.14 W
San Juan de la Vega 234 20.38 N 100.46 W
San Juan del César 246 10.46 N 73.01 W
San Juan de Lima, Punta ≻ 234 18.36 N 103.42 W
San Juan de Limay 236 13.10 N 86.37 W
San Juan del Monte 269f 14.36 N 121.02 E
San Juan del Norte 236 10.55 N 83.42 W
San Juan del Oro ≏ 248 21.02 S 65.19 W
San Juan de los Cayos 246 11.10 N 68.25 W
San Juan de los Lagos 234 21.15 N 102.18 W
San Juan de los Lagos ≏ 234 21.18 N 102.33 W
San Juan de los Morros 246 9.55 N 67.21 W
San Juan del Piray 248 20.37 S 64.09 W
San Juan del Río, Méx. 232 24.47 N 104.27 W
San Juan del Río, Méx. 234 20.23 N 100.00 W
San Juan del Río ≏ 234 20.40 N 99.30 W
San Juan del Salado 234 23.18 N 101.56 W
San Juan del Sur 236 11.15 N 85.52 W
San Juan de Micay ≏ 246 3.05 N 77.32 W
San Juan de Payara 246 7.39 N 67.36 W
San Juan de Pirque 286e 33.38 S 70.30 W
San Juan de Sabinas 196 27.55 N 101.18 W
San Juan Evangelista 234 17.54 N 95.08 W
San Juanico, Isla I 234 21.43 N 106.38 W
San Juanillo 236 10.02 N 85.44 W
San Juan Indian Reservation ◆[4] 200 36.03 N 106.04 W
San Juan Island I 224 48.32 N 123.05 W
San Juan Island National Historical Park ♦ 224 48.28 N 123.00 W
San Juan Islands II 224 48.36 N 122.50 W
San Juan Ixcaquixtla 234 18.27 N 97.49 W
San Juan Ixtayopan ◆[8] 286a 19.14 N 99.00 W
San Juan Lachao 234 16.14 N 97.09 W
San Juan Mazatlán 234 17.02 N 95.25 W
San Juan Mountains ∧ 200 37.35 N 107.10 W
San Juan Naval Station ■ 240m 18.28 N 66.06 W
San Juan Nepomuceno, Col. 246 9.57 N 75.05 W
San Juan Nepomuceno, Para. 252 26.06 S 55.58 W
San Juan Peyotán 234 22.24 N 104.21 W
San Juan Quiahije 234 16.17 N 97.20 W
San Juan Sacatepéquez 236 14.43 N 90.39 W
San Juan Sayultepec 234 17.27 N 97.17 W
San Juan y Martínez 240p 22.16 N 83.50 W
San Judas 234 23.15 N 100.52 W
San Julián, Arg. 254 49.18 S 67.43 W
San Julián, Méx. 234 21.01 N 102.10 W
San Julian, Pil. 116 11.45 N 125.27 E
San Julian, Quebrada ≏ 286c 10.37 N 66.51 W
San Justo, Arg. 252 30.47 S 60.35 W
San Justo, Arg. 258 34.40 S 58.33 W
San Justo, Aeródromo ≋ 288 34.44 S 58.36 W
Sankanbiaiwa ∧ 150 8.56 N 10.48 W
Sankarani ≏ 150 12.01 N 8.19 W
Sankarankovil 122 9.10 N 77.33 E
Sankarpur 272b 22.51 N 88.27 E
Sānkdaha 126 22.46 N 89.10 E
Sankeng 100 23.36 N 112.48 E
Sankertown 214 40.28 N 78.35 W
Sankeshu 104 42.38 N 122.25 E
Sankeshwar 122 16.16 N 74.29 E
Sankey Brook ≏ 262 53.22 N 2.38 W
Sankh ≏ 124 22.15 N 84.48 E
Sankheda 120 22.10 N 73.35 E
Sankhosh ≏ 124 26.48 N 89.56 E
Sānkra 120 21.18 N 82.39 E
Sānkrāil 272b 22.34 N 88.14 E
Sankt Aegyd am Neuwalde 61 47.52 N 15.35 E
Sankt Andrä 61 46.46 N 14.49 E
Sankt Andrä vor dem Hagenthale 264b 48.19 N 16.13 E
Sankt Andreasberg 54 51.43 N 10.31 E
Sankt Anton am Arlberg 58 47.08 N 10.16 E
Sankt Antönien 58 46.58 N 9.49 E
Sankt Augustin 56 50.40 N 7.16 E
Sankt Bartholomä ●[1] 64 47.32 N 12.58 E
Sankt Blasien 58 47.46 N 8.07 E
Sankt Christopher-Nevis → Saint Christopher-Nevis □[1] 238 17.20 N 62.45 W
Sankt Egidien 54 50.47 N 12.36 E
Sankt Florian ●[1] 61 48.12 N 14.23 E
Sankt Gallen, Öst. 61 47.41 N 14.37 E
Sankt Gallen, Schw. 58 47.25 N 9.23 E
Sankt Gallen □[3] 58 47.10 N 9.08 E
Sankt Gallenkirch 58 47.01 N 9.59 E
Sankt Georgen, B.R.D. 58 48.07 N 8.20 E
Sankt Georgen, B.R.D. 58 47.59 N 7.47 E
Sankt Georgen, Öst. 61 46.43 N 14.55 E
Sankt Georgen im Attergau 64 47.56 N 13.29 E
Sankt Gertraud → Santa Gertrude 64 46.29 N 10.53 E
Sankt Gertrud ◆[8] 54 53.52 N 10.47 E
Sankt Gilgen 64 47.46 N 13.22 E
Sankt Goar 56 50.09 N 7.43 E
Sankt Goarshausen 56 50.09 N 7.44 E
Sankt Helena → Saint Helena □[2] 8 15.57 S 5.42 W
Sankt Hubert 56 51.23 N 6.26 E
Sankt Ingbert 56 49.17 N 7.06 E
Sankt Jakob → San Giacomo 64 46.57 N 11.36 E
Sankt Jakob im Lesachtal 64 46.41 N 12.56 E
Sankt Jakob im Rosental 61 46.33 N 14.03 E
Sankt Jakob in Defereggen 64 46.55 N 12.20 E
Sankt Johann → San Giovanni 64 46.38 N 11.44 E
Sankt Johann am Tauern 61 47.22 N 14.29 E
Sankt Johann im Pongau 64 47.21 N 13.12 E
Sankt Johann im Walde 64 46.54 N 12.37 E
Sankt Johann in Tirol 64 47.31 N 12.26 E
Sankt Kanzian 61 46.37 N 14.34 E
Sankt Leonhard → San Leonardo 64 46.49 N 11.15 E
Sankt Leonhard Am Forst 61 48.09 N 15.17 E
Sankt Leonhard im Pitztal 58 47.04 N 10.51 E
Sankt Lorenz ◆[8] 52 51.57 N 10.40 E
Sankt Lorenz → Saint Lawrence ≏ 176 49.30 N 67.00 W
Sankt Lorenzen → San Lorenzo di Sebato 64 46.47 N 11.54 E
Sankt Lorenzen im Lesachtal 64 46.42 N 12.47 E
Sankt Lorenz-Golf → Saint Lawrence, Gulf of c 186 48.00 N 62.00 W
Sankt Lorenz-Insel → Saint Lawrence Island I 180 63.30 N 170.30 W
Sankt Mang 58 47.44 N 10.21 E
Sankt Margarethen an der Raab 61 47.03 N 15.45 E
Sankt Märgen 58 48.00 N 8.05 E
Sankt Margrethen 58 47.27 N 9.36 E
Sankt Martin 64 47.28 N 13.23 E
Sankt Martin an der Raab 61 46.55 N 16.08 E
Sankt Martin in Gsies → San Martino in Casies 64 46.49 N 12.14 E
Sankt Mauritz 52 51.57 N 7.39 E
Sankt Michael im Lungau 64 47.06 N 13.38 E
Sankt Michael in Obersteiermark 61 47.20 N 15.01 E
Sankt Michel → Mikkeli 26 61.41 N 27.15 E
Sankt Moritz 58 46.30 N 9.50 E
Sankt Niklaus → San Nicolò d'Ultimo, It. 64 46.30 N 10.55 E
Sankt Niklaus, Schw. 58 46.11 N 7.48 E
Sankt Oswald 60 48.54 N 13.25 E
Sankt Paul im Lavanttal 61 46.42 N 14.52 E
Sankt Peter, B.R.D. 30 54.18 N 8.38 E
Sankt Peter, B.R.D. 58 48.01 N 8.01 E
Sankt Peter ●[1] 263 51.37 N 7.12 E
Sankt Peter am Kammersberg 61 47.11 N 14.11 E
Sankt Peter am Ottersbach 61 46.48 N 15.45 E
Sankt Peter in der Au 61 48.03 N 14.37 E
Sankt Pölten 61 48.12 N 15.37 E
Sankt-Quirinus-Dom ●[1] 263 51.12 N 6.42 E
Sankt Stefan an der Gail 64 46.37 N 13.31 E
Sankt Stefan im Rosental 61 46.54 N 15.42 E
Sankt Ulrich → Ortisei 64 46.34 N 11.40 E
Sankt Valentin 61 48.10 N 14.32 E
Sankt Veit an der Glan 61 46.46 N 14.21 E
Sankt Veit an der Gölsen 61 48.03 N 15.40 E
Sankt Veit im Pongau 64 47.20 N 13.09 E
Sankt-Viktors-Dom ●[1] 263 51.40 N 6.27 E
Sankt Vincent → Saint Vincent and the Grenadines □[1] 241h 13.15 N 61.12 W
Sankt Wallburg → Santa Valburga 64 46.33 N 11.00 E
Sankt Wendel 56 49.28 N 7.10 E
Sankt-Willibrodi-Dom ●[1] 263 51.40 N 6.37 E
Sankt Wolfgang im Salzkammergut 64 47.44 N 13.27 E
Sankuru ≏ 152 4.17 S 20.25 E
San Lázaro 252 22.10 S 57.55 W
San Lázaro, Cabo ≻ 232 24.48 N 112.19 W
San Lazaro Race Track ♦ 269f 14.37 N 120.59 E
San Lazzaro di Savena 64 44.28 N 11.25 E
San Leandro 226 37.43 N 122.09 W
San Leandro Creek ≏ 282 37.45 N 122.12 W
San Leo 66 43.54 N 12.21 E
San Leon 222 29.29 N 94.55 W
San Leonardo (Sankt Leonhard), It. 64 46.49 N 11.15 E
San Leonardo, Méx. 196 27.28 N 104.55 W
San Leonardo ≏ 70 37.59 N 13.41 E
San Leone 70 37.16 N 13.35 E
Sanlicheng 100 31.48 N 114.12 E
Sanlidian 100 30.48 N 118.15 E
Sanlifan 100 30.51 N 115.15 E
Sanlintang 106 31.08 N 121.29 E
Sanlipu 106 31.46 N 119.03 E
Sanliuji 100 32.08 N 116.19 E
San Lope 246 6.12 N 71.56 W
San Lorenzo, Arg. 252 28.08 S 58.46 W
San Lorenzo, Arg. 252 32.45 S 60.44 W
San Lorenzo, Bol. 248 21.26 S 64.47 W
San Lorenzo, Ec. 246 1.17 N 78.50 W
San Lorenzo, Hond. 236 13.25 N 87.27 W
San Lorenzo, It. 68 38.01 N 15.50 E
San Lorenzo, Méx. 196 25.37 N 97.35 W
San Lorenzo, Méx. 232 25.32 N 102.11 W
San Lorenzo, Nic. 236 12.23 N 85.40 W
San Lorenzo, P.R. 240m 18.11 N 65.58 W
San Lorenzo, Ca., U.S. 226 37.40 N 122.07 W
San Lorenzo, Ven. 246 9.47 N 71.04 W
San Lorenzo ≏, Méx. 232 24.15 N 107.24 W
San Lorenzo ≏, Méx. 286a 19.28 N 99.16 W
San Lorenzo → Saint Lawrence ≏, N.A. 176 49.30 N 67.00 W
San Lorenzo ≏, Ca., U.S. 226 36.58 N 122.01 W
San Lorenzo, Bahía c 236 13.19 N 87.30 W
San Lorenzo, Cabo ≻ 246 1.04 S 80.56 W
San Lorenzo, Cerro ∧ 254 47.37 S 72.19 W
San Lorenzo, Golfo del → Saint Lawrence, Gulf of c 186 48.00 N 62.00 W
San Lorenzo, Isla I, Méx. 232 28.38 N 112.51 W
San Lorenzo, Isla I, Perú 248 12.05 S 77.15 W
San Lorenzo Bellizzi 68 39.53 N 16.20 E
San Lorenzo Creek ≏ 226 36.12 N 120.38 W
San Lorenzo Creek ≏, Ca., U.S. 282 37.39 N 122.09 W
San Lorenzo de El Escorial 34 40.35 N 4.09 W
San Lorenzo de la Parrilla 34 39.51 N 2.22 W
San Lorenzo del Vallo 68 39.40 N 16.18 E
San Lorenzo di Sebato (Sankt Lorenzen) 64 46.47 N 11.54 E
San Lorenzo in Campo 66 43.36 N 12.56 E
San Lorenzo Nuovo 66 42.41 N 11.54 E
San Lorenzo Tenoxtitlan ⊥ 234 17.44 N 94.45 W
San Lorenzo Tezonco ◆[8] 286a 19.18 N 99.04 W
San Luca 68 38.09 N 16.04 E
Sanlúcar de Barrameda 34 36.47 N 6.21 W
Sanlúcar la Mayor 34 37.23 N 6.12 W
San Lucas, Bol. 248 20.06 S 65.07 W
San Lucas, Ec. 246 3.45 S 79.15 W
San Lucas, Méx. 232 24.13 N 103.04 W
San Lucas, Méx. 232 22.53 N 109.54 W
San Lucas, Ca., U.S. 226 36.08 N 121.01 W
San Lucas, Cabo ≻ 232 22.52 N 109.53 W
San Lucas, Serranía de ∧ 246 8.00 N 74.20 W
San Luis, Arg. 252 33.18 S 66.21 W
San Luis, Cuba 240p 20.12 N 75.51 W
San Luis, Cuba 240p 22.17 N 83.46 W
San Luis, Guat. 236 16.14 N 89.27 W
San Luis, Az., U.S. 200 32.04 N 111.57 W
San Luis, Co., U.S. 200 37.12 N 105.25 W
San Luis, Ven. 246 11.07 N 69.42 W
San Luis □[4] 252 34.00 S 66.00 W
San Luis ◆[8] 286b 23.05 N 82.21 W
San Luis, Arroyo ≏ 258 34.10 S 57.44 W
San Luis, Laguna ⊜ 248 13.45 S 64.00 W
San Luis, Sierra de ∧ 252 32.40 S 65.50 W
San Luis Acatlán 234 16.48 N 98.45 W
San Luis Creek ≏ 200 37.42 N 105.44 W
San Luis de la Loma 234 17.18 N 100.55 W
San Luis de la Paz 234 21.18 N 100.31 W
San Luis del Cordero 232 25.26 N 104.18 W
San Luis del Palmar 252 27.31 S 58.34 W
San Luis Gonzaga 232 24.55 N 111.16 W
San Luis Gonzaga, Bahía c 232 29.48 N 114.22 W
San Luis Jilotepeque 236 14.39 N 89.44 W
San Luis Obispo 226 35.16 N 120.39 W
San Luis Obispo □[6] 226 35.30 N 120.30 W
San Luis Pass c 222 29.05 N 95.08 W
San Luis Peak ∧ 200 37.59 N 106.56 W
San Luis Potosí 234 22.09 N 100.59 W
San Luis Potosí □[3] 234 22.30 N 100.30 W
San Luis Reservoir ⊜[1] 226 37.07 N 121.05 W
San Luis Rey 228 33.14 N 117.20 W
San Luis Rey ≏ 204 33.12 N 117.24 W
San Luis Rey, Mission ●[1] 228 33.14 N 117.20 W
San Luis Río Colorado 232 32.29 N 114.48 W
San Luis Soyatlán 234 20.12 N 103.18 W
San Luis State Recreation Area ♦ 226 37.04 N 121.05 W
San Luis Valley V 200 37.25 N 106.00 W
Sanluri 71 39.34 N 8.54 E
San Macario 266b 45.36 N 8.47 E
Sanmaiden 270 34.34 N 135.51 E
San Mamete 58 46.02 N 9.04 E
San Mango d'aquino 68 39.03 N 16.11 E
San Manuel, Arg. 252 37.47 S 58.50 W
San Manuel, Méx. 234 17.37 N 93.24 W
San Manuel, Az., U.S. 200 32.35 N 110.37 W
San Marcelino, El Sal. 236 13.22 N 89.03 W
San Marcelino, Pil. 116 14.58 N 120.09 E
San Marcello Pistoiese 66 44.03 N 10.47 E
San Marcial, Punta ≻ 232 25.30 N 111.01 W
San Marco 286e 33.37 S 70.38 W
San Marco, Capo ≻, It. 70 37.30 N 13.01 E
San Marco, Capo ≻, It. 71 39.51 N 8.26 E
San Marco Argentano 68 39.33 N 16.07 E
San Marco dei Cavoti 68 41.18 N 14.53 E
San Marco in Lamis 68 41.43 N 15.38 E
San Marco la Catola 68 41.31 N 15.00 E
San Marcos, Chile 252 30.56 S 71.03 W
San Marcos, Col. 246 8.39 N 75.08 W
San Marcos, C.R. 236 9.40 N 84.01 W
San Marcos, El Sal. 236 13.39 N 89.11 W
San Marcos, Guat. 236 14.58 N 91.48 W
San Marcos, Hond. 236 14.24 N 88.56 W
San Marcos, Hond. 236 15.17 N 88.23 W
San Marcos, Méx. 234 16.48 N 99.21 W
San Marcos, Méx. 234 20.02 N 99.20 W
San Marcos, Méx. 234 20.47 N 104.11 W
San Marcos, Ca., U.S. 228 33.08 N 117.09 W
San Marcos, Tx., U.S. 196 29.52 N 97.56 W
San Marcos □[5] 236 15.00 N 91.55 W
San Marcos ≏, Méx. 234 20.17 N 97.32 W
San Marcos ≏, Tx., U.S. 196 29.29 N 97.28 W
San Marcos, Estadio de ♦ 286d 12.04 S 77.05 W
San Marcos, Isla I 232 27.13 N 112.06 W
San Marcos, Laguna de ⊜ 234 20.17 N 103.23 W
San Marcos, Universidad de ●[2] 286d 12.03 S 77.05 W
San Marcos Arteaga 234 17.45 N 97.58 W
San Marcos de Colón 236 13.26 N 86.48 W
San Marino, S. Mar. 66 43.55 N 12.28 E
San Marino, Ca., U.S. 280 34.07 N 118.06 W
San Marino □[1] 22 43.56 N 12.25 E
San Marino □[1], Europe 66 43.56 N 12.25 E
San Martín, Arg. 252 29.14 S 65.46 W
San Martín, Arg. 252 33.04 S 68.28 W
San Martín → General San Martín, Arg. 258 34.34 S 58.32 W
San Martín, Col. 246 3.42 N 73.42 W
San Martin, Ca., U.S. 226 37.05 N 121.37 W
San Martín □[5] 258 33.45 S 57.37 W
San Martín □[5] 248 7.00 S 76.50 W
San Martín ≏ 248 13.08 S 63.43 W
San Martín ●[3] 9 68.07 S 67.08 W
San Martín, Arroyo ≏ 258 33.49 S 57.44 W
San Martín, Cerro ∧[1] 234 18.19 N 94.48 W
San Martín, Cuchilla ∧[2] 258 33.45 S 57.54 W
San Martín, Lago (Lago O'Higgins) ⊜ 254 49.00 S 72.40 W
San Martín, Volcán ∧[1] 234 18.33 N 95.12 W
San Martín de Bolaños 234 21.29 N 103.58 W
San Martín [de las Pirámides] 234 19.42 N 98.50 W
San Martín de las Vacas 196 25.30 N 101.20 W
San Martín de los Andes 254 40.10 S 71.21 W
San Martín de Valdeiglesias 34 40.21 N 4.24 W
San Martín Hidalgo 234 20.27 N 103.57 W
San Martino, It. 62 45.27 N 8.47 E
San Martino, It. 64 45.25 N 10.35 E
San Martino (Sankt Martin), It. 64 46.47 N 11.13 E
San Martino Buon Albergo 64 45.25 N 11.05 E
San Martino d'agri 68 40.14 N 16.04 E
San Martino di Castrozza 64 46.16 N 11.48 E
San Martino di Lupari 64 45.39 N 11.51 E
San Martino in Badia (Saint Martin) 64 46.41 N 11.52 E
San Martino in Casies (Sankt Martin in Gsies) 64 46.49 N 12.14 E
San Martino in Rio 64 44.44 N 10.48 E
San Martino Valle Caudina 68 41.01 N 14.39 E
San Martín Peras 234 17.19 N 98.15 W
San Marzano di San Giuseppe 68 40.27 N 17.30 E
San Marzano sul Sarno 66 40.46 N 14.35 E
San Mateo, Méx. 234 22.59 N 103.30 W
San Mateo, Pil. 269f 14.42 N 121.07 E
San Mateo, Ca., U.S. 226 37.33 N 122.19 W
San Mateo, Fl., U.S. 192 29.36 N 81.35 W
San Mateo, N.M., U.S. 200 35.19 N 107.38 W
San Mateo, Ven. 246 9.45 N 64.33 W
San Mateo □[6] 226 37.25 N 122.20 W
San Mateo ≏ 286a 19.30 N 99.17 W
San Mateo Atenco 234 19.16 N 99.32 W
San Mateo Bridge ◆[5] 282 37.36 N 122.13 W
San Mateo Canyon V 228 33.23 N 117.36 W
San Mateo Creek ≏ 282 37.34 N 122.18 W
San Mateo del Mar 234 16.12 N 95.00 W
San Mateo Ixtatán 236 15.50 N 91.29 W
San Mateo Memorial Park ♦ 282 37.17 N 122.18 W
San Mateo Point ≻ 228 33.23 N 117.36 W
San Mateo Tecoloapan 286a 19.34 N 99.14 W
San Matías 248 16.22 S 58.24 W
San Matías, Golfo c 254 41.30 S 64.15 W
San Mauro Castelverde 70 37.55 N 14.11 E
San Mauro Forte 68 40.29 N 16.15 E
San Mauro la Bruca 68 40.07 N 15.17 E
San Mauro Marchesato 68 39.06 N 16.56 E
San Mauro Torinese 62 45.06 N 7.46 E
San Medi, Arroyo de ≏ 266d 41.28 N 2.06 E
Sanmen 100 29.06 N 121.24 E
San Menaio 68 41.56 N 15.58 E
Sanmen Wan c 100 29.08 N 121.44 E
Sanmenxia (Shanxian) 102 34.45 N 111.05 E
San Michele, Sacra di ●[1] 62 45.11 N 7.21 E
San Michele all'Adige 64 46.12 N 11.08 E
San Michele al Tagliamento 64 45.46 N 12.59 E
San Michele di Ganzaria 70 37.17 N 14.26 E
San Michele Mondovì 62 44.23 N 7.54 E
San Michele Salentino 68 40.38 N 17.37 E
San Miguel, Arg. 252 28.00 S 57.36 W
San Miguel → General Sarmiento, Arg. 258 34.33 S 58.43 W
San Miguel, Bol. 248 16.42 S 61.01 W
San Miguel, Chile 286e 33.30 S 70.40 W
San Miguel, Ec. 246 1.44 S 79.01 W
San Miguel, El Sal. 236 13.29 N 88.11 W
San Miguel, Esp. 148 28.05 N 16.37 W
San Miguel, Méx. 232 29.10 N 101.28 W
San Miguel, Méx. 234 23.23 N 98.10 W
San Miguel, Pan. 236 8.27 N 78.56 W
San Miguel, Perú 248 13.01 S 73.58 W
San Miguel, Perú 286d 12.06 S 77.07 W
San Miguel, Pil. 116 15.09 N 120.59 E
San Miguel, Ca., U.S. 226 35.45 N 120.41 W
San Miguel ≏, Bol. 248 13.52 S 63.56 W
San Miguel ≏, Méx. 232 29.16 N 110.53 W
San Miguel ≏, Méx. 234 18.16 N 100.40 W
San Miguel (Cuilco) ≏, N.A. 236 15.56 N 92.10 W
San Miguel ≏, S.A. 248 19.15 S 59.20 W
San Miguel ≏, Co., U.S. 200 38.23 N 108.48 W
San Miguel, Cerro ∧[2] 248 19.19 S 60.36 W
San Miguel, Golfo de c 246 8.22 N 78.17 W
San Miguel, Volcán de ∧[1] 236 13.26 N 88.16 W
San Miguel Arcángel, Mission ●[1] 226 35.44 N 120.42 W
San Miguel Bay c 116 13.50 N 123.10 E
San Miguel Canoa 234 19.09 N 98.05 W
San Miguel Chimalapa 234 16.43 N 94.41 W
San Miguel Creek ≏ 196 28.30 N 98.25 W
San Miguel de Allende 234 20.55 N 100.45 W
San Miguel de Cruces 232 24.25 N 105.51 W
San Miguel del Monte 258 35.27 S 58.48 W
San Miguel del Padrón ◆[8] 286b 23.05 N 82.19 W
San Miguel de Pallaques 248 7.00 S 78.51 W
San Miguel de Salcedo 246 1.02 S 78.34 W
San Miguel de Tucumán 252 26.49 S 65.13 W
San Miguel el Alto 234 21.01 N 102.21 W
San Miguel Island I, Pil. 116 13.23 N 123.48 E
San Miguel Island I, Ca., U.S. 204 34.02 N 120.22 W
San Miguel Islands II 116 7.45 N 118.28 E
San Miguelito 236 11.24 N 84.54 W
San Miguel Ixtahuacán 236 15.15 N 91.45 W
San Miguel Mountain ∧ 228 32.42 N 116.56 W
San Miguel Octopan 234 20.34 N 100.44 W
San Miguel Talea de Castro 234 17.22 N 96.15 W
San Miguel Tenango 234 16.16 N 95.36 W
San Miguel Totolapan 234 18.08 N 100.23 W
Sanming 100 26.14 N 117.36 E
San Miniato 66 43.41 N 10.51 E
San Murezzan → Sankt Moritz 58 46.30 N 9.50 E
Sannahed 40 59.06 N 15.09 E
Sannan 96 35.04 N 135.02 E
Sannār 140 13.33 N 33.38 E
San Narciso, Pil. 116 13.34 N 122.34 E
San Narciso, Pil. 116 15.01 N 120.05 E
Sannazzaro de'Burgondi 62 45.06 N 8.54 E
Sannicandro di Bari 68 41.00 N 16.48 E
Sannicandro Garganico 68 41.50 N 15.34 E
Sannicola 68 40.05 N 18.04 E
San Nicola, Isola I 66 42.07 N 15.30 E
San Nicola, Monte ∧ 68 38.35 N 16.24 E
San Nicola Arcella 68 39.51 N 15.48 E
San Nicola da Crissa 68 38.40 N 16.17 E
San Nicolás, Esp. 148 27.59 N 15.46 W
San Nicolás, Hond. 236 15.00 N 88.45 W
San Nicolás, Méx. 234 16.26 N 98.32 W
San Nicolás, Méx. 234 19.05 N 101.07 W
San Nicolás, Perú 248 15.13 S 75.12 W
San Nicolas, Pil. 116 18.09 N 120.38 E
San Nicolás ≏ 234 19.40 N 105.14 W
San Nicolás de Bari 240p 22.47 N 81.55 W
San Nicolás de los Arroyos 252 33.20 S 60.13 W
San Nicolás de los Garzas 196 25.45 N 100.18 W
San Nicolas Island I 204 33.15 N 119.31 W
San Nicolò di Comelico 64 46.35 N 12.31 E
San Nicolò d'Ultimo (Sankt Nikolaus) 64 46.30 N 10.55 E
San Nicolò Ferrarese 64 44.42 N 11.42 E
San Nicolò Gerrei 71 39.30 N 9.18 E
Sannieshof 158 26.30 S 25.47 E
Sannikova, proliv ⲓ 74 74.30 N 140.00 E
Sannīn, Jabal ∧ 132 33.57 N 35.52 E
Sannio, Monti del ∧ 68 41.30 N 14.45 E
Sanniquellie 150 7.22 N 8.43 W
Sannohe 92 40.22 N 141.15 E
Sannois 261 48.58 N 2.15 E
Sannūr, Wādī V 142 28.58 N 31.03 E
Sano 94 36.19 N 139.35 E
Sañogasta 252 29.18 S 67.36 W
Sanok 30 49.34 N 22.13 E
Sânon ≏ 58 48.38 N 6.20 E
San Onofre 246 9.44 N 75.32 W
San Onofre Mountain ∧ 228 33.22 N 117.30 W
San Pablo, Chile 254 40.24 S 73.01 W
San Pablo, Col. 246 1.40 N 77.00 W
San Pablo, Pil. 116 7.40 N 123.27 E
San Pablo, Pil. 116 14.04 N 121.19 E
San Pablo, Ca., U.S. 226 37.57 N 122.20 W
San Pablo ≏, Bol. 248 14.52 S 63.42 W
San Pablo ≏, Pan. 236 7.51 N 81.10 W
San Pablo, Point ≻ 282 37.58 N 122.26 W
San Pablo Autopan 234 19.21 N 99.40 W
San Pablo Balleza 232 26.57 N 106.21 W
San Pablo Bay c 226 38.06 N 122.22 W
San Pablo Creek ≏ 282 37.58 N 122.30 W
San Pablo de Tiquina 248 16.13 S 68.52 W
San Pablo Huitzo 234 17.15 N 96.52 W
San Pablo Huixtepec 234 16.50 N 96.46 W
San Pablo Ostotepec ◆[8] 286a 19.11 N 99.04 W
San Pablo Reservoir ⊜[1] 282 37.56 N 122.15 W
San Pablo Ridge ∧ 282 37.55 N 122.15 W
San Pablo Strait ⲓ 282 37.58 N 122.26 W
San Pablo Villa de Mitla 234 16.55 N 96.24 W
Sanpādā 272c 19.04 N 73.01 E
San Pancrazio Salentino 68 40.25 N 17.50 E
San Paolo 64 46.29 N 11.15 E
San Paolo di Civitate 68 41.44 N 15.15 E
San Pascual 116 13.08 N 122.59 E
San Pasqual Indian Reservation ◆[4] 228 33.12 N 116.58 W
San Pedrillo, Punta ≻ 236 8.39 N 83.45 W
San Pedro, Arg. 252 33.40 S 59.40 W
San Pedro, Arg. 252 24.14 S 64.52 W
San Pedro, Arg. 252 27.57 S 65.10 W
San Pedro, Bol. 248 14.20 S 64.50 W
San Pedro, Chile 252 33.54 S 71.28 W
San Pedro, Chile 252 21.57 S 68.34 W
San Pedro, Col. 246 9.24 N 75.04 W
San Pedro, C.R. 236 9.56 N 84.03 W
San Pedro, C. Iv. 150 4.44 N 6.37 W
San Pedro, Para. 252 24.07 S 56.59 W
San Pedro, Tx., U.S. 196 27.47 N 97.40 W
San Pedro, Ur. 258 34.21 S 57.51 W
San Pedro, Ven. 246 8.50 N 71.58 W
San Pedro □[5] 252 24.15 S 56.30 W
San Pedro ◆[8], Cuba 286b 23.03 N 82.27 W
San Pedro ◆[8], Ca., U.S. 280 33.44 N 118.17 W
San Pedro ≏, Cuba 240p 21.09 N 78.30 W
San Pedro ≏, Méx. 234 21.45 N 105.30 W
San Pedro ≏, N.A. 200 32.59 N 110.47 W
San Pedro ≏, N.A. 236 17.45 N 91.25 W
San Pedro ≏, Ven. 286c 10.35 N 66.48 W
San Pedro, Arroyo ≏ 258 34.21 S 57.56 W
San Pedro, Point ≻, Ca., U.S. 282 37.59 N 122.27 W
San Pedro, Point ≻, Ca., U.S. 282 37.35 N 122.31 W
San Pedro, Punta ≻ 252 25.30 S 70.38 W
San Pedro, Volcán ∧[1] 252 21.53 S 68.25 W
San Pedro Apóstol 234 16.44 N 96.44 W
San Pedro Ayampuc 236 14.47 N 90.27 W
San Pedro Bay c, Pil. 116 11.11 N 125.05 E
San Pedro Bay c, Ca., U.S. 228 33.45 N 118.11 W
San Pedro Breakwater ◆[5] 280 33.42 N 118.16 W
San Pedro Carchá 236 15.29 N 90.16 W
San Pedro Channel ⲓ 228 33.35 N 118.25 W
San Pedro Creek ≏, Ca., U.S. 282 37.36 N 122.30 W
San Pedro Creek ≏, Tx., U.S. 222 31.34 N 95.14 W
San Pedro de Arriba 258 34.18 S 57.47 W
San Pedro de Atacama 252 22.55 S 68.13 W
San Pedro de Buena Vista 248 18.13 S 65.59 W

Symbols in the index entries represent the broad categories identified in the key at the right. Symbols with superior numbers (∧[1]) identify subcategories (see complete key on page *I · 1).*

Symbole im Register stellen die rechts im Schlüssel erklärten Kategorien dar. Symbole mit hochgestellten Ziffern (∧[1]) bezeichnen Unterabteilungen einer Kategorie (vgl. vollständiger Schlüssel auf Seite *I · 1).*

Los símbolos incluidos en el texto del índice representan las grandes categorías identificadas con la clave a la derecha. Los símbolos con numeros en su parte superior (∧[1]) identifican las subcategorías (véase la clave completa en la página *I · 1).*

Les symboles de l'index représentent les catégories indiquées dans la légende à droite. Les symboles suivis d'un indice (∧[1]) représentent des souscatégories (voir légende complète à la page *I · 1).*

Os símbolos incluídos no texto do índice representam as grandes categorias identificadas com a chave à direita. Os símbolos com números em sua parte superior (∧[1]) identificam as subcategorias (veja-se a chave completa à página *I · 1).*

∧ Mountain	Berg	Montaña	Montagne	Montanha
∧ Mountains	Gebirge	Montañas	Montagnes	Montanhas
)(Pass	Paß	Paso	Col	Passo
V Valley, Canyon	Tal, Cañon	Valle, Cañón	Vallée, Canyon	Vale, Canhão
⊐ Plain	Ebene	Llano	Plaine	Planície
≻ Cape	Kap	Cabo	Cap	Cabo
I Island	Insel	Isla	Île	Ilha
II Islands	Inseln	Islas	Îles	Ilhas
≛ Other Topographic Features	Andere Topographische Objekte	Otros Elementos Topográficos	Autres données topographiques	Outros acidentes topográficos

ESPAÑOL Nombre Página Lat.°′ Long.°′ W = Oeste
FRANÇAIS Nom Page Lat.°′ Long.°′ W = Ouest
PORTUGUÊS Nome Página Lat.°′ Long.°′ W = Oeste
Sanp-Sant I · 155

San Pedro de la Cueva 232 29.18 N 109.44 W
San Pedro de las Colonias 232 25.45 N 102.59 W
San Pedro del Gallo 232 25.33 N 104.18 W
San Pedro de Lloc 248 7.26 S 79.31 W
San Pedro del Norte 236 13.04 N 84.33 W
San Pedro del Paraná 252 26.46 S 56.15 W
San Pedro de Macorís 238 18.27 N 69.18 W
San Pedro El Alto 234 16.01 N 96.28 W
San Pedro Huamelula 234 16.02 N 95.40 W
San Pedro Jicayán 234 16.25 N 97.59 W
San Pedro Juchatengo 234 16.21 N 97.06 W
San Pedro Mártir ◆[8] 286a 19.16 N 99.10 W
San Pedro Mártir, Sierra ∧ 232 30.45 N 115.13 W
San Pedro Mixtepec 234 16.00 N 97.07 W
San Pedro Peaks ∧ 200 36.07 N 106.49 W
San Pedro Piedra Gorda 234 22.27 N 102.21 W
San Pedro Pinula 236 14.40 N 89.51 W
San Pedro Sacatepéquez 236 14.58 N 91.46 W
San Pedro Sula 236 15.27 N 88.02 W
San Pedro Tapanatepec 234 16.21 N 94.12 W
San Pedro Xalostoc 286a 19.32 N 99.05 W
San Pedro y Miquelón → Saint Pierre and Miquelon □[2] 186 46.55 N 56.20 W
San Pelayo 246 8.58 N 75.51 W
San Pellegrino 62 45.50 N 9.40 E
San Piero a Grado 66 43.41 N 10.21 E
San Piero in Bagno 66 43.51 N 11.58 E
San Pierre 216 41.12 N 86.53 W
San Pietro (Sankt Peter) 64 47.01 N 12.03 E
San Pietro, Isola di I 71 39.08 N 8.17 E
San Pietro a Maida 68 38.50 N 16.20 E
San Pietro di Cadore 64 46.34 N 12.35 E
San Pietro in Casale 64 44.42 N 11.24 E
San Pietro in Gu 64 45.37 N 11.40 E
San Pietro in Guarano 68 39.20 N 16.19 E
San Pietro in Palazzi 66 43.20 N 10.30 E
San Pietro in Vaticano ✝[1] 267a 41.54 N 12.28 E
San Pietro Vara 62 44.20 N 9.35 E
San Pietro Vernotico 68 40.29 N 18.00 E
San Pitch ≃ 200 39.03 N 111.51 W
Sanpoil ≃ 202 47.53 N 118.41 W
San Policarpio 116 12.11 N 125.30 E
San Polo d'Enza 64 44.38 N 10.26 E
Sanpu 98 34.09 N 117.10 E
Sanqiao 106 30.35 N 119.58 E
San Quentin 282 37.56 N 122.29 W
San Quentin State Prison ✝ 282 37.56 N 122.28 W
Sanquhar 44 55.22 N 3.56 W
San Quintin 116 16.00 N 120.50 E
San Quintín, Bahía de ⊂ 232 30.22 N 115.55 W
San Quintín, Cabo ≻ 232 30.21 N 116.00 W
San Quintín, Ventisquero ⋒ 254 46.52 S 74.05 W
San Quirico d'Orcia 66 43.03 N 11.36 E
Sanqutan 100 27.17 N 115.04 E
Sanquzhen 107 29.39 N 105.37 E
San Rafael, Arg. 252 34.36 S 68.20 W
San Rafael, Chile 252 35.19 S 71.32 W
San Rafael, Méx. 232 28.34 N 111.42 W
San Rafael, Méx. 232 25.01 N 100.33 W
San Rafael, Méx. 234 20.12 N 96.51 W
San Rafael, Ca., U.S. 226 37.58 N 122.31 W
San Rafael, N.M., U.S. 200 35.06 N 107.52 W
San Rafael, Ven. 246 10.58 N 71.44 W
San Rafael ≃, Bol. 248 18.38 S 58.55 W
San Rafael ≃, Ut., U.S. 200 38.47 N 110.07 W
San Rafael Bay ⊂ 282 37.58 N 122.28 W
San Rafael de Arriba 232 31.05 N 116.05 W
San Rafael de las Tortillas 196 26.49 N 99.32 W
San Rafael del Norte 236 13.12 N 86.06 W
San Rafael del Sur 236 11.51 N 86.27 W
San Rafael Desert ◆[2] 200 38.40 N 110.30 W
San Rafael Hills ∧[2] 280 34.10 N 118.12 W
San Rafael Mountains ∧ 204 34.45 N 119.50 W
San Rafael Oriente 236 13.23 N 88.21 W
San Rafael Swell ∧[1] 200 38.40 N 110.45 W
San Ramón, Arg. 252 27.42 S 64.17 W
San Ramón, Bol. 248 13.17 S 64.43 W
San Ramón, C.R. 236 10.06 N 84.28 W
San Ramón, Hond. 236 14.41 N 84.43 W
San Ramón, Perú 248 11.08 S 75.20 W
San Ramon, Pil. 116 13.16 N 124.05 E
San Ramon, Ca., U.S. 282 37.47 N 121.59 W
San Ramón, Ur. 252 34.18 S 55.58 W
San Ramón, Bahía ⊂ 232 30.45 N 116.03 W
San Ramon Creek ≃ 282 37.54 N 122.03 W
San Ramón de la Nueva Orán 252 23.08 S 64.20 W
San Ramon Valley ∨ 282 37.46 N 121.58 W
Sanrao 100 23.59 N 116.50 E
San-rei ∧ 96 33.50 N 133.59 E
San Remigio 116 11.05 N 123.56 E
San Remo, Austl. 169 38.31 S 145.22 E
San Remo, It. 62 43.49 N 7.46 E
San Remo, N.Y., U.S. 210 40.52 N 73.13 W
San Roberto 68 38.18 N 15.44 E
San Rodrigo ≃ 196 28.54 N 100.37 W
San Román ≃ 236 16.21 N 90.26 W
San Román, Cabo ≻ 246 12.12 N 70.00 W
San Roque, Arg. 252 30.17 S 68.41 W
San Roque, Arg. 252 28.34 S 58.43 W
San Roque, Esp. 34 36.13 N 5.24 W
San Roque, Pil. 269f 14.29 N 120.54 E
San Roque, T.T.P.I. 174n 15.15 N 145.47 E
San Roque, Cabo → São Roque, Cabo de ≻ 250 5.29 S 35.16 W
San Roque, Punta ≻ 232 27.11 N 114.26 W
San Rosendo 252 37.16 S 72.43 W
San Rufo 68 40.26 N 15.28 E
San Saba 196 31.11 N 98.43 W
San Saba ≃ 196 31.15 N 98.35 W
San Saep, Khlong ≅ 269a 13.45 N 100.36 E
San Salvador, Arg. 252 31.37 S 58.30 W
San Salvador, Arg. 252 29.16 S 57.31 W
San Salvador, El Sal. 236 13.42 N 89.12 W
San Salvador (Watling Island) I 238 24.02 N 74.28 W
San Salvador ≃ 258 33.37 S 58.06 W
San Salvador, Cuchilla de ∧[2] 258 33.56 S 57.45 W
San Salvador, Isla I 246a 0.14 S 90.45 W
San Salvador, Volcán de ∧[1] 236 13.44 N 89.17 W
San Salvador de Jujuy 252 24.11 S 65.18 W
San Salvador el Seco 234 19.08 N 97.39 W
San Salvatore, Monte ∧ 70 37.50 N 14.03 E
San Salvatore Monferrato 62 44.59 N 8.34 E
San Salvatore Telesino 68 41.14 N 14.30 E
San Salvo 66 42.03 N 14.44 E
Sansanné-Mango 150 10.21 N 0.28 E
Sans Bois Creek ≃ 196 35.20 N 94.50 W
San Sebastián 236 13.44 N 88.50 W
San Sebastián → Donostia 34 43.19 N 1.59 W
San Sebastián, Guat. 236 14.34 N 91.39 W
San Sebastián, Hond. 236 14.24 N 88.42 W
San Sebastián, Méx. 234 21.26 N 102.21 W
San Sebastián, Méx. 234 20.47 N 104.51 W
San Sebastián, Méx. 234 22.10 N 104.19 W
San Sebastián, P.R. 240m 18.20 N 66.59 W
San Sebastián, Bahía ⊂ 254 53.12 S 68.20 W
San Sebastián de la Gomera 148 28.06 N 17.06 W
San Sebastián de los Reyes 266a 40.33 N 3.38 W
San Sebastián de Yalí 236 13.18 N 86.11 W
San Sebastiano 64 45.38 N 10.16 E
San Sebastiano Curone 62 44.47 N 9.04 E
San Secondo Parmense 64 44.55 N 10.14 E
Sansepolcro 66 43.34 N 12.08 E
San Severino Lucano 68 40.01 N 16.08 E
San Severino Marche 66 43.13 N 13.10 E
San Severo 68 41.41 N 15.23 E
Sansha 100 26.58 N 120.12 E
Sanshengchang 89 44.51 N 120.21 E
Sanshierzhan 89 53.16 N 121.49 E
Sanshijia, Zhg. 98 41.44 N 119.15 E
Sanshijia, Zhg. 98 41.05 N 119.03 E
Sanshilibao 98 39.15 N 121.48 E
Sanshiling 106 30.51 N 119.29 E
Sanshisanzhan 89 53.10 N 121.27 E
Sanshui 100 23.11 N 112.53 E
San Sigismondo (Sankt Sigmund) 64 46.49 N 11.46 E
San Simeon 226 35.39 N 121.11 W
San Simon, Méx. 204 30.30 N 115.58 W
San Simon, Az., U.S. 200 32.16 N 109.13 W
San Simón ≃, Bol. 248 13.13 S 63.31 W
San Simon ≃, Az., U.S. 200 32.50 N 109.39 W
San Simon Wash ↳ 200 31.45 N 112.25 W
San Siro ◆[8] 266b 45.29 N 9.07 E
Sanski Most 36 44.46 N 16.40 E
Sanso 150 11.43 N 6.51 W
San Solano 252 31.29 S 65.55 W
Sansom Park Village 222 32.48 N 97.24 W
Sanson 172 40.13 S 175.25 E
San Sosti 68 39.40 N 16.02 E
San Sperate 71 39.21 N 9.00 E
Sans Souci 274a 33.59 S 151.08 E
Sans-Souci ⊥ 238 19.37 N 72.12 W
Sanssouci, Schloss ✝ 54 52.24 N 13.02 E
San Stefano Ticino 266b 45.29 N 8.55 E
Santa, Perú 248 8.59 S 78.36 W
Santa, Pil. 116 17.29 N 120.26 E
Santa ≃ 248 8.58 S 78.39 W
Santa, Isla de I 248 9.02 S 78.40 W
Santa Adélia 255 21.16 S 48.48 W
Santa Albertina 255 20.02 S 50.44 W
Santa Amalia 34 39.01 N 6.01 W
Santa Ana, Arg. 252 27.22 S 55.34 W
Santa Ana, Bol. 248 15.31 S 67.30 W
Santa Ana, Bol. 248 13.45 S 65.35 W
Santa Ana, Bol. 248 18.43 S 58.44 W
Santa Ana, Col. 246 9.19 N 74.35 W
Santa Ana, Ec. 246 1.13 S 80.23 W
Santa Ana, El Sal. 236 13.59 N 89.34 W
Santa Ana, Méx. 232 24.04 N 100.30 W
Santa Ana, Méx. 232 30.33 N 111.07 W
Santa Ana, Méx. 234 18.15 N 93.28 W
Santa Ana, Méx. 234 19.19 N 98.11 W
Santa Ana, Ca., U.S. 228 33.44 N 117.52 W
Santa Ana, Ven. 246 9.19 N 64.39 W
Santa Ana ≃ 228 33.38 N 117.57 W
Santa Ana, Volcán de ∧[1] 236 13.50 N 89.38 W
Santa Ana Canyon ∨ 280 33.53 N 117.43 W
Santa Ana de Chena 286e 33.34 S 70.47 W
Santa Ana Heights 228 33.39 N 117.54 W
Santa Ana Indian Reservation ◆[4] 200 35.28 N 106.37 W
Santa Ana Island I 175e 10.50 S 162.28 E
Santa Ana Maya 234 20.00 N 101.01 W
Santa Ana Mountains ∧ 228 33.45 N 117.35 W
Santa Ana Pacueco 234 20.22 N 102.00 W
Santa Ana Race Track ◆ 269f 14.35 N 121.01 E
Santa Ana Tlacotenco ◆[8] 286a 19.10 N 98.59 W
Santa Anita 234 20.33 N 103.27 W
Santa Anita Canyon ∨ 280 34.12 N 118.01 W
Santa Anita Park ◆ 280 34.08 N 118.03 W
Santa Anna 196 31.44 N 99.19 W
Santa Apolonia 196 25.38 N 97.59 W
Santa Bábara 255 11.57 S 38.58 W
Santa Bárbara, Chile 252 37.40 S 72.01 W
Santa Bárbara, Col. 246 5.53 N 75.35 W
Santa Bárbara, Hond. 236 14.53 N 88.14 W
Santa Bárbara, Méx. 232 26.48 N 105.49 W
Santa Bárbara, Méx. 234 18.52 N 101.07 W
Santa Barbara, Ca., U.S. 204 34.25 N 119.42 W
Santa Bárbara, Ven. 246 3.57 N 67.06 W
Santa Bárbara, Ven. 246 7.47 N 71.10 W
Santa Bárbara □[5] 236 15.10 N 88.20 W
Santa Barbara □[6] 228 33.28 N 119.02 W
Santa Bárbara ≃ 248 16.58 S 61.39 W
Santa Bárbara, Morro de ∧ 287a 22.57 S 43.28 W
Santa Bárbara, Ribeirão ≃ 256 22.00 S 45.43 W
Santa Bárbara, Túnel ◆[5] 287a 22.56 S 43.12 W
Santa Barbara Channel ᴗ 204 34.15 N 119.55 W
Santa Bárbara de Samaná 238 19.13 N 69.19 W
Santa Bárbara do Monte Verde 256 21.58 S 43.42 W
Santa Bárbara do Sul 252 28.22 S 53.15 W
Santa Barbara Island I 228 33.28 N 119.02 W
Santa Branca 256 23.24 S 45.53 W
Santa Branca, Represa @[1] 256 23.20 S 45.50 W
Santaca 158 26.36 S 32.32 E
Santa Catalina, Arg. 252 21.57 S 66.04 W
Santa Catalina, Pan. 236 8.47 N 81.20 W
Santa Catalina, Pil. 116 9.20 N 122.51 E
Santa Catalina, Ur. 258 33.49 S 57.29 W
Santa Catalina, Arroyo ≃ 288 34.46 S 58.27 W
Santa Catalina, Gulf of ⊂ 228 33.20 N 117.45 W
Santa Catalina, Isla I 232 25.40 N 110.47 W
Santa Catalina, Laguna @ 288 34.46 S 58.27 W
Santa Catalina Island I 228 33.23 N 118.24 W
Santa Catarina, Méx. 204 31.37 N 115.48 W
Santa Catarina, Méx. 232 25.41 N 100.28 W
Santa Catarina, Méx. 234 19.18 N 101.10 W
Santa Catarina □[3] 252 27.00 S 50.00 W
Santa Catarina, Ilha de I 252 27.36 S 48.30 W
Santa Catarina Yosonotú 234 16.59 N 97.39 W
Santa Caterina di Pittinuri 71 40.06 N 8.30 E
Santa Caterina Valfurva 64 46.25 N 10.29 E
Santa Caterina Villarmosa 70 37.35 N 14.02 E
Santa Cecília 252 26.56 S 50.27 W
Santa Cesarea Terme 68 40.02 N 18.29 E
Santa Clara, Arg. 252 29.33 S 68.31 W
Santa Clara, Col. 246 2.43 S 69.43 W
Santa Clara, Cuba 240p 22.24 N 79.58 W
Santa Clara, Méx. 232 29.17 N 107.01 W
Santa Clara, Méx. 234 19.41 N 101.30 W
Santa Clara, Ca., U.S. 226 37.20 N 121.56 W
Santa Clara, Ut., U.S. 200 37.07 N 113.39 W
Santa Clara □[6] 226 37.20 N 121.53 W
Santa Clara ≃, Ca., U.S. 228 34.14 N 119.16 W
Santa Clara ≃, Ut., U.S. 200 37.05 N 113.36 W
Santa Clara, Bahía de ⊂ 240p 23.05 N 80.30 W
Santa Clara, University of ✝[2] 282 37.21 N 121.56 W
Santa Clara Coatitla 286a 19.34 N 99.04 W
Santa Clara de Olimar 252 32.55 S 54.58 W
Santa Clara Indian Reservation ◆[4] 200 35.59 N 106.10 W
Santa Clara Valley ∨ 226 37.10 N 121.40 W
Santa Clarita 286d 12.00 S 77.01 W
Santa Clotilde 246 2.34 S 73.44 W
Santa Coloma de Cervelló 266d 41.22 N 2.01 E
Santa Coloma de Farners 34 41.52 N 2.40 E
Santa Coloma de Gramanet 266d 41.27 N 2.13 E
Santa Comba 34 43.02 N 8.49 W
Santa Comba Dão 34 40.24 N 8.08 W
Santa Cristina 64 46.34 N 11.43 E
Santa Cristina d'aspromonte 68 38.15 N 15.58 E
Santa Croce 64 46.05 N 12.18 E
Santa Croce, Capo ≻ 70 37.14 N 15.15 E
Santa Croce, Lago di @ 64 46.10 N 12.20 E
Santa Croce Camerina 70 36.50 N 14.31 E
Santa Croce del Sannio 68 41.23 N 14.43 E
Santa Croce di Magliano 66 41.42 N 14.59 E
Santa Croce Sull'Arno 66 43.42 N 10.47 E
Santa Cruz, Bol. 248 17.48 S 63.10 W
Santa Cruz, Bra. 250 6.13 S 36.01 W
Santa Cruz, Bra. 255 19.56 S 40.09 W
Santa Cruz, Chile 252 34.38 S 71.22 W
Santa Cruz, C.R. 236 10.16 N 85.36 W
Santa Cruz, Méx. 200 31.14 N 110.35 W
Santa Cruz, Méx. 234 23.05 N 97.50 W
Santa Cruz, Perú 248 6.37 S 78.57 W
Santa Cruz, Pil. 116 14.17 N 121.25 E
Santa Cruz, Pil. 116 13.04 N 120.43 E
Santa Cruz, Pil. 116 6.50 N 125.25 E
Santa Cruz, Pil. 116 13.29 N 122.02 E
Santa Cruz (Tubajon), Pil. 116 10.19 N 125.33 E
Santa Cruz, Pil. 116 15.46 N 119.55 E
Santa Cruz, Ca., U.S. 226 36.58 N 122.01 W
Santa Cruz, Ven. 246 8.25 N 71.39 W
Santa Cruz, Ven. 286c 10.26 N 67.01 W
Santa Cruz □[4] 254 49.00 S 70.00 W
Santa Cruz □[5] 248 17.30 S 61.30 W
Santa Cruz □[6] 226 36.58 N 122.01 W
Santa Cruz ◆[8], Bra. 256 22.56 S 43.41 W
Santa Cruz ◆[8], India 272c 19.05 N 72.50 E
Santa Cruz ≃, Arg. 254 50.08 S 68.20 W
Santa Cruz ≃, Cuba 286b 23.04 N 82.29 W
Santa Cruz ≃, N.A. 200 32.42 N 111.33 W
Santa Cruz, Ilha I 287a 22.52 S 43.07 W
Santa Cruz, Isla I 246a 0.38 S 90.23 W
Santa Cruz, Sierra de ∧ 236 15.40 N 89.15 W
Santa Cruz Basin ◆[1] 14 12.00 S 163.00 E
Santa Cruz Cabrália 255 16.17 S 39.02 W
Santa Cruz da Graciosa 148a 39.05 N 28.01 W
Santa Cruz das Flores 148a 39.27 N 31.07 W
Santa Cruz da Vitória 255 14.57 S 39.48 W
Santa Cruz de el Seibo 238 18.46 N 69.02 W
Santa Cruz de Goiás 255 17.19 S 48.30 W
Santa Cruz de Juventino Rosas 234 20.39 N 101.00 W
Santa Cruz de la Palma 148 28.41 N 17.45 W
Santa Cruz de la Zarza 34 39.58 N 3.10 W
Santa Cruz del Norte 240p 23.09 N 81.55 W
Santa Cruz del Quiché 236 15.02 N 91.08 W
Santa Cruz del Sur 240p 20.43 N 78.00 W
Santa Cruz de Mudela 34 38.38 N 3.28 W
Santa Cruz de Tenerife 148 28.27 N 16.14 W
Santa Cruz de Tenerife □[4] 148 28.15 N 17.00 W
Santa Cruz do Capibaribe 250 7.57 S 36.12 W
Santa Cruz do Piauí 250 7.09 S 41.48 W
Santa Cruz do Prata 256 21.12 S 46.45 W
Santa Cruz do Rio Abaixo 256 23.18 S 45.24 W
Santa Cruz do Rio Pardo 255 22.55 S 49.37 W
Santa Cruz do Sul 252 29.43 S 52.26 W
Santa Cruz International Airport ✈ 272c 19.05 N 72.52 E
Santa Cruz Island I 204 34.01 N 119.45 W
Santa Cruz Islands II 14 11.00 S 166.15 E
Santa Cruz Meyehualco ◆[8] 286a 19.20 N 99.03 W
Santa Cruz Mountains ∧ 226 37.15 N 122.00 W
Santa Cruz Point ≻ 116 15.44 N 119.52 E
Santa Cruz Tacache Mina 234 17.51 N 98.07 W
Santadi 71 39.05 N 8.43 E
Santa Domenica Talao 68 39.49 N 15.51 E
Santa Domenica Vittoria 70 37.55 N 14.58 E
Sant Adrià de Besòs 266d 41.25 N 2.14 E
Santa Eduviges 286e 33.33 S 70.39 W
Santa Elena, Arg. 252 30.57 S 59.48 W
Santa Elena, Ec. 246 2.14 S 80.51 W
Santa Elena, El Sal. 236 13.22 N 88.25 W
Santa Elena, Méx. 196 27.59 N 103.56 W
Santa Elena, Méx. 232 27.28 N 102.33 W
Santa Elena, Méx. 234 18.39 N 101.34 W
Santa Elena ≃ 248 15.42 S 67.13 W
Santa Elena, Bahía de ⊂ 246 2.06 S 80.53 W
Santa Elena, Golfo de ⊂ 236 10.59 N 85.50 W
Santa Elena, Punta ≻, C.R. 236 10.54 N 85.57 W
Santa Elena, Punta ≻, Ec. 246 2.11 S 81.00 W
Santa Elena del Gomero 286e 33.29 S 70.46 W
Santa Elena de Uairén 246 4.37 N 61.08 W
Santa Elisabetta 70 37.26 N 13.33 E
Santa Emilia 286e 33.23 S 70.39 W
Santa Eufemia 34 38.36 N 4.54 W
Santa Eugenia 34 42.33 N 9.00 W
Santa Eulalia, Esp. 34 40.34 N 1.19 W
Santa Eulalia, Guat. 236 15.45 N 91.29 W
Santa Eulària del Riu 34 38.59 N 1.31 E
Santa Fe, Arg. 252 31.38 S 60.42 W
Santa Fé, Bra. 255 15.40 S 51.16 W
Santa Fé, Bra. 255 23.01 S 51.48 W
Santa Fé, Cuba 240p 21.45 N 82.45 W
Santa Fe, Esp. 34 37.11 N 3.43 W
Santa Fé, Hond. 236 15.55 N 86.05 W
Santa Fé, Pan. 236 8.31 N 81.05 W
Santa Fe, Pil. 116 11.09 N 123.47 E
Santa Fe, Pil. 116 16.10 N 120.57 E
Santa Fe, Pil. 116 12.10 N 122.00 E
Santa Fe, Mo., U.S. 219 39.22 N 91.49 W
Santa Fe, N.M., U.S. 200 35.41 N 105.56 W
Santa Fe □[4] 252 31.00 S 61.00 W
Santa Fé ◆[8] 286b 23.05 N 82.31 W
Santa Fe ≃, Fl., U.S. 192 29.53 N 82.53 W
Santa Fe ≃, N.M., U.S. 200 35.36 N 106.20 W
Santa Fé, Aeropuerto ✈ 286b 23.04 N 82.28 W
Santa Fe, Isla I 246a 0.49 S 90.04 W
Santa Fé, Ribeirão ≃ 287b 23.24 S 46.48 W
Santa Fe Baldy ∧ 200 35.50 N 105.46 W
Santa Fe Dam ◆[6] 280 34.07 N 117.58 W
Santa Fé do Sul 255 20.13 S 50.56 W
Santa Fe Flood Control Basin ≃[1] 280 34.07 N 117.58 W
Santa Fe Springs 280 33.56 N 118.04 W
Santa Filomena 250 9.07 S 45.56 W
Santa Fiora 66 42.50 N 11.35 E
Santa Flavia 70 38.05 N 13.31 E
Sant'Agata Bolognese 64 44.40 N 11.08 E
Sant'Agata de'Goti 68 41.05 N 14.30 E
Sant'Agata del Bianco 68 38.05 N 16.05 E
Sant'Agata di Militello 70 38.04 N 14.38 E
Sant'Agata di Puglia 68 41.09 N 15.23 E
Sant'Agata Feltria 66 43.52 N 12.12 E
Sant'Agata sul Santerno 66 44.26 N 11.51 E
Santa Gertrude (Sankt Gertraud) 64 46.29 N 10.53 E
Santa Gertrudis 196 26.09 N 98.44 W
Santa Giusta, Stagno di @ 71 39.52 N 8.35 E
Sant'Agostino 64 44.48 N 11.23 E
Sāntāhār 124 24.48 N 88.59 E
Santa Helena 250 2.14 S 45.18 W
Santa Helena de Goiás 255 17.43 S 50.35 W
Santai, Zhg. 85 39.14 N 77.42 E
Santai, Zhg. 86 44.35 N 81.18 E
Santai, Zhg. 102 31.10 N 105.02 E
Santai, Zhg. 104 41.48 N 121.53 E
Santai, Zhg. 104 41.56 N 123.11 E
Santai, Zhg. 105 38.58 N 115.46 E
Santa Inês 255 13.17 S 39.48 W
Santa Inés, Bahía ⊂ 232 26.59 N 111.59 W
Santa Inés, Isla I 254 53.45 S 72.45 W
Santa Inês Ahuatempan 234 18.25 N 98.01 W
Santa Inés Zacatelco 234 19.13 N 98.14 W
Santa Iria de Azóia 266c 38.51 N 9.05 W
Santa Isabel, Arg. 252 33.54 S 61.42 W
Santa Isabel, Arg. 252 36.15 S 66.56 W
Santa Isabel, Bra. 256 23.19 S 46.14 W
Santa Isabel, Ec. 246 3.21 S 79.19 W
Santa Isabel → Malabo, Gui. Ecu. 152 3.45 N 8.47 E
Santa Isabel, P.R. 240m 17.58 N 66.24 W
Santa Isabel I 175e 8.00 S 159.00 E
Santa Isabel ≃ 236 15.59 N 90.00 W
Santa Isabel, Pico de ∧ 152 3.35 N 8.46 E
Santa Isabel Creek ≃ 196 27.39 N 99.38 W
Santa Isabel de las Lajas 240p 22.25 N 80.18 W
Santa Isabel de Sihuas 248 16.20 S 72.06 W
Santa Isabel do Araguaia 250 6.07 S 48.19 W
Santa Isabel do Rio Prêto 256 22.14 S 44.05 W
Santaizi 104 41.21 N 121.36 E
Santa Josefa 116 8.02 N 125.57 E
Santa Julia 286e 33.30 S 70.38 W
Santa Juliana 255 19.19 S 47.32 W
Sant'Alberto 66 44.32 N 12.09 E
Santa Leopoldina 255 20.06 S 40.32 W
Sant'Alfio 70 37.44 N 15.08 E
Sāntalpur 120 23.45 N 71.10 E
Santa Luce 66 43.28 N 10.34 E
Santa Lucía, Arg. 252 31.32 S 68.29 W
Santa Lucía, Arg. 252 28.59 S 59.06 W
Santa Lucía, Cuba 240p 21.02 N 76.00 W
Santa Lucía, Cuba 240p 22.40 N 83.58 W
Santa Lucía, Cuba 240p 20.59 N 77.25 W
Santa Lucia, It. 64 46.28 N 10.21 E
Santa Lucía, Ur. 258 34.27 S 56.24 W
Santa Lucía, Ven. 246 8.07 N 69.46 W
Santa Lucia → Saint Lucia □[1] 241f 13.53 N 60.58 W
Santa Lucía ≃ 258 34.48 S 56.22 W
Santa Lucía, Cabo → Saint Lucia, Cape ≻ 158 28.25 S 32.25 E
Santa Lucía, Cuchilla ∧[2] 258 34.09 S 56.11 W
Santa Lucía Chico ≃ 258 34.21 S 56.20 W
Santa Lucía Cotzumalguapa 236 14.20 N 91.01 W
Santa Lucia Creek ≃ 226 36.13 N 121.30 W
Santa Lucía del Mela 70 38.09 N 15.17 E
Santa Lucia di Piave 64 45.51 N 12.17 E
Santa Lucia Range ∧ 226 36.00 N 121.20 W
Santa Lugarda, Punta ≻ 232 26.44 N 109.48 W
Santa Luísa de Baixo 256 22.46 S 45.49 W
Santaluz 250 11.15 S 39.22 W
Santa Luzia, Bra. 250 6.53 S 36.56 W
Santa Luzia, Port. 34 37.44 N 8.24 W
Santa Luzia I 150a 16.46 N 24.45 W
Santa Magdalena 252 34.30 S 63.56 W
Santa Magdalena, Isla I 232 24.55 N 112.15 W
Santa-Manza, Golfu di ⊂ 71 41.37 N 9.22 E
Santa Margarita 226 35.23 N 120.36 W
Santa Margarita ≃ 228 33.14 N 117.25 W
Santa Margarita, Isla de I 232 24.27 N 111.50 W
Santa Margarita Lake @[1] 226 35.20 N 120.28 W
Santa Margarita Mountains ∧ 228 33.30 N 117.25 W
Santa Margherita di Belice 70 37.41 N 13.01 E
Santa Margherita Ligure 62 44.20 N 9.12 E
Santa María, Arg. 252 26.41 S 66.02 W
Santa Maria, Bra. 252 29.41 S 53.48 W
Santa Maria, C.V. 150a 16.36 N 22.54 W
Santa María, C.R. 236 9.39 N 83.57 W
Santa María, Méx. 196 28.02 N 101.38 W
Santa María, Pan. 236 8.07 N 80.40 W
Santa María, Perú 286d 11.59 S 77.00 W
Santa Maria, Pil. 116 17.22 N 120.29 E
Santa Maria, Pil. 116 18.09 N 121.30 E
Santa Maria, Schw. 58 46.36 N 10.26 E
Santa Maria, Schw. 58 46.36 N 10.24 E
Santa Maria, Ca., U.S. 204 34.57 N 120.26 W
Santa Maria I, Port. 148a 36.58 N 25.06 W
Santa Maria I, Vanuatu 175f 14.15 S 167.30 E
Santa Maria ≃, Bra. 252 29.48 S 54.56 W
Santa Maria ≃, Bra. 252 21.50 S 54.53 W
Santa María ≃, Méx. 232 31.00 N 107.14 W
Santa María ≃, Méx. 234 21.48 N 99.10 W
Santa María ≃, Pan. 236 8.06 N 80.29 W
Santa Maria ≃, Az., U.S. 200 34.19 N 113.31 W
Santa María, Bahía de ⊂ 232 25.04 N 108.06 W
Santa Maria, Cabo → Sainte-Marie, Cap ≻, Madag. 157b 25.36 S 45.08 E
Santa Maria, Cabo ≻, Ur. 252 34.40 S 54.10 W
Santa Maria, Cabo de ≻, Ang. 152 13.25 S 12.32 E
Santa Maria, Cabo de ≻, Port. 34 36.58 N 7.54 W
Santa María, Cape ≻ 238 23.41 N 75.19 W
Santa María, Cayo I 240p 22.40 N 79.00 W
Santa María, Cerro ∧ 286d 11.56 S 76.57 W
Santa Maria, Giogo di (Pass Umbrail))(64 46.34 N 10.25 E
Santa María, Isla I, Chile 252 37.02 S 73.33 W
Santa María, Isla I, Ec. 246a 1.17 S 90.26 W
Santa Maria, Isola I 71 41.17 N 9.22 E
Santa María, Laguna de @ 232 31.07 N 107.16 W
Santa Maria, Ribeirão ≃, Bra. 250 7.10 S 49.13 W
Santa Maria, Ribeirão ≃, Bra. 250 8.08 S 43.02 W
Santa María, Volcán ∧[1] 236 14.45 N 91.33 W
Santa María Ajoloapan 234 19.58 N 99.03 W
Santa Maria a Monte 66 43.42 N 10.42 E
Santa Maria a Vico 68 41.02 N 14.29 E
Santa Maria Capua Vetere 68 41.05 N 14.15 E
Santa María Chimalapa 234 16.55 N 94.41 W
Santa María Colotepec 234 15.53 N 96.55 W
Santa Maria da Boa Vista 250 8.49 S 39.49 W
Santa Maria da Vitória 255 13.24 S 44.12 W
Santa Maria degli Angeli 66 43.03 N 12.34 E
Santa María de Ipire 246 8.49 N 65.19 W
Santa Maria de Itabira 255 19.27 S 43.08 W
Santa Maria del Cedro 68 39.45 N 15.50 E
Santa Maria della Versa 62 44.59 N 9.18 E
Santa María delle Grazie ✝[1] 266b 45.27 N 9.10 E
Santa María del Oro 232 25.56 N 105.22 W
Santa María de los Ángeles 234 22.11 N 103.14 W
Santa María del Refugio 234 23.44 N 101.14 W
Santa María del Río 234 21.48 N 100.45 W
Santa María del Valle 234 20.54 N 102.22 W
Santa Maria di Galeria ◆[8] 267a 42.01 N 12.19 E
Santa Maria di Leuca, Capo ≻ 68 39.47 N 18.22 E
Santa Maria di Licodia 70 37.37 N 14.53 E
Santa Maria di Siponto ✝[1] 68 41.40 N 15.51 E
Santa Maria do Suaçuí 255 18.12 S 42.25 W
Santa María Jalapa [del Marqués] 234 16.30 N 95.28 W
Santa Maria la Real de Nieva 34 41.04 N 4.24 W
Santa Maria Madalena 255 21.57 S 42.01 W
Santa María Magdalena [Cahuacán] 234 19.38 N 99.25 W
Santa Maria Maggiore 58 46.08 N 8.28 E
Santa Maria Maggiore ✝[1] 267a 41.53 N 12.30 E
Santa Maria Nuova 66 43.29 N 13.18 E
Santa-Maria-Siché 36 41.52 N 8.59 E
Santa María Tulpetlac 286a 19.34 N 99.03 W
Santa María Zoquitlán 234 16.33 N 96.23 W
Santa Marinella 66 42.02 N 11.51 E
Santa Marta, Col. 246 11.15 N 74.13 W
Santa Marta, Guat. 236 13.58 N 91.18 W
Santa Marta, Cabo de ≻, Ang. 152 13.52 S 12.25 E
Santa Marta, Cabo de ≻, Moç. 158 26.05 S 32.58 E
Santa Marta Grande, Cabo de ≻ 252 28.38 S 48.45 W
Sant'Ambrogio 64 45.31 N 10.50 E
Santa Mónica, Méx. 196 28.12 N 100.37 W
Santa Monica, Ca., U.S. 228 34.01 N 118.29 W
Santa Mónica ◆[8] 286c 10.29 N 66.53 W
Santa Monica Bay ⊂ 228 33.54 N 118.25 W
Santa Monica Beach State Park ◆ 280 34.01 N 118.30 W
Santa Monica Mountains ∧ 228 34.05 N 118.40 W
Santa Monica Mountains National Recreation Area ◆ 228 34.05 N 118.45 W
Santa Monica Municipal Airport ✈ 280 34.01 N 118.27 W
Santan 112 0.03 S 117.28 E
Santana 255 12.59 S 44.03 W
Santana ◆[8] 287b 23.29 S 46.38 W
Santana ≃, Bra. 250 8.35 S 44.01 W
Santana ≃, Bra. 255 19.43 S 51.02 W
Santana, Cachoeira ↳ 255 14.45 S 49.10 W
Santana, Coxilha de ∧[2] 252 31.15 S 55.15 W
Santana, Ribeirão ≃ 250 9.47 S 50.13 W
Santana, Serra de ∧ 256 22.30 S 42.35 W
Santana da Boa Vista 252 30.52 S 53.07 W
Santana da Vargem 256 21.15 S 45.30 W
Santana de Caldas 256 21.50 S 46.24 W
Santana de Cataguases 256 21.17 S 42.33 W
Santana de Parnaíba 256 23.27 S 46.55 W
Santana de Parnaíba □[7] 287b 23.27 S 46.54 W
Santana do Acaraú 250 3.27 S 40.12 W
Santana do Capivari 256 22.14 S 44.56 W
Santana do Cariri 250 7.11 S 39.44 W
Santana do Deserto 256 21.57 S 43.11 W
Santana do Garambéu 256 21.36 S 44.06 W
Santana do Ipanema 250 9.22 S 37.14 W
Santana do Livramento 252 30.53 S 55.31 W
Santana do Matos 250 5.57 S 36.39 W
Santander, Col. 246 3.01 N 76.28 W
Santander, Esp. 34 43.28 N 3.48 W
Santander, Pil. 116 9.25 N 123.20 E
Santander □[5] 246 7.00 N 73.15 W
Santander, Norte de □[3] 238 9.15 N 73.00 W
Santander Jiménez 232 24.13 N 98.28 W
Sant'andrea, Isola I 68 40.03 N 17.57 E
Sant'Andrea Frius 71 39.29 N 9.10 E
Sant Andreu de la Barca 266d 41.27 N 1.59 E
Santa Nella 226 37.03 N 121.02 W
Santanésia 256 22.30 S 43.49 W
Santang 100 28.44 N 116.32 E
Sant'Angelo, Castel ⊥ 267a 41.55 N 12.28 E
Sant'Angelo, Monte ∧ 267a 41.56 N 12.49 E
Sant'Angelo dei Lombardi 68 40.56 N 15.11 E
Sant'Angelo in Vado 66 43.40 N 12.25 E
Sant'Angelo Lodigiano 62 45.14 N 9.24 E
Sant'Angelo Muxard 70 37.28 N 13.32 E
Sant'Angelo Romano 267a 42.02 N 12.42 E
Santanghu 102 44.13 N 93.22 E
Santanilla, Islas II 238 17.25 N 83.55 W
Santa Ninfa 70 37.46 N 12.53 E
Sant'Antimo 68 40.56 N 14.14 E
Sant'antine, Nuraghe ⊥ 71 40.29 N 8.46 E
Sant'Antioco 71 39.04 N 8.27 E
Sant'antioco, Isola di I 71 39.02 N 8.25 E
Sant Antoni de Portmany 34 38.58 N 1.18 E
Sant'Antonio Abate 68 40.43 N 14.32 E
Sant'Antonio di Santadi 71 39.43 N 8.29 E
Sant'Antonio Morignone 64 46.24 N 10.21 E
Santanyí 34 39.22 N 3.07 E
Santa Panagia, Capo ≻ 70 37.07 N 15.18 E
Santa Paula 228 34.21 N 119.03 W
Santa Paula Creek ≃ 228 34.21 N 119.03 W
Santa Perpètua de Mogoda 266d 41.32 N 2.11 E
Santapogue Creek ≃ 276 40.40 N 73.21 W
Santa Pola, Cap de ≻ 34 38.12 N 0.31 W
Sant'Apollinare in Classe ✝[1] 66 44.22 N 12.15 E
Santaquin 200 39.58 N 111.47 W
Santa Quitéria 250 4.20 S 40.10 W
Santa Quitéria do Maranhão 250 3.31 S 42.32 W
Sant'Arcangelo 68 40.15 N 16.17 E
Santarcangelo di Romagna 66 44.04 N 12.27 E
Sant'Arcangelo Trimonte 68 41.10 N 14.56 E
Santarém, Bra. 250 2.26 S 54.42 W
Santarém, Port. 34 39.14 N 8.41 W
Santarém □[5] 266c 38.50 N 8.56 W
Santarém Novo 250 0.56 S 47.23 W
Santaren Channel ᴗ 238 24.00 N 79.30 W
Santa Rita, Bra. 250 7.08 S 34.58 W
Santa Rita, Bra. 287a 22.41 S 43.28 W
Santa Rita, Col. 246 1.04 N 73.58 W
Santa Rita, Hond. 236 15.09 N 87.53 W
Santa Rita, Méx. 196 27.29 N 100.33 W
Santa Rita, Pil. 116 11.27 N 124.56 E
Santa Rita, Mt., U.S. 182 48.42 N 112.19 W
Santa Rita, Ven. 246 10.32 N 71.32 W
Santa Rita, Riacho ≃ 255 12.49 S 43.21 W
Santa Rita de Caldas 256 22.02 S 46.20 W
Santa Rita de Catuna 252 30.57 S 66.13 W
Santa Rita de Jacutinga 256 22.09 S 44.06 W
Santa Rita del Rucio 234 23.04 N 100.19 W
Santa Rita do Araguaia 255 17.20 S 53.12 W
Santa Rita do Ibitipoca 256 21.33 S 43.55 W
Santa Rita do Sapucaí 256 22.15 S 45.42 W
Santa Rita do Weil 246 3.29 S 69.19 W
Santa Rita Park 226 37.02 N 120.35 W
Santa Rosa, Arg. 252 28.02 S 67.37 W
Santa Rosa, Arg. 252 32.20 S 65.12 W
Santa Rosa, Arg. 252 23.22 S 64.30 W
Santa Rosa, Arg. 252 36.37 S 64.17 W
Santa Rosa, Bol. 248 17.07 S 63.35 W
Santa Rosa, Bol. 248 10.36 S 67.25 W
Santa Rosa, Bol. 248 14.10 S 66.53 W
Santa Rosa, Bra. 252 27.52 S 54.29 W
Santa Rosa, Bra. 255 15.01 S 47.13 W
Santa Rosa, Col. 246 2.31 N 68.13 W
Santa Rosa, C.R. 236 10.51 N 85.38 W
Santa Rosa, Ec. 246 3.27 S 79.58 W
Santa Rosa, Méx. 204 31.59 N 116.45 W
Santa Rosa, Méx. 234 19.41 N 100.02 W
Santa Rosa, Méx. 234 22.18 N 104.24 W
Santa Rosa, Para. 248 21.46 S 61.43 W
Santa Rosa, Para. 252 26.52 S 56.49 W
Santa Rosa, Perú 286d 12.00 S 77.06 W
Santa Rosa, Ca., U.S. 226 38.26 N 122.42 W
Santa Rosa, N.M., U.S. 196 34.56 N 104.40 W
Santa Rosa, Tx., U.S. 196 26.15 N 97.50 W
Santa Rosa, Ur. 258 34.30 S 56.03 W
Santa Rosa, Ven. 246 8.26 N 69.24 W
Santa Rosa, Ven. 286c 10.30 N 66.46 W
Santa Rosa □[5] 236 14.10 N 90.18 W
Santa Rosa, Mount ∧[2] 174p 13.32 N 144.55 E
Santa Rosa, Presa @[1] 234 20.58 N 103.35 W
Santa Rosa Beach 194 30.23 N 86.13 W
Santa Rosa Creek ≃ 226 35.34 N 121.06 W
Santa Rosa de Aguán 236 15.57 N 85.43 W
Santa Rosa de Amanadona 246 1.29 N 66.55 W
Santa Rosa de Cabal 246 4.52 N 75.38 W
Santa Rosa [de Copán] 236 14.47 N 88.46 W
Santa Rosa de Huechuraba 286e 33.21 S 70.41 W
Santa Rosa de la Roca 248 16.04 S 61.32 W
Santa Rosa de Leales 252 27.09 S 65.15 W
Santa Rosa de Lima 236 13.37 N 87.53 W
Santa Rosa de Locobe 286e 33.26 S 70.33 W
Santa Rosa del Palmar 248 16.54 S 62.24 W
Santa Rosa de Osos 246 6.39 N 75.28 W
Santa Rosa de Río Primero 252 31.09 S 63.23 W
Santa Rosa de Sucumbíos 246 0.22 N 77.10 W
Santa Rosa de Viterbo 246 5.53 N 72.59 W
Santa Rosa Indian Reservation ◆[4] 204 33.35 N 116.35 W
Santa Rosa Island I, Ca., U.S. 204 33.58 N 120.06 W
Santa Rosa Island I, Fl., U.S. 194 30.22 N 86.55 W
Santa Rosa Jáuregui 234 20.44 N 100.27 W
Santa Rosalía, Méx. 196 26.08 N 98.59 W
Santa Rosalía, Méx. 232 27.19 N 112.17 W
Santa Rosalía, Ven. 246 9.02 N 69.01 W
Santa Rosalía, Bahía ⊂ 232 28.37 N 114.13 W
Santa Rosa Range ∧ 204 41.35 N 117.40 W
Santa Rosa Wash ∨ 200 33.00 N 112.00 W
Santa Rosita 286d 12.03 S 76.59 W
Sant'Arsenio 68 40.28 N 15.29 E
Santarskije ostrova II 74 55.00 N 137.36 E
Santa Severa 66 42.02 N 11.57 E
Santa Severina 68 39.09 N 16.55 E
Santa Sofia 66 43.57 N 11.54 E
Santa Susana 228 34.16 N 118.43 W
Santa Susana Mountains ∧ 228 34.20 N 118.42 W
Santa Sylvina 252 27.49 S 61.09 W
Santa Tecla → Nueva San Salvador 236 13.41 N 89.17 W
Santa Teresa, Arg. 252 33.26 S 60.47 W
Santa Teresa, Bra. 255 19.55 S 40.36 W

≃ River	Fluß	Río	Rivière	Rio	
≅ Canal	Kanal	Canal	Canal	Canal	
↳ Waterfall, Rapids	Wasserfall, Stromschnellen	Cascada, Rápidos	Chute d'eau, Rapides	Cascata, Rápidos	
ᴗ Strait	Meeresstraße	Estrecho	Détroit	Estreito	
⊂ Bay, Gulf	Bucht, Golf	Bahía, Golfo	Baie, Golfe	Baía, Golfo	
@ Lake, Lakes	See, Seen	Lago, Lagos	Lac, Lacs	Lago, Lagos	
≚ Swamp	Sumpf	Pantano	Marais	Pântano	
⋒ Ice Features, Glacier	Eis- und Gletscherformen	Accidentes Glaciales	Formes glaciaires	Acidentes glaciares	
ᴛ Other Hydrographic Features	Andere Hydrographische Objekte	Otros Elementos Hidrográficos	Autres données hydrographiques	Outros acidentes hidrográficos	
◆ Submarine Features	Untermeerische Objekte	Accidentes Submarinos	Formes de relief sous-marin	Acidentes submarinos	
□ Political Unit	Politische Einheit	Unidad Política	Entité politique	Unidade política	
✝ Cultural Institution	Kulturelle Institution	Institución Cultural	Institution culturelle	Instituição cultural	
⊥ Historical Site	Historische Stätte	Sitio Histórico	Site historique	Sitio histórico	
◆ Recreational Site	Erholungs- und Ferienort	Sitio de Recreo	Centre de loisirs	Area de Lazer	
✈ Airport	Flughafen	Aeropuerto	Aéroport	Aeroporto	
■ Military Installation	Militäranlage	Instalación Militar	Installation militaire	Instalação militar	
◆ Miscellaneous	Verschiedenes	Misceláneo	Divers	Diversos	

I · 156 Sant-Sara

ENGLISH — Name Page Lat.°′ Long.°′
DEUTSCH — Name Seite Breite°′ Länge°′ E = Ost

Santa Teresa, Méx. 196 29.34 N 104.39 W
Santa Teresa, Méx. 200 30.52 N 111.33 W
Santa Teresa, Méx. 234 22.28 N 104.44 W
Santa Teresa ≃ 255 11.47 S 48.37 W
Santa Teresa, Embalse de ⊜1 34 40.40 N 5.30 W
Santa Teresa de Goiás 255 13.38 S 49.01 W
Santa Teresa de lo Ovalle 286e 33.23 S 70.47 W
Santa Teresa del Tuy 246 10.14 N 66.40 W
Santa Teresa di Riva 70 37.57 N 15.22 E
Santa Teresa Gallura 71 41.14 N 9.11 E
Santa Teresinha 255 12.45 S 39.32 W
Santa Valburga (Sankt Wallburg) 64 46.33 N 11.00 E
Santa Venerina 70 37.41 N 15.08 E
Santa Venetia 226 38.01 N 122.31 W
Santa Vitória 255 18.50 S 50.08 W
Santa Vitória do Palmar 252 33.31 S 53.21 W
Santa Vittoria, Monte ʌ 71 39.45 N 9.18 E
Santa Vittoria in Matenano 66 43.01 N 13.29 E
Santa Ynez ≃ 204 34.41 N 120.36 W
Santa Ynez Canyon V 280 34.04 N 118.34 W
Santa Ysabel Indian Reservation ◆4 204 33.11 N 116.41 W
Sant Bartomeu de la Quadra 266d 41.26 N 2.02 E
Sant Boi de Llobregat 266d 41.21 N 2.03 E
Sant Carles de la Ràpita 34 40.37 N 0.36 E
Sant Climent de Llobregat 266d 41.20 N 2.00 E
Sant Cugat del Vallès 266d 41.28 N 2.05 E
Santee 228 32.50 N 116.58 W
Santee ≃ 192 33.14 N 79.28 W
Santee Dam ◆6 192 33.24 N 80.12 W
Santee Indian Reservation ◆4 198 42.45 N 97.50 W
Sant'Egidio alla Vibrata 66 42.49 N 13.42 E
Sant'Elena 64 45.12 N 11.43 E
Sant'Elia a Pianisi 66 41.38 N 14.52 E
Sant'Elia Fiumerapido 66 41.32 N 13.52 E
San Telmo, Bahía de c 234 18.38 N 103.42 W
San Telmo, Cerro ʌ 234 18.37 N 103.37 W
Sant'Elpidio a Mare 66 43.14 N 13.41 E
Santena 62 44.57 N 7.45 E
Santenay 58 46.55 N 4.41 E
Santeny 261 48.43 N 2.34 E
San Teodoro, It. 70 37.51 N 14.42 E
San Teodoro, It. 71 40.46 N 9.39 E
Santermo in Colle 68 40.48 N 16.45 E
Santerno ≃ 66 44.34 N 11.58 E
Santerre ▫9 50 49.40 N 2.40 E
Sant'eufemia, Golfo di c 68 38.50 N 16.00 E
Sant'Eufemia a Maiella 66 42.07 N 14.02 E
Sant'Eufemia d'Aspromonte 68 38.16 N 15.52 E
Sant'Eufemia Lamezia 68 38.55 N 16.15 E
Sant Feliu de Guíxols 34 41.47 N 3.02 E
Sant Feliu de Llobregat 266d 41.23 N 2.03 E
Sant Fost de Campsentelles 266d 41.31 N 2.14 E
Sānthia, Bngl. 126 24.03 N 89.33 E
Santhià, It. 62 45.22 N 8.10 E
Santiago, Bol. 248 18.19 S 59.34 W
Santiago, Bra. 252 29.11 S 54.53 W
Santiago, Chile 252 33.27 S 70.40 W
Santiago, Chile 286e 33.27 S 70.40 W
Santiago, C.R. 236 9.51 N 84.18 W
Santiago → Santiago de Compostela, Esp. 34 42.53 N 8.33 W
Santiago, Méx. 232 25.25 N 100.09 W
Santiago, Méx. 232 23.28 N 109.43 W
Santiago, Pan. 236 8.06 N 80.59 W
Santiago, Para. 252 27.09 S 56.47 W
Santiago, Perú 248 14.11 S 75.44 W
Santiago, Pil. 116 16.41 N 121.33 E
Santiago I 150a 15.05 N 23.40 W
Santiago ≃, Arg. 288 34.50 S 57.57 W
Santiago ≃, S.A. 246 4.27 S 77.38 W
Santiago, Cape ≻ 116 13.46 N 120.39 E
Santiago, Cerro ʌ 236 8.33 N 81.44 W
Santiago, Isla I 288 34.50 S 57.53 W
Santiago, Río de ≃ 232 25.11 N 105.26 W
Santiago, Serranía de ⋏ 248 18.25 S 59.25 W
Santiago Apóstol 234 16.49 N 96.42 W
Santiago Atitlán 236 14.38 N 91.14 W
Santiago Creek ≃, Ca., U.S. 228 35.06 N 119.17 W
Santiago Creek ≃, Ca., U.S. 228 33.46 N 117.54 W
Santiago Dam ◆6 280 33.47 N 117.43 W
Santiago de Cao 248 7.58 S 79.15 W
Santiago de Chocorvos 248 13.50 S 75.16 W
Santiago de Chuco 248 8.09 S 78.11 W
Santiago de Compostela 34 42.53 N 8.33 W
Santiago de Cuba 240p 20.01 N 75.49 W
Santiago de Cuba ▫4 240p 20.10 N 75.55 W
Santiago de Huata 248 16.06 S 68.53 W
Santiago de la Peña 234 20.57 N 97.24 W
Santiago de las Vegas ◆8 286b 22.58 N 82.23 W
Santiago del Estero 252 27.47 S 64.16 W
Santiago del Estero ▫4 252 28.00 S 63.30 W
Santiago [de los Caballeros] 238 19.27 N 70.42 W
Santiago de Machaca 248 17.05 S 69.16 W
Santiago do Cacém 34 38.01 N 8.42 W
Santiago Island I 116 16.24 N 119.56 E
Santiago Ixcuintla 234 21.49 N 105.13 W
Santiago Ixtayutla 234 16.33 N 97.39 W
Santiago Lachiguiri 234 16.41 N 95.32 W
Santiago Larre 258 35.34 S 59.10 W
Santiago Maravatío 234 20.10 N 101.00 W
Santiago Papasquiaro 232 25.03 N 105.25 W
Santiago Peak ʌ, Ca., U.S. 228 33.42 N 117.32 W
Santiago Peak ʌ, Tx., U.S. 196 29.47 N 103.25 W
Santiago Reservoir ⊜1 228 33.47 N 117.43 W
Santiago Tepalcatlapan ◆8 286a 19.15 N 99.08 W
Santiago Tulantepec 234 20.02 N 98.22 W
Santiago Tutla 234 17.10 N 95.26 W
Santiago Tuxtla 234 18.28 N 95.18 W
Santiago Vázquez 258 34.48 S 56.21 W
Santiago Yaveo 234 17.19 N 95.42 W
Santiago Zacatepec 234 17.11 N 95.51 W
Santiaguillo, Laguna de ⊜ 232 24.48 N 104.48 W
Santiam Pass)(202 44.25 N 121.51 W
San Tian Zhu (Three Indian Temples) ◆1 106 30.15 N 120.08 E
Santiao Chiao ≻ 100 25.02 N 121.59 E
Santiaoqiao 106 31.36 N 121.22 E
Santi Filippo e Giacomo 70 37.51 N 12.31 E
Santiguila 150 12.42 N 7.26 W
Sant'Ilario d'Enza 64 44.46 N 10.27 E
San Timoteo 246 9.48 N 71.04 W
San Timoteo Canyon V 228 34.04 N 117.17 W
Säntis ʌ 58 47.15 N 9.21 E
Santissima Trinita di Saccargia ◆1 71 40.41 N 8.42 E
Santissimo ◆8 287a 22.53 S 43.31 W
Santisteban del Puerto 34 38.15 N 3.12 W
Sant Joan de Labritja 34 39.05 N 1.30 E
Sant Joan Despí 266d 41.22 N 2.04 E
Sant Jordi, Golf de c 34 40.53 N 1.00 E
Sant Just Desvern 266d 41.23 N 2.05 E
Sant Mateu del Maestrat 34 40.28 N 0.11 E
Santō, Nihon 94 35.21 N 136.22 E
Santō, Nihon 96 35.19 N 134.53 E
Santo, Tx., U.S. 196 32.36 N 98.13 W
Santo, Vanuatu 175f 15.32 S 167.08 E
Santo Aleixo 256 22.34 S 43.04 W
Santo Amaro, Bra. 250 2.33 S 43.14 W
Santo Amaro, Bra. 255 12.32 S 38.43 W
Santo Amaro ◆8 287b 23.39 S 46.42 W
Santo Amaro, Ilha de I 256 23.57 S 46.14 W
Santo Amaro das Brotas 250 10.47 S 37.04 W
Santo Anastácio 255 21.58 S 51.39 W
Santo Anastácio ≃ 255 21.49 S 52.11 W
Santo André 256 23.40 S 46.31 W
Santo Ângelo 252 28.18 S 54.16 W
Santo Antão I 150a 17.05 N 25.10 W
Santo Antônio, Bra. 250 6.18 S 35.27 W
Santo Antônio, Bra. 252 29.50 S 50.32 W
Santo Antônio, S. Tom./P. 152 1.39 N 7.26 E
Santo Antônio ≃, Bra. 250 11.31 S 48.37 W
Santo Antônio ≃, Bra. 255 17.30 S 45.37 W
Santo Antônio ≃, Bra. 287a 22.42 S 43.37 W
Santo Antônio, Cachoeira ⌊ 248 9.46 S 60.35 W
Santo Antônio, Igarapé ≃ 246 1.32 S 59.48 W
Santo Antônio, Ilha de I 156 21.58 S 35.28 E
Santo Antônio da Boa Vista 255 15.52 S 44.09 W
Santo Antônio da Charneca 266c 38.37 N 9.02 W
Santo Antônio da Jesus 255 12.58 S 39.16 W
Santo Antônio de Posse 256 22.36 S 46.55 W
Santo Antônio do Amparo 255 20.57 S 44.55 W
Santo Antônio do Aventureiro 256 21.45 S 42.49 W
Santo Antônio do Içá 246 3.05 S 67.57 W
Santo Antônio do Jardim 256 22.07 S 46.41 W
Santo Antônio do Leverger 248 15.52 S 56.05 W
Santo Antônio do Pinhal 256 22.47 S 45.41 W
Santo Antônio do Rio Verde 255 17.57 S 47.27 W
Santo Antônio do Sudoeste 252 26.02 S 53.44 W
Santo Augusto 252 27.51 S 53.47 W
Santo Corazón 248 17.59 S 58.51 W
Santo Cristo 252 27.50 S 54.40 W
Santo Domingo, Arg. 252 29.16 S 63.56 W
Santo Domingo, Cuba 240p 22.35 N 80.15 W
Santo Domingo, Méx. 196 25.38 N 101.05 W
Santo Domingo, Méx. 196 25.48 N 104.28 W
Santo Domingo, Méx. 232 25.32 N 112.02 W
Santo Domingo, Méx. 234 23.20 N 101.44 W
Santo Domingo, Nic. 236 12.16 N 85.05 W
Santo Domingo, Rep. Dom. 238 18.28 N 69.54 W
Santo Domingo ≃, Méx. 234 16.41 N 93.00 W
Santo Domingo ≃, Méx. 234 17.40 N 98.07 W
Santo Domingo ≃, Méx. 234 18.10 N 96.08 W
Santo Domingo ≃, Méx. 236 16.15 N 91.17 W
Santo Domingo, Arroyo ≃, Méx. 204 30.43 N 116.03 W
Santo Domingo, Arroyo ≃, Méx. 232 25.29 N 112.05 W
Santo Domingo, Isla → Hispaniola I 238 19.00 N 71.00 W
Santo Domingo de la Calzada 34 42.26 N 2.57 W
Santo Domingo de los Colorados 246 0.15 S 79.09 W
Santo Domingo Indian Reservation ◆4 200 35.30 N 106.25 W
Santo Domingo Nuxaá 234 17.08 N 97.02 W
Santo Domingo Pueblo 200 35.30 N 106.21 W
Santo Domingo Teojomulco 234 16.36 N 97.14 W
Santo Estevão 255 12.26 S 39.13 W
Sant'Olcese 62 44.30 N 8.58 E
Santolea, Embalse de ⊜1 34 40.47 N 0.19 W
Santo / Malo ▫8 175f 15.20 S 166.55 E
San Tomé 246 8.58 N 64.08 W
San Tommaso 66 42.11 N 13.58 E
Sant'Omobono Imagna 62 45.48 N 9.32 E
Santoña 34 43.27 N 3.27 W
Santong ≃ 98 42.39 N 126.03 E
Santo Niño Island I 116 11.55 N 124.27 E
Sant' Onofrio ◆8 267a 41.56 N 12.25 E
Santo Onofre ≃ 255 12.34 S 43.12 W
Santop, Pic ʌ 175f 18.39 S 169.03 E
Sant'Oreste 66 42.14 N 12.32 E
Santorini → Thíra I 38 36.24 N 25.29 E
Santorso 64 45.44 N 11.23 E
Santos 256 23.57 S 46.20 W
Santos, Arroyo de los ≃ 258 35.28 S 57.29 W
Santos, Baía de c 256 24.00 S 46.21 W
Santos Dumont 256 21.28 S 43.34 W
Santos Dumont, Aeroporto ◆ 256 22.55 S 43.10 W
Santoshpur 272b 22.40 N 88.10 E
Santo Stefano, Isola I 66 40.47 N 13.27 E
Santo Stefano Belbo 62 44.43 N 8.14 E
Santo Stefano d'Aveto 62 44.33 N 9.27 E
Santo Stefano di Cadore 64 46.33 N 12.32 E
Santo Stefano di Camastra 70 38.01 N 14.21 E
Santo Stefano di Magra 64 44.10 N 9.55 E
Santo Stefano Quisquina 70 37.37 N 13.29 E
Santo Stino di Livenza 64 45.44 N 12.41 E
Santo Tirso 34 41.21 N 8.28 W
Santo Tomás, Col. 246 10.46 N 74.45 W
Santo Tomás, Méx. 232 31.33 N 116.24 W
Santo Tomás, Nic. 236 12.04 N 85.05 W
Santo Tomás, Perú 248 6.36 S 77.48 W
Santo Tomás, Perú 248 14.29 S 72.06 W
Santo Tomas, Pil. 116 7.29 N 125.38 E
Santo Tomás, Ven. 246 8.53 N 64.33 W
Santo Tomás ≃, Méx. 204 31.32 N 116.40 W
Santo Tomás ≃, Perú 248 13.47 S 72.09 W
Santo Tomás, Punta ≻ 232 31.34 N 116.42 W
Santo Tomas, University of ◆2 269f 14.37 N 120.59 E
Santo Tomás, Volcán ʌ1 246a 0.48 S 91.07 W
Santo Tomás de Nance 236 13.11 N 86.56 W
Santo Tomás Ocotepec 234 17.08 N 97.46 W
Santo Tomás y Principe → Sao Tome and Principe ▫1 152 1.00 N 7.00 E
Santo Tomé, Arg. 252 31.40 S 60.46 W
Santo Tomé, Arg. 252 28.33 S 56.03 W
Santo Tomé de Guayana → Ciudad Guayana 246 8.22 N 62.40 W
Sant' Pietro, Lago di ⊜ 68 41.01 N 15.30 E
Santpoort 52 52.25 N 4.38 E
Sant Quirze de la Serra 266d 41.32 N 2.05 E
Santuanjiang 106 30.54 N 121.43 E
Santu Lussurgiu 71 40.08 N 8.39 E
Santunying 105 40.14 N 118.12 E
Sant Vicenç dels Horts 266d 41.24 N 2.01 E
San Ubaldo 236 11.51 N 85.20 W
Sanuki 268 35.16 N 139.53 E
Sanuki-sammyaku ⋏ 96 34.09 N 134.11 E
Sānūr 132 32.21 N 35.15 E
San Valentín, Cerro ʌ 254 46.36 S 73.20 W
San Valentino in Abruzzo Citeriore 66 42.14 N 13.59 E
San Valentino Torio 68 40.48 N 14.36 E
San Venanzo 66 42.52 N 12.16 E
San Vendemiano 64 45.54 N 12.20 E
San Vicente, Arg. 252 28.30 S 64.09 W
San Vicente, Arg. 258 34.58 S 58.22 W
San Vicente, El Sal. 236 13.38 N 88.48 W
San Vicente, Méx. 232 31.20 N 116.15 W
San Vicente ▫5 288 34.56 S 58.24 W
San Vicente → Saint Vincent and the Grenadines ▫1 241h 13.15 N 61.12 W
San Vicente, Cabo de → São Vicente, Cabo de ≻ 34 37.01 N 9.00 W
San Vicente, Volcán de ʌ1 236 13.36 N 88.51 W
San Vicente Creek ≃ 282 37.32 N 122.31 W
San Vicente de Alcántara 34 39.21 N 7.08 W
San Vicente de Cañete 248 13.05 S 76.24 W
San Vicente de Chucurí 246 6.54 N 73.25 W
San Vicente de la Barquera 34 43.26 N 4.24 W
San Vicente del Caguán 246 2.07 N 74.46 W
San Vicente de Tagua-Tagua 252 34.26 S 71.05 W
San Vicente Mountain ʌ 280 34.08 N 118.31 W
San Vicente Reservoir ⊜1 228 32.55 N 116.55 W
San Vicente Tancuayalab 234 21.44 N 98.34 W
San Vigilio 64 45.34 N 10.41 E
San Vigilio ◆1 64 46.37 N 11.07 E
San Vincenzo 66 43.06 N 10.32 E
San Vito, C.R. 236 8.50 N 82.58 W
San Vito, It. 71 39.26 N 9.32 E
San Vito, Capo ≻ 70 38.11 N 12.44 E
San Vito, Serralta di ʌ 68 38.46 N 16.22 E
San Vito al Tagliamento 64 45.54 N 12.52 E
San Vito Chietino 66 42.18 N 14.27 E
San Vito dei Normanni 68 40.39 N 17.42 E
San Vito lo Capo 70 38.10 N 12.45 E
San Vito Romano 66 41.53 N 12.59 E
San Vito sullo Ionio 68 38.43 N 16.25 E
Sanwa, Nihon 94 37.07 N 138.21 E
Sanwa, Nihon 94 36.12 N 139.49 E
Sanwa, Nihon 96 34.42 N 133.15 E
San Xavier Indian Reservation ◆4 200 32.05 N 111.08 W
Sanxi, Zhg. 100 30.22 N 118.25 E
Sanxi, Zhg. 100 27.42 N 120.04 E
Sanxing, Zhg. 100 31.47 N 121.35 E
Sanxing, Zhg. 106 31.58 N 121.07 E
Sanxingchang, Zhg. 107 30.19 N 104.09 E
Sanxingchang, Zhg. 107 30.32 N 104.38 E
Sanxingjie 106 32.06 N 121.01 E
Sanyang, Zhg. 100 28.37 N 116.15 E
Sanyang, Zhg. 100 31.20 N 113.10 E
Sanyang, Zhg. 100 27.57 N 114.22 E
Sanyangzhen 106 31.55 N 121.29 E
Sanyanjing 104 41.28 N 122.27 E
Sanyanqiao 100 28.39 N 113.43 E
Sanyati ≃ 154 16.49 S 28.45 E
San Ygnacio 196 27.03 N 99.27 W
Sanyō, Nihon 94 36.25 N 138.40 E
Sanyō, Nihon 96 34.02 N 131.10 E
Sanyuan 102 34.35 N 108.54 E
Sanyuanpu 98 42.02 N 125.44 E
Sanyuhao 98 42.30 N 117.34 E
Sanyuzhen 106 32.08 N 121.19 E
Sanza 68 40.15 N 15.33 E
Sanzao Dao I 100 22.03 N 113.21 E
Sanza Pombo 152 7.19 S 15.59 E
Sanzar ≃ 85 40.00 N 67.40 E
San Zeno di Montagna 64 45.37 N 10.43 E
Sanzha 98 41.44 N 114.39 E
Sanzhan, Zhg. 89 49.42 N 125.20 E
Sanzhan, Zhg. 89 49.36 N 126.38 E
Sanzuodian 98 41.36 N 118.49 E
São Benedito 250 4.03 S 40.53 W
São Benedito ≃ 250 9.11 S 57.02 W
São Benedito das Areias 256 21.19 S 47.02 W
São Benedito do Rio Prêto 250 3.20 S 43.35 W
São Bento, Bra. 246 3.02 N 60.30 W
São Bento, Bra. 250 2.42 S 44.50 W
São Bento ≃ 256 21.42 S 45.18 W
São Bento, Mosteiro e Igreja de ◆1 287a 22.54 S 43.11 W
São Bento de Caldas 256 22.08 S 46.18 W
São Bento do Norte 250 5.04 S 36.02 W
São Bento do Sapucaí 256 22.42 S 45.43 W
São Bento do Sul 252 26.15 S 49.23 W
São Bento do Una 250 8.32 S 36.22 W
São Bernardino 287a 22.40 S 43.26 W
São Bernardo 250 3.22 S 42.24 W
São Bernardo do Campo 256 23.42 S 46.33 W
São Bernardo do Campo ▫7 287b 23.44 S 46.33 W
São Borja 252 28.39 S 56.00 W
São Brás 250 10.05 S 36.55 W
São Brás de Alportel 34 37.09 N 7.53 W
São Braz, Cabo de ≻ 152 9.59 S 13.19 E
São Caetano de Odivelas 250 0.45 S 48.02 W
São Caetano do Sul 256 23.36 S 46.34 W
São Caetano do Sul ▫7 287b 23.37 S 46.33 W
São Caitano 250 8.21 S 36.06 W
São Carlos, Bra. 252 27.04 S 52.59 W
São Carlos, Bra. 255 22.01 S 47.54 W
São Cristóvão 250 11.01 S 37.12 W
São Cristóvão ◆8 287a 22.54 S 43.14 W
Saodatun 104 42.02 N 123.31 E
São Domingos, Bra. 252 26.34 S 52.32 W
São Domingos, Bra. 255 13.24 S 46.19 W
São Domingos, Bra. 256 21.41 S 42.47 W
São Domingos, Gui.-B. 150 12.22 N 16.08 W
São Domingos ≃, Bra. 248 12.28 S 64.13 W
São Domingos ≃, Bra. 255 13.24 S 47.12 W
São Domingos ≃, Bra. 255 19.13 S 50.44 W
São Domingos ≃, Bra. 255 20.03 S 53.13 W
São Domingos da Bocaina 256 21.50 S 44.01 W
São Domingos do Capim 250 1.41 S 47.47 W
São Domingos do Maranhão 250 5.42 S 44.22 W
São Félix 250 11.36 S 50.39 W
São Félix de Balsas 250 7.08 S 44.52 W
São Félix do Piauí 250 5.56 S 42.07 W
São Filipe, Bra. 255 14.49 S 41.23 W
São Filipe, C.V. 150a 14.54 N 24.31 W
São Francisco, Bra. 255 15.57 S 44.52 W
São Francisco, Bra. 256 22.36 S 45.18 W
São Francisco ≃, Bra. 242 10.30 S 36.24 W
São Francisco ≃, Bra. 255 16.09 S 40.39 W
São Francisco ≃, Bra. 255 18.41 S 50.17 W
São Francisco ≃, Bra. 256 21.50 S 42.42 W
São Francisco ≃, Bra. 287a 22.57 S 43.20 W
São Francisco, Baía de c 252 26.10 S 48.34 W
São Francisco, Ilha de I 252 26.18 S 48.37 W
São Francisco de Assis 252 29.33 S 55.08 W
São Francisco de Goiás 255 15.55 S 49.16 W
São Francisco de Paula 252 29.27 S 50.35 W
São Francisco do Croará 287a 22.42 S 43.08 W
São Francisco do Maranhão 250 6.15 S 42.52 W
São Francisco do Piauí 250 7.15 S 42.32 W
São Francisco do Sul 252 26.14 S 48.39 W
São Francisco Xavier 256 22.54 S 45.58 W
São Gabriel 252 30.20 S 54.19 W
São Gabriel da Palha 255 19.01 S 40.32 W
São Gabriel de Goiás 255 15.12 S 47.34 W
São Gonçalo, Bra. 256 21.36 S 46.19 W
São Gonçalo, Bra. 256 22.51 S 43.04 W
São Gonçalo ▫7 287a 22.48 S 43.01 W
São Gonçalo do Abaeté 255 18.20 S 45.49 W
São Gonçalo do Amarante 250 3.36 S 38.58 W
São Gonçalo do Pará 255 19.59 S 44.51 W
São Gonçalo do Sapucaí 256 21.54 S 45.36 W
São Gonçalo dos Campos 255 12.25 S 38.58 W
Sao Hill 154 8.20 S 35.12 E
São Jerônimo 252 29.58 S 51.43 W
São Jerônimo, Serra de ʌ1 255 17.00 S 54.50 W
São Jerônimo da Serra 255 23.43 S 50.44 W
São João 150 11.32 N 15.26 W
São João ≃, Bra. 255 12.27 S 51.07 W
São João ≃, Bra. 256 22.33 S 42.29 W
São João ≃, Bra. 287b 23.31 S 46.51 W
São João, Ribeirão ≃ 256 21.28 S 42.49 W
São João da Aliança 255 14.42 S 47.32 W
São João da Barra 255 21.38 S 41.03 W
São João da Boa Vista 256 21.58 S 46.47 W
São João da Madeira 34 40.54 N 8.30 W
São João da Mata 256 21.56 S 45.56 W
São João da Ponte 255 15.56 S 44.01 W
São João da Serra 256 21.28 S 43.27 W
São João das Lampas 266c 38.52 N 9.24 W
São João de Côrtes 250 2.12 S 44.32 W
São João del Rei 255 21.09 S 44.16 W
São João de Meriti 256 22.48 S 43.22 W
São João de Meriti ▫7 287a 22.48 S 43.21 W
São João de Meriti ≃ 287a 22.48 S 43.18 W
São João de Pirabas 250 0.46 S 47.10 W
São João do Araguaia 250 5.23 S 48.46 W
São João do Caiuá 255 22.48 S 52.22 W
São João do Cariri 250 7.23 S 36.31 W
São João do Jaguaribe 250 5.16 S 38.16 W
São João do Paraíso 255 15.19 S 42.01 W
São João do Piauí 250 8.21 S 42.15 W
São João do Sabugi 250 6.43 S 37.12 W
São João dos Patos 250 6.30 S 43.42 W
São João do Triunfo 252 25.40 S 50.20 W
São João Evangelista 255 18.32 S 42.45 W
São João Nepomuceno 256 21.33 S 43.01 W
São João Nôvo 256 23.33 S 47.01 W
São Joaquim 252 28.18 S 49.56 W
São Joaquim, Parque Nacional de ◆ 252 28.15 S 49.57 W
São Joaquim da Barra 255 20.35 S 47.53 W
São Joaquim dos Melos 250 5.48 S 44.44 W
São Jorge 255 23.24 S 52.17 W
São Jorge I 148a 38.38 N 28.03 W
São Jorge, Castelo de ◆1 266c 38.43 N 9.08 W
São José 252 27.38 S 48.39 W
São José ≃, Bra. 255 19.10 S 40.12 W
São José ≃, Bra. 287a 22.39 S 43.27 W
São José, Ponta de ≻ 152 12.36 S 13.12 E
São José da Lagoa Tapada 250 6.57 S 38.10 W
São José da Laje 250 9.01 S 36.03 W
São José das Palmeiras 256 22.33 S 47.12 W
São José de Anauá 246 1.00 N 61.23 W
São José de Encoge 152 7.38 S 14.41 E
São José de Mipibu 250 6.05 S 35.15 W
São José de Piranhas 250 7.07 S 38.30 W
São José do Alegre 256 22.19 S 45.32 W
São José do Barreiro 256 22.38 S 44.35 W
São José do Belmonte 250 7.52 S 38.46 W
São José do Calçado 255 21.02 S 41.40 W
São José do Campestre 250 6.18 S 35.42 W
São José do Cedro 252 26.30 S 53.30 W
São José do Egito 250 7.28 S 37.16 W
São José do Goiabal 255 19.56 S 42.42 W
São José do Gurupi 250 1.36 S 46.13 W
São José do Norte 252 32.01 S 52.03 W
São José do Peixe 250 7.24 S 42.34 W
São José do Piriá 250 1.17 S 46.18 W
São José do Rio Pardo 256 21.36 S 46.54 W
São José do Rio Prêto, Bra. 255 20.48 S 49.23 W
São José do Rio Prêto, Bra. 256 22.10 S 42.57 W
São José dos Campos, Bra. 256 22.10 S 45.06 W
São José dos Campos, Bra. 256 23.11 S 45.53 W
São José dos Lopes 256 21.48 S 43.53 W
São José dos Pinhais 252 25.31 S 49.13 W
São José do Turvo 256 22.21 S 43.59 W
São Julião da Barra 266c 38.40 N 9.21 W
São Julião do Tojal 266c 38.51 N 9.08 W
São Leopoldo 252 29.46 S 51.09 W
São Lourenço 256 22.07 S 45.03 W
São Lourenço ≃ 248 17.53 S 57.27 W
São Lourenço, Pantanal de ⩸ 248 17.30 S 56.30 W
São Lourenço da Serra 256 23.52 S 46.57 W
São Lourenço d'Oeste 252 26.24 S 52.46 W
São Lourenço do Ipixuna 250 4.28 S 44.54 W
São Lourenço do Sul 252 31.22 S 51.58 W
São Luís 250 2.31 S 44.16 W
São Luís de Montes Belos 255 16.32 S 50.20 W
São Luís do Curu 250 3.40 S 39.14 W
São Luís Do Paraitinga 256 23.14 S 45.20 W
São Luís do Quitunde 250 9.20 S 35.33 W
São Luís do Tocantins 255 14.17 S 47.59 W
São Luís Gonzaga 252 28.24 S 54.58 W
São Mamede 250 6.56 S 37.06 W
São Manuel 255 22.44 S 48.34 W
São Manuel ≃ 242 7.21 S 58.03 W
São Marcos ≃ 255 18.15 S 47.37 W
São Mateus, Bra. 255 18.44 S 39.51 W
São Mateus, Bra. 256 22.49 S 43.23 W
São Mateus, Port. 148a 38.26 N 28.27 W
São Mateus ≃ 255 13.48 S 46.54 W
São Mateus, Braço Norte ≃ 255 18.37 S 40.05 W
São Mateus, Braço Sul ≃ 255 18.37 S 40.05 W
São Mateus de Minas 256 22.46 S 46.03 W
São Mateus do Sul 252 25.52 S 50.23 W
São Miguel 250 6.13 S 38.30 W
São Miguel I 148a 37.47 N 25.30 W
São Miguel ≃ 255 16.26 S 41.00 W
São Miguel do Anta 255 20.42 S 42.43 W
São Miguel do Araguaia 255 13.19 S 50.13 W
São Miguel d'Oeste 252 26.45 S 53.34 W
São Miguel do Guamá 250 1.37 S 47.27 W
São Miguel dos Campos 250 9.47 S 36.05 W
São Miguel dos Macacos 250 1.11 S 50.28 W
São Miguel do Tapuio 250 5.30 S 41.20 W
São Miguel Paulista (Baquiriru) ◆8 287b 23.30 S 46.26 W
Saona, Isla I 238 18.09 N 68.40 W
Saonara 64 45.22 N 11.59 E
Saône ≃ 58 45.44 N 4.50 E
Saône-et-Loire ▫5 32 46.42 N 4.45 E
Saonek 164 0.28 S 130.47 E
Saoner 120 21.23 N 78.54 E
São Nicolau I 150a 16.35 N 24.15 W
São Nicolau ≃ 250 5.45 S 42.02 W
São Paulo, Bra. 256 23.32 S 46.37 W
São Paulo, Bra. 287b 23.32 S 46.37 W
São Paulo ▫3 255 22.00 S 49.00 W
São Paulo ▫7 287b 23.33 S 46.38 W
São Paulo, Ribeirão de ≃ 256 22.16 S 46.37 W
São Paulo de Olivença 246 3.27 S 68.48 W
São Paulo do Potengi 250 5.55 S 35.45 W
São Pedro, Bra. 255 19.53 S 51.55 W
São Pedro, Bra. 256 22.12 S 46.46 W
São Pedro ≃ 250 16.30 S 41.17 W
São Pedro de Viseu 250 2.33 S 49.33 W
São Pedro do Estoril 266c 38.42 N 9.22 W
São Pedro do Ivaí 255 23.51 S 51.51 W
São Pedro do Piauí 250 5.56 S 42.43 W
São Pedro do Sul, Bra. 252 29.37 S 54.10 W
São Pedro do Sul, Port. 34 40.45 N 8.04 W
São Rafael 250 5.47 S 36.55 W
São Raimundo das Mangabeiras 250 7.01 S 45.29 W
São Raimundo de Codó 250 4.21 S 43.37 W
São Raimundo Nonato 250 9.01 S 42.42 W
Saorge 62 43.59 N 7.33 E
Saori 94 35.11 N 136.44 E
São Romão 255 16.22 S 45.04 W
São Roque 256 23.32 S 47.08 W
São Roque, Cabo de ≻ 250 5.29 S 35.16 W
São Roque da Fartura 256 21.51 S 46.45 W
São Roque do Paraguaçu 255 12.51 S 38.51 W
São Salvador → Salvador 255 12.59 S 38.31 W
São Sebastião 256 23.48 S 45.25 W
São Sebastião, Canal de ꓵ 256 23.48 S 45.23 W
São Sebastião, Ilha de I 256 23.50 S 45.18 W
São Sebastião, Pico de ʌ 256 23.52 S 45.23 W
São Sebastião, Ponta ≻ 156 22.07 S 35.30 E
São Sebastião da Bela Vista 256 22.10 S 45.45 W
São Sebastião da Boa Vista 250 1.42 S 49.31 W
São Sebastião da Grama 256 21.43 S 46.49 W
São Sebastião da Vitória 256 21.14 S 44.25 W
São Sebastião do Barreado 256 22.04 S 43.38 W
São Sebastião do Maranhão 255 18.05 S 42.35 W
São Sebastião do Paraíso 255 20.55 S 47.00 W
São Sebastião do Rio Claro 255 15.45 S 51.30 W
São Sebastião do Rio Verde 256 22.13 S 44.58 W
São Sebastião dos Peitudos 256 22.19 S 46.29 W
São Sebastião dos Robertos 256 22.13 S 46.32 W
São Sebastião do Umbuzeiro 250 8.09 S 37.01 W
São Sepé 252 30.10 S 53.34 W
São Simão, Bra. 255 18.56 S 50.30 W
São Simão, Bra. 255 21.30 S 47.33 W
São Simão ≃ 248 12.40 S 63.04 W
São Tiago 255 20.55 S 44.30 W
São Timóteo 255 13.51 S 42.11 W
São Tomé, Bra. 250 5.58 S 36.04 W
São Tomé, S. Tom./P. 152 0.20 N 6.44 E
São Tomé I 152 0.12 N 6.39 E
São Tomé ≃ 250 8.10 S 58.13 W
São Tomé, Cabo de ≻ 255 21.59 S 40.59 W
São Tomé, Pico de ʌ 152 0.16 N 6.33 E
São Tomé, Ribeirão ≃ 256 21.26 S 46.02 W
Sao Tome and Principe (São Tomé e Principe) ▫1, Afr. 138 1.00 N 7.00 E
Sao Tome and Principe (São Tomé e Principe) ▫1, Afr. 152 1.00 N 7.00 E
São Tomé das Letras 256 21.43 S 44.59 W
Sao Tomé-et-Principe → Sao Tome and Principe ▫1 152 1.00 N 7.00 E
Saou 62 44.39 N 5.04 E
Saoura, Oued V 148 29.00 N 0.55 W
São Valério ≃ 250 11.20 S 48.28 W
São Vicente, Bra. 250 6.13 S 36.41 W
São Vicente, Bra. 256 23.58 S 46.23 W
São Vicente I 150a 16.50 N 25.00 W
São Vicente, Cabo de (Cape Saint Vincent) ≻ 34 37.01 N 9.00 W
São Vicente, Ribeirão ≃ 256 21.59 S 45.40 W
São Vicente de Minas 256 21.42 S 44.27 W
São Vicente Ferrer, Bra. 250 2.53 S 44.52 W
São Vicente Ferrer, Bra. 250 7.35 S 35.30 W
Sa Pa 110 22.21 N 103.50 E
Sápai 38 41.02 N 25.41 E
Sapallanga 248 12.09 S 75.11 W
Sapanca 130 40.41 N 30.16 E
Sapang Baho ≃ 269f 14.33 N 121.06 E
Sapao 116 10.01 N 126.02 E
Sapão ≃ 250 11.01 S 45.32 W
Saparua, Pulau I 164 3.34 S 128.40 E
Sapatgrām 124 26.20 N 90.08 E
Sapé, Bra. 250 7.06 S 35.13 W
Sapé, Bra. 256 22.16 S 46.34 W
Sape, Indon. 115b 8.34 S 118.59 E
Sapé ≃ 287a 22.52 S 43.02 W
Sape, Selat ꓵ 115b 8.39 S 119.18 E
Sapeaçu 255 12.44 S 39.13 W
Sapele 150 5.54 N 5.41 E
Sapello ≃ 200 35.47 N 104.59 W
Sapelo Island I 192 31.28 N 81.15 W
Saperkino 80 54.05 N 51.38 E
Şaphane 130 39.01 N 29.14 E
Sapian Bay c 116 11.33 N 122.37 E
Sapindji 152 9.39 S 23.12 E
Sapitwa ʌ 154 15.57 S 35.36 E
Šapki 76 59.36 N 31.14 E
Šapkina ≃ 24 66.44 N 52.25 E
Šapkino 80 51.42 N 42.24 E
Šapkovo, S.S.S.R. 76 55.47 N 33.20 E
Sapkovo, S.S.S.R. 82 54.34 N 39.10 E
Sa Pobla 34 39.46 N 3.01 E
Sapodilla Cays I 236 16.08 N 88.15 W
Saponara 70 38.11 N 15.26 E
Saponé 150 12.03 N 1.36 W
Sap'o-ri 98 40.49 N 129.31 E
Sap'ornaja 265a 59.46 N 30.41 E
Saporoschje → Zaporožje 78 47.50 N 35.10 E
Saposoa 248 6.56 S 76.48 W
Sapou 175c 7.18 N 151.53 E
Sapožok 80 53.56 N 40.41 E
Sappa Creek ≃ 198 40.07 N 99.38 W
Sappa Creek, Middle Fork ≃ 198 39.40 N 100.53 W
Sappa Creek, North Fork ≃ 198 39.47 N 100.35 W
Sappa Creek, South Fork ≃ 198 39.47 N 100.35 W
Sappada 64 46.34 N 12.41 E
Sapphire Mountains ⋏ 202 46.20 N 113.45 W
Sappho 224 48.04 N 124.16 W
Sappington 219 38.32 N 90.22 W
Sapporo 92a 43.03 N 141.21 E
Sapri 68 40.04 N 15.38 E
Šapša 76 60.34 N 34.01 E
Sap Songkhla, Thale c 110 7.13 N 100.30 E
Šapsugskaja 78 44.45 N 38.05 E
Saptakośī ≃ 124 26.31 N 86.58 E
Sapta-ri 271b 37.43 N 126.44 E
Sapu 152 12.29 S 19.26 E
Sapucaí 256 22.19 S 46.42 W
Sapucaí ≃ 256 21.33 S 45.40 W
Sapucaia 256 22.00 S 42.54 W
Sapucaí-Mirim 256 22.44 S 45.45 W
Sapucaí-Mirim ≃ 256 22.12 S 45.53 W
Sapudi, Pulau I 115a 7.06 S 114.20 E
Sapulpa 196 35.59 N 96.06 W
Sapulu 115a 6.54 S 112.57 E
Sapuran 115a 7.28 S 109.58 E
Sapwe 154 10.57 S 28.10 E
Sāq, Jabal ʌ2 128 26.17 N 43.16 E
Sāqiat al-ʿAbd 140 20.48 N 30.19 E
Sāqiyat Makkī 142 30.00 N 31.13 E
Ṣaqqārah 142 29.51 N 31.13 E
Ṣaqqārah (Step Pyramid) ⊥ 142 29.52 N 31.13 E
Saqqez 128 36.14 N 46.16 E
Saquarema 256 22.56 S 42.30 W
Saquarema, Lagoa de c 256 22.55 S 42.33 W
Saquena 248 4.40 S 73.31 W
Saquish Neck ≻1 283 42.00 N 70.37 W
Saquisilí 246 0.51 S 78.40 W
Sāra, Bngl. 126 24.07 N 89.02 E
Sara, Burkina 150 11.43 N 3.50 W
Sara, Pil. 116 11.16 N 123.01 E
Sara, S.S.S.R. 80 54.38 N 46.46 E
Sarāb 128 37.56 N 47.32 E
Sarabia 234 20.31 N 101.05 W
Sarabia ≃ 234 17.11 N 94.56 W
Sarābiyūm 142 30.23 N 32.17 E
Saraburi 110 14.32 N 100.55 E
Saracena 68 39.46 N 16.09 E
Saraceno, Monte ʌ 66 41.27 N 14.44 E
Saracura ≃ 255 12.18 S 40.07 W
Saracuruna ≃ 287a 22.41 S 43.13 W
Saraféré 150 15.50 N 3.42 W
Saragosa 196 31.01 N 103.39 W
Saragossa → Zaragoza 34 41.38 N 0.53 W
Saraguay ◆8 275a 45.31 N 73.45 W
Saraguro 246 3.36 S 79.13 W
Sarai 80 53.44 N 41.00 E
Sarāi Alamgir 123 32.54 N 73.45 E
Saraikela 124 22.43 N 85.57 E
Sarāi Naurang 123 32.50 N 70.47 E
Saraipāli 120 21.20 N 83.00 E
Säräisniemi 26 64.27 N 26.47 E
Sarajas de Madrid ◆8 266a 40.28 N 3.35 W
Sarajčik 80 47.30 N 51.43 E
Sarajevo 38 43.52 N 18.25 E
Saraj-Gir 80 53.36 N 53.24 E
Saraji 166 22.21 S 148.18 E
Sarajskij 80 47.19 N 40.45 E
Sarakhs 128 36.32 N 61.11 E
Saraktaš 86 51.50 N 56.22 E
Sarala 86 54.52 N 89.14 E
Saraland 194 30.49 N 88.04 W
Šaraldaj 88 51.01 N 107.38 E
Saralžinskaja 80 49.12 N 48.55 E
Saramacca ▫5 250 4.45 N 56.00 W
Saramacca ≃ 250 5.51 N 55.53 W
Saramaguacán ≃ 240p 21.30 N 77.17 W
Saran, Fr. 50 47.57 N 1.53 E
Šaran, S.S.S.R. 80 54.49 N 54.00 E
Saran', S.S.S.R. 86 49.46 N 72.52 E
Saran, Gunung ʌ 112 0.25 S 111.18 E
Saranac 216 42.55 N 85.12 W
Saranac ≃ 188 44.42 N 73.27 W
Saranac Lake 188 44.19 N 74.07 W
Saranakan, gora ʌ 88 52.35 N 113.50 E
Saranap 226 37.53 N 122.06 W
Šaranbaš-Kn'azevo 80 54.58 N 54.09 E
Saranda 154 5.43 S 34.59 E
Sarandapótamos ≃ 267c 38.26 N 23.54 E
Sarandë 38 39.52 N 20.00 E

Symbols in the index entries represent the broad categories identified in the key at the right. Symbols with superior numbers (⋏1) identify subcategories (see complete key on page *I · 1).*

Symbole im Register stellen die rechts im Schlüssel erklärten Kategorien dar. Symbole mit hochgestellten Ziffern (⋏1) bezeichnen Unterabteilungen einer Kategorie (vgl. vollständiger Schlüssel auf Seite *I · 1).*

Los símbolos incluídos en el texto del índice representan las grandes categorias identificadas con la clave a la derecha. Los símbolos con numeros en su parte superior (⋏1) identifican las subcategorías (véase la clave completa en la página *I · 1).*

Les symboles de l'index représentent les catégories indiquées dans la légende à droite. Les symboles suivis d'un indice (⋏1) représentent des sous-catégories (voir légende complète à la page *I · 1).*

Os símbolos incluídos no texto do índice representam as grandes categorias identificadas com a chave à direita. Os símbolos com números em sua parte superior (⋏1) identificam as subcategorias (veja-se a chave completa à página *I · 1).*

ʌ	Mountain	Berg	Montaña	Montagne	Montanha
⋏	Mountains	Gebirge	Montañas	Montagnes	Montanhas
)(	Pass	Paß	Paso	Col	Passo
V	Valley, Canyon	Tal, Cañon	Valle, Cañón	Vallée, Canyon	Vale, Canhão
≚	Plain	Ebene	Llano	Plaine	Planície
≻	Cape	Kap	Cabo	Cap	Cabo
I	Island	Insel	Isla	Île	Ilha
II	Islands	Inseln	Islas	Îles	Ilhas
⊥	Other Topographic Features	Andere Topographische Objekte	Otros Elementos Topográficos	Autres données topographiques	Outros acidentes topográficos

ESPAÑOL

Nombre	Página	Lat.°′	Long.°′ W = Oeste
Sarandi	252	27.56 S	52.55 W
Sarandí ✦[8]	253	34.40 S	58.21 W
Sarandí del Yi	252	33.21 S	55.38 W
Sarandí Grande	253	33.44 S	56.20 W
Şarandira	253	21.50 S	43.11 W
Šaranga	80	57.11 N	46.34 E
Sarangani Bay ⊂	116	5.57 N	125.11 E
Sarangani Island I	116	5.27 N	125.28 E
Sarangani Islands II	116	5.25 N	125.26 E
Sarangani Strait Ʉ	116	5.31 N	125.23 E
Sārangarh	120	21.36 N	83.05 E
Sārangpur	124	23.34 N	76.28 E
Sārankhola	126	22.18 N	89.47 E
Saranley	144	2.22 N	42.17 E
Saranpaul'	24	64.14 N	60.53 E
Saransk	80	54.11 N	45.11 E
Sarantina, Valle V	64	46.35 N	11.25 E
Sara Peak ∧	150	9.41 N	9.17 E
Saraphi	110	18.43 N	99.03 E
Sarapiquí ≃	236	10.43 N	83.56 W
Şarapó ≃	287a	22.46 S	43.37 W
Šarapovo, S.S.S.R.	80	55.17 N	44.42 E
Šarapovo, S.S.S.R.	82	55.11 N	37.16 E
Sarapuí ≃	287a	22.46 S	43.24 W
Sarapuí, Canal ≊	287a	22.44 S	43.16 W
Sarapul	80	56.28 N	53.48 E
Sarapul'skaja vozvyšennost' ⟑[1]	80	56.15 N	53.30 E
Sarapul'skoje	89	48.52 N	135.59 E
Sarāqib	130	35.52 N	36.48 E
Sarare	246	9.47 N	69.10 W
Sarar Plain ≚	144	9.25 N	46.17 E
Sará-Sará	256	23.40 S	47.05 W
Sara Sara, Nevado ∧	248	15.19 S	73.27 W
Sarasota	220	27.20 N	82.31 W
Sarasota □[6]	220	27.10 N	82.21 W
Sarasota Bay ⊂	220	27.23 N	82.39 W
Sarasota-Bradenton Airport ⊠	220	27.24 N	82.33 W
Sarasota Springs	220	27.17 N	82.28 W
Saraswati ≃	272b	22.59 N	88.22 E
Sarata	78	46.02 N	29.38 E
Sarath	126	24.14 N	86.50 E
Saratoga, Austl.	170	33.28 S	151.21 E
Saratoga, Ca., U.S.	226	37.15 N	122.01 W
Saratoga, In., U.S.	216	40.14 N	84.55 W
Saratoga, Tx., U.S.	222	30.17 N	94.31 W
Saratoga, Wy., U.S.	200	41.27 N	106.48 W
Saratoga □[6]	210	43.00 N	73.51 W
Saratoga Battlefield Monument ⊥	210	43.05 N	75.36 W
Saratoga Creek ≃	282	37.25 N	121.58 W
Saratoga Lake ⊜	210	43.01 N	73.39 W
Saratoga National Historical Park ♠	210	43.00 N	73.38 W
Saratoga Passage Ʉ	224	48.10 N	122.30 W
Saratoga Spa State Park ♠	210	43.03 N	73.50 W
Şaratoga Springs	210	43.04 N	73.47 W
Šara-Togot	88	53.01 N	106.43 E
Saratok	112	1.44 N	111.20 E
Saratov	80	51.34 N	46.02 E
Saratov □[4]	76	52.00 N	42.40 E
Saratovka	86	51.12 N	54.54 E
Saratovskoje vodochranilišče ⊜[1]	80	52.45 N	48.30 E
Saraurcu ∧	246	0.06 S	77.55 W
Sarāvān, Īrān	128	27.15 N	62.40 E
Saravan, Lao	110	15.43 N	106.25 E
Sarawak □[3]	112	2.30 N	113.30 E
Saray	130	41.26 N	27.55 E
Saraya, Guinée	150	10.46 N	10.24 W
Saraya, Sén.	150	12.50 N	11.45 W
Sarāyān	128	33.51 N	58.31 E
Saraycık	130	40.57 N	35.08 E
Saraydüzü	130	41.20 N	34.52 E
Sarā-ye Aḥmadī	128	27.56 N	56.42 E
Sarayevo → Sarajevo	38	43.52 N	18.25 E
Sarayköy	130	37.55 N	28.58 E
Sarayönü	130	38.17 N	32.25 E
Sarbaj	80	53.39 N	51.34 E
Sarbāz	128	26.39 N	61.15 E
Sarbinowo	54	52.40 N	14.40 E
Sárbogárd	30	46.53 N	18.38 E
Sarca ≃	64	45.52 N	10.52 E
Sarce ≃	50	48.09 N	4.18 E
Sarcee Indian Reserve ✦[4]	182	50.58 N	114.06 W
Sarcelle, Passe de la Ʉ	175l	22.29 S	167.12 E
Sarcelles	50	49.00 N	2.23 E
Sarche di Calavino	64	46.03 N	10.57 E
Sarcidano ✦[1], It.	36	39.55 N	9.05 E
Şarcidano ✦[1], It.	71	39.49 N	9.10 E
Šarčino	86	53.09 N	81.45 E
Sarclet	46	58.22 N	3.07 W
Sarcoxie	194	37.04 N	94.06 W
Sārda (Mahākālī) ≃	124	27.22 N	81.23 E
Sard āb)(	123	36.40 N	71.32 E
Sārda Canal ≊	124	28.08 N	80.24 E
Sardagna	64	46.03 N	11.06 E
Sardah	124	24.18 N	88.44 E
Sardaq	128	34.48 N	58.07 E
Sardara	71	39.37 N	8.49 E
Sardār Chāh	128	27.58 N	64.50 E
Sardārpur	120	22.39 N	74.59 E
Sardārshahr	120	28.26 N	74.29 E
Sar Dasht, Īrān	128	36.09 N	45.28 E
Sar Dasht, Īrān	128	32.32 N	48.52 E
Sardegna □[4]	71	40.00 N	9.00 E
Sardegna (Sardinia) I	71	40.00 N	9.00 E
Sardeh Band	120	33.17 N	68.39 E
Sardhana	124	29.09 N	77.37 E
Sardiha	126	22.22 N	87.09 E
Sardina	246	2.02 N	67.07 W
Sardinal	236	10.31 N	85.39 W
Sardinata	246	8.05 N	72.48 W
Sardinia, N.Y., U.S.	210	42.32 N	78.31 W
Sardinia, Oh., U.S.	218	39.00 N	83.48 W
Sardinia → Sardegna I	71	40.00 N	9.00 E
Sardinien → Sardegna I	71	40.00 N	9.00 E
Sardis, B.C., Can.	224	49.08 N	121.57 W
Sardis, Al., U.S.	194	32.17 N	86.59 W
Sardis, Ga., U.S.	192	32.58 N	81.45 W
Sardis, Ky., U.S.	218	38.31 N	83.57 W
Sardis, Ms., U.S.	194	34.26 N	89.55 W
Sardis, Pa., U.S.	279b	40.29 N	79.42 W
Sardis, Tn., U.S.	194	35.27 N	88.18 W
Sardis Lake ⊜[1]	194	34.27 N	89.43 W
Şardona, Piz ∧	58	46.55 N	9.15 E
Šardonem'	24	63.56 N	44.37 E
Sarek ∧	24	67.25 N	17.46 E
Sareks Nationalpark ♠	24	67.15 N	17.30 E
Sārenga, India	126	22.46 N	87.02 E
Sārenga, India	272b	22.31 N	88.13 E
Sarentino (Sarnthein)	64	46.38 N	11.21 E
Sar-e Pol	120	36.14 N	65.55 E
Sarepta	194	32.53 N	93.26 W
Sarezzo	64	45.39 N	10.12 E
Sargans	58	47.03 N	9.26 E
Sargatskoje	86	55.37 N	73.30 E
Sargé-lès-le-Mans	50	48.02 N	0.14 E
Sargent, Ga., U.S.	192	33.25 N	84.52 W
Sargent, Ne., U.S.	198	41.38 N	99.22 W
Sargent Creek ≃	226	35.57 N	120.52 W
Sargodha	123	32.05 N	72.40 E
Šargol'džin	88	52.21 N	114.42 E
Šargorod	78	48.44 N	28.05 E
Sargou ≃	85	43.25 N	73.50 E
Šargul', ozero ⊜	86	54.35 N	78.51 E
Šargun	85	38.37 N	67.53 E
Sarh	146	9.09 N	18.23 E
Sarhli, Djebel ∧	34	36.06 N	0.40 E
Sārī	128	36.34 N	53.04 E
Saría I	38	35.50 N	27.15 E
Saribi, Tanjung ›	164	1.36 S	135.25 E

FRANÇAIS

Nom	Page	Lat.°′	Long.°′ W = Ouest
Sanbuğday	130	40.35 N	35.35 E
Sáric	232	31.08 N	111.23 W
Saricumbe	152	12.12 S	19.46 E
Sarigan I	108	16.42 N	145.47 E
Sarıgazi ✦[8]	267b	41.01 N	29.12 E
Sarıgöl	130	38.14 N	28.43 E
Sarıkamış	130	40.20 N	42.35 E
Sarıkaya, Tür.	130	39.30 N	35.24 E
Sarıkaya, Tür.	130	38.47 N	32.15 E
Sarikei	112	2.07 N	111.31 E
Sarıköy	130	40.12 N	27.36 E
Sarilhos Grandes	266c	38.41 N	8.58 W
Sarilhos Pequenos	266c	38.41 N	8.59 W
Sarim	154	0.23 S	40.58 E
Sarimbun, Pulau I	271c	1.26 N	103.41 E
Sarina	166	21.26 S	149.13 E
Sarine ≃	58	46.54 N	7.14 E
Sariñena	34	41.48 N	0.10 W
Sarıoğlan	130	39.05 N	35.59 E
Saripul'	85	38.26 N	70.08 E
Sarīr	146	27.36 N	22.32 E
Sarısu	84	39.01 N	42.55 E
Sarita	196	27.13 N	97.47 W
Sariwŏn	98	38.31 N	125.44 E
Sarıyar Barajı ⊜[1]	130	40.02 N	31.40 E
Şarız	130	38.30 N	36.30 E
Šarja	80	58.24 N	45.30 E
Sarju (Babaī) ≃	124	27.42 N	81.16 E
Sark I	43b	49.26 N	2.21 W
Sark ≃	44	54.58 N	3.04 W
Şarkad	30	46.44 N	21.23 E
Šarkan	80	57.18 N	53.53 E
Sarkand	86	45.26 N	79.54 E
Şarkikaraağaç	130	38.04 N	31.23 E
Şarkışla	130	39.21 N	36.26 E
Šarkovščina	76	55.22 N	27.28 E
Şarköy	130	40.37 N	27.06 E
Šarlat-la-Canéda	32	44.53 N	1.13 E
Šarlauk	128	38.13 N	55.38 E
Şarles	198	48.56 N	98.59 W
Šarlyk	86	52.55 N	54.35 E
Sarmakovo	84	43.43 N	43.12 E
Sarmanovo	80	55.15 N	52.36 E
Sărmaşu	38	46.46 N	24.11 E
Sarmathura	124	26.31 N	77.22 E
Sarmatskaja ≃	83	47.20 N	38.48 E
Sármellék	30	46.44 N	17.10 E
Sarmi	164	1.51 S	138.44 E
Sarmiento	254	45.36 S	69.05 W
Sarmiento ≃	288	34.25 S	58.35 W
Sarmiento, Cerro ∧	254	54.27 S	70.50 W
Sarmiento, Lago ⊜	254	51.04 S	72.45 W
Särna	26	61.41 N	13.08 E
Sarna, ozero ⊜	80	48.24 N	44.38 E
Sarnano	66	43.02 N	13.18 E
Sārnāth ⊥	124	25.24 N	83.01 E
Sarnen	58	46.54 N	8.15 E
Sârnena ⟑	38	42.35 N	25.10 E
Sarner See ⊜	58	46.52 N	8.13 E
Sarnia	214	42.58 N	82.23 W
Sarnico	64	45.40 N	9.57 E
Sarno	68	40.49 N	14.37 E
Sarnow	54	53.45 N	13.37 E
Sarnowa	30	51.38 N	16.54 E
Sarnthein → Sarentino	64	46.38 N	11.21 E
Šarnutovskij	80	47.40 N	43.46 E
Sarny	78	51.21 N	26.36 E
Şaroako	112	2.31 S	121.22 E
Šaroargun ≃	84	43.02 N	45.44 E
Sarolangun	112	2.18 S	102.42 E
Saroma-ko ⊜	92a	44.08 N	143.50 E
Saron	158	33.11 S	19.01 E
Saronikós Kólpos ⊂	38	37.54 N	23.12 E
Saronno	62	45.38 N	9.02 E
Saros Körfezi ⊂	130	40.30 N	26.20 E
Şárospatak	30	48.19 N	21.34 E
Šarovka	78	50.01 N	35.27 E
Sarowbī	120	34.36 N	69.43 E
Sarpa	80	47.07 N	45.29 E
Şarpa, ozero ⊜	80	47.18 N	45.20 E
Šarpajevka	78	48.34 N	40.59 E
Sar Passage Ʉ	175b	7.12 N	134.23 E
Şarpinskije ozera ⊜	80	47.30 N	45.00 E
Šar Planina ⟑	38	42.05 N	20.50 E
Sarpsborg	26	59.17 N	11.07 E
Sarpy Creek ≃	202	46.15 N	107.09 W
Sárrabus ✦[1]	71	39.23 N	9.21 E
Sarralbe	56	49.00 N	7.01 E
Sarras	62	45.11 N	4.48 E
Sarrath, Oued V	36	35.59 N	8.23 E
Sarratt	260	51.41 N	0.29 W
Sarre	62	45.43 N	7.15 E
Sarre (Saar) ≃	56	49.42 N	6.34 E
Sarre Blanche ≃	56	48.41 N	7.01 E
Sarrebourg	58	48.44 N	7.03 E
Sarrebruck → Saarbrücken	56	49.14 N	6.59 E
Sarreguemines	56	49.06 N	7.03 E
Sarre Rouge ≃	56	48.41 N	7.01 E
Sarre-Union	56	48.56 N	7.05 E
Sarria	34	42.47 N	7.24 W
Sarriá ✦[8]	266d	41.24 N	2.08 E
Sarro	150	13.43 N	5.15 W
Sarroch	71	39.04 N	9.00 E
Sars	86	56.33 N	57.07 E
Sarsfield	212	45.27 N	75.21 W
Sarsina	66	43.55 N	12.08 E
Sarsol	272c	19.02 N	73.01 E
Sarstedt	52	52.14 N	9.51 E
Sarstein ∧	64	47.36 N	13.41 E
Sarstoon ≃	236	15.53 N	88.55 W
Sarsuna	272b	22.28 N	88.18 E
Sart	56	50.31 N	5.56 E
Sartang ≃	74	67.44 N	133.12 E
Sarteano	66	42.59 N	11.52 E
Sartell	190	45.37 N	94.12 W
Sartène	36	41.36 N	8.59 E
Sarthe □[5]	32	48.00 N	0.05 E
Sarthe ≃	32	47.30 N	0.32 W
Sartičala	84	41.43 N	45.10 E
Sartilly	32	48.45 N	1.27 W
Sartirana Lomellina	62	45.07 N	8.39 E
Sartlan, ozero ⊜	86	55.00 N	78.35 E
Sartol'gen	80	48.57 N	47.03 E
Sartrouville	261	48.57 N	2.10 E
Saru	85	42.20 N	77.55 E
Sarufutsu	92a	45.16 N	142.12 E
Saruhanlı	130	38.44 N	27.34 E
Şarūr	128	23.22 N	58.07 E
Šar Us ≃	88	47.08 N	97.38 E
Saru-shima I	268	35.17 N	139.42 E
Sarvadyk	80	46.07 N	44.07 E
Sárvár	30	47.15 N	16.57 E
Sarver	214	40.44 N	79.45 W
Sarvestān	128	29.16 N	53.13 E
Sárvíz ≃	30	46.24 N	18.41 E
Saryagač	85	41.27 N	69.10 E
Saryassija	85	38.25 N	67.57 E
Sarybarak	85	43.24 N	71.30 E
Sarybasat	86	46.38 N	60.27 E
Sarybulak, S.S.S.R.	85	40.54 N	73.49 E
Sarybulak, S.S.S.R.	86	49.27 N	76.27 E
Saryč, mys ›	78	44.23 N	33.45 E
Sarychosor	85	38.32 N	69.49 E
Sarydala	85	41.11 N	70.27 E
Saryg-Sep	88	51.30 N	95.36 E
Sary-Išikotrau ✦[2]	86	45.30 N	76.00 E
Sarykoby	85	43.44 N	72.35 E
Sarykol'skij chrebet ⟑	120	38.00 N	74.30 E
Sarykomej	86	45.12 N	74.11 E
Sarykopa, ozero ⊜	86	50.22 N	64.08 E
Sarymogol	85	39.55 N	72.47 E
Sarymoin, ozero ⊜	86	51.36 N	64.30 E
Šaryozek	86	44.22 N	77.59 E
Šarypovo	86	55.33 N	89.12 E
Saryšagan	86	46.07 N	73.38 E
Sarysu	86	48.23 N	69.59 E
Sarysu ≃	86	45.12 N	66.36 E
Sary-Taš	85	39.44 N	73.15 E

PORTUGUÊS

Nome	Página	Lat.°′	Long.°′ W = Oeste
Sarytau	86	49.54 N	76.41 E
Saryžaz	72	42.55 N	79.38 E
Sarzana	64	44.07 N	9.58 E
Sarzanello, Fortezza di ⊥	64	44.08 N	9.58 E
Sarzeau	32	47.32 N	2.46 W
S'as' ≃	76	60.09 N	32.30 E
Sa'sa', Sūrīy.	132	33.17 N	36.02 E
Sasa, Yis.	132	33.02 N	35.24 E
Sasabe	200	31.27 N	111.31 W
Sasabe ≃	200	30.41 N	111.56 W
Sasabeneh	144	7.55 N	43.39 E
Sasaga-mine ∧	96	33.49 N	133.17 E
Sasaginnigak Lake ⊜	184	51.36 N	95.40 W
Sasago-tunnel ✦[5]	94	35.38 N	138.47 E
Sasaguri	96	33.37 N	130.32 E
Sasak	110	0.01 S	99.42 E
Sasakwa	196	34.56 N	96.31 W
Sasamungga	175e	7.02 S	156.47 E
Sasao	270	34.57 N	135.20 E
Sasar, Tanjung ›	115b	9.17 S	119.56 E
Sāsarām	124	24.57 N	84.02 E
Sasayama	96	35.04 N	135.13 E
Sasa-yama ∧	96	33.03 N	132.40 E
Sasbach	58	48.08 N	7.37 E
Sasco Brook ≃	276	41.07 N	73.18 W
Sásd	30	46.15 N	18.06 E
Sasebo	92	33.10 N	129.43 E
Sasebo Naval Base ■	92	33.09 N	129.45 E
Saseenos	224	48.24 N	123.40 W
Saseginaga, Lac ⊜	190	47.06 N	78.35 W
Sashalom ✦[8]	264c	47.31 N	19.11 E
Sas-hegy ∧[2]	264c	47.23 N	19.18 E
Sashiki	174m	26.10 N	127.47 E
Sashima	94	36.08 N	139.51 E
Saskatchewan □[4], Can.	176	54.00 N	105.00 W
Saskatchewan □[4], Can.	184	54.00 N	105.00 W
Saskatchewan ≃	184	53.12 N	99.16 W
Saskatoon	184	52.07 N	106.38 W
Saskylach	74	71.55 N	114.01 E
Saslaya, Cerro ∧	238	13.45 N	85.03 W
Sasmik, Cape ›	180	51.36 N	177.55 W
Sāsni	124	27.43 N	78.05 E
Sasolburg	158	26.48 S	27.45 E
Sason	130	38.20 N	41.25 E
Sasovo	80	54.21 N	41.54 E
Saspamco	196	29.14 N	98.18 W
Saspul Gompa	123	34.15 N	77.09 E
Sassafras, Austl.	274b	37.52 S	145.21 E
Sassafras, Ky., U.S.	192	37.14 N	83.06 W
Sassafras ≃	208	39.23 N	76.02 W
Sassafras Mountain ∧	192	35.03 N	82.48 W
Sassafras Neck ›[1]	208	39.25 N	75.55 W
Sassandra	150	4.58 N	6.05 W
Sassandra ≃	150	4.58 N	6.05 W
Sassano	68	40.20 N	15.33 E
Sassari	71	40.44 N	8.33 E
Sassari □[4]	71	40.40 N	9.00 E
Sassbach ≃	61	46.43 N	15.48 E
Sasse ≃	62	44.15 N	5.55 E
Sassello	62	44.29 N	8.30 E
Sassenage	62	45.12 N	5.40 E
Sassenberg	52	51.59 N	8.02 E
Sassenheim	52	52.13 N	4.31 E
Sassnitz	54	54.31 N	13.38 E
Sassocorvaro	66	43.47 N	12.30 E
Sasso di Castalda	68	40.30 N	15.40 E
Sassoferrato	66	43.26 N	12.51 E
Sasso Marconi	64	44.24 N	11.15 E
S'as'stroj	76	60.08 N	32.34 E
Sassuolo	64	44.33 N	10.47 E
Sastobe	85	42.34 N	70.00 E
Sastown	150	4.40 N	8.26 W
Sastre	252	31.45 S	61.50 W
Sas van Gent	52	51.14 N	3.47 E
Sasyk, ozero ⊜	78	45.12 N	33.31 E
Sasykkol', ozero ⊜	86	46.35 N	81.00 E
Şasykoli	80	47.33 N	47.00 E
Šat ≃	82	54.08 N	37.47 E
Satadougou	150	12.21 N	10.07 W
Satah Mountain ∧	182	52.29 N	124.41 W
Şatakunta ✦[1]	26	61.30 N	23.00 E
Šatalovka	78	51.09 N	38.16 E
Šatalovo	76	54.20 N	32.27 E
Sata-misaki ›	92	30.59 N	130.40 E
Satāna	122	20.35 N	74.12 E
Satanov	78	49.15 N	26.16 E
Satanta	198	37.26 N	100.59 W
Sátão	34	40.44 N	7.44 W
Sātāra, India	122	17.41 N	73.59 E
Satara, S. Afr.	156	24.29 S	31.47 E
Sataua	175a	13.28 S	172.40 W
Sātbāria, Bngl.	126	23.52 N	89.26 E
Sātbāria, India	272b	22.25 N	88.33 E
Satellite Beach	220	28.10 N	80.35 W
Satellite Channel Ʉ	224	48.43 N	123.30 W
Satema	152	4.18 N	21.42 E
Satengar, Pulau I	112	7.31 S	117.17 E
Säter	40	60.21 N	15.45 E
Sātgāchia	126	23.16 N	88.08 E
Sātghara	272b	22.44 N	88.21 E
Saticoy	228	34.17 N	119.09 W
Satilla ≃	192	30.59 N	81.28 W
Satilpa Creek ≃	194	31.39 N	88.05 W
Satin	222	31.21 N	97.02 W
Satipo	248	11.16 S	74.37 W
Sátiro Dias	250	11.36 S	38.36 W
Satis	80	55.02 N	43.48 E
Satīt (Tekeze) ≃	140	14.20 N	35.50 E
Satka	86	55.03 N	59.01 E
Satkānia	120	22.04 N	92.03 E
Şātkhira	124	22.43 N	89.06 E
Šatki	80	55.11 N	44.08 E
Satla Bīl ⁝⁝	126	22.54 N	90.04 E
Satluj → Sutlej ≃	120	29.23 N	71.02 E
Satna	124	24.35 N	80.50 E
Sato, Cañada de ≃	288	34.35 S	58.38 W
Satomi	94	36.43 N	140.30 E
Şátoraljaújhely	30	48.24 N	21.39 E
Šatov	61	48.48 N	16.01 E
Šatovo	82	54.56 N	37.14 E
Satow	54	53.59 N	11.51 E
Sātpura Range ⟑	122	22.00 N	78.00 E
Sätrabrunn	40	59.51 N	16.27 E
Şatriano di Lucania	68	40.33 N	15.33 E
Šatrovo	86	56.31 N	64.38 E
Satrup	41	54.41 N	9.35 E
Satsop ≃	224	47.03 N	123.30 W
Satsop, Middle Fork ≃	224	47.05 N	123.30 W
Satsop, West Fork ≃	224	47.02 N	123.32 W
Satsuma	194	30.51 N	88.03 W
Satsuma-hantō ›[1]	92	31.25 N	130.25 E
Satsunan-shotō II	93b	29.00 N	130.00 E
Sattahip	110	12.40 N	100.54 E
Sāttānkulam	122	8.27 N	77.56 E
Satte	94	36.04 N	139.43 E
Sattel	58	47.05 N	8.42 E
Sattenapalle	122	16.24 N	80.11 E
Satthwa	110	17.46 N	94.30 E
Sattledt	61	48.04 N	14.03 E
Satui	112	3.47 S	115.27 E
Sātuli	272b	22.33 N	88.34 E
Satu Mare	38	47.48 N	22.53 E
Satu Mare □[6]	38	47.40 N	23.00 E
Şatun	110	6.37 N	100.04 E
Šatura	80	55.34 N	39.32 E
Saturna	224	48.43 N	123.11 W
Saturna Island I	224	48.47 N	123.08 W
Şaturnino M. Laspiur	252	31.42 S	62.29 W
Šaturtorf	76	55.34 N	39.26 E
Satus Creek ≃	202	46.16 N	120.07 W
Satus Peak ∧	224	46.15 N	120.45 W
Satyamangalam	122	11.31 N	77.15 E
Satzkorn	264a	52.29 N	12.59 E
Sau ≃	269c	10.46 N	106.48 E

Sauble ≃	212	44.40 N	81.17 W
Sauce, Arg.	252	30.05 S	58.46 W
Sauce, Perú	248	6.44 S	76.10 W
Sauce, Ur.	258	34.39 S	56.04 W
Sauce, Arroyo del ≃, Arg.	288	34.41 S	58.50 W
Sauce, Arroyo del ≃, Ur.	258	34.26 S	57.28 W
Sauce Chico ≃	252	38.47 S	62.18 W
Sauce Corto, Arroyo ≃	252	36.55 S	61.48 W
Sauce Grande ≃	252	38.59 S	61.07 W
Saucier	194	30.38 N	89.08 W
Saucillo	232	28.01 N	105.17 W
Sauda	26	59.39 N	6.20 E
Saudade	256	21.56 S	43.03 W
Sauđárkrókur	24a	65.46 N	19.41 W
Saúde	250	10.56 S	40.24 W
Saúde ✦[8]	287b	23.37 S	46.37 W
Saudi Arabia (Al-'Arabīyah as-Su'ūdīyah) □[1]	118	25.00 N	45.00 E
Saudi-Arabien → Saudi Arabia □[1]	118	25.00 N	45.00 E
Saudron	58	48.30 N	5.20 E
Sauer (Sûre) ≃, Europe	56	49.44 N	6.31 E
Sauer ≃, Europe	56	48.55 N	8.10 E
Sauerkohl-Berge ⟑[2]	264a	52.20 N	13.45 E
Sauerlach	64	47.58 N	11.38 E
Sauerland ✦[1]	52	51.10 N	8.00 E
Sauêruiná ≃	248	12.00 S	58.43 W
Sauêuiná ≃	248	12.24 S	58.40 W
Saug ≃	116	7.27 N	125.44 E
Saugatuck, Ct., U.S.	276	41.08 N	73.23 W
Saugatuck, Mi., U.S.	216	42.39 N	86.12 W
Saugatuck ≃	276	41.07 N	73.22 W
Saugatuck Reservoir ⊜[1]	207	41.16 N	73.22 W
Saugeen ≃	190	44.30 N	81.22 W
Saugeen Indian Reserve ✦[4]	212	44.33 N	81.18 W
Saugerties	210	42.04 N	73.57 W
Saughall	262	53.13 N	2.58 W
Saugor → Sāgar	124	23.50 N	78.43 E
Saugstad, Mount ∧	182	52.15 N	126.31 W
Saugus, Ca., U.S.	228	34.24 N	118.32 W
Saugus, Ma., U.S.	207	42.27 N	71.00 W
Saugus ≃	283	42.28 N	70.58 W
Saugus Iron Works National Historical Site ⊥	283	42.28 N	71.01 W
Sauh, Tanjong ›	114	3.46 N	100.49 E
Saujil	252	28.11 S	66.14 W
Saujon	32	45.40 N	0.56 W
Sauk ≃, Mn., U.S.	198	45.36 N	94.10 W
Sauk ≃, Wa., U.S.	224	48.30 N	121.37 W
Sauk Centre	198	45.44 N	94.57 W
Sauk City	190	43.16 N	89.43 W
Sauk Rapids	190	45.35 N	94.09 W
Sauksaj ≃	85	39.11 N	72.15 E
Sauk Village	216	41.29 N	87.34 W
Saukville	190	43.22 N	87.56 W
Saül	250	3.37 N	53.12 W
Şaulape ⟑	61	46.55 N	14.40 E
Šaul'der	85	42.47 N	68.24 E
Sauldre ≃	50	47.16 N	1.30 E
Sauldre, Canal de la ≊	50	47.36 N	2.06 E
Saulgau	58	48.01 N	9.30 E
Saulgrub	64	47.40 N	11.01 E
Saulheim	56	49.51 N	8.09 E
Saulieu	50	47.16 N	4.14 E
Saulkrasti	76	57.17 N	24.25 E
Saulnot	58	47.34 N	6.38 E
Sault-au-Mouton	186	48.33 N	69.15 W
Sault au Récollet ✦[8]	275a	45.34 N	73.39 W
Sault aux Cochons, Rivière du ≃	186	48.44 N	69.04 W
Sault-de-Vaucluse	62	44.05 N	5.25 E
Saulteaux ≃	182	55.16 N	114.25 W
Saulteaux Indian Reserve ✦[4]	184	53.08 N	108.18 W
Sault-lès-Rethel	50	49.30 N	4.22 E
Sault Sainte Marie, On., Can.	190	46.31 N	84.20 W
Sault Sainte Marie, Mi., U.S.	190	46.29 N	84.20 W
Saulx ≃, Fr.	56	48.45 N	4.35 E
Saulx ≃, Fr.	261	48.41 N	2.19 E
Saulx-de-Vesoul	58	47.42 N	6.17 E
Saulx-les-Chartreux	261	48.42 N	2.16 E
Saulxures-sur-Moselotte	58	47.57 N	6.46 E
Šaum'ani	84	41.21 N	44.46 E
Šaum'anovsk	84	40.26 N	46.34 E
Saumarez Reef ✣[2]	166	21.50 S	153.40 E
Saumlaki	164	7.57 S	131.19 E
Saumon, Rivière au ≃	206	45.41 N	71.27 W
Saumons, Rivíere aux ≃	186	49.25 N	62.15 W
Saumur	32	47.16 N	0.05 W
Saundatti	122	15.47 N	75.07 E
Saundersfoot	42	51.43 N	4.43 W
Saunders Island I, Falk. Is.	9	57.47 S	26.27 W
Saunders Island I, Falk. Is.	254	51.20 S	60.10 W
Saunders Point ∧[2]	162	27.52 S	125.38 E
Saunderstown	207	41.30 N	71.25 W
Saunemin	216	40.54 N	88.24 W
Saupite	152	13.54 S	17.43 E
Sauquoit	210	43.00 N	75.16 W
Sauquoit Creek ≃	210	43.08 N	75.16 W
Saura	84	44.14 N	50.50 E
Sauran	85	43.29 N	67.50 E
Saurimo	152	9.39 S	20.24 E
Saur-Mogila ⊥	83	47.56 N	38.46 E
Sausalito	226	37.51 N	122.29 W
Sausar	120	21.39 N	78.47 E
Sauškin	80	49.30 N	43.32 E
Sausset-les-Pins	62	43.20 N	5.07 E
Saussy	58	47.28 N	4.57 E
Sausu	112	1.00 S	120.30 E
Saútar	152	11.06 S	18.27 E
Sauteurs	241k	12.14 N	61.38 W
Sauteurs Bay ⊂	241k	12.14 N	61.38 W
Sauvas	62	44.19 N	4.09 E
Sauve	62	43.56 N	3.57 E
Sauveterre	62	44.02 N	4.48 E
Sauveterre-de-Béarn	34	43.24 N	0.56 W
Sauveterre-de-Guyenne	32	44.42 N	0.05 W
Sauvie Island I	224	45.41 N	122.49 W
Sauvo	26	60.21 N	22.42 E
Sauwald ✦[3]	60	48.28 N	13.40 E
Sauzal	200	31.37 N	106.18 W
Sauze di Cesana	62	44.56 N	6.51 E
Sauze d'Oulx	62	45.02 N	6.52 E
Sava, It.	68	40.24 N	17.34 E
S'ava, S.S.S.R.	80	58.01 N	46.22 E
Sava ≃	38	44.50 N	20.26 E
Sävaån ≃	40	59.45 N	17.24 E
Savage, Md., U.S.	208	39.08 N	76.49 W
Savage, Mt., U.S.	198	47.27 N	104.20 W
Savai'i I	175a	13.35 S	172.25 W
Savala ≃	80	51.03 N	41.30 E
Savalen ⊜	26	62.15 N	10.29 E
Savalou	150	7.56 N	1.58 E
Savana Island I	240m	18.20 N	65.05 W
Savana Passage Ʉ	240m	18.21 N	65.04 W
Savane ≃	186	51.08 N	71.26 W
Savanna, Il., U.S.	190	42.05 N	90.09 W
Savanna, Ok., U.S.	196	34.49 N	95.50 W
Savannah, Ga., U.S.	192	32.05 N	81.06 W
Savannah, Mo., U.S.	194	39.56 N	94.49 W
Savannah, N.Y., U.S.	210	43.04 N	76.45 W
Savannah, Oh., U.S.	214	40.57 N	82.21 W
Savannah, Tn., U.S.	194	35.13 N	88.14 W
Savannah ≃	192	32.02 N	80.53 W
Savannah River Plant ʊ[3]	192	33.15 N	81.40 W
Savannah Sound	192	25.06 N	76.09 W
Savannakhét	110	16.33 N	104.45 E
Savanna-la-Mar	241q	18.13 N	78.08 W
Savanna Portage State Park ♠	190	46.51 N	93.10 W
Sāvantvādi	122	15.54 N	73.49 E
Savanūr	122	14.58 N	75.21 E
Sävar	26	63.54 N	20.34 E
Savara ≃	62	45.42 N	7.12 E
Savasse ≃	62	45.03 N	5.02 E
Savaştepe	130	39.22 N	27.40 E
Savat	130	38.21 N	40.38 E
Savcılıbüyükoba	130	39.14 N	33.41 E
Savé	150	8.02 N	2.29 E
Save (Sabi) ≃, Afr.	156	21.00 S	35.02 E
Save ≃, Fr.	32	43.47 N	1.17 E
Sāveh	128	35.01 N	50.20 E
Savelli	68	39.19 N	16.47 E
Savelugu	150	9.37 N	0.49 W
Savenay	32	47.22 N	1.57 W
Săveni	38	47.57 N	26.52 E
Saverdun	32	43.14 N	1.35 E
Savernake Forest ✦[3]	42	51.24 N	1.38 W
Saverne	56	48.44 N	7.22 E
Savery Creek ≃	200	41.01 N	107.27 W
Saviči, S.S.S.R.	76	52.25 N	29.03 E
Saviči, S.S.S.R.	78	51.37 N	30.17 E
Savick Brook ≃	262	53.49 N	2.37 W
Savièse	58	46.16 N	7.20 E
Savigliano	62	44.38 N	7.40 E
Savignano Irpino	68	41.14 N	15.11 E
Savignano sul Panaro	64	44.29 N	11.02 E
Savignano sul Rubicone	66	44.05 N	12.24 E
Savignone	62	44.34 N	8.58 E
Savigny-lès-Beaune	58	47.04 N	4.49 E
Savigny-le-Temple	261	48.35 N	2.35 E
Savigny-sur-Braye	50	47.53 N	0.49 E
Savigny-sur-Orge	50	48.40 N	2.21 E
Savill Gardens ♠	260	51.27 N	0.36 E
Savincy	78	49.24 N	37.04 E
Savines	62	44.32 N	6.24 E
Savinjske Alpe ⟑	61	46.23 N	14.35 E
Savinka, S.S.S.R.	80	50.06 N	47.06 E
Savinka, S.S.S.R.	82	54.27 N	38.52 E
Savino	80	56.35 N	41.13 E
Savino-Borisovskaja	24	62.38 N	44.34 E
Savinsk	89	52.10 N	140.23 E
Savinskij	24	62.58 N	40.08 E
Savio	66	44.18 N	12.18 E
Savio ≃	66	44.19 N	12.20 E
Saviore dell'Adamello	64	46.05 N	10.24 E
Săvîrşin	38	46.01 N	22.14 E
Şavitaipale	26	61.12 N	27.42 E
Šavnik	38	42.57 N	19.05 E
Savognin	58	46.36 N	9.36 E
Savoie □[5]	32	45.30 N	6.25 E
Savo Island I	175e	9.08 S	159.49 E
Savolaks ✦[1]	26	62.00 N	28.00 E
Sav'olovo	82	56.52 N	37.22 E
Sav'olovo Station ✦[5]	265b	55.48 N	37.35 E
Savona, B.C., Can.	182	50.45 N	120.50 W
Savona, It.	62	44.17 N	8.30 E
Savona, N.Y., U.S.	210	42.17 N	77.13 W
Savona □[4]	62	44.18 N	8.16 E
Savonlinna	26	61.52 N	28.53 E
Savonnières	50	47.21 N	0.33 E
Savonranta	26	62.11 N	29.12 E
Savoonga	180	63.42 N	170.27 W
Savory Creek ≃	162	23.22 S	122.37 E
Savoureuse ≃	58	47.31 N	6.51 E
Savoy	196	33.34 N	96.21 W
Savran'	78	48.09 N	30.04 E
Savruši	80	55.02 N	50.40 E
Sävsjö	26	57.25 N	14.40 E
S'avta	24	67.08 N	61.45 E
Savu Basin ✣[1]	14	9.15 S	123.15 E
Savudrija	64	45.30 N	13.30 E
Savur	130	37.33 N	40.53 E
Savusavu	175g	16.16 S	179.21 E
Savusavu Bay ⊂	175g	16.45 S	179.15 E
Savu Sea → Sawu, Laut ⍑[2]	112	9.40 S	122.00 E
Savuto ≃	68	39.02 N	16.06 E
Savvatejevka	88	52.20 N	103.39 E
Savvino, S.S.S.R.	82	55.43 N	36.48 E
Savvino, S.S.S.R.	82	56.33 N	37.47 E
Savvo-Borz'a	88	50.46 N	118.18 E
Şawāb, Wādī aş- V	130	34.36 N	40.25 E
Sawabala Point ›	164	10.10 S	151.15 E
Sawah	112	2.23 N	115.14 E
Sawahlunto	112	0.40 S	100.47 E
Sawai	164	2.58 S	129.09 E
Sawai, Teluk ⊂	164	2.52 S	129.12 E
Sawāi Mādhopur	124	25.59 N	76.22 E
Sawākin	140	19.07 N	37.20 E
Sawal, Gunung ∧	115a	7.12 S	108.16 E
Sawan, Indon.	115b	8.08 S	115.11 E
Sawan, Mya.	110	24.30 N	96.19 E
Sawang	114	0.45 N	103.21 E
Sawankhalok	110	17.19 N	99.50 E
Sawara	94	35.53 N	140.30 E
Sawata	92	38.00 N	138.16 E
Sawatch Range ⟑	200	39.10 N	106.25 W
Sawbridgeworth	42	51.50 N	0.09 E
Sawdā', Jabal as- ⟑[2]	146	28.40 N	15.30 E
Sawdā', Qurnat as- ∧	130	34.18 N	36.07 E
Sawdirī	140	14.25 N	29.05 E
Sawel Mountain ∧	48	54.49 N	7.02 W
Sawhāj	140	26.33 N	31.42 E
Sawi	110	10.14 N	99.07 E
Sawin, Lac ⊜	206	46.32 N	73.54 W
Sawknah	146	29.04 N	15.47 E
Şawl	142	29.21 N	31.14 E
Sawla	150	9.17 N	2.25 W
Saw Log Creek ≃	198	38.07 N	99.42 W
Saw Mill ≃	276	40.56 N	73.53 W
Sawmill Brook ≃, Ma., U.S.	283	42.34 N	70.46 W
Sawmill Brook ≃, N.J., U.S.	276	40.28 N	74.26 W
Sawmill Creek ≃, N.J., U.S.	276	40.46 N	74.05 W
Sawmill Creek ≃, Pa., U.S.	279b	40.10 N	79.58 W
Sawmill Pond Brook ≃	276	41.10 N	74.23 W
Sawmill Run ≃	285	40.07 N	75.21 W
Sawmills	154	19.31 S	28.02 E
Şawqirah, Ghubbat ⊂	118	18.35 N	57.00 E
Sawston	42	52.07 N	0.10 E
Sawtayr ⍑[4]	140	17.03 N	30.24 E
Sawtooth National Recreation Area ♠	202	44.00 N	114.55 W
Sawtry	42	52.27 N	0.17 W
Sawu, Laut (Savu Sea) ⍑[2]	112	9.40 S	122.00 E
Sawu, Pulau I	112	10.30 S	121.54 E
Sawyer, Mi., U.S.	216	41.53 N	86.35 W
Sawyer, N.D., U.S.	198	48.05 N	101.03 W
Sawyers Hill ∧[2]	186	47.11 N	53.52 W
Sawyers Valley	168a	31.54 S	116.13 E
Sawyerville, P.Q., Can.	206	45.20 N	71.34 W
Sawyerville, Il., U.S.	219	39.05 N	89.48 W
Sawyerwood	214	41.02 N	81.27 W
Saxby ≃	166	18.25 S	140.53 E
Saxdalen	40	60.09 N	14.57 E
Saxen ⊜	40	59.46 N	14.25 E
Saxike	120	30.44 N	86.22 E
Saxilby	44	53.17 N	0.40 W
Saxis	208	37.55 N	75.43 W
Saxmundham	42	52.13 N	1.29 E
Saxon, Schw.	58	46.09 N	7.11 E
Saxon, Wi., U.S.	190	46.29 N	90.24 W
Saxonburg	214	40.45 N	79.49 W
Saxon Woods Park ♠	276	40.59 N	73.45 W
Saxony → Sachsen □[9]	30	52.45 N	9.30 E
Saxton	214	40.12 N	78.14 W
Say	150	13.07 N	2.21 E
Sāy, Jazīrat I	140	20.42 N	30.20 E
Saya de Malha Bank ✣[4]	12	10.30 S	61.30 E
Sayama, Nihon	94	35.51 N	139.24 E
Sayama, Nihon	270	34.31 N	135.34 E
Sayama-kyūryō ⟑[2]	268	35.47 N	139.24 E
Sayán	248	11.08 S	77.12 W
Sayan Mountains (Sajany) ⟑	88	52.45 N	96.00 E
Sayansk	88	54.02 N	102.06 E
Sayaxché	232	16.31 N	90.10 W
Saybrook, Il., U.S.	216	40.25 N	88.31 W
Saybrook, Oh., U.S.	214	41.50 N	80.51 W
Saybrook Manor	207	41.17 N	72.23 W
Sayda, D.D.R.	54	50.43 N	13.25 E
Şaydā (Sidon), Lubnān	132	33.33 N	35.22 E
Şaydā □[4]	132	33.15 N	35.15 E
Şaydnāyā	132	33.42 N	36.22 E
Sayghān	120	35.11 N	67.42 E
Sayḥūt	144	15.12 N	51.14 E
Sayil ⊥	232	20.16 N	89.42 W
Saylah	142	29.21 N	30.58 E
Saylorsburg	210	40.54 N	75.19 W
Saylorville Lake ⊜[1]	190	41.48 N	93.46 W
Saylūn, Khirbat (Shiloh) ⊥	132	32.03 N	35.17 E
Säynätsalo	26	62.08 N	25.46 E
Sayō	96	35.00 N	134.22 E
Şayqal, Baḥr ⊜	132	33.40 N	37.06 E
Sayram Hu ⊜	86	44.36 N	81.13 E
Sayre, Ok., U.S.	196	35.17 N	99.38 W
Sayre, Pa., U.S.	210	41.58 N	76.30 W
Sayreville	208	40.27 N	74.21 W
Sayula, Méx.	232	29.22 N	111.33 W
Sayula, Méx.	234	19.52 N	103.37 W
Sayula, Laguna de ⊜	234	20.03 N	103.31 W
Sayula de Alemán	234	17.52 N	94.57 W
Sayville	210	40.44 N	73.04 W
Sayward	182	50.22 N	125.55 W
Saywūn	144	15.56 N	48.47 E
Saza	92	33.14 N	129.39 E
Sazanit I	38	40.30 N	19.16 E
Sazdy, S.S.S.R.	80	46.57 N	49.19 E
Sazdy, S.S.S.R.	86	47.22 N	61.48 E
Saze	62	43.56 N	4.41 E
Sažino	86	56.20 N	58.11 E
Sazlijka ≃	38	42.02 N	25.52 E
Şazonovo	76	59.04 N	35.14 E
Šazud	120	37.43 N	72.11 E
Sazykul', ozero ⊜	86	55.22 N	67.34 E
Sba	148	28.13 N	0.08 W
Sbeïtla	148	35.14 N	9.08 E
Sbiba	36	35.33 N	9.05 E
Scaddan	162	33.27 S	121.43 E
Scaër	32	48.02 N	3.42 W
Scafati	68	40.45 N	14.31 E
Scafell Pikes ∧	44	54.27 N	3.12 W
Scaggsville	208	39.09 N	76.54 W
Scajaquada Creek ≃	284a	42.56 N	78.53 W
Scala, Teatro alla ʊ	266b	45.28 N	9.11 E
Scala Coeli	68	39.27 N	16.53 E
Scalasaig	46	56.04 N	6.11 W
Scalby	44	54.18 N	0.27 W
Scalea	68	39.49 N	15.48 E
Scaletta Zanclea	70	38.03 N	15.28 E
Scalloway	46a	60.08 N	1.18 W
Scalpay I, Scot., U.K.	46	57.52 N	6.40 W
Scalpay I, Scot., U.K.	46	57.17 N	5.59 W
Scalp Level	214	40.14 N	78.50 W
Scalp Mountain ∧[2]	48	55.04 N	7.24 W
Scammon	198	37.16 N	94.49 W
Scammon Bay	180	61.53 N	165.38 W
Scammon Bay ⊂	180	61.53 N	165.54 W
Scammonden Water ⊜[1]	262	53.38 N	1.56 W
Scampton	44	53.18 N	0.34 W
Scandale	68	39.07 N	16.57 E
Scandia	198	39.47 N	97.47 W
Scandiano	64	44.36 N	10.43 E
Scandicci	66	43.45 N	11.11 E
Scanlon	190	46.42 N	92.25 W
Scanno	66	41.54 N	13.53 E
Scansano	66	42.41 N	11.20 E
Scantic ≃	207	41.52 N	72.38 W
Scapa	182	51.52 N	111.59 W
Scapa Flow ⊂	46	58.55 N	3.06 W
Scapegoat Mountain ∧	202	47.19 N	112.50 W
Ščapino	74	55.19 N	159.25 E
Ščapov	80	51.01 N	51.11 E
Ščapovo	82	55.09 N	38.11 E
Scappoose	224	45.45 N	122.52 W
Şcar ≃	44	55.13 N	3.46 W
Ščara ≃	76	53.27 N	24.45 E
Scaramia, Capo ›	70	36.47 N	14.29 E
Scarba I	46	56.11 N	5.43 W
Scarborough, Austl.	168a	31.54 S	115.45 E
Scarborough, On., Can.	212	43.47 N	79.15 W
Scarborough, Trin.	241r	11.11 N	60.44 W
Scarborough, Eng., U.K.	44	54.17 N	0.24 W
Scarborough Centre ✦[9]	275b	43.47 N	79.16 W
Scarborough Point ›	171a	27.12 S	153.07 E
Scarborough Reef ✣[2]	116	15.08 N	117.46 E
Scardroy	46	57.31 N	4.59 W
Scargill	172	42.56 S	172.57 E
Scarinish	46	56.29 N	6.48 W
Scarisbrick	262	53.37 N	2.56 W
Scărişoara	38	44.00 N	24.35 E
Scarlino	66	42.54 N	10.51 E
Scarp I	46	58.02 N	7.08 W
Scarpe ≃	50	50.30 N	3.27 E
Scarperia	66	44.00 N	11.21 E
Scarper Peak ∧	282	37.32 N	122.26 W
Scarriff	48	52.55 N	8.31 W
Scarsdale, Austl.	169	37.40 S	143.40 E
Scarsdale, N.Y., U.S.	210	40.59 N	73.49 W
Scartaglin	48	52.10 N	9.26 W
Scarth Hill	262	53.33 N	2.52 W
Sčastje	83	48.44 N	39.14 E
Scatarie Island I	186	46.00 N	59.44 W
Scatter Creek ≃	224	46.48 N	123.06 W
Scauri, It.	66	41.15 N	13.42 E
Scauri, It.	70	36.45 N	11.58 E
Scavaig, Loch ⊂	46	57.09 N	6.10 W
Scawfell Island I	166	20.52 S	149.36 E
Sceaux	50	48.47 N	2.17 E
Sceaux, Château de ⊥	261	48.46 N	2.18 E
Ščedrin	76	52.53 N	29.33 E
Ščedrovka	83	49.30 N	40.17 E
Ščeglovo	265a	60.02 N	30.46 E
Ščeljajur	24	65.21 N	53.21 E
Ščelkan ≃	80	50.47 N	43.33 E
Ščelkovo	76	55.55 N	38.00 E
Ščemilovo	265b	55.48 N	38.05 E
Scena	64	46.41 N	11.12 E
Scenery Hill	214	40.05 N	80.04 W
Sceptre	184	50.51 N	109.15 W
Ščerbakovo, S.S.S.R.	74	65.15 N	160.30 E
Ščerbakovo, S.S.S.R.	86	56.01 N	73.29 E
Ščerbakty	86	52.29 N	78.09 E
Ščerbinka	82	55.31 N	37.35 E
Ščerbinovka	83	48.26 N	37.50 E
Scerni	66	42.07 N	14.34 E
Scey-sur-Saône-et-Saint-Albin	58	47.40 N	5.58 E
Schaale ≃	54	53.21 N	10.49 E
Schaalsee ⊜	54	53.35 N	10.57 E
Schaan	58	47.10 N	9.31 E

≃	River	Fluß	Río	Rivière	Rio
≊	Canal	Kanal	Canal	Canal	Canal
⌊	Waterfall, Rapids	Wasserfall, Stromschnellen	Cascada, Rápidos	Chute d'eau, Rapides	Cascata, Rápidos
Ʉ	Strait	Meeresstraße	Estrecho	Détroit	Estreito
⊂	Bay, Gulf	Bucht, Golf	Bahía, Golfo	Baie, Golfe	Baía, Golfo
⊜	Lake, Lakes	See, Seen	Lago, Lagos	Lac, Lacs	Lago, Lagos
⁝⁝	Swamp	Sumpf	Pantano	Marais	Pântano
⍐	Ice Features, Glacier	Eis- und Gletscherformen	Accidentes Glaciales	Formes glaciaires	Acidentes glaciares
⍑	Other Hydrographic Features	Andere Hydrographische Objekte	Otros Elementos Hidrográficos	Autres données hydrographiques	Outros acidentes hidrográficos

✣	Submarine Features	Untermeerische Objekte	Accidentes Submarinos	Formes de relief sous-marin	Acidentes submarinos
□	Political Unit	Politische Einheit	Unidad Politica	Entité politique	Unidade política
ʊ	Cultural Institution	Kulturelle Institution	Institución Cultural	Institution culturelle	Instituição cultural
⊥	Historical Site	Historische Stätte	Sitio Histórico	Site historique	Sitio histórico
♠	Recreational Site	Erholungs- und Ferienort	Sitio de Recreo	Centre de loisirs	Area de Lazer
⊠	Airport	Flughafen	Aeropuerto	Aéroport	Aeroporto
■	Military Installation	Militäranlage	Instalación Militar	Installation militaire	Instalação militar
✦	Miscellaneous	Verschiedenes	Misceláneo	Divers	Diversos

Name	Page	Lat.°′	Long.°′
Schabs → Sciaves	64	46.46 N	11.40 E
Schachendorf	61	47.16 N	16.26 E
Schaefferstown	208	40.17 N	76.17 W
Schaephuysen	263	51.26 N	6.29 E
Schaerbeek	50	50.51 N	4.23 E
Schafberg ∧	64	47.47 N	13.27 E
Schäferberg ∧ [2]	264a	52.25 N	13.08 E
Schaffhausen	58	47.42 N	8.38 E
Schaffhausen □ [3]	58	47.40 N	8.35 E
Schafstädt	54	51.23 N	11.46 E
Schäftlarn	64	47.59 N	11.28 E
Schagen	52	52.46 N	4.47 E
Schaghticoke	210	42.54 N	73.35 W
Schalchen	60	48.07 N	13.10 E
Schale	52	52.26 N	7.37 E
Schalkau	54	50.24 N	11.00 E
Schalke ◆ [8]	263	51.31 N	7.05 E
Schälker Heide ◆ [3]	263	51.24 N	7.36 E
Schalksmühle	56	51.14 N	7.31 E
Schaller	198	42.30 N	95.18 W
Schanck, Cape >	169	38.30 S	144.53 E
S-Chanf	58	46.36 N	9.59 E
Schanfigg V	58	46.51 N	9.38 E
Schanghai → Shanghai	106	31.14 N	121.28 E
Schangnau	58	46.50 N	7.52 E
Schapbach	58	48.22 N	8.17 E
Schapen	52	52.24 N	7.33 E
Schaprode	54	54.31 N	13.10 E
Scharbeutz	54	54.03 N	10.44 E
Schardenberg	60	48.32 N	13.30 E
Schardenberg ∧ [2]	263	51.27 N	6.28 E
Schärding	60	48.27 N	13.26 E
Scharhörn I	52	53.57 N	8.25 E
Schari → Chari ≃	146	12.58 N	14.31 E
Scharl	263	51.06 N	7.40 E
Scharmützelsee ⊜	54	52.15 N	14.03 E
Scharnhorst ◆ [8]	263	51.32 N	7.32 E
Scharnitz	64	47.23 N	11.17 E
Scharnitzer Klause)(	64	47.24 N	11.16 E
Scharrel	52	53.04 N	7.42 E
Scharzfeld	52	51.37 N	10.22 E
Schässburg → Sighișoara	38	46.13 N	24.48 E
Schauinsland ∧	58	47.55 N	7.54 E
Schaumburg	216	42.02 N	88.05 W
Schaut	84	43.43 N	42.32 E
Schebeli → Shabeelle ≃	144	0.12 S	42.45 E
Scheessel	52	53.10 N	9.29 E
Schefferville	176	54.48 N	66.50 W
Scheggia	66	43.24 N	12.40 E
Scheggino	66	42.43 N	12.50 E
Scheibbs	61	48.00 N	15.10 E
Scheiblingstein	264b	48.16 N	16.13 E
Scheidegg	58	47.35 N	9.51 E
Scheifling	61	47.09 N	14.24 E
Scheinfeld	56	49.40 N	10.27 E
Schelde (Escaut) ≃	50	51.22 N	4.15 E
Schelklingen	58	48.22 N	9.44 E
Schell Creek Range ⩘	204	39.10 N	114.40 W
Schellenberg ∧	60	48.18 N	13.03 E
Schellsburg	214	40.03 N	78.39 W
Schelsen ◆ [8]	263	51.09 N	6.31 E
Schenectady	210	42.48 N	73.56 W
Schenectady □ [6]	210	42.47 N	73.53 W
Schenefeld	52	53.36 N	9.49 E
Schenevus	210	42.32 N	74.49 W
Schenevus Creek ≃	210	42.29 N	74.59 W
Schenkendorf	264a	52.16 N	13.35 E
Schenkenhorst	264a	52.20 N	13.12 E
Schenklengsfeld	56	50.49 N	9.50 E
Schenley	214	40.41 N	79.40 W
Schenley Park ♠	279b	40.26 N	79.56 W
Schepsdorf-Lohne	52	52.30 N	7.16 E
Schererville	216	41.30 N	87.27 W
Scherfede	52	51.32 N	9.02 E
Scherlebeck	263	51.37 N	7.08 E
Schermbeck	52	51.41 N	6.52 E
Schermerhorn	52	52.36 N	4.52 E
Schermützelsee ⊜	54	52.34 N	14.04 E
Scherpenheuvel	56	50.59 N	4.59 E
Scherpenzeel	52	52.05 N	5.30 E
Schertz	196	29.33 N	98.16 W
Schesch, Erg → Chech, Erg ◆ [2]	148	25.00 N	2.15 W
Schesslitz	60	49.59 N	11.01 E
Schevelinger-Stausee ⊜ [1]	263	51.08 N	7.26 E
Scheveningen ◆ [8]	52	52.06 N	4.18 E
Schiedam	52	51.55 N	4.24 E
Schieder	52	51.55 N	9.09 E
Schiefbahn	56	51.14 N	6.31 E
Schiehallion ∧	46	56.40 N	4.06 W
Schierke	54	51.46 N	10.40 E
Schierling	60	48.50 N	12.08 E
Schiermonnikoog	52	53.24 N	6.10 E
Schiermonnikoog I	52	53.28 N	6.15 E
Schiers	58	46.59 N	9.41 E
Schiessen	58	48.18 N	10.14 E
Schiffdorf	52	53.32 N	8.39 E
Schiffenensee ⊜	58	46.50 N	7.10 E
Schifferstadt	56	49.23 N	8.22 E
Schiffshebewerk ◆ [5]	263	51.37 N	7.19 E
Schihkiatschwang → Shijiazhuang	98	38.03 N	114.28 E
Schijndel	52	51.37 N	5.25 E
Schikoku → Shikoku I	92	33.45 N	133.30 E
Schildau	54	51.27 N	12.56 E
Schilde	56	51.14 N	4.34 E
Schilde ≃	54	53.26 N	10.53 E
Schildow	54	52.38 N	13.23 E
Schildwolde	52	53.14 N	6.49 E
Schiller Park	216	41.57 N	87.52 W
Schillingsfürst	56	49.17 N	10.15 E
Schillingstedt	54	51.14 N	11.11 E
Schilpario	64	46.01 N	10.09 E
Schiltach	58	48.17 N	8.20 E
Schiltigheim	58	48.36 N	7.45 E
Schimborn	56	50.03 N	9.11 E
Schimmert	56	50.55 N	5.50 E
Schinveld	56	50.57 N	5.59 E
Schinznach Bad	58	47.27 N	8.10 E
Schio	64	45.43 N	11.21 E
Schipbeek ≃	52	52.14 N	6.09 E
Schiphol, Luchthaven ⊠	52	52.17 N	4.40 E
Schipkau	54	51.31 N	13.53 E
Schippenbeil → Sępopol	30	54.15 N	21.00 E
Schirgiswalde	54	51.05 N	14.27 E
Schirmeck	58	48.29 N	7.13 E
Schirnding	54	50.05 N	12.13 E
Schisuoka → Shizuoka	94	34.58 N	138.23 E
Schivelbein → Świdwin	30	53.47 N	15.47 E
Schjetman Reef ✤ [2]	14	15.10 N	178.40 W
Schkeuditz	54	51.24 N	12.13 E
Schkoder-See → Scutari, Lake ⊜	38	42.12 N	19.18 E
Schkölen	54	51.02 N	11.49 E
Schkopau	54	51.23 N	11.59 E
Schladen	54	52.01 N	10.32 E
Schladming	64	47.23 N	13.41 E
Schlanders → Silandro	64	46.38 N	10.46 E
Schlangen	52	51.49 N	8.50 E
Schlangenbad	56	50.05 N	8.05 E
Schlänitz-See ⊜	264a	52.27 N	12.57 E
Schlanstedt	54	52.00 N	11.02 E
Schlater	194	33.38 N	90.20 W
Schlegel Lake ⊜	276	40.59 N	74.03 W
Schlei c	41	54.36 N	9.51 E
Schleiden	56	50.31 N	6.28 E
Schleife	54	51.32 N	14.32 E
Schleinitz Range ⩘	164	3.10 S	151.40 E
Schleithal	56	48.59 N	8.02 E
Schleitheim	58	47.45 N	8.29 E
Schleiz	54	50.34 N	11.49 E
Schlema	54	50.40 N	12.40 E
Schlepzig	54	52.01 N	13.53 E
Schlesien → Silesia □ [9]	30	51.00 N	16.45 E
Schlesischer (Ost) Bahnhof ◆ [5]	264a	52.30 N	13.26 E
Schleswig, B.R.D.	41	54.31 N	9.33 E
Schleswig, Ia., U.S.	198	42.09 N	95.26 W
Schleswig-Holstein □ [3]	30	54.20 N	9.40 E
Schlettau	54	50.33 N	12.56 E
Schlettstadt → Sélestat	58	48.16 N	7.27 E
Schleusingen	54	50.31 N	10.45 E
Schlichtingsheim → Szlichtyngowa	30	51.43 N	16.15 E
Schlicke ∧	58	47.31 N	10.37 E
Schlieben	54	51.43 N	13.23 E
Schliengen	58	47.46 N	7.35 E
Schlieren	58	47.24 N	8.27 E
Schliersee	64	47.44 N	11.51 E
Schlitz	56	50.40 N	9.33 E
Schlochau → Człuchów	30	53.41 N	17.21 E
Schloppe → Człopa	30	53.06 N	16.08 E
Schloss Holte	52	51.52 N	8.35 E
Schloss Neuhaus	52	51.44 N	8.43 E
Schlossvippach	54	51.06 N	11.08 E
Schloss Zeil	64	47.52 N	10.00 E
Schlotheim	54	51.14 N	10.39 E
Schluchsee	58	47.49 N	8.10 E
Schluchsee ⊜	58	47.49 N	8.10 E
Schlucht, Col de la)(	58	48.04 N	7.02 E
Schlüchtern	56	50.20 N	9.31 E
Schluderns → Sluderno	64	46.40 N	10.35 E
Schlüsselburg	52	52.29 N	9.04 E
Schlüsselfeld	56	49.45 N	10.37 E
Schlutup ◆ [8]	54	53.53 N	10.48 E
Schmachtendorf ◆ [8]	263	51.32 N	6.49 E
Schmalfeld	52	53.52 N	9.58 E
Schmalkalden	54	50.43 N	10.26 E
Schmallenberg	56	51.09 N	8.17 E
Schmalnau	56	50.27 N	9.47 E
Schmannewitz	54	51.24 N	12.58 E
Schmarsau	54	52.54 N	11.21 E
Schmelz	56	49.27 N	6.51 E
Schmida ≃	61	48.21 N	16.09 E
Schmidmühlen	60	49.16 N	11.56 E
Schmidt	56	50.39 N	6.25 E
Schmidtsdrif	158	28.41 S	24.02 E
Schmiedeberg	54	50.50 N	13.40 E
Schmiedefeld	54	50.37 N	10.49 E
Schmilka	54	50.53 N	14.14 E
Schmöckwitz ◆ [8]	264a	52.23 N	13.39 E
Schmölln	54	50.53 N	12.20 E
Schmutter ≃	58	48.42 N	10.46 E
Schnabelwaid	60	49.49 N	11.35 E
Schnackenburg	54	53.02 N	11.32 E
Schnait	56	48.47 N	9.23 E
Schnaitsee	60	48.04 N	12.22 E
Schnaittach	60	49.31 N	11.19 E
Schnaittenbach	60	49.33 N	12.01 E
Schnakenbek	52	53.23 N	10.30 E
Schnecksville	208	40.41 N	75.36 W
Schneealpe ⩘	61	47.41 N	15.36 E
Schneeberg	54	50.36 N	12.38 E
Schneeberg ∧, B.R.D.	54	50.03 N	11.51 E
Schneeberg ∧, Öst.	61	47.47 N	15.47 E
Schneidemühl → Piła	30	53.10 N	16.44 E
Schneider	216	41.11 N	87.26 W
Schneifel ⩘ [1]	56	50.15 N	6.25 E
Schneverdingen	52	53.07 N	9.47 E
Schney	56	50.10 N	11.04 E
Schober Gruppe ⩘	64	46.55 N	12.42 E
Schobüll	41	54.30 N	9.00 E
Schöckl ∧	61	47.11 N	15.28 E
Schodn'a	82	55.57 N	37.18 E
Schodn'a ≃	265b	55.50 N	37.25 E
Schoenbrunn Village State Memorial ⊥	214	40.27 N	81.24 W
Schofield	190	44.54 N	89.36 W
Schofield Barracks ■	229c	21.30 N	158.04 W
Schofields	274a	33.42 S	150.52 E
Schöftland	58	47.18 N	8.03 E
Schoharie	210	42.39 N	74.18 W
Schoharie □ [6]	210	42.40 N	74.19 W
Schoharie Creek ≃	210	42.57 N	74.18 W
Schoharie Reservoir ⊜ [1]	210	42.22 N	74.26 W
Scholen	52	52.44 N	8.46 E
Scholes	44	53.49 N	1.25 W
Schollene	54	52.41 N	12.13 E
Schöllenen V	58	46.40 N	8.35 E
Schöller ◆ [8]	263	51.14 N	7.01 E
Schöllkrippen	56	50.05 N	9.14 E
Schöllnach	60	48.45 N	13.11 E
Scholls	224	45.24 N	122.55 W
Scholven ◆ [8]	263	51.36 N	7.01 E
Schömberg, B.R.D.	56	48.47 N	8.38 E
Schömberg, B.R.D.	58	48.13 N	8.46 E
Schomberg, On., Can.	212	44.00 N	79.41 W
Schonach	58	48.08 N	8.11 E
Schönaich	56	48.39 N	9.03 E
Schönau, B.R.D.	56	49.26 N	8.49 E
Schönau, B.R.D.	58	47.47 N	7.53 E
Schönau, B.R.D.	64	47.37 N	12.59 E
Schönau → Świerzawa	30	51.01 N	15.54 E
Schönbeck	54	53.34 N	13.34 E
Schönberg, B.R.D.	54	54.23 N	10.22 E
Schönberg, B.R.D.	60	48.50 N	13.20 E
Schönberg, D.D.R.	54	50.11 N	12.19 E
Schönberg, D.D.R.	54	50.31 N	11.57 E
Schönberg, D.D.R.	54	53.50 N	11.38 E
Schönberger Strand	54	54.25 N	10.24 E
Schönberg im Stubaital	64	47.11 N	11.25 E
Schönbrunn	54	50.32 N	10.53 E
Schönbrunn, Schloss ♥	264b	48.11 N	16.19 E
Schönbrunner Schlosspark ♠	264b	48.11 N	16.19 E
Schondra ≃	56	50.07 N	9.44 E
Schönebeck, D.D.R.	54	53.03 N	12.13 E
Schönebeck, D.D.R.	54	52.01 N	11.44 E
Schönebeck ◆ [8]	263	51.28 N	6.56 E
Schöneberg ◆ [8]	264a	52.29 N	13.21 E
Schöneck, B.R.D.	56	50.13 N	8.52 E
Schöneck, D.D.R.	54	50.23 N	12.20 E
Schönecken	56	50.09 N	6.27 E
Schönefeld	264a	52.23 N	13.30 E
Schöneiche	54	52.28 N	13.41 E
Schönenwerd	58	47.22 N	8.00 E
Schönerlinde	264a	52.39 N	13.27 E
Schönewalde	54	51.49 N	13.13 E
Schönfeld	264a	52.41 N	13.44 E
Schönfliess	264a	52.39 N	13.20 E
Schongau	58	47.49 N	10.54 E
Schönhagen, B.R.D.	41	54.38 N	10.01 E
Schönhagen, B.R.D.	52	51.41 N	9.33 E
Schönhausen, B.R.D.	263	51.37 N	7.38 E
Schönhausen, D.D.R.	54	52.35 N	12.02 E
Schönheide	54	50.30 N	12.31 E
Schönholthausen	56	51.11 N	8.00 E
Schöningen	54	52.08 N	10.58 E
Schönkirchen	54	54.20 N	10.15 E
Schönlanke → Trzcianka	30	53.03 N	16.28 E
Schönmünzach	56	48.36 N	8.22 E
Schonnebeck ◆ [8]	263	51.29 N	7.04 E
Schönningstedt	52	53.32 N	10.15 E
Schönow	54	52.40 N	13.32 E
Schönsee	60	49.31 N	12.33 E
Schönthal	60	49.21 N	12.36 E
Schonungen	56	50.03 N	10.18 E
Schönwald, B.R.D.	54	50.12 N	12.05 E
Schönwald, B.R.D.	58	48.06 N	8.11 E
Schönwalde, B.R.D.	54	54.11 N	10.45 E
Schönwalde, D.D.R.	54	52.37 N	13.07 E
Schönwalde, D.D.R.	54	52.40 N	13.26 E
Schönwies	58	47.11 N	10.39 E
Schoodic Lake ⊜	188	45.21 N	68.54 W
Schoolcraft	216	42.06 N	85.38 W
Schoolhouse Run ≃	285	40.13 N	75.27 W
Schoombee	158	31.28 S	25.30 E
Schoondijke	52	51.21 N	3.32 E
Schoonebeek	52	52.29 N	6.52 E
Schoonhoven	52	51.56 N	4.51 E
Schoorl	52	52.42 N	4.41 E
Schopfheim	58	47.39 N	7.49 E
Schopfloch	56	49.07 N	10.18 E
Schopp	56	49.21 N	7.41 E
Schöppenstedt	54	52.08 N	10.46 E
Schöppingen	52	52.05 N	7.14 E
Schorfheide	54	52.56 N	13.43 E
Schorfheide ◆ [3]	54	52.55 N	13.35 E
Schörfling	64	47.56 N	13.36 E
Schorndorf	56	48.48 N	9.31 E
Schortens	52	53.31 N	7.56 E
Schoten	50	51.15 N	4.30 E
Schötmar	52	52.04 N	8.45 E
Schotten	56	50.30 N	9.07 E
Schottland → Scotland □ [8]	28	57.00 N	4.00 W
Schouten, Kepulauan II	164	0.55 S	135.55 E
Schouten Island I	166	42.19 S	148.17 E
Schouten Islands II	164	3.30 S	144.40 E
Schouwen I	52	51.43 N	3.50 E
Schrader Creek ≃	210	41.43 N	76.30 W
Schrader Range ⩘	164	5.05 S	144.15 E
Schramberg	58	48.13 N	8.23 E
Schram City	219	39.09 N	89.27 W
Schrankogel ∧	64	47.02 N	11.06 E
Schraplau	54	51.26 N	11.40 E
Schreiber	190	48.48 N	87.15 W
Schrems	61	48.47 N	15.04 E
Schrick	61	48.30 N	16.37 E
Schriever	194	29.44 N	90.48 W
Schrobenhausen	60	48.33 N	11.17 E
Schröcken	58	47.15 N	10.05 E
Schroffenstein ∧	158	27.11 S	18.42 E
Schroon ≃	188	43.29 N	73.49 W
Schroon Lake ⊜	188	43.47 N	73.46 W
Schrozberg	56	49.20 N	9.59 E
Schruns	58	47.04 N	9.55 E
Schulenburg, B.R.D.	52	52.12 N	9.47 E
Schulenburg, Tx., U.S.	222	29.40 N	96.54 W
Schuls → Scuol	58	46.48 N	10.18 E
Schultz Lake ⊜	176	64.45 N	97.30 W
Schulzendorf	54	52.22 N	13.35 E
Schulzenhöhe	264a	52.29 N	13.47 E
Schumacher	190	48.28 N	81.18 W
Schüpfheim	58	46.57 N	8.01 E
Schüren ◆ [8]	263	51.30 N	7.32 E
Schussen ≃	58	47.37 N	9.32 E
Schussenried	58	48.00 N	9.40 E
Schüttenberg ∧ [2]	61	48.05 N	16.44 E
Schutter ≃	58	48.34 N	7.50 E
Schüttorf	52	52.19 N	7.13 E
Schützenbruch → Kalety	30	50.34 N	18.54 E
Schuyler, Ne., U.S.	198	41.26 N	97.03 W
Schuyler, Va., U.S.	192	37.47 N	78.41 W
Schuyler □ [6], Il., U.S.	219	40.07 N	90.34 W
Schuyler □ [6], N.Y., U.S.	210	42.23 N	76.52 W
Schuyler Lake	210	42.47 N	75.02 W
Schuylerville	210	43.06 N	73.34 W
Schuylkill □ [6]	210	40.41 N	76.12 W
Schuylkill ≃	208	39.53 N	75.12 W
Schuylkill Canal ≊	285	40.14 N	75.42 W
Schuylkill Haven	208	40.37 N	76.10 W
Schwaan	54	53.56 N	12.06 E
Schwabach	60	49.20 N	11.01 E
Schwaben □ [5]	58	48.15 N	10.30 E
Schwaben □ [9]	30	48.10 N	9.25 E
Schwabing ◆ [8]	60	48.10 N	11.34 E
Schwäbische Alb ⩘	58	48.25 N	9.30 E
Schwäbisch Gmünd	56	48.48 N	9.47 E
Schwäbisch Hall	56	49.07 N	9.44 E
Schwabmünchen	58	48.11 N	10.45 E
Schwabstedt	41	54.23 N	9.11 E
Schwadorf	264b	48.04 N	16.35 E
Schwafheim	263	51.25 N	6.39 E
Schwagstorf	52	52.31 N	7.45 E
Schwaigern	56	49.08 N	9.03 E
Schwalenberg	52	51.52 N	9.11 E
Schwalm ≃	56	51.10 N	9.25 E
Schwalmstadt	56	50.55 N	9.11 E
Schwalmtal	56	51.13 N	6.16 E
Schwanden	58	47.00 N	9.04 E
Schwandorf	60	49.20 N	12.08 E
Schwanebeck, D.D.R.	54	52.37 N	13.32 E
Schwanebeck, D.D.R.	54	51.58 N	11.07 E
Schwanenstadt	60	48.03 N	13.46 E
Schwanenwerder ◆ [8]	264a	52.27 N	13.10 E
Schwaner, Pegunungan ⩘	112	0.40 S	112.40 E
Schwanewede	52	53.14 N	8.35 E
Schwangau	58	47.35 N	10.44 E
Schwansen ◆ [1]	41	54.35 N	9.50 E
Schwante	264a	52.44 N	13.05 E
Schwarme	52	52.54 N	9.01 E
Schwarmstedt	52	52.40 N	9.37 E
Schwartau ≃	54	53.56 N	10.41 E
Schwarza, D.D.R.	54	50.38 N	10.32 E
Schwarza, D.D.R.	54	50.41 N	11.19 E
Schwarza ≃, D.D.R.	54	50.41 N	11.19 E
Schwarza ≃, Öst.	61	47.43 N	16.13 E
Schwarzach, B.R.D.	60	48.55 N	12.49 E
Schwarzach, Öst.	58	47.27 N	9.45 E
Schwarzach ≃	60	49.36 N	12.08 E
Schwarzach im Pongau	64	47.19 N	13.09 E
Schwarzbach ≃, B.R.D.	56	49.16 N	7.18 E
Schwarzbach ≃, B.R.D.	263	51.19 N	6.44 E
Schwarzburg	54	50.38 N	11.12 E
Schwarze Elster ≃	54	51.49 N	12.51 E
Schwarze Laber ≃	60	49.00 N	12.03 E
Schwarzenbach am Wald	54	50.17 N	11.37 E
Schwarzenbach an der Saale	54	50.13 N	11.56 E
Schwarzenbek	52	53.30 N	10.29 E
Schwarzenberg	54	50.32 N	12.47 E
Schwarzenberg ◆ [8]	263	51.24 N	6.42 E
Schwarzenberg Park ♠	264b	48.14 N	16.15 E
Schwarzenborn	56	50.37 N	9.58 E
Schwarzenbruck	60	49.21 N	11.14 E
Schwarzenburg	58	46.49 N	7.21 E
Schwarzenfeld	60	49.23 N	12.08 E
Schwarze Pumpe	54	51.32 N	14.20 E
Schwarzer Berg ∧ [2]	263	51.41 N	7.12 E
Schwarzer Mann ∧	56	50.15 N	6.21 E
Schwarzer Regen ≃	60	49.10 N	12.50 E
Schwarzes Meer → Black Sea ⊤ [2]	22	43.00 N	35.00 E
Schwarzheide	54	51.29 N	13.51 E
Schwarzkogel ∧	61	47.25 N	15.25 E
Schwarzrand ⩘	156	25.37 S	16.50 E
Schwarzriegel ∧	60	49.14 N	12.56 E
Schwarzsee	58	46.40 N	7.20 E
Schwarzwald (Black Forest) ⩘	58	48.00 N	8.15 E
Schwarzwälder Hochwald ◆ [3]	56	49.39 N	6.55 E
Schwatka Mountains ⩘	180	67.25 N	157.00 W
Schwaz	64	47.20 N	11.42 E
Schwechat	264b	48.08 N	16.29 E
Schwechat ≃	264b	48.08 N	16.34 E
Schweden → Sweden □ [1]	24	62.00 N	15.00 E
Schwedeneck	41	54.27 N	10.05 E
Schwedt	54	53.03 N	14.17 E
Schweez	54	53.53 N	12.24 E
Schweflinghausen	263	51.16 N	7.25 E
Schwegenheim	56	49.16 N	8.20 E
Schwei	52	53.24 N	8.21 E
Schweich	56	49.49 N	6.45 E
Schweidnitz → Świdnica	30	50.51 N	16.29 E
Schweighausen	58	48.13 N	7.57 E
Schweighouse-sur-Moder	56	48.49 N	7.44 E
Schweinfurt	56	50.03 N	10.14 E
Schweinitz	54	51.48 N	13.01 E
Schweinrich	54	53.10 N	12.37 E
Schweiz → Switzerland □ [1]	58	47.00 N	8.00 E
Schweizer Nationalpark ♠	58	46.38 N	10.11 E
Schweizer-Reneke	158	27.11 S	25.18 E
Schwelm	56	51.17 N	7.17 E
Schwendi	58	48.10 N	9.58 E
Schwenke	263	51.11 N	7.26 E
Schwenksville	285	40.16 N	75.28 W
Schwepnitz	54	51.20 N	13.57 E
Schwerin, B.R.D.	263	51.33 N	7.20 E
Schwerin, D.D.R.	54	53.38 N	11.25 E
Schwerin □ [5]	54	53.30 N	11.30 E
Schwerin an der Warthe → Skwierzyna	30	52.36 N	15.30 E
Schweriner See ⊜	54	53.45 N	11.28 E
Schwertberg	61	48.16 N	14.35 E
Schwerte	56	51.26 N	7.34 E
Schwetzingen	56	49.23 N	8.34 E
Schweyen	56	49.10 N	7.24 E
Schwieberdingen	56	48.52 N	9.04 E
Schwiebus → Świebodzin	30	52.15 N	15.32 E
Schwielochsee ⊜	54	52.03 N	14.12 E
Schwielowsee ⊜	54	52.20 N	12.57 E
Schwitten	263	51.27 N	7.48 E
Schwyz	58	47.02 N	8.40 E
Schwyz □ [3]	58	47.05 N	8.40 E
Sciacca	70	37.31 N	13.03 E
Sciara	70	37.55 N	13.45 E
Sciaves (Schabs)	64	46.46 N	11.40 E
Scicli	70	36.47 N	14.42 E
Scie ≃	50	49.55 N	1.02 E
Science and Industry, Museum of ♥	278	41.47 N	87.35 W
Sciez	58	46.20 N	6.23 E
Scigliano	68	39.08 N	16.19 E
Ščigry	78	51.53 N	36.55 E
Scilla	68	38.15 N	15.44 E
Scilly, Isles of II	42a	49.55 N	6.20 W
Ścinawa	30	51.25 N	16.27 E
Scio, N.Y., U.S.	210	42.10 N	77.59 W
Scio, Oh., U.S.	214	40.23 N	81.05 W
Scio, Or., U.S.	202	44.42 N	122.50 W
Scionzier	58	46.03 N	6.34 E
Sciota	210	40.56 N	75.19 W
Scioto □ [6]	218	38.48 N	83.01 W
Scioto ≃	188	38.44 N	83.01 W
Scioto Brush Creek ≃	218	38.50 N	83.01 W
Scipio, In., U.S.	218	39.05 N	85.43 W
Scipio, Ut,. U.S.	200	39.14 N	112.06 W
Scipio Center	210	42.47 N	76.34 W
Scippo Creek ≃	218	39.31 N	82.59 W
Šćit ∧	36	44.02 N	17.47 E
Ščitkoviči	76	53.13 N	27.59 E
Scituate	207	42.11 N	70.43 W
Scituate Reservoir ⊜ [1]	207	41.47 N	71.36 W
Sclafani Bagni	70	37.49 N	13.51 E
Scobey	202	48.47 N	105.25 W
Scoffera, Passo della)(	62	44.29 N	9.07 E
Scofield Reservoir ⊜ [1]	200	39.47 N	111.09 W
Scoglitti ◆ [8]	70	36.53 N	14.26 E
Ščokino	76	54.01 N	37.31 E
Scole	42	52.22 N	1.10 E
Ščolkovo	82	55.55 N	38.00 E
Scoltenna ≃	64	44.15 N	10.50 E
Scolt Head >	42	52.58 N	0.42 E
Scone	166	32.03 S	150.52 E
Scooba	194	32.49 N	88.28 W
Scopello	62	45.46 N	8.06 E
Scordia	70	37.18 N	14.51 E
Scoresby	274b	37.54 S	145.14 E
Scorrano, It.	66	42.35 N	13.49 E
Scorrano, It.	68	40.05 N	18.18 E
Ščors	78	51.49 N	31.59 E
Ščorsk	78	48.22 N	34.06 E
Scorzè	64	45.34 N	12.06 E
Scotch ≃	206	45.27 N	74.59 W
Scotch Plains	210	40.39 N	74.23 W
Scotchtown	210	41.29 N	74.21 W
Scotia, Ne., U.S.	198	41.27 N	98.42 W
Scotia, N.Y., U.S.	210	42.49 N	73.57 W
Scotia Lake ⊜	190	47.05 N	81.23 W
Scotia Ridge ✤ [3]	18	54.00 S	50.00 W
Scotia Sea ⊤ [2]	9	56.00 S	40.00 W
Scotland, On., Can.	212	43.01 N	80.22 W
Scotland, Pa., U.S.	208	39.58 N	77.35 W
Scotland, S.D., U.S.	198	43.08 N	97.43 W
Scotland, Tx., U.S.	196	33.40 N	98.28 W
Scotland □ [8]	28	57.00 N	4.00 W
Scotland Neck	192	36.07 N	77.25 W
Scotland Run ≃	285	39.39 N	75.03 W
Scotlandville	194	30.31 N	91.10 W
Ščot'ovo	83	48.09 N	39.04 E
Scotrun	210	41.04 N	75.19 W
Scotsburn	186	45.39 N	62.51 W
Scotstown	206	45.32 N	71.17 W
Scott, Sk., Can.	184	52.23 N	108.50 W
Scott, Ms., U.S.	194	33.35 N	91.04 W
Scott, Oh., U.S.	216	40.59 N	84.35 W
Scott □ [6], Il., U.S.	219	39.38 N	90.27 W
Scott □ [6], In., U.S.	218	38.41 N	85.46 W
Scott □ [6], Ky., U.S.	218	38.18 N	84.35 W
Scott ≃	204	41.48 N	123.02 W
Scott, Cape >	182	50.47 N	128.26 W
Scott, Mount ∧, Ok., U.S.	196	34.44 N	98.32 W
Scott, Mount ∧, Or., U.S.	202	42.56 N	122.01 W
Scott Air Force Base ■	219	38.32 N	89.52 W
Scott Base ♥ [3]	9	77.50 S	166.25 E
Scottburgh	158	30.19 S	30.40 E
Scott City, Ks., U.S.	198	38.28 N	100.54 W
Scott City, Mo., U.S.	194	37.13 N	89.31 W
Scott Cove c	276	41.03 N	73.28 W
Scott Creek ≃	226	37.02 N	122.13 W
Scottdale, Mi., U.S.	216	42.03 N	86.27 W
Scottdale, Pa., U.S.	214	40.06 N	79.35 W
Scotter	44	53.29 N	0.40 W
Scott Glacier ⍓, Ant.	9	66.15 S	100.05 E
Scott Glacier ⍓, Ant.	9	85.45 S	153.00 W
Scott Haven	279b	40.15 N	79.47 W
Scott Island I	212	44.36 N	76.20 W
Scott Islands II	182	50.48 N	128.40 W
Scott Lake	220	25.56 N	80.13 W
Scott Mountain ∧	202	44.11 N	115.47 W
Scott Peak ∧	202	44.21 N	112.50 W
Scott Reef ✤ [2]	160	14.00 S	121.50 E
Scott Run ≃	284c	38.58 N	77.12 W
Scotts	216	42.11 N	85.24 W
Scottsbluff	198	41.52 N	103.40 W
Scotts Bluff National Monument ♠	198	41.49 N	103.41 W
Scottsboro	194	34.40 N	86.02 W
Scottsburg, In., U.S.	218	38.41 N	85.46 W
Scottsburg, N.Y., U.S.	210	42.40 N	77.43 W
Scottsdale, Austl.	166	41.10 S	147.31 E
Scottsdale, Az., U.S.	200	33.30 N	111.53 W
Scotts Flat Reservoir ⊜ [1]	226	39.17 N	120.55 W
Scotts Head >	240d	15.13 N	61.23 W
Scotts Hill	194	35.31 N	88.15 W
Scotts Level Branch ≃	284b	39.22 N	76.45 W
Scottsmoor	220	28.46 N	80.53 W
Scotts Valley	226	37.03 N	122.00 W
Scottsville, Ky., U.S.	194	36.45 N	86.11 W
Scottsville, N.Y., U.S.	210	43.01 N	77.44 W
Scott Township	279b	40.32 N	80.11 W
Scottville, Il., U.S.	219	39.29 N	90.06 W
Scottville, Mi., U.S.	190	43.57 N	86.16 W
Scourie	46	58.20 N	5.08 W
Scout Lake	184	49.22 N	106.00 W
Scrabster	46	58.37 N	3.32 W
Scranton, Ia., U.S.	198	42.01 N	94.32 W
Scranton, N.Y., U.S.	210	42.44 N	78.50 W
Scranton, N.D., U.S.	198	46.08 N	103.08 W
Scranton, Pa., U.S.	210	41.24 N	75.39 W
Scremerston	44	55.44 N	1.59 W
Screven	192	31.29 N	82.01 W
Screw ≃	164	3.55 S	142.50 E
Scribner	198	41.40 N	96.39 W
Scridain, Loch c	46	56.21 N	6.07 W
Scripps Institution of Oceanography ♥ [3]	228	32.52 N	117.15 W
Scrivia ≃	62	45.03 N	8.54 E
Scroggins	222	32.58 N	95.11 W
Scrooby	44	53.25 N	1.01 W
Scrub Island I	240m	18.28 N	64.31 W
Ščučin	76	53.36 N	24.45 E
Ščučinsk	86	52.56 N	70.12 E
Ščučje, S.S.S.R.	78	51.45 N	40.29 E
Ščučje, S.S.S.R.	80	51.46 N	40.29 E
Ščučje, S.S.S.R.	86	55.17 N	63.59 E
Ščučje Ozero	86	56.28 N	56.38 E
Scugog ≃	212	44.24 N	78.45 W
Scugog, Lake ⊜	212	44.10 N	78.51 W
Scugog Indian Reserve ◆ [4]	212	44.11 N	78.54 W
Scugog Island I	212	44.10 N	78.53 W
Ščukino	82	54.28 N	37.01 E
Scunthorpe	44	53.36 N	0.38 W
Scuol (Schuls)	58	46.48 N	10.18 E
Scuppernong ≃	216	42.54 N	88.42 W
Scurcola Marsicana	66	42.03 N	13.20 E
Ščurovo	82	55.03 N	38.49 E
Scurrival Point >	46	57.04 N	7.31 W
Scurry	222	32.31 N	96.23 W
Scutari → Shkodër	38	42.05 N	19.30 E
Scutari, Lake ⊜	38	42.12 N	19.18 E
Sé ◆ [8]	287b	23.33 S	46.37 W
Seabeck	224	47.38 N	122.51 W
Sea Bird Island I	224	49.15 N	121.45 W
Seabird Island Indian Reserve ◆ [4]	182	49.17 N	121.42 W
Seaboard	192	36.29 N	77.26 W
Sea Bright	276	40.21 N	73.58 W
Seabrook, Md., U.S.	284c	38.58 N	76.50 W
Seabrook, N.J., U.S.	208	39.30 N	75.13 W
Seabrook, Tx., U.S.	222	29.33 N	95.01 W
Seabrook, Lake ⊜	162	30.56 S	119.40 E
Sea Cliff	210	40.50 N	73.38 W
Seacock Swamp ≃	208	36.48 N	76.51 W
Seacombe	262	53.25 N	3.01 W
Sea Dog Island I	276	40.36 N	73.35 W
Seadrift	196	28.30 N	96.47 W
Seaford, Eng., U.K.	42	50.46 N	0.06 E
Seaford, De., U.S.	208	38.38 N	75.36 W
Seaford, N.Y., U.S.	276	40.39 N	73.29 W
Seaford, Va., U.S.	208	37.11 N	76.26 W
Seaford Creek ≃	276	40.38 N	73.29 W
Seaforth, Austl.	274a	33.48 S	151.15 E
Seaforth, On., Can.	190	43.33 N	81.24 W
Seaforth, Eng., U.K.	262	53.28 N	3.01 W
Seaforth, Loch c	46	57.54 N	6.40 W
Seafox Seamount ✤ [3]	14	30.30 S	172.45 W
Seager Wheeler Lake ⊜	184	54.27 N	103.30 W
Seagoville	222	32.38 N	96.32 W
Seagraves	196	32.56 N	102.33 W
Seaham	44	54.52 N	1.21 W
Seaholme	274b	37.52 S	144.50 E
Seahorse Breakers ✤ [2]	112	5.30 N	112.37 E
Seahorse Point >	176	63.47 N	80.09 W
Seahouses	44	55.35 N	1.38 W
Seahurst	224	47.28 N	122.22 W
Sea Island I	224	49.12 N	123.10 W
Sea Islands II	192	31.20 N	81.20 W
Sea Isle City	208	39.09 N	74.41 W
Seal	260	51.17 N	0.14 E
Seal ≃	176	59.04 N	94.48 W
Seal, Cape >	158	34.07 S	23.25 E
Sea Lake	166	35.30 S	142.51 E
Sealand	262	53.12 N	2.58 W
Sealark Channel ⊔	175e	9.18 S	160.20 E
Seal Bay c	9	71.40 S	12.25 W
Seal Beach	228	33.44 N	118.06 W
Seal Beach National Wildlife Refuge ◆ [4]	280	33.45 N	118.03 W
Seal Cove, N.B., Can.	186	44.39 N	66.51 W
Seal Cove, Nf., Can.	186	49.56 N	56.23 W
Sealdah Railroad Station ◆ [5]	272b	22.34 N	88.23 E
Seale	194	32.17 N	85.10 W
Sealevel	192	34.51 N	76.23 W
Seal Island I	186	43.25 N	66.01 W
Seal Islands II	282	38.03 N	122.03 W
Seal Lake ⊜	176	54.18 N	61.40 W
Seal Rocks II [1]	282	37.47 N	122.31 W
Sealston	208	38.15 N	77.19 W
Sealy	222	29.46 N	96.09 W
Seaman	218	38.56 N	83.34 W
Seamer	44	54.14 N	0.26 W
Seanor	214	40.13 N	78.54 W
Seara	252	27.07 S	52.17 W
Searchlight	204	35.27 N	114.55 W
Searcy	194	35.15 N	91.44 W
Searles Lake ⊜	204	35.43 N	117.20 W
Sears Lake ⊜	281	42.35 N	83.39 W
Searsport	188	44.27 N	68.55 W
Sears Tower ♥	278	41.53 N	87.38 W
Searsville Lake ⊜	282	37.24 N	122.14 W
Seascale	44	54.24 N	3.29 W
Seashore State Park ♠	208	36.54 N	76.02 W
Seaside, Ca., U.S.	226	36.36 N	121.51 W
Seaside, Or., U.S.	224	45.59 N	123.55 W
Seaside Park	208	39.55 N	74.04 W
Seaside Park ♠	276	41.10 N	73.12 W
Seaton, Eng., U.K.	42	50.43 N	3.05 W
Seaton, Eng., U.K.	44	54.41 N	3.33 W
Seaton, Eng., U.K.	44	53.54 N	0.14 W
Seaton ≃	42	50.22 N	4.22 W
Seaton Delaval	44	55.04 N	1.31 W
Seaton Sluice	44	55.05 N	1.28 W
Seat Pleasant	284c	38.53 N	76.54 W
Seattle	224	47.36 N	122.19 W
Seattle, Mount ∧	180	60.06 N	139.11 W
Seattle Heights	224	47.48 N	122.20 W
Seattle-Tacoma International Airport ⊠	224	47.27 N	122.18 W
Seatuck National Wildlife Refuge ◆ [4]	276	40.43 N	73.13 W
Seaview, Eng., U.K.	42	50.43 N	1.06 W
Sea View, Ma., U.S.	283	42.08 N	70.42 W
Seaview, N.Y., U.S.	276	40.39 N	73.09 W
Seaview, Wa., U.S.	224	46.20 N	124.03 W
Seaward Kaikoura Range ⩘	172	42.14 S	173.39 E
Seaward Roads ⊔	174g	28.13 N	177.25 W
Seawell Airport ⊠	241g	13.04 N	59.29 W
Sea World ♠, Fl., U.S.	220	28.25 N	81.28 W
Sea World ♠, Oh., U.S.	214	41.21 N	81.23 W
Seba	112	10.29 S	121.50 E
Sébaco	236	12.51 N	86.06 W
Sebago Lake ⊜	188	43.50 N	70.35 W
Se Bai ≃	110	15.13 N	104.47 E
Sebakor, Teluk c	164	3.35 S	132.50 E
Sebakung	112	1.37 S	116.26 E
Šebalin	80	47.22 N	43.36 E
Šebalino, S.S.S.R.	80	48.16 N	43.21 E
Šebalino, S.S.S.R.	86	51.17 N	85.40 E
Sebanga	114	1.24 N	101.10 E
Sebangan, Teluk c	112	3.15 S	113.30 E
Sebangka, Pulau I	112	0.07 N	104.36 E
Sébaou, Oued ≃	34	36.55 N	3.55 E
Sebarok, Pulau I	271c	1.13 N	103.48 E
Sebastian, Fl., U.S.	220	27.46 N	80.29 W
Sebastian, Tx., U.S.	196	26.20 N	97.47 W
Sebastian, Cape >	202	42.19 N	124.26 W
Sebastian Inlet c	220	27.51 N	80.26 W
Sebastián Vizcaíno, Bahía c	232	28.00 N	114.30 W
Sebastião de Lacerda	256	22.17 S	43.35 W
Sebastopol, Austl.	169	37.36 S	143.51 E
Sebastopol, Ca., U.S.	204	38.24 N	122.49 W
Sebastopol, Ms., U.S.	194	32.34 N	89.20 W
Sebatik, Pulau I	112	4.10 N	117.45 E
Sebba	150	13.26 N	0.32 E
Sebderat	144	15.26 N	36.40 E
Sébé ≃	152	1.02 S	13.06 E
Sebec Lake ⊜	188	45.18 N	69.18 W
Sebeka	198	46.38 N	95.05 W
Šebekino	78	50.25 N	36.56 E
Sébékoro	150	12.57 N	8.59 W
Šebelinka	78	49.27 N	36.30 E
Seben	130	40.24 N	31.34 E
Sebenico → Šibenik	36	43.44 N	15.54 E
Sebera, Punta ∧	71	39.03 N	8.50 E
Seberi	252	27.29 S	53.24 W
Seberida	112	0.43 S	102.31 E
Šeberta	88	54.40 N	99.54 E
Sebeș	38	45.58 N	23.34 E
Sebesi, Pulau I	115a	5.57 S	105.30 E
Sebes Körös (Crișul Repede) ≃	38	46.55 N	20.59 E
Sebewaing	190	43.43 N	83.27 W
Sebež	76	56.17 N	28.29 E
Sebille Manor	281	42.39 N	82.49 W
Şebinkarahisar	130	40.18 N	38.26 E
Sebiș	38	46.23 N	22.08 E
Sebnitz	54	50.58 N	14.16 E
Sebou, Oued ≃	148	34.15 N	6.40 W
Sebree	194	37.36 N	87.31 W
Sebrell	208	36.47 N	77.07 W
Sebring, Fl., U.S.	220	27.29 N	81.26 W
Sebring, Oh., U.S.	214	40.55 N	81.01 W
Sebringville	212	43.24 N	81.04 W
Sebuku	112	4.03 N	116.56 E
Sebuku, Pulau I, Indon.	112	3.30 S	116.22 E
Sebuku, Pulau I, Indon.	115a	5.53 S	105.31 E
Sebuku, Teluk c	112	4.00 N	118.26 E
Šebunino	89	46.27 N	141.51 E
Seč	60	49.36 N	13.30 E
Sêca, Ilha I	287a	22.50 S	43.11 W
Secane	285	39.55 N	75.18 W
Secang	115a	7.23 S	110.15 E
Secas, Islas II	236	7.58 N	82.02 W
Secaucus	276	40.47 N	74.03 W
Secchia ≃	64	45.04 N	11.00 E
Sečenovo	80	55.13 N	45.54 E
Secesh ≃	202	45.02 N	115.43 W
Séchault	56	49.16 N	4.44 E
Sechelt	182	49.28 N	123.45 W
Šechman'	76	52.32 N	40.29 E
Sechura	248	5.33 S	80.51 W
Sechura, Bahía de c	248	5.42 S	81.00 W
Sechura, Desierto de ◆ [2]	248	5.50 S	80.40 W
Seckach	56	49.26 N	9.20 E
Seckau	61	47.16 N	14.47 E
Seckau ♥ [1]	61	47.16 N	14.47 E
Seckauer Alpen ⩘	61	47.20 N	14.40 E
Seckauer Zinken ∧	61	47.20 N	14.44 E
Seclantas	252	25.18 S	66.15 W
Seclin	50	50.33 N	3.02 E
Seco ≃, Arg.	252	23.08 S	63.57 W
Seco ≃, Arg.	254	48.34 S	67.02 W
Seco ≃, Esp.	266d	41.30 N	2.09 E
Seco, Arroyo ≃, Ca., U.S.	226	36.25 N	121.20 W
Seco, Arroyo ≃, Ca., U.S.	280	34.05 N	118.13 W
Seco Creek ≃, N.M., U.S.	200	32.59 N	107.18 W
Seco Creek ≃, Tx., U.S.	196	29.02 N	99.08 W
Seco Island I	116	11.19 N	121.40 E
Second ≃	276	40.47 N	74.09 W
Second Cliff ⩪ [4]	283	42.12 N	70.43 W
Second Han-gang Bridge ◆ [5]	271b	37.34 N	126.54 E
Second Herring Brook ≃	283	42.09 N	70.47 W
Second Lake ⊜	206	45.09 N	71.10 W
Second Mountain ∧	208	40.33 N	76.30 W
Second San Diego Aqueduct ≊ [1]	228	32.41 N	117.01 W
Second Swamp ≃	208	37.08 N	77.12 W
Second Valley	168b	35.33 S	138.14 E
Second Watchung Mountain ∧	276	40.55 N	74.13 W
Sečovce	30	48.43 N	21.40 E
Sečovská Polianka	30	48.47 N	21.42 E
Secretário, Ribeirão do ≃	256	22.14 S	43.25 W
Secretary	208	38.36 N	75.56 W
Secretary Island I	172	45.15 S	166.55 E
Section	194	34.34 N	85.59 W
Secubun Island I	116	5.06 N	120.18 E
Sécure ≃	248	15.10 S	64.52 W
Security	198	38.45 N	104.44 W
Security Square ◆ [9]	284b	39.19 N	76.45 W
Séd ≃	30	47.00 N	18.31 E
Seda, S.S.S.R.	76	56.10 N	22.04 E
Seda, S.S.S.R.	76	57.40 N	25.46 E
Seda, Zhg.	102	32.20 N	100.41 E
Seda ≃	76	57.47 N	25.15 E
Sedah	112	10.46 S	123.12 E
Sedalia, Ab., Can.	184	51.41 N	110.40 W
Sedalia, In., U.S.	216	40.25 N	86.31 W
Sedalia, Mo., U.S.	194	38.42 N	93.13 W
Sedalia, Oh., U.S.	218	39.44 N	83.29 W
Sedan, Austl.	168b	34.35 S	139.18 E
Sedan, Fr.	56	49.42 N	4.57 E
Sedan, Ks., U.S.	198	37.07 N	96.11 W
Sedanka, Cape >	180	53.49 N	166.06 W
Sedanka Island I	180	53.50 N	166.10 W
Sedano	34	42.43 N	3.45 W
Sedano, Tanjung >	115a	7.49 S	114.27 E
Sedanovo	88	56.58 N	101.22 E
Sedari, Tanjung >	115a	5.57 S	107.18 E
Sedayu	115a	6.59 S	112.33 E
Sedbergh	44	54.20 N	2.31 W
Sedco Hills	228	33.39 N	117.24 W
Seddin	54	52.16 N	13.01 E
Seddin-Berg ∧ [2]	264a	52.24 N	13.40 E
Seddinsee ⊜	264a	52.23 N	13.41 E
Seddon	172	41.40 S	174.05 E
Seddonville	172	41.33 S	171.59 E
Sedé Boqér	132	30.52 N	34.47 E
Sedel'nikovo	86	56.57 N	75.18 E
Séderon	62	44.12 N	5.32 E
Sederot	132	31.31 N	34.35 E

Symbols in the index entries represent the broad categories identified in the key at the right. Symbols with superior numbers (⩘ [1]) identify subcategories (see complete key on page *I · 1)*.

Symbole im Register stellen die rechts im Schlüssel erklärten Kategorien dar. Symbole mit hochgestellten Ziffern (⩘ [1]) bezeichnen Unterabteilungen einer Kategorie (vgl. vollständiger Schlüssel auf Seite *I · 1)*.

Los símbolos incluídos en el texto del índice representan las grandes categorias identificadas con la clave a la derecha. Los símbolos con numeros en su parte superior (⩘ [1]) identifican las subcategorías (véase la clave completa en la página *I · 1)*.

Les symboles de l'index représentent les catégories indiquées dans la légende à droite. Les symboles suivis d'un indice (⩘ [1]) représentent des sous-catégories (voir légende complète à la page *I · 1)*.

Os símbolos incluídos no texto do índice representam as grandes categorias identificadas com a chave à direita. Os símbolos com números em sua parte superior (⩘ [1]) identificam as subcategorias (veja-se a chave completa à página *I · 1)*.

	English	Deutsch	Español	Français	Português
∧	Mountain	Berg	Montaña	Montagne	Montanha
⩘	Mountains	Gebirge	Montañas	Montagnes	Montanhas
)(	Pass	Paß	Paso	Col	Passo
V	Valley, Canyon	Tal, Cañon	Valle, Cañón	Vallée, Canyon	Vale, Canhão
≃	Plain	Ebene	Llano	Plaine	Planície
>	Cape	Kap	Cabo	Cap	Cabo
I	Island	Insel	Isla	Île	Ilha
II	Islands	Inseln	Islas	Îles	Ilhas
⩪	Other Topographic Features	Andere Topographische Objekte	Otros Elementos Topográficos	Autres données topographiques	Outros acidentes topográficos

ESPAÑOL Nombre / FRANÇAIS Nom / PORTUGUÊS Nome	Página / Page / Página	Lat.°′	Long.°′ W = Oeste / W = Ouest
Sedgefield, Eng., U.K.	44	54.39 N	1.26 W
Sedgefield, N.J., U.S.	276	40.51 N	74.28 W
Sedgefield, N.C., U.S.	192	35.10 N	80.51 W
Sedge Island I	276	40.21 N	73.59 W
Sedgewick	182	52.46 N	111.41 W
Sedgwick, Co., U.S.	198	40.56 N	102.31 W
Sedgwick, Ks., U.S.	198	37.55 N	97.25 W
Sedgwick, Mount ∧	200	35.11 N	108.06 W
Sédhiou	150	12.44 N	15.33 W
Sedico	64	46.06 N	12.06 E
Sedilo	71	40.10 N	8.55 E
Sedini	71	40.51 N	8.49 E
Sedlčany	30	49.40 N	14.26 E
Sedley	208	36.46 N	76.59 W
Sedlice	60	49.23 N	13.56 E
Sedlitz	54	51.33 N	14.03 E
Sedlo ∧	54	50.36 N	14.17 E
Sedn'ov	78	51.39 N	31.34 E
Šedok	84	44.13 N	40.52 E
Sedom (Sodom) ⊥	132	31.04 N	35.23 E
Sedona	200	34.52 N	111.45 W
Sedot Yam	132	32.29 N	34.53 E
Sedova, pik ∧	72	73.29 N	54.58 E
Sedovo	83	47.03 N	38.10 E
Sedovo-Vasiljevka	83	47.14 N	38.08 E
Sedrata	36	36.08 N	7.32 E
Sedriano	62	45.29 N	8.58 E
Sedrina	62	45.47 N	9.38 E
Sedro Woolley	224	48.30 N	122.14 W
Sedrun	58	46.41 N	8.46 E
Sedtim	24	66.25 N	56.20 E
Šeduva	76	55.46 N	23.46 E
Sędziszów	30	50.04 N	21.41 E
See, Öst.	58	47.05 N	10.28 E
See, Öst.	64	47.48 N	13.27 E
Seebad Ahlbeck	54	53.56 N	14.11 E
Seebad Bansin	54	53.57 N	14.07 E
Seebad Heringsdorf	54	53.56 N	14.08 E
Seeberg, D.D.R.	264a	52.33 N	13.41 E
Seeberg, Schw.	58	47.09 N	7.40 E
Seebergsattel)(	61	47.38 N	15.18 E
Seeber Lake ⊜	184	53.52 N	93.03 W
Seeboden	64	46.49 N	13.30 E
Seebruck	64	47.56 N	12.28 E
Seebrugg	58	47.49 N	8.13 E
Seeburg, D.D.R.	264a	52.31 N	13.07 E
Seeburg → Jeziorany, Pol.	30	53.58 N	20.46 E
Seefeld, B.R.D.	52	53.27 N	8.21 E
Seefeld, D.D.R.	54	52.37 N	13.40 E
Seefeld in Tirol	64	47.20 N	11.11 E
Seefin ∧[2]	48	52.18 N	8.32 W
Seeg	58	47.38 N	10.36 E
Seege ≃	54	53.04 N	11.23 E
Seehausen, D.D.R.	54	52.53 N	11.45 E
Seehausen, D.D.R.	54	52.06 N	11.17 E
Seeheim	156	26.50 S	17.45 E
Seeheim-Jugenheim	56	49.45 N	8.38 E
Seehof	264a	52.24 N	13.17 E
Seeis	156	22.29 S	17.39 E
Seekaskootch Indian Reserve ✦[4]	184	53.43 N	109.55 W
Seekoegat	158	33.03 S	22.31 E
Seekoei ≃	158	30.18 S	25.01 E
Seekonk	207	41.48 N	71.20 W
Seelbach	58	48.18 N	7.56 E
Seeley Lake	202	47.10 N	113.29 W
Seeleys Bay	212	44.29 N	76.14 W
Seelingstädt	54	50.46 N	12.14 E
Seelow	54	52.32 N	14.23 E
Seelyville, In., U.S.	194	39.29 N	87.16 W
Seelyville, Pa., U.S.	210	41.35 N	75.17 W
Seelze	52	52.24 N	9.35 E
Seemade	144	7.10 N	48.36 E
Seemalik Butte ∧	180	60.09 N	167.08 W
Seemenbach ≃	56	50.17 N	8.59 E
Seemore Downs	162	30.42 S	125.15 E
Seen	58	47.29 N	8.46 E
Seengen	58	47.19 N	8.13 E
Seeon	64	47.58 N	12.26 E
Seer Green	260	51.37 N	0.36 W
Seergu	102	32.00 N	103.33 E
Seerhausen	54	51.16 N	13.15 E
Sées	50	48.36 N	0.10 E
Seesen	52	51.53 N	10.10 E
Seeshaupt	64	47.49 N	11.18 E
Seest	41	55.29 N	9.27 E
Seetal	61	47.09 N	13.57 E
Seetaler Alpen ⋏	61	47.05 N	14.35 E
Seevetal	52	53.23 N	9.59 E
Seewalchen am Attersee	64	47.57 N	13.35 E
Seewiesen	61	47.37 N	15.16 E
Seewinkel ✦[1]	61	47.48 N	16.49 E
Seewis	58	47.00 N	9.32 E
Séez	62	45.37 N	6.48 E
Seez ≃	58	47.07 N	9.18 E
Şefaatli	130	39.31 N	34.46 E
Sefadu	150	8.39 N	10.59 W
Sefar ⊥	148	24.27 N	9.16 E
Sefare	156	23.02 S	27.28 E
Seferihisar	130	38.11 N	26.51 E
Séféto	150	14.08 N	9.49 W
Seffern	56	50.04 N	6.30 E
Seffner	220	27.59 N	82.17 W
Sefīd ≃	128	37.26 N	49.55 E
Sefīd Ābeh	128	30.56 N	60.35 E
Sefrou	148	33.50 N	4.50 W
Sefton, N.Z.	172	43.15 S	172.40 E
Sefton, Eng., U.K.	262	53.30 N	2.58 W
Sefton □[8]	262	53.34 N	3.14 W
Sefton, Mount ∧	172	43.41 S	170.03 E
Sefton Park ♦	262	53.23 N	2.56 W
Segag	144	7.40 N	42.50 E
Segaliud ≃	116	5.43 N	117.55 E
Segama ≃	112	5.27 N	118.48 E
Segamat	114	2.30 N	102.49 E
Segang	100	31.58 N	114.18 E
Segangane	34	35.09 N	3.00 W
Şegarcea	38	44.06 N	23.45 E
Šegarka ≃	86	57.16 N	84.05 E
Segbana	150	10.56 N	3.42 E
Segbwema	150	8.00 N	10.57 W
Segen ≃	144	4.49 N	36.57 E
Segera	164	8.15 S	143.30 E
Segeri	112	4.39 S	119.33 E
Segesta ⊥	70	37.56 N	12.50 E
Segesvár → Sighișoara	38	46.13 N	24.48 E
Segeža	24	63.44 N	34.19 E
Seggiano	66	42.56 N	11.33 E
Seggueur, Oued es V	148	31.39 N	2.26 E
Šegmas	24	64.43 N	49.14 E
Segni	66	41.41 N	13.01 E
Segno	222	30.35 N	94.41 W
Segorbe	34	39.51 N	0.29 W
Ségou	150	13.27 N	6.16 W
Ségou □[4]	150	14.00 N	5.40 E
Šegovary	24	62.23 N	42.57 E
Segovia, Col.	246	7.07 N	74.42 W
Segovia, Esp.	34	40.57 N	4.07 W
Segozero, ozero ⊜	24	63.18 N	33.45 E
Segrate	266b	45.29 N	9.19 E
Segré	32	47.41 N	0.53 W
Segre ≃	34	41.40 N	0.43 E
Seguam Island I	180	52.17 N	172.30 W
Seguam Pass ʯ	180	52.08 N	172.45 W
Séguédine	146	20.12 N	12.59 E
Séguéla, C. Iv.	150	7.57 N	6.40 W
Séguéla, Mali	150	14.07 N	6.44 W
Séguélon	150	9.25 N	7.09 W
Séguénéga	150	13.27 N	1.58 W
Seguí	252	31.57 S	60.08 W
Seguin	196	29.34 N	97.57 W
Seguin ≃	212	45.21 N	80.01 W
Seguine Point ›	276	40.31 N	74.12 W
Segula Island I	181a	52.01 N	178.07 E
Segundo	198	37.07 N	104.45 W
Segundo ≃	252	31.21 S	62.59 W
Seguntur	112	1.54 N	117.47 E
Segura	34	39.50 N	6.59 W
Segura ≃	34	38.06 N	0.38 W
Segura, Sierra de ⋏	34	38.00 N	2.43 W
Sehāni Kalān	272a	28.41 N	77.25 E
Sehāni Khurd	272a	28.42 N	77.25 E
Sehāra Bāzār	126	23.06 N	87.49 E
Sehithwa	156	20.23 S	22.45 E
Sehlabathebe	158	29.53 S	29.05 E
Sehlabathebe National Park ♦	158	29.53 S	29.06 E
Sehma	54	50.32 N	13.00 E
Sehnde	52	52.18 N	9.57 E
Sehnkwehn	150	5.13 N	9.12 W
Sehnkwehn ≃	150	5.12 N	9.21 W
Sehore	124	23.12 N	77.05 E
Sehwān	120	26.26 N	67.52 E
Sehyŏn-ni	98	38.20 N	127.41 E
Seia	34	40.25 N	7.42 W
Seibert	198	39.18 N	102.52 W
Seibu	268	35.50 N	139.22 E
Seiches-sur-le-Loir	32	47.35 N	0.22 W
Seidan	96	34.19 N	134.45 E
Seidersville	210	40.35 N	75.23 W
Seiersberg	61	47.01 N	15.24 E
Seiffen	54	50.39 N	13.26 E
Seifhennersdorf	54	50.56 N	14.36 E
Seignelay	50	47.54 N	3.36 E
Seigneurial, Lac ⊜	275a	45.33 N	73.20 W
Seika	270	34.46 N	135.48 E
Seikpyu	110	20.55 N	94.47 E
Seil I	46	56.18 N	5.39 W
Seiland I	24	70.25 N	23.15 E
Seilhac	32	45.22 N	1.42 E
Seiling	196	36.08 N	98.55 W
Seillans	62	43.38 N	6.38 E
Seille ≃, Fr.	56	49.07 N	6.11 E
Seille ≃, Fr.	58	46.31 N	4.56 E
Seilo	140	12.20 N	23.50 E
Seim → Sejm ≃	78	51.27 N	32.34 E
Sein, Île de I	32	48.02 N	4.51 W
Seinaiji	94	35.30 N	137.42 E
Seinäjoki	26	62.47 N	22.50 E
Seine □[5]	50	48.50 N	2.10 E
Seine ≃, Mb., Can.	184	49.54 N	97.07 W
Seine ≃, On., Can.	190	48.40 N	92.49 W
Seine ≃, Fr.	32	49.26 N	0.26 E
Seine, Baie de la ⊂	32	49.30 N	0.30 W
Seine-et-Marne □[5]	50	48.30 N	3.00 E
Seine-et-Oise □[5]	50	48.45 N	2.00 E
Seine-Maritime □[5]	50	49.45 N	1.00 E
Seine-Port	50	48.33 N	2.33 E
Seine-Saint-Denis □[5]	261	48.55 N	2.30 E
Seip Mound State Memorial ⊥	218	39.15 N	83.13 W
Seipstown	208	40.35 N	75.40 W
Seis de Septiembre → Morón	258	34.39 S	58.37 W
Seishin → Ch'ŏngjin	98	41.47 N	129.50 E
Seitenstetten	61	48.02 N	14.39 E
Seitovka	80	46.43 N	48.03 E
Seitsemisen kansallispuisto ♦	26	61.58 N	23.20 E
Seiwa	94	34.29 N	136.30 E
Seixal	34	38.38 N	9.06 W
Seiz	61	47.23 N	14.55 E
Seize Îles, Lac des ⊜	206	45.54 N	74.28 W
Sejaka	112	3.34 S	116.12 E
Sejerø I	41	55.53 N	11.09 E
Sejerø Bugt ⊂	41	55.50 N	11.15 E
Sejm ≃	78	51.27 N	32.34 E
Sejmčan	74	62.53 N	152.26 E
Šejno	80	53.22 N	43.12 E
Sejny	30	54.07 N	23.20 E
Sejorong	115b	9.02 S	116.48 E
Sejs	41	56.09 N	9.36 E
Sekači	80	50.30 N	43.37 E
Sekadau	112	0.01 S	110.54 E
Sekake	158	29.58 S	28.27 E
Sekampung ≃	115a	5.36 S	105.50 E
Sekayam ≃	112	0.07 N	110.38 E
Sekayu	112	2.51 S	103.51 E
Seke, Ityo.	144	9.56 N	38.19 E
Seke, Tan.	154	3.20 S	33.31 E
Seke-Banza	152	5.20 S	13.16 E
Sekeladi	112	2.38 S	102.14 E
Sekenke	154	4.16 S	34.10 E
Şekerli	130	37.33 N	39.22 E
Seki, Nihon	94	35.29 N	136.55 E
Seki, Nihon	94	34.51 N	136.24 E
Šeki (Nucha), S.S.S.R.	84	41.12 N	47.12 E
Seki, Tür.	130	36.24 N	29.13 E
Sekidō-san ∧	94	36.58 N	136.59 E
Sekigahara	94	35.22 N	136.28 E
Sekigane	96	35.22 N	133.46 E
Sekijō	94	36.14 N	139.55 E
Sekima	112	1.41 S	111.31 E
Sekinomiya	96	35.22 N	134.38 E
Sekiu	224	48.15 N	124.18 W
Sekiya	270	34.27 N	135.42 E
Sekiyado	94	36.06 N	139.47 E
Seki-zaki ›	96	33.15 N	131.54 E
Sekoma	156	24.41 S	23.50 E
Sekondi-Takoradi	150	4.59 N	1.43 W
Sekota	144	12.38 N	39.03 E
Sekpiegu	150	9.33 N	0.02 W
Sekretaris ≃	269e	6.10 S	106.47 E
Şekretarka	80	52.36 N	44.11 E
Šekšema	80	58.22 N	45.11 E
Šeksna	76	59.13 N	38.30 E
Sekudai	114	1.32 N	103.40 E
Sela ≃[1]	126	21.54 N	89.39 E
Sela, Ponta da ›	256	23.54 S	45.27 W
Šelabolicha	86	53.25 N	82.37 E
Sela Dingay	144	9.59 N	39.33 E
Šelagskij, mys ›	74	70.06 N	170.26 E
Selah	202	46.39 N	120.31 W
Selai ≃	114	2.13 N	103.26 E
Šelajevo	88	56.56 N	97.42 E
Selama	114	5.13 N	100.42 E
Šelanger	80	56.13 N	48.16 E
Selangor □[3]	114	3.20 N	101.30 E
Selangor ≃	114	3.20 N	101.15 E
Selaön I	40	59.24 N	17.12 E
Selaphum	110	16.02 N	103.57 E
Selargius	71	39.16 N	9.10 E
Selaru, Pulau I	164	8.09 S	131.00 E
Selatan, Tanjung ›	112	4.10 S	114.38 E
Sel'atin	78	47.53 N	25.12 E
Selatpanjang	114	1.00 N	102.43 E
Selawik	180	66.37 N	160.03 W
Selawik ≃	180	66.36 N	160.20 W
Selawik Lake ⊜	180	66.30 N	160.40 W
Selayar, Pulau I	112	6.05 S	120.30 E
Selayar, Selat ʯ	112	5.42 S	120.28 E
Selb	54	50.10 N	12.08 E
Selbeck ✦[8]	263	51.22 N	6.52 E
Selbecke ✦[8]	263	51.20 N	7.28 E
Selbitz	54	50.19 N	11.44 E
Selborne	42	51.06 N	0.56 W
Selbu	26	63.13 N	11.02 E
Selbusjøen ⊜	26	63.14 N	10.54 E
Selby, Austl.	274b	37.55 S	145.22 E
Selby, Eng., U.K.	44	53.48 N	1.04 W
Selby, S.D., U.S.	198	45.30 N	100.01 W
Selby ✦[8]	273d	26.13 S	28.02 E
Selbyville	208	38.27 N	75.13 W
Selchow	264a	52.21 N	13.28 E
Sel'co, S.S.S.R.	24	63.18 N	41.22 E
Sel'co, S.S.S.R.	76	53.22 N	34.06 E
Selcourt	273d	26.18 S	28.27 E
Selčuga ≃	89	49.42 N	133.20 E
Selçuk	130	37.56 N	27.22 E
Sel'cy, S.S.S.R.	76	57.57 N	35.59 E
Sel'cy, S.S.S.R.	265a	59.57 N	30.43 E
Selden, Ks., U.S.	198	39.32 N	100.34 W
Selden, N.Y., U.S.	210	40.51 N	73.02 W
Seldovia	180	59.27 N	151.43 W
Sele ≃	68	40.29 N	14.56 E
Sele, Piana del ≚	68	40.33 N	14.57 E
Sele, Selat ʯ	164	1.10 S	131.05 E
Sele, Tanjung ›	164	1.26 S	130.55 E
Selebi Phikwe	156	22.00 S	27.50 E
Selec	76	52.33 N	33.35 E
Şelec-Cholopejev	76	53.23 N	30.24 E
Šelechov	88	52.13 N	104.08 E
Selečn'a	76	52.23 N	34.23 E
Selection Park	273d	26.18 S	28.27 E
Selegas	71	39.34 N	9.06 E
Selemadeg	115b	8.29 S	115.02 E
Selembao	273b	4.22 S	15.17 E
Selemdža ≃	89	51.42 N	128.53 E
Şelemdžinsk	89	52.36 N	131.08 E
Šelemeti	80	57.27 N	48.07 E
Selendi	130	38.45 N	28.53 E
Selenduma	88	50.55 N	106.10 E
Selenga (Selenge) ≃	88	52.16 N	106.16 E
Selenge, Mong.	88	49.25 N	103.59 E
Selenge, Zaïre	152	1.58 S	18.11 E
Selenge □[4]	88	49.30 N	106.30 E
Selenge (Selenga) ≃	88	52.16 N	106.16 E
Selenginsk	88	52.06 N	107.01 E
Selenicë	38	40.32 N	19.38 E
Selenn'ach ≃	74	67.48 N	144.54 E
Selent	54	54.17 N	10.26 E
Selenter See ⊜	54	54.17 N	10.28 E
Sélestat (Schlettstadt)	58	48.16 N	7.27 E
Seletar ≃	271c	1.25 N	103.52 E
Seletar, Pulau I	271c	1.27 N	103.52 E
Seletar Airport ⊠	271c	1.16 N	103.53 E
Seletar Hills	271c	1.23 N	103.53 E
Seletar Reservoir ⊜[1]	271c	1.24 N	103.48 E
Selety ≃	86	53.06 N	73.22 E
Seletyteniz, ozero ⊜	86	53.15 N	73.15 E
Selezen'ovo, S.S.S.R.	26	60.45 N	28.39 E
Selezen'ovo, S.S.S.R.	76	59.12 N	42.18 E
Selezni, S.S.S.R.	76	55.39 N	31.29 E
Selezni, S.S.S.R.	80	52.48 N	41.15 E
Selezn'ovo	76	60.45 N	28.39 E
Self Defense Fleet Headquarters ■	268	35.18 N	139.38 E
Selfoss	24a	63.56 N	20.57 W
Selfridge	198	46.02 N	100.55 W
Selfridge Air National Guard Base ■	281	42.36 N	82.49 W
Selghar	272c	18.57 N	73.02 E
Sel'gon	89	49.36 N	135.26 E
Sélibaby	150	15.10 N	12.11 W
Şelichino	89	50.22 N	137.38 E
Šelichova, zaliv ⊂	74	60.00 N	158.00 E
Šelichovo	88	55.42 N	97.41 E
Selidovo	83	48.08 N	37.18 E
Seligenthal	54	50.45 N	10.28 E
Seliger, ozero ⊜	76	57.13 N	33.05 E
Seligman, Az., U.S.	200	35.19 N	112.52 W
Seligman, Mo., U.S.	194	36.31 N	93.56 W
Selim	114	3.51 N	101.29 E
Selimbau	112	0.37 N	112.08 E
Selimiye	130	37.24 N	27.40 E
Selim River	114	3.50 N	101.24 E
Selínia	267c	37.56 N	23.32 E
Selinsgrove	208	40.47 N	76.51 W
Selinunte ⊥, It.	36	37.35 N	12.49 E
Selinunte ⊥, It.	70	37.35 N	12.49 E
Seliščе, S.S.S.R.	24	64.58 N	46.18 E
Seliščе, S.S.S.R.	76	56.53 N	33.16 E
Selitrennoje	80	47.11 N	47.27 E
Selivanovskaja	80	48.52 N	41.42 E
Seližarovo	76	56.51 N	33.27 E
Selje	26	62.03 N	5.22 E
Seljord	26	59.29 N	8.37 E
Selkämeri (Bottenhavet) ⊂	26	62.00 N	20.00 E
Selke ≃	54	51.52 N	11.14 E
Selkirk, Mb., Can.	184	50.09 N	96.52 W
Selkirk, On., Can.	212	42.49 N	79.56 W
Selkirk, Scot., U.K.	46	55.33 N	2.50 W
Selkirk, N.Y., U.S.	210	42.32 N	73.48 W
Selkirk Mountains ⋏	182	51.00 N	117.40 W
Selkirk Provincial Park ♦	212	42.49 N	79.58 W
Selkirk Shores State Park ♦	212	43.33 N	76.12 W
Šelkovka	82	55.32 N	36.22 E
Šelkovskaja	84	43.30 N	46.22 E
Sella	64	46.00 N	11.25 E
Sella, Monte ∧	64	46.40 N	12.02 E
Sella, Paso di)(	64	46.30 N	11.45 E
Sella di Corno	66	42.21 N	13.14 E
Sellano	66	42.54 N	12.55 E
Selle ≃	50	49.54 N	2.17 E
Selle, Chaîne de la ∧	238	18.22 N	71.59 W
Seller Lake ⊜	184	55.00 N	94.32 W
Sellero	64	46.03 N	10.20 E
Sellers	192	34.17 N	79.28 W
Sellersburg	218	38.23 N	85.45 W
Sellersville	208	40.21 N	75.18 W
Selles-sur-Cher	50	47.16 N	1.33 E
Sellia Marina	68	38.55 N	16.45 E
Sellières	58	46.50 N	5.34 E
Sellin	54	54.22 N	13.41 E
Sells	200	31.54 N	111.52 W
Selly Oak ✦[8]	42	52.25 N	1.52 W
Selm	52	51.42 N	7.28 E
Selma, Al., U.S.	194	32.24 N	87.01 W
Selma, Ca., U.S.	226	36.34 N	119.36 W
Selma, In., U.S.	218	40.11 N	85.16 W
Selma, N.C., U.S.	192	35.32 N	78.17 W
Selman City	222	32.11 N	94.58 W
Selmer	194	35.10 N	88.35 W
Selmigerheide ✦[8]	263	51.38 N	7.47 E
Selmont	194	32.23 N	87.01 W
Selmsdorf	54	53.48 N	10.50 E
Şelommes	50	47.45 N	1.12 E
Šelon' ≃	76	58.14 N	30.50 E
Seloncourt	58	47.28 N	6.52 E
Selong	115b	8.39 S	116.32 E
Şelongey	58	47.35 N	5.10 E
Šelopugino	88	51.39 N	117.33 E
Selouane	34	35.04 N	2.58 W
Selous, Mount ∧	180	62.57 N	132.31 W
Selous Game Reserve ✦[4]	154	9.10 S	37.10 E
Selsdon ✦[8]	260	51.21 N	0.04 W
Selsey	42	50.44 N	0.48 W
Selsey Bill ›	42	50.43 N	0.48 W
Selsingen	52	53.22 N	9.13 E
Selston	42	53.04 N	1.20 W
Selters	56	50.32 N	7.44 E
Selty	80	57.19 N	52.10 E
Seltz	56	48.53 N	8.06 E
Selu, Pulau I	164	7.32 S	130.54 E
Selva, Arg.	252	29.46 S	62.03 W
Selva, It.	64	46.33 N	11.46 E
Sel'vačevo	82	55.25 N	37.57 E
Selva di Cadore	64	46.27 N	12.02 E
Selvagens, Ilhas II	148	30.05 N	15.55 W
Selvas ✦[3]	242	5.00 S	68.00 W
Selvino	62	45.48 N	9.45 E
Selway ≃	202	46.08 N	115.36 W
Selwyn	166	21.32 S	140.30 E
Selwyn, Mount ∧	182	55.59 N	123.36 W
Selwyn, Passage ʯ	175f	16.03 S	168.12 E
Selwyn Lake ⊜	176	59.55 N	104.35 W
Selwyn Mountains ⋏	180	63.10 N	130.20 W
Selwyn Range ⋏	166	21.35 S	140.35 E
Şelz ≃	56	49.59 N	8.02 E
Šemacha, S.S.S.R.	84	40.38 N	48.39 E
Šemacha, S.S.S.R.	86	56.15 N	59.16 E
Semai, Pulau I	164	3.08 S	132.30 E
Semakau, Pulau I	271c	1.12 N	103.46 E
Seman ≃	38	40.56 N	19.24 E
Semanggol	114	4.57 N	100.38 E
Şemangka, Teluk ⊂	112	5.36 S	104.42 E
Šemanicha	80	57.18 N	45.24 E
Semans	184	51.25 N	104.44 W
Semanu	115a	8.00 S	110.39 E
Semarang	115a	6.58 S	110.25 E
Semaria	124	24.16 N	79.54 E
Sematan	112	1.48 N	109.46 E
Semau, Pulau I	112	10.13 S	123.22 E
Semayang, Kenohan ⊜	112	0.14 S	116.28 E
Sembabule	154	0.05 S	31.27 E
Sembadel	62	45.16 N	3.41 E
Sembakung ≃	112	3.47 N	117.30 E
Sembawang	271c	1.27 N	103.50 E
Sembé	152	1.39 N	14.36 E
Semberong ≃	114	2.27 N	103.37 E
Semblançay	50	47.30 N	0.35 E
Sembo ≃	152	7.42 S	13.01 E
Semcy	76	52.51 N	33.28 E
Şemdinli	128	37.18 N	44.35 E
Šemejkino	83	48.19 N	39.32 E
Semeliškės	76	54.40 N	24.40 E
Semenanjung Malaysia □[9]	114	4.00 N	102.00 E
Semendua	152	3.11 S	18.05 E
Semène ≃	62	45.23 N	4.13 E
Semenicului, Munții ⋏	38	45.05 N	22.05 E
Semenyih	114	2.57 N	101.51 E
Semertak	89	52.57 N	132.34 E
Şemeru, Gunung ∧	115a	8.06 S	112.55 E
Šemetovo	82	54.28 N	38.30 E
Semeževo	76	52.58 N	27.00 E
Semiahmoo Bay ⊂	224	48.58 N	122.48 W
Semibalki	83	47.00 N	39.03 E
Semibratovo	80	57.18 N	39.32 E
Semibugry	80	46.11 N	48.16 E
Semichi Islands II	181a	52.42 N	174.00 E
Semides'atnoje	78	51.21 N	38.44 E
Semidi Islands II	180	56.07 N	156.44 W
Semigorsk	88	56.42 N	104.41 E
Semijarka	86	50.54 N	78.20 E
Semikarakorsk	80	47.31 N	40.48 E
Semilej	80	53.57 N	45.21 E
Semilovo	80	55.04 N	42.10 E
Semiluki	78	51.41 N	39.02 E
Semily	30	50.36 N	15.20 E
Seminara	68	38.20 N	15.52 E
Seminary	194	31.33 N	89.29 W
Seminoe Reservoir ⊜[1]	200	42.00 N	106.50 W
Seminoe State Park ♦	202	42.05 N	106.55 W
Seminole, Fl., U.S.	220	27.50 N	82.47 W
Seminole, Ok., U.S.	196	35.13 N	96.40 W
Seminole, Tx., U.S.	196	32.43 N	102.38 W
Seminole □[6]	220	28.45 N	81.13 W
Seminole, Lake ⊜[1]	192	30.46 N	84.50 W
Seminole Draw V	196	32.27 N	102.20 W
Seminole Park	220	27.52 N	82.45 W
Seminskij chrebet ⋏	86	51.05 N	85.50 E
Semiozerje	88	49.52 N	110.23 E
Semioz'ornoje	86	52.22 N	64.08 E
Semioz'ornyj	88	53.44 N	120.25 E
Semipalatinsk	86	50.28 N	80.13 E
Semipolka	86	54.07 N	67.16 E
Semipolki	78	50.43 N	30.56 E
Semirara Island I	116	12.04 N	121.23 E
Semisopochnoi Island I	181a	52.00 N	179.35 E
Semitau	112	0.33 N	111.58 E
Semizbugy	86	50.12 N	74.48 E
Semizbugy, gora ∧	86	50.10 N	74.56 E
Semjany	80	56.02 N	45.59 E
Semli Kalān	124	24.10 N	76.39 E
Seml'ovo	76	55.03 N	33.58 E
Semmens Lake ⊜	184	55.03 N	94.11 W
Semmering	61	47.38 N	15.49 E
Semnān	128	35.33 N	53.24 E
Semnān □[4]	128	35.30 N	54.00 E
Şemois ≃	56	49.53 N	4.45 E
Šemonaicha	86	50.39 N	81.54 E
Sem'ono-Aleksandrovka	78	51.03 N	40.12 E
Sem'onov	24	56.48 N	44.30 E
Sem'onovka, S.S.S.R.	78	52.10 N	32.35 E
Sem'onovka, S.S.S.R.	78	49.36 N	33.10 E
Sem'onovka, S.S.S.R.	85	42.43 N	77.32 E
Sem'onovka, S.S.S.R.	86	51.20 N	70.46 E
Sem'onovskoje, S.S.S.R.	82	55.03 N	37.46 E
Sem'onovskoje, S.S.S.R.	82	55.18 N	38.21 E
Šemordan	80	56.11 N	50.26 E
Sempach	58	47.08 N	8.11 E
Sempacher See ⊜	58	47.09 N	8.09 E
Sempang Mangayau, Tanjong ›	112	7.02 N	116.45 E
Semple Lake ⊜	184	55.02 N	95.38 W
Sempol	115a	8.01 S	114.08 E
Semporna	112	4.28 N	118.36 E
Sempu, Pulau I	115a	8.26 S	112.42 E
Semuda	112	2.51 S	112.58 E
Semuliki ≃	154	1.14 N	30.28 E
Şemur-en-Auxois	50	47.29 N	4.20 E
Šemurša	80	54.53 N	47.32 E
Šemyšejka	80	52.54 N	45.24 E
Semža	24	66.09 N	44.08 E
Sên ≃	110	12.32 N	104.28 E
Sena, Bol.	248	11.32 S	67.11 W
Seňa, Česko.	30	48.34 N	21.15 E
Sena, Moç.	154	17.27 S	35.00 E
Sena → Seine ≃	32	49.26 N	0.26 E
Senador Amaral	256	22.35 S	46.11 W
Senador Canedo	255	16.43 S	49.05 W
Senador Côrtes	256	21.48 S	42.56 W
Senador Firmino	255	20.55 S	43.06 W
Senador José Bento	256	22.10 S	46.10 W
Senador José Porfirio	250	2.39 S	51.55 W
Senador Pompeu	250	5.35 S	39.22 W
Senago	266b	45.35 N	9.07 E
Senahú	236	15.24 N	89.50 W
Senai	114	1.36 N	103.39 E
Senainville	261	48.30 N	1.37 E
Senaja	112	6.45 N	117.03 E
Senale	64	46.31 N	11.06 E
Senales, Val di V	64	46.45 N	10.50 E
Sena Madureira	248	9.04 S	68.40 W
Senamaninik	114	0.45 N	100.47 E
Senanayake Samudra ⊜[1]	122	7.11 N	81.29 E
Senang, Pulau I	271c	1.11 N	103.44 E
Senanga	152	16.06 S	23.16 E
Sénart, Forêt de ♦	261	48.40 N	2.30 E
Sénas	62	43.45 N	5.05 E
Senate	184	49.18 N	109.41 W
Senath	194	36.08 N	90.09 W
Şenatobia	194	34.37 N	89.58 W
Šenbertal	86	48.43 N	60.20 E
Senča	78	50.16 N	33.20 E
Send	260	51.17 N	0.31 W
Sendafa	144	9.07 N	39.00 E
Sendai, Nihon	92	31.49 N	130.18 E
Sendai, Nihon	92	38.15 N	140.53 E
Sendai ≃, Nihon	92	31.51 N	130.12 E
Sendai ≃, Nihon	96	35.32 N	134.11 E
Sendai-heiya ≚	92	38.15 N	141.00 E
Sendelingsdrif	156	28.12 S	16.53 E
Senden, B.R.D.	52	51.51 N	7.29 E
Senden, B.R.D.	58	48.19 N	10.03 E
Şendenhorst	52	51.50 N	7.49 E
Šender	86	49.46 N	66.09 E
Sendhwa	120	21.41 N	75.06 E
Sêndo	102	31.42 N	95.16 E
Sendurjana	120	21.32 N	78.17 E
Senduruhan	112	1.00 S	110.46 E
Sene ≃	150	7.30 N	0.33 W
Senebui, Tanjung ›	114	2.17 N	101.03 E
Senec	30	48.14 N	17.24 E
Seneca, Il., U.S.	216	41.18 N	88.36 W
Seneca, Ks., U.S.	198	39.50 N	96.03 W
Seneca, Md., U.S.	284c	39.04 N	77.17 W
Seneca, Mo., U.S.	194	36.50 N	94.36 W
Seneca, Or., U.S.	202	44.08 N	118.58 W
Seneca, Pa., U.S.	214	41.23 N	79.42 W
Seneca, S.C., U.S.	192	34.41 N	82.57 W
Seneca □[6], N.Y., U.S.	210	42.54 N	76.52 W
Seneca □[6], Oh., U.S.	214	41.07 N	83.11 W
Seneca ≃	210	43.12 N	76.17 W
Seneca, Mount ∧	210	42.01 N	78.49 W
Seneca Castle	210	42.53 N	77.06 W
Seneca Caverns •[5]	214	41.11 N	82.53 W
Seneca Creek ⊂	284b	39.19 N	76.22 W
Seneca Creek ≃	196	36.36 N	102.52 W
Seneca Falls	210	42.54 N	76.47 W
Seneca Lake ⊜	210	42.40 N	76.57 W
Seneca Mall ✦[9]	284a	42.50 N	78.47 W
Seneca State Park ♦	208	39.08 N	77.15 W
Senecaville Lake ⊜[1]	188	39.55 N	81.25 W
Senecú	232	31.43 N	106.23 W
Seneffe	50	50.31 N	4.15 E
Senegal (Sénégal) □[1], Afr.	134	14.00 N	14.00 W
Senegal (Sénégal) □[1], Afr.	150	14.00 N	14.00 W
Sénégal ≃	150	15.48 N	16.32 W
Seneghe	71	40.05 N	8.36 E
Senekal	158	28.19 S	27.36 E
Senerchia	68	40.44 N	15.12 E
Senetosa, Capu di ›	71	41.33 N	8.47 E
Sénez	62	43.55 N	6.24 E
Senežskoje, ozero ⊜	82	56.12 N	37.00 E
Senftenberg	54	51.31 N	14.00 E
Senga Hill	154	9.22 S	31.12 E
Sengbachstausee ⊜[1]	263	51.08 N	7.09 E
Şengejskij, ostrov I	24	68.27 N	51.05 E
Šengel'šij	86	48.33 N	57.28 E
Sengés	255	24.06 S	49.29 W
Senggarang	114	1.45 N	103.03 E
Sênggê ≃	120	32.28 N	79.44 E
Senghenydd	42	51.36 N	3.16 W
Sengilej	80	53.58 N	48.46 E
Sengkamang	114	0.42 N	101.55 E
Sengsengbirge ⋏	61	47.47 N	14.15 E
Senguerr ≃	254	45.32 S	68.54 W
Sengwa ≃	154	17.07 S	28.05 E
Sengwarden	52	53.35 N	8.02 E
Senhāti	126	22.53 N	89.33 E
Senhora do Pôrto	255	18.53 S	43.06 W
Senhor do Bonfim	250	10.27 S	40.11 W
Senica	30	48.41 N	17.22 E
Senigallia	66	43.43 N	13.13 E
Senirkent	130	38.07 N	30.33 E
Senise	68	40.09 N	16.18 E
Senj	36	44.59 N	14.54 E
Senja I	24	69.20 N	17.30 E
Senjitu	98	41.56 N	116.25 E
Senjō-san ∧	96	35.26 N	133.36 E
Senkevičevka	78	50.32 N	25.02 E
Senkobo	154	17.38 S	25.58 E
Sen'kovo	83	49.31 N	37.43 E
Şenköy	130	36.05 N	36.05 E
Šenkursk	24	62.08 N	42.53 E
Senlac	184	52.29 N	109.41 W
Şenlikköy ✦[8]	267b	40.59 N	28.47 E
Šenlis	50	49.12 N	2.35 E
Senlisse	261	48.41 N	1.59 E
Senmonorom	110	12.27 N	107.12 E
Senn, Dahr ou •[4]	150	18.30 N	11.00 W
Sennaja	78	45.15 N	37.01 E
Sennan	96	34.22 N	135.17 E
Senne(Zenne) ≃	50	51.04 N	4.26 E
Sennecey-le-Grand	58	46.39 N	4.52 E
Senne II → Sennestadt	52	51.59 N	8.37 E
Sennen	42	50.04 N	5.42 W
Sennestadt	52	51.59 N	8.37 E
Senneterre	190	48.23 N	77.15 W
Senneville	275a	45.27 N	73.57 W
Sennevoy-le-Bas	50	47.48 N	4.17 E
Senno	76	54.49 N	29.43 E
Sennoj, S.S.S.R.	80	52.11 N	46.57 E
Sennoj, S.S.S.R.	80	50.16 N	43.37 E
Sennokura-yama ∧	94	36.49 N	138.50 E
Sennori	71	40.47 N	8.35 E
Sennwald	58	47.16 N	9.30 E
Sennybridge	42	51.57 N	3.34 W
Senoia	192	33.18 N	84.33 W
Senonches	50	48.33 N	1.02 E
Senones	58	48.24 N	6.59 E
Senorbì	71	39.32 N	9.08 E
Sénou	150	12.31 N	6.56 W
Sénouire ≃	62	45.16 N	3.25 E
Şenpazar	130	41.48 N	33.16 E
Senqu → Orange ≃	156	28.41 S	16.28 E
Senqunyane ≃	158	30.03 S	28.10 E
Senriyama	270	34.47 N	135.30 E
Sens	50	48.12 N	3.17 E
Sensburg → Mrągowo	30	53.52 N	21.19 E
Sense ≃	58	46.54 N	7.14 E
Sensée ≃	50	50.16 N	3.06 E
Sensée, Canal de la ≋	50	50.14 N	3.17 E
Sensuntepeque	236	13.52 N	88.38 W
Şenta	38	45.56 N	20.04 E
Šentala	80	54.27 N	51.29 E
Sentani, Danau ⊜	164	2.36 S	140.34 E
Sentarum, Danau ⊜	112	0.51 N	112.06 E
Sentas	86	49.19 N	82.28 E
Sentelek	86	51.13 N	83.44 E
Şentery	154	5.22 S	25.45 E
Šentilj	61	46.41 N	15.40 E
Sentinel	196	35.09 N	99.10 W
Sentinel Butte ∧	198	46.53 N	103.50 W
Sentinel Peak ∧	182	54.54 N	121.57 W
Sentinel Range ⋏	9	78.10 S	85.30 W
Şentino ≃	66	43.24 N	12.59 E
Šentjur	36	46.13 N	15.24 E
Sentolo	115a	7.50 S	110.13 E
Sentosa I	271c	1.15 N	103.50 E
Sento Sé	250	9.40 S	41.18 W
Sentsū-zan ∧	96	35.09 N	133.11 E
Senyavin Islands II	14	6.55 N	158.00 E
Senye	152	1.34 N	9.50 E
Şenyurt	130	37.06 N	40.40 E
Šenzaki-wan ⊂	96	34.24 N	131.15 E
Sen-zan ∧	96	34.21 N	134.51 E
Senzig	54	52.17 N	13.39 E
Senzu-dake ∧	270	34.57 N	135.52 E
Seo de Urgel	34	42.21 N	1.28 E
Seohāra	124	29.13 N	78.35 E
Seolag-san Kukrip Kongwŏn ♦	98	38.09 N	128.24 E
Seon	58	47.21 N	8.10 E
Seonāth ≃	122	21.44 N	82.28 E
Seoni	124	22.05 N	79.32 E
Seoni Mālwa	124	22.27 N	77.28 E
Seorīnārāyan	120	21.44 N	82.35 E
Seoul → Sŏul	98	37.33 N	126.58 E
Seoul Bridge ✦[5]	271b	37.32 N	126.56 E
Seoul National University ◗[2]	271b	37.28 N	126.57 E
Seoul Stadium ♦	271b	37.35 N	127.02 E
Seoul Station ✦[5]	271b	37.34 N	126.58 E
Sepahat	114	1.34 N	101.53 E
Sepang	114	2.42 N	101.45 E
Sepanjang, Pulau I	112	7.10 S	115.50 E
Separation Creek ≃	200	41.59 N	107.28 W
Separation Point ›	172	40.47 S	173.00 E
Sepasu	112	0.43 N	117.35 E
Sepatini ≃	248	7.36 S	65.24 W
Sépeaux	50	47.57 N	3.14 E
Sepetiba ✦[8]	256	22.58 S	43.42 W
Şepetiba, Baía de ⊂	256	23.00 S	43.48 W
Šepetovka	78	50.11 N	27.04 E
Sepi	175e	8.33 S	159.50 E
Sepik ≃	164	3.51 S	144.34 E
Sepino	66	41.24 N	14.37 E
Sep'o	98	38.39 N	127.22 E
Sępólno Krajeńskie	30	53.28 N	17.32 E
Sépone → Muang Xépôn	110	16.41 N	106.14 E
Sepopa	156	18.13 S	22.13 E
Sępopol	30	54.15 N	21.00 E
Sepoti ≃	248	6.43 S	61.38 W
Sepotuba ≃	248	15.56 S	57.39 W
Seppeltsfield	168b	34.30 S	138.54 E
Seppenrade	52	51.46 N	7.23 E
Sepphoris → Zippori	132	32.45 N	35.17 E
Seppois-le-Bas	58	47.33 N	7.10 E
Septeuil	261	48.54 N	1.41 E
Sept Frères, Lac des ⊜	206	46.20 N	75.10 W
Sept-Îles (Seven Islands)	186	50.12 N	66.23 W
Septvaux	50	49.34 N	3.23 E
Sepulga ≃	194	31.11 N	86.46 W
Sepúlveda	34	41.18 N	3.45 W
Sepulveda ✦[8]	280	34.13 N	118.28 W
Sepulveda Dam ✦[6]	280	34.10 N	118.29 W
Sepulveda Flood Control Basin ≚[1]	228	34.11 N	118.29 W
Seputih ≃	112	4.42 S	105.54 E
Sepyč	80	58.11 N	54.08 E
Sequals	64	46.10 N	12.50 E
Sequatchie ≃	192	35.02 N	85.38 W
Sequeros	34	40.31 N	6.01 W
Sequillo ≃	34	41.45 N	5.30 W
Sequim	224	48.04 N	123.06 W
Sequim Bay ⊂	224	48.03 N	123.02 W
Sequoia National Park ♦	204	36.30 N	118.30 W
Sera	96	34.36 N	133.03 E
Şera, Pulau I	164	7.40 S	131.05 E
Šerabad	128	37.40 N	67.01 E
Serachs	128	36.32 N	61.13 E
Serafettin Dağları ⋏	130	39.05 N	41.10 E
Şerafimovič	80	49.36 N	42.43 E
Šeragul	88	54.29 N	100.56 E
Seraidi	36	36.55 N	7.41 E
Seraing	56	50.36 N	5.29 E
Seraja ≃	82	56.15 N	38.45 E
Seram (Ceram) I	164	3.00 S	129.00 E
Seram, Laut (Ceram Sea) ⊤[2]	108	2.30 S	128.00 E
Serampore	126	22.45 N	88.21 E
Serang	115a	6.07 S	106.09 E
Serang ≃	115a	6.43 S	110.35 E
Serangoon	271c	1.22 N	103.54 E
Serangoon ≃	271c	1.24 N	103.56 E
Serangoon, Pulau I	271c	1.25 N	103.56 E
Serangoon Harbour ⊂	271c	1.23 N	103.57 E
Serapo	66	41.13 N	13.34 E
Serasan, Pulau I	112	2.30 N	109.03 E
Serasan, Selat ʯ	112	2.20 N	109.00 E
Seravalle Sesia	62	45.41 N	8.19 E
Seravezza	64	43.59 N	10.13 E
Seraya, Pulau I	271c	1.16 N	103.43 E
Serayevo → Sarajevo	38	43.52 N	18.25 E
Şerayu ≃	115a	7.41 S	109.06 E
Šerbakul'	86	54.38 N	72.24 E
Serbeulangit, Pegunungan ⋏	114	3.45 N	97.50 E
Serbia → Srbija □[3]	38	44.00 N	21.00 E
Serchio ≃	64	43.47 N	10.16 E
Serdce-Kamen', mys ›	180	66.57 N	171.40 W
Serdež	80	57.17 N	48.17 E
Serditoje	83	48.02 N	38.24 E
Serdo	144	11.58 N	41.18 E
Serdoba ≃	80	52.34 N	44.01 E
Serdobsk	80	52.28 N	44.13 E
Séré'ama, Mont ∧	175f	13.47 S	167.29 E
Serebr'anka, S.S.S.R.	83	48.55 N	38.08 E
Serebr'anka, S.S.S.R.	86	57.13 N	70.42 E
Serebr'anka, S.S.S.R.	265b	55.45 N	37.55 E
Serebr'anka ≃	265b	55.47 N	37.42 E
Serebr'ansk	86	49.43 N	83.20 E
Serebr'anyj Bor ✦[8]	265b	55.48 N	37.25 E
Serebr'anyje Prudy	82	54.28 N	38.44 E
Serebrovo	88	55.24 N	97.52 E
Serechoviči	78	51.25 N	24.40 E
Sered'	30	48.17 N	17.44 E
Sereda, S.S.S.R.	76	55.54 N	35.31 E
Şereda, S.S.S.R.	80	58.00 N	40.27 E
Šeredar' ≃	82	55.56 N	39.04 E
Seredejskij	76	54.03 N	35.14 E
Seredič̌i	76	53.35 N	35.51 E
Seredina-Buda	78	52.11 N	34.01 E
Serednikovo, S.S.S.R.	80	55.15 N	39.40 E
Serednikovo, S.S.S.R.	265b	55.56 N	37.14 E
Seredn'ovo	265b	55.35 N	37.18 E
Seredžius	76	55.05 N	23.25 E
Şereflikoçhisar	130	38.56 N	33.33 E
Šereges̆	86	52.57 N	88.02 E
Seregno	62	45.39 N	9.12 E
Serein ≃	50	47.55 N	3.31 E
Şeremban	114	2.43 N	101.56 E
Šeremetjevka	80	55.23 N	51.32 E
Šeremetjevo, Aeroport ⊠	82	55.59 N	37.24 E
Šeremetjevskij	82	55.59 N	37.30 E
Seremuk ≃	164	1.36 S	131.46 E
Serena	216	41.29 N	88.44 W
Seren del Grappa	64	45.59 N	11.51 E
Serengeti National Park ♦	154	2.20 S	34.50 E
Serengeti Plain ≚	154	2.50 S	35.00 E
Serengka	112	1.40 S	110.40 E
Serenje	154	13.15 S	30.14 E
Şereno	256	21.19 S	42.39 W
Šereševo	76	52.33 N	24.13 E
Seret ≃	78	48.38 N	25.52 E
Serfaus	58	47.02 N	10.36 E
Ser'ga	86	57.46 N	56.52 E
Sergač	80	55.32 N	45.28 E
Sergeant	214	41.38 N	78.45 W
Sergeant Bluff	198	42.24 N	96.21 W
Sergeja Kirova, ostrova II	74	77.12 N	89.30 E
Sergejeviči	76	53.30 N	27.45 E
Sergejevka, S.S.S.R.	83	48.40 N	37.22 E
Sergejevka, S.S.S.R.	86	53.51 N	67.25 E
Sergejevka, S.S.S.R.	86	51.39 N	68.13 E
Sergejevka, S.S.S.R.	89	44.22 N	131.39 E
Sergejevka, S.S.S.R.	89	43.21 N	133.22 E
Sergejevo	86	57.18 N	86.02 E
Sergen	130	41.42 N	27.42 E
Sergijevka	78	51.46 N	41.05 E
Sergijevskaja, S.S.S.R.	76	60.16 N	43.54 E
Sergijevskaja, S.S.S.R.	80	50.16 N	43.47 E
Sergijevskij	80	51.56 N	51.54 E
Sergili	85	41.13 N	69.14 E
Sergines	50	48.20 N	3.15 E
Sergino	72	62.30 N	65.38 E
Sergipe □[3]	250	10.30 S	37.30 W
Sergokala	84	42.27 N	47.40 E
Sergozero, ozero ⊜	24	66.47 N	36.42 E
Seria	112	4.39 N	114.23 E
Serian	112	1.10 N	110.34 E
Seriana, Valle V	64	45.55 N	9.55 E

Symbol	English	Deutsch	Español	Français	Português
≃	River	Fluß	Río	Rivière	Rio
≋	Canal	Kanal	Canal	Canal	Canal
⌊	Waterfall, Rapids	Wasserfall, Stromschnellen	Cascada, Rápidos	Chute d'eau, Rapides	Cascata, Rápidos
ʯ	Strait	Meeresstraße	Estrecho	Détroit	Estreito
⊂	Bay, Gulf	Bucht, Golf	Bahía, Golfo	Baie, Golfe	Baía, Golfo
⊜	Lake, Lakes	See, Seen	Lago, Lagos	Lac, Lacs	Lago, Lagos
⠿	Swamp	Sumpf	Pantano	Marais	Pântano
⊓	Ice Features, Glacier	Eis- und Gletscherformen	Accidentes Glaciales	Formes glaciaires	Acidentes glaciares
⊤	Other Hydrographic Features	Andere Hydrographische Objekte	Otros Elementos Hidrográficos	Autres données hydrographiques	Outros acidentes hidrográficos
✧	Submarine Features	Untermeerische Objekte	Accidentes Submarinos	Formes de relief sous-marin	Acidentes submarinos
□	Political Unit	Politische Einheit	Unidad Politica	Entité politique	Unidade política
◗	Cultural Institution	Kulturelle Institution	Institución Cultural	Institution culturelle	Institução cultural
⊥	Historical Site	Historische Stätte	Sitio Histórico	Site historique	Sitio histórico
♦	Recreational Site	Erholungs- und Ferienort	Sitio de Recreo	Centre de loisirs	Area de Lazer
⊠	Airport	Flughafen	Aeropuerto	Aéroport	Aeroporto
■	Military Installation	Militäranlage	Instalación Militar	Installation militaire	Instalação militar
✦	Miscellaneous	Verschiedenes	Misceláneo	Divers	Diversos

Name	Page	Lat.°'	Long.°'	Name	Seite	Breite°'	Länge°' E = Ost

Left index (continuous reading order)

```
Seriate                        62   45.41 N    9.43 E
Seribu, Kepulauan II          115a   5.36 S  106.33 E
Seribudolok, Indon.           114    2.56 N   98.37 E
Seribudolok, Indon.           114    2.51 N   99.04 E
Sericho                       154    1.05 N   39.05 E
Seridó ≃                      250    6.12 S   37.10 W
Sérifontaine                   50   49.21 N    1.46 E
Sérifos                        38   37.09 N   24.31 E
Sérifos I                      38   37.11 N   24.31 E
Sérignan-du-Comtat             62   44.11 N    4.51 E
Sérigny                       176   56.47 N   66.00 W
Serik                         130   36.55 N   31.06 E
Seringa, Serra da ⩘¹          250    7.00 S   50.40 W
Seringat, Pulau I            271c    1.14 N  103.51 E
Serino                         68   40.51 N   14.52 E
Serinyol                      130   36.24 N   36.11 E
Serio ≃                        62   45.16 N    9.45 E
Seritinga                     256   21.54 S   44.30 W
Serjol                         24   60.02 N   48.58 E
Serkhe, Cerro ⩘               248   17.22 S   69.22 W
Serkout, Djebel ⩘            148   23.30 N    6.48 E
Serkovo                        82   54.28 N   38.46 E
Serles ⩘                       64   47.08 N   11.20 E
Šerlovaja Gora                 88   50.34 N  116.15 E
Serm ⊶⁸                       263   51.21 N    6.42 E
Sermaise                      261   48.32 N    2.05 E
Sermaises                      50   48.18 N    2.12 E
Sermaize-les-Bains             56   48.47 N    4.55 E
Serman                         80   53.34 N   46.22 E
Sermata, Pulau I              164    8.13 S  128.55 E
Sermide                        64   45.00 N   11.18 E
Sermilik C²                   176   65.37 N   38.03 W
Sermizelles                    56   47.32 N    3.48 E
Sermoneta                      66   41.33 N   12.59 E
Serna ≃                        82   55.51 N   38.34 E
Sernambitiba                 287a   22.41 S   42.59 W
Sernambitiba, Pontal de ➤    287a   23.02 S   43.27 W
Serniki                        78   51.49 N   26.14 E
Sernovodsk                     80   56.56 N   49.09 E
Sernur                         82   56.54 N   48.50 E
Sernyj Zavod                  128   39.59 N   58.50 E
Séro                          150   14.48 N   11.04 W
Serodino                      252   32.37 S   60.57 W
Ser'odka                       76   58.10 N   28.12 E
Serogiazka                     80   47.01 N   47.29 E
Ser'ogovo                      24   62.60 N   50.36 E
Serooskerke                    52   51.42 N    3.50 E
Seropédica                    256   22.44 S   43.43 W
Serovo                         85   40.27 N   71.12 E
Serowe                         80   22.25 S   26.44 E
Ser'oža ≃                      80   55.34 N   42.29 E
Serpa                          34   37.56 N    7.36 W
Serpa, Ilha de I              246    3.07 S   58.19 W
Serpeddi, Punta ⩘             71   39.22 N    9.18 E
Serpejsk                       76   54.20 N   34.59 E
Serpent, Rivière au ≃        186   49.31 N   71.14 W
Serpentine                   168a   32.22 S  115.59 E
Serpentine ≃, Austl.         168a   32.33 S  115.46 E
Serpentine ≃, B.C., Can.     224   49.05 N  122.50 W
Serpentine Lakes ☒           162   28.32 S  129.29 E
Serpentine National Park ☒   168a   32.22 S  116.01 E
Serpentine Reservoir ☒       168a   32.25 S  116.08 E
Serpent Mound State Memorial I 218  39.02 N   83.26 W
Serpents Mouth ⩴             241r   10.00 N   62.00 W
Serpnevoje                     82   46.18 N   29.02 E
Serpuchov                      82   54.55 N   37.25 E
Serpukhov → Serpuchov          82   54.55 N   37.25 E
Serqo → Sark I                43b   49.26 N    2.21 W
Serra                         255   20.07 S   40.18 W
Serra, Monte ⩘                64   43.46 N   10.33 E
Serra Branca                  250    7.29 S   36.40 W
Serracapriola                  68   41.48 N   15.09 E
Serrada                        66   45.53 N   11.09 E
Serra d'aiello                 68   39.05 N   16.08 E
Serra de'Conti                 66   43.33 N   13.02 E
Serra di Corvo, Lago di ☒¹    68   40.51 N   16.14 E
Serradifalco                   70   37.27 N   13.53 E
Serra do Navio                250    0.59 N   52.03 W
Serra do Salitre              255   19.06 S   46.41 W
Serra dos Órgãos, Parque Nacional da ☒ 256 22.26 S 43.02 W
Serra Grande                  250    7.15 S   38.19 W
Sérrai                         38   41.05 N   23.32 E
Serramanna                     71   39.25 N    8.55 E
Serramazzoni                   64   44.25 N   10.47 E
Serramonte Center ⊶          282   37.40 N  122.28 W
Serrana                       250   21.14 S   47.36 W
Serrana Bank ⩘⁴              236   14.23 N   80.12 W
Serra Negra                   250   22.36 S   46.42 W
Serra Negra do Norte          250    6.40 S   37.24 W
Serrania                      250   21.33 S   46.03 W
Serranilla Bank ⩘⁴          236   15.51 N   79.50 W
Serrano, Isla I               254   48.30 S   74.45 W
Serranópolis                  255   18.16 S   52.00 W
Serranos                      256   21.51 S   44.30 W
Serra Preta                   250   12.09 S   39.20 W
Serrara                        68   40.42 N   13.54 E
Serraria, Bra.                250    6.49 S   35.38 W
Serraria, Bra.                256   22.01 S   43.12 W
Serra San Bruno                68   38.35 N   16.20 E
Serra San Quirico              66   43.27 N   13.01 E
Serrastretta                   68   39.01 N   16.25 E
Serrat, Cap ➤                  36   37.14 N    9.13 E
Serra Talhada                 250    7.59 S   38.18 W
Serravalle, It.                66   42.47 N   13.01 E
Serravalle, It.                64   43.57 N   12.30 E
Serravalle all'Adige           64   45.53 N   11.01 E
Serravalle Scrivia             62   44.43 N    8.51 E
Serre                          56   40.35 N   15.11 E
Serre ≃                        50   49.41 N    3.23 E
Serre-Ponçon                   71   39.24 N    8.58 E
Serre-Ponçon, Barrage de ⊶⁶   62   44.33 N    6.30 E
Serre-Ponçon, Lac de ☒¹       62   44.30 N    6.17 E
Serres                        248   24.06 N    5.43 E
Serrezuela                    252   30.38 S   65.23 W
Serri                          71   39.42 N    9.08 E
Serrières                      62   45.19 N    4.45 E
Serriola, Bocca ⩗             66   43.31 N   12.21 E
Serris                        261   48.51 N    2.47 E
Serrita                       250    7.56 S   39.19 W
Sêrro                         255   18.37 S   43.23 W
Serrote ≃                     254   27.27 S   54.40 W
Sersale                        68   39.01 N   16.44 E
Serstin                        52   52.39 N   31.03 E
Šerstobitovo                   86   57.16 N   78.52 E
Sertã                          34   39.48 N    8.06 W
Sertaneja                     250   23.03 S   50.50 W
Sertânia                      250    8.05 S   37.16 W
Sertãozinho                   256   22.19 S   46.03 W
Sertig-Dörfli                 259   46.43 N    9.51 E
Sertung, Pulau I             115a    6.06 S  105.24 E
Seru                          144    7.50 N   40.28 E
Šerua, Pulau I                164    6.18 S  130.02 E
Serudj-Nura ⩘                 80   52.16 N  112.59 E
Serui                         164    1.53 S  136.14 E
Seruini ≃                     248    7.42 S   66.42 W
Serule                         80   21.57 S   27.20 E
Serutu, Pulau I               112    1.42 S  108.45 E
Seruwai                       114    3.57 N   98.04 E
Servia                         38   40.11 N   22.00 E
Servi Burnu ➤                 130   41.40 N   28.06 E
Servigliano                    66   43.05 N   13.29 E
Servon                        261   48.43 N    2.35 E
Servoz                         58   45.56 N    6.46 E
Serwaru                       112    8.10 S  127.42 E
Sêrxü                         102   33.04 N   97.45 E
Seryševo                       89   51.08 N  128.20 E
```

```
Šes, Muntele ⩗                 38   47.05 N   22.30 E
Šešan                         180   46.59 N  171.26 W
Sesayap ≃                     112    3.36 N  117.15 E
Sesayap Lama                  112    3.36 N  117.03 E
Sešča                          76   53.45 N   33.23 E
Sese Islands II               154    0.20 S   32.20 E
Seseke ≃                      263   51.37 N    7.32 E
Sesefontein                   156   19.07 S   13.39 E
Seseheke                      152   17.28 S   24.18 E
Seshu                         105   39.33 N  115.37 E
Sesia ≃                        62   45.05 N    8.37 E
Sesia, Val V                   62   45.47 N    8.05 E
Sesibu                        112    4.02 N  116.33 E
Sesimbra                       34   38.26 N    9.06 W
Seskar, ostrov I               76   60.02 N   28.23 E
Seškarö                        26   65.44 N   23.44 E
Sešma ≃                        80   55.27 N   51.05 E
Sesmarias ≃                   256   22.28 S   44.27 W
Sesoko-jima I                147m   26.38 N  127.52 E
Sespe                         228   34.23 N  118.58 W
Sespe Creek ≃                 204   34.23 N  118.57 W
Sessa                         152   13.56 S   20.38 E
Sessa Aurunca                  68   41.14 N   13.56 E
Séssé                          34   39.16 N    3.03 E
Sessenheim                     56   48.48 N    7.59 E
Šesta Godano                   62   44.17 N    9.40 E
Šestakovka                     78   48.32 N   31.58 E
Šestakovo, S.S.S.R.            82   56.21 N   35.49 E
Šestakovo, S.S.S.R.            88   56.29 N  103.59 E
Šestao                         34   43.18 N    3.00 W
Šestern'a                      64   47.33 N   33.16 E
Šestino                        66   43.42 N   12.18 E
Sesto (Sexten)                 64   46.42 N   12.21 E
Sesto Calende                  62   45.44 N    8.38 E
Sesto Fiorentino               64   43.50 N   11.12 E
Sestola                        64   44.14 N   10.46 E
Sesto San Giovanni             62   45.32 N    9.14 E
Sestra ≃, S.S.S.R.             82   52.11 N   49.36 E
Sestra ≃, S.S.S.R.             82   56.43 N   37.14 E
Sestriere                      62   44.57 N    6.53 E
Sestri Levante                 62   44.16 N    9.24 E
Sestri Ponente                 62   44.25 N    8.51 E
Šestroreck                     76   60.06 N   29.58 E
Šestroreckij Razliv, ozero ☒ 265a   60.04 N   30.00 E
Šestu                          71   39.18 N    9.05 E
Šešupe ≃                       76   55.03 N   22.12 E
Šešurga                        80   57.29 N   47.35 E
Šešuvis ≃                      76   55.15 N   22.58 E
Šeta, Nihon                   270   34.58 N  135.55 E
Šeta, S.S.S.R.                 76   55.17 N   24.15 E
Šeta, S.S.S.R.                 82   55.17 N   24.15 E
Setagaya ⊶⁸                   268   35.39 N  139.40 E
Setail ≃                      115a    8.30 S  114.21 E
Setaka                         96   33.09 N  130.28 E
Setana                         92   42.26 N  139.51 E
Setapak                       114    3.11 N  101.42 E
Setauket                      210   40.57 N   73.07 W
Sète                           62   43.24 N    3.41 E
Sete Barras                   252   24.23 S   47.55 W
Sete Cidades, Parque Nacional de 250  3.50 S 41.40 W
Sete de Setembro ≃            250   12.56 S   52.51 W
Sete Lagoas                   255   19.27 S   44.14 W
Sete Pontes                   256   22.51 S   43.05 W
Sete Quedas, Cachoeira das ⅃ 250   22.57 S   56.41 W
Sete Quedas, Parque Nacional de 252 24.02 S 54.12 W
Sete Quedas, Salto das ⅃     252   24.02 S   54.16 W
Sete Rios ⊶⁸                 266c   38.45 N    9.12 E
Setesdal V                     26   59.25 N    7.25 E
Seth Ward                     196   34.13 N  101.42 W
Setif                         124   29.15 N   81.06 E
Setl ≃²                       124   28.58 N   81.06 E
Setlagodi                     158   26.16 S   25.06 E
Seto, Nihon                    94   35.14 N  137.06 E
Seto, Nihon                    96   33.27 N  132.15 E
Seto, Nihon                    94   34.44 N  134.02 E
Seto-naikai C                  96   34.18 N  133.05 E
Seto-naikai C²                 96   34.20 N  133.30 E
Seton Hall University ⋁²     276   40.45 N   74.15 W
Seton Lake ☒                  182   50.45 N  122.05 W
Seton Portage                 182   50.45 N  122.05 W
Seto-saki ➤                    96   34.40 N  135.00 E
Setouchi                      93b   28.10 N  129.15 E
Seto-zaki ➤                    78   49.23 N   40.49 E
Setta ≃                        64   44.33 N   11.14 E
Settat                        148   33.05 N    7.30 W
Settat □⁴                     148   33.05 N    7.30 W
Setté Bagni ⊶                267a   42.00 N   12.31 E
Setté Cama                    152    2.32 S    9.45 E
Settecamini ⊶⁸               267a   41.56 N   12.37 E
Sette-Daban, chrebet ⩘        74   62.00 N  138.00 E
Settee Lake ☒                 184   57.03 N   96.55 W
Settepani, Monte ⩘            64   44.15 N    8.12 E
Settimo Milanese             266b   45.29 N    9.03 E
Settimo San Pietro             71   39.17 N    9.11 E
Settimo Torinese               62   45.09 N    7.46 E
Settimo Vittone                62   45.33 N    7.50 E
Setting Lake ☒                184   55.00 N   98.38 W
Settle                         44   54.04 N    2.16 W
Settlement Point ➤            169   38.25 S  145.25 E
Settlers                      156   25.02 S   28.30 E
Settlers Cabin Regional Park ⊶ 279b 40.26 N 80.10 W
Settons, Lac des ☒            56   47.11 N    4.04 E
Settsu                         96   34.46 N  135.33 E
Setúbal                        34   38.32 N    8.54 W
Setúbal □⁴                   266c   38.37 N    9.00 W
Setúbal, Baía de ⊂            34   38.27 N    8.53 W
Seui                           71   39.50 N    9.19 E
Seúl → Sŏul                    98   37.33 N  126.58 E
Seul, Lac ☒                   184   50.20 N   92.30 W
Seul Choix Point ➤            190   45.55 N   85.52 W
Seulimeum                     114    5.22 N   95.21 E
Seulo                          71   39.52 N    9.14 E
Seumanyam                     114    3.35 N   96.35 E
Seurre                         58   47.00 N    5.09 E
Seuzach                        62   47.30 N    8.44 E
Sev ≃¹                         76   52.24 N   34.10 E
Sevan                          78   52.24 N   34.44 E
Sevan, ozero ☒                78   40.30 N   45.20 E
Sévaré                        150   14.32 N    4.06 W
Sevastopol'                    82   44.36 N   33.32 E
Sevastopol'skij                86   53.08 N   65.44 E
Ševčenko                       78   43.35 N   51.05 E
Ševčenkovo, S.S.S.R.           76   47.01 N   27.10 E
Ševčenkovo, S.S.S.R.           78   49.41 N   39.20 E
Ševčenkovo Vtoroje             82   51.40 N   33.39 E
Sevelen, B.R.D.               263   51.35 N    6.25 E
Sevelen, Schweiz              259   47.07 N    9.28 E
Ševelevskij Majdan             82   54.25 N   42.15 E
Seven Caves ⊶⁵               218   39.13 N   83.23 W
Seven Creeks ≃                169   36.43 S  145.53 E
Seven Harbors                 214   42.36 N   83.25 W
Sevenhill                     168b   33.53 S  138.38 E
Seven Hills, Austl.          168b   33.46 S  150.56 E
Seven Hills, Oh., U.S.        214   41.23 N   81.40 W
Seven Islands → Sept-Îles    186   50.12 N   66.23 W
Seven Kings ⊶⁸                50   51.34 N    0.06 E
Seven Mile                    218   39.28 N   84.33 W
Seven Mile Beach National Park ⊶ 170 34.49 S 150.46 E
Sevenmile Bridge ⊶⁵          220   24.41 N   81.11 W
Sevenmile Creek ≃            218   39.28 N   84.33 W
Sevenoaks, Eng., U.K.         42   51.16 N    0.12 E
Seven Oaks, Tx., U.S.        222   30.51 N   94.51 W
Sevenoaks ⊂²⁸                156   51.18 N    0.10 E
Sevenoaks Weald              260   51.18 N    0.12 E
Seven Palm Lake ☒            220   25.12 N   80.44 W
Seven Persons                184   49.52 N  110.54 W
Seven Sisters                184   51.46 N    3.43 W
Seven Sisters Peaks ⩘        182   54.58 N  128.10 W
Seventy Mile House           182   51.18 N  121.24 W
Seven Valleys                208   39.51 N   76.46 W
Sévérac-le-Château            32   44.19 N    3.04 E
Severance Center ⊶⁸          279a   41.31 N   81.33 W
Ser'anskij les ➤              82   48.55 N   38.00 E
Severka ≃                      82   55.10 N   38.45 E
Severn, S. Afr.              158   26.36 S   22.52 E
Severn, Md., U.S.            208   39.08 N   76.41 W
Severn, Va., U.S.            208   37.17 N   76.24 W
Severn ≃, On., Can.          176   56.02 N   87.36 W
Severn ≃, On., Can.          212   44.52 N   79.51 W
Severn ≃, U.K.                42   51.35 N    2.40 W
Severn, Mouth of the ⩴        42   51.25 N    3.00 W
Severnaja Dvina ≃             24   64.32 N   40.30 E
Severnaja Sos'va ≃            72   64.10 N   65.28 E
Severnaja Zeml'a II           74   79.30 N   98.00 E
Severna Park                  208   39.04 N   76.32 W
Severn Bridge ⊶⁵             42   51.39 N    2.42 W
Severn Lake ☒                184   53.54 N   90.48 W
Severnoje, S.S.S.R.           80   58.02 N   41.26 E
Severnoje, S.S.S.R.           80   54.06 N   52.32 E
Severnoje, S.S.S.R.           83   48.04 N   38.44 E
Severnoje, S.S.S.R.           83   49.11 N   42.51 E
Severnoje, S.S.S.R.           86   56.21 N   78.23 E
Severnoje ≃ (Severn River) ≃, Md., U.S. 208 38.58 N 76.28 W
Severn River ≃, Va., U.S.    208   37.19 N   76.25 W
Severnyj, S.S.S.R.            24   67.38 N   64.06 E
Severnyj, S.S.S.R.          265b   55.56 N   37.33 E
Severnyje uvaly ⩘²           24   59.30 N   49.00 E
Severnyj Kommunar             84   58.23 N   54.02 E
Severnyj Prijut               84   43.16 N   41.51 E
Severnyj Ural ≃               24   63.00 N   59.00 E
Severo-Bajkal'skoje nagorje ⩘  88  57.00 N  111.00 E
Severočeský Kraj □⁴           30   50.30 N   14.00 E
Severodoneck                   83   48.58 N   38.27 E
Severodvinsk                   24   64.34 N   39.50 E
Severo-Jenisejskij            74   60.22 N   93.01 E
Severo-Kazachstanskaja Oblast' □⁴ 86 54.30 N 69.00 E
Severo-Kuril'sk               74   50.40 N  156.08 E
Severomorावskij Kraj □⁴       30   44.19 N   17.50 E
Severomorsk                    24   69.05 N   33.24 E
Severo-Mujskij chrebet ⩘      88   56.30 N  114.00 E
Severo-Osetinskaja Avtonomnaja Sovetskaja Socialističeskaja Respublika □⁴ 78 43.00 N 44.15 E
Severo-Sibirskaja nizmennost' ⩝ 74 73.00 N 100.00 E
Severo-Zadonsk                82   54.06 N   38.24 E
Severskaja                    78   44.51 N   38.42 E
Severskij Donec ≃             72   47.35 N   40.54 E
Severskij Donec–Donbass, kanal ≃ 83 48.55 N 37.45 E
Severucha                     88   48.18 N   63.25 E
Severy                        198   37.37 N   96.13 W
Seveso                         62   45.39 N    9.09 E
Seveso ≃                     266b   45.30 N    9.12 E
Ševetín                        61   49.06 N   14.35 E
Ševětín                       264b   48.20 N   16.29 E... (see right column)
```

```
Seven Mile Beach National Park ⊶  170  34.49 S  150.46 E
Sevnica → Šadrinsk            86   56.05 N   63.38 E
Shady Cove                    202   42.04 N  122.36 W
Shady Grove, Fl., U.S.        192   30.17 N   83.37 W
Shady Grove, Tx., U.S.        222   32.48 N   97.01 W
Shady Hills                   226   28.25 N   82.34 W
Shady Shores                  222   33.09 N   97.02 W
Shady Side                    208   38.50 N   76.31 W
Sha'i                         132   32.38 N   35.11 E
Shafer, Lake ☒                218   40.47 N   86.46 W
Shafir                        132   31.42 N   34.44 E
Shaft                         158   27.12 S   25.39 E
Shaftesbury                    42   51.01 N    2.12 W
Shafton                        42   53.36 N    1.26 W
Shaftsburg                    214   42.48 N   84.18 W
Shafu                         100   22.25 N  113.01 E
Shagamu                       150   6.51 N     3.39 E
Shagaluk                      180   62.36 N  159.32 W
Shag Rocks II                244   53.33 S   42.02 W
Shaguotun                     104   41.10 N  120.38 E
Shāhābād, India              122   17.08 N   76.56 E
Shāhābād, India              124   27.39 N   79.57 E
Shāhābād, India              122   28.38 N   76.09 E
Shāhābād, Īrān               272c   37.32 N   56.54 E
Shāhāda                       124   21.33 N   74.28 E
Shah Alam                     114    3.04 N  101.33 E
Shāhbandar                    124   24.10 N   67.56 E
Shāhbāzpur ≃                  124   22.10 N   90.50 E
Shahdād, Namakzār-e ≃        128   30.30 N   58.30 E
Shāhdādkot                   124   27.51 N   67.54 E
Shāhdādpur                   124   25.56 N   68.37 E
Shahdara                     272a   28.41 N   77.18 E
Shāhdol                      124   23.18 N   81.21 E
Shāhe ≃                      105   40.10 N  114.38 E
Shāhepu                      102   37.30 N  103.04 E
Shaheji                      105   33.38 N  114.59 E
Shāhganj                     124   26.03 N   82.41 E
Shāhgarh                     124   27.08 N   69.48 E
Shāhhāt                      146   32.49 N   21.52 E
Shāhī Kowt                   123   34.16 N   70.34 E
Shāhjahānpur                 123   27.53 N   79.55 E
Shāh Jūy                     123   32.31 N   67.25 E
Shāh Kot                     123   31.34 N   73.29 E
Shāh Kūh ⩘                   123   31.37 N   59.16 E
Shāhpura, India             122   16.42 N   76.50 E
Shāhpura, Pāk.               123   28.43 N   68.25 E
Shāhpura, Pāk.               123   32.17 N   72.26 E
Shāhpura, India             124   25.38 N   74.56 E
Shāhpura, India             124   27.23 N   75.58 E
Shāhpura, India             124   23.11 N   80.42 E
Shāhrak                      120   34.06 N   64.18 E
Shahr-e Bābak                128   30.07 N   55.09 E
Shahr-e Kord                 128   32.19 N   50.50 E
Shahr-e Monjān               128   36.02 N   70.46 E
Shahr-e Şafā                 128   31.50 N   66.22 E
Shahrestān                   128   32.20 N   66.47 E
Shahr-e Şafā... 
Shāhrūd                      128   36.40 N   49.25 E
Shāh Kūh ⩘ ...
Shaiki                       150   8.39 N     3.25 E
Shajianzi                    104   41.01 N  125.26 E
Shajiazhuang                 105   32.13 N  120.53 E
Shajing                      100   22.43 N  113.48 E
Shajingzi                    102   37.42 N  105.09 E
Shakaga-dake ⩘                95   33.11 N  130.53 E
Shakaga-take-tunnel          95   33.11 N  130.53 E
Shakardarra                  123   33.27 N   71.30 E
Shakargarh                   123   32.16 N   75.10 E
Shakarpura                 272a   28.46 N   77.21 E
Shakarpur Khās ⊶            272a   28.38 N   77.17 E
Shakaskraal                  158   29.26 S   31.14 E
Shakawe                      156   18.23 S   21.50 E
Shaker Heights               214   41.28 N   81.32 W
Shaker Heights Park ⊶        279a   41.28 N   81.33 W
Shakespeare                  212   43.22 N   80.49 W
Shakhtin                     128   32.27 N   35.01 E
Shakhty → Šachty              83   47.42 N   40.13 E
Shaki                        150   8.39 N     3.25 E
Shakotan-hantō ➤             92a   43.20 N  140.30 E
Shakou                       100   24.25 N  113.32 E
Shaktoolik                   180   64.20 N  161.09 W
Shakūjī ⊶⁸                   268   35.45 N  139.37 E
Shakūrpur ⊶⁸                272a   28.41 N   77.09 E
Shala, Lake ☒                144    7.25 N   38.30 E
Shalalth                     182   50.44 N  122.13 W
Shalatayn, Bi'r ⥋            146   23.07 N   35.36 E
Shalateli Dao I              101   11.12 N  108.44 E
Shaler Mountains ⩘           176   72.35 N  110.45 W
Shaleshanto                  158   19.09 S   23.58 E
Shalford                     260   51.13 N    0.34 W
Shālimar                     192   30.26 N   86.34 W
Shalimar Railroad Station ⊶ 272b  22.33 N   88.19 E
Shaling, Zhg.                104   41.20 N  123.01 E
Shaling, Zhg.                104   41.09 N  122.22 E
Shalingzi                    105   38.25 N   77.16 E
Shache (Yarkand)             104   38.25 N   77.16 E
Shacheng                     105   40.25 N  115.31 E
Shacheng Gang C              100   27.10 N  120.24 E
Shackan Indian Reserve ⊶     182   50.17 N  121.12 W
Shackleton Ice Shelf ⬙         9    66.00 S  100.00 E
Shackleton Range ⩘             9   80.40 S   26.00 W
Shade Gap                    208   40.11 N   77.52 W
Shadehill Reservoir ☒        198   45.45 N  102.15 W
Shades Glen                  208   40.34 N   79.40 W
Shade Mountain ⩘             208   40.34 N   77.20 W
Shadi                        100   26.08 N  114.49 E
Shadian                       98   35.30 N  114.26 E
Shading                       98   31.20 N   94.40 E
Shadow Lake ☒, On., Can.     212   44.43 N   78.48 W
Shadow Lake ☒, Ma., U.S.     285   40.21 N   74.24 W
Shadow Lake ≃                218   40.21 N   74.35 W
Shadow-Wood Village          214   40.35 N   79.12 W
Shadrinsk → Šadrinsk          86   56.05 N   63.38 E
Shadui                       102   31.30 N  100.10 E
Shafter                      204   35.30 N  119.16 W
Shagang                      100   27.10 N  118.55 E
Shager                      279b   40.17 N   79.47 W
Shanesville                  214   40.31 N   81.39 W
Shangalinge                  158   19.47 S   29.22 E
Shang'ao                      98   30.41 N  119.25 E
Shangbahe                    100   30.40 N  114.48 E
Shangbancheng                104   40.19 N  118.00 E
Shangcai                      98   33.16 N  114.15 E
Shangcheng                    98   31.48 N  115.24 E
Shangchuan Dao I             100   21.38 N  112.47 E
Shangdu                       98   41.32 N  113.32 E
Shangdunji                    98   33.26 N  115.20 E
Shangdundang                 100   22.56 N  110.13 E
Shangdundu                   104   26.09 N  117.19 E
Shanggao                     100   28.15 N  114.55 E
Shanggudui                   104   23.26 N  116.31 E
Shanghai, Va., U.S.          208   37.37 N   76.47 W
Shanghai, Zhg.               106   31.14 N  121.28 E
Shanghai, Zhg.               106   31.14 N  121.28 E
Shanghai, Zhg.              269b   31.14 N  121.28 E
Shanghailingtou             104   41.57 N  120.55 E
Shanghai Museum ⬙           269b   31.13 N  121.28 E
Shanghai Shi (Shanghai Shih) □⁷ 106 31.10 N 121.20 E
Shanghai Station ⊶⁵         269b   31.15 N  121.28 E
Shanghang                    100   25.06 N  116.25 E
Shanghe                       98   37.19 N  117.07 E
Shanghekou                   104   40.26 N  124.47 E
Shanghetou                   105   39.12 N  116.59 E
Shanghewantun                104   44.12 N  123.23 E
Shang Hu ⬙                   105   31.39 N  120.41 E
Shanghuang                   106   31.33 N  119.34 E
Shanghuangqi                  98   41.29 N  116.31 E
Shanghuocun                  105   40.35 N  115.45 E
Shangjiao                    100   28.26 N  117.58 E
  → Shangrao                 100   28.26 N  117.58 E
Shangjiahe                   104   41.18 N  121.10 E
Shangjiahe                   104   33.59 N  113.01 E
Shangkasa                    120   33.45 N   80.12 E
Shangkou                      98   36.59 N  118.53 E
Shangli                      100   27.52 N  113.46 E
Shanglin                     100   23.36 N  114.06 E
Shanglin, Zhg.               102   38.19 N  116.05 E
Shanglin, Zhg.               100   24.43 N  116.27 E
Shangliba                    104   41.31 N  122.14 E
Shanglianghezi               104   44.28 N  123.12 E
Shanglin                     104   41.02 N  123.13 E
Shangluli                    104   41.33 N  119.55 E
Shangmagushan                105   39.22 N  117.15 E
Shangmatai                   105   39.22 N  117.15 E
Shangmengjian                106   31.12 N  118.57 E
Shangmingju                  105   39.41 N  115.12 E
Shangnan                     102   33.31 N  110.45 E
Shangpandaoling              104   41.42 N  121.14 E
Shangpeibu                   100   25.57 N  117.33 E
Shangping, Zhg.              100   24.43 N  115.27 E
Shangping, Zhg.              100   24.29 N  114.38 E
Shangpuzi                    104   41.37 N  121.25 E
Shangqianou                  106   31.20 N  120.04 E
Shangqiao                    105   31.02 N  117.42 E
Shangqiu                      98   34.28 N  115.40 E
Shangqiu Shuiku ⊚¹           100   25.49 N  114.50 E
Shangqiyao                   102   38.15 N  105.61 E
Shangquan                    102   33.33 N  114.34 E
Shangqunzhen                 104   41.17 N  120.51 E
Shangquyou                   102   32.09 N  107.57 E
Shangtan                     106   30.27 N  118.42 E
Shangtang                    100   23.23 N  118.02 E
Shangtuan                    106   30.29 N  119.21 E
Shangweinuchang              104   40.54 N  120.44 E
Shangxingzhen                102   31.32 N  119.15 E
Shangxinhe                   102   38.15 N  113.20 E
Shangxinqiu                  104   42.27 N  121.37 E
Shangyangbao                 106   30.48 N  118.40 E
Shangye                      106   30.48 N  119.59 E
Shangying                    104   44°10 N  127.17 E
Shangyinku                   102   32.52 N  103.04 E
Shangyou                     100   25.51 N  114.38 E
Shangyou ≃                   100   25.49 N  114.50 E
Shangyuan                    102   34.01 N  109.40 E
Shangzhaoshougou             104   42.12 N  121.58 E
Shangzhen                    100   31.40 N  117.59 E
Shangzhenxuang               104   40.52 N  117.42 E
Shangzhi                     105   45.13 N  127.59 E
Shangzhou                    102   33.52 N  109.58 E
Shangzhuang                  105   34.11 N  115.25 E
Shanhaiguan                   98   40.01 N  119.44 E
  → Shanhaiguan              98   40.01 N  119.44 E
Shanhecun                     98   38.50 N   75.36 E
  → Shanhaiguan
Shanjiazhuang                105   38.52 N  128.27 E
Shanjing                     102   31.04 N  104.25 E
Shanklin                      42   50.38 N    1.10 W
Shankou, Zhg.                100   26.40 N  117.46 E
Shankou, Zhg.                100   28.58 N  115.12 E
Shanlenggang                 102   28.13 N  107.25 E
Shanli                       104   29.52 N  117.21 E
Shanmenjie                   100   30.42 N  120.19 E
Shanmulong                   102   24.39 N   96.05 E
Shannan                      102   31.36 N  116.52 E
Shannock                     211b   55.54 N  148.58 E
Shannon, Ire.                42   52.43 N    8.37 W
Shannon, Ga., U.S.           192   34.20 N   85.04 W
Shannon, Il., U.S.           218   42.09 N   89.44 W
Shannon, Ms., U.S.           194   34.07 N   88.42 W
Shannon, N.Z.                172   40.33 S  175.25 E
Shannon, S. Afr.             158   29.08 S   26.18 E
Shannon ≃                     42   52.36 N    9.41 W
Shannon, Lake ☒              224   48.37 N  121.42 W
Shannon, Mouth of the ⩴       42    9.50 W
Shannon Airport ⟋             50   52.41 N    8.55 W
Shannon Flat                171b   35.54 S  148.58 E
Shannonville                 192   33.53 N   80.21 W
Shannonville                 212   44.12 N   77.13 W
Shanp                        279b   40.44 N   79.29 W
Shanrendong                   89   46.50 N  123.08 E
Shanshan                     180   31.16 N   20.27 E
Shanshanmiao                 105   40.45 N  117.11 E
Shanshui                     100   23.10 N  112.58 E
Shantan                      102   38.21 N  105.12 E
Shantarskije ostrova II       74   55.00 N  137.36 E
Shanting                     105   35.05 N  117.10 E
Shantou (Swatow)             100   23.23 N  116.41 E
Shantung
  → Shandong □⁴              98   36.00 N  118.00 E
Shantung Peninsula
  → Shandong Bandao ➤¹       98   37.00 N  121.00 E
Shanwei                      100   22.47 N  115.20 E
Shanxi (Shansi) □⁴           102   37.00 N  112.00 E
Shānxian                     98   34.48 N  116.03 E
  → Sanmenxia, Zhg.          98
Shanyang                     102   33.32 N  109.52 E
Shanyin                      102   39.33 N  112.50 E
Shaodong                     100   27.15 N  111.45 E
Shaoguan                     100   24.48 N  113.37 E
Shaoguang                    104   41.30 N  123.37 E
Shaowu                       100   27.21 N  117.29 E
Shaoxing                      98   30.00 N  120.35 E
Shaoyang                     100   27.14 N  111.28 E
Shaozhai                     104   41.38 N  121.34 E
Shaoyuingari                 104   41.33 N  120.27 E
```

Bottom legend

Symbols in the index entries represent the broad categories identified in the key at the right. Symbols with superior numbers (⩘¹) identify subcategories (see complete key on page I · 1).

Symbole im Register stellen die rechts im Schlüssel erklärten Kategorien dar. Symbole mit hochgestellten Ziffern (⩘¹) bezeichnen Unterabteilungen einer Kategorie (vgl. vollständiger Schlüssel auf Seite I · 1).

Los símbolos incluídos en el texto del índice representan las grandes categorías identificadas con la clave a la derecha. Los símbolos con números en su parte superior (⩘¹) identifican las subcategorías (véase la clave completa en la página I · 1).

Les symboles de l'index représentent les catégories indiquées dans la légende à droite. Les symboles suivis d'un indice (⩘¹) identifient des sous-catégories (voir légende complète à la page I · 1).

Os símbolos incluídos no texto do índice representam as grandes categorias identificadas com a chave à direita. Os símbolos com números em sua parte superior (⩘¹) identificam as subcategorias (veja-se a chave completa à página I · 1).

Symbol	English	Deutsch	Español	Français	Português
⩘	Mountain	Berg	Montaña	Montagne	Montanha
⩘	Mountains	Gebirge	Montañas	Montagnes	Montanhas
				Col	Passo
⩗	Valley, Canyon	Tal, Cañon	Valle, Cañón	Vallée, Canyon	Vale, Canhão
⩝	Plain	Ebene	Llano	Plaine	Planície
➤	Cape	Kap	Cabo	Cap	Cabo
I	Island	Insel	Isla	Île	Ilha
II	Islands	Inseln	Islas	Îles	Ilhas
±	Other Topographic Features	Andere Topographische Objekte	Otros Elementos Topográficos	Autres données topographiques	Outros acidentes topográficos

ESPAÑOL Nombre	Página	Lat. °′	Long. °′ W = Oeste
Shaohing → Shaoxing	100	30.00 N	120.35 E
Shaohsing → Shaoxing	100	30.00 N	120.35 E
Shaojiaolou	106	31.05 N	121.32 E
Shaokuan → Shaoguan	100	24.50 N	113.37 E
Shaowu	100	27.20 N	117.28 E
Shaoxing	100	30.00 N	120.35 E
Shaoyang, Zhg.	102	27.15 N	111.28 E
Shaoyang, Zhg.	102	27.00 N	111.18 E
Shaoyun	107	29.30 N	105.57 E
Shaozihe	98	40.13 N	123.33 E
Shap	44	54.32 N	2.41 W
Shapinsay I	46	59.03 N	2.53 W
Shāpūr ≃	128	29.39 N	51.03 E
Shaqʿah, Ra's ash- ›	130	34.19 N	35.41 E
Shaqqā	132	32.53 N	36.42 E
Shaqq al-Juʿayfir, Wādī ∨	140	15.16 N	26.00 E
Shaqrā', Ar. Su.	128	25.15 N	45.15 E
Shaqrā', J.Y.D.S.	144	13.21 N	45.42 E
Shaqrā, Lubnān	132	33.12 N	35.28 E
Shaqrā', Sūrīy.	132	32.54 N	36.14 E
Shaquan	86	44.33 N	83.25 E
Shaquzhen	107	30.33 N	103.45 E
Sharafābād	272a	28.36 N	77.23 E
Sharafkhāneh	128	38.11 N	45.29 E
Sharan Jogīzai	120	31.02 N	68.33 E
Sharatin Mountain ∧	180	57.49 N	152.41 W
Sharbatāt, Ra's ash- ›	118	17.56 N	56.21 E
Sharbīn, Jabal ∧	132	33.43 N	36.21 E
Sharbot Lake	212	44.46 N	76.41 W
Sharbot Lake ⊝	212	44.46 N	76.41 W
Share	150	8.50 N	4.56 E
Shari	92a	43.55 N	144.50 E
Shari-dake ∧	92a	43.46 N	144.43 E
Sharīṭah, Ra's ›	128	26.23 N	56.23 E
Shark ≃	220	25.21 N	81.05 W
Shark Bay c	162	25.30 S	113.30 E
Shark Point ›, Austl.	274a	33.55 S	151.17 E
Shark Point ›, Fl., U.S.	220	25.23 N	81.09 W
Shark River Hills	208	40.12 N	74.03 W
Sharktooth Mountain ∧	180	58.35 N	127.57 W
Sharm ash-Shaykh	140	27.51 N	34.17 E
Sharnbrook	42	52.13 N	0.32 W
Sharnūb	142	31.01 N	30.35 E
Sharon, On., Can.	214	42.53 N	81.22 W
Sharon, Ct., U.S.	207	41.52 N	73.28 W
Sharon, Ma., U.S.	207	42.07 N	71.10 W
Sharon, N.D., U.S.	198	47.35 N	97.53 W
Sharon, Pa., U.S.	214	41.13 N	80.29 W
Sharon, Tn., U.S.	194	36.14 N	88.49 W
Sharon, Wi., U.S.	216	42.30 N	88.43 W
Sharon Center	214	41.06 N	81.44 W
Sharon Hill	285	39.54 N	75.16 W
Sharon Park	218	39.23 N	84.35 W
Sharon Springs, Ks., U.S.	198	38.53 N	101.45 W
Sharon Springs, N.Y., U.S.	210	42.48 N	74.37 W
Sharon Valley	207	41.53 N	73.29 W
Sharonville	218	39.16 N	84.24 W
Sharpe, Lake ⊝[1]	198	44.05 N	99.55 W
Sharpe Lake ⊝	184	54.24 N	93.30 W
Sharpes	220	28.25 N	80.45 W
Sharp Island I	271d	22.22 N	114.17 E
Sharpley	285	39.48 N	75.33 W
Sharp Park ♠	282	37.37 N	122.29 W
Sharp Peak ∧	116	5.58 N	125.31 E
Sharpsburg, Il., U.S.	219	39.37 N	89.21 W
Sharpsburg, Ky., U.S.	218	38.12 N	83.55 W
Sharpsburg, Pa., U.S.	279b	40.29 N	79.55 W
Sharps Hill	279b	40.30 N	79.56 W
Sharps Run ≃	285	39.54 N	74.49 W
Sharpsville, In., U.S.	216	40.22 N	86.05 W
Sharpsville, Pa., U.S.	214	41.15 N	80.28 W
Sharptown, Md., U.S.	208	38.32 N	75.43 W
Sharptown, N.J., U.S.	285	39.39 N	75.21 W
Sharqī, Al-Jabal ash- (Anti-Lebanon) ⋀	132	33.35 N	36.00 E
Sharqīyah, Aṣ-Ṣaḥrā' ash- (Arabian Desert) ◆[2]	140	28.00 N	32.00 E
Sharqpur	123	31.28 N	74.06 E
Sharshar, Jabal ∧[2]	140	23.52 N	30.20 E
Shartlesville	208	40.31 N	76.06 W
Shārūnah	142	28.36 N	30.51 E
Shārūnah, Wādī ∨	142	28.36 N	30.52 E
Shasha	144	6.20 N	35.57 E
Shashe ≃	156	22.14 S	29.20 E
Shashemene	144	7.12 N	38.43 E
Shashi	102	30.19 N	112.14 E
Shashibu	100	25.48 N	114.54 E
Shasi → Shashi	102	30.19 N	112.14 E
Shasta	204	40.36 N	122.29 W
Shasta ≃	204	41.50 N	122.35 W
Shasta, Mount ∧[1]	204	41.20 N	122.20 W
Shasta Lake ⊝[1]	204	40.50 N	122.25 W
Shatangjiang	106	31.25 N	120.01 E
Shaṭānūf	142	30.14 N	31.04 E
Shatawī	140	14.39 N	32.06 E
Shāṭi', Wādī ash- ∨	146	27.30 N	13.15 E
Shatian, Zhg.	100	25.53 N	113.44 E
Shatian, Zhg.	100	23.59 N	113.56 E
Shatila	132	33.51 N	35.30 E
Sha Tin	271d	22.23 N	114.11 E
Shatt al-Arab → Arab, Shatt al- ≃	128	29.57 N	48.34 E
Shattuck	196	36.16 N	99.52 W
Shatuji	98	35.18 N	115.45 E
Shatuosi	102	31.20 N	108.51 E
Shauck	214	40.37 N	82.40 W
Shaunavon	184	49.40 N	108.25 W
Shaver Lake	226	37.09 N	119.18 W
Shaver Lake ⊝[1]	226	37.08 N	119.17 W
Shavertown	210	41.19 N	75.55 W
Shavé Ẕiyyon	132	32.59 N	35.05 E
Shavington	44	53.04 N	2.27 W
Shaw, Eng., U.K.	44	53.34 N	2.05 W
Shaw, Eng., U.K.	262	53.35 N	2.06 W
Shaw, Ms., U.S.	194	33.36 N	90.46 W
Shaw ≃	162	20.20 S	119.17 E
Shaw Air Force Base ▪	192	33.58 N	80.29 W
Shawan, Zhg.	86	44.34 N	85.48 E
Shawan, Zhg.	100	27.52 N	119.28 E
Shawan, Zhg.	107	29.25 N	103.33 E
Shawanaga Inlet c	190	45.32 N	80.24 W
Shawangunk Kill ≃	210	41.41 N	74.10 W
Shawangunk Mountains ⋀	210	41.35 N	74.30 W
Shawano	190	44.46 N	88.36 W
Shawbury	42	52.47 N	2.39 W
Shaw Creek ≃	192	33.34 N	81.30 W
Shawhan	218	38.18 N	84.16 W
Shawinigan	206	46.33 N	72.45 W
Shawinigan ≃	206	46.32 N	72.46 W
Shawinigan, Lac ⊝	206	46.41 N	73.10 W
Shawinigan Falls → Shawinigan	206	46.33 N	72.45 W
Shawinigan-Sud	206	46.31 N	72.45 W
Shaw Island I	224	48.34 N	122.57 W
Shawmarī, Wādī ash- ∨	132	30.21 N	36.25 E
Shawmere ≃	190	48.20 N	82.28 W
Shawnee, Ks., U.S.	198	39.02 N	94.43 W
Shawnee, Oh., U.S.	188	39.36 N	82.12 W
Shawnee, Ok., U.S.	196	35.19 N	96.55 W
Shawnee, Lake ⊝	276	40.58 N	74.35 W
Shawnee Hills	214	40.07 N	83.09 W
Shawnee On Delaware	210	41.01 N	75.07 W
Shawnee State Park ♠	218	38.43 N	83.10 W

FRANÇAIS Nom	Page	Lat. °′	Long. °′ W = Ouest
Shawneetown	194	37.42 N	88.11 W
Shawnī	142	30.45 N	30.55 E
Shawnigan Lake	224	48.38 N	123.35 W
Shawnigan Lake ⊝	224	48.37 N	123.37 W
Shawo, Som.	144	3.26 N	45.21 E
Shawo, Zhg.	98	34.28 N	114.37 E
Shawo, Zhg.	100	28.52 N	114.47 E
Shawo, Zhg.	100	31.44 N	115.08 E
Shawsheen ≃	283	42.42 N	71.08 W
Shawsheen Village	283	42.40 N	71.09 W
Shawtown	279b	40.20 N	79.42 W
Shawville	188	45.36 N	76.30 W
Shaxi, Zhg.	100	28.34 N	118.06 E
Shaxi, Zhg.	100	26.53 N	115.34 E
Shaxi, Zhg.	100	24.38 N	113.42 E
Shaxi, Zhg.	106	31.34 N	121.04 E
Shaxian	100	26.24 N	117.47 E
Shaxikou	100	26.33 N	118.02 E
Shaximiao	107	29.57 N	106.19 E
Shayang	100	30.42 N	112.33 E
Shaybārā I	128	25.27 N	36.48 E
Shay Gap	162	20.25 S	120.03 E
Shaykh, Jabal ash- (Mount Hermon) ∧	132	33.26 N	35.51 E
Shaykh, Wādī ash- ∨	142	28.48 N	30.55 E
Shaykh Al-Ḥadīd	130	36.30 N	36.35 E
Shaykh Miskīn	132	32.49 N	36.09 E
Shaykh Saʿd	128	32.34 N	46.17 E
Shaykh ʿUthmān	144	12.52 N	44.59 E
Shayuan	100	27.45 N	120.38 E
Shazhen	98	36.23 N	115.47 E
Shazhou	106	31.52 N	120.32 E
Shazihe	102	32.12 N	106.42 E
Shchekino → Ščokino	76	54.01 N	37.31 E
Shchelkovo → Ščolkovo	76	55.55 N	38.00 E
Shcherbakov → Rybinsk	76	58.03 N	38.52 E
She ≃	100	30.41 N	114.32 E
Sheaf ≃	44	53.23 N	1.26 W
Shea Island I	276	41.03 N	73.24 W
Sheakleyville	214	41.27 N	80.13 W
Shea Stadium ♠	276	40.45 N	73.51 W
Shebele	144	9.43 N	42.43 E
Shebele (Shabeelle) ≃	144	0.12 S	42.45 E
Sheberghān	120	36.41 N	65.45 E
Shebeshekong ≃	212	45.26 N	80.19 W
Sheboygan	190	43.45 N	87.42 W
Sheboygan ≃	190	43.45 N	87.42 W
Sheboygan Falls	190	43.43 N	87.48 W
Shebu	100	27.40 N	112.48 E
Shechem → Nābulus	132	32.13 N	35.16 E
Shechem ⊥	132	32.13 N	35.15 E
Shecheng	102	37.14 N	113.05 E
Shedd Canyon ∨	226	35.39 N	120.26 W
Shedden	214	42.44 N	81.21 W
Shediac	186	46.13 N	64.32 W
Shedin Peak ∧	182	55.55 N	127.32 W
Sheekh	144	9.56 N	45.11 E
Sheelin, Lough ⊝	48	53.48 N	7.22 W
Sheenjek ≃	180	66.45 N	144.33 W
Sheep ≃	182	50.44 N	113.51 W
Sheep Creek ≃, Ab., Can.	182	54.04 N	119.00 W
Sheep Creek ≃, U.S.	202	42.27 N	115.36 W
Sheep Creek ≃, Ut,. U.S.	200	40.55 N	109.39 W
Sheep Creek ≃, Wy., U.S.	200	42.03 N	106.04 W
Sheep Haven c	48	55.10 N	7.52 W
Sheepmoor	158	26.42 S	30.13 E
Sheep Mountain ∧, Az., U.S.	200	32.32 N	114.14 W
Sheep Mountain ∧, Wy., U.S.	200	43.33 N	110.32 W
Sheep Peak ∧	196	31.14 N	104.59 W
Sheepranch	226	38.13 N	120.28 W
Sheep Range ⋀	204	36.45 N	115.05 W
Sheepshead Bay ◆[8]	276	40.35 N	73.56 W
's-Heerenberg	52	51.53 N	6.15 E
's-Heerenhoek	52	51.27 N	3.46 E
Sheerness	42	51.27 N	0.45 E
Sheet Harbour	186	44.55 N	62.32 W
Shefarʿam	132	32.48 N	35.10 E
Sheffield, N.Z.	172	43.23 S	172.01 E
Sheffield, Eng., U.K.	44	53.23 N	1.28 W
Sheffield, Al., U.S.	194	34.45 N	87.41 W
Sheffield, Il., U.S.	190	41.21 N	89.44 W
Sheffield, Ia., U.S.	190	42.53 N	93.12 W
Sheffield, Ma., U.S.	207	42.06 N	73.21 W
Sheffield, Oh., U.S.	214	41.25 N	82.05 W
Sheffield, Pa., U.S.	214	41.42 N	79.02 W
Sheffield, Tx., U.S.	196	30.41 N	101.49 W
Sheffield Island I	276	41.03 N	73.25 W
Sheffield Island Harbor c	276	41.03 N	73.25 W
Sheffield Lake	214	41.29 N	82.06 W
Sheffield Lake ⊝	186	49.20 N	56.35 W
Shefford	42	52.02 N	0.20 W
Shefford □[6]	206	45.25 N	72.30 W
Shefu	100	26.11 N	115.22 E
Shegangshi	100	28.32 N	113.36 E
Shegaon	122	20.47 N	76.41 E
Sheho	184	51.38 N	103.12 W
Shehong	102	30.56 N	105.22 E
Shehongmiao	107	30.44 N	106.03 E
Shehuen ≃	254	49.35 S	69.34 W
Shehy Mountains ⋀	48	51.48 N	9.15 W
Sheikh Hasan	144	12.04 N	35.53 E
Sheikhpura	124	25.09 N	85.51 E
Shekatika	186	51.17 N	58.20 W
Shekhūpura	123	31.42 N	73.59 E
Sheki → Šeki	84	41.12 N	47.12 E
Shekki → Zhongshan	100	22.31 N	113.22 E
Shek Kong	271d	22.26 N	114.06 E
Shek Kong Airfield ⊠	271d	22.27 N	114.05 E
Shek Kwu Chau I	271d	22.12 N	113.59 E
Shekou	100	30.44 N	114.20 E
Shek Uk Shan ∧	271d	22.27 N	114.18 E
Shelagyote Peak ∧	182	55.58 N	127.12 W
Shelbina	219	39.41 N	92.02 W
Shelbourne	169	36.52 S	144.01 E
Shelburn	194	39.11 N	87.24 W
Shelburne, N.S., Can.	186	43.46 N	65.19 W
Shelburne, On., Can.	212	44.04 N	80.12 W
Shelburne Bay c	164	11.49 S	143.00 E
Shelburne Falls	207	42.36 N	72.44 W
Shelby, In., U.S.	216	41.11 N	87.20 W
Shelby, Ia., U.S.	198	41.30 N	95.27 W
Shelby, Mi., U.S.	190	43.36 N	86.21 W
Shelby, Ms., U.S.	194	33.57 N	90.46 W
Shelby, Mt., U.S.	202	48.30 N	111.51 W
Shelby, Ne., U.S.	198	41.11 N	97.25 W
Shelby, N.C., U.S.	192	35.17 N	81.32 W
Shelby, Oh., U.S.	214	40.52 N	82.39 W
Shelby □[6], Il., U.S.	219	39.24 N	88.48 W
Shelby □[6], In., U.S.	218	39.31 N	85.47 W
Shelby □[6], Ky., U.S.	218	38.15 N	85.13 W
Shelby □[6], Mo., U.S.	219	39.49 N	92.03 W
Shelby □[6], Oh., U.S.	216	40.17 N	84.09 W
Shelby Village	281	42.38 N	83.04 W
Shelbyville, Il., U.S.	219	39.24 N	88.47 W
Shelbyville, In., U.S.	218	39.31 N	85.46 W
Shelbyville, Ky., U.S.	218	38.12 N	85.13 W
Shelbyville, Mo., U.S.	219	39.48 N	92.02 W
Shelbyville, Tn., U.S.	194	35.29 N	86.27 W
Shelbyville, Lake ⊝[1]	219	39.30 N	88.40 W
Sheldon, Il., U.S.	216	40.46 N	87.33 W
Sheldon, Ia., U.S.	198	43.10 N	95.51 W
Sheldon, Mi., U.S.	216	42.17 N	83.28 W
Sheldon, Mo., U.S.	194	37.39 N	94.17 W
Sheldon, Tx., U.S.	222	29.52 N	95.08 W
Sheldon Brook ≃	276	41.03 N	73.52 W
Sheldon Creek ≃	212	44.07 N	79.53 W
Sheldon Point	180	62.32 N	164.52 W

PORTUGUÊS Nome	Página	Lat. °′	Long. °′ W = Oeste
Sheldon Reservoir ⊝[1]	222	29.52 N	95.10 W
Sheldonville	283	42.02 N	71.23 W
Sheldrake ≃	276	40.57 N	73.44 W
Sheldrake Lake ⊝, On., Can.	212	44.49 N	77.16 W
Sheldrake Lake ⊝, N.Y., U.S.	276	40.57 N	73.46 W
Shelikof Strait ʊ	180	57.30 N	155.00 W
Shell ≃	184	50.58 N	101.24 W
Shell, Loch c	46	58.00 N	6.30 W
Shellbrook	184	53.13 N	106.24 W
Shell Brook ≃	184	53.21 N	106.00 W
Shell Creek ≃, U.S.	200	40.56 N	108.37 W
Shell Creek ≃, Ne., U.S.	198	41.27 N	96.58 W
Shell Creek ≃, N.D., U.S.	198	47.59 N	102.17 W
Shell Creek ≃, Wy., U.S.	202	44.31 N	108.03 W
Shellen	146	9.54 N	12.00 E
Shelley, B.C., Can.	182	54.00 N	122.37 W
Shelley, Id., U.S.	202	43.22 N	112.07 W
Shellharbour	170	34.35 S	150.52 E
Shell Lake, Sk., Can.	184	53.18 N	107.04 W
Shell Lake, Wi., U.S.	190	45.44 N	91.55 W
Shell Lakes ⊝	162	29.21 S	127.25 E
Shellman	192	31.45 N	84.36 W
Shellmouth Dam ◆[6]	184	50.58 N	101.25 W
Shellow Bowells	260	51.45 N	0.20 E
Shell Rock	190	42.42 N	92.34 W
Shell Rock ≃	190	42.38 N	92.30 W
Shellrock Peak ∧	224	46.43 N	121.14 W
Shellsburg	190	42.05 N	91.52 W
Shelocta	214	40.39 N	79.18 W
Shelter, Port c	271d	22.21 N	114.17 E
Shelter Island	207	41.04 N	72.20 W
Shelter Island I, H.K.	271d	22.20 N	114.17 E
Shelter Island I, N.Y., U.S.	207	41.04 N	72.20 W
Shelter Island Heights	207	41.05 N	72.21 W
Shelter Island Sound ʊ	207	41.03 N	72.22 W
Shelton, Ct., U.S.	207	41.18 N	73.05 W
Shelton, Ne., U.S.	198	40.47 N	98.44 W
Shelton, Wa., U.S.	224	47.13 N	123.06 W
Shemanker ≃	150	8.12 N	9.45 E
Shemogue	186	46.09 N	64.11 W
Shemya Station	181a	52.43 N	174.05 E
Shenandoah, Ia., U.S.	198	40.45 N	95.22 W
Shenandoah, Pa., U.S.	208	40.49 N	76.12 W
Shenandoah, Va., U.S.	188	38.29 N	78.37 W
Shenandoah ≃	188	39.19 N	77.44 W
Shenandoah, North Fork ≃	188	38.57 N	78.12 W
Shenandoah, South Fork ≃	188	38.57 N	78.12 W
Shenandoah Heights	210	40.49 N	76.12 W
Shenandoah National Park ♠	188	38.48 N	78.12 W
Shenango	214	41.23 N	80.24 W
Shenango ≃	214	40.57 N	80.23 W
Shenango River Lake ⊝[1]	214	41.22 N	80.28 W
Shenchi	102	39.09 N	112.19 E
Shencottah	122	8.58 N	77.16 E
Shencun	106	31.04 N	118.51 E
Shendam	150	8.53 N	9.32 E
Shendang	106	30.34 N	120.49 E
Shending Shan ∧	89	46.38 N	133.28 E
Shenduncun	106	30.48 N	120.25 E
Shenfield	260	51.38 N	0.19 E
Shengang, Zhg.	100	27.20 N	116.18 E
Shengang, Zhg.	106	31.54 N	120.08 E
Shenge	150	7.55 N	12.57 W
Shengfang	105	39.04 N	116.42 E
Shenggongjing	106	31.07 N	119.48 E
Shenghongqing	100	30.12 N	114.56 E
Shengjiachi	107	30.28 N	105.03 E
Shengjiaqiao	106	31.27 N	121.24 E
Shengjiatun	104	41.14 N	121.22 E
Shengjin'gao	104	42.04 N	120.43 E
Shengou	100	34.08 N	113.13 E
Shengqing	104	41.34 N	121.36 E
Shengshan	106	30.50 N	120.15 E
Shengshui	98	35.45 N	119.39 E
Shengshuihezi	98	42.27 N	125.59 E
Shengsi Liedao II	100	30.42 N	122.20 E
Shengtian	100	27.14 N	113.06 E
Shengxian	100	29.36 N	120.48 E
Shengze	106	30.55 N	120.39 E
Shengzigou	104	41.35 N	124.04 E
Shenhu	100	24.38 N	118.39 E
Shenipsit Lake ⊝	207	41.53 N	72.26 W
Shenji	98	34.47 N	115.09 E
Shenjia	89	46.06 N	126.46 E
Shenjiadian	89	46.35 N	130.38 E
Shenjiatai	104	41.22 N	120.50 E
Shenjiawan	106	31.43 N	121.19 E
Shenjiazhuang	106	32.18 N	120.26 E
Shenjing, Zhg.	102	21.59 N	112.28 E
Shenjing, Zhg.	105	40.24 N	114.49 E
Shenjingzi	104	41.47 N	123.41 E
Shenk'eng	269d	25.00 N	121.36 E
Shenkou	100	28.42 N	116.02 E
Shenley	260	51.41 N	0.17 W
Shenmu	102	38.56 N	110.19 E
Shennan	105	38.59 N	114.56 E
Shenorock	210	41.20 N	73.44 W
Shenqiu	100	33.24 N	115.02 E
Shenquan	100	22.59 N	116.20 E
Shenquan Gang c	100	22.54 N	116.18 E
Shensi → Shaanxi □[4]	102	35.00 N	109.00 E
Shenton, Mount ∧	162	28.00 S	123.22 E
Shentuan	98	35.30 N	119.17 E
Shenxian, Zhg.	98	38.01 N	115.33 E
Shenxian, Zhg.	98	36.15 N	115.41 E
Shenxing	105	39.02 N	115.19 E
Shenyang (Mukden)	104	41.48 N	123.27 E
Shenze	98	38.11 N	115.11 E
Sheoganj	120	25.09 N	73.04 E
Sheokhāla	126	22.46 N	88.10 E
Sheopur	124	25.40 N	76.42 E
Shepard	182	50.57 N	113.55 W
Shepard Island I	9	74.25 S	132.30 W
Shepards Brook ≃	283	42.08 N	71.25 W
Shepaug ≃	207	41.28 N	73.19 W
Shepherd, Mi., U.S.	190	43.31 N	84.41 W
Shepherd, Tx., U.S.	222	30.30 N	95.01 W
Shepherd □[8]	175f	17.05 S	168.25 E
Shepherd, Îles II	175f	16.55 S	168.36 E
Shepherdstown	188	39.25 N	77.48 W
Shepherdsville	194	37.59 N	85.42 W
Sheppard Air Force Base ▪	196	33.58 N	98.30 W
Sheppard Peak ∧	180	57.41 N	132.37 W
Sheppard Pond ⊝	276	41.08 N	74.13 W
Shepparton	166	36.23 S	145.25 E
Shepperd, Lake ⊝	162	29.55 S	123.09 E
Shepperton	260	51.24 N	0.27 W
Sheppey, Isle of I	42	51.24 N	0.50 E
Sheppler Hill ∧[2]	279b	40.09 N	79.49 W
Sheppton	210	40.53 N	76.07 W
Shepshed	42	52.47 N	1.18 W
Shepton Mallet	42	51.12 N	2.33 W
Shepway	260	51.15 N	0.33 E
Sheqi	100	33.03 N	112.57 E
Sherab	140	10.43 N	24.47 E
Sherada	144	7.21 N	36.32 E
Sheraden ◆[8]	279b	40.28 N	80.05 W
Sherard, Cape ›	176	74.36 N	80.25 W
Sherborn	283	42.14 N	71.22 W
Sherborne	42	50.57 N	2.31 W
Sherborne Lake ⊝	212	45.11 N	78.47 W
Sherborne Saint John	42	51.18 N	1.07 W

Sherbro ≃	150	7.45 N	12.55 W
Sherbro Island I	150	7.45 N	12.55 W
Sherbrooke, N.S., Can.	186	45.08 N	61.59 W
Sherbrooke, P.Q., Can.	206	45.25 N	71.54 W
Sherbrooke □[6]	206	45.25 N	71.55 W
Sherbrooke Lake ⊝	186	44.40 N	64.35 W
Sherburn	198	43.39 N	94.43 W
Sherburne	210	42.40 N	75.29 W
Sherburne Reef ✣[2]	164	3.20 S	148.00 E
Sherburn in Elmet	44	53.48 N	1.15 W
Shercock	48	54.00 N	6.54 W
Shere	260	51.13 N	0.28 W
Sheridan, Ar., U.S.	194	34.18 N	92.24 W
Sheridan, Ca., U.S.	226	38.59 N	121.22 W
Sheridan, Il., U.S.	216	41.32 N	88.41 W
Sheridan, In., U.S.	218	40.08 N	86.13 W
Sheridan, Mt., U.S.	202	45.27 N	112.11 W
Sheridan, Or., U.S.	202	45.05 N	123.23 W
Sheridan, Pa., U.S.	208	40.21 N	76.14 W
Sheridan, Tx., U.S.	222	29.29 N	96.40 W
Sheridan, Wy., U.S.	202	44.47 N	106.57 W
Sheridan, Mount ∧	202	44.16 N	110.32 W
Sheridan Park ♠	284a	42.59 N	78.54 W
Sheringa	162	33.51 S	135.15 E
Sheringham	42	52.57 N	1.12 E
Sherkston	284a	42.53 N	79.08 W
Sherlock ≃	162	20.44 S	117.35 E
Sherman, Ct., U.S.	207	41.34 N	73.29 W
Sherman, Il., U.S.	219	39.54 N	89.36 W
Sherman, Ky., U.S.	218	38.44 N	84.36 W
Sherman, Ms., U.S.	194	34.21 N	88.50 W
Sherman, N.Y., U.S.	214	42.09 N	79.35 W
Sherman, Tx., U.S.	196	33.38 N	96.36 W
Sherman □[6]	224	45.25 N	120.49 W
Sherman Creek ≃	208	40.23 N	77.02 W
Sherman Mills	188	45.52 N	68.23 W
Sherman Mountain ∧	194	36.01 N	93.17 W
Sherman Oaks ◆[8]	280	34.09 N	118.26 W
Sherman Reservoir ⊝[1]	198	41.20 N	98.55 W
Sherman Station	188	45.53 N	68.25 W
Sherpur, Bngl.	124	24.41 N	89.25 E
Sherpur, Bngl.	124	25.01 N	90.01 E
Sher Qila	123	36.06 N	74.03 E
Sherrard	190	41.19 N	90.31 W
Sherridon	184	55.07 N	101.05 W
Sherrill	210	43.04 N	75.35 W
Sherri Park	278	42.02 N	87.51 W
Sherrodsville	214	40.29 N	81.14 W
Sher Shāh	123	30.06 N	71.21 E
Shertallai	122	9.42 N	76.20 E
's-Hertogenbosch	52	51.41 N	5.19 E
Sherway Centre ◆[9]	275b	43.37 N	79.33 W
Sherwood, On., Can.	275b	43.50 N	79.31 W
Sherwood, P.E., Can.	186	46.17 N	63.08 W
Sherwood, Ar., U.S.	194	34.48 N	92.13 W
Sherwood, Md., U.S.	208	38.36 N	76.19 W
Sherwood, Mi., U.S.	216	42.00 N	85.14 W
Sherwood, N.D., U.S.	198	48.57 N	101.37 W
Sherwood, Oh., U.S.	216	41.17 N	84.33 W
Sherwood, Or., U.S.	224	45.21 N	122.50 W
Sherwood, Tn., U.S.	194	35.04 N	85.55 W
Sherwood, Lake ⊝	281	42.36 N	83.33 W
Sherwood Forest, Ca., U.S.	226	37.57 N	122.17 W
Sherwood Forest, Md., U.S.	284c	39.05 N	77.01 W
Sherwood Forest ◆[3]	44	53.08 N	1.08 W
Sherwood Island State Park ♠	276	41.07 N	73.20 W
Sherwood Manor	207	42.01 N	72.38 W
Sherwood Park, Ab., Can.	182	53.31 N	113.19 W
Sherwood Park, De., U.S.	285	39.44 N	75.39 W
Sherwood Park, N.Y., U.S.	210	42.36 N	73.43 W
Sherwood Park ♠	275b	43.43 N	79.24 W
Sherwood Point ›	276	41.07 N	73.20 W
Sherwood Shores	196	30.36 N	98.22 W
She Shan ∧[2]	106	31.06 N	121.11 E
Sheshea ≃	248	9.36 S	74.10 W
Shesh Gāv	120	33.45 N	68.33 E
Shet Bandar	272c	18.58 N	72.56 E
Shetek, Lake ⊝	198	44.08 N	95.42 W
Shetland □[4]	46a	60.30 N	1.15 W
Shetland del Sur, Islas → South Shetland Islands II	9	62.00 S	58.00 W
Shetland Islands II	46a	60.30 N	1.15 W
Shetou	106	31.39 N	119.27 E
Shetrunji ≃	120	21.19 N	72.07 E
Shetucket ≃	207	41.31 N	72.05 W
Sheva	272c	18.56 N	72.57 E
Sheva Nhava	272c	18.58 N	72.58 E
Shevaroy Hills ⋀[2]	122	11.50 N	78.16 E
Shevington	262	53.34 N	2.42 W
Shevington Moor	262	53.35 N	2.41 W
Shewa □[4]	144	9.00 N	39.00 E
Shewa Gimira	144	7.00 N	35.50 E
Shexian, Zhg.	98	36.33 N	113.40 E
Shexian, Zhg.	100	29.53 N	118.26 E
Sheyang, Zhg.	100	33.20 N	119.38 E
Sheyang, Zhg.	100	33.46 N	120.18 E
Sheyenne	198	47.49 N	99.07 W
Sheyenne ≃	198	47.05 N	96.50 W
Sheykhābād	120	34.05 N	68.45 E
Shey-Phoksundo National Park ♠	124	29.30 N	82.45 E
Shezhu	106	31.19 N	119.16 E
Shḥīm	132	33.37 N	35.29 E
Shi ≃, Zhg.	100	32.18 N	114.31 E
Shi ≃, Zhg.	100	32.32 N	115.52 E
Shiant, Sound of ʊ	46	57.55 N	6.25 W
Shiant Islands II	46	57.53 N	6.21 W
Shiawassee □[6]	216	42.56 N	84.09 W
Shiawassee ≃	216	43.06 N	84.10 W
Shiawassee, South Branch ≃	216	42.49 N	83.56 W
Shiba	100	32.45 N	118.07 E
Shiba ≃	268	35.47 N	139.44 E
Shibadu	102	28.01 N	110.51 E
Shibakawa	94	35.13 N	138.33 E
Shibām	144	15.56 N	48.38 E
Shiban	107	30.18 N	104.28 E
Shibanxi	107	29.17 N	103.51 E
Shibaocheng	102	39.48 N	96.10 E
Shibarni	140	14.50 N	24.25 E
Shibasaki	268	35.39 N	139.34 E
Shibata	92	37.57 N	139.20 E
Shibayama	94	35.41 N	140.25 E
Shibayama-gata ⊝	94	36.21 N	136.23 E
Shibden Hall	262	53.44 N	1.51 W
Shibecha	92a	43.17 N	144.36 E
Shibetsu, Nihon	92a	43.40 N	145.08 E
Shibetsu, Nihon	92a	44.10 N	142.23 E
Shibi	100	26.43 N	120.02 E
Shibīn al-Kawm	142	30.33 N	31.01 E
Shibīn al-Qanāṭir	142	30.19 N	31.19 E
Shibing	102	26.50 N	108.04 E
Shibishan	100	29.21 N	116.45 E
Shiblanjah	142	30.28 N	31.16 E
Shibu	98	36.45 N	119.27 E
Shibukawa	94	36.29 N	139.00 E
Shibure-yama ∧	270	34.45 N	135.05 E
Shibushi	92	31.28 N	131.07 E
Shibutsu-san ∧	94	36.54 N	139.11 E
Shibuya ◆[8]	268	35.40 N	139.42 E
Shibuzi	98	36.09 N	119.06 E
Shicha	100	28.24 N	115.50 E
Shichangyu	104	41.12 N	123.14 E
Shicheng, Zhg.	98	40.39 N	124.17 E
Shicheng, Zhg.	100	25.18 N	119.21 E
Shicheng, Zhg.	100	26.22 N	116.22 E
Shicheng Dao I	98	39.31 N	123.02 E
Shichisō	94	35.33 N	137.07 E
Shickley	198	40.25 N	97.43 W

Shickshinny	210	41.09 N	76.09 W
Shidai	100	30.20 N	117.56 E
Shidao	98	36.53 N	122.23 E
Shideng	102	26.44 N	99.11 E
Shidler	196	36.46 N	96.39 W
Shido	96	34.19 N	134.10 E
Shidong, Zhg.	107	28.59 N	105.27 E
Shidong, Zhg.	107	30.25 N	105.20 E
Shidongzigou	105	40.41 N	118.23 E
Shiel, Loch ⊝	46	56.47 N	5.35 W
Shiel Bridge	46	57.12 N	5.25 W
Shieldaig	46	57.31 N	5.39 W
Shieldhill	46	55.58 N	3.46 W
Shields ≃	202	45.43 N	110.28 W
Shiercun	106	30.31 N	119.34 E
Shi'er Shan ∧	100	29.18 N	118.08 E
Shi'erwei	106	32.15 N	119.14 E
Shifang	100	25.01 N	116.14 E
Shifnal	42	52.40 N	2.21 W
Shifo	107	29.58 N	103.50 E
Shifobao	104	41.28 N	121.27 E
Shifochang	107	30.19 N	105.07 E
Shifodian	100	32.06 N	115.46 E
Shifosi	104	42.08 N	123.20 E
Shifoya	98	40.12 N	123.10 E
Shiga, Nihon	94	36.20 N	137.59 E
Shiga, Nihon	94	35.09 N	135.55 E
Shiga □[5]	96	35.15 N	136.00 E
Shigaib	140	15.01 N	23.36 E
Shigang, Zhg.	100	32.13 N	120.58 E
Shigang, Zhg.	106	32.14 N	121.00 E
Shigangmen	269b	31.21 N	121.17 E
Shigaopu	107	30.16 N	104.01 E
Shigar ≃, Asia	123	34.39 N	75.51 E
Shigar ≃, Pāk.	123	34.39 N	75.51 E
Shigaraki	94	34.52 N	136.03 E
Shigaraki-gū ♥[1]	94	34.54 N	136.04 E
Shigenobu	96	33.48 N	132.50 E
Shigenobu ≃	96	33.48 N	132.41 E
Shigezhuang, Zhg.	105	38.57 N	116.19 E
Shigezhuang, Zhg.	105	38.59 N	115.36 E
Shigezhuang, Zhg.	105	39.18 N	116.53 E
Shigouyi	102	37.44 N	106.26 E
Shigu, Zhg.	100	29.27 N	117.14 E
Shigu, Zhg.	102	26.50 N	99.55 E
Shiguaigou	102	40.42 N	110.20 E
Shiguantun	104	41.38 N	123.39 E
Shigulingyu	105	40.38 N	116.54 E
Shīḥān ∧	132	31.23 N	35.44 E
Shihch'i → Zhongshan	100	22.31 N	113.22 E
Shihchiachuang → Shijiazhuang	98	38.03 N	114.28 E
Shihe	98	39.19 N	121.52 E
Shihengyuanyu	106	31.50 N	121.45 E
Shihezi	86	44.18 N	86.02 E
Shihkiachwang → Shijiazhuang	98	38.03 N	114.28 E
Shihlin ◆[8]	269d	25.06 N	121.31 E
Shihti	269d	25.02 N	121.44 E
Shihting	269d	24.59 N	121.39 E
Shihu, Zhg.	98	41.29 N	126.18 E
Shihu, Zhg.	105	40.04 N	117.17 E
Shihuajie	102	32.20 N	111.25 E
Shihudang	106	30.58 N	121.07 E
Shihuixi	107	29.02 N	105.04 E
Shihuiyaozi	104	42.08 N	123.47 E
Shihuxia	105	40.48 N	117.22 E
Shiida	96	33.39 N	131.04 E
Shijiaba	107	30.18 N	104.46 E
Shijiagangzi	104	42.19 N	123.34 E
Shijiagou	104	42.27 N	123.28 E
Shijiao	100	23.36 N	112.59 E
Shijiaqiao, Zhg.	106	32.18 N	119.26 E
Shijiaqiao, Zhg.	106	30.46 N	120.06 E
Shijiawu	105	39.21 N	116.15 E
Shijiaxiang	107	29.38 N	104.59 E
Shijiayaozhuang	106	32.13 N	120.29 E
Shijiazhai, Zhg.	98	38.56 N	114.18 E
Shijiazhai, Zhg.	269b	31.23 N	121.30 E
Shijiazhen	106	31.51 N	121.10 E
Shijiazhuang	98	38.03 N	114.28 E
Shijiazi, Zhg.	104	42.39 N	122.06 E
Shijiazi, Zhg.	104	42.07 N	122.18 E
Shijiedu	106	30.57 N	119.13 E
Shijing, Zhg.	98	35.30 N	118.57 E
Shijing, Zhg.	100	24.40 N	118.24 E
Shijing, Zhg.	105	39.54 N	114.58 E
Shijingshan	105	39.56 N	116.07 E
Shijiu Hu ⊝	106	31.28 N	118.53 E
Shijiusuo	98	35.24 N	119.29 E
Shijiu Tuo I	98	39.11 N	118.56 E
Shijōnawate	270	34.45 N	135.39 E
Shijūmagari-tōge)(	96	35.11 N	133.32 E
Shika	94	37.01 N	136.47 E
Shikami-yama ∧	270	34.47 N	135.10 E
Shikano	96	35.28 N	134.04 E
Shikārpur, India	122	14.16 N	75.21 E
Shikārpur, India	124	28.17 N	78.01 E
Shikārpur, Pāk.	120	27.57 N	68.38 E
Shikatsu	94	35.14 N	136.53 E
Shikengkong ∧	100	24.56 N	113.00 E
Shikewusumiao	102	40.13 N	108.52 E
Shiki	94	35.50 N	139.35 E
Shikishima	94	35.41 N	138.32 E
Shikohābād	124	27.06 N	78.36 E
Shikoku I	92	33.45 N	133.30 E
Shikoku-sanchi ⋀	96	33.47 N	133.30 E
Shikoma	268	35.11 N	139.56 E
Shikotsu-ko ⊝	92a	42.45 N	141.20 E
Shikotsu-Tōya-kokuritsu-kōen ♠	92a	42.47 N	141.00 E
Shikuang	106	31.54 N	121.24 E
Shil	272c	19.09 N	73.03 E
Shilabo	144	6.05 N	44.48 E
Shilbottle	44	55.23 N	1.42 W
Shildon	44	54.38 N	1.39 W
Shiliangji	100	33.54 N	115.14 E
Shilibao	105	39.55 N	116.29 E
Shiliguri	124	26.42 N	88.26 E
Shilihe	104	41.31 N	123.22 E
Shiling	106	30.26 N	119.35 E
Shilipeng	106	31.14 N	119.35 E
Shilipu, Zhg.	105	39.29 N	116.18 E
Shilipu, Zhg.	105	39.11 N	115.59 E
Shilipu, Zhg.	105	40.15 N	117.58 E
Shiliuban	100	24.08 N	117.33 E
Shillelagh	48	52.45 N	6.32 W
Shillingstone	42	50.54 N	2.14 W
Shillington	208	40.18 N	75.57 W
Shillong	120	25.34 N	91.53 E
Shilo, Canadian Forces Base ▪	184	49.49 N	99.38 W
Shiloh, Il., U.S.	219	38.34 N	89.54 W
Shiloh, N.J., U.S.	208	39.27 N	75.17 W
Shiloh, Oh., U.S.	214	40.58 N	82.36 W
Shiloh, Oh., U.S.	218	39.49 N	84.13 W
Shiloh, Oh., U.S.	218	39.49 N	84.13 W
Shiloh, Pa., U.S.	208	39.59 N	76.49 W
Shiloh → Saylūn, Khirbat ⊥	132	32.03 N	35.17 E
Shiloh National Military Park ♠	194	35.06 N	88.21 W
Shilong, Zhg.	100	23.07 N	113.48 E
Shilong, Zhg.	102	23.54 N	109.40 E
Shilong, Zhg.	107	30.15 N	106.34 E
Shilou	100	22.58 N	113.29 E
Shima, Nihon	92	34.13 N	136.51 E
Shima, Nihon	270	34.59 N	135.20 E
Shima, Zhg.	100	24.27 N	117.49 E
Shima, Zhg.	107	29.38 N	105.50 E
Shimabara	92	32.47 N	130.22 E
Shimachang, Zhg.	107	28.59 N	105.55 E
Shimachang, Zhg.	107	29.03 N	105.36 E
Shimada, Nihon	94	34.49 N	138.11 E
Shimada, Nihon	268	35.59 N	139.25 E
Shimagahara	94	34.46 N	136.03 E
Shima-hantō ›[1]	94	34.26 N	136.33 E
Shimamiao	106	32.08 N	119.20 E

Shimamoto	96	34.53 N	135.40 E
Shimane □[5]	96	35.00 N	132.30 E
Shimane-hantō ›[1]	96	35.30 N	133.00 E
Shimantan	100	33.17 N	113.28 E
Shimanto ≃	96	32.56 N	133.00 E
Shimata ≃	96	33.57 N	131.55 E
Shimber Berris ∧	144	10.44 N	47.15 E
Shimei	106	32.14 N	120.10 E
Shimen, Zhg.	98	39.44 N	118.52 E
Shimen, Zhg.	102	29.28 N	111.17 E
Shimen, Zhg.	105	40.06 N	117.42 E
Shimen, Zhg.	106	30.37 N	120.26 E
Shimen, Zhg.	107	29.09 N	106.02 E
Shimen, Zhg.	107	29.36 N	106.27 E
Shimencun, Zhg.	106	31.21 N	119.34 E
Shimencun, Zhg.	106	30.23 N	119.41 E
Shimendong	100	28.16 N	120.07 E
Shimengou	104	40.40 N	123.43 E
Shimenjie	100	29.34 N	116.44 E
Shimenlou	100	28.58 N	114.51 E
Shimenying	105	39.54 N	116.05 E
Shimenzi	89	48.30 N	121.31 E
Shimian	102	29.18 N	102.22 E
Shimiaozi	104	40.39 N	123.31 E
Shimizu → Tosa-shimizu	92	32.46 N	132.57 E
Shimizu, Nihon	92	35.01 N	138.29 E
Shimizu, Nihon	92a	43.01 N	142.53 E
Shimizu, Nihon	94	36.02 N	136.09 E
Shimizu, Nihon	94	35.01 N	138.29 E
Shimizu, Nihon	96	34.05 N	135.26 E
Shimizu-tunnel ◆[5]	94	36.52 N	138.55 E
Shimla	123	31.06 N	77.10 E
Shimminato	94	36.47 N	137.04 E
Shimobe	94	35.27 N	138.29 E
Shimoda	94	34.40 N	138.57 E
Shimodate	94	36.18 N	139.59 E
Shimofusa	94	35.52 N	140.21 E
Shimofusa-daichi ⋀[1]	268	35.45 N	139.58 E
Shimofusa-kōkūkichi, Kaijō-jieitai- ▪	94	35.50 N	140.05 E
Shimofusa Naval Air Base ▪	268	35.48 N	140.01 E
Shimoga	122	13.55 N	75.34 E
Shimogawara	268	35.56 N	139.21 E
Shimogōri	268	35.21 N	140.03 E
Shimogyō ◆[8]	270	34.59 N	135.45 E
Shimohōya	268	35.45 N	139.34 E
Shimoichi	96	34.22 N	135.47 E
Shimoigusa ◆[8]	268	35.43 N	139.37 E
Shimoji	175d	24.45 N	125.16 E
Shimoji-jima I	175d	24.49 N	125.09 E
Shimojō	94	35.24 N	137.47 E
Shimokawa	92a	44.18 N	142.39 E
Shimokita-hantō ›[1]	92	41.15 N	141.00 E
Shimomatsu	270	34.27 N	135.23 E
Shimomizo	268	35.31 N	139.23 E
Shimoni	154	4.39 S	39.23 E
Shimoniikura	268	35.47 N	139.38 E
Shimonita	94	36.13 N	138.47 E
Shimonoseki	96	33.57 N	130.57 E
Shimookudomi	268	35.53 N	139.26 E
Shimoryūzu-zaki ›	96	33.30 N	133.34 E
Shimosakamoto	270	35.03 N	135.53 E
Shimosuwa	94	36.04 N	138.05 E
Shimotajiri	270	34.57 N	135.28 E
Shimotomi	268	35.50 N	139.29 E
Shimotsu	96	34.10 N	135.08 E
Shimotsuchidana	268	35.24 N	139.27 E
Shimotsui	96	34.26 N	133.47 E
Shimotsuma	94	36.11 N	139.58 E
Shimotsuruma	268	35.29 N	139.28 E
Shimoya	268	35.23 N	139.21 E
Shimoyama	94	35.02 N	137.19 E
Shimoyugi	268	35.38 N	139.23 E
Shimura ◆[8]	268	35.46 N	139.41 E
Shin, Loch ⊝	46	58.06 N	4.34 W
Shinagawa ◆[8]	268	35.37 N	139.45 E
Shinan	102	22.43 N	109.54 E
Shinano	94	36.48 N	138.13 E
Shinano ≃	92	37.56 N	139.03 E
Shinarā	142	28.47 N	30.46 E
Shināṣ	128	24.46 N	56.28 E
Shinawari	123	33.32 N	70.48 E
Shinbārī	273c	30.07 N	31.09 E
Shīndand	128	33.18 N	62.08 E
Shindenbaru-kichi, Kōkū-jieitai- ▪	92	32.04 N	131.30 E
Shindo	268	35.21 N	139.21 E
Shiner	222	29.25 N	97.10 W
Shingbwiyang	110	26.41 N	96.13 E
Shingishū → Sinŭiju	98	40.05 N	124.24 E
Shinglehouse	214	41.57 N	78.11 W
Shingle Springs	226	38.40 N	120.56 W
Shing Mun Reservoir ⊝[1]	271d	22.23 N	114.08 E
Shingo	96	34.59 N	133.23 E
Shingū, Nihon	92	33.44 N	135.59 E
Shingū, Nihon	96	33.56 N	133.38 E
Shingū, Nihon	96	34.55 N	134.33 E
Shingwidzi	156	23.05 S	31.25 E
Shingwidzi (Singuédeze) ≃	156	23.53 S	32.17 E
Shinichi	96	34.33 N	133.16 E
Shining Tor ∧	262	53.16 N	2.01 W
Shinīrah	132	32.22 N	36.45 E
Shinji	96	35.24 N	132.54 E
Shinji-ko ⊝	96	35.27 N	132.58 E
Shinjō, Nihon	92	38.46 N	140.18 E
Shinjō, Nihon	270	34.30 N	135.44 E
Shinjuku ◆[8]	268	35.41 N	139.42 E
Shinkawa	94	35.09 N	136.50 E
Shīnkay	120	31.57 N	67.26 E
Shinkolobwe	154	11.02 S	26.35 E
Shinmachi	94	36.16 N	139.07 E
Shinminato ≃	270	34.38 N	135.09 E
Shinnārah, Minqār ⊓[4]	142	28.52 N	30.38 E
Shinnayō	96	34.04 N	131.47 E
Shinnecock Bay c	207	40.52 N	72.28 W
Shinnel Water ≃	44	55.13 N	3.49 W
Shinness	46	58.05 N	4.28 W
Shinnston	188	39.23 N	80.18 W
Shino-jima I	94	34.39 N	137.00 E
Shinsai-bashi ◆[8]	270	34.40 N	135.31 E
Shinshār	130	34.36 N	36.44 E
Shinshiro	94	34.54 N	137.30 E
Shinshū-shinmachi	94	36.34 N	138.01 E
Shintone	94	35.50 N	140.20 E
Shinyanga	154	3.40 S	33.26 E
Shinyanga □[4]	154	3.45 S	33.00 E
Shin-yōdo ≃[1]	270	34.41 N	135.26 E
Shio	94	36.52 N	136.48 E
Shiobara	94	36.58 N	139.49 E
Shiocton	190	44.26 N	88.34 W
Shiogama	92	38.19 N	141.01 E
Shiojiri	94	36.06 N	137.58 E
Shiojiri-tōge)(	94	36.05 N	138.02 E
Shiomi-dake ∧	94	35.34 N	138.12 E
Shionoe	96	34.10 N	134.05 E
Shiono-misaki ›	92	33.26 N	135.45 E
Shioya	94	36.46 N	139.51 E
Shioya ◆[8]	270	34.38 N	135.06 E
Shioya-zaki ›, Nihon	92	33.26 N	135.45 E
Shioya-zaki ›, Nihon	94	36.59 N	140.59 E
Shiozawa	94	37.02 N	138.51 E
Shipai, Zhg.	100	23.08 N	113.21 E
Shipai, Zhg.	106	31.30 N	120.55 E
Shipanpu	107	30.28 N	104.23 E
Shipantuo	107	30.25 N	106.13 E
Ship Bottom	208	39.38 N	74.10 W
Shipbourne	260	51.15 N	0.17 E
Ship Cove	186	47.06 N	54.05 W
Shipdham	42	52.37 N	0.53 E
Shiping, Zhg.	102	28.20 N	107.42 E
Shiping, Zhg.	102	23.47 N	102.30 E
Shipley	44	53.50 N	1.47 W
Shipman, Il., U.S.	219	39.07 N	90.03 W
Shipman, Va., U.S.	192	37.43 N	78.50 W
Shippan Point ›	276	41.01 N	73.32 W

	English	Deutsch	Español	Français	Português
≃	River	Fluß	Río	Rivière	Rio
≍	Canal	Kanal	Canal	Canal	Canal
⌊	Waterfall, Rapids	Wasserfall, Stromschnellen	Cascada, Rápidos	Chute d'eau, Rapides	Cascata, Rápidos
ʊ	Strait	Meeresstraße	Estrecho	Détroit	Estreito
c	Bay, Gulf	Bucht, Golf	Bahía, Golfo	Baie, Golfe	Baía, Golfo
⊝	Lake, Lakes	See, Seen	Lago, Lagos	Lac, Lacs	Lago, Lagos
≡	Swamp	Sumpf	Pantano	Marais	Pântano
⊓	Ice Features, Glacier	Eis- und Gletscherformen	Accidentes Glaciales	Formes glaciaires	Acidentes glaciares
⊤	Other Hydrographic Features	Andere Hydrographische Objekte	Otros Elementos Hidrográficos	Autres données hydrographiques	Outros acidentes hidrográficos
✣	Submarine Features	Untermeerische Objekte	Accidentes Submarinos	Formes de relief sous-marin	Acidentes submarinos
□	Political Unit	Politische Einheit	Unidad Politica	Entité politique	Unidade política
♥	Cultural Institution	Kulturelle Institution	Institución Cultural	Institution culturelle	Instituição cultural
⊥	Historical Site	Historische Stätte	Sitio Histórico	Site historique	Sitio histórico
♠	Recreational Site	Erholungs- und Ferienort	Sitio de Recreo	Centre de loisirs	Area de Lazer
⊠	Airport	Flughafen	Aeropuerto	Aéroport	Aeroporto
▪	Military Installation	Militäranlage	Instalación Militar	Installation militaire	Instalação militar
◆	Miscellaneous	Verschiedenes	Misceláneo	Divers	Diversos

Column 1

Name	Page	Lat.°'	Long.°'
Shippegan	186	47.45 N	64.42 W
Shippensburg	208	40.03 N	77.31 W
Shippenville	214	41.15 N	79.28 W
Shippingport	214	40.38 N	80.25 W
Shippō	94	35.10 N	136.48 E
Shiprock	200	36.47 N	108.41 W
Ship Rock ▲	200	36.42 N	108.50 W
Shipshaw ≃	186	48.27 N	71.12 W
Shipshewana	216	41.40 N	85.34 W
Shipston-on-Stour	42	52.04 N	1.37 W
Shipton-under-Wychwood	42	51.51 N	1.35 W
Shipu, Zhg.	100	29.13 N	121.55 E
Shipu, Zhg.	106	31.15 N	121.03 E
Shiqi → Zhongshan	100	22.31 N	113.22 E
Shiqian	100	27.31 N	108.20 E
Shiqiao, Zhg.	100	26.58 N	114.23 E
Shiqiao, Zhg.	100	33.12 N	112.36 E
Shiqiao, Zhg.	100	30.30 N	119.11 E
Shiqiao, Zhg.	107	30.25 N	104.31 E
Shiqiaopu	100	30.05 N	105.23 E
Shiqiaozi	104	41.27 N	123.43 E
Shiqma ≃	132	31.36 N	34.30 E
Shiquan, Zhg.	102	33.03 N	108.17 E
Shiquan, Zhg.	106	30.30 N	120.48 E
Shirahama, Nihon	94	34.54 N	139.54 E
Shirahama, Nihon	94	33.40 N	135.20 E
Shirahata-yama ▲	96	34.54 N	134.23 E
Shiraitono-taki ∟	94	33.28 N	131.08 E
Shirakami-misaki ⊁	92a	41.24 N	140.12 E
Shirakawa, Nihon	94	37.07 N	140.13 E
Shirakawa, Nihon	94	35.35 N	137.12 E
Shirakawa, Nihon	96	36.16 N	136.54 E
Shirakawa-no-seki-ato ⊥	94	37.03 N	140.15 E
Shirakawa-tōge ⚹²	270	34.42 N	135.07 E
Shirakoi	94	35.26 N	140.23 E
Shirākol	128	22.18 N	88.16 E
Shirakura-yama ▲	94	35.00 N	137.46 E
Shiramine	96	34.01 N	135.23 E
Shirane-san ▲, Nihon	94	36.10 N	136.37 E
Shirane-san ▲, Nihon	96	35.38 N	138.22 E
Shirane-san (Kita-dake) ▲, Nihon	94	35.40 N	138.15 E
Shiranuka	92a	42.57 N	144.05 E
Shiraoi	92a	42.33 N	141.21 E
Shiraoka	94	36.01 N	139.40 E
Shirarone	272e	19.03 N	73.01 E
Shirasawa	94	36.40 N	139.08 E
Shirase Glacier ⊠	9	70.10 S	38.35 E
Shirati	154	1.08 S	33.59 E
Shīrāz	128	29.36 N	52.32 E
Shirbin	142	31.11 N	31.32 E
Shirdley Hill	262	53.36 N	2.58 W
Shire (Chire) ≃	154	17.42 S	35.19 E
Shirebrook	44	53.12 N	1.13 W
Shiremanstown	208	40.13 N	76.57 W
Shiretoko-hantō ⊁¹	92a	44.00 N	145.00 E
Shiretoko-kokuritsu-kōen ♦	92a	44.08 N	145.10 E
Shiretoko-misaki ⊁	92a	44.14 N	145.17 E
Shirin ≃	128	36.49 N	65.01 E
Shīr Wādī ≃	128	31.34 N	54.34 E
Shirland	216	42.27 N	89.12 W
Shirley, B.C., Can.	224	48.23 N	123.54 W
Shirley, Il., U.S.	216	40.24 N	89.04 W
Shirley, In., U.S.	216	39.53 N	85.34 W
Shirley, Ma., U.S.	207	42.32 N	71.39 W
Shirley Plantation ⊥	208	37.21 N	77.15 W
Shirleysburg	214	40.18 N	77.53 W
Shiro	222	30.37 N	95.53 W
Shiroi	94	35.48 N	140.04 E
Shiroishi	94	38.00 N	140.37 E
Shirokawa	96	33.23 N	132.46 E
Shirone	92	37.46 N	139.01 E
Shirotori, Nihon	94	35.53 N	136.52 E
Shirotori, Nihon	96	34.15 N	134.20 E
Shirouma-dake ▲	96	36.45 N	137.46 E
Shiroyama	94	35.35 N	139.19 E
Shiro-yama ▲	270	34.38 N	133.15 E
Shirpur	100	21.21 N	74.53 E
Shirrell Heath	42	50.55 N	1.12 W
Shirshābah	142	30.47 N	31.10 E
Shīrvān	128	37.24 N	57.55 E
Shisaka-jima I	96	34.07 N	133.11 E
Shisanling	105	40.16 N	116.16 E
Shi San Ling (Ming Tombs) ⊥	105	40.19 N	116.13 E
Shisanzhan	100	49.21 N	125.43 E
Shisha Hai ⊜	271a	39.57 N	116.22 E
Shishaldin Volcano ▲¹	180	54.45 N	163.57 W
Shishan	100	24.48 N	118.38 E
Shishi	100	24.44 N	117.54 E
Shishi Shan ▲	100	33.34 N	134.18 E
Shishmaref	180	66.14 N	166.09 W
Shishmaref Inlet c	180	66.07 N	165.50 W
Shishou	102	29.43 N	112.19 E
Shisht al-An'ām	142	30.52 N	30.44 E
Shisiazhan	100	50.26 N	125.42 E
Shisixian	104	40.53 N	122.59 E
Shisler Point ⊁	284a	42.12 N	79.26 W
Shisui	94	35.43 N	140.16 E
Shitai	100	30.13 N	117.27 E
Shitan, Zhg.	100	27.44 N	112.42 E
Shitan, Zhg.	100	23.10 N	113.47 E
Shitang, Zhg.	100	28.16 N	121.36 E
Shitang, Zhg.	100	25.38 N	110.50 E
Shitangwan	106	31.40 N	120.13 E
Shitara	94	35.06 N	137.35 E
Shithāthah	128	32.33 N	43.29 E
Shiting, Zhg.	102	28.30 N	113.16 E
Shiting, Zhg.	100	39.31 N	115.41 E
Shitougouzi	89	48.38 N	126.08 E
Shitougouzi	89	49.19 N	125.55 E
Shitoumiao	102	41.41 N	106.50 E
Shitoumiaozi	100	41.38 N	121.26 E
Shitoushan	104	41.38 N	116.13 E
Shitoushuangmiao	100	44.01 N	108.05 E
Shituan	107	30.09 N	105.01 E
Shitunwei	104	41.07 N	121.31 E
Shiv	120	26.11 N	71.15 E
Shivalya	126	23.50 N	89.47 E
Shively	218	38.12 N	85.49 W
Shivering, Mount ▲	170	34.08 S	150.02 E
Shivpuri	124	25.26 N	77.39 E
Shivta, Horvot (Subeita) ⊥	132	30.53 N	34.38 E
Shivwits Plateau ▲¹	200	35.16 N	113.40 W
Shiwaku-shotō II	96	34.20 N	133.45 E
Shiwan, Zhg.	100	28.12 N	113.49 E
Shiwan, Zhg.	102	23.01 N	113.04 E
Shiwan, Zhg.	100	27.17 N	112.57 E
Shiwan, Zhg.	107	37.35 N	109.01 E
Shiwenchang	104	41.43 N	123.54 E
Shiwu	89	43.48 N	124.13 E
Shixi, Zhg.	100	28.16 N	117.45 E
Shixi, Zhg.	100	25.14 N	117.46 E
Shixia	105	40.20 N	114.59 E
Shixian	89	43.05 N	129.47 E
Shixiancun	89	31.12 N	120.29 E
Shixiechang	100	29.51 N	106.41 E
Shixing	100	24.55 N	114.04 E
Shixun	100	24.44 N	118.11 E
Shiyanchang	100	27.42 N	105.30 E
Shiyan, Zhg.	102	32.38 N	110.44 E
Shiyan, Zhg.	107	30.42 N	105.57 E
Shiyangqiao	102	29.56 N	105.37 E
Shiyiwei	31	31.59 N	120.43 E
Shiyizhan	89	51.13 N	125.32 E
Shiyu	107	29.46 N	106.06 E
Shizhangzi	98	40.24 N	119.48 E
Shizheng	104	24.32 N	115.50 E
Shizhenjie	100	28.51 N	116.56 E
Shizhong, Zhg.	100	24.57 N	117.06 E

Column 2

Name	Page	Lat.°'	Long.°'
Shizhong, Zhg.	106	30.44 N	120.16 E
Shizhongtan	107	30.26 N	104.35 E
Shizhu	100	28.48 N	120.06 E
Shizhuang	100	32.08 N	120.31 E
Shizhuangzi, Zhg.	104	42.24 N	122.53 E
Shizhuangzi, Zhg.	105	40.38 N	116.50 E
Shizhuzi	104	41.18 N	121.35 E
Shizichang	107	29.32 N	106.14 E
Shizigu	105	39.23 N	118.08 E
Shizikou	100	24.12 N	113.38 E
Shizilin	106	31.26 N	121.25 E
Shizipo	105	40.21 N	115.07 E
Shizipu	106	30.59 N	119.07 E
Shizuchi-kokutei-kōen ♦	96	33.45 N	133.08 E
Shizugawa	92	38.40 N	141.27 E
Shizui, Zhg.	89	43.08 N	126.06 E
Shizui, Zhg.	98	38.52 N	113.42 E
Shizuma ≃	96	35.12 N	132.28 E
Shizunai	92a	42.20 N	142.22 E
Shizuoka	94	34.58 N	138.23 E
Shizuoka □⁵	94	35.00 N	138.00 E
Shkodër	38	42.05 N	19.30 E
Shkumbin ≃	38	41.01 N	19.26 E
Shō ≃	94	36.47 N	137.04 E
Shoal ≃	194	30.41 N	86.39 W
Shoal Cape ⊁	194	33.53 S	121.07 E
Shoal Creek ≃, U.S.	194	34.50 N	87.33 W
Shoal Creek ≃, U.S.	194	37.05 N	94.42 W
Shoal Creek ≃, U.S.	194	42.06 N	92.42 W
Shoal Creek ≃, Il., U.S.	219	38.28 N	89.35 W
Shoal Creek ≃, Mo., U.S.	219	39.44 N	93.32 W
Shoal Creek, East Fork ≃	219	38.51 N	89.30 W
Shoal Creek, Middle Fork ≃	219	39.05 N	89.43 W
Shoal Creek, West Fork ≃	219	39.05 N	89.33 W
Shoal Harbour	186	48.11 N	53.59 W
Shoalhaven ≃	170	34.52 S	150.44 E
Shoalhaven Bight c³	170	34.52 S	150.47 E
Shoal Lake	184	52.26 N	100.34 W
Shoal Lake	184	49.32 N	95.00 W
Shoal Point ⊁	276	41.08 N	73.15 W
Shoals	194	38.39 N	86.47 W
Shoals, Bay of c	168b	35.37 S	137.37 E
Shoalwater Bay c	166	22.02 S	150.25 E
Shō ≃	96	36.06 N	133.01 E
Shōbara	96	35.06 N	134.01 E
Shobonier	219	38.52 N	89.05 W
Shōbu	94	36.04 N	139.36 E
Shōdai	270	34.51 N	135.42 E
Shōdo-shima I	96	34.34 N	134.17 E
Shoeburyness	42	51.32 N	0.48 E
Shoe Cove	186	49.55 N	55.33 W
Shoemakersville	208	40.30 N	75.58 W
Shōgawa ≃	94	36.34 N	136.59 E
Shogunle	273a	6.35 N	3.21 E
Shohola	210	41.28 N	74.55 W
Shohola Creek ≃	210	41.28 N	74.55 W
Shokambetsu-dake ▲	92a	43.43 N	141.31 E
Shokan	210	41.58 N	74.13 W
Shōkawa	94	36.02 N	136.57 E
Sholingnur	122	13.07 N	79.25 E
Shomera	132	33.05 N	35.17 E
Shomolu	273a	6.32 N	3.23 E
Shōnyō-no-taki ∟	96	35.36 N	137.24 E
Shona, Eilean I	46	56.47 N	5.52 W
Shōnai ≃	94	35.11 N	131.26 E
Shongum	276	40.50 N	74.33 W
Shongum Lake ⊜	276	40.51 N	74.32 W
Shōō	96	35.04 N	134.05 E
Shooters Hill	170	33.54 S	149.52 E
Shooters Island I	276	40.39 N	74.10 W
Shopiere	216	42.34 N	88.57 W
Shoranūr	122	10.46 N	76.17 E
Shorapur	122	16.31 N	76.45 E
Shoreacres, B.C., Can.	182	49.26 N	117.32 W
Shore Acres, Ca., U.S.	238	38.02 N	121.58 W
Shore Acres, Ma., U.S.	283	42.12 N	70.44 W
Shore Acres, N.J., U.S.	208	40.01 N	74.06 W
Shoreacres, Tx., U.S.	232	29.37 N	95.01 W
Shoreditch ⊥	260	51.32 N	0.05 W
Shoreham, Austl.	168	38.25 S	145.03 E
Shoreham, Eng., U.K.	260	51.20 N	0.11 E
Shoreham, Mi., U.S.	216	42.03 N	86.30 W
Shoreham-by-Sea	42	50.49 N	0.16 W
Shorewood, Il., U.S.	216	41.32 N	88.12 W
Shorewood, Wi., U.S.	216	43.05 N	87.53 W
Shorewood Hills	216	43.05 N	89.27 W
Shorkot	123	30.50 N	72.15 E
Shorkot Road	123	30.47 N	72.15 E
Shorne	260	51.25 N	0.26 E
Short Acres	226	36.21 N	119.38 W
Short Beach	207	41.15 N	72.50 W
Short Creek ≃	210	40.06 N	80.46 W
Shortland Islands II	175e	6.55 S	155.53 E
Short Mountain ▲	192	36.23 N	83.10 W
Shortsville	210	42.57 N	77.13 W
Shoshone	202	42.56 N	114.24 W
Shoshone ≃	202	44.52 N	108.11 W
Shoshone, North Fork ≃	202	44.29 N	109.18 W
Shoshone, South Fork ≃	202	44.29 N	109.14 W
Shoshone Lake ⊜	202	44.22 N	110.43 W
Shoshone Mountains ⚹	204	39.00 N	117.30 W
Shoshone Peak ▲	204	36.56 N	116.16 W
Shoshone Range ⚹	204	40.30 N	116.50 W
Shoshong	156	22.59 S	26.30 E
Shoshoni	202	43.14 N	108.06 W
Shostka → Šostka	78	51.52 N	33.30 E
Shotley Gate	42	51.58 N	1.15 E
Shotton Colliery	44	54.44 N	1.20 W
Shotts	46	55.49 N	3.48 W
Shotwick	262	51.14 N	3.02 W
Shou'anzhen	107	30.16 N	103.37 E
Shoufang	100	29.22 N	119.13 E
Shouguang	98	36.52 N	118.44 E
Shoushan	107	31.12 N	103.43 E
Shouwangfen	105	40.35 N	117.48 E
Shouxian	100	32.34 N	116.47 E
Shouyang	98	37.59 N	113.09 E
Shouzhang	98	35.47 N	116.03 E
Show Low	200	34.15 N	110.01 W
Shqipëri → Albania □¹	38	41.00 N	20.00 E
Shreve	214	40.41 N	82.01 W
Shreveport	222	32.30 N	93.45 W
Shrewsbury, Eng., U.K.	42	52.43 N	2.45 W
Shrewsbury, Ma., U.S.	207	42.17 N	71.42 W
Shrewsbury, N.J., U.S.	208	40.19 N	74.03 W
Shrewsbury, Pa., U.S.	208	39.46 N	76.40 W
Shrewsbury River c	276	40.21 N	74.00 W
Shrewton	42	51.12 N	1.55 W
Shri Dūngargarh	120	28.05 N	74.00 E
Shri Mohangarh	120	27.17 N	71.14 E

Column 3

Name	Page	Lat.°'	Long.°'
Shriner Mountain ▲	210	40.56 N	77.20 W
Shrīrangapattana	122	12.25 N	76.42 E
Shrivenham	42	51.36 N	1.39 W
Shropshire □⁶	42	52.40 N	2.40 W
Shropshire Union Canal ≋	262	53.17 N	2.53 W
Shrub Oak	210	41.20 N	73.49 W
Shrule	48	53.30 N	9.08 W
Shu ≃	98	34.07 N	118.30 E
Shuajingsi	102	32.00 N	103.05 E
Shuanfeng Shan ▲	107	29.26 N	105.47 E
Shuang ≃	269d	25.00 N	121.31 E
Shuangbai	102	24.54 N	101.32 E
Shuangcheng	89	45.21 N	126.17 E
Shuangchengzi	105	40.11 N	118.03 E
Shuangdun	106	32.13 N	121.08 E
Shuangfeng, Zhg.	89	43.08 N	126.06 E
Shuangfeng, Zhg.	106	31.31 N	121.01 E
Shuangfeng, Zhg.	106	31.31 N	121.02 E
Shuangfeng Shan ▲	100	24.28 N	114.43 E
Shuangfengyi	107	29.27 N	105.09 E
Shuangfu	105	39.48 N	117.44 E
Shuangfuchang, Zhg.	107	29.41 N	103.31 E
Shuangfuchang, Zhg.	100	30.08 N	103.32 E
Shuanggang, Zhg.	89	45.07 N	122.59 E
Shuanggang, Zhg.	100	28.11 N	117.30 E
Shuangfengtun	89	48.58 N	129.57 E
Shuanggou, Zhg.	98	34.03 N	117.37 E
Shuanggou, Zhg.	100	32.12 N	112.21 E
Shuanggou, Zhg.	98	33.16 N	118.10 E
Shuanggufen	100	29.38 N	104.11 E
Shuanghe, Zhg.	100	31.41 N	112.46 E
Shuanghe, Zhg.	100	31.33 N	116.46 E
Shuanghe, Zhg.	107	29.40 N	104.48 E
Shuanghe, Zhg.	107	30.07 N	105.10 E
Shuanghechang, Zhg.	107	28.51 N	104.51 E
Shuanghechang, Zhg.	107	29.25 N	106.17 E
Shuanghechang, Zhg.	107	29.12 N	105.43 E
Shuangji ≃	100	34.05 N	114.24 E
Shuangjiang, Zhg.	100	26.48 N	116.28 E
Shuangjiang, Zhg.	102	23.37 N	99.41 E
Shuangjiang, Zhg.	100	30.13 N	105.45 E
Shuangjiang, Zhg.	100	29.38 N	104.11 E
Shuangjiaji	105	33.12 N	116.40 E
Shuangjingzi	104	42.28 N	123.42 E
Shuangliao	89	43.31 N	123.30 E
Shuangliao	100	30.47 N	120.19 E
Shuanglingzi, Zhg.	104	40.54 N	124.10 E
Shuanglingzi, Zhg.	105	40.53 N	123.06 E
Shuangliu	107	30.34 N	103.55 E
Shuangliushu	107	31.56 N	115.12 E
Shuanglongchang	104	40.56 N	122.39 E
Shuangmiao, Zhg.	100	38.24 N	120.45 E
Shuangmiao, Zhg.	100	32.09 N	116.52 E
Shuangmiaozi, Zhg.	104	42.02 N	122.17 E
Shuangpai	100	25.57 N	111.32 E
Shuangqiao, Zhg.	106	31.24 N	118.59 E
Shuangqiao, Zhg.	100	32.29 N	116.41 E
Shuangqiao, Zhg.	89	39.54 N	116.37 E
Shuangqiaozi	100	40.09 N	118.47 E
Shuangshanzi	98	40.21 N	119.08 E
Shuangshiqiao	107	29.14 N	104.42 E
Shuangshiqiao, Zhg.	89	29.22 N	105.51 E
Shuangshiqiao, Zhg.	99	29.23 N	104.29 E
Shuangshu	89	39.34 N	117.01 E
Shuangtaizi ≃	104	40.50 N	121.15 E
Shuangtaizi, Zhg.	104	41.11 N	121.21 E
Shuangtaizi, Zhg.	104	41.34 N	121.12 E
Shuangtangdian	106	30.59 N	118.51 E
Shuangtangxi	100	27.01 N	119.03 E
Shuangtaizihe Kou ⌣	104	40.55 N	121.52 E
Shuangyang, Zhg.	89	43.32 N	125.42 E
Shuangyangdian	104	41.07 N	121.16 E
Shuangyangaocun	105	38.55 N	117.03 E
Shuanji, Zhg.	106	32.41 N	119.25 E
Shubenacadie	186	45.05 N	63.25 W
Shubrā al-Khaymah	142	30.06 N	31.15 E
Shubrā Bābil	142	30.54 N	31.11 E
Shubrā Khalfūn	142	31.02 N	30.43 E
Shubrā Khīt	142	31.11 N	30.43 E
Shubuta	194	31.51 N	88.41 W
Shufu	89	39.27 N	75.52 E
Shufuka Shan ▲	102	27.57 N	104.21 E
Shuheyingzi	104	41.18 N	121.16 E
Shuhezhen	105	31.35 N	121.35 E
Shūhō	96	34.13 N	131.18 E
Shuibatang	102	28.39 N	107.03 E
Shuibei, Zhg.	100	25.17 N	115.01 E
Shuidong, Zhg.	100	21.34 N	111.00 E
Shuidong, Zhg.	100	31.23 N	119.37 E
Shuidongkou	100	39.23 N	106.09 E
Shuiduixia	100	30.17 N	110.50 E
Shuihai	102	29.22 N	105.34 E
Shuihouling	100	24.28 N	115.25 E
Shuijiahu	100	32.17 N	117.01 E
Shuijiangbo	100	24.38 N	104.35 E
Shuijingtang	102	25.54 N	109.06 E
Shuikou, Zhg.	100	29.29 N	103.42 E
Shuikou, Zhg.	100	26.59 N	118.41 E
Shuikouchang	107	31.03 N	107.06 E
Shuikouguan	102	22.06 N	106.54 E
Shuimenzi	98	39.36 N	122.19 E
Shuimoqipan	85	37.10 N	76.42 E
Shuiquan'gou	104	41.58 N	121.50 E
Shuiquanzi, Zhg.	104	42.15 N	121.43 E
Shuiquanzi, Zhg.	104	42.15 N	121.20 E
Shuiting	100	29.10 N	119.14 E
Shuitou	100	24.43 N	118.16 E
Shuitouwei	107	26.06 N	106.31 E
Shuiyang ≃	106	31.14 N	118.47 E
Shuizhai	98	36.54 N	114.42 E
Shujaābād	123	29.53 N	71.18 E

Column 4

Name	Page	Lat.°'	Long.°'
Shujālpur	124	23.24 N	76.43 E
Shujāwazi	100	42.20 N	121.57 E
Shuksan, Mount ▲	224	48.50 N	121.36 W
Shulan	89	44.27 N	126.57 E
Shulaps Peak ▲	182	50.57 N	122.31 W
Shule	85	39.23 N	76.06 E
Shule	102	40.50 N	94.10 E
Shūlgareh	120	36.19 N	66.53 E
Shullsburg	190	42.34 N	90.13 W
Shulu (Xinji)	98	37.54 N	115.13 E
Shumagin Islands II	180	55.07 N	159.45 W
Shumatsucacant ≃	283	42.03 N	70.51 W
Shumen	38	43.16 N	26.55 E
Shūnah, Wādī ash- ≃	142	29.38 N	32.13 E
Shun'an	100	30.57 N	117.57 E
Shūnat Nimrīn	132	31.54 N	35.37 E
Shunayn, Sabkhat ⊜	146	30.30 N	21.00 E
Shunchang	100	26.50 N	117.48 E
Shunde	100	22.50 N	113.14 E
Shundian	100	34.15 N	113.20 E
Shundianqiao	100	31.24 N	120.41 E
Shunge	100	25.28 N	95.27 E
Shungnak	180	66.53 N	157.02 W
Shunhechang	107	29.57 N	104.42 E
Shunlongchang	100	30.04 N	103.27 E
Shunshanpu	100	42.08 N	122.21 E
Shuntianhu	100	24.08 N	114.48 E
Shunyi	105	40.08 N	116.38 E
Shuoduozong	102	30.48 N	95.47 E
Shuojiaji	100	33.42 N	119.44 E
Shuping	107	29.19 N	104.43 E
Shupiyan	123	33.43 N	74.50 E
Shuqayyiqah, Nafūd ⊥⁸	128	25.45 N	43.55 E
Shuqualak	194	32.58 N	88.34 W
Shūr ≃, Īrān	128	30.57 N	57.42 E
Shūr ≃, Īrān	128	31.45 N	55.15 E
Shūr ≃, Īrān	128	35.57 N	56.24 E
Shūr ≃, Īrān	128	34.38 N	51.46 E
Shuri	174m	26.13 N	127.43 E
Shurkhua	110	22.15 N	93.38 E
Shurugwi	154	19.40 S	30.00 E
Shūsf	128	31.48 N	60.01 E
Shūsh	128	32.11 N	48.15 E
Shushan	210	43.05 N	73.21 W
Shushan Hu ⊜	105	35.36 N	116.27 E
Shūshtar	128	32.03 N	48.51 E
Shuswap ≃	182	50.50 N	119.00 W
Shuswap Lake ⊜	182	50.57 N	119.15 W
Shutab	142	20.08 N	31.14 E
Shutendōji-yama ▲	96	33.06 N	130.54 E
Shuteye Peak ▲	226	37.21 N	119.25 W
Shutlingsloe ▲	262	53.13 N	2.02 W
Shūtō	96	34.05 N	132.05 E
Shuwak	140	14.23 N	35.52 E
Shuwaykah	132	32.20 N	35.02 E
Shuya	174m	26.40 N	128.06 E
Shuya → Šuja	46	56.51 N	41.23 E
Shuyak Island I	180	58.35 N	152.30 W
Shuyang	100	34.08 N	118.47 E
Shuzenji	94	34.58 N	138.56 E
Shwangliao → Liaoyuan	89	42.54 N	125.07 E
Shwebo	110	22.34 N	95.42 E
Shwegun	110	17.09 N	97.39 E
Shwegyin	110	17.55 N	96.53 E
Shweli (Longchuan) ≃	102	23.56 N	96.17 E
Shwenyaung	110	20.46 N	96.57 E
Shyamdih	126	23.47 N	86.56 E
Shyok	120	34.11 N	78.08 E
Shyok ≃	120	35.13 N	75.53 E
Sia	164	8.49 S	134.19 E
Siabu	114	1.01 N	99.29 E
Siachen Glacier ⊠	123	35.30 N	77.00 E
Siād Kuh, Kavīr-e ≃	128	32.40 N	53.52 E
Siahan Range ⚹	128	27.25 N	64.30 E
Siāhān Kūh, Selseleh-ye ⚹	128	34.00 N	64.00 E
Siak ≃	114	1.13 N	102.09 E
Siak Kecil ≃	114	1.16 N	102.08 E
Siak Sri Indrapura	114	0.46 N	102.04 E
Sialang	114	1.31 N	99.27 E
Siălejavska P'atina ⊜	76	53.49 N	44.22 E
Sialkot	123	32.30 N	74.31 E
Sialsūk	126	23.24 N	92.45 E
Siam → Thailand □¹	110	15.00 N	100.00 E
Siam, Gulf of → Thailand, Gulf of c	110	10.00 N	101.00 E
Siamanna	71	39.55 N	8.46 E
Sian → Xi'an, Zhg.	102	34.15 N	108.52 E
Si'an, Zhg.	106	30.54 N	119.39 E
Siangtan	102	27.51 N	112.54 E
Sianhala	150	10.03 N	6.51 W
Sianów	30	54.15 N	16.16 E
Siantan, Pulau I	114	3.10 N	106.15 E
Sianzhuang	105	33.05 N	119.13 E
Siapa ≃	246	2.07 N	66.28 W
Siargao Island I	116	9.52 N	126.03 E
Siasconset	207	41.15 N	69.58 W
Siasi	116	5.33 N	120.49 E
Siaton	116	9.04 N	123.02 E
Siaton Point ⊁	116	9.02 N	123.02 E
Siau, Pulau I	116	2.42 N	125.24 E
Siaugues-Saint-Romain	62	45.04 N	3.38 E
Šiauliai	76	55.56 N	23.19 E
Siazan'	84	41.05 N	49.06 E
Sibago Island I	116	6.45 N	122.24 E
Sibā'ī, Jabal as- ▲	140	25.43 N	34.09 E
Sibay	82	52.42 N	58.39 E
Sibayi, Lake ⊜	156	27.20 S	32.42 E
Sibay Island I	116	11.51 N	121.29 E
Sibbald	184	51.23 N	110.09 W
Sibbald Point Provincial Park ♦	212	44.19 N	79.19 W
Sibbo (Sipoo)	18	60.22 N	25.16 E
Šibbchar	126	23.21 N	90.09 E
Sibenik	36	43.44 N	15.54 E
Siberia → Sibir' □¹	74	65.00 N	110.00 E
Siberia Occidental, Llanura de → Sibirskaja ravnina	72	60.00 N	75.00 E
Siberia Occidental, Dépression de la → Zapadno-Sibirskaja ravnina	72	60.00 N	75.00 E
Siberut, Pulau I	114	1.20 S	98.55 E
Sibi	120	29.33 N	67.53 E
Sibidiri	164	9.00 S	142.15 E
Sibigo	114	2.51 N	95.55 E
Sibillini, Monti ⚹¹	34	42.51 N	13.13 E
Sibir' ≃¹	74	65.00 N	110.00 E
Sibir'akova, ostrov I	84	72.50 N	79.00 E

Column 5 / Bilingual English–German

Name (English)	Page	Lat.°'	Long.°'	Name (Deutsch)	Seite	Breite°'	Länge°'
Sibircevo	89	44.12 N	132.26 E	Sieber	52	51.42 N	10.25 E
Sibiti	152	3.41 S	13.21 E	Siebnen	58	47.11 N	8.54 E
Sibiti ≃	154	3.49 S	34.46 E	Siedenbollentin	54	53.44 N	13.23 E
Sibiu	38	45.48 N	24.09 E	Siedenburg	52	52.41 N	8.36 E
Sibiu □⁶	38	46.00 N	24.15 E	Siedlce	30	52.11 N	22.16 E
Sible Hedingham	42	51.58 N	0.35 E	Siedlce □⁴	30	52.15 N	22.00 E
Sibley, Ia., U.S.	216	40.35 N	88.23 W	Sieg ≃	56	50.45 N	7.05 E
Sibley, Ia., U.S.	198	43.23 N	95.45 W	Siegburg	56	50.47 N	7.12 E
Sibley, La., U.S.	194	32.33 N	93.18 W	Siegen	56	50.52 N	8.02 E
Sibley, Ms., U.S.	194	31.22 N	91.23 W	Siegenburg	60	48.45 N	11.51 E
Sibley Peninsula ⊁¹	190	48.25 N	88.45 W	Siegendorf im Burgenland	61	47.47 N	16.33 E
Sibley Provincial Park ♦	190	48.25 N	88.49 W	Siegenfeld	264b	48.02 N	16.10 E
Siboa	112	0.16 N	120.32 E	Sieghartskirchen	61	48.15 N	16.02 E
Sibochi	107	28.50 N	104.32 E	Siegler Springs	226	38.54 N	122.39 W
Sibolga	114	1.45 N	98.48 E	Siegsdorf	64	47.46 N	12.39 E
Siborang	114	1.08 N	99.26 E	Sielbeck	54	54.11 N	10.37 E
Siborongborong	114	2.13 N	98.59 E	Sielenbach	60	48.24 N	11.10 E
Sibpur, Bngl.	124	22.02 N	90.44 E	Siemens, Cape ⊁	116	1.21 S	149.34 E
Sibpur, India	272b	22.24 N	88.33 E	Siemensstadt ⊢⁸	264a	52.32 N	13.17 E
Sibpur, India	272b	22.50 N	88.19 E	Siemianowice Śląskie	30	50.19 N	19.01 E
Sibsa ≃	126	22.01 N	89.30 E	Siemiatycze	30	52.26 N	22.53 E
Sibsāgar	120	26.59 N	94.38 E	Siempang	110	14.07 N	106.23 E
Sibu	112	2.18 N	111.49 E	Siennrėab	110	13.22 N	103.51 E
Sibu, Pulau I	114	2.13 N	104.04 E	Siems-Dänischburg ⊢⁸	—	—	—
Sibuatan, Gunung ▲	114	2.56 N	98.24 E	Siena	66	43.19 N	11.21 E
Sibuguey ≃	116	7.38 N	122.48 E	Siena □⁴	66	43.13 N	11.24 E
Sibuguey Bay c	116	7.30 N	122.40 E	Sieniawa	30	50.11 N	22.36 E
Sibut	152	5.44 N	19.05 E	Sienna → Siena	66	43.19 N	11.21 E
Sibuti	112	4.03 N	113.48 E	Sienyang → Xianyang	102	34.22 N	108.42 E
Sibutu Island I	112	4.46 N	119.29 E	Sieradz	30	51.36 N	18.45 E
Sibutu Passage ⋃	112	4.50 N	119.35 E	Sieradz □⁴	30	51.40 N	18.45 E
Sibuyan Island I	116	12.25 N	122.34 E	Sieraków	30	52.39 N	16.04 E
Sibuyan Sea ⊤²	116	12.50 N	122.40 E	Sierck-les-Bains	56	49.26 N	6.21 E
Sibyón	98	38.19 N	126.41 E	Sierksdorf	54	54.04 N	10.46 E
Sicamous	182	50.50 N	119.00 W	Sierning	61	48.03 N	14.19 E
Sicapoo, Mount ▲	116	18.01 N	120.56 E	Sierpc	30	52.52 N	19.41 E
Sicasica	248	17.22 S	67.45 W	Si'erpu	104	40.47 N	120.41 E
Siccus ≃	166	31.26 S	139.30 E	Sičany	80	52.07 N	47.13 E
Sichakou	98	41.39 N	116.26 E	Sierra □⁶	204	39.35 N	120.30 W
Sichang	94	35.07 N	137.04 E	Sierra Blanca	200	31.11 N	105.21 W
Si Chon	110	9.00 N	99.54 E	Sierra Blanca Peak ▲	200	33.23 N	105.48 W
Sichote-Alin' ⚹	89	48.00 N	138.00 E	Sierra-Bullones	116	9.51 N	124.20 E
Sichote-Alinskij zapovednik ♦	89	45.15 N	136.15 E	Sierra Chica	252	36.50 S	60.13 W
Šichtovo	76	55.43 N	32.18 E	Sierra City	226	39.33 N	120.37 W
Sichuan (Szechwan) □⁴	102	30.00 N	105.00 E	Sierra Colorada	254	40.35 S	67.48 W
Sichuan Pendi ≃¹	102	30.00 N	105.00 E	Sierra de Agua	232	17.32 N	88.54 W
Sichuanzhai	102	32.00 N	101.44 E	Sierra del Carmen, Parque Nacional ♦	232	29.15 N	102.42 W
Sicié, Cap ⊁	62	43.03 N	5.51 E	Sierra de Outes	32	42.51 N	8.54 W
Sicignano degli Alburni	68	40.34 N	15.18 E	Sierra Gorda	252	22.54 S	69.19 W
Sicilia → Sicily I	36	37.30 N	14.00 E	Sierra Leone → Sierra Leone □¹	150	8.30 N	11.30 W
Sicilia □⁴	36	37.30 N	14.00 E	Sierra Leone □¹, Afr.	134	8.30 N	11.30 W
Sicilia (Sicily) I	70	37.30 N	14.00 E	Sierra Leone □¹, Afr.	150	8.30 N	11.30 W
Sicilia, Isla de → Sicilia I	70	37.30 N	14.00 E	Sierra Leone Rise ◆³	10	5.00 N	17.00 W
Sicily I	70	37.30 N	14.00 E	Sierra Madre	228	34.09 N	118.03 W
→ Sicilia I	70	37.30 N	14.00 E	Sierra Mojada	196	27.17 N	103.42 W
Sicily, Strait of ⋃	36	37.30 N	11.20 E	Sierra Nevada, Parque Nacional ♦	246	8.36 N	70.50 W
Sicily Island	194	31.50 N	91.39 W	Sierra Peak ▲	280	33.51 N	117.39 W
Siciliamühle	263	54.47 N	7.07 E				
Sickerville	208	39.43 N	74.58 W				
Sicogon Island I	116	11.27 N	123.16 E				
Sico Tinto ≃	236	15.58 N	84.58 W				
Sicuani	248	14.16 S	71.13 W	Sierra San Pedro Mártir, Parque Nacional ♦	204	31.00 N	115.30 W
Siculiana	70	37.20 S	13.18 E	Sierra Bayas	252	36.57 S	60.09 W
Šid	38	45.08 N	19.13 E	Sierravelle	226	39.35 N	120.21 W
Sidah, Qārat ▲³	142	30.16 N	29.58 E	Sierra Vista	200	31.33 N	110.18 W
Sidamo □⁴	144	5.00 N	39.00 E	Sierre	58	46.18 N	7.32 E
Sidao	271a	39.51 N	116.26 E	Siersleben	54	51.36 N	11.32 E
Sidareja	115a	7.29 S	108.47 E	Siesta Key	220	27.16 N	82.34 W
Sidcup ⊢⁸	260	51.25 N	0.06 E	Siesta Key I	220	27.16 N	82.33 W
Siddeburen	52	53.25 N	6.52 E	Sieste Puntas	252	23.34 S	61.12 W
Siddhapur	120	23.55 N	72.23 E	Siethener See ⊜	264a	52.17 N	13.12 E
Siddinghausen	263	51.32 N	7.48 E	Sietow	54	53.29 N	12.33 E
Siddipet	262	53.14 N	2.14 W	Sieve ≃	66	43.46 N	11.26 E
Sideia Island I	164	10.35 S	150.50 E	Sievering ◆⁸	264b	48.15 N	16.22 E
Sidel'kino	80	54.32 N	51.08 E	Sieversen	264a	53.26 N	9.48 E
Sidéradougou	150	10.40 N	4.15 W	Sifang, Zhg.	98	36.10 N	120.21 E
Siderno	68	38.16 N	16.18 E	Sifangtai, Zhg.	104	41.02 N	121.19 E
Siderópolis	252	28.35 S	49.26 W	Sifangtai, Zhg.	104	41.02 N	122.46 E
Šiderty ≃, S.S.S.R.	82	50.10 N	75.00 E	Sifangtai, Zhg.	104	41.22 N	122.57 E
Šiderty ≃, S.S.S.R.	82	50.10 N	52.20 E	Sifen	144	12.16 N	40.21 E
Sidhauli	124	27.17 N	80.50 E	Sifentoudun	98	32.18 N	121.21 E
Sidheros, Ákra ⊁	39	35.19 N	26.19 E	Sifie ≃	116	17.12 N	121.48 E
Sidhi	124	24.25 N	81.53 E	Sifié	150	7.59 N	6.55 W
Sifnos I	39	36.59 N	24.40 E				
Sidhirókastron	38	41.14 N	23.22 E	Sifón Villanueva	196	27.17 N	100.17 W
Slđī 'Abd ar-Rahmān	140	30.58 N	29.44 E	Sig, Alg.	148	35.32 N	0.12 W
Sīdī Aïch	148	36.37 N	4.42 E	Sig. ≃, S.S.S.R.	46	55.35 N	34.13 E
Sīdī Aïssa	148	35.53 N	3.48 E	Sig Galangang	114	1.15 N	99.20 E
Sīdī Akacha	148	36.28 N	1.18 E	Sigal	152	4.22 N	43.02 E
Sidi Ali, Oued V	148	34.07 N	2.05 W	Sigean	62	43.02 N	2.59 E
Sīdī Ali Ben Nasrallah	148	35.54 N	9.37 E	Sigel	214	41.17 N	79.07 W
Sīdī Barrāni	140	31.36 N	25.55 E	Sigges	263	51.15 N	7.57 E
Sīdī Bel Abbès	148	35.13 N	0.37 W	Sighetu Marmației	38	47.56 N	23.54 E
Sīdī Bel Abbès □⁵	148	35.00 N	0.10 W	Sighişoara	38	46.13 N	24.48 E
Sīdī Bennour	148	32.38 N	8.30 W	Sighty Crag ▲	44	55.09 N	2.37 W
Sīdī Bou Zid	148	35.02 N	9.37 E	Sigli	114	5.23 N	95.57 E
Sīdī Bou Zid □⁵	148	35.05 N	9.30 E	Sigli, Cap ⊁	148	36.54 N	4.46 E
Sīdī Daoud	148	36.53 N	10.55 E	Siglistorf	58	47.34 N	8.21 E
Sīdī el Hani, Sebkhet ⊜	148	35.33 N	10.25 E	Sigiriya	122	7.57 N	80.45 E
Sīdī Ghāzī	142	31.31 N	30.58 E	Sigloan	114	3.12 N	103.02 E
Sīdī Hunaysh	142	31.10 N	27.37 E	Siglufjördur	16a	66.09 N	18.55 W
Sīdī Ifni	148	29.24 N	10.12 W	Sigly, Cap ⊁	148	36.54 N	4.46 E
Sīdī Kacem	148	34.15 N	5.39 W	Sigmaringen	56	48.05 N	9.13 E
Sīdī Sālim	142	31.17 N	30.48 E	Sigmaringendorf	58	48.03 N	9.15 E
Sīdī Slimane	148	34.16 N	5.58 W	Signal Hill National Historic Park ♦	186	47.35 N	52.40 W
Sīdī Smaīl	148	32.49 N	8.30 W	Signau	58	46.55 N	7.43 E
Sidlaghatta	122	13.23 N	77.52 E	Signal Mountain	192	35.07 N	85.20 W
Sidlaw Hills ⚹²	44	56.30 N	3.10 W	Signal Mountain ▲	202	43.50 N	110.40 W
Sidley, Mount ▲	9	77.02 S	126.06 W	Signal Peak ▲	200	37.19 N	113.29 W
Sidman	214	40.21 N	78.45 W	Signau	58	46.55 N	7.43 E
Sidmouth	42	50.41 N	3.15 W	Signes	62	43.17 N	5.52 E
Sidnaw	190	46.30 N	88.42 W	Signy-l'Abbaye	56	49.42 N	4.25 E
Sidney, B.C., Can.	224	48.39 N	123.24 W	Signy-Le-Petit	56	49.54 N	4.17 E
Sidney, Il., U.S.	216	40.01 N	88.04 W	Sigony	80	53.20 N	49.24 E
Sidney, Ia., U.S.	216	40.45 N	95.39 W	Sigri ≃	114	1.45 N	102.10 E
Sidney, Mt., U.S.	202	47.43 N	104.09 W	Sigriswil	58	46.43 N	7.42 E
Sidney, Ne., U.S.	198	41.08 N	102.58 W	Sigröwl	16a	65.05 N	18.13 W
Sidney, N.Y., U.S.	208	42.18 N	75.23 W	Sigtuna	40	59.37 N	17.43 E
Sidney, Oh., U.S.	212	40.17 N	84.09 W				
Sidney Center	210	42.17 N	75.15 W	Siguanea, Ensenada de la c	240p	21.38 N	83.05 W
Sidney Lanier, Lake ⊜¹	192	34.15 N	83.57 W	Siguatepeque	236	14.36 N	87.51 W
Sido	150	11.40 N	7.36 W	Sigüenza	34	41.04 N	2.38 W
Sidoan	112	0.16 N	120.12 E	Sigüés	32	42.37 N	0.59 W
Sidoarjo	115a	7.27 S	112.43 E	Sigulda	76	57.09 N	24.51 E
→ Saydā	128	33.33 N	35.22 E	Sihai	104	41.33 N	116.40 E
Sidorovo	194	56.48 N	89.12 W	Sihabuhabu, Dolok ▲	114	2.10 N	99.21 E
Sidra, Ra's as- ⊁	128	29.36 N	32.40 E	Sihala	123	33.34 N	73.14 E
Sidra, Gulf of → Surt, Khalīj c	146	31.30 N	18.00 E	Sihanoukville → Kâmpóng Saôm	110	10.38 N	103.30 E
Sidrolândia	255	20.55 S	54.58 W	Sihecun	104	39.56 N	117.07 E
Sidu, Zhg.	100	23.48 N	117.18 E	Sihepu	104	42.53 N	122.33 E
Sidu, Zhg.	100	24.51 N	115.15 E	Sihong	114	1.06 N	99.27 E
Siduan	106	30.59 N	121.48 E	Sihlsee ⊜	58	47.08 N	8.46 E
Siebengebirge ⚹²	56	50.40 N	7.13 E	Sihlepu	158	27.42 S	32.06 E
Siebenlehn	54	51.01 N	13.18 E	Sihong	100	33.28 N	118.11 E

Nombre | Página | Lat.°′ | Long.°′ W = Oeste
Nom | Page | Lat.°′ | Long.°′ W = Ouest
Nome | Página | Lat.°′ | Long.°′ W = Oeste

Sihor 120 21.42 N 71.58 E
Sihorā 124 23.29 N 80.07 E
Sihu 98 34.38 N 117.59 E
Sihuas 248 8.34 S 77.37 W
Sihui 102 23.19 N 112.40 E
Şihŭng ◈[8] 271b 37.28 N 126.54 E
Šiiči 78 52.15 N 29.14 E
Siikajoki ≃ 26 64.50 N 24.44 E
Siilinjärvi 26 63.05 N 27.40 E
Si'īr 132 31.35 N 35.09 E
Siirt 130 37.56 N 41.57 E
Siirt □[4] 128 38.00 N 42.00 E
Sija 24 63.38 N 41.38 E
Sijā ≃ 124 29.08 N 81.35 E
Sijbekarspel 52 52.43 N 4.59 E
Sijiaba 106 32.02 N 121.18 E
Sijianfang 104 42.29 N 122.17 E
Sijiao Shan I 100 30.41 N 122.28 E
Sijiazi 98 41.47 N 120.06 E
Sijing 106 31.07 N 121.16 E
Sijunjung 112 0.42 S 100.58 E
Sijupu 107 30.02 N 106.18 E
Sik 114 5.49 N 100.44 E
Sika 115b 8.45 S 122.12 E
Sikalongo 154 16.46 S 27.07 E
Sikandarābād 124 28.27 N 77.42 E
Sikandarpur, India 272a 28.42 N 77.21 E
Sikandarpur, India 272b 22.57 N 88.12 E
Sikandra 124 24.57 N 86.02 E
Sikandra Rao 124 27.42 N 78.24 E
Sikanni Chief ≃ 176 58.20 N 121.50 W
Sikao 110 7.34 N 99.21 E
Sīkar 120 27.37 N 75.09 E
Sikarpur 272b 22.36 N 88.32 E
Sikasso 150 11.19 N 5.40 W
Sikasso □[4] 150 10.55 N 7.00 W
Sikéai 38 36.46 N 22.56 E
Sikelenge 152 14.50 S 24.14 E
Sikeli 112 5.16 S 121.48 E
Sikensi 150 5.40 N 4.34 W
Sikeshu 86 44.25 N 84.14 E
Sikeston 194 36.52 N 89.35 W
Sikfors 40 59.48 N 14.35 E
Si Khiu 110 14.53 N 101.44 E
Sikiá 38 40.02 N 23.56 E
Sikiang → Xi ≃ 102 22.25 N 113.23 E
Sikijang 114 4.22 N 98.02 E
Siking → Xi'an 102 34.15 N 108.52 E
Síkinos 38 36.39 N 25.06 E
Síkinos I 38 36.39 N 25.06 E
Sikión ⊥ 38 37.59 N 22.44 E
Sikkim □[3] 124 27.35 N 88.35 E
Siklós ⊥ 30 45.52 N 18.28 E
Sikonge 154 5.38 S 32.46 E
Şikosi 156 17.59 S 23.19 E
Šikotan, ostrov (Shikotan-tō) I 92a 43.47 N 146.45 E
Sikrod 272a 28.43 N 77.11 E
Sikt'ach 74 69.55 N 125.02 E
Sikuati 112 6.53 N 116.40 E
Sikutu 112 0.53 N 120.37 E
Şil ≃ 34 42.27 N 7.43 W
Šila 86 56.33 N 93.02 E
Silacayoapan 234 17.30 N 98.09 W
Sila Grande ⋏ 68 39.22 N 16.30 E
Sila Greca ⋏ 68 39.30 N 16.30 E
Silai ≃ 126 22.41 N 87.46 E
Šilalahi 114 2.48 N 98.32 E
Šilalė 76 55.28 N 22.12 E
Silam, Gunong ∧ 116 4.58 N 118.10 E
Silāmpur ◈[8] 272a 28.40 N 77.16 E
Silandro (Schlanders) 64 46.38 N 10.46 E
Silang 116 14.14 N 120.58 E
Silangcheng 98 42.19 N 115.43 E
Silanus 71 40.17 N 8.53 E
Silao 234 20.56 N 101.26 W
Sila Piccola ⋏ 68 39.05 N 16.35 E
Silas 194 31.45 N 88.19 W
Silat 112 0.21 N 111.47 E
Silat az-Zahr 132 32.19 N 35.11 E
Silau ≃ 114 2.58 N 99.48 E
Silaut 112 2.22 S 101.08 E
Silaw Aihagam, Gunung ∧ 114 5.25 N 95.40 E
Silay 116 10.48 N 122.58 E
Silay, Mount ∧ 116 10.47 N 123.14 E
Silba 36 44.23 N 14.42 E
Silbertal 58 47.05 N 9.59 E
Silchar 120 24.49 N 92.48 E
Şilda, India 126 22.37 N 86.49 E
Šil'da, S.S.S.R. 86 51.46 N 59.45 E
Şile 130 41.11 N 29.36 E
Šile ≃ 64 45.33 N 12.27 E
Sileby 42 52.43 N 1.06 W
Šilega 24 64.03 N 44.01 E
Silenrieux 50 50.14 N 4.24 E
Silent Lake ⊜ 212 44.55 N 78.04 W
Silent Lake Provincial Park ♠ 212 44.54 N 78.05 W
Siler City 192 35.43 N 79.27 W
Sileru ≃ 122 17.47 N 81.24 E
Silesia □[9] 30 51.00 N 16.45 E
Silet 148 22.44 N 4.37 E
Siletz 202 44.43 N 123.55 W
Siletz ≃ 202 44.54 N 124.00 W
Silex 219 39.07 N 91.03 W
Silgadhī 124 29.16 N 80.59 E
Silghāt 120 26.37 N 92.56 E
Silhouette I 138 4.29 S 55.14 E
Siliana 148 36.05 N 9.22 E
Siliana □[8] 148 36.00 N 9.20 E
Siliana, Oued ≃ 36 36.33 N 9.25 E
Silifke 130 36.22 N 33.56 E
Şilijiang 105 39.43 N 117.28 E
Šilikty 86 47.10 N 84.32 E
Silingan, Mount ∧ 116 7.46 N 122.30 E
Siling Co ⊜ 120 31.50 N 89.00 E
Siliqua 71 39.18 N 8.48 E
Silistra 38 44.07 N 27.16 E
Şilivri 130 41.04 N 28.15 E
Šiljak ∧ 38 43.45 N 21.50 E
Siljan ⊜ 26 60.50 N 14.45 E
Siljansnäs 26 60.45 N 14.42 E
Šilka 88 51.51 N 116.02 E
Šilka ≃ 74 53.22 N 121.32 E
Silkāripāra 126 24.14 N 87.28 E
Silkeborg 41 56.10 N 9.34 E
Silkworth 210 41.16 N 76.05 W
Sill ≃ 64 47.16 N 11.25 E
Sillamäe 76 59.24 N 27.45 E
Sillānwāli 123 31.50 N 72.33 E
Sillaro ≃ 66 44.34 N 11.51 E
Sille 130 37.56 N 32.26 E
Sillem Island I 176 70.55 N 71.30 W
Sillen ⊜ 40 58.59 N 17.22 E
Sillenstede 52 53.34 N 7.59 E
Sillery, P.Q., Can. 206 46.46 N 71.15 W
Sillery, Fr. 50 49.12 N 4.08 E
Silli 150 11.36 N 2.30 W
Sillian 64 46.45 N 12.25 E
Sillil 144 10.59 N 43.26 E
Sillon de Talbert ≻[1] 32 48.53 N 3.05 W
Silloth 44 54.52 N 3.23 W
Sillustani ⊥ 248 15.45 S 70.05 W
Silly-le-Long 261 49.06 N 2.48 E
Sil'naja Balka 80 50.34 N 49.01 E
Silnice 60 48.54 N 13.44 E
Siloam Springs 194 36.11 N 94.32 W
Siloam Springs State Park ♠ 219 39.53 N 90.54 W
Şilogui 110 1.14 S 99.00 E
Šilovići 76 55.24 N 32.33 E
Šilovka 80 54.03 N 48.40 E
Šilovo, S.S.S.R. 76 55.00 N 33.46 E
Šilovo, S.S.S.R. 80 54.19 N 40.53 E
Silowana Plains ≡ 152 17.00 S 23.15 E
Silphuh 126 23.44 N 86.22 E
Silsbee 194 30.20 N 94.10 W
Silsby Lake ⊜ 184 55.29 N 95.46 W
Silschede 263 51.21 N 7.19 E
Silsden 44 53.55 N 1.55 W
Sils im Engadin 58 46.22 N 9.46 E
Silton 184 50.48 N 104.55 W
Siluas 112 1.17 N 109.51 E
Şiluko 150 6.31 N 5.09 E
Šilutė 76 55.21 N 21.29 E
Silvacane, Abbaye de ♥[1] 62 43.44 N 5.20 E
Silva Jardim 255 22.39 S 42.23 W
Silvan (Miyafarkin) 130 38.08 N 41.01 E
Silvana 224 48.12 N 122.15 W
Sīlvāneh 128 37.25 N 44.51 E
Silvânia 255 16.42 S 48.38 W
Silvano d'Orba 62 44.41 N 8.40 E
Silvan Reservoir ⊜[1] 169 37.50 S 145.25 E
Silvaplana 58 46.26 N 9.47 E
Silvassa 122 20.17 N 73.00 E
Silveiras, Bra. 256 22.33 S 46.55 W
Silveiras, Bra. 256 22.40 S 44.52 W
Silver 196 32.04 N 100.40 W
Silverado 228 33.45 N 117.35 W
Silver Bank ✢[2] 238 20.30 N 69.45 W
Silver Bank Passage ⊔ 238 20.45 N 70.15 W
Silver Bay 190 47.17 N 91.15 W
Silver Bell 200 32.23 N 111.29 W
Silver City, N.M., U.S. 200 32.46 N 108.16 W
Silver City, N.C., U.S. 192 35.00 N 79.12 W
Silver Creek, Ms., U.S. 194 31.36 N 89.59 W
Silver Creek, Ne., U.S. 198 41.18 N 97.39 W
Silver Creek, N.Y., U.S. 214 42.32 N 79.10 W
Silver Creek ≃, Az., U.S. 200 34.44 N 110.02 W
Silver Creek ≃, Ca., U.S. 226 38.47 N 120.35 W
Silver Creek ≃, Ca., U.S. 226 36.36 N 120.41 W
Silver Creek ≃, Il., U.S. 219 38.20 N 89.52 W
Silver Creek ≃, Il., U.S. 278 41.54 N 87.50 W
Silver Creek ≃, In., U.S. 218 38.17 N 85.47 W
Silver Creek ≃, In., U.S. 218 39.36 N 84.59 W
Silver Creek ≃, Ky., U.S. 192 37.48 N 84.30 W
Silver Creek ≃, Or., U.S. 202 43.16 N 119.13 W
Silver Creek ≃, Wa., U.S. 224 46.32 N 121.55 W
Silver Creek, Muddy Fork ≃ 218 38.25 N 86.44 W
Silver Creek, South Fork ≃ 226 38.49 N 120.27 W
Silverdale, B.C., Can. 224 49.09 N 122.24 W
Silverdale, N.Z. 172 36.37 S 174.40 E
Silverdale, Eng., U.K. 44 54.10 N 2.49 W
Silverdale, Pa., U.S. 208 40.21 N 75.16 W
Silverdale, Wa., U.S. 224 47.38 N 122.41 W
Silverdalen 26 57.32 N 15.44 E
Silverdome ♠ 281 42.39 N 83.15 W
Silver End 42 51.51 N 0.37 E
Silver Falls State Park ♠ 202 44.48 N 122.50 W
Silverfields 273d 26.07 S 27.49 E
Silver Fork ≃ 219 39.06 N 92.21 W
Silver Grove 218 39.02 N 84.23 W
Silver Hill 284c 38.50 N 76.56 W
Silverhope Creek ≃ 224 49.18 N 121.27 W
Silver Lake, Ca., U.S. 226 38.38 N 120.07 W
Silver Lake, In., U.S. 216 41.04 N 85.53 W
Silver Lake, Ks., U.S. 198 39.06 N 95.51 W
Silver Lake, Ma., U.S. 207 42.34 N 71.11 W
Silver Lake, Mn., U.S. 190 44.54 N 94.11 W
Silver Lake, Oh., U.S. 214 41.09 N 81.27 W
Silver Lake, Or., U.S. 202 43.07 N 121.02 W
Silverlake, Wa., U.S. 224 46.17 N 122.48 W
Silver Lake, Wi., U.S. 216 42.32 N 88.09 W
Silver Lake ⊜, Ca., U.S. 226 38.39 N 120.07 W
Silver Lake ⊜, De., U.S. 208 39.11 N 75.32 W
Silver Lake ⊜, Ma., U.S. 283 42.01 N 70.48 W
Silver Lake ⊜, N.Y., U.S. 210 42.42 N 78.02 W
Silver Lake ⊜, N.Y., U.S. 276 41.03 N 73.45 W
Silver Lake ⊜, Or., U.S. 202 43.06 N 120.53 W
Silver Lake ⊜, Or., U.S. 202 43.22 N 119.24 W
Silver Lake ⊜, Wa., U.S. 224 46.17 N 122.47 W
Silver Lake ⊜, Wa., U.S. 224 48.58 N 122.04 W
Silver Lake Park ♠ 276 41.03 N 73.45 W
Silver Lake Reservoir ⊜[1], Ca., U.S. 280 34.06 N 118.16 W
Silver Lake Reservoir ⊜[1], N.Y., U.S. 276 40.37 N 74.06 W
Silvermine ≃ 276 41.08 N 73.26 W
Silver Mine Bay ⊂ 271d 22.16 N 114.00 E
Silvermine Brook ≃ 276 41.08 N 73.27 W
Silvermine Mountains ⋏ 48 52.45 N 8.15 W
Silvermines 48 52.47 N 8.13 W
Silver Mountain ∧ 280 34.12 N 117.52 W
Silver Peak ∧ 228 33.28 N 118.35 W
Silver Peak Range ⋏ 204 37.35 N 117.45 W
Silver Spring, Md., U.S. 208 38.59 N 77.01 W
Silver Spring, Pa., U.S. 208 40.04 N 76.26 W
Silver Springs, Nv., U.S. 226 39.24 N 119.13 W
Silver Springs, N.Y., U.S. 210 42.39 N 78.05 W
Silver Springs State Park ♠ 216 41.38 N 88.32 W
Silver Star Mountain ∧ 224 48.33 N 120.35 W
Silver Star Provincial Park ♠ 182 50.22 N 119.05 W
Silverstone 42 52.05 N 1.02 W
Silver Streams 158 28.20 S 23.33 E
Silverthrone Mountain ∧ 182 51.31 N 126.06 W
Silvertip Mountain ∧ 202 47.47 N 113.15 W
Silverton, Austl. 166 31.53 S 141.13 E
Silverton, B.C., Can. 182 49.57 N 117.21 W
Silverton, Eng., U.K. 42 50.48 N 3.28 W
Silverton, Co., U.S. 200 37.48 N 107.39 W
Silverton, N.J., U.S. 208 40.00 N 74.08 W
Silverton, Oh., U.S. 218 39.12 N 84.24 W
Silverton, Or., U.S. 224 45.00 N 122.46 W
Silverton, Tx., U.S. 196 34.28 N 101.19 W
Silverwood Lake ⊜[1] 228 34.18 N 117.19 W
Silves 34 37.11 N 8.26 W
Silvi 66 42.34 N 14.05 E
Silvia 246 2.37 N 76.21 W
Silvianópolis 256 22.02 S 45.50 W
Silvícola 164 8.39 S 126.59 E
Silvies ≃ 202 43.22 N 118.48 W
Silview 285 39.42 N 75.37 W
Silvolde 52 51.54 N 6.53 E
Silvretta Gruppe ⋏ 58 46.50 N 10.10 E
Sim 86 54.59 N 57.41 E
Sim, Cap ≻ 148 31.23 N 9.51 W
Sima, Comores 157a 12.11 S 44.17 E
Sima, S.S.S.R. 80 56.41 N 39.33 E
Simaltala 124 24.43 N 86.33 E
Simanggang 112 1.15 N 111.26 E
Simangumban 114 1.42 N 99.10 E
Şimanoviči 76 53.05 N 28.38 E
Šimanovsk 89 52.00 N 127.42 E
Simao 102 22.50 N 101.00 E
Simão Dias 250 10.44 S 37.49 W
Simão Pereira 256 21.58 S 43.19 W
Simara Island I 116 12.48 N 122.03 E
Simard, Lac ⊜ 190 47.37 N 78.41 W
Simaria Kalān 124 24.04 N 84.56 E
Simatang, Pulau I 112 1.04 N 120.23 E
Simav 130 39.05 N 28.59 E
Simav ≃ 130 40.23 N 28.31 E
Simav Gölü ⊜ 130 39.09 N 28.55 E
Simaxis 71 39.56 N 8.41 E
Simba, Kenya 154 2.10 S 37.36 E
Simba, Tan. 154 1.44 S 34.13 E
Simba, Zaïre 152 0.36 N 22.55 E
Simbach 60 48.34 N 12.45 E
Simbach am Inn 60 48.16 N 13.01 E
Simbal 248 7.58 S 78.49 W
Simbario 68 38.37 N 16.20 E
Simberi Island I 164 2.40 S 152.00 E
Simbirsk → Uljanovsk 80 54.20 N 48.24 E
Simbo, Tan. 154 4.40 S 33.27 E
Simbo, Tan. 154 4.53 S 29.44 E
Simbo Island I 175e 8.17 S 156.33 E
Simbruini, Monti ⋏ 66 41.55 N 13.15 E
Simcoe 212 42.50 N 80.18 W
Simcoe □[6] 212 44.25 N 79.50 W
Simcoe, Lake ⊜ 212 44.20 N 79.20 W
Simcoe Creek ≃ 224 46.22 N 120.36 W
Simcoe Island I 212 44.10 N 76.31 W
Simcoe Point ≻ 275b 43.49 N 79.01 W
Simdega 124 22.37 N 84.31 E
Simeiz 78 44.26 N 34.01 E
Simen 104 40.44 N 123.49 E
Simeng 107 29.56 N 103.44 E
Simen Mountains National Park ♠ 144 13.08 N 38.15 E
Simenti 150 13.00 N 13.25 W
Simeri ≃ 68 38.52 N 16.43 E
Simeria 38 45.51 N 23.01 E
Simeto ≃ 70 37.24 N 15.06 E
Simeulue, Pulau I 114 2.33 N 96.05 E
Simferopol' 78 44.57 N 34.06 E
Sími 38 36.36 N 27.50 E
Sími I 38 36.35 N 27.52 E
Simi, Arroyo ≃ 228 34.16 N 118.39 W
Simiane 62 43.25 N 5.26 E
Simianshan 107 28.49 N 105.09 E
Simikoṭ 124 29.58 N 81.50 E
Similkameen ≃ 182 48.56 N 119.26 W
Simingchang 107 29.02 N 105.45 E
Simiri 150 14.08 N 2.08 E
Simisa Island I 116 5.57 N 121.35 E
Simití 246 7.58 N 73.57 W
Simi Valley 228 34.16 N 118.47 W
Simiyu ≃ 154 2.33 S 33.25 E
Simizu → Shimizu 94 35.01 N 138.29 E
Simla, India 272b 22.47 N 88.16 E
Simla, India 272b 22.54 N 88.22 E
Simla, Co., U.S. 198 39.08 N 104.05 W
Simla ◈[8] 272b 22.35 N 88.22 E
Simlāpāl 126 22.55 N 87.05 E
Şimleu Silvaniei 38 47.14 N 22.48 E
Şimlipālgarh 126 21.51 N 86.23 E
Simme ≃ 58 46.41 N 7.38 E
Simmelsdorf 60 49.36 N 11.21 E
Simmental V 58 46.37 N 7.25 E
Simmerath 56 50.36 N 6.18 E
Simmerberg 58 47.35 N 9.56 E
Simmering ◈[8] 264b 48.11 N 16.25 E
Simmern 56 49.59 N 7.31 E
Simmesport 194 30.59 N 91.48 W
Simmie 184 49.57 N 108.06 W
Simmons Island I 282 38.06 N 121.58 W
Simmons Point ≻ 282 38.03 N 121.56 W
Simmonswood Moss ◈[3] 262 53.30 N 2.50 W
Simms 202 47.29 N 111.55 W
Simnas 76 54.24 N 23.39 E
Simoca 252 27.16 S 65.21 W
Simões 250 7.36 S 40.49 W
Simojärvi ⊜ 26 66.06 N 27.03 E
Simojoki ≃ 26 65.37 N 25.03 E
Simojovel de Allende 234 17.12 N 92.38 W
Simon, Lac ⊜, P.Q., Can. 206 46.10 N 74.45 W
Simon, Lac ⊜, P.Q., Can. 206 45.58 N 75.05 W
Simón Bolívar, Parque Nacional → Sierra Nevada, Parque Nacional ♠ 246 8.36 N 70.50 W
Simoneti 84 42.14 N 42.52 E
Simonette ≃ 182 55.07 N 118.00 W
Simonhouse Lake ⊜ 184 54.30 N 101.10 W
Simonicha 80 56.31 N 53.50 E
Simoniči 78 51.53 N 28.04 E
Simonoseki → Shimonoseki 96 33.57 N 130.57 E
Simonsbath 42 51.09 N 3.45 W
Simonson Brook ≃ 276 40.26 N 74.37 W
Simonstone 262 53.48 N 2.20 W
Simonstorp 40 58.47 N 16.09 E
Simon's Town 158 34.14 S 18.26 E
Simonton Lake 216 41.44 N 85.59 W
Şimoom Sound 182 50.45 N 126.29 W
Šimorskoje 80 55.19 N 42.02 E
Simpang, Indon. 112 1.16 S 104.05 E
Simpang, Indon. 112 1.03 S 110.06 E
Simpang, Indon. 112 0.09 N 103.15 E
Simpangampat 114 2.55 N 99.43 E
Simpang Empat 114 6.20 N 100.11 E
Simpang-kanan ≃ 114 2.21 N 97.51 E
Simpang-kiri ≃ 114 2.21 N 97.51 E
Simpang Rengam 114 1.50 N 103.19 E
Simpangtiga 114 2.23 N 99.47 E
Simpangulim 114 5.06 N 97.32 E
Simpele 26 61.26 N 29.22 E
Simplicío Mendes 250 7.51 S 41.54 W
Simplon Pass)(58 46.15 N 8.02 E
Simplon Tunnel ◈[5] 58 46.15 N 8.05 E
Simpnäs 40 59.52 N 19.04 E
Simp'o-ri 98 38.36 N 127.41 E
Simpson, La., U.S. 194 31.14 N 93.00 W
Simpson, Pa., U.S. 210 41.35 N 75.29 W
Simpson ≃ 254 45.25 S 72.32 W
Simpson, Isla I 254 45.53 S 73.48 W
Simpson Desert ◈[2] 162 25.00 S 137.00 E
Simpson Desert National Park ♠ 162 25.40 S 138.15 E
Simpson Island I 190 48.48 N 87.40 W
Simpson Lake ⊜ 180 68.10 N 126.35 W
Simpson Peak ∧ 180 59.44 N 131.27 W
Simpson Peninsula ≻[1] 176 68.34 N 88.45 W
Simpsons Gap National Park ♠ 162 23.40 S 133.45 E
Simpson Strait ⊔ 176 68.27 N 97.45 W
Simpsonville, Ky., U.S. 218 38.13 N 85.21 W
Simpsonville, Md., U.S. 208 39.11 N 76.52 W
Simpsonville, S.C., U.S. 192 34.44 N 82.15 W
Simrishamn 26 55.33 N 14.20 E
Sims 216 40.30 N 85.51 W
Şimsbury 207 41.52 N 72.48 W
Šimsk 76 58.13 N 30.43 E
Simssee ⊜ 64 47.52 N 12.14 E
Simunjan 112 1.23 N 110.45 E
Simurāli 126 23.03 N 88.30 E
Simušir, ostrov I 74 46.58 N 152.02 E
Sīnā' □[4] 142 30.15 N 32.40 E
Sīna ≃ 122 17.22 N 75.54 E
Sīnā', Shibh Jazīrat (Sinai Peninsula) ≻[1] 140 29.30 N 34.00 E
Sinabang 114 2.29 N 96.23 E
Sinabelkirchen 61 47.06 N 15.50 E
Sinabung, Gunung ∧ 114 3.10 N 98.24 E
Sinadhago 144 5.22 N 46.20 E
Sinagra 70 38.05 N 14.51 E
Sinai, Mount → Mūsā, Jabal ∧ 140 28.32 N 33.59 E
Sinaia 38 45.21 N 25.33 E
Sinai Peninsula → Sīnā', Shibh Jazīrat ≻[1] 140 29.30 N 34.00 E
Sin'aja ≃, S.S.S.R. 74 61.06 N 126.50 E
Sin'aja ≃, S.S.S.R. 76 57.10 N 28.31 E
Sinajana 174p 13.28 N 144.45 E
Sinako, Mount ∧ 116 7.30 N 125.17 E
Sinaloa □[3] 232 25.00 N 107.30 W
Sinaloa ≃ 232 25.18 N 108.30 W
Sinalunga 66 43.12 N 11.44 E
Sinamaica 246 11.05 N 71.51 W
Sinan, Tür. 130 37.52 N 41.00 E
Sinan, Zhg. 102 27.54 N 108.18 E
Sinanju 98 39.36 N 125.36 E
Sinanpaşa 130 38.45 N 30.15 E
Sīnarū 142 29.22 N 30.45 E
Sinatle 84 42.28 N 43.04 E
Sin'avka, S.S.S.R. 76 52.58 N 26.29 E
Sin'avka, S.S.S.R. 83 47.17 N 39.17 E
Sīnāwin 146 31.02 N 10.36 E
Sinbad Creek ≃ 282 37.35 N 121.53 W
Sinbaungwe 110 19.43 N 95.10 E
Sinbo 110 24.46 N 97.03 E
Sinbokchang 98 41.01 N 128.54 E
Sincan, Tür. 130 39.28 N 37.54 E
Sincan, Tür. 130 39.59 N 32.26 E
Sincé 246 9.15 N 75.09 W
Sincelejo 246 9.18 N 75.24 W
Sinch'ang, C.M.I.K. 98 40.19 N 125.27 E
Sinch'ang, C.M.I.K. 98 40.07 N 128.28 E
Sinch'ŏn 98 38.22 N 125.28 E
Sinch'ŏn-ni 271b 37.27 N 126.48 E
Sinclair 200 41.46 N 107.06 W
Sinclair, Lake ⊜[1] 192 33.11 N 83.16 W
Sinclair, Point ≻ 162 32.06 S 133.00 E
Sinclair Island I 224 48.37 N 122.40 W
Sinclair Mills 182 54.02 N 121.41 W
Sinclair's Bay ⊂ 46 58.30 N 3.07 W
Sinclairville 214 42.15 N 79.15 W
Sind □[4] 120 25.30 N 69.00 E
Sind ≃ 124 26.26 N 79.13 E
Sinda 89 48.57 N 136.18 E
Sindal 26 57.28 N 10.13 E
Sindangan 116 8.14 N 123.00 E
Sindangan ≃ 116 8.13 N 123.00 E
Sindangan Bay ⊂ 116 8.11 N 122.50 E
Sindangan Point ≻ 116 8.10 N 122.40 E
Sindangbarang 115a 7.27 S 107.08 E
Sindara 152 1.02 S 10.40 E
Sindari 120 25.35 N 71.55 E
Sindelfingen 56 48.42 N 9.00 E
Sindèr 150 14.29 N 1.22 E
Sindhnūr 122 15.47 N 76.46 E
Sindhulī Māḿdi 124 27.16 N 85.58 E
Sindi 76 58.24 N 24.40 E
Sindia 71 40.18 N 8.39 E
Sindingale 110 18.17 N 94.25 E
Sındıran 130 39.17 N 32.41 E
Sındırgı 130 39.14 N 28.10 E
Sindiyūn 142 30.15 N 31.12 E
Sin-do I 98 39.48 N 124.14 E
Sindŏk 98 36.47 N 126.10 E
Sindor 24 62.50 N 51.57 E
Sindou 150 10.40 N 5.10 W
Sindri 126 23.45 N 86.42 E
Sind Sāgar Doāb ⋏[1] 123 31.30 N 71.30 E
Sine V 150 14.10 N 16.28 W
Sinegorje 24 59.42 N 50.40 E
Sinegorsk 89 47.10 N 142.30 E
Şinegorskij 78 48.00 N 40.53 E
Šine-Ider 88 48.56 N 99.33 E
Sinekçi 130 40.16 N 27.24 E
Sinekli 130 41.14 N 28.12 E
Sinel'nikovo 78 48.20 N 35.31 E
Sinendé 150 10.21 N 2.23 E
Sinen'kije 80 51.15 N 45.46 E
Sinepuxent Bay ⊂ 208 38.16 N 75.09 W
Sines 34 37.57 N 8.52 W
Sines, Cabo de ≻ 34 37.57 N 8.53 W
Sinevir 78 48.30 N 23.38 E
Sinevka 78 50.33 N 34.06 E
Sinewit, Mount ∧ 164 4.40 S 152.00 E
Sinez'orki 76 53.02 N 34.26 E
Sinfra 150 6.37 N 5.55 W
Singair 126 23.49 N 90.08 E
Singako 146 9.50 N 19.29 E
Singal 123 36.06 N 73.53 E
Singalamwe 156 17.41 S 23.23 E
Singālila ∧ 124 27.13 N 88.01 E
Singālila Range ⋏ 124 27.25 N 88.05 E
Singaparna 115a 7.21 S 108.06 E
Singapore, Sing. 114 1.17 N 103.51 E
Singapore, Sing. 271c 1.17 N 103.51 E
Singapore □[1], Asia 108 1.22 N 103.48 E
Singapore □[1], Asia 114 1.22 N 103.48 E
Singapore I 271c 1.23 N 103.48 E
Singapore ≃ 271c 1.17 N 103.51 E
Singapore, National University of ♥[2] 271c 1.18 N 103.46 E
Singapore Station ◈[5] 271c 1.17 N 103.50 E
Singapore Strait ⊔ 112 1.15 N 104.00 E
Singapour → Singapore □[1] 114 1.22 N 103.48 E
Singapur → Singapore 114 1.17 N 103.51 E
Singapur → Singapore □[1] 114 1.22 N 103.48 E
Singaraja 115b 8.07 S 115.06 E
Singarka ≃ 265a 59.53 N 29.54 E
Singāti 126 22.44 N 89.43 E
Singatoka 175g 18.08 S 177.30 E
Sing Buri 110 14.53 N 100.25 E
Singe 272b 22.57 N 88.26 E
Singen (Hohentwiel) 58 47.46 N 8.50 E
Singer 194 30.39 N 93.24 W
Singhi 126 23.37 N 87.48 E
Singida 154 4.49 S 34.45 E
Singida □[4] 154 5.30 S 34.30 E
Singing, India 102 28.59 N 94.50 E
Singing, India 120 28.53 N 94.47 E
Singing Tower ♠ 220 27.57 N 81.34 W
Singkaling Hkāmti 110 26.00 N 95.42 E
Singkang 112 4.08 S 120.01 E
Singkawang 112 0.54 N 109.00 E
Singkep, Pulau I 112 0.30 S 104.25 E
Singkil 114 2.17 N 97.49 E
Singkuang 114 1.03 N 98.56 E
Singleton, Austl. 170 32.34 S 151.10 E
Singleton, Eng., U.K. 42 50.55 N 0.46 W
Singleton, Mount ∧, Austl. 162 22.00 S 130.49 E
Singleton, Mount ∧, Austl. 162 29.28 S 117.18 E
Singleton Ditch ≍ 216 41.10 N 87.37 W
Singlewell or Ifield 260 51.25 N 0.23 E
Singö 40 60.10 N 18.44 E
Singö I 40 60.11 N 18.46 E
Singora → Songkhla 110 7.12 N 100.36 E
Şingorkai 164 5.55 S 146.55 E
Šingoža 86 47.45 N 80.40 E
Singpāra 272b 22.40 N 88.31 E
Singrāmau 124 25.57 N 82.23 E
Singuédeze (Shingwidzi) ≃ 156 23.53 S 32.17 E
Singur 126 22.49 N 88.14 E
Sin'gye 98 38.36 N 126.30 E
Sinhai → Lianyungang 98 34.39 N 119.16 E
Sinh Ho 110 22.22 N 103.14 E
Sinhŭng 98 40.11 N 127.34 E
Siniaka-Minia, Réserve de ■ 146 10.30 N 18.00 E
Sinicha 83 49.31 N 37.34 E
Sinička ≃ 265b 55.50 N 37.19 E
Sinije gory ⋏[2] 80 51.10 N 49.25 E
Sinije Lip'agi 78 51.23 N 38.29 E
Siniloan 116 14.25 N 121.27 E
Sining → Xining 102 36.38 N 101.55 E
Siniscola 71 40.34 N 9.41 E
Sinj 36 43.42 N 16.38 E
Sinjah 140 13.09 N 33.56 E
Sinjai 112 5.07 S 120.15 E
Sinjang-ni 98 39.04 N 127.46 E
Sinjār 128 36.19 N 41.52 E
Sinjār, Jabal ⋏ 130 36.25 N 41.40 E
Sinji-do I 98 34.20 N 126.50 E
Sinkan 110 24.08 N 97.01 E
Sinkāt 140 18.50 N 36.50 E
Sinkiang → Xinjiang Uygur Zizhiqu □[4] 90 40.00 N 85.00 E
Sinking ≃ 48 53.37 N 8.52 W
Sinking Creek ≃ 210 40.51 N 77.34 W
Sinking Spring, Oh., U.S. 218 39.04 N 83.23 W
Sinking Spring, Pa., U.S. 208 40.19 N 76.02 W
Şin'kok-ni 271b 37.37 N 126.46 E
Šinkovo, S.S.S.R. 76 56.03 N 31.31 E
Sin'kovo, S.S.S.R. 82 54.37 N 38.56 E
Sin'kovo, S.S.S.R. 82 56.26 N 36.04 E
Sin'kovo, S.S.S.R. 82 56.23 N 37.19 E
Sinks Canyon State Park ♠ 200 42.45 N 108.50 W
Sin-le-Noble 50 50.22 N 3.07 E
Sinmak 98 38.25 N 126.14 E
Sinmi-do I 98 39.33 N 124.53 E
Sinn ≃ 56 50.03 N 9.42 E
Sinnahwā 142 30.25 N 31.21 E
Sínnai 71 39.18 N 9.12 E
Sinnamahoning 214 41.19 N 78.06 W
Sinnamary 250 5.23 N 52.57 W
Sinnamary ≃ 250 5.27 N 53.00 W
Sinnar 122 19.51 N 74.00 E
Sinnemahoning Creek ≃ 210 41.15 N 77.54 W
Sinnemahoning Creek, Bennett Branch ≃ 210 41.20 N 78.08 W
Sinnemahoning Creek, Driftwood Branch ≃ 210 41.20 N 78.08 W
Sinnemahoning Creek, First Fork ≃ 210 41.19 N 78.05 W
Sinnersdorf 56 51.01 N 6.49 E
Sinnes 26 58.56 N 6.50 E
Sinni ≃ 68 40.09 N 16.42 E
Sînnicolau Mare 38 46.05 N 20.38 E
Sinntal 56 50.18 N 9.38 E
Sinnūris 142 29.25 N 30.52 E
Sinnyŏng 98 36.04 N 128.46 E
Sinoie, Lacul ⊜ 38 44.38 N 28.53 E
Sinop 130 42.01 N 35.09 E
Sinop □[4] 130 41.40 N 34.50 E
Sinop Burnu ≻ 130 42.02 N 35.12 E
Sinp'a 98 41.24 N 127.46 E
Sinp'o 98 40.03 N 128.12 E
Sins 58 47.11 N 8.23 E
Sinsang 98 39.38 N 127.25 E
Sinsen 263 51.40 N 7.11 E
Sinsheim 56 49.15 N 8.53 E
Sinsiang → Xinxiang 98 35.20 N 113.51 E
Sinsin 56 50.17 N 5.15 E
Sinsi-ri 98 39.59 N 124.58 E
Sinskoje 74 61.08 N 126.48 E
Sinspelt 56 49.58 N 6.19 E
Sint-Amandsberg 50 51.04 N 3.45 E
Sintana 38 46.21 N 21.30 E
Sint-Andries 50 51.12 N 3.10 E
Sintang 112 0.04 N 111.30 E
Sint Annaland 52 51.36 N 4.06 E
Sint Annaparochie 52 53.16 N 5.39 E
Sint Anthonis 52 51.37 N 5.52 E
Sint Christoffelberg ∧ 241s 12.20 N 69.08 W
Sint-Denijs-Westrem 50 51.01 N 3.40 E
Sint Eustatius I 238 17.30 N 62.59 W
Sint-Gillis-Waas 50 51.13 N 4.08 E
Sint Helenabaai ⊂ 158 32.43 S 18.05 E
Sint-Joris-Weert 56 50.48 N 4.39 E
Sint-Joris-Winge 56 50.55 N 4.52 E
Sint-Katelijne-Waver 56 51.04 N 4.32 E
Sint-Kruis, Bel. 50 51.13 N 3.15 E
Sint Kruis, Ned. Ant. 241s 12.18 N 69.08 W
Sint-Lenaarts 56 51.21 N 4.41 E
Sint Maarten 52 52.46 N 4.44 E
Sint Maarten (Saint-Martin) I 238 18.04 N 63.04 W
Sint Maartensdijk 52 51.33 N 4.05 E
Sint-Michiels 50 51.11 N 3.12 E
Sint Michielsgestel 52 51.38 N 5.21 E
Sint Nicolaas 241s 12.27 N 69.52 W
Sint-Niklaas (Saint-Nicolas) 50 51.10 N 4.08 E
Sint-Oedenrode 52 51.34 N 5.27 E
Sinton 196 28.02 N 97.30 W
Sintong 114 1.31 N 100.58 E
Sint Pancras 52 52.39 N 4.46 E
Sint-Pieters-Leeuw 50 50.47 N 4.14 E
Sintra 34 38.48 N 9.23 W
Sintra, Serra de ⋏[2] 266c 38.47 N 9.25 W
Sintra Granjo do Marquez, Aeroporto ⊠ 266c 38.49 N 9.20 W
Sint-Truiden 56 50.48 N 5.12 E
Sint Willebrord 52 51.33 N 4.35 E
Sinú ≃ 246 9.24 N 75.49 W
Sin'ucha ≃, S.S.S.R. 78 48.03 N 30.51 E
Sin'ucha ≃, S.S.S.R. 84 44.45 N 40.58 E
Sin'uga 88 57.45 N 115.13 E
Sinŭiju 98 40.05 N 124.24 E
Sinujif 144 8.33 N 48.59 E
Sinŭp, C.M.I.K. 98 39.54 N 126.47 E
Sinŭp, Taehan 98 37.54 N 127.12 E
Sinwŏn-ni 98 38.13 N 125.44 E
Sinzig 56 50.32 N 7.15 E
Sinzing 60 49.00 N 12.02 E
Sió ≃, Magy. 30 46.20 N 18.55 E
Sio ≃, Togo 150 6.17 N 1.13 E
Siocon 116 7.42 N 122.08 E
Siófok 30 46.54 N 18.04 E
Sioma 152 16.39 S 23.30 E
Sioma Ngweze National Park ♠ 152 17.15 S 23.20 E
Sion (Sitten) 58 46.14 N 7.21 E
Sionascaig, Loch ⊜ 46 58.04 N 5.11 W
Sion Mills 48 54.47 N 7.29 W
Sioule ≃ 32 46.22 N 3.19 E
Sioux Center 198 43.04 N 96.10 W
Sioux City 198 42.30 N 96.24 W
Sioux Falls 198 43.33 N 96.42 W
Sioux Lookout 184 50.06 N 91.55 W
Sioux Narrows 184 49.25 N 94.06 W
Sioux Rapids 198 42.53 N 95.09 W
Sipalay 116 9.45 N 122.24 E
Sipalay ≃ 116 9.46 N 122.24 E
Sipaliwini ≃ 250 2.22 N 56.50 W
Sipaozi 104 41.26 N 122.13 E
Sipapo ≃ 246 5.03 N 67.48 W
Siparia 241r 10.08 N 61.30 W
Šipčenski prohod)(38 42.46 N 25.19 E
Şipek 130 40.14 N 41.29 E
Şipes 220 28.48 N 81.14 W
Şipesville 214 40.06 N 79.06 W
Šipicyno, S.S.S.R. 24 61.17 N 46.28 E
Šipicyno, S.S.S.R. 86 56.04 N 77.18 E
Šipilovo 82 54.49 N 37.32 E
Siping 89 43.12 N 124.20 E
Sipingjie 98 42.31 N 125.08 E
Sipirok 114 1.37 N 99.16 E
Sipitang 112 5.05 N 115.33 E
Sipiwesk 184 55.27 N 97.24 W
Sipiwesk Lake ⊜ 184 55.05 N 97.35 W
Siple ♥[3] 9 75.56 S 84.15 W
Siple, Mount ∧ 9 73.15 S 126.06 W
Siple Coast ⫠[2] 9 82.00 S 153.00 W
Sipocot 116 13.46 N 122.58 E
Sipofaneni 158 26.41 S 31.41 E
Sipot 114 4.31 N 96.02 E
Şipoteny 78 47.18 N 28.11 E
Šipovatoje 78 49.56 N 37.24 E
Sipplingen 58 47.47 N 9.05 E
Si Prachan 110 14.37 N 100.09 E
Sipsey ≃ 194 33.00 N 88.10 W
Sipsey Creek ≃ 194 33.53 N 88.17 W
Sipu 98 40.48 N 113.43 E
Şipul 164 5.50 S 148.45 E
Šipunovo 86 52.13 N 82.17 E
Šipunskij, mys ≻ 74 53.06 N 160.02 E
Sipupus 114 1.25 N 99.31 E
Sipura, Pulau I 112 2.12 S 99.40 E
Siqian, Zhg. 100 22.31 N 112.52 E
Siqian, Zhg. 100 24.40 N 114.06 E
Siqueira Campos 255 23.42 S 49.50 W
Siquia ≃ 236 12.09 N 84.13 W
Siquijor 116 9.13 N 123.30 E
Siquijor □[4] 116 9.11 N 123.34 E
Siquijor Island I 116 9.11 N 123.34 E
Siquirres 236 10.06 N 83.30 W
Siquisique 246 10.34 N 69.42 W
Sīra, India 122 13.45 N 76.54 E
Şira, Nor. 26 58.25 N 6.38 E
Šira, S.S.S.R. 86 54.29 N 89.56 E
Sira ≃ 26 58.17 N 6.24 E
Si Racha 110 13.10 N 100.56 E
Siracuas 248 21.03 S 61.46 W
Siracusa (Syracuse) 70 37.04 N 15.17 E
Siracusa □[4] 70 37.03 N 15.00 E
Sir Adam Beck II Reservoir ⊜[1] 284a 43.08 N 79.04 W
Şirāhā 124 26.39 N 86.12 E
Šir'aj 80 49.34 N 44.07 E
Šir'ajevo 78 47.23 N 30.13 E
Sirājganj 124 24.27 N 89.43 E
Sir Alexander, Mount ∧ 182 53.56 N 120.23 W
Sirāmpur 126 24.08 N 86.20 E
Şiran 130 40.12 N 39.08 E
Sirasso 150 9.16 N 6.06 W
Sirault 50 50.30 N 3.47 E
Siraway 116 7.34 N 122.08 E
Sirba ≃ 150 13.46 N 1.40 E
Şīr Banī Yās I 128 24.19 N 52.37 E
Sir Colin Mackenzie Wildlife Sanctuary ◈[4] 169 37.40 S 145.32 E
Sirdalsvatn ⊜ 26 58.33 N 6.41 E
Sīrdān 128 36.39 N 49.12 E
Şirdar 182 49.15 N 116.37 W
Širdkoje 78 48.08 N 34.49 E
Sir Douglas, Mount ∧ 182 50.44 N 115.20 W
Sire 144 9.00 N 36.55 E
Sir Edward Pellew Group II 164 15.40 S 136.48 E
Širega 76 60.10 N 41.15 E
Sireniki 180 64.25 N 173.57 W
Sirente, Monte ∧ 66 42.09 N 13.36 E
Siret 38 47.57 N 26.04 E
Siret ≃ 38 45.24 N 28.01 E
Sirevåg 26 58.30 N 5.47 E
Sir Francis Drake, Mount ∧ 182 50.48 N 124.47 W
Sir Francis Drake Channel ⊔ 240m 18.25 N 64.30 W
Sirghāyā 132 33.48 N 36.09 E
Sirḥān, Wādī as- V 128 30.30 N 38.00 E
Sirhind 124 30.39 N 76.23 E
Sirhind Canal ≍ 123 30.47 N 76.01 E
Siria → Syria □[1] 128 35.00 N 38.00 E
Sirik, Tanjong ≻ 112 2.46 N 111.19 E
Sirikit Reservoir ⊜[1] 110 17.50 N 100.30 E
Şírina I 130 36.21 N 26.42 E
Širinguši 80 53.51 N 42.46 E
Sirino, Monte ∧ 68 40.08 N 15.50 E
Siriya-zaki ≻ 92 41.26 N 141.28 E
Sir James MacBrien, Mount ∧ 180 62.07 N 127.41 W
Sīrjān 128 29.27 N 55.40 E
Sir Joseph Banks Group II 166 34.32 S 136.17 E
Sirkābād 126 23.16 N 86.12 E
Sirkeli 130 40.09 N 32.52 E
Sirmaur 124 24.51 N 81.23 E
Şirmione 64 45.30 N 10.36 E
Širmovka 78 49.34 N 29.06 E
Sirnach 58 47.28 N 9.00 E
Siro, Jabal ∧ 140 14.23 N 24.23 E
Şirohi 120 24.54 N 72.51 E
Širokaja Pad' 89 50.14 N 142.09 E
Širokij 89 49.45 N 129.30 E
Širokij Bujerak 80 52.07 N 47.46 E
Širokino 83 47.06 N 37.49 E
Širokoje, S.S.S.R. 78 47.41 N 33.14 E
Širokoje, S.S.S.R. 83 47.58 N 38.13 E
Širokolanovka 78 47.10 N 31.24 E
Širokovo 88 55.27 N 99.23 E
Sirolo 66 43.32 N 13.37 E
Sirombu 114 0.57 N 97.25 E
Sironj 124 24.06 N 77.42 E
Síros → Ermoúpolis 38 37.26 N 24.56 E
Síros I 38 37.26 N 24.54 E
Sirotino, S.S.S.R. 76 55.23 N 29.37 E
Sirotino, S.S.S.R. 83 48.55 N 38.31 E
Sirotinskaja 80 49.16 N 43.39 E
Siroua, Jebel ∧ 148 30.41 N 7.37 W
Sırpsındığı 130 41.46 N 26.29 E
Sirrah, Nafūd as- ⫠[8] 128 23.05 N 44.25 E
Sīrrī, Jazīreh-ye I 128 25.55 N 54.32 E
Sirsa, India 123 29.32 N 75.01 E
Sirsa, India 126 22.14 N 86.38 E
Sirsāganj 124 27.03 N 78.42 E
Sirs al-Layyānah 142 30.26 N 30.58 E
Sir Sandford, Mount ∧ 182 51.40 N 117.52 W
Sirsi 122 14.37 N 74.51 E
Sirsilla 122 18.23 N 78.50 E
Sirsinā, Mişr 142 29.24 N 30.58 E
Sirsinā, Mişr 142 30.36 N 30.54 E
Sirsiri 154 4.24 N 31.53 E
Sir Thomas, Mount ∧ 162 27.10 S 129.45 E
Siruma 116 14.00 N 123.15 E
Şirvan 130 38.02 N 42.00 E
Šīrvān (Diyālā) ≃ 128 33.14 N 44.31 E
Širvanskaja ravnina ≡ 84 40.15 N 48.00 E
Širvintos 76 55.03 N 24.57 E
Sir Wilfrid Laurier, Mount ∧ 182 52.47 N 119.45 W
Sir Wilfrid Laurier's Birthplace National Historic Site ⊥ 206 45.51 N 73.45 W
Sirykrabet ⊥ 86 44.07 N 62.35 E
Sís ≃, Guat. 236 14.09 N 91.39 W
Šiš ≃, S.S.S.R. 86 57.19 N 73.23 E
Sisa, Mount ∧ 164 6.08 S 142.45 E
Sisaba ∧ 154 6.09 S 29.48 E
Sisaiya Thāna 124 27.35 N 81.20 E
Sisak 36 45.29 N 16.23 E
Şi Sa Ket 110 15.07 N 104.20 E
Šišaki 78 49.53 N 34.00 E
Šišakovo 76 60.02 N 41.30 E
Şi Satchanalai 110 17.31 N 99.46 E
Šišchid (Kyzyl-Chem) ≃ 88 51.21 N 96.58 E
Šiševka 76 58.52 N 38.52 E

≃ River	Fluß	Río	Rivière	Rio
≍ Canal	Kanal	Canal	Canal	Canal
⌞ Waterfall, Rapids	Wasserfall, Stromschnellen	Cascada, Rápidos	Chute d'eau, Rapides	Cascata, Rápidos
⊔ Strait	Meeresstraße	Estrecho	Détroit	Estreito
⊂ Bay, Gulf	Bucht, Golf	Bahía, Golfo	Baie, Golfe	Baía, Golfo
⊜ Lake, Lakes	See, Seen	Lago, Lagos	Lac, Lacs	Lago, Lagos
≡ Swamp	Sumpf	Pantano	Marais	Pântano
⩀ Ice Features, Glacier	Eis- und Gletscherformen	Accidentes Glaciales	Formes glaciaires	Acidentes glaciares
⫪ Other Hydrographic Features	Andere Hydrographische Objekte	Otros Elementos Hidrográficos	Autres données hydrographiques	Outros acidentes hidrográficos
✢ Submarine Features	Untermeerische Objekte	Accidentes Submarinos	Formes de relief sous-marin	Acidentes submarinos
□ Political Unit	Politische Einheit	Unidad Politica	Entité politique	Unidade política
♥ Cultural Institution	Kulturelle Institution	Institución Cultural	Institution culturelle	Instituição cultural
⊥ Historical Site	Historische Stätte	Sitio Histórico	Site historique	Sitio histórico
♠ Recreational Site	Erholungs- und Ferienort	Sitio de Recreo	Centre de loisirs	Area de Lazer
⊠ Airport	Flughafen	Aeropuerto	Aéroport	Aeroporto
■ Military Installation	Militäranlage	Instalación Militar	Installation militaire	Instalação militar
◈ Miscellaneous	Verschiedenes	Misceláneo	Divers	Diversos

Name	Page	Lat.°′	Long.°′
Sishangcun	105	40.16 N	116.33 E
Sishen	158	27.55 S	22.59 E
Sishili	106	32.09 N	120.45 E
Sishilijie	100	29.08 N	116.44 E
Sishilipu	105	40.12 N	118.08 E
Sishuang Liedao II	100	26.42 N	120.24 E
Sishui	98	35.39 N	117.15 E
Sisian	84	39.32 N	46.02 E
Sisib Lake ◎	184	52.35 N	99.22 W
Šišicy	76	53.13 N	27.32 E
Sisikon	58	46.57 N	8.42 E
Sisim ≃	88	55.09 N	91.54 E
Sisipuk Lake ◎	184	55.45 N	101.50 W
Šiškejevo	80	54.12 N	44.45 E
Šiškino	88	52.18 N	113.35 E
Siskiyou Mountains ⋏	204	41.55 N	123.15 W
Siskiyou Pass)(	202	42.03 N	122.36 W
Şişli ⬥[8]	267b	41.04 N	28.59 E
Šišlovo	82	54.14 N	38.33 E
Sison	116	9.40 N	125.31 E
Sisŏphŏn	110	13.35 N	102.59 E
Sisquoc ≃	204	34.54 N	120.18 W
Sissa ≃	115b	8.29 S	121.18 E
Sissach	58	47.28 N	7.49 E
Sissano	164	3.00 S	142.05 E
Sisséla	150	10.49 N	10.37 W
Sisseton	198	45.39 N	97.02 W
Sisseton Indian Reservation ⬥[4]	198	45.40 N	97.02 W
Sissili ≃	150	10.16 N	1.15 W
Sisson Branch Reservoir ◎[1]	186	47.16 N	67.20 W
Sissonne	50	49.34 N	3.54 E
Sissonville	188	38.31 N	81.37 W
Sīstān ⬥[1]	128	30.30 N	62.00 E
Sīstān va Balūchestān □[4]	128	28.30 N	60.30 E
Sister Bay	190	45.11 N	87.07 W
Sister Lakes	216	42.05 N	86.12 W
Sisteron	62	44.12 N	5.56 E
Sisters	202	44.17 N	121.32 W
Sistersville	188	39.33 N	80.59 W
Sistig	56	50.29 N	6.30 E
Sisto ≃	66	41.18 N	13.10 E
Sistranda	26	63.43 N	8.50 E
Sit' ≃, S.S.S.R.	76	59.59 N	40.10 E
Sit' ≃, S.S.S.R.	76	58.16 N	37.54 E
Sitabamba	248	8.02 S	77.44 W
Sitai, Zhg.	85	39.23 N	77.56 E
Sitai, Zhg.	98	41.16 N	114.23 E
Sitaizi, Zhg.	104	42.29 N	123.20 E
Sitaizi, Zhg.	104	41.17 N	122.16 E
Sitaizui	105	40.49 N	115.20 E
Sitakili	150	13.07 N	11.14 W
Sitalike	154	6.38 S	31.08 E
Sitalkuchi	124	26.10 N	89.11 E
Sītāmarhi	124	26.36 N	85.29 E
Sitampiky	157b	16.41 S	46.06 E
Si Tangkay	112	4.40 N	119.24 E
Sītāpur	124	27.34 N	80.41 E
Sītāpur Branch ≅	124	28.10 N	80.25 E
Sitārāmpur	126	23.43 N	86.53 E
Siteki	158	26.32 S	31.58 E
Sites	226	39.19 N	122.20 W
Si Thep ⊥	110	15.30 N	101.10 E
Sithoniá	38	35.12 N	26.07 E
Sithoniá ≻[1]	38	40.10 N	23.47 E
Sitidgi Lake ◎	180	68.32 N	132.42 W
Sítio da Abadia	255	14.48 S	46.16 W
Sítio Nôvo do Grajaú	250	5.51 S	46.43 W
Sitionuevo	246	10.47 N	74.43 W
Sitka	180	57.03 N	135.02 W
Sitkalidak Island I	180	57.10 N	153.14 W
Sitka National Historical Park ♠	180	57.05 N	135.15 W
Sitka Point ≻	180	57.00 N	135.49 W
Sitka Sound ʊ	180	57.00 N	135.30 W
Sitkinak Island I	180	56.35 N	154.12 W
Sitkinak Strait ʊ	180	56.39 N	154.06 W
Šitkino	88	56.23 N	98.21 E
Sitkovcy	78	48.54 N	29.12 E
Sitna ≃	38	47.37 N	27.08 E
Sitn'a-Ščelkanovo	82	54.58 N	37.59 E
Sitnica ≃	38	42.45 N	21.01 E
Sitniki	80	56.27 N	44.06 E
Sitnikovo	86	56.23 N	67.53 E
Sitobela	158	26.53 S	31.36 E
Sitona	144	14.28 N	37.27 E
Sitrah	128	26.09 N	50.38 E
Sitrah ⊤[4]	140	28.42 N	26.54 E
Sittard	56	51.00 N	5.53 E
Sitten → Sion	58	46.14 N	7.21 E
Sittendorf	264b	48.05 N	16.10 E
Sittensen	52	53.17 N	9.30 E
Sitter ≃	58	47.29 N	9.14 E
Sittingbourne	42	51.21 N	0.44 E
Sittoung ≃	110	17.10 N	96.58 E
Sittwe (Akyab)	110	20.09 N	92.54 E
Situ	105	39.20 N	115.39 E
Situbondo	115a	7.42 S	114.00 E
Siufaalele Point ≻	174y	14.17 S	169.29 W
Si'ufage	174y	14.14 S	169.32 W
Siulakderas	112	1.55 S	101.18 E
Siu Lek Yuen	271d	22.23 N	114.12 E
Siumbatu	112	2.45 S	122.03 E
Siumpu, Pulau I	112	5.40 S	122.31 E
Siuna	236	13.44 N	84.46 W
Siurgus Donigala	71	39.35 N	9.12 E
Siuri	126	23.55 N	87.32 E
Siusi (Seis)	64	46.32 N	11.34 E
Siuslaw ≃	202	44.01 N	124.08 W
Siva ≃	80	56.48 N	53.55 E
Sivaganga	122	9.52 N	78.29 E
Sivakāsi	122	9.27 N	77.49 E
Sivaki	89	52.39 N	126.45 E
Sīvand ≃	128	29.51 N	52.46 E
Sivas	130	39.45 N	37.02 E
Sivas □[4]	130	39.30 N	37.15 E
Sivaš ʊ	78	46.00 N	34.30 E
Sivaslı	130	38.30 N	29.42 E
Sivašskoje	78	46.23 N	34.34 E
Sivé	150	15.42 N	13.12 W
Šiveluč, vulkan ∧[1]	74	56.39 N	161.18 E
Siverek	130	37.45 N	39.19 E
Siverskij	76	59.21 N	30.05 E
Sivkovo	82	55.26 N	35.53 E
Sivomaskinskij	24	66.40 N	62.35 E
Sivri Ada I	267b	40.54 N	28.59 E
Sivrice	130	38.27 N	39.19 E
Sivrihisar	130	39.27 N	31.34 E
Sivry-Courtry	261	48.32 N	2.45 E
Sivry-sur-Meuse	56	49.19 N	5.16 E
Sīwah	140	29.12 N	25.31 E
Sīwah, Wāḥat ⊤[4]	140	29.12 N	25.31 E
Siwalik Range ⋏	120	31.00 N	78.00 E
Siwān	124	26.13 N	84.22 E
Siwang ≃	107	29.25 N	103.50 E
Sixaola ≃	236	9.34 N	82.34 W
Six Flags Great America ♠	216	42.21 N	87.55 W
Six Flags over Mid-America ♠	219	38.31 N	90.40 W
Six Flags Over Texas ♠	222	32.45 N	97.05 W
Six-Fours-la-Plage	62	43.06 N	5.51 E
Sixian	100	33.30 N	117.56 E
Sixitou	100	27.31 N	119.57 E
Six Mile Creek ≃, On., Can.	284a	43.15 N	79.10 W
Sixmile Creek ≃, Ky., U.S.	218	38.26 N	84.58 W
Sixmile Creek ≃, N.Y., U.S.	284a	43.17 N	78.58 W
Sixmilecross	48	54.34 N	7.08 W
Six Mile Lake ◎	212	44.55 N	79.45 W
Sixmile Run ≃	276	40.28 N	74.35 W
Six Mile Water ≃	48	54.42 N	6.14 W
Six Nations Indian Reserve ⬥[4]	212	43.03 N	80.07 W
Sixshooter Draw V	196	30.51 N	102.33 W
Sixteen Mile Creek ≃, On., Can.	275b	43.27 N	79.40 W
Sixteenmile Creek ≃, Mt., U.S.	202	46.06 N	111.23 W
Sixth Cataract → Sablūkah, Ash-Shallāl as- ᒪ	140	16.20 N	32.42 E
Siyāl, Jazā'ir II	140	22.47 N	36.12 E
Siyāna	124	28.38 N	78.03 E
Siyang	100	33.43 N	118.41 E
Si Yat ≃	110	13.42 N	101.26 E
Siyeteb	140	18.00 N	35.01 E
Siz'absk	24	65.05 N	53.49 E
Sizaja	88	58.07 N	100.38 E
Sizhijian	98	42.25 N	114.36 E
Siziano	62	45.20 N	9.12 E
Sizilien → Sicilia I	70	37.30 N	14.00 E
Siziman	89	50.43 N	140.26 E
Siziwang Qi	102	41.33 N	111.31 E
Sizun	32	48.24 N	4.05 W
Sizuoka → Shizuoka	94	34.58 N	138.23 E
Sjælland I	41	55.30 N	11.45 E
Sjællands Odde ≻[1]	41	55.58 N	11.22 E
Själevad	26	63.18 N	18.36 E
Sjanovo	82	54.59 N	37.25 E
Sjenica	38	43.16 N	20.00 E
Sjeništa ∧	38	43.42 N	18.37 E
Sjoa ≃	26	61.41 N	9.33 E
Sjöbo	41	55.38 N	13.42 E
Sjøholt	26	62.29 N	6.48 E
Sjösa	40	58.46 N	17.04 E
Sjötorp	40	58.50 N	13.59 E
Skaby	264a	52.19 N	13.51 E
Skaby-Berge ⋏[2]	264a	52.19 N	13.49 E
Skåde	41	56.06 N	10.13 E
Skadovsk	78	46.08 N	32.54 E
Skælskør	41	55.15 N	11.19 E
Skærbæk, Dan.	41	55.31 N	9.38 E
Skærbæk, Dan.	41	55.09 N	8.46 E
Skævinge	41	55.55 N	12.10 E
Skaftafell National Park ♠	24a	64.15 N	17.00 W
Skaftung	26	62.07 N	21.22 E
Skagafjörður c	24a	65.55 N	19.35 W
Skagen	26	57.44 N	10.36 E
Skagern ◎	40	58.59 N	14.17 E
Skagerrak ʊ	26	57.45 N	9.00 E
Skagersvik	40	58.58 N	14.06 E
Skaggs Creek ≃	194	36.54 N	86.04 W
Skagit □[6]	224	48.29 N	121.45 W
Skagit ≃	224	48.20 N	122.25 W
Skagit Bay c	224	48.19 N	122.24 W
Skagway	180	59.28 N	135.19 W
Skaidi	24	70.25 N	24.30 E
Skaistkalne	76	56.23 N	24.39 E
Skála Oropoú	38	38.20 N	23.46 E
Skala-Podol'skaja	78	48.51 N	26.12 E
Skalat	78	49.26 N	25.59 E
Skalbmierz	30	50.19 N	20.25 E
Skälderviken	41	56.17 N	12.50 E
Skälderviken c	41	56.18 N	12.38 E
Skalica	30	48.51 N	17.14 E
Skalino	76	58.32 N	40.13 E
Skalistaja, gora ∧	84	42.48 N	40.59 E
Skalistyj, gora ∧	180	68.12 N	178.10 E
Skalistyj chrebet ⋏	84	43.15 N	43.00 E
Skalistyj Golec, gora ∧	88	56.24 N	119.12 E
Skalka ◎	24	66.50 N	18.46 E
Skalka, údolní nádrž ◎[1]	54	50.06 N	12.19 E
Skalná	54	50.07 N	12.23 E
Skal'nyj	86	58.22 N	57.59 E
Skamania	224	45.37 N	122.02 W
Skamania □[6]	224	45.58 N	121.53 W
Skamlingsbanke ∧[2]	41	55.25 N	9.34 E
Skamokawa	224	46.16 N	123.27 W
Skanderborg	41	56.02 N	9.56 E
Skanderborg Sø ◎	41	56.01 N	9.56 E
Skåne □[9]	41	55.59 N	13.30 E
Skaneateles	210	42.56 N	76.25 W
Skaneateles Falls	210	43.00 N	76.27 W
Skaneateles Lake ◎	210	42.53 N	76.24 W
Skånevik	26	59.44 N	5.59 E
Skänninge	26	58.24 N	15.05 E
Skanör	26	55.25 N	12.52 E
Skara	26	58.22 N	13.25 E
Skaraborgs Län □[6]	26	58.20 N	13.30 E
Skaramagás	267c	38.01 N	23.36 E
Skärblacka	40	58.34 N	15.54 E
Skarð	24a	64.03 N	19.50 W
Skardhø ∧	26	62.30 N	8.45 E
Skārdu	123	35.18 N	75.37 E
Skärhamn	26	58.00 N	11.33 E
Skarhult	41	55.49 N	13.23 E
Skarnes	26	60.15 N	11.41 E
Skarø I	41	55.00 N	10.29 E
Skärplinge	40	60.28 N	17.46 E
Skarszewy	30	54.05 N	18.27 E
Skårup	41	55.05 N	10.42 E
Skaryszew	30	51.19 N	21.15 E
Skarżysko-Kamienna	30	51.08 N	20.53 E
Skášov	60	49.31 N	13.26 E
Skate Creek ≃	224	46.37 N	121.41 W
Skattkärr	40	59.25 N	13.41 E
Skaudvilė	76	55.24 N	22.35 E
Skaugum	26	59.51 N	10.26 E
Skawina	30	49.59 N	19.49 E
Skebobruk	40	59.58 N	18.36 E
Skebokvarn	40	59.04 N	16.42 E
Skedviken ◎	40	59.46 N	18.16 E
Skedvisjön ◎	40	59.35 N	15.40 E
Skeena ≃	182	54.09 N	130.02 W
Skeena Crossing	182	55.06 N	127.49 W
Skeena Mountains ⋏	176	57.00 N	128.30 W
Skeen Peak ∧	222	32.59 N	97.48 W
Skegness	44	53.10 N	0.21 E
Skegrie	41	55.24 N	13.04 E
Skei	26	61.38 N	6.30 E
Skeikampen	26	61.20 N	10.07 E
Skelde	41	54.51 N	9.44 E
Skeldon	246	5.53 N	57.08 W
Skeleton Coast ⌓[2]	156	19.15 S	12.30 E
Skeleton Coast Park ♠	156	19.25 S	12.55 E
Skeleton Creek ≃	196	35.58 N	97.25 W
Skeleton Lake ◎	212	45.15 N	79.27 W
Skellefteå	26	64.46 N	20.57 E
Skellefteälven ≃	26	64.42 N	21.06 E
Skelleftehamn	26	64.41 N	21.14 E
Skellig Rocks II[1]	48	51.48 N	10.31 W
Skellytown	196	35.34 N	101.11 W
Skelmersdale	44	53.33 N	2.48 W
Skelmorlie	46	55.51 N	4.53 W
Skelton, Eng., U.K.	44	54.33 N	0.59 W
Skelton, Eng., U.K.	44	54.43 N	2.51 W
Skene	26	57.29 N	12.38 E
Skene, Mount ∧	169	37.25 S	146.23 E
Skepptuna	40	59.43 N	18.05 E
Skerne ≃	44	54.29 N	1.34 W
Skerpioensdrif	158	31.05 S	21.33 E
Skerries	48	53.35 N	6.07 W
Skerryvore I[2]	46	56.19 N	7.07 W
Skewen	42	51.40 N	3.51 W
Skhíza I	38	36.44 N	21.46 E
Ski	26	59.43 N	10.50 E
Skíathos	38	39.10 N	23.29 E
Skíathos I	38	39.10 N	23.28 E
Skiatook	196	36.22 N	96.00 W
Skibbereen	48	51.33 N	9.15 W
Skibby	41	55.45 N	11.58 E
Skibotn	24	69.24 N	20.16 E
Skiddaw ∧	44	54.38 N	3.08 W
Skidegate	182	53.15 N	132.00 W
Skidegate Inlet c	182	53.14 N	132.00 W
Skidel'	76	53.34 N	24.15 E
Skidmore	196	28.15 N	97.41 W
Skien	26	59.12 N	9.36 E
Skierniewice	30	51.58 N	20.08 E
Skierniewice □[4]	30	52.10 N	20.15 E
Skiftet ʊ	26	60.15 N	21.05 E
Skihist Mountain ∧	182	50.11 N	121.54 W
Skikda (Philippeville)	148	36.50 N	6.58 E
Skikda □[5]	148	36.45 N	7.00 E
Skilak Lake ◎	180	60.25 N	150.25 W
Skillet Fork ≃	194	38.08 N	88.07 W
Skillingaryd	26	57.26 N	14.05 E
Skillman	276	40.25 N	74.42 W
Škin'	82	55.11 N	38.30 E
Skinnastaður	24a	66.07 N	16.24 W
Skinner Reservoir ◎[1]	228	33.35 N	117.03 W
Skinnskatteberg	40	59.50 N	15.41 E
Skippack	285	40.14 N	75.24 W
Skippack Creek ≃	285	40.09 N	75.27 W
Skippack Creek, West Branch ≃	285	40.14 N	75.23 W
Skippers	208	36.37 N	77.38 W
Skipskop	158	34.33 S	20.25 E
Skipton, Austl.	169	37.41 S	143.22 E
Skipton, Eng., U.K.	44	53.58 N	2.01 W
Skirfare ≃	44	54.07 N	2.01 W
Skirmish Point ≻	171a	27.05 S	153.13 E
Skíros	38	38.53 N	24.33 E
Skíros I	38	38.53 N	24.32 E
Skivarp	41	55.25 N	13.34 E
Skive	26	56.34 N	9.02 E
Skjálfandafljót ≃	24a	65.57 N	17.38 W
Skjálfandi c	24a	66.08 N	17.38 W
Skjeberg	26	59.14 N	11.12 E
Skjern	26	55.57 N	8.30 E
Skjern Å ≃	41	55.57 N	8.40 E
Sklad	74	71.55 N	123.33 E
Šklov	76	54.13 N	30.18 E
Skniga ≃	82	54.53 N	37.24 E
Skobeleva, pik ∧	85	39.49 N	72.44 E
Skoby	40	60.02 N	18.01 E
Škocjanske jame ⌓[7]	36	45.40 N	14.00 E
Skodborg	41	55.25 N	9.09 E
Skodsborg	41	55.49 N	12.34 E
Skoenmakerskop	158	34.02 S	25.33 E
Škofije	64	45.34 N	13.48 E
Škofja Loka	36	46.10 N	14.18 E
Skoganvarre	24	69.47 N	25.06 E
Skoghall	40	59.19 N	13.26 E
Skogstorp	40	59.20 N	16.28 E
Skokholm Island I	42	51.42 N	5.16 W
Skoki	30	52.41 N	17.10 E
Skokie	216	42.02 N	87.44 W
Skokie ≃	216	42.05 N	87.46 W
Skokie Lagoons c	278	42.07 N	87.47 W
Skokloster ⊥	40	59.42 N	17.37 E
Skokomish, North Fork ≃	224	47.18 N	123.14 W
Skokomish, South Fork ≃	224	47.18 N	123.14 W
Skokomish Indian Reservation ⬥[4]	224	47.21 N	123.12 W
Sköldinge	40	59.02 N	16.26 E
Skole	78	49.02 N	23.29 E
Sköllersta	40	59.09 N	15.20 E
Skolsta	40	59.40 N	17.14 E
Skolwin	54	53.32 N	14.35 E
Skomer Island I	42	51.44 N	5.17 W
Skomoroški, S.S.S.R.	78	49.20 N	29.26 E
Skomoroški, S.S.S.R.	82	54.05 N	36.57 E
Skón	110	12.04 N	105.04 E
Skookumchuck ≃	224	46.41 N	123.00 W
Skookumchuck Reservoir ◎[1]	224	47.47 N	122.42 W
Skoonspruit ≃	158	27.00 S	26.38 E
Skootamatta ≃	212	44.32 N	77.20 W
Skootamatta Lake ◎	212	44.50 N	77.15 W
Skópelos, Ellás	38	39.02 N	26.26 E
Skópelos, Ellás	38	39.07 N	23.43 E
Skópelos I	38	39.10 N	23.40 E
Skopin	76	53.51 N	39.33 E
Skopje	38	41.59 N	21.26 E
Skórcz	30	53.48 N	18.32 E
Skorodnoje, S.S.S.R.	78	51.05 N	37.14 E
Skorodnoje, S.S.S.R.	78	51.38 N	28.49 E
Skørping	26	56.50 N	9.53 E
Skotfoss	26	59.12 N	9.30 E
Skotovataja	83	48.13 N	37.54 E
Škotovo	89	43.20 N	132.21 E
Skotterud	26	59.59 N	12.07 E
Skovby	41	54.53 N	10.00 E
Skövde	26	58.24 N	13.50 E
Skovlund	41	55.44 N	8.43 E
Skovorodino	89	53.59 N	123.55 E
Skowhegan	188	44.45 N	69.43 W
Skownan	184	51.57 N	99.36 W
Skradin	36	43.49 N	15.56 E
Skreen	48	54.15 N	8.45 W
Skreia	26	60.39 N	10.56 E
Skriplivka	76	57.32 N	30.38 E
Skrīveri	76	56.39 N	25.08 E
Skromberga	41	56.00 N	12.58 E
Skrudaļiena	76	55.49 N	26.43 E
Skrunda	76	56.41 N	22.01 E
Skruv	26	56.41 N	15.22 E
Skrydstrup	41	55.14 N	9.15 E
Skudeneshavn	26	59.09 N	5.17 E
Skukuza	156	25.01 S	31.38 E
Skuleberget ∧[2]	26	63.05 N	18.21 E
Skulforp	26	58.21 N	13.49 E
Skull	48	51.32 N	9.33 W
Skull Creek ≃	222	29.32 N	96.24 W
Skull Valley	200	34.30 N	112.41 W
Skull Valley Indian Reservation ⬥[4]	200	40.24 N	112.45 W
Skultuna	40	59.43 N	16.25 E
Skuna ≃	194	33.54 N	89.41 W
Skunk ≃	190	40.42 N	91.07 W
Škunovka	86	50.45 N	55.27 E
Skuodas	76	56.16 N	21.32 E
Škuratovskij	82	54.07 N	37.36 E
Škurinskaja	78	46.35 N	39.22 E
Skurišenskaja	80	49.52 N	42.57 E
Skurup	41	55.28 N	13.30 E
Skutskär	40	60.38 N	17.25 E
Skvira	78	49.44 N	29.40 E
Skwentna	180	61.58 N	151.11 W
Skwentna ≃	180	62.00 N	151.08 W
Skwierzyna	30	52.36 N	15.30 E
Skye, Island of I	46	57.18 N	6.15 W
Sky Harbor Airport ⊠	278	42.09 N	87.51 W
Skykomish	224	47.42 N	121.21 W
Skykomish ≃	224	47.50 N	122.03 W
Skykomish, North Fork ≃	224	47.47 N	121.33 W
Skykomish, South Fork ≃	224	47.47 N	121.33 W
Sky Lake	220	28.28 N	81.24 W
Sky Lake ◎	212	44.48 N	81.15 W
Skyland, Nv., U.S.	226	39.01 N	119.56 W
Skyland, N.C., U.S.	192	35.29 N	82.31 W
Skylight	218	38.25 N	85.31 W
Skyline	284c	38.50 N	76.54 W
Skyline Lakes ◎	276	41.04 N	74.16 W
Skyllberg	40	58.57 N	14.59 E
Skyring, Península ≻[1]	254	45.58 S	74.53 W
Skyring, Seno ʊ	254	52.35 S	72.00 W
Sky Sailing Airport ⊠	282	37.30 N	121.58 W
Skytop	210	41.14 N	75.15 W
Skyttorp	40	60.05 N	17.44 E
Skyway	224	47.29 N	122.14 W
Slackhall	262	53.20 N	1.53 W
Slackwood	208	40.15 N	74.44 W
Slade Green ⬥[8]	260	51.28 N	0.12 E
Sladkij	80	46.10 N	42.17 E
Sladkovo	86	55.32 N	70.20 E
Slagelse	41	55.24 N	11.22 E
Slagnäs	24	65.34 N	18.05 E
Slagovišči	76	53.57 N	35.54 E
Slaithwaite	262	53.37 N	1.53 W
Slamannan	46	55.56 N	3.50 W
Slamet, Gunung ∧	115a	7.14 S	109.12 E
Slancy	76	59.06 N	28.04 E
Slaney ≃	48	52.21 N	6.30 W
Slangerup	41	55.51 N	12.11 E
Slănic	38	45.15 N	25.57 E
Slănic Moldova	38	46.13 N	26.26 E
Slano	36	42.47 N	17.54 E
Slanské vrchy ⋏	30	48.50 N	21.30 E
Slaný	54	50.11 N	14.04 E
Šlapanice	30	49.10 N	16.44 E
Slaščevskaja	80	49.52 N	42.21 E
Śląsk → Silesia □[9]	30	51.00 N	16.45 E
Slastucha	80	51.57 N	44.32 E
Slate Bottom Creek ≃	284a	42.53 N	78.45 W
Slate Creek ≃, Ks., U.S.	198	37.08 N	97.09 W
Slate Creek ≃, Pa., U.S.	279b	40.28 N	79.32 W
Slatedale	208	40.45 N	75.40 W
Slate Hill	210	41.23 N	74.29 W
Slater, Ia., U.S.	190	41.52 N	93.40 W
Slater, Mo., U.S.	194	39.13 N	93.04 W
Slater Creek ≃	200	40.59 N	107.23 W
Slatersville	207	42.00 N	71.34 W
Slaterville Springs	210	42.24 N	76.21 W
Slatina	38	44.26 N	24.22 E
Slatington	208	40.44 N	75.36 W
Slatino	78	50.12 N	36.11 E
Slaton	196	33.26 N	101.38 W
Slattocks	262	53.35 N	2.10 W
Slaughter	194	30.43 N	91.08 W
Slaung	115a	8.02 S	111.24 E
Slautnoje	74	63.00 N	167.59 E
Slava	89	52.08 N	129.24 E
Slav'anka, S.S.S.R.	78	48.24 N	36.43 E
Slav'anka, S.S.S.R.	85	40.40 N	68.32 E
Slav'anka, S.S.S.R.	89	42.53 N	131.21 E
Slav'anka ≃	265a	59.50 N	30.32 E
Slav'anogorsk	83	49.02 N	37.31 E
Slav'anoserbsk	83	48.42 N	38.59 E
Slav'ansk	83	48.52 N	37.37 E
Slav'ansk-na-Kubani	78	45.15 N	38.08 E
Slave ≃	176	61.18 N	113.39 W
Slave Coast ⌓[2]	150	6.25 N	3.00 E
Slave Lake	182	55.17 N	114.46 W
Slavgorod, S.S.S.R.	76	53.27 N	31.00 E
Slavgorod, S.S.S.R.	78	48.06 N	35.31 E
Slavgorod, S.S.S.R.	78	50.36 N	35.21 E
Slavgorod, S.S.S.R.	86	53.00 N	78.40 E
Slavitino	82	56.41 N	39.13 E
Slavkino	80	52.58 N	47.11 E
Slavkoviči	76	57.39 N	29.05 E
Slavkovský les ⋏	54	50.07 N	12.45 E
Slavkov u Brna	61	49.09 N	16.52 E
Slavnoje	76	54.18 N	29.27 E
Slavonia → Slavonija □[9]	36	45.00 N	18.00 E
Slavonice	61	49.00 N	15.21 E
Slavonija □[9]	36	45.00 N	18.00 E
Slavonska Požega	36	45.20 N	17.41 E
Slavonski Brod	38	45.10 N	18.01 E
Slavsk	76	55.03 N	21.41 E
Slavskoje	78	48.49 N	23.24 E
Slavuta	78	50.18 N	26.52 E
Sława	30	51.53 N	16.04 E
Slawi	115a	6.59 S	109.08 E
Sławno	30	54.22 N	16.40 E
Slayton	198	43.59 N	95.45 W
Slea ≃	42	53.03 N	0.12 W
Sleaford	42	53.00 N	0.24 W
Slea Head ≻	48	52.06 N	10.27 W
Sleat, Point of ≻	46	57.01 N	6.02 W
Sleat, Sound of ʊ	46	57.06 N	5.49 W
Sledge	194	34.25 N	90.13 W
Sledge Island I	180	64.29 N	166.13 W
Sled Lake ◎	184	54.27 N	107.25 W
Sledmere	44	54.04 N	0.35 W
Slednevo	82	56.25 N	38.36 E
Sled'uki	76	53.35 N	30.22 E
Sleen	52	52.46 N	6.48 E
Sleeping Bear Dunes National Lakeshore ♠	190	44.50 N	86.08 W
Sleeping Giant State Park ♠	207	41.25 N	72.53 W
Sleepy Eye	198	44.17 N	94.43 W
Sleepy Hollow, Ca., U.S.	226	38.00 N	122.34 W
Sleepy Hollow, Ca., U.S.	280	33.57 N	117.47 W
Sleepy Hollow, Il., U.S.	216	42.06 N	88.24 W
Sleetmute	180	61.42 N	157.11 W
Sleidinge	50	51.08 N	3.41 E
Sleights	44	54.27 N	0.40 W
Sleman	115a	7.42 S	110.20 E
Slepino	76	59.11 N	29.02 E
Ślesin	30	52.23 N	18.19 E
Slessor Glacier ⊓	9	79.50 S	28.30 W
Slickville	214	40.27 N	79.31 W
Slidell	194	30.16 N	89.46 W
Slide Mountain ∧	210	42.00 N	74.23 W
Sliderock Mountain ∧	202	46.35 N	113.33 W
Sliedrecht	52	51.49 N	4.45 E
Slieve Aughty Mountains ⋏	48	53.05 N	8.35 W
Slieve Bloom Mountains ⋏	48	53.05 N	7.35 W
Slievekimalta ∧	48	52.45 N	8.16 W
Slievenamon ∧	48	52.25 N	7.34 W
Sligeach → Sligo	48	54.17 N	8.28 W
Sligo (Sligeach), Ire.	48	54.17 N	8.28 W
Sligo, Pa., U.S.	214	41.06 N	79.29 W
Sligo □[6]	48	54.10 N	8.40 W
Sligo Bay c	48	54.20 N	8.40 W
Sligo Creek ≃	284c	38.57 N	76.58 W
Slikkerveer	52	51.53 N	4.37 E
Slingebeek ≃	52	51.56 N	6.17 E
Slinger	190	43.20 N	88.17 W
Šlino, ozero ◎	76	57.40 N	33.23 E
Slioch ∧	46	57.41 N	5.22 W
Slippery Rock	214	41.03 N	80.03 W
Slippery Rock Creek ≃	214	40.51 N	80.15 W
Slite	26	57.43 N	18.48 E
Slīteres Rezervāts ♠	76	57.38 N	22.25 E
Sliven	38	42.40 N	26.19 E
Slivnica	38	42.51 N	23.02 E
Sloan, Ia., U.S.	198	42.13 N	96.13 W
Sloan, Nv., U.S.	204	35.56 N	115.12 W
Sloan, N.Y., U.S.	210	42.53 N	78.47 W
Sloan Peak ∧	224	48.03 N	121.20 W
Sloansville	210	42.46 N	74.20 W
Sloatsburg	210	41.09 N	74.11 W
Sloboda, S.S.S.R.	76	55.30 N	31.51 E
Sloboda, S.S.S.R.	76	53.58 N	28.08 E
Sloboda, S.S.S.R.	78	51.09 N	40.17 E
Sloboda, S.S.S.R.	78	51.11 N	33.37 E
Slobodka, S.S.S.R.	76	55.41 N	27.11 E
Slobodka, S.S.S.R.	78	47.53 N	29.21 E
Slobodka, S.S.S.R.	82	54.22 N	37.33 E
Slobodskoj	86	58.42 N	50.12 E
Slobodzeja	78	46.44 N	29.43 E
Slobodzeja-Mare	78	45.34 N	28.12 E
Slobozia, Rom.	38	44.34 N	27.23 E
Slobozia, Rom.	38	43.51 N	25.54 E
Slocan	182	49.46 N	117.28 W
Slocan Lake ◎	182	49.56 N	117.22 W
Slochteren	52	53.12 N	6.47 E
Slocomb	194	31.06 N	85.35 W
Slocum	207	41.32 N	71.31 W
Slocum Mountain ∧	228	35.18 N	117.13 W
Słomniki	30	50.15 N	20.06 E
Slonim	76	53.06 N	25.19 E
Slonovka	78	50.39 N	37.45 E
Słońsk	54	52.35 N	14.50 E
Sloop Channel ʊ	276	40.36 N	73.31 W
Sloping Hills	276	40.42 N	74.34 W
Slosh Indian Reserve ⬥[4]	182	50.44 N	122.13 W
Sloten	52	52.54 N	5.38 E
Sloten ⬥[8]	52	52.21 N	4.48 E
Slotermeer ◎	52	52.55 N	5.40 E
Slough	42	51.31 N	0.36 W
Slough □[8]	260	51.32 N	0.35 W
Slough Brook ≃	276	40.45 N	74.21 W
Sloughhouse	226	38.30 N	121.12 W
Slovakia → Slovensko □[9]	30	48.50 N	20.00 E
Slovan	214	40.21 N	80.23 W
Slovečna ≃	78	51.41 N	29.41 E
Slovečno	78	51.23 N	28.21 E
Slovenia → Slovenija □[3]	36	46.15 N	15.10 E
Slovenija □[3]	36	46.15 N	15.10 E
Slovenj Gradec	61	46.31 N	15.05 E
Slovenska Bistrica	61	46.23 N	15.34 E
Slovenská Socialistická Republika □[3]	30	48.30 N	20.00 E
Slovenske Gorice ⋏[2]	61	46.35 N	15.55 E
Slovenské rudohorie ⋏	30	48.45 N	20.00 E
Slovensko □[9]	30	48.50 N	20.00 E
Slovinka	80	58.02 N	43.07 E
Slowakei → Slovensko □[9]	30	48.50 N	20.00 E
Słowiński Park Narodowy ♠	30	54.40 N	17.25 E
Słubice	54	52.20 N	14.32 E
Sluč' ≃, S.S.S.R.	76	52.08 N	27.31 E
Sluč' ≃, S.S.S.R.	78	51.37 N	26.38 E
Sluck	76	53.01 N	27.33 E
Sl'ud'anka	88	51.38 N	103.42 E
Sluderno (Schluderns)	64	46.40 N	10.35 E
Sludy	76	58.52 N	36.52 E
Sluis	52	51.18 N	3.24 E
Sluiskil	52	51.16 N	3.50 E
Šluknov	54	51.00 N	14.27 E
Slunj	36	45.07 N	15.35 E
Słupca	30	52.19 N	17.52 E
Słupia ≃	30	54.35 N	16.50 E
Słupsk (Stolp)	30	54.28 N	17.01 E
Słupsk □[4]	30	54.10 N	17.15 E
Slurry	156	25.49 S	25.52 E
Šl'uz-Mokr'aki	86	59.17 N	88.50 E
Sly, Oued ≃	34	36.04 N	1.08 E
Smachtino	82	54.51 N	36.25 E
Smackover	194	33.21 N	92.43 W
Smackover Creek ≃	194	33.22 N	92.24 W
Småland □[9]	26	57.20 N	15.00 E
Smålandsfarvandet ʊ	41	55.05 N	11.20 E
Smålandsstenar	26	57.10 N	13.24 E
Smalininkai	76	55.05 N	22.35 E
Smallbridge	262	53.38 N	2.08 W
Smalleytown	276	40.39 N	74.28 W
Smallwood	210	41.40 N	74.49 W
Smallwood Reservoir ◎[1]	176	54.05 N	64.30 W
Smallwood State Park ♠	208	38.33 N	77.12 W
Smara	148	26.44 N	11.41 W
Smartt Syndicate Dam ◎[1]	158	30.40 S	23.18 E
Smartville	226	39.12 N	121.18 W
Smeaton	184	53.30 N	104.49 W
Smeaton Bay c	182	55.20 N	130.50 W
Smečno	54	50.10 N	14.03 E
Smedby	40	58.33 N	16.16 E
Smědeč	61	48.56 N	14.09 E
Smederevo	38	44.40 N	20.56 E
Smederevska Palanka	38	44.22 N	20.58 E
Smedjebacken	40	60.08 N	15.25 E
Smela	78	49.14 N	31.53 E
Smeloje	78	50.55 N	33.36 E
Šmel'ovka	80	54.47 N	49.11 E
Smelt Brook ≃, Ma., U.S.	283	42.13 N	70.58 W
Smelt Brook ≃, Ma., U.S.	283	42.00 N	70.43 W
Smelt Pond ◎	283	41.58 N	70.43 W
Smeralda, Costa ⌓[2]	71	41.04 N	9.30 E
Smerwick Harbour c	48	52.12 N	10.24 W
Smethport	214	41.48 N	78.26 W
Smethwick	42	52.30 N	1.58 W
Smicksburg	214	40.52 N	79.10 W
Smidovič	89	48.36 N	133.49 E
Šmidta → Mys Šmidta	180	68.56 N	179.26 W
Šmidta, mys ≻	180	68.56 N	179.30 W
Šmidta, ostrov I	74	81.08 N	90.48 E
Šmidta, poluostrov ≻[1]	89	54.10 N	142.40 E
Śmigiel	30	52.01 N	16.32 E
Smilde	52	52.56 N	5.27 E
Smile	218	38.15 N	83.29 W
Smiley, Sk., Can.	184	51.37 N	109.29 W
Smiley, Tx., U.S.	222	29.16 N	97.38 W
Smiloviči	76	53.45 N	28.01 E
Smiltene	76	57.26 N	25.56 E
Smirnovskij	86	54.31 N	69.25 E
Smirnych	89	49.43 N	142.38 E
Smith	182	55.10 N	114.02 W
Smith □[6]	222	32.20 N	95.15 W
Smith ≃, U.S.	192	36.29 N	79.45 W
Smith ≃, Ca., U.S.	204	41.56 N	124.12 W
Smith ≃, Mt., U.S.	202	47.25 N	111.29 W
Smith ≃, Or., U.S.	202	43.43 N	124.05 W
Smith, Cape ≻	190	45.48 N	81.35 W
Smith Arm c	180	66.15 N	124.00 W
Smith Bay c	180	70.51 N	154.25 W
Smithboro, Il., U.S.	219	38.54 N	89.20 W
Smithboro, N.Y., U.S.	210	42.02 N	76.24 W
Smith Canyon V	198	37.46 N	103.26 W
Smith Center	198	39.46 N	98.47 W
Smith Creek ≃, S.D., U.S.	198	43.58 N	99.20 W
Smith Creek ≃, Wa., U.S.	224	46.45 N	123.53 W
Smithdale	279b	40.14 N	79.48 W
Smithers, B.C., Can.	182	54.47 N	127.10 W
Smithers, W.V., U.S.	188	38.10 N	81.18 W
Smithers Lake ◎[1]	222	29.29 N	95.38 W
Smithfield, Austl.	168b	34.41 S	138.41 E
Smithfield, Austl.	274a	33.51 S	150.57 E
Smithfield, On., Can.	212	44.04 N	77.41 W
Smithfield, S. Afr.	158	30.09 S	26.30 E
Smithfield, Eng., U.K.	44	54.59 N	2.52 W
Smithfield, N.C., U.S.	192	35.30 N	78.20 W
Smithfield, Oh., U.S.	214	40.16 N	80.46 W
Smithfield, Pa., U.S.	214	39.48 N	79.48 W
Smithfield, Ut,. U.S.	200	41.50 N	111.49 W
Smithfield, Va., U.S.	208	36.58 N	76.37 W
Smithflat	226	38.44 N	120.45 W
Smith Haven Mall ⬥[9]	276	40.52 N	73.08 W
Smithills Hall ⊥	262	53.36 N	2.27 W
Smith Island I, B.A.T.	9	62.59 S	62.32 W
Smith Island I, N.C., U.S.	192	33.52 N	77.59 W
Smith Island I, Va., U.S.	208	37.10 N	75.51 W
Smith Island I, Wa., U.S.	224	48.19 N	122.50 W
Smith Island II	208	38.01 N	76.02 W
Smithland	194	37.08 N	88.24 W
Smithmill	214	40.46 N	78.25 W
Smith Mountain ∧	280	34.17 N	117.52 W
Smith Mountain Lake ◎[1]	192	37.10 N	79.40 W
Smith Peak ∧	202	48.50 N	116.39 W
Smith Peninsula ≻[1]	9	74.25 S	61.15 W
Smith Point	222	29.27 N	94.45 W
Smith Point ≻, N.S., Can.	186	45.51 N	63.25 W
Smith Point ≻, Tx., U.S.	222	29.32 N	94.46 W
Smith Point ≻, Va., U.S.	208	37.53 N	76.14 W
Smithport	214	40.50 N	78.52 W
Smith River	204	41.55 N	124.08 W
Smiths	194	32.32 N	85.05 W
Smithsburg	208	39.39 N	77.34 W

Name	Seite	Breite°′	Länge°′ E = Ost
Smiths Creek	214	42.55 N	82.36 W
Smiths Falls	212	44.54 N	76.01 W
Smiths Fork ≃	202	41.23 N	110.12 W
Smiths Grove	194	37.03 N	86.12 W
Smiths Mills	276	41.01 N	74.22 W
Smith Sound ʊ	182	51.18 N	127.43 W
Smithton, Austl.	166	40.51 S	145.07 E
Smithton, Il., U.S.	219	38.24 N	89.59 W
Smithton, Mo., U.S.	194	38.40 N	93.05 W
Smithton, Pa., U.S.	279b	40.09 N	79.44 W
Smithtown	210	40.52 N	73.13 W
Smithtown Bay c	276	40.57 N	73.12 W
Smith Valley	218	39.36 N	86.12 W
Smithville, On., Can.	212	43.06 N	79.33 W
Smithville, Ga., U.S.	192	31.54 N	84.15 W
Smithville, In., U.S.	218	39.04 N	86.30 W
Smithville, Ms., U.S.	194	34.04 N	88.23 W
Smithville, Mo., U.S.	194	39.23 N	94.34 W
Smithville, N.J., U.S.	208	39.59 N	74.44 W
Smithville, N.J., U.S.	285	39.29 N	74.27 W
Smithville, Oh., U.S.	214	40.51 N	81.51 W
Smithville, Tn., U.S.	194	35.57 N	85.48 W
Smithville, Tx., U.S.	222	30.00 N	97.09 W
Smithville Flats	210	42.24 N	75.49 W
Smithville Lake ◎[1]	194	39.25 N	94.30 W
Smögen	26	58.21 N	11.13 E
Smoke Creek ≃, Mt., U.S.	198	48.18 N	104.41 W
Smoke Creek ≃, N.Y., U.S.	284a	42.49 N	78.52 W
Smoke Creek, South Branch ≃	284a	42.49 N	78.49 W
Smoke Creek Desert ⬥[2]	204	40.30 N	119.40 W
Smoke Lake ◎	212	45.32 N	78.41 W
Smokeless	214	40.24 N	76.02 W
Smokerun	214	40.48 N	78.26 W
Smoketown	208	40.02 N	76.12 W
Smokey, Cape ≻	186	46.38 N	60.21 W
Smokey Dome ∧	202	43.29 N	114.56 W
Smoky ≃	182	56.10 N	117.21 W
Smoky Bay	162	32.22 S	133.56 E
Smoky Cape ≻	166	30.56 S	153.05 E
Smoky Hill ≃	198	39.03 N	96.48 W
Smoky Hill, North Fork ≃	198	38.55 N	101.17 W
Smoky Lake	182	54.07 N	112.28 W
Smøla I	24	63.24 N	8.00 E
Smol'anica	76	52.42 N	24.38 E
Smol'aninovo	89	43.19 N	132.28 E
Smol'any	76	54.36 N	30.04 E
Smolensk	76	54.47 N	32.03 E
Smolenskaja vozvyšennost' ⋏[1]	76	54.30 N	33.00 E
Smolenskoje	86	52.20 N	85.05 E
Smoleviči	76	54.02 N	28.05 E
Smólikas ∧	38	40.06 N	20.52 E
Smoljan	38	41.35 N	24.41 E
Smolny ⊍	265a	59.57 N	30.24 E
Smolovka	76	55.33 N	30.13 E
Smoot	200	42.37 N	110.54 W
Smoothstone ≃	184	55.20 N	106.39 W
Smoothstone Lake ◎	184	54.40 N	106.50 W
Smorgon'	76	54.29 N	26.24 E
Smorodovka	76	57.08 N	29.52 E
Smotrič	78	48.56 N	26.34 E
Smotrič ≃	78	48.34 N	26.38 E
Smuškovoje	80	47.20 N	45.55 E
Smyčka	82	56.04 N	35.56 E
Smygehamn	41	55.21 N	13.22 E
Smygehuk ≻	41	55.21 N	13.23 E
Smyley, Cape ≻	9	72.26 S	78.10 W
Smyrna → İzmir	130	38.25 N	27.09 E
Smyrna, De., U.S.	208	39.17 N	75.36 W
Smyrna, Ga., U.S.	192	33.53 N	84.30 W
Smyrna, N.Y., U.S.	210	42.41 N	75.34 W
Smyrna, Tn., U.S.	194	35.58 N	86.31 W
Smyrna ≃	208	39.22 N	75.31 W
Smyšl'ajevka	80	53.15 N	50.22 E
Smyth, Canal ʊ	254	52.15 S	73.40 W
Smythe, Mount ∧	176	57.54 N	124.53 W
Smythe Park ♠	275b	43.41 N	79.30 W
Smythesdale	169	37.38 S	143.41 E
Sn'adin	78	52.04 N	28.19 E
Snæfell ∧, Ísland	24a	64.48 N	15.32 W
Snaefell ∧, I. of Man	44	54.16 N	4.27 W
Snæfellness ≻[1]	24a	64.50 N	23.00 W
Snag	180	62.24 N	140.22 W
Snaght, Slieve ∧	48	55.12 N	7.20 W
Snagost'	78	51.21 N	34.54 E
Snahapish ≃	224	47.38 N	124.11 W
Snaith	44	53.41 N	1.02 W
Šn'ajevo	80	52.34 N	46.11 E
Snake ≃, Yk., Can.	180	65.58 N	134.10 W
Snake ≃, U.S.	202	46.12 N	119.02 W
Snake ≃, Ca., U.S.	226	39.07 N	121.43 W
Snake ≃, Mn., U.S.	190	45.49 N	92.46 W
Snake ≃, Mn., U.S.	198	48.26 N	97.07 W
Snake ≃, Ne., U.S.	198	42.47 N	100.48 W
Snake Bight c[3]	220	25.10 N	80.50 W
Snake Brook ≃	283	42.18 N	71.22 W
Snake Creek ≃, Mt., U.S.	202	48.32 N	108.53 W
Snake Creek ≃, Ne., U.S.	198	42.01 N	102.45 W
Snake Creek ≃, S.D., U.S.	198	44.58 N	98.29 W
Snake Creek, South Fork ≃	198	45.02 N	98.36 W
Snake Creek Canal ≅	220	25.57 N	80.11 W
Snake Indian ≃	182	53.11 N	118.00 W
Snake Range ⋏	204	39.00 N	114.15 W
Snake Rapids ᒪ	212	45.14 N	77.20 W
Snake River Plain ≚	202	43.00 N	113.00 W
Snake Valley	169	37.37 S	143.35 E
Snake Valley V	204	39.20 N	113.55 W
Snape	42	52.11 N	1.30 E
Snaptun	41	55.49 N	10.04 E
Snares Islands II	9	48.00 S	166.30 E
Snasahögarna ∧	26	63.13 N	12.21 E
Sn'atyn	78	48.28 N	25.34 E
Snay Pôl	110	11.40 N	105.13 E
Sneads	192	30.42 N	84.55 W
Snedsted	26	56.54 N	8.32 E
Sneedville	192	36.31 N	83.13 W
Sneek	52	53.02 N	5.40 E
Sneekermeer ◎	52	53.02 N	5.45 E
Snee-osh-Beach	224	48.24 N	122.33 W
Sneeuberg ∧	158	32.25 S	19.12 E
Sneeuberg ⋏	158	31.46 S	24.20 E
Snekkersten	41	56.00 N	12.36 E
Snelgrove	275b	43.44 N	79.49 W
Snelling	204	37.31 N	120.26 W
Snettisham	42	52.53 N	0.30 E
Snežnaja ≃	88	51.28 N	104.38 E
Snežnik ∧	36	45.35 N	14.27 E
Snežnoje	83	48.01 N	38.46 E
Śniardwy, Jezioro ◎	30	53.46 N	21.44 E
Snicarte	219	40.07 N	90.14 W
Snicarte Island I	219	40.08 N	90.12 W
Snigir'ovka	78	47.06 N	32.47 E
Snina	30	48.59 N	22.07 E
Snipe Keys II	220	24.40 N	81.38 W
Snipe Lake ◎	182	55.07 N	116.46 W
Snizort, Loch c	46	57.34 N	6.28 W
Snøde	41	55.05 N	10.55 E
Snodland	42	51.20 N	0.27 E
Snoghøj	41	55.31 N	9.43 E
Snøhetta ∧	26	62.20 N	9.17 E
Snohomish	224	47.54 N	122.05 W
Snohomish □[6]	224	48.02 N	121.41 W
Snohomish ≃	224	48.01 N	122.13 W
Snønipa ∧	26	61.42 N	6.41 E
Snook	222	30.29 N	96.28 W
Snoqualmie	224	47.31 N	121.49 W
Snoqualmie ≃	224	47.50 N	122.03 W
Snoqualmie, Middle Fork ≃	224	47.31 N	121.46 W
Snoqualmie, North Fork ≃	224	47.31 N	121.46 W

Symbols in the index entries represent the broad categories identified in the key at the right. Symbols with superior numbers (⋏[1]) identify subcategories (see complete key on page *I · 1).*

Symbole im Register stellen die rechts im Schlüssel erklärten Kategorien dar. Symbole mit hochgestellten Ziffern (⋏[1]) bezeichnen Unterabteilungen einer Kategorie (vgl. vollständiger Schlüssel auf Seite *I · 1).*

Los símbolos incluídos en el texto del índice representan las grandes categorias identificadas con la clave a la derecha. Los símbolos con numeros en su parte superior (⋏[1]) identifican las subcategorías (véase la clave completa en la página *I · 1).*

Les symboles de l'index représentent les catégories indiquées dans la légende à droite. Les symboles suivis d'un indice (⋏[1]) représentent des souscatégories (voir légende complète à la page *I · 1).*

Os símbolos incluídos no texto do índice representam as grandes categorias identificadas com a chave à direita. Os símbolos com números em sua parte superior (⋏[1]) identificam as subcategorias (vejase a chave completa à página *I · 1).*

ENGLISH	DEUTSCH	ESPAÑOL	FRANÇAIS	PORTUGUÊS
∧ Mountain	Berg	Montaña	Montagne	Montanha
⋏ Mountains	Gebirge	Montañas	Montagnes	Montanhas
)(Pass	Paß	Paso	Col	Passo
V Valley, Canyon	Tal, Cañon	Valle, Cañón	Vallée, Canyon	Vale, Canhão
≚ Plain	Ebene	Llano	Plaine	Planície
≻ Cape	Kap	Cabo	Cap	Cabo
I Island	Insel	Isla	Île	Ilha
II Islands	Inseln	Islas	Îles	Ilhas
⌓ Other Topographic Features	Andere Topographische Objekte	Otros Elementos Topográficos	Autres données topographiques	Outros acidentes topográficos

ESPAÑOL — Nombre / Página / Lat.°′ / Long.°′ W = Oeste
FRANÇAIS — Nom / Page / Lat.°′ / Long.°′ W = Ouest
PORTUGUÊS — Nome / Página / Lat.°′ / Long.°′ W = Oeste

≃ River	Fluß	Río	Rivière	Rio		
≋ Canal	Kanal	Canal	Canal	Canal		
⌞ Waterfall, Rapids	Wasserfall, Stromschnellen	Cascada, Rápidos	Chute d'eau, Rapides	Cascata, Rápidos		
ʮ Strait	Meeresstraße	Estrecho	Détroit	Estreito		
c Bay, Gulf	Bucht, Golf	Bahía, Golfo	Baie, Golfe	Baía, Golfo		
⊜ Lake, Lakes	See, Seen	Lago, Lagos	Lac, Lacs	Lago, Lagos		
⊞ Swamp	Sumpf	Pantano	Marais	Pântano		
⌗ Ice Features, Glacier	Eis- und Gletscherformen	Accidentes Glaciales	Formes glaciaires	Acidentes glaciares		
⊤ Other Hydrographic Features	Andere Hydrographische Objekte	Otros Elementos Hidrográficos	Autres données hydrographiques	Outros acidentes hidrográficos		
✢ Submarine Features	Untermeerische Objekte	Accidentes Submarinos	Formes de relief sous-marin	Acidentes submarinos		
□ Political Unit	Politische Einheit	Unidad Política	Entité politique	Unidade política		
⊍ Cultural Institution	Kulturelle Institution	Institución Cultural	Institution culturelle	Instituição cultural		
⊥ Historical Site	Historische Stätte	Sitio Histórico	Site historique	Sítio histórico		
♠ Recreational Site	Erholungs- und Ferienort	Sitio de Recreo	Centre de loisirs	Area de Lazer		
⊠ Airport	Flughafen	Aeropuerto	Aéroport	Aeroporto		
■ Military Installation	Militäranlage	Instalación Militar	Installation militaire	Instalação militar		
◆ Miscellaneous	Verschiedenes	Misceláneo	Divers	Diversos		

Name	Page	Lat.°′	Long.°′
Sörfjärden ⊂	40	59.24 N	16.50 E
Sørfjorden ⊂[2]	26	60.24 N	6.40 E
Sørfold	24	67.28 N	15.22 E
Sörforsa	26	61.40 N	17.00 E
Sorge ≃	41	54.21 N	9.25 E
Sorgono	71	40.01 N	9.06 E
Sorgues	62	44.00 N	4.52 E
Sorgun	130	39.49 N	35.11 E
Sori	62	44.22 N	9.06 E
Soria	34	41.46 N	2.28 W
Soriano	252	33.24 S	58.19 W
Soriano □[5]	258	33.45 S	57.45 W
Soriano Calabro	68	38.36 N	16.14 E
Soriano nel Cimino	66	42.25 N	12.14 E
Sorico	58	46.10 N	9.22 E
Sorido	164	1.09 S	136.03 E
Sori-do I	98	34.26 N	127.48 E
Sørli	26	64.15 N	13.45 E
Sormonne ≃	56	49.46 N	4.40 E
Sorn	46	55.30 N	4.18 W
Sorne ≃	58	47.22 N	7.22 E
Sorø, Dan.	41	55.26 N	11.34 E
Soro, India	120	21.17 N	86.40 E
Soro, Monte ∧	70	37.56 N	14.42 E
Sorocaba	255	23.29 S	47.27 W
Sorocá-Buçu ≃	256	23.38 S	47.13 W
Soročinka	80	47.30 N	51.44 E
Soročinsk	80	52.26 N	53.10 E
Soročkino	86	57.02 N	68.52 E
Soroco	240m	18.22 N	65.38 W
Sorok	88	52.20 N	100.12 E
Sorok ≃	61	47.07 N	16.50 E
Soroki	78	48.09 N	28.17 E
Sorokino, S.S.S.R.	86	53.45 N	84.58 E
Sorokino, S.S.S.R.	86	54.13 N	91.31 E
Sorokošiči	78	51.12 N	30.35 E
Soroksár ◆[8]	264c	47.24 N	19.07 E
Sorol I[1]	108	8.08 N	140.23 E
Soron	124	27.53 N	78.45 E
Sorong	164	0.53 S	131.15 E
Sororó ≃	250	5.24 S	49.07 W
Sorot' ≃	76	57.04 N	28.50 E
Soroti	154	1.43 N	33.37 E
Sorovskije	86	59.53 N	71.34 E
Sørøya I	24	70.36 N	22.46 E
Sorpestausee ⊜[1]	56	51.20 N	7.56 E
Sorraia ≃	34	38.56 N	8.53 W
Sorrento, Austl.	169	38.20 S	144.45 E
Sorrento, It.	68	40.37 N	14.22 E
Sorrento, Fl., U.S.	220	28.48 N	81.33 W
Sorrento, La., U.S.	194	30.11 N	90.51 W
Sorris Sorris	156	20.57 S	14.50 E
Sør Rondane Mountains ⋏	9	72.00 S	25.00 E
Sorsakoski	26	62.27 N	27.39 E
Sorsatunturi ∧	24	67.24 N	29.38 E
Sorsele	24	65.30 N	17.30 E
Sorsk	86	54.01 N	90.12 E
Sorso	71	40.48 N	8.34 E
Sorsogon	116	12.58 N	124.00 E
Sorsogon □[4]	116	12.50 N	123.55 E
Sorsogon Bay ⊂	116	12.55 N	123.55 E
Sörstafors	40	59.35 N	16.13 E
Šorsu	85	40.17 N	70.48 E
Sort	34	42.24 N	1.08 E
Šortandy	86	51.42 N	71.00 E
Sortat	46	58.33 N	3.13 W
Sortavala	24	61.42 N	30.41 E
Sortino	70	37.09 N	15.02 E
Sortland	24	68.40 N	15.20 E
Sør-Trøndelag □[6]	26	63.00 N	10.40 E
Sorunda	40	59.01 N	17.48 E
Sörup	41	54.43 N	9.40 E
Sõrve neem ›	76	57.54 N	22.03 E
Sörvik	40	60.11 N	15.09 E
Sorviži	80	57.52 N	48.32 E
Sosa, D.D.R.	54	50.30 N	12.39 E
Sosa, Taehan	271b	37.29 N	126.47 E
Šoša ≃	82	56.31 N	36.05 E
Sŏsan	98	36.47 N	126.26 E
Sösdala	41	56.02 N	13.40 E
Sos del Rey Católico	34	42.30 N	1.13 W
Sosedka	80	53.15 N	42.40 E
Sosedno	76	58.14 N	28.42 E
Sosenka ≃, S.S.S.R.	265b	55.35 N	37.23 E
Sosenka ≃, S.S.S.R.	265b	55.47 N	37.42 E
Sosenki	82	55.34 N	37.26 E
Sösetalsperre ◆[6]	52	51.44 N	10.20 E
Soshigaya ◆[8]	268	35.39 N	139.36 E
Sösjöfjällen ⋏	26	63.53 N	13.15 E
Šoška	24	62.42 N	50.40 E
Soskovo	76	52.45 N	35.23 E
Sosna ≃	76	52.42 N	38.55 E
Sosneado, Cerro ∧	252	34.45 S	69.59 W
Sosnica	78	51.32 N	32.28 E
Sosnicy	76	57.38 N	30.25 E
Sosnogorsk	24	63.37 N	53.51 E
Sosnovaja Maza	80	52.30 N	47.53 E
Sosnovaja Pol'ana ◆[8]	265a	59.50 N	30.09 E
Sosnovec	24	64.26 N	34.27 E
Sosnovica	76	60.21 N	40.50 E
Sosnovka, S.S.S.R.	24	66.30 N	40.32 E
Sosnovka, S.S.S.R.	80	56.17 N	51.17 E
Sosnovka, S.S.S.R.	80	52.26 N	43.29 E
Sosnovka, S.S.S.R.	80	53.14 N	41.22 E
Sosnovka, S.S.S.R.	80	56.13 N	47.13 E
Sosnovka, S.S.S.R.	80	57.16 N	53.31 E
Sosnovka, S.S.S.R.	80	57.48 N	51.43 E
Sosnovka, S.S.S.R.	80	54.06 N	46.38 E
Sosnovka, S.S.S.R.	82	54.54 N	38.41 E
Sosnovka, S.S.S.R.	82	54.31 N	38.08 E
Sosnovka, S.S.S.R.	85	42.40 N	73.55 E
Sosnovka, S.S.S.R.	86	59.10 N	81.18 E
Sosnovka, S.S.S.R.	86	51.26 N	79.28 E
Sosnovka, S.S.S.R.	88	54.09 N	109.35 E
Sosnovo, S.S.S.R.	76	60.33 N	30.15 E
Sosnovo, S.S.S.R.	80	56.42 N	54.35 E
Sosnovoborsk	80	53.18 N	46.16 E
Sosnovoje	78	50.49 N	27.00 E
Sosnovo-Oz'orskoje	88	52.31 N	111.30 E
Sosnovskij	86	54.36 N	73.10 E
Sosnovskoje	80	55.48 N	43.10 E
Sosnovyj Bor, S.S.S.R.	76	59.55 N	29.07 E
Sosnovyj Bor, S.S.S.R.	76	52.32 N	29.36 E
Sosnovyj Bor, S.S.S.R.	86	57.07 N	55.03 E
Sosnovyj Solonec	80	53.17 N	49.33 E
Sosnowiec	30	50.18 N	19.08 E
Soso	194	31.45 N	89.16 W
Sosok	112	0.17 N	110.14 E
Sospel	62	43.53 N	7.27 E
Sospirolo	64	46.09 N	12.04 E
Sossusvlei ⊜	156	24.40 S	15.23 E
Šoštanj	61	46.23 N	15.03 E
Šostka	78	51.52 N	33.30 E
Sŏsura	98	42.16 N	130.37 E
Sos'va, S.S.S.R.	72	63.40 N	62.06 E
Sos'va, S.S.S.R.	86	59.10 N	61.50 E
Sos'va ≃	86	59.32 N	62.20 E
Sosyka ≃	78	46.35 N	39.05 E
Sot' ≃	80	58.00 N	40.39 E
Sota ≃	150	11.52 N	3.24 E
Sotério ≃	248	11.36 S	65.10 W
Sotik	154	0.41 S	35.21 E
Sotkamo	26	64.08 N	28.25 E
Sotnicyno	80	54.17 N	41.49 E
Soto de Aldovea	266a	40.26 N	3.27 W
Soto de Pajares	266a	40.17 N	3.32 W
Soto la Marina	234	23.46 N	98.13 W
Soto la Marina ≃	234	23.45 N	97.45 W
Sotomayor	248	19.18 S	65.03 W
Sotonera, Embalse de ⊜[1]	34	42.05 N	0.48 W
Sotouboua	150	8.34 N	0.59 E
Sotta, Fr.	71	41.32 N	9.12 E
Sotta, Fr.	71	41.32 N	9.12 E
Sottens	58	46.39 N	6.44 E
Sottern ⊜	40	59.02 N	15.29 E
Sotteville	50	49.25 N	1.06 E
Sottile, Punta ›	70a	35.30 N	12.38 E
Sottomarina	64	45.13 N	12.17 E
Sottrum	52	53.06 N	9.14 E
Sottrup	41	54.57 N	9.43 E
Sottunga I	26	60.08 N	20.40 E
Souain-Perthes-lès-Hurlus	56	49.11 N	4.32 E
Souanké	152	2.05 N	14.03 E
Soubakaniédougou	150	10.28 N	5.01 W
Soubré	150	5.47 N	6.36 W
Soudan	166	20.05 S	137.00 E
Soudan → Sudan □[1]	140	15.00 N	30.00 E
Soude ≃	50	48.52 N	4.10 E
Soudersburg	208	40.01 N	76.09 W
Souderton	208	40.18 N	75.19 W
Souesmes	50	47.27 N	2.10 E
Soufflay	152	2.01 N	14.54 E
Soufflenheim	56	48.50 N	7.58 E
Soufflot, Lac ⊜	190	47.24 N	78.31 W
Souflíon	38	41.12 N	26.18 E
Soufrière	241f	13.52 N	61.04 W
Soufrière ∧, Guad.	241o	16.03 N	61.40 W
Soufrière ∧, St. Vin.	241h	13.20 N	61.11 W
Soufrière Bay ⊂, Dom.	240d	15.14 N	61.22 W
Soufrière Bay ⊂, St. Luc.	241f	13.51 N	61.04 W
Sougahatchee Creek ≃	194	32.38 N	85.50 W
Sougne-Remouchamps	56	50.29 N	5.40 E
Souguer	148	35.12 N	1.30 E
Souhegan ≃	188	42.51 N	71.29 W
Souillac	32	44.54 N	1.29 E
Souilly	56	49.01 N	5.17 E
Souk-el-Arba-des-Beni-Hassan	34	35.16 N	5.20 W
Souk-Khemis-du-Sahel	34	35.17 N	6.05 W
Souk Larbat Gharb	148	34.43 N	6.01 W
Sŏul (Seoul), Taehan	98	37.33 N	126.58 E
Sŏul (Seoul), Taehan	271b	37.33 N	126.58 E
Sŏul □[4]	98	37.34 N	127.00 E
Soulac-sur-Mer	32	45.31 N	1.07 W
Soulaines-Dhuys	58	48.22 N	4.44 E
Soulanges □[6]	206	45.20 N	74.15 W
Soulanges, Canal de ≋	275a	45.20 N	73.58 W
Soulougou	150	13.01 N	0.23 E
Soulsbyville	226	37.59 N	120.16 W
Soultzeren	58	48.04 N	7.06 E
Soultz-Haut-Rhin	58	47.53 N	7.14 E
Soultzmatt	58	47.58 N	7.14 E
Soultz-sous-Forêts	56	48.56 N	7.53 E
Soummam, Oued ≃	34	36.45 N	5.04 E
Sound Beach	210	40.57 N	72.58 W
Sounding Creek ≃	184	52.06 N	110.28 W
Sounding Lake ⊜	184	52.08 N	110.29 W
Sound View Park ♠	276	40.49 N	73.52 W
Soúnion, Ákra ›	38	37.39 N	24.02 E
Soup Harbour ⊂	212	43.51 N	77.11 W
Souppes-sur-Loing	50	48.11 N	2.44 E
Souq Ahras	148	36.23 N	8.00 E
Sources, Mont aux ∧	158	28.46 S	28.52 E
Soure, Bra.	250	0.44 S	48.31 W
Soure, Port.	34	40.03 N	8.38 W
Sour el Ghozlane	148	36.10 N	3.45 E
Souris, Mb., Can.	184	49.38 N	100.15 W
Souris, P.E., Can.	186	46.21 N	62.15 W
Souris ≃	198	49.39 N	99.34 W
Sourlake	194	30.09 N	94.25 W
Sourland Mountain ∧[2]	208	40.29 N	74.43 W
Sourou ≃	150	12.45 N	3.25 W
Souroukaha	150	8.13 N	5.08 W
Souš	54	50.32 N	13.34 E
Sous, Oued V	148	30.27 N	9.31 W
Sousa	250	6.45 S	38.14 W
Sousânia	255	16.11 S	49.05 W
Sousas	256	22.52 S	46.59 W
Sousel	34	38.57 N	7.40 W
Sous-le-Vent, Îles → Leeward Islands II	238	17.00 N	63.00 W
Sousse	148	35.49 N	10.38 E
Sousse □[8]	148	35.40 N	10.30 E
Sout ≃, S. Afr.	158	31.35 S	18.24 E
Sout ≃, S. Afr.	158	28.56 S	20.40 E
Sout ≃, S. Afr.	158	33.03 S	23.28 E
South ≃, Ia., U.S.	190	41.29 N	93.20 W
South ≃, Ma., U.S.	283	42.10 N	70.43 W
South ≃, Mo., U.S.	219	39.52 N	91.26 W
South ≃, N.J., U.S.	208	40.29 N	74.23 W
South ≃, N.C., U.S.	192	34.20 N	78.03 W
South ≃, Va., U.S.	192	37.46 N	79.23 W
South ≃, Va., U.S.	208	38.02 N	77.23 W
South Acton	207	42.27 N	71.27 W
South Africa (Suid-Afrika) □[1], Afr.	138	30.00 S	26.00 E
South Africa (Suid-Afrika) □[1], Afr.	156	30.00 S	26.00 E
Southall ◆[8]	260	51.31 N	0.23 W
South Alligator ≃	164	12.15 S	132.24 E
Southam	42	52.15 N	1.23 W
South Amboy	208	40.28 N	74.17 W
South America ≗[1]	4	15.00 S	60.00 W
South America ≗[1]	18	15.00 S	60.00 W
South Amherst, Ma., U.S.	207	42.20 N	72.30 W
South Amherst, Oh., U.S.	214	41.22 N	82.14 W
Southampton, N.S., Can.	186	45.35 N	64.15 W
Southampton, On., Can.	212	44.29 N	81.23 W
Southampton, Eng., U.K.	42	50.55 N	1.25 W
Southampton, Ma., U.S.	207	42.13 N	72.43 W
Southampton, N.Y., U.S.	207	40.53 N	72.23 W
Southampton, Pa., U.S.	285	40.10 N	75.02 W
Southampton □[6]	208	36.42 N	77.05 W
Southampton (Eastleigh) Airport ⊠	42	50.57 N	1.21 W
Southampton, Cape ›	176	62.09 N	83.40 W
Southampton Island I	176	64.20 N	84.40 W
South Andaman I	110	11.45 N	92.45 E
South Anna ≃	192	37.48 N	77.25 W
South Apopka	220	28.39 N	81.31 W
Southard	208	40.08 N	74.14 W
Southards Pond ⊜	276	40.43 N	73.20 W
South Ashburnham	207	42.36 N	71.56 W
South Aulatsivik Island I	176	56.45 N	61.30 W
South Australia □[3]	162	30.00 S	135.00 E
South Australian Basin ✧[1]	14	38.00 S	126.00 E
Southaven	194	34.59 N	90.02 W
South Bald Mountain ∧	200	40.45 N	105.41 W
South Baldy ∧	200	33.59 N	107.11 W
South Banda Basin ✧[1]	14	6.30 S	127.30 E
Southbank	182	54.02 N	125.46 W
South Barre	207	42.23 N	72.05 W
South Barrington	278	42.06 N	88.07 W
South Barrule ∧[2]	44	54.12 N	4.40 W
South Bass Island I	214	41.39 N	82.49 W
South Bay	220	26.39 N	80.42 W
South Bay ⊂, Mb., Can.	184	56.43 N	99.00 W
South Bay ⊂, N.T., Can.	176	63.58 N	83.30 W
South Bay ⊂, On., Can.	190	45.38 N	81.50 W
South Bay ⊂, On., Can.	212	43.55 N	77.03 W
South Bay ⊂, On., Can.	212	44.52 N	79.47 W
South Bay ⊂, Fl., U.S.	220	26.42 N	80.45 W
South Bay ⊂, Va., U.S.	208	37.14 N	75.52 W
South Bay ⊂, Wa., U.S.	224	46.53 N	124.04 W
South Baymouth	190	45.33 N	82.01 W
South Beach ♠	276	40.35 N	74.05 W
South Beacon Mountain ∧	210	41.29 N	73.57 W
South Bedias Creek ≃	222	30.54 N	95.42 W
South Bellingham	207	42.03 N	71.28 W
South Belmar	208	40.10 N	74.02 W
South Beloit	216	42.29 N	89.02 W
South Bend, In., U.S.	216	41.41 N	86.15 W
South Bend, Wa., U.S.	224	46.40 N	123.48 W
South Benfleet	42	51.33 N	0.34 E
South Bentinck Arm ⊂	182	52.15 N	126.50 W
South Bethlehem	214	41.00 N	79.20 W
South Bihar Plains ≍	124	25.15 N	84.30 E
South Bloomfield	218	39.43 N	82.59 W
Southborough, Eng., U.K.	42	51.10 N	0.15 E
Southborough, Ma., U.S.	207	42.18 N	71.31 W
South Bosque ≃	222	31.29 N	97.16 W
South Boston	192	36.41 N	78.54 W
South Boston ◆[8]	283	42.20 N	71.03 W
South Bound Brook	276	40.33 N	74.32 W
South Bradenton	220	27.27 N	82.35 W
South Branch, Nf., Can.	186	47.55 N	59.02 W
South Branch, N.J., U.S.	276	40.33 N	74.42 W
South Brent	42	50.25 N	3.50 W
Southbridge, N.Z.	172	43.49 S	172.15 E
Southbridge, Ma., U.S.	207	42.04 N	72.02 W
South Britain	207	41.28 N	73.15 W
Southbrook, Austl.	171a	27.41 S	151.43 E
Southbrook, N.Z.	172	43.20 S	172.36 E
South Brook ≃	285	39.52 N	75.44 W
South Brookfield	186	44.23 N	64.58 W
South Brooklyn ◆[8]	276	40.41 N	73.59 W
South Bruny Island I	166	43.23 S	147.17 E
South Buganda □[5]	154	0.30 S	31.35 E
South Burlington	188	44.28 N	73.10 W
Southbury	207	41.28 N	73.12 W
South Butler	210	43.08 N	76.46 W
South Byfield	283	42.44 N	70.54 W
South Byron	210	43.03 N	78.04 W
South Cairo	210	42.17 N	73.57 W
South Canaan	210	41.30 N	75.25 W
South Cape ›	175g	17.01 S	179.55 E
South Carolina □[3], U.S.	178	34.00 N	81.00 W
South Carolina □[3], U.S.	192	34.00 N	81.00 W
South Carver	207	41.50 N	70.44 W
South Castor ≃	212	45.15 N	75.23 W
South Cave	44	53.46 N	0.35 W
South Cerney	42	51.40 N	1.56 W
South Chagrin Reservation ♠	279a	41.25 N	81.25 W
South Channel ų, Pil.	116	14.20 N	120.37 E
South Channel ų, Mi., U.S.	190	45.38 N	84.32 W
South Channel ≃[1]	281	42.32 N	82.40 W
South Chaplin	207	41.46 N	72.07 W
South Charleston, Oh., U.S.	218	39.49 N	83.38 W
South Charleston, W.V., U.S.	188	38.22 N	81.41 W
South Chatham	207	41.40 N	70.01 W
South Chelmsford	283	42.34 N	71.23 W
South Chicago ◆[8]	278	41.44 N	87.33 W
South China Basin ✧[1]	12	15.00 N	115.00 E
South China Sea ⊤[2]	108	10.00 N	113.00 E
South Cle Elum	224	47.11 N	120.56 W
South Coast Botanic Garden ♠	280	33.47 N	118.21 W
South Coatesville	208	39.58 N	75.49 W
South Coffeyville	196	36.59 N	95.37 W
South Concho ≃	196	31.21 N	100.28 W
South Corinth	210	43.12 N	73.51 W
South Corning	210	42.07 N	77.02 W
South Cotabato □[4]	116	6.15 N	125.00 E
South Creek ≃	170	33.36 S	150.50 E
South Crest	273d	26.15 S	28.07 E
South Dakota □[3], U.S.	178	44.15 N	100.00 W
South Dakota □[3], U.S.	198	44.15 N	100.00 W
South Dandalup ≃	168a	32.35 S	115.53 E
South Dandalup Dam ◆[6]	168a	32.38 S	116.04 E
South Darenth	260	51.24 N	0.15 E
South Dartmouth	207	41.35 N	70.56 W
South Dayton	210	42.21 N	79.03 W
South Deerfield	207	42.28 N	72.36 W
South Dennis, Ma., U.S.	207	41.41 N	70.09 W
South Dennis, N.J., U.S.	208	39.10 N	74.49 W
South Dorset	210	43.13 N	73.04 W
South Dorset Downs ⋏[1]	42	50.40 N	2.25 W
South Dos Palos	226	36.57 N	120.39 W
South Downs ⋏[1]	42	50.55 N	0.25 W
South Dum Dum	126	22.37 N	88.25 E
South Duxbury	207	42.01 N	70.41 W
South East □[5]	156	25.00 S	25.45 E
Southeast Asia Treaty Organization Headquarters ʊ	269a	13.45 N	100.31 E
South East Cape ›, Austl.	166	43.39 S	146.50 E
Southeast Cape ›, Ak., U.S.	180	62.55 N	169.42 W
Southeast Indian Ridge ✧[3]	6	50.00 S	110.00 E
South East Mountain ∧	241k	12.05 N	61.40 W
South Easton	207	42.02 N	71.04 W
Southeast Pacific Basin ✧[1]	6	60.00 S	115.00 W
South East Point ›, Austl.	166	39.00 S	146.20 E
South East Point ›, Kiribati	174o	1.40 N	157.10 W
South Egg Harbor	208	39.31 N	74.39 W
South Egremont	207	42.09 N	73.25 W
South Elgin	216	41.59 N	88.17 W
South Elkhorn Creek ≃	218	38.13 N	84.48 W
South El Monte	280	34.03 N	118.02 W
Southend	44	55.20 N	5.38 W
Southend Municipal Airport ⊠	42	51.34 N	0.41 E
Southend-on-Sea	42	51.33 N	0.43 E
Southend-on-Sea □[8]	260	51.33 N	0.41 E
Southend Pier ◆[5]	260	51.31 N	0.44 E
South English ≃	190	41.30 N	91.56 W
Southern □[4], Malawi	154	15.30 S	35.00 E
Southern □[4], S.L.	150	8.00 N	12.15 W
Southern □[4], Zam.	154	16.30 S	27.00 E
Southern □[5], Bots.	156	24.45 S	24.00 E
Southern □[5], Ug.	154	0.30 S	30.30 E
Southern Alps ⋏	172	43.30 S	170.30 E
Southern California, University of ʊ[2]	280	34.02 N	118.17 W
Southern Cook Islands II	14	20.00 S	159.00 W
Southern Cross	162	31.13 S	119.19 E
Southern Ghāts ⋏	122	9.30 N	77.00 E
Southern Highlands □[5]	164	6.00 S	143.30 E
Southern Indian Lake ⊜	176	57.10 N	98.40 W
Southern Leyte □[4]	116	10.50 N	124.55 E
Southern Lueti ≃	152	16.14 S	23.13 E
Southern Ocean ⊤[1]	4	50.00 S	135.00 E
Southern Pines	192	35.10 N	79.23 W
Southern Ute Indian Reservation ◆[4]	200	37.05 N	107.45 W
Southern View	219	39.46 N	89.39 W
Southern Yemen → Yemen □[1]	144	15.00 N	47.00 E
Southery	42	52.32 N	0.23 E
South Esk ≃, Austl.	166	41.25 S	147.08 E
South Esk ≃, Scot., U.K.	46	56.42 N	2.32 W
South Esk ≃, Scot., U.K.	46	55.53 N	3.04 W
Southesk Tablelands ⋏[1]	162	20.50 S	126.40 E
South Essex	207	42.38 N	70.46 W
South Euclid	214	41.31 N	81.31 W
Southey	184	50.56 N	104.30 W
South Fabius ≃	219	39.54 N	91.30 W
South Fallsburg	210	41.42 N	74.37 W
South Farmbridge	260	51.38 N	0.41 E
South Farmingdale	276	40.43 N	73.26 W
Southfield, Ma., U.S.	207	42.06 N	73.14 W
Southfield, Mi., U.S.	216	42.28 N	83.13 W
Southfields	210	41.15 N	74.11 W
South Fiji Basin ✧[1]	14	26.00 S	175.00 E
Southfleet	260	51.25 N	0.19 E
South Floral Park	276	40.43 N	73.42 W
South Foreland ›	42	51.09 N	1.23 E
South Fork, Co., U.S.	200	37.40 N	106.38 W
South Fork, Pa., U.S.	214	40.22 N	78.47 W
South Fort George	182	53.54 N	122.45 W
South Forty Foot Drain ≋	42	52.56 N	0.15 W
South Fox Island I	190	45.25 N	85.50 W
South Fulton	194	36.30 N	88.52 W
South Gate, Ca., U.S.	228	33.57 N	118.12 W
Southgate, Fl., U.S.	220	27.18 N	82.32 W
Southgate, Mi., U.S.	216	42.12 N	83.11 W
Southgate, Wa., U.S.	224	47.10 N	122.30 W
Southgate ◆[8]	260	51.38 N	0.08 W
Southgate U.S.A. ◆[9]	279a	41.25 N	81.32 W
South Georgia I	244	54.15 S	36.45 W
South Gibson	210	41.44 N	75.38 W
South Glamorgan □[6]	42	51.30 N	3.25 W
South Glastonbury	207	41.40 N	72.35 W
South Glens Falls	210	43.17 N	73.38 W
South Grafton	207	42.11 N	71.42 W
South Grand ≃	194	38.18 N	93.28 W
South Grand Island Bridge ◆[5]	284a	43.00 N	78.56 W
South Green	260	51.37 N	0.26 E
South Greensburg	214	40.17 N	79.33 W
South Hackensack	276	40.51 N	74.02 W
South Hadley, Ma., U.S.	188	42.15 N	72.34 W
South Hadley, Ma., U.S.	207	42.15 N	72.34 W
South Hadley Falls	207	42.13 N	72.36 W
South Hamilton	207	42.36 N	70.52 W
South Hams ≍	42	50.22 N	3.50 W
South Hanningfield	260	51.39 N	0.31 E
South Hanover	283	42.05 N	70.51 W
South Harbor ⊂	269f	14.33 N	120.58 E
South Hartford	210	43.21 N	73.25 W
South Harwich	207	41.40 N	70.02 W
South Hātia Island I	124	22.19 N	91.07 E
South Haven, In., U.S.	216	41.32 N	87.08 W
South Haven, Ks., U.S.	198	37.03 N	97.24 W
South Haven, Mi., U.S.	216	42.24 N	86.16 W
South Hayling	42	50.47 N	0.59 W
South Head ›, Austl.	274a	33.50 S	151.17 E
South Head ›, N.Z.	172	36.26 S	174.14 E
South Heart ≃	182	55.34 N	116.11 W
South Heights	279b	40.35 N	80.14 W
South Hempstead	276	40.41 N	73.37 W
South Henderson	192	36.17 N	78.25 W
South Henik Lake ⊜	176	61.30 N	97.30 W
South Hero	188	44.38 N	73.18 W
South Hetton	44	54.48 N	1.24 W
South Hill, N.Y., U.S.	210	42.25 N	76.33 W
South Hill, Va., U.S.	192	36.43 N	78.07 W
South Hills ◆[8]	273d	26.15 S	28.05 E
South Hills Village ◆[9]	279b	40.21 N	80.03 W
South Hingham	207	42.11 N	70.52 W
South Hogan Creek ≃	218	39.03 N	84.54 W
South Holland	216	41.36 N	87.36 W
South Holston Lake ⊜[1]	192	36.35 N	82.00 W
South Honcut Creek ≃	226	39.19 N	121.35 W
South Honshu Ridge ✧[3]	14	24.00 N	142.00 E
South Hopkinton	207	41.24 N	71.45 W
South Horr	154	2.06 N	36.55 E
South Houston	222	29.39 N	95.14 W
South Huntington	276	40.49 N	73.23 W
South Indian Basin ✧[1]	6	60.00 S	120.00 E
South Indian Lake	184	56.46 N	98.57 W
Southington, Ct., U.S.	207	41.35 N	72.52 W
Southington, Oh., U.S.	214	41.19 N	80.57 W
South International Falls	190	48.35 N	93.23 W
South Ionia	216	42.57 N	85.04 W
South Island I, India	122	10.03 N	72.17 E
South Island I, Kenya	154	2.38 N	36.36 E
South Island I, N.Z.	172	43.00 S	171.00 E
South Island I, Micron.	175c	6.59 N	151.59 E
South Islet I	116	8.44 N	119.49 E
South Jacksonville	219	39.42 N	90.13 W
South Kemptville Creek ≃	212	44.54 N	75.41 W
South Kenosha	216	42.32 N	87.50 W
South Kensington Museums ʊ	260	51.30 N	0.11 W
South Kent	207	41.40 N	73.28 W
South Kirkby	44	53.34 N	1.20 W
South Konkan Hills ⋏[2]	122	17.00 N	73.30 E
South Korea → Korea, South □[1]	98	36.30 N	128.00 E
South Ladder Creek ≃	198	38.41 N	101.34 W
South Laguna	228	33.30 N	117.45 W
Southlake	222	32.57 N	97.09 W
South Lake ⊜, On., Can.	212	44.26 N	76.13 W
South Lake ⊜, Fl., U.S.	220	28.37 N	80.52 W
South Lake Tahoe	226	38.56 N	119.58 W
South Lancaster	207	42.26 N	71.41 W
Southland, Ky., U.S.	218	38.01 N	84.31 W
Southland, Mi., U.S.	216	42.13 N	84.24 W
Southland, Tx., U.S.	196	33.22 N	101.33 W
Southland ◆[9]	282	37.39 N	122.06 W
South Laurel	284c	39.05 N	76.52 W
Southlawn, Il., U.S.	219	39.45 N	89.37 W
South Lawn, Md., U.S.	284c	38.48 N	76.59 W
South Layhill	284c	39.04 N	77.03 W
South Lebanon	218	39.22 N	84.12 W
South Lee	207	42.16 N	73.16 W
South Lima	210	42.51 N	77.41 W

ENGLISH

Name	Page	Lat.°′	Long.°′
South Line Island I	276	40.37 N	73.30 W
South Llano ≃	196	30.30 N	99.46 W
South Lockport	284a	43.09 N	78.42 W
South Lorain	279a	41.27 N	82.08 W
South Loup ≃	198	41.04 N	98.40 W
South Luangwa National Park ♠	154	12.50 S	31.45 E
South Luconia Shoals ✧[2]	112	5.00 N	112.42 E
South Lynnfield	283	42.31 N	71.00 W
South Lyon	216	42.27 N	83.39 W
South Macmillan ≃	180	63.03 N	133.18 W
South Magnetic Pole ◆	9	65.18 S	139.30 E
South Malosmadulu Atoll I[1]	122	5.10 N	72.58 E
South Manitou Island I	190	45.01 N	86.07 W
South Marsh Island I	208	38.06 N	76.02 W
South Medford	202	42.18 N	122.50 W
South Media	285	39.54 N	75.23 W
South Melbourne	274b	37.50 S	144.57 E
South Merrimack	207	42.48 N	71.33 W
South Miami	220	25.42 N	80.17 W
South Miami Heights	220	25.35 N	80.22 W
South Middleboro	207	41.49 N	70.49 W
South Milford	216	41.31 N	85.16 W
South Mills	192	36.26 N	76.19 W
South Milwaukee	216	42.54 N	87.51 W
South Mimms	260	51.42 N	0.14 W
Southminster	42	51.40 N	0.50 E
South Modesto	226	37.38 N	120.58 W
South Mokelumne ≃	226	38.08 N	121.35 W
South Molton	42	51.01 N	3.50 W
South Monroe	216	41.54 N	83.25 W
Southmont	214	40.18 N	78.56 W
South Montrose	210	41.48 N	75.53 W
South Moose Lake ⊜	184	53.46 N	100.08 W
South Mountain	208	39.51 N	77.29 W
South Mountain ∧, U.S.	208	39.40 N	77.30 W
South Mountain ∧, Id., U.S.	202	42.44 N	116.54 W
South Mountain Reservation ♠	276	40.45 N	74.18 W
South Mount Vernon	214	40.23 N	82.23 W
South Nahanni ≃	176	61.03 N	123.20 W
South Naknek	180	58.43 N	157.00 W
South Nation ≃	188	45.34 N	75.06 W
South Negril Point ›	241q	18.15 N	78.22 W
South New Berlin	210	42.31 N	75.23 W
South New Castle	214	40.58 N	80.21 W
South New River Canal ≋	220	26.04 N	80.12 W
South Norfolk → Chesapeake	208	36.43 N	76.15 W
South Normanton	44	53.06 N	1.20 W
South Norwalk Reservoir ⊜[1]	276	41.11 N	73.27 W
South Norwood ◆[8]	260	51.24 N	0.04 W
South Nutfield	260	51.14 N	0.08 W
South Nyack	276	41.04 N	73.55 W
South Ockendon	42	51.32 N	0.18 E
South Ogden	200	41.11 N	111.58 W
Southold	207	41.03 N	72.25 W
South Onondaga	210	42.56 N	76.13 W
South Orange	276	40.47 N	74.15 W
South Orkney Islands II	9	60.35 S	45.30 W
South Oroville	226	39.30 N	121.33 W
South Otselic	210	42.38 N	75.46 W
Southowram	262	53.43 N	1.50 W
South Oxhey	260	51.38 N	0.23 W
South Oyster Bay ⊂	276	40.38 N	73.28 W
South Palo Duro Creek ≃	196	36.06 N	101.29 W
South Para ≃	168b	34.36 S	138.45 E
South Para Reservoir ⊜[1]	168b	34.42 S	138.52 E
South Paris	188	44.13 N	70.30 W
South Park	216	41.44 N	88.18 W
South Park ♠, N.Y., U.S.	284a	42.50 N	78.50 W
South Park ♠, Pa., U.S.	279b	40.19 N	80.01 W
South Pasadena, Ca., U.S.	280	34.06 N	118.08 W
South Pasadena, Fl., U.S.	220	27.46 N	82.43 W
South Pass)(	200	42.22 N	108.55 W
South Pass ų	175c	7.14 N	151.48 E
South Passage ų, Austl.	171a	27.22 S	153.26 E
South Passage ų, Oh., U.S.	214	41.35 N	82.45 W
South Patrick Shores	220	28.12 N	80.35 W
South Pekin	190	40.29 N	89.39 W
South Pender	224	48.45 N	123.14 W
South Pender Island I	224	48.45 N	123.10 W
South Perth	168a	31.59 S	115.52 E
South Petherton	42	50.58 N	2.49 W
South Philadelphia ◆[8]	285	39.56 N	75.10 W
South Philipsburg	214	40.53 N	78.13 W
South Pittsburg	194	35.00 N	85.42 W
South Plainfield	210	40.34 N	74.24 W
South Platte ≃	178	41.07 N	100.42 W
South Platte, North Fork ≃	200	39.25 N	105.10 W
South Point ›, Ba.	238	22.50 N	74.52 W
South Point ›, Barb.	241g	13.02 N	59.31 W
South Point ›, Pil.	116	10.24 N	122.30 E
South Pole ◆	9	90.00 S	0.00
South Porcupine	190	48.28 N	81.13 W
Southport, Austl.	166	43.25 S	146.59 E
Southport, Austl.	171a	27.58 S	153.25 E
Southport, Eng., U.K.	44	53.39 N	3.01 W
Southport, Ct., U.S.	207	41.08 N	73.17 W
Southport, Fl., U.S.	194	30.17 N	85.38 W
Southport, In., U.S.	218	39.39 N	86.07 W
Southport, N.Y., U.S.	210	42.03 N	76.49 W
Southport, N.C., U.S.	192	33.55 N	78.01 W
South Portland	188	43.38 N	70.14 W
South Portsmouth	218	38.43 N	83.00 W
South Pottstown	208	40.14 N	75.39 W
South Prairie Creek ≃	224	47.08 N	122.10 W
South Raisin ≃	206	45.08 N	74.35 W
South Range	190	47.04 N	88.38 W
South Renovo	214	41.19 N	77.44 W
South Reservoir ⊜[1]	283	42.27 N	71.07 W
South Ribble □[8]	262	53.45 N	2.42 W
South River, On., Can.	190	45.50 N	79.23 W
South River, N.J., U.S.	208	40.26 N	74.23 W
South River ⊂	208	38.57 N	76.29 W
South Rockwood	216	42.04 N	83.16 W
South Ronaldsay I	46	58.46 N	2.58 W
South Roxana	219	38.50 N	90.04 W
South Royalston	207	42.37 N	72.08 W
South Rukuru ≃	154	10.46 S	34.14 E
South Russell	214	41.25 N	81.21 W
South Salmara	124	25.55 N	90.01 E
South Sand Bluff ›	158	31.19 S	30.01 E
South Sandwich Islands II	18	57.45 S	26.30 W
South Sandwich Trench ✧[1]	18	56.30 S	25.00 W
South Sandy Creek ≃	212	43.43 N	76.12 W
South San Francisco	226	37.39 N	122.24 W
South San Gabriel	280	34.03 N	118.05 W
South San Jose Hills	280	34.01 N	117.55 W
South San Ramon Creek ≃	282	37.42 N	121.55 W
South Santiam ≃	202	44.41 N	123.00 W
South Saskatchewan ≃	184	53.15 N	105.05 W
South Saugeen ≃	212	44.08 N	81.02 W

DEUTSCH

Name	Seite	Breite°′	Länge°′ E = Ost
South Seaville	208	39.10 N	74.45 W
South Setauket	210	40.54 N	73.06 W
South Shafter	226	35.28 N	119.17 W
South Shetland Islands II	9	62.00 S	58.00 W
South Shields	44	55.00 N	1.25 W
South Shore	218	38.43 N	82.59 W
South Shore ◆[8]	278	41.46 N	87.35 W
South Shore Mall ◆[9]	276	40.44 N	73.15 W
South Shore Plaza ◆[9]	283	42.13 N	71.01 W
Southside	174h	2.49 S	171.43 W
South Side ◆[8]	279b	40.26 N	79.58 W
Southside Place	222	29.42 N	95.26 W
South Sioux City	198	42.28 N	96.24 W
South Skunk ≃	190	41.15 N	92.02 W
South Slocan	182	49.28 N	117.32 W
South Solon	218	39.44 N	83.36 W
South Sound ų	48	53.02 N	9.28 W
South Spicer Island I	176	68.06 N	79.13 W
South Standard	219	39.21 N	89.47 W
South Station ◆[5]	283	42.21 N	71.04 W
South Sterling	210	41.17 N	75.21 W
South Stickney	278	41.45 N	87.46 W
South Stony Brook	276	40.53 N	73.07 W
South Stradbroke Island I	171a	27.51 S	153.25 E
South Streator	216	40.39 N	88.23 W
South Suburban → Behāla	126	22.31 N	88.19 E
South Sulphur ≃	196	33.23 N	95.18 W
South Sunday Creek ≃	202	46.27 N	105.54 W
South Superior	200	41.45 N	108.57 W
South Swansea	207	41.43 N	71.12 W
South Taranaki Bight ⊂[3]	172	39.40 S	174.10 E
South Tasman Rise ✧[3]	6	49.00 S	148.00 E
South Temple	208	40.24 N	75.55 W
South Thompson ≃	182	50.41 N	120.21 W
South Toms River	208	39.56 N	74.12 W
South Torrington	198	42.02 N	104.10 W
South Towanda	210	41.45 N	76.27 W
South Tucson	200	32.11 N	110.58 W
South Turkeyfoot Creek ≃	216	41.25 N	83.58 W
South Turlock	226	37.29 N	120.51 W
South Twillingate Island I	186	49.37 N	54.47 W
South Tyne ≃	44	54.59 N	2.08 W
South Ubian	116	5.11 N	120.30 E
South Uist I	46	57.15 N	7.21 W
South Umpqua ≃	202	43.20 N	123.25 W
South Valley	210	42.42 N	74.43 W
South Valley Hills ⋏[2]	285	40.00 N	75.40 W
South Valley Stream	276	40.38 N	73.44 W
South Venice	220	27.03 N	82.25 W
South Ventana Cone ∧	204	36.17 N	121.38 W
South Vestal	210	42.01 N	76.00 W
South Vietnam → Vietnam □[1]	108	16.00 N	108.00 E
Southview	214	40.20 N	80.16 W
Southview Apartments	284c	38.50 N	77.00 W
South Wabasca Lake ⊜	182	55.54 N	113.45 W
South Wales	210	42.43 N	78.35 W
South Walpole	283	42.06 N	71.15 W
Southwark ◆[8]	42	51.30 N	0.06 W
South Warren Reservoir ⊜[1]	168b	34.43 S	138.55 E
Southwater	42	51.01 N	0.21 W
South Waverly	210	41.59 N	76.32 W
South Weald	260	51.37 N	0.16 E
Southwell	44	53.05 N	0.58 W
South Wellfleet	207	41.55 N	69.59 W
South Wellington	224	49.06 N	123.53 W
Southwest	214	40.12 N	79.32 W
South West Bay ⊂	240b	25.00 N	77.32 W
Southwest Branch ≃	284c	38.53 N	76.48 W
South Westbury	276	40.45 N	73.35 W
South West Cape ›, Austl.	166	43.34 S	146.02 E
South West Cape ›, N.Z.	172	47.17 S	167.28 E
Southwest Cape ›, Ak., U.S.	180	63.18 N	171.27 W
Southwest Cape ›, Vir. Is., U.S.	241n	17.41 N	64.54 W
Southwest Channel ų	220	27.34 N	82.45 W
South West City	194	36.30 N	94.36 W
South Westerlo	210	42.27 N	74.02 W
Southwest Greensburg	214	40.17 N	79.33 W
Southwest Harbor	188	44.16 N	68.19 W
Southwest Indian Ridge ✧[3]	6	30.00 S	60.00 E
Southwest Miramichi ≃	186	46.58 N	65.35 W
Southwest Museum ʊ	280	34.06 N	118.13 W
Southwest National Park ♠	166	43.15 S	146.15 E
Southwest Pacific Basin ✧[1]	6	40.00 S	150.00 W
Southwest Point ›, Ba.	238	25.51 N	77.13 W
South West Point ›, Kiribati	174o	1.52 N	157.33 W
Southwest Point ›, Pap. N. Gui.	164	2.14 S	146.34 E
Southwest Road ų	240m	18.20 N	65.00 W
South Weymouth	283	42.10 N	70.57 W
South Weymouth Naval Air Station ■	207	42.09 N	70.57 W
South Whitley	216	41.05 N	85.37 W
South Whittier	280	33.57 N	118.02 W
South Wichita ≃	196	33.43 N	99.29 W
Southwick, Eng., U.K.	42	50.50 N	0.13 W
Southwick, Ma., U.S.	207	42.03 N	72.46 W
South Williamson	192	37.40 N	82.17 W
South Williamsport	210	41.13 N	76.59 W
South Wilmington	216	41.10 N	88.16 W
South Windham	188	43.44 N	70.25 W
South Windsor	207	41.49 N	72.37 W
Southwold	42	52.20 N	1.40 E
Southwood	210	42.59 N	76.08 W
Southwood Acres	207	41.59 N	72.32 W
South Woodham Ferrers	42	51.39 N	0.37 E
South Woodslee	214	42.14 N	82.43 W
South Woodstock	207	41.56 N	71.57 W
Southworth	224	47.31 N	122.30 W
South Yadkin ≃	192	35.45 N	80.27 W
South Yamhill ≃	224	45.13 N	123.08 W
South Yarmouth	207	41.40 N	70.11 W
South Yarra	274b	37.51 S	145.00 E
South Yorkshire □[6]	44	53.30 N	1.15 W
South Yuba ≃	226	39.17 N	121.12 W
South Zeal	42	50.44 N	3.54 W
Soutpan	158	28.43 S	26.04 E
Soutpansberg ⋏	156	22.55 S	29.30 E
Souttouf, Adrar ⋏	148	22.15 N	15.40 W
Souvigny	32	46.32 N	3.11 E
Souzy-la-Briche	261	48.32 N	2.09 E
Sovata	38	46.35 N	25.04 E
Soverato	68	38.41 N	16.33 E
Sovere	64	45.49 N	10.01 E
Sovereign Hill Historical Park ⊥	169	37.37 S	143.51 E
Sovereign Mountain ∧	180	62.08 N	148.36 W
Soveria Mannelli	68	39.05 N	16.22 E
Sövestad	41	55.30 N	13.47 E
Sovetabad	85	40.48 N	72.58 E
Sovetašen, S.S.S.R.	84	39.50 N	45.03 E
Sovetašen, S.S.S.R.	84	40.06 N	44.33 E

Symbols in the index entries represent the broad categories identified in the key at the right. Symbols with superior numbers (⋏[1]) identify subcategories (see complete key on page *I · 1).*

Symbole im Register stellen die rechts im Schlüssel erklärten Kategorien dar. Symbole mit hochgestellten Ziffern (⋏[1]) bezeichnen Unterabteilungen einer Kategorie (vgl. vollständiger Schlüssel auf Seite *I · 1).*

Los símbolos incluídos en el texto del índice representan las grandes categorias identificadas con la clave a la derecha. Los símbolos con numeros en su parte superior (⋏[1]) identifican las subcategorías (véase la clave completa en la página *I · 1).*

Les symboles de l'index représentent les catégories indiquées dans la légende à droite. Les symboles suivis d'un indice (⋏[1]) représentent des sous-catégories (voir légende complète à la page *I · 1).*

Os símbolos incluídos no texto do índice representam as grandes categorias identificadas com a chave à direita. Os símbolos com números em sua parte superior (⋏[1]) identificam as subcategorias (veja-se a chave completa à página *I · 1).*

∧ Mountain	Berg	Montaña	Montagne	Montanha
⋏ Mountains	Gebirge	Montañas	Montagnes	Montanhas
)(Pass	Paß	Paso	Col	Passo
V Valley, Canyon	Tal, Cañon	Valle, Cañón	Vallée, Canyon	Vale, Canhão
≍ Plain	Ebene	Llano	Plaine	Planície
› Cape	Kap	Cabo	Cap	Cabo
I Island	Insel	Isla	Île	Ilha
II Islands	Inseln	Islas	Îles	Ilhas
≗ Other Topographic Features	Andere Topographische Objekte	Otros Elementos Topográficos	Autres données topographiques	Outros acidentes topográficos

Sove-Stan *I* · *167*

ESPAÑOL — Nombre / Página / Lat.°′ / Long.°′ W = Oeste

FRANÇAIS — Nom / Page / Lat.°′ / Long.°′ W = Ouest

PORTUGUÊS — Nome / Página / Lat.°′ / Long.°′ W = Oeste

Nombre	Página	Lat.°′	Long.°′
Sovetka	83	47.30 N	39.15 E
Sovetsk, S.S.S.R.	76	53.56 N	37.39 E
Sovetsk, S.S.S.R.	76	55.05 N	21.53 E
Sovetsk, S.S.S.R.	80	57.37 N	48.58 E
Sovetskaja, S.S.S.R.	80	49.00 N	42.07 E
Sovetskaja, S.S.S.R.	84	44.46 N	41.11 E
Sovetskaja, S.S.S.R.	84	44.02 N	44.03 E
Sovetskaja Gavan'	89	48.58 N	140.18 E
Sovetskich Oficerov, pik ∧	85	38.26 N	73.18 E
Sovetskij, S.S.S.R.	76	60.32 N	28.41 E
Sovetskij, S.S.S.R.	78	45.20 N	34.56 E
Sovetskij, S.S.S.R.	80	56.46 N	48.32 E
Sovetskij, S.S.S.R.	85	40.11 N	71.19 E
Sovetskij, S.S.S.R.	85	38.02 N	69.35 E
Sovetskij, S.S.S.R.	86	51.04 N	56.29 E
Sovetskoje, S.S.S.R.	78	50.21 N	39.01 E
Sovetskoje, S.S.S.R.	80	47.18 N	44.31 E
Sovetskoje, S.S.S.R.	80	51.27 N	46.44 E
Sovetskoje, S.S.S.R.	84	42.52 N	45.41 E
Sovetskoje, S.S.S.R.	84	43.19 N	43.36 E
Sovetskoje, S.S.S.R.	85	42.17 N	70.15 E
Šovgenovskij	78	45.02 N	40.14 E
Sovicille	66	43.17 N	11.13 E
Sovico	266b	45.39 N	9.16 E
Soviet Union → Union of Soviet Socialist Republics □[1]	72	60.00 N	80.00 E
Søvik	26	62.33 N	6.18 E
Søvind	41	55.54 N	10.01 E
Sovpolje	24	65.18 N	43.55 E
Sow ≃	42	52.48 N	2.00 W
Sowa Pan ≚	156	20.45 S	26.00 E
Sowek	164	0.49 S	135.30 E
Sowerby, Eng., U.K.	44	54.13 N	1.21 W
Sowerby, Eng., U.K.	262	53.42 N	1.56 W
Sowerby Bridge	44	53.43 N	1.54 W
Soweto	158	26.14 S	27.54 E
Sowjetisches Ehrenmal ⊥	264a	52.29 N	13.28 E
Sowjetunion → Union of Soviet Socialist Republics □[1]	72	60.00 N	80.00 E
Soy	56	50.17 N	5.31 E
Sōya-kaikyō → La Perouse Strait ʊ	89	45.45 N	142.00 E
Sōya-misaki ›	92a	45.31 N	141.56 E
Soyang-chŏsuji ⊜[1]	98	37.56 N	127.53 E
Soyapango	236	13.42 N	89.09 W
Soyers Lake ⊜	212	45.02 N	78.37 W
Soyet	124	24.12 N	76.10 E
Soyland Moor ◆[3]	262	53.40 N	2.02 W
Soyo	152	6.07 S	12.18 E
Soyons	62	44.53 N	4.51 E
Sož ≃, S.S.S.R.	78	51.57 N	30.48 E
Soz' ≃, S.S.S.R.	82	56.48 N	36.44 E
Şozimskij	24	59.44 N	52.16 E
Šožma	24	61.56 N	40.15 E
Sozopol	38	42.25 N	27.42 E
Sozzago	266b	45.24 N	8.43 E
Spa	56	50.30 N	5.52 E
Space Needle ⊍	224	47.38 N	122.23 W
Space Obelisk ⊥	265b	55.49 N	37.38 E
Spadafora	70	38.13 N	15.22 E
Spada Lake ⊜[1]	224	47.57 N	121.40 W
Spaden	52	53.34 N	8.38 E
Spahl	56	50.39 N	9.55 E
Spaichingen	58	48.04 N	8.44 E
Spain (España) □[1], Europe	22	40.00 N	4.00 W
Spain (España) □[1], Europe	34	40.00 N	4.00 W
Spakenburg	52	52.15 N	5.23 E
Spalato → Split	36	43.31 N	16.27 E
Spalding, Austl.	166	33.30 S	138.37 E
Spalding, Sk., Can.	184	52.20 N	104.30 W
Spalding, Eng., U.K.	42	52.47 N	0.10 W
Spalding, Mo., U.S.	219	39.38 N	91.32 W
Spalding, Ne., U.S.	198	41.41 N	98.21 W
Spalt	56	49.10 N	10.55 E
Spam Island I	174h	2.48 S	171.43 W
Spanaway	224	47.06 N	122.26 W
Spandau ◆[8]	54	52.33 N	13.12 E
Spandau, Berliner Forst ◆[3]	264a	52.35 N	13.11 E
Spandau, Berliner Forst ♠	264a	52.35 N	13.10 E
Spang	41	54.56 N	9.50 E
Spangenberg	56	51.07 N	9.40 E
Spangler	214	40.38 N	78.46 W
Spaniard's Bay	186	47.37 N	53.17 W
Spanien → Spain □[1]	34	40.00 N	4.00 W
Spanish	190	46.12 N	82.21 W
Spanish ≃	190	46.11 N	82.19 W
Spanish Camp	222	29.23 N	96.10 W
Spanish Fork	200	40.06 N	111.39 W
Spanish Lake	219	38.47 N	90.12 W
Spanish North Africa □[2], Afr.	34	35.53 N	5.19 W
Spanish North Africa □[2], Afr.	134	35.53 N	5.19 W
Spanish Peak ∧	202	44.24 N	119.46 W
Spanish Point ›	240a	32.18 N	64.48 W
Spanish Sahara → Western Sahara □[2]	134	24.30 N	13.00 W
Spanish Town	241q	17.59 N	76.57 W
Spannberg	61	48.27 N	16.44 E
Sparagio, Monte ∧	70	38.03 N	12.46 E
Sparbach	264b	48.04 N	16.11 E
Spargi, Isola I	71	41.14 N	9.21 E
Sparkford	42	51.02 N	2.34 W
Sparkill	276	41.02 N	73.56 W
Sparkle Lake	210	41.18 N	73.47 W
Sparkman	194	33.55 N	92.50 W
Sparks, Ga., U.S.	192	31.10 N	83.26 W
Sparks, Nv., U.S.	226	39.32 N	119.45 W
Sparland	190	41.02 N	89.26 W
Sparlingville	214	42.58 N	82.30 W
Sparneck	54	50.09 N	11.50 E
Sparreholm	40	59.04 N	16.49 E
Sparrow Bush	210	41.23 N	74.43 W
Sparrow Lake ⊜	212	44.49 N	79.24 W
Sparrowpit	262	53.19 N	1.52 W
Sparrows Point	208	39.13 N	76.28 W
Sparrows Point ›	284b	39.12 N	76.30 W
Sparta, On., Can.	212	42.42 N	81.05 W
Sparta → Spárti, Ellás	38	37.05 N	22.27 E
Sparta, Ga., U.S.	192	33.16 N	82.58 W
Sparta, Il., U.S.	194	38.07 N	89.42 W
Sparta, Ky., U.S.	218	38.40 N	84.54 W
Sparta, Mi., U.S.	190	43.09 N	85.42 W
Sparta, N.J., U.S.	210	41.02 N	74.38 W
Sparta, N.C., U.S.	192	36.30 N	81.07 W
Sparta, Oh., U.S.	214	40.24 N	82.42 W
Sparta, Tn., U.S.	194	35.55 N	85.27 W
Sparta, Wi., U.S.	190	43.56 N	90.48 W
Sparta Brook ≃	276	41.08 N	73.52 W
Spartak Garden ♠	265a	59.51 N	30.30 E
Sparta Lake	210	41.03 N	74.34 W
Spartanburg, In., U.S.	218	40.03 N	84.51 W
Spartanburg, S.C., U.S.	192	34.56 N	81.55 W
Spartansburg	214	41.49 N	79.41 W
Spartel, Cap ›	34	35.48 N	5.56 W
Spárti (Sparta)	38	37.05 N	22.27 E
Spartivento, Capo ›, It.	68	37.55 N	16.04 E
Spartivento, Capo ›, It.	71	38.53 N	8.50 E
Spas-Demensk	76	54.25 N	34.01 E
Spas-Klepiki	80	55.08 N	40.13 E
Spass	82	55.55 N	35.55 E
Spassk-Dal'nij	89	44.37 N	132.48 E
Spasskij	86	53.42 N	59.12 E
Spasskij Zavod	86	49.32 N	73.17 E
Spasskoje, S.S.S.R.	76	53.06 N	36.24 E
Spasskoje, S.S.S.R.	80	55.52 N	45.42 E
Spasskoje, S.S.S.R.	82	54.05 N	38.28 E
Spassk-R'azanskij	80	54.24 N	40.23 E
Spas-Zaulok	82	56.29 N	36.34 E
Spáta	267c	38.00 N	21.31 E
Spátha, Ákra ›	38	35.42 N	23.44 E
Spaulding	219	39.52 N	89.32 W
Spaulding, Lake ⊜[1]	226	39.20 N	120.37 W
Speaks	222	29.15 N	96.42 W
Spean, Glen V	46	56.53 N	4.45 W
Spean Bridge	46	56.53 N	4.54 W
Spear, Cape ›	186	47.32 N	52.32 W
Spearfish	198	44.29 N	103.51 W
Spearman	196	36.11 N	101.11 W
Spearsville	218	39.21 N	86.11 W
Spearville	198	37.51 N	99.45 W
Spearwood	168a	32.07 S	115.47 E
Speas Artemidos (Rock Tombs) ⊥	142	27.54 N	30.52 E
Specchia	68	39.57 N	18.18 E
Spechtsbrunn	54	50.30 N	11.14 E
Spectacle Island I	283	42.19 N	70.59 W
Spectrum ♠	285	39.54 N	75.10 W
Spectrum Range ⋀	180	57.30 N	130.40 W
Spednic Lake ⊜	186	45.36 N	67.35 W
Speed	218	38.24 N	85.45 W
Speed ≃	212	43.23 N	80.22 W
Speedway	218	39.48 N	86.16 W
Speicher	58	47.24 N	9.27 E
Speichersee ⊜	60	48.13 N	11.45 E
Speightstown	241g	13.15 N	59.39 W
Speigletown	210	42.48 N	73.38 W
Speikkogel ∧	61	47.14 N	15.03 E
Speinshart	60	49.47 N	11.49 E
Speising ◆[8]	264b	48.10 N	16.17 E
Speke ◆[8]	262	53.21 N	2.51 W
Speke Gulf ⊂	154	2.20 S	33.15 E
Speke Hall ⊥	262	53.20 N	2.52 W
Speldorf ◆[8]	263	51.25 N	6.52 E
Spellen	263	51.37 N	6.37 E
Spello	66	42.59 N	12.40 E
Spelthorne □[8]	260	51.25 N	0.28 W
Spelve, Loch ⊂	46	56.22 N	5.46 W
Spenard	180	61.11 N	149.55 W
Spence Bay	176	69.32 N	93.31 W
Spencer, In., U.S.	194	39.17 N	86.45 W
Spencer, Ia., U.S.	198	43.08 N	95.08 W
Spencer, Ma., U.S.	207	42.14 N	71.59 W
Spencer, Ne., U.S.	198	42.52 N	98.42 W
Spencer, N.Y., U.S.	210	42.12 N	76.29 W
Spencer, N.C., U.S.	192	35.41 N	80.26 W
Spencer, Oh., U.S.	214	41.06 N	82.07 W
Spencer, S.D., U.S.	198	43.43 N	97.35 W
Spencer, Tn., U.S.	194	35.44 N	85.28 W
Spencer, W.V., U.S.	188	38.48 N	81.21 W
Spencer, Wi., U.S.	190	44.45 N	90.17 W
Spencer, Cape ›, Austl.	166	35.18 S	136.53 E
Spencer, Cape ›, N.B., Can.	186	45.12 N	65.55 W
Spencer, Cape ›, Ak., U.S.	180	58.14 N	136.40 W
Spencer, Mount ∧	224	49.03 N	124.38 W
Spencer, Point ›	180	65.18 N	166.50 W
Spencer Brook ≃	283	42.28 N	71.22 W
Spencer Creek ≃, On., Can.	212	43.17 N	79.54 W
Spencer Creek ≃, Mo., U.S.	219	39.33 N	91.20 W
Spencer Field ⊠	281	42.31 N	83.33 W
Spencer Gulf ⊂	166	34.00 S	137.00 E
Spencer Lake ⊜	224	47.16 N	122.57 W
Spencerport	210	43.11 N	77.48 W
Spencertown	210	42.20 N	73.33 W
Spencerville, On., Can.	212	44.51 N	75.33 W
Spencerville, In., U.S.	216	41.16 N	84.55 W
Spencerville, Md., U.S.	208	39.06 N	76.58 W
Spencerville, Oh., U.S.	216	40.42 N	84.21 W
Spences Bridge	182	50.25 N	121.21 W
Spenge	52	52.08 N	8.28 E
Spennymoor	44	54.42 N	1.35 W
Spenser Mountains ⋀	172	42.15 S	172.30 E
Sperenberg	54	52.08 N	13.22 E
Sperillen ⊜	26	60.28 N	10.03 E
Sperling	224	49.08 N	122.33 W
Sperlinga	70	37.46 N	14.21 E
Sperlonga	66	41.15 N	13.26 E
Spermaceti Cove ⊂	276	40.26 N	73.59 W
Sperone, Capo ›	71	38.57 N	8.25 E
Sperrin Mountains ⋀	48	54.50 N	7.05 W
Sperry Creek ≃	279a	41.29 N	81.53 W
Sperry Rand Corporation ⊍[3]	276	40.45 N	73.42 W
Sperryville	188	38.39 N	78.13 W
Spessart ◆[1]	56	50.10 N	9.20 E
Spesutie Island I	208	39.27 N	76.05 W
Spétsai I	38	37.16 N	23.08 E
Spevakovka	83	49.03 N	38.54 E
Spexard	52	51.52 N	8.24 E
Spey ≃	46	57.40 N	3.06 W
Spey Bay ⊂	46	57.41 N	3.00 W
Speyer	56	49.19 N	8.26 E
Speyerbach ≃	56	49.19 N	8.27 E
Speyside	241r	11.18 N	60.32 W
Spezia → La Spezia	62	44.07 N	9.50 E
Spezzano Albanese	68	39.40 N	16.19 E
Spezzano della Sila	68	39.18 N	16.20 E
Sphinx → Abū al-Hawl ⊥	142	29.59 N	31.08 E
Spiazzo	64	46.07 N	10.40 E
Spiceland	218	39.50 N	85.26 W
Spicer	198	45.13 N	94.56 W
Spicer Creek ≃	284a	43.02 N	78.53 W
Spicer Meadow Reservoir ⊜[1]	226	38.23 N	119.59 W
Spicheren	56	49.12 N	6.58 E
Spickard	194	40.14 N	93.35 W
Spicket ≃	283	42.42 N	71.09 W
Spieka	52	53.45 N	8.35 E
Spiekeroog I	52	53.46 N	7.42 E
Spiess Seamount ✥[3]	8	54.40 S	0.15 E
Spiez	58	46.41 N	7.39 E
Şpijkenisse	52	51.21 N	4.20 E
Špikov	78	48.46 N	28.35 E
Spilamberto	64	44.32 N	11.01 E
Spilimbergo	64	46.07 N	12.54 E
Spilinga	68	38.37 N	15.54 E
Spillersboda	40	59.42 N	18.51 E
Spillimacheen ≃	182	50.55 N	116.20 W
Spillville	190	43.12 N	91.57 W
Spilsby	44	53.11 N	0.06 E
Spinazzola	68	40.58 N	16.06 E
Spīn Būldak	120	31.01 N	66.24 E
Spincourt	56	49.20 N	5.40 E
Spindale	192	35.21 N	81.55 W
Spindoli	66	43.12 N	12.54 E
Spinea-Orgnano	64	45.29 N	12.10 E
Spinetta Marengo	62	44.53 N	8.41 E
Spinnerstown	208	40.26 N	75.26 W
Spinoso	68	40.16 N	15.58 E
Spires → Speyer	56	49.19 N	8.26 E
Spirit Lake, Id., U.S.	202	47.57 N	116.52 W
Spirit Lake, Ia., U.S.	198	43.25 N	95.06 W
Spirit Lake ⊜	224	46.16 N	122.08 W
Spirit River	182	55.47 N	118.50 W
Spiritwood	184	53.22 N	107.31 W
Spiro	194	35.14 N	94.37 W
Spirovo	76	57.26 N	34.59 E
Spišská Nová Ves	30	48.57 N	20.34 E
Spitak	84	40.51 N	44.16 E
Spital am Pyhrn	61	47.39 N	14.20 E
Spithead ›	42	50.45 N	1.05 W
Spit Point ›	162	20.02 S	119.00 E
Spitsbergen I	12	78.45 N	16.00 E
Spitsbergen Bank ✥[4]	12	76.00 N	23.00 E
Spittal an der Drau	64	46.48 N	13.30 E
Spittal of Glenshee	46	56.48 N	3.28 W
Spitz	61	48.22 N	15.25 E
Spitzbergen und Jan Mayen → Svalbard □[2]	12	78.00 N	20.00 E
Spitzer Berg ∧[2]	264a	52.38 N	13.35 E
Spixworth	42	52.40 N	1.20 E
Spjelkavik	26	62.28 N	6.23 E
Splavnucha	80	51.05 N	45.22 E
Splendora	222	30.14 N	95.10 W
Split	36	43.31 N	16.27 E
Split, Cape ›	186	45.20 N	64.30 W
Split Lake ⊜	184	56.08 N	96.15 W
Splitrock Reservoir ⊜[1]	276	40.58 N	74.27 W
Spluga, Passo della (Splügenpass) ⟩⟨	58	46.30 N	9.20 E
Splügen	58	46.33 N	9.20 E
Splügenpass (Passo della Spluga) ⟩⟨	58	46.30 N	9.20 E
Spodsbjerg	41	54.56 N	10.50 E
Spofford	196	29.11 N	100.25 W
Spoği	76	56.05 N	26.44 E
Spokane	202	47.39 N	117.25 W
Spokane ≃	202	47.54 N	118.20 W
Spokane, Mount ∧	202	47.55 N	117.07 W
Spokane Indian Reservation ◆[4]	202	47.55 N	118.00 W
Şpokojnaja	84	44.15 N	41.25 E
Špola	78	49.01 N	31.24 E
Spoleto	66	42.44 N	12.44 E
Spoltore	66	42.27 N	14.08 E
Spondigna	64	46.38 N	10.37 E
Spondon	42	52.54 N	1.25 W
Sponds Hill ∧[2]	262	53.19 N	2.03 W
Spóng	110	13.27 N	105.34 E
Spoon ≃	194	40.18 N	90.04 W
Spooner	190	45.49 N	91.53 W
Spořice	54	50.26 N	13.25 E
Spornitz	54	53.24 N	11.43 E
Spornoje	74	62.20 N	151.03 E
Sporovo	76	52.25 N	25.20 E
Spørring	41	56.18 N	10.09 E
Sportforum ♠	264a	52.33 N	13.29 E
Sport Hill	207	41.14 N	73.16 W
Sporting Hill	208	40.09 N	76.26 W
Sportsman's Park Race Track ♠	278	41.50 N	87.46 W
Spotorno	62	44.14 N	8.25 E
Spot Pond ⊜	283	42.27 N	71.06 W
Spotswood, Austl.	274b	37.50 S	144.53 E
Spotswood, N.J., U.S.	208	40.23 N	74.23 W
Spotsylvania	208	38.12 N	77.35 W
Spotsylvania □[6]	208	38.15 N	77.30 W
Spotsylvania Court House Battlefield ⊥	208	38.15 N	77.35 W
Sprague, Mb., Can.	184	49.02 N	95.38 W
Sprague, Wa., U.S.	202	47.18 N	117.58 W
Sprague ≃	202	42.34 N	121.51 W
Sprague, North Fork ≃	202	42.26 N	121.07 W
Sprague, South Fork ≃	202	42.26 N	121.07 W
Spragueville	207	41.53 N	71.32 W
Sprain Ridge Park ♠	276	40.59 N	73.51 W
Sprankle Mills	214	41.00 N	79.07 W
Spratly Islands II	108	10.00 N	114.00 E
Spratt Point ›	212	44.36 N	80.01 W
Spray	202	44.50 N	119.47 W
Spray Lakes Reservoir ⊜[1]	182	50.55 N	115.20 W
Spreča ≃	38	44.45 N	18.06 E
Spreckels	226	36.36 N	121.34 W
Spreckelsville	229a	20.53 N	156.24 W
Spree ≃	54	52.32 N	13.13 E
Spreenhagen	54	52.20 N	13.52 E
Spreeufontein	158	33.22 S	20.45 E
Spreewald ◆[1]	54	51.50 N	14.05 E
Spremberg	54	51.34 N	14.22 E
Sprendlingen	56	49.51 N	7.59 E
Spresiano	64	45.46 N	12.16 E
Spring	222	30.04 N	95.25 W
Spring ≃, U.S.	194	36.52 N	94.44 W
Spring ≃, Ar., U.S.	194	36.08 N	91.05 W
Spring, North Fork ≃	194	37.18 N	94.21 W
Spring, South Fork ≃	194	36.19 N	91.30 W
Spring Arbor	216	42.12 N	84.33 W
Spring Bay ⊂	200	41.40 N	112.50 W
Springbok	156	29.43 S	17.55 E
Springboro, Oh., U.S.	218	39.33 N	84.14 W
Springboro, Pa., U.S.	214	41.48 N	80.22 W
Spring Branch ≃	284b	39.26 N	76.35 W
Springbrook, On., Can.	275b	43.39 N	79.47 W
Springbrook, Md., U.S.	284c	39.03 N	77.00 W
Spring Brook, N.Y., U.S.	210	42.49 N	78.40 W
Spring Brook ≃	278	41.58 N	87.59 W
Springbrook Forest	284c	39.03 N	77.01 W
Springburn	172	43.40 S	171.28 E
Spring City, Pa., U.S.	208	40.10 N	75.32 W
Spring City, Tn., U.S.	192	35.41 N	84.51 W
Spring City, Ut,. U.S.	200	39.28 N	111.29 W
Spring Coulee V	198	48.31 N	100.54 W
Spring Creek, N.Z.	172	41.28 S	173.58 E
Spring Creek, Pa., U.S.	214	41.53 N	79.32 W
Spring Creek ≃, Austl.	166	24.12 S	140.58 E
Spring Creek ≃, U.S.	198	40.30 N	101.21 W
Spring Creek ≃, Ga., U.S.	192	30.54 N	84.45 W
Spring Creek ≃, Il., U.S.	216	40.49 N	87.50 W
Spring Creek ≃, Il., U.S.	219	39.52 N	89.37 W
Spring Creek ≃, Il., U.S.	278	41.32 N	88.04 W
Spring Creek ≃, Mo., U.S.	219	38.21 N	91.10 W
Spring Creek ≃, Nv., U.S.	204	39.55 N	117.50 W
Spring Creek ≃, N.D., U.S.	198	47.15 N	101.48 W
Spring Creek ≃, Pa., U.S.	214	41.24 N	78.57 W
Spring Creek ≃, Pa., U.S.	214	40.56 N	77.47 W
Spring Creek ≃, S.D., U.S.	198	45.54 N	100.18 W
Spring Creek ≃, S.D., U.S.	198	43.52 N	102.42 W
Spring Creek ≃, Tx., U.S.	222	30.02 N	95.16 W
Springdale, Nf., Can.	186	49.30 N	56.04 W
Springdale, Ar., U.S.	194	36.11 N	94.07 W
Springdale, Oh., U.S.	218	39.17 N	84.28 W
Springdale, Pa., U.S.	214	40.32 N	79.47 W
Springdale, S.C., U.S.	192	33.57 N	81.06 W
Springdale, Ut,. U.S.	200	37.11 N	112.59 W
Springdale, Wa., U.S.	202	48.03 N	117.44 W
Spring Dale, W.V., U.S.	192	37.52 N	80.48 W
Springe	52	52.12 N	9.32 E
Springer	196	36.21 N	104.35 W
Springers Brook ≃	285	39.44 N	74.41 W
Springerville	200	34.08 N	109.17 W
Springfield, N.S., Can.	186	44.38 N	64.52 W
Springfield, On., Can.	212	42.50 N	80.56 W
Springfield, N.Z.	172	43.20 S	171.55 E
Springfield, S. Afr.	158	29.02 S	22.53 E
Springfield, Co., U.S.	198	37.24 N	102.36 W
Springfield, Fl., U.S.	194	30.09 N	85.36 W
Springfield, Ga., U.S.	192	32.22 N	81.18 W
Springfield, Il., U.S.	219	39.48 N	89.38 W
Springfield, Ky., U.S.	194	37.41 N	85.13 W
Springfield, Ma., U.S.	207	42.06 N	72.35 W
Springfield, Mi., U.S.	216	42.19 N	85.14 W
Springfield, Mn., U.S.	198	44.14 N	94.58 W
Springfield, Mo., U.S.	194	37.12 N	93.17 W
Springfield, N.J., U.S.	276	40.43 N	74.18 W
Springfield, Oh., U.S.	218	39.55 N	83.48 W
Springfield, Or., U.S.	202	44.02 N	123.01 W
Springfield, Pa., U.S.	285	39.55 N	75.19 W
Springfield, S.C., U.S.	192	33.29 N	81.16 W
Springfield, S.D., U.S.	198	42.51 N	97.53 W
Springfield, Tn., U.S.	194	36.30 N	86.53 W
Springfield, Vt., U.S.	188	43.17 N	72.28 W
Springfield, Va., U.S.	284c	38.45 N	77.13 W
Springfield, Lake ⊜[1]	219	39.44 N	89.36 W
Springfield Center	210	42.50 N	74.53 W
Springfield Estates	284c	38.47 N	77.11 W
Springfield Lake ⊜	285	40.11 N	75.00 W
Springfield Lake ⊜[1]	222	31.36 N	96.33 W
Springfield Mall ◆[9]	284c	38.46 N	77.11 W
Springfield Plateau ⋀[1]	194	37.10 N	93.30 W
Springfontein	158	30.19 S	25.36 E
Spring Garden	246	6.59 N	58.31 W
Spring Garden Brook ≃	276	40.46 N	74.23 W
Spring Garden Township	208	39.57 N	76.44 W
Spring Glen, N.Y., U.S.	210	41.40 N	74.26 W
Spring Glen, Pa., U.S.	208	40.38 N	76.37 W
Spring Glen, Ut,. U.S.	200	39.39 N	110.51 W
Spring Green	190	43.10 N	90.04 W
Spring Grove, Il., U.S.	216	42.26 N	88.13 W
Spring Grove, Mn., U.S.	190	43.33 N	91.38 W
Spring Grove, Pa., U.S.	208	39.52 N	76.51 W
Springhill, N.S., Can.	186	45.39 N	64.03 W
Spring Hill, Ca., U.S.	226	39.15 N	121.03 W
Spring Hill, Fl., U.S.	220	28.33 N	82.27 W
Springhill, La., U.S.	194	33.00 N	93.28 W
Spring Hill, Pa., U.S.	214	40.23 N	78.40 W
Spring Hill, Tn., U.S.	194	35.45 N	86.55 W
Spring Hill, Tx., U.S.	222	32.34 N	94.48 W
Springhills	216	40.16 N	83.22 W
Spring Hope	192	35.56 N	78.06 W
Springhouse, B.C., Can.	182	51.55 N	122.07 W
Spring House, Pa., U.S.	285	40.11 N	75.14 W
Spring Lake, Mi., U.S.	216	43.04 N	86.11 W
Spring Lake, N.J., U.S.	208	40.09 N	74.01 W
Spring Lake, N.C., U.S.	192	35.10 N	78.58 W
Spring Lake ⊜, Mi., U.S.	216	43.06 N	86.11 W
Spring Lake ⊜, N.J., U.S.	276	40.35 N	74.25 W
Spring Lake Heights	208	40.09 N	74.01 W
Spring Mill, Oh., U.S.	214	40.54 N	82.36 W
Spring Mill, Pa., U.S.	285	40.04 N	75.17 W
Spring Mill Reservoir ⊜[1]	262	53.39 N	2.13 W
Spring Mills	210	40.51 N	77.34 W
Spring Mill State Park ♠	218	38.43 N	86.25 W
Spring Mount	208	40.17 N	75.28 W
Spring Mountains ⋀	204	36.10 N	115.40 W
Spring Pond ⊜	283	42.30 N	70.57 W
Springport, In., U.S.	218	40.03 N	85.24 W
Springport, Mi., U.S.	216	42.22 N	84.41 W
Spring Run	214	40.09 N	83.47 W
Springs	158	26.13 S	28.25 E
Springs □[5]	273d	26.14 S	28.30 E
Springs Aerodrome ⊠	273d	26.15 S	28.24 E
Springside	285	40.04 N	74.51 W
Springs Junction	172	42.19 S	172.11 E
Springsure	166	24.07 S	148.05 E
Springton	168b	34.43 S	139.05 E
Springtown	222	32.58 N	97.41 W
Springvale, Austl.	162	17.48 S	127.41 E
Springvale, Austl.	166	23.33 S	140.42 E
Springvale, Austl.	169	37.57 S	145.09 E
Springvale, Me., U.S.	188	43.28 N	70.47 W
Springvale South	274b	37.58 S	145.09 E
Spring Valley, Ca., U.S.	228	32.44 N	116.59 W
Spring Valley, Il., U.S.	190	41.19 N	89.11 W
Spring Valley, Mn., U.S.	190	43.41 N	92.23 W
Spring Valley, N.Y., U.S.	210	41.06 N	74.02 W
Spring Valley, Oh., U.S.	218	39.36 N	84.00 W
Spring Valley, Tx., U.S.	222	29.47 N	95.31 W
Spring Valley, Wi., U.S.	190	44.50 N	92.14 W
Spring Valley V	204	39.15 N	114.25 W
Spring Valley Creek ≃	204	39.20 N	114.25 W
Springview	198	42.49 N	99.44 W
Springville, Al., U.S.	194	33.46 N	86.28 W
Springville, Ca., U.S.	204	36.08 N	118.49 W
Springville, Ia., U.S.	190	42.03 N	91.26 W
Springville, N.J., U.S.	285	39.56 N	74.52 W
Springville, N.Y., U.S.	210	42.30 N	78.40 W
Springville, Pa., U.S.	210	41.42 N	75.55 W
Springville, Ut,. U.S.	200	40.09 N	111.36 W
Springwater	210	42.38 N	77.35 W
Springwood	170	33.42 S	150.33 E
Sprint ≃	44	54.22 N	2.45 W
Sprite Creek ≃	210	43.08 N	74.44 W
Sproat Lake ⊜	182	49.16 N	125.03 W
Sprockhövel	56	51.22 N	7.15 E
Sprogels Run ≃	285	40.14 N	75.37 W
Sprogø I	41	55.20 N	10.58 E
Sprottau → Szprotawa	30	51.34 N	15.33 E
Sprötze	52	53.18 N	9.49 E
Sproul	214	40.16 N	78.28 W
Sprout Brook ≃	276	40.54 N	74.05 W
Spruce ≃	184	53.15 N	105.43 W
Spruce Brook	186	48.45 N	58.11 W
Spruce Creek	214	40.37 N	78.08 W
Spruce Creek ≃	210	43.07 N	74.46 W
Spruce Grove	182	53.32 N	113.55 W
Spruce Knob ∧	188	38.42 N	79.32 W
Spruce Knob-Seneca Rocks National Recreation Area ♠	188	38.50 N	79.20 W
Spruce Lake	184	53.32 N	109.05 W
Spruce Mountain ∧, Az., U.S.	200	34.28 N	112.24 W
Spruce Mountain ∧, Nv., U.S.	204	40.33 N	114.49 W
Spruce Pine, Al., U.S.	194	34.23 N	87.43 W
Spruce Pine, N.C., U.S.	192	35.54 N	82.03 W
Spruce Run Reservoir ⊜[1]	210	40.40 N	74.57 W
Spruce Run State Park ♠	210	40.40 N	74.56 W
Spruce Woods Provincial Park ♠	184	49.42 N	99.05 W
Spry	208	39.55 N	76.41 W
Spry Lake ⊜	212	44.44 N	81.15 W
Spulico, Capo ›	68	39.58 N	16.39 E
Spur	196	33.28 N	100.51 W
Spurfield	182	55.13 N	114.16 W
Spurger	194	30.42 N	94.11 W
Spurn Head ›	44	53.34 N	0.07 E
Spurr, Mount ∧	180	61.18 N	152.15 W
Sputendorf	264a	52.20 N	13.13 E
Spuzzum	182	49.41 N	121.25 W
Spy Hill	184	50.36 N	101.41 W
Spy Pond ⊜	283	42.24 N	71.09 W
Squally Channel ʊ	182	53.10 N	129.15 W
Squamish	182	49.42 N	123.09 W
Squamish ≃	182	49.45 N	123.09 W
Squam Lake ⊜	188	43.45 N	71.32 W
Square Butte Creek ≃	198	46.55 N	100.55 W
Square Lake ⊜	186	47.03 N	68.20 W
Squatec	186	47.53 N	68.43 W
Squaw Cap Mountain ∧	186	47.53 N	66.53 W
Squaw Creek ≃, Id., U.S.	202	43.51 N	116.22 W
Squaw Creek ≃, Il., U.S.	278	42.21 N	88.07 W
Squaw Creek ≃, Or., U.S.	202	44.27 N	121.20 W
Squaw Creek Lake ⊜[1]	222	32.19 N	97.47 W
Squaw Harbor	180	55.11 N	160.30 W
Squaw Hill ∧	200	41.48 N	105.02 W
Squaw Island I	284a	42.56 N	78.54 W
Squaw Peak ∧, Ca., U.S.	226	39.11 N	120.16 W
Squaw Peak ∧, Mt., U.S.	202	47.10 N	114.21 W
Squaw Rapids	184	53.41 N	103.20 W
Squaw Rapids Dam ◆[6]	184	53.40 N	103.25 W
Squaw Run ≃	279b	40.29 N	79.52 W
Squaw Valley State Recreation Area ♠	226	39.12 N	120.15 W
Squibnocket Point ›	207	41.18 N	70.47 W
Squilax	182	50.52 N	119.35 W
Squillace	68	38.47 N	16.31 E
Squillace, Golfo di ⊂	68	38.50 N	16.50 E
Squinzano	68	40.26 N	18.03 E
Squire	192	37.14 N	81.36 W
Squires, Mount ∧	162	26.12 S	127.28 E
Squirrel ≃	180	66.57 N	160.27 W
Squirrel Hill ◆[8]	279b	40.26 N	79.55 W
Squirrel Hill Tunnel ◆[5]	279b	40.26 N	79.55 W
Squirrel's Heath ◆[8]	260	51.35 N	0.13 E
Şragen	115a	7.26 S	111.02 E
Šramkovka	78	50.10 N	32.05 E
Srbija (Serbia) □[3]	38	44.00 N	21.00 E
Srbija □[9]	38	43.00 N	21.00 E
Srbobran	38	45.33 N	19.48 E
Srê Âmbĕl	110	11.07 N	103.46 E
Sredinnyj chrebet ⋀	74	56.00 N	158.00 E
Sredna Gora ⋀	38	42.30 N	25.00 E
Sredn'aja Achtuba	80	48.43 N	44.52 E
Sredn'aja Mokla ≃	88	55.01 N	119.37 E
Sredn'aja Nanaki, gora ∧	89	52.26 N	132.50 E
Sredn'aja Ol'okma	88	55.26 N	120.33 E
Srednegorje	76	60.34 N	29.25 E
Sredneje Kujto, ozero ⊜	24	65.08 N	31.15 E
Srednekolymsk	74	67.27 N	153.41 E
Srednerusskaja vozvyšennost' ⋀[1]	72	52.00 N	38.00 E
Srednesibirskoje ploskogorje ⋀[1]	74	65.00 N	105.00 E
Srednij Ikorec	78	51.05 N	39.45 E
Srednij Kalar	88	55.51 N	117.24 E
Srednij Ural ⋀	86	58.00 N	59.00 E
Srednij Urgal	89	51.09 N	132.59 E
Srednij Vas'ugan	86	59.16 N	78.15 E
Srednyj	83	48.09 N	39.50 E
Srê Khtŭm	110	12.10 N	106.52 E
Śrem	30	52.08 N	17.01 E
Srê Moăt	110	13.18 N	107.10 E
Sremska Mitrovica	38	44.58 N	19.37 E
Sremski Karlovci	38	45.12 N	19.57 E
Srêng ≃	110	13.21 N	103.27 E
Srêpŏk ≃	110	13.33 N	106.16 E
Sretensk	88	52.15 N	117.43 E
Sretenskoje	88	56.28 N	96.25 E
Srīdharpur	126	23.04 N	89.25 E
Sri Hargobindpur	123	31.41 N	75.39 E
Sri Jayawardenepura (Kotte)	122	6.54 N	79.54 E
Srīkākulam	122	18.18 N	83.54 E
Sri Kālahasti	122	13.45 N	79.43 E
Sri Lanka □[1], Asia	118	7.00 N	81.00 E
Sri Lanka □[1], Asia	122	7.00 N	81.00 E
Srīnagar, Bngl.	126	23.32 N	90.18 E
Srīnagar, India	123	34.05 N	74.49 E
Srīnagar, India	124	30.13 N	78.47 E
Srīnagar Airport ⊠	123	34.00 N	74.52 E
Srīpur, Bngl.	126	23.36 N	89.24 E
Srīpur, Bngl.	126	24.12 N	90.29 E
Srīrampur, India	122	19.34 N	74.34 E
Srirāmpur, India	272b	22.49 N	88.29 E
Srīrangam	122	10.52 N	78.41 E
Srīvardhan	122	18.02 N	73.01 E
Srīvilliputtūr	122	9.31 N	77.38 E
Środa Śląska	30	51.10 N	16.36 E
Środa Wielkopolski	30	52.14 N	17.17 E
Srpska Crnja	38	45.43 N	20.42 E
Ssangmun-ni ◆[8]	271b	37.39 N	127.02 E
Ssuchunghsi	100	22.06 N	120.44 E
Ssup'ing → Siping	89	43.12 N	124.20 E
Staaken ◆[8]	264a	52.32 N	13.08 E
Staaten ≃	164	16.24 S	141.17 E
Staaten River National Park ♠	164	16.40 S	143.00 E
Staatsburg	210	41.50 N	73.55 W
Staatz	61	48.40 N	16.29 E
Stabbursdalen Nasjonalpark ♠	24	70.06 N	24.30 E
Staberhuk ›	54	54.24 N	11.19 E
Stabroek	50	51.20 N	4.22 E
Stachanov	83	48.34 N	38.40 E
Stachy	60	49.06 N	13.40 E
Stack, Loch ⊜	46	58.20 N	4.55 W
Stackpoie Head ›	42	51.37 N	4.54 W
Stack Skerry I[2]	46	59.01 N	4.31 W
Stacksteads	262	53.41 N	2.13 W
Stacyville	190	43.26 N	92.46 W
Stad-Delden	52	52.16 N	6.42 E
Stade	52	53.36 N	9.28 E
Staden, Bel.	50	50.59 N	3.01 E
Staden, B.R.D.	56	50.20 N	8.54 E
Städjan ∧	26	61.55 N	12.52 E
Stadl an der Mur	61	47.05 N	13.58 E
Stadlandet ›[1]	26	62.07 N	5.18 E
Stadlau ◆[8]	264b	48.14 N	16.28 E
Stadl-Paura	64	48.05 N	13.53 E
Stadskanaal	52	53.00 N	6.55 E
Stadtallendorf	56	50.50 N	9.01 E
Stadtbergen	58	48.22 N	10.50 E
Stadt Haag	30	48.07 N	14.34 E
Stadthagen	52	52.19 N	9.13 E
Stadtilm	54	50.47 N	11.05 E
Städtische Rahmede	263	51.17 N	7.40 E
Stadtkyll	56	50.21 N	6.32 E
Stadtlauringen	56	50.11 N	10.22 E
Stadtlengsfeld	56	50.47 N	10.07 E
Stadtlohn	52	51.59 N	6.55 E
Stadtoldendorf	52	51.53 N	9.37 E
Stadtprozelten	56	49.47 N	9.25 E
Stadtroda	54	50.51 N	11.44 E
Stadtsteinach	54	50.09 N	11.30 E
Stadt Wehlen	54	50.58 N	14.02 E
Stadum	41	54.44 N	9.03 E
Stäfa	58	47.15 N	8.44 E
Staffa I	46	56.25 N	6.20 W
Staffanstorp	41	55.38 N	13.13 E
Staffelberg ∧	56	50.06 N	11.02 E
Staffelde	264a	52.44 N	13.00 E
Staffelsee ⊜	64	47.42 N	11.10 E
Staffelstein	56	50.06 N	11.00 E
Staffin	46	57.37 N	6.12 W
Staffora ≃	62	45.04 N	9.01 E
Stafford, Eng., U.K.	42	52.48 N	2.07 W
Stafford, Ct., U.S.	207	41.59 N	72.17 W
Stafford, Ks., U.S.	198	37.57 N	98.36 W
Stafford, N.Y., U.S.	210	42.59 N	78.04 W
Stafford, Tx., U.S.	222	29.37 N	95.34 W
Stafford, Va., U.S.	208	38.25 N	77.24 W
Stafford □[6]	208	38.25 N	77.30 W
Staffordshire □[6]	28	52.50 N	2.00 W
Stafford Springs	207	41.57 N	72.18 W
Staffordsville	188	37.49 N	82.50 W
Staffordville	207	41.59 N	72.15 W
Stagen	112	3.18 S	116.10 E
Stag Pond ⊜	276	40.59 N	74.42 W
Stahl-Berg ∧[2]	264a	52.21 N	13.46 E
Stahlbrode	54	54.14 N	13.17 E
Stahle	52	51.50 N	9.25 E
Stahnsdorf	54	52.23 N	13.13 E
Stahringen	58	47.47 N	8.58 E
Staicele	76	57.50 N	24.45 E
Staines	42	51.26 N	0.31 W
Staines Reservoirs ⊜[1]	260	51.27 N	0.30 W
Stainforth	44	53.36 N	1.01 W
Staining	44	53.49 N	2.59 W
Stainland	262	53.40 N	1.53 W
Stainmore Forest ◆[3]	44	54.30 N	2.10 W
Stains	261	48.57 N	2.23 E
Stainz	61	46.54 N	15.16 E
Stairtown	222	29.43 N	97.44 W
Stajki	78	50.05 N	30.54 E
Staked Plain → Estacado, Llano ≚	196	33.30 N	102.40 W
Stäket	40	59.28 N	17.48 E
Stakroge	41	55.53 N	8.51 E
Stalać	38	43.40 N	21.25 E
Stalbridge	42	50.58 N	2.23 W
Stalden	58	46.14 N	7.52 E
Stalettì	68	38.46 N	16.32 E
Stalham	42	52.47 N	1.31 E
Stalheim	26	60.50 N	6.40 E
Stalhofen	61	47.05 N	15.16 E
Stalin → Varna, Blg.	38	43.13 N	27.55 E
Stalin → Brașov, Rom.	38	45.39 N	25.37 E
Stalin (Kuçovë), Shq.	38	40.48 N	19.54 E
Stalinabad → Dušanbe	85	38.35 N	68.48 E
Stalingrad → Volgograd	80	48.44 N	44.25 E
Stalino → Doneck	83	48.00 N	37.48 E
Stalinogorsk → Novomoskovsk	82	54.05 N	38.13 E
Stalinogród → Katowice	30	50.16 N	19.00 E
Stalinsk → Novokuzneck	86	53.45 N	87.06 E
Stallarholmen	40	59.22 N	17.12 E
Ställberg	40	59.59 N	14.55 E
Ställdalen	40	59.56 N	14.56 E
Stallwang	60	49.03 N	12.40 E
Stalowa Wola	30	50.35 N	22.02 E
Stalybridge, Eng., U.K.	44	53.29 N	2.03 W
Stalybridge, Eng., U.K.	262	53.29 N	2.04 W
Stambaugh	190	46.04 N	88.37 W
Stamford, Austl.	166	21.16 S	143.49 E
Stamford, Eng., U.K.	42	52.39 N	0.29 W
Stamford, Ct., U.S.	207	41.03 N	73.32 W
Stamford, N.Y., U.S.	210	42.24 N	74.36 W
Stamford, Tx., U.S.	196	32.56 N	99.48 W
Stamford, Vt., U.S.	207	42.45 N	73.04 W
Stamford, Lake ⊜[1]	196	33.05 N	99.35 W
Stamford Bridge	44	53.59 N	0.55 W
Stamford Brige Stadium ♠	260	51.29 N	0.11 W
Stamford Harbor ⊂	276	41.02 N	73.32 W
Stamford Museum ⊍	276	41.07 N	73.33 W
Stammbach	54	50.09 N	11.41 E
Stammersdorf ◆[8]	264b	48.18 N	16.25 E
Stammham	60	48.15 N	12.53 E
Stammheim, B.R.D.	56	48.41 N	8.46 E
Stammheim, Schw.	58	47.38 N	8.47 E
Stampede Reservoir ⊜[1]	226	39.29 N	120.07 W
Stamping Ground	218	38.16 N	84.41 W
Stampriet	156	24.20 S	18.28 E
Stamps	194	33.21 N	93.29 W
Stams	64	47.16 N	10.59 E
Stanaford	188	37.48 N	81.09 W
Stanardsville	188	38.17 N	78.26 W
Stanberry	194	40.13 N	94.32 W
Stanborough	260	51.47 N	0.13 W
Stancija-Gorčakovo	85	40.25 N	71.45 E
Stancionno-Ojašinskij	86	55.28 N	83.53 E
Standard, Ab., Can.	182	51.07 N	112.59 W
Standard, Ak., U.S.	180	64.47 N	148.32 W
Standard, Ca., U.S.	226	37.59 N	120.20 W
Standard, Pa., U.S.	214	40.10 N	79.32 W
Standard Oil Company Refinery ⊍[3]	282	37.57 N	122.24 W
Standard Shaft	279b	40.10 N	79.32 W
Standedge Canal Tunnel ◆[5]	262	53.34 N	2.00 W
Standedge Railway Tunnel ◆[5]	262	53.34 N	2.00 W
Standerton	158	26.58 S	29.07 E
Standiford Field ⊠	218	38.11 N	85.44 W
Standing Rock Indian Reservation ◆[4]	198	45.50 N	101.10 W
Standing Stone Creek ≃	214	40.30 N	78.00 W
Standing Stones ⊥	46	58.12 N	6.48 W
Standish, Eng., U.K.	44	53.36 N	2.41 W
Standish, Mi., U.S.	190	43.58 N	83.57 W
Standish Monument ⊥	283	42.01 N	70.41 W
Standon	42	51.53 N	0.02 E
Stanfield, Az., U.S.	200	32.52 N	111.57 W
Stanfield, Or., U.S.	202	45.46 N	119.12 W
Stanford, S. Afr.	158	34.26 S	19.29 E
Stanford, Ca., U.S.	226	37.25 N	122.08 W
Stanford, Ky., U.S.	192	37.31 N	84.39 W
Stanford, Mt., U.S.	202	47.09 N	110.13 W
Stanford Center ◆[9]	282	37.27 N	122.10 W
Stanford Heights	210	42.46 N	73.53 W
Stanford le Hope	42	51.31 N	0.26 E
Stanford Linear Accelerator ⊍[3]	282	37.25 N	122.12 W
Stanford Rivers	260	51.41 N	0.13 E
Stanford University ⊍[2]	282	37.26 N	122.10 W
Stanfordville	210	41.52 N	73.43 W
Stånga	26	57.17 N	18.28 E
Stångån ≃	26	58.27 N	15.37 E
Stångby	41	55.46 N	13.10 E
Stange	26	60.43 N	11.11 E
Stanger	158	29.27 S	31.14 E
Stanghella	64	45.08 N	11.45 E
Stanhope, Eng., U.K.	44	54.45 N	2.01 W
Stanhope, Ia., U.S.	190	42.17 N	93.47 W
Stanhope, N.J., U.S.	210	40.54 N	74.42 W
Staničnо-Luganskoje	83	48.39 N	39.30 E
Stanislaus □[6]	226	37.39 N	121.00 W
Stanislaus ≃	226	37.40 N	121.14 W
Stanislaus, Clark Fork ≃	226	38.22 N	119.52 W
Stanislaus, Middle Fork ≃	226	38.09 N	120.21 W
Stanislaus, North Fork ≃	226	38.09 N	120.21 W

Symbol	English	Deutsch	Español	Français	Português
≃	River	Fluß	Río	Rivière	Rio
⩧	Canal	Kanal	Canal	Canal	Canal
⌞	Waterfall, Rapids	Wasserfall, Stromschnellen	Cascada, Rápidos	Chute d'eau, Rapides	Cascata, Rápidos
ʊ	Strait	Meeresstraße	Estrecho	Détroit	Estreito
⊂	Bay, Gulf	Bucht, Golf	Bahía, Golfo	Baie, Golfe	Baía, Golfo
⊜	Lake, Lakes	See, Seen	Lago, Lagos	Lac, Lacs	Lago, Lagos
≝	Swamp	Sumpf	Pantano	Marais	Pântano
⍓	Ice Features, Glacier	Eis- und Gletscherformen	Accidentes Glaciales	Formes glaciaires	Acidentes glaciares
≚	Other Hydrographic Features	Andere Hydrographische Objekte	Otros Elementos Hidrográficos	Autres données hydrographiques	Outros acidentes hidrográficos
✥	Submarine Features	Untermeerische Objekte	Accidentes Submarinos	Formes de relief sous-marin	Acidentes submarinos
□	Political Unit	Politische Einheit	Unidad Politica	Entité politique	Unidade política
⊍	Cultural Institution	Kulturelle Institution	Institución Cultural	Institution culturelle	Instituição cultural
⊥	Historical Site	Historische Stätte	Sitio Histórico	Site historique	Sitio histórico
♠	Recreational Site	Erholungs- und Ferienort	Sitio de Recreo	Centre de loisirs	Area de Lazer
⊠	Airport	Flughafen	Aeropuerto	Aéroport	Aeroporto
■	Military Installation	Militäranlage	Instalación Militar	Installation militaire	Instalação militar
◆	Miscellaneous	Verschiedenes	Misceláneo	Divers	Diversos

Name / Name	Page / Seite	Lat.°′ / Breite°′	Long.°′ / Länge°′ E = Ost
Stanislaus, South Fork ≃	226	38.04 N	120.25 W
Stanislav, S.S.S.R.	78	46.34 N	32.09 E
Stanislav → Ivano-Frankovsk, S.S.S.R.	78	48.55 N	24.43 E
Stanislavčik	78	48.58 N	28.07 E
Stanisławów → Ivano-Frankovsk	78	48.55 N	24.43 E
Stanke Dimitrov	38	42.16 N	23.07 E
Staňkov	60	49.34 N	13.04 E
Stanley, Austl.	166	40.46 S	145.18 E
Stanley, N.B., Can.	186	46.17 N	66.44 W
Stanley, Falk. Is.	254	51.42 S	57.51 W
Stanley, H.K.	271d	22.13 N	114.12 E
Stanley, Eng., U.K.	44	54.52 N	1.42 W
Stanley, Scot., U.K.	46	56.28 N	3.27 W
Stanley, N.Y., U.S.	210	42.49 N	77.06 W
Stanley, N.C., U.S.	192	35.21 N	81.05 W
Stanley, N.D., U.S.	198	48.19 N	102.23 W
Stanley, Va., U.S.	188	38.34 N	78.30 W
Stanley, Wi., U.S.	190	44.57 N	90.56 W
Stanley ≃	171a	27.09 S	152.32 E
Stanley, Mont ∧[2]	273b	4.19 S	15.15 E
Stanley Bay ⊂	271d	22.12 N	114.12 E
Stanley Falls ⌞	154	0.30 N	25.12 E
Stanley Mills	275b	43.46 N	79.44 W
Stanley Mound ∧	271d	22.14 N	114.12 E
Stanley Park ♦, B.C., Can.	224	49.19 N	123.09 W
Stanley Park ♦, Eng., U.K.	262	53.26 N	2.57 W
Stanley Park ♦, Eng., U.K.	262	53.49 N	3.02 W
Stanley Reservoir ⊜[1]	122	11.54 N	77.50 E
Stanleyville → Kisangani	154	0.30 N	25.12 E
Stanlow	44	53.17 N	2.52 W
Stanmore ✦[8]	260	51.37 N	0.19 W
Stannards	210	42.05 N	77.55 W
Stann Creek	232	16.58 N	88.13 W
Stannington	44	55.06 N	1.40 W
Stanovoj chrebet ✱	74	56.20 N	126.00 E
Stanovoje nagorje (Stanovoy Mountains) ✱	88	56.00 N	114.00 E
Stanovoj Kolodez'	76	52.51 N	36.16 E
Stanovoy Mountains → Stanovoje nagorje ✱	88	56.00 N	114.00 E
Stans	58	46.57 N	8.22 E
Stansbury	168b	34.55 S	137.47 E
Stansmore Range ✱	162	21.23 S	128.33 E
Stansstad	58	46.59 N	8.20 E
Stanstead	206	45.01 N	72.05 W
Stanstead □[6]	206	45.10 N	72.00 W
Stanstead Abbots	42	51.47 N	0.01 E
Stansted	260	51.20 N	0.18 E
Stansted Mountfitchet	42	51.54 N	0.12 E
Stanthorpe	166	28.39 S	151.57 E
Stanton, Eng., U.K.	42	52.19 N	0.53 E
Stanton, Ca., U.S.	228	33.48 N	117.59 W
Stanton, De., U.S.	208	39.43 N	75.37 W
Stanton, Ia., U.S.	198	41.05 N	95.11 W
Stanton, Ky., U.S.	192	37.50 N	83.51 W
Stanton, Mi., U.S.	190	43.17 N	85.04 W
Stanton, Mo., U.S.	219	38.16 N	91.06 W
Stanton, Ne., U.S.	198	41.57 N	97.13 W
Stanton, N.D., U.S.	198	47.19 N	101.22 W
Stanton, Tn., U.S.	194	35.27 N	89.24 W
Stanton, Tx., U.S.	196	32.07 N	101.47 W
Stantonsburg	192	35.36 N	77.49 W
Stanwell	260	51.27 N	0.29 W
Stanwell Moor	260	51.28 N	0.30 W
Stanwood	224	48.14 N	122.22 W
Stanwood Gardens	285	40.07 N	74.57 W
Stanwyck Estates	285	39.42 N	75.33 W
Stanzach	58	47.23 N	10.34 E
Stanz im Mürztal	61	47.28 N	15.30 E
Stapelburg	54	51.53 N	10.40 E
Stapelfeld	52	53.36 N	10.13 E
Staphorst	52	52.37 N	6.12 E
Stapleford	42	52.56 N	1.16 W
Stapleford Abbotts	260	51.38 N	0.10 E
Stapleford Aerodrome ⊠	260	51.39 N	0.08 E
Stapleford Tawney	260	51.40 N	0.11 E
Staplehurst	42	51.10 N	0.33 E
Staples	198	46.21 N	94.47 W
Stapleton, Al., U.S.	194	30.44 N	87.47 W
Stapleton, Ne., U.S.	198	41.28 N	100.30 W
Staporków	30	51.09 N	20.34 E
Star', S.S.S.R.	76	53.37 N	34.09 E
Star, Ms., U.S.	194	32.05 N	90.02 W
Star, N.C., U.S.	192	35.24 N	79.47 W
Stará Boleslav	54	50.12 N	14.42 E
Starachowice	30	51.03 N	21.04 E
Stara Fužina	64	46.17 N	13.54 E
Staraja	265a	59.55 N	30.38 E
Staraja Belica, S.S.S.R.	76	54.42 N	29.38 E
Staraja Belica, S.S.S.R.	78	51.59 N	35.13 E
Staraja Belogorka	82	52.05 N	53.17 E
Staraja Derevn'a ✦[8]	265a	59.59 N	30.15 E
Staraja Duginka	82	54.20 N	38.45 E
Staraja Kriuša	78	50.12 N	41.09 E
Staraja Kulatka	80	52.43 N	47.37 E
Staraja Kupavna	82	55.48 N	38.10 E
Staraja Majačka	78	46.30 N	33.11 E
Staraja Majna	80	54.36 N	48.57 E
Staraja Poltavka	80	50.28 N	46.28 E
Staraja Porubežka	80	52.03 N	49.11 E
Staraja Račejka	80	53.22 N	48.03 E
Staraja Rudn'a	76	52.50 N	30.17 E
Staraja Russa	76	58.00 N	31.23 E
Staraja Ruza	82	55.39 N	36.20 E
Staraja Sachča	80	54.25 N	49.58 E
Staraja Sin'ava	78	49.36 N	27.37 E
Staraja Sitn'a	82	54.56 N	38.09 E
Staraja Terizmorga	80	54.16 N	44.32 E
Staraja Toropa	76	56.17 N	31.40 E
Staraja Ušica	78	48.35 N	27.07 E
Staraja Veduga	78	51.48 N	38.31 E
Staraja Vičuga	80	57.16 N	41.53 E
Staraja Vyževka	78	51.27 N	24.24 E
Staranzano	64	45.49 N	13.30 E
Stara Pazova	38	44.59 N	20.10 E
Stara Planina (Balkan Mountains) ✱	38	42.45 N	25.00 E
Stará Role	54	50.14 N	12.47 E
Starav, Ben ∧	46	56.32 N	5.03 W
Stará Voda	60	50.00 N	12.36 E
Stara Zagora	38	42.25 N	25.38 E
Starbejevo	265b	55.55 N	37.26 E
Starbrick	214	41.50 N	79.12 W
Starbuck, Mb., Can.	184	49.46 N	97.36 W
Starbuck, Mn., U.S.	198	45.36 N	95.31 W
Starbuck, Wa., U.S.	202	46.31 N	118.07 W
Starbuck I	14	5.37 S	155.53 W
Starčenkovo	78	47.17 N	36.59 E
Star City, Sk., Can.	184	52.53 N	104.21 W
Star City, Ar., U.S.	194	33.56 N	91.50 W
Star City, In., U.S.	216	40.58 N	86.33 W
Starcross	42	50.38 N	3.27 W
Stare Czarnowo	54	53.16 N	14.45 E
Staré Sedliště	60	49.45 N	12.42 E
Starford	214	40.42 N	78.58 W
Stargard Szczeciński (Stargard in Pommern)	30	53.20 N	15.02 E
Stargo	200	33.04 N	109.21 W
Star Harbour ⊂	175e	10.47 S	162.18 E
Stari Bar	38	42.06 N	19.08 E
Starica, S.S.S.R.	76	56.30 N	34.56 E
Starica, S.S.S.R.	76	59.04 N	29.30 E
Starica, S.S.S.R.	80	48.13 N	45.56 E
Stari Grad	36	43.11 N	16.36 E
Starij R'ad	76	58.05 N	34.54 E
Starina	76	59.37 N	44.42 E
Stari Vlah ✦[1]	38	43.35 N	20.15 E
Star Junction	214	40.04 N	79.46 W
Stark □[6]	214	40.48 N	81.22 W
Starke	192	29.56 N	82.06 W
Starke □[6]	216	41.18 N	86.37 W
Starkey	210	42.32 N	76.56 W
Starkville	194	33.27 N	88.49 W
Star Lake	224	47.22 N	122.18 W
Star Mountains ✱	164	5.05 S	141.05 E
Starnberg	60	48.00 N	11.20 E
Starnberger See ⊜	64	47.55 N	11.18 E
Starnikovo	82	55.22 N	38.24 E
Staroalejskoje	86	51.00 N	82.01 E
Starobačaty	86	54.14 N	86.07 E
Starobaltačevo	86	56.01 N	55.56 E
Starobel'sk	83	49.16 N	38.56 E
Starobeševo	83	47.44 N	38.03 E
Starobin	76	52.44 N	27.28 E
Staročerkasskaja	83	47.15 N	40.03 E
Starocuruchajtuj	88	50.12 N	119.15 E
Staroderev'ankovskaja	78	46.08 N	38.58 E
Starodub	76	52.35 N	32.46 E
Starod'umejevo	80	55.16 N	54.22 E
Starogan'kino	80	53.55 N	52.15 E
Starogard Gdański	30	53.59 N	18.33 E
Staroignatjevka	83	47.32 N	37.47 E
Staroje	76	59.16 N	40.40 E
Staroje Bajsarovo	80	55.31 N	53.54 E
Staroje Drožžanoje	80	54.44 N	47.34 E
Staroje Ibrajkino	80	54.52 N	51.02 E
Staroje Jaškino	80	52.49 N	52.57 E
Staroje Jermakovo	80	54.04 N	51.59 E
Staroje Olenčevo	80	45.34 N	47.11 E
Staroje Rachino	76	58.08 N	32.39 E
Staroje Šajgovo	80	54.18 N	44.26 E
Staroje Šajmurzino	80	54.45 N	47.58 E
Staroje Selo	76	55.14 N	29.54 E
Staroje Sindrovo	80	54.25 N	44.06 E
Staroje Slavkino	80	52.34 N	45.08 E
Staroje Ustje	80	53.28 N	41.51 E
Starojurjevo	80	53.21 N	40.42 E
Starokazačje	78	46.21 N	29.59 E
Starokonstantinov	78	49.46 N	27.13 E
Starokuručevo	80	55.09 N	54.04 E
Starolaspa	83	47.34 N	37.59 E
Staroleuškovskaja	78	45.59 N	39.44 E
Starominskaja	83	47.58 N	37.36 E
Starominskaja	78	46.31 N	39.04 E
Staromlinovka	78	47.42 N	36.49 E
Staromušta	80	55.49 N	54.14 E
Staronikolajevo	82	55.37 N	36.16 E
Staropodgorodneje	82	54.46 N	38.57 E
Staropokrovka	85	42.50 N	75.18 E
Staroščerbinovskaja	78	46.37 N	38.40 E
Staroseslavino	80	53.12 N	40.25 E
Starošešminsk	80	55.22 N	51.15 E
Starosiedle	54	51.50 N	14.50 E
Starosoldatskoje	86	56.12 N	72.37 E
Starosubchangulovo	86	53.06 N	57.26 E
Starotimoškino	80	53.43 N	47.32 E
Starotitarovskaja	78	45.14 N	37.09 E
Staroutkinsk	86	57.14 N	59.20 E
Staroverovka	78	49.33 N	35.42 E
Starožilovo	80	54.14 N	39.55 E
Starožil'sk	86	50.34 N	47.17 E
Star Peak ∧	204	40.32 N	118.10 W
Starr	214	41.32 N	79.22 W
Starrucca	210	41.54 N	75.28 W
Start Bay ⊂	42	50.17 N	3.36 W
Start Point ≻	42	50.13 N	3.38 W
Startup	224	47.52 N	121.44 W
Starvation Reservoir ⊜[1]	200	40.15 N	110.30 W
Starved Rock State Park ♦	216	41.19 N	88.58 W
Staryj Ajbesi	80	54.57 N	47.03 E
Staryj-Ajdar	83	48.43 N	39.11 E
Staryj Bagr'až	80	56.54 N	51.39 E
Staryj Bir'uz'ak	84	44.47 N	46.54 E
Staryj Bol'ševik	265b	55.57 N	37.47 E
Staryj Čartorijsk	78	51.15 N	25.54 E
Staryj Chop'or	80	51.30 N	42.58 E
Staryj Čindant	88	50.33 N	115.33 E
Staryje Burasy	80	52.16 N	46.09 E
Staryje Dorogi	76	53.02 N	28.16 E
Staryje Maty	80	55.14 N	53.55 E
Staryje Popel'uchi	78	48.18 N	28.55 E
Staryje Senžary	78	49.25 N	34.27 E
Staryje Turdaki	80	53.55 N	45.29 E
Staryje Z'atcy	80	57.21 N	52.39 E
Staryj Kazangal	80	50.15 N	47.39 E
Staryj Kistruss	80	54.28 N	40.34 E
Staryj Krym, S.S.S.R.	78	45.03 N	35.05 E
Staryj Krym, S.S.S.R.	83	47.10 N	37.30 E
Staryj Lesken	84	43.20 N	43.55 E
Staryj Medved'	76	58.18 N	30.30 E
Staryj Merčik	78	50.00 N	35.35 E
Staryj Oskol	78	51.19 N	37.51 E
Staryj Sambor	78	49.27 N	22.59 E
Staryj Terek ≃	84	44.00 N	47.24 E
Staryj Tukšum	80	53.42 N	48.33 E
Starý Plzenec	60	49.42 N	13.28 E
Stary Sącz	30	49.34 N	20.38 E
Stary Zamość	54	51.51 N	14.54 E
Staszów	30	50.34 N	21.20 E
State Center	190	42.01 N	93.09 W
State College	214	40.47 N	77.51 W
State Fair Grounds ♦	284b	39.27 N	76.38 W
Stateline, Ca., U.S.	226	38.57 N	119.57 W
State Line, Ms., U.S.	194	31.26 N	88.28 W
Stateline, Nv., U.S.	204	38.58 N	119.56 W
Staten Island I	276	40.35 N	74.09 W
Staten Island Mall ✦[9]	276	40.35 N	74.10 W
Statenville	192	30.42 N	83.01 W
State Park Place	219	38.38 N	90.03 W
State Road	192	36.19 N	80.52 W
Statesboro	192	32.26 N	81.47 W
Statesville	192	35.46 N	80.53 W
Stateville Correctional Center ✦	278	41.35 N	88.06 W
Station Peak	162	21.10 S	118.11 E
Statte	68	40.34 N	17.12 E
Statue of Liberty National Monument ♦	210	40.41 N	74.03 W
Staubbachfall ⌞	58	46.35 N	7.55 E
Staufen	58	47.53 N	7.44 E
Staufenberg	56	50.40 N	8.43 E
Staughton Vale	169	37.51 S	144.17 E
Staunton, Il., U.S.	219	39.00 N	89.47 W
Staunton, Va., U.S.	188	38.08 N	79.04 W
Staunton → Roanoke ≃	192	35.56 N	76.43 W
Stavanger	26	58.58 N	5.45 E
Stave ≃	224	49.10 N	122.26 W
Stave Lake ⊜	182	49.15 N	122.21 W
Staveley	44	53.16 N	1.20 W
Stavelot	50	50.23 N	5.56 E
Stavely, Ab., Can.	182	50.10 N	113.38 W
Stavely, Eng., U.K.	44	54.22 N	2.49 W
Staveren	52	52.53 N	5.22 E
Stavern	26	59.00 N	10.02 E
Stavišče	78	49.23 N	30.12 E
Stavnoje	78	48.59 N	22.40 E
Stavropol', S.S.S.R.	72	45.02 N	41.59 E
Stavropol' → Tol'atti, S.S.S.R.	80	53.31 N	49.26 E
Stavropol' □[8]	84	44.38 N	43.30 E
Stavrovo	80	56.08 N	40.00 E
Stawell	166	37.04 S	142.46 E
Stawell ≃	166	20.38 S	142.55 E
Stawiski	30	53.23 N	22.09 E
Stawiszyn	30	51.55 N	18.07 E
Staxigoe	46	58.28 N	3.04 W
Stayner	212	44.25 N	80.05 W
Stayton	202	44.48 N	122.47 W
Stazzema	64	43.59 N	10.19 E
Steamboat	226	39.22 N	119.44 W
Steamboat Creek ≃	226	39.31 N	119.42 W
Steamboat Mountain ∧	200	41.58 N	108.58 W
Steamboat Slough ≃	226	38.11 N	121.40 W
Steamboat Springs	200	40.29 N	106.49 W
Steamburg	210	42.07 N	78.54 W
Stearns	192	36.41 N	84.28 W
Stearns Pond ⊜	283	42.37 N	71.04 W
Stębark	30	53.30 N	20.08 E
Stebbins	180	63.32 N	162.18 W
Stebl'ov	78	49.24 N	31.06 E
Stechow	54	52.38 N	12.28 E
Steckborn	58	47.40 N	8.55 E
Stederdorf	52	52.21 N	10.15 E
Stedten	54	51.26 N	11.41 E
Stedum	52	53.18 N	6.41 E
Steeg	58	47.14 N	10.17 E
Steel ≃	190	48.46 N	86.54 W
Steel City	210	40.38 N	75.20 W
Steele, Mo., U.S.	194	36.05 N	89.49 W
Steele, N.D., U.S.	198	46.51 N	99.54 W
Steele ✦[8]	263	51.27 N	7.05 E
Steele, Mount ∧	200	41.50 N	107.00 W
Steele Creek ≃, Tx., U.S.	222	31.13 N	96.19 W
Steele Creek ≃, Tx., U.S.	222	32.01 N	97.28 W
Steeles Corners	275b	43.48 N	79.25 W
Steeleville	194	38.00 N	89.39 W
Steelhead	224	49.13 N	122.19 W
Steel's Drift	158	27.21 S	29.30 E
Steels Point ≻	174c	29.02 S	168.00 E
Steels Run ≃	279b	40.25 N	79.38 W
Steelton, N.Y., U.S.	284a	42.47 N	78.49 W
Steelton, Pa., U.S.	208	40.14 N	76.50 W
Steelville	194	37.58 N	91.21 W
Steenbergen	52	51.35 N	4.19 E
Steenburg Lake ⊜	212	44.50 N	77.41 W
Steenderen	52	52.04 N	6.11 E
Steens Mountain ✱	202	42.35 N	118.40 W
Steenvoorde	50	50.48 N	2.35 E
Steenwijk	52	52.47 N	6.08 E
Steepbank ≃	184	57.01 N	111.28 W
Steephill Lake ⊜	184	55.58 N	103.08 W
Steep Holm I	42	51.21 N	3.07 W
Steeping ≃	44	53.06 N	0.18 E
Steeple Claydon	42	51.56 N	0.59 W
Steep Point ≻	162	26.08 S	113.08 E
Steep Rock	184	51.26 N	98.48 W
Stefanie, Lake (Chew Bahir) ⊜	144	4.40 N	36.50 E
Stefansson Island I	176	73.20 N	105.45 W
Ştefan Vodă	38	44.19 N	27.19 E
Steffisburg	58	46.47 N	7.39 E
Steg	58	47.21 N	8.56 E
Stegalovka	76	52.24 N	38.19 E
Stege	41	54.59 N	12.18 E
Stegeborg	26	58.26 N	16.35 E
Stege Bugt ⊂	41	55.01 N	12.50 E
Stegelitz	54	53.08 N	13.51 E
Steger	216	41.28 N	87.38 W
Stegersbach	61	47.10 N	16.10 E
Steglitz ✦[8]	264a	52.28 N	13.19 E
Stehag	41	55.54 N	13.23 E
Stehekin	224	48.18 N	120.39 W
Stehekin ≃	224	48.21 N	120.40 W
Steiermark □[3]	30	47.10 N	15.10 E
Steigerwald ✱	56	49.40 N	10.20 E
Steigra	54	51.18 N	11.39 E
Steilacoom	224	47.10 N	122.36 W
Steimbke	52	52.40 N	9.22 E
Stein, B.R.D.	60	49.25 N	11.01 E
Stein, Ned.	56	50.57 N	5.46 E
Stein, Schw.	58	47.33 N	7.58 E
Steina	54	51.12 N	14.01 E
Steinach, B.R.D.	58	48.18 N	8.04 E
Steinach, D.D.R.	54	50.25 N	11.10 E
Steinach, Öst.	64	47.05 N	11.28 E
Steinach ≃	56	50.11 N	11.12 E
Steinamanger → Szombathely	61	47.14 N	16.38 E
Stein am Rhein	58	47.40 N	8.51 E
Steinau	56	50.23 N	9.27 E
Steinau → Ścinawa	30	51.25 N	16.27 E
Steinbach, B.R.D.	56	48.43 N	8.10 E
Steinbach, Mb., Can.	184	49.32 N	96.41 W
Steinbach-Hallenberg	54	50.42 N	10.34 E
Steinberg ∧[2]	263	51.05 N	7.27 E
Steinberger Slough ≃	282	37.33 N	122.13 W
Steinbourg	56	48.46 N	7.25 E
Steindorf	61	46.42 N	14.01 E
Steinen	58	47.38 N	7.44 E
Steinernes Meer ✱	64	47.30 N	12.58 E
Steinfeld, B.R.D.	52	52.35 N	8.12 E
Steinfeld, D.D.R.	54	50.22 N	10.44 E
Steinfeld, Öst.	64	46.45 N	13.15 E
Steinfort	56	49.40 N	5.55 E
Steinforth	263	51.09 N	6.32 E
Steinfurt	52	52.09 N	7.21 E
Steingaden	58	47.42 N	10.51 E
Steinhagen, B.R.D.	52	52.00 N	8.24 E
Steinhagen, D.D.R.	54	54.13 N	12.59 E
Steinhatchee ≃	192	29.40 N	83.24 W
Steinhausen	156	21.49 S	18.20 E
Steinhausen ✦[1]	58	48.01 N	9.41 E
Steinheid	54	50.28 N	11.04 E
Steinheim, B.R.D.	52	51.52 N	9.05 E
Steinheim, B.R.D.	56	48.58 N	9.16 E
Steinheim, B.R.D.	58	48.01 N	10.09 E
Steinhöfel	54	52.24 N	14.10 E
Steinhöring	60	48.05 N	12.02 E
Steinhude	52	52.27 N	9.21 E
Steinhuder Meer ⊜	52	52.28 N	9.19 E
Steinkjer	26	64.01 N	11.30 E
Steinkopf	156	29.18 S	17.43 E
Steinloge	52	52.54 N	8.19 E
Stein-Neukirch	56	50.41 N	8.03 E
Steinpass)(	64	47.39 N	12.45 E
Steinsdorf	54	52.02 N	14.40 E
Steinshamn	26	62.47 N	6.29 E
Steinstücken ✦[8]	264a	52.23 N	13.08 E
Steinwiesen	54	50.17 N	11.28 E
Stekene	50	51.12 N	4.02 E
Stekl'anka	76	59.08 N	41.37 E
Steklino	76	56.51 N	32.10 E
Steksovo	80	55.17 N	43.25 E
Stella, It.	62	44.24 N	8.30 E
Stella, S. Afr.	158	26.38 S	24.48 E
Stella, Ne., U.S.	198	40.13 N	95.46 W
Stella Niagara	210	43.12 N	79.02 W
Stella-Plage	50	50.29 N	1.35 E
Stellaquo Indian Reserve ✦[4]	182	54.03 N	124.55 W
Stellarton	186	45.34 N	62.40 W
Stelle	52	53.23 N	10.06 E
Stellenbosch	158	33.58 S	18.50 E
Steller, Mount ∧	180	60.32 N	143.02 W
Stelvio, Parco Nazionale dello ♦	58	46.30 N	10.40 E
Stelvio, Passo dello)(	58	46.32 N	10.27 E
Stemwede	52	52.25 N	8.27 E
Stenay	56	49.29 N	5.11 E
Stendal	54	52.36 N	11.51 E
Stende	76	57.09 N	22.33 E
Stenden	263	51.25 N	6.27 E
Stenhammar slott ⊥	40	59.03 N	16.31 E
Stenhouse Bay	166	35.17 S	136.56 E
Stenhousemuir	46	56.02 N	3.48 W
Stenico	64	46.03 N	10.51 E
Stenlille	41	55.32 N	11.36 E
Stenløse	41	55.46 N	12.12 E
Stenness, Loch of ⊜	46	59.00 N	3.15 W
Stenón	267c	37.58 N	23.20 E
Stenón Návstathmou	267c	37.58 N	23.33 E
Stensätra	40	60.36 N	16.44 E
Stensele	24	65.05 N	17.09 E
Stenstorp	26	58.16 N	13.43 E
Stenstrup	41	55.07 N	10.31 E
Stentrop	263	51.30 N	7.49 E
Stenungsund	26	58.05 N	11.49 E
Stepan'	78	51.10 N	26.18 E
Stepanakert	84	39.49 N	46.44 E
Stepanavan	84	41.00 N	44.23 E
Stepancevo, S.S.S.R.	80	56.08 N	41.42 E
Stepancevo, S.S.S.R.	82	56.22 N	36.10 E
Stepancy	78	49.42 N	31.18 E
Stepano-Krynka	83	47.55 N	38.21 E
Stepanovka, S.S.S.R.	78	50.58 N	34.37 E
Stepanovka, S.S.S.R.	80	52.04 N	53.02 E
Stepanovka, S.S.S.R.	86	57.13 N	67.26 E
Stepanovo	82	55.43 N	38.28 E
Stepanovskoje	265b	55.47 N	37.10 E
Stepan Razin	84	40.24 N	49.59 E
Stepanščino	82	55.15 N	38.30 E
Stepenitz ≃	54	53.48 N	11.10 E
Stephans-Dom ✦[1]	264b	48.12 N	16.23 E
Stephanskirchen	64	47.51 N	12.11 E
Stephen	198	48.27 N	96.52 W
Stephen A. Forbes State Park ♦	219	38.44 N	88.46 W
Stephen F. Austin State Historic Park ♦	222	29.48 N	96.05 W
Stephens	194	33.24 N	93.04 W
Stephens, Cape ≻	172	40.42 S	173.57 E
Stephens, Port ⊂	166	32.45 S	152.05 E
Stephens City	188	39.05 N	78.13 W
Stephens Creek	166	31.50 S	141.30 E
Stephens Island I	182	54.10 N	130.45 W
Stephens Knob ∧[2]	192	36.37 N	84.20 W
Stephens Lake ⊜[1]	184	56.26 N	95.07 W
Stephens Mills	210	42.23 N	77.38 W
Stephenson	190	45.24 N	87.36 W
Stephenson, Lake ⊜	222	29.35 N	94.40 W
Stephenson, Mount ∧	9	69.49 S	69.43 W
Stephens Passage ⊻	180	57.50 N	133.50 W
Stephentown	210	42.33 N	73.23 W
Stephentown Center	210	42.34 N	73.25 W
Stephenville, Nf., Can.	186	48.33 N	58.35 W
Stephenville, Tx., U.S.	196	32.13 N	98.12 W
Stephenville Crossing	186	48.30 N	58.26 W
Stepn'ak	86	52.50 N	70.50 E
Stepney ✦[8]	260	51.31 N	0.02 W
Stepnica	54	53.40 N	14.36 E
Stepnoj	80	48.56 N	45.36 E
Stepnoje, S.S.S.R.	80	51.24 N	46.52 E
Stepnoje, S.S.S.R.	84	44.17 N	44.36 E
Step Pyramid → Şaqqārah ⊥	142	29.52 N	31.14 E
Steps Point ≻	174u	14.22 S	170.45 W
Steptoe Valley ∨	204	39.25 N	114.45 W
Stepurino	76	56.24 N	35.16 E
Sterdyń	30	52.35 N	22.18 E
Sterkaar	158	31.05 S	23.42 E
Sterkrade ✦[8]	263	51.31 N	6.51 E
Sterkspruit	158	30.32 S	27.22 E
Sterkstroom	158	31.32 S	26.32 E
Sterlibaševo	86	53.28 N	55.15 E
Sterling, S. Afr.	158	31.16 S	21.28 E
Sterling, Ak., U.S.	180	60.32 N	150.48 W
Sterling, Co., U.S.	198	40.37 N	103.12 W
Sterling, Ct., U.S.	207	41.42 N	71.49 W
Sterling, Il., U.S.	190	41.47 N	89.41 W
Sterling, Ks., U.S.	198	38.12 N	98.12 W
Sterling, Ma., U.S.	207	42.26 N	71.45 W
Sterling, Mi., U.S.	190	44.02 N	84.01 W
Sterling, Ne., U.S.	198	40.27 N	96.22 W
Sterling, N.Y., U.S.	210	43.20 N	76.39 W
Sterling, Oh., U.S.	214	40.58 N	81.51 W
Sterling, Ok., U.S.	196	34.45 N	98.10 W
Sterling, Va., U.S.	208	39.00 N	77.25 W
Sterling City	196	31.50 N	100.59 W
Sterling Creek ≃	210	43.20 N	76.42 W
Sterling Forest Lake ⊜	276	41.10 N	74.16 W
Sterling Heights	214	42.34 N	83.01 W
Sterling Junction	207	42.24 N	71.46 W
Sterling Park	282	37.41 N	122.26 W
Sterling Run	214	41.25 N	78.12 W
Sterlington	194	32.41 N	92.05 W
Sterlitamak	86	53.37 N	55.58 E
Sternberg	54	53.43 N	11.49 E
Sternberg in der Neumark → Torzym	30	52.20 N	15.04 E
Šternberk	30	49.44 N	17.18 E
Şternstein ∧	61	48.34 N	14.16 E
Šterovka	83	48.19 N	38.57 E
Sterup	41	54.44 N	9.44 E
Sterzing → Vipiteno	64	46.54 N	11.26 E
Stęszew	30	52.18 N	16.42 E
Štětí	54	50.25 N	14.23 E
Stetson Pond ⊜	283	42.02 N	70.50 W
Stetten am kalten Markt	58	48.07 N	9.04 E
Stettin → Szczecin	30	53.24 N	14.32 E
Stettler	182	52.19 N	112.43 W
Steuben □[6], In., U.S.	216	41.38 N	85.00 W
Steuben □[6], N.Y., U.S.	210	42.20 N	77.19 W
Steubenville	214	40.22 N	80.38 W
Stevenage	42	51.55 N	0.14 W
Stevens, N.J., U.S.	285	40.05 N	74.49 W
Stevens, Pa., U.S.	208	40.13 N	76.09 W
Stevens, Lake ⊜	224	48.01 N	122.05 W
Stevens, Mount ∧	172	40.48 S	172.27 E
Stevens Creek ≃, Ca., U.S.	282	37.26 N	122.05 W
Stevens Creek ≃, S.C., U.S.	192	33.34 N	82.03 W
Stevens Creek Park ♦	282	37.17 N	122.04 W
Stevens Creek Reservoir ⊜[1]	282	37.17 N	122.05 W
Stevens Institute of Technology ✦[2]	276	40.44 N	74.02 W
Stevenson, Al., U.S.	194	34.52 N	85.50 W
Stevenson, Md., U.S.	284b	39.25 N	76.43 W
Stevenson, Wa., U.S.	224	45.42 N	121.53 W
Stevenson Creek ≃	162	27.06 S	135.33 E
Stevenson Entrance ⊻	180	58.45 N	152.20 W
Stevenson Lake ⊜	184	53.56 N	96.09 W
Stevens Pass)(	224	47.45 N	121.04 W
Stevens Peak ∧	202	47.27 N	115.46 W
Stevens Point	190	44.31 N	89.34 W
Stevenston	46	55.39 N	4.45 W
Stevens Village	180	66.00 N	149.05 W
Stevensville, On., Can.	284a	42.57 N	79.04 W
Stevensville, Md., U.S.	208	38.58 N	76.18 W
Stevensville, Mi., U.S.	216	42.00 N	86.31 W
Stevensville, Mt., U.S.	202	46.30 N	114.05 W
Stevensville, Pa., U.S.	210	41.46 N	76.11 W
Stevinson	226	37.20 N	120.51 W
Stevns Klint ⊥[4]	41	55.18 N	12.27 E
Steward	216	41.51 N	89.01 W
Stewardson	219	39.15 N	88.37 W
Stewart, B.C., Can.	182	55.56 N	129.59 W
Stewart, Mn., U.S.	198	44.43 N	94.29 W
Stewart ≃	180	63.18 N	139.25 W
Stewart, Cape ≻	164	11.57 S	134.45 E
Stewart, Isla I	254	54.52 S	71.12 W
Stewart, Mount ∧	166	20.12 S	145.29 E
Stewart Island I	172	47.00 S	167.50 E
Stewart Islands II	175e	8.25 S	162.52 E
Stewart Lake ⊜	219	39.09 N	90.16 W
Stewart Manor	276	40.43 N	73.41 W
Stewarton	46	55.41 N	4.31 W
Stewartstown, N. Ire., U.K.	48	54.35 N	6.41 W
Stewartstown, Pa., U.S.	208	39.45 N	76.35 W
Stewartsville, Mo., U.S.	194	39.45 N	94.29 W
Stewartsville, N.J., U.S.	208	40.41 N	75.06 W
Stewartsville, Pa., U.S.	279b	40.21 N	79.46 W
Stewart Valley	184	50.36 N	107.50 W
Stewartville	190	43.51 N	92.29 W
Stewiacke	186	45.08 N	63.21 W
Steyerberg	52	52.34 N	9.01 E
Steyning	42	50.53 N	0.20 W
Steynsburg	158	31.15 S	25.49 E
Steynsrus	158	27.58 S	27.33 E
Steyr	61	48.03 N	14.25 E
Steyr ≃	61	48.02 N	14.25 E
Steyregg	61	48.17 N	14.22 E
Steytlerville	158	33.21 S	24.21 E
Stežki	80	53.06 N	41.13 E
Stezzano	62	45.38 N	9.39 E
Sthal	126	24.12 N	89.44 E
Ştia	66	43.48 N	11.42 E
Štiavnické vrchy ✱	30	48.40 N	18.45 E
Stickle Pond ⊜	276	40.59 N	74.25 W
Stickney, Eng., U.K.	44	53.05 N	0.01 E
Stickney, Il., U.S.	216	41.49 N	87.46 W
Stickney, S.D., U.S.	198	43.35 N	98.26 W
Stidsvig	41	56.12 N	13.08 E
Stiefingbach ≃	61	46.47 N	15.35 E
Stiege	54	51.40 N	10.53 E
Stiene	76	57.26 N	24.34 E
Stienitzfliess ≃	264a	52.33 N	13.43 E
Stienitz-See ⊜	264a	52.30 N	13.49 E
Stiens	52	53.15 N	5.45 E
Stiepel ✦[8]	263	51.25 N	7.15 E
Stif	148	36.09 N	5.26 E
Stif □[5]	148	36.15 N	5.10 E
Stiftskirche ✦[1]	263	51.23 N	7.00 E
Stige	41	55.26 N	10.25 E
Stigler	196	35.15 N	95.07 W
Stigliano	68	40.24 N	16.14 E
Stigtomta	40	58.48 N	16.47 E
Stikine ≃	180	56.40 N	132.30 W
Stikine Ranges ✱	180	58.45 N	130.00 W
Stiklestad	26	63.48 N	11.33 E
Stilbaai	158	34.24 S	21.26 E
Stiles	210	40.40 N	75.30 W
Stiles Pond ⊜	283	42.41 N	71.02 W
Stilesville	210	42.05 N	75.24 W
Stilfontein	158	26.50 S	26.50 E
Stilís	38	38.55 N	22.36 E
Still	148	34.20 N	5.51 E
Stillaguamish ≃	224	48.11 N	122.22 W
Stillaguamish, North Fork ≃	224	48.11 N	122.07 W
Stillaguamish, South Fork ≃	224	48.11 N	122.07 W
Stillhouse Hollow Lake ⊜[1]	222	31.00 N	97.35 W
Stilling	41	56.04 N	10.00 E
Stillman Valley	216	42.07 N	89.11 W
Stillmore	192	32.26 N	82.12 W
Still Pond	208	39.19 N	76.02 W
Still Run ≃	285	39.49 N	75.18 W
Stillwater, B.C., Can.	182	49.46 N	124.18 W
Stillwater, Mn., U.S.	190	45.03 N	92.48 W
Stillwater, N.J., U.S.	210	41.02 N	74.52 W
Stillwater, N.Y., U.S.	210	42.56 N	73.39 W
Stillwater, Oh., U.S.	214	40.20 N	81.18 W
Stillwater, Ok., U.S.	196	36.06 N	97.03 W
Stillwater, Pa., U.S.	210	41.09 N	76.22 W
Stillwater ≃, Mt., U.S.	202	45.38 N	109.17 W
Stillwater ≃, Oh., U.S.	218	39.47 N	84.12 W
Stillwater Creek ≃	214	40.25 N	81.22 W
Stillwater Range ✱	204	39.50 N	118.15 W
Stillwell, Il., U.S.	219	40.13 N	91.11 W
Stillwell, Ok., U.S.	194	35.49 N	94.38 W
Stilo	68	38.29 N	16.28 E
Stilo, Punta ≻	68	38.28 N	16.36 E
Stimberg ∧[2]	263	51.40 N	7.15 E
Stimigliano	66	42.18 N	12.34 E
Stimson, Mount ∧	202	48.31 N	113.36 W
Stînca-Costeşti, Lacul (vodochranilišče Kostešty-Stynka) ⊜[1]	38	47.55 N	27.10 E
Stinchar ≃	44	55.06 N	5.00 W
Stinear Nunataks ✱	9	69.42 S	64.40 E
Stine Canal ≅	226	35.15 N	119.08 W
Stine Mountain ∧	202	45.44 N	113.07 W
Stingray Point ≻	208	37.33 N	76.18 W
Stînişoarei, Munţii ✱	38	47.10 N	26.00 E
Stinking Water Creek ≃	198	40.22 N	101.07 W
Stinnett	196	35.49 N	101.26 W
Stintino	71	40.56 N	8.13 E
Stintonville	273d	26.14 S	28.13 E
Štip	38	41.44 N	22.12 E
Stiperstones ∧	42	52.35 N	2.56 W
Stiring-Wendel	56	49.12 N	6.56 E
Stírka ∧	60	49.24 N	13.34 E
Stirling, Austl.	162	21.44 S	133.45 E
Stirling, Austl.	168a	31.54 S	115.47 E
Stirling, Austl.	168b	35.00 S	138.43 E
Stirling, Ab., Can.	182	49.30 N	112.31 W
Stirling, On., Can.	212	44.18 N	77.33 W
Stirling, Scot., U.K.	46	56.07 N	3.57 W
Stirling, N.J., U.S.	210	40.40 N	74.29 W
Stirling, Mount ∧	162	31.50 S	117.38 E
Stirling Castle ⊥	46	56.07 N	3.57 W
Stirling City	204	39.54 N	121.31 W
Stirling Range ✱	162	34.23 S	117.50 E
Stirling Range National Park ♦	162	34.22 S	118.00 E
Stirling Reservoir ⊜[1]	168a	33.08 S	116.03 E
Stirrat	192	37.43 N	82.00 W
Stissing Mountain ∧	210	41.57 N	73.42 W
Štitary	61	48.56 N	15.51 E
Stittsville	212	45.15 N	75.55 W
Stittville	210	43.13 N	75.17 W
Stjärnhov	40	59.05 N	17.00 E
Stjärnsund, Sve.	40	60.26 N	16.12 E
Stjärnsund, Sve.	40	58.51 N	14.55 E
Stjernøya I	24	70.18 N	22.45 E
Stjørdalshalsen	26	63.28 N	10.56 E
Stöberhai ∧	54	51.39 N	10.34 E
Stochod ≃	78	51.52 N	25.38 E
Stock	260	51.40 N	0.27 E
Stock, Étang du ⊜	56	48.45 N	6.55 E
Stockach	58	47.51 N	9.00 E
Stöckalp	58	46.48 N	8.17 E
Stockamöllan	41	55.57 N	13.22 E
Stockbridge, Eng., U.K.	42	51.07 N	1.29 W
Stockbridge, Ga., U.S.	192	33.32 N	84.14 W
Stockbridge, Ma., U.S.	207	42.17 N	73.19 W
Stockbridge, Mi., U.S.	216	42.27 N	84.10 W
Stockbridge Bowl ⊜	207	42.20 N	73.19 W
Stockbridge Indian Reservation ✦[4]	190	44.52 N	88.53 W
Stockbury	260	51.20 N	0.39 E
Stockby	40	59.20 N	17.41 E
Stockdale, Oh., U.S.	218	38.57 N	82.51 W
Stockdale, Tx., U.S.	196	29.14 N	97.57 W
Stockdorf	60	48.05 N	11.24 E
Stöcken	52	53.00 N	10.40 E
Stockerau	61	48.23 N	16.13 E
Stockertown	210	40.45 N	75.15 W
Stockett	202	47.21 N	111.09 W
Stockheim	56	50.19 N	9.01 E
Stockheim bei Braunschweig	52	52.12 N	10.31 E
Stockholm, Sve.	40	59.20 N	18.03 E
Stockholm, Me., U.S.	186	47.02 N	68.08 W
Stockholm, N.J., U.S.	210	41.05 N	74.31 W
Stockholm, Lake ⊜	276	41.04 N	74.32 W
Stockholms Län □[6]	40	59.30 N	18.20 E
Stock Island	220	24.34 N	81.45 W
Stockland	216	40.37 N	87.36 W
Stockport, Eng., U.K.	44	53.25 N	2.10 W
Stockport, N.Y., U.S.	210	42.19 N	73.45 W
Stockport □[8]	262	53.23 N	2.08 W
Stocksbridge	44	53.27 N	1.34 W
Stockstadt	56	49.48 N	8.28 E
Stocksund	40	59.23 N	18.04 E
Stockton, Austl.	170	32.55 S	151.47 E
Stockton, Al., U.S.	194	30.59 N	87.51 W
Stockton, Ca., U.S.	226	37.57 N	121.17 W
Stockton, Il., U.S.	190	42.20 N	90.00 W
Stockton, Ks., U.S.	198	39.26 N	99.15 W
Stockton, Md., U.S.	208	38.03 N	75.24 W
Stockton, Mo., U.S.	194	37.41 N	93.47 W
Stockton, N.J., U.S.	208	40.24 N	74.58 W
Stockton, N.Y., U.S.	214	42.19 N	79.22 W
Stockton, Ut,. U.S.	200	40.27 N	112.21 W
Stockton Heath, Eng., U.K.	44	53.22 N	2.34 W
Stockton Heath, Eng., U.K.	262	53.22 N	2.35 W
Stockton Metropolitan Airport ⊠	226	37.54 N	121.15 W
Stockton-on-Tees	44	54.34 N	1.19 W
Stockton Plateau ✱[1]	196	30.30 N	102.30 W
Stockton Reservoir ⊜[1]	194	37.40 N	93.45 W
Stockton Springs	188	44.29 N	68.51 W
Stockum, B.R.D.	52	51.40 N	7.42 E
Stockum, B.R.D.	263	51.28 N	7.22 E
Stockum, B.R.D.	263	51.32 N	7.47 E
Stockum, B.R.D.	263	51.36 N	6.39 E
Stockum ✦[8]	263	51.16 N	6.44 E
Stockville	198	40.31 N	100.22 W
Stockwell	216	40.17 N	86.46 W
Stockwell, Lake ⊜	285	39.51 N	74.47 W
Stoco Lake ⊜	212	44.28 N	77.18 W
Stoczek Łukowski	30	51.58 N	21.58 E
Stod	60	49.39 N	13.10 E
Stoddard Mountain ∧	228	34.42 N	117.07 W
Stöde	26	62.25 N	16.35 E
Stodoliči	78	51.44 N	28.30 E
Stodolišče	76	54.11 N	32.39 E
Stœng Tréng	110	13.31 N	105.58 E
Stoer	46	58.12 N	5.20 W
Stoer, Point of ≻	46	58.15 N	5.21 W
Stoffberg	156	25.29 S	29.49 E
Stoj, gora ∧	78	48.37 N	23.11 E
Stojba	89	52.49 N	131.43 E
Stoke	260	51.27 N	0.37 E
Stoke ≃	206	45.35 N	71.58 W
Stoke, Monts ✱	206	45.33 N	71.42 W
Stoke D'Abernon	260	51.19 N	0.23 W
Stoke Golding	42	52.34 N	1.24 W
Stokenchurch	42	51.40 N	0.55 W
Stoke Newington ✦[8]	260	51.34 N	0.05 W
Stoke-on-Trent	42	53.00 N	2.10 W
Stoke Poges	260	51.33 N	0.35 W
Stokes, Mount ∧	172	41.06 S	174.06 E
Stokes Inlet ⊂	162	33.50 S	121.08 E
Stokesley	44	54.28 N	1.11 W
Stokes Point ≻	166	40.10 S	143.56 E
Stokes Range ✱[2]	164	15.46 S	130.57 E
Stokkemarke	41	54.50 N	11.23 E
Stokksnes ≻	24a	64.17 N	14.54 W
Stol ∧	38	44.13 N	22.14 E
Stolac	36	43.05 N	17.58 E
Stolbcy	76	53.29 N	26.44 E
Stolberg, B.R.D.	56	50.46 N	6.13 E
Stolberg, D.D.R.	54	51.34 N	10.57 E
Stolbišči	80	55.39 N	49.14 E
Stolboucha	86	49.59 N	84.30 E
Stolbovo	76	52.38 N	34.47 E
Stolbovoj, ostrov I	74	74.05 N	136.00 E
Stolbun	76	52.48 N	31.25 E
Stolby, zapovednik ♦	88	55.45 N	92.45 E
Stolin	78	51.53 N	26.51 E
Stollberg	54	50.42 N	12.47 E
Stöllet	26	60.24 N	13.16 E
Stol'noje	78	51.31 N	31.55 E
Stolp → Słupsk	30	54.28 N	17.01 E
Stolpe	264a	52.40 N	13.16 E
Stolpen	54	51.05 N	14.04 E
Stolper Heide ✦[3]	264a	52.39 N	13.14 E
Stolpino	80	57.24 N	42.55 E
Stolpmünde → Ustka	30	54.35 N	16.50 E
Stolzenau	52	52.31 N	9.04 E
Ston	36	42.50 N	17.42 E
Stondon Massey	260	51.41 N	0.18 E
Stone, Eng., U.K.	42	52.54 N	2.10 W
Stone, Eng., U.K.	260	51.27 N	0.16 E
Stoneboro	214	41.20 N	80.06 W
Stone Canyon Reservoir ⊜[1]	280	34.07 N	118.28 W
Stone Corral Creek ≃	226	39.16 N	122.06 W
Stone Creek	214	40.24 N	81.34 W
Stonecutters Island I	271d	22.19 N	114.08 E
Stonefort	194	37.37 N	88.42 W
Stoneham, Ma., U.S.	283	42.28 N	71.06 W
Stoneham, Pa., U.S.	214	41.49 N	79.07 W
Stone Harbor	208	39.03 N	74.45 W
Stonehaven	46	56.38 N	2.13 W
Stonehenge	166	24.22 S	143.17 E
Stonehenge ⊥	42	51.11 N	1.49 W
Stonehill College ✦[2]	283	42.03 N	71.05 W
Stonehouse, Eng., U.K.	42	51.45 N	2.17 W
Stonehouse, Scot., U.K.	46	55.43 N	4.00 W
Stone Indian Reserve ✦[4]	182	51.54 N	123.12 W
Stoneleigh	42	52.21 N	1.31 W
Stonelick Creek ≃	218	39.07 N	84.13 W
Stonelick State Park ♦	218	39.13 N	84.04 W
Stone Mountain	192	33.48 N	84.10 W
Stone Mountain ∧, Pa., U.S.	210	40.37 N	77.48 W
Stone Mountain ∧, Vt., U.S.	188	44.34 N	71.40 W
Stone Mountain Memorial State Park ♦	192	33.49 N	84.06 W
Stone Park	278	41.45 N	87.53 W
Stoner	182	53.36 N	122.40 W
Stoner Creek ≃	218	38.18 N	84.14 W
Stone Ridge	210	41.51 N	74.09 W
Stonerstown	214	40.13 N	78.16 W
Stones, East Fork ≃	194	35.59 N	86.27 W
Stones, West Fork ≃	194	35.59 N	86.27 W
Stones River National Battlefield ♦	194	35.52 N	86.26 W
Stonestown ✦[9]	282	37.44 N	122.28 W
Stonevilla	279b	40.18 N	79.31 W
Stoneville	192	36.27 N	79.54 W
Stonewall, Mb., Can.	184	50.09 N	97.21 W
Stonewall, La., U.S.	194	32.16 N	93.49 W
Stonewall, Ms., U.S.	194	32.07 N	88.47 W
Stonewall, Ok., U.S.	196	34.39 N	96.31 W
Stonewall Manor	284c	38.53 N	77.14 W
Stoney Creek	212	43.13 N	79.46 W
Stoney Point ≻	214	42.18 N	82.34 W
Stonington, Ct., U.S.	207	41.20 N	71.54 W
Stonington, Il., U.S.	219	39.38 N	89.11 W
Stonington, Me., U.S.	188	44.09 N	68.40 W
Stony ≃, Ak., U.S.	180	61.45 N	156.35 W
Stony ≃, Mn., U.S.	190	47.44 N	91.47 W
Stony Brook	210	40.55 N	73.08 W
Stony Brook ≃, Ct., U.S.	276	41.10 N	73.22 W
Stony Brook ≃, Ct., U.S.	276	41.04 N	73.28 W
Stony Brook ≃, Ma., U.S.	283	42.38 N	71.22 W

Symbols in the index entries represent the broad categories identified in the key at the right. Symbols with superior numbers (✱[1]) identify subcategories (see complete key on page I · 1).

Symbole im Register stellen die rechts im Schlüssel erklärten Kategorien dar. Symbole mit hochgestellten Ziffern (✱[1]) bezeichnen Unterabteilungen einer Kategorie (vgl. vollständiger Schlüssel auf Seite I · 1).

Los símbolos incluidos en el texto del índice representan las grandes categorías identificadas con la clave a la derecha. Los símbolos con numeros en su parte superior (✱[1]) identifican las subcategorías (véase la clave completa en la página I · 1).

Les symboles de l'index représentent les catégories indiquées dans la légende à droite. Les symboles suivis d'un indice (✱[1]) représentent des sous-catégories (voir légende complète à la page I · 1).

Os símbolos incluídos no texto do índice representam as grandes categorias identificadas com a chave à direita. Os símbolos com números em sua parte superior (✱[1]) identificam as subcategorias (veja-se a chave completa à página I · 1).

English	Deutsch	Español	Français	Português
∧ Mountain	Berg	Montaña	Montagne	Montanha
✱ Mountains	Gebirge	Montañas	Montagnes	Montanhas
)(Pass	Paß	Paso	Col	Passo
∨ Valley, Canyon	Tal, Cañon	Valle, Cañón	Vallée, Canyon	Vale, Canhão
≃ Plain	Ebene	Llano	Plaine	Planície
≻ Cape	Kap	Cabo	Cap	Cabo
I Island	Insel	Isla	Île	Ilha
II Islands	Inseln	Islas	Îles	Ilhas
✦ Other Topographic Features	Andere Topographische Objekte	Otros Elementos Topográficos	Autres données topographiques	Outros acidentes topográficos

ESPAÑOL — Nombre | Página | Lat.°′ | Long.°′ W = Oeste

FRANÇAIS — Nom | Page | Lat.°′ | Long.°′ W = Ouest

PORTUGUÊS — Nome | Página | Lat.°′ | Long.°′ W = Oeste

Nombre / Nom / Nome	Página	Lat.°′	Long.°′
Stony Brook ≃, Ma., U.S.	283	42.22 N	71.16 W
Stony Brook ≃, N.J., U.S.	276	40.19 N	74.41 W
Stony Brook ≃, N.J., U.S.	276	40.56 N	74.26 W
Stony Brook Harbor c	276	40.54 N	73.10 W
Stony Brook Reservation ♦	283	42.16 N	71.09 W
Stony Creek, Ct., U.S.	207	41.15 N	72.44 W
Stony Creek, Mi., U.S.	281	42.42 N	83.07 W
Stony Creek, Va., U.S.	208	36.56 N	77.24 W
Stony Creek ≃, Ca., U.S.	204	39.41 N	121.58 W
Stony Creek ≃, Il., U.S.	278	41.41 N	87.51 W
Stony Creek ≃, Mi., U.S.	216	41.57 N	83.18 W
Stony Creek ≃, Mi., U.S.	216	43.00 N	84.55 W
Stony Creek ≃, N.Y., U.S.	212	43.49 N	76.14 W
Stony Creek ≃, Pa., U.S.	285	40.07 N	75.21 W
Stony Creek ≃, Va., U.S.	208	36.56 N	77.23 W
Stony Creek, Middle Fork ≃	226	39.25 N	122.31 W
Stony Creek, North Fork ≃	226	39.22 N	122.37 W
Stony Creek, South Fork ≃	226	39.22 N	122.39 W
Stony Creek Indian Reserve ◆[4]	182	53.57 N	124.07 W
Stony Creek Mills	208	40.21 N	75.52 W
Stonyford	226	39.22 N	122.32 W
Stony Gorge Reservoir ⊜[1]	226	39.34 N	122.31 W
Stony Indian Reserve ◆[4]	182	51.10 N	114.55 W
Stony Island I, Mi., U.S.	281	42.07 N	83.08 W
Stony Island I, N.Y., U.S.	212	43.53 N	76.25 W
Stony Kill ≃	210	42.24 N	73.38 W
Stony Lake ⊜, Mb., Can.	176	58.51 N	98.35 W
Stony Lake ⊜, On., Can.	212	44.33 N	78.05 W
Stony Plain	182	53.32 N	114.00 W
Stony Plain Indian Reserve ◆[4]	182	53.30 N	113.45 W
Stony Point, Austl.	169	38.22 S	145.13 E
Stony Point, Mi., U.S.	216	41.57 N	83.16 W
Stony Point, N.Y., U.S.	210	41.13 N	73.59 W
Stony Point, N.C., U.S.	192	35.51 N	81.02 W
Stony Point ≻	284a	42.50 N	78.52 W
Stony Point ≻[1]	212	43.52 N	76.15 W
Stony Prairie	214	41.21 N	83.10 W
Stony Rapids	176	59.16 N	105.50 W
Stony Ridge	214	41.30 N	83.30 W
Stony River	180	61.47 N	156.41 W
Stony Run	284b	39.11 N	76.42 W
Stony Run ≃	285	40.09 N	75.32 W
Stony Stratford	42	52.04 N	0.52 W
Stoober Bach ≃	61	47.27 N	16.35 E
Stop ≃	283	42.10 N	71.19 W
Stopnica	30	50.27 N	20.57 E
Stoppenberg ◆[8]	263	51.29 N	7.02 E
Stör ≃	54	53.50 N	11.29 E
Storå	40	59.43 N	15.08 E
Storå ≃	26	56.19 N	8.19 E
Stora Alvaret ≚	26	56.30 N	16.30 E
Stora Gla ⊜	26	59.30 N	12.30 E
Stora Kloten ⊜	40	59.52 N	15.16 E
Stora Le ⊜	26	59.05 N	11.53 E
Stora Lulevatten ⊜	24	67.10 N	19.16 E
Stora Mellösa	40	59.13 N	15.30 E
Stora Möja I, Sve.	26	59.26 N	18.55 E
Stora Möja I, Sve.	40	59.26 N	18.55 E
Stora Norn ⊜	40	60.14 N	15.42 E
Stora Sjöfallets Nationalpark ♦	24	67.44 N	18.16 E
Stora Skedvi	40	60.24 N	15.48 E
Stora Sundby	40	59.16 N	16.07 E
Storavan ⊜	24	65.40 N	18.15 E
Stora Vika	40	58.56 N	17.48 E
Storby	26	60.13 N	19.34 E
Stord I	26	59.53 N	5.25 E
Store Andst	41	55.29 N	9.14 E
Storebælt ᵾ	41	55.30 N	11.00 E
Store Heddinge	41	55.19 N	12.25 E
Store Magleby	41	55.36 N	12.38 E
Store Merløse	41	55.33 N	11.40 E
Støren	26	63.02 N	10.18 E
Store Sotra I	26	60.18 N	5.05 E
Storeton	262	53.21 N	3.03 W
Storey □[6]	226	39.28 N	119.30 W
Storfjärden ⊜	40	60.30 N	17.23 E
Storfjorden c[2]	26	62.25 N	6.30 E
Storfors	40	59.32 N	14.16 E
Störitzsee ⊜	264a	52.23 N	13.51 E
Störkanal ≅	54	53.36 N	11.30 E
Storkerson Bay c	176	73.00 N	124.50 W
Storkerson Peninsula ≻[1]	176	72.30 N	106.30 W
Storkow, D.D.R.	54	52.15 N	13.56 E
Storkow, D.D.R.	54	53.19 N	14.17 E
Storlien	26	63.19 N	12.06 E
Stormarn ◆[1]	52	53.45 N	10.20 E
Storm Bay c	166	43.10 S	147.32 E
Stormberg ∧	158	30.57 S	26.41 E
Stormberge ⋀	158	31.27 S	26.55 E
Storm King Mountain ∧	224	46.39 N	122.10 W
Storm Lake	198	42.38 N	95.12 W
Storm Mountain ∧	180	59.37 N	150.35 W
Stormont-Dundas and Glengarry □[6]	206	45.10 N	75.00 W
Štormovo	83	49.06 N	38.55 E
Stormsrivier	158	33.59 S	23.52 E
Stormsvlei	158	34.05 S	20.06 E
Stormville	210	41.34 N	73.45 W
Stornara	68	41.17 N	15.46 E
Stornarella	68	41.15 N	15.44 E
Stornorrforsen	26	63.52 N	20.03 E
Stornoway	46	58.12 N	6.23 W
Storo	64	45.51 N	10.35 E
Storoževaja	84	43.53 N	41.27 E
Storoževsk	24	61.57 N	52.16 E
Storožinec	78	48.10 N	25.43 E
Storrensjön ⊜	26	63.38 N	12.34 E
Storrington	42	50.55 N	0.28 W
Storrs	207	41.48 N	72.15 W
Storsjøen ⊜, Nor.	26	60.23 N	11.40 E
Storsjøen ⊜, Nor.	26	61.35 N	11.12 E
Storsjön ⊜, Sve.	26	62.48 N	13.07 E
Storsjön ⊜, Sve.	26	63.12 N	14.18 E
Storsjön ⊜, Sve.	40	59.04 N	17.12 E
Storsjön ⊜, Sve.	40	60.34 N	16.44 E
Storsteinsfjellet ∧	24	68.14 N	17.52 E
Storstrøm □[6]	41	55.00 N	11.55 E
Storstrømmen ᵾ	41	54.58 N	11.55 E
Storstrømsbroen ◆[5]	41	54.58 N	11.50 E
Stort ≃	260	51.46 N	0.01 E
Storthoaks	184	49.22 N	101.38 W
Storuman	24	65.06 N	17.06 E
Storuman ⊜[1]	24	65.14 N	16.54 E
Storuman-See → Storavan ⊜	24	65.40 N	18.15 E
Storvarts gruve	26	62.38 N	11.31 E
Storvätteshågna ∧	26	62.07 N	12.27 E
Storvik	40	60.35 N	16.32 E
Storvindeln ⊜	24	65.43 N	17.05 E
Storvreta	40	59.58 N	17.42 E
Story	202	44.34 N	106.53 W
Story City	190	42.11 N	93.35 W
Stosch, Isla I	254	49.09 S	75.26 W
Stössen	54	51.06 N	11.55 E
Stotfold	42	52.01 N	0.14 W
Stotternheim	54	51.03 N	11.02 E
Stottville	210	42.17 N	73.44 W
Stouchsburg	208	40.23 N	76.14 W
Stough Park ♦	280	34.12 N	118.18 W
Stoughton, Sk., Can.	184	49.41 N	103.03 W
Stoughton, Eng., U.K.	260	51.15 N	0.35 W
Stoughton, Ma., U.S.	207	42.07 N	71.06 W
Stoughton, Wi., U.S.	216	42.55 N	89.13 W
Stoumont	56	50.25 N	5.48 E
Stoŭng ≃	110	12.50 N	104.19 E
Stour ≃, Eng., U.K.	42	51.18 N	1.22 E
Stour ≃, Eng., U.K.	42	51.52 N	1.16 E
Stour ≃, Eng., U.K.	42	50.43 N	1.46 W
Stour ≃, Eng., U.K.	42	52.20 N	2.15 W
Stourbridge	42	52.27 N	2.09 W
Stourport-on-Severn	42	52.21 N	2.16 W
Stout Lake ⊜	184	52.08 N	94.33 W
Stoutsville	219	39.33 N	91.51 W
Stover	194	38.26 N	92.59 W
Stow, Ma., U.S.	207	42.26 N	71.30 W
Stow, N.Y., U.S.	214	42.09 N	79.25 W
Stow, Oh., U.S.	214	41.10 N	81.27 W
Stowe, Pa., U.S.	208	40.15 N	75.40 W
Stowe, Vt., U.S.	188	44.27 N	72.41 W
Stowell	194	29.47 N	94.23 W
Stowe Township	279b	40.29 N	80.04 W
Stow Maries	260	51.40 N	0.39 E
Stowmarket	42	52.11 N	1.00 E
Stow-on-the-Wold	42	51.56 N	1.44 W
Stowupland	42	52.12 N	1.01 E
Stoyoma Mountain ∧	182	49.59 N	121.13 W
Stoystown	214	40.06 N	78.57 W
Stožec	60	48.51 N	13.50 E
Stra	64	45.25 N	12.00 E
Straach	54	51.57 N	12.35 E
Strabane, N. Ire., U.K.	48	54.49 N	7.27 W
Strabane, Pa., U.S.	214	40.15 N	80.11 W
Straberg	263	51.05 N	6.45 E
Strachan	46	57.01 N	2.32 W
Strachan Island I	164	9.00 S	142.10 E
Strachur	46	56.10 N	5.04 W
Stradbally	48	53.00 N	7.08 W
Stradbroke	42	52.19 N	1.16 E
Stradeč'	78	51.56 N	23.40 E
Stradella	62	45.05 N	9.18 E
Stradone	48	53.58 N	7.14 W
Stradovn'a, ozero ⊜	82	56.53 N	36.18 E
Straelen	56	51.27 N	6.16 E
Strafford	285	40.03 N	75.25 W
Straffordville	212	42.45 N	80.47 W
Strahan	166	42.09 S	145.19 E
Straight Creek ≃	218	38.46 N	83.55 W
Strakonice	60	49.16 N	13.55 E
Stralsund	54	54.19 N	13.05 E
Strambino	62	45.23 N	7.53 E
Strand	158	34.06 S	18.50 E
Stranda	26	62.19 N	6.54 E
Strande	54	54.26 N	10.12 E
Strandhill	48	54.17 N	8.36 W
Stranger Creek ≃	198	39.00 N	95.01 W
Strangford	48	54.22 N	5.34 W
Strangford Lough ⊜	48	54.28 N	5.35 W
Strängnäs	40	59.23 N	17.02 E
Strångsjö	40	58.54 N	16.12 E
Strangways ≃	164	14.52 S	133.50 E
Strangways, Mount ∧	162	23.02 S	133.51 E
Stranorlar	48	54.48 N	7.46 W
Stranraer	44	54.55 N	5.02 W
Strasbourg, Sk., Can.	184	51.04 N	104.57 W
Strasbourg, Fr.	58	48.35 N	7.45 E
Strasbourg, Aéroport ⊠	58	48.32 N	7.38 E
Strasburg, D.D.R.	54	53.30 N	13.44 E
Strasburg, Co., U.S.	198	39.44 N	104.20 W
Strasburg, N.D., U.S.	198	46.08 N	100.09 W
Strasburg, Oh., U.S.	214	40.35 N	81.31 W
Strasburg, Pa., U.S.	208	39.58 N	76.11 W
Strasburg, Va., U.S.	188	38.59 N	78.21 W
Straševiči	76	56.49 N	34.36 E
Strašín	60	49.08 N	13.38 E
Stråssa	40	59.45 N	15.13 E
Strassburg → Strasbourg	58	48.35 N	7.45 E
Strasshof an der Nordbahn	61	48.19 N	16.39 E
Strasskirchen	60	48.50 N	12.43 E
Strata Florida Abbey Ʊ[1]	42	52.16 N	3.51 W
Stratford, On., Can.	212	43.22 N	80.57 W
Stratford, N.Z.	172	39.20 S	174.17 E
Stratford, Ca., U.S.	226	36.11 N	119.49 W
Stratford, Ct., U.S.	207	41.11 N	73.08 W
Stratford, De., U.S.	285	39.40 N	75.38 W
Stratford, Ia., U.S.	190	42.16 N	93.55 W
Stratford, N.J., U.S.	208	39.49 N	75.00 W
Stratford, N.Y., U.S.	210	43.11 N	74.42 W
Stratford, Ok., U.S.	196	34.47 N	96.57 W
Stratford, Tx., U.S.	196	36.20 N	102.04 W
Stratford, Wi., U.S.	190	44.48 N	90.04 W
Stratford Centre	206	45.47 N	71.16 W
Stratford Point ≻	276	41.09 N	73.06 W
Stratford-upon-Avon	42	52.12 N	1.41 W
Strathalbyn	168b	35.16 S	138.54 E
Strathaven	46	55.40 N	4.04 W
Strathbogie Ranges ⋀	169	36.55 S	145.45 E
Strathclair	184	50.24 N	100.24 W
Strathclyde □[4]	46	56.00 N	5.15 W
Strathcona Provincial Park ♦	182	49.40 N	125.50 W
Strathdearn V	46	57.15 N	4.05 W
Strathdon	46	57.11 N	3.02 W
Strathearn V	46	56.18 N	3.45 W
Strathfield	170	33.52 S	151.06 E
Strathgordon	166	42.46 S	146.03 E
Strath Kanaird	46	57.59 N	5.11 W
Strathlorne	186	46.11 N	61.17 W
Strathminglo	46	56.16 N	3.16 W
Strathmoor ◆[8]	281	42.23 N	83.11 W
Strathmore, Ab., Can.	182	51.03 N	113.23 W
Strathmore, Ca., U.S.	204	36.08 N	119.03 W
Strathmore, N.J., U.S.	276	40.24 N	74.13 W
Strathmore V	46	56.39 N	3.00 W
Strathpeffer	46	57.35 N	4.33 W
Strathpine	171a	27.19 S	152.59 E
Strathroy	214	42.57 N	81.38 W
Strathy ≃	46	58.34 N	4.00 W
Strathy Point ≻	46	58.35 N	4.02 W
Strattanville	214	41.12 N	79.19 W
Stratton, Eng., U.K.	42	51.44 N	1.59 W
Stratton, Eng., U.K.	42	50.50 N	4.31 W
Stratton, Co., U.S.	198	39.18 N	102.36 W
Stratton, Me., U.S.	188	45.08 N	70.26 W
Stratton, Ne., U.S.	198	40.08 N	101.13 W
Stratton, Oh., U.S.	214	40.32 N	80.38 W
Stratton Mountain ∧	188	43.05 N	72.56 W
Stratton Saint Margaret	42	51.35 N	1.45 W
Straubing	60	48.53 N	12.34 E
Strauch	263	51.09 N	6.56 E
Straumen	26	63.52 N	11.18 E
Straupitz	54	51.54 N	14.07 E
Strausberg	54	52.35 N	13.53 E
Straus-Berger Stadtforst ♦	264a	52.34 N	13.52 E
Strausberg-Vorstadt	264a	52.32 N	13.51 E
Straussberg	54	51.23 N	10.44 E
Straussee ⊜	264a	52.35 N	13.53 E
Straussfurt	54	51.09 N	10.59 E
Strausstown	208	40.30 N	76.11 W
Stravignano	66	43.05 N	12.49 E
Strawberry	226	38.13 N	118.35 W
Strawberry ≃, Ar., U.S.	194	35.53 N	91.13 W
Strawberry ≃, Ut., U.S.	200	40.10 N	110.24 W
Strawberry Island I	284a	42.57 N	78.55 W
Strawberry Mountain ∧	202	44.19 N	118.43 W
Strawberry Point, Ca., U.S.	282	37.54 N	122.31 W
Strawberry Point, Ia., U.S.	190	42.41 N	91.32 W
Strawberry Point ≻	283	42.15 N	70.46 W
Strawberry Reservoir ⊜[1]	200	40.11 N	111.08 W
Strawberry Valley	226	39.34 N	121.06 W
Strawbridge Lake ⊜	285	39.57 N	74.57 W
Strawn	196	32.33 N	98.29 W
Straw Pump	279b	40.19 N	79.40 W
Stráž	61	49.04 N	14.54 E
Strážnice	30	48.54 N	17.18 E
Strážov	60	49.18 N	13.15 E
Strážske	30	48.53 N	21.50 E
Streaky Bay	162	32.48 S	134.13 E
Streaky Bay c	162	32.36 S	134.08 E
Streamwood	216	42.01 N	88.10 W
Streatham, Austl.	169	37.41 S	143.04 E
Streatham, B.C., Can.	182	53.52 N	126.12 W
Streatham ◆[8]	260	51.26 N	0.08 W
Streator	216	41.07 N	88.50 W
Strebersdorf ◆[8]	264b	48.18 N	16.23 E
Středočeský Kraj □[4]	30	49.55 N	14.30 E
Stredoslovenský Kraj □[4]	30	48.50 N	19.10 E
Street	42	51.07 N	2.42 W
Streeter	198	46.39 N	99.21 W
Streetman	222	31.53 N	96.19 W
Streetsboro	214	41.14 N	81.20 W
Streets Run ≃	279b	40.23 N	79.56 W
Streetsville	212	43.35 N	79.42 W
Strehaia	38	44.37 N	23.12 E
Strehla	54	51.21 N	13.13 E
Strehlen → Strzelin	30	50.47 N	17.03 E
Streitberg	60	49.49 N	11.13 E
Střela ≃	60	49.55 N	13.33 E
Strelasund ᵾ	54	54.20 N	13.05 E
Strel'covka	83	49.18 N	39.52 E
Streleckaja Step', zapovednik ♦	83	49.16 N	40.05 E
Streleckije Vyselki	82	54.12 N	38.57 E
Strelica	78	51.37 N	38.55 E
Střelice	61	49.09 N	16.30 E
Strelitzalt	54	53.20 N	13.05 E
Strelka	86	58.05 N	93.01 E
Strelka ≃	265a	59.52 N	30.03 E
Strelka-Čun'a	74	61.45 N	102.48 E
Strelkovo	82	55.28 N	37.37 E
Strelkovoje	78	45.54 N	34.53 E
Strel'na, S.S.S.R.	24	66.06 N	38.40 E
Strel'na, S.S.S.R.	76	59.51 N	30.02 E
Strel'na ≃	24	66.04 N	38.39 E
Strel'skaja	24	59.28 N	47.47 E
Střelské Hoštice	60	49.18 N	13.46 E
Strem ≃	61	47.00 N	16.31 E
Strembo	64	46.09 N	10.44 E
Stremilovo	82	55.09 N	37.09 E
Strenči	76	57.37 N	25.41 E
Strengen	58	47.08 N	10.27 E
Strensall	44	54.03 N	1.02 W
Stresa	62	45.53 N	8.32 E
Strešen'	78	47.08 N	28.36 E
Strešin	76	52.43 N	30.05 E
Stretford	44	53.27 N	2.19 W
Stretton, Austl.	162	32.32 S	117.41 E
Stretton, Eng., U.K.	42	52.44 N	0.35 W
Stretton, Eng., U.K.	44	53.21 N	2.35 W
Streu ≃	56	50.21 N	10.16 E
Strib	41	55.32 N	9.47 E
Striberg	40	59.33 N	14.56 E
Stříbro	60	49.46 N	13.00 E
Strichen	46	57.34 N	2.05 W
Strickherdicke	263	51.29 N	7.43 E
Strickland ≃	164	6.00 S	142.05 E
Striegau → Strzegom	30	50.57 N	16.21 E
Strigno	64	46.04 N	11.31 E
Strijen	52	51.45 N	4.33 E
Striker, Lake ⊜[1]	222	31.57 N	94.59 W
Strimón (Struma) ≃	38	40.47 N	23.51 E
Stringtown	218	40.05 N	86.29 W
Striven, Loch c	46	55.58 N	5.09 W
Strižament, gora ∧	84	44.46 N	42.01 E
Strižavka	78	49.19 N	28.28 E
Striži	80	58.30 N	49.13 E
Strjama ≃	38	42.10 N	24.56 E
Strobel	252	32.03 S	60.37 W
Strobel, Lago ⊜	254	48.22 S	71.12 W
Strobl	64	47.43 N	13.29 E
Strobleton	214	41.22 N	79.25 W
Strøby	41	55.23 N	12.18 E
Stroeder	254	40.11 S	62.37 W
Strofádhes, Nísoi II	38	37.15 N	21.00 E
Strogino ◆[8]	265b	55.49 N	37.25 E
Strogonof Point ≻	180	56.53 N	158.49 W
Stroh	216	41.34 N	85.11 W
Ströhen	52	52.32 N	8.41 E
Stroitel'	78	50.47 N	36.26 E
Strokestown	48	53.47 N	8.08 W
Strom ≃	54	53.15 N	13.50 E
Stroma I	46	58.41 N	3.08 W
Stromberg, B.R.D.	52	51.48 N	8.12 E
Stromberg, B.R.D.	56	49.57 N	7.46 E
Stromboli, Isola I	70	38.47 N	15.13 E
Strome	182	52.48 N	112.04 W
Stromeferry	46	57.21 N	5.34 W
Strömkendorf	54	53.58 N	11.29 E
Stromness	46	58.57 N	3.18 W
Strömsberg	40	60.24 N	17.35 E
Strömsbro	40	60.42 N	17.10 E
Strömsbruk	26	61.53 N	17.19 E
Stromsburg	198	41.06 N	97.35 W
Strömsholm	40	59.32 N	16.15 E
Strömsnäsbruk	26	56.33 N	13.43 E
Strömstad	26	58.56 N	11.10 E
Strömsund	26	63.51 N	15.35 E
Strömsvattudal ⊜	26	63.56 N	15.28 E
Stromyn'	82	56.03 N	38.29 E
Strong	194	33.06 N	92.20 W
Strong ≃	194	31.51 N	90.08 W
Strong City	198	38.23 N	96.32 W
Stronghurst	190	40.44 N	90.54 W
Strongoli	68	39.15 N	17.03 E
Strongs Creek ≃	276	40.40 N	73.22 W
Strongs Neck ≻[1]	276	40.58 N	73.07 W
Strongstown	214	40.33 N	78.55 W
Strongsville	214	41.18 N	81.50 W
Strongsville Airport ⊠	279a	41.19 N	81.52 W
Stronsay I	46	59.07 N	2.37 W
Stronsay Firth ᵾ	46	59.02 N	2.41 W
Stronsdorf	61	48.39 N	16.18 E
Strontian	46	56.41 N	5.44 W
Strood	42	51.24 N	0.28 E
Stropkov	30	49.12 N	21.40 E
Stropnice ≃	61	48.52 N	14.30 E
Stroppiana	62	45.14 N	8.27 E
Stroud, Austl.	166	32.20 S	151.56 E
Stroud, Eng., U.K.	42	51.45 N	2.12 W
Stroud, Ok., U.S.	196	35.44 N	96.39 W
Stroudsburg	210	40.59 N	75.11 W
Strövelstorp	41	56.09 N	12.49 E
Strubenvale	273d	26.16 S	28.28 E
Strücklingen	52	53.07 N	7.40 E
Struer	26	56.29 N	8.37 E
Struga	38	41.11 N	20.40 E
Strugi-Krasnyje	76	58.17 N	29.06 E
Struisbaai	158	34.49 S	20.04 E
Struisbult	273d	26.19 S	28.29 E
Strule ≃	48	54.43 N	7.25 W
Strum	190	44.32 N	91.23 W
Struma (Strimón) ≃	38	40.47 N	23.51 E
Strumble Head ≻	42	52.02 N	5.04 W
Strumica	38	41.26 N	22.38 E
Strümp	263	51.17 N	6.40 E
Strunino	82	56.23 N	38.34 E
Strupna	82	54.43 N	38.48 E
Struthers	214	41.03 N	80.36 W
Struy	46	57.24 N	4.39 W
Strydenburg	158	29.58 S	23.40 E
Strydomsvlei	158	33.10 S	23.03 E
Strydpoort	158	27.00 S	25.58 E
Stryj	78	49.15 N	23.51 E
Stryj ≃	78	49.24 N	24.13 E
Stryker, Mt., U.S.	182	48.40 N	114.46 W
Stryker, Oh., U.S.	216	41.30 N	84.24 W
Strykersville	210	42.42 N	78.27 W
Stryków	30	51.55 N	19.37 E
Stryn	26	61.55 N	6.47 E
Strynø I	41	54.54 N	10.37 E
Strypa ≃	78	48.52 N	25.26 E
Strzegom	30	50.57 N	16.21 E
Strzegowo-Osada	30	52.55 N	20.18 E
Strzelce Krajeńskie	30	52.53 N	15.32 E
Strzelce Opolskie	30	50.31 N	18.19 E
Strzelecki Creek ≃	166	29.37 S	139.59 E
Strzelecki Desert ◆[2]	162	28.00 S	140.10 E
Strzeleckie, Mount ∧	162	21.10 S	133.53 E
Strzelecki National Park ♦	166	40.14 S	148.06 E
Strzelin	30	50.47 N	17.03 E
Strzelno	30	52.38 N	18.11 E
Strzyżów	30	49.52 N	21.47 E
Stuart, Fl., U.S.	220	27.11 N	80.15 W
Stuart, Ia., U.S.	198	41.30 N	94.19 W
Stuart, Ne., U.S.	198	42.35 N	99.08 W
Stuart, Va., U.S.	192	36.38 N	80.15 W
Stuart ≃	182	54.00 N	123.32 W
Stuart, Central Mount ∧	162	21.54 S	133.27 E
Stuart, Mount ∧	224	47.29 N	120.54 W
Stuart Channel ᵾ	224	48.55 N	123.45 W
Stuart Island I, Ak., U.S.	180	63.35 N	162.30 W
Stuart Island I, Wa., U.S.	224	48.42 N	123.12 W
Stuart Lake ⊜	182	54.32 N	124.35 W
Stuart Mountains ⋀	172	45.00 S	167.37 E
Stuart Range ⋀	162	29.10 S	134.56 E
Stuarts Draft	192	38.01 N	79.02 W
Stubai V	64	47.06 N	11.19 E
Stubaier Alpen ⋀	64	47.10 N	11.05 E
Stubalpe ⋀	61	47.06 N	14.54 E
Stübbecken	263	51.23 N	7.36 E
Stubbekøbing	41	54.53 N	12.03 E
Stubbenfelde	54	54.02 N	14.01 E
Stubbenkammer	54	54.35 N	13.40 E
Stubbington	42	50.50 N	1.13 W
Stubbins	262	53.39 N	2.19 W
Stubbs Bay c	241h	13.08 N	61.10 W
Stubenberg	61	47.14 N	15.48 E
Stubla ≃	78	50.50 N	26.04 E
Stubner Kogel ∧	64	47.07 N	13.06 E
Stučka	76	56.38 N	25.13 E
Studená	61	49.11 N	15.17 E
Studenec	80	54.52 N	48.16 E
Studenica, Manastir Ʊ[1]	38	43.21 N	20.35 E
Studen Kladenec, jazovir ⊜[1]	38	41.37 N	25.30 E
Studholme Junction	172	44.44 S	171.08 E
Studland	42	50.39 N	1.58 W
Studley	42	52.16 N	1.52 W
Stud'onoje, S.S.S.R.	80	51.36 N	53.10 E
Stud'onoje, S.S.S.R.	86	53.37 N	77.31 E
Stud'onok	78	51.42 N	34.07 E
Studsvik	40	58.46 N	17.23 E
Stugudal	26	62.54 N	11.52 E
Stugun	26	63.10 N	15.36 E
Stuhleck ∧	61	47.34 N	15.47 E
Stühlingen	58	47.44 N	8.26 E
Stuhlweissenburg → Székesfehérvár	30	47.12 N	18.25 E
Stuhm → Sztum	30	53.56 N	19.01 E
Stuhr	52	53.01 N	8.45 E
Stuie	182	52.22 N	126.02 W
Stukely, Lac ⊜	206	45.22 N	72.15 W
Stukenbrock	52	51.54 N	8.39 E
Stull ≃	184	55.10 N	92.39 W
Stull Lake ⊜	184	54.23 N	92.34 W
Stülpe	54	52.02 N	13.19 E
Stumm	64	47.17 N	11.53 E
Stump Creek	214	41.01 N	78.50 W
Stump Creek ≃	276	40.28 N	74.16 W
Stumpf	263	51.06 N	7.13 E
Stump Lake ⊜	198	47.54 N	98.24 W
Stumsdorf	54	51.37 N	12.03 E
Stuorre Tjõure ∧	26	63.56 N	13.30 E
Stupart ≃	184	56.00 N	93.22 W
Stupava	61	48.17 N	17.02 E
Stupino	82	54.53 N	38.05 E
Stuppach	56	49.27 N	9.44 E
Stura di Ala ≃	62	45.18 N	7.24 E
Stura di Demonte ≃	62	44.40 N	7.53 E
Stura di Lanzo ≃	62	45.06 N	7.44 E
Stura di Val Grande ≃	62	45.18 N	7.24 E
Stura di Viù ≃	62	45.16 N	7.26 E
Sturbridge	207	42.06 N	72.04 W
Sturdee	162	31.52 S	132.23 E
Sturge Island I	9	67.27 S	164.18 E
Sturgeon, Mo., U.S.	219	39.14 N	92.16 W
Sturgeon, Pa., U.S.	279b	40.23 N	80.13 W
Sturgeon ≃, On., Can.	190	46.19 N	79.58 W
Sturgeon ≃, Sk., Can.	184	53.12 N	105.53 W
Sturgeon ≃, Mi., U.S.	190	45.50 N	86.41 W
Sturgeon ≃, Mi., U.S.	190	47.02 N	88.30 W
Sturgeon ≃, Mi., U.S.	190	45.24 N	84.38 W
Sturgeon Bay	190	44.50 N	87.22 W
Sturgeon Bay c	184	52.00 N	97.50 W
Sturgeon Falls	190	46.22 N	79.55 W
Sturgeon Lake ⊜, Ab., Can.	182	55.06 N	117.30 W
Sturgeon Lake ⊜, On., Can.	184	55.25 N	90.55 W
Sturgeon Lake ⊜, On., Can.	212	44.28 N	78.42 W
Sturgeon Lake ⊜, Wa., U.S.	224	45.44 N	122.48 W
Sturgeon Lake Indian Reserve ◆[4], Ab., Can.	182	55.04 N	117.29 W
Sturgeon Lake Indian Reserve ◆[4], Sk., Can.	184	53.25 N	106.05 W
Sturgeon Landing	184	54.16 N	101.49 W
Sturgeon Point ≻	212	42.42 N	79.03 W
Sturgis, Sk., Can.	184	51.58 N	102.32 W
Sturgis, Ky., U.S.	194	37.32 N	87.59 W
Sturgis, Mi., U.S.	216	41.47 N	85.25 W
Sturgis, Ms., U.S.	194	33.20 N	89.02 W
Sturgis, S.D., U.S.	198	44.24 N	103.30 W
Sturla	62	44.24 N	8.59 E
Sturminster Newton	42	50.50 N	2.19 W
Štúrovo	30	47.48 N	18.49 E
Sturry	42	51.18 N	1.07 E
Sturt, Mount ∧	166	29.33 S	141.42 E
Sturt Creek	162	19.10 S	128.10 E
Sturt Creek ≃	162	20.08 S	127.24 E
Sturtevant	216	42.41 N	87.53 W
Sturt National Park ♦	166	29.00 S	141.40 E
Sturt Stony Desert ◆[2]	166	28.30 S	141.00 E
Sturup flygplats ⊠	41	55.34 N	13.21 E
Stürzelberg	263	51.08 N	6.49 E
Stutterheim	158	32.33 S	27.28 E
Stuttgart, B.R.D.	56	48.46 N	9.11 E
Stuttgart, Ar., U.S.	194	34.30 N	91.33 W
Stuttgart □[5]	56	49.00 N	9.45 E
Stuttgart, Flughafen ⊠	56	48.41 N	9.12 E
Stützengrün	54	50.32 N	12.31 E
Stützerbach	54	50.38 N	10.51 E
Stuyvesant	210	42.24 N	73.47 W
Stuyvesant Falls	210	42.21 N	73.44 W
Stviga ≃	78	52.04 N	27.54 E
Styal	262	53.21 N	2.15 W
Stykkishólmur	24a	65.06 N	22.48 W
Styla	83	47.41 N	37.50 E
Styr' ≃	78	52.07 N	26.35 E
Styrum ◆[8]	263	51.27 N	6.51 E
Styx ≃, On., Can.	212	44.11 N	80.57 W
Styx ≃, Al., U.S.	194	30.31 N	87.27 W
Suaçuí Grande ≃	255	18.50 S	41.46 W
Suai	112	3.48 N	113.38 E
Suain	164	3.20 S	142.55 E
Suaita	246	6.07 N	73.27 W
Suakin Archipelago II	140	18.42 N	38.30 E
Sual	116	16.04 N	120.05 E
Suan	98	38.42 N	126.22 E
Suao, T'aiwan	100	24.36 N	121.51 E
Su'ao, Zhg.	100	25.38 N	119.42 E
Suaqui Grande	232	28.24 N	109.54 W
Suār	124	29.02 N	79.03 E
Suātala	124	23.09 N	79.02 E
Suatima	114	4.13 N	96.04 E
Šubač	76	60.22 N	38.14 E
Subačius	76	55.46 N	24.47 E
Subah	115a	6.58 S	109.52 E
Subaio	256	22.35 S	42.52 W
Subang	115a	6.34 S	107.45 E
Subansiri ≃	120	26.48 N	93.50 E
Šubarkuduk	86	49.13 N	56.34 E
Subar Laut, Pulau I	271c	1.13 N	103.50 E
Subarnapur	272b	22.58 N	88.34 E
Subarnarekha ≃	120	21.34 N	87.24 E
Šubarši	86	48.35 N	57.12 E
Subashi	85	38.22 N	74.57 E
Subasio, Monte ∧	66	43.03 N	12.40 E
Subata	76	56.01 N	25.56 E
Subay', 'Urūq as- ◆[2]	144	22.15 N	43.05 E
Subbiano	66	43.34 N	11.52 E
Subbotino	86	53.04 N	91.55 E
Subchankulovo	80	54.34 N	53.49 E
Subei	102	39.27 N	95.03 E
Subeita → Shivta, Ḥorvot ⊥	132	30.53 N	34.38 E
Suben	60	48.25 N	13.26 E
Subhepur	272a	28.45 N	77.16 E
Subi, Pulau I	112	2.55 N	108.50 E
Subiaco	66	41.55 N	13.06 E
Subic	116	14.53 N	120.14 E
Subic Bay c	116	14.45 N	120.13 E
Subic Bay Naval Base (U.S.) ■	116	14.47 N	120.16 E
Subipur	272b	22.54 N	88.08 E
Subk al-Ahad	142	30.18 N	31.02 E
Sublette	198	37.28 N	100.50 W
Sublett Range ⋀	202	42.20 N	112.50 W
Sublime	222	29.29 N	96.48 W
Subotica	38	46.06 N	19.39 E
Suburban Airport ⊠	284c	39.05 N	76.50 W
Suburban Village	285	39.58 N	75.34 W
Suca	144	6.31 N	39.14 E
Sucarnoochee ≃	194	32.25 N	88.02 W
Succasunna	210	40.52 N	74.38 W
Succor Creek ≃	202	43.38 N	116.56 W
Suceava	38	47.39 N	26.19 E
Suceava □[6]	38	47.30 N	25.45 E
Suceava ≃	38	47.32 N	26.32 E
Sucha [Beskidzka]	30	49.44 N	19.36 E
Suchaja	88	52.32 N	107.06 E
Suchaja Volnovacha ≃	83	47.37 N	38.01 E
Suchań	30	53.17 N	15.19 E
Suchan → Partizansk	89	43.08 N	133.09 E
Suchana	74	68.45 N	118.00 E
Suchang	107	30.34 N	103.34 E
Süchbaatar	88	50.15 N	106.12 E
Süchbaatar □[4]	102	45.30 N	114.00 E
Suchdol ◆[8]	54	50.08 N	14.21 E
Suchdol nad Lužnicí	61	48.54 N	14.53 E
Suchedniów	30	51.03 N	20.51 E
Suchetgarh	123	32.34 N	74.40 E
Suchiapa	234	16.37 N	93.05 W
Suchiapa ≃	234	16.36 N	93.01 W
Súchil	234	23.38 N	103.55 W
Suchilquitongo	234	17.15 N	96.53 W
Suchiniči	76	54.06 N	35.20 E
Suchitepéquez □[5]	236	14.25 N	91.20 W
Suchitlán	234	19.22 N	103.43 W
Suchitoto	236	13.56 N	89.02 W
Suchobezvodnoje	80	57.03 N	44.50 E
Suchoborka	24	59.06 N	49.58 E
Suchodol, S.S.S.R.	80	53.55 N	51.14 E
Suchodol, S.S.S.R.	82	54.27 N	37.22 E
Suchodol'skij	76	53.43 N	38.17 E
Suchodrev ≃	82	54.44 N	35.59 E
Suchoj	80	47.06 N	41.21 E
Suchoj Jelančik ≃	83	47.16 N	38.25 E
Suchoj Log	86	56.55 N	62.01 E
Suchoj Pit	86	58.48 N	92.49 E
Suchoj Sambek ≃	83	47.23 N	39.07 E
Suchoj Torec ≃	83	48.49 N	37.36 E
Suchona ≃	24	60.46 N	46.24 E
Suchorečka	80	52.49 N	52.27 E
Suchotinka	80	52.31 N	41.35 E
Suchou → Suzhou	106	31.18 N	120.37 E
Suchoverkovo	76	56.37 N	35.35 E
Suchov Pervyj	80	49.59 N	43.28 E
Süchow → Xuzhou	98	34.16 N	117.11 E
Süchteln	56	51.17 N	6.22 E
Suchumi	84	43.01 N	41.02 E
Sucio ≃, Col.	246	7.27 N	77.07 W
Sucio ≃, El Sal.	236	14.02 N	89.17 W
Suck ≃	48	53.16 N	8.03 W
Sucker Creek ≃	212	44.09 N	77.08 W
Sucker Creek Indian Reserve ◆[4]	182	55.28 N	116.10 W
Sucker Lake ⊜	212	44.46 N	78.16 W
Suckling, Mount ∧	164	9.45 S	148.55 E
Sucre, Arg.	258	34.30 S	59.07 W
Sucre, Bol.	248	19.02 S	65.17 W
Sucre, Col.	246	8.49 N	74.44 W
Sucre, Ec.	246	1.16 S	80.26 W
Sucre □[3]	246	10.25 N	63.30 W
Sucre □[5], Col.	246	9.00 N	75.00 W
Sucre □[5], Ven.	286c	10.25 N	66.50 W
Sucúa	246	2.28 S	78.10 W
Sucuaro	246	4.34 N	68.50 W
Sucunduri ≃	248	5.50 S	59.32 W
Sucuriju	250	1.39 N	49.57 W
Sucuriú ≃	255	20.47 S	51.38 W
Sucy-en-Brie	50	48.46 N	2.32 E
Sud, Canal du ᵾ	238	18.40 N	73.05 W
Sud, Grand Récif ✥[2]	175f	23.00 S	167.02 E
Sud, Pointe ≻	157a	11.53 S	43.49 E
Sud, Rivière du ≃	206	45.08 N	73.15 W
Suda	76	59.09 N	37.33 E
Suda ≃	76	59.11 N	37.30 E
Südafrika → South Africa □[1]	156	30.00 S	26.00 E
Sudaj	76	58.58 N	43.08 E
Sudak	78	44.52 N	34.59 E
Südamerika → South America •[1]	18	15.00 S	60.00 W
Sudan	196	34.04 N	102.31 W
Sudan (As-Sūdān) □[1], Afr.	136	15.00 N	30.00 E
Sudan (As-Sūdān) □[1], Afr.	140	15.00 N	30.00 E
Sudan ◆[1]	10	10.00 N	20.00 E
Sudarsan	272b	22.59 N	88.17 E
Südbahnhof ◆[5]	264b	48.11 N	16.23 E
Sudberg ◆[8]	263	51.11 N	7.08 E
Sudbišči	76	52.57 N	37.39 E
Sud'bodarovka	80	52.19 N	54.07 E
Südbrookmerland	52	53.29 N	7.24 E
Sudbury, On., Can.	190	46.30 N	81.00 W
Sudbury, Eng., U.K.	42	52.02 N	0.44 E
Sudbury, Ma., U.S.	207	42.23 N	71.25 W
Sudbury ≃	283	42.28 N	71.22 W
Sudbury Center	283	42.23 N	71.25 W
Sudbury Reservoir ⊜[1]	207	42.19 N	71.31 W
Südchinesisches Meer → South China Sea ⍑[2]	108	10.00 N	113.00 E
Sudd → As-Sudd ◆[1]	140	8.00 N	31.00 E
Sud Dakota → South Dakota □[3]	198	44.15 N	100.00 W
Sudd an-Na'ām, Jabal ∧	142	29.49 N	31.43 E
Suddie	246	7.07 N	58.29 W
Sude ≃	54	53.22 N	10.45 E
Süderbrarup	41	54.38 N	9.46 E
Süderlügum	41	54.52 N	8.55 E
Suderwich	263	51.37 N	7.15 E
Sudeten → Sudety ⋀	30	50.30 N	16.00 E
Sudety ⋀	30	50.30 N	16.00 E
Süd-Georgien → South Georgia I	244	54.15 S	36.45 W
Sudi	154	10.06 S	39.57 E
Sudislavl'	80	57.53 N	41.43 E
Südkamen	263	51.35 N	7.39 E
Süd-Korea → Korea, South □[1]	98	36.30 N	128.00 E
Sudlersville	208	39.11 N	75.51 W
Südlicher Bug → Južnyj Bug ≃	78	46.59 N	31.58 E
Südlicher Indianer-See → Southern Indian Lake ⊜	176	57.10 N	98.40 W
Sudnikovo	82	55.53 N	36.02 E
Sudočje, ozero ⊜	86	43.25 N	58.30 E
Sudogda	80	55.57 N	40.50 E
Sudomskaja vozvyšennost' ⋀[1]	76	57.25 N	29.25 E
Sudong, Pulau I	271c	1.13 N	103.44 E
Süd-Orkney-Inseln → South Orkney Islands II	9	60.35 S	45.30 W
Sudost' ≃	76	52.19 N	33.24 E
Sud-Ouest □[4]	152	5.10 N	9.00 E
Sud-Ouest, Pointe du ≻	186	49.23 N	63.36 W
Sudovaja Višn'a	78	49.49 N	23.22 E
Südradde ≃	52	52.41 N	7.34 E
Süd-Sandwich-Inseln → South Sandwich Islands II	18	57.45 S	26.30 W
Süd-Shetland-Inseln → South Shetland Islands II	9	62.00 S	58.00 W
Sudūd	142	30.25 N	30.54 E
Südwest-Kap → South West Cape ≻	166	43.34 S	146.02 E
Sudweyhe	52	52.59 N	8.53 E
Sudža	78	51.12 N	35.16 E
Sue	96	33.35 N	130.30 E
Sue ≃	140	7.41 N	28.03 E
Sueca	34	39.12 N	0.19 W
Suecia → Sweden □[1]	24	62.00 N	15.00 E
Sue Creek c	284b	39.17 N	76.24 W
Suedberg	208	40.32 N	76.28 W
Suède → Sweden □[1]	24	62.00 N	15.00 E
Suemez Island I	182	55.17 N	133.21 W
Suèvres	50	47.40 N	1.28 E
Suez → As-Suways	142	29.58 N	32.33 E
Suez, Gulf of → Suways, Khalīj as- c	140	29.00 N	32.50 E
Suez Canal → Suways, Qanāt as- ≅	142	29.55 N	32.33 E
Sūf	132	32.19 N	35.50 E
Şufaynah	128	23.09 N	40.32 E
Suffern	210	41.06 N	74.09 W
Suffern Park	276	41.07 N	74.07 W
Suffield, Ab., Can.	184	50.12 N	111.10 W
Suffield, Ct., U.S.	207	41.58 N	72.39 W
Suffield, Oh., U.S.	214	41.01 N	81.21 W
Suffield, Canadian Forces Base ■	184	50.15 N	111.10 W
Suffolk	208	36.43 N	76.35 W
Suffolk □[6], Eng., U.K.	42	52.10 N	1.00 E
Suffolk □[6], Ma., U.S.	207	42.21 N	71.04 W
Suffolk □[6], N.Y., U.S.	210	40.55 N	72.40 W
Suffolk, Ruisseau ≃	206	45.48 N	74.59 W
Suffolk Downs Race Track ♦	283	42.23 N	71.00 W
Şūfīān	128	38.17 N	45.59 E
Sufi-Kurgan	85	40.02 N	73.30 E
Sufu → Kashi	85	39.29 N	75.59 E
Suga-jima I	94	34.29 N	136.53 E
Sugana, Val V	64	46.00 N	11.40 E
Sugandha	272b	22.54 N	88.20 E
Sugandy	85	43.27 N	74.38 E
Sugano	268	35.44 N	139.56 E
Sugar ≃, U.S.	190	42.26 N	89.12 W
Sugar ≃, N.H., U.S.	188	43.24 N	72.24 W
Sugar ≃, N.Y., U.S.	212	43.31 N	75.19 W
Sugar City	202	43.52 N	111.44 W
Sugarcreek, Oh., U.S.	214	40.30 N	81.39 W
Sugarcreek, Pa., U.S.	214	41.25 N	79.52 W
Sugar Creek ≃, U.S.	216	40.47 N	87.45 W
Sugar Creek ≃, Il., U.S.	194	40.09 N	89.38 W
Sugar Creek ≃, Il., U.S.	219	38.28 N	89.37 W
Sugar Creek ≃, Il., U.S.	219	39.48 N	89.32 W
Sugar Creek ≃, In., U.S.	194	39.51 N	87.21 W
Sugar Creek ≃, In., U.S.	218	39.21 N	86.00 W
Sugar Creek ≃, Mi., U.S.	281	42.06 N	83.36 W
Sugar Creek ≃, N.Y., U.S.	210	42.38 N	77.09 W
Sugar Creek ≃, Oh., U.S.	214	40.31 N	81.28 W
Sugar Creek ≃, Oh., U.S.	216	40.57 N	84.11 W
Sugar Creek ≃, Oh., U.S.	218	39.27 N	83.25 W
Sugar Creek ≃, Ok., U.S.	196	35.05 N	98.10 W
Sugar Creek ≃, Pa., U.S.	210	41.47 N	76.27 W
Sugar Creek ≃, Wi., U.S.	216	42.43 N	88.19 W
Sugar Grove, Il., U.S.	216	41.45 N	88.27 W
Sugargrove, Pa., U.S.	214	41.59 N	79.21 W
Sugar Grove, Va., U.S.	192	36.46 N	81.24 W
Sugar Hill	192	34.06 N	84.02 W
Sugar Island I, On., Can.	212	44.26 N	77.17 W
Sugar Island I, Mi., U.S.	190	46.25 N	84.12 W

Symbol	English	Deutsch	Español	Français	Português
≃	River	Fluß	Río	Rivière	Rio
≅	Canal	Kanal	Canal	Canal	Canal
∟	Waterfall, Rapids	Wasserfall, Stromschnellen	Cascada, Rápidos	Chute d'eau, Rapides	Cascata, Rápidos
ᵾ	Strait	Meeresstraße	Estrecho	Détroit	Estreito
c	Bay, Gulf	Bucht, Golf	Bahía, Golfo	Baie, Golfe	Baía, Golfo
⊜	Lake, Lakes	See, Seen	Lago, Lagos	Lac, Lacs	Lago, Lagos
≚	Swamp	Sumpf	Pantano	Marais	Pântano
⍓	Ice Features, Glacier	Eis- und Gletscherformen	Accidentes Glaciales	Formes glaciaires	Acidentes glaciares
⍑	Other Hydrographic Features	Andere Hydrographische Objekte	Otros Elementos Hidrográficos	Autres données hydrographiques	Outros acidentes hidrográficos
✥	Submarine Features	Untermeerische Objekte	Accidentes Submarinos	Formes de relief sous-marin	Acidentes submarinos
□	Political Unit	Politische Einheit	Unidad Politica	Entité politique	Unidade política
Ʊ	Cultural Institution	Kulturelle Institution	Institución Cultural	Institution culturelle	Institução cultural
⊥	Historical Site	Historische Stätte	Sitio Histórico	Site historique	Sitio histórico
♦	Recreational Site	Erholungs- und Ferienort	Sitio de Recreo	Centre de loisirs	Area de Lazer
⊠	Airport	Flughafen	Aeropuerto	Aéroport	Aeroporto
■	Military Installation	Militäranlage	Instalación Militar	Installation militaire	Instalação militar
◆	Miscellaneous	Verschiedenes	Misceláneo	Divers	Diversos

Name	Page	Lat.°′	Long.°′
Sugar Land	**222**	29.37 N	95.38 W
Sugar Loaf	**210**	41.19 N	74.17 W
Sugar Loaf → Pão de Açúcar ∧	**287a**	22.57 S	43.09 W
Sugarloaf ∧[2]	**214**	41.24 N	81.06 W
Sugarloaf Hill ∧[2]	**274b**	37.58 S	145.19 E
Sugarloaf Key I	**220**	24.40 N	81.32 W
Sugarloaf Mountain ∧, Ky., U.S.	**218**	38.13 N	83.32 W
Sugarloaf Mountain ∧, Me., U.S.	**188**	45.01 N	70.22 W
Sugar Loaf Mountain ∧, Md., U.S.	**208**	39.16 N	77.23 W
Sugar Loaf Mountain ∧, Ok., U.S.	**194**	35.02 N	94.28 W
Sugarloaf Mountain ∧[2]	**220**	28.39 N	81.44 W
Sugarloaf Peak ∧	**280**	34.14 N	117.38 W
Sugarloaf Point ›, Austl.	**166**	32.26 S	152.33 E
Sugar Loaf Point ›, On., Can.	**284a**	42.52 N	79.17 W
Sugarloaf Reservoir ⊜[1]	**169**	37.41 S	145.18 E
Sugarloaf Ridge State Park ♦	**226**	38.26 N	122.29 W
Sugar Notch	**210**	41.11 N	75.55 W
Sugar Pine Point State Park ♦	**226**	39.03 N	120.07 W
Sugartown	**285**	40.00 N	75.31 W
Sugauli	**124**	26.46 N	84.44 E
Sugbai Passage ⊔	**116**	5.22 N	120.33 E
Sugbay	**116**	7.31 N	123.19 E
Sugbuhan Point ›	**116**	10.04 N	126.04 E
Suggi Lake ⊜	**184**	54.22 N	102.47 W
Suginami ◈[8]	**268**	35.42 N	139.38 E
Sugita ◈[8]	**268**	35.23 N	139.38 E
Sugito	**94**	36.02 N	139.44 E
Şuğla Gölü ⊜	**130**	37.20 N	32.02 E
Šugnou	**85**	38.35 N	70.20 E
Sugod	**116**	12.03 N	124.09 E
Sugoj ≃	**74**	64.15 N	154.29 E
Šugonovo	**82**	54.41 N	36.41 E
Šugozero	**76**	59.55 N	34.12 E
Šugurovo, S.S.S.R.	**80**	53.25 N	46.29 E
Šugurovo, S.S.S.R.	**80**	54.31 N	52.06 E
Sugut ≃	**112**	6.26 N	117.43 E
Suguta ≃	**154**	2.03 N	36.33 E
Suguti	**154**	1.44 S	33.39 E
Suhai Hu ⊜	**102**	38.50 N	94.00 E
Suhaitu	**102**	44.50 N	93.39 E
Şuḥār	**128**	24.22 N	56.45 E
Suheli Island I[1]	**122**	10.03 N	72.17 E
Suhl	**54**	50.37 N	10.41 E
Suhl □[5]	**54**	50.40 N	10.30 E
Suhlendorf	**54**	52.55 N	10.46 E
Suhopolje	**36**	45.48 N	17.30 E
Suhr	**58**	47.22 N	8.05 E
Suhr ≃	**58**	47.25 N	8.04 E
Suhum	**150**	6.05 N	0.27 W
Şuhut	**130**	38.32 N	30.33 E
Sūi	**120**	28.37 N	69.19 E
Suia-Miçu ≃	**250**	11.13 S	53.15 W
Suianzhan	**89**	53.07 N	125.20 E
Suiattle ≃	**224**	48.20 N	121.33 W
Suichang	**100**	28.34 N	119.14 E
Suichuan	**100**	26.26 N	114.32 E
Suichuan ≃	**100**	26.30 N	114.45 E
Suid Afrika → South Africa □[1]	**156**	30.00 S	26.00 E
Suide	**102**	37.32 N	110.12 E
Suiding	**86**	44.03 N	80.49 E
Suido-suigenchi ⊜[1]	**270**	34.54 N	135.17 E
Suidvaal	**158**	26.52 S	29.47 E
Suifenhe	**89**	44.24 N	131.10 E
Suifu, Nihon	**94**	36.37 N	140.29 E
Suifu → Yibin, Zhg.	**107**	28.47 N	104.38 E
Suigō-kokutei-kōen ♦	**94**	36.05 N	140.20 E
Suigō-Tsukuba-kokutei-kōen ♦	**94**	36.00 N	140.20 E
Suihua	**89**	46.37 N	127.00 E
Suijiang	**102**	28.31 N	104.07 E
Suileng	**89**	47.18 N	127.10 E
Suining, Zhg.	**100**	33.54 N	117.56 E
Suining, Zhg.	**102**	26.21 N	110.00 E
Suining, Zhg.	**107**	30.31 N	105.34 E
Suipacha	**252**	34.45 S	59.41 W
Suiping	**100**	33.10 N	113.57 E
Suippe ≃	**50**	49.25 N	3.57 E
Suippes	**56**	49.08 N	4.32 E
Suir ≃	**48**	52.15 N	7.00 W
Suisse → Switzerland □[1]	**58**	47.00 N	8.00 E
Suisun Bay ⊂	**226**	38.06 N	122.00 W
Suisun City	**226**	38.14 N	122.02 W
Suisun Creek ≃	**226**	38.12 N	122.06 W
Suita	**96**	34.45 N	135.32 E
Suitland	**284c**	38.50 N	76.55 W
Suixi, Zhg.	**100**	33.56 N	116.46 E
Suixi, Zhg.	**102**	21.25 N	110.15 E
Suixian, Zhg.	**98**	34.26 N	115.05 E
Suixian, Zhg.	**100**	31.42 N	113.20 E
Suiyang, Zhg.	**89**	44.26 N	130.53 E
Suiyang, Zhg.	**102**	27.56 N	107.18 E
Suiyangdian	**100**	32.04 N	112.55 E
Suiza → Switzerland □[1]	**58**	47.00 N	8.00 E
Suize ≃	**58**	48.08 N	5.08 E
Şuizhong	**98**	40.20 N	120.19 E
Šuja, S.S.S.R.	**24**	61.55 N	34.12 E
Šuja, S.S.S.R.	**80**	56.50 N	41.23 E
Šuja ≃, S.S.S.R.	**24**	61.54 N	34.15 E
Šuja ≃, S.S.S.R.	**80**	57.56 N	43.15 E
Sujānagar	**126**	23.57 N	89.25 E
Sujāngarh	**120**	27.42 N	74.28 E
Sujāwal	**120**	24.36 N	68.05 E
Suji	**107**	29.35 N	103.37 E
Sujiabu	**100**	31.38 N	116.22 E
Sujiaqiao	**105**	39.24 N	116.10 E
Sujiatun	**104**	41.40 N	123.22 E
Sujiawan	**107**	29.48 N	104.57 E
Sujiawu	**105**	39.17 N	115.55 E
Şujiazui	**100**	33.40 N	119.29 E
Šujskoje	**76**	59.22 N	40.59 E
Sujutkina Kosa, mys ›	**84**	44.13 N	47.15 E
Sukabihanawa	**112**	9.30 S	124.57 E
Sukabumi	**115a**	6.55 S	106.56 E
Sukadana, Indon.	**112**	1.15 S	109.57 E
Sukadana, Indon.	**115a**	5.05 S	105.33 E
Sukadana, Teluk ⊂	**112**	1.24 S	109.50 E
Sukagawa	**92**	37.17 N	140.23 E
Sukamandi	**115a**	6.20 S	107.39 E
Sukamara	**112**	2.43 S	111.11 E
Sukanegara	**115a**	7.06 S	107.07 E
Sukapura	**115a**	7.52 S	113.03 E
Sukaraja, Indon.	**112**	2.21 S	110.37 E
Sukaraja, Indon.	**115a**	7.27 S	108.12 E
Sukaraja, Indon.	**115a**	7.27 S	109.17 E
Sukarno, Pegunungan → Jaya, Puncak ∧	**164**	4.05 S	137.11 E
Sukau	**112**	5.32 N	118.17 E
Sukchar	**272b**	22.42 N	88.22 E
Sukch'ŏn	**98**	39.24 N	125.38 E
Sukematsu	**270**	34.31 N	135.26 E
Sukeva	**26**	63.52 N	27.26 E
Sukhnah, 'Ayn ⊤[4]	**142**	29.35 N	32.15 E
Sukhothai	**110**	17.01 N	99.49 E
Sukhumi → Suchumi	**84**	43.01 N	41.02 E
Sukkertoppen (Maniitsoq)	**176**	65.25 N	52.53 W
Sukkozero	**24**	63.11 N	32.18 E
Sukkur	**120**	27.42 N	68.52 E
Sukkwan Island I	**182**	55.05 N	132.45 W
Suklāra	**126**	23.11 N	86.21 E
Sukmanovka	**78**	51.47 N	41.34 E
Sukodadi	**115a**	7.06 S	112.19 E
Sukoharjo	**115a**	7.41 S	110.50 E
Sukovo	**82**	54.54 N	38.19 E
Sukroml'a	**76**	56.53 N	34.44 E
Sukses	**156**	21.01 S	16.52 E
Suksun	**86**	57.07 N	57.24 E
Sukumo	**92**	32.56 N	132.44 E
Sukun, Pulau I	**115b**	8.07 S	122.08 E
Sukunka ≃	**182**	55.37 N	121.37 W
Sul, Baía do ⊂	**252**	27.40 S	48.35 W
Sul, Canal do ⊔	**250**	0.10 S	49.30 W
Sula I	**26**	61.08 N	4.55 E
Sula ≃, S.S.S.R.	**24**	67.16 N	52.07 E
Sula ≃, S.S.S.R.	**78**	49.40 N	32.41 E
Sula, Kepulauan II	**112**	1.52 S	125.22 E
Sulaco ≃	**236**	14.58 N	87.45 W
Sulaimān Khel	**123**	33.41 N	71.01 E
Sulaimān Range ⋏	**120**	30.30 N	70.10 E
Sulak, S.S.S.R.	**80**	51.52 N	48.21 E
Sulak, S.S.S.R.	**84**	43.16 N	47.32 E
Sulak ≃	**84**	43.20 N	47.34 E
Sulakyurt	**130**	40.10 N	33.44 E
Sulang	**115a**	6.48 S	111.23 E
Sulat	**116**	11.49 N	125.27 E
Sulauan Point ›	**116**	8.37 N	124.29 E
Sulawesi (Celebes) I	**112**	2.00 S	121.00 E
Sulawesi Selatan □[4]	**112**	3.30 S	120.00 E
Sulawesi Tengah □[4]	**112**	1.00 N	123.00 E
Sulawesi Tenggara □[4]	**112**	4.00 S	122.00 E
Sulawesi Utara □[4]	**112**	0.30 N	124.00 E
Sulaymān, Birak (Solomon's Pools) ⊥	**132**	31.41 N	35.10 E
Sulby	**44**	54.18 N	4.29 W
Sulcis ◈[1]	**71**	39.04 N	8.41 E
Suldalsvatnet ⊜	**26**	59.35 N	6.45 E
Sūldeh	**128**	36.34 N	52.01 E
Sulechów	**30**	52.06 N	15.37 E
Sulęcin	**30**	52.26 N	15.08 E
Suleja	**86**	55.09 N	58.50 E
Sulejów	**30**	51.22 N	19.53 E
Sulejówek	**30**	52.14 N	21.17 E
Sulen, Mount ∧	**164**	3.25 S	142.15 E
Sule Skerry I[2]	**46**	59.05 N	4.26 W
Suleymaniye Mosque ✝[1]	**267b**	41.00 N	28.57 E
Süleymanlı	**130**	37.54 N	36.50 E
Şülfeld	**52**	53.48 N	10.14 E
Šul'ginka	**83**	49.08 N	38.56 E
Şulğino, S.S.S.R.	**82**	55.50 N	35.55 E
Šul'gino, S.S.S.R.	**82**	54.33 N	37.35 E
Sulia	**154**	1.32 S	26.33 E
Suliki	**112**	0.06 S	100.27 E
Sulima	**150**	6.58 N	11.35 W
Sulin	**83**	48.54 N	40.07 E
Sulina	**38**	45.09 N	29.40 E
Sulina, Brațul ≃[1]	**38**	45.09 N	29.41 E
Sulincheer	**102**	42.41 N	109.20 E
Sulingen	**52**	52.41 N	8.47 E
Sulinskij	**83**	47.52 N	40.06 E
Sulitelma ∧	**24**	67.08 N	16.24 E
Sulkava	**26**	61.47 N	28.23 E
Sullana	**248**	4.53 S	80.41 W
Sullane ≃	**48**	51.53 N	8.56 W
Sulligent	**194**	33.54 N	88.08 W
Sullivan, Il., U.S.	**194**	39.35 N	88.36 W
Sullivan, In., U.S.	**194**	39.06 N	87.24 W
Sullivan, Mo., U.S.	**219**	38.12 N	91.09 W
Sullivan, Oh., U.S.	**214**	41.02 N	82.13 W
Sullivan, Wi., U.S.	**216**	43.00 N	88.35 W
Sullivan □[6], N.Y., U.S.	**210**	41.39 N	74.42 W
Sullivan □[6], Pa., U.S.	**210**	41.25 N	76.29 W
Sullivan Canyon V	**280**	34.03 N	118.30 W
Sullivan Creek ≃	**226**	37.53 N	120.25 W
Sullivan Lake ⊜	**182**	52.00 N	112.00 W
Sullivan Stadium ♦	**283**	42.05 N	71.16 W
Sullivanville	**210**	42.14 N	76.46 W
Sully-sur-Loire	**50**	47.46 N	2.22 E
Sulm ≃	**61**	46.45 N	15.34 E
Sulmona	**66**	42.03 N	13.55 E
Sulot' ≃	**82**	56.41 N	38.01 E
Sulphur, Yk., Can.	**180**	63.47 N	138.53 W
Sulphur, In., U.S.	**218**	38.14 N	86.28 W
Sulphur, Ky., U.S.	**218**	38.29 N	85.16 W
Sulphur, La., U.S.	**194**	30.14 N	93.22 W
Sulphur, Ok., U.S.	**196**	34.30 N	96.58 W
Sulphur ≃, Ab., Can.	**182**	53.50 N	119.10 W
Sulphur ≃, U.S.	**194**	33.07 N	93.52 W
Sulphur Creek ≃	**198**	44.46 N	102.25 W
Sulphur Draw V	**196**	33.12 N	102.17 W
Sulphur Springs, In., U.S.	**218**	40.00 N	85.26 W
Sulphur Springs, Oh., U.S.	**214**	40.52 N	82.52 W
Sulphur Springs, Tx., U.S.	**222**	33.08 N	95.36 W
Sulphur Springs Draw V	**196**	32.12 N	101.36 W
Sulphur Springs Valley V	**200**	31.50 N	109.50 W
Sulsul	**144**	5.06 N	44.55 E
Sultan	**224**	47.51 N	121.48 W
Sultan ≃	**224**	47.52 N	121.49 W
Sultana	**226**	36.33 N	119.20 W
Sultanahmet Mosque ✝[1]	**267b**	41.00 N	28.58 E
Sultan Alonto, Lake ⊜	**116**	7.53 N	124.15 E
Sultana Point ›	**168b**	35.08 S	137.45 E
Sulṭanatābād ◈[8]	**267d**	35.46 N	51.28 E
Sultançiftligi ◈[8]	**267b**	41.02 N	29.13 E
Sultandağı	**130**	38.32 N	31.14 E
Sultan Dağı ∧	**130**	38.58 N	27.26 E
Sultanhanı	**130**	38.15 N	33.33 E
Sultanhisar	**130**	37.53 N	28.10 E
Sultan Kudarat	**116**	7.17 N	124.16 E
Sultan Kudarat □[4]	**116**	6.20 N	124.20 E
Sultan Mosque ✝[1]	**271c**	1.18 N	103.52 E
Sultānpur, India	**123**	31.13 N	75.11 E
Sultānpur, India	**124**	26.16 N	82.04 E
Sultānpur Dabās ◈[8]	**272a**	28.46 N	77.03 E
Sultan sa Barongis	**116**	6.46 N	124.38 E
Sultan-Saly	**83**	47.21 N	39.35 E
Sulu	**164**	5.25 S	151.00 E
Sulu □[4]	**116**	6.00 N	121.00 E
Suluan Island I	**116**	10.46 N	125.57 E
Sulu Archipelago II	**116**	6.00 N	121.00 E
Sulu Basin ✣[1]	**12**	8.00 N	121.30 E
Sulu Chi ⊜	**124**	30.12 N	86.20 E
Sülüklü	**130**	39.05 N	30.58 E
Sul'ukta	**85**	39.56 N	69.34 E
Sululta	**144**	9.10 N	38.48 E
Suluntah	**146**	32.36 N	21.43 E
Suluova (Suluca)	**130**	40.47 N	35.42 E
Sulūq	**146**	31.39 N	20.15 E
Sulusaj	**85**	38.50 N	67.05 E
Sulusaray	**130**	40.00 N	36.06 E
Sulu Sea ⊤[2]	**116**	8.00 N	120.00 E
Suly	**86**	53.45 N	66.30 E
Sulz	**58**	48.18 N	7.51 E
Sulz am Neckar	**58**	48.21 N	8.37 E
Sulzano	**64**	45.41 N	10.05 E
Sulzbach	**56**	49.18 N	7.07 E
Sulzbach ≃	**60**	48.36 N	13.02 E
Sulzbach am Kocher	**56**	48.58 N	9.50 E
Sulzbach-Rosenberg	**60**	49.30 N	11.45 E
Sulzberger Bay ⊂	**9**	77.00 S	152.00 W
Sulzbrunn	**58**	47.41 N	10.20 E
Sulzburg	**58**	47.50 N	7.42 E
Şülze	**52**	52.46 N	10.02 E
Šum, S.S.S.R.	**76**	59.52 N	31.46 E
Šum, S.S.S.R.	**88**	54.51 N	95.18 E
Şuma ◈[8]	**270**	34.39 N	135.08 E
Šum'ači	**76**	53.52 N	32.25 E
Šumadija ◈[1]	**38**	44.10 N	20.50 E
Sumalata	**112**	0.59 N	122.30 E
Sumallo ≃	**224**	49.14 N	121.05 W
Şumampa	**252**	29.22 S	63.28 W
Šumanaj	**86**	42.37 N	59.08 E
Sumangat, Tanjong ›	**116**	6.35 N	117.33 E
Sumano-ura ♦	**96**	34.38 N	135.08 E
Sūmār	**128**	33.52 N	45.39 E
Sumarokovo	**82**	55.46 N	35.55 E
Sumas	**202**	49.00 N	122.15 W
Sumas ≃	**224**	49.09 N	122.12 W
Sumatera (Sumatra) I	**108**	0.05 S	102.00 E
Sumatera Barat □[4]	**112**	0.30 S	100.30 E
Sumatera Selatan □[4]	**112**	3.00 S	104.00 E
Sumatera Utara □[4]	**114**	2.20 N	99.00 E
Sum'atino	**82**	55.00 N	36.21 E
Sumatou	**107**	30.28 N	104.03 E
Sumatra → Sumatera I	**108**	0.05 S	102.00 E
Sumaúma	**248**	7.50 S	60.02 W
Sumava Resorts	**216**	41.10 N	87.26 W
Sumayḥ	**140**	12.43 N	30.50 E
Sumba I	**115b**	10.00 S	120.00 E
Sumba, Île I	**152**	1.44 N	19.32 E
Sumba, Selat ⊔	**115b**	9.05 S	120.00 E
Sumbar ≃	**128**	38.00 N	55.17 E
Sumbawa I	**115b**	8.40 S	118.00 E
Sumbawa Besar	**115b**	8.30 S	117.26 E
Sumbawanga	**154**	7.58 S	31.37 E
Sumbay	**248**	15.58 S	71.23 W
Sumbe	**152**	11.13 S	13.50 E
Sümber	**90**	46.21 N	108.20 E
Sumbilla	**34**	43.10 N	1.40 W
Sumbing, Gunung ∧	**115a**	7.23 S	110.04 E
Sumbu National Park ♦	**154**	8.50 S	30.25 E
Sumburgh Head ›	**46a**	59.53 N	1.20 W
Şumburgh Roost ⊔	**46a**	59.49 N	1.19 W
Šumbut	**80**	55.33 N	50.41 E
Sumbuya	**150**	7.39 N	11.58 W
Sumdo	**120**	35.01 N	78.41 E
Sumé	**250**	7.39 S	36.55 W
Sumedang	**115a**	6.52 S	107.55 E
Şümeg	**30**	46.59 N	17.17 E
Šumek	**86**	48.42 N	85.32 E
Šumen	**38**	43.16 N	26.55 E
Sumène	**62**	43.59 N	3.43 E
Şumenep	**115a**	7.01 S	113.52 E
Šumerl'a	**80**	55.30 N	46.26 E
Sumgait	**84**	40.36 N	49.38 E
Şumgait ≃	**84**	40.37 N	49.37 E
Šumicha	**86**	55.14 N	63.19 E
Sumida ◈[8]	**268**	35.42 N	139.48 E
Sumida ≃	**268**	35.40 N	139.47 E
Sumidouro	**256**	22.03 S	42.41 W
Şumilao	**116**	8.18 N	124.57 E
Šumilino	**76**	55.18 N	29.37 E
Šumilinskaja	**80**	49.58 N	41.26 E
Suminoe ◈[8]	**270**	34.36 N	135.28 E
Sumisu-jima I	**90**	31.27 N	140.03 E
Sumiswald	**58**	47.02 N	7.45 E
Sumiyoshi ◈[8]	**270**	34.36 N	135.31 E
Sumki	**86**	55.03 N	65.44 E
Sumkino	**86**	58.09 N	68.21 E
Sumlog ≃	**116**	6.53 N	126.02 E
Summer Bridge	**44**	54.03 N	1.41 W
Summerdale	**208**	40.18 N	76.56 W
Summerfield, Fl., U.S.	**220**	29.00 N	82.02 W
Summerfield, Mo., U.S.	**219**	38.17 N	91.49 W
Summerfield, N.C., U.S.	**192**	36.12 N	79.54 W
Summerford, Nf., Can.	**186**	49.29 N	54.47 W
Summerford, Oh., U.S.	**218**	39.55 N	83.29 W
Summerhill, Ire.	**48**	53.29 N	6.44 W
Summerhill, Pa., U.S.	**214**	40.22 N	78.46 W
Summer Island I	**190**	45.34 N	86.39 W
Summer Isles II	**46**	58.02 N	5.28 W
Summer Lake ⊜	**202**	42.50 N	120.45 W
Summerland	**182**	49.36 N	119.41 W
Summerland Reserve ◈[4]	**169**	38.31 S	145.10 E
Sümmern	**56**	51.25 N	7.43 E
Summer Palace ✝	**265a**	59.53 N	29.55 E
Summerseat	**262**	53.38 N	2.19 W
Summerside	**186**	46.24 N	63.47 W
Summersville, Mo., U.S.	**194**	37.10 N	91.39 W
Summersville, W.V., U.S.	**188**	38.16 N	80.51 W
Summerton	**192**	33.36 N	80.21 W
Summertown	**194**	35.26 N	87.18 W
Summerville, On., Can.	**275b**	43.37 N	79.34 W
Summerville, Ga., U.S.	**192**	34.28 N	85.20 W
Summerville, Pa., U.S.	**214**	41.06 N	79.11 W
Summerville, S.C., U.S.	**192**	33.00 N	80.11 W
Summit, Eng., U.K.	**262**	53.40 N	2.05 W
Summit, Ak., U.S.	**180**	63.20 N	149.08 W
Summit, Ca., U.S.	**228**	34.20 N	117.25 W
Summit, Il., U.S.	**216**	41.47 N	87.48 W
Summit, Ms., U.S.	**194**	31.17 N	90.28 W
Summit, N.J., U.S.	**210**	40.44 N	74.21 W
Summit, N.Y., U.S.	**210**	42.35 N	74.35 W
Summit, S.D., U.S.	**198**	45.18 N	97.02 W
Summit, Wa., U.S.	**224**	47.10 N	122.21 W
Summit □[6]	**214**	41.05 N	81.31 W
Summit Creek ≃	**224**	46.00 N	121.10 W
Summit Farms	**284b**	39.19 N	76.32 W
Summit Hill	**210**	40.49 N	75.52 W
Summit Lake	**182**	54.17 N	122.38 W
Summit Lake ⊜	**224**	47.04 N	123.07 W
Summit Mountain ∧	**204**	39.23 N	116.28 W
Summit Park	**276**	41.09 N	74.03 W
Summit Park Mall ◈[9]	**284a**	43.05 N	78.56 W
Summit Peak ∧	**200**	37.21 N	106.42 W
Summit Rock ∧	**172**	45.25 S	170.04 E
Summit Station	**208**	40.34 N	76.12 W
Summitville, In., U.S.	**216**	40.20 N	85.38 W
Summitville, N.Y., U.S.	**210**	41.37 N	74.27 W
Summitville, Oh., U.S.	**214**	40.41 N	80.53 W
Summt	**264a**	52.41 N	13.22 E
Şummter See ⊜	**264a**	52.42 N	13.23 E
Šumná	**61**	48.56 N	15.52 E
Sumnal	**120**	35.45 N	78.40 E
Sumner, Ia., U.S.	**190**	42.50 N	92.05 W
Sumner, Ms., U.S.	**194**	33.58 N	90.22 W
Sumner, Wa., U.S.	**224**	47.12 N	122.14 W
Sumner, Lake ⊜	**172**	42.42 S	172.13 E
Sumner, Lake ⊜[1]	**196**	34.38 N	104.25 W
Sumner Lake State Park ♦	**196**	34.38 N	104.24 W
Sumner Strait ⊔	**180**	56.15 N	133.45 W
Sumoto	**96**	34.21 N	134.54 E
Şumpangbinangae	**112**	4.24 S	119.36 E
Šumperk	**30**	49.58 N	16.58 E
Sumpiuh	**115a**	7.37 S	109.21 E
Sumprabum	**110**	26.33 N	97.34 E
Sumpter	**281**	42.10 N	83.29 W
Sumrall	**194**	31.25 N	89.32 W
Sumsar	**85**	41.18 N	71.19 E
Ş'umsi	**80**	57.07 N	51.37 E
Šumskij	**88**	54.48 N	99.09 E
Şumskij Posad	**24**	64.15 N	35.25 E
Šumskoje	**78**	50.07 N	26.07 E
Šumšu, ostrov I	**74**	50.45 N	156.20 E
Sumter	**192**	33.55 N	80.20 W
Sumter □[6]	**220**	28.38 N	82.08 W
Sumusṭā al-Waqf	**142**	28.55 N	30.51 E
Sumy	**78**	50.55 N	34.45 E
Sumy □[4]	**76**	52.10 N	33.40 E
Sumzom	**102**	29.45 N	96.10 E
S'un' ≃, S.S.S.R.	**80**	55.44 N	54.16 E
Sun ≃, Mt., U.S.	**202**	47.30 N	111.19 W
Sun ≃, Zhg.	**107**	29.13 N	106.21 E
Suna, Kenya	**154**	1.05 S	34.26 E
Suna, S.S.S.R.	**80**	57.51 N	50.05 E
Suna ≃	**24**	62.08 N	34.12 E
Sunagawa	**92a**	43.29 N	141.55 E
Sun al-Heteimi ⊤[4]	**132**	31.05 N	34.00 E
Sun' al-Menī'i ⊤[4]	**132**	31.07 N	34.12 E
Sunām	**123**	30.08 N	75.48 E
Sunāmganj	**120**	25.04 N	91.24 E
Sunami	**94**	35.25 N	136.40 E
Sunan	**98**	39.13 N	125.41 E
Sunapee Lake ⊜	**188**	43.23 N	72.03 W
Sunart, Loch ⊜	**46**	56.41 N	5.43 W
Sunashinden	**268**	35.53 N	139.30 E
Sunbāt	**142**	30.48 N	31.12 E
Sunbright	**192**	36.14 N	84.40 W
Sunburst	**202**	48.52 N	111.54 W
Sunbury, Austl.	**169**	37.35 S	144.44 E
Sunbury, Eng., U.K.	**260**	51.25 N	0.26 W
Sunbury, N.C., U.S.	**192**	36.26 N	76.36 W
Sunbury, Oh., U.S.	**214**	40.14 N	82.51 W
Sunbury, Pa., U.S.	**210**	40.51 N	76.47 W
Sunchales	**252**	30.56 S	61.34 W
Sunch'ang	**98**	35.23 N	127.07 E
Sunchild Indian Reserve ◈[4]	**182**	52.43 N	115.24 W
Sünching	**60**	48.53 N	12.21 E
Suncho Corral	**252**	27.56 S	63.27 W
Sunch'ŏn, C.M.I.K.	**98**	39.26 N	125.54 E
Sunch'ŏn, Taehan	**98**	34.57 N	127.28 E
Sun City, Az., U.S.	**200**	33.35 N	112.16 W
Sun City, Ca., U.S.	**228**	33.42 N	117.11 W
Sun City, Fl., U.S.	**220**	27.40 N	82.28 W
Sun City Center	**220**	27.43 N	82.21 W
Suncook	**188**	43.07 N	71.27 W
Suncook ≃	**188**	43.08 N	71.28 W
Sunda, Selat (Sunda Strait) ⊔	**112**	6.00 S	105.45 E
Sundance	**198**	44.24 N	104.22 W
Sundar	**112**	4.54 N	115.12 E
Sundar ∧	**124**	28.26 N	84.20 E
Sundarbans ◈[1]	**126**	22.00 N	89.00 E
Sundargarh	**124**	22.07 N	84.02 E
Sundarnagar	**123**	31.32 N	76.53 E
Sunda Shelf ✣[4]	**14**	5.00 N	107.00 E
Sunda Strait → Sunda, Selat ⊔	**112**	6.00 S	105.45 E
Sunday Creek ≃	**169**	37.02 S	145.05 E
Sundby, Dan.	**41**	54.42 N	11.48 E
Sundby, Sve.	**40**	59.23 N	17.03 E
Sundbyberg	**40**	59.22 N	17.58 E
Sundbyholm	**40**	59.27 N	16.37 E
Sundbyholm slott ⊥	**40**	59.27 N	16.37 E
Sunde	**26**	59.50 N	5.43 E
Sunderland, On., Can.	**212**	44.16 N	79.04 W
Sunderland, Eng., U.K.	**44**	54.55 N	1.23 W
Sunderland, Ma., U.S.	**207**	42.28 N	72.34 W
Sunderland, Vt., U.S.	**210**	43.06 N	73.06 W
Sundern	**56**	51.20 N	8.00 E
Sünderup	**41**	54.46 N	9.27 E
Sundhausen	**54**	50.56 N	10.40 E
Sundhouse	**58**	48.15 N	7.36 E
Sundi-Lutete	**152**	4.34 S	14.14 E
Sundown, Austl.	**162**	26.14 S	133.12 E
Sundown, N.Y., U.S.	**210**	41.53 N	74.28 W
Sundown, Tx., U.S.	**196**	33.27 N	102.29 W
Sundra	**273d**	26.11 S	28.33 E
Sundre	**182**	51.48 N	114.38 W
Sundridge, On., Can.	**190**	45.46 N	79.24 W
Sundridge, Eng., U.K.	**260**	51.17 N	0.18 E
Sunds	**41**	56.12 N	9.01 E
Sundsbruk	**26**	62.27 N	17.22 E
Sundsvall	**26**	62.23 N	17.18 E
Sundwig	**263**	51.23 N	7.47 E
Suneori	**268**	35.56 N	139.24 E
Sunfield	**216**	42.45 N	84.59 W
Sunfish Creek ≃	**218**	39.01 N	83.03 W
Sunflower	**194**	33.32 N	90.32 W
Sunflower, Mount ∧	**198**	39.04 N	102.01 W
Sungaianyar	**112**	2.55 S	116.18 E
Sungaiapit	**114**	1.09 N	102.10 E
Sungaibamban	**114**	3.26 N	99.09 E
Sungaibatu	**112**	0.48 N	110.45 E
Sungai Bayor	**114**	5.15 N	100.47 E
Sungaibuntu	**115a**	6.03 S	107.24 E
Sungaidareh	**112**	0.58 S	101.30 E
Sungaigerong	**112**	2.59 S	104.52 E
Sungaiguntung	**112**	0.18 N	103.37 E
Sungaikakap	**112**	0.04 S	109.10 E
Sungai Kolok	**114**	6.02 N	101.58 E
Sungailangsat	**112**	0.52 S	101.18 E
Sungai Lembing	**114**	3.55 N	103.02 E
Sungailiat	**112**	1.51 S	106.08 E
Sungailimau	**112**	0.31 S	100.03 E
Sungaimanasip	**114**	1.49 N	100.54 E
Sungainipah	**114**	0.57 N	98.57 E
Sungaipakning	**114**	1.20 N	102.09 E
Sungaipenuh	**112**	2.05 S	101.23 E
Sungaipenyu	**112**	0.16 N	109.04 E
Sungai Petani	**114**	5.39 N	100.30 E
Sungaipinang	**112**	0.48 S	114.04 E
Sungairampah	**114**	3.29 N	99.09 E
Sungairotan, Indon.	**112**	1.39 S	102.51 E
Sungairotan, Indon.	**112**	3.06 S	104.18 E
Sungaisalak	**112**	0.27 S	102.59 E
Sungaiselan	**112**	2.24 S	105.59 E
Sungai Siput	**114**	4.49 N	101.04 E
Sungaitampang	**114**	2.20 N	100.07 E
Şungaitiram	**112**	0.47 S	117.12 E
Šungaj	**80**	48.32 N	46.46 E
Sungari → Songhua ≃	**89**	47.44 N	132.32 E
Sungchiang → Songjiang	**106**	31.01 N	121.14 E
Sungezhuang	**105**	40.15 N	116.39 E
Sungguminasa	**112**	5.12 S	119.27 E
Sungi ≃	**115b**	8.38 S	115.06 E
Sungi Point ›	**116**	10.55 N	125.50 E
Sungkai	**114**	4.00 N	101.19 E
Sung Kong I	**271d**	22.11 N	114.17 E
Sung Noen	**110**	14.54 N	101.50 E
Sungsang	**112**	2.22 S	104.56 E
Sungshan Domestic Airport ⊠	**269d**	25.04 N	121.33 E
Sungurlu	**130**	40.10 N	34.23 E
Sunhezhen	**105**	40.03 N	116.31 E
Suni	**71**	40.17 N	8.33 E
Suning	**98**	38.25 N	115.50 E
Sunjiabu	**106**	30.55 N	118.54 E
Sunjiadizi	**104**	42.09 N	124.09 E
Sunjiagou	**104**	40.45 N	120.39 E
Sunjiajiang	**105**	40.10 N	115.32 E
Sunjiakanzi	**104**	40.42 N	123.02 E
Sunjiawan	**104**	41.59 N	121.42 E
Sunjiazhai	**106**	30.55 N	121.52 E
Sunjikāy	**140**	12.20 N	29.46 E
Sunkar, gora ∧	**86**	44.15 N	73.50 E
Sunken Meadow State Park ♦	**207**	40.54 N	73.16 W
Sunkoši ≃	**124**	26.55 N	87.09 E
Sunland ◈[8]	**280**	34.16 N	118.19 W
Sunland Park	**200**	32.15 N	106.45 W
Sunlight Creek ≃	**202**	44.47 N	109.23 W
Sunlongwan	**104**	41.19 N	122.57 E
Sunman	**218**	39.14 N	85.05 W
Sunnansjö	**40**	60.13 N	14.57 E
Sunndalsøra	**26**	62.40 N	8.33 E
Sunne	**26**	59.50 N	13.09 E
Sunnemo	**40**	59.53 N	13.43 E
Sunnersta	**40**	59.48 N	17.39 E
Sunnī, Khawr V	**140**	7.09 N	28.41 E
Sunningdale	**260**	51.24 N	0.38 W
Sunninghill	**42**	51.25 N	0.40 W
Sunnybrae	**186**	45.24 N	62.30 W
Sunny Corner	**170**	33.23 S	149.53 E
Sunny Crest	**278**	41.33 N	87.42 W
Sunnydale	**224**	47.28 N	122.20 W
Sunnyland	**220**	27.17 N	82.29 W
Sunnylvsfjorden ⊂[2]	**26**	62.17 N	7.01 E
Sunnymead	**228**	33.56 N	117.14 W
Sunnynook	**182**	51.17 N	111.40 W
Sunnyridge	**273d**	26.10 S	28.11 E
Sunnyside, Nf., Can.	**186**	47.51 N	53.55 W
Sunnyside, Ca., U.S.	**226**	32.40 N	117.01 W
Sunny Side, Tx., U.S.	**222**	29.54 N	96.04 W
Sunnyside, Ut,. U.S.	**200**	39.33 N	110.23 W
Sunnyside, Wa., U.S.	**202**	46.19 N	120.00 W
Sunnyside ⊥	**276**	41.03 N	73.52 W
Sunnyslope, Ab., Can.	**182**	51.40 N	113.32 W
Sunnyslope, Wa., U.S.	**224**	47.30 N	122.44 W
Sunnyvale, Ca., U.S.	**226**	37.22 N	122.02 W
Sunnyvale, Tx., U.S.	**222**	32.48 N	96.33 W
Sunol	**282**	37.36 N	121.53 W
Sunol Ridge ∧	**282**	37.38 N	121.56 W
Sun Prairie	**216**	43.11 N	89.12 W
Sunray	**196**	36.01 N	101.49 W
Sunrise, Ky., U.S.	**218**	38.33 N	84.14 W
Sunrise, Tx., U.S.	**222**	31.17 N	96.53 W
Sunrise, Wy., U.S.	**200**	42.19 N	104.42 W
Sunrise Heights	**216**	42.18 N	85.09 W
Sunrise Mall ◈[9]	**276**	40.41 N	73.26 W
Sunrise Manor	**204**	36.08 N	115.04 W
Sunrise Peak ∧	**224**	46.20 N	121.46 W
Sun River Terrace	**216**	41.06 N	87.45 W
Sunset, La., U.S.	**194**	30.24 N	92.04 W
Sunset, Tx., U.S.	**196**	33.27 N	97.46 W
Sunset ◈[8]	**282**	37.45 N	122.30 W
Sunset Bay	**214**	42.11 N	79.24 W
Sunset Beach, Ca., U.S.	**280**	33.43 N	118.04 W
Sunset Beach, Hi., U.S.	**229c**	21.40 N	158.02 W
Sunset Country ◈[1]	**166**	35.00 S	141.30 E
Sunset Crater National Monument ♦	**200**	35.18 N	111.21 W
Sunset Heights	**196**	31.53 N	102.22 W
Sunset Hill	**276**	40.26 N	74.35 W
Sunset Hills	**279b**	40.35 N	80.15 W
Sunset Peak ∧	**280**	34.13 N	117.42 W
Sunset Prairie	**182**	55.50 N	120.48 W
Sunset Trailer Park	**278**	42.06 N	87.48 W
Sunset Valley	**214**	40.18 N	79.44 W
Sunshine, Austl.	**166**	37.47 S	144.50 E
Sunshine, Austl.	**169**	37.47 S	144.50 E
Sunshine, Ak., U.S.	**180**	62.10 N	150.04 W
Sunshine Island I	**271d**	22.16 N	114.03 E
Sunshine Point ›	**281**	42.36 N	82.47 W
Sunshine Skyway Bridge ◈[5]	**220**	27.37 N	82.39 W
Suntai ≃	**146**	8.05 N	10.04 E
Suntar	**74**	62.10 N	117.40 E
Suntar-Chajata, chrebet ⋏	**74**	62.00 N	143.00 E
Suntaug Lake ⊜	**283**	42.32 N	71.00 W
Süntel ⋏	**52**	52.12 N	9.25 E
Sun Temple ✝[1]	**273c**	29.55 N	31.11 E
Sunter ◈[8]	**269e**	6.09 S	106.50 E
Sunter, Kali ≍	**269e**	6.07 S	106.50 E
Sunti ≃	**272b**	22.37 N	88.34 E
Suntrana	**180**	63.51 N	148.51 W
Suntsar	**128**	25.31 N	62.00 E
Suntu	**144**	8.06 N	36.57 E
Sun Valley, Id., U.S.	**202**	43.41 N	114.21 W
Sun Valley, Nv., U.S.	**226**	39.34 N	119.47 W
Sun Valley ◈[8]	**280**	34.14 N	118.21 W
SunValley Center ◈[9]	**282**	37.58 N	122.03 W
Sun Village	**228**	34.35 N	118.03 W
Sunwapta ≃	**182**	52.32 N	117.41 W
Sunwi-do I	**98**	37.44 N	125.15 E
Sunwu	**89**	49.27 N	127.20 E
Sunwui → Jiangmen	**100**	22.35 N	113.05 E
Sunyani	**150**	7.20 N	2.20 W
Sunying	**98**	34.30 N	114.21 E
Sunža ≃	**84**	43.26 N	46.08 E
Sunženskij chrebet ⋏	**84**	43.21 N	45.00 E
Sun Zhong Shan Ling (Tomb of Sun Yat Sen) ⊥	**106**	32.10 N	118.56 E
Suojarvi	**24**	62.05 N	32.21 E
Suolahti	**26**	62.34 N	25.52 E
Suomenlahti → Finland, Gulf of ⊂	**26**	60.00 N	27.00 E
Suomenselkä ∧	**26**	63.59 N	27.00 E
Suomi → Finland □[1]	**24**	64.00 N	26.00 E
Suomussalmi	**26**	64.53 N	29.05 E
Suō-nada ⊤[2]	**96**	33.50 N	131.30 E
Suonenjoki	**26**	62.37 N	27.08 E
Suontee ⊜	**26**	61.40 N	26.30 E
Suordach	**74**	66.43 N	132.04 E
Suoshu	**106**	31.57 N	119.00 E
Supamo ≃	**246**	6.48 N	61.50 W
Supaul	**124**	26.07 N	86.36 E
Supe	**144**	8.37 N	35.38 E
Superbe ≃	**50**	48.35 N	3.53 E
Superga, Basilica di ✝[1]	**62**	45.05 N	7.46 E
Superior, Az., U.S.	**200**	33.17 N	111.05 W
Superior, Mt., U.S.	**202**	47.11 N	114.53 W
Superior, Ne., U.S.	**198**	40.01 N	98.04 W
Superior, Wi., U.S.	**190**	46.43 N	92.06 W
Superior, Laguna ⊂	**234**	16.20 N	94.55 W
Superior, Lake ⊜	**190**	48.00 N	88.00 W
Superior Lake ⊜	**228**	35.15 N	117.02 W
Superior Valley V	**228**	35.16 N	117.00 W
Supersano	**68**	40.01 N	18.14 E
Supetar	**36**	43.23 N	16.33 E
Suphan Buri	**110**	14.28 N	100.07 E
Suphan Buri ≃	**110**	13.29 N	100.17 E
Süphan Dağı ∧	**84**	38.56 N	42.50 E
Supino	**66**	41.37 N	13.14 E
Supiori I	**164**	0.45 S	135.30 E
Sūpkhār	**124**	22.12 N	80.56 E
Supoj ≃	**78**	49.38 N	31.48 E
Suponevo	**76**	53.12 N	34.18 E
Supoqiao	**107**	30.40 N	103.59 E
Süpplingen	**54**	52.14 N	10.54 E
Supraśl	**30**	53.13 N	23.20 E
Supraśl ≃	**30**	53.04 N	22.56 E
Sup'ung	**98**	40.27 N	124.57 E
Sup'ung-chŏsuji ⊜[1]	**98**	40.30 N	125.05 E
Supur	**126**	23.01 N	86.52 E
Suputinskij zapovednik ♦	**89**	43.40 N	132.20 E
Sūq-'Abs	**144**	15.59 N	43.04 E
Sūq ash-Shuyūkh	**128**	30.53 N	46.28 E
Suq'at al-Jamal	**140**	12.48 N	27.42 E
Suqian	**100**	33.59 N	118.18 E
Suqiao, Zhg.	**100**	34.08 N	113.47 E
Suqiao, Zhg.	**105**	39.03 N	116.29 E
Sūq Suwayq	**128**	24.23 N	38.27 E
Suquamish	**224**	47.43 N	122.33 W
Suquṭrā (Socotra) I	**118**	12.30 N	54.00 E
Şūr (Tyre), Lubnān	**132**	33.16 N	35.11 E
Şūr, 'Umān	**118**	22.35 N	59.31 E
Sur, Cabo ›	**174z**	27.12 S	109.26 W
Sur, Point ›	**226**	36.18 N	121.54 W
Sur, Punta ›	**252**	36.52 S	56.40 W
Sura	**80**	53.53 N	45.45 E
Sura ◈[8]	**272b**	22.33 N	88.25 E
Sura ≃	**80**	56.06 N	46.00 E
Sura, Cape ›	**144**	11.10 N	47.30 E
Şūrāb, Pāk.	**120**	28.29 N	66.16 E
Šurab, S.S.S.R.	**85**	40.03 N	70.33 E
Surabaya	**115a**	7.15 S	112.45 E
S'urachi, Nuraghe ⊥	**71**	40.01 N	8.33 E
Şurad	**142**	30.59 N	30.54 E
Surag-san ∧	**271b**	37.42 N	127.04 E
Surahammar	**40**	59.43 N	16.13 E
Sūrak	**128**	25.43 N	58.48 E
Surakarta	**115a**	7.35 S	110.50 E
Suramana	**112**	0.50 S	119.33 E
Surami	**84**	42.01 N	43.34 E
Şūrān, Īrān	**128**	27.18 N	62.04 E
Šuran, S.S.S.R.	**80**	55.22 N	49.50 E
Şūrān, Sūrīy.	**130**	36.34 N	37.13 E
Şūrān, Sūrīy.	**130**	35.17 N	36.45 E
Şuran ≃	**58**	46.02 N	5.19 E
Šurany	**30**	48.06 N	18.14 E
Surar	**144**	7.27 N	40.57 E
Surat, Austl.	**166**	27.09 S	149.04 E
Sūrat, India	**120**	21.10 N	72.50 E
Sūratgarh	**123**	29.19 N	73.54 E
Surat Thani (Ban Don)	**110**	9.08 N	99.19 E
Surava	**80**	52.57 N	41.18 E
Suraż, Pol.	**30**	52.58 N	22.58 E
Suraž, S.S.S.R.	**76**	53.01 N	32.24 E
Suraž, S.S.S.R.	**76**	55.25 N	30.44 E
Surbiton ◈[8]	**260**	51.24 N	0.18 W
Surbo	**68**	40.24 N	18.08 E
Surbourg	**56**	48.55 N	7.51 E
Surchan	**80**	46.39 N	49.38 E
Surchandarja ≃	**85**	37.58 N	67.50 E
Surchandarjinskaja Oblast' □[4]	**85**	38.00 N	67.30 E
Surchdara	**85**	38.37 N	69.55 E
Şurchob ≃	**85**	38.53 N	70.03 E
Šurči	**85**	37.59 N	67.47 E
Surco	**286d**	12.09 S	77.01 W
Surco ≃	**286d**	12.13 S	77.03 W
Surdulica	**38**	42.41 N	22.10 E
Sûre (Sauer) ≃	**56**	49.44 N	6.31 E
Şureanu, Munții ⋏	**38**	45.38 N	23.27 E
Šureksor, ozero ⊜	**86**	52.16 N	75.50 E
Surendorf	**41**	54.28 N	10.04 E
Surendranagar	**120**	22.42 N	71.41 E
Suresnes	**261**	48.52 N	2.14 E
Suretka	**236**	9.34 N	82.56 W
Surf City	**208**	39.39 N	74.09 W
Surfers Paradise	**171a**	28.00 S	153.26 E
Surfside, Fl., U.S.	**220**	25.52 N	80.07 W
Surfside, Tx., U.S.	**222**	28.57 N	95.17 W
Surgères	**32**	46.07 N	0.45 W
Surgidero	**240p**	22.41 N	82.18 W
Surgijn ≃	**88**	47.20 N	95.50 E
Surgoinsville	**192**	36.28 N	82.51 W
Sürgü	**130**	38.01 N	37.59 E
Sürgücü	**130**	37.35 N	40.44 E
Surgut	**74**	61.14 N	73.20 E
Surhuisterveen	**52**	53.10 N	6.10 E
Suri	**164**	7.10 S	143.55 E
Suria	**272b**	22.51 N	88.33 E
Suriāpet	**122**	17.09 N	79.37 E
Suribachi-yama ∧[2]	**174f**	24.45 N	141.17 E
Suribao ≃	**116**	11.33 N	125.28 E
Surigao	**116**	9.45 N	125.30 E
Surigao del Norte □[4]	**116**	9.35 N	125.36 E
Surigao del Sur □[4]	**116**	9.00 N	126.00 E
Surigao Strait ⊔	**116**	10.15 N	125.23 E
Surikova	**86**	56.59 N	91.31 E
Surin	**110**	14.53 N	103.29 E
Surinam → Suriname □[1]	**250**	4.00 N	55.00 W
Suriname □[5]	**250**	5.30 N	55.00 W
Suriname □[1], S.A.	**242**	4.00 N	56.00 W
Şuriname □[1], S.A.	**250**	4.00 N	56.00 W
Šurinda	**88**	55.13 N	113.23 E
Suring	**190**	44.59 N	88.22 W
Sūrīyah → Syria □[1]	**128**	35.00 N	38.00 E
S'urkum	**89**	50.08 N	140.31 E
Ş'urkum, mys ›	**89**	50.05 N	140.41 E
Šurma	**80**	56.58 N	50.21 E
Sūrmaq	**128**	31.03 N	52.48 E
Surmelin ≃	**50**	49.04 N	3.13 E
Surnadalsøra	**26**	62.59 N	8.39 E
Surodadi	**115a**	6.53 S	109.15 E
Surovaticha	**80**	55.45 N	43.56 E
Surovikino	**80**	48.36 N	42.51 E
Surovo	**88**	55.37 N	105.36 E
Surprise	**200**	33.37 N	112.19 W
Surprise, Lake ⊜	**222**	29.33 N	94.41 W
Surprise Valley V	**204**	41.35 N	120.05 W
Surquillo	**286d**	12.07 S	77.02 W
Surrency	**192**	31.43 N	82.11 W
Surrey	**198**	48.14 N	101.07 W
Surrey □[6]	**42**	51.10 N	0.20 W
Surrey, University of ✝[2]	**260**	51.14 N	0.36 W
Surrey Heath □[8]	**260**	51.23 N	0.35 W
Surry	**208**	37.08 N	76.50 W
Surry □[6]	**208**	37.10 N	76.50 W
Sursee	**58**	47.10 N	8.06 E
Sursés V	**58**	46.34 N	9.38 E
Sursk	**80**	53.04 N	45.42 E
Surskij Majdan	**80**	55.01 N	46.32 E
Surskoje	**80**	54.30 N	46.44 E
Surt	**146**	31.12 N	16.35 E
Surt, Khalīj (Gulf of Sidra) ⊂	**146**	31.30 N	18.00 E
Surtainville	**28**	49.25 N	1.50 W
Surtanāhu	**120**	26.22 N	70.00 E
Surte	**26**	57.49 N	12.01 E
Surtsey I	**24a**	63.16 N	20.32 W
Suru	**164**	6.50 S	144.45 E
Suru ≃	**123**	34.45 N	76.12 E
Surubim ≃	**250**	11.15 S	48.27 W
Surubiú ≃	**250**	3.58 S	48.52 W
Sürüç	**130**	36.58 N	38.24 E
Suruga-wan ⊂	**94**	34.51 N	138.33 E
Suruí	**256**	22.40 S	43.07 W
Suruí ≃	**287a**	22.42 S	43.07 W
Surulangun	**112**	2.37 S	102.45 E
Suru-Lere ◈[8]	**273a**	6.31 N	3.22 E
Surumu ≃	**246**	3.22 N	60.19 W
Surveyor Creek ≃	**198**	40.20 N	102.38 W
Surveyor Point ›	**168b**	34.47 S	137.51 E
Survilliers	**261**	49.06 N	2.33 E
Surwold	**52**	53.00 N	7.30 E
Şury-le-Comtal	**62**	45.32 N	4.10 E
Šuryškary	**74**	65.54 N	65.22 E
Susa, It.	**62**	45.08 N	7.03 E
Susa, Nihon	**96**	34.37 N	131.36 E
Suså ≃	**41**	55.11 N	11.46 E
Susa, Valle di V	**62**	45.09 N	7.10 E
Sūsah	**146**	32.54 N	21.58 E
Susak, Otok I	**36**	44.31 N	14.18 E
Susaki	**96**	33.22 N	133.17 E
Susami	**96**	33.33 N	135.30 E
Susamyr	**85**	42.09 N	73.58 E
Susamyr ≃	**85**	42.08 N	74.03 E
Susamyrtau, chrebet ⋏	**85**	42.08 N	73.15 E
Susan	**208**	37.22 N	76.19 W
Susan ≃	**204**	40.19 N	120.17 W
Susan, Port ⊂	**224**	48.10 N	122.25 W
Susana Knolls	**228**	34.16 N	118.41 W
Sūsangerd	**128**	31.34 N	48.11 E
Susanino, S.S.S.R.	**76**	59.30 N	30.22 E
Susanino, S.S.S.R.	**80**	58.09 N	41.36 E
Susanino, S.S.S.R.	**89**	52.47 N	140.06 E
Şusanville	**204**	40.24 N	120.39 W
Šušary, S.S.S.R.	**265a**	59.48 N	30.23 E
Šušary, S.S.S.R.	**265a**	59.46 N	30.21 E
Susch	**58**	46.46 N	10.04 E
Susegana	**64**	45.51 N	12.15 E
Suşehri	**130**	40.11 N	38.06 E
Şüsel	**54**	54.04 N	10.43 E
Šušenskoje	**86**	53.19 N	91.58 E
Sušice	**60**	49.14 N	13.32 E
Susitna	**180**	61.33 N	150.31 W
Susitna ≃	**180**	61.16 N	150.30 W
Susleny	**78**	47.25 N	28.59 E
Suslonger	**80**	56.18 N	48.13 E
Sušn'aki Pervoje	**86**	57.53 N	88.47 E
Susobana ≃	**94**	36.37 N	138.11 E
Susoh	**114**	3.43 N	96.50 E
Susong	**100**	30.09 N	116.06 E
Susono	**94**	35.09 N	138.54 E
Suspiro del Moro, Puerto del)(	**34**	37.04 N	3.39 W
Susquehanna	**210**	41.56 N	75.36 W
Susquehanna □[6]	**210**	41.50 N	75.50 W
Susquehanna ≃	**188**	39.33 N	76.05 W
Susquehanna, West Branch ≃	**210**	40.53 N	76.47 W
Susquehanna State Park ♦	**208**	39.36 N	76.09 W
Susques	**252**	23.25 S	66.29 W

Symbols in the index entries represent the broad categories identified in the key at the right. Symbols with superior numbers (⋏[1]) identify subcategories (see complete key on page *I · 1)*.

Symbole im Register stellen die rechts im Schlüssel erklärten Kategorien dar. Symbole mit hochgestellten Ziffern (⋏[1]) bezeichnen Unterabteilungen einer Kategorie (vgl. vollständiger Schlüssel auf Seite *I · 1)*.

Los símbolos incluídos en el texto del índice representan las grandes categorias identificadas con la clave a la derecha. Los símbolos con numeros en su parte superior (⋏[1]) identifican las subcategorías (véase la clave completa en la página *I · 1)*.

Les symboles de l'index représentent les catégories indiquées dans la légende à droite. Les symboles suivis d'un indice (⋏[1]) représentent des sous-catégories (voir légende complète à la page *I · 1)*.

Os símbolos incluídos no texto do índice representam as grandes categorias identificadas com a chave à direita. Os símbolos com números em sua parte superior (⋏[1]) identificam as subcategorias (veja-se a chave completa à página *I · 1)*.

	English	Deutsch	Español	Français	Português
∧	Mountain	Berg	Montaña	Montagne	Montanha
⋏	Mountains	Gebirge	Montañas	Montagnes	Montanhas
)(	Pass	Paß	Paso	Col	Passo
V	Valley, Canyon	Tal, Cañon	Valle, Cañón	Vallée, Canyon	Vale, Canhão
≚	Plain	Ebene	Llano	Plaine	Planície
›	Cape	Kap	Cabo	Cap	Cabo
I	Island	Insel	Isla	Île	Ilha
II	Islands	Inseln	Islas	Îles	Ilhas
⩟	Other Topographic Features	Andere Topographische Objekte	Otros Elementos Topográficos	Autres données topographiques	Outros acidentes topográficos

ESPAÑOL — Nombre / Página / Lat.°′ / Long.°′ W = Oeste

FRANÇAIS — Nom / Page / Lat.°′ / Long.°′ W = Ouest

PORTUGUÊS — Nome / Página / Lat.°′ / Long.°′ W = Oeste

Sussa ≐ 152 7.22 S 17.05 E
Süssen 56 48.41 N 9.45 E
Süssenbrunn ◆[8] 264b 48.17 N 16.30 E
Süsser See ⊜ 54 51.30 N 11.40 E
Sussex, N.B., Can. 186 45.43 N 65.31 W
Sussex, N.J., U.S. 210 41.12 N 74.36 W
Sussex, Va., U.S. 208 36.54 N 77.16 W
Sussex, Wi., U.S. 216 43.08 N 88.13 W
Sussex □[6], De., U.S. 208 38.42 N 75.23 W
Sussex □[6], N.J., U.S. 210 41.08 N 74.41 W
Sussex □[6], Va., U.S. 208 36.50 N 77.15 W
Sussex, East □[6] 42 50.55 N 0.15 E
Sussex, Vale of V 42 50.57 N 0.17 W
Sussex Inlet 170 35.11 S 150.36 E
Sussey 50 47.13 N 4.22 E
Sustenhorn ∧ 58 46.42 N 8.28 E
Susten Pass)(58 46.44 N 8.27 E
Susteren 52 51.04 N 5.51 E
Šustikovo 82 55.17 N 35.59 E
Susu 174m 26.47 N 128.19 E
Susubona 175e 8.18 S 159.27 E
Susui 112 4.56 N 116.41 E
Susuman 74 62.47 N 148.10 E
Susurluk 130 39.54 N 28.10 E
Susuzmüsellim 130 41.06 N 27.03 E
Šušvė ≐ 76 55.10 N 23.49 E
Susz 30 53.44 N 19.20 E
Sutāhāta 126 22.08 N 88.07 E
Sutak 123 33.12 N 77.28 E
Sutama 94 35.47 N 138.25 E
Sut-Chol' 86 51.24 N 91.17 E
Sütçüler 130 37.30 N 30.59 E
Sutera 70 37.31 N 13.44 E
Sutersville 214 40.14 N 79.48 W
Suthat, Wat ʋ[1] 269a 13.45 N 100.30 E
Sutherland, Austl. 170 34.02 S 151.04 E
Sutherland, S. Afr. 158 32.24 S 20.40 E
Sutherland, Ia., U.S. 198 42.58 N 95.29 W
Sutherland, Ne., U.S. 198 41.09 N 101.07 W
Sutherland ≐ 182 54.29 N 125.05 W
Sutherland, Lake ⊜ 224 48.05 N 123.42 W
Sutherland Falls ∟ 172 44.48 S 167.44 E
Sutherlands 168b 34.10 S 139.13 E
Sutherlin 202 43.23 N 123.18 W
Suthiāna 272a 28.31 N 77.26 E
Sutjeska Nacionalni Park ♠ 38 43.22 N 18.45 E
Sutlej (Satluj) (Langqên) ≐ 120 29.23 N 71.02 E
Sutri 66 42.14 N 12.13 E
Sutrio 64 46.31 N 12.59 E
Sütschou → Xuzhou, Zhg. 98 34.16 N 117.11 E
Sutschou → Suzhou, Zhg. 106 31.18 N 120.37 E
Sutter 226 39.10 N 121.45 W
Sutter □[6] 226 39.08 N 121.37 W
Sutter Buttes ∧ 226 39.12 N 121.50 W
Sutter Bypass ≐ 226 38.47 N 121.38 W
Sutter Creek 226 38.23 N 120.48 W
Sutter Creek ≐ 226 38.22 N 120.59 W
Sutton, Austl. 171b 35.10 S 149.15 E
Sutton, P.Q., Can. 206 45.06 N 72.37 W
Sutton, Eng., U.K. 42 52.23 N 0.07 E
Sutton, Eng., U.K. 260 51.12 N 0.26 W
Sutton, Ak., U.S. 180 61.43 N 148.53 W
Sutton, Ma., U.S. 207 42.09 N 71.45 W
Sutton, Ne., U.S. 198 40.36 N 97.51 W
Sutton, W.V., U.S. 188 38.39 N 80.42 W
Sutton ◆[8] 42 51.22 N 0.12 W
Sutton, Monts ⩘ 206 45.05 N 72.30 W
Sutton-at-Home 260 51.25 N 0.14 E
Sutton Bridge 42 52.46 N 0.12 E
Sutton Coldfield 42 52.34 N 1.48 W
Sutton Courtenay 42 51.39 N 1.17 W
Sutton Forest 170 34.35 S 150.19 E
Sutton in Ashfield 44 53.08 N 1.15 W
Sutton Lake ⊜[1] 188 38.40 N 80.40 W
Sutton Lane Ends 262 53.14 N 2.06 W
Sutton Leach 262 53.26 N 2.42 W
Sutton on Sea 44 53.19 N 0.17 E
Sutton on Trent 44 53.10 N 0.49 W
Sutton Park 276 40.49 N 74.42 W
Sutton Place ⊥ 260 51.16 N 0.33 W
Suttons Bay 190 44.58 N 85.39 W
Sutton Scotney 42 51.10 N 1.21 W
Sutton Valence 42 51.12 N 0.36 E
Sutton Veny 42 51.11 N 2.08 W
Sutton Weaver 262 53.18 N 2.41 W
Sutton West 212 44.18 N 79.22 W
Suttor ≐ 166 21.25 S 147.45 E
Suttrop 56 51.27 N 8.22 E
Suttsu 92a 42.48 N 140.14 E
Sutwik Island I 180 56.34 N 157.05 W
Suunduk ≐ 86 51.46 N 58.46 E
Suurberge ⩘ 158 33.18 S 25.32 E
Suurbraak 158 34.00 S 20.39 E
Suure-Jaani 76 58.33 N 25.28 E
Suur Pakri I 76 59.20 N 23.55 E
Suva 175g 18.08 S 178.25 E
Suvainiškis 76 56.10 N 25.17 E
Šuvalovo Oz'orki ◆[8] 265a 60.02 N 30.18 E
Suva Planina ⩘ 38 43.10 N 22.10 E
Suvarlı 130 37.32 N 37.38 E
Suvasvesi ⊜ 26 62.39 N 28.12 E
Šuvel'an 84 40.30 N 50.09 E
Suvereto 66 43.05 N 10.40 E
Suvo 88 53.39 N 110.00 E
Suvorka 88 56.33 N 103.24 E
Suvorov 82 54.07 N 36.30 E
Suvorovo, S.S.S.R. 78 45.34 N 28.59 E
Suvorovo, S.S.S.R. 82 56.07 N 35.54 E
Suwa, Ityo. 144 14.17 N 41.06 E
Suwa, Nihon 94 36.02 N 138.08 E
Suwa-ko ⊜ 94 36.05 N 138.05 E
Suwałki 30 54.07 N 22.56 E
Suwałki □[4] 30 54.10 N 22.15 E
Suwannaphum 110 15.33 N 103.47 E
Suwannee ≐ 192 29.18 N 83.09 W
Suwannee Lake ⊜ 184 56.08 N 100.10 W
Suwanose-jima I 93b 29.38 N 129.43 E
Suwanose-suidō ʉ 93b 29.32 N 129.40 E
Suwarrow I[1] 14 13.15 S 163.05 W
Suwaydah 130 35.46 N 39.38 E
Şuwaylih 132 32.02 N 35.50 E
Suways, Khalīj as- (Gulf of Suez) c 140 29.00 N 32.50 E
Suways, Qanāt as- (Suez Canal) ≖ 142 29.55 N 32.33 E
Suwŏn 98 37.17 N 127.01 E
Suwon-dong 98 41.54 N 129.43 E
Suxi 100 29.25 N 120.07 E
Suxian 100 33.38 N 116.58 E
Suya 150 9.28 N 3.11 E
Suykbulak 86 49.48 N 80.50 E
Suyo 246 4.30 S 80.00 W
Suzak 86 44.07 N 68.28 E
Suzaka 94 36.39 N 138.19 E
Suzano 256 23.32 S 46.20 W
Suzano □[7] 287b 23.35 S 46.18 W
Suzdal' 80 56.25 N 40.26 E
Suze ≐ 58 47.08 N 7.14 E
Suze-la-Rousse 62 44.17 N 4.51 E
Suzhi 98 42.17 N 113.42 E
Suzhou (Soochow) 106 31.18 N 120.37 E
Suzhuang 105 40.04 N 116.44 E
Suzi ≐ 98 41.55 N 124.17 E
Suzigou 98 40.25 N 123.25 E
S'uzikozero 24 61.48 N 37.20 E
Suz'omka 76 52.19 N 34.05 E
Suzu 92 37.25 N 137.17 E
Suzuka 94 34.51 N 136.35 E
Suzuka ≐ 94 34.54 N 136.39 E
Suzuka-kokutei-kōen ♠ 94 35.00 N 136.25 E
Suzuka-sammyaku ⩘ 94 35.00 N 136.25 E
Suzuki 268 35.43 N 139.31 E
S'uz'um 80 58.02 N 47.32 E
Suzu-misaki › 92 37.31 N 137.21 E
Suzun 86 53.47 N 82.19 E
Suzzara 64 45.00 N 10.45 E
Sværdborg 41 55.05 N 11.54 E
Sval'ava 78 48.33 N 22.59 E
Svalbard □[2] 12 78.00 N 20.00 E
Svalöv 41 55.55 N 13.06 E
Svaneholm 41 55.30 N 13.28 E
Svaneke 26 55.08 N 15.09 E
Svanetskij chrebet ⩘ 84 42.55 N 42.42 E
Svängsta 26 56.16 N 14.46 E
Svanninge 41 55.07 N 10.15 E
Svanskog 26 59.11 N 12.33 E
Svapa ≐ 78 51.44 N 34.56 E
Svappavaara 24 67.39 N 21.04 E
Švarcevskij 82 54.06 N 37.59 E
Svärdsjö 26 60.45 N 15.55 E
Švaricha 80 57.33 N 49.37 E
Svartå 40 59.08 N 14.31 E
Svartälven ≐ 40 59.19 N 14.35 E
Svartån ≐ 40 59.37 N 16.33 E
Svarte 41 55.25 N 13.43 E
Svartenhuk ›[1] 176 71.55 N 55.00 W
Svärtinge 40 58.39 N 16.00 E
Svartisen ⌗ 24 66.38 N 14.00 E
Svartlöga I 40 59.34 N 19.03 E
Svartsjölandet I 40 59.22 N 17.41 E
Svataj 74 67.57 N 151.54 E
Svatava 54 50.11 N 12.35 E
Svatava ≐ 54 50.32 N 12.07 E
Sv'atica ≐ 80 58.22 N 51.43 E
Sv'atogorskaja 83 49.04 N 37.32 E
Sv'atoj Nos, mys ›, S.S.S.R. 24 68.10 N 39.45 E
Sv'atoj Nos, mys ›, S.S.S.R. 74 72.52 N 140.42 E
Sv'atoj Nos, poluostrov ›[1] 88 53.40 N 108.50 E
Sv'atoslavka 80 51.20 N 43.26 E
Svatovo 83 49.23 N 38.13 E
Svay Chék 110 13.48 N 102.58 E
Svay Riěng 110 11.05 N 105.48 E
Sveafallen ∟ 40 59.10 N 14.22 E
Svebølle 41 55.38 N 11.20 E
Sveča 80 58.16 N 47.32 E
Svedala 41 55.30 N 13.14 E
Svėdasai 76 55.41 N 25.22 E
Sveg 26 62.02 N 14.21 E
Svegssjön ⊜[1] 26 62.03 N 14.10 E
Švėkšna 76 55.31 N 21.37 E
Svelgen 26 61.47 N 5.15 E
Svelvik 26 59.37 N 10.24 E
Sven' 76 53.09 N 34.21 E
Švenčionėliai 76 55.10 N 26.00 E
Švenčionys 76 55.07 N 26.10 E
Svendborg 41 55.03 N 10.37 E
Svenljunga 26 57.30 N 13.07 E
Svennevad 40 59.01 N 15.22 E
Svensen 224 46.10 N 123.39 W
Svenstorp 41 55.46 N 13.15 E
Svenstrup 26 56.59 N 9.52 E
Šventoji 76 56.02 N 21.05 E
Šventoji ≐ 76 55.06 N 24.22 E
Sverbejevo 89 53.36 N 123.15 E
Sverdlovo, S.S.S.R. 80 51.16 N 44.34 E
Sverdlovo, S.S.S.R. 82 56.38 N 36.37 E
Sverdlovsk, S.S.S.R. 83 48.05 N 39.40 E
Sverdlovsk, S.S.S.R. 86 56.51 N 60.36 E
Sverdrup, ostrov I 74 74.35 N 79.30 E
Sverige → Sweden □[1] 24 62.00 N 15.00 E
Sverkestaån ≐ 40 59.28 N 15.28 E
Švermov 54 50.09 N 14.05 E
Svessa 78 51.57 N 33.54 E
Sveti Arhandjel Mihajlo ʋ[1] 38 42.07 N 21.28 E
Sveti Jovan Bigorski ʋ[1] 38 41.38 N 20.37 E
Svetilovići 76 52.48 N 31.19 E
Sveti Nikole 38 41.52 N 21.58 E
Sveti Petar u Šumi 64 45.11 N 13.52 E
Svetlaja 89 46.33 N 138.18 E
Světlá nad Sázavou 30 49.40 N 15.25 E
Svetlanovo 83 48.42 N 38.28 E
Svetlogorsk, S.S.S.R. 76 54.57 N 20.10 E
Svetlogorsk, S.S.S.R. 76 52.38 N 29.42 E
Svetlograd 72 45.20 N 42.40 E
Svetloje 80 57.03 N 53.38 E
Svetlovodsk 78 49.04 N 33.15 E
Svetlyj, S.S.S.R. 76 54.41 N 20.08 E
Svetlyj, S.S.S.R. 86 50.47 N 60.53 E
Svetlyj, S.S.S.R. 88 58.26 N 115.55 E
Svetlyj Jar 80 48.29 N 44.46 E
Svetogorsk 24 61.07 N 28.51 E
Svetozarevo 38 43.58 N 21.16 E
Svežen'kaja 80 54.01 N 42.26 E
Svidník 30 49.18 N 21.35 E
Švihov 60 49.29 N 13.17 E
Svijaga ≐ 80 55.47 N 48.40 E
Svilajnac 38 44.14 N 21.13 E
Svilengrad 38 41.46 N 26.12 E
Svindal 26 58.30 N 7.28 E
Svinecea Mare, Vîrful ∧ 38 44.48 N 22.09 E
Svinesund 26 59.06 N 11.16 E
Svinninge 41 55.43 N 11.28 E
Svir' 76 54.51 N 26.24 E
Svir' ≐ 76 60.30 N 32.48 E
Svirica 76 60.29 N 32.51 E
Svirsk 88 53.04 N 103.21 E
Svir'stroj 76 60.48 N 33.43 E
Sviščovka 80 52.51 N 43.44 E
Svisloč', S.S.S.R. 76 53.02 N 24.06 E
Svisloč', S.S.S.R. 76 53.26 N 28.59 E
Svisloč' ≐ 76 53.26 N 28.59 E
Svištov 38 43.37 N 25.20 E
Svistunovka 83 49.29 N 38.20 E
Svit 30 49.03 N 20.12 E
Svitávka 30 49.30 N 16.37 E
Svitavy 30 49.45 N 16.27 E
Svitino 82 54.54 N 35.49 E
Svoboda, S.S.S.R. 78 51.58 N 36.17 E
Svoboda, S.S.S.R. 78 47.12 N 40.39 E
Svobodnaja 89 46.48 N 143.23 E
Svobodnoje 83 47.32 N 37.34 E
Svobodnyj, S.S.S.R. 80 52.20 N 46.22 E
Svobodnyj, S.S.S.R. 89 51.24 N 128.08 E
Svobodnyj Port 78 46.20 N 31.51 E
Svoge 38 42.58 N 23.21 E
Svojna 82 54.09 N 36.39 E
Svol'na ≐ 76 55.43 N 28.02 E
Svolvær 24 68.14 N 14.34 E
Svor 54 50.47 N 14.36 E
Svorkmo 26 63.10 N 9.45 E
Svratka ≐ 61 49.11 N 16.38 E
Svržno 60 49.35 N 12.46 E
Svullrya 26 60.25 N 12.24 E
Swābi 123 34.07 N 72.28 E
Swadlincote 42 52.47 N 1.33 W
Swaffham 42 52.39 N 0.41 E
Swain 210 42.29 N 77.51 W
Swain Reefs ✤[2] 166 21.40 S 152.15 E
Swainsboro 192 32.35 N 82.20 W
Swains Island I[1] 14 11.03 S 171.05 W
Swakop ≐ 156 22.38 S 14.36 E
Swakopmund 156 22.41 S 14.34 E
Swakopmund □[5] 156 23.00 S 15.00 E
Swale □[8] 260 51.21 N 0.41 E
Swale ≐ 44 54.06 N 1.20 W
Swale Canyon V 224 45.49 N 121.05 W
Swale Creek ≐ 224 45.49 N 121.05 W
Swaledale V 44 54.25 N 1.47 W
Swallowfield 218 38.21 N 84.51 W
Swalmen 52 51.15 N 6.02 E
Swamp City 222 32.29 N 94.56 W
Swampscott 207 42.28 N 70.55 W
Swan 222 32.26 N 95.22 W
Swan ≐, Austl. 168a 32.03 S 115.45 E
Swan ≐, Can. 184 52.30 N 100.47 W
Swan ≐, Ab., Can. 182 55.31 N 115.17 W
Swan ≐, Mn., U.S. 190 47.01 N 93.16 W
Swan ≐, Mt., U.S. 202 48.04 N 114.05 W
Swan Acres 279b 40.33 N 80.02 W
Swanage 42 50.37 N 1.58 W
Swan Bay c 169 38.14 S 144.40 E
Swan Creek ≐, Austl. 171a 28.08 S 152.13 E
Swan Creek ≐, Mi., U.S. 216 41.58 N 85.19 W
Swan Creek ≐, Mi., U.S. 216 41.58 N 83.17 W
Swan Creek ≐, Oh., U.S. 216 41.39 N 83.32 W
Swan Creek ≐, S.D., U.S. 198 45.19 N 100.15 W
Swan Creek, North Branch ≐ 281 42.06 N 83.23 W
Swan Creek Point › 281 42.40 N 82.39 W
Swanee → Suwannee ≐ 192 29.18 N 83.09 W
Swan Hill 166 35.21 S 143.34 E
Swan Hills 182 54.43 N 115.24 W
Swan Hills ⩘[2] 182 54.48 N 115.52 W
Swanington 216 40.35 N 87.17 W
Swan Island I 169 38.15 S 144.41 E
Swan Islands → Santanilla, Islas II 238 17.25 N 83.55 W
Swank Creek ≐ 224 47.07 N 120.45 W
Swan Lake, Mb., Can. 184 49.24 N 98.46 W
Swan Lake, Mt., U.S. 202 47.55 N 113.50 W
Swan Lake, N.Y., U.S. 210 41.45 N 74.47 W
Swan Lake ⊜, Mb., Can. 184 52.30 N 100.45 W
Swan Lake ⊜, On., Can. 184 54.17 N 91.12 W
Swan Lake ⊜, Il., U.S. 219 38.57 N 90.33 W
Swan Lake ⊜, Mn., U.S. 190 44.19 N 94.15 W
Swanland 44 53.44 N 0.29 W
Swanley 42 51.24 N 0.12 E
Swanlinbar 48 54.10 N 7.42 W
Swannanoa 192 35.36 N 82.23 W
Swannanoa, Lake ⊜ 276 41.01 N 74.31 W
Swan Peak ∧ 202 47.43 N 113.38 W
Swanquarter 192 35.24 N 76.20 W
Swan Range ⩘ 202 47.50 N 113.40 W
Swan Reach 166 34.34 S 139.36 E
Swan River 184 52.06 N 101.16 W
Swansboro 192 34.41 N 77.07 W
Swanscombe 260 51.26 N 0.18 E
Swansea, Austl. 166 42.08 S 148.04 E
Swansea, Austl. 170 33.05 S 151.38 E
Swansea, Wales, U.K. 42 51.38 N 3.57 W
Swansea, Il., U.S. 219 38.32 N 89.59 W
Swansea, Ma., U.S. 207 41.44 N 71.11 W
Swansea, S.C., U.S. 192 33.44 N 81.05 W
Swansea ◆[8] 275b 43.38 N 79.28 W
Swansea Bay c 42 51.35 N 3.52 W
Swans Island I 188 44.10 N 68.25 W
Swanson Lake ⊜[1] 198 40.09 N 101.06 W
Swanton, Oh., U.S. 216 41.35 N 83.53 W
Swanton, Vt., U.S. 206 44.55 N 73.07 W
Swanville 190 45.54 N 94.38 W
Swanzey Center 207 42.49 N 72.10 W
Swartberg 158 30.15 S 29.23 E
Swarthmore 208 39.54 N 75.21 W
Swarthmore College ʋ[2] 285 39.54 N 75.21 W
Swart-Kei ≐ 158 32.09 S 27.24 E
Swart-Mfolozi ≐ 158 28.22 S 31.58 E
Swartplaas 158 26.08 S 26.57 E
Swartruggens 156 25.40 S 26.42 E
Swartruggens ⩘ 158 33.02 S 19.35 E
Swartswood Lake 210 41.04 N 74.51 W
Swartswood State Park ♠ 210 41.05 N 74.50 W
Swartz Creek 216 42.57 N 83.49 W
Swarupkāti 126 22.45 N 90.06 E
Swarupnagar 126 22.49 N 88.52 E
Swarzędz 30 52.26 N 17.05 E
Swasey Peak ∧ 200 39.23 N 113.19 W
Swasey Wash V 200 39.15 N 112.53 W
Swasiland → Swaziland □[1] 158 26.30 S 31.30 E
Swāt ≐ 123 34.20 N 71.34 E
Swatara Creek ≐ 208 40.11 N 76.44 W
Swa-Tenda 152 7.09 S 17.07 E
Swatow → Shantou 100 23.23 N 116.41 E
Swauger Creek ≐ 226 38.16 N 119.16 W
Swauk Pass)(224 47.21 N 120.40 W
Sway 42 50.47 N 1.37 W
Swayzee 216 40.30 N 85.49 W
Swaziland □[1], Afr. 138 26.30 S 31.30 E
Swaziland □[1], Afr. 158 26.30 S 31.30 E
Swea City 190 43.23 N 94.19 W
Swede Hill 279b 40.17 N 79.34 W
Swedeland 285 40.05 N 75.20 W
Sweden (Sverige) □[1], Europe 22 62.00 N 15.00 E
Sweden (Sverige) □[1], Europe 24 62.00 N 15.00 E
Sweden Valley 214 41.45 N 77.56 W
Swede Run ≐ 285 40.02 N 74.58 W
Swedesboro 208 39.44 N 75.18 W
Swedesburg 285 40.06 N 75.20 W
Swedish Knoll ∧ 200 39.16 N 111.26 W
Swedru 150 5.32 N 0.43 W
Sween, Loch c 46 55.59 N 5.39 W
Sweeney Plan 279b 40.11 N 79.48 W
Sweeny 222 29.02 N 95.41 W
Sweeny Park ♠ 284a 43.02 N 78.52 W
Sweet Briar 192 37.33 N 79.04 W
Sweetgrass 182 49.00 N 111.57 W
Sweet Grass Creek ≐ 202 45.47 N 109.47 W
Sweetgrass Hills ⩘[2] 202 48.55 N 111.30 W
Sweet Grass Indian Reserve ◆[4] 184 52.44 N 108.45 W
Sweetheart Abbey ʋ[1] 44 54.59 N 3.38 W
Sweet Home, Or., U.S. 202 44.23 N 122.44 W
Sweet Home, Tx., U.S. 222 29.21 N 97.04 W
Sweetsers 216 40.34 N 85.46 W
Sweet Springs 194 38.57 N 93.24 W
Sweet Valley 210 41.17 N 76.09 W
Sweetwater, Fl., U.S. 220 25.46 N 80.21 W
Sweet Water, Il., U.S. 219 40.03 N 89.42 W
Sweetwater, Tn., U.S. 192 35.36 N 84.27 W
Sweetwater, Tx., U.S. 196 32.28 N 100.24 W
Sweetwater ≐ 200 42.31 N 107.02 W
Sweetwater Creek 220 27.59 N 82.33 W
Sweetwater Creek ≐, U.S. 196 35.18 N 99.57 W
Sweetwater Creek ≐, Tx., U.S. 196 32.40 N 100.06 W
Sweetwater Mountains ⩘ 226 38.30 N 119.17 W
Swellendam 158 34.02 S 20.26 E
Swepsonville 192 36.01 N 79.21 W
Swerdlowsk → Sverdlovsk 86 56.51 N 60.36 E
Świdnica (Schweidnitz) 30 50.51 N 16.29 E
Świdnik 30 51.14 N 22.41 E
Świdwin 30 53.47 N 15.47 E
Świebodzice 30 50.52 N 16.19 E
Świebodzin 30 52.15 N 15.32 E
Świecie 30 53.25 N 18.28 E
Świerzawa 30 51.01 N 15.54 E
Świerzno 54 53.57 N 14.59 E
Święta 54 53.35 N 14.36 E
Świętokrzyskie, Góry ⩘ 30 50.55 N 21.00 E
Świętokrzyski Park Narodowy ♠ 30 50.55 N 21.00 E
Swift ≐, Eng., U.K. 42 52.23 N 1.16 W
Swift ≐, Ak., U.S. 180 61.53 N 156.18 W
Swift ≐, Ma., U.S. 207 42.12 N 72.22 W
Swift Creek ≐, Al., U.S. 194 32.25 N 86.38 W
Swift Creek ≐, N.C., U.S. 192 35.57 N 77.35 W
Swift Creek ≐, N.C., U.S. 192 35.12 N 77.05 W
Swift Creek ≐, Va., U.S. 208 37.17 N 77.15 W
Swift Current 184 50.17 N 107.50 W
Swift Current Creek ≐ 184 50.40 N 107.44 W
Swifton 194 35.49 N 91.07 W
Swift Reservoir ⊜[1] 224 46.04 N 122.05 W
Swiftwater 210 41.06 N 75.20 W
Swilly ≐ 48 54.57 N 7.42 W
Swilly, Lough c 48 55.10 N 7.38 W
Swimming ≐ 276 40.21 N 74.05 W
Swimming River Reservoir ⊜[1] 276 40.19 N 74.07 W
Świna ≐[1] 54 53.55 N 14.17 E
Swinburne, Cape › 176 71.14 N 98.34 W
Swinden Reservoirs ⊜[1] 262 53.48 N 2.10 W
Swindle Island I 182 52.32 N 128.35 W
Swindon 42 51.34 N 1.47 W
Swinemünde → Świnoujście 30 53.53 N 14.14 E
Swineshead 42 52.56 N 0.09 W
Swinford 48 53.57 N 8.57 W
Swinging Bridge Reservoir ⊜[1] 210 41.37 N 74.48 W
Swinomish Indian Reservation ◆[4] 224 48.25 N 122.33 W
Świnoujście (Swinemünde) 30 53.53 N 14.14 E
Swinton, Eng., U.K. 44 53.28 N 1.20 W
Swinton, Eng., U.K. 262 53.31 N 2.20 W
Swinton, Scot., U.K. 46 55.43 N 2.15 W
Swissvale 279b 40.25 N 79.52 W
Swisttal 56 50.40 N 6.54 E
Switzerland □[6] 218 38.45 N 85.04 W
Switzerland □[1], Europe 22 47.00 N 8.00 E
Switzerland □[1], Europe 58 47.00 N 8.00 E
Swona I 46 58.45 N 3.03 W
Swordfish Seamount ✤[3] 14 18.25 N 158.25 W
Swords 48 53.28 N 6.13 W
Swords Range ⩘ 166 21.57 S 141.32 E
Swormville 284a 43.02 N 78.42 W
Sworton Heath 262 53.21 N 2.28 W
Swoyerville 210 41.18 N 75.52 W
Syalach 74 66.12 N 124.00 E
Syam 58 46.42 N 5.57 E
Syāmnagar 126 22.21 N 89.07 E
Syāmpur, India 126 22.18 N 88.02 E
Syampur, India 272b 22.29 N 88.13 E
Sybille Creek ≐ 198 42.07 N 105.02 W
Syburg ◆[8] 263 51.25 N 7.29 E
Sycamore, Ga., U.S. 192 31.40 N 83.38 W
Sycamore, Il., U.S. 216 41.59 N 88.41 W
Sycamore, Oh., U.S. 214 40.56 N 83.10 W
Sycamore Creek ≐, Az., U.S. 200 33.38 N 111.40 W
Sycamore Creek ≐, Mi., U.S. 216 42.43 N 84.32 W
Sycamore Creek ≐, Oh., U.S. 214 40.59 N 83.12 W
Sycamore Creek ≐, Tx., U.S. 196 29.14 N 100.48 W
Sycamore Gardens 285 39.42 N 75.42 W
Sycamore Island I 279b 40.29 N 79.52 W
Sycamore Slough ≐ 226 38.48 N 121.44 W
Sycan ≐ 202 42.27 N 121.15 W
Sycaway 210 42.44 N 73.39 W
Syčova 86 57.35 N 69.20 E
Syčovka 76 55.50 N 34.17 E
Syców 30 51.19 N 17.43 E
Sydenham, Austl. 274b 37.42 S 144.46 E
Sydenham, On., Can. 212 44.25 N 76.36 W
Sydenham ◆[8], S. Afr. 273d 26.09 S 28.06 E
Sydenham ◆[8], Eng., U.K. 260 51.26 N 0.03 W
Sydenham ≐, On., Can. 190 42.33 N 82.25 W
Sydenham ≐, On., Can. 212 44.35 N 80.57 W
Sydenham Lake ⊜ 212 44.25 N 76.35 W
Sydenham West 274b 37.41 S 144.39 E
Sydney, Austl. 170 33.52 S 151.13 E
Sydney, Austl. 274a 33.52 S 151.13 E
Sydney, N.S., Can. 186 46.09 N 60.11 W
Sydney, Fl., U.S. 220 27.58 N 82.12 W
Sydney, University of ʋ[2] 274a 33.53 S 151.11 E
Sydney Bay c, On., Can. 212 44.54 N 81.05 W
Sydney Bay c, Norf. I. 174c 29.04 S 167.57 E
Sydney Bay Bluff ⍊[4] 212 44.54 N 81.07 W
Sydney Harbour Bridge ◆[5] 170 33.52 S 151.12 E
Sydney Lake ⊜ 184 50.40 N 94.24 W
Sydney Mines 186 46.14 N 60.14 W
Sydney Point › 174d 0.53 S 169.36 E
Syferbult 158 26.00 S 27.20 E
Sygan 279b 40.21 N 80.08 W
Syke 52 52.54 N 8.49 E
Sykesville, Md., U.S. 208 39.22 N 76.58 W
Sykesville, Pa., U.S. 214 41.03 N 78.49 W
Sykkylven 26 62.24 N 6.35 E
Syktyvkar 24 61.40 N 50.46 E
Sylacauga 194 33.10 N 86.15 W
Sylarna ∧ 26 63.02 N 12.13 E
Sylhet 120 24.54 N 91.52 E
Syloga 24 63.50 N 43.39 E
Sylt I 30 54.54 N 8.20 E
Sylva 192 35.22 N 83.13 W
Sylva ≐ 86 57.39 N 56.54 E
Sylvan 224 45.30 N 122.41 W
Sylvan Beach 210 43.11 N 75.43 W
Sylvan Glen 285 40.11 N 75.42 W
Sylvan Grove 198 39.00 N 98.23 W
Sylvan Hills 194 34.50 N 92.13 W
Sylvania, Austl. 274a 34.01 S 151.07 E
Sylvania, Ga., U.S. 192 32.45 N 81.38 W
Sylvania, Oh., U.S. 214 41.43 N 83.42 W
Sylvania, Pa., U.S. 210 41.48 N 76.51 W
Sylvania Heights 274a 34.02 S 151.06 E
Sylvan Lake, Ab., Can. 182 52.19 N 114.05 W
Sylvan Lake, Il., U.S. 278 42.15 N 88.03 W
Sylvan Lake, Mi., U.S. 281 42.37 N 83.20 W
Sylvan Lake ⊜, Ab., Can. 182 52.21 N 114.10 W
Sylvan Lake ⊜, In., U.S. 216 41.29 N 85.20 W
Sylvan Lake ⊜, Mi., U.S. 281 42.37 N 83.20 W
Sylvan Pass)(202 44.28 N 110.08 W
Sylvan Shores 220 28.49 N 81.41 W
Sylvensteinsee ⊜[1] 64 47.34 N 11.32 E
Sylvester, Ga., U.S. 192 31.31 N 83.50 W
Sylvester, Tx., U.S. 196 32.43 N 100.15 W
Sylvester, Mount ∧[2] 186 48.11 N 55.04 W
Sylvia 198 37.57 N 98.24 W
Sym 74 60.20 N 88.23 E
Symmes Creek ≐ 188 38.26 N 82.27 W
Syn'a 24 65.22 N 57.42 E
Syndal 274b 37.53 S 145.09 E
Synkovo 82 55.21 N 37.38 E
Synnyr, chrebet ⩘ 88 56.50 N 111.10 E
Syntul 80 55.00 N 41.18 E
Synžereja 78 47.38 N 28.09 E
Syon House ⊥ 260 51.29 N 0.19 W
Syosset 210 40.49 N 73.30 W
Syowa ʋ[3] 9 69.00 S 39.35 E
Syracuse → Siracusa, It. 70 37.04 N 15.18 E
Syracuse, In., U.S. 216 41.25 N 85.45 W
Syracuse, Ks., U.S. 198 37.58 N 101.45 W
Syracuse, Ne., U.S. 198 40.39 N 96.11 W
Syracuse, N.Y., U.S. 210 43.02 N 76.08 W
Syracuse Hancock International Airport ⊠, N.Y., U.S. 210 43.07 N 76.07 W
Syracuse Hancock International Airport ⊠, N.Y., U.S. 212 43.07 N 76.07 W
Syrčan 80 57.22 N 50.15 E
Syrdarja 85 40.52 N 68.38 E
Syrdarja (Syr Darya) ≐ 72 46.03 N 61.00 E
Syrdarjinskaja Oblast' □[4] 85 40.40 N 68.45 E
Syr-Darya → Syrdarja ≐ 72 46.03 N 61.00 E
Syre 46 58.22 N 4.14 W
Syre ≐ 56 49.35 N 6.08 E
Syria (As-Sūrīyah) □[1], Asia 118 35.00 N 38.00 E
Syria (Sūrīyah) □[1], Asia 128 35.00 N 38.00 E
Syriam 110 16.46 N 96.15 E
Syrian Desert → Shām, Bādiyat ash- ◆[2] 128 32.00 N 40.00 E
Syrie → Syria □[1] 128 35.00 N 38.00 E
Syrien → Syria □[1] 128 35.00 N 38.00 E
Syrskij 76 52.34 N 39.29 E
Sysert' 86 56.29 N 60.49 E
Sysmä 26 61.30 N 25.41 E
Sysola ≐ 24 61.42 N 50.53 E
Sysslebäck 26 60.44 N 12.52 E
Syston 42 52.42 N 1.04 W
Systyg-Chem 88 52.40 N 95.30 E
Syt'kovo 76 56.31 N 34.01 E
Sytykanskij, porog ∟ 88 57.49 N 118.33 E
Syukunoshō 270 34.50 N 135.32 E
Syväri ⊜ 26 63.16 N 28.06 E
Syzran' 80 53.09 N 48.27 E
Syzran' ≐ 80 53.04 N 48.26 E
Szabadka → Subotica 38 46.06 N 19.39 E
Szabolcs-Szatmár □[6] 30 48.00 N 22.10 E
Szada 264c 47.38 N 19.19 E
Szamocin 30 53.02 N 17.08 E
Szamos (Someș) ≐ 38 48.07 N 22.20 E
Szamotuły 30 52.37 N 16.35 E
Szarvas 30 46.52 N 20.34 E
Szatmárnémeti → Satu Mare 38 47.48 N 22.53 E
Százhalombatta 264c 47.20 N 18.56 E
Szczawnica 30 49.26 N 20.30 E
Szczecin (Stettin) 30 53.24 N 14.32 E
Szczecin □[4] 30 53.45 N 15.00 E
Szczecinek (Neustettin) 30 53.43 N 16.42 E
Szczeciński, Zalew (Oderhaff) c 54 53.46 N 14.14 E
Szczekociny 30 50.38 N 19.50 E
Szczuczyn 30 53.34 N 22.18 E
Szczytno 30 53.34 N 21.00 E
Szechwan → Sichuan □[4] 102 31.00 N 105.00 E
Szechwan Basin → Sichuan Pendi ≚[1] 102 30.00 N 105.00 E
Szécsény 30 48.06 N 19.31 E
Szeged 30 46.15 N 20.09 E
Szeghalom 30 47.01 N 21.11 E
Székesfehérvár 30 47.12 N 18.25 E
Szekszárd 30 46.21 N 18.42 E
Szemenyecsörnye 61 46.30 N 16.37 E
Szentendre 30 47.40 N 19.05 E
Szentendrei-Duna ≐[1] 264c 47.36 N 19.05 E
Szentendrei-sziget I 264c 47.39 N 19.07 E
Szentes 30 46.39 N 20.16 E
Szentgotthárd 61 46.57 N 16.17 E
Szentpéterfa 61 47.06 N 16.29 E
Szeping → Siping 89 43.12 N 124.20 E
Szépművészeti Museum ʋ 264c 47.31 N 19.05 E
Szerencs 30 48.09 N 21.13 E
Szigethalom 264c 47.20 N 19.00 E
Szigetszentmiklós 264c 47.21 N 19.03 E
Szilas-patak ≐ 264c 47.36 N 19.06 E
Szlichtyngowa 30 51.43 N 16.15 E
Szob 30 47.50 N 18.52 E
Szolnok 30 47.10 N 20.12 E
Szolnok □[6] 30 47.12 N 20.11 E
Szombathely 61 47.14 N 16.38 E
Szprotawa 30 51.34 N 15.33 E
Sztum 30 53.56 N 19.01 E
Szubin 30 53.00 N 17.44 E
Szydłowiec 30 51.14 N 20.51 E
Szypliszki 30 54.15 N 23.05 E

T

Ta ≐ 94 36.17 N 139.54 E
Taacyn ≐ 102 45.09 N 101.27 E
Taal 116 13.53 N 120.55 E
Taal, Lake ⊜ 116 13.55 N 121.00 E
Taalintehdas → Dalsbruk 26 60.02 N 22.31 E
Taan ≐ 100 24.24 N 120.36 E
Taancan Point › 116 10.00 N 125.01 E
Taavetti 26 60.55 N 27.34 E
Tabacal 252 23.16 S 64.15 W
Tabacal, Quebrada ≐ 286c 10.31 N 67.02 W
Tabaco 116 13.23 N 123.44 E
Tabacundo 246 0.03 N 78.12 W
Tabai ≐ 164 3.01 S 135.52 E
Tabalosos 248 6.21 S 76.41 W
Tabanan 115b 8.32 S 115.08 E
Tabango 116 11.19 N 124.22 E
Tabankulu 158 30.58 S 29.19 E
Tábara 34 41.49 N 5.57 W
Tabar Island I 164 2.55 S 152.05 E
Tabar Islands II 164 2.50 S 152.00 E
Tabarka 148 36.57 N 8.45 E
Tabarz 54 50.52 N 10.31 E
Ţabas 128 33.36 N 56.54 E
Tabasará ≐ 236 8.00 N 81.39 W
Tabasco 232 32.35 N 114.55 W
Tabasco □[3] 232 18.15 N 93.00 W
Ţabas Masīnā 128 32.48 N 60.14 E
Tabat 86 52.57 N 90.43 E
Tabatinga ≐ 255 17.24 S 43.18 W
Tabayama 94 35.47 N 138.55 E
Tabayin 110 22.42 N 95.19 E
Tabb 208 37.08 N 76.29 W
Tabei 98 39.44 N 122.29 E
Tabelbala 148 29.23 N 3.15 W
Tabelbala, Kahal ⍊[8] 148 28.30 N 2.00 W
Taber 182 49.47 N 112.08 W
Taberg, Sve. 26 57.41 N 14.05 E
Taberg, Sve. 40 59.50 N 14.08 E
Taberg, N.Y., U.S. 210 43.18 N 75.37 W
Tabernacle 285 39.50 N 74.42 W
Tabi 152 8.10 S 13.18 E
Tabiang 174d 0.52 S 169.35 E
Tabiano Terme 64 44.48 N 10.21 E
Tabira 250 7.35 S 37.33 W
Tabiteuea 174t 1.25 N 173.07 E
Tabiteuea I[1] 14 1.20 S 174.50 E
Tabla 150 13.46 N 3.01 E
Tabla, Cerro de la ∧ 240m 18.03 N 66.08 W
Tablada 288 34.42 S 58.32 W
Tablas, Cabo › 252 31.51 S 71.34 W
Tablas Island I 116 12.24 N 122.02 E
Tablas Plateau ⩘[1] 116 9.43 N 122.43 E
Tablas Strait ʉ 116 12.40 N 121.48 E
Tablat 34 36.24 N 3.19 E
Table Bay c 158 33.53 S 18.27 E
Table Cape › 172 39.06 S 178.00 E
Tableland 162 17.17 S 127.00 E
Table Mountain ∧, Nf., Can. 186 47.43 N 59.13 W
Table Mountain ∧, S. Afr. 158 33.57 S 18.25 E
Table Mountain ∧, Az., U.S. 200 32.49 N 110.31 W
Table Rock 198 40.10 N 96.05 W
Table Rock Lake ⊜[1] 194 36.35 N 93.30 W
Tabletop ∧, Austl. 162 22.32 S 123.55 E
Table Top ∧, Az., U.S. 200 32.46 N 112.07 W
Tabletop Mountain ∧ 171b 35.58 S 148.30 E
Tabley Mere ⊜ 262 53.17 N 2.25 W
Tabligbo 150 6.35 N 1.30 E
Tablones 240m 18.15 N 65.45 W
Taboan ≐ 116 17.57 N 122.11 E
Taboão, Ribeirão do ≐ 287b 23.40 S 46.28 W
Taboão da Serra 256 23.38 S 46.46 W
Taboco ≐ 248 19.53 S 55.58 W
Taboga 236 8.48 N 79.33 W
Tabogon 116 10.57 N 124.02 E
Tábor, Česko. 30 49.25 N 14.41 E
Tabor, S.S.S.R. 74 71.16 N 150.12 E
Tabor, Ia., U.S. 198 40.53 N 95.40 W
Tabor, N.J., U.S. 276 40.52 N 74.29 W
Tabor, S.D., U.S. 198 42.56 N 97.39 W
Tabor, Mount → Tavor, Har ∧ 132 32.41 N 35.23 E
Tabora 154 5.01 S 32.48 E
Tabora □[4] 154 5.15 S 32.45 E
Tabor City 192 34.08 N 78.52 W
Tabory 86 58.31 N 64.33 E
Tabou 150 4.25 N 7.21 W
Tabrīz 128 38.05 N 46.18 E
Tábua, Riacho da ≐ 250 9.12 S 44.25 W
Tabuaço 34 41.07 N 7.34 W
Tabuaeran I[1] 14 3.52 N 159.20 W
Tabuão 256 21.59 S 44.02 W
Tábuas 256 22.12 S 43.37 W
Tabu-dong 98 36.03 N 128.31 E
Tabuelan 116 10.49 N 123.52 E
Tabūk, Ar. Su. 128 28.23 N 36.35 E
Tabuk, Pil. 116 17.24 N 121.25 E
Tabuleiro 256 21.22 S 43.15 W
Tabuleiro do Norte 250 5.15 S 38.07 W
Tabuny 86 52.46 N 78.45 E
Tabuse 96 33.57 N 132.03 E
Tabuyung 114 0.51 N 99.00 E
Tabwémasana, Mont ∧ 175f 15.20 S 166.44 E
Täby 40 59.30 N 18.03 E
Tacagua, Quebrada ≐ 286c 10.37 N 67.02 W
Tacámbaro ≐ 234 18.29 N 101.07 W
Tacámbaro de Codallos 234 19.14 N 101.28 W
Tacaná 236 15.14 N 92.05 W
Tacaná, Volcán ∧[1] 236 15.08 N 92.06 W
Tacañitas 252 28.38 S 62.36 W
Tacaratu 250 9.06 S 38.10 W
Taceno 58 46.02 N 9.21 E
T'ačev 78 48.02 N 23.34 E
Taché, Lac ⊜ 176 64.00 N 120.00 W
Tacheng (Qoqek) 86 46.45 N 82.57 E
Tacherting 60 48.05 N 12.34 E
Tachia 100 24.21 N 120.37 E
Tachia ≐ 100 24.20 N 120.33 E
Tachiaochang Airport ⊠ 107 32.01 N 118.47 E
Tachiataš 72 42.22 N 59.35 E
Tachibana, Nihon 96 33.54 N 132.17 E
Tachibana, Nihon 96 33.11 N 130.36 E
Tachie ≐ 182 54.40 N 124.50 W
Tachikawa 94 35.42 N 139.25 E
Tachikawa Air Base ■ 268 35.43 N 139.25 E
Tachinger See ⊜ 60 47.58 N 12.45 E
Táchira □[3] 246 7.50 N 72.05 W
Tachoshui 100 24.20 N 121.44 E
Tachov 60 49.48 N 12.38 E
Tachta, S.S.S.R. 80 45.54 N 42.07 E
Tachta, S.S.S.R. 89 53.08 N 139.53 E
Tachta-Bazar 128 35.57 N 62.50 E
Tachtabrod 86 52.38 N 67.34 E
Tachtakupyr 86 43.02 N 60.17 E
Tachtamygda 89 54.06 N 123.34 E
Tacima 250 6.30 S 35.39 W
Tacina ≐ 68 38.56 N 16.53 E
Tacinskij 80 48.13 N 41.17 E
Taciuã, Lago ≐ 246 4.29 S 60.35 W
Tacloban 116 11.15 N 125.00 E
Taclobo 116 12.20 N 122.34 E
Tacna, Perú 248 18.01 S 70.15 W
Tacna, Az., U.S. 200 32.41 N 113.57 W
Tacna □[5] 248 17.40 S 70.20 W
Tacoignières 261 48.50 N 1.40 E
Tacoma 224 47.15 N 122.26 W
Tacoma Narrows Bridge ◆[5] 224 47.16 N 122.33 W
Taconic 207 42.02 N 73.24 W
Taconic Range ⩘ 210 42.30 N 73.20 W
Taconic State Park ♠ 210 42.05 N 73.34 W
Tacony ◆[8] 285 40.02 N 75.03 W
Tacony Creek ≐ 285 40.01 N 75.06 W
Tacony Creek Park ♠ 285 40.02 N 75.07 W
Tacony Palmyra Bridge ◆[5] 285 40.01 N 75.02 W
Taco Pozo 252 25.37 S 63.17 W
Tacotalpa 234 17.36 N 92.49 W
Tacotalpa ≐ 234 17.50 N 92.52 W
Tacuarembó 252 31.44 S 55.59 W
Tacuarembó ≐ 252 32.25 S 55.29 W
Tacuarí ≐ 252 32.46 S 53.18 W
Tacuatí 252 23.27 S 56.35 W
Tacuba ◆[8] 286a 19.28 N 99.12 W
Tacubaya 232 28.20 N 104.34 W
Tacubaya ◆[8] 286a 19.25 N 99.12 W
Tacurong 116 6.42 N 124.42 E
Tacurú, Laguna ⊜ 258 34.58 S 58.25 W
Tacutu (Takutu) ≐ 246 3.01 N 60.29 W
Tadain 270 34.52 N 135.24 E
Tadami 92 37.21 N 139.19 E
Tadaoka 270 34.29 N 135.24 E
Tadasuni 71 40.06 N 8.53 E
Tadcaster 44 53.53 N 1.16 W
Tademaït, Plateau du ⩘[1] 148 28.30 N 2.00 E
Tadenac Lake ⊜ 212 45.03 N 79.56 W
Tādepallegūdem 122 16.50 N 81.30 E
Tadía, Ciénaga de ⊜ 246 6.48 N 76.49 W
Tadine 175f 21.33 S 167.52 E
Tadio, Lagune c 150 5.11 N 5.15 W
Tadjemout 148 25.37 N 3.48 E
Tadjenanet 34 36.08 N 5.59 E
Tadjeraout, Oued V 148 21.17 N 1.19 E
Tadjoura 144 11.47 N 42.54 E
Tadjoura, Golfe de c 144 11.42 N 43.00 E
Tadley 42 51.21 N 1.08 W
Tado 94 35.08 N 136.38 E
Tadok 114 3.58 N 96.19 E
Tadotsu 96 34.16 N 133.45 E
Tadoule Lake ⊜ 176 58.36 N 98.20 W
Tadoussac 186 48.09 N 69.43 W
Tādpatri 122 14.55 N 78.01 E
Taduno 112 1.55 S 123.05 E
Tadworth 42 51.17 N 0.14 W
Tadžikabad 85 39.07 N 70.50 E

Symbol	English	Deutsch	Español	Français	Português
≐	River	Fluß	Río	Rivière	Rio
≖	Canal	Kanal	Canal	Canal	Canal
∟	Waterfall, Rapids	Wasserfall, Stromschnellen	Cascada, Rápidos	Chute d'eau, Rapides	Cascata, Rápidos
ʉ	Strait	Meeresstraße	Estrecho	Détroit	Estreito
c	Bay, Gulf	Bucht, Golf	Bahía, Golfo	Baie, Golfe	Baía, Golfo
⊜	Lake, Lakes	See, Seen	Lago, Lagos	Lac, Lacs	Lago, Lagos
⊞	Swamp	Sumpf	Pantano	Marais	Pântano
⌗	Ice Features, Glacier	Eis- und Gletscherformen	Accidentes Glaciales	Formes glaciaires	Acidentes glaciares
⊤	Other Hydrographic Features	Andere Hydrographische Objekte	Otros Elementos Hidrográficos	Autres données hydrographiques	Outros acidentes hidrográficos
✤	Submarine Features	Untermeerische Objekte	Accidentes Submarinos	Formes de relief sous-marin	Acidentes submarinos
□	Political Unit	Politische Einheit	Unidad Política	Entité politique	Unidade política
ʋ	Cultural Institution	Kulturelle Institution	Institución Cultural	Institution culturelle	Instituição cultural
⊥	Historical Site	Historische Stätte	Sitio Histórico	Site historique	Sítio histórico
♠	Recreational Site	Erholungs- und Ferienort	Sitio de Recreo	Centre de loisirs	Area de Lazer
⊠	Airport	Flughafen	Aeropuerto	Aéroport	Aeroporto
■	Military Installation	Militäranlage	Instalación Militar	Installation militaire	Instalação militar
◆	Miscellaneous	Verschiedenes	Misceláneo	Divers	Diversos

ESPAÑOL Nombre	Página	Lat.°′	Long.°′ W = Oeste
Tamir	88	50.24 N	107.25 E
Tamiryn ≃	88	47.48 N	102.36 E
Tamiš (Timiş) ∼	38	44.51 N	20.39 E
Tamitatoala ≃	255	11.56 S	53.36 W
Tāmīyah	142	29.29 N	30.58 E
Tamkūhi	124	26.41 N	84.11 E
Tam Ky	110	15.34 N	108.29 E
Tamlūk	126	22.18 N	87.55 E
Tämma	120	25.11 N	93.42 E
Tammaro ≃	68	41.09 N	14.50 E
Tammerfors → Tampere	25	61.30 N	23.45 E
Tammisaari → Ekenäs	25	59.58 N	23.26 E
Tamms	194	37.14 N	89.16 W
Tammūh	273c	29.56 N	31.16 E
Tämna	126	23.15 N	86.21 E
Tämnarän ≃	40	60.31 N	17.39 E
Tämnaren ☉	40	60.10 N	17.20 E
Tamnun	144	15.07 N	50.49 E
Tamon ☀	270	34.39 N	135.04 E
Tamós, Laguna de ☉	234	22.10 N	98.02 W
Tampa, Ang.	152	15.30 S	13.27 E
Tampa, Fl., U.S.	220	27.56 N	82.27 W
Tampa Bay c	220	27.45 N	82.35 W
Tampa International Airport ≖	220	27.59 N	82.32 W
Tampamachoco, Laguna ☉	234	21.00 N	97.21 W
Tampang	112	5.54 S	104.43 E
Tampaon ≃	234	21.59 N	98.36 W
Tamparani	116	8.27 N	117.13 E
Tampere	26	61.30 N	23.45 E
Tampico, Méx.	234	22.13 N	97.51 W
Tampico, Il., U.S.	190	41.37 N	89.47 W
Tampico, In., U.S.	218	38.48 N	85.58 W
Tampin	114	2.28 N	102.14 E
Tampoc ≃	250	3.27 N	54.00 W
Tampulonanjing, Gunung ⋀	114	1.46 N	99.24 E
Tam Quan	110	14.35 N	109.03 E
Tamra	132	32.51 N	35.12 E
Tamrau, Pegunungan ⋌	164	0.30 S	132.27 E
Tamri	148	30.43 N	9.43 W
Tamsagbulag	88	47.14 N	117.21 E
Tamsalu	76	59.10 N	26.06 E
Tamshiyacu	246	4.05 S	72.58 W
Tamsweg	64	47.08 N	13.48 E
Tamu	110	24.13 N	94.18 E
Tamuín	234	21.59 N	98.45 W
Tamuin ≃	234	21.59 N	98.36 W
Tamuk Island I	116	6.27 N	121.49 E
Tamuning	174p	13.29 N	144.46 E
Tamura	268	35.22 N	139.22 E
Tamusuke	85	38.03 N	76.53 E
Tamworth, Austl.	166	31.05 S	150.55 E
Tamworth, On., Can.	212	44.29 N	77.00 W
Tamworth, Eng., U.K.	42	52.39 N	1.40 W
Tamyang	98	35.21 N	126.58 E
Tan ⌖	100	23.57 N	115.17 E
Tana, Chile	248	19.27 S	69.57 W
Tana, Nor.	24	70.28 N	28.18 E
Tana ≃, Cuba	240p	20.42 N	77.25 W
Tana (Teno) ≃, Europe	24	70.30 N	28.23 E
T'an'a ≃, S.S.S.R.	88	58.40 N	120.30 E
Tana, Lake ☉	144	12.00 N	37.20 E
Tanabe, Nihon	96	34.49 N	135.46 E
Tanabe, Nihon	96	33.44 N	135.22 E
Tanabi	255	20.37 S	49.37 W
Tanacross	180	63.23 N	143.21 W
Tanafjorden c²	24	70.54 N	28.40 E
Tanaga Island I	180	51.50 N	178.00 W
Tanaga Volcano ⋀¹	180	51.55 N	178.09 W
Tanagro ≃	68	40.38 N	15.14 E
Tanaguarena	106	10.37 N	66.49 W
Tanagura	94	37.02 N	140.23 E
Tanah, Tanjung ⋗	115a	6.29 S	108.32 E
Tanahbala, Pulau I	110	0.25 S	98.25 E
Tanahgrogot	112	1.55 S	116.12 E
Tanahjampea, Pulau I	112	7.05 S	120.42 E
Tanahmasa, Pulau I	110	0.12 S	98.27 E
Tanahmerah, Indon.	114	34.11 N	117.31 E
Tanahmerah, Indon.	164	6.05 S	140.17 E
Tanah Merah, Malay.	114	5.48 N	102.09 E
Tanah Merah, Malay.	114	2.36 N	101.48 E
Tanahputih	114	1.41 N	101.03 E
Tanaka ☀⁸	270	34.42 N	134.59 E
Tanakeke, Pulau I	112	5.30 S	119.16 E
Tanakpur	124	29.05 N	80.07 E
Tan'am	128	23.09 N	58.07 E
Tanami	162	19.59 S	129.43 E
Tanami Desert ≃²	162	20.00 S	129.30 E
Tanān, Mişr	142	30.15 N	31.14 E
Tan An, Viet.	110	10.32 N	106.25 E
Tan An, Viet.	110	8.46 N	105.11 E
Tanana	180	65.10 N	152.05 W
Tanana ≃	180	65.09 N	151.55 W
Tananarive → Antananarivo	157b	18.55 S	47.31 E
Tanapag, Lagunar c	174n	15.14 N	145.45 E
Tanapag ≃	62	45.01 N	8.47 E
Tanärūt, Wādi ∿	146	30.08 N	9.59 E
Tanashi	94	35.44 N	139.33 E
Tanat ≃	52	52.46 N	3.07 W
Tanauan	116	11.07 N	125.01 E
Tanbar	166	25.50 S	141.55 E
Tanbidī	142	28.38 N	30.47 E
Tan Binh	269c	10.48 N	106.40 E
Tanbu, Zhg.	98	33.51 N	118.17 E
Tanbu, Zhg.	100	28.08 N	114.12 E
Tancarville, Canal de ≖	50	49.28 N	0.28 E
Tancha	174m	26.28 N	121.52 E
Tan Chau	110	10.48 N	105.15 E
Tancheng	98	34.37 N	118.23 E
Tanchipa, Sierra de ⋌	234	22.40 N	98.50 W
Tanchoj	88	51.33 N	105.07 E
Tanch'ŏn	98	40.27 N	128.54 E
Tancitaro	234	19.20 N	102.22 W
Tancitaro, Pico de ⋀	234	19.23 N	102.13 W
Tancochapa ≃	234	17.59 N	94.04 W
Tanda, C. Iv.	150	7.48 N	3.10 W
Tända, India	123	31.42 N	75.38 E
Tända, India	124	28.02 N	78.56 E
Tända, India	124	26.33 N	82.39 E
Tända, Pāk.	123	32.42 N	74.22 E
Tandag	116	9.04 N	126.12 E
Tandah	142	27.41 N	30.46 E
Tandai	154	19.36 S	32.48 E
Tandaj	80	47.33 N	51.30 E
Tandala	154	9.23 S	34.14 E
Tandaltī	148	13.01 N	31.52 E
Tandarei	38	44.38 N	27.40 E
Tandaué	152	17.00 S	18.06 E
Tandian	98	40.39 N	124.46 E
Tandil	252	37.19 S	59.09 W
Tandjilé ≃⁵	146	9.45 N	16.30 E
Tandlianwāla	123	31.02 N	73.08 E
Tando Ādam	120	25.46 N	68.40 E
Tando Allāhyār	120	25.28 N	68.43 E
Tando Bāgo	120	24.47 N	68.58 E
Tando Muhammad Khān	120	25.08 N	68.32 E
Tandou Bougou	152	3.32 S	10.53 E
Tandou Lake ☉	166	32.38 S	142.05 E
Tandovo, ozero ☉	86	55.07 N	78.02 E
Tando Zinze	152	5.22 S	12.16 E
Tandragee	48	54.20 N	6.25 W
Tandridge	260	51.14 N	0.02 W
Tandridge ☉⁸	260	51.14 N	0.05 W
Tanduas	41	54.55 N	9.52 E
Tandubatu Island I	116	5.10 N	120.20 E
Tändula Tank ☉¹	122	20.40 N	81.12 E

FRANÇAIS Nom	Page	Lat.°′	Long.°′ W = Ouest
Tandun	112	0.36 N	100.38 E
Tändür	122	17.14 N	77.35 E
Tanduy ☉	115a	7.41 S	108.47 E
Taneatua	172	38.04 S	177.01 E
Tanega-shima I	93b	30.40 N	131.00 E
Taneichi	92	40.26 N	141.43 E
Tan Emellel	148	27.30 N	9.45 E
Tanete	112	4.32 S	119.36 E
Taneum Creek ≃	224	47.10 N	120.40 W
Tanew ≃	30	50.31 N	22.16 E
Taneytown	208	39.39 N	77.10 W
Tanezrouft ⁂²	148	24.00 N	0.45 W
Tanezzuft, Wādī ∿	146	25.51 N	10.19 E
Tanforan Park ⋆⁹	282	37.38 N	122.25 W
Targ ≃, Zhg.	98	38.45 N	115.35 E
Targ ≃, Zhg.	100	32.09 N	112.25 E
Targ ≃, Zhg.	100	33.18 N	117.46 E
Targ ≃, Zhg.	104	41.15 N	123.21 E
Targ ≃, Zhg.	106	40.43 N	116.38 E
Targ ≃, Zhg.	98	41.25 N	120.52 E
Targainony	157b	22.42 S	47.45 E
Tanga Islands II	1	3.30 S	153.15 E
Targalla	122	6.01 N	80.48 E
Tangamandapio	232	19.57 N	102.26 W
Tangamong Lake ☉	212	44.43 N	77.51 W
Tangancicuaro [de Arista]	234	19.54 N	102.08 W
Tanganika, Lago → Tanganyika, Lake ☉	154	6.00 S	29.30 E
Tanganika-See → Tanganyika, Lake ☉	154	6.00 S	29.30 E
Tanganyika, Lake ☉	154	6.00 S	29.30 E
Tangarana ≃	252	27.08 S	51.13 W
Tangara ≃	246	3.02 S	75.08 W
Tangarare	175e	9.35 S	159.39 E
Tanga-shima I	96	34.40 N	134.35 E
Tangba	107	30.00 N	105.46 E
Tangchi	89	47.00 N	123.46 E
Tangchigou	104	41.04 N	124.11 E
Tangcun ≃, Zhg.	100	29.50 N	118.54 E
Tangcun, Zhg.	100	25.26 N	113.10 E
Tangdaohe	98	40.38 N	118.58 E
Tanger (Tangier)	148	35.48 N	5.45 W
Tanger ☉⁴	54	52.33 N	11.59 E
Tangerhütte	54	52.26 N	11.48 E
Tangerine	220	28.47 N	81.38 W
Tang'erli	105	39.09 N	116.43 E
Tangermünde	54	52.32 N	11.58 E
Tangfang, Zhg.	102	27.00 N	101.08 E
Tangfang, Zhg.	104	41.20 N	120.34 E
Tangfang, Zhg.	105	39.29 N	118.01 E
Tangfangqiao	106	31.45 N	120.50 E
Tangga ≃	98	38.07 N	115.30 E
Tanggangzi	104	41.01 N	122.54 E
Tanggeasinua, Pegunungan ⋌	112	3.24 S	121.42 E
Tanggengtou	106	30.55 N	119.03 E
Tanggu	105	39.01 N	117.40 E
Tangguantun	98	38.43 N	116.55 E
Tanggul	115a	8.10 S	113.26 E
Tanggulashan (Tuotuoheyan)	120	34.05 N	92.45 E
Tanggula Shan ⋌	120	33.00 N	92.00 E
Tanggula Shankou ⋋	120	32.59 N	91.45 E
Tanggushiluke	120	38.45 N	80.55 E
Tanghe	100	32.43 N	112.48 E
Tanghekou	105	40.44 N	116.38 E
Tanghu	100	39.11 N	115.24 E
Tanghuang	106	31.41 N	119.25 E
Tangi, N.S., Can.	218	34.18 N	90.40 W
Tangier, N.S., Can.	186	44.48 N	62.42 W
Tangier → Tanger, Magreb	148	35.48 N	5.45 W
Tangier, Va., U.S.	208	37.49 N	75.59 W
Tangier Island I	208	37.50 N	76.00 W
Tangier Sound ╚	208	38.02 N	75.58 W
Tangjiahua ☉	99	29.36 N	106.39 E
Tangjiapaboa ≃	194	30.20 N	90.18 W
Tangjia	100	22.23 N	113.36 E
Tangjiang	100	25.51 N	114.44 E
Tangjiapao	100	33.00 N	92.00 E
Tangjiaxu	100	32.59 N	91.45 E
Tangjiqiaozhen	106	31.13 N	121.31 E
Tangkak	114	2.16 N	102.33 E
Tangkou	100	30.06 N	118.11 E
Tanglewood, Fl., U.S.	115b	8.47 S	115.35 E
Tanglewood, Tx., U.S.	226	26.37 N	81.53 W
Tanglewood ⋆	207	42.21 N	73.20 W
Tangling	100	26.14 N	119.24 E
Tanglitun	105	43.15 N	123.57 E
Tangmai	102	30.08 N	95.11 E
Tangmazhai	100	41.10 N	122.44 E
Tang Nhon Phu	269c	10.50 N	106.47 E
Tang-ni	98	34.12 N	126.52 E
Tango	96	35.40 N	135.10 E
Tango-hantō ⋗¹	96	35.40 N	135.10 E
Tangpu, Zhg.	100	29.51 N	120.47 E
Tangpu, Zhg.	100	28.28 N	114.58 E
Tangqiao	106	30.29 N	120.11 E
Tangra Yumco ☉	120	31.13 N	119.15 E
Tangshan	120	30.40 N	86.20 E
Tangsanying	105	41.38 N	117.40 E
Tangshan → Tangshan	105	39.38 N	118.11 E
Tangxia	100	5.01 N	95.55 E
Tangshan, Zhg.	100	39.38 N	118.11 E
Tangshan, Zhg.	106	32.05 N	119.03 E
Tang Shan ⋀	106	32.03 N	119.02 E
Tangshi	100	31.33 N	120.51 E
Tangtou, Zhg.	98	35.16 N	118.35 E
Tangtou, Zhg.	100	27.42 N	108.17 E
Tangtou, Zhg.	100	31.38 N	120.19 E
Tangtouxia	100	22.50 N	114.06 E
Tangtse	123	34.02 N	78.11 E
Tanguá	256	22.44 S	42.43 W
Tangub	116	8.03 N	123.44 E
Tanguieta	150	10.37 N	1.16 E
Tanguip Point ⋗	116	7.43 N	126.32 E
Tanguy	88	55.23 N	100.58 E
Tangwu, Telukan c	116	5.27 N	119.54 E
Tangwu	99	46.40 N	129.54 E
Tangxian	100	29.04 N	119.23 E
Tangxianzhen	100	30.58 N	114.58 E
Tangy ☉	100	36.32 N	115.47 E
Tangyin, Zhg.	98	35.55 N	114.21 E
Tangyin, Zhg.	106	32.36 N	116.16 E
Tangyuan	89	46.42 N	129.55 E
Tanhaçu	255	13.44 S	41.15 W
Taniantaweng Shan ⋌	102	30.00 N	98.00 E
Tanigawa-dake ⋀	94	36.50 N	138.56 E
Tanimbar, Kepulauan II	164	7.30 S	131.30 E
Taninges	60	46.07 N	6.36 E
Tanintharyi ≃⁴	110	12.00 N	99.00 E
Tanis (Zoan) ⋈	142	30.57 N	31.53 E

PORTUGUÊS Nome	Página	Lat.°′	Long.°′ W = Oeste
Tanishpa ⋀	120	31.10 N	68.24 E
Tanjay	116	9.31 N	123.09 E
Tanjiafang	98	36.41 N	118.36 E
Tanjiahe	100	31.58 N	113.56 E
Tanjiang	100	24.07 N	116.32 E
Tanjiang ≃	100	30.11 N	118.15 E
Tanjil ☉	169	38.08 S	146.17 E
Tanjong Dawai	114	5.41 N	100.22 E
Tanjong Malim	114	3.41 N	101.31 E
Tanjore → Thanjāvūr	122	10.48 N	79.09 E
Tanjung, Indon.	112	2.11 S	115.23 E
Tanjung, Indon.	115a	6.52 S	108.52 E
Tanjung, Indon.	115b	8.21 S	116.09 E
Tanjungbalai	114	2.58 N	99.48 E
Tanjungbatu, Indon.	112	0.45 N	117.26 E
Tanjungbatu, Indon.	112	2.17 N	118.05 E
Tanjungbatu, Indon.	112	0.38 N	103.26 E
Tanjungenim	112	3.45 S	103.48 E
Tanjungkarang-Telukbetung	115a	5.27 S	105.16 E
Tanjunglabu	112	2.57 S	106.54 E
Tanjungmedan, Indon.	114	2.06 N	100.14 E
Tanjungmedan, Indon.	114	1.26 N	100.34 E
Tanjungmengedar	112	2.39 N	100.01 E
Tanjungpandan	112	2.45 S	107.39 E
Tanjungpinang	112	0.55 N	104.27 E
Tanjungpriok ⋆⁸	269e	6.06 S	106.53 E
Tanjungpura	114	3.54 N	98.26 E
Tanjungpusu	112	4.11 N	101.16 E
Tanjungraja	112	3.21 S	104.40 E
Tanjungredep	112	2.09 N	117.29 E
Tanjungsamak	112	0.52 N	103.03 E
Tanjungselor	112	2.51 N	117.22 E
Tanjungslamat	114	3.49 N	98.20 E
Tanjunguban	112	1.03 N	104.14 E
Tankapirtti	24	68.12 N	27.20 E
Tan Kena	148	26.38 N	9.35 E
Tan Kien	269c	10.42 N	106.35 E
Tankou	100	25.48 N	114.50 E
Tankwa ≃	158	32.20 S	19.33 E
Tanlay	50	47.50 N	4.05 E
Tann	56	50.38 N	10.01 E
Tänna	54	50.38 N	11.52 E
Tanna I	175f	19.30 S	169.20 E
Tannan	96	35.05 N	135.10 E
Tännäs	26	62.27 N	12.40 E
Tann-tunnel ⋆⁵	94	35.06 N	139.00 E
Tannay	50	47.21 N	3.36 E
Tanner	194	34.43 N	86.58 W
Tanner, Mount ⋀	182	49.40 N	118.34 W
Tannersville, N.Y., U.S.	210	42.12 N	74.08 W
Tannersville, Pa., U.S.	210	41.03 N	75.18 W
Tännesberg	60	49.32 N	12.22 E
Tännforsen ∿	26	63.27 N	12.44 E
Tannila	26	65.29 N	25.59 E
Tannis Bugt c	26	57.40 N	10.15 E
Tannu-Ola, chrebet ⋌	88	51.00 N	94.00 E
Tannūrah, Ra's ⋗	128	26.40 N	50.10 E
Tano, Nihon	96	33.26 N	134.00 E
Tano, Nihon	270	34.57 N	135.36 E
Tano ≃	150	5.07 N	2.54 W
Tanon Strait ╚	116	10.20 N	123.30 E
Tānout	150	14.58 N	8.53 E
Tanque de Dolores	234	23.40 N	101.10 W
Tanque Grande, Ribeirão ≃	287b	23.25 S	46.28 W
Tan Qui Dong	269c	10.44 N	106.42 E
Tanquinho, Bra.	255	11.58 S	39.06 W
Tanquinho, Bra.	255	22.48 S	47.00 W
T'an' San' → Tien Shan ⋌	90	42.00 N	80.00 E
Tansania → Tanzania ☐¹	154	6.00 S	35.00 E
Tansboro	285	39.46 N	74.55 W
Tänsen	124	27.52 N	83.33 E
Tanshui	100	25.10 N	121.26 E
Tanshuia	150	12.26 N	4.23 W
Tánsin, Isla de I	236	15.17 N	83.54 W
Tánsin, Laguna de ☉	236	15.18 N	83.55 W
Tan Son Nhut Airport ≖	269c	10.49 N	106.40 E
Tansyk	86	47.20 N	79.52 E
Tantā	142	30.47 N	31.00 E
Tantabogue Creek ≃	222	31.00 N	95.21 W
Tan-Tan	148	28.26 N	11.06 W
Tantangara Reservoir ☉¹	171b	35.45 S	148.39 E
Tan Thoi Nhut	269c	10.50 N	106.38 E
Tan Thuan Dong	269c	10.45 N	106.44 E
Tântipāra	126	23.54 N	87.22 E
Tantoli	96	35.29 S	150.09 E
Tantonville	58	48.28 N	6.08 E
Tantou, Zhg.	100	29.07 N	121.08 E
Tantou, Zhg.	106	26.03 N	119.35 E
Tantou Shan I	100	29.11 N	122.01 E
Tantoyuca	234	21.21 N	98.14 W
Tantura	132	32.36 N	34.55 E
Tanuma	94	36.22 N	139.35 E
Tanumshede	26	58.44 N	11.19 E
Tanunda	168b	34.32 S	138.57 E
Tan'uner ≃	180	64.44 N	174.15 E
Tanvald	30	50.45 N	15.19 E
Tanwax Creek ≃	224	46.52 N	122.27 W
Tanworth-in-Arden	42	52.20 N	1.50 W
Tanxi	100	28.58 N	115.38 E
Tanxia	100	23.58 N	115.34 E
Tanxu Shan I	106	30.37 N	121.37 E
Tanyang	98	35.39 N	119.02 E
Tanyeri	130	39.37 N	39.50 E
Tanyi	100	34.13 N	118.09 E
Tanymas ≃	85	38.25 N	72.39 E
Tanzania ☐¹, Afr.	138	6.00 S	35.00 E
Tanzania ☐¹, Afr.	154	6.00 S	35.00 E
Tanzawa-Ōyama-kokutei-kōen ⋆	94	35.30 N	139.10 E
Tanzawa-san ⋀	94	35.28 N	139.10 E
Tao ≃, Zhg.	102	35.52 N	103.16 E
Tao, Ko I	110	10.05 N	99.52 E
Taochang	100	23.04 N	122.47 E
Taochong	102	25.07 N	111.06 E
Taocun	98	37.10 N	121.05 E
Taodigou	105	40.52 N	116.14 E
Tao'er ≃	105	45.42 N	124.05 E
Taohong	102	30.03 N	111.09 E
Taohua	106	31.23 N	120.04 E
Taohuachiyingzi	104	42.18 N	121.06 E
Taohua Dao I	106	29.48 N	122.17 E
Taohuawu	106	30.53 N	120.02 E
Taohuwan	100	30.45 N	106.52 E
Taohulbigai	104	40.53 N	121.29 E
Taoji	100	34.40 N	120.00 E
Taojiang	100	28.33 N	112.09 E
Taojiaqu	102	30.55 N	115.06 E
Taojialing	102	30.51 N	115.02 E
Taolanaro	157b	25.02 S	46.59 E
Taolaizhao	105	44.55 N	125.57 E
Taolepa	105	32.05 S	85.22 E
Taonan	104	45.20 N	122.47 E
Taoshu	100	34.30 N	118.30 E
Taoling	106	30.41 N	121.08 E

PORTUGUÊS Nome (cont.)	Página	Lat.°′	Long.°′ W = Oeste
Taoluo	98	35.17 N	119.24 E
T'aonan → Tao'an	89	45.22 N	122.47 E
Taongi I¹	14	14.37 N	168.58 E
Taormina	70	37.51 N	15.17 E
Taos, Mo., U.S.	219	38.30 N	92.04 W
Taos, N.M., U.S.	200	36.24 N	105.34 W
Taos Pueblo	200	36.26 N	105.32 W
Taoudenni	148	22.40 N	4.00 W
Taougrite	34	36.15 N	0.55 E
Taounate	148	34.35 N	4.39 W
Taounate ☉⁴	148	34.30 N	4.40 W
Taoura	148	36.09 N	8.03 E
Taourirt	148	34.25 N	2.53 W
Taourirt ≃	148	24.03 N	5.02 E
Taoussa	150	16.55 N	0.35 W
Taowu	106	31.47 N	118.46 E
Taoxi, Zhg.	100	31.33 N	117.00 E
Taoxi, Zhg.	100	25.18 N	116.05 E
Taoxi, Zhg.	100	28.44 N	119.36 E
Taoxiantun	104	41.39 N	123.27 E
Taoyuan, Zhg.	100	25.48 N	117.32 E
Taoyuan, Zhg.	102	28.46 N	111.20 E
Taozhu	100	28.50 N	121.31 E
Taozhuang	106	30.58 N	120.48 E
Tapa, India	123	30.19 N	75.21 E
Tapa, S.S.S.R.	76	59.16 N	25.58 E
Tapaan Island I	116	5.28 N	120.44 E
Tapacarí	248	17.31 S	66.36 W
Tapachula	232	14.54 N	92.17 W
Tapaga, Cape ⋗	175a	14.01 S	171.23 W
Tapah Road	114	4.10 N	101.12 E
Tapaje ≃	246	2.44 N	78.07 W
Tapajós ≃	250	2.24 S	54.41 W
Tapaktuan	114	3.16 N	97.11 E
Tapalpa	234	19.57 N	103.46 W
Tapalquén	252	36.21 S	60.01 W
Tapan	112	2.10 S	101.04 E
Tapanahony ≃	250	4.22 N	54.27 W
Tapanui	172	45.57 S	169.16 E
Tapanuli, Teluk c	114	1.38 N	98.45 E
Tapasi	126	23.40 N	87.08 E
Tapauá	248	5.45 S	63.04 W
Tapauá ≃	248	5.40 S	64.21 W
Tapawera	172	41.23 S	172.49 E
Tapaz	116	11.16 N	122.32 E
Tapejara	252	28.04 S	52.00 W
Tapera	252	28.38 S	52.52 W
Taperoá, Bra.	250	7.12 S	36.49 W
Taperoá, Bol.	255	13.31 S	39.06 W
Tapeta	150	6.29 N	8.51 W
Taphan Hin	110	16.13 N	100.26 E
Taphoen ≃	110	14.07 N	99.25 E
Ta Pi ≃, India	120	21.06 N	72.41 E
Ta Pi ≃, Thai	110	9.05 N	99.12 E
Tapiales	288	34.42 S	58.31 W
Tapiantana Channel ╚	116	6.23 N	122.00 E
Tapiantana Island I	116	6.18 N	121.59 E
Tapiche ≃	248	4.59 S	73.51 W
Tapili	154	3.25 N	27.40 E
Tapilula	234	17.14 N	93.02 W
Taping (Daying) ≃	102	24.17 N	97.14 E
Tapini	164	8.20 S	146.59 E
Tapirai	255	19.52 S	46.01 W
Tapirapé ≃	250	10.41 S	50.38 W
Tapiratiba	255	21.28 S	46.45 W
Tapis, Gunong ⋀	114	4.03 N	102.54 E
Tapolca	30	46.53 N	17.27 E
Taquaíra	112	11.12 N	119.16 E
Tapoa ≃	150	12.36 N	2.29 E
Tapol	146	8.31 N	15.35 E
Tapolca	30	46.53 N	17.27 E
Tappahannock	208	37.55 N	76.51 W
Tappal	124	28.03 N	77.31 E
Tappan, Lake ☉¹	285	41.01 N	73.59 W
Tappan Lake ☉¹	214	40.21 N	81.11 W
Tappan Zee c	285	41.06 N	73.53 W
Tappan Zee Bridge ⋈	285		
Tappen	198	46.52 N	99.38 W
Tappernøje	41	55.10 N	11.58 E
Tarbolton	46	55.31 N	4.24 W
Tarboro	192	35.53 N	77.32 W
Tarčaului, Munţii ⋌	38	46.45 N	26.20 E
Tarcento	64	46.13 N	13.13 E
Tarchankut, mys ⋗	78	45.21 N	32.30 E
Tarcoola	166	30.41 S	134.33 E
Tarcoola	166	30.15 S	146.43 E
Tarcutta Creek ≃	171b	35.08 S	147.36 E
Tardajos	62	42.21 N	3.49 W
Tardoki-Jani, gora ⋀	89	48.53 N	138.04 E
Tardun	162	28.48 S	115.48 E
Tare	124	29.39 S	150.47 E
Taree	166	31.54 S	152.28 E
Taremt-N-Akli, Oued ∿	148	25.49 N	1.37 E
Tårendö	24	67.10 N	22.38 E
Tarent, Golf von → Taranto, Golfo di c	68	40.10 N	17.20 E
Tarentum	214	40.36 N	79.45 W
Tarf, Garaet et ☉	148	35.40 N	7.10 E
Tarfâ, Batn at ∿	128	23.50 N	51.27 E
Tarfâ, Ra's at ⋗	144	16.30 N	42.30 E
Tarfâ, Wādī at ∿	142	28.38 N	30.50 E
Tarfawi, Bi'r ⋇, Mişr	142	22.57 N	28.53 E
Tarfawi, Bi'r ⋇	143		
Targ ≃, S.S.S.R.	192	35.33 N	77.05 W
Tara, Austl.	166	27.17 S	150.28 E
Tara ≃, On., Can.	212	44.28 N	81.09 W
Tara ≃, Zam.	154	16.56 S	26.47 E
Tara ≃	38	43.55 N	19.11 E
Tara ≃, Jugo.	72	43.21 N	18.51 E
Tara ≃, S.S.S.R.	86	56.42 N	74.36 E
Taraba ≃	150	8.30 N	10.15 E
Tarabine, Oued tin-n ∿	148	20.50 N	7.25 E
Tarabuco	248	19.10 S	64.57 W
Tarābulus (Tripoli), Lībiyā	146	32.54 N	13.11 E
Tarābulus (Tripoli), Lubnān	132	34.26 N	35.51 E
Tarābulus (Tripolitania) ☐⁹	146	31.00 N	15.00 E
Tarabya ⋆⁸	267b	41.08 N	29.03 E
Tarach ≃	154	4.09 N	34.56 E
Taradale	172	39.36 S	176.51 E
Taragh	52	52.41 N	9.32 W
Taraghin	146	26.00 N	14.27 E
Tarago	171b	35.04 S	149.39 E
Tarahumara, Sierra ⋌	232	27.00 N	107.30 W
Tarai ≃⁴	124	28.30 N	80.00 E
Taraia	124	26.05 N	84.53 E
Tara Hills	282	37.58 N	122.24 W
Taraira ≃	248	0.33 N	69.40 W
Tara Island I	164	1.20 S	152.22 E
Tarakan	112	3.18 N	117.38 E
Tarakan, Pulau I	112	3.21 N	117.35 E
Tarakki	120	32.52 N	68.00 E
Taraklija, S.S.S.R.	78	45.54 N	28.38 E
Taraklija, S.S.S.R.	78	46.34 N	29.06 E
Taralga	170	34.24 S	149.49 E
Tarama	175d	24.40 N	124.41 E
Taramakau ≃	172	42.35 S	171.08 E
Tarama-shima I	175d	24.39 N	124.42 E
Tarana	170	33.32 S	149.54 E
Tārānagar	123	28.41 N	75.02 E
Taranaki, Mount ⋀	172	39.18 S	174.04 E
Tarancón	34	40.01 N	3.00 W
Tarandacuao	234	19.59 N	100.32 W
Taranga Island I	172	35.58 S	174.43 E
Tarangire National Park ⋆	154	4.00 S	36.00 E
Tarango, Presa de ☉¹	286a	19.22 N	99.13 W
Taranovka	78	49.37 S	36.08 E
Taransay I	46	57.54 N	7.01 W
Taranta Peligna	68	42.01 N	14.10 E
Tarante, Murge ⋗¹	68	40.22 N	17.40 E
Taranto	68	40.28 N	17.15 E
Taranto ☉⁴	68	40.37 N	17.15 E
Taranto, Golfo di c	68	40.10 N	17.20 E
Tarapacá	246	2.52 S	69.44 W
Tarapacá ☐⁴	248	20.30 S	69.50 W
Tarapoto	248	6.30 S	76.25 W
Taraq al-Ḥbâri ⋖¹	130	34.17 N	39.16 E
Taraq an-Na'jah ⋖¹	130	34.16 N	39.53 E
Taraq Sidâoui ⋖¹	130	34.33 N	39.54 E
Taraquá	246	0.06 N	68.28 W
Tarare	58	45.54 N	4.26 E
Tararua Range ⋌	172	40.45 S	175.23 E
Tārāsa Dwīp I	110	8.15 N	93.10 E
Tarašča	78	49.34 N	30.29 E
Tarāsh	78	49.34 N	30.29 E
Tarascon, Fr.	58	43.51 N	1.36 E
Tarascon, Fr.	62	43.48 N	4.40 E
Tarasht ⋆⁸	267d	35.42 N	51.21 E
Tarasovka, S.S.S.R.	83	49.40 N	38.23 E
Tarasovka, S.S.S.R.	83	48.21 N	37.33 E
Tarasovka, S.S.S.R.	83	49.28 N	40.05 E
Tarasovo, S.S.S.R.	24	66.13 N	46.39 E
Tarasovo, S.S.S.R.	24	62.49 N	41.10 E
Tarasovskij	78	48.43 N	40.22 E
Tarasp	58	46.48 N	10.25 E
Tarat, Oued ∿	148	26.09 N	9.20 E
Tarata, Bol.	248	17.37 S	66.01 W
Tarata, Perú	248	17.28 S	70.02 W
Taratanr	126	23.80 N	86.29 E
Taratabuluh	112	0.23 N	101.27 E
Tarauacá	248	8.10 S	70.46 W
Tarauacá ≃	248	6.42 S	69.48 W
Taravao, Baie de c	175f	17.43 S	149.17 W
Taravo, Isthme de ╚	66	41.48 N	8.49 E
Taravo ≃	66	41.42 N	8.49 E
Tarawa I¹	174t	1.25 N	173.00 E
Tarawera	172	39.02 S	176.35 E
Tarawera, Lake ☉	172	38.12 S	176.27 E
Tarazona de la Mancha	34	39.15 N	1.55 W
Tarba	246	1.35 S	75.15 W
Tårbæk	41	55.47 N	12.36 E
Tarbagataj, S.S.S.R.	88	51.30 N	107.22 E
Tarbagataj, S.S.S.R.	88	52.07 N	109.12 E
Tarbagataj, chrebet ⋌	86	47.12 N	83.00 E
Tarbat Ness ⋗	46	57.51 N	3.47 W
Tarbela	123	34.08 N	72.49 E
Tarbela Reservoir ☉¹	123	34.14 N	72.50 E
Tarbert, Ire.	52	52.34 N	9.23 W
Tarbert, Scot., U.K.	46	55.52 N	5.26 W
Tarbert, Scot., U.K.	46	57.54 N	6.49 W
Tarbert, East Loch c	46	57.52 N	6.43 W
Tarbert, Loch c	46	55.57 N	6.00 W
Tarbert, West Loch c	46	57.55 N	6.54 W
Tarbes	58	43.14 N	0.05 E
Tarija ☐⁴	248	21.43 S	64.20 W
Tarim	144	16.03 N	48.59 E
Tarim ≃	90	40.23 N	84.32 E
Tarime	154	1.21 S	34.20 E
Tarim Pendi ✦¹	90	39.00 N	83.00 E
Taring	114	3.50 N	97.33 E
Tarín Kowt	120	32.52 N	65.38 E
Taritatu ≃	164	2.54 S	138.27 E
Tarituba	256	23.02 S	44.36 W
Tarjannevesi ☉	26	62.07 N	24.03 E
Tarka, Vallée de ✧	150	14.00 N	6.00 E
Tarkastad	158	32.00 S	26.16 E
Tarkazy	80	53.52 N	53.39 E
Tarkhūrān	128	34.41 N	50.00 E
Tarki	84	42.56 N	47.30 E
Tarkiln	207	41.57 N	71.36 W
Tarkington Bayou ≃	222	30.10 N	94.59 W
Tarko-Sale	74	64.55 N	77.49 E
Tarkwa	150	5.19 N	1.59 W
Tarlac	116	15.29 N	120.35 E
Tarlac ☐⁴	116	15.30 N	120.25 E
Tarlac ≃	116	15.45 N	120.27 E
Tarleton	42	53.41 N	2.50 W
Tärlevo	265a	59.42 N	30.27 E
Tarlo	170	34.28 S	150.04 E
Tarlo River National Park ⋆	170	34.31 S	149.55 E
Tarlscough	262	53.37 N	2.52 W
Tarm	26	55.55 N	8.32 E
Tarma	248	11.25 S	75.42 W
Tarmstedt	52	53.13 N	9.04 E
Tarn ☐⁵	32	43.50 N	2.00 E
Tarn ≃	32	44.05 N	1.06 E
Tarn ≃	58	44.05 N	1.06 E
Tarnaby	24	65.43 N	15.16 E
Tarnak ≃	120	31.26 N	65.31 E
Tarna Mare, Rom.	38	47.59 N	23.10 E
Tarna Mare, Rom.	38	48.04 N	23.12 E
Tårnby	41	55.38 N	12.36 E
Tarneit	169	37.52 S	144.41 E
Tarn-et-Garonne ☐⁵	32	44.05 N	1.20 E
Tarnobrzeg	54	53.58 N	11.14 E
Tarnobrzeg ☐⁴	30	50.35 N	21.41 E
Tarnobrzeg ☐⁴	30	50.45 N	21.50 E
Tarnogród	30	50.23 N	22.45 E
Tarnogskij Gorodok	24	60.29 N	43.33 E
Tarnopol → Ternopol'	78	49.34 N	25.36 E
Tarnów, Pol.	30	50.01 N	21.00 E
Tarnów, Pol.	54	52.47 N	14.58 E
Tarnów, Pol.	30	50.00 N	21.00 E
Tarnowskie Góry	30	50.27 N	18.52 E
Tarnsjö	40	60.09 N	16.56 E
Tarō	92	39.44 N	141.58 E
Tarō ≃	36	45.00 N	10.15 E
Tarom Tārān	123	31.27 N	74.55 E
Tarp	41	54.40 N	9.23 E
Tarpey	282	36.47 N	119.41 W
Tarpon, Lake ☉	220	28.07 N	82.44 W
Tarpon Springs	220	28.09 N	82.45 W
Tarporley	42	53.09 N	2.40 W
Tarqui	246	2.28 S	78.59 W
Tarquinia	68	42.15 N	11.45 E
Tarqūmiyah	132	31.35 N	35.01 E
Tarra ≃	246	9.05 N	72.30 W
Tarrabool Lake ☉	162	18.15 S	135.04 E
Tarrafal, C.V.	150a	16.58 N	25.10 W
Tarrafal, C.V.	150a	15.17 N	23.46 W
Tarragona	34	41.07 N	1.15 E
Tarraleah	166	42.18 S	146.27 E
Tarrant ☐⁶	222	32.47 N	97.18 W
Tarrant, Ala.	194	33.34 N	86.46 W
Tarrant Hinton	44	50.53 N	2.05 W
Tarrasa Creek ≃	208	36.31 N	77.10 W
Tàrrega	34	41.39 N	1.09 E
Tarri	144	0.42 N	41.38 E
Tarrington	262	53.45 N	2.47 W
Tarrs	214	40.10 N	79.35 W
Tarryall Creek ≃	200	39.05 N	105.19 W
Tarrytown	192	41.04 N	73.51 W
Tarrytown Reservoir ☉¹	276	41.05 N	73.51 W
Tarso	150	36.55 N	34.53 E
Tarsus	128	36.55 N	34.53 E
Tartagal, Arg.	252	22.32 S	63.49 W
Tartagal, Arg.	252	28.65 S	59.47 W
Tartas	58	43.50 N	0.48 W
Tartu	76	58.23 N	26.43 E
Tartūs	132	34.53 N	35.53 E
Tartūs ☐⁴	130	34.55 N	36.00 E
Tartus ≃	256	21.37 S	42.56 W
Tarum ≃	34	35.22 N	16.30 E
Tarumi	115a	5.59 S	107.03 E
Tarumirim	255	19.16 S	41.59 W
Tarumizu	93	31.29 N	130.42 E
Tarusa	82	54.43 N	37.11 E
Tarutao, Ko I	114	6.35 N	99.40 E
Tarutino, S.S.S.R.	78	46.12 N	29.09 E
Tarutung	114	2.01 N	98.58 E
Tarvagatajn nuruu ⋌	88	48.20 N	99.00 E
Tarves	46	57.22 N	2.13 W
Tarvisio	64	46.30 N	13.35 E
Tarvin	42	53.12 N	2.46 W
Tarwin, East Branch ≃	169	38.42 S	145.50 E
Tarwin, West Branch ≃	169	38.38 S	146.12 E
Tarza	24	62.32 N	40.25 E
Tarzan	170	32.18 N	101.43 W
Tarzana ☀⁸	280	34.10 N	118.32 W
Tarzo	64	45.58 N	12.14 E
Tas	42	52.36 N	1.18 E
Taşçı	130	36.55 N	34.53 E
Tasajera	106	9.48 N	75.35 W
Taşanta	86	49.43 N	89.11 E
Tašauz	84	41.50 N	59.58 E
Tašauz ☐⁴	84	42.00 N	59.30 E
Tasāwah	146	26.00 N	13.30 E
Tasbuget	84	44.48 N	65.33 E
Taschkent → Taškent	85	41.20 N	69.18 E
Taščagol	86	52.47 N	87.53 E
Tasejeva ≃	88	58.06 N	94.01 E
Tasejevo	86	57.12 N	94.54 E
Taseko ≃	182	52.00 N	123.40 W
Taseko Lakes ☉	182	51.15 N	123.35 W
Taseko Mountain ⋀	182	51.14 N	123.28 W
Taseyevo	88	57.12 N	94.54 E
Tasgaon	122	17.02 N	74.36 E
Tashi Gang Dzong	124	27.19 N	91.34 E
Tashk, Daryācheh-ye ☉	128	29.45 N	53.30 E
Tashkent → Taškent	85	41.20 N	69.18 E
Tašir	84	41.07 N	44.16 E
Tasikmalaya	115a	7.20 S	108.12 E
Tasil	132	32.50 N	35.58 E

I · 174 **Tasi-Tend**

ENGLISH — Name | Page | Lat.°′ | Long.°′
DEUTSCH — Name | Seite | Breite°′ | Länge°′ E = Ost

Tåsinge I 41 55.00 N 10.36 E
Taširovo 82 55.25 N 36.39 E
Tasitan 85 39.17 N 76.07 E
Tåsjö 26 64.13 N 15.54 E
Tåsjön ⊜ '26 64.15 N 15.47 E
Taskajevo 86 55.06 N 78.36 E
Taškent, S.S.S.R. 85 41.20 N 69.18 E
Taşkent, Tür. 130 36.55 N 32.31 E
Taškent □[4] 85 41.00 N 69.30 E
Taškepri 128 36.18 N 62.38 E
Taşkesen 130 39.43 N 41.29 E
Taskesken 86 47.15 N 80.44 E
Taşköprü 130 41.30 N 34.14 E
Taskul 164 2.35 S 150.25 E
Taš-Kumyr 85 41.21 N 72.14 E
Taškyja 85 40.16 N 74.19 E
Tašla 80 51.47 N 52.46 E
Taşlı ≃ 267b 41.03 N 28.56 E
Tasman, Mount ∧ 172 43.34 S 170.09 E
Tasman Basin ✢[1] 6 43.00 S 158.00 E
Tasman Bay C 172 41.00 S 173.20 E
Tasmania □[3] 166 43.00 S 147.00 E
Tasmania I 166 42.00 S 147.00 E
Tasmanien → Tasmania I 166 42.00 S 147.00 E
Tasman Mountains ⋏ 172 41.07 S 172.33 E
Tasman Peninsula ›[1] 166 43.05 S 147.50 E
Tasman Sea ⊤[2] 14 40.00 S 163.00 E
T'asmin ≃ 78 49.05 N 32.48 E
Tăşnad 38 47.29 N 22.35 E
Tasoba 80 49.47 N 49.52 E
Taşova 130 40.46 N 36.20 E
Tasrār Sharīf 123 33.52 N 74.46 E
Taşrumi 84 38.48 N 44.04 E
Tassajara Creek ≃ 282 37.41 N 121.53 W
Tassara 150 16.48 N 5.39 E
Tassdorf 264a 52.30 N 13.47 E
Tassialouc, Lac ⊜ 176 59.03 N 74.00 W
Tassin-la-Demi-Lune 62 45.46 N 4.47 E
Tasso Lake ⊜ 212 45.27 N 78.56 W
Tassu, Serra di lu ∧ 71 41.01 N 9.08 E
Taštagol 86 52.47 N 87.53 E
Tastiota 232 28.22 N 111.23 W
Tåstrup 41 55.39 N 12.19 E
Taštyp 86 52.48 N 89.54 E
Taşucu 130 36.19 N 33.53 E
Tasutkol'skoje vodochranilišče ⊜[1] 85 43.22 N 74.00 E
Tata, Magreb 148 29.44 N 7.56 W
Tata, Magy. 30 47.39 N 18.18 E
Tata □[4] 148 29.40 N 7.45 W
T'at'a, vulkan ∧[1] 92a 44.21 N 146.15 E
Tataa, Pointe › 174s 17.34 S 149.37 W
Tatabánya 30 47.34 N 18.26 E
Tatahuicapan 234 18.14 N 94.45 W
Tatal 80 47.17 N 46.16 E
Tatalin ≃ 102 37.30 N 95.28 E
Tata Mailau ∧ 112 8.55 S 125.30 E
Tatamy 208 40.44 N 75.15 W
Tataouine 148 32.56 N 10.27 E
Tata Raphael, Camp ■ 273b 4.18 S 15.17 E
Tatarbunary 78 45.49 N 29.36 E
Tatarinka 76 55.58 N 33.54 E
Tatarino 78 50.36 N 39.07 E
Tatarinovo, S.S.S.R. 82 55.13 N 37.56 E
Tatarinovo, S.S.S.R. 82 56.34 N 38.25 E
Tatarischer Sund → Tatarskij proliv ⊔ 89 50.00 N 141.15 E
Tatarka, S.S.S.R. 76 53.16 N 28.48 E
Tatarka, S.S.S.R. 86 53.58 N 75.05 E
Tatarlar 130 41.46 N 26.55 E
Tatarovo ◆[8] 265b 55.46 N 37.26 E
Tātārpur ◆[8] 272a 28.39 N 77.07 E
Tatarsk 86 55.13 N 75.58 E
Tatarskaja Avtonomnaja Sovetskaja Socialističeskaja Respublika □[3] 80 55.00 N 51.00 E
Tatarskij Kandyz 80 54.07 N 53.07 E
Tatarskij proliv (Tatar Strait) ⊔ 89 50.00 N 141.15 E
Tatarskij Sajman 80 53.18 N 47.07 E
Tatarskoje-Maklakovo 80 55.48 N 45.34 E
Tatar Strait → Tatarskij proliv ⊔ 89 50.00 N 141.15 E
Tatau ≃ 112 3.07 N 112.49 E
Tatau Island I 164 2.50 S 152.00 E
Tataurovo, S.S.S.R. 76 58.44 N 43.20 E
Tataurovo, S.S.S.R. 80 57.48 N 49.34 E
Tataurovo, S.S.S.R. 88 51.37 N 112.56 E
Tate 192 34.25 N 84.22 W
Tate ≃ 166 17.22 S 143.44 E
Tatebayashi 94 36.15 N 139.32 E
Tate Gallery ʊ 260 51.29 N 0.08 W
Tateishi-misaki › 94 35.46 N 136.01 E
Tateiwa 94 37.05 N 139.32 E
Tateiwa-chosuichi ⊜[1] 96 34.33 N 132.10 E
Tateshina 94 36.16 N 138.19 E
Tateyama, Nihon 94 34.59 N 139.52 E
Tateyama, Nihon 94 36.40 N 137.19 E
Tate-yama ∧ 94 36.35 N 137.37 E
Tathlina Lake ⊜ 176 60.32 N 117.32 W
Tathlīth, Wādī V 144 20.44 N 44.17 E
Tathong Point › 271d 22.14 N 114.17 E
Tathra 166 36.44 S 149.59 E
Tatikawa → Tachikawa 94 35.42 N 139.25 E
Tatiščevo, S.S.S.R. 80 51.40 N 45.35 E
Tatiščevo, S.S.S.R. 82 56.24 N 37.31 E
Tatitlek 180 60.52 N 146.41 W
Tatla Lake 182 51.55 N 124.36 W
Tatla Lake ⊜ 182 52.00 N 124.25 W
Tatlayoko Lake 182 51.39 N 124.24 W
Tatlayoko Lake ⊜ 182 51.30 N 124.25 W
Tatlow, Mount ∧ 182 51.23 N 123.52 W
Tatnam, Cape › 176 57.16 N 91.00 W
Tatomi 94 35.36 N 138.31 E
Tatoosh Island I 224 48.24 N 124.44 W
Tatrang 120 38.28 N 85.35 E
Tatranský národní park ♠ 30 49.10 N 20.05 E
Tatrzański Park Narodowy ♠ 30 49.15 N 20.00 E
Tatsfield 260 51.18 N 0.02 E
Tatsuno, Nihon 94 35.59 N 137.59 E
Tatsuno, Nihon 96 34.52 N 134.33 E
Tatsunokuchi 94 36.27 N 136.35 E
Tatsuruhama 94 37.04 N 136.53 E
Tatsuyama 94 34.58 N 137.49 E
Tatta 120 24.45 N 67.55 E
Tattenhall 44 53.06 N 2.46 W
Tatton Hall ⊥ 262 53.20 N 2.23 W
Tatton Mere ⊜ 262 53.19 N 2.22 W
Tatton Park ♠ 262 53.20 N 2.22 W
Tatty 85 43.12 N 73.19 E
Tatu ≃ 100 24.12 N 120.29 E
Tatuapé ◆[8] 287b 23.32 S 46.34 W
Tatuk Lake ⊜ 182 53.32 N 124.15 W
Tatum, N.M., U.S. 196 33.15 N 103.19 W
Tatum, Tx., U.S. 222 32.19 N 94.31 W
Tat'ung → Datong 102 40.05 N 113.18 E
Tat'un Shan ∧ 269d 25.11 N 121.31 E
Tatvan 130 38.30 N 42.16 E
Tatzuli ≃ 100 24.08 N 121.39 E
Tau, Am. Sam. 174y 14.14 S 169.32 W
Tau, Nor. 26 59.04 N 5.54 E
Tau, S.S.S.R. 80 49.40 N 47.17 E
Tau I 174y 14.15 S 169.30 W
Tauá 250 6.01 S 40.26 W
Taualap Pass ⊔ 175c 7.28 N 151.36 E
Tauari 250 1.07 S 47.04 W
Taubaté 256 23.02 S 45.33 W
Tauber ≃ 56 49.46 N 9.31 E
Tauberbischofsheim 56 49.37 N 9.40 E
Taucha 54 51.23 N 12.30 E
Taučik 72 44.21 N 51.19 E
Tauern-Tunnel ◆[5] 64 47.05 N 13.05 E
Täuffelen 58 47.04 N 7.12 E
Taufkirchen 60 48.21 N 12.08 E
Taufstein ∧ 56 50.31 N 9.14 E
Taughannock Creek ≃ 210 42.33 N 76.36 W
Taughannock Falls State Park ♠ 210 42.32 N 76.35 W
Tauini ≃ 246 0.30 N 58.22 W
Taujskaja guba C 74 59.20 N 150.20 E
Taukum ◆[2] 86 44.50 N 75.30 E
Taulabé 236 14.38 N 87.59 W
Taulihawā 124 27.32 N 83.03 E
Taulov 41 55.33 N 9.37 E
Taumarunui 172 38.52 S 175.17 E
Taumaturgo 248 8.57 S 72.48 W
Taum Sauk Mountain ∧ 194 37.34 N 90.44 W
Taunay 248 20.18 S 56.05 W
Taunay, Cascatinha ∟ 287a 22.57 S 43.17 W
Taung 158 27.33 S 24.47 E
Taungbon 110 15.25 N 97.50 E
Taungdwingyi 110 20.01 N 95.33 E
Taunggon 110 23.38 N 96.32 E
Taunggyi 110 20.47 N 97.02 E
Taungnyo Range ⋏ 110 15.38 N 97.56 E
Taungup 110 18.51 N 94.14 E
Taungup Pass)(110 18.40 N 94.45 E
Taunsa 123 30.42 N 70.39 E
Taunsa Barrage ◆[6] 123 30.31 N 70.51 E
Taunton, Eng., U.K. 42 51.01 N 3.06 W
Taunton, Ma., U.S. 207 41.54 N 71.05 W
Taunton, N.Y., U.S. 210 43.01 N 76.13 W
Taunton ≃ 207 41.42 N 71.10 W
Taunton, Vale of V 42 51.02 N 3.08 W
Taunton Lake ⊜ 285 39.51 N 74.51 W
Taunton Lakes 285 39.51 N 74.51 W
Taunus ⋏ 56 50.10 N 8.15 E
Taunusstein 56 50.08 N 8.08 E
Taupiri 172 37.37 S 175.11 E
Tauplitz 61 47.33 N 14.00 E
Taupo 172 38.41 S 176.05 E
Taupo, Lake ⊜ 172 38.49 S 175.55 E
Tauragė 76 55.15 N 22.17 E
Taurak 86 51.35 N 85.01 E
Tauranga 172 37.42 S 176.10 E
Taurasi 68 41.00 N 14.57 E
Taureau, Réservoir ⊜[1] 206 46.46 N 73.50 W
Tauri ≃ 164 8.08 S 146.06 E
Taurianova 68 38.21 N 16.01 E
Tauripampa 248 12.35 S 76.07 W
Taurisano 68 39.57 N 18.13 E
Taurisma 248 15.10 S 72.51 W
Tauroa Point › 172 35.10 S 173.04 E
Taurovo 86 59.36 N 73.18 E
Taurus Mountains → Toros Dağları ⋏ 130 37.00 N 33.00 E
Tauste 34 41.55 N 1.15 W
Tautira 174s 17.44 S 149.09 W
Tauxigny 50 47.13 N 0.50 E
Tauz 84 41.00 N 45.38 E
Tavaí 252 26.07 S 55.32 W
Tavajvaam ≃ 180 64.56 N 177.30 E
Tavajza 89 45.12 N 136.44 E
Ţavālesh, Kūhhā-ye → Talish Mountains ⋏ 128 38.42 N 48.18 E
Tavanasa 58 46.45 N 9.04 E
Tavannes 58 47.13 N 7.12 E
Tavant 50 47.07 N 0.23 E
Tavares, Bra. 250 7.38 S 37.54 W
Tavares, Fl., U.S. 220 28.48 N 81.43 W
Tavares, Ilha dos I 287a 22.49 S 43.06 W
Tavarnelle Val di Pesa 66 43.33 N 11.10 E
Tavas 130 37.34 N 29.04 E
Tavastehus → Hämeenlinna 26 61.00 N 24.27 E
Tavaux 58 47.02 N 5.24 E
Tavda 86 58.03 N 65.15 E
Tavda ≃ 72 57.47 N 67.16 E
Tave ≃ 62 44.07 N 4.42 E
Tavera ≃ 64 46.29 N 11.21 E
Taverham 42 52.41 N 1.12 E
Taverna 68 39.01 N 16.35 E
Tavern Creek ≃ 194 38.19 N 92.18 W
Tavernelle, It. 64 44.18 N 10.04 E
Tavernelle, It. 66 43.00 N 12.09 E
Tavernes 62 43.36 N 6.01 E
Tavernes de Valldigna 34 39.04 N 0.16 W
Tavernier 220 25.00 N 80.30 W
Tavernole sul Mella 64 45.45 N 10.14 E
Taverny 50 49.02 N 2.13 E
Taveta, Kenya 154 3.24 S 37.41 E
Taveta, Tan. 154 9.01 S 35.37 E
Taveuni I 175g 16.51 S 179.58 W
Taviano 68 39.59 N 18.05 E
Tavil'dara 85 38.43 N 70.28 E
Tavira 34 37.07 N 7.39 W
Tavistock, On., Can. 212 43.19 N 80.50 W
Tavistock, Eng., U.K. 42 50.33 N 4.08 W
Tavn-Gašun 80 46.01 N 45.55 E
Tavolara, Isola I 71 40.54 N 9.42 E
Tavoliere ◆[1] 68 41.35 N 15.25 E
Tavolžan 86 52.44 N 77.27 E
Tavor, Har (Mount Tabor) ∧ 132 32.41 N 35.23 E
Távora ≃ 34 41.09 N 7.35 W
Tavoy → Dawei 110 14.05 N 98.12 E
Tavoy Point › 110 13.32 N 98.10 E
Tavričanka 89 43.22 N 131.52 E
Tavričeskoje 86 54.35 N 73.38 E
Tavry 265a 59.55 N 30.42 E
Tavsalayihüseynan 130 38.38 N 40.32 E
Tavşanlı 130 39.33 N 29.30 E
Tavua 175g 17.27 S 177.51 E
Tavy ≃ 42 50.16 N 4.10 W
Taw ≃ 42 51.04 N 4.11 W
Tawa 172 41.10 S 174.51 E
Tawa ≃ 124 22.48 N 77.48 E
Tawaeli 112 0.43 S 119.51 E
Tawakoni, Lake ⊜[1] 222 32.55 N 96.00 W
Tawara 270 34.27 N 135.57 E
Tawarada 268 35.19 N 140.04 E
Tawaramoto 96 34.33 N 135.48 E
Tawas City 190 44.16 N 83.30 W
Tawau 112 4.15 N 117.54 E
Tawd ≃ 262 53.36 N 2.48 W
Tāwi ≃ 123 32.40 N 74.41 E
Ţawīlah, Juzur II 140 27.35 N 33.46 E
Tawi-Tawi □[4] 116 5.20 N 120.00 E
Tawi-Tawi Group II 116 5.10 N 120.15 E
Tawi-Tawi Island I 116 5.10 N 120.00 E
Ţawkar 140 18.26 N 37.44 E
Tawu 100 22.22 N 120.54 E
Ţāwūq 128 35.08 N 44.27 E
Tāwurghā' 146 32.02 N 15.09 E
Ţawwah Banī Ibrāhīm 142 28.05 N 30.41 E
Taxco de Alarcón 234 18.33 N 99.36 W
Taxenbach 64 47.17 N 12.58 E
Taxi 89 49.26 N 126.08 E
Taxila 123 33.44 N 72.49 E
Taxisco 236 14.04 N 90.28 W
Taxkorgan Tajik Zizhixian 120 37.49 N 75.14 E
Taxusi 102 32.58 N 98.10 E
Tay ≃, On., Can. 212 44.53 N 76.07 W
Tay ≃, Yk., Can. 180 62.34 N 134.22 W
Tay ≃, Scot., U.K. 46 56.22 N 3.21 W
Tay, Firth of C[1] 46 56.26 N 3.00 W
Tay, Lake ⊜ 162 32.55 S 120.48 E
Tay, Loch ⊜ 46 56.31 N 4.10 W
Tayabamba 248 8.17 S 77.18 W
Tayabas 116 14.01 N 121.35 E
Tayabas Bay C 116 13.45 N 121.45 E
Tayan 112 0.02 S 110.07 E
Tayandu, Kepulauan II 164 5.30 S 132.15 E
Tayayi 105 39.25 N 115.03 E
Tayeegle 144 4.02 N 44.31 E
Taylor, B.C., Can. 182 56.10 N 120.41 W
Taylor, Az., U.S. 200 34.27 N 110.05 W
Taylor, Ar., U.S. 194 33.06 N 93.27 W
Taylor, Mi., U.S. 216 42.14 N 83.16 W
Taylor, Mo., U.S. 219 39.56 N 91.32 W
Taylor, Ne., U.S. 198 41.46 N 99.22 W
Taylor, Pa., U.S. 210 41.23 N 75.42 W
Taylor, Tx., U.S. 222 30.34 N 97.24 W
Taylor ≃ 200 38.40 N 106.51 W
Taylor, Mount ∧, N.Z. 172 43.30 S 171.19 E
Taylor, Mount ∧, N.M., U.S. 200 35.14 N 107.37 W
Taylor Creek ≃, On., Can. 275b 43.42 N 79.20 W
Taylor Creek ≃, Il., U.S. 219 39.13 N 90.18 W
Taylor Lake Village 222 29.36 N 95.03 W
Taylor Mountain ∧ 202 44.53 N 114.13 W
Taylor Mountains ⋏ 180 60.50 N 157.20 W
Taylor Run ≃ 285 39.57 N 75.39 W
Taylors 192 34.55 N 82.17 W
Taylors Bush Park ♠ 275b 43.42 N 79.19 W
Taylors Island 208 38.28 N 76.17 W
Taylor Springs 219 39.08 N 89.30 W
Taylors Run ≃ 279b 40.11 N 79.57 W
Taylorstown 214 40.10 N 80.23 W
Taylorsville, In., U.S. 218 39.17 N 85.57 W
Taylorsville, Ky., U.S. 194 38.01 N 85.20 W
Taylorsville, Ms., U.S. 194 31.49 N 89.25 W
Taylorsville, N.C., U.S. 192 35.55 N 81.10 W
Taylorsville Dam ◆[6] 218 39.53 N 84.10 W
Taylortown, N.J., U.S. 276 40.56 N 74.24 W
Taylortown, Oh., U.S. 214 40.28 N 80.40 W
Taylortown Reservoir ⊜[1] 276 40.58 N 74.22 W
Taylorville 219 39.32 N 89.17 W
Taylorville, Lake ⊜[1] 219 39.30 N 89.15 W
Taymā' 128 27.38 N 38.29 E
Taymouth 186 46.11 N 66.37 W
Taymyr Peninsula → Tajmyr, poluostrov ›[1] 74 76.00 N 104.00 E
Tay Ninh 110 11.18 N 106.06 E
Taynuilf 46 56.25 N 5.14 W
Tayoltita 232 24.05 N 105.56 W
Tayport 46 57.27 N 2.53 W
Táyros 267c 37.58 N 23.42 E
Tayside □[4] 46 56.30 N 3.30 W
Taytay, Pil. 116 10.49 N 119.31 E
Taytay, Pil. 116 14.34 N 121.08 E
Taytay Bay C 116 10.55 N 119.35 E
Tayu 115a 6.32 S 111.02 E
Tayüan, T'aiwan 100 25.04 N 121.11 E
Tayuan, Zhg. 89 51.27 N 124.16 E
Tayyārah 140 13.12 N 30.47 E
Ţayyebāt 128 34.44 N 60.45 E
Taz ≃ 72 67.32 N 78.40 E
Taza 148 34.16 N 4.01 W
Taza □[4] 148 34.05 N 3.45 W
Tazawa-ko ⊜ 92 39.43 N 140.40 E
Tazenakht 148 30.35 N 7.12 W
Tazewell, Tn., U.S. 192 36.27 N 83.34 W
Tazewell, Va., U.S. 192 37.06 N 81.31 W
Tazhuang 105 39.55 N 117.13 E
Tazicheng 89 46.35 N 123.06 E
Tazigou ≃ 104 41.44 N 121.30 E
Tazin ≃ 176 60.26 N 110.45 W
Tazin Lake ⊜ 176 59.47 N 109.03 W
T'ažinskij 86 56.07 N 88.31 E
Tāzirbū ⊤[4] 146 25.45 N 21.00 E
Tazishan 107 29.28 N 104.14 E
Tazlina 180 62.04 N 145.25 W
Tazlina Lake ⊜ 180 61.50 N 146.30 W
Tazoult-Lambese 34 35.29 N 6.15 E
Tazovskaja guba C 74 69.05 N 76.00 E
Tazovskij 74 67.28 N 78.42 E
Tazovskij poluostrov ›[1] 72 68.35 N 76.00 E
Tazrouk 148 23.25 N 6.16 E
Tazumal ⊥ 236 13.59 N 89.41 W
Tāzumuddin 126 22.29 N 90.53 E
Tazungdām 102 28.02 N 97.35 E
Tbessa 148 35.28 N 8.09 E
Tbessa □[5] 148 35.10 N 8.00 E
Tbilisi 84 41.43 N 44.49 E
Tbilisskaja 78 45.23 N 40.12 E
Tchad → Chad □[1] 146 15.00 N 19.00 E
Tchad, Lac (Lake Chad) ⊜ 146 13.20 N 14.00 E
Tchaguine Golo 146 10.03 N 16.19 E
Tchamba 150 9.02 N 1.25 E
Tch'ang-Cha → Changsha 100 28.12 N 112.58 E
Tchaourou 150 8.53 N 2.36 E
Tchécoslovaquie → Czechoslovakia □[1] 30 49.30 N 17.00 E
Tchefuncta ≃ 194 30.22 N 90.10 W
Tchékapika 152 1.17 S 16.11 E
Tcheliabinsk → Čel'abinsk 86 55.10 N 61.24 E
Tcheng-Tcheou → Zhengzhou 102 34.48 N 113.39 E
Tchentlo Lake ⊜ 182 55.11 N 125.00 W
Tchériba 150 12.16 N 3.05 W
Tchesinkut Lake ⊜ 182 54.05 N 125.40 W
Tchetti 150 7.50 N 1.40 E
Tchibanga 152 2.51 S 11.02 E
Tchigaï, Plateau du ⋏[1] 146 21.30 N 14.50 E
Tchikala-Tcholohanga 152 12.38 S 16.03 E
Tchin-Tabáradene 150 15.58 N 5.50 E
Tchitondi 152 4.33 S 12.08 E
Tchollíré 146 8.24 N 14.10 E
Tchong-K'ing → Chongqing 107 29.34 N 106.35 E
Tchořovice 60 49.27 N 13.48 E
Tchula 194 33.10 N 90.13 W
T.C. Steele State Memorial ⊥ 218 39.08 N 86.20 W
Tczew 30 54.06 N 18.47 E
Té ≃ 110 12.27 N 106.02 E
Te, Kinh ≍ 269c 10.45 N 106.42 E
Tea ≃ 246 0.30 S 65.09 W
Teaca 38 46.55 N 24.31 E
Teacapán 234 22.33 N 105.45 W
Tea Creek ≃ 284a 43.02 N 79.06 W
Teaehoa, Pointe › 174x 9.51 S 139.01 W
Teague 222 31.37 N 96.17 W
Teahupoo 174s 17.51 S 149.13 W
Te Anau 172 45.25 S 167.43 E
Te Anau, Lake ⊜ 172 45.12 S 167.48 E
Teanaway ≃ 224 47.10 N 120.50 W
Teanaway, Middle Fork ≃ 224 47.15 N 120.53 W
Teanaway, North Fork ≃ 224 47.22 N 120.53 W
Teaneck 210 40.53 N 74.00 W
Teangue 46 57.07 N 5.50 W
Teano 68 41.15 N 14.04 E
Teapa 234 17.33 N 92.57 W
Teapa ≃ 234 17.58 N 92.54 W
Te Araroa 172 37.38 S 178.22 E
Tearinibai 174t 1.35 N 172.58 E
Te Aroha 172 37.33 S 175.43 E
Teaticket 207 41.33 N 70.35 W
Tea Tree 162 22.11 S 133.17 E
Tea Tree Gully 168b 34.49 S 138.44 E
Te Atukura ∧ 174k 21.14 S 159.45 W
Te Awamutu 172 38.01 S 175.19 E
Teba, Esp. 34 36.58 N 4.56 W
Teba, Indon. 164 1.29 S 137.54 E
Tebakang 112 1.06 N 110.30 E
Tebas 256 21.35 S 42.44 W
Tebay 44 54.26 N 2.35 W
Tebbetts 219 38.37 N 91.57 W
Teberda 84 43.28 N 41.45 E
Teberdinskij zapovednik ♠ 84 43.20 N 41.45 E
Tebes 286d 12.07 S 77.00 W
Tebicuary ≃ 252 26.36 S 58.16 W
Tebicuary-Mí ≃ 252 26.26 S 56.51 W
Tebingbulan 112 3.03 S 103.44 E
Tebingtinggi, Indon. 112 0.36 N 101.36 E
Tebingtinggi, Indon. 112 3.36 S 103.05 E
Tebingtinggi, Indon. 114 3.20 N 99.09 E
Tebingtinggi, Pulau I 114 0.54 N 102.45 E
Tébourba 36 36.49 N 9.51 E
Téboursouk 148 36.28 N 9.15 E
Téboursouk, Monts de ⋏ 36 36.30 N 9.10 E
Tebra ≃ 76 56.51 N 21.12 E
Tebstrup 41 55.59 N 9.53 E
Tebulosmta, gora ∧ 84 42.33 N 45.19 E
Tebza ≃ 80 58.23 N 41.19 E
Tecalitlán 234 19.26 N 103.15 W
Tecamachalco 234 18.53 N 97.44 W
Tecate 232 32.34 N 116.38 W
Tech ≃ 32 42.36 N 3.03 E
Teche, Bayou ≃ 194 29.43 N 91.13 W
Techendorf 64 46.43 N 13.17 E
Techiman 150 7.35 N 1.56 W
Techimentia 150 7.11 N 2.02 W
Techirghiol 38 44.03 N 28.36 E
Techlé 148 21.35 N 14.58 W
Techny 278 42.07 N 87.49 W
Techou → Dezhou 98 37.27 N 116.18 E
Techtin 76 53.51 N 29.44 E
Tecka 254 43.29 S 70.48 W
Tecka ≃ 254 42.37 S 70.25 W
Tecklenburg 52 52.13 N 7.48 E
Teckomatorp 41 55.52 N 13.05 E
Tecolote Creek ≃ 200 35.22 N 105.15 W
Tecolotlán 234 20.13 N 104.03 W
Tecolutla ≃ 234 20.29 N 97.00 W
Tecomán 234 18.55 N 103.53 W
Tecomate, Laguna C 234 16.35 N 99.25 W
Tecomaxtlahuaca 234 17.21 N 98.02 W
Tecominoacán 234 17.53 N 93.37 W
Tecopa 204 35.50 N 116.13 W
Tecozautla 234 20.32 N 99.38 W
Tecpan de Galeana 234 17.15 N 100.41 W
Tecpán Guatemala 236 14.46 N 91.00 W
Tecpatán 234 17.08 N 93.18 W
Tecuala 234 22.23 N 105.27 W
Tecuamburro, Volcán ∧[1] 236 14.09 N 90.24 W
Tecuantepec ≃ 234 20.16 N 97.27 W
Tecuci 38 45.50 N 27.26 E
Tecumseh, On., Can. 214 42.19 N 82.54 W
Tecumseh, Mi., U.S. 216 42.00 N 83.56 W
Tecumseh, Ne., U.S. 198 40.22 N 96.11 W
Tecumseh, Ok., U.S. 196 35.15 N 96.56 W
Ted Ceidaar Dabole 144 4.24 N 43.55 E
Teddington ◆[8] 260 51.25 N 0.20 W
Tédji 146 11.46 N 21.19 E
Tedori ≃ 94 36.29 N 136.28 E
Tedrow 216 41.37 N 84.13 W
Tedžen 128 37.23 N 60.31 E
Tedžen (Harīrūd) ≃ 128 37.24 N 60.38 E
Tedženstroj 128 36.55 N 60.53 E
Teec Nos Pos 200 36.56 N 109.42 W
Teeli 86 51.07 N 90.14 E
Teels Marsh ≋ 204 38.12 N 118.21 W
Teen ⊜ 40 59.07 N 14.40 E
Teerijärvi → Terjärv 26 63.32 N 23.30 E
Tees ≃ 44 54.34 N 1.16 W
Tees Bay C 44 54.39 N 1.07 W
Teesdale V 44 54.38 N 2.07 W
Teesside → Middlesbrough 44 54.35 N 1.14 W
Tees-Side Airport ⊠ 44 54.31 N 1.25 W
Teeswater 212 44.00 N 81.17 W
Teeswater ≃ 212 44.18 N 81.17 W
Tefé 246 3.22 S 64.42 W
Tefé ≃ 242 3.35 S 64.47 W
Tefé, Lago de ⊜ 246 3.27 S 64.47 W
Tefenni 130 37.18 N 29.47 E
Tefft 216 41.12 N 86.58 W
Tefle 150 5.59 N 0.35 E
Tegal 115a 6.52 S 109.08 E
Tegalombo 115a 8.04 S 111.17 E
Tégama ◆[1] 150 15.50 N 8.12 E
Tega-numa ⊜ 268 35.51 N 140.04 E
Tegel ◆[8] 264a 52.35 N 13.17 E
Tegel, Berliner Forst ◆[3] 264a 52.37 N 13.16 E
Tegelen 52 51.21 N 6.09 E
Tegeler See ⊜ 264a 52.35 N 13.15 E
Tegernsee 64 47.43 N 11.45 E
Tegernsee ⊜ 64 47.42 N 11.45 E
Teggiano 68 40.23 N 15.32 E
Teghra 124 25.29 N 85.57 E
Tegid, Llyn ⊜ 42 52.53 N 3.36 W
Tegina 150 10.05 N 6.14 E
Tegineneng 112 5.12 S 105.10 E
Tegistyk 85 44.02 N 68.22 E
Teglio 64 46.10 N 10.04 E
Tégua I 175f 13.15 S 166.37 E
Tegualda 254 41.02 S 73.26 W
Tegucigalpa 236 14.06 N 87.13 W
Tegul'det 86 57.19 N 88.10 E
Tehachapi 228 35.07 N 118.26 W
Tehachapi Creek ≃ 228 35.17 N 118.38 W
Tehachapi Mountains ⋏ 228 35.00 N 118.40 W
Tehachapi Pass)(228 35.06 N 118.18 W
Tehamiyam 140 18.20 N 36.32 E
Te Hapua 172 34.31 S 172.54 E
Tehar ◆[8] 272a 28.38 N 77.07 E
Te Haroto 172 39.08 S 176.36 E
Tehata 126 23.43 N 88.32 E
Tehek Lake ⊜ 176 64.55 N 95.38 W
Teheran → Tehrān 128 35.40 N 51.26 E
Téhini 150 9.36 N 3.40 W
Tehoohaivei, Cap › 174x 9.49 S 138.54 W
Te Hope O Te Keho, Cap › 174x 10.02 S 139.06 W
Tehoru 164 3.23 S 129.30 E
Tehrān, Īrān 128 35.40 N 51.26 E
Tehrān, Īrān 267d 35.40 N 51.26 E
Tehrān □[4] 128 35.30 N 51.30 E
Tehrān, University of ʊ[2] 267d 35.42 N 51.24 E
Tehran International Airport ⊠ 267d 35.41 N 51.19 E
Tehrān Pārs ◆[8] 267d 35.44 N 51.32 E
Tehrathum 124 27.07 N 87.32 E
Tehri 124 30.23 N 78.29 E
Tehuacán 234 18.27 N 97.23 W
Tehuacana 222 31.44 N 96.33 W
Tehuacana Creek ≃, Tx., U.S. 222 31.31 N 97.02 W
Tehuacana Creek ≃, Tx., U.S. 222 31.50 N 95.59 W
Tehuantepec, Méx. 234 16.20 N 95.14 W
Tehuantepec, Méx. 234 18.41 N 103.17 W
Tehuantepec ≃ 234 16.10 N 95.07 W
Tehuantepec, Golfo de C 234 16.00 N 94.50 W
Tehuantepec, Istmo de ⊥[3] 234 17.00 N 95.00 W
Tehuantepec Ridge ✢[3] 16 13.30 N 98.00 W
Tehuelches 254 46.56 S 67.27 W
Tehuipango 234 18.31 N 97.04 W
Tehuitzingo 234 18.21 N 98.17 W
Teià 266d 41.30 N 2.19 E
Teichl ≃ 61 47.46 N 14.10 E
Teichröda 54 50.45 N 11.18 E
Teichwolframsdorf 54 50.43 N 12.14 E
Teide, Parque Nacional del ♠ 148 28.15 N 16.30 W
Teide, Pico de ∧ 148 28.16 N 16.38 W
Teifi ≃ 42 52.07 N 4.42 W
Teifiside ◆[1] 42 52.02 N 4.22 W
Teiga Plateau ⋏[1] 140 15.38 N 25.40 E
Teign ≃ 42 50.33 N 3.29 W
Teignmouth 42 50.33 N 3.30 W
Teise ≃ 260 51.13 N 0.25 E
Teisendorf 64 47.51 N 12.49 E
Teisnach 60 49.02 N 13.00 E
Teita 234 17.05 N 97.25 W
Teith ≃ 46 56.08 N 3.59 W
Teitipac 234 16.54 N 96.34 W
Teixeira 250 7.13 S 37.15 W
Teixeira Pinto 150 12.10 N 13.55 W
Teixeiras 255 20.39 S 42.51 W
Teixeira Soares 252 25.22 S 50.27 W
Tejakula 115b 8.08 S 115.20 E
Tejamén 232 24.48 N 105.07 W
Tejkovo 80 56.52 N 40.34 E
Tejo → Tagus ≃ 34 38.40 N 9.24 W
Tejon Creek ≃ 228 35.08 N 118.53 W
Tejon Pass)(228 34.48 N 118.52 W
Tejupan, Punta › 234 18.20 N 103.32 W
Tejupilco de Hidalgo 234 18.54 N 100.09 W
Te Kaha 172 37.44 S 177.41 E
Tekai ≃ 114 4.14 N 102.23 E
Tékakwitha, Île I 275a 45.25 N 73.42 W
Tekam ≃ 114 3.52 N 102.27 E
Tekamah 198 41.46 N 96.13 W
Te Kao 172 34.39 S 172.57 E
Tekapo, Lake ⊜ 172 43.53 S 170.31 E
Te Karaka 172 38.28 S 177.52 E
Tekāri 124 24.56 N 84.50 E
Te Kauwhata 172 37.24 S 175.09 E
Tekax de Álvaro Obregón 232 20.12 N 89.17 W
Teke 130 41.04 N 29.39 E
Teke, ozero ⊜ 86 53.48 N 73.00 E
Teke Burnu › 130 38.05 N 26.36 E
Tekeli 86 44.48 N 78.57 E
Tekeli Dağı ∧ 130 40.09 N 37.28 E
Tekes 86 43.10 N 81.43 E
Tekes ≃ 86 43.36 N 82.32 E
Tekeze (Satīt) ≃ 140 14.20 N 35.50 E
Tekirdağ 130 40.59 N 27.31 E
Tekirdağ □[4] 130 41.00 N 27.30 E
Tekkali 122 18.37 N 84.14 E
Tekke 130 40.43 N 36.12 E
Tekke Burnu › 130 40.02 N 26.10 E
Tekkiraz 130 40.59 N 37.08 E
Tekman 130 39.38 N 41.31 E
Tekoa 202 47.13 N 117.04 W
Tekong, Pulau I 271c 1.24 N 104.03 E
Tekong Kechil, Pulau I 271c 1.25 N 104.01 E
Tekonsha 216 42.05 N 84.59 W
Te Kopuru 172 36.02 S 173.56 E
Tekouiat, Oued V 148 22.25 N 2.35 E
Tékro ⊤[4] 146 19.30 N 20.58 E
Tekstil'ščiki 82 55.57 N 37.49 E
Tekstil'ščiki ◆[8] 265b 55.42 N 37.44 E
Teku 112 0.46 S 123.26 E
Te Kuiti 172 38.20 S 175.10 E
Tekukor, Pulau I 271c 1.14 N 103.50 E
Tel ≃ 122 20.50 N 83.54 E
Tela, Hond. 236 15.44 N 87.27 W
Tela, India 272a 28.44 N 77.20 E
Tela, Bahía de C 236 15.48 N 87.30 W
Telaga 116 6.51 N 117.03 E
Telaga, Teluk C 114 2.10 N 98.00 E
Telaga-kulon 115a 6.58 S 108.18 E
Télagh 148 34.47 N 0.34 W
Telaopengsha Shan ∧ 120 30.33 N 86.25 E
Tel Ashqelon ⊥ 132 31.39 N 34.32 E
Telavåg 26 60.16 N 4.49 E
Telavi 84 41.55 N 45.28 E
Tel Aviv □[5] 132 32.05 N 34.48 E
Tel Aviv-Yafo 132 32.03 N 34.46 E
Telč 30 49.11 N 15.27 E
Tel'čje 76 53.21 N 36.20 E
Telde 148 28.00 N 15.25 W
Tele ≃, Afr. 158 30.26 S 27.33 E
Tele ≃, Zaïre 152 2.48 N 23.54 E
Telechany 76 52.31 N 25.51 E
Teleckoje, ozero ⊜ 86 51.35 N 87.40 E
Telefomin 164 5.10 S 141.35 E
Telegapulang 112 2.55 S 112.25 E
Telegino 80 52.55 N 44.34 E
Telegrafo, Pizzo ∧ 70 37.37 N 13.10 E
Telegraph Canyon V 280 33.55 N 117.45 W
Telegraph Cove 182 50.33 N 126.50 W
Telegraph Creek 180 57.55 N 131.10 W
Telemark □[6] 26 59.30 N 8.40 E
Telemba 88 52.43 N 113.16 E
Telembí ≃ 246 1.50 N 78.16 W
Telén 252 36.16 S 65.30 W
Telen ≃ 112 0.26 S 116.42 E
Telenešty 78 47.30 N 28.22 E
Teleno ∧ 34 42.21 N 6.23 W
Teleorman □[6] 38 44.00 N 25.15 E
Teleorman ≃ 38 43.52 N 25.26 E
Téléphone, Île du I 273b 4.20 S 15.12 E
Telerig 38 43.51 N 27.40 E
Telertheba, Djebel ∧ 148 24.10 N 6.51 E
Telescope Peak ∧ 204 36.10 N 117.05 W
Telescope Point › 241k 12.08 N 61.36 W
Telese 68 41.13 N 14.32 E
Telesterion ⊥ 267c 38.02 N 23.32 E
Telferner 222 28.51 N 96.53 W
Telfes 64 47.10 N 11.22 E
Telford, Eng., U.K. 42 52.40 N 2.28 W
Telford, Pa., U.S. 208 40.19 N 75.19 W
Telfs 64 47.18 N 11.04 E
Telgte 52 51.59 N 7.47 E
Telica ≃ 236 14.43 N 86.08 W
Telica, Volcán ∧[1] 236 12.36 N 86.50 W
Telida 180 63.23 N 153.16 W
Telikovka 80 52.35 N 48.17 E
Télimélé 150 10.54 N 13.02 W
Telixtlahuaca 234 17.18 N 96.54 W
Telizi 265a 59.42 N 29.59 E
Teljo, Jabal ∧ 140 14.42 N 25.56 E
Telkwa 182 54.42 N 127.03 W
Telkwa ≃ 182 54.41 N 127.02 W
Tel Lakhish ⊥ 132 31.34 N 34.51 E
Tellaro ≃ 70 36.50 N 15.06 E
Tell City 194 37.57 N 86.46 W
Teller 180 65.16 N 166.22 W
Tellicherry 122 11.45 N 75.32 E
Tellico ≃ 192 35.36 N 84.13 W
Tellico Plains 192 35.21 N 84.17 W
Tellier 254 47.39 S 66.03 W
Tellier, Lac ⊜ 206 46.23 N 74.00 W
Tello 246 3.04 N 75.08 W
Telluride 200 37.56 N 107.48 W
Tel'ma 88 52.43 N 103.41 E
Tel'mana 83 48.30 N 39.18 E
Tel'manovo 83 47.24 N 38.02 E
Tel Megiddo (Armageddon) ⊥ 132 32.35 N 35.11 E
Telmen 88 48.38 N 97.37 E
Telmen nuur ⊜ 88 48.50 N 97.18 E
Tel Mond 132 32.15 N 34.56 E
Tel'novskij 89 49.22 N 142.05 E
Telo 110 0.03 N 98.16 E
Teloekbetoeng → Tanjungkarang-Telukbetung 115a 5.27 S 105.16 E
Telogia Creek ≃ 192 30.16 N 84.44 W
Telok Anson 114 4.02 N 101.01 E
Telok Datok 114 2.49 N 101.31 E
Teloloapan 234 18.21 N 99.51 W
Telpaneca 236 13.32 N 86.17 W
Telsen 254 42.24 S 66.57 W
Telsen, Arroyo ≃ 254 42.51 S 66.48 W
Telšiai 76 55.59 N 22.15 E
Telti 71 40.52 N 9.21 E
Teltow 54 52.23 N 13.16 E
Teltow ◆[1] 264a 52.18 N 13.25 E
Teltower Hochfläche ⋏[1] 264a 52.22 N 13.20 E
Teltowkanal ≍ 264a 52.26 N 13.35 E
Telukbatang 112 1.00 S 109.46 E
Telukbayur, Indon. 112 2.09 N 117.24 E
Telukbayur, Indon. 112 1.00 S 100.22 E
Telukbrombang 114 2.03 N 100.52 E
Telukbutun 112 4.13 N 108.12 E
Telukdalem 114 0.34 N 97.49 E
Teluklanjut 112 0.09 N 103.29 E
Teluklecak 114 1.51 N 101.44 E
Telukmerbau 114 2.04 N 100.38 E
Telukpambang 114 1.28 N 102.28 E
Teluk Punggur, Ujung › 112 3.53 S 102.17 E
Telumengtang Shan ∧ 120 30.33 N 86.27 E
Teluša 76 53.03 N 29.31 E
Tem' 88 55.21 N 100.44 E
Tema 150 5.38 N 0.01 E
Temae 174s 17.29 S 149.46 W
Temagami, Lake ⊜ 190 47.00 N 80.05 W
Temaju, Pulau I 112 0.29 N 108.52 E
Temalacacingo 234 17.52 N 98.41 W
Temalı Bendi ◆[6] 267b 41.04 N 29.06 E
Te Manga ∧ 174k 21.13 S 159.45 W
Temangan Baharu 114 5.42 N 102.09 E
Temangga 112 0.27 N 111.21 E
Temanggung 115a 7.18 S 110.10 E
Temascal, Méx. 234 23.24 N 104.14 W
Temascal, Méx. 234 18.15 N 96.20 W
Temascaltepec ≃ 234 18.47 N 100.41 W
Tem'asovo 86 52.59 N 58.06 E
Temastián 234 21.53 N 103.28 W
Tematagi I[1] 14 21.41 S 140.40 W
Temax 232 21.09 N 88.56 W
Tembakul, Pulau I 271c 1.14 N 103.52 E
Tembe 154 0.16 S 28.14 E
Tembe ≃ 158 26.03 S 32.26 E
Tembeling 114 4.04 N 102.19 E
Tembeling ≃ 114 4.04 N 102.20 E
Tembenči ≃ 74 64.36 N 99.58 E
Tembesi ≃ 112 1.43 S 103.06 E
Tembilahan 112 0.19 S 103.09 E
Tembisa 158 25.58 S 28.14 E
Temblador 246 8.59 N 62.44 W
Tembleque 34 39.42 N 3.30 W
Temblor Range ⋏ 226 35.20 N 119.55 W
Tembo Aluma 152 7.42 S 17.17 E
Tembuè 154 14.52 S 32.58 E
Tembuland □[9] 158 31.30 S 27.40 E
Teme ≃ 42 52.09 N 2.18 W
Temecula 228 33.29 N 117.08 W
Temecula Creek ≃ 228 33.28 N 117.08 W
Temelli 130 39.44 N 32.22 E
Temengor 114 5.19 N 101.22 E
Temengor, Tasek ⊜[1] 114 5.30 N 101.20 E
Temerin 38 45.24 N 19.53 E
Temerloh 114 3.27 N 102.25 E
Temescal Canyon V 280 34.04 N 118.32 W
Temescal Wash V 228 33.40 N 117.20 W
Temesvár → Timișoara 38 45.45 N 21.13 E
Temiang, Pulau I 112 0.19 N 104.23 E
Teminaabuan 164 1.26 S 132.01 E
Temir 86 49.08 N 57.06 E
Temir ≃ 86 48.31 N 57.27 E
Temirgojevskaja 78 45.07 N 40.16 E
Temirlanovka 85 42.36 N 69.17 E
Temirtau, S.S.S.R. 86 53.08 N 87.28 E
Temirtau, S.S.S.R. 86 50.05 N 72.56 E
Témiscamie, Lac ⊜ 186 51.11 N 72.12 W
Témiscaming 190 46.43 N 79.06 W
Témiscouata, Lac ⊜ 186 47.41 N 68.47 W
Temixco 234 18.50 N 99.14 W
Temnik ≃ 88 51.00 N 106.18 E
Temnikov 80 54.38 N 43.12 E
Temnikovo 265b 55.43 N 38.01 E
Temo ≃ 71 40.21 N 8.47 E
Temoaya 234 19.28 N 99.35 W
Temora 166 34.26 S 147.32 E
Temósachic 232 28.57 N 107.51 W
Tempe 200 33.24 N 111.54 W
Tempe, Danau ⊜ 112 4.06 S 119.57 E
Tempelburg → Czaplinek 30 53.34 N 16.14 E
Tempelfelde 264a 52.43 N 13.43 E
Tempelhof ◆[8] 264a 52.28 N 13.23 E
Temperance 216 41.46 N 83.34 W
Temperanceville 208 37.53 N 75.32 W
Temperley ◆[8] 258 34.47 S 58.24 W
Tempest, Mount ∧[2] 171a 27.10 S 153.26 E
Tempilang 112 2.07 S 105.40 E
Tempino 112 1.44 S 103.29 E
Tempio di Clitunno ⊥ 66 42.48 N 12.45 E
Tempio Pausania 71 40.54 N 9.06 E
Tempisque ≃ 236 10.12 N 85.14 W
Temple, Ok., U.S. 196 34.16 N 98.14 W
Temple, Pa., U.S. 208 40.24 N 75.55 W
Temple, Tx., U.S. 222 31.05 N 97.20 W
Temple City 228 34.06 N 118.03 W
Templecombe 42 51.00 N 2.25 W
Temple Ewell 42 51.09 N 1.16 E
Temple Hills Park 284c 38.48 N 76.57 W
Templemore 48 52.48 N 7.50 W
Templers 168b 34.28 S 138.45 E
Temple Sowerby 44 54.39 N 2.35 W
Templestowe 169 37.45 S 145.07 E
Temple Terrace 220 28.02 N 82.23 W
Templeton, P.Q., Can. 212 45.29 N 75.36 W
Templeton, Ca., U.S. 226 35.33 N 120.42 W
Templeton, In., U.S. 216 40.31 N 87.12 W
Templeton, Ma., U.S. 207 42.33 N 72.04 W
Templeton, Pa., U.S. 214 40.55 N 79.27 W
Templeton ≃ 166 21.14 S 138.13 E
Temple University ʊ[2] 285 39.59 N 75.09 W
Templeuve, Bel. 50 50.38 N 3.16 E
Templeuve, Fr. 50 50.32 N 3.10 E
Templi, Valle dei ⊥ 70 37.17 N 13.35 E
Templin 54 53.07 N 13.30 E
Templiner See ⊜ 264a 52.22 N 13.01 E
Templo Island I 116 13.09 N 122.52 E
Tempoal 234 21.31 N 98.23 W
Tempoal ≃ 234 21.47 N 98.27 W
Tempy 82 56.38 N 37.18 E
Temr'uk 78 45.17 N 37.23 E
Temr'ukskij zaliv C 78 45.24 N 37.20 E
Temse 50 51.08 N 4.13 E
Temù 64 46.15 N 10.28 E
Temuco 252 38.44 S 72.36 W
Temuka 172 44.15 S 171.17 E
Temwen I 174r 6.52 N 158.19 E
Tena 246 0.59 S 77.49 W
Tenabo 232 20.03 N 90.14 W
Tenacatita, Bahía C 234 19.17 N 104.50 W
Tenafly 210 40.55 N 73.57 W
Tenaha 194 31.57 N 94.15 W
Tenakee Springs 180 57.47 N 135.13 W
Tenakill Brook ≃ 276 40.59 N 73.58 W
Tena Kourou ∧[2] 150 10.45 N 5.25 W
Tenāli 122 16.15 N 80.35 E
Tenamaxtlán 234 20.13 N 104.10 W
Tenancingo [de Degollado] 234 18.58 N 99.36 W
Tenango del Valle 234 19.07 N 99.33 W
Tenantongo, Presa ⊜[1] 286a 19.28 N 99.16 W
Tenasillahe Island I 224 46.14 N 123.27 W
Tenasserim 110 12.05 N 99.01 E
Tenay 58 45.55 N 5.30 E
Tenaya Creek ≃ 226 37.44 N 119.35 W
Tenbury Wells 42 52.19 N 2.35 W
Tenby 42 51.41 N 4.43 W
Tence 62 45.07 N 4.17 E
Tench Island I 164 1.40 S 150.40 E
Tencin 62 45.19 N 5.58 E
Tenda, Colle di (Col de Tende))(62 44.09 N 7.34 E

Symbols in the index entries represent the broad categories identified in the key at the right. Symbols with superior numbers (⋏[1]) identify subcategories (see complete key on page *I · 1).*

Symbole im Register stellen die rechts im Schlüssel erklärten Kategorien dar. Symbole mit hochgestellten Ziffern (⋏[1]) bezeichnen Unterabteilungen einer Kategorie (vgl. vollständiger Schlüssel auf Seite *I · 1).*

Los símbolos incluídos en el texto del índice representan las grandes categorias identificadas con la clave a la derecha. Los símbolos con numeros en su parte superior (⋏[1]) identifican las subcategorías (véase la clave completa en la página *I · 1).*

Les symboles de l'index représentent les catégories indiquées dans la légende à droite. Les symboles suivis d'un indice (⋏[1]) représentent des sous-catégories (voir légende complète à la page *I · 1).*

Os símbolos incluídos no texto do índice representam as grandes categorias identificadas com a chave à direita. Os símbolos com números em sua parte superior (⋏[1]) identificam as subcategorias (veja-se a chave completa à página *I · 1).*

	English	Deutsch	Español	Français	Português
∧	Mountain	Berg	Montaña	Montagne	Montanha
⋏	Mountains	Gebirge	Montañas	Montagnes	Montanhas
)(	Pass	Paß	Paso	Col	Passo
V	Valley, Canyon	Tal, Cañon	Valle, Cañón	Vallée, Canyon	Vale, Canhão
≚	Plain	Ebene	Llano	Plaine	Planície
›	Cape	Kap	Cabo	Cap	Cabo
I	Island	Insel	Isla	Île	Ilha
II	Islands	Inseln	Islas	Îles	Ilhas
⊥	Other Topographic Features	Andere Topographische Objekte	Otros Elementos Topográficos	Autres données topographiques	Outros acidentes topográficos

ESPAÑOL

Nombre	Página	Lat.°′	Long.°′ W = Oeste
Tendaho	144	11.48 N	40.52 E
Tendai-san ∧	270	34.55 N	135.28 E
Tende	62	44.05 N	7.36 E
Tende, Col de (Colle di Tenda))(	62	44.09 N	7.34 E
Tende, Tunnel de ◆[5]	62	44.09 N	7.34 E
Ten Degree Channel ʊ	110	10.00 N	93.00 E
Tendeka	158	27.44 S	30.54 E
Tendō	92	38.21 N	140.22 E
Tendrara	148	33.04 N	1.59 W
Tendrovskaja kosa ›[2]	78	46.12 N	31.50 E
Tendrovskij zaliv c	78	46.15 N	31.55 E
Tendürek Dağı ∧	84	39.22 N	43.52 E
Ténenkou	150	14.28 N	4.55 W
Tenente Marques ≃	248	11.10 S	59.56 W
Tenente Portela	252	27.22 S	53.45 W
Tenentes	256	22.48 S	46.20 W
Ténéré ◆[2]	146	19.00 N	10.30 E
Ténéré, Erg du ⌓[8]	146	17.35 N	10.55 E
Tenerife I	148	28.19 N	16.34 W
Ténès	148	36.31 N	1.14 E
Ténès, Cap ›	34	36.33 N	1.21 E
Tenexpa	234	17.11 N	100.43 W
Tenextepango	234	18.43 N	98.57 W
Teng ≃	110	19.52 N	97.45 E
Tengah, Kepulauan II	112	7.30 S	117.30 E
Teng'aopu	104	41.05 N	122.49 E
Tengchong	102	25.04 N	98.29 E
Tengeh Reservoir ⊜[1]	271c	1.21 N	103.39 E
Tengen	58	47.49 N	8.40 E
Tenggara, Nusa (Lesser Sunda Islands) II	108	9.00 S	120.00 E
Tenggarong	112	0.24 S	116.58 E
Tengger Shamo ◆[2]	102	38.00 N	104.40 E
Tenggol, Pulau I	114	4.48 N	103.38 E
Tenghilan	112	6.14 N	116.19 E
Tengi ≃	114	3.24 N	101.10 E
Tengiz, ozero ⊜	86	50.24 N	68.57 E
Tengjiabao	100	31.10 N	115.29 E
Tengqiao	110	18.22 N	109.46 E
Tengra	272b	22.48 N	88.32 E
Tengréla	150	10.29 N	6.24 W
Tengtian	100	27.04 N	115.40 E
Tengtiao (Na) ≃	110	22.05 N	103.09 E
Ten'guševo	80	54.46 N	42.44 E
Tengxian, Zhg.	98	35.08 N	117.10 E
Tengxian, Zhg.	102	23.21 N	110.53 E
Teniente Rodolfo Marsh ᴗ[3]	9	62.12 S	58.54 W
Tenigerbad	58	46.42 N	8.57 E
Tenino	224	46.51 N	122.51 W
Tenis, ozero ⊜	86	56.09 N	71.56 E
Teniya-zaki ›	174m	26.33 N	128.09 E
Teniz, ozero ⊜	86	54.08 N	64.34 E
Tenjin ≃	96	35.30 N	133.53 E
Tenjo, Mount ∧[2]	174p	13.25 N	144.42 E
Tenkāsi	122	8.58 N	77.18 E
Tenke, Zaïre	154	10.35 S	26.07 E
Tenke, Zaïre	154	11.26 S	26.45 E
Tenkeli	74	70.01 N	140.58 E
Tenkergynpil'gyn, laguna c	180	68.30 N	178.00 W
Ten'ki	80	55.26 N	49.00 E
Tenkiller Ferry Lake ⊜[1]	196	35.43 N	95.00 W
Tenkodogo	150	11.47 N	0.22 W
Tenmile ≃, Ma., U.S.	283	41.58 N	71.20 W
Tenmile ≃, N.Y., U.S.	210	41.40 N	73.31 W
Ten Mile Creek ≃, On., Can.	284a	43.07 N	79.11 W
Ten Mile Creek ≃, Ky., U.S.	218	38.43 N	84.46 W
Tenmile Creek ≃, Oh., U.S.	216	41.42 N	83.33 W
Tenmile Creek ≃, Pa., U.S.	188	40.08 N	80.22 W
Tenmile Creek ≃, Tx., U.S.	222	32.34 N	96.34 W
Ten Mile Lake ⊜	186	51.06 N	56.41 W
Tenmile Run ≃	276	40.27 N	74.35 W
Tenmile Wash V	200	32.52 N	113.28 W
Tenmoku-san ∧	94	35.52 N	139.03 E
Tenna ≃	66	43.14 N	13.47 E
Tennant Creek	162	19.40 S	134.10 E
Tennenbronn	58	48.11 N	8.20 E
Tennengau ◆[1]	64	47.40 N	13.15 E
Tennen-Gebirge ⋀	64	47.30 N	13.15 E
Tennent	208	40.16 N	74.20 W
Tennent Pond ⊜	276	40.26 N	74.20 W
Tennessee □[3]	178	35.50 N	85.30 W
Tennessee ≃	178	37.04 N	88.33 W
Tennessee Colony	222	31.50 N	95.50 W
Tenneville	56	50.06 N	5.32 E
Tennille	192	32.56 N	82.48 W
Tenno	64	45.55 N	10.49 E
Tennōji ◆[8]	270	34.39 N	135.31 E
Teno	252	34.52 S	71.11 W
Teno (Tana) ≃	24	70.30 N	28.23 E
Tenom	112	5.08 N	115.57 E
Ténos, Pointe ›	240e	14.48 N	61.00 W
Tenosique	232	17.29 N	91.26 W
Tenri	96	34.36 N	135.51 E
Tenryū, Nihon	94	35.16 N	137.51 E
Tenryū, Nihon	94	34.52 N	137.49 E
Tenryū ≃	94	34.39 N	137.47 E
Tensas ≃	194	31.38 N	91.49 W
Tensed	202	47.09 N	116.55 W
Tensift, Oued ≃	148	32.02 N	9.22 W
Ten Sleep	202	44.02 N	107.27 W
Tensta	40	60.02 N	17.40 E
Tente ◆[8]	263	51.18 N	7.14 E
Tenteksor ⁝	80	47.18 N	53.24 E
Tentena	112	1.47 S	120.39 E
Tenterden	42	51.05 N	0.42 E
Tenterfield	166	29.03 S	152.01 E
Tent Hill	171a	27.36 S	152.14 E
Tenthill Creek ≃	171a	27.34 S	152.14 E
Ten Thousand Islands II	220	25.50 N	81.33 W
Tentolomatinan, Gunung ∧	112	0.56 N	121.48 E
Tentugal	250	1.19 S	46.59 W
Tentulia	272b	22.50 N	88.28 E
Teocaltiche	234	21.26 N	102.35 W
Teocelo	234	19.23 N	96.58 W
Teocuitatlán de Corona	234	20.07 N	103.24 W
Teocuitlapa	234	17.22 N	98.58 W
Teodelina	252	34.11 S	61.32 W
Teófilo Cunha	287a	22.39 S	43.34 W
Teófilo Otoni	255	17.51 S	41.30 W
Teofipol'	78	49.50 N	26.25 E
Teohotepapa, Pointe ›	174x	9.46 S	138.48 W
Teohotupa, Pointe ›	174x	9.46 S	138.50 W
Teo Lakes ⊜	184	51.30 N	109.21 W
Teolo	64	45.21 N	11.40 E
Teomabal Island I	116	6.20 N	120.51 E
Teor	64	45.51 N	13.03 E
Teora	68	40.51 N	15.15 E
Teotihuacán ⊥	234	19.44 N	98.50 W
Teotitlán del Camino	234	18.08 N	97.05 W
Teotitlán del Valle	234	17.02 N	96.30 W
Tepa, Ghana	150	7.00 N	2.10 W
Tepa, Indon.	164	7.52 S	129.31 E
Tepalcatepec	234	19.11 N	102.51 W
Tepalcatepec ≃	234	18.50 N	102.05 W
Tepalcatepec, Arroyo ≃	234	17.25 N	100.40 W
Tepalcingo	234	18.36 N	98.51 W
Tepa Point ›	174v	19.07 S	169.56 W
Tepatepec	234	20.14 N	99.05 W
Tepatitlán [de Morelos]	234	20.49 N	102.44 W
Tepatlaxco [de Hidalgo]	234	19.04 N	97.58 W
Tepe	130	37.48 N	40.47 E

FRANÇAIS

Nom	Page	Lat.°′	Long.°′ W = Ouest
Tepeaca	234	18.58 N	97.54 W
Tepeapulco	234	19.47 N	98.33 W
Tepebaşı	130	36.40 N	32.45 E
Tepechitlán	234	21.40 N	103.20 W
Tepecoacuilco [de Trujano]	234	18.18 N	99.29 W
Tepecoacuilo ≃	234	17.59 N	99.47 W
Tepeguaje, Méx.	196	25.40 N	99.50 W
Tepeguaje, Méx.	234	23.30 N	97.50 W
Tepehan	130	38.06 N	38.45 E
Tepehuanes	232	25.21 N	105.44 W
Tepehuanes, Río los ≃	232	25.10 N	105.25 W
Tepeji del Río	234	19.54 N	99.21 W
Tepelenë	38	40.18 N	20.01 E
Tepelmeme [de Morelos]	234	17.51 N	97.21 W
Tepelská vrchovina ⋀[1]	60	50.00 N	13.00 E
Tepeören	130	41.04 N	35.30 E
Tepepan ◆[8]	286a	19.16 N	99.08 W
Tepe Saif	267d	35.36 N	51.18 E
Tepetixtla	234	17.13 N	100.08 W
Tepetlixpa	234	19.02 N	98.49 W
Tepi	144	7.10 N	35.23 E
Tepic	234	21.30 N	104.54 W
Tepko	168b	34.58 S	139.11 E
Teplá	60	49.59 N	12.52 E
Teplá ≃	54	50.14 N	12.52 E
Teplice	54	50.39 N	13.48 E
Teplik	78	48.40 N	29.44 E
Teplitz → Teplice	54	50.39 N	13.48 E
Teplooz'orsk	89	49.00 N	131.48 E
Teplovka	80	51.33 N	51.33 E
Teplovo	80	55.25 N	42.56 E
Tepoca, Bahía de c	232	30.15 N	112.50 W
Te Pohue	172	39.15 S	176.41 E
Tepopa, Cabo ›	232	29.22 N	112.27 W
Teposcolula	234	17.31 N	97.29 W
Te Puia	172	38.04 S	178.18 E
Te Puke	172	37.47 S	176.20 E
Tepuxtepec, Presa ⊜[1]	234	20.02 N	100.13 W
Tepuzhuacán	234	20.53 N	104.33 W
Tequepa, Bahía de c	234	17.17 N	101.05 W
Tequila	234	20.54 N	103.47 W
Tequisquiac	234	19.55 N	99.09 W
Tequisquita Slough ≃	226	36.58 N	121.27 W
Tequma	132	31.27 N	34.35 E
Ter ≃, Esp.	34	42.01 N	3.12 E
Ter ≃, Ityo.	144	7.20 N	42.11 E
Ter ≃, Eng., U.K.	42	51.50 N	0.36 E
Téra	150	14.01 N	0.45 E
Tera ≃	34	41.54 N	5.44 W
Teradomari	92	37.38 N	138.46 E
Terai	94	36.26 N	136.30 E
Teraina I	14	4.43 N	160.24 W
Ter'ajevo	82	56.11 N	36.07 E
Terakhāda	126	22.56 N	89.40 E
Teralba	170	32.58 S	151.37 E
Teramo	66	42.39 N	13.42 E
Teramo □[6]	66	42.39 N	13.41 E
Terán	234	16.45 N	93.10 W
Terang	169	38.14 S	142.55 E
Teranum	114	3.44 N	101.49 E
Ter Apel	52	52.53 N	7.04 E
Teraruma	164	8.00 S	141.50 E
Teras	114	3.45 N	101.49 E
Teratak	112	0.46 S	110.32 E
Terborg	52	51.55 N	6.21 E
Terbuny	76	52.08 N	38.17 E
Tercan	130	39.47 N	40.24 E
Terceira I	148a	38.43 N	24.13 W
Tercero ≃	252	32.55 S	62.19 W
Tercero de Febrero, Parque ♦	288	34.34 S	58.25 W
Terdal	122	16.30 N	75.03 E
Terdoppio, Torrente ≃	266b	45.30 N	8.37 E
Terebovl'a	78	49.18 N	25.43 E
Terebuš	82	54.16 N	38.09 E
Terebutinec	76	59.01 N	33.39 E
Terechovka	78	52.13 N	31.27 E
Terechovo	82	55.50 N	35.45 E
Te Rehunga	172	40.13 S	176.01 E
Tereida	140	10.35 N	31.17 E
Terek, S.S.S.R.	84	43.29 N	44.08 E
Terek, S.S.S.R.	85	40.01 N	73.33 E
Terek ≃	84	43.44 N	46.33 E
Terekli-Mekteb	84	44.10 N	45.53 E
Terek-Saj	85	41.32 N	71.09 E
Terektinskij chrebet ⋀	86	50.30 N	86.00 E
Terekty	80	48.34 N	49.02 E
Terempa	112	3.14 N	106.14 E
Terence Bay	186	44.28 N	63.43 W
Teren'ga	80	53.42 N	48.24 E
Terengganu □[3]	114	5.00 N	103.00 E
Terengganu ≃	114	5.17 N	103.05 E
Terenino	76	54.31 N	33.35 E
Terenkuduk	80	48.24 N	47.11 E
Terenni ⊥	150	16.30 N	9.35 W
Terenos	255	20.26 S	54.50 W
Terensaj	86	51.36 N	59.31 E
Terenuzek	86	45.05 N	64.59 E
Teresina	250	5.05 S	42.49 W
Tereška ≃	80	51.48 N	46.26 E
Teresópolis	256	22.26 S	42.59 W
Terespol	30	52.05 N	23.36 E
Teresva	78	48.01 N	23.42 E
Terevaka, Cerro ∧	174z	27.05 S	109.23 W
Terezín	54	50.31 N	14.08 E
Tergauči	85	41.11 N	71.30 E
Tergnier	50	49.39 N	3.18 E
Tergun Daba Shan ⋀	102	38.25 N	95.55 E
Terhorne	52	53.02 N	5.46 E
Teriang	114	3.14 N	102.25 E
Teriang ≃	114	3.19 N	102.31 E
Teribe ≃	236	9.22 N	82.32 W
Terib'orka	24	69.08 N	35.08 E
Terihi I	174x	10.02 S	138.49 W
Terio	164	8.25 S	143.00 E
Terjärv (Teerijärvi)	26	63.32 N	23.30 E
Terlago	64	46.06 N	11.02 E
Terlano	64	46.32 N	11.15 E
Terlingua	196	29.19 N	103.37 W
Terlingua Creek ≃	196	29.10 N	103.36 W
Terlizzi	68	41.08 N	16.32 E
Termas de Río Hondo	252	27.29 S	64.52 W
Terme	130	41.12 N	36.59 E
Terme del Brennero (Brennerbad)	64	46.58 N	11.29 E
Terme di Stigliano	66	42.09 N	12.01 E
Terme di Suio	68	41.18 N	13.51 E
Terme di Valdieri	62	44.12 N	7.16 E
Termeno (Tramin)	64	46.20 N	11.14 E
Termez	72	37.14 N	67.16 E
Termignon	62	45.17 N	6.49 E
Terminal	258	34.09 S	57.31 W
Terminal Island I	280	33.45 N	118.15 W
Terminal Island Coast Guard Base ■	280	33.43 N	118.17 W
Termini Imerese	70	37.59 N	13.42 E
Termini Imerese, Golfo di c	70	38.01 N	13.45 E
Terminillo, Monte ∧	66	42.28 N	13.00 E
Términos, Laguna de c	232	18.37 N	91.33 W
Termit, Massif de ⋀	146	16.15 N	11.17 E
Termoli	66	42.00 N	15.00 E
Termonde → Dendermonde	50	51.02 N	4.07 E
Termsdorf	264a	52.16 N	13.07 E
Tern ≃	42	52.47 N	2.32 W
Ternate, Indon.	108	0.48 N	127.24 E
Ternate, Pil.	116	14.17 N	120.43 E
Ternberg	61	47.58 N	14.22 E
Ternej	89	45.03 N	136.37 E
Terneuzen	52	51.20 N	3.50 E

PORTUGUÊS

Nome	Página	Lat.°′	Long.°′ W = Oeste
Terni	66	42.34 N	12.37 E
Terni □[4]	66	42.41 N	12.19 E
Ternitz	61	47.44 N	16.03 E
Ternoise ≃	50	50.23 N	2.01 E
Ternopol'	78	49.34 N	25.36 E
Ternovatoje	78	47.50 N	36.09 E
Ternovka, S.S.S.R.	78	51.40 N	41.37 E
Ternovka, S.S.S.R.	78	47.02 N	32.01 E
Ternovka, S.S.S.R.	78	48.32 N	29.58 E
Ternovka, S.S.S.R.	80	51.19 N	42.56 E
Ternovka, S.S.S.R.	80	53.09 N	45.02 E
Ternovoje	80	51.03 N	43.43 E
Ternovskaja	78	45.53 N	40.24 E
Terolak	114	3.53 N	101.23 E
Terong	114	4.43 N	100.44 E
Terontola	66	43.13 N	12.02 E
Terpe	54	51.32 N	14.19 E
Terpenija, mys ›	89	48.39 N	144.44 E
Terpenija, zaliv c	89	49.00 N	143.30 E
Terra Alta	188	39.26 N	79.32 W
Terra Bella	204	35.58 N	119.03 W
Terra Boa	255	23.45 S	52.27 W
Terrace	182	54.31 N	128.35 W
Terrace Bay	190	48.47 N	87.06 W
Terracina	66	41.17 N	13.15 E
Terra del Sole	66	44.11 N	11.57 E
Terral	196	33.53 N	97.56 W
Terralba	71	39.43 N	8.39 E
Terra Linda	226	38.01 N	122.32 W
Terranova → Newfoundland □[4]	176	52.00 N	56.00 W
Terra Nova Bay c	9	74.45 S	164.30 E
Terranova da Sibari	68	39.39 N	16.20 E
Terranova di Pollino	68	39.59 N	16.18 E
Terranova di Sicilia → Gela	70	37.04 N	14.15 E
Terra Nova Lake ⊜	186	48.30 N	54.20 W
Terra Nova National Park ♦	186	48.37 N	53.56 W
Terranuova Bracciolini	66	43.33 N	11.35 E
Terra Rica	255	22.43 S	52.38 W
Terrarossa, Foce di)(	64	44.12 N	10.26 E
Terra Roxa d'Oeste	252	24.08 S	53.59 W
Terras, Pinhal do ◆[3]	266c	38.39 N	9.02 W
Terra Santa	250	2.06 S	56.29 W
Terrasini	70	38.09 N	13.05 E
Terrassa	34	41.34 N	2.01 E
Terrasse-Vaudreuil	206	45.24 N	73.59 W
Terrasson-la-Villedieu	32	45.08 N	1.18 E
Terravecchia	68	39.29 N	16.58 E
Terrebonne	206	45.42 N	73.38 W
Terrebonne □[6]	206	46.00 N	74.10 W
Terrebonne Bay c	194	29.09 N	90.35 W
Terre Ceia	220	27.35 N	82.35 W
Terre-de-Bas	241o	15.51 N	61.39 W
Terre-de-Bas I	241o	15.52 N	61.38 W
Terre de Feu → Tierra del Fuego, Isla Grande de I	254	54.00 S	69.00 W
Terre-de-Haut	241o	15.58 N	61.35 W
Terre-de-Haut I	241o	15.52 N	61.35 W
Terre des Hommes ♦	275a	45.31 N	73.32 W
Terre Haute	194	39.28 N	87.24 W
Terre Hill	208	40.09 N	76.03 W
Terrell	222	32.44 N	96.16 W
Terrell, Lake ⊜	224	48.52 N	122.41 W
Terrell Hills	196	29.28 N	98.27 W
Terrenceville	186	47.40 N	54.44 W
Terre-Neuve → Newfoundland □[4]	176	52.00 N	56.00 W
Terre Noire Creek ≃	194	33.49 N	92.55 W
Terre Rouge Creek ≃	194	33.49 N	93.11 W
Terres australes et antarctiques françaises → French Southern and Antarctic Territories □[2]	6	49.30 S	69.30 E
Terrey Hills	170	33.41 S	151.14 E
Terrigal	170	33.27 S	151.27 E
Terrington Saint Clement	42	52.45 N	0.18 E
Territoires du Nord-Ouest → Northwest Territories □[4]	176	70.00 N	100.00 W
Territorio Británico de la Antártica → British Antarctic Territory □[2]	9	60.00 S	45.00 W
Territorio Británico del Océano Índico → British Indian Ocean Territory □[2]	12	7.00 S	72.00 E
Territorios del Noroeste → Northwest Territories □[4]	176	70.00 N	100.00 W
Terror Point ›	182	53.10 N	129.56 W
Terrugem	266c	38.51 N	9.20 W
Terry, Ms., U.S.	194	32.05 N	90.17 W
Terry, Mt., U.S.	198	46.47 N	105.18 W
Terry Peak ∧	198	44.19 N	103.50 W
Terryville, Ct., U.S.	207	41.40 N	73.00 W
Terryville, N.Y., U.S.	210	40.54 N	73.03 W
Tersa, S.S.S.R.	80	52.05 N	47.32 E
Tersa, S.S.S.R.	80	50.53 N	43.48 E
Tersa ≃	80	50.46 N	44.40 E
Tersakan Gölü ⊜	130	38.35 N	33.06 E
Tersakkan ≃	86	51.15 N	67.10 E
Terschelling I	52	53.24 N	5.20 E
Tersiva, Punta ∧	62	45.37 N	7.28 E
Terskej-Alatau, chrebet ⋀	85	41.55 N	77.00 E
Terskij chrebet ⋀	84	43.32 N	45.00 E
Terslev	41	55.22 N	11.59 E
Tersløse	41	55.31 N	11.30 E
Tertenia	71	39.42 N	9.34 E
Terter ≃	84	40.35 N	47.22 E
Teru	123	36.11 N	72.45 E
Teruel, Col.	246	2.44 N	75.33 W
Teruel, Esp.	34	40.21 N	1.06 W
Terujak	114	4.23 N	97.31 E
Tervakoski	26	60.48 N	24.37 E
Tervel	38	43.45 N	27.24 E
Tervola	26	66.05 N	24.48 E
Tervuren	56	50.49 N	4.31 E
Terwagne	56	50.27 N	5.20 E
Terwolde	52	52.16 N	6.06 E
Terzaghi Dam ◆[6]	182	50.49 N	122.12 W
Terzigno	68	40.48 N	14.29 E
Teržola	84	42.12 N	42.59 E
Tes	88	50.27 N	93.30 E
Tésa, Magy.	30	48.02 N	18.51 E
Teša, S.S.S.R.	80	55.30 N	42.50 E
Tesalia	246	2.29 N	75.44 W
Tešanj	38	44.37 N	18.00 E
Tes-Chem (Tesijn) ≃	88	50.28 N	93.04 E
Teschen → Český Těšín	30	49.45 N	18.37 E
Teschendorf	54	52.51 N	13.10 E
Tescott	198	39.00 N	97.52 W
Tesdrero, Cerro ∧	234	22.47 N	103.04 W
Teseney	144	15.07 N	36.41 E
Tesero	64	46.17 N	11.31 E
Teshekpuk Lake ⊜	180	70.35 N	153.30 W
Teshikaga	92a	43.29 N	144.28 E
Te-shima I, Nihon	96	34.24 N	133.40 E
Te-shima I, Nihon	96	34.29 N	134.05 E
Teshio	92a	44.53 N	141.44 E
Teshio ≃	92a	44.53 N	141.44 E
Teshio-sanchi ⋀	92a	44.15 N	142.05 E
Tešig	88	49.56 N	102.34 E
Tesijn (Tes-Chem) ≃	88	50.28 N	93.04 E

Tesimo (Tisens)	64	46.34 N	11.10 E
Teslić	38	44.37 N	17.51 E
Teslin	180	60.09 N	132.45 W
Teslin ≃	180	61.34 N	134.54 W
Teslin Lake ⊜	180	60.15 N	132.57 W
Tesouras ≃	255	14.36 S	50.51 W
Tesouro	255	16.04 S	53.34 W
Tesovo	82	55.34 N	36.05 E
Tesperhude	52	53.24 N	10.26 E
Tessa, Oued ≃	36	36.34 N	8.54 E
Tessa-Araral, Oued V	148	26.18 N	1.58 E
Tessala, Djebel ∧	34	35.17 N	0.48 W
Tessala, Monts du ⋀	34	35.25 N	0.45 W
Tessalit	150	20.12 N	1.00 E
Tessancourt-sur-Aubette	261	49.02 N	1.55 E
Tessaoua	150	13.45 N	7.59 E
Tessei	96	34.56 N	133.20 E
Tessenderlo	56	51.04 N	5.05 E
Tesserete	58	46.04 N	8.58 E
Tessin	54	54.01 N	12.28 E
Tessin → Ticino □[3]	58	46.20 N	8.45 E
Tessy-sur-Vire	32	48.58 N	1.04 W
Test ≃	42	50.55 N	1.29 W
Testa, Capo ›	71	41.14 N	9.08 E
Teston, On., Can.	275b	43.52 N	79.32 W
Teston, Eng., U.K.	260	51.15 N	0.26 E
Testour	36	36.33 N	9.27 E
Tesuque	200	35.45 N	105.55 W
Têt ≃	32	42.44 N	3.02 E
Tetachuck Lake ⊜	182	53.20 N	125.50 W
Tetagouche ≃	186	47.38 N	65.41 W
Tetas, Punta ›	252	23.31 S	70.38 W
Tetbury	42	51.39 N	2.10 W
Tete	154	16.13 S	33.35 E
Tete □[5]	154	15.15 S	32.40 E
Tété ≃	146	9.12 N	20.29 E
Tête-à-la-Baleine	186	50.41 N	59.20 W
Tête du Parmelan ∧	58	45.57 N	6.14 E
Tête-Jaune-Cache	182	52.57 N	119.26 W
Te Teko	172	38.02 S	176.48 E
Tetepare Island I	175e	8.43 S	157.33 E
Tétépisca, Lac ⊜	186	51.00 N	69.25 W
Teterboro	276	40.52 N	74.03 W
Teterboro Airport ⊠	276	40.51 N	74.04 W
Téterchen	56	49.14 N	6.34 E
Tetere ≃	88	59.30 N	105.00 E
Teterev ≃	78	51.01 N	30.05 E
Teterow	54	53.46 N	12.34 E
Teteven	38	42.55 N	24.16 E
Tetiaroa I[1]	14	17.05 S	149.32 W
Tetica ∧	34	37.15 N	2.25 W
Tetijev	78	49.23 N	29.41 E
Tetla	234	19.26 N	98.06 W
Tetlin	180	63.08 N	142.31 W
Tetlin Lake ⊜	180	63.05 N	142.45 W
Teton	202	43.53 N	111.40 W
Teton ≃, Id., U.S.	202	43.54 N	111.51 W
Teton ≃, Mt., U.S.	202	47.56 N	110.31 W
Tetonia	202	43.49 N	111.09 W
Teton Range ⋀	202	43.45 N	110.50 W
Tétouan	148	35.34 N	5.23 W
Tétouan □[4]	148	35.30 N	5.30 W
Tetovo	38	42.01 N	20.58 E
Tétreauville ◆[8]	275a	45.36 N	73.32 W
Tetri-Ckaro	84	41.34 N	44.28 E
Tetschen → Děčín	54	50.48 N	14.13 E
Tetsuta	96	34.56 N	133.28 E
Tettau	54	50.28 N	11.15 E
Tettenhall	42	52.36 N	2.09 W
Tettens	52	53.38 N	7.53 E
Tettnang	58	47.40 N	9.35 E
Tetuán → Tétouan	148	35.34 N	5.23 W
Tetufera, Mont ∧	174s	17.40 S	149.26 W
Tetulbāria	126	21.58 N	90.03 E
Tetulia ≃[1]	126	22.15 N	90.37 E
Teturi	154	1.04 N	29.08 E
Tet'uši	80	54.57 N	48.50 E
Tet'ušskoje	80	54.18 N	48.03 E
Teublitz	60	49.13 N	12.05 E
Teuchern	54	51.07 N	12.01 E
Teuco ≃	252	25.38 S	60.12 W
Teufelshöhle ⌓[5]	60	49.45 N	11.25 E
Teufels-Insel → Diable, Île du I	250	5.17 N	52.35 W
Teufelsmoor ◆[3]	52	53.15 N	8.50 E
Teufen	58	47.23 N	9.23 E
Teufenbach	61	47.08 N	14.21 E
Teulada	71	38.58 N	8.46 E
Teulada, Capo ›	71	38.52 N	8.38 E
Teúl de González Ortega	234	21.28 N	103.29 W
Teulon	184	50.23 N	97.16 W
Teun, Pulau I	164	6.59 S	129.08 E
Teunom ≃	114	4.26 N	95.48 E
Teunz	60	49.29 N	12.23 E
Teupitz	54	52.08 N	13.36 E
Teuplitz → Tuplice	30	51.41 N	14.50 E
Teureubangan-cut	114	3.12 N	97.18 E
Teuri-tō I	92a	44.25 N	141.19 E
Teuschnitz	54	50.24 N	11.23 E
Teutleben	54	50.57 N	10.33 E
Teutli, Cerro del ∧	286a	19.14 N	99.01 W
Teutoburger Wald ◆[3]	52	52.10 N	8.15 E
Teutopolis	194	39.07 N	88.28 W
Teutschenthal	54	51.27 N	11.46 E
Teuva	26	62.29 N	21.44 E
Tevere ≃	66	41.44 N	12.14 E
Teverya (Tiberias)	132	32.47 N	35.32 E
Teviot ≃	44	55.36 N	2.26 W
Teviot Brook ≃	171a	27.51 S	152.57 E
Teviotdale V	44	55.25 N	2.50 W
Teviothead	44	55.21 N	2.56 W
Tevli	76	52.20 N	24.15 E
Tevriz	86	57.34 N	72.24 E
Te Waewae Bay c	172	46.15 S	167.30 E
Tewah	112	1.05 S	113.42 E
Te Whaiti	172	38.35 S	176.47 E
Tewkesbury	42	51.59 N	2.09 W
Tewksbury	207	42.36 N	71.14 W
Tew-Mac Airport ⊠	283	42.36 N	71.12 W
Têwo	102	34.02 N	103.05 E
Texada Island I	182	49.40 N	124.24 W
Texana, Lake ⊜[1]	222	28.58 N	96.32 W
Texarkana, Ar., U.S.	194	33.26 N	94.02 W
Texarkana, Tx., U.S.	194	33.25 N	94.02 W
Texas, Austl.	166	28.51 S	151.11 E
Texas, Oh., U.S.	216	41.26 N	83.57 W
Texas □[3], U.S.	178	31.30 N	99.00 W
Texas □[3], U.S.	196	31.30 N	99.00 W
Texas City	222	29.23 N	94.54 W
Texcaltitlán	234	18.54 N	99.55 W
Texcoco □[7]	286a	19.28 N	99.01 W
Texcoco, Lago de ⊜	234	19.30 N	99.00 W
Texcoco [de Mora]	234	19.31 N	98.53 W
Texel I	52	53.05 N	4.45 E
Texhoma	196	36.30 N	101.46 W
Texico	196	34.23 N	103.03 W
Texistepec	234	17.53 N	94.47 W
Texline	196	36.23 N	103.01 W
Texoma, Lake ⊜[1]	196	33.55 N	96.37 W
Teyateyaneng	158	29.07 S	27.34 E
Teyéa ⊥	38	37.29 N	22.24 E
Teylān	120	35.32 N	64.47 E
Teynham	42	51.20 N	0.50 E
Teywarah	120	33.21 N	64.25 E
Teza ≃	80	56.32 N	41.53 E
Teziutlán	234	19.49 N	97.21 W
Težler, gora ∧	84	40.42 N	44.37 E
Tezoatlán [de Segura y Luna]	234	17.42 N	97.49 W
Tezpur	120	26.37 N	92.48 E
Tezu	120	27.53 N	96.11 E
Tezzeron Lake ⊜	182	54.41 N	124.25 W

Tha ≃	110	20.07 N	100.36 E
Tha-anne ≃	176	60.31 N	94.37 W
Thabana-Ntlenyana ∧	158	29.28 S	29.16 E
Thaba Nchu	158	29.17 S	26.52 E
Thabankulu ∧	158	27.30 S	30.20 E
Thaba-Putsoa Range ⋀	158	29.45 S	27.55 E
Thabaung	110	17.02 N	94.48 E
Thabawleikkyi	110	12.01 N	99.12 E
Thabazimbi	156	24.41 S	27.21 E
Thabor, Mont ∧	62	45.07 N	6.34 E
Thabyu	110	15.36 N	98.29 E
Thacher Island I	207	42.38 N	70.35 W
Thādiq	128	25.18 N	45.52 E
Thagyettaw	110	13.45 N	98.09 E
Thai Binh	110	20.27 N	106.20 E
Thailand (Prathet Thai) □[1], Asia	108	15.00 N	100.00 E
Thailand (Prathet Thai) □[1], Asia	110	15.00 N	100.00 E
Thailand, Gulf of c	110	10.00 N	101.00 E
Thaïlande → Thailand □[1]	110	15.00 N	100.00 E
Thailandia → Thailand □[1]	110	15.00 N	100.00 E
Thai Muang	110	8.24 N	98.16 E
Thai Nguyen	110	21.36 N	105.50 E
Thak	120	30.32 N	70.13 E
Thakhek → Muang Khammouan	110	17.24 N	104.48 E
Thākurdwāra	124	29.12 N	78.51 E
Thākurdwāri	272b	22.34 N	88.28 E
Thākurgaon	124	26.02 N	88.28 E
Thākurpukur	272b	22.28 N	88.19 E
Thākurvādi	272c	18.54 N	73.04 E
Thal, D.D.R.	54	50.55 N	10.23 E
Thal, Pāk.	123	33.22 N	70.33 E
Tha'l, Jabal ∧	140	14.13 N	24.14 E
Thala	36	35.35 N	8.40 E
Thalang	110	8.01 N	98.19 E
Thal-Assling	64	46.47 N	12.38 E
Thalāthah	142	30.35 N	32.20 E
Thal Desert ◆[2]	123	31.30 N	71.40 E
Thale	54	51.45 N	11.02 E
Thalfang	56	49.45 N	6.59 E
Thalgau	64	47.50 N	13.15 E
Thalheim	54	50.42 N	12.51 E
Thalheim bei Wels	61	48.09 N	14.02 E
Tha Li	110	17.37 N	101.25 E
Thalia	196	33.59 N	99.32 W
Thālith, Ash-Shallāl ath- (Third Cataract) ∟	140	19.49 N	30.19 E
Thalitter	56	51.13 N	8.53 E
Thalkirch	58	46.38 N	9.16 E
Thallon	166	28.38 S	148.52 E
Thallwitz	54	51.26 N	12.40 E
Thalmah, Marsā c	142	29.03 N	32.38 E
Thalmässing	60	49.05 N	11.13 E
Thalwil	58	47.17 N	8.34 E
Thamar, Jabal ∧	144	13.53 N	45.12 E
Thame	42	51.45 N	0.59 W
Thames	172	37.08 S	175.33 E
Thames ≃, On., Can.	190	42.19 N	82.27 W
Thames ≃, Eng., U.K.	42	51.28 N	0.43 E
Thames ≃, Ct., U.S.	207	41.18 N	72.05 W
Thames, Firth of c	172	37.00 S	175.25 E
Thames Barrier ◆[6]	260	51.29 N	0.03 E
Thames Ditton	260	51.23 N	0.21 W
Thames Estuary c[1]	260	51.30 N	0.40 W
Thamesford	212	43.04 N	81.00 W
Thames Haven	260	51.30 N	0.31 E
Thamesville	214	42.33 N	81.59 W
Thāmit, Wādī V	146	31.15 N	16.06 E
Thammasat University ᴗ[2]	269a	13.45 N	100.30 E
Thamūd, Bi'r ⊤[4]	144	17.17 N	49.56 E
Thāna, India	122	19.12 N	72.58 E
Thāna, Pāk.	128	28.55 N	63.45 E
Thāna Creek c	272c	19.00 N	72.57 E
Thāna Gāzi	124	27.25 N	76.19 E
Thāna Kasba	124	25.13 N	77.20 E
Thanbyuzayat	110	15.58 N	97.44 E
Thandaung	110	19.04 N	96.41 E
Thānedārwāla	123	32.36 N	71.07 E
Thānesar	124	29.59 N	76.49 E
Thanet, Isle of I	42	51.22 N	1.20 E
Thanet Lake ⊜	212	44.47 N	77.46 W
Thang Binh	110	15.44 N	108.22 E
Thangoo	162	18.10 S	122.22 E
Thangool	166	24.29 S	150.35 E
Thanh Hoa	110	19.48 N	105.46 E
Thanh My Tay	269c	10.49 N	106.46 E
Thanh Pho Ho Chi Minh (Saigon), Viet.	110	10.45 N	106.40 E
Thanh Pho Ho Chi Minh (Saigon), Viet.	269c	10.45 N	106.40 E
Thanjāvūr	122	10.48 N	79.09 E
Thann	58	47.49 N	7.05 E
Thannhausen	58	48.17 N	10.28 E
Thāno Bula Khān	120	25.22 N	67.50 E
Than Uyen	110	22.00 N	103.54 E
Thaoge ≃	156	20.27 S	22.36 E
Thaon-les-Vosges	58	48.15 N	6.25 E
Tha Pla	110	17.48 N	100.32 E
Thap Than ≃	110	15.21 N	104.06 E
Tharabwin West	110	12.17 N	99.03 E
Tharād	120	24.24 N	71.38 E
Tharandt	54	50.59 N	13.35 E
't Harde	52	52.25 N	5.53 E
Thar Desert (Great Indian Desert) ◆[2]	120	27.00 N	71.00 E
Thargomindah	166	28.00 S	143.49 E
Thāri Pātan ∧	124	28.58 N	82.04 E
Thar Nhom	140	7.26 N	30.29 E
Tharptown	210	40.48 N	76.34 W
Tharr, Wüste → Thar Desert ◆[2]	120	27.00 N	71.00 E
Tharrawaddy	110	17.39 N	95.48 E
Tharrawaw	110	17.41 N	95.28 E
Tharros ⊥	71	39.52 N	8.26 E
Tharsuinn, Beinn ∧	46	57.47 N	4.21 W
Tharthār, Buḩayrat ath- ⊜	128	34.00 N	43.05 E
Tharthār, Wādī ath- V	128	33.59 N	43.12 E
Tharwa	171b	35.31 S	149.04 E
Tha Sala	110	8.40 N	99.56 E
Thásos	38	40.47 N	24.42 E
Thásos I	38	40.41 N	24.47 E
Thásos ⊥	38	40.46 N	24.33 E
Tha Tako	110	15.38 N	100.29 E
Thatcham	42	51.25 N	1.15 W
Thatch Cay I	240m	18.22 N	64.52 W
Thatcher	200	32.50 N	109.45 W
Thatch Island I	276	40.38 N	73.23 W
That Khe	110	22.16 N	106.28 E
Thaton	110	16.55 N	97.22 E
That Phanom	110	16.57 N	104.44 E
Thatto Heath	262	53.26 N	2.45 W
Tha Tum	110	15.19 N	103.41 E
Thau, Bassin de c	32	43.23 N	3.36 E
Thaungdut	110	24.26 N	94.42 E
Thaungyin ≃	110	17.50 N	97.42 E
Tha Uthen	110	17.34 N	104.36 E
Thawville	216	40.41 N	88.07 W
Thaxted	42	51.57 N	0.20 E
Thaya (Dyje) ≃	61	48.37 N	16.56 E
Thayawthadangyi Kyun I	110	12.20 N	98.00 E
Thayer, Il., U.S.	219	39.32 N	89.46 W
Thayer, In., U.S.	216	41.10 N	87.20 W
Thayer, Ks., U.S.	198	37.29 N	95.28 W
Thayer, Mo., U.S.	194	36.31 N	91.32 W
Thayetchaung	110	13.52 N	98.16 E
Thayetmyo	110	19.19 N	95.11 E
Thayngen	58	47.45 N	8.42 E
Thazi	110	20.51 N	96.05 E

The Aldermen Islands II	172	36.58 S	176.05 E
Theale	42	51.27 N	1.04 W
Thealka	192	37.49 N	82.47 W
The Basin	274b	37.51 S	145.19 E
Thebes → Thívai	38	38.21 N	23.19 E
Thebes	194	37.13 N	89.28 W
Thebes ⊥	140	25.42 N	32.37 E
The Bight	238	24.19 N	75.24 W
The Birket ≃	262	53.24 N	3.01 W
The Bluffs ⌓[4]	210	43.22 N	76.40 W
The Bourne ≃	260	51.22 N	0.29 W
The Calvados Chain II	164	11.10 S	152.40 E
The Camels Hump ∧	169	37.23 S	144.35 E
The Capital ᴗ	284c	38.53 N	77.00 W
The Cheviot ∧	44	55.28 N	2.09 W
The Citadel ⊥, Magy.	264c	47.29 N	19.03 E
The Citadel ⊥, Mişr	273c	30.02 N	31.15 E
The Cloisters ᴗ	276	40.52 N	73.56 W
The Colony	222	33.05 N	96.52 W
The Coorong c	168b	35.40 S	139.15 E
The Coteau ⋀[2]	184	51.10 N	107.30 W
The Curragh ♦	48	53.10 N	6.52 W
The Dalles	224	45.35 N	121.10 W
The Dalles Dam ◆[6]	224	45.37 N	121.08 W
The Deeps c	46a	60.09 N	1.23 W
Thedford	198	41.58 N	100.34 W
Thedinghausen	52	52.58 N	9.01 E
The Downs ⊤[3]	42	51.13 N	1.27 E
Theebine	166	25.57 S	152.33 E
The English Companys Islands II	164	11.50 S	136.32 E
The Entrance	170	33.21 S	151.30 E
Theessen	54	52.14 N	12.02 E
The Everglades ⁝	220	26.00 N	80.40 W
The Fens ◆[1]	42	52.38 N	0.02 E
The Fishing Lakes ⊜	184	50.45 N	103.51 W
The Flash ⊜	262	53.29 N	2.33 W
The Flat Tops ⋀	200	40.00 N	107.10 W
The Forest of Nisene Marks State Park ♦	226	37.03 N	121.53 W
The Glenkens ◆[1]	44	55.10 N	4.15 W
Thègon	110	18.39 N	95.25 E
The Granites	162	20.35 S	130.21 E
The Granites ∧	162	20.35 S	130.20 E
The Graves II	283	42.22 N	70.52 W
The Grove	222	31.16 N	97.32 W
The Hague → 's-Gravenhage	52	52.06 N	4.18 E
The Heads ›	202	42.44 N	124.31 W
The Hermitage ᴗ	265a	59.56 N	30.20 E
The Home Park ♦	260	51.28 N	0.36 W
The Hunters Hills ⋀[2]	172	44.30 S	170.50 E
Theinkun	110	11.53 N	99.09 E
The Isles Lagoon c	174o	1.50 N	157.23 W
Theiss → Tisa ≃	38	45.15 N	20.17 E
Theissen	54	51.05 N	12.06 E
The Key Indian Reserve ◆[4]	184	51.45 N	102.08 W
The Lake Fleet Islands II	212	44.18 N	76.07 W
The Lakes National Park ♦	166	38.05 S	147.40 E
The Little Minch ʊ	46	57.35 N	6.55 W
Thelon ≃	176	64.16 N	96.05 W
The Long Mynd ∧	42	52.35 N	2.48 W
The Lower Hope ≃[1]	260	51.28 N	0.28 E
Thelwall	262	53.23 N	2.32 W
The Lynd	166	18.56 S	144.30 E
Them	41	56.06 N	9.33 E
The Machars ◆[1]	44	54.50 N	4.33 W
The Mall in Columbia ◆[9]	284b	39.13 N	76.52 W
Themar	54	50.30 N	10.37 E
The Meadows Race Track ♦	279b	40.13 N	80.12 W
The Mere ⊜	262	53.20 N	2.24 W
Théméricourt	261	49.05 N	1.54 E
The Minch ʊ	46	58.10 N	5.50 W
The Mumbles	42	51.34 N	4.00 W
Then	123	32.26 N	75.44 E
The Narrows ʊ	276	40.37 N	74.03 W
The Navy Islands II	212	44.21 N	76.03 W
The Naze ›	42	51.53 N	1.16 E
The Needles ›	42	50.39 N	1.34 W
Thénezay	32	46.43 N	0.02 W
Thenia	148	36.43 N	3.34 E
Theniet el Hadd	148	35.47 N	2.01 E
The Oa ›[1]	46	55.37 N	6.16 W
The Oaks, Austl.	170	34.04 S	150.34 E
The Oaks, Ca., U.S.	226	39.13 N	121.05 W
Theodore, Austl.	166	24.57 S	150.05 E
Theodore, Sk., Can.	184	51.25 N	102.54 W
Theodore, Al., U.S.	194	30.32 N	88.10 W
Theodore Francis Green Airport ⊠	207	41.44 N	71.26 W
Theodore Roosevelt Inaugural National Historical Site ⊥	284a	42.54 N	78.52 W
Theodore Roosevelt Island I	284c	38.54 N	77.03 W
Theodore Roosevelt Lake ⊜[1]	200	33.42 N	111.07 W
Theodore Roosevelt National Park (North Unit) ♦, N.D., U.S.	198	47.34 N	103.24 W
Theodore Roosevelt National Park (South Unit) ♦, N.D., U.S.	198	46.55 N	103.26 W
Theodor-Heuss-Brücke ◆[5]	263	51.15 N	6.45 E
Theog	123	31.07 N	77.21 E
Theólogos	38	40.39 N	24.41 E
The Orchards	284b	39.18 N	76.50 W
Théoule-sur-Mer	62	43.31 N	6.57 E
The Oval ⊥	260	51.29 N	0.07 W
The Pages II	168b	35.47 S	138.17 E
The Paps ∧	48	52.00 N	9.17 W
The Pas	184	53.50 N	101.15 W
The Peak ∧	192	36.24 N	81.39 W
Thepha	110	6.52 N	100.58 E
The Pinnacle ∧[2]	219	39.22 N	90.55 W
Thérain ≃	50	49.15 N	2.27 E
The Rajah ∧	182	53.15 N	118.31 W
The Rand → Witwatersrant ◆[1]	158	26.00 S	27.00 E
The Range	154	19.00 S	31.04 E
Theresa	212	44.12 N	75.47 W
Theresa Creek ≃	166	23.26 S	148.09 E
Theresa Park	274a	34.01 S	150.39 E
Theresienstadt → Terezín	54	50.31 N	14.08 E
The Rhins ›[1]	44	54.50 N	5.00 W
The Rip c	169	38.17 S	144.37 E
Thermaïkós Kólpos c	38	40.23 N	22.47 E
Thermalito	226	39.31 N	121.36 W
Thermopílai ⊥	38	38.48 N	22.33 E
Thermopolis	200	43.38 N	108.12 W
Thermopylae → Thermopílai ⊥	38	38.48 N	22.33 E
The Road c	42a	49.56 N	6.20 W
The Rock	166	35.16 S	147.07 E
The Rockies ∧	224	46.39 N	122.22 W
Theron Mountains ⋀	9	79.05 S	28.15 W
The Rope ⌓[4]	174e	25.04 S	130.05 W
Thérouanne	50	50.38 N	2.15 E
The Savannahs ⊜	220	27.19 N	80.17 W
Theseion ⊥	267c	37.58 N	23.43 E
Thesiger Bay c	176	71.30 N	124.05 W
The Sisters ∧[2]	162	26.17 S	126.40 E
The Slot → New Georgia Sound ʊ	175e	8.00 S	158.10 E

Symbol	English	Deutsch	Español	Français	Português
≃	River	Fluß	Río	Rivière	Rio
≡	Canal	Kanal	Canal	Canal	Canal
∟	Waterfall, Rapids	Wasserfall, Stromschnellen	Cascada, Rápidos	Chute d'eau, Rapides	Cascata, Rápidos
ʊ	Strait	Meeresstraße	Estrecho	Détroit	Estreito
c	Bay, Gulf	Bucht, Golf	Bahía, Golfo	Baie, Golfe	Baía, Golfo
⊜	Lake, Lakes	See, Seen	Lago, Lagos	Lac, Lacs	Lago, Lagos
⁝	Swamp	Sumpf	Pantano	Marais	Pântano
⊓	Ice Features, Glacier	Eis- und Gletscherformen	Accidentes Glaciales	Formes glaciaires	Acidentes glaciares
⊤	Other Hydrographic Features	Andere Hydrographische Objekte	Otros Elementos Hidrográficos	Autres données hydrographiques	Outros acidentes hidrográficos
✢	Submarine Features	Untermeerische Objekte	Accidentes Submarinos	Formes de relief sous-marin	Acidentes submarinos
□	Political Unit	Politische Einheit	Unidad Politica	Entité politique	Unidade política
ᴗ	Cultural Institution	Kulturelle Institution	Institución Cultural	Institution culturelle	Instituição cultural
⊥	Historical Site	Historische Stätte	Sitio Histórico	Site historique	Sitio histórico
♦	Recreational Site	Erholungs- und Ferienort	Sitio de Recreo	Centre de loisirs	Area de Lazer
⊠	Airport	Flughafen	Aeropuerto	Aéroport	Aeroporto
■	Military Installation	Militäranlage	Instalación Militar	Installation militaire	Instalação militar
◆	Miscellaneous	Verschiedenes	Misceláneo	Divers	Diversos

I · 176 **Thes-Timi**

ENGLISH — Name, Page, Lat.°′, Long.°′ | DEUTSCH — Name, Seite, Breite°′, Länge°′ E = Ost

Name	Page	Lat.°′	Long.°′
The Sluice ≚	262	53.41 N	2.57 W
The Sny ≃	219	39.16 N	90.44 W
The Solent Ц	42	50.46 N	1.20 W
The Sound (Øresund) Ц	41	55.50 N	12.40 E
The Springs	207	40.52 N	72.32 W
Thesprotikón	38	39.15 N	20.47 E
Thessalía □[9]	38	39.30 N	22.00 E
Thessalon	190	46.15 N	83.34 W
Thessaloníki (Salonika)	38	40.38 N	22.56 E
Thessalonique → Thessaloníki	38	40.38 N	22.56 E
The Storr ∧	46	57.31 N	6.12 W
The Swale Ц	42	51.22 N	0.56 E
Thet ≃	42	52.27 N	0.33 E
The Tauride Palace ♜	265a	59.57 N	30.23 E
The Terraces ⊥[4]	162	28.40 S	121.30 E
Thetford	42	52.25 N	0.45 E
Thetford-Mines	206	46.05 N	71.18 W
The Thorofare Ц	208	37.15 N	75.54 W
The Thumbs ∧	172	43.36 S	170.44 E
Thetis Island	224	49.59 N	123.40 W
Thetis Island I	224	49.00 N	123.41 W
The Twelve Pins ∧	48	53.31 N	9.50 W
The Twins ∧	172	41.14 S	172.39 E
Theunissen	158	28.30 S	26.41 E
Theux	56	50.32 N	5.49 E
The Valley	238	18.13 N	63.04 W
Thevenard	162	32.09 S	133.38 E
Thevenard Island I	162	21.27 S	115.00 E
The Wash ⊂	42	52.55 N	0.15 E
The Weald ◆[1]	42	51.05 N	0.05 E
The Whirlpool ≃	284a	43.07 N	79.04 W
The Winehead ∧	210	40.58 N	77.28 W
The Woodlands	222	30.09 N	95.27 W
The Wrekin ∧[2]	42	52.41 N	2.34 W
Theydon Bois	260	51.40 N	0.06 E
Theys	62	45.18 N	6.00 E
Thiais	261	48.46 N	2.23 E
Thiant	50	50.18 N	3.27 E
Thiaucourt-Regniéville	56	48.57 N	5.52 E
Thibaudeau	184	57.05 N	94.08 W
Thiberville	50	49.08 N	0.27 E
Thibodaux	194	29.47 N	90.49 W
Thicket	222	30.24 N	94.38 W
Thicket Portage	184	55.19 N	97.42 W
Thiéblemont-Farémont	58	48.41 N	4.44 E
Thief ≃	198	48.08 N	96.10 W
Thief Lake ⊜	198	48.30 N	95.55 W
Thief River Falls	198	48.07 N	96.10 W
Thiéle ≃	58	47.03 N	7.05 E
Thiel Mountains ⋏	9	85.15 S	91.00 W
Thielsen, Mount ∧	202	43.09 N	122.04 W
Thiendorf	54	51.17 N	13.44 E
Thiene	64	45.42 N	11.29 E
Thiensville	216	43.14 N	87.58 W
Thier	263	51.05 N	7.22 E
Thiérache, Collines de la ⋏[2]	50	49.50 N	3.50 E
Thierhaupten	56	48.34 N	10.54 E
Thiers	62	45.51 N	3.34 E
Thiersheim	54	50.04 N	12.07 E
Thierville-sur-Meuse	56	49.10 N	5.21 E
Thiès	150	14.48 N	16.56 W
Thiès □[4]	150	14.45 N	16.50 W
Thiesi	71	40.31 N	8.43 E
Thiessow	54	54.16 N	13.43 E
Thieux	261	49.01 N	2.40 E
Thieveley Pike ∧[2]	262	53.45 N	2.12 W
Thika	154	1.03 S	37.05 E
Thikombia Island I	175g	15.44 S	179.55 W
Thilay	56	49.52 N	4.49 E
Thilenius, Cape ›	164	1.35 S	149.57 E
Thimphu	124	27.28 N	89.39 E
Thines	62	44.29 N	4.03 E
Thingvallavatn ⊜	24a	64.12 N	21.10 W
Thingvellir	24a	64.17 N	21.07 W
Thingvellir National Park ♦	24a	64.17 N	21.06 W
Thio	175f	21.37 S	166.14 E
Thionville	56	49.22 N	6.10 E
Thiou	150	13.48 N	2.40 W
Thíra	38	36.25 N	25.26 E
Thíra I	38	36.24 N	25.29 E
Third ≃	276	40.49 N	74.08 W
Third Cataract → Thālith, Ash-Shallāl ath- ʟ	140	19.49 N	30.19 E
Third Cliff ⊥[4]	283	42.11 N	70.43 W
Third Creek ≃, Mo., U.S.	219	38.26 N	91.40 W
Third Creek ≃, N.C., U.S.	192	35.47 N	80.31 W
Third Han-gang Bridge ◆[5]	271b	37.32 N	127.00 E
Third Herring Brook ≃	283	42.07 N	70.48 W
Third Lake ⊜	206	45.14 N	71.12 W
Third Street Station ◆[5]	282	37.46 N	122.23 W
Thirlmere	170	34.12 S	150.34 E
Thirlmere ⊜	44	54.33 N	3.04 W
Thirlmere Lakes National Park ♦	170	34.14 S	150.32 E
Thiron	50	48.19 N	0.59 E
Thironne ≃	50	48.17 N	1.15 E
Thirroul	170	34.19 S	150.56 E
Thirsk	44	54.14 N	1.20 W
Thirtieth Street Station ◆[5]	285	39.57 N	75.11 W
Thirtymile Creek ≃	198	46.22 N	102.03 W
Thirtymile Point ›	210	43.22 N	78.29 W
Thiruvārūr	122	10.46 N	79.39 E
Thisted	26	56.57 N	8.42 E
Thistilfjörđur ⊂	24a	66.20 N	15.25 W
Thistledown Race Track ♦	279a	41.26 N	81.32 W
Thistle Island I	166	35.00 S	136.09 E
Thistletown ◆[8]	275b	43.44 N	79.33 W
Thithia Island I	175g	17.45 S	179.18 W
Thívai (Thebes)	38	38.21 N	23.19 E
Thiverval-Grignon	261	48.51 N	1.55 E
Thiviers	32	45.25 N	0.56 E
Thizy	32	46.02 N	4.19 E
Thjórsá ≃	24a	63.47 N	20.48 W
Thlewiaza ≃	176	60.28 N	94.45 W
Thoa ≃	176	60.30 N	109.47 W
Tho Chu, Dao II	110	9.20 N	103.28 E
Thoen	110	17.36 N	99.12 E
Thohoyandou	156	23.00 S	30.29 E
Thoi Binh	110	9.21 N	105.05 E
Thoirette	58	46.16 N	5.32 E
Thoiry	261	48.52 N	1.48 E
Thoissey	58	46.10 N	4.48 E
Tholen	52	51.32 N	4.12 E
Tholen I	52	51.35 N	4.05 E
Tholey	56	49.29 N	7.02 E
Thollon	58	46.23 N	6.43 E
Thomas, Ok., U.S.	196	35.44 N	98.44 W
Thomas, Pa., U.S.	279b	40.15 N	80.06 W
Thomas, Wa., U.S.	224	47.21 N	122.13 W
Thomas, W.V., U.S.	188	39.08 N	79.29 W
Thomasboro	216	40.15 N	88.11 W
Thomas Creek ≃	202	44.40 N	122.56 W
Thomas Hill Reservoir ⊜[1]	194	39.40 N	92.40 W
Thomas J. O'Brien Lock and Dam ◆[5]	278	41.39 N	87.35 W
Thomas Lake ⊜	184	57.00 N	96.43 W
Thomas Mountains ⋏	9	75.32 S	70.57 W
Thomas Point ›	208	38.54 N	76.28 W
Thomaston, Al., U.S.	194	32.15 N	87.37 W
Thomaston, Ct., U.S.	207	41.40 N	73.04 W
Thomaston, Ga., U.S.	192	32.53 N	84.19 W
Thomaston, Me., U.S.	188	44.04 N	69.10 W
Thomaston, N.Y., U.S.	276	40.47 N	73.43 W
Thomaston, Tx., U.S.	222	29.00 N	97.09 W
Thomastown, Austl.	274b	37.41 S	145.01 E
Thomastown, Ire.	48	52.31 N	7.08 W
Thomasville, Al., U.S.	194	31.54 N	87.44 W
Thomasville, Ga., U.S.	192	30.50 N	83.58 W
Thomasville, N.C., U.S.	192	35.52 N	80.04 W
Thomasville, Pa., U.S.	208	39.56 N	76.51 W
Thomes Creek ≃	204	39.59 N	122.06 W
Thom Lake ⊜	184	55.24 N	96.08 W
Thomlinson, Mount ∧	182	55.33 N	127.29 W
Thompson, Mb., Can.	184	55.45 N	97.45 W
Thompson, Ct., U.S.	207	41.57 N	71.51 W
Thompson, Ia., U.S.	190	43.22 N	93.46 W
Thompson, Mo., U.S.	219	39.11 N	91.59 W
Thompson, N.D., U.S.	198	47.46 N	97.06 W
Thompson, Oh., U.S.	214	41.41 N	81.03 W
Thompson, Pa., U.S.	210	41.52 N	75.31 W
Thompson ≃, B.C., Can.	182	50.15 N	121.33 W
Thompson ≃, U.S.	194	39.45 N	93.36 W
Thompson Creek ≃, U.S.	198	45.04 N	104.25 W
Thompson Creek ≃, Ms., U.S.	194	31.10 N	88.54 W
Thompson Falls	202	47.35 N	115.20 W
Thompson Island I	283	42.23 N	71.01 W
Thompson Pass)(	180	61.08 N	145.45 W
Thompson Peak ∧	204	41.00 N	123.03 W
Thompson Place	224	47.03 N	122.45 W
Thompson Ridge	210	41.34 N	74.20 W
Thompson Run ≃	279b	40.24 N	79.50 W
Thompsons	222	29.30 N	95.36 W
Thompsons Creek ≃	284a	43.03 N	79.08 W
Thompson Sound Ц	172	45.09 S	166.57 E
Thompsontown	208	40.33 N	77.14 W
Thompsonville	190	44.31 N	85.56 W
Thomsen ≃	176	74.08 N	119.35 W
Thomson, Ga., U.S.	192	33.28 N	82.30 W
Thomson, Il., U.S.	190	41.58 N	90.06 W
Thomson, N.Y., U.S.	210	43.07 N	73.35 W
Thomson ≃, Austl.	166	25.11 S	142.53 E
Thomson ≃, Austl.	169	37.58 S	146.32 E
Thomson, Lake ⊜[1]	169	37.45 S	146.22 E
Thomson Lake ⊜[1]	184	49.45 N	106.35 W
Thon ≃	50	49.53 N	3.55 E
Thon Buri	110	13.43 N	100.29 E
Thônes	62	45.53 N	6.20 E
Thong	260	51.24 N	0.24 E
Thong Hoe	271c	1.25 N	103.42 E
Thong Tay Hoi	269c	10.50 N	106.39 E
Thongwa	110	16.46 N	96.32 E
Thon Lac Nghiep	110	11.20 N	108.54 E
Thonnance-lès-Joinville	58	48.27 N	5.10 E
Thonon-les-Bains	58	46.22 N	6.29 E
Thonotosassa	220	28.03 N	82.18 W
Thonze	110	17.38 N	95.47 E
Thorah Island I	212	44.27 N	79.14 W
Thorame-Haute	62	44.06 N	6.33 E
Thorburn	186	45.34 N	62.33 W
Thoreau	200	35.24 N	108.13 W
Thorembais-les-Béguines	56	50.40 N	4.49 E
Thorenc	62	43.48 N	6.49 E
Thorens-Glières	58	45.59 N	6.15 E
Thorez → Torez	83	48.01 N	38.37 E
Thorhild	182	54.10 N	113.07 W
Thorial	140	8.40 N	29.56 E
Thorigny-sur-Marne	261	48.53 N	2.42 E
Thorigny-sur-Oreuse	50	48.17 N	3.24 E
Thórisvatn ⊜	24a	64.50 N	19.26 W
Thörl	61	47.31 N	15.13 E
Thorlákshöfn	24a	63.53 N	21.18 W
Thormanby	44	54.10 N	1.14 W
Thorn, Ned.	52	51.10 N	5.50 E
Thorn → Toruń, Pol.	30	53.02 N	18.35 E
Thornaby-on-Tees	44	54.34 N	1.18 W
Thornapple ≃, Mi., U.S.	216	42.56 N	85.28 W
Thornapple ≃, Wi., U.S.	190	45.28 N	91.16 W
Thornapple Lake ⊜	216	42.37 N	85.11 W
Thornburg	279b	40.26 N	80.05 W
Thornbury, Austl.	274b	37.45 S	145.00 E
Thornbury, On., Can.	212	44.34 N	80.26 W
Thornbury, N.Z.	172	46.17 S	168.06 E
Thornbury, Eng., U.K.	42	51.37 N	2.32 W
Thorn Creek ≃	278	41.36 N	87.35 W
Thorndale, On., Can.	212	43.06 N	81.08 W
Thorndale, Tx., U.S.	222	30.36 N	97.12 W
Thorndike	207	42.11 N	72.20 W
Thorndon	42	52.17 N	1.08 E
Thorne	44	53.37 N	0.58 W
Thorne ≃	184	54.56 N	90.35 W
Thorne Bay	182	55.44 N	132.32 W
Thorney	42	52.37 N	0.07 W
Thorngumbald	44	53.43 N	0.10 W
Thornhill, On., Can.	275b	43.48 N	79.25 W
Thornhill, S. Afr.	273d	26.07 S	28.09 E
Thornhill, Scot., U.K.	44	55.15 N	3.46 W
Thornhurst	210	41.11 N	75.35 W
Thornleigh	274a	33.44 S	151.05 E
Thornton, Austl.	171a	27.49 S	152.23 E
Thornton, Eng., U.K.	44	53.53 N	3.02 W
Thornton, Eng., U.K.	262	53.30 N	3.00 W
Thornton, Eng., U.K.	262	53.47 N	1.51 W
Thornton, Scot., U.K.	46	56.10 N	3.09 W
Thornton, Ar., U.S.	194	33.46 N	92.29 W
Thornton, Ca., U.S.	226	38.14 N	121.25 W
Thornton, Co., U.S.	200	39.52 N	104.58 W
Thornton, Il., U.S.	278	41.35 N	87.37 W
Thornton, Pa., U.S.	285	39.54 N	75.32 W
Thornton, Tx., U.S.	222	31.24 N	96.34 W
Thornton Beach ♦	282	37.42 N	122.30 W
Thornton Dale	44	54.14 N	0.43 W
Thornton Hough	262	53.19 N	3.03 W
Thornton-le-Moors	262	53.16 N	2.50 W
Thorntonville	196	31.34 N	102.55 W
Thornwood	210	41.07 N	73.46 W
Thornwood Common	260	51.43 N	0.08 E
Thorny Mountain ∧[2]	194	37.06 N	91.10 W
Thorofare	285	39.50 N	75.11 W
Thorold	212	43.07 N	79.12 W
Thorold South	284a	43.06 N	79.12 W
Thoronet, Abbaye du ♜[1]	62	43.28 N	6.16 E
Thorp, Wa., U.S.	224	47.04 N	120.40 W
Thorp, Wi., U.S.	190	44.57 N	90.47 W
Thorpe	260	51.24 N	0.32 W
Thorpe-le-Soken	42	51.52 N	1.10 E
Thorp Spring	222	32.28 N	97.49 W
Thorsby, Ab., Can.	182	53.14 N	114.03 W
Thorsby, Al., U.S.	194	32.54 N	86.42 W
Thorshavn → Tórshavn	22	62.01 N	6.46 W
Thórshöfn	24a	66.13 N	15.17 W
Thorsø	41	56.18 N	9.48 E
Thorsteinson Lake ⊜	184	57.15 N	97.30 W
Thorton Moor Reservoir ⊜[1]	262	53.47 N	1.55 W
Thot Not	110	10.16 N	105.32 E
Thouars	32	46.59 N	0.13 W
Thouin, Cape ›	162	20.20 S	118.12 E
Thoune → Thun	58	46.45 N	7.37 E
Thourotte	50	49.29 N	2.53 E
Thousand Islands II	212	44.15 N	76.12 W
Thousand Islands International Bridge ◆[5]	212	44.20 N	75.58 W
Thousand Lake Mountain ∧	200	38.25 N	111.29 W
Thousand Oaks	228	34.10 N	118.50 W
Thousand Ships Bay ⊂	175e	8.25 S	159.40 E
Thousand Springs Creek ≃	200	41.17 N	113.51 W
Thowa ≃	154	1.33 S	40.03 E
Thowgla Creek ≃	171b	36.10 S	147.57 E
Thrace □[9]	38	41.20 N	26.45 E
Thrakikón Pélagos ⩡[2]	38	40.15 N	24.28 E
Thrall	222	30.35 N	97.18 W
Thrapston	42	52.24 N	0.32 W
Thrasher Lake ⊜	212	44.55 N	78.58 W
Thread Creek ≃	216	43.01 N	83.42 W
Thredbo Village	171b	36.29 S	148.19 E
Three Bridges	208	40.31 N	74.47 W
Three Brothers ∧	224	47.23 N	120.45 W
Three Brothers Mountain ∧	224	49.10 N	120.46 W
Three Creek ≃	208	36.47 N	77.10 W
Three Fathoms Cove ⊂	271d	22.26 N	114.17 E
Three Fingered Jack ∧	202	44.29 N	121.50 W
Three Fingers ∧	224	48.10 N	121.41 W
Three Fools Creek ≃	224	48.53 N	120.57 W
Three Forks	202	45.53 N	111.33 W
Three Hills	182	51.42 N	113.16 W
Three Hummock Island I	166	40.26 S	144.55 E
Three Kings Islands II	172	34.10 S	172.05 E
Three Lakes	190	45.47 N	89.09 W
Three M Airport ⊠	285	40.08 N	74.51 W
Three Mile Bay	212	44.04 N	76.11 W
Three Mile Plains	186	44.58 N	64.07 W
Three Oaks	216	41.47 N	86.36 W
Three Pagodas Pass)(	110	15.18 N	98.23 E
Threepoint Lake ⊜	184	55.41 N	98.56 W
Three Points, Cape ›	150	4.45 N	2.06 W
Three Rivers, Austl.	162	25.07 S	119.09 E
Three Rivers → Trois-Rivières, P.Q., Can.	206	46.21 N	72.33 W
Three Rivers, Ma., U.S.	207	42.10 N	72.21 W
Three Rivers, Mi., U.S.	216	41.56 N	85.37 W
Three Rivers, Tx., U.S.	196	28.27 N	98.10 W
Three Rivers □[8]	260	51.40 N	0.27 W
Three Sisters	158	31.54 S	23.06 E
Three Sisters ∧	202	44.10 N	121.46 W
Three Sisters Islands II	175e	10.10 S	161.57 E
Three Springs, Austl.	162	29.32 S	115.45 E
Three Springs, Pa., U.S.	214	40.12 N	77.59 W
Threlkeld	44	54.38 N	3.03 W
Throat ≃	184	51.48 N	93.30 W
Throckley	44	54.59 N	1.45 W
Throckmorton	196	33.10 N	99.10 W
Throgs Neck ◆[8]	276	40.49 N	73.49 W
Throgs Neck Bridge ◆[5]	276	40.48 N	73.48 W
Throgs Point ›	276	40.48 N	73.48 W
Throop	210	41.27 N	75.36 W
Throssel, Lake ⊜	162	27.27 S	124.16 E
Throssell Range ⋏	162	22.03 S	121.43 E
Thrushel ≃	42	50.39 N	4.15 W
Thruway Mall ◆[9]	284a	42.55 N	78.46 W
Thu, Cu Lao I	110	10.33 N	108.57 E
Thuan Chau	110	21.26 N	103.41 E
Thu Dau Mot	110	10.58 N	106.39 E
Thu Duc	269c	10.51 N	106.45 E
Thueyts	62	44.41 N	4.13 E
Thuilley-aux-Groseilles	58	48.34 N	5.58 E
Thuin	50	50.20 N	4.17 E
Thul	120	28.14 N	68.46 E
Thulaythiwāt, Tilāl ath- ∧	132	30.58 N	36.40 E
Thulba ≃	56	50.11 N	9.52 E
Thule	16	76.34 N	68.47 W
Thulī Bherī ≃	124	28.42 N	82.16 E
Thum	54	50.40 N	12.57 E
Thumb Peak ∧	116	9.48 N	118.36 E
Thumby	41	54.35 N	9.54 E
Thun	58	46.45 N	7.37 E
Thun Chang	110	19.25 N	100.53 E
Thunder Bay	190	48.23 N	89.15 W
Thunder Bay ⊂, On., Can.	190	48.24 N	89.00 W
Thunder Bay ⊂, On., Can.	212	44.48 N	80.03 W
Thunder Bay ⊂, Mi., U.S.	190	45.00 N	83.22 W
Thunder Bay ≃	190	45.04 N	83.25 W
Thunder Bay, North Branch ≃	190	45.08 N	83.35 W
Thunderbird, Lake ⊜[1]	196	35.15 N	97.20 W
Thunderbolt	192	32.02 N	81.03 W
Thunder Butte ∧	198	45.19 N	101.53 W
Thunder Butte Creek ≃	198	45.13 N	101.42 W
Thunder Creek ≃, Sk., Can.	184	50.23 N	105.32 W
Thunder Creek ≃, Wa., U.S.	224	48.40 N	121.05 W
Thunder Hills ⋏[2]	184	54.30 N	106.00 W
Thunder Mountain ∧[2]	216	42.16 N	86.20 W
Thundersley	260	51.34 N	0.35 E
Thunersee ⊜	58	46.40 N	7.45 E
Thüngen	56	49.56 N	9.51 E
Thung Song	110	8.09 N	99.41 E
Thung Wa	110	7.06 N	99.46 E
Thur ≃, Fr.	58	48.05 N	7.23 E
Thur ≃, Schw.	58	47.36 N	8.35 E
Thurcroft	44	53.24 N	1.16 W
Thurgau □[3]	58	47.35 N	9.00 E
Thurgovie → Thurgau □[3]	58	47.35 N	9.00 E
Thüringen	58	47.12 N	9.45 E
Thüringen □[9]	54	51.00 N	11.00 E
Thüringer Wald ⋏	30	50.40 N	10.50 E
Thürkow	54	53.50 N	12.33 E
Thurles	48	52.41 N	7.49 W
Thurmont	208	39.37 N	77.24 W
Thurn, Pass)(	64	47.19 N	12.24 E
Thurnau	60	50.01 N	11.23 E
Thurnham	260	51.17 N	0.36 E
Thurnscoe	44	53.31 N	1.19 W
Thurnwald Range ⋏	164	4.45 S	141.15 E
Thurø	41	55.03 N	10.40 E
Thurrock □[8]	260	51.30 N	0.21 E
Thursby	44	54.51 N	3.03 W
Thursday Island	164	10.35 S	142.13 E
Thurso, P.Q., Can.	206	45.36 N	75.15 W
Thurso, Scot., U.K.	46	58.35 N	3.32 W
Thurso ≃	46	58.36 N	3.30 W
Thurstaston	262	53.21 N	3.08 W
Thurston	42	52.15 N	0.49 E
Thurston □[6]	224	46.59 N	122.42 W
Thurston Island I	9	72.20 S	99.00 W
Thusis	58	46.42 N	9.26 E
Thwaites Ice Tongue ⌂	9	74.45 S	106.30 W
Thy ◆[1]	26	57.00 N	8.30 E
Thyborøn	26	56.42 N	8.13 E
Thylungra	166	26.04 S	143.28 E
Thyolo	154	16.10 S	35.10 E
Thyregod	41	55.54 N	9.16 E
Thysville → Mbanza-Ngungu	152	5.15 S	14.52 E
Tiadiaye	150	14.25 N	16.42 W
Tiahuanacu	248	16.33 S	68.42 W
Tía Juana	246	10.16 N	71.22 W
Tian ≃	105	40.42 N	116.33 E
Tiana, Esp.	266d	44.29 N	2.16 E
Tiana, It.	71	40.04 N	9.08 E
Tian'anmen Square ⊥	271a	39.55 N	116.23 E
Tianbao	100	24.36 N	117.35 E
Tianchang	100	32.41 N	119.01 E
Tiancunpu	105	39.06 N	115.41 E
Tiandeng	102	23.09 N	107.10 E
Tiandong	102	23.36 N	107.08 E
Tian'e	102	25.01 N	107.20 E
Tianeti	84	42.07 N	44.59 E
Tianfanjie	100	29.20 N	116.50 E
Tiangang, Zhg.	89	43.24 N	125.54 E
Tiangang, Zhg.	89	43.55 N	127.00 E
Tiangongsi	105	39.14 N	115.53 E
Tianguá	250	3.44 S	40.59 W
Tianhe	100	27.01 N	114.30 E
Tianhekou	100	32.08 N	113.25 E
Tianhelong	89	43.56 N	120.39 E
Tianhuang	98	35.29 N	117.18 E
Tianjara, Mount ∧	170	35.11 S	150.18 E
Tianjia, Zhg.	104	41.07 N	122.03 E
Tianjia, Zhg.	107	29.40 N	105.08 E
Tianjiaba	102	32.08 N	110.03 E
Tianjiatun	104	41.39 N	123.44 E
Tianjiawopu	104	42.28 N	122.38 E
Tianjiazhen	100	29.56 N	115.26 E
Tianjin (Tientsin)	105	39.08 N	117.12 E
Tianjing	106	31.27 N	120.46 E
Tianjin Shi (Tientsin Shih) □[7]	98	39.30 N	117.15 E
Tianjun	102	37.25 N	98.58 E
Tiankai	105	39.38 N	115.51 E
Tiankoura	150	10.46 N	3.16 W
Tiankoye	150	12.35 N	12.40 W
Tianlin, Zhg.	102	24.14 N	106.03 E
Tianlin, Zhg.	107	29.49 N	105.19 E
Tian Ling ∧	89	44.22 N	129.52 E
Tianmashan	106	31.04 N	121.08 E
Tianmen	100	30.39 N	113.06 E
Tianmu Shan ⋏	100	30.25 N	119.30 E
Tianpu	106	31.56 N	121.07 E
Tianqiaochang	104	40.52 N	121.02 E
Tianqiaoling	89	43.26 N	129.38 E
Tianquan	102	30.10 N	102.48 E
Tian Shan → Tien Shan ⋏	90	42.00 N	80.00 E
Tianshenggang	106	32.03 N	120.45 E
Tianshifu	98	41.17 N	124.21 E
Tianshui	102	34.30 N	105.58 E
Tianshuijing, Zhg.	102	40.17 N	95.21 E
Tianshuijing, Zhg.	104	41.19 N	121.48 E
Tianshuituo	105	39.20 N	118.12 E
Tianshuizhan	104	41.00 N	123.34 E
Tiantai	100	29.09 N	121.02 E
Tiantang	102	22.32 N	111.55 E
Tiantou, Zhg.	100	28.48 N	120.39 E
Tiantou, Zhg.	100	26.19 N	115.57 E
Tianwangsi	106	31.45 N	119.12 E
Tianxin, Zhg.	100	27.53 N	113.06 E
Tianxin, Zhg.	100	28.11 N	114.35 E
Tianxin, Zhg.	102	27.21 N	111.00 E
Tianxingqiao	106	32.05 N	119.57 E
Tianxiyang	100	26.31 N	118.33 E
Tianyang	102	23.51 N	106.34 E
Tianyangping	107	29.11 N	105.16 E
Tianyar	115b	8.12 S	115.30 E
Tianzhen	98	40.28 N	114.06 E
Tianzhongying	100	33.13 N	115.22 E
Tianzhu, Zhg.	102	37.14 N	102.59 E
Tianzhu, Zhg.	102	26.50 N	109.00 E
Tianzhuang, Zhg.	100	25.43 N	113.40 E
Tianzhuang, Zhg.	105	39.25 N	117.54 E
Tianzhuangtai	104	40.50 N	122.08 E
Tiao ≃	106	30.56 N	120.11 E
Tiaodengchang	107	30.47 N	106.22 E
Tiarel	174s	17.32 S	149.20 W
Tiarno	64	45.53 N	10.40 E
Tiaro	166	25.44 S	152.35 E
Tiassalé	150	5.54 N	4.50 W
Tiati ∧	154	1.19 N	35.56 E
Ti'avea	175a	13.57 S	171.24 W
Tiawichi Creek ≃	222	32.19 N	94.44 W
Tiba → Chiba	94	35.36 N	140.07 E
Tibagi	252	24.30 S	50.24 W
Tibaji ≃	252	22.47 S	51.01 W
Tibari	154	5.01 N	31.43 E
Tibasti, Sarīr ◆[2]	146	24.00 N	17.00 E
Tibati	152	6.27 N	12.38 E
Tibbermore	46	56.22 N	3.32 W
Tibbie	194	31.21 N	88.14 W
Tibe	144	9.03 N	37.08 E
Tibel'ti	88	51.46 N	103.11 E
Tiber → Tevere ≃	66	41.44 N	12.14 E
Tiberias → Teverya	132	32.47 N	35.32 E
Tiberias, Lake → Kinneret, Yam ⊜	132	32.48 N	35.35 E
Tiberina, Val V	66	43.31 N	12.10 E
Tibesti ⋏	146	21.30 N	17.30 E
Tibet → Xizang Zizhiqu □[4]	90	32.00 N	88.00 E
Tibet, Lake ⊜	220	28.27 N	81.31 W
Tibet, Plateau of → Qing Zang Gaoyuan ⋏[1]	12	33.00 N	92.00 E
Tibiao	116	11.17 N	122.02 E
Tibiao Point ›	116	11.18 N	122.02 E
Tibidabo ∧	266d	41.25 N	2.07 E
Tibiri, Niger	150	13.34 N	7.04 E
Tibiri, Niger	150	13.06 N	4.00 E
Tibiriçá ≃	255	21.43 S	50.15 W
Tibirke	41	56.03 N	12.07 E
Tiblawan	116	6.29 N	126.06 E
Tiblemont, Lac ⊜	190	48.14 N	77.18 W
Tibnah	132	32.59 N	36.13 E
Tibnīn	132	33.12 N	35.25 E
Tibooburra	166	29.26 S	142.01 E
Tibro	26	58.26 N	14.10 E
Tiburon	226	37.52 N	122.27 W
Tiburón, Cabo ›	246	8.42 N	77.24 W
Tiburón, Isla I	232	29.00 N	112.23 W
Tiburon Peninsula ›[1]	282	37.53 N	122.28 W
Tiča, jazovir ⊜[1]	38	43.05 N	26.45 E
Ticao Island I	116	12.31 N	123.42 E
Ticao Pass Ц	116	12.38 N	123.47 E
Tice	220	26.40 N	81.48 W
Tice Creek ≃	282	37.53 N	122.03 W
Ticehurst	42	51.03 N	0.25 E
Tichigan	216	42.50 N	88.12 W
Tichigan Lake ⊜	216	42.49 N	88.13 W
Tîchît	150	18.28 N	9.30 W
Tîchît, Ḍahr ⊥[4]	150	18.30 N	9.25 W
Tichmenevo, S.S.S.R.	76	58.00 N	38.36 E
Tichmenevo, S.S.S.R.	89	49.12 N	142.54 E
Ticho	144	7.50 N	39.32 E
Tichon	24	59.23 N	46.38 E
Tichonova Pustyn'	82	54.38 N	36.09 E
Tichonoviči	78	51.56 N	32.09 E
Tichonovka	88	53.13 N	104.13 E
Tichookeanskij	89	43.00 N	132.24 E
Tichoreck	78	45.51 N	40.09 E
Tichtozero	24	65.35 N	30.27 E
Tichvin	76	59.39 N	33.31 E
Tichvinskaja gr'ada ∧	76	59.30 N	34.30 E
Ticino □[3]	58	46.20 N	8.45 E
Ticino ≃	36	45.09 N	9.14 E
Tickfaw	194	30.34 N	90.28 W
Tickfaw ≃	194	30.20 N	90.28 W
Tickhill	44	53.26 N	1.06 W
Ticomán ◆[8]	286a	19.31 N	99.08 W
Ticonderoga	188	43.50 N	73.25 W
Ticul	232	20.24 N	89.32 W
Tīdah	142	31.15 N	30.50 E
Tidaholm	26	58.11 N	13.57 E
Tidan ≃	40	58.42 N	13.58 E
Tiddim	110	23.23 N	93.39 E
Tide Lake ⊜	184	50.33 N	111.20 W
Tideswell	44	53.16 N	1.46 W
Tidewater	208	37.51 N	76.42 W
Tidewater ◆[1]	208	37.45 N	77.00 W
Tidikelt ≚	148	26.54 N	1.20 E
Tidioute	214	41.41 N	79.24 W
Tidirhine, Jebel ∧	148	34.50 N	4.30 W
Tidjidit, Erg ◆[2]	148	23.30 N	1.00 E
Tidjikja	150	18.33 N	11.25 W
Tidö	40	59.30 N	16.28 E
Tidone ≃	62	45.04 N	9.32 E
Tidore	108	0.40 N	127.26 E
Tiébissou	150	7.10 N	5.13 W
Tiechang, Zhg.	98	41.44 N	126.11 E
Tiechang, Zhg.	100	24.10 N	115.30 E
Tiechang, Zhg.	102	26.34 N	103.58 E
Tiechang, Zhg.	105	40.04 N	118.12 E
Tiechangpu	107	29.29 N	104.20 E
Tiefenbach	60	49.26 N	12.35 E
Tiefenbroich	263	51.18 N	6.49 E
Tiefencastel	58	46.40 N	9.35 E
Tiefensee	54	52.41 N	13.50 E
Tiefo	107	29.45 N	104.33 E
Tiegenhof → Nowy Dwór Gdański	30	54.13 N	19.06 E
T'iehling → Tieling	104	42.18 N	123.49 E
Tiekou	98	37.16 N	121.13 E
Tiel	52	51.54 N	5.25 E
Tieli	89	46.59 N	128.02 E
Tieling	104	42.18 N	123.49 E
Tielt	50	51.00 N	3.19 E
Tieluotou	100	27.49 N	115.48 E
Tiémé	150	9.33 N	7.19 W
T'ienching → Tianjin	105	39.08 N	117.12 E
T'ienchung	100	23.52 N	120.35 E
Tienen	56	50.48 N	4.57 E
Tiengen	58	47.38 N	8.16 E
Tiénigboué	150	8.11 N	5.43 W
Tienko	150	10.14 N	7.29 W
Tien Shan ⋏	90	42.00 N	80.00 E
T'ienshui → Tianshui	102	34.30 N	105.58 E
Tientsin → Tianjin	105	39.08 N	117.12 E
Tien Yen	110	21.20 N	107.24 E
Tiepido ≃	64	44.30 N	10.59 E
Tie Plant	194	33.44 N	89.47 W
Tierga	34	41.37 N	1.36 W
Tiergarten ◆[8]	264a	52.31 N	13.21 E
Tiergarten ♦	264a	52.31 N	13.21 E
Tieroko, Tarso ∧	146	20.45 N	17.52 E
Tierp	40	60.20 N	17.30 E
Tierpark ♦	264a	52.30 N	13.32 E
Tierra Amarilla, Chile	252	27.29 S	70.17 W
Tierra Amarilla, N.M., U.S.	200	36.42 N	106.32 W
Tierra Blanca, Méx.	196	27.12 N	104.53 W
Tierra Blanca, Méx.	234	18.25 N	96.20 W
Tierra Blanca ≃	234	21.02 N	99.50 W
Tierra Blanca Creek ≃	196	34.58 N	101.55 W
Tierra Buena	226	39.09 N	121.40 W
Tierra Colorada, Méx.	234	17.56 N	92.39 W
Tierra Colorada, Méx.	234	17.10 N	99.35 W
Tierra Colorada, Bajo de la ≚[1]	254	42.52 S	66.48 W
Tierra de Campos ◆[1]	34	42.10 N	4.50 W
Tierra del Fuego □[8]	254	54.00 S	67.00 W
Tierra del Fuego, Isla Grande de I	254	54.00 S	69.00 W
Tierra del Fuego, Parque Nacional ♦	254	54.39 S	68.30 W
Tierra del Norte → Severnaja Zeml'a II	74	79.30 N	98.00 E
Tierralta	246	8.11 N	76.04 W
Tierra Nueva	234	17.47 N	93.28 W
Tierra Redonda Mountain ∧	226	35.47 N	120.59 W
Tierras Australes y Antárticas Francesas → French Southern and Antarctic Territories □[2]	6	49.30 S	69.30 E
Tierras Coloradas	234	22.24 N	104.35 W
Tieshan	100	30.14 N	114.52 E
Tieshanguan	100	23.30 N	113.54 E
Tiétar ≃	34	39.50 N	6.01 W
Tietê	255	23.07 S	47.43 W
Tietê ≃	255	20.40 S	51.35 W
Tiéti	175f	20.57 S	165.19 E
Tieton	224	46.42 N	120.45 W
Tieton ≃	224	46.45 N	120.45 W
Tieton, South Fork ≃	224	46.38 N	121.08 W
Tietzow	264a	52.43 N	12.56 E
Tif	148	27.00 N	1.37 E
Tiffany Mountain ∧	202	48.40 N	119.56 W
Tiffin	214	41.07 N	83.11 W
Tiffin ≃	216	41.17 N	84.23 W
Tiflis → Tbilisi	84	41.43 N	44.49 E
Tifton	192	31.27 N	83.30 W
Tiftona	192	35.05 N	85.10 W
Tiga, Île I	175f	21.07 S	167.49 E
Tiga, Pulau I	112	5.43 N	115.39 E
Tigalda Island I	180	54.05 N	165.05 W
Tigapuluh, Pegunungan ⋏	112	1.05 S	102.30 E
Tigard	224	45.25 N	122.46 W
Tigasaki → Chigasaki	94	35.19 N	139.24 E
Tigbauan	116	10.41 N	122.22 E
Tigeaux	261	48.50 N	2.54 E
Tiger Lake ⊜	220	27.53 N	81.22 W
Tiger Stadium ♦	281	42.20 N	83.04 W
Tigery	261	48.38 N	2.31 E
Tighennif	148	35.20 N	0.21 E
Tighvein ∧[2]	46	55.30 N	5.10 W
Tigil'	74	57.48 N	158.40 E
Tiglid	148	28.31 N	10.15 W
Tiglione ≃	62	44.48 N	8.27 E
Tignale	64	45.44 N	10.44 E
Tignall	192	33.52 N	82.44 W
Tignère	152	7.22 N	12.39 E
Tignes	62	45.30 N	6.55 E
Tignish	186	46.57 N	64.02 W
Tignousti, Jebel ∧	148	31.31 N	6.44 W
Tigoda ≃	76	59.22 N	31.54 E
Tigray □[4]	144	13.40 N	40.00 E
Tigre	258	34.25 S	58.34 W
Tigre □[5]	288	34.24 S	58.37 W
Tigre ∧	234	19.53 N	102.59 W
Tigre ≃, Arg.	288	34.25 S	58.35 W
Tigre → Tigris ≃, Asia	128	31.00 N	47.25 E
Tigre ≃, Méx.	234	22.43 N	97.51 W
Tigre ≃, Perú	246	4.26 S	74.05 W
Tigre ≃, Ven.	246	9.20 N	62.30 W
Tigre, Cerro ∧	236	8.31 N	83.28 W
Tigre, Isla del I	258	34.47 S	56.23 W
Tigre, Punta del ›	258	34.46 S	56.33 W
Tigres, Baía dos ⊂	152	16.38 S	11.46 E
Tigris (Dicle) (Dijlah) ≃	128	31.00 N	47.25 E
Tiguabos	240p	20.14 N	75.21 W
Tiguentourine	148	27.50 N	9.18 E
Tiguesmat ⋏[2]	148	24.54 N	8.14 W
Tigy	50	47.48 N	2.12 E
Tigyaing	110	23.46 N	96.08 E
Tigzert, Oued V	148	28.20 N	9.35 W
Tigzirt	34	36.54 N	4.08 E
Tīh, Jabal at- ⋏[1]	140	29.30 N	34.00 E
Tihāmah ≚	128	26.00 N	36.30 E
Tihany ⊥	30	46.54 N	17.53 E
Tihert	148	35.28 N	1.21 E
Tihert □[5]	148	35.00 N	1.45 E
Tiḥnāwī, Wādī aṭ- V	142	28.11 N	30.46 E
Tihua → Ürümqi	86	43.48 N	87.35 E
Tihuatlán	234	20.43 N	97.32 W
Tiilikkajärven kansallispuisto ♦	26	63.38 N	28.20 E
Tijamuchi ≃	248	14.10 S	64.58 W
Tijesno	36	43.48 N	15.39 E
Tījī	146	32.01 N	11.22 E
Tijuana	232	32.32 N	117.01 W
Tijuana ≃	204	32.33 N	117.07 W
Tijuca ◆[8]	287a	22.56 S	43.14 W
Tijuca, Barra da Ц	287a	23.01 S	43.18 W
Tijuca, Floresta da ♦	287a	22.56 S	43.17 W
Tijuca, Lagoa da ⊂	287a	22.59 S	43.20 W
Tijuca, Pico da ∧	287a	22.56 S	43.17 W
Tijucas	252	27.14 S	48.38 W
Tijucas do Sul	252	25.55 S	49.12 W
Tijuco ≃	255	18.40 S	50.05 W
Tijuco Prêto	256	22.56 S	46.40 W
Tikal ⊥	232	17.20 N	89.39 W
Tikamgarh	124	24.44 N	78.50 E
Tikaré	150	13.17 N	1.43 W
Tikchik Lakes ⊜	180	60.07 N	158.35 W
Tikei, Île I	14	14.58 S	144.32 W
Tikhand ◆[8]	272a	28.31 N	77.17 E
Tikhoretsk → Tichoreck	78	45.51 N	40.09 E
Tikitiki	172	37.48 S	178.24 E
Tiko	152	4.05 N	9.22 E
Tikokino	172	39.49 S	176.27 E
Tikrīt	128	34.36 N	43.42 E
Tikša	24	64.07 N	32.27 E
Tikšeozero, ozero ⊜	24	66.16 N	31.53 E
Tiksi	74	71.36 N	128.48 E
Tiku	112	0.24 S	99.56 E
Til	130	38.44 N	41.49 E
Tiladummati Atoll I[1]	122	6.50 N	73.05 E
Tilamuta	112	0.30 N	122.20 E
Tilape ≃	234	18.06 N	94.31 W
Tilarán	236	10.28 N	84.59 W
Tilbalakan, Laguna ⊂	236	15.30 N	84.17 W
Tilbānah	142	30.59 N	31.27 E
Tilburg	52	51.34 N	5.05 E
Tilbury, On., Can.	214	42.16 N	82.26 W
Tilbury, Eng., U.K.	42	51.28 N	0.23 E
Tilcara	252	23.34 S	65.22 W
Tilcha	166	29.36 S	140.54 E
Til-Châtel	58	47.31 N	5.10 E
Tilden, Il., U.S.	219	38.12 N	89.40 W
Tilden, Ne., U.S.	198	42.02 N	97.50 W
Tilden, Tx., U.S.	196	28.28 N	98.33 W
Tilden Lake ⊜	226	38.07 N	119.36 W
Tilden Woods	284c	39.03 N	77.09 W
Tilemsès	150	15.37 N	4.44 E
Tilemsi, Vallée du V	150	16.15 N	0.02 E
Tilff	56	50.34 N	5.35 E
Tilghman Island I	208	38.42 N	76.20 W
Tilhar	124	27.59 N	79.44 E
Tilia, Oued V	148	27.27 N	0.01 W
Tiligul ≃	78	47.04 N	30.57 E
Tiligulo-Berezanka	78	46.52 N	31.24 E
Tiligul'skij liman ⊜	78	46.48 N	31.08 E
Tiliktino	82	56.06 N	36.36 E
Tilimsen	148	34.52 N	1.15 W
Tilimsen □[5]	148	35.00 N	2.00 W
Tilin	110	21.42 N	94.04 E
Tilisarao	252	32.44 S	65.18 W
Till ≃, Eng., U.K.	44	53.16 N	0.37 W
Till ≃, Eng., U.K.	44	55.41 N	2.12 W
Tillaberi	150	14.13 N	1.27 E
Tillamook	202	45.27 N	123.50 W
Tillamook □[6]	224	45.25 N	123.39 W
Tillamook ≃	224	45.28 N	123.53 W
Tillamook Bay ⊂	224	45.30 N	123.53 W
Tillamook Head ›	224	45.57 N	124.00 W
Tillanchāng Dwīp I	110	8.30 N	93.37 E
Tillberga	40	59.41 N	16.37 E
Tille ≃	58	47.07 N	5.21 E
Tillery, Lake ⊜[1]	192	35.17 N	80.05 W
Tilley	182	50.27 N	111.39 W
Tilli	126	23.57 N	89.57 E
Tillia	150	16.08 N	4.47 E
Tillicoultry	46	56.09 N	3.45 W
Tillicum	224	47.08 N	122.33 W
Tillières-sur-Avre	50	48.46 N	1.04 E
Tilling Bourne ≃	260	51.13 N	0.34 W
Tillmans Corner	194	30.43 N	88.05 W
Tillson	210	41.49 N	74.04 W
Tillsonburg	212	42.51 N	80.44 W
Tillyfourie	46	57.11 N	2.35 W
Tilogne	150	15.58 N	13.36 W
Tilomar	112	9.21 S	125.08 E
Tílos I	38	36.25 N	27.25 E
Tilpa	166	30.57 S	144.24 E
Tilrhemt	148	33.10 N	3.21 E
Tilsit → Sovetsk	76	55.05 N	21.53 E
Tilt ≃	46	56.46 N	3.50 W
Tilton, Il., U.S.	194	40.05 N	87.38 W
Tilton, Ky., U.S.	218	38.22 N	83.45 W
Tilton, N.H., U.S.	188	43.26 N	71.35 W
Tilton ≃	224	46.33 N	122.33 W
Tiltonsville	214	40.10 N	80.41 W
Tilzapotla	234	18.29 N	99.16 W
Tim	78	51.37 N	37.07 E
Tim ≃	76	52.15 N	37.22 E
Timā	140	26.54 N	31.26 E
Timah, Bukit ∧[2]	271c	1.21 N	103.47 E
Timahoe	48	53.20 N	6.49 W
Timaná	246	1.58 N	75.56 W
Timane ≃	248	20.34 S	59.15 W
Timanskij kr'až ∧	24	65.00 N	51.00 E
Timar	84	38.49 N	43.27 E
Timaricha	80	57.33 N	44.47 E
Timaru	172	44.24 S	171.15 E
Timaševo, S.S.S.R.	80	53.21 N	51.12 E
Timaševo, S.S.S.R.	82	55.08 N	36.29 E
Timaševsk	78	45.37 N	38.57 E
Timau, It.	64	46.35 N	13.00 E
Timau, Kenya	154	0.05 N	37.14 E
Timavo San Giovanni	64	45.48 N	13.37 E
Timay al-Amdīd	142	30.57 N	31.32 E
Timbákion	38	35.04 N	24.46 E
Timbalier Bay ⊂	194	29.10 N	90.20 W
Timbaúba	250	7.31 S	35.19 W
Timbavati Game Reserve ◆[4]	156	24.27 S	31.27 E
Timbedgha	150	16.15 N	8.10 W
Timber	224	45.43 N	123.17 W
Timber Creek	164	15.39 S	130.29 E
Timber Creek ≃	198	44.49 N	98.17 W
Timber Lake, Il., U.S.	278	42.14 N	88.07 W
Timberlake, Oh., U.S.	214	41.41 N	81.25 W
Timber Lake, S.D., U.S.	198	45.26 N	101.04 W
Timber Run ≃	284b	39.27 N	76.52 W
Timber Trails	278	41.52 N	87.57 W
Timberview	284b	39.13 N	76.45 W
Timbío	246	2.20 N	76.40 W
Timbira ≃	287a	22.41 S	43.13 W
Timbiras	250	4.15 S	43.57 W
Timblin	214	40.58 N	79.12 W
Timbó, Bra.	252	26.50 S	49.18 W
Timbo, Guinée	150	10.38 N	11.50 W
Timbo, Liber.	150	5.37 N	9.43 W
Timbó ≃	287a	22.52 S	43.16 W
Timboon	169	38.29 S	142.59 E
Timbuctoo	285	40.00 N	74.49 W
Timbuktu → Tombouctou	150	16.46 N	3.01 W
Timbun Mata, Pulau I	112	4.39 N	118.28 E
Timel'ga	86	58.53 N	76.42 E
Timelkam	60	48.00 N	13.36 E
Times Square ♦	276	40.45 N	74.00 W
Timétrine	150	19.27 N	0.26 W
Timétrine ⋏	150	19.20 N	0.42 W
Timeu Creek ≃	182	54.28 N	114.27 W
Timewell	219	40.00 N	90.52 W
Timgad ⊥	148	35.29 N	6.28 E
Timilpan	234	19.52 N	99.45 W
Timimoun	148	29.14 N	0.16 E
Timimoun, Sebkha de ⊜	148	29.00 N	0.05 E
Timinar	140	19.02 N	30.29 E

Symbols in the index entries represent the broad categories identified in the key at the right. Symbols with superior numbers (⋏[1]) identify subcategories (see complete key on page *I · 1).*

Symbole im Register stellen die rechts im Schlüssel erklärten Kategorien dar. Symbole mit hochgestellten Ziffern (⋏[1]) bezeichnen Unterabteilungen einer Kategorie (vgl. vollständiger Schlüssel auf Seite *I · 1).*

Los símbolos incluídos en el texto del índice representan las grandes categorías identificadas con la clave a la derecha. Los símbolos con numeros en su parte superior (⋏[1]) identifican las subcategorías (véase la clave completa en la página *I · 1).*

Les symboles de l'index représentent les catégories indiquées dans la légende à droite. Les symboles suivis d'un indice (⋏[1]) représentent des sous-catégories (voir légende complète à la page *I · 1).*

Os símbolos incluídos no texto do índice representam as grandes categorias identificadas com a chave à direita. Os símbolos com números em sua parte superior (⋏[1]) identificam as subcategorias (veja-se a chave completa à página *I · 1).*

∧ Mountain	Berg	Montaña	Montagne	Montanha
⋏ Mountains	Gebirge	Montañas	Montagnes	Montanhas
)(Pass	Paß	Paso	Col	Passo
V Valley, Canyon	Tal, Cañon	Valle, Cañón	Vallée, Canyon	Vale, Canhão
≚ Plain	Ebene	Llano	Plaine	Planície
› Cape	Kap	Cabo	Cap	Cabo
I Island	Insel	Isla	Île	Ilha
II Islands	Inseln	Islas	Îles	Ilhas
⊥ Other Topographic Features	Andere Topographische Objekte	Otros Elementos Topográficos	Autres données topographiques	Outros acidentes topográficos

ESPAÑOL Nombre	Página	Lat.	Long. W=Oeste
FRANÇAIS Nom	Page	Lat.	Long. W=Ouest
PORTUGUÊS Nome	Página	Lat.	Long. W=Oeste

Column 1 (ESPAÑOL)

Nombre	Página	Lat.	Long.
Timi Ouli, Ehi ▲	146	21.08 N	16.31 E
Timir'azevo	76	55.05 N	21.37 E
Timir'azevskij	86	56.29 N	84.54 E
Timirevo	82	55.08 N	39.10 E
Timirist, Rås ⏵	150	19.23 N	16.32 W
Timiş □⁶	38	44.51 N	21.20 E
Timiş (Tamiš) ≃	38	44.51 N	20.39 E
Timiskaming, Lake ◎	190	47.10 N	79.25 W
Timişoara	38	45.45 N	21.13 E
Timkoviči	76	53.03 N	27.00 E
Timkovo	82	55.56 N	38.37 E
Timmendorfer Strand	54	54.00 N	10.46 E
Timmernabben	26	56.58 N	16.26 E
Timmins	190	48.28 N	81.20 W
Timmonsville	192	34.08 N	79.56 W
Timms Hill ▲²	190	45.27 N	90.11 W
Timok ≃	38	44.13 N	22.40 E
Timon	250	5.06 S	42.49 W
Timonovo	82	56.13 N	37.02 E
Timor I	112	9.00 S	125.00 E
Timor Sea ▽²	112	11.00 S	128.00 E
Timor Timur □⁴	112	8.35 S	126.00 E
Timor Trough ⬥¹	14	9.50 S	126.00 E
Timošino, S.S.S.R.	76	60.05 N	36.10 E
Timošino, S.S.S.R.	30	57.50 N	44.25 E
Timotes	246	8.59 N	70.44 W
Timothy Lake ◎¹	224	45.07 N	121.47 W
Timoudi	148	29.19 N	1.09 W
Timousserarène ≃	150	16.21 N	8.07 E
Timpanogos Cave National Monument ⬥	200	40.18 N	111.52 W
Timpas Creek ≃	198	38.02 N	103.38 W
Timpaus, Pulau I	112	1.51 S	124.01 E
Timperley	262	53.24 N	2.19 W
Timpia ≃	248	11.35 S	72.58 W
Timpson	194	31.54 N	94.23 W
Timpton ≃	74	58.43 N	127.12 E
Timra	26	62.31 N	17.22 E
Timsâh, Buhayrat at- (Lake Timsah) ◎	142	30.34 N	32.17 E
Timsah, Lake → Timsâh, Buhayrat at- ◎	142	30.34 N	32.17 E
Timšer	24	62.06 N	54.40 E
Tims Ford Lake ◎¹	194	35.15 N	86.10 W
Timur	85	42.50 N	68.26 E
Timur, Banjaran ⋌	114	5.00 N	102.30 E
Timurni	124	22.22 N	77.22 E
Tin, Ra's at- ⏵	146	32.37 N	23.08 E
Tina ≃	158	31.18 S	29.14 E
Tina Point ⏵	146	5.33 N	125.20 E
Tinaco	246	9.42 N	68.26 W
Tinaga Island I	116	14.28 N	122.56 E
Tinah, Khalij at- ⊂	140	31.08 N	32.40 E
Tinahely	48	52.48 N	6.28 W
Tinaja, Punta ⏵	248	16.14 S	73.39 W
Tinajas, Cerro de las ▲	232	29.57 N	112.12 W
Tinalmud	116	13.36 N	122.53 E
Tinambac	116	13.49 N	123.19 E
Tinambung	112	3.31 S	119.01 E
Ti-n-Amzi ∨	150	18.20 N	4.32 E
Tinapagee	166	29.28 S	144.23 E
Tinaquillo	246	9.55 N	68.18 W
Tindari, Capo ⏵	70	38.10 N	15.03 E
Tinderry Peak ▲	171b	35.42 S	149.16 E
Tindila	151b	10.16 N	8.15 W
Tindis	125	21.35 N	86.42 E
Tindivanam	122	12.15 N	79.39 E
Tindouf	143	27.50 N	8.04 W
Tindouf, Hamada de ⬥¹	143	27.30 N	9.00 W
Tindouf, Sebkha de ≃	143	27.45 N	7.15 W
Tineba, Pegunungan ⋌	112	1.40 S	120.25 E
Tinée ≃	62	43.55 N	7.11 E
Tineg ≃	116	17.38 N	120.37 E
Tineo	34	43.20 N	6.25 W
Ting ≃	100	24.24 N	116.35 E
Tinga ▲	146	9.21 N	23.38 E
Tingambato	234	19.30 N	101.52 W
Tinggi, Pulau I	114	2.18 N	104.07 E
Tingha	166	29.57 S	151.13 E
Tinghert, Hamâdat (Plateau du Tinghert) ⬥¹	148	29.00 N	9.00 E
Tinghert, Plateau du (Hamâdat Tinghert) ⬥¹	148	29.00 N	9.00 E
Tinghsien → Dingxian	98	38.32 N	114.59 E
Tingkar ▲	116	5.20 N	117.06 E
Ting Kau	271d	22.22 N	114.05 E
Tingkou	96	36.34 N	119.46 E
Tinglev	26	54.56 N	9.15 E
Tinglin	106	30.53 N	121.17 E
Tingliuhe	98	39.34 N	118.49 E
Tingloy	116	13.40 N	120.52 E
Tingmerkpuk Mountain ▲	180	68.34 N	162.28 W
Tingo de Saposoa	248	7.07 S	76.38 W
Tingo María	248	9.09 S	75.56 W
Tingqian	100	30.10 N	115.54 E
Tingri, Zhg.	120	28.38 N	87.04 E
Tingri, Zhg.	120	28.35 N	86.38 E
Tingsiqiao	100	29.50 N	114.12 E
Tingsryd	26	56.32 N	14.59 E
Tingstäde	26	57.44 N	18.36 E
Tingsted	51	54.49 N	11.56 E
Tinguá	256	22.36 S	43.26 W
Tingüindín	234	19.45 N	102.29 W
Tinguipaya	248	19.11 S	65.51 W
Tingvoll	26	62.54 N	8.12 E
Tingvollfjorden c²	26	62.50 N	8.11 E
Tingwick	206	45.50 N	71.58 W
Tingwon Group II	164	2.35 S	149.45 E
Tingzitou	150	30.12 N	119.46 E
Tinharé, Ilha de I	255	13.30 S	38.58 W
Tinh Bien	110	10.36 N	104.57 E
Tinian I	174n	14.58 N	145.38 E
Tinian Harbor ⊂	174n	14.57 N	145.36 E
Tinié	150	14.20 N	1.28 W
Tiniguiban	116	11.22 N	119.30 E
Tinitian	110	10.04 N	119.12 E
Tinjar ≃	112	4.04 N	114.18 E
Tinjil, Pulau I	115a	6.58 S	105.47 E
Tinker Air Force Base ⬥	196	35.25 N	97.24 W
Tinkers Creek ≃, Md., U.S.	284c	38.46 N	76.57 W
Tinkers Creek ≃, Oh., U.S.	284	41.22 N	81.37 W
Tinkisso ≃	150	11.21 N	9.10 W
Tinley Creek ≃	278	41.39 N	87.45 W
Tinley Creek Woods ⬥	278	41.41 N	87.47 W
Tinley Park	216	41.34 N	87.47 W
Tinniswood, Mount ▲	182	50.19 N	123.50 W
Tinnsjø ◎	26	59.43 N	9.02 E
Tinogasta	252	28.04 S	67.34 W
Tinompo	112	2.09 S	121.17 E
Tinos	38	37.32 N	25.10 E
Tinos I	38	37.38 N	25.10 E
Tin Rerhoh, Tassili ⬥¹	148	21.18 N	1.40 E
Tinrhir	148	31.31 N	5.10 W
Tin Sam	271d	22.22 N	114.11 E
Tinskoj	86	56.10 N	96.55 E
Tinsley	194	32.43 N	90.27 W
Tintagel, B.C., Can.	182	54.01 N	125.29 W
Tintagel, Eng., U.K.	42	50.40 N	4.46 W
Tintagel Head ⏵	42	50.41 N	4.46 W
Tintaldra	171b	36.03 S	147.56 E

Column 2 (FRANÇAIS)

Nom	Page	Lat.	Long.
Tintas, Rio das ≃	287a	22.52 S	43.28 W
Tinte, Cerro ▲	248	22.40 S	67.02 W
Tintern Abbey ⛪¹	42	51.41 N	2.40 W
Tintern Parva	42	51.42 N	2.40 W
Tintigny	56	49.41 N	5.31 E
Tintina	252	27.02 S	62.43 W
Tintinara	166	35.54 S	140.03 E
Tintioulé	150	10.13 N	9.12 W
Tinto ≃	46	55.36 N	3.39 W
Tinto ⊼	34	37.12 N	6.55 W
Ti-n-Toumma ⬥¹	146	16.04 N	12.40 E
Tintwistle	262	53.28 N	1.58 W
Tinui	172	40.53 S	176.04 E
Tinwald	172	43.55 S	171.43 E
Ti-n-Zaouatene	150	19.55 N	2.52 E
Tinzap ≃	120	38.23 N	77.24 E
Tio	144	14.42 N	40.58 E
Tioga, Il., U.S.	219	40.13 N	91.21 W
Tioga, N.D., U.S.	198	48.23 N	102.56 W
Tioga, Pa., U.S.	210	41.55 N	77.08 W
Tioga □⁶, N.Y., U.S.	210	42.06 N	76.16 W
Tioga □⁶, Pa., U.S.	210	41.45 N	77.17 W
Tioga ≃⁸	285	40.00 N	75.10 W
Tioga ≃	210	42.09 N	77.05 W
Tioga Center	210	42.04 N	76.21 W
Tioga Pass)(	226	37.54 N	119.16 W
Tioga Terrace	210	42.03 N	76.07 W
Tiojala	24	61.10 N	23.52 E
Tioman, Pulau I	114	2.48 N	104.10 E
Tione	214	41.45 N	79.03 W
Tione di Trento	64	46.02 N	10.43 E
Tionesta	214	41.30 N	79.27 W
Tionesta Creek ≃	214	41.28 N	79.22 W
Tionesta Lake ◎¹	214	41.28 N	79.28 W
Tioor, Pulau I	164	4.45 S	131.45 E
Tior	140	6.23 N	31.11 E
Tioro	112	4.41 S	122.36 E
Tioro, Selat ⊔	112	4.40 S	122.20 E
Tioroniaradougou	150	9.21 N	5.38 W
Tioughnioga ≃	210	42.14 N	75.51 W
Tioughnioga, East Branch ≃	210	42.36 N	76.10 W
Tipac, Monte ▲²	250	3.34 N	51.20 W
Tipasa	34	36.35 N	2.27 E
Tipitapa	128	12.12 N	86.06 W
Tipp City	218	39.57 N	84.10 W
Tippecanoe, In., U.S.	216	41.12 N	86.06 W
Tippecanoe, Oh., U.S.	214	40.16 N	81.17 W
Tippecanoe □⁶	216	40.25 N	86.53 W
Tippecanoe ≃	216	40.31 N	86.47 W
Tippecanoe, Lake ◎	216	41.20 N	85.46 W
Tippecanoe River Battlefield State Memorial ⬥	216	40.31 N	86.52 W
Tippecanoe River State Park ⬥	216	41.07 N	86.36 W
Tipperary, Austl.	164	14.54 S	131.02 E
Tipperary, Ire.	48	52.29 N	8.10 W
Tipperary □⁶	48	52.40 N	8.20 W
Tipton, Eng., U.K.	42	52.32 N	2.05 W
Tipton, Ca., U.S.	226	36.03 N	119.18 W
Tipton, In., U.S.	216	40.16 N	86.02 W
Tipton, Ia., U.S.	190	41.46 N	91.07 W
Tipton, Mi., U.S.	216	42.01 N	84.04 W
Tipton, Mo., U.S.	216	38.39 N	92.46 W
Tipton, Ok., U.S.	196	34.30 N	99.08 W
Tipton, Pa., U.S.	214	40.38 N	78.18 W
Tipton □⁶	216	40.17 N	86.02 W
Tipton, Mount ▲	200	35.32 N	114.12 W
Tiptonville	194	36.22 N	89.28 W
Tip Top Mountain ▲	42	51.49 N	0.45 E
Tiptree	122	13.16 N	76.20 E
Tiputini ≃	246	0.47 S	75.32 W
Tiquicheo	234	18.53 N	100.44 W
Tiquisate	132	14.17 N	91.22 W
Tira	132	32.14 N	34.57 E
Tiracambu, Serra do ⬥¹	250	3.55 S	46.30 W
Tira Chapéu, Morro ⏵	256	22.45 S	44.39 W
Tiradentes	255	21.07 S	44.11 W
Tiradero ▲	232	17.47 N	91.10 W
Tirán, Bahr ⋈	142	31.03 N	31.15 E
Tiran I	128	27.56 N	34.34 E
Tiran, Madîq ⊔	142	27.56 N	34.28 E
Tiran, Strait of → Tirân, Madîq ⊔	140	27.58 N	34.28 E
Tirana → Tiranë	38	41.20 N	19.50 E
Tiranë	38	41.20 N	19.50 E
Tiraque	248	17.25 S	65.44 W
Tirari Desert ⬥²	162	28.00 S	138.20 E
Tiraspol ⬥	78	46.51 N	29.38 E
Tirat Karmel	132	32.46 N	34.58 E
Tirat Zevi	132	32.25 N	35.32 E
Tirau	172	37.59 S	175.45 E
Tire	130	38.04 N	27.45 E
Tirebolu	130	41.00 N	38.48 E
Tiree I	46	56.31 N	6.49 W
Tire Hill	214	40.16 N	78.55 W
Tires (Tiers), It.	64	46.28 N	11.31 E
Tires, Port.	266c	38.43 N	9.21 W
Tirgoviste →	38	44.55 N	25.27 E
Tirgovište	38	44.56 N	25.27 E
Tirgu Bujor	38	45.52 N	27.54 E
Tîrgu-Cărbuneşti	38	44.58 N	23.31 E
Tirgu-Frumos	38	47.13 N	27.00 E
Tirgu Jiu	38	45.02 N	23.17 E
Tîrgu-Lăpuş	38	47.27 N	23.52 E
Tîrgu-Neamţ	38	47.12 N	26.22 E
Tirgu Ocna	38	46.15 N	26.37 E
Tirgu Secuiesc	38	46.00 N	26.08 E
Tîrgusor	38	44.28 N	28.25 E
Tirhahart, Oued ∨	148	24.00 N	3.14 E
Tiria, Monte ▲	71	40.23 N	9.15 E
Tirich Mir ▲	123	36.15 N	71.50 E
Tiris ⬥¹	150	20.17 N	8.39 W
Tiris Zemmour □⁴	148	24.10 N	9.30 W
Tirl'anskij	86	54.11 N	58.35 E
Tiroungou	150	18.04 N	76.57 E
Tir Pol	128	34.36 N	61.15 E
Tirrenia	66	43.38 N	10.17 E
Tirreno, Mare → Tyrrhenian Sea ▽²	36	40.00 N	12.00 E
Tirry ≃	46	58.02 N	4.26 W
Tirsã, Misr	142	29.35 N	31.12 E
Tirschenreuth	54	49.53 N	12.21 E
Tirschtiegel → Trzciel	30	52.23 N	15.52 E
Tirso ≃	71	39.53 N	8.32 E
Tirsö	71	44.41 N	11.07 E
Tirua Point ⏵	172	38.23 S	174.38 E
Tiruchchiráppalli	122	10.49 N	78.41 E
Tiruchengōdu	122	12.57 N	77.56 E
Tirukkalukkunram	122	12.37 N	80.04 E
Tirukkōyilūr	122	11.58 N	79.12 E
Tirulai	76	55.47 N	23.12 E
Tirumangalam	122	9.50 N	77.59 E
Tirunelveli	122	8.44 N	77.42 E

Column 3 (PORTUGUÊS)

Nome	Página	Lat.	Long.
Tirupati	122	13.39 N	79.25 E
Tiruppattūr, India	122	12.30 N	78.34 E
Tiruppattūr, India	122	12.06 N	78.37 E
Tiruppur	122	11.06 N	77.21 E
Tirūr	122	10.54 N	75.55 E
Tiruttani	122	13.11 N	79.38 E
Tiruttaraippūndi	122	10.32 N	79.39 E
Tiruvalla	122	9.23 N	76.34 E
Tiruvallūr	122	13.09 N	79.55 E
Tiruvannāmalai	122	12.13 N	79.04 E
Tiruvettipuram	122	12.20 N	79.33 E
Tirūvōttiyūr	122	13.09 N	80.18 E
Tiruvur	122	17.06 N	80.38 E
Tisa (Tisza) ≃	38	45.15 N	20.17 E
Tis'ah	142	30.02 N	32.35 E
Tisaiyanvilai	122	8.20 N	77.53 E
Tisaren ≃	40	59.00 N	15.08 E
Tisbury	42	51.04 N	2.03 W
Tisdale	184	52.51 N	104.04 W
Tishomingo, Ms., U.S.	194	34.38 N	88.13 W
Tishomingo, Ok., U.S.	196	34.14 N	96.40 W
Tisisat Falls ∟	144	11.29 N	37.35 E
Tisijah	132	32.24 N	36.27 E
Tisjön ◎	26	60.55 N	12.58 E
Tiskilwa	190	41.17 N	89.30 W
Tiskino	86	58.05 N	83.10 E
Tiškovka	78	48.29 N	30.56 E
Tiškovo, S.S.S.R.	80	64.48 N	43.14 E
Tiškovo, S.S.S.R.	82	56.05 N	37.44 E
Tisma	236	12.05 N	86.01 W
Tisnaren ≃	40	58.57 N	15.57 E
Tišnov	30	49.21 N	16.25 E
Tišnov	30	48.43 N	19.57 E
Tissa	146	7.26 N	10.16 E
Tissemsilt	148	35.35 N	1.50 E
Tissø ◎	51	55.35 N	11.18 E
Tista ≃	126	25.23 N	89.43 E
Tisul'	86	55.46 N	88.19 E
Tisvildeleje	51	56.03 N	12.05 E
Tisza (Tisa) ≃	38	45.15 N	20.17 E
Tiszaföldvár	30	46.59 N	20.15 E
Tiszafüred	30	47.37 N	20.46 E
Tiszavasvári	30	47.58 N	21.22 E
Titaf	148	27.26 N	0.13 W
Titâgarh	126	22.45 N	88.22 E
Titano, Monte ▲	66	43.55 N	12.28 E
Titao	150	13.46 N	2.04 W
Tit-Ary	74	71.58 N	127.01 E
Titel	38	45.12 N	20.18 E
Tithwâl	123	34.24 N	73.47 E
Titicaca, Lago ◎	248	15.50 S	69.20 W
Titicus	207	41.18 N	73.30 W
Titi Karangan	114	5.31 N	100.37 E
Titikaveka	174k	21.15 S	159.45 W
Titilâgarh	126	20.18 N	83.09 E
Titisee-Neustadt	54	47.54 N	8.13 E
Titlis ▲	58	46.47 N	8.25 E
Titograd	38	42.26 N	19.14 E
Titonka	190	43.14 N	94.02 W
Titou	100	24.52 N	112.42 E
Titova Korenica	36	44.45 N	15.43 E
Titova Mitrovica	38	42.53 N	20.52 E
Titovka	83	43.59 S	39.44 E
Titovo, S.S.S.R.	80	53.17 N	43.41 E
Titovo, S.S.S.R.	82	54.19 N	36.56 E
Titovo Užice	38	43.51 N	19.51 E
Titov Veles	38	41.42 N	21.48 E
Titov vrh ▲	38	42.00 N	20.51 E
Titran	26	63.40 N	8.18 E
Tittabawassee ≃	190	43.23 N	83.59 W
Titteri ≃	34	36.00 N	3.30 E
Tittling	60	48.43 N	13.23 E
Tittmoning	60	48.04 N	12.46 E
Titu	38	44.41 N	25.32 E
Titule	154	3.17 N	25.32 E
Titusville, Fl., U.S.	220	28.36 N	80.48 W
Titusville, N.J., U.S.	208	40.18 N	74.52 W
Titusville, Pa., U.S.	214	41.37 N	79.40 W
Titz	56	51.01 N	6.25 E
Tiu Chung Chau I	271d	22.20 N	114.19 E
Tiumpan Head ⏵	46	58.16 N	6.09 W
Tiva ≃	154	2.20 S	38.48 E
Tivaouane	150	14.57 N	16.49 W
Tiveden ⬥¹	26	58.45 N	14.40 E
Tiverton, Eng., U.K.	42	50.55 N	3.29 W
Tiverton, R.I., U.S.	207	41.37 N	71.13 W
Tivoli, Grén.	241k	12.10 N	61.37 W
Tivoli, It.	66	41.58 N	12.48 E
Tivoli, N.Y., U.S.	207	42.03 N	73.54 W
Tivoli, Tx., U.S.	196	28.27 N	96.53 W
Tivoli ⬥	41	15.40 N	12.34 E
Tiwāl, Wādī ∨	146	10.22 N	22.43 E
Tiwai al-'Abã ≃	148	30.00 N	10.10 E
Tiwi, Phl.	116	13.27 N	123.41 E
Tiwi, 'Umān	128	22.49 N	59.16 E
Tiworónto	115b	8.48 S	120.09 E
Tixtla [de Guerrero]	234	17.34 N	99.24 W
Tiyās	134	34.33 N	37.40 E
Tiyo, Pegunungan ⋌	164	4.00 S	135.30 E
Tizapán el Alto	234	20.10 N	103.04 W
Tizatlán ⬥	234	19.21 N	98.15 W
Tizayuca	234	19.50 N	98.58 W
Tizimín	232	21.10 N	88.10 W
Tizi-Ouzou	148	36.44 N	4.05 E
Tizi Ouzou □³	148	36.40 N	4.10 E
Tizmant ash-Sharqīyah	142	29.03 N	31.03 E
Tiznados ≃	246	8.16 N	67.47 W
Tiznit	148	29.29 N	9.30 W
Tiznit □⁴	148	29.40 N	9.45 W
Tjämträsk ◎	22	66.10 N	19.20 E
Tjaldkemær ≃	255	54.05 S	5.50 E
Tjilatjap → Cilacap	115a	7.44 S	109.00 E
Tjirebon → Cirebon	115a	6.44 S	108.34 E
Tjolotjo	156	19.47 S	27.46 E
Tjome I	26	59.08 N	10.24 E
Tjörn I	26	58.00 N	11.38 E
Tjörnarp	26	55.58 N	13.23 E
Tjuratam → Leninsk	84	45.38 N	63.32 E
Tjutši	82	56.25 N	41.43 E

Column 4

Name	Page	Lat.	Long.
Tlalnepantla	234	19.32 N	99.12 W
Tlalpan ⬝⁸	286a	19.17 N	99.10 W
Tlalpujahua	234	19.48 N	100.10 W
Tlaltenango de Sánchez Román	234	21.47 N	103.19 W
Tlaltenco ⬝⁸	286a	19.17 N	99.01 W
Tl'ančetamak	80	55.28 N	52.37 E
Tlapa	234	17.33 N	98.33 W
Tlapacoyan	234	19.58 N	97.13 W
Tlapaneco ≃	234	18.05 N	98.48 W
Tlapehuala	234	18.13 N	100.31 W
Tlapeng	156	23.15 S	21.49 E
Tlaquepaque	234	20.39 N	103.19 W
Tl'arata	84	42.07 N	46.22 E
Tlatlauqui	234	19.51 N	97.29 W
Tlaxcala □³	234	19.25 N	98.10 W
Tlaxcala [de Xicotēncatl]	234	19.19 N	98.14 W
Tlaxco [de Morelos]	234	19.37 N	98.07 W
Tlaxiaco	234	17.16 N	97.41 W
Tlaxmalac	234	18.21 N	99.25 W
Tlaxzalaca	234	19.58 N	102.04 W
Tletat ed Douair	34	35.59 N	2.55 E
Tlété Ouâte Gharbî, Jabal ▲	134	35.20 N	39.13 E
Tlevak Strait ⊔	182	55.03 N	132.58 W
Tlhakgameng	158	26.27 S	24.21 E
Tločniá ▲	84	42.38 N	46.28 E
Tlučín ≃	60	49.44 N	13.14 E
Tlumač	78	48.52 N	25.01 E
Tluszcz	30	52.26 N	21.26 E
Tmassah	146	26.22 N	15.47 E
Tmīlsān ≃	146	27.32 N	13.19 E
Tnâot ≃	110	11.29 N	104.57 E
Tnekvejem ≃	180	65.50 N	177.31 E
Toa, Cuchillas de ⋌	240p	20.27 N	74.58 W
Toa Alta	240m	18.23 N	66.15 W
Toab	46a	59.53 N	1.19 W
Toa Baja	240m	18.27 N	66.15 W
Toabré ≃	236	8.56 N	80.33 W
Toachi ≃	246	0.08 N	79.18 W
Toahayaná	232	26.08 N	107.44 W
Toamasina	157b	18.10 S	49.23 E
Toamasina □⁴	157b	18.00 S	48.40 E
Toandonggu	98	40.33 N	127.35 E
Toandos Peninsula ⏵¹	224	47.43 N	122.47 W
Toano, It.	64	44.23 N	10.34 E
Toano, Va., U.S.	208	37.23 N	76.48 W
Toano Draw ∨	204	41.27 N	114.35 W
Toano Range ⋌	204	40.50 N	114.20 W
Toast	192	36.30 N	80.37 W
Toay	252	36.40 S	64.21 W
Toba, Mali	151	14.52 N	7.28 W
Toba, Nihon	104	34.29 N	136.51 E
Toba, Zhg.	102	31.18 N	97.40 E
Toba ≃	182	50.30 N	124.15 W
Toba, Danau ◎	114	2.35 N	98.50 E
Tōgō-ike ◎	104	35.28 N	133.54 E
Tobacco ≃	216	43.36 N	84.24 W
Tobacco Plains Indian Reserve ⬝⁴	182	49.04 N	115.06 W
Tobacco Root Mountains ⋌	202	45.35 N	112.00 W
Tobago I	241r	11.15 N	60.40 W
Toba Inlet c	182	50.20 N	124.50 W
Toba Kākar Range ⋌	123	31.15 N	68.00 E
Tobali, Pulau I	164	1.37 S	128.20 E
Tobara	34	38.35 N	1.41 W
Tobas	252	28.08 S	62.42 W
Tobašino	86	56.56 N	47.40 E
Toba Tek Singh	123	30.58 N	72.29 E
Tobe	96	33.44 N	132.47 E
Tobejuba, Isla I	246	9.30 N	60.52 W
Tobekuduk	286	49.50 N	54.15 E
Tobelo	108	1.44 N	128.01 E
Tobelombang	112	0.57 S	122.00 E
Tobercurry	48	54.03 N	8.43 W
Tobermore	166	22.15 S	138.00 E
Tobermory, Austl.	166	27.15 S	143.41 E
Tobermory, On., Can.	190	45.15 N	81.40 W
Tobermory, Scot., U.K.	46	56.37 N	6.05 W
Toberonochy	46	56.13 N	5.38 W
Tōbetsu	92a	43.13 N	141.31 E
Tobias	198	40.25 N	97.20 W
Tobias Barreto	250	11.11 S	38.01 W
Tobiishi-bana ⏵	104	34.45 N	131.17 E
Tobin, Mount ▲	204	40.22 N	117.32 W
Tobin Lake ◎	166	21.45 S	125.49 E
Tobin Lake ◎, Sk., Can.	184	53.40 N	103.35 W
Toboali	114	3.00 S	106.30 E
Tobol	86	52.40 N	62.39 E
Tobol ≃	86	58.10 N	68.12 E
Toboli	112	0.43 S	120.05 E
Tobol'sk	86	58.12 N	68.16 E
Tobong-san ▲	271d	37.42 N	127.01 E
Toboso	116	10.43 N	123.31 E
Toboso	116	10.12 N	2.08 E
Tobruk → Tubruq	146	32.05 N	23.59 E
Tobseda	24	68.36 N	52.14 E
Tobyhanna	210	41.11 N	75.25 W
Tobyhanna Creek ≃	210	41.10 N	75.39 W
Tobyhanna State Park ⬥	210	41.13 N	75.25 W

Column 5

Name	Page	Lat.	Long.
Toddington	42	51.57 N	0.32 W
Todd Point ⏵	284b	39.15 N	76.27 W
Todville, Md., U.S.	208	38.17 N	76.04 W
Todville, N.Y., U.S.	210	41.17 N	73.53 W
Todenyang	154	4.32 N	35.56 E
Todi	66	42.47 N	12.24 E
Todi ▲	58	46.49 N	8.56 E
Todmorden, Austl.	162	27.08 S	134.48 E
Todmorden, Eng., U.K.	44	53.43 N	2.05 W
Todohokke	92a	41.47 N	140.46 E
Todoga-saki ⏵	92	39.33 N	142.05 E
Todoroki	270	34.53 N	135.28 E
Todos Santos, Bol.	248	16.48 S	65.08 W
Todos Santos, Méx.	232	23.27 N	110.13 W
Todos Santos, Bahia c	232	31.48 N	116.42 W
Todro	154	3.21 N	30.14 E
Todtenhausen	58	52.20 N	8.56 E
Todtmoos	58	47.44 N	8.00 E
Todtmoos Au	58	47.42 N	7.58 E
Todtnau	58	47.50 N	7.56 E
Toe Head ⏵	46	57.50 N	7.08 W
Tōei	96	35.04 N	137.41 E
T'oejo	98	39.54 N	127.46 E
Toetoes Bay c	172	46.38 S	168.43 E
Tofield	182	53.22 N	112.40 W
Tofino	182	49.09 N	125.54 W
Tofino	94	36.27 N	137.02 E
Tofta	26	57.11 N	12.11 E
Toften ◎	58	59.03 N	14.36 E
Tofterup	51	55.39 N	8.50 E
Toftlund	51	55.11 N	9.04 E
Tōga	94	36.27 N	137.02 E
Togakushi	96	36.44 N	138.05 E
Togakushi-yama ▲	94	36.46 N	138.04 E
Toganas	80	50.49 N	52.02 E
Togane	94	35.33 N	140.22 E
Togauchi	96	34.34 N	132.13 E
Togcheer □⁴	144	9.00 N	46.00 E
Toggenburg V	58	47.15 N	9.10 E
Togho	152	6.01 N	17.26 E
Togiak	180	59.04 N	160.24 W
Togiak Bay c	180	58.45 N	160.24 W
Togian, Kepulauan II	112	0.20 S	122.00 E
Togian, Pulau I	112	0.22 S	121.56 E
Togian and Inn	60	48.15 N	12.35 E
Togliatti → Tol'jatti	80	53.31 N	49.26 E
Togni	144	18.04 N	35.13 E
Togo, Nihon	94	35.05 N	137.03 E
Togo, Nihon	96	35.28 N	133.53 E
Togo □¹, Afr.	134	8.00 N	1.10 E
Togo ◎¹, Afr.	152	8.00 N	1.10 E
Togochale	144	9.33 N	43.18 E
Togou	150	14.26 N	4.08 W
Togrog, Mong.	102	45.46 N	94.48 E
Tögrög, Mong.	102	45.32 N	102.59 E
Togtoh	102	40.22 N	111.11 E
Toguín	150	12.22 N	0.28 W
Togton ≃	102	34.24 N	92.25 E
Toguzak ≃	80	54.06 N	62.50 E
Tögüy-san Kukrip Kongwon ♦	98	35.52 N	127.45 E
Togyz	86	47.34 N	60.33 E
Tohakum Peak ▲	204	40.11 N	119.27 W
Tohatchi	200	35.51 N	108.45 W
Tohea, Mont ▲	174s	17.33 S	149.49 W
Tohma ≃	130	38.31 N	38.25 E
Toholampi	24	63.46 N	24.15 E
Tohopekaliga, Lake ◎	220	28.12 N	81.23 W
T'ohor, Tanjong ⏵	114	1.51 N	102.42 E
Toi, Niue	174v	18.57 S	169.51 W
Toi, Niue	174v	19.04 S	169.51 W
Toijala	24	61.10 N	23.52 E
Toija	26	60.11 N	23.06 E
Toi-misaki ⏵	92	31.20 N	131.20 E
Toinya	140	6.17 N	29.44 E
Toi Sar	120	31.06 N	69.54 E
Toiyabe Range ⋌	204	39.10 N	117.10 W
Tojkan	98	40.01 N	120.32 E
Tōjō, Indon.	112	1.17 S	121.11 E
Tōjō, Nihon	96	34.53 N	133.16 E
Tōjō, Nihon	270	34.31 N	135.18 E
Tojl-san → Dobbiaco	64	46.44 N	12.14 E
Toka, Indon.	164	3.34 S	130.11 E
Tojus	85	41.00 N	75.29 E
Toka, Guy.	246	1.40 N	59.03 W
Tōkai, Nihon	94	35.02 N	136.54 E
Tōkai, Nihon	96	33.57 N	130.35 E
Tokaj, Magy.	30	48.08 N	21.25 E
Tokamachi	94	37.08 N	138.46 E
Tokanui	172	46.34 S	168.57 E
Tokar	144	18.26 N	37.44 E
Tokara-kaikyō ⊔	93b	30.10 N	130.10 E
Tokara-rettō II	93b	29.30 N	129.30 E
Tokarevka	82	52.08 N	41.18 E
Tokar Game Reserve ♦	144	18.15 N	37.45 E
Tokat	130	40.19 N	36.34 E
Tokat □⁴	130	40.15 N	36.30 E
Tokat ≃	98	38.22 N	127.14 E
Tokch'ŏn	98	39.45 N	126.18 E
Tokelau □²	14	9.00 S	171.45 W
Tokelau-Inseln → Tokelau II	174e	9.00 S	171.45 W
Toklat ≃	180	65.30 N	151.00 W
Toklat, North Fork ≃	180	63.40 N	150.30 W
Tokmak	84	42.50 N	75.18 E
Tŏkok-kundo II	98	34.30 N	126.11 E
Toko	172	39.19 S	174.24 E
Tokola	150	5.38 N	8.32 W
Tokomaru Bay	172	38.08 S	178.18 E
Tokoname	94	34.53 N	136.51 E
Tokoroa	172	38.13 S	175.52 E
Tokoro	92a	44.07 N	144.05 E
Tokoro ≃	92a	44.08 N	144.05 E
Tokorozawa	94	35.47 N	139.28 E
Tokra → Tukrah	146	32.32 N	20.34 E
Tokrau ≃	86	46.18 N	74.20 E
Toksook Bay	180	60.32 N	165.06 W

Column 6

Name	Page	Lat.	Long.
Toksovo	76	60.09 N	30.31 E
Tok-to (Take-shima) II	92	37.17 N	131.53 E
Toktogul	85	41.50 N	72.50 E
Toktogul'skoje vodochranilišče ◎¹	85	41.50 N	72.55 E
Toku Island I	14	18.10 S	174.11 W
Tokuji	96	34.11 N	131.40 E
Tokul Creek ≃	224	47.33 N	121.53 W
Tokuno-shima I	93b	27.45 N	128.58 E
Tokur	89	53.10 N	132.53 E
Tokura	270	34.58 N	135.18 E
Tokura-tōge)(	96	35.17 N	134.31 E
Tokusaga-mine ▲	96	34.26 N	131.41 E
Tokushima	96	34.04 N	134.34 E
Tokushima □⁵	96	33.45 N	134.00 E
Tokuyama, Nihon	94	35.42 N	136.29 E
Tokuyama, Nihon	96	34.03 N	131.49 E
Tokwe ≃	154	21.09 S	31.30 E
Tōkyō, Nihon	94	35.42 N	139.46 E
Tōkyō, Nihon	268	35.42 N	139.46 E
Tōkyō □⁵	94	35.42 N	139.46 E
Tokyo Bay → Tōkyō-wan c	94	35.25 N	139.47 E
Tōkyō-daigaku-uchūkūkan-kenkyūsho ◎³	92	31.17 N	131.05 E
Tokyo Disneyland ♦	268	35.37 N	139.53 E
Tōkyō-kō c	268	35.37 N	139.46 E
Tōkyō-kokusai-kūkō	94	35.45 N	140.21 E
Tokyo Station ⬥⁵	268	35.41 N	139.46 E
Tokyo Tower ⬥¹	268	35.39 N	139.45 E
Tokyo University of Education ⬥²	268	35.43 N	139.44 E
Tōkyō-wan (Tokyo Bay) c	94	35.25 N	139.47 E
Tokzār	123	35.52 N	66.26 E
Tol I	175c	7.22 N	151.37 E
Tolaga Bay	172	38.22 S	178.18 E
Tolala	112	2.56 S	121.06 E
Tolang	114	1.56 N	99.26 E
Tolbert	52	53.10 N	6.21 E
Tolbo Nuur ◎	86	48.25 N	90.17 E
Tolbuhin	38	43.34 N	27.50 E
Tolbuhin	83	43.34 N	27.50 E
Tolderol Point ⏵	168b	35.22 S	139.10 E
Tolé, Pan.	236	8.14 N	81.41 W
Toledo, Bra.	252	24.44 S	53.45 W
Toledo, Col.	246	7.19 N	72.28 W
Toledo, Esp.	34	39.52 N	4.01 W
Toledo, Il., U.S.	194	39.16 N	88.14 W
Toledo, Ia., U.S.	190	41.59 N	92.34 W
Toledo, Oh., U.S.	214	41.39 N	83.33 W
Toledo, Or., U.S.	202	44.37 N	123.56 W
Toledo, Wa., U.S.	224	46.26 N	122.51 W
Toledo □³	34	39.45 N	4.30 W
Toledo, Montes de ⋌	34	39.33 N	4.20 W
Toledo Bend Reservoir ◎¹	194	31.30 N	93.45 W
Toledo Express Airport ⬥	216	41.35 N	83.49 W
Tolentino	66	43.12 N	13.17 E
Tolfa	66	42.09 N	11.56 E
Tolfa, Monti della ⋌	66	42.08 N	11.54 E
Tolga, Alg.	148	34.46 N	5.22 E
Tolga, Nor.	26	62.25 N	11.00 E
Toliara	157b	23.21 S	43.40 E
Toliara □⁴	157b	24.00 S	45.00 E
Tolima ⬝⁵	246	3.45 N	75.15 W
Tolima, Nevado del ▲	246	4.40 N	75.19 W
Tolimán, Méx.	234	19.36 N	103.55 W
Tolimán, Méx.	234	20.55 N	99.56 W
Tolitoli	112	1.02 N	120.49 E
Toljatti (Togliatti)	80	53.31 N	49.26 E
Tol'ka	74	64.02 N	81.55 E
Tolkmicko	30	54.19 N	19.31 E
Tolland	207	41.52 N	72.22 W
Tolland □⁶	207	41.52 N	72.22 W
Tollarp	26	55.54 N	13.58 E
Tollense ≃	54	53.54 N	13.02 E
Tollensesee ◎	54	53.33 N	13.11 E
Tollesboro	218	38.33 N	83.34 W
Tollesbury	42	51.46 N	0.51 E
Tolleson	200	33.27 N	112.15 W
Tollhouse	226	37.01 N	119.24 W
Tolloche	252	25.30 S	63.32 W
Tølløse	51	55.37 N	11.45 E
Tollygunge ⬝⁸	272b	22.30 N	88.21 E
Tolmačí	82	57.52 N	36.11 E
Tolmezzo	64	46.24 N	13.01 E
Tolmin	36	46.11 N	13.44 E
Tolna, Magy.	30	46.26 N	18.47 E
Tolna, N.D., U.S.	198	47.50 N	98.26 W
Tolna □⁶	30	46.30 N	18.30 E
Tolo, Teluk c	112	2.00 S	122.30 E
Tolochin	76	54.25 N	29.42 E
Tolocko	76	50.03 N	37.45 E
Tolomato ≃	221	29.54 N	81.20 W
Tolonao	194	31.50 N	91.42 W
Tolosa	34	43.08 N	2.04 W
Tolox	34	36.42 N	4.55 W
Tolsona	180	62.07 N	146.00 W
Tolstoj, Mys ⏵	74	54.23 N	155.43 E
Tolstoj, mys ⏵	74	59.10 N	155.12 E
Tolstopal'cevo	265b	55.38 N	37.13 E
Toltén	254	39.13 S	73.14 W
Toltén ≃	254	39.13 S	73.14 W
Toltry ⬥¹	78	49.00 N	26.10 E
Tolú	246	9.31 N	75.35 W
Toluca, Nevado de ▲¹	234	19.08 N	99.44 W
Toluca [de Lerdo]	234	19.17 N	99.40 W
Tolun → Dolonnur	98	42.11 N	116.28 E
Tolvajarvi	24	62.17 N	31.27 E
Tolve	68	40.42 N	16.01 E
Tolvadjärvi	32	62.17 N	31.27 E
Tolworth ⬝⁸	263	51.23 N	0.17 W
Tolyatti → Toljatti	80	53.31 N	49.26 E
Tom ≃, S.S.S.R.	74	50.23 N	127.00 E
Tom ≃, S.S.S.R.	86	56.50 N	84.27 E
Tomah	190	43.58 N	90.30 W
Tomahawk	190	45.28 N	89.43 W
Tomakomai	92a	42.38 N	141.36 E
Tomamae	92a	44.19 N	141.39 E
Tomanivi ▲	175g	17.37 S	178.01 E
Tomar	34	39.36 N	8.25 W
Tomari, S.S.S.R.	89	47.46 N	142.04 E
Tomari, Nihon	92a	43.04 N	140.28 E
Tomás Barrón (Eucalyptus)	248	17.35 S	67.31 W
Tomasboda	40	59.24 N	14.58 E

Footer legend

| ≃ River / Fluß / Rio / Rivière / Rio |
| ≈ Canal / Kanal / Canal / Canal / Canal |
| ∟ Waterfall, Rapids / Wasserfall, Stromschnellen / Cascada, Rápidos / Chute d'eau, Rapides / Cascata, Rápidos |
| ⊔ Strait / Meeresstraße / Estrecho / Détroit / Estreito |
| c Bay, Gulf / Bucht, Golf / Bahía, Golfo / Baie, Golfe / Baía, Golfo |
| ◎ Lake, Lakes / See, Seen / Lago, Lagos / Lac, Lacs / Lago, Lagos |
| ⧈ Swamp / Sumpf / Pantano / Marais / Pântano |
| ❄ Ice Features, Glacier / Eis- und Gletscherformen / Accidentes Glaciales / Formes glaciaires / Acidentes glaciares |
| ▽ Other Hydrographic Features / Andere Hydrographische Objekte / Otros Elementos Hidrográficos / Autres données hydrographiques / Outros acidentes hidrográficos |
| ⬥ Submarine Features / Untermeerische Objekte / Accidentes Submarinos / Formes de relief sous-marin / Acidentes submarinos |
| □ Political Unit / Politische Einheit / Unidad Política / Entité politique / Unidade política |
| ⛪ Cultural Institution / Kulturelle Institution / Institución Cultural / Institution culturelle / Instituição cultural |
| ⬥ Historical Site / Historische Stätte / Sitio Histórico / Site historique / Sítio histórico |
| ♦ Recreational Site / Erholungs- und Ferienort / Sitio de Recreo / Centre de loisirs / Área de Lazer |
| ⬝ Airport / Flughafen / Aeropuerto / Aéroport / Aeroporto |
| ⬥ Military Installation / Militäranlage / Instalación Militar / Installation militaire / Instalação militar |
| ⬥ Miscellaneous / Verschiedenes / Misceláneo / Divers / Diversos |

ENGLISH | DEUTSCH

Name	Page	Lat.°′	Long.°′
Tomás Gomensoro	252	30.26 S	57.26 W
Tomašgorod	78	51.19 N	27.02 E
Tomasine ≃	190	46.40 N	76.16 W
Tomás Jofré	258	34.43 S	59.19 W
Tomášov	61	48.09 N	17.16 E
Tomašpol'	78	48.33 N	28.31 E
Tomaszów Lubelski	30	50.28 N	23.25 E
Tomaszów Mazowiecki	30	51.32 N	20.01 E
Tomatin	46	57.20 N	3.59 W
Tomatlán	234	19.56 N	105.15 W
Tomatlán ≃	234	19.50 N	105.23 W
Tomave	248	20.06 S	66.35 W
Tomazina	255	23.46 S	49.58 W
Tomba di Nerone ◆[8]	267a	41.57 N	12.27 E
Tombadonkéa	150	11.00 N	14.23 W
Tombador, Serra do ⋀[1]	248	12.00 S	57.40 W
Tomball	222	30.06 N	95.37 W
Tombe	140	5.49 N	31.41 E
Tombigbee ≃	194	31.04 N	87.58 W
Tombo, Punta >	254	44.03 S	65.11 W
Tombôco	152	6.48 S	13.18 E
Tombolo	64	45.38 N	11.50 E
Tombos	255	20.55 S	42.02 W
Tombouctou (Timbuktu)	150	16.46 N	3.01 W
Tombouctou □[4]	150	18.20 N	3.50 W
Tombs of the Caliphs ⊥	273c	30.03 N	31.17 E
Tombstone	200	31.42 N	110.04 W
Tombstone Mountain ∧	180	64.25 N	138.30 W
Tombua	152	15.49 S	11.53 E
Tom Burke	156	23.05 S	28.00 E
Tomdoun	46	57.04 N	5.03 W
Tomé	252	36.37 S	72.57 W
Tomea, Pulau I	112	5.45 S	123.56 E
Tomé-Açu	250	2.25 S	48.09 W
Tömek	130	38.02 N	32.41 E
Tomelilla	26	55.33 N	13.57 E
Tomelloso	34	39.10 N	3.01 W
Tomerong	170	35.04 S	150.35 E
Tomhannock Reservoir ⊜[1]	210	42.51 N	73.33 W
Tomi ≃	152	5.07 N	19.19 E
Tomich	46	57.18 N	4.48 W
Tomichi Creek ≃	200	38.31 N	106.58 W
Tomifobia ≃	206	45.11 N	72.02 W
Tomiko Lake ⊜	190	46.32 N	79.49 W
Tomilino	265b	55.39 N	37.57 E
Tomini	112	0.30 N	120.32 E
Tomini, Teluk ⊂	112	0.20 S	121.00 E
Tominian	150	13.17 N	4.35 W
Tomintoul	46	57.14 N	3.22 W
Tomio ≃	270	34.35 N	135.44 E
Tomioka	94	36.15 N	138.54 E
Tomisato	94	35.44 N	140.19 E
Tomiura	94	35.03 N	139.50 E
Tomiyama, Nihon	94	35.11 N	137.48 E
Tomiyama, Nihon	94	35.05 N	139.51 E
Tomizawa	94	35.14 N	138.29 E
T'omkino	76	55.05 N	35.01 E
Tomkins Cove	210	41.15 N	73.59 W
Tomkinson Ranges ⋀	162	26.11 S	129.05 E
Tomkinsville	208	38.19 N	76.53 W
Tomlinson Run State Park ♠	214	40.33 N	80.34 W
Tommerup Stationsby	41	55.19 N	10.13 E
Tommot	74	58.58 N	126.19 E
Tomnavoulin	46	57.18 N	3.19 W
T'omnyj	88	53.24 N	118.31 E
Tomo ≃	246	5.20 N	67.48 W
Tomobe	94	36.20 N	140.20 E
Tomogashima-suidō ⋓	96	34.17 N	135.00 E
Tomohon	112	1.19 N	124.49 E
Tömör Bulag	88	49.16 N	100.15 E
Tomori	174m	26.08 N	127.44 E
Tomori, Teluk ⊂	112	1.58 S	121.28 E
Tompa	88	55.08 N	109.47 E
Tompkins, Nf., Can.	186	47.48 N	59.13 W
Tompkins, Sk., Can.	184	50.04 N	108.47 W
Tompkins □[6]	210	42.27 N	76.30 W
Tompkins County Airport ⊠	210	42.29 N	76.57 W
Tompkinsville	194	36.42 N	85.41 W
Tompo	112	0.56 N	120.20 E
Tom Price	162	22.41 S	117.43 E
Tom Price, Mount ∧	162	22.39 S	117.40 E
Tomptokan	74	57.06 N	133.59 E
Tomra	26	62.35 N	6.56 E
Toms ≃	208	39.57 N	74.07 W
Toms, Ridgeway Branch ≃	208	40.00 N	74.14 W
Toms Cove ⊂	208	37.53 N	75.22 W
Toms Creek ≃	208	39.38 N	77.17 W
Tomsk	86	56.30 N	84.58 E
Toms River	208	39.58 N	74.12 W
Tom Steed Reservoir ⊜[1]	196	34.45 N	99.00 W
Tomtabacken ∧[2]	26	57.30 N	14.28 E
Tömük	130	36.41 N	34.22 E
Tomuzlovka ≃	84	44.46 N	44.10 E
Ton	64	46.15 N	11.04 E
Tonadico	64	46.11 N	11.50 E
Tonaki-shima I	93b	26.21 N	127.09 E
Tonalá, Méx.	234	16.04 N	93.45 W
Tonalá, Méx.	234	20.37 N	103.14 W
Tonalá ≃	234	18.13 N	94.25 W
Tonale, Passo del)(	64	46.16 N	10.35 E
Tonami	94	36.38 N	136.54 E
Tonantins	246	2.47 S	67.47 W
Tonantins ≃	246	2.47 S	67.47 W
Tonara	71	40.02 N	9.10 E
Tonasket	202	48.42 N	119.26 W
Tonatico	234	18.47 N	99.41 W
Tonawanda	210	43.01 N	78.52 W
Tonawanda Channel ≃[1]	284a	43.04 N	79.00 W
Tonawanda Creek ≃	210	43.02 N	78.53 W
Tonawanda Indian Reservation ◆[4]	210	43.05 N	78.27 W
Tonawanda Island I	284a	43.02 N	78.53 W
Tonbara	96	35.05 N	132.47 E
Tonbo	110	18.31 N	95.05 E
Tonbridge	42	51.12 N	0.16 E
Tonbridge and Malling □[8]	260	51.16 N	0.20 E
Tonda	270	34.50 N	135.36 E
Tonda ≃	96	33.38 N	135.24 E
Tondabayashi	96	34.30 N	135.36 E
Tondano	112	1.19 N	124.54 E
Tønder	41	54.56 N	8.54 E
Tondhre	272c	19.05 N	73.08 E
Tondi	122	9.44 N	79.01 E
Tondibi	150	16.39 N	0.14 W
Tondidji	150	13.06 N	10.20 W
Tondi Kiwindi	150	14.28 N	2.02 E
Tondoro	156	17.45 S	18.50 E
Tone, Nihon	94	36.42 N	139.13 E
Tone, Nihon	94	35.51 N	140.09 E
Tone ≃	94	35.44 N	140.51 E
Tonekābon	128	36.49 N	50.53 E
Tone-unga ≍	268	35.54 N	139.53 E
Tonež	78	51.49 N	27.48 E
Tonga, Cam.	152	4.58 N	10.42 E
Tonga, Sūd.	140	9.28 N	31.03 E
Tonga □[1]	14	20.00 S	175.00 W
Tongaat	158	29.37 S	31.03 E
Tonga Islands II	14	20.00 S	175.00 W
Tong'an	100	24.46 N	118.08 E
Tonganoxie	198	39.06 N	95.05 W
Tong'anqiao	106	31.22 N	120.27 E
Tonga Ridge ✥[3]	14	21.00 S	175.00 W
Tongariro, Mount ∧	172	39.08 S	175.38 E
Tongariro National Park ♠	172	39.15 S	175.30 E
Tongas	115a	7.44 S	113.06 E
Tongatapu □[8]	174w	21.10 S	175.10 W
Tongatapu I	174w	21.10 S	175.10 W
Tongatapu Group II	14	21.10 S	175.10 W
Tonga Trench ✥[1]	14	20.00 S	173.00 W
Tongbai, Zhg.	100	32.22 N	113.24 E
Tongbai, Zhg.	105	39.35 N	116.44 E
Tongbai Shan ∧	100	32.20 N	113.14 E
Tongbai Shan ⋀	100	32.20 N	113.15 E
Tongbei	89	47.45 N	126.46 E
Tongcheng, Zhg.	100	32.53 N	118.58 E
Tongcheng, Zhg.	100	31.03 N	116.58 E
Tongcheng, Zhg.	100	29.11 N	113.49 E
Tongchengzha	100	31.30 N	118.07 E
Tongchengzhuang	105	39.22 N	117.36 E
T'ongch'ŏn	98	38.54 N	127.54 E
Tongchuan	102	35.01 N	109.01 E
Tongdao	102	26.23 N	109.23 E
Tongde	102	35.17 N	100.42 E
Tongerbao	104	41.26 N	123.02 E
Tongeren	56	50.47 N	5.28 E
Tongerlo	56	51.07 N	4.54 E
Tonggou	98	41.53 N	125.46 E
Tonggu, Zhg.	100	28.33 N	114.21 E
Tonggu, Zhg.	100	21.53 N	112.55 E
Tongguan, Zhg.	100	28.29 N	112.48 E
Tongguan, Zhg.	102	34.38 N	110.20 E
Tongguan, Zhg.	102	23.18 N	101.23 E
Tongguanyi	107	29.20 N	106.23 E
Tonghai	102	24.07 N	102.49 E
Tonghaikou	100	30.14 N	113.08 E
Tonghe, Zhg.	89	45.59 N	128.45 E
Tonghe, Zhg.	100	32.56 N	112.45 E
Tongho-ri	98	35.49 N	127.54 E
Tonghua (Kuaidamao), Zhg.	98	41.40 N	125.44 E
Tonghua, Zhg.	98	41.41 N	125.55 E
Tonghui ≃	271a	39.53 N	116.41 E
Tongi	126	23.53 N	90.24 E
Tong Island I	164	2.05 S	147.50 E
Tongjiang, Zhg.	89	47.40 N	132.30 E
Tongjiang, Zhg.	102	31.58 N	107.14 E
Tongjiangchang	107	29.37 N	103.43 E
Tongjiangkou	104	42.37 N	123.41 E
Tongjing	100	31.47 N	118.33 E
Tongjosŏn-man ⊂	98	39.30 N	128.00 E
Tongjuzhen	98	38.36 N	117.11 E
Tongken ≃	89	46.31 N	126.22 E
Tongli	106	31.10 N	120.43 E
Tongliang	107	29.51 N	106.03 E
Tongliao	89	43.39 N	122.14 E
Tongling, Zhg.	100	30.53 N	117.46 E
Tongling, Zhg.	102	23.28 N	109.40 E
Tonglu	100	29.48 N	119.40 E
Tonglü Yunhe ≍	106	32.04 N	121.40 E
Tongmang-ni	98	37.37 N	126.26 E
Tongmu, Zhg.	100	27.57 N	113.55 E
Tongmu, Zhg.	102	24.09 N	110.04 E
Tongnae	98	35.12 N	129.05 E
Tongnan	107	30.11 N	105.48 E
Tongno-gang ≃	98	40.58 N	126.04 E
Tongo	166	30.30 S	143.45 E
Tongoa I	175f	16.54 S	168.34 E
Tongobory	157b	23.32 S	44.20 E
Tongololo Creek ≃	162	22.06 S	121.08 E
Tongoy	252	30.15 S	71.30 W
Tongqin	100	28.52 N	119.56 E
Tongquansi	107	30.23 N	104.50 E
Tongquil Island I	116	6.02 N	121.51 E
Tongren, Zhg.	102	27.38 N	109.03 E
Tongren, Zhg.	102	35.32 N	101.54 E
Tongrengchang	107	30.02 N	106.42 E
Tongsa ≃	124	26.52 N	90.57 E
Tongsa Dzong	124	27.31 N	90.30 E
Tongsan-ni	271b	37.38 N	126.53 E
Tongshan	100	29.38 N	114.29 E
Tongshi	98	35.26 N	117.43 E
Tongshuping	100	27.17 N	114.54 E
Tongta	110	21.20 N	99.16 E
Tongtai	100	32.38 N	120.47 E
Tongtan	107	28.56 N	105.17 E
Tongtian ≃	102	33.25 N	96.32 E
Tongue	46	58.28 N	4.25 W
Tongue ≃, U.S.	202	46.24 N	105.52 W
Tongue ≃, N.D., U.S.	198	48.56 N	97.18 W
Tongue ≃, Tx., U.S.	196	34.07 N	100.25 W
Tongue, Kyle of ⊂	46	58.30 N	4.26 W
Tongue of the Ocean ✥[1]	238	24.30 N	77.30 W
Tongue River Reservoir ⊜[1]	202	45.06 N	106.47 W
Tongwei	102	35.07 N	105.27 E
Tongxi	107	29.59 N	106.08 E
Tongxian	105	39.55 N	116.39 E
Tongxianchang	107	30.14 N	105.24 E
Tongxiang	106	30.38 N	120.32 E
Tongxin	102	37.02 N	106.09 E
Tongxinchang	107	29.42 N	106.26 E
Tongxing	107	30.35 N	106.12 E
Tongxu	98	34.29 N	114.28 E
Tongyang-ni	98	39.08 N	126.52 E
Tongyang Yunhe ≍	106	32.02 N	120.48 E
Tongyu	89	44.48 N	123.05 E
Tongyuan, Zhg.	100	28.04 N	116.08 E
Tongyuan, Zhg.	106	30.28 N	120.52 E
Tongyuanpu	104	40.49 N	123.54 E
Tongzhaipu	100	32.48 N	112.44 E
Tongzi	102	28.08 N	106.49 E
Tongzidixia	104	41.08 N	120.34 E
Tonica	216	41.12 N	89.04 W
Tónichi	232	28.35 N	109.34 W
Tonila	234	19.26 N	103.31 W
Tönisberg	263	51.25 N	6.30 E
Tönisheide	263	51.19 N	7.03 E
Tönisvorst	56	51.19 N	6.29 E
Tonj	140	7.17 N	28.45 E
Tonk	120	26.10 N	75.47 E
Tonkawa	196	36.40 N	97.18 W
Tonkin → Bac Phan □[9]	110	22.00 N	105.00 E
Tonkin, Gulf of ⊂	110	20.00 N	108.00 E
Tonkino	80	57.23 N	46.28 E
Tonkou, Mont ∧	150	7.27 N	7.39 W
Tonkwa	110	23.36 N	96.58 E
Tônlé Sab, Bœng ⊜	110	13.00 N	104.00 E
Tonle Sap → Tônlé Sab, Bœng ⊜	110	13.00 N	104.00 E
Tonnay-Boutonne	32	45.58 N	0.42 W
Tonneins	32	44.23 N	0.19 E
Tonner Canyon V	280	33.58 N	117.48 W
Tonnerre	50	47.51 N	3.58 E
Tönnet	40	60.14 N	13.30 E
Tönning	41	54.19 N	8.56 E
Tōno	92	39.19 N	141.32 E
Tonogaya	268	35.46 N	139.22 E
Tonopah	204	38.04 N	117.13 W
Tōnoshō, Nihon	94	35.49 N	140.42 E
Tonoshō, Nihon	96	34.29 N	134.11 E
Tonosí	246	7.24 N	80.27 W
Tonota	156	21.29 S	27.29 E
Tonquish Creek ≃	281	42.21 N	83.22 W
Tons ≃	124	25.17 N	82.04 E
Tonšajevo	80	57.44 N	47.00 E
Tønsberg	26	59.17 N	10.25 E
Tönsholt	263	51.38 N	6.58 E
Tonstad	26	58.40 N	6.43 E
Tonto ≃	234	18.10 N	96.08 W
Tonto Creek ≃	200	33.46 N	111.15 W
Tontogany	216	41.25 N	83.44 W
Tonto National Monument ♠	200	33.34 N	111.02 W
Tonya	130	40.53 N	39.16 E
Tonypandy	42	51.38 N	3.27 W
Tonyrefail	42	51.36 N	3.25 W
Toobeah	166	28.25 S	149.52 E
Toodyay	168a	31.33 S	116.28 E
Tooele	200	40.31 N	112.17 W
Toogoolawah	171a	27.06 S	152.23 E
Tool	222	32.16 N	96.10 W
Toolik ≃	180	69.55 N	149.30 W
Tooma	171b	35.58 S	148.03 E
Tooma ≃	171b	36.04 S	148.00 E
Tooma Reservoir ⊜[1]	171b	36.04 S	148.16 E
Toomebridge	48	54.45 N	6.27 W
Toompine	166	27.13 S	144.22 E
Toomsboro	192	32.49 N	83.04 W
Toomyvara	48	52.50 N	8.02 W
Toongabbie	274a	33.47 S	150.57 E
Toora	169	38.40 S	146.20 E
Toora-Chem	88	52.28 N	96.17 E
Toorak	274b	37.51 S	145.01 E
Toormakeady	48	53.39 N	9.24 W
Toosey Indian Reserve ◆[4]	182	51.56 N	122.29 W
Toot Hill	260	51.42 N	0.12 E
Tootias	144	3.57 N	43.57 E
Tootie, Mount ∧	170	33.28 S	150.30 E
Tootsi	76	58.34 N	24.47 E
Toowoomba	171a	27.33 S	151.57 E
Topanga	228	34.06 N	118.36 W
Topanga Canyon V	280	34.05 N	118.36 W
Topanga State Park ♠	280	34.06 N	118.33 W
Topar	86	49.32 N	72.50 E
Topawa	200	31.48 N	111.49 W
Topaz Lake ⊜	226	38.41 N	119.32 W
Topçam	130	40.38 N	37.48 E
Topchānchi	126	23.54 N	86.12 E
Töpchin	54	52.10 N	13.34 E
Topčicha	86	52.49 N	83.10 E
Topeka, In., U.S.	216	41.32 N	85.32 W
Topeka, Ks., U.S.	198	39.02 N	95.40 W
Töpen	54	50.23 N	11.52 E
Topia	232	25.13 N	106.34 W
Topilejo ◆[8]	286a	19.12 N	99.09 W
Topino ≃	66	43.02 N	12.30 E
Topkanovo	82	54.43 N	38.29 E
Topkapı ◆[8]	267b	41.02 N	28.54 E
Topkapi Palace ⊥	267b	41.00 N	28.59 E
Topki	86	55.16 N	85.36 E
Topko, gora ∧	74	57.08 N	137.24 E
Topl'a ≃	30	48.45 N	21.45 E
Topley	182	54.30 N	126.18 W
Toplica ≃	38	43.13 N	21.49 E
Toplița	38	46.55 N	25.21 E
T'oploje, S.S.S.R.	76	53.13 N	38.53 E
T'oploje, S.S.S.R.	76	53.37 N	37.36 E
T'oploje ≃	83	48.47 N	39.19 E
T'oplyj Stan	80	53.58 N	50.10 E
T'oplyj Stan ◆[8]	265b	55.37 N	37.30 E
Topo, Quebrada ≃	286c	10.33 N	67.00 W
Topocalma, Punta >	252	34.08 S	72.01 W
Top of Hebers	262	53.34 N	2.12 W
Topo Infiernito ∧	286c	10.33 N	66.55 W
Topol'čany	30	48.34 N	18.10 E
Topoli	80	47.59 N	51.36 E
Topolobampo	232	25.36 N	109.03 W
Topolog	38	44.53 N	28.22 E
Topolovățu Mare	38	45.46 N	21.37 E
Topolovgrad	38	42.05 N	26.20 E
Toporok	76	58.33 N	33.28 E
Topozero, ozero ⊜	24	65.40 N	32.00 E
Toppenish	202	46.22 N	120.18 W
Toppenish Creek ≃	202	46.20 N	120.11 W
Toppenish Ridge ∧	224	46.18 N	120.40 W
Toppings	262	53.37 N	2.25 W
Toprakkale	130	37.06 N	36.07 E
Tops, Mount ∧	162	21.50 S	134.00 E
Topsa	24	62.39 N	43.34 E
Topsfield	207	42.38 N	70.57 W
Topsham, Eng., U.K.	42	50.41 N	3.27 W
Topsham, Me., U.S.	188	43.55 N	69.58 W
Top Springs	164	16.38 S	131.50 E
Topton	208	40.30 N	75.42 W
Toquima Range ⋀	204	38.45 N	116.55 W
Toquop Wash V	204	36.45 N	114.11 W
Tor	144	7.51 N	33.35 E
Torahime	94	35.25 N	136.16 E
Torano Castello	68	39.30 N	16.08 E
Torawitan, Tanjung >	112	1.46 N	124.58 E
Toraya	248	14.03 S	73.18 W
Torbalı	130	38.10 N	27.21 E
Torbat-e Ḥeydarīyeh	128	35.16 N	59.13 E
Torbat-e Jām	128	35.14 N	60.36 E
Torbay	186	47.40 N	52.44 W
Torbay □[9]	42	50.26 N	3.34 W
Tor Bay ⊂	42	50.25 N	3.30 W
Torbejevo, S.S.S.R.	80	54.05 N	43.15 E
Torbejevo, S.S.S.R.	82	54.44 N	36.11 E
Torbert, Mount ∧	180	61.25 N	152.24 W
Torbino	76	58.35 N	32.53 E
Torbole	64	45.52 N	10.52 E
Torbreck, Mount ∧	169	37.21 S	145.57 E
Torbrook	186	44.55 N	64.59 W
Torch ≃	184	53.50 N	103.05 W
Torchany	80	55.34 N	46.36 E
Torchiarolo	68	40.29 N	18.03 E
Torch Lake ⊜	190	45.00 N	85.19 W
Torčin	78	50.46 N	24.59 E
Torcy	261	48.51 N	2.39 E
Torda → Turda	38	46.34 N	23.47 E
Tordera ≃	34	41.39 N	2.47 E
Tordesillas	34	41.30 N	5.00 W
Tordino ≃	66	42.44 N	13.59 E
Tor di Quinto ◆[8]	267a	41.56 N	12.28 E
Töre	26	65.54 N	22.39 E
Töreboda	40	58.43 N	14.08 E
Torej	88	50.33 N	104.50 E
Torekov	26	56.26 N	12.37 E
Toreno	34	42.42 N	6.30 W
Torez	83	48.01 N	38.37 E
Torfou	261	48.32 N	2.14 E
Torgau	54	51.34 N	13.00 E
Torgelow	54	53.37 N	14.00 E
Torgelower See ⊜	54	53.34 N	12.47 E
Torgo	88	58.28 N	119.50 E
Torgun ≃	80	50.15 N	46.18 E
Torhamn	26	56.05 N	15.50 E
Torhout	50	51.04 N	3.06 E
Toribero ≃	250	10.59 S	49.48 W
Toribulu	112	0.19 S	120.01 E
Toride	94	35.53 N	140.04 E
Torigakubi-misaki >	94	37.10 N	138.06 E
Torigoe	94	36.21 N	136.36 E
Toriido	270	34.25 N	135.43 E
Torii-tōge)(	94	36.29 N	138.24 E
Toriki	265a	59.47 N	30.07 E
Torín	232	27.34 N	110.14 W
Torino (Turin)	62	45.03 N	7.40 E
Torino □[4]	62	45.08 N	7.22 E
Torino di Sangro Marina	66	42.11 N	14.32 E
Torío ≃	34	42.35 N	5.34 W
Toriparu	255	16.20 S	53.55 W
Torit	154	4.24 N	32.34 E
Toritto	68	41.00 N	16.41 E
Toriya	94	36.59 N	136.54 E
Torjun	115a	7.10 S	113.13 E
Torkestān, Selseleh-ye Band-e ⋀	128	35.25 N	64.15 E
Torkoviči	76	58.52 N	30.20 E
Torlino	86	58.53 N	63.46 E
Torment, Point >	162	17.02 S	123.36 E
Tormentine, Cape >	186	46.07 N	63.47 W
Tormes ≃	34	41.18 N	6.29 W
Tormestorp	41	56.07 N	13.44 E
Tormey	282	38.03 N	122.15 W
Tormini	64	45.36 N	10.29 E
Tormosin	80	48.12 N	42.42 E
Torna	24	68.04 N	44.10 E
Torna ∧	122	18.16 N	73.37 E
Tornado Mountain ∧	182	49.58 N	114.39 W
Tornareccio	66	42.02 N	14.24 E
Tornberget ∧[2]	40	59.08 N	18.01 E
Torne ≃	44	53.36 N	0.44 W
Torneälven (Tornionjoki) ≃	24	65.48 N	24.08 E
Torne Brook ≃	276	41.08 N	74.10 W
Tornesch	52	53.41 N	9.43 E
Torneträsk ⊜	24	68.20 N	19.10 E
Torngat Mountains ⋀	176	59.00 N	64.00 W
Tornillo	200	31.27 N	106.05 W
Tornillo Creek ≃	196	29.11 N	103.00 W
Tornimparte	66	42.17 N	13.18 E
Torning	41	56.17 N	9.20 E
Tornio	26	65.51 N	24.08 E
Tornionjoki (Torneälven) ≃	24	65.48 N	24.08 E
Tornquist	252	38.06 S	62.14 W
T'orny, S.S.S.R.	78	48.09 N	33.33 E
T'orny, S.S.S.R.	78	50.59 N	33.59 E
T'orny, S.S.S.R.	83	49.05 N	37.57 E
Tornyiszentmiklós	61	46.31 N	16.34 E
Toro	34	41.31 N	5.24 W
Torö I	40	58.50 N	17.50 E
Toro, Arroyo ≃	288	34.27 S	58.52 W
Toro, Cañada del ≃	258	35.16 S	59.05 W
Toro, Cerro ∧	234	19.10 N	104.27 W
Toro, Lago del ⊜	254	51.14 S	72.45 W
Toro, Punta >	252	33.47 S	71.49 W
Torobuku	112	4.25 S	122.26 E
Torodi	150	13.18 N	1.40 E
Toro-iseki ⊥	94	34.57 N	138.24 E
Torok	146	10.03 N	14.33 E
Torokina	175e	6.14 S	155.03 E
Törökszentmiklós	30	47.11 N	20.25 E
Torola ≃	236	13.52 N	88.30 W
Torom	89	54.32 N	135.50 E
Torom ≃	89	54.36 N	135.46 E
Toroni, Nevado ∧	248	19.43 S	68.41 W
Toronto, Austl.	170	33.01 S	151.36 E
Toronto, On., Can.	212	43.39 N	79.23 W
Toronto, On., Can.	275b	43.39 N	79.23 W
Toronto, Ks., U.S.	198	37.47 N	95.56 W
Toronto, Oh., U.S.	214	40.27 N	80.36 W
Toronto, S.D., U.S.	198	44.34 N	96.38 W
Toronto □[6]	275b	43.44 N	79.24 W
Toronto, Canadian Forces Base ■	212	43.45 N	79.28 W
Toronto, University of ʊ[2]	275b	43.40 N	79.24 W
Toronto Harbour ⊂	275b	43.38 N	79.22 W
Toronto Island Airport ⊠	275b	43.38 N	79.24 W
Toronto Lake ⊜[1]	198	37.46 N	95.57 W
Toronto Reservoir ⊜[1]	210	41.38 N	74.51 W
Toronto Zoo, Metro ♠	275b	43.49 N	79.11 W
Toro Peak ∧	204	33.32 N	116.25 W
Toropec	76	56.30 N	31.39 E
Toropovo	82	54.21 N	36.07 E
Tororo	154	0.42 N	34.11 E
Toros Dağları (Taurus Mountains) ⋀	130	37.00 N	33.00 E
Torošino	76	57.56 N	28.36 E
Torosozero	24	62.30 N	38.10 E
Torotoro	248	18.07 S	65.46 W
Toroume ∧[2]	174k	21.15 S	159.45 W
Torpa ⊥	26	57.39 N	13.16 E
Torpè	71	40.38 N	9.40 E
Torphins	46	57.06 N	2.37 W
Tor Pignatara ◆[8]	267a	41.52 N	12.32 E
Torpo	26	60.40 N	8.43 E
Torpoint	42	50.22 N	4.11 W
Torpy ≃	182	53.44 N	120.55 W
Torquay, Austl.	169	38.21 S	144.19 E
Torquay, Sk., Can.	184	49.08 N	103.31 W
Torquay, Eng., U.K.	42	50.28 N	3.30 W
Torquemada	34	42.02 N	4.19 W
Torraca	68	40.07 N	15.38 E
Torraccia, Fosso ≃	267a	42.00 N	12.30 E
Torrance, Ca., U.S.	228	33.50 N	118.20 W
Torrance, Pa., U.S.	214	40.25 N	79.14 W
Torrance Lake ⊜	184	57.04 N	98.12 W
Torrance Municipal Airport ⊠	280	33.48 N	118.20 W
Torrão	34	38.18 N	8.13 W
Torre Annunziata	68	40.45 N	14.27 E
Torre Baja	34	40.07 N	1.15 W
Torrebelvicino	64	45.43 N	11.18 E
Torre Beretti	62	45.04 N	8.40 E
Torreblanca	34	40.13 N	0.12 E
Torrebruna	66	41.52 N	14.33 E
Torrecilla ∧	34	37.36 N	2.31 W
Torrecilla en Cameros	34	42.16 N	2.37 W
Torre del Campo	34	37.46 N	3.53 W
Torre del Greco	68	40.47 N	14.22 E
Torre del Lago Puccini	66	43.50 N	10.17 E
Torre de Moncorvo	34	41.10 N	7.03 W
Torre de'Passeri	66	42.14 N	13.56 E
Torre di Mosto	64	45.41 N	12.43 E
Torre di Santa Maria	64	46.14 N	9.51 E
Torredonjimeno	34	37.46 N	3.57 W
Torre Faro ◆[8]	70	38.16 N	15.39 E
Torre Gaia ◆[8]	267a	41.51 N	12.39 E
Torregrotta	70	38.11 N	15.21 E
Torrejon Air Base ■	266a	40.28 N	3.28 W
Torrejoncillo	34	39.54 N	6.28 W
Torrejón de Ardoz	34	40.27 N	3.29 W
Torrejón-Tajo, Embalse de ⊜[1]	34	39.50 N	5.50 W
Torrelaguna	34	40.50 N	3.32 W
Torrelavega	34	43.21 N	4.03 W
Torrellas, Riera de ≃	266d	41.23 N	2.01 E
Torrelles de Llobregat	266d	41.21 N	1.59 E
Torrelletes	266d	41.21 N	1.57 E
Torremaggiore	68	41.41 N	15.17 E
Torremolinos	34	36.37 N	4.30 W
Torrenieri	66	43.05 N	11.33 E
Torrens ≃	168b	34.56 S	138.30 E
Torrens, Lake ⊜	166	31.00 S	137.50 E
Torrens, Mount ∧	168b	34.52 S	138.56 E
Torrens Creek	166	20.46 S	145.02 E
Torrens Creek ≃	166	22.22 S	145.09 E
Torrens Island I	168b	34.48 S	138.32 E
Torrent, Arg.	252	28.50 S	56.28 W
Torrent, Esp.	34	39.26 N	0.28 W
Torreões	256	21.52 S	43.33 W
Torreón	232	25.33 N	103.26 W
Torre Orsaia	68	40.08 N	15.28 E
Torre Pedrera	66	44.06 N	12.31 E
Torre Pellice	62	44.49 N	7.13 E
Torreperogil	34	38.02 N	3.17 W
Torres, Arg.	258	34.26 S	59.08 W
Tôrres, Bra.	252	29.21 S	49.44 W
Torres, Arroyo ≃	288	34.39 S	58.45 W
Torres, Îles II	175f	13.15 S	166.37 E
Torre Santa Susanna	68	40.28 N	17.44 E
Torresdale ◆[8]	285	40.03 N	75.00 W
Torres de Alcalá	34	35.10 N	4.16 W
Torres Martinez Indian Reservation ◆[4]	204	33.35 N	116.02 W
Torres Novas	34	39.29 N	8.32 W
Torres Strait ⋓	164	10.25 S	142.10 E
Torres Vedras	34	39.06 N	9.16 W
Torretta	68	38.08 N	13.14 E
Torrette di Fano	66	43.47 N	13.07 E
Torrevella	34	37.59 N	0.41 W
Torricella	68	40.21 N	17.29 E
Torricella in Sabina	66	42.16 N	12.52 E
Torricella Peligna	66	42.01 N	14.15 E
Torricella Sicura	66	42.39 N	13.39 E
Torricelli Mountains ⋀	164	3.25 S	142.20 E
Torridge ≃	42	51.03 N	4.11 W
Torridon	46	57.33 N	5.31 W
Torridon, Loch ⊂	46	57.35 N	5.46 W
Torriglia	62	44.31 N	9.10 E
Torrijos, Esp.	34	39.59 N	4.17 W
Torrijos, Pil.	116	13.19 N	122.05 E
Torrild	41	55.59 N	10.04 E
Torrimpietra ◆[8]	267a	41.56 N	12.13 E
Torrin	46	57.12 N	6.02 W
Tørring	41	55.51 N	9.29 E
Torrington, Ct., U.S.	207	41.48 N	73.07 W
Torrington, Wy., U.S.	198	42.03 N	104.10 W
Torrinha	255	22.26 S	48.09 W
Torrita di Siena	66	43.10 N	11.46 E
Torröjen ⊜	26	63.55 N	12.56 E
Torrox	34	36.46 N	3.58 W
Torrvarpen ⊜	40	59.42 N	14.30 E
Torsåker	40	60.31 N	16.29 E
Tor Sapienza ◆[8]	267a	41.54 N	12.35 E
Torsås	26	56.24 N	16.00 E
Torsburgen ⊥	26	57.25 N	18.43 E
Torsby	26	60.08 N	13.00 E
Tors Cove	186	47.13 N	52.51 W
Torshälla	40	59.25 N	16.28 E
Tórshavn	22	62.01 N	6.46 W
Torside Reservoir ⊜[1]	262	53.29 N	1.54 W
Torsö	40	58.47 N	13.48 E
Torsö I	40	58.48 N	13.50 E
Torteval	43b	49.27 N	2.38 W
Torto ≃	70	37.58 N	13.46 E
Tortola I	240m	18.27 N	64.36 W
Tortolì	71	39.55 N	9.39 E
Tortona	62	44.54 N	8.52 E
Tortora	68	39.56 N	15.48 E
Tortoreto	66	42.48 N	13.55 E
Tortorici	70	38.02 N	14.49 E
Tortosa	34	40.48 N	0.31 E
Tortosa, Cap de >	34	40.43 N	0.55 E
Tortue ≃	186	50.18 N	65.23 W
Tortue, Île de la I	238	20.04 N	72.49 W
Tortue, Rivière de la ≃	206	45.24 N	73.32 W
Tortugas, Laguna ⊜	234	22.20 N	98.07 W
Tortuguero ≃	236	10.34 N	83.31 W
Tortuguero, Laguna ⊂	240m	18.28 N	66.26 W
Tortuguero, Puerto del ⊂	240m	18.29 N	66.28 W
Tortuguitas	288	34.28 S	58.46 W
Tortum	130	40.19 N	41.35 E
Toru ≃	114	1.26 N	98.46 E
Toruajgyr	85	42.32 N	76.26 E
Torue	112	0.58 S	120.18 E
Torugart, pereval)(	85	40.33 N	75.20 E
Torul	130	40.35 N	39.18 E
Toruń	30	53.02 N	18.35 E
Toruń □[4]	30	53.20 N	19.00 E
Torunos	246	8.30 N	70.04 W
Torup, Sve.	26	56.58 N	13.05 E
Torup, Sve.	41	55.34 N	13.12 E
Tõrva	76	58.00 N	25.56 E
Tory	88	51.47 N	103.00 E
Tory Island I	48	55.16 N	8.14 W
Torysa ≃	30	48.39 N	21.21 E
Tory Sound ⋓	48	55.14 N	8.14 W
Toržok	76	57.03 N	34.58 E
Torzym	30	52.20 N	15.04 E
Tosa, Nihon	96	33.44 N	133.32 E
Tosa, Nihon	96	33.29 N	133.25 E
T'oša ≃	80	55.38 N	42.09 E
T'osan	98	38.18 N	126.43 E
Tosari	115a	7.53 S	112.54 E
Tosa-shimizu	92	32.46 N	132.57 E
Tosa-wan ⊂	96	33.20 N	133.40 E
Tosayama	96	33.38 N	133.32 E
Tosa-yamada	96	33.36 N	133.41 E
Tosca	156	25.53 S	23.58 E
Toscaig	46	57.24 N	5.50 W
Toscana (Tuscany) □[4]	36	43.25 N	11.00 E
Toscolano	64	45.38 N	10.37 E
Tösens	58	47.01 N	10.36 E
Toses, Collada de)(	34	42.19 N	2.01 E
Tōshi-jima I	94	34.31 N	136.53 E
Toshima ◆[8]	268	35.44 N	139.43 E
To-shima I	94	34.31 N	139.17 E
Tōshō-gū ʊ[1]	94	36.46 N	139.36 E
Tosi, Indon.	115b	9.35 S	118.57 E
Tosi, It.	66	43.45 N	11.31 E
Tosilei	144	1.25 N	41.24 E
Toškalykaja, gora ∧	86	50.38 N	89.30 E
Toškovskij	83	48.46 N	38.34 E
Tosna ≃	265a	59.46 N	30.46 E
Tosno	76	59.33 N	30.53 E
Toson Cengel	88	48.47 N	98.15 E
Toson Hu ⊜	102	35.18 N	98.54 E
T'osovo	76	55.37 N	34.30 E
T'osovo-Netyl'skij	76	58.57 N	31.04 E
T'osovskij	76	58.48 N	30.52 E
Töss ≃	58	47.33 N	8.33 E
Tossens	52	53.34 N	8.16 E
Tossicia	66	42.33 N	13.39 E
Tost → Toszek	30	50.28 N	18.32 E
Tostado	252	29.14 S	61.46 W
Tõstamaa	76	58.20 N	24.00 E
Tostedt	52	53.17 N	9.42 E
Tosterön I	40	59.25 N	17.00 E
Tostu	85	41.34 N	71.34 E
Tost uul ⋀	102	43.15 N	100.30 E
Tosu	96	33.22 N	130.31 E
Tosya	130	41.01 N	34.02 E
Totagatic ≃	190	46.05 N	92.11 W
Totak ⊜	26	59.42 N	7.57 E
Totana	34	37.46 N	1.30 W
Totānāla	126	22.05 N	87.40 E
Totatiche	234	21.56 N	103.27 W
Totban	80	46.47 N	49.06 E
Toteng	156	20.22 S	22.58 E
Tôtes	50	49.41 N	1.03 E
Totes Gebirge ⋀	30	47.42 N	13.55 E
T'otkino	78	51.17 N	34.16 E
Tot'ma	76	59.57 N	42.45 E
Totnes	42	50.25 N	3.41 W
Totness	250	5.53 N	56.19 W
Toto	152	7.08 S	14.16 E
Totonicapán	236	14.55 N	91.22 W
Totonicapán □[5]	236	15.00 N	91.20 W
Totopotomoy Creek ≃	208	37.41 N	77.13 W
Totora, Bol.	248	17.42 S	65.09 W
Totora, Bol.	248	17.49 S	68.07 W
Totora Palca	248	19.55 S	65.26 W
Totoras	252	32.35 S	61.11 W
Totos	248	13.31 S	74.30 W
Tototlán	234	20.33 N	102.48 W
Totowa	210	40.54 N	74.12 W
Totoya Island I	175g	18.57 S	179.50 W
Totson Mountain ∧	180	64.26 N	157.15 W
Totsuka ◆[8]	268	35.24 N	139.32 E
Totten Glacier ⊓	9	66.45 S	116.10 E
Tottenham, Austl.	166	32.14 S	147.21 E
Tottenham, On., Can.	212	44.01 N	79.49 W
Tottenham ◆[8]	260	51.35 N	0.04 W
Tottenham Hotspur Football Ground ♠	260	51.36 N	0.04 W
Totten Inlet ⊂	224	47.07 N	123.02 W
Tottenville ◆[8]	276	40.31 N	74.15 W
Totteridge ◆[8]	260	51.38 N	0.12 W
Tottington	44	53.37 N	2.20 W
Totton	42	50.56 N	1.29 W
Tottori	96	35.30 N	134.14 E
Tottori □[5]	96	35.30 N	134.00 E
Tottori-sakyū ∧[2]	96	35.31 N	134.15 E
Totuskey Creek ≃	208	37.52 N	76.45 W
Tou, Motu I	174k	21.11 S	159.48 W
Touba, C. Iv.	150	8.17 N	7.41 W
Touba, Sén.	150	14.51 N	15.53 W
Toubei	100	26.44 N	116.05 E
Toubéré Bafal	150	14.23 N	13.32 W
Toubkal, Jebel ∧	148	31.05 N	7.55 W
Toubkal, Parc National du ♠	148	31.05 N	7.55 W
Toubori	146	13.59 N	12.18 E
Touboro	152	7.43 N	15.12 E
T'ouch'eng	100	24.52 N	121.49 E
Touchet ≃	202	46.02 N	118.41 W
Touchwood Hills ⋀[2]	184	51.35 N	104.17 W
Touchwood Lake ⊜, Ab., Can.	182	54.50 N	111.23 W
Touchwood Lake ⊜, Mb., Can.	184	54.29 N	95.00 W
Toucy	50	47.44 N	3.18 E
Toudao ≃	98	42.36 N	127.11 E
Toudaogou, Zhg.	98	42.46 N	129.12 E
Toudaogou, Zhg.	104	41.37 N	121.40 E
Toudaogou, Zhg.	105	40.58 N	117.59 E
Touët-sur-Var	62	43.57 N	7.00 E
Tougan	150	13.04 N	3.04 W
Touggourt	148	33.10 N	6.00 E
Toughkenamon	285	39.50 N	75.46 W
Tougouri	150	13.19 N	0.31 W
Tougué	150	11.27 N	11.41 W
Touho	175f	20.47 S	165.14 E
Touiel, Oued V	148	31.30 N	4.46 E
Touil, Oued V	148	35.30 N	2.33 E
Touisset	207	41.43 N	71.13 W
Toukansi	100	29.22 N	119.06 E
Toukley	170	33.16 S	151.33 E
Toukoto	150	13.27 N	9.53 W
Toul	58	48.41 N	5.54 E
Toulépleu	150	6.35 N	8.25 W
Touliu	100	23.43 N	120.32 E
Toulnustouc ≃	186	49.35 N	68.24 W
Toulnustouc Nord-Est ≃	186	50.56 N	67.44 W
Toulon, Fr.	62	43.07 N	5.56 E
Toulon, Il., U.S.	190	41.05 N	89.51 W
Toulon Lake ⊜	204	40.01 N	118.40 W
Toulon-sur-Arroux	32	46.42 N	4.08 E
Touloubre ≃	62	43.33 N	5.02 E
Toulourenc ≃	62	44.14 N	5.09 E
Toulouse	32	43.36 N	1.26 E
Toumen Shan I	100	28.41 N	121.46 E
Toumfafi	150	15.02 N	5.38 E
Toumodi	150	6.33 N	5.01 W
Tounan	100	23.41 N	120.28 E
Tounassine, Hamada ◆[2]	148	28.30 N	5.00 W
Toungo	146	8.07 N	12.03 E
Toungoo	110	18.56 N	96.26 E
Toupeng	106	30.19 N	120.31 E
Touques	50	49.22 N	0.06 E
Touques ≃	50	49.22 N	0.06 E
Tour, Étang de la ⊜	261	48.40 N	1.53 E
Toura, Monts du ⋀	150	7.40 N	7.25 W
Touraine	188	45.34 N	75.47 W
Touraine □[9]	50	47.12 N	1.30 E
Tourakom	110	18.26 N	102.32 E
Tourane → Da Nang	108	16.04 N	108.13 E
Tourassine ⍑[4]	148	24.37 N	11.23 W
Tourbe ≃	56	49.10 N	4.52 E
Tourcoing	50	50.43 N	3.09 E
Touriñan, Cabo >	34	43.03 N	9.18 W
Tournai	50	50.36 N	3.23 E
Tournan-en-Brie	50	48.44 N	2.46 E
Tourndo, Oued V	148	22.15 N	10.28 E
Tournesac ≃	50	47.15 N	4.12 E
Tournhout	56	51.19 N	4.57 E
Tournon	62	45.04 N	4.50 E
Tournus	58	46.34 N	4.54 E
Touros	250	5.12 S	35.28 W
Tou Rout	110	16.24 N	107.00 E
Tourouvre	50	48.35 N	0.40 E
Tourrette-Levens	62	43.47 N	7.16 E
Tours	50	47.23 N	0.41 E
Tours-sur-Marne	50	49.03 N	4.07 E
Tours-sur-Meymont	62	45.40 N	3.35 E
Tourteron	56	49.32 N	4.39 E
Tourves	62	43.24 N	5.56 E
Toury	50	48.12 N	1.56 E
Toussaint Creek ≃	214	41.35 N	83.04 W
Toussidé, Pic ∧	146	21.02 N	16.25 E
Toussoro, Mont ∧	146	9.18 N	23.23 E
Toussus-le-Noble	261	48.45 N	2.07 E
Toussus-le-Noble, Aéroport de ⊠	261	48.45 N	2.10 E
Toustain	36	36.40 N	8.15 E
Toutai, Zhg.	89	45.40 N	124.50 E
Toutai, Zhg.	104	41.41 N	121.11 E
Toutaizi	104	42.19 N	122.49 E
Toutle	224	46.20 N	122.41 W
Toutle ≃	224	46.17 N	122.55 W
Toutle, North Fork ≃	224	46.23 N	122.34 W
Toutle, South Fork ≃	224	46.20 N	122.44 W
Toutle Mountain Range ⋀	224	46.20 N	122.30 W
Toutuohe	100	31.06 N	116.25 E
Touws ≃	158	33.45 S	21.11 E
Touwsrivier	158	33.20 S	20.00 E
Touzhan	89	49.27 N	119.41 E
Toužim	60	50.04 N	13.00 E
Töv □[4]	88	47.30 N	106.30 E
Tova	24	65.58 N	40.45 E
Tovar	246	8.20 N	71.46 W
Tovarkovo	82	54.42 N	35.57 E
Tovarkovskij	76	53.40 N	38.14 E
Tove ≃	42	52.05 N	0.38 W
Tovey	219	39.35 N	89.27 W
Tow	196	30.53 N	98.28 W
Tōwa	96	33.13 N	132.53 E
Towaco	210	40.55 N	74.20 W
Towada	92	40.37 N	141.13 E
Towada-Hachimantai-kokuritsu-kōen ♠	92	40.35 N	140.53 E
Towada-ko ⊜	92	40.28 N	140.55 E
Towai	172	35.29 S	174.08 E
Towamencin Creek ≃	285	40.13 N	75.23 W
Towanda, Il., U.S.	216	40.34 N	88.54 W
Towanda, Ks., U.S.	198	37.47 N	96.59 W
Towanda, Pa., U.S.	210	41.46 N	76.26 W
Towanda Creek ≃	210	41.45 N	76.26 W
Towan Head >	42	50.25 N	5.07 W
Towar Gardens	216	42.45 N	84.28 W
Towari	112	4.36 S	121.29 E
Towcester	42	52.08 N	1.00 W
Tower	190	47.48 N	92.16 W
Tower City, N.D., U.S.	198	46.55 N	97.40 W
Tower City, Pa., U.S.	208	40.35 N	76.33 W
Tower Hamlets ◆[8]	42	51.32 N	0.03 W
Tower Hill, Austl.	166	22.03 S	144.36 E
Tower Hill, Il., U.S.	219	39.23 N	88.57 W
Towerhill Creek ≃	166	22.29 S	144.39 E
Tower of London ⊥	260	51.30 N	0.05 W
Tower Peak ∧	226	38.09 N	119.33 W
Towers of Silence ʊ[1]	272c	18.58 N	72.48 E
Tower Soudan State Park ♠	190	47.50 N	92.15 W
Towla, Mount ∧	154	21.22 S	29.52 E
Tow Law	44	54.44 N	1.49 W
Towlī	84	39.11 N	47.32 E
Town ≃	283	42.00 N	70.57 W
Town and Country	202	47.42 N	117.23 W
Town Bank	208	39.00 N	74.56 W
Town Creek ≃, Al., U.S.	194	34.24 N	86.11 W
Town Creek ≃, Al., U.S.	194	34.46 N	87.25 W
Town Creek ≃, Oh., U.S.	216	41.05 N	84.25 W
Town Creek Manor	208	38.19 N	76.27 W
Towneley Hall ⊥	262	53.46 N	2.13 W
Towner	198	48.20 N	100.24 W
Town Estates	285	40.04 N	74.52 W
Town Hill ∧[2]	240a	32.19 N	64.44 W
Townline Tunnel ◆[5]	284a	42.57 N	79.15 W
Town of Niagara	284a	43.06 N	78.59 W
Town of Pines	216	41.41 N	86.58 W
Town of Tonawanda	210	42.59 N	78.52 W
Townsend, On., Can.	212	42.54 N	80.07 W
Townsend, De., U.S.	208	39.23 N	75.41 W
Townsend, Ma., U.S.	207	42.40 N	71.42 W
Townsend, Mt., U.S.	202	46.19 N	111.31 W
Townsend, Va., U.S.	208	37.11 N	75.57 W
Townsend, Mount ∧	171b	36.25 S	148.15 E
Townsend Island I	276	40.38 N	73.26 W
Townsends Inlet ⊂	208	39.07 N	74.43 W
Townshend Island I	166	22.15 S	150.30 E
Township Line Run ≃	279b	40.13 N	79.33 W
Townsville	166	19.16 S	146.48 E
Townville	214	41.41 N	79.53 W
Towrang	170	34.42 S	149.51 E
Towrang, Mount ∧	170	34.46 S	149.51 E
Towra Point >	274a	34.00 S	151.10 E
Towr Kham	123	34.08 N	71.05 E

Symbols in the index entries represent the broad categories identified in the key at the right. Symbols with superior numbers (⋀[1]) identify subcategories (see complete key on page *I · 1*).

Symbole im Register stellen die rechts im Schlüssel erklärten Kategorien dar. Symbole mit hochgestellten Ziffern (⋀[1]) bezeichnen Unterabteilungen einer Kategorie (vgl. vollständiger Schlüssel auf Seite *I · 1*).

Los símbolos incluídos en el texto del índice representan las grandes categorías identificadas con la clave a la derecha. Los símbolos con numeros en su parte superior (⋀[1]) identifican las subcategorías (véase la clave completa en la página *I · 1*).

Les symboles de l'index représentent les catégories indiquées dans la légende à droite. Les symboles suivis d'un indice (⋀[1]) représentent des sous-catégories (voir légende complète à la page *I · 1*).

Os símbolos incluídos no texto do índice representam as grandes categorias identificadas com a chave à direita. Os símbolos com números em sua parte superior (⋀[1]) identificam as subcategorias (veja-se a chave completa à página *I · 1*).

	English	Deutsch	Español	Français	Português
∧	Mountain	Berg	Montaña	Montagne	Montanha
⋀	Mountains	Gebirge	Montañas	Montagnes	Montanhas
)(	Pass	Paß	Paso	Col	Passo
V	Valley, Canyon	Tal, Cañon	Valle, Cañón	Vallée, Canyon	Vale, Canhão
≚	Plain	Ebene	Llano	Plaine	Planície
>	Cape	Kap	Cabo	Cap	Cabo
I	Island	Insel	Isla	Île	Ilha
II	Islands	Inseln	Islas	Îles	Ilhas
⊥	Other Topographic Features	Andere Topographische Objekte	Otros Elementos Topográficos	Autres données topographiques	Outros acidentes topográficos

ESPAÑOL

Nombre	Página	Lat.°′	Long.°′ W = Oeste
Towrzī, Afg.	120	30.11 N	65.59 E
Towrzī, Afg.	128	32.38 N	65.53 E
Towson	208	39.24 N	76.36 W
Towson State College ᵿ[2]	284b	39.24 N	76.37 W
Towuti, Danau ⊜	112	2.45 S	121.32 E
Toxkan (Aksaj) ≃, Asia	85	40.55 N	78.16 E
Toxkan ≃, Zhg.	90	41.08 N	80.11 E
Toyah	196	31.19 N	103.47 W
Toyah Creek ≃	196	31.18 N	103.27 W
Tōya-ko ⊜	92a	42.35 N	140.51 E
Toyama	94	36.41 N	137.13 E
Toyama □[5]	94	36.30 N	137.30 E
Toyama-heiya ≚	94	36.40 N	137.15 E
Toyama-wan ⊂	94	36.50 N	137.10 E
Toyapakeh	115b	8.41 S	115.29 E
Tōyō, Nihon	96	33.30 N	134.16 E
Tōyo, Nihon	96	33.55 N	133.05 E
Toyo ≃	94	34.47 N	137.20 E
Toyoake	94	35.03 N	137.01 E
Toyoda, Nihon	94	34.45 N	137.49 E
Toyoda, Nihon	268	35.39 N	139.23 E
Toyofuta	268	35.53 N	139.57 E
Toyohama	96	34.04 N	133.38 E
Toyohara	175d	24.15 N	123.48 E
Toyohashi	94	34.46 N	137.23 E
Toyohira	96	34.40 N	132.24 E
Toyokawa	94	34.49 N	137.24 E
Toyo-kawa-yōsui ≊	94	34.35 N	137.03 E
Toyonaka, Nihon	96	34.09 N	133.42 E
Toyonaka, Nihon	96	34.47 N	135.28 E
Toyone	94	35.09 N	137.43 E
Toyono	94	36.43 N	138.16 E
Toyooka, Nihon	94	34.50 N	137.52 E
Toyooka, Nihon	94	35.33 N	137.54 E
Toyooka, Nihon	96	35.32 N	134.50 E
Toyooka, Nihon	268	35.11 N	139.58 E
Toyosaka, Nihon	92	37.56 N	139.13 E
Toyosaka, Nihon	96	34.34 N	132.50 E
Toyosato	94	36.06 N	140.02 E
Toyoshina	94	36.18 N	137.54 E
Toyota, Nihon	94	35.05 N	137.09 E
Toyota, Nihon	94	36.46 N	138.19 E
Toyota, Nihon	96	34.12 N	131.04 E
Toyota-ko ⊜	96	34.14 N	131.08 E
Toyotomi	94	35.34 N	138.33 E
Toyotsu	96	33.40 N	130.58 E
Toyoura	96	34.08 N	130.58 E
Toy's Hill	260	51.14 N	0.06 E
Tozer, Mount ∧	164	12.45 S	143.13 E
Tozeur	148	33.55 N	8.08 E
Tozi, Mount ∧	180	65.41 N	150.58 W
Tozitna ≃	180	65.08 N	152.23 W
Tpig	84	41.47 N	47.36 E
Traar ◆[8]	263	51.23 N	6.36 E
Trabaria, Bocca)(	66	43.36 N	12.14 E
Traben-Trarbach	56	49.57 N	7.06 E
Trabia	70	37.59 N	13.39 E
Trabiju	255	22.03 S	48.18 W
Trabuco, Arroyo ≃	228	33.31 N	117.40 W
Trabzon	130	41.00 N	39.43 E
Trabzon □[4]	130	40.50 N	39.50 E
Tracadie	186	47.31 N	64.54 W
Tracajá, Cachoeira ∟	248	10.29 S	64.05 W
Trachenberg → Żmigród	30	51.29 N	16.55 E
Trachselwald	58	47.01 N	7.45 E
Tra Cu	110	9.42 N	106.16 E
Tracuateua	250	1.05 S	46.54 W
Tracy, P.Q., Can.	206	46.01 N	73.09 W
Tracy, Ca., U.S.	226	37.44 N	121.25 W
Tracy, Mn., U.S.	198	44.14 N	95.37 W
Tracy City	194	35.15 N	85.44 W
Tracyton	224	47.36 N	122.39 W
Tradate	62	45.43 N	8.54 E
Trade Lake ⊜	184	55.22 N	103.44 W
Tradewater ≃	194	37.31 N	88.03 W
Trading Bay ⊂	212	45.15 N	78.55 W
Tradinghouse Creek Reservoir ⊜[1]	222	31.35 N	96.55 W
Traditional Cultures, Museum of ᵿ	269f	14.31 N	121.00 E
Trælleborg ⊥	41	55.23 N	11.17 E
Traer	190	42.11 N	92.27 W
Traessu, Monte ∧	71	40.28 N	8.40 E
Trafalgar, Austl.	169	38.12 S	146.09 E
Trafalgar, On., Can.	275b	43.29 N	79.43 W
Trafalgar, In., U.S.	218	39.24 N	86.09 W
Trafalgar, Cabo ›	34	36.11 N	6.02 W
Trafaria	266c	38.40 N	9.14 W
Trafford	214	40.23 N	79.45 W
Trafford □[8]	262	53.24 N	2.21 W
Trafford, Lake ⊜	220	26.25 N	81.30 W
Trafford Park	262	53.28 N	2.20 W
Trafoi	64	46.33 N	10.31 E
Tragacete	34	40.21 N	1.51 W
Tragliata ◆[8]	267a	41.58 N	12.15 E
Tragwein	61	48.20 N	14.37 E
Traição, Córrego ≃	287b	23.36 S	46.41 W
Traid	34	40.40 N	1.49 W
Traiguén	252	38.15 S	72.41 W
Traiguén, Isla I	254	45.35 S	73.42 W
Trail	182	49.06 N	117.42 W
Trail Creek	216	41.41 N	86.51 W
Trailer Estates	220	27.24 N	82.34 W
Trail Ridge ∧	192	30.35 N	82.05 W
Traînel	50	48.25 N	3.27 E
Trainer	285	39.50 N	75.25 W
Traipu	250	9.58 S	37.01 W
Traíra (Taraira) ≃	246	1.04 S	69.26 W
Trairão ≃	250	7.20 S	51.14 W
Traíras ≃	255	14.07 S	48.31 W
Trairi	250	3.17 S	39.15 W
Traisen	61	48.02 N	15.37 E
Traisen ≃	61	48.22 N	15.46 E
Traiskirchen	61	48.01 N	16.18 E
Traismauer	61	48.21 N	15.44 E
Traîtres, Baie des ⊂	174x	9.50 S	139.02 W
Trajouce	266c	38.44 N	9.20 W
Trakai	76	54.38 N	24.56 E
Trakt	24	62.44 N	51.11 E
Träkvista	40	59.16 N	17.47 E
Tralee	48	52.16 N	9.42 W
Tralee Bay ⊂	48	52.15 N	9.59 W
Trá Lí → Tralee	48	52.16 N	9.42 W
Tramatza	71	40.00 N	8.39 E
Tramayes	58	46.18 N	4.36 E
Tramelan	58	47.13 N	7.06 E
Tra Mi	110	15.20 N	108.13 E
Tramin → Termeno	64	46.20 N	11.14 E
Trammel	192	37.00 N	82.17 W
Trammel Creek ≃	194	36.52 N	86.23 W
Tramonti di sopra	64	46.18 N	12.47 E
Tramore	48	52.10 N	7.10 W
Tramperos Creek (Punta de Agua Creek) ≃	196	35.32 N	102.27 W
Tramping Lake ⊜	184	52.08 N	108.49 W
Tramutola	68	40.19 N	15.47 E
Trân	38	42.50 N	22.39 E
Tranås	26	58.03 N	14.59 E
Trancão ≃	266c	38.48 N	9.06 W
Trancas	252	26.13 S	65.17 W
Trancoso, Méx.	234	22.44 N	102.22 W
Trancoso, Port.	34	40.47 N	7.21 W
Trand	123	34.38 N	72.59 E
Tranderup	41	54.52 N	10.22 E
Tranebjerg	41	55.50 N	10.36 E
Tranekær	41	55.00 N	10.51 E
Tranemo	26	57.29 N	13.21 E
Tranent	46	55.57 N	2.58 W
Tränental	158	27.09 S	19.33 E
Trang	110	7.33 N	99.36 E
Trangahy	157b	19.07 S	44.43 E
Trangan, Pulau I	164	6.35 S	134.20 E
Trangie	166	32.02 S	147.59 E
Tran Grande ≃	116	6.43 N	124.01 E

FRANÇAIS

Nom	Page	Lat.°′	Long.°′ W = Ouest
Trängslet	26	61.25 N	13.40 E
Trani	68	41.17 N	16.26 E
Tranmere	262	53.23 N	3.01 W
Trannon ≃	42	52.31 N	3.25 W
Tranoroa	157b	24.42 S	45.04 E
Tranquebar	122	11.02 N	79.51 E
Tranqueira ≃	250	7.15 S	42.12 W
Tranqueras	252	31.12 S	55.45 W
Tranquility	218	38.58 N	83.32 W
Tranquilla	236	8.30 N	80.14 W
Tranquillity	226	36.38 N	120.15 W
Transantarctic Mountains ⋏	9	85.00 S	175.00 W
Trans-en-Provence	62	43.30 N	6.29 E
Transfer	214	41.20 N	80.26 W
Transit Airport ⊠	284a	43.06 N	78.44 W
Transkei □[1], Afr.	138	31.20 S	29.00 E
Transkei □[1], Afr.	158	31.20 S	29.00 E
Transquaking ≃	208	38.22 N	76.00 W
Transsylvanische Alpen → Carpații Meridionali ⋏	38	45.30 N	24.15 E
Transtrand	26	61.05 N	13.19 E
Transtrandsfjällen ∧	26	61.17 N	13.00 E
Transvaal □[4]	156	25.00 S	29.00 E
Transylvania □[9]	38	46.30 N	24.00 E
Transylvanian Alps → Carpații Meridionali ⋏	38	45.30 N	24.15 E
Tranters Creek ≃	192	35.33 N	77.05 W
Traona	58	46.09 N	9.31 E
Trapalcó, Salinas de ≚	254	39.45 S	66.45 W
Trapani	70	38.01 N	12.31 E
Trapani □[4]	70	37.50 N	12.40 E
Traphole Brook ≃	283	42.10 N	71.11 W
Trappe, Md., U.S.	208	38.39 N	76.03 W
Trappe, Pa., U.S.	208	40.12 N	75.29 W
Trappenkamp	54	54.03 N	10.16 E
Trapper Peak ∧	202	45.54 N	114.18 W
Trappes	50	48.47 N	2.00 E
Trappeto	70	38.04 N	13.03 E
Trapuá ≃	287b	23.36 S	46.17 W
Traralgon	169	38.12 S	146.32 E
Traralgon Creek ≃	169	38.10 S	146.31 E
Traras, Monts des ⋏	34	35.10 N	1.40 W
Trarza □[4]	150	17.45 N	15.45 W
Trârza ◆[1]	150	18.00 N	15.00 W
Trasacco	66	41.57 N	13.32 E
Trasadingen	58	47.40 N	8.26 E
Trascăului, Munții ⋏	38	46.23 N	23.33 E
Trasimeno, Lago ⊜	66	43.08 N	12.06 E
Trask ≃	224	45.28 N	123.53 W
Träslövsläge	26	57.04 N	12.16 E
Trasna	82	54.45 N	38.42 E
Trás-os-Montes □[9]	34	41.30 N	7.15 W
Trassem	56	49.34 N	6.31 E
Trâstenik	38	43.31 N	24.28 E
Trat	110	12.14 N	102.30 E
Tratalias	71	39.06 N	8.34 E
Tratzberg, Schloss ⊥	64	47.23 N	11.44 E
Trauchgau	58	47.38 N	10.49 E
Traun	61	48.13 N	14.14 E
Traun ≃, B.R.D.	60	48.00 N	12.32 E
Traun ≃, Öst.	30	48.16 N	14.22 E
Traunkirchen	64	47.50 N	13.47 E
Traunreut	64	47.56 N	12.35 E
Traunsee ⊜	64	47.51 N	13.48 E
Traunstein, B.R.D.	64	47.52 N	12.38 E
Traunstein, Öst.	61	48.26 N	15.07 E
Traunstein ∧	64	47.52 N	13.50 E
Trautenstein	54	51.41 N	10.43 E
Travagliato	64	45.31 N	10.05 E
Trave ≃	54	53.54 N	10.50 E
Travedona	62	45.48 N	8.40 E
Travellers Lake ⊜	166	33.18 S	142.00 E
Travemünde ◆[8]	54	53.57 N	10.52 E
Traver	226	36.27 N	119.29 W
Travers, Mount ∧	172	42.01 S	172.44 E
Travers, Val de V	58	46.57 N	6.38 E
Traverse, Lake ⊜	198	45.43 N	96.40 W
Traverse Bay ⊂	184	50.40 N	96.25 W
Traverse City	190	44.45 N	85.37 W
Traversella	62	45.30 N	7.45 E
Traverse Peak ∧	180	65.10 N	159.12 W
Traversetolo	64	44.38 N	10.23 E
Travers Reservoir ⊜[1]	182	50.14 N	112.51 W
Travesía ⊥	236	15.20 N	87.53 W
Tra Vinh	110	9.56 N	106.20 E
Travis	222	31.08 N	97.00 W
Travis □[6]	222	30.18 N	97.40 W
Travis, Lake ⊜[1]	196	30.27 N	98.00 W
Travis Air Force Base ■	226	38.16 N	121.55 W
Travnik	36	44.14 N	17.40 E
Trawalla	169	37.26 S	143.29 E
Trawbreaga Bay ⊂	48	55.17 N	7.18 W
Trawick	222	31.46 N	94.45 W
Trawsfynydd	42	52.54 N	3.55 W
Trayning	162	31.07 S	117.48 E
Trazegnies	50	50.28 N	4.19 E
Trbovlje	36	46.10 N	15.03 E
Treadwell	210	42.21 N	75.03 W
Treales	262	53.47 N	2.51 W
Treasure Island	220	27.46 N	82.46 W
Treasure Island I	226	37.48 N	122.22 W
Treasure Island Naval Station ■	282	37.49 N	122.22 W
Trebatsch	54	52.05 N	14.09 E
Trebbia ≃	62	45.04 N	9.41 E
Trebbin	54	52.13 N	13.13 E
Třebechovice pod Orebem	30	50.12 N	16.00 E
Trebel	54	52.59 N	11.20 E
Trebel ≃	54	53.55 N	13.01 E
Trebelsee ⊜	54	52.28 N	12.47 E
Třebenice	54	50.29 N	14.00 E
Trebgast	60	50.04 N	11.33 E
Třebíč	30	49.13 N	15.53 E
Trebinje	38	42.43 N	18.20 E
Trebisacce	68	39.52 N	16.32 E
Trebišov	30	48.40 N	21.47 E
Trebitz	54	51.45 N	12.44 E
Trebizond → Trabzon	130	41.00 N	39.43 E
Trebjerg ∧[2]	41	55.10 N	10.14 E
Třebkov	60	49.22 N	14.04 E
Treble Mountain ∧	182	55.50 N	129.51 W
Treblinka	30	52.39 N	22.03 E
Trebnitz → Trzebnica	30	51.19 N	17.03 E
Třeboň	61	49.00 N	14.47 E
Třebouň ∧	60	50.01 N	12.59 E
Trebsen	54	51.17 N	12.45 E
Trebur	56	49.56 N	8.25 E
Trecastagni	70	37.37 N	15.05 E
Trecate	62	45.26 N	8.44 E
Trecchina	68	40.02 N	15.46 E
Trece Martires	116	14.16 N	120.50 E
Trecenta	64	45.02 N	11.28 E
Tred Avon River ⊂	208	38.42 N	76.08 W
Tredegar	42	51.47 N	3.16 W
Tredici Archi, Ponte ◆[5]	66	41.32 N	14.57 E
Treene ≃	41	54.22 N	9.05 E
Trees Mills	279b	40.23 N	80.13 W
Treffen	64	46.40 N	13.52 E
Treffort	58	46.16 N	5.22 E
Treffurt	56	51.08 N	10.14 E
Trèfle, Lac du ⊜	206	46.36 N	73.55 W
Tregaron	42	52.13 N	3.55 W
Tregnago	64	45.31 N	11.10 E
Tregosse Islets II	166	17.41 S	150.43 E
Tregubovo	76	58.59 N	31.33 E
Tréguier	32	48.47 N	3.14 W
Treharris	42	51.41 N	3.16 W
Treherne	184	49.38 N	98.41 W
Trehörningsjö	26	63.42 N	18.48 E
Treia, B.R.D.	41	54.30 N	9.17 E

PORTUGUÊS

Nome	Página	Lat.°′	Long.°′ W = Oeste
Treia, It.	66	43.19 N	13.19 E
Treig, Loch ⊜[1]	46	56.50 N	4.44 W
Treinta y Tres	252	33.14 S	54.23 W
Treis	56	50.10 N	7.17 E
Trekkopje	156	22.18 S	14.53 E
Trélazé	32	47.27 N	0.28 W
Trelde Næs ›	41	55.37 N	9.52 E
Trelew	254	43.15 S	65.18 W
Trelleborg	41	55.22 N	13.10 E
Treloar	219	38.39 N	91.10 W
Tremadog	42	52.56 N	4.09 W
Tremadog Bay ⊂	42	52.52 N	4.15 W
Tremblant, Lac ⊜	206	46.15 N	74.38 W
Tremblant, Mont ∧	206	46.16 N	74.35 W
Tremblay, Hippodrome du ♠	261	48.50 N	2.29 E
Tremblay-lès-Gonesse	261	48.59 N	2.34 E
Trembleur Lake ⊜	182	54.51 N	125.07 W
Tremedal	255	14.58 S	41.24 W
Tremembé	256	22.58 S	45.33 W
Tremezzo	58	45.59 N	9.15 E
Tremino	88	56.42 N	98.04 E
Tremiti, Isole II	66	42.07 N	15.30 E
Tremo La)(	124	27.44 N	89.12 E
Tremont, Il., U.S.	190	40.31 N	89.29 W
Tremont, In., U.S.	216	41.39 N	87.02 W
Tremont, Pa., U.S.	208	40.37 N	76.23 W
Tremont ◆[8]	276	40.51 N	73.55 W
Tremont City	218	40.00 N	83.50 W
Tremonton	200	41.42 N	112.09 W
Třemošna	60	49.49 N	13.20 E
Třemošná ≃	60	49.52 N	13.32 E
Tremp	34	42.10 N	0.54 E
Trempealeau	190	44.00 N	91.26 W
Trempealeau ≃	190	44.02 N	91.32 W
Tremsbüttel	52	53.44 N	10.18 E
Trena	144	10.45 N	40.38 E
Trenčín	30	48.54 N	18.04 E
Trendelburg	52	51.34 N	9.25 E
Trenel	252	35.42 S	64.08 W
Trêng	110	12.49 N	102.54 E
Trenggalek	115a	8.03 S	111.43 E
Trenque Lauquen	252	35.58 S	62.42 W
Trent, D.D.R.	54	54.31 N	13.15 E
Trent → Trento, It.	64	46.04 N	11.08 E
Trent ≃, On., Can.	212	44.06 N	77.34 W
Trent ≃, Eng., U.K.	28	53.42 N	0.41 W
Trent ≃, N.C., U.S.	192	35.05 N	77.02 W
Trent, Vale of V	42	52.44 N	1.50 W
Trent and Mersey Canal ≊	262	53.19 N	2.39 W
Trente et un Milles, Lac des ⊜	188	46.12 N	75.49 W
Trentham	169	37.23 S	144.19 E
Trentino-Alto Adige □[4]	64	46.30 N	11.20 E
Trento	64	46.04 N	11.08 E
Trento □[4]	64	46.08 N	11.07 E
Trentola-Ducenta	68	40.59 N	14.10 E
Trenton, N.S., Can.	186	45.37 N	62.38 W
Trenton, On., Can.	212	44.06 N	77.35 W
Trenton, Fl., U.S.	192	29.36 N	82.49 W
Trenton, Ga., U.S.	192	34.52 N	85.30 W
Trenton, Il., U.S.	219	38.36 N	89.40 W
Trenton, Ky., U.S.	194	36.43 N	87.15 W
Trenton, Mi., U.S.	216	42.08 N	83.10 W
Trenton, Mo., U.S.	194	40.04 N	93.36 W
Trenton, Ne., U.S.	198	40.10 N	101.00 W
Trenton, N.J., U.S.	208	40.13 N	74.44 W
Trenton, N.C., U.S.	192	35.04 N	77.21 W
Trenton, Oh., U.S.	218	39.29 N	84.28 W
Trenton, Tn., U.S.	194	35.58 N	88.56 W
Trenton, Tx., U.S.	196	33.26 N	96.20 W
Trenton, Canadian Forces Base ■	190	44.07 N	77.33 W
Trenton Channel ≃[1]	281	42.06 N	83.11 W
Trentwood	202	47.42 N	117.13 W
Trepalade	64	45.34 N	12.24 E
Trepassey	186	46.44 N	53.22 W
Trepassey Bay ⊂	186	46.37 N	53.20 W
Treptow ◆[8]	54	52.29 N	13.29 E
Treptow an der Rega → Trzebiatów	30	54.04 N	15.14 E
Trepuzzi	68	40.24 N	18.05 E
Trequanda	66	43.11 N	11.40 E
Tresa ≃	58	46.00 N	8.43 E
Tres Algarrobos	252	35.12 S	62.46 W
Tres Árboles	252	32.24 S	56.43 W
Tres Arroyos	252	38.23 S	60.17 W
Tres Cerros	254	48.13 S	67.33 W
Treščevo	82	54.11 N	37.55 E
Tresckow	210	40.54 N	75.58 W
Tresco I	42a	49.57 N	6.19 W
Três Corações	256	21.42 S	45.16 W
Trescore Balneario	62	45.41 N	9.50 E
Três Coroas	252	29.32 S	50.48 W
Tres de Febrero → Caseros	258	34.36 S	58.33 W
Tres de Febrero □[5]	288	34.36 S	58.35 W
Três de Maio	252	27.47 S	54.14 W
Tresenda	64	46.10 N	10.05 E
Tres Esquinas	246	0.43 N	75.16 W
Três Fronteiras	255	20.13 S	50.55 W
Treshnish Isles II	46	56.30 N	6.24 W
Treshnish Point ›	46	56.33 N	6.21 W
Tre Signori, Picco dei (Dreiherrnspitze) ∧	64	47.04 N	12.15 E
Três Ilhas	256	22.04 S	43.29 W
Tresinaro ≃	64	44.39 N	10.47 E
Tres Isletas	252	26.21 S	60.26 W
Treskino	80	52.40 N	44.40 E
Três Lagoas	255	20.48 S	51.43 W
Tres Lagos	254	49.37 S	71.30 W
Três Marias, Represa ⊜[1]	255	18.12 S	45.15 W
Tres Montes, Golfo ⊂	254	46.54 S	75.00 W
Tres Montes, Península ›[1]	254	46.50 S	75.30 W
Tres Montosas ∧	200	34.06 N	107.28 W
Tresnuraghes	71	40.15 N	8.31 E
Tres Palacios ≃	196	28.45 N	96.09 W
Três Passos	252	27.27 S	53.56 W
Tres Picos	234	15.52 N	93.32 W
Tres Picos, Cerro ∧, Arg.	252	38.09 S	61.57 W
Tres Picos, Cerro ∧, Méx.	234	16.36 N	94.13 W
Tres Pinos	226	36.48 N	121.19 W
Tres Pinos Creek ≃	226	36.47 N	121.21 W
Três Pontas	256	21.22 S	45.31 W
Três Pontas, Cabo das ›	152	10.23 S	13.32 E
Tres Puntas, Cabo ›	254	47.06 S	65.53 W
Três Ranchos	255	18.22 S	47.47 W
Tres Reyes Islands II	116	13.14 N	121.51 E
Três Rios, Bra.	256	22.07 S	43.12 W
Tres Ríos, C.R.	236	9.54 N	83.58 W
Tressancourt	261	48.55 N	2.00 E
Třešť	30	49.18 N	15.30 E
Tresta	46a	60.14 N	1.21 W
Tres Valles	234	18.15 N	96.08 W
Tres Zapotes ⊥	234	18.28 N	95.24 W
Tret'akovskaja Galereja ᵿ	265b	55.45 N	37.37 E
Tretet	114	4.40 N	96.51 E
Trets	62	43.27 N	5.41 E
Tretten	26	61.19 N	10.19 E
Treuburg → Olecko	30	54.03 N	22.30 E
Treuchtlingen	56	48.57 N	10.54 E
Treuen	54	50.32 N	12.18 E
Treuenbrietzen	54	52.06 N	12.52 E
Treuhandgebiet Pazifische Inseln → Trust Territory of the Pacific Islands □[2]	14	5.00 N	137.00 E
Trevelín	254	43.04 S	71.28 W
Trèves → Trier	56	49.45 N	6.38 E
Trevi	66	42.52 N	12.45 E
Treviglio	62	45.31 N	9.35 E
Trevignano Romano	66	42.09 N	12.15 E
Treviño	34	42.44 N	2.45 W
Treviso	64	45.40 N	12.15 E
Treviso □[4]	64	45.50 N	12.13 E
Trevor	216	42.30 N	88.07 W
Trevorton	208	40.46 N	76.40 W
Trevose	208	40.08 N	74.58 W
Trevose Head ›	42	50.33 N	5.01 W
Trevose Heights	285	40.09 N	74.59 W
Trévoux	58	45.56 N	4.46 E
Trexlertown	208	40.33 N	75.36 W
Treze Quedas ∟	250	0.07 N	56.55 W
Trezevant	194	36.00 N	88.37 W
Trezzano sul Naviglio	266b	45.25 N	9.04 E
Trezzo sull'Adda	62	45.36 N	9.31 E
Trgovište	38	42.21 N	22.05 E
Trhomné	60	49.55 N	13.05 E
Trhové Sviny	61	48.51 N	14.39 E
Triabunna	166	42.30 S	147.55 E
Triadelphia Reservoir ⊜[1]	208	39.13 N	77.01 W
Trialeti	84	41.33 N	44.07 E
Trialetskij chrebet ⋏	84	41.45 N	43.50 E
Triana	66	42.47 N	11.33 E
Triánda	38	36.24 N	28.10 E
Triangle, Eng., U.K.	262	53.42 N	1.56 W
Triangle, Va., U.S.	208	38.32 N	77.20 W
Triangle Lake	210	42.32 N	74.13 W
Triangul'atorov, pik ∧	88	53.45 N	97.00 E
Triángulos, Arrecifes ✢[2]	232	20.57 N	92.16 W
Triaucourt-en-Argonne	56	48.59 N	5.04 E
Tribeni	126	22.59 N	88.24 E
Triberg	58	48.08 N	8.13 E
Tribes Hill	210	42.57 N	74.17 W
Tribobó	287a	22.52 S	43.01 W
Triborough Bridge ◆[5]	276	40.47 N	73.55 W
Tri Brata, porog ∟	86	57.25 N	95.39 E
Tribsees	54	54.05 N	12.45 E
Tribugá, Golfo de ⊂	246	5.45 N	77.20 W
Tribune, Sk., Can.	184	49.15 N	103.50 W
Tribune, Ks., U.S.	198	38.28 N	101.45 W
Tribune Channel Ա	182	50.50 N	126.16 W
Tribuswinkel	264b	48.00 N	16.16 E
Tricao Malal	252	37.03 S	70.19 W
Tricarico	68	40.37 N	16.09 E
Tricase	68	39.56 N	18.22 E
Tricesimo	64	46.10 N	13.13 E
Trichardt	158	26.28 S	29.13 E
Trichiana	64	46.05 N	12.07 E
Trichinopoly → Tiruchchirāppalli	122	10.49 N	78.41 E
Trichūr	122	10.31 N	76.13 E
Tri Cities	222	32.09 N	95.56 W
Tricot	50	49.34 N	2.35 E
Tri County Supply Canal ≊	198	40.49 N	100.06 W
Trida	166	33.01 S	145.01 E
Trident Peak ∧	204	41.54 N	118.25 W
Triduby	78	48.06 N	30.24 E
Trieben	61	47.29 N	14.30 E
Triebes	54	50.41 N	12.01 E
Triel-sur-Seine	261	48.59 N	2.00 E
Trient → Trento	64	46.04 N	11.08 E
Triepkendorf	54	53.17 N	13.20 E
Trier	56	49.45 N	6.38 E
Trier □[5]	56	50.00 N	6.40 E
Triesen	58	47.06 N	9.31 E
Trieste (Triest)	64	45.40 N	13.46 E
Trieste □[4]	64	45.30 N	13.50 E
Trieste, Gulf of ⊂	64	45.40 N	13.35 E
Triesting ≃	264b	48.05 N	16.24 E
Trieux	56	49.20 N	5.56 E
Triftern	60	48.24 N	13.01 E
Trigal	248	18.17 S	64.08 W
Triggiano	68	41.04 N	16.55 E
Triglav ∧	64	46.23 N	13.50 E
Triglitz	54	53.12 N	12.05 E
Trigna, Pizzo ∧	70	37.58 N	13.34 E
Trigno ≃	66	42.04 N	14.48 E
Trigueros	34	37.23 N	6.50 W
Trikala	38	39.34 N	21.46 E
Trikhonís, Límni ⊜	38	38.34 N	21.28 E
Trikora, Puncak (Wilhelmina Peak) ∧	164	4.15 S	138.45 E
Tri-Lakes	216	41.14 N	85.26 W
Trilbardou	261	48.57 N	2.48 E
Trilby	220	28.27 N	82.11 W
Trilesy	78	49.59 N	29.50 E
Trillick	48	54.27 N	7.30 W
Trilport	50	48.57 N	2.57 E
Trim	48	53.34 N	6.47 W
Triman	120	29.38 N	69.05 E
Trimbach	58	47.22 N	7.54 E
Trimble □[6]	218	38.37 N	85.20 W
Trim Creek ≃	216	41.10 N	87.38 W
Trimdon	44	54.42 N	1.25 W
Trimont	198	43.45 N	94.42 W
Trimonte	256	21.43 S	42.35 W
Trin	58	46.50 N	9.22 E
Trinchera Creek ≃	200	37.19 N	105.45 W
Trincheras, Méx.	196	25.37 N	101.55 W
Trincheras, Méx.	232	30.24 N	111.32 W
Trincomalee	122	8.34 N	81.14 E
Trincomali Channel Ա	224	48.02 N	123.30 W
Trindade	255	16.40 S	49.30 W
Trindade I	244	20.31 S	29.19 W
Třinec	30	49.41 N	18.40 E
Tring	42	51.48 N	0.40 W
Trinidad, Bol.	248	14.47 S	64.47 W
Trinidad, Col.	246	5.25 N	71.40 W
Trinidad, Cuba	240p	21.48 N	79.59 W
Trinidad, Hond.	236	14.57 N	88.45 W
Trinidad, Co., U.S.	198	37.10 N	104.30 W
Trinidad, Tx., U.S.	222	32.08 N	96.05 W
Trinidad, Ur.	252	33.32 S	56.54 W
Trinidad I	241r	10.30 N	61.15 W
Trinidad, Golfo ⊂	254	49.55 S	75.25 W
Trinidad, Isla I	252	39.08 S	61.58 W
Trinidad, Río la ≃	234	17.49 N	95.09 W
Trinidad and Tobago □[1], N.A.	230	11.00 N	61.00 W
Trinidad and Tobago □[1], N.A.	241r	11.00 N	61.00 W
Trinità	62	44.30 N	7.45 E
Trinità, Lago della ⊜	70	37.43 N	12.46 E
Trinità d'agultu	71	40.59 N	8.54 E
Trinitapoli	68	41.21 N	16.05 E
Trinitaria	232	16.07 N	92.03 W
Trinité, Havre de la ⊂	240e	14.44 N	60.58 W
Trinity, Nf., Can.	186	48.59 N	53.55 W
Trinity, Tx., U.S.	222	30.56 N	95.22 W
Trinity □[6]	222	31.07 N	95.10 W
Trinity ≃, Ca., U.S.	204	41.11 N	123.42 W
Trinity ≃, Tx., U.S.	222	29.47 N	94.42 W
Trinity, Clear Fork ≃	196	32.46 N	97.21 W
Trinity, East Fork ≃	222	32.30 N	96.30 W
Trinity, Elm Fork ≃	222	32.47 N	96.54 W
Trinity, South Fork ≃	204	40.54 N	123.35 W
Trinity, West Fork ≃	196	32.48 N	96.51 W
Trinity Bay ⊂, Nf., Can.	186	48.00 N	53.40 W
Trinity Bay ⊂, Tx., U.S.	222	29.40 N	94.45 W
Trinity Islands II	180	56.33 N	154.25 W
Trinity Mountain ∧	202	43.36 N	115.26 W
Trinity Mountains ⋏	204	41.00 N	122.30 W
Trinity Park ♠	275b	43.39 N	79.25 W
Trinity Peak ∧	204	40.14 N	118.45 W
Trinity Site ⊥	200	33.41 N	106.28 W
Trinkat Island I	110	8.05 N	93.30 E
Trinkitat	140	18.41 N	37.43 E
Trino	62	45.12 N	8.18 E
Trins	64	47.05 N	11.25 E
Trinway	214	40.08 N	82.00 W
Triolet	157c	20.03 S	57.32 E
Triolo ≃	66	41.40 N	15.34 E
Trion	192	34.32 N	85.18 W
Trionto ≃	68	39.37 N	16.45 E
Trionto, Capo ›	68	39.37 N	16.45 E
Triora	62	43.59 N	7.46 E
Tripa ≃	114	3.53 N	96.23 E
Tripi	70	38.03 N	15.06 E
Triplett Creek ≃	218	38.10 N	83.27 W
Triplett Creek, North Fork ≃	218	38.10 N	83.31 W
Tripoli → Ṭarābulus, Lībiyā	146	32.54 N	13.11 E
Tripoli → Ṭarābulus, Lubnān	130	34.26 N	35.51 E
Tripoli	190	42.48 N	92.15 W
Trípolis	38	37.31 N	22.21 E
Tripolis → Ṭarābulus	146	32.54 N	13.11 E
Tripolis ⊥	130	37.58 N	28.59 E
Tripolitania → Ṭarābulus □[9]	146	31.00 N	15.00 E
Tripolje	78	50.07 N	30.46 E
Triponzo	66	42.50 N	12.56 E
Tripp	198	43.13 N	97.57 W
Trips Subdivision	281	42.34 N	83.25 W
Triptis	54	50.44 N	11.52 E
Tripura □[3]	120	24.00 N	92.00 E
Triquet, Lac ⊜	186	50.42 N	59.47 W
Trisanna ≃	58	47.07 N	10.30 E
Tristan da Cunha Group II	10	37.15 S	12.30 W
Tristan Island I	10	37.05 S	12.17 W
Tristán Suárez	258	34.53 S	58.34 W
Tristao, Îles II	150	10.53 N	14.58 W
Tristate Village	278	41.44 N	87.57 W
Triste	34	42.23 N	0.43 W
Triste, Golfo ⊂	246	10.40 N	68.10 W
Triśuli Gaṅgā ≃	124	27.49 N	84.47 E
Tri Ton	110	10.25 N	105.00 E
Tritriva	157b	22.46 S	46.07 E
Trittau	52	53.37 N	10.25 E
Trittenheim	56	49.49 N	6.54 E
Triuggio	266b	45.40 N	9.16 E
Triumph	194	29.20 N	89.28 W
Triunfo	250	7.50 S	38.07 W
Triunfo, Igarapé ≃	250	6.22 S	52.25 W
Triunfo de Madero	234	16.52 N	93.48 W
Trivandrum	122	8.29 N	76.55 E
Trivento	66	41.47 N	14.33 E
Trivero	62	45.40 N	8.10 E
Trivigno	68	40.35 N	15.59 E
Trkmanka ≃	61	48.47 N	16.50 E
Trnava	30	48.23 N	17.35 E
Trnovo → Veliko Târnovo	38	43.04 N	25.39 E
Tr'ochgolovyj Golec, gora ∧	88	53.22 N	107.03 E
Tr'ochizbenka	83	48.45 N	38.58 E
Tr'ochsv'atskoje	82	56.29 N	37.03 E
Trochtelfingen	58	48.18 N	9.14 E
Trochu	182	51.50 N	113.13 W
Troense	41	55.02 N	10.39 E
Trofa, Arroyo de ≃	266a	40.30 N	3.45 W
Trofaich	61	47.25 N	15.00 E
Trofarello	62	44.59 N	7.44 E
Trögd ›[1]	40	59.31 N	17.15 E
Trogen	58	47.24 N	9.28 E
Trogir	36	43.31 N	16.15 E
Troglav ∧	36	43.57 N	16.36 E
Tröglitz	54	51.04 N	12.11 E
Troia	68	41.22 N	15.18 E
Troica	76	54.24 N	40.14 E
Troice-Lykovo ◆[8]	265b	55.47 N	37.24 E
Troick, S.S.S.R.	86	54.06 N	61.35 E
Troick, S.S.S.R.	88	57.25 N	94.50 E
Troickaja	78	45.08 N	38.07 E
Troickij, S.S.S.R.	80	50.14 N	43.05 E
Troickij, S.S.S.R.	80	50.14 N	43.03 E
Troickij, S.S.S.R.	86	50.41 N	54.38 E
Troickij, S.S.S.R.	86	57.03 N	63.43 E
Troickij, S.S.S.R.	88	54.36 N	113.09 E
Troickije Rosl'ai	80	53.21 N	41.24 E
Troickij Sungur	80	53.17 N	47.37 E
Troickij Zavod	88	53.27 N	102.09 E
Troicko-Charcyzsk	83	47.58 N	38.16 E
Troickoje, S.S.S.R.	78	51.17 N	41.28 E
Troickoje, S.S.S.R.	78	49.55 N	38.19 E
Troickoje, S.S.S.R.	78	47.38 N	30.19 E
Troickoje, S.S.S.R.	80	53.22 N	48.23 E
Troickoje, S.S.S.R.	80	46.26 N	44.15 E
Troickoje, S.S.S.R.	80	53.06 N	52.32 E
Troickoje, S.S.S.R.	80	53.23 N	52.48 E
Troickoje, S.S.S.R.	82	54.52 N	37.07 E
Troickoje, S.S.S.R.	82	55.23 N	37.25 E
Troickoje, S.S.S.R.	83	48.32 N	38.23 E
Troickoje, S.S.S.R.	83	47.22 N	38.53 E
Troickoje, S.S.S.R.	86	52.19 N	56.23 E
Troickoje, S.S.S.R.	86	52.58 N	84.40 E
Troickoje, S.S.S.R.	86	59.07 N	58.25 E
Troickoje, S.S.S.R.	89	49.27 N	136.36 E
Troicko-Pečorsk	24	62.44 N	56.06 E
Troina	70	37.47 N	14.36 E
Troina ≃	70	37.49 N	14.46 E
Troisdorf	56	50.49 N	7.08 E
Trois Fourches, Cap des ›	148	35.26 N	2.58 W
Trois-Îlets	240e	14.32 N	61.02 W
Trois-Pistoles	186	48.07 N	69.10 W
Trois Pitons, Morne ∧	240d	15.22 N	61.20 W
Trois Ponts	56	50.22 N	5.52 E
Trois-Rivières, P.Q., Can.	206	46.21 N	72.33 W
Trois-Rivières, Guad.	241o	15.59 N	61.39 W
Trois-Rivières-Ouest	206	46.19 N	72.35 W
Troisvierges	56	50.08 N	6.00 E
Trojan	38	42.51 N	24.43 E
Trojanov	78	50.07 N	28.31 E
Trojanova Tabla ⊥	38	44.37 N	22.20 E
Trojanovka	78	51.20 N	25.17 E
Trojebratskij	86	54.28 N	66.01 E
Trojekurovo, S.S.S.R.	76	53.00 N	38.58 E
Trojekurovo, S.S.S.R.	76	53.25 N	39.43 E
Troldhede	41	55.59 N	8.45 E
Trolleholm	41	55.54 N	13.15 E
Trollhättan	26	58.16 N	12.18 E
Trollheimen ∧	26	62.51 N	9.05 E
Trombay ◆[8]	272c	19.02 N	72.57 E
Trombetas ≃	250	1.55 S	55.35 W
Trombudo Central	252	27.18 S	49.47 W
Tromelin, Île I	138	15.52 S	54.25 E
Tromello	62	45.12 N	8.52 E
Tromper Wiek ⊂	54	54.37 N	13.24 E
Trompia, Val V	64	45.44 N	10.12 E
Trompsburg	158	30.01 S	25.46 E
Troms □[6]	24	69.15 N	19.40 E
Tromsø	24	69.40 N	18.58 E
Trona	204	35.45 N	117.22 W
Tronador, Monte ∧	254	41.10 S	71.54 W
Trondheim	26	63.25 N	10.25 E
Trondheimsfjorden ⊂[2]	26	63.39 N	10.49 E
Trondheimsleia Ա	26	63.30 N	9.00 E
Tronto ≃	66	42.54 N	13.55 E
Tronville-en-Barrois	56	48.43 N	5.17 E
Tronzano Vercellese	62	45.21 N	8.10 E
Troo	50	47.47 N	0.47 E
Troödos	130	34.55 N	32.53 E
Trooilapspan	158	28.40 S	21.25 E
Troon, Eng., U.K.	42	50.12 N	5.16 W
Troon, Scot., U.K.	46	55.32 N	4.40 W
Trooper	285	40.09 N	75.24 W
Troparevo	82	55.23 N	35.54 E
Tropar'ovo ◆[8]	265b	55.39 N	37.29 E
Tropas, Rio das ≃	250	6.07 S	57.28 W
Tropea	68	38.41 N	15.54 E
Trophy Mountain ∧	182	51.47 N	119.48 W
Tropic	200	37.37 N	112.04 W
Tropojë	38	42.24 N	20.10 E
Troppau → Opava	30	49.56 N	17.54 E
Trosa	40	58.54 N	17.33 E
Troškovo	80	57.19 N	46.05 E
Troškūnai	76	55.36 N	24.51 E
Trosna	76	52.26 N	35.46 E
Trossingen	58	48.04 N	8.38 E
Trostan ∧	48	55.03 N	6.09 W
Trost'anec, S.S.S.R.	78	48.31 N	29.12 E
Trost'anec, S.S.S.R.	78	50.28 N	34.59 E
Tröstau	60	50.01 N	11.57 E
Trostberg	60	48.01 N	12.32 E
Trostenskoje, ozero ⊜	82	55.52 N	36.29 E
Trotha ◆[8]	54	51.31 N	11.58 E
Trottiscliffe	260	51.19 N	0.21 E
Trotuș ≃	38	46.03 N	27.14 E
Trotwood	218	39.47 N	84.18 W
Troublesome Creek ≃	219	39.54 N	91.37 W
Troubridge Point ›	168b	35.11 S	137.41 E
Trou-du-Nord	238	19.38 N	72.01 W
Troumasse ⊂	241f	13.49 N	60.54 W
Troup	222	32.08 N	95.07 W
Troup Head ›	46	57.41 N	2.18 W
Troupsburg	210	42.03 N	77.33 W
Trout	194	31.41 N	92.10 W
Trout ≃, N.T., Can.	176	61.19 N	119.51 W
Trout ≃, N.A.	206	45.05 N	74.10 W
Trout Brook ≃, Ma., U.S.	283	42.16 N	71.18 W
Trout Brook ≃, Ma., U.S.	283	42.39 N	71.16 W
Trout Creek, Mi., U.S.	190	46.28 N	89.00 W
Trout Creek, Mt., U.S.	182	47.50 N	115.35 W
Trout Creek, N.Y., U.S.	210	42.12 N	75.17 W
Trout Creek ≃, Az., U.S.	200	34.56 N	113.36 W
Trout Creek ≃, Or., U.S.	202	44.48 N	121.03 W
Trout Creek ≃, Or., U.S.	202	42.23 N	118.36 W
Trout Creek ≃, Pa., U.S.	285	40.07 N	75.24 W
Trout Creek ≃, Wa., U.S.	224	46.02 N	121.12 W
Trout Creek Pass)(	200	38.54 N	105.58 W
Troutdale	224	45.32 N	122.23 W
Trout Lake	224	45.59 N	121.31 W
Trout Lake ⊜, B.C., Can.	182	50.35 N	117.26 W
Trout Lake ⊜, N.T., Can.	176	60.35 N	121.10 W
Trout Lake ⊜, On., Can.	184	51.13 N	93.20 W
Trout Lake ⊜, On., Can.	190	46.18 N	79.20 W
Trout Lake ⊜, On., Can.	190	46.13 N	80.35 W
Trout Lake Creek ≃	224	46.00 N	121.30 W
Trout Peak ∧	202	44.36 N	109.32 W
Trout River	186	49.29 N	58.08 W
Trout Run	210	41.23 N	77.03 W
Troutville, Pa., U.S.	214	41.02 N	78.47 W
Troutville, Va., U.S.	192	37.25 N	79.52 W
Trouville-sur-Mer	50	49.22 N	0.05 E
Trowbridge	42	51.20 N	2.13 W
Troxelville	210	40.48 N	77.12 W
Troy, Al., U.S.	194	31.48 N	85.58 W
Troy, Id., U.S.	202	46.44 N	116.46 W
Troy, Il., U.S.	219	38.43 N	89.52 W
Troy, In., U.S.	194	37.59 N	86.47 W
Troy, Ks., U.S.	198	39.46 N	95.05 W
Troy, Mi., U.S.	214	42.34 N	83.09 W
Troy, Mo., U.S.	219	38.58 N	90.58 W
Troy, Mt., U.S.	202	48.27 N	115.53 W
Troy, N.H., U.S.	207	42.49 N	72.10 W
Troy, N.Y., U.S.	210	42.43 N	73.41 W
Troy, N.C., U.S.	192	35.21 N	79.53 W
Troy, Oh., U.S.	218	40.02 N	84.12 W
Troy, Pa., U.S.	210	41.47 N	76.47 W
Troy, Tn., U.S.	194	36.20 N	89.09 W
Troy, Tx., U.S.	222	31.12 N	97.18 W
Troy → Truva ⊥	130	39.57 N	26.15 E
Troy Brook ≃	276	40.50 N	74.22 W
Troyes	50	48.18 N	4.05 E
Troy Grove	216	41.28 N	89.05 W
Troy Hills	210	40.51 N	74.23 W
Troy Lake ⊜	204	34.49 N	116.33 W
Troy Meadows ☷	276	40.50 N	74.22 W
Troy Peak ∧	204	38.19 N	115.30 W
Trpanj	36	43.00 N	17.17 E
Trst → Trieste	64	45.40 N	13.46 E
Trstená	30	49.22 N	19.37 E
Trstenik	38	43.37 N	21.00 E
Truax	184	49.55 N	104.58 W
Trubč'ovsk	76	52.37 N	33.44 E
Trubetčino	76	52.53 N	39.33 E
Trubino, S.S.S.R.	82	54.58 N	36.42 E
Trubino, S.S.S.R.	82	55.59 N	38.08 E
Trub'ož ≃	82	56.44 N	38.51 E
Truchas	200	36.02 N	105.48 W
Truchas Peak ∧	200	35.58 N	105.39 W
Truchtersheim	58	48.40 N	7.36 E
Trucial States → United Arab Emirates □[1]	128	24.00 N	54.00 E
Truckee	226	39.19 N	120.10 W
Truckee ≃	204	39.51 N	119.24 W
Trucksville	210	41.18 N	75.56 W
Trud	76	57.37 N	33.58 E
Trudfront	80	45.56 N	47.41 E
Trudnovo	86	56.39 N	91.30 E
Trudovaja	83	48.21 N	38.04 E
Trudovoj	80	51.42 N	52.43 E
Trues Creek ≃	276	40.41 N	73.17 W
Truganina	274b	37.49 S	144.43 E
Truim ≃	46	57.02 N	4.10 W
Truite, Lac à la ⊜	190	47.16 N	78.17 W
Trujillo, Col.	246	4.10 N	76.19 W
Trujillo, Esp.	34	39.28 N	5.53 W
Trujillo, Hond.	236	15.55 N	86.00 W
Trujillo, Perú	248	8.07 S	79.02 W
Trujillo, Ven.	246	9.22 N	70.26 W
Trujillo □[3]	246	9.25 N	70.30 W
Trujillo Alto	240m	18.22 N	66.01 W
Trujillo Creek ≃	196	35.28 N	102.52 W
Truk Islands II	175c	7.25 N	151.47 E
Truk Lagoon ⊂	175c	7.25 N	151.45 E
Trull Brook ≃	283	42.39 N	71.15 W
Truman	198	43.49 N	94.26 W
Trumann	194	35.40 N	90.30 W
Trumansburg	210	42.32 N	76.39 W
Trumbauersville	208	40.25 N	75.23 W
Trumbull	207	41.14 N	73.12 W
Trumbull □[6]	214	41.14 N	80.52 W
Trumbull, Mount ∧	200	36.25 N	113.10 W
Trumon	114	2.49 N	97.38 E
Trun, Fr.	50	48.51 N	0.02 E
Trun, Schw.	58	46.45 N	8.58 E
Trundle	166	32.55 S	147.43 E
Trung Luong	110	13.57 N	109.15 E
Trung Phan □[9]	110	15.00 N	108.00 E
Trunovskoje	80	45.29 N	42.08 E
Truro, Austl.	168b	34.25 S	139.07 E
Truro, N.S., Can.	186	45.22 N	63.16 W
Truro, Eng., U.K.	42	50.16 N	5.03 W
Truro, Ma., U.S.	207	41.59 N	70.03 W
Trusan ≃	112	4.58 N	115.11 E
Truscott	196	33.45 N	99.49 W

≃	River	Fluß	Río	Rivière	Rio
≊	Canal	Kanal	Canal	Canal	Canal
∟	Waterfall, Rapids	Wasserfall, Stromschnellen	Cascada, Rápidos	Chute d'eau, Rapides	Cascata, Rápidos
Ա	Strait	Meeresstraße	Estrecho	Détroit	Estreito
⊂	Bay, Gulf	Bucht, Golf	Bahía, Golfo	Baie, Golfe	Baía, Golfo
⊜	Lake, Lakes	See, Seen	Lago, Lagos	Lac, Lacs	Lago, Lagos
☷	Swamp	Sumpf	Pantano	Marais	Pântano
⍓	Ice Features, Glacier	Eis- und Gletscherformen	Accidentes Glaciales	Formes glaciaires	Acidentes glaciares
⍑	Other Hydrographic Features	Andere Hydrographische Objekte	Otros Elementos Hidrográficos	Autres données hydrographiques	Outros acidentes hidrográficos
✢	Submarine Features	Untermeerische Objekte	Accidentes Submarinos	Formes de relief sous-marin	Acidentes submarinos
□	Political Unit	Politische Einheit	Unidad Politica	Entité politique	Unidade política
ᵿ	Cultural Institution	Kulturelle Institution	Institución Cultural	Institution culturelle	Institução cultural
⊥	Historical Site	Historische Stätte	Sitio Histórico	Site historique	Sitio histórico
♠	Recreational Site	Erholungs- und Ferienort	Sitio de Recreo	Centre de loisirs	Area de Lazer
⊠	Airport	Flughafen	Aeropuerto	Aéroport	Aeroporto
■	Military Installation	Militäranlage	Instalación Militar	Installation militaire	Instalação militar
◆	Miscellaneous	Verschiedenes	Misceláneo	Divers	Diversos

Name	Page	Lat.°′	Long.°′
Trušeny	78	47.04 N	28.41 E
Trușești	38	47.46 N	27.01 E
Trusetal	54	50.47 N	10.25 E
Truskavec	78	49.16 N	23.33 E
Truslejka	80	53.54 N	46.24 E
Trus Madi, Gunong ∧	112	5.33 N	116.31 E
Trust Territory of the Pacific Islands □[2]	14	10.00 N	155.00 E
Truth or Consequences (Hot Springs)	200	33.07 N	107.15 W
Trutnov	30	50.34 N	15.55 E
Truva (Troy) ⊥	130	39.57 N	26.15 E
Truxall	279b	40.33 N	79.33 W
Truxton, Mo., U.S.	219	39.00 N	91.14 W
Truxton, N.Y., U.S.	210	42.43 N	76.02 W
Truxton Wash V	200	35.38 N	114.04 W
Truyère ≃	32	44.39 N	2.34 E
Trwyn Cilan ›	42	52.46 N	4.30 W
Tryon, Ne., U.S.	198	41.33 N	100.57 W
Tryon, N.C., U.S.	192	35.12 N	82.14 W
Tryonville	214	41.42 N	79.47 W
Trysil	26	61.19 N	12.16 E
Trysilelva (Klarälven) ≃	26	59.23 N	13.32 E
Tryškiai	76	56.04 N	22.35 E
Tryweryn ≃	42	52.55 N	3.35 W
Trzcianka	30	53.03 N	16.28 E
Trzciel	30	52.23 N	15.52 E
Trzcińsko-Zdrój	30	52.58 N	14.35 E
Trzebiatów	30	54.04 N	15.14 E
Trzebiel	54	51.37 N	14.50 E
Trzebież	30	53.42 N	14.31 E
Trzebinia	30	50.10 N	19.18 E
Trzebnica	30	51.19 N	17.03 E
Trzemeszno	30	52.35 N	17.50 E
Trzęsacz	54	54.05 N	14.58 E
Tržič	61	46.22 N	14.19 E
Tsacha Lake ⊜	182	53.05 N	124.40 W
Tsala Apopka Lake ⊜	220	28.52 N	82.20 W
Tsamkong → Zhanjiang	102	21.16 N	110.28 E
Tsandi	156	17.42 S	14.50 E
Tsangano	154	15.08 S	34.32 E
Ts'anghsien → Cangzhou	98	38.19 N	116.51 E
T'sangwu → Wuzhou	102	23.30 N	111.27 E
Ts'aot'un	100	23.59 N	120.41 E
Tsarabaria	157b	13.46 S	49.58 E
Tsaramandroso	157b	16.22 S	47.02 E
Tsaratanana	157b	16.47 S	47.39 E
Tsaratanana, Massif du ⋏	157b	14.00 S	49.00 E
Tsaraxaibis	158	27.25 S	19.22 E
Tsaritsyn → Volgograd	80	48.44 N	44.25 E
Tsau	156	20.12 S	22.22 E
Tsaukaib	156	26.37 S	15.31 E
Tsavo	154	2.59 S	38.28 E
Tsavo East National Park ♠	154	2.11 S	38.25 E
Tsavo West National Park ♠	154	2.55 S	37.55 E
Tsawwassen	224	49.01 N	123.06 W
Tsaydaychuz Peak ∧	182	53.02 N	126.35 W
Tsayta Lake ⊜	182	55.25 N	125.30 W
Tschad → Chad □[1]	146	15.00 N	19.00 E
Tschad-See → Chad, Lake ⊜	146	13.20 N	14.00 E
Tschagguns	58	47.05 N	9.54 E
Tschamut	58	46.40 N	8.42 E
Tschangscha → Changsha	100	28.12 N	112.58 E
Tschangtschun → Changchun	89	43.53 N	125.19 E
Tschechoslowakei → Czechoslovakia □[1]	30	49.30 N	17.00 E
Tscheljuskin, Kap → Čel'uskin, mys ›	74	77.45 N	104.20 E
Tschengtu → Chengdu	107	30.39 N	104.04 E
Tschenstochau → Częstochowa	30	50.49 N	19.06 E
Tschernitz	54	51.35 N	14.37 E
Tscheschkaja-Bucht → Češskaja guba ⊂	24	67.30 N	46.30 E
Tschida, Lake ⊜[1]	198	46.36 N	101.54 W
Tschingtau → Qingdao	98	36.06 N	120.19 E
Tschittagong → Chittagong	120	22.20 N	91.50 E
Tschuktschen-Meer → Chukchi Sea ▾[2]	16	69.00 N	171.00 W
Tschungking → Chongqing	107	29.34 N	106.35 E
Tsekanyani	156	19.52 S	26.39 E
Tsembeyi	158	31.36 S	27.03 E
Ts'engwen ≃	100	23.03 N	120.03 E
Tsenke ≃	273b	4.24 S	15.26 E
Tses	156	25.58 S	18.08 E
Tsévié	150	6.25 N	1.13 E
Tshabong	156	26.03 S	22.29 E
Tshabuta	152	7.47 S	23.16 E
Tshane	156	24.05 S	21.54 E
Tshaneni	158	26.00 S	31.47 E
Tshangalele, Lac ⊜	154	10.55 S	27.03 E
Tshangu ≃	273b	4.25 S	15.23 E
Tshela	152	4.59 S	12.56 E
Tshesebe	156	21.51 S	27.35 E
Tshibeke	154	2.44 S	28.36 E
Tshibinda	154	2.19 S	28.45 E
Tshibomba	152	9.02 S	22.34 E
Tshidilamolomo	156	25.50 S	24.41 E
Tshikapa	152	6.25 S	20.48 E
Tshilenge	152	6.15 S	23.46 E
Tshimbulu	152	6.29 S	22.51 E
Tshindjamba	152	10.54 S	22.41 E
Tshinota	152	7.01 S	20.57 E
Tshinsenda	154	12.18 S	27.58 E
Tshisuku	152	6.26 S	19.55 E
Tshitadi	152	6.45 S	21.45 E
Tshoa	152	5.34 S	12.41 E
Tshofa	154	5.14 S	25.15 E
Tshopo ≃	154	0.33 N	25.07 E
Tshuapa ≃	152	0.14 S	20.42 E
Tshukudu	156	22.30 S	23.22 E
Tshumbiri	152	2.39 S	16.14 E
Tshwaane	156	22.29 S	22.03 E
Tsiafajavona ∧	157b	19.21 S	47.15 E
Tsianaloka	157b	18.08 S	44.50 E
Tsiémé ≃	273b	4.15 S	15.18 E
Tsiga	152	1.32 S	10.11 E
Tsihombe	157b	25.18 S	45.29 E
Tsilmamo	144	6.01 N	35.17 E
Tsimanampetsotsa, Lac ⊜	157b	24.08 S	43.46 E
Tsimilofo	157b	24.59 S	45.10 E
Tsimpsean Indian Reserve ◆[4]	182	54.30 N	130.22 W
Tsinan → Jinan	98	36.40 N	116.57 E
Tsineng	158	27.06 S	23.04 E
Tsinghai → Qinghai □[4]	90	36.00 N	96.00 E
Tsingkiang → Qingjiang	100	33.35 N	119.02 E
Tsingtao → Qingdao	98	36.06 N	120.19 E
Tsing Yi I	271d	22.21 N	114.05 E
Tsingyuan → Baoding	105	38.52 N	115.29 E
Tsining → Jining	98	35.25 N	116.36 E
Tsinjoarivo	157b	19.37 S	47.40 E
Tsinjomitondraka	157b	15.36 S	47.08 E
Tsinling Shan → Qin Ling ⋏	102	34.00 N	108.00 E
Tsintsabis	156	18.45 S	17.51 E
Tsiribihina ≃	157b	19.42 S	44.31 E
Tsiroanomandidy	157b	18.46 S	46.02 E
Tsitondroina	157b	21.19 S	46.00 E
Tsitsihar → Qiqihar	89	47.19 N	123.55 E
Tsitsikama Forest and Coastal National Park ♠	158	33.57 S	23.53 E
Tsitsutl Peak ∧	182	52.44 N	125.47 W
Tsivory	157b	24.04 S	46.05 E
Tskhinvali → Cchinvali	84	42.13 N	43.56 E
Tsna → Cna ≃	80	54.32 N	42.05 E
Tsobis	156	19.27 S	17.30 E
Tsolo	158	31.18 S	28.37 E
Tsomo	158	32.00 S	27.42 E
Tsomo ≃	158	32.25 S	27.50 E
Tsoying	100	22.41 N	120.17 E
Tsu	94	34.43 N	136.31 E
Tsubakuro-dake ∧	94	36.24 N	137.42 E
Tsubame	92	37.39 N	138.56 E
Tsubata	94	36.40 N	136.44 E
Tsuboro-suigenchi ⊜[1]	270	34.24 N	135.54 E
Tsuchiura	94	36.05 N	140.12 E
Tsuchiyama	94	34.56 N	136.17 E
Tsuda, Nihon	96	34.17 N	134.15 E
Tsuda, Nihon	270	34.49 N	135.43 E
Tsuen Wan (Quanwan)	271d	22.22 N	114.07 E
Tsugaru-hantō ›[1]	92	41.00 N	140.30 E
Tsugaru-heiya ≚	92	40.49 N	140.27 E
Tsugaru-kaikyō)(	92a	41.35 N	141.00 E
Tsuge	94	34.37 N	135.57 E
Tsugu	94	35.10 N	137.37 E
Tsuha	174m	26.14 N	127.47 E
Tsuiki	96	33.40 N	131.03 E
Tsujidō	268	35.20 N	139.27 E
Tsukahara	268	35.18 N	139.58 E
Tsukechi	94	35.38 N	137.26 E
Tsuken-jima I	174m	26.15 N	127.57 E
Tsukigase	94	34.42 N	136.02 E
Tsukinowa-kofun ⊥	96	34.55 N	134.11 E
Tsukiyono	94	36.41 N	138.59 E
Tsukuba	94	36.13 N	140.06 E
Tsukuba-san ∧	94	36.13 N	140.06 E
Tsukude	94	34.59 N	137.25 E
Tsukui	94	35.35 N	139.16 E
Tsukumi	96	33.04 N	131.52 E
Tsukumono ◆[8]	270	34.50 N	135.11 E
Tsukushi-heiya ≚	96	33.20 N	130.30 E
Tsukushi-sanchi ⋏	92	33.30 N	130.30 E
Tsumagoi	94	36.31 N	138.32 E
Tsumeb	156	19.13 S	17.42 E
Tsumeb □[5]	156	19.00 S	17.30 E
Tsumeki-zaki ›	94	34.39 N	138.59 E
Tsumis Park	156	23.43 S	17.28 E
Tsumkwe	156	19.41 S	20.30 E
Tsuna	96	34.26 N	134.54 E
Tsunan	94	37.01 N	138.39 E
Tsunashima ◆[8]	268	35.32 N	139.38 E
Tsunekami-misaki ›	94	35.38 N	135.49 E
Tsuni → Zunyi	102	27.39 N	106.57 E
Tsuno-shima I	96	34.21 N	130.51 E
Tsuru	94	35.33 N	138.55 E
Tsuruga	94	35.39 N	136.04 E
Tsurugaoka-hachimangu Shrine ʊ[1]	268	35.19 N	139.33 E
Tsurugashima	268	35.56 N	139.24 E
Tsuruga-wan ⊂	94	35.45 N	136.04 E
Tsurugi	94	36.27 N	136.38 E
Tsurugi-dake ∧	94	36.37 N	137.37 E
Tsurugi-san ∧	96	33.51 N	134.06 E
Tsurugi-san-kokutei-kōen ♠	96	33.50 N	134.06 E
Tsuruhara	270	34.26 N	135.20 E
Tsuruma	268	35.51 N	139.33 E
Tsurumi ◆[8]	268	35.30 N	139.41 E
Tsurumi ≃	94	35.29 N	139.41 E
Tsurumi-dake ∧	96	33.17 N	131.26 E
Tsuruoka	92	38.44 N	139.50 E
Tsushima, Nihon	94	35.10 N	136.43 E
Tsushima, Nihon	96	33.05 N	132.30 E
Tsushima II	92	34.30 N	129.22 E
Tsushima-kaikyō (Eastern Channel))(	92	34.00 N	129.00 E
Tsuwano	96	34.28 N	131.46 E
Tsuyama	96	35.03 N	134.00 E
Tsuyazaki	96	33.47 N	130.28 E
Ttruchchendūr	122	8.29 N	78.07 E
Tu → Tsu	94	34.43 N	136.31 E
Tua	152	3.38 S	16.36 E
Tua ≃	34	41.13 N	7.26 W
Tua, Tanjung ›	115a	5.54 S	105.44 E
Tua Chau	110	21.55 N	103.21 E
Tuakau	172	37.16 S	174.57 E
Tual	164	5.40 S	132.45 E
Tualatin	224	45.23 N	122.45 W
Tualatin ≃	224	45.20 N	122.39 W
Tuam	48	53.31 N	8.50 W
Tuamarina	172	41.26 S	173.57 E
Tuamotu, Îles (Tuamotu Archipelago) II	14	19.00 S	142.00 W
Tuamotu Ridge ◆[3]	14	17.00 S	145.00 W
Tuan, Tanjong ›	114	2.23 N	101.52 E
Tuanan	112	2.07 S	114.24 E
Tuanfeng	100	30.38 N	114.51 E
Tuan Giao	110	21.35 N	103.25 E
Tuangku, Pulau I	114	2.10 N	97.16 E
Tuanlin	98	39.35 N	119.15 E
Tuannian	107	29.55 N	106.03 E
Tuanpi	100	30.44 N	115.13 E
Tuanshan	98	40.02 N	123.34 E
Tuanwang	98	36.45 N	120.38 E
Tuanxi	102	27.28 N	107.08 E
Tuapa	174v	18.57 S	169.54 W
Tuapeka Mouth	172	46.01 S	169.31 E
Tuapse	84	44.07 N	39.05 E
Tuaran	112	6.11 N	116.14 E
Tuas	114	1.19 N	103.38 E
Tuasivi	175a	13.40 S	172.07 W
Tuasivi, Cape ›	175a	13.40 S	172.07 W
Tuatapere	172	46.08 S	167.41 E
Tuath, Loch)(	46	56.30 N	6.12 W
Tuba	88	57.24 N	102.48 E
Tuba ≃	86	53.57 N	91.31 E
Tubac	200	31.36 N	111.02 W
Tuba City	200	36.08 N	111.14 W
T'ub'ak-Čekurča	80	56.05 N	49.56 E
Tubalan Head ›	116	6.30 N	125.35 E
Tuban	115a	6.54 S	112.03 E
Tubarão	252	28.30 S	49.01 W
Ṭūbās	132	32.19 N	35.22 E
Tubau	112	3.08 N	113.42 E
Tubbataha Reefs ◆[2]	116	8.51 N	119.56 E
Tubbergen	52	52.25 N	6.46 E
Tubbs Island I	282	38.08 N	122.26 W
Ṭubhār	142	29.19 N	30.42 E
Tubig ≃	116	11.54 N	125.25 E
Tubigan Island I	116	6.26 N	120.47 E
Tubingantan Point ›	116	5.54 N	120.55 E
Tübingen	58	48.31 N	9.02 E
Tübingen □[5]	58	48.10 N	9.30 E
Tubinskij	86	52.53 N	58.13 E
Tubize	50	50.41 N	4.12 E
T'ub-Karagan, mys ›	84	44.39 N	50.18 E
T'ub-Karagan, poluostrov ›[1]	84	44.30 N	50.30 E
Tubli	116	13.56 N	124.09 E
Tubod	116	8.03 N	123.48 E
Tubre	64	46.39 N	10.27 E
Ṭubruq (Tobruk)	146	32.05 N	23.59 E
Tuburan, Pil.	116	10.44 N	123.49 W
Tuburan, Pil.	116	6.39 N	122.16 E
Tubusereia	164	9.33 S	147.18 E
Tubutama	200	30.53 N	111.29 W
Tucacas	246	10.48 N	68.19 W
Tucacas, Punta ›	246	10.50 N	68.14 W
Tucalota Creek ≃	228	33.32 N	117.10 W
Tucannon ≃	202	46.33 N	118.11 W
Tucano	250	10.58 S	38.48 W
Tucavaca ≃	248	18.37 S	58.59 W
T'uch'ang	100	24.35 N	121.29 E
Tucheim	54	52.17 N	12.11 E
Tüchen	54	53.04 N	12.05 E
T'uch'eng, T'aiwan	269d	24.59 N	121.26 E
Tucheng, Zhg.	98	38.53 N	121.15 E
Tucheng, Zhg.	102	28.12 N	105.58 E
Tuchengzi, Zhg.	98	40.29 N	124.24 E
Tuchengzi, Zhg.	98	41.20 N	116.29 E
Tuchengzi, Zhg.	104	42.27 N	122.44 E
Tuchengzicun	104	41.52 N	120.41 E
Tuchengziwuhao	98	40.56 N	113.58 E
Tuchlovice	54	50.06 N	14.00 E
Tuchola	30	53.35 N	17.50 E
Tuchów	30	49.54 N	21.03 E
T'uchtet	86	56.32 N	89.19 E
Tuckahoe, N.J., U.S.	208	39.17 N	74.45 W
Tuckahoe, N.Y., U.S.	276	40.57 N	73.49 W
Tuckahoe ≃	208	39.17 N	74.39 W
Tuckahoe Creek ≃	208	38.49 N	75.53 W
Tuckanarra	162	27.07 S	118.05 E
Tucker Heights	210	42.55 N	73.55 W
Tuckerman	194	35.43 N	91.11 W
Tuckernuck Island I	207	41.18 N	70.15 W
Tuckerton, N.J., U.S.	208	39.36 N	74.20 W
Tuckerton, Pa., U.S.	208	40.25 N	75.57 W
Tuckfield, Mount ∧	162	18.44 S	124.54 E
Tučkovo	82	55.36 N	36.28 E
Tucson	200	32.13 N	110.55 W
Tucumã, Paraná ≃[1]	246	3.58 S	66.26 W
Tucumán → San Miguel de Tucumán	252	26.49 S	65.13 W
Tucumán □[4]	252	27.00 S	65.30 W
Tucumcari	196	35.10 N	103.43 W
Tucumcari Mountain ∧	196	35.08 N	103.42 W
Tucunduva	252	27.39 S	54.27 W
Tucunuco	252	30.36 S	68.38 W
Tucuparé, Cachoeira do ∟	250	5.20 S	55.50 W
Tucupido	246	9.17 N	65.47 W
Tucupita	246	9.04 N	62.03 W
Tucuruí	250	3.42 S	49.27 W
Tucuruvi ◆[8]	287b	23.28 S	46.35 W
Tuczna	30	51.54 N	23.26 E
Tud ≃	42	52.38 N	1.15 E
Tudameda	112	10.52 S	122.55 E
Tudcum	252	30.14 S	69.15 W
Tudeå ≃	41	55.23 N	11.13 E
Tudela, Esp.	34	42.05 N	1.36 W
Tudela, Pil.	116	8.15 N	123.50 E
Tudela de Duero	34	41.35 N	4.35 W
Tudian	106	30.35 N	120.37 E
Tudichang	107	30.06 N	103.56 E
Tuditang	100	30.12 N	114.18 E
Tudmur (Palmyra)	130	34.33 N	38.17 E
Tudu	76	59.11 N	26.51 E
Tudweiliog	42	52.54 N	4.35 W
Tuela ≃	34	41.30 N	7.12 W
Tuen Mun	271d	22.24 N	113.58 E
Tuenno	64	46.20 N	11.01 E
Tueré ≃	250	2.48 S	50.59 W
Tuergate	85	40.28 N	75.21 E
Tufanbeyli	130	38.16 N	36.13 E
Tufānganj	124	26.19 N	89.40 E
Tuffé	50	48.07 N	0.31 E
Tufi	164	9.05 S	149.20 E
Tufo	68	41.00 N	14.47 E
Tufts University ʊ[2]	283	42.24 N	71.07 W
Tufu Point ›	174y	14.13 S	169.32 W
Tugaske	184	50.53 N	106.16 W
Tugela	158	29.09 S	31.29 E
Tugela ≃	158	29.14 S	31.30 E
Tugela Falls ∟	158	28.45 S	28.58 E
Tugela Ferry	158	28.44 S	30.27 E
Tug Fork ≃	192	38.06 N	82.36 W
Tuggerah Lake ⊂	170	33.18 S	151.30 E
Tughlakābād ◆[8]	272a	28.31 N	77.16 E
Tugidak Island I	180	56.30 N	154.36 W
Tuğköyü	130	38.27 N	42.16 E
Tuglie	68	40.04 N	18.05 E
Tugnug Point ›	116	11.21 N	125.38 E
Tugolesskij Bor	80	55.33 N	39.49 E
Tugolukovo	80	51.56 N	41.40 E
Tugubun Point ›	116	7.00 N	126.27 E
Tuguegarao	116	17.37 N	121.44 E
Tugulym	86	57.04 N	64.39 E
Tugun	171a	28.09 S	153.30 E
Tugur	89	53.48 N	136.48 E
Tugur ≃	89	53.48 N	136.44 E
Tugúrio	256	21.15 S	43.35 W
Tugurskij poluostrov ›[1]	89	54.00 N	137.24 E
Tuguša	88	55.57 N	96.26 E
Tugutuj	88	52.40 N	104.50 E
Tuhai ≃	98	37.55 N	118.05 E
Tuhepu	104	40.54 N	122.49 E
Tuhuangba	102	31.40 N	108.21 E
Tuibo	89	44.01 N	127.47 E
Tuichi ≃	248	14.36 S	67.35 W
Tuim	86	54.20 N	89.55 E
Tuineje	148	28.19 N	14.03 W
Tuirc, Beinn an ∧[2]	46	55.34 N	5.34 W
Tuitán	234	21.08 N	103.48 W
Tuitui	256	22.47 S	46.42 W
Tuj ≃	86	57.33 N	72.31 E
T'ujabuguz	85	40.58 N	69.15 E
Tujemojnak	86	49.20 N	62.55 E
Tuji-ri	98	41.31 N	127.12 E
Tujmazy	80	54.36 N	53.42 E
Tüjn Gol ≃	102	45.04 N	100.46 E
Tujunga ◆[8]	280	34.15 N	118.17 W
Tujunga Valley V	280	34.17 N	118.20 W
Tujunga Wash V	280	34.09 N	118.24 W
Tukaj	86	55.24 N	90.49 E
T'ukalinsk	86	55.52 N	72.12 E
Tukan	86	53.50 N	57.26 E
Tukan ≃	86	60.02 N	71.36 E
Tukangbesi, Kepulauan II	112	5.40 S	123.50 E
Ṭūkh, Miṣr	142	27.41 N	30.49 E
Ṭūkh, Miṣr	142	30.21 N	31.12 E
Ṭūkh al-Aqlām	142	30.52 N	31.26 E
Ṭūkh al-Khayl	142	28.06 N	30.40 E
Tukituki ≃	172	39.36 S	176.57 E
Tuk Méas	110	10.40 N	104.34 E
Tukolon'	88	55.24 N	107.42 E
Tukosméra, Mont ∧	175f	19.35 S	169.22 E
Tukpo	154	4.25 N	25.52 E
Tūkrah	146	32.32 N	20.34 E
Tuktoyaktuk	180	69.27 N	133.02 W
Tuktoyaktuk Peninsula ›[1]	180	69.45 N	131.20 W
Tukuj-Mekteb	84	44.20 N	45.11 E
Tukums	76	57.00 N	23.10 E
Tukuran	116	7.51 N	123.35 E
Tukuringra, chrebet ⋏	89	54.20 N	126.20 E
Tukuyu	154	9.15 S	33.39 E
T'uk'u Yüeh ∧	269d	25.02 N	121.38 E
Tukwila	224	47.28 N	122.15 W
Tula, Am. Sam.	174u	14.15 S	170.34 W
Tula, It.	71	40.44 N	8.59 E
Tula, Méx.	234	23.00 N	99.43 W
Tula, Nig.	146	9.50 N	11.28 E
Tula, S.S.S.R.	82	54.12 N	37.37 E
Tula □[4]	82	54.23 N	37.47 E
Tula ≃, Kenya	154	0.50 S	39.51 E
Tula ≃, Méx.	234	20.40 N	99.30 W
Tula ⊥	234	20.06 N	99.19 W
Tula de Allende	234	20.03 N	99.21 W
Tulaghi	175e	9.06 S	160.09 E
Tulagt Ar ≃	120	36.35 N	92.20 E
Tulai Nanshan ⋏	102	38.44 N	98.20 E
Tūlak	128	33.58 N	63.44 E
Tulalip Indian Reservation ◆[4]	224	48.06 N	122.15 W
Tulancingo	234	20.05 N	98.22 W
Tulangbawang ≃	112	4.24 S	105.52 E
Tulaodian	104	41.13 N	121.27 E
T'ul'apsy	86	57.28 N	89.38 E
Tulare, Ca., U.S.	226	36.12 N	119.20 W
Tulare, S.D., U.S.	198	44.44 N	98.30 W
Tulare □[6]	226	36.20 N	119.18 W
Tulare Canal ≅	226	36.08 N	119.25 W
Tulare Lake Bed ⊜	226	36.03 N	119.49 W
Tulare Lake Canal ≅	226	36.04 N	119.39 W
Tularosa	200	33.04 N	106.01 W
Tularosa ≃	200	33.41 N	108.46 W
Tularosa Valley ≚[1]	200	32.45 N	106.10 W
Tulbagh	158	33.17 S	19.09 E
Tulbing	264b	48.16 N	16.09 E
Tulbinger Kogel ∧	264b	48.17 N	16.09 E
Tulcán	246	0.48 N	77.43 W
Tulcea	38	45.11 N	28.48 E
Tulcea □[6]	38	45.00 N	29.00 E
Tul'čin	78	48.39 N	28.52 E
Tulcingo de Valle	234	18.03 N	98.26 W
Tule ≃, Nic.	236	11.20 N	84.52 W
Tule ≃, Ca., U.S.	226	36.03 N	119.50 W
Tule, North Branch ≃	226	36.06 N	119.22 W
Tule, South Branch ≃	226	36.05 N	119.29 W
Tule Canal ≅	226	38.37 N	121.35 W
Tule Creek ≃	196	34.40 N	101.14 W
T'ulek	85	41.56 N	75.41 E
Tulelake	204	41.57 N	121.29 W
Tule Lake Sump ⊜[1]	204	41.54 N	121.32 W
Tulemalu Lake ⊜	176	62.58 N	99.25 W
T'ulenij, mys ›	84	40.12 N	50.22 E
T'ulenij, ostrov I	84	44.28 N	47.30 E
Tule River Indian Reservation ◆[4]	204	36.02 N	118.42 W
Tulette	62	44.17 N	4.56 E
Tule Valley V	200	39.20 N	113.25 W
T'ul'gan	86	52.22 N	56.12 E
Tul'goviči	78	51.47 N	29.38 E
Tuli	154	21.59 S	29.15 E
Tuli ≃	154	21.48 S	29.04 E
Tulia	196	34.32 N	101.45 W
Tuliahan ≃	269f	14.41 N	120.58 E
Tulica ≃	82	54.12 N	37.37 E
Tulik Volcano ∧[1]	180	53.22 N	168.03 W
Tulillo	234	22.30 N	104.05 W
Tuling	100	25.11 N	118.50 E
Tuliszków	30	52.05 N	18.17 E
Ṭūlkarm	132	32.19 N	35.02 E
T'ul'kino	86	59.49 N	56.30 E
T'ul'kubas	85	42.28 N	70.02 E
Tulla	48	52.52 N	8.45 W
Tullahoma	194	35.21 N	86.12 W
Tullamarine	274b	37.41 S	144.52 E
Tullamarine International Airport ⊠, Austl.	169	37.40 S	144.50 E
Tullamarine International Airport ⊠, Austl.	274b	37.40 S	144.50 E
Tullamore, Austl.	166	32.38 S	147.34 E
Tullamore, On., Can.	275b	43.47 N	79.46 W
Tullamore, Ire.	48	53.16 N	7.30 W
Tullaroop Creek ≃	169	36.53 S	143.53 E
Tullaroop Reservoir ⊜[1]	169	37.07 S	143.52 E
Tull Bay ⊂	208	36.30 N	76.04 W
Tulle	32	45.16 N	1.46 E
Tullgarn	40	58.57 N	17.35 E
Tullibigeal	166	33.25 S	146.44 E
Tullinge	40	59.12 N	17.53 E
Tullins	62	45.18 N	5.29 E
Tulln	61	48.20 N	16.03 E
Tullner Feld ◆[1]	264b	48.19 N	16.10 E
Tulloch Reservoir ⊜[1]	226	37.53 N	120.35 W
Tullock Creek ≃	202	46.08 N	107.27 W
Tullos	194	31.49 N	92.19 W
Tullow	48	52.48 N	6.44 W
Tullus	140	11.03 N	24.33 E
Tully, Austl.	166	17.56 S	145.56 E
Tully, N.Y., U.S.	210	42.47 N	76.06 W
Tully Dam ◆[6]	207	42.39 N	72.11 W
Tullytown	208	40.09 N	74.49 W
Ṭulmaythah	146	32.43 N	20.57 E
Tuloma ≃	24	68.52 N	32.49 E
Tulpfontein	158	32.44 S	19.43 E
Tulsa	196	36.09 N	95.59 W
Tulsequah	176	58.35 N	133.35 W
Tulsī Lake ⊜	272c	19.11 N	72.55 E
Tulsīpur	124	28.07 N	82.18 E
Tulsk	48	53.47 N	8.16 W
Tul'skij	84	44.31 N	40.10 E
Tulstrup	41	56.07 N	9.46 E
Tultepec	234	19.41 N	99.08 W
Tultitlán □[7]	286a	19.39 N	99.09 W
Tultitlán de Mariano Escobedo	286a	19.39 N	99.09 W
Tuluá	246	4.06 N	76.11 W
Tuluksak	180	61.06 N	160.58 W
Tulum	232	20.13 N	87.28 W
Tulum ⊥	232	20.12 N	87.26 W
Tulumaya (Lavalle)	252	32.43 S	68.35 W
Tulumayo ≃	248	11.10 S	75.16 W
Tulun	88	54.35 N	100.33 E
Tulungagung	115a	8.04 S	111.54 E
Tulungselapan	112	3.15 S	105.19 E
Tuluran Island I	116	10.59 N	119.17 E
Tulu Welel ∧	144	8.53 N	34.47 E
Tulyehualco ◆[8]	286a	19.15 N	99.01 W
Tum	164	3.38 S	130.23 E
Tuma	80	55.09 N	40.34 E
Tuma ≃	236	13.03 N	84.44 W
Tumacacori National Monument ♠	200	31.25 N	111.01 W
Tumaco	246	1.49 N	78.46 W
Tumaco, Ensenada de ⊂	246	1.55 N	78.45 W
Tumak	80	46.14 N	48.31 E
Tumalykol'	86	48.21 N	60.03 E
Tuman'an	84	41.00 N	44.40 E
Tuman-gang (Tumen) ≃	98	42.18 N	130.41 E
Tumannaja, gora ∧	180	66.33 N	179.43 E
Tumanovo	76	55.25 N	34.39 E
Tumanšet ≃	88	55.53 N	97.30 E
Tumanskij	180	63.58 N	178.12 E
Tumany	74	60.56 N	155.56 E
Tumarbong	116	10.23 N	119.27 E
T'um'ati → Sklad	74	71.55 N	123.33 E
Tumatumari	246	5.22 N	59.00 W
Tumauini	116	17.17 N	121.49 E
Tumba	40	59.12 N	17.49 E
Tumba, Lac ⊜	152	0.48 S	18.03 E
Tumbarumba	171b	35.47 S	148.01 E
Tumbarumba Creek ≃	171b	35.58 S	148.03 E
Tumbaya	252	23.51 S	65.28 W
Tumbes	246	3.34 S	80.28 W
Tumbes □[4]	246	3.50 N	80.30 W
Tumbes (Puyango) ≃	246	3.30 S	80.27 W
Tumbes, Punta ›	252	36.37 S	73.07 W
Tumbiscatio de Ruiz	234	18.31 N	102.21 W
Tumble Mountain ∧	202	45.19 N	110.02 W
Tumbler Ridge	182	55.07 N	120.55 W
Tumblong	171b	35.09 S	148.00 E
Tumbotino	80	55.59 N	43.02 E
Tumbur	154	4.20 N	31.34 E
Tumby Bay	166	34.22 S	136.06 E
Tumča ≃	24	66.36 N	30.48 E
Tŭmch'on-ni ◆[8]	271b	37.34 N	126.51 E
T'umen', S.S.S.R.	86	57.09 N	65.32 E
Tumen, Zhg.	98	42.58 N	129.49 E
Tumen (Tuman-gang) ≃	98	42.18 N	130.41 E
T'umen'-Aryk	86	44.02 N	67.01 E
T'umencevo	86	53.20 N	81.31 E
T'umenec, porog ∟	88	56.38 N	99.00 E

ENGLISH Name	Page	Lat.°′	Long.°′
Tumenpu	107	29.49 N	103.39 E
T'umenskaja Oblast' □[4]	24	65.00 N	62.00 E
Tumenskoje	82	55.00 N	38.32 E
Tumenzi	102	37.43 N	103.09 E
Tumeremo	246	7.18 N	61.30 W
Tumiritinga	255	18.58 S	41.38 W
Tumkūr	122	13.21 N	77.05 E
Tummel ≃	46	56.38 N	3.40 W
Tumnin ≃	89	49.18 N	140.22 E
Tumon Bay ⊂	174p	13.31 N	144.48 E
Tumos ≃	156	22.55 S	14.37 E
Tumoteqi	102	40.52 N	111.28 E
Tumpang	115a	8.00 S	112.46 E
Tumpat	114	6.12 N	102.10 E
Tumsar	120	21.23 N	79.44 E
Tumtum	182	47.53 N	117.40 W
Tumu, Ghana	150	10.52 N	1.59 W
Tumu, Zhg.	105	40.23 N	115.36 E
Tumuc-Humac Mountains ⋏	250	2.20 N	55.00 W
Tumupasa	248	14.09 S	67.55 W
Tumut	171b	35.18 S	148.13 E
Tumut ≃	171b	35.07 S	148.13 E
Tumut Pond Reservoir ⊜[1]	171b	35.59 S	148.25 E
Tumutuk	80	55.02 N	53.19 E
Tumwater	224	47.00 N	122.54 W
Tun ≃	110	17.25 N	98.42 E
Tuña ≃	246	1.30 N	73.55 W
Tuna Canyon V	280	34.03 N	118.36 W
Tunago Lake ⊜	180	66.18 N	125.50 W
Tuna-Hästberg	40	60.20 N	15.11 E
Tunapuna	241r	10.38 N	61.23 W
Tunari, Cerro ∧	248	17.18 S	66.22 W
Tunas Creek ≃	196	31.01 N	102.11 W
Tunas de Zaza	240p	21.38 N	79.33 W
Tūnat al-Jabal, Miṣr	142	27.46 N	30.44 E
Tūnat al-Jabal, Miṣr	142	28.13 N	30.43 E
Tunaydah	140	25.31 N	29.21 E
Tunbridge Wells → Royal Tunbridge Wells	42	51.08 N	0.16 E
Tunçbilek	130	39.37 N	29.29 E
Tunceli	130	39.07 N	39.32 E
Tunceli □[4]	130	39.10 N	39.30 E
Tunchang	110	19.28 N	110.08 E
T'unch'i → Tunxi	100	29.44 N	118.18 E
Tunda, Pulau I	115a	5.49 S	106.16 E
Tundazi ∧	154	17.33 S	28.05 E
Tündern	52	52.04 N	9.22 E
Tūndla	124	27.12 N	78.17 E
Tundubai ▾[4]	140	18.31 N	28.33 E
Tunduru	154	11.07 S	37.21 E
Tundyk ≃	86	51.04 N	77.24 E
Tundža ≃	38	41.40 N	26.34 E
Tune	41	55.36 N	12.11 E
Tunesien → Tunisia □[1]	148	34.00 N	9.00 E
T'unež, S.S.S.R.	82	54.37 N	38.29 E
Túnez → Tunis, Tun.	148	36.48 N	10.11 E
Túnez → Tunisia □[1]	148	34.00 N	9.00 E
T'ung ≃	74	63.46 N	121.35 E
Tunga	150	8.00 N	9.19 E
Tunga ≃	122	14.00 N	75.41 E
Tungabhadra ≃	122	15.57 N	78.15 E
Tungabhadra Reservoir ⊜[1]	122	15.16 N	76.21 E
Tungaru	140	10.14 N	30.42 E
Tungauan Bay ⊂	116	7.28 N	122.21 E
Tungchi University ʊ[2]	269b	31.18 N	121.29 E
Tungchi Yü I	100	23.15 N	119.40 E
T'ungchou → Tongxian	105	39.55 N	116.39 E
T'ungch'uan → Tongchuan	102	35.01 N	109.01 E
Tungch'üan Tao I	100	25.58 N	119.58 E
Tungelsta	40	59.06 N	18.02 E
Tung Hai → East China Sea ▾[2]	90	30.00 N	126.00 E
Tungho	100	22.58 N	121.18 E
T'unghsien → Tongxian	105	39.55 N	116.39 E
T'unghua → Tonghua	98	41.41 N	125.55 E
Tunghwa → Tonghua	98	41.41 N	125.55 E
Tungir ≃	88	55.24 N	120.32 E
Tungirskij chrebet ⋏	88	54.40 N	119.40 E
Tungkal ≃	112	0.49 S	103.29 E
Tungkang	100	22.28 N	120.26 E
Tungkillo	168b	34.49 S	139.04 E
Tungku	112	5.01 N	118.53 E
Tungla	236	13.18 N	84.26 W
T'ungliao → Tongliao	89	43.39 N	122.14 E
Tung Lung Island I	271d	22.15 N	114.17 E
Tung O	271d	22.12 N	114.08 E
Tungokočen	88	53.33 N	115.36 E
Tungsha Tao (Pratas Island) I	90	20.42 N	116.43 E
Tungshih	100	24.15 N	120.49 E
Tungsten	180	61.57 N	128.16 W
Tungsunga, Jabal ∧	140	11.29 N	23.21 E
Tungting Tao I	100	24.10 N	118.14 E
Tungurahua □[4]	246	1.15 S	78.35 W
Tungyin Tao I	100	26.22 N	120.30 E
Tuni	122	17.21 N	82.33 E
Tunia ≃	246	1.13 N	72.44 W
Tunica	194	34.41 N	90.22 W
Tunis	148	36.48 N	10.11 E
Tunis □[8]	148	36.50 N	10.15 E
Tūnis → Tunisia □[1]	148	34.00 N	9.00 E
Tunis, Golfe de ⊂	36	37.00 N	10.30 E
Tunis et Banlieue □[8]	36	36.48 N	10.10 E
Tunisia (Tunisie) □[1], Afr.	134	34.00 N	9.00 E
Tunisia (Tunisie) □[1], Afr.	148	34.00 N	9.00 E
Tunisie → Tunisia □[1]	148	34.00 N	9.00 E
Tunis Sud □[8]	148	36.30 N	10.00 E
Tunitas Creek ≃	282	37.21 N	122.24 W
Tunja	246	5.31 N	73.22 W
Tunjang	114	6.16 N	100.21 E
Tunka	88	51.45 N	102.32 E
Tunkás	232	20.54 N	88.45 W
Tunkhannock	210	41.32 N	75.56 W
Tunkhannock Creek ≃	210	41.32 N	75.57 W
Tunkhannock Creek, East Branch ≃	210	41.38 N	75.43 W
Tunliu	102	36.19 N	112.54 E
Tunnel	210	42.13 N	75.44 W
Tunnel Hill, Ga., U.S.	192	34.50 N	85.02 W
Tunnelhill, Pa., U.S.	214	40.29 N	78.33 W
Tunnelton, In., U.S.	218	38.46 N	86.21 W
Tunnelton, W.V., U.S.	188	39.23 N	79.44 W
Tunnsjøen ⊜	24	64.43 N	13.24 E
Tunø I	41	55.57 N	10.26 E
Tuntenhausen	64	47.56 N	12.01 E
Tuntum	250	5.14 S	44.39 W
Tuntutuliak	180	60.22 N	162.38 W
Tununak	180	60.35 N	165.16 W
Tunungayualok Island I	176	56.05 N	61.05 W
Tunuyán	252	33.34 S	69.01 W
Tunuyán ≃	252	34.03 S	66.45 W
Tunxi	100	29.44 N	118.18 E
Tuo ≃, Zhg.	100	33.16 N	117.45 E
Tuo ≃, Zhg.	102	28.57 N	105.27 E
Tuobalage	120	31.37 N	88.10 E
Tuobuja	74	62.00 N	122.02 E
Tuocheng	100	24.05 N	115.13 E
Tuoe Shan ∧	102	24.20 N	103.32 E
Tuoheji	100	33.26 N	117.26 E

DEUTSCH Name	Seite	Breite°′	Länge°′ E = Ost
Tuoj-Chaja	74	62.32 N	111.18 E
Tuoji Dao I	98	38.09 N	120.14 E
Tuokedingling	120	32.45 N	84.55 E
Tuokusidawan Ling ∧	120	37.14 N	85.47 E
Tuoli	105	39.46 N	116.01 E
Tuolumne	226	37.57 N	120.14 W
Tuolumne □[6]	226	37.59 N	120.23 W
Tuolumne ≃	226	37.36 N	121.10 W
Tuolumne, Lyell Fork ≃	226	37.53 N	119.23 W
Tuolumne, North Fork ≃	226	37.54 N	120.15 W
Tuolumne, South Fork ≃	226	37.50 N	120.03 W
Tuolunduo	89	50.35 N	120.05 E
Tuong Duong	110	19.16 N	104.27 E
Tuotuo ≃	120	34.15 N	93.11 E
Tuowu	102	28.58 N	102.13 E
T'up	85	42.44 N	78.22 E
Tupã	255	21.56 S	50.30 W
Tupaciguara	255	18.35 S	48.42 W
Tupana ≃	246	4.25 S	60.05 W
Tupanciretã	252	29.05 S	53.51 W
Tuparro ≃	246	5.13 N	67.50 W
Tupelo, Ms., U.S.	194	34.15 N	88.42 W
Tupelo, Ok., U.S.	196	34.36 N	96.25 W
Tupelo National Battlefield ⊥	194	34.13 N	88.44 W
Tupi	116	6.19 N	124.57 E
Tupičov	78	51.46 N	31.26 E
Tupik	88	54.26 N	119.57 E
Tupilac	116	7.40 N	122.30 E
Tupinambarana, Ilha I	246	3.00 S	58.00 W
Tupi Paulista	255	21.24 S	51.34 W
Tupiraçaba	255	14.29 S	48.34 W
Tupirama	250	8.58 S	48.12 W
Tupiza	248	21.27 S	65.43 W
Tuplice	30	51.41 N	14.50 E
Tupman	226	35.17 N	119.21 W
Tupper	182	55.31 N	120.02 W
Tupper Lake	188	44.13 N	74.29 W
Tupperville	214	42.36 N	82.16 W
Tupuai, Île I	14	23.18 S	149.30 W
Tupungato	252	33.22 S	69.08 W
Tupungato, Cerro ∧	252	33.22 S	69.47 W
Tuqiao, Zhg.	106	31.56 N	119.03 E
Tuqiao, Zhg.	106	31.39 N	120.24 E
Tuqiao, Zhg.	107	30.24 N	105.28 E
Tuqiaozhen	107	30.32 N	104.50 E
Tuquan	89	45.26 N	121.50 E
Túquerres	246	1.05 N	77.37 W
Tuquiaochang	107	29.47 N	106.01 E
Tura, India	124	25.31 N	90.13 E
Ṭurā, Miṣr	142	29.56 N	31.16 E
Tura, S.S.S.R.	74	64.17 N	100.15 E
Tura ≃, S.S.S.R.	86	57.12 N	66.56 E
Tura ≃, S.S.S.R.	88	51.36 N	114.09 E
Turabah	144	21.13 N	41.39 E
Turabah ▾[4]	128	28.15 N	42.55 E
Turābah, 'Ayn at- ▾[4]	132	31.36 N	35.25 E
Turāg ≃	126	23.45 N	90.21 E
Turaiyūr	122	11.10 N	78.37 E
Turakina	172	40.02 S	175.13 E
Turakina ≃	172	40.04 S	175.08 E
Turama ≃	164	6.50 S	143.05 E
Turambhe	272c	19.04 N	73.01 E
Turan, S.S.S.R.	88	51.38 N	101.40 E
Turan, S.S.S.R.	88	52.08 N	93.55 E
Turangi	172	39.00 S	175.49 E
Turano ≃	66	42.26 N	12.47 E
Turanskaja nizmennost' ≚	86	44.30 N	63.00 E
Ṭurāq al-'Ilab ⋏[2]	130	33.55 N	38.18 E
Turate	266b	45.39 N	9.00 E
Tur'at Ghunaym	142	31.16 N	31.29 E
Ṭurayf	128	31.44 N	38.33 E
Turbaco	246	10.20 N	75.25 W
Turbacz ∧	30	49.33 N	20.08 E
Turbat	128	25.59 N	63.04 E
Turbenthal	58	47.27 N	8.51 E
Turbigo	62	45.32 N	8.44 E
Turbio ≃	234	20.19 N	101.37 W
Turbo	246	8.06 N	76.43 W
Turbotville	210	41.06 N	76.46 W
Turbov	78	49.21 N	28.44 E
Turčasovo	24	63.06 N	39.12 E
Turchi, Balata dei ›	70	36.43 N	12.02 E
Turčiansky Svätý Martin → Martin	30	49.05 N	18.55 E
Turckheim	58	48.05 N	7.17 E
Turda	38	46.34 N	23.47 E
Turdej	76	53.22 N	38.01 E
Turee Creek	162	23.37 S	118.39 E
Turee Creek ≃	162	23.35 S	117.25 E
Turek	30	52.02 N	18.30 E
Turen	115a	8.10 S	112.41 E
Turenki	26	60.55 N	24.38 E
Turfan → Turpan	86	42.56 N	89.10 E
Turfan Depression → Turpan Pendi ▴[7]	86	42.40 N	89.10 E
Turffontein ◆[8]	273d	26.15 S	28.02 E
Turffontein Race Course ♠	273d	26.14 S	28.03 E
Turgaj, S.S.S.R.	86	49.38 N	63.28 E
Turgaj, S.S.S.R.	86	51.46 N	72.44 E
Turgaj ≃	86	48.01 N	62.45 E
Turgajskaja ložbina V	86	51.00 N	64.30 E
Turgajskaja Oblast' □[4]	86	50.00 N	65.20 E
Turgajskoje plato ⋏[1]	86	51.00 N	64.00 E
Türgen, Mong.	86	50.04 N	91.36 E
Turgen', S.S.S.R.	85	43.24 N	77.36 E
Turgen' ≃	85	43.50 N	77.38 E
Turgenevka	88	53.02 N	105.41 E
Turgenevo	80	54.50 N	46.19 E
Turginovo	82	56.30 N	36.00 E
Turgojak	86	55.10 N	60.07 E
Turgoš	76	59.18 N	35.10 E
Tŭrgovishte → Târgovište	38	43.15 N	26.34 E
Turgut, Tür.	130	37.22 N	28.02 E
Turgut, Tür.	130	38.37 N	31.49 E
Turgutlu	130	38.30 N	27.43 E
Turgwi ≃	154	20.28 S	32.18 E
Turhal	130	40.24 N	36.06 E
Turi, It.	68	40.55 N	17.01 E
Türi, S.S.S.R.	76	58.48 N	25.26 E
Turia ≃	34	39.27 N	0.19 W
Turiaçu	250	1.41 S	45.21 W
Turiaçu ≃	250	1.36 S	45.19 W
Turiančajskij zapovednik ♠	84	40.40 N	47.35 E
Turij Rog	89	45.14 N	131.58 E
Turijsk	78	51.07 N	24.31 E
Turilovka	83	49.06 N	40.13 E
Turimetta Head ›	274a	33.42 S	151.19 E
Turimiquire, Cerro ∧	246	10.07 N	63.53 W
Turin, Ab., Can.	182	49.58 N	112.31 W
Turin → Torino, It.	62	45.03 N	7.40 E
Turin, N.Y., U.S.	212	43.38 N	75.25 W
Turinge	40	59.12 N	17.27 E
Turinsk	86	58.03 N	63.42 E
Turinskaja Sloboda	86	57.37 N	64.25 E
Turja ≃	78	51.48 N	24.52 E
Turka, S.S.S.R.	78	49.10 N	23.02 E
Turka, S.S.S.R.	88	52.57 N	108.13 E
Turka ≃	88	52.56 N	108.13 E
Turkana, Lake → Rudolf, Lake ⊜	144	3.30 N	36.05 E
Türkei → Turkey □[1]	22	39.00 N	35.00 E
Türkeli Adası I	130	40.30 N	27.30 E
Turkestan	85	43.18 N	68.15 E
Turkestanskij chrebet ⋏	85	39.35 N	69.15 E
Turkestanskij kanal ≅	85	42.44 N	69.00 E

Symbols in the index entries represent the broad categories identified in the key at the right. Symbols with superior numbers (⋏[1]) identify subcategories (see complete key on page I · 1).

Symbole im Register stellen die rechts im Schlüssel erklärten Kategorien dar. Symbole mit hochgestellten Ziffern (⋏[1]) bezeichnen Unterabteilungen einer Kategorie (vgl. vollständiger Schlüssel auf Seite I · 1).

Los símbolos incluídos en el texto del índice representan las grandes categorias identificadas con la clave a la derecha. Los símbolos con numeros en su parte superior (⋏[1]) identifican las subcategorías (véase la clave completa en la página I · 1).

Les symboles de l'index représentent les catégories indiquées dans la légende à droite. Les symboles suivis d'un indice (⋏[1]) représentent des sous-catégories (voir légende complète à la page I · 1).

Os símbolos incluídos no texto do índice representam as grandes categorias identificadas com a chave à direita. Os símbolos com números em sua parte superior (⋏[1]) identificam as subcategorias (veja-se a chave completa à página I · 1).

	English	Deutsch	Español	Français	Português
∧	Mountain	Berg	Montaña	Montagne	Montanha
⋏	Mountains	Gebirge	Montañas	Montagnes	Montanhas
)(	Pass	Paß	Paso	Col	Passo
V	Valley, Canyon	Tal, Cañon	Valle, Cañón	Vallée, Canyon	Vale, Canhão
≚	Plain	Ebene	Llano	Plaine	Planície
›	Cape	Kap	Cabo	Cap	Cabo
I	Island	Insel	Isla	Île	Ilha
II	Islands	Inseln	Islas	Îles	Ilhas
▴	Other Topographic Features	Andere Topographische Objekte	Otros Elementos Topográficos	Autres données topographiques	Outros acidentes topográficos

ESPAÑOL

Nombre	Página	Lat.°′	Long.°′ W = Oeste
Túrkeve	30	47.06 N	20.45 E
Turkey	196	34.23 N	100.53 W
Turkey (Türkiye) □[1], Asia	22	39.00 N	35.00 E
Turkey (Türkiye) □[1], Asia	130	39.00 N	35.00 E
Turkey ≏	190	42.43 N	91.01 W
Turkey Branch ≏	284c	38.52 N	76.48 W
Turkey City	214	41.11 N	79.37 W
Turkey Creek	164	17.02 S	128.12 E
Turkey Creek ≏, On., Can.	281	42.14 N	83.06 W
Turkey Creek ≏, U.S.	198	39.58 N	96.02 W
Turkey Creek ≏, In., U.S.	278	41.31 N	87.18 W
Turkey Creek ≏, Ia., U.S.	198	41.20 N	95.05 W
Turkey Creek ≏, Ks., U.S.	198	38.53 N	97.11 W
Turkey Creek ≏, Ne., U.S.	198	40.23 N	96.53 W
Turkey Creek ≏, Ok., U.S.	196	35.58 N	97.56 W
Turkey Creek ≏, Tx., U.S.	222	30.39 N	97.05 W
Turkey Island I	284c	38.58 N	77.12 W
Turkey Point ≻, On., Can.	212	42.40 N	80.21 W
Turkey Point ≻, Fl., U.S.	220	25.26 N	80.19 W
Turkey Point Provincial Park ♠	212	42.40 N	80.22 W
Turkey Run State Park ♠	194	39.54 N	87.13 W
Turkeytown	279b	40.12 N	79.44 W
Türkheim	58	48.03 N	10.38 E
Turki	80	51.59 N	43.16 E
Türkiye → Turkey □[1]	22	39.00 N	35.00 E
Turkmān Deh	267d	35.40 N	51.36 E
Turkmenistan → Turkmenskaja Sovetskaja Socialističeskaja Respublika □[3]	72	40.00 N	60.00 E
Turkmen-Kala	128	37.26 N	62.20 E
Turkmenskaja Sovetskaja Socialističeskaja Respublika □[3]	72	40.00 N	60.00 E
Turkmenskij zaliv ⊂	128	38.54 N	53.48 E
Turk Mine	154	19.45 S	28.50 E
Türkoğlu	130	37.31 N	36.49 E
Turks and Caicos Islands □[2], N.A.	230	21.45 N	71.35 W
Turks and Caicos Islands □[2], N.A.	238	21.45 N	71.35 W
Turks Island Passage ⋓	238	21.25 N	71.19 W
Turks Islands II	238	21.24 N	71.07 W
Turks-und Caicos-Inseln → Turks and Caicos Islands □[2]	238	21.45 N	71.35 W
Turku (Åbo)	26	60.27 N	22.17 E
Turkwel ≏	154	3.06 N	36.06 E
Turlan	85	43.36 N	69.03 E
Turley	196	36.14 N	95.58 W
Turlock	226	37.29 N	120.50 W
Turlock Lake ⊜[1]	226	42.17 N	73.21 W
Turmalina	255	17.17 S	42.45 W
Turmantas	76	55.42 N	26.27 E
Turmerito, Quebrada ≏	286c	10.26 N	66.55 W
Turnagain ≏	180	59.06 N	127.35 W
Turnagain, Cape ≻	172	40.29 S	176.37 E
Turnagain Arm ⊂	180	61.00 N	150.00 W
Turnagain Island I	164	9.34 S	142.18 E
Turna nad Bodvou	30	48.37 N	20.53 E
Turnau	61	47.33 N	15.20 E
Turnbull, Mount ∧	200	33.04 N	110.16 W
Turnbull, Mount ∧[2]	162	21.03 S	131.57 E
Turneffe Islands II	232	17.22 N	87.51 W
Turner, Austl.	162	17.50 S	128.17 E
Turner, Mt., U.S.	202	48.50 N	108.24 W
Turner, Or., U.S.	202	44.50 N	122.57 W
Turner ≏	162	20.21 S	118.25 E
Turner Field ⊠	285	40.13 N	75.13 W
Turners Falls	207	42.36 N	72.33 W
Turners Peninsula ≻[1]	150	7.22 N	12.22 W
Turnersville, N.J., U.S.	285	39.46 N	75.03 W
Turnersville, Tx., U.S.	222	31.37 N	97.44 W
Turner Valley	182	50.40 N	114.17 W
Turnhout	52	51.19 N	4.57 E
Türnitz	61	47.57 N	15.30 E
Turnor Lake ⊜	184	56.32 N	108.38 W
Turnov	30	50.35 N	15.10 E
Tŭrnovo → Veliko Târnovo	38	43.04 N	25.39 E
Turnpike Lake ⊜	283	42.01 N	71.19 W
Turnu-Măgurele	38	43.45 N	24.53 E
Turnu Roşu, Pasul)(	38	45.33 N	24.16 E
Turnu-Severin → Drobeta-Turnu Severin	38	44.38 N	22.39 E
Turobin	30	50.50 N	22.45 E
Turočak	86	52.16 N	87.08 E
Turon	198	37.48 N	98.25 W
Turon ≏	170	33.03 S	149.43 E
Turopin	78	51.00 N	24.27 E
Turopolje ⍓	36	45.40 N	16.05 E
Tuross ≏	171b	36.09 S	149.39 E
Turov	78	52.04 N	27.44 E
Turovo	82	54.52 N	37.49 E
Turpan	86	42.56 N	89.10 E
Turpan Pendi (Turfan Depression) ⌣[7]	86	42.40 N	89.10 E
Turques et Caicos, Îles → Turks and Caicos Islands □[2]	238	21.45 N	71.35 W
Turquía → Turkey □[1]	22	39.00 N	35.00 E
Turquie → Turkey □[1]	22	39.00 N	35.00 E
Turquino, Pico ∧	240p	19.59 N	76.50 W
Turrach	64	46.57 N	13.52 E
Turramurra	274a	33.44 S	151.08 E
Turrell	194	35.22 N	90.15 W
Turret Peak ∧	200	34.15 N	111.53 W
Turriaco	64	45.49 N	13.26 E
Turrialba	236	9.54 N	83.41 W
Turrialba, Volcán ∧[1]	236	10.02 N	83.46 W
Turriers	62	44.24 N	6.10 E
Turriff	46	57.32 N	2.28 W
Turritano ◆[1]	71	40.45 N	8.35 E
Turrubares, Cerro ∧	236	9.47 N	84.28 W
Tursi	68	40.15 N	16.28 E
Tursunzade	85	38.32 N	68.13 E
Turtas ≏	86	59.06 N	68.52 E
Turtipār	124	26.10 N	83.54 E
Turtle ≏, Mb., Can.	184	51.07 N	99.39 W
Turtle ≏, On., Can.	184	48.51 N	92.45 W
Turtle, North Branch ≏	198	47.57 N	97.35 W
Turtle Creek, N.B., Can.	186	45.58 N	64.53 W
Turtle Creek, Pa., U.S.	214	40.24 N	79.49 W
Turtle Creek ≏, Pa., U.S.	279b	40.23 N	79.51 W
Turtle Creek ≏, S.D., U.S.	198	44.55 N	98.29 W
Turtle Creek ≏, Wi., U.S.	216	42.29 N	89.03 W
Turtle-Flambeau Flowage ⊜[1]	190	46.05 N	90.11 W
Turtleford	184	53.23 N	108.56 W

FRANÇAIS

Nom	Page	Lat.°′	Long.°′ W = Ouest
Turtle Harbor Channel ⋓	220	25.15 N	80.18 W
Turtle Islands II	150	7.37 N	13.02 W
Turtle Lake, N.D., U.S.	198	47.31 N	100.53 W
Turtle Lake, Wi., U.S.	190	45.23 N	92.08 W
Turtle Lake ⊜	184	53.35 N	108.40 W
Turtle Mountain ∧[2]	184	49.00 N	100.15 W
Turtle Mountain Indian Reservation ◆[4]	198	48.51 N	99.45 W
Turtle Mountain Provincial Park ♠	184	49.03 N	100.15 W
Turtmann	58	46.18 N	7.41 E
Turton and Entwistle Reservoir ⊜[1]	262	53.39 N	2.25 W
Turton Bottoms	262	53.38 N	2.24 W
Turton Moor ◆[3]	262	53.40 N	2.29 W
Turton Tower ✦	262	53.38 N	2.25 W
Turu ≏	74	64.38 N	100.00 E
Turua	172	37.14 S	175.34 E
Turuchan ≏	74	65.56 N	87.42 E
Turuchansk	74	65.49 N	87.59 E
Turuntajevo, S.S.S.R.	86	56.38 N	85.59 E
Turuntajevo, S.S.S.R.	88	52.12 N	107.37 E
Turusele ∧	71	40.09 N	9.34 E
Turvânia	255	16.39 S	50.09 W
Turvo	252	28.56 S	49.41 W
Turvo ≏, Bra.	255	17.46 S	50.12 W
Turvo ≏, Bra.	255	19.56 S	49.55 W
Turvo ≏, Bra.	256	22.04 S	45.42 W
Turvo ≏, Bra.	256	22.29 S	44.15 W
Turvo ≏, Bra.	256	21.32 S	44.26 W
Turvo Grande ≏	256	21.42 S	44.22 W
Turvo Pequeno ≏	256	21.42 S	44.22 W
Turyu-san ∧	98	41.10 N	128.47 E
Turzovka	30	49.25 N	18.39 E
Tusa	70	37.59 N	14.14 E
Tusa ≏	70	38.01 N	14.16 E
Tusas, Rio ≏	200	36.23 N	106.03 W
Tuscaloosa	194	33.12 N	87.34 W
Tuscaloosa, Lake ⊜[1]	194	33.20 N	87.35 W
Tuscania	66	42.25 N	11.52 E
Tuscany → Toscana □[4]	36	43.25 N	11.00 E
Tuscarawas	214	40.24 N	81.25 W
Tuscarawas □[6]	214	40.30 N	81.27 W
Tuscarawas ≏	214	40.17 N	81.52 W
Tuscarora, N.Y., U.S.	210	42.38 N	77.52 W
Tuscarora, Pa., U.S.	208	40.46 N	76.02 W
Tuscarora Creek ≏, N.Y., U.S.	210	42.07 N	77.14 W
Tuscarora Creek ≏, Pa., U.S.	208	40.32 N	77.23 W
Tuscarora Creek, North Branch ≏	210	42.05 N	77.18 W
Tuscarora Indian Reservation ◆[4]	210	43.09 N	78.57 W
Tuscarora Mountain ∧	188	40.10 N	77.45 W
Tuscarora Mountains ⋏	204	41.00 N	116.20 W
Tuscarora State Park ♠	208	40.48 N	76.01 W
Tuscarora Tunnel ◆[5]	214	40.05 N	77.50 W
Tuscola, Il., U.S.	194	39.47 N	88.16 W
Tuscola, Tx., U.S.	196	32.12 N	99.48 W
Tuscolo ⊥	267a	41.48 N	12.42 E
Tuscumbia, Al., U.S.	194	34.43 N	87.42 W
Tuscumbia, Mo., U.S.	194	38.13 N	92.27 W
Tuse	41	55.43 N	11.37 E
Tushan	98	34.14 N	117.51 E
Tušino ◆[8]	265b	55.50 N	37.26 E
Tuskegee	194	32.25 N	85.41 W
Tusker Rock II[1]	42	51.27 N	3.40 W
Tussey Mountain ∧	214	40.25 N	78.07 W
Tüssling	60	48.13 N	12.36 E
Tustin	228	33.44 N	117.49 W
Tustin Marine Corps Air Station (Helicopter) ■	280	33.43 N	117.50 W
Tustumena Lake ⊜	180	60.12 N	150.50 W
Tuszyn	30	51.37 N	19.34 E
Tut	130	37.48 N	37.55 E
Tuta	152	14.37 S	20.45 E
Tutaekuri ≏	172	39.30 S	176.54 E
Tutaizi	104	41.01 N	122.38 E
Tutajev	80	57.53 N	39.32 E
Tutak	84	39.32 N	42.46 E
Tutang	100	29.21 N	116.24 E
Tutbury	42	52.51 N	1.41 W
Tuthills Creek ≏	276	40.45 N	73.02 W
Tuticorin	122	8.47 N	78.08 E
Tutin	38	42.59 N	20.20 E
Tutkaul	85	38.18 N	69.17 E
T'ut'kovo	82	54.37 N	38.32 E
Tutóia	250	2.45 S	42.16 W
Tutoko, Mount ∧	172	44.36 S	168.00 E
Tutong	112	4.50 N	114.40 E
Tutova ≏	38	46.06 N	27.32 E
Tutrakan	38	44.03 N	26.37 E
Tuttle, N.D., U.S.	198	47.08 N	99.59 W
Tuttle, Ok., U.S.	196	35.17 N	97.48 W
Tuttle Creek Lake ⊜[1]	198	39.22 N	96.40 W
Tuttlingen	58	47.59 N	8.49 E
Tutuala	112	8.24 S	127.15 E
Tutuban Station ◆[5]	269f	14.37 N	120.58 E
Tutu Bay ⊂	116	5.55 N	121.12 E
Tutubu	154	5.30 S	32.41 E
Tutuila I	174u	14.18 S	170.42 W
Tuṭūn	142	29.09 N	30.46 E
Tütüncü	130	40.04 N	27.43 E
Tutupaca, Volcán ∧[1]	248	17.01 S	70.22 W
Tutura	88	54.46 N	105.15 E
Tututalak Mountain ∧	180	67.46 N	161.10 W
Tututepec	234	16.09 N	97.38 W
Tutwiler	194	34.00 N	90.25 W
Tutzing	64	47.54 N	11.17 E
Tuul ≏	90	48.57 N	104.48 E
Tuupovaara	26	62.29 N	30.36 E
Tuurun-Poorin lääni □[4]	26	61.20 N	22.30 E
Tuusniemi	26	62.49 N	28.30 E
Tuutapu, Cerro ∧	174z	27.08 S	109.24 W
T'uva-Guba	24	69.08 N	33.32 E
Tuvalu □[1]	14	8.00 S	178.00 E
Tuvinskaja Avtonomnaja Sovetskaja Socialističeskaja Respublika □[3]	88	53.00 N	96.00 E
Tuvutha Island I	175g	17.40 S	178.48 W
Tuwang	107	29.06 N	105.48 E
Ṭuwayq, Jabal ⋏	118	23.00 N	46.00 E
Ṭuwayyil ash-Shihāq ∧[2]	132	30.36 N	36.08 E
Tuxedo Park, De., U.S.	285	39.43 N	75.37 W
Tuxedo Park, N.Y., U.S.	210	41.11 N	74.11 W
Tuxer Hauptkamm ∧	64	47.10 N	11.45 E
Tuxer Vorberge ⋏	64	47.10 N	11.45 E
Tuxford, Sk., Can.	184	50.35 N	105.35 W
Tuxford, Eng., U.K.	44	53.13 N	0.53 W
Tuxiaqiao	100	28.47 N	121.29 E
Tuxpan, Méx.	234	19.33 N	103.24 W
Tuxpan, Méx.	234	21.37 N	104.07 W
Tuxpan, Méx.	234	19.34 N	100.28 W
Tuxpan, Méx.	234	21.57 N	105.18 W
Tuxpan, Méx.	234	20.57 N	97.24 W
Tuxpan ≏	234	20.59 N	97.18 W
Tuxsun	86	42.47 N	88.38 E
Tuxtepec	234	18.06 N	96.07 W
Tuxtla Chico	232	14.57 N	92.10 W
Tuxtla Gutiérrez	234	16.45 N	93.07 W
Tuy	34	42.03 N	8.38 W
Tuy ≏	246	10.24 N	65.59 W
Tuy An	110	13.17 N	109.16 E
Tuyen Hoa	110	17.50 N	106.10 E
Tuyen Quang	110	21.49 N	105.13 E

PORTUGUÊS

Nome	Página	Lat.°′	Long.°′ W = Oeste
Tuy Hoa	110	13.05 N	109.18 E
Tūysarkān	128	34.33 N	48.27 E
Tuyün → Duyun	102	26.12 N	107.31 E
Ṭuyūr, Burj aṭ- ∧[2]	140	20.55 N	27.55 E
Tuža	80	57.37 N	47.57 E
Tuzamapan	234	19.24 N	96.51 W
T'uzašu, pereval)(	85	42.21 N	73.48 E
T'uzbel'	85	40.34 N	73.21 E
Tuzdykol', ozero ⊜	80	49.36 N	52.20 E
Tuz Gölü ⊜	130	38.45 N	33.25 E
Tuzigoot National Monument ♠	200	34.49 N	112.01 W
Ṭūz Khurmātū	128	34.53 N	44.38 E
Tuzla, Jugo.	38	44.32 N	18.41 E
Tuzla, Tür.	130	36.42 N	35.05 E
Tuzla ≏	130	39.43 N	40.16 E
Tuzla Gölü ⊜	130	39.02 N	35.50 E
Tuzlagözü	130	38.11 N	41.34 E
Tuzlov ≏	83	47.23 N	40.08 E
Tuzluca	84	40.03 N	43.40 E
Tuzlukçu	130	38.28 N	31.38 E
Tuzly	78	45.52 N	30.05 E
Tvârdica, Blg.	38	43.42 N	25.52 E
Tvardica, S.S.S.R.	78	46.09 N	28.58 E
Tvedestrand	26	58.37 N	8.55 E
Tveitsund	26	59.01 N	8.32 E
Tver → Kalinin	82	56.52 N	35.55 E
Tverca ≏	76	56.52 N	35.55 E
Twain Harte	226	38.02 N	120.14 W
Twann	58	47.06 N	7.10 E
Twardogóra	30	51.22 N	17.28 E
Tweed	212	44.29 N	77.19 W
Tweed ≏	44	55.46 N	2.00 W
Tweeddale V	46	55.40 N	3.10 W
Tweede Exloërmond	52	52.55 N	6.58 E
Tweed Heads	171a	28.10 S	153.31 E
Tweedmouth	44	55.45 N	2.01 W
Tweedsmuir Provincial Park ♠	182	52.55 N	126.05 W
Tweedy Mountain ∧	202	45.29 N	112.58 W
Tweeling	158	27.38 S	28.31 E
Twee Rivieren	158	26.27 S	20.37 E
Tweespruit	158	29.11 S	27.01 E
Twello	52	52.14 N	6.06 E
Twelve Mile	216	40.52 N	86.13 W
Twelve Mile Creek ≏, On., Can.	212	43.11 N	79.16 W
Twelvemile Creek ≏, N.Y., U.S.	210	43.18 N	78.51 W
Twelvemile Island I	279b	40.32 N	79.51 W
Twelve Mile Lake ⊜, On., Can.	212	45.02 N	78.43 W
Twelve Mile Lake ⊜, Sk., Can.	184	49.29 N	106.14 W
Tweng	64	47.11 N	13.36 E
Twente ◆[1]	52	52.17 N	6.40 E
Twentekanaal ≍	52	52.15 N	6.40 E
Twentieth Century Fox Studios ✦[3]	280	34.03 N	118.25 W
Twentyfive Mile Wash V	200	37.33 N	111.07 W
Twenty Mile Creek ≏	212	43.10 N	79.22 W
Twentynine Palms	204	34.08 N	116.03 W
Twentynine Palms Marine Corps Center ■	204	34.25 N	116.10 W
Tweya	152	0.54 S	19.05 E
Twickenham ◆[8]	260	51.27 N	0.20 W
Twilight Cove ⊂	162	32.16 S	126.03 E
Twilight Park	210	42.11 N	74.05 W
Twillingate	186	49.39 N	54.46 W
Twin Beach	216	42.34 N	83.24 W
Twinberg	61	46.55 N	14.50 E
Twin Bridge Farm	285	39.57 N	75.33 W
Twin Bridges	202	45.32 N	112.19 W
Twin Butte Creek ≏	198	38.46 N	100.56 W
Twin Buttes ∧	202	44.20 N	122.15 W
Twin Buttes Reservoir ⊜[1]	196	31.20 N	100.35 W
Twin City	192	32.34 N	82.09 W
Twin Creek ≏	218	39.33 N	84.21 W
Twin Falls	202	42.33 N	114.27 W
Twin Heads ⋏	162	20.13 S	126.30 E
Twin Hills	180	59.23 N	159.58 W
Twin Lakes, Ca., U.S.	226	36.58 N	122.00 W
Twin Lakes, Ga., U.S.	192	30.42 N	83.12 W
Twin Lakes, In., U.S.	216	41.19 N	86.23 W
Twin Lakes, Mi., U.S.	216	42.02 N	86.04 W
Twin Lakes, Oh., U.S.	214	41.11 N	81.21 W
Twin Lakes, Pa., U.S.	210	41.24 N	74.54 W
Twin Lakes, Wi., U.S.	216	42.31 N	88.14 W
Twin Lakes ⊜, Ca., U.S.	226	38.09 N	119.21 W
Twin Lakes ⊜, Ct., U.S.	207	42.02 N	73.26 W
Twin Lakes ⊜, Wa., U.S.	224	47.55 N	120.51 W
Twin Oaks, Il., U.S.	278	42.03 N	87.50 W
Twin Oaks, Pa., U.S.	208	39.51 N	75.26 W
Twin Peak Islands II	162	34.00 S	122.50 E
Twin Peaks	228	34.12 N	117.12 W
Twin Peaks ⋏, Ca., U.S.	282	37.45 N	122.27 W
Twin Peaks ⋏, Id., U.S.	202	44.35 N	114.29 W
Twin Rocks, Or., U.S.	224	45.36 N	123.57 W
Twin Rocks, Pa., U.S.	214	40.29 N	78.51 W
Twinsburg	214	41.18 N	81.26 W
Twin Valley	198	47.15 N	96.15 W
Twisp	202	48.21 N	120.07 W
Twiss Green	262	53.27 N	2.32 W
Twist	52	52.38 N	7.03 E
Twiste ≏	52	51.29 N	9.09 E
Twistringen	52	52.48 N	8.38 E
Twitchell Reservoir ⊜[1]	204	35.00 N	120.19 W
Twitya ≏	180	64.10 N	128.12 W
Two, Channel ⋓	220	24.50 N	80.45 W
Two Butte Creek ≏	198	38.02 N	102.08 W
Twofold Bay ⊂	166	37.06 S	149.55 E
Two Harbors	190	47.01 N	91.40 W
Two Hills	182	53.43 N	111.45 W
Two Lakes ⊜	224	46.22 N	121.27 W
Two Medicine ≏	202	48.29 N	112.14 W
Two Mile Creek ≏, On., Can.	284a	43.16 N	79.06 W
Twomile Creek ≏, N.Y., U.S.	284a	43.01 N	78.55 W
Twong	140	8.18 N	28.20 E
Two Penny Run ≏	285	39.41 N	75.26 W
Two River Lake ⊜	184	53.52 N	91.27 W
Two Rivers	190	44.09 N	87.34 W
Two Rivers Reservoir ⊜[1]	196	33.17 N	104.45 W
Two Thumb Range ⋏	172	43.45 S	170.43 E
Two Wells	168b	34.36 S	138.30 E
Twrch ≏, Wales, U.K.	42	51.46 N	3.46 W
Twrch ≏, Wales, U.K.	42	52.42 N	3.29 W
Twyford, Eng., U.K.	42	51.29 N	0.53 W
Twyford, Eng., U.K.	42	51.01 N	1.19 W
Twymyn ≏	42	52.38 N	3.44 W
Tyabb	169	38.16 S	145.11 E
Tybee Island	192	32.01 N	80.51 W
Tybju	24	60.37 N	50.20 E
Tychy	30	50.09 N	18.59 E
Tyczyn	30	49.58 N	22.02 E
Tydal	26	63.04 N	11.34 E
Tye	196	32.27 N	99.52 W
Tyende Creek ≏	200	36.50 N	109.43 W
Tyendinaga Indian Reserve ◆[4]	212	44.11 N	77.07 W
Tyers ≏	169	38.10 S	145.26 E
Tyfors	40	60.09 N	14.12 E
Tygarts Creek ≏	218	38.43 N	82.57 W
Tygda	89	53.07 N	126.20 E
Tygda ≏	89	52.35 N	127.55 E
Tygelsjö	41	55.31 N	13.00 E
Tygh Valley	224	45.14 N	121.10 W
Tyin ⊜	26	61.17 N	8.13 E
Tyja ≏	88	55.36 N	109.20 E
Tylden	158	32.07 S	27.05 E
Tyldesley	44	53.31 N	2.28 W
Tyler, Mn., U.S.	198	44.16 N	96.08 W
Tyler, Pa., U.S.	214	41.14 N	78.32 W
Tyler, Tx., U.S.	222	32.21 N	95.18 W
Tyler □[6]	222	30.47 N	94.32 W
Tyler, Lake ⊜[1]	222	32.13 N	95.10 W
Tyler East, Lake ⊜[1]	222	32.15 N	95.10 W
Tyler Park	284c	38.52 N	77.12 W
Tylersburg	214	41.23 N	79.19 W
Tyler State Park ♠, Pa., U.S.	208	40.14 N	74.59 W
Tyler State Park ♠, Tx., U.S.	222	32.29 N	95.14 W
Tylersville	210	41.00 N	77.25 W
Tylerton	208	37.58 N	76.01 W
Tylertown	194	31.06 N	90.08 W
Tylla	40	60.28 N	15.33 E
Tylösand	26	56.39 N	12.44 E
Tylöskog ⋏[2]	40	58.45 N	15.20 E
Tylovaj	80	57.30 N	53.47 E
Tym ≏, S.S.S.R.	74	59.25 N	80.04 E
Tym' ≏, S.S.S.R.	89	51.51 N	143.10 E
Tymna, laguna ⊂	180	64.00 N	178.30 E
Tymochtee Creek ≏	214	40.57 N	83.16 W
Tymovskoje	89	50.51 N	142.39 E
Tymsk	86	59.24 N	80.18 E
Tynagh	48	53.09 N	8.22 W
Tyndall	198	42.59 N	97.51 W
Tyndall Air Force Base ■	194	30.04 N	85.35 W
Tyndaris ⊥	70	38.09 N	15.03 E
Tyndinskij	74	55.10 N	124.43 E
Tyndrum	46	56.27 N	4.44 W
Tyne ≏, Eng., U.K.	44	55.01 N	1.26 W
Tyne ≏, Scot., U.K.	46	56.01 N	2.37 W
Tyne and Wear □[6]	44	54.55 N	1.35 W
Tynemouth	44	55.01 N	1.24 W
Tyner	216	41.24 N	86.24 W
Tyngsboro	283	42.40 N	71.25 W
Tyngsjö	40	60.18 N	13.53 E
Tynica	78	51.08 N	32.54 E
Týn nad Vltavou	30	49.14 N	14.26 E
Tynnelsö	40	59.25 N	17.06 E
Tynset	26	62.17 N	10.47 E
Tyonek	180	61.02 N	151.17 W
Typta	88	54.35 N	104.31 E
Tyr	89	52.57 N	139.48 E
Tyre → Ṣūr	132	33.16 N	35.11 E
Tyre	214	40.26 N	80.16 W
Tyresö	40	59.14 N	18.18 E
Tyret'	88	53.41 N	102.19 E
Tyrgetuj	88	51.27 N	113.46 E
Tyrifjorden ⊜	26	60.02 N	10.08 E
Tyringe	41	56.10 N	13.35 E
Tyringham	207	42.14 N	73.12 W
Tyrka	88	54.30 N	107.09 E
Tyrma	89	50.03 N	132.12 E
Tyrma ≏	89	50.29 N	131.18 E
Tyrnovo	78	48.10 N	27.40 E
Tyrnyauz	84	43.23 N	42.56 E
Tyrone, Ky., U.S.	218	38.01 N	84.50 W
Tyrone, N.Y., U.S.	210	42.25 N	77.03 W
Tyrone, Ok., U.S.	196	36.57 N	101.03 W
Tyrone, Pa., U.S.	214	40.40 N	78.14 W
Tyrone Lake ⊜	281	42.42 N	83.43 W
Tyrrell, Lake ⊜	166	35.21 S	142.50 E
Tyrrellspass	48	53.23 N	7.22 W
Tyrrhenian Sea (Mare Tirreno) ⊤[2]	36	40.00 N	12.00 E
Tyrrhenisches Meer → Tyrrhenian Sea ⊤[2]	36	40.00 N	12.00 E
Tysmenica	78	48.54 N	24.49 E
Tysnesøy I	26	60.00 N	5.35 E
Tysons Corner	284c	38.55 N	77.14 W
Tysons Corner Center ◆[9]	284c	38.55 N	77.13 W
Tysons Green	284c	38.55 N	77.15 W
Tysse	26	60.22 N	5.45 E
Tyssedal	26	60.07 N	6.34 E
Tysslingen ⊜	40	59.19 N	15.02 E
Tystberga	40	58.52 N	17.15 E
Tystrup Sø ⊜	41	55.22 N	11.35 E
Tytherington	262	53.17 N	2.08 W
Tytuvėnai	76	55.36 N	23.12 E
Ty Ty	192	31.28 N	83.38 W
Tyumen → T'umen'	86	57.09 N	65.32 E
Tyvrov	78	49.01 N	28.30 E
Tywa ≏	54	53.13 N	14.29 E
Tywardreath	42	50.22 N	4.41 W
Tywi ≏	42	51.46 N	4.22 W
Tywyn	42	52.35 N	4.05 W
Tzanconeja ≏	232	16.35 N	91.35 W
Tzaneen	156	23.50 S	30.09 E
Tzekung → Zigong	107	29.24 N	104.47 E
Tzeliutsing → Zigong	107	29.24 N	104.47 E
Tzimol	236	16.16 N	92.16 W
Tzintzuntzan ⊥	234	19.38 N	101.34 W
Tzucacab	232	20.04 N	89.03 W
Tzukung → Zigong	107	29.24 N	104.47 E
Tzupo → Boshan, Zhg.	98	36.29 N	117.50 E
Tzupo → Zibo, Zhg.	98	36.47 N	118.01 E

U

Uaboe	174b	0.31 S	166.55 E
Uac, Mount ∧	116	12.12 N	123.40 E
Uaçá ≏	250	4.13 N	51.32 W
Uagadugu → Ouagadougou	150	12.22 N	1.31 W
Uamba	152	7.12 S	16.25 E
Uamba (Wamba) ≏, Afr.	152	3.56 S	17.12 E
Uamba ≏, Ang.	152	7.58 S	17.09 E
Uampochane	158	26.23 S	32.41 E
Uaoa Bay ⊂	229a	20.56 N	156.16 W
Uaran → Ouarâne ◆[1]	134	21.00 N	10.30 W
Uato-Lari	112	8.45 S	126.34 E
Uatumã ≏	246	2.26 S	57.37 W
Uauá	250	9.50 S	39.28 W
Uaupés (Vaupés) ≏	246	0.02 N	67.16 W
Uaxactún ⊥	232	17.24 N	89.39 W
Ubá	255	21.07 S	42.56 W
Uba ≏	86	50.15 N	81.41 E
Übach-Palenberg	56	50.55 N	6.07 E
Ubagan ≏	86	54.24 N	64.45 E
Ubai	164	5.40 S	150.40 E
Ubaidullaganj	124	22.59 N	77.36 E
Ubaíra	255	13.16 S	39.39 W
Ubaitaba	255	14.18 S	39.20 W
Ubajara	250	3.51 S	40.56 W
Ubajara, Parque Nacional de ♠	250	3.47 S	40.56 W
Ubangi (Oubangui) ≏	152	0.30 S	17.42 E
Ubatã	255	14.12 S	39.31 W
Ubaté	246	5.19 N	73.49 W
Ubatuba	256	23.26 S	45.04 W
Ubatuba, Baía de ⊂	256	23.27 S	45.02 W
Ubauro	120	28.10 N	69.44 E
Ubay	116	10.03 N	124.28 E
Ubaye	62	44.28 N	6.22 E
Ubaye ≏	62	44.28 N	6.18 E
Ubayyiḍ, Wādī al- V	128	32.34 N	43.48 E
Ubby	41	55.37 N	11.13 E
Ube	96	33.56 N	131.15 E
Ubed' ≏	78	51.27 N	32.29 E
Úbeda	34	38.01 N	3.22 W
Uberaba	255	19.45 S	47.55 W
Uberaba ≏	255	20.07 S	48.31 W
Uberaba, Lagoa ⊜	248	17.30 S	57.45 W
Überackern	60	48.11 N	12.52 E
Über dem Wind, Inseln → Leeward Islands II	238	17.00 N	63.00 W
Uberlândia	255	18.56 S	48.18 W
Überlingen	58	47.46 N	9.10 E
Überlinger See ⊂	58	47.45 N	9.09 E
Übersee	64	47.49 N	12.28 E
Ubiaja	150	6.38 N	6.21 E
Ubili	154	1.07 S	26.55 E
Ubin, Pulau I	271c	1.24 N	103.58 E
Ubinskoje	86	55.19 N	79.41 E
Ubinskoje, ozero ⊜	86	55.30 N	80.05 E
Ubl'a	30	48.55 N	22.23 E
Ubly	190	43.42 N	82.55 W
Uboldo	266b	45.37 N	9.00 E
Ubombo	158	27.33 S	32.00 E
Ubondo	154	0.52 S	25.37 E
Ubon Ratchathani	110	15.14 N	104.54 E
Úborsko	60	49.20 N	13.09 E
Ubort' ≏	78	52.06 N	28.28 E
Ubrique	34	36.41 N	5.27 W
Ubudiah, Masjid ✦[1]	114	4.46 N	100.56 E
Ubundu (Ponthierville)	154	0.21 S	25.29 E
Ubur-Tochtor	88	50.06 N	113.37 E
Uča ≏, S.S.S.R.	82	56.02 N	37.37 E
Uča ≏, S.S.S.R.	265b	55.56 N	37.57 E
Ucacha	252	33.02 S	63.31 W
Uč-Adži	128	38.05 N	62.48 E
Učaly	86	54.19 N	59.27 E
Učami	74	63.50 N	96.29 E
Učaral	86	46.10 N	80.56 E
Ucayali □[4]	248	9.00 S	74.00 W
Ucayali ≏	242	4.30 S	73.27 W
Uccellina, Monti dell' ⋏	66	42.38 N	11.05 E
Uccle	50	50.48 N	4.19 E
Uch	123	29.14 N	71.03 E
Uchab	156	19.47 S	17.42 E
Uchāna	124	29.28 N	76.10 E
Uchaud	62	43.45 N	4.16 E
Uchee Creek ≏	192	32.18 N	84.57 W
Uchihara	94	36.22 N	140.21 E
Uchihata	270	34.25 N	135.27 E
Uchiko	96	33.33 N	132.39 E
Uchi Lake	184	51.05 N	92.35 W
Uchinada	94	36.39 N	136.39 E
Uchinomi	96	34.30 N	134.20 E
Uchinoura	92	31.16 N	131.05 E
Uchiumi	96	33.01 N	132.30 E
Uchiura-wan ⊂	92a	42.20 N	140.40 E
Uchiza	248	8.29 S	76.23 W
Uchoa	255	20.56 S	49.13 W
Ucholovo	80	53.47 N	40.29 E
Uchra ≏	80	58.20 N	39.00 E
Uchta, S.S.S.R.	24	61.12 N	38.32 E
Uchta, S.S.S.R.	24	63.33 N	53.38 E
Uchte	52	52.30 N	8.54 E
Uchte ≏	54	52.46 N	11.45 E
Uchtoma	76	60.10 N	38.02 E
Uchtspringe	54	52.32 N	11.36 E
Učinskij Rybovčastok	86	60.02 N	65.10 E
Učinskoje vodochranilišče ⊜[1]	82	56.02 N	37.45 E
Uckange	56	49.18 N	6.09 E
Ückendorf ◆[8]	263	51.30 N	7.07 E
Uckermark ◆[1]	54	53.10 N	13.35 E
Uckfield	42	50.58 N	0.06 E
Üçköşe	130	40.13 N	41.00 E
Uckro	54	51.51 N	13.37 E
Učkupr'uk	85	40.33 N	71.04 E
Učkurgan	85	41.07 N	72.05 E
Ucluelet	182	48.57 N	125.33 W
Ucon	202	43.35 N	111.57 W
Üçpınar	130	37.08 N	32.16 E
Ucria	70	38.03 N	14.53 E
Üçtepeler ∧	130	39.39 N	42.41 E
Účterek	85	41.45 N	73.12 E
Úcua ≏	152	8.35 S	13.40 E
Učujevskij Majdan	80	54.33 N	44.30 E
Učur ≏	74	58.48 N	130.35 E
Uda ≏, S.S.S.R.	88	56.05 N	99.34 E
Uda ≏, S.S.S.R.	88	51.47 N	107.33 E
Uda ≏, S.S.S.R.	89	54.42 N	135.14 E
Udagamandalam	122	11.24 N	76.42 E
Udaipur	120	24.35 N	73.41 E
Udaj ≏	78	50.05 N	33.07 E
Udala	126	21.35 N	86.34 E
Udalguri	120	26.46 N	92.08 E
Udall	198	37.23 N	97.06 W
Udamalpet	122	10.35 N	77.15 E
Udankudi	122	8.26 N	78.01 E
Udaquiola	252	36.34 S	58.31 W
Udarnyj	89	49.07 N	142.09 E
Udaypur	124	26.56 N	86.31 E
Udbina	36	44.32 N	15.46 E
Udby	41	55.05 N	11.57 E
Uddeholm	40	60.01 N	13.37 E
Uddel	52	52.15 N	5.46 E
Uddevalla	26	58.21 N	11.55 E
Uddingston	46	55.50 N	4.06 W
Uddjaure ⊜	24	65.55 N	17.49 E
Udel'naja	82	55.38 N	38.03 E
Udel'naja ◆[8]	265a	60.01 N	30.19 E
Uden	52	51.40 N	5.36 E
Udenhout	52	51.37 N	5.08 E
Uder	56	51.22 N	10.05 E
Üdersdorf	56	50.09 N	6.49 E
Udgīr	122	18.23 N	77.07 E
Udhampur	123	32.56 N	75.08 E
Udhruḥ	132	30.20 N	35.36 E
Udi	150	6.19 N	7.25 E
Udimskij	24	61.09 N	45.52 E
Udine	64	46.03 N	13.14 E
Udine □[4]	64	46.10 N	13.00 E
Udmurtskaja Avtonomnaja Sovetskaja Socialističeskaja Respublika □[3]	80	57.00 N	53.00 E
Udokan, chrebet ⋏	88	56.20 N	118.10 E
Udoml'a	76	57.52 N	35.01 E
Udone-jima I	94	34.28 N	139.18 E
Udono	92	33.44 N	136.01 E
Udon Thani	110	17.26 N	102.46 E
Udor, Mount ∧	162	23.30 S	131.01 E
Udot I	175c	7.23 N	151.43 E
Udskaja guba ⊂	89	54.50 N	135.45 E
Udskoje	89	54.32 N	134.26 E
Udubo	146	11.57 N	10.38 E
Udupi	122	13.21 N	74.45 E
Udy	78	50.24 N	36.03 E
Udyl', ozero ⊜	89	52.06 N	139.48 E
Udža	74	71.14 N	117.10 E
Udžary	84	40.31 N	47.39 E
Uebigau	54	51.35 N	13.18 E
Uebonti	112	0.55 S	121.38 E
Uebonti, Teluk ⊂	112	0.50 S	121.45 E
Uecker ≏	54	53.45 N	14.04 E
Ueckeritz	54	54.00 N	14.02 E
Ueckermünde	54	53.44 N	14.03 E
Ueckermünder Heide ◆[3]	54	53.40 N	14.10 E
Ueda	94	36.24 N	138.16 E
Uedem	52	51.40 N	6.16 E
Uedesheim	263	51.10 N	6.48 E
Uegō	268	35.13 N	139.56 E
Ueharu	175d	24.25 N	123.46 E
Uehlfeld	56	49.40 N	10.43 E
Uele ≏	136	4.09 N	22.26 E
Uelen	180	66.10 N	169.48 W
Uel'kal'	180	65.32 N	179.17 W
Uelsen	52	52.30 N	6.53 E
Uelzen, B.R.D.	52	52.58 N	10.33 E
Uelzen, B.R.D.	263	51.33 N	7.44 E
Ueno, Nihon	94	36.05 N	138.47 E
Ueno, Nihon	94	34.45 N	136.08 E
Ueno, Nihon	270	34.53 N	135.14 E
Uenohara	94	35.37 N	139.07 E
Ueno Park ♠	268	35.43 N	139.46 E
Uenoshiba	270	34.33 N	135.28 E
Uerdingen ◆[8]	263	51.21 N	6.39 E
Uere ≏	154	3.42 N	25.24 E
Uetersen	52	53.41 N	9.39 E
Uettingen	56	49.48 N	9.43 E
Uetz	264a	52.28 N	12.56 E
Uetze	52	52.28 N	10.11 E
Ufa	86	54.44 N	55.56 E
Ufa ≏	86	54.40 N	56.00 E
Ufala, Punta ≻	70	38.22 N	14.59 E
Uffculme	42	50.54 N	3.20 W
Uffenheim	56	49.32 N	10.14 E
Ufita ≏	68	41.09 N	14.56 E
Ufra	128	40.00 N	53.02 E
Uft'uga ≏	76	59.46 N	39.21 E
Ugab ≏	156	21.08 S	13.40 E
Ugak Bay ⊂	180	57.25 N	152.45 W
Ugāle	76	57.16 N	22.02 E
Ugalla ≏	154	5.08 S	30.42 E
Ugamskij chrebet ⋏	85	42.00 N	70.20 E
Uganda □[1]	154	1.00 N	32.00 E
Uganik Island I	180	57.53 N	153.28 W
Ugârčin	38	43.06 N	24.25 E
Ugarit ⊥	130	35.35 N	35.45 E
Ugashik	180	57.32 N	157.25 W
Ugashik Bay ⊂	180	57.34 N	157.38 W
Ugatkyn ≏	180	68.24 N	171.30 E
Ugento	68	39.56 N	18.10 E
Ugep	150	5.48 N	8.05 E
Ugerløse	41	55.35 N	11.40 E
Uggiano la Chiesa	68	40.06 N	18.27 E
Ughaybish	140	10.52 N	31.05 E
Ughelli	150	5.29 N	5.59 E
Ugie	158	31.10 S	28.13 E
Ugie ≏	46	57.30 N	1.47 W
Ugíjar	34	36.57 N	3.03 W
Ugine	62	45.45 N	6.25 E
Uglegorsk, S.S.S.R.	83	48.19 N	38.17 E
Uglegorsk, S.S.S.R.	89	49.02 N	142.03 E
Uglekamensk	89	43.13 N	133.11 E
Uglezavodsk	89	47.21 N	142.38 E
Uglič	76	57.32 N	38.19 E
Ugljan, Otok I	36	44.05 N	15.10 E
Uglovaja	80	57.01 N	52.57 E
Uglovka	76	58.14 N	33.31 E
Uglovoje	89	43.20 N	132.06 E
Uglovskoje	86	51.23 N	80.12 E
Ugly-Zavod	78	52.11 N	32.53 E
Ugnev	78	50.23 N	23.44 E
Ugodiči	80	57.10 N	39.30 E
Ugodskij Zavod	82	55.02 N	36.45 E
Ugol'naja, buchta ⊂	180	63.00 N	179.20 E
Ugolnyy	180	62.58 N	179.17 E
Ugoma ∧	154	4.00 S	28.45 E
Ugovizza	64	46.31 N	13.29 E
Ugra	76	54.47 N	34.17 E
Ugra ≏	82	54.30 N	36.07 E
Ugrojedy	78	50.52 N	35.17 E
Ugr'umovo	82	55.09 N	37.40 E
Ugtaal Cajdam	88	48.17 N	105.25 E
Uguj	86	56.02 N	76.03 E
Uğurludağ	130	40.27 N	34.28 E
Ug'ut	85	41.24 N	74.50 E
Ugyak, Cape ≻	180	58.17 N	154.04 W
Uh (Už) ≏	30	48.34 N	22.00 E
Uha-dong	98	40.41 N	125.38 E
Uḥayjibah, Jabal al- ∧	132	30.11 N	34.33 E
Uherčice	61	48.55 N	15.38 E
Uherské Hradiště	30	49.05 N	17.28 E
Uherský Brod	30	49.02 N	17.39 E
Uhingen	56	48.42 N	9.35 E
Úhlava ≏	60	49.43 N	13.23 E
Uhlenhorst	156	23.45 S	17.55 E
Ühlingen	58	47.43 N	8.19 E
Uhlman Lake ⊜	184	56.40 N	98.23 W
Uhlstädt	54	50.44 N	11.28 E
Uhrichsville	214	40.23 N	81.20 W
Uhyst, D.D.R.	54	51.11 N	14.13 E
Uhyst, D.D.R.	54	51.24 N	14.30 E
Uiche	152	12.03 S	21.02 E
Ui-do I	98	34.37 N	125.51 E
Uig	46	57.35 N	6.22 W
Uíge	152	7.37 S	15.03 E
Uíge □[5]	152	7.00 S	15.30 E
Ŭijŏngbu	98	37.44 N	127.03 E
Ŭiju	98	40.12 N	124.32 E
Uil	86	49.05 N	54.40 E
Uil ≏	80	48.36 N	52.30 E
Uilpata, gora ∧	84	42.48 N	43.48 E
Uimaharju	26	62.55 N	30.15 E
Uiñaimarca, Lago ⊜	248	16.20 S	68.50 W
Uinebona ≏	246	5.04 N	63.01 W
Uinskoje	86	56.53 N	56.35 E
Uinta ≏	200	40.14 N	109.51 W
Uintah and Ouray Indian Reservation ◆[4]	200	40.20 N	110.20 W
Uinta Mountains ⋏	200	40.45 N	110.05 W
Uiraúna	250	6.31 S	38.25 W
Uis	156	21.08 S	14.49 E
Ŭisŏng	98	36.22 N	128.41 E
Uitenhage	158	33.40 S	25.28 E
Uitgeest	52	52.32 N	4.43 E
Uithoorn	52	52.14 N	4.50 E
Uithuizen	52	53.24 N	6.40 E
Uithuizermeeden	52	53.24 N	6.42 E
Uitspanning	158	26.46 S	29.56 E
Uj ≏, S.S.S.R.	86	57.06 N	74.12 E
Uj ≏, S.S.S.R.	86	54.17 N	64.58 E
Ujae I[1]	14	9.05 N	165.40 E
Ujaly	86	44.37 N	60.57 E
Ujandina ≏	74	68.23 N	145.50 E
Ujar	86	55.48 N	94.20 E
Ujarrás ⊥	236	9.51 N	83.50 W
Ujedinenija, ostrov I	72	77.28 N	82.28 E
Ujelang I[1]	14	9.49 N	160.55 E
Ujemskij	24	64.29 N	40.50 E
Újezd, Česko.	54	50.03 N	14.44 E
Újezd, Česko.	60	49.26 N	13.27 E
Újezd u Brna	61	49.06 N	16.45 E
Újfehértó	30	47.48 N	21.40 E
Ujgursaj	85	40.53 N	71.03 E
Ujhāni	124	28.01 N	79.01 E
Uji	96	34.53 N	135.48 E
Uji ≏	96	34.53 N	135.42 E
Uji-guntō II	92	31.11 N	129.27 E
Ujiie	94	36.41 N	139.58 E
Ujiji	154	4.55 S	29.41 E
Uji-tawara	96	34.51 N	135.52 E
Uji-yamada → Ise	94	34.29 N	136.42 E
Ujjain	120	23.11 N	75.46 E
Újkér	61	47.28 N	16.49 E
'Ujmān	128	25.25 N	55.27 E
Újpest ◆[8]	264c	47.34 N	19.06 E
Ujście	30	53.04 N	16.43 E
Ujskoje	86	54.22 N	60.00 E
Ujum	85	38.22 N	70.51 E
Ujung	112	7.04 S	120.46 E
Ujungbatu	114	0.43 N	100.31 E
Ujungbatu, Pulau I	114	2.20 N	97.24 E
Ujungberung	115a	6.55 S	107.42 E
Ujunggading	110	0.16 N	99.33 E
Ujunggenteng	115a	7.22 S	106.24 E
Ujungkulon, Semenanjung ≻[1]	115a	6.45 S	105.20 E
Ujungkulon National Park ♠	115a	6.40 S	105.20 E
Ujunglamuru	112	4.40 S	119.58 E

Symbol	English	Deutsch	Español	Français	Português
≏	River	Fluß	Río	Rivière	Rio
≍	Canal	Kanal	Canal	Canal	Canal
∟	Waterfall, Rapids	Wasserfall, Stromschnellen	Cascada, Rápidos	Chute d'eau, Rapides	Cascata, Rápidos
⋓	Strait	Meeresstraße	Estrecho	Détroit	Estreito
⊂	Bay, Gulf	Bucht, Golf	Bahía, Golfo	Baie, Golfe	Baía, Golfo
⊜	Lake, Lakes	See, Seen	Lago, Lagos	Lac, Lacs	Lago, Lagos
⍓	Swamp	Sumpf	Pantano	Marais	Pântano
⌓	Ice Features, Glacier	Eis- und Gletscherformen	Accidentes Glaciales	Formes glaciaires	Acidentes glaciares
⊤	Other Hydrographic Features	Andere Hydrographische Objekte	Otros Elementos Hidrográficos	Autres données hydrographiques	Outros acidentes hidrográficos

Symbol	English	Deutsch	Español	Français	Português
✧	Submarine Features	Untermeerische Objekte	Accidentes Submarinos	Formes de relief sous-marin	Acidentes submarinos
□	Political Unit	Politische Einheit	Unidad Politica	Entité politique	Unidade política
✦	Cultural Institution	Kulturelle Institution	Institución Cultural	Institution culturelle	Instituição cultural
⊥	Historical Site	Historische Stätte	Sitio Histórico	Site historique	Sitio histórico
♠	Recreational Site	Erholungs- und Ferienort	Sitio de Recreo	Centre de loisirs	Area de Lazer
⊠	Airport	Flughafen	Aeropuerto	Aéroport	Aeroporto
■	Military Installation	Militäranlage	Instalación Militar	Installation militaire	Instalação militar
◆	Miscellaneous	Verschiedenes	Misceláneo	Divers	Diversos

Name	Page	Lat.°′	Long.°′
Ujungpandang (Makasar)	112	5.07 S	119.24 E
Újvidék → Novi Sad	38	45.15 N	19.50 E
Uk	88	55.04 N	98.52 E
Uka, Nihon	174m	26.48 N	128.14 E
Uka, S.S.S.R.	74	57.50 N	162.06 E
Ukamas	158	28.02 S	19.45 E
Ukara Island I	154	1.50 S	33.03 E
Ukerewe Island I	154	2.03 S	33.00 E
Ukhayḍir, Wādī V	132	30.55 N	37.01 E
Ukhra	126	23.39 N	87.14 E
Ukhrul	120	25.07 N	94.22 E
Ukhta → Uchta	24	63.33 N	53.38 E
Ukiah, Ca., U.S.	204	39.09 N	123.12 W
Ukiah, Or., U.S.	202	45.08 N	118.55 W
Ukibaru-jima I	174m	26.18 N	128.00 E
Ukiha	96	33.19 N	130.47 E
Uki Ni Masi Island I	175e	10.15 S	161.45 E
Ukmergė	76	55.15 N	24.45 E
Ukolnoi Island I	180	55.14 N	161.34 W
Ukraine → Ukrainskaja Sovetskaja Socialističeskaja Respublika □[3]	78	49.00 N	32.00 E
Ukrainka	86	54.39 N	71.20 E
Ukrainsk	83	48.06 N	37.18 E
Ukrainskaja Sovetskaja Socialističeskaja Respublika □[3]	78	49.00 N	32.00 E
Ukrina ≃	36	45.05 N	17.56 E
Uks'anskoje	86	55.57 N	63.01 E
Uktuz	86	55.38 N	68.30 E
Uktym	24	62.38 N	48.52 E
Uku	152	11.24 S	14.15 E
Ukui	112	0.09 S	102.11 E
Ukurejskij	88	52.24 N	116.49 E
Ukuti	154	3.39 N	33.32 E
Ukyō ✦[8]	270	35.03 N	135.42 E
Ukyr	88	49.28 N	108.52 E
Ula, India	272b	22.43 N	88.33 E
Ula, Tür.	130	37.05 N	28.26 E
Ula ≃	86	54.40 N	56.00 E
Ulaanbaatar	88	47.55 N	106.53 E
Ulaanbaatar □[8]	88	47.55 N	106.53 E
Ulaanbadrach	102	44.07 N	110.11 E
Ulaan Chus	86	49.02 N	89.23 E
Ulaangom	86	49.58 N	92.02 E
Ulaan nuur ⊜	102	44.30 N	103.35 E
Ulaan Tajga ⋏	88	50.45 N	98.30 E
Ula-Chuduk	80	47.39 N	45.34 E
Ulak Island I	181a	51.22 N	179.00 W
Ulakmedan	114	2.43 N	99.38 E
Ulamba	152	9.07 S	23.40 E
Ulamona	164	5.00 S	151.15 E
Ulan, Austl.	166	32.17 S	149.44 E
Ulan, Zhg.	102	36.59 N	98.26 E
Ulan Bator → Ulaanbaatar	88	47.55 N	106.53 E
Ulanbel'	86	44.48 N	71.10 E
Ulan Buh Shamo ✦[2]	102	40.00 N	106.30 E
Ulan-Burgasy, chrebet ⋏	88	52.45 N	109.00 E
Ulan-Erge	80	46.19 N	44.53 E
Ulang ≃	236	14.27 N	83.14 W
Ulanhot → Horqin Youyi Qianqi	89	46.05 N	122.05 E
Ulānia	126	22.12 N	90.29 E
Ulanov	78	49.42 N	28.08 E
Ulanovo	78	51.46 N	34.18 E
Ulanovskij	82	54.04 N	37.51 E
Ulanów	30	50.30 N	22.16 E
Ulansuhai Nur ⊜	102	40.56 N	108.49 E
Ulan-Ude	88	51.50 N	107.37 E
Ulan Ul Hu ⊜	120	34.45 N	90.25 E
Ulan-Ušotej	88	50.45 N	105.29 E
Ular, Pulau I	271c	1.14 N	103.45 E
Ulaş	130	39.27 N	37.03 E
Ul'ašovo	24	65.27 N	56.57 E
Ulatis Creek ≃	226	38.18 N	121.00 W
Ul'atuj	88	51.09 N	116.14 E
Ulawa Island I	175e	9.46 S	161.57 E
Ulawun, Mount ʌ	164	5.03 S	151.20 E
Ulaya	154	7.04 S	36.54 E
Ułazów	30	50.17 N	23.00 E
Ul'ba	86	50.16 N	83.22 E
Ul'banskij zaliv c	89	53.45 N	137.50 E
Ulchin	98	36.59 N	129.23 E
Ul'chun-Partija	88	49.56 N	112.46 E
Ulcinj	38	41.55 N	19.11 E
Ulco	158	28.21 S	24.15 E
Ulcombe	260	51.12 N	0.39 E
Ulcumayo	248	11.01 S	75.55 W
Uldum	41	55.51 N	9.36 E
Uldz ≃	88	49.56 N	115.31 E
Uleåborg → Oulu	26	65.01 N	25.28 E
Ulefoss	26	59.17 N	9.16 E
Ulen	198	47.04 N	96.15 W
Ulety	88	51.22 N	112.29 E
Ulfborg	26	56.16 N	8.20 E
Ulft	52	51.54 N	6.23 E
Ulgajsyn	86	49.38 N	60.17 E
Ulgueira	266c	38.47 N	9.28 W
Ulhās ≃	272c	19.13 N	73.01 E
Ulhāsnagar	122	19.13 N	73.07 E
Uliast	86	48.57 N	91.17 E
Uliastaj (Džavchlant)	88	47.45 N	96.49 E
Úlice	60	49.45 N	13.09 E
Ulindi ≃	154	1.40 S	25.52 E
Ulingan	164	4.30 S	145.25 E
Ulithi I[1]	108	9.58 N	139.40 E
Ulja	74	58.51 N	141.50 E
Uljanino	82	55.21 N	38.26 E
Uljanovka, S.S.S.R.	76	59.38 N	30.46 E
Uljanovka, S.S.S.R.	78	48.20 N	30.13 E
Uljanovka, S.S.S.R.	78	50.58 N	34.18 E
Uljanovo, S.S.S.R.	76	53.43 N	35.32 E
Uljanovo, S.S.S.R.	85	40.07 N	68.30 E
Uljanovsk	80	54.20 N	48.24 E
Uljanovskoje, S.S.S.R.	86	50.02 N	73.42 E
Uljanovskoje, S.S.S.R.	89	46.17 N	142.13 E
Uljuan tekojärvi ⊜	26	64.19 N	25.57 E
Ul'kajak ≃	86	48.54 N	62.00 E
Ul'kan	88	57.14 N	107.19 E
Ul'kan ≃	88	55.53 N	107.45 E
Ul'ken-Karoj, ozero ⊜	86	54.00 N	71.58 E
Ulla	76	55.14 N	29.15 E
Ulla ≃, Esp.	34	42.39 N	8.44 W
Ulla ≃, S.S.S.R.	76	55.14 N	29.14 E
Ulladulla	170	35.21 S	150.29 E
Ulladulla Head ›	170	35.22 S	150.30 E
Ullāpāra	126	24.19 N	89.34 E
Ullapool	46	57.54 N	5.10 W
Ullastrell	266d	41.31 N	1.58 E
Üllendahl ✦[8]	263	51.19 N	7.18 E
Ullerslev	41	55.22 N	10.40 E
Ullervad	40	58.40 N	13.52 E
Ullin	194	37.17 N	89.11 W
Üllő	264c	47.23 N	19.21 E
Ullswater ⊜	44	54.34 N	2.54 W
Ullučaj ≃	84	42.18 N	48.08 E
Ullún	252	31.28 S	68.42 W
Ullŭng-do I	92	37.29 N	130.52 E
Ullvettern ⊜	40	59.27 N	14.16 E
Ullvi	40	59.42 N	16.37 E
Ulm, B.R.D.	58	48.24 N	10.00 E
Ulm, Mt., U.S.	202	47.25 N	111.30 W
Ulma	38	47.53 N	25.18 E
Ul'ma ≃	89	51.54 N	129.18 E
Ulmarra	166	29.37 S	153.02 E
Ulmen	56	50.13 N	6.59 E
Ulmeni	38	45.04 N	26.39 E
Ulmer, Mount ʌ	9	77.35 S	86.09 W
Ulmeu-Meisereich	56	50.13 N	6.58 E
Ulongué	154	14.37 S	34.19 E
Ulpur	126	23.04 N	89.50 E
Ulricehamn	26	57.47 N	13.25 E
Ulrichskirchen	61	48.24 N	16.29 E
Ulrichstein	56	50.34 N	9.11 E
Ulrum	52	53.22 N	6.20 E
Ulsan	98	35.34 N	129.19 E
Ulsta	46a	60.30 N	1.09 W
Ulsteinvik	26	62.20 N	5.53 E
Ulster	210	41.51 N	76.30 W
Ulster □[6]	210	41.56 N	74.00 W
Ulster □[9]	48	54.35 N	7.00 W
Ulster ≃	56	50.51 N	9.59 E
Ulster Canal ≍	48	54.08 N	7.22 W
Ultimo, Val d' V	64	46.35 N	11.00 E
Ultraoriental, Cordillera (Serra do Divisor) ⋏	248	8.20 S	73.30 W
Ulu, Indon.	112	2.45 N	125.24 E
Ulu, S.S.S.R.	74	60.19 N	127.24 E
Ulu, Sūd.	140	10.43 N	33.29 E
Ulúa ≃	236	15.53 N	87.44 W
Ulubāria	126	22.28 N	88.06 E
Ulubat Gölü ⊜	130	40.10 N	28.35 E
Ulubey, Tür.	130	38.25 N	29.18 E
Ulubey, Tür.	130	40.53 N	37.43 E
Uluborlu	130	38.05 N	30.28 E
Uluçınar	130	36.27 N	35.51 E
Uludağ ʌ	130	40.04 N	29.13 E
Uludāngar	272b	22.51 N	88.31 E
Uludere	128	37.27 N	42.51 E
Ulugan Bay c	116	10.07 N	118.47 E
Ulugqat	85	39.48 N	74.21 E
Uluinggalau ʌ	175g	16.54 S	179.59 E
Ulujul ≃	86	57.46 N	85.30 E
Ulukışla, Kıbrıs	130	35.13 N	33.37 E
Ulukışla, Tür.	130	37.33 N	34.30 E
Ulul I	14	8.35 N	149.40 E
Ulu Laho, Bukit ʌ	114	5.43 N	101.27 E
Ulunchan	88	54.51 N	111.02 E
Ulundi	158	28.17 S	31.26 E
Ulunga	89	46.31 N	136.56 E
Ulungur ≃	86	46.59 N	87.27 E
Ulungur Hu ⊜	86	47.15 N	87.20 E
Ulurijskij Golec, gora ʌ	88	50.12 N	111.45 E
Uluru National Park ♦	162	25.20 S	131.00 E
Ulus	130	41.35 N	32.39 E
Ulusara	126	24.16 N	90.36 E
Ulut ≃	116	12.00 N	125.27 E
Ulutau	86	48.39 N	67.01 E
Ulutau, gora ʌ	86	48.39 N	66.56 E
Ulutau, gory ⋏	86	49.00 N	67.00 E
Ulu Tiram	114	1.36 N	103.49 E
Ulu Yam	114	3.27 N	101.38 E
Ulva	272c	18.59 N	73.02 E
Ulva I	46	56.29 N	6.14 W
Ulvenhout	52	51.34 N	4.48 E
Ulverston	44	54.12 N	3.06 W
Ulverstone	166	41.09 S	146.10 E
Ulvöarna II	26	63.01 N	18.40 E
Ulvshale ›[1]	41	55.02 N	12.16 E
Ulvshyttan	40	60.18 N	15.22 E
Ulvsund ʯ	41	54.59 N	12.11 E
Ulyanovsk → Uljanovsk	80	54.20 N	48.24 E
Ulysses, Ks., U.S.	198	37.34 N	101.21 W
Ulysses, Ne., U.S.	198	41.04 N	97.12 W
Ulysses, Pa., U.S.	214	41.54 N	77.46 W
Uly-Žilanšik ≃	86	48.51 N	63.47 E
Ulzë	38	41.41 N	19.54 E
Uma	89	52.36 N	120.37 E
Umag	64	45.25 N	13.32 E
Umaji	96	33.33 N	134.03 E
Umal'tinskij	89	51.56 N	133.36 E
Umán, Méx.	232	20.53 N	89.45 W
Uman', S.S.S.R.	78	48.44 N	30.14 E
'Umān → Oman □[1]	118	22.00 N	58.00 E
Uman I	175c	7.18 N	151.53 E
Umanak	176	70.40 N	52.07 W
Umanak Fjord c[2]	176	70.55 N	53.00 W
Umancevo	80	47.44 N	44.16 E
Umargāon	122	20.12 N	72.45 E
Umari	250	6.38 S	38.42 W
'Umarī, Qā' al- ⊜	132	31.42 N	36.57 E
Umaria	124	23.32 N	80.50 E
Umarizal	250	5.59 S	37.49 W
Umarkot	120	25.22 N	69.44 E
Umatac	174p	13.18 N	144.39 E
Umatilla, Fl., U.S.	220	28.55 N	81.39 W
Umatilla, Or., U.S.	202	45.55 N	119.20 W
Umatilla ≃	202	45.55 N	119.20 W
Umatilla, Lake ⊜[1]	202	45.44 N	120.35 W
Umatilla Indian Reservation ✦[4]	202	45.41 N	118.31 W
Umayan ≃	116	8.13 N	125.50 E
Umaze	270	34.57 N	135.03 E
Umba	24	66.41 N	34.15 E
Umbagog Lake ⊜	188	44.45 N	71.05 W
Umbai	114	2.10 N	102.20 E
Umbaúba	250	11.22 S	37.39 W
Umbelasha ≃	140	9.51 N	24.50 E
Umbertide	66	43.18 N	12.20 E
Umbogintwini	158	30.00 S	30.58 E
Umboi Island I	164	5.36 S	148.00 E
Umbrail, Pass (Giogo di Santa Maria))(	64	46.34 N	10.25 E
Umbria □[4]	66	43.00 N	12.30 E
Umbriatico	68	39.21 N	16.55 E
Umbroli	272c	19.11 N	73.06 E
Umbukul	164	2.30 S	150.00 E
Umbuzeiro	250	7.41 S	35.40 W
Umbuzero, ozero ⊜	24	67.43 N	34.25 E
Ume ≃	154	16.40 S	28.26 E
Umeå	26	63.50 N	20.15 E
Umeälven ≃	24	63.47 N	20.16 E
Umedani	270	34.44 N	135.51 E
Umedpur	126	22.31 N	89.59 E
Umfolozi Game Reserve ✦[4]	158	28.19 S	31.50 E
Umfors	24	65.56 N	15.00 E
Umfreville Lake ⊜	184	50.18 N	94.45 W
Umfuli ≃	154	17.30 S	29.23 E
Umgungundhlovu ⊥	158	28.27 S	31.28 E
Umguza	154	19.25 S	27.51 E
Umhausen	64	47.08 N	10.56 E
Umhlanga Rocks	158	29.43 S	31.06 E
Umi	96	33.34 N	130.30 E
Umingan	116	15.56 N	120.50 E
Umkomaas	158	30.15 S	30.42 E
Umm ad-Daraj, Jabal ʌ	132	32.19 N	35.48 E
Umm 'Ajārim •[8]	142	30.50 N	32.49 E
Umm al-Abīd	146	27.31 N	15.02 E
Umm al-'Arā'is, Wādī V	146	26.26 N	13.55 E
Umm al-Arānib	146	26.08 N	14.45 E
Umm al-Birak	128	23.25 N	39.13 E
Umm al-Ḥawāyā, Jabal ʌ	142	28.41 N	31.06 E
Umm al-Jimāl, Khirbat ⊥	132	32.20 N	36.22 E
Umm al-Khashab	144	17.21 N	42.32 E
Umm al-Qaywayn	128	25.35 N	55.34 E
Umm al-Qiṭṭayn	132	32.19 N	36.38 E
Umm al-Quṣūr	142	27.23 N	30.54 E
Ummanz	54	54.28 N	13.10 E
Umm Artah, Wādī V	142	28.41 N	32.37 E
Umm as-Sa'd ⊥	132	33.16 N	36.47 E
Umm Badr	140	14.14 N	27.57 E
Umm Balad, Wādī V	142	27.40 N	32.39 E
Umm Bayyū'd	140	12.05 N	31.40 E
Umm Bel	140	13.32 N	28.04 E
Umm Boim	140	11.43 N	25.57 E
Umm Dabbī	140	14.37 N	30.23 E
Umm Dam	140	13.45 N	30.59 E
Umm Dhibbān, Sūd.	140	14.14 N	29.37 E
Umm Dhibbān, Sūd.	140	15.26 N	32.51 E
Umm Digulgulaya	140	10.29 N	24.57 E
Umm Dīnār	142	30.12 N	31.04 E
Umm Durmān (Omdurman)	140	15.38 N	32.30 E
Umm el Faḥm	132	32.31 N	35.09 E
Ummeln	52	51.58 N	8.27 E
Ummendorf	54	52.09 N	11.11 E
Umm Habwah, Jabal ʌ[2]	142	27.23 N	31.29 E
Umm Ḥamāṭ	132	31.02 N	35.46 E
Umm Jamālah	140	11.27 N	28.12 E
Umm Kaddādah	140	13.36 N	26.42 E
Umm Khunān	273c	29.55 N	31.15 E
Umm Khushayb, Wādī V	142	30.24 N	32.43 E
Umm Kuwaykah	140	13.00 N	32.17 E
Umm Lajj	128	25.04 N	37.13 E
Umm Marahik, Jabal ʌ[2]	140	13.40 N	26.53 E
Umm Mirdi	140	18.59 N	33.32 E
Umm Mitmān •[8]	142	30.41 N	32.30 E
Umm Qantur	140	14.17 N	31.22 E
Umm Qaṣr	128	30.02 N	47.56 E
Umm Qurayn	140	9.58 N	28.55 E
Umm Quṣayr	132	31.40 N	35.53 E
Umm Raqm, Jabal ʌ	142	30.14 N	31.52 E
Umm Rīshah, Birkat ⊜	142	30.21 N	30.22 E
Umm Rumaylah ⊽[4]	140	16.55 N	31.40 E
Umm Ruwābah	140	12.54 N	31.13 E
Umm Saggāt, Wādī V	140	15.15 N	23.12 E
Umm Saysabān, Jabal ʌ	132	29.45 N	35.10 E
Umm Sayyālah	140	14.25 N	31.10 E
Umm Shalīl	140	10.51 N	23.42 E
Umm Shanqah	140	13.14 N	27.14 E
Umm Shuṭūr	140	7.17 N	33.14 E
Umm Sidr, Wādī V	142	27.54 N	32.33 E
Umm Sughra ⊽[4]	140	15.03 N	27.12 E
Umm 'Umayd, Ra's ʌ	142	27.50 N	32.19 E
Umm 'Umayyid, Bi'r ⊽[4]	142	27.53 N	32.30 E
Umm 'Umayyid, Wādī V	142	27.37 N	32.41 E
Umm Urūmah I	128	25.46 N	36.32 E
Umm Walad	132	32.39 N	36.26 E
Umm Zaytah, Jabal ʌ[2]	142	29.49 N	32.16 E
Umnak	180	53.17 N	168.20 W
Umnak Island I	180	53.25 N	168.10 W
Umnak Pass ʯ	180	53.20 N	167.45 W
Umnäs	24	65.24 N	16.10 E
Umniati	154	18.39 S	29.49 E
Umniati ≃	154	17.30 S	29.23 E
Um'ot, S.S.S.R.	80	54.08 N	42.42 E
Um'ot, S.S.S.R.	80	52.31 N	42.58 E
Umpferstedt	54	50.59 N	11.25 E
Umpqua ≃	202	43.42 N	124.03 W
Umpulo	152	12.38 S	17.42 E
'Umrān	144	15.50 N	43.56 E
'Umrānī, Wādī al- V	142	27.37 N	30.53 E
Umraniye	130	39.10 N	31.15 E
Umraniye ✦[8]	267b	41.01 N	29.05 E
Umred	122	20.51 N	79.20 E
Umreth	120	22.42 N	73.07 E
Umsini, Gunung ʌ	164	1.22 S	133.45 E
Ŭmsŏng	98	36.56 N	127.41 E
Umstead State Park ♦	192	35.52 N	78.47 W
Umtanum Creek ≃	224	46.52 N	120.35 W
Umtata	158	31.35 S	28.47 E
Umtentweni	158	30.42 S	30.28 E
Umuahia	150	5.33 N	7.29 E
Umuarama	255	23.45 S	53.20 W
Umurbey	130	40.14 N	26.36 E
Umurlu	130	37.50 N	27.58 E
Umzimkulu	158	30.16 S	29.56 E
Umzingwani ≃	154	22.12 S	29.56 E
Umzinto	158	30.22 S	30.33 E
Una, Bra.	255	15.18 S	39.04 W
Una, India	120	20.49 N	71.02 E
Una, India	123	31.29 N	76.17 E
Una ≃	36	45.16 N	16.55 E
Una, Mount ʌ	172	42.13 S	172.35 E
Una, Ribeirão ≃	287b	23.31 S	46.18 W
Unac ≃	36	44.30 N	16.09 E
Uña de Gato	196	25.58 N	99.41 W
Unadilla, Ga., U.S.	192	32.15 N	83.44 W
Unadilla, N.Y., U.S.	210	42.19 N	75.18 W
Unadilla ≃	210	42.20 N	75.25 W
Unaí	255	16.23 S	46.53 W
Unakami	94	35.46 N	140.45 E
Unalakleet	180	63.53 N	160.47 W
Unalaska	180	53.52 N	166.32 W
Unalaska Island I	180	53.45 N	166.45 W
Unanderra	170	34.27 S	150.52 E
Unango	154	12.50 S	35.20 E
Únanov	61	48.54 N	16.04 E
Unao	124	25.35 N	78.36 E
Unare ≃	246	10.03 N	65.14 W
Unauna, Pulau I	112	0.10 S	121.35 E
Unayyir, Ḥarrat al- •[9]	128	25.20 N	37.45 E
'Unayzah, Ar. Su.	128	26.06 N	43.56 E
'Unayzah, Urd.	132	30.29 N	35.48 E
'Unayzah, Jabal ʌ, Asia	128	32.12 N	39.18 E
'Unayzah, Jabal ʌ, Urd.	132	30.30 N	35.47 E
Unazuki	94	36.49 N	137.35 E
Uncasville	207	41.26 N	72.06 W
Unchahra	124	24.23 N	80.47 E
Ŭnch'ŏn	98	38.34 N	125.26 E
Uncia	248	18.27 S	66.37 W
Uncompahgre ≃	200	38.45 N	108.06 W
Uncompahgre Peak ʌ	200	38.04 N	107.28 W
Uncompahgre Plateau ⋏[1]	200	38.30 N	108.25 W
Uncukul'	84	42.42 N	46.48 E
Uncular	130	40.28 N	41.28 E
Unda	88	51.42 N	116.56 E
Unda ≃	88	51.25 N	116.05 E
Unden ⊜	40	58.47 N	14.26 E
Undenäs	40	58.39 N	14.25 E
Underberg	158	29.50 S	29.22 E
Under River	260	51.15 N	0.14 E
Undersåker	26	63.20 N	13.23 E
Underwood, In., U.S.	218	38.36 N	85.46 W
Underwood, N.D., U.S.	198	47.27 N	101.08 W
Underwood, Wa., U.S.	224	45.43 N	121.31 W
Undløse	41	55.36 N	11.35 E
Undory	80	54.37 N	48.25 E
Undu, Tanjung ›	115b	10.05 S	120.51 E
Undu Point ›	175g	16.08 S	179.57 W
Undva nina ›	76	58.32 N	21.55 E
Unea Island I	164	4.55 S	149.10 E
Uneča	76	52.50 N	32.40 E
Uneča ≃	76	52.50 N	31.56 E
Uneiuxi ≃	246	0.37 S	65.34 W
Úněšov	60	49.53 N	13.09 E
Unga Island I	180	55.15 N	160.45 W
Ungama Bay c	154	2.45 S	40.20 E
Ungaran	115a	7.07 S	110.24 E
Ungarie	166	33.38 S	146.58 E
Ungarn → Hungary □[1]	30	47.00 N	20.00 E
Ungava, Péninsule d' ›[1]	176	60.00 N	74.00 W
Ungava Bay c	176	59.30 N	67.30 W
Ungch'ŏn	98	35.07 N	128.44 E
Ungeny	78	47.12 N	27.48 E
Unggi	98	42.20 N	130.24 E
Ungurkuj	88	50.27 N	106.58 E
Ungvár → Užgorod	78	48.37 N	22.18 E
Unhos	266c	38.50 N	9.07 W
Unhošť	54	50.04 N	14.08 E
Uni	80	57.46 N	51.30 E
União	250	4.35 S	42.52 W
União da Vitória	252	26.13 S	51.05 W
União dos Palmares	250	9.10 S	36.02 W
Unica	24	62.38 N	34.38 E
Unicoi	192	36.11 N	82.20 W
Unicorn Branch ≃	208	39.15 N	75.52 W
Unidad Santa Fe ✦[8]	286a	19.23 N	99.15 W
Uniejów	30	51.58 N	18.49 E
Unieux	62	45.24 N	4.16 E
Unije, Otok I	36	44.38 N	14.15 E
Unimak Island I	180	54.50 N	164.00 W
Unimak Pass ʯ	180	54.35 N	164.43 W
Unini ≃	246	1.41 S	61.31 W
Unión, Arg.	252	35.09 S	65.57 W
Union, On., Can.	212	42.42 N	81.12 W
Unión, Para.	252	24.48 S	56.33 W
Union, Il., U.S.	216	42.14 N	88.33 W
Union, Ia., U.S.	190	42.14 N	93.03 W
Union, Ky., U.S.	218	38.56 N	84.40 W
Union, La., U.S.	194	30.06 N	90.54 W
Union, Ms., U.S.	194	32.34 N	89.07 W
Union, Mo., U.S.	219	38.26 N	91.00 W
Union, N.J., U.S.	210	40.41 N	74.15 W
Union, Oh., U.S.	218	39.53 N	84.18 W
Union, Or., U.S.	202	45.12 N	117.51 W
Union, S.C., U.S.	192	34.42 N	81.37 W
Union, Wa., U.S.	224	47.21 N	123.06 W
Union, W.V., U.S.	192	37.35 N	80.32 W
Union □[6], In., U.S.	218	39.38 N	84.56 W
Union □[6], N.J., U.S.	208	40.40 N	74.11 W
Union □[6], Oh., U.S.	214	40.18 N	83.19 W
Union □[6], Pa., U.S.	210	40.58 N	76.54 W
Unión ✦[8]	258	34.53 S	56.08 W
Union Bay	182	49.35 N	124.53 W
Union Beach	208	40.26 N	74.10 W
Union Bridge	208	39.34 N	77.10 W
Union Center	210	42.09 N	76.04 W
Union City, Ca., U.S.	226	37.35 N	122.04 W
Union City, Ga., U.S.	192	33.35 N	84.32 W
Union City, In., U.S.	194	40.07 N	85.05 W
Union City, Mi., U.S.	216	42.04 N	85.09 W
Union City, N.J., U.S.	276	40.46 N	74.01 W
Union City, Oh., U.S.	216	40.11 N	84.48 W
Union City, Pa., U.S.	214	41.53 N	79.50 W
Union City, Tn., U.S.	194	36.25 N	89.03 W
Union City Dam ✦[6]	214	41.55 N	79.54 W
Uniondale, S. Afr.	158	33.40 S	23.08 E
Uniondale, In., U.S.	216	40.50 N	85.15 W
Uniondale, N.Y., U.S.	276	40.42 N	73.35 W
Union Dale, Pa., U.S.	210	41.43 N	75.30 W
Unión de Repúblicas Socialistas Soviéticas → Union of Soviet Socialist Republics □[1]	72	60.00 N	80.00 E
Unión de Reyes	240p	22.48 N	81.32 W
Unión de San Antonio	234	21.06 N	101.58 W
Union des Émirats Arabes → United Arab Emirates □[1]	128	24.00 N	54.00 E
Union des Républiques socialistes soviétiques → Union of Soviet Socialist Republics □[1]	72	60.00 N	80.00 E
Unión de Tula	234	19.58 N	104.16 W
Union Flat Creek ≃	202	46.50 N	117.59 W
Union Gap	202	46.33 N	120.28 W
Union Grove, Tx., U.S.	222	32.34 N	94.55 W
Union Grove, Wi., U.S.	216	42.41 N	88.03 W
Unión Hidalgo	234	16.28 N	94.50 W
Union Hill	210	43.13 N	77.23 W
Union Lake	216	42.36 N	83.26 W
Union Lake ⊜, Mi., U.S.	216	42.03 N	85.11 W
Union Lake ⊜, Mi., U.S.	281	42.37 N	83.26 W
Union Lake ⊜, N.J., U.S.	208	39.25 N	75.03 W
Union Mills	216	41.29 N	86.46 W
Union of Soviet Socialist Republics □[1], Europe	72	60.00 N	80.00 E
Union of Soviet Socialist Republics □[1], Europe	74	60.00 N	100.00 E
Union Park	220	28.30 N	81.15 W
Union Pier	216	41.49 N	86.41 W
Union Point	192	33.36 N	83.04 W
Unionport, In., U.S.	218	40.07 N	85.06 W
Unionport, Oh., U.S.	214	40.21 N	80.51 W
Union Seamount ✦[3]	16	49.35 N	132.45 W
Union Springs, Al., U.S.	194	32.08 N	85.42 W
Union Springs, N.Y., U.S.	210	42.50 N	76.41 W
Union Station ✦[5], On., Can.	275b	43.39 N	79.23 W
Union Station ✦[5], Ca., U.S.	280	34.04 N	118.14 W
Union Station ✦[5], D.C., U.S.	284c	38.54 N	77.00 W
Union Station ✦[5], Il., U.S.	278	41.53 N	87.38 W
Uniontown, Al., U.S.	194	32.26 N	87.30 W
Uniontown, Ky., U.S.	194	37.46 N	87.55 W
Uniontown, Md., U.S.	208	39.35 N	77.06 W
Uniontown, Oh., U.S.	214	40.58 N	81.24 W
Uniontown, Pa., U.S.	188	39.54 N	79.44 W
Union Valley Reservoir ⊜[1]	226	38.50 N	120.26 W
Union Village	207	41.59 N	71.32 W
Unionville, On., Can.	275b	43.52 N	79.18 W
Unionville, Ct., U.S.	207	41.45 N	72.53 W
Unionville, In., U.S.	218	39.14 N	86.25 W
Unionville, Mi., U.S.	190	43.39 N	83.27 W
Unionville, Mo., U.S.	194	40.28 N	93.00 W
Unionville, N.J., U.S.	285	40.01 N	74.46 W
Unionville, N.Y., U.S.	210	41.18 N	74.34 W
Unionville, Oh., U.S.	214	41.47 N	81.00 W
Unionville, Pa., U.S.	285	39.54 N	75.44 W
Unionville Center	214	40.08 N	83.21 W
Uniopolis	216	40.36 N	84.05 W
Unipouheos Indian Reserve ✦[4]	184	53.52 N	110.21 W
Unisan	116	13.51 N	121.59 E
United	214	40.13 N	79.29 W
United Arab Emirates (Al-Imārāt al-'Arabīyah al-Muttaḥidah) □[1], Asia	118	24.00 N	54.00 E
United Arab Emirates (Al-Imārāt al-'Arabīyah al-Muttaḥidah) □[1], Asia	128	24.00 N	54.00 E
United Arab Republic → Egypt □[1]	140	27.00 N	30.00 E
United Kingdom □[1], Europe	22	54.00 N	2.00 W
United Kingdom □[1], Europe	28	54.00 N	2.00 W
United Kingdom Sovereign Base Area ■	130	35.00 N	33.45 E
United Nations Headquarters ✪	276	40.45 N	73.58 W
United States □[1]	178	38.00 N	97.00 W
United States Air Force Academy ■	200	39.00 N	104.55 W
United States Coast Guard Academy ■	207	41.22 N	72.06 W
United States Merchant Marine Academy ✪[2]	276	40.48 N	73.46 W
United States Military Academy ■	210	41.23 N	73.58 W
United States Naval Academy ■	208	38.59 N	76.30 W
United States Steel Corporation (Lorain Plant) ✪[3], Oh., U.S.	279a	41.27 N	82.07 W
United States Steel Corporation ✪[3], Pa. U.S.	279b	40.20 N	79.54 W
United States Steel Corporation ✪[3], Pa., U.S.	279b	40.25 N	79.54 W
United States Steel Corporation Fairless Works ✪[3]	285	40.09 N	74.45 W
Unity	184	52.27 N	109.10 W
Unity Reservoir ⊜[1]	279b	40.17 N	79.30 W
Universal City	196	29.32 N	98.17 W
Universal City ✪[3]	280	34.09 N	118.21 W
Universal Mall ✦[9]	281	42.30 N	83.05 W
Università Degli Studi ✪[2]	266b	45.28 N	9.14 E
Universitaria, Ciudad ✪[2]	266d	41.23 N	2.08 E
University	194	34.21 N	89.32 W
University City	219	38.39 N	90.19 W
University Gardens	276	40.46 N	73.43 W
University Heights, Ca., U.S.	226	37.26 N	122.12 W
University Heights, Oh., U.S.	279a	41.29 N	81.32 W
University Park, Il., U.S.	216	41.36 N	87.39 W
University Park, Md., U.S.	284c	38.58 N	76.57 W
University Park, N.M., U.S.	200	32.06 N	106.39 W
University Park, Tx., U.S.	222	32.52 N	96.47 W
University Place	224	47.14 N	122.32 W
University View	218	40.00 N	83.03 W
Unjha	120	23.48 N	72.24 E
Unkel	56	50.35 N	7.13 E
Unken	64	47.39 N	12.43 E
Unkurda	86	55.48 N	59.24 E
Unley	168b	34.57 S	138.35 E
Unna	52	51.32 N	7.41 E
'Unnāb, Jabal al- ʌ	132	29.57 N	36.55 E
'Unnāb, Wādī al- V	132	30.11 N	36.39 E
Unnão	124	26.32 N	80.30 E
Uno, Canal Numero ≍	252	36.17 S	57.08 W
Uno, Ilha I	150	11.12 N	16.15 W
Unoke	94	36.43 N	136.42 E
Ŭnp'a	98	38.26 N	125.45 E
Unpenji-san ʌ	96	34.02 N	133.44 E
Unqua Point ›	276	40.39 N	73.26 W
Unquillo	252	31.14 S	64.19 W
Ŭnsan	98	39.25 N	126.01 E
Unseburg	54	51.56 N	11.30 E
Unserfrau → Madonna	64	46.43 N	10.52 E
Unseleben	56	50.22 N	10.15 E
Unst I	46a	60.45 N	0.53 W
Unstrut ≃	54	51.10 N	11.48 E
Un't	88	49.07 N	102.50 E
Unten	174m	26.41 N	128.00 E
Unterägeri	58	47.08 N	8.35 E
Unterbach, B.R.D.	263	51.12 N	6.54 E
Unterbäch, Schw.	58	46.17 N	7.48 E
Unter dem Wind, Inseln → Windward Islands II	238	13.00 N	61.00 W
Unterelchingen	58	48.27 N	10.07 E
Unterföhring	60	48.12 N	11.38 E
Unterfranken □[5]	56	50.10 N	10.00 E
Untergermaringen	58	47.56 N	10.40 E
Unterglottertal	58	48.03 N	7.56 E
Untergriesbach	60	48.35 N	13.40 E
Untergröningen	56	48.55 N	9.53 E
Untergrüne	263	51.22 N	7.39 E
Unterhaching	60	48.04 N	11.38 E
Unterhausen	58	48.26 N	9.16 E
Unterinntal V	64	47.24 N	11.47 E
Unterjettenberg	64	47.41 N	12.49 E
Unterlaa ✦[8]	264b	48.08 N	16.25 E
Unterlüss	52	52.50 N	10.17 E
Untermauerbach	264b	48.14 N	16.12 E
Untermünkheim	56	49.09 N	9.44 E
Untermünstertal	58	47.51 N	7.46 E
Unteröwisheim	56	49.08 N	8.40 E
Unterrath ✦[8]	263	51.16 N	6.47 E
Unterschächen	58	46.52 N	8.47 E
Unterschwaningen	56	49.04 N	10.37 E
Unterseen	58	46.41 N	7.51 E
Untertauern	64	47.18 N	13.30 E
Unterterzen	58	47.07 N	9.15 E
Unterthingau	58	47.46 N	10.31 E
Unterueckersee ⊜	54	53.17 N	13.51 E
Unteruhldingen	58	47.43 N	9.14 E
Unterwasser	58	47.12 N	9.19 E
Unterweissbach	54	50.37 N	11.10 E
Unterwellenborn	54	50.39 N	11.26 E
Unterwössen	64	47.44 N	12.27 E
Unterzeiring	61	47.15 N	14.31 E
Untraverket	40	60.25 N	17.18 E
Unuli Horog	120	35.06 N	91.51 E
Ünye	130	41.08 N	37.17 E
Unža	80	58.01 N	44.01 E
Unža ≃	80	57.20 N	43.08 E
Unzen-Amakusa-kokuritsu-kōen ♦	92	32.45 N	130.17 E
Unzen-dake ʌ	92	32.45 N	130.17 E
Unže-Pavinskaja	86	58.53 N	64.02 E
Uojan	88	56.07 N	111.38 E
Uono ≃	94	37.15 N	138.53 E
Uo-shima I	96	34.11 N	133.19 E
Uozu	94	36.48 N	137.24 E
Upa ≃	76	54.02 N	36.15 E
Upala	236	10.47 N	85.02 W
Upanema	250	5.38 S	37.15 W
Upano ≃	246	2.45 S	78.12 W
Upata	246	8.01 N	62.24 W
Upatoi Creek ≃	192	32.22 N	84.58 W
Upavon	42	51.18 N	1.49 W
Ŭpchŏ-ri	98	37.53 N	125.09 E
Upchurch	260	51.23 N	0.39 E
Upemba, Lac ⊜	154	8.36 S	26.26 E
Upemba, Parc National de l' ♦	154	9.10 S	26.35 E
Upernavik	176	72.47 N	56.10 W
Upgant-Schott	52	53.30 N	7.16 E
Uphal	140	6.58 N	34.16 E
Upham	198	48.34 N	100.43 W
Up Holland	262	53.33 N	2.44 W
Uphusen	52	53.01 N	8.58 E
Upi	116	6.57 N	124.09 E
Upía ≃	246	4.18 N	72.45 W
Upington	158	28.25 S	21.15 E
Upire ≃	246	11.27 N	68.58 W
Upland, Ca., U.S.	228	34.05 N	117.38 W
Upland, In., U.S.	216	40.28 N	85.29 W
Upland, Ne., U.S.	198	40.19 N	98.54 W
Upland, Pa., U.S.	285	39.51 N	75.23 W
Upleta	120	21.44 N	70.17 E
Upnuk Lake ⊜	180	60.21 N	158.58 W
Upolu I	175a	13.55 S	171.45 W
Upolu Point ›	229d	20.16 N	155.51 W
Uporovo	86	56.18 N	66.17 E
Upper □[4]	150	10.30 N	1.30 W
Upper Arlington	218	40.00 N	83.03 W
Upper Arrow Lake ⊜	182	50.30 N	117.55 W
Upper Artichoke Reservoir ⊜[1]	283	42.48 N	70.57 W
Upper Bay c	276	40.41 N	74.03 W
Upper Beaconsfield	274b	38.01 S	145.25 E
Upper Berkshire Valley	276	40.56 N	74.35 W
Upper Beverley Lake ⊜	212	44.37 N	76.05 W
Upper Black Eddy	210	40.35 N	75.07 W
Upper Blackville	186	46.39 N	65.52 W
Upper Brookville	276	40.51 N	73.34 W
Upper Canada Village ⊥	206	44.57 N	75.03 W
Upper Castlereagh	274a	33.43 S	150.40 E
Upperco	208	39.33 N	76.50 W
Upper Coliban Reservoir ⊜[1]	169	37.18 S	144.23 E
Upper Crystal Springs Reservoir ⊜[1]	282	37.30 N	122.20 W
Upper Darby	208	39.55 N	75.16 W
Upper des Lacs Lake ⊜[1]	198	48.50 N	102.07 W
Upper Egypt → Aṣ-Ṣa'īd □[9]	140	26.00 N	32.00 E
Upper End	262	53.17 N	1.52 W
Upper Erskine Lake ⊜	276	41.06 N	74.15 W
Upper Fairmount	208	38.06 N	75.47 W
Upper Falls	284b	39.26 N	76.24 W
Upper Ferntree Gully	274b	37.54 S	145.19 E
Upper Fraser	182	54.07 N	121.56 W
Upper Ganga Canal ≍	124	29.57 N	78.12 E
Upper Gap ʯ	212	44.06 N	76.50 W
Upper Goose Lake ⊜	184	51.44 N	92.44 W
Upper Greenwood Lake	276	41.10 N	74.22 W
Upper Greenwood Lake ⊜	276	41.11 N	74.23 W
Upper Hat Creek	182	50.38 N	121.35 W
Upper Humber ≃	186	49.10 N	57.28 W
Upper Hutt	172	41.08 S	175.04 E
Upper Iowa ≃	190	43.29 N	91.14 W
Upper Island Cove	186	47.39 N	53.12 W
Upper Keechi Creek ≃	222	31.23 N	95.42 W
Upper Klamath Lake ⊜	202	42.23 N	122.55 W
Upper Lake	204	39.10 N	122.54 W
Upper Lake ⊜	204	41.44 N	120.08 W
Upper Lehigh	210	41.02 N	75.55 W
Upper Liard	180	60.02 N	128.55 W
Upper Machodoc Creek ≃	208	38.18 N	77.02 W
Upper Manitou Lake ⊜	184	49.24 N	92.48 W
Upper Marlboro	208	38.48 N	76.45 W
Upper Matecumbe Key I	220	24.55 N	80.39 W
Upper Moutere	172	41.16 S	173.00 E
Upper Musquodoboit	186	45.08 N	62.57 W
Upper Mystic Lake ⊜	283	42.27 N	71.09 W
Upper Nyack	210	41.07 N	73.55 W
Upper Peirce Reservoir ⊜[1]	271c	1.22 N	103.48 E
Upper Red Lake ⊜	198	48.10 N	94.40 W
Upper Rideau Lake ⊜	212	44.41 N	76.20 W
Upper River Rouge ≃	281	42.23 N	83.16 W
Upper Saddle River	276	41.03 N	74.05 W
Upper Saint Clair	279b	40.21 N	80.05 W
Upper Sandusky	214	40.49 N	83.16 W
Upper San Leandro Reservoir ⊜[1]	226	37.47 N	122.07 W
Upper Sheila	186	47.28 N	64.56 W
Upper Straits Lake ⊜	281	42.35 N	83.24 W
Upper Sumas	224	49.01 N	122.12 W
Upper Swan	168a	31.46 S	116.01 E
Upper Takaka	172	41.02 S	172.50 E
Upper Tean	42	52.57 N	1.58 W
Upper Tooting ✦[8]	260	51.26 N	0.10 W
Upper Ugashik Lake ⊜	180	57.40 N	156.43 W
Upper Volta → Burkina Faso □[1]	150	13.00 N	1.30 W
Upper Windigo Lake ⊜	184	52.30 N	91.35 W
Upper Yarra Reservoir ⊜[1]	169	37.41 S	145.56 E
Upper Yosemite Fall ⌊	226	37.45 N	119.36 W
Uppingham	42	52.35 N	0.43 W
Uppland □[9]	40	59.59 N	17.48 E
Upplanda	40	60.14 N	17.44 E
Upplands Väsby	40	59.31 N	17.54 E
Uppsala	40	59.52 N	17.38 E
Uppsala Län □[6]	40	60.00 N	17.45 E
Upright, Cape ›	180	60.17 N	172.15 W
Upsala → Uppsala	40	59.52 N	17.38 E
Upshi	120	33.50 N	77.49 E
Upshur □[6]	222	32.45 N	94.55 W
Upstart, Cape ›	166	19.42 S	147.45 E
Upton, P.Q., Can.	206	45.39 N	72.41 W
Upton, Eng., U.K.	44	53.37 N	1.17 W
Upton, Eng., U.K.	260	51.30 N	0.35 W
Upton, Eng., U.K.	262	53.13 N	2.52 W
Upton, Eng., U.K.	262	53.23 N	3.06 W
Upton, Ky., U.S.	194	37.27 N	85.53 W
Upton, Ma., U.S.	207	42.10 N	71.36 W
Upton, Wy., U.S.	198	44.05 N	104.37 W
Upton Hill ʌ[2]	169	36.52 S	145.27 E
Upton upon Severn	42	52.04 N	2.13 W
Uptown ✦[8]	278	41.58 N	87.40 W
Upwell	42	52.36 N	0.12 E
Upwey	274b	37.54 S	145.20 E
Uquía, Cerro ʌ	246	4.22 N	63.46 W
Ur → Tall al-Muqayyar ⊥	128	30.57 N	46.09 E
Urabá, Golfo de c	246	8.25 N	76.53 W
Urachi	84	42.21 N	47.36 E
Uracoa	246	9.00 N	62.21 W
Urad	54	52.15 N	14.45 E
Uradome-kaigan ♦	96	35.35 N	134.21 E
Urad Zhonghou Lianheqi	102	41.42 N	108.49 E
Uraga	268	35.15 N	139.43 E
Uraga-kō c	268	35.14 N	139.44 E
Uraga-suidō ʯ	94	35.13 N	139.45 E
Uragawara	94	37.09 N	138.26 E
Urahoro	92a	42.48 N	143.39 E
Uraj	86	60.08 N	64.48 E
Urakan	88	58.38 N	106.01 E
Urakawa	92a	42.09 N	142.47 E
Ural ≃	72	47.00 N	51.48 E
Uralla	166	30.39 S	151.30 E
Ural Mountains → Ural'skije gory ⋏	72	60.00 N	60.00 E
Uralo-Kl'uči	88	56.03 N	97.28 E
Uralovo	78	52.11 N	33.34 E
Ural'sk	80	51.14 N	51.22 E
Ural'skij	80	51.36 N	51.40 E
Ural'skije gory (Ural Mountains) ⋏	72	60.00 N	60.00 E
Urambo	154	5.04 S	32.03 E
Uran	272c	18.52 N	72.56 E
Urana	166	35.20 S	146.16 E
Urandangi	166	21.36 S	138.18 E
Urandi	255	14.46 S	42.38 W
Urangan	166	25.18 S	152.54 E
Urania, Austl.	168b	34.31 S	137.36 E
Urania, La., U.S.	194	31.51 N	92.17 W
Uranium City	176	59.34 N	108.36 W
Uranquinty	171b	35.12 S	147.15 E
Urarey	162	27.26 S	122.18 E
Urariá, Paraná ≃[1]	246	3.03 S	57.43 W
Uraricaá ≃	246	3.20 N	61.56 W
Uraricoera	246	3.27 N	60.59 W
Uraricoera ≃	246	3.02 N	60.30 W
Uras	71	39.42 N	8.42 E
Urasaki	174m	26.40 N	127.53 E
Urasoe	174m	26.15 N	127.43 E
Ura-T'ube	85	39.55 N	68.59 E
Uravakonda	122	14.57 N	77.16 E
Uravan	200	38.22 N	108.44 W

Symbols in the index entries represent the broad categories identified in the key at the right. Symbols with superior numbers (⋏[1]) identify subcategories (see complete key on page *I* · *1*).

Symbole im Register stellen die rechts im Schlüssel erklärten Kategorien dar. Symbole mit hochgestellten Ziffern (⋏[1]) bezeichnen Unterabteilungen einer Kategorie (vgl. vollständiger Schlüssel auf Seite *I* · *1*).

Los símbolos incluídos en el texto del índice representan las grandes categorias identificadas con la clave a la derecha. Los símbolos con numeros en su parte superior (⋏[1]) identifican las subcategorías (véase la clave completa en la página *I* · *1*).

Les symboles de l'index représentent les catégories indiquées dans la légende à droite. Les symboles suivis d'un indice (⋏[1]) représentent des sous-catégories (voir légende complète à la page *I* · *1*).

Os símbolos incluídos no texto do índice representam as grandes categorias identificadas com a chave à direita. Os símbolos com números em sua parte superior (⋏[1]) identificam as subcategorias (veja-se a chave completa à página *I* · *1*).

ʌ	Mountain	Berg	Montaña	Montagne	Montanha
⋏	Mountains	Gebirge	Montañas	Montagnes	Montanhas
)(	Pass	Paß	Paso	Col	Passo
V	Valley, Canyon	Tal, Cañon	Valle, Cañón	Vallée, Canyon	Vale, Canhão
≚	Plain	Ebene	Llano	Plaine	Planície
›	Cape	Kap	Cabo	Cap	Cabo
I	Island	Insel	Isla	Île	Ilha
II	Islands	Inseln	Islas	Îles	Ilhas
•	Other Topographic Features	Andere Topographische Objekte	Otros Elementos Topográficos	Autres données topographiques	Outros acidentes topográficos

ESPAÑOL Nombre	Página	Lat.°′	Long.°′ W = Oeste
Urawa	94	35.51 N	139.39 E
Urayasu	94	35.39 N	139.54 E
'Urayfan Nāqah, Jabal ▲	132	30.22 N	34.27 E
'Urayyidah, Bi'r ▼⁴	142	29.00 N	31.58 E
Urazmetovo	86	53.49 N	55.25 E
Urazovka	80	55.24 N	45.38 E
Urazovo	78	50.07 N	38.04 E
Urbach	56	50.53 N	7.05 E
Urban	224	48.38 N	122.40 W
Urbana, Ar., U.S.	194	33.09 N	92.26 W
Urbana, Il., U.S.	194	40.06 N	88.12 W
Urbana, In., U.S.	216	40.53 N	85.47 W
Urbana, Mo., U.S.	194	37.50 N	93.10 W
Urbana, Oh., U.S.	218	40.06 N	83.45 W
Urbancrest	218	39.53 N	83.05 W
Urbandale, Ia., U.S.	190	41.37 N	93.42 W
Urbandale, Mi., U.S	216	44.09 N	85.11 W
Urbania	66	43.40 N	12.31 E
Urbanna	208	37.38 N	76.34 W
Urbano Santos	250	3.12 S	43.23 W
Urbe	62	44.29 N	8.36 E
Urbe, Aeroporto dell' ⊛¹	267a	41.57 N	12.30 E
Urbiña, Peña ▲	54	43.01 N	5.57 W
Urbino	66	43.43 N	12.38 E
Urbisaglia	66	43.12 N	13.23 E
Urcos	248	13.42 S	71.38 W
Urda	88	48.47 N	47.26 E
Urdaneta	116	15.59 N	120.34 E
Urdenbach ⌂⁸	252	51.09 N	6.53 E
Urdinarrain	252	32.41 S	58.53 W
Urdoma	24	61.47 N	48.32 E
Urdžar	86	47.05 N	81.38 E
Uré	246	7.46 N	75.31 W
Ure ≃, Fr.	50	48.45 N	0.11 E
Ure ≃, Eng., U.K.	44	54.01 N	1.12 W
Urečje	56	52.57 N	27.54 E
Ürein	142	30.58 N	30.42 E
Ureki	84	41.59 N	41.46 E
Ureliki	180	64.23 N	173.15 W
Uren'	80	57.28 N	45.49 E
Urén ⊜	40	58.59 N	16.44 E
Ureña	246	7.55 N	72.28 W
Urenui	172	39.00 S	174.23 E
Ureparapara I	175l	13.32 S	167.20 E
Ures	232	29.26 N	110.24 W
Ureshino, Nihon	92	33.06 N	129.59 E
Ureshino, Nihon	94	34.37 N	136.29 E
Ureterp	52	53.05 N	6.10 E
Urewera National Park ♦	172	38.40 S	177.00 E
Urfa	130	37.08 N	38.46 E
Urfa	130	37.20 N	39.15 E
Urft ≃	56	50.35 N	6.30 E
Urga → Ulaanbaatar	88	47.55 N	106.53 E
Urga ≃	88	43.35 N	58.30 E
Urgamal	88	48.29 N	94.20 E
Urgenč	72	41.33 N	60.38 E
Urgano	62	45.35 N	9.41 E
Urgučenskij Golec, gora ▲	88	53.30 N	118.08 E
Ürgüp	130	38.38 N	34.56 E
Urgut	86	39.23 N	67.15 E
Urho	88	46.48 N	89.45 E
Urho Kekkosen kansallispuisto ♦	26	68.10 N	28.30 E
Uri, India	123	34.05 N	74.02 E
Uri, It.	70	40.38 N	8.29 E
Uri □³	58	46.50 N	8.40 E
Uriah	194	31.18 N	87.30 W
Uriangato	234	20.09 N	101.11 W
Uribante ≃	246	7.18 N	70.44 W
Uribe	246	3.13 N	74.24 W
Uribelarrea	258	35.09 S	58.54 W
Uribia	246	11.43 N	72.16 W
Urich ⌂⁸	194	38.27 N	94.00 W
Urick ⌂⁸	265a	59.50 N	30.11 E
Urickij	86	53.19 N	65.34 E
Urickoje	78	52.02 N	38.11 E
Urie ≃	44	57.19 N	2.30 W
Urimba	158	10.56 S	16.32 E
Urión, Canal ≃¹	258	54.24 S	71.30 W
Urique	232	27.13 N	107.55 W
Urique ≃	232	26.29 N	107.58 W
Uri-Rotstock ▲	58	46.52 N	8.33 E
Urituyacu ≃	246	4.45 S	75.28 W
Uriuana	250	2.47 S	50.29 W
Uizura	94	36.30 N	140.27 E
Urjala	26	61.05 N	23.32 E
Urk	52	52.39 N	5.36 E
Urkan ≃	89	53.27 N	126.56 E
Urkarach	84	42.11 N	47.38 E
Urla	130	38.18 N	26.46 E
Urlaţi	38	44.59 N	26.14 E
Urlingford	48	52.42 N	7.35 W
Urlins	240c	17.02 N	61.52 W
Urluk	88	50.03 N	107.55 E
Urma	126	23.10 N	86.15 E
Urman, S.S.S.R.	86	54.52 N	56.52 E
'Urmān, Sūriy.	132	32.30 N	36.45 E
Urmary	80	55.42 N	47.57 E
Urmetan	86	39.27 N	68.47 E
Urmi ≃	89	48.44 N	134.16 E
Urmia → Orūmīyeh	128	37.33 N	45.04 E
Urmia, Lake → Orūmīyeh, Daryācheh-ye ⊜	128	37.40 N	45.30 E
Urmston	44	53.27 N	2.21 W
Urnäsch	58	47.19 N	9.17 E
Urnersee ⊜	58	46.55 N	8.37 E
Uróm	264c	47.36 N	19.01 E
Uromi	150	6.44 N	6.18 E
Uroševac	80	42.22 N	21.09 E
Uroyán, Montañas de ☆	240m	18.14 N	67.02 W
Urožajnoje, S.S.S.R.	84	43.43 N	44.13 E
Urožajnoje, S.S.S.R.	84	44.47 N	44.15 E
Urquhart, Glen ∨	44	57.20 N	4.35 W
Urr ≃	44	54.53 N	3.49 W
Urr Water ≃	44	54.53 N	3.49 W
Ursa	219	40.04 N	91.22 W
Ursel	52	51.09 N	3.24 E
Uršel'skij	80	55.41 N	40.13 E
Ursensollen	60	49.24 N	11.46 E
Ursk	86	54.27 N	85.24 E
Urspring	60	48.33 N	9.48 E
Urt Moron ≃	88	52.12 N	58.50 E
Uru ⊜	255	15.24 S	49.36 W
Uruaçu	250	14.30 S	49.10 W
Uruana	255	15.30 S	49.41 W
Uruapan	204	31.38 N	116.15 W
Uruapan [del Progreso]	234	19.25 N	102.04 W
Uruará ≃	250	2.06 S	53.38 W
Urubamba	248	13.18 S	72.07 W
Urubamba ≃	248	10.44 S	73.45 W
Urubaxi ≃	246	0.31 S	64.50 W
Urubu ≃	246	2.55 S	58.25 W
Urubu, Cachoeira do ⭢⁵	255	12.52 S	48.13 W
Urubu Grande ≃	250	10.51 S	49.47 W
Uruburetama	250	3.38 S	39.30 W
Urucará	250	2.32 S	57.45 W
Uruch ≃	84	43.28 N	44.06 E
Urucu ≃	246	4.53 S	63.36 W
Urucuca	255	14.35 S	39.16 W
Uruçuí	250	7.14 S	44.33 W
Uruçuí, Serra da ▲²	250	9.00 S	44.45 W
Urucuia ≃	255	16.08 S	45.05 W
Uruçuí-Prêto ≃	250	7.20 S	44.30 W
Urucurituba	250	2.41 S	57.40 W
Urugi	94	35.16 N	137.42 E
Uruguaiana	252	29.45 S	57.05 W
Uruguay □¹	244	33.00 S	56.00 W
Uruguay □¹, S.A.	252	33.00 S	56.00 W
Uruguay (Uruguai) ≃	252	34.12 S	58.18 W

FRANÇAIS Nom	Page	Lat.°′	Long.°′ W = Ouest
Urugudejevskij Golec, gora ▲	88	51.25 N	102.09 E
Urul'ga	88	51.45 N	114.47 E
Urul'unguj ≃	88	50.24 N	119.08 E
Ur'um, ozero ⊜	86	54.33 N	78.30 E
Urumchi → Ürümqi	90	43.48 N	87.35 E
Ürümqi	90	43.48 N	87.35 E
Ur'umkan ≃	88	52.35 N	120.08 E
Ürümqi	90	43.48 N	87.35 E
Urundel	252	23.33 S	64.25 W
Ur'ung-Chaja	74	72.48 N	113.23 E
Uruoca	250	3.20 S	40.32 W
Urup	84	43.52 N	41.09 E
Urup ≃	84	44.49 N	41.10 E
Urup, gora ▲	84	43.38 N	40.58 E
Urup, ostrov I	74	46.00 N	150.00 E
Urupá ≃	248	10.54 S	61.57 W
Urupadi ≃	250	3.51 S	57.21 W
Urupês	255	21.13 S	49.17 W
Urussu	80	54.36 N	53.24 E
Urutai	255	17.28 S	48.12 W
Urutai, Ilha I	250	1.07 S	51.17 W
Urutaú	252	25.42 S	63.04 W
Uruti	172	38.57 S	174.32 E
Uruwira	154	6.27 S	31.21 E
Uryl'-yama ▲	270	35.05 N	135.48 E
Uryv	78	51.07 N	39.10 E
Urzajbaš	86	54.43 N	54.23 E
Urziceni	38	44.43 N	26.38 E
Ürzig	56	49.59 N	7.01 E
Urzulei	70	40.06 N	9.30 E
Uržum	80	57.08 N	50.00 E
Us ≃	261	49.06 N	1.58 E
Us ≃	86	52.07 N	92.15 E
Usakos	156	22.01 S	15.32 E
Ušakovka ≃	83	48.49 N	39.48 E
Ušakovo, S.S.S.R.	89	51.55 N	126.34 E
Usambara Mountains ☆			
Usangu Flats ≃	154	8.30 S	34.15 E
Usanovy	86	51.29 N	73.24 E
Ušaral	85	43.54 N	70.42 E
Usarp Mountains ☆	9	71.10 S	160.00 E
Ušava ≃	89	49.46 N	12.40 E
Usaymir, Wādī al-	273c	30.04 N	31.23 E
Usbas, gora ▲	84	43.08 N	42.40 E
Usbas ≃	85	43.55 N	69.39 E
Usborne, Mount ▲	254	51.41 S	58.50 W
Ušče	38	43.28 N	20.37 E
Uščerpье	76	52.43 N	31.53 E
Uscio	62	44.25 N	9.10 E
Usedom (Uznam) I	54	54.00 N	14.00 E
Useldange	56	49.47 N	5.59 E
Usellus	71	39.48 N	8.51 E
Usen' ≃	80	54.44 N	53.38 E
'Usfān	144	21.55 N	39.21 E
Ushaa	152	14.55 S	23.18 E
Ushant → Ouessant, Île d'			
Ushashi	154	2.01 S	33.57 E
'Ushayrah	144	21.46 N	40.38 E
Ushetu	154	4.10 S	32.16 E
Ushibuka	92	32.11 N	130.01 E
Ushiku	94	35.58 N	140.08 E
Ushimado	96	34.37 N	134.10 E
Ushuaia	254	54.48 S	68.18 W
Usibelli	180	63.51 N	148.47 W
Ušica ≃	78	48.35 N	27.08 E
Usingen	56	50.20 N	8.32 E
Usini	71	40.40 N	8.32 E
Usinsk	24	65.58 N	56.39 E
Usisya	154	11.09 S	34.11 E
Usk, B.C., Can.	182	54.38 N	128.25 W
Usk, Wales, U.K.	44	51.36 N	2.58 W
Usk, Wa., U.S.	202	48.18 N	117.16 W
Usk ≃	44	51.36 N	2.58 W
Uskanij kr'až ▲	180	65.15 N	178.35 E
Uskedal	26	59.56 N	5.52 E
Usken ≃	88	50.29 N	15.01 E
Uskovo	265b	55.56 N	37.19 E
Üsküb → Skopje	38	41.59 N	21.26 E
Üskümru ⌂⁸	267b	41.12 N	29.01 E
Uslar	56	51.39 N	9.38 E
Úslava ≃	60	49.45 N	13.24 E
Usmajac	234	19.52 N	103.34 W
Usman', S.S.S.R.	76	52.02 N	39.44 E
Usman' ≃	78	51.29 N	39.08 E
Usmanka ≃	80	52.49 N	51.42 E
Usmānpur ⌂⁸	272a	28.41 N	77.15 E
Usmas ezers ⊜	76	57.11 N	22.10 E
Usmat Velate	62	39.44 N	67.40 E
Usmynskij Golec, gora ▲	89	51.40 N	118.35 E
Usmyn'	76	55.43 N	31.09 E
Usoke	154	5.06 S	32.20 E
Usolje, S.S.S.R.	80	59.23 N	49.05 E
Usolje, S.S.S.R.	80	59.25 N	56.41 E
Usolje-Sibirskoje	88	52.47 N	103.38 E
Usolka ≃	86	58.42 N	56.38 E
Uson	116	12.13 N	123.47 E
Usoro ≃	150	5.17 N	7.52 E
Usovo	265b	55.44 N	37.13 E
Uspallata	252	32.35 S	69.20 W
Uspanapa ≃	234	17.58 N	94.29 W
Uspenka ≃	80	50.38 N	44.28 W
Uspenka, S.S.S.R.	82	48.23 N	39.10 E
Uspenka, S.S.S.R.	85	52.45 N	77.25 E
Uspenovka ≃	80	51.16 N	53.36 E
Uspenskij	85	48.45 N	72.42 E
Uspenskoje	80	52.00 N	40.32 E
Usri ≃	126	24.03 N	86.23 E
Ussassai	71	39.49 N	9.23 E
Usseglio	62	45.14 N	7.13 E
Ussel	32	45.33 N	2.18 E
Ussel ≃	56	48.44 N	11.04 E
Ushers Creek ≃	284a	43.03 N	79.02 W
Usson-en-Forez	32	45.39 N	3.56 E
Ussure	154	4.39 S	34.23 E
Ussuri (Wusuli) ≃	89	48.28 N	135.04 E
Ust-'Aldan	74	61.58 N	131.59 E
Usta ≃	80	57.26 N	45.40 E
Ust-'Ajsk	74	56.08 N	57.04 E
Ustaritz	32	43.24 N	1.27 W
Ust-'Bagar'ak	86	56.15 N	61.36 E
Ust-'Barguzin	88	53.27 N	108.59 E
Ust-'Belaja	180	65.30 N	173.20 E
Ust-'Bol'šereck	74	52.50 N	156.14 E
Ust-'B-ur'	88	53.49 N	90.15 E
Ust-'Buzulukskaja	80	50.12 N	42.10 E

PORTUGUÊS Nome	Página	Lat.°′	Long.°′ W = Oeste
Ust'-Bystr'anskaja	80	47.49 N	41.03 E
Ust'-Čaja	88	58.17 N	82.38 E
Ust'-Čaryšskaja Pristan'	86	52.24 N	83.39 E
Ust'-Čaun	74	68.47 N	170.30 E
Ust'-Choperskaja	80	49.36 N	42.24 E
Ust'-Cil'ma	24	65.27 N	52.06 E
Ust'-Čižapka	86	59.02 N	79.37 E
Ust'-Čorna	78	48.18 N	23.56 E
Ust'-Čornaja	88	52.57 N	119.02 E
Ust'-Dolyssy	76	56.09 N	29.39 E
Ust'-Doneckij	80	47.39 N	40.52 E
Ust'-Džegutinskaja	84	44.05 N	41.58 E
Uštěk	54	50.36 N	14.20 E
Ust'-Elegest	88	51.32 N	94.05 E
Uster	58	47.21 N	8.43 E
Ust'-Gr'aznucha	80	50.28 N	45.26 E
Ustica	70	3.51 S	57.21 W
Ustica, Isola di I	70	38.42 N	13.11 E
Ust'-Il'ga	88	56.55 N	105.02 E
Ust'-Ilimsk	88	58.00 N	102.39 E
Ust'-Ilimskoje vodochranilišče ⊜¹	88	57.00 N	102.15 E
Ustilug	78	50.51 N	24.09 E
Ust'-Ilyč	24	62.32 N	56.41 E
Ust' nad Labem	54	50.40 N	14.02 E
Usti nad Orlicí	30	49.58 N	16.24 E
Ustinovka, S.S.S.R.	78	47.57 N	32.32 E
Ustinovka, S.S.S.R.	83	48.49 N	38.34 E
Ust'-Išim	86	57.44 N	71.10 E
Ust'-Izes	86	55.56 N	76.56 E
Ust'-Ižora	265a	59.48 N	30.36 E
Ustja ≃	24	61.30 N	42.36 E
'Ust'-Jayron'ga ≃	24	63.25 N	44.21 E
Ustje, S.S.S.R.	76	60.49 N	32.49 E
Ustje, S.S.S.R.	76	59.38 N	39.43 E
Ustje, S.S.S.R.	80	57.47 N	39.47 E
Ustje ≃	82	55.36 N	20.20 E
Ustje-Kirovskoje	88	57.46 N	94.42 E
Ustka	30	54.35 N	16.50 E
Ust'-K'achta	88	50.32 N	106.16 E
Ust'-Kajtym	88	57.23 N	95.28 E
Ust'-Kalmanka	86	52.07 N	83.19 E
Ust'-Kamčatsk	74	56.15 N	162.30 E
Ust'-Kamenogorsk	86	49.58 N	82.38 E
Ust'-Kan, S.S.S.R.	86	50.57 N	84.45 E
Ust'-Kan, S.S.S.R.	86	56.31 N	93.48 E
Ust'-Karenga	88	54.26 N	116.30 E
Ust'-Karsk	88	52.43 N	118.48 E
Ust'-Katav	86	54.56 N	58.10 E
Ust'-Kemčug	88	56.11 N	90.30 E
Ust'-Kil'mez'	80	56.57 N	50.30 E
Ust'-Kišert'	86	57.22 N	57.15 E
Ust'-Koksa	86	50.18 N	85.36 E
Ust'-Kujda	74	70.01 N	135.36 E
Ust'-Kulom	24	61.43 N	53.40 E
Ust'-Kurd'um	80	51.39 N	46.12 E
Ust'-Kurenga	88	57.27 N	75.34 E
Ust'-Kut	88	56.46 N	105.40 E
Ust'-Labinsk	78	45.13 N	39.42 E
Ust'-Lubija	88	52.36 N	120.16 E
Ust'-Luga	76	59.40 N	28.15 E
Ust'-Lyža	24	65.26 N	56.32 E
Ust'-Manja	86	62.25 N	134.32 E
Ust'-Maya	72	62.11 N	56.32 E
Ust'-Naryk	86	54.20 N	87.25 E
Ust'-Nemda	80	57.55 N	50.22 E
Ust'-Nera	74	64.34 N	143.12 E
Ust'-Niman	89	51.23 N	132.42 E
Ust'-N'ukža	88	56.33 N	121.37 E
Ustobe	86	45.16 N	78.00 E
Ust'-Omčug	74	61.09 N	149.38 E
Ust'-Ordynskij	88	52.48 N	104.45 E
Ust'-Ordynskij Bur'atskij Nacional'nyj Okrug □⁴	88	53.30 N	104.00 E
Ust'-Oz'ornaja	88	58.54 N	87.48 E
Ust'-Oz'ornoje	88	58.54 N	87.48 E
Ust'-Paden'ga ≃	24	61.53 N	42.36 E
Ust'-Pečengskoje	76	59.47 N	42.37 E
Ust'-Pinega	24	64.11 N	41.56 E
Ust'-Pit	88	58.59 N	91.44 E
Ust'-Pogožje	80	49.28 N	44.38 E
Ust'reka	76	58.38 N	34.33 E
Ust'-Reki	24	62.12 N	46.45 E
Ustroń	30	49.43 N	18.49 E
Ustrzyki Dolne	30	49.26 N	22.37 E
Ust'-Šara	76	60.13 N	33.57 E
Ust'-Ščerbedino	80	51.53 N	42.52 E
Ust'-Slav'anka ⌂⁸	265a	59.50 N	30.32 E
Ust'-Šonoša	24	61.10 N	41.18 E
Ust'-Sumy	76	54.48 N	80.26 E
Ust'-Tarka	86	55.34 N	75.42 E
Ust'-Tašino	80	54.19 N	42.00 E
Ust'-Tygda	89	52.35 N	127.53 E
Ust'-Tym	86	59.20 N	80.08 E
Ust'-Tyrma	89	50.29 N	131.18 E
Ust'uckoje	76	58.35 N	35.31 E
Ust'-Uda	88	54.10 N	103.03 E
Ustürkan	130	39.16 N	41.17 E
Ust'-Ulagan	86	50.38 N	87.58 E
Ust'-Umal'ta	89	51.39 N	133.18 E
Ust'-Undurga	88	51.29 N	118.04 E
Ust'-Unja	24	61.48 N	57.48 E
Ustupo Yantupo	246	9.27 N	78.34 W
Ust'-Urgal	89	51.03 N	132.33 E
Ust'-urt, plato ⭢¹	72	43.00 N	56.00 E
Ust'-Usa	24	65.59 N	56.54 E
Ust'-Uza	80	52.58 N	45.17 E
Ust'-Vichoreva	88	56.47 N	101.24 E
Ust'-Voja	24	64.27 N	57.40 E
Ust'-Vojskaja ≃	24	62.14 N	50.24 E
Ust'-Vym'	24	62.14 N	50.24 E
Ust'-Zaza	88	53.10 N	111.40 E
Ust'-Žuja	88	58.48 N	118.12 E
Usuda	94	36.14 N	138.29 E
Usugli	88	54.12 N	117.48 E
Usui ≃	94	33.39 N	130.42 E
Usuki	96	33.08 N	131.49 E
Usuki-wan c	96	33.00 N	131.52 E
Usulután	236	13.21 N	88.27 W
Usumacinta ≃	232	18.24 N	92.38 W
Usumbura → Bujumbura	154	3.23 S	29.22 E
Ušumun	89	52.49 N	126.27 E
Ušur	88	57.47 N	92.58 E
Usuyòng	98	34.35 N	126.18 E
Usva	86	58.41 N	57.35 E
Usvjaty	76	55.45 N	30.45 E
Uta	71	39.17 N	8.57 E
'Utaybah, Buhayrat al- ⊜	132	33.32 N	36.37 E
Ute	198	42.03 N	95.42 W
Ute Creek ≃	196	35.21 N	103.50 W
Utegi	154	1.34 S	34.35 E
Utena	76	55.30 N	25.36 E
Ute Mountain Indian Reservation ⭢⁴	200	37.10 N	108.35 W
Utengule	154	8.57 S	35.02 E

≃ River	Fluß	Rio	Rivière	Rio	⟷ Submarine Features	Untermeerische Objekte	Accidentes Submarinos	Formes de relief sous-marin	Acidentes submarinos
≊ Canal	Kanal	Canal	Canal	Canal	□ Political Unit	Politische Einheit	Unidad Politica	Entité politique	Unidade política
⌄ Waterfall, Rapids	Wasserfall, Stromschnellen	Cascada, Rápidos	Chute d'eau, Rapides	Cascata, Rápidos	⌂ Cultural Institution	Kulturelle Institution	Institución Cultural	Institution culturelle	Instituição cultural
⌣ Strait	Meeresstraße	Estrecho	Détroit	Estreito	⏚ Historical Site	Historische Stätte	Sitio Histórico	Site historique	Sítio histórico
c Bay, Gulf	Bucht, Golf	Bahía, Golfo	Baie, Golfe	Baía, Golfo	⊛ Recreational Site	Erholungs- und Ferienort	Sitio de Recreo	Centre de loisirs	Área de Lazer
⊜ Lake, Lakes	See, Seen	Lago, Lagos	Lac, Lacs	Lago, Lagos	⊕ Airport	Flughafen	Aeropuerto	Aéroport	Aeroporto
⌻ Swamp	Sumpf	Pantano	Marais	Pântano	⊗ Military Installation	Militäranlage	Instalación Militar	Installation militaire	Instalação militar
⌸ Ice Features, Glacier	Eis- und Gletscherformen	Accidentes Glaciales	Formes glaciaires	Acidentes glaciares	⊙ Miscellaneous	Verschiedenes	Misceláneo	Divers	Diversos
⊤ Other Hydrographic Features	Andere Hydrographische Objekte	Otros Elementos Hidrográficos	Autres données hydrographiques	Outros acidentes hidrográficos					

Name	Page	Lat.°′	Long.°′
Valla	40	59.02 N	16.23 E
Valladares	196	26.53 N 100.37 W	
Valladolid, Ec.	246	4.33 S	79.08 W
Valladolid, Esp.	34	41.39 N	4.43 W
Valladolid, Méx.	232	20.41 N	88.12 W
Vallage ‣ ¹	58	48.24 N	5.00 E
Vallåkra	41	55.58 N	12.52 E
Vallarsa	64	45.47 N	11.07 E
Vallata	68	41.02 N	15.15 E
Vallauris	62	43.35 N	7.03 E
Vallco Fashion Park ⚫⁹	282	37.19 N 122.01 W	
Valldal	26	62.20 N	7.21 E
Valldoreix	266d	41.28 N	2.04 E
Valle, Esp.	34	43.14 N	4.18 W
Valle, It.	64	46.04 N	10.25 E
Valle, S.S.S.R.	76	56.30 N	24.44 E
Valle ⏚⁵	236	13.30 N	87.35 W
Valle, Arroyo ⏚	282	37.39 N 121.54 W	
Vallecas ⚫⁸	266a	40.23 N	3.37 W
Valle Castellana	66	42.44 N	13.29 E
Vallecillo	196	26.40 N	99.58 W
Vallecito	226	38.07 N 120.27 W	
Vallecitos	200	36.05 N 106.20 W	
Vallecitos Creek ⏚	282	37.36 N 121.53 W	
Vallecorsa	66	41.27 N	13.24 E
Valle Crucis Abbey ⬩¹	42	52.59 N	3.12 W
Valle d'Aosta ⏚⁴	62	45.45 N	7.25 E
Valle de Bravo	234	19.11 N 100.08 W	
Valle de Guadalupe	234	21.00 N 102.37 W	
Valle de Guanape	246	9.54 N	65.41 W
Valle de Juárez	234	19.53 N 102.51 W	
Valle de la Pascua	246	9.13 N	66.00 W
Valle del Cauca ⏚⁵	246	3.45 N	76.30 W
Valle de Olivos	232	27.12 N 106.17 W	
Valle de San José	234	23.20 N	98.24 W
Valle de Santiago	234	20.23 N 101.12 W	
Valle de Zaragoza	232	27.25 N 105.49 W	
Valle di Cadore	64	46.24 N	12.20 E
Valle di Sotto	64	46.25 N	10.21 E
Valledolmo	70	37.45 N	13.49 E
Valledupar	246	10.29 N	73.15 W
Valle Edén	252	31.50 S	56.09 W
Vallefiorita	68	38.46 N	16.27 E
Vallegrande	248	18.29 S	64.06 W
Valle Hermoso, Arg.	252	31.07 S	64.26 W
Valle Hermoso, Méx.	196	25.39 N	97.52 W
Vallehermoso, Pil.	116	10.20 N 123.19 E	
Vallejo	226	38.06 N 122.15 W	
Valle Lomellina	62	45.09 N	8.37 E
Vallelunga Pratameno	70	37.41 N	13.50 E
Valle Mosso	62	45.38 N	8.09 E
Vällen ⚫⁸	40	60.03 N	18.20 E
Vallenar	252	28.35 S	70.46 W
Vallendar	56	50.24 N	7.37 E
Vallensbæk	41	55.38 N	12.22 E
Vallentuna	40	59.32 N	18.05 E
Vallepietra	66	41.55 N	13.14 E
Valleraugue	62	44.05 N	3.38 E
Valle Redonda	204	32.31 N 116.46 W	
Vallerotonda	71	39.22 N	8.48 E
Valleroy	66	41.31 N	13.55 E
Valles	56	49.12 N	5.55 E
Valles → Ciudad de Valles	234	21.59 N	99.01 W
Valles Caldera ⏚⁶	200	35.52 N 106.33 W	
Vallet	32	47.10 N	1.16 W
Valletta	36	35.54 N	14.31 E
Valley, Al., U.S.	194	32.49 N	85.11 W
Valley, Ne., U.S.	186	41.18 N	96.20 W
Valley, Wa., U.S.	182	48.10 N 117.43 W	
Valley ⏚	184	51.21 N	99.55 W
Valley Bend	188	38.46 N	79.56 W
Valley Center, Ca., U.S.	204	33.13 N 117.02 W	
Valley Center, Ks., U.S.	198	37.50 N	97.22 W
Valley City, N.D., U.S.	198	46.55 N	97.59 W
Valley City, Oh., U.S.	214	41.14 N	81.56 W
Valley Cottage	210	41.07 N	73.57 W
Valley Creek ⏚, Pa., U.S.	285	40.06 N	75.28 W
Valley Creek ⏚, Tx., U.S.	285	39.58 N	75.40 W
Valleydale	280	34.06 N 117.56 W	
Valley Falls, Ks., U.S.	198	39.20 N	95.27 W
Valley Falls, N.Y., U.S.			
Valley Falls, R.I., U.S.	207	41.54 N	71.23 W
Valley Farms	182	32.59 N 111.36 W	
Valleyfield	186	49.08 N	53.37 W
Valley Forge	208	40.05 N	75.28 W
Valley Forge Estates	285	40.05 N	75.26 W
Valley Forge National Historical Park ◆	208	40.06 N	75.27 W
Valley Grove	214	40.05 N	80.34 W
Valley Head, Al., U.S.	194	34.34 N	85.36 W
Valley Head, W.V., U.S.	188	38.32 N	80.02 W
Valley Home	226	37.50 N 120.55 W	
Valley Mede	284b	39.17 N	76.50 W
Valley Mills	222	31.39 N	97.28 W
Valley of Desolation National Monument ◆	158	32.17 S	24.30 E
Valley of Fire State Park ◆	204	36.26 N 114.30 W	
Valley of the Kings ⬩	140	25.41 S	32.37 E
Valley Park	219	38.32 N	90.29 W
Valley Plaza ⚫⁹	280	34.11 N 118.24 W	
Valley Springs, Ca., U.S.	226	38.12 N 120.50 W	
Valley Springs, S.D., U.S.	198	43.34 N	96.28 W
Valley Station	194	38.06 N	85.52 W
Valley Stream	210	40.39 N	73.42 W
Valley Stream ⏚	285	40.39 N	73.45 W
Valley Stream State Park ◆	285	40.41 N	73.42 W
Valleyview, Ab., Can.	182	55.04 N 117.17 W	
Valley View, Il., U.S.	216	41.50 N	88.03 W
Valley View, Oh., U.S.	279a	41.23 N	81.37 W
Valley View, Pa., U.S.	210	40.38 N	76.32 W
Valley View, Tx., U.S.	196	33.29 N	97.10 W
Valley View Park	234	34.13 N 117.20 W	
Vallgrund I	26	63.12 N	21.14 E
Valliant	196	34.00 N	95.05 W
Valli del Pasubio	64	45.41 N	11.15 E
Vallières	34	41.41 N	1.20 W
Vallimanca, Arroyo ⏚	252	35.40 S	60.02 W
Vallio	266d	41.23 N	10.23 E
Vallirana	266d	41.23 N	1.56 E
Vallo	41	55.24 N	12.15 E
Vallo della Lucania	68	40.14 N	15.16 E
Valloire	62	45.10 N	6.26 E
Vallombrosa	64	43.44 N	11.32 E
Vallon-Pont-d'Arc	62	44.24 N	4.24 E
Vallorbe	58	46.43 N	6.22 E
Vallorcine	62	46.02 N	6.56 E
Vallouise	62	44.51 N	6.29 E
Valtromanes	266d	41.32 N	2.18 E
Valls	34	41.17 N	1.15 E
Valluga ⋀	64	47.09 N	10.12 E
Vallvidrera ⚫⁸	266d	41.25 N	2.07 E
Vallvidrera, Riera de ⏚	266d	41.25 N	2.01 E
Val-Maribel	184	49.14 N 107.44 W	
Valmaseda	34	43.12 N	3.12 W
Valmeyer	219	38.17 N	90.18 W
Valmiera	76	57.33 N	25.24 E
Valmondois	261	49.06 N	2.11 E
Valmont	50	49.44 N	0.31 E
Valmontone	66	41.46 N	12.57 E
Valmy	261	49.05 N	4.46 E

Name	Page	Lat.°′	Long.°′
Valognes	32	49.31 N	1.28 W
Valois	210	43.20 N	76.53 W
Valois, Baie de ⊂	275a	45.26 N	73.47 W
Valok	78	45.47 N	34.57 E
Valona → Vlorë	38	40.27 N	19.30 E
Valongo	34	41.11 N	8.30 W
Valoria la Buena	34	41.48 N	4.32 W
Valpäarai	122	10.22 N	76.58 E
Valparaíso, Bra.	255	21.13 S	50.51 W
Valparaíso, Chile	252	33.02 S	71.38 W
Valparaíso, Méx.	234	22.46 N 103.34 W	
Valparaiso, Fl., U.S.	194	30.30 N	86.29 W
Valparaiso, In., U.S.	216	41.28 N	87.03 W
Valparaiso, Ne., U.S.	198	41.04 N	96.49 W
Valparaíso ⏚⁴	252	32.45 S	71.20 W
Valparaíso ⏚	234	22.33 N 103.39 W	
Valpelline V	62	45.50 N	7.25 E
Valpolicella ⚫¹	64	45.25 N	10.52 E
Valprato Soana	62	45.31 N	7.33 E
Valréas	62	44.23 N	4.59 E
Valrico	220	27.57 N	82.16 W
Val Roveto V	66	41.52 N	13.30 E
Vals, Tanjung ‣	164	8.26 S 137.38 E	
Val-Saint-Michel	206	46.52 N	71.27 W
Valsbaai ⊂	158	34.12 S	18.40 E
Valsequillo, Presa ⊜¹	234	18.55 N	98.10 W
Valserine ⏚	58	46.06 N	5.50 E
Valserrhein ⏚	58	46.42 N	9.10 E
Valsertal V	58	47.01 N	11.30 E
Valsetz	202	44.50 N 123.39 W	
Valsinni	68	40.10 N	16.26 E
Valsjöbyn	26	64.04 N	14.08 E
Valskog	40	59.27 N	15.57 E
Vals-les-Bains	62	44.40 N	4.22 E
Vals Platz	58	46.37 N	9.11 E
Vals-Près-le-Puy	62	45.01 N	3.52 E
Valstagna	64	45.51 N	11.39 E
Val-Suzon ⏚	58	47.25 N	4.54 E
Valtellina V	64	46.11 N	9.55 E
Valthermond	52	52.53 N	6.59 E
Valtice	61	48.44 N	16.45 E
Valtellinilla	234	20.32 N 101.08 W	
Valtimo	26	63.40 N	28.48 E
Valtorta	58	45.59 N	9.32 E
Valtournanche	62	45.53 N	7.37 E
Valujec	76	52.46 N	33.23 E
Valuevo	265b	55.35 N	37.21 E
Valujevka	80	46.44 N	43.43 E
Valujevo	265b	55.35 N	37.21 E
Valuyki	78	50.13 N	38.08 E
Valvason	64	45.59 N	12.52 E
Valverde	148	27.48 N	17.55 W
Valverde del Camino	34	37.34 N	6.45 W
Val Verde Park	228	34.27 N 118.40 W	
Valyermo	228	34.26 N 117.50 W	
Van, Saun Mill Brook ⏚	276	7.27 S	14.17 E
Vamdrup	41	55.25 N	9.17 E
Vämhus	26	61.08 N	14.28 E
Vamizi, Ilha I	154	11.02 S	40.40 E
Vammala	26	61.20 N	22.54 E
Vamori Wash V	200	31.57 N 112.21 W	
Van, Tür.	128	38.28 N	43.20 E
Van, Ar., U.S.	214	41.19 N	79.40 W
Van, Tx., U.S.	222	32.31 N	95.38 W
Van ⊐ ²	128	39.00 N	43.45 E
Vanajavesi ⊜	26	61.09 N	24.15 E
Vanak ⚫⁸	267d	35.45 N	51.23 E
Van Alstyne	196	33.25 N	96.34 W
Vanapa ⏚	164	9.05 S 147.10 E	
Vanault-les-Dames	56	48.51 N	4.46 E
Vanavana I	14	20.47 S 139.09 W	
Vanavara	74	60.22 N 102.16 E	
Van Buren, Ar., U.S.	222	29.01 N	94.20 W
Van Buren, In., U.S.	216	40.37 N	85.30 W
Van Buren, Me., U.S.	186	47.09 N	67.56 W
Van Buren, Mo., U.S.	216	36.59 N	91.00 W
Van Buren, Oh., U.S.	216	41.08 N	83.38 W
Van Buren ⏚²	216	42.14 N	86.04 W
Van Buren Point ‣	214	42.27 N	79.25 W
Vanč ⏚	85	38.23 N	71.26 E
Vanč ⏚	85	38.18 N	71.19 E
Vance Air Force Base ✈	196	36.21 N	97.55 W
Vanceboro	188	45.33 N	67.25 W
Vanceburg	218	38.35 N	83.19 W
Vancleave	194	30.32 N	88.41 W
Van Cortland Park ⚫	276	40.54 N	73.53 W
Van Cortlandtville	276	41.19 N	73.54 W
Vancouver, B.C., Can.	182	49.16 N 123.07 W	
Vancouver, Wa., U.S.	224	45.38 N 122.39 W	
Vancouver, Cape ‣, Austl.	162	35.01 S 118.12 E	
Vancouver, Cape ‣, Ak., U.S.	180	60.33 N 165.27 W	
Vancouver, Mount ⋀	180	60.20 N 139.40 W	
Vancouver International Airport ✈	224	49.39 N 123.26 W	
Vancouver Island I	182	49.45 N 126.00 W	
Vancouver Island Ranges ⋀	182	49.25 N 125.25 W	
Van Daalen ⏚	164	3.05 S 138.09 E	
Vandalia, Il., U.S.	219	38.57 N	89.05 W
Vandalia, Mi., U.S.	216	41.55 N	85.55 W
Vandalia, Mo., U.S.	216	39.18 N	91.29 W
Vandalia, Oh., U.S.	218	39.53 N	84.11 W
Vandalia Lake ⊜¹	219	39.01 N	89.09 W
Vandam	84	40.57 N	47.57 E
Vandanävasi	122	12.30 N	79.37 E
Vanderbeerckhove Lake ⊜	184	57.02 N 101.25 W	
Vandel	41	55.43 N	9.13 E
Vandenberg Air Force Base ✈	204	34.43 N 120.28 W	
Van den Bosch, Tanjung ‣	164	4.06 S 132.55 E	
Vandenesse	58	47.13 N	4.37 E
Vanderbijlpark	158	26.42 S	27.54 E
Vanderbilt, Mi., U.S.	216	45.08 N	84.39 W
Vanderbilt, Tx., U.S.	196	28.49 N	96.37 W
Vanderbilt Mansion National Historic Site ⬩	210	41.47 N	73.56 W
Vanderbilt Museum ⚫	276	40.54 N	73.22 W
Vandercook Lake	216	42.11 N	84.23 W
Vandergrift	214	40.36 N	79.33 W
Vanderhoof	182	54.01 N 124.01 W	
Vanderlin Island I	164	15.44 S 137.02 E	
Vandervoort	194	34.22 N	94.21 W
Van Diemen, Cape ‣, Austl.	164	11.10 S 130.23 E	
Van Diemen, Cape ‣, Austl.	164	16.31 S 139.41 E	
Van Diemen Gulf ⊂	164	11.50 S 132.00 E	
Vandling	210	41.33 N	75.29 W
Vandoeuvre-lès-Nancy	58	48.39 N	6.11 E
Vandoies (Vintl)	64	46.49 N	11.43 E
Vändra	76	58.39 N	25.02 E
Van Duzen ⏚	204	40.33 N 124.08 W	
Vändykpark	273d	26.16 S	28.19 E
Vandžiogala	76	55.07 N	24.01 E
Vanegas	234	23.51 N 100.52 W	
Vänern ⊜	26	58.55 N	13.30 E
Vänersborg	26	58.22 N	12.19 E
Van Etten	210	42.12 N	76.33 W
Vang, Mount ⋀	182	73.58 S	63.89 E
Vanga	154	4.39 S	39.13 E
Vängaindrano	157b	23.21 S	47.36 E
Van Gölü ⊜²	128	38.33 N	42.46 E
Vangsnes	26	61.11 N	6.38 E
Vanguard	184	49.55 N 107.20 W	
Vangunu, Mount ⋀	175e	8.42 S 158.00 E	

Name	Page	Lat.°′	Long.°′
Vangunu Island I	175e	8.38 S 158.00 E	
Van Hook Arm ⊂	198	47.50 N 102.25 W	
Van Horn	196	31.02 N 104.49 W	
Van Horne	190	42.00 N	92.05 W
Van Hornesville	210	42.54 N	74.50 W
Vani	84	42.06 N	42.30 E
Vanier	212	45.26 N	75.40 W
Vanikolo I	14	11.39 S 166.54 E	
Vanikōy ⚫⁸	267b	41.04 N	29.04 E
Vanimo	164	2.40 S 141.20 E	
Vanino	89	49.05 N 140.15 E	
Vänivilåsa Sågara ⊜¹	122	13.52 N	76.26 E
Väniyambädi	122	12.41 N	78.37 E
Vankalai	122	8.40 N	76.50 E
Vankarem	180	67.51 N 175.50 W	
Vankarem ⏚	180	67.42 N 176.17 W	
Vankarem, laguna ⊂	180	67.40 N 176.00 W	
Vankaremskaja nizmennost' ⏚	180	67.30 N 176.00 W	
Van Kleef Aquarium ⚫	271c	1.18 N 103.51 E	
Vankleek Hill	206	45.31 N	74.39 W
Vanlay	58	48.02 N	4.01 E
Van Lear	192	37.46 N	82.45 W
Vanlue	216	40.58 N	83.28 W
Vanna I	24	70.09 N	19.51 E
Vänndale	194	35.18 N	90.46 W
Vanne ⏚	56	48.12 N	3.16 E
Vanne et du Loing, Aqueduc de ⊟¹	261	48.36 N	2.26 E
Vannes	32	47.39 N	2.46 W
Vannes-sur-Cosson	57	47.43 N	2.13 E
Van Ninh	110	12.42 N 109.14 E	
Van Norman Lakes ⊜¹	228	34.18 N 118.28 W	
Vannovka	85	42.32 N	70.21 E
Van Nuys ⚫⁸	280	34.11 N 118.29 W	
Van Nuys Airport ⚙	280	34.12 N 118.29 W	
Van Nuys-Sherman Oaks War Memorial Park ◆	280	34.10 N 118.27 W	
Vanoi ⏚	64	46.06 N	11.45 E
Vanoise, Massif de la ⋀			
Vanoise, Parc National de la ◆	62	45.20 N	6.40 E
Van Ormer	214	40.41 N	78.30 W
Van Phong, Vung ⊂	110	12.30 N 109.18 E	
Vanport	214	40.41 N	80.20 W
Van Reenen	158	28.22 S	29.24 E
Van Reenen's Plaats	158	30.55 S	21.14 E
Van Rees, Pegunungan ⋀	164	2.35 S 138.15 E	
Vanrhynsdorp	158	31.36 S	18.44 E
Vanrook	166	16.57 S 141.57 E	
Vanryndam ⊐¹	286	26.09 S	28.21 E
Vansant	192	37.13 N	82.05 W
Vansbro	40	60.31 N	14.13 E
Van Sciver Lake ⊜	285	40.09 N	74.48 W
Van Sickle Island I	282	38.04 N 121.53 W	
Vansittart Island I	176	65.50 N	84.00 W
Vansjøn ⊜	40	59.59 N	16.57 E
Vansköp	76	58.56 N	36.52 E
Vanstadensrus	158	29.59 S	27.02 E
Vantaa (Vanda)	26	60.16 N	25.03 E
Vantaa ⏚	26	60.13 N	24.59 E
Vanthali	120	21.29 N	70.20 E
Vanua Lava I	175f	13.48 S 167.28 E	
Vanua Levu I	175g	16.33 S 179.15 E	
Vanua Mbalavu Island I	175f	17.40 S 178.57 W	
Vanuatu ⊐¹, Oc.	14	16.00 S 167.00 E	
Vanuatu ⊐¹, Oc.	175f	16.00 S 167.00 E	
Vanves	261	48.50 N	2.18 E
Van Vleck	222	29.01 N	95.53 W
Van Voorhis	279b	40.10 N	79.58 W
Van Wert	216	40.52 N	84.35 W
Van Wert ⏚⁸	216	40.52 N	84.35 W
Vanwyksdorp	158	33.46 S	21.28 E
Vanwyksvlei	158	30.18 S	21.49 E
Vanzaghello	266b	45.35 N	8.47 E
Vanzandt ⊐⁶	222	32.35 N	95.50 W
Vanzylsrus	158	26.52 S	22.04 E
Vao	175f	22.39 S 167.32 E	
Vapn'arka	78	48.33 N	28.45 E
Vaprio d'Adda	62	45.35 N	9.34 E
Vaqueros Creek ⏚	226	36.16 N 121.20 W	
Var ⊐⁵	62	43.30 N	6.20 E
Var ⏚	62	43.39 N	7.12 E
Vaşcău	34	46.28 N	22.28 E
Vara	26	58.16 N	12.57 E
Vara ⏚	64	44.09 N	9.53 E
Varada ⏚	122	14.55 N	75.40 E
Varades	32	47.23 N	1.02 W
Varages	62	43.36 N	5.58 E
Varaita ⏚	62	44.49 N	7.36 E
Varaita, Valle V	62	44.35 N	7.10 E
Varaklāni	76	56.37 N	26.44 E
Varallo, It.	62	45.49 N	8.15 E
Varallo, It.	266b	45.40 N	8.38 E
Väränäm	180	35.20 N 179.39 E	
Väränasi (Benares)	124	25.20 N	83.00 E
Varandej	74	68.49 N	57.46 E
Varangerfjorden ⊂²	24	70.00 N	30.00 E
Varangerhalvøya ¹	24	70.25 N	29.30 E
Varängeville	58	48.38 N	6.19 E
Varano, Lago Di ⊂	68	41.53 N	15.45 E
Varano de' Melegari	64	44.41 N	10.01 E
Varapodio	68	38.18 N	15.59 E
Varaždin	70	46.18 N	16.21 E
Varazze	62	44.22 N	8.34 E
Varberg	26	57.06 N	12.15 E
Varces	62	45.05 N	5.41 E
Varcissne	84	42.08 N	43.32 E
Vardak ⊐⁸	120	34.15 N	68.00 E
Vardaman	194	33.52 N	89.10 W
Vardar (Axiós) ⏚	38	40.35 N	22.50 E
Varde	26	55.38 N	8.29 E
Varde ⏚	41	55.38 N	8.09 E
Vardenik	84	40.08 N	45.43 E
Vardenikovskaja	84	40.11 N	45.43 E
Vardenskij chrebet ⋀	84	40.08 N	45.27 E
Vardhoúsia Óri ⋀	38	38.44 N	22.07 E
Vardø	24	70.21 N	31.02 E
Varduj ⏚	84	37.01 N	70.47 E
Varegovo	62	45.36 N	9.09 E
Varéna	76	54.13 N	24.34 E
Varengeville-sur-Mer	50	49.55 N	0.59 E
Varennikovskaja	78	45.07 N	37.37 E
Varennes	58	46.19 N	9.17 E
Varennes-en-Argonne	56	49.14 N	5.02 E
Varennes-Jarcy	261	48.41 N	2.34 E
Varennes-Saint-Sauveur	58	46.29 N	5.15 E
Varennes-sur-Allier	62	46.19 N	3.24 E
Vareš	70	44.10 N	18.19 E
Varese	62	45.48 N	8.48 E
Varese, Lago di ⊜	64	45.49 N	8.45 E
Varese Ligure	64	44.22 N	9.36 E
Varfolomejevka	92	44.25 N 134.18 E	
Vårgårda	26	58.02 N	12.49 E
Vargem	255	22.53 S	46.25 W
Vargem, Riacho da ⏚	258	8.42 S 39.09 W	
Vargem Alegre	250	19.32 S 41.59 W	
Vargem do Laje	258	12.08 S 40.44 W	
Vargem Grande, Bra.	250	3.33 S 43.56 W	

Name	Page	Lat.°′	Long.°′
Vargem Grande, Bra.	256	22.59 S	45.17 W
Vargem Grande ⚫⁸	287a	22.59 S	43.29 W
Vargem Grande ⏚	250	22.17 S	45.40 W
Vargem Grande do Sul	256	21.50 S	46.53 W
Varginha	256	21.33 S	45.26 W
Vargón	26	58.22 N	12.22 E
Vargotti	62	44.11 N	8.24 E
Vargträsk ⊜¹	40	59.26 N	15.23 E
Varirata National Park ◆	164	9.20 S 147.20 E	
Varjão	255	17.03 S	49.37 W
Varkallai	122	8.40 N	76.50 E
Varkaus	26	62.19 N	27.55 E
Varkhän ⏚	128	32.55 N	65.30 E
Varlamovo	86	54.38 N	60.40 E
Värmdölandet I	40	59.20 N	18.33 E
Värmeln ⊜	26	59.32 N	12.54 E
Värmland ⏚ ⁴	26	59.48 N	13.03 E
Värmlands Län ⊐ ⁶	26	59.48 N	13.20 E
Värmlandsnäs ‣¹	26	59.00 N	13.10 E
Varna, Blg.	38	43.13 N	27.55 E
Varna (Vahm), It.	64	46.44 N	11.38 E
Varna, S.S.S.R.	86	53.24 N	60.58 E
Varna, N.Y., U.S.	210	42.27 N	76.26 W
Varnamo	26	57.11 N	14.02 E
Varnavino	76	57.24 N	45.04 E
Varnenski zaliv ⊂	38	43.11 N	27.56 E
Varner-Hogg Plantation State Historic Park ◆	222	29.09 N	95.37 W
Varnhem ⬩	26	58.23 N	13.39 E
Varnai	76	55.45 N	22.22 E
Varnsdorf	54	50.52 N	14.40 E
Värö	192	32.51 N	81.04 W
Väröbacken	41	57.16 N	12.11 E
Városliget ⚫¹	264c	47.31 N	19.06 E
Varpaisjärvi	26	63.22 N	27.45 E
Varpan ⊜	40	60.38 N	15.36 E
Varramista ⬩	64	43.39 N	10.42 E
Vars, On., Can.	212	45.21 N	75.21 W
Vars, Fr.	62	44.37 N	6.41 E
Vars, Col de ⋎	62	44.32 N	6.42 E
Värşec	38	43.40 N	9.51 E
Varsi	62	44.49 N	9.51 E
Varsinais-Suomi ⚫¹	26	60.40 N	22.30 E
Vartan	76	57.58 N	27.38 E
Varšava → Warszawa	30	52.15 N	21.00 E
Varsseveld	52	51.57 N	6.28 E
Varto	128	39.10 N	41.28 E
Värtsilä, S.S.S.R.	24	62.11 N	30.41 E
Värtsilä, Suomi	26	62.15 N	30.40 E
Varty Lake ⊜	212	44.23 N	76.48 W
Varuna ⏚	124	25.21 N	83.03 E
Varvarin	38	43.43 N	21.19 E
Varvarovka, S.S.S.R.	78	49.33 N	35.12 E
Varvarovka, S.S.S.R.	80	48.42 N	36.02 E
Varvarovka, S.S.S.R.	83	49.05 N	38.24 E
Varvarovka ⬩	83	49.05 N	38.24 E
Varysburg	210	42.46 N	78.19 W
Várzea, Rio da ⏚	252	27.13 S	53.19 W
Várzea Alegre	250	6.47 S	39.17 W
Várzea da Palma	255	17.36 S	44.44 W
Várzea das Moças ⚫⁸	287a	22.57 S	42.58 W
Várzea de Sintra ⚫⁸	266c	38.49 N	9.23 W
Várzea Grande	248	15.39 S	56.08 W
Varzelão	250	24.34 S	49.26 W
Várzea Paulista	256	23.12 S	46.50 W
Varzi, It.	62	44.49 N	9.12 E
Varzi, S.S.S.R.	86	56.03 N	52.50 E
Varzino	24	68.19 N	38.19 E
Varzob	85	38.46 N	68.49 E
Varzob ⏚	85	38.50 N	68.45 E
Varzuga	24	67.24 N	36.32 E
Varzy	58	47.22 N	3.23 E
Vas ⏚⁶	61	47.10 N	16.55 E
Vas ⏚⁶	64	45.56 N	11.56 E
Vasa → Vaasa	26	63.06 N	21.36 E
Vasai (Bassein)	122	19.21 N	72.48 E
Vasalemma	76	59.14 N	24.18 E
Vāshi ⚫⁸	272c	19.04 N	72.59 E
Vashon	224	47.26 N 122.27 W	
Vashon Heights	224	47.30 N 122.28 W	
Vashon Island I	224	47.24 N 122.27 W	
Vasilevičí	76	52.14 N	29.49 E
Vasiliká	76	64.34 N 178.33 E	
Vasiliškī	76	53.47 N	24.51 E
Vasiljevka, S.S.S.R.	78	52.15 N	31.31 E
Vasiljevka, S.S.S.R.	78	47.26 N	35.16 E
Vasiljevo, S.S.S.R.	80	53.40 N	40.36 E
Vasiljevo, S.S.S.R.	86	55.52 N	48.42 E
Vasiljevskij Moch	76	57.01 N	35.55 E
Vasiljevskoje, S.S.S.R.	80	56.31 N	45.49 E
Vasiljevskoje, S.S.S.R.	86	57.50 N	45.49 E
Vasiľkov	78	50.12 N	30.19 E
Vasiľsursk	86	56.08 N	46.01 E
Vasis	72	47.18 N	23.48 E
Vaskelovo	76	60.25 N	30.27 E
Vaskess Bay ⊂	174o	1.51 N 157.31 W	
Vaskojoki ⏚	24	68.46 N	25.57 E
Vaškovcy	78	48.21 N	25.30 E
Vaslui	72	46.38 N	27.45 E
Vaso	192	29.55 N	82.19 W
Vason	40	60.11 N	15.04 E
Vaso	192	35.15 N	79.16 W

Name	Page	Lat.°′	Long.°′
Vašutino	265b	55.56 N	37.26 E
Vašutkiny ozera ⊜	24	68.06 N	61.18 E
Vašvár	61	47.03 N	16.49 E
Veedersburg	194	40.06 N	87.15 W
Veen	263	51.37 N	6.27 E
Veendam	52	53.06 N	6.58 E
Veenendaal	52	52.02 N	5.34 E
Veenhuizen	52	53.03 N	6.24 E
Veenoord	52	52.42 N	6.50 E
Veere	52	51.34 N	3.40 E
Veert	52	51.33 N	6.17 E
Vefsna ⏚	24	65.50 N	13.12 E
Vega	196	35.15 N 102.26 W	
Vega I	24	65.39 N	11.50 E
Vega, Arroyo de la ⏚	266a	40.31 N	3.33 W
Vega Alta	240m	18.25 N	66.20 W
Vega Baja	240m	18.27 N	66.23 W
Vega Point ‣	181a	51.49 N 177.16 E	
Vegår ⊜	26	58.48 N	8.47 E
Vegesack ⚫⁸	52	53.10 N	8.37 E
Veghel	52	51.37 N	5.33 E
Voglie	266	40.20 N	17.58 E
Vegreville	182	53.30 N 112.03 W	
Veguita	200	34.30 N 106.46 W	
Vehär Lake ⊜¹	272c	19.09 N	72.55 E
Vehlefanz	264a	52.43 N	13.06 E
Vatnejri	24a	65.38 N	23.57 W
Vätti I	40	59.49 N	18.57 E
Veigne	50	47.17 N	0.44 E
Veil, Loch ⊜	46	56.20 N	4.25 W
Veilsdorf	54	50.24 N	10.48 E
Veinte de Noviembre	196	25.47 N	97.33 W
Veinticinco de Agosto	258	34.24 S	56.25 W
Veinticinco de Mayo, Arg.	252	34.35 S	68.33 W
Veinticinco de Mayo, Arg.	252	35.26 S	60.10 W
Veinticinco de Mayo, Ur.	258	34.12 S	56.22 W
Veintiocho de Mayo	246	3.50 S	78.52 W
Veintiocho de Noviembre	254	51.39 S	72.18 W
Veintisiete de Abril	236	10.15 N	85.45 W
Veires	66	42.02 N	12.24 E
Veiros	250	2.25 S	52.10 W
Veisiejai	76	54.06 N	23.42 E
Veitsbronn	56	49.31 N	10.53 E
Veitsch	61	47.35 N	15.30 E
Veitschalpe ⋀	61	47.39 N	15.30 E
Veitshöchheim	56	49.50 N	9.52 E
Vejbystrand	41	56.19 N	12.45 E
Vejdelevka	78	50.09 N	38.27 E
Vejen	41	55.29 N	9.09 E
Vejer de la Frontera	34	36.15 N	5.58 W
Vejlby	41	56.12 N	10.13 E
Vejle	41	55.45 N	9.32 E
Vejle Fjord ⊂	41	55.40 N	9.50 E
Vejprty	54	50.30 N	13.02 E
Vejrhøj ⋀ ²	41	55.47 N	11.24 E
Vejro I	41	55.02 N	11.24 E
Vekšor	24	60.33 N	49.26 E
Vel'a ⏚	264	56.31 N	37.41 E
Veladero, Cerro ⋀	234	16.55 N	99.54 W
Velača	70	44.48 N	16.43 E
Velapåda	272c	18.59 S	73.04 E
Velardeña	232	25.04 N 103.44 W	
Velas	148a	38.41 N	28.13 W
Velas, Cabo ‣	236	10.22 N	85.53 W
Velázquez	258	34.02 S	54.17 W
Velber	56	51.20 N	7.02 E
Velburg	56	49.14 N	11.40 E
Velddrif	158	32.47 S	18.11 E
Velden, B.R.D.	56	49.40 N	11.41 E
Velden, B.R.D.	56	48.22 N	12.16 E
Velden, Öst.	61	46.37 N	14.03 E
Veldhoven	52	51.24 N	5.24 E
Veleben	54	52.41 N	11.27 E
Velebitski Kanal ⊔	70	44.45 N	14.50 E
Velegož	264	54.52 N	37.16 E
Veleka ⏚	38	42.04 N	27.58 E
Velemin	54	50.32 N	13.59 E
Velen	52	51.53 N	6.59 E
Velencei-tó ⊜	30	47.12 N	18.35 E
Velenje	70	46.22 N	15.07 E
Veleš	38	41.43 N	21.46 E
Velešin	61	48.50 N	14.28 E
Velestínon	38	39.23 N	22.45 E
Velet'ma	86	55.20 N	42.25 E
Veleveština	84	41.54 N	44.02 E
Vélez	246	6.01 N	73.41 W
Vélez de la Gomera, Peñón de ‣	34	35.11 N	4.20 W
Vélez-Málaga	34	36.47 N	4.06 W
Vélez Rubio	34	37.39 N	2.04 W
Velgast	54	54.16 N	12.48 E
Vel'gija, Canal do ⏚	287a	22.43 S	43.22 W
Velhas, Rio das ⏚	255	17.13 S	44.49 W
Veličkovo	84	45.43 N	36.16 E
Velika Gorica	70	45.43 N	16.05 E
Velika, S.S.S.R.	180	64.04 N 176.12 E	
Velika, S.S.S.R.	76	57.48 N	28.20 E
Velika ⏚ → Aleksandrovka	78	47.20 N	33.18 E
Velikaja Bagačka	78	49.47 N	33.43 E
Velikaja Beloz'erka	78	47.16 N	34.62 E
Velikaja Danilovka ⚫⁸	265d	50.00 N	36.17 E
Velika Kapela ⋀	70	45.16 N	15.02 E
Velika Morava ⏚	38	44.43 N	21.03 E
Velika Plana	38	44.20 N	21.00 E
Velikaja, S.S.S.R.	180	44.50 N 147.40 E	
Veliki Bečkerek → Zrenjanin	38	45.23 N	20.24 E
Velikije Bor'oznyj	78	51.13 N	30.49 E
Veliki Bor	78	51.30 N	29.34 E
Veliki Burluk	83	49.50 N	37.25 E
Veliki Crljeni	38	44.33 N	20.26 E
Veliki Gradište	38	44.45 N	21.26 E
Velikija, S.S.S.R.	92	58.04 N 159.95 E	
Velika Plana	38	44.33 S	21.09 E
Velikolukskij kanal ⟘	76	55.49 N	21.07 E
Velikij Ust'ug	24	60.46 N	46.18 E
Velikije Luki	76	56.20 N	30.32 E
Velikije Mosty	76	50.05 N	24.09 E
Velikije Soročincy	78	50.01 N	33.58 E
Veliki Glubočok	78	49.41 N	25.50 E
Veliki Vitoróg ⋀	70	44.08 N	17.03 E
Velikoarchangel'skoje	83	47.42 N	37.23 E
Velikoarchangel'skoje	78	47.42 N	37.23 E
Velikoarch-angel'skoje	78	50.51 N	34.03 E
Velico-oko-doje	78	50.51 N	40.46 E
Velikodolinskoje	78	46.21 N	30.35 E
Veliko Gradište	38	44.45 N	21.26 E
Velikoknjažeskoje	83	47.42 N	37.23 E

ESPAÑOL

Nombre	Página	Lat.°′	Long.°′ W = Oeste
Velikoje, ozero ⊜, S.S.S.R.	80	55.13 N	40.10 E
Velikonda Hills ⋏[2]	122	14.45 N	79.10 E
Velikookt'abr'skij	76	57.26 N	33.49 E
Velikoploskoje	78	47.01 N	29.40 E
Velikorusskoje	86	54.39 N	74.38 E
Veliko Târnovo	38	43.04 N	25.39 E
Velikovisočnoje	24	67.16 N	52.01 E
Velikovo	76	59.18 N	42.08 E
Velilla de San Antonio	266a	40.22 N	3.29 W
Veli Lošinj	36	44.31 N	14.30 E
Velimče	78	51.36 N	24.44 E
Vélingara, Sén.	150	15.00 N	14.40 W
Vélingara, Sén.	150	13.09 N	14.07 W
Velingrad	38	42.04 N	24.00 E
Velino ≃	66	42.33 N	12.43 E
Velino, Monte ∧	66	42.09 N	13.23 E
Veli Stol (Hochstuhl) ∧	61	46.26 N	14.10 E
Velìž	76	55.38 N	31.12 E
Velìžany	86	57.34 N	65.49 E
Vélizy-Villacoublay	261	48.47 N	2.10 E
Veljaminovo, S.S.S.R.	82	55.12 N	37.52 E
Veljaminovo, S.S.S.R.	82	55.53 N	36.52 E
Velká Bíteš	30	49.17 N	16.13 E
Vel'ké Kapušany	30	48.33 N	22.04 E
Velké Meziříčí	30	49.21 N	16.00 E
Velké Němčie	61	48.59 N	16.40 E
Velké Pavlovice	61	48.54 N	16.19 E
Velký Bor	60	49.22 N	13.42 E
Velký Šenov	54	51.00 N	14.25 E
Vellach ≃	61	46.35 N	14.29 E
Vella Gulf ⋓	175e	8.00 S	156.50 E
Vella Lavella I	175e	7.45 S	156.40 E
Vellano	66	43.57 N	10.43 E
Vellār ≃	122	11.29 N	79.46 E
Vellberg	56	49.05 N	9.53 E
Vellechevreux-et-Courbenans	58	47.33 N	6.32 E
Velletri	66	41.41 N	12.47 E
Vellinge	41	55.28 N	13.01 E
Vellmar	56	51.21 N	9.28 E
Vellore, On., Can.	275b	43.50 N	79.34 W
Vellore, India	122	12.56 N	79.08 E
Velm	264b	48.03 N	16.27 E
Velma	196	34.27 N	97.40 W
Vel'maj ≃	180	67.26 N	175.28 W
Velmede	56	51.21 N	8.22 E
Velo d'Astico	64	45.43 N	11.23 E
Velp	52	52.00 N	5.59 E
Velp ≃	56	50.58 N	5.05 E
Velpke	54	52.24 N	10.56 E
Velsen	52	52.27 N	4.39 E
Vel'sk	24	61.05 N	42.05 E
Vel't	24	68.03 N	49.55 E
Velten	54	52.41 N	13.10 E
Veltheim	52	52.11 N	8.58 E
Veltrusy	54	50.14 N	14.18 E
Veluwe ◆[1]	52	52.12 N	5.45 E
Veluwemeer ⊜	52	52.22 N	5.38 E
Velva, It.	62	44.16 N	9.33 E
Velva, N.D., U.S.	198	48.03 N	100.55 W
Velvary	54	50.15 N	14.15 E
Vémars	261	49.04 N	2.34 E
Vemdalen	26	62.27 N	13.52 E
Vemmenæs	41	54.59 N	10.40 E
Ven I	41	55.54 N	12.41 E
Venachar, Loch ⊜	46	56.13 N	4.19 W
Venaco	36	42.14 N	9.10 E
Venadillo	246	4.43 N	74.55 W
Venado	234	22.56 N	101.05 W
Venado, Isla I	241r	10.00 N	62.25 W
Venado Tuerto	252	33.45 S	61.58 W
Venafiorita, Aeroporto di ⊠	71	40.53 N	9.30 E
Venafro	66	41.29 N	14.02 E
Venalzio	62	45.09 N	7.01 E
Venâncio Aires	252	29.36 S	52.11 W
Venango	214	41.46 N	80.07 W
Venango □[6]	214	41.24 N	79.50 W
Venanson	62	44.03 N	7.15 E
Venant	261	48.30 N	2.06 E
Venarey-les-Laumes	58	47.32 N	4.26 E
Venaria	62	45.08 N	7.38 E
Venasca	62	44.33 N	7.24 E
Venasque	62	43.59 N	5.09 E
Vence	62	43.43 N	7.07 E
Venceslau Brás	255	23.51 S	49.48 W
Vencimont	56	50.02 N	4.55 E
Venda □[1], Afr.	138	23.00 S	30.30 E
Venda □[1], Afr.	156	23.00 S	30.30 E
Venda Nova	34	41.40 N	7.58 W
Vendargues	62	43.39 N	3.58 E
Vendas Novas	34	38.41 N	8.28 W
Vendée □[5]	32	46.40 N	1.20 W
Vendéen, Bocage ◆[1]	32	46.40 N	1.30 W
Vendel	40	60.10 N	17.36 E
Vendelsö	40	59.12 N	18.12 E
Vendeuvre-sur-Barse	58	48.14 N	4.28 E
Vendičany	78	48.37 N	27.48 E
Vendin-lès-Béthune	50	50.32 N	2.37 E
Vendin-le-Vieil	50	50.28 N	2.52 E
Vendôme	50	47.48 N	1.04 E
Vendsyssel ◆[1]	26	57.20 N	10.00 E
Venecia, C.R.	236	10.22 N	84.17 W
Venecia → Venezia, It.	64	45.27 N	12.21 E
Venedig → Venezia	64	45.27 N	12.21 E
Venedocia	216	40.44 N	84.25 W
Venedy	219	38.24 N	89.39 W
Veneta, Laguna ⊂	64	45.25 N	12.19 E
Venetia	214	40.15 N	80.03 W
Venetian Village	216	42.24 N	88.02 W
Venetie	180	67.01 N	146.25 W
Veneto □[4]	64	45.30 N	11.45 E
Venev	82	54.21 N	38.16 E
Venezia (Venice)	64	45.27 N	12.21 E
Venezia □[4]	64	45.35 N	12.34 E
Venezuela □[1], S.A.	242	8.00 N	66.00 W
Venezuela □[1], S.A.	246	8.00 N	66.00 W
Venezuela, Golfo de ⊂	246	11.30 N	71.00 W
Venezuelan Basin ✢[1]	16	15.00 N	68.00 W
Veng	41	56.07 N	9.53 E
Vengerovka	83	48.43 N	38.24 E
Vengerovo	86	55.41 N	76.45 E
Vengurla	122	15.52 N	73.38 E
Veniaminof, Mount ∧	180	56.13 N	159.18 W
Venice → Venezia, It.	64	45.27 N	12.21 E
Venice, Fl., U.S.	220	27.05 N	82.27 W
Venice, Il., U.S.	219	38.40 N	90.10 W
Venice, La., U.S.	194	29.16 N	89.21 W
Venice, Oh., U.S.	214	41.27 N	82.46 W
Venice, Pa., U.S.	279b	40.19 N	80.14 W
Venice ◆[8]	228	34.00 N	118.29 W
Venice, Gulf of ⊂	64	45.15 N	13.00 E
Venice Gardens	220	27.04 N	82.26 W
Venise → Venezia	64	45.27 N	12.21 E
Vénissieux	62	45.41 N	4.53 E
Venjan	26	60.57 N	13.55 E
Venjansjön ⊜	26	60.54 N	14.00 E
Venkatagiri	122	13.58 N	79.35 E
Venlo	52	51.24 N	6.10 E
Vennesla	26	58.17 N	7.59 E
Vennhausen ◆[8]	263	51.13 N	6.51 E
Venosa	68	40.57 N	15.49 E
Vénosc	62	44.59 N	6.07 E
Venosta, Val V	64	46.40 N	10.35 E
Venoste, Alpi (Ötztaler Alpen) ⋏	64	46.45 N	10.55 E
Venray	52	51.32 N	5.59 E
Vent	64	46.52 N	10.56 E

FRANÇAIS

Nom	Page	Lat.°′	Long.°′ W = Ouest
Vent, Îles du → Windward Islands II	238	13.00 N	61.00 W
Venta ≃	76	57.24 N	21.33 E
Venta, Río de la ≃	234	16.59 N	93.46 W
Ventanas	246	1.23 S	79.25 W
Ventasso, Monte ∧	64	44.23 N	10.17 E
Ventersburg	158	28.09 S	27.08 E
Ventersdorp	158	26.17 S	26.48 E
Venterspos	273d	26.18 S	27.39 E
Venterstad	158	30.47 S	25.48 E
Venticano	68	41.05 N	14.50 E
Ventimiglia	62	43.47 N	7.36 E
Ventimiglia di Sicilia	70	37.55 N	13.34 E
Ventnor	42	50.36 N	1.11 W
Ventnor City	208	39.20 N	74.28 W
Ventotene	66	40.48 N	13.26 E
Ventotene, Isola I	66	40.47 N	13.25 E
Ventoux, Mont ∧	62	44.10 N	5.17 E
Ventry	48	52.08 N	10.22 W
Ventspils	76	57.24 N	21.36 E
Ventuari ≃	246	3.58 N	67.02 W
Ventura (San Buenaventura)	228	34.16 N	119.17 W
Ventura □[6]	228	34.30 N	119.00 W
Ventura ≃	228	34.16 N	119.18 W
Venturina	66	43.02 N	10.36 E
Venus, Fl., U.S.	220	27.04 N	81.21 W
Venus, Pa., U.S.	214	41.22 N	79.29 W
Venus, Tx., U.S.	222	32.26 N	97.06 W
Vénus, Pointe ›	174s	17.29 S	149.29 W
Venus Bay ⊂	169	38.40 S	145.43 E
Venustiano Carranza, Méx.	232	16.21 N	92.33 W
Venustiano Carranza, Méx.	234	19.44 N	103.47 W
Venustiano Carranza, Méx.	234	20.31 N	97.38 W
Venustiano Carranza □[7]	286a	19.27 N	99.06 W
Venustiano Carranza, Presa ⊜[1]	232	27.30 N	100.40 W
Venzone	64	46.20 N	13.09 E
Véore ≃	62	44.49 N	4.49 E
Vép	61	47.14 N	16.44 E
Veprik	78	50.23 N	34.11 E
Vepsovskaja vozvyšennost' ⋏[1]	76	60.20 N	35.15 E
Ver ≃	42	51.42 N	0.20 W
Vera, Arg.	252	29.28 S	60.13 W
Vera, Esp.	34	37.15 N	1.52 W
Vera, Il., U.S.	219	39.02 N	89.07 W
Veracruz, Méx.	200	32.25 N	115.05 W
Vera Cruz, Pa., U.S.	208	40.30 N	75.30 W
Veracruz □[3]	234	19.20 N	96.40 W
Veracruz [Llave]	234	19.12 N	96.08 W
Veraguas □[4]	236	8.30 N	81.00 W
Verano Brianza	266b	45.41 N	9.14 E
Veranópolis	252	28.57 S	51.33 W
Verava	256	23.47 S	47.05 W
Verāval	120	20.54 N	70.22 E
Verba	78	50.17 N	25.37 E
Verbania	58	45.56 N	8.33 E
Verbank	210	41.44 N	73.43 W
Verbeek, Pegunungan ⋏	112	2.35 S	121.25 E
Verberg ◆[8]	263	51.22 N	6.36 E
Verberie	50	49.19 N	2.44 E
Verbicaro	68	39.45 N	15.55 E
Verbier	58	46.06 N	7.13 E
Verbilki	82	56.32 N	37.36 E
Verbinskij	83	47.53 N	40.02 E
Verbl'užka	78	48.23 N	32.54 E
Verbovskij	80	55.32 N	42.00 E
Vercelli	62	45.19 N	8.25 E
Vercelli □[4]	62	45.37 N	8.10 E
Vercel-Villedieu-le-Camp	58	47.11 N	6.24 E
Verch'aja Irmen'	86	54.35 N	82.14 E
Verchazovka	80	50.56 N	48.46 E
Vercheje Talyzino	80	55.06 N	45.49 E
Verchères	206	45.47 N	73.21 W
Verchères □[6]	206	45.45 N	73.20 W
Verchn'ačka	78	48.49 N	30.02 E
Verchn'aja Amga	74	59.30 N	126.08 E
Verchn'aja Angara ≃	88	55.42 N	109.54 E
Verchn'aja Balkarija	84	43.06 N	43.24 E
Verchn'aja Buzinovka	80	49.04 N	43.12 E
Verchn'aja Čebula	86	56.02 N	87.36 E
Verchn'aja Chava	78	51.50 N	39.56 E
Verchn'aja Chila	88	52.06 N	115.54 E
Verchn'aja Chortica	78	47.51 N	35.01 E
Verchn'aja Čuginka	83	48.55 N	39.39 E
Verchn'aja Dobrinka	80	50.46 N	45.03 E
Verchn'aja Gniluša	78	50.16 N	40.23 E
Verchn'aja Grajvoronka	78	51.41 N	37.46 E
Verchn'aja Inta	24	66.00 N	60.20 E
Verchn'aja Maza	80	52.58 N	47.56 E
Verchn'aja Orl'anka	80	53.44 N	51.04 E
Verchn'aja Pyšma	86	56.55 N	60.37 E
Verchn'aja Salda	86	58.02 N	60.33 E
Verchn'aja Serebr'akovka	80	47.21 N	42.14 E
Verchn'aja Sin'ačicha	86	57.59 N	61.40 E
Verchn'aja Sysert'	86	56.26 N	60.46 E
Verchn'aja Tajmyra ≃	74	74.15 N	99.48 E
Verchn'aja Tarka	86	56.37 N	77.30 E
Verchnaja Tereška	80	52.54 N	47.24 E
Verchn'aja Tišanka	78	51.19 N	40.32 E
Verchn'aja Tojma	24	62.13 N	45.00 E
Verchn'aja Troica	76	57.15 N	37.08 E
Verchn'aja Tura	86	58.22 N	59.49 E
Verchn'aja Zaimka	88	55.51 N	110.09 E
Verchn'aja Zima	88	53.48 N	101.47 E
Verchneaks'onovskij	80	48.21 N	42.38 E
Verchneangarskij chrebet ⋏	88	56.20 N	111.30 E
Verchne-Anikin	83	48.09 N	39.59 E
Verchnebakanskij	78	44.52 N	37.39 E
Verchneber'ozovskij	86	50.17 N	82.13 E
Verchnebuzanskij	80	46.38 N	48.02 E
Verchnecaricynskij	80	48.23 N	43.57 E
Verchnedneprovsk	78	48.39 N	34.21 E
Verchnedneprovskij	76	54.59 N	33.21 E
Verchneduvannyj	78	48.20 N	39.48 E
Verchnedvinsk	76	55.47 N	27.56 E
Verchneimbatskoje	74	63.11 N	87.58 E
Verchnejarkejevo	80	55.27 N	54.19 E
Verchneje	78	48.53 N	38.28 E
Verchneje ◆[8]	83	48.53 N	38.28 E
Verchneje Šachlovo	82	55.02 N	37.15 E
Verchneje Sinevidnoje	78	49.06 N	23.34 E
Verchnekarabachskij kanal ≅	84	39.44 N	47.57 E
Verchnemakejevka	78	49.10 N	41.03 E
Verchnemulomskoje vodochranilišče ⊜[1]	24	68.30 N	31.05 E
Verchnesadovoje	78	44.42 N	33.42 E
Verchnesjezžeje	80	52.44 N	51.15 E
Verchnespasskoje	80	52.39 N	41.47 E
Verchne-T'oploje	83	48.51 N	39.26 E
Verchnetulomskij	24	68.38 N	31.45 E
Verchneural'sk	86	53.53 N	59.13 E
Verchneusinskoje	86	52.14 N	93.01 E
Verchnevil'ujsk	74	63.27 N	120.18 E
Verchnevolynskoje	85	40.43 N	68.51 E
Verchnij Amyl	88	53.08 N	94.30 E
Verchnij Avz'an	86	53.32 N	57.33 E
Verchnij Balyklej	80	49.34 N	45.10 E
Verchnij Baskunčak	80	48.14 N	46.44 E
Verchnij Byk	78	50.43 N	41.14 E
Verchnije Dvoriki	82	56.28 N	38.22 E
Verchnije Kigi	86	55.25 N	58.37 E
Verchnije Korobki	80	50.19 N	44.38 E
Verchnije Lipki	80	49.38 N	43.51 E
Verchnije Tatyšly	86	56.17 N	55.52 E
Verchnij Ikorec	78	51.11 N	39.46 E

PORTUGUÊS

Nome	Página	Lat.°′	Long.°′ W = Oeste
Verchnij Karačan	80	51.24 N	41.46 E
Verchnij Krasnyj Pereval	89	46.33 N	134.37 E
Verchnij Kužebar	86	53.22 N	93.15 E
Verchnij Landech	80	56.51 N	42.36 E
Verchnij Leb'ažinskij	80	46.45 N	47.50 E
Verchnij Lomov	80	53.28 N	43.34 E
Verchnij Lomovec	76	52.13 N	38.37 E
Verchnij Mamon	78	50.10 N	40.23 E
Verchnij Most	76	57.31 N	28.50 E
Verchnij Nejvinskij	86	57.17 N	60.09 E
Verchnij Petr'ak	86	57.29 N	77.30 E
Verchnij Rogačik	78	47.14 N	34.21 E
Verchnij Šergol'džin	88	50.12 N	108.20 E
Verchnij Tagil	86	57.22 N	59.56 E
Verchnij Takermen'	80	55.39 N	52.43 E
Verchnij Trojanov Val (Upper Trajan's Wall) ⊥	78	46.35 N	29.00 E
Verchnij Ufalej	86	56.04 N	60.14 E
Verchnij Ul'chun	88	49.34 N	112.32 E
Verchnij Uslon	80	55.47 N	48.57 E
Verchnij Zub, gora ∧	86	53.45 N	89.15 E
Verchnyje Nikul'asy	76	60.25 N	30.45 E
Verchnyj Jenisej (Ulug-Chem) ≃	88	51.47 N	92.00 E
Verchnyj Nagol'čik	83	48.05 N	39.06 E
Verchojansk	74	67.35 N	133.27 E
Verchojanskij chrebet ⋏	74	67.00 N	129.00 E
Vercholensk	88	54.06 N	105.35 E
Verchopuja	24	61.34 N	41.31 E
Verchošižemje	80	58.01 N	49.07 E
Verchososna	78	50.44 N	38.14 E
Verchoturje	86	58.52 N	60.48 E
Verchoturovo	86	58.22 N	95.21 E
Verchovažje	24	60.45 N	42.00 E
Verchovcevo	78	48.29 N	34.14 E
Verchovina	78	48.09 N	24.47 E
Verchovino	76	59.33 N	43.19 E
Verchovje	76	52.49 N	37.14 E
Verchovl'an'	82	55.03 N	38.21 E
Verchozim	80	52.56 N	46.23 E
Verchubinka	86	50.29 N	82.26 E
Verclause	62	44.23 N	5.26 E
Vercors ◆[1]	62	44.57 N	5.25 E
Verdalsøra	26	63.48 N	11.29 E
Verde ≃, Bra.	248	11.54 S	55.48 W
Verde ≃, Bra.	248	13.33 S	58.01 W
Verde ≃, Bra.	250	10.11 S	42.24 W
Verde ≃, Bra.	255	15.07 S	48.40 W
Verde ≃, Bra.	255	17.05 S	46.05 W
Verde ≃, Bra.	255	18.01 S	50.14 W
Verde ≃, Bra.	255	19.11 S	50.44 W
Verde ≃, Bra.	255	19.55 S	49.45 W
Verde ≃, Bra.	255	21.12 S	51.53 W
Verde ≃, Bra.	256	21.38 S	47.03 W
Verde ≃, Bra.	256	21.34 S	45.31 W
Verde ≃, Méx.	234	21.37 N	99.15 W
Verde ≃, Méx.	234	20.42 N	103.14 W
Verde ≃, Para.	252	23.09 S	57.37 W
Verde ≃, S.A.	248	13.59 S	60.24 W
Verde ≃, Az., U.S.	200	33.33 N	111.40 W
Verde, Arroyo ≃, Arg.	254	41.56 S	65.03 W
Verde, Arroyo ≃, Bol.	248	11.25 S	66.20 W
Verde, Costa ⏊[2]	71	39.34 N	8.28 E
Verde Grande ≃	255	14.35 S	43.53 W
Verde Island I	116	13.33 N	121.05 E
Verde Island Passage ⋓	116	13.34 N	120.51 E
Verdello	62	45.36 N	9.37 E
Verden, B.R.D.	52	52.55 N	9.13 E
Verden, Ok., U.S.	196	35.05 N	98.05 W
Verde Pequeno ≃	255	14.48 S	43.31 W
Verdesela, Pinhal da ♠	266c	38.37 N	9.08 W
Verdi	226	39.31 N	119.59 W
Verdigre	198	42.35 N	98.02 W
Verdigre Creek ≃	198	42.42 N	98.03 W
Verdigris ≃	196	35.48 N	95.19 W
Verdinho ≃	255	17.29 S	50.27 W
Verdon	198	40.08 N	95.42 W
Verdon ≃	62	43.43 N	5.46 E
Verdon, Canal du ≅	62	43.43 N	5.57 E
Verdoy	210	42.46 N	73.48 W
Verduga	76	58.46 N	29.12 E
Verdugo Mountains ⋏	280	34.13 N	118.18 W
Verdun, P.Q., Can.	206	45.27 N	73.34 W
Verdun, Fr.	32	43.52 N	1.14 E
Verdun-sur-le-Doubs	58	46.54 N	5.01 E
Verdun-sur-Meuse	56	49.10 N	5.23 E
Verdura ≃	70	37.28 N	13.12 E
Vereb'jo	76	58.41 N	32.42 E
Vereeniging	158	26.38 S	27.57 E
Veregin	184	51.35 N	102.05 W
Vereinigte Arabische Emirate → United Arab Emirates □[1]	128	24.00 N	54.00 E
Vereinigte Königreich → United Kingdom □[1]	28	54.00 N	2.00 W
Vereinigte Staaten → United States □[1]	178	38.00 N	97.00 W
Vereja, S.S.S.R.	82	55.21 N	36.11 E
Vereja, S.S.S.R.	82	55.46 N	39.06 E
Vereja, S.S.S.R.	265b	55.37 N	38.02 E
Veremejki	76	53.46 N	31.15 E
Vereščagino, S.S.S.R.	74	64.14 N	87.37 E
Vereščagino, S.S.S.R.	80	58.05 N	54.40 E
Veresegyház	264c	47.39 N	19.17 E
Veresoč'	78	51.19 N	31.46 E
Veretje	82	54.08 N	36.17 E
Véretz	50	47.22 N	0.48 E
Verga	285	39.52 N	75.10 W
Verga, Cap ›	150	10.12 N	14.27 W
Vergara	252	32.56 S	53.57 W
Vergato	64	44.17 N	11.07 E
Vergel	196	25.39 N	103.32 W
Vergeletto	58	46.14 N	8.36 E
Vergemont Creek ≃	166	24.12 S	143.17 E
Vergennes	188	44.10 N	73.15 W
Verghereto	66	43.47 N	12.00 E
Vergiate	62	45.43 N	8.42 E
Vergons	62	43.55 N	6.35 E
Vergt	32	45.02 N	0.43 E
Vergulevka	83	48.24 N	38.32 E
Verigino	82	56.42 N	38.08 E
Verín	34	41.56 N	7.26 W
Veringenstadt	58	48.11 N	9.12 E
Verin Talin	84	40.23 N	43.53 E
Veriora	76	58.00 N	27.21 E
Veríssimo	255	19.42 S	48.18 W
Verkeerdevlei	158	28.48 S	26.48 E
Verkhneudinsk → Ulan-Ude	88	51.50 N	107.37 E
Verkhniy Ufaley → Verchnij Ufalej	86	56.04 N	60.14 E
Verkhnyaya Salda → Verchn'aja Salda	86	58.02 N	60.33 E
Verkhoyansk → Verchojansk	74	67.35 N	133.27 E
Verkykerskop	158	27.54 S	29.17 E
Verl (Senne I)	52	51.53 N	8.31 E
Vermaaklikheid	158	34.19 S	21.01 E
Vermaas	158	26.30 S	25.59 E
Vermand	50	49.52 N	3.09 E
Vermejo ≃	196	36.30 N	104.33 W
Vermelho ≃, Bra.	250	9.16 S	47.23 W
Vermelho ≃, Bra.	250	7.44 S	47.17 W
Vermelho ≃, Bra.	250	5.33 S	49.14 W
Vermelho ≃, Bra.	255	14.54 S	51.06 W
Vermenton	50	47.40 N	3.44 E
Vermette Lake ⊜	184	55.40 N	109.05 W

Vermezzo	266b	45.24 N	8.59 E
Vermiglio	64	46.18 N	10.42 E
Vermilion, Ab., Can.	182	53.22 N	110.51 W
Vermilion, Oh., U.S.	214	41.25 N	82.21 W
Vermilion □[6]	216	40.08 N	87.37 W
Vermilion ≃, Ab., Can.	184	53.44 N	110.18 W
Vermilion ≃, On., Can.	190	46.16 N	81.41 W
Vermilion ≃, Il., U.S.	216	41.19 N	89.04 W
Vermilion ≃, La., U.S.	194	29.46 N	92.09 W
Vermilion ≃, Mn., U.S.	190	48.16 N	92.30 W
Vermilion ≃, Oh., U.S.	214	41.26 N	82.22 W
Vermilion, Middle Fork ≃	216	40.12 N	87.45 W
Vermilion, North Fork ≃, Il., U.S.	216	40.49 N	88.30 W
Vermilion, North Fork ≃, Il., U.S.	216	40.13 N	87.39 W
Vermilion, South Fork ≃	216	40.49 N	88.30 W
Vermilion Bay	184	49.51 N	93.24 W
Vermilion Bay ⊂	194	29.40 N	92.00 W
Vermilion Lake ⊜, On., Can.	184	50.03 N	92.13 W
Vermilion Lake ⊜, Mn., U.S.	190	47.53 N	92.25 W
Vermilion Pass)(	182	51.14 N	116.03 W
Vermillion	198	42.46 N	96.55 W
Vermillion ≃	198	42.44 N	96.53 W
Vermillion, East Fork ≃	198	43.44 N	97.03 W
Vermillion, West Fork ≃	198	43.44 N	97.03 W
Vermillion Bluffs ⏊[4]	200	40.50 N	108.30 W
Vermillion Creek ≃, U.S.	200	40.46 N	108.53 W
Vermillion Creek ≃, Ks., U.S.	198	39.12 N	96.13 W
Vermont, Austl.	274b	37.50 S	145.12 E
Vermont, Il., U.S.	194	40.17 N	90.25 W
Vermont □[3], U.S.	178	43.50 N	72.45 W
Vermont □[3], U.S.	188	43.50 N	72.45 W
Vermontville	216	42.37 N	85.01 W
Vernà, Pizzo di ∧	70	38.01 N	15.15 E
Vernaison	62	45.39 N	4.49 E
Vernal	200	40.27 N	109.31 W
Vernalis	226	37.37 N	121.17 W
Vernante	62	44.15 N	7.32 E
Vernayaz	58	46.08 N	7.02 E
Vernazza	62	44.08 N	9.41 E
Verndale	198	46.24 N	95.01 W
Verne	52	51.41 N	8.34 E
Verner	190	46.25 N	80.07 W
Verneuil	32	48.44 N	0.56 E
Verneuil-L'Étang	261	48.39 N	2.50 E
Verneuil-sur-Avre	50	48.44 N	0.56 E
Verneuil-sur-Seine	50	48.59 N	1.59 E
Verneukpan	158	30.00 S	21.00 E
Verneukpan ≡	158	30.00 S	21.10 E
Vernier	58	46.13 N	6.06 E
Verninge	41	55.18 N	10.13 E
Vernio	66	44.03 N	11.09 E
Vernole	68	40.17 N	18.18 E
Vernon, B.C., Can.	182	50.16 N	119.16 W
Vernon, On., Can.	212	45.10 N	75.28 W
Vernon, Fr.	50	49.05 N	1.29 E
Vernon, Al., U.S.	194	33.45 N	88.06 W
Vernon, Ca., U.S.	280	34.01 N	118.13 W
Vernon, Ct., U.S.	207	41.49 N	72.28 W
Vernon, Fl., U.S.	194	30.37 N	85.42 W
Vernon, Il., U.S.	219	38.48 N	89.05 W
Vernon, In., U.S.	218	38.59 N	85.36 W
Vernon, Mi., U.S.	216	42.56 N	84.02 W
Vernon, N.J., U.S.	210	41.11 N	74.29 W
Vernon, N.Y., U.S.	210	43.05 N	75.32 W
Vernon, Oh., U.S.	214	41.23 N	80.34 W
Vernon, Tx., U.S.	196	34.09 N	99.15 W
Vernon, Ut,. U.S.	200	40.05 N	112.25 W
Vernon, Lake ⊜	212	45.20 N	79.17 W
Vernon Dam ◆[6]	207	42.46 N	72.31 W
Vernon Hills	278	42.13 N	87.58 W
Vernonia	224	45.51 N	123.11 W
Vernon Lake ⊜[1]	194	31.15 N	93.25 W
Vernon River	186	46.12 N	62.50 W
Vernouillet	261	48.58 N	1.59 E
Vernoux-en-Vivarais	62	44.54 N	4.39 E
Verny	56	49.01 N	6.12 E
Vero ≃	34	42.00 N	0.10 E
Vero Beach	220	27.38 N	80.23 W
Véroia	38	40.31 N	22.12 E
Verolanuova	64	45.19 N	10.04 E
Verolavecchia	64	45.19 N	10.03 E
Veroli	66	41.41 N	13.25 E
Verona, On., Can.	212	44.29 N	76.42 W
Verona, It.	64	45.27 N	11.00 E
Verona, Ky., U.S.	218	38.49 N	84.39 W
Verona, Ms., U.S.	194	34.11 N	88.43 W
Verona, N.J., U.S.	276	40.49 N	74.14 W
Verona, N.Y., U.S.	210	43.08 N	75.34 W
Verona, Oh., U.S.	218	39.54 N	84.29 W
Verona, Pa., U.S.	279b	40.30 N	79.50 W
Verona, Wi., U.S.	216	42.59 N	89.31 W
Verona □[4]	64	45.25 N	11.02 E
Verona Beach	210	43.12 N	75.44 W
Verona Beach State Park ♠	210	43.14 N	75.44 W
Verona Park	216	42.21 N	85.09 W
Verónica	258	35.22 S	57.20 W
Verperluda, ostrov I	265a	59.59 N	30.01 E
Verplanck	210	41.15 N	73.58 W
Verran	166	33.51 S	136.18 E
Verrazano-Narrows Bridge ◆[5]	210	40.36 N	74.03 W
Verrès	62	45.40 N	7.42 E
Verrettes	238	19.03 N	72.28 W
Verrey-sous-Salmaise	58	47.26 N	4.40 E
Verrières, Bois de ♠	261	48.45 N	2.15 E
Verrières-le-Buisson	261	48.45 N	2.16 E
Versa ≃	62	44.54 N	8.16 E
Versailles, Fr.	50	48.48 N	2.08 E
Versailles, Il., U.S.	194	39.53 N	90.39 W
Versailles, In., U.S.	218	39.04 N	85.15 W
Versailles, Ky., U.S.	218	38.03 N	84.43 W
Versailles, Mo., U.S.	194	38.25 N	92.50 W
Versailles, N.Y., U.S.	210	42.31 N	78.59 W
Versailles, Oh., U.S.	216	40.13 N	84.29 W
Versailles, Pa., U.S.	279b	40.21 N	79.51 W
Versailles ◆[8]	288	34.38 S	58.31 W
Versailles, Château de ⊥	261	48.48 N	2.07 E
Versailles, Parc de ♠	261	48.49 N	2.06 E
Versailles State Park ♠	218	39.04 N	85.13 W
Verse ≃	263	51.15 N	7.46 E
Versec → Vršac	38	45.07 N	21.18 E
Versestausee ⊜[1]	263	51.11 N	7.41 E
Versien	158	27.05 S	27.52 E
Veršina Tei	86	53.20 N	89.36 E
Veršino-Darasunskij	88	52.20 N	115.32 E
Veršino-Šachtaminskij	88	51.21 N	117.50 E
Versmold	52	52.02 N	8.09 E
Versoix	58	46.16 N	6.10 E
Ver-sur-Launette	261	49.06 N	2.41 E
Vert	261	48.57 N	1.41 E
Vert, Cap ›	150	14.43 N	17.30 W
Vert'ačij	80	48.57 N	43.53 E
Verte, Île I, P.Q., Can.	186	48.02 N	69.26 W
Verte, Île I, P.Q., Can.	275a	45.34 N	73.30 W
Vertedero	240m	18.05 N	66.15 W
Verteillac	32	45.21 N	0.22 E
Vertentes	250	7.54 S	35.59 W
Vertientes	240p	21.16 N	78.09 W
Vertijevka	78	51.10 N	31.51 E

Vertkovo	82	56.07 N	36.25 E
Vert-le-Grand	261	48.34 N	2.22 E
Vert-le-Petit	261	48.33 N	2.22 E
Vertlinskoje	82	56.14 N	36.58 E
Vertou	32	47.10 N	1.29 W
Vertova	62	45.48 N	9.50 E
Vert-Saint-Denis	261	48.34 N	2.37 E
Vertus	50	48.54 N	4.00 E
Verucchio	66	43.59 N	12.25 E
Verulam	158	29.45 S	31.02 E
Verulamium ⊥	260	51.45 N	0.22 W
Verviers	56	50.35 N	5.52 E
Vervins	50	49.50 N	3.54 E
Verwall Gruppe ⋏	58	47.02 N	10.10 E
Verwood	42	50.53 N	1.52 W
Veryan	42	50.13 N	4.54 W
Verzasca ≃	58	46.09 N	8.52 E
Verzegnis	64	46.25 N	12.59 E
Verzenay	50	49.10 N	4.09 E
Verzino	68	39.19 N	16.51 E
Verzuolo	62	44.36 N	7.29 E
Verzy	50	49.09 N	4.10 E
Vesanto	26	62.56 N	26.25 E
Vesava ◆[8]	272c	19.08 N	72.48 E
Vescovato, Fr.	36	42.30 N	9.26 E
Vescovato, It.	64	45.10 N	10.10 E
Vescovo di Squillace, Roccelletta del ⊥	68	38.48 N	16.35 E
Vesdre ≃	56	50.37 N	5.37 E
Veseja	76	53.04 N	27.41 E
Veselí nad Lužnicí	30	49.11 N	14.43 E
Veselí nad Moravou	30	48.58 N	17.22 E
Veselinovo	78	47.21 N	31.14 E
Veselovskoje	86	54.00 N	78.43 E
Veselovskoje vodochranilišče ⊜[1]	80	47.00 N	41.18 E
Vésenaz	58	46.14 N	6.12 E
Vešenskaja	80	49.38 N	41.43 E
Vesgre ≃	50	48.48 N	1.36 E
Vesijärvi ⊜	26	61.06 N	25.32 E
Vesjegonsk	76	58.40 N	37.16 E
Veškajma, S.S.S.R.	80	54.04 N	47.02 E
Veškajma, S.S.S.R.	80	54.03 N	47.08 E
Veški	265b	55.56 N	37.37 E
Vesle ≃	50	49.23 N	3.38 E
Vešn'aki ◆[8]	265b	55.44 N	37.49 E
Ves'olaja Gora	83	48.43 N	39.16 E
Ves'olaja Rošča	86	53.47 N	76.22 E
Vesole, Monte ∧	68	40.24 N	15.10 E
Ves'oloje, S.S.S.R.	78	47.01 N	34.55 E
Ves'oloje, S.S.S.R.	80	50.17 N	45.15 E
Ves'oloje, S.S.S.R.	83	47.10 N	38.45 E
Ves'oloje, S.S.S.R.	85	43.19 N	77.06 E
Ves'olo-Voznesenka	83	47.09 N	38.20 E
Ves'olyj, S.S.S.R.	80	47.06 N	40.45 E
Ves'olyj, S.S.S.R.	83	47.20 N	39.18 E
Ves'olyje Terny	78	48.07 N	33.32 E
Ves'olyj Jar, S.S.S.R.	86	51.18 N	81.07 E
Ves'olyj Jar, S.S.S.R.	89	43.57 N	135.28 E
Ves'olyj Podol, S.S.S.R.	78	49.36 N	33.16 E
Ves'olyj Podol, S.S.S.R.	86	53.31 N	65.54 E
Ves'olyj Pos'olok ◆[8]	265a	59.54 N	30.28 E
Vesoul	58	47.38 N	6.10 E
Vespasiano	255	19.40 S	43.55 W
Vespolate	62	45.21 N	8.40 E
Vesta	236	9.43 N	83.03 W
Vest-Agder □[6]	26	58.30 N	7.10 E
Vestal	210	42.05 N	76.03 W
Vestal Center	210	42.02 N	76.01 W
Vestavia Hills	194	33.26 N	86.46 W
Vestbygd	26	58.06 N	6.35 E
Vesterålen II	24	68.45 N	15.00 E
Vester Egede	41	55.16 N	11.59 E
Vesterø Havn	26	57.18 N	10.56 E
Vester Skerninge	41	55.03 N	10.28 E
Vester Sottrup	41	54.57 N	9.43 E
Vestfjorden ⊂[2]	24	68.08 N	15.00 E
Vestfold □[6]	26	59.15 N	10.10 E
Vestmannaeyjar	24a	63.26 N	20.12 W
Vestone	64	45.42 N	10.24 E
Vestreno	58	46.06 N	9.18 E
Vestsjælland □[6]	41	55.35 N	11.30 E
Vestvågøya I	24	68.15 N	13.50 E
Vésubie ≃	62	43.52 N	7.12 E
Vesubio → Vesuvio ∧[1]	68	40.49 N	14.26 E
Vesuv → Vesuvio ∧[1]	68	40.49 N	14.26 E
Vesuvio (Vesuvius) ∧[1]	68	40.49 N	14.26 E
Vesuvius → Vesuvio ∧[1]	68	40.49 N	14.26 E
Vesuvius Bay	224	48.53 N	123.35 W
Veszprém	30	47.06 N	17.55 E
Veszprém □[6]	30	46.50 N	17.30 E
Vésztő	30	46.55 N	21.16 E
Vet ≃	158	27.40 S	25.40 E
Vetapālem	122	15.47 N	80.19 E
Vetčin	76	52.27 N	28.10 E
Veterans Stadium ♠	285	39.54 N	75.10 W
Vétheuil	50	49.04 N	1.42 E
Vetju	24	62.57 N	50.44 E
Vetka	76	52.33 N	31.10 E
Vetlanda	26	57.26 N	15.04 E
Vetl'anka	80	52.52 N	51.09 E
Vetluga	80	57.51 N	45.47 E
Vetluga ≃	80	56.18 N	46.24 E
Vetlužskij, S.S.S.R.	80	58.23 N	45.26 E
Vetlužskij, S.S.S.R.	80	57.11 N	45.07 E
Vetoškino	80	57.18 N	49.44 E
Vetovo	38	43.42 N	26.16 E
Vetralla	66	42.19 N	12.03 E
Vetren	38	42.16 N	24.03 E
Vetrino	76	55.25 N	28.28 E
Vetriolo	64	46.02 N	11.18 E
Vetrișoaia	38	46.26 N	28.13 E
Větřni	61	48.46 N	14.17 E
Vetschau	54	51.47 N	14.04 E
Vettisfossen ∟	26	61.22 N	7.55 E
Vetto	64	44.29 N	10.20 E
Vettore, Monte ∧	66	42.49 N	13.16 E
Vetulonia	66	42.51 N	10.58 E
Veules-les-Roses	50	49.52 N	0.48 E
Veulettes-sur-Mer	50	49.51 N	0.36 E
Veurne (Furnes)	50	51.04 N	2.40 E
Vevay	218	38.44 N	85.04 W
Vevelstad	24	65.43 N	12.30 E
Veveno, Khawr V	140	6.40 N	32.58 E
Vevey	58	46.28 N	6.51 E
Vex	58	46.13 N	7.24 E
Veyle ≃	58	46.18 N	4.50 E
Veynes	62	44.32 N	5.49 E
Veyrier	62	45.53 N	6.10 E
Vézelay	50	47.28 N	3.44 E
Vézelise	58	48.29 N	6.05 E
Vézénobres	62	44.03 N	4.09 E
Vézère ≃	32	44.53 N	0.53 E
Vezirköprü	130	41.09 N	35.28 E
Vezouze ≃	58	48.35 N	6.29 E
Vezza d'Oglio	64	46.14 N	10.24 E
Vezzana, Cima della ∧	64	46.17 N	11.50 E
Vezzano	64	46.05 N	11.00 E
Vezzano Ligure	64	44.09 N	9.52 E
Viacha	248	16.39 S	68.18 W
Viadana	64	44.56 N	10.31 E
Viadutos	252	27.34 S	52.01 W
Viale	252	31.53 S	60.01 W
Vialonga	266c	38.52 N	9.05 W
Via Mala V	58	46.40 N	9.26 E
Viamão	252	30.05 S	51.02 W
Viamonte	252	33.44 S	63.06 W
Vian	196	35.29 N	94.58 W
Viana	250	3.13 S	45.00 W
Viana, Ilha do I	287a	22.52 S	43.08 W
Viana del Bollo	34	42.11 N	7.06 W
Viana do Alentejo	34	38.20 N	8.00 W
Viana do Castelo	34	41.42 N	8.50 W

Vianden	56	49.57 N	6.11 E
Vianen	52	52.00 N	5.05 E
Viangchan (Vientiane)	110	17.58 N	102.36 E
Viangphoukha	110	20.41 N	101.04 E
Viar ≃	34	37.36 N	5.50 W
Viareggio	64	43.52 N	10.14 E
Viarmes	50	49.08 N	2.22 E
Viatka → Kirov	80	58.38 N	49.42 E
Viaur ≃	32	44.08 N	2.23 E
Vibank	184	50.20 N	103.55 W
Víboras, Arroyo de las ≃	258	33.57 S	58.21 W
Viborg, Dan.	26	56.26 N	9.24 E
Viborg → Vyborg, S.S.S.R.	76	60.42 N	28.45 E
Viborg, S.D., U.S.	198	43.10 N	97.04 W
Viborg □[6]	41	56.18 N	9.27 E
Vibo Valentia	68	38.40 N	16.06 E
Vibraye	50	48.03 N	0.44 E
Viburnum	194	37.42 N	91.08 W
Viby	41	55.33 N	12.02 E
Viby ◆[8]	41	56.07 N	10.10 E
Vic (Vich)	34	41.56 N	2.15 E
Vic, Étang de ⊂	62	43.29 N	3.50 E
Vicálvaro ◆[8]	266a	40.24 N	3.36 W
Vicarello	66	42.10 N	12.12 E
Vicari	70	37.49 N	13.34 E
Vicchio	66	43.56 N	11.28 E
Vicco	192	37.12 N	83.03 W
Vic-en-Bigorre	32	43.23 N	0.03 E
Vicência	250	7.40 S	35.20 W
Vicente, Point ›	280	33.44 N	118.25 W
Vicente Casares	258	34.57 S	58.38 W
Vicente de Carvalho	256	23.56 S	46.19 W
Vicente Guerrero, Méx.	232	30.45 N	116.00 W
Vicente Guerrero, Méx.	234	18.24 N	92.53 W
Vicente Guerrero, Méx.	234	19.08 N	98.10 W
Vicente López	258	34.32 S	58.28 W
Vicente López □[5]	288	34.32 S	58.30 W
Vicente Noble	238	18.23 N	71.11 W
Vicenza	64	45.33 N	11.33 E
Vicenza □[4]	64	45.40 N	11.27 E
Viceroy	184	49.27 N	105.22 W
Vichada □[5]	246	5.00 N	69.30 W
Vichada ≃	246	4.55 N	67.50 W
Vichadero	252	31.48 S	54.43 W
Vichigasta	252	29.29 S	67.31 W
Vichoreva ≃	88	56.47 N	101.22 E
Vichorevka	88	56.12 N	101.09 E
Vichra ≃	76	54.01 N	31.52 E
Vichuga → Vičuga	80	57.13 N	41.56 E
Vichuquén	252	34.53 S	72.00 W
Vichy	32	46.08 N	3.26 E
Vici	196	36.08 N	99.17 W
Vickery	214	41.23 N	82.56 W
Vicksburg, Mi., U.S.	216	42.07 N	85.31 W
Vicksburg, Ms., U.S.	194	32.21 N	90.52 W
Vicksburg, Pa., U.S.	210	40.56 N	76.59 W
Vicksburg National Military Park ♠	194	32.24 N	90.52 W
Vico	36	42.10 N	8.48 E
Vico, Lago di ⊜	66	42.19 N	12.10 E
Vico Canavese	62	45.30 N	7.47 E
Vico del Gargano	68	41.54 N	15.57 E
Vico Equense	68	40.40 N	14.25 E
Vicoforte	62	44.21 N	7.54 E
Vicopisano	66	43.42 N	10.35 E
Viçosa, Bra.	250	9.24 S	36.14 W
Viçosa, Bra.	255	20.45 S	42.53 W
Viçosa do Ceará	250	3.34 S	41.05 W
Vicosoprano	58	46.22 N	9.37 E
Vicovaro	66	42.01 N	12.54 E
Vicq	261	48.49 N	1.50 E
Vic-Sur-Aisne	50	49.24 N	3.07 E
Vic-sur-Cère	32	44.59 N	2.37 E
Vic-sur-Seille	56	48.47 N	6.32 E
Victor, Ca., U.S.	226	38.08 N	121.12 W
Victor, Id., U.S.	202	43.36 N	111.06 W
Victor, Ia., U.S.	190	41.43 N	92.17 W
Victor, Mt., U.S.	202	46.25 N	114.08 W
Victor, N.Y., U.S.	210	42.58 N	77.24 W
Victor, Lac ⊜	186	50.35 N	61.50 W
Victorbur	52	53.29 N	7.20 E
Victor Harbor	168b	35.34 S	138.37 E
Victoria, Arg.	252	32.37 S	60.10 W
Victoria → Vitória, Bra.	255	20.19 S	40.21 W
Victoria, Cam.	152	4.01 N	9.12 E
Victoria, B.C., Can.	224	48.25 N	123.22 W
Victoria, P.E., Can.	186	46.13 N	63.29 W
Victoria, Chile	252	38.13 S	72.20 W
Victoria, Gren.	241k	12.12 N	61.42 W
Victoria, Guinée	150	10.50 N	14.33 W
Victoria (Xianggang), H.K.	271d	22.17 N	114.09 E
Victoria, Malay.	112	5.17 N	115.15 E
Victoria → Ciudad Victoria, Méx.	234	23.44 N	99.08 W
Victoria, Pil.	116	15.35 N	120.41 E
Victoria, Pil.	116	13.12 N	121.15 E
Victoria, Rom.	38	45.45 N	24.41 E
Victoria, Sey.	138	4.38 S	55.27 E
Victoria, Ks., U.S.	198	38.51 N	99.08 W
Victoria, Tx., U.S.	196	28.48 N	97.00 W
Victoria, Va., U.S.	192	36.59 N	78.13 W
Victoria □[3]	166	38.00 S	145.00 E
Victoria □[4]	154	20.54 S	31.21 E
Victoria □[6], On., Can.	212	44.35 N	78.50 W
Victoria □[6], Tx., U.S.	222	28.55 N	97.00 W
Victoria ◆[8]	288	34.28 S	58.31 W
Victoria ≃, Austl.	160	15.12 S	129.43 E
Victoria ≃, Nf., Can.	186	48.45 N	56.40 W
Victoria, Isla I	254	45.18 S	73.58 W
Victoria, Lake ⊜, Afr.	154	1.00 S	33.00 E
Victoria, Lake ⊜, Austl.	166	34.00 S	141.16 E
Victoria, Mount ∧, Mya.	110	21.14 N	93.55 E
Victoria, Mount ∧, Pap. N. Gui.	164	8.55 S	147.35 E
Victoria, Pont ◆[5]	275a	45.29 N	73.32 W
Victoria and Albert Museum ⊎	272c	18.59 N	72.50 E
Victoria Beach	184	50.43 N	96.33 W
Victoria Beach ⏊[2]	273a	6.25 N	3.25 E
Victoria de Durango → Durango	234	24.02 N	104.40 W
Victoria de las Tunas	240p	20.58 N	76.57 W
Victoria Falls	154	17.56 S	25.50 E
Victoria Falls ∟	154	17.55 S	25.51 E
Victoria Falls National Park ♠	154	17.55 S	25.40 E
Victoria Gardens ♠	272c	18.59 N	72.50 E
Victoria Harbour	212	44.45 N	79.46 W
Victoria International Airport ⊠	224	48.39 N	123.26 W
Victoria Island I, N.T., Can.	176	71.00 N	110.00 W
Victoria Island I, Nig.	273a	6.26 N	3.26 E
Victoria Lake ⊜	273d	26.14 S	28.09 E
Victoria Lake ⊜[1]	186	48.18 N	57.30 W
Victoria Land ◆[1]	9	75.00 S	163.00 E
Victoria Lawn Tennis Association Courts ♠	274b	37.51 S	145.02 E
Victoria Memorial Hall ⊎	271c	1.17 N	103.51 E
Victoria Memorial Museum ⊎	272b	22.33 N	88.21 E
Victoria Nile ≃	154	2.14 N	31.26 E
Victoria Park	168a	31.58 S	115.55 E
Victoria Park ♠, H.K.	271d	22.17 N	114.11 E

Symbol	English	Deutsch	Español	Français	Português
≃	River	Fluß	Río	Rivière	Rio
≅	Canal	Kanal	Canal	Canal	Canal
∟	Waterfall, Rapids	Wasserfall, Stromschnellen	Cascada, Rápidos	Chute d'eau, Rapides	Cascata, Rápidos
⋓	Strait	Meeresstraße	Estrecho	Détroit	Estreito
⊂	Bay, Gulf	Bucht, Golf	Bahía, Golfo	Baie, Golfe	Baía, Golfo
⊜	Lake, Lakes	See, Seen	Lago, Lagos	Lac, Lacs	Lago, Lagos
≡	Swamp	Sumpf	Pantano	Marais	Pântano
⍓	Ice Features, Glacier	Eis- und Gletscherformen	Accidentes Glaciales	Formes glaciaires	Acidentes glaciares
⊤	Other Hydrographic Features	Andere Hydrographische Objekte	Otros Elementos Hidrográficos	Autres données hydrographiques	Outros acidentes hidrográficos
✢	Submarine Features	Untermeerische Objekte	Accidentes Submarinos	Formes de relief sous-marin	Acidentes submarinos
□	Political Unit	Politische Einheit	Unidad Politica	Entité politique	Unidade política
⊎	Cultural Institution	Kulturelle Institution	Institución Cultural	Institution culturelle	Institução cultural
⊥	Historical Site	Historische Stätte	Sitio Histórico	Site historique	Sitio histórico
♠	Recreational Site	Erholungs- und Ferienort	Sitio de Recreo	Centre de loisirs	Area de Lazer
⊠	Airport	Flughafen	Aeropuerto	Aéroport	Aeroporto
■	Military Installation	Militäranlage	Instalación Militar	Installation militaire	Instalação militar
◆	Miscellaneous	Verschiedenes	Misceláneo	Divers	Diversos

ENGLISH — Name / Page / Lat.°′ / Long.°′
DEUTSCH — Name / Seite / Breite°′ / Länge°′ E = Ost

Victoria Park ♦, Eng., U.K. **262** 53.23 N 2.34 W
Victoria Peak ∧, Belize **232** 16.48 N 88.37 W
Victoria Peak ∧, B.C., Can. **182** 50.03 N 126.06 W
Victoria Peak ∧, H.K. **271d** 22.17 N 114.08 E
Victoria Peaks ⋏ **116** 9.22 N 118.20 E
Victoria Point **171a** 27.35 S 153.18 E
Victoria Range ⋏, N.Z. **172** 42.09 S 172.08 E
Victoria Range ⋏, Pil. **116** 9.32 N 118.23 E
Victoria River **164** 15.37 S 131.08 E
Victoria River Downs **164** 16.24 S 131.00 E
Victorias **116** 10.54 N 123.05 E
Victoria State Car Club Race Circuit ♦ **274b** 37.45 S 145.11 E
Victoria Station ◆[5], Eng., U.K. **260** 51.29 N 0.09 W
Victoria Station ◆[5], Eng., U.K. **262** 53.29 N 2.15 W
Victoria Strait ʯ **176** 69.15 N 100.30 W
Victoria Terminus ◆[5] **272c** 18.57 N 72.50 E
Victoria University of Manchester υ[2] **262** 53.28 N 2.14 W
Victoriaville **206** 46.03 N 71.57 W
Victoria West **158** 31.25 S 23.04 E
Victorica **252** 36.13 S 65.27 W
Victorino **246** 2.48 N 67.50 W
Victorino de la Plaza **252** 36.36 S 62.40 W
Victor Manuel Bueno **232** 24.20 N 98.58 W
Victorville **228** 34.32 N 117.17 W
Victory, Mount ∧ **164** 9.10 S 149.05 E
Victory Gardens **276** 40.52 N 74.32 W
Victory Heights **214** 41.22 N 79.46 W
Victory Hills **279b** 40.11 N 79.53 W
Victory Mills **210** 43.05 N 73.36 W
Victory Monument ⊥ **269a** 13.46 N 100.33 E
Vičuga **80** 57.13 N 41.56 E
Vicuña **252** 30.02 S 70.44 W
Vicuña Mackenna **252** 33.54 S 64.23 W
Vidal, Kaap › **158** 28.09 S 32.33 E
Vidalia, Ga., U.S. **192** 32.13 N 82.24 W
Vidalia, La., U.S. **194** 31.33 N 91.25 W
Vidal Ramos **252** 27.23 S 49.22 W
Vidauban **62** 43.26 N 6.26 E
Videbæk **26** 56.05 N 8.38 E
Videira **252** 27.00 S 51.08 W
Videle **38** 44.16 N 25.31 E
Vidigueira **34** 38.13 N 7.48 W
Vidim, Česko. **54** 50.28 N 14.31 E
Vidim, S.S.S.R. **88** 56.29 N 103.09 E
Vidin **38** 43.59 N 22.52 E
Vidisha **124** 23.32 N 77.49 E
Vidlica **24** 61.10 N 32.21 E
Vidnoje **82** 55.34 N 37.41 E
Vidogošči **82** 56.42 N 36.23 E
Vidor **194** 30.07 N 94.00 W
Vidos ≃ **267b** 40.58 N 28.53 E
Vidöstern ⊜ **26** 57.04 N 14.01 E
Vidourle ≃ **62** 43.32 N 4.08 E
Vidra, Rom. **38** 44.16 N 26.11 E
Vidra, Rom. **38** 45.55 N 26.54 E
Vidsel **24** 65.51 N 20.24 E
Vidzeme □[9] **76** 57.10 N 25.30 E
Vidzy **76** 55.24 N 26.38 E
Vie ≃ **50** 49.05 N 0.04 E
Viecht **60** 48.30 N 12.04 E
Viechtach **60** 49.05 N 12.53 E
Viedma **254** 40.48 S 63.00 W
Viedma, Lago ⊜ **254** 49.35 S 72.35 W
Viehberg ∧ **61** 48.33 N 14.37 E
Viehhausen **60** 48.59 N 11.58 E
Vieil Armand ♦ **58** 47.52 N 7.10 E
Vieillard, Lac du ⊜ **190** 47.23 N 78.02 W
Vieille Case **240d** 15.36 N 61.24 W
Vieira do Minho **34** 41.39 N 8.09 W
Viejo ≃ **236** 12.28 N 86.21 W
Viejo, Cerro ∧ **246** 4.49 S 79.27 W
Viekšniai **76** 56.16 N 22.31 E
Vielank **54** 53.15 N 11.08 E
Viella **34** 42.42 N 0.48 E
Vielle-Eglise-en-Yvelines **261** 48.40 N 1.53 E
Vielsalm **56** 50.17 N 5.55 E
Viels-Maisons **50** 48.54 N 3.24 E
Viena → Vienne ≃ **32** 47.13 N 0.05 E
Vienenburg **54** 51.57 N 10.34 E
Vienna, On., Can. **212** 42.41 N 80.48 W
Vienna → Wien, Öst. **61** 48.13 N 16.20 E
Vienna, Ga., U.S. **192** 32.05 N 83.47 W
Vienna, Il., U.S. **194** 37.25 N 88.54 W
Vienna, In., U.S. **218** 38.39 N 85.46 W
Vienna, Md., U.S. **208** 38.29 N 75.49 W
Vienna, Mo., U.S. **194** 38.11 N 91.56 W
Vienna, N.J., U.S. **210** 40.52 N 74.53 W
Vienna, Oh., U.S. **214** 41.14 N 80.40 W
Vienna, S.D., U.S. **198** 44.42 N 97.30 W
Vienna, Va., U.S. **208** 38.54 N 77.15 W
Vienna, Va., U.S. **208** 38.29 N 75.49 W
Vienna, W.V., U.S. **188** 39.19 N 81.32 W
Vienne, Fr. **62** 45.31 N 4.52 E
Vienne → Wien, Öst. **61** 48.13 N 16.20 E
Vienne □[5] **32** 46.35 N 0.30 E
Vienne ≃ **32** 47.13 N 0.05 E
Vienne-en-Arthies **261** 49.04 N 1.44 E
Vienne-le-Château **56** 49.11 N 4.53 E
Vientiane → Viangchan **110** 17.58 N 102.36 E
Vientos, Paso de los → Windward Passage ʯ **238** 20.00 N 73.50 W
Vieques **240m** 18.09 N 65.27 W
Vieques, Isla de I **240m** 18.08 N 65.25 W
Vieques, Pasaje de ʯ **240m** 18.11 N 65.37 W
Vieques, Sonda de ʯ **240m** 18.15 N 65.23 W
Vière ≃ **56** 48.46 N 4.41 E
Viereck **54** 53.32 N 14.02 E
Vieremä **26** 63.45 N 27.01 E
Vierfontein **158** 27.03 S 26.46 E
Vierhouten **52** 52.20 N 5.50 E
Vieringhausen ◆[8] **263** 51.11 N 7.10 E
Vierlande ◆[1] **52** 53.26 N 10.14 E
Viernau **54** 50.40 N 10.32 E
Viernheim **56** 49.32 N 8.34 E
Vierraden **54** 53.06 N 14.17 E
Viersen **56** 51.15 N 6.23 E
Vierumäki **26** 61.06 N 25.57 E
Vierwaldstättersee ⊜ **58** 47.00 N 8.28 E
Vierzehnheiligen υ[1] **56** 50.08 N 11.02 E
Vierzon **50** 47.13 N 2.05 E
Viesca **232** 25.21 N 102.48 W
Viesecke **54** 53.01 N 12.01 E
Vieselbach **54** 51.00 N 11.08 E
Viesīte **76** 56.21 N 25.33 E
Vieste **68** 41.53 N 16.10 E
Vietgest **54** 53.45 N 12.20 E
Vietnam □[1], Asia **108** 16.00 N 108.00 E
Vietnam □[1], Asia **110** 16.00 N 108.00 E
Vietnam Veterans Memorial ⊥ **284c** 38.53 N 77.03 W
Vietri di Potenza **68** 40.36 N 15.30 E
Vietri sul Mare **68** 40.40 N 14.44 E
Viet Tri **110** 21.18 N 105.26 E
Vietz → Witnica **30** 52.40 N 14.55 E
Vieux-Condé **50** 50.27 N 3.34 E
Vieux-Ferette **58** 47.30 N 7.18 E
Vieux-Fort, P.Q., Can. **186** 51.26 N 57.49 W
Vieux-Fort, Guad. **241o** 15.57 N 61.43 W
Vieux Fort, St. Luc. **241f** 13.44 N 60.57 W
Vieux-Fort, Pointe du › **241o** 15.57 N 61.43 W
Vieux Fort Bay ⊂ **241f** 13.44 N 60.58 W
Vieux-Habitants **241o** 16.04 N 61.46 W
Vieux-Thann **58** 47.48 N 7.08 E
Vievis **76** 54.46 N 24.48 E
View Park **280** 34.00 N 118.20 W
Vieytes **258** 35.16 S 57.35 W
Vif **62** 45.03 N 5.40 E
Vig **41** 55.51 N 11.36 E
Viga ≃ **76** 59.14 N 43.41 E
Vigala **76** 58.43 N 24.22 E
Vigan **116** 17.34 N 120.23 E
Vigarano Mainarda **64** 44.50 N 11.30 E
Vigatto **64** 44.43 N 10.20 E
Vigeland **26** 58.05 N 7.18 E
Vigentino ◆[8] **266b** 45.25 N 9.11 E
Vigersted **41** 55.29 N 11.54 E
Vigese, Monte ∧ **64** 44.12 N 11.06 E
Vigésima Quinta de Abril, Ponte ◆[5] **266c** 38.41 N 9.11 W
Vigevano **62** 45.19 N 8.51 E
Viggianello **68** 39.58 N 16.05 E
Viggiano **68** 40.20 N 15.54 E
Viggiù **62** 45.52 N 8.54 E
Vigia **250** 0.48 S 48.08 W
Vigie Airport ⊠ **241f** 14.01 N 60.59 W
Vignacourt **50** 50.01 N 2.12 E
Vignale **62** 45.01 N 8.24 E
Vignanello **66** 42.23 N 12.17 E
Vigneulles-lès-Hattonchâtel **56** 48.59 N 5.43 E
Vigneux-sur-Seine **261** 48.42 N 2.25 E
Vignola **64** 44.29 N 11.00 E
Vignory **58** 48.17 N 5.06 E
Vignot **56** 48.46 N 5.36 E
Vigny **261** 49.05 N 1.56 E
Vigo **34** 42.14 N 8.43 W
Vigo, Ría de ⊂[1] **34** 42.15 N 8.45 W
Vigodarzere **64** 45.27 N 11.53 E
Vigo di Fassa **64** 46.25 N 11.40 E
Vigolzone **62** 44.55 N 9.40 E
Vigone **62** 44.51 N 7.30 E
Vigonovo **64** 45.23 N 12.00 E
Vigo-Rendena **64** 46.05 N 10.43 E
Vigrestad **26** 58.34 N 5.42 E
Viguzzolo **62** 44.54 N 8.55 E
Vigy **56** 49.12 N 6.18 E
Vihanti **26** 64.29 N 25.00 E
Vihāri **123** 30.02 N 72.21 E
Vihiers **32** 47.09 N 0.32 W
Vihowa **123** 31.08 N 70.30 E
Vihren ∧ **38** 41.46 N 23.24 E
Vihti **26** 60.25 N 24.20 E
Viiala **26** 61.13 N 23.47 E
Viinijärvi **26** 62.39 N 29.14 E
Viinijärvi ⊜ **26** 62.44 N 29.17 E
Viipuri → Vyborg **76** 60.42 N 28.45 E
Viitasaari **26** 63.04 N 25.52 E
Viivikonna **76** 59.19 N 27.42 E
Vijāpur **120** 23.34 N 72.45 E
Vijayawāda **122** 16.31 N 80.37 E
Vijosë (Aóös) ≃ **38** 40.37 N 19.20 E
Vik **40** 59.44 N 17.28 E
Vik ⊥ **40** 59.44 N 17.27 E
Vika **40** 60.31 N 15.42 E
Vikajärvi **24** 66.37 N 26.12 E
Vikārābād **122** 17.20 N 77.54 E
Vikbolandet ›[1] **40** 58.32 N 16.40 E
Vikeke **112** 8.52 S 126.22 E
Viken **41** 56.09 N 12.34 E
Viken ⊜ **26** 58.39 N 14.20 E
Vikern ⊜ **40** 59.30 N 14.55 E
Vikersund **26** 59.59 N 10.02 E
Vikhroli ◆[8] **272c** 19.07 N 72.56 E
Viking **182** 53.06 N 111.46 W
Viking Village **218** 39.05 N 84.18 W
Vikmanshyttan **40** 60.17 N 15.49 E
Vikna **24** 64.57 N 10.58 E
Vikna I **24** 64.57 N 10.58 E
Vikramasingapuram **122** 8.43 N 77.24 E
Viksøyri **26** 61.05 N 6.35 E
Viktor **24** 66.09 N 58.07 E
Viktorovka **86** 52.51 N 62.32 E
Viktring **61** 46.35 N 14.16 E
Vikulovo **86** 56.49 N 70.37 E
Vil'a **80** 55.15 N 42.13 E
Vila Alferes Chamusca **156** 24.29 S 33.00 E
Vila Augusta **287b** 23.28 S 46.32 W
Vila Boacaya ◆[8] **287b** 23.29 S 46.44 W
Vila Brasil **248** 22.22 S 54.34 W
Vila Caldas Xavier **154** 15.59 S 34.12 E
Vila da Maganja **154** 17.18 S 37.30 E
Vila da Ribeira Brava **150a** 16.37 N 24.18 W
Viladecans **266d** 41.19 N 2.00 E
Viladecavalls del Vallès **266d** 41.33 N 1.58 E
Vila de Manica **156** 18.56 S 32.53 E
Vila de Rei **34** 39.40 N 8.09 W
Vila do Bispo **34** 37.05 N 8.55 W
Vila do Conde **34** 41.21 N 8.45 W
Vila do Porto **148a** 36.56 N 25.09 W
Vila Flor **34** 41.18 N 7.09 W
Vila Fontes **156** 17.50 S 35.21 E
Vila Formosa ◆[8] **287b** 23.34 S 46.33 W
Vilafranca del Penedès **34** 41.21 N 1.42 E
Vila Franca de Xira **34** 38.57 N 8.59 W
Vila Galvão **287b** 23.27 S 46.33 W
Vila Gamito **154** 14.12 S 33.00 E
Vila Gomes da Costa **156** 24.19 S 33.38 E
Vila Gouveia **156** 18.03 S 33.11 E
Vila Guilherme ◆[8] **287b** 23.30 S 46.36 W
Vilaine ≃ **32** 47.30 N 2.27 W
Vila Isabel ◆[8] **287a** 22.55 S 43.15 W
Vila Jaguára ◆[8] **287b** 23.31 S 46.45 W
Viļaka **76** 57.11 N 27.41 E
Vila Luísa **156** 25.44 S 32.40 E
Vilama, Laguna de ⊜ **252** 22.36 S 66.55 W
Vila Machado **156** 19.18 S 34.11 E
Vila Madalena ◆[8] **287b** 23.33 S 46.42 W
Vila Maria ◆[8] **287b** 23.31 S 46.34 W
Vila Mariana ◆[8] **287b** 23.35 S 46.38 W
Vila Matilde ◆[8] **287b** 23.32 S 46.31 W
Vila Muriqui **256** 22.56 S 43.57 W
Vilanculos **156** 22.01 S 35.19 E
Viļāni **76** 56.33 N 26.57 E
Vila Nova ≃ **250** 0.04 S 51.13 W
Vila Nova de Famalicão **34** 41.25 N 8.32 W
Vila Nova de Foz Côa **34** 41.05 N 7.12 W
Vila Nova de Gaia **34** 41.08 N 8.37 W
Vilanova de la Roca **266d** 41.33 N 2.17 E
Vilanova i la Geltrú **34** 41.14 N 1.44 E
Vila Novo de Ourém **34** 39.39 N 8.35 W
Vila Paiva de Andrada **156** 18.44 S 34.03 E
Vila Progresso **287a** 22.55 S 43.03 W
Vila Prudente ◆[8] **287b** 23.35 S 46.33 W
Vila-real, Esp. **34** 39.56 N 0.06 W
Vila Real, Port. **34** 41.18 N 7.45 W
Vila Real de Santo António **34** 37.12 N 7.25 W
Vilar Formoso **34** 40.37 N 6.50 W
Vila Rica **246** 3.40 S 61.02 W
Vilarinho do Monte **250** 1.37 S 52.01 W
Vilassar de Dalt **266d** 41.31 N 2.22 E
Vilassar de Mar **266d** 41.30 N 2.24 E
Vila Vasco da Gama **154** 14.54 S 32.14 E
Vila Velha, Bra. **250** 3.13 N 51.13 W
Vila Velha, Bra. **255** 20.20 S 40.17 W
Vila Velha de Ródão **34** 39.38 N 7.40 W
Vila Verde, Port. **34** 41.39 N 8.26 W
Vila Verde, Port. **266c** 38.50 N 9.22 W
Vila Viçosa **34** 38.47 N 8.13 W
Vil'ča **78** 51.22 N 29.24 E
Vîlcea □[6] **38** 45.19 N 24.00 E
Vildbjerg **41** 56.12 N 8.46 E
Vilejka **76** 54.30 N 26.53 E
Vilelas **252** 27.57 S 62.38 W
Vilenki **82** 54.16 N 38.55 E
Vil'gort, S.S.S.R. **24** 60.34 N 56.24 E
Vil'gort, S.S.S.R. **24** 61.35 N 50.40 E
Vilhelmina **26** 64.37 N 16.39 E
Vilhena **248** 12.43 S 60.07 W
Vilija ≃ **76** 54.54 N 25.35 E
Viljandi **76** 58.22 N 25.36 E
Viljoensdrif **158** 26.44 S 27.55 E
Viljoenshof **158** 34.40 S 19.42 E
Viljoenskroon **158** 27.12 S 27.00 E
Viljoenspos **158** 27.35 S 30.30 E
Vilkaviškis **76** 54.39 N 23.02 E
Vil'kickogo, ostrov I, S.S.S.R. **72** 73.29 N 75.50 E
Vil'kickogo, ostrov I, S.S.S.R. **74** 75.44 N 152.20 E
Vil'kickogo, proliv ʯ **74** 77.55 N 103.00 E
Vilkija **76** 55.03 N 23.35 E
Vilkovo **78** 45.25 N 29.35 E
Villa Abecia **248** 21.00 S 65.23 W
Villa Aberastain **252** 31.39 S 68.35 W
Villa Acuña → Ciudad Acuña **232** 29.18 N 100.55 W
Villa Adelina ◆[8] **288** 34.31 S 58.32 W
Villa Adriana ⊥ **66** 41.56 N 12.45 E
Villa Ahumada **232** 30.37 N 106.31 W
Villa Alberdi **252** 27.35 S 65.37 W
Villa Alejandrina **258** 33.46 S 58.21 W
Villa Alemana **252** 33.03 S 71.23 W
Villa Allende **252** 31.18 S 64.18 W
Villa Alta **234** 17.21 N 96.09 W
Villa Ana **252** 28.29 S 59.37 W
Villa Ángela **252** 27.35 S 60.43 W
Villa Atamisqui **252** 28.29 S 63.48 W
Villa Atuel **252** 34.50 S 67.54 W
Villaba **116** 11.13 N 124.23 E
Villa Ballester ◆[8] **258** 34.32 S 58.33 W
Villabassa (Niederdorf) **64** 46.44 N 12.10 E
Villabate **70** 38.04 N 13.26 E
Villabé **261** 48.35 N 2.27 E
Villa Bella **248** 10.23 S 65.24 W
Villa Berthet **252** 27.17 S 60.25 W
Villablino **34** 42.56 N 6.19 W
Villa Borghese υ **267a** 41.55 N 12.29 E
Villa Bosch ◆[8] **288** 34.35 S 58.34 W
Villa Bruzual **246** 9.20 N 69.06 W
Villa Bustos **252** 29.17 S 67.02 W
Villa Cañás, Arg. **252** 34.00 S 61.36 W
Villacañas, Esp. **34** 39.38 N 3.20 W
Villa Carlos Paz **252** 31.24 S 64.31 W
Villacarriedo **34** 43.14 N 3.48 W
Villacarrillo **34** 38.07 N 3.05 W
Villa Castelli, Arg. **252** 29.00 S 68.11 W
Villa Castelli, It. **68** 40.35 N 17.28 E
Villacastín **34** 40.47 N 4.25 W
Villach **64** 46.36 N 13.50 E
Villacidro **71** 39.27 N 8.44 E
Villa Ciudadela ◆[8] **258** 34.38 S 58.34 W
Villa Clara □[4] **240p** 22.30 N 80.00 W
Villa Colón **234** 20.48 N 100.03 W
Villa Concepción del Tío **252** 31.19 S 62.50 W
Villa Constitución **252** 33.14 S 60.20 W
Villa Corona **234** 20.25 N 103.41 W
Villa Cortese **266b** 45.34 N 8.53 E
Villacoublay, Aérodrome de ⊠ **261** 48.45 N 2.10 E
Villa Creek ≃ **226** 35.27 N 120.58 W
Villa Cuauhtémoc, Méx. **234** 19.24 N 99.34 W
Villa Cuauhtémoc, Méx. **234** 22.11 N 97.50 W
Villada **34** 42.15 N 4.58 W
Villa de Apaseo el Alto **234** 20.27 N 100.37 W
Villa de Arriaga **234** 21.54 N 101.23 W
Villadeati **62** 45.04 N 8.10 E
Villa de Comaltitlán **236** 15.13 N 92.35 W
Villa de Cos **234** 23.17 N 102.21 W
Villa de Cura **246** 10.02 N 67.29 W
Villa de Guadalupe **234** 23.22 N 100.46 W
Villa del Carmen **252** 32.57 S 65.03 W
Villa Delgado **236** 13.43 N 89.10 W
Villa del Pueblito **234** 20.32 N 100.27 W
Villa del Río **34** 37.59 N 4.17 W
Villa del Rosario, Arg. **252** 31.35 S 63.32 W
Villa del Rosario, Arg. **252** 30.47 S 57.55 W
Villa de María **252** 29.54 S 63.43 W
Villa de Mayo **258** 34.30 S 58.41 W
Villa de Méndez **232** 25.07 N 98.34 W
Villa de Nova Sintra **150a** 14.52 N 24.43 W
Villa de Reyes **234** 21.48 N 100.56 W
Villa de San Antonio **236** 14.16 N 87.36 W
Villa de San Francisco **236** 14.10 N 86.58 W
Villa de Soto **252** 30.51 S 64.59 W
Villa d'Este ⊥ **267a** 41.57 N 12.48 E
Villa Devoto ◆[8] **288** 34.36 S 58.31 W
Villa Diamante ◆[8] **288** 34.41 S 58.26 W
Villa di Chiavenna **58** 46.20 N 9.29 E
Villa Diego, Arg. **252** 33.01 S 60.37 W
Villadiego, Esp. **34** 42.31 N 4.00 W
Villa Dolores **252** 31.56 S 65.12 W
Villa Domínico ◆[8] **258** 34.41 S 58.19 W
Villadose **64** 45.04 N 11.53 E
Villadossola **58** 46.04 N 8.16 E
Villa El Alto **252** 28.18 S 65.22 W
Villa el Carmen **236** 11.59 N 86.31 W
Villa Elisa **252** 32.10 S 58.24 W
Villa Elisa ◆[8] **258** 34.50 S 58.05 W
Villa Escalante **234** 19.24 N 101.39 W
Villa Eufronio Viscarra **248** 17.59 S 65.36 W
Villa Flores **234** 16.14 N 93.14 W
Villa Florida **252** 26.23 S 57.09 W
Villafranca d'Asti **62** 44.55 N 8.02 E
Villafranca del Bierzo **34** 42.36 N 6.48 W
Villafranca de los Barros **34** 38.34 N 6.20 W
Villafranca di Verona **64** 45.21 N 10.50 E
Villafranca in Lunigiana **64** 44.17 N 9.57 E
Villafranca Piemonte **62** 44.47 N 7.33 E
Villafranca Sicula **70** 37.35 N 13.17 E
Villafranca Tirrena **70** 38.14 N 15.26 E
Villafrati **70** 37.54 N 13.29 E
Villa Frontera **232** 26.56 N 101.27 W
Villagarcía, Esp. **34** 42.36 N 8.45 W
Villa García, Méx. **234** 22.10 N 101.57 W
Village **196** 35.33 N 97.33 W
Village Creek ≃ **194** 35.28 N 91.19 W
Village Green **285** 39.52 N 75.26 W
Villa General Roca **252** 32.39 S 66.28 W
Village of Drummond Hill **285** 39.43 N 75.42 W
Village of the Branch **276** 40.51 N 73.11 W
Villa Giambruno **288** 34.48 S 58.13 W
Villa González **234** 22.50 N 98.27 W
Villa González Ortega **234** 22.30 N 101.55 W
Villagrán, Méx. **232** 24.29 N 99.29 W
Villagrán, Méx. **234** 20.31 N 100.59 W
Villagrande Strisaili **71** 39.58 N 9.30 E
Villa Grazia **70** 38.09 N 13.10 E
Villagrazia ◆[8] **70** 38.05 N 13.20 E
Villa Grove **194** 39.51 N 88.09 W
Villaguay **252** 31.51 S 59.01 W
Villa Guerrero, Méx. **234** 21.59 N 103.36 W
Villa Guerrero, Méx. **234** 18.52 N 99.39 W
Villa Guillermina **252** 28.14 S 59.28 W
Villa Hayes **252** 25.06 S 57.34 W
Villahermosa **234** 17.59 N 92.55 W
Villa Hernandarias **252** 31.13 S 59.59 W
Villa Hidalgo, Méx. **204** 30.59 N 116.10 W
Villa Hidalgo, Méx. **234** 21.40 N 102.36 W
Villa Hidalgo, Méx. **234** 21.44 N 105.15 W
Villa Huidobro **252** 34.50 S 64.35 W
Villaines-la-Juhel **32** 48.21 N 0.17 W
Villa Iris **252** 38.10 S 63.15 W
Villa Jiménez **234** 19.55 N 101.35 W
Villa José L. Suárez ◆[8] **288** 34.32 S 58.35 W
Villa Juárez, Méx. **232** 27.10 N 109.50 W
Villa Juárez, Méx. **234** 22.20 N 100.17 W
Villa Krause **252** 31.34 S 68.32 W
Villa La Angostura **254** 40.47 S 71.40 W
Villalago **66** 41.56 N 13.50 E
Villa La Paz **252** 33.27 S 67.38 W
Villa Larca **252** 32.37 S 64.59 W
Villa Larroque **252** 33.02 S 59.01 W
Villalba, Esp. **34** 43.18 N 7.41 W
Villalba, It. **70** 37.39 N 13.50 E
Villalba, P.R. **240m** 18.08 N 66.30 W
Villa Lia **258** 34.07 S 59.26 W
Villalon **116** 11.31 N 124.22 E
Villalon ◆[8] **286b** 23.03 N 82.26 W
Villalón de Campos **34** 42.06 N 5.02 W
Villalonga **254** 39.53 S 62.35 W
Villa López **232** 27.00 N 105.02 W
Villalpando **34** 41.52 N 5.24 W
Villa Lugano ◆[8] **288** 34.41 S 58.28 W
Villalvernia **62** 44.49 N 8.51 E
Villa Lynch ◆[8] **288** 34.36 S 58.31 W
Villa Madero, Arg. **288** 34.42 S 58.30 W
Villa Madero, Méx. **234** 19.24 N 101.16 W
Villa Mainero **232** 24.32 N 99.38 W
Villamar **71** 39.37 N 8.59 E
Villa María, Arg. **252** 32.25 S 63.15 W
Villa Maria, Pa., U.S. **214** 41.05 N 80.30 W
Villa María Grande **252** 31.39 S 59.54 W
Villa Martín, Bol. **248** 20.46 S 67.47 W
Villamartín, Esp. **34** 36.52 N 5.38 W
Villamarzana **64** 45.01 N 11.41 E
Villamassargia **71** 39.16 N 8.38 E
Villa Matoque **252** 25.49 S 63.49 W
Villa Mazán **252** 28.40 S 66.34 W
Villa Media Agua **252** 31.59 S 68.25 W
Villa Mercedes **252** 30.07 S 68.42 W
Villamil **246a** 0.56 S 91.01 W
Villa Minozzo **64** 44.22 N 10.28 E
Villa Montes **248** 21.15 S 63.30 W
Villa Morelos **234** 20.00 N 101.25 W
Villandraut **32** 44.28 N 0.23 W
Villa Nova, Md., U.S. **284b** 39.21 N 76.44 W
Villa Nova, Oh., U.S. **216** 40.33 N 84.26 W
Villanova, Pa., U.S. **208** 40.02 N 75.20 W
Villanova d'Asti **62** 44.57 N 7.56 E
Villanova Mondovì **62** 44.21 N 7.45 E
Villanova Monferrato **62** 45.11 N 8.28 E
Villanova Monteleone **71** 40.30 N 8.28 E
Villanova sull'Arda **64** 45.01 N 10.00 E
Villanova Tulo **71** 39.47 N 9.13 E
Villanova University υ[2] **285** 40.02 N 75.21 W
Villa Nueva, Arg. **252** 32.54 S 68.47 W
Villa Nueva, Arg. **252** 32.26 S 63.15 W
Villanueva, Col. **246** 10.37 N 72.59 W
Villa Nueva, Guat. **236** 14.31 N 90.35 W
Villanueva, Hond. **236** 15.17 N 88.00 W
Villanueva, Méx. **234** 22.21 N 102.53 W
Villanueva, Nic. **236** 12.58 N 86.49 W
Villanueva, N.M., U.S. **200** 35.16 N 105.21 W
Villanueva de Córdoba **34** 38.20 N 4.37 W
Villanueva de la Serana **34** 38.58 N 5.48 W
Villanueva de la Sierra **34** 40.12 N 6.24 W
Villanueva de los Infantes **34** 38.44 N 2.59 W
Villanueva del Río y Minas **34** 37.39 N 5.42 W
Villa Numancia **288** 34.55 S 58.24 W
Villa Obregón **234** 21.07 N 102.42 W
Villa Obregón ◆[8] **286a** 19.21 N 99.12 W
Villa Ocampo **252** 28.28 S 59.22 W
Villa Ojo de Agua **252** 29.31 S 63.42 W
Villa Oliva **252** 26.01 S 57.53 W
Villa Opicina **64** 45.40 N 13.49 E
Villa Orestes Pereyra **232** 26.31 N 105.40 W
Villa Ottone (Uttenheim) **64** 46.52 N 11.57 E
Villa Papale υ **267a** 41.45 N 12.39 E
Villa Park, Ca., U.S. **228** 33.48 N 117.48 W
Villa Park, Il., U.S. **278** 41.53 N 87.59 W
Villa Park Dam ◆[6] **280** 33.48 N 117.46 W
Villa Pérez **240m** 18.12 N 66.47 W
Villapiana **68** 39.51 N 16.28 E
Villapiana Lido **68** 39.48 N 16.29 E
Villapinzón **246** 5.13 N 73.36 W
Villa Potenza **66** 43.19 N 13.25 E
Villaputzu **71** 39.26 N 9.34 E
Villa Quinteros **252** 27.14 S 65.33 W
Villa Quintilio Varo ⊥ **267a** 41.58 N 12.47 E
Villa Ramírez **252** 32.11 S 60.12 W
Villarcayo **34** 42.56 N 3.34 W
Villar-d'Arène **62** 45.02 N 6.20 E
Villard-Bonnot **62** 45.14 N 5.53 E
Villard-de-Lans **62** 45.04 N 5.33 E
Villardefrades **34** 41.43 N 5.15 W
Villar del Arzobispo **34** 39.44 N 0.49 W
Villareal **116** 11.34 N 124.56 E
Villa Real ◆[8] **288** 34.37 S 58.31 W
Villa Regina **252** 39.06 S 67.04 W
Villa Reynolds **252** 33.43 S 65.23 W
Villa Rica **192** 33.43 N 84.55 W
Villa Rivero **248** 17.37 S 65.48 W
Villaroche **261** 48.37 N 2.39 E
Villaroche ■ **261** 48.37 N 2.40 E
Villa Romana del Casale ⊥ **70** 37.22 N 14.20 E
Villa Rosa, Arg. **258** 34.25 S 58.52 W
Villarosa, It. **70** 37.35 N 14.10 E
Villar Pellice **62** 44.48 N 7.09 E
Villar Perosa **62** 44.56 N 7.15 E
Villarreales **196** 26.07 N 100.20 W
Villarrica, Chile **254** 39.16 S 72.13 W
Villarrica, Col. **246** 3.58 N 74.37 W
Villarrica, Para. **252** 25.45 S 56.26 W
Villarrica, Lago ⊜ **254** 39.15 S 72.06 W
Villarrobledo **34** 39.16 N 2.36 W
Villarrubia de los Ojos **34** 39.13 N 3.36 W
Villars, Arg. **258** 34.50 S 58.56 W
Villars, Schw. **58** 46.18 N 7.04 E
Villars-Colmars **62** 44.10 N 6.36 E
Villars-en-Azois **58** 48.04 N 4.45 E
Villars-les-Dombes **58** 46.00 N 5.01 E
Villars-sur-Var **62** 43.56 N 7.06 E
Villa Ruiz **258** 34.25 S 59.15 W
Villas **208** 39.01 N 74.56 W
Villa Sáenz Peña ◆[8] **288** 34.36 S 58.31 W
Villa San Andrés ◆[8] **288** 34.33 S 58.32 W
Villa Sandino **236** 12.03 N 84.59 W
Villa San Giovanni **68** 38.13 N 15.38 E
Villa San José **252** 32.12 S 58.13 W
Villa San Martín **252** 28.18 S 64.12 W
Villasanta **62** 45.37 N 9.18 E
Villa Santa, Montaña ∧ **236** 14.12 N 86.27 W
Villa Santa Maria **66** 41.57 N 14.21 E
Villa Santina **64** 46.24 N 12.55 E
Villa Santos Lugares ◆[8] **288** 34.36 S 58.32 W
Villasayas **34** 41.21 N 2.37 W
Villa Serrano **248** 19.06 S 64.22 W
Villasimius **71** 39.08 N 9.31 E
Villasis **116** 15.54 N 120.35 E
Villasor **71** 39.23 N 8.56 E
Villa Tunari **248** 16.55 S 65.25 W
Villa Turdera ◆[8] **288** 34.48 S 58.25 W
Villa Unión, Arg. **252** 29.18 S 68.12 W
Villa Unión, Arg. **252** 29.24 S 62.47 W
Villa Unión, Méx. **232** 28.15 N 100.43 W
Villa Unión, Méx. **234** 23.58 N 104.02 W
Villa Unión, Méx. **234** 23.12 N 106.14 W
Villa Vaca Guzmán **248** 19.54 S 63.48 W
Villa Valeria **252** 34.20 S 64.55 W
Villa Vallelonga **66** 41.52 N 13.37 E
Villa Vázquez **238** 19.45 N 71.27 W
Villaverde ◆[8] **266a** 40.21 N 3.42 W
Villaverla **64** 45.39 N 11.29 E
Villa Verona **226** 39.28 N 121.33 W
Villavicencio **246** 4.09 N 73.37 W
Villa Vicente Guerrero **234** 23.45 N 103.59 W
Villaviciosa **34** 43.29 N 5.26 W
Villaviciosa de Córdoba **34** 38.05 N 5.01 W
Villa Victoria **234** 18.47 N 103.24 W
Villa Vomano **66** 42.37 N 13.46 E
Villazón **248** 22.06 S 65.36 W
Villa Zorraquín **252** 31.19 S 58.02 W
Villé **58** 48.20 N 7.18 E
Villebon, Lac ⊜ **190** 47.58 N 77.17 W
Villebon-sur-Yvette **261** 48.42 N 2.15 E
Villeconin **261** 48.31 N 2.08 E
Villecresnes **261** 48.43 N 2.32 E
Villecroze **62** 43.35 N 6.16 E
Ville-d'Avray **261** 48.50 N 2.11 E
Ville-de-Laval → Laval **206** 45.35 N 73.45 W
Villedieu **32** 48.50 N 1.13 W
Ville-en-Tardenois **50** 49.11 N 3.48 E
Villefort **62** 44.26 N 3.56 E
Villefranche **58** 45.59 N 4.43 E
Villefranche-de-Rouergue **32** 44.21 N 2.02 E
Villefranche-Sur-Cher **50** 47.18 N 1.46 E
Villefranche-sur-Mer **62** 43.42 N 7.19 E
Villejuif **50** 48.48 N 2.22 E
Villejust **261** 48.41 N 2.14 E
Ville-Marie **190** 47.19 N 79.26 W
Villemaur-sur-Vanne **50** 48.15 N 3.44 E
Villemeux-sur-Eure **50** 48.40 N 1.28 E
Villemoisson-sur-Orge **261** 48.40 N 2.19 E
Villemomble **261** 48.53 N 2.31 E
Villena **34** 38.38 N 0.51 W
Villenauxe-la-Grande **50** 48.35 N 3.33 E
Villeneuve, It. **62** 45.42 N 7.14 E
Villeneuve, Schw. **58** 46.24 N 6.55 E
Villeneuve-d'Ascq **50** 50.37 N 3.10 E
Villeneuve-d'Aveyron **32** 44.26 N 2.02 E
Villeneuve-de-Berg **62** 44.33 N 4.30 E
Villeneuve-la-Garenne **261** 48.56 N 2.20 E
Villeneuve-la-Guyard **50** 48.20 N 3.04 E
Villeneuve-l'Archevêque **50** 48.14 N 3.33 E
Villeneuve-le-Comte **261** 48.49 N 2.50 E
Villeneuve-le-Roi **50** 48.44 N 2.25 E
Villeneuve-lès-Avignon **62** 43.58 N 4.48 E
Villeneuve-lès-Maguelonne **62** 43.32 N 3.52 E
Villeneuve-Saint-Denis **261** 48.49 N 2.48 E
Villeneuve-Saint-Georges **50** 48.44 N 2.27 E
Villeneuve-sous-Dammartin **261** 49.02 N 2.39 E
Villeneuve-sur-Lot **32** 44.25 N 0.42 E
Villeneuve-sur-Yonne **50** 48.05 N 3.18 E
Villennes-sur-Seine **261** 48.56 N 2.00 E
Villenoy **50** 48.57 N 2.52 E
Villeny **50** 47.37 N 1.45 E
Villeparisis **50** 48.56 N 2.37 E
Villepinte **261** 48.58 N 2.32 E
Ville Platte **194** 30.41 N 92.16 W
Villepreux **261** 48.50 N 2.01 E
Villequier **50** 49.31 N 0.40 E
Villeron **261** 49.03 N 2.33 E
Villeroy **50** 48.59 N 2.47 E
Villers-Bocage, Fr. **32** 49.05 N 0.39 W
Villers-Bocage, Fr. **50** 49.59 N 2.20 E
Villers-Bretonneux **50** 49.52 N 2.31 E
Villers-Carbonnel **50** 49.52 N 2.54 E
Villers-Cotterêts **50** 49.15 N 3.05 E
Villers-devant-Orval **56** 49.37 N 5.19 E
Villers-en-Arthies **261** 49.05 N 1.44 E
Villersexel **58** 47.33 N 6.26 E
Villers-Farlay **58** 47.00 N 5.45 E
Villers-la-Ville **50** 50.35 N 4.32 E
Villers-le-Lac **58** 47.04 N 6.40 E
Villers-lès-Nancy **58** 48.40 N 6.09 E
Villers-lès-Pots **58** 47.13 N 5.21 E
Villers-Outréaux **50** 50.02 N 3.18 E
Villers-Saint-Paul **50** 49.17 N 2.29 E
Villers-Semeuse **56** 49.44 N 4.45 E
Villerupt **56** 49.28 N 5.56 E
Villerville **50** 49.24 N 0.08 E
Ville-Saint-Georges → Saint-Georges **188** 46.07 N 70.40 W
Villes-sur-Auzon **62** 44.03 N 5.14 E
Ville-sur-Tourbe **56** 49.11 N 4.47 E
Villeta **246** 5.01 N 74.28 W
Villetta Barrea **66** 41.47 N 13.56 E
Villeurbanne **62** 45.46 N 4.53 E
Villevaudé **261** 48.55 N 2.39 E
Villeziers **261** 48.40 N 2.10 E
Villiers **158** 27.03 S 28.35 E
Villiers-Adam **261** 49.04 N 2.14 E
Villiersdorp **158** 34.00 S 19.19 E
Villiers-le-Bâcle **261** 48.44 N 2.08 E
Villiers-le-Bel **261** 49.00 N 2.23 E
Villiers-le-Sec **261** 49.04 N 2.23 E
Villiers-Saint-Frédéric **261** 48.49 N 1.54 E
Villiers-Saint-Georges **50** 48.39 N 3.25 E
Villiers-sur-Marne **261** 48.50 N 2.33 E
Villiers-sur-Morin **261** 48.52 N 2.53 E
Villigst **263** 51.26 N 7.35 E
Villingen-Schwenningen **30** 48.04 N 8.28 E
Villisca **198** 40.55 N 94.58 W
Villmanstrand → Lappeenranta **26** 61.04 N 28.11 E
Villmergen **58** 47.21 N 8.15 E
Villorba **64** 45.44 N 12.14 E
Villoresi, Canale ≅ **62** 45.33 N 9.31 E
Villotta **64** 45.52 N 12.45 E
Vilm I **54** 54.19 N 13.32 E
Vilmnitz **54** 54.21 N 13.31 E
Vilna, Ab., Can. **182** 54.07 N 111.55 W
Vilna → Vilnius, S.S.S.R. **76** 54.41 N 25.19 E
Vilnius **76** 54.41 N 25.19 E
Vilosnes-sur-Meuse **56** 49.20 N 5.14 E
Vilppula **26** 62.01 N 24.31 E
Vils **58** 47.33 N 10.38 E
Vils ≃, B.R.D. **60** 48.37 N 13.11 E
Vils ≃, B.R.D. **60** 49.09 N 11.58 E
Vils ≃, Europe **58** 47.33 N 10.40 E
Vilsandi saar I **76** 58.23 N 21.52 E
Vilsbiburg **60** 48.27 N 12.12 E
Vilseck **60** 49.37 N 11.48 E
Vilsheim **60** 48.27 N 12.07 E
Vilshofen **60** 48.39 N 13.12 E
Vil'uj ≃ **74** 64.24 N 126.26 E
Vil'ujsk **74** 63.45 N 121.35 E
Vil'ujskoje vodochranilišče ⊜[1] **74** 62.30 N 111.00 E
Viluppuram **122** 11.56 N 79.29 E
Vil'va **86** 58.37 N 56.52 E
Vilvoorde **50** 50.56 N 4.26 E
Vimercate **62** 45.37 N 9.22 E
Vimianzo **34** 43.07 N 9.02 W
Vimmerby **26** 57.40 N 15.51 E
Vimodrone **266b** 45.31 N 9.17 E
Vimoutiers **50** 48.55 N 0.12 E
Vimpeli **26** 63.09 N 23.48 E
Vimperk **60** 49.03 N 13.47 E
Vimy **50** 50.22 N 2.49 E
Vina **204** 39.55 N 122.03 W
Vina ≃ **146** 7.45 N 15.36 E
Viñac **248** 12.56 S 75.47 W
Viña del Mar **252** 33.02 S 71.34 W
Vinadi **58** 46.55 N 10.29 E
Vinadio **62** 44.18 N 7.10 E
Viñales **240p** 22.37 N 83.43 W
Vinalhaven **188** 44.02 N 68.49 W
Vinalhaven Island I **188** 44.05 N 68.52 W
Vinantes **261** 49.01 N 2.44 E
Vina Roni, Mount ∧ **175e** 8.10 S 157.28 E
Vinaròs **34** 40.28 N 0.29 E
Vinay **62** 45.13 N 5.24 E
Vinazco ≃ **234** 20.56 N 97.44 W
Vincennes, Fr. **50** 48.51 N 2.26 E
Vincennes, In., U.S. **194** 38.40 N 87.31 W
Vincennes, Bois de ♦ **261** 48.50 N 2.25 E
Vincennes, Château de ⊥ **261** 48.51 N 2.26 E
Vincennes, Étang de ⊜ **261** 48.47 N 2.45 E
Vincennes Bay ⊂ **9** 66.30 S 109.30 E
Vincent **194** 33.22 N 86.22 W
Vincent, Point › **174c** 29.00 S 167.55 E
Vincentown **208** 39.56 N 74.44 W
Vinces **246** 1.32 S 79.45 W
Vinces ≃ **246** 1.39 S 79.47 W
Vinchiaturo **66** 41.29 N 14.35 E
Vinchina **252** 28.46 S 68.10 W
Vinchos **248** 13.16 S 74.21 W
Vinci **66** 43.47 N 10.55 E
Vinco **214** 40.25 N 78.52 W
Vindeby **41** 55.03 N 10.38 E
Vindelälven ≃ **24** 63.54 N 19.52 E
Vindeln **26** 64.12 N 19.44 E
Vinden, Mount ∧ **162** 27.01 S 115.38 E
Vinderslev **41** 56.15 N 9.26 E
Vinderup **26** 56.29 N 8.47 E
Vindhya Range ⋏ **120** 23.00 N 77.00 E
Vinding **41** 55.41 N 9.35 E
Vindinge **41** 55.19 N 10.45 E
Vine Brook ≃ **283** 42.27 N 71.13 W
Vinegar Hill ∧ **202** 44.43 N 118.34 W
Vine Grove **194** 37.48 N 85.58 W
Vine Hill **282** 38.00 N 122.06 W
Vineland, Mi., U.S. **216** 42.03 N 86.30 W
Vineland, N.J., U.S. **208** 39.29 N 75.01 W
Vinemont **194** 34.14 N 86.51 W
Vine Valley **210** 42.43 N 77.20 W
Vineyard Canyon V **226** 35.46 N 120.41 W
Vineyard Haven **207** 41.27 N 70.36 W
Vineyard Lake ⊜ **216** 42.05 N 84.13 W
Vineyard Sound ʯ **207** 41.25 N 70.46 W
Vingåker **40** 59.02 N 15.52 E
Vingeanne ≃ **58** 47.21 N 5.29 E
Ving Ngün **110** 22.37 N 99.16 E
Vinh **110** 18.40 N 105.40 E
Vinhais **34** 41.50 N 7.00 W
Vinhas, Ribeira das ≃ **266c** 38.42 N 9.25 W
Vinh Chau **110** 9.19 N 105.59 E
Vinhedo **256** 23.01 S 46.59 W
Vinh Loc **269c** 10.49 N 106.34 E
Vinh Long **110** 10.15 N 105.58 E
Vinh Tuy, Viet. **110** 17.24 N 106.36 E
Vinh Tuy, Viet. **110** 9.37 N 105.22 E
Vinica **36** 45.28 N 15.15 E
Vinita **196** 36.38 N 95.09 W
Vînju Mare **38** 44.26 N 22.52 E
Vinkekuil **158** 32.42 S 20.27 E
Vinkeveen **52** 52.13 N 4.54 E
Vinkovci **38** 45.17 N 18.49 E
Vin'kovcy **78** 49.02 N 27.14 E
Vinnhorst **52** 52.25 N 9.43 E
Vinnica **78** 49.14 N 28.29 E
Vinnica □[4] **38** 48.30 N 28.30 E
Vinniki **78** 49.48 N 24.08 E
Vinnitsa → Vinnica **78** 49.14 N 28.29 E
Vinnum **263** 51.41 N 7.24 E
Vinogradov **78** 48.09 N 23.02 E
Vinogradovo, S.S.S.R. **82** 55.25 N 38.32 E
Vinogradovo, S.S.S.R. **82** 55.57 N 37.32 E
Vinogrobol' **78** 51.51 N 36.26 E
Vinön I **40** 59.12 N 15.43 E
Vinon-sur-Verdon **62** 43.43 N 5.48 E
Vinovo **62** 44.57 N 7.38 E
Vinslöv **26** 56.06 N 13.55 E
Vinson Massif ∧ **9** 78.35 S 85.25 W
Vinstra **26** 61.36 N 9.45 E
Vintilă Vodă **38** 45.28 N 26.44 E
Vinton, Ia., U.S. **190** 42.10 N 92.01 W
Vinton, La., U.S. **194** 30.11 N 93.34 W
Vinton, Va., U.S. **192** 37.16 N 79.53 W
Vintondale **214** 40.28 N 78.55 W
Vintrosa **40** 59.15 N 14.57 E
Viñuelas, Arroyo de ≃ **266a** 40.33 N 3.33 W
Viny **76** 58.22 N 32.13 E
Vinzelberg **54** 52.33 N 11.40 E
Vinzili **86** 56.58 N 65.46 E
Viola, Il., U.S. **190** 41.12 N 90.35 W
Viola, N.Y., U.S. **276** 41.08 N 74.05 W
Viola, Wi., U.S. **190** 43.30 N 90.40 W
Viola, Val V **64** 46.27 N 10.15 E
Violín, Isla I **236** 8.51 N 83.39 W
Viols-le-Fort **62** 43.45 N 3.42 E
Viosne ≃ **261** 49.03 N 2.06 E
Vipava **36** 45.51 N 13.58 E
Vipava ≃ **64** 45.54 N 13.33 E
Vipiteno (Sterzing) **64** 46.54 N 11.26 E
Vipos **252** 26.29 S 65.22 W
Vipperow **54** 53.19 N 12.41 E
Vir, Otok I **36** 44.18 N 15.04 E
Vira **58** 46.08 N 8.51 E
Virac **116** 13.35 N 124.15 E
Viracopos, Aeroporto de ⊠ **256** 23.00 S 47.08 W
Virac Point › **116** 13.31 N 124.13 E
Viradouro **255** 20.53 S 48.18 W
Virago Sound ʯ **182** 54.00 N 132.36 W
Viramgām **120** 23.07 N 72.02 E
Virandozero **24** 64.05 N 35.58 E
Viranşehir **130** 37.13 N 39.45 E
Vīrarājendrapet **122** 12.12 N 75.48 E
Virbalis **76** 54.38 N 22.49 E
Virden, Mb., Can. **184** 49.51 N 100.55 W
Virden, Il., U.S. **219** 39.30 N 89.46 W
Virden, N.M., U.S. **200** 32.41 N 109.00 W
Vire **32** 48.50 N 0.53 W
Vire ≃ **32** 49.20 N 1.07 W
Virelles **50** 50.04 N 4.20 E
Virelles, Étang de ⊜ **50** 50.04 N 4.21 E
Vireux-Molhain **56** 50.05 N 4.43 E
Vîrfurile **38** 46.19 N 22.31 E
Virgem da Lapa **255** 16.49 S 42.21 W
Virgen **64** 47.00 N 12.27 E
Vírgen del San Cristóbal υ[1] **286e** 33.26 S 70.39 W
Vírgenes, Cabo › **254** 52.22 S 68.20 W
Vírgenes, Islas → Virgin Islands □[2], N.A. **240m** 18.20 N 64.50 W
Vírgenes, Islas → British Virgin Islands □[2], N.A. **240m** 18.30 N 64.30 W
Virgen Tal V **64** 47.00 N 12.25 E
Virgil, On., Can. **284a** 43.13 N 79.08 W
Virgil, Ks., U.S. **198** 37.58 N 96.00 W
Virgil, N.Y., U.S. **210** 42.31 N 76.12 W
Virgilina **192** 36.33 N 78.52 W
Virgilio **64** 45.07 N 10.47 E
Virgin ≃ **200** 36.31 N 114.20 W
Virgin, North Fork ≃ **200** 37.10 N 113.01 W
Virginal-Samme **50** 50.38 N 4.12 E
Virgin Gorda I **240m** 18.30 N 64.24 W
Virgin Gorda Peak ∧ **240m** 18.30 N 64.24 W
Virginia, Austl. **168b** 34.40 S 138.34 E
Virgínia, Bra. **256** 22.20 S 45.06 W
Virginia, Ire. **48** 53.49 N 7.04 W
Virginia, S. Afr. **158** 28.12 S 26.49 E
Virginia, Il., U.S. **219** 39.57 N 90.12 W
Virginia, Mn., U.S. **190** 47.31 N 92.32 W
Virginia □[3] **178** 37.30 N 78.45 W
Virginia Beach **208** 36.51 N 75.58 W
Virginia City, Mt., U.S. **202** 45.17 N 111.56 W
Virginia City, Nv., U.S. **226** 39.18 N 119.38 W
Virginia Creek ≃ **226** 38.13 N 119.14 W
Virginia Falls ʟ **180** 61.38 N 125.42 W
Virginia Gardens **220** 25.49 N 80.17 W
Virginia Hills **208** 38.47 N 77.06 W
Virginia Key I **220** 25.44 N 80.09 W
Virginia Peak ∧ **204** 39.45 N 119.28 W

Symbols in the index entries represent the broad categories identified in the key at the right. Symbols with superior numbers (⋏[1]) identify subcategories (see complete key on page *I · 1).*

Symbole im Register stellen die rechts im Schlüssel erklärten Kategorien dar. Symbole mit hochgestellten Ziffern (⋏[1]) bezeichnen Unterabteilungen einer Kategorie (vgl. vollständiger Schlüssel auf Seite *I · 1).*

Los símbolos incluídos en el texto del índice representan las grandes categorias identificadas con la clave a la derecha. Los símbolos con numeros en su parte superior (⋏[1]) identifican las subcategorías (véase la clave completa en la página *I · 1).*

Les symboles de l'index représentent les catégories indiquées dans la légende à droite. Les symboles suivis d'un indice (⋏[1]) représentent des sous-catégories (voir légende complète à la page *I · 1).*

Os símbolos incluídos no texto do índice representam as grandes categorias identificadas com a chave à direita. Os símbolos com números em sua parte superior (⋏[1]) identificam as subcategorias (veja-se a chave completa à página *I · 1).*

∧ Mountain	Berg	Montaña	Montagne	Montanha
⋏ Mountains	Gebirge	Montañas	Montagnes	Montanhas
)(Pass	Paß	Paso	Col	Passo
V Valley, Canyon	Tal, Cañon	Valle, Cañón	Vallée, Canyon	Vale, Canhão
≚ Plain	Ebene	Llano	Plaine	Planície
› Cape	Kap	Cabo	Cap	Cabo
I Island	Insel	Isla	Île	Ilha
II Islands	Inseln	Islas	Îles	Ilhas
⊥ Other Topographic Features	Andere Topographische Objekte	Otros Elementos Topográficos	Autres données topographiques	Outros acidentes topográficos

ESPAÑOL

Nombre	Página	Lat.°′	Long.°′ W = Oeste
Virginia Ranch Reservoir ⊜[1]	226	39.20 N	121.19 W
Virginia Range ⋌	226	39.18 N	119.30 W
Virginiatown	190	48.08 N	79.35 W
Virginia Water	260	51.24 N	0.34 W
Virginie occidentale → West Virginia □[3]	188	38.45 N	80.30 W
Virgin Islands □[2], N.A.	230	18.20 N	64.50 W
Virgin Islands □[2], N.A.	240m	18.20 N	64.50 W
Virgin Islands II	240m	18.00 N	64.40 W
Virgin Islands National Park ♠	240m	18.20 N	64.45 W
Virginópolis	255	18.45 S	42.45 W
Virgin Passage c[1]	240m	18.20 N	65.10 W
Virginville	208	40.31 N	75.52 W
Virgolândia	255	18.27 S	42.18 W
Virieu	62	45.29 N	5.28 E
Virieu-le-Grand	62	45.51 N	5.39 E
Virihaure ⊜	24	67.20 N	16.35 E
Virje	36	46.04 N	16.59 E
Virkkala	26	60.12 N	24.01 E
Virklund	41	56.07 N	9.34 E
Virneburg	56	50.20 N	7.04 E
Virôchey	110	13.59 N	106.49 E
Viroflay	50	48.48 N	2.10 E
Viroin ≃	56	50.05 N	4.43 E
Virojoki	26	60.35 N	27.42 E
Víron	267c	37.57 N	23.45 E
Vironvay	50	49.12 N	1.13 E
Viroqua	190	43.33 N	90.53 W
Virovitica	36	45.50 N	17.23 E
Virpazar	38	42.15 N	19.05 E
Virrat	26	62.14 N	23.47 E
Virsbo	40	59.52 N	16.02 E
Virserum	26	57.19 N	15.35 E
Virtaniemi	24	68.53 N	28.27 E
Virton	56	49.34 N	5.32 E
Vîrtopu	38	44.12 N	23.21 E
Virtsu	76	58.34 N	23.31 E
Virú	248	8.25 S	78.45 W
Virudunagar	122	9.36 N	77.58 E
Viru-Jaagupi	76	59.15 N	26.28 E
Virulento	196	28.52 N	104.21 W
Virunga, Parc National de ♠	154	1.00 S	29.15 E
Virungu	154	7.04 S	29.46 E
Viru-Nigula	76	59.27 N	26.41 E
Virvyčia ≃	76	56.13 N	22.34 E
Viry-Châtillon	50	48.40 N	2.23 E
Vis	36	43.03 N	16.12 E
Vis ≃, Fr.	62	43.56 N	3.42 E
Vis (Fish) ≃, Namibia	156	28.07 S	17.45 E
Vis ≃, S. Afr.	158	30.53 S	20.23 E
Vis, Otok I	36	43.02 N	16.11 E
Visale	175e	9.15 S	159.42 E
Visalia	226	36.19 N	119.17 W
Visalia Airport ⊠	226	36.19 N	119.23 W
Visayan Islands II	12	11.00 N	123.30 E
Visayan Sea ✢[2]	116	11.35 N	123.51 E
Visbek	52	52.48 N	8.19 E
Visby	26	57.38 N	18.18 E
Viscaya, Bahía de → Biscay, Bay of c	32	44.00 N	4.00 W
Viscount	184	51.57 N	105.39 W
Viscount Melville Sound ⟗	176	74.10 N	108.00 W
Visé	56	50.44 N	5.42 E
Višegrad	38	43.47 N	19.17 E
Vis-en-Artois	50	50.15 N	2.56 E
Višera ≃	76	58.34 N	31.24 E
Viserba	66	44.05 N	12.32 E
Viseu, Bra.	250	1.12 S	46.07 W
Viseu, Port.	34	40.39 N	7.55 W
Vișeu ≃	38	47.55 N	24.09 E
Vișeu de Sus	38	47.44 N	24.22 E
Vishākhapatnam	122	17.42 N	83.18 E
Vishoek	158	34.08 S	18.26 E
Visim	86	57.39 N	59.30 E
Visingsö I	26	58.03 N	14.20 E
Visitation, Île de la I	275a	45.35 N	73.40 W
Viskafors	26	57.38 N	12.50 E
Viskan ≃	26	57.14 N	12.12 E
Viškil'	80	58.05 N	48.19 E
Viskinge	41	55.40 N	11.16 E
Visl'ajevo	82	54.25 N	36.43 E
Vislanda	26	56.47 N	14.27 E
Vislinskij zaliv c	30	54.27 N	19.40 E
Vismen ⊜	40	59.17 N	14.17 E
Visnagar	120	23.42 N	72.33 E
Višn'aki	265b	55.47 N	37.54 E
Višn'akovo	82	55.45 N	38.10 E
Višnevčik	78	49.02 N	26.28 E
Visnevo	76	54.08 N	26.14 E
Višnevoje, S.S.S.R.	78	48.27 N	33.56 E
Višnevoje, S.S.S.R.	80	52.38 N	43.26 E
Višňové	61	48.59 N	16.09 E
Višn'ovec	78	49.54 N	25.45 E
Višn'ovka, S.S.S.R.	78	46.20 N	28.26 E
Višn'ovka, S.S.S.R.	86	50.49 N	72.12 E
Viso, Monte ∧	62	44.40 N	7.07 E
Visoki Dečani, Manastir ⊕[1]	38	42.30 N	20.31 E
Visoko	38	43.59 N	18.11 E
Visokoi Island I	18	56.42 S	27.12 W
Visp	58	46.18 N	7.53 E
Vispa ≃	58	46.18 N	7.52 E
Visrivier	158	31.55 S	25.25 E
Vissefjärda	26	56.32 N	15.35 E
Visselhövede	52	52.59 N	9.35 E
Vissenbjerg	41	55.23 N	10.08 E
Visso	66	42.56 N	13.05 E
Vissoie	58	46.13 N	7.36 E
Vista, Ca., U.S.	228	33.12 N	117.14 W
Vista, N.Y., U.S.	210	41.12 N	73.31 W
Vista Alegre, Arg.	252	38.45 S	68.11 W
Vista Alegre, Bra.	256	21.27 S	42.35 W
Vista Alegre, Chile	286e	33.30 S	70.43 W
Vista Alegre, Perú	286d	12.09 S	77.00 W
Vista Flores	252	33.38 S	69.09 W
Vista Hermosa, Méx.	234	19.38 N	103.22 W
Vista Hermosa, Méx.	234	20.16 N	102.29 W
Vista La Mesa	228	32.35 N	117.01 W
Vista Park	228	35.21 N	118.55 W
Vistina	76	59.47 N	28.29 E
Vistre ≃	62	43.40 N	4.15 E
Vistula → Wisła ≃	30	54.22 N	18.55 E
Visun' ≃	78	47.07 N	32.53 E
Vit ≃	38	43.41 N	24.45 E
Vita, Mb., Can.	184	49.08 N	96.34 W
Vita, It.	70	37.52 N	12.49 E
Vita ≃	246	6.11 N	67.31 W
Vitacura	286e	33.24 S	70.36 W
Vitali	116	7.22 N	122.18 E
Vitanje	36	46.23 N	15.18 E
Vitarte	248	12.02 S	76.56 W
Vit'azevka	78	48.01 N	31.53 E
Vite	122	17.17 N	74.33 E
Vitebsk	76	55.12 N	30.11 E
Vitebsk Station ◆[5]	265a	59.55 N	30.21 E
Vitel, Laguna ⊜	258	35.32 S	58.07 W
Viterbo	66	42.25 N	12.06 E
Viterbo □[4]	66	42.25 N	12.05 E
Vitiaz Strait ⟗	164	5.50 S	147.20 E
Vitichi	248	20.13 S	65.29 W
Vitigudino	34	41.01 N	6.26 W
Viti Levu I	175g	18.00 S	178.00 E
Vitim	74	59.28 N	112.34 E
Vitim ≃	74	59.26 N	112.34 E
Vitimskij	88	58.14 N	113.18 E
Vitimskoje ploskogorje ⋌[1]	88	54.00 N	113.30 E
Vitinia ◆[8]	267a	41.47 N	12.24 E
Vitis	61	48.45 N	15.10 E
Vítkov	30	49.46 N	17.45 E
Vito	175e	6.02 S	155.24 E
Vítor	248	16.26 S	71.49 W

FRANÇAIS

Nom	Page	Lat.°′	Long.°′ W = Ouest
Vitor ≃	248	16.37 S	72.19 W
Vitória, Bra.	250	2.54 S	52.01 W
Vitória, Bra.	255	20.19 S	40.21 W
Vitoria (Gasteiz), Esp.	34	42.51 N	2.40 W
Vitória, Ilha da I	256	23.45 S	45.01 W
Vitória da Conquista	255	14.51 S	40.51 W
Vitória de Santo Antão	250	8.07 S	35.18 W
Vitória do Mearim	250	3.28 S	44.53 W
Vitorino Freire	250	4.04 S	45.10 W
Vitravo ≃	68	39.11 N	17.05 E
Vitré	28	48.08 N	1.12 W
Vitrey-sur-Mance	58	47.49 N	5.45 E
Vitry-aux-Loges	50	47.56 N	2.16 E
Vitry-en-Artois	50	50.20 N	2.59 E
Vitry-la-Ville	50	48.50 N	4.28 E
Vitry-le-François	56	48.44 N	4.35 E
Vitry [-sur-Seine]	50	48.48 N	2.24 E
Vitshumbi	154	0.41 S	29.23 E
Vittangi	24	67.41 N	21.36 E
Vitte	54	54.34 N	13.06 E
Vitteaux	58	47.24 N	4.32 E
Vittel	58	48.12 N	5.57 E
Vittinge	40	59.54 N	17.04 E
Vittoria, On., Can.	212	42.46 N	80.19 W
Vittoria, It.	70	36.57 N	14.32 E
Vittorio Veneto	64	45.59 N	12.18 E
Vittsjö	26	56.20 N	13.40 E
Vitulano	68	41.10 N	14.38 E
Vitznau	58	47.01 N	8.29 E
Viù	62	45.14 N	7.22 E
Vivarais □[9]	62	44.40 N	4.30 E
Vivarais, Monts du ⋌	62	44.55 N	4.15 E
Viver	34	39.55 N	0.36 W
Vivero	34	43.40 N	7.35 W
Viverols	62	45.26 N	3.53 E
Viverone, Lago di ⊜	62	45.25 N	8.02 E
Vivi ≃	74	63.52 N	97.50 E
Vivian	194	32.52 N	93.59 W
Viviers	62	44.29 N	4.41 E
Viviers-du-Lac	62	45.39 N	5.54 E
Vivione, Passo del)(	64	46.02 N	10.12 E
Vivonne	32	46.26 N	0.16 E
Vivoratá	252	37.40 S	57.39 W
Vivorillo, Cayos II	236	15.50 N	83.18 W
Viwa I	175g	17.08 S	176.54 E
Vizagapatam → Vishākhapatnam	122	17.42 N	83.18 E
Vizcaíno, Desierto de ◆[2]	232	27.40 N	114.40 W
Vizcaíno, Isla I	258	33.47 S	59.15 W
Vize	130	41.34 N	27.45 E
Vize, ostrov I	72	79.30 N	77.00 E
Vizianagaram	122	18.07 N	83.25 E
Vizille	62	45.05 N	5.46 E
Vižinada	36	45.20 N	13.46 E
Vizinga	24	61.05 N	50.04 E
Vižnica	78	48.15 N	25.12 E
Vizzini	70	37.10 N	14.53 E
Vizzola	266b	45.38 N	8.42 E
Vjulka ≃	82	56.53 N	37.57 E
Vjunka ≃	265b	55.42 N	38.01 E
Vjuny	86	55.31 N	82.55 E
Vlaanderen → Flanders □[9]	50	51.00 N	3.00 E
Vlaardingen	52	51.54 N	4.21 E
Vlachovo Březí	60	49.05 N	13.57 E
Vladař ∧	54	50.05 N	13.14 E
Vlădeasa, Vîrful ∧	38	46.45 N	22.48 E
Vlădeni	38	47.25 N	27.20 E
Vladičin Han	38	42.42 N	22.04 E
Vladikavkaz → Ordžonikidze	84	43.03 N	44.40 E
Vladimir	80	56.10 N	40.25 E
Vladimir □[4]	82	56.15 N	39.00 E
Vladimirec	78	51.25 N	26.08 E
Vladimirovka, S.S.S.R.	78	47.32 N	32.55 E
Vladimirovka, S.S.S.R.	80	50.51 N	51.08 E
Vladimirovka, S.S.S.R.	83	47.44 N	37.23 E
Vladimirovka, S.S.S.R.	86	53.28 N	64.02 E
Vladimirskij Tupik	76	55.42 N	33.18 E
Vladimirskoje	80	56.49 N	45.07 E
Vladimir-Volynskij	78	50.51 N	24.20 E
Vladivostok	89	43.10 N	131.56 E
Vladyčnoje	76	58.49 N	39.29 E
Vladykino ◆[8]	265b	55.52 N	37.36 E
Vlasenica	38	44.11 N	18.56 E
Vlašim	30	49.42 N	14.54 E
Vlaskovo	82	56.11 N	36.31 E
Vlasotince	38	42.58 N	22.08 E
Vlasovo, S.S.S.R.	74	70.48 N	135.00 E
Vlasovo, S.S.S.R.	82	56.38 N	38.14 E
Vlazoviči	76	53.01 N	32.18 E
Vledder	52	52.52 N	6.12 E
Vleesbaai c	158	34.16 S	21.57 E
Vleikolk	158	29.43 S	20.50 E
Vleuten	52	52.05 N	5.02 E
Vlieland I	52	53.15 N	5.00 E
Vlijmen	52	51.42 N	5.15 E
Vlissingen (Flushing)	52	51.26 N	3.35 E
Vlodrop	52	51.08 N	6.05 E
Vloesberg → Flobecq	50	50.44 N	3.44 E
Vlonë → Vlorë	38	40.27 N	19.30 E
Vlorë	38	40.27 N	19.30 E
Vlorës, Gji i c	38	40.25 N	19.25 E
Vlotho	52	52.10 N	8.51 E
Vltava ≃	30	50.21 N	14.30 E
Vluyn	52	51.26 N	6.32 E
Vnukovo	82	55.38 N	37.16 E
Vnukovo Airport ⊠	265b	55.37 N	37.17 E
Voca	196	31.01 N	99.11 W
Vochrinka	82	55.24 N	38.18 E
Vochtoga	76	58.47 N	41.07 E
Vočin	36	45.37 N	17.32 E
Vöckla ≃	64	48.00 N	13.36 E
Vöcklabruck	60	48.01 N	13.39 E
Vöcklamarkt	60	48.00 N	13.29 E
Vodla ≃	24	61.49 N	36.00 E
Vodlozero, ozero ⊜	24	62.20 N	36.55 E
Vodňany	30	49.09 N	14.11 E
Vodnjan	64	44.57 N	13.51 E
Vodnyj	24	63.32 N	53.18 E
Vodo	64	46.25 N	12.14 E
Vodosalma	24	64.29 N	30.44 E
Vodovatovo	80	55.24 N	43.34 E
Vodzimonje	80	56.49 N	51.38 E
Voël ≃	158	33.07 S	25.07 E
Voerde, B.R.D.	52	51.35 N	6.41 E
Voerde, B.R.D.	263	51.18 N	7.24 E
Voesch	263	51.24 N	6.26 E
Vogelenzang	52	52.19 N	4.35 E
Vogelheim ◆[8]	263	51.29 N	6.59 E
Vogelkop → Doberai, Jazirah ›[1]	164	1.30 S	132.30 E
Vogel Peak → Dimlang ∧	146	8.24 N	11.47 E
Vogelsang, B.R.D.	56	50.35 N	6.27 E
Vogelsang, D.D.R.	54	53.43 N	14.09 E
Vogelsberg ⋌	56	50.30 N	9.15 E
Vogesen → Vosges ⋌	58	48.30 N	7.10 E
Voghera	62	44.59 N	9.01 E
Vognema	76	59.59 N	38.10 E
Vogogna	58	46.01 N	8.17 E
Vogtland ◆[1]	54	50.30 N	12.05 E
Voh	175f	20.58 S	164.42 E
Vohburg an der Donau	60	48.46 N	11.37 E
Vohenstrauss	60	49.37 N	12.21 E
Vohibinany	157b	18.49 S	49.04 E
Vohilava	157b	21.04 S	48.00 E
Vohimarina	157b	13.21 S	50.02 E
Vohipeno	157b	22.22 S	47.51 E

PORTUGUÊS

Nome	Página	Lat.°′	Long.°′ W = Oeste
Vohitsora	157b	23.54 S	44.17 E
Võhma	76	58.38 N	25.33 E
Vöhringen, B.R.D.	58	48.20 N	8.40 E
Vöhringen, B.R.D.	58	48.16 N	10.04 E
Vöhringen, B.R.D.	58	48.02 N	8.18 E
Vöhrum	52	52.20 N	10.10 E
Vohwinkel ◆[8]	263	51.14 N	7.09 E
Voi	154	3.23 S	38.34 E
Void	58	48.41 N	5.37 E
Voight Creek ≃	224	47.06 N	122.10 W
Voikkaa	26	60.56 N	26.37 E
Voinești	38	47.05 N	27.26 E
Voinjama	150	8.25 N	9.45 W
Voinka	78	45.52 N	33.59 E
Voire ≃	58	48.27 N	4.25 E
Voiron	62	45.22 N	5.35 E
Voise	50	48.24 N	1.43 E
Voise ≃	50	48.35 N	1.35 E
Voisenon	261	48.34 N	2.40 E
Voisins-le-Bretonneux	50	48.45 N	2.03 E
Voiteur	58	46.45 N	5.37 E
Voitsberg	61	47.03 N	15.10 E
Voja ≃	80	57.23 N	49.55 E
Vojens	41	55.15 N	9.19 E
Vojevodskoje	86	52.47 N	85.35 E
Vojkovice	54	50.15 N	13.02 E
Vojkovo, S.S.S.R.	78	45.31 N	33.52 E
Vojkovo, S.S.S.R.	83	48.00 N	38.02 E
Vojkovskij	83	47.46 N	38.20 E
Vojmsjön ⊜	26	64.55 N	16.40 E
Vojnić	36	45.19 N	15.42 E
Vojnica	24	65.12 N	30.15 E
Vojnilov	78	49.08 N	24.30 E
Vojtanov	54	50.06 N	12.19 E
Vojvodina □[4]	38	45.00 N	20.00 E
Voj-Vož, S.S.S.R.	24	64.20 N	55.03 E
Voj-Vož, S.S.S.R.	24	62.56 N	54.56 E
Vokeo Island I	164	3.10 S	144.05 E
Volano	66	45.55 N	11.03 E
Volant	214	41.07 N	80.16 W
Volary	60	48.55 N	13.54 E
Volcán	252	23.54 S	65.27 W
Volcancillo ∧	234	19.02 N	103.36 W
Volcán de Colima, Parque Nacional ♠	234	19.30 N	103.35 W
Volčanka	80	52.33 N	49.59 E
Volcano, Ca., U.S.	226	38.26 N	120.37 W
Volcano, Hi., U.S.	229d	19.25 N	155.14 W
Volcano Island I	116	14.00 N	121.00 E
Volcano Islands → Kazan-rettō II	14	25.00 N	141.00 E
Volčansk, S.S.S.R.	78	50.18 N	36.57 E
Volčansk, S.S.S.R.	86	59.56 N	60.04 E
Volčejarovka	83	48.50 N	38.22 E
Volčenskij	83	48.14 N	40.07 E
Volchonka-Zil ◆[8]	265b	55.40 N	37.37 E
Volchov	76	59.55 N	32.20 E
Volchov ≃	76	60.08 N	32.20 E
Volčicha	86	52.02 N	80.23 E
Volčij Nos, mys ›	76	60.31 N	32.35 E
Volčja ≃	78	48.00 N	36.08 E
Volčje	78	49.14 N	22.53 E
Volčki	80	52.29 N	40.42 E
Volda	26	62.09 N	6.06 E
Volders	64	47.17 N	11.34 E
Volendam	52	52.30 N	5.04 E
Volga, S.S.S.R.	76	57.57 N	38.24 E
Volga, Ia., U.S.	190	42.48 N	91.32 W
Volga, S.D., U.S.	198	44.19 N	96.55 W
Volga ≃, S.S.S.R.	72	45.55 N	47.52 E
Volga ≃, Ia., U.S.	190	42.45 N	91.17 W
Volga-Baltic Canal → Volgo-Baltijskij kanal ≅	24	59.00 N	38.00 E
Volgino	76	58.27 N	33.52 E
Volgo, ozero ⊜	76	56.55 N	33.10 E
Volgo-Baltijskij kanal ≅	24	59.00 N	38.00 E
Volgodonsk	80	47.33 N	42.08 E
Volgo-Donskoj sudochodnyj kanal imeni V.I. Lenina ≅	80	48.40 N	43.37 E
Volgograd (Stalingrad)	80	48.44 N	44.25 E
Volgogradskoje vodochranilišče ⊜[1]	80	49.20 N	45.00 E
Volgorečensk	76	57.30 N	41.02 E
Volissós	38	38.29 N	25.58 E
Vol'ka	76	52.47 N	25.39 E
Volkach	56	49.52 N	10.13 E
Volkel	52	51.38 N	5.40 E
Völkermarkt	61	46.39 N	14.38 E
Völkermarkter Stausee ⊜[1]	61	46.39 N	14.38 E
Völkerschlacht-Denkmal ⊥	54	51.18 N	12.24 E
Völklingen	56	49.15 N	6.50 E
Volkmarsen	56	51.24 N	9.07 E
Volkovincy	78	49.13 N	27.39 E
Volkovo, S.S.S.R.	76	59.15 N	41.27 E
Volkovo, S.S.S.R.	82	55.46 N	36.15 E
Volkovo Cemetery ◆	265a	59.54 N	30.22 E
Volkovskoje	82	54.49 N	37.13 E
Volkovysk	76	53.10 N	24.28 E
Volksdorf ◆[8]	52	53.39 N	10.10 E
Völksen	52	52.13 N	9.37 E
Volksrust	158	27.24 S	29.53 E
Vollenhove	52	52.41 N	5.58 E
Vollersode	52	53.18 N	8.56 E
Vollme	263	51.10 N	7.36 E
Vollore-Montagne	62	45.47 N	3.41 E
Vollore-Ville	62	45.47 N	3.36 E
Vollsjö	41	55.42 N	13.46 E
Volma ≃	76	53.35 N	28.19 E
Volmarstein	56	51.22 N	7.23 E
Volme ≃	263	51.24 N	7.27 E
Volmerange-les-Mines	56	49.27 N	6.05 E
Volmerswerth ◆[8]	263	51.11 N	6.46 E
Volmunster	56	49.07 N	7.21 E
Vol'naja Gorka	76	58.43 N	30.51 E
Volnay	58	47.00 N	4.47 E
Vol'nogorsk	78	48.29 N	34.01 E
Vol'noje, S.S.S.R.	80	47.09 N	47.38 E
Vol'noje, S.S.S.R.	86	54.17 N	71.21 E
Volnovacha	83	47.36 N	37.31 E
Vol'nyj	80	45.55 N	45.14 E
Vol'nyj, ostrov I	265a	59.58 N	30.14 E
Voločajevka Vtoraja	89	48.34 N	134.34 E
Voločanka	74	71.00 N	94.28 E
Voločisk	78	49.32 N	26.11 E
Volockaja	76	60.17 N	42.59 E
Volodarka, S.S.S.R.	78	49.31 N	29.55 E
Volodarka, S.S.S.R.	86	52.43 N	83.38 E
Volodarsk, S.S.S.R.	76	56.13 N	43.10 E
Volodarsk, S.S.S.R.	83	48.06 N	39.35 E
Volodarskij, S.S.S.R.	80	46.24 N	48.32 E
Volodarskij, S.S.S.R.	82	55.30 N	37.57 E
Volodarskij ◆[8]	265a	59.49 N	30.05 E
Volodarskoje, S.S.S.R.	83	47.12 N	37.20 E
Volodarskoje, S.S.S.R.	86	53.18 N	68.08 E
Volodarsk-Volynskij	78	50.37 N	28.25 E
Volodino	86	57.06 N	83.54 E
Vologda	76	59.12 N	39.55 E
Vologda ≃	76	59.17 N	40.13 E
Voloje	76	54.09 N	34.35 E
Volokolamsk	82	56.02 N	35.57 E
Volokonovka	78	50.29 N	37.51 E
Volokovaja	24	66.28 N	48.10 E
Volonga	24	67.07 N	47.41 E
Volonne	62	44.07 N	6.01 E
Volontirovka	78	46.26 N	29.37 E
Vólos	38	39.21 N	22.56 E
Vološino, S.S.S.R.	83	48.55 N	39.56 E
Vološino, S.S.S.R.	83	47.31 N	39.40 E
Vološka	24	61.20 N	40.06 E
Vološn'a ≃	82	55.51 N	35.54 E
Vološno	76	58.29 N	28.29 E
Volosoviči	76	54.46 N	28.50 E
Volosovo	76	59.26 N	29.29 E
Volosskaja Balaklejka	83	49.37 N	37.20 E
Volot	76	57.56 N	30.42 E
Volovec	78	48.43 N	23.11 E
Volovo, S.S.S.R.	76	53.35 N	38.02 E
Volovo, S.S.S.R.	78	52.03 N	37.53 E
Voložin	76	54.05 N	26.32 E
Volpago del Montello	64	45.47 N	12.07 E
Volpedo	62	44.53 N	8.59 E
Volpiano	62	45.12 N	7.46 E
Völpke	54	52.08 N	11.09 E
Völs → Fiè	64	46.31 N	11.30 E
Volsini, Monti ⋌	66	42.40 N	11.55 E
Vol'sk	80	52.02 N	47.23 E
Volstruisleegte	158	33.05 S	23.28 E
Volta □[4]	150	7.00 N	0.30 E
Volta ≃	150	5.46 N	0.41 E
Volta, Lake ⊜[1]	150	7.30 N	0.15 E
Volta, Riacho da ≃	250	7.24 S	44.51 W
Volta Blanche (White Volta) ≃	150	9.10 N	1.15 W
Voltaggio	62	44.37 N	8.50 E
Voltago	64	46.16 N	12.00 E
Volta Grande	256	21.46 S	42.32 W
Voltaire, Cape ›	164	14.16 S	125.35 E
Volta Mantovana	64	45.19 N	10.39 E
Volta Noire (Black Volta) ≃	150	8.41 N	1.33 W
Volta Redonda	256	22.32 S	44.07 W
Volta Rouge ≃	150	10.34 N	0.30 W
Volterra	66	43.24 N	10.51 E
Vol'teva	24	64.30 N	44.12 E
Voltri	62	44.26 N	8.45 E
Volturara Appula	68	41.30 N	15.03 E
Volturara Irpina	68	40.53 N	14.55 E
Volturino	68	41.28 N	15.07 E
Volturino, Monte ∧	68	40.25 N	15.49 E
Volturno ≃	68	41.01 N	13.55 E
Volubilis ⊥	148	34.00 N	5.30 W
Voluntown	207	41.34 N	71.52 W
Volusia □[6]	220	28.51 N	81.05 W
Vólvi, Límni ⊜	38	40.41 N	23.23 E
Volx	62	43.53 N	5.51 E
Volyncy, S.S.S.R.	76	55.42 N	28.11 E
Volyncy, S.S.S.R.	80	57.48 N	45.28 E
Volyně	60	49.10 N	13.53 E
Volynka	78	51.37 N	32.26 E
Volyňka ≃	60	49.16 N	13.54 E
Volynskaja Oblast' □[4]	78	51.00 N	25.00 E
Volynskoje Polesje ◆[1]	78	51.10 N	26.00 E
Volzhskiy → Volžskij	80	48.50 N	44.44 E
Volžsk	80	55.53 N	48.21 E
Volžskij, S.S.S.R.	80	53.27 N	50.07 E
Volžskij, S.S.S.R.	80	48.50 N	44.44 E
Vom	150	9.41 N	8.42 E
Vomano ≃	66	42.39 N	14.02 E
Vombsjön ⊜	41	55.41 N	13.36 E
Vomp	64	47.20 N	11.41 E
Vonavona Island I	175e	8.15 S	157.05 E
Vonda	184	52.19 N	106.06 W
Vondanka	24	59.07 N	47.49 E
Vondrozo	157b	22.49 S	47.20 E
Von Frank Mountain ∧	180	63.33 N	154.20 W
Võnnu	76	58.17 N	27.05 E
Vonozero	76	60.22 N	34.26 E
Vonsild	41	55.27 N	9.29 E
Von Treuer Tableland ⋌[1]	162	26.38 S	122.53 E
Voorburg	52	52.05 N	4.23 E
Voordeelspan	158	29.05 S	21.32 E
Voorheesville	210	42.39 N	73.56 W
Voorne I	52	51.55 N	4.00 E
Voorschoten	52	52.07 N	4.27 E
Voorst	52	52.10 N	6.09 E
Voorthuizen	52	52.12 N	5.35 E
Vop' ≃	76	54.56 N	32.44 E
Vopnafjörður	24a	65.47 N	14.44 W
Vopnafjörður c	24a	65.52 N	14.40 W
Vörå (Vöyri)	26	63.09 N	22.15 E
Vor'a ≃, S.S.S.R.	76	54.54 N	35.01 E
Vor'a ≃, S.S.S.R.	82	55.52 N	38.13 E
Vor'a ≃, S.S.S.R.	265b	55.56 N	38.13 E
Vorarlberg □[3]	64	47.15 N	9.55 E
Vorau	61	47.25 N	15.54 E
Vorbach	60	49.49 N	11.45 E
Vorbasse	41	55.38 N	9.05 E
Vorbjovo	88	57.23 N	102.18 E
Vorchdorf	60	48.00 N	13.55 E
Vörden, B.R.D.	52	52.28 N	8.05 E
Vorden, Ned.	52	52.07 N	6.18 E
Vorder-Grauspitz ∧	58	47.03 N	9.36 E
Vorderkrimmi	64	47.14 N	12.12 E
Vordernberg	61	47.28 N	15.00 E
Vorderrhein ≃	58	46.49 N	9.25 E
Vorderriss	64	47.33 N	11.26 E
Vordingborg	41	55.01 N	11.55 E
Voreifel ⋌	56	50.15 N	7.10 E
Voreppe	62	45.18 N	5.38 E
Vorey	62	45.11 N	3.54 E
Vorga	76	53.45 N	32.45 E
Vorhalle ◆[8]	263	51.23 N	7.28 E
Vorhelm	52	51.48 N	7.56 E
Voríai Sporádhes II	38	39.17 N	23.23 E
Vøringsfossen ʟ	26	60.26 N	7.15 E
Vórios Evvoïkós Kólpos c	38	38.40 N	23.15 E
Vorkuta	24	67.27 N	63.58 E
Vorlich, Ben ∧	46	56.20 N	4.14 W
Vorma ≃	26	60.09 N	11.27 E
Vormholz	263	51.24 N	7.18 E
Vormsi I	76	59.00 N	23.20 E
Vorn'any	76	54.44 N	26.01 E
Vorobjevo, S.S.S.R.	82	56.11 N	35.45 E
Vorobjevo, S.S.S.R.	86	56.08 N	76.32 E
Vorobji	82	55.09 N	36.48 E
Vorobjovka	80	50.38 N	40.56 E
Vorob'jovo, S.S.S.R.	76	59.38 N	40.55 E
Vorob'jovo, S.S.S.R.	78	45.20 N	33.15 E
Vorochta	78	48.18 N	24.36 E
Voron'	76	55.00 N	28.39 E
Voron, porog ʟ	88	57.05 N	98.40 E
Vorona ≃	80	51.22 N	42.03 E
Voroncovka, S.S.S.R.	78	50.37 N	40.21 E
Voroncovka, S.S.S.R.	78	45.51 N	33.47 E
Voroncovka, S.S.S.R.	86	59.39 N	60.14 E
Voroncovka, S.S.S.R.	86	48.49 N	81.32 E
Voroncovka, S.S.S.R.	88	58.51 N	112.56 E
Voroncovo, S.S.S.R.	76	57.18 N	28.42 E
Voroncovo, S.S.S.R.	80	55.16 N	40.27 E
Voronej → Voronež	78	51.40 N	39.10 E
Voronež, S.S.S.R.	78	51.40 N	39.10 E
Voronež, S.S.S.R.	78	51.46 N	33.28 E
Voronež □[4], S.S.S.R.	76	51.55 N	40.00 E
Voronež □[4], S.S.S.R.	83	49.40 N	40.00 E
Voronež ≃	76	51.56 N	39.25 E
Voronezh → Voronež	78	51.40 N	39.10 E
Voronežskij Zapovednik ◆[4]	76	51.56 N	39.37 E
Voronino	82	56.24 N	36.52 E
Voronja ≃	24	69.10 N	35.50 E
Voronjo, S.S.S.R.	24	68.27 N	35.21 E
Voronjo, S.S.S.R.	80	58.00 N	42.01 E
Voron'ki, S.S.S.R.	78	50.14 N	33.02 E
Voronki, S.S.S.R.	82	55.48 N	37.16 E
Voronkovo	78	47.43 N	29.08 E
Voronok	76	52.23 N	32.40 E
Voronov, mys ›	76	60.15 N	32.05 E
Voronovica	78	49.06 N	28.41 E
Voronovkova Niva	76	57.04 N	29.16 E
Voronovo, S.S.S.R.	76	54.09 N	25.19 E
Voronovo, S.S.S.R.	82	55.19 N	37.10 E
Voronovo, S.S.S.R.	86	56.01 N	83.52 E
Voropajevo	76	55.09 N	27.13 E
Voroshilov → Ussurijsk	89	43.48 N	131.59 E
Voroshilovsk → Stavropol', S.S.S.R.	72	45.02 N	41.59 E
Voroshilovsk → Kommunarsk, S.S.S.R.	83	48.30 N	38.47 E
Vorošilovgrad (Lugansk)	83	48.34 N	39.20 E
Vorošilovgrad □[4]	83	49.00 N	39.00 E
Vorotajevka	80	51.56 N	47.16 E
Vorotynec	80	56.04 N	45.52 E
Vorotynsk	82	54.25 N	36.05 E
Vorovskolesskaja	84	44.23 N	42.25 E
Vorožba	78	51.12 N	34.14 E
Vorožejka	86	58.12 N	90.02 E
Vorpommern □[9]	54	53.40 N	13.45 E
Vorra	60	49.33 N	11.30 E
Vorsfelde	54	52.26 N	10.49 E
Vorskla ≃	78	48.53 N	34.06 E
Vorsma	80	55.59 N	43.16 E
Vorst, Bel.	56	51.04 N	5.01 E
Vorst, B.R.D.	56	51.18 N	6.25 E
Vørterkaka Nunatak ∧	9	72.20 S	27.29 E
Võrtsjärv ⊜	76	58.16 N	26.03 E
Võru	76	57.50 N	27.01 E
Voruch	85	39.52 N	70.35 E
Vorzel'	78	50.33 N	30.09 E
Vosburg	158	30.33 S	22.52 E
Voschod	80	47.24 N	41.50 E
Vösendorf	61	48.07 N	16.20 E
Vosges □[5]	58	48.10 N	6.20 E
Vosges ⋌	58	48.30 N	7.10 E
Vosja	76	59.01 N	41.11 E
Voskresenka, S.S.S.R.	80	51.01 N	46.28 E
Voskresenka, S.S.S.R.	88	53.15 N	119.31 E
Voskresenki	82	54.57 N	38.04 E
Voskresenovskoje	265a	59.43 N	30.47 E
Voskresensk	82	55.19 N	38.42 E
Voskresenskoje, S.S.S.R.	76	58.54 N	38.36 E
Voskresenskoje, S.S.S.R.	76	53.12 N	38.43 E
Voskresenskoje, S.S.S.R.	76	59.26 N	37.56 E
Voskresenskoje, S.S.S.R.	76	57.49 N	37.40 E
Voskresenskoje, S.S.S.R.	78	47.02 N	32.09 E
Voskresenskoje, S.S.S.R.	80	56.51 N	45.26 E
Voskresenskoje, S.S.S.R.	80	51.51 N	46.56 E
Voskresenskoje, S.S.S.R.	82	54.07 N	37.07 E
Voskresenskoje, S.S.S.R.	82	56.20 N	38.29 E
Voskresenskoje, S.S.S.R.	86	53.08 N	56.10 E
Voslapp	52	53.36 N	8.05 E
Voss	26	60.39 N	6.26 E
Vosselaar	56	51.19 N	4.53 E
Vossijatskoje	78	47.41 N	32.07 E
Vossman's Beacon	158	26.11 S	30.40 E
Vostočnaja Kambal'nica	24	68.18 N	46.00 E
Vostočno-Kazachstanskaja Oblast' □[4]	86	49.00 N	84.00 E
Vostočno-Kounradskij	86	47.02 N	75.07 E
Vostočno-Sibirskoje more (East Siberian Sea) ✢[2]	12	74.00 N	166.00 E
Vostočnyj, S.S.S.R.	82	55.47 N	37.52 E
Vostočnyj, S.S.S.R.	86	58.48 N	61.52 E
Vostočnyj, S.S.S.R.	89	53.29 N	143.03 E
Vostočnyj, S.S.S.R.	89	48.17 N	142.34 E
Vostočnyj Sajan ⋌	88	53.00 N	97.00 E
Vostok I	14	10.06 S	152.23 W
Vostok ⊕[3]	9	78.30 S	106.50 E
Vostr'akovo	82	55.23 N	37.49 E
Vostrecovo	89	45.53 N	134.58 E
Vostrovo	86	52.09 N	80.38 E
Vosves	261	48.31 N	2.36 E
Votaw	222	30.26 N	94.41 W
Votice	30	49.38 N	14.39 E
Votkinsk	80	57.03 N	53.59 E
Votkinskoje vodochranilišče ⊜[1]	86	57.00 N	54.30 E
Vot'pa	86	60.13 N	62.57 E
Votuporanga	255	20.24 S	49.59 W
Voué	50	48.28 N	4.07 E
Vouga ≃	34	40.41 N	8.40 W
Vougba	152	5.10 N	23.06 E
Vougeot	58	47.10 N	4.58 E
Vouillé	32	46.39 N	0.10 E
Voujeaucourt	58	47.28 N	6.46 E
Voulangis	261	48.51 N	2.54 E
Voulou	146	8.33 N	22.36 E
Voulx	50	48.17 N	2.58 E
Voulzie ≃	50	48.25 N	3.12 E
Voutenay-sur-Cure	50	47.33 N	3.47 E
Vouvray	50	47.25 N	0.48 E
Vouvry	58	46.20 N	6.53 E
Vouziers	56	49.24 N	4.42 E
Voves	50	48.16 N	1.38 E
Vovodo ≃	140	5.40 N	24.21 E
Vowinckel	214	41.25 N	79.14 W
Voxnan ≃	26	61.17 N	16.26 E
Voyageurs National Park ♠	190	48.30 N	93.00 W
Voyeykov Ice Shelf ⊓	9	66.20 S	124.38 E
Vöyri → Vörå	26	63.09 N	22.15 E
Voža ≃	82	54.38 N	39.10 E
Vožajol'	24	62.50 N	51.17 E
Vožď Proletariata	76	55.26 N	39.19 E
Vozdviženka, S.S.S.R.	78	47.46 N	36.05 E
Vozdviženka, S.S.S.R.	80	53.10 N	54.14 E
Vozdviženskoje, S.S.S.R.	80	56.58 N	45.37 E
Vozdviženskoje, S.S.S.R.	80	45.50 N	43.40 E
Vozdviženskoje, S.S.S.R.	82	56.12 N	38.04 E
Vože, ozero ⊜	24	60.30 N	39.00 E
Vožega	76	60.29 N	40.12 E
Vožega ≃	76	60.33 N	39.11 E
Vožgaly	80	58.09 N	50.11 E
Vožgora	24	64.32 N	48.25 E
Voznesenje	24	61.01 N	35.27 E
Voznesenka, S.S.S.R.	78	46.51 N	35.26 E
Voznesenka, S.S.S.R.	86	52.24 N	70.12 E
Voznesenovka	80	46.16 N	44.21 E
Voznesensk	78	47.34 N	31.20 E
Voznesenskoje, S.S.S.R.	80	54.54 N	42.46 E
Voznesenskoje, S.S.S.R.	80	45.49 N	43.25 E
Vozroždenija, ostrov I	86	45.03 N	59.12 E
Vozroždenije	80	52.42 N	48.12 E
Vozžajevka	89	50.44 N	128.41 E
Vrå	26	57.21 N	9.57 E
Vráble	30	48.15 N	18.19 E
Vraca	38	43.12 N	23.33 E
Vračevo	82	54.53 N	39.10 E
Vrådal	26	59.20 N	8.25 E
Vrancea □[6]	38	45.45 N	27.00 E
Vrancei, Munții ⋌	38	46.00 N	26.30 E
Vrangel'a, mys ›	89	54.17 N	138.39 E
Vrangel'a, ostrov I	74	71.00 N	179.30 W
Vranje	38	42.33 N	21.54 E
Vranov	61	48.54 N	15.49 E
Vranov [nad Topl'ou]	30	48.54 N	21.41 E
Vrbas	38	45.35 N	19.39 E
Vrbas ≃	36	45.06 N	17.31 E
Vrbovec	36	45.53 N	16.25 E
Vrbovsko	36	45.23 N	15.05 E
Vrchlabí	30	50.38 N	15.37 E
Vrede	158	27.30 S	29.06 E
Vredefort	158	27.05 S	27.16 E
Vreden	52	52.02 N	6.52 E
Vredenburg	158	32.54 S	17.59 E
Vredenburgh	194	31.49 N	87.19 W
Vredendal	158	31.41 S	18.35 E
Vreed en Hoop	246	6.48 N	58.11 W
Vreeswijk	52	52.01 N	5.05 E
Vrena	40	58.52 N	16.41 E
Vresse	56	49.52 N	4.56 E
Vreta kloster ⊕[1]	26	58.28 N	15.29 E
Vretstorp	40	59.02 N	14.52 E
Vrginmost	36	45.21 N	15.52 E
Vrhnika	36	45.58 N	14.18 E
Vriddhāchalam	122	11.30 N	79.20 E
Vriendschaps ≃	164	5.28 S	138.53 E
Vries	52	53.04 N	6.35 E
Vriezenveen	52	52.25 N	6.38 E
Vrigne-Meuse	56	49.42 N	4.51 E
Vrigstad	26	57.21 N	14.28 E
Vrilissia	267c	38.02 N	23.50 E
Vrille ≃	50	47.31 N	2.52 E
Vrin	58	46.39 N	9.06 E
Vrin ≃	50	48.00 N	3.20 E
Vrindāvan	124	27.35 N	77.42 E
Vrlika	36	43.55 N	16.24 E
Vrnograč	36	45.10 N	15.57 E
Vroeggedeel	158	28.02 S	22.32 E
Vron	50	50.19 N	1.45 E
Vrondádhes	38	38.24 N	26.08 E
Vroomshoop	52	52.27 N	6.34 E
Vrouenspan	158	27.50 S	20.24 E
Vroutek	54	50.08 N	13.24 E
Vršac	38	45.07 N	21.18 E
Vrsar	64	45.08 N	13.37 E
Vršič)(	64	46.26 N	13.44 E
Vrubovka	83	48.44 N	38.20 E
Vrubovskij	83	48.26 N	39.07 E
Vrútky	30	49.07 N	18.55 E
Vryburg	158	26.55 S	24.45 E
Vryheid	158	27.46 S	30.48 E
Vschody	76	54.42 N	34.06 E
Vselug, ozero ⊜	76	57.03 N	32.42 E
Všepadly	60	49.28 N	13.06 E
Vsetín	30	49.21 N	17.59 E
Vsevidof, Mount ∧	180	53.07 N	168.43 W
Vsevoložsk	76	60.01 N	30.40 E
Vtoroje Potapovo	265b	55.56 N	37.58 E
Vtoryje Levyje Lamki	80	53.17 N	41.04 E
Vuadil'	85	40.11 N	71.43 E
Vuanggava Island I	175g	18.52 S	178.54 W
Vučitrn	38	42.49 N	20.58 E
Vudor, gora ∧	85	38.13 N	71.49 E
Vue-des-Alpes)(	58	47.04 N	6.53 E
Vught	52	51.40 N	5.17 E
Vuillafans	58	47.04 N	6.13 E
Vuitebœuf	58	46.37 N	6.34 E
Vukovar	38	45.21 N	19.00 E
Vulcan, Ab., Can.	182	50.24 N	113.15 W
Vulcan, Rom.	38	45.23 N	23.17 E
Vulcan, Mi., U.S.	190	45.46 N	87.51 W
Vulcano, Bocche di ⟗	70	38.26 N	14.57 E
Vulcano, Isola I, It.	36	38.27 N	14.58 E
Vulcano, Isola I, It.	70	38.24 N	14.58 E
Vulcano, Monte ∧	70a	35.51 N	12.52 E
Vulci ⊥	66	42.25 N	11.35 E
Vulkanešty	78	45.41 N	28.24 E
Vulkaničeskij chrebet ⋌	78	48.30 N	23.00 E
Vulture, Monte ∧	68	40.57 N	15.38 E
Vul'vyvejem ≃	180	66.58 N	179.10 W
Vung Tau	110	10.21 N	107.04 E
Vunindawa	175g	17.49 S	178.19 E
Vunisea Station	175g	19.03 S	178.09 E
Vuoggatjålme	24	66.36 N	16.22 E
Vuohijärvi	26	61.05 N	26.48 E
Vuohijärvi ⊜	26	61.12 N	26.42 E
Vuokatti ∧[2]	26	64.07 N	28.14 E
Vuoksa ≃	26	61.03 N	30.11 E
Vuoksa, ozero ⊜	76	60.40 N	29.50 E
Vuoksenniska	26	61.13 N	28.49 E
Vuotso	24	68.08 N	27.08 E
Vurnary	80	55.29 N	46.58 E
Vuturu, Pizzo ∧	70	37.56 N	14.13 E
Vuya	154	5.21 N	29.40 E
Vuyyūru	122	16.22 N	80.51 E
Vuzenica	61	46.36 N	15.10 E
Vvedenka	86	54.03 N	63.45 E
Vvedenovka	89	51.19 N	128.12 E
Vvedenskoje	82	55.42 N	36.54 E
Vyāra	120	21.07 N	73.24 E
Vyatka → Kirov	80	58.38 N	49.42 E
Vyaz'ma → V'az'ma	76	55.13 N	34.18 E
Vyazniki → V'azniki	80	56.15 N	42.10 E
Vyborg	76	60.42 N	28.45 E
Vyborgskij zaliv c	76	60.35 N	28.24 E
Výčapy	61	49.09 N	15.53 E
Vyčegda ≃	24	61.18 N	46.36 E
Vyčegodskij	24	61.16 N	46.48 E
Vychino ◆[8]	265b	55.43 N	37.48 E
Východočeský Kraj □[4]	30	50.10 N	16.00 E
Východoslovenský Kraj □[4]	30	49.00 N	21.15 E
Vydrino, S.S.S.R.	88	51.27 N	104.39 E
Vydrino, S.S.S.R.	88	56.50 N	99.02 E
Vygoda	78	48.56 N	23.55 E
Vygoniči	76	53.08 N	34.05 E
Vygonišči	76	52.37 N	25.55 E
Vygozero, ozero ⊜	24	63.35 N	34.42 E
Vyjezdnoje	80	55.23 N	43.47 E
Vyjezžij Log	86	54.58 N	93.57 E
Vyksa	80	55.18 N	42.11 E
Vylkovo	86	53.05 N	81.26 E
Vym' ≃	24	62.13 N	50.25 E
Vyntja	86	60.31 N	67.18 E
Vypolzovo	76	57.53 N	33.42 E
Vyrica	76	59.25 N	30.21 E
Vyrnwy, Lake ⊜	42	52.47 N	3.30 W
Vyša	80	53.52 N	42.24 E
Vyša ≃	80	54.02 N	42.06 E
Vyšehrad ◆[8]	54	50.01 N	14.27 E
Vyšelej	80	53.26 N	45.29 E
Vyselki	78	45.35 N	39.38 E
Vyšesteblijevskaja	78	45.12 N	37.00 E
Vyšgorodok	76	57.02 N	28.01 E
Vyška, S.S.S.R.	76	57.31 N	35.57 E
Vyška, S.S.S.R.	128	39.20 N	54.08 E
Vyskod'	76	57.46 N	30.04 E
Vyškov, Česko.	30	49.16 N	17.00 E
Vyškov, S.S.S.R.	76	52.29 N	31.41 E
Vyškovskij, pereval)(	78	48.42 N	23.38 E
Vyšná Radvaň	30	49.07 N	21.56 E
Vyšneol'šanoje	76	52.08 N	37.39 E
Vyšnevolockoje vodochranilišče ⊜[1]	76	57.35 N	34.28 E
Vyšnij Voločok	76	57.35 N	34.34 E
Vysočany ◆[8]	54	50.05 N	14.31 E
Vysock, S.S.S.R.	76	60.36 N	28.34 E
Vysock, S.S.S.R.	78	51.43 N	26.39 E
Vysokaja, gora ∧	89	45.59 N	136.35 E
Vysokaja Gora	80	55.56 N	49.19 E
Vysoké Mýto	30	49.57 N	16.10 E
Vysoké Tatry ⋌	30	49.12 N	20.05 E
Vysokiniči	82	54.54 N	36.55 E
Vysokogornyj	89	50.09 N	139.09 E
Vysokogorsk	89	44.23 N	135.23 E
Vysokoje, S.S.S.R.	76	56.43 N	34.55 E
Vysokoje, S.S.S.R.	76	54.02 N	33.44 E
Vysokoje, S.S.S.R.	76	52.22 N	23.22 E

	English	Deutsch	Español	Français	Português
≃	River	Fluß	Río	Rivière	Rio
≅	Canal	Kanal	Canal	Canal	Canal
ʟ	Waterfall, Rapids	Wasserfall, Stromschnellen	Cascada, Rápidos	Chute d'eau, Rapides	Cascata, Rápidos
⟗	Strait	Meeresstraße	Estrecho	Détroit	Estreito
c	Bay, Gulf	Bucht, Golf	Bahía, Golfo	Baie, Golfe	Baía, Golfo
⊜	Lake, Lakes	See, Seen	Lago, Lagos	Lac, Lacs	Lago, Lagos
☷	Swamp	Sumpf	Pantano	Marais	Pântano
⊓	Ice Features, Glacier	Eis- und Gletscherformen	Accidentes Glaciales	Formes glaciaires	Acidentes glaciares
✢	Other Hydrographic Features	Andere Hydrographische Objekte	Otros Elementos Hidrográficos	Autres données hydrographiques	Outros acidentes hidrográficos

	English	Deutsch	Español	Français	Português
✣	Submarine Features	Untermeerische Objekte	Accidentes Submarinos	Formes de relief sous-marin	Acidentes submarinos
□	Political Unit	Politische Einheit	Unidad Politica	Entité politique	Unidade política
⊕	Cultural Institution	Kulturelle Institution	Institución Cultural	Institution culturelle	Instituição cultural
⊥	Historical Site	Historische Stätte	Sitio Histórico	Site historique	Sitio histórico
♠	Recreational Site	Erholungs- und Ferienort	Sitio de Recreo	Centre de loisirs	Area de Lazer
⊠	Airport	Flughafen	Aeropuerto	Aéroport	Aeroporto
■	Military Installation	Militäranlage	Instalación Militar	Installation militaire	Instalação militar
◆	Miscellaneous	Verschiedenes	Misceláneo	Divers	Diversos

Column 1:

Name	Page	Lat.	Long.
Vysokoje, S.S.S.R.	82	54.30 N	37.03 E
Vysokoje, S.S.S.R.	85	42.30 N	70.32 E
Vysokoje, S.S.S.R.	265b	55.59 N	37.09 E
Vysokopolje	78	47.29 N	33.32 E
Vysokovsk	82	56.19 N	36.33 E
Vysoký kámen ▲	61	49.06 N	15.13 E
Vyšší Dubečn'a	78	50.44 N	30.40 E
Vyšší Brod	61	48.37 N	14.19 E
Vystupoviči	78	51.34 N	29.04 E
Vytebet'	76	53.53 N	35.38 E
Vytegra	24	61.00 N	36.24 E
Vyževka ≃	78	51.41 N	24.35 E
Vzmorje	89	47.51 N	142.31 E
Vzvad	76	58.10 N	31.29 E

W

Name	Page	Lat.	Long.
W., Parc National du ♦	150	12.50 N	2.30 W
Wa	150	10.04 N	2.29 W
Waabs	41	54.32 N	9.58 E
Waackaack Creek ≃	276	40.27 N	74.08 W
Waadt → Vaud □³	58	46.40 N	6.30 E
Waajid	144	3.48 N	43.15 E
Waakirchen	58	47.46 N	11.40 E
Waal	58	48.00 N	10.46 E
Waalre	52	51.24 N	5.26 E
Waalwijk	52	51.42 N	5.04 E
Waar	102	24.20 N	104.40 E
Waar, Meos I	164	2.05 S	134.23 E
Waarschoot	52	51.09 N	3.36 E
Waasmunster	50	51.06 N	4.05 E
Wabag	164	5.30 S	143.40 E
Wabamun Indian Reserve ▲⁴	182	53.30 N	114.30 W
Wabamun Lake ◎	182	53.33 N	114.35 W
Waban	283	42.20 N	71.14 W
Waban, Lake ◎	283	42.17 N	71.17 W
Wabana	182	47.38 N	52.57 W
Wabasca ≃	182	56.00 N	113.53 W
Wabasca	176	58.22 N	115.20 W
Wabasca Indian Reserve ▲⁴	182	55.53 N	113.32 W
Wabash, In., U.S.	216	40.47 N	85.49 W
Wabash, Oh., U.S.	216	40.03 N	84.45 W
Wabash ≃⁶	216	40.48 N	85.49 W
Wabash ≃	194	37.46 N	88.02 W
Wabasha	190	44.23 N	92.01 W
Wabasso, Fl., U.S.	220	27.44 N	80.26 W
Wabasso, Mn., U.S.	198	44.24 N	95.15 W
Wabatongushi Lake ◎	190	48.26 N	84.15 W
Wabe Gestro ≃	144	4.17 N	42.02 E
Wabe Mena ≃	144	5.32 N	41.11 E
Wabeno	190	45.26 N	88.39 W
Wabera	144	6.26 N	40.42 E
Wabern	56	51.06 N	9.20 E
Wabigoon Lake ◎	184	49.44 N	92.44 W
Wabowden	184	54.55 N	98.38 W
Wabrah ≃⁴	128	27.26 N	47.22 E
Wabrzeźno	30	53.17 N	18.57 E
Wabu	100	32.17 N	116.55 E
Wabu Hu ◎	100	32.23 N	116.54 E
Wabuska	226	39.09 N	119.10 W
W.A.C. Bennett Dam ≃⁶	182	56.01 N	122.10 W
Waccamaw ≃	192	33.21 N	79.16 W
Waccamaw, Lake ◎	192	34.17 N	78.30 W
Waccasassa Bay c	192	29.06 N	82.52 W
Wachapreague	208	37.36 N	75.41 W
Wachapreague Inlet c	208	37.35 N	75.36 W
Wachau ≃¹	61	48.18 N	15.24 E
Wachenheim	56	49.26 N	8.10 E
Wachi	96	35.15 N	135.24 E
Wachock, Klasztory ☨¹	30	51.05 N	21.01 E
Wachtberg	56	50.37 N	7.11 E
Wachtendonk	56	51.24 N	6.20 E
Wächtersbach	56	50.15 N	9.17 E
Wachusett Mountain ▲	207	42.29 N	71.53 W
Wachusett Reservoir ◎¹	207	42.23 N	71.43 W
Wackersdorf	60	49.19 N	12.11 E
Waco	222	31.32 N	97.08 W
Waco Lake ◎¹	222	31.34 N	97.13 W
Waconia	190	44.51 N	93.47 W
Waconda Lake ◎¹	198	39.30 N	98.24 W
Wacouno ≃	190	51.04 N	66.22 E
Wacousta	216	42.49 N	84.42 W
Wad	120	27.21 N	66.22 E
Wada, Nihon	96	35.02 N	140.01 E
Wada, Nihon	94	36.12 N	138.13 E
Wada, Nihon	268	35.12 N	139.38 E
Wada, Nihon	96	34.33 N	135.55 E
Wadagou	104	42.27 N	120.58 E
Wad Al-Ḥaddād	140	13.49 N	33.32 E
Wadamago	144	8.55 N	46.17 E
Wada-misaki ▸	96	34.39 N	135.11 E
Wādat Ga	120	26.57 N	97.37 E
Wadayama	96	35.19 N	134.52 E
Wad Bandah	140	13.06 N	27.57 E
Wad Ban Naqa	140	16.30 N	33.08 E
Wadbilliga National Park ♦	166	36.20 S	149.35 E
Waddān, Jabal ⱬ²	146	29.10 N	16.08 E
Waddeneilanden II	52	53.30 N	5.30 E
Waddenzee ▾²	52	53.15 N	5.15 E
Wadderin	162	32.00 S	118.27 E
Waddingham	44	53.28 N	0.31 W
Waddington, Eng., U.K.	44	53.10 N	0.32 W
Waddington, N.Y., U.S.	212	44.51 N	75.12 W
Waddington, Mount ▲	182	51.23 N	125.15 W
Waddinxveen	52	52.03 N	4.40 E
Waddy ≃	218	38.08 N	85.04 W
Wade, Mount ▲	9	84.51 S	174.15 E
Wadebridge	42	50.32 N	4.50 W
Wadena, Sk., Can.	184	51.57 N	103.47 W
Wadena, In., U.S.	216	40.43 N	87.16 W
Wadena, Mn., U.S.	198	46.26 N	95.08 W
Wädenswil	58	47.14 N	8.40 E
Wadern	56	49.32 N	6.53 E
Wadersloh	52	51.44 N	8.15 E
Wadesboro	192	34.58 N	80.04 W
Wadeville	273d	26.16 S	28.11 E
Wadeye	164	14.13 S	129.32 E
Wadgassen	56	49.16 N	6.47 E
Wad Ḥāmid	146	16.30 N	32.48 E
Wadham Islands II	186	49.34 N	53.50 W
Wadhams	182	51.30 N	127.31 W
Wadhurst	42	51.04 N	0.21 E
Wadian	100	32.48 N	112.30 E
Wādī as-Sīr	132	31.57 N	35.49 E
Wādī Ḥalfā	140	21.56 N	31.20 E
Wādī Mūsā	132	30.19 N	35.29 E
Wading ≃, Ma., U.S.	283	41.56 N	71.13 W
Wading, West Branch ≃	208	39.40 N	74.32 W
Wading River	207	40.57 N	72.50 W
Wādī Rashrāsh, Bi'r ≃	142	29.36 N	31.31 E
Wadley, Al., U.S.	194	33.07 N	85.33 W
Wadley, Ga., U.S.	192	32.52 N	82.24 W
Wad Madanī	140	14.25 N	33.28 E
Wadowice	30	49.53 N	19.30 E
Wadsworth, Il., U.S.	216	42.26 N	87.56 W

Column 2:

Name	Page	Lat.	Long.
Wadsworth, Nv., U.S.	204	39.38 N	119.17 W
Wadsworth, N.Y., U.S.	210	42.49 N	77.54 W
Wadsworth, Oh., U.S.	214	41.01 N	81.43 W
Wadsworth Moor ⊹	262	53.48 N	2.02 W
Wadu I	122	5.51 N	72.58 E
Waegwan	98	35.58 N	128.24 E
Waelder	222	29.42 N	97.18 W
Waenhuiskrans	158	34.41 S	20.14 E
Wafang	98	41.44 N	118.54 E
Wafania	152	1.21 S	20.20 E
Wafrah	128	28.33 N	48.02 E
Wagadugu → Ouagadougou	150	12.22 N	1.31 W
Wāgah	123	31.36 N	74.33 E
Wagait Aboriginal Reserve ▲⁴	164	13.00 S	130.20 E
Wagang	102	28.04 N	103.10 E
Wagenborgen	52	53.15 N	6.56 E
Wagenfeld-Haßlingen	52	52.33 N	8.34 E
Wageningen, Ned.	52	51.58 N	5.40 E
Wageningen, Sur.	250	5.46 N	56.41 W
Wager Bay c	176	65.26 N	88.40 W
Wagerup	168a	32.55 S	115.54 E
Waggaman Heights	284c	38.49 N	76.57 W
Wagga Wagga	171b	35.07 S	147.22 E
Waggoner	219	39.23 N	89.39 W
Waghäusel	56	49.14 N	8.31 E
Wagin	162	33.18 S	117.21 E
Waging am See	64	47.56 N	12.43 E
Waginger See ◎	64	47.52 N	12.44 E
Wagitaler See ◎	58	47.06 N	8.55 E
Waglan Island I	271d	22.11 N	114.18 E
Wagna	61	46.46 N	15.34 E
Wagner	198	43.04 N	98.17 W
Wagner College ⱴ²	276	40.37 N	74.07 W
Wagoner	196	35.57 N	95.22 W
Wagon Mound	196	36.00 N	104.42 W
Wagontire Mountain ▲	202	43.21 N	119.53 W
Wagontown	208	40.01 N	75.51 W
Wagrain	61	47.20 N	13.18 E
Wagram → Deutsch Wagram	61	48.18 N	16.34 E
Wagrien ≃¹	54	54.15 N	10.45 E
Wagrowiec	30	52.49 N	17.11 E
Waha	146	28.16 N	19.54 E
Wahādürgañj	124	27.32 N	82.50 E
Wahai	164	2.48 S	129.30 E
Waharoa	172	37.46 S	175.46 E
Wāh Cantonment	123	33.48 N	72.42 E
Wahiawa	229c	21.30 N	158.01 W
Wāhid	142	30.19 N	32.20 E
Wahkiakum ▫⁶	224	46.16 N	123.28 W
Wahlen	56	49.37 N	8.51 E
Wahlstedt	54	53.57 N	10.12 E
Wahnbachtalsee ◎¹	56	50.48 N	7.19 E
Wahneta	220	27.57 N	81.44 W
Wahoo	198	41.12 N	96.37 W
Wahpeton	198	46.15 N	96.36 W
Wahran (Oran)	148	35.43 N	0.43 W
Wahran ≃³	148	35.30 N	0.30 E
Wahrenbrück	54	51.33 N	13.22 E
Wahrenholz	54	52.36 N	10.36 E
Währing ⱴ⁸	264b	48.14 N	16.21 E
Wahroonga	274a	33.43 S	151.07 E
Wahweap Creek ≃	200	37.02 N	111.29 W
Wai, Indon.	122	17.56 N	73.54 E
Wai, Indon.	164	1.42 S	127.59 E
Waialeale ▲	229b	22.04 N	159.30 W
Waialua	229c	21.36 N	158.07 W
Waialua Bay c	229c	21.36 N	158.07 W
Waianae	229c	21.26 N	158.11 W
Waianae Range ⱬ	229c	21.30 N	158.11 W
Waiananapanapa State Park ♦	229a	20.47 N	156.01 W
Waiatoto ≃	172	43.59 S	168.47 E
Waiau ≃, N.Z.	172	42.39 S	173.03 E
Waiau ≃, N.Z.	172	38.58 S	177.24 E
Waiau ≃, N.Z.	172	46.12 S	167.38 E
Waibaikul	115b	39.36 S	119.35 E
Waibeem	164	0.28 S	132.58 E
Waiblingen	56	48.50 N	9.19 E
Waibstadt	56	49.18 N	8.54 E
Waichagoumen	98	40.54 N	125.45 E
Waidbruck → Ponte Gardena	64	46.36 N	11.32 E
Waidhān	124	24.04 N	82.20 E
Waidhofen an der Thaya	61	48.49 N	15.18 E
Waidhofen an der Ybbs	61	47.58 N	14.47 E
Waidmannslust ⱴ⁸	264a	52.36 N	13.20 E
Waidring	64	47.36 N	12.34 E
Waigang	229a	20.55 N	156.30 W
Waigatsch → Vajgač, ostrov I	106	31.22 N	121.11 E
Waigeo, Pulau I	164	0.14 S	130.45 E
Waigoumen	98	41.24 N	116.13 E
Waihao Downs	172	44.48 S	170.55 E
Waihau Bay	172	37.37 S	177.55 E
Waihee	229a	20.56 N	156.30 W
Waiheke Point ≽	229a	20.57 N	156.31 W
Waiheke Island I	172	36.48 S	175.06 E
Waihi	172	37.23 S	175.51 E
Waihola	172	46.02 S	170.06 E
Waihopai ≃	172	41.31 S	173.44 E
Waihou ≃	172	37.12 S	175.32 E
Waihuntan	106	30.25 N	118.40 E
Waika	154	2.21 S	25.43 E
Waikabubak	115b	9.38 S	119.25 E
Waikaia	172	45.43 S	168.51 E
Waikanae	172	40.53 S	175.04 E
Waikapu	229a	20.51 N	156.30 W
Waikare, Lake ◎	172	37.26 S	175.13 E
Waikaremoana, Lake ◎	172	38.46 S	177.07 E
Waikari	172	42.58 S	172.41 E
Waikato ≃	172	37.23 S	174.43 E
Waikeria	115b	9.29 S	119.14 E
Waikiki Beach ♦	229c	21.17 N	157.50 W
Waikino	172	37.25 S	175.46 E
Waikouaiti	172	45.36 S	170.41 E
Waikuatang	106	31.20 N	120.41 E
Waikui	144	9.25 N	48.55 E
Wailua	229b	22.03 N	159.20 W
Wailua River State Park ♦	229b	22.02 N	159.21 W
Wailuku	229a	20.53 N	156.30 W
Waimahaka	172	46.31 S	168.49 E
Waimakariri ≃	172	43.24 S	172.42 E
Waimamaku	172	35.35 S	173.29 E
Waimana	172	38.09 S	177.05 E
Waimanalo	229c	21.21 N	157.43 W
Waimangaroa	172	41.43 S	171.46 E
Waimangura	115b	9.30 S	119.14 E
Waimea, Hi., U.S.	229c	21.57 N	159.40 W
Waimea, Hi., U.S.	229b	20.01 N	155.40 W
Waimea Canyon V	229b	22.04 N	159.39 W
Waimea Canyon State Park ♦	229b	22.04 N	159.40 W
Wainfleet All Saints	44	53.06 N	0.07 E
Waingapu	115b	9.39 S	120.16 E
Waini ≃	246	8.24 N	59.51 W
Wainstalls	262	53.45 N	1.56 W

Column 3:

Name	Page	Lat.	Long.
Wainuiomata	172	41.16 S	174.57 E
Wainunu Bay c	175g	16.55 S	178.53 E
Wainwright, Ab., Can.	182	52.49 N	110.52 W
Wainwright, Ak., U.S.	180	70.38 N	160.01 W
Waiohau	172	38.14 S	176.51 E
Waiotira	172	35.56 S	174.12 E
Waiouru	172	39.29 S	175.40 E
Waipa ≃	172	37.41 S	175.09 E
Waipahi	172	46.07 S	169.15 E
Waipahu	229c	21.23 N	158.00 W
Waipaoa ≃	172	38.32 S	177.54 E
Waipara	172	43.04 S	172.45 E
Waipara ≃	172	43.09 S	172.48 E
Waipawa	172	39.56 S	176.36 E
Waipiata	172	45.11 S	170.10 E
Waipio Acres	229c	21.28 N	158.00 W
Waipio Bay c	229a	20.55 N	156.13 W
Waipiro	172	38.01 S	178.20 E
Waipu	172	35.59 S	174.27 E
Waipukurau	172	40.00 S	176.34 E
Wairakei	172	38.38 S	176.06 E
Wairarapa, Lake ◎	172	41.13 S	175.15 E
Wairau ≃	172	41.30 S	174.04 E
Wairau Valley	172	41.34 S	173.32 E
Wairio	172	46.00 S	168.02 E
Wairoa	172	39.02 S	177.25 E
Wairoa ≃	172	39.04 S	177.26 E
Waisanzao	106	30.57 N	121.52 E
Waischenfeld	60	49.51 N	11.21 E
Waisisi	175f	19.30 S	169.22 E
Waitahanui	172	38.47 S	176.05 E
Waitahuna	172	45.59 S	169.46 E
Waitakaruru	172	37.15 S	175.23 E
Waitaki ≃	172	44.57 S	171.09 E
Waitara, Austl.	274a	33.43 S	151.07 E
Waitara, N.Z.	172	39.00 S	174.13 E
Waitara ≃	172	38.59 S	174.14 E
Waitarere	172	40.33 S	175.12 E
Waita Reservoir ◎¹	229b	21.55 N	159.27 W
Waitati	172	45.45 S	170.34 E
Waita-zan ▲	96	33.08 N	131.10 E
Waite Hill	214	41.37 N	81.22 W
Waitemata c	172	36.56 S	174.42 E
Waite Park	190	45.33 N	94.13 W
Waitoa	172	37.37 S	175.38 E
Waitotara	172	39.48 S	174.44 E
Waitotara ≃	172	39.51 S	174.41 E
Waitpinga	168b	35.37 S	138.29 E
Waitsburg	202	46.16 N	118.09 W
Waitzen → Vác	30	47.47 N	19.08 E
Waiuku	172	37.15 S	174.45 E
Waiuta	172	42.18 S	171.49 E
Waiwera South	172	46.13 S	169.30 E
Waiwo	164	0.56 S	131.03 E
Waiya	164	3.13 S	128.55 E
Waizenkirchen	61	48.20 N	13.52 E
Wajiki	96	33.51 N	134.30 E
Wajima	92	37.24 N	136.54 E
Waka, Ityo.	144	1.45 N	40.04 E
Waka, Tx., U.S.	196	36.17 N	101.03 W
Waka, Zaïre	152	1.01 N	20.13 E
Wakajabi	144	5.38 S	134.24 E
Wakakusa	96	34.38 N	138.29 E
Wakakusa-yama ▲²	270	34.42 N	135.52 E
Wakamatsu → Aizu-wakamatsu	92	37.30 N	139.56 E
Wakami ≃	190	47.43 N	82.22 W
Wakami Lake ◎	190	47.29 N	82.51 W
Wakanya	154	3.44 N	130.37 E
Wakano-ura ◄	96	34.11 N	135.11 E
Wakarusa	216	41.32 N	86.03 W
Wakarusa ≃	198	38.57 N	95.05 W
Wakasa	96	35.25 N	134.24 E
Wakasa-wan c	92	35.45 N	135.40 E
Wakatipu, Lake ◎	172	45.05 S	168.34 E
Wakatomika Creek ≃	214	40.07 N	82.00 W
Wakato-ōhashi ≃⁵	96	33.54 N	130.49 E
Wakaw	184	52.39 N	105.44 W
Wakaw Lake ◎	184	52.40 N	105.35 W
Wakayama	96	34.13 N	135.11 E
Wakayama ▫⁵	96	34.00 N	135.20 E
Wakayanagi	92	38.46 N	141.08 E
Wake, Nihon	96	34.48 N	134.08 E
Wake, Zaïre	152	0.48 S	20.10 E
Wakefield, Eng., U.K.	44	53.42 N	1.29 W
Wakefield, Eng., U.K.	44	41.24 S	173.03 E
Wakefield, Ma., U.S.	198	39.12 N	97.00 W
Wakefield, Ma., U.S.	207	42.30 N	71.04 W
Wakefield, Mi., U.S.	218	38.59 N	83.01 W
Wakefield, Oh., U.S.	214	41.21 N	90.25 W
Wakefield, R.I., U.S.	207	41.26 N	71.30 W
Wakefield, Va., U.S.	208	36.58 N	76.59 W
Wakefield ≃	168b	34.10 S	138.10 E
Wakefield Forest	284c	38.50 N	77.14 W
Wake Forest	192	35.58 N	78.30 W
Wake Island □², Oc.	14	19.17 N	166.36 E
Wake Island I², Oc.	14	19.17 N	166.36 E
Wake Island I	14	19.18 N	166.38 E
Wake Island Air Force Base □	174a	19.17 N	166.37 E
Wake Lagoon c	174a	19.16 N	166.38 E
Wakema	110	16.36 N	95.11 E
Wakeman	214	41.15 N	82.23 W
Wakeman ≃	182	51.00 N	126.30 W
Wakema Creek ≃	194	33.19 N	93.16 W
Wake Village	194	33.26 N	94.07 W
Wakhān ≃¹	120	37.00 N	73.00 E
Wakhān → Vākhān ▲	120	36.40 N	71.00 E
Wakis	164	6.13 S	150.17 E
Wakita	196	36.53 N	97.55 W
Wakkanai	92a	45.25 N	141.40 E
Wakkerstroom	158	27.24 S	30.10 E
Wakō, Nihon	268	35.47 N	139.37 E
Wako, Pap. N. Gui.	164	6.05 S	149.05 E
Wakondiosi	152	46.28 S	81.47 E
Wakonda ▾	198	43.00 N	97.06 W
Wakre	164	0.19 S	131.09 E
Waku Kundo	154	11.28 S	15.07 E
Wakunai	175e	5.52 S	155.13 E
Wala ≃	154	5.46 S	32.04 E
Walamba	154	13.29 S	28.45 E
Walano	234	23.00 N	106.15 W
Walanae ≃	112	4.08 S	119.58 E
Walba	144	28.33 N	100.54 E
Walbeck	122	6.06 N	81.01 E
Walberswick	42	52.19 N	1.40 E
Walbran Creek ≃	224	48.40 N	124.46 W
Walbridge	214	41.35 N	83.29 W
Wałbrzych (Waldenburg)	30	50.46 N	16.17 E
Walbury Hill ▲²	42	51.21 N	1.28 W
Walcha	166	30.59 S	151.36 E
Walchensee ◎	64	47.36 N	11.20 E
Walcheren ≃¹	52	51.33 N	3.35 E
Walcott	202	41.46 N	106.51 W
Walcott, B.C., Can.	182	54.31 N	126.51 W
Walcott, Ia., U.S.	190	41.35 N	90.46 W
Walcott, N.D., U.S.	198	46.32 N	96.56 W
Walcott, Lake ◎¹	202	42.40 N	113.23 W
Walcz	30	53.17 N	16.28 E
Wald ≃	56	50.15 N	4.25 E
Wald	263	51.11 N	7.03 E

Column 4:

Name	Page	Lat.	Long.
Waldaist ≃	61	48.19 N	14.34 E
Wald am Schoberpass	61	47.27 N	14.40 E
Waldbauer ⱴ⁸	263	51.18 N	7.28 E
Waldbillig	56	49.47 N	6.18 E
Waldböckelheim	56	49.49 N	7.43 E
Waldbröl	56	50.53 N	7.37 E
Waldbronn	56	48.56 N	8.29 E
Waldburg	58	47.45 N	9.43 E
Waldeck, B.R.D.	56	51.12 N	9.04 E
Waldeck, B.R.D.	60	49.52 N	11.57 E
Walden, Co., U.S.	200	40.44 N	106.16 W
Walden, N.Y., U.S.	210	41.33 N	74.11 W
Walden, Lake ◎	221	42.39 N	83.46 W
Waldenbuch	56	48.38 N	9.07 E
Waldenburg, B.R.D.	56	49.11 N	9.38 E
Waldenburg, Schw.	58	47.23 N	7.45 E
Walden Pond ◎, Ma., U.S.	283	42.26 N	71.20 W
Walden Pond ◎, Ma., U.S.	283	42.28 N	71.00 W
Waldfischbach	56	49.17 N	7.40 E
Waldhaim, Sk., Can.	184	52.37 N	106.38 W
Waldheim, D.D.R.	54	51.04 N	13.01 E
Waldighoffen	58	47.33 N	7.19 E
Wald im Pinzgau	64	47.15 N	12.14 E
Waldkappel	56	51.08 N	9.52 E
Waldkirch	58	48.05 N	7.57 E
Waldkirchen	60	48.44 N	13.37 E
Waldkirchen am Wesen	61	48.26 N	13.49 E
Waldkraiburg	60	48.12 N	12.28 E
Waldmohr	56	49.23 N	7.20 E
Waldmünchen	60	49.23 N	12.43 E
Waldnaab ≃	60	49.36 N	12.08 E
Waldo, B.C., Can.	182	49.13 N	115.13 W
Waldo, Ar., U.S.	194	33.21 N	93.17 W
Waldo, Fl., U.S.	192	29.47 N	82.10 W
Waldoboro	188	44.05 N	69.22 W
Waldo Lake ◎	283	42.07 N	71.03 W
Waldo Lake ◎	202	43.44 N	122.03 W
Waldon ≃	42	50.51 N	4.15 W
Waldorf	208	38.37 N	76.56 W
Waldport	202	44.25 N	124.04 W
Waldron, Sk., Can.	184	50.51 N	102.30 W
Waldron, Ar., U.S.	194	34.53 N	94.05 W
Waldron, In., U.S.	218	39.27 N	85.40 W
Waldron, Mi., U.S.	216	41.43 N	84.25 W
Waldron Island I	224	48.43 N	123.02 W
Waldsassen	60	50.00 N	12.18 E
Waldshut	58	47.37 N	8.13 E
Waldstatt	58	47.21 N	9.17 E
Waldthurn	60	49.40 N	12.20 E
Waldviertel ≃¹	61	48.40 N	15.40 E
Waldwick	276	41.00 N	74.07 W
Wales, Ak., U.S.	180	65.36 N	168.05 W
Wales, Ma., U.S.	207	42.04 N	72.13 W
Wales, Wi., U.S.	216	43.00 N	88.23 W
Wales Center	210	42.46 N	78.33 W
Wales Island I, B.C., Can.	182	54.45 N	130.30 W
Wales Island I, N.T., Can.	176	68.00 N	86.43 W
Walewale	150	10.21 N	0.48 W
Walgett	166	30.01 S	148.07 E
Walgreen Coast ⊾²	9	75.15 S	105.00 W
Walhachin	182	50.45 N	120.59 W
Walhalla, N.D., U.S.	198	48.55 N	97.55 W
Walhalla, S.C., U.S.	192	34.45 N	83.03 W
Walhalla ⸊	60	49.03 N	12.14 E
Walheim	56	50.42 N	6.10 E
Walhonding ≃	214	40.22 N	82.09 W
Walhonding ≃	214	40.18 N	81.53 W
Wali	105	39.42 N	118.20 E
Walia	144	3.47 S	138.32 E
Walikale	154	1.25 S	28.03 E
Walincourt	52	50.04 N	3.20 E
Walis Island I	164	3.15 S	143.20 E
Walkaway	162	28.57 S	114.48 E
Walkden	44	53.32 N	2.24 W
Walken-ned ≃	56	51.35 N	10.37 E
Walker, Ia., U.S.	190	42.17 N	91.46 W
Walker, Mi., U.S.	216	43.00 N	85.46 W
Walker, Mn., U.S.	190	47.06 N	94.35 W
Walker, N.Y., U.S.	210	43.18 N	77.52 W
Walker ≃, Or., U.S.	204	39.07 N	118.53 W
Walker ≃, Tx., U.S.	222	32.38 N	97.00 W
Walker Basin Creek ≃	228	35.20 N	118.47 W
Walker Bay c	158	34.30 S	19.20 E
Walker Creek ≃, Az., U.S.	200	36.58 N	109.42 W
Walker Creek ≃, Ma., U.S.	283	42.38 N	70.44 W
Walker Creek ≃, Wy., U.S.	200	44.11 N	108.53 W
Walker Lake ◎, Mb., Can.	184	54.42 N	96.57 W
Walker Lake ◎, Ak., U.S.	180	67.10 N	154.26 W
Walker Lake ◎, Nv., U.S.	204	38.44 N	118.43 W
Walker Mill	279b	40.24 N	80.08 W
Walker Point ≽	158	22.57 N	57.04 W
Walker River Indian Reservation ▲⁴	204	39.00 N	118.40 W
Walkers Mill	279b	40.24 N	80.08 W
Walkersville	208	39.29 N	77.21 W
Walkerton, On., Can.	212	44.07 N	81.09 W
Walkerton, In., U.S.	216	41.28 N	86.28 W
Walkerton, Va., U.S.	208	37.43 N	77.02 W
Walkertown	192	36.10 N	80.09 W
Walker Valley	210	41.36 N	74.18 W
Walkerville	166	38.52 S	146.27 E
Wali Mik	122	8.52 N	82.17 W
Wall, Pa., U.S.	279b	40.24 N	79.47 W
Wall, S.D., U.S.	198	43.59 N	102.14 W
Wallace, Ca., U.S.	228	38.12 N	120.59 W
Wallace, Id., U.S.	202	47.28 N	115.55 W
Wallace, Ne., U.S.	198	40.50 N	101.09 W
Wallace, N.Y., U.S.	210	42.33 N	77.15 W
Wallace, Ky., U.S.	218	38.41 N	82.58 W
Wallace ≃	164	16.31 S	143.42 E
Wallaceburg	214	42.36 N	82.24 W
Wallace Lake ◎¹	279a	41.12 N	81.52 W
Wallacetown	214	40.57 N	78.17 W
Wallaceton	214	40.57 N	78.17 W
Wallal Downs	162	19.47 S	120.40 E
Wallam Creek ≃	166	28.40 S	147.20 E
Wallangarra	166	28.56 S	151.56 E
Wallaroo	168b	33.56 S	137.38 E
Wallaroo Mines	168b	33.57 S	137.41 E
Wallasey	44	53.26 N	3.03 W
Wallbeck	42	52.49 N	0.49 W
Wall Creek ≃	166	30.08 S	142.02 E
Wall Disney World ♦	220	28.22 N	81.34 W
Wallenfels	60	50.18 N	11.17 E
Wallenhorst	52	52.21 N	8.01 E

Column 5:

Name	Page	Lat.	Long.
Wallenpaupack, Lake ◎	210	41.25 N	75.12 W
Waller	222	30.04 N	95.56 W
Waller ≃⁶	222	30.00 N	96.00 W
Wallerawang	170	33.25 S	150.04 E
Wallers im Eurgenland	61	47.43 N	16.56 E
Wallers	50	50.22 N	3.24 E
Wallersdorf	60	48.44 N	12.45 E
Wallersee ◎	64	47.55 N	13.11 E
Wallerstein	58	48.53 N	10.28 E
Wallgau	64	47.31 N	11.16 E
Wallgrove	274a	33.47 S	150.51 E
Waltz	216	42.06 N	83.23 W
Walupt Lake ◎	224	46.25 N	121.28 W
Walvisbaai (Walvis Bay)	156	22.59 S	14.31 E
Walvisbaai c	156	22.57 S	14.30 E
Walvis Bay → Walvisbaai	156	22.59 S	14.31 E
Walvis Bay ⸆⁸	156	22.57 S	14.31 E
Walvis Ridge ⊹³	10	28.00 S	3.00 E
Walwa	171b	35.58 S	147.45 E
Walwen	262	53.14 N	3.15 W
Walworth, N.Y., U.S.	210	43.08 N	77.17 W
Walworth, Wi., U.S.	216	42.31 N	88.35 W
Walworth ▫⁶	216	42.41 N	88.32 W
Walyunga National Park ♦	168a	31.44 S	116.04 E
Walyungup, Lake ◎	168a	32.21 S	115.47 E
Walze	263	51.16 N	7.31 E
Walzin, Château de ☨	152	12.14 S	15.33 E
Wama	219	38.31 N	89.08 W
Wamac	219	38.31 N	89.08 W
Wamba, Kenya	154	0.59 N	37.19 E
Wamba, Nig.	150	8.58 N	8.36 E
Wamba (Uamba) ≃	152	3.56 S	17.12 E
Wamba ⸆⁸	263	51.32 N	7.32 E
Wamego	198	39.12 N	96.18 W
Wamel	52	51.53 N	5.28 E
Wamesit	283	42.37 N	71.15 W
Wami ≃	154	6.08 S	38.49 E
Wamiao	100	30.49 N	116.59 E
Wamsasa	204	45.13 N	121.16 W
Wamsutter	200	41.40 N	107.58 W
Wana	123	32.19 N	69.34 E
Wanaaring	166	29.42 S	144.09 E
Wanaka	172	44.42 S	169.09 E
Wanakah	210	42.45 N	78.54 W
Wanamassa	208	40.14 N	74.02 W
Wanamie	210	41.10 N	76.02 W
Wan'an, Zhg.	100	26.56 N	114.49 E
Wan'an, Zhg.	106	26.30 N	114.48 E
Wan'anchang	107	30.39 N	104.25 E
Wanapiri	164	4.33 S	135.59 E
Wanapitei ≃	190	46.02 N	80.51 W
Wanapitei Lake ◎	190	46.45 N	80.45 W
Wanapum Lake ◎¹	202	47.00 N	120.00 W
Wanaque	210	41.02 N	74.17 W
Wanaque Reservoir ◎¹	276	41.05 N	74.17 W
Wanatah	216	41.26 N	86.53 W
Wanau	164	1.22 S	132.42 E
Wanbaoshan	89	44.12 N	125.11 E
Wanbi	166	34.46 S	140.19 E
Wanblee	198	43.34 N	101.40 W
Wanborough	42	51.33 N	1.42 W
Wanchangzhai	107	29.43 N	104.45 E
Wanchese	192	35.50 N	75.38 W
Wanda	158	29.36 S	24.28 E
Wandai	164	3.43 S	136.41 E
Wandana	162	32.04 S	133.49 E
Wandawega	216	42.45 N	88.40 W
Wande	98	36.21 N	116.56 E
Wandel ⸆⁸	158	19.37 S	29.56 E
Wandering	168a	32.45 S	116.42 E
Wandiwash	122	12.30 N	79.36 E
Wandlitz	54	52.45 N	13.28 E
Wandlitzer See ◎	264a	52.44 N	13.28 E
Wando I	98	34.18 N	126.44 E
Wando	98	34.23 N	126.40 E
Wan-do I	98	34.18 N	126.42 E
Wandoan	166	26.09 S	149.57 E
Wandsbek ⸆⁸	265	53.34 N	10.04 E
Wandsworth ⸆⁸	265c	51.27 N	0.12 W
Waneta Lake ◎	210	42.27 N	77.06 W
Wang ≃	110	17.40 N	100.43 E
Wangal	164	5.58 S	134.29 E
Wangamaty, Mount ▲	172	44.23 S	168.42 E
Wanganui	172	39.56 S	175.03 E
Wanganui ≃	172	37.12 S	175.11 E
Wang anzhen	98	37.45 N	116.58 E
Wangaratta	166	36.22 S	146.20 E
Wangary	168b	34.33 S	135.29 E
Wangbenying	104	40.18 N	116.06 E
Wangbenyuan	104	38.53 N	115.07 E
Wangcang	100	32.11 N	106.23 E
Wangchuangzi	105	39.05 N	118.45 E
Wangcun	110	28.23 N	112.48 E
Wangdain	120	29.32 N	91.38 E
Wang Hin, Khlong ≃	269a	13.48 N	100.35 E
Wanghu	100	29.52 N	115.33 E
Wangjing	105	39.59 N	116.29 E
Wanglaizhuang	105	38.56 N	117.25 E
Wangqi	106	38.50 N	117.42 E
Wangqing	89	43.15 N	129.45 E
Wangjiang	100	30.08 N	116.42 E
Wängi	58	47.29 N	8.57 E
Wangjia	104	39.54 N	116.27 E
Wangjiatun	104	41.42 N	121.14 E
Wanguan	104	40.47 N	114.42 E
Wangjing	104	40.00 N	116.28 E

Column 6 (DEUTSCH):

Name	Seite	Breite	Länge E
Walton on the Hill	260	51.17 N	0.15 W
Walton-on-the-Naze	42	51.51 N	1.16 E
Walton Run ≃	285	40.05 N	74.59 W
Waltonville	219	38.13 N	89.02 W
Waltrop	52	51.37 N	7.23 E
Walt Whitman Bridge ≃⁵	285	39.54 N	75.08 W
Walt Whitman Homes	285	39.52 N	75.11 W
Walt Whitman House State Historic Site ☩	276	40.49 N	73.25 W
Walt Whitman Mall	276	40.50 N	73.25 W

Bottom key section:

Symbol	ENGLISH	DEUTSCH	(Español)	FRANÇAIS	(Português)
▲	Mountain	Berg	Montaña	Montagne	Montanha
ⱬ	Mountains	Gebirge	Montañas	Montagnes	Montanhas
ⱶ	Pass	Paß	Paso	Col	Passo
V	Valley, Canyon	Tal, Cañon	Valle, Cañón	Vallée, Canyon	Vale, Canhão
≃	Plain	Ebene	Llano	Plaine	Planície
▸	Cape	Kap	Cabo	Cap	Cabo
I	Island	Insel	Isla	Île	Ilha
II	Islands	Inseln	Islas	Îles	Ilhas
⸆	Other Topographic Features	Andere Topographische Objekte	Otros Elementos Topográficos	Autres données topographiques	Outros acidentes topográficos

Wang-Wavr I · 189

ESPAÑOL: Nombre · Página · Lat.°′ · Long.°′ W = Oeste
FRANÇAIS: Nom · Page · Lat.°′ · Long.°′ W = Ouest
PORTUGUÊS: Nome · Página · Lat.°′ · Long.°′ W = Oeste

Nombre	Página	Lat.°′	Long.°′
Wangiwangi, Pulau I	112	5.20 S	123.35 E
Wangji, Zhg.	100	33.52 N	118.44 E
Wangji, Zhg.	100	34.00 N	117.46 E
Wangjia, Zhg.	106	31.59 N	121.13 E
Wangjia, Zhg.	106	32.07 N	120.59 E
Wangjiadian, Zhg.	100	31.26 N	113.58 E
Wangjiadian, Zhg.	105	40.03 N	117.29 E
Wangjiagou	104	42.33 N	123.16 E
Wangjiajing, Zhg.	98	37.49 N	115.23 E
Wangjiajing, Zhg.	98	39.56 N	122.11 E
Wangjiang	100	30.09 N	116.41 E
Wangjiangjing	106	30.53 N	120.43 E
Wang Jian Mu (Tomb of Wang Jian) ⊥	107	30.38 N	104.04 E
Wangjiaputun	104	40.39 N	122.50 E
Wangjiapuzi, Zhg.	104	40.41 N	122.24 E
Wangjiapuzi, Zhg.	104	41.05 N	123.34 E
Wangjiaqiao	106	30.50 N	119.18 E
Wangjiashan	105	40.19 N	114.45 E
Wangjiashao	102	23.57 N	102.18 E
Wangjiatai	105	39.17 N	117.29 E
Wangjiaying, Zhg.	105	40.36 N	116.34 E
Wangjiaying, Zhg.	105	39.06 N	115.59 E
Wangjiazhai	106	31.21 N	121.37 E
Wangjiazui	106	31.16 N	120.18 E
Wangkantou	100	29.12 N	120.09 E
Wangkou	105	38.56 N	116.44 E
Wangkui	89	46.50 N	126.30 E
Wanglanzhuang	105	39.26 N	118.01 E
Wangling	100	27.13 N	113.26 E
Wangliu	100	32.25 N	115.40 E
Wangmiao	100	26.50 N	112.52 E
Wangmulazi	104	41.42 N	124.02 E
Wang Noi	110	14.13 N	100.44 E
Wangong	89	49.10 N	118.53 E
Wangpan Shan II	106	30.30 N	121.15 E
Wangpan Yang ⊂	100	30.30 N	121.46 E
Wangpingchang	107	29.17 N	105.45 E
Wangqing	89	43.20 N	129.48 E
Wangqingmen	98	41.42 N	125.23 E
Wangqingtuo	105	39.11 N	116.53 E
Wangqinzhuang	105	39.15 N	117.05 E
Wangqucun	106	31.22 N	120.19 E
Wangs	58	47.02 N	9.26 E
Wang Saphung	110	17.18 N	101.46 E
Wangshanhutun	104	42.03 N	122.37 E
Wangshi	100	33.11 N	116.04 E
Wangsi	98	38.00 N	116.55 E
Wangsim-ni ◆[8]	271b	37.36 N	127.03 E
Wangsiying	107	30.34 N	103.29 E
Wangtai, Zhg.	98	36.05 N	119.59 E
Wangtai, Zhg.	100	26.39 N	117.57 E
Wangtan	100	29.45 N	120.40 E
Wang Thong	110	16.50 N	100.26 E
Wangtian	100	25.59 N	116.04 E
Wangting	106	31.26 N	120.26 E
Wangtongshitai	104	42.05 N	123.11 E
Wangtuan, Zhg.	98	37.32 N	116.08 E
Wangtuan, Zhg.	98	37.17 N	122.04 E
Wangtuanji	100	33.12 N	116.21 E
Wangu	107	30.19 N	106.05 E
Wanguzhen	107	29.41 N	105.57 E
Wangwenzhuang	105	38.53 N	117.15 E
Wangxiangshang	106	31.29 N	120.15 E
Wangxiangtai	105	40.02 N	115.09 E
Wangxiuqiao	106	31.38 N	121.03 E
Wangyangzhen	107	29.44 N	104.14 E
Wangyedian	98	41.36 N	118.17 E
Wangyefu	98	41.50 N	118.23 E
Wangyehmiao → Horqin Youyi Qianqi	89	46.05 N	122.05 E
Wangyiguantun	104	42.36 N	123.19 E
Wangzhai	98	34.09 N	116.47 E
Wangzhimawo	105	39.39 N	117.40 E
Wangzhong	98	35.08 N	116.58 E
Wangzhuang	100	33.07 N	117.29 E
Wangzhuangbu	98	39.27 N	113.56 E
Wangzhuangji	98	34.09 N	118.23 E
Wangzhuangzi	105	39.17 N	118.14 E
Wanham	182	55.44 N	118.24 W
Wanhedian	100	32.16 N	113.16 E
Wanheimerort ◆[8]	263	51.24 N	6.46 E
Wanhsien → Wanxian	102	30.52 N	108.22 E
Wanhuyu	102	38.24 N	110.40 E
Wani	122	20.04 N	78.57 E
Wani, Gunung ∧	112	4.29 S	123.01 E
Wani, Laguna ⊂	236	14.45 N	83.20 W
Wanie-Rukula	154	0.15 N	25.32 E
Wanigela	164	9.22 S	149.10 E
Wanipigow ≃	184	51.11 N	96.18 W
Wanjiabu	100	28.51 N	115.39 E
Wanjiaqiao	106	30.25 N	119.07 E
Wanjiatun	98	40.03 N	119.51 E
Wanjindian	100	32.50 N	114.46 E
Wānkāner	120	22.37 N	70.56 E
Wankendorf	54	54.07 N	10.13 E
Wankum	56	51.24 N	6.20 E
Wanle Weyne	144	2.37 N	44.54 E
Wanli, T'aiwan	269d	25.11 N	121.41 E
Wanli, Zhg.	106	31.06 N	120.16 E
Wanna	52	53.44 N	8.46 E
Wanna Lakes ⊜	162	28.30 S	128.27 E
Wān Namton	110	22.03 N	99.33 E
Wanne-Eickel	52	51.32 N	7.09 E
Wanneroo	168a	31.45 S	115.48 E
Wannery Creek ≃	162	22.47 S	115.43 E
Wannian	100	28.42 N	117.03 E
Wanning	110	18.53 N	110.26 E
Wannsee ◆[8]	264a	52.25 N	13.09 E
Wanon Niwat	110	17.38 N	103.46 E
Wanouchi	94	35.17 N	136.38 E
Wānow	120	32.38 N	65.54 E
Wanparti	122	16.22 N	78.04 E
Wanquan	98	40.52 N	114.45 E
Wansdorf	264a	52.38 N	13.05 E
Wan-See → Van Gölü ⊜	128	38.33 N	42.46 E
Wansen → Wiązów	30	50.49 N	17.11 E
Wanshan	107	30.23 N	106.06 E
Wanshouchang	107	29.26 N	105.55 E
Wanstead	172	40.08 S	176.32 E
Wanstead ◆[8]	260	51.34 N	0.02 E
Wantage	42	51.36 N	1.25 W
Wantagh	210	40.41 N	73.30 W
Wantan	102	30.03 N	110.18 E
Wantirna	274b	37.51 S	145.14 E
Wantirna South	274b	37.52 S	145.14 E
Wanxian, Zhg.	102	30.52 N	108.22 E
Wanxian, Zhg.	105	38.50 N	115.09 E
Wanyuan	102	32.04 N	108.02 E
Wanzai	100	28.06 N	114.27 E
Wanzarīk	146	27.31 N	13.29 E
Wanzhuang	105	39.34 N	116.36 E
Wanzleben	54	52.03 N	11.26 E
Wapack Range ⩚	207	42.48 N	71.52 W
Wapakoneta	216	40.34 N	84.11 W
Wapanucka	196	34.22 N	96.25 W
Wapato	202	46.26 N	120.25 W
Wapawekka Hills ⩚[2]	184	54.45 N	104.20 W
Wapawekka Lake ⊜	184	54.55 N	104.40 W
Wapella, Sk., Can.	184	50.15 N	102.00 W
Wapella, Il., U.S.	219	40.13 N	88.58 W
Wapello	190	41.10 N	91.11 W
Wapenamanda	164	5.35 S	143.55 E
Wapesi Lake ⊜	184	50.34 N	92.21 W
Wāpi	122	20.22 N	72.54 E
Wapinda	152	3.41 N	22.48 E
Wapinitia Pass)(	224	45.14 N	121.42 W
Wapisu Lake ⊜	184	55.47 N	99.11 W
Wapiti ≃	182	55.08 N	118.18 W
Wapizagonke, Lac ⊜	206	46.43 N	73.02 W
Waples	222	32.29 N	97.43 W
Wapoga ≃	164	2.42 S	136.06 E
Wappapello, Lake ⊜[1]	194	36.58 N	90.20 W
Wapping	207	41.50 N	72.33 W
Wappinger Creek ≃	210	41.35 N	73.57 W
Wappingers Falls	210	41.35 N	73.54 W
Wapsipinicon ≃	190	41.44 N	90.20 W
Waptus Lake ⊜	224	47.30 N	121.10 W
Wapus ≃	190	47.11 N	76.06 W
Wapus Lake ⊜	184	56.27 N	102.12 W
Waqf aṣ-Ṣawwān, Jibāl ⩚	132	30.53 N	36.48 E
Wāqid	142	30.42 N	30.44 E
Waqqāṣ	132	32.33 N	35.36 E
War	192	37.18 N	81.41 W
Wara	94	35.45 N	137.05 E
Warabi	94	35.49 N	139.41 E
Wārāh	120	27.27 N	67.48 E
Warakaraket I	164	2.15 S	130.36 E
Waramaug, Lake ⊜	207	41.42 N	73.22 W
Warangal	122	18.00 N	79.35 E
Wararisbari, Tanjung >	164	1.05 S	136.23 E
Wārāseoni	120	21.45 N	80.02 E
Waratah, Austl.	166	41.27 S	145.32 E
Waratah, Austl.	170	32.54 S	151.44 E
Waratah Bay ⊂	166	38.51 S	146.04 E
Warboys	42	52.24 N	0.04 W
Warbreccan	166	24.18 S	142.51 E
Warburg	52	51.29 N	9.08 E
Warburton, Austl.	162	26.07 S	126.35 E
Warburton, Austl.	169	37.46 S	145.41 E
Warburton, Pāk.	123	31.33 N	73.50 E
Warburton, Eng., U.K.	262	53.24 N	2.27 W
Warburton Aboriginal Reserve ◆[4], Austl.	162	26.20 S	127.00 E
Warburton Aboriginal Reserve ◆[4], Austl.	162	24.00 S	128.15 E
Warburton Bay ⊂	176	63.50 N	111.30 W
Warburton Creek ≃	166	27.55 S	137.28 E
Warchha	123	32.25 N	71.59 E
Ward, N.Z.	172	41.50 S	174.08 E
Ward, Pa., U.S.	285	39.53 N	75.31 W
Ward ≃	166	26.32 S	146.06 E
Ward, Mount ∧, Ant.	9	71.55 S	66.00 W
Ward, Mount ∧, N.Z.	172	43.52 S	169.50 E
Warda	222	30.03 N	96.55 W
Wardcliff	216	42.43 N	84.28 W
Ward Cove	182	55.24 N	131.44 W
Warden, S. Afr.	158	27.56 S	29.00 E
Warden, Wa., U.S.	202	46.58 N	119.02 W
Wardenburg	52	53.04 N	8.11 E
Warder	54	53.59 N	10.22 E
Wardersee ⊜	54	53.58 N	10.26 E
Wardha	122	20.45 N	78.37 E
Wardha ≃	122	19.38 N	79.48 E
Ward Hill ∧[2], Scot., U.K.	46	58.57 N	3.09 W
Ward Hill ∧[2], Scot., U.K.	46	58.54 N	3.20 W
Ward Hunt, Cape >	164	8.05 S	149.55 E
Ward Hunt Strait ʊ	164	9.25 S	149.55 E
Wardle	44	53.39 N	2.08 W
Wardlow	182	50.54 N	111.33 W
Ward Mountain ∧	202	46.10 N	114.17 W
Wardner	182	49.25 N	115.26 W
Wardour, Vale of V	42	51.05 N	2.00 W
Wards Chapel	284b	39.24 N	76.52 W
Wards Island I	276	40.47 N	73.56 W
Ward's Stone ∧	44	54.02 N	2.38 W
Wardsville, On., Can.	214	42.39 N	81.45 W
Wardsville, Mo., U.S.	219	38.29 N	92.10 W
Wardswell Draw V	196	32.39 N	102.35 W
Wardt	52	51.41 N	6.25 E
Ware, Eng., U.K.	42	51.49 N	0.02 W
Ware, Ma., U.S.	207	42.15 N	72.14 W
Ware ≃	207	42.11 N	72.22 W
War Eagle Creek ≃	194	36.14 N	94.00 W
Waregem	50	50.53 N	3.25 E
Wareham, Eng., U.K.	42	50.41 N	2.07 W
Wareham, Ma., U.S.	207	41.45 N	70.43 W
Warehouse Point	207	41.55 N	72.37 W
Waremme	56	50.41 N	5.15 E
Waren, D.D.R.	54	53.31 N	12.40 E
Waren, Indon.	164	2.16 S	136.20 E
Warenai ≃	164	2.52 S	135.55 E
Warenda	166	22.37 S	140.32 E
Warendorf	52	51.57 N	7.59 E
Ware River ⊂	208	37.23 N	76.27 W
Ware Shoals	192	34.23 N	82.14 W
Waretown	208	39.47 N	74.11 W
Warffum	52	53.23 N	6.34 E
Warfusée-Abancourt	50	49.52 N	2.35 E
Warga	52	53.08 N	5.51 E
Wargalo	144	6.17 N	47.31 E
Wargla	148	31.59 N	5.25 E
Wargla □[5]	148	29.00 N	8.00 E
Warialda	166	29.32 S	150.34 E
Wariap	164	1.34 S	134.11 E
Warilau	164	5.24 S	134.30 E
Warilau, Pulau I	164	5.23 S	134.33 E
Warin	54	53.48 N	11.42 E
Warinanco Park ♠	276	40.39 N	74.14 W
Warin Chamrap	110	15.12 N	104.53 E
Waring Mountains ⩚	180	66.50 N	159.00 W
Wāris Alīganj	124	25.01 N	85.38 E
Warka	30	51.47 N	21.10 E
Warkopi	164	1.08 S	134.07 E
Warks Burn ≃	44	55.03 N	2.08 W
Warkworth, On., Can.	212	44.12 N	77.53 W
Warkworth, N.Z.	172	36.24 S	174.40 E
Warkworth, Eng., U.K.	44	55.21 N	1.36 W
Warland, Eng., U.K.	262	53.41 N	2.05 W
Warland, Mt., U.S.	182	48.30 N	115.17 W
Warland Reservoir ⊜[1]	262	53.41 N	2.04 W
Warley → Smethwick	42	52.30 N	1.58 W
Warley Moor Reservoir ⊜[1]	262	53.47 N	1.57 W
Warlingham	42	51.19 N	0.04 W
Warlington	42	51.39 N	1.01 W
Warman	184	52.20 N	106.34 W
Warmandi	164	0.22 S	132.39 E
Warmbad, Namibia	156	28.29 S	18.41 E
Warmbad, S. Afr.	156	24.55 S	28.15 E
Warm Baths → Warmbad	156	24.55 S	28.15 E
Warm Beach	224	48.10 N	122.21 W
War Memorial Cross ⊥	169	37.20 S	144.36 E
Warmenhuizen	52	52.43 N	4.44 E
Warmensteinach	60	49.59 N	11.47 E
Warmeriville	50	49.21 N	4.13 E
Warmington	42	52.08 N	1.24 W
Warminster, Eng., U.K.	42	51.13 N	2.12 W
Warminster, Pa., U.S.	208	40.12 N	75.06 W
Warminster Naval Air Development Center ■	285	40.12 N	75.09 W
Warm Springs, Ga., U.S.	192	32.53 N	84.40 W
Warm Springs, Mt., U.S.	202	46.11 N	112.48 W
Warm Springs, Or., U.S.	202	44.45 N	121.15 W
Warm Springs, Va., U.S.	192	38.02 N	79.47 W
Warm Springs ≃	202	44.52 N	121.04 W
Warm Springs Indian Reservation ◆[4]	224	45.00 N	121.25 W
Warm Springs Reservoir ⊜[1]	202	43.37 N	118.14 W
Warnbro Sound ʊ	168a	32.20 S	115.40 E
Warnemünde ◆[8]	54	54.10 N	12.04 E
Warner, Ab., Can.	182	49.17 N	112.12 W
Warner, N.H., U.S.	188	43.16 N	71.49 W
Warner, Ok., U.S.	196	35.29 N	95.18 W
Warner Lakes ⊜	202	42.25 N	119.50 W
Warner Mountains ⩚	204	41.40 N	120.20 W
Warner Peak ∧	202	42.27 N	119.44 W
Warner Ranch	228	33.56 N	117.13 W
Warner Robins	192	32.37 N	83.36 W
Warners	210	43.05 N	76.20 W
Warners Pond ⊜	283	42.28 N	71.24 W
Warnerville	210	42.34 N	74.30 W
Warnes, Arg.	252	34.55 S	60.31 W
Warnes, Bol.	248	17.30 S	63.10 W
Warnes Brook ≃	276	40.25 N	74.18 W
Warneton	50	50.45 N	2.57 E
Warngau	64	47.50 N	11.41 E
Warnicken → Primorje	76	54.57 N	20.02 E
Warnkenhagen	54	54.00 N	11.04 E
Warnow ≃	54	54.06 N	12.09 E
Warns	52	52.52 N	5.25 E
Warnsveld	52	52.08 N	6.13 E
Waroona	168a	32.50 S	115.55 E
Warpath ≃	184	52.21 N	98.26 W
Warra	166	26.56 S	150.55 E
Warrabri Aboriginal Reserve ◆[4]	162	21.00 S	134.20 E
Warracknabeal	166	36.15 S	142.24 E
Warr Acres	196	35.31 N	97.37 W
Warragamba Dam ◆[6]	170	33.54 S	150.36 E
Warragul	169	38.10 S	145.56 E
Warrandyte	274b	37.45 S	145.13 E
Warrandyte South	274b	37.46 S	145.14 E
Warrāq al-ʻArab	273c	30.06 N	31.12 E
Warrāq al-Ḥaḍar, Jazīrat I	273c	30.07 N	31.13 E
Warrāq al-Hadar wa Ambūtbah wa Mīt an-Naṣārā	273c	30.06 N	31.13 E
Warrawagine	162	20.51 S	120.42 E
Warrawee	274a	33.44 S	151.07 E
Warrawolong, Mount ∧	170	33.03 S	151.15 E
Warrawong	170.	34.29 S	150.53 E
Warrego ≃	166	30.24 S	145.21 E
Warrego Range ⩚	166	25.00 S	146.30 E
Warren, Austl.	166	31.42 S	147.50 E
Warren, Eng., U.K.	262	53.14 N	2.10 W
Warren, Ar., U.S.	194	33.36 N	92.03 W
Warren, Il., U.S.	190	42.29 N	89.59 W
Warren, In., U.S.	216	40.40 N	85.25 W
Warren, Ma., U.S.	207	42.12 N	72.11 W
Warren, Mi., U.S.	216	42.28 N	83.01 W
Warren, Mn., U.S.	198	48.11 N	96.46 W
Warren, Mo., U.S.	219	39.47 N	91.45 W
Warren, N.J., U.S.	276	40.37 N	74.30 W
Warren, Oh., U.S.	214	41.14 N	80.49 W
Warren, Or., U.S.	224	45.49 N	122.50 W
Warren, Pa., U.S.	214	41.50 N	79.08 W
Warren, R.I., U.S.	207	41.43 N	71.16 W
Warren □[6], In., U.S.	216	40.21 N	87.17 W
Warren □[6], Mo., U.S.	219	38.45 N	91.09 W
Warren □[6], N.J., U.S.	210	40.49 N	75.05 W
Warren □[6], N.Y., U.S.	210	43.26 N	73.43 W
Warren □[6], Oh., U.S.	218	39.26 N	84.13 W
Warren □[6], Pa., U.S.	214	41.51 N	79.08 W
Warren ≃	162	34.35 S	115.50 E
Warren City	222	32.33 N	94.54 W
Warrendale	214	40.39 N	80.04 W
Warren Dunes State Park ♠	216	41.56 N	86.36 W
Warren H. Manning State Park ♠	283	42.34 N	71.18 W
Warren Park	218	39.46 N	86.03 W
Warren Peaks ⩚	198	44.29 N	104.28 W
Warrenpoint	48	54.06 N	6.15 W
Warren Point >	180	69.44 N	132.30 W
Warrens	190	44.07 N	90.29 W
Warrensburg, Il., U.S.	219	39.56 N	89.04 W
Warrensburg, Mo., U.S.	194	38.45 N	93.44 W
Warrensburg, N.Y., U.S.	188	43.29 N	73.46 W
Warrensville	210	41.19 N	76.57 W
Warrensville Heights	214	41.26 N	81.32 W
Warrenton, S. Afr.	158	28.09 S	24.47 E
Warrenton, Ga., U.S.	192	33.24 N	82.39 W
Warrenton, Mo., U.S.	219	38.48 N	91.08 W
Warrenton, N.C., U.S.	192	36.23 N	78.09 W
Warrenton, Or., U.S.	224	46.09 N	123.55 W
Warrenton, Tx., U.S.	222	30.01 N	96.44 W
Warrenton, Va., U.S.	188	38.42 N	77.47 W
Warrenville	216	41.49 N	88.10 W
Warrenzin	54	53.54 N	12.57 E
Warri	150	5.31 N	5.45 E
Warriedar Hill ∧[2]	162	29.06 S	117.06 E
Warriewood	274a	33.42 S	151.18 E
Warrill Creek ≃	171a	27.39 S	152.44 E
Warrington, N.Z.	172	45.43 S	170.35 E
Warrington, Eng., U.K.	44	53.24 N	2.37 W
Warrington, Fl., U.S.	194	30.23 N	87.16 W
Warrington, Pa., U.S.	285	40.15 N	75.08 W
Warrington □[8]	262	53.24 N	2.33 W
Warrington Airport ⊠	285	40.16 N	75.09 W
Warrior	194	33.48 N	86.48 W
Warrior Creek ≃	192	31.15 N	83.34 W
Warrior Reefs ✧[2]	164	9.35 S	143.10 E
Warriors Mark	214	40.42 N	78.08 W
Warrnambool	166	38.23 S	142.29 E
Warroad	198	48.54 N	95.18 W
Warrumbungle National Park ♠	166	31.20 S	149.00 E
Warsak	123	34.10 N	71.25 E
Warsaw → Warszawa, Pol.	30	52.15 N	21.00 E
Warsaw, Il., U.S.	190	40.21 N	91.26 W
Warsaw, In., U.S.	216	41.14 N	85.51 W
Warsaw, Ky., U.S.	218	38.47 N	84.54 W
Warsaw, Mo., U.S.	194	38.14 N	93.22 W
Warsaw, N.Y., U.S.	210	42.44 N	78.07 W
Warsaw, N.C., U.S.	192	34.59 N	78.05 W
Warsaw, Oh., U.S.	214	40.20 N	82.00 W
Warsaw, Va., U.S.	208	37.57 N	76.45 W
Warsaw Station ◆[5]	265a	59.54 N	30.19 E
Warschau → Warszawa	30	52.15 N	21.00 E
Warscheneck ∧	61	47.39 N	14.14 E
Warshiikh	144	2.18 N	45.48 E
Warsop	44	53.13 N	1.09 W
Warspite	182	54.06 N	112.37 W
Warstein	56	51.26 N	8.21 E
Warszawa (Warsaw)	30	52.15 N	21.00 E
Warszawa □[4]	30	52.15 N	21.00 E
Warta	30	51.42 N	18.38 E
Warta ≃	30	52.35 N	14.39 E
Wartburg, S. Afr.	158	29.25 S	30.35 E
Wartburg, Tn., U.S.	192	36.06 N	84.35 W
Wartburg ⊥	54	50.58 N	10.18 E
Wartenberg	60	48.24 N	11.59 E
Wartenberg ◆[8]	264a	52.34 N	13.31 E
Warth	58	47.15 N	10.11 E
Warthan Creek ≃	226	36.08 N	120.20 W
Warthe → Warta ≃	30	52.35 N	14.39 E
Wartin	54	53.15 N	14.09 E
Warton, Eng., U.K.	44	54.09 N	2.47 W
Warton, Eng., U.K.	262	53.45 N	2.54 W
Warton Aerodrome ⊠	262	53.45 N	2.54 W
Wartrace	194	35.31 N	86.20 W
Wartsberg ∧[2]	263	51.25 N	6.29 E
Waru	164	3.24 S	130.40 E
Warud	120	21.28 N	78.16 E
Warunta, Laguna ⊜	236	15.22 N	84.09 W
Waruta ≃	164	3.18 S	140.08 E
Warwick, Austl.	171a	28.13 S	152.02 E
Warwick, P.Q., Can.	206	45.56 N	71.59 W
Warwick, Eng., U.K.	42	52.17 N	1.34 W
Warwick, Md., U.S.	208	39.25 N	75.46 W
Warwick, N.Y., U.S.	210	41.15 N	74.21 W
Warwick, R.I., U.S.	207	41.41 N	71.22 W
Warwick ≃	208	37.05 N	76.33 W
Warwick Castle ⊥	42	52.17 N	1.34 W
Warwick Channel ʊ	164	13.51 S	136.16 E
Warwick Farm Racecourse and Motor Race Track ♠	274a	33.55 S	150.57 E
Warwickshire □[6]	42	52.13 N	1.37 W
Warza	54	51.00 N	10.41 E
Wasaga Beach	212	44.31 N	80.01 W
Wasagu	150	11.25 N	5.49 E
Wasatch Mountain State Park ♠	200	40.33 N	111.31 W
Wasatch Plateau ⩚[1]	200	39.20 N	111.30 W
Wasatch Range ⩚	200	40.40 N	111.35 W
Wasāwewāla	123	30.28 N	73.40 E
Wasbank	158	28.24 S	30.05 E
Wasbister	46	59.10 N	3.07 W
Wascana Creek ≃	184	50.39 N	104.55 W
Wäschenbeuren	56	48.46 N	9.41 E
Wasco, Ca., U.S.	226	35.35 N	119.20 W
Wasco, Or., U.S.	224	45.35 N	120.41 W
Wasco □[6]	224	45.10 N	121.12 W
Wase	150	9.06 N	9.59 E
Wase ≃	146	8.27 N	10.06 E
Waseca	190	44.04 N	93.30 W
Waseda University ▿[2]	268	35.42 N	139.43 E
Wasekamio Lake ⊜	184	56.45 N	108.45 W
Wasen	58	47.03 N	7.48 E
Wasgomuwa National Park ♠	122	7.40 N	80.45 E
Washademoak Lake ⊜	186	45.48 N	65.58 W
Washago	212	44.45 N	79.20 W
Washburn, Il., U.S.	190	40.55 N	89.17 W
Washburn, Me., U.S.	186	46.47 N	68.09 W
Washburn, N.D., U.S.	198	47.17 N	101.01 W
Washburn, Wi., U.S.	190	46.40 N	90.53 W
Washburn ≃	44	53.54 N	1.39 W
Washburn, Mount ∧	202	44.48 N	110.25 W
Washburn Lake ⊜	176	70.03 N	106.50 W
Washdyke	172	44.21 S	171.14 E
Washicoutai	186	50.17 N	60.42 W
Washiga-take ∧	94	35.56 N	136.58 E
Wāshīm	122	20.06 N	77.09 E
Washimiya	94	36.06 N	139.40 E
Washington, Eng., U.K.	44	54.55 N	1.30 W
Washington, Ca., U.S.	226	39.22 N	120.48 W
Washington, Ct., U.S.	207	41.37 N	73.18 W
Washington, D.C., U.S.	208	38.53 N	77.02 W
Washington, D.C., U.S.	284c	38.53 N	77.02 W
Washington, Ga., U.S.	192	33.44 N	82.44 W
Washington, Il., U.S.	190	40.42 N	89.24 W
Washington, In., U.S.	194	38.39 N	87.10 W
Washington, Ia., U.S.	190	41.17 N	91.41 W
Washington, Ks., U.S.	198	39.49 N	97.03 W
Washington, Ky., U.S.	218	38.36 N	83.48 W
Washington, La., U.S.	194	30.36 N	92.03 W
Washington, Mi., U.S.	214	42.44 N	83.02 W
Washington, Mo., U.S.	219	38.33 N	91.01 W
Washington, N.J., U.S.	210	40.45 N	74.58 W
Washington, N.C., U.S.	192	35.31 N	77.01 W
Washington, Pa., U.S.	214	40.10 N	80.14 W
Washington, Tx., U.S.	222	30.20 N	96.10 W
Washington, Ut,. U.S.	200	37.07 N	113.30 W
Washington, Va., U.S.	188	38.42 N	78.09 W
Washington □[6], Il., U.S.	219	38.21 N	89.23 W
Washington □[6], In., U.S.	218	38.36 N	86.06 W
Washington □[6], N.Y., U.S.	210	43.15 N	73.27 W
Washington □[6], Or., U.S.	224	45.33 N	123.07 W
Washington □[6], Pa., U.S.	214	40.10 N	80.15 W
Washington □[6], R.I., U.S.	207	41.28 N	71.35 W
Washington □[6], Tx., U.S.	222	30.15 N	96.20 W
Washington □[6], Wi., U.S.	216	43.14 N	88.15 W
Washington □[3], U.S.	178	47.30 N	120.30 W
Washington □[3], U.S.	202	47.30 N	120.30 W
Washington, Lake ⊜, Fl., U.S.	220	28.07 N	80.45 W
Washington, Lake ⊜, Wa., U.S.	224	47.37 N	122.15 W
Washington, Mount ∧	188	44.15 N	71.15 W
Washington Court House	218	39.32 N	83.26 W
Washington Crossing	208	40.17 N	74.52 W
Washington Crossing State Historic Site ⊥	208	40.17 N	74.53 W
Washington Depot	207	41.38 N	73.18 W
Washington Heights ◆[8]	276	40.52 N	73.56 W
Washington Island	190	45.23 N	86.55 W
Washington Island I	190	45.23 N	86.55 W
Washington Memorial Chapel ▿[1]	285	40.06 N	75.26 W
Washington Mills	210	43.03 N	75.16 W
Washington Monument ♠	284c	38.53 N	77.03 W
Washington Monument State Park ♠	208	39.30 N	77.38 W
Washington National Airport ⊠	208	38.51 N	77.02 W
Washington-on-the-Brazos State Historic Park ♠	222	30.20 N	96.09 W
Washington Park	219	38.38 N	90.05 W
Washington Park ♠, Il., U.S.	278	41.48 N	87.37 W
Washington Park ♠, Oh., U.S.	279a	41.27 N	81.40 W
Washington Pass)(	224	48.32 N	120.39 W
Washington Place	218	39.47 N	86.01 W
Washington Rock State Park ♠	276	40.37 N	74.28 W
Washington's Headquarters ⊥	285	40.06 N	75.28 W
Washington Terrace	200	41.10 N	111.58 W
Washington Township	276	40.54 N	74.00 W
Washington Valley	276	40.48 N	74.32 W
Washington Valley Reservoir ⊜[1]	276	40.36 N	74.34 W
Washingtonville, N.Y., U.S.	210	41.26 N	74.10 W
Washingtonville, Oh., U.S.	214	40.54 N	80.46 W
Washingtonville, Pa., U.S.	210	41.03 N	76.40 W
Washita ≃	196	34.12 N	96.50 W
Washoe □[6]	226	39.22 N	119.43 W
Washoe Lake ⊜	226	39.16 N	119.48 W
Washougal	224	45.34 N	122.21 W
Washougal ≃	224	45.35 N	122.23 W
Washow Bay ⊂	184	51.22 N	96.47 W
Washtenaw □[6]	216	42.15 N	83.50 W
Washtucna	202	46.45 N	118.18 W
Wāshuk	128	27.44 N	64.48 E
Wasian	164	1.54 S	133.17 E
Wasilków	30	53.12 N	23.12 E
Wasilla	180	61.35 N	149.26 W
Wasior	164	2.43 S	134.30 E
Wasiri	112	7.35 S	126.38 E
Wāsiṭ □[4]	128	32.45 N	45.25 E
Waskada	184	49.06 N	100.46 W
Waskaganish	176	51.30 N	78.45 W
Waskahigan ≃	182	54.45 N	117.12 W
Waskaiowaka Lake ⊜	184	56.30 N	96.20 W
Waskatenau	182	54.07 N	112.47 W
Waskesiu Lake ⊜	184	53.56 N	106.10 W
Waskom	194	32.29 N	94.04 W
Wąsosz	30	51.34 N	16.42 E
Waspam	236	14.44 N	83.58 W
Waspuk ≃	236	14.38 N	84.26 W
Wasquehal	50	50.40 N	3.09 E
Wassaic	210	41.48 N	73.35 W
Wasselonne	58	48.38 N	7.27 E
Wassen	58	46.42 N	8.36 E
Wassenaar	52	52.07 N	4.24 E
Wassenberg	56	51.06 N	6.08 E
Wasseralfingen	56	48.52 N	10.06 E
Wasserbillig	56	49.44 N	6.30 E
Wasserburg am Inn	60	48.04 N	12.13 E
Wasserkuppe ∧	56	50.30 N	9.56 E
Wasserkurl	263	51.33 N	7.38 E
Wasserleben	54	51.55 N	10.44 E
Wassertrüdingen	56	49.02 N	10.35 E
Wassigny	50	50.01 N	3.36 E
Wass Lake ⊜	184	53.40 N	95.25 W
Wassmannsdorf	264a	52.22 N	13.28 E
Wassou	150	10.02 N	13.39 W
Wassy	58	48.30 N	4.57 E
Wast Water ⊜	44	54.26 N	3.18 W
Wasu	164	6.00 S	147.15 E
Wasum	164	6.05 S	149.20 E
Wasungen	54	50.40 N	10.22 E
Watabeag Lake ⊜	190	48.14 N	80.32 W
Watampone (Bone)	112	4.32 S	120.20 E
Watamu Marine National Park ♠	154	3.23 S	40.00 E
Waṭan, Wādī al- V	142	30.26 N	31.49 E
Watansopeng	112	4.21 S	119.53 E
Watapi Lake ⊜	184	55.18 N	109.35 W
Watarai	94	34.26 N	136.37 E
Watarase ≃	94	36.13 N	139.42 E
Wataru I	122	5.43 N	73.23 E
Watatic, Mount ∧	207	42.42 N	71.53 W
Watauga	222	32.51 N	97.15 W
Watchet	42	51.12 N	3.20 W
Watch Hill	207	41.18 N	71.51 W
Watchung	276	40.38 N	74.27 W
Watchung Reservation ♠	276	40.41 N	74.23 W
Water	262	53.44 N	2.14 W
Waterbeach	42	52.16 N	0.11 E
Waterberg	156	20.28 S	17.13 E
Waterberge ⩚	156	24.30 S	28.00 E
Waterberg Plateau Park ♠	156	20.30 S	17.00 E
Waterbury, Ct., U.S.	207	41.33 N	73.02 W
Waterbury, Vt., U.S.	188	44.20 N	72.45 W
Waterdale	158	30.40 S	24.02 E
Wateree ≃	192	33.45 N	80.37 W
Wateree Lake ⊜[1]	192	34.25 N	80.50 W
Waterend, Eng., U.K.	260	51.47 N	0.30 W
Water End, Eng., U.K.	262	53.41 N	2.15 W
Waterfall, Austl.	170	34.08 S	151.00 E
Waterfall, Pa., U.S.	214	40.08 N	78.04 W
Waterford, On., Can.	212	42.56 N	80.17 W
Waterford (Port Láirge), Ire.	48	52.15 N	7.06 W
Waterford, S. Afr.	158	33.05 S	25.00 E
Waterford, Ca., U.S.	226	37.38 N	120.46 W
Waterford, Ct., U.S.	207	41.20 N	72.09 W
Waterford, In., U.S.	216	41.40 N	86.50 W
Waterford, Mi., U.S.	216	42.42 N	83.24 W
Waterford, N.Y., U.S.	210	42.47 N	73.40 W
Waterford, Pa., U.S.	214	41.56 N	79.59 W
Waterford, Wi., U.S.	216	42.45 N	88.12 W
Waterford □[6]	48	52.10 N	7.40 W
Waterford Harbour ⊂	48	52.10 N	6.55 W
Waterford Mills	216	41.33 N	85.50 W
Waterford Works	208	39.43 N	74.50 W
Watergate Bay ⊂	42	50.27 N	5.05 W
Watergrasshill	48	52.01 N	8.21 W
Watergrove Reservoir ⊜[1]	262	53.39 N	2.08 W
Waterhen ≃	184	54.38 N	107.47 W
Waterhen Lake ⊜, Mb., Can.	184	52.06 N	99.34 W
Waterhen Lake ⊜, Sk., Can.	184	54.28 N	108.25 W
Waterhouse Range ⩚	162	24.01 S	133.25 E
Wateringbury	260	51.15 N	0.25 E
Wateringen	52	52.02 N	4.16 E
Water Island	276	40.41 N	73.02 W
Waterkloof	158	30.19 S	25.18 E
Waterloo, Austl.	164	16.38 S	129.18 E
Waterloo, Austl.	168a	33.20 S	115.47 E
Waterloo, Austl.	168b	33.59 S	138.53 E
Waterloo, Bel.	50	50.43 N	4.23 E
Waterloo, On., Can.	212	43.28 N	80.31 W
Waterloo, P.Q., Can.	206	45.21 N	72.31 W
Waterloo, S.L.	150	8.20 N	13.04 W
Waterloo, Eng., U.K.	44	53.28 N	3.02 W
Waterloo, Al., U.S.	194	34.55 N	88.03 W
Waterloo, Il., U.S.	219	38.20 N	90.08 W
Waterloo, In., U.S.	216	41.25 N	85.01 W
Waterloo, Ia., U.S.	190	42.29 N	92.20 W
Waterloo, N.Y., U.S.	210	42.54 N	76.51 W
Waterloo, Wi., U.S.	216	43.11 N	88.59 W
Waterloo □[6]	212	43.30 N	80.30 W
Waterloo Bay ⊂	168b	35.08 S	137.26 E
Waterloo State Recreation Area ♠	216	42.22 N	84.20 W
Waterloo Station ◆[5]	260	51.30 N	0.07 W
Waterlooville	42	50.53 N	1.02 W
Waterman, Il., U.S.	216	41.46 N	88.46 W
Waterman, Wa., U.S.	224	47.34 N	122.35 W
Waterman Mountain ∧	228	34.20 N	117.56 W
Waterman Wash V	200	33.21 N	112.31 W
Water Mill	207	40.55 N	72.21 W
Waterport	210	43.20 N	78.16 W
Waterport Pond ⊜[1]	212	43.19 N	78.16 W
Waterproof	194	31.48 N	91.23 W
Waterside	214	40.11 N	78.23 W
Waterside Park	276	40.56 N	73.20 W
Watersmeet	190	46.16 N	89.10 W
Waterton ≃	182	49.32 N	113.16 W
Waterton-Glacier International Peace Park ♠	202	48.47 N	113.45 W
Waterton Lakes National Park ♠	182	49.05 N	113.50 W
Watertown, Ct., U.S.	207	41.36 N	73.07 W
Watertown, Ma., U.S.	207	42.22 N	71.11 W
Watertown, N.Y., U.S.	212	43.58 N	75.54 W
Watertown, S.D., U.S.	198	44.53 N	97.06 W
Watertown, Wi., U.S.	216	43.11 N	88.43 W
Waterval-Boven	156	25.40 S	30.20 E
Watervale	168b	33.57 S	138.38 E
Water Valley, Ms., U.S.	194	34.09 N	89.37 W
Water Valley, N.Y., U.S.	284a	42.42 N	78.51 W
Water View	208	37.43 N	76.36 W
Waterville, N.S., Can.	186	45.03 N	64.41 W
Waterville, P.Q., Can.	206	45.16 N	71.54 W
Waterville, Ire.	48	51.49 N	10.13 W
Waterville, Ks., U.S.	198	39.41 N	96.44 W
Waterville, Me., U.S.	188	44.33 N	69.37 W
Waterville, Ma., U.S.	207	42.40 N	72.04 W
Waterville, Mn., U.S.	190	44.13 N	93.34 W
Waterville, N.Y., U.S.	210	42.55 N	75.22 W
Waterville, Oh., U.S.	216	41.30 N	83.43 W
Waterville, Pa., U.S.	210	41.19 N	77.22 W
Waterville, Wa., U.S.	202	47.38 N	120.04 W
Watervliet, Mi., U.S.	216	42.11 N	86.15 W
Watervliet, N.Y., U.S.	210	42.43 N	73.42 W
Watervliet Reservoir ⊜[1]	210	42.43 N	73.58 W
Wates, Indon.	114	1.00 N	100.16 E
Wates, Indon.	115a	7.55 S	112.07 E
Wates, Indon.	115a	7.51 S	110.10 E
Watford, On., Can.	214	42.57 N	81.53 W
Watford, Eng., U.K.	42	51.40 N	0.25 W
Watford □[8]	260	51.40 N	0.25 W
Watford City	198	47.48 N	103.16 W
Waʻth	140	8.10 N	32.07 E
Wathaman ≃	184	57.16 N	102.52 W
Wathaman Lake ⊜	184	56.55 N	103.43 W
Wathena	198	39.45 N	94.56 W
Watheroo	162	30.17 S	116.04 E
Watheroo National Park ♠	162	30.14 S	115.52 E
Wathlingen	52	52.32 N	10.09 E
Wath upon Dearne	44	53.29 N	1.20 W
Wati	120	28.02 N	96.59 E
Watino	182	55.43 N	117.37 W
Watkins Glen	210	42.22 N	76.52 W
Watkins Glen International Raceway ♠	210	42.20 N	76.55 W
Watkins Glen State Park ♠	210	42.22 N	76.55 W
Watkins Island I	284c	39.02 N	77.17 W
Watkins Lake ⊜	281	42.40 N	83.22 W
Watkinsville	192	33.51 N	83.24 W
Watlaar	164	5.28 S	133.07 E
Watling Island → San Salvador I	238	24.02 N	74.28 W
Watlington	42	51.37 N	1.00 W
Watoga State Park ♠	188	38.07 N	80.05 W
Watonga	196	35.50 N	98.24 W
Watonwan ≃	198	44.04 N	94.07 W
Watopeka ≃	206	45.34 N	72.00 W
Watou	50	50.51 N	2.37 E
Wat Phai Tan, Khlong ≋	269a	13.48 N	100.33 E
Watrous, Sk., Can.	184	51.40 N	105.28 W
Watrous, N.M., U.S.	200	35.47 N	104.58 W
Watsa	154	3.03 N	29.32 E
Watseka	216	40.46 N	87.44 W
Watsi Kengo	152	0.48 S	20.33 E
Watson, Austl.	162	30.29 S	131.31 E
Watson, Sk., Can.	184	52.07 N	104.31 W
Watson, In., U.S.	218	38.22 N	85.41 W
Watsonia	274b	37.43 S	145.05 E
Watson Lake	180	60.07 N	128.48 W
Watsons Bay	274a	33.51 S	151.17 E
Watsons Creek	274b	37.40 S	145.13 E
Watsons Creek ≃	274b	37.43 S	145.16 E
Watsontown	210	41.05 N	76.51 W
Watsonville	226	36.54 N	121.45 W
Watt	222	31.39 N	96.51 W
Watten	50	50.50 N	2.13 E
Watten, Loch ⊜	46	58.29 N	3.19 W
Wattens	64	47.17 N	11.36 E
Wattenscheid	56	51.29 N	7.08 E
Wattenwil	58	46.46 N	7.30 E
Wattignies	50	50.35 N	3.03 E
Wattiwarriganna ≃	162	28.57 S	136.10 E
Wattle Flat	170	33.08 S	149.41 E
Wattle Glen	274b	37.40 S	145.11 E
Wattle Park ♠	274b	37.50 S	145.07 E
Watt Mountain ∧	240d	15.19 N	61.19 W
Watton	42	52.35 N	0.48 E
Wattrelos	50	50.42 N	3.13 E
Watts ◆[8]	280	33.56 N	118.15 W
Watts Bar Lake ⊜[1]	192	35.48 N	84.39 W
Watts Branch ≃	284c	39.03 N	77.15 W
Wattsburg	214	42.00 N	79.49 W
Watts Island I	208	37.48 N	75.53 W
Watts Mills	192	34.31 N	82.02 W
Wattville	273d	26.13 S	28.18 E
Wattwil	58	47.18 N	9.06 E
Watu	152	3.18 S	20.03 E
Watubela, Kepulauan II	164	4.35 S	131.40 E
Wat Wat	164	4.29 S	152.21 E
Watzekopf ∧	58	46.59 N	10.48 E
Watzmann ∧	64	47.33 N	12.55 E
Wau	164	7.20 S	146.45 E
Waubach	56	50.55 N	6.03 E
Waubaushene	212	44.45 N	79.42 W
Waubaushene Channel ʊ	212	44.46 N	79.45 W
Waubay	198	45.19 N	97.18 W
Waubay Lake ⊜	198	45.25 N	97.25 W
Waubesa, Lake ⊜	216	43.01 N	89.20 W
Waubra	169	37.21 S	143.39 E
Waubuno Creek ≃	212	42.58 N	81.08 W
Wauchope, Austl.	162	20.36 S	134.15 E
Wauchope, Austl.	166	31.27 S	152.44 E
Wauchula	220	27.32 N	81.48 W
Wauconda, Il., U.S.	216	42.15 N	88.08 W
Wauconda, Wa., U.S.	182	48.43 N	119.00 W
Wauconda, Wa., U.S.	202	48.43 N	119.00 W
Waugh	184	49.40 N	95.13 W
Waugh Mountain ∧	202	45.29 N	114.47 W
Waukara, Bukit ∧	112	1.15 S	119.42 E
Waukaringa	166	32.18 S	139.26 E
Waukarlycarly, Lake ⊜	162	21.25 S	121.50 E
Waukegan	216	42.21 N	87.50 W
Waukena	226	36.08 N	119.31 W
Waukesha	216	43.00 N	88.13 W
Waukesha □[6]	216	43.02 N	88.20 W
Waukomis	196	36.16 N	97.53 W
Waukon	190	43.16 N	91.28 W
Waulsort	56	50.13 N	4.52 E
Wauna	224	47.22 N	122.38 W
Waunakee	216	43.11 N	89.27 W
Wauneta	198	40.25 N	101.22 W
Waupaca	190	44.21 N	89.05 W
Waupecan Creek ≃	216	41.20 N	88.28 W
Waupoos Island I	212	43.59 N	76.58 W
Waupun	190	43.38 N	88.43 W
Wauregan	207	41.44 N	71.54 W
Waurika	196	34.10 N	97.59 W
Waurika Lake ⊜[1]	196	34.15 N	98.05 W
Wausa	198	42.29 N	97.32 W
Wausau	190	44.57 N	89.37 W
Wausaukee	190	45.22 N	87.57 W
Wauseon	216	41.32 N	84.08 W
Waushakum Pond ⊜	283	42.16 N	71.26 W
Wautoma	190	44.04 N	89.17 W
Wauwa	154	3.27 N	27.21 E
Wauwatosa	216	43.02 N	88.00 W
Wauzeka	190	43.05 N	90.52 W
Wave Hill	162	17.29 S	130.57 E
Waveland, Ma., U.S.	283	42.17 N	70.53 W
Waveland, Ms., U.S.	194	30.17 N	89.22 W
Waveney ≃	42	52.28 N	1.45 E
Waver ≃	44	54.52 N	3.17 W
Waverley, Austl.	169	37.53 S	145.10 E
Waverley, Austl.	274a	33.54 S	151.16 E
Waverley, N.Z.	172	39.46 S	174.38 E
Waverley, S. Afr.	158	31.58 S	26.28 E
Waverley, Ma., U.S.	283	42.23 N	71.11 W
Waverley ◆[8]	273d	26.08 S	28.04 E
Waverly, Al., U.S.	194	32.44 N	85.35 W
Waverly, Fl., U.S.	220	27.59 N	81.37 W
Waverly, Il., U.S.	219	39.35 N	89.57 W
Waverly, Ia., U.S.	190	42.43 N	92.28 W
Waverly, Ks., U.S.	198	38.23 N	95.36 W
Waverly, Mi., U.S.	216	42.44 N	84.33 W
Waverly, Mn., U.S.	190	45.04 N	93.57 W
Waverly, Mo., U.S.	194	39.12 N	93.31 W
Waverly, Ne., U.S.	198	40.55 N	96.31 W
Waverly, N.Y., U.S.	210	42.00 N	76.31 W
Waverly, Oh., U.S.	218	39.07 N	82.59 W
Waverly, Pa., U.S.	210	41.32 N	75.42 W
Waverly, Tn., U.S.	194	36.05 N	87.47 W
Waverly, Va., U.S.	208	37.02 N	77.05 W
Waverly Hall	192	32.41 N	84.44 W
Wavre	56	50.43 N	4.37 E
Wavrin	50	50.34 N	2.55 E

Symbol	English	Deutsch	Español	Français	Português
≃	River	Fluß	Río	Rivière	Rio
≋	Canal	Kanal	Canal	Canal	Canal
ᒪ	Waterfall, Rapids	Wasserfall, Stromschnellen	Cascada, Rápidos	Chute d'eau, Rapides	Cascata, Rápidos
ʊ	Strait	Meeresstraße	Estrecho	Détroit	Estreito
⊂	Bay, Gulf	Bucht, Golf	Bahía, Golfo	Baie, Golfe	Baía, Golfo
⊜	Lake, Lakes	See, Seen	Lago, Lagos	Lac, Lacs	Lago, Lagos
⁞⁞	Swamp	Sumpf	Pantano	Marais	Pântano
⊓	Ice Features, Glacier	Eis- und Gletscherformen	Accidentes Glaciales	Formes glaciaires	Acidentes glaciares
⊤	Other Hydrographic Features	Andere Hydrographische Objekte	Otros Elementos Hidrográficos	Autres données hydrographiques	Outros acidentes hidrográficos
✧	Submarine Features	Untermeerische Objekte	Accidentes Submarinos	Formes de relief sous-marin	Acidentes submarinos
□	Political Unit	Politische Einheit	Unidad Politica	Entité politique	Unidade política
▿	Cultural Institution	Kulturelle Institution	Institución Cultural	Institution culturelle	Instituição cultural
⊥	Historical Site	Historische Stätte	Sitio Histórico	Site historique	Sitio histórico
♠	Recreational Site	Erholungs- und Ferienort	Sitio de Recreo	Centre de loisirs	Area de Lazer
⊠	Airport	Flughafen	Aeropuerto	Aéroport	Aeroporto
■	Military Installation	Militäranlage	Instalación Militar	Installation militaire	Instalação militar
◆	Miscellaneous	Verschiedenes	Misceláneo	Divers	Diversos

Name	Page	Lat.	Long.
Wäw ≃	140	7.42 N	28.00 E
Wäw ≃	140	7.03 N	27.13 E
Wawa, On., Can.	190	47.59 N	84.47 W
Wawa, Nig.	150	9.55 N	4.25 E
Wawa, Süd.	140	20.26 N	30.21 E
Wawa ≃	236	13.53 N	83.28 W
Wawaka	216	41.27 N	85.28 W
Wāw al-Kabīr	146	25.20 N	16.43 E
Wawanesa	184	49.36 N	99.41 W
Wawarsing	210	41.46 N	74.21 W
Wawasee, Lake ⊜	216	41.24 N	85.41 W
Wawayanda State Park ♦	276	41.11 N	74.26 W
Wawiag ≃	190	48.25 N	91.07 W
Wawol ≃	164	8.01 S	143.33 E
Waworada, Teluk c	115b	8.44 S	118.51 E
Wawota	184	49.55 N	102.00 W
Waxahachie	222	32.23 N	96.50 W
Waxahachie, Lake ⊜¹	222	32.20 N	96.49 W
Waxhaw	192	34.55 N	80.44 W
Waxuecun	106	31.07 N	121.38 E
Waxweiler	56	50.05 N	6.22 E
Waya I	175g	17.18 S	177.08 E
Wayabula	216	2.17 N	128.12 E
Wayaopu	106	30.33 N	118.53 E
Waycross	192	31.12 N	82.21 W
Wayi	154	5.11 N	30.10 E
Wayland, Ia., U.S.	192	41.08 N	91.39 W
Wayland, Ky., U.S.	283	37.26 N	82.48 W
Wayland, Ma., U.S.	216	42.21 N	71.21 W
Wayland, Mi., U.S.	216	42.40 N	85.38 W
Wayland, N.Y., U.S.	210	42.34 N	77.35 W
Wayland, Oh., U.S.	214	41.10 N	81.04 W
Waylyn	192	32.51 N	79.59 W
Waymansville	218	39.04 N	86.03 W
Waymart	210	41.34 N	75.24 W
Wayne, Ab., Can.	182	51.23 N	112.39 W
Wayne, Mi., U.S.	216	42.16 N	83.23 W
Wayne, Ne., U.S.	198	42.13 N	97.01 W
Wayne, N.J., U.S.	210	40.55 N	74.16 W
Wayne, N.Y., U.S.	210	42.28 N	77.06 W
Wayne, Oh., U.S.	214	41.18 N	83.28 W
Wayne, Ok., U.S.	196	34.55 N	97.18 W
Wayne, Pa., U.S.	208	40.02 N	75.23 W
Wayne, W.V., U.S.	188	38.13 N	82.26 W
Wayne □⁶, Il., U.S.	219	38.25 N	88.40 W
Wayne □⁶, In., U.S.	218	39.50 N	84.54 W
Wayne □⁶, Mi., U.S.	216	42.14 N	83.12 W
Wayne □⁶, N.Y., U.S.	210	43.04 N	77.00 W
Wayne □⁶, Oh., U.S.	214	40.54 N	81.56 W
Wayne □⁶, Pa., U.S.	210	41.34 N	75.16 W
Wayne City	194	38.20 N	88.35 W
Wayne Lakes	218	40.01 N	84.39 W
Waynesboro, Ga., U.S.	192	33.05 N	82.00 W
Waynesboro, Ms., U.S.	194	31.40 N	88.38 W
Waynesboro, Pa., U.S.	208	39.45 N	77.34 W
Waynesboro, Tn., U.S.	194	35.19 N	87.45 W
Waynesboro, Va., U.S.	192	38.04 N	78.53 W
Waynesburg, Oh., U.S.	214	40.40 N	81.15 W
Waynesburg, Pa., U.S.	188	39.53 N	80.10 W
Waynesfield	218	40.36 N	83.59 W
Wayne State University ʋ²	281	42.21 N	83.04 W
Waynesville, Il., U.S.	194	40.15 N	89.08 W
Waynesville, Mo., U.S.	194	37.49 N	92.12 W
Waynesville, N.C., U.S.	192	35.29 N	82.59 W
Waynesville, Oh., U.S.	218	39.32 N	84.05 W
Waynoka	196	36.34 N	98.52 W
Waynoka, Lake ⊜¹	218	38.55 N	83.47 W
Wayoh Reservoir ⊜¹	262	53.39 N	2.24 W
Waza	146	11.25 N	14.34 E
Waza, Parc National de ♦	146	11.20 N	13.40 E
Wazah	120	33.22 N	69.26 E
Wāzah Khwāh	120	32.12 N	68.21 E
Waziers	50	50.23 N	3.07 E
Wāzin	146	31.57 N	10.40 E
Wazīrābād	123	32.27 N	74.07 E
Wazīrābād ⊶⁸	272a	28.41 N	77.14 E
Wāzirpur ⊶⁸	272a	28.41 N	77.10 E
Wazuka	96	34.47 N	135.55 E
Wazuka □³	264	34.45 N	135.53 E
Wda ≃	30	53.25 N	18.29 E
We, Pulau I	114	5.51 N	95.18 E
Wea Creek ≃	204	38.26 N	86.57 W
Weagamow Lake ⊜	184	52.53 N	91.22 W
Weald Park ♦	260	51.38 N	0.14 E
Wealdstone ⊶⁸	260	51.36 N	0.20 W
Weam	164	8.40 S	141.08 E
Wear ≃	44	54.55 N	1.22 W
Wearhead	44	54.45 N	2.13 W
Wearyan ≃	164	15.57 S	136.51 E
Weatherford, Ok., U.S.	196	35.31 N	98.42 W
Weatherford, Tx., U.S.	222	32.45 N	97.47 W
Weatherford, Lake ⊜¹	222	32.47 N	97.41 W
Weatherly	210	40.56 N	75.50 W
Weatogue	207	41.51 N	72.49 W
Weaubleau	194	37.53 N	93.32 W
Weaver, Austl.	168b	34.56 S	137.40 E
Weaver, Al., U.S.	194	33.45 N	85.48 W
Weaver, Tx., U.S.	222	33.10 N	95.25 W
Weaver ≃	44	53.19 N	2.44 W
Weaver ≃	262	53.19 N	2.45 W
Weaverham	44	53.16 N	2.35 W
Weaver Lake ⊜	184	54.38 N	94.23 W
Weavertown	279b	40.16 N	80.11 W
Weaverville, Ca., U.S.	204	40.43 N	122.56 W
Weaverville, N.C., U.S.	192	35.41 N	82.33 W
Webau	54	51.10 N	12.04 E
Webb, Sk., Can.	184	50.11 N	108.12 W
Webb, Ms., U.S.	194	33.56 N	90.20 W
Webb Brook ≃	283	42.32 N	71.14 W
Webb City	194	37.08 N	94.27 W
Webber Lake ⊜	184	54.28 N	94.00 W
Webberville	216	42.40 N	84.10 W
Webbwood	190	46.16 N	81.53 W
Weber	200	41.13 N	112.16 W
Weber, Mount ∧	182	55.32 N	128.31 W
Weber City	188	36.37 N	82.33 W
Weber Creek ≃	226	38.46 N	121.00 W
Weber Hill	279	38.27 N	90.34 W
Weberi Bekera ≃	144	9.39 N	39.03 E
Webster, Ab., Can.	182	55.26 N	118.42 W
Webster, Fl., U.S.	220	28.36 N	82.03 W
Webster, In., U.S.	218	39.54 N	84.57 W
Webster, Ma., U.S.	207	42.03 N	71.52 W
Webster, N.Y., U.S.	210	43.12 N	77.25 W
Webster, Pa., U.S.	214	40.11 N	79.50 W
Webster, S.D., U.S.	198	45.19 N	97.31 W
Webster, Wi., U.S.	190	45.52 N	92.22 W
Webster City	190	42.27 N	93.48 W
Webster Crossing	210	42.40 N	77.38 W
Webster Groves	279	38.35 N	90.21 W
Webster Lake ⊜	216	41.12 N	85.41 W
Websters Corners, B.C., Can.	224	49.13 N	122.30 W
Websters Corners, N.Y., U.S.	284a	41.47 N	78.45 W
Webster Springs	188	38.28 N	80.24 W
Weches	222	31.33 N	95.14 W
Wechmar	54	50.53 N	10.47 E
Wechselburg	54	51.00 N	12.47 E
Weda	108	0.21 N	127.52 E
Wedau ⊶⁸	56	51.24 N	6.48 E
Wedau, Sportpark ♦	263	51.25 N	6.47 E

Name	Page	Lat.	Long.
Weddell Island I	254	51.55 S	61.00 W
Weddell Sea ≃²	9	72.00 S	45.00 W
Wedderburn	166	36.25 S	143.37 E
Wedding ⊶⁸	264a	52.33 N	13.22 E
Weddinghofen	263	51.36 N	7.37 E
Wedel	52	53.35 N	9.41 E
Wedemark	52	52.33 N	9.44 E
Wedge, Central Mount ∧	162	22.51 S	131.50 E
Wedge Mountain ∧	182	50.10 N	122.50 W
Wedgeport	186	43.44 N	65.59 W
Wedgewood	219	38.47 N	90.17 W
Wedmore	42	51.14 N	2.49 W
Wedowee	194	33.18 N	85.29 W
Wedron	216	41.26 N	88.46 W
Weduar, Tanjung ⟩	164	6.00 S	132.50 E
Wedwell	140	9.00 N	27.12 E
Wedza	154	18.35 S	31.35 E
Weebo	162	28.01 S	121.03 E
Weed	204	41.25 N	122.23 W
Weed Heights	226	38.59 N	119.12 W
Weedon	206	45.42 N	71.28 W
Weedon Beck	42	52.14 N	1.05 W
Weedon Island I	220	27.51 N	82.36 W
Weed Patch	228	35.19 N	118.55 W
Weed Patch Hill ∧²	218	39.10 N	86.13 W
Weedsport	210	43.02 N	76.33 W
Weedville	214	41.17 N	78.30 W
Weehawken	276	40.46 N	74.01 W
Weeim, Pulau I	164	1.29 S	130.14 E
Wee Jasper	171b	35.09 S	148.41 E
Weekapauq	207	41.20 N	71.45 W
Weeki Wachee Spring ⋄			
Weeki Wachee Swamp ⊟	220	28.31 N	82.37 W
Weeks Point ⟩	276	40.53 N	73.39 W
Weekstown	208	39.35 N	74.36 W
Weelde	50	51.25 N	5.00 E
Weeley	42	51.51 N	1.07 E
Weel Shimbirro ∧	144	2.23 N	44.16 E
Weems	208	37.39 N	76.26 W
Weende	52	51.33 N	9.55 E
Weenen	158	28.57 S	30.03 E
Weener	52	53.10 N	7.21 E
Weeney Bay c	274a	34.01 S	151.10 E
Weeping Water	198	40.52 N	96.08 W
Weequahic Lake ⊜	276	40.42 N	74.12 W
Weert	52	51.15 N	5.43 E
Weesatche	222	28.51 N	97.27 W
Weesby	41	54.50 N	9.08 E
Weesow	264a	52.39 N	13.43 E
Weesp	52	52.17 N	5.02 E
Weetfeld ⊶⁸	263	51.38 N	7.49 E
Weethalle	166	33.53 S	146.38 E
Weeting	42	52.27 N	0.37 E
Weeton	262	53.48 N	2.56 W
Weetulta	168b	34.15 S	137.38 E
Wee Waa	166	30.14 S	149.26 E
Weeze	52	51.37 N	6.12 E
Wefensleben	54	52.11 N	11.09 E
Weferlingen	54	52.19 N	11.02 E
Wegberg	56	51.08 N	6.16 E
Wegdraai	158	28.50 S	21.52 E
Wegeleben	54	51.53 N	11.10 E
Wegendorf	264a	52.36 N	13.45 E
Wegenstedt	54	52.23 N	11.11 E
Wegeringhausen	56	51.07 N	7.45 E
Weggis	58	47.02 N	8.26 E
Wegliniec	30	51.17 N	15.13 E
Wegorzewo	30	54.14 N	21.44 E
Węgorzyno	30	53.32 N	15.33 E
Węgrów	30	52.25 N	22.01 E
Wegscheid	60	48.36 N	13.48 E
Wehdel	52	53.30 N	8.48 E
Wehebach Stausee ⊜¹			
Wehingen	58	48.10 N	8.48 E
Wehnrein ⊶⁸	263	51.32 N	6.46 E
Wehr	58	47.37 N	7.54 E
Wehringhausen ⊶⁸	263	51.21 N	7.27 E
Wehrsdorf	54	51.03 N	14.22 E
Weiwan	98	37.05 N	119.28 E
Wei ≃, Zhg.	98	36.51 N	115.43 E
Wei ≃, Zhg.	102	34.30 N	110.20 E
Weichang (Zhuizishan)	98	42.00 N	117.32 E
Weichsel → Wisła ≃	30	54.22 N	18.55 E
Weichselboden	60	47.40 N	15.10 E
Weichuan	102	29.33 N	104.39 E
Weicun	106	31.59 N	119.55 E
Weida	54	50.45 N	12.04 E
Weida ≃	54	50.47 N	12.06 E
Weiden am See	60	47.55 N	16.52 E
Weidenberg	60	49.57 N	11.43 E
Weiden in der Oberpfalz	60	49.41 N	12.10 E
Weidenstetten	56	48.33 N	9.59 E
Weiding	60	49.16 N	12.46 E
Weidling	264b	48.17 N	16.19 E
Weidlingau ⊶⁸	264b	48.16 N	16.13 E
Weidlingbach ⊶⁸	264b	48.18 N	16.20 E
Weifang	98	36.42 N	119.04 E
Weigelstown	208	39.59 N	76.49 W
Weihai	98	37.28 N	122.07 E
Weihaiwei → Weihai	98	37.28 N	122.07 E
Weihnachtsinsel → Christmas Island □²	112	10.30 S	105.40 E
Wei Island I	98	3.20 S	144.25 E
Weijiagou	105	40.28 N	115.08 E
Weijiahe	106	29.15 S	118.55 E
Weijiazhuang	105	39.37 N	116.22 E
Weijiazui	100	30.29 N	117.22 E
Weijingtang	106	31.27 N	120.39 E
Weikersheim	56	49.29 N	9.54 E
Weil ≃	56	50.28 N	8.16 E
Weil am Rhein	58	47.37 N	7.38 E
Weilburg	56	50.29 N	8.15 E
Weiler an der Stadt	58	48.45 N	8.52 E
Weiler	58	47.36 N	9.55 E
Weilerbach	56	49.29 N	7.37 E
Weilerswist	56	50.45 N	6.50 E
Weilheim	56	47.50 N	11.08 E
Weilheim an der Teck	56	48.37 N	9.32 E
Weilmoringle	166	29.15 S	146.51 E
Weilmünster	56	50.26 N	8.22 E
Weimar, B.R.D.	56	50.59 N	11.19 E
Weimar, D.D.R.	54	50.59 N	11.19 E
Weimar, Ca., U.S.	226	39.02 N	120.58 W
Weimar, Tx., U.S.	222	29.42 N	96.46 W
Weinan	102	34.30 N	109.29 E
Weinböhla	54	51.10 N	13.34 E
Weinel Cross Roads	279b	40.37 N	79.37 W
Weiner	194	35.37 N	90.53 W
Weinfelden	58	47.34 N	9.06 E
Weingarten, B.R.D.	56	49.05 N	8.31 E
Weingarten, B.R.D.	56	47.48 N	9.39 E
Weinheim	56	49.33 N	8.39 E
Weining, B.R.D.	102	26.53 N	104.18 E
Weining, Zhg.	98	41.21 N	123.49 E
Weinsberg	56	49.10 N	9.17 E
Weinsberger Wald ⊾	60	48.30 N	14.50 E
Weinviertel ⊾¹	61	48.30 N	16.25 E
Weipa	164	12.41 S	141.52 E
Weippe	200	46.22 N	115.56 W
Weir, India	122	27.01 N	77.11 E
Weir ≃, Austl.	166	28.10 S	149.06 E
Weir ≃, Ms., Can.	184	56.54 S	93.21 W
Weir ≃, Mb., Can.	184	56.54 N	93.21 W
Weir, Ms., U.S.	194	33.16 N	89.17 W
Weira	54	50.38 N	11.38 E
Weir River	184	56.49 N	94.06 W
Weirsdale	220	29.00 N	81.57 W
Weirton	214	40.25 N	80.35 W

Name	Page	Lat.	Long.
Weisberg			
→ Monguelfo	64	46.45 N	12.06 E
Weisburd	252	27.18 S	62.36 W
Weisburg	218	39.13 N	85.03 W
Weischlitz	54	50.26 N	12.02 E
Weisendorf	56	49.37 N	10.49 E
Weiser	202	44.15 N	116.58 W
Weiser ≃	202	44.15 N	116.59 W
Weishan (Xiazhen), Zhg.	98	34.52 N	117.09 E
Weishan, Zhg.	100	29.20 N	120.25 E
Weishan, Zhg.	100	29.41 N	120.48 E
Weishan, Zhg.	102	25.15 N	100.20 E
Weishancheng	100	32.34 N	113.24 E
Weishanhe	104	40.47 N	123.31 E
Weishan Hu ⊜	98	34.40 N	117.15 E
Weishanzhuang	105	39.40 N	116.25 E
Weishi	98	34.25 N	114.11 E
Weismain	54	50.05 N	11.14 E
Weiser Mountain ∧	194	34.02 N	85.40 W
Weissach	56	48.50 N	8.55 E
Weissbriach	64	46.41 N	13.15 E
Weisse Elster ≃	54	51.26 N	11.57 E
Weissenbach	264b	48.05 N	16.13 E
Weissenborn am Lech	58	48.26 N	10.39 E
Weissenberg	54	51.11 N	14.40 E
Weissenborn	54	52.52 N	13.25 E
Weissenbrunn	54	50.12 N	11.20 E
Weissenburg	58	46.39 N	7.28 E
Weissenburg in Bayern	56	49.01 N	10.58 E
Weissenfels	54	51.12 N	11.58 E
Weissenhorn	58	48.18 N	10.09 E
Weissensee	54	51.11 N	11.04 E
Weissensee ⊶⁸	264a	52.33 N	13.27 E
Weissensee ⊜	64	46.42 N	13.22 E
Weissenstadt	54	50.06 N	11.53 E
Weissenstein, B.R.D.	56	48.42 N	9.53 E
Weissenstein, Öst.	64	46.41 N	13.44 E
Weissenstein ∧	58	47.15 N	7.31 E
Weissenstein Tunnel ⊶⁵	58	47.12 N	7.23 E
Weissenthurm	56	50.24 N	7.27 E
Weisser Main ≃	54	50.04 N	11.24 E
→ White Nile ≃	140	15.38 N	32.31 E
Weisser See			
→ Beloje, ozero ⊜	26	60.11 N	37.37 E
Weisser Stein ∧	56	50.23 N	6.20 E
Weisses Meer			
→ Beloje more ≃²	24	65.30 N	38.00 E
Weisse Spitze ∧	64	46.52 N	12.21 E
Weissflüh ∧	58	46.50 N	9.48 E
Weisshorn ∧	58	46.06 N	7.42 E
Weissig	54	51.05 N	13.52 E
Weisskugel (Palla Bianca) ∧	64	46.49 N	10.44 E
Weiss Lake ⊜	192	34.15 N	85.35 W
Weissmeer-Ostsee Kanal			
→ Belomorsko-Baltijskij kanal ⊟	24	62.48 N	34.48 E
Weissport	210	40.50 N	75.42 W
Weisstannen	58	46.59 N	9.21 E
Weisswasser	54	51.30 N	14.38 E
Weisweiler	56	50.50 N	6.19 E
Weitang	105	40.24 N	117.24 E
Weitang ≃	104	42.19 N	122.18 E
Weitendorf	54	53.54 N	12.16 E
Weitensfeld	61	46.51 N	14.11 E
Weiterstadt	56	49.54 N	8.35 E
Weitian	100	27.10 N	113.18 E
Weitin	54	53.34 N	13.12 E
Weiting	106	31.22 N	120.47 E
Weitmar ⊶⁸	263	51.27 N	7.12 E
Weitnau	58	47.38 N	10.07 E
Weitou	100	24.34 N	118.34 E
Weitra	61	48.42 N	14.54 E
Weituo	107	30.03 N	106.08 E
Weitzgrund	54	52.11 N	12.32 E
Weiwan	98	33.46 N	115.54 E
Weixdorf	54	51.09 N	13.48 E
Weixi, Zhg.	102	27.14 N	99.12 E
Weixi, Zhg.	107	30.16 N	106.39 E
Weixian, Zhg.	98	36.57 N	115.15 E
Weixian, Zhg.	98	36.22 N	114.56 E
Weixian (Hanting), Zhg.	98	36.50 N	119.07 E
Weixin	102	27.48 N	105.06 E
Weiyuan	107	29.33 N	104.39 E
Weiyuan ≃	102	22.50 N	100.20 E
Weiyuankou	100	30.09 N	115.15 E
Weiyuanpu	104	41.30 N	124.16 E
Weiz	61	47.13 N	15.37 E
Weizhen	98	37.17 N	114.44 E
Weizhou Dao I	102	21.03 N	109.04 E
Weizhou Wan c	100	24.34 N	118.30 E
Weizhuang	105	39.02 N	115.20 E
Weizi	104	41.05 N	120.13 E
Weizigou, Zhg.	104	42.25 N	122.47 E
Weizigou, Zhg.	104	41.05 N	120.38 E
Weizigou, Zhg.	104	41.29 N	126.07 E
Weizigoumen	105	41.58 N	116.49 E
Weizigou	98	41.29 N	124.31 E
Weiherowo	30	54.37 N	18.15 E
Wekiva ≃	220	28.52 N	81.23 W
Wekiwa Springs State Park ♦	220	28.43 N	81.27 W
Wekomew Punt ⟩	241s	12.14 N	68.53 W
Wekusko Lake ⊜	184	54.45 N	99.50 W
Wekwela	152	9.28 N	81.40 W
Welbourn Hill	162	27.21 S	134.06 E
Welch, Ok., U.S.	196	36.52 N	95.05 W
Welch, Tx., U.S.	196	32.56 N	102.08 W
Welch, W.V., U.S.	188	37.26 N	81.35 W
Welch Creek ≃	282	37.32 N	121.51 W
Welches	224	45.19 N	121.57 W
Welch Peak ∧	182	31.27 N	121.36 W
Welcome, On., U.S.	284a	43.58 N	78.21 W
Welcome, Mn., U.S.	198	43.40 N	94.37 W
Welcome, S.C., U.S.	192	34.49 N	82.26 W
Welcome Lake ⊜	212	45.25 N	78.25 W
Welcome Monument I	269e	6.11 S	106.49 E
Welda	56	51.28 N	9.08 E
Weldiya	144	11.50 N	39.41 E
Weldon, Sk., Can.	184	53.00 N	105.08 W
Weldon, Ca., U.S.	228	35.40 N	118.17 W
Weldon, N.C., U.S.	192	36.25 N	77.35 W
Weldon, Tx., U.S.	222	31.00 N	95.34 W
Weldon ≃	194	40.00 N	93.05 W
Weldona	198	40.20 N	103.58 W
Weldon Brook ≃	276	40.58 N	74.35 W
Weleetka	196	35.20 N	96.08 W
Welega □⁴	144	9.30 N	35.30 E
Welele Jaja			
→ Velikaja ≃	76	57.48 N	28.20 E
Welkenraedt	50	50.40 N	5.59 E
Welker Seamount ⌄³	16	55.07 N	140.20 W
Welkite	144	8.17 N	37.50 E
Welkom	158	27.59 S	26.45 E
Well	56	51.34 N	6.06 E
Welland	204	50.41 N	79.15 W
Welland ≃, On., Can.	212	43.04 N	79.03 W
Welland ≃, Eng., U.K.	42	52.53 N	0.02 E
Welland Canal ⊟	212	43.01 N	79.14 W
Welland Junction	284a	42.57 N	79.14 W
Wellaune	54	51.34 N	12.33 E
Wellborn, Fl., U.S.	192	30.13 N	82.49 W
Wellborn, Tx., U.S.	222	30.39 N	96.18 W
Wellerode	56	51.14 N	9.34 E

Name	Page	Lat.	Long.
Wellers Bay c	212	44.00 N	77.34 W
Wellers Creek ≃	278	42.03 N	87.53 W
Wellesbourne	42	52.12 N	1.35 W
Welles Harbor c	174g	28.12 N	177.26 W
Wellesley, On., Can.	212	43.28 N	80.45 W
Wellesley, Ma., U.S.	207	42.17 N	71.17 W
Wellesley College ʋ²	283	42.18 N	71.19 W
Wellesley Hills	283	42.19 N	71.17 W
Wellesley Island I	212	44.19 N	75.58 W
Wellesley Islands II	164	16.42 S	139.30 E
Wellesley Island State Park ♦	212	44.19 N	76.01 W
Wellesley Lake ⊜	180	62.30 N	139.50 W
Wellfleet	207	41.56 N	70.02 W
Well Hill	260	51.21 N	0.09 E
Wellin	56	50.05 N	5.07 E
Welling ⊶⁸	260	51.28 N	0.07 E
Wellingborough	42	52.19 N	0.42 W
Wellinghofen ⊶⁸	263	51.28 N	7.29 E
Wellington, Austl.	166	32.33 S	148.57 E
Wellington, B.C., Can.	224	49.13 N	124.01 W
Wellington, N.Z.	172	41.18 S	174.47 E
Wellington, S. Afr.	158	33.38 S	18.57 E
Wellington, Eng., U.K.	42	52.43 N	2.31 W
Wellington, Eng., U.K.	42	50.59 N	3.14 W
Wellington, Co., U.S.	200	40.42 N	105.00 W
Wellington, Il., U.S.	216	40.32 N	87.41 W
Wellington, Ks., U.S.	198	37.15 N	97.22 W
Wellington, Mo., U.S.	194	39.08 N	93.58 W
Wellington, Nv., U.S.	226	38.45 N	119.22 W
Wellington, Oh., U.S.	214	41.10 N	82.13 W
Wellington, Tx., U.S.	196	34.51 N	100.12 W
Wellington, Ut., U.S.	200	39.32 N	110.44 W
Wellington □⁶	212	43.50 N	80.30 W
Wellington, Isla I	254	49.20 S	74.40 W
Wellington Bay c, N.T., Can.	176	69.30 N	106.30 W
Wellington Bay c, On., Can.	212	43.56 N	77.21 W
Wellington Channel ⋃	176	75.00 N	93.00 W
Wellington Point ⟩	171a	27.29 S	153.15 E
Wellington Reservoir ⊜¹			
Wellington Station	186	46.27 N	64.00 W
Wellman, Ia., U.S.	190	41.27 N	91.50 W
Wellman, Tx., U.S.	196	33.03 N	102.26 W
Wells, B.C., Can.	182	53.06 N	121.34 W
Wells, Eng., U.K.	42	51.13 N	2.39 W
Wells, Mi., U.S.	190	45.47 N	87.04 W
Wells, Mn., U.S.	190	43.44 N	93.43 W
Wells, Nv., U.S.	204	41.06 N	114.57 W
Wells, N.Y., U.S.	210	43.24 N	74.17 W
Wells, Tx., U.S.	222	31.29 N	94.56 W
Wells, Lake ⊜	162	26.43 S	123.10 E
Wells, Mount ∧	162	32.42 S	116.20 E
Wells, Mount ∧²	162	17.26 S	127.14 E
Wellsboro	210	41.44 N	77.18 W
Wells Bridge	210	42.22 N	75.15 W
Wellsburg, Ia., U.S.	190	42.26 N	92.55 W
Wellsburg, N.Y., U.S.	210	42.00 N	76.43 W
Wellsburg, W.V., U.S.	214	40.16 N	80.36 W
Wells Cathedral ʋ¹	42	51.13 N	2.39 W
Wellsford	172	36.17 S	174.31 E
Wells Gray Provincial Park ♦	182	52.20 N	120.00 W
Wells-next-the-Sea	42	52.58 N	0.51 E
Wells Point ⟩	284b	39.17 N	76.23 W
Wells State Park ♦	214	42.09 N	72.05 W
Wells Tannery	214	40.05 N	78.10 W
Wellston, Oh., U.S.	188	39.07 N	82.31 W
Wellston, Ok., U.S.	196	35.41 N	97.03 W
Wellsville, Ks., U.S.	198	38.43 N	95.04 W
Wellsville, Mo., U.S.	219	39.04 N	91.34 W
Wellsville, N.Y., U.S.	210	42.07 N	77.56 W
Wellsville, Oh., U.S.	214	40.36 N	80.38 W
Wellsville, Pa., U.S.	208	40.03 N	76.56 W
Wellsville, Ut., U.S.	200	41.38 N	111.55 W
Wellton	200	32.40 N	114.08 W
Welmel ≃	144	5.38 N	40.47 E
Welna ≃	263	51.39 N	23.16 E
Welney	42	52.31 N	0.15 E
Welo □⁴	144	11.50 N	40.00 E
Welper	263	51.25 N	7.12 E
Wels	61	48.10 N	14.02 E
Welschbillig	56	49.51 N	6.34 E
Welse ≃	54	53.10 N	14.18 E
Welsh	194	30.14 N	92.49 W
Welshpool, Austl.	169	38.39 S	146.26 E
Welshpool, Wales, U.K.	42	52.40 N	3.09 W
Welsleben	54	51.54 N	11.38 E
Welt-Aspe	54	52.10 N	8.43 E
Welterhausen	54	51.19 N	9.41 E
Welver	56	51.38 N	7.57 E
Welverdiend	158	26.25 S	27.16 E
Welwitschia	156	20.21 S	14.57 E
Welwyn Garden City	42	51.50 N	0.13 W
Welwyn Hatfield □⁸	260	51.47 N	0.12 W
Welzheim	56	48.53 N	9.38 E
Welzow	54	51.34 N	14.10 E
Wem	42	52.51 N	2.44 W
Wema	152	0.26 S	21.38 E
Wembere ≃	154	4.10 S	34.11 E
Wembley, Austl.	182	55.09 N	119.08 W
Wembley ⊶⁸	260	51.33 N	0.18 W
Wembley Stadium ♦, S. Afr.	273d	26.14 S	28.03 E
Wembley Stadium ♦, Eng., U.K.	260	51.33 N	0.17 W
Wemding	56	48.52 N	10.43 E
Wemindji	184	53.01 N	78.49 W
Wemmel	56	50.55 N	4.18 E
Wemmershoek ≃	158	33.50 S	19.04 E
Wemperhardt	56	50.09 N	6.05 E
Wemyss Bay	46	55.53 N	4.53 W
Wen ≃, Zhg.	98	36.00 N	118.32 E
Wen ≃, Zhg.	105	38.54 N	117.24 E
Wen'an	105	38.52 N	116.28 E
Wen an Wa ⊜	105	38.54 N	116.20 E
Wenas Creek ≃	224	46.42 N	120.35 W
Wenatchee	202	47.25 N	120.19 W
Wenatchee ≃	202	47.27 N	120.19 W
Wenatchee, Lake ⊜	202	47.49 N	120.47 W
Wenatchee Mountains ∧	202	47.20 N	120.45 W
Wencheng	100	27.50 N	120.05 E
Wenchi	150	7.42 N	2.07 W
Wenchow → Wenzhou	100	28.01 N	120.39 E
Wendaohezi	98	41.46 N	124.09 E
Wendel	279b	40.18 N	79.41 W
Wendell, Id., U.S.	200	42.46 N	114.42 W
Wendell, N.C., U.S.	192	35.46 N	78.22 W
Wenden	198	35.46 N	78.22 W
Wenden, B.R.D.	56	50.58 N	7.51 E
Wenden, Ariz., U.S.	200	33.49 N	113.32 W
Wenden, Az., U.S.	200	33.49 N	113.32 W
Wendisch Baggendorf	54	54.04 N	12.56 E
Wendlingen	152	9.04 S	31.10 E
Wendlingou	104	41.41 N	126.23 E
Wendo	144	6.38 N	38.27 E
Wendover, Eng., U.K.	42	51.46 N	0.45 W
Wendover, Ut., U.S.	200	40.44 N	114.02 W
Weneebegon ≃	190	46.53 N	83.12 W

Name	Page	Lat.	Long.
Wenebegon Lake ⊜	190	47.24 N	83.08 W
Werfang	100	28.02 N	117.19 E
Werg	60	48.40 N	12.23 E
Werg ≃	100	24.10 N	113.24 E
Werg'an	102	26.53 N	107.22 E
Wergbo	120	31.23 N	86.40 E
Wengcheng	100	24.23 N	113.51 E
Wengding	124	28.50 N	90.03 E
Wenge	152	0.03 N	24.01 E
Wengen, B.R.D.	58	47.41 N	10.09 E
Wengen, Schw.	58	46.36 N	7.56 E
Wengern	263	51.24 N	7.21 E
Wengjiabu	106	30.23 N	120.21 E
Wengjiang ≃	100	25.42 N	116.45 E
Wenghen	100	25.42 N	116.45 E
Wenheng	100	25.42 N	116.45 E
Wenhe ≃	98	35.35 N	116.58 E
Wenhi	124	28.21 N	83.34 E
Wenigzell	61	47.26 N	15.47 E
Wenjiechang	107	30.41 N	103.55 E
Wenjiezhen	100	30.42 N	103.49 E
Wenjiengban	100	26.01 N	117.51 E
Wenjiezhen	100	28.20 N	116.05 E
Wenling	100	28.22 N	121.20 E
Wenlock	164	13.06 S	142.58 E
Wenlock ≃	164	12.02 S	141.55 E
Wenlock Edge ∧⁴	42	52.30 N	2.40 W
Wenningsen	263	51.20 N	7.05 W
Wenringsi	102	52.16 N	9.34 E
Wenning ≃	44	54.07 N	2.39 W
Wennington ⊶⁸	260	51.30 N	0.13 E
Wennu	100	24.18 N	104.31 E
Wenns	58	47.10 N	10.44 E
Wenona, Il., U.S.	216	41.03 N	89.03 W
Wenona, Md., U.S.	208	38.08 N	75.57 W
Wenonah	208	39.47 N	75.08 W
Wenquan, Zhg.	100	23.37 N	113.43 E
Wenquansi	102	41.20 N	124.04 E
Wenshan	102	23.30 N	104.20 E
Wensnang	98	36.44 N	116.29 E
Wenshui, Zhg.	100	28.28 N	106.30 E
Wenshui, Zhg.	98	37.28 N	112.01 E
Wenskendorf	264a	52.45 N	13.23 E
Wensleydale ∨	44	54.19 N	2.00 W
Went ≃	44	53.39 N	0.59 W
Wentzel ≃	182	52.37 N	1.19 E
Wentworth, Austl.	166	34.07 S	141.55 E
Wentworth, N.C., J.S.	192	36.24 N	79.46 W
Wentworth, S.D., J.S.	198	43.59 N	96.57 W
Wentworth Falls	274a	33.43 S	150.22 E
Wentworth Park	273d	26.07 S	27.48 E
Wentwville	214	33.48 S	150.58 E
Wentzville	219	38.48 N	90.51 W
Wenxian	102	35.26 N	111.11 E
Wenxingchang	107	29.52 N	106.29 E
Wenyu ≃	105	39.56 N	116.40 E
Wenzenbach	60	49.06 N	12.12 E
Wenzhou	100	28.01 N	120.39 E
Wenzhuangzicun	104	42.16 N	123.51 E
Weobley	42	52.09 N	2.51 W
Weohyakapka, Lake ⊜	220	27.49 N	81.25 W
Wepener	158	29.46 S	27.02 E
Wepion	56	50.25 N	4.52 E
Weppersdorf	61	47.35 N	16.26 E
Wequetequock	207	41.21 N	71.52 W
Wera ≃	115b	8.20 S	120.43 E
Werbellinsee ⊜	54	52.54 N	13.43 E
Werben	54	52.52 N	11.58 E
Werbomont	56	50.23 N	5.41 E
Werchojansker Gebirge → Verchojanskij chrebet ∧	74	67.00 N	129.00 E
Werda	156	25.15 S	23.16 E
Werdau	54	50.44 N	12.22 E
Werden ≃	263	51.23 N	7.00 E
Werder, D.D.R.	54	52.23 N	12.56 E
Werder, Ityo.	144	6.58 N	45.20 E
Werdohl	56	51.15 N	7.45 E
Werfen ≃	64	47.28 N	13.11 E
Wergen	56	51.09 N	9.18 E
Werkendam	56	51.49 N	4.53 E
Werl	56	51.33 N	7.55 E
Werlaburgdorf	54	52.06 N	10.31 E
Werlau	56	50.10 N	7.43 E
Werlohausen	54	51.19 N	9.44 E
Wermelskirchen	56	51.09 N	7.13 E
Wermsdorf	54	51.17 N	12.57 E
Werms	56	49.38 N	8.22 E
Wernberg	60	49.32 N	12.10 E
Werne	56	51.40 N	7.38 E
Werneck	56	49.59 N	10.06 E
Werneuchen	54	52.38 N	13.44 E
Wernigerode	54	51.50 N	10.47 E
Wernitz ≃	56	48.47 N	10.53 E
Wernsdorfer See ⊜	264a	52.20 N	13.41 E
Werra ≃	54	51.26 N	9.39 E
Werra-Meissner-Kreis □⁶	54	51.10 N	9.40 E
Werre ≃	56	52.13 N	8.38 E
Werribee	169	37.54 S	144.40 E
Werribee ≃	169	37.59 S	144.41 E
Werribee Gorge State Park ♦	169	37.40 S	144.21 E
Werribee South	169	37.56 S	144.42 E
Werriwa ≃	166	35.15 S	150.36 E
Werris Creek	166	31.21 S	150.39 E
Werschweiler	56	49.27 N	7.13 E
Wersen	56	52.18 N	7.59 E
Werste ⊶⁸	263	52.14 N	8.44 E
Wertach	58	47.36 N	10.25 E
Wertach ≃	56	48.24 N	10.53 E
Wertheim	56	49.45 N	9.31 E
Wertingen	56	48.33 N	10.41 E
Wervershoof	50	52.43 N	5.09 E
Wervik	50	50.47 N	3.02 E
Werra ≃	50	49.43 N	6.38 E
Wesel	56	51.40 N	6.37 E
Wesel-Datteln-Kanal ⊟	56	51.38 N	6.36 E
Wesenberg	54	53.17 N	12.58 E
Wesendorf	54	52.34 N	10.34 E
Wesenufer ⊶⁸	264a	52.30 N	13.15 E
Weser ≃	52	53.32 N	8.34 E
Weser-Elbe-Kanal (Mittellandkanal) ⊟	54	52.16 N	11.41 E
Weser-Ems □³	52	52.45 N	8.10 E
Wesergebirge ∧	52	52.15 N	9.10 E
Weslaco	222	26.09 N	97.59 W
Weslemkoon Lake ⊜	212	45.02 N	77.25 W

Name	Page	Lat.	Long.
Wesley, Dom.	240d	15.34 N	61.19 W
Wesley, Ia., U.S.	190	43.05 N	93.59 W
Wesleyville, Nf., Can.	186	49.09 N	53.34 W
Wesleyville, Pa., U.S.	214	42.08 N	79.59 W
Wessel, Cape ⟩	164	10.59 S	136.46 E
Wesseling	56	50.49 N	6.58 E
Wessel Islands II	164	11.30 S	136.25 E
Wesselsbron	158	27.50 S	25.23 E
Wesselskerri	158	27.23 S	23.47 E
Wessington	198	44.27 N	98.41 W
Wessington Springs	198	44.04 N	98.34 W
Wessobrunn	64	47.52 N	11.01 E
Wesson	194	31.42 N	90.23 W
Wessum	52	52.05 N	6.58 E
West, Ms., U.S.	194	33.11 N	89.46 W
West, Tx., U.S.	222	31.48 N	97.05 W
West ≃, N.Y., U.S.	210	42.41 N	77.22 W
West ≃, Vt., U.S.	188	42.52 N	72.33 W
West Abington	207	42.05 N	70.58 W
Westacres	216	42.35 N	83.26 W
West Acton	283	42.29 N	71.28 W
West Alexander	214	40.06 N	80.31 W
West Alexandria	218	39.44 N	84.31 W
Westall, Point ⟩	162	32.55 S	134.04 E
West Allen ≃	44	54.55 N	2.19 W
West Allis	216	43.01 N	88.00 W
Westalton	219	38.51 N	90.13 W
West Amityville	276	40.41 N	73.26 W
West Andover	207	42.39 N	71.09 W
West Athens	280	33.55 N	118.18 W
West Atlantic City	208	39.23 N	74.28 W
West Babylon	276	40.43 N	73.21 W
Westbahnhof ⊶⁵	264b	48.11 N	16.20 E
West Baines ≃	164	15.36 S	129.58 E
West Bangor	210	40.52 N	75.14 W
Westbank	182	49.50 N	119.38 W
West Bank □⁹	132	31.40 N	35.15 E
West Barnstable	207	41.42 N	70.22 W
West Barrington	207	41.44 N	71.20 W
West Bay, N.S., Can.	186	45.43 N	61.10 W
Westbay, Fl., U.S.	194	30.17 N	85.52 W
West Bay c, Fl., U.S.	194	30.16 N	85.47 W
West Bay c, Tx., U.S.	222	29.12 N	94.57 W
West Bay Shore	276	40.42 N	73.16 W
West Belmar	208	40.10 N	74.02 W
West Bend, In., U.S.	218	39.20 N	84.26 W
West Bend, Wi., U.S.	190	43.25 N	88.11 W
West Bengal □³	124	24.00 N	88.00 E
West Bergholt	42	51.55 N	0.51 E
West-Berlin → Berlin (West), B.R.D.	54	52.30 N	13.20 E
West Berlin, N.J., U.S.	208	39.48 N	74.56 W
West Berlin, U.S.	208	52.30 N	13.15 E
West Bernard Creek ≃	222	29.23 N	95.58 W
West Bhādrath Plain ∧¹	126	23.30 N	88.00 E
West Bijou Creek ≃	198	39.51 N	104.08 W
West Billerica	283	42.33 N	71.19 W
West Blocton	194	33.07 N	87.07 W
West Bloomfield	210	42.54 N	77.26 W
West Bolivar	194	40.23 N	79.10 W
Westborough	207	42.16 N	71.37 W
Westbourne	184	50.09 N	98.35 W
West Bow Creek ≃	198	42.46 N	97.08 W
West Boxford	283	42.42 N	71.04 W
West Boylston	207	42.22 N	71.47 W
West Bradenton	220	27.30 N	82.37 W
West Branch ≃, In., U.S.	190	41.40 N	91.20 W
West Branch, Mi., U.S.	190	44.16 N	84.14 W
West Branch Reservoir ⊜¹	210	41.25 N	73.42 W
West Branch State Park ♦	214	41.07 N	81.05 W
Westbridge	182	49.10 N	118.59 W
West Bridgewater	207	42.00 N	71.00 W
West Bridgford	42	52.56 N	1.08 W
West Bristol	285	40.06 N	74.53 W
West Bromwich	42	52.31 N	1.56 W
Westbrook, Austl.	171a	27.36 S	151.52 E
Westbrook, On., Can.	212	44.16 N	76.38 W
West Brook ≃	276	41.16 N	74.18 W
West Brookfield	207	42.14 N	72.08 W
Westbrookville	210	41.30 N	74.34 W
West Burlington, Ia., U.S.	190	40.49 N	91.09 W
West Burlington, N.Y., U.S.	210	42.42 N	75.13 W
West Burra I	46a	60.05 N	1.21 W
Westbury, Eng., U.K.	42	51.16 N	2.11 W
Westbury, Eng., U.K.	42	52.41 N	2.57 W
Westbury, N.Y., U.S.	276	40.45 N	73.35 W
Westbury-on-Severn	42	51.50 N	2.24 W
West Butte ∧	202	48.24 N	111.32 W
West Canada Creek ≃	210	43.01 N	74.58 W
West Cape ⟩	188	43.01 N	74.58 W
West Cape Howe ⟩	162	35.08 S	117.36 E
West Cape May	208	38.56 N	74.56 W
West Carlisle	196	33.35 N	101.56 W
West Caroline Basin ⌄¹	14	4.00 N	138.00 E
West Carrollton	218	39.40 N	84.15 W
West Carson	280	33.50 N	118.23 W
West Carthage	212	43.59 N	75.36 W
West Catfish Creek ≃			
West Channel ⊟	180	68.51 N	136.10 W
West Chelmsford	283	42.37 N	71.23 W
West Chester, Pa., U.S.	208	39.57 N	75.36 W
Westchester, Va., U.S.	284c	38.51 N	77.16 W
Westchester □⁶	210	41.20 N	73.45 W
Westchester ⊶⁸, Ca., U.S.	280	33.56 N	118.25 W
Westchester ⊶⁸, N.Y., U.S.	276	40.51 N	73.52 W
West Chester Airport ⟨			
Westchester County Airport ⟨	210	41.04 N	73.42 W
Westchester Creek ≃	276	40.48 N	73.51 W
Westchester Estates	284c	38.47 N	76.55 W
Westchester Station	196	33.40 N	101.54 W
Westchester University of Pennsylvania ʋ²	285	39.57 N	75.36 W
West Chicago	216	41.53 N	88.12 W
West Clandon	260	51.15 N	0.30 W
West Clarksville	210	42.06 N	78.13 W
West Clear Creek ≃	200	34.34 N	111.51 W
West Cliddau ≃	263	51.46 N	4.54 W
Westcliffe	200	38.08 N	105.27 W
Westcliff-on-Sea	273d	26.11 S	28.02 E
Westcliff-on-Sea	260	51.32 N	0.41 E
West College Corner	218	39.34 N	84.48 W
West Collingswood Heights	285	39.59 N	75.07 W

∧ Mountain	Berg	Montaña	Montagne	Montanha
∧ Mountains	Gebirge	Montañas	Montagnes	Montanhas
⋉ Pass	Paß	Paso	Col	Passo
∨ Valley, Canyon	Tal, Cañon	Valle, Cañón	Vallée, Canyon	Vale, Canhão
⊑ Plain	Ebene	Llano	Plaine	Planicie
⟩ Cape	Kap	Cabo	Cap	Cabo
I Island	Insel	Isla	Île	Ilha
II Islands	Inseln	Islas	Îles	Ilhas
≃ Other Topographic Features	Andere Topographische Objekte	Otros Elementos Topográficos	Autres données topographiques	Outros acidentes topográficos

West-Whit I · 191

ESPAÑOL — Nombre | Página | Lat.°′ | Long.°′ W = Oeste
FRANÇAIS — Nom | Page | Lat.°′ | Long.°′ W = Ouest
PORTUGUÊS — Nome | Página | Lat.°′ | Long.°′ W = Oeste

Nombre / Nom / Nome	Página / Page	Lat.°′	Long.°′
West Columbia, S.C., U.S.	192	33.59 N	81.04 W
West Columbia, Tx., U.S.	222	29.08 N	95.38 W
West Concord, Ma., U.S.	207	42.27 N	71.23 W
West Concord, Mn., U.S.	190	44.09 N	92.53 W
West Conshohocken	285	40.04 N	75.19 W
West Cote Blanche Bay c	194	29.40 N	91.45 W
Westcott	260	51.13 N	0.22 W
Westcott Cove c	276	41.02 N	73.30 W
West Covina	228	34.04 N	117.56 W
West Creek	208	39.38 N	74.18 W
West Creek ≃, In., U.S.	216	41.12 N	87.30 W
West Creek ≃, Pa., U.S.	214	41.30 N	78.15 W
Westdale, Ma., U.S.	283	42.01 N	70.59 W
Westdale, N.Y., U.S.	210	43.23 N	75.49 W
West Danby	210	42.19 N	76.32 W
West Davenport	210	42.27 N	74.58 W
West Deane Park ♠	275b	43.40 N	79.34 W
West Decatur	214	40.56 N	78.17 W
West Delaware Aqueduct ≊[1]	210	41.52 N	74.31 W
West Demerara-Essequibo Coast □[5]	246	7.00 N	58.40 W
Westdene ◆[8]	273d	26.11 S	27.59 E
West Dennis	207	41.39 N	70.10 W
West Derby ◆[8]	262	53.26 N	2.54 W
West Derry	214	40.20 N	79.20 W
West Des Moines	190	41.34 N	93.42 W
West Ditch ≊	276	40.56 N	74.19 W
West Dolores ≃	200	37.35 N	108.21 W
West Drayton ◆[8]	260	51.30 N	0.29 W
West Duffins Creek ≃	212	43.51 N	79.04 W
West Duxbury	283	42.03 N	70.47 W
West Easton	210	40.41 N	75.14 W
West Eaton	210	42.51 N	75.39 W
Westecunk Creek ≃	208	39.37 N	74.16 W
West Edmeston	210	42.46 N	75.17 W
West Edmondale	284b	39.18 N	76.43 W
West Elizabeth	279b	40.17 N	79.54 W
West Elk Mountains ⋏	200	38.40 N	107.15 W
West Elk Peak ∧	200	38.43 N	107.13 W
West Elkton	218	39.35 N	84.33 W
West Ellicott	214	42.05 N	79.16 W
West Elmira	210	42.04 N	76.50 W
West End, Ba.	238	26.41 N	78.58 W
West End, Eng., U.K.	260	51.44 N	0.04 W
West End, Eng., U.K.	260	51.20 N	0.38 W
West End, Ar., U.S.	194	34.13 N	92.03 W
West End, Il., U.S.	216	42.17 N	89.09 W
West End, N.Y., U.S.	210	42.28 N	75.05 W
West End, N.C., U.S.	192	35.14 N	79.34 W
West End ◆[8], Eng., U.K.	260	51.32 N	0.24 W
West End ◆[8], Pa., U.S.	279b	40.27 N	80.02 W
Westende, Bel.	50	51.10 N	2.46 E
Westende, B.R.D.	263	51.25 N	7.24 E
Westendorf	64	47.26 N	12.13 E
Westenfeld ◆[8]	263	51.28 N	7.09 E
Westenholz	52	51.45 N	8.28 E
Westenschouwen	52	51.41 N	3.42 E
Westerbauer ◆[8]	263	51.20 N	7.23 E
Westerblokker	52	52.39 N	5.08 E
Westerbönen	263	51.36 N	7.46 E
Westerbork	52	52.51 N	6.37 E
Westerburg	56	50.33 N	7.58 E
Westercelle	52	52.36 N	10.05 E
Westerdale	46	58.27 N	3.30 W
Westeregeln	54	51.57 N	11.23 E
Westerham	42	51.16 N	0.05 E
Westerhausen	54	51.48 N	11.03 E
Westerholt	52	51.36 N	7.05 E
Westerholz ◆[3]	263	51.32 N	7.28 E
Westerich □[9]	56	49.15 N	7.20 E
Westerkappeln	52	52.18 N	7.52 E
Westerland	30	54.54 N	8.18 E
Westerlo, Bel.	56	51.05 N	4.55 E
Westerlo, N.Y., U.S.	210	42.31 N	74.03 W
Westerly	207	41.22 N	71.49 W
Western	198	40.23 N	97.11 W
Western □[4], Ghana	150	5.30 N	2.30 W
Western □[4], Kenya	154	0.30 N	34.35 E
Western □[4], Sol.Is.	175e	8.00 S	157.00 E
Western □[4], Zam.	152	16.00 S	24.00 E
Western □[5], Pap. N. Gui.	164	7.00 S	142.00 E
Western □[5], Ug.	154	1.00 N	31.00 E
Western ≃	166	22.22 S	142.25 E
Western Area □[4]	150	8.20 N	13.00 W
Western Australia □[3]	160	25.00 S	122.00 E
Western Branch ≃	284c	38.55 N	76.48 W
Western Canal ≊	226	39.28 N	121.35 W
Western Channel ⊔	98	34.40 N	129.00 E
Western Cove c	168b	35.43 S	137.38 E
Western Desert → Gharbīyah, Aş-Şaḥrā' al- ◆[2]	140	27.00 N	27.00 E
Western Division □[5]	175g	18.00 S	177.30 E
Western Ghāts ⋏	122	14.00 N	75.00 E
Western Highlands □[5]	164	5.45 S	144.30 E
Western Isles □[4]	46	57.40 N	7.00 W
Westernport	188	39.29 N	79.02 W
Western Port c	169	38.22 N	145.20 E
Western Port Bay c	169	38.15 S	145.20 E
Western Sahara □[2], Afr.	134	24.30 N	13.00 W
Western Sahara □[2], Afr.	148	24.30 N	13.00 W
Western Samoa □[1], Oc.	14	13.55 S	172.00 W
Western Samoa □[1], Oc.	175a	13.55 S	172.00 W
Western Sayans → Zapadnyj Sajan ⋏	74	53.00 N	94.00 E
Western Shore	186	44.32 N	64.19 W
Western Springs	278	41.48 N	87.54 W
Westernville	210	43.18 N	75.23 W
Westerschelde c[1]	52	51.25 N	3.45 E
Westerstede	52	53.15 N	7.55 E
Westervelt	219	39.29 N	88.52 W
Westerville	214	40.07 N	82.55 W
Westerwald ⋏	56	50.40 N	7.55 E
West European Basin ✦[1]	10	47.00 N	15.00 W
West Exeter	210	42.48 N	75.09 W
West Fairview	208	40.16 N	76.54 W
Westfalen □[9]	52	51.50 N	7.30 E
Westfalenhalle ⊍	263	51.30 N	7.27 E
West Falkland I	254	51.50 S	60.00 W
West Falls	210	42.42 N	78.41 W
West Falmouth	207	41.36 N	70.38 W
West Fargo	198	46.52 N	96.54 W
West Farleigh	260	51.15 N	0.27 E
West Farmington	214	41.23 N	80.58 W
Westfield, Eng., U.K.	42	50.55 N	0.35 E
Westfield, Il., U.S.	194	39.27 N	88.01 W
Westfield, In., U.S.	218	40.02 N	86.07 W
Westfield, Ma., U.S.	207	42.07 N	72.45 W
Westfield, N.J., U.S.	210	40.39 N	74.20 W
Westfield, N.Y., U.S.	214	42.19 N	79.34 W
Westfield, Pa., U.S.	210	41.55 N	77.32 W
Westfield, Tx., U.S.	222	30.01 N	95.24 W
Westfield, Wi., U.S.	190	43.53 N	89.29 W
Westfield ≃	207	42.05 N	72.35 W
Westfield, Middle Branch ≃	207	42.16 N	72.52 W
Westfield, West Branch ≃	207	42.13 N	72.52 W
Westfield Center	214	41.01 N	81.55 W
West Fiord c[2]	176	76.02 N	90.00 W
Westford, Ma., U.S.	283	42.34 N	71.26 W
Westford, N.Y., U.S.	210	42.39 N	74.48 W
West Fork	194	35.55 N	94.11 W
West Foxboro	283	42.05 N	71.17 W
West Frankfort	194	37.53 N	88.55 W
West Friesland ◆[1]	52	52.45 N	4.50 E
West Frisian Islands → Waddeneilanden II	52	53.26 N	5.30 E
West Fulton	210	42.34 N	74.28 W
Westgate, Austl.	166	26.35 S	146.12 E
Westgate, Mi., U.S.	216	43.03 N	85.42 W
Westgate on Sea	42	51.23 N	1.21 E
West Genesee Terrace	210	43.03 N	76.16 W
West Germany → Germany, Federal Republic of □[1]	30	51.00 N	9.00 E
West-Ghats → Western Ghāts ⋏	122	14.00 N	75.00 E
West Gilgo Beach	276	40.37 N	73.25 W
West Glacier	202	48.29 N	113.58 W
West Glamorgan □[6]	42	51.35 N	3.35 W
West Glens Falls	210	43.18 N	73.43 W
West Glenville	210	42.56 N	74.04 W
West Goshen	207	41.49 N	73.15 W
West Granby	207	41.57 N	72.50 W
West Grand Lake ◎	188	45.15 N	67.50 W
West Groton	207	42.36 N	71.37 W
West Grove	208	39.49 N	75.49 W
Westham	208	37.35 N	77.32 W
West Ham ◆[8]	260	51.31 N	0.01 E
West Hamburg	208	40.33 N	76.00 W
West Ham Football Club ♠	260	51.32 N	0.02 E
Westham Island I	224	49.05 N	123.10 W
West Hamlin	188	38.17 N	82.11 W
Westhampton, N.Y., U.S.	207	40.49 N	72.39 W
Westhampton, Va., U.S.	284c	38.54 N	77.11 W
West Hanningfield	260	51.40 N	0.30 E
West Hanover	283	42.07 N	70.53 W
West Harbor c	276	40.54 N	73.32 W
West Harrison	218	39.15 N	84.49 W
West Hartford	207	41.45 N	72.44 W
West Hartland	207	42.00 N	72.58 W
Westhausen	56	48.53 N	10.11 E
Westhaven, Ca., U.S.	204	41.03 N	124.06 W
West Haven, Ct., U.S.	207	41.16 N	72.57 W
Westhaven, Il., U.S.	278	41.35 N	87.51 W
West Haverstraw	210	41.12 N	73.59 W
West Hazleton	210	40.57 N	75.59 W
Westhead	262	53.34 N	2.51 W
West Hebron	210	43.14 N	73.22 W
West Heidelberg	274b	37.45 S	145.02 E
Westheim	56	49.03 N	9.44 E
West Helena	194	34.33 N	90.38 W
Westhemmerde	263	51.33 N	7.47 E
West Hempstead	276	40.42 N	73.39 W
West Henrietta	210	43.02 N	77.40 W
West Hickory	214	41.34 N	79.25 W
Westhill	46	57.09 N	2.17 W
West Hill ◆[8]	275b	43.46 N	79.11 W
Westhofen	263	51.25 N	7.31 E
Westhoff	222	29.12 N	97.28 W
Westhoffen	58	48.36 N	7.26 E
West Hollywood, Ca., U.S.	228	34.05 N	118.21 W
West Hollywood, Fl., U.S.	220	26.01 N	80.10 W
Westholme	224	49.52 N	123.42 W
West Homestead	279b	40.24 N	79.55 W
Westhope, N.D., U.S.	198	48.54 N	101.01 W
Westhope, Oh., U.S.	216	41.18 N	83.57 W
West Horndon	260	51.34 N	0.21 E
West Horsley	260	51.16 N	0.27 W
Westhoughton	262	53.33 N	2.32 W
West Hoxton	274a	33.55 S	150.49 E
West Humber ≃	212	43.44 N	79.33 W
West Humble	260	51.15 N	0.20 W
West Huntington	276	40.42 N	73.18 W
West Hurley	210	42.00 N	74.06 W
Westhuyzen	158	27.30 S	25.27 E
West Hyde	260	51.37 N	0.30 W
West Ice Shelf ⊓	9	67.00 S	85.00 E
Westick	263	51.35 N	7.38 E
Westig	263	51.22 N	7.45 E
West Indies II	230	19.00 N	70.00 W
Westindische Inseln → West Indies II	230	19.00 N	70.00 W
West Irian → Irian Jaya □[4]	164	5.00 S	138.00 E
West Island I, Austl.	164	15.36 S	136.34 E
West Island I, Ma., U.S.	207	41.36 N	70.50 W
West Islip	210	40.42 N	73.18 W
West Jan Mayen Ridge ✦[3]	10	71.00 N	13.00 W
West Jefferson, N.C., U.S.	192	36.24 N	81.29 W
West Jefferson, Oh., U.S.	218	39.56 N	83.16 W
West Jordan	200	40.36 N	111.56 W
Westkapelle, Bel.	50	51.19 N	3.18 E
Westkapelle, Ned.	52	51.32 N	3.27 E
West Keansburg	276	40.27 N	74.09 W
West Kettle ≃	182	49.07 N	119.00 W
West Kilbride	46	55.42 N	4.51 W
West Kill	210	42.13 N	74.31 W
West Kingsdown	42	51.21 N	0.17 E
West Kingston	207	41.28 N	71.33 W
West Kirby	44	53.22 N	3.10 W
Westkirchen	52	51.53 N	8.02 E
West Kittanning	214	40.49 N	79.32 W
West Lafayette, In., U.S.	216	40.25 N	86.54 W
West Lafayette, Oh., U.S.	214	40.16 N	81.45 W
Westlake, La., U.S.	194	30.15 N	93.15 W
Westlake, Oh., U.S.	214	41.27 N	81.55 W
Westlake, Tx., U.S.	222	32.59 N	97.12 W
West Lake ◎, On., Can.	212	43.56 N	77.17 W
West Lake ◎, Fl., U.S.	220	25.12 N	80.49 W
West Lake ◎, N.J., U.S.	276	40.58 N	74.22 W
West Lamma Channel ⊔	271d	22.13 N	114.04 E
West Lancashire □[8]	262	53.35 N	2.50 W
Westland, Mi., U.S.	216	42.19 N	83.24 W
Westland, Pa., U.S.	214	40.17 N	80.16 W
Westland Center ◆[9]	281	42.20 N	83.23 W
Westland National Park ♠	172	43.30 S	170.10 E
Westlands	207	42.37 N	71.20 W
West Lanham Hills	284c	38.57 N	76.53 W
West Laramie	200	41.18 N	105.37 W
West Lawn	284c	38.52 N	77.11 W
West Lebanon, In., U.S.	216	40.16 N	87.23 W
West Lebanon, Pa., U.S.	214	40.35 N	79.22 W
West Leechburg	214	40.37 N	79.37 W
Westleigh, S. Afr.	158	27.31 S	27.21 E
Westleigh, Eng., U.K.	262	53.30 N	2.31 W
West Leipsic	216	41.07 N	84.00 W
Westley	226	37.33 N	121.12 W
West Leyden	212	43.28 N	75.28 W
West Liberty, Ia., U.S.	190	41.34 N	91.15 W
West Liberty, Ky., U.S.	192	37.55 N	83.15 W
West Liberty, Oh., U.S.	216	40.15 N	83.45 W
West Liberty, Pa., U.S.	214	41.00 N	80.03 W
West Liberty, W.V., U.S.	214	40.10 N	80.35 W
West Liberty ◆[8]	279b	40.24 N	80.01 W
Westliche Sahara → Western Sahara □[2]	148	24.30 N	13.00 W
Westliche Sierra Madre → Madre Occidental, Sierra ⋏	232	25.00 N	105.00 W
Westline	214	41.47 N	78.46 W
West Linn	224	45.21 N	122.36 W
West Linton	46	55.46 N	3.22 W
West Little Owyhee ≃	202	42.28 N	117.15 W
Westlock	182	54.09 N	113.52 W
West Lorne	214	42.36 N	81.36 W
West Los Angeles ◆[8]	280	34.03 N	118.28 W
West Lulworth	42	50.38 N	2.15 W
West Lunga ≃	154	13.06 S	24.39 E
West Lunga National Park ♠	154	12.55 S	25.10 E
West Malling	42	51.18 N	0.25 E
West Malling Aerodrome ⊠	260	51.16 N	0.24 E
West Manayunk	285	40.01 N	75.14 W
West Manchester	218	39.54 N	84.37 W
West Mansfield, Ma., U.S.	207	41.59 N	71.14 W
West Mansfield, Oh., U.S.	216	40.24 N	83.32 W
West Mariana Basin ✦[1]	14	15.00 N	137.00 E
West Mayfield	214	40.47 N	80.20 W
West Meadowview	216	41.08 N	87.52 W
Westmeath □[6]	48	53.30 N	7.30 W
West Medway	207	42.08 N	71.25 W
West Melbourne	220	28.04 N	80.39 W
West Memphis	194	35.08 N	90.11 W
West Meon	42	51.01 N	1.05 W
Westmere	210	42.41 N	73.52 W
West Mersea	42	51.47 N	0.55 E
West Miami	220	25.45 N	80.17 W
West Middlesex	214	41.10 N	80.27 W
West Middletown	214	40.15 N	80.25 W
West Midlands □[6]	42	52.30 N	2.00 W
West Mifflin	214	40.22 N	79.52 W
West Milford	210	41.07 N	74.22 W
West Millbury	207	42.11 N	71.48 W
West Mill Creek ≃	222	29.55 N	96.17 W
West Milton, Oh., U.S.	218	39.57 N	84.19 W
West Milton, Pa., U.S.	210	41.01 N	76.52 W
West Milwaukee	216	43.00 N	87.58 W
West Mineola	222	32.41 N	95.31 W
Westminster, Ca., U.S.	228	33.45 N	118.02 W
Westminster, Co., U.S.	200	39.50 N	105.02 W
Westminster, Md., U.S.	208	39.34 N	76.59 W
Westminster, Ma., U.S.	207	42.32 N	71.54 W
Westminster, Oh., U.S.	216	40.42 N	83.58 W
Westminster, S.C., U.S.	192	34.39 N	83.05 W
Westminster Abbey ⊍[1]	260	51.30 N	0.07 W
Westminster Mall ◆[9]	280	33.45 N	118.01 W
West Modesto	226	37.37 N	121.02 W
West Monroe	194	32.31 N	92.08 W
Westmont, Ca., U.S.	280	33.56 N	118.18 W
Westmont, Il., U.S.	278	41.47 N	87.58 W
Westmont, N.J., U.S.	285	39.54 N	75.02 W
Westmont, Pa., U.S.	214	40.18 N	78.57 W
West Monterey	214	41.03 N	79.39 W
West Montreal ≃	190	47.56 N	80.39 W
West Moors	42	50.49 N	1.55 W
Westmoreland, Ks., U.S.	198	39.23 N	96.24 W
Westmoreland, N.Y., U.S.	210	43.07 N	75.24 W
Westmoreland, Tn., U.S.	194	36.33 N	86.14 W
Westmoreland, Va., U.S.	208	38.04 N	76.34 W
Westmoreland □[6], Pa., U.S.	214	40.18 N	79.33 W
Westmoreland □[6], Va., U.S.	208	38.10 N	76.50 W
Westmoreland City	214	40.20 N	79.41 W
Westmoreland State Park ♠	208	38.09 N	76.50 W
Westmorland	204	33.02 N	115.37 W
Westmount	206	45.29 N	73.36 W
West Mountain ∧	188	43.51 N	74.43 W
West Mud Creek ≃	222	32.07 N	95.10 W
West Mustang Creek ≃	222	29.04 N	96.26 W
West Nab ∧	262	53.35 N	1.53 W
West Nanticoke	210	40.13 N	76.01 W
West New Britain □[5]	164	5.45 S	149.30 E
West Newbury	207	42.48 N	70.59 W
West Newton, Ma., U.S.	283	42.21 N	71.14 W
West Newton, Pa., U.S.	214	40.12 N	79.46 W
West New York	276	40.47 N	74.00 W
West Nicholson	154	21.06 S	29.25 E
West Nishnabotna ≃	198	40.39 N	95.37 W
West Nodaway ≃	194	40.38 N	95.01 W
West Norriton	208	40.08 N	75.22 W
West Norwood ◆[8]	260	51.26 N	0.06 W
West Novaya Zemlya Trough ✦[1]	10	73.30 N	50.00 E
West Nueces ≃	196	29.16 N	99.56 W
West Nyack	210	41.06 N	73.58 W
West Okaw ≃	219	39.32 N	88.42 W
Weston, Austl.	170	32.49 S	151.28 E
Weston, Malay.	112	5.13 N	115.36 E
Weston, Eng., U.K.	262	53.19 N	2.44 W
Weston, Co., U.S.	200	37.07 N	104.50 W
Weston, Ct., U.S.	207	41.12 N	73.22 W
Weston, Id., U.S.	202	42.02 N	111.58 W
Weston, Ma., U.S.	207	42.22 N	71.18 W
Weston, Mi., U.S.	216	41.46 N	84.06 W
Weston, Mo., U.S.	194	39.24 N	94.54 W
Weston, Ne., U.S.	198	41.11 N	96.44 W
Weston, Oh., U.S.	216	41.20 N	83.47 W
Weston, Or., U.S.	202	45.48 N	118.25 W
Weston, Pa., U.S.	210	40.57 N	76.09 W
Weston, W.V., U.S.	188	39.02 N	80.28 W
Weston □[8]	275b	43.43 N	79.31 W
Westonaria	273d	26.19 S	27.39 E
West Oneonta	210	42.28 N	75.07 W
Westönnen	52	51.33 N	7.58 E
Weston Reservoir ◎[1]	283	42.21 N	71.18 W
Westons Mill Pond ◎	276	40.28 N	74.25 W
Westons Mills	210	42.04 N	78.23 W
Weston-super-Mare	42	51.21 N	2.59 W
Weston upon Trent	42	52.45 N	2.02 W
West Orange, N.J., U.S.	276	40.47 N	74.14 W
West Orange, Tx., U.S.	194	30.05 N	93.46 W
Westover, Md., U.S.	208	38.07 N	75.42 W
Westover, Pa., U.S.	214	40.45 N	78.40 W
Westover, Tn., U.S.	194	35.36 N	88.52 W
Westover, W.V., U.S.	188	39.38 N	79.58 W
Westover Air Force Base ■	207	42.12 N	72.33 W
Westoverledingen	52	53.10 N	7.28 E
Westowne	284b	39.17 N	76.43 W
West Palm Beach	220	26.42 N	80.03 W
West Palm Beach Canal ≊	220	26.38 N	80.03 W
West Paris	188	44.19 N	70.34 W
West Park	210	41.48 N	73.58 W
West Paterson	276	40.53 N	74.11 W
West Pawlet	210	43.21 N	73.15 W
West Peckham	260	51.15 N	0.22 E
West Pensacola	194	30.25 N	87.16 W
Westphalia, Ks., U.S.	198	38.10 N	95.29 W
Westphalia, Mi., U.S.	216	42.55 N	84.47 W
Westphalia, Mo., U.S.	219	38.26 N	91.59 W
West Pittsburg, Ca., U.S.	226	38.01 N	121.56 W
West Pittsburg, Pa., U.S.	214	40.55 N	80.21 W
West Pittston	210	41.19 N	75.47 W
West Plains	194	36.43 N	91.51 W
West Point, Ca., U.S.	226	38.23 N	120.31 W
West Point, Ga., U.S.	192	32.52 N	85.11 W
Westpoint, In., U.S.	216	40.21 N	87.03 W
West Point, Ia., U.S.	190	40.43 N	91.27 W
West Point, Ky., U.S.	194	37.59 N	85.56 W
West Point, Ms., U.S.	194	33.36 N	88.39 W
West Point, Ne., U.S.	198	41.50 N	96.42 W
West Point, N.Y., U.S.	210	41.23 N	73.57 W
West Point, Oh., U.S.	214	40.43 N	80.42 W
West Point, Pa., U.S.	285	40.12 N	75.18 W
West Point, Va., U.S.	208	37.31 N	76.47 W
West Point ∧	180	64.57 N	144.40 W
West Point ›, Austl.	166	35.01 S	135.57 E
West Point ›, P.E., Can.	186	46.37 N	64.25 W
West Point Lake ◎[1]	192	33.00 N	85.10 W
West Pond ◎	276	40.53 N	73.38 W
Westport, Nf., Can.	186	49.47 N	56.38 W
Westport, N.S., Can.	186	44.16 N	66.21 W
Westport, On., Can.	212	44.41 N	76.26 W
Westport, Ire.	48	53.48 N	9.32 W
Westport, N.Z.	172	41.45 S	171.36 E
Westport, Ct., U.S.	207	41.08 N	73.21 W
Westport, In., U.S.	218	39.10 N	85.34 W
Westport, Ky., U.S.	218	38.28 N	85.28 W
Westport, Ma., U.S.	207	41.37 N	71.04 W
Westport, Or., U.S.	224	46.07 N	123.22 W
Westport, Pa., U.S.	214	41.18 N	77.51 W
Westport, Wa., U.S.	224	46.53 N	124.06 W
West Portland	224	45.25 N	122.45 W
West Portland Park	224	45.21 N	122.37 W
Westport Point	207	41.31 N	71.04 W
West Portsmouth	218	38.45 N	83.01 W
West Prairie ≃	182	55.30 N	116.31 W
West Puente Valley	280	34.04 N	117.59 W
West Pullman ◆[8]	278	41.41 N	87.39 W
Westpunt ›	241s	12.37 N	70.03 W
West Pymble	274a	33.46 S	151.08 E
West Quoddy Head ›	188	44.49 N	66.57 W
West Rand	273d	26.07 S	27.45 E
Westray I	46	59.18 N	3.00 W
Westray Firth ⊔	46	59.12 N	2.55 W
West Redding	207	41.19 N	73.26 W
Westrem	50	50.58 N	3.52 E
West Richfield	214	41.14 N	81.39 W
West Richland	202	46.18 N	119.20 W
West River c	208	38.52 N	76.31 W
West Road ≃	182	53.19 N	122.52 W
West Rosebud Creek ≃	202	45.29 N	109.27 W
West Roxbury ◆[8]	283	42.17 N	71.09 W
West Rupert	210	43.14 N	73.14 W
West Rutland	188	43.35 N	73.02 W
West Ryde	274a	33.48 S	151.05 E
West Sacramento	226	38.34 N	121.31 W
West Saint Marys ≃	186	45.15 N	62.04 W
West Saint Modeste	186	51.36 N	56.42 W
West Salem, Il., U.S.	194	38.31 N	88.00 W
West Salem, Oh., U.S.	214	40.58 N	82.06 W
West Salem, Wi., U.S.	190	43.53 N	91.04 W
West Salt Creek ≃	200	39.13 N	108.54 W
Westsamoa → Western Samoa □[1]	175a	13.55 S	172.00 W
West Sand Lake	210	42.39 N	73.37 W
West Saugerties	210	42.07 N	74.03 W
West Sayville	276	40.43 N	73.05 W
West Sayville County Park ♠	276	40.43 N	73.06 W
West Scenic Park	220	27.55 N	81.39 W
West Scotia Basin ✦[1]	18	57.00 S	53.00 W
West Seneca	210	42.50 N	78.45 W
West Sepik □[5]	164	4.00 S	141.30 E
West Shoal Lake ◎	184	50.20 N	97.41 W
West Siberian Plain → Zapadno-Sibirskaja ravnina ≚	72	60.00 N	75.00 E
Westsibirisches Flachland → Zapadno-Sibirskaja ravnina ≚	72	60.00 N	75.00 E
West Side Canal ≊	226	35.19 N	119.23 W
West Side Tennis Club ♠	276	40.43 N	73.51 W
West Simsbury	207	41.52 N	72.51 W
West Slope	224	45.29 N	122.45 W
West Spanish Peak ∧	200	37.23 N	104.59 W
West Springfield, Ma., U.S.	207	42.06 N	72.37 W
West Springfield, Pa., U.S.	214	41.57 N	80.29 W
West Springfield, Va., U.S.	208	38.46 N	77.13 W
West Stewartstown	206	44.59 N	71.31 W
West Stockbridge	207	42.20 N	73.22 W
West Stony Creek ≃	210	43.15 N	74.13 W
West Suffield	207	41.59 N	72.41 W
West Sunbury	214	41.00 N	79.54 W
West Sussex □[6]	42	50.55 N	0.35 W
West Swanzey	207	42.52 N	72.20 W
West Terre Haute	194	39.27 N	87.27 W
West-Terschelling	52	53.21 N	5.13 E
West Thompson Lake ◎[1]	207	41.57 N	71.54 W
West Thurrock	260	51.29 N	0.16 E
West Tiana	207	40.52 N	72.33 W
West Tilbury	260	51.29 N	0.24 E
West Tisbury	207	41.22 N	70.40 W
West Toodyay	168a	31.33 S	116.27 E
West Torrens	168b	34.56 S	138.32 E
Westtown, N.Y., U.S.	210	41.20 N	74.32 W
Westtown, Pa., U.S.	285	39.56 N	75.33 W
West Townsend	207	42.40 N	71.44 W
West Turffontein ◆[8]	273d	26.16 S	28.02 E
West Union, Ia., U.S.	190	42.57 N	91.48 W
West Union, Oh., U.S.	218	38.47 N	83.32 W
West Union, W.V., U.S.	188	39.17 N	80.46 W
West Union Creek ≃	282	37.25 N	122.16 W
West Unity	216	41.35 N	84.26 W
West University Place	222	29.43 N	95.26 W
West Upton	207	42.10 N	71.37 W
Westvale	210	43.02 N	76.13 W
West Valley, Mt., U.S.	202	46.08 N	113.01 W
West Valley, N.Y., U.S.	210	42.24 N	78.37 W
West Valley City	200	40.42 N	111.57 W
West Vancouver	182	49.22 N	123.12 W
West View	214	40.31 N	80.02 W
West View Amusement Park ♠	279b	40.31 N	80.02 W
Westview Heights	207	41.33 N	73.05 W
Westville, N.S., Can.	186	45.34 N	62.43 W
Westville, In., U.S.	216	41.32 N	86.54 W
Westville, N.H., U.S.	207	42.49 N	71.07 W
Westville, N.J., U.S.	285	39.52 N	75.07 W
Westville, Oh., U.S.	218	40.07 N	83.51 W
Westville, Ok., U.S.	194	35.59 N	94.34 W
Westville, Pa., U.S.	214	41.13 N	78.50 W
Westville Center	206	44.57 N	74.24 W
Westville Grove	285	39.51 N	75.07 W
Westville Lake ◎[1]	207	42.05 N	72.05 W
Westville Oaks	285	39.51 N	75.08 W
West Virginia □[3], U.S.	178	38.45 N	80.30 W
West Virginia □[3], U.S.	188	38.45 N	80.30 W
West-Vlaanderen □[4]	50	51.00 N	3.00 E
West Walker ≃	226	38.53 N	119.10 W
West Wallsend	170	32.54 S	151.35 E
Westward Ho!	42	51.02 N	4.15 W
West Wareham	207	41.47 N	70.45 W
West Warren	207	42.12 N	72.14 W
West Warwick	207	41.42 N	71.31 W
West Water ≃	46	56.47 N	2.38 W
West Webster	210	43.12 N	77.29 W
Westwego	194	29.54 N	90.08 W
West Wellow	42	50.58 N	1.35 W
West Whittier	280	33.59 N	118.03 W
West Wickham ◆[8]	260	51.22 N	0.01 W
West Willington	207	41.52 N	72.18 W
West Willow	216	42.14 N	83.34 W
West Windsor	210	42.06 N	74.46 W
West Winfield, N.Y., U.S.	210	42.53 N	75.11 W
West Winfield, Pa., U.S.	214	40.48 N	79.42 W
Westwold	182	50.28 N	119.45 W
Westwood, Ca., U.S.	204	40.18 N	121.00 W
Westwood, In., U.S.	218	39.55 N	85.25 W
Westwood, Ma., U.S.	207	42.12 N	71.14 W
Westwood, Mi., U.S.	216	42.18 N	85.38 W
Westwood, N.J., U.S.	210	40.59 N	74.01 W
Westwood, Pa., U.S.	214	40.18 N	78.56 W
Westwood ◆[8]	280	34.04 N	118.27 W
Westwood Lakes	220	25.44 N	80.22 W
Westworth Village	222	32.45 N	97.25 W
West Wyalong	166	33.55 S	147.13 E
West Wycombe	42	51.39 N	0.49 W
West Yarmouth	207	41.39 N	70.14 W
West Yegua Creek ≃	222	30.20 N	96.52 W
West Yellow Creek ≃	194	39.38 N	93.04 W
West Yellowstone	202	44.39 N	111.06 W
West York	208	39.57 N	76.45 W
West Yorkshire □[6]	44	53.45 N	1.40 W
Wetan, Pulau I	164	7.54 S	129.32 E
Wetar, Pulau I	112	7.48 S	126.18 E
Wetar, Selat ⊔	112	8.20 S	126.30 E
Wetaskiwin	182	52.58 N	113.22 W
Wete	154	5.04 S	39.43 E
Wethau	54	51.08 N	11.52 E
Wetherby	44	53.56 N	1.23 W
Wetherill Park	274a	33.51 S	150.54 E
Wethersfield	207	41.43 N	72.40 W
Wethmar	263	51.37 N	7.33 E
Wetiko Hills ⋏[2]	184	54.30 N	92.20 W
Wetluga → Vetluga ≃	80	56.18 N	46.24 E
Wetmore	198	39.38 N	95.48 W
Wet Mountains ⋏	200	38.00 N	105.10 W
Weto	152	7.57 N	7.50 E
Wetten	52	51.34 N	6.17 E
Wetter, B.R.D.	56	51.23 N	7.23 E
Wetter, B.R.D.	56	50.54 N	8.43 E
Wetter ≃	56	50.18 N	8.49 E
Wetterau □[9]	56	50.15 N	8.50 E
Wetteren	50	51.00 N	3.53 E
Wetterhorn ∧	58	46.39 N	8.08 E
Wetterstein Gebirge ⋏	64	47.25 N	11.05 E
Wettigan	110	18.57 N	95.21 E
Wettin	54	51.35 N	11.48 E
Wettingen	58	47.28 N	8.19 E
Wettringen	52	52.12 N	7.19 E
Wetumka	196	35.14 N	96.14 W
Wetumpka	194	32.32 N	86.12 W
Wetwang	44	54.01 N	0.34 W
Wetzikon	58	47.19 N	8.47 E
Wetzlar	56	50.33 N	8.29 E
Wetzstein ∧[2]	54	50.27 N	11.27 E
Wevelgem	50	50.48 N	3.10 E
Wevelinghoven	56	51.06 N	6.37 E
Wewahitchka	192	30.06 N	85.12 W
Wewak	164	3.35 S	143.40 E
Wewelsfleth	52	53.50 N	9.24 E
Wewer	52	51.41 N	8.42 E
Wewoka	196	35.09 N	96.29 W
Wexford, Ire.	48	52.20 N	6.27 W
Wexford, Pa., U.S.	214	40.38 N	80.03 W
Wexford □[6]	48	52.20 N	6.40 W
Wexford ◆[8]	275b	43.45 N	79.18 W
Wexford Harbour c	48	52.20 N	6.24 W
Wey ≃	42	51.23 N	0.28 W
Weyakwin Lake ◎	184	54.30 N	106.00 W
Weyanoke	284c	38.48 N	77.09 W
Weyarn	64	47.51 N	11.48 E
Weyauwega	190	44.19 N	88.56 W
Weybridge	42	51.23 N	0.28 W
Weyburn	184	49.41 N	103.52 W
Weyer ◆[8]	263	51.10 N	7.01 E
Weyer Markt	61	47.52 N	14.41 E
Weyersheim	56	48.43 N	7.48 E
Weyhausen	52	52.47 N	10.23 E
Weyhe	52	52.59 N	8.52 E
Weymouth, N.S., Can.	186	44.25 N	66.00 W
Weymouth, Eng., U.K.	42	50.36 N	2.28 W
Weymouth, Ma., U.S.	207	42.13 N	70.56 W
Weymouth, N.J., U.S.	208	39.30 N	74.46 W
Weymouth, Cape ›	164	12.37 S	143.27 E
Weymouth Back ≃	283	42.15 N	70.55 W
Weymouth Fore ≃	283	42.16 N	70.56 W
Weymouth Great Pond ◎	283	42.12 N	71.02 W
Wezemaal	56	50.57 N	4.46 E
Wezep	52	52.27 N	6.00 E
Whakatane	172	37.58 S	177.00 E
Whakatane ≃	172	37.57 S	177.00 E
Whalan	274a	33.45 S	150.49 E
Whale Creek ≃	276	40.27 N	74.13 W
Whales, Bay of c	9	78.30 S	164.20 W
Whaley Bridge	44	53.20 N	1.59 W
Whaley Lake	210	41.33 N	73.40 W
Whaleysville	208	38.23 N	75.18 W
Whaleyville	208	36.37 N	76.41 W
Whalley	44	53.50 N	2.24 W
Whalom	207	42.34 N	71.44 W
Whalsay I	46a	60.20 N	0.59 W
Whangaehu ≃	172	40.03 S	175.06 E
Whangamata	172	37.12 S	175.52 E
Whangamomona	172	39.09 S	174.44 E
Whanganui National Park ♠	172	39.20 S	175.00 E
Whangara	172	38.34 S	178.13 E
Whangarei	172	35.43 S	174.19 E
Whangaruru Harbour c	172	35.22 S	174.21 E
Whaplode	42	52.48 N	0.02 W
Wharfe ≃	44	53.51 N	1.07 W
Wharfedale V	44	54.01 N	1.56 W
Wharles	262	53.49 N	2.50 W
Wharton, N.J., U.S.	210	40.53 N	74.34 W
Wharton, Oh., U.S.	214	40.52 N	83.21 W
Wharton, Tx., U.S.	222	29.18 N	96.06 W
Wharton, W.V., U.S.	188	37.54 N	81.40 W
Wharton □[6]	222	29.17 N	96.13 W
Wharton Basin ✦[1]	12	21.00 S	100.00 E
Wharton Lake ◎	176	64.00 N	99.55 W
Wharton State Forest ♠	285	39.45 N	74.40 W
Whataroa	172	43.17 S	170.25 E
Whatatutu	172	38.23 S	177.50 E
What Cheer	190	41.24 N	92.21 W
Whatcom □[6]	224	48.48 N	121.59 W
Whatcom, Lake ◎	224	48.43 N	122.20 W
Whately	207	42.26 N	72.38 W
Whatley	194	31.39 N	87.42 W
Whatshan Lake ◎	182	50.00 N	118.03 W
Whauphill	44	54.49 N	4.29 W
Wheao ≃	172	38.34 S	176.39 E
Wheatfield	216	40.33 N	87.06 W
Wheathampstead	42	51.49 N	0.17 W
Wheatland, Ca., U.S.	226	39.00 N	121.25 W
Wheatland, Ia., U.S.	190	41.49 N	90.50 W
Wheatland, Pa., U.S.	214	41.12 N	80.28 W
Wheatland, Wy., U.S.	200	42.03 N	104.57 W
Wheatland Hills	208	40.02 N	76.21 W
Wheatland Reservoir ◎[1]	200	41.52 N	105.36 W
Wheatley, On., Can.	214	42.06 N	82.27 W
Wheatley, Eng., U.K.	42	51.44 N	1.08 W
Wheatley, Ar., U.S.	194	34.54 N	91.06 W
Wheatley Hill	44	54.45 N	1.23 W
Wheaton, Il., U.S.	216	41.51 N	88.06 W
Wheaton, Md., U.S.	208	39.02 N	77.03 W
Wheaton, Mn., U.S.	198	45.48 N	96.29 W
Wheaton Plaza ◆[9]	284c	39.02 N	77.03 W
Wheaton Regional Park ♠	284c	39.03 N	77.02 W
Wheat Ridge	200	39.45 N	105.04 W
Wheelbarrow Peak ∧	204	37.27 N	116.05 W
Wheeler, In., U.S.	216	41.30 N	87.10 W
Wheeler, Ms., U.S.	194	34.34 N	88.36 W
Wheeler, Tx., U.S.	196	35.26 N	100.16 W
Wheeler ≃, P.Q., Can.	176	57.02 N	67.13 W
Wheeler ≃, Sk., Can.	184	57.20 N	105.30 W
Wheeler Air Force Base ■	229c	21.29 N	158.03 W
Wheeler Dam ◆[6]	283	42.48 N	71.12 W
Wheeler Island I	282	38.05 N	121.56 W
Wheeler Lake ◎[1]	194	34.40 N	87.05 W
Wheeler Peak ∧, Ca., U.S.	226	38.25 N	119.17 W
Wheeler Peak ∧, Nv., U.S.	204	38.59 N	114.19 W
Wheeler Peak ∧, N.M., U.S.	200	36.34 N	105.25 W
Wheeler Ridge	228	35.06 N	119.01 W
Wheelersburg	218	38.43 N	82.51 W
Wheelers Hill	274b	37.55 S	145.11 E
Wheeling, Il., U.S.	216	42.08 N	87.55 W
Wheeling, W.V., U.S.	214	40.03 N	80.43 W
Wheeling Creek ≃	214	40.03 N	80.41 W
Wheelock	222	30.54 N	96.24 W
Wheelock ≃	44	53.12 N	2.26 W
Wheelton	262	53.41 N	2.36 W
Wheelwright, Arg.	252	33.47 S	61.13 W
Wheelwright, Ky., U.S.	192	37.19 N	82.43 W
Wheelwright Park ♠	283	42.15 N	70.49 W
Wheeny Creek ≃	170	33.26 S	150.50 E
Whela Creek ≃	162	26.17 S	116.50 E
Whelan, Mount ∧[2]	166	23.25 S	138.54 E
Whelpleyhill	260	51.44 N	0.33 W
Whernside ∧	44	54.14 N	2.23 W
Whetstone Creek ≃	214	40.23 N	83.03 W
Whetstone Gulf State Park ♠	212	43.44 N	75.27 W
Whickham	44	54.56 N	1.41 W
Whidbey Island I	224	48.15 N	122.40 W
Whidbey Island Naval Air Station ■	224	48.17 N	122.37 W
Whiddon Down	42	50.43 N	3.51 W
Whigham	192	30.52 N	84.19 W
Whigville	207	41.43 N	72.56 W
Whim Creek	162	20.50 S	117.50 E
Whinham, Mount ∧	162	26.04 S	130.15 E
Whippany	210	40.49 N	74.25 W
Whippany ≃	276	40.51 N	74.21 W
Whirl Creek ≃	212	43.28 N	81.12 W
Whirlwind Reefs ✦[2]	164	4.42 S	148.16 E
Whiskey Peak ∧	200	42.18 N	107.35 W
Whiskeytown-Shasta-Trinity National Recreation Area ♠	204	40.45 N	122.15 W
Whisky Chitto Creek ≃	194	30.31 N	92.55 W
Whiston	262	53.25 N	2.50 W
Whitacres	207	41.48 N	72.39 W
Whitaker	279b	40.24 N	79.53 W
Whitakers	192	36.06 N	77.42 W
Whitbourne	186	47.25 N	53.32 W
Whitburn, Eng., U.K.	44	54.57 N	1.22 W
Whitburn, Scot., U.K.	46	55.52 N	3.42 W
Whitby, On., Can.	212	43.52 N	78.56 W
Whitby, Eng., U.K.	44	54.29 N	0.37 W
Whitby, Eng., U.K.	262	53.17 N	2.54 W
Whitby Abbey ⊍[1]	44	54.28 N	0.38 W
Whitchurch, Eng., U.K.	42	51.53 N	0.51 W
Whitchurch, Eng., U.K.	42	51.14 N	1.20 W
Whitchurch, Eng., U.K.	42	51.52 N	2.39 W
Whitchurch, Eng., U.K.	42	52.58 N	2.41 W
Whitchurch-Stouffville	212	43.58 N	79.15 W
Whitcombe, Mount ∧	172	43.13 S	170.55 E
White, Ga., U.S.	192	34.16 N	84.44 W
White, S.D., U.S.	198	44.26 N	96.38 W
White □[6]	216	40.45 N	86.46 W
White ≃, B.C., Can.	182	50.23 N	115.35 W
White ≃, On., Can.	190	48.33 N	86.16 W
White ≃, N.A.	180	63.11 N	139.36 W
White ≃, U.S.	194	33.53 N	91.03 W
White ≃, U.S.	198	43.45 N	99.30 W
White ≃, U.S.	200	40.04 N	109.41 W
White ≃, Az., U.S.	200	33.44 N	110.13 W
White ≃, In., U.S.	194	38.25 N	87.44 W
White ≃, Mi., U.S.	190	43.25 N	86.21 W
White ≃, Nv., U.S.	204	37.42 N	115.10 W
White ≃, Or., U.S.	224	45.14 N	121.04 W
White ≃, Tx., U.S.	196	33.14 N	100.56 W
White ≃, Vt., U.S.	188	43.37 N	72.20 W
White ≃, Wa., U.S.	224	47.12 N	122.15 W
White ≃, Wa., U.S.	224	47.50 N	120.49 W
White ≃, Wi., U.S.	190	46.36 N	90.42 W
White ≃, Wi., U.S.	216	42.41 N	88.17 W
White, East Fork ≃, Az., U.S.	200	33.47 N	110.00 W
White, East Fork ≃, In., U.S.	194	38.33 N	87.14 W
White, Lake ◎	162	21.05 S	129.00 E
White, Lake ◎[1]	218	39.07 N	83.02 W
White, North Fork ≃, Az., U.S.	200	33.47 N	110.00 W
White, North Fork ≃, Co., U.S.	200	39.58 N	107.38 W
White, South Fork ≃	200	39.58 N	107.38 W
White, West Fork ≃	224	47.07 N	121.37 W
White Bay c	186	50.00 N	56.30 W
White Bear Indian Reserve ◆[4]	184	49.45 N	102.15 W
White Bear Lake	190	45.03 N	93.00 W
Whitebear Lake ◎	184	51.05 N	108.05 W
White Bluff	194	36.06 N	87.13 W
White Breast Creek ≃	190	41.24 N	93.02 W
White Butte ∧	198	46.23 N	103.19 W
Whitecap Lake ◎	184	56.54 N	95.14 W
White Cap Mountain ∧	188	45.35 N	69.13 W
White Castle	194	30.10 N	91.08 W
White Center	224	47.31 N	122.21 W
White Chuck ≃	224	48.11 N	121.27 W
White City, Fl., U.S.	220	29.53 N	85.13 W
White City, Ks., U.S.	198	38.47 N	96.44 W
White City Stadium ♠	260	51.31 N	0.14 W
White Clay Creek ≃, U.S.	198	43.12 N	102.48 W
White Clay Creek ≃, U.S.	285	39.42 N	75.37 W
White Cliffs, Austl.	162	28.26 S	122.57 E

Symbol	English	Deutsch	Español	Français	Português
≃	River	Fluß	Río	Rivière	Rio
≊	Canal	Kanal	Canal	Canal	Canal
L	Waterfall, Rapids	Wasserfall, Stromschnellen	Cascada, Rápidos	Chute d'eau, Rapides	Cascata, Rápidos
⊔	Strait	Meeresstraße	Estrecho	Détroit	Estreito
c	Bay, Gulf	Bucht, Golf	Bahía, Golfo	Baie, Golfe	Baía, Golfo
◎	Lake, Lakes	See, Seen	Lago, Lagos	Lac, Lacs	Lago, Lagos
≡	Swamp	Sumpf	Pantano	Marais	Pântano
⊓	Ice Features, Glacier	Eis- und Gletscherformen	Accidentes Glaciales	Formes glaciaires	Acidentes glaciares
⫪	Other Hydrographic Features	Andere Hydrographische Objekte	Otros Elementos Hidrográficos	Autres données hydrographiques	Outros acidentes hidrográficos
✦	Submarine Features	Untermeerische Objekte	Accidentes Submarinos	Formes de relief sous-marin	Acidentes submarinos
□	Political Unit	Politische Einheit	Unidad Politica	Entité politique	Unidade política
⊍	Cultural Institution	Kulturelle Institution	Institución Cultural	Institution culturelle	Institução cultural
⊥	Historical Site	Historische Stätte	Sitio Histórico	Site historique	Sitio histórico
♠	Recreational Site	Erholungs- und Ferienort	Sitio de Recreo	Centre de loisirs	Area de Lazer
⊠	Airport	Flughafen	Aeropuerto	Aéroport	Aeroporto
■	Military Installation	Militäranlage	Instalación Militar	Installation militaire	Instalação militar
◆	Miscellaneous	Verschiedenes	Misceláneo	Divers	Diversos

Column 1

White Cliffs, Austl. 166 30.51 S 143.05 E
White Cloud 190 43.33 N 85.46 W
White Cloud Island I 212 44.50 N 80.58 W
Whitecoomb ʌ, N.Z. 172 45.36 S 169.05 E
White Coomb ʌ, Scot., U.K. 44 55.26 N 3.20 W
Whitecourt 182 54.09 N 115.41 W
White Creek ≃, In., U.S. 218 42.58 N 73.18 W
White Creek ≃, Wa., U.S. 224 46.01 N 121.08 W
White Deer, Pa., U.S. 210 41.05 N 76.52 W
White Deer, Tx., U.S. 196 35.26 N 101.10 W
White Deer Creek ≃ 210 41.05 N 76.53 W
White Earth ≃ 198 48.09 N 102.42 W
White Earth Indian Reservation ◄⁴ 198 47.18 N 95.50 W
White Esk ≃ 44 55.12 N 3.10 W
Whiteface ≃ 190 33.36 N 102.37 W
Whiteface ʌ 190 46.58 N 92.48 W
Whiteface Mountain ʌ 188 44.22 N 73.54 W
Whitefield, Eng., U.K. 44 53.33 N 2.18 W
Whitefield, Eng., U.K. 262 53.33 N 2.18 W
Whitefield, N.H., U.S. 188 44.22 N 71.36 W
Whitefish 202 48.24 N 114.20 W
Whitefish ≃ 190 45.55 N 86.57 W
Whitefish Bay 216 43.06 N 87.54 W
Whitefish Bay c, On., Can. 184 49.26 N 94.14 W
Whitefish Bay c, N.A. 190 46.40 N 84.50 W
Whitefish Lake ⊜, Ab., Can. 182 54.22 N 111.55 W
Whitefish Lake ⊜, Mb., Can. 184 55.34 N 93.13 W
Whitefish Lake ⊜, N.T., Can. 176 62.41 N 106.48 W
Whitefish Lake ⊜, On., Can. 190 48.03 N 84.29 W
Whitefish Lake ⊜, On., Can. 212 45.18 N 79.47 W
Whitefish Lake ⊜, On., Can. 212 44.70 N 76.14 W
Whitefish Lake ⊜, Ak., U.S. 180 61.21 N 160.00 W
Whitefish Lake ⊜, Mt., U.S. 202 48.27 N 114.22 W
White Fish Lake Indian Reserve ◄⁴ 182 54.20 N 111.45 W
Whitefish Point 190 46.45 N 84.59 W
Whitefish Point ⊁ 190 46.45 N 85.00 W
Whitefish Range ⱅ 202 48.40 N 114.26 W
Whiteford 208 39.42 N 76.20 W
Whiteford Point ⊁ 42 51.38 N 4.14 W
White Fox 184 53.27 N 104.05 W
White Fox ≃ 184 53.32 N 104.00 W
Whitegate 48 51.50 N 8.14 W
White Gull Creek ≃ 184 53.44 N 104.20 W
Whitehall (Paulstown), Ire. 48 52.41 N 7.01 W
Whitehall, Scot., U.K. 46 59.07 N 2.37 W
White Hall, Ar., U.S. 194 34.16 N 92.05 W
White Hall, Il., U.S. 219 39.26 N 90.24 W
White Hall, Md., U.S. 208 39.37 N 76.37 W
Whitehall, Mt., U.S. 190 43.24 N 86.20 W
Whitehall, Mt., U.S. 202 45.52 N 112.05 W
Whitehall, N.Y., U.S. 188 43.33 N 73.24 W
Whitehall, Oh., U.S. 218 39.58 N 82.53 W
Whitehall, Pa., U.S. 214 40.21 N 79.59 W
Whitehall, Wi., U.S. 190 44.22 N 91.18 W
Whitehaven, Eng., U.K. 44 54.33 N 3.35 W
White Haven, Pa., U.S. 210 41.03 N 75.46 W
Whitehead 48 54.46 N 5.43 W
White Holme Reservoir ⊜¹ 262 53.41 N 2.02 W
Whitehorse, Yk., Can. 180 60.43 N 135.03 W
White Horse, N.J., U.S. 208 40.11 N 74.42 W
White Horse, Vale of ⊻ 42 51.37 N 1.37 W
Whitehorse Hill ʌ² 42 51.34 N 1.34 W
Whitehouse, Scot., U.K. 46 57.13 N 2.37 W
Whitehouse, N.J., U.S. 208 40.37 N 74.46 W
Whitehouse, Oh., U.S. 218 41.31 N 83.48 W
White House, Tn., U.S. 194 36.35 N 86.49 W
White House, Tx., U.S. 222 32.13 N 95.14 W
White House ⊻ 284c 38.54 N 77.02 W
White House Station 210 40.36 N 74.46 W
White Island I, Ant. 9 66.44 S 48.35 E
White Island I, N.T., Can. 176 65.00 N 84.50 W
White Island I, N.Z. 172 37.31 S 177.11 E
White Lake, Mi., U.S. 281 42.41 N 83.03 W
White Lake, N.Y., U.S. 210 41.40 N 74.50 W
White Lake, S.D., U.S. 198 43.43 N 98.42 W
White Lake ⊜, On., Can. 190 45.09 N 84.46 W
White Lake ⊜, On., Can. 212 44.27 N 77.03 W
White Lake ⊜, On., Can. 212 45.18 N 76.31 W
White Lake ⊜, Mi., U.S. 281 42.40 N 83.34 W
Whiteland 218 39.33 N 86.05 W
Whitelaw 190 44.09 N 87.38 W
Whiteley Village 260 51.21 N 0.26 W
White Lick Creek ≃ 218 39.30 N 86.23 W
White Lick Creek, East Fork ≃ 218 39.35 N 86.22 W
White Lick Creek, West Fork ≃ 218 39.38 N 86.23 W
Whiteman Air Force Base 194 38.44 N 93.34 W
Whiteman Airpark ⊠ 280 34.15 N 118.25 W
Whiteman Range ⱅ 164 5.50 S 149.55 E
Whitemans Creek ≃ 212 43.10 N 80.21 W
Whitemark 166 40.07 S 148.01 E
White Marsh 284b 39.23 N 76.26 W
Whitemans Run ⊜ 284b 39.22 N 76.25 W
White Meadow Lake 210 40.55 N 74.31 W
White Meadow Lake ⊜ 276 40.55 N 74.31 W
White Mills 210 41.32 N 75.12 W
White Mountain 180 64.41 N 163.24 W
White Mountain Peak ʌ 204 37.38 N 118.15 W
White Mountains ⱅ, U.S. 188 44.10 N 71.35 W
White Mountains ⱅ, Az., U.S. 200 33.58 N 109.40 W
White Mountains ⱅ, N.H., U.S. 188 44.10 N 71.15 W
Whitemouth 184 49.57 N 95.59 W
Whitemouth ≃ 184 50.07 N 96.02 W
Whitemouth Lake ⊜ 184 49.14 N 95.40 W
Whitemud ≃ 184 50.15 N 98.37 W
Whiten Head ⊁ 46 58.34 N 4.36 W
White Nile (Al-Bahr al-Abyad) ≃ 140 15.38 N 32.31 E
White Nile Dam → Jabal al-Awliyā', Khazzān ◄⁶ 146 15.14 N 32.29 E
White Oak, Md., U.S. 284c 39.02 N 77.00 W
White Oak, Pa., U.S. 279b 40.20 N 79.48 W
White Oak, Tx., U.S. 222 32.32 N 94.52 W

Column 2

White Oak ≃ 192 34.40 N 77.07 W
White Oak Creek ≃, Oh., U.S. 218 38.47 N 83.57 W
White Oak Creek ≃, Tx., U.S. 194 33.16 N 94.39 W
White Oak Creek, East Fork ≃ 218 39.00 N 83.53 W
White Oak Creek, North Fork ≃ 218 39.00 N 83.53 W
White Oak Lake ⊜¹ 194 33.40 N 93.10 W
White Oak Regional Park ◆ 279a 40.21 N 79.47 W
White Pass ⱅ, N.A. 180 59.38 N 135.05 W
White Pass ⱅ, Wa., U.S. 224 46.38 N 121.24 W
White Pigeon 216 41.47 N 85.38 W
White Pine, Mi., U.S. 190 46.45 N 89.35 W
Whitepine, Mt., U.S. 182 47.45 N 115.29 W
White Pine, Tn., U.S. 192 36.06 N 83.17 W
White Pines, Ca., U.S. 226 38.18 N 120.21 W
White Pines, Il., U.S. 218 41.57 N 87.57 W
White Plains, Md., U.S. 208 38.35 N 76.56 W
White Plains, N.Y., U.S. 210 41.02 N 73.45 W
White Plains, W.V., U.S. 192 36.36 N 80.38 W
White Pond ⊜ 283 42.26 N 71.23 W
White River, On., Can. 190 48.35 N 85.15 W
Whiteriver, Az., U.S. 200 33.50 N 109.57 W
White River, S.D., U.S. 198 43.34 N 100.44 W
White River Junction 188 43.38 N 72.19 W
White Rock 224 49.02 N 122.49 W
White Rock Creek ≃, Ks., U.S. 198 39.55 N 97.51 W
White Rock Creek ≃, Tx., U.S. 222 30.54 N 95.16 W
White Rock Lake ⊜¹ 222 32.43 N 96.44 W
White Rocks ʌ 192 36.40 N 83.27 W
Whiterocks ≃ 200 40.26 N 109.55 W
White Roding 260 51.48 N 0.16 E
White Russia → Belorusskaja Sovetskaja Socialističeskaja Respublika ◻³ 76 53.50 N 28.00 E
Whiteseal Lake ⊜ 182 53.30 N 127.00 W
White Salmon 224 45.43 N 121.29 W
White Salmon ≃ 224 45.43 N 121.31 W
Whitesand ≃ 184 51.34 N 101.55 W
White Sands Beach ◄ 207 41.18 N 72.09 W
White Sands Missile Range ◄ 200 32.23 N 106.28 W
White Sands National Monument ◆ 200 32.46 N 106.20 W
Whitesboro, N.J., U.S. 208 39.02 N 74.51 W
Whitesboro, N.Y., U.S. 210 43.07 N 75.17 W
Whitesboro, Tx., U.S. 196 33.39 N 96.54 W
Whitesburg 192 37.07 N 82.49 W
White Sea → Beloje more ≃² 24 65.30 N 38.00 E
White Settlement 222 32.45 N 97.27 W
Whiteshell Provincial Park ◆ 184 50.00 N 95.25 W
Whiteside 219 39.11 N 91.01 W
Whiteside, Canal x 254 53.55 N 109.57 W
White's Landing 214 41.25 N 82.54 W
White Springs 192 30.19 N 82.45 W
White Stone 192 37.38 N 76.23 W
Whitestone ◄⁸ 276 40.47 N 73.49 W
White Stone Lake ⊜ 184 56.25 N 97.31 W
Whitestown 218 39.59 N 86.20 W
White Sulphur Springs, Mt., U.S. 202 46.32 N 110.54 W
White Sulphur Springs, N.Y., U.S. 210 41.48 N 74.50 W
White Sulphur Springs, W.V., U.S. 192 37.47 N 80.17 W
Whites Valley 210 41.42 N 75.22 W
Whitesville, Ky., U.S. 194 37.40 N 86.52 W
Whitesville, N.J., U.S. 210 40.02 N 77.45 W
Whitesville, W.V., U.S. 210 37.58 N 81.31 W
White Swan 224 46.22 N 120.43 W
Whiteswan Lakes ⊜ 184 54.05 N 105.10 W
Whitevale 212 43.53 N 79.09 W
White Valley 214 40.25 N 79.36 W
Whiteville, N.C., U.S. 192 34.20 N 78.42 W
Whiteville, Tn., U.S. 194 35.19 N 89.08 W
White Volta (Volta Blanche) ≃ 150 9.10 N 1.15 W
Whitewater, Ks., U.S. 196 37.57 N 97.08 W
Whitewater, Mt., U.S. 202 48.45 N 107.37 W
Whitewater, Wi., U.S. 218 42.50 N 88.43 W
Whitewater ≃, Ca., U.S. 228 33.44 N 117.28 W
Whitewater ≃, In., U.S. 204 33.30 N 116.03 W
Whitewater, Mo., U.S. 194 37.01 N 89.43 W
Whitewater, Dry Fork ≃ 218 39.11 N 84.47 W
Whitewater, East Fork ≃ 218 39.24 N 85.01 W
Whitewater, Greens Fork ≃ 218 39.45 N 85.07 W
Whitewater, Nolands Fork ≃ 218 39.41 N 85.07 W
Whitewater Baldy ʌ 200 33.20 N 108.39 W
Whitewater Bay c 220 25.16 N 81.00 W
Whitewater Creek ≃, N.A. 200 48.30 N 107.11 W
Whitewater Creek ≃, Ga., U.S. 192 32.21 N 84.03 W
White Oak Creek ≃, Wi., U.S. 216 42.52 N 88.45 W
Whitewater Lake ⊜, Mb., Can. 184 49.15 N 100.20 W
Whitewater Lake ⊜, Wi., U.S. 216 42.47 N 88.42 W
Whitewater State Park ◆ 184 44.04 N 88.58 W
White Woman Creek ≃ 198 38.25 N 100.54 W
Whitewood, Austl. 166 21.28 S 143.36 E
Whitewood, Sk., Can. 184 50.20 N 102.15 W
Whitewood, S.D., U.S. 198 44.27 N 103.38 W
Whitewood, Lake ⊜ 184 44.20 N 97.18 W
Whitewright 196 33.30 N 96.23 W
Whitfield 58 50.09 N 1.18 E
Whitford, Jam. 241q 18.15 N 78.02 W
Whithorn, Scot., U.K. 44 54.44 N 4.25 W
Whitianga 172 36.50 S 175.42 E
Whiting, In., U.S. 218 41.40 N 87.29 W
Whiting, Ks., U.S. 198 39.35 N 95.36 W
Whiting, N.J., U.S. 208 39.57 N 74.22 W
Whiting, Wi., U.S. 190 44.29 N 89.33 W
Whiting Bay 44 55.29 N 5.06 W
Whiting Field Naval Air Station ⊠ 194 30.43 N 87.02 W
Whittingham 207 42.47 N 72.53 W
Whittinsville 207 42.06 N 71.40 W
Whitland 42 51.50 N 4.37 W
Whitley ◻⁶ 216 41.10 N 85.29 W
Whitley Bay 44 55.03 N 1.25 W
Whitley City 192 36.43 N 84.28 W
Whitley Row 207 51.15 N 0.09 E
Whitman 207 42.05 N 70.56 W
Whitman Mission National Historic Site ◆ 202 46.01 N 118.30 W

Column 3

Whitmans Pond ⊜ 283 42.12 N 70.57 W
Whitman Square 208 39.45 N 75.03 W
Whitmire 192 34.30 N 81.36 W
Whitmore Lake 216 42.25 N 83.46 W
Whitmore Lake ⊜ 281 42.26 N 83.45 W
Whitmore Mountains ⱅ 9 82.35 S 104.30 W
Whitmore Village 229c 21.30 N 158.01 W
Whitner Heights 226 36.37 N 119.32 W
Whitney, On., Can. 212 45.30 N 78.14 W
Whitney, Tx., U.S. 214 40.15 N 79.24 W
Whitney, Tx., U.S. 222 31.57 N 97.19 W
Whitney, Lake ⊜¹ 222 31.55 N 97.23 W
Whitney, Mount ʌ 204 36.35 N 118.18 W
Whitney Point 210 42.19 N 75.58 W
Whitney Point Lake ⊜¹ 210 42.25 N 75.55 W
Whitney Woods Reservation ◆ 283 42.13 N 70.51 W
Whitstable 42 51.22 N 1.02 E
Whitsunday Island I 166 20.17 S 148.59 E
Whittaker 281 42.08 N 83.36 W
Whittemore, Ia., U.S. 198 43.03 N 94.25 W
Whittemore, Mi., U.S. 190 44.14 N 83.48 W
Whittier, Ak., U.S. 180 60.47 N 148.42 W
Whittier, Ca., U.S. 228 33.58 N 118.01 W
Whittier, N.C., U.S. 192 35.26 N 83.22 W
Whittier Narrows Dam ◄¹ 280 34.01 N 118.04 W
Whittier Narrows Flood Control Basin ◄¹ 280 34.02 N 118.04 W
Whittingham 44 55.24 N 1.54 W
Whittington ʌ² 200 35.16 N 106.06 W
Whittle, Cap ⊁ 186 50.11 N 60.08 W
Whittle Hill ʌ² 262 53.40 N 2.16 W
Whittle-le-Woods 262 53.41 N 2.38 W
Whittlesea, Austl. 169 37.31 S 145.07 E
Whittlesea, Ciskei 158 32.10 S 26.50 E
Whittlesey 42 52.34 N 0.08 W
Whittlesey, Mount ʌ 190 46.18 N 90.37 W
Whitwell 194 35.12 N 85.31 W
Whitworth 44 52.44 N 1.21 W
Whitworth Peak ʌ 224 49.05 N 121.13 W
Wholdaia Lake ⊜ 176 60.43 N 104.10 W
Whonock 224 49.11 N 122.28 W
W. Howard Frankland Bridge ◄⁵ 220 27.56 N 82.35 W
Whyalla 166 33.02 S 137.35 E
Whycocomagh 186 45.59 N 61.07 W
Whymper, Mount ʌ 224 48.57 N 124.10 W
Wiang Pa Pao 110 19.22 N 99.30 E
Wiang Phan 110 20.26 N 99.53 E
Wiarton 212 44.45 N 81.09 W
Wiasi 150 11.26 N 2.04 W
Wiau Lake ⊜ 182 55.23 N 111.18 W
Wiawso 150 6.12 N 2.29 W
Wiay I 46 57.23 N 7.13 W
Wiązów 30 50.49 N 17.11 E
Wibaux 198 46.59 N 104.11 W
Wichian Buri 110 15.39 N 101.07 E
Wichita 196 37.41 N 97.20 W
Wichita ≃ 196 34.00 N 98.10 W
Wichita Falls 196 33.54 N 98.29 W
Wichita Mountains ⱅ 196 34.45 N 98.40 W
Wichlinghofen ◄⁸ 263 51.27 N 7.30 E
Wick ≃ 58 58.26 N 3.06 W
Wick 46 58.26 N 3.05 W
Wickatunk 276 40.21 N 74.14 W
Wickede 219 39.29 N 7.52 E
Wickede ◄⁸ 263 51.32 N 7.37 E
Wickenburg 200 33.58 N 112.43 W
Wickepin 162 32.46 S 117.30 E
Wicker Memorial Park ◆ 278 41.34 N 87.28 W
Wickett 196 31.34 N 102.59 W
Wickford 42 51.38 N 0.31 E
Wickham, Austl. 162 20.31 N 117.08 E
Wickham, P.Q., Can. 206 45.45 N 72.30 W
Wickham, Eng., U.K. 42 50.54 N 1.11 W
Wickham ≃ 164 16.22 S 131.06 E
Wickham, Cape ⊁ 166 39.36 S 143.57 E
Wickham Bishops 260 51.47 N 0.40 E
Wickford 42 52.09 N 1.22 E
Wickiup Reservoir ⊜¹ 202 43.40 N 121.43 W
Wickliffe, Ky., U.S. 194 36.58 N 89.05 W
Wickliffe, Oh., U.S. 214 41.06 N 80.43 W
Wickliffe, Oh., U.S. 214 41.36 N 81.27 W
Wicklow 48 52.59 N 6.03 W
Wicklow ◻⁶ 48 53.00 N 6.30 W
Wicklow Head ⊁ 48 52.58 N 5.59 W
Wicklow Mountains ⱅ 48 53.02 N 6.24 W
Wickrath 56 51.07 N 6.24 E
Wicksteed Lake ⊜ 190 46.46 N 79.40 W
Wicomico ◻⁶ 208 38.22 N 75.36 W
Wicomico ≃ 208 38.22 N 75.36 W
Wicomico ≃ 208 38.19 N 77.20 W
Wicomico Church 208 37.49 N 76.23 W
Wiconisco 208 40.34 N 76.41 W
Wiconisco Creek ≃ 208 40.32 N 76.58 W
Wid ≃ 262 51.45 N 0.27 E
Widas 115a 7.30 S 112.08 E
Widden Brook ≃ 170 32.32 S 150.22 E
Widdern 52 49.43 N 9.32 E
Widdert ◄⁸ 263 51.08 N 7.04 E
Widdop Reservoir ⊜¹ 262 53.48 N 2.06 W
Widdrington Station 44 55.15 N 1.36 W
Wide Bay c, Pap. N. Gui. 164 5.05 S 152.05 E
Wide Bay c, Ak., U.S. 180 57.20 N 156.25 W
Widecombe in the Moor 42 50.35 N 3.48 W
Widemouth Bay 42 50.47 N 4.32 W
Widen 188 38.29 N 80.51 W
Widener College ʌ² 285 39.52 N 75.21 W
Wide Open 44 55.03 N 1.38 W
Widerøe, Mount ʌ 9 72.08 S 23.30 E
Wide Ruin Wash ⅴ 200 35.13 N 109.52 W
Widford 260 51.48 N 0.27 E
Widgeegoara Creek ≃ 166 27.30 S 145.55 E
Widgiemooltha 162 31.30 S 121.34 E
Widnes 44 53.22 N 2.44 W
Wi-do I 88 35.36 N 126.17 E
Widodaren 115a 7.25 S 111.14 E
Widuchowa 54 53.10 N 14.25 E
Vidur 124 27.55 N 85.10 E
Wiebelskirchen 56 53.22 N 7.20 E
Wiebork 30 53.22 N 17.30 E
Wieck 54 54.06 N 13.26 E
Wied ≃ 56 50.26 N 7.27 E
Wieda 54 51.38 N 10.34 E
Wiedenritzsch 54 51.24 N 12.22 E
Wiedelstedt 58 47.15 N 8.07 E
Wiefelstede 52 53.15 N 8.07 E
Wiehe 54 51.16 N 11.25 E
Wiehengebirge ⱅ 52 52.19 N 8.40 E
Wiehengebirge, Naturpark ◆ 52 52.20 N 8.20 E
Wiehl 56 50.57 N 7.31 E
Wiek 54 54.37 N 13.17 E
Wielbark 30 53.24 N 20.56 E
Wieliczka 30 50.00 N 20.04 E
Wielichowo 30 52.08 N 16.21 E
Wielkopolska ◄⁹ 30 52.15 N 16.50 E
Wielkopolski Park Narodowy ◆ 30 52.15 N 16.50 E
Wieluń 30 51.14 N 18.34 E
Wiełowieś 30 50.10 N 18.34 E
Wiemelhausen ◄⁸ 263 51.28 N 7.13 E
Wien (Vienna), Öst. 61 48.13 N 16.22 E
Wien (Vienna), Öst. 264b 48.12 N 16.22 E
Wien ◻³ 264b 48.10 N 16.23 E
Wien, Universität ʌ² 264b 48.13 N 16.23 E
Wiener Berg ʌ² 264b 48.10 N 16.23 E
Wienerherberg 264b 48.03 N 16.33 E
Wiener Neustadt 61 47.49 N 16.15 E

Column 4

Wiener Neustädter Kanal x 61 48.05 N 16.22 E
Wienerwald ⱅ 61 48.10 N 16.00 E
Wienhagen ʌ² 263 51.08 N 7.33 E
Wienhausen 52 52.35 N 10.11 E
Wien-Schwechat, Flughafen ⊠ 264b 48.07 N 16.33 E
Wiepke 54 52.36 N 11.20 E
Wieprz ≃ 30 51.34 N 21.49 E
Wieprza ≃ 30 54.26 N 16.22 E
Wieprz-Krzna, Kanał x 30 51.56 N 22.56 E
Wiera ≃ 56 50.55 N 9.10 E
Wierden 52 52.22 N 6.35 E
Wieren 54 52.53 N 10.39 E
Wiergate 194 31.00 N 93.42 W
Wieringermeer ◄¹ 52 52.51 N 5.00 E
Wieringerwerf 52 52.51 N 5.02 E
Wieruszów 30 51.18 N 18.08 E
Wierzyca ≃ 30 53.51 N 18.50 E
Wies 61 46.43 N 15.16 E
Wies ʌ¹ 58 47.40 N 10.53 E
Wiesa 54 50.36 N 13.01 E
Wiesbaden 56 50.05 N 8.14 E
Wiesbaden ◻⁵ 56 50.20 N 8.20 E
Wiescheid ◄⁸ 263 51.08 N 6.59 E
Wiesecherhöfen ◄⁸ 263 51.39 N 7.46 E
Wiese ≃ 58 47.35 N 7.35 E
Wiesede 52 53.27 N 7.46 E
Wieselburg 61 48.08 N 15.09 E
Wiesen 58 46.43 N 9.43 E
Wiesenburg 54 52.07 N 12.26 E
Wiesenfeld 56 51.16 N 10.06 E
Wiesensteig 56 48.34 N 9.37 E
Wiesent ≃ 60 49.42 N 11.05 E
Wiesentheid 56 49.47 N 10.20 E
Wieseth ≃ 56 49.10 N 10.39 E
Wiesloch 56 49.17 N 8.42 E
Wiesmoor 52 53.25 N 7.43 E
Wieting 61 46.52 N 14.32 E
Wietmarschen 52 52.31 N 7.07 E
Wietze 52 52.39 N 9.50 E
Wietzen 52 52.43 N 9.04 E
Wigan 44 53.33 N 2.38 W
Wigan ◻⁸ 262 53.32 N 2.38 W
Wiggensbach 58 47.44 N 10.14 E
Wigger ≃ 58 47.18 N 7.53 E
Wiggins, Co., U.S. 198 40.13 N 104.04 W
Wiggins, Ms., U.S. 194 30.51 N 89.08 W
Wiggins Fork ≃ 202 43.27 N 109.28 W
Wigglesworth 44 54.01 N 2.17 W
Wight, Isle of I 42 50.40 N 1.20 W
Wigmore, Eng., U.K. 42 52.19 N 2.51 W
Wigmore, Eng., U.K. 260 51.21 N 0.35 E
Wignehies 56 50.01 N 4.00 E
Wigston 42 52.36 N 1.05 W
Wigton 44 54.49 N 3.09 W
Wigtown 44 54.52 N 4.26 W
Wigtown Bay c 44 54.46 N 4.15 W
Wijalpuā 124 26.55 N 85.51 E
Wijchen 52 51.48 N 5.43 E
Wijhe 52 52.24 N 6.07 E
Wijk aan Zee 52 52.29 N 4.35 E
Wijk bij Duurstede 52 51.58 N 5.20 E
Wilbarger Creek ≃ 222 30.11 N 97.23 W
Wilber 198 40.28 N 96.57 W
Wilberforce, Austl. 170 33.33 S 150.50 E
Wilberforce, Oh., U.S. 218 39.42 N 83.52 W
Wilberforce Falls L 176 67.07 N 108.47 W
Wilbraham 207 42.07 N 72.25 W
Wilbur 202 47.45 N 118.42 W
Wilburton 196 34.55 N 95.18 W
Wilcannia 166 31.34 S 143.23 E
Wilcock, Península ⊁¹ 254 50.40 S 74.00 W
Wilcox, Sk., Can. 184 50.07 N 104.44 W
Wilcox, Ne., U.S. 198 40.21 N 99.10 W
Wilcox, Pa., U.S. 214 41.34 N 78.41 W
Wilcox, Tx., U.S. 222 30.27 N 96.22 W
Wilcox, Mount ʌ 207 42.13 N 73.16 W
Wildalpen 61 47.39 N 14.59 E
Wildau 54 52.19 N 13.38 E
Wildbad im Schwarzwald 56 48.45 N 8.32 E
Wildberg, B.R.D. 56 48.37 N 8.44 E
Wildberg, D.D.R. 54 52.52 N 12.37 E
Wildboarclough 262 53.13 N 2.02 W
Wildcat Canyon Regional Park ◆ 282 37.56 N 122.17 W
Wildcat Creek ≃, Ca., U.S. 282 37.57 N 122.23 W
Wildcat Creek ≃, In., U.S. 216 40.28 N 86.52 W
Wildcat Creek, Middle Fork ≃ 216 40.26 N 86.48 W
Wildcat Creek, South Fork ≃ 216 40.26 N 86.48 W
Wildcat Hill ʌ² 184 53.11 N 102.30 W
Wild Coast ʌ² 158 32.30 S 28.45 E
Wilde ʌ² 288 34.42 S 58.20 W
Wildegg 58 47.25 N 8.11 E
Wildeman ≃ 164 5.33 S 139.13 E
Wildenbruch 54 52.18 N 13.13 E
Wildenfels 54 50.40 N 12.35 E
Wildenrath 54 51.09 N 10.17 E
Wildenstein 58 47.59 N 6.58 E
Wildenthal 54 50.27 N 12.37 E
Wilder 202 43.40 N 116.54 W
Wilderness 158 34.00 S 22.36 E
Wilderness of Judaea (Midbar Yehuda) ⊻ 132 31.30 N 35.18 E
Wilderness State Park ◆ 190 45.42 N 84.57 W
Wildervank 52 53.04 N 6.51 E
Wildeshausen 52 52.54 N 8.26 E
Wildfield 212 43.49 N 79.44 W
Wildflecken 56 50.23 N 9.54 E
Wildfontein 158 31.04 S 24.50 E
Wildhaus 58 47.12 N 9.21 E
Widhay ʌ² 124 30.24 N 69.25 E
Wildhorn ʌ 58 54.02 N 117.20 W
Wildhorse Creek ≃, U.S. 198 40.36 N 102.00 W
Wildhorse Creek ≃, Ok., U.S. 196 34.32 N 97.10 W
Wild Horse Creek ≃, Wy., U.S. 202 43.00 N 106.08 W
Wild Horse Draw ⅴ 196 31.11 N 104.50 W
Wild Horse Hill ʌ² 168a 33.12 S 116.40 E
Wild Horse Lake ⊜ 202 38.52 N 116.00 W
Wild Horse Plains 168b 34.22 S 138.17 E
Wildnest Lake ⊜ 184 55.00 N 102.20 W
Wild Rice ≃, Mn., U.S. 198 47.20 N 96.50 W
Wild Rice ≃, N.D., U.S. 198 46.53 N 96.35 W
Wild Rice, South Branch ≃ 198 46.42 N 96.47 W
Wildrose, N.D., U.S. 198 48.37 N 103.11 W
Wildrose, Wi., U.S. 190 44.10 N 89.14 W
Wildseeloder ʌ 64 52.16 N 12.32 E
Wildspitze ʌ 58 46.53 N 10.52 E
Wildstrubel ʌ 58 46.24 N 7.32 E
Wildwood, Ab., Can. 182 53.37 N 115.14 W
Wildwood, Fl., U.S. 220 28.52 N 82.02 W
Wildwood, N.J., U.S. 208 38.58 N 74.48 W
Wildwood, Pa., U.S. 214 40.36 N 79.58 W
Wild Wood Beach 284b 39.15 N 76.25 W
Wildwood Crest 208 38.58 N 74.50 W
Wiley 224 46.33 N 120.39 W
Wilfersdorf 61 48.35 N 16.38 E

Column 5

Wilge ≃ S. Afr. 158 27.03 S 28.20 E
Wilge ≃ S. Afr. 158 25.34 S 29.10 E
Wilgena 162 30.46 S 134.44 E
Wilgespruit ≃ 273d 26.07 S 27.52 E
Wilhelm, Lake ⊜¹ 214 41.23 N 80.08 W
Wilhelm, Mount ʌ 164 5.45 S 145.05 E
Wilhelmina Gebergte ⱅ 250 3.45 N 56.30 W
Wilhelminakanaal ≃¹ 52 51.47 N 4.51 E
Wilhelminaoord 52 52.53 N 6.10 E
Wilhelmina Peak → Trikora, Puncak ʌ 164 4.15 S 138.45 E
Wilhelm-Pieck-Stadt Guben¹ 54 51.57 N 14.43 E
Wilhelmsburg 61 48.06 N 15.36 E
Wilhelmsburg ◄⁸ 52 53.30 N 10.00 E
Wilhelmshaven 52 53.31 N 8.08 E
Wilhelmshöhe, Schloss ⊥ 56 51.21 N 9.22 E
Wilhelmsthorst 52 52.19 N 13.03 E
Wilhelmstadt ◄⁸ 264a 52.31 N 13.11 E
Wilhelmsthal 156 21.54 S 16.19 E
Wilis, Gunung ʌ 115a 7.52 S 111.48 E
Wilkau-Hasslau 54 50.40 N 12.31 E
Wilkerson Pass ⱅ 200 39.02 N 105.32 W
Wilkes-Barre 212 41.14 N 75.52 W
Wilkes-Barre Scranton Airport ⊠ 210 41.20 N 75.45 W
Wilkesboro 192 36.08 N 81.09 W
Wilkas Island I 174a 19.18 N 166.34 E
Wilkes Land ◄¹ 9 69.00 S 120.00 E
Wilkeson 224 47.06 N 122.02 W
Wilket Creek ≃ 275b 43.43 N 79.21 W
Wilket Creek Park ◆ 275b 43.43 N 79.21 W
Wilkhaven 46 57.52 N 3.45 W
Wilkie 184 52.25 N 108.43 W
Wilkinsburg 214 40.26 N 79.51 W
Wilkinson 190 39.53 N 85.36 W
Wilkinson Lakes ⊜ 162 29.40 S 132.39 E
Wilkins Sound ⊔ 9 70.15 S 73.00 W
Wilkins Township 279b 40.25 N 79.50 W
Will ◻⁶ 216 41.32 N 88.05 W
Will, Mount ʌ 180 57.31 N 128.46 W
Willacoochee 192 31.20 N 83.02 W
Willamette ≃ 202 45.39 N 122.46 W
Willamette, Middle Fork ≃ 202 43.44 N 123.01 W
Willamette, North Fork ≃ 202 43.46 N 122.32 W
Willamette, North Fork ≃ 202 43.46 N 122.32 W
Willandra Billabong Creek ≃ 166 33.08 S 144.06 E
Willapa ≃ 224 46.40 N 123.50 W
Willapa Bay c 224 46.37 N 124.00 W
Willar ≃ 194 36.37 N 93.25 W
Willard, N.M., U.S. 200 34.35 N 106.01 W
Willard, Oh., U.S. 214 41.03 N 82.44 W
Willard, Ut., U.S. 204 41.24 N 112.02 W
Willard, Wa., U.S. 224 45.48 N 121.38 W
Willards 208 38.23 N 75.20 W
Willaston, Austl. 168b 34.36 S 138.45 E
Willaston, Eng., U.K. 262 53.18 N 3.00 W
Willaumez Peninsula ⊁¹ 164 5.05 S 150.05 E
Willcox 200 32.15 N 109.49 W
Willcox Playa ⊜ 200 32.08 N 109.51 W
Willebadessen 52 51.37 N 9.02 E
Willebroek 52 51.04 N 4.22 E
Willem Pretorius Game Reserve ◆ 158 28.16 S 27.13 E
Willemstad, Ned. 52 51.42 N 4.26 E
Willemstad, Ned. Ant. 241s 12.06 N 68.56 W
Willenhall 42 52.36 N 2.02 W
Willerby 44 53.59 N 0.22 W
Willesden ◄⁸ 260 51.33 N 0.14 W
Willet 210 42.28 N 75.55 W
Willey Pond ⊜ 283 42.11 N 71.14 W
Willey Creek ≃ 279a 41.25 N 79.21 W
William, Lac ⊜ 206 46.07 N 71.34 W
William, Mount ʌ, Austl. 169 37.17 S 142.36 E
William, Mount ʌ, Austl. 170 33.13 S 144.47 E
William, Mount ʌ² 168a 32.57 S 116.07 E
William "Bill" Dannelly Reservoir ◄¹ 192 32.00 N 87.10 W
William Boyce Regional Park ◆ 279b 40.28 N 79.45 W
William Girling Reservoir ◄¹ 260 51.37 N 0.02 W
William H. Harsha Lake ⊜¹ 218 39.02 N 84.07 W
William Lake ⊜ 184 53.50 N 99.25 W
Williamnagar 124 25.30 N 90.35 E
William Patterson College ʌ² 276 40.56 N 74.12 W
William P. Gleason Park ◆ 278 41.33 N 87.21 W
William Preston Lane Jr. Memorial Bridge ◄⁵ 208 39.00 N 76.28 W
Williams, Austl. 168a 33.01 S 116.52 E
Williams, Az., U.S. 200 35.14 N 112.11 W
Williams, Ca., U.S. 226 39.09 N 122.08 W
Williams, Ia., U.S. 198 42.29 N 93.32 W
Williams, Mn., U.S. 198 48.46 N 94.57 W
Williams ◻⁸ 166 41.35 N 84.33 W
Williams ≃, Austl. 168a 33.01 S 116.55 E
Williams ≃, Austl. 170 32.45 S 151.45 E
Williams, Cape ⊁ 9 70.29 S 164.05 E
Williams Air Force Base ⊠ 200 33.18 N 111.40 W
Williams Bay 216 42.34 N 88.32 W
Williamsburg, On., Can. 212 44.58 N 75.15 W
Williamsburg, In., U.S. 218 39.57 N 84.59 W
Williamsburg, Ia., U.S. 190 41.39 N 92.00 W
Williamsburg, Ky., U.S. 192 36.44 N 84.09 W
Williamsburg, Ma., U.S. 207 42.23 N 72.43 W
Williamsburg, N.D., U.S. 218 38.55 N 91.42 W
Williamsburg, Oh., U.S. 218 39.03 N 84.03 W
Williamsburg, Pa., U.S. 214 40.27 N 78.12 W
Williamsburg, Va., U.S. 208 37.16 N 76.42 W
Williamsburg Bridge ◄⁵ 276 40.43 N 73.58 W
Williams Center 216 41.26 N 84.36 W
Williams Creek ≃, Austl. 274a 33.57 S 150.58 E
Williams Creek ≃, U.S. 218 39.50 N 85.47 W
Williamsdale 171b 35.35 S 149.09 E
Williamsfield, Oh., U.S. 214 41.32 N 80.32 W
Williams Fork ≃ 200 40.01 N 107.27 W
Williams Lake 182 52.08 N 122.09 W
Williams Lake Indian Reserve ◄⁴ 182 52.07 N 122.00 W
Williamson, W.V., U.S. 192 37.40 N 82.16 W
Williamson ◻⁶ 222 30.40 N 97.32 W
Williamson ʌ 202 42.28 N 121.57 W
Williamson Head ⊁ 9 69.09 S 157.49 E
Williamsport, Nf., Can. 186 50.32 N 56.19 W
Williamsport, Oh., U.S. 216 40.17 N 87.17 W
Williamsport, Pa., U.S. 214 39.35 N 83.07 W
Williamsport, Pa., U.S. 210 41.14 N 77.00 W
Williamston, Mi., U.S. 216 42.41 N 84.16 W
Williamston, N.C., U.S. 192 35.51 N 77.03 W
Williamston, S.C., U.S. 192 34.37 N 82.28 W
Williamstown, Austl. 169 37.52 S 144.54 E
Williamstown, Ky., U.S. 206 45.08 N 74.35 W
Williamstown, Ma., U.S. 218 38.38 N 84.33 W
Williamstown, N.J., U.S. 207 42.42 N 73.12 W
Williamstown, N.Y., U.S. 210 39.41 N 74.59 W
Williamstown, Pa., U.S. 212 43.26 N 75.54 W
Williamstown, Pa., U.S. 208 40.34 N 76.37 W
Williamstown, Vt., U.S. 188 44.07 N 72.32 W
Williamstown, W.V., U.S. 188 39.24 N 81.27 W
Williamstown Junction 285 39.45 N 74.56 W
Williamstown Lake ⊜¹ 218 38.41 N 84.32 W
Williamsville, Il., U.S. 219 39.57 N 89.32 W
Williamsville, N.Y., U.S. 210 42.57 N 78.44 W
Williamton 170 32.49 S 151.50 E
Willich 56 51.16 N 6.33 E
Willingboro 208 40.03 N 74.54 W
Willingdon, Ab., Can. 182 53.50 N 112.08 W
Willingdon, Eng., U.K. 42 50.47 N 0.15 E
Willingdon, Mount ʌ 182 51.49 N 116.15 W
Willingen 56 51.17 N 8.37 E
Willington, Eng., U.K. 44 54.43 N 1.41 W
Willington, Eng., U.K. 42 52.50 N 1.33 W
Willis, Mi., U.S. 281 42.09 N 83.33 W
Willis, Tx., U.S. 222 30.25 N 95.28 W
Willisau 58 47.07 N 8.00 E
Willis Group II 164 16.18 S 150.00 E
Willis Island I 166 48.48 N 53.42 W
Williston, S. Afr. 158 31.20 S 20.53 E
Williston, Fl., U.S. 220 29.23 N 82.26 W
Williston, N.D., U.S. 198 48.08 N 103.38 W
Williston, S.C., U.S. 192 33.24 N 81.25 W
Williston Lake ⊜¹ 175 56.00 N 123.40 W
Williston Park 276 40.45 N 73.38 W
Willisville 194 45.49 N 89.35 W
Willits 226 39.24 N 123.21 W
Willmar 204 45.07 N 95.02 W
Willmersdorf 264a 52.40 N 13.41 E
Willmore Wilderness Provincial Park ◆ 182 53.45 N 119.00 W
Willoughby, Austl. 170 33.48 S 151.12 E
Willoughby, Oh., U.S. 214 41.38 N 81.25 W
Willoughby, Cape ⊁ 166 35.51 S 138.07 E
Willoughby Bay c 240c 17.02 N 61.44 W
Willoughby Hills 214 41.35 N 81.25 W
Willow, Ak., U.S. 180 61.45 N 150.03 W
Willow, Mi., U.S. 216 40.07 N 83.24 W
Willow, N.Y., U.S. 210 42.05 N 74.14 W
Willow ≃, Can. 182 55.58 N 115.55 W
Willow ≃, N.A. 216 40.05 N 122.21 W
Willow ≃, Wa., U.S. 224 46.59 N 92.46 W
Willowbrook, Sk., Can. 184 51.13 N 102.47 W
Willow Brook, Ca., U.S. 280 33.54 N 118.14 W
Willow Brook ≃, In., U.S. 278 41.46 N 87.56 W
Willow Brook ≃, Oh., U.S. 212 42.32 N 80.16 W
Willow Brook ≃, U.S. 42 52.32 N 0.24 W
Willowbrook Mall ⁹ 276 40.53 N 74.15 W
Willowbrook Park ◆ 276 40.36 N 74.09 W
Willow Bunch 184 49.24 N 105.37 W
Willow Bunch Lake ⊜ 184 49.27 N 105.28 W
Willow City 198 48.36 N 100.17 W
Willow Creek, Ca., U.S. 226 40.56 N 123.38 W
Willow Creek, Mt., U.S. 202 45.49 N 111.38 W
Willow Creek ≃, Ab., Can. 182 53.50 N 112.08 W
Willow Creek ≃, U.S. 198 49.46 N 113.21 W
Willow Creek ≃, U.S. 212 44.25 N 79.53 W
Willow Creek ≃, U.S. 204 41.30 N 116.35 W
Willow Creek ≃, Nv., U.S. 204 38.10 N 116.35 W
Willow Creek, North Fork ≃ 226 39.32 N 122.10 W
Willow Creek, South Fork ≃ 226 39.32 N 122.10 W
Willowdale State Forest ◆ 283 43.47 N 79.26 W
Willowemoc Creek ≃ 210 41.54 N 74.48 W
Willow Glen ◄⁸ 282 37.18 N 121.53 W
Willow Grove 208 40.08 N 75.06 W
Willow Grove Naval Air Station ⊠ 285 40.12 N 75.08 W
Willow Grove Park ◆ 285 40.08 N 75.08 W
Willow Hill 214 40.03 N 77.48 W
Willowick 214 41.37 N 81.28 W
Willow Lake 198 44.37 N 97.38 W

ESPAÑOL — Nombre | Página | Lat.°′ | Long.°′ W = Oeste

FRANÇAIS — Nom | Page | Lat.°′ | Long.°′ W = Ouest

PORTUGUÊS — Nome | Página | Lat.°′ | Long.°′ W = Oeste

Nombre / Nom / Nome	Página / Page	Lat.°′	Long.°′
Willow Lake ⊜, N.T., Can.	176	62.11 N	119.10 W
Willow Lake ⊜, N.Y., U.S.	276	40.43 N	73.50 W
Willowlake ≃	176	62.52 N	123.08 W
Willow Metropolitan Park ♦	281	42.08 N	83.22 W
Willowmore	158	33.17 S	23.29 E
Willow Park	222	32.45 N	97.39 W
Willowra	162	21.15 S	132.35 E
Willowra Aboriginal Reserve ◆ 4	162	21.15 S	132.35 E
Willow Reservoir ⊜ 1	190	45.45 N	89.50 W
Willow Ridge Estates	284a	43.01 N	78.49 W
Willow River	182	54.04 N	122.28 W
Willow Run, De., U.S.	285	39.44 N	75.37 W
Willow Run, Mi., U.S.	216	42.14 N	83.35 W
Willow Run, Va., U.S.	284c	38.49 N	77.10 W
Willow Run Airport ⊠	281	42.14 N	83.32 W
Willows	226	39.31 N	122.11 W
Willow Springs, Ca., U.S.	228	34.53 N	118.18 W
Willow Springs, Il., U.S.	278	41.44 N	87.51 W
Willow Springs, Mo., U.S.	194	36.59 N	91.58 W
Willow Springs, Pa., U.S.	279b	40.19 N	79.44 W
Willow Street	208	39.59 N	76.17 W
Willowvale	158	32.16 S	28.30 E
Willow Woods	284c	38.50 N	77.16 W
Will Rogers Beach State Park ♦	280	34.01 N	118.30 W
Will Rogers State Park ♦	280	34.03 N	118.31 W
Willroth	56	50.34 N	7.31 E
Wills, Lake ⊜	162	21.25 S	128.51 E
Wills Creek ≃, Austl.	166	22.43 S	140.02 E
Wills Creek ≃, Oh., U.S.	188	40.09 N	81.55 W
Wills Creek Lake ⊜ 1	214	40.08 N	81.45 W
Willseyville	210	42.17 N	76.23 W
Willshire	216	40.45 N	84.48 W
Wills Point	222	32.43 N	96.01 W
Willston	284c	38.52 N	77.09 W
Willunga	168b	35.17 S	138.33 E
Wilmar	194	33.37 N	91.55 W
Wilmer, Al., U.S.	194	30.49 N	88.21 W
Wilmer, Pa., U.S.	285	40.07 N	75.32 W
Wilmer, Tx., U.S.	222	32.35 N	96.41 W
Wilmerding	279b	40.23 N	79.48 W
Wilmersdorf ◆ 8	264a	52.30 N	13.19 E
Wilmette	216	42.04 N	87.43 W
Wilmington, Austl.	166	32.39 S	138.07 E
Wilmington, Eng., U.K.	260	51.26 N	0.12 E
Wilmington, De., U.S.	208	39.44 N	75.32 W
Wilmington, Il., U.S.	216	41.18 N	88.08 W
Wilmington, Ma., U.S.	207	42.32 N	71.10 W
Wilmington, N.C., U.S.	192	34.13 N	77.56 W
Wilmington, Oh., U.S.	218	39.26 N	83.49 W
Wilmington, Vt., U.S.	188	42.52 N	72.52 W
Wilmington ◆ 8	280	33.47 N	118.16 W
Wilmington Manor	285	39.41 N	75.35 W
Wilmington Manor Gardens	285	39.40 N	75.34 W
Wilmore, Ky., U.S.	192	37.51 N	84.39 W
Wilmore, Pa., U.S.	214	40.23 N	78.43 W
Wilmot, Ar., U.S.	194	33.03 N	91.34 W
Wilmot, Oh., U.S.	214	40.39 N	81.38 W
Wilmot, S.D., U.S.	198	45.24 N	96.51 W
Wilmot, Wi., U.S.	216	42.31 N	88.11 W
Wilmot Woods ♦	278	42.18 N	87.56 W
Wilmslow	44	53.20 N	2.15 W
Wilna → Vilnius	76	54.41 N	25.19 E
Wilnecote	42	52.36 N	1.40 W
Wilnsdorf	56	50.49 N	8.09 E
Wilpattu National Park ♦	122	8.20 N	80.00 E
Wilpen	214	40.17 N	79.12 W
Wilpshire	262	53.47 N	2.28 W
Wilsall	202	45.59 N	110.39 W
Wilsdruff	54	51.05 N	13.32 E
Wilseder Berg ∧ 2	52	53.10 N	9.56 E
Wilseyville	226	38.23 N	120.31 W
Wilshamstead	42	52.05 N	0.27 W
Wilson, Austl.	166	32.00 S	138.22 E
Wilson, Ar., U.S.	194	35.34 N	90.02 W
Wilson, Ct., U.S.	207	41.48 N	72.38 W
Wilson, Il., U.S.	278	42.21 N	87.54 W
Wilson, Ks., U.S.	198	38.49 N	98.28 W
Wilson, La., U.S.	194	30.55 N	91.06 W
Wilson, N.Y., U.S.	210	43.18 N	78.49 W
Wilson, N.C., U.S.	192	35.43 N	77.54 W
Wilson, Ok., U.S.	196	34.09 N	97.25 W
Wilson, Pa., U.S.	208	40.41 N	75.14 W
Wilson, Tx., U.S.	196	33.19 N	101.44 W
Wilson ≃, Austl.	164	16.47 S	128.17 E
Wilson ≃, Austl.	166	27.38 S	141.24 E
Wilson ≃, Or., U.S.	224	45.28 N	123.53 W
Wilson, Cape ≻	176	66.59 N	81.28 W
Wilson, Mount ∧, Az., U.S.	200	35.59 N	114.37 W
Wilson, Mount ∧, Ca., U.S.	280	34.13 N	118.04 W
Wilson, Mount ∧, Co., U.S.	200	37.51 N	107.59 W
Wilson, Mount ∧, Nv., U.S.	204	38.15 N	114.23 W
Wilson, Mount ∧, Or., U.S.	224	45.04 N	121.39 W
Wilson, Mount ∧ 2, Austl.	162	20.14 S	127.39 E
Wilson, Mount ∧ 2, Austl.	168b	35.13 S	138.38 E
Wilson, Point ≻, Austl.	169	38.05 S	144.30 E
Wilson, Point ≻, Wa., U.S.	224	48.08 N	122.45 W
Wilson Cliffs ⩡ 4	162	22.03 S	127.09 E
Wilson Creek ≃, Tx., U.S.	222	33.07 N	96.35 W
Wilson Creek ≃, Wa., U.S.	202	47.25 N	119.07 W
Wilson Lake ⊜ 1, Al., U.S.	194	34.49 N	87.30 W
Wilson Lake ⊜ 1, Ks., U.S.	198	38.57 N	98.40 W
Wilson Range ⋌	162	28.50 S	124.25 E
Wilson Run ≃, De., U.S.	285	39.48 N	75.35 W
Wilson Run ≃, Pa., U.S.	279b	40.13 N	79.37 W
Wilsons Beach	186	44.56 N	66.56 W
Wilson's Creek National Battlefield ♦	194	37.06 N	93.27 W
Wilsons Promontory ≻	166	38.55 S	146.20 E
Wilsons Promontory National Park ♦	166	39.00 S	146.25 E
Wilsonville, Il., U.S.	219	39.04 N	89.51 W
Wilsonville, Ne., U.S.	198	40.06 N	100.06 W
Wilsonville, Or., U.S.	224	45.18 N	122.46 W
Wilster	52	53.55 N	9.22 E
Wilthen	54	51.06 N	14.24 E
Wilton, Eng., U.K.	42	51.05 N	1.52 W
Wilton, Ct., U.S.	207	41.11 N	73.26 W
Wilton, Me., U.S.	188	44.35 N	70.13 W
Wilton, N.H., U.S.	207	42.50 N	71.44 W
Wilton, N.Y., U.S.	210	43.11 N	73.45 W
Wilton, N.D., U.S.	198	47.09 N	100.46 W
Wilton, Wi., U.S.	190	43.48 N	90.31 W
Wilton ≃	164	14.45 S	134.33 E
Wilton Creek ≃	212	44.12 N	76.56 W
Wilton Farm Acres	284b	39.18 N	76.50 W
Wilton Manors	220	26.09 N	80.08 W
Wiltshire □ 6	42	51.15 N	1.50 W
Wiltz	56	49.48 N	5.55 E
Wiluna	162	26.36 S	120.13 E
Wimapedi ≃	184	55.27 N	99.07 W
Wimauma	220	27.42 N	82.17 W
Wimberley	196	30.00 N	98.06 W
Wimbledon	198	47.10 N	98.27 W
Wimbledon ◆ 8	260	51.25 N	0.12 W
Wimbledon Common ♦	260	51.26 N	0.14 W
Wimborne Minster	42	50.48 N	1.59 W
Wimereux	50	50.46 N	1.37 E
Wimmelburg	54	51.31 N	11.30 E
Wimmenau	56	48.55 N	7.25 E
Wimmera ≃	169	36.55 S	142.56 E
Wimmis	58	46.41 N	7.38 E
Winagami Lake ⊜	182	55.38 N	116.45 W
Winam ⊂	154	0.15 S	34.35 E
Winamac	216	41.03 N	86.36 W
Winburg	158	28.37 S	27.00 E
Winburne	214	40.57 N	78.08 W
Wincanton	42	51.04 N	2.25 W
Wincham	262	53.16 N	2.29 W
Winchcombe	42	51.57 N	1.58 W
Winchelsea, Austl.	169	38.15 S	143.59 E
Winchelsea, Eng., U.K.	42	50.55 N	0.42 E
Winchendon	207	42.41 N	72.02 W
Winchester, On., Can.	212	45.06 N	75.21 W
Winchester, N.Z.	172	44.12 S	171.17 E
Winchester, Eng., U.K.	42	51.04 N	1.19 W
Winchester, Ca., U.S.	228	33.42 N	117.05 W
Winchester, Id., U.S.	202	46.14 N	116.37 W
Winchester, Il., U.S.	219	39.37 N	90.27 W
Winchester, In., U.S.	218	40.10 N	84.58 W
Winchester, Ky., U.S.	192	37.59 N	84.10 W
Winchester, Ma., U.S.	283	42.27 N	71.08 W
Winchester, N.H., U.S.	207	42.46 N	72.23 W
Winchester, Oh., U.S.	218	38.56 N	83.39 W
Winchester, Tn., U.S.	194	35.11 N	86.06 W
Winchester, Tx., U.S.	222	30.01 N	97.01 W
Winchester, Va., U.S.	188	39.11 N	78.10 W
Winchester Cathedral ᵾ 1	42	51.04 N	1.19 W
Winchmore Hill	260	51.39 N	0.39 W
Winchmore Hill ◆ 8	260	51.38 N	0.06 W
Wind ≃, Yk., Can.	180	65.49 N	135.18 W
Wind ≃, Wa., U.S.	224	45.43 N	121.47 W
Wind ≃, Wy., U.S.	202	43.35 N	108.13 W
Windang	170	34.32 S	150.53 E
Windau → Ventspils	76	57.24 N	21.36 E
Windber	214	40.14 N	78.50 W
Wind Cave National Park ♦	198	43.32 N	103.25 W
Windeck	56	50.48 N	7.37 E
Winder	192	33.59 N	83.43 W
Winder, Lake ⊜	220	28.15 N	80.51 W
Windera	166	26.03 S	151.50 E
Windermere, B.C., Can.	182	50.30 N	115.58 W
Windermere, Eng., U.K.	44	54.23 N	2.54 W
Windermere, Fl., U.S.	220	28.30 N	81.32 W
Windermere ⊜	44	54.22 N	2.56 W
Windermere Lake ⊜	190	47.56 N	83.47 W
Winder Village	285	40.06 N	74.52 W
Windfall, Ab., Can.	182	54.11 N	116.15 W
Windfall, In., U.S.	216	40.21 N	85.57 W
Windgap	210	40.51 N	75.18 W
Windham, Ct., U.S.	207	41.41 N	72.09 W
Windham, N.H., U.S.	283	42.48 N	71.18 W
Windham, N.Y., U.S.	210	42.19 N	74.15 W
Windham, Oh., U.S.	214	41.14 N	81.02 W
Windham □ 6, Ct., U.S.	207	41.55 N	71.55 W
Windham □ 6, Vt., U.S.	207	42.50 N	72.43 W
Windham Manor	284c	39.04 N	77.00 W
Windhoek	156	22.34 S	17.06 E
Windhoek □ 5	156	22.30 S	17.00 E
Windigo ≃	184	53.22 N	91.48 W
Windigo Lake ⊜	184	52.35 N	91.32 W
Windisch	58	47.29 N	8.13 E
Windischeschenbach	60	49.48 N	12.09 E
Windischgarsten	61	47.44 N	14.20 E
Wind Lake	216	42.49 N	88.09 W
Wind Lake ⊜	216	42.50 N	88.09 W
Windlass Run ≃	284b	39.24 N	76.24 W
Windleite ∧	54	51.22 N	10.56 E
Windlesham	260	51.22 N	0.40 W
Windley Key I	220	24.57 N	80.35 W
Windmill Point ≻, On., Can.	284a	42.52 N	79.01 W
Windmill Point ≻, Mi., U.S.	281	42.22 N	82.55 W
Windmill Point ≻, Va., U.S.	208	37.37 N	76.17 W
Windom, Mn., U.S.	198	43.51 N	95.07 W
Windom, N.Y., U.S.	210	42.47 N	78.48 W
Windom Peak ∧	200	37.37 N	107.35 W
Windorah	166	25.26 S	142.39 E
Windorf, B.R.D.	60	48.37 N	13.13 E
Windorf, Öst.	61	48.27 N	14.02 E
Window Rock	200	35.40 N	109.03 W
Wind Point	216	42.47 N	87.45 W
Wind River Indian Reservation ◆ 4	202	43.26 N	109.00 W
Wind River Peak ∧	200	42.42 N	109.07 W
Wind River Range ⋌	200	43.05 N	109.25 W
Windrush ≃	42	51.42 N	1.25 W
Windsbach	56	49.14 N	10.50 E
Windsor, Austl.	168b	34.25 S	138.20 E
Windsor, Austl.	170	33.37 S	150.49 E
Windsor, Nf., Can.	186	48.57 N	55.40 W
Windsor, N.S., Can.	186	44.59 N	64.08 W
Windsor, On., Can.	214	42.18 N	83.01 W
Windsor, On., Can.	281	42.18 N	83.01 W
Windsor, P.Q., Can.	206	45.34 N	72.00 W
Windsor, Eng., U.K.	42	51.29 N	0.38 W
Windsor, Ca., U.S.	204	38.33 N	122.49 W
Windsor, Co., U.S.	200	40.28 N	104.54 W
Windsor, Ct., U.S.	207	41.51 N	72.38 W
Windsor, Il., U.S.	194	39.26 N	88.35 W
Windsor, In., U.S.	218	40.09 N	85.12 W
Windsor, Mo., U.S.	194	38.31 N	93.31 W
Windsor, N.J., U.S.	208	40.15 N	74.35 W
Windsor, N.Y., U.S.	210	42.05 N	75.39 W
Windsor, N.C., U.S.	192	35.59 N	76.56 W
Windsor, Oh., U.S.	214	41.32 N	80.56 W
Windsor, Pa., U.S.	208	39.54 N	76.35 W
Windsor, Vt., U.S.	188	43.29 N	72.23 W
Windsor, Va., U.S.	208	36.48 N	76.44 W
Windsor, Wi., U.S.	216	43.13 N	89.20 W
Windsor, Gare ◆ 5	275a	45.30 N	73.34 W
Windsor, University of ᵾ 2	281	42.18 N	83.04 W
Windsor Airport ⊠	214	42.17 N	82.58 W
Windsor and Maidenhead □ 8	260	51.28 N	0.37 W
Windsor Castle ⊥	42	51.29 N	0.36 W
Windsor Forest	192	31.58 N	81.07 W
Windsor Forest ◆ 3	42	51.27 N	0.43 W
Windsor Great Park ♦	260	51.27 N	0.37 W
Windsor Heights	214	40.12 N	80.40 W
Windsor Hills	280	33.59 N	118.21 W
Windsor Locks	207	41.55 N	72.37 W
Windsor Race Course ♦	260	51.29 N	0.39 W
Windsor Raceway ♦	281	42.15 N	83.05 W
Windsor Terrace	284b	39.19 N	76.43 W
Windsorton	158	28.16 S	24.44 E
Windsorville	207	41.53 N	72.32 W
Windthorst	196	33.34 N	98.26 W
Windward Islands II	238	13.00 N	61.00 W
Windward Passage ⊔	238	20.00 N	73.50 W
Windy Hills	285	39.48 N	75.35 W
Windy Lake ⊜	184	54.22 N	102.35 W
Windy Peak ∧, Co., U.S.	200	38.21 N	106.16 W
Windy Peak ∧, Wa., U.S.	202	48.56 N	119.58 W
Windy Run ≃	284c	38.54 N	77.05 W
Winefred ≃	184	56.02 N	110.36 W
Winefred Lake ⊜	182	55.30 N	110.35 W
Winejok	140	9.01 N	27.34 E
Winesburg	214	40.37 N	81.42 W
Winfield, Ab., Can.	182	52.58 N	114.26 W
Winfield, Al., U.S.	194	33.55 N	87.49 W
Winfield, Il., U.S.	216	41.52 N	88.10 W
Winfield, Ia., U.S.	190	41.07 N	91.26 W
Winfield, Ks., U.S.	198	37.14 N	96.59 W
Winfield, Mo., U.S.	219	38.59 N	90.44 W
Winfield, N.J., U.S.	276	40.38 N	74.17 W
Winfield, Tx., U.S.	222	33.10 N	95.07 W
Winfield, W.V., U.S.	188	38.31 N	81.53 W
Wing	198	47.08 N	100.16 W
Wing ≃	198	46.29 N	94.58 W
Wingate, Eng., U.K.	44	55.44 N	1.23 W
Wingate, Md., U.S.	208	38.16 N	76.04 W
Wingate, N.C., U.S.	192	34.59 N	80.26 W
Wingate Mountains ⋌	164	14.29 S	130.42 E
Wingates	262	53.34 N	2.32 W
Wingdale	210	41.39 N	73.34 W
Wingecarribee ≃	170	34.23 S	150.07 E
Wingecarribee Reservoir ⊜ 1	170	34.34 S	150.30 E
Wingello	170	34.42 S	150.09 E
Wingene	50	51.04 N	3.16 E
Wingen-sur-Moder	56	48.55 N	7.22 E
Wingerworth	44	53.12 N	1.26 W
Wingham, Austl.	166	31.52 S	152.22 E
Wingham, On., Can.	212	43.53 N	81.19 W
Wingham, Eng., U.K.	42	51.17 N	1.13 E
Wing Lake Shores	281	42.33 N	83.17 W
Wingles	50	50.29 N	2.51 E
Wingo	194	36.38 N	88.44 W
Wings Field ⊠	285	40.08 N	75.16 W
Wingst	52	53.43 N	9.03 E
Winhole Channel ⊔	276	43.37 N	73.48 W
Winhöring	60	48.16 N	12.39 E
Winifred	202	47.33 N	109.22 W
Winifreda	252	36.15 S	64.14 W
Winisk	176	55.15 N	85.12 W
Winisk ≃	176	55.17 N	85.05 W
Winisk Lake ⊜	176	52.55 N	87.22 W
Wink	196	31.45 N	103.06 W
Winkana	110	15.44 N	98.01 E
Winkelman	200	32.59 N	110.46 W
Winkelpos	158	27.35 S	26.49 E
Winkler, Mb., Can.	184	49.11 N	97.56 W
Winkler, Tx., U.S.	222	31.56 N	96.13 W
Winklern	64	46.52 N	12.52 E
Winlaw	182	49.37 N	117.34 W
Winlock	224	46.29 N	122.56 W
Winneba	150	5.25 N	0.36 W
Winnebago, Il., U.S.	190	42.15 N	89.14 W
Winnebago, Mn., U.S.	190	43.46 N	94.09 W
Winnebago, Ne., U.S.	198	42.14 N	96.28 W
Winnebago □ 6	216	42.17 N	89.06 W
Winnebago ≃	190	43.03 N	92.57 W
Winnebago, Lake ⊜	190	44.00 N	88.25 W
Winnebago Indian Reservation ◆ 4, Ne., U.S.	198	42.15 N	96.31 W
Winnebago Indian Reservation ◆ 4, Wi., U.S.	190	44.15 N	90.38 W
Winnecke, Mount ∧ 2	162	18.47 S	130.20 E
Winnecke Creek ≃	162	18.35 S	131.34 E
Winneconne	190	44.06 N	88.42 W
Winneconnet	283	41.59 N	71.08 W
Winneconnet Pond ⊜	283	41.58 N	71.08 W
Winnekendonk	52	51.36 N	6.17 E
Winnekenni Park ♦	283	42.47 N	71.04 W
Winnemucca	204	40.58 N	117.44 W
Winnemucca Lake ⊜	204	40.09 N	119.20 W
Winnenden	56	48.53 N	9.24 E
Winner	198	43.22 N	99.51 W
Winnetka	216	42.06 N	87.44 W
Winnetka ◆ 8	280	34.13 N	118.35 W
Winnett	202	47.00 N	108.21 W
Winnfield	194	31.55 N	92.38 W
Winnibigoshish, Lake ⊜	190	47.27 N	94.12 W
Winnie	194	29.49 N	94.23 W
Winning	162	23.09 S	114.32 E
Winningen, B.R.D.	56	50.18 N	7.31 E
Winningen, D.D.R.	54	51.49 N	11.26 E
Winnipeg	184	49.53 N	97.09 W
Winnipeg ≃	184	50.38 N	96.19 W
Winnipeg, Lake ⊜	184	52.00 N	97.00 W
Winnipeg Beach	184	50.31 N	96.58 W
Winnipegosis	184	51.39 N	99.56 W
Winnipegosis, Lake ⊜	184	52.30 N	100.00 W
Winnipesaukee, Lake ⊜	188	43.35 N	71.20 W
Winnsboro, La., U.S.	194	32.09 N	91.43 W
Winnsboro, S.C., U.S.	192	34.22 N	81.05 W
Winnsboro, Tx., U.S.	222	32.57 N	95.17 W
Winnsboro, Lake ⊜ 1	222	32.55 N	95.21 W
Winnsboro Mills	192	34.21 N	81.05 W
Winnweiler	56	49.34 N	7.51 E
Winona, Ks., U.S.	198	39.03 N	101.14 W
Winona, Mi., U.S.	190	46.52 N	88.55 W
Winona, Mn., U.S.	190	44.03 N	91.38 W
Winona, Ms., U.S.	194	33.28 N	89.43 W
Winona, Mo., U.S.	194	37.00 N	91.19 W
Winona, Oh., U.S.	214	40.50 N	80.54 W
Winona, Tx., U.S.	222	32.29 N	95.10 W
Winona Lake, In., U.S.	216	41.13 N	85.49 W
Winona Lake, N.Y., U.S.	210	41.31 N	74.03 W
Winona Lake ⊜	216	41.13 N	85.50 W
Winooski	188	44.29 N	73.11 W
Winooski ≃	188	44.30 N	73.15 W
Winooski, North Branch ≃	188	44.15 N	72.35 W
Winschoten	52	53.08 N	7.02 E
Winscombe	42	51.18 N	2.50 W
Winsen, B.R.D.	52	52.41 N	9.54 E
Winsen, B.R.D.	52	53.22 N	10.12 E
Winsford, Eng., U.K.	42	51.06 N	3.33 W
Winsford, Eng., U.K.	44	53.12 N	2.32 W
Winshill	42	52.48 N	1.36 W
Winside	198	42.10 N	97.10 W
Winslow, Eng., U.K.	42	51.57 N	0.54 W
Winslow, Az., U.S.	200	35.01 N	110.41 W
Winslow, Me., U.S.	188	44.32 N	69.37 W
Winslow, N.J., U.S.	285	39.39 N	74.52 W
Winslow Reef ✥ 2	14	1.36 S	174.57 W
Winsted, Ct., U.S.	207	41.55 N	73.03 W
Winsted, Mn., U.S.	190	44.57 N	94.02 W
Winston, Fl., U.S.	220	28.01 N	82.00 W
Winston, Or., U.S.	202	43.07 N	123.24 W
Winston Churchill Memorial ᵾ	219	38.52 N	91.58 W
Winston Creek ≃	224	46.30 N	122.40 W
Winston-Salem	192	36.05 N	80.14 W
Winsum	52	53.19 N	6.31 E
Wintego Lake ⊜	184	55.33 N	102.52 W
Winter	190	45.49 N	91.00 W
Winter Beach	220	27.43 N	80.25 W
Winterberg, B.R.D.	56	51.11 N	8.32 E
Winterberg, B.R.D.	263	51.17 N	7.18 E
Winterberg ∧ 2	263	51.20 N	7.13 E
Winterberge ⋌	158	32.28 S	26.15 E
Winterbourne Abbas	42	50.43 N	2.34 W
Winter Creek ≃	280	34.12 N	118.02 W
Winterfeld	54	52.44 N	11.14 E
Winter Garden	220	28.33 N	81.35 W
Winter Gardens	228	32.50 N	116.56 W
Winter Harbor	188	44.23 N	68.05 W
Winter Harbour	182	50.31 N	128.02 W
Winterhaven, Ca., U.S.	204	32.44 N	114.38 W
Winter Haven, Fl., U.S.	220	28.01 N	81.43 W
Winter Hill ∧ 2	262	53.38 N	2.31 W
Wintering ≃	198	48.12 N	100.34 W
Wintering Lake ⊜	184	55.24 N	97.42 W
Winter Island I, N.T., Can.	176	66.14 N	83.04 W
Winter Island I, Ca., U.S.	282	38.03 N	121.51 W
Winter Island I, Ma., U.S.	283	42.32 N	70.52 W
Winterlingen	58	48.11 N	9.07 E
Winter Park, Fl., U.S.	220	28.35 N	81.20 W
Winter Park, N.C., U.S.	192	34.12 N	77.53 W
Winterport	188	44.38 N	68.51 W
Winters, Ca., U.S.	226	38.31 N	121.58 W
Winters, Tx., U.S.	196	31.57 N	99.57 W
Winters Bayou ≃	222	30.22 N	95.06 W
Winters Canal ≌	226	38.32 N	121.58 W
Wintersdorf	54	51.03 N	12.21 E
Winterset, Ia., U.S.	190	41.19 N	94.00 W
Winterset, Oh., U.S.	214	40.06 N	81.25 W
Winter Springs	220	28.41 N	81.18 W
Winters Run ≃	208	39.26 N	76.18 W
Winterstown	208	39.50 N	76.37 W
Wintersville	214	40.22 N	80.42 W
Winterswijk	52	51.58 N	6.44 E
Winterthur, Schw.	58	47.30 N	8.43 E
Winterthur, De., U.S.	285	39.48 N	75.35 W
Winterthur Museum ᵾ	285	39.48 N	75.36 W
Winterton, Nf., Can.	186	47.58 N	53.20 W
Winterton, S. Afr.	158	28.46 S	29.35 E
Winterton, Eng., U.K.	44	53.39 N	0.36 W
Winterton-on-Sea	42	52.43 N	1.42 E
Winterville, Ga., U.S.	192	33.58 N	83.16 W
Winterville, Ms., U.S.	194	33.30 N	91.03 W
Winterville, N.C., U.S.	192	35.31 N	77.24 W
Winthrop, Ct., U.S.	207	41.21 N	72.29 W
Winthrop, Ia., U.S.	190	42.28 N	91.44 W
Winthrop, Me., U.S.	188	44.18 N	69.58 W
Winthrop, Ma., U.S.	283	42.22 N	70.59 W
Winthrop, Mn., U.S.	190	44.32 N	94.21 W
Winthrop, Wa., U.S.	182	48.28 N	120.11 W
Winthrop, Lake ⊜	283	42.11 N	71.25 W
Winthrop Harbor	216	42.28 N	87.49 W
Wintinna	162	27.44 S	134.07 E
Wintinna Creek ≃	162	27.47 S	134.14 E
Winton, Austl.	166	22.23 S	143.02 E
Winton, N.Z.	172	46.09 S	168.20 E
Winton, S. Afr.	158	27.29 S	22.34 E
Winton, Ca., U.S.	226	37.23 N	120.37 W
Winton, N.C., U.S.	192	36.23 N	76.55 W
Winton, Wa., U.S.	224	47.44 N	120.44 W
Wintzenheim	58	48.04 N	7.17 E
Winwick	262	53.26 N	2.36 W
Winz	263	51.23 N	7.09 E
Winzenberg	263	51.06 N	7.38 E
Winzer	60	48.44 N	13.04 E
Winzermark	263	51.23 N	7.08 E
Wipper ≃, B.R.D.	263	51.07 N	7.24 E
Wipper ≃, D.D.R.	54	51.47 N	11.42 E
Wipper ≃, D.D.R.	54	51.17 N	11.10 E
Wipperdorf	54	51.28 N	10.42 E
Wipperfeld	263	51.05 N	7.19 E
Wipperfürth	56	51.07 N	7.23 E
Wippra	54	51.34 N	11.16 E
Wirāṭnagar	124	26.29 N	87.17 E
Wīrendranagar	124	28.35 N	81.38 E
Wireton, Il., U.S.	278	41.40 N	87.42 W
Wireton, Pa., U.S.	279b	40.34 N	80.14 W
Wīrgañj	124	27.00 N	84.52 E
Wiriagar ≃	164	2.17 S	132.52 E
Wirksworth	44	53.05 N	1.34 W
Wirosari	115a	7.05 S	111.05 E
Wirral □ 8	262	53.22 N	3.05 W
Wirral ≻ 1	44	53.20 N	3.03 W
Wirraminna	166	31.12 S	136.15 E
Wirrulla	162	32.24 S	134.31 E
Wisbech	42	52.40 N	0.10 E
Wisby → Visby	26	57.38 N	18.18 E
Wiscasset	188	44.00 N	69.39 W
Wische ◆ 1	54	52.50 N	11.55 E
Wischhafen	52	53.46 N	9.19 E
Wisconsin □ 3, U.S.	178	44.45 N	89.30 W
Wisconsin □ 3, U.S.	190	44.45 N	89.30 W
Wisconsin ≃	190	43.00 N	91.10 W
Wisconsin, Lake ⊜ 1	190	43.24 N	89.43 W
Wisconsin Dells	190	43.37 N	89.46 W
Wisconsin Dells V	190	43.41 N	89.49 W
Wisconsin Rapids	190	44.23 N	89.49 W
Wiscoy	210	42.30 N	78.05 W
Wisdom	202	45.37 N	113.27 W
Wisdom, Lake ⊜	164	5.20 S	147.05 E
Wise	192	36.58 N	82.34 W
Wise □ 6	222	33.07 N	97.40 W
Wise ≃	202	45.48 N	112.57 W
Wiseman	180	67.25 N	150.06 W
Wisemans Ferry	170	33.24 S	150.59 E
Wises Landing	218	38.35 N	85.25 W
Wishart	184	51.34 N	104.00 W
Wishaw	46	55.47 N	3.56 W
Wishek	198	46.16 N	99.33 W
Wishkah ≃	224	46.58 N	123.45 W
Wishram	224	45.39 N	120.57 W
Wisła	30	49.40 N	18.52 E
Wisła ≃	30	54.22 N	18.55 E
Wisley Aerodrome ⊠	260	51.18 N	0.28 W
Wisley Gardens ♦	260	51.19 N	0.29 W
Wisłok ≃	30	50.13 N	22.32 E
Wisłoka ≃	30	50.27 N	21.23 E
Wismar, D.D.R.	54	53.53 N	11.28 E
Wismar, Guy.	246	6.00 N	58.18 W
Wismarbucht ⊂	54	53.57 N	11.25 E
Wisner, La., U.S.	194	31.58 N	91.39 W
Wisner, Ne., U.S.	198	41.59 N	96.54 W
Wissahickon Creek ≃	285	40.01 N	75.12 W
Wissant	50	50.53 N	1.40 E
Wissembourg	56	49.02 N	7.57 E
Wissen	56	50.47 N	7.43 E
Wissenkerke	52	51.35 N	3.45 E
Wissey ≃	42	52.33 N	0.21 E
Wissinoming ◆ 8	285	40.01 N	75.04 W
Wissmar	56	50.38 N	8.41 E
Wissous	261	48.44 N	2.20 E
Wister	194	34.58 N	94.43 W
Wisznice	30	51.48 N	23.12 E
Witbank	158	25.56 S	29.07 E
Witberge ⋌	158	30.45 S	27.32 E
Witbooisvlei	156	25.04 S	18.27 E
Witchekan Lake ⊜	184	53.25 N	107.35 W
Witches Falls National Park ♦	171a	27.56 S	153.10 E
Witch Hazel	224	45.30 N	122.46 W
Witdraai	158	26.58 S	20.45 E
Witfield	273d	26.11 S	28.12 E
Witham	42	51.48 N	0.38 E
Witham ≃	44	53.06 N	0.13 W
Withamsville	218	39.03 N	84.16 W
Withens Clough Reservoir ⊜ 1	262	53.42 N	2.02 W
Witheridge	42	50.55 N	3.42 W
Withernsea	44	53.44 N	0.02 E
Witherspoon, Mount ∧	180	61.23 N	147.12 W
Withington ◆ 8	262	53.26 N	2.14 W
Withington Green	262	53.14 N	2.18 W
Withlacoochee ≃, U.S.	192	30.24 N	83.10 W
Withlacoochee ≃, Fl., U.S.	192	29.00 N	82.45 W
Withnell	262	53.42 N	2.34 W
Withokspruit ≃	273d	26.19 S	28.21 E
Witjira National Park ♦	162	26.25 S	135.40 E
Wit-Kei ≃	158	32.09 S	27.24 E
Witkoppies ∧	158	27.44 S	29.20 E
Witkowo	30	52.27 N	17.47 E
Witless Bay	186	47.16 N	52.50 W
Witley	42	51.09 N	0.38 W
Wit-Mfolozi ≃	158	28.22 S	31.58 E
Witney	42	51.48 N	1.29 W
Witnica	30	52.40 N	14.55 E
Wit Nossob ≃	156	23.05 S	18.45 E
Witpoort	158	27.10 S	26.08 E
Witrivier	156	24.40 S	31.00 E
Witry-lès-Reims	50	49.18 N	4.07 E
Witsand	158	34.24 S	20.50 E
Witt	219	39.15 N	89.20 W
Wittabrenna Creek ≃	166	29.20 S	142.43 E
Witteberg ⋌	158	28.40 S	28.02 E
Witteberge ⋌	158	33.18 S	20.36 E
Wittelsheim	58	47.49 N	7.15 E
Witten	56	51.26 N	7.20 E
Wittenau ◆ 8	264a	52.35 N	13.20 E
Wittenberg, D.D.R.	54	51.52 N	12.39 E
Wittenberg, Wi., U.S.	190	44.49 N	89.10 W
Wittenberge	54	53.00 N	11.44 E
Wittenburg	54	53.31 N	11.04 E
Wittenheim	58	47.49 N	7.20 E
Wittenoom	162	22.17 S	118.19 E
Wittensee ⊜	41	54.23 N	9.45 E
Wittering	42	52.37 N	0.27 W
Wittgensdorf	54	50.53 N	12.52 E
Wittichenau	54	51.23 N	14.14 E
Wittingen	54	52.43 N	10.44 E
Wittislingen	56	48.37 N	10.25 E
Wittlaer	56	51.19 N	6.44 E
Wittlich	56	49.59 N	6.53 E
Wittman	208	38.47 N	76.17 W
Wittmar	54	52.07 N	10.38 E
Wittmund	52	53.34 N	7.47 E
Witton Park ♦	262	53.45 N	2.31 W
Wittow ≻ 1	54	54.38 N	13.19 E
Wittstock	54	53.10 N	12.29 E
Witu	154	2.23 S	40.26 E
Witu Islands II	164	4.40 S	149.25 E
Witvlai	156	22.23 S	18.32 E
Witwatersrand, University of the ᵾ 2	273d	26.12 S	28.02 E
Witwatersrand Gold Mine ◆ 7	273d	26.12 S	28.11 E
Witwatersrant ◆ 1	158	26.00 S	27.00 E
Witzenhausen	56	51.20 N	9.51 E
Witzhelden	263	51.07 N	7.06 E
Witzputz	156	27.25 S	17.43 E
Wiveliscombe	42	51.03 N	3.19 W
Wivenhoe	42	51.52 N	0.58 E
Wivenhoe Reservoir ⊜ 1	171a	27.20 S	152.35 E
Wiwa Creek ≃	184	50.02 N	106.31 W
Wixom	216	42.31 N	83.32 W
Wiżajny	30	54.23 N	22.51 E
Wizernes	50	50.43 N	2.14 E
Wjatka → V'atka ≃	80	55.36 N	51.30 E
W. J. van Blommestein Meer ⊜ 1	250	4.45 N	55.00 W
W. Kerr Scott Reservoir ⊜ 1	192	36.07 N	81.15 W
Wkra ≃	30	52.27 N	20.44 E
Wladiwostok → Vladivostok	89	43.10 N	131.56 E
Władysławowo	30	54.49 N	18.25 E
Wleń	30	51.01 N	15.40 E
Wlingi	115a	8.05 S	112.19 E
Włocławek	30	52.39 N	19.02 E
Włocławek □ 4	30	52.30 N	19.05 E
Włodawa	30	51.34 N	23.32 E
Włoszczowa	30	50.52 N	19.59 E
Wnion ≃	42	52.45 N	3.54 W
Woady Yaloak ≃	169	38.06 S	143.33 E
Wobaer	85	39.19 N	75.32 E
Wöbbelin	54	53.24 N	11.30 E
Woburn	207	42.28 N	71.09 W
Woburn ◆ 8	275b	43.46 N	79.13 W
Woburn Sands	42	52.01 N	0.39 W
Woden, Austl.	171b	35.22 S	149.08 E
Woden, Tx., U.S.	222	31.30 N	94.32 W
Wodgina	162	21.11 S	118.40 E
Wodonga	166	36.07 S	146.54 E
Wodzisław Śląski	30	50.00 N	18.28 E
Woensdrecht	52	51.26 N	4.18 E
Woerdeke	85	39.41 N	77.53 E
Woerden	52	52.05 N	4.54 E
Woerth	56	48.56 N	7.45 E
Woëvre ◆ 1	56	49.05 N	5.40 E
Wofosi	105	40.09 N	115.18 E
Wo Fo Si (Temple of the Sleeping Buddha) ᵾ 1	105	40.01 N	116.12 E
Wognum	52	52.41 N	5.01 E
Wohlau → Wołów	30	51.21 N	16.39 E
Wohlde	41	54.24 N	9.17 E
Wohlen	58	47.21 N	8.17 E
Wohlensee ⊜	58	46.58 N	7.20 E
Wohlford, Lake ⊜ 1	228	33.10 N	116.59 W
Wohlthat Mountains ⋌	9	71.35 S	12.20 E
Wohra ≃	56	50.49 N	8.55 E
Woi	140	7.53 N	31.10 E
Woincourt	50	50.04 N	1.32 E
Woippy	56	49.09 N	6.09 E
Wojcieszów	30	50.58 N	15.56 E
Wokalup	168a	33.06 S	115.53 E
Wokam, Pulau I	164	5.37 S	134.30 E
Wokha	120	26.06 N	94.16 E
Woking, Ab., Can.	182	55.35 N	118.46 W
Woking, Eng., U.K.	42	51.20 N	0.34 W
Woking □ 8	260	51.19 N	0.32 W
Wokingham	42	51.25 N	0.51 W
Wokingham Creek ≃	166	22.19 S	142.30 E
Wolbach	198	41.24 N	98.24 W
Wolbeck	52	51.55 N	7.43 E
Wolbrom	30	50.24 N	19.46 E
Wolcott, Ct., U.S.	207	41.36 N	72.59 W
Wolcott, In., U.S.	216	40.45 N	87.02 W
Wolcott, N.Y., U.S.	210	43.13 N	76.48 W
Wolcott Creek ≃	210	43.17 N	76.50 W
Wolcottsburg	210	43.04 N	78.38 W
Wolcottsville	210	43.07 N	78.31 W
Wolcottville	216	41.32 N	85.22 W
Wołcza ≃	54	53.58 N	14.53 E
Wołczenica ≃	54	53.52 N	14.44 E
Wołczyn	30	51.01 N	18.03 E
Woldberg ⋌ 1	52	52.25 N	5.55 E
Woldegk	54	53.27 N	13.35 E
Woldenburg → Dobiegniew	30	52.59 N	15.47 E
Woldingham	260	51.17 N	0.02 W
Wolds, The ⋌ 2	44	53.20 N	0.10 W
Woleai I 1	108	7.21 N	143.52 E
Woleu-Ntem □ 4	152	1.30 N	12.00 E
Wolf ≃, On., Can.	190	48.49 N	88.30 W
Wolf ≃, U.S.	194	35.09 N	90.04 W
Wolf ≃, Ks., U.S.	198	39.54 N	95.11 W
Wolf ≃, Ms., U.S.	194	30.21 N	89.18 W
Wolf ≃, Wi., U.S.	190	44.11 N	88.48 W
Wolf, Isla I	246a	1.23 N	91.49 W
Wolf, Volcán ∧ 1	246a	0.02 N	91.20 W
Wolfach	58	48.17 N	8.13 E
Wolf-Bay	186	50.16 N	60.08 W
Wolf Creek, Mt., U.S.	202	47.00 N	112.04 W
Wolf Creek, Or., U.S.	202	42.41 N	123.23 W
Wolf Creek ≃, U.S.	196	36.35 N	99.30 W
Wolf Creek ≃, Ca., U.S.	226	39.02 N	121.08 W
Wolf Creek ≃, Co., U.S.	200	40.12 N	108.29 W
Wolf Creek ≃, In., U.S.	216	41.15 N	87.07 W
Wolf Creek ≃, Ia., U.S.	190	42.20 N	92.09 W
Wolf Creek ≃, Mt., U.S.	198	48.05 N	105.40 W
Wolf Creek ≃, Mt., U.S.	202	47.37 N	109.38 W
Wolf Creek ≃, Oh., U.S.	214	41.16 N	83.11 W
Wolf Creek ≃, Pa., U.S.	214	41.03 N	80.07 W
Wolf Creek ≃, S.D., U.S.	198	43.21 N	97.37 W
Wolf Creek ≃, S.D., U.S.	198	44.42 N	98.40 W
Wolf Creek Lake ⊜ 1	198	38.14 N	95.41 W
Wolf Creek Pass)(	200	37.29 N	106.48 W
Wolf Creek State Park ♦	219	39.30 N	88.41 W
Wolfdale	214	40.12 N	80.17 W
Wolfe □ 6	206	45.45 N	71.30 W
Wolfeboro	188	43.35 N	71.12 W
Wolfe City	196	33.22 N	96.04 W
Wolfegg	58	47.49 N	9.47 E
Wolfe Island	212	44.12 N	76.26 W
Wolfe Island I	212	44.12 N	76.20 W
Wolfe Lake ⊜	212	44.40 N	76.30 W
Wolfen	54	51.40 N	12.16 E
Wolfenbüttel	52	52.10 N	10.32 E
Wolfenden, Mount ∧	182	50.26 N	127.33 W
Wolfenschiessen	58	46.55 N	8.24 E
Wolfertschwenden	58	47.53 N	10.16 E
Wolfforth	196	33.30 N	102.01 W
Wolfgangsee ⊜	64	47.44 N	13.26 E
Wolfhagen	56	51.19 N	9.10 E
Wölfis	54	50.48 N	10.46 E
Wolf Island I	212	44.33 N	78.15 W
Wolflake, In., U.S.	216	41.20 N	85.30 W
Wolf Lake, Mi., U.S.	216	43.15 N	86.06 W
Wolf Lake ⊜, Ab., Can.	182	54.42 N	110.59 W
Wolf Lake ⊜, On., Can.	212	44.44 N	78.11 W
Wolf Lake ⊜, Yk., Can.	180	60.40 N	131.40 W
Wolf Lake ⊜, U.S.	278	41.40 N	87.31 W
Wolf Lake ⊜, N.J., U.S.	276	40.57 N	74.42 W
Wolf Mountain ∧	180	65.17 N	154.02 W
Wolfpassing	264b	48.19 N	16.11 E
Wolf Point	202	48.05 N	105.38 W
Wolframs-Eschenbach	56	49.14 N	10.43 E
Wolfratshausen	64	47.54 N	11.25 E
Wolf Rock I 2	28	49.57 N	5.49 W
Wolf Run	214	40.30 N	80.54 W
Wolfsberg	61	46.51 N	14.51 E
Wolfsberg ∧ 2	263	51.38 N	6.27 E
Wolfsburg	54	52.25 N	10.47 E
Wolf's Castle	42	51.54 N	4.58 W
Wolfsegg am Hausruck	60	48.06 N	13.40 E
Wolfstein	56	49.35 N	7.36 E
Wolftrap Creek ≃	284c	38.58 N	77.17 W
Wolf Trap Farms for the Performing Arts ♦	284c	38.56 N	77.16 W
Wolfurt	58	47.28 N	9.45 E
Wolfville	186	45.05 N	64.22 W
Wolga → Volga ≃	72	45.55 N	47.52 E
Wolgan ≃	170	33.12 S	150.28 E
Wolgast	54	54.03 N	13.46 E
Wolgograd → Volgograd	80	48.44 N	44.25 E
Wolgograder Stausee → Volgogradskoje vodochranilišče ⊜ 1	80	49.20 N	45.00 E
Wolhusen	58	47.04 N	8.04 E
Wolin	30	53.50 N	14.35 E
Wolin I	54	53.55 N	14.31 E
Woliński Park Narodowy ♦	30	53.55 N	14.30 E
Wolkenstein	54	50.39 N	13.04 E
Wolkersdorf	61	48.23 N	16.31 E
Wölkisch	54	51.13 N	13.21 E
Wolkramshausen	54	51.25 N	10.44 E
Wollangambe ≃	170	33.21 S	150.35 E
Wollaston	42	52.15 N	0.40 W
Wollaston, Islas II	254	55.40 S	67.30 W
Wollaston Beach ⩡ 2	283	42.17 N	71.01 W
Wollaston Lake ⊜, On., Can.	212	44.50 N	77.50 W
Wollaston Lake ⊜, Sk., Can.	176	58.15 N	103.20 W
Wollaston Peninsula ≻ 1	176	70.00 N	115.00 W
Wollemi Creek ≃	170	33.13 S	150.31 E
Wollemi National Park ♦	166	32.50 S	150.30 E
Wollogorang	166	17.13 S	137.57 E
Wollombi	170	32.56 S	151.09 E
Wollombi Brook ≃	170	32.33 S	151.04 E
Wollondilly ≃	170	33.57 S	150.26 E
Wollongong	170	34.25 S	150.54 E
Wöllstein	56	49.49 N	7.58 E
Wolmaransstad	158	27.12 S	26.13 E
Wolmirsleben	54	51.57 N	11.29 E
Wolmirstedt	54	52.15 N	11.37 E
Wolnzach	60	48.36 N	11.37 E
Wołomin	30	52.21 N	21.14 E
Wołów	30	51.21 N	16.39 E
Wolowaru	115b	8.46 S	121.54 E
Wolseley, Sk., Can.	184	50.25 N	103.19 W
Wolseley, S. Afr.	158	33.26 S	19.12 E
Wolsey	198	44.24 N	98.28 W
Wolsingham	44	54.44 N	1.52 W
Wolsztyn	30	52.08 N	16.06 E
Wolterdingen	52	53.02 N	9.50 E
Woltersdorf, D.D.R.	54	52.24 N	12.22 E
Woltersdorf, D.D.R.	54	52.26 N	13.45 E
Woluogu	105	39.40 N	117.46 E
Wolvega	52	52.53 N	6.00 E
Wolverhampton	42	52.36 N	2.08 W
Wolverine	190	45.16 N	84.36 W
Wolverine Lake	281	42.33 N	83.29 W
Wolverine Loon Lake ⊜	281	42.33 N	83.30 W
Wolverine Mountain ∧	180	65.20 N	149.51 W
Wolvertem	50	50.57 N	4.18 E
Wolverton	42	52.04 N	0.50 W
Wolwehoek	158	26.55 S	27.48 E
Wölzerbach ≃	61	47.08 N	14.23 E
Wolziger See ⊜	54	52.16 N	13.50 E
Woman ≃	190	47.57 N	82.19 W
Wombarra	170	34.16 S	150.58 E
Wombat, Mount ∧	169	36.51 S	145.40 E
Wombeyan Caves ⩡ 5	170	34.18 S	149.56 E
Wombourne	42	52.32 N	2.11 W
Wombwell	44	53.31 N	1.24 W
Womelsdorf	208	40.22 N	76.11 W
Women's Rights National Historical Park ♦	210	42.54 N	76.47 W
Wommels	52	53.06 N	5.36 E
Wompatuck State Park ♦	283	42.13 N	70.51 W
Wonarah	162	19.55 S	136.20 E
Wondai	166	26.19 S	151.52 E
Wondelgem	50	51.05 N	3.43 E
Wonderfonteinspruit ≃	273d	26.16 S	27.42 E
Wonderkop	158	27.50 S	27.26 E
Wonder Lake	216	42.25 N	88.21 W
Wonderland	204	40.24 N	121.19 W
Wonderland Center ◆ 9	281	42.22 N	83.20 W
Wonderland Dog Track ♦	283	42.25 N	71.00 W
Wondinong	162	27.52 S	118.25 E
Wŏndong-ni	98	34.23 N	126.40 E
Wonersh	260	51.12 N	0.33 W
Wonewoc	190	43.39 N	90.13 W

Symbol	English	Deutsch	Español	Français	Português
≃	River	Fluß	Río	Rivière	Rio
≌	Canal	Kanal	Canal	Canal	Canal
ᒪ	Waterfall, Rapids	Wasserfall, Stromschnellen	Cascada, Rápidos	Chute d'eau, Rapides	Cascata, Rápidos
⊔	Strait	Meeresstraße	Estrecho	Détroit	Estreito
⊂	Bay, Gulf	Bucht, Golf	Bahía, Golfo	Baie, Golfe	Baía, Golfo
⊜	Lake, Lakes	See, Seen	Lago, Lagos	Lac, Lacs	Lago, Lagos
≡	Swamp	Sumpf	Pantano	Marais	Pântano
⊡	Ice Features, Glacier	Eis- und Gletscherformen	Accidentes Glaciales	Formes glaciaires	Acidentes glaciares
⊤	Other Hydrographic Features	Andere Hydrographische Objekte	Otros Elementos Hidrográficos	Autres données hydrographiques	Outros acidentes hidrográficos
✥	Submarine Features	Untermeerische Objekte	Accidentes Submarinos	Formes de relief sous-marin	Acidentes submarinos
□	Political Unit	Politische Einheit	Unidad Política	Entité politique	Unidade política
ᵾ	Cultural Institution	Kulturelle Institution	Institución Cultural	Institution culturelle	Instituição cultural
⊥	Historical Site	Historische Stätte	Sitio Histórico	Site historique	Sitio histórico
♦	Recreational Site	Erholungs- und Ferienort	Sitio de Recreo	Centre de loisirs	Area de Lazer
⊠	Airport	Flughafen	Aeropuerto	Aéroport	Aeroporto
■	Military Installation	Militäranlage	Instalación Militar	Installation militaire	Instalação militar
◆	Miscellaneous	Verschiedenes	Misceláneo	Divers	Diversos

ENGLISH — Name / Page / Lat.°′ / Long.°′
DEUTSCH — Name / Seite / Breite°′ / Länge°′ E = Ost

Wong ≃ 124 27.10 N 89.30 E
Wongan Hills 162 30.53 S 116.42 E
Wonga Park 274b 37.44 S 145.16 E
Wonga-Wongué, Parc National de ♦ 152 0.30 S 9.30 E
Wonggarasi 112 0.33 N 121.36 E
Wong Ka Wai 271d 22.24 N 113.58 E
Woniushi 104 42.31 N 123.03 E
Wŏnjang-ni 98 39.05 N 125.32 E
Wŏnju 98 37.22 N 127.58 E
Wonogiri 115a 7.49 S 110.55 E
Wonokromo 115a 7.18 S 112.44 E
Wonosari 115a 7.58 S 110.35 E
Wonosegoro 115a 7.18 S 110.39 E
Wonosobo 115a 7.22 S 109.54 E
Wonotobo Vallen ⌞ 250 4.22 N 57.58 W
Wonreli 112 8.05 S 127.09 E
Wŏnsan 98 39.09 N 127.25 E
Wonthaggi 169 38.36 S 145.35 E
Woocalla 166 31.42 S 137.13 E
Wood, Pa., U.S. 214 40.10 N 78.08 W
Wood, S.D., U.S. 198 43.29 N 100.28 W
Wood □[6], Oh., U.S. 216 41.22 N 83.39 W
Wood □[6], Tx., U.S. 222 32.48 N 95.20 W
Wood ≃, B.C., Can. 182 52.10 N 118.30 W
Wood ≃, Sk., Can. 184 50.08 N 106.10 W
Wood ≃, U.S. 207 41.26 N 71.43 W
Wood ≃, Ak., U.S. 180 64.35 N 148.41 W
Wood ≃, Ne., U.S. 198 41.02 N 98.05 W
Wood ≃, Wy., U.S. 202 44.07 N 108.58 W
Wood, Mount ∧, Yk., Can. 180 61.14 N 140.31 W
Wood, Mount ∧, Mt., U.S. 202 45.17 N 109.49 W
Woodacre 226 38.05 N 122.36 W
Woodall Mountain ∧[2] 194 34.45 N 88.11 W
Wood Bay ⊂ 180 69.45 N 129.00 W
Woodberry Forest 284c 38.48 N 76.56 W
Woodbine, Ga., U.S. 192 30.57 N 81.43 W
Woodbine, Ia., U.S. 198 41.44 N 95.42 W
Woodbine, Md., U.S. 208 39.21 N 77.03 W
Woodbine, N.J., U.S. 208 39.14 N 74.48 W
Woodbourne, N.Y., U.S. 210 41.45 N 74.35 W
Woodbourne, Oh., U.S. 218 39.38 N 84.10 W
Woodbourne, Pa., U.S. 285 40.12 N 74.53 W
Woodbridge, Eng., U.K. 42 52.06 N 1.19 E
Woodbridge, Ca., U.S. 226 38.09 N 121.18 W
Woodbridge, Ct., U.S. 207 41.21 N 73.00 W
Woodbridge, N.J., U.S. 210 40.33 N 74.17 W
Woodbridge, Va., U.S. 208 38.39 N 77.15 W
Woodbridge Center ◆[9] 276 40.33 N 74.18 W
Woodbridge Creek ≃ 276 40.32 N 74.15 W
Woodbridge Island I 283 42.48 N 70.50 W
Woodburn, Il., U.S. 219 39.03 N 90.00 W
Woodburn, In., U.S. 216 41.07 N 84.51 W
Woodburn, Or., U.S. 224 45.08 N 122.51 W
Woodbury, Eng., U.K. 42 50.41 N 3.24 W
Woodbury, Ct., U.S. 207 41.32 N 73.12 W
Woodbury, Ga., U.S. 192 32.59 N 84.34 W
Woodbury, Mi., U.S. 216 42.46 N 85.05 W
Woodbury, N.J., U.S. 208 39.50 N 75.09 W
Woodbury, N.Y., U.S. 276 40.49 N 73.28 W
Woodbury, Pa., U.S. 214 40.14 N 78.22 W
Woodbury, Tn., U.S. 194 35.49 N 86.04 W
Woodbury Creek ≃ 285 39.52 N 75.11 W
Woodbury Heights 285 39.49 N 75.09 W
Woodchester 168b 35.13 S 138.57 E
Woodchopper 180 65.18 N 143.25 W
Woodchurch 42 51.05 N 0.46 E
Woodcliff Lake 276 41.01 N 74.04 W
Woodcliff Lake ⊜ 276 41.01 N 74.03 W
Woodcock 214 41.45 N 80.05 W
Woodcock, Mount ∧ 162 19.16 S 134.02 E
Woodcrest, Ca., U.S. 228 33.52 N 117.21 W
Woodcrest, Pa., U.S. 285 39.59 N 75.35 W
Wood Dale 278 41.57 N 87.58 W
Woodenbong 166 28.23 S 152.37 E
Woodend 169 37.22 S 144.32 E
Woodfibre 182 49.40 N 123.15 W
Woodfield ◆[9] 278 42.03 N 88.03 W
Woodford, Austl. 171a 26.57 S 152.47 E
Woodford, Ire. 48 53.03 N 8.23 W
Woodford, Eng., U.K. 262 53.21 N 2.10 W
Woodford □[6], Il., U.S. 216 40.43 N 89.16 W
Woodford □[6], Ky., U.S. 218 38.06 N 84.15 W
Woodford ◆[8] 260 51.36 N 0.02 E
Woodford Aerodrome ⊠ 262 53.20 N 2.09 W
Woodford Bridge ◆[8] 260 51.36 N 0.04 E
Woodford Halse 42 52.10 N 1.12 W
Wood Green ◆[8] 260 51.36 N 0.07 W
Woodhall Spa 44 53.09 N 0.13 W
Woodham 260 51.21 N 0.30 W
Woodham Ferrers 260 51.40 N 0.36 E
Woodham Mortimer 260 51.43 N 0.37 E
Woodham Walter 260 51.44 N 0.37 E
Woodhaven 216 42.08 N 83.14 W
Woodhaven ◆[8] 276 40.41 N 73.51 W
Woodhead Reservoir ⊜[1] 262 53.30 N 1.52 W
Woodhill 275b 43.45 N 79.41 W
Wood Hill ∧[2] 283 42.39 N 71.13 W
Woodhull, Il., U.S. 190 41.10 N 90.18 W
Woodhull, N.Y., U.S. 210 42.05 N 77.25 W
Woodinville 224 47.45 N 122.09 W
Wood Islands 186 45.58 N 62.45 W
Woodlake, Ca., U.S. 204 36.25 N 119.06 W
Wood Lake, Ne., U.S. 198 42.38 N 100.14 W
Woodlake, Tx., U.S. 222 31.01 N 95.02 W
Wood Lake ⊜, On., Can. 212 45.01 N 79.05 W
Wood Lake ⊜, Sk., Can. 184 55.17 N 103.17 W
Woodland, Ca., U.S. 226 38.40 N 121.46 W
Woodland, Ga., U.S. 192 32.47 N 84.33 W
Woodland, Il., U.S. 216 40.43 N 87.44 W
Woodland, Me., U.S. 188 45.09 N 67.24 W
Woodland, Mi., U.S. 216 42.43 N 85.08 W
Woodland, N.C., U.S. 192 36.19 N 77.12 W
Woodland, Pa., U.S. 214 40.59 N 78.20 W
Woodland, Wa., U.S. 224 45.54 N 122.44 W
Woodland Beach 216 41.57 N 83.19 W
Woodland Heights 214 41.25 N 79.43 W
Woodland Hills ◆[8] 280 34.11 N 118.35 W
Woodland Hills Park ♦ 279a 41.28 N 81.36 W
Woodland Park, Co., U.S. 200 38.59 N 105.03 W
Woodland Park, Pa., U.S. 210 41.18 N 77.03 W
Woodlands, N.Z. 172 46.22 S 168.33 E
Woodlands, Sing. 271c 1.27 N 103.46 E
Woodlands, N.Y., U.S. 276 41.01 N 73.50 W
Woodlawn, Il., U.S. 219 38.20 N 89.02 W
Woodlawn, Ky., U.S. 194 37.02 N 88.34 W
Woodlawn, Md., U.S. 284b 39.19 N 76.43 W
Woodlawn, Md., U.S. 284c 38.57 N 76.53 W
Woodlawn, Wa., U.S. 224 47.01 N 123.48 W
Woodlawn ◆[8] 278 41.47 N 87.36 W
Woodlawn Beach 210 42.48 N 78.51 W
Woodlawn Heights 284b 39.11 N 76.39 W
Woodley 42 51.28 N 0.54 W
Woodlyn 285 39.52 N 75.20 W
Woodlynne 285 39.55 N 75.05 W
Woodmansey 44 53.50 N 0.29 W
Woodmansterne 260 51.19 N 0.10 W
Woodmere, N.Y., U.S. 210 40.37 N 73.42 W
Woodmere, Oh., U.S. 279a 41.28 N 81.29 W
Woodmoor 284b 39.20 N 76.44 W
Wood Mountain ∧ 184 49.14 N 106.20 W
Wood Mountain Indian Reserve ◆[4] 184 49.21 N 106.24 W
Woodplumpton 262 53.48 N 2.47 W
Woodport 276 40.59 N 74.36 W
Woodrarung Range ⋏ 162 27.10 S 115.30 E
Woodridge, Austl. 171a 27.38 S 153.06 E
Woodridge, Mb., Can. 184 49.17 N 96.09 W
Woodridge, Il., U.S. 216 41.44 N 88.03 W
Wood-Ridge, N.J., U.S. 276 40.50 N 74.05 W
Woodridge, N.Y., U.S. 210 41.43 N 74.34 W
Wood River, Ak., U.S. 180 59.04 N 158.26 W
Wood River, Il., U.S. 219 38.51 N 90.05 W
Wood River, Ne., U.S. 198 40.49 N 98.35 W
Wood River Lakes ⊜ 180 59.30 N 158.45 W
Wood River Mountains ⋏ 180 59.32 N 159.30 W
Woodroffe ≃ 166 21.28 S 137.58 E
Woodroffe, Mount ∧ 162 26.20 S 131.45 E
Woodrow 192 35.08 N 77.05 W
Woodrow Wilson Memorial Bridge ◆[5] 284c 38.48 N 77.02 W
Woodruff, Az., U.S. 200 34.46 N 110.02 W
Woodruff, S.C., U.S. 192 34.44 N 82.02 W
Woodruff, Wi., U.S. 190 45.53 N 89.41 W
Woodruff Creek ≃ 281 42.21 N 83.43 W
Woods 168b 34.15 S 138.31 E
Woods, Lake ⊜ 162 17.50 S 133.30 E
Woods, Lake of the ⊜ 184 49.15 N 94.45 W
Woods Bay ⊂ 212 45.08 N 80.00 W
Woodsboro, Md., U.S. 208 39.31 N 77.18 W
Woodsboro, Tx., U.S. 196 28.14 N 97.19 W
Woodsburgh 276 40.37 N 73.42 W
Woods Creek ≃, N.Y., U.S. 276 40.39 N 73.24 W
Woods Creek ≃, N.Y., U.S. 284a 43.04 N 78.58 W
Woodsfield 188 39.45 N 81.06 W
Woods Hole 207 41.31 N 70.40 W
Woodside, Austl. 166 38.31 S 146.52 E
Woodside, Austl. 168b 34.57 S 138.52 E
Woodside, Eng., U.K. 260 51.45 N 0.11 W
Woodside, Ca., U.S. 226 37.25 N 122.15 W
Woodside, De., U.S. 208 39.04 N 75.34 W
Woodside, Pa., U.S. 285 40.13 N 74.53 W
Woodside ◆[8] 276 40.45 N 73.55 W
Woodside National Historic Park ♦ 212 43.26 N 80.08 W
Woodson, Il., U.S. 219 39.38 N 90.13 W
Woodson, Tx., U.S. 196 33.01 N 99.03 W
Woods Point 169 37.35 S 146.15 E
Woods Reservoir ⊜[1] 194 35.20 N 86.00 W
Woodstock, Austl. 166 22.15 S 141.57 E
Woodstock, N.B., Can. 186 46.09 N 67.34 W
Woodstock, On., Can. 212 43.08 N 80.45 W
Woodstock, Eng., U.K. 42 51.52 N 1.21 W
Woodstock, Ct., U.S. 207 41.56 N 71.58 W
Woodstock, Il., U.S. 216 42.18 N 88.26 W
Woodstock, Md., U.S. 284b 39.19 N 76.52 W
Woodstock, N.Y., U.S. 210 42.02 N 74.07 W
Woodstock, Oh., U.S. 218 40.10 N 83.32 W
Woodstock, Vt., U.S. 188 43.37 N 72.31 W
Woodstock, Va., U.S. 188 38.52 N 78.30 W
Woodstown 208 39.39 N 75.19 W
Wood Street 260 51.15 N 0.38 W
Woodsville 188 44.09 N 72.02 W
Woodvale Airfield ⊠ 262 53.35 N 3.03 W
Woodview Manor 278 42.06 N 87.53 W
Wood Village 224 45.32 N 122.19 W
Woodville, Austl. 168b 34.53 S 138.32 E
Woodville, On., Can. 212 44.24 N 78.59 W
Woodville, N.Z. 172 40.20 S 175.52 E
Woodville, Al., U.S. 194 34.38 N 86.16 W
Woodville, Ca., U.S. 226 36.06 N 119.12 W
Woodville, Fl., U.S. 192 30.20 N 84.15 W
Woodville, Ga., U.S. 192 33.40 N 83.06 W
Woodville, Ma., U.S. 207 42.14 N 71.33 W
Woodville, Mi., U.S. 216 43.39 N 85.40 W
Woodville, Ms., U.S. 194 31.06 N 91.17 W
Woodville, N.Y., U.S. 210 42.40 N 77.22 W
Woodville, Oh., U.S. 214 41.27 N 83.21 W
Woodville, Tx., U.S. 194 30.46 N 94.24 W
Woodward, Ia., U.S. 190 41.51 N 93.55 W
Woodward, Ok., U.S. 196 36.26 N 99.23 W
Woodward, Pa., U.S. 210 40.54 N 77.21 W
Woodward Reservoir ⊜[1] 226 37.51 N 120.52 W
Woodway, Tx., U.S. 222 31.30 N 97.12 W
Woodway, Wa., U.S. 224 47.47 N 122.23 W
Woodworth, Oh., U.S. 214 40.59 N 80.40 W
Woodworth, Wi., U.S. 216 42.34 N 88.00 W
Woody ≃ 184 52.30 N 100.51 W
Woody Creek ≃ 202 47.27 N 106.21 W
Woody Head > 166 29.22 S 153.22 E
Woody Island 180 57.47 N 152.22 W
Wool 42 50.41 N 2.14 W
Woolacombe 42 51.10 N 4.13 W
Woolamai, Cape > 169 38.34 S 145.21 E
Wool Bay 168b 35.00 S 137.45 E
Wooldridge 158 33.13 S 27.15 E
Wooler 44 55.33 N 2.01 W
Woolford 208 38.30 N 76.11 W
Woolgangie 162 31.10 S 120.32 E
Woolgoolga 166 30.07 S 153.12 E
Woollahra 274a 33.53 S 151.15 E
Woolmarket 194 30.28 N 88.59 W
Woolooware Bay ⊂ 274a 34.02 S 151.09 E
Woolpit 42 52.13 N 0.54 E
Woolrich 210 41.12 N 77.23 W
Woolsey Peak ∧ 200 33.10 N 112.53 W
Woolston 262 53.24 N 2.32 W
Woolton ◆[8] 262 53.23 N 2.52 W
Woolwich ◆[8] 260 51.29 N 0.04 E
Woomargama 171b 35.50 S 147.15 E
Woomera 166 31.31 S 137.10 E
Woomera Prohibited Area ◆[4] 162 29.45 S 134.30 E
Woonona 170 34.21 S 150.55 E
Woonsocket, R.I., U.S. 207 42.00 N 71.30 W
Woonsocket, S.D., U.S. 198 44.03 N 98.16 W
Woorabinda 166 24.08 S 149.28 E
Wooramel 162 25.44 S 114.17 E
Wooramel ≃ 162 25.47 S 114.10 E
Woorim 171a 27.08 S 153.12 E
Wooroloo 168a 31.48 S 116.19 E
Wooster 214 40.48 N 81.56 W
Wootton 42 52.11 N 0.53 W
Wootton Bassett 42 51.33 N 1.54 W
Wootton Wawen 42 52.16 N 1.47 W
Woqooyi Gelbeed □[4] 144 10.00 N 44.00 E
Worb 58 46.56 N 7.34 E
Worbis 54 51.25 N 10.21 E
Worcester, S. Afr. 158 33.39 S 19.27 E
Worcester, Eng., U.K. 42 52.11 N 2.13 W
Worcester, Ma., U.S. 207 42.15 N 71.48 W
Worcester, N.Y., U.S. 210 42.35 N 74.45 W
Worcester, Pa., U.S. 285 40.12 N 75.21 W
Worcester □[6], Md., U.S. 208 38.11 N 75.24 W
Worcester □[6], Ma., U.S. 207 42.16 N 71.48 W
Worcester Municipal Airport ⊠ 207 42.16 N 71.52 W
Worden, Il., U.S. 219 38.55 N 89.50 W
Worden, Mt., U.S. 202 45.57 N 108.09 W
Worden Pond ⊜ 207 41.26 N 71.35 W
Wördern 61 48.20 N 16.13 E
Wörgl 64 47.29 N 12.04 E
Workai, Pulau I 164 6.40 S 134.40 E
Work Channel ⊔ 182 54.30 N 130.15 W
Workers' Stadium ♦ 271a 39.55 N 116.27 E
Workington 44 54.39 N 3.35 W
Worksop 44 53.18 N 1.07 W
Workum 52 52.57 N 5.26 E
Worland 202 44.01 N 107.57 W
World End Pond ⊜ 283 42.45 N 71.12 W
Worli ◆[8] 272c 19.01 N 72.50 E
Wörlitz 54 51.50 N 12.25 E
Wormditt → Orneta 30 54.08 N 20.08 E
Wormerveer 52 52.28 N 4.46 E
Wormhoudt 50 50.53 N 2.28 E
Wormit 46 56.25 N 2.59 W
Wormley 260 51.44 N 0.01 W
Worms 56 49.38 N 8.22 E
Worms Head > 42 51.34 N 4.20 W
Wormshill 260 51.17 N 0.42 E
Wörnitz ≃ 56 48.42 N 10.45 E
Woronesch → Voronež 78 51.40 N 39.10 E
Woronoco 207 42.09 N 72.49 W
Woronora 274a 34.01 S 151.03 E
Woronora ≃ 274a 34.00 S 151.04 E
Woronora Reservoir ⊜[1] 170 34.08 S 150.56 E
Worplesdon 260 51.16 N 0.37 W
Worpswede 52 53.13 N 8.56 E
Wörrstadt 56 49.50 N 8.07 E
Wörsbach ≃ 56 50.22 N 8.09 E
Worsbrough 44 53.31 N 1.29 W
Worsley 262 53.30 N 2.23 W
Worsthorne 262 53.47 N 2.11 W
Wörth, B.R.D. 56 49.48 N 9.09 E
Worth, B.R.D. 263 51.13 N 7.39 E
Worth, Il., U.S. 216 41.41 N 87.47 W
Worth, Lake ⊜[1] 222 32.48 N 97.28 W
Wortham 222 31.47 N 96.27 W
Wörth am Rhein 56 49.03 N 8.16 E
Wörth an der Donau 60 49.00 N 12.25 E
Wörth an der Isar 60 48.37 N 12.24 E
Worthen 42 52.38 N 3.00 W
Wörther See ⊜ 61 46.37 N 14.10 E
Worthing 42 50.48 N 0.23 W
Worthington, In., U.S. 194 39.07 N 86.58 W
Worthington, Md., U.S. 284b 39.14 N 76.47 W
Worthington, Mn., U.S. 198 43.37 N 95.35 W
Worthington, N.Y., U.S. 276 41.02 N 73.50 W
Worthington, Oh., U.S. 214 40.05 N 83.01 W
Worthington, Pa., U.S. 214 40.50 N 79.37 W
Worthington Peak ∧ 204 37.55 N 115.37 W
Wörthsee ⊜ 60 48.03 N 11.10 E
Worthville, Ky., U.S. 218 38.36 N 85.04 W
Worthville, Pa., U.S. 214 41.02 N 79.08 W
Worton 208 39.16 N 76.05 W
Wŏrun-dong 98 39.36 N 125.20 E
Wosimi 164 2.54 S 134.31 E
Wostok → Vostok ʊ[3] 9 78.30 S 106.50 E
Wosu 112 2.21 S 121.50 E
Wotap, Pulau I 164 7.21 S 131.16 E
Wotho I[1] 14 10.06 N 165.59 E
Wotje I[1] 14 9.27 N 170.02 E
Wotton, P.Q., Can. 206 45.44 N 71.48 W
Wotton, Eng., U.K. 260 51.13 N 0.23 W
Wotton-under-Edge 42 51.39 N 2.21 W
Wotu 112 2.35 S 120.48 E
Woudenberg 52 52.05 N 5.25 E
Woudrichem 52 51.49 N 5.00 E
Woudsend 52 52.56 N 5.36 E
Wouldham 260 51.21 N 0.28 E
Wounded Knee 198 43.08 N 102.21 W
Wounded Knee Creek ≃ 198 43.26 N 102.32 W
Wounta 236 13.33 N 83.32 W
Wounta, Laguna de ⊂ 236 13.38 N 83.34 W
Wour 146 21.21 N 15.57 E
Wouri ≃ 152 4.06 N 9.43 E
Woutchaba 152 5.13 N 13.05 E
Wouw 52 51.32 N 4.24 E
Wowan 166 23.55 S 150.12 E
Wowoni, Pulau I 112 4.08 S 123.06 E
Woyla ≃ 114 4.18 N 95.56 E
Woy Woy 170 33.30 S 151.20 E
Woźniki 30 50.36 N 19.03 E
Wragby 44 53.18 N 0.19 W
Wrangel Island → Vrangel'a, ostrov I 74 71.00 N 179.30 W
Wrangell 180 56.28 N 132.23 W
Wrangell, Cape > 181a 52.50 N 172.26 E
Wrangell, Mount ∧ 180 62.00 N 144.06 W
Wrangell Island I 180 56.15 N 132.10 W
Wrangell Mountains ⋏ 180 62.00 N 143.00 W
Wrangell-Saint Elias National Park ♦ 180 61.00 N 142.00 W
Wrath, Cape > 46 58.37 N 5.01 W
Wray 198 40.04 N 102.13 W
Wraysbury 260 51.27 N 0.33 W
Wrea Green 262 53.46 N 2.55 W
Wreck Bay ⊂ 170 35.11 S 150.40 E
Wreck Island I 208 37.16 N 75.48 W
Wreck Reef ✢[2] 166 22.13 S 155.17 E
Wrecks, Bay of ⊂ 174o 1.52 N 157.17 W
Wredenhagen 54 53.17 N 12.31 E
Wremen 52 53.39 N 8.30 E
Wren 216 40.48 N 84.46 W
Wrens 192 33.12 N 82.23 W
Wrentham, Ab., Can. 182 49.32 N 112.10 W
Wrentham, Eng., U.K. 42 52.23 N 1.40 E
Wrentham, Ma., U.S. 207 42.04 N 71.19 W
Wrentham State Forest ♦ 283 42.02 N 71.20 W
Wrexham 44 53.03 N 3.00 W
Wriezen 54 52.43 N 14.08 E
Wright 278 41.31 N 87.21 W
Wright, Mount ∧, Austl. 166 31.12 S 142.26 E
Wright, Mount ∧, Mt., U.S. 202 47.58 N 112.49 W
Wright Brothers National Memorial ⊥ 192 35.55 N 75.50 W
Wright City, Mo., U.S. 219 38.49 N 91.01 W
Wright City, Ok., U.S. 194 34.03 N 95.00 W
Wright City, Tx., U.S. 222 32.12 N 94.59 W
Wrightington Bar 262 53.37 N 2.42 W
Wright Patman Lake ⊜[1] 194 33.16 N 94.14 W
Wright-Patterson Air Force Base ■ 218 39.49 N 84.03 W
Wright Peak ∧ 204 38.59 N 122.46 W
Wrights 219 39.23 N 90.18 W
Wrightsboro 222 29.22 N 97.34 W
Wrights Corners 210 43.13 N 78.46 W
Wrightson, Mount ∧ 200 31.42 N 110.50 W
Wrightstown, N.J., U.S. 208 40.02 N 74.37 W
Wrightstown, Pa., U.S. 208 40.17 N 74.58 W
Wrightstown, Wi., U.S. 190 44.19 N 88.09 W
Wrightsville, Ga., U.S. 192 32.43 N 82.43 W
Wrightsville, Pa., U.S. 214 40.01 N 76.31 W
Wrightsville Beach 192 34.12 N 77.47 W
Wrightwood 228 34.21 N 117.37 W
Wrigley, N.T., Can. 180 63.16 N 123.37 W
Wrigley, Tn., U.S. 194 35.54 N 87.20 W
Wrigley Field ♦ 278 41.57 N 87.39 W
Wrigley Gulf ⊂ 9 74.00 S 129.00 W
Writtle 42 51.44 N 0.26 E
Wrocław (Breslau) 30 51.06 N 17.00 E
Wrocław □[4] 30 51.15 N 17.00 E
Wrong Lake ⊜ 184 52.38 N 96.10 W
Wronki 30 52.43 N 16.23 E
Wrotham 42 51.19 N 0.19 E
Wrotham Heath 260 51.18 N 0.21 E
Wrottesley, Cape > 176 74.33 N 121.32 W
Wroughton 42 51.31 N 1.46 W
Wroxham 42 52.42 N 1.24 E
Wroxton 184 51.14 N 101.53 W
Września 30 52.20 N 17.34 E
Wschowa 30 51.48 N 16.19 E
Wu ≃, Zhg. 98 34.25 N 117.55 E
Wu ≃, Zhg. 100 28.57 N 116.39 E
Wu ≃, Zhg. 100 24.48 N 113.35 E
Wu ≃, Zhg. 102 27.12 N 109.48 E
Wu ≃, Zhg. 102 29.43 N 107.24 E
Wu ≃, Zhg. 102 27.03 N 109.53 E
Wu'an 98 36.40 N 114.12 E
Wubaozhen 107 29.14 N 104.29 E
Wubin 162 30.06 S 116.38 E
Wubu 102 37.33 N 110.39 E
Wuchagou 89 46.46 N 120.16 E
Wuchang, Zhg. 89 44.54 N 127.08 E
Wuchang → Wuhan, Zhg. 100 30.36 N 114.17 E
Wuchang Hu ⊜ 100 30.17 N 116.47 E
Wucheng (Jiucheng), Zhg. 98 37.13 N 116.02 E
Wucheng, Zhg. 98 37.09 N 115.53 E
Wucheng, Zhg. 100 29.36 N 118.10 E
Wucheng, Zhg. 100 33.28 N 113.44 E
Wucheng, Zhg. 100 29.10 N 115.59 E
Wuch'i 100 24.16 N 120.31 E
Wuchin → Changzhou 106 31.47 N 119.57 E
Wuch'iu Yü I 100 25.00 N 119.27 E
Wuchow → Wuzhou 102 23.30 N 111.27 E
Wuchuan, Zhg. 102 21.25 N 110.40 E
Wuchuan, Zhg. 102 28.25 N 107.56 E
Wuchuan, Zhg. 102 41.05 N 111.23 E
Wuchung → Wuzhong 102 37.57 N 106.10 E
Wucun 105 38.57 N 115.19 E
Wuda 102 39.30 N 106.40 E
Wudao 98 39.28 N 121.28 E
Wudaogou, Zhg. 98 41.43 N 127.05 E
Wudaogou, Zhg. 98 42.08 N 125.51 E
Wudaoliang 120 35.11 N 93.35 E
Wudaolianggou 104 40.59 N 120.35 E
Wudi 98 37.44 N 117.35 E
Wudian, Zhg. 100 32.42 N 117.18 E
Wudian, Zhg. 100 31.57 N 112.46 E
Wuding 102 25.32 N 102.23 E
Wuding ≃ 102 37.05 N 110.20 E
Wudinna 166 33.03 S 135.28 E
Wudu, Zhg. 100 27.37 N 119.00 E
Wudu, Zhg. 100 28.23 N 118.14 E
Wudu, Zhg. 102 33.24 N 104.50 E
Wuduhe 102 31.03 N 111.03 E
Wuerqihan 89 49.37 N 121.45 E
Wufeng 102 30.11 N 110.33 E
Wufeng Shan I 106 31.07 N 120.16 E
Wufengxi 107 30.37 N 104.29 E
Wufu 100 30.06 N 120.58 E
Wugang 102 26.44 N 110.38 E
Wugong 102 34.20 N 108.04 E
Wugong Shan ∧ 100 27.35 N 114.18 E
Wugong Shan ⋏ 100 27.21 N 113.50 E
Wugouying 100 33.28 N 114.08 E
Wugunuoer 89 49.10 N 119.19 E
Wuhai 102 39.39 N 106.41 E
Wuhan 100 30.36 N 114.17 E
Wuhe, Zhg. 100 33.10 N 117.54 E
Wuhe, Zhg. 100 24.26 N 115.25 E
Wuhle ≃ 264a 52.29 N 13.34 E
Wuhsi → Wuxi 106 31.35 N 120.18 E
Wuhsing → Huzhou 106 30.52 N 120.06 E
Wuhu, Zhg. 100 31.11 N 118.35 E
Wuhu, Zhg. 100 31.21 N 118.22 E
Wuhua 100 23.57 N 115.48 E
Wuhuanchi 104 42.20 N 121.51 E
Wuhuang 107 29.58 N 104.46 E
Wuhudongmiao 102 38.19 N 107.20 E
Wüjang 120 33.38 N 79.50 E
Wuji, Zhg. 98 38.13 N 114.57 E
Wuji, Zhg. 98 34.12 N 119.02 E
Wujia ≃ 102 41.10 N 108.45 E
Wujiabeigou 104 40.57 N 123.50 E
Wujiang, Zhg. 100 27.14 N 115.15 E
Wujiang, Zhg. 100 31.52 N 118.28 E
Wujiang, Zhg. 106 31.10 N 120.38 E
Wujiangdu 102 27.16 N 106.48 E
Wujianpu 107 29.10 N 105.50 E
Wujiapai 105 39.32 N 117.18 E
Wujiapu 105 38.52 N 117.07 E
Wujiazhen 107 29.38 N 105.24 E
Wujiazhuang, Zhg. 105 40.35 N 115.20 E
Wujiazhuang, Zhg. 106 32.18 N 120.10 E
Wujiazi, Zhg. 89 46.27 N 123.34 E
Wujiazi, Zhg. 104 42.13 N 122.08 E
Wujiazi, Zhg. 104 42.30 N 121.10 E
Wujing 100 25.16 N 114.36 E
Wukang 106 30.33 N 119.58 E
Wukari 150 7.51 N 9.47 E
Wukeshu, Zhg. 89 46.02 N 123.45 E
Wukeshu, Zhg. 89 44.48 N 126.08 E
Wulai 100 24.52 N 121.33 E
Wulajia 89 48.23 N 129.58 E
Wulanheduojia 102 42.40 N 113.20 E
Wulanhutong 98 41.44 N 114.49 E
Wulanmutou 104 42.23 N 121.21 E
Wulanwusu, Zhg. 86 44.20 N 85.50 E
Wulanwusu, Zhg. 102 41.39 N 107.48 E
Wular Lake ⊜ 123 34.20 N 74.33 E
Wulasitai, Zhg. 89 43.15 N 121.27 E
Wulasitai, Zhg. 89 43.28 N 122.44 E
Wulateqianqi 102 40.39 N 109.05 E
Wulaxi 102 28.38 N 101.40 E
Wuleidao Wan ⊂ 98 36.55 N 122.00 E
Wulfen 52 51.43 N 7.00 E
Wülfrath 56 51.17 N 7.02 E
Wulfsen 52 53.18 N 10.08 E
Wulfsode 52 53.04 N 10.13 E
Wulften 52 51.40 N 10.10 E
Wulian (Hongning) 98 35.47 N 119.15 E
Wulian Feng ⋏ 102 28.03 N 103.57 E
Wuliangdian 104 41.52 N 122.16 E
Wuliang Shan ⋏ 102 24.30 N 100.45 E
Wuliaru, Pulau I 164 7.27 S 131.04 E
Wulichuan 102 33.49 N 111.08 E
Wulie ≃ 105 40.54 N 117.55 E
Wuling 98 35.53 N 114.36 E
Wuling Shan ∧ 105 40.36 N 117.29 E
Wulitaizi 104 41.28 N 123.21 E
Wulizhuang 100 33.49 N 118.57 E
Wulka ≃ 61 47.52 N 16.40 E
Wüllen 52 52.04 N 6.58 E
Wullwye Creek ≃ 171b 36.30 S 148.49 E
Wulong, Zhg. 102 29.20 N 107.43 E
Wulong, Zhg. 104 41.39 N 124.13 E
Wulong ≃ 98 36.35 N 120.56 E
Wulongbei 98 40.21 N 124.16 E
Wulsdorf ◆[8] 52 53.30 N 8.35 E
Wultschau 61 48.42 N 14.50 E
Wulu ≃ 85 39.38 N 74.38 E
Wuluhan 115a 8.21 S 113.33 E
Wuluhayingzi 104 42.20 N 121.34 E
Wulumuch'i → Ürümqi 90 43.48 N 87.35 E
Wulumuqi → Ürümqi 90 43.48 N 87.35 E
Wuluo 102 26.09 N 108.15 E
Wulur 164 7.09 S 128.39 E
Wulu Station ◆[5] 271a 39.56 N 116.16 E
Wum 152 6.23 N 10.04 E
Wumang Dao I 98 39.14 N 123.03 E
Wumiaoxiang 107 30.23 N 104.17 E
Wuming 102 23.10 N 108.18 E
Wümme ≃ 52 53.10 N 8.44 E
Wunamu 86 46.06 N 85.44 E
Wundowie 168a 31.46 S 116.22 E
Wundwin 110 21.05 N 96.02 E
Wuneba 154 4.50 N 30.20 E
Wungong Brook ≃ 168a 32.06 S 115.59 E
Wuning 100 29.17 N 115.06 E
Wünnenberg 52 51.31 N 8.42 E
Wunnummin Lake ⊜ 176 52.55 N 89.10 W
Wun Rog 140 9.00 N 28.21 E
Wünschendorf 54 50.48 N 12.05 E
Wünsdorf 54 52.10 N 13.28 E
Wunsiedel 60 50.02 N 12.01 E
Wunstorf 52 52.25 N 9.26 E
Wuntho 110 23.54 N 95.41 E
Wunuer 89 48.53 N 121.15 E
Wupaowan 107 29.50 N 103.59 E
Wupatki National Monument ♦ 200 35.24 N 111.14 W
Wuping 100 25.08 N 116.06 E
Wupper ≃ 263 51.05 N 7.00 E
Wuppertal, B.R.D. 56 51.16 N 7.11 E
Wuppertal, B.R.D. 263 51.16 N 7.11 E
Wuppertal, S. Afr. 158 32.15 S 19.15 E
Wuqi, Zhg. 100 27.10 N 120.23 E
Wuqi, Zhg. 102 37.08 N 108.10 E
Wuqia 85 39.42 N 75.13 E
Wuqiang (Xiaofan) 98 38.03 N 115.58 E
Wuqing (Yangcun) 105 39.23 N 117.04 E
Wuraming 168a 32.48 S 116.16 E
Wurarga 162 28.25 S 116.17 E
Würenlingen 58 47.32 N 8.16 E
Wurgwitz 54 51.01 N 13.37 E
Wurm ≃, B.R.D. 56 51.08 N 6.10 E
Würm ≃, B.R.D. 56 48.53 N 8.42 E
Würm ≃, B.R.D. 60 48.10 N 11.28 E
Wurmannsquick 60 48.21 N 12.47 E
Wurmberg ∧ 54 51.45 N 10.37 E
Wurno 150 13.17 N 5.24 E
Wurong 164 6.07 S 140.47 E
Würselen 56 50.49 N 6.08 E
Wurtsboro 210 41.35 N 74.29 W
Wurtsboro Hills 210 41.36 N 74.30 W
Wurtsmith Air Force Base ■ 190 44.27 N 83.23 W
Wuruf 164 6.43 S 146.25 E
Wuryantoro 115a 7.54 S 110.51 E
Wurzbach 54 50.28 N 11.32 E
Würzburg 56 49.48 N 9.56 E
Wurzen 54 51.22 N 12.44 E
Wusanga 152 3.22 S 22.50 E
Wusha 100 30.39 N 117.18 E
Wushan, Zhg. 100 32.04 N 117.03 E
Wushan, Zhg. 102 34.38 N 105.04 E
Wushan, Zhg. 102 31.05 N 109.48 E
Wushan, Zhg. 106 31.44 N 118.58 E
Wusheng, Zhg. 100 29.56 N 119.25 E
Wusheng, Zhg. 107 30.21 N 106.17 E
Wushengchang 107 29.00 N 103.43 E
Wushenqi 102 38.58 N 109.01 E
Wushi, Zhg. 102 22.11 N 110.11 E
Wushi, Zhg. 106 31.44 N 120.59 E
Wushishi 150 9.46 N 6.07 E
Wushu 100 26.20 N 114.56 E
Wusi 175f 15.22 S 166.36 E
Wusih → Wuxi 106 31.35 N 120.18 E
Wuskwatim Lake ⊜ 184 55.32 N 98.32 W
Wusong 106 31.23 N 121.29 E
Wusong ≃ 106 31.15 N 121.29 E
Wust 54 52.33 N 12.07 E
Wüsten 52 52.06 N 8.47 E
Wüstensachsen 56 50.30 N 10.00 E
Wusterhausen 54 52.54 N 12.28 E
Wusterhusen 54 54.07 N 13.37 E
Wustermark 54 52.33 N 12.56 E
Wüstermarke 54 51.49 N 13.36 E
Wusterwitz 54 52.22 N 12.18 E
Wüsting 52 53.07 N 8.20 E
Wustrow, B.R.D. 54 52.55 N 11.07 E
Wustrow, D.D.R. 54 54.05 N 11.34 E
Wustrow >[1] 54 54.05 N 11.34 E
Wusuli (Ussuri) ≃ 89 48.27 N 135.04 E
Wusuo 100 25.02 N 116.02 E
Wuta 106 31.31 N 120.39 E
Wutach ≃ 58 47.37 N 8.15 E
Wutai, Zhg. 85 39.28 N 78.09 E
Wutai, Zhg. 86 44.36 N 82.06 E
Wutai, Zhg. 98 41.18 N 113.59 E
Wutai, Zhg. 102 38.44 N 113.17 E
Wutai Shan ∧ 98 39.04 N 113.35 E
Wutai Shan ⋏ 98 39.13 N 113.45 E
Wutaizi 104 42.27 N 123.17 E
Wutan 102 28.29 N 111.40 E
Wutanchang 107 29.15 N 106.04 E
Wutang 106 31.31 N 119.10 E
Wutangdun 106 30.38 N 120.08 E
Wutangjie 100 29.59 N 122.22 E
Wuteve, Mount ∧ 150 8.09 N 9.56 W
Wutianzhen 100 30.23 N 117.12 E
Wutong 102 25.18 N 110.01 E
Wutonghaolai 89 42.55 N 120.15 E
Wutongqiao 107 29.26 N 103.51 E
Wutongwozi 102 42.27 N 95.17 E
Wutsin → Changzhou 106 31.47 N 119.57 E
Wutun 100 27.51 N 118.04 E
Wut'ungch'iao → Wutongqiao 107 29.26 N 103.51 E
Wutungkiao → Wutongqiao 107 29.26 N 103.51 E
Wutuohuo 102 40.51 N 101.48 E
Wuustwezel 50 51.23 N 4.36 E
Wuvulu Island I 164 1.45 S 142.50 E
Wuwei, Zhg. 100 31.18 N 117.54 E
Wuwei (Liangzhou), Zhg. 102 37.58 N 102.49 E
Wuxi, Zhg. 102 31.25 N 109.34 E
Wuxi, Zhg. 106 31.20 N 118.39 E
Wuxi (Wuhsi), Zhg. 106 31.35 N 120.18 E
Wuxi ≃ 100 29.00 N 118.56 E
Wuxiang 102 36.51 N 113.00 E
Wuxingchang 106 31.13 N 119.23 E
Wuxuan 102 23.36 N 109.42 E
Wuyang, Zhg. 100 33.26 N 113.34 E
Wuyang, Zhg. 100 25.41 N 115.55 E
Wuyang, Zhg. 102 26.41 N 110.20 E
Wuyi, Zhg. 98 37.49 N 115.54 E
Wuyi, Zhg. 100 32.13 N 118.26 E
Wuyi, Zhg. 100 28.54 N 119.48 E
Wuying 89 48.05 N 129.15 E
Wuyi Shan ⋏ 90 27.52 N 117.40 E
Wuyuan, Zhg. 100 29.15 N 117.49 E
Wuyuan, Zhg. 102 41.06 N 108.29 E
Wuyun 89 49.16 N 129.37 E
Wuyunqiao 100 26.02 N 114.52 E
Wuyur ≃ 89 47.00 N 124.10 E
Wuzaizi 104 42.28 N 123.57 E
Wuzhai 102 38.58 N 111.55 E
Wuzhan 89 45.51 N 126.17 E
Wuzhen 106 30.46 N 120.29 E
Wuzhi Shan ∧, Zhg. 105 40.29 N 118.00 E
Wuzhi Shan ∧, Zhg. 110 18.57 N 109.43 E
Wuzhong 102 38.00 N 106.10 E
Wuzhou (Wuchow) 102 23.30 N 111.27 E
Wuzong 106 32.14 N 121.03 E
Wyaaba Creek ≃ 164 16.27 S 141.35 E
Wyaconda 194 40.23 N 91.55 W
Wyaconda ≃ 194 40.04 N 91.30 W
Wyalkatchem 162 31.10 S 117.22 E
Wyalusing 210 41.40 N 76.15 W
Wyalusing Creek ≃ 210 41.40 N 76.16 W
Wyandanch 276 40.45 N 73.21 W
Wyandot 214 40.44 N 83.08 W
Wyandot □[6] 214 40.50 N 83.17 W
Wyandotte 216 42.12 N 83.09 W
Wyandotte Cave ⊥[5] 218 38.14 N 86.18 W
Wyandotte National Wildlife Refuge ◆[4] 281 42.14 N 83.08 W
Wyandra 166 27.15 S 145.59 E
Wyangala, Lake ⊜[1] 166 33.58 S 148.55 E
Wyano 214 40.12 N 79.42 W
Wyatt, In., U.S. 216 41.31 N 86.10 W
Wyatt, Mo., U.S. 194 36.54 N 89.13 W
Wycheproof 166 36.05 S 143.14 E
Wychwood 273d 26.12 S 28.08 E
Wyckoff 210 41.00 N 74.10 W
Wydgee 162 28.51 S 117.49 E
Wydgelee 158 34.23 S 20.26 E
Wy-Dit-Joli-Village 261 49.06 N 1.50 E
Wye 42 51.11 N 0.56 E
Wye ≃, On., Can. 212 44.44 N 79.52 W
Wye ≃, U.K. 42 51.37 N 2.39 W
Wye ≃, Eng., U.K. 44 53.12 N 1.37 W
Wyee 170 33.11 S 151.29 E
Wye Lake ⊜ 212 44.43 N 79.52 W
Wyemandoo ∧ 162 28.31 S 118.32 E
Wyeville 190 44.01 N 90.23 W
Wyhl 58 48.09 N 7.39 E
Wyhra ≃ 54 51.09 N 12.27 E
Wyk 30 54.42 N 8.34 E
Wyke Regis 42 50.36 N 2.29 W
Wykoff 190 43.42 N 92.16 W
Wylandville 279b 40.12 N 80.08 W
Wyleswood Lake ⊜ 279a 41.20 N 81.55 W
Wylie, Pa., U.S. 279b 40.27 N 79.59 W
Wylie, Tx., U.S. 222 33.01 N 96.32 W
Wylie, Lake ⊜[1] 192 35.07 N 81.02 W
Wylye ≃ 42 51.04 N 1.52 W
Wymah 171b 36.02 S 147.17 E
Wymark 184 50.07 N 107.44 W
Wymeswold 42 52.47 N 1.06 W
Wymondham 42 52.34 N 1.07 E
Wymore 198 40.07 N 96.39 W
Wynantskill 210 42.42 N 73.39 W
Wynberg 158 34.02 S 18.28 E
Wynbring 162 30.33 S 133.32 E
Wyncote 285 40.05 N 75.08 W
Wyndham, Austl. 164 15.28 S 128.06 E
Wyndham, N.Z. 172 46.20 S 168.51 E
Wyndmere 198 46.16 N 97.07 W
Wyndmoor 285 40.04 N 75.11 W
Wynigen 58 47.06 N 7.40 E
Wynndel 182 49.11 N 116.33 W
Wynne 194 35.13 N 90.47 W
Wynnewood, Ok., U.S. 196 34.38 N 97.09 W
Wynnewood, Pa., U.S. 285 40.00 N 75.16 W
Wynniatt Bay ⊂ 176 72.55 N 110.30 W
Wynnum 171a 27.27 S 153.10 E
Wynona 196 36.32 N 96.19 W
Wynoochee ≃ 224 46.58 N 123.35 W
Wynoochee Lake ⊜[1] 224 47.25 N 123.35 W
Wynot 198 42.44 N 97.10 W
Wynyard, Austl. 166 40.59 S 145.41 E
Wynyard, Sk., Can. 184 51.47 N 104.10 W
Wyocena 190 43.29 N 89.18 W
Wyodak 198 44.17 N 105.22 W
Wyola Lake ⊜ 162 29.08 S 130.17 E
Wyoming, On., Can. 190 42.57 N 82.07 W
Wyoming, De., U.S. 208 39.07 N 75.33 W
Wyoming, Il., U.S. 190 41.03 N 89.46 W
Wyoming, Ia., U.S. 190 42.03 N 91.00 W
Wyoming, Mi., U.S. 216 42.54 N 85.42 W
Wyoming, N.Y., U.S. 210 42.49 N 78.05 W
Wyoming, Oh., U.S. 218 39.13 N 84.27 W
Wyoming, Pa., U.S. 210 41.18 N 75.50 W
Wyoming, R.I., U.S. 207 41.30 N 71.42 W
Wyoming □[6], N.Y., U.S. 210 42.44 N 78.08 W
Wyoming □[6], Pa., U.S. 210 41.32 N 75.57 W
Wyoming □[3] 178 43.00 N 107.30 W
Wyoming Peak ∧ 200 42.36 N 110.37 W
Wyomissing 208 40.19 N 75.57 W
Wyong 170 33.17 S 151.25 E
Wyong ≃ 170 33.18 S 151.28 E
Wyperfield National Park ♦ 166 35.30 S 142.00 E
Wyre ≃ 44 53.55 N 3.00 W
Wyreema 171a 27.39 S 151.52 E
Wyre Forest ◆[3] 42 52.23 N 2.23 W
Wyrzysk 30 53.10 N 17.15 E
Wyśmierzyce 30 51.38 N 20.49 E
Wysoka 30 53.11 N 17.05 E
Wysokie Mazowieckie 30 52.56 N 22.32 E
Wysox 210 41.46 N 76.24 W
Wyszków 30 52.36 N 21.28 E
Wyszogród 30 52.23 N 20.11 E
Wythenshawe ◆[8] 262 53.24 N 2.17 W
Wythenshawe Hall ⊥ 262 53.24 N 2.17 W
Wytheville 192 36.56 N 81.05 W
Wytschegda → Vyčegda ≃ 24 61.18 N 46.36 E
Wyvis, Ben ∧ 46 57.42 N 4.35 W

X

Xaafuun 144 10.25 N 51.16 E
Xàbia 34 38.47 N 0.10 E
Xabregas ◆[8] 266c 38.44 N 9.07 W
Xá-Cassau 152 9.02 S 20.14 E
Xaclbal ≃ 236 16.06 N 90.58 W
Xadani 234 15.56 N 96.04 W
Xaidulla 120 36.21 N 78.02 E
Xainza 120 30.57 N 88.38 E
Xaitongmoin 124 29.22 N 88.15 E
Xai-Xai 156 25.02 S 33.34 E
Xalin 144 9.06 N 48.37 E
Xalpatláhuac 234 17.01 N 99.18 W
Xaltianguis 234 17.04 N 99.50 W
Xam (Chu) ≃ 110 19.53 N 105.45 E
Xambioá 250 6.25 S 48.40 W
Xambrê ≃ 255 24.02 S 53.59 W
Xam Nua 110 20.25 N 104.02 E
Xá-Muteba 152 9.34 S 17.50 E
Xan (San) ≃ 110 13.32 N 105.58 E
Xang ≃ 124 29.22 N 89.09 E
Xangongo 152 16.43 S 15.01 E
Xanten 52 51.39 N 6.26 E
Xánthi 38 41.08 N 24.53 E
Xanxerê 252 26.53 S 52.23 W
Xapecó ≃ 252 27.06 S 53.01 W
Xapuri 248 10.39 S 68.31 W
Xapuri ≃ 248 10.39 S 68.30 W
Xarardheere 144 4.39 N 47.51 E
Xar Moron ≃, Zhg. 90 43.25 N 121.41 E
Xar Moron ≃, Zhg. 102 43.02 N 111.20 E
Xarrama ≃ 34 38.14 N 8.20 W
Xàtiva (Játiva) 34 38.59 N 0.31 W
Xau, Lake ≚ 156 21.15 S 24.38 E
Xauen → Chaouen 148 35.10 N 5.16 W
Xavantes ≃ 250 10.40 S 50.41 W
Xavantina 255 21.15 S 52.48 W
Xa Vo Dat 110 11.09 N 107.31 E
Xaxim 252 26.56 S 52.31 W
X-Can 232 20.50 N 87.43 W
Xelva 34 39.45 N 0.59 W
Xenia, Il., U.S. 219 38.38 N 88.38 W
Xenia, Oh., U.S. 218 39.41 N 83.55 W
Xénô 110 16.35 N 104.50 E
Xercavins, Arroyo de ≃ 266d 41.30 N 2.02 E
Xerém 256 22.33 S 43.18 W
Xeres → Jerez de la Frontera 34 36.41 N 6.08 W

Symbols in the index entries represent the broad categories identified in the key at the right. Symbols with superior numbers (⋏[1]) identify subcategories (see complete key on page I · 1).

Symbole im Register stellen die rechts im Schlüssel erklärten Kategorien dar. Symbole mit hochgestellten Ziffern (⋏[1]) bezeichnen Unterabteilungen einer Kategorie (vgl. vollständiger Schlüssel auf Seite I · 1).

Los símbolos incluídos en el texto del índice representan las grandes categorias identificadas con la clave a la derecha. Los símbolos con numeros en su parte superior (⋏[1]) identifican las subcategorías (véase la clave completa en la página I · 1).

Les symboles de l'index représentent les catégories indiquées dans la légende à droite. Les symboles suivis d'un indice (⋏[1]) représentent des sous-catégories (voir légende complète à la page I · 1).

Os símbolos incluídos no texto do índice representam as grandes categorias identificadas com a chave à direita. Os símbolos com números em sua parte superior (⋏[1]) identificam as subcategorias (veja-se a chave completa à página I · 1).

∧ Mountain	Berg	Montaña	Montagne	Montanha
⋏ Mountains	Gebirge	Montañas	Montagnes	Montanhas
× Pass	Paß	Paso	Col	Passo
V Valley, Canyon	Tal, Cañon	Valle, Cañón	Vallée, Canyon	Vale, Canhão
≚ Plain	Ebene	Llano	Plaine	Planície
> Cape	Kap	Cabo	Cap	Cabo
I Island	Insel	Isla	Île	Ilha
II Islands	Inseln	Islas	Îles	Ilhas
⊥ Other Topographic Features	Andere Topographische Objekte	Otros Elementos Topográficos	Autres données topographiques	Outros acidentes topográficos

ESPAÑOL: Nombre · Página · Lat.°′ · Long.°′ W = Oeste
FRANÇAIS: Nom · Page · Lat.°′ · Long.°′ W = Ouest
PORTUGUÊS: Nome · Página · Lat.°′ · Long.°′ W = Oeste

Xertigny	58	48.03 N	6.24 E
Xhumo	156	21.07 S	24.42 E
Xi ≃, Zhg.	100	30.21 N	115.06 E
Xi ≃, Zhg.	100	24.34 N	117.30 E
Xi ≃, Zhg.	100	25.14 N	118.03 E
Xi ≃, Zhg.	102	42.20 N	100.20 E
Xi ≃, Zhg.	102	22.25 N	113.23 E
Xi ≃, Zhg.	104	41.15 N	123.32 E
Xi ≃, Zhg.	104	41.30 N	121.26 E
Xi ≃, Zhg.	107	30.26 N	103.48 E
Xiaang	106	30.45 N	120.07 E
Xiaba	100	24.54 N	116.06 E
Xiabai, Zhg.	106	30.29 N	120.00 E
Xiabai, Zhg.	106	31.12 N	119.50 E
Xiabanghu	100	30.31 N	112.38 E
Xiabian	104	40.51 N	120.30 E
Xiabuji	100	28.19 N	116.20 E
Xiacang	105	39.47 N	117.24 E
Xiache	100	24.40 N	115.08 E
Xiachengzi	89	44.41 N	130.27 E
Xiachuan Dao I	102	21.40 N	112.37 E
Xiacun	105	40.21 N	116.14 E
Xiadao	100	26.34 N	118.16 E
Xiadian, Zhg.	98	37.06 N	120.19 E
Xiadian, Zhg.	100	31.26 N	114.17 E
Xiadian, Zhg.	105	39.57 N	116.55 E
Xiadianjie	100	25.13 N	118.27 E
Xiafeidi	98	42.18 N	124.21 E
Xiafu, Zhg.	100	25.01 N	113.41 E
Xiafu, Zhg.	100	23.52 N	115.45 E
Xiagaixin	102	22.36 N	99.59 E
Xiagang	106	31.55 N	120.13 E
Xiagezhuang	98	36.41 N	120.25 E
Xiaguan, Zhg.	98	39.07 N	114.09 E
Xiaguan, Zhg.	102	25.34 N	100.14 E
Xiaguan, Zhg.	106	32.06 N	118.44 E
Xiaguanjunchang	104	41.28 N	121.40 E
Xiaguanpi	100	24.04 N	117.06 E
Xiagucheng	102	36.47 N	102.53 E
Xiagucun	106	30.56 N	119.09 E
Xiahada	104	41.58 N	124.08 E
Xiahailangzhai	104	41.35 N	123.46 E
Xiahe	102	35.18 N	102.30 E
Xiahuangjintun	104	41.57 N	123.48 E
Xiahuayuan	105	40.29 N	115.17 E
Xiajiabaozi	98	42.16 N	124.37 E
Xiajialou	104	42.25 N	123.39 E
Xiajiang	100	27.32 N	115.08 E
Xiajiangdun	106	31.14 N	120.24 E
Xiajiangwu	106	30.29 N	119.00 E
Xiajiayuan	106	32.13 N	120.38 E
Xiajiezi	102	27.28 N	101.35 E
Xiajin	98	36.55 N	115.57 E
Xiakou	100	28.28 N	118.31 E
Xialianggang	105	39.14 N	115.07 E
Xialufang	102	31.11 N	103.38 E
Xiamaguan	102	37.14 N	106.28 E
Xiamen (Amoy)	100	24.28 N	118.07 E
Xiamen Gang ⊂	100	24.19 N	118.10 E
Xiamianzhen	107	30.08 N	106.32 E
Xiamin'ansutai	104	41.54 N	120.53 E
Xiamocun	106	31.09 N	119.22 E
Xi'an (Sian)	102	34.15 N	108.52 E
Xian ≃	107	29.22 N	104.44 E
Xianchenggu	98	36.53 N	115.17 E
Xiandu	100	25.04 N	117.44 E
Xianfeng, Zhg.	100	25.42 N	117.53 E
Xianfeng, Zhg.	102	29.41 N	109.02 E
Xiang ≃, Zhg.	100	25.35 N	115.49 E
Xiang ≃, Zhg.	102	29.00 N	112.56 E
Xiang'an	100	31.12 N	117.46 E
Xiangcheng, Zhg.	100	33.28 N	114.53 E
Xiangcheng, Zhg.	100	33.53 N	113.29 E
Xiangcheng, Zhg.	102	28.59 N	99.45 E
Xiangcheng, Zhg.	106	31.29 N	120.44 E
Xiangfan	102	32.03 N	112.01 E
Xiangfuguan	100	28.30 N	115.26 E
Xiangfusi	107	30.06 N	104.24 E
Xianggang → Victoria	271d	22.17 N	114.09 E
Xianggongshi	100	28.25 N	113.32 E
Xianggongzhuang	105	39.48 N	118.19 E
Xianghe	105	39.46 N	116.59 E
Xiangheguan	100	33.08 N	113.26 E
Xianghuazhen	106	31.31 N	121.43 E
Xiangjia, Zhg.	106	31.20 N	120.31 E
Xiangjia, Zhg.	106	31.19 N	120.23 E
Xiangjiachang	107	30.08 N	104.18 E
Xiangkhoang	110	19.20 N	103.22 E
Xiangkhoang, Plateau de ⩘[1]	110	19.30 N	103.10 E
Xiangning	102	36.01 N	110.45 E
Xiangride	102	36.02 N	98.08 E
Xiangshan, Zhg.	100	29.28 N	121.51 E
Xiangshan, Zhg.	105	39.59 N	116.12 E
Xiangshan Gang ⊂	100	29.38 N	121.48 E
Xiangshizhen	107	29.17 N	105.09 E
Xiangshui, Zhg.	100	23.15 N	114.10 E
Xiangshui, Zhg.	100	34.12 N	119.34 E
Xiangtan	100	27.51 N	112.54 E
Xiangtang	100	28.26 N	115.58 E
Xiangxiang	102	27.43 N	112.27 E
Xiangyang	105	39.13 N	115.25 E
Xiangyangkou	105	40.06 N	115.47 E
Xiangyin	100	28.40 N	112.53 E
Xiangyuan	102	36.32 N	113.00 E
Xiangyun	102	25.30 N	100.30 E
Xiangzhenpu	100	30.52 N	117.21 E
Xiangzhou, Zhg.	98	36.12 N	119.24 E
Xiangzhou, Zhg.	102	23.55 N	109.49 E
Xiangzhu	100	29.02 N	120.04 E
Xianinggang	100	28.20 N	112.56 E
Xianjiang	100	27.48 N	120.30 E
Xianju	100	28.51 N	120.44 E
Xianning	100	29.53 N	114.13 E
Xiannongtan Stadium ♠	271a	39.52 N	116.23 E
Xiannübu	100	25.36 N	114.40 E
Xianru	89	43.11 N	128.02 E
Xianshichang	107	28.43 N	105.44 E
Xianshui ≃	102	30.05 N	110.59 E
Xianshuigu	105	38.59 N	117.23 E
Xiantan, Zhg.	107	29.21 N	104.53 E
Xiantan, Zhg.	107	28.50 N	106.12 E
Xiantang	100	23.48 N	114.46 E
Xianxia Ling ⩘	100	28.30 N	118.46 E
Xianxian	98	38.13 N	116.06 E
Xianyang, Zhg.	100	28.02 N	118.30 E
Xianyang, Zhg.	102	34.22 N	108.42 E
Xianyou	100	25.23 N	118.40 E
Xianzhong	100	28.36 N	113.48 E
Xiao ≃	100	28.11 N	120.14 E
Xiao'an ≃	107	29.59 N	106.13 E
Xiao'ao	100	26.14 N	119.39 E
Xiaoazhang	102	23.42 N	104.58 E
Xiaobangniulu	104	41.34 N	122.46 E
Xiaobeigou	104	41.55 N	120.46 E
Xiaobeihe, Zhg.	104	42.39 N	123.58 E
Xiaobeihe, Zhg.	104	41.22 N	122.50 E
Xiaocaohu	86	43.06 N	88.30 E
Xiaochangshan Dao I	98	39.12 N	122.41 E
Xiaocheng	100	26.20 N	119.47 E
Xiaochengdu	106	30.59 N	120.04 E
Xiaochengzi, Zhg.	89	46.33 N	122.54 E
Xiaochengzi, Zhg.	89	42.56 N	123.12 E
Xiaochi	100	30.33 N	116.23 E
Xiaochikou	100	29.46 N	115.59 E
Xiaodanyang	106	31.38 N	118.43 E
Xiaodong	102	22.14 N	108.39 E
Xiao'ergou	89	49.12 N	123.42 E
Xiaofangshen	104	42.13 N	123.54 E
Xiaofanshan	105	40.16 N	115.19 E
Xiaofen	106	31.45 N	119.39 E
Xiaofeng	106	30.36 N	119.32 E
Xiaogan	100	30.55 N	113.54 E
Xiaogangkou	100	28.14 N	115.50 E
Xiaogaojiatun	104	41.02 N	121.59 E
Xiaogencaigangzi	104	41.48 N	122.42 E
Xiaogu	107	29.08 N	104.01 E
Xiaoguai	86	45.13 N	85.02 E
Xiaogushan	98	39.49 N	123.12 E
Xiaohaizhen	106	31.58 N	120.59 E
Xiaohaladaokou	98	42.37 N	119.32 E
Xiaohan	98	35.48 N	114.52 E
Xiaohe	106	32.01 N	119.52 E
Xiaohei Shan ∧	102	24.42 N	98.55 E
Xiaohekou	102	33.19 N	107.25 E
Xiaoheyan	98	42.26 N	119.38 E
Xiaoheying	102	32.37 N	104.23 E
Xiao Hinggan Ling (Lesser Khingan Range) ⩘	89	48.45 N	127.00 E
Xiaohongmen	271a	39.49 N	116.26 E
Xiaohu	100	27.20 N	118.14 E
Xiaohuying	98	41.09 N	117.13 E
Xiaoji, Zhg.	98	36.45 N	121.01 E
Xiaoji, Zhg.	100	27.08 N	113.15 E
Xiaoji, Zhg.	100	32.38 N	119.48 E
Xiaojiachang	107	30.18 N	106.28 E
Xiaojiagang	100	31.06 N	113.55 E
Xiaojialing	100	29.35 N	116.32 E
Xiaojiang	100	25.08 N	114.59 E
Xiaojianji	100	33.23 N	116.29 E
Xiaojiawu	105	39.36 N	116.36 E
Xiaojiayingzi	98	40.17 N	118.47 E
Xiaojieling	100	31.36 N	115.09 E
Xiaojin	102	31.00 N	102.21 E
Xiaojingfang	105	39.22 N	116.34 E
Xiaojiu	89	45.15 N	127.47 E
Xiaokaoshantun	104	42.10 N	123.53 E
Xiaokuli	89	50.18 N	120.20 E
Xiaokunshan	106	31.02 N	121.07 E
Xiaolan	100	22.41 N	113.14 E
Xiaoliangshan	104	42.05 N	122.32 E
Xiaoling, Zhg.	89	45.20 N	127.18 E
Xiaoling, Zhg.	104	42.18 N	123.23 E
Xiaoling ≃	104	41.06 N	121.07 E
Xiaolingzi	104	41.07 N	123.19 E
Xiaolinzhuang	104	41.36 N	124.01 E
Xiaolipu	98	36.24 N	116.35 E
Xiaolongtan	102	23.51 N	103.10 E
Xiaoluan ≃	98	41.36 N	117.05 E
Xiaolüzhuang	106	31.57 N	119.25 E
Xiaomei	100	27.50 N	118.58 E
Xiaomei Guan)(	100	25.17 N	114.17 E
Xiaomiaozi	98	41.24 N	114.25 E
Xiaonanhai	107	29.23 N	106.27 E
Xiaopikou	98	35.47 N	115.53 E
Xiaopingyang	102	23.22 N	109.13 E
Xiao Qaidam He ⊜	102	37.30 N	95.12 E
Xiaoqiao	100	26.57 N	118.30 E
Xiaoqiaotou	106	30.43 N	119.27 E
Xiaoqing ≃	98	37.17 N	118.52 E
Xiaoqingchuizi	104	42.30 N	123.39 E
Xiaoquandong	102	41.14 N	95.26 E
Xiaosanjiazi	104	42.34 N	123.23 E
Xiaosha ≃	104	41.13 N	122.45 E
Xiaoshakou	100	29.58 N	113.16 E
Xiaoshan	106	30.10 N	120.15 E
Xiaoshangqiao	100	33.43 N	113.58 E
Xiaoshi	100	27.27 N	116.49 E
Xiaoshixiang	100	30.36 N	116.38 E
Xiaoshu	106	30.48 N	119.46 E
Xiaoshun	100	29.11 N	119.51 E
Xiaosigou	98	40.53 N	118.33 E
Xiaosijia	104	42.24 N	120.46 E
Xiaotang	98	41.38 N	119.33 E
Xiaotanghe	98	42.04 N	127.10 E
Xiaotao	100	25.46 N	117.08 E
Xiaotazi	104	42.17 N	123.08 E
Xiaotian	100	31.12 N	116.33 E
Xiaotianji	100	32.45 N	115.36 E
Xiaotun	104	42.24 N	123.44 E
Xiaotunzicun	104	41.14 N	123.20 E
Xiaowa	104	41.03 N	122.04 E
Xiaowan	100	26.53 N	116.36 E
Xiaowangmiao	100	29.41 N	121.21 E
Xiaowutai Shan ∧	105	39.51 N	115.09 E
Xiaowutai Shan ⩘	105	39.50 N	115.00 E
Xiaoxi	100	25.48 N	115.21 E
Xiaoxi ≃	106	32.15 N	120.24 E
Xiaoxian	98	34.11 N	116.56 E
Xiaoxincheng	105	39.24 N	115.11 E
Xiaoxintian	271a	39.58 N	116.22 E
Xiaoxizhen	106	30.51 N	119.50 E
Xiaoyangjiadian	104	42.23 N	122.24 E
Xiaoyangqi	89	50.48 N	124.12 E
Xiaoyantai	104	41.26 N	123.10 E
Xiaoyaozhen	100	33.46 N	114.16 E
Xiaoyi	102	37.10 N	111.46 E
Xiaoying, Zhg.	98	37.18 N	118.04 E
Xiaoying, Zhg.	105	40.12 N	116.33 E
Xiaoyingcun	105	39.28 N	116.41 E
Xiaoyuan	107	30.00 N	104.56 E
Xiaozhan	105	38.55 N	117.25 E
Xiaozhang ≃	105	39.47 N	117.22 E
Xiaozhongdian	102	27.40 N	99.46 E
Xiaozhuang	104	41.30 N	121.27 E
Xiaozhujiawan	106	31.24 N	121.01 E
Xiapu, Zhg.	100	26.52 N	120.01 E
Xiapu, Zhg.	100	27.49 N	114.26 E
Xiaqialafangzi	104	41.48 N	121.44 E
Xiaqi Dao I	100	29.42 N	122.15 E
Xiaqiubao	98	37.01 N	119.54 E
Xiasantumen	105	38.50 N	114.48 E
Xiashe	106	30.33 N	120.11 E
Xiashesi	100	27.46 N	112.57 E
Xiashi → Haining	106	30.32 N	120.41 E
Xiashu	106	32.11 N	119.10 E
Xiashuerfowei	89	50.23 N	120.47 E
Xiashuiquan	104	41.52 N	123.38 E
Xiataizi	105	40.37 N	117.45 E
Xiatang, Zhg.	100	33.45 N	112.39 E
Xiatang, Zhg.	106	31.29 N	118.41 E
Xiatangtian	106	30.55 N	120.12 E
Xiataohuatu	104	41.42 N	120.36 E
Xiawa	98	42.39 N	120.35 E
Xiawajiang	106	30.59 N	121.51 E
Xiawaziyu	104	41.15 N	123.38 E
Xiaxi	106	31.43 N	119.45 E
Xiaxian	102	35.11 N	111.15 E
Xiaxiangcheng	102	28.42 N	99.59 E
Xiaxikou	100	26.15 N	118.59 E
Xiaxinhe	106	31.40 N	119.31 E
Xiayang, Zhg.	100	28.48 N	119.41 E
Xiayang, Zhg.	100	26.46 N	117.59 E
Xiayang, Zhg.	100	24.39 N	116.52 E
Xiayi	98	34.14 N	116.06 E
Xiaying, Zhg.	98	37.03 N	119.25 E
Xiaying, Zhg.	105	40.10 N	117.25 E
Xiayunling	105	39.43 N	115.44 E
Xiazhang	98	36.08 N	116.57 E
Xiazhen	100	28.39 N	118.21 E
Xiazhuang, Zhg.	98	35.28 N	118.43 E
Xiazhuang, Zhg.	100	27.22 N	119.01 E
Xiazhuang, Zhg.	105	39.54 N	117.01 E
Xiazhuang, Zhg.	105	39.38 N	115.26 E
Xiazikou	105	39.01 N	115.25 E
Xiban	107	30.32 N	106.12 E
Xibaqianmou	104	40.59 N	121.35 E
Xibeiyingzi	104	41.55 N	121.38 E
Xibo ≃	98	42.17 N	118.57 E
Xibu	100	31.46 N	118.17 E
Xicang	106	31.34 N	120.29 E
Xichang, Zhg.	102	27.58 N	102.13 E
Xichang, Zhg.	104	42.15 N	124.12 E
Xicheng	89	48.10 N	125.29 E
Xichong	102	31.00 N	105.52 E
Xicicun	105	39.29 N	116.08 E
Xico	234	19.25 N	97.00 W
Xicoténcatl	234	23.00 N	98.56 W
Xicotepec de Juárez	234	20.17 N	97.57 W
Xicun	100	27.46 N	114.14 E
Xidachuan	98	41.46 N	127.34 E
Xidapo	89	43.12 N	130.02 E
Xidaying	105	39.41 N	116.14 E
Xidian	100	29.32 N	121.26 E
Xiditou	105	39.16 N	117.23 E
Xidongting Shan ∧	106	31.07 N	120.16 E
Xié ≃	246	0.54 N	67.11 W
Xiecun	105	39.00 N	115.31 E
Xiedian	100	33.27 N	113.28 E
Xiefang	100	26.12 N	116.41 E
Xieji	98	34.32 N	115.29 E
Xiejia	98	42.24 N	125.42 E
Xiejiagangzi	104	41.55 N	122.20 E
Xiejiapu	106	31.15 N	119.09 E
Xiejunmiao	107	30.15 N	103.40 E
Xielipuke	120	31.30 N	82.45 E
Xiemachang	107	29.46 N	106.22 E
Xiemata Shan ∧	89	50.28 N	120.47 E
Xiepu	100	30.02 N	121.37 E
Xieqiao, Zhg.	106	30.29 N	120.34 E
Xieqiao, Zhg.	106	32.03 N	120.22 E
Xietang	106	31.18 N	120.44 E
Xiexi	106	31.54 N	118.54 E
Xiexinggou	104	41.51 N	121.05 E
Xifei ≃	100	32.38 N	116.39 E
Xifeng, Zhg.	98	42.43 N	124.40 E
Xifeng, Zhg.	102	27.02 N	106.30 E
Xifengkou	105	40.24 N	118.19 E
Xifocun	104	41.26 N	122.33 E
Xigangzi	89	49.58 N	127.20 E
Xigaolizhuangzi	104	41.40 N	122.55 E
Xigaotan	98	38.18 N	116.13 E
Xigaotun	98	40.27 N	122.36 E
Xigazê	120	29.17 N	88.53 E
Xiguanjiatun	104	42.35 N	123.10 E
Xiguanyingzi	104	41.50 N	120.37 E
Xihaikou	104	40.50 N	121.05 E
Xihan ≃	102	33.30 N	106.02 E
Xihe, Zhg.	100	31.41 N	113.27 E
Xihe, Zhg.	100	31.01 N	118.28 E
Xihe, Zhg.	102	34.01 N	105.17 E
Xiheying	105	39.53 N	114.42 E
Xihezhuang	105	39.20 N	118.02 E
Xi Hu ⊜	106	30.15 N	120.08 E
Xihua	100	33.47 N	114.31 E
Xihuangcang	106	31.43 N	121.40 E
Xihuanzidong	104	41.31 N	122.28 E
Xihuashan, Zhg.	100	25.28 N	114.20 E
Xihuashan, Zhg.	105	40.07 N	116.54 E
Xihuishan	104	41.41 N	122.38 E
Xiis	144	10.53 N	46.54 E
Xiji, Zhg.	102	35.58 N	105.44 E
Xiji, Zhg.	105	39.49 N	116.52 E
Xijialong	102	23.31 N	103.51 E
Xijiang	100	25.50 N	115.49 E
Xijianshanzi	104	40.47 N	120.48 E
Xi Jiao Airfield ⊠	271a	39.58 N	116.15 E
Xijiapuzitun	104	41.26 N	123.50 E
Xijir Ulan Hu ⊜	120	35.12 N	90.18 E
Xikou, Zhg.	89	46.40 N	120.40 E
Xikou, Zhg.	100	29.11 N	114.23 E
Xikou, Zhg.	100	25.26 N	118.45 E
Xikou, Zhg.	100	29.44 N	118.02 E
Xikou, Zhg.	100	29.14 N	114.24 E
Xikou, Zhg.	100	28.52 N	119.11 E
Xikou, Zhg.	106	30.40 N	118.41 E
Xikouxu	100	25.24 N	117.03 E
Xikouzi	89	53.06 N	120.40 E
Xilai	107	30.20 N	103.29 E
Xilaiqiao	106	32.03 N	119.54 E
Xilaizhen	106	32.07 N	120.25 E
Xilin	120	28.33 N	87.48 E
Xi Ling (Western Tombs) ⊥	105	39.24 N	115.18 E
Xilintuo	120	30.08 N	88.04 E
Xilitla	234	21.20 N	98.58 W
Xiliuhe	105	38.58 N	116.32 E
Xiliushuyingzi	104	42.25 N	121.54 E
Xilókastron	38	38.05 N	22.38 E
Xiluga ≃	98	42.21 N	118.38 E
Xiluncun	89	47.08 N	126.26 E
Ximagou	105	40.16 N	117.50 E
Ximakou	100	30.33 N	113.47 E
Ximalatu	89	47.00 N	122.01 E
Ximalin	98	40.48 N	114.29 E
Ximiao	102	41.09 N	100.17 E
Ximucheng	104	40.42 N	122.54 E
Xin ≃	100	28.37 N	116.40 E
Xin'an, Zhg.	89	43.46 N	125.40 E
Xin'an, Zhg.	100	23.02 N	114.56 E
Xin'an, Zhg.	100	26.44 N	116.13 E
Xinan, Zhg.	100	25.26 N	117.35 E
Xin'an, Zhg.	105	39.09 N	116.38 E
Xin'an, Zhg.	106	31.30 N	120.22 E
Xin'an, Zhg.	106	31.47 N	120.09 E
Xin'an ≃	100	29.33 N	118.58 E
Xin'andian	100	32.37 N	114.03 E
Xin'andu	100	30.52 N	116.53 E
Xin'anji	100	33.22 N	115.13 E
Xin'anjiang Shuiku ⊜[1]	100	29.27 N	119.06 E
Xin'anpu	104	42.39 N	123.27 E
Xin'anqiao	106	32.16 N	121.07 E
Xin'ansuo	102	23.16 N	103.27 E
Xin'anzhen, Zhg.	89	44.06 N	123.46 E
Xin'anzhen, Zhg.	105	39.45 N	117.32 E
Xi'nanzhuang	105	40.48 N	118.23 E
Xinavane	156	25.02 S	32.47 E
Xinba, Zhg.	98	34.27 N	119.09 E
Xinba, Zhg.	100	30.24 N	116.52 E
Xinba, Zhg.	106	32.08 N	120.39 E
Xinba, Zhg.	106	32.16 N	119.45 E
Xinbao'an	105	40.27 N	115.24 E
Xin Barag Youqi (Altan Emel)	88	48.41 N	116.53 E
Xin Barag Zuoqi (Amgalang)	88	48.14 N	118.18 E
Xinbin, Zhg.	98	41.42 N	125.02 E
Xinbin, Zhg.	106	30.56 N	121.04 E
Xinbo	98	42.19 N	117.44 E
Xincai	100	32.44 N	114.59 E
Xincang, Zhg.	106	30.25 N	120.42 E
Xincang, Zhg.	106	30.44 N	121.11 E
Xinchang, Zhg.	100	29.30 N	120.53 E
Xinchang, Zhg.	102	28.03 N	103.46 E
Xinchang, Zhg.	102	25.10 N	104.18 E
Xinchang, Zhg.	106	31.42 N	121.46 E
Xinchang, Zhg.	106	31.02 N	121.38 E
Xinchang, Zhg.	107	29.20 N	104.15 E
Xinchang, Zhg.	107	30.29 N	106.21 E
Xinchang, Zhg.	107	29.38 N	104.33 E
Xinchang, Zhg.	107	30.16 N	104.29 E
Xinchangzi	107	29.40 N	103.46 E
Xincheng, Zhg.	100	25.34 N	114.36 E
Xincheng, Zhg.	102	24.09 N	108.46 E
Xincheng (Gaobeidian), Zhg.	105	39.20 N	115.51 E
Xincheng, Zhg.	105	38.59 N	117.33 E
Xincheng, Zhg.	106	30.48 N	120.36 E
Xincheng, Zhg.	106	32.17 N	119.14 E
Xinchengzi	104	42.03 N	123.30 E
Xinchepaizi	86	44.55 N	84.30 E
Xincunji	100	32.53 N	115.31 E
Xindai	106	30.49 N	121.05 E
Xindi	104	42.21 N	120.31 E
Xindian, Zhg.	89	45.55 N	127.50 E
Xindian, Zhg.	98	37.07 N	114.49 E
Xindian, Zhg.	98	37.29 N	118.28 E
Xindian, Zhg.	100	29.40 N	113.40 E
Xindian, Zhg.	100	33.07 N	112.38 E
Xindian, Zhg.	100	31.33 N	115.16 E
Xindian, Zhg.	100	33.38 N	113.51 E
Xindian, Zhg.	105	40.11 N	116.11 E
Xindian, Zhg.	105	40.47 N	116.49 E
Xindian, Zhg.	105	39.10 N	116.27 E
Xindian, Zhg.	107	29.19 N	105.40 E
Xindianbu	100	32.24 N	116.22 E
Xindianzi, Zhg.	105	40.04 N	118.01 E
Xindianzi, Zhg.	107	29.52 N	106.06 E
Xindianzi, Zhg.	107	28.49 N	103.35 E
Xindianzi, Zhg.	107	29.46 N	105.11 E
Xindianzi, Zhg.	107	29.03 N	103.46 E
Xindianzi, Zhg.	107	29.43 N	104.01 E
Xindu	102	23.59 N	111.46 E
Xinfatuncun	104	41.13 N	122.28 E
Xinfeng, Zhg.	100	24.05 N	116.53 E
Xinfeng, Zhg.	100	25.24 N	114.56 E
Xinfeng, Zhg.	100	27.26 N	116.40 E
Xinfeng, Zhg.	100	33.19 N	120.30 E
Xinfeng, Zhg.	100	24.04 N	114.12 E
Xinfeng, Zhg.	106	31.09 N	118.40 E
Xinfeng, Zhg.	106	32.05 N	119.34 E
Xinfeng, Zhg.	106	30.43 N	120.55 E
Xinfeng ≃	100	23.42 N	114.42 E
Xinfeng Shuiku ⊜[1]	100	23.52 N	114.30 E
Xing'an, Zhg.	89	48.49 N	121.45 E
Xing'an, Zhg.	102	25.37 N	110.31 E
Xingang, Zhg.	106	32.03 N	120.25 E
Xin'gang, Zhg.	106	31.56 N	120.57 E
Xing'antun	89	51.31 N	120.08 E
Xingcheng	104	40.37 N	120.43 E
Xingguo	100	26.21 N	115.19 E
Xinghai	102	35.31 N	99.36 E
Xinghe	98	40.48 N	113.58 E
Xinghua	100	32.57 N	119.50 E
Xinghua Wan ⊂	100	25.20 N	119.20 E
Xingjing	102	29.43 N	102.59 E
Xingkai Hu (ozero Chanka) ⊜	89	45.00 N	132.24 E
Xingliu	100	33.04 N	115.41 E
Xinglong, Zhg.	100	32.05 N	112.51 E
Xinglong, Zhg.	102	35.38 N	106.08 E
Xinglong, Zhg.	105	40.26 N	117.34 E
Xinglong, Zhg.	107	30.20 N	106.07 E
Xinglong, Zhg.	107	30.36 N	106.20 E
Xinglongchang, Zhg.	107	30.25 N	104.06 E
Xinglongchang, Zhg.	107	29.34 N	106.09 E
Xinglongchang, Zhg.	107	29.54 N	105.26 E
Xinglongcun	89	49.50 N	125.12 E
Xinglongdian, Zhg.	104	42.16 N	124.00 E
Xinglongdian, Zhg.	104	41.59 N	123.03 E
Xinglonggou, Zhg.	104	41.46 N	120.38 E
Xinglonggou, Zhg.	104	40.45 N	123.08 E
Xinglongpao	89	46.27 N	125.47 E
Xinglongtai	104	42.30 N	123.48 E
Xingning	100	24.09 N	115.45 E
Xingou, Zhg.	100	30.41 N	113.57 E
Xingou, Zhg.	100	30.08 N	112.56 E
Xingren	102	25.27 N	105.13 E
Xingrenbu	102	37.06 N	105.12 E
Xingshanbao	89	45.30 N	125.45 E
Xingtai	98	37.04 N	114.29 E
Xingtan	100	22.46 N	113.07 E
Xingtang	98	38.26 N	114.33 E
Xingtian	100	27.30 N	118.02 E
Xingu ≃	242	1.30 S	51.53 W
Xinguan	100	33.38 N	118.05 E
Xingwenping	102	29.24 N	103.23 E
Xingxian	102	38.36 N	111.15 E
Xingxing	106	30.39 N	121.09 E
Xingyi, Zhg.	98	38.18 N	115.01 E
Xingyi, Zhg.	102	25.06 N	104.58 E
Xingzhuangzi	105	40.34 N	115.00 E
Xingzi	100	29.28 N	116.01 E
Xinhe, Zhg.	98	37.32 N	115.14 E
Xinhe, Zhg.	100	28.30 N	121.27 E
Xinhe, Zhg.	105	39.03 N	117.37 E
Xinhe, Zhg.	106	31.59 N	121.21 E
Xinhekou	89	48.22 N	130.45 E
Xinheng	100	23.38 N	116.18 E
Xinhezhen	106	31.35 N	121.31 E
Xinhezhuang	106	31.10 N	118.46 E
Xinhua	102	27.37 N	111.02 E
Xinhuai ≃	100	34.23 N	120.05 E
Xinhuang	106	30.37 N	120.55 E
Xinhui	100	22.32 N	113.02 E
Xining (Sining)	102	36.38 N	101.55 E
Xiniu, Zhg.	100	24.10 N	113.07 E
Xiniu, Zhg.	106	31.25 N	120.07 E
Xiniuguchengzi	104	41.01 N	122.24 E
Xinji, Zhg.	98	35.19 N	115.36 E
Xinji, Zhg.	100	33.24 N	114.44 E
Xinji, Zhg.	105	40.04 N	118.21 E
Xinji, Zhg.	105	39.52 N	117.10 E
Xinjiaji	98	36.56 N	116.59 E
Xinjian, Zhg.	100	28.34 N	115.47 E
Xinjian, Zhg.	100	28.46 N	120.02 E
Xinjian, Zhg.	106	31.33 N	119.39 E
Xinjiang, Zhg.	100	24.29 N	113.52 E
Xinjiang, Zhg.	102	35.40 N	111.11 E
Xinjiang, Zhg.	106	32.05 N	120.40 E
Xinjianglang	106	30.58 N	120.54 E
Xinjiang Uygur Zizhiqu (Sinkiang) □[4]	90	40.00 N	85.00 E
Xinjiapu	105	40.32 N	115.57 E
Xinjiazhuang	105	40.31 N	114.58 E
Xinjie	102	26.48 N	101.15 E
Xinjieji	89	52.08 N	126.24 E
Xinjin (Pulandian), Zhg.	98	39.24 N	121.58 E
Xinjin, Zhg.	107	30.25 N	103.49 E
Xinjingzi	86	42.13 N	87.36 E
Xinjuntun	105	39.39 N	117.57 E
Xinkai ≃	89	43.37 N	123.36 E
Xinkaigang	106	31.55 N	120.56 E
Xinkengdong	100	26.09 N	113.46 E
Xinle (Dongchangshou)	98	38.24 N	114.47 E
Xinli	89	44.41 N	126.45 E
Xinlitun, Zhg.	89	43.34 N	125.18 E
Xinlitun, Zhg.	104	42.15 N	122.51 E
Xinlitun, Zhg.	104	42.00 N	122.09 E
Xinlizhuang	105	39.17 N	116.10 E
Xinmin	104	42.00 N	122.48 E
Xinmintun	104	41.39 N	123.02 E
Xinning	102	26.19 N	110.45 E
Xinping	102	24.06 N	101.58 E
Xinpu	100	24.31 N	116.08 E
Xinqianhu	98	37.59 N	118.15 E
Xinqiao, Zhg.	106	31.04 N	121.18 E
Xinqiao, Zhg.	106	31.32 N	119.04 E
Xinqiao, Zhg.	107	29.32 N	106.28 E
Xinqiao, Zhg.	107	30.10 N	103.50 E
Xinqiao, Zhg.	107	30.33 N	105.33 E
Xinqiaotou	106	31.00 N	119.24 E
Xinqiaozhen	107	29.36 N	103.39 E
Xinqiu	98	41.53 N	119.41 E
Xinqizhou	100	28.56 N	115.50 E
Xinqu	86	44.57 N	85.15 E
Xinquan	100	25.23 N	116.38 E
Xinsanyu	106	31.58 N	120.07 E
Xinshao	102	27.11 N	111.20 E
Xinshengzhen	107	29.29 N	104.39 E
Xinshi, Zhg.	106	30.37 N	120.19 E
Xinshi, Zhg.	106	32.04 N	120.02 E
Xinshizhen, Zhg.	102	28.39 N	104.02 E
Xinshizhen, Zhg.	107	30.20 N	104.35 E
Xinshu ≃	98	34.41 N	119.12 E
Xintai	98	35.54 N	117.44 E
Xintaimen	98	40.50 N	120.23 E
Xintaizi, Zhg.	104	41.06 N	122.42 E
Xintaizi, Zhg.	104	42.07 N	123.36 E
Xintang, Zhg.	100	23.08 N	113.36 E
Xintang, Zhg.	102	30.13 N	109.30 E
Xintang, Zhg.	106	31.02 N	119.59 E
Xintangcun	106	31.53 N	119.31 E
Xintanpu	100	29.43 N	114.54 E
Xintian	102	25.53 N	112.05 E
Xintun	104	42.11 N	123.45 E
Xinvi	105	40.04 N	118.21 E
Xinwei	100	25.21 N	115.48 E
Xinwen (Suncun)	98	35.53 N	117.40 E
Xinxian, Zhg.	100	31.38 N	114.51 E
Xinxian, Zhg.	102	38.25 N	112.48 E
Xinxiang	98	35.20 N	113.51 E
Xinxim ≃	250	7.57 S	53.20 W
Xinxing, Zhg.	89	43.16 N	129.48 E
Xinxing, Zhg.	100	22.40 N	112.52 E
Xinxing, Zhg.	102	19.57 N	109.32 E
Xinxu, Zhg.	100	24.57 N	117.34 E
Xinxu, Zhg.	100	22.52 N	114.20 E
Xinyang	100	32.08 N	114.04 E
Xinyao	100	27.39 N	118.52 E
Xinye	100	32.33 N	112.21 E
Xinyi (Xin'anzhen), Zhg.	98	34.22 N	118.21 E
Xinyi (Dongzhen), Zhg.	102	22.13 N	110.50 E
Xinyi ≃	100	34.29 N	119.49 E
Xinying	102	36.03 N	105.35 E
Xinyu	100	27.49 N	114.57 E
Xinyuan	86	43.08 N	82.31 E
Xinzao	100	23.02 N	113.26 E
Xinzha	102	23.41 N	101.09 E
Xinzhai, Zhg.	98	36.24 N	118.37 E
Xinzhai, Zhg.	98	39.24 N	118.46 E
Xinzhai, Zhg.	102	24.33 N	99.08 E
Xinzhan	100	33.33 N	114.50 E
Xinzhang	105	39.05 N	116.46 E
Xinzhangzi	105	40.45 N	117.50 E
Xinzhao	102	39.32 N	107.52 E
Xinzhazhen	106	31.50 N	119.52 E
Xinzhen, Zhg.	98	35.37 N	114.03 E
Xinzhen, Zhg.	105	39.01 N	116.22 E
Xinzhen, Zhg.	106	31.24 N	121.24 E
Xinzheng	100	34.25 N	113.43 E
Xinzhou, Zhg.	100	30.50 N	114.47 E
Xinzhou, Zhg.	102	19.48 N	109.18 E
Xinzhuang, Zhg.	98	35.05 N	117.56 E
Xinzhuang, Zhg.	271a	39.56 N	116.31 E
Xinzhuangtou	105	39.25 N	115.45 E
Xinzhuangzi, Zhg.	104	41.05 N	121.23 E
Xinzhuangzi, Zhg.	105	40.14 N	116.59 E
Xinzhuangzi, Zhg.	105	40.32 N	115.10 E
Xinzhuangzi, Zhg.	105	38.52 N	117.21 E
Xinzhuangzi, Zhg.	105	39.20 N	118.25 E
Xinzo de Limia	34	42.03 N	7.43 W
Xiongdi Yu II	100	23.33 N	117.40 E
Xiongjiachang	102	26.31 N	105.39 E
Xiongxian	105	38.59 N	116.05 E
Xiongyuecheng	98	40.10 N	122.08 E
Xipamanu ≃	248	10.43 S	67.50 W
Xiping, Zhg.	100	33.23 N	114.02 E
Xiping, Zhg.	100	28.27 N	119.29 E
Xiping'anhe	104	40.47 N	122.01 E
Xiqia	106	31.03 N	119.37 E
Xiqilichiquan	89	49.59 N	119.27 E
Xiqin	100	26.33 N	118.06 E
Xiqing Shan ⩘	102	35.30 N	101.30 E
Xique-Xique	250	10.50 S	42.44 W
Xiriri, Lago ⊜	250	1.37 S	55.56 W
Xiruá ≃	248	6.03 S	67.50 W
Xisanshilipu	100	32.40 N	117.31 E
Xisantai	98	39.38 N	121.37 E
Xishan, Zhg.	100	28.34 N	115.37 E
Xishan, Zhg.	105	39.38 N	118.10 E
Xishanqiao	106	31.57 N	118.43 E
Xishanxicun	105	40.01 N	116.50 E
Xisha Qundao (Paracel Islands) II	108	16.30 N	112.15 E
Xishijiazi	104	41.46 N	120.55 E
Xishiqiao	106	31.53 N	120.06 E
Xishu	98	36.41 N	113.49 E
Xishui	100	30.27 N	115.13 E
Xishuiyu	105	40.25 N	116.16 E
Xisuhupu	104	41.41 N	123.14 E
Xitai	98	40.37 N	120.12 E
Xitan	100	23.47 N	117.08 E
Xitang	106	30.57 N	120.53 E
Xitangqiao, Zhg.	106	31.49 N	120.38 E
Xitangqiao, Zhg.	106	30.37 N	121.01 E
Xitaoyuan	104	40.57 N	122.11 E
Xiti	120	33.27 N	82.48 E
Xitianmu Shan ∧	106	30.21 N	119.25 E
Xitiao ≃	106	30.57 N	120.10 E
Xiting	106	32.07 N	121.00 E
Xitole	150	11.43 N	14.50 W
Xituan	105	39.29 N	115.47 E
Xiu ≃	100	29.13 N	115.56 E
Xiujiangpu	104	41.17 N	123.02 E
Xiuning	100	29.47 N	118.10 E
Xiushan	102	28.29 N	108.52 E
Xiushui	100	29.04 N	114.33 E
Xiushui ≃	104	42.03 N	122.58 E
Xiushuihe	104	42.22 N	123.01 E
Xiuyan	98	40.17 N	123.18 E
Xiva	34	39.28 N	0.43 W
Xiwei	100	25.22 N	117.46 E
Xiweizigou	104	42.01 N	121.59 E
Xiwenquan	107	29.42 N	106.07 E
Xiwu	100	29.40 N	121.30 E
Xiwukou	106	30.24 N	118.54 E
Xixabangma Feng ∧	124	28.22 N	85.50 E
Xixi	100	26.45 N	118.42 E
Xixia	102	33.22 N	111.28 E
Xixian, Zhg.	100	32.21 N	114.44 E
Xixian, Zhg.	102	36.43 N	110.52 E
Xixiang	102	32.48 N	107.55 E
Xixiangyang	105	39.33 N	116.02 E
Xixiaojie	104	40.42 N	122.12 E
Xixiashu	106	31.57 N	119.49 E
Xixing	106	30.11 N	120.13 E
Xixona	34	38.32 N	0.30 W
Xiyang, Zhg.	98	37.37 N	113.42 E
Xiyang, Zhg.	100	25.50 N	117.25 E
Xiyang, Zhg.	106	31.49 N	120.43 E
Xiyang, Zhg.	106	31.52 N	119.23 E
Xiyang Dao I	100	26.32 N	120.04 E
Xiyangji	100	33.25 N	116.22 E
Xiyangjiao	106	31.43 N	120.23 E
Xiyangshugou	104	40.41 N	122.44 E
Xiyangzhuang	106	31.50 N	119.22 E
Xiyingzi	104	41.55 N	122.34 E
Xiyou	98	37.24 N	119.56 E
Xiyushi	106	30.36 N	119.26 E
Xizang Zizhiqu (Tibet) □[4]	90	32.00 N	88.00 E
Xizhi ≃	100	23.04 N	114.31 E
Xizhimen Station ⬥[5]	271a	39.56 N	116.21 E
Xizhong Dao I	98	39.26 N	121.17 E
Xizhou	100	29.29 N	121.39 E
Xizi	98	41.48 N	119.16 E
Xkalak	232	18.16 N	87.50 W
Xochapa	234	17.39 N	95.46 W
Xochimilco □[7]	286a	19.14 N	99.05 W
Xochimilco ⬥[8]	286a	19.16 N	99.06 W
Xochimilco, Lago de ⊜	286a	19.16 N	99.06 W
Xochipala	234	17.48 N	99.39 W
Xochistlahuaca	234	16.47 N	98.15 W
Xochitlán	234	19.59 N	97.36 W
Xoka	120	29.58 N	93.48 E
Xom Binh Phuoc	269c	10.40 N	106.47 E
Xom Xoai Minh	269c	10.42 N	106.50 E
Xoxocotla	234	18.41 N	99.15 W
Xu ≃	100	28.17 N	116.05 E
Xuancheng	106	30.58 N	118.45 E
Xuan'en	102	30.00 N	109.20 E
Xuanfeng	100	27.42 N	114.08 E
Xuang ≃	110	19.58 N	102.15 E
Xuanhan	102	31.24 N	107.43 E
Xuanhua	105	40.37 N	115.03 E
Xuanhuadian	100	31.42 N	114.29 E
Xuanhui ≃	98	38.07 N	117.45 E
Xuanjiabao	106	32.17 N	120.01 E
Xuanjiangying	98	41.25 N	116.45 E
Xuan Loc	110	10.56 N	107.14 E
Xuantan	107	29.12 N	105.34 E
Xuan Thoi Thuong	269c	10.52 N	106.34 E
Xuanwei	102	26.07 N	104.05 E
Xuanzhuang	105	39.29 N	118.07 E
Xubu	98	40.02 N	113.43 E
Xuchang, Zhg.	100	34.03 N	113.49 E
Xuchang, Zhg.	107	29.06 N	104.31 E
Xucheng	98	35.56 N	116.27 E
Xucun	106	30.27 N	120.22 E
Xudazhuang	100	33.44 N	117.53 E
Xuddun	144	9.09 N	47.28 E
Xuddur	144	4.07 N	43.54 E
Xueao	100	29.27 N	121.30 E
Xuebu	106	31.43 N	119.22 E
Xuecheng	98	34.50 N	117.16 E
Xuedian, Zhg.	100	34.04 N	113.04 E
Xuedian, Zhg.	100	34.30 N	113.44 E
Xuefanggou	104	41.57 N	121.01 E
Xuefeng	100	33.21 N	118.22 E
Xuehu	98	34.08 N	116.27 E
Xueshan Zhang ∧	100	24.24 N	113.37 E
Xueshuiwen	89	49.10 N	129.45 E
Xuetangpuzi	104	40.38 N	123.53 E
Xueyanqiao	106	31.30 N	120.06 E
Xuezhen	106	31.35 N	118.38 E
Xuguanzhen	106	31.23 N	120.30 E
Xuguichenxiaodian	106	32.07 N	121.20 E
Xuguit Qi (Yakeshi)	89	49.17 N	120.41 E
Xuji	100	31.50 N	116.22 E
Xujiabu	100	29.27 N	116.18 E
Xujiadong	100	25.54 N	113.02 E
Xujiadu	100	28.18 N	114.44 E
Xujiagou	104	42.17 N	124.04 E
Xujiapuzi	104	40.44 N	123.18 E
Xujiatou	106	31.19 N	119.25 E
Xujiazhai, Zhg.	106	31.11 N	121.46 E
Xujiazhai, Zhg.	269b	31.23 N	121.17 E
Xuliying	105	39.28 N	116.02 E
Xun ≃, Zhg.	89	49.27 N	128.55 E
Xun ≃, Zhg.	102	23.28 N	111.18 E
Xungru	120	29.15 N	84.49 E
Xunhe	89	49.18 N	128.04 E
Xunhua	102	35.49 N	102.26 E
Xunjiansi	105	40.50 N	116.04 E
Xunke	89	49.35 N	128.25 E
Xunle	102	25.17 N	108.12 E
Xunmukou	98	34.03 N	114.42 E
Xunshansuo	98	37.10 N	122.29 E
Xunwu	100	24.58 N	115.38 E
Xunwu ≃	100	24.28 N	115.26 E
Xunxian	98	35.43 N	114.31 E
Xupu, Zhg.	102	27.44 N	110.24 E
Xupu, Zhg.	106	31.45 N	120.54 E
Xushe	106	31.24 N	119.39 E
Xushi	106	31.40 N	120.57 E
Xushui	105	39.02 N	115.39 E
Xutian	98	34.10 N	114.03 E
Xuwan	100	27.55 N	116.31 E
Xuwen	102	20.21 N	110.11 E
Xuxiandai	106	30.40 N	120.47 E
Xuxiang	106	31.33 N	120.13 E
Xuyen Moc	110	10.34 N	107.25 E
Xuyi	100	33.01 N	118.29 E
Xuyong	102	28.10 N	105.24 E
Xuzhou (Süchow)	98	34.16 N	117.11 E
Xuzhuang	106	31.09 N	120.32 E
Y			
Yaak	182	48.50 N	115.42 W
Yaan	102	30.03 N	103.02 E
Yaapeet	166	35.46 S	142.03 E
Yaaq-Baraawe	144	1.57 N	43.11 E
Yaba ⬥[8]	273a	6.30 N	3.23 E
Yaba College of Technology ⛉[2]	273a	6.32 N	3.23 E
Ya'bad	132	32.27 N	35.10 E
Yabakei	96	33.27 N	131.07 E
Yabassi	152	4.28 N	9.58 E
Yabe	96	33.09 N	130.49 E
Yabe ≃	96	33.06 N	130.26 E
Yabelo	144	4.54 N	38.05 E
Yablis	236	14.10 N	83.49 W
Yablonovy Range → Jablonovyj chrebet ⩘	88	53.30 N	115.00 E
Yabrīn ⊤[4]	128	23.17 N	48.58 E
Yabrūd	130	33.58 N	36.40 E
Yabu, Nihon	96	35.22 N	134.47 E
Yabu, Nihon	174m	26.36 N	127.57 E
Yabucoa	240m	18.03 N	65.53 W
Yabuki	94	37.12 N	140.19 E
Yabuli	89	44.55 N	128.35 E
Yacambu, Parque Nacional ♠	246	9.40 N	69.42 W
Yacaré Norte, Riacho ≃	252	22.43 S	58.14 W
Yacheng	110	18.25 N	109.11 E
Yachi ≃	102	27.18 N	107.15 E
Yachimata	94	35.39 N	140.19 E
Yachiyo, Nihon	94	35.43 N	140.07 E
Yachiyo, Nihon	94	36.10 N	139.53 E
Yaciretá, Isla I	252	27.25 S	56.30 W
Yaco	248	17.09 S	67.24 W
Yaco (Iaco) ≃	248	9.03 S	68.34 W
Yacolt	224	45.51 N	122.24 W
Yacuiba	248	22.02 S	63.45 W
Yacuma ≃	248	13.38 S	65.23 W
Yada ≃	96	35.38 N	134.37 E
Yādgīr	122	16.46 N	77.08 E
Yadkin ≃	192	35.23 N	80.03 W
Yadkinville	192	36.08 N	80.39 W
Yad Mordekhay	132	31.35 N	34.34 E
Yadong	124	27.29 N	88.55 E
Yādūdah	132	32.40 N	36.04 E
Yaenengu	152	2.28 N	23.15 E
Yaeyama-rettō II	175d	24.20 N	124.00 E
Yāfā	132	32.41 N	35.17 E
Yafran	146	32.04 N	12.31 E
Yaftābād	267d	35.39 N	51.19 E
Yafuquan	85	39.12 N	76.09 E
Yagachi-shima I	174m	26.40 N	128.01 E
Yağcılar	130	39.25 N	28.23 E
Yageg	144	3.16 N	44.00 E
Yagi	96	35.04 N	135.32 E
Yagishiri-tō I	92a	44.26 N	141.25 E
Yağlıca Dağı ∧	84	40.18 N	43.18 E
Yago	234	21.50 N	105.04 W
Yagonde	152	0.02 N	22.41 E
Yagoona	274a	33.55 S	151.02 E
Yagoua	146	10.20 N	15.14 E
Yagradagzê Shan ∧	120	35.12 N	95.20 E
Yaguachi	246	2.07 S	79.41 W
Yaguachi ≃	246	2.02 S	79.44 W
Yaguajay	240p	22.19 N	79.14 W
Yaguala ≃	236	15.25 N	86.40 W
Yaguará	246	2.40 N	75.31 W
Yaguaraparo	246	10.34 N	62.49 W
Yaguarí	252	31.31 S	54.58 W
Yaguarón (Jaguarão) ≃	252	32.39 S	53.12 W
Yaguas ≃	246	2.45 S	70.04 W
Yagur	132	32.44 N	35.04 E
Yahagi ≃	94	34.50 N	136.59 E
Yahagong	102	28.24 N	99.11 E
Yahara ≃	190	42.48 N	89.07 W
Yahata → Kitakyūshū	96	33.53 N	130.50 E
Yahe, Zhg.	89	45.24 N	130.24 E
Yahe, Zhg.	106	31.44 N	119.52 E
Yahila	152	0.13 N	24.28 E
Yahk	182	49.05 N	116.05 W
Yahmūm al-Asmar, Jabal ∧	142	29.56 N	31.38 E
Yaho	268	35.41 N	139.27 E
Yahōga-take ∧	96	33.04 N	130.50 E
Yahongqiao	105	39.45 N	117.51 E
Yahualica	234	21.08 N	102.51 W
Yahuma	152	1.05 N	23.13 E
Yahyalı	130	38.07 N	35.22 E
Yai ≃	114	5.02 N	101.47 E
Yai, Khao ∧, Asia	110	12.27 N	99.26 E
Yai, Khao ∧, Thai	110	15.25 N	99.20 E
Yainax Butte ∧	202	42.20 N	121.16 W
Yaita, Nihon	94	36.48 N	139.56 E
Yaita, Nihon	268	35.57 N	140.03 E
Yaitopya → Ethiopia □[1]	144	9.00 N	39.00 E
Yaizu	94	34.52 N	138.20 E
Yajiang	102	30.02 N	101.05 E
Yaka	130	41.15 N	34.01 E
Yakacık	130	36.47 N	36.10 E
Yakacık ⬥[8]	267b	40.55 N	29.13 E
Yakage	96	34.37 N	133.35 E
Yakak, Cape ›	180	51.38 N	177.00 W

≃	River	Fluß	Río	Rivière	Rio
≅	Canal	Kanal	Canal	Canal	Canal
⌊	Waterfall, Rapids	Wasserfall, Stromschnellen	Cascada, Rápidos	Chute d'eau, Rapides	Cascata, Rápidos
⌣	Strait	Meeresstraße	Estrecho	Détroit	Estreito
⊂	Bay, Gulf	Bucht, Golf	Bahía, Golfo	Baie, Golfe	Baía, Golfo
⊜	Lake, Lakes	See, Seen	Lago, Lagos	Lac, Lacs	Lago, Lagos
≡	Swamp	Sumpf	Pantano	Marais	Pântano
⌂	Ice Features, Glacier	Eis- und Gletscherformen	Accidentes Glaciales	Formes glaciaires	Acidentes glaciares
⊤	Other Hydrographic Features	Andere Hydrographische Objekte	Otros Elementos Hidrográficos	Autres données hydrographiques	Outros acidentes hidrográficos
⊹	Submarine Features	Untermeerische Objekte	Accidentes Submarinos	Formes de relief sous-marin	Acidentes submarinos
□	Political Unit	Politische Einheit	Unidad Politica	Entité politique	Unidade política
⛉	Cultural Institution	Kulturelle Institution	Institución Cultural	Institution culturelle	Instituição cultural
⊥	Historical Site	Historische Stätte	Sitio Histórico	Site historique	Sitio histórico
♠	Recreational Site	Erholungs- und Ferienort	Sitio de Recreo	Centre de loisirs	Area de Lazer
⊠	Airport	Flughafen	Aeropuerto	Aéroport	Aeroporto
■	Military Installation	Militäranlage	Instalación Militar	Installation militaire	Instalação militar
⬥	Miscellaneous	Verschiedenes	Misceláneo	Divers	Diversos

ENGLISH — Name, Page, Lat.°′, Long.°′ / DEUTSCH — Name, Seite, Breite°′, Länge°′ E = Ost

Name	Page	Lat.°′	Long.°′
Yakapınar	130	37.00 N	35.36 E
Yakarta → Jakarta	115a	6.10 S	106.48 E
Yake-dake ∧	94	36.14 N	137.35 E
Yake-yama ∧	94	36.55 N	138.03 E
Yakhchāl, Afg.	120	31.47 N	64.41 E
Yakhchāl, Afg.	128	31.47 N	64.41 E
Yakima	202	46.36 N	120.30 W
Yakima □[6]	224	46.34 N	121.03 W
Yakima ≃	202	46.15 N	119.02 W
Yakima Firing Center ■	202	46.44 N	120.10 W
Yakima Indian Reservation ◆[4]	224	46.16 N	121.03 W
Yakkan ≃	96	33.34 N	131.22 E
Yakmach	128	28.45 N	63.51 E
Yako	150	12.58 N	2.16 W
Yakō ◆[8]	268	35.32 N	139.41 E
Yakobi Island I	180	58.00 N	136.30 W
Yakoma	152	4.05 N	22.27 E
Yakou	100	24.46 N	118.46 E
Yakuendai	268	35.43 N	140.03 E
Yakuluku	154	4.20 N	28.48 E
Yakumo	92a	42.15 N	140.16 E
Yakuno	96	35.19 N	135.00 E
Yakushi-dake ∧	94	36.28 N	137.33 E
Yakushi-ji ɞ[1]	94	36.25 N	139.53 E
Yaku-shima I	93b	30.20 N	130.30 E
Yakutat	180	59.33 N	139.44 W
Yakutat Bay ⊂	180	59.40 N	140.00 W
Yakutat Seamount ✣[3]	16	35.15 N	48.00 W
Yakutsk → Jakutsk	74	62.00 N	129.40 E
Yala, Ghana	150	10.07 N	1.52 W
Yala, Thai	110	6.33 N	101.18 E
Yalaha	220	28.44 N	81.48 W
Yalahán, Laguna de ⊂	232	21.30 N	87.15 W
Yalakdere	130	40.36 N	29.33 E
Yalata	162	31.29 S	131.52 E
Yalata Aboriginal Reserve ◆[4]	162	31.30 S	131.45 E
Yalca, Laguna ⊜	258	35.34 S	57.55 W
Yalding	260	51.13 N	0.26 E
Yale, B.C., Can.	182	49.34 N	121.26 W
Yale, Mi., U.S.	190	43.07 N	82.47 W
Yale, Ok., U.S.	196	36.06 N	96.41 W
Yale, Va., U.S.	208	36.50 N	77.17 W
Yale, Lake ⊜	220	28.54 N	81.45 W
Yale, Mount ∧	200	38.51 N	106.18 W
Yale Lake ⊜[1]	224	46.00 N	122.12 W
Yalgar ≃	162	26.09 S	117.57 E
Yalgoo	162	28.20 S	116.41 E
Yalgorup National Park ♦	168a	32.55 S	115.41 E
Yali	152	0.04 N	21.03 E
Yaliji	98	36.06 N	114.56 E
Yalikamba	152	1.17 S	22.30 E
Yalinga	152	6.31 N	23.15 E
Yalisere	152	0.11 N	22.33 E
Yalleroi	166	24.04 S	145.45 E
Yallourn	169	38.11 S	146.21 E
Yallourn North	169	38.09 S	146.22 E
Yalnızçam Dağları ⩕	84	41.10 N	42.25 E
Yalobusha ≃	194	33.33 N	90.10 W
Yaloká	152	5.19 N	17.05 E
Yalong ≃	102	26.37 N	101.48 E
Yalova	130	40.39 N	29.15 E
Yalta → Jalta	78	44.30 N	34.10 E
Yalu	89	48.34 N	122.09 E
Yalu (Amnok-kang) ≃, Asia	98	39.55 N	124.22 E
Yalu ≃, Zhg.	89	46.56 N	123.30 E
Yalufi	152	0.45 N	24.26 E
Yalvaç	130	38.17 N	31.11 E
Yalwal Creek ≃	170	34.50 S	150.23 E
Yamachiche	206	46.16 N	72.50 W
Yamachiche ≃	206	46.16 N	72.48 W
Yamada, Nihon	92	39.28 N	141.57 E
Yamada, Nihon	94	35.49 N	140.36 E
Yamada, Nihon	94	36.34 N	137.05 E
Yamada → Tosa-yamada	96	33.36 N	133.41 E
Yamada, Nihon	96	33.33 N	130.47 E
Yamada, Nihon	174m	26.26 N	127.47 E
Yamada, Nihon	270	34.31 N	135.39 E
Yamada, Nihon	270	34.48 N	135.32 E
Yamada ≃	270	34.47 N	135.04 E
Yamaga, Nihon	96	33.01 N	130.41 E
Yamaga, Nihon	96	33.27 N	131.30 E
Yamagata, Nihon	92	38.15 N	140.20 E
Yamagata, Nihon	94	36.38 N	140.24 E
Yamagata, Nihon	94	36.10 N	137.52 E
Yamagawa	92	31.12 N	130.39 E
Yamaguchi, Nihon	94	35.33 N	137.33 E
Yamaguchi, Nihon	96	34.10 N	131.29 E
Yamaguchi, Nihon	270	34.50 N	135.15 E
Yamaguchi □[5]	96	34.20 N	131.30 E
Yamaguchi-chosuichi ⊜[1]	268	35.46 N	139.25 E
Yama-Hita-Hiko-san-kokutei-kōen ♦	96	33.25 N	131.02 E
Yamakawa	96	34.04 N	134.15 E
Yamakita	94	35.21 N	139.05 E
Yamakuni	96	33.24 N	131.02 E
Yamakuni ≃	96	33.37 N	131.12 E
Yamām, Jabal al- ∧	132	30.02 N	35.28 E
Yamamoto, Nihon	96	34.07 N	133.44 E
Yamamoto, Nihon	270	34.38 N	135.38 E
Yamanaka	94	36.15 N	136.22 E
Yamanakako	94	35.24 N	138.52 E
Yamanaka-ko ⊜	94	35.25 N	138.52 E
Yamanashi	94	35.40 N	138.40 E
Yamanashi □[5]	94	35.30 N	138.30 E
Yamanouchi	94	36.44 N	138.25 E
Yamasaki	96	35.00 N	134.33 E
Yamashina ◆[8]	270	34.58 N	135.49 E
Yamashiro, Nihon	94	34.45 N	135.49 E
Yamashiro, Nihon	96	33.57 N	133.45 E
Yamaska (Saint-Michel)	206	46.00 N	72.55 W
Yamaska □[6]	206	46.00 N	72.45 W
Yamaska ≃	206	46.06 N	72.56 W
Yamaska, Mont ∧[2]	206	45.27 N	72.52 W
Yamaska Nord ≃	206	45.17 N	72.51 W
Yamaska Sud-Est ≃	206	45.17 N	72.55 W
Yamate	270	34.30 N	135.27 E
Yamatengwumulu	102	38.38 N	97.05 E
Yamato, Nihon	94	35.48 N	136.54 E
Yamato, Nihon	94	35.29 N	139.29 E
Yamato, Nihon	94	37.10 N	138.56 E
Yamato, Nihon	96	33.08 N	130.26 E
Yamato ≃	96	34.36 N	135.26 E
Yamato-Aogaki-kokutei-kōen ♦	94	34.40 N	135.50 E
Yamato-kōriyama	96	34.38 N	135.47 E
Yamato-takada	96	34.31 N	135.45 E
Yamatsuri	94	36.52 N	140.25 E
Yamazaki	268	35.56 N	139.54 E
Yamba	166	29.26 S	153.22 E
Yambata	152	2.26 N	21.58 E
Yambéring	150	11.49 N	12.21 W
Yambio	154	4.34 N	28.23 E
Yambol → Jambol	38	42.29 N	26.30 E
Yambou Head ≻	241h	13.09 N	61.09 W
Yamboyo	152	0.40 N	22.18 E
Yambrasbamba	248	5.45 S	77.54 W
Yambuya	154	1.16 N	24.33 E
Yamdena, Pulau I	164	7.36 S	131.25 E
Yame	96	33.28 N	130.34 E
Ya Men ⊂	100	22.09 N	113.05 E
Yamenkou	105	39.53 N	116.12 E
Yamenying	89	43.25 N	122.19 E
Yamethin	110	20.26 N	96.09 E
Yamhill	224	45.21 N	123.11 W
Yamhill □[6]	224	45.15 N	123.20 W
Yamhill ≃	224	45.14 N	123.00 W
Yamia	150	13.24 N	10.18 E
Yamizo-san ∧	94	36.56 N	140.17 E
Yamma Yamma, Lake ⊜	166	26.20 S	141.25 E
Yamoussoukro	150	6.49 N	5.17 W
Yampa	200	40.09 N	106.54 W
Yampa ≃	200	40.32 N	108.59 W
Yampa Plateau ⩕[1]	200	40.25 N	109.00 W
Yamparáez	248	19.10 S	65.10 W
Yamsay Mountain ∧	202	42.56 N	121.22 W
Yamu	102	43.48 N	94.48 E
Yamuna ≃	120	25.25 N	81.50 E
Yamuna Bridge ◆[5]	272a	28.40 N	77.14 E
Yamunānagar	124	30.07 N	77.18 E
Yamzho Yumco ⊜	120	28.58 N	90.44 E
Yan	114	5.48 N	100.22 E
Yan ≃, S. Lan.	122	8.55 N	81.01 E
Yan ≃, Zhg.	102	36.24 N	110.28 E
Yanac	166	36.08 S	141.26 E
Yanacachi	248	16.23 S	67.43 W
Yanadani	96	33.32 N	133.01 E
Yanagawa	96	33.10 N	130.24 E
Yanagi	270	34.25 N	135.56 E
Yanagimoto	270	34.34 N	135.51 E
Yanahara	96	34.55 N	134.05 E
Yanaha-shima I	174m	26.54 N	127.56 E
Yanahuara	248	16.24 S	71.33 W
Yanai	96	33.58 N	132.07 E
Yanaka	268	35.24 N	140.01 E
Yanam	122	16.44 N	82.13 E
Yan'an	102	36.36 N	109.28 E
Yanaoca	248	14.13 S	71.26 W
Yanarsu	130	38.02 N	41.33 E
Yanbian	102	26.55 N	101.30 E
Yanbu	100	23.05 N	113.10 E
Yanbuʻal-Baḥr	128	24.05 N	38.03 E
Yanbutou	100	29.52 N	115.04 E
Yanceyville	192	36.24 N	79.20 W
Yanchang	102	36.31 N	110.08 E
Yancheng, Zhg.	100	33.36 N	113.57 E
Yancheng, Zhg.	100	33.24 N	120.09 E
Yanchep	168a	31.33 S	115.41 E
Yanchep National Park ♦	168a	31.32 S	115.40 E
Yanchi, Zhg.	102	37.52 N	107.22 E
Yanchi, Zhg.	105	40.02 N	115.53 E
Yanchuan	102	36.56 N	110.05 E
Yanco	166	34.36 S	146.25 E
Yanco Creek ≃	166	35.16 S	145.07 E
Yanda Creek ≃	166	30.28 S	145.45 E
Yandal	162	27.33 S	121.07 E
Yandama Creek ≃	166	30.00 S	140.10 E
Yandé, Île I	175f	20.03 S	163.49 E
Yande Aboriginal Reserve ◆[4]	162	21.35 S	118.45 E
Yandev	150	7.20 N	9.01 E
Yandina	175e	9.07 S	159.13 E
Yandja	152	1.41 S	17.43 E
Yandongi	152	2.51 N	22.16 E
Yandoon	110	17.02 N	95.39 E
Yandua Island I	175g	16.49 S	178.18 E
Yandun	102	42.20 N	94.09 E
Yanfeng	102	25.53 N	101.01 E
Yanfolila	150	11.11 N	8.09 W
Yang ≃, Thai	110	15.44 N	104.00 E
Yang ≃, Zhg.	105	40.24 N	115.20 E
Yanga	234	18.50 N	96.48 W
Yangambi	154	0.47 N	24.28 E
Yangan, Austl.	171a	28.12 S	152.13 E
Yang'an, Zhg.	98	37.38 N	117.09 E
Yan'gang	100	26.02 N	116.22 E
Yangarakata	154	3.01 N	30.28 E
Yangasa Levu I	175g	18.57 S	178.26 W
Yangbajain	120	30.06 N	90.33 E
Yangce	100	32.58 N	113.14 E
Yangcha	98	41.11 N	126.15 E
Yangchang	107	30.22 N	103.42 E
Yangcheng, Zhg.	102	35.29 N	112.25 E
Yangcheng, Zhg.	106	31.24 N	120.47 E
Yangcheng Hu ⊜	106	31.26 N	120.47 E
Yangchiang → Yangjiang	102	21.51 N	111.56 E
Yangch'ŏn ◆[8]	271b	37.34 N	126.51 E
Yangchow → Yangzhou	100	32.24 N	119.26 E
Yangchu	98	37.11 N	120.47 E
Yangch'üan → Yangquan	98	37.52 N	113.36 E
Yangchun	102	22.10 N	111.46 E
Yangcun, Zhg.	100	28.07 N	117.40 E
Yangcun, Zhg.	100	23.26 N	114.30 E
Yangcun, Zhg.	105	39.09 N	115.50 E
Yangcunqiao	100	29.36 N	119.28 E
Yangdachengzi	89	43.59 N	124.25 E
Yangdalinzi	98	42.38 N	125.07 E
Yangdang	100	32.23 N	112.39 E
Yangdian	106	31.08 N	119.45 E
Yang'erzhuang	98	38.18 N	117.30 E
Yangfang	105	40.07 N	116.07 E
Yangfangpu	105	40.48 N	115.01 E
Yangfengang	105	39.07 N	116.52 E
Yangfenzhen	106	30.28 N	120.03 E
Yanggang Do □[4]	98	41.15 N	128.00 E
Yangganzhen	106	31.00 N	119.15 E
Yanggao	98	40.25 N	113.44 E
Yanggezhuang	105	40.09 N	116.48 E
Yanggong-ni	271b	37.39 N	126.37 E
Yanggu, Taehan	98	38.06 N	127.59 E
Yanggu, Zhg.	98	34.44 N	114.48 E
Yanggu, Zhg.	98	36.08 N	115.48 E
Yangguanpu	100	32.13 N	115.31 E
Yanghang	106	31.22 N	121.26 E
Yanghe	100	33.47 N	118.23 E
Yanghexi	102	29.39 N	108.40 E
Yanghu	100	32.34 N	116.30 E
Yanghua	107	30.11 N	104.45 E
Yanghua ≃	107	30.09 N	104.42 E
Yangi-Yul' → Jangijul'	85	41.07 N	69.03 E
Yangji, Zhg.	98	34.25 N	116.06 E
Yangji, Zhg.	98	36.44 N	113.56 E
Yangji, Zhg.	100	34.19 N	119.28 E
Yangjia, Zhg.	98	34.19 N	119.28 E
Yangjia, Zhg.	106	30.41 N	120.15 E
Yangjiachang, Zhg.	107	29.23 N	104.21 E
Yangjiachang, Zhg.	107	29.45 N	105.21 E
Yangjiafeng	100	30.49 N	112.47 E
Yangjiagou	105	39.18 N	117.54 E
Yangjiajie	107	30.18 N	104.39 E
Yangjian	106	31.39 N	120.33 E
Yangjiang	102	21.51 N	111.56 E
Yangjiaogou	98	37.16 N	118.50 E
Yangjiaqiao, Zhg.	100	27.44 N	112.46 E
Yangjiaqiao, Zhg.	106	32.02 N	121.26 E
Yangjiaqiao, Zhg.	106	31.53 N	121.42 E
Yangjiatao	105	39.49 N	117.51 E
Yangjiawopu	104	42.21 N	122.57 E
Yangjiazeng	105	40.12 N	117.04 E
Yangjiazhangzi	104	40.48 N	120.33 E
Yangjie	102	24.49 N	100.22 E
Yangjishi	100	26.39 N	113.14 E
Yangkou	100	26.47 N	117.51 E
Yangkoushi	100	28.39 N	118.53 E
Yanglinjie	100	29.07 N	113.27 E
Yangliupu, Zhg.	100	30.52 N	118.37 E
Yangliupu, Zhg.	107	30.09 N	104.03 E
Yangliuqing	105	39.08 N	117.01 E
Yangloudong	100	29.31 N	113.44 E
Yanglousi	100	29.30 N	113.38 E
Yangluo	100	30.41 N	114.34 E
Yangluomayu	104	40.47 N	122.54 E
Yangmachang	107	30.39 N	103.45 E
Yangma Dao I	98	37.28 N	121.37 E
Yangmahe	107	30.29 N	104.31 E
Yangmeisi	100	25.42 N	114.30 E
Yangmiao, Zhg.	98	34.11 N	114.53 E
Yangmiao, Zhg.	106	30.51 N	120.49 E
Yangmingshan ◆[8]	269d	25.09 N	121.33 E
Yangming Shan ∧	102	26.03 N	111.56 E
Yangmugou, Zhg.	98	40.36 N	124.28 E
Yangmugou, Zhg.	104	41.11 N	123.50 E
Yangmulin	105	40.06 N	115.12 E
Yangon (Rangoon)	110	16.47 N	96.10 E
Yangon □[8]	110	16.50 N	96.10 E
Yangor	174b	0.31 S	166.54 E
Yangpingguan	102	32.51 N	106.09 E
Yangpu	100	27.14 N	119.08 E
Yangp'yŏng	98	37.30 N	127.29 E
Yangp'yŏng-ni	98	40.53 N	127.58 E
Yangqi	106	31.23 N	119.57 E
Yangquan	98	37.52 N	113.36 E
Yangriwan	102	31.37 N	110.49 E
Yangsan	98	35.21 N	129.03 E
Yangshan, Zhg.	98	41.13 N	120.24 E
Yangshan, Zhg.	98	35.13 N	116.13 E
Yangshan, Zhg.	102	24.28 N	112.38 E
Yangshigangzi	104	41.42 N	122.59 E
Yangshitun	104	42.06 N	123.44 E
Yangshu	106	31.39 N	120.08 E
Yangshugemen	105	40.55 N	118.18 E
Yangshugoudonggou	104	41.43 N	120.41 E
Yangshuling	98	41.02 N	118.47 E
Yangshuo	102	24.45 N	110.24 E
Yangtan	106	30.42 N	119.11 E
Yangtian Zhang ∧	100	24.37 N	115.38 E
Yangting	98	37.24 N	122.07 E
Yangtou	100	23.26 N	115.24 E
Yangtze → Chang ≃	90	31.48 N	121.10 E
Yanguan	106	30.26 N	120.32 E
Yangwan, Zhg.	100	28.22 N	116.46 E
Yangwan, Zhg.	106	31.03 N	120.22 E
Yangxi, Zhg.	100	30.11 N	118.39 E
Yangxi, Zhg.	100	27.18 N	114.10 E
Yangxian	102	33.03 N	107.47 E
Yangxiang, Zhg.	106	31.29 N	119.35 E
Yangxiang, Zhg.	106	31.12 N	121.01 E
Yangxiangtun	104	40.58 N	122.48 E
Yangxiaodian	100	31.46 N	116.45 E
Yangximu ≃	104	42.04 N	123.00 E
Yangxin, Zhg.	98	37.39 N	117.34 E
Yangxin, Zhg.	100	29.51 N	115.12 E
Yangxiudian	271a	39.44 N	116.32 E
Yangyang	98	38.04 N	128.36 E
Yangyuan (Xicheng)	98	40.01 N	114.10 E
Yangze	100	26.57 N	118.23 E
Yangzhong	106	32.16 N	119.49 E
Yangzhou	100	32.24 N	119.26 E
Yangzhuang	100	33.36 N	118.58 E
Yangzhujuanzi	104	41.38 N	122.46 E
Yangzi	100	31.19 N	112.36 E
Yangzishao	98	42.28 N	126.09 E
Yanhaiyingzi	104	41.52 N	123.05 E
Yanhe, Zhg.	100	31.16 N	115.07 E
Yanhe, Zhg.	102	28.37 N	108.35 E
Yanhecheng	105	40.04 N	115.43 E
Yanheying	98	40.02 N	119.03 E
Yanhui	98	37.54 N	113.51 E
Yanina → Ioánnina	38	39.40 N	20.50 E
Yanji, Zhg.	98	34.17 N	115.39 E
Yanji, Zhg.	98	34.41 N	115.27 E
Yanji, Zhg.	98	42.57 N	129.32 E
Yanji (Longjing), Zhg.	98	42.47 N	129.26 E
Yanjia	104	40.57 N	121.41 E
Yanjiabao	106	32.19 N	120.07 E
Yanjiadian	98	39.48 N	121.49 E
Yanjiahe	100	31.48 N	114.50 E
Yanjiajie	104	41.02 N	121.32 E
Yanjiao	105	39.56 N	116.48 E
Yanjiapu	105	39.52 N	118.00 E
Yanjiatuozi	104	42.27 N	123.47 E
Yanjiawopeng	104	40.59 N	121.17 E
Yanjin	98	35.11 N	114.11 E
Yanjing, Zhg.	102	29.00 N	98.34 E
Yanjing, Zhg.	107	29.56 N	106.21 E
Yankalilla	168b	35.28 S	138.21 E
Yankalilla Bay ⊂	168b	35.28 S	138.15 E
Yankari Game Reserve ◆[4]	146	9.45 N	10.30 E
Yankdŏk	98	39.14 N	126.41 E
Yankee Lake	210	41.35 N	74.33 W
Yankee Springs State Recreation Area ♦	216	42.38 N	85.30 W
Yankee Stadium ♦	276	40.50 N	73.56 W
Yankeetown	220	29.01 N	82.42 W
Yankton	198	42.52 N	97.23 W
Yankton Indian Reservation ◆[4]	198	43.10 N	98.22 W
Yanling, Zhg.	98	34.07 N	114.11 E
Yanling, Zhg.	106	31.54 N	119.30 E
Yanliumiao	100	32.01 N	116.52 E
Yanmeimeizi	105	39.42 N	115.03 E
Yanna	166	26.56 S	146.03 E
Yannarie ≃	162	22.28 S	114.48 E
Yanqi	90	42.00 N	86.15 E
Yanqian, Zhg.	100	24.54 N	116.14 E
Yanqian, Zhg.	100	26.15 N	117.28 E
Yanqianhu	104	42.16 N	123.12 E
Yanqiao	106	31.41 N	120.17 E
Yanqidoumen	106	31.17 N	118.42 E
Yanqing	105	40.28 N	115.58 E
Yanque	248	15.39 S	71.39 W
Yanrey	162	22.31 S	114.48 E
Yanshan, Zhg.	98	38.05 N	117.13 E
Yanshan, Zhg.	100	28.18 N	117.41 E
Yanshan, Zhg.	102	23.41 N	104.21 E
Yan Shan ⩕	105	40.20 N	117.40 E
Yanshankou	105	39.59 N	117.42 E
Yanshi	100	25.17 N	117.10 E
Yanshi ≃	100	25.20 N	117.17 E
Yanshou	89	45.28 N	128.20 E
Yansi	100	29.48 N	118.20 E
Yanṭā	132	33.36 N	35.57 E
Yantabulla	166	29.21 S	145.00 E
Yantai (Chefoo), Zhg.	98	37.33 N	121.20 E
Yantai, Zhg.	105	39.47 N	116.38 E
Yantan, Zhg.	100	28.28 N	120.44 E
Yantan, Zhg.	100	28.55 N	120.11 E
Yantan, Zhg.	107	29.17 N	104.52 E
Yantian, Zhg.	100	26.53 N	119.53 E
Yantian, Zhg.	100	27.21 N	114.22 E
Yantic ≃	207	41.31 N	72.05 W
Yantietang ≊	106	31.49 N	120.46 E
Yanting	102	31.19 N	105.23 E
Yantis	222	32.56 N	95.35 W
Yantongshan, Zhg.	89	43.17 N	126.00 E
Yantongshan, Zhg.	105	40.42 N	115.06 E
Yanu	164	9.57 S	148.25 E
Yanwangshan	104	41.36 N	123.57 E
Yanweigang	98	34.30 N	119.48 E
Yanxi	100	24.46 N	117.47 E
Yanxia	100	29.34 N	114.50 E
Yanxidu	100	26.51 N	114.58 E
Yanxing	102	25.23 N	101.42 E
Yan Yean Reservoir ⊜[1]	169	37.33 S	145.08 E
Yanyegongsi	106	32.02 N	121.41 E
Yanyuan	102	27.29 N	101.32 E
Yanzhou	98	35.33 N	116.50 E
Yanziji	106	32.09 N	118.49 E
Yanzijiao	102	23.38 N	100.12 E
Yanzikou	102	27.31 N	105.21 E
Yao, Centraf.	152	5.19 N	19.36 E
Yao, Nihon	96	34.37 N	135.36 E
Yao, Tchad	146	12.51 N	17.34 E
Yao Airport ⊠	270	34.36 N	135.36 E
Yao'an	102	25.32 N	101.12 E
Yaoba	107	28.45 N	105.39 E
Yaocun, Zhg.	98	36.12 N	113.50 E
Yaocun, Zhg.	98	35.41 N	116.57 E
Yaocun, Zhg.	105	39.09 N	115.32 E
Yaodafangshen	104	42.27 N	122.59 E
Yaoerwan	105	40.49 N	115.27 E
Yaogongbu	100	29.51 N	120.18 E
Yaohongcaopao	104	40.55 N	122.26 E
Yaohuamen	106	32.08 N	118.52 E
Yaohuangdi	104	41.32 N	122.48 E
Yaojiaji	100	31.14 N	114.22 E
Yaojiaqiao	106	32.10 N	119.46 E
Yaojiatun	104	41.18 N	121.57 E
Yaojiawopeng	104	41.47 N	122.25 E
Yaojie	102	36.26 N	102.59 E
Yaoling	100	24.49 N	113.58 E
Yaolugou	98	40.34 N	119.24 E
Yaoluzi	104	41.26 N	121.34 E
Yaopi	100	26.52 N	113.38 E
Yaopu	100	32.14 N	118.20 E
Yaoqianhutun	104	41.32 N	123.36 E
Yaoshizhen	107	30.11 N	105.30 E
Yaotou	100	26.38 N	114.48 E
Yaotsu	94	35.28 N	137.09 E
Yaotun, Zhg.	89	49.28 N	127.30 E
Yaotun, Zhg.	104	40.59 N	122.18 E
Yaotutun	104	42.06 N	123.29 E
Yaoundé	152	3.52 N	11.31 E
Yaowan	98	34.12 N	118.03 E
Yaowangmiao	98	40.47 N	120.10 E
Yaoxian	102	34.56 N	108.53 E
Yaoya ≃	236	13.28 N	84.14 W
Yao Yai, Ko I	110	8.00 N	98.35 E
Yaozhan	89	52.53 N	125.13 E
Yap I	174q	9.31 N	138.06 E
Yapacaní	248	16.45 S	64.18 W
Yapacani ≃	248	16.00 S	64.25 W
Yapakopra	164	4.24 S	135.05 E
Yapehe	152	0.13 S	24.27 E
Yapei (Tamale Port)	150	9.10 N	1.10 W
Yapen, Pulau I	164	1.45 S	136.15 E
Yapen, Selat ʯ	164	1.30 S	136.10 E
Yapero	164	4.59 S	137.11 E
Yapeyú	252	29.28 S	56.49 W
Yaphank	207	40.50 N	72.56 W
Yappar ≃	166	18.22 S	141.16 E
Yapraklı	130	40.46 N	33.47 E
Yap Trench ✣[1]	14	8.30 N	138.00 E
Yaqian	100	26.38 N	114.30 E
Yaʻqūb	140	12.29 N	25.11 E
Yaque del Norte ≃	238	19.51 N	71.41 W
Yaqui	232	27.19 N	110.01 W
Yaqui ≃	232	27.37 N	110.39 W
Yaquina ≃	202	44.37 N	124.04 W
Yara	240p	20.16 N	76.57 W
Yaracuy □[3]	246	10.20 N	69.10 W
Yaraka	166	24.53 S	144.04 E
Yaratuar	164	2.58 S	134.40 E
Yarbasan	130	38.59 N	28.49 E
Yarcombe	42	50.52 N	3.05 W
Yardea	166	32.23 S	135.32 E
Yardımcı	130	37.00 N	38.59 E
Yardımcı Burnu ≻	130	36.13 N	30.25 E
Yardley	208	40.14 N	74.50 W
Yardville	208	40.10 N	74.39 W
Yare ≃	42	52.35 N	1.44 E
Yarí ≃	246	0.23 S	72.16 W
Yariga-take ∧	94	36.20 N	137.39 E
Yārik	123	32.06 N	70.47 E
Yarīm	144	14.29 N	44.21 E
Yaring	110	6.52 N	101.22 E
Yaritagua	246	10.05 N	69.08 W
Yarkand → Shache	120	38.25 N	77.16 E
Yarkand → Yarkant ≃	90	40.28 N	80.52 E
Yarkant (Yarkand) ≃	90	40.28 N	80.52 E
Yarker	212	44.23 N	76.46 W
Yarkhūn ≃	123	36.17 N	72.30 E
Yarlarweelor	162	25.35 S	117.59 E
Yarle Lakes ⊜	162	30.15 S	131.27 E
Yarloop	168a	32.57 S	115.54 E
Yarlung → Brahmaputra ≃	120	24.02 N	90.59 E
Yarma	130	37.49 N	32.54 E
Yarmouth, N.S., Can.	186	43.50 N	66.07 W
Yarmouth, Eng., U.K.	42	50.42 N	1.29 W
Yarmouth → Great Yarmouth, Eng., U.K.	42	52.37 N	1.44 E
Yarmouth, Me., U.S.	188	43.48 N	70.11 W
Yarmouth, Ma., U.S.	207	41.42 N	70.13 W
Yarmu	164	4.18 S	142.17 E
Yarmūk, Nahr al- ≃	132	32.38 N	35.34 E
Yaroupi ≃	250	2.47 N	52.28 W
Yarra ≃	169	37.51 S	144.54 E
Yarra Bend Park ♦	274b	37.48 S	145.01 E
Yarra Glen	169	37.40 S	145.23 E
Yarragon	169	38.12 S	146.04 E
Yarra Junction	169	37.47 S	145.37 E
Yarraloola	162	21.34 S	115.52 E
Yarram	166	38.33 S	146.41 E
Yarraman	171a	26.50 S	151.59 E
Yarrangobilly	171b	35.39 S	148.28 E
Yarrangobilly ≃	171b	35.48 N	148.23 E
Yarrangobilly Caves ⩲[5]	171b	35.44 S	148.29 E
Yarraville	274b	37.49 S	144.53 E
Yarrawonga	166	36.01 S	146.00 E
Yarra Yarra Lakes ⊜	162	29.40 S	115.47 E
Yarrow, B.C., Can.	224	49.05 N	122.02 W
Yarrow, Scot., U.K.	46	55.32 N	3.01 W
Yarrow ≃	262	53.40 N	2.49 W
Yarrowee ≃	169	37.48 S	143.56 E
Yarrow Point	224	47.39 N	122.13 W
Yarrow Reservoir ⊜[1]	262	53.38 N	2.34 W
Yarrow Water ≃	44	55.34 N	2.51 W
Yarrunga, Lake ⊜[1]	170	34.45 S	150.20 E
Yarty ≃	42	50.47 N	3.01 W
Yarumal	246	6.58 N	75.24 W
Yarvicoya, Cerro ∧	248	20.07 S	69.00 W
Yasa	152	3.42 S	21.24 E
Yasaka, Nihon	96	35.39 N	135.07 E
Yasaka, Nihon	96	34.46 N	132.04 E
Yasa-Lokwa	152	5.15 S	19.24 E
Yasato	94	36.14 N	140.12 E
Yasawa I	175g	16.47 S	177.31 E
Yasawa Group II	175g	17.00 S	177.23 E
Yasendu	152	0.27 N	24.20 E
Yashanjie	106	30.51 N	119.03 E
Yashbum	144	14.19 N	46.56 E
Yashi	150	12.23 N	7.54 E
Yashikera	150	9.46 N	3.28 E
Ya-shima I	96	33.44 N	132.09 E
Yashima ♦	96	34.23 N	134.08 E
Yashio	268	35.49 N	139.51 E
Yashiro	96	34.55 N	134.58 E
Yashiro-jima I	96	33.55 N	132.15 E
Yāsīn	123	36.21 N	73.19 E
Yasku	146	12.20 N	12.30 E
Yasothon	110	15.45 N	104.08 E
Yass	166	34.50 S	148.55 E
Yassıada I	267b	40.51 N	29.00 E
Yassy → Iaşi	38	47.10 N	27.35 E
Yasu, Nihon	94	35.03 N	136.01 E
Yasu, Nihon	96	33.32 N	133.45 E
Yasuda	96	33.26 N	133.59 E
Yasugi	96	35.26 N	133.15 E
Yāsūj	128	30.40 N	51.36 E
Yasun Burnu ≻	130	41.08 N	37.41 E
Yasuni ≃	246	0.56 S	75.23 W
Yasuoka	94	35.22 N	137.50 E
Yasuura	96	34.17 N	132.45 E
Yasuzuka	94	37.08 N	138.28 E
Yata	248	13.20 S	66.35 W
Yata ≃, Bol.	248	10.29 S	65.26 W
Yata ≃, Centraf.	146	10.23 N	22.45 E
Yatabe	94	36.02 N	140.04 E
Yatağan	130	37.20 N	28.09 E
Yatakala	150	14.48 N	0.22 E
Yata-Ngaya, Réserve de Faune de la ◆[4]	146	9.15 N	23.30 W
Yāṭar	132	33.09 N	35.20 E
Yatate-yama ∧	92	34.10 N	129.10 E
Yaté	175f	22.09 S	166.57 E
Yates □[6]	210	42.40 N	77.03 W
Yatesboro	214	40.48 N	79.20 W
Yates Center	198	37.52 N	95.43 W
Yates City	190	40.46 N	90.00 W
Yathata Island I	175g	17.15 S	179.32 W
Yathkyed Lake ⊜	176	62.41 N	98.00 W
Yating	102	25.03 N	106.05 E
Yatomi	94	35.06 N	136.43 E
Yatsuga-take ∧	94	35.59 N	138.23 E
Yatsuga-take-chūshin-kōgen-kokutei-kōen ♦	94	36.03 N	138.20 E
Yatsuka	96	35.17 N	133.42 E
Yatsuo	94	36.34 N	137.08 E
Yatsushiro	92	32.30 N	130.36 E
Yatsushiro-kai ⊂	92	32.20 N	130.25 E
Yaṭṭah	132	31.27 N	35.05 E
Yatta Plateau ⩕[1]	154	2.00 S	38.00 E
Yatton	42	51.24 N	2.49 W
Yatua ≃	246	1.43 N	66.30 W
Yatusiro → Yatsushiro	92	32.30 N	130.36 E
Yauca	248	15.40 S	74.32 W
Yauca ≃	248	15.41 S	74.31 W
Yauco	240m	18.02 N	66.51 W
Yauco ≃	240m	17.59 N	66.48 W
Yauco, Embalse de ⊜[1]	240m	18.07 N	66.50 W
Yauli	248	11.41 S	76.06 W
Yaundé → Yaoundé	152	3.52 N	11.31 E
Yaupi	246	2.59 S	77.50 W
Yautepec	234	18.53 N	99.04 W
Yau Tong	271d	22.18 N	114.13 E
Yauyos	248	12.24 S	75.57 W
Yāval	120	21.10 N	75.42 E
Yavarí (Javari) ≃	242	4.21 S	70.02 W
Yavarí Mirim ≃	246	4.31 S	71.44 W
Yavaros	232	26.42 N	109.31 W
Yavatmāl	122	20.24 N	78.08 E
Yaven Yaven Creek ≃	171b	35.06 S	147.46 E
Yavero ≃	248	12.06 S	72.57 W
Yavi	130	39.48 N	36.13 E
Yaví, Cerro ∧	246	5.32 N	65.59 W
Yavita	246	2.55 N	67.26 W
Yaviza	246	8.11 N	77.41 W
Yavne	132	31.53 N	34.45 E
Yavuzeli	130	37.20 N	37.33 E
Yavuzkemal	130	40.43 N	38.21 E
Yaw ≃	110	20.55 N	94.49 E
Yawahara	268	35.59 N	140.01 E
Yawata → Kitakyūshū, Nihon	96	33.53 N	130.50 E
Yawata, Nihon	96	34.52 N	135.42 E
Yawata, Nihon	268	35.32 N	140.08 E
Yawatahama	96	33.27 N	132.24 E
Yaxchilan ⊥	232	16.54 N	90.58 W
Yaxi	102	27.32 N	106.45 E
Yaxian	110	18.20 N	109.30 E
Yaxigang	106	31.23 N	119.10 E
Yaxley	42	52.31 N	0.16 W
Yayama	152	1.16 S	23.07 E
Yayladağı	130	35.56 N	36.01 E
Yayladere	130	39.14 N	40.03 E
Yaylak	130	37.23 N	38.20 E
Yayouta	150	8.11 N	8.30 W
Yayuan	98	41.47 N	126.11 E
Yazd	128	31.53 N	54.25 E
Yazd □[4]	128	32.00 N	54.30 E
Yazi	98	37.04 N	121.17 E
Yazichangcun	104	41.16 N	122.26 E
Yazıhan	130	38.36 N	38.11 E
Yazmān	123	29.08 N	71.45 E
Yazoo ≃	194	32.22 N	91.00 W
Yazoo City	194	32.51 N	90.24 W
Ybbs ≃	61	48.10 N	15.06 E
Ybbs an der Donau	61	48.11 N	15.05 E
Ybbsitz	61	47.56 N	14.53 E
Ybor City	220	27.57 N	82.27 W
Ybycuí	252	26.01 S	57.03 W
Yding Skovhøj ∧[2]	41	56.00 N	9.48 E
Ydstebøhavn	26	59.08 N	5.15 E
Ydžid Parma ⩕	24	63.06 N	58.15 E
Ye	110	15.15 N	97.51 E
Yea	169	37.13 S	145.26 E
Yea ≃	169	37.11 S	145.23 E
Yeading ◆[8]	260	51.32 N	0.24 W
Yeadon, Eng., U.K.	44	53.52 N	1.41 W
Yeadon, Pa., U.S.	285	39.56 N	75.15 W
Yeagertown	208	40.38 N	77.34 W
Yealm ≃	42	50.18 N	4.03 W
Yealmpton	42	50.21 N	3.59 W
Yebawgyi	110	18.40 N	94.35 E
Yebbi-Bou	146	20.58 N	18.04 E
Yébigué, Enneri V	146	22.04 N	17.49 E
Yèbles	261	48.38 N	2.46 E
Yebyu	110	14.15 N	98.12 E
Yecapixtla	234	18.53 N	98.52 W
Yecheng	120	37.54 N	77.25 E
Yech'ŏn	98	36.40 N	128.26 E
Yecla	34	38.37 N	1.07 W
Yécora	232	28.20 N	108.58 W
Yedashe	110	19.09 N	96.21 E
Yedi Göller Milli Parkı ♦	130	40.50 N	31.30 E
Yedikule ◆[8]	267b	40.59 N	28.55 E
Yedikule ⊥	267b	40.59 N	28.55 E
Yédinga, Ouadi V	146	15.46 N	20.05 E
Yedseram ≃	146	12.30 N	14.05 E
Yeed	144	4.33 N	43.02 E
Yeeda	162	17.36 S	123.39 E
Yeelanna	166	34.09 S	135.45 E
Yeelirrie	162	27.17 S	120.06 E
Yeernuozha Hu ⊜	120	32.30 N	89.30 E
Yegor'yevsk → Jegorjevsk	82	55.23 N	39.02 E
Yegros	252	26.24 S	56.25 W
Yegua Creek ≃	222	30.23 N	96.18 W
Yeguas, Río de las ≃	34	37.22 N	4.45 W
Yehliu	269d	25.12 N	121.41 E
Yehliu Chia ≻	269d	25.13 N	121.42 E
Yehud	132	32.02 N	34.53 E
Yei	154	4.05 N	30.40 E
Yei ≃	140	6.15 N	30.13 E
Yeji, Ghana	150	8.13 N	0.39 W
Yeji, Zhg.	100	31.52 N	115.55 E
Yekaterinburg → Sverdlovsk	86	56.51 N	60.36 E
Yekaterinodar → Krasnodar	78	45.02 N	39.00 E
Yekaterinoslav → Dnepropetrovsk	78	48.27 N	34.59 E
Yekokora ≃	152	1.20 N	20.21 E
Yekumbo	152	1.02 S	23.27 E
Ye Kyun I	110	18.37 N	93.47 E
Yela Island I	160	11.21 S	154.09 E
Yelarbon	166	28.34 S	150.45 E
Yele	150	8.25 N	11.50 W
Yelets → Jelec	76	52.37 N	38.30 E
Yélimané	150	15.08 N	10.34 W
Yell I	46a	60.36 N	1.06 W
Yellandu	122	17.36 N	80.20 E
Yellow ≃, U.S.	194	30.33 N	87.00 W
Yellow ≃, In., U.S.	216	41.16 N	86.50 W
Yellow ≃, Ia., U.S.	190	43.05 N	91.11 W
Yellow ≃, Wi., U.S.	190	44.58 N	91.18 W
Yellow ≃, Wi., U.S.	190	43.59 N	90.03 W
Yellow ≃, Wi., U.S.	190	46.01 N	92.22 W
Yellow → Huang ≃	90	37.32 N	118.19 E
Yellow Breeches Creek ≃	208	40.13 N	76.51 W
Yellow Creek ≃, U.S.	194	33.34 N	88.20 W
Yellow Creek ≃, Co., U.S.	200	40.10 N	108.24 W
Yellow Creek ≃, Oh., U.S.	214	40.34 N	80.40 W
Yellow Creek ≃, Tn., U.S.	194	36.26 N	87.34 W
Yellow Creek, North Fork ≃	214	40.33 N	80.42 W
Yellow Creek State Park ♦	214	40.35 N	79.02 W
Yellowdine	162	31.18 S	119.39 E
Yellow Grass	184	49.49 N	104.08 W
Yellowhead Pass)(	182	52.53 N	118.28 W
Yellow House Draw V	196	33.35 N	101.50 W
Yellowknife	176	62.27 N	114.21 W
Yellowknife ≃	176	62.31 N	114.19 W
Yellow Lake ⊜	212	44.20 N	75.36 W
Yellow Medicine ≃	198	44.44 N	95.25 W
Yellow Mountain ∧	166	32.30 S	146.51 E
Yellow Sea ≂[2]	90	36.00 N	123.00 E
Yellow Springs	218	39.48 N	83.53 W
Yellowstone ≃	178	47.58 N	103.59 W
Yellowstone, Clarks Fork ≃	202	45.39 N	108.43 W
Yellowstone Falls ∟	202	44.43 N	110.30 W
Yellowstone Lake ⊜	202	44.25 N	110.22 W
Yellowstone National Park	202	44.59 N	110.42 W
Yellowstone National Park ♦	202	44.30 N	110.35 W
Yellowtail Dam ◆[6]	202	45.12 N	107.57 W
Yell Sound ʯ	46a	60.32 N	1.15 W
Yellville	194	36.13 N	92.41 W
Yelm	224	46.56 N	122.36 W
Yelma	162	26.30 S	121.40 E
Yelvertoft	166	20.13 S	138.53 E
Yelverton	42	50.30 N	4.05 W
Yelwa	150	10.51 N	4.46 E
Yema ≃	102	41.25 N	95.10 E
Yemadu	86	43.36 N	81.50 E
Yemagong	124	29.28 N	89.06 E
Yemaotai	104	42.20 N	122.53 E
Yemassee	192	32.41 N	80.51 W
Yematan	102	34.40 N	98.16 E
Yemen (Al-Yaman) □[1], Asia	118	15.00 N	47.00 E
Yemen (Al-Yaman) □[1], Asia	144	15.00 N	47.00 E
Yemen, People's Democratic Republic of → Yemen □[1]	118	15.00 N	47.00 E
Yemen, República Popular Democrática del → Yemen □[1]	144	15.00 N	47.00 E
Yémen, République démocratique populaire du → Yemen □[1]	144	15.00 N	47.00 E
Yen	152	2.27 N	12.41 E
Yenagoa	150	4.55 N	6.19 E
Yenakiyevo → Jenakijevo	83	48.14 N	38.13 E
Yenangyaung	110	20.28 N	94.52 E
Yenanma	110	19.46 N	94.48 E
Yen Bai	110	21.42 N	104.52 E
Yen Chau	110	21.03 N	104.18 E
Yench'eng → Yancheng	100	33.24 N	120.09 E
Yenchi → Yanji	98	42.57 N	129.32 E
Yenda	166	34.15 S	146.11 E
Yende Millimou	150	8.53 N	10.11 W
Yendéré	150	10.12 N	4.58 W
Yendi	150	9.26 N	0.01 W
Ye-ngan	110	21.09 N	96.27 E
Yenge ≃	152	0.55 S	20.40 E
Yengema	150	8.43 N	11.10 W
Yengisar	85	38.57 N	76.03 E
Yengo	152	0.22 N	15.29 E
Yengo, Mount ∧	170	32.59 S	150.51 E
Yéni	150	13.26 N	2.59 E
Yeniçağa	130	40.46 N	32.02 E
Yenice, Tür.	130	39.45 N	28.55 E
Yenice, Tür.	130	41.11 N	32.19 E
Yenice, Tür.	130	39.55 N	27.18 E
Yenice, Tür.	130	36.59 N	35.03 E
Yenice ≃	130	41.35 N	32.03 E
Yenicekale	130	37.37 N	36.37 E
Yeniceoba	130	38.53 N	32.48 E
Yenierenköy	130	35.32 N	34.11 E
Yenifoça	130	38.44 N	26.51 E
Yenikapı ◆[8]	267b	41.00 N	28.57 E
Yeniköy	130	39.46 N	28.00 E
Yeniköy ◆[8]	267b	40.59 N	28.53 E
Yenimehmetli	130	39.26 N	32.10 E
Yenipazar, Tür.	130	37.48 N	28.12 E
Yenipazar, Tür.	130	40.11 N	30.31 E
Yenişehir	130	40.16 N	29.39 E
Yenisey → Jenisej ≃	72	71.50 N	82.40 E
Yennadon	224	49.14 N	122.34 W
Yenne	62	45.42 N	5.46 E
Yennora	274a	33.52 S	150.58 E
Yenshuichen	100	23.20 N	120.16 E
Yentna ≃	180	61.34 N	150.28 W
Yeo ≃	42	51.02 N	2.49 W
Yeola	122	20.02 N	74.29 E
Yeo Lake ⊜	162	28.04 S	124.23 E
Yeoman	216	40.40 N	86.43 W
Yeoval	166	32.45 S	148.40 E
Yeovil	42	50.57 N	2.39 W
Yeoville ◆[8]	273d	26.12 S	28.04 E
Yepachic	232	28.26 N	108.23 W
Yeppoon	166	23.08 S	150.45 E
Yerba Buena, Montaña ∧	236	14.05 N	87.26 W
Yerba Buena Island I	282	37.48 N	122.22 W
Yères ≃	50	50.02 N	1.19 E
Yerevan → Jerevan	84	40.11 N	44.30 E
Yerilla	162	29.28 S	121.49 E
Yering	274b	37.41 S	145.23 E
Yerington	226	38.59 N	119.09 W
Yerington Indian Reservation ◆[4]	226	39.05 N	119.12 W
Yerkes	285	40.10 N	75.27 W
Yerkes Astronomical Observatory ɞ[3]	216	42.34 N	88.34 W
Yerkesik	130	37.07 N	28.17 E
Yerköy	130	39.38 N	34.29 E
Yerlisu	130	40.46 N	26.39 E
Yermasóyia	130	34.43 N	33.05 E
Yermenonville	261	48.33 N	1.37 E
Yermo	204	34.54 N	116.49 W
Yeroḥam	132	31.00 N	34.55 E
Yerolimín	38	36.28 N	22.24 E
Yèrre ≃	50	48.01 N	1.16 E
Yerres	50	48.43 N	2.30 E
Yerres ≃	50	48.43 N	2.27 E
Yerseke	52	51.29 N	4.02 E
Yerupaja, Nevado ∧	248	10.16 S	76.54 W
Yerushalayim (Al-Quds) (Jerusalem)	132	31.46 N	35.14 E
Yerushalayim □[5]	132	31.45 N	35.00 E
Yerville	50	49.40 N	0.54 E
Yesa, Embalse de ⊜[1]	34	42.36 N	1.09 W
Yesan	98	36.41 N	126.50 E
Yeshenpu	104	40.51 N	122.32 E
Yeshiva University ɞ[2]	276	40.51 N	73.55 W
Yeshvi	272c	18.55 N	73.03 E
Yeşil ≃	130	41.24 N	36.35 E
Yeşilçonlu	130	40.13 N	28.06 E
Yeşildere	130	37.09 N	33.31 E
Yeşilhisar	130	38.21 N	35.06 E
Yeşilkent	130	36.59 N	36.10 E
Yeşilköy	130	40.57 N	28.49 E
Yeşilköy Burnu ≻	267b	40.57 N	28.50 E
Yeşilova	130	37.30 N	29.46 E
Yeşiltepe	130	37.12 N	33.02 E
Yeşilyazı	130	39.20 N	39.05 E
Yeşilyurt	130	38.18 N	38.15 E

Symbols in the index entries represent the broad categories identified in the key at the right. Symbols with superior numbers (⩕[1]) identify subcategories (see complete key on page I · 1).

Symbole im Register stellen die rechts im Schlüssel erklärten Kategorien dar. Symbole mit hochgestellten Ziffern (⩕[1]) bezeichnen Unterabteilungen einer Kategorie (vgl. vollständiger Schlüssel auf Seite I · 1).

Los símbolos incluídos en el texto del índice representan las grandes categorias identificadas con la clave a la derecha. Los símbolos con numeros en su parte superior (⩕[1]) identifican las subcategorías (véase la clave completa en la página I · 1).

Les symboles de l'index représentent les catégories indiquées dans la légende à droite. Les symboles suivis d'un indice (⩕[1]) représentent des sous-catégories (voir légende complète à la page I · 1).

Os símbolos incluídos no texto do índice representam as grandes categorias identificadas com a chave à direita. Os símbolos com números em sua parte superior (⩕[1]) identificam as subcategorias (veja-se a chave completa à página I · 1).

	English	Deutsch	Español	Français	Português
∧	Mountain	Berg	Montaña	Montagne	Montanha
⩕	Mountains	Gebirge	Montañas	Montagnes	Montanhas
)(	Pass	Paß	Paso	Col	Passo
V	Valley, Canyon	Tal, Cañon	Valle, Cañón	Vallée, Canyon	Vale, Canhão
≚	Plain	Ebene	Llano	Plaine	Planície
≻	Cape	Kap	Cabo	Cap	Cabo
I	Island	Insel	Isla	Île	Ilha
II	Islands	Inseln	Islas	Îles	Ilhas
⩲	Other Topographic Features	Andere Topographische Objekte	Otros Elementos Topográficos	Autres données topographiques	Outros acidentes topográficos

Symbol	English	Deutsch	Español	Français	Português
≃	River	Fluß	Río	Rivière	Rio
≊	Canal	Kanal	Canal	Canal	Canal
∟	Waterfall, Rapids	Wasserfall, Stromschnellen	Cascada, Rápidos	Chute d'eau, Rapides	Cascata, Rápidos
⊔	Strait	Meeresstraße	Estrecho	Détroit	Estreito
⊂	Bay, Gulf	Bucht, Golf	Bahía, Golfo	Baie, Golfe	Baía, Golfo
⊜	Lake, Lakes	See, Seen	Lago, Lagos	Lac, Lacs	Lago, Lagos
≡	Swamp	Sumpf	Pantano	Marais	Pântano
⊓	Ice Features, Glacier	Eis- und Gletscherformen	Accidentes Glaciales	Formes glaciaires	Acidentes glaciares
∓	Other Hydrographic Features	Andere Hydrographische Objekte	Otros Elementos Hidrográficos	Autres données hydrographiques	Outros acidentes hidrográficos
✣	Submarine Features	Untermeerische Objekte	Accidentes Submarinos	Formes de relief sous-marin	Acidentes submarinos
□	Political Unit	Politische Einheit	Unidad Politica	Entité politique	Unidade política
♁	Cultural Institution	Kulturelle Institution	Institución Cultural	Institution culturelle	Instituição cultural
⊥	Historical Site	Historische Stätte	Sitio Histórico	Site historique	Sitio histórico
♠	Recreational Site	Erholungs- und Ferienort	Sitio de Recreo	Centre de loisirs	Area de Lazer
⊠	Airport	Flughafen	Aeropuerto	Aéroport	Aeroporto
■	Military Installation	Militäranlage	Instalación Militar	Installation militaire	Instalação militar
✦	Miscellaneous	Verschiedenes	Misceláneo	Divers	Diversos

ENGLISH — Name, Page, Lat.°′, Long.°′
DEUTSCH — Name, Seite, Breite°′, Länge°′ E = Ost

Symbols in the index entries represent the broad categories identified in the key at the right. Symbols with superior numbers (⋏[1]) identify subcategories (see complete key on page *I · 1).*

Symbole im Register stellen die rechts im Schlüssel erklärten Kategorien dar. Symbole mit hochgestellten Ziffern (⋏[1]) bezeichnen Unterabteilungen einer Kategorie (vgl. vollständiger Schlüssel auf Seite *I · 1).*

Los símbolos incluídos en el texto del índice representan las grandes categorias identificadas con la clave a la derecha. Los símbolos con numeros en su parte superior (⋏[1]) identifican las subcategorías (véase la clave completa en la página *I · 1).*

Les symboles de l'index représentent les catégories indiquées dans la légende à droite. Les symboles suivis d'un indice (⋏[1]) représentent des sous-catégories (voir légende complète à la page *I · 1).*

Os símbolos incluídos no texto do índice representam as grandes categorias identificadas com a chave à direita. Os símbolos com números em sua parte superior (⋏[1]) identificam as subcategorias (veja-se a chave completa à página *I · 1).*

	English	Deutsch	Español	Français	Português
∧	Mountain	Berg	Montaña	Montagne	Montanha
⋏	Mountains	Gebirge	Montañas	Montagnes	Montanhas
)(	Pass	Paß	Paso	Col	Passo
V	Valley, Canyon	Tal, Cañon	Valle, Cañón	Vallée, Canyon	Vale, Canhão
≚	Plain	Ebene	Llano	Plaine	Planície
›	Cape	Kap	Cabo	Cap	Cabo
I	Island	Insel	Isla	Île	Ilha
II	Islands	Inseln	Islas	Îles	Ilhas
±	Other Topographic Features	Andere Topographische Objekte	Otros Elementos Topográficos	Autres données topographiques	Outros acidentes topográficos

ESPAÑOL				FRANÇAIS				PORTUGUÊS			
Nombre	**Página**	**Lat.°'**	**Long.°' W = Oeste**	**Nom**	**Page**	**Lat.°'**	**Long.°' W = Ouest**	**Nome**	**Página**	**Lat.°'**	**Long.°' W = Oeste**

Column 1 (ESPAÑOL)

Nombre	Página	Lat.	Long.
Zhangji	98	34.08 N	117.24 E
Zhangjiachang, Zhg.	107	29.26 N	104.34 E
Zhangjiachang, Zhg.	107	29.33 N	104.54 E
Zhangjiadian	105	29.57 N	103.48 E
Zhangjiadian	105	39.44 N	114.54 E
Zhangjiagou	100	30.18 N	113.22 E
Zhangjiaji	102	32.09 N	112.23 E
Zhangjiajie	104	41.28 N	124.08 E
Zhangjiakou (Kalgan)	105	40.50 N	114.53 E
Zhangjiapang	100	30.25 N	115.47 E
Zhangjiaqiao, Zhg.	107	41.18 N	122.02 E
Zhangjiaqiao, Zhg.	106	31.36 N	120.36 E
Zhangjiaqiao, Zhg.	107	30.02 N	104.15 E
Zhangjiatou	100	31.38 N	119.05 E
Zhangjiatun, Zhg.	104	41.05 N	121.44 E
Zhangjiatun, Zhg.	105	40.37 N	114.57 E
Zhangjiawa	105	40.10 N	117.52 E
Zhangjiawan	100	39.51 N	116.41 E
Zhangjiawopu	104	41.10 N	122.17 E
Zhangjiawngzi	104	42.04 N	120.57 E
Zhangjingqiao	106	31.39 N	120.27 E
Zhangjinhe	100	30.14 N	112.35 E
Zhangliangdian	100	33.42 N	113.02 E
Zhangliantang	100	31.01 N	121.02 E
Zhangling	98	36.32 N	119.29 E
Zhangli	98	36.16 N	115.33 E
Zhangmang	100	32.03 N	114.32 E
Zhangming	102	31.49 N	104.51 E
Zhangmuqiao	100	31.26 N	116.44 E
Zhangmushi	100	27.01 N	112.38 E
Zhangmutou	100	22.55 N	114.05 E
Zhangping	100	25.19 N	117.25 E
Zhangpu, Zhg.	100	24.09 N	117.36 E
Zhangpu, Zhg.	106	31.17 N	120.57 E
Zhangqiangzhen	98	42.39 N	122.59 E
Zhangqiao	100	32.21 N	117.38 E
Zhangqiu (Mingshui)	98	36.43 N	117.30 E
Zhangsanta	102	39.37 N	110.14 E
Zhangsanying	104	41.34 N	117.39 E
Zhangshan	102	41.50 N	122.51 E
Zhangshuping	102	31.20 N	111.02 E
Zhangshuxia	102	25.54 N	112.45 E
Zhangtaitai	104	40.59 N	121.05 E
Zhangting	104	41.22 N	123.16 E
Zhangwan	100	30.02 N	121.19 E
Zhangwenpu	105	26.43 N	119.36 E
Zhangwu, Zhg.	104	40.26 N	116.04 E
Zhangwu, Zhg.	104	42.22 N	122.31 E
Zhangwutaimen	100	30.47 N	119.33 E
Zhangxinliuji	104	42.16 N	122.42 E
Zhangyan, Zhg.	100	33.43 N	115.48 E
Zhangyan, Zhg.	106	31.48 N	119.44 E
Zhangyangongtun	104	40.58 N	120.46 E
Zhangze	102	38.56 N	100.27 E
Zhangze	100	30.55 N	121.15 E
Zhangzhishan	106	31.56 N	121.01 E
Zhangzhou (Longxi)	100	24.33 N	117.39 E
Zhangzhu	106	31.16 N	119.37 E
Zhangzhuang, Zhg.	98	36.02 N	118.01 E
Zhangzhuang, Zhg.	98	37.03 N	116.32 E
Zhangzhuang, Zhg.	98	31.57 N	119.52 E
Zhangzi Dao I	98	39.00 N	122.44 E
Zhanhua (Fuguo)	98	37.42 N	118.08 E
Zhanji	98	34.14 N	115.52 E
Zhanjiang	107	29.15 N	104.55 E
Zhanjiang	100	21.16 N	110.28 E
Zhanjiaqiao, Zhg.	100	29.19 N	113.34 E
Zhanjiaqiao, Zhg.	100	30.25 N	120.08 E
Zhanyang	100	25.30 N	119.28 E
Zhanyi	100	25.38 N	103.43 E
Zhao'an	89	24.31 N	122.37 E
Zhao'an	100	23.47 N	117.12 E
Zhao'an Wan c	100	23.38 N	117.19 E
Zhaobeikou	100	38.55 N	116.14 E
Zhaocun	100	40.41 N	115.18 E
Zhaodong	100	39.35 N	116.14 E
Zhaodong	89	46.05 N	125.59 E
Zhaogezhuang, Zhg.	98	37.27 N	120.37 E
Zhaogezhuang, Zhg.	100	39.45 N	118.24 E
Zhaoguang	89	48.07 N	126.43 E
Zhaohe	100	33.12 N	112.49 E
Zhaohuazhen	100	32.29 N	105.08 E
Zhaojiagou	104	40.47 N	123.27 E
Zhaojiapuzi	104	40.51 N	123.49 E
Zhaojiaqiao	104	30.44 N	121.12 E
Zhaojiatang	104	42.07 N	122.57 E
Zhaojiatun	104	41.24 N	121.53 E
Zhaojiawopeng	104	42.30 N	123.06 E
Zhaojiaying	105	38.58 N	116.42 E
Zhaojue	100	28.15 N	102.50 E
Zhaomaozhuang	105	39.28 N	117.59 E
Zhaomutun	104	41.10 N	121.38 E
Zhaoping	102	24.03 N	110.52 E
Zhaoqiao	100	28.42 N	114.45 E
Zhaoqiao (Gaoyao)	100	23.03 N	112.27 E
Zhaosu	89	43.06 N	81.08 E
Zhaotan	100	29.42 N	116.48 E
Zhaotong	102	27.19 N	103.48 E
Zhaotun	104	41.54 N	121.59 E
Zhaoxian, Zhg.	93	37.45 N	114.46 E
Zhaoxian, Zhg.	98	34.45 N	118.55 E
Zhaoxing	98	47.43 N	131.19 E
Zhaoya	100	29.00 N	105.35 E
Zhaoyi	105	39.55 N	116.43 E
Zhaoyuan, Zhg.	89	45.31 N	125.09 E
Zhaoyuan, Zhg.	98	37.22 N	120.24 E
Zhaozhou	89	45.41 N	125.21 E
Zhaozhuang, Zhg.	98	34.14 N	116.38 E
Zhaozhuang, Zhg.	98	34.45 N	116.27 E
Zhaozhuangzi	106	39.10 N	117.20 E
Zhapu	106	30.36 N	121.05 E
Zhari Namco ⊜	120	31.05 N	85.35 E
Zhaxi Co ⊜	120	32.10 N	85.05 E
Zhaxigang	102	32.32 N	79.41 E
Zhayi	102	28.34 N	99.09 E
Zhdanov	83	47.06 N	37.33 E
— Mariupol'			
Zhecheng	98	34.06 N	115.19 E
Zhegao	100	31.46 N	117.45 E
Zhegu	120	28.43 N	91.43 E
Zhêhôr	102	31.41 N	100.24 E
Zhejiang (Chekiang) □⁴	100	29.00 N	120.00 E
Zhelang	100	22.43 N	115.32 E
Zhelin, Zhg.	100	29.14 N	115.30 E
Zhelin, Zhg.	100	23.36 N	117.06 E
Zhen ≈	100	30.50 N	121.29 E
Zhen'an	102	24.55 N	113.44 E
Zhen'an	102	33.27 N	109.01 E
Zhenbeikou	98	39.15 N	106.17 E
Zhenbancheng	104	40.10 N	115.49 E
Zhenchang, Zhg.	98	38.47 N	115.24 E
Zhenchang, Zhg.	102	32.04 N	121.02 E
Zhenfeng	102	25.23 N	105.41 E
Zheng'an	102	28.31 N	107.29 E
Zheng'anpu	104	41.43 N	121.56 E
Zhengding	98	38.10 N	114.34 E
Zhengdongyu	100	31.59 N	120.10 E
Zhengfang	100	28.42 N	117.53 E
Zhengguanchang	107	29.54 N	106.35 E
Zhengguo	100	23.25 N	113.53 E
Zhenghe	100	27.22 N	118.50 E
Zhengjiadiancun	100	31.48 N	120.20 E
Zhengjiaqiao	100	29.29 N	120.05 E
Zhenglan Qi (Dund Hot)	98	42.16 N	116.03 E
Zhengning	102	35.22 N	108.24 E
Zhengyang	98	32.36 N	114.46 E
Zhen'quosi	271a	39.51 N	116.21 E
Zhengxiangbai Qi (Qagan Nur)	98	42.16 N	114.52 E
Zhengyangguan	102	32.37 N	116.33 E
Zhengyi	106	31.23 N	120.52 E

Column 2 (FRANÇAIS)

Nom	Page	Lat.	Long.
Zhengzhou (Chengchow)	102	34.48 N	113.39 E
Zhengzhuang	100	28.11 N	119.01 E
Zhengzi	107	29.22 N	104.16 E
Zhengzichang	107	29.08 N	104.56 E
Zhenhai, Zhg.	100	29.57 N	121.42 E
Zhenhai, Zhg.	100	24.16 N	118.06 E
Zhenhai, Zhg.	102	21.53 N	112.25 E
Zhenjiang, Zhg.	98	40.44 N	125.28 E
Zhenjiang, Zhg.	106	32.13 N	119.26 E
Zhenjiangguan	102	32.25 N	103.35 E
Zhenjiaqiao	106	32.08 N	120.49 E
Zhenqiao	106	30.12 N	104.22 E
Zhenkang	102	24.06 N	99.16 E
Zhenlai	89	45.52 N	123.14 E
Zhenning	102	26.05 N	105.46 E
Zhenping	102	33.08 N	112.19 E
Zhenru	106	31.15 N	121.24 E
Zhentou	100	27.04 N	114.56 E
Zhentou	102	32.58 N	114.24 E
Zhentoudian	100	29.10 N	117.29 E
Zhentoushi	100	28.01 N	113.20 E
Zhenxi	100	29.29 N	104.33 E
Zhenxiaguan	100	27.12 N	120.28 E
Zhenxing	98	42.38 N	124.53 E
Zhenxiong	102	27.24 N	104.50 E
Zhenyu	100	27.08 N	120.18 E
Zhenyuan, Zhg.	102	35.46 N	107.18 E
Zhenyuan, Zhg.	102	26.53 N	108.19 E
Zhenze	106	30.55 N	120.30 E
Zhenzhumen	98	41.53 N	126.45 E
Zhenzichang, Zhg.	107	29.59 N	105.11 E
Zhenzichang, Zhg.	107	29.52 N	104.12 E
Zhenzichang, Zhg.	107	30.38 N	104.20 E
Zhenzijie	107	28.48 N	106.40 E
Zhenziling	104	42.10 N	124.12 E
Zheqiao	100	26.27 N	112.48 E
Zherong	100	27.16 N	119.54 E
Zheshan	106	30.15 N	120.24 E
Zhetang	106	31.45 N	118.55 E
Zhidan	102	37.00 N	108.40 E
Zhidoi	102	33.08 N	94.50 E
Zhierling	98	40.26 N	114.16 E
Zhigou	98	35.55 N	119.13 E
Zhijiang	102	27.27 N	109.41 E
Zhijin	102	26.41 N	105.37 E
Zhili	106	30.52 N	120.16 E
Zhitan	100	29.35 N	117.16 E
Zhitang, Zhg.	106	31.33 N	121.01 E
Zhitang, Zhg.	106	31.36 N	120.58 E
Zhitomir → Žitomir	78	50.16 N	28.40 E
Zhitouji	100	33.28 N	118.18 E
Zhiwucun	106	30.38 N	119.47 E
Zhixi	100	23.57 N	114.33 E
Zhixia	100	29.42 N	119.36 E
Zhixi.qiao	100	31.49 N	119.29 E
Zhiyang	102	33.47 N	113.07 E
Zhizushan	104	41.50 N	121.24 E
Zhob	120	31.20 N	69.27 E
Zhob ≈	120	32.04 N	69.50 E
Zhonganpu	104	41.37 N	121.58 E
Zhong'aozhen	107	29.46 N	105.41 E
Zhongba, Zhg.	120	23.43 N	115.22 E
Zhongba, Zhg.	120	29.38 N	84.13 E
Zhongbu → Žukovskij	100	31.25 N	117.45 E
Zhulanbu	100	31.40 N	117.45 E
Zhongchuan	106	28.50 N	117.16 E
Zhongcun	102	26.58 N	119.27 E
Zhongdai	102	33.27 N	110.05 E
Zhongdan	106	30.46 N	120.59 E
Zhongdian	102	27.50 N	99.40 E
Zhongdu, Zhg.	106	24.56 N	116.26 E
Zhongdu, Zhg.	107	28.46 N	103.58 E
Zhongduan	106	25.17 N	116.41 E
Zhongerdong	104	38.31 N	115.45 E
Zhonggang	100	23.58 N	121.55 E
Zhonggong	98	36.30 N	117.01 E
Zhonggoumen	98	41.00 N	116.25 E
Zhongu	104	42.27 N	124.00 E
Zhongguo → China □¹	90	35.00 N	105.00 E
Zhonghe	100	22.31 N	103.52 E
Zhonghechang	107	30.12 N	104.49 E
Zhongheying	102	23.48 N	103.36 E
Zhonghezhen	107	30.34 N	104.06 E
Zhonghuamen	106	32.01 N	118.46 E
Zhonghupu	100	31.58 N	113.59 E
Zhongjianchang	107	29.46 N	106.13 E
Zhongjia	107	31.00 N	106.18 E
Zhongjiatai	100	40.48 N	122.46 E
Zhonglou	98	35.24 N	119.02 E
Zhongluotan	100	23.23 N	113.23 E
Zhongluyantai	104	41.32 N	123.17 E
Zhongmeihe	100	29.32 N	105.40 E
Zhongmou	98	34.46 N	114.01 E
Zhongnan	100	34.37 N	114.46 E
Zhongpingchang	102	31.15 N	110.10 E
Zhongqiao	106	31.03 N	119.11 E
Zhongshan	100	26.24 N	116.36 E
Zhongshan, Zhg. (Shiqizhen), Zhg.	100	22.31 N	113.22 E
Zhongshan Park ⋆	269b	31.13 N	121.25 E
Zhongtiao Shan ⋊	102	35.00 N	111.35 E
Zhongtou	104	34.00 N	113.21 E
Zhongwei	98	37.33 N	105.10 E
Zhongwopu	104	38.30 N	102.59 E
Zhongxian	102	30.17 N	108.04 E
Zhongxian, Zhg.	100	22.31 N	113.22 E
Zhongxiangzhen	107	30.49 N	104.34 E
Zhongxin, Zhg.	100	23.16 N	113.38 E
Zhongxin, Zhg.	102	23.38 N	111.48 E
Zhongxing, Zhg.	100	32.17 N	119.34 E
Zhongxing, Zhg.	102	30.12 N	103.32 E
Zhongxingchang	107	30.30 N	104.03 E
Zhongxinzhen	107	30.30 N	106.13 E
Zhongyang	98	37.21 N	111.09 E
Zhongyangqu	89	26.53 N	112.13 E
Zhongyi	98	31.08 N	114.52 E
Zhongzangcun	107	29.38 N	117.06 E
Zhongzhan	100	25.16 N	114.24 E
Zhongzhuang	100	31.23 N	114.47 E
Zhou ≈	100	39.47 N	117.23 E
Zhouba	107	29.06 N	103.43 E
Zhoubachang	107	28.59 N	103.52 E
Zhoudao	100	36.40 N	105.48 E
Zhoudangfan	100	30.34 N	114.31 E
Zhouiachang	100	30.33 N	114.25 E
Zhoujiadu	100	31.11 N	121.30 E
Zhoujiajing	106	31.11 N	121.29 E
Zhoujiatun, Zhg.	104	41.34 N	121.05 E
Zhoujiatun, Zhg.	104	42.05 N	121.40 E
Zhoujiayao	104	41.19 N	122.48 E
Zhoujiaxiang	106	31.46 N	120.11 E
Zhoukouzhen	105	39.55 N	116.01 E
Zhoukoudianzhen	105	39.55 N	115.59 E
Zhoupi	105	39.24 N	115.58 E
Zhoupu	107	29.48 N	104.10 E
Zhouqu	102	33.43 N	104.21 E
Zhoushan Dao I	100	30.00 N	122.00 E
Zhoushan Qundao II	100	30.00 N	122.00 E

Column 3 (PORTUGUÊS)

Nome	Página	Lat.	Long.
Zhouxi	100	29.13 N	116.20 E
Zhouxiang	100	30.10 N	121.08 E
Zhouxinzhen	106	31.30 N	120.18 E
Zhouzhai	106	32.02 N	121.31 E
Zhouzhi	102	34.12 N	108.10 E
Zhuzhuang, Zhg.	105	39.09 N	115.18 E
Zhuzhuang, Zhg.	106	31.06 N	120.51 E
Zhuzhuang, Zhg.	106	32.15 N	120.08 E
Zhuanghang	106	30.54 N	121.23 E
Zhuanghe	98	39.43 N	123.01 E
Zhuangji	98	34.20 N	115.15 E
Zhuanglang	102	34.58 N	106.07 E
Zhuangtou	105	34.58 N	117.57 E
Zhuangtouyingzi, Zhg.	104	41.43 N	120.32 E
Zhuangtouyingzi, Zhg.			
Zhuangxi	107	30.33 N	104.31 E
Zhuangyuanqiao	107	27.54 N	119.08 E
Zhuanping Shan ⋀	107	29.07 N	103.37 E
Zhuanqiao	106	31.04 N	121.23 E
Zhuantouwan	106	31.29 N	122.24 E
Zhuanwantai	104	41.20 N	122.22 E
Zhuao	100	29.05 N	121.16 E
Zhucang	102	27.18 N	107.26 E
Zhucheng	98	36.00 N	119.24 E
Zhudi	269b	31.12 N	121.18 E
Zhudian	100	30.33 N	115.12 E
Zhuergan	89	52.04 N	120.48 E
Zhufengzhen	106	30.35 N	118.56 E
Zhufuo	107	29.02 N	105.51 E
Zhugan ≈	100	31.18 N	114.42 E
Zhugao	102	32.13 N	114.39 E
Zhuge, Zhg.	98	36.00 N	118.32 E
Zhuge, Zhg.	100	29.15 N	119.18 E
Zhugentan	107	29.55 N	103.50 E
Zhugou	98	36.52 N	120.15 E
Zhugouzhen	102	32.47 N	113.42 E
Zhuhe	100	29.44 N	113.06 E
Zhuhongyu	104	40.48 N	123.00 E
Zhuji	100	29.43 N	120.14 E
Zhujiabeng	106	31.21 N	120.41 E
Zhujiabian	106	31.38 N	119.11 E
Zhujiachang, Zhg.	107	29.48 N	104.20 E
Zhujiachang, Zhg.	107	30.03 N	104.13 E
Zhujiadang	106	31.42 N	120.40 E
Zhujiahang	106	30.51 N	121.19 E
Zhujiahe	100	31.08 N	120.53 E
Zhujia Jian I	100	29.54 N	122.24 E
Zhujiajiao	106	31.24 N	121.11 E
Zhujiaxou	100	22.36 N	113.44 E
Zhujiang Kou c¹	100	22.18 N	114.44 E
Zhujiangqing	100	27.18 N	119.03 E
Zhujiaqiao	106	32.06 N	119.03 E
Zhujiawan, Zhg.	100	32.28 N	117.29 E
Zhujiawan, Zhg.	100	40.08 N	114.56 E
Zhujiawopeng	104	42.27 N	122.13 E
Zhujiesi	102	33.34 N	97.21 E
Zhukeng	100	23.49 N	112.55 E
Zhukou, Zhg.	98	34.07 N	115.04 E
Zhukou, Zhg.	100	27.41 N	118.53 E
Zhukou, Zhg.	100	26.58 N	117.16 E

Column 4

	Página	Lat.	Long.
Ziftâ	142	30.43 N	31.15 E
Žigajlovka	78	50.38 N	35.07 E
Žigalgan	84	44.36 N	50.46 E
Žigalovo	88	54.48 N	105.08 E
Žigansk	74	66.45 N	123.20 E
Zigazinskij	86	53.50 N	57.20 E
Zigong (Tzukung)	107	29.24 N	104.47 E
Ziguéy	146	14.43 N	15.47 E
Zigui	102	31.00 N	110.31 E
Ziguinchor	150	12.35 N	16.16 W
Ziguinchor □⁴	150	12.45 N	16.20 W
Žigulevsk	80	53.25 N	49.27 E
Žiguli ↗	80	53.22 N	49.19 E
Žigutaicun	80	53.20 N	49.40 E
Zihedian	104	42.10 N	121.16 E
Zihuatanejo	98	36.48 N	118.22 E
Zihukou, Zhg.	234	17.38 N	101.33 W
Zihukou, Zhg.	100	28.44 N	112.33 E
Ziiyang	100	28.55 N	118.08 E
Žijančurino	102	32.31 N	108.48 E
Žijankum	86	51.33 N	56.55 E
Žijiao	85	42.50 N	69.00 E
Zijin	98	37.21 N	117.25 E
Zijingguan	100	23.40 N	115.11 E
Zijin Shan ⋀²	105	39.23 N	115.12 E
Zikhron Ya'aqov	106	32.04 N	118.51 E
Zikoufang	132	32.34 N	34.57 E
Zilair	100	26.22 N	117.24 E
Žilaja Kosa	86	52.14 N	57.30 E
Žilaja Tambica	86	46.49 N	53.12 E
Zilina	24	62.32 N	36.09 E
Žilino	130	40.18 N	35.54 E
Zilah, Lībīyā	130	26.50 N	100.27 E
Zilah, Wa., U.S.	146	28.33 N	17.35 E
Ziller ≈	202	46.24 N	120.15 W
Zillertal V	64	47.24 N	11.50 E
Zillertaler Alpen (Alpi Aurine) ⋊	64	47.20 N	11.50 E
Zillis	64	47.00 N	11.55 E
Zillisheim	58	46.38 N	9.27 E
Zilly	58	47.41 N	7.16 E
Zirne	144	51.56 N	10.49 E
Žilo, ostrov I	106	16.25 N	43.49 E
Žiloj Bor	78	40.19 N	50.36 E
Žil'ovo	76	59.06 N	34.37 E
Ziltendorf	82	54.59 N	38.02 E
Zilupe	54	52.12 N	14.37 E
Zilwaukee	76	56.23 N	28.07 E
Zima	190	43.28 N	83.55 W
Zima, gora ⋀	88	53.52 N	102.04 E
Zimapán	88	53.18 N	107.38 E
Zimatlán de Alvarez	234	20.45 N	99.21 W
Zimba	234	16.52 N	96.47 W
Zimbabwe □¹, Afr.	154	17.19 S	26.13 E
Zimbabwe □¹, Afr.	138	20.00 S	30.00 E
Zimbor	38	44.20 N	9.16 E
Zimella	38	47.00 N	23.16 E
Zimi	150	7.19 N	11.18 W
Zimljansker-Stausee → Ciml'anskoje vodochranilišče ⊜¹	80	48.00 N	43.00 E
Zimmara, Monte ⋀	70	37.45 N	14.16 E
Zimn'ackij	80	49.44 N	42.53 E
Zimnicea	38	43.39 N	25.21 E
Zimogorje	88	48.35 N	38.56 E
Zimonino	76	53.47 N	31.52 E
Zimovniki	80	47.08 N	42.28 E
Zimovskoje	86	57.31 N	86.52 E
Zin, Nahal V	132	30.57 N	35.19 E
Zinacatepec	234	18.20 N	97.15 W
Zinal	58	46.08 N	7.38 E
Zinapécuaro [de Figueroa]	234	19.52 N	100.49 W
Zinave, Parque Nacional de ♦	156	21.35 S	33.35 E
Zinder	146	13.48 N	8.59 E
Zinder □⁵	146	15.00 N	10.30 E
Zinga	152	3.43 N	18.35 E
Zinga Mulike	154	9.09 S	38.44 E
Zingaro, Passo dello ⟍	70	37.43 N	14.50 E
Zingst	54	54.26 N	12.41 E
Zingst ↗¹	54	54.25 N	12.50 E
Zingiwanda	140	7.10 N	27.56 E
Ziniare	150	12.35 N	1.18 W
Žiniške ≈	88	43.14 N	78.30 E
Zinkgruvan	40	58.49 N	15.05 E
Zin'kov	78	50.13 N	33.59 E
Zinnik → Soignies	54	50.35 N	4.04 E
Zinnowitz	54	54.04 N	13.55 E
Zinswiller	58	48.55 N	7.35 E
Zion, II., U.S.	188	42.26 N	87.49 W
Zion, Md., U.S.	208	40.29 N	75.57 W
Zionhill	208	40.29 N	75.24 W
Zion National Park ♦	200	37.10 N	113.00 W
Zionz Lake ⊜	218	50.51 N	96.15 W
Zippori	132	32.45 N	35.17 E
Zipsendorf	54	51.02 N	12.16 E
Ziqlāb, Wādī V	132	32.30 N	35.34 E
Zira	120	30.59 N	32.31 E
Zirahuén, Laguna ⊜	234	19.27 N	101.44 W
Žirándaro	234	18.27 N	100.59 W
Žir'atino	76	53.15 N	33.44 E
Zírcholzkogel ⋀	64	47.04 N	14.34 E
Zirchow	54	53.52 N	14.08 E
Zirgan	86	53.14 N	55.55 E
Zirl, Otok I	36	43.40 N	15.39 E
Zirl	64	47.17 N	11.14 E
Žirnov	78	49.26 N	36.21 E
Žirnov	80	48.13 N	41.06 E
Žiro	38	27.38 N	98.21 E
Žiroškino	76	55.22 N	38.03 E
Zirovnice	54	49.15 N	15.11 E
Žirtsy	80	52.55 N	37.15 E
Zisterdorf	54	48.32 N	16.45 E
Zisterzienserabtei ↗¹	54	50.38 N	9.47 E
Zisuntang	100	30.38 N	118.42 E
Žitácuaro	234	19.24 N	100.22 W
Žitácuaro ≈	234	18.51 N	100.44 W
Žiteli	36	42.52 N	18.18 E
Žitenice	54	50.35 N	14.08 E
Žit'kovci	78	51.13 N	27.54 E
Žitomir	78	50.15 N	28.40 E
Zittau	54	50.54 N	14.48 E
Zitundo	156	26.45 S	32.50 E
Ziwa Magharibi □⁴	154	2.00 S	31.30 E
Ziway, Lake ⊜	148	8.00 N	38.50 E
Zixi	100	27.42 N	117.01 E
Zixi, Zhg.	98	28.01 N	117.46 E
Ziya ≈	98	39.09 N	117.10 E
Ziyang	102	30.07 N	104.39 E
Ziyuan	102	26.02 N	110.40 E
Ziz, Oued V	148	30.39 N	4.26 W
Zizdra	76	53.46 N	34.44 E
Žiž'akovo	82	54.14 N	36.12 E

Column 5

	Página	Lat.	Long.
Zizers	58	46.56 N	9.34 E
Zizhong	107	29.48 N	104.50 E
Zizhou	102	37.37 N	109.41 E
Žízkovce, ozero ⊜	76	56.14 N	31.15 E
Žizma ≈	76	53.54 N	25.36 E
Zlata Koruna ↗¹	61	48.52 N	14.22 E
Zlatar	36	46.06 N	16.05 E
Zlaté Moravce	30	48.25 N	18.24 E
Zlatica	38	42.43 N	24.08 E
Zlatograd	38	41.23 N	25.06 E
Zlatoust	86	55.10 N	59.40 E
Zlatoustovsk	89	52.58 N	133.38 E
Zlín	30	49.13 N	17.41 E
— Gottwaldov			
Zlītan	146	32.28 N	14.34 E
Žlobin	82	52.54 N	30.03 E
Złoczew	30	51.25 N	18.36 E
Złocieniec	30	53.33 N	16.01 E
Złonice	54	50.15 N	14.07 E
Złotoryja	30	51.08 N	15.55 E
Złotów	30	53.22 N	17.02 E
Žlutice	54	50.03 N	13.10 E
Zlydnev	30	48.46 N	45.48 E
Žlynka, S.S.S.R.	76	52.25 N	31.44 E
Žlynka, S.S.S.R.	78	48.28 N	31.32 E
Zmeinogorsk	86	51.10 N	82.13 E
Žmenyj, ostrov I	78	45.15 N	30.12 E
Žmerinka	78	49.02 N	28.06 E
Žmigród	30	51.29 N	16.55 E
Žminj	36	45.09 N	13.55 E
Zmiʼovka	76	52.40 N	36.23 E
Zna ≈			
— Cna ≈	80	54.32 N	42.05 E
Znaim → Znojmo	61	48.52 N	16.02 E
Znamenka, S.S.S.R.	76	54.54 N	34.34 E
Znamenka, S.S.S.R.	88	48.43 N	32.40 E
Znamenka, S.S.S.R.	80	52.24 N	41.26 E
Znamenka, S.S.S.R.	83	48.51 N	31.02 E
Znamenka, S.S.S.R.	86	53.10 N	79.30 E
Znamenka, S.S.S.R.	86	53.32 N	91.54 E
Znamenka Vtoraja	88	54.42 N	104.50 E
Znamenskaja, S.S.S.R.	76	54.37 N	2ʼ.13 E
Znamenskaja, S.S.S.R.	80	53.17 N	35.41 E
Znamenskoje, S.S.S.R.	80	53.19 N	42.57 E
Znamenskoje, S.S.S.R.	86	57.08 N	73.55 E
Znin	30	52.45 N	17.43 E
Znob'-Novgorodskoje	78	52.27 N	33.36 E
Znojmo	61	48.52 N	16.02 E
Zoagli	62	44.20 N	9.16 E
Zoar	38	44.00 N	8.31 E
Zoar Village State Memorial ⊥	214	40.36 N	81.27 W
Zoarville	214	40.19 N	81.24 W
Zobia	154	2.58 N	25.56 E
Zöblitz	54	50.39 N	13.14 E
Zocca	64	44.21 N	10.59 E
Zochova, ostrov I	74	76.04 N	152.40 E
Žod	84	40.12 N	45.52 E
Žodino	54	54.06 N	28.21 E
Žodiški	76	54.38 N	26.26 E
Zoétélé	152	3.15 N	11.53 E
Zoetermeer	52	52.03 N	4.30 E
Zofingen	58	47.18 N	7.57 E
Zogang	102	29.55 N	97.44 E
Zogno	62	45.48 N	9.40 E
Zográfos	267c	37.59 N	23.46 E
Zohar	132	31.36 N	34.42 E
Zohar, Mizpé ⋀²	132	31.13 N	35.21 E
Zohreh ≈	128	30.04 N	49.31 E
Zola Predosa	64	44.29 N	11.12 E
Zolder	52	51.01 N	5.18 E
Zoldo Alto	64	46.22 N	12.06 E
Zolfo Springs	220	27.29 N	81.47 W
Zolka ≈	80	43.42 N	43.52 E
Żółkiewka	30	50.55 N	22.51 E
Zollhaus	58	50.17 N	8.04 E
Zollikofen	58	47.00 N	7.28 E
Zollikon	58	47.20 N	8.35 E
Zol'noje	80	53.27 N	49.48 E
Zoločov, S.S.S.R.	78	50.17 N	24.53 E
Zoločov, S.S.S.R.	78	50.17 N	35.59 E
Zolotaja Gora	89	54.16 N	126.36 E
Zolotaja Lipa ≈	78	49.25 N	25.04 E
Zolotari	30	53.04 N	45.20 E
Zolotar'ovka	80	53.04 N	25.08 E
Zolotkovo	76	55.45 N	41.14 E
Zolotoje	80	50.41 N	46.50 E
Zolotoje Koldoec	86	54.08 N	69.31 E
Zolotoj Potok	89	58.50 N	130.53 E
Zolotonoša	78	49.40 N	32.03 E
Zolotucha	80	51.32 N	41.54 E
Zolotuchino	80	51.55 N	36.27 E
Zol'tje, S.S.S.R.	80	53.35 N	39.07 E
Zol'tje, S.S.S.R.	80	48.48 N	44.38 E
Žoltyje Vody	78	48.20 N	33.31 E
Zólymbet	86	51.45 N	71.44 E
Zomba	154	15.23 S	35.18 E
Zomergem	54	51.07 N	3.33 E
Zompi	154	1.20 S	29.35 E
Zonay	30	49.34 N	18.25 E
Zonguldak	130	41.27 N	31.49 E
Zongolica	234	18.40 N	97.00 W
Zongwe	154	5.05 S	28.55 E
Zonhoven	54	50.59 N	5.22 E
Zonnebeke	54	50.52 N	2.59 E
Zontehuitz, Cerro ⋀	234	16.50 N	92.38 W
Zoo, Bahnhof ⋆⁵	264c	52.30 N	13.20 E
Zooafskolk	158	28.56 S	20.28 E
Zoppot	30	54.26 N	18.34 E
Zopten am Berge → Sobótka	30	50.55 N	16.45 E
Zörbig	54	51.37 N	12.07 E
Zorge	54	51.38 N	10.39 E
Zorgo	150	12.15 N	0.37 W
Zorgongo	150	12.16 N	0.48 W
Zorita	34	39.17 N	5.42 W
Žorkul', ozero ⊜	118	37.27 N	73.30 E
Žorn ≈	88	50.56 N	91.02 E
Žorn, N.M., U.S.	200	33.16 N	105.10 E
Žorn, Va., U.S.	208	36.51 N	76.49 W
Zorra, Arroyo de la ≈	196	29.31 N	101.13 W
Zorritos	246	3.40 S	80.40 W
Zorzor	150	7.46 N	9.28 W
Zossen	54	52.13 N	13.27 E
Žoti	38	41.53 N	20.37 E
Zottegem	54	50.52 N	3.49 E
Zou □⁵	150	7.30 N	2.15 E
Zou ≈	150	7.24 N	2.06 E

Column 6

	Página	Lat.	Long.
Zoumagang	107	29.28 N	106.18 E
Zoumayi	98	39.07 N	114.34 E
Zouping	98	36.53 N	117.42 E
Zourma	150	11.22 N	0.49 W
Zousfana, Oued V	148	30.29 N	2.17 W
Zoutelande	52	51.30 N	3.30 E
Zoutkamp	52	53.20 N	6.18 E
Zova	132	31.48 N	35.06 E
Zovka	76	58.26 N	28.52 E
Žovnino	78	49.23 N	32.41 E
Žovten', S.S.S.R.	78	49.23 N	24.45 E
Žovten', S.S.S.R.	78	47.14 N	30.20 E
Žovtnevoje, S.S.S.R.	78	49.39 N	34.09 E
Žovtnevoje, S.S.S.R.	78	52.02 N	32.02 E
Žovtnevoje, S.S.S.R.	78	50.57 N	34.22 E
Žovtnevoje, S.S.S.R.	78	51.15 N	28.07 E
Zozaya, Picacho de ⋀	232	27.10 N	102.34 W
Zozov	78	49.19 N	29.01 E
Zrenjanin	38	45.23 N	20.24 E
Žriba	36	36.20 N	10.16 E
Zrmanja ≈	36	44.15 N	15.32 E
Zruč nad Sázavou	30	49.45 N	15.07 E
Zscherndorf	54	51.36 N	12.15 E
Zschieren ⋆⁸	54	51.00 N	13.52 E
Zschopau	54	50.44 N	13.04 E
Zschopau ≈	54	51.08 N	13.03 E
Zschorlau	54	50.34 N	12.38 E
Zschornewitz	54	51.43 N	12.25 E
Zschortau	54	51.28 N	12.21 E
Žuanbalyk	86	45.04 N	61.51 E
Žuantobe	86	44.05 N	68.54 E
Zuarungu	150	10.47 N	0.48 W
Zuata ≈	248	9.06 S	64.44 W
Zuazua	54	54.15 N	13.20 E
Zubaydīyah, Jabal az- ⋀	132	37.02 E
Zubayr, Jazāʼir az- II	144	15.05 N	42.08 E
Zubayr, Wādī V	142	27.27 N	32.41 E
Zubcov		56.10 N	34.34 E
Zubkovičí	78	51.22 N	27.41 E
Zubova Pol'ana	80	54.04 N	42.51 E
Zubovka	80	54.16 N	51.06 E
Zubovo, S.S.S.R.	76	60.19 N	36.57 E
Zubovo, S.S.S.R.	80	56.52 N	44.08 E
Zubovo, S.S.S.R.	76	54.37 N	33.29 E
Zuccarello	62	44.07 N	8.07 E
Zuccone, Monte ⋀	62	44.26 N	9.37 E
Zuchwil	58	47.12 N	7.33 E
Zuckerhütl ⋀	64	46.58 N	11.10 E
Zudañez	248	19.06 S	64.44 W
Žuel	54	54.15 N	13.20 E
Z'udev, ostrov I	80	45.35 N	47.58 E
Zuénoula	150	7.26 N	6.03 W
Zuera	34	41.52 N	0.47 W
Zufār ⇄¹	118	17.00 N	54.10 E
Zufayt Mashtūl	142	30.20 N	31.21 E
Zug	58	47.00 N	8.31 E
Zug □³	58	47.10 N	8.30 E
Zugdeli	88	55.03 N	111.10 E
Zugdidi	84	42.30 N	41.53 E
Zugersee ⊜	58	47.08 N	8.30 E
Zug Island I	281	42.17 N	83.07 W
Zugló ⋆⁵	264c	47.31 N	19.08 E
Zugres	83	48.01 N	38.15 E
Zugspitze ⋀	64	47.25 N	10.59 E
Zugurrma Game Reserve ♦⁴	150	9.55 N	5.00 E
Zühlsdorf	264a	52.44 N	13.24 E
Zui	70	40.56 N	31.37 E
Zuid-Beijerland	52	51.45 N	4.22 E
Zuid-Beveland I	52	51.25 N	3.45 E
Zuidbroek	52	53.10 N	6.52 E
Zuidelijk Flevoland			
⊥	52	52.22 N	5.20 E
Zuiderzee → IJsselmeer ⇄²	52	52.40 N	5.25 E
Zuid-Holland □⁴	52	52.00 N	4.30 E
Zuidhorn	52	53.14 N	6.24 E
Zuidlaren	52	53.06 N	6.41 E
Zuid-Willemsvaart ⊠	52	51.12 N	5.52 E
Zuidwolde	52	53.15 N	6.35 E
Zuja ≈	78	45.03 N	34.20 E
Zuja ≈	58	48.45 N	118.11 E
Žujatun	88	39.01 N	5.47 W
Zújar, Embalse del ⊜¹	34	38.50 N	5.20 W
Zújevka, S.S.S.R.	80	58.24 N	51.07 E
Zújevka, S.S.S.R.	80	58.12 N	54.43 E
Z'ukajka	80	58.12 N	54.52 E
Žukopa ≈	76	56.32 N	33.44 E
Zukovka, S.S.S.R.	76	55.32 N	33.44 E
Žukovka, S.S.S.R.	76	53.32 N	33.44 E
Žukovka, S.S.S.R.	265b	55.44 N	37.15 E
Žukovskij	76	55.35 N	38.07 E
Žukovskaja	80	47.05 N	41.21 E
Žukovo	80	56.05 N	41.21 E
Žuljevo	36	43.24 N	18.22 E
Žulidny	144	15.11 N	39.41 E
Žula	234	20.21 N	102.46 W
Zula	144	15.11 N	39.41 E
Žulia □⁴	246	10.00 N	72.10 W
Žulia ≈	246	9.04 N	72.18 W

Column 7

	Página	Lat.	Long.
Zulichau → Sulechów	30	52.06 N	15.37 E
Žüls	50	50.46 N	6.37 E
Züls → Biała	30	50.23 N	17.40 E
Zulueta	240p	22.22 N	79.34 W
Zuland ⇄¹	158	28.10 S	32.00 E
Zul'al'za	98	52.33 N	116.13 E
Zumaia	34	43.17 N	2.15 W
Zumarraga	118	13.38 N	124.50 E
Zumate, Cerro ⋀	234	20.10 N	98.40 W
Zumba	246	4.52 S	79.08 W
Zumbo	154	15.36 S	30.25 E
Zumbro, North Fork ≈	190	44.15 N	91.56 W
Zumbro, South Fork ≈	190	44.15 N	92.29 W
Zumbrota	190	44.17 N	92.40 W
Zumpango	234	19.48 N	99.06 W
Zumpango, Lago de ⊜	234	19.46 N	99.03 W
Zumpango del Río	234	17.39 N	99.30 W
Zundert	52	51.28 N	4.39 E
Zungbi	118	10.05 N	55.11 W
Zungeru	150	9.48 N	6.09 E
Zuni	200	35.04 N	108.51 W
Zuni ≈	200	34.34 N	109.40 W
Zuni Indian Reservation ♦⁴	200	35.15 N	108.20 W
Zuni Mountains ⋊	200	35.10 N	108.00 W
Zunyi	102	27.42 N	106.55 E
Zuo ≈	102	22.34 N	108.04 E
Zuoerfu	102	33.30 N	97.00 E
Zuojiawu	104	40.08 N	118.07 E
Zuojulaimiao	98	48.02 N	114.18 E
Zuoquan	98	37.04 N	113.22 E
Zuoyun	98	40.00 N	112.42 E
Zuozhou	102	22.20 N	107.22 E
Zwartsluis	52	52.38 N	6.05 E

≈	River	Fluß	Río	Rivière	Rio	⊸	Submarine Features	Untermeerische Objekte	Accidentes Submarinos	Formes de relief sous-marin	Acidentes submarinos
⊠	Canal	Kanal	Canal	Canal	Canal	⊥	Political Unit	Politische Einheit	Unidad Política	Entité politique	Unidade política
ʟ	Waterfall, Rapids	Wasserfall, Stromschnellen	Cascada, Rápidos	Chute d'eau, Rapides	Cascata, Rápidos	ɷ	Cultural Institution	Kulturelle Institution	Institución Cultural	Institution culturelle	Instituição cultural
ม	Strait	Meeresstraße	Estrecho	Détroit	Estreito	⊥	Historical Site	Historische Stätte	Sitio Histórico	Site historique	Sitio histórico
c	Bay, Gulf	Bucht, Golf	Bahía, Golfo	Baie, Golfe	Baía, Golfo	♦	Recreational Site	Erholungs- und Ferienort	Sitio de Recreo	Centre de loisirs	Area de Lazer
⊜	Lake, Lakes	See, Seen	Lago, Lagos	Lac, Lacs	Lago, Lagos	⊁	Airport	Flughafen	Aeropuerto	Aéroport	Aeroporto
ᴴ	Swamp	Sumpf	Pantano	Marais	Pântano	■	Military Installation	Militäranlage	Instalación Militar	Installation militaire	Instalação militar
ㄴ	Ice Features, Glacier	Eis- und Gletscherformen	Accidentes Glaciales	Formes glaciaires	Acidentes glaciares	●	Miscellaneous	Verschiedenes	Misceláneo	Divers	Diversos
ㅜ	Other Hydrographic Features	Andere Hydrographische Objekte	Otros Elementos Hidrográficos	Autres données hydrographiques	Outros acidentes hidrográficos						

Name	Page	Lat.°'	Long.°'
Zuoyun	102	40.02 N	112.54 E
Zuoz	58	46.36 N	9.58 E
Županja	38	45.04 N	18.42 E
Zûq Muşbiḥ	132	33.58 N	35.37 E
Žura, S.S.S.R.	78	47.31 N	29.04 E
Zura, S.S.S.R.	80	57.37 N	53.26 E
Žūrābād	128	38.49 N	44.35 E
Žuraviči, S.S.S.R.	76	53.15 N	30.33 E
Žuraviči, S.S.S.R.	78	50.59 N	25.43 E
Žuravl'ovka, S.S.S.R.	83	48.13 N	38.58 E
Žuravl'ovka, S.S.S.R.	86	51.57 N	69.56 E
Žurayghit	128	26.29 N	40.33 E
Žurban	89	54.12 N	127.56 E
Zurich, On., Can.	190	43.26 N	81.37 W
Zürich, Ned.	52	53.06 N	5.23 E
Zürich, Schw.	58	47.23 N	8.32 E
Zürich □³	58	47.25 N	8.40 E
Zürich, Flughafen ≋	58	47.27 N	8.33 E
Zurich, Lake �container	278	42.12 N	88.06 W
Zürichsee �container	58	47.13 N	8.45 E
Zurigo → Zürich			
Zurmi	150	12.46 N	6.48 E
Zuromin	30	53.04 N	19.55 E
Zurq, Al-Qārāt az- ▲²	142	29.00 N	29.55 E
Zürs	58	47.10 N	10.10 E
Zuru	150	11.27 N	5.12 E
Zurzach	58	47.35 N	8.18 E
Zuša ≃	76	53.27 N	36.23 E
Zusam ≃	56	48.42 N	10.45 E
Žusandala ◆²	86	44.20 N	75.00 E
Zushi	94	35.18 N	139.35 E
Zusmarshausen	58	48.24 N	10.35 E
Züssow	54	53.59 N	13.32 E
Žut, Otok I	36	43.52 N	15.19 E
Zutiua ≃	250	3.43 S	45.29 W
Žutovo Vtoroje	80	47.49 N	43.51 E
Zutphen	52	52.08 N	6.12 E
Zützen	54	51.57 N	13.38 E
Zuwārah	146	32.56 N	12.06 E
Zuwayzā	132	31.42 N	35.55 E
Z'uzel'skij	86	56.29 N	60.07 E
Žužemberk	36	45.50 N	14.56 E
Z'uzino	265b	55.40 N	38.07 E
Z'uzino ◆⁸	265b	55.39 N	37.35 E
Žužymdyk	85	43.05 N	69.08 E
Zv'agino	265b	55.59 N	37.48 E
Zvannoje	78	51.23 N	34.33 E
Zvenigorod	82	55.44 N	36.51 E
Zvenigorodka	78	49.04 N	30.57 E
Zvenigovo	80	55.58 N	48.02 E
Zverevo	83	48.01 N	40.07 E
Zverinogolovskoje	86	54.28 N	64.50 E
Zvezdec	38	42.07 N	27.25 E
Zvezdnyj	88	56.49 N	106.27 E
Zvikovec	60	49.56 N	13.42 E
Zvishavane	154	20.20 S	30.02 E
Zvolen	30	48.35 N	19.08 E
Zvon ▲	60	49.33 N	12.39 E
Zvornik	38	44.23 N	19.06 E
Zwaag	52	52.40 N	5.05 E
Zwaagwesteinde	52	53.15 N	6.04 E
Zwadiba	152	3.04 N	14.02 E
Zwanenburg	52	52.23 N	4.45 E
Zwartemeer	52	52.43 N	7.03 E
Zwarte Meer �container	52	52.37 N	5.57 E
Zwartsluis	52	52.37 N	6.04 E
Zweckel ◆⁸	263	51.36 N	6.59 E
Zwedru	150	6.04 N	8.08 W
Zweibrücken	56	49.15 N	7.21 E
Zweifall	56	50.43 N	6.15 E
Zweisimmen	58	46.33 N	7.22 E
Zweite Wiener Hochquellenleitung ≂¹	61	48.10 N	16.14 E
Zwenkau	54	51.13 N	12.19 E
Zwentendorf	61	48.21 N	15.55 E
Zwesten	56	51.03 N	9.10 E
Zwettl	61	48.37 N	15.10 E
Zwevegem	50	50.48 N	3.20 E
Zwevezele	50	51.02 N	3.12 E
Zwickau	54	50.44 N	12.29 E
Zwickauer Mulde ≃	54	51.10 N	12.48 E
Zwiefalten	58	48.14 N	9.28 E
Zwiefaltendorf	58	48.13 N	9.31 E
Zwierzyniec	30	50.37 N	22.58 E
Zwiesel	60	49.01 N	13.14 E
Zwieselstein	64	46.56 N	11.02 E
Zwijndrecht	52	51.49 N	4.39 E
Zwillbrock	52	52.04 N	6.42 E
Zwingenberg, B.R.D.	56	49.25 N	9.02 E
Zwingenberg, B.R.D.	56	49.43 N	8.37 E
Zwischenahner Meer �container	52	53.12 N	8.01 E
Zwochau	54	51.28 N	12.16 E
Zwoleń	30	51.22 N	21.35 E
Zwölfaxing	264b	48.06 N	16.28 E
Zwolle, Ned.	52	52.30 N	6.05 E
Zwolle, La., U.S.	194	31.37 N	93.38 W
Zwönitz	54	50.38 N	12.49 E
Zwota	54	50.21 N	12.25 E
Żychlin	30	52.15 N	19.39 E
Zyr'anka	74	65.45 N	150.51 E
Zyr'anovsk	86	49.43 N	84.20 E
Zyr'anovskij	86	57.46 N	61.42 E
Zyr'anskoje	86	56.50 N	86.38 E
Żyrardów	30	52.04 N	20.25 E
Zyryanovsk → Zyr'anovsk	86	49.43 N	84.20 E
Żyrzyn	30	51.30 N	22.07 E
Żywiec	30	49.41 N	19.12 E